NELSON'S COMPACT™ SERIES

THE NEW
STRONG'S®
COMPACT BIBLE CONCORDANCE

JAMES STRONG, LL.D., S.T.D.

THOMAS NELSON
Since 1798

NASHVILLE DALLAS MEXICO CITY RIO DE JANEIRO BEIJING

Nelson's Compact™ Series

The New
Strong's®
Compact Bible Concordance

James Strong, LL.D., S.T.D.

Thomas Nelson
Since 1798

NASHVILLE DALLAS MEXICO CITY RIO DE JANEIRO BEIJING

Library of Congress Cataloging-in Publication Data

Strong, James, 1822-1894.

   [New exhaustive concordance of the Bible]

   The new Strong's concordance of the Bible: compact edition / James Strong.

     p.   cm.

   ISBN-10: 0-7852-5250-9 (pb)

   ISBN-13: 978-0-7852-5250-4 (pb)

   1. Bible—Concordance, English. 2. Hebrew language—Dictionaries—English. 3. Bible—Index. 4. Greek language, Biblical—Dictionaries—English. I. Title.

BS425.S83 1996

220.5'2033—dc20   96-19866

                                        CIP

Printed in the United States of America

9 10 11 12 13 —10 09 08

PREFACE

For over a century, Bible readers have relied on *Strong's Exhaustive Concordance of the Bible* to guide them to any passage in the Bible. Recently this standard reference work has been completely re-typeset and corrected as *The New Strong's™ Exhaustive Concordance of the Bible*. *The New Strong's™* family of reference works continues the Strong's tradition of dependable information and clear presentation.

The New Strong's™ Compact Bible Concordance contains not only the clear typography of the Exhaustive edition but other special features as well. Proper names for people and places that share the same name have been separated and grouped under the appropriate entry. Variant spellings of proper names from other versions of the Bible have been listed and cross-referenced, allowing this concordance to be used with modern translations.

The *Compact* edition is designed to serve better the needs of the average reader. It preserves the excellent scholarship of Dr. James Strong in a more convenient format, providing a complete concordance without the Hebrew and Greek detail. It is easily portable, with clear, legible type.

To accomplish this more manageable size, this edition eliminates 168 words that the reader is not likely to use in searching for particular passages in Scripture:

a	been	for	I
about	before	forth	if
according	both	from	in
after	brought	given	into
again	but	go	is
against	by	good	it
all	came	great	land
also	cast	had	let
am	cause	hand	like
among	children	hast	made
an	city	hath	make
and	come	have	man
any	days	he	many
are	did	her	may
art	do	high	me
as	done	him	men
at	down	himself	mine
away	even	his	more
be	every	how	my
because	fathers	hundred	neither

no	said	their	unto
nor	saith	them	up
not	same	themselves	upon
now	saw	then	us
O	say	there	was
of	saying	therefore	way
off	see	therein	we
on	sent	thereof	went
one	set	thereon	were
ones	shall, shalt	thereto	what
or	she	these	when
our	should	they	which
out	so	thine	who
over	sons	thing(s)	whom
own	sought	this	will
part	spake	those	with
parts	speak	thou	ye
pass	take	thy	yea
people	than	time	yet
place	that	to	you
places	the	took	your
put	thee	two	

Entries for the following forty words have been condensed by retaining the more important passages enabling the user to quickly find specific verses:

Aaron	Egypt	house	Moses
another	evil	Israel	name
behold	father	Jerusalem	servant
bring	give	Jesus	servants
called	God	Judah	son
Christ	hear	king	together
David	heard	know	voice
day	heart	lord	word
earth	heaven	midst	words
eat	holy	might	years

CONCORDANCE

A See PREFACE.

AARON (a'-ur-un) See PREFACE. SEE ALSO
AARON'S, AARONITES. *First high priest of
Israel; brother of Moses.*
Is not A the Levite thy brother *a* .... Ex 4:14
A went in, and told Pharaoh, Thus.......... Ex 5:1
A cast down his rod before..................... Ex 7:10
LORD spake unto Moses, Say unto A ...... Ex 7:19
A did so, as the LORD commanded......... Ex 7:20
and A and Hur stayed up his hands, ... Ex 17:12
take thou unto thee A thy brother.......... Ex 28:1
me in the priest's office, even A .... Ex 28:1
ears, and brought them unto A .... Ex 32:3
when A saw it, he built an altar .... Ex 32:5
they made the calf, which A made......... Ex 32:35
Take A and his sons with him, and......... Lev 8:2
And Moses brought A and his sons, ... Lev 8:6
And the LORD spake unto A, saying, ... Lev 10:8
A and his sons shall go in, and.............. Num 4:19
against Moses and against A................... Num 16:3
the rod of A for the house of .... Num 17:8
LORD spake unto Moses and A .... Num 20:12
A died there in the top of the................ Num 20:28
But A and his sons offered upon.......... 1Chr 6:49
and A whom he had chosen.................... Ps 105:26
wife was of the daughters of A .... Lk 1:5
Saying unto A, Make us gods to go..... Acts 7:40
that is called of God, as was A............. Heb 5:4
be called after the order of A .... Heb 7:11

AARONITES (a'-ur-un-ites) *Priests; Aaron's
descendants.*
Jehoiada was the leader of the A......... 1Chr 12:27
of the A, Zadok 1Chr 27:17

AARON'S (a'-ur-uns)
Eleazar A son took him one of the .... Ex 6:25
but A rod swallowed up their rods .... Ex 7:12
Abihu, Eleazar and Ithamar, A sons, ... Ex 28:1
that they may make A garments to .... Ex 28:3
and they shall be upon A heart .... Ex 28:30
And it shall be upon A forehead .... Ex 28:38
for A sons thou shalt make coats, ... Ex 28:40
of the ram of a consecration .... Ex 29:26
And it shall be A and his sons' by.......... Ex 29:28
A sons shall bring the blood, and............ Lev 1:5
A sons shall lay the parts, the.................. Lev 1:8
A sons shall sprinkle his blood .... Lev 1:11
bring it to A sons the priests................... Lev 2:2
the meat offerings shall be A .... Lev 2:3
of the meat offering shall be A .... Lev 2:10
A sons the priests shall sprinkle .... Lev 3:2
A sons shall burn it on the altar............. Lev 3:5
A sons shall sprinkle the blood .... Lev 3:8
but the breast shall be A .... Lev 7:31
of the anointing oil upon A head .... Lev 8:12
And Moses brought A sons, and put ..... Lev 8:13
it upon the tip of A right ear................... Lev 8:23
And he brought A sons, and Moses ...... Lev 8:24
And he put all upon A hands................. Lev 8:27
A sons presented unto him the............. Lev 9:12
A sons presented unto him the............. Lev 9:18
And it shall be A and his sons'.............. Lev 24:9
thou shalt write A name upon the....... Num 17:3
Bring A rod again before the .... Num 17:10
down upon the beard, even A beard..... Ps 133:2
A rod that budded, and the tables........ Heb 9:4

ABADDON (ab-ad'-dun) *Angel of the Abyss.*
name in the Hebrew tongue is A........... Rev 9:11

ABAGTHA (ab-ag'-thah) *Servant of King
Ahasuerus.*
Biztha, Harbona, Bigtha, and A .... Est 1:10

ABANA (ab-ay'-nah) *A river in Syria.*
Are not A and Pharpar, rivers of......... 2Kin 5:12

ABANAH See ABANA.

ABARIM (ab'-ar-im) See IJE-ABARIM. *A
mountain range in Moab.*
Get thee up into this mount A .... Num 27:12
and pitched in the mountains of A .... Num 33:47
departed from the mountains of A .... Num 33:48
Get thee up into this mountain A......... Deut 32:49

ABASE
every one that is proud, and a him....... Job 40:11
nor a himself for the noise of .... Is 31:4
is low, and a him that is high............... Eze 21:26
walk in pride he is able to a .... Dan 4:37

ABASED
shall exalt himself shall be a .... Mt 23:12
exalteth himself shall be a .... Lk 14:11

---

that exalteth himself shall be a .... Lk 18:14
I know both how to be a, and I............. Phil 4:12

ABASING
Have I committed an offence in a......... 2Cor 11:7

ABATED
and fifty days were a .... Gen 8:3
to see if the waters were a from............. Gen 8:8
waters were a from off the earth.......... Gen 8:11
it shall be a from thy estimation .... Lev 27:18
not dim, nor his natural force a............ Deut 34:7
Then their anger was a toward him...... Judg 8:3

ABBA (ab'-bah) *Aramaic for "Father."*
And he said, A, Father, all things........... Mk 14:36
of adoption, whereby we cry, A............. Rom 8:15
Son into your hearts, crying, A .... Gal 4:6

ABDA (ab'-dah)
1. Father of Adoniram.
Adoniram the son of A was over............ 1Kin 4:6
2. A chief Levite after the exile.
A the son of Shammua, the son of ...... Neh 11:17

ABDEEL (ab-de-el) *Father of Shelemiah.*
Azriel, and Shelemiah the son of A ..... Jer 36:26

ABDI (ab'-di)
1. Levite grandfather of Ethan.
the son of Kishi, the son of A 1Chr 6:44
sons of Merari, Kish the son of A 2Chr 29:12
2. Married a foreigner while in exile.
Zechariah, and Jehiel, and A .... Ezr 10:26

ABDIEL (ab'-de-el) *Son of Guni.*
Ahi the son of A, the son of Guni........... 1Chr 5:15

ABDON (ab'-dun)
1. Levitical city in Asher.
her suburbs, A with her suburbs, ... Josh 21:30
suburbs, and A with her suburbs, ... 1Chr 6:74
2. A judge of Israel.
after him A the son of Hillel, a .... Judg 12:13
And A the son of Hillel the, ... Judg 12:15
3. A Benjamite in Jerusalem.
And A, and Zichri, and Hanan,............. 1Chr 8:23
4. Son of Jehiel.
And his firstborn son A, and Zur,......... 1Chr 8:30
And his firstborn son A, then Zur,........ 1Chr 9:36
5. Son of Micah.
A the son of Micah, and Shaphan....... 2Chr 34:20

ABED-NEGO (ab-ed'-ne-go) *A companion of
Daniel in captivity.*
and to Azariah, of A................................ Dan 1:7
and set Shadrach, Meshach, and A ...... Dan 2:49
Babylon, Shadrach, Meshach, and A..... Dan 3:12
to bring Shadrach, Meshach, and A..... Dan 3:13
true, O Shadrach, Meshach, and A ...... Dan 3:14
Shadrach, Meshach, and A, answered... Dan 3:16
against Shadrach, Meshach, and A...... Dan 3:19
to bind Shadrach, Meshach, and A ..... Dan 3:20
took up Shadrach, Meshach, and A ..... Dan 3:22
men, Shadrach, Meshach, and A .... Dan 3:23
and said, Shadrach, Meshach, and A... Dan 3:26
Then Shadrach, Meshach, and A .... Dan 3:26
God of Shadrach, Meshach, and A....... Dan 3:28
God of Shadrach, Meshach, and A....... Dan 3:29
promoted Shadrach, Meshach, and A.. Dan 3:30

ABEL (a'-bel)
1. Second son of Adam.
And she again bare his brother A .... Gen 4:2
A was a keeper of sheep, but Cain........ Gen 4:2
And A, he also brought of........................ Gen 4:4
And the LORD had respect unto A......... Gen 4:4
And Cain talked with A his brother ...... Gen 4:8
rose up against A his brother.................. Gen 4:8
unto Cain, Where is A thy brother .... Gen 4:9
me another seed instead of A .... Gen 4:25
from the blood of righteous A .... Mt 23:35
the blood of A unto the........................ Lk 11:51
By faith A offered unto God a.............. Heb 11:4
better things than that of A .... Heb 12:24
2. Great stone near Beth-shemesh.
even unto the great stone of A 1Sa 6:18
3. A city in Naphtali.
all the tribes of Israel unto A 2Sa 20:14
besieged him in A of Beth-maachah ... 2Sa 20:15
shall surely ask counsel at A 2Sa 20:18

ABEL ACACIA GROVE See ABEL-SHITTIM.

ABEL BETH MAACAH See BETH-MAACHAH.

ABEL-BETH-MAACHAH (a'-bel-beth-ma'-a-
kah) *A city in northern Israel.*
and smote Ijon, and Dan, and A 1Kin 15:20
of Assyria, and took Ijon, and A 2Kin 15:29

ABEL-MAIM (a'-bel-ma'-im) *Another name
for Abel-beth-maachah.*
and they smote Ijon, and Dan, and A. 2Chr 16:4

ABEL-MEHOLAH (a'-bel-me-ho'-lah) *A city
in Issachar.*
Zererath, and to the border of A .... Judg 7:22
Jezreel, the son of Shaphat of A 1Kin 4:12
Elisha the son of Shaphat of A 1Kin 19:16

ABEL-MIZRAIM (a'-bel-miz'-ra-im) *A place
east of the Jordan River.*
the name of it was called A .... Gen 50:11

ABEL-SHITTIM (a'-bel-shit'-tim) *A place in
Moab.*
even unto A in the plains of Moab ...... Num 33:49

ABEZ (a'-bez) *A place in Issachar.*
And Rabbith, and Kishion, and .... Josh 19:20

ABHOR
and my soul shall not a you .... Lev 26:11
or if your soul a my judgments, ... Lev 26:15
idols, and my soul shall a you .... Lev 26:30
them away, neither will I a them............ Lev 26:44
it, and thou shalt utterly a it................. Deut 7:26
Thou shalt not a an Edomite .... Deut 23:7
thou shalt not a an Egyptian .... Deut 23:7
people Israel utterly to a him 1Sa 27:12
and mine own clothes shall a me .... Job 9:31
They a me, they flee far from me,........ Job 30:10
Wherefore I a myself, and repent......... Job 42:6
the LORD will a the bloody .... Ps 5:6
I hate and a lying .... Ps 119:163
people curse, nations shall a him...... Prov 24:24
Do not a us, for thy name's sake, ... Jer 14:21
gate, and they a him that speaketh.... Amos 5:10
I a the excellency of Jacob, and........... Amos 6:8
that a judgment, and pervert all .... Mic 3:9
A that which is evil.................................. Rom 12:9

ABHORRED
to be a in the eyes of Pharaoh .... Ex 5:21
things, and therefore I a them .... Lev 20:23
because their soul a my statutes .... Lev 26:43
he a them, because of the .... Deut 32:19
for men a the offering of the .... Deut 32:19
that thou art a of their fathers' 2Sa 16:21
he a Israel, and reigned over............... 1Kin 11:25
All my inward friends a me................... Job 19:19
For he hath not despised nor a .... Ps 22:24
he was wroth, and greatly a Israel...... Ps 78:59
But thou hast cast off and a .... Ps 89:38
insomuch that he a his own................ Ps 106:40
he that is a of the LORD shall.............. Prov 22:14
he hath a his sanctuary, he hath .... Lam 2:7
and hast made thy beauty to be a ...... Eze 16:25
them, and their soul also a me .... Zec 11:8

ABHORREST
the land that thou a shall be .... Is 7:16
thou that a idols, dost thou .... Rom 2:22

ABHORRETH
So that his life a bread, and his .... Job 33:20
the covetous, whom the LORD a .... Ps 10:3
he a not evil... Ps 36:4
Their soul a all manner of meat......... Ps 107:18
to him whom the nation a .... Is 49:7

ABHORRING
they shall be an a unto all flesh........... Is 66:24

ABI (a'-bi) See ABI-ALBON, ABI-EZER. *Mother of
King Hezekiah.*
His mother's name was also A 2Kin 18:2

ABIA (a-bi'-ah) See ABIAH, ABIJAH, ABIJAM.
1. A son of Rehoboam.
Rehoboam, A his son, Asa his son, ... 1Chr 3:10
and Roboam begat A .... Mt 1:7
and A begat Asa... Mt 1:7
2. A priest.
Zacharias, of the course of A .... Lk 1:5

ABIAH (ab-i'-ah) See ABIA.
1. Son of Samuel.
and the name of his second, A.............. 1Sa 8:2
the firstborn Vashni, and A 1Chr 6:28
2. Mother of Ashur.
then A Hezron's wife bare him 1Chr 2:24

3. *Son of Becher.*
and Omri, and Jerimoth, and A 1Chr 7:8

ABI-ALBON (ab'-i-al'-bun) A "mighty man" of David.
A the Arbathite, Azmaveth the.............. 2Sa 23:31

ABIASAPH (ab-i'-as-af) See EBI-ASAPH. A son of Korah.
Assir, and Elkanah, and A .... Ex 6:24

ABIATHAR (ab-i'-uth-ur) See ABITHAR's. High Priest during David's reign.
the son of Ahitub, named A................. 1Sa 22:20
A shewed David that Saul had............. 1Sa 22:21
And David said unto A, I knew it 1Sa 22:22
when A the son of Ahimelech fled......... 1Sa 23:6
and he said to A the priest.................... 1Sa 23:9
And David said to A the priest............... 1Sa 30:7
A brought thither the ephod to 1Sa 30:7
Ahitub, and Ahimelech the son of A 2Sa 8:17
A went up, until all the people............. 2Sa 15:24
thy son, and Jonathan the son of A 2Sa 15:27
A carried the ark of God again to......... 2Sa 15:29
with thee Zadok and A the priests......... 2Sa 15:35
tell it to Zadok and A the priests 2Sa 15:35
to A the priests, Thus and thus............. 2Sa 15:36
to A the priests, saying, Speak............. 2Sa 19:11
and Zadok and A were the priests 2Sa 20:25
of Zeruiah, and with A the priest.......... 1Kin 1:7
A the priest, and Joab the captain 1Kin 1:19
of the host, and A the priest................. 1Kin 1:25
the son of A the priest came 1Kin 1:42
for A the priest, and for Joab 1Kin 2:22
unto A the priest said the king............. 1Kin 2:26
So Solomon thrust out A from.............. 1Kin 2:27
did the king put in the room of A........ 1Kin 2:35
and Zadok and A were the priests........ 1Kin 4:4
A the priests, and for the Levites........ 1Chr 15:11
Ahitub, and Ahimelech the son of A 1Chr 18:16
priest, and Ahimelech the son of A 1Chr 24:6
Jehoiada the son of Benaiah, and A 1Chr 27:34
in the days of A the high priest............ Mk 2:26

ABIATHAR'S (ab-i'-uth-urs)
Zadok's son, and Jonathan A son 2Sa 15:36

ABIB (ab'-bib) See TEL-ABIB. First month of the Hebrew year.
day came ye out in the month A.......... Ex 13:4
the time appointed of the month A....... Ex 23:15
thee, in the time of the month A........... Ex 34:18
for in the month A thou camest........... Ex 34:18
Observe the month of A, and keep....... Deut 16:1
for in the month of A the LORD............. Deut 16:1

ABIDA (ab'-id-ah) See ABIDAH. A son of Midian.
and Epher, and Hanoch, and A 1Chr 1:33

ABIDAN (ab'-id-ah) See ABIDA. Same as Abida. Ephah, and Epher, and Hanoch, and A Gen 25:4

ABIDAN (ab'-id-an) Son of Gideoni.
A the son of Gideoni............................. Num 1:11
shall be A the son of Gideoni............... Num 2:22
On the ninth day A the son of.............. Num 7:60
offering of A the son of Gideoni........... Num 7:65
Benjamin was A the son of Gideoni...... Num 10:24

ABIDE
but we will a in the street all .... Gen 19:2
young men, A ye here with the ass...... Gen 22:5
Let the damsel a with us a few.............. Gen 24:55
a with me .... Gen 29:19
let thy servant a instead of the............ Gen 44:33
a ye every man in his place, let............ Ex 16:29
Therefore shall ye a at the door .... Lev 8:35
a with thee all night until the .... Lev 19:13
earth, and they a over against me........ Num 22:5
do ye a without the camp seven.......... Num 31:19
Every thing that may a the fire............. Num 31:23
he shall a in it unto the death.............. Num 35:25
shall a in your cities which I................. Deut 3:19
Judah shall a in their coast on............. Josh 18:5
the house of Joseph shall a in.............. Josh 18:5
but a here fast by my maidens............. Ruth 2:8
the LORD, and there a for ever.............. Ps 61:7
God of Israel shall not a with us 1Sa 5:7
a in a secret place, and hide................ 1Sa 19:2
unto David, and in the hold 1Sa 22:5
A thou with me, fear not....................... 1Sa 22:23
made also to a at the brook Besor 1Sa 30:21
And Israel, and Judah, a in tents 2Sa 11:11
to thy place, and a with the king.......... 2Sa 15:19
will I be, and with him will I a 2Sa 16:18
place for thee to a in for ever 1Kin 8:13
a now at home....................................... 2Chr 25:19
that ye a in the siege in....................... 2Chr 32:10
nor a in the paths thereof .... Job 24:13
a in the covert to lie in wait .... Job 38:40
to serve thee, or a by thy crib............. Job 39:9
who shall a in thy tabernacle .... Ps 15:1
I will a in thy tabernacle for................. Ps 61:4
He shall a before God for ever .... Ps 61:7
shall a under the shadow of the .... Ps 91:1
her feet a not in her house .... Prov 7:11
he that hath it shall a satisfied .... Prov 19:23
for that shall a with him of his............ Eccl 8:15
not be able to a his indignation............ Jer 10:10
If ye will still a in this land................... Jer 42:10
the LORD, no man shall a there............. Jer 49:18
there shall no man a there.................... Jer 49:33
so shall no man a there, neither .... Jer 50:40

Thou shalt a for me many days............. Hos 3:3
shall a many days without a king......... Hos 3:4
the sword shall a on his cities .... Hos 11:6
and who can a it .... Joel 2:11
and they shall a .... Mic 5:4
who can a in the fierceness of............. Nah 1:6
But who may a the day of his............... Mal 3:2
there a till ye go thence .... Mt 10:11
there a till ye depart from that .... Mk 6:10
house ye enter into, there a .... Lk 9:4
for to day I must a at thy house............ Lk 19:5
him, saying, A with us .... Lk 24:29
on me should not a in darkness........... Jn 12:46
that he may a with you for ever............ Jn 14:16
A in me, and I in you............................. Jn 15:4
itself, except it a in the vine .... Jn 15:4
no more can ye, except ye a in me ...... Jn 15:4
If a man a not in me, he is cast........... Jn 15:6
If ye a in me, and my words a .... Jn 15:7
a in me, and my words a in you .... Jn 15:7
ye shall a in my love .... Jn 15:10
commandments, and a in his love .... Jn 15:10
it pleased Silas to a there still.............. Acts 15:34
come into my house, and a there......... Acts 16:15
that bonds and afflictions a me............ Acts 20:23
Except these a in the ship .... Acts 27:31
If they a not still in unbelief................. Rom 11:23
If any man's work a which he hath 1Cor 3:14
good for them if they a even as I 1Cor 7:8
Let every man a in the same................ 1Cor 7:20
he is called, therein a with God 1Cor 7:24
But she is happier if she so a 1Cor 7:40
And it may be that I will a 1Cor 16:6
Nevertheless to a in the flesh is........... Phil 1:24
confidence, I know that I shall a .... Phil 1:25
the to a still at Ephesus 1Ti 1:3
Let that therefore a in you.................... 1Jn 2:24
taught you, ye shall a in him 1Jn 2:27
And now, little children, a in him 1Jn 2:28

ABIDETH
all that a not the fire ye shall .... Num 31:23
king, Behold, he is at Jerusalem 2Sa 16:3
a on the rock, upon the crag of .... Job 39:28
man being in honour a not .... Ps 49:12
them, even he that a of old................... Ps 55:19
established the earth, and it a .... Ps 119:90
cannot be removed, but a for ever .... Ps 125:1
reproof of life a among the wise........... Prov 15:31
but the earth a for ever .... Eccl 1:4
He that a in this city shall die.............. Jer 21:9
but the wrath of God a on him .... Jn 3:36
the servant a not in the house............. Jn 8:35
but the Son a ever................................ Jn 8:35
the ground and die, it a alone.............. Jn 12:24
of the law that Christ a for ever .... Jn 12:34
He that a in me, and I in him, the .... Jn 15:5
now a faith, hope, charity, these 1Cor 13:13
we believe not, yet he a faithful 2Ti 2:13
a a priest continually .... Heb 7:3
God, which liveth and a for ever 1Pet 1:23
He that saith he a in him ought........... 1Jn 2:6
loveth his brother a in the light 1Jn 2:10
and the word of God a in you 1Jn 2:14
doeth the will of God a for ever 1Jn 2:17
ye have received of him a in you 1Jn 2:27
Whosoever a in him sinneth not........... 1Jn 3:6
loveth not his brother a in death......... 1Jn 3:14
And hereby we know that he a in us 1Jn 3:24
a not in the doctrine of Christ,............. 2Jn 9
He that a in the doctrine of 2Jn 9

ABIDING
he saw Israel a in his tents................... Num 24:2
a with her in the chamber .... Judg 16:9
liers in wait a in the chamber .... Judg 16:12
driven me out this day from a in.......... 1Sa 26:19
as a shadow, and there is none a 1Chr 29:15
country shepherds a in the field............ Lk 2:8
And ye have not his word a in you........ Jn 5:38
were in that city a certain days .... Acts 16:12
hath eternal life a in him 1Jn 3:15

ABIEL (a'-bi-el)
1. Grandfather of King Saul.
whose name was Kish, the son of A..... 1Sa 9:1
father of Abner was the son of A.......... 1Sa 14:51
2. A "mighty man" of David.
brooks of Gaash, A the Arbathite,........ 1Chr 11:32

ABI-EZER (ab-i-e'-zur) See ABIEZRITE, JEEZER.
1. A descendant of Manasseh.
and A was gathered after him .... Judg 6:34
better than the vintage of A .... Judg 8:2

ABIEZER
for the children of A, and for the .... Josh 17:2
A the Anethothite, Mebunnai the 2Sa 23:27
Hammoleketh bare Ishod, and A 1Chr 7:18
the Tekoite, A the Antothite,................. 1Chr 11:28
ninth month was A the Anetothite 1Chr 27:12

ABI-EZRITE (ab-i-ez'-rite) See ABI-EZRITES. A descendant of Abiezer.
that pertained unto Joash the A........... Judg 6:11

ABI-EZRITES (ab-i-ez'-rites)
day it is yet in Ophrah of the A............ Judg 6:24
his father, in Ophrah of the A............... Judg 8:32

ABIGAIL (ab'-e-gul)
1. A wife of David.
and the name of his wife A................... 1Sa 25:3
But one of the young men told A........... 1Sa 25:14

Then A made haste, and took two....... 1Sa 25:18
when A saw David, she hasted, and 1Sa 25:23
And David said to A, Blessed be 1Sa 25:32
And A came to Nabal 1Sa 25:36
sent and communed with A 1Sa 25:39
of David were come to A to Carmel..... 1Sa 25:40
A hasted, and arose, and rode upon... 1Sa 25:42
the Carmelitess, Nabal's wife 1Sa 27:3
A the wife of Nabal the Carmelite 1Sa 30:5
A Nabal's wife the Carmelite................ 2Sa 2:2
A of A the wife of Nabal the................. 2Sa 3:3
Daniel, of A the Carmelitess................. 1Chr 3:1
2. Mother of Amasa.
that went in to A the daughter of 2Sa 17:25
Whose sisters were Zeruiah, and A 1Chr 2:16
And A bare Amasa 1Chr 2:17

ABIHAIL (ab-e-ha'-il)
1. Head of Levital family of Merari.
of Merari was Zuriel the son of A .... Num 3:35
2. Wife of Abishur.
name of the wife of Abishur was A 1Chr 2:29
3. Chief of a family of Gad.
the children of A the son of Huri.......... 1Chr 5:14
4. Descendant of Eliab.
A the daughter of Eliab the son 2Chr 11:18
5. Father of Esther.
the daughter of A the uncle of .... Est 2:15
the queen, the daughter of A .... Est 9:29

ABIHU (a-bi'-hew) A son of Aaron.
and she bare him Nadab, and A .... Ex 6:23
LORD, thou, and Aaron, Nadab, and A .. Ex 24:1
up Moses, and Aaron, Nadab, and A .... Ex 24:9
office, even Aaron, Nadab and A .... Ex 28:1
And Nadab and A, the sons of Aaron,... Lev 10:1
Nadab the firstborn, and A .... Num 3:2
A died before the LORD, when they ...... Num 3:4
unto Aaron was born Nadab, and A ..... Num 26:60
A died, when they offered strange....... Num 26:61
Nadab, and A, Eleazar, and Ithamar 1Chr 6:3
Nadab, and A, Eleazar, and Ithamar 1Chr 24:1
A died before their father, and............ 1Chr 24:2

ABIHUD (a-bi'-hud) A son of Bela.
Bela were, Addar, and Gera, and A 1Chr 8:3

ABIJAH (a-bi'-jah) See ABIA, ABIJAM.
1. A son of Jeroboam I.
At that time A the son of 1Kin 14:1
2. A priest during David's reign.
to Hakkoz, the eighth to A 1Chr 24:10
3. A son of Rehoboam.
which bare him A, and Attai, and......... 2Chr 11:20
Rehoboam made A the son of............... 2Chr 11:22
A his son reigned in his stead 2Chr 12:16
began A to reign over Judah 2Chr 13:1
And there was war between A 2Chr 13:2
A set the battle in array with an.......... 2Chr 13:3
A stood up upon mount Zemaraim, ... 2Chr 13:4
Jeroboam and all Israel before A 2Chr 13:15
A and his people slew them.................. 2Chr 13:17
A pursued after Jeroboam, and took.... 2Chr 13:19
strength again in the days of A 2Chr 13:20
But A waxed mighty, and married......... 2Chr 13:21
And the rest of the acts of A 2Chr 13:22
So A slept with his fathers, and 2Chr 14:1
4. Mother of King Hezekiah.
And his mother's name was A 2Chr 29:1
5. A priest in Nehemiah's time.
Meshullam, A, Mijamin,........................ Neh 10:7
6. A person who returned from Exile under Zerubbabel.
Iddo, Ginnetho, A,................................. Neh 12:4
Of A, Zichri,... Neh 12:17

ABIJAM (a-bi'-jum) Son and successor of King Rehoboam.
A his son reigned in his stead 1Kin 14:31
son of Nebat reigned A over Judah 1Kin 15:1
Now the rest of the acts of A 1Kin 15:7
and there was war between A 1Kin 15:7
And A slept with his fathers.................. 1Kin 15:8

ABILENE (ab-i-le'-ne) A Roman tetrarchy in northern Palestine.
and Lysanias the tetrarch of A .... Lk 3:1

ABILITY
according to his a that vowed............... Lev 27:8
They gave after their a into the............ Ezr 2:69
We after our a have redeemed our ...... Neh 5:8
such as had a in them to stand in........ Dan 1:4
man according to his several .... Mt 25:15
every man according to his a .... Acts 11:29
it as of the a which God giveth............. 1Pet 4:11

ABIMAEL (a-bim'-ah-el) A son of Joktan in Arabia.
And Obal, and A, and Sheba,................ Gen 10:28
And Ebal, and A, and Sheba,................ 1Chr 1:22

ABIMELECH (a-bim'-e-lek) See ABIMELECH'S.
1. Philistine king in Abraham's time.
A king of Gerar sent, and took............. Gen 20:2
But God came to A in a dream by .... Gen 20:3
But A had not come near her................ Gen 20:4
Therefore A rose early in the................ Gen 20:8
Then A called Abraham, and said .... Gen 20:9
A said unto Abraham, What sawest ...... Gen 20:10
A took sheep, and oxen, and................ Gen 20:14
A said, Behold, my land is before .... Gen 20:15
And God healed A, and his wife, and ... Gen 20:17
all the wombs of the house of A.......... Gen 20:18

came to pass at that time, that *A*..... Gen 21:22
Abraham reproved *A* because of a..... Gen 21:25
A said, I wot not who hath done..... Gen 21:26
and oxen, and gave them unto *A*..... Gen 21:27
A said unto Abraham, What mean..... Gen 21:29
then *A* rose up, and Phichol the..... Gen 21:32
Isaac went unto *A* king of the..... Gen 26:1
that *A* king of the Philistines..... Gen 26:8
A called Isaac, and said, Behold,..... Gen 26:9
A said, What is this thou hast..... Gen 26:10
A charged all his people, saying,..... Gen 26:11
A said unto Isaac, Go from us..... Gen 26:16
Then *A* went to him from Gerar, and..... Gen 26:26
  2. Son of Gideon.
him a son, whose name he called *A*..... Judg 8:31
A the son of Jerubbaal went to..... Judg 9:1
their hearts inclined to follow *A*..... Judg 9:3
wherewith *A* hired vain and light..... Judg 9:4
of Millo, and went, and made *A* king..... Judg 9:6
in that ye have made *A* king...... Judg 9:16
upon one stone, and have made *A*..... Judg 9:18
this day, then rejoice ye in *A*..... Judg 9:19
if not, let fire come out from *A*..... Judg 9:20
the house of Millo, and devour *A*..... Judg 9:20
there, for fear of *A* his brother..... Judg 9:21
When *A* had reigned three years..... Judg 9:22
God sent an evil spirit between *A*..... Judg 9:23
dealt treacherously with *A*..... Judg 9:23
he laid upon *A* their brother..... Judg 9:24
and it was told *A*..... Judg 9:25
and did eat and drink, and cursed *A*..... Judg 9:27
the son of Ebed said, Who is *A*..... Judg 9:28
then would I remove *A*..... Judg 9:29
And he said to *A*, Increase thine..... Judg 9:29
he sent messengers after *A* privily..... Judg 9:31
A rose up, and all the people that..... Judg 9:33
A rose up, and the people that..... Judg 9:35
wherewith thou saidst, Who is *A*..... Judg 9:38
men of Shechem, and fought with *A*..... Judg 9:39
A chased him, and he fled before..... Judg 9:40
And *A* dwelt at Arumah..... Judg 9:41
and they told *A*..... Judg 9:41
And *A*, and the company that was..... Judg 9:44
A fought against the city all..... Judg 9:45
And it was told *A*, that all the..... Judg 9:47
A gat him up to mount Zalmon, he..... Judg 9:48
A took an axe in his hand, and..... Judg 9:48
man his bough, and followed *A*..... Judg 9:49
Then went *A* to Thebez, and..... Judg 9:50
A came unto the tower, and fought..... Judg 9:52
men of Israel saw that *A* was dead..... Judg 9:55
God rendered the wickedness of *A*..... Judg 9:56
after *A* there arose to defend..... Judg 10:1
Who smote *A* the son of..... 2Sa 11:21
  3. Son of Abiathar the High Priest.
A the son of Abiathar, were the..... 1Chr 18:16
  4. Used in title of Psalm 34.
he changed his behaviour before *A*..... Ps 34:t

ABIMELECH'S (a-bim'-e-leks)
which *A* servants had violently..... Gen 21:25
piece of a millstone upon *A* head..... Judg 9:53

ABINADAB (a-bin'-ah-dab)
  1. A Levite of Kirjath-jearim.
into the house of *A* in the hill..... 1Sa 7:1
the house of *A* that was in Gibeah..... 2Sa 6:3
and Uzzah and Ahio, the sons of *A*..... 2Sa 6:3
house of *A* which was at Gibeah..... 2Sa 6:4
a new cart out of the house of *A*..... 1Chr 13:7
  2. A brother of David.
Then Jesse called *A*, and made him..... 1Sa 16:8
first born, and next unto him *A*..... 1Sa 17:13
A the second, and Shimma the third... 1Chr 2:13
  3. A son of King Saul.
Philistines slew Jonathan, and *A*..... 1Sa 31:2
Jonathan, and Malchi-shua, and *A*..... 1Chr 8:33
Jonathan, and Malchi-shua, and *A*..... 1Chr 9:39
Philistines slew Jonathan, and *A*..... 1Chr 10:2
  4. Father of an officer of Solomon.
The son of *A*, in all the region..... 1Kin 4:11

ABINOAM (a-bin'-o-am) *Father of Barak.*
son of *A* out of Kedesh-naphtali...... Judg 4:6
of *A* was gone up to mount Tabor...... Judg 4:12
and Barak the son of *A* on that day..... Judg 5:1
captivity captive, thou son of *A*..... Judg 5:12

ABIRAM (a-bi'-rum)
  1. A conspirator against Moses.
the son of Levi, and Dathan and *A*..... Num 16:1
sent to call Dathan and *A*..... Num 16:12
tabernacle of Korah, Dathan, and *A*..... Num 16:24
went unto Dathan and *A*..... Num 16:25
tabernacle of Korah, Dathan, and *A*..... Num 16:27
A came out, and stood in the door..... Num 16:27
Nemuel, and Dathan, and *A*..... Num 26:9
This is that Dathan and *A*, which..... Num 26:9
And what he did unto Dathan and *A*..... Deut 11:6
and covered the company of *A*..... Ps 106:17
  2. Son of Hiel the Bethelite.
thereof in *A* his firstborn..... 1Kin 16:34

ABISHAG (a-bi'-shag) *An attendant of David.*
found *A* a Shunammite, and brought..... 1Kin 1:3
the Shunammite ministered unto..... 1Kin 1:15
that he give me *A* the Shunammite..... 1Kin 2:17
Let *A* the Shunammite be given to..... 1Kin 2:21
And why dost thou ask *A* the..... 1Kin 2:22

ABISHAI (a-bi'-e-shahee) *David's nephew.*
to *A* the son of Zeruiah, brother..... 1Sa 26:6
A said, I will go down with thee..... 1Sa 26:6

A came to the people by night..... 1Sa 26:7
Then said *A* to David, God hath..... 1Sa 26:8
And David said to *A*, Destroy him..... 1Sa 26:9
sons of Zeruiah there, Joab, and *A*..... 2Sa 2:18
and *A* pursued after Abner..... 2Sa 2:24
A his brother slew Abner, because..... 2Sa 3:30
into the hand of *A* his brother..... 2Sa 10:10
then fled they also before *A*..... 2Sa 10:14
Then said *A* the son of Zeruiah..... 2Sa 16:9
And David said to *A*, and to all his..... 2Sa 16:11
the hand of *A* the son of Zeruiah..... 2Sa 18:2
And the king commanded Joab and *A*..... 2Sa 18:5
the king charged thee and *A*..... 2Sa 18:12
But *A* the son of Zeruiah answered..... 2Sa 19:21
And David said to *A*, Now shall..... 2Sa 20:6
A his brother pursued after Sheba..... 2Sa 20:10
But *A* the son of Zeruiah..... 2Sa 21:17
And *A*, the brother of Joab, the..... 2Sa 23:18
A, and Joab, and Asahel, these..... 1Chr 2:16
A the brother of Joab, he was..... 1Chr 11:20
The son Zeruiah slew of the..... 1Chr 18:12
unto the hand of *A* his brother..... 1Chr 19:11
fled before *A* his brother..... 1Chr 19:15

ABISHALOM (a-bish'-ah-lum) See ABSALOM.
Father of Maachah.
was Maachah, the daughter of *A*..... 1Kin 15:2
was Maachah, the daughter of *A*..... 1Kin 15:10

ABISHUA (a-bish'-u-ah) *Son of Phinehas.*
begat Phinehas, Phinehas begat *A*..... 1Chr 6:4
A begat Bukki, and Bukki begat..... 1Chr 6:5
son, Phinehas his son, *A* his son,..... 1Chr 6:50
And *A*, and Naaman, and Ahoah,..... 1Chr 8:4
The son of *A*, the son of Phinehas..... Ezr 7:5

ABISHUR (ab'-e-shur) *A son of Shammai.*
Nadab, and *A*..... 1Chr 2:28
name of the wife of *A* was Abihail..... 1Chr 2:29

ABITAL (ab'-e-tal) *A wife of David.*
fifth; Shephatiah the son of *A*..... 2Sa 3:4
The fifth, Shephatiah of *A*..... 1Chr 3:3

ABITUB (ab'-e-tub) *Son of Shaharaim.*
And of Hushim he begat *A*, and..... 1Chr 8:11

ABIUD (a-bi'-ud) *A descendant of Zerubbabel;*
ancestor of Jesus.
And Zorobabel begat *A*..... Mt 1:13
and *A* begat Eliakim..... Mt 1:13

ABJECTS
the *A* gathered themselves..... Ps 35:15

ABLE
the land was not *A* to bear them..... Gen 13:6
if thou be *a* to number them..... Gen 15:5
me and the children be *a* to endure..... Gen 33:14
one cannot be *a* to see the earth..... Ex 10:5
thou art not *a* to perform it..... Ex 18:18
out of all the people *a* men..... Ex 18:21
then thou shalt be *a* to endure..... Ex 18:23
Moses chose *a* men out of all..... Ex 18:25
Moses was not *a* to enter into the..... Ex 40:35
if he be not *a* to bring a lamb,..... Lev 5:7
But if he be not *a* to bring two,..... Lev 5:11
if she be not *a* to bring a lamb,..... Lev 12:8
pigeons, such as he is *a* to get..... Lev 14:22
Even such as he is *a* to get..... Lev 14:31
whose hand is not *a* to get that..... Lev 14:32
himself be *a* to redeem it..... Lev 25:26
But if he be not *a* to restore it..... Lev 25:28
or if he be *a*, he may redeem..... Lev 25:49
all that are *a* to go forth to *a*..... Num 1:3
all that were *a* to go forth to..... Num 1:20
all that were *a* to go forth to..... Num 1:22
all that were *a* to go forth to..... Num 1:24
all that were *a* to go forth to..... Num 1:26
all that were *a* to go forth to..... Num 1:28
all that were *a* to go forth to..... Num 1:30
all that were *a* to go forth to..... Num 1:32
all that were *a* to go forth to..... Num 1:34
all that were *a* to go forth to..... Num 1:36
all that were *a* to go forth to..... Num 1:38
all that were *a* to go forth to..... Num 1:40
all that were *a* to go forth to..... Num 1:42
all that were *a* to go forth to..... Num 1:45
I am not *a* to bear all this..... Num 11:14
for we are well *a* to overcome it..... Num 13:30
We be not *a* to go up against the..... Num 13:31
Because the LORD was not *a* to..... Num 14:16
I shall be *a* to overcome them,..... Num 22:11
am I not *a* indeed to promote thee..... Num 22:37
all that are *a* to go to war in..... Num 26:2
I am not *a* to bear you myself..... Deut 1:9
no man be *a* to stand before thee..... Deut 7:24
Because the LORD was not *a* to..... Deut 9:28
no man be *a* to stand before you..... Deut 11:25
that thou art not *a* to carry it..... Deut 14:24
Every man shall give as he is *a*..... Deut 16:17
then I shall be *a* to drive them..... Josh 14:12
no man hath been *a* to stand..... Josh 23:9
what was I *a* to do in comparison..... Judg 8:3
Who is *a* to stand before this..... 1Sa 6:20
If he be *a* to fight with me, and..... 1Sa 17:9
Thou art not *a* to go against this..... 1Sa 17:33
for who is *a* to judge this thy so..... 1Kin 3:9
were not *a* utterly to destroy..... 1Kin 9:21
all that were *a* to put on armour..... 1Kin 3:21
if thou be *a* on thy part to set..... 2Kin 18:23
for he shall not be *a* to deliver..... 2Kin 18:29

men to bear buckler and sword,..... 1Chr 5:18
very *a* men for the work of the..... 1Chr 9:13
a men for strength for the..... 1Chr 26:8
that we should be *a* to offer so..... 1Chr 29:14
But who is *a* to build him an..... 2Chr 2:6
a to receive the burnt offerings..... 2Chr 7:7
so that none is *a* to withstand..... 2Chr 20:6
they were not *a* to go to Tarshish..... 2Chr 20:37
a to go forth to war, that could..... 2Chr 25:5
The LORD is *a* to give thee much..... 2Chr 25:9
a to deliver their lands out of..... 2Chr 32:13
that your God should be *a* to..... 2Chr 32:14
a to deliver his people out of..... 2Chr 32:15
we are not *a* to stand without,..... Ezr 10:13
we are not *a* to build the wall..... Neh 4:10
who then is *a* to stand before me..... Job 41:10
them that they were not *a* to rise..... Ps 18:38
which they are not *a* to perform..... Ps 21:11
down, and shall not be *a* to rise..... Ps 36:12
me, so that I am not *a* to look up..... Ps 40:12
but who is *a* to stand before envy..... Prov 27:4
yet shall he not be *a* to find it..... Eccl 8:17
if thou be *a* on thy part to set..... Is 36:8
he shall not be *a* to deliver you..... Is 36:14
thou shalt not be *a* to put it off..... Is 47:11
so thou shalt be *a* to profit..... Is 47:12
not be *a* to abide his indignation..... Jer 10:10
they shall not be *a* to escape..... Jer 11:11
he shall not be *a* to hide himself..... Jer 49:10
from whom I am not *a* to rise up..... Lam 1:14
their gold shall not be *a* to..... Eze 7:19
a to live for his righteousness..... Eze 33:12
lambs as he shall be *a* to give..... Eze 46:5
to the lambs as he is *a* to give..... Eze 46:11
Art thou *a* to make known unto me..... Dan 2:26
our God whom we serve is *a* to..... Dan 3:17
not *a* to make known unto me the..... Dan 4:18
but thou art *a*..... Dan 4:18
walk in pride he is *a* to abase..... Dan 4:37
a to deliver thee from the lions..... Dan 6:20
the land is not *a* to bear all his..... Amos 7:10
a to deliver them in the day of..... Zeph 1:18
that God is *a* of these stones to..... Mt 3:9
Believe ye that I am *a* to do this..... Mt 9:28
but are not *a* to kill the soul..... Mt 10:28
which is *a* to destroy both soul..... Mt 10:28
He that is *a* to receive it, let..... Mt 19:12
Are ye *a* to drink of the cup that..... Mt 20:22
They say unto him, We are *a*..... Mt 20:22
no man was *a* to answer him a word... Mt 22:46
I am *a* to destroy the temple of..... Mt 26:61
them, as they were *a* to hear it..... Mk 4:33
not *a* to speak, until the day..... Lk 1:20
That God is *a* of these stones to..... Lk 3:8
If ye then be not *a* to do that..... Lk 12:26
to enter in, and shall not be *a*..... Lk 13:24
is not *a* to finish it, all that..... Lk 14:29
to build, and was not *a* to finish..... Lk 14:30
consulteth whether he be *a* with..... Lk 14:31
not be *a* to gainsay nor resist..... Lk 21:15
no man is *a* to pluck them out of..... Jn 10:29
now they were not *a* to draw it..... Jn 21:6
they were not *a* to resist the..... Acts 6:10
our fathers nor were *a* to bear..... Acts 15:10
which is *a* to build you up, and to..... Acts 20:32
said he, which among you are *a*..... Acts 25:5
he was *a* also to perform..... Rom 4:21
shall be *a* to separate us from..... Rom 8:39
for God is *a* to graft them in..... Rom 11:23
for God is *a* to make him stand..... Rom 14:4
a also to admonish one another..... Rom 15:14
hitherto ye were not *a* to bear it..... 1Cor 3:2
neither yet now are ye *a*..... 1Cor 3:2
not one that shall be *a* to judge..... 1Cor 6:5
to be tempted above that ye are *a*..... 1Cor 10:13
that ye may be *a* to bear it..... 1Cor 10:13
that we may be *a* to comfort them..... 2Cor 1:4
Who also hath made us *a* ministers..... 2Cor 3:6
God is *a* to make all grace abound..... 2Cor 9:8
May be *a* to comprehend with all..... Eph 3:18
Now unto him that is *a* to do..... Eph 3:20
that ye may be *a* to stand against..... Eph 6:11
that ye may be *a* to withstand in..... Eph 6:13
wherewith ye shall be *a* to quench..... Eph 6:16
to the working whereby he is *a*..... Phil 3:21
am persuaded that he is *a* to keep..... 2Ti 1:12
who shall be *a* to teach others..... 2Ti 2:2
never *a* to come to the knowledge..... 2Ti 3:7
which are *a* to make thee wise..... 2Ti 3:15
that he may be *a* by sound..... Titus 1:9
he is *a* to succour them that are..... Heb 2:18
that was *a* to save him from death..... Heb 5:7
Wherefore he is *a* also to save..... Heb 7:25
that God was *a* to raise him up..... Heb 11:19
which is *a* to save your souls..... Jas 1:21
a also to bridle the whole body..... Jas 3:2
who is *a* to save and to destroy..... Jas 4:12
a after my decease to have these..... 2Pet 1:15
Now unto him that is *a* to keep,..... Jude 24
was *a* to open the book, neither..... Rev 5:3
and who shall be *a* to stand..... Rev 6:17
who is *a* to make war with him..... Rev 13:4
no man was *a* to enter into the..... Rev 15:8

ABNER (ab'-nur) See ABNER'S. *King Saul's*
military commander.
of the captain of his host was *A*..... 1Sa 14:50
Ner the father of *A* was the son..... 1Sa 14:51
the Philistine, he said unto *A*..... 1Sa 17:55
the captain of the host, *A*..... 1Sa 17:55
A said, As thy soul liveth, O..... 1Sa 17:55

A took him, and brought him before... 1Sa 17:57
A sat by Saul's side, and David's..... 1Sa 20:25
A the son of Ner, the captain of 1Sa 26:5
but *A* and the people lay round........ 1Sa 26:7
to *A* the son of Ner, saying,........... 1Sa 26:14
Answerest thou not, *A*................... 1Sa 26:14
Then *A* answered and said, Who art .. 1Sa 26:14
And David said to *A*, Art not thou.... 1Sa 26:15
But *A* the son of Ner, captain of 2Sa 2:8
A the son of Ner, and the servants ... 2Sa 2:12
A said to Joab, Let the young men 2Sa 2:14
A was beaten, and the men of 2Sa 2:17
And Asahel pursued after *A* 2Sa 2:19
nor to the left from following *A* 2Sa 2:19
Then *A* looked behind him, and said .. 2Sa 2:20
A said to him, Turn thee aside to 2Sa 2:21
A said again to Asahel, Turn thee..... 2Sa 2:22
wherefore *A* with the hinder end 2Sa 2:23
also and Abishai pursued after *A* 2Sa 2:24
themselves together after *A* 2Sa 2:25
Then *A* called to Joab, and said, ... 2Sa 2:26
And *A* and his men walked all that ... 2Sa 2:29
And Joab returned from following *A*... 2Sa 2:30
that *A* made himself strong for 2Sa 3:6
and Ish-bosheth said to *A*, ... 2Sa 3:7
Then was *A* very wroth for the 2Sa 3:8
So do God to *A*, and more also,........ 2Sa 3:9
could not answer *A* a word again 2Sa 3:11
A sent messengers to David on his 2Sa 3:12
Then said *A* unto him, Go, return 2Sa 3:16
A had communication with the 2Sa 3:17
A also spake in the ears of 2Sa 3:19
A went also to speak in the ears 2Sa 3:19
So *A* came to David to Hebron, and ... 2Sa 3:20
And David made *A* and the men that .. 2Sa 3:20
A said unto David, I will arise......... 2Sa 3:21
And David sent *A* away................... 2Sa 3:21
but *A* was not with David in 2Sa 3:22
A the son of Ner came to the king 2Sa 3:23
behold, *A* came unto thee 2Sa 3:24
Thou knowest *A* the son of Ner, ... 2Sa 3:25
David, he sent messengers after *A* 2Sa 3:26
when *A* was returned to Hebron, ... 2Sa 3:27
the blood of *A* the son of Ner 2Sa 3:28
and Abishai his brother slew *A* 2Sa 3:30
with sackcloth, and mourn before *A* ... 2Sa 3:31
And they buried *A* in Hebron........... 2Sa 3:32
voice, and wept at the grave of *A* 2Sa 3:32
And the king lamented over *A* 2Sa 3:33
and said, Died *A* as a fool dieth....... 2Sa 3:33
the king to slay *A* the son of Ner 2Sa 3:37
heard that *A* was dead in Hebron 2Sa 4:1
in the sepulchre of *A* in Hebron 2Sa 4:12
unto *A* the son of Ner, and unto 1Kin 2:5
A the son of Ner, captain of the 1Kin 2:32
A the son of Ner, and Joab the son ... 1Chr 26:28
of Benjamin, Jaasiel the son of *A* 1Chr 27:21

ABNER'S (*ab'-nurs*)
of *A* men, so that three hundred 2Sa 2:31

ABOARD
over unto Phenicia, we went *a* .... Acts 21:2

ABODE
he *a* with him the space of *a* .... Gen 29:14
But his bow *a* in strength.............. Gen 49:24
of the LORD *a* upon mount Sinai........ Ex 24:16
because the cloud *a* thereon............ Ex 40:35
and in the place where the cloud *a* .... Num 9:17
as long as the cloud *a* upon the .... Num 9:18
of the LORD they *a* in their tents ...... Num 9:20
when the cloud *a* from even unto ...... Num 9:21
of Israel *a* in their tents .... Num 9:22
and *a* at Hazeroth........................ Num 11:35
And the people *a* in Kadesh .... Num 20:1
the princes of Moab *a* with Balaam .... Num 22:8
Israel *a* in Shittim, and the .... Num 25:1
So ye *a* in Kadesh many days,.......... Deut 1:46
unto the days that ye *a* there .... Deut 1:46
So we *a* in the valley over .... Deut 3:29
then I *a* in the mount forty days .... Deut 9:9
a there three days, until the.......... Josh 2:22
that they *a* in their places in......... Josh 8:9
a between Beth-el and Ai, on the ...... Josh 8:9
Gilead *a* beyond Jordan................. Judg 5:17
sea shore, and *a* in his breaches ...... Judg 5:17
and Israel *a* in Kadesh .... Judg 11:17
and he *a* with him three days .... Judg 19:4
a in the rock Rimmon four months..... Judg 20:47
where *a* thine ass .... Judg 21:2
So the woman *a*, and gave her son 1Sa 1:23
while the ark *a* in Kirjath-jearim 1Sa 7:2
them, *a* in Gibeah of Benjamin 1Sa 13:16
(now Saul *a* in Gibeah under a 1Sa 22:6
David *a* in the wilderness in 1Sa 23:14
David *a* in the wood, and Jonathan 1Sa 23:18
a in the wilderness of Maon 1Sa 23:25
two hundred *a* by the stuff 1Sa 25:13
But David *a* in the wilderness, and 1Sa 26:3
for two hundred *a* behind, which 1Sa 30:10
David had *a* two days in Ziklag........ 2Sa 1:1
So Uriah *a* in Jerusalem that day,..... 2Sa 11:12
vow while I *a* at Geshur in Syria 2Sa 15:8
him up into a loft, where he *a* 1Kin 17:19
But I know thy *a*, and thy going....... 2Kin 19:27
where he is tents there days,............ 2Sa 6:11 (?)
Jerusalem, and *a* there three days...... Ezr 8:32
But I know thy *a*, and thy going .... Is 37:28
So Jeremiah *a* in the court of the ..... Jer 38:28
And while they *a* in Galilee........... Mt 17:22
Mary *a* with her about three............ Lk 1:56

neither *a* in any house, but in......... Lk 8:27
a in the mount that is called the...... Lk 21:37
like a dove, and it *a* upon him......... Jn 1:32
he dwelt, and *a* with him that day ..... Jn 1:39
and he *a* there two days................ Jn 4:40
unto them, he *a* still in Galilee....... Jn 7:9
a not in the truth, because there ..... Jn 8:44
and there he *a* .... Jn 10:40
he *a* two days still in the same........ Jn 11:6
unto him, and make our *a* with him ..... Jn 14:23
where *a* both Peter, and James, and.... Acts 1:13
Judaea to Caesarea, and there *a* .... Acts 12:19
Long time therefore *a* they............. Acts 14:3
there they *a* long time with the .... Acts 14:28
Silas and Timotheus *a* there still...... Acts 17:14
he *a* with them, and wrought........... Acts 18:3
And there *a* three months............... Acts 20:3
where we *a* seven days.................. Acts 20:6
brethren, and *a* with them one day ..... Acts 21:7
of the seven; and *a* with him.......... Acts 21:8
Peter, and *a* with him fifteen days .... Gal 1:18
Erastus *a* at Corinth 2Ti 4:20

ABODEST
Why *a* thou among the sheepfolds, ... Judg 5:16

ABOLISH
And the idols he shall utterly *a*........ Is 2:18

ABOLISHED
my righteousness shall not be *a* .... Is 51:6
cut down, and your works may be *a* ..... Eze 6:6
to the end of that which is *a* 2Cor 3:13
Having *a* in his flesh the enmity,..... Eph 2:15
Jesus Christ, who hath *a* death 2Ti 1:10

ABOMINABLE
or any *a* unclean thing, and eat of..... Lev 7:21
a with any creeping thing that .... Lev 11:43
not any one of these *a* customs........ Lev 18:30
at all on the third day, it is *a* ...... Lev 19:7
not make your souls *a* by beast .... Lev 20:25
Thou shalt not eat any *a* thing .... Deut 14:3
for the king's word was *a* to Joab 1Chr 21:6
put away the *a* idols out of all........ 2Chr 15:8
How much more *a* and filthy is man, ... Job 15:16
corrupt, they have done *a* works........ Ps 14:1
are they, and have done *a* iniquity..... Ps 53:1
out of thy grave like an *a* branch...... Is 14:19
broth of *a* things is in their......... Is 65:4
of their detestable and *a* things ...... Jer 16:18
do not this *a* thing that I hate .... Jer 44:4
neither came there *a* flesh into .... Eze 4:14
a beasts, and all the idols of the .... Eze 8:10
hast committed more *a* than they....... Eze 16:52
and the scant measure that is *a* .... Mic 6:10
I will cast *a* filth upon thee, and .... Nah 3:6
in works they deny him, being *a* .... Titus 1:16
banquetings, and *a* idolatries 1Pet 4:3
fearful, and unbelieving, and the *a* ... Rev 21:8

ABOMINABLY
he did very *a* in following idols,...... 1Kin 21:26

ABOMINATION
for that is an *a* unto the.............. Gen 43:32
is an *a* unto the Egyptians............. Gen 46:34
for we shall sacrifice the *a* of .... Ex 8:26
shall we sacrifice the *a* of the .... Ex 8:26
it shall be an *a*, and the soul .... Lev 7:18
they shall be *a* unto you............... Lev 11:10
They shall be even an *a* unto you,...... Lev 11:11
ye shall have their carcases in *a* ..... Lev 11:11
that shall be an *a* unto you............ Lev 11:12
shall have in *a* among the fowls........ Lev 11:13
shall not be eaten, they are an *a* ..... Lev 11:13
all four, shall be an *a* unto you....... Lev 11:20
four feet, shall be an *a* unto you ..... Lev 11:23
upon the earth shall be an *a* .... Lev 11:41
for they are an *a*...................... Lev 11:42
with womankind: it is *a* .... Lev 18:22
both of them have committed an *a* ...... Lev 20:13
for it is an *a* to the LORD thy .... Deut 7:25
thou bring an *a* into thine house ...... Deut 7:26
for every *a* to the LORD, which he ..... Deut 12:31
that such a is wrought among you .... Deut 13:14
for that is an *a* unto the LORD........ Deut 17:1
such a is wrought in Israel .... Deut 17:4
things are an *a* unto the LORD......... Deut 18:12
do so are *a* unto the LORD thy God..... Deut 22:5
these are *a* unto the LORD thy God ..... Deut 23:18
for that is a before the LORD........... Deut 24:4
are an *a* unto the LORD thy God .... Deut 25:16
an *a* unto the LORD, the work of .... Deut 27:15
was had in *a* with the Philistines..... 1Sa 13:4
Milcom the *a* of the Ammonites......... 1Kin 11:5
the *a* of Moab, in the hill that....... 1Kin 11:7
the *a* of the children of Ammon 1Kin 11:7
Ashtoreth the *a* of the Zidonians 2Kin 23:13
for Chemosh the *a* of the Moabites...... 2Kin 23:13
for Milcom the *a* of the children 2Kin 23:13
thou hast made me an *a* unto them....... Ps 88:8
For the froward is *a* to the LORD ...... Prov 3:32
yea, seven are an *a* unto him .... Prov 6:16
and wickedness is an *a* to my lips ..... Prov 8:7
A false balance is *a* to the LORD ...... Prov 11:1
a froward heart are *a* to the LORD ..... Prov 11:20
Lying lips are *a* to the LORD.......... Prov 12:22
but it is *a* to fools to depart .... Prov 13:19
of the wicked is an *a* to the LORD ..... Prov 15:8
the wicked is an *a* unto the LORD....... Prov 15:9
the wicked are an *a* to the LORD .... Prov 15:26
in heart is an *a* to the LORD.......... Prov 16:5

It is an *a* to kings to commit.......... Prov 16:12
even they both are *a* to the LORD....... Prov 17:15
of them are alike *a* to the LORD........ Prov 20:10
weights are an *a* unto the LORD .... Prov 20:23
The sacrifice of the wicked is *a* ...... Prov 21:27
and the scorner is an *a* to men......... Prov 24:9
law, even his prayer shall be *a* .... Prov 28:9
An unjust man is an *a* to the just...... Prov 29:27
in the way is *a* to the wicked......... Prov 29:27
incense is an *a* unto me .... Is 1:13
an *a* is he that chooseth you .... Is 41:24
I make the residue thereof an *a* .... Is 44:19
eating swine's flesh, and the *a* .... Is 66:17
land, and made mine heritage an *a* ..... Jer 2:7
ashamed when they had committed *a* ..... Jer 6:15
ashamed when they had committed *a*...... Jer 8:12
mind, that they should do this *a*....... Jer 32:35
haughty, and committed *a* before me .... Eze 16:50
to the idols, hath committed *a* .... Eze 18:12
one hath committed *a* with his.......... Eze 22:11
stand upon your sword, ye work *a* ...... Eze 33:26
place the *a* that maketh desolate ...... Dan 11:31
the *a* that maketh desolate set up...... Dan 12:11
an *a* is committed in Israel and in .... Mal 2:11
shall see the *a* of desolation .... Mt 24:15
ye shall see the *a* of desolation ...... Mk 13:14
men is *a* in the sight of God.......... Lk 16:15
neither whatsoever worketh *a* .... Rev 21:27

ABOMINATIONS
shall not commit any of these *a* .... Lev 18:26
(For all these *a* have the men of ...... Lev 18:27
shall commit any of these *a* .... Lev 18:29
do after the *a* of those nations .... Deut 18:9
because of these *a* the LORD thy .... Deut 18:12
you not to do after all their *a* .... Deut 20:18
And ye have seen their *a*, and their ... Deut 29:17
with *a* provoked they him to anger..... Deut 32:16
a of the nations which the LORD 1Kin 14:24
according to the *a* of the heathen...... 2Kin 16:3
after the *a* of the heathen, whom 2Kin 21:2
king of Judah hath done these *a* 2Kin 21:11
all the *a* that were spied in the 2Kin 23:24
after the *a* of the heathen whom 2Chr 28:3
like unto the *a* of the heathen,........ 2Chr 33:2
Josiah took away all the *a* of 2Chr 34:33
his *a* which he did, and that which 2Chr 36:8
after all the *a* of the heathen 2Chr 36:14
lands, doing according to their *a* ..... Ezr 9:1
people of the lands, with their *a* ..... Ezr 9:11
with the people of these *a* .... Ezr 9:14
there are seven *a* in his heart......... Prov 26:25
their soul delighteth in their *a* ...... Is 66:3
put away thine *a* out of my sight ...... Jer 4:1
are delivered to do all these *a* .... Jer 7:10
they have set their *a* in the.......... Jer 7:30
thine *a* on the hills in the........... Jer 13:27
But they set their *a* in the house...... Jer 32:34
because of the *a* which ye have .... Jer 44:22
the like, because of all thine *a* ...... Eze 5:9
things, and with all thine *a* .... Eze 5:11
have committed in all their *a* .... Eze 6:9
Alas for all the evil *a* of the .... Eze 6:11
recompense upon thee all thine *a* ...... Eze 7:3
thine *a* shall be in the midst of ...... Eze 7:4
recompense thee for all thine *a* .... Eze 7:8
thine *a* that are in the midst of ...... Eze 7:9
they made the images of their *a* .... Eze 7:20
even the great *a* that the house .... Eze 8:6
and thou shalt see greater *a*........... Eze 8:6
the wicked *a* that they do here......... Eze 8:9
shalt see greater *a* that they do....... Eze 8:13
shalt see greater *a* than these .... Eze 8:15
the *a* which they commit here.......... Eze 8:17
that cry for all the *a* that be .... Eze 9:4
all the *a* thereof from thence......... Eze 11:18
detestable things and their *a* .... Eze 11:21
a among the heathen whither they ...... Eze 12:16
away your faces from all your *a* .... Eze 14:6
cause Jerusalem to know her *a* .... Eze 16:2
And in all thine *a* and thy............ Eze 16:22
and with all the idols of thy *a* .... Eze 16:36
this lewdness above all thine *a* .... Eze 16:43
ways, nor done after their *a* .... Eze 16:47
multiplied thine *a* more than they ..... Eze 16:51
all thine *a* which thou hast done ...... Eze 16:51
borne thy lewdness and thine *a* .... Eze 16:58
he hath done all these *a* .... Eze 18:13
the *a* that the wicked man doeth........ Eze 18:24
to know the *a* of their fathers........ Eze 20:4
away every man the *a* of his eyes....... Eze 20:7
man cast away the *a* of their eyes...... Eze 20:8
commit ye whoredom after their *a* ...... Eze 20:30
thou shalt shew her all her *a* .... Eze 22:2
yea, declare unto them their *a* .... Eze 23:36
their *a* which they have committed ..... Eze 33:29
for your iniquities and for your *a* .... Eze 36:31
their *a* that they have committed ...... Eze 43:8
let it suffice you of all your *a* ...... Eze 44:6
my covenant because of all your *a* ..... Eze 44:7
their *a* which they have committed,..... Dan 9:27
for the overspreading of *a* he .... Dan 9:27
their *a* were according as they .... Hos 9:10
his *a* from between his teeth........... Zec 9:7
golden cup in her hand full of *a* ...... Rev 17:4
AND *A* OF THE EARTH.................... Rev 17:5

ABOUND
man shall *a* with blessings .... Prov 28:20
and because iniquity shall *a* .... Mt 24:12
entered, that the offence might *a* ..... Rom 5:20

ABOUNDED

abounded, grace did much more a.......	Rom 5:20
continue in sin, that grace may a........	Rom 6:1
believing, that ye may a in hope.........	Rom 15:13
the sufferings of Christ a in us.........	2Cor 1:5
as ye a in every thing, in faith,.........	2Cor 8:7
see that ye a in these grace also........	2Cor 8:7
to make all grace a toward you..........	2Cor 9:8
things, may a to every good work.......	2Cor 9:8
that your love may a yet more...........	Phil 1:9
to be abased, and I know how to a......	Phil 4:12
full and to be hungry, both to a........	Phil 4:12
fruit that may a to your account........	Phil 4:17
But I have all, and a.....................	Phil 4:18
a in love one toward another, and......	1Th 3:12
to please God, so ye would a more......	1Th 4:1
if these things be in you, and a.........	2Pet 1:8

ABOUNDED

a through my lie unto his glory.........	Rom 3:7
Jesus Christ, hath a unto many.........	Rom 5:15
But where sin a, grace did much........	Rom 5:20
their deep poverty a unto the............	2Cor 8:2
Wherein he hath a toward us in.........	Eph 1:8

ABOUNDETH

a furious man a in transgression.......	Prov 29:22
our consolation also a by Christ........	2Cor 1:5
of you all toward each other a..........	2Th 1:3

ABOUNDING

were no fountains a with water........	Prov 8:24
always a in the work of the Lord,......	1Cor 15:58
a therein with thanksgiving............	Col 2:7

ABOUT See PREFACE.

ABOVE

waters which were a the firmament....	Gen 1:7
fowl that may fly a the earth in.........	Gen 1:20
thou art cursed a all cattle..............	Gen 3:14
a every beast of the field................	Gen 3:14
in a cubit shalt thou finish it a.........	Gen 6:16
and it was lift up a the earth............	Gen 7:17
and of the dew of heaven from a.......	Gen 27:39
And, behold, the LORD stood a it.......	Gen 28:13
the one portion a thy brethren.........	Gen 48:22
thee with blessings of heaven a........	Gen 49:25
of thy father have prevailed a..........	Gen 49:26
they dealt proudly he was a them......	Ex 18:11
treasure unto me a all people..........	Ex 19:5
of any thing that is in heaven a........	Ex 20:4
put the mercy seat a upon the ark......	Ex 25:21
with thee from a the mercy seat.......	Ex 25:22
a covering of badgers' skins a.........	Ex 26:14
a the head of it unto one ring..........	Ex 26:24
the curious girdle of the ephod........	Ex 28:27
that it may be a the curious............	Ex 28:28
and the caul that is a the liver.........	Ex 29:13
the caul a the liver, and the two.......	Ex 29:22
from twenty years old and a............	Ex 30:14
covering of badgers' skins a that......	Ex 36:19
a the curious girdle of the ephod......	Ex 39:20
that it might be a the curious..........	Ex 39:21
covering of the tent a upon it...........	Ex 40:19
put the mercy seat a upon the ark.....	Ex 40:20
the caul a the liver, with the..........	Lev 3:4
the caul a the liver, with the..........	Lev 3:10
the caul a the liver, with the..........	Lev 3:15
the caul a the liver, with the..........	Lev 4:9
and the caul that is a the liver........	Lev 7:4
the caul a the liver, and the two......	Lev 8:16
the caul a the liver, and the two......	Lev 9:10
the caul a the liver of the sin.........	Lev 9:19
kidneys, and the caul a the liver......	Lev 9:19
which have legs a their feet...........	Lev 11:21
it be from sixty years old and a.......	Lev 27:7
a them that were redeemed by the....	Num 3:49
badgers' skins that is a upon it.......	Num 4:25
a all the men which were upon the....	Num 12:3
then lift ye up yourselves a the.......	Num 16:3
the LORD he is God in heaven a........	Deut 4:39
of any thing that is in heaven a.......	Deut 5:8
a all people that are upon the.........	Deut 7:6
shalt be blessed a all people.........	Deut 7:14
even you a all people, as it is.......	Deut 10:15
a all the nations that are upon.......	Deut 14:2
be not lifted up a his brethren.......	Deut 17:20
beat him a these with many...........	Deut 25:3
to make thee high a all nations......	Deut 26:19
high a all nations of the earth......	Deut 28:1
and thou shalt be a only, and thou...	Deut 28:13
shalt get up a thee very high........	Deut 28:43
and multiply thee a thy fathers......	Deut 30:5
your God, he is God in heaven a......	Josh 2:11
the waters that came down from a.....	Josh 3:13
which came down from a Jordan.......	Josh 3:16
Blessed a women shall Jael the.......	Judg 5:24
shall she be a women in the tent......	Judg 5:24
and honourest thy sons a the.........	1Sa 2:29
He sent from a, he took me...........	2Sa 22:17
a them that rose up against me.......	2Sa 22:49
with cedar a upon the beams.........	1Kin 7:3
a were costly stones, after the......	1Kin 7:11
pillars had pomegranates also a.....	1Kin 7:20
and the sea was set a upon them.....	1Kin 7:25
the ledges there was a base a.......	1Kin 7:29
the chapiter and a was a cubit......	1Kin 7:31
the ark and the staves thereof a.....	1Kin 8:7
is no God like thee, in heaven a.....	1Kin 8:23
But hast done evil a all that........	1Kin 14:9
a all that their fathers had done....	1Kin 14:22
LORD a all that were before him......	1Kin 16:30
hath done wickedly a all that thou....	2Kin 21:11

set his throne a the throne of.........	2Kin 25:28
Judah prevailed a his brethren.......	1Chr 5:2
also is to be feared a all gods........	1Chr 16:25
from twenty years old and a..........	1Chr 23:27
among the thirty, and a the thirty....	1Chr 27:6
a all that I have prepared for.........	1Chr 29:3
and thou art exalted as head of all...	1Chr 29:11
for great is our God a all gods........	2Chr 2:5
and the sea was set a upon them.....	2Chr 4:4
the ark and the staves thereof a.....	2Chr 5:9
of Absalom a all his wives............	2Chr 11:21
priest, which stood a the people.....	2Chr 24:20
them from twenty years old and a....	2Chr 25:5
images, that were on high a them....	2Chr 34:4
From a the horse gate repaired......	Neh 3:28
man, and feared God a many..........	Neh 7:2
(for he was a all the people...........	Neh 8:5
which is exalted a all blessing......	Neh 9:5
a the house of David, even unto......	Neh 12:37
from a the gate of Ephraim, and.....	Neh 12:39
a the old gate, and a the fish.......	Neh 12:39
king loved Esther a all the women....	Est 2:17
set his seat a all the princes........	Est 3:1
he had advanced him a the princes...	Est 5:11
let not God regard it from a.........	Job 3:4
a shall his branch be cut off.........	Job 18:16
the price of wisdom is a rubies......	Job 28:18
portion of God is there from a.......	Job 31:2
have denied the God that is a........	Job 31:28
hast set thy glory a the heavens.....	Ps 8:1
are far a out of his sight..............	Ps 10:5
He sent from a, he took me, he......	Ps 18:16
thou liftest me up a those that......	Ps 18:48
up a mine enemies round about me...	Ps 27:6
the oil of gladness a thy fellows.....	Ps 45:7
shall call to the heavens from a.....	Ps 50:4
exalted, O God, a the heavens.......	Ps 57:5
let thy glory be a all the earth......	Ps 57:5
exalted, O God, a the heavens.......	Ps 57:11
let thy glory be a all the earth......	Ps 57:11
had commanded the clouds from a....	Ps 78:23
God, and a great King a all gods.....	Ps 95:3
he is to be feared a all gods.........	Ps 96:4
LORD, art high a all the earth........	Ps 97:9
thou art exalted far a all gods.......	Ps 97:9
he is high a all the people...........	Ps 99:2
as the heaven is high a the earth....	Ps 103:11
the waters stood a the mountains....	Ps 104:6
thy mercy is great a the heavens.....	Ps 108:4
exalted, O God, a the heavens.......	Ps 108:5
thy glory a all the earth..............	Ps 108:5
The LORD is high a all nations.......	Ps 113:4
and his glory a the heavens..........	Ps 113:4
I love thy commandments a gold.....	Ps 119:127
yea, a fine gold.........................	Ps 119:127
and that our Lord is a all gods......	Ps 135:5
out the earth a the waters...........	Ps 136:6
not Jerusalem a my chief joy........	Ps 137:6
magnified thy word a all thy name..	Ps 138:2
Send thine hand from a..............	Ps 144:7
ye waters that be a the heavens.....	Ps 148:4
his glory is a the earth and..........	Ps 148:13
When he established the clouds a....	Prov 8:28
The way of life is a to the wise......	Prov 15:24
for her price is far a rubies..........	Prov 31:10
small cattle a all that were in.......	Eccl 2:7
man hath no preeminence a beast...	Eccl 3:19
and shall be exalted a the hills.....	Is 2:2
A it stood the seraphims.............	Is 6:2
in the depth, or in the height a......	Is 7:11
my throne a the stars of God........	Is 14:13
I will ascend a the heights of.......	Is 14:14
Drop down, ye heavens, from a......	Is 45:8
mourn, and the heavens a be black..	Jer 4:28
to me a the sand of the seas........	Jer 15:8
heart is deceitful a all things......	Jer 17:9
If heaven a can be measured, and...	Jer 31:37
which was a the chamber of..........	Jer 35:4
set his throne a the throne of.......	Jer 52:32
From a hath he sent fire into my.....	Lam 1:13
forth over their heads a..............	Eze 1:22
a the firmament that was over.......	Eze 1:26
the appearance of a man a upon it...	Eze 1:26
in the firmament that was a the......	Eze 10:1
The God of Israel was over them a...	Eze 10:19
the God of Israel was over them a...	Eze 11:22
lewdness a all thine abominations...	Eze 16:47
itself any more a the nations........	Eze 29:15
his height was exalted a all the.....	Eze 31:5
them, and the skin covered them a..	Eze 37:8
To that a the door, even unto the....	Eze 41:17
From the ground unto a the door.....	Eze 41:20
was preferred a the presidents......	Dan 6:3
and he shall be strong a him........	Dan 11:5
and magnify himself a every god....	Dan 11:36
he shall magnify himself a all......	Dan 11:37
yet I destroyed his fruit from a......	Amos 2:9
it shall be exalted a the hills........	Mic 4:1
merchants a the stars of heaven.....	Nah 3:16
The disciple is not a his master.....	Mt 10:24
nor the servant a his lord............	Mt 10:24
Added yet this a all, that he..........	Lk 3:20
The disciple is not a his master.....	Lk 6:40
were sinners a all the Galileans....	Lk 13:2
a all men that dwelt in Jerusalem...	Lk 13:4
that cometh from a is a all..........	Jn 3:31
that cometh from heaven is a all....	Jn 3:31
a unto them that had eaten..........	Jn 6:23
I am from a.............................	Jn 8:23

except it were given thee from a.....	Jn 19:11
I will shew wonders in heaven a.....	Acts 2:19
For the man was a forty years old....	Acts 4:22
the brightness of the sun,............	Acts 26:13
is, to bring Christ down from a.......	Rom 10:6
man esteemeth one day a another....	Rom 14:5
of men a that which is written........	1Cor 4:6
to be tempted a that ye are able.....	1Cor 10:13
he was seen of a five hundred.......	1Cor 15:6
a strength, insomuch that we........	2Cor 1:8
abundant, in stripes a measure......	2Cor 11:23
in Christ a fourteen years ago.......	2Cor 12:2
me a that which he seeth me to be..	2Cor 12:6
lest I should be exalted a............	2Cor 12:7
I should be exalted a measure.......	2Cor 12:7
a many my equals in mine own.......	Gal 1:14
But Jerusalem which is a is free.....	Gal 4:26
Far a all principality, and power,....	Eph 1:21
a all that we ask or think............	Eph 3:20
and Father of all, who is a all.......	Eph 4:6
ascended up far a all heavens.......	Eph 4:10
A all, taking the shield of faith......	Eph 6:16
him a name which is a every name...	Phil 2:9
seek those things which are a.......	Col 3:1
Set your affection on things a.......	Col 3:2
a all these things put on charity....	Col 3:14
exalteth himself a all that is........	2Th 2:4
but a a servant, a brother............	Phlm 16
the oil of gladness a thy fellows....	Heb 1:9
A when he said, Sacrifice and.......	Heb 10:8
and every perfect gift is from a.....	Jas 1:17
This wisdom descendeth not from a..	Jas 3:15
that is from a is first pure...........	Jas 3:17
But a all things, my brethren,.......	Jas 5:12
a all things have fervent charity....	1Pet 4:8
I wish a all things that thou.........	3Jn 2

ABRAHAM (a'-bra-ham) See ABRAHAM'S,
ABRAM. Father of the nation of Israel.

Abram, but thy name shall be A......	Gen 17:5
And God said unto A, Thou shalt.....	Gen 17:9
And God said unto A, As for Sarai...	Gen 17:15
Then A fell upon his face, and.......	Gen 17:17
A said unto God, O that Ishmael.....	Gen 17:18
with him, and God went up from A...	Gen 17:22
A took Ishmael his son, and all.....	Gen 17:23
A was ninety years old and nine,....	Gen 17:24
selfsame day was A circumcised.....	Gen 17:26
A hastened into the tent unto........	Gen 18:6
A ran unto the herd, and fetcht a....	Gen 18:7
Now A and Sarah were old and well..	Gen 18:11
And the LORD said unto A,............	Gen 18:13
A went with them to bring them on..	Gen 18:16
Shall I hide from A that thing.......	Gen 18:17
Seeing that A shall surely become...	Gen 18:18
A that which he hath spoken of......	Gen 18:19
but A stood yet before the LORD.....	Gen 18:22
A drew near, and said, Wilt thou....	Gen 18:23
A answered and said, Behold now, I..	Gen 18:27
as he had left communing with A....	Gen 18:33
A returned unto his place............	Gen 18:33
A gat up early in the morning to.....	Gen 19:27
the plain, that God remembered A...	Gen 19:29
A journeyed from thence toward.....	Gen 20:1
A said of Sarah his wife, She is.....	Gen 20:2
Then Abimelech called A, and said..	Gen 20:9
And Abimelech said unto A, What....	Gen 20:10
A said, Because I thought, Surely....	Gen 20:11
and gave them unto A, and restored..	Gen 20:14
So A prayed unto God................	Gen 20:17
bare A a son in his old age, at.......	Gen 21:2
A called the name of his son that....	Gen 21:3
A circumcised his son Isaac being..	Gen 21:4
A was an hundred years old, when...	Gen 21:5
said, Who would have said unto A...	Gen 21:7
A made a great feast the same day...	Gen 21:8
which she had born unto A...........	Gen 21:9
Wherefore she said unto A...........	Gen 21:10
And God said unto A, Let it not be...	Gen 21:12
A rose up early in the morning,......	Gen 21:14
captain of his host spake unto A....	Gen 21:22
And A said, I will swear..............	Gen 21:24
A reproved Abimelech because of a..	Gen 21:25
A took sheep and oxen, and gave....	Gen 21:27
A set seven ewe lambs of the........	Gen 21:28
And Abimelech said unto A, What....	Gen 21:29
A planted a grove in Beer-sheba,....	Gen 21:33
A sojourned in the Philistines'......	Gen 21:34
things, that God did tempt A.........	Gen 22:1
and said unto him, A..................	Gen 22:1
A rose up early in the morning,......	Gen 22:3
third day A lifted up his eyes.......	Gen 22:4
A said unto his young men, Abide...	Gen 22:5
A took the wood of the burnt........	Gen 22:6
And Isaac spake unto A his father...	Gen 22:7
A said, My son, God will provide.....	Gen 22:8
A built an altar there, and laid......	Gen 22:9
A stretched forth his hand, and.....	Gen 22:10
of heaven, and said, A, A............	Gen 22:11
A lifted up his eyes, and looked,....	Gen 22:13
A went and took the ram, and........	Gen 22:13
A called the name of that place.....	Gen 22:14
A out of heaven the second time....	Gen 22:15
So A returned unto his young men,..	Gen 22:19
and A dwelt at Beer-sheba...........	Gen 22:19
these things, that it was told A......	Gen 22:20
A came to mourn for Sarah, and to..	Gen 23:2
A stood up from before his dead,....	Gen 23:3
the children of Heth answered A....	Gen 23:5
A stood up, and bowed himself to....	Gen 23:7
Ephron the Hittite answered A in....	Gen 23:10

A bowed down himself before the...... Gen 23:12
And Abraham answered *A*, saying unto Gen 23:14
And *A* hearkened unto Ephron............ Gen 23:16
A weighed to Ephron the silver,........ Gen 23:16
Unto *A* for a possession in the............ Gen 23:18
A buried Sarah his wife in the............ Gen 23:19
were made sure unto *A* for a............ Gen 23:20
A was old, and well stricken in........ Gen 24:1
LORD had blessed *A* in all things........ Gen 24:1
A said unto his eldest servant of...... Gen 24:2
A said unto him, Beware thou that...... Gen 24:6
under the thigh of *A* his master...... Gen 24:9
said, O LORD God of my master *A*,...... Gen 24:12
kindness unto my master *A*............ Gen 24:12
be the LORD God of my master *A*,...... Gen 24:27
said, O LORD God of my master *A*,...... Gen 24:42
the LORD God of my master *A*............ Gen 24:48
Then again *A* took a wife, and her...... Gen 25:1
A gave all that he had unto Isaac...... Gen 25:5
of the concubines, which *A* had...... Gen 25:6
A gave gifts, and sent them away...... Gen 25:6
Then *A* gave up the ghost, and died..... Gen 25:8
The field which *A* purchased of........ Gen 25:10
there was *A* buried, and Sarah his...... Gen 25:10
came to pass after the death of *A*...... Gen 25:11
Sarah's handmaid, bare unto *A*........ Gen 25:12
A begat Isaac............................ Gen 25:19
famine that was in the days of *A*...... Gen 26:1
which I sware unto *A* thy father........ Gen 26:3
Because that *A* obeyed my voice,...... Gen 26:5
in the days of *A* his father............ Gen 26:15
in the days of *A* his father............ Gen 26:18
stopped them after the death of *A*...... Gen 26:18
I am the God of *A* thy father............ Gen 26:24
And give thee the blessing of *A*...... Gen 28:4
a stranger, which God gave unto *A*...... Gen 28:4
I am the LORD God of *A* thy father...... Gen 28:13
God of my father, the God of *A*........ Gen 31:42
The God of *A*, and the God of Nahor..... Gen 31:53
Jacob said, O God of my father *A*...... Gen 32:9
And the land which I gave *A*............ Gen 35:12
Arbah, which is Hebron, where *A*...... Gen 35:27
God, before whom my fathers *A*........ Gen 48:15
them, and the name of my fathers *A*...... Gen 48:16
which *A* bought with the field for...... Gen 49:30
There they buried *A* and Sarah his...... Gen 49:31
which *A* bought with the field for...... Gen 50:13
unto the land which he sware to *A*...... Gen 50:24
remembered his covenant with *A*...... Ex 2:24
God of thy father, the God of *A*........ Ex 3:6
God of your fathers, the God of *A*...... Ex 3:15
God of your fathers, the God of *A*...... Ex 3:16
of their fathers, the God of *A*............ Ex 4:5
And I appeared unto *A*, unto Isaac,..... Ex 6:3
which I did swear to give it to *A*........ Ex 6:8
Remember *A*, Isaac, and Israel, thy.... Ex 32:13
the land which I sware unto *A*.......... Ex 33:1
covenant with *A* will I remember...... Lev 26:42
see the land which I sware unto *A*...... Num 32:11
sware unto your fathers, *A*,............ Deut 1:8
he sware unto thy fathers, to *A*........ Deut 6:10
LORD sware unto thy fathers, to *A*...... Deut 9:5
Remember thy servants, *A*, Isaac,...... Deut 9:27
hath sworn unto thy fathers, to *A*...... Deut 29:13
LORD sware unto thy fathers, to *A*...... Deut 30:20
is the land which I sware unto *A*...... Deut 34:4
time, even Terah, the father of *A*...... Josh 24:2
I took your father *A* from the.......... Josh 24:3
came near, and said, LORD God of *A*..... 1Kin 18:36
because of his covenant with *A*........ 2Kin 13:23
Abram; the same is *A*.................... 1Chr 1:27
The sons of *A*; Isaac, and.............. 1Chr 1:28
And *A* begat Isaac...................... 1Chr 1:34
the covenant which he made with *A*... 1Chr 16:16
O LORD God of *A*, Isaac, and of...... 1Chr 29:18
the seed of *A* thy friend for ever...... 2Chr 20:7
turn again unto the LORD God of *A*...... 2Chr 30:6
and gavest him the name of *A*........ Neh 9:7
even the people of the God of *A*........ Ps 47:9
O ye seed of *A* his servant.............. Ps 105:6
Which covenant he made with *A*...... Ps 105:9
holy promise, and *A* his servant...... Ps 105:42
saith the LORD, who redeemed *A*...... Is 29:22
chosen, the seed of *A* my friend...... Is 41:8
Look unto *A* your father, and unto...... Is 51:2
though *A* be ignorant of us, and...... Is 63:16
to be rulers over the seed of *A*........ Jer 33:26
A was one, and he inherited the...... Eze 33:24
truth to Jacob, and the mercy to *A*... Mic 7:20
the son of David, the son of *A*........ Mt 1:1
A begat Isaac.......................... Mt 1:2
from *A* to David are fourteen........ Mt 1:17
We have *A* to our father.............. Mt 3:9
to raise up children unto *A*.......... Mt 3:9
and west, and shall sit down with *A*... Mt 8:11
I am the God of *A*, and the God of...... Mt 22:32
him, saying, I am the God of *A*...... Mk 12:26
As he spake to our fathers, to *A*...... Lk 1:55
which he sware to our father *A*........ Lk 1:73
We have *A* to our father.............. Lk 3:8
to raise up children unto *A*.......... Lk 3:8
of Isaac, which was the son of *A*...... Lk 3:34
this woman, being a daughter of *A*... Lk 13:16
of teeth, when ye shall see *A*.......... Lk 13:28
seeth *A* afar off, and Lazarus in...... Lk 16:23
And he cried and said, Father *A*...... Lk 16:24
But *A* said, Son, remember that...... Lk 16:25
A saith unto him, They have Moses...... Lk 16:29
And he said, Nay, father *A*............ Lk 16:30
as he also is a son of *A*................ Lk 19:9

he calleth the Lord the God of *A*...... Lk 20:37
and said unto him, *A* is our father...... Jn 8:39
ye would do the works of *A*............ Jn 8:39
of God: this did not *A*.................. Jn 8:40
A is dead, and the prophets............ Jn 8:52
thou greater than our father *A*........ Jn 8:53
Your father *A* rejoiced to see my...... Jn 8:56
years old, and hast thou seen *A*........ Jn 8:57
I say unto you, Before *A* was.......... Jn 8:58
The God of *A*, and of Isaac, and of..... Acts 3:13
with our fathers, saying unto *A*...... Acts 3:25
glory appeared unto our father *A*...... Acts 7:2
so *A* begat Isaac, and circumcised...... Acts 7:8
laid in the sepulchre that *A*............ Acts 7:16
nigh, which God had sworn to *A*...... Acts 7:17
God of thy fathers, the God of *A*...... Acts 7:32
children of the stock of *A*.............. Acts 13:26
we say then that *A* our father.......... Rom 4:1
For if *A* were justified by works,...... Rom 4:2
A believed God, and it was counted...... Rom 4:3
reckoned to *A* for righteousness...... Rom 4:9
of that faith of our father *A*............ Rom 4:12
heir of the world, was not to *A*...... Rom 4:13
also which is of the faith of *A*........ Rom 4:16
because they are the seed of *A*........ Rom 9:7
am an Israelite, of the seed of *A*...... Rom 11:1
Are they the seed of *A*................ 2Cor 11:22
Even as *A* believed God, and it was...... Gal 3:6
the same are the children of *A*........ Gal 3:7
preached before the gospel unto *A*...... Gal 3:8
faith are blessed with faithful *A*...... Gal 3:9
That the blessing of *A* might come...... Gal 3:14
Now to *A* and his seed were the...... Gal 3:16
but God gave it to *A* by promise...... Gal 3:18
that *A* had two sons, the one by a...... Gal 4:22
but he took on him the seed of *A*...... Heb 2:16
For when God made promise to *A*...... Heb 6:13
who met *A* returning from the........ Heb 7:1
To whom also *A* gave a tenth part...... Heb 7:2
A gave the tenth of the spoils.......... Heb 7:4
they come out of the loins of *A*........ Heb 7:5
from them received tithes of *A*........ Heb 7:6
tithes, payed tithes in *A*.............. Heb 7:9
By faith *A*, when he was called to...... Heb 11:8
By faith *A*, when he was tried,........ Heb 11:17
Was not *A* our father justified by...... Jas 2:21
A believed God, and it was imputed...... Jas 2:23
Even as Sarah obeyed *A*, calling...... 1Pet 3:6

ABRAHAM'S (*a´-bra-hams*)
male among the men of *A* house...... Gen 17:23
because of Sarah *A* wife.............. Gen 20:18
in *A* sight because of his son.......... Gen 21:11
did bear to Nahor, *A* brother.......... Gen 22:23
a brother, with her pitcher upon...... Gen 24:15
And he said, I am *A* servant............ Gen 24:34
when *A* servant heard their words,...... Gen 24:52
nurse, and *A* servant, and his men..... Gen 24:59
years of *A* life which he lived.......... Gen 25:7
A son, whom Hagar the Egyptian,...... Gen 25:12
the generations of Isaac, *A* son........ Gen 25:19
thy seed for my servant *A* sake........ Gen 26:24
the daughter of Ishmael *A* son........ Gen 28:9
the sons of Keturah, *A* concubine...... 1Chr 1:32
by the angels into *A* bosom............ Lk 16:22
They answered him, We be *A* seed...... Jn 8:33
I know that ye are *A* seed.............. Jn 8:37
unto them, If ye were *A* children...... Jn 8:39
be Christ's, then are ye *A* seed........ Gal 3:29

ABRAM (*a´-brum*) See ABRAHAM, ABRAM'S.
Abraham's original name.
lived seventy years, and begat *A*...... Gen 11:26
Terah begat *A*, Nahor, and Haran...... Gen 11:27
And *A* and Nahor took them wives...... Gen 11:29
And Terah took *A* his son, and Lot...... Gen 11:31
Now the LORD had said unto *A*........ Gen 12:1
So *A* departed, as the LORD had........ Gen 12:4
A was seventy and five years old...... Gen 12:4
A took Sarai his wife, and Lot his...... Gen 12:5
A passed through the land unto........ Gen 12:6
And the LORD appeared unto *A*........ Gen 12:7
A journeyed, going on still............ Gen 12:9
A went down into Egypt to sojourn..... Gen 12:10
when *A* was come into Egypt, the...... Gen 12:14
he entreated *A* well for her sake...... Gen 12:16
And Pharaoh called *A*, and said,...... Gen 12:18
A went up out of Egypt, he, and........ Gen 13:1
A was very rich in cattle, in.......... Gen 13:2
there a called on the name of the...... Gen 13:4
And Lot also, which went with *A*...... Gen 13:5
A said unto Lot, Let there be no........ Gen 13:8
A dwelled in the land of Canaan,...... Gen 13:12
And the LORD said unto *A*, after........ Gen 13:14
Then *A* removed his tent, and came..... Gen 13:18
had escaped, and told *A* the Hebrew... Gen 14:13
and these were confederate with *A*..... Gen 14:13
when *A* heard that his brother was..... Gen 14:14
Blessed be *A* of the most high God...... Gen 14:19
And the king of Sodom said unto *A*..... Gen 14:21
A said to the king of Sodom, I........ Gen 14:22
shouldest say, I have made *A* rich..... Gen 14:23
the LORD came unto *A* in a vision...... Gen 15:1
in a vision, saying, Fear not, *A*...... Gen 15:1
A said, LORD God, what wilt thou........ Gen 15:2
A said, Behold, to me thou hast........ Gen 15:3
the carcases, *A* drove them away...... Gen 15:11
down, a deep sleep fell upon *A*........ Gen 15:12
And he said unto *A*, Know of a........ Gen 15:13
the LORD made a covenant with *A*...... Gen 15:18
And Sarai said unto *A*, Behold, now..... Gen 16:2

A hearkened to the voice of Sarai...... Gen 16:2
after *A* had dwelt ten years in........ Gen 16:3
to her husband *A* to be his wife...... Gen 16:3
And Sarai said unto *A*, My wrong be..... Gen 16:5
But *A* said unto Sarai, Behold,...... Gen 16:6
And Hagar bare *A* a son.............. Gen 16:15
A called his son's name, which........ Gen 16:15
A was fourscore and six years old,...... Gen 16:16
old, when Hagar bare Ishmael to *A*..... Gen 16:16
when *A* was ninety years old and...... Gen 17:1
and nine, the LORD appeared to *A*...... Gen 17:1
And *A* fell on his face................ Gen 17:3
thy name any more be called *A*........ Gen 17:5
A; the same is Abraham............ 1Chr 1:27
LORD the God, who didst choose *A*...... Neh 9:7

ABRAM'S (*a´-brums*)
the name of *A* wife was Sarai........ Gen 11:29
daughter in law, his son *A* wife...... Gen 11:31
plagues because of Sarai *A* wife...... Gen 12:17
between the herdmen of *A* cattle...... Gen 13:7
A brother's son, who dwelt in........ Gen 14:12
Now Sarai *A* wife bare him no........ Gen 16:1
Sarai *A* wife took Hagar her maid...... Gen 16:3

ABROAD
of the Canaanites spread *a*............ Gen 10:18
lest we be scattered *a* upon the...... Gen 11:4
So the LORD scattered them *a* from..... Gen 11:8
did the LORD scatter them *a* upon...... Gen 11:9
And he brought him forth *a*............ Gen 15:5
they had brought them forth *a*........ Gen 19:17
thou shalt spread *a* to the west........ Gen 28:14
a throughout all the land of.......... Ex 5:12
I will spread *a* my hands unto the...... Ex 9:29
spread *a* his hands unto the LORD...... Ex 9:33
of the flesh *a* out of the house...... Ex 12:46
walk *a* upon his staff, then shall...... Ex 21:19
he spread *a* the tent over the........ Ex 40:19
scab spread much *a* in the skin........ Lev 13:7
a leprosy break out *a* in the skin...... Lev 13:12
if it spread much *a* in the skin...... Lev 13:22
it be spread much *a* in the skin...... Lev 13:27
shall tarry *a* out of his tent.......... Lev 14:8
she be born at home, or born *a*........ Lev 18:9
they spread them all *a* for............ Num 11:32
shall he go *a* out of the camp.......... Deut 23:10
whither thou shalt go forth *a*........ Deut 23:12
be, when thou wilt ease thyself *a*...... Deut 23:13
Thou shalt stand *a*, and the man to..... Deut 24:11
bring out the pledge *a* unto thee...... Deut 24:11
her young, spreadeth *a* her wings...... Deut 32:11
thirty daughters, whom he sent *a*...... Judg 12:9
daughters from *a* for his sons........ Judg 12:9
out both of them, he and Samuel, *a*..... 1Sa 9:26
they were spread *a* upon the........ 1Sa 30:16
the street, and did spread them *a*...... 2Sa 22:43
walkest *a* any whither, that thou...... 1Kin 2:42
borrow thee vessels *a* of all thy...... 2Kin 4:3
let us send *a* unto our brethren...... 1Chr 13:2
spread themselves *a* in the valley...... 1Chr 14:13
his name spread *a* even to the........ 2Chr 26:8
And his name spread far *a*............ 2Chr 26:15
to carry it out *a* into the brook...... 2Chr 29:16
as soon as the commandment came *a*..... 2Chr 31:5
scatter you *a* among the nations...... Neh 1:8
queen shall come *a* unto all women..... Est 1:17
is a certain people scattered *a*........ Est 3:8
lion's whelps are scattered *a*.......... Job 4:11
He wandereth *a* for bread, saying,...... Job 15:23
Cast *a* the rage of thy wrath.......... Job 40:11
when he goeth *a*, he telleth it........ Ps 41:6
thine arrows also went *a*............ Ps 77:17
Let thy fountains be dispersed *a*...... Prov 5:16
scattereth *a* the inhabitants.......... Is 24:1
doth he not cast *a* the fitches........ Is 28:25
that spreadeth *a* the earth by........ Is 44:24
pour it out upon the children *a*...... Jer 6:11
a fire sword bereaveth, at home...... Lam 1:20
till ye have scattered them *a*........ Eze 34:21
prosperity shall yet be spread *a*...... Zec 1:17
for I have spread you *a* as the........ Zec 2:6
hereof went *a* into all that land...... Mt 9:26
spread *a* his fame in all that........ Mt 9:31
they fainted, and were scattered *a*..... Mt 9:36
not with me scattereth *a*............ Mt 12:30
of the flock shall be scattered *a*...... Mt 26:31
immediately his fame spread *a*........ Mk 1:28
to blaze *a* the matter, insomuch...... Mk 1:45
secret, but that it should come *a*...... Mk 4:22
(for his name was spread *a*.......... Mk 6:14
all these sayings were noised *a*...... Lk 1:65
they made known *a* the saying........ Lk 2:17
more went there a fame *a* of him...... Lk 5:15
that shall not be known and come *a*..... Lk 8:17
of God that were scattered *a*.......... Jn 11:52
this saying *a* among the brethren...... Jn 21:23
Now when this was noised *a*.......... Acts 2:6
they were all scattered *a*............ Acts 8:1
they that were scattered *a* went...... Acts 8:4
Now they which were scattered *a*...... Acts 11:19
a in our hearts by the Holy Ghost...... Rom 5:5
obedience is come *a* unto all men...... Rom 16:19
is written, He hath dispersed *a*...... 2Cor 9:9
faith to God-ward is spread *a*........ 1Th 1:8
tribes which are scattered *a*.......... Jas 1:1

ABRONAH See EBRONAH.

ABSALOM (*ab´-sal-um*) *A son of David.*
A the son of Maacah the daughter...... 2Sa 3:3
that *A* the son of David had a.......... 2Sa 13:1

A her brother said unto her, Hath....... 2Sa 13:20
A spake unto his brother Amnon......... 2Sa 13:22
for A hated Amnon, because he had 2Sa 13:22
that A had sheepshearers in 2Sa 13:23
A invited all the king's sons............... 2Sa 13:23
A came to the king, and said,.............. 2Sa 13:24
And the king said to A, Nay, my 2Sa 13:25
Then said A, If not, I pray thee,.......... 2Sa 13:26
But A pressed him, that he let 2Sa 13:27
Now A had commanded his servants,... 2Sa 13:28
the servants of A did unto Amnon....... 2Sa 13:29
as A had commanded.......................... 2Sa 13:29
A hath slain all the king's sons,.......... 2Sa 13:30
for by the appointment of A this......... 2Sa 13:32
But A fled... 2Sa 13:34
But A fled, and went to Talmai,........... 2Sa 13:37
So A fled, and went to Geshur, and..... 2Sa 13:38
David longed to go forth unto A.......... 2Sa 13:39
the king's heart was toward A............. 2Sa 14:1
bring the young man A again 2Sa 14:21
A prepared him chariots and 2Sa 14:25
A rose up early, and stood beside....... 2Sa 15:2
then A called unto him, and said,........ 2Sa 15:2
A said unto him, See, thy matters....... 2Sa 15:3
A said moreover, Oh that I were.......... 2Sa 15:4
on this manner did A to all................. 2Sa 15:6
so A stole the hearts of the men 2Sa 15:6
that A said unto the king, I pray......... 2Sa 15:7
But A sent spies throughout all 2Sa 15:10
shall say, A reigneth in Hebron 2Sa 15:10
with A went two hundred men out 2Sa 15:11
A sent for Ahithophel the 2Sa 15:12
increased continually with A 2Sa 15:12
of the men of Israel are after A 2Sa 15:13
we shall not else escape from A 2Sa 15:14
is among the conspirators with A....... 2Sa 15:31
return to the city, and say unto A........ 2Sa 15:34
city, and A came into Jerusalem 2Sa 15:37
into the hand of A thy son.................. 2Sa 16:8
And A, and all the people the men 2Sa 16:15
David's friend, was come unto A......... 2Sa 16:16
A, that Hushai said unto A 2Sa 16:16
A said to Hushai, Is this thy............... 2Sa 16:17
And Hushai said unto A, Nay 2Sa 16:18
Then said A to Ahithophel, Give......... 2Sa 16:20
And Ahithophel said unto A 2Sa 16:21
So they spread A a tent upon the 2Sa 16:22
A went in unto his father's................. 2Sa 16:22
both with David and with A 2Sa 16:23
Moreover Ahithophel said unto A 2Sa 17:1
And the saying pleased A well 2Sa 17:4
Then said A, Call now Hushai the....... 2Sa 17:5
And when Hushai was come to A......... 2Sa 17:6
A spake unto him, saying,................... 2Sa 17:6
And Hushai said unto A, The.............. 2Sa 17:7
among the people that follow A 2Sa 17:9
And A and all the men of Israel 2Sa 17:14
the LORD might bring evil upon A........ 2Sa 17:14
and thus did Ahithophel counsel A..... 2Sa 17:15
a lad saw them, and told A 2Sa 17:18
A passed over Jordan, he and all......... 2Sa 17:24
A made Amasa captain of the host...... 2Sa 17:25
A pitched in the land of Gilead 2Sa 17:26
with the young man, even with A 2Sa 18:5
the captains charge concerning A....... 2Sa 18:5
A met the servants of David 2Sa 18:9
A rode upon a mule, and the mule...... 2Sa 18:9
Behold, I saw A hanged in an oak 2Sa 18:10
that none touch the young man A 2Sa 18:12
them through the heart of A 2Sa 18:14
compassed about and smote A........... 2Sa 18:15
And they took A, and cast him into..... 2Sa 18:17
Now A in his lifetime had taken.......... 2Sa 18:18
said, Is the young man A safe.............. 2Sa 18:29
Cushi, Is the young man A safe 2Sa 18:32
my son A, my son, my son A 2Sa 18:33
God I had died for thee, O A 2Sa 18:33
king weepeth and mourneth for A 2Sa 19:1
loud voice, O my son A, O A 2Sa 19:4
that if A had lived, and all we............. 2Sa 19:6
he is fled out of the land for A 2Sa 19:9
And A, whom we anointed over us,...... 2Sa 19:10
Bichri do us more harm than did A 2Sa 20:6
and his mother bare him after A 1Kin 1:6
I fled because of A thy brother 1Kin 2:7
though he turned not after A 1Kin 2:28
A the son of Maachah the daughter 1Chr 3:2
he took Maachah the daughter of A.... 2Chr 11:20
daughter of A above all his wives........ 2Chr 11:21
when he fled from A his son .... Ps 3:t

ABSALOM'S (ab′-sal-ums)
I love Tamar, my brother A sister....... 2Sa 13:4
desolate in her brother A house......... 2Sa 13:20
A servants set the field on fire........... 2Sa 14:30
when A servants came to the woman .. 2Sa 17:20
is called unto this day, A place 2Sa 18:18

ABSENCE
them in the a of the multitude .... Lk 22:6
only, but now much more in my a........ Phil 2:12

ABSENT
when we are a one from another........ Gen 31:49
as a in body, but present in 1Cor 5:3
the body, we are a from the Lord 2Cor 5:6
rather to be a from the body.............. 2Cor 5:8
that, whether present or a 2Cor 5:9
but being a am bold toward you......... 2Cor 10:1
in word by letters when we are a 2Cor 10:11
being a now I write to them which 2Cor 13:2
I write these things being a............... 2Cor 13:10
I come and see you, or else be a .... Phil 1:27
For though I be a in the flesh .... Col 2:5

ABSTAIN
that they a from pollutions of............. Acts 15:20
That ye a from meats offered to .... Acts 15:29
that ye should a from fornication........ 1Th 4:3
A from all appearance of evil.............. 1Th 5:22
and commanding to a from meats....... 1Ti 4:3
a from fleshly lusts, which war 1Pet 2:11

ABSTINENCE
But after long a Paul stood forth......... Acts 27:21

ABUNDANCE
of heart, for the a of all things .... Deut 28:47
shall suck of the a of the seas............. Deut 33:19
for out of the a of my complaint.......... 1Sa 1:16
the spoil of the city in great a 2Sa 12:30
oxen and fat cattle and sheep in a 1Kin 1:19
oxen and fat cattle and sheep in a 1Kin 1:25
there came no more such a of 1Kin 10:10
trees that are in the vale, for a 1Kin 10:27
for there is a sound of a of rain.......... 1Kin 18:41
David prepared iron in a for the......... 1Chr 22:3
brass in a without weight 1Chr 22:3
Also cedar trees in a.......................... 1Chr 22:4
there are workmen with thee in a 1Chr 22:15
stones, and marble stones in a 1Chr 29:2
sacrifices in a for all Israel................. 1Chr 29:21
trees that are in the vale for a 2Chr 1:15
Even to prepare me timber in a 2Chr 2:9
made all these vessels in great a 2Chr 4:18
that bare spices, and gold in a............ 2Chr 9:1
of gold, and of spices great a 2Chr 9:9
that are in the low plains in a 2Chr 9:27
and he gave them victual in a............. 2Chr 11:23
carried away sheep and camels in a ... 2Chr 14:15
fell to him out of Israel in a 2Chr 15:9
and he had riches and honour in a 2Chr 17:5
had riches and honour in a 2Chr 18:1
killed sheep and oxen for him in a 2Chr 18:2
they found among them in a both....... 2Chr 20:25
by day, and gathered money in a........ 2Chr 24:11
the burnt offerings were in a 2Chr 29:35
in a the firstfruits of corn 2Chr 31:5
and made darts and shields in a 2Chr 32:5
of flocks and herds in a 2Chr 32:29
oliveyards, and fruit trees in a .... Neh 9:25
from another,) and royal wine in a ..... Est 1:7
and a of waters cover these................ Job 22:11
he giveth meat in a .... Job 36:31
that a of waters may cover these........ Job 38:34
themselves in the a of peace.............. Ps 37:11
trusted in the a of his riches.............. Ps 52:7
a of peace so long as the moon.......... Ps 72:7
land brought forth frogs in a.............. Ps 105:30
he that loveth a with increase .... Eccl 5:10
but the a of the rich will not.............. Eccl 5:12
Therefore the a they have gotten,...... Is 15:7
and for the great a of thine .... Is 47:9
because the a of the sea shall be .... Is 60:5
delighted with the a of her glory........ Is 66:11
reveal unto them the a of peace......... Jer 33:6
a of idleness was in her and in .... Eze 16:49
By reason of the a of his horses......... Eze 26:10
and silver, and apparel, in great a...... Zec 14:14
for out of the a of the heart the .... Mt 12:34
be given, and he shall have more a ..... Mt 13:12
be given, and he shall have a............. Mt 25:29
all they did cast in of their a .... Mk 12:44
for of the a of the heart his............... Lk 6:45
in the a of the things which he.......... Lk 12:15
For all these have of their a .... Lk 21:4
they which receive a of grace .... Rom 5:17
of affliction the a of their joy............. 2Cor 8:2
that now at this time your a may 2Cor 8:14
that their a also may be a supply 2Cor 8:14
a which is administered by us 2Cor 8:20
through the a of the revelations,........ 2Cor 12:7
through the a of her delicacies.......... Rev 18:3

ABUNDANT
and in goodness and truth,................ Ex 34:6
be as this day, and much more a .... Is 56:12
a in treasures, thine end is come....... Jer 51:13
these we bestow upon a honour 1Cor 12:23
parts have more a comeliness 1Cor 12:24
having given more a honour to 1Cor 12:24
that the a grace might through........... 2Cor 4:15
affection is more a toward you 2Cor 7:15
the saints, but is also by many 2Cor 9:12
in labours more a, in stripes.............. 2Cor 11:23
in Jesus Christ for me by my .... Phil 1:26
Lord was exceeding a with faith 1Ti 1:14
which according to his a mercy 1Pet 1:3

ABUNDANTLY
Let the waters bring forth a the .... Gen 1:20
which the waters brought forth a....... Gen 1:21
they may breed a in the earth............ Gen 8:17

bring forth a in the earth, and .... Gen 9:7
were fruitful, and increased a............ Ex 1:7
river shall bring forth frogs a............. Ex 8:3
and the water came out a, and the ..... Num 20:11
wine, and oil, and oxen, and sheep a .. 1Chr 12:40
David prepared a before his death 1Chr 22:5
saying, Thou hast shed blood a 1Chr 22:8
of all things brought they in a........... 1Chr 31:5
into whose hand God bringeth a .... Job 12:6
do drop and distil upon man a .... Job 36:28
They shall be a satisfied with............ Ps 36:8
watereth the ridges thereof a .... Ps 65:10
I will a bless her provision .... Ps 132:15
They shall a utter the memory of....... Ps 145:7
drink, yea, drink a, O beloved .... Song 5:1
every one shall howl, weeping a .... Is 15:3
It shall blossom a, and rejoice........... Is 35:2
to our God, for he will a pardon......... Is 55:7
and that they might have it more a .... Jn 10:10
I laboured more a than they all.......... 1Cor 15:10
toward you, and that to you-ward 2Cor 1:12
love which I have more a unto you 2Cor 2:4
by you according to our rule a........... 2Cor 10:15
though the more a I love you 2Cor 12:15
that is able to do exceeding a............ Eph 3:20
endeavoured the more a to see.......... 1Th 2:17
Which he shed on us a through.......... Titus 3:6
willing more a to shew unto the......... Heb 6:17
shall be ministered unto you a 2Pet 1:11

ABUSE
and thrust me through, and a me....... 1Sa 31:4
these uncircumcised come and a me... 1Chr 10:4
that I a not my power in the 1Cor 9:18

ABUSED
a her all the night until the .... Judg 19:25

ABUSERS
nor a of themselves with mankind,.... 1Cor 6:9

ABUSING
that use this world, as not a it........... 1Cor 7:31

ACBOR See ACHBOR.

ACCAD (ak′-kad) A city of Shinar.
was Babel, and Erech, and A............. Gen 10:10

ACCEPT
peradventure he will a of me.............. Gen 32:20
the owner of it shall a thereof .... Ex 22:11
then then a of the punishment of ...... Lev 26:41
they shall a of the punishment of ..... Lev 26:43
and a the work of his hands .... Deut 33:11
against me, let him a an offering........ 1Sa 26:19
the king, The LORD thy God a thee 2Sa 24:23
Will ye a his person .... Job 13:8
you, if ye do secretly a persons......... Job 13:10
a any man's person, neither let......... Job 32:21
for him will I a .... Job 42:8
and a thy burnt sacrifice................... Ps 20:3
a the persons of the wicked............... Ps 82:2
A, I beseech thee, the freewill........... Ps 119:108
It is not good to a the person of .... Prov 18:5
the LORD doth not a a person.............. Jer 14:10
and an oblation, I will not a them ...... Jer 14:12
there will I a them, and there .... Eze 20:40
I will a you with your sweet............... Eze 20:41
and I will a you, saith the Lord.......... Eze 43:27
meat offerings, I will not a them .... Amos 5:22
with thee, or a thy person.................. Mal 1:8
neither will I a an offering at............. Mal 1:10
should I a this of your hand............... Mal 1:13
We a it always, and in all places,....... Acts 24:3

ACCEPTABLE
for it shall not be a for you .... Lev 22:20
let him be a to his brethren, and....... Deut 33:24
be a in thy sight, O Lord, my............. Ps 19:14
unto thee, O LORD, in an a time .... Ps 69:13
of the righteous know what is a......... Prov 10:32
judgment is more a to the LORD.......... Prov 21:3
sought to find out a words .... Eccl 12:10
In an a time have I heard thee,.......... Is 49:8
a fast, and an a day to the LORD......... Is 58:5
To proclaim the a year of the............ Is 61:2
your burnt offerings are not a .... Jer 6:20
let my counsel be a unto thee............ Dan 4:27
To preach the a year of the Lord........ Lk 4:19
a unto God, which is your.................. Rom 12:1
may prove what is that good, and a ... Rom 12:2
things serveth Christ is a to God .... Rom 14:18
up of the Gentiles might be a .... Rom 15:16
Proving what is a unto the Lord......... Eph 5:10
of a sweet smell, a sacrifice a............ Phil 4:18
a in the sight of God our Saviour....... 1Ti 2:3
for that is good and a before God 1Ti 5:4
a to God by Jesus Christ.................... 1Pet 2:5
it patiently, this is a with God........... 1Pet 2:20

ACCEPTABLY
we may serve God a with reverence... Heb 12:28

ACCEPTANCE
come up with a on mine altar............ Is 60:7

ACCEPTATION
saying, and worthy of all a 1Ti 1:15
saying and worthy of all a 1Ti 4:9

ACCEPTED
doest well, shalt thou not be a .... Gen 4:7
I have a thee concerning this............. Gen 19:21
they may be a before the LORD........... Ex 28:38
it shall be a for him to make .... Lev 1:4

the third day, it shall not be a .... Lev 7:18
should it have been a in the .... Lev 10:19
it shall not be a .... Lev 19:7
it shall be perfect to be a .... Lev 22:21
but for a vow it shall not be a .... Lev 22:23
they shall not be a for you .... Lev 22:25
thenceforth it shall be a for an .... Lev 22:27
before the LORD, to be a for you .... Lev 23:11
he was a in the sight of all the 1Sa 18:5
thy voice, and have a thy person 1Sa 25:35
a of the multitude of his .... Est 10:3
the LORD also a Job .... Job 42:9
shall be a upon mine altar .... Is 56:7
I pray thee, be a before thee .... Jer 37:20
our supplication be a before thee .... Jer 42:2
No prophet is a in his own .... Lk 4:24
righteousness, is a with him .... Acts 10:35
Jerusalem may be a of the saints .... Rom 15:31
or absent, we may be a of it 2Cor 5:9
I have heard thee in a time a 2Cor 6:2
behold, now is the a time a 2Cor 6:2
it is a according to that a man 2Cor 8:12
For indeed he a the exhortation 2Cor 8:17
gospel, which ye have not a 2Cor 11:4
he hath made us a in the beloved .... Eph 1:6

ACCEPTEST
neither a thou the person of any, ... Lk 20:21

ACCEPTETH
How much less to him that a not .... Job 34:19
for God now a thy works. .... Eccl 9:7
but the LORD a them not .... Hos 8:13
God a no man's person .... Gal 2:6

ACCEPTING
were tortured, not a deliverance .... Heb 11:35

ACCESS
By whom also we have a by faith .... Rom 5:2
For through him we both have a by .... Eph 2:18
a with confidence by the faith of .... Eph 3:12

ACCHO (ak′-ko) A coastal city in Asher.
drive out the inhabitants of A .... Judg 1:31

ACCO See ACCHO.

ACCOMPANIED
certain brethren from Joppa a him .... Acts 10:23
Moreover these six brethren a me. .... Acts 11:12
there a him into Asia Sopater of .... Acts 20:4
And they a him unto the ship .... Acts 20:38

ACCOMPANY
you, and things that a salvation .... Heb 6:9

ACCOMPANYING
was at Gibeah, the ark of God. 2Sa 6:4

ACCOMPLISH
unto the LORD to a his vow .... Lev 22:21
and thou shalt a my desire 1Kin 5:9
that he may rest, till he shall a .... Job 14:6
they a a diligent search. .... Ps 64:6
but it shall a that which I .... Is 55:11
ye will surely a your vows .... Jer 44:25
thus will I a my fury upon them .... Eze 6:12
thee, and a mine anger upon thee .... Eze 7:8
Thus will I a my wrath against them .... Eze 13:15
to a my anger against them in the .... Eze 20:8
to a my anger against them in the .... Eze 20:21
that he would a seventy years in .... Dan 9:2
which he should a at Jerusalem .... Lk 9:31

ACCOMPLISHED
the mouth of Jeremiah might be a 2Chr 36:22
the days of their purifications a .... Est 2:12
It shall be a before his time, and .... Job 15:32
The desire a is sweet to the soul .... Prov 13:19
unto her, that her warfare is a .... Is 40:2
to pass, when seventy years are a .... Jer 25:12
and of your dispersions are a .... Jer 25:34
be a at Babylon I will visit you. .... Jer 29:10
they shall be a in that day .... Jer 39:16
The LORD hath a his fury .... Lam 4:11
punishment of thine iniquity is a .... Lam 4:22
And when thou hast a them, lie. .... Eze 4:6
Thus shall mine anger be a .... Eze 5:13
when I have a my fury in them. .... Eze 5:13
prosper till the indignation be a .... Dan 11:36
when he shall have a to scatter .... Dan 12:7
days of his ministration were a .... Lk 1:23
the days were a that she should .... Lk 2:6
when eight days were a for the .... Lk 2:21
to the law of Moses were a .... Lk 2:22
how am I straitened till it be a .... Lk 12:50
The Son of man shall be a .... Lk 18:31
is written must yet be a in me. .... Lk 22:37
that all things were now a .... Jn 19:28
And when we had a those days .... Acts 21:5
a in your brethren that are in 1Pet 5:9

ACCOMPLISHING
tabernacle, a the service of God .... Heb 9:6

ACCOMPLISHMENT
to signify the a of the days of .... Acts 21:26

ACCORD
a of thy harvest thou shalt not .... Lev 25:5
Joshua and with Israel, with one a .... Josh 9:2
continued with one a in prayer .... Acts 1:14
were all with one a in one place .... Acts 2:1
daily with one a in the temple. .... Acts 2:46
up their voice to God with one a .... Acts 4:24
all with one a in Solomon's porch .... Acts 5:12

ears, and ran upon him with one a ...... Acts 7:57
the people with one a gave heed. .... Acts 8:6
which opened to them of his own a .... Acts 12:10
but they came with one a to him .... Acts 12:20
us, being assembled with one a .... Acts 15:25
with one a against Paul, and .... Acts 18:12
with one a into the theatre .... Acts 19:29
of his own a he went unto thee, ... 2Cor 8:17
the same love, being of one a .... Phil 2:2

ACCORDING See PREFACE.

ACCORDINGLY
a he will repay, fury to his .... Is 59:18

ACCOUNT
of every one that passeth the a 2Kin 12:4
was the number put in the a of 1Chr 27:24
to the number of their a by the 2Chr 26:11
for he giveth not a of any of his .... Job 33:13
of man, that thou makest a of him .... Ps 144:3
one by one, to find out the a .... Eccl 7:27
they shall give a thereof in the .... Mt 12:36
would take a of his servants .... Mt 18:23
given an a of thy stewardship .... Lk 16:2
may give an a of this concourse .... Acts 19:40
us shall give a of himself to God .... Rom 14:12
Let a man so a of us, as of the 1Cor 4:1
fruit that may abound to your a .... Phil 4:17
thee ought, put that on mine a .... Philem 18
souls, as they that must give a. .... Heb 13:17
Who shall give a to him that is 1Pet 4:5
a that the longsuffering of our 2Pet 3:15

ACCOUNTED
Which also were a giants, as the .... Deut 2:11
(That also was a land of giants .... Deut 2:20
it was nothing a of in the days 1Kin 10:21
it was not any thing a of in the 2Chr 9:20
it shall be a to the Lord for a .... Ps 22:30
for wherein is he to be a of. .... Is 2:22
are a to rule over the Gentiles. .... Mk 10:42
But they which shall be a worthy .... Lk 20:35
that ye may be a worthy to escape .... Lk 21:36
of them should be a the greatest .... Lk 22:24
we are a as sheep for the .... Rom 8:36
it was a to him for righteousness. .... Gal 3:6

ACCOUNTING
A that God was able to raise him .... Heb 11:19

ACCOUNTS
princes might give a unto them. .... Dan 6:2

ACCURSED
for he that is hanged is a of God .... Deut 21:23
And the city shall be a, even it, ... Josh 6:17
keep yourselves from the a thing .... Josh 6:18
lest ye make yourselves a .... Josh 6:18
when ye take of the a thing. .... Josh 6:18
a trespass in the a thing. .... Josh 7:1
of Judah, took of the a thing. .... Josh 7:1
have even taken of the a thing. .... Josh 7:11
enemies, because they were a .... Josh 7:12
ye destroy the a from among you .... Josh 7:12
There is an a thing in the midst. .... Josh 7:13
away the a thing from among you. .... Josh 7:13
a thing shall be burnt with fire .... Josh 7:15
commit a trespass in the a thing .... Josh 22:20
who transgressed in the a thing 1Chr 2:7
an hundred years old shall be a .... Is 65:20
a from Christ for my brethren .... Rom 9:3
the Spirit of God calleth Jesus a 1Cor 12:3
preached unto you, let him be a. .... Gal 1:8
ye have received, let him be a .... Gal 1:9

ACCUSATION
wrote they unto him an a against .... Ezr 4:6
up over his head his a written .... Mt 27:37
of his a was written over .... Mk 15:26
they might find an a against him .... Lk 6:7
any thing from any man by false a .... Lk 19:8
What a bring ye against this man .... Jn 18:29
they brought none a of such .... Acts 25:18
Against an elder receive not an a 1Ti 5:19
bring not railing a against them. 2Pet 2:11
not bring against him a railing a .... Jude 9

ACCUSE
A not a servant unto his master, ... Prov 30:10
that they might a him .... Mt 12:10
that they might a him .... Mk 3:2
to no man, neither a any falsely. .... Lk 3:14
his mouth, that they might a him. .... Lk 11:54
And they began to a him, saying, ... Lk 23:2
those things whereof ye a him .... Lk 23:14
that I will a you to the Father .... Jn 5:45
that they might have to a him. .... Jn 8:6
forth, Tertullus began to a him. .... Acts 24:2
these things, whereof we a him .... Acts 24:8
the things whereof they now a me .... Acts 24:13
a this man, if there be any .... Acts 25:5
these things whereof these a me .... Acts 25:11
I had ought to a my nation of .... Acts 28:19
a your good conversation in. 1Pet 3:16

ACCUSED
came near, and a the Jews. .... Dan 3:8
those men which had a Daniel .... Dan 6:24
men that a him of the chief .... Mk 15:3
the chief priests a him of many. .... Mk 15:3
the same was a unto him that he .... Lk 16:1
scribes stood and vehemently a him ..... Lk 23:10
wherefore he was a of the Jews. .... Acts 23:28
the cause wherefore they a him .... Acts 23:28

Whom I perceived to be a of .... Acts 23:29
before that he which is a have .... Acts 25:16
things whereof I am a of the Jews. .... Acts 26:2
king Agrippa, I am a of the Jews. .... Acts 26:7
children not a of riot or unruly .... Titus 1:6
which a them before our God day. .... Rev 12:10

ACCUSER
for the a of our brethren is cast .... Rev 12:10

ACCUSERS
Woman, where are those thine a .... Jn 8:10
gave commandment to his a also to ...... Acts 23:30
when thine a are also come .... Acts 23:35
Commanding his a to come unto. .... Acts 24:8
accused have the a face to face .... Acts 25:16
Against whom when the a stood up ..... Acts 25:18
affection, trucebreakers, false a 2Ti 3:3
as becometh holiness, not false a .... Titus 2:3

ACCUSETH
there is one that a you, even. .... Jn 5:45

ACCUSING
a or else excusing one another .... Rom 2:15

ACCUSTOMED
do good, that are a to do evil .... Jer 13:23

ACELDAMA (as-el′-dam-ah) A burial ground
bought with Judas′ betrayal money.
called in their proper tongue, A .... Acts 1:19

ACHAIA (ah-ah′-yah) Roman province in
Greece.
when Gallio was the deputy of A .... Acts 18:12
he was disposed to pass into A .... Acts 18:27
through Macedonia and A. .... Acts 19:21
A to make a certain contribution .... Rom 15:26
the firstfruits of A unto Christ. .... Rom 16:5
that A was ready a year ago 1Cor 16:15
all the saints which are in all A 2Cor 1:1
that A was ready a year ago 2Cor 9:2
this boasting in the regions of A 2Cor 11:10
that believe in Macedonia and A 1Th 1:7
Lord not only in Macedonia and A 1Th 1:8

ACHAICUS (ak-ah′-yah-cus) A Corinthian
who visited Paul in Philippi
of Stephanas and Fortunatus and A. 1Cor 16:17
by Stephanus, and Fortunatus, and A. ... 1Cor s

ACHAN (a′-kan) See ACHAR. Soldier under
Joshua executed for disobedience.
for A, the son of Carmi, the son .... Josh 7:1
and A, the son of Carmi, the son .... Josh 7:18
And Joshua said unto A, My son, ... Josh 7:19
A answered Joshua, and said, ... Josh 7:20
took A the son of Zerah, and the .... Josh 7:24
Did not A the son of Zerah commit ..... Josh 22:20

ACHAR (a′-kar) See ACHAN. A form of Achan.
A, the troubler of Israel, who............ 1Chr 2:7

ACHAZ (a′-kaz) See AHAZ. The Greek form of
Ahaz.
and Joatham begat A .... Mt 1:9
And A begat Ezekias .... Mt 1:9

ACHBOR (ak′-bor)
1. Father of an Edomite king.
the son of A reigned in his stead. .... Gen 36:38
And Baal-hanan the son of A died. .... Gen 36:39
the son of A reigned in his stead 1Chr 1:49
2. A messenger of Josiah to Huldah.
A the son of Michaiah, and Shaphan 2Kin 22:12
the priest, and Ahikam, and A 2Kin 22:14
3. Father of Elnathan.
namely, Elnathan the son of A .... Jer 26:22
and Elnathan the son of A .... Jer 36:12

ACHIM (a′-kim) Son of Sadoc; ancestor of
Jesus.
and Sadoc begat A .... Mt 1:14
A begat Eliud .... Mt 1:14

ACHISH (a′-kish)
1. A king of Gath who aided David.
went to a the king of Gath 1Sa 21:10
the servants of A said unto him 1Sa 21:11
sore afraid of A the king of Gath 1Sa 21:12
Then said A unto his servants, Lo, ... 1Sa 21:14
men that were with him unto A 1Sa 21:14
And David dwelt with A at Gath 1Sa 27:3
And David said unto A, If I have 1Sa 27:5
Then A gave him Ziklag that day 1Sa 27:6
and returned, and came to A 1Sa 27:9
A said, Whither have ye made a 1Sa 27:10
A believed David, saying, He hath 1Sa 27:12
A said unto David, Know thou 1Sa 28:1
And David said to A, Surely thou 1Sa 28:2
A said to David, Therefore will I 1Sa 28:2
passed on in the rereward with A 1Sa 29:2
A said unto the princes of the 1Sa 29:3
Then A called David, and said unto. 1Sa 29:6
And David said unto A, But what 1Sa 29:8
A answered and said to David, I 1Sa 29:9
2. A king of Gath during Solomon's reign.
of Shimei ran away unto A son of 1Kin 2:39
went to Gath to A to seek his. 1Kin 2:40

ACHMETHA (ak′-meth-ah) A city in Media.
And there was found at A, in the .... Ezr 6:2

ACHOR (a′-kor) A valley near Jericho.
brought them unto the valley of A. ...... Josh 7:24
place was called, The valley of A .... Josh 7:26

toward Debir from the valley of A .... Josh 15:7
the valley of A a place for the.......... Is 65:10
the valley of A for a door of .... Hos 2:15

ACHSA (ak'-sah) See ACHSAH. *Daughter of Caleb.*
and the daughter of Caleb was A 1Chr 2:49

ACHSAH (ak'-sah) See ACHSA. *A form of Achsa.*
to him will I give A my daughter .... Josh 15:16
he gave him A his daughter to .... Josh 15:17
to him will I give A my daughter....... Judg 1:12
he gave him A his daughter to .... Judg 1:13

ACHSHAPH (ak'-shaf) *A Phoenician city in Asher.*
of Shimron, and to the king of A .... Josh 11:1
the king of A, one.......................... Josh 12:20
Helkath, and Hali, and Beten, and A .. Josh 19:25

ACHZIB (ak'-zib) See CHEZIB.
1. A town in western Judah.
And Keilah, and A, and Mareshah.... Josh 15:44
the houses of A shall be a lie to ...... Mic 1:14
2. A coastal city in Asher.
at the sea from the coast of A .... Josh 19:29
of Zidon, nor of Ahlab, nor of A....... Judg 1:31

ACKNOWLEDGE
But he shall a the men of the .... Deut 21:17
neither did he a his brethren............ Deut 33:9
For I a my transgressions .... Ps 51:3
In all thy ways a him, and he .... Prov 3:6
and, ye that are near, a my might ...... Is 33:13
all that see them shall a them .... Is 61:9
of us, and Israel a us not................. Is 63:16
Only a thine iniquity, that thou........ Jer 3:13
We a, O LORD, our wickedness, and .. Jer 14:20
so will I a them that are carried .... Jer 24:5
a strange god, whom he shall a .... Dan 11:39
till they a their offence, and............ Hos 5:15
let him a that the things that I 1Cor 14:37
therefore a ye them that are such 1Cor 16:18
unto you, than what ye read or a 2Cor 1:13
trust ye shall a even to the end......... 2Cor 1:13

ACKNOWLEDGED
And Judah a them, and said, She ...... Gen 38:26
I a my sin unto thee, and mine......... Ps 32:5
As also ye have a us in part 2Cor 1:14

ACKNOWLEDGEMENT
to the a of the mystery of God,......... Col 2:2

ACKNOWLEDGETH
[but] he that a the Son hath........... 1Jn 2:23

ACKNOWLEDGING
repentance to the a of the truth........ 2Ti 2:25
the a of the truth which is after .... Titus 1:1
may become effectual by the a of ..... Philem 6

ACQUAINT
A now thyself with him, and be at..... Job 22:21

ACQUAINTANCE
it to them, every man of his a........... 2Kin 12:5
receive no more money of your a 2Kin 12:7
mine a are verily estranged from ...... Job 19:13
that had been of his a before............ Job 42:11
neighbours, and a fear to mine a ...... Ps 31:11
mine equal, my guide, and mine a .... Ps 55:13
hast put away mine a far from me..... Ps 88:8
from me, and mine a into darkness.... Ps 88:18
him among their kinsfolk and a .... Lk 2:44
And all his a, and the women that..... Lk 23:49
a to minister or come unto him .... Acts 24:23

ACQUAINTED
down, and art a with all my ways ..... Ps 139:3
a man of sorrows, and a with grief .... Is 53:3

ACQUAINTING
yet a mine heart with wisdom .... Eccl 2:3

ACQUIT
thou wilt not a me from mine........... Job 10:14
and will not at all a the wicked......... Nah 1:3

ACRE
as it were an half a of land.............. 1Sa 14:14

ACRES
ten a of vineyard shall yield one....... Is 5:10

ACSAH See ACHSA.

ACSHAPH See ACHSHAPH.

ACT
to pass this a, his strange a.............. Is 28:21
the a of violence is in their .... Is 59:6
taken in adultery, in the very a .... Jn 8:4

ACTIONS
and by him a are weighed 1Sa 2:3

ACTIVITY
knowest any men of a among them ... Gen 47:6

ACTS
And his miracles, and his a .... Deut 11:3
great a of the LORD which he did ...... Deut 11:7
the righteous a of the LORD............... Judg 5:11
even the righteous a toward the .... Judg 5:11
all the righteous a of the LORD 1Sa 12:7
of Kabzeel, who had done many a 2Sa 23:20
I heard in mine own land of thy a 1Kin 10:6
And the rest of the a of Solomon...... 1Kin 11:41

in the book of the a of Solomon........ 1Kin 11:41
Now the rest of the a of Jeroboam.... 1Kin 14:19
Now the rest of the a of Rehoboam... 1Kin 14:29
Now the rest of the a of Abijam 1Kin 15:7
The rest of all the a of Asa.............. 1Kin 15:23
Now the rest of the a of Nadab........ 1Kin 15:31
Now the rest of the a of Baasha....... 1Kin 16:5
Now the rest of the a of Elah 1Kin 16:14
Now the rest of the a of Zimri.......... 1Kin 16:20
Now the rest of the a of Omri.......... 1Kin 16:27
Now the rest of the a of Ahab 1Kin 22:39
the rest of the a of Jehoshaphat 1Kin 22:45
Now the rest of the a of Ahaziah...... 2Kin 1:18
And the rest of the a of Joram.......... 2Kin 8:23
Now the rest of the a of Jehu 2Kin 10:34
And the rest of the a of Joash 2Kin 12:19
And the rest of the a of Jehoahaz..... 2Kin 13:8
And the rest of the a of Joash 2Kin 13:12
Now the rest of the a of Jehoash 2Kin 14:15
And the rest of the a of Amaziah...... 2Kin 14:18
Now the rest of the a of Jeroboam.... 2Kin 14:28
And the rest of the a of Azariah 2Kin 15:6
And the rest of the a of Zachariah.... 2Kin 15:11
And the rest of the a of Shallum....... 2Kin 15:15
And the rest of the a of Menahem.... 2Kin 15:21
And the rest of the a of Pekahiah..... 2Kin 15:26
And the rest of the a of Pekah 2Kin 15:31
Now the rest of the a of Jotham 2Kin 15:36
Now the rest of the a of Ahaz.......... 2Kin 16:19
Now the rest of the a of Hezekiah.... 2Kin 20:20
And the rest of the a of Manasseh.... 2Kin 21:17
Now the rest of the a of Amon......... 2Kin 21:25
the a that he had done in Beth-el 2Kin 23:19
Now the rest of the a of Josiah 2Kin 23:28
the rest of the a of Jehoiakim........... 2Kin 24:5
Of Kabzeel, who had done many a 1Chr 11:22
Now the a of David the king,........... 1Chr 29:29
heard in mine own land of thine a 2Chr 9:5
Now the rest of the a of Solomon..... 2Chr 9:29
Now the a of Rehoboam, first and..... 2Chr 12:15
And the rest of the a of Abijah 2Chr 13:22
the a of Asa, first and last, lo,.......... 2Chr 16:11
the rest of the a of Jehoshaphat 2Chr 20:34
Now the rest of the a of Amaziah..... 2Chr 25:26
Now the rest of the a of Uzziah 2Chr 26:22
Now the rest of the a of Jotham 2Chr 27:7
Now the rest of his a and of all 2Chr 28:26
Now the rest of the a of Jehoash...... 2Chr 32:32
Now the rest of the a of Manasseh.... 2Chr 33:18
Now the rest of the a of Josiah 2Chr 35:26
the rest of the a of Jehoiakim........... 2Chr 36:8
all the a of his power and of his....... Est 10:2
his a unto the children of Israel........ Ps 103:7
utter the mighty a of the LORD .... Ps 106:2
and shall declare thy mighty a .... Ps 145:4
of the might of thy terrible a............ Ps 145:6
to the sons of men his mighty a .... Ps 145:12
Praise him for his mighty a.............. Ps 150:2

ACZIB See ACHZIB.

ADADAH (ad'-ad-ah) *A city in southern Judah.*
And Kinah, and Dimonah, and A...... Josh 15:22

ADAH (a'-dah)
1. A wife of Lamech.
the name of the one was A .... Gen 4:19
And A bare Jabal .... Gen 4:20
And Lamech said unto his wives, A ... Gen 4:23
2. A wife of Esau.
The daughter of Elon the................. Gen 36:2
And A bare to Esau Eliphaz............. Gen 36:4
A the wife of Esau......................... Gen 36:10
were the sons of A Esau's wife......... Gen 36:12
these were the sons of A .... Gen 36:16

ADAIAH (ad-a-i'-yah)
1. Grandfather of King Josiah.
the daughter of A of Boscath........... 2Kin 22:1
2. A Levite descendant of Gershon.
the son of Zerah, the son of A 1Chr 6:41
3. A son of Shimhi.
And A, and Beraiah, and Shimrath,.... 1Chr 8:21
4. A Levite of Jerusalem.
the son of Jeroham, the son of A...... 1Chr 9:12
5. Father of Maaseiah.
Of Obed, and Maaseiah the son of A .. 2Chr 23:1
6. Married a foreign wife in Exile.
Meshullam, Malluch, and A, Jashub,.. Ezr 10:29
7. Married a foreign wife in Exile.
And Shelemiah, and Nathan, and A... Ezr 10:39
8. A descendant of Pharez.
the son of Hazaiah, the son of A ...... Neh 11:5
9. An Aaronite Levite.
the son of Jeroham, the son of A ...... Neh 11:12

ADALIA (ad-a-li'-yah) *A son of Haman.*
And Poratha, and A, and Aridatha,.... Est 9:8

ADAM (ad'-um) See ADAM'S.
1. First man created by God.
brought them unto A to see what...... Gen 2:19
whatsoever A called every living....... Gen 2:19
A gave names to all cattle, and to ..... Gen 2:20
but for A there was not found an ...... Gen 2:20
a deep sleep to fall upon A .... Gen 2:21
A said, This is now bone of my .... Gen 2:23
and A and his wife had themselves.... Gen 3:8
And the LORD God called unto A ...... Gen 3:9
unto A he said, Because thou hast .... Gen 3:17
A called his wife's name Eve .... Gen 3:20
Unto A also and to his wife did .... Gen 3:21
And A knew Eve his wife................. Gen 4:1

And A knew his wife again............... Gen 4:25
the book of the generations of A ...... Gen 5:1
them, and called their name A.......... Gen 5:2
A lived an hundred and thirty .... Gen 5:3
the days of a after he had .... Gen 5:4
all the days that A lived were .... Gen 5:5
when he separated the sons of .... Deut 32:8
A, Sheth, Enosh,............................ 1Chr 1:1
I covered my transgressions as A ...... Job 31:33
of Seth, which was the son of A .... Lk 3:38
death reigned from A to Moses......... Rom 5:14
For as in A all die, even so in.......... 1Cor 15:22
The first man A was made a living..... 1Cor 15:45
the last A was made a quickening..... 1Cor 15:45
For A was first formed, then Eve 1Ti 2:13
A was not deceived, but the woman .. 1Ti 2:14
And Enoch also, the seventh from A .. Jude 14
2. A town in Manasseh.
an heap very far from the city A ...... Josh 3:16

ADAMAH (ad'-am-ah) *A walled city in Naphtali.*
And A, and Ramah, and Hazor,........ Josh 19:36

ADAMANT
As an a harder than flint have I........ Eze 3:9
made their hearts as an a stone .... Zec 7:12

ADAMI (ad'-am-i) *A variant of Adamah.*
from Allon to Zaanannim, and A...... Josh 19:33

ADAMI NEKEB See NEKEB.

ADAM'S (ad'-ums)
the similitude of A transgression....... Rom 5:14

ADAR (a'-dar) See ADDAR, ATABOTH-ADAR.
1. A city in southern Judah.
along to Hezron, and went up to A.... Josh 15:3
2. Twelfth month of the Hebrew year.
on the third day of the month A .... Ezr 6:15
month, that is, the month A.............. Est 3:7
month, which is the month A............ Est 3:13
month, which is the month A............ Est 8:12
month, that is, the month A.............. Est 9:1
day also of the month A, and slew .... Est 9:15
the thirteenth day of the month A ..... Est 9:17
of the month A a day of gladness..... Est 9:19
the fourteenth day of the month A .... Est 9:21

ADBEEL (ad'-be-el) *Son of Ishmael.*
and Kedar, and A, and Mibsam,....... Gen 25:13
then Kedar, and A, and Mibsam,....... 1Chr 1:29

ADD
The LORD shall a to me another .... Gen 30:24
shall a the fifth part thereto,............. Lev 5:16
shall a the fifth part more............... Lev 6:5
then he shall a a fifth part .... Lev 27:13
then he shall a the fifth part of .... Lev 27:15
then he shall a the fifth part of .... Lev 27:19
shall a a fifth part of it................... Lev 27:27
he shall a thereto the fifth part .... Lev 27:31
a unto it the fifth part thereof,.......... Num 5:7
and to them ye shall a forty............. Num 35:6
Ye shall not a unto the word .... Deut 4:2
thou shalt not a thereto, nor............ Deut 12:32
then shalt thou a three cities............ Deut 19:9
to a drunkenness to thirst .... Deut 29:19
LORD thy God a unto the people 2Sa 24:3
heavy yoke, I will a to your yoke 1Kin 12:11
heavy, and I will a to your yoke 1Kin 12:14
I will a unto thy days fifteen 2Kin 20:6
and thou mayest a thereto 1Chr 22:14
yoke heavy, but I will a thereto 2Chr 10:14
ye intend to a more to our sins........ 2Chr 28:13
A iniquity unto their iniquity............ Ps 69:27
and peace, shall they a to thee......... Prov 3:2
A thou not unto his words, lest .... Prov 30:6
a year to year................................ Is 29:1
that they may a sin to sin .... Is 30:1
I will a unto thy days fifteen .... Is 38:5
can a one cubit unto his stature .... Mt 6:27
can a to his stature one cubit .... Lk 12:25
supposing to a affliction to my .... Phil 1:16
diligence, a to your faith virtue 2Pet 1:5
If any man shall a unto these .... Rev 22:18
God shall a unto him the plagues...... Rev 22:18

ADDAN (ad'-dan) *Home of some Exiles in Babylon.*
Tel-melah, Tel-harsa, Cherub, A....... Ezr 2:59

ADDAR (ad'-dar) See ADAR, ATAROTH-ADDAR. *Son of Bela.*
And the sons of Bela were, A........... 1Chr 8:3

ADDED
and he a no more........................... Deut 5:22
for we have a unto all our sins......... 1Sa 12:19
there were a besides unto them .... Jer 36:32
for the LORD hath a grief to my........ Jer 45:3
excellent majesty was a unto me ...... Dan 4:36
these things shall be a unto you........ Mt 6:33
A yet this above all, that he .... Lk 3:20
these things shall be a unto you .... Lk 12:31
as they heard these things, he a .... Lk 19:11
the same day there were a unto......... Acts 2:41
the Lord a to the church daily .... Acts 2:47
were the more a to the Lord............. Acts 5:14
much people was a unto the Lord ..... Acts 11:24
in conference a nothing to me .... Gal 2:6
It was a because of......................... Gal 3:19

ADDER
an *a* in the path, that biteth the......... Gen 49:17
the deaf *a* that stoppeth her ear......... Ps 58:4
shalt tread upon the lion and *a*......... Ps 91:13
a serpent, and stingeth like an *a*...... Prov 23:32

ADDERS'
a poison is under their lips......... Ps 140:3

ADDETH
For he a rebellion unto his sin,......... Job 34:37
rich, and he a no sorrow with it......... Prov 10:22
mouth, and a learning to his lips......... Prov 16:23
no man disannulleth, or a thereto...... Gal 3:15

ADDI (ad'-di) Son of Cozam; ancestor of Jesus.
of Melchi, which was the son of A......... Lk 3:28

ADDICTED
that they have a themselves to.......... 1Cor 16:15

ADDITION
molten, at the side of every a......... 1Kin 7:30

ADDITIONS
were certain a made of thin work......... 1Kin 7:29
of every one, and a round about......... 1Kin 7:36

ADDON (ad'-don) A form of Addan.
Tei-melah, Tel-haresha, Cherub, A......... Neh 7:61

ADER (a'-dur) A son of Beriah.
And Zebadiah, and Arad, and A......... 1Chr 8:15

ADIEL (a'-de-el)
1. A descendant of Simeon.
and Jeshohaiah, and Asaiah, and A...... 1Chr 4:36
2. Father of Maasiai.
and Maasiai the son of A, the son... 1Chr 9:12
3. Father of Azmaveth.
was Azmaveth the son of A........ 1Chr 27:25

ADIN (a'-din)
1. Family who returned from exile.
The children of A, four hundred......... Ezr 2:15
The children of A, six hundred......... Neh 7:20
2. Family who sealed the covenant with Nehemiah.
Adonijah, Bigvai, A,......... Neh 10:16
3. An exilic family with Ezra.
Of the sons also of A......... Ezr 8:6

ADINA (ad'-in-ah) A "mighty man" of David.
A the son of Shiza the Reubenite,..... 1Chr 11:42

ADINO (a'-din-o) A "mighty man" of David.
the same was A the Eznite......... 2Sa 23:8

ADITHAIM (ad-ith-a'-im) A city in the plain of Judah.
Sharaim, and A, and Gederah......... Josh 15:36

ADJURE
How many times shall I a thee......... 1Kin 22:16
How many times shall I a thee......... 2Chr 18:15
I a thee by the living God, that......... Mt 26:63
I a thee by God, that thou......... Mk 5:7
We a you by Jesus whom Paul......... Acts 19:13

ADJURED
Joshua a them at that time,......... Josh 6:26
for Saul had a the people......... 1Sa 14:24

ADLAI (ad'-la-i) Father of Shapat.
valleys was Shaphat the son of A... 1Chr 27:29

ADMAH (ad'-mah) A city destroyed with Sodom and Gomorrah.
unto Sodom, and Gomorrah, and A.... Gen 10:19
of Gomorrah, Shinab king of A......... Gen 14:2
of Gomorrah, and the king of A...... Gen 14:8
of Sodom, and Gomorrah, A, and ... Deut 29:23
how shall I make thee as A......... Hos 11:8

ADMATHA (ad'-math-ah) A prince of Persia.
unto him was Carshena, Shethar, A..... Est 1:14

ADMINISTERED
which is a by us to the glory of......... 2Cor 8:19
this abundance which is a by us...... 2Cor 8:20

ADMINISTRATION
For the a of this service not......... 2Cor 9:12

ADMINISTRATIONS
And there are differences of......... 1Cor 12:5

ADMIRATION
persons in a because of advantage......... Jude 16
saw her, I wondered with great a...... Rev 17:6

ADMIRED
to be a in all them that believe......... 2Th 1:10

ADMONISH
able also to a one another......... Rom 15:14
over you in the Lord, and a you...... 1Th 5:12
an enemy, but a him as a brother...... 2Th 3:15

ADMONISHED
king, who will no more be a......... Eccl 4:13
further, by these, my son, be a......... Eccl 12:12
that I have a you this day......... Jer 42:19
was now already past, Paul a them... Acts 27:9
as Moses was a of God when he was... Heb 8:5

ADMONISHING
a one another in psalms and hymns ..... Col 3:16

ADMONITION
and they are written for our a......... 1Cor 10:11
in the nurture and a of the Lord......... Eph 6:4

the first and second a reject......... Titus 3:10

ADNA (ad'-nah) See ADNAH.
1. Married a foreigner while in exile.
And Chelal, Benaiah, Maaseiah, ... Ezr 10:30
2. A priest during Joiakim's reign.
Of Harim, A......... Neh 12:15

ADNAH (ad'-nah) See ADNA.
1. A captain in David's army.
there fell to him of Manasseh, A... 1Chr 12:20
2. A commander in Jehoshaphat's army.
A the chief, and with him mighty... 2Chr 17:14

ADO
unto them, Why make ye this a......... Mk 5:39

ADONI-BEZEK (ad'-on-i-be'-zek) A lord of a Canaanite city.
And they found A in Bezek......... Judg 1:5
But A fled......... Judg 1:6
A said, Threescore and ten kings,...... Judg 1:7

ADONIJAH (ad-on-i'-jah) See TOB-ADONIJAH.
1. A son of David.
the fourth, A the son of Haggith......... 2Sa 3:4
Then A the son of Haggith exalted...... 1Kin 1:5
and they following A helped him 1Kin 1:7
to David, were not with A......... 1Kin 1:8
A slew sheep and oxen and fat......... 1Kin 1:9
Hast thou not heard that A the...... 1Kin 1:11
why then doth A reign......... 1Kin 1:13
And now, behold, A reigneth......... 1Kin 1:18
a shall reign after me, and he......... 1Kin 1:24
him, and say, God save king A......... 1Kin 1:25
And A and all the guests that were... 1Kin 1:41
And A said unto him, Come in......... 1Kin 1:42
answered and said to A......... 1Kin 1:43
that were with A were afraid......... 1Kin 1:49
A feared because of Solomon, and... 1Kin 1:50
Behold, A feareth king Solomon...... 1Kin 1:51
A the son of Haggith came to......... 1Kin 2:13
Solomon, to speak unto him for A... 1Kin 2:19
be given to A thy brother to wife ... 1Kin 2:21
ask Abishag the Shunammite for A... 1Kin 2:22
if A have not spoken this word......... 1Kin 2:23
A shall be put to death this day...... 1Kin 2:24
for Joab had turned after A......... 1Kin 2:28
the fourth, A the son of Haggith...... 1Chr 3:2
2. A Levite under King Jehoshaphat.
Shemiramoth, and Jehonathan, and A 2Chr 17:8
3. A clan leader who sealed the covenant with Nehemiah.
Adonijah, Adin,......... Neh 10:16

ADONIKAM (ad-on-i'-kam) A family in exile.
The children of A, six hundred......... Ezr 2:13
And of the last sons of A, whose...... Ezr 8:13
The children of A, six hundred...... Neh 7:18

ADONIRAM (ad-on-i'-ram) See ADORAM.
A tribute officer under Solomon.
A the son of Abda was over the 1Kin 4:6
and A was over the levy......... 1Kin 5:14

ADONI-ZEDEK (ad-on'-i-ze'-dek) Canaanite king slain by Joshua.
when A king of Jerusalem had......... Josh 10:1
Wherefore A king of Jerusalem ...... Josh 10:3

ADOPTION
ye have received the Spirit of a......... Rom 8:15
ourselves, waiting for the a......... Rom 8:23
to whom pertaineth the a, and the...... Rom 9:4
we might receive the a of sons......... Gal 4:5
predestinated us unto the a of......... Eph 1:5

ADORAM (ad-o-ra'-im) A city built by Rehoboam.
And A, and Lachish, and Azekah,...... 2Chr 11:9

ADORAM (ad-o'-ram) See ADONIRAM.
1. A tribute officer under David.
And A was over the tribute......... 2Sa 20:24
2. A tribute officer under Solomon.
Then king Rehoboam sent A......... 1Kin 12:18

ADORN
that women a themselves in modest 1Ti 2:9
that they may a the doctrine of...... Titus 2:10

ADORNED
shalt again be a with thy tabrets......... Jer 31:4
how it was a with goodly stones,...... Lk 21:5
a themselves, being in subjection 1Pet 3:5
as a bride a for her husband......... Rev 21:2

ADORNETH
as a bride a herself with her......... Is 61:10

ADORNING
Whose a let it not be that......... 1Pet 3:3
outward a of plaiting the hair......... 1Pet 3:3

ADRAMMELECH (a-dram'-mel-ek)
1. A god of the Avites.
burnt their children in fire to A 2Kin 17:31
2. A son of Sennacherib.
house of Nisroch his god, that A...... 2Kin 19:37
house of Nisroch his god, that A... Is 37:38

ADRAMYTTIAN See ADRAMYTTIUM.

ADRAMYTTIUM (a-dram-mit'-te-um) A seaport of Mysia in Asia Minor.
And entering into a ship of A......... Acts 27:2

ADRIA (a'-dre-ah) The Adriatic Sea.
as we were driven up and down in A Acts 27:27

ADRIATIC See ADRIA.

ADRIEL (a'-dre-el) Husband of Merab, Saul's daughter.
unto A the Meholathite to wife......... 1Sa 18:19
whom she brought up for A the son ... 2Sa 21:8

ADULLAM (a-dul'-lam) See ADULLAMITE.
1. A city south of Jerusalem.
the king of A, one......... Josh 12:15
Jarmuth, and A, Socoh, and Azekah,.. Josh 15:35
And Beth-zur, and Shoco, and A......... 2Chr 11:7
Zanoah, A, and in their villages,...... Neh 11:30
he shall come unto A the glory of ...... Mic 1:15
2. A cave near the city of Adullam.
thence, and escaped to the cave of A.. 1Sa 22:1
harvest time unto the cave of A...... 2Sa 23:13
rock to David, into the cave of A ... 1Chr 11:15

ADULLAMITE (a-dul'-lam-ite) A native of Adullam.
and turned in to a certain A......... Gen 38:1
he and his friend Hirah the A......... Gen 38:12
by the hand of his friend the A...... Gen 38:20

ADULTERER
with his neighbour's wife, the a......... Lev 20:10
The eye also of the a waiteth for...... Job 24:15
the sorceress, the seed of the a...... Is 57:3

ADULTERERS
him, and hast been partaker with a ... Ps 50:18
for they be all a, an assembly of......... Jer 9:2
For the land is full of a......... Jer 23:10
They are all a, as an oven heated ...... Hos 7:4
the sorcerers, and against the a......... Mal 3:5
men are, extortioners, unjust, a......... Lk 18:11
fornicators, nor idolaters, nor a......... 1Cor 6:9
whoremongers and a God will judge... Heb 13:4
for a and adulteresses, know ye not... Jas 4:4

ADULTERESS
the a shall surely be put to......... Lev 20:10
the a will hunt for the precious......... Prov 6:26
beloved of her friend, yet an a......... Hos 3:1
man, she shall be called an a......... Rom 7:3
so that she is no a, though she......... Rom 7:3

ADULTERESSES
judge them after the manner of a...... Eze 23:45
because they are a, and blood is...... Eze 23:45
Ye adulterers and a, know ye not...... Jas 4:4

ADULTERIES
I have seen thine a, and thy......... Jer 13:27
said I unto her that was old in a ...... Eze 23:43
her a from between her breasts......... Hos 2:2
proceed evil thoughts, murders, a...... Mt 15:19
of men, proceed evil thoughts, a...... Mk 7:21

ADULTEROUS
Such is the way of an a woman......... Prov 30:20
a generation seeketh after a sign...... Mt 12:39
a generation seeketh after a sign...... Mt 16:4
of me and of my words in this a...... Mk 8:38

ADULTERY
Thou shalt not commit a......... Ex 20:14
a with another man's wife......... Lev 20:10
even he that committeth a with......... Lev 20:10
Neither shalt thou commit a......... Deut 5:18
committeth a with a woman lacketh ... Prov 6:32
committed a I had put her away......... Jer 3:8
committed a with stones and with ...... Jer 3:9
the full, they then committed a......... Jer 5:7
ye steal, murder, and commit a......... Jer 7:9
they commit a, and walk in lies......... Jer 23:14
have committed a with their......... Jer 29:23
But as a wife that committeth a......... Eze 16:32
That they have committed a......... Eze 23:37
their idols have they committed a ... Eze 23:37
and stealing, and committing a......... Hos 4:2
and your spouses shall commit a...... Hos 4:13
your spouses when they commit a...... Hos 4:14
old time, Thou shalt not commit a...... Mt 5:27
a with her already in his heart......... Mt 5:28
causeth her to commit a......... Mt 5:32
her that is divorced committeth a... Mt 5:32
shall marry another, committeth a... Mt 19:9
which is put away doth commit a...... Mt 19:9
murder, Thou shalt not commit a...... Mt 19:18
another, committeth a against her... Mk 10:11
to another, she committeth a......... Mk 10:12
the commandments, Do not commit a Mk 10:19
and marrieth another, committeth a... Lk 16:18
from her husband committeth a......... Lk 16:18
the commandments, Do not commit a... Lk 18:20
unto him a woman taken in a......... Jn 8:3
Master, this woman was taken in a ... Jn 8:4
sayest a man should not commit a ... Rom 2:22
dost thou commit a......... Rom 2:22
For this, Thou shalt not commit a...... Rom 13:9
A, fornication, uncleanness,......... Gal 5:19
For he that said, Do not commit a ... Jas 2:11
Now if thou commit no a, yet if......... Jas 2:11
Having eyes full of a, and that......... 2Pet 2:14
them that commit a with her into...... Rev 2:22

ADUMMIM (a-dum'-mim)
that is before the going up to A......... Josh 15:7
is over against the going up of A ... Josh 18:17

ADVANCED

It is the LORD that *a* Moses 1Sa 12:6
a him, and set his seat above all .... Est 3:1
how he had *a* him above the .... Est 5:11
whereunto the king *a* him .... Est 10:2

ADVANTAGE

What *a* will it be unto thee .... Job 35:3
What *a* then hath the Jew .... Rom 3:1
Lest Satan should get an *a* of us 2Cor 2:11
in admiration because of *a* .... Jude 16

ADVANTAGED

For what is a man, if he gain .... Lk 9:25

ADVANTAGETH

what *a* it me, if the dead rise 1Cor 15:32

ADVENTURE

which would not *a* to set the sole ...... Deut 28:56
not *a* himself into the theatre .... Acts 19:31

ADVENTURED

a his life far, and delivered you .... Judg 9:17

ADVERSARIES

and an adversary unto thine *a* .... Ex 23:22
lest their *a* should behave .... Deut 32:27
and will render vengeance to his *a* .. Deut 32:43
Art thou for us, or for our *a* .... Josh 5:13
The *a* of the LORD shall be broken 1Sa 2:10
ye should this day be *a* unto me 2Sa 19:22
Now when the *a* of Judah and .... Ezr 4:1
our *a* said, They shall not know .... Neh 4:11
render evil for good are mine *a* .... Ps 38:20
mine *a* are all before thee .... Ps 69:19
and consumed that are *a* to my soul .. Ps 71:13
and turned my hand against their *a* .. Ps 81:14
set up the right hand of his *a* .... Ps 89:42
For my love they are my *a* .... Ps 109:4
reward of mine *a* from the LORD .... Ps 109:20
Let mine *a* be clothed with shame, .. Ps 109:29
Ah, I will ease me of mine *a* .... Is 1:24
set up the *a* of Rezin against him ...... Is 9:11
the *a* of Judah shall be cut off .... Is 11:13
he will repay, fury to his *a* .... Is 59:18
our *a* have trodden down thy .... Is 63:18
to make thy name known to thine *a* .. Is 64:2
and all thine *a*, every one of them .... Jer 30:16
that he may avenge him of his *a* .... Jer 46:10
and their *a* said, We offend not, ... Jer 50:7
Her *a* are the chief, her enemies .... Lam 1:5
the *a* saw her, and did mock at her ... Lam 1:7
that his *a* should be round about ...... Lam 1:17
hath set up the horn of thine *a* .... Lam 2:17
shall be lifted up upon thine *a* .... Mic 5:9
LORD will take vengeance on his *a* ..... Nah 1:2
things, all his *a* were ashamed .... Lk 13:17
which all your *a* shall not be .... Lk 21:15
unto me, and there are many *a* 1Cor 16:9
And in nothing terrified by your *a* .... Phil 1:28
which shall devour the *a* .... Heb 10:27

ADVERSARY

an *a* unto thine adversaries .... Ex 23:22
in the way for an *a* against him .... Num 22:22
her *a* also provoked her sore, for 1Sa 1:6
in the battle he be an *a* to us 1Sa 29:4
is neither *a* nor evil occurrent 1Kin 5:4
LORD stirred up an *a* unto Solomon... 1Kin 11:14
And God stirred him up another *a*. 1Kin 11:23
he was an *a* to Israel all the 1Kin 11:25
And Esther said, The *a* and enemy is. Est 7:6
that mine *a* had written a book .... Job 31:35
how long shall the *a* reproach .... Ps 74:10
who is mine *a* .... Is 50:8
The *a* hath spread out his hand .... Lam 1:10
stood with his right hand as an *a* ...... Lam 2:4
not have believed that the *a* .... Lam 4:12
An *a* there shall be even round .... Amos 3:11
Agree with thine *a* quickly .... Mt 5:25
lest at any time the *a* deliver .... Mt 5:25
with thine *a* to the magistrate .... Lk 12:58
him, saying, Avenge me of mine *a* .... Lk 18:3
to the *a* to speak reproachfully 1Ti 5:14
because your *a* the devil, as 1Pet 5:8

ADVERSITIES

saved you out of all your *a* 1Sa 10:19
thou hast known my soul in *a* .... Ps 31:7

ADVERSITY

redeemed my soul out of all *a* 2Sa 4:9
for God did vex them with all *a* 2Chr 15:6
for I shall never be in *a* .... Ps 10:6
But in mine *a* they rejoiced, and, ... Ps 35:15
give him rest from the days of *a* .... Ps 94:13
times, and a brother is born for *a* ...... Prov 17:17
If thou faint in the day of *a* .... Prov 24:10
but in the day of *a* consider .... Eccl 7:14
the Lord give you the bread of *a* .... Is 30:20
and them which suffer *a*, as being .... Heb 13:3

ADVERTISE

I will *a* thee what this people .... Num 24:14
And I thought to *a* thee, saying, ... Ruth 4:4

ADVICE

consider of it, take *a*, and speak .... Judg 19:30
give here your *a* and counsel .... Judg 20:7
And blessed be thy *a*, and blessed 1Sa 25:33
that our *a* should not be first 2Sa 19:43
What *a* give ye that we return 2Chr 10:9
them after the *a* of the young men ... 2Chr 10:14
Then Amaziah king of Judah took *a*. 2Chr 25:17

and with good *a* make war .... Prov 20:18
And herein I give my *a* 2Cor 8:10

ADVISE

now *a*, and see what answer I shall.... 2Sa 24:13
How do ye *a* that I may answer 1Kin 12:6
Now therefore *a* thyself what word .. 1Chr 21:12

ADVISED

but with the well *a* is wisdom .... Prov 13:10
the more part *a* to depart thence....... Acts 27:12

ADVISEMENT

Philistines upon *a* sent him away 1Chr 12:19

ADVOCATE

we have an *a* with the Father, ... 1Jn 2:1

AENEAS

(e'-ne-as) *A paralytic healed by Peter.*
he found a certain man named A .... Acts 9:33
And Peter said unto him, A .... Acts 9:34

AENON

(e'-non) *A place in the valley of Shechem.*
was baptizing in A near to Salim.......... Jn 3:23

AFAR

his eyes, and saw the place *a* off .... Gen 22:4
And when they saw him *a* off .... Gen 37:18
And his sister stood *a* off .... Ex 2:4
it, they removed, and stood *a* off ...... Ex 20:18
And the people stood *a* off .... Ex 20:21
and worship ye *a* off .... Ex 24:1
a off from the camp, and called it ..... Ex 33:7
body, or be in a journey *a* off .... Num 9:10
stood on the top of an hill *a* off 1Sa 26:13
went, and stood to view *a* off 2Kin 2:7
when the man of God saw her *a* off .. 2Kin 4:25
and the noise was heard *a* off .... Ezr 3:13
of Jerusalem was heard even *a* off .... Neh 12:43
they lifted up their eyes *a* off .... Job 2:12
I will fetch my knowledge from *a* ...... Job 36:3
man may behold it *a* off .... Job 36:25
and he smelleth the battle *a* off .... Job 39:25
prey, and her eyes behold *a* off .... Job 39:29
Why standest thou *a* off, O LORD ..... Ps 10:1
and my kinsmen stand *a* off .... Ps 38:11
them that are *a* off upon the sea .... Ps 65:5
but the proud he knoweth *a* off .... Ps 138:6
understandest my thought *a* off .... Ps 139:2
the bringeth her food from *a* .... Prov 31:14
shall carry her *a* off to sojourn .... Is 23:7
and justice standeth *a* off .... Is 59:14
the LORD, and not a God *a* off .... Jer 23:23
for, lo, I will save thee from *a* .... Jer 30:10
and declare it in the isles *a* off .... Jer 31:10
I will save thee from *a* off .... Jer 46:27
remember the LORD *a* off, and let ..... Jer 51:50
and rebuke strong nations *a* off .... Mic 4:3
But Peter followed him *a* off unto ..... Mt 26:58
women were there beholding *a* off. ... Mt 27:55
But when he saw Jesus *a* off .... Mk 5:6
a fig tree *a* off having leaves .... Mk 11:13
And Peter followed him *a* off .... Mk 14:54
were also women looking on *a* off ..... Mk 15:40
torments, and seeth Abraham *a* off ... Lk 16:23
were lepers, which stood *a* off .... Lk 17:12
And the publican, standing *a* off .... Lk 18:13
And Peter followed *a* off .... Lk 22:54
him from Galilee, stood *a* off .... Lk 23:49
and to all that are *a* off .... Acts 2:39
peace to you which were *a* off .... Eph 2:17
but having seen them *a* off .... Heb 11:13
is blind, and cannot see *a* off 2Pet 1:9
Standing *a* off for the fear of .... Rev 18:10
shall stand *a* off for the fear of .... Rev 18:15
many as trade by sea, stood *a* off ...... Rev 18:17

AFFAIRS

to God, and *a* of the king 1Chr 26:32
will guide his *a* with discretion .... Ps 112:5
over the *a* of the province of .... Dan 2:49
the *a* of the province of Babylon. ...... Dan 3:12
But that ye also may know my *a* .... Eph 6:21
purpose, that ye might know our *a* .... Eph 6:22
be absent, I may hear of your *a* .... Phil 1:27
himself with the *a* of this life 2Ti 2:4

AFFECT

They zealously *a* you, but not .... Gal 4:17
exclude you, that ye might *a* them .... Gal 4:17

AFFECTED

minds evil *a* against the brethren ...... Acts 14:2
a always in a good thing, and not ...... Gal 4:18

AFFECTETH

Mine eye *a* mine heart because of .... Lam 3:51

AFFECTION

because I have set my *a* to the 1Chr 29:3
without natural *a*, implacable, ... Rom 1:31
his inward *a* is more abundant 2Cor 7:15
Set your *a* on things above, not, ... Col 3:2
uncleanness, inordinate *a* .... Col 3:5
Without natural *a*, trucebreakers, ... 2Ti 3:3

AFFECTIONATELY

So being *a* desirous of you, we, ... 1Th 2:8

AFFECTIONED

Be kindly *a* one to another with......... Rom 12:10

AFFECTIONS

God gave them up unto vile *a* .... Rom 1:26
crucified the flesh with the *a* .... Gal 5:24

AFFINITY

Solomon made *a* with Pharaoh king ... 1Kin 3:1
abundance, and joined *a* with Ahab. .. 2Chr 18:1
join in *a* with the people of .... Ezr 9:14

AFFIRM

as some *a* that we say,) Let us do ...... Rom 3:8
what they say, nor whereof they *a* 1Ti 1:7
I will that thou *a* constantly .... Titus 3:8

AFFIRMED

hour after another confidently *a* .... Lk 22:59
But she constantly *a* that it was......... Acts 12:15
was dead, whom Paul *a* to be alive.... Acts 25:19

AFFLICT

they shall *a* them four hundred .... Gen 15:13
If thou shalt *a* my daughters .... Gen 31:50
to *a* them with their burdens .... Ex 1:11
Ye shall not *a* any widow, or .... Ex 22:22
If thou *a* them in any wise, and .... Ex 22:23
ye shall *a* your souls, and do no .... Lev 16:29
ye shall *a* your souls, by *a* .... Lev 16:31
ye shall *a* your souls, and offer .... Lev 23:27
of rest, and ye shall *a* your souls....... Lev 23:32
a Asshur, and shall *a* Eber .... Num 24:24
and ye shall *a* your souls .... Num 29:7
every binding oath to *a* the soul .... Num 30:13
that we may bind him to *a* him .... Judg 16:5
thou mightest be bound to *a* thee, ... Judg 16:6
and she began to *a* him, and his, ... Judg 16:19
of wickedness *a* them any more 2Sa 7:10
I will for this *a* the seed of 1Kin 11:39
their sin, when thou dost *a* them 2Chr 6:26
that we might *a* ourselves before ...... Ezr 8:21
he will not *a* .... Job 37:23
how thou didst *a* the people .... Ps 44:2
a them, even he that abideth of .... Ps 55:19
nor the son of wickedness *a* him ...... Ps 89:22
O LORD, and thine heritage. .... Ps 94:5
destroy all them that *a* my soul .... Ps 143:12
a her by the way of the sea .... Is 9:1
into the land of them that *a* thee. ..... Is 51:23
a day for a man to *a* his soul .... Is 58:5
hold thy peace, and *a* us very sore .... Is 64:12
down, and to destroy, and to *a* .... Jer 31:28
For he doth not *a* willingly nor .... Lam 3:33
they *a* the just, they take *a* .... Amos 5:12
they shall *a* you from the .... Amos 6:14
then, I will *a* thee no more .... Nah 1:12
time I will undo all that *a* thee .... Zeph 3:19

AFFLICTED

But the more they *a* them, the .... Ex 1:12
shall not be *a* in that same day .... Lev 23:29
Wherefore hast thou *a* thy servant ... Num 11:11
a us, and laid upon us hard .... Deut 26:6
me, and the Almighty hath *a* me ...... Ruth 1:21
the *a* people thou wilt save 2Sa 22:28
because thou hast been *a* in all 1Kin 2:26
in all wherein my father was *a* 1Kin 2:26
a them, and delivered them into 2Kin 17:20
To him that is *a* pity should be .... Job 6:14
a me, they have also let loose .... Job 30:11
and he heareth the cry of the *a* .... Job 34:28
For thou wilt save the *a* people .... Ps 18:27
abhorred the affliction of the *a* .... Ps 22:24
for I am desolate and *a* .... Ps 25:16
do justice to the *a* and needy .... Ps 82:3
thou hast *a* me with all thy waves.... Ps 88:7
I am *a* and ready to die from my .... Ps 88:15
the days wherein thou hast *a* us. ...... Ps 90:15
A Prayer of the *a*, when he is .... Ps 102:t
of their iniquities, are *a* .... Ps 107:17
I was greatly *a* .... Ps 116:10
Before I was *a* I went astray .... Ps 119:67
is good for me that I have been *a* ...... Ps 119:71
thou in faithfulness hast *a* me. .... Ps 119:75
I am *a* very much .... Ps 119:107
time have they *a* me from my youth . Ps 129:1
time have they *a* me from my youth . Ps 129:2
will maintain the cause of the *a* .... Ps 140:12
All the days of the *a* are evil .... Prov 15:15
neither oppress the *a* in the gate. ..... Prov 22:22
hateth those that are *a* by spirit. ...... Prov 26:28
the judgment of any of the *a* .... Prov 31:5
the lightly *a* the land of Zebulun ...... Is 9:1
and will have mercy upon his *a* .... Is 49:13
Therefore hear now this, thou *a* .... Is 51:21
stricken, smitten of God, and *a* .... Is 53:4
He was oppressed, and he was *a* ...... Is 53:7
O thou *a*, tossed with tempest, and .. Is 54:11
wherefore have we *a* our soul .... Is 58:3
the hungry, and satisfy the *a* soul. ... Is 58:10
The sons also of them that *a* thee. .... Is 60:14
In all their affliction he was *a* .... Is 63:9
priests sigh, her virgins are *a* .... Lam 1:4
for the LORD hath *a* her for the .... Lam 1:5
wherewith the LORD hath *a* me in.... Lam 1:12
driven out, and her that I have *a* .... Mic 4:6
Though I have *a* thee, I will .... Nah 1:12
leave in the midst of thee an *a* .... Zeph 3:12
shall they deliver you up to be *a* .... Mt 24:9
And ye shall be *a*, and ye shall 2Cor 1:6
feet, if she have relieved the *a* 1Ti 5:10
being destitute, *a*, tormented, ... Heb 11:37
Be *a*, and mourn, and weep .... Jas 4:9
is any among you *a* .... Jas 5:13

AFFLICTEST

from their sin, when thou *a* them 1Kin 8:35

AFFLICTION

because the LORD hath heard thy *a*. .. Gen 16:11
the LORD hath looked upon my *a* ...... Gen 29:32

God hath seen mine *a* and the............ Gen 31:42
be fruitful in the land of my *a*........... Gen 41:52
I have surely seen the *a* of my........... Ex 3:7
a of Egypt unto the land of the.......... Ex 3:17
that he had looked upon their *a*......... Ex 4:31
therewith, even the bread of *a*........... Deut 16:3
our voice, and looked on our *a*.......... Deut 26:7
look on the *a* of thine handmaid........ 1Sa 1:11
that the LORD will look on mine *a*....... 2Sa 16:12
bread of *a* and with water of *a*......... 1Kin 22:27
For the LORD saw the *a* of Israel........ 2Kin 14:26
bread of *a* and with water of *a*......... 2Chr 18:26
house,) and cry unto thee in our *a*...... 2Chr 20:9
And when he was in *a*, he besought.... 2Chr 33:12
in the province are in great *a*............. Neh 1:3
didst see the *a* of our fathers in......... Neh 9:9
Although *a* cometh not forth of........... Job 5:6
therefore see thou mine *a*................. Job 10:15
the days of *a* have taken hold............ Job 30:16
the days of *a* prevented me.............. Job 30:27
and be holden in cords of *a*.............. Job 36:8
He delivereth the poor in his *a*......... Job 36:15
hast thou chosen rather than *a*......... Job 36:21
abhorred the *a* of the afflicted.......... Ps 22:24
Look upon mine *a* and my pain......... Ps 25:18
thy face, and forgettest our *a*........... Ps 44:24
thou laidst *a* upon our loins............. Ps 66:11
Mine eye mourneth by reason of *a*..... Ps 88:9
Nevertheless he regarded their *a*....... Ps 106:44
shadow of death, being bound in *a*..... Ps 107:10
brought low through oppression, *a*..... Ps 107:39
he the poor on high from *a*.............. Ps 107:41
This is my comfort in my *a*.............. Ps 119:50
then have perished in mine *a*............ Ps 119:92
Consider mine *a*, and deliver me........ Ps 119:153
of adversity, and the water of *a*......... Is 30:20
chosen thee in the furnace of *a*......... Is 48:10
In all their *a* was afflicted............... Is 63:9
publisheth *a* from mount Ephraim...... Jer 4:15
time of evil and in the time of *a*......... Jer 15:11
and my refuge in the day of *a*........... Jer 16:19
Why criest thou for thine *a*.............. Jer 30:15
to come, and his *a* hasteth fast......... Jer 48:16
gone into captivity because of *a*........ Lam 1:3
remembered in the days of her *a*....... Lam 1:7
O LORD, behold my *a*..................... Lam 1:9
seen *a* by the rod of his wrath.......... Lam 3:1
Remembering mine *a* and my misery,.. Lam 3:19
in their *a* they will seek me............. Hos 5:15
not grieved for the *a* of Joseph......... Amos 6:6
not have looked on their *a* in the...... Obad 13
by reason of mine *a* unto the LORD..... Jonah 2:2
a shall not rise up the second.......... Nah 1:9
I saw the tents of Cushan in *a*......... Hab 3:7
and they helped forward the *a*.......... Zec 1:15
out or came in because of the *a*........ Zec 8:10
shall pass through the sea with *a*....... Zec 10:11
when *a* or persecution ariseth for...... Mk 4:17
For in those days shall be *a*............. Mk 13:19
of Egypt and Chanaan, and great *a*.... Acts 7:11
I have seen the *a* of my people......... Acts 7:34
For out of much *a* and anguish of...... 2Cor 2:4
For our light *a*, which is but for......... 2Cor 4:17
of *a* the abundance of their joy........ 2Cor 8:2
supposing to add *a* to my bonds........ Phil 1:16
that ye did communicate with my *a*.... Phil 4:14
received the word in much *a*............ 1Th 1:6
comforted over you in all our *a*......... 1Th 3:7
suffer *a* with the people of God......... Heb 11:25
fatherless and widows in their *a*........ Jas 1:27
for an example of suffering *a*........... Jas 5:10

AFFLICTIONS

Many are the *a* of the righteous......... Ps 34:19
remember David, and all his *a*........... Ps 132:1
And delivered him out of all his *a*...... Acts 7:10
saying that bonds and *a* abide me...... Acts 20:23
of God, in much patience, in *a*.......... 2Cor 6:4
a of Christ in my flesh for his........... Col 1:24
no man should be moved by these *a*.... 1Th 3:3
but be thou partaker of the *a*........... 2Ti 1:8
Persecutions, *a*, which came unto...... 2Ti 3:11
thou in all things, endure *a*.............. 2Ti 4:5
ye endured a great fight of *a*............ Heb 10:32
both by reproaches and *a*................ Heb 10:33
knowing that the same *a* are............ 1Pet 5:9

AFFORDING

be full, *a* all manner of store............ Ps 144:13

AFFRIGHT

to *a* them, and to trouble them.......... 2Chr 32:18

AFFRIGHTED

Thou shalt not be *a* at their.............. Deut 7:21
as they that went before were *a*........ Job 18:20
He mocketh at fear, and is not *a*........ Job 39:22
My heart panted, fearfulness *a* me..... Is 21:4
fire, and the men of war are *a*........... Jer 51:32
and they were *a*........................... Mk 16:5
And he saith unto them, Be not *a*....... Mk 16:6
But they were terrified and *a*............ Lk 24:37
and the remnant were *a*, and gave..... Rev 11:13

AFOOT

ran *a* thither out of all cities............. Mk 6:33
minding himself to go *a*................... Acts 20:13

AFORE

a Isaiah was gone out into the........... 2Kin 20:4
which withereth *a* it groweth up......... Ps 129:6
For *a* the harvest, when the bud........ Is 18:5
a he that was escaped came............. Eze 33:22

(Which he had promised *a* by his........ Rom 1:2
which he had *a* prepared unto........... Rom 9:23
(as I wrote *a* in few words,............... Eph 3:3

AFOREHAND

she is come *a* to anoint my body....... Mk 14:8

AFORETIME

where *a* they laid the meat............... Neh 13:5
and *a* I was as a tabret.................... Job 17:6
My people went down *a* into Egypt..... Is 52:4
Their children also shall be as *a*........ Jer 30:20
before his God, as he did *a*.............. Dan 6:10
Pharisees him that *a* was blind.......... Jn 9:13
a were written for our learning.......... Rom 15:4

AFRAID

voice in the garden, and I was *a*........ Gen 3:10
for she was *a*............................... Gen 18:15
and the men were sore *a*................. Gen 20:8
And he was *a*, and said, How........... Gen 28:17
and said to Laban, Because I was *a*.... Gen 31:31
Then Jacob was greatly *a* and.......... Gen 32:7
heart failed them, and they were *a*.... Gen 42:28
the bundles of money, they were *a*.... Gen 42:35
And the men were *a*, because they..... Gen 43:18
for he was *a* to look upon God.......... Ex 3:6
and they were sore *a*..................... Ex 14:10
The people shall hear, and be *a*........ Ex 15:14
they were *a* to come nigh him.......... Ex 34:30
down, and none shall make you *a*...... Lev 26:6
wherefore then were ye not *a* to....... Num 12:8
And Moab was *a* of the people.......... Num 22:3
ye shall not be *a* of the face of........ Deut 1:17
Dread not, neither be *a* of them........ Deut 1:29
and they shall be *a* of you................ Deut 2:4
for ye were *a* by reason of the.......... Deut 5:5
Thou shalt not be *a* of them............. Deut 7:18
all the people of whom thou art *a*...... Deut 7:19
For I was *a* of the anger and hot....... Deut 9:19
thou shalt not be *a* of him............... Deut 18:22
more than thou, be not *a* of them...... Deut 20:1
and they shall be *a* of thee.............. Deut 28:10
of Egypt, which thou wast *a* of......... Deut 28:60
fear not, nor be *a* of them............... Deut 31:6
be not *a*, neither be thou................ Josh 1:9
therefore we were sore *a* of our........ Josh 9:24
Joshua, Be not *a* because of them..... Josh 11:6
saying, Whosoever is fearful and *a*.... Judg 7:3
at midnight, that the man was *a*........ Ruth 3:8
And the Philistines were *a*............... 1Sa 4:7
they were the *a* of the Philistines...... 1Sa 7:7
they were dismayed, and were *a*........ 1Sa 17:11
fled from him, and were sore *a*......... 1Sa 17:24
And Saul was *a* of David, because...... 1Sa 18:12
very wisely, he was *a* of him............ 1Sa 18:15
Saul was yet the more *a* of David...... 1Sa 18:29
Ahimelech was *a* at the meeting of.... 1Sa 21:1
was sore *a* of Achish the king of....... 1Sa 21:12
Behold, we be *a* here in Judah.......... 1Sa 23:3
host of the Philistines, he was *a*........ 1Sa 28:5
the king said unto her, Be not *a*........ 1Sa 28:13
along on the earth, and was sore *a*.... 1Sa 28:20
for he was sore *a*.......................... 1Sa 31:4
How wast thou not *a* to stretch........ 2Sa 1:14
David was *a* of the LORD that day,...... 2Sa 6:9
because the people have made me *a*... 2Sa 14:15
weak handed, and will make him *a*..... 2Sa 17:2
floods of ungodly men made me *a*...... 2Sa 22:5
they shall be *a* out of their.............. 2Sa 22:46
that were with Adonijah were *a*......... 1Kin 1:49
be not *a* of him............................. 2Kin 1:15
But they were exceedingly *a*............ 2Kin 10:4
Be not *a* of the words which thou...... 2Kin 19:6
for they were *a* of the Chaldees........ 2Kin 25:26
for he was sore *a*.......................... 1Chr 10:4
David was *a* of God that day,............ 1Chr 13:12
for he was *a* because of the sword..... 1Chr 21:30
Be not *a* nor dismayed by reason...... 2Chr 20:15
be not *a* nor dismayed for the.......... 2Chr 32:7
Then I was very sore *a*................... Neh 2:2
the people, Be not ye *a* of them........ Neh 4:14
For they all made us *a*, saying,......... Neh 6:9
was he hired, that I should be *a*........ Neh 6:13
Then Haman was *a* before the king.... Est 7:6
that which I was *a* of is come........... Job 3:25
neither shalt thou be *a* of............... Job 5:21
neither shalt thou be *a* of the........... Job 5:22
ye see my casting down, and are *a*.... Job 6:21
I am *a* of all my sorrows, I know....... Job 9:28
down, and none shall make thee *a*..... Job 11:19
not his excellency make you *a*.......... Job 13:11
and let not thy dread make me *a*....... Job 13:21
and anguish shall make him *a*........... Job 15:24
shall make him *a* on every side......... Job 18:11
Be ye *a* of the sword...................... Job 19:29
Even when I remember I am *a*........... Job 21:6
when I consider, I am *a* of him.......... Job 23:15
wherefore I was *a*, and durst not...... Job 32:6
my terror shall not make thee *a*........ Job 33:7
thou make him *a* as a grasshopper.... Job 39:20
up himself, the mighty are *a*............. Job 41:25
I will not be *a* of ten thousands........ Ps 3:6
floods of ungodly men made me *a*...... Ps 18:4
be *a* out of their close places........... Ps 18:45
of whom shall I be *a*...................... Ps 27:1
Be not thou *a* when one is made....... Ps 49:16
What time I am *a*, I will trust in........ Ps 56:3
I will not be *a* what man can do........ Ps 56:11
parts are *a* at thy tokens................. Ps 65:8
they were *a*................................. Ps 77:16
make them *a* with thy storm............ Ps 83:15

Thou shalt not be *a* for the.............. Ps 91:5
He shall not be *a* of evil tidings........ Ps 112:7
is established, he shall not be *a*......... Ps 112:8
and I am *a* of thy judgments............ Ps 119:120
liest down, thou shalt not be *a*......... Prov 3:24
Be not *a* of sudden fear, neither........ Prov 3:25
She is not *a* of the snow for her........ Prov 31:21
shall be *a* of that which is high......... Eccl 12:5
fear ye their fear, nor be *a*.............. Is 8:12
in Zion, be not *a* of the Assyrian....... Is 10:24
Ramah is *a*.................................. Is 10:29
I will trust, and not be *a*................. Is 12:2
And they shall be *a*....................... Is 13:8
down, and none shall make them *a*.... Is 17:2
and it shall be *a* and fear because..... Is 19:16
thereof shall be *a* in himself............ Is 19:17
And they shall be *a* and ashamed of... Is 20:5
he will not be *a* of their voice.......... Is 31:4
princes shall be *a* of the ensign........ Is 31:9
The sinners in Zion are *a*................ Is 33:14
Be not *a* of the words that thou........ Is 37:6
lift it up, be not *a*......................... Is 40:9
the ends of the earth were *a*........... Is 41:5
Fear ye not, neither be *a*................ Is 44:8
of men, neither be ye *a* of their........ Is 51:7
that thou shouldest be *a* of a man..... Is 51:12
whom hast thou been *a* or feared...... Is 57:11
Be not *a* of their faces................... Jer 1:8
at this, and be horribly.................... Jer 2:12
Be not *a* of them.......................... Jer 10:5
when Urijah heard it, he was *a*......... Jer 26:21
quiet, and none shall make him *a*...... Jer 30:10
the words, they were *a* both one....... Jer 36:16
Yet they were not *a*, nor rent........... Jer 36:24
I am *a* of the Jews that are............. Jer 38:19
of the men of whom thou art *a*......... Jer 39:17
for they were *a* of them, because...... Jer 41:18
Be not *a* of the king of Babylon,....... Jer 42:11
of whom ye are *a*.......................... Jer 42:11
be not *a* of him, saith the LORD........ Jer 42:11
and the famine, whereof ye were *a*.... Jer 42:16
at ease, and none shall make him *a*... Jer 46:27
be not *a* of them.......................... Eze 2:6
neither be *a* of their words,............. Eze 2:6
be not *a* of their words, nor be......... Eze 2:6
and their kings shall be sore *a*......... Eze 27:35
to make the careless Ethiopians *a*..... Eze 30:9
shall be horribly *a* for them............. Eze 32:10
safely, and none shall make them *a*... Eze 34:28
their land, and none made them *a*..... Eze 39:26
I saw a dream which made me *a*........ Dan 4:5
and when he came, I was *a*, and fell.. Dan 8:17
Be not *a*, ye beasts of the field........ Joel 2:22
the city, and the people not be *a*....... Amos 3:6
Then the mariners were *a*, and......... Jonah 1:5
Then were the men exceedingly *a*...... Jonah 1:10
and none shall make them *a*............ Mic 4:4
they shall be *a* of the LORD our........ Mic 7:17
lion's whelp, and none made them *a*... Nah 2:11
of beasts, which made them *a*.......... Hab 2:17
I have heard thy speech, and was *a*... Hab 3:2
down, and none shall make them *a*.... Zeph 3:13
me, and was a before my name.......... Mal 2:5
Herod, he was *a* to go thither........... Mt 2:22
be not *a*..................................... Mt 14:27
saw the wind boisterous, he was *a*.... Mt 14:30
on their face, and were sore *a*.......... Mt 17:6
them, and said, Arise, and be not *a*.... Mt 17:7
And I was *a*, and went and hid thy..... Mt 25:25
said Jesus unto them, Be not *a*........ Mt 28:10
and they were *a*........................... Mk 5:15
ruler of the synagogue, Be not *a*....... Mk 5:36
be not *a*..................................... Mk 6:50
for they were sore *a*..................... Mk 9:6
that saying, and were *a* to ask him.... Mk 9:32
and as they followed, they were *a*..... Mk 10:32
thing to any man for they were *a*...... Mk 16:8
and they were sore *a*..................... Lk 2:9
And they being *a* wondered, saying... Lk 8:25
and they were *a*........................... Lk 8:35
Be not *a* of them that kill............... Lk 12:4
And as they were *a*, and bowed down. Lk 24:5
and they were *a*........................... Jn 6:19
be not *a*..................................... Jn 6:20
be troubled, neither let it be *a*.......... Jn 14:27
that saying, he was the more *a*......... Jn 19:8
but they were all *a* of him............... Acts 9:26
when he looked on him, he was *a*...... Acts 10:4
the night by a vision, Be not *a*......... Acts 18:9
saw indeed the light, and were *a*...... Acts 22:9
and the chief captain also was *a*....... Acts 22:29
thou then not be *a* of the power....... Rom 13:3
thou do that which is evil, be *a*........ Rom 13:4
I am *a* of you, lest I have............... Gal 4:11
they were not *a* of the king's.......... Heb 11:23
are not *a* with any amazement......... 1Pet 3:6
be not *a* of their terror, neither........ 1Pet 3:14
they are not *a* to speak evil of......... 2Pet 2:10

AFRESH

to themselves the Son of God *a*......... Heb 6:6

AFTER See PREFACE.

AFTERNOON

And they tarried until *a*, and they...... Judg 19:8

AFTERWARD

a were the families of the................ Gen 10:18
a shall they come out with great....... Gen 15:14
me, and *a* I will see his face............ Gen 32:20
a came out his brother, that had....... Gen 38:30

a Moses and Aaron went in, and told ... Ex 5:1
a all the children of Israel came ... Ex 34:32
a he shall kill the burnt ... Lev 14:18
the priest shall go in to see ... Lev 14:36
in water, and *a* come into the camp ... Lev 16:26
a he shall come into the camp ... Lev 16:28
shall *a* eat of the holy things ... Lev 22:7
a shall cause the woman to drink ... Num 5:26
a the people removed from ... Num 12:16
a he shall come into the camp, and ... Num 19:7
a shalt thou be gathered unto thy ... Num 31:2
a ye shall come into the camp ... Num 31:24
then *a* ye shall return, and be ... Num 32:22
a the hands of all the people ... Deut 17:7
thou shalt not glean it *a* ... Deut 24:21
and *a* may ye go your way ... Josh 2:16
a he read all the words of the ... Josh 8:34
a Joshua smote them, and slew them Josh 10:26
and *a* I brought you out ... Josh 24:5
a the children of Judah went down ... Judg 1:9
and *a* shall thine hands be ... Judg 7:11
And it came to pass *a* that he ... Judg 16:4
morsel of bread, and *a* go your way ... Judg 19:5
And it came to pass *a*, that ... 1Sa 24:5
David also arose *a*, and went out ... 1Sa 24:8
a when David heard it, he said, I ... 2Sa 3:28
a Hezron went in to the daughter ... 1Chr 2:21
a they made ready for themselves, ... 2Chr 35:14
a offered the continual burnt ... Ezr 3:5
A I came unto the house of ... Neh 6:10
counsel, and *a* receive me to glory ... Ps 73:24
a thou shalt be called, The city ... Is 1:26
a did more grievously afflict her ... Is 9:1
And *a*, saith the LORD, I will, ... Jer 21:7
But *a* they turned, and caused the ... Jer 34:11
a it shall be inhabited, as in ... Jer 46:26
And *a* I will bring again the ... Jer 49:6
A he brought me to the temple, and ... Eze 41:1
A he brought me to the gate, even ... Eze 43:1
A he brought me again unto the ... Eze 47:1
A he measured a thousand ... Eze 47:5
a I rose up, and did the king's ... Dan 8:27
A shall the children of Israel ... Hos 3:5
And it shall come to pass *a* ... Joel 2:28
forty nights, he was *a* hungred ... Mt 4:2
but *a* he repented, and went ... Mt 21:29
ye had seen it, repented not *a* ... Mt 21:32
A came also the other virgins, ... Mt 25:11
a, when affliction or persecution ... Mk 4:17
A he appeared unto the eleven as ... Mk 16:14
they were ended, he *a* hungered ... Lk 4:2
And it came to pass *a*, that he ... Lk 8:1
a thou shalt eat and drink ... Lk 17:8
but *a* he said within himself, ... Lk 18:4
A Jesus findeth him in the temple ... Jn 5:14
And *a* they desired a king ... Acts 13:21
a they that are Christ's at his ... 1Cor 15:23
a that which is spiritual ... 1Cor 15:46
then would he not *a* have spoken ... Heb 4:8
nevertheless *a* it yieldeth the ... Heb 12:11
For ye know how that *a*, when he ... Heb 12:17
a destroyed them that believed ... Jude 5

AFTERWARDS
a she bare a daughter, and called ... Gen 30:21
a he will let you go hence ... Ex 11:1
the hand of *a* all the people ... Deut 13:9
a they eat that be bidden ... 1Sa 9:13
mark, and *a* we will speak ... Job 18:2
but *a* his mouth shall be filled ... Prov 20:17
and *a* build thine house ... Prov 24:27
He that rebuketh a man *a* shall ... Prov 28:23
a wise man keepeth it in till *a* ... Prov 29:11
A the spirit took me up, and ... Eze 11:24
but thou shalt follow me *a* ... Jn 13:36
A I came into the regions of ... Gal 1:21
faith which should *a* be revealed ... Gal 3:23

AGABUS (*ag'-ab-us*) A Christian prophet.
stood up one of them named A ... Acts 11:28
Judaea a certain prophet, named A ... Acts 21:10

AGAG (*a'-gag*) See **AGAGITE**. A king of Amalek
during Exodus.
his king shall be higher than A ... Num 24:7
he took A the king of the ... 1Sa 15:8
But Saul and the people spared A ... 1Sa 15:9
have brought A the king of Amalek ... 1Sa 15:20
Bring ye hither to me A the king ... 1Sa 15:32
A came unto him delicately ... 1Sa 15:32
a said, Surely the bitterness of ... 1Sa 15:32
Samuel hewed A in pieces before ... 1Sa 15:33

AGAGITE (*ag'-ag-ite*) A member of an
Amalekite tribe.
Haman the son of Hammedatha the ... Est 3:1
Haman the son of Hammedatha the A ... Est 3:10
away the mischief of Haman the A ... Est 8:3
Haman the son of Hammedatha the A ... Est 8:5
the son of Hammedatha, the A ... Est 9:24

AGAIN See PREFACE.

AGAINST See PREFACE.

AGAR (*a'-gar*) See **HAGAR**. Greek form of
Hagar.
gendereth to bondage, which is A ... Gal 4:24
For this A is mount Sinai in, ... Gal 4:25

AGATE
And the third row a ligure, an *a*... Ex 28:19
And the third row, a ligure, an *a* ... Ex 39:12
and fine linen, and coral, and *a* ... Eze 27:16

AGATES
And I will make thy windows of *a* ... Is 54:12

AGE
shalt be buried in a good old *a* ... Gen 15:15
were old and well stricken in *a* ... Gen 18:11
bare Abraham a son in his old *a* ... Gen 21:2
have born him a son in his old *a* ... Gen 21:7
was old, and well stricken in *a* ... Gen 24:1
ghost, and died in a good old *a* ... Gen 25:8
he was the son of his old *a* ... Gen 37:3
old man, and a child of his old *a* Gen 44:20
so the whole *a* of Jacob was an ... Gen 47:28
the eyes of Israel were dim for *a* ... Gen 48:10
from the *a* of fifty years they ... Num 8:25
Joshua waxed old and stricken in *a* ... Josh 23:1
them, I am old and stricken in *a* ... Josh 23:2
to a good old *a* died in a good old *a* ... Judg 8:32
and a nourisher of thine old *a* ... Ruth 4:15
die in the flower of their *a* ... 1Sa 2:33
eyes were set by reason of his *a* ... 1Kin 14:4
in the time of his old *a* he was ... 1Kin 15:23
from the *a* of thirty years ... 1Chr 23:3
from the *a* of twenty years and ... 1Chr 23:24
And he died in a good old *a* ... 1Chr 29:28
man, or him that stooped for *a* ... 2Chr 36:17
come to thy grave in a full *a* ... Job 5:26
I pray thee, of the former *a* ... Job 8:8
thine *a* shall be clearer than the ... Job 11:17
in whom old *a* was perished ... Job 30:2
mine *a* is as nothing before thee ... Ps 39:5
me not off in the time of old *a* ... Ps 71:9
still bring forth fruit in old *a* ... Ps 92:14
Mine *a* is departed, and is removed ... Is 38:12
And even to your old *a* I am he ... Is 46:4
his staff in his hand for very *a* ... Zec 8:4
she was of the *a* of twelve years ... Mk 5:42
also conceived a son in her old *a* ... Lk 1:36
she was of a great *a*, and had ... Lk 2:36
to be about thirty years of *a* ... Lk 3:23
daughter, about twelve years of *a* ... Lk 8:42
he is of *a* ... Jn 9:21
said his parents, He is of *a* ... Jn 9:23
if she pass the flower of her *a* ... 1Cor 7:36
to them that are of full *a* ... Heb 5:14
of a child when she was past *a* ... Heb 11:11

AGED
Now Barzillai was a very *a* man ... 2Sa 19:32
away the understanding of the *a* ... Job 12:20
both the *a* and very a men ... Job 15:10
and the *a* arose, and stood up ... Job 29:8
neither do the *a* understand ... Job 32:9
the *a* with him that is full of ... Jer 6:11
That the *a* men be sober, grave, ... Titus 2:2
The *a* women likewise, that they ... Titus 2:3
being such an one as Paul the *a* ... Philem 9

AGEE (*ag'-ee*) Father of a "mighty man" of
David.
Shammah the son of A the Hararite ... 2Sa 23:11

AGES
That in the *a* to come he might ... Eph 2:7
Which in other *a* was not made ... Eph 3:5
by Christ Jesus throughout all *a* ... Eph 3:21
which hath been hid from *a* ... Col 1:26

AGO
asses that were lost three days *a* ... 1Sa 9:20
heard long *a* how I have done it ... 2Kin 19:25
was builded these many years *a* ... Ezr 5:11
unto him that fashioned it long *a* ... Is 22:11
Hast thou not heard long *a* ... Is 37:26
have repented long *a* in sackcloth ... Mt 11:21
How long is it *a* since this came ... Mk 9:21
they had a great while *a* repented ... Lk 10:13
Four days *a* I was fasting until ... Acts 10:30
while *a* God made choice among us ... Acts 15:7
but also to be forward a year *a* ... 2Cor 8:10
that Achaia was ready a year *a* ... 2Cor 9:2
in Christ above fourteen years *a* ... 2Cor 12:2

AGONE
because three days *a* I fell sick ... 1Sa 30:13

AGONY
being in an *a* he prayed more ... Lk 22:44

AGREE
A with thine adversary quickly, ... Mt 5:25
That if two of you shall *a* on ... Mt 18:19
didst not thou *a* with me for a ... Mt 20:13
so did their witness *a* together ... Mk 14:59
to this *a* the words of the ... Acts 15:15
and these three *a* in one ... 1Jn 5:8
to fulfil his will, and to *a* ... Rev 17:17

AGREED
walk together, except they be *a* ... Amos 3:3
when he had *a* with the labourers ... Mt 20:2
but their witness *a* not together ... Mk 14:56
for the Jews had *a* already ... Jn 9:22
How is it that ye have *a* together ... Acts 5:9
And to him they *a* ... Acts 5:40
The Jews have *a* to desire thee ... Acts 23:20
when they *a* not among themselves, ... Acts 28:25

AGREEMENT
Make an *a* with me by a present, ... 2Kin 18:31
and ye will make an *a* with me by ... Is 28:16
year, and hell shall not stand ... Is 28:18
Make an *a* with me by a present, ... Is 36:16
king of the north to make an *a* ... Dan 11:6
what *a* hath the temple of God ... 2Cor 6:16

AGREETH
and thy speech *a* thereto ... Mk 14:70
out of the new *a* not with the old ... Lk 5:36

AGRIPPA (*ag-rip'-pah*) Great-grandson of
Herod the Great.
And after certain days king A ... Acts 25:13
Then A said unto Festus, I would ... Acts 25:22
when A was come, and Bernice, with ... Acts 25:23
And Festus said, King A, and all ... Acts 25:24
specially before thee, O king A ... Acts 25:26
Then A said unto Paul, Thou art ... Acts 26:1
I think myself happy, king A ... Acts 26:2
For which hope's sake, king A ... Acts 26:7
Whereupon, O king A, I was not ... Acts 26:19
King A, believest thou the ... Acts 26:27
Then A said unto Paul, Almost ... Acts 26:28
Then said A unto Festus, This man ... Acts 26:32

AGROUND
two seas met, they ran the ship *a* ... Acts 27:41

AGUE
consumption, and the burning *a* ... Lev 26:16

AGUR (*a'-gur*) Son of Jakeh.
The words of A the son of Jakeh, ... Prov 30:1

AH
them not say in their hearts, A ... Ps 35:25
A sinful nation, a people laden, ... Is 1:4
the mighty One of Israel, A ... Is 1:24
Then said I, A, Lord God ... Jer 1:6
Then said I, A, Lord God ... Jer 4:10
Then said I, A, Lord God ... Jer 14:13
for him, saying, A my brother ... Jer 22:18
or, A sister ... Jer 22:18
lament for him, saying, A lord ... Jer 22:18
or, A his glory ... Jer 22:18
A Lord God ... Jer 32:17
will lament thee, saying, A lord ... Jer 34:5
Then said I, A Lord God ... Eze 4:14
and cried, and said, A Lord God ... Eze 9:8
a loud voice, and said, A Lord God ... Eze 11:13
Then said I, A Lord God ... Eze 20:49
a ... Eze 21:15
wagging their heads, and saying, A ... Mk 15:29

AHA
wide against me, and said, A, a, ... Ps 35:21
shame that say unto me, A, a, ... Ps 40:15
of their shame that say, A, a, ... Ps 70:3
he warmeth himself, and saith, A, ... Is 44:16
Because thou saidst, A, against ... Eze 25:3
hath said against Jerusalem, A, ... Eze 26:2
enemy hath said against you, A, ... Eze 36:2

AHAB (*a'-hab*) See **AHAB'S**.
1. A king of Israel.
And son reigned in his stead ... 1Kin 16:28
A the son of Omri to reign over ... 1Kin 16:29
A the son of Omri reigned over ... 1Kin 16:29
A the son of Omri did evil in the ... 1Kin 16:30
And A made a grove ... 1Kin 16:33
A did more to provoke the LORD ... 1Kin 16:33
of Gilead, said unto A, As the ... 1Kin 17:1
saying, Go, shew thyself unto A ... 1Kin 18:1
went to shew himself unto A ... 1Kin 18:2
A called Obadiah, which was the ... 1Kin 18:3
A said unto Obadiah, Go into the ... 1Kin 18:5
A went one way by himself, and ... 1Kin 18:6
thy servant into the hand of A ... 1Kin 18:9
and so when I come and tell A ... 1Kin 18:12
So Obadiah went to meet A ... 1Kin 18:16
and A went to meet Elijah ... 1Kin 18:16
when A saw Elijah, that A said ... 1Kin 18:17
So A sent unto all the children ... 1Kin 18:20
And Elijah said unto A, Get thee ... 1Kin 18:41
So A went up to eat and to drink ... 1Kin 18:42
And he said, Go up, say unto A ... 1Kin 18:44
A rode, and went to Jezreel ... 1Kin 18:45
And A told Jezebel all that Elijah ... 1Kin 19:1
ran before A to the entrance of ... 1Kin 18:46
A told Jezebel all that Elijah ... 1Kin 19:1
he sent messengers to A king of ... 1Kin 20:2
a prophet unto A king of Israel ... 1Kin 20:13
And A said, By whom ... 1Kin 20:14
Then said A, I will send thee ... 1Kin 20:34
the palace of A king of Samaria ... 1Kin 21:1
A spake unto Naboth, saying, Give ... 1Kin 21:2
And Naboth said to A, The LORD ... 1Kin 21:3
A came into his house heavy and ... 1Kin 21:4
was dead, that Jezebel said to A ... 1Kin 21:15
when A heard that Naboth was dead ... 1Kin 21:16
that A rose up to go down to the ... 1Kin 21:18
go down to meet A king of Israel ... 1Kin 21:18
A said to Elijah, Hast thou found ... 1Kin 21:20
will cut off from A him that ... 1Kin 21:21
Him that dieth of A in the city ... 1Kin 21:24
But there was none like unto A ... 1Kin 21:25
when A heard those words, that he ... 1Kin 21:27
Seest thou how A humbleth himself ... 1Kin 21:29
LORD said, Who shall persuade A ... 1Kin 22:20
Now the rest of the acts of A ... 1Kin 22:39
So A slept with his fathers ... 1Kin 22:40
fourth year of A king of Israel ... 1Kin 22:41
the son of A unto Jehoshaphat ... 1Kin 22:49
Ahaziah the son of A began to ... 1Kin 22:51
2.
Israel after the death of A ... 2Kin 1:1
Now Jehoram the son of A began to ... 2Kin 3:1
when A was dead, that the king of ... 2Kin 3:5
Joram the son of A king of Israel ... 2Kin 8:16
of Israel, as did the house of A ... 2Kin 8:18
the daughter of A was his wife ... 2Kin 8:18

year of Joram the son of A king........... 2Kin 8:25
in the way of the house of A 2Kin 8:27
the LORD, as did the house of A 2Kin 8:27
the son in law of the house of A 2Kin 8:27
he went with Joram the son of A 2Kin 8:28
see Joram the son of A in Jezreel 2Kin 8:29
smite the house of A thy master.......... 2Kin 9:7
the whole house of A shall perish........ 2Kin 9:8
I will cut off from A him that 2Kin 9:8
I will make the house of A like 2Kin 9:9
rode together after A his father 2Kin 9:25
year of Joram the son of A began........ 2Kin 9:29
A had seventy sons in Samaria 2Kin 10:1
spake concerning the house of A 2Kin 10:10
of the house of A in Jezreel................ 2Kin 10:11
that remained unto A in Samaria......... 2Kin 10:17
unto them, A served Baal a little......... 2Kin 10:18
hast done unto the house of A 2Kin 10:30
a grove, as did A king of Israel........... 2Kin 21:3
and the plummet of the house of A 2Kin 21:13
and joined affinity with A 2Chr 18:1
he went down to A to Samaria 2Chr 18:2
A killed sheep and oxen for him in...... 2Chr 18:2
A king of Israel said unto 2Chr 18:3
Who shall entice A king of Israel 2Chr 18:19
like as did the house of A 2Chr 21:6
he had the daughter of A to wife......... 2Chr 21:6
the whoredoms of the house of A 2Chr 21:13
in the ways of the house of A 2Chr 22:3
of the LORD like the house of A 2Chr 22:4
went with Jehoram the son of A 2Chr 22:5
Jehoram the son of A at Jezreel.......... 2Chr 22:6
to cut off the house of A 2Chr 22:7
judgment upon the house of A 2Chr 22:8
all the works of the house of A .... Mic 6:16
  2. A false prophet during the Exile.
of the son of Kolaiah, and like............ Jer 29:21
them like Zedekiah and like A .... Jer 29:22

AHAB'S (a'-habs)
So she wrote letters in A name............ 1Kin 21:8
them that brought up A children.......... 2Kin 10:1

AHARAH (a-har'-ah) See AHER, AHIRAM, EHI.
  Third son of Benjamin.
the second, and A the third,................ 1Chr 8:1

AHARHEL (a-har'-hel) A descendant of Judah.
  the families of A the son of 1Chr 4:8

AHASAI (a-ha'-sai) Family of returned exiles.
  the son of Azareel, the son of A......... Neh 11:13

AHASBAI (a-has'-ba-i) Father of a "mighty
  man" of David.
Eliphelet the son of A, ... 2Sa 23:34

AHASUERUS (a-has-u-e'-rus) See AHASUERUS'.
  1. A Persian king, Cambyses.
And in the reign of A, the................... Ezr 4:6

AHASUERUS' (a-has-u-e'-rus) Refers to
  Ahasuerus 1.
And he wrote in the king A name......... Est 8:10

AHASUERUS (a-has-u-e'-rus)
  1. A Persian king, Cambyses.
And in the reign of A, the................... Ezr 4:6
  2. Father of Darius the Meda.
first year of Darius the son of A.......... Dan 9:1
  3. A king of Persia, Xerxes.
it came to pass in the days of A .... Est 1:1
(this is A which reigned from .... Est 1:1
when the king A sat on the throne .... Est 1:2
house which belonged to king A .... Est 1:9
in the presence of A king, ... Est 1:10
of the king A by the chamberlains ...... Est 1:15
all the provinces of the king A............ Est 1:16
The king A commanded Vashti the....... Est 1:17
Vashti come no more before king A ..... Est 1:19
the wrath of king A was appeased....... Est 2:1
turn was come to go in to king A......... Est 2:12
A into his house royal in the .... Est 2:16
sought to lay hand on the king A .... Est 2:21
king A promote Haman the son of .... Est 3:1
throughout the whole kingdom of A ..... Est 3:6
in the twelfth year of king A .... Est 3:7
And Haman said unto king A .... Est 3:8
the name of king A was written.......... Est 3:12
sought to lay hand on the king A .... Est 6:2
Then the king A answered and said..... Est 7:5
On that day did the king A give........... Est 8:1
Then the king A said unto Esther........ Est 8:7
in all the provinces of king A .... Est 8:12
all the provinces of the king A............ Est 9:2
all the provinces of the king A............ Est 9:20
provinces of the kingdom of A .... Est 9:30
And king A laid a tribute upon .... Est 10:1
the Jew was next unto king A .... Est 10:3

AHAVA (a-ha'-vah) See IVA. A river of
  Babylon.
to the river than runneth to A.............. Ezr 8:15
a fast there, at the river of A .... Ezr 8:21
we departed from the river of A .... Ezr 8:31

AHAZ (a'-haz) See also AHAZ.
  1. A king of Judah.
A his son reigned in his stead............ 2Kin 15:38
of Pekah the son of Remaliah A........... 2Kin 16:1
Twenty years old was A when he 2Kin 16:2
and they besieged A, but could not..... 2Kin 16:5
So A sent messengers to 2Kin 16:7
A took the silver and gold that........... 2Kin 16:8
king A went to Damascus to meet....... 2Kin 16:10
king A sent to Urijah the priest 2Kin 16:10
king A had sent from Damascus 2Kin 16:11

against king A came from Damascus 2Kin 16:11
king A commanded Urijah the............. 2Kin 16:15
to all that king A commanded............. 2Kin 16:16
king A cut off the borders of the......... 2Kin 16:17
of the acts of A which he did.............. 2Kin 16:19
A slept with his fathers, and was 2Kin 16:20
In the twelfth year of A king of 2Kin 17:1
that Hezekiah son of A began to 2Kin 18:1
it had gone down in the dial of A 2Kin 20:11
the top of the upper chamber of A 2Chr 23:12
A his son, Hezekiah his son,............... 1Chr 3:13
A his son reigned in his stead............ 2Chr 27:9
A was twenty years old when he 2Chr 28:1
At that time did king A send unto........ 2Chr 28:16
low because of A king of Israel 2Chr 28:19
For A took away a portion out of......... 2Chr 28:21
this is that king A 2Chr 28:22
A gathered together the vessels.......... 2Chr 28:24
A slept with his fathers, and they 2Chr 28:27
which king A in his reign did............... 2Chr 29:19
in the days of Uzziah, Jotham, A .... Is 1:1
the days of A the son of Jotham .... Is 7:1
Isaiah, Go forth now to meet A .... Is 7:3
the LORD spake again unto A.............. Is 7:10
But A said, I will not ask, ... Is 7:12
that king A died was this burden .... Is 14:28
is gone down in the sun dial of A........ Is 38:8
in the days of Uzziah, Jotham, A .... Hos 1:1
in the days of Jotham, A, and............. Mic 1:1
  2. A Benjaminite and relative of Saul.
Pirathon, and Melech, and Tarea, and A 1Chr 8:35
And A begat Jehoadah 1Chr 8:36
and Melech, and Tahrea, and A 1Chr 9:41
And A begat Jarah.............................. 1Chr 9:42

AHAZIAH (a-haz-i'-ah) See AZARIAH,
  JEHOAHAZ.
  1. A king of Israel.
A his son reigned in his stead............ 1Kin 22:40
Then said A the son of Ahab unto........ 1Kin 22:49
A the son of Ahab began to reign 1Kin 22:51
A fell down through a lattice in 2Kin 1:2
of the acts of A which he did.............. 2Kin 1:18
A his son, Joash his son, ... 1Chr 3:11
himself with A king of Israel 2Chr 20:35
thou hast joined thyself with A 2Chr 20:37
  *2. Son and successor of King Jehoram of
  Judah.*
A his son reigned in his stead............ 2Kin 8:24
did A the son of Jehoram king of 2Kin 8:25
twenty years old was A when he 2Kin 8:26
A the son of Jehoram king of 2Kin 8:29
A king of Judah was come down to 2Kin 9:16
A king of Judah went out, each in 2Kin 9:21
his hands, and fled, and said to A 2Kin 9:23
There is treachery, O A 2Kin 9:23
But when A the king of Judah saw 2Kin 9:27
Ahab began A to reign over Judah....... 2Kin 9:29
the brethren of A asked of 2Kin 10:13
We are the brethren of A 2Kin 10:13
of A saw that her son was dead 2Kin 11:1
of king Joram, sister of A 2Kin 11:2
took Joash the son of A 2Kin 11:2
Jehosaphat, and Jehoram, and A 2Kin 12:18
year of Joash the son of A king........... 2Kin 13:1
the son of Jehoash the son of A 2Kin 14:13
A his youngest son king in his 2Chr 21:17
So A the son of Jehoram king of 2Chr 22:1
two years old was A king when he began.. 2Chr 22:2
the destruction of A was of God.......... 2Chr 22:7
and the sons of the brethren of A 2Chr 22:8
that ministered to A 2Chr 22:8
And he sought A 2Chr 22:9
So the house of A had no power to 2Chr 22:9
of A saw that her son was dead 2Chr 22:10
the king, took Joash the son of A 2Chr 22:11
(for she was the sister of A 2Chr 22:11

AHBAN (ah'-ban) A descendant of Pharez.
  was Abihail, and she bare him A......... 1Chr 2:29

AHER (a'-hur) See AHARAH. A descendant of
  Benjamin.
of Ir, and Hushim, the sons of A.......... 1Chr 7:12

AHI (a'-hi)
  1. Son of Abdiel.
A the son of Abdiel, the son of............ 1Chr 5:15
  2. A chief of the Asherites.
A, and Rohgah, Jehubbah, and Aram ... 1Chr 7:34

AHIAH (a-hi'-ah) See AHIJAH.
  1. Grandson of Phinehas.
And A, the son of Ahitub, ... 1Sa 14:3
and Saul said unto A, Bring hither....... 1Sa 14:18
  2. A scribe of Solomon.
Elihoreph and A, the sons of 1Kin 4:3
  3. A descendant of Benjamin.
and Naaman, and A, and Gera, he....... 1Chr 8:7

AHIAM (a-hi'-am) Son of Shemidah.
A the son of Sharar the Hararite, ... 2Sa 23:33
A the son of Sacar the Hararite, ... 1Chr 11:35

AHIAN (a-hi'-an)
And the sons of Shemidah were, A 1Chr 7:19

AHIEZER (a-hi-e'-zer)
  1. One who numbered the people.
A the son of Ammishaddai .... Num 1:12
shall be A the son of Ammishaddai ..... Num 2:25
On the tenth day A the son of............. Num 7:66
of A the son of Ammishaddai .... Num 7:71
over his host was A the son of .... Num 10:25

  2. A chief of the Benjamites.
The chief was A, then Joash, the......... 1Chr 12:3

AHIHUD (a-hi'-hud)
  1. A prince of Asher.
of Asher, A the son of Shelomi .... Num 34:27
  2. A Benjamite of the Ehud family.
removed them, and begat Uzza, and A. 1Chr 8:7

AHIJAH (a-hi'-jah) See AHIAH, AHIMAELECH.
  *1. A prophet during the reigns of Solomon
  and Rehoboam.*
that the prophet A the Shilonite 1Kin 11:29
A caught the new garment that was 1Kin 11:30
which the LORD spake by A the 1Kin 12:15
there is A the prophet, which.............. 1Kin 14:2
Shiloh, and came to the house of A 1Kin 14:4
But A could not see........................... 1Kin 14:4
And the LORD said unto A, Behold,...... 1Kin 14:5
when A heard the sound of her 1Kin 14:6
hand of his servant A the prophet 1Kin 14:18
by his servant A the Shilonite 1Kin 15:29
the prophecy of A the Shilonite 2Chr 9:29
A the Shilonite to Jeroboam the 2Chr 10:15
  2. Father of Baasha.
And Baasha the son of A, of the 1Kin 15:27
of A to reign over all Israel in 1Kin 15:33
the house of Baasha the son of A 1Kin 21:22
the house of Baasha the son of A 2Kin 9:9
  3. Son of Jerahmeel.
and Oren, and Ozem, and A 1Chr 2:25
  4. A "mighty man" of David.
the Mecherathite, A the Pelonite,........ 1Chr 11:36
  5. A treasury official under David.
A was over the treasures of the 1Chr 26:20
  6. A Levite who renewed the covenant.
And A, Hanan, Anan,......................... Neh 10:26

AHIKAM (a-hi'-kam) An officer in Josiah's
  court.
A the son of Shaphan, and Achbor....... 2Kin 22:12
So Hilkiah the priest, and A 2Kin 22:14
he made Gedaliah the son of A 2Kin 25:22
A the son of Shaphan, and Abdon........ 2Chr 34:20
Nevertheless the hand of A the .... Jer 26:24
the son of A the son of Shaphan .... Jer 39:14
the son of A the son of Shaphan .... Jer 40:5
Gedaliah the son of A to Mizpah.......... Jer 40:6
the son of A governor in the land......... Jer 40:7
Gedaliah the son of A the son of .... Jer 40:9
the son of A the son of Shaphan .... Jer 40:11
the son of A believed them not .... Jer 40:14
But Gedaliah the son of A said .... Jer 40:16
Gedaliah the son of A to Mizpah.......... Jer 41:1
smote Gedaliah the son of A .... Jer 41:2
Come to Gedaliah the son of A .... Jer 41:6
to Gedaliah the son of A .... Jer 41:10
had slain Gedaliah the son of A .... Jer 41:16
had slain Gedaliah the son of A .... Jer 41:18
the son of A the son of Shaphan .... Jer 43:6

AHILUD (a-hi'-lud) Father of a recorder under
  David and Solomon.
the son of A was recorder 2Sa 8:16
the son of A was recorder 2Sa 20:24
Jehoshaphat the son of A, the 1Kin 4:3
Baana the son of A 1Kin 4:12
and Jehoshaphat the son of A 1Chr 18:15

AHIMAAZ (a-him'-a-az)
  1. Father of Ahinoam.
was Ahinoam, the daughter of A.......... 1Sa 14:50
  2. Son of Zadok.
A thy son, and Jonathan the son of...... 2Sa 15:27
of Zadok's son, and Jonathan 2Sa 15:36
Jonathan and A stayed by En-rogel...... 2Sa 17:17
the house, they said, Where is A 2Sa 17:20
Then said A the son of Zadok, Let 2Sa 18:19
Then said A the son of Zadok yet 2Sa 18:22
Then A ran by the way of the.............. 2Sa 18:23
the running of A the son of Zadok 2Sa 18:27
A called, and said unto the king,......... 2Sa 18:28
A answered, When Joab sent the 2Sa 18:29
begat Zadok, and Zadok begat A 1Chr 6:8
A begat Azariah, and Azariah begat 1Chr 6:9
Zadok his son, A his son..................... 1Chr 6:53
  3. An officer of Solomon.
A was in Naphtali.............................. 1Kin 4:15

AHIMAN (a-hi'-man)
  1. A giant of Anak.
where A, Sheshai, and Talmai, the ...... Num 13:22
three sons of Anak, Sheshai, and A ..... Josh 15:14
and they slew Sheshai, and A .... Judg 1:10
  2. A Levite Temple servant.
and Akkub, and Talmon, and A 1Chr 9:17

AHIMELECH (a-him'-el-ek)
  1. A priest.
came David to Nob to A the priest 1Sa 21:1
A was afraid at the meeting of 1Sa 21:1
And David said unto A the priest,........ 1Sa 21:2
And David said unto A, And is there..... 1Sa 21:8
to Nob, to A the son of Ahitub............. 1Sa 22:9
king sent to call A the priest 1Sa 22:11
Then A answered the king, and said 1Sa 22:14
said, Thou shalt surely die, A 1Sa 22:16
the sons of A the son of Ahitub 1Sa 22:20
son of A fled to David to Keilah 1Sa 23:6
A the son of Abiathar, were the 2Sa 8:17
A the son of Ithamar,........................ 1Chr 24:3
A the son of Abiathar, and before 1Chr 24:6
of David the king, and Zadok, and A 1Chr 24:31

David is come to the house of A ...... Ps 52:t
2. A Hittite officer.
said to A the Hittite, and to................ 1Sa 26:6

AHIMELECH'S (a-him'-el-eks) Refers to Ahimelech 1.
A son, I pray thee, bring me........... 1Sa 30:7

AHIMOTH
Amasai, and A.................................. 1Chr 6:25

AHINADAB (a-hin'-ad-ab) A son of Iddo.
A the son of Iddo had Mahanaim 1Kin 4:14

'AHINOAM (a-hin'-o-am)
1. A wife of King Saul.
And the name of Saul's wife was A 1Sa 14:50
2. A wife of David.
David also took A of Jezreel.............. 1Sa 25:43
A the Jezreelitess, and Abigail 1Sa 27:3
A the Jezreelitess, and Abigail 1Sa 30:5
A the Jezreelitess, and Abigail 2Sa 2:2
was Amnon, of A the Jezreelitess 2Sa 3:2
Amnon, of A the Jezreelitess 1Chr 3:1

AHIO (a-hi'-o)
1. A son of Abinadab.
and Uzzah and A, the sons of 2Sa 6:3
and A went before the ark................... 2Sa 6:4
and Uzza and A drave the cart........... 1Chr 13:7
2. A son of Beriah the Benjamite.
And A, Shashak, and Jeremoth,......... 1Chr 8:14
3. A son of Jehiel.
And Gedor, and A, and Zacher.......... 1Chr 8:31
and A, and Zechariah......................... 1Chr 9:37

AHIRA (a-hi'-rah) A chief of Naphtali.
A the son of Enan.............................. Num 1:15
shall be A the son of Enan................. Num 2:29
the twelfth day A the son of Enan...... Num 7:78
the offering of A the son of Enan....... Num 7:83
of Naphtali was A the son of Enan .... Num 10:27

AHIRAM (a-hi'-rum) See AHARAH, AHIRAMITES.
A descendant of Benjamin.
of A, the family of the .... Num 26:38

AHIRAMITES (a-hi'-rum-ites) Descendants of Ahiram.
of Ahiram, the family of the A .... Num 26:38

AHISAMACH (a-his'-am-ak) Father of Aholiab.
with him Aholiab, the son of A .... Ex 31:6
both he, and Aholiab, the son of A .... Ex 35:34
And with him was Aholiab, son of A .. Ex 38:23

AHISHAHAR (a-hish'-a-har) A son of Bilhan.
and Zethan, and Tharshish, and A 1Chr 7:10

AHISHAR (a-hi'-shar) Governor of the palace under Solomon.
And A was over the household............ 1Kin 4:6

AHITHOPHEL (a-hith'-o-fel) A counsellor of David.
Absalom sent for A the Gilonite 2Sa 15:12
A is among the conspirators with 2Sa 15:31
the counsel of A into foolishness....... 2Sa 15:31
for me defeat the counsel of A 2Sa 15:34
came to Jerusalem, and A with him ... 2Sa 16:15
Then said Absalom to A, Give........... 2Sa 16:20
A said unto Absalom, Go in unto 2Sa 16:21
And the counsel of A, which he 2Sa 16:23
the counsel of A both with David 2Sa 16:23
Moreover A said unto Absalom, Let ... 2Sa 17:1
A hath spoken after this manner........ 2Sa 17:6
The counsel that A hath given is 2Sa 17:7
is better than the counsel of A 2Sa 17:14
to defeat the good counsel of A 2Sa 17:14
thus did A counsel Absalom and the .. 2Sa 17:15
for thus hath A counselled................ 2Sa 17:21
when A saw that his counsel was 2Sa 17:23
Eliam the son of A the Gilonite.......... 2Sa 23:34
A was the king's counsellor................ 1Chr 27:33
after A was Jehoiada the son of 1Chr 27:34

AHITUB (a-hi'-tub)
1. The son of Phinehas.
And Ahiah, the son of A,.................... 1Sa 14:3
to Nob, to Ahimelech the son of A 1Sa 22:9
the priest, the son of A, and all.......... 1Sa 22:11
said, Hear now, thou son of A............ 1Sa 22:12
sons of Ahimelech the son of A.......... 1Sa 22:20
2. Father of the high priest during David's reign.
And Zadok the son of A, and 2Sa 8:17
begat Amariah, and Amariah begat A . 1Chr 6:7
A begat Zadok, and Zadok begat........ 1Chr 6:8
son, Amariah his son, A his son,....... 1Chr 6:52
And Zadok the son of A, and 1Chr 18:16
the son of Zadok, the son of A .... Ezr 7:2
3. A priest seven generations later than Ahitub 2.
begat Amariah, and Amariah begat A . 1Chr 6:11
A begat Zadok, and Zadok begat........ 1Chr 6:12
4. A priest in Nehemiah's time.
the son of Meraioth, the son of A 1Chr 9:11
the son of Meraioth, the son of A ...... Neh 11:11

AHLAB (ah'-lab) A city of Asher.
inhabitants of Zidon, nor of A .... Judg 1:31

AHLAI (ah'-lahee)
1. A daughter of Sheshan.
And the children of Sheshan; A 1Chr 2:31
2. Father of a "mighty man" of David.

the Hittite, Zabad the son of A........... 1Chr 11:41

AHOAH (a-ho'-ah) See AHOHITE. The son of Bela.
And Abishua, and Naaman, and A 1Chr 8:4

AHOHITE (a-ho'-hite)
1. A descendant of Ahoah.
Zalmon the A, Maharai the................ 2Sa 23:28
Eleazar the son of Dodo, the A 1Chr 11:12
the Hushathite, Ilai the A.................. 1Chr 11:29
the second month was Dodai an A 1Chr 27:4
2. A rendering of "son of Ahohi."
was Eleazar the son of Dodo the A 2Sa 23:9

AHOLAH (a-ho'-lah) A name for Samaria and the Ten Tribes.
names of them were A the elder .... Eze 23:4
Samaria is A, and Jerusalem.............. Eze 23:4
A played the harlot when she was ...... Eze 23:5
Son of man, with thou judge A .... Eze 23:36
so went they in unto A and unto .... Eze 23:44

AHOLIAB (a-ho'-lee-ab) A Danite craftsman.
behold, I have given with him a.......... Ex 31:6
that he may teach, both he, and A ..... Ex 35:34
Then wrought Bezaleel and A .... Ex 36:1
And Moses called Bezaleel and A ...... Ex 36:2
And with him was A, son of .... Ex 38:23

AHOLIBAH (a-ho'-lib-ah) A name for Jerusalem and Judah.
Aholah the elder, and A her sister ..... Eze 23:4
Samaria is Aholah, and Jerusalem A .. Eze 23:4
And when her sister A saw this.......... Eze 23:11
Therefore, O A, thus saith the .... Eze 23:22
man, wilt thou judge Aholah and A .... Eze 23:36
they in unto Aholah and unto A .... Eze 23:44

AHOLIBAMAH (a-ho'-ib-a'-mah)
1. A wife of Esau.
A the daughter of Anah the .... Gen 36:2
A bare Jeush, and Jaalam, and Korah.. Gen 36:5
And these were the sons of A............ Gen 36:14
are the sons of A Esau's wife .... Gen 36:18
came of A the daughter of Anah........ Gen 36:18
Dishon, and A the daughter of Anah . Gen 36:25
2. A chief from Esau.
Duke A, duke Elah, duke Pinon,........ Gen 36:41
Duke A, duke Elah, duke Pinon,........ 1Chr 1:52

AHUMAI (a-hoo'-mahee) Grandson of Shobal.
and Jahath begat A, and Lahad......... 1Chr 4:2

AHUZAM (a-hoo'-zam) A son of Ashur.
And Naarah bare him A, and Hepher,.. 1Chr 4:6

AHUZZAM See AHUZAM.

AHUZZATH (a-huz'-zath) A friend of Ahimelech the Philistine king.
A one of his friends, and Phichol....... Gen 26:26

AI (a'-i) See AIATH, AIJA, HAI. A city near Bethel in Benjamin.
Joshua sent men from Jericho to A .... Josh 7:2
And the men went up and viewed A .... Josh 7:2
thousand men go up and smite A ...... Josh 7:3
and they fled before the men of A ...... Josh 7:4
the men of A smote of them about ..... Josh 7:5
with thee, and arise, go up to A .... Josh 8:1
given into thy hand the king of A ...... Josh 8:1
And thou shalt do to A and her king,.. Josh 8:2
people of war, to go up against A ...... Josh 8:3
and A, on the west side of A .... Josh 8:9
of Israel, before the people to A .... Josh 8:10
and pitched on the north side of A ..... Josh 8:11
was a valley between them and A ...... Josh 8:11
in ambush between Bethel and A .... Josh 8:12
pass, when the king of A saw it......... Josh 8:14
all the people that were in A .... Josh 8:16
not a man left in A or Beth-el .... Josh 8:17
that is in thy hand toward A .... Josh 8:18
when the men of A looked behind ...... Josh 8:20
again, and slew the men of A .... Josh 8:21
the king of A they took alive, and...... Josh 8:23
the inhabitants of A in the field.......... Josh 8:24
the Israelites returned unto A .... Josh 8:24
thousand, even all the men of A .... Josh 8:25
all the inhabitants of A .... Josh 8:26
And Joshua burnt A, and made it an.. Josh 8:28
the king of A he hanged on a tree ...... Josh 8:29
had done unto Jericho and to A .... Josh 9:3
had heard how Joshua had taken A .... Josh 10:1
and her king, so he had done to A ..... Josh 10:1
and because it was greater than A ..... Josh 10:2
the king of A, which is beside .... Josh 12:9
The men of Beth-el and A, two.......... Ezr 2:28
The men of Beth-el and A, an............ Neh 7:32
Howl, O Heshbon, for A is spoiled ..... Jer 49:3

AIAH (a'-i-ah) See AJAH.
1. A son of Zibeon the Horite.
A, and Anah..................................... 1Chr 1:40
2. The father of Saul's concubine.
was Rizpah, the daughter of A 2Sa 3:7
sons of Rizpah the daughter of A 2Sa 21:8
the daughter of A took sackcloth 2Sa 21:10
what Rizpah the daughter of A 2Sa 21:11

AIATH (a'i-ath) See AI. A form of Ai.
He is come to A, he is passed to ...... Is 10:28

AIDED
which a him in the killing of his .... Judg 9:24

AIJA (a'i-jah) See AI. A form of Ai.
dwelt at Michmash, and A .... Neh 11:31

AIJALON (a'i-el-on) See AJALON.
1. A Levitical city in Dan.
A with her suburbs, Gath-rimmon .... Josh 21:24

would dwell in mount Heres in A .... Judg 1:35
2. A place in Zebulun.
was buried in A in the country of ...... Judg 12:12
3. A town between Benjamin and Judah.
that day from Michmash to A 1Sa 14:31
fathers of the inhabitants of A 1Chr 8:13
Zorah, and A, and Hebron................. 2Chr 11:10
4. A Levitical city in Ephraim.
And A with her suburbs, and............. 1Chr 6:69

AIJELETH (a-ij'-el-eth) A musical notation.
the chief Musician upon A Shahar ..... Ps 22:t

AILED
What a thee, O thou sea, that .... Ps 114:5

AILETH
and said unto her, What a thee .... Gen 21:17
and said unto Micah, What a thee ..... Judg 18:23
that ye say unto me, What a thee ...... Judg 18:24
What a the people that they weep...... 1Sa 11:5
king said unto her, What a thee 2Sa 14:5
king said unto her, What a thee 2Kin 6:28
What a thee now, that thou art.......... Is 22:1

AIN (ah'-yin) See EN.
1. A place between Riblah and the Sea of Chinneroth.
to Riblah, on the east side of A .... Num 34:11
2. A Levitical city in Simeon.
And Lebaoth, and Shilhim, and A ...... Josh 15:32
A, Remmon, and Ether, and Ashan..... Josh 19:7
A with her suburbs, and Juttah .... Josh 21:16
their villages were, Etam, and A 1Chr 4:32

AIR
sea, and over the fowl of the a.......... Gen 1:26
sea, and over the fowl of the a.......... Gen 1:28
earth, and to every fowl of the a........ Gen 1:30
the field, and every fowl of the a .... Gen 2:19
cattle, and to the fowl of the a .... Gen 2:20
thing, and the fowls of the a.............. Gen 6:7
Of fowls also of the a by sevens........ Gen 7:3
and upon every fowl of the a.............. Gen 9:2
winged fowl that flieth in the a .... Deut 4:17
be meat unto all fowls of the a .... Deut 28:26
thy flesh unto the fowls of the a 1Sa 17:44
this day unto the fowls of the a 1Sa 17:46
of the a to rest on them by day.......... 2Sa 21:10
shall the fowls of the a eat 1Kin 14:11
shall the fowls of the a eat 1Kin 16:4
shall the fowls of the a eat 1Kin 21:24
and the fowls of the a, and they .... Job 12:7
close from the fowls of the a............. Job 28:21
that no a can come between them....... Job 41:16
The fowl of the a, and the fish of ...... Ps 8:8
The way of an eagle in the a .... Prov 30:19
for a bird of the a shall carry .... Eccl 10:20
Behold the fowls of the a.................. Mt 6:26
and the birds of the a have nests....... Mt 8:20
so that the birds of the a come.......... Mt 13:32
side, and the fowls of the a devoured . Mk 4:4
so that the fowls of the a may .... Mk 4:32
and the fowls of the a devoured it...... Lk 8:5
and birds of the a have nests .... Lk 9:58
the fowls of the a lodged in the .... Lk 13:19
things, and fowls of the a .... Acts 10:12
things, and fowls of the a .... Acts 11:6
clothes, and threw dust into the a ..... Acts 22:23
I, not as one that beateth the a 1Cor 9:26
for ye shall speak into the a 1Cor 14:9
the prince of the power of the a .... Eph 2:2
clouds, to meet the Lord in the a 1Th 4:17
the a were darkened by reason of ...... Rev 9:2
poured out his vial into the a............. Rev 16:17

AJAH (a'-jah) See AIAH. A son of Zibeon the Horite.
both A, and Anah.............................. Gen 36:24

AJALON (aj'-a-lon) See AIJALON.
1. A valley of Dan.
and thou, Moon, in the valley of A ..... Josh 10:12
2. A Levitical city in Dan.
And Shaalabbin, and A, and Jethlah,.. Josh 19:42
3. A town between Benjamin and Judah.
and had taken Beth-shemesh, and A . 2Chr 28:18

AKAN (a'-kan) See JAAKAN, JAKAN. A son of Ezer.
Bilhan, and Zaavan, and A................. Gen 36:27

AKEL DAMA See ACELDAMA.

AKKAD See ACCAD.

AKKUB (ak'-kub)
1. A descendant of David.
and Eliashib, and Pelaiah, and A 1Chr 3:24
2. A Levitical gatekeeper.
the porters were, Shallum, and A 1Chr 9:17
Moreover the porters, Talmon,........... Neh 11:19
Obadiah, Meshullam, Talmon, A .... Neh 12:25
3. A family of Levitical porters.
of Talmon, the children of A .... Ezr 2:42
of Talmon, the children of A .... Neh 7:45
4. A family of returned exiles.
of Hagabah, the children of A .... Ezr 2:45
5. A priest in Ezra's time.
and Bani, and Sherebiah, Jamin, A .... Neh 8:7

AKRABBIM (ac-rab'-bim) See MAALE-ACRABBIM, an ascent on the south of the Dead Sea.
from the south to the ascent of A ...... Num 34:4
was from the going up to A .... Judg 1:36

ALABASTER
a box of very precious ointment.......... Mt 26:7
an box of ointment of spikenard .... Mk 14:3

brought an a box of ointment,............ Lk 7:37

ALAMETH (al'-am-eth) A son of Becher.
and Abiah, and Anathoth, and A 1Chr 7:8

ALAMMELECH (a-lam'-mel-ek) A town in Asher.
And A, and Amad, and Misheal .... Josh 19:26

ALAMOTH (al'-am-oth) A musical notation.
and Benaiah, with psalteries on A 1Chr 15:20
the sons of Korah, A Song upon a .... Ps 46:t

ALARM
When ye blow an a, then the camps..... Num 10:5
When ye blow an a the second time...... Num 10:6
blow an a for their journeys .... Num 10:6
blow, but ye shall not sound an a .... Num 10:7
shall blow an a with the trumpets....... Num 10:9
trumpets to cry a against you............ 2Chr 13:12
of the trumpet, the a of war .... Jer 4:19
that I will cause an a of war to .... Jer 49:2
sound an a in my holy mountain........ Joel 2:1
a against the fenced cities, and......... Zeph 1:16

ALAS
And Aaron said unto Moses, A........... Num 12:11
took up his parable, and said, A........ Num 24:23
And Joshua said, A, O Lord God,........ Josh 7:7
angel of the LORD, Gideon said, A...... Judg 6:22
he rent his clothes, and said, A......... Judg 11:35
they mourned over him, saying, A..... 1Kin 13:30
And the king of Israel said, A.......... 2Kin 3:10
and he cried, and said, A, master...... 2Kin 6:5
And his servant said unto him, A...... 2Kin 6:15
A! for that day is great................. Jer 30:7
A for all the evil abominations......... Eze 6:11
A for the day .... Joel 1:15
say in all the highways, A! a!.......... Amos 5:16
fear of her torment, saying, A......... Rev 18:10
a that great city Babylon, that........ Rev 18:10
And saying, A, a that great .... Rev 18:16
weeping and wailing, saying, A........ Rev 18:19
a that great city, wherein were .... Rev 18:19

ALBEIT
a I have not spoken .... Eze 13:7
a I do not say to thee how thou........ Philem 19

ALEMETH (al-e'-meth)
1. A Levitical city in Benjamin.
A with her suburbs, and Anathoth 1Chr 6:60
2. A descendant of Jonathan.
and Jehoadah begat A 1Chr 8:36
and Jarah begat A 1Chr 9:42

ALEXANDER (al-ex-an'-dur)
1. Son of Simeon who bore Jesus'cross.
of the country, the father of A .... Mk 15:21
2. A Christian leader in Jerusalem.
and Caiaphas, and John, and A .... Acts 4:6
3. A participant in the Ephesian riot.
they drew A out of the multitude,....... Acts 19:33
A beckoned with the hand, and......... Acts 19:33
4. An opponent of Paul.
Of whom is Hymenaeus and A 1Ti 1:20
the coppersmith did me much 2Ti 4:14

ALEXANDRIA (al-ex-an'-dree-ah) See ALEXANDRIANS. A city in Egypt.
Jew named Apollos, born at A .... Acts 18:24
a ship of A sailing into Italy .... Acts 27:6
months we departed in a ship of A .... Acts 28:11

ALEXANDRIAN See ALEXANDRIA.

ALEXANDRIANS (al-ex-an'-dree-uns) Residents of Alexandria
Libertines, and Cyrenians, and A...... Acts 6:9

ALGUM
trees, and a trees, out of Lebanon 2Chr 2:8
gold from Ophir, brought a trees 2Chr 9:10
the king made of the a trees 2Chr 9:11

ALIAH (a-li'-ah) See ALVAH. A chief of Edom.
duke Timnah, duke A, duke Jetheth ... 1Chr 1:51

ALIAN (a-li'-un) See ALVAN. A son of Shobal.
A, and Manahath, and Ebal, Shephi,... 1Chr 1:40

ALIEN
I have been an a in a strange .... Ex 18:3
or thou mayest sell it unto an a........ Deut 14:21
I am an a in thine sight .... Job 19:15
an a unto my mother's children........ Ps 69:8
the sons of the a shall be your .... Is 61:5

ALIENATE
nor a the firstfruits of the land .... Eze 48:14

ALIENATED
them, and her mind was a from them. Eze 23:17
then my mind was a from her......... Eze 23:18
as my mind was a from her sister..... Eze 23:18
thee, from whom thy mind is a .... Eze 23:22
of them from whom thy mind is a .... Eze 23:28
being a from the life of God .... Eph 4:18
And you, that were sometime a .... Col 1:21

ALIENS
to strangers, our houses to a .... Lam 5:2
being a from the commonwealth of ... Eph 2:12
to flight the armies of the a .... Heb 11:34

ALIKE
and the clean shall eat of them a...... Deut 12:22
the clean person shall eat it a......... Deut 15:22
they shall part a 1Sa 30:24

They shall lie down a in the dust ...... Job 21:26
He fashioneth their hearts a .... Ps 33:15
and the light are both a to thee .... Ps 139:12
both of them are a abomination to ... Prov 20:10
day and a contentious woman are a... Prov 27:15
All things come a to all .... Eccl 9:2
whether they both shall be a good .... Eccl 11:6
another esteemeth every day a .... Rom 14:5

ALIVE
the ark, to keep them a with thee .... Gen 6:19
come unto thee, to keep them a .... Gen 6:20
to keep seed a upon the face of....... Gen 7:3
and Noah only remained a, and they.. Gen 7:23
me, but they will save thee a .... Gen 12:12
saying, Is your father yet a .... Gen 43:7
Is he yet a .... Gen 43:27
is in good health, he is yet a .... Gen 43:28
told him, saying, Joseph is yet a .... Gen 45:26
Joseph my son is yet a .... Gen 45:28
thy face, because thou art yet a ..... Gen 46:30
this day, to save much people a ..... Gen 50:20
but saved the men children a .... Ex 1:17
and have saved the men children a .. Ex 1:18
and every daughter ye shall save a .. Ex 1:22
and see whether they be yet a .... Ex 4:18
be certainly found in his hand a ..... Ex 22:4
sons of Aaron which were left a ..... Lev 10:16
is to be cleansed two birds a .... Lev 14:4
be presented a before the LORD ..... Lev 16:10
upon them that are left a of you ..... Lev 26:36
went down a into the pit, and the ... Num 16:33
until there was none left him a ..... Num 21:35
I had slain thee, and saved thee a .. Num 22:33
Have ye saved all the women a ..... Num 31:15
with him, keep a for yourselves .... Num 31:18
are a every one of you this day..... Deut 4:4
who are all of us here a this day.... Deut 5:3
that he might preserve us a .... Deut 6:24
thou shalt save a nothing that ..... Deut 20:16
while I am yet a with you this ...... Deut 31:27
I kill, and I make a .... Deut 32:39
And that ye will save a my father... Josh 2:13
Joshua saved Rahab the harlot a.... Josh 6:25
And the king of Ai they took a ..... Josh 8:23
behold, the LORD hath kept me a ... Josh 14:10
liveth, if ye had saved them a ..... Judg 8:19
a of the women of Jabesh-gilead ... Judg 21:14
The LORD killeth, and maketh a 1Sa 2:6
Agag the king of the Amalekites a.. 1Sa 15:8
and left neither man nor woman a... 1Sa 27:9
saved neither man nor woman a 1Sa 27:11
and with one full line to keep a 2Sa 8:2
Behold, while the child was yet a .. 2Sa 12:18
for the child, while it was a 2Sa 12:21
said, While the child was yet a 2Sa 12:22
while he was yet a in the midst..... 2Sa 18:14
to save the horses and mules a 1Kin 18:5
come out for peace, take them a ... 1Kin 20:18
be come out for war, take them a .. 1Kin 20:18
And he said, Is he yet a 1Kin 20:32
for Naboth is not a, but dead 1Kin 21:15
Am I God, to kill and to make a 2Kin 5:7
if they save us a, we shall live 2Kin 7:4
the city, we shall catch them a 2Kin 7:12
And he said, Take them a 2Kin 10:14
And they took them a 2Kin 10:14
other ten thousand left a did the .. 2Chr 25:12
and none can keep a his own soul .. Ps 22:29
thou hast kept me a, that I .... Ps 30:3
and to keep them a in famine ...... Ps 33:19
will preserve him, and keep him a.. Ps 41:2
us swallow them up a as the grave.. Prov 1:12
than the living which are yet a ..... Eccl 4:2
children, I will preserve them a .... Jer 49:11
is sold, although they were yet a... Eze 13:18
the souls a that come unto you ..... Eze 13:18
to save the souls a that should .... Eze 13:19
right, he shall save his soul a ...... Eze 18:27
and whom he would he kept a ...... Dan 5:19
deceiver said, while he was a ...... Mt 27:63
when they had heard that he was a.. Mk 16:11
my son was dead, and is a again.... Lk 15:24
brother was dead, and is a again.... Lk 15:32
angels, which said that he was a ... Lk 24:23
a after his passion by many .... Acts 1:3
saints and widows, presented her a.. Acts 9:41
And they brought the young man a .. Acts 20:12
dead, whom Paul affirmed to be a .. Acts 25:19
but a unto God through Jesus....... Rom 6:11
as those that are a from the dead... Rom 6:13
For I was a without the law once.... Rom 7:9
so in Christ shall all be made a 1Cor 15:22
of the Lord, that we which are a ... 1Th 4:15
Then we which are a and remain ... 1Th 4:17
I am a for evermore, Amen .... Rev 1:18
the last, which was dead, and is a.. Rev 2:8
These both were cast a into a ...... Rev 19:20

ALL See PREFACE.

ALLAMMELECH See ALAMMELECH.

ALLEGING
Opening a, that Christ must .... Acts 17:3

ALLEGORY
Which things are an a .... Gal 4:24

ALLELUIA (al-le-loo'-yah) Greek form of Hallelujah.
much people in heaven, saying, A ... Rev 19:1
And again they said, A .... Rev 19:3

saying, Amen; A .... Rev 19:4
of mighty thunderings, saying, A .... Rev 19:6

ALLIED
of our God, was a unto Tobiah ...... Neh 13:4

ALLON (al'-lon) See ALLON-BACHUTH, ELON.
1. A city in Naphtali.
from A to Zaanannim, and Adami,... Josh 19:33
2. A chief of a Simeonite family.
the son of Shiphi, the son of A 1Chr 4:37

ALLON-BACHUTH (al'-lon-bak'-ooth) A place near Bethel.
and the name of it was called A ..... Gen 35:8

ALLOW
ye a the deeds of your fathers ...... Lk 11:48
which they themselves also a .... Acts 24:15
For that which I do I a not .... Rom 7:15

ALLOWANCE
his a was a continual a 2Kin 25:30

ALLOWED
But as we were a of God to be put... 1Th 2:4

ALLOWETH
himself in that thing which he ...... Rom 14:22

ALLURE
Therefore, behold, I will a her ...... Hos 2:14
they a through the lusts of the 2Pet 2:18

ALMIGHTY A term for God meaning sufficient or all-powerful.
and said unto him, I am the A, God.. Gen 17:1
God A bless thee, and make thee .... Gen 28:3
And God said unto him, I am God A.. Gen 35:11
God A give you mercy before the ... Gen 43:14
God A appeared unto me at Luz in .. Gen 48:3
and by the A, who shall bless thee... Gen 49:25
unto Jacob, by the name of God A .. Ex 6:3
which saw the vision of the A ...... Num 24:4
which saw the vision of the A ...... Num 24:16
for the A hath dealt very .... Ruth 1:20
me, and the A hath afflicted me .... Ruth 1:21
not thou the chastening of the A ... Job 5:17
the arrows of the A are within me... Job 6:4
he forsaketh the fear of the A ...... Job 6:14
or doth the A pervert justice .... Job 8:3
and make thy supplication to the A.. Job 8:5
find out the A unto perfection ...... Job 11:7
Surely I would speak to the A ...... Job 13:3
himself against the A .... Job 15:25
What is the A, that we should ...... Job 21:15
shall drink of the wrath of the A ... Job 21:20
Is it any pleasure to the A .... Job 22:3
and what can the A do for them .... Job 22:17
If thou return to the A, thou .... Job 22:23
the A shall be thy defence, and..... Job 22:25
thou have thy delight in the A ...... Job 22:26
heart soft, and the A troubleth me.. Job 23:16
times are not hidden from the A .... Job 24:1
and the A, who hath vexed my soul.. Job 27:2
Will he delight himself in the A .... Job 27:10
is with the A will I not conceal..... Job 27:11
which they shall receive of the A ... Job 27:13
When the A was yet with me, when.. Job 29:5
inheritance of the A from on high .. Job 31:2
that the A would answer me, and ... Job 31:35
the inspiration of the A giveth ..... Job 32:8
the breath of the A hath given..... Job 33:4
and from the A, that he should ..... Job 34:10
will the A pervert judgment .... Job 34:12
neither will the A regard it .... Job 35:13
Touching the A, we cannot find .... Job 37:23
with the a instruct him .... Job 40:2
When the A scattered kings in it,... Ps 68:14
abide under the shadow of the A.... Ps 91:1
come as a destruction from the A ... Is 13:6
waters, as the voice of the A .... Eze 1:24
as the voice of the A God when he.. Eze 10:5
from the A shall it come .... Joel 1:15
and daughters, saith the Lord A 2Cor 6:18
was, and which is to come, the A ... Rev 1:8
Holy, holy, holy, Lord God A .... Rev 4:8
We give thee thanks, O Lord God A.. Rev 11:17
are thy works, Lord God A .... Rev 15:3
altar say, Even so, Lord God A ..... Rev 16:7
battle of that great day of God A ... Rev 16:14
the fierceness and wrath of A God.. Rev 19:15
for the Lord God A and the Lamb... Rev 21:22

ALMODAD (al-mo'-dad) A descendant of Shem.
And Joktan begat A .... Gen 10:26
And Joktan begat A 1Chr 1:20

ALMON (al'-mon) A Levitical town in Benjamin.
suburbs, and A with her suburbs.... Josh 21:18

ALMOND
the a tree shall flourish, and the ... Eccl 12:5
I said, I see a rod of an a tree ...... Jer 1:11

ALMON-DIBLATHAIM (al'-mon-dib-lath-a'-im) An encampment of Israel in the Wilderness.
from Dibon-gad, and encamped in A.. Num 33:46
And they removed from A, and ...... Num 33:47

ALMONDS
spices, and myrrh, nuts, and a ...... Gen 43:11
Three bowls made like unto a .... Ex 25:33
made like a in the other branch ..... Ex 25:33

be four bowls made like unto a............ Ex 25:34
the fashion of a in one branch........... Ex 37:19
made like a in another branch............ Ex 37:19
were four bowls made like a................ Ex 37:20
and bloomed blossoms, and yielded a.. Num 17:8

ALMOST

they be a ready to stone me.................. Num 14:40
as for me, my feet were a gone............ Ps 73:2
my soul had a dwelt in silence.............. Ps 94:17
They had a consumed me upon earth.. Ps 119:87
I was a in all evil in the midst.............. Prov 5:14
the next sabbath day came a the....... Acts 13:44
but a throughout all Asia, this........... Acts 19:26
when the seven days were a ended..... Acts 21:27
A thou persuadest me to be a............ Acts 26:28
hear me this day, were both a............ Acts 26:29
a all things are by the law................. Heb 9:22

ALMS

that ye do not your a before men...... Mt 6:1
Therefore when thou doest thine a..... Mt 6:2
But when thou doest a, let not......... Mt 6:3
That thine a may be in secret............ Mt 6:4
But rather give a of such things......... Lk 11:41
Sell that ye have, and give a............. Lk 12:33
to ask a of them that entered........... Acts 3:2
to go into the temple asked an a....... Acts 3:3
a at the Beautiful gate of the............. Acts 3:10
which gave much a to the people........ Acts 10:2
thine a are come up for a................. Acts 10:4
thine a are had in remembrance in..... Acts 10:31
I came to bring a to my nation.......... Acts 24:17

ALMSDEEDS

of good works and a which she did ... Acts 9:36

ALMUG

Ophir great plenty of a trees............. 1Kin 10:11
the king made of the a trees.............. 1Kin 10:12
there came no such a trees............... 1Kin 10:12

ALOES

as the trees of lign a which the......... Num 24:6
thy garments smell of myrrh, and a... Ps 45:8
perfumed my bed with myrrh, a......... Prov 7:17
myrrh and a, with all the chief........... Song 4:14
brought a mixture of myrrh and a...... Jn 19:39

ALONE

not good that the man should be a.... Gen 2:18
And Jacob was left a......................... Gen 32:24
brother is dead, and he is left a........ Gen 42:38
he is left of his mother, and............. Gen 44:20
thee in Egypt, saying, Let us a.......... Ex 14:12
why sittest thou thyself a................. Ex 18:14
not able to perform it thyself a......... Ex 18:18
Moses a shall come near the LORD..... Ex 24:2
Now therefore let me a, that my...... Ex 32:10
he shall dwell a............................... Lev 13:46
able to bear all this people a............ Num 11:14
that thou bear it not thyself a.......... Num 11:17
lo, the people shall dwell a............... Num 23:9
am not able to bear you myself a...... Deut 1:9
How can I myself a bear your........... Deut 1:12
Let me a, that I may destroy them .... Deut 9:14
So the LORD a did lead him, and........ Deut 32:12
then shall dwell in safety a............... Deut 33:28
perished not a in his iniquity............ Josh 22:20
which he had for himself a................ Judg 3:20
let me a two months, that I may...... Judg 11:37
and said unto him, Why art thou a.... 1Sa 21:1
let him a, and let him curse............. 2Sa 16:11
looked, and behold a man running a.. 2Sa 18:24
And the king said, If he be a.............. 2Sa 18:25
Behold another man running a........... 2Sa 18:26
and they two were a in the field....... 1Kin 11:29
And the man of God said, Let her a... 2Kin 4:27
thou art the God, even thou a.......... 2Kin 19:15
And he said, Let him a...................... 2Kin 23:18
So they let his bones a, with the...... 2Kin 23:18
whom a God hath chosen, is yet....... 1Chr 29:1
the work of this house of God a........ Ezr 6:7
Thou, even thou, art LORD a............. Neh 9:6
scorn to lay hands on Mordecai a...... Est 3:6
I only am escaped a to tell thee........ Job 1:15
I only am escaped a to tell thee........ Job 1:16
I only am escaped a to tell thee........ Job 1:17
I only am escaped a to tell thee........ Job 1:19
let me a.. Job 7:16
nor let me a till I swallow down........ Job 7:19
Which a spreadeth out the heavens... Job 9:8
cease then, and let me a, that I....... Job 10:20
Hold your peace, let me a................ Job 13:13
Unto whom a the earth was given,.... Job 15:19
Or have eaten my morsel myself a..... Job 31:17
thou, whose name a is JEHOVAH....... Ps 83:18
thou art God a.................................. Ps 86:10
am as a sparrow a upon the house .... Ps 102:7
To him who a doeth great wonders.... Ps 136:4
for his name a is excellent................ Ps 148:13
scornest, thou a shalt bear it........... Prov 9:12
There is one a, and there is not a..... Eccl 4:8
to him that is a when he falleth........ Eccl 4:10
but how can one be warm a.............. Eccl 4:11
the LORD a shall be exalted in.......... Is 2:11
the LORD a shall be exalted in.......... Is 2:17
that they may be placed a in the...... Is 5:8
none shall be a in his appointed....... Is 14:31
thou art the God, even thou a.......... Is 37:16
stretcheth forth the heavens a.......... Is 44:24
Behold, I was left a......................... Is 49:21
for I called him, and blessed.............. Is 51:2

I have trodden the winepress a......... Is 63:3
I sat a because of thy hand.............. Jer 15:17
gates our hars, which dwell a........... Jer 49:31
He sitteth a and keepeth silence,...... Lam 3:28
I Daniel a saw the vision.................. Dan 10:7
Therefore I was left a, and saw........ Dan 10:8
leth him a....................................... Hos 4:17
Assyria, a wild ass a by himself........ Hos 8:9
Man shall not live by bread a............ Mt 4:4
evening was come, he was there a..... Mt 14:23
Let them a...................................... Mt 15:14
his fault between thee and him a...... Mt 18:15
Saying, Let us a.............................. Mk 1:24
And when he was a, they that were.. Mk 4:10
and when they were a, he expounded.. Mk 4:34
of the sea, and he a on the land....... Mk 6:47
And Jesus said, Let her a................. Mk 14:6
gave him to drink, saying, Let a........ Mk 15:36
man shall not live by bread a............ Lk 4:4
Saying, Let us a.............................. Lk 4:34
Who can forgive sins, but God a........ Lk 5:21
to eat but for the priests a............... Lk 6:4
came to pass, as he was a praying.... Lk 9:18
voice was past, Jesus was found a.... Lk 9:36
my sister hath left me to serve a...... Lk 10:40
let it a this year also, till I.............. Lk 13:8
again into a mountain himself a......... Jn 6:15
his disciples were gone away a.......... Jn 6:22
and Jesus was left a, and the woman.. Jn 8:9
for I am not a, but I and the............ Jn 8:16
the Father hath not left me a........... Jn 8:29
If we let him thus a, all men............ Jn 11:48
Then said Jesus, Let her a................ Jn 12:7
the ground and die, it abideth a....... Jn 12:24
to his own, and shall leave me a....... Jn 16:32
and yet I am not a, because the........ Jn 16:32
Neither pray I for these a.................. Jn 17:20
from these men, and let them a........ Acts 5:38
that not a at Ephesus, but almost..... Acts 19:26
it was not written for his sake a....... Rom 4:23
and I am left a, and they seek my.... Rom 11:3
he have rejoicing in himself a............ Gal 6:4
it good to be left at Athens a............ 1Th 3:1
the high priest a once every year...... Heb 9:7
hath not works, is dead, being a........ Jas 2:17

ALONG

her maidens walked a by the............ Ex 2:5
the fire ran a upon the ground.......... Ex 9:23
but we will go a by the king's........... Num 21:22
of Zin a by the coast of Edom.......... Num 34:3
I will go a by the high way, I............ Deut 2:27
chased them a the way that goeth.... Josh 10:10
and passed a to Zin, and ascended.... Josh 15:3
passed a to Hezron, and went up to.. Josh 15:3
and passed a by the north of........... Josh 15:6
passed a unto the side of mount....... Josh 15:10
passed a to mount Baalah, and went. Josh 15:11
passeth a unto the borders of........... Josh 16:2
the border went a on the right.......... Josh 17:7
passed a toward the side over.......... Josh 18:18
the border passed a to the side........ Josh 18:19
from thence passeth on a on the....... Josh 19:13
the children of the east lay a in........ Judg 7:12
it, that the tent lay a.................... Judg 7:13
all that came a that way by them..... Judg 8:25
another company come a by the........ Judg 9:37
Then they went a through the.......... Judg 11:16
that be a by the coasts of Arnon....... Judg 11:26
liers in wait drew themselves a......... Judg 20:37
went a the highway, lowing as........... 1Sa 6:12
straightway all a on the earth........... 1Sa 28:20
her husband went with her a............ 2Sa 3:16
Shimei went a on the hill's side........ 2Sa 16:13
a by the altar and the temple.......... 2Kin 11:11
a by the altar and the temple, by..... 2Chr 23:10
them, weeping all a as he went......... Jer 41:6

ALOOF

my friends stand a from my sore....... Ps 38:11

ALOTH
(a'-loth) See BEALOTH. A region near
Asher.
of Hushai was in Asher and in A........ 1Kin 4:16

ALOUD

And he wept a................................ Gen 45:2
mocked them, and said, Cry a........... 1Kin 18:27
And they cried a, and cut................. 1Kin 18:28
and many shouted a for joy............. Ezr 3:12
I cry a, but there is no judgment...... Job 19:7
shall sing a of thy righteousness...... Ps 51:14
and at noon, will I pray, and cry a.... Ps 55:17
I will sing a of thy mercy in the........ Ps 59:16
Sing a unto God our strength........... Ps 81:1
her saints shall shout a for joy......... Ps 132:16
let them sing a upon their beds........ Ps 149:5
they shall cry a from the sea........... Is 24:14
forth into singing, and cry a.............. Is 54:1
Cry a, spare not, lift up thy............. Is 58:1
Then an herald cried a, To you it...... Dan 3:4
He cried a, and said thus, Hew......... Dan 4:14
The king cried a to bring in the........ Dan 5:7
cry a at Beth-aven, after thee, O...... Hos 5:8
Now why dost thou cry out a............ Mic 4:9
the multitude crying a began to........ Mk 15:8

ALPHA (al'-fah) First letter of Greek alphabet.
I am A and Omega, the beginning and.. Rev 1:8
Saying, I am A and Omega, the.......... Rev 1:11
I am A and Omega, the beginning and. Rev 21:6
I am A and Omega........................... Rev 22:13

ALPHAEUS (al-fe'-us) See CLEOPAS.
  1. Father of the apostle James.
James the son of A, and Lebbaeus,.... Mt 10:3
and Thomas, and James the son of A. Mk 3:18
and Thomas, James the son of A ...... Lk 6:15
and Matthew, James the son of A ..... Acts 1:13
  2. Father of the apostle Levi.
he saw Levi the son of A sitting........ Mk 2:14

ALREADY
have offended against the LORD a..... 2Chr 28:13
are brought unto bondage a.............. Neh 5:5
it hath been a of old time................ Eccl 1:10
even that which hath been a done..... Eccl 2:12
that which is to be hath a been........ Eccl 3:15
I praised the dead which are a.......... Eccl 4:2
That which hath been is named a...... Eccl 6:10
yea, I have cursed them a................ Mal 2:2
adultery with her a in his heart........ Mt 5:28
unto you, That Elias is come a......... Mt 17:12
marvelled if he were a dead.............. Mk 15:44
what will I, if it be a kindled............ Lk 12:49
that believeth not is condemned a.... Jn 3:18
for they are white a to harvest......... Jn 4:35
for the Jews had agreed a................ Jn 9:22
answered them, I have told you a...... Jn 9:27
had lain in the grave four days a...... Jn 11:17
Jesus, and saw that he was there a... Jn 19:33
there were three men a come unto .... Acts 11:11
because the fast was now a past....... Acts 27:9
present in spirit, have judged a......... 1Cor 5:3
bewail many which have sinned a...... 2Cor 12:21
Not as though I had a attained......... Phil 3:12
attained, either were a perfect.......... Phil 3:12
whereto we have a attained.............. Phil 3:16
mystery of iniquity doth a work........ 2Th 2:7
For some are a turned aside after..... 1Ti 5:15
that the resurrection is past a.......... 2Ti 2:18
even now a is it in the world............ 1Jn 4:3
ye have a hold fast till I come......... Rev 2:25

ALSO See PREFACE.

ALTAR

Noah builded an a unto the LORD...... Gen 8:20
offered burnt offerings on the a......... Gen 8:20
builded he an a unto the LORD.......... Gen 12:7
he builded an a unto the LORD.......... Gen 12:8
Unto the place of the a, which he..... Gen 13:4
and built there an a unto the LORD... Gen 13:18
and Abraham built an a there............ Gen 22:9
laid him on the a upon the wood...... Gen 22:9
And he builded an a there, and......... Gen 26:25
And he erected there an a, and......... Gen 33:20
and make there an a unto God......... Gen 35:1
I will make there an a unto God....... Gen 35:3
And he built there an a, and called... Gen 35:7
And Moses built an a, and called...... Ex 17:15
An a of earth thou shalt make.......... Ex 20:24
thou wilt make me an a of stone...... Ex 20:25
thou go up by steps unto mine a...... Ex 20:26
thou shalt take him from mine a....... Ex 21:14
builded an a under the hill, and........ Ex 24:4
the blood he sprinkled on the a......... Ex 24:6
shalt make an a of shittim wood....... Ex 27:1
the a shall be foursquare................. Ex 27:1
the compass of the a beneath.......... Ex 27:5
may be even to the midst of the a.... Ex 27:5
thou shalt make staves for the a...... Ex 27:6
be upon the two sides of the a......... Ex 27:7
a to minister in the holy place......... Ex 28:43
horns of the a with thy finger.......... Ex 29:12
blood beside the bottom of the a...... Ex 29:12
them, and burn them upon the a...... Ex 29:13
it round about upon the a................ Ex 29:16
burn the whole ram upon the a........ Ex 29:18
the blood upon the a round about..... Ex 29:20
of the blood that is upon the a......... Ex 29:21
burn them upon the a for a burnt..... Ex 29:25
and thou shalt cleanse the a............ Ex 29:36
shalt make an atonement for the a.... Ex 29:37
and it shall be an a most holy.......... Ex 29:37
toucheth the a shall be holy............. Ex 29:37
which thou shalt offer upon the a..... Ex 29:38
of the congregation, and the a......... Ex 29:44
thou shalt make an a to burn........... Ex 30:1
of the congregation and the a.......... Ex 30:18
come near to the a to minister......... Ex 30:20
his vessels, and the a of incense,...... Ex 30:27
the a of burnt offering with all........ Ex 30:28
furniture, and the a of incense,........ Ex 31:8
the a of burnt offering with all........ Ex 31:9
saw it, he built an a before it........... Ex 32:5
And the incense a, and his staves,..... Ex 35:15
The a of burnt offering, with his....... Ex 35:16
the incense a of shittim wood.......... Ex 37:25
he made the a of burnt offering........ Ex 38:1
he made all the vessels of the a....... Ex 38:3
he made for the a a brasen grate...... Ex 38:4
the rings on the sides of the a......... Ex 38:7
he made the a hollow with boards..... Ex 38:7
the congregation, and the brasen a... Ex 38:30
it, and all the vessels of the a.......... Ex 38:30
And the golden a, and the anointing.. Ex 39:38
The brasen a, and his grate of......... Ex 39:39
thou shalt set the a of gold for........ Ex 40:5
thou shalt set the a of the burnt..... Ex 40:6
of the congregation and the a.......... Ex 40:7
the a of the burnt offering.............. Ex 40:10
his vessels, and sanctify the a.......... Ex 40:10
and it shall be an a most holy.......... Ex 40:10
he put the golden a in the tent....... Ex 40:26

he put the *a* of burnt offering by .... Ex 40:29
tent of the congregation and the *a* ...... Ex 40:30
and when they came near unto the *a* .... Ex 40:32
about the tabernacle and the *a* .... Ex 40:33
the *a* that is by the door of the .... Lev 1:5
priest shall put fire upon the *a* .... Lev 1:7
on the fire which is upon the *a* .... Lev 1:8
priest shall burn all on the *a* .... Lev 1:9
the *a* northward before the LORD .... Lev 1:11
his blood round about upon the *a* .... Lev 1:11
on the fire which is upon the *a* .... Lev 1:12
it all, and burn it upon the *a* .... Lev 1:13
priest shall bring it unto the *a* .... Lev 1:15
off his head, and burn it on the *a* .... Lev 1:15
be wrung out at the side of the *a* .... Lev 1:15
it beside the *a* on the east part .... Lev 1:16
priest shall burn it upon the *a* .... Lev 1:17
the memorial of it upon the *a* .... Lev 2:2
he shall bring it unto the *a* .... Lev 2:8
and shall burn it upon the *a* .... Lev 2:9
burnt on the *a* for a sweet savour .... Lev 2:12
the blood upon the *a* round about .... Lev 3:2
on the *a* upon the burnt sacrifice .... Lev 3:5
thereof round about upon the *a* .... Lev 3:8
priest shall burn it upon the *a* .... Lev 3:11
thereof upon the *a* round about .... Lev 3:13
priest shall burn them upon the *a* .... Lev 3:16
the *a* of sweet incense before the .... Lev 4:7
of the *a* of the burnt offering .... Lev 4:7
upon the *a* of the burnt offering .... Lev 4:10
of the *a* which is before the LORD .... Lev 4:18
of the *a* of the burnt offering .... Lev 4:18
from him, and burn it upon the *a* .... Lev 4:19
horns of the *a* of burnt offering .... Lev 4:25
bottom of the *a* of burnt offering .... Lev 4:25
shall burn all his fat upon the *a* .... Lev 4:26
horns of the *a* of burnt offering .... Lev 4:30
thereof at the bottom of the *a* .... Lev 4:30
the *a* for a sweet savour unto the .... Lev 4:31
horns of the *a* of burnt offering .... Lev 4:34
thereof at the bottom of the *a* .... Lev 4:34
priest shall burn them upon the *a* .... Lev 4:35
offering upon the side of the *a* .... Lev 5:9
wrung out at the bottom of the *a* .... Lev 5:9
thereof, and burn it on the *a* .... Lev 6:12
the *a* all night unto the morning .... Lev 6:9
the fire of the *a* shall be .... Lev 6:9
with the burnt offering on the *a* .... Lev 6:10
and he shall put them beside the *a* .... Lev 6:10
the fire upon the *a* shall be .... Lev 6:12
shall ever be burning upon the *a* .... Lev 6:13
it before the LORD, before the *a* .... Lev 6:14
it upon the *a* for a sweet savour .... Lev 6:15
sprinkle round about upon the *a* .... Lev 7:2
a for an offering made by fire .... Lev 7:5
shall burn the fat upon the *a* .... Lev 7:31
thereof upon the *a* seven times .... Lev 8:11
seven times, and anointed the *a* .... Lev 8:11
the *a* round about with his finger .... Lev 8:15
his finger, and purified the *a* .... Lev 8:15
the blood at the bottom of the *a* .... Lev 8:15
and Moses burned it upon the *a* .... Lev 8:16
the blood upon the *a* round about .... Lev 8:19
burnt the whole ram upon the *a* .... Lev 8:21
the blood upon the *a* round about .... Lev 8:24
burnt them on the *a* upon the .... Lev 8:28
of the blood which was upon the *a* .... Lev 8:30
said unto Aaron, Go unto the *a* .... Lev 9:7
Aaron therefore went unto the *a* .... Lev 9:8
and put it upon the horns of the *a* .... Lev 9:9
the blood at the bottom of the *a* .... Lev 9:9
sin offering, he burnt upon the *a* .... Lev 9:10
sprinkled round about upon the *a* .... Lev 9:12
and he burnt them upon the *a* .... Lev 9:13
upon the burnt offering on the *a* .... Lev 9:14
thereof, and burnt it upon the *a* .... Lev 9:17
sprinkled upon the *a* round about .... Lev 9:18
and he burnt the fat upon the *a* .... Lev 9:20
consumed upon the *a* the burnt .... Lev 9:24
it without leaven beside the *a* .... Lev 10:12
and the meat offering upon the *a* .... Lev 14:20
from off the *a* before the LORD .... Lev 16:12
the *a* that is before the LORD .... Lev 16:18
the horns of the *a* round about .... Lev 16:18
of the congregation, and the *a* .... Lev 16:20
offering shall he burn upon the *a* .... Lev 16:25
of the congregation, and for the *a* .... Lev 16:33
sprinkle the blood upon the *a* of .... Lev 17:6
a to make an atonement for your .... Lev 17:11
vail, nor come nigh unto the *a* .... Num 21:23
of them upon the *a* unto the LORD .... Num 22:22
by the *a* round about, and the .... Num 23:26
upon the golden *a* they shall .... Num 4:11
take away the ashes from the *a* .... Num 4:13
basons, all the vessels of the *a* .... Num 4:14
by the *a* round about, and their .... Num 4:26
the LORD, and offer it unto the *a* .... Num 5:25
thereof, and burn it upon the *a* .... Num 5:26
instruments thereof, both the *a* .... Num 7:1
offered for dedicating of the *a* .... Num 7:10
their offering before the *a* .... Num 7:10
day, for the dedicating of the *a* .... Num 7:84
This was the dedication of the *a* .... Num 7:84
This was the dedication of the *a* .... Num 7:88
plates for a covering of the *a* .... Num 16:38
plates for a covering of the *a* .... Num 16:39
put fire therein from off the *a* .... Num 16:46
vessels of the sanctuary and the *a* .... Num 18:3
sanctuary, and the charge of the *a* .... Num 18:5
office for every thing of the *a* .... Num 18:7

sprinkle their blood upon the *a* .... Num 18:17
offered on every *a* a bullock .... Num 23:2
offered upon every *a* a bullock .... Num 23:4
a bullock and a ram on every *a* .... Num 23:14
a bullock and a ram on every *a* .... Num 23:30
upon the *a* of the LORD thy God .... Deut 12:27
upon the *a* of the LORD thy God .... Deut 12:27
unto the *a* of the LORD thy God .... Deut 16:21
before the *a* of the LORD thy God .... Deut 26:4
there shalt thou build an *a* .... Deut 27:5
the LORD thy God, an *a* of stones .... Deut 27:5
Thou shalt build the *a* of the .... Deut 27:6
burnt sacrifice upon thine *a* .... Deut 33:10
Then Joshua built an *a* unto the .... Josh 8:30
an *a* of whole stones, over which .... Josh 8:31
for the *a* of the LORD, even unto .... Josh 9:27
a by Jordan, a great *a* .... Josh 22:10
a over against the land of Canaan .... Josh 22:11
in that ye have builded you an *a* .... Josh 22:16
an *a* beside the *a* of the LORD .... Josh 22:19
That we have built us an *a* to .... Josh 22:23
us now prepare to build us an *a* .... Josh 22:26
the pattern of the *a* of the LORD .... Josh 22:28
to build an *a* for burnt offerings .... Josh 22:29
beside the *a* of the LORD our God .... Josh 22:29
children of Gad called the *a* Ed .... Josh 22:34
built an *a* there unto the LORD .... Judg 6:24
throw down the *a* of Baal that thy .... Judg 6:25
build an *a* unto the LORD thy God .... Judg 6:26
the *a* of Baal was cast down, and .... Judg 6:28
offered upon the *a* that was built .... Judg 6:28
he hath cast down the *a* of Baal .... Judg 6:30
because one hath cast down his *a* .... Judg 6:31
because he hath thrown down his *a* ...... Judg 6:32
up toward heaven from off the *a* .... Judg 13:20
ascended in the flame of the *a* .... Judg 13:20
rose early, and built there an *a* .... Judg 21:4
my priest, to offer upon mine *a* 1Sa 2:28
I shall not cut off from mine *a* 1Sa 2:33
there he built an *a* unto the LORD 1Sa 7:17
And Saul built an *a* unto the LORD 1Sa 14:35
the same was the first *a* that he 1Sa 14:35
rear an *a* unto the LORD in the 2Sa 24:18
to build an *a* unto the LORD, that 2Sa 24:21
built there an *a* unto the LORD 2Sa 24:25
caught hold on the horns of the *a* 1Kin 1:50
caught hold on the horns of the *a* 1Kin 1:51
they brought him down from the *a* 1Kin 1:53
caught hold on the horns of the *a* 1Kin 2:28
and, behold, he is by the *a* 1Kin 2:29
did Solomon offer upon that *a* 1Kin 3:4
so covered the *a* which was of 1Kin 6:20
also the whole *a* that was by the 1Kin 6:22
the *a* of gold, and the table of 1Kin 7:48
Solomon stood before the *a* of the 1Kin 8:22
come before thine *a* in this house 1Kin 8:31
from before the *a* of the LORD 1Kin 8:54
because the brasen *a* that was 1Kin 8:64
peace offerings upon the *a* which 1Kin 9:25
the *a* that was before the LORD 1Kin 9:25
Judah, and he offered upon the *a* 1Kin 12:32
So he offered upon the *a* which he 1Kin 12:33
and he offered upon the *a*, and 1Kin 12:33
stood by the *a* to burn incense 1Kin 13:1
he cried against the *a* in the 1Kin 13:2
of the LORD, and said, O *a*, *a* 1Kin 13:2
the *a* shall be rent, and the ashes 1Kin 13:3
cried against the *a* in Beth-el 1Kin 13:4
he put forth his hand from the *a* 1Kin 13:4
The *a* also was rent 1Kin 13:5
the ashes poured out from the *a* 1Kin 13:5
the LORD against the *a* in Beth-el 1Kin 13:32
he reared up an *a* for Baal in the 1Kin 16:32
leaped upon the *a* which was made 1Kin 18:26
he repaired the *a* of the LORD 1Kin 18:30
an *a* in the name of the LORD 1Kin 18:32
and he made a trench about the *a* 1Kin 18:35
the water ran round about the *a* 1Kin 18:35
of the temple, along by the *a* 2Kin 11:11
lid of it, and set it beside the *a* 2Kin 12:9
saw an *a* that was at Damascus 2Kin 16:10
the priest the fashion of the *a* 2Kin 16:10
Urijah the priest built an *a* 2Kin 16:11
from Damascus, the king saw the *a* 2Kin 16:12
and the king approached to the *a* 2Kin 16:12
his peace offerings, upon the *a* 2Kin 16:13
And he brought also the brasen *a* 2Kin 16:14
of the house, from between the *a* 2Kin 16:14
put it on the north side of the *a* 2Kin 16:14
Upon the great *a* burn the morning 2Kin 16:15
the brasen *a* shall be for me to 2Kin 16:15
before this *a* in Jerusalem 2Kin 18:22
to the *a* of the LORD in Jerusalem 2Kin 23:9
Moreover the *a* that was at 2Kin 23:15
to sin, had made, both that *a* 2Kin 23:15
and burned them upon the *a* 2Kin 23:16
done against the *a* of the Beth-el 2Kin 23:17
upon the *a* of the burnt offering 1Chr 6:49
on the *a* of incense, and were 1Chr 6:49
upon the *a* of the burnt offering 1Chr 16:40
set up an *a* unto the LORD in the 1Chr 21:18
that I may build an *a* therein 1Chr 21:22
built there an *a* unto the LORD 1Chr 21:26
fire upon the *a* of burnt offering 1Chr 21:26
the *a* of the burnt offering, were 1Chr 21:29
this is the *a* of the burnt 1Chr 22:1
for the *a* of incense refined gold 1Chr 28:18
Moreover the brasen *a*, that 2Chr 1:5
to the brasen *a* before the LORD 2Chr 1:6
Moreover he made an *a* of brass 2Chr 4:1

house of God, the golden *a* also 2Chr 4:19
stood at the east end of the *a* 2Chr 5:12
he stood before the *a* of the LORD 2Chr 6:12
come before thine *a* in this house 2Chr 6:22
because the brasen *a* which 2Chr 7:7
dedication of the *a* seven days 2Chr 7:9
the LORD on the *a* of the LORD 2Chr 8:12
and renewed the *a* of the LORD 2Chr 15:8
of the temple, along by the *a* 2Chr 23:10
incense upon the *a* of incense 2Chr 26:16
LORD, from beside the incense *a* 2Chr 26:19
the *a* of burnt offering, with all 2Chr 29:18
they are before the *a* of the LORD 2Chr 29:19
offer them on the *a* of the LORD 2Chr 29:21
blood, and sprinkled it on the *a* 2Chr 29:22
sprinkled the blood upon the *a* 2Chr 29:22
sprinkled the blood upon the *a* 2Chr 29:22
with their blood upon the *a* 2Chr 29:24
the burnt offering upon the *a* 2Chr 29:27
Ye shall worship before one *a* 2Chr 32:12
And he repaired the *a* of the LORD 2Chr 33:16
offerings upon the *a* of the LORD 2Chr 35:16
builded the *a* of the God of .... Ezr 3:2
they set the *a* upon his bases .... Ezr 3:3
offer them upon the *a* of the .... Ezr 7:17
to burn upon the *a* of the LORD .... Neh 10:34
so will I compass thine *a* .... Ps 26:6
Then will I go unto the *a* of God .... Ps 43:4
they offer bullocks upon thine *a* .... Ps 51:19
even unto the horns of the *a* .... Ps 118:27
with the tongs from off the *a* .... Is 6:6
In that day shall there be an *a* .... Is 19:19
as a chalkstones that are beaten .... Is 27:9
Ye shall worship before this *a* .... Is 36:7
shall be accepted upon mine *a* .... Is 56:7
come up with acceptance on mine *a* ..... Is 60:7
The Lord hath cast off his *a* .... Lam 2:7
northward at the gate of the *a* .... Eze 8:5
LORD, between the porch and the *a* ...... Eze 8:16
in, and stood beside the brasen *a* .... Eze 9:2
keepers of the charge of the *a* .... Eze 40:46
the *a* that was before the house .... Eze 40:47
The *a* of wood was three cubits............ Eze 41:22
of the *a* after the cubits .... Eze 43:13
be the higher place of the *a* .... Eze 43:13
So the *a* shall be four cubits .... Eze 43:15
and from the *a* and upward shall be .... Eze 43:15
the *a* shall be twelve cubits long .... Eze 43:16
a in the day when they shall make ...... Eze 43:18
and they shall cleanse the *a* .... Eze 43:22
Seven days shall they purge the *a* .... Eze 43:26
your burnt offerings upon the *a* .... Eze 43:27
corners of the settle of the *a* .... Eze 45:19
house, at the south side of the *a* .... Eze 47:1
howl, ye ministers of the *a* .... Joel 1:13
weep between the porch and the *a* .... Joel 2:17
clothes laid to pledge by every *a* .... Amos 2:8
horns of the *a* shall be cut off .... Amos 3:14
saw the Lord standing upon the *a* .... Amos 9:1
bowls, and as the corners of the *a* .... Zec 9:15
be like the bowls before the *a* .... Zec 14:20
offer polluted bread upon mine *a* .... Mal 1:7
kindle fire on mine *a* for nought .... Mal 1:10
covering the *a* of the LORD with .... Mal 2:13
if thou bring thy gift to the *a* .... Mt 5:23
Leave there thy gift before the *a* .... Mt 5:24
Whosoever shall swear by the *a* .... Mt 23:18
or the *a* that sanctifieth the .... Mt 23:19
therefore shall swear by the *a* .... Mt 23:20
slew between the temple and the *a* ...... Mt 23:35
right side of the *a* of incense............... Lk 1:11
which perished between the *a* .... Lk 11:51
devotions, I found an *a* with this .... Acts 17:23
a are partakers with the *a* 1Cor 9:13
the sacrifices partakers of the *a* 1Cor 10:18
no man gave attendance at the *a* .... Heb 7:13
We have an *a*, whereof they have .... Heb 13:10
offered Isaac his son upon the *a* .... Jas 2:21
I saw under the *a* the souls of .... Rev 6:9
angel came and stood at the *a* .... Rev 8:3
a which was before the throne .... Rev 8:3
and filled it with fire of the *a* .... Rev 8:5
the golden *a* which is before God .... Rev 9:13
the temple of God, and the *a* .... Rev 11:1
another angel came out from the *a* ...... Rev 14:18
I heard another out of the *a* say .... Rev 16:7

ALTARS

But ye shall destroy their *a* .... Ex 34:13
and the candlestick, and the *a* .... Num 3:31
unto Balak, Build me here seven *a* .... Num 23:1
unto him, I have prepared seven *a* .... Num 23:4
top of Pisgah, and built seven *a* .... Num 23:14
unto Balak, Build me here seven *a* .... Num 23:29
ye shall destroy their *a*, and .... Deut 7:5
And ye shall overthrow their *a* .... Deut 12:3
ye shall throw down their *a* .... Judg 2:2
thy covenant, thrown down thine *a* 1Kin 19:10
thy covenant, thrown down thine *a* 1Kin 19:14
his *a* and his images brake they in 2Kin 11:18
the priest of Baal before the *a* 2Kin 11:18
whose *a* Hezekiah hath taken away, ... 2Kin 18:22
he built *a* in the house of the LORD 2Kin 21:4
he built *a* for all the host of 2Kin 21:5
he built a for all the host of 2Kin 21:5
the *a* that were on the top of the 2Kin 23:12
the *a* which Manasseh had made in 2Kin 23:12
places that were there upon the *a* 2Kin 23:20
away the *a* of the strange gods 2Chr 14:3
and brake it down, and brake his *a* 2Chr 23:17
the priest of Baal before the *a* 2Chr 23:17

he made him a in every corner of...... 2Chr 28:24
took away the a that were in............ 2Chr 30:14
all the a for incense took they........... 2Chr 30:14
the a out of all Judah and................. 2Chr 31:1
away his high places and his a........... 2Chr 32:12
and he reared up a for Baalim............ 2Chr 33:3
Also he built a in the house of........... 2Chr 33:4
he built a for all the host of.............. 2Chr 33:5
all the a that he had built in.............. 2Chr 33:15
they brake down the a of Baalim........ 2Chr 34:4
bones of the priests upon their a....... 2Chr 34:5
And when he had broken down the a... 2Chr 34:7
may lay her young, even thine a......... Ps 84:3
And he shall not look to the a........... Is 17:8
whose a Hezekiah hath taken away,..... Is 36:7
burneth incense upon a of brick......... Is 65:3
set up a to that shameful thing.......... Jer 11:13
even a to burn incense unto Baal........ Jer 11:13
and upon the horns of your a............ Jer 17:1
their children remember their a.......... Jer 17:2
your a shall be desolate, and your...... Eze 6:4
your bones round about your a.......... Eze 6:5
that your a may be laid waste and...... Eze 6:6
their idols round about their a........... Eze 6:13
Ephraim hath made many a to sin...... Hos 8:11
a shall be unto him to sin................. Hos 8:11
his fruit he hath increased the a........ Hos 10:1
he shall break down their a............... Hos 10:2
thistle shall come up on their a.......... Hos 10:8
their a are as heaps in the................ Hos 12:11
will also visit the a of Beth-el........... Amos 3:14
prophets, and digged down thine a..... Rom 11:3

ALTASCHITH
To the chief Musician, A, Michtam ...... Ps 57:t
To the chief Musician, A, Michtam ...... Ps 58:t
To the chief Musician, A, Michtam ...... Ps 59:t
To the chief Musician, A, A Psalm....... Ps 75:t

AL-TASHHETH See AL-TASCHITH.

ALTER
He shall not a it, nor change it,.......... Lev 27:10
that whosoever shall a this word......... Ezr 6:11
that shall put to their hand to a......... Ezr 6:12
nor a the thing that is gone out......... Ps 89:34

ALTERED
and the Medes, that it be not a......... Est 1:19
fashion of his countenance was a....... Lk 9:29

ALTERETH
Medes and Persians, which a not .... Dan 6:8
Medes and Persians, which a not .... Dan 6:12

ALTHOUGH
the Philistines, a that was near.......... Ex 13:17
a there was a plague in the............... Josh 22:17
A my house be not so with God......... 2Sa 23:5
desire, a he make it not to grow........ 2Sa 23:5
A I have sent unto thee, saying,........ 1Kin 20:5
a the enemy could not countervail..... Est 7:4
a thou movedst me against him, to..... Job 2:3
A affliction cometh not forth of........ Job 5:6
A thou sayest thou shalt not see....... Job 35:14
a I was an husband unto them,........... Jer 31:32
is sold, a they were yet alive............ Eze 7:13
A I have cast them far off among...... Eze 11:16
a I have scattered them among the.... Eze 11:16
A the fig tree shall not blossom,....... Hab 3:17
A all shall be offended, yet will .... Mk 14:29
a the works were finished from......... Heb 4:3

ALTOGETHER
done a according to the cry of it....... Gen 18:21
surely thrust you out hence a.......... Ex 11:1
And mount Sinai was a on a smoke,.. Ex 19:18
make thyself a a prince over us....... Num 16:13
behold, thou hast blessed them a..... Num 23:11
thou hast a blessed them these....... Num 24:10
But if her husband a hold his......... Num 30:14
That which is a just shalt thou...... Deut 16:20
that he would not destroy him a...... 2Chr 12:12
For if thou a holdest thy peace...... Est 4:14
that ye would a hold your peace..... Job 13:5
why then are ye thus a vain.......... Job 27:12
the LORD are true and righteous a... Ps 19:9
man at his best state is a vanity..... Ps 39:5
I was a such an one as thyself....... Ps 50:21
they are a become filthy.............. Ps 53:3
they are a lighter than vanity........ Ps 62:9
to, O LORD, thou knowest it a....... Ps 139:4
yea, he is a lovely..................... Song 5:16
saith, Are not my princes a kings... Is 10:8
but these have a broken the yoke,... Jer 5:5
But they are a brutish and foolish ... Jer 10:8
wilt thou be a unto me as a liar,..... Jer 15:18
will not leave thee a unpunished..... Jer 30:11
he that shall a go unpunished........ Jer 49:12
Thou wast a born in sins, and dost..... Jn 9:34
a such as I am, except these........ Acts 26:29
Yet not a with the fornicators of ... 1Cor 5:10
Or saith he it a for our sakes........ 1Cor 9:10

ALUSH (a'-lush) An Israelite encampment
   during the Exodus.
from Dophkah, and encamped in A .. Num 33:13
And they removed from A, and....... Num 33:14

ALVAH (al'-vah) See ALIAH. An Edomite chief.
duke Timnah, duke A, duke Jetheth .. Gen 36:40

ALVAN (al'-van) See ALIAN. A son of Shobal
   the Horite.
A, and Manahath, and Ebal, Shepho, . Gen 36:23

ALWAY
the table shewbread before me a...... Ex 25:30
So it was a............................... Num 9:16
and his commandments, a.............. Deut 11:1
be only oppressed and crushed a..... Deut 28:33
son shall eat bread a at my table..... 2Sa 9:10
a light a before me in Jerusalem...... 1Kin 11:36
him to give him a a light.............. 2Kin 8:19
I would not live a....................... Job 7:16
needy shall not a be forgotten....... Ps 9:18
heart to perform thy statutes a...... Ps 119:112
Happy is the man that feareth a...... Prov 28:14
and, lo, I am with you a, even....... Mt 28:20
but your time is a ready............... Jn 7:6
to the people, and prayed to God a... Acts 10:2
not see, and bow down their back a.. Rom 11:10
For we which live are a delivered.... 2Cor 4:11
As sorrowful, yet a rejoicing......... 2Cor 6:10
Rejoice in the Lord a................... Phil 4:4
Let your speech be a with grace..... Col 4:6
be saved, to fill up their sins a...... 1Th 2:16
to give thanks a to God for you..... 2Th 2:13
said, The Cretians are a liars......... Titus 1:12
They do a err in their heart.......... Heb 3:10

ALWAYS
shall not a strive with man............ Gen 6:3
to cause the lamp to burn a.......... Ex 27:20
it shall be a upon his forehead,...... Ex 28:38
keep all my commandments a......... Deut 5:29
the LORD our God, for our good a... Deut 6:24
of the LORD thy God are a upon it .. Deut 11:12
learn to fear the LORD thy God a.... Deut 14:23
Be ye mindful a of his covenant..... 1Chr 16:15
good unto me, but a evil.............. 2Chr 18:7
will he a call upon God................ Job 27:10
Great men are not a wise............. Job 32:9
His ways are a grievous............... Ps 10:5
I have set the LORD a before me..... Ps 16:8
He will not a chide..................... Ps 103:9
be thou ravished a with her love..... Prov 5:19
delight, rejoicing a before him....... Prov 8:30
Let thy garments be a white.......... Eccl 9:8
ever, neither will I be a wroth....... Is 57:16
and her womb to be a great with me... Jer 20:17
Israel, which have been a............. Eze 38:8
do a behold the face of my Father... Mt 18:10
For ye have the poor a with you..... Mt 26:11
but me ye have not a................... Mt 26:11
And a, night and day, he was in the.. Mk 5:5
For ye have the poor with you a..... Mk 14:7
but me ye have not a................... Mk 14:7
end, that men ought a to pray....... Lk 18:1
Watch ye therefore, and pray a...... Lk 21:36
for I do a those things that........... Jn 8:29
And I knew that thou hearest me a .. Jn 11:42
For the poor a ye have with you..... Jn 12:8
but me ye have not a................... Jn 12:8
temple, whither the Jews a resort... Jn 18:20
foresaw the Lord a before my face.. Acts 2:25
ye do a resist the Holy Ghost....... Acts 7:51
We accept it a, and in all places,.... Acts 24:3
to have a a conscience void of....... Acts 24:16
mention of you a in my prayers...... Rom 1:9
I thank my God a on your behalf..... 1Cor 1:4
a abounding in the work of the....... 1Cor 15:58
which a causeth us to triumph in..... 2Cor 2:14
A bearing about in the body the...... 2Cor 4:10
Therefore we are a confident......... 2Cor 5:6
a having all sufficiency in all........ 2Cor 9:8
affected a in a good thing............. Gal 4:18
Giving thanks a for all things........ Eph 5:20
Praying a with all prayer and........ Eph 6:18
A in every prayer of mine for you... Phil 1:4
but that with all boldness, as a...... Phil 1:20
my beloved, as ye have a obeyed.... Phil 2:12
Jesus Christ, praying a for you....... Col 1:3
a labouring fervently for you in....... Col 4:12
give thanks to God a for you all..... 1Th 1:2
ye have good remembrance of us a.. 1Th 3:6
are bound to thank God a for you.... 2Th 1:3
Wherefore also we pray a for you.... 2Th 1:11
give you peace a by all means....... 2Th 3:16
mention of thee a in my prayers..... Philem 4
the priests went a into the first..... Heb 9:6
be ready a to give an answer to..... 1Pet 3:15
not be negligent to put you a in..... 2Pet 1:12
these things a in remembrance....... 2Pet 1:15

AM See PREFACE.

AMAD (a'-mad) A town on the border of Asher.
And Alammelech, and A.................. Josh 19:26

AMAL (a'-mal) A descendant of Asher.
and Imna, and Shelesh, and A.......... 1Chr 7:35

AMALEK (am'-al-ek) See AMALEKITE.
   1. The son of Eliphaz.
and she bare to Eliphaz A.............. Gen 36:12
duke Gatam, and duke A................ Gen 36:16
and Gatam, Kenaz, and Timna, and A 1Chr 1:36
   2. Descendants of Amalek.
Then came A, and fought with......... Ex 17:8
out men, and go out, fight with A.... Ex 17:9
had said to him, and fought with A... Ex 17:10
he let down his hand, A prevailed.... Ex 17:11
And Joshua discomfited A and his.... Ex 17:13
of A from under heaven................ Ex 17:14
the LORD will have war with A........ Ex 17:16
And when he looked on A, he took... Num 24:20
A was the first of the nations........ Num 24:20
Remember what A did unto thee by.. Deut 25:17

of A from under heaven................ Deut 25:19
him the children of Ammon and A.... Judg 3:13
there a root of them against A ...... Judg 5:14
that which A did to Israel.............. 1Sa 15:2
Now go and smite A, and utterly..... 1Sa 15:3
And Saul came to a city of A.......... 1Sa 15:5
have brought Agag the king of A..... 1Sa 15:20
his fierce wrath upon A,............... 1Sa 28:18
from the Philistines, and from A...... 2Sa 8:12
from the Philistines and, from A...... 1Chr 18:11
Gebal, and Ammon, and A.............. Ps 83:7

AMALEKITE (am'-al-ek-ite) See AMALEKITES.
   A descendant of Amalek.
man of Egypt, servant to an A........ 1Sa 30:13
And I answered him, I am an A........ 2Sa 1:8
I am the son of a stranger, an A...... 2Sa 1:13

AMALEKITES (am'-al-ek-ites)
and smote all the country of the A... Gen 14:7
The A dwell in the land of the........ Num 13:29
(Now the A and the Canaanites...... Num 14:25
For the A and the Canaanites are .... Num 14:43
Then the A came down, and the...... Num 14:45
the Midianites came up, and the A... Judg 6:3
Then all the Midianites and the A.... Judg 6:33
And the Midianites and the A......... Judg 7:12
The Zidonians also, and the A........ Judg 10:12
of Ephraim, in the mount of the A... Judg 12:15
gathered an host, and smote the A... 1Sa 14:48
get you down from among the A...... 1Sa 15:6
Kenites departed from among the A... 1Sa 15:6
Saul smote the A from Havilah........ 1Sa 15:7
took Agag the king of the A alive.... 1Sa 15:8
They have brought them from the A.. 1Sa 15:15
utterly destroy the sinners the A..... 1Sa 15:18
and have utterly destroyed the A..... 1Sa 15:20
to me Agag the king of the A......... 1Sa 15:32
and the Gezrites, and the A........... 1Sa 27:8
that the A had invaded the south,.... 1Sa 30:1
all that the A had carried away....... 1Sa 30:18
from the slaughter of the A........... 2Sa 1:1
rest of the A that were escaped...... 1Chr 4:43

AMAM (a'-mam) A city near Shema and
   Moladah.
A, and Shema, and Moladah,........... Josh 15:26

AMANA (am-a'-nah) A city in southern Judah.
look from the top of A, from the..... Song 4:8

AMARIAH (am-a-ri'-ah)
   1. A descendant of Aaron.
begat A, and A begat Ahitub,.......... 1Chr 6:7
A his son, Ahitub his son,.............. 1Chr 6:52
The son of A, the son of Azariah,.... Ezr 7:3
   2. A High Priest during Solomon's reign.
begat Amariah, and A begat Ahitub,.. 1Chr 6:11
   3. A descendant of Kohath.
A the second, Jahaziel the third,..... 1Chr 23:19
A the second, Jahaziel the third,..... 1Chr 24:23
   4. Chief priest during Jehoshaphat's reign.
A the chief priest is over you in..... 2Chr 19:11
   5. A Levite in Hezekiah's time.
and Jeshua, and Shemaiah, a......... 2Chr 31:15
   6. Married a foreign wife in Exile.
Shallum, A, and Joseph................. Ezr 10:42
   7. A priest who sealed the covenant with
   Nehemiah.
Pashur, A, Malchijah,................... Neh 10:3
A, Malluch, Hattush,................... Neh 12:2
of A, Jehohanan....................... Neh 12:13
   8. A descendant of Judah.
son of Zechariah, the son of A....... Neh 11:4
   9. An ancestor of Zephaniah the prophet.
the son of Gedaliah, the son of A.... Zeph 1:1

AMASA (am'-a-sah)
   1. David's nephew.
Absalom made A captain of the....... 2Sa 17:25
which A was a man's son, whose...... 2Sa 17:25
And say ye to A, Art thou not of..... 2Sa 19:13
Then said the king to A, Assemble... 2Sa 20:4
So A went to assemble the men of... 2Sa 20:5
is in Gibeon, A went before them..... 2Sa 20:8
And Joab said to A, Art thou in...... 2Sa 20:9
And Joab took A by the beard with .. 2Sa 20:9
But A took no heed to the sword..... 2Sa 20:10
A wallowed in blood in the midst..... 2Sa 20:12
he removed A out of the highway..... 2Sa 20:12
unto A the son of Jether, whom he.. 1Kin 2:5
A the son of Jether, captain of....... 1Kin 2:32
And Abigail bare A..................... 1Chr 2:17
the father of A was Jether the....... 1Chr 2:17
   2. An Ephraimite who opposed the slavery of
   the Jews.
the son of Hadlai, stood up 2Chr 28:12

AMASAI (am'-as-ahee)
   1. A descendant of Kohath.
the son of Mahath, the son of A...... 1Chr 6:25
arose, Mahath the son of A............ 1Chr 6:35
   2. A captain in David's army.
Then the spirit came upon A 1Chr 12:18
   3. A Levite who helped relocate the Ark.
Jehoshaphat, and Nethaneel, and A... 1Chr 15:24

AMASHAI (am'-ash-ahee) A priest of the
   Emmer family.
A the son of Azareel, the son of ..... Neh 11:13

AMASHSAI See AMASHAI.

AMASIAH (am-a-si'-ah) *Chief captain of Jehoshaphat's army.*
next him was A the son of Zichri, ... 2Chr 17:16

AMAZED
Then the dukes of Edom shall be a ..... Ex 15:15
again, the men of Benjamin were a.... Judg 20:41
They were a, they answered no .... Job 32:15
they shall be a one at another................ Is 13:8
I will make many people a at thee ..... Eze 32:10
And all the people were a, and said..... Mt 12:23
heard it, they were exceedingly a ...... Mt 19:25
And they were all a, insomuch that...... Mk 1:27
insomuch that they were all a .... Mk 2:12
they were sore a in themselves.......... Mk 6:51
they beheld him, were greatly a......... Mk 9:15
and they were a .... Mk 10:32
and John, and began to be sore a ...... Mk 14:33
for they trembled and were a .... Mk 16:8
And when they saw him, they were a .. Lk 2:48
And they were all a, and spake .... Lk 4:36
And they were all a, and they............. Lk 5:26
they were all a of the mighty............... Lk 9:43
And they were all a and marvelled...... Acts 2:7
And they were all a, and were in......... Acts 2:12
But all that heard him were a .... Acts 9:21

AMAZEMENT
a at that which had happened unto...... Acts 3:10
and are not afraid with any a 1Pet 3:6

AMAZIAH (am-a-zi'-ah)
1. Son and successor of King Joash of Judah.
A his son reigned in his stead 2Kin 12:21
he fought against A king of Judah..... 2Kin 13:12
A the son of Joash king of Judah....... 2Kin 14:1
Then A sent messengers to Jehoash... 2Kin 14:8
of Israel sent to A king of Judah........ 2Kin 14:9
But A would not hear.......................... 2Kin 14:11
A king of Judah looked one............... 2Kin 14:11
of Israel took A king of Judah............ 2Kin 14:13
he fought with A king of Judah.......... 2Kin 14:15
A the son of Joash king of Judah....... 2Kin 14:17
And the rest of the acts of A.............. 2Kin 14:18
him king instead of his father A......... 2Kin 14:21
In the fifteenth year of A the............. 2Kin 14:23
son of A king of Judah to reign.......... 2Kin 15:1
to all that his father A had done 2Kin 15:3
A his son, Azariah his son, ... 1Chr 3:12
A his son reigned in his stead 2Chr 24:27
A was twenty and five years old......... 2Chr 25:1
Moreover A gathered Judah 2Chr 25:5
But A said to the man of God, But...... 2Chr 25:9
Then A separated them, to wit, ... 2Chr 25:10
A strengthened himself, and led......... 2Chr 25:11
of the army which A sent back............ 2Chr 25:13
after that A was come from the 2Chr 25:14
of the LORD was kindled against A..... 2Chr 25:15
Then A king of Judah took advice, ... 2Chr 25:17
of Israel sent to A king of Judah 2Chr 25:18
But A would not hear.......................... 2Chr 25:20
A king of Judah, at Beth-shemesh,..... 2Chr 25:21
of Israel took A king of Judah............ 2Chr 25:23
A the son of Joash king of Judah....... 2Chr 25:25
Now the rest of the acts of A.............. 2Chr 25:26
Now after the time that A did 2Chr 25:27
king in the room of his father A 2Chr 26:1
to all that his father A did 2Chr 26:4
2. A Simeonite.
Jamlech, and Joshah the son of A 1Chr 4:34
3. A Levite from the Merari family.
son of Hashabiah, the son of A 1Chr 6:45
4. Priest of the idols at Bethel.
Then A the priest of Beth-el sent ...... Amos 7:10
Also A said unto Amos, O thou .... Amos 7:12
Then answered Amos, and said to A ... Amos 7:14

AMBASSADOR
but a faithful a is health .... Prov 13:17
an a is sent unto the heathen,............ Jer 49:14
an a is sent among the heathen,......... Obad 1
For which I am an a in bonds.............. Eph 6:20

AMBASSADORS
and made as if they had been a.......... Josh 9:4
the a of the princes of Babylon 2Chr 32:31
But he sent a to him, saying, ... 2Chr 35:21
That sendeth a by the sea................... Is 18:2
at Zoan, and his a came to Hanes....... Is 30:4
the a of peace shall weep .... Is 33:7
him in sending his a into Egypt,......... Eze 17:15
Now then we are a for Christ 2Cor 5:20

AMBASSAGE
a great way off, he sendeth an a .... Lk 14:32

AMBER
midst thereof as the colour of a .... Eze 1:4
And I saw as the colour of a .... Eze 1:27
of brightness, as the colour of a .... Eze 8:2

AMBUSH
lay them an a for the city behind .... Josh 8:2
Then ye shall rise up from the a .... Josh 8:7
and they went to lie in a, and .... Josh 8:9
them to lie in a between Beth-el......... Josh 8:12
in a against him behind the city .... Josh 8:14
the a arose quickly out of their........... Josh 8:19
saw that the a had taken the city .... Josh 8:21

AMBUSHES
up the watchmen, prepare the a......... Jer 51:12

AMBUSHMENT
But Jeroboam caused an a to come.... 2Chr 13:13
Judah, and the a was behind them..... 2Chr 13:13

AMBUSHMENTS
the LORD set a against the................. 2Chr 20:22

AMEN
1. A term meaning "so be it."
And the woman shall say, A, a........... Num 5:22
the people shall answer and say, A ... Deut 27:15
and all the people shall say, A .... Deut 27:16
And all the people shall say, A .... Deut 27:17
And all the people shall say, A .... Deut 27:18
And all the people shall say, A .... Deut 27:19
And all the people shall say, A .... Deut 27:20
And all the people shall say, A .... Deut 27:21
And all the people shall say, A .... Deut 27:22
And all the people shall say, A .... Deut 27:23
And all the people shall say, A .... Deut 27:24
And all the people shall say, A .... Deut 27:25
And all the people shall say, A .... Deut 27:26
answered the king, and said, A 1Kin 1:36
And all the people said, A 1Chr 16:36
And all the congregation said, A .... Neh 5:13
all the people answered, A, A, ... Neh 8:6
A, and A. .... Ps 41:13
A, and A. .... Ps 72:19
A, and A. .... Ps 89:52
and let all the people say, A. .... Ps 106:48
Even the prophet Jeremiah said, A .... Jer 28:6
and the glory, for ever. A.................... Mt 6:13
the end of the world. A....................... Mt 28:20
with signs following. A....................... Mk 16:20
praising and blessing God. A............. Lk 24:53
that should be written. A................... Jn 21:25
who is blessed for ever. A.................. Rom 1:25
God blessed for ever. A...................... Rom 9:5
to whom be glory for ever. A............. Rom 11:36
peace be with you all. A. .... Rom 15:33
Jesus Christ be with you. A............... Rom 16:20
Jesus Christ be with you all. A........... Rom 16:24
through Jesus Christ for ever. A......... Rom 16:27
say A at thy giving of thanks 1Cor 14:16
and of Christ Jesus. A. 1Cor 16:24
God in him are yea, and in him A 2Cor 1:20
Holy Ghost, be with you all. A............ 2Cor 13:14
be glory for ever and ever. A............. Gal 1:5
Christ be with your spirit. A. .... Gal 6:18
all ages, world without end. A. .... Eph 3:21
Lord Jesus Christ in sincerity. A. .... Eph 6:24
be glory for ever and ever. A............. Phil 4:20
Jesus Christ be with you all. A........... Phil 4:23
Grace be with you. A. .... Col 4:18
Jesus Christ be with you. A............... 1Th 5:28
Jesus Christ be with you all. A........... 2Th 3:18
glory for ever and ever. A. 1Ti 1:17
honour and power everlasting. A....... 1Ti 6:16
Grace be with thee. A. 1Ti 6:21
be glory for ever and ever. A............. 2Ti 4:18
Grace be with you. A. 2Ti 4:22
Christ be with your spirit. A............... Philem 25
be glory for ever and ever. A............. Heb 13:21
Grace be with you all. A. .... Heb 13:25
dominion for ever and ever. A. 1Pet 4:11
dominion for ever and ever. A. 1Pet 5:11
all that are in Christ Jesus. A. 1Pet 5:14
glory both now and for ever. A. 2Pet 3:18
keep yourselves from idols. A............ 1Jn 5:21
thy elect sister greet thee. A. 2Jn 13
power, both now and ever. A............. Jude 25
dominion for ever and ever. A. .... Rev 1:6
Even so, A .... Rev 1:7
I am alive for evermore, A.................. Rev 1:18
And the four beasts said, A. .... Rev 5:14
Saying, A: Blessing, and glory .... Rev 7:12
Our God for ever and ever. A. .... Rev 7:12
sat on the throne, saying, A;.............. Rev 19:4
Surely I come quickly. A. .... Rev 22:20
Jesus Christ be with you all. A. .... Rev 22:21
2. A title of Christ.
These things saith the A, the............. Rev 3:14

AMEND
LORD, to repair and a the house 2Chr 34:10
A your ways and your doings, and I ... Jer 7:3
For if ye throughly a your ways.......... Jer 7:5
Therefore now a your ways................. Jer 26:13
a your doings, and be not after .... Jer 35:15
them the hour when he began to a..... Jn 4:52

AMENDS
he shall make a for the harm that ...... Lev 5:16

AMERCE
they shall a him in an hundred .... Deut 22:19

AMETHYST
row a ligure, an agate, and an a......... Ex 28:19
row, a ligure, an agate, and an a........ Ex 39:12
the twelfth, an a................................. Rev 21:20

AMI (a'-mi) *A family of returned exiles.*
of Zebaim, the children of A .... Ezr 2:57

AMIABLE
How a are thy tabernacles, O LORD ... Ps 84:1

AMINADAB (a-min'-a-dab) See AMMINADAB.
Son of Aram; ancestor of Jesus.
And Aram begat A .... Mt 1:4

and A begat Naasson............................ Mt 1:4
Which was the son of A, which was ..... Lk 3:33

AMISS
We have sinned, we have done a........ 2Chr 6:37
which speak any thing a against.......... Dan 3:29
but this man hath done nothing a....... Lk 23:41
and receive not, because ye ask a...... Jas 4:3

AMITTAI (a-mit'-tahee) *Father of Jonah.*
his servant Jonah, the son of A 2Kin 14:25
LORD came unto Jonah the son of A... Jonah 1:1

AMMAH (am'-mah) See METHEG-AMMAH. *A hill near Gibeon.*
they were come to the hill of A 2Sa 2:24

AMMI (am'-mi) See AMMI-NADIB, BEN-AMMI, LO-AMMI. *A name given to Israel by Hosea meaning "my people."*
Say ye unto your brethren, A .... Hos 2:1

AMMIEL (am'-me-el) See ELIAM.
1. A spy for Moses.
of Dan, A the son of Gemalli .... Num 13:12
2. A Manassehite of Lodebar.
the house of Machir, the son of A....... 2Sa 9:4
the house of Machir, the son of A....... 2Sa 9:5
Machir the son of A of Lo-debar 2Sa 17:27
3. Father of a wife of David.
of Bath-shua the daughter of A.......... 1Chr 3:5
4. A Levite Tabernacle servant.
A the sixth, Issachar the seventh 1Chr 26:5

AMMIHUD (am-mi'-hud)
1. Father of Elishama.
Elishama the son of A.......................... Num 1:10
shall be Elishama the son of A .... Num 7:48
seventh day Elishama the son of A..... Num 7:48
offering of Elishama the son of A........ Num 7:53
host was Elishama the son of A .... Num 10:22
A his son, Elishama his son,................. 1Chr 7:26
2. A Simeonite.
of Simeon, Shemuel the son of A....... Num 34:20
3. A Naphtalite.
of Naphtali, Pedahel the son of A ...... Num 34:28
4. Father of the king of Geshur.
and went to Talmai, the son of A 2Sa 13:37
5. A son of Omri.
Uthai the son of A, the son of 1Chr 9:4

AMMINADAB (am-min'-a-dab) See AMINADAB, AMMI-NADIB.
1. Aaron's father-in-law.
took him Elisheba, daughter of A .... Ex 6:23
2. A prince of Judah.
Nahshon the son of A........................... Num 1:7
Nahshon the son of A shall be............. Num 2:3
day was Nahshon the son of A .... Num 7:12
offering of Nahshon the son of A......... Num 7:17
his host was Nahshon the son of A...... Num 10:14
Hezron begat Ram, and Ram begat A.. Ruth 4:19
A begat Nahshon................................. Ruth 4:20
And Ram begat A 1Chr 2:10
a begat Nahshon, prince of the........... 1Chr 2:10
3. A son of Kohath.
A his son, Korah his son, Assir............ 1Chr 6:22
4. A Levite who relocated the Ark.
A the chief, and his brethren an.......... 1Chr 15:10
and Joel, Shemaiah, and Eliel, and A 1Chr 15:11

AMMI-NADIB
made me like the chariots of A .... Song 6:12

AMMISHADDAI (am-mi-shad'-dahee) *Father of the chief of the tribe of Dan.*
Ahiezer the son of A .... Num 1:12
Dan shall be Ahiezer the son of A....... Num 2:25
tenth day Ahiezer the son of A .... Num 7:66
offering of Ahiezer the son of A.......... Num 7:71
his host was Ahiezer the son of A....... Num 10:25

AMMIZABAD (am-miz'-a-bad) *Son of a captain of David.*
and in his course was A his son.......... 1Chr 27:6

AMMON (am'-mon)
1. Territory in Jordan.
the children of A unto this day............ Gen 19:38
even unto the children of A .... Num 21:24
of the children of A was strong.......... Num 21:24
over against the children of A .... Deut 2:19
the children of A any possession........ Deut 2:19
the children of A thou camest not....... Deut 2:37
in Rabbath of the children of A .... Deut 3:11
the border of the children of A .... Deut 3:16
the border of the children of A .... Josh 12:2
the border of the children of A .... Josh 13:10
the land of the children of A .... Josh 13:25
unto him the children of A .... Judg 3:13
and the gods of the children of A .... Judg 10:6
the hands of the children of A .... Judg 10:7
Moreover the children of A passed..... Judg 10:9
Amorites, from the children of A .... Judg 10:11
Then the children of A were .... Judg 10:17
fight against the children of A .... Judg 10:18
that the children of A made war .... Judg 11:4
of A made war against Israel.............. Judg 11:5
may fight with the children of A .... Judg 11:6
fight against the children of A .... Judg 11:8
fight against the children of A .... Judg 11:9
the king of the children of A .... Judg 11:12
the king of the children of A .... Judg 11:13
the king of the children of A .... Judg 11:14
nor the land of the children of A .... Judg 11:15

of Israel and the children of A............ Judg 11:27
the king of the children of A............ Judg 11:28
over unto the children of A............ Judg 11:29
the children of A into mine hands..... Judg 11:30
in peace from the children of A........ Judg 11:31
of A to fight against them............... Judg 11:32
Thus the children of A were............. Judg 11:33
even of the children of A............... Judg 11:36
fight against the children of A........ Judg 12:1
strife with the children of A.......... Judg 12:2
over against the children of A........ Judg 12:3
children of A came against you........ 1Sa 11:11
and against the children of A......... 1Sa 14:47
of Moab, and the children of A........ 2Sa 8:12
king of the children of A died........ 2Sa 10:1
the land of the children of A.......... 2Sa 10:2
of A said unto Hanun their lord....... 2Sa 10:3
when the children of A saw that...... 2Sa 10:6
David, the children of A sent.......... 2Sa 10:6
And the children of A came out....... 2Sa 10:8
array against the children of A........ 2Sa 10:10
of A be too strong for thee............. 2Sa 10:11
when the children of A saw that...... 2Sa 10:14
returned from the children of A....... 2Sa 10:14
help the children of A any more....... 2Sa 10:19
they destroyed the children of A...... 2Sa 11:1
the sword of the children of A........ 2Sa 12:9
Rabbah of the children of A........... 2Sa 12:26
the cities of the children of A......... 2Sa 12:31
of Rabbah of the children of A........ 1Chr 17:27
abomination of the children of A...... 1Kin 11:7
the god of the children of A........... 1Kin 11:33
abomination of the children of A...... 2Kin 23:13
and bands of the children of A........ 2Kin 24:2
Moab, and from the children of A..... 1Chr 18:11
king of the children of A died........ 1Chr 19:1
of the children of A to Hanun......... 1Chr 19:2
the children of A said to Hanun....... 1Chr 19:3
when the children of A saw that...... 1Chr 19:6
the children of A sent a thousand..... 1Chr 19:6
the children of A gathered............. 1Chr 19:7
And the children of A came out....... 1Chr 19:9
array against the children of A........ 1Chr 19:11
of A be too strong for thee............. 1Chr 19:12
when the children of A saw that...... 1Chr 19:15
help the children of A any more....... 1Chr 19:19
the country of the children of A....... 1Chr 20:1
the cities of the children of A......... 1Chr 20:1
of Moab, and the children of A........ 1Chr 20:1
And now, behold, the children of A.... 2Chr 20:10
against the children of A............... 2Chr 20:22
For the children of A and Moab....... 2Chr 20:23
the children of A gave him the........ 2Chr 27:5
the children of A pay unto him........ 2Chr 27:5
had married wives of Ashdod, of A.... Neh 13:23
Gebal, and A, and Amalek............. Ps 83:7
the children of A shall obey them..... Is 11:14
and Edom, and the children of A...... Jer 9:26
and Moab, and the children of A...... Jer 25:21
captivity of the children of A.......... Jer 49:6
and the chief of the children of A..... Dan 11:41
of the children of A, and for four..... Amos 1:13
revilings of the children of A.......... Zeph 2:8
and the children of A as Gomorrah.... Zeph 2:9

AMMONITE (am'-mon-ite) See AMMONITES,
AMMONITESS. A descendant of Ammon.
An A or Moabite shall not enter...... Deut 23:3
Then Nahash the A came up........... 1Sa 11:1
Nahash the A answered them, On..... 1Sa 11:2
Zelek the A, Naharai the.............. 2Sa 23:37
Zelek the A, Naharai the.............. 1Chr 11:39
and Tobiah the servant, the A......... Neh 2:10
and Tobiah the servant, the A......... Neh 2:19
Now Tobiah the A was by him......... Neh 4:3
was found written, that the A......... Neh 13:1

AMMONITES (am'-mon-ites)
the A call them Zamzummims........ Deut 2:20
slew the A until the heat of the...... 1Sa 11:11
Pharaoh, women of the Moabites, A... 1Kin 11:1
Milcom the abomination of the A...... 1Kin 11:5
and with them other beside the A..... 2Chr 20:1
the A gave gifts to Uzziah............. 2Chr 26:8
also with the king of the A............ 2Chr 27:5
Perizzites, the Jebusites, the A........ Ezr 9:1
Tobiah, and the Arabians, and the A... Neh 4:7
of Moab, and to the king of the A..... Jer 27:3
that were in Moab, and among the A... Jer 40:11
that Baalis the king of the A.......... Jer 40:14
and departed to go over to the A...... Jer 41:10
with eight men, and went to the A..... Jer 41:15
Concerning The A, thus saith the..... Jer 49:1
to be heard in Rabbah of the A........ Jer 49:2
may come to Rabbah of the A.......... Eze 21:20
The Lord God concerning the A........ Eze 21:28
man, set thy face against the A........ Eze 25:2
And say unto the, A, Hear the word... Eze 25:3
the A a couchingplace for flocks...... Eze 25:5
the men of the east with the A........ Eze 25:10
that the A may not be remembered.... Eze 25:10

AMMONITESS (am'-mon-i-tess)
name was Naamah an A................ 1Kin 14:21
name was Naamah an A................ 1Kin 14:31
name was Naamah an A................ 2Chr 12:13
Zabad the son of Shimeath an A....... 2Chr 24:26

AMNON (am'-non) See AMNON's.
1. A son of David.
and his firstborn was A, of............ 2Sa 3:2
A the son of David loved her.......... 2Sa 13:1

A was so vexed, that he fell sick...... 2Sa 13:2
A thought it hard for him to do....... 2Sa 13:2
But A had a friend, whose name....... 2Sa 13:3
A said unto him, I love Tamar, my.... 2Sa 13:4
So A lay down, and made himself..... 2Sa 13:6
A said unto the king, I pray thee...... 2Sa 13:6
A said, Have out all men from me..... 2Sa 13:9
A said unto Tamar, Bring the meat.... 2Sa 13:10
into the chamber to A her brother..... 2Sa 13:10
Then A hated her exceedingly.......... 2Sa 13:15
A said unto her, Arise, be gone........ 2Sa 13:15
Hath A thy brother been with thee.... 2Sa 13:20
brother A neither good nor bad........ 2Sa 13:22
for Absalom hated A, because he...... 2Sa 13:22
thee, let my brother A go with us...... 2Sa 13:26
pressed him, that he let A............. 2Sa 13:27
and when I say unto you, Smite A..... 2Sa 13:28
unto A as Absalom had commanded... 2Sa 13:29
for A only is dead..................... 2Sa 13:32
for A only is dead..................... 2Sa 13:33
for he was comforted concerning A.... 2Sa 13:39
the firstborn A, of Ahinoam the....... 1Chr 3:1
2. A son of Shimon.
And the sons of Shimon were,......... 1Chr 4:20

AMNON'S (am'-nons) Refers to Amnon 1.
Go now to thy brother A house........ 2Sa 13:7
A said unto the king, Let Tamar....... 2Sa 13:7
Mark ye now when A heart is merry... 2Sa 13:28

AMOK (a'-mok) A priest who returned from
Exile under Zerubbabel.
Sallu, A, Hilkiah, Jedaiah,............. Neh 12:7
of A, Eber............................ Neh 12:20

AMON (a'-mon)
1. A governor of Samaria.
carry him back unto A the............. 1Kin 22:26
carry him back to A the governor..... 2Chr 18:25
2. Son and successor of King Manasseh of
Judah.
A his son reigned in his stead......... 2Kin 21:18
A was twenty and two years old....... 2Kin 21:19
the servants of A conspired............ 2Kin 21:23
that had conspired against king A..... 2Kin 21:24
of the acts of A which he did.......... 2Kin 21:25
A his son, Josiah his son.............. 1Chr 3:14
A his son reigned in his stead......... 2Chr 33:20
A was two and twenty years old....... 2Chr 33:21
for a sacrificed unto all the........... 2Chr 33:22
but A trespassed more and more....... 2Chr 33:23
that had conspired against the A....... 2Chr 33:25
Josiah the son of A king of Judah..... Jer 1:2
Josiah the son of A king of Judah..... Jer 25:3
the days of Josiah the son of A........ Zeph 1:1
and Manasseh begat A................. Mt 1:10
and A begat Josias.................... Mt 1:10
3. A descendant of Solomon who returned
from the Exile under Zerubbabel.
of Zebaim, the children of A........... Neh 7:59

AMONG See PREFACE.

AMONGST
God at the trees of the garden......... Gen 3:8
of a buryingplace a you................ Gen 23:9

AMORITE (am'-o-rite) A descendant of
Canaan, Ham's son.
And the Jebusite, and the A........... Gen 10:16
dwelt in the plain of Mamre the A..... Gen 14:13
the hand of the A with my sword...... Gen 48:22
drive out the Canaanite, the A......... Ex 33:2
I drive out before thee the A.......... Ex 34:11
the A which was in..................... Num 32:39
given into thine hand Sihon the A..... Deut 2:24
Lebanon, the Hittite, and the A........ Josh 9:1
east and on the west, and to the A..... Josh 11:3
The Jebusite also, and the A........... 1Chr 1:14
thy father was an A, and thy.......... Eze 16:3
an Hittite, and your father an A....... Eze 16:45
Yet destroyed I the A before him...... Amos 2:9
to possess the land of the A........... Amos 2:10

AMORITES (am'-o-rites)
of the Amalekites, and also the A...... Gen 14:7
iniquity of the A is not yet full....... Gen 15:16
And the A, and the Canaanites, and... Gen 15:21
the Hittites, and the A................. Ex 3:8
and the Hittites, and the A............ Ex 3:17
and the Hittites, and the A............ Ex 13:5
thee, and bring thee in unto the A..... Ex 23:23
and the Jebusites, and the A........... Num 13:29
cometh out of the coasts of the A...... Num 21:13
of Moab, between Moab and the A..... Num 21:13
unto Sihon king of the A, saying,...... Num 21:21
dwelt in all the cities of the A......... Num 21:25
city of Sihon the king of the A......... Num 21:26
unto Sihon king of the A.............. Num 21:29
Israel dwelt in the land of the A....... Num 21:31
drove out the A that were there....... Num 21:32
didst unto Sihon king of the A......... Num 21:34
all that Israel had done to the A....... Num 22:2
kingdom of Sihon king of the A....... Num 32:33
had slain Sihon the king of the A..... Deut 1:4
and go to the mount of the A.......... Deut 1:7
the way of the mountain of the A...... Deut 1:19
come unto the mountain of the A...... Deut 1:20
deliver us into the hand of the A...... Deut 1:27
And the A, which dwelt in that........ Deut 1:44
didst unto Sihon king of the A......... Deut 3:2
hand of the two kings of the A......... Deut 3:8
and the A call it Shenir................ Deut 3:9

---

the land of Sihon king of the A........ Deut 4:46
of Bashan, two kings of the A......... Deut 4:47
the Girgashites, and the A............. Deut 7:1
namely, the Hittites, and the A........ Deut 20:17
to Sihon and to Og, kings of the A.... Deut 31:4
did unto the two kings of the A........ Josh 2:10
and the Girgashites, and the A......... Josh 3:10
pass, when all the kings of the A...... Josh 5:1
deliver us into the hand of the A...... Josh 7:7
he did to the two kings of the A....... Josh 9:10
Therefore the five kings of the A...... Josh 10:5
for all the kings of the A that......... Josh 10:6
A before the children of Israel......... Josh 10:12
Sihon king of the A, who dwelt in..... Josh 12:2
the Hittites, the A, and the............ Josh 12:8
Aphek, to the borders of the A......... Josh 13:4
the cities of Sihon king of the A....... Josh 13:10
kingdom of Sihon king of the A........ Josh 13:21
you into the land of the A............. Josh 24:8
Jericho fought against you, the A...... Josh 24:11
you, even the two kings of the A...... Josh 24:12
the flood, on the gods of the A........ Josh 24:15
even the A which dwelt in the......... Josh 24:18
the A forced the children of Dan...... Judg 1:34
But the A would dwell in mount....... Judg 1:35
the coast of the A was from the....... Judg 1:36
the Canaanites, Hittites, and A........ Judg 3:5
fear not the gods of the A............. Judg 6:10
side Jordan in the land of the A....... Judg 10:8
from the Egyptians, and from the A... Judg 10:11
unto Sihon king of the A, king........ Judg 11:19
possessed all the land of the A........ Judg 11:21
possessed all the coasts of the A...... Judg 11:22
A from before his people Israel........ Judg 11:23
was peace between Israel and the A... 1Sa 7:14
but of the remnant of the A........... 2Sa 21:2
country of Sihon king of the A......... 1Kin 4:19
people that were left of the A......... 1Kin 9:20
to all things as did the A.............. 1Kin 21:26
wickedly above all that A did.......... 2Kin 21:11
left of the Hittites, and the A.......... 2Chr 8:7
Moabites, the Egyptians, and the A... Ezr 9:1
Canaanites, the Hittites, and the A.... Neh 9:8
Sihon king of the A, and Og king..... Ps 135:11
Sihon king of the A.................... Ps 136:19

AMOS (a'-mos)
1. A prophet during the reign of Uzziah.
The words of A, who was among the.. Amos 1:1
And the LORD said unto me, A........ Amos 7:8
A hath conspired against thee in....... Amos 7:10
For thus A saith, Jeroboam shall...... Amos 7:11
Also Amaziah said unto A, O thou..... Amos 7:12
Then answered A, and said to......... Amos 7:14
And he said, A what seest thou....... Amos 8:2
2. Son of Naum; an ancestor of Jesus.
which was the son of A, which........ Lk 3:25

AMOUNTING
gold, a to six hundred talents.......... 2Chr 3:8

AMOZ (a'-moz) Father of Isaiah.
Isaiah the prophet the son of A........ 2Kin 19:2
the son of A sent to Hezekiah......... 2Kin 19:20
Isaiah the son of A came to him...... 2Kin 20:1
Isaiah the prophet, the son of A....... 2Chr 26:22
the prophet Isaiah the son of A........ 2Chr 32:20
Isaiah the prophet, the son of A....... 2Chr 32:32
The vision of Isaiah the son of A...... Is 1:1
the son of A saw concerning Judah.... Is 2:1
which Isaiah the son of A did see..... Is 13:1
the Lord by Isaiah the son of A....... Is 20:2
Isaiah the prophet the son of A........ Is 37:2
the son of A sent unto Hezekiah...... Is 37:21
the son of A came unto him........... Is 38:1

AMPHIPOLIS (am-fip'-o-lis) A city in
Macedonia.
when they had passed through A....... Acts 17:1

AMPLIAS (am'-ple-as) A Christian
acquaintance of Paul's.
Greet A my beloved in the Lord....... Rom 16:8

AMRAM (am'-ram) See AMRAMITES, AMRAM'S,
HEMDAN.
1. Father of Moses and Aaron.
A, and Izhar, and Hebron, and Uzziel.. Ex 6:18
A took him Jochebed his father's...... Ex 6:20
of the life of A were an hundred...... Ex 6:20
A, and Izehar, Hebron, and Uzziel..... Num 3:19
And Kohath begat A................... Num 26:58
bare unto A Aaron and Moses......... Num 26:59
A, Izhar, and Hebron, and Uzziel..... 1Chr 6:2
And the children of A.................. 1Chr 6:3
And the sons of Kohath were, A....... 1Chr 6:18
A, Izhar, Hebron, and Uzziel, four.... 1Chr 23:12
The sons of A.......................... 1Chr 23:13
Of the sons of A....................... 1Chr 24:20
2. Married a foreign wife in Exile.
Maadai, A, and Uel,................... Ezr 10:34
3. A son of Dishon.
and Eshban, and Ithran, and.......... 1Chr 1:41

AMRAMITES (am'-ram-ites) Descendants of
Amram 1.
of Kohath was the family of the A.... Num 3:27
Of the A, and the Izharites, the....... 1Chr 26:23

AMRAM'S (am'-rams)
the name of A wife was Jochebed,.... Num 26:59

AMRAPHEL (am'-raf-el) King of Shinar in
Abraham's time.
in the days of A king of Shinar,....... Gen 14:1

A king of Shinar, and Arioch king ...... Gen 14:9

AMZI (am´-zi)
  1. A son of Merari.
  The son of A, the son of Bani, ... 1Chr 6:46
  2. Ancestor of Adaiah.
  the son of Pelaliah, the son of A .... Neh 11:12

AN See PREFACE.

ANAB (a´-nab) *A Canaanite city.*
  from Hebron, from Debir, from A .... Josh 11:21
  And A, and Eshtemoh, and Anim, ... Josh 15:50

ANAH (a´-nah)
  1. A daughter of Zibeon.
  of A the daughter of Zibeon the .... Gen 36:2
  the daughter of A the daughter of ...... Gen 36:14
  of Aholibamah the daughter of A .... Gen 36:18
  And the children of A were these .... Gen 36:25
  and Aholibamah the daughter of A ...... Gen 36:25
  2. A son of Seir.
  Shobal, and Zibeon, and A .... Gen 36:20
  duke Shobal, duke Zibeon, duke A .... Gen 36:29
  Shobal, and Zibeon, and A 1Chr 1:38
  3. A son of Zibeon.
  both Ajah, and A .... Gen 36:24
  this was that A that found the .... Gen 36:24
  Ajah, and A 1Chr 1:40
  The sons of A 1Chr 1:41

ANAHARATH (an-a-ha´-rath) *A town in Issachar.*
  And Haphraim, and Shihon, and A .... Josh 19:19

ANAIAH (an-a-i´-ah)
  1. A priest who assisted Ezra.
  stood Mattithiah, and Shema, and A ... Neh 8:4
  2. A Jew who sealed the covenant.
  Pelatiah, Hanan, A .... Neh 10:22

ANAK (a´-nak) See ANAKIMS. *The son of Arba.*
  and Talmai, the children of A .... Num 13:22
  we saw the children of A there .... Num 13:28
  we saw the giants, the sons of A .... Num 13:33
  stand before the children of A .... Deut 9:2
  the city of Arba the father of A .... Josh 15:13
  drove thence the three sons of A .... Josh 15:14
  and Talmai, the children of A .... Josh 15:14
  the city of Arba the father of A .... Josh 21:11
  thence the three sons of A .... Judg 1:20

ANAKIM See ANAKIMS.

ANAKIMS (an´-ak-ims) *Descendants of Anak.*
  have seen the sons of the A there .... Deut 1:28
  great, and many, and tall, as the A ...... Deut 2:10
  were accounted giants, as the A .... Deut 2:11
  great, and many, and tall, as the A ...... Deut 2:21
  and tall, the children of the A .... Deut 9:2
  cut off the A from the mountains, ... Josh 11:21
  There was none of the A left in .... Josh 11:22
  in that day how the A were there .... Josh 14:12
  Arba was a great man among the A .... Josh 14:15

ANAKITES See ANAKIMS.

ANAMIM (an´-am-im) *A people of northern Egypt.*
  And Mizraim begat Ludim, and A .... Gen 10:13
  And Mizraim begat Ludim, and A 1Chr 1:11

ANAMITES See ANAMIM.

ANAMMELECH (a-nam´-mel-ek) *A god of the Babylonians.*
  in fire to Adrammelech and A 2Kin 17:31

ANAN (a´-nan) *An Israelite who sealed the covenant under Nehemiah.*
  And Ahijah, Hanan, A .... Neh 10:26

ANANI (a-na´-ni) *A son of Elioenai.*
  and Johanan, and Dalaiah, and A 1Chr 3:24

ANANIAH (an-an-i´-ah) See ANANIAS.
  1. Grandfather of Azariah.
  the son of A by his house .... Neh 3:23
  2. A town in Benjamin.
  And at Anathoth, Nob, A .... Neh 11:32

ANANIAS (an-an-i´-as) See ANANIAH.
  1. A Christian who tried to deceive the apostles.
  But a certain man named A .... Acts 5:1
  But Peter said, A, why hath Satan .... Acts 5:3
  A hearing these words fell down, ... Acts 5:5
  2. A Christian who aided Paul.
  disciple at Damascus, named A .... Acts 9:10
  him said the Lord in a vision, A .... Acts 9:10
  a vision a man named A coming in .... Acts 9:12
  Then A answered, Lord, I have .... Acts 9:13
  A went his way, and entered into .... Acts 9:17
  And one A, a devout man according ..... Acts 22:12
  3. The High Priest who interrogated Paul.
  the high priest A commanded them ...... Acts 23:2
  after five days A the high priest .... Acts 24:1

ANATH (a´-nath) See BETH-ANATH. *Father of Shamgar the Judge.*
  him was Shamgar the son of A .... Judg 3:31
  the days of Shamgar the son of A .... Judg 5:6

ANATHEMA (a-nath´-em-ah) *Greek word for "accursed."*
  Christ, let him be A Maranatha 1Cor 16:22

ANATHOTH (an´-a-thoth) See ANETOTHITE.
  1. A Levitical city in Benjamin.
  A with her suburbs, and Almon .... Josh 21:18
  said the king, Get thee to A 1Kin 2:26
  suburbs, and A with her suburbs 1Chr 6:60
  The men of A, an hundred twenty .... Ezr 2:23
  The men of A, an hundred twenty .... Neh 7:27
  And at A, Nob, Ananiah, ... Neh 11:32
  to be heard unto Laish, O poor A .... Is 10:30
  were in A in the land of Benjamin .... Jer 1:1
  saith the LORD of the men of A .... Jer 11:21
  will bring evil upon the men of A .... Jer 11:23
  thou not reproved Jeremiah of A .... Jer 29:27
  Buy thee my field that is in A .... Jer 32:8
  field, I pray thee, that is in A .... Jer 32:8
  my uncle's son, that was in A .... Jer 32:9
  2. A son of Becher.
  Omri, and Jerimoth, and Abiah, and A . 1Chr 7:8
  3. An Israelite who sealed the covenant under Nehemiah.
  Hariph, A, Nebai, ... Neh 10:19

ANATHOTHITE See ANTOTHITE.

ANCESTORS
  remember the covenant of their a .... Lev 26:45

ANCHOR
  hope we have as an a of the soul .... Heb 6:19

ANCHORS
  they cast four a out of the stern .... Acts 27:29
  have cast a out of the foreship. .... Acts 27:30
  And when they had taken up the a ...... Acts 27:40

ANCIENT
  chief things of the a mountains .... Deut 33:15
  that a river, the river Kishon .... Judg 5:21
  of a times that I have formed it 2Kin 19:25
  And these are a things, ... 1Chr 4:22
  of the fathers, who were a men .... Ezr 3:12
  With the a in wisdom .... Job 12:12
  days of old, the years of a times, ... Ps 77:5
  Remove not the a landmark. .... Prov 22:28
  prophet, and the prudent, and the a ... Is 3:2
  himself proudly against the a .... Is 3:5
  The a and honourable, he is the .... Is 9:15
  of the wise, the son of a kings .... Is 19:11
  whose antiquity is of a days .... Is 23:7
  of a times, that I have formed it .... Is 37:26
  since I appointed the a people. .... Is 44:7
  hath declared this from a time .... Is 45:21
  from a times the things that are .... Is 46:10
  upon the a hast thou very heavily ...... Is 47:6
  awake, as in the a days, in the .... Is 51:9
  mighty nation, it is an a nation .... Jer 5:15
  in their ways from the a paths. .... Jer 18:15
  Then they began at the a men. .... Eze 9:6
  even the a high places are ours .... Eze 36:2
  the A of days did sit, whose .... Dan 7:9
  heaven, and came to the a of days ..... Dan 7:13
  Until the A of days came, and .... Dan 7:22

ANCIENTS
  As saith the proverb of the a 1Sa 24:13
  I understand more than the a .... Ps 119:100
  judgment with the a of his people ...... Is 3:14
  and before his a gloriously .... Is 24:23
  take of the a of the people. .... Jer 19:1
  and of the a of the priests .... Jer 19:1
  the priest, and counsel from the a ...... Eze 7:26
  of the a of the house of Israel— .... Eze 8:11
  hast thou seen what the a of the .... Eze 8:12
  The a of Gebal and the wise men .... Eze 27:9

ANCLE
  a bones received strength .... Acts 3:7

ANCLES
  the waters were to the a .... Eze 47:3

AND See PREFACE.

ANDREW (an´-drew) *One of the twelve disciples.*
  A his brother, casting a net into .... Mt 4:18
  is called Peter, and A his brother— ...... Mt 10:2
  A his brother casting a net into .... Mk 1:16
  into the house of Simon and A .... Mk 1:29
  And A, and Philip, and Bartholomew,... Mk 3:18
  and John and A asked him privately,... Mk 13:3
  A his brother, James and John, ... Lk 6:14
  speak, and followed him, was A .... Jn 1:40
  was of Bethsaida, the city of A .... Jn 1:44
  One of his disciples, A, Simon .... Jn 6:8
  Philip cometh and telleth A .... Jn 12:22
  and again A and Philip tell Jesus .... Jn 12:22
  Peter, and James, and John, and A ..... Acts 1:13

ANDRONICUS (an-dro-ni´-cus) *A relative of Paul.*
  Salute A and Junia, my kinsmen, and . Rom 16:7

ANEM (a´-nem) See EN-GANNIM. *A Levitical city in Issachar.*
  suburbs, and A with her suburbs 1Chr 6:73

ANER (a´-ner)
  1. An ally of Abraham.
  of Eshcol, and brother of A .... Gen 14:13
  of the men which went with me, A ...... Gen 14:24
  2. A Levitical city in Manasseh.
  A with her suburbs, and Bileam 1Chr 6:70

ANETHOTHITE (a-neth-o-thite) See ANETOTHITE. *A native of Anathoth.*
  Abiezer the A, Mebunnai 2Sa 23:27

ANETOTHITE (an´-e-toth-ite) See ANETHOTHITE, ANTOTHITE. *Same as Anethothite.*
  the ninth month was Abiezer the A... 1Chr 27:12

ANGEL
  the a of the LORD found her by a .... Gen 16:7
  the a of the LORD said unto her,.......... Gen 16:9
  the a of the LORD said unto her,.......... Gen 16:10
  the a of the LORD said unto him,.......... Gen 16:11
  the a of God called to Hagar out.......... Gen 21:17
  the a of the LORD called unto him .... Gen 22:11
  the a of the LORD called unto.............. Gen 22:15
  he shall send his a before thee............ Gen 24:7
  I walk, will send his a with thee........... Gen 24:40
  the a of God spake unto me in a .... Gen 31:11
  The a which redeemed me from all ...... Gen 48:16
  the a of the LORD appeared unto .... Ex 3:2
  the a of God, which went before .... Ex 14:19
  I send an A before thee, to keep.......... Ex 23:20
  For mine A shall go before thee,.......... Ex 23:23
  mine A shall go before thee................. Ex 32:34
  And I will send an a before thee.......... Ex 33:2
  he heard our voice, and sent an a .... Num 20:16
  the a of the LORD stood in the............. Num 22:22
  the ass saw the a of the LORD............. Num 22:23
  But the a of the LORD stood in a.......... Num 22:24
  the ass saw the a of the LORD............. Num 22:25
  the a of the LORD went further,.......... Num 22:26
  the ass saw the a of the LORD............. Num 22:27
  he saw the a of the LORD standing....... Num 22:31
  the a of the LORD said unto him,.......... Num 22:32
  said unto the a of the LORD................. Num 22:34
  the a of the LORD said unto................ Num 22:35
  an a of the LORD came up from........... Judg 2:1
  when the a of the LORD spake.............. Judg 2:4
  said the a of the LORD, curse ye .... Judg 5:23
  And there came an a of the LORD......... Judg 6:11
  the a of the LORD appeared unto .... Judg 6:12
  the a of God said unto him, Take .... Judg 6:20
  Then the a of the LORD put forth.......... Judg 6:21
  Then the a of the LORD departed. .... Judg 6:21
  that he was an a of the LORD. .... Judg 6:22
  the a of the LORD face to face .... Judg 6:22
  the a of the LORD appeared unto .... Judg 13:3
  the countenance of an a of God........... Judg 13:6
  the a of God came again unto the .... Judg 13:9
  the a of the LORD said unto .... Judg 13:13
  said unto the a of the LORD................. Judg 13:15
  the a of the LORD said unto................ Judg 13:16
  not that he was an a of the LORD........ Judg 13:16
  said unto the a of the LORD................ Judg 13:17
  the a of the LORD said unto him,......... Judg 13:18
  and the a did wondrously, ... Judg 13:19
  that the a of the LORD ascended.......... Judg 13:20
  But the a of the LORD did no more .... Judg 13:21
  knew that he was an a of the LORD ..... Judg 13:21
  good in my sight, as an a of God 1Sa 29:9
  for as an a of God, so is my lord 2Sa 14:17
  to the wisdom of an a of God 2Sa 14:20
  lord the king is as an a of God 2Sa 19:27
  when the a stretched out his hand 2Sa 24:16
  said to the a that destroyed the 2Sa 24:16
  the a of the LORD was by the 2Sa 24:16
  saw the a that smote the people......... 2Sa 24:17
  an a spake unto me by the word of...... 1Kin 13:18
  then an a touched him, and said 1Kin 19:5
  the a of the LORD came again the 1Kin 19:7
  But the a of the LORD said to 2Kin 1:3
  the a of the LORD said 2Kin 1:15
  that the a of the LORD went out,......... 2Kin 19:35
  the a of the LORD destroying 1Chr 21:12
  God sent an a unto Jerusalem to 1Chr 21:15
  said to the a that destroyed, It 1Chr 21:15
  the a of the LORD stood by the............ 1Chr 21:15
  saw the a of the LORD stand 1Chr 21:16
  Then the a of the LORD commanded. 1Chr 21:18
  Ornan turned back, and saw the a 1Chr 21:20
  And the LORD commanded the a 1Chr 21:27
  of the sword of the a of the LORD........ 1Chr 21:30
  And the LORD sent an a, which cut 2Chr 32:21
  The a of the LORD encampeth round.... Ps 34:7
  let the a of the LORD chase them .... Ps 35:5
  let the a of the LORD persecute.......... Ps 35:6
  neither say thou before the a .... Eccl 5:6
  Then the a of the LORD went forth ...... Is 37:36
  the a of his presence saved them .... Is 63:9
  and Abed-nego, who hath sent his a ... Dan 3:28
  My God hath sent his a, and hath .... Dan 6:22
  Yea, he had power over the a .... Hos 12:4
  the a that talked with me said .... Zec 1:9
  they answered the a of the LORD .... Zec 1:11
  Then the a of the LORD answered........ Zec 1:12
  the LORD answered the a that............. Zec 1:13
  So the a that communed with me .... Zec 1:14
  I said unto the a that talked .... Zec 1:19
  the a that talked with me went .... Zec 2:3
  another a went out to meet him, ... Zec 2:3
  standing before the a of the LORD .... Zec 3:1
  garments, and stood before the a .... Zec 3:4
  the a of the LORD stood by................. Zec 3:5
  the a of the LORD protested unto .... Zec 3:6
  the a that talked with me came.......... Zec 4:1
  spake to the a that talked with .... Zec 4:4
  Then the a that talked with me .... Zec 4:5
  Then the a that talked with me .... Zec 4:5
  Then said I to the a that talked .... Zec 5:5
  said unto the a that talked with......... Zec 6:4
  the a answered and said unto me, ... Zec 6:5
  as the a of the LORD before them, ... Zec 12:8
  the a of the Lord appeared unto.......... Mt 1:20

the *a* of the Lord had bidden him .... Mt 1:24
the *a* of the Lord appeareth to .... Mt 2:13
an *a* of the Lord appeareth in a .... Mt 2:19
for the *a* of the Lord descended .... Mt 28:2
the *a* answered and said unto the .... Mt 28:5
there appeared unto him an *a* of .... Lk 1:11
But the *a* said unto him, Fear not .... Lk 1:13
and Zacharias said unto the *a* .... Lk 1:18
the *a* answering said unto him, I .... Lk 1:19
in the sixth month the *a* Gabriel .... Lk 1:26
the *a* came in unto her, and said, ... Lk 1:28
the *a* said unto her, Fear not, ... Lk 1:30
Then said Mary unto the *a* .... Lk 1:34
the *a* answered and said unto her, ... Lk 1:35
And the *a* departed from her .... Lk 1:38
the *a* of the Lord came upon them, ... Lk 2:9
the *a* said unto them, Fear not .... Lk 2:10
the *a* a multitude of the heavenly .... Lk 2:13
which was so named of the *a* .... Lk 2:21
there appeared an *a* unto him from .... Lk 22:43
For an *a* went down at a certain .... Jn 5:4
others said, An *a* spake to him .... Jn 12:29
But the *a* of the Lord by night .... Acts 5:19
as it had been the face of an *a* .... Acts 6:15
a of the Lord in a flame of fire .... Acts 7:30
a which appeared to him in the *a* .... Acts 7:35
in the wilderness with the *a* .... Acts 7:38
the *a* of the Lord spake unto .... Acts 8:26
day an *a* of God coming in to him .... Acts 10:3
when the *a* which spake unto .... Acts 10:7
was warned from God by an holy *a* .... Acts 10:22
how he had seen an *a* in his house .... Acts 11:13
the *a* of the Lord came upon him, ... Acts 12:7
the *a* said unto him, Gird thyself. .... Acts 12:8
was true which was done by the *a* .... Acts 12:9
forthwith the *a* departed from him .... Acts 12:10
that the Lord hath sent his *a* .... Acts 12:11
Then said they, It is his *a* .... Acts 12:15
immediately the *a* of the Lord .... Acts 12:23
is no resurrection, neither *a* .... Acts 23:8
spirit or an *a* hath spoken to him .... Acts 23:9
by me this night the *a* of God .... Acts 27:23
is transformed into an *a* of light 2Cor 11:14
or an *a* from heaven, preach any .... Gal 1:8
but received me as an *a* of God .... Gal 4:14
signified it by his *a* unto his .... Rev 1:1
Unto the *a* of the church of .... Rev 2:1
unto the *a* of the church in .... Rev 2:8
to the *a* of the church in .... Rev 2:12
unto the *a* of the church in .... Rev 2:18
unto the *a* of the church in .... Rev 3:1
to the *a* of the church .... Rev 3:7
unto the *a* of the church of the. .... Rev 3:14
I saw a strong *a* proclaiming with .... Rev 5:2
I saw another *a* ascending from .... Rev 7:2
And another *a* came and stood at the .... Rev 8:3
the *a* took the censer, and filled .... Rev 8:5
The first *a* sounded, and there .... Rev 8:7
And the second *a* sounded, and as I .... Rev 8:8
And the third *a* sounded, and there .... Rev 8:10
And the fourth *a* sounded, and the .... Rev 8:12
heard an *a* flying through the .... Rev 8:13
And the fifth *a* sounded, and I saw .... Rev 9:1
which is the *a* of the bottomless .... Rev 9:11
And the sixth *a* sounded, and I .... Rev 9:13
Saying to the sixth *a* which had .... Rev 9:14
I saw another mighty *a* come down .... Rev 10:1
the *a* which I saw stand upon the .... Rev 10:5
of the voice of the seventh *a* .... Rev 10:7
is open in the hand of the *a* .... Rev 10:8
And I went unto the *a*, and said .... Rev 10:9
the *a* stood, saying, Rise, and .... Rev 11:1
And the seventh *a* sounded .... Rev 11:15
I saw another *a* fly in the midst. .... Rev 14:6
And there followed another *a* .... Rev 14:8
the third *a* followed them, saying .... Rev 14:9
another *a* came out of the temple. .... Rev 14:15
another *a* came out of the temple .... Rev 14:17
another *a* came out from the altar .... Rev 14:18
the *a* thrust in his sickle into .... Rev 14:19
the second *a* poured out his vial .... Rev 16:3
the third *a* poured out his vial .... Rev 16:4
I heard the *a* of the waters say, ... Rev 16:5
the fourth *a* poured out his vial .... Rev 16:8
the fifth *a* poured out his vial .... Rev 16:10
the sixth *a* poured out his vial .... Rev 16:12
the seventh *a* poured out his vial .... Rev 16:17
the *a* said unto me, Wherefore .... Rev 17:7
another *a* come down from heaven. .... Rev 18:1
a mighty *a* took up a stone like a .... Rev 18:21
I saw an *a* standing in the sun .... Rev 19:17
I saw an *a* come down from heaven, ... Rev 20:1
of man, that is, of the *a* .... Rev 21:17
a to shew unto his servants the *a* .... Rev 22:6
a which shewed me these things .... Rev 22:8
I Jesus have sent mine *a* to .... Rev 22:16

ANGEL'S

up before God out of the *a* hand .... Rev 8:4
the little book out of the *a* hand .... Rev 10:10

ANGELS

there came two *a* to Sodom at even .... Gen 19:1
then the *a* hastened Lot, saying .... Gen 19:15
behold the *a* of God ascending and .... Gen 28:12
his way, and the *a* of God met him .... Gen 32:1
his *a* he charged with folly .... Job 4:18
him a little lower than the *a* .... Ps 8:5
thousand, even thousands of *a* .... Ps 68:17
by sending evil *a* among them .... Ps 78:49
shall give his *a* charge over thee .... Ps 91:11

Bless the Lord, ye his *a*, that .... Ps 103:20
Who maketh his *a* spirits .... Ps 104:4
Praise ye him, all his *a* .... Ps 148:2
He shall give his *a* charge .... Mt 4:6
a came and ministered unto him .... Mt 4:11
and the reapers are the *a* .... Mt 13:39
Son of man shall send forth his *a* .... Mt 13:41
the *a* shall come forth, and sever .... Mt 13:49
glory of his Father with his *a* .... Mt 16:27
That in heaven their *a* do always .... Mt 18:10
but are as the *a* of God in heaven .... Mt 22:30
he shall send his *a* with a great .... Mt 24:31
not the *a* of heaven, but my .... Mt 24:36
glory, and all the holy *a* with .... Mt 25:31
prepared for the devil and his *a* .... Mt 25:41
me more than twelve legions of *a* .... Mt 26:53
the *a* ministered unto him .... Mk 1:13
of his Father with the holy *a* .... Mk 8:38
but are as the *a* which are in .... Mk 12:25
And then shall he send his *a* .... Mk 13:27
not the *a* which are in heaven, ... Mk 13:32
as the *a* were gone away from them .... Lk 2:15
shall give his *a* charge over thee .... Lk 4:10
in his Father's, and of the holy *a* .... Lk 9:26
also confess before the *a* of God .... Lk 12:8
be denied before the *a* of God .... Lk 12:9
the *a* of God over one sinner that .... Lk 15:10
was carried by the *a* into .... Lk 16:22
for they are equal unto the *a* .... Lk 20:36
they had also seen a vision of *a* .... Lk 24:23
the *a* of God ascending and .... Jn 1:51
seeth two *a* in white sitting, the .... Jn 20:12
the law by the disposition of *a* .... Acts 7:53
neither death, nor life, nor *a* .... Rom 8:38
spectacle unto the world, and to *a* 1Cor 4:9
Know ye not that we shall judge *a* 1Cor 6:3
on her head because of the *a* 1Cor 11:10
with the tongues of men and of *a* 1Cor 13:1
it was ordained by *a* in the hand .... Gal 3:19
humility and worshipping of *a* .... Col 2:18
from heaven with his mighty *a* 2Th 1:7
in the Spirit, seen of *a* 1Ti 3:16
Lord Jesus Christ, and the elect *a* 1Ti 5:21
made so much better than the *a* .... Heb 1:4
of the *a* said he at any time .... Heb 1:5
let all the *a* of God worship him .... Heb 1:6
of the *a* he saith .... Heb 1:7
Who maketh his *a* spirits .... Heb 1:7
But to which of the *a* said he at .... Heb 1:13
the word spoken by *a* was stedfast .... Heb 2:2
For unto the *a* hath he not put in .... Heb 2:5
him a little lower than the *a* .... Heb 2:7
the *a* for the suffering of death .... Heb 2:9
took not on him the nature of *a* .... Heb 2:16
and to an innumerable company of *a* .... Heb 12:22
some have entertained *a* unawares .... Heb 13:2
which things the *a* desire to look 1Pet 1:12
a and authorities and powers being 1Pet 3:22
God spared not the *a* that sinned 2Pet 2:4
Whereas *a*, which are greater in 2Pet 2:11
the *a* which kept not their first .... Jude 6
are the *a* of the seven churches .... Rev 1:20
before my Father, and before his *a* .... Rev 3:5
of many *a* round about the throne .... Rev 5:11
after these things I saw four *a* .... Rev 7:1
with a loud voice to the four *a* .... Rev 7:2
all the *a* stood round about the .... Rev 7:11
I saw the seven *a* which stood .... Rev 8:2
the seven *a* which had the seven .... Rev 8:6
of the trumpet of the three *a* .... Rev 8:13
Loose the four *a* which are bound. .... Rev 9:14
the four *a* were loosed, which .... Rev 9:15
his *a* fought against the dragon .... Rev 12:7
and the dragon fought and his *a* .... Rev 12:7
his *a* were cast out with him .... Rev 12:9
in the presence of the holy *a* .... Rev 14:10
seven *a* having the seven last .... Rev 15:1
the seven *a* came out of the .... Rev 15:6
a seven golden vials full of the .... Rev 15:7
of the seven *a* were fulfilled .... Rev 15:8
the temple saying to the seven *a* .... Rev 16:1
seven *a* which had the seven vials .... Rev 17:1
came unto me one of the seven *a* .... Rev 21:9
gates, and at the gates twelve *a* .... Rev 21:12

ANGELS'

Man did eat *a* food .... Ps 78:25

ANGER

brother's *a* turn away from thee. .... Gen 27:45
Jacob's *a* was kindled against .... Gen 30:2
let not thine *a* burn against thy .... Gen 44:18
for in their *a* they slew a man, ... Gen 49:6
Cursed be their *a*, for it .... Gen 49:7
the *a* of the Lord was kindled .... Ex 4:14
out from Pharaoh in a great *a* .... Ex 11:8
Moses' *a* waxed hot, and he cast. .... Ex 32:19
Let not the *a* of my lord wax hot .... Ex 32:22
and his *a* was kindled .... Num 11:10
the *a* of the Lord was kindled .... Num 11:10
the *a* of the Lord was kindled .... Num 12:9
God's *a* was kindled because he .... Num 22:22
Balaam's *a* was kindled, and he .... Num 22:27
Balak's *a* was kindled against .... Num 24:10
the *a* of the Lord was kindled .... Num 25:3
that the fierce *a* of the Lord may .... Num 25:4
the Lord's *a* was kindled the same .... Num 32:10
the Lord's *a* was kindled against .... Num 32:13
a of the Lord toward Israel .... Num 32:14
Lord thy God, to provoke him to *a* .... Deut 4:25
a of the Lord thy God be kindled .... Deut 6:15

---

so will the *a* of the Lord be .... Deut 7:4
of the Lord, to provoke him to *a* .... Deut 9:18
For I was afraid of the *a* .... Deut 9:19
turn from the fierceness of his *a* .... Deut 13:17
him, but then the *a* of the Lord .... Deut 29:20
which the Lord overthrew in his *a* .... Deut 29:23
meaneth the heat of this great *a* .... Deut 29:24
the *a* of the Lord was kindled .... Deut 29:27
them out of their land in *a* .... Deut 29:28
Then my *a* shall be kindled .... Deut 31:17
to provoke him to *a* through the .... Deut 31:29
provoked they him to *a* .... Deut 32:16
me to *a* with their vanities .... Deut 32:21
them to *a* with a foolish nation .... Deut 32:21
For a fire is kindled in mine *a* .... Deut 32:22
the *a* of the Lord was kindled .... Josh 7:1
from the fierceness of his *a* .... Josh 7:26
then shall the *a* of the Lord be. .... Josh 23:16
them, and provoked the Lord to *a* .... Judg 2:12
the *a* of the Lord was hot against .... Judg 2:14
the *a* of the Lord was kindled .... Judg 2:20
Therefore the *a* of the Lord was .... Judg 3:8
Let not thine *a* be hot against me .... Judg 6:39
Then their *a* was abated toward .... Judg 8:3
son of Ebed, his *a* was kindled .... Judg 9:30
the *a* of the Lord was kindled .... Judg 10:7
his *a* was kindled, and he went up .... Judg 14:19
his *a* was kindled greatly 1Sa 11:6
Eliab's *a* was kindled against 1Sa 17:28
Then Saul's *a* was kindled against 1Sa 20:30
arose from the table in fierce *a* 1Sa 20:34
the *a* of the Lord was kindled 2Sa 6:7
David's *a* was greatly kindled 2Sa 12:5
again the *a* of the Lord was 2Sa 24:1
molten images, to provoke me to *a* 1Kin 14:9
groves, provoking the Lord to *a* 1Kin 14:15
the Lord God of Israel to *a* 1Kin 15:30
provoke me to *a* with their sins. 1Kin 16:2
in provoking him to *a* with the 1Kin 16:7
Israel to *a* with their vanities. 1Kin 16:13
Israel to *a* with their vanities. 1Kin 16:26
the Lord God of Israel to *a* than 1Kin 16:33
thou hast provoked me to *a* 1Kin 21:22
provoked to *a* the Lord God of 1Kin 22:53
the *a* of the Lord was kindled 2Kin 13:3
things to provoke the Lord to *a* 2Kin 17:11
of the Lord, to provoke him to *a* 2Kin 17:17
of the Lord, to provoke him to *a* 2Kin 21:6
sight, and have provoked me to *a* 2Kin 21:15
to *a* with all the works of their 2Kin 22:17
had made to provoke the Lord to *a* 2Kin 23:19
wherewith his *a* was kindled 2Kin 23:26
For through the *a* of the Lord it 2Kin 24:20
the *a* of the Lord was kindled 1Chr 13:10
wherefore their *a* was greatly 2Chr 25:10
and they returned home in great *a* 2Chr 25:10
Wherefore the *a* of the Lord was 2Chr 25:15
provoked to *a* the Lord God of his 2Chr 28:25
of the Lord, to provoke him to *a* 2Chr 33:6
to *a* with all the works of their 2Chr 34:25
thee to *a* before the builders .... Neh 4:5
gracious and merciful, slow to *a* .... Neh 9:17
wroth, and his *a* burned in him .... Est 1:12
which overturneth them in his *a* .... Job 9:5
If God will not withdraw his *a* .... Job 9:13
He teareth himself in his *a* .... Job 18:4
God distributeth sorrows in his *a* .... Job 21:17
not so, he hath visited in his *a* .... Job 35:15
O Lord, rebuke me not in thine *a* .... Ps 6:1
Arise, O Lord, in thine *a* .... Ps 7:6
fiery oven in the time of thine *a* .... Ps 21:9
put not thy servant away in *a* .... Ps 27:9
For his *a* endureth but a moment. .... Ps 30:5
Cease from *a*, and forsake wrath .... Ps 37:8
in my flesh because of thine *a* .... Ps 38:3
in thine *a* cast down the people. .... Ps 56:7
let thy wrathful *a* take hold of .... Ps 69:24
why doth thine *a* smoke against. .... Ps 74:1
hath he in *a* shut up his tender .... Ps 77:9
a also came up against Israel .... Ps 78:21
many a time turned he his *a* away .... Ps 78:38
upon them the fierceness of his *a* .... Ps 78:49
He made a way to his *a* .... Ps 78:50
him to *a* with their high places .... Ps 78:58
from the fierceness of thine *a* .... Ps 85:3
cause thine *a* toward us to cease. .... Ps 85:4
out thine *a* to all generations. .... Ps 85:5
For we are consumed by thine *a* .... Ps 90:7
Who knoweth the power of thine *a* .... Ps 90:11
merciful and gracious, slow to *a* .... Ps 103:8
will he keep his *a* for ever .... Ps 103:9
him to *a* with their inventions. .... Ps 106:29
slow to *a*, and of great mercy. .... Ps 145:8
but grievous words stir up *a* .... Prov 15:1
is slow to *a* appeaseth strife .... Prov 15:18
He that is slow to *a* is better .... Prov 16:32
of man deferreth his *a* .... Prov 19:11
whoso provoketh him to *a* sinneth .... Prov 20:2
A gift in secret pacifieth *a* .... Prov 21:14
and the rod of his *a* shall fail. .... Prov 22:8
is cruel, and *a* is outrageous .... Prov 27:4
for *a* resteth in the bosom of .... Eccl 7:9
the Holy One of Israel unto *a* .... Is 1:4
Therefore is the *a* of the Lord .... Is 5:25
For all this his *a* is not turned. .... Is 5:25
for the fierce *a* of Rezin with .... Is 7:4
For all this his *a* is not turned. .... Is 9:12
For all this his *a* is not turned. .... Is 9:17
For all this his *a* is not turned. .... Is 9:21
For all this his *a* is not turned. .... Is 10:4

O Assyrian, the rod of mine *a*............ Is 10:5
mine *a* in their destruction................. Is 10:25
thine *a* is turned away, and thou........ Is 12:1
called my mighty ones for mine *a*...... Is 13:3
cruel both with wrath and fierce *a*..... Is 13:9
and in the day of his fierce *a*............ Is 13:13
he that ruled the nations in *a*............ Is 14:6
from far, burning with his *a*............... Is 30:27
with the indignation of his *a*.............. Is 30:30
poured upon him the fury of his *a*..... Is 42:25
name's sake will I defer mine *a*.......... Is 48:9
for I will tread them in mine *a*.......... Is 63:3
tread down the people in mine *a*........ Is 63:6
me to a continually to my face............ Is 65:5
to render his *a* with fury.................... Is 66:15
surely his *a* shall turn from me.......... Jer 2:35
Will he reserve his *a* for ever............ Jer 3:5
not cause mine *a* to fall upon you...... Jer 3:12
and I will not keep *a* for ever............ Jer 3:12
for the fierce *a* of the LORD............... Jer 4:8
of the LORD, and by his fierce *a*........ Jer 4:26
that they may provoke me to *a*.......... Jer 7:18
Do they provoke me to *a*................... Jer 7:19
Behold, mine *a* and my fury shall...... Jer 7:20
me to *a* with their graven images...... Jer 8:19
not in thine *a*, lest thou bring.......... Jer 10:24
themselves to provoke me to *a* in...... Jer 11:17
of the fierce *a* of the LORD............... Jer 12:13
for a fire is kindled in mine *a*........... Jer 15:14
ye have kindled a fire in mine *a*........ Jer 17:4
with them in the time of thine *a*....... Jer 18:23
and with a strong arm, even in *a*....... Jer 21:5
The *a* of the LORD shall not............... Jer 23:20
provoke me not to *a* with the............ Jer 25:6
that ye might provoke me to *a*.......... Jer 25:7
of the fierce *a* of the LORD............... Jer 25:37
and because of his fierce *a*................ Jer 25:38
The fierce *a* of the LORD shall.......... Jer 30:24
other gods, to provoke me to *a*......... Jer 32:29
to *a* with the work of their hands...... Jer 32:30
destroy them in *a* from under the...... Jer 32:31
they have done to provoke me to *a*... Jer 32:32
I have driven them in mine *a*............ Jer 32:37
men, whom I have slain in mine *a*..... Jer 33:5
for great is the *a* and the fury.......... Jer 36:7
As mine *a* and my fury hath been...... Jer 42:18
have committed to provoke me to *a*.. Jer 44:3
mine *a* was poured forth, and was..... Jer 44:6
evil upon them, even my fierce *a*....... Jer 49:37
from the fierce *a* of the LORD........... Jer 51:45
For through the *a* of the LORD it....... Jer 52:3
me in the day of his fierce *a*............. Lam 1:12
of Zion with a cloud in his *a*............ Lam 2:1
his footstool in the day of his *a*........ Lam 2:1
fierce *a* all the horn of Israel............. Lam 2:3
the indignation of his *a* the king........ Lam 2:6
slain them in the day of thine *a*......... Lam 2:21
a none escaped nor remained............... Lam 2:22
Thou hast covered with *a*, and.......... Lam 3:43
destroy them in *a* from under the...... Lam 3:66
he hath poured out his fierce *a*......... Lam 4:11
The *a* of the LORD hath divided......... Lam 4:16
Thus shall mine *a* be accomplished.... Eze 5:13
execute judgments in thee in *a*.......... Eze 5:15
and I will send mine *a* upon thee....... Eze 7:3
and accomplish mine *a* upon thee...... Eze 7:8
have returned to provoke me to *a*...... Eze 8:17
an overflowing shower in mine *a*....... Eze 13:13
thy whoredoms, to provoke me to *a*.. Eze 16:26
to accomplish my *a* against them....... Eze 20:8
to accomplish my *a* against them....... Eze 20:21
so will I gather you in mine *a*............ Eze 22:20
do in Edom according to mine *a*........ Eze 25:14
will even do according to thine *a*....... Eze 35:11
I have consumed them in mine *a*....... Eze 43:8
I beseech thee, let thine *a*................. Dan 9:16
shall be destroyed, neither in *a*......... Dan 11:20
mine *a* is kindled against them.......... Hos 11:9
execute the fierceness of mine *a*........ Hos 11:9
provoked him to a most bitterly........... Hos 12:14
I gave thee a king in mine *a*.............. Hos 13:11
for mine *a* is turned away from.......... Hos 14:4
gracious and merciful, slow to *a*........ Joel 2:13
his *a* did tear perpetually, and he...... Amos 1:11
and turn away from his fierce *a*......... Jonah 3:9
God, and merciful, slow to *a*............. Jonah 4:2
And I will execute vengeance in *a*..... Mic 5:15
he retaineth not his *a* for ever.......... Mic 7:18
The LORD is slow to *a*, and great....... Nah 1:3
abide in the fierceness of his *a*.......... Nah 1:6
was thine *a* against the rivers............ Hab 3:8
didst thresh the heathen in *a*............ Hab 3:12
before the fierce *a* of the LORD......... Zeph 2:2
day of the LORD's come upon you........ Zeph 2:2
be hid in the day of the LORD's *a*...... Zeph 2:3
indignation, even all my fierce *a*....... Zeph 3:8
Mine *a* was kindled against the.......... Zec 10:3
looked round about on them with *a*... Mk 3:5
by a foolish nation I will *a* you......... Rom 10:19
all bitterness, and wrath, and *a*......... Eph 4:31
a, wrath, malice, blasphemy,............. Col 3:8
provoke not your children to *a*.......... Col 3:21

ANGERED

They *a* him also at the waters of....... Ps 106:32

ANGLE

all they that cast *a* into the............... Is 19:8
take up all of them with the *a*........... Hab 1:15

ANGRY

him, Oh let not the LORD be *a*........... Gen 18:30
he said, Oh let not the Lord be *a*....... Gen 18:32

---

nor *a* with yourselves, that ye........... Gen 45:5
he was *a* with Eleazar and Ithamar,... Lev 10:16
Also the LORD was *a* with me for....... Deut 1:37
LORD was *a* with me for your sakes.... Deut 4:21
so that the LORD was *a* with you........ Deut 9:8
the LORD was very *a* with Aaron to.... Deut 9:20
lest *a* fellows run upon thee, and....... Judg 18:25
then be ye *a* for this matter............... 2Sa 19:42
thou be *a* with them, and deliver........ 1Kin 8:46
And the LORD was *a* with Solomon..... 1Kin 11:9
the LORD was very *a* with Israel......... 2Kin 17:18
thou be *a* with them, and deliver........ 2Chr 6:36
wouldest not thou be *a* with us.......... Ezr 9:14
I was very *a* when I heard their.......... Neh 5:6
Kiss the Son, lest he be *a*.................. Ps 2:12
God is *a* with the wicked every.......... Ps 7:11
in thy sight when once thou art *a*...... Ps 76:7
wilt thou be *a* for ever....................... Ps 79:5
how long wilt thou be *a* against......... Ps 80:4
Wilt thou be *a* with us for ever.......... Ps 85:5
He that is soon *a* dealeth................... Prov 14:17
with a contentious and an *a* woman... Prov 21:19
Make no friendship with an *a* man..... Prov 22:24
so doth an *a* countenance a............... Prov 25:23
A man stirreth up strife, and a............. Prov 29:22
should God be *a* at thy voice.............. Eccl 5:6
not hasty in thy spirit to be *a*........... Eccl 7:9
mother's children were *a* with me...... Song 1:6
though thou wast *a* with me.............. Is 12:1
be quiet, and will be no more *a*......... Eze 16:42
For this cause the king was *a*............ Dan 2:12
exceedingly, and he was very *a*.......... Jonah 4:1
The LORD, Doest thou well to be *a*.... Jonah 4:4
thou well to be *a* for the gourd.......... Jonah 4:9
And he said, I do well to be *a*............ Jonah 4:9
That whosoever is *a* with his............. Mt 5:22
house being *a* said to his servant....... Lk 14:21
And he was *a*, and would not go in.... Lk 15:28
are ye *a* at me, because I have........... Jn 7:23
Be ye *a*, and sin not.......................... Eph 4:26
not selfwilled, not soon *a*.................. Titus 1:7
And the nations were *a*, and thy........ Rev 11:18

ANGUISH

in that we saw the *a* of his soul......... Gen 42:21
not unto Moses for *a* of spirit............ Ex 6:9
and be in *a* because of thee............... Deut 2:25
for *a* is come upon me, because my.... 1Sa 1:9
will speak in the *a* of my spirit.......... Job 7:11
and *a* shall make him afraid............... Job 15:24
because his *a* cometh upon you.......... Ps 119:143
distress and *a* cometh upon you......... Prov 1:27
trouble and darkness, dimness of *a*.... Is 8:22
into the land of trouble and *a*........... Is 30:6
the *a* as of her that bringeth............. Jer 4:31
a hath taken hold of us, and pain,........ Jer 6:24
and sorrows have taken her; as a......... Jer 49:24
a took hold of him, and pangs as........ Jer 50:43
she remembereth no more the *a*........ Jn 16:21
Tribulation and *a*, upon every soul..... Rom 2:9
of *a* heart I wrote unto you with........ 2Cor 2:4

ANIAM (a'-ne-am) A son of Shemida.

Shechem, and Likhi, and A.................. 1Chr 7:19

ANIM (a'-nim) A city in Judah.

And Anab, and Eshtemoh, and A......... Josh 15:50

ANISE

for ye pay tithe of mint and *a*............ Mt 23:23

ANNA (an'-nah) A prophetess.

And there was one A, a prophetess,..... Lk 2:36

ANNAS (an'-nas) A High Priest during Jesus' ministry.

And Caiaphas being the high............... Lk 3:2
And led him away to A first................. Jn 18:13
Now A had sent him bound unto.......... Jn 18:24
A the high priest, and Caiaphas,.......... Acts 4:6

ANOINT

and shalt *a* them, and consecrate....... Ex 28:41
pour it upon his head, and *a* him....... Ex 29:7
for it, and thou shalt *a* it................... Ex 29:36
thou shalt *a* the tabernacle of............ Ex 30:26
And thou shalt *a* Aaron and his sons. Ex 30:30
a the tabernacle, and all that is......... Ex 40:9
thou shalt *a* the altar of the.............. Ex 40:10
And thou shalt *a* the laver................. Ex 40:11
and *a* him, and sanctify him.............. Ex 40:13
And thou shalt *a* them,...................... Ex 40:15
as thou didst *a* their father................ Ex 40:15
And the priest, whom he shall *a*......... Lev 16:32
but thou shalt not *a* thyself with........ Deut 28:40
on a time to *a* a king over them........ Judg 9:8
If in truth ye *a* me king over you....... Judg 9:15
a thee, and put thy raiment upon....... Ruth 3:3
thou shalt *a* him to be captain........... 1Sa 9:16
The LORD sent me to *a* thee to be..... 1Sa 15:1
thou shalt *a* unto me him whom I...... 1Sa 16:3
And the LORD said, Arise, *a* him........ 1Sa 16:12
a not thyself with oil, but as............... 2Sa 14:2
Nathan the prophet *a* him there......... 1Kin 1:34
a Hazael to be king over Syria.............. 1Kin 19:15
thou *a* to be king over Israel............. 1Kin 19:16
thou *a* to be prophet in thy room...... 1Kin 19:16
ye princes, and *a* the shield............... Is 21:5
prophecy, and to *a* the most Holy...... Dan 9:24
neither did I *a* myself at all............... Dan 10:3
a themselves with the chief................. Amos 6:6
thou shalt not *a* thee with oil............ Mic 6:15
a thine head, and wash thy face.......... Mt 6:17
to *a* my body to the burying.............. Mk 14:8

---

that they might come and *a* him........ Mk 16:1
My head with oil thou didst not *a*..... Lk 7:46
a thine eyes with eyesalve, that........... Rev 3:18

ANOINTED

and wafers unleavened *a* with oil....... Ex 29:2
to be a therein, and to be................... Ex 29:29
or unleavened wafers *a* with oil......... Lev 2:4
If the priest that is *a* do sin............. Lev 4:3
the priest that is *a* shall take............ Lev 4:5
the priest that is *a* shall bring........... Lev 4:16
the LORD in the day when he is *a*...... Lev 6:20
is *a* in his stead shall offer it............ Lev 6:22
and unleavened wafers *a* with oil....... Lev 7:12
Israel, in the day that he *a* them....... Lev 7:36
a the tabernacle and that that was.... Lev 8:10
a the altar and all his vessels,........... Lev 8:11
head, and *a* him, to sanctify him....... Lev 8:12
Aaron, the priests which were *a*......... Num 3:3
of unleavened bread *a* with oil.......... Num 6:15
up the tabernacle, and had *a* it......... Num 7:1
had *a* them, and sanctified them....... Num 7:1
altar in the day that it was *a*............. Num 7:10
altar, in the day when it was *a*.......... Num 7:84
of the altar, after that it was *a*.......... Num 7:88
which was *a* with the holy oil............ Num 35:25
king, and exalt the horn of his *a*....... 1Sa 2:10
shall walk before mine *a* for ever....... 1Sa 2:35
a thee to be captain over his.............. 1Sa 10:1
before the LORD, and before his *a*..... 1Sa 12:3
his *a* is witness this day, that............ 1Sa 12:5
the LORD the king over Israel............. 1Sa 15:17
Surely the LORD's *a* is before him..... 1Sa 16:6
a him in the midst of his.................... 1Sa 16:13
unto my master, the LORD's *a*........... 1Sa 24:6
seeing he is the *a* of the LORD.......... 1Sa 24:6
for he is the LORD's *a*....................... 1Sa 24:10
his hand against the LORD's *a*........... 1Sa 26:9
mine hand against the LORD's *a*......... 1Sa 26:11
kept your master, the LORD's *a*.......... 1Sa 26:16
mine hand against the LORD's *a*......... 1Sa 26:23
hand to destroy the LORD's *a*............ 2Sa 1:14
saying, I have slain the LORD's *a*....... 2Sa 1:16
though he had not been *a* with oil..... 2Sa 1:21
there they *a* David king over the........ 2Sa 2:4
of Judah have *a* me king over them... 2Sa 2:7
I am this day weak, though *a* king..... 2Sa 3:39
they *a* David king over Israel............. 2Sa 5:3
they had *a* David king over Israel...... 2Sa 5:17
I *a* thee king over Israel, and I.......... 2Sa 12:7
a himself, and changed his apparel...... 2Sa 12:20
And Absalom, whom we *a* over us...... 2Sa 19:10
because he cursed the LORD's *a*......... 2Sa 19:21
and sheweth mercy to his *a*............... 2Sa 22:51
the *a* of the God of Jacob, and the.... 2Sa 23:1
of the tabernacle, and *a* Solomon...... 1Kin 1:39
prophet have *a* him king in Gihon...... 1Kin 1:45
had *a* him king in the room of his..... 1Kin 5:1
I have *a* thee king over Israel............ 2Kin 9:3
I have *a* thee king over the............... 2Kin 9:6
I have *a* thee king over Israel............ 2Kin 9:12
and they made him king, and *a* him... 2Kin 11:12
a him, and made him king in his......... 2Kin 23:30
they *a* David king over Israel............. 1Chr 11:3
David was *a* king over all Israel......... 1Chr 14:8
Saying, Touch not mine *a*, and do..... 1Chr 16:22
a him unto the LORD to be the............ 1Chr 29:22
turn not away the face of thine *a*...... 2Chr 6:42
whom the LORD had *a* to cut off....... 2Chr 22:7
And Jehoiada and his sons *a*.............. 2Chr 23:11
a them, and carried all the feeble,....... 2Chr 28:15
the LORD, and against his *a*.............. Ps 2:2
and sheweth mercy to his *a*............... Ps 18:50
know I that the LORD saveth his *a*.... Ps 20:6
is the saving strength of his *a*........... Ps 28:8
hath *a* thee with the oil of............... Ps 45:7
and look upon the face of thine *a*...... Ps 84:9
with my holy oil have I *a* him........... Ps 89:20
thou hast been wroth with thine *a*.... Ps 89:38
the footsteps of thine *a*.................... Ps 89:51
I shalt be *a* with fresh oil................. Ps 92:10
Saying, Touch not mine *a*, and do..... Ps 105:15
turn not away the face of thine *a*...... Ps 132:10
I have ordained a lamp for mine *a*..... Ps 132:17
Thus saith the LORD to his *a*............ Is 45:1
because the LORD hath *a* me to........ Is 61:1
the *a* of the LORD, was taken in........ Lam 4:20
from thee, and I *a* thee with oil........ Eze 16:9
Thou art the *a* cherub that............... Eze 28:14
even for salvation with thine *a*.......... Hab 3:13
said he, These are the two *a* ones...... Zec 4:14
a with oil many that were sick,........... Mk 6:13
because he hath *a* me to preach........ Lk 4:18
feet, and *a* them with the ointment... Lk 7:38
but this woman hath *a* my feet.......... Lk 7:46
My head with oil thou didst not *a*..... Lk 7:46
a mine eyes, and said unto me, Go...... Jn 9:11
which *a* the Lord with ointment,....... Jn 11:2
a the feet of Jesus, and wiped his....... Jn 12:3
child Jesus, whom thou hast.............. Acts 4:27
How God *a* Jesus of Nazareth with... Acts 10:38
with you in Christ, and hath *a* us...... 2Cor 1:21
hath *a* thee with the oil of............... Heb 1:9

ANOINTEDST

Beth-el, where thou *a* the pillar......... Gen 31:13

ANOINTEST

thou *a* my head with oil.................... Ps 23:5

ANOINTING

for the light, spices for a *a* oil........... Ex 25:6
Then shalt thou take the *a* oil............ Ex 29:7

upon the altar, and of the *a* oil .... Ex 29:21
it shall be an holy *a* oil .... Ex 30:25
This shall be an holy *a* oil unto .... Ex 30:31
And the *a* oil, and sweet incense .... Ex 31:11
the light, and spices for *a* oil .... Ex 35:8
and his staves, and the *a* oil .... Ex 35:15
for the light, and for the *a* oil .... Ex 35:28
And he made the holy *a* oil .... Ex 37:29
And the golden altar, and the *a* oil .... Ex 39:38
And thou shalt take the *a* oil .... Ex 40:9
for their *a* shall surely be an .... Ex 40:15
is the portion of the *a* of Aaron .... Lev 7:35
of the *a* of his sons, out of the .... Lev 7:35
and the garments, and the *a* oil .... Lev 8:2
And Moses took the *a* oil, and .... Lev 8:10
he poured of the *a* oil upon .... Lev 8:12
And Moses took of the *a* oil .... Lev 8:30
for the *a* oil of the LORD is upon .... Lev 10:7
whose head the *a* oil was poured .... Lev 21:10
for the crown of the *a* oil of his .... Lev 21:12
daily meat offering, and the *a* oil .... Num 4:16
I given them by reason of the *a* .... Num 18:8
be destroyed because of the *a* .... Is 10:27
a him with oil in the name of the .... Jas 5:14
But the *a* which ye have received 1Jn 2:27
but as the same *a* teacheth you of 1Jn 2:27

ANON

word, and *a* with joy receiveth it .... Mt 13:20
fever, and *a* they tell him of her .... Mk 1:30

ANOTHER See PREFACE.

and shalt be turned into *a* man 1Sa 10:6
mine eyes shall behold, and not *a* .... Job 19:27
and let *a* take his office .... Ps 109:8
and discover not *a* secret to a .... Prov 25:9
Let *a* man praise thee, and not .... Prov 27:2
and my glory will I not give to *a* .... Is 42:8
and call his servants by *a* name .... Is 65:15
and thou shalt not be for *a* man .... Hos 3:3
let no man strive, nor reprove *a* .... Hos 4:4
should come, or do we look for *a* .... Mt 11:3
Then said he to *a*, And how much .... Lk 16:7
and he shall give you a Comforter .... Jn 14:16
he that cometh preacheth *a* Jesus 2Cor 11:4
Which is not *a* .... Gal 1:7
in himself alone, and not in *a* .... Gal 6:4
But exhort one *a* daily, while it .... Heb 3:13

ANOTHER'S

may not understand one *a* speech .... Gen 11:7
And if one man's ox hurt *a* .... Ex 21:35
ye also ought to wash one *a* feet .... Jn 13:14
his own, but every man *a* wealth 1Cor 10:24
Bear ye one *a* burdens, and so .... Gal 6:2

ANSWER

a for me in time to come, when it .... Gen 30:33
shall give Pharaoh an *a* of peace .... Gen 41:16
And his brethren could not *a* him .... Gen 45:3
be, if it make thee *a* of peace .... Deut 20:11
And they shall *a* and say, Our hands .... Deut 21:7
and spit in his face, and shall *a* .... Deut 25:9
And all the people shall *a* .... Deut 27:15
Then ye shall *a* them, That the .... Josh 4:7
yea, she returned *a* to herself .... Judg 5:29
then he would *a* him, Nay 1Sa 2:16
what if thy father *a* thee roughly 1Sa 20:10
he could not *a* Abner a word again 2Sa 3:11
see what *a* I shall return to him 2Sa 24:13
And they shall *a*, Because they 1Kin 9:9
advise that I may *a* this people 1Kin 12:6
a them, and speak good words to 1Kin 12:7
give ye that we may *a* this people 1Kin 12:9
was neither voice, nor any to *a* 1Kin 18:29
any salute thee, *a* him not again 2Kin 4:29
was, saying, A him not 2Kin 18:36
ye me to return *a* to this people 2Chr 10:6
we may return *a* to this people 2Chr 10:9
Thus shalt thou *a* the people that 2Chr 10:10
Then sent the king an *a* unto .... Ezr 4:17
then they returned *a* by letter .... Ezr 5:5
Thus they returned us *a* .... Ezr 5:11
peace, and found nothing to *a* .... Neh 5:8
Mordecai commanded to *a* Esther .... Est 4:13
bade them return Mordecai this *a* .... Est 4:15
if there be any that will *a* thee .... Job 5:1
he cannot *a* him one of a thousand .... Job 9:3
How much less shall I *a* him .... Job 9:14
were righteous, yet would I not *a* .... Job 9:15
man, as I am, that I should *a* him .... Job 9:32
Then call thou, and I will *a* .... Job 13:22
or let me speak, and *a* thou me .... Job 13:22
Thou shalt call, and I will *a* thee .... Job 14:15
my servant, and he gave me no *a* .... Job 19:16
do my thoughts cause me to *a* .... Job 20:2
my understanding causeth me to *a* .... Job 20:3
the words which he would *a* me .... Job 23:5
he visiteth, what shall I *a* him .... Job 31:14
is, that the Almighty would *a* me .... Job 31:35
these three men ceased to *a* Job .... Job 32:1
because they had found no *a* .... Job 32:3
Elihu saw that there was in *a* .... Job 32:5
neither will I *a* him with your .... Job 32:14
I will *a* also my part, I also .... Job 32:17
I will open my lips and *a* .... Job 32:20
If thou canst *a* me, set thy words .... Job 33:5
I will *a* thee, that God is .... Job 33:12
thou hast any thing to say, *a* me .... Job 33:32
I will *a* thee, and thy companions .... Job 35:4
There they cry, but none giveth *a* .... Job 35:12
will demand of thee, and *a* thou me .... Job 38:3

that reproveth God, let him *a* thee .... Job 40:2
what shall I *a* thee .... Job 40:4
but I will not *a* .... Job 40:5
have mercy also upon me, and *a* me .... Ps 27:7
in righteousness wilt thou *a* us .... Ps 65:5
for thou wilt *a* me .... Ps 86:7
call upon me, and I will *a* him .... Ps 91:15
the day when I call *a* me speedily .... Ps 102:2
save with thy right hand, and *a* me .... Ps 108:6
to *a* him that reproacheth me .... Ps 119:42
in thy faithfulness *a* me, and in .... Ps 143:1
call upon me, but I will not *a* .... Prov 1:28
A soft *a* turneth away wrath .... Prov 15:1
hath joy by the *a* of his mouth .... Prov 15:23
of the righteous studieth to *a* .... Prov 15:28
the *a* of the tongue, is from the .... Prov 16:1
that thou mightest *a* the words of .... Prov 22:21
his lips that giveth a right *a* .... Prov 24:26
A not *a* fool according to his .... Prov 26:4
A *a* fool according to his folly .... Prov 26:5
that I may *a* him that reproacheth .... Prov 27:11
he understand he will not *a* .... Prov 29:19
I called him, but he gave me no *a* .... Song 5:6
What shall one then *a* the .... Is 14:32
he shall hear it, he will *a* thee .... Is 30:19
was, saying, A him not .... Is 36:21
I asked of them, could *a* a word .... Is 41:28
cry unto him, yet can he not *a* .... Is 46:7
I called, was there none to *a* .... Is 50:2
thou call, and the LORD shall *a* .... Is 58:9
when I called, ye did not *a* .... Is 65:12
that before they call, I will *a* .... Is 65:24
because when I called, none did *a* .... Is 66:4
then shalt thou *a* them, Like as .... Jer 5:19
but they will not *a* thee .... Jer 7:27
Then they shall *a*, Because they .... Jer 22:9
Call unto me, and I will *a* thee .... Jer 33:3
thing the LORD shall *a* you .... Jer 42:4
people which had given him that *a* .... Jer 44:20
I the LORD will *a* him that cometh .... Eze 14:4
I the LORD will *a* him by myself .... Eze 14:7
that thou shalt *a*, For the .... Eze 21:7
careful to *a* thee in this matter .... Dan 3:16
Yea, the LORD will *a* and say unto .... Joel 2:19
for there is no *a* of God .... Mic 3:7
what I shall *a* when I am reproved .... Hab 2:1
beam out of the timber shall *a* it .... Hab 2:11
Then he shall *a*, Those with which .... Zec 13:6
no man was able to *a* him a word .... Mt 22:46
Then shall the righteous *a* him .... Mt 25:37
And the King shall *a* and say unto .... Mt 25:40
Then shall they also *a* him .... Mt 25:44
And he *a* them, saying .... Mt 25:45
a me, and I will tell you by what .... Mk 11:29
a me .... Mk 11:30
neither wist they what to *a* him .... Mk 14:40
And he from within shall *a* .... Lk 11:7
how or what thing ye shall *a* .... Lk 12:11
and he shall *a* and say unto you, I .... Lk 13:25
they could not *a* him again to .... Lk 14:6
and *a* me .... Lk 20:3
and they marvelled at his *a* .... Lk 20:26
meditate before what ye shall *a* .... Lk 21:14
I also ask you, ye will not *a* me .... Lk 22:68
that we may give an *a* to them .... Jn 1:22
But Jesus gave him no *a* .... Jn 19:9
the more cheerfully *a* for himself .... Acts 24:10
have licence to *a* for himself .... Acts 25:16
because I shall *a* for myself this .... Acts 26:2
what saith the *a* of God unto him .... Rom 11:4
Mine *a* to them that do examine me 1Cor 9:3
that ye may have somewhat to *a* 2Cor 5:12
know how ye ought to *a* every man .... Col 4:6
At my first *a* no man stood with 2Ti 4:16
be ready always to give an *a* to 1Pet 3:15
but the *a* of a good conscience 1Pet 3:21

ANSWERABLE

to the hangings of the court .... Ex 38:18

ANSWERED

And Abraham *a* and said .... Gen 18:27
And the children of Heth *a* Abraham .... Gen 23:5
Ephron the Hittite *a* Abraham in .... Gen 23:10
Ephron *a* Abraham, saying unto him .... Gen 23:14
Then Laban and Bethuel *a* and said .... Gen 24:50
And Isaac *a* and said unto Esau .... Gen 27:37
And Isaac his father *a* and said .... Gen 27:39
And Rachel and Leah *a* .... Gen 31:14
And Jacob *a* and said to Laban .... Gen 31:31
and Jacob *a* and said to Laban, What .... Gen 31:36
And Laban *a* and said unto Jacob .... Gen 31:43
And the sons of Jacob *a* Shechem .... Gen 34:13
who *a* me in the day of my .... Gen 35:3
And Joseph *a* and said, This is the .... Gen 40:18
Joseph *a* Pharaoh, saying, It is .... Gen 41:16
And Reuben *a* them, saying, Spake I .... Gen 42:22
And they *a*, Thy servant our father .... Gen 43:28
And Moses *a* and said, But, behold .... Ex 4:1
And Miriam *a* them, Sing ye to the .... Ex 15:21
And all the people *a* together .... Ex 19:8
spake, and God *a* him by a voice .... Ex 19:19
all the people *a* with one voice .... Ex 24:3
of Moses, one of his young men, *a* .... Num 11:28
And Balaam *a* and said unto the .... Num 22:18
And he *a* and said, Must I not take .... Num 23:12
But Balaam *a* and said unto Balak .... Num 23:26
Gad and the children of Reuben *a* .... Num 32:31
And ye *a* me, and said, The thing .... Deut 1:14
Then ye *a* and said unto me, We .... Deut 1:41
they *a* Joshua, saying, All that .... Josh 1:16
And the men *a* her, Our life for .... Josh 2:14

Achan *a* Joshua, and said, Indeed I .... Josh 7:20
And Joshua *a* them, If thou be a .... Josh 9:24
Who *a*, Give me a blessing .... Josh 15:19
And Joshua *a* them, If thou be a .... Josh 17:15
and the half tribe of Manasseh *a* .... Josh 22:21
And the people *a* and said, God .... Josh 24:16
Her wise ladies *a* her, yea, she .... Judg 5:29
And his fellow *a* and said, This is .... Judg 7:14
the men of Penuel *a* him as he .... Judg 8:8
as the men of Succoth had *a* him .... Judg 8:8
And they *a*, As thou art, so were .... Judg 8:18
And they *a*, We will willingly give .... Judg 8:25
king of the children of Ammon *a* .... Judg 11:13
And they *a*, Samson, the son in law .... Judg 15:6
And they *a*, To bind Samson are we .... Judg 15:10
That the five men that went to .... Judg 18:14
But none *a* .... Judg 19:28
of the woman that was slain, *a* .... Judg 20:4
And they *a* him, The LORD bless .... Ruth 2:4
that was set over the reapers *a* .... Ruth 2:6
And Boaz *a* and said unto her, It .... Ruth 2:11
And she *a*, I am Ruth thine .... Ruth 3:9
And Hannah *a* and said, No, my lord 1Sa 1:15
Then Eli *a* and said, Go in peace 1Sa 1:17
and he *a*, Here am I 1Sa 3:4
then Samuel *a*, Speak 1Sa 3:10
And he *a*, Here am I 1Sa 3:16
and the messenger *a* and said 1Sa 4:17
But she *a* not, neither did she 1Sa 4:20
And they *a*, Let the ark of the God 1Sa 6:4
They *a*, Five golden emerods, and 1Sa 6:4
And the servant *a* Saul again 1Sa 9:8
And they *a* them, and said, He is 1Sa 9:12
And Samuel *a* Saul, and said, I am 1Sa 9:19
And Saul *a* and said, Am not I a 1Sa 9:21
And one of the same place *a* 1Sa 10:12
And the LORD *a*, Behold, he hath 1Sa 10:22
And Nahash the Ammonite *a* them 1Sa 11:2
And they *a*, He is witness 1Sa 12:5
men of the garrison *a* Jonathan 1Sa 14:12
Then *a* one of the people, and said 1Sa 14:28
But he *a* him not that day 1Sa 14:37
among all the people that *a* him 1Sa 14:39
And Saul *a*, God do so and more also 1Sa 14:44
Then *a* one of the servants, and 1Sa 16:18
the people *a* him after this 1Sa 17:27
the people *a* him again after the 1Sa 17:30
And David *a*, I am the son of thy 1Sa 17:58
the women *a* one another as they 1Sa 18:7
And Michal *a* Saul, He said unto me 1Sa 19:17
And Jonathan *a* Saul, David 1Sa 20:28
Jonathan *a* Saul his father, and 1Sa 20:32
And the priest *a* David, and said 1Sa 21:4
David *a* the priest, and said unto 1Sa 21:5
Then *a* Doeg the Edomite, which 1Sa 22:9
And he *a*, Here I am, my lord 1Sa 22:12
Then Ahimelech *a* the king 1Sa 22:14
And the LORD *a* him and said, Arise 1Sa 23:4
Nabal *a* David's servants, and said 1Sa 25:10
Then *a* David and said to Ahimelech 1Sa 26:6
Then Abner *a* and said, Who art 1Sa 26:14
And David *a* and said, Behold the 1Sa 26:22
of the LORD, the LORD *a* him not 1Sa 28:6
And Saul *a*, I am sore distressed 1Sa 28:15
And Achish *a* and said to David, I 1Sa 29:9
And he *a* him, Pursue 1Sa 30:8
Then *a* all the wicked men and men 1Sa 30:22
And he *a*, That the people are fled 2Sa 1:4
And I *a*, Here am I 2Sa 1:7
I *a* him, I am an Amalekite 2Sa 1:8
And he *a*, I am the son of a 2Sa 1:13
And he *a*, I am 2Sa 1:20
David *a* Rechab and Baanah his 2Sa 4:9
And he *a*, Behold thy servant 2Sa 9:6
And she *a* him, Nay, my brother, do 2Sa 13:12
son of Shimeah David's brother, *a* 2Sa 13:32
And she *a*, I am indeed a widow 2Sa 14:5
Then the king *a* and said unto the 2Sa 14:18
And the woman *a* and said, As thy 2Sa 14:19
And Absalom *a* Joab, Behold, I sent 2Sa 14:32
Ittai *a* the king, and said, As the 2Sa 15:21
But the people *a*, Thou shalt not 2Sa 18:3
And Ahimaaz *a*, When Joab sent the 2Sa 18:29
And Cushi *a*, The enemies of my 2Sa 18:32
But Abishai the son of Zeruiah *a* 2Sa 19:21
And he *a*, My lord, O king, my 2Sa 19:26
men of Judah *a* the men of Israel 2Sa 19:42
men of Israel *a* the men of Judah 2Sa 19:43
And he, I am 2Sa 20:17
And he *a*, I am 2Sa 20:17
And Joab *a* and said, Far be it, far 2Sa 20:20
And the LORD *a*, It is for Saul, and 2Sa 21:1
they *a* the king, The man that 2Sa 21:5
unto the LORD, but he *a* them not 2Sa 22:42
Then king David *a* and said, Call 1Kin 1:28
the son of Jehoiada *a* the king 1Kin 1:36
And Jonathan *a* and said to Adonijah 1Kin 1:43
And king Solomon *a* and said unto 1Kin 2:22
Thus said Joab, and thus he *a* me 1Kin 2:30
Then the king *a* and said, Give her 1Kin 3:27
And he *a*, Nothing 1Kin 11:22
the king *a* the people roughly, and 1Kin 12:13
unto them, the people *a* the king 1Kin 12:16
And the king *a* and said unto the 1Kin 13:6
And he *a* him, I am 1Kin 18:8
And he *a*, I have not troubled 1Kin 18:18
the people *a* him not a word 1Kin 18:21
And all the people *a* and said, It 1Kin 18:24

was no voice, nor any that a............ 1Kin 18:26
And the king of Israel a and said.... 1Kin 20:4
And the king of Israel a and said,.. 1Kin 20:11
And he a, Thou........................... 1Kin 20:14
and he a, I will not give thee my ... 1Kin 21:6
And he a, I have found thee............ 1Kin 21:20
And he a him, Go, and prosper......... 1Kin 22:15
And they a him, He was an hairy 2Kin 1:8
And Elijah a and said to the.......... 2Kin 1:10
And he a and said unto him, O man .. 2Kin 1:11
And Elijah a and said unto them, If .. 2Kin 1:12
And he a, Yea, I know it................. 2Kin 2:5
And he a, The way through the........ 2Kin 3:8
the king of Israel's servants a 2Kin 3:11
And she a, I dwell among mine own... 2Kin 4:13
And Gehazi a, Verily she hath no..... 2Kin 4:14
And she a, It is well.................... 2Kin 4:26
And he a, Go ye........................... 2Kin 6:2
And he a, I will go....................... 2Kin 6:3
And he a, Fear not....................... 2Kin 6:16
And he a, Thou shalt not smite 2Kin 6:22
And she a, This woman said unto me. 2Kin 6:28
the king leaned a the man of God 2Kin 7:2
And one of his servants a and said,... 2Kin 7:13
that lord a the man of God, and....... 2Kin 7:19
And he a, Because I know the evil 2Kin 8:12
And Elisha a, The LORD hath shewed . 2Kin 8:13
And he a, He told me that thou........ 2Kin 8:14
And Jehu a, What hast thou to do 2Kin 9:19
And he a, What peace, so long as 2Kin 9:22
And they a, We are the brethren of .. 2Kin 10:13
And Jehonadab a, It is 2Kin 10:15
their peace, and a him not a word 2Kin 18:36
And Hezekiah a, It is a light............ 2Kin 20:10
And Hezekiah a, All the things......... 2Kin 20:15
David went out to meet them, and a . 1Chr 12:17
And Joab a, The LORD make his 1Chr 21:3
he a him from heaven by fire upon ... 1Chr 21:26
David saw that the LORD had a him . 1Chr 21:28
the king of Tyre a in writing........... 2Chr 2:11
And it shall be so, Because they 2Chr 7:22
And the king a them roughly........... 2Chr 10:13
a them after the advice of the......... 2Chr 10:14
unto them, the people a the king..... 2Chr 10:16
he a him, I am as thou art, and my .. 2Chr 18:3
And the man of God a, The LORD is.. 2Chr 25:9
Then Hezekiah a and said, Now ye... 2Chr 29:31
of the house of Zadok a him........... 2Chr 31:10
And Hilkiah a and said to Shaphan.. 2Chr 34:15
she a them, Thus saith the LORD 2Chr 34:23
one of the sons of Elam, a............. Ezr 10:2
Then all the congregation a........... Ezr 10:12
Then a I them, and said unto them,.. Neh 2:20
I a them after the same manner....... Neh 6:4
And all the people a, Amen, Amen,... Neh 8:6
Memucan a before the king and the .. Est 1:16
And Esther a, If it seem good unto... Est 5:4
Then a Esther, and said, My........... Est 5:7
Haman a the king, For the man....... Est 6:7
Then Esther the queen a and said,... Est 7:3
Then the king Ahasuerus a .... Est 7:5
Then Satan a the LORD, and.......... Job 1:7
Then Satan a the LORD, and said,.... Job 1:9
Satan a the LORD, and said, From ... Job 2:2
Satan a the LORD, and said, Skin .... Job 2:4
Then Eliphaz the Temanite a .... Job 4:1
But Job a and said,...................... Job 6:1
Then a Bildad the Shuhite,............. Job 8:1
Then Job a and said,..................... Job 9:1
If I had called, and he had a me ..... Job 9:16
Then a Zophar the Naamathite, and .. Job 11:1
not the multitude of words be a ...... Job 11:2
And Job a and said,...................... Job 12:1
Then a Eliphaz the Temanite, and ... Job 15:1
Then Job a and said,..................... Job 16:1
Then a Bildad the Shuhite, and....... Job 18:1
Then Job a and said,..................... Job 19:1
Then a Zophar the Naamathite, and .. Job 20:1
But Job a and said,...................... Job 21:1
Then Eliphaz the Temanite a .... Job 22:1
Then Job a and said,..................... Job 23:1
Then a Bildad the Shuhite, and....... Job 25:1
But Job a and said,...................... Job 26:1
the son of Barachel the Buzite a ..... Job 32:6
Job, or that a his words................. Job 32:12
They were amazed, they a no more.. Job 32:15
but stood still, and a no more......... Job 32:16
Furthermore Elihu a and said,........ Job 34:1
Then the LORD a Job out of the ...... Job 38:1
Moreover the LORD a Job, and said.. Job 40:1
Then Job a the LORD, and said,...... Job 40:3
Then a the LORD unto Job out of .... Job 40:6
Then Job a the LORD, and said,...... Job 42:1
unto the LORD, but he a them not .... Ps 18:41
I a thee in the secret place of .... Ps 81:7
upon the LORD, and he a them .... Ps 99:6
the LORD a me, and set me in a ...... Ps 118:5
And he a, Until the cities be.......... Is 6:11
And he a and said, Babylon is......... Is 21:9
their peace, and a him not a word ... Is 36:21
And Hezekiah a, All that is in .... Is 39:4
and I called you, but ye a not .... Jer 7:13
Then a I, and said, So be it, O........ Jer 11:5
his brother, What hath the LORD a .. Jer 23:35
What hath the LORD a thee............ Jer 23:37
unto them, but they have not a .... Jer 35:17
Then Baruch a them, He pronounced .. Jer 36:18
in Pathros, a Jeremiah, saying,....... Jer 44:15
Then I a them, The word of them .... Eze 24:20
And I a, O Lord GOD, thou knowest.. Eze 37:3

The king a and said to the............ Dan 2:5
They a again and said, Let the......... Dan 2:7
The king a and said, I know of........ Dan 2:8
The Chaldeans a before the king,.... Dan 2:10
Then Daniel a with counsel and....... Dan 2:14
He a and said to Arioch the king's ... Dan 2:15
Daniel a and said, Blessed be the .... Dan 2:20
The king a and said to Daniel,......... Dan 2:26
Daniel a in the presence of the........ Dan 2:27
The king a unto Daniel, and said,..... Dan 2:47
Meshach, and Abed-nego, a............ Dan 3:16
They a and said unto the king,........ Dan 3:24
He a and said, Lo, I see four men ..... Dan 3:25
Belteshazzar a and said, My lord,..... Dan 4:19
Then Daniel a and said before the ... Dan 5:17
Then Daniel a and said, The thing is.. Dan 6:12
Then a they and said before the...... Dan 6:13
Then a Amos, and said to Amaziah,.. Amos 7:14
what Balaam the son of Beor a ...... Mic 6:5
And he a me, and said, Write.......... Hab 2:2
And the priests a and said, No......... Hag 2:12
And the priests a and said, It.......... Hag 2:13
Then a Haggai, and said, So is........ Hag 2:14
stood among the myrtle trees a .... Zec 1:10
they a the angel of the LORD that.... Zec 1:11
Then the angel of the LORD a .... Zec 1:12
the LORD the angel that talked....... Zec 1:13
And he a me, These are the horns .... Zec 1:19
And he a and spake unto those that .. Zec 3:4
So I a and spake to the angel that .... Zec 4:4
the angel that talked with me a .... Zec 4:5
Then he a and spake unto me,........ Zec 4:6
Then a I, and said unto him, What ... Zec 4:11
I a again, and said unto him, What ... Zec 4:12
And he a me and said, Knowest thou.. Zec 4:13
And I a, I see a flying roll.............. Zec 5:2
Then I a and said unto the angel .... Zec 6:4
And the angel a and said unto me,.. Zec 6:5
But he a and said, It is written,....... Mt 4:4
The centurion a and said, Lord, I .... Mt 8:8
Jesus a and said unto them, Go and.. Mt 11:4
At that time Jesus a and said, I ...... Mt 11:25
the scribes and of the Pharisees a .. Mt 12:38
But he a and said unto them, An..... Mt 12:39
But he a and said unto them that .... Mt 12:48
He a and said unto them, Because ... Mt 13:11
He a and said unto them, He that ... Mt 13:37
And Peter a him and said, Lord, if .. Mt 14:28
But he a and said unto them, Why .. Mt 15:3
And Jesus a and said, Every man,.... Mt 15:13
Then a Peter and said unto him,...... Mt 15:15
But he a not a word..................... Mt 15:23
But he a and said, I am not sent ..... Mt 15:24
But he a and said, It is not meet ..... Mt 15:26
Then Jesus a and said unto her, O .. Mt 15:28
He a and said unto them, When it ... Mt 16:2
And Simon Peter a and said, Thou... Mt 16:16
And Jesus a and said unto him,...... Mt 16:17
a Peter, and said unto Jesus,......... Mt 17:4
And Jesus a and said unto them,.... Mt 17:11
Then Jesus a and said, O faithless... Mt 17:17
And he a and said unto them, Have . Mt 19:4
And Peter a and said unto him,....... Mt 19:27
But he a one of them, and said,....... Mt 20:13
But Jesus a and said, Ye know not ... Mt 20:22
Jesus a and said unto them, My...... Mt 21:21
And Jesus a and said unto them, I ... Mt 21:24
they a Jesus, and said, We cannot ... Mt 21:27
He a and said, I will not................ Mt 21:29
And he a and said, I go sir............. Mt 21:30
And Jesus a and spake unto them.... Mt 22:1
Jesus a and said unto them, Ye do... Mt 22:29
And Jesus a and said unto them,..... Mt 24:4
But the wise a, saying, Not so......... Mt 25:9
But he a and said, Verily I say........ Mt 25:12
His lord a and said unto him, Thou .. Mt 25:26
And he a and said, He that dippeth .. Mt 26:23
Then Judas, which betrayed him, a.. Mt 26:25
Peter a and said unto him, Though... Mt 26:33
And the high priest a and said unto.. Mt 26:63
They a and said, He is guilty of ...... Mt 26:66
priests and elders, he a nothing ...... Mt 27:12
And he a him to never a word .... Mt 27:14
The governor a and said unto them.. Mt 27:21
Then a all the people, and said,....... Mt 27:25
And the angel a and said unto the .. Mt 28:5
he a them, saying, Who is my .... Mk 3:33
And he a, saying, My name is .... Mk 5:9
He a and said unto them, Give ye ... Mk 6:37
And he a and said unto them, Well .. Mk 7:6
And she a and said unto him, Yes,.. Mk 7:28
And his disciples a him, From .... Mk 8:4
And they a, John the Baptist........... Mk 8:28
And Peter a and said to Jesus,....... Mk 9:5
And he a and told them, Elias........ Mk 9:12
And one of the multitude a............ Mk 9:17
And John a him, saying, Master, we.. Mk 9:38
And he a and said unto them, What.. Mk 10:3
And Jesus a and said unto them, For. Mk 10:5
And he a and said unto him, Master, Mk 10:20
And Jesus a and said, Verily I say.... Mk 10:29
And Jesus a and said unto him, What. Mk 10:51
And Jesus a and said unto it, No .... Mk 11:14
And he a and said unto them, I....... Mk 11:29
And they a and said unto Jesus, We.. Mk 11:33
that he had a them well, asked........ Mk 12:28
And Jesus a him, The first of all..... Mk 12:29
Jesus saw that he a discreetly........ Mk 12:34
And Jesus a and said, while he....... Mk 12:35
And he a and said unto them, It is... Mk 14:20

And Jesus a and said unto them, Are.. Mk 14:48
he held his peace, and a nothing .... Mk 14:61
but he a nothing......................... Mk 15:3
But Jesus yet a nothing................ Mk 15:5
But Pilate a them, saying, Will........ Mk 15:9
And Pilate a and said again unto.... Mk 15:12
And the angel a and said unto her,.. Lk 1:35
And his mother a and said, Not so .. Lk 1:60
John a, saying unto them all, I .... Lk 3:16
And Jesus a him, saying, It is .... Lk 4:4
And Jesus a and said unto him, Get.. Lk 4:8
Simon a and said, I suppose that .... Lk 7:43
And he a and said unto them, My ... Lk 8:21
he a him, saying, Fear not............. Lk 8:50
And John a and said, Master, we saw.. Lk 9:49
said unto him, Thou hast a right .... Lk 10:28
And Jesus a and said unto him,...... Lk 10:41
Then a one of the lawyers, and....... Lk 11:45
the synagogue a with indignation ... Lk 13:14
The Lord then a him, and said,....... Lk 13:15
a them, saying, Which of you......... Lk 14:5
he a them and said, The kingdom of.. Lk 17:20
And they a and said unto him, Where.. Lk 17:37
And he a and said unto them, I tell ... Lk 19:40
And he a and said unto them, I will.. Lk 20:3
And they a, that they could not....... Lk 20:7
They a and said, Caesar's.............. Lk 20:24
And Jesus a and said, Suffer ye...... Lk 22:51
he a him and said, Thou sayest it ... Lk 23:3
but he a him nothing.................... Lk 23:9
And he a, No.............................. Jn 1:21
John a them, saying, I baptize......... Jn 1:26
Jesus a and said unto him, Before... Jn 1:48
Nathanael a and saith unto him,..... Jn 1:49
Jesus a and said unto him, Because .. Jn 1:50
Jesus a and said unto him, Verily,.... Jn 2:18
Jesus a and said unto them,........... Jn 2:19
Jesus a and said unto him, Verily,.... Jn 3:3
Jesus a, Verily, verily, I say .... Jn 3:5
Nicodemus a and said unto him, How.. Jn 3:9
Jesus a and said unto him, Art thou .. Jn 3:10
John a and said, A man can receive .. Jn 3:27
Jesus a and said unto her, If thou.... Jn 4:10
Jesus a and said unto her,............. Jn 4:13
The woman a and said, I have no .... Jn 4:17
The impotent man a him, Sir, I........ Jn 5:7
He a them, He that made me whole,.. Jn 5:11
But Jesus a them, My Father.......... Jn 5:17
Jesus a and said unto them, Verily .. Jn 5:19
Philip a him, Two hundred............. Jn 6:7
Jesus a them and said, Verily,........ Jn 6:26
Jesus a and said unto them, This.... Jn 6:29
Jesus therefore a and said unto...... Jn 6:43
Then Simon Peter a him, Lord, to.... Jn 6:68
Jesus a them, Have not I chosen .... Jn 6:70
Jesus a them, and said, My .... Jn 7:16
The people a and said, Thou hast a.. Jn 7:20
Jesus a and said unto them, I have .. Jn 7:21
The officers a, Never man spake..... Jn 7:46
Then a them the Pharisees, Are ye .. Jn 7:47
They a and said unto him, Art thou . Jn 7:52
Jesus a and said unto them, Though .. Jn 8:14
Jesus a, Ye neither know me, nor .... Jn 8:19
They a him, We be Abraham's seed,.. Jn 8:33
Jesus a them, Verily, verily, I .... Jn 8:34
They a and said unto him, Abraham .. Jn 8:39
Then a the Jews, and said unto him.. Jn 8:48
Jesus a, I have not a devil............. Jn 8:49
Jesus a, If I honour myself, my....... Jn 8:54
Jesus a, Neither hath this man....... Jn 9:3
He a and said, A man that is.......... Jn 9:11
His parents a them and said, We .... Jn 9:20
Jesus a and said, Whether he be a .. Jn 9:25
He a them, I have told you............. Jn 9:27
The man a and said unto him, Why .. Jn 9:30
They a and said unto him, Thou ..... Jn 9:34
He a and said, Who is he, Lord,...... Jn 9:36
Jesus a them, I told you, and ye ..... Jn 10:25
The Jews a him, saying, For a........ Jn 10:33
Jesus a them, Is it not written .... Jn 10:34
Jesus a, Are there not twelve......... Jn 11:9
And Jesus a them, saying, The hour .. Jn 12:23
Jesus a and said, This voice came... Jn 12:30
The people a him, We have heard.... Jn 12:34
Jesus a and said unto him, What I ... Jn 13:7
Jesus a him, If I wash thee not,...... Jn 13:8
Jesus a, He it is, to whom I............ Jn 13:26
Jesus a him, Whither I go, thou ..... Jn 13:36
Jesus a him, Wilt thou lay down ..... Jn 13:38
Jesus a and said unto him, If a ...... Jn 14:23
Jesus a them, Do ye now believe .... Jn 16:31
Jesus a, I am Jesus of Nazareth..... Jn 18:5
Jesus a, I have told you that I........ Jn 18:8
Jesus a him, I spake openly to .... Jn 18:20
Jesus a him, If I have spoken......... Jn 18:23
Jesus a and said unto him, If he ..... Jn 18:30
Jesus a him, Sayest thou this......... Jn 18:34
Pilate a, Am I a Jew.................... Jn 18:35
Jesus a, My kingdom is not of........ Jn 18:36
Jesus a, Thou sayest that I am a .... Jn 18:37
The Jews a him, We have a law, and.. Jn 19:7
Jesus a, Thou couldest have no ..... Jn 19:11
The chief priests a, We have no...... Jn 19:15
Pilate a, What I have written I........ Jn 19:22
And Thomas a and said unto him, My .. Jn 20:28
They a him, No........................... Jn 21:5
he a unto the people, Ye men of ..... Acts 3:12
But Peter and John a and said unto .. Acts 4:19
Peter a unto her, Tell me whether ... Acts 5:8

Peter and the other apostles *a*............ Acts 5:29
Then *a* Simon, and said, Pray ye to ..... Acts 8:24
And the eunuch *a* Philip, and said,...... Acts 8:34
And he *a* and said, I believe that......... Acts 8:37
Then Ananias *a*, Lord, I have .... Acts 9:13
Then *a* Peter,................................... Acts 10:46
But the voice *a* me again from .... Acts 11:9
had held their peace, James *a* .... Acts 15:13
And the evil spirit *a* and said,............. Acts 19:15
Then Paul *a*, What mean ye to weep. Acts 21:13
And *a*, Who art thou, Lord................... Acts 22:8
And the chief captain *a*, With a.......... Acts 22:28
had beckoned unto him to speak, *a* .. Acts 24:10
to come, Felix trembled, and *a*.......... Acts 24:25
But Festus *a*, that Paul should be...... Acts 25:4
While he *a* for himself, Neither .... Acts 25:8
a Paul, and said, Wilt thou go up...... Acts 25:9
had conferred with the council, *a*...... Acts 25:12
To whom I *a*, It is not the manner ..... Acts 25:16
forth the hand, and *a* for himself....... Acts 26:1
And one of the elders *a*, saying......... Rev 7:13

ANSWEREDST
Thou *a* them, O LORD our God........... Ps 99:8
In the day when I cried thou *a* me .... Ps 138:3

ANSWEREST
of Ner, saying, *A* thou not, Abner...... 1Sa 26:14
that emboldenest thee that thou *a* .... Job 16:3
and said unto him, *A* thou nothing..... Mt 26:62
Jesus, saying, *A* thou nothing............ Mk 14:60
him again, saying, *A* thou nothing..... Mk 15:4
A thou the high priest so................... Jn 18:22

ANSWERETH
a me no more, neither by prophets.... 1Sa 28:15
and the God that *a* by fire 1Kin 18:24
who calleth upon God, and he *a* him. Job 12:4
He that *a* a matter before he............. Prov 18:13
but the rich *a* roughly....................... Prov 18:23
As in water face *a* to face .... Prov 27:19
because God *a* him in the joy of .... Eccl 5:20
but money *a* all things...................... Eccl 10:19
And Peter *a* and saith unto him,....... Mk 8:29
He *a* him, and saith, O faithless .... Mk 9:19
But Jesus *a* again, and saith unto..... Mk 10:24
He *a* and saith unto them, He that .... Lk 3:11
a to Jerusalem which now is, and....... Gal 4:25

ANSWERING
Jesus *a* said unto him, Suffer it......... Mt 3:15
Jesus *a* saith unto them, Have .... Mk 11:22
Jesus *a* saith unto them, Neither ...... Mk 11:33
Jesus *a* saith unto them, Render to ... Mk 12:17
Jesus *a* said unto them, Do ye not ... Mk 12:24
Jesus *a* said unto him, Seest thou.... Mk 13:2
Jesus them began to say, Take .... Mk 13:5
he *a* said unto him, Thou sayest .... Mk 15:2
the angel *a* said unto him, I am......... Lk 1:19
Jesus *a* said unto him, It is said .... Lk 4:12
Simon *a* said unto him, Master, we ... Lk 5:5
he *a* said unto them, What reason .... Lk 5:22
Jesus *a* said unto them, They that .... Lk 5:31
Jesus *a* them said, Have ye not .... Lk 6:3
Then Jesus *a* said unto them, Go...... Lk 7:22
Jesus *a* said unto him, Simon, ... Lk 7:40
They *a* said, John the Baptist............ Lk 9:19
Peter *a* said, The Christ of God......... Lk 9:20
And Jesus *a* said, O Jerusalem .... Lk 9:41
he *a* said, Thou shalt love the .... Lk 10:27
And Jesus *a* said, A certain man ...... Lk 10:30
Jesus *a* said unto them, Suppose..... Lk 13:2
he *a* said unto him, Lord, let it.......... Lk 13:8
Jesus *a* spake unto the lawyers and . Lk 14:3
he *a* said to his father, Lo,............... Lk 15:29
And Jesus *a* said, Were there not ..... Lk 17:17
Jesus *a* said unto them, The............. Lk 20:34
certain of the scribes *a* said............. Lk 20:39
But the other *a* rebuked him............. Lk 23:40
Jesus *a* said unto him, Art thou only *a* .. Lk 24:18
not *a* again .... Titus 2:9

ANSWERS
seeing in your *a* there remaineth....... Job 21:34
because of his *a* for wicked men .... Job 34:36
at his understanding and *a* .... Lk 2:47

ANT
Go to the *a*, thou sluggard................ Prov 6:6

ANTHOTHIJAH See ANTOTHIJAH.

ANTICHRIST
ye have heard that *a* shall come........ 1Jn 2:18
He is *a*, that denieth the Father......... 1Jn 2:22
and this is that spirit of *a* 1Jn 4:3
This is a deceiver and an *a*............... 2Jn 7

ANTICHRISTS
come, even now are there many *a* 1Jn 2:18

ANTIOCH (*an'-te-ok*)
1. A city in Syria.
and Nicolas a proselyte of *A*............. Acts 6:5
far as Phenice, and Cyprus, and *A*... Acts 11:19
which, when they were come to *A*..... Acts 11:20
that he should go as far as *A*............ Acts 11:22
found him, he brought him unto *A*..... Acts 11:26
were called Christians first in *A*........ Acts 11:26
prophets from Jerusalem unto *A*....... Acts 11:27
that was at *A* certain prophets.......... Acts 13:1
And thence sailed to *A*, from .... Acts 14:26
their own company to *a* with Paul..... Acts 15:22
which are of the Gentiles in *A* .... Acts 15:23
were dismissed, they came to *A*....... Acts 15:30

also and Barnabas continued in *A*.... Acts 15:35
the church, he went down to *A* .... Acts 18:22
But when Peter was come to *A*.......... Gal 2:11
2. A city in Pisidia.
Perga, they came to *A* in Pisidia...... Acts 13:14
came thither certain Jews from *A*..... Acts 14:19
to Lystra, and to Iconium, and *A* ...... Acts 14:21
which came unto me at *A*, at............ 2Ti 3:11

ANTIPAS (*an'-tip-as*) A Christian martyr.
wherein *A* was my faithful martyr..... Rev 2:13

ANTIPATRIS (*an-tip'-at-ris*) A city in northern Palestine.
and brought him by night to *A*.......... Acts 23:31

ANTIQUITY
whose *a* is of ancient days............... Is 23:7

ANTIOCHAB (*an-to-thi'-jah*) Son of Shashak.
And Hananiah, and Elam, and *A*....... 1Chr 8:24

ANTOTHITE (*an'-to-thite*) See ANETOTHITE. A native of Anathoth.
Ikkesh the Tekoite, Abiezer the *A*..... 1Chr 11:28
and Berachah, and Jehu the *A*.......... 1Chr 12:3

ANTS
The *a* are a people not strong, ... Prov 30:25

ANUB (*a'-nub*) A descendant of Judah.
And Coz begat *A*, and Zobebah, and . 1Chr 4:8

ANVIL
the hammer him that smote the *a*...... Is 41:7

ANY See PREFACE.

APACE
And he came *a*, and drew near 2Sa 18:25
Kings of armies did flee *a* .... Ps 68:12
are beaten down, and are fled *a*........ Jer 46:5

APART
That thou shalt set *a* unto the........... Ex 13:12
she shall be put *a* seven days........... Lev 15:19
she is put *a* for her uncleanness ...... Lev 18:19
a him that is godly for himself .... Ps 4:3
her that was set *a* for pollution .... Eze 22:10
family of the house of David *a* .... Zec 12:12
of David *a*, and their wives *a* .... Zec 12:12
of Nathan *a*, and their wives *a* .... Zec 12:12
of Levi *a*, and their wives *a*............ Zec 12:13
of Shimei *a*, and their wives *a* .... Zec 12:13
family *a*, and their wives *a*............. Zec 12:14
by ship into a desert place *a*............. Mt 14:13
went up into a mountain to pray .... Mt 14:23
them up into an high mountain *a* ...... Mt 17:1
came the disciples to Jesus *a* .... Mt 17:19
the twelve disciples *a* in the way...... Mt 20:17
Come ye yourselves *a* into a .... Mk 6:31
an high mountain *a* by themselves.... Mk 9:2
Wherefore lay *a* all filthiness and..... Jas 1:21

APELLES (*a-pel'-leze*) A Christian acquaintance of Paul.
Salute *A* approved in Christ .... Rom 16:10

APES
gold, and silver, ivory, and *a*............. 1Kin 10:22
gold, and silver, ivory, and *a*............. 2Chr 9:21

APHARSACHITES (*a-far'-sak-ites*) See APHARSATHCHITES, an Assyrian tribe.
and his companions the *A*, which ...... Ezr 5:6
and your companions the *A*............... Ezr 6:6

APHARSATHCHITES (*a-far'-sath-kites*) See APHARSATHCHITES, APHARSITES. Same as Apharsachites.
the Dinaites, the *A*,.......................... Ezr 4:9

APHARSITES (*a-far'-sites*) See APHARSATHCHITES. Same as Apharsachites
the Tarpelites, the *A*......................... Ezr 4:9

APHEK (*a'-fek*) See APHIK.
1. A Canaanite city.
The king of *A*, one .... Josh 12:18
and the Philistines pitched in *A* 1Sa 4:1
together all their armies to *A* 1Sa 29:1
2. A city in Asher.
is beside the Sidonians, unto *A* .... Josh 13:4
Ummah also, and *A*, and Rehob....... Josh 19:30
3. Place where Ahab defeated Benhadad.
the Syrians, and went up to *A* 1Kin 20:26
But the rest fled to *A*, into the.......... 1Kin 20:30
thou shalt smite the Syrians in *A*...... 2Kin 13:17

APHEKAH (*a-fe'-kah*) A city in Judah.
and Beth-tappuah, and *A*................. Josh 15:53

APHIAH (*af-i'-ah*) An ancestor of Saul.
son of Bechorath, the son of *A*........ 1Sa 9:1

APHIK (*a'-fik*) See APHEK. Same as Aphek 2.
Achzib, nor of Helbah, nor of *A*....... Judg 1:31

APHRAH (*af'-rah*) See BETH-LEAPHRAH, OPHRAH. A city in Benjamin.
in the house of *A* roll thyself in........ Mic 1:10

APHSES (*af'-seze*) A Levite chief.
to Hezir, the eighteenth to *A* 1Chr 24:15

APIECE
take five shekels by the poll .... Num 3:47
incense, weighing ten shekels *a* ...... Num 7:86
of their princes gave him a rod *a* ..... Num 17:6
brass, of eighteen cubits high *a* 1Kin 7:15

Every one had four faces *a*............... Eze 10:21
And the doors had two leaves *a* .... Eze 41:24
neither have two coats *a*.................. Lk 9:3
containing two or three firkins *a*....... Jn 2:6

APOLLONIA (*ap-ol-lo'-ne-ah*) A city in Macedonia.
passed through Amphipolis and *A*.... Acts 17:1

APOLLOS (*ap-ol'-los*) A Christian Jew from Alexandria.
And a certain Jew named *A*, born at. Acts 18:24
while *A* was at Corinth, Paul.............. Acts 19:1
and I of *A*....................................... 1Cor 1:12
and another, I am of *A*..................... 1Cor 3:4
Who then is Paul, and who is *A*........ 1Cor 3:5
I have planted, *A* watered 1Cor 3:6
Whether Paul, or *A*, or Cephas, or ... 1Cor 3:22
to myself and to *A* for your sakes..... 1Cor 4:6
As touching our brother *A* 1Cor 16:12
A on their journey diligently,............. Titus 3:13

APOLLYON (*ap-ol'-le-on*) The angel of the Abyss.
the Greek tongue hath his name *A*.... Rev 9:11

APOSTLE
Jesus Christ, called to be an *a*......... Rom 1:1
as I am the *a* of the Gentiles............ Rom 11:13
called to be an *a* of Jesus Christ...... 1Cor 1:1
Am I not an *a*................................... 1Cor 9:1
If I be not an *a* unto others............... 1Cor 9:2
am not meet to be called an *a* 1Cor 15:9
an *a* of Jesus Christ by the will........ 2Cor 1:1
Truly the signs of an *a* were 2Cor 12:12
Paul, an *a*, (not of men, neither .... Gal 1:1
an *a* of Jesus Christ by the will........ Eph 1:1
an *a* of Jesus Christ by the will........ Col 1:1
an *a* of Jesus Christ by the.............. 1Ti 1:1
I am ordained a preacher, and an *a* .. 1Ti 2:7
an *a* of Jesus Christ by the will........ 2Ti 1:1
am appointed a preacher, and an *a* .. 2Ti 1:11
an *a* of Jesus Christ, according .... Titus 1:1
heavenly calling, consider the *A*....... Heb 3:1
an *a* of Jesus Christ, to them 1Pet 1:1
an *a* of Jesus Christ, to them 2Pet 1:1

APOSTLES
names of the twelve *a* are these .... Mt 10:2
the *a* gathered themselves .... Mk 6:30
twelve, whom also he named *a* .... Lk 6:13
And the *a*, when they were returned.. Lk 9:10
I will send them prophets and *a*........ Lk 11:49
the *a* said unto the Lord,.................. Lk 17:5
down, and the twelve *a* with him ...... Lk 22:14
told these things unto the *a* .... Lk 24:10
unto the *a* whom he had chosen ...... Acts 1:2
he was numbered with the eleven *a* . Acts 1:26
Peter and to the rest of the *a* .... Acts 2:37
and signs were done by the *a* .... Acts 2:43
with great power gave the *a* .... Acts 4:33
who by the *a* was surnamed............. Acts 4:36
hands of the *a* were many signs....... Acts 5:12
And laid their hands on the *a* .... Acts 5:18
Peter and the other *a* answered .... Acts 5:29
to put the *a* forth a little space......... Acts 5:34
and when they had called the *a* .... Acts 5:40
Whom they set before the *a* .... Acts 6:6
Judaea and Samaria, except the *a*.... Acts 8:1
Now when the *a* which were at .... Acts 8:14
took him, and brought him to the *a* .. Acts 9:27
And the *a* and brethren that were in . Acts 11:1
with the Jews, and part with the *a* .... Acts 14:4
Which when the *a*, Barnabas and ..... Acts 14:14
go up to Jerusalem unto the *a* .... Acts 15:2
of the church, and of the *a* .... Acts 15:4
And the *a* and elders came together.. Acts 15:6
Then pleased it the *a* and elders,...... Acts 15:22
The *a* and elders and brethren send.. Acts 15:23
from the brethren unto the *a*............. Acts 15:33
keep, that were ordained of the *a*..... Acts 16:4
who are of note among the *a* .... Rom 16:7
God hath set forth us the *a* last........ 1Cor 4:9
a wife, as well as other *a*................. 1Cor 9:5
set some in the church, first *a* 1Cor 12:28
Are all *a*? 1Cor 12:29
then of all the *a* 1Cor 15:7
For I am the least of the *a* 1Cor 15:9
a whit behind the very chiefest *a* 2Cor 11:5
For such are false *a*, deceitful 2Cor 11:13
themselves into the *a* of Christ......... 2Cor 11:13
am I behind the very chiefest *a*......... 2Cor 12:11
to them which were a before me .... Gal 1:17
But other of the *a* saw I none .... Gal 1:19
upon the foundation of the *a*............. Eph 2:20
is now revealed unto his holy *a* .... Eph 3:5
And he gave some, *a*,....................... Eph 4:11
burdensome, as the *a* of Christ........ 1Th 2:6
of us the *a* of the Lord and............... 2Pet 3:2
of the *a* of our Lord Jesus Christ...... Jude 17
tried them which say they are *a* .... Rev 2:2
her, thou heaven, and ye holy *a*....... Rev 18:20
the twelve *a* of the Lamb................. Rev 21:14

APOSTLES'
stedfastly in the *a* doctrine............... Acts 2:42
And laid them down at the *a* feet...... Acts 4:35
money, and laid it at the *a* feet......... Acts 4:37
part, and laid it at the *a* feet............. Acts 5:2
that through laying on of the *a* .... Acts 8:18

APOSTLESHIP
take part of this ministry and *a* .... Acts 1:25
whom we have received grace and *a* .. Rom 1:5
seal of mine *a* are ye in the Lord 1Cor 9:2
to the *a* of the circumcision .... Gal 2:8

APOTHECARIES
Hananiah the son of one of the *a*. ...... Neh 3:8

APOTHECARIES'
of spices prepared by the art 2Chr 16:14

APOTHECARY
compound after the art of the *a*........ Ex 30:25
confection after the art of the *a*........ Ex 30:35
according to the work of the *a*............ Ex 37:29
a to send forth a stinking savour ...... Eccl 10:1

APPAIM (*ap'-pa-im*) A son of Nadab.
Seled, and *A* 1Chr 2:30
And the sons of *A* 1Chr 2:31

APPAREL
by the year, and a suit of *a*............ Judg 17:10
asses, and the camels, and the *a*...... 1Sa 27:9
on ornaments of gold upon your *a* 2Sa 1:24
himself, and changed his *a* 2Sa 12:20
mourner, and put on now mourning *a*.. 2Sa 14:2
of his ministers, and their *a* 1Kin 10:5
of his ministers, and their *a* 2Chr 9:4
his cupbearers also, and their *a* 2Chr 9:4
priests in their *a* with trumpets........ Ezr 3:10
that Esther put on her royal *a* .... Est 5:1
Let the royal *a* be brought which ...... Est 6:8
And let this *a* and horse be .... Est 6:9
Haman, Make haste, and take the *a*.. Est 6:10
Then took Haman the *a* and the........ Est 6:11
of the king in royal *a* of blue .... Est 8:15
The changeable suits of *a*.................. Is 3:22
our own bread, and wear our own *a* .... Is 4:1
this that is glorious in his *a* .... Is 63:1
Wherefore art thou red in thine *a* ...... Is 63:2
work, and in chests of rich *a*.......... Eze 27:24
as are clothed with strange *a*.......... Zeph 1:8
together, gold, and silver, and *a* ...... Zec 14:14
two men stood by them in white *a* .... Acts 1:10
set day Herod, arrayed in royal *a* .... Acts 12:21
no man's silver, or gold, or *a* .... Acts 20:33
adorn themselves in modest *a*............ 1Ti 2:9
man with a gold ring, in goodly *a* ...... Jas 2:2
of gold, or of putting on of *a* 1Pet 3:3

APPARELLED
daughters that were virgins *a* 2Sa 13:18
they which are gorgeously *a* .... Lk 7:25

APPARENTLY
I speak mouth to mouth, even *a*...... Num 12:8

APPEAL
I *a* unto Caesar .... Acts 25:11
was constrained to *a* unto Caesar .... Acts 28:19

APPEALED
answered, Hast thou *a* unto Caesar .. Acts 25:12
But when Paul had *a* to be................ Acts 25:21
he himself had *a* to Augustus .... Acts 25:25
if he had not *a* unto Caesar .... Acts 26:32

APPEAR
one place, and let the dry land *a* .... Gen 1:9
made the white *a* which was in the.... Gen 30:37
none shall *a* before me empty............ Ex 23:15
males shall *a* before the Lord God...... Ex 23:17
none shall *a* before me empty............ Ex 34:20
children *a* before the Lord .... Ex 34:23
when thou shalt go up to a before ...... Ex 34:24
to day the Lord will *a* unto you.......... Lev 9:4
of the Lord shall *a* unto you.............. Lev 9:6
if it a still in the garment,.................... Lev 13:57
for I will *a* in the cloud upon .... Lev 16:2
in a year shall all thy males *a*.......... Deut 16:16
they shall not *a* before the Lord........ Deut 16:16
When all Israel is come to *a* .... Deut 31:11
the Lord no more *a* to Manoah........ Judg 13:21
that he may *a* before the Lord, and.... Judg 1:22
Did I plainly *a* unto the house of 1Sa 2:27
that night did God *a* unto Solomon .. 2Chr 1:7
when shall I come and *a* before God .. Ps 42:2
Let thy work *a* unto thy servants,...... Ps 90:16
up Zion, he shall *a* in his glory........ Ps 102:16
The flowers *a* on the earth................ Song 2:12
goats, that *a* from mount Gilead........ Song 4:1
flock of goats that *a* from Gilead...... Song 6:5
whether the tender grape *a* .... Song 7:12
When ye come to *a* before me .... Is 1:12
but he shall *a* to your joy.................... Is 66:5
thy face, that thy shame may *a*........ Jer 13:26
in all your doings your sins do *a*...... Eze 21:24
that they may *a* unto men to fast...... Mt 6:16
That thou *a* not unto men to fast...... Mt 6:18
which indeed a beautiful outward,...... Mt 23:27
outwardly *a* righteous unto men ...... Mt 23:28
then shall *a* the sign of the Son........ Mt 24:30
for ye are as graves which *a* not........ Lk 11:44
of God should immediately *a* .... Lk 19:11
priests and all their council to *a* ...... Acts 22:30
in the which I will *a* unto thee .... Acts 26:16
But sin, that it might *a* sin................ Rom 7:13
For we must all *a* before the 2Cor 5:10
the sight of God might *a* unto you 2Cor 7:12
not that we should *a* approved.......... 2Cor 13:7
Christ, who is our life, shall *a*............ Col 3:4
shall ye also *a* with him in glory........ Col 3:4
thy profiting may *a* to all 1Ti 4:15

now to *a* in the presence of God .... Heb 9:24
he *a* the second time without sin ...... Heb 9:28
not made of things which do *a* .... Heb 11:3
shall the ungodly and the sinner *a* 1Pet 4:18
when the chief Shepherd shall *a* 1Pet 5:4
that, when he shall *a*, we may 1Jn 2:28
it doth not yet *a* what we shall.......... 1Jn 3:2
but we know that, when he shall *a* 1Jn 3:2
shame of thy nakedness do not *a* ...... Rev 3:18

APPEARANCE
as it were the *a* of fire, until.............. Num 9:15
by day, and the *a* of fire by night ...... Num 9:16
for man looketh on the outward *a*...... 1Sa 16:7
And this was their *a* .... Eze 1:5
their *a* was like burning coals of .... Eze 1:13
and like the *a* of lamps .... Eze 1:13
returned as the *a* of a flash of .... Eze 1:14
The *a* of the wheels and their work .. Eze 1:16
and their *a* and their work was as .... Eze 1:16
as the *a* of a sapphire stone.............. Eze 1:26
as the *a* of a man above upon it .... Eze 1:26
as the *a* of fire round about .... Eze 1:27
from the *a* of his loins even .... Eze 1:27
from the *a* of his loins even .... Eze 1:27
I saw as it were the *a* of fire .... Eze 1:27
As the *a* of the bow that is in .... Eze 1:28
so was the *a* of the brightness .... Eze 1:28
This was the *a* of the likeness of ...... Eze 1:28
and lo a likeness as the *a* of fire ...... Eze 8:2
from the *a* of his loins even .... Eze 8:2
as the *a* of brightness, as the............ Eze 8:2
as the *a* of the likeness of a .... Eze 10:1
the *a* of the wheels was as the.......... Eze 10:9
whose *a* was like the .... Eze 40:3
the *a* of the one as the *a* .... Eze 41:21
the *a* of the chambers which were .... Eze 42:11
it was according to the *a* of the.......... Eze 43:3
stood before me as the *a* of a man.... Dan 8:15
and his face as the *a* of lightning...... Dan 10:6
me one like the *a* of a man................ Dan 10:18
a of them is as the *a* of horses ...... Joel 2:4
Judge not according to the *a* .... Jn 7:24
to answer them which glory in *a*........ 2Cor 5:12
on things after the outward *a* 2Cor 10:7
Abstain from all *a* of evil 1Th 5:22

APPEARANCES
And as for their *a*, they four had ...... Eze 10:10
by the river of Chebar, their *a* .... Eze 10:22

APPEARED
the Lord *a* unto Abram, and said,...... Gen 12:7
unto the Lord, who *a* unto him .... Gen 12:7
old and nine, the Lord *a* to Abram...... Gen 17:1
The Lord *a* unto him in the plains ...... Gen 18:1
And the Lord *a* unto him, and said,.... Gen 26:2
the Lord *a* unto him the same............ Gen 26:24
that *a* unto thee when thou................ Gen 35:1
because there God *a* unto him............ Gen 35:7
God *a* unto Jacob again, when he ...... Gen 35:9
God Almighty *a* unto me at Luz in...... Gen 48:3
the angel of the Lord *a* unto him........ Ex 3:2
a unto me, saying, I have surely .... Ex 3:16
The Lord hath not *a* unto thee............ Ex 4:1
God of Jacob, hath *a* unto thee.......... Ex 4:5
a unto Abraham, unto Isaac, and...... Ex 6:3
his strength when the morning *a* .... Ex 14:27
glory of the Lord *a* in the cloud.......... Ex 16:10
of the Lord *a* unto all the people........ Lev 9:23
the glory of the Lord *a* in the .... Num 14:10
the glory of the Lord *a* unto them...... Num 16:19
it, and the glory of the Lord *a*............ Num 16:42
the glory of the Lord *a* unto them...... Num 20:6
the Lord *a* in the tabernacle in a ...... Deut 31:15
the angel of the Lord *a* unto him........ Judg 6:12
a unto the woman................................ Judg 13:3
Behold, the man hath *a* unto me........ Judg 13:10
the Lord *a* again in Shiloh.................... 1Sa 3:21
And the channels of the sea *a* 2Sa 22:16
In Gibeon the Lord *a* to Solomon........ 1Kin 3:5
That the Lord *a* to Solomon the.......... 1Kin 9:2
as he had *a* unto him at Gibeon 1Kin 9:2
which had *a* unto him twice................ 1Kin 11:9
there *a* a chariot of fire, and.............. 2Kin 2:11
where the Lord *a* unto David his........ 2Chr 3:1
the Lord *a* to Solomon by night.......... 2Chr 7:12
of the morning till the stars *a* .... Neh 4:21
The Lord hath *a* of old unto me,.......... Jer 31:3
a over them as it were a sapphire...... Eze 10:1
there *a* in the cherubims the form...... Eze 10:8
she *a* in her height with the .... Eze 19:11
days their countenances *a* fairer ...... Dan 1:15
Belshazzar a vision *a* unto me .... Dan 8:1
after that which *a* unto me at the ...... Dan 8:1
of the Lord *a* unto him in a dream...... Mt 1:20
diligently what time the star *a* .... Mt 2:7
fruit, then *a* the tares also.................. Mt 13:26
there *a* unto them Moses and Elias.... Mt 17:3
the holy city, and *a* unto many.......... Mt 27:53
there *a* unto them Elias with .... Mk 9:4
he *a* first to Mary Magdalene, out .... Mk 16:9
After that he *a* in another form.......... Mk 16:12
Afterward he *a* unto the eleven as .... Mk 16:14
there *a* unto him an angel of the........ Lk 1:11
And of some, that Elias had *a* .... Lk 9:8
Who *a* in glory, and spake of his .... Lk 9:31
there *a* an angel unto him from .... Lk 22:43
risen indeed, and hath *a* to Simon .... Lk 24:34
there *a* unto them cloven tongues ...... Acts 2:3
The God of glory *a* unto our................ Acts 7:2
there *a* to him in the wilderness .... Acts 7:30

angel which *a* to him in the bush........ Acts 7:35
that *a* unto thee in the way as............ Acts 9:17
a vision *a* to Paul in the night............ Acts 16:9
for I have *a* unto thee for this............ Acts 26:16
sun nor stars in many days *a*............ Acts 27:20
salvation hath *a* to all men .... Titus 2:11
of God our Saviour toward man *a* ...... Titus 3:4
hath he *a* to put away sin by the ...... Heb 9:26
there *a* a great wonder in heaven...... Rev 12:1
there *a* another wonder in heaven...... Rev 12:3

APPEARETH
But when raw flesh *a* in him.............. Lev 13:14
as the leprosy *a* in the skin of .... Lev 13:43
him into thy hand, as *a* this day .... Deut 2:30
one of them in Zion *a* before God ...... Ps 84:7
The hay *a*, and the tender grass........ Prov 27:25
for evil *a* out of the north, and .... Jer 6:1
and who shall stand when he *a*.......... Mal 3:2
the Lord *a* to Joseph in a dream........ Mt 2:13
an angel of the Lord *a* in a dream...... Mt 2:19
that *a* for a little time, and then.......... Jas 4:14

APPEARING
until the *a* of our Lord Jesus.............. 1Ti 6:14
the *a* of our Saviour Jesus Christ........ 2Ti 1:10
the quick and the dead at his *a*.......... 2Ti 4:1
all them also that love his *a* 2Ti 4:8
the glorious *a* of the great God .... Titus 2:13
glory at the *a* of Jesus Christ.............. 1Pet 1:7

APPEASE
I will *a* him with the present.............. Gen 32:20

APPEASED
the wrath of king Ahasuerus was *a*...... Est 2:1
the townclerk had *a* the people.......... Acts 19:35

APPEASETH
he that is slow to anger *a* strife........ Prov 15:18

APPERTAIN
up, with all that *a* unto them.............. Num 16:30
for to thee doth it *a* .... Jer 10:7

APPERTAINED
and all the men that *a* unto Korah...... Num 16:32
They, and all that *a* to them .... Num 16:33
the palace which *a* to the house........ Neh 2:8

APPERTAINETH
and give it unto him to whom it *a*........ Lev 6:5
It *a* not unto thee, Uzziah, to 2Chr 26:18

APPETITE
or fill the *a* of the young lions,............ Job 38:39
if thou be a man given to *a* .... Prov 23:2
mouth, and yet the *a* is not filled........ Eccl 6:7
he is faint, and his soul hath *a*.......... Is 29:8

APHIAH (*af'-fee-ah*) A Christian acquaintance
of Paul.
And to our beloved *A*, and Archippus.. Philem 2

APPII (*ap'-pee-i*) A place south of Rome.
came to meet us as far as *A* forum .... Acts 28:15

APPIUS See APPII.

APPLE
he kept him as the *a* of his eye .... Deut 32:10
Keep me as the *a* of the eye .... Ps 17:8
and my law as the *a* of thine eye ...... Prov 7:2
As the *a* tree among the trees of .... Song 2:3
I raised thee up under the *a* tree........ Song 8:5
let not the *a* of thine eye cease .... Lam 2:18
the *a* tree, even all the trees of .... Joel 1:12
you toucheth the *a* of his eye .... Zec 2:8

APPLES
A word fitly spoken is like *a* of............ Prov 25:11
with flagons, comfort me with *a* .... Song 2:5
and the smell of thy nose like *a* .... Song 7:8

APPLIED
I *a* mine heart to know, and to .... Eccl 7:25
a my heart unto every work that .... Eccl 8:9
When I *a* mine heart to know .... Eccl 8:16

APPLY
that we may *a* our hearts unto .... Ps 90:12
a thine heart to understanding .... Prov 2:2
a thine heart unto my knowledge ...... Prov 22:17
A thine heart unto instruction,............ Prov 23:12

APPOINT
A me thy wages, and I will give it .... Gen 30:28
let him *a* officers over the land,.......... Gen 41:34
then I will *a* thee a place .... Ex 21:13
shalt *a* it for the service of the .... Ex 30:16
I will even *a* over you terror,.............. Lev 26:16
But thou shalt *a* the Levites over ...... Num 1:50
And thou shalt *a* Aaron and his sons.. Num 3:10
a them every one to his service .... Num 4:19
ye shall *a* unto them in charge.......... Num 4:27
refuge, which ye shall *a* for the.......... Num 35:6
Then ye shall *a* you cities to be.......... Num 35:11
A out for you cities of refuge, ... Josh 20:2
a them for himself, for his.................. 1Sa 8:11
he will *a* him captains over 1Sa 8:12
to *a* me ruler over the people of 2Sa 6:21
Moreover I will *a* a place for my 2Sa 7:10
my lord the king shall *a* 2Sa 15:15
to all that thou shalt *a* 1Kin 5:6
the place that thou shalt *a* me............ 1Kin 5:9
to *a* their brethren to be the 1Chr 15:16
the watches of the inhabitants of .... Neh 7:3
let the king *a* officers in all .... Est 2:3

thou wouldest a me a set time............ Job 14:13
salvation wilt God a for walls................... Is 26:1
To a unto them that mourn in Zion ... Is 61:3
I will a over them four kinds,............... Jer 15:3
chosen man, that I may a over her....... Jer 49:19
and who will a me the time............... Jer 49:19
chosen man, that I may a over her....... Jer 50:44
and who will a me the time............... Jer 50:44
a captain against her............................ Jer 51:27
a thee two ways, that the sword.......... Eze 21:19
A a way, that the sword may come...... Eze 21:20
to a captains, to open the mouth......... Eze 21:22
to a battering rams against the .... Eze 21:22
ye shall a the possession of it,............ Eze 45:6
a themselves one head, and they......... Hos 1:11
a him his portion with the.................... Mt 24:51
will a him his portion with the .... Lk 12:46
I a unto you a kingdom, as my .... Lk 22:29
whom we may a over this business ..... Acts 6:3

APPOINTED

hath a me another seed instead of ...... Gen 4:25
At the time a I will return unto............ Gen 18:14
thou hast a for thy servant Isaac........ Gen 24:14
hath a out for my master's son............ Gen 24:44
the LORD a a set time, saying, To....... Ex 9:5
in the time a of the month Abib .... Ex 23:15
keep the passover at his a season........ Num 9:2
ye shall keep it in his a season .... Num 9:3
a season among the children of........... Num 9:7
of the LORD in his a season............... Num 9:13
he and all his people, at a time in...... Josh 8:14
they a Kedesh in Galilee in mount....... Josh 20:7
These were the cities a for all............ Josh 20:9
six hundred men a with weapons of .... Judg 18:11
the six hundred men a with their........ Judg 18:16
that were a with weapons of war .... Judg 18:17
Now there was an a sign between........ Judg 20:38
to the set time that Samuel had a....... 1Sa 13:8
thou camest not within the days a 1Sa 13:11
and Samuel standing as a over them .. 1Sa 19:20
field at the time a with David............. 1Sa 20:35
I have a my servants to such and....... 1Sa 21:2
shall have a thee ruler over.............. 1Sa 25:30
his place which thou hast a him.......... 2Sa 17:14
For the Lord had a to defeat the......... 2Sa 17:14
the set time which he had a him......... 2Sa 20:5
the morning even to the time a........... 2Sa 24:15
I have a him to be ruler over.............. 1Kin 1:35
a him victuals, and gave him land...... 1Kin 11:18
the third day, as the king had a......... 1Kin 12:12
man whom I a to utter destruction..... 1Kin 20:42
the king a the lord on whose hand..... 2Kin 7:17
So the king a unto her a certain........ 2Kin 8:6
Jehu a fourscore men without, and...... 2Kin 10:24
the priest a officers over the.............. 2Kin 11:18
the king of Assyria a unto............... 2Kin 18:14
a unto all manner of service of.......... 1Chr 6:48
were a for all the work of the............ 1Chr 9:13
were a to oversee the vessels.............. 1Chr 9:29
So the Levites a Heman the son of 1Chr 15:17
were a to sound with cymbals of........ 1Chr 15:19
he a certain of the Levites to............. 1Chr 16:4
And he a, according to the order......... 2Chr 8:14
he a singers unto the LORD, and......... 2Chr 20:21
Also Jehoiada a the offices of............ 2Chr 23:18
Hezekiah a the courses of................ 2Chr 31:2
He a also the king's portion of 2Chr 31:3
and they that the king had a............ 2Chr 34:22
a the Levites, from twenty years......... Ezr 3:8
the princes had a a for the service ..... Ezr 8:20
in our cities came at a time.............. Neh 5:14
from the time that I was a to be......... Neh 5:14
thou hast also a prophets to.............. Neh 6:7
the singers and the Levites were a..... Neh 7:1
their in rebellion a a captain to......... Neh 9:17
at times a year by year, to burn........ Neh 10:34
a two great companies of them .... Neh 12:31
at that time were some a over the...... Neh 12:44
a the wards of the priests and the...... Neh 13:30
for the wood offering, at times a....... Neh 13:31
for so the king had a to all the.......... Est 1:8
the keeper of the women, a............... Est 2:15
whom he had a to attend upon her,.... Est 4:5
to their a time every year .... Est 9:27
days of Purim in their times a .... Est 9:31
Is there not an a time to man........... Job 7:1
and wearisome nights are a to me...... Job 7:3
thou hast a his bounds that he......... Job 14:5
the days of my a time will I wait....... Job 14:14
the heritage a unto him by God......... Job 20:29
the thing that is a for me................ Job 23:14
to the house a for all living............... Job 30:23
given us like sheep a for meat........... Ps 44:11
a a law in Israel, which he.............. Ps 78:5
thou chose that are a to die.............. Ps 79:11
in the new moon, in the time a.......... Ps 81:3
loose those that are a to death.......... Ps 102:20
He a the moon for seasons................ Ps 104:19
and will come home at the day a....... Prov 7:20
when he a the foundations of the....... Prov 8:29
all such as are a to destruction......... Prov 31:8
your a feasts my soul hateth.............. Is 1:14
shall be alone in his a times............. Is 14:31
the a barley and the rie in their........ Is 28:25
since I a the ancient people.............. Is 44:7
us the a weeks of the harvest........... Jer 5:24
in the heaven knoweth her a times .... Jer 8:7
if I have not a the ordinances of........ Jer 33:25
he hath passed the time a................ Jer 46:17

there hath he a it.......................... Jer 47:7
I have a thee each day for a year ...... Eze 4:6
which have a my land into their......... Eze 36:5
it in the a place of the house............ Eze 43:21
the king a them a daily provision ...... Dan 1:5
who hath a your meat and your......... Dan 1:10
for at the time a the end shall.......... Dan 8:19
was true, but the time a was long...... Dan 10:1
the end shall be at the time a.......... Dan 11:27
At the time a he shall return, and..... Dan 11:29
because it is yet for a time a............ Dan 11:35
hear ye the rod, and who hath a it.... Mic 6:9
the vision is yet for an a time........... Hab 2:3
disciples did as Jesus had a them...... Mt 26:19
potter's field, as the Lord a them...... Mt 27:10
a mountain where Jesus had a them... Mt 28:16
no more than that which is a you...... Lk 3:13
the Lord a other seventy also........... Lk 10:1
as my Father hath a unto me........... Lk 22:29
And they a two, Joseph called............ Acts 1:23
in the wilderness, as he had a.......... Acts 7:44
determined the times before a.......... Acts 17:26
Because he hath a a day, in the........ Acts 17:31
for so had he a, minding himself....... Acts 20:13
things which are a for thee to do....... Acts 22:10
And when they had a him a day .... Acts 28:23
last, as it were a to death.............. 1Cor 4:9
until the time a of the father........... Gal 4:2
know that we are a thereunto............ 1Th 3:3
For God hath not a us to wrath......... 1Th 5:9
Whereunto I am a a preacher............ 2Ti 1:11
in every city, as I had a thee............ Titus 1:5
whom he hath a heir of all things..... Heb 1:2
was faithful to him that a him.......... Heb 3:2
as it is a unto men once to die,......... Heb 9:27
whereunto also they were a................ 1Pet 2:8

APPOINTETH

that he a over it whomsoever thou ..... Dan 5:21

APPOINTMENT

At the a of Aaron and his sons.......... Num 4:27
for by the a of Absalom this hath...... 2Sa 13:32
according to the a of the priests........ Ezr 6:9
for they had made an a together........ Job 2:11

APPREHEND

with a garrison, desirous to a me....... 2Cor 11:32
if that I may a that for which............ Phil 3:12

APPREHENDED

And when he had a him, he put him... Acts 12:4
which also I am a of Christ Jesus....... Phil 3:12
I count not myself to have a.............. Phil 3:13

APPROACH

None of you shall a to any that......... Lev 18:6
thou shalt not a to his wife.............. Lev 18:14
Also thou shalt not a unto a............. Lev 18:14
if a woman a unto any beast, and..... Lev 20:16
let him not a to offer the bread......... Lev 21:17
hath a blemish, he shall not a.......... Lev 21:18
when they a unto the most holy........ Num 4:19
battle, that the priest shall a........... Deut 20:2
ye a this day unto battle against....... Deut 20:3
thy days a that thou must die........... Deut 31:14
are with me, will a unto the city....... Josh 8:5
can make his sword to a unto him..... Job 40:19
and causest to a unto thee............... Ps 65:4
draw near, and he shall a unto me .... Jer 30:21
engaged his heart to a unto me......... Jer 30:21
where the priests that a unto thee..... Eze 42:13
shall a to those things which are...... Eze 42:14
which a unto me, to minister unto..... Eze 43:19
the light which no man can a unto.... 1Ti 6:16

APPROACHED

Wherefore a ye so nigh unto the........ 2Sa 11:20
the king a to the altar, and.............. 2Kin 16:12

APPROACHETH

faileth not, where no thief a............. Lk 12:33

APPROACHING

they take delight in a to God............ Is 58:2
the more, as ye see the day a........... Heb 10:25

APPROVE

their posterity a their sayings........... Ps 49:13
ye shall a by your letters................. 1Cor 16:3
That ye may a things that are.......... Phil 1:10

APPROVED

a man a of God among you by........... Acts 2:22
is acceptable to God, and a of men.... Rom 14:18
Salute Apelles a in Christ............... Rom 16:10
that they which are a may be made.. 1Cor 11:19
In all things ye have a................... 2Cor 7:11
he that commendeth himself is a...... 2Cor 10:18
not that we should appear a............ 2Cor 13:7
Study to shew thyself a unto God..... 2Ti 2:15

APPROVEST

a the things that are more.............. Rom 2:18

APPROVETH

man in his cause, the Lord a not..... Lam 3:36

APPROVING

But in all things a ourselves as....... 2Cor 6:4

APRONS

together, and made themselves a ..... Gen 3:7
unto the sick handkerchiefs or a...... Acts 19:12

APT

a for war, even them the king of 2Kin 24:16
of them that were a to the war........ 1Chr 7:40
given to hospitality, a to teach......... 1Ti 3:2
all men, a to teach, patient,............. 2Ti 2:24

AQUILA (ac'-quil-ah) *A Christian acquaintance of Paul.*
And found a certain Jew named A...... Acts 18:2
Syria, and with him Priscilla and A.. Acts 18:18
whom when A and Priscilla had....... Acts 18:26
A my helpers in Christ Jesus............ Rom 16:3
A and Priscilla salute you much in ... 1Cor 16:19
Salute Prisca and A, and the........... 2Ti 4:19

AR (ar) *The capital of Moab.*
goeth down to the dwelling of A ...... Num 21:15
it hath consumed A of Moab............ Num 21:28
because I have given A unto the........ Deut 2:9
Thou art to pass over through A....... Deut 2:18
and the Moabites which dwell in A ... Deut 2:29
Because in the night A of Moab is..... Is 15:1

ARA (a'-rah) *A son of Jether.*
Jephunneh, and Pispah, and A.......... 1Chr 7:38

ARAB (a'-rab) See ARBITE. *A city in Judah.*
A, and Dumah, and Eshean,............ Josh 15:52

ARABAH (ar'-ab-ah) See BETH-ARABAH. *The Jordan Valley.*
the side over against A northward..... Josh 18:18
and went down unto A..................... Josh 18:18

ARABIA (a-ra'-be-ah) *The northern part of the Arabian peninsula.*
and of all the kings of A................. 1Kin 10:15
And all the kings of A.................... 2Chr 9:14
The burden upon A........................ Is 21:13
In the forest in a shall ye lodge....... Is 21:13
And all the kings of A, and all the.... Jer 25:24
A, and all the princes of Kedar,........ Eze 27:21
but I went into A, and returned........ Gal 1:17
For this Agar is mount Sinai in A..... Gal 4:25

ARABIAN (a-ra'-be-un) See ARABIANS. *An inhabitant of Arabia.*
the Ammonite, and Geshem the A..... Neh 2:19
and Tobiah, and Geshem the A......... Neh 6:1
shall the A pitch tent there.............. Is 13:20
as the A in the wilderness.............. Jer 3:2

ARABIANS (a-ra'-be-uns)

the A brought him flocks, seven,...... 2Chr 17:11
of the Philistines, and of the A......... 2Chr 21:16
to the camp had slain all the........... 2Chr 22:1
against the A that dwelt in.............. 2Chr 26:7
Sanballat, and Tobiah, and the A...... Neh 4:7
Cretes and A, we do hear them,........ Acts 2:11

ARABS See ARABIANS.

ARAD (a'-rad)
1. A Canaanite king.
when king A the Canaanite, which.... Num 21:1
king A the Canaanite, which dwelt.... Num 33:40
2. A district in Judah.
the king of A, one.......................... Josh 12:14
which lieth in the south of A............ Judg 1:16
3. A son of Beriah.
And Zebadiah, and A, and Ader,....... 1Chr 8:15

ARAH (a'-rah)
1. A son of Ulla.
A, and Haniel, and Rezia................. 1Chr 7:39
2. A family of exiles who returned under Zerubbabel.
The children of A, seven hundred...... Ezr 2:5
The children of A, six hundred.......... Neh 7:10
3. Grandfather of Tobiah's wife.
in law of Shechaniah the son of A..... Neh 6:18

ARAM (a'-ram) See ARAMITESS, ARAM-NAHARAIM, ARAM-ZOBAH, BETH-ARAM, PADAN-ARAM, SYRIA.
1. The son of Shem.
Arphaxad, and Lud, and A................ Gen 10:22
And the children of A....................... Gen 10:23
Arphaxad, and Lud, and A............... 1Chr 1:17
2. The son of Kemuel.
and Kemuel the father of A............. Gen 22:21
3. Another name for Syria.
of Moab hath brought me from A ...... Num 23:7
4. A district of Canaan.
And he took Geshur, and A, with the. 1Chr 2:23
5. The son of Shamer.
Ahi, and Rohgah, Jehubbah, and A.... Mt 1:3
and Esrom begat A......................... Mt 1:4
And A begat Aminadab.................... Mt 1:4
Aminadab, which was the son of A.... Lk 3:33

ARAMEAN See ARAMITESS.

ARAMITESS (a'-ram-i-tes) See SYRIAN.
Manasseh's concubine.
(but his concubine the A bare.......... 1Chr 7:14

ARAM-NAHARAIM (a'-ram-na-ha-ra'-im) See MESOPOTAMIA. *The area between the Tigris and Euphrates rivers.*
when he strove with A...................... Ps 60:t

ARAM-ZOBAH (a'-ram-zo'-bah) *The area between the Orontes and Euphrates rivers.*
with Aram-naharaim and with A........ Ps 60:t

ARAN (a'-ran) See BETH-ARAN. *The son of Seir the Horite.*
of Dishan are these; Uz, and A .... Gen 36:28
sons of Dishan; Uz, and A 1Chr 1:42

ARARAT (ar'-ar-at) See ARMENIA. *A district in Armenia.*
month, upon the mountains of A .... Gen 8:4
against her the kingdoms of A .... Jer 51:27

ARAUNAH (a-raw'-nah) See ORNAN. *A Jebusite.*
threshingplace of A the Jebusite 2Sa 24:16
threshingfloor of A the Jebusite 2Sa 24:18
A looked, and saw the king and his 2Sa 24:20
A went out, and bowed himself 2Sa 24:20
A said, Wherefore is my lord the 2Sa 24:21
A said unto David, Let my lord 2Sa 24:22
All these things did A, as a king 2Sa 24:23
A said unto the king, The LORD 2Sa 24:23
And the king said unto A, Nay 2Sa 24:24

ARBA (ar'-bah) See ARBAH, ARBATHITE, ARBITE, KIRJATH-ABBA. *Father of Anakim.*
even the city of A the father of .... Josh 15:13
the city of A the father of Anak .... Josh 21:11

ARBAH (ar'-bah) See ARBA. *Another name for Hebron.*
unto Mamre, unto the city of A .... Gen 35:27

ARBATHITE (ar'-bath-ite) *A native of Arbah.*
Abi-albon the A, Azmaveth the 2Sa 23:31
the brooks of Gaash, Abiel the A 1Chr 11:32

ARBITE (ar'-bite) *A native of Arab.*
the Carmelite, Paarai the A 2Sa 23:35

ARCHANGEL
a shout, with the voice of the a 1Th 4:16
Yet Michael the a, when .... Jude 9

ARCHELAUS (ar-ke-la'-us) *A son of Herod the Great.*
But when he heard that A did .... Mt 2:22

ARCHER
in the wilderness, and became an a .... Gen 21:20
bendeth let the a bend his bow .... Jer 51:3

ARCHERS
The a have sorely grieved him, and... ... Gen 49:23
a in the places of drawing water .... Judg 5:11
against Saul, and the a hit him 1Sa 31:3
and he was sore wounded of the a 1Sa 31:3
Ulam were mighty men of valour, a 1Chr 8:40
the a hit him 1Chr 10:3
and he was wounded of the a 1Chr 10:3
the a shot at king Josiah 2Chr 35:23
His a compass me round about, he .... Job 16:13
And the residue of the number of a .... Is 21:17
together, they are bound by the a .... Is 22:3
together the a against Babylon .... Jer 50:29

ARCHES
round about, and likewise to the a .... Eze 40:16
the a thereof were after the .... Eze 40:22
And their windows, and their a .... Eze 40:22
the a thereof were before them .... Eze 40:22
the a thereof according to these .... Eze 40:22
in the a thereof round about,... .... Eze 40:25
the a thereof were before them .... Eze 40:26
the a thereof, according to these .... Eze 40:29
in the a thereof round about .... Eze 40:29
the a round about were five and .... Eze 40:30
the a thereof were toward the .... Eze 40:31
the a thereof, were according to .... Eze 40:33
in the a thereof round about .... Eze 40:33
the a thereof were toward the .... Eze 40:34
the a thereof, and the windows to .... Eze 40:36

ARCHEVITES (ar'-ke-vites) *Chaldean settlers in Samaria.*
Tarpelites, the Apharsites, the A .... Ezr 4:9

ARCHI (ar'-kee) See ARCHITE. *A border city of Ephraim.*
unto the borders of A to Ataroth .... Josh 16:2

ARCHIPPUS (ar-kip'-pus) *A Christian acquaintance of Paul.*
And say to A, Take heed to the .... Col 4:17
A our fellowsoldier, and to the .... Philem 2

ARCHITE (ar'-kite) See ARCHI. *A friend of David.*
Hushai the A came to meet him... .... 2Sa 15:32
came to pass, when Hushai the A 2Sa 16:16
Call now Hushai the A also 2Sa 17:5
The counsel of Hushai the A is 2Sa 17:14
Hushai the A was the king's 1Chr 27:33

ARCHITES See ARCHITE.

ARCTURUS (ark-tu'-rus) *Another name for "the Great Bear."*
Which maketh A, Orion, and... .... Job 9:9
canst thou guide A with his sons .... Job 38:32

ARD (ard) See ARDITES.
1. A son of Benjamin.
Muppim, and Huppim, and A .... Gen 46:21
2. A son of Bela.
And the sons of Bela were A .... Num 26:40
of A, the family of the Ardites... .... Num 26:40

ARDITES (ar'-dites) *Descendants of Bela.*
of Ard, the family of the A .... Num 26:40

ARDON (ar'-don) *A son of Caleb.*
Jesher, and Shobab, and A 1Chr 2:18

ARE See PREFACE.

ARELI (a-re'-li) See ARELITES. *A son of Gad.*
and Ezbon, Eri, and Arodi, and A .... Gen 46:16
of A, the family of the Arelites... ...... Num 26:17

ARELITES (a-re'-lites) See ARELI. *Descendants of Areli.*
of Areli, the family of the A .... Num 26:17

AREOPAGITE (a-re-op'-a-jite) *A title of Dionysius.*
the which was Dionysius the A .... Acts 17:34

AREOPAGUS (a-re-op'-a-gus) See AREOPAGITE, MARS'-HILL. *A plaza in Athens.*
took him, and brought him unto A .... Acts 17:19

ARETAS (ar'-e-tas) *A north Arabian ruler.*
A the king kept the city of the 2Cor 11:32

ARGOB (ar'-gob)
1. A district of Og in Bashan.
cities, all the region of A .... Deut 3:4
all the region of A, with all .... Deut 3:13
took all the country of A unto .... Deut 3:14
also pertained the region of A 1Kin 4:13
2. An official of King Pekah of Israel.
of the king's house, with A 2Kin 15:25

ARGUING
but what doth your a reprove .... Job 6:25

ARGUMENTS
him, and fill my mouth with a .... Job 23:4

ARIDAI (a-rid'-a-i) *A son of Haman.*
And Parmashta, and Arisai, and .... Est 9:9

ARIDATHA (a-rid'-a-thah) *A son of Haman.*
And Poratha, and Adalia, and A .... Est 9:8

ARIEH (a-ri'-eh) *A companion of Argob.*
the king's house, with Argob and A .. 2Kin 15:25

ARIEL (a'-re-el) See JERUSALEM.
1. An emissary of Ezra.
Then sent I for Eliezer, for A .... Ezr 8:16
2. A name for Jerusalem.
Woe to Ariel, to A, the city .... Is 29:1
Yet I will distress A, and there .... Is 29:2
and it shall be unto me as A .... Is 29:2
the nations that fight against A .... Is 29:7

ARIGHT
a will I shew the salvation of .... Ps 50:23
that set not their heart a .... Ps 78:8
of the wise useth knowledge a .... Prov 15:2
the cup, when it moveth itself a .... Prov 23:31
and heard, but they spake not a .... Jer 8:6

ARIMATHAEA (ar-im-ath-e'-ah) *Another name for Ramah.*
come, there came a rich man of A .... Mt 27:57
Joseph of A, an honourable... .... Mk 15:43
he was of A, a city of the Jews .... Lk 23:51
And after this Joseph of A .... Jn 19:38

ARIMATHEA See ARIMATHAEA.

ARIOCH (a'-re-ok)
1. King of Ellasar in Assyria.
A king of Ellasar, Chedorlaomer... .... Gen 14:1
of Shinar, and A king of Ellasar .... Gen 14:9
2. Captain of Nebuchadnezzar's guard.
wisdom to A the captain of the .... Dan 2:14
said to A the king's captain, Why ...... Dan 2:15
Then A made the thing known to .... Dan 2:25
Therefore Daniel went in unto a .... Dan 2:24
Then A brought in Daniel before .... Dan 2:25

ARISAI (a-ris'-a-i) *A son of Haman.*
And Parmashta, and A, and Aridai, and.. Est 9:9

ARISE
A, walk through the land in the .... Gen 13:17
angels hastened Lot, saying, A .... Gen 19:15
A, lift up the lad, and hold him... .... Gen 21:18
a, I pray thee, sit and eat of my ...... Gen 27:19
unto his father, Let my father a .... Gen 27:31
and a, flee thou to Laban my .... Gen 27:43
A, go to Padan-aram, to the house ...... Gen 28:2
now a, get thee out from this .... Gen 31:13
And God said unto Jacob, A .... Gen 35:1
And let us a, and go up to Beth-el ..... Gen 35:3
there shall a after them seven... ...... Gen 41:30
the lad with me, and we will a .... Gen 43:8
Take also your brother, and a .... Gen 43:13
And the LORD said unto me, A .... Deut 9:12
And the LORD said unto me, A .... Deut 10:11
If there a among you a prophet,... ..... Deut 13:1
If there a a matter too hard for .... Deut 17:8
then shalt thou a, and get thee up ..... Deut 17:8
now therefore a, go over this .... Josh 1:2
the people of war with thee, and a ..... Josh 8:1
a, Barak, and lead thy captivity... .... Judg 5:12
that the LORD said unto him, A .... Judg 7:9
the host of Israel, and said, A .... Judg 7:15
And they said, A, that we may go .... Judg 18:9
to a up out of the city with a .... Judg 20:40
of the servants with thee, and a 1Sa 9:3
And the LORD said, A, anoint him 1Sa 16:12
The LORD answered him and said, A 1Sa 23:4

to Joab, Let the young men now a 2Sa 2:14
And Joab said, Let them a 2Sa 2:14
Abner said unto David, I will a 2Sa 2:14
if so be that the king's wrath a 2Sa 11:20
And Amnon said unto her, A 2Sa 13:15
were with him at Jerusalem, A 2Sa 15:14
twelve thousand men, and I will a 2Sa 17:1
king David, and said unto David, A 2Sa 17:21
Now therefore a, go forth, and 2Sa 19:7
them, that they could not a 2Sa 22:39
thee shall any a like unto thee 1Kin 3:12
And Jeroboam said to his wife, A 1Kin 14:2
A thou therefore, get thee to... ...... 1Kin 14:12
A, get thee to Zarephath, which... .... 1Kin 17:9
touched him, and said unto him, A 1Kin 19:5
time, and touched him, and said, A 1Kin 19:7
and eat and bread, and let them 1Kin 21:7
that Jezebel said to Ahab, A 1Kin 21:15
A, go down to meet Ahab king of 1Kin 21:18
said to Elijah the Tishbite, A 2Kin 1:3
had restored to life, saying, A 2Kin 8:1
make him a up from among his... .... 2Kin 9:2
A therefore, and be doing, and the 1Chr 22:16
a therefore, and build ye the 1Chr 22:19
Now therefore a, O LORD God, into... .. 2Chr 6:41
A .... Ezr 10:4
therefore we his servants will a ...... Neh 2:20
Thus shall there a too much .... Est 1:18
deliverance a to the Jews from... ..... Est 4:14
I lie down, I say, When shall I a ..... Job 7:4
and upon whom doth not his light a .... Job 25:3
A, O LORD .... Ps 3:7
A, O LORD, in thine anger, lift .... Ps 7:6
A, O LORD .... Ps 9:19
A, O LORD .... Ps 10:12
of the needy, now will I a .... Ps 12:5
A, O LORD, disappoint him, cast... .... Ps 17:13
a, cast us not off for ever .... Ps 44:23
A for our help, and redeem us for ..... Ps 44:26
Let God a, let his enemies be... ...... Ps 68:1
A, O God, plead thine own cause .... Ps 74:22
who should a and declare them to ...... Ps 78:6
A, O God, judge the earth .... Ps 82:8
shall the dead a and praise thee... ... Ps 88:10
when the waves thereof a, thou .... Ps 89:9
Thou shalt a, and have mercy upon ..... Ps 102:13
when they a, let them be ashamed... ... Ps 109:28
A, O LORD, into thy rest... .... Ps 132:8
when wilt thou a out of thy sleep... .. Prov 6:9
Her children a up, and call her .... Prov 31:28
A, my love, my fair one, and come... .. Song 2:13
a, ye princes, and anoint the .... Is 21:5
a, pass over to Chittim .... Is 23:12
with my dead body shall they a .... Is 26:19
but will a against the house of .... Is 31:2
of rulers, Kings shall see and a ...... Is 49:7
a, and sit down, O Jerusalem... .... Is 52:2
A, shine .... Is 60:1
but the LORD shall a upon thee... ..... Is 60:2
therefore gird up thy loins, and a .... Jer 1:17
of their trouble they will say, A ..... Jer 2:28
let them a, if they can save thee ..... Jer 2:28
a, and let us go up at noon... .... Jer 6:4
a, and let us go by night, and let .... Jer 6:5
Shall they fall, and not a .... Jer 8:4
which is upon thy loins, and a .... Jer 13:4
a, and go unto the potter's... .... Jer 18:2
A ye, and let us go up to Zion .... Jer 31:6
and they said, A, and let us go... .... Jer 46:16
A ye, go up to Kedar, and spoil .... Jer 49:28
A, get you up unto the wealthy... ..... Jer 49:31
A, cry out in the night... .... Lam 2:19
and he said unto me, A, go forth... ... Eze 3:22
after these shall a another... .... Dan 2:39
and they said thus unto it, A .... Dan 7:5
which shall a out of the earth... ..... Dan 7:17
are ten kings that shall a .... Dan 7:24
shall a tumult a among thy people... .. Hos 10:14
by whom shall Jacob a... .... Amos 7:2
by whom shall Jacob a... .... Amos 7:5
A ye, and let us rise up against... .... Obad 1
A, go to Nineveh, that great city... .. Jonah 1:2
a, call upon thy God, if so be... ..... Jonah 1:6
A, go unto Nineveh, that great... ..... Jonah 3:2
came to pass, when the sun did a ...... Jonah 4:8
A ye, and depart... .... Mic 2:10
A and friends, O daughter of Zion... .. Mic 4:13
A, contend thou before the... .... Mic 6:1
when I fall, I shall a .... Mic 7:8
to the dumb stone, A, it shall... ..... Hab 2:19
a with healing in his wings... .... Mal 4:2
to Joseph in a dream, saying, A .... Mt 2:13
Saying, A, and take the young... ...... Mt 2:20
or to say, A, and walk .... Mt 9:5
he to the sick of the palsy,) A .... Mt 9:6
came and touched them, and said, A .... Mt 17:7
For there shall a false Christs... .... Mt 24:24
or to say, A, and take up thy bed... .. Mk 2:9
I say unto thee, A, and take up... .... Mk 2:11
Damsel, I say unto thee, a... .... Mk 5:41
of the palsy,) I say unto thee, A ..... Lk 5:24
Young man, I say unto thee, A... ...... Lk 7:14
hand, and called, saying, Maid, a ..... Lk 8:54
I will a and go to my father, and ..... Lk 15:18
And he said unto them, A, go thy... ... Lk 17:19
why do thoughts a in your hearts... ... Lk 24:38
A, let us go hence... .... Jn 14:31
Lord spake unto Philip, saying, A ..... Acts 8:26
And the Lord said unto him, A... ...... Acts 9:6

And the Lord said unto him, A... Acts 9:11
a, and make thy bed... Acts 9:34
him to the body said, Tabitha, a... Acts 9:40
A therefore, and get thee down, and. Acts 10:20
I heard a voice saying unto me, A... Acts 11:7
him up, saying, A up quickly... Acts 12:7
of your own selves shall men a... Acts 20:30
And the Lord said unto me, A... Acts 22:10
a, and be baptized, and wash away... Acts 22:16
a from the dead, and Christ shall... Eph 5:14
the day star a in your hearts... 2Pet 1:19

ARISETH
there a a little cloud out of the... 1Kin 18:44
The sun a, they gather themselves... Ps 104:22
there a light in the darkness... Ps 112:4
The sun also a, and the sun goeth... Eccl 1:5
when he a to shake terribly the... Is 2:19
when he a to shake terribly the... Is 2:21
but when the sun a they flee away... Nah 3:17
persecution a because of the word... Mt 13:21
persecution a for the word's sake. Mk 4:17
for out of Galilee a no prophet... Jn 7:52
there a another priest... Heb 7:15

ARISING
the king a from the banquet of... Est 7:7

ARISTARCHUS (ar-is-tar'-cus) A companion
of Paul.
and having caught Gaius and A... Acts 19:29
and of the Thessalonians, A... Acts 20:4
one A, a Macedonian of... Acts 27:2
A my fellowprisoner saluteth you,.. Col 4:10
Marcus, A, Demas, Lucas, my... Philem 24

ARISTOBULUS See ARISTOBULUS'.

ARISTOBULUS' (a-rus-to-bu'-luz) A Christian
acquaintance of Paul.
them which are of A household... Rom 16:10

ARK
Make thee an a of gopher wood... Gen 6:14
rooms shalt thou make in the a... Gen 6:14
The length of the a shall be... Gen 6:15
A window shalt thou make to the a... Gen 6:16
the door of the a shalt thou set... Gen 6:16
and thou shalt come into the a... Gen 6:18
sort shalt thou bring into the a... Gen 6:19
thou and all thy house into the a... Gen 7:1
sons' wives with him, into the a... Gen 7:7
two and two unto Noah into the a... Gen 7:9
of his sons with them, into the a... Gen 7:13
they went in unto Noah into the a... Gen 7:15
increased, and bare up the a... Gen 7:17
the a went upon the face of the... Gen 7:18
they that were with him in the a... Gen 7:23
cattle that was with him in the a... Gen 8:1
the a rested in the seventh month... Gen 8:4
window of the a which he had made... Gen 8:6
she returned unto him into the a... Gen 8:9
pulled her in unto him into the a... Gen 8:9
sent forth the dove out of the a... Gen 8:10
removed the covering of the a... Gen 8:13
Go forth of the a, thou, and thy... Gen 8:16
kinds, went forth out of the a... Gen 8:19
from all that go out of the a... Gen 8:19
of Noah, that went forth of the a... Gen 9:10
took for him an a of bulrushes... Ex 2:3
she saw the a among the flags... Ex 2:5
shall make an a of shittim wood... Ex 25:10
the rings by the sides of the a... Ex 25:14
that the a may be borne with them... Ex 25:14
shall be in the rings of the a... Ex 25:15
thou shalt put into the a the... Ex 25:16
the mercy seat above upon the a... Ex 25:21
in the a thou shalt put the... Ex 25:21
are upon the a of the testimony... Ex 25:22
the vail the a of the testimony... Ex 26:33
and the mercy seat upon the a of... Ex 26:34
that is by the a of the testimony... Ex 30:6
and the a of the testimony, and... Ex 30:26
the a of the testimony, and the... Ex 30:26
The a, and the staves thereof,... Ex 35:12
made the a of shittim wood... Ex 37:1
sides of the a, to bear the a... Ex 37:5
The a of the testimony, and the... Ex 39:35
therein the a of the testimony... Ex 40:3
cover the a with the vail... Ex 40:3
before the a of the testimony... Ex 40:5
and put the testimony into the a... Ex 40:20
and set the staves on the a... Ex 40:20
the mercy seat above upon the a... Ex 40:20
he brought the a unto the... Ex 40:21
covered the a of the testimony... Ex 40:21
mercy seat, which is upon the a... Lev 16:2
And their charge shall be the a... Num 3:31
cover the a of testimony with it... Num 4:5
that was upon the a of testimony... Num 7:89
the a of the covenant of the LORD... Num 10:33
when the a set forward, that... Num 10:35
nevertheless the a of the... Num 14:44
mount, and make thee an a of wood... Deut 10:1
and thou shalt put them in the a... Deut 10:2
I made an a of shittim wood, and... Deut 10:3
tables in the a which I had made... Deut 10:5
to bear the a of the covenant of... Deut 10:8
which bare the a of the covenant... Deut 31:9
which bare the a of the covenant... Deut 31:25
put it in the side of the a of... Deut 31:26
When ye see the a of the covenant,. Josh 3:3
Take up the a of the covenant... Josh 3:6

took up the a of the covenant... Josh 3:6
that bear the a of the covenant... Josh 3:8
the a of the covenant of the Lord... Josh 3:11
the priests bearing the a of the... Josh 3:13
bare the a were come unto Jordan... Josh 3:15
of the priests that bare the a... Josh 3:15
the priests that bare the a... Josh 3:17
Pass over before the a of the... Josh 4:5
the a of the covenant of the LORD... Josh 4:7
bare the a of the covenant stood... Josh 4:9
a stood in the midst of Jordan... Josh 4:10
that the a of the LORD passed over... Josh 4:11
that bear the a of the testimony... Josh 4:16
of a seven trumpets of rams' horns... Josh 6:4
Take up the a of the covenant, and... Josh 6:6
horns before the a of the LORD... Josh 6:6
pass on before the a of the LORD... Josh 6:7
the a of the covenant of the LORD... Josh 6:8
and the renward came after the a... Josh 6:9
So the a of the LORD compassed... Josh 6:11
priests took up the a of the LORD... Josh 6:12
of rams' horns before the a of... Josh 6:13
came after the a of the LORD... Josh 6:13
the a of the LORD until the eventide... Josh 8:33
judges, stood on this side the a... Josh 8:33
which bare the a of the covenant... Josh 8:33
(for the a of the covenant of God... Judg 20:27
where the a of God was, and Samuel... 1Sa 3:3
Let us fetch the a of the... 1Sa 4:3
might bring from thence the a of... 1Sa 4:4
were there with the a of the... 1Sa 4:4
when the a of the covenant of the... 1Sa 4:5
they understood that the a of the... 1Sa 4:6
And the a of God was taken... 1Sa 4:11
heart trembled for the a of God... 1Sa 4:13
dead, and the a of God is taken... 1Sa 4:17
he made mention of the a of God... 1Sa 4:18
that the a of God was taken... 1Sa 4:19
because the a of God was taken,... 1Sa 4:21
for the a of God is taken... 1Sa 4:22
the Philistines took the a of God... 1Sa 5:1
the Philistines took the a of God... 1Sa 5:2
earth before the a of the LORD... 1Sa 5:3
ground before the a of the LORD... 1Sa 5:4
The a of the God of Israel shall... 1Sa 5:7
with the a of the God of Israel... 1Sa 5:8
Let the a of the God of Israel be... 1Sa 5:8
they carried the a of the God of... 1Sa 5:8
they sent the a of God to Ekron... 1Sa 5:10
as the a of God came to Ekron,... 1Sa 5:10
the a of the God of Israel to us... 1Sa 5:10
Send away the a of the God of... 1Sa 5:11
for the a of the LORD was in the... 1Sa 6:1
shall we do to the a of the LORD... 1Sa 6:2
If ye send away the a of God of... 1Sa 6:3
take the a of the LORD, and lay it... 1Sa 6:8
they laid the a of the LORD upon... 1Sa 6:11
up their eyes, and saw the a... 1Sa 6:13
took down the a of the LORD... 1Sa 6:15
they set down the a of the LORD... 1Sa 6:18
had looked into the a of the LORD... 1Sa 6:19
brought again the a of the LORD... 1Sa 6:21
and brought up the a of the LORD... 1Sa 7:1
his son to keep the a of the LORD... 1Sa 7:1
to pass, while the a abide in... 1Sa 7:2
Ahiah, bring hither the a of God... 1Sa 14:18
For the a of God was at that time... 1Sa 14:18
bring up from thence the a of God... 2Sa 6:2
the a of God upon a new... 2Sa 6:3
Gibeah, accompanying the a of God... 2Sa 6:3
and Ahio went before the a... 2Sa 6:4
forth his hand to the a of God... 2Sa 6:6
and there he died by the a of God. 2Sa 6:7
How shall the a of the LORD come... 2Sa 6:9
a of the LORD unto him into the... 2Sa 6:10
the a of the LORD continued in... 2Sa 6:11
unto him, because of the a of God... 2Sa 6:12
brought up the a of God from the... 2Sa 6:12
that when they bare the a of the... 2Sa 6:13
the a of the LORD with shouting... 2Sa 6:15
as the a of the LORD came into... 2Sa 6:16
they brought in the a of the LORD... 2Sa 6:17
but the a of God dwelleth within... 2Sa 7:2
And Uriah said unto David, The a... 2Sa 11:11
bearing the a of the covenant of... 2Sa 15:24
and they set down the a of God... 2Sa 15:24
Carry back the a of God into the... 2Sa 15:25
Abiathar carried the a of God... 2Sa 15:29
because thou barest the a of the... 1Kin 2:26
stood before the a of the... 1Kin 3:15
to set there the a of the... 1Kin 6:19
that they might bring up the a of... 1Kin 8:1
and the priests took up the a... 1Kin 8:3
they brought up the a of the... 1Kin 8:4
him, were with him before the a... 1Kin 8:5
the priests brought in the a of... 1Kin 8:6
two wings over the place of the a... 1Kin 8:7
and the cherubims covered the a... 1Kin 8:7
There was nothing in the a save... 1Kin 8:9
have set there a place for the a... 1Kin 8:21
LORD, after that a had rest... 1Chr 6:31
again the a of our God is not... 1Chr 13:3
to bring the a of God from... 1Chr 13:5
up thence the a of God the LORD... 1Chr 13:6
they carried the a of God in a... 1Chr 13:7
put forth his hand to hold the a... 1Chr 13:9
because he put his hand to the a... 1Chr 13:10
I bring the a of God home to me... 1Chr 13:12

So David brought not the a home... 1Chr 13:13
the a of God remained with the... 1Chr 13:14
prepared a place for the a of God... 1Chr 15:1
the a of God but the Levites... 1Chr 15:2
LORD chosen to carry the a of God... 1Chr 15:2
to bring up the a of the LORD... 1Chr 15:3
that ye may bring up the a of the... 1Chr 15:12
the a of the LORD God of Israel... 1Chr 15:14
of the Levites bare the a of God... 1Chr 15:15
were doorkeepers for the a... 1Chr 15:23
the trumpets before the a of... 1Chr 15:24
Jehiah were doorkeepers for the a. 1Chr 15:24
went to bring up the a of the... 1Chr 15:25
the Levites that bare the a of... 1Chr 15:26
all the Levites that bare the a... 1Chr 15:27
the a of the covenant of the LORD... 1Chr 15:28
as the a of the covenant of the... 1Chr 15:29
So they brought the a of God... 1Chr 16:1
minister before the a of God... 1Chr 16:4
the a of the covenant of God... 1Chr 16:6
the a of the covenant of the LORD... 1Chr 16:37
minister before the a continually... 1Chr 16:37
but the a of the covenant of the... 1Chr 17:1
to bring the a of the covenant of... 1Chr 22:19
the a of the covenant of the LORD... 1Chr 28:2
covered the a of the covenant of... 1Chr 28:18
But the a of God had David... 2Chr 1:4
to bring up the a of the covenant... 2Chr 5:2
and the Levites took up the a... 2Chr 5:4
And they brought up the a, and the... 2Chr 5:5
assembled unto him before the a... 2Chr 5:6
the priests brought in the a of... 2Chr 5:7
wings over the place of the a... 2Chr 5:8
and the cherubims covered the a... 2Chr 5:8
they drew out the staves of the a... 2Chr 5:9
seen from the a before the oracle... 2Chr 5:9
There was nothing in the a save... 2Chr 5:10
And in it have I put the... 2Chr 6:11
thou, and the a of thy strength... 2Chr 6:41
whereunto the a of the LORD hath... 2Chr 8:11
Put the holy a in the house which. 2Chr 35:3
thou, and the a of thy strength... Ps 132:8
The a of the covenant of the LORD... Jer 3:16
day that Noe entered into the a... Mt 24:38
day that Noe entered into the a... Lk 17:27
the a of the covenant overlaid... Heb 9:4
prepared an a to the saving of... Heb 11:7
while the a was a preparing... 1Pet 3:20
his temple the a of his testament... Rev 11:19

ARKITE (ar'-kite) A tribe descended from
Canaan.
And the Hivite, and the A, and the... Gen 10:17
And the Hivite, and the A, and the... 1Chr 1:15

ARKITES See ARCHI.

ARM
redeem you with a stretched out a... Ex 6:6
by the greatness of thine a they... Ex 15:16
A some of yourselves unto the war... Num 31:3
hand, and by a stretched out a... Deut 4:34
hand and by a stretched out a... Deut 5:15
hand, and the stretched out a... Deut 7:19
power and by thy stretched out a... Deut 9:29
hand, and his stretched out a... Deut 11:2
hand, and with an outstretched a... Deut 26:8
teareth the a with the crown of... Deut 33:20
come, that I will cut off thine a. 1Sa 2:31
the a of thy father's house, that... 1Sa 2:31
and the bracelet that was on his a... 2Sa 1:10
hand, and of thy stretched out a... 1Kin 8:42
great power and a stretched out a... 2Kin 17:36
hand, and thy stretched out a... 2Chr 6:32
With his is an a of flesh... 2Chr 32:8
how savest thou the a that hath... Job 26:2
Then let mine a fall from my... Job 31:22
mine a be broken from the bone... Job 31:22
by reason of the a of the mighty... Job 35:9
the high a shall be broken... Job 38:15
Hast thou an a like God... Job 40:9
Break thou the a of the wicked... Ps 10:15
neither did their own a save them... Ps 44:3
but thy right hand, and thine a... Ps 44:3
with thine a redeemed thy people... Ps 77:15
thine enemies with thy strong a... Ps 89:10
Thou hast a mighty a... Ps 89:13
mine a also shall strengthen him... Ps 89:21
his right hand, and his holy a... Ps 98:1
hand, and with a stretched out a... Ps 136:12
heart, as a seal upon thine a... Song 8:6
every man the flesh of his own a... Is 9:20
and reapeth the ears with his a... Is 17:5
shew the lighting down of his a... Is 30:30
be thou their a every morning... Is 33:2
hand, and his a shall rule for him... Is 40:10
shall gather the lambs with his a... Is 40:11
his a shall be on the Chaldeans... Is 48:14
on mine a shall they trust... Is 51:5
put on strength, O a of the LORD... Is 51:9
LORD hath made bare his holy a in... Is 52:10
to whom is the a of the LORD... Is 53:1
therefore his a brought salvation... Is 59:16
by the a of his strength, Surely... Is 62:8
therefore mine own a brought... Is 63:5
hand of Moses with his glorious a... Is 63:12
in man, and maketh flesh his a... Jer 17:5
hand and with a strong a, even in... Jer 27:5
power and by my outstretched a... Jer 27:5
great power and stretched out a... Jer 32:17
hand, and with a stretched out a... Jer 32:21
his a is broken, saith the LORD... Jer 48:25

thine a shall be uncovered, and............ Eze 4:7
hand, and with a stretched out a.......... Eze 20:33
hand, and with a stretched out a.......... Eze 20:34
I have broken the a of Pharaoh............ Eze 30:21
and they that were his a, that.............. Eze 31:17
not retain the power of the a.............. Dan 11:6
neither shall he stand, nor his a.......... Dan 11:6
the sword shall be upon his a............. Zec 11:17
his a shall be clean dried up, and........ Zec 11:17
hath shewed strength with his a.......... Lk 1:51
to whom hath the a of the Lord............ Jn 12:38
with an high a brought he them............ Acts 13:17
a yourselves likewise with the............. 1Pet 4:1

ARMAGEDDON (ar-mag-ed'-don) Scene of
the last great battle of time.
called in the Hebrew tongue A............ Rev 16:16

ARMED
he a his trained servants, born............ Gen 14:14
tribe, twelve thousand a for war.......... Num 31:5
a before the children of Israel............. Num 32:17
if ye will go a before the LORD............ Num 32:20
will go all of you a over Jordan............ Num 32:21
pass over, every man a for war............ Num 32:27
Jordan, every man a to battle............. Num 32:29
will not pass over with you a............... Num 32:30
We will pass over a before the............. Num 32:32
ye shall pass over a before your.......... Deut 3:18
shall pass before your brethren a........ Josh 1:14
passed over a before the children........ Josh 4:12
let him that is a pass on before........... Josh 6:7
the a men went before the priests........ Josh 6:9
the a men went before them................ Josh 6:13
the a men that were in the host........... Judg 7:11
he was a with a coat of mail............... 1Sa 17:5
Saul a David with his armour, and........ 1Sa 17:38
also he a him with a coat of mail.......... 1Sa 17:38
They were a with bows, and could....... 1Chr 12:2
that were ready a to the war............... 1Chr 12:23
eight hundred, ready a to the war........ 1Chr 12:24
with him a men with bow and shield...... 2Chr 17:17
So the a men left the captives and....... 2Chr 28:14
he goeth on to meet the a men........... Job 39:21
The children of Ephraim, being a......... Ps 78:9
and thy want an a man...................... Prov 6:11
and thy want as an a man.................. Prov 24:34
therefore is a soldiers of Moab............. Is 15:4
When a strong man a keepeth his........ Lk 11:21

ARMENIA (ar-me'-ne-ah) A region between
the lower ends of the Black and Caspian
seas.
they escaped into the land of A........... 2Kin 19:37
they escaped into the land of A........... Is 37:38

ARMHOLES
under thine a under the cords............. Jer 38:12
women that sew pillows to all a........... Eze 13:18

ARMIES
of Egypt according to their a............... Ex 6:26
upon Egypt, and bring forth mine a...... Ex 7:4
day have I brought your a out of.......... Ex 12:17
of the land of Egypt by their a............ Ex 12:51
shall number them by their a.............. Num 1:3
of Judah pitch throughout their a........ Num 2:3
four hundred, throughout their a......... Num 2:9
of Reuben according to their a........... Num 2:10
and fifty, throughout their a............... Num 2:16
of Ephraim according to their a.......... Num 2:18
and an hundred, throughout their a..... Num 2:24
be on the north side by their a........... Num 2:25
of Judah according to their a............. Num 10:14
set forward according to their a.......... Num 10:18
set forward according to their a.......... Num 10:22
of Israel according to their a.............. Num 10:25
their a under the hand of Moses.......... Num 33:1
of the a to lead the people................. Deut 20:9
together their a to battle.................... 1Sa 17:1
and cried unto the a of Israel.............. 1Sa 17:8
I defy the a of Israel this day.............. 1Sa 17:10
out of the a of the Philistines............. 1Sa 17:23
defy the a of the living God................ 1Sa 17:26
defied the a of the living God............. 1Sa 17:36
hosts, the God of the a of Israel.......... 1Sa 17:45
against the a of the Philistines............ 1Sa 23:3
their a together for warfare................. 1Sa 28:1
together all their a to Aphek............... 1Sa 29:1
And when all the captains of the a...... 2Kin 25:23
great, and the captains of the a.......... 2Kin 25:26
the valiant men of the a were............. 1Chr 11:26
sent the captains of his a.................. 2Chr 16:4
Is there any number of his a............... Job 25:3
and goest not forth with our a............. Ps 44:9
which didst not go out with our a........ Ps 60:10
Kings of a did flee apace................... Ps 68:12
As it were the company of two a......... Song 6:13
and his fury upon all their a................ Is 34:2
and he sent forth his a, and............... Mt 22:7
see Jerusalem compassed with a......... Lk 21:20
to fight the a of the aliens................. Heb 11:34
the a which were in heaven................ Rev 19:14
kings of the earth, and their a............ Rev 19:19

ARMONI (ar-mo'-ni) A son of King Saul.
Aiah, whom she bare unto Saul, A....... 2Sa 21:8

ARMOUR
the young man that bare his a............ 1Sa 14:1
to the young man that bare his a......... 1Sa 14:6
And Saul armed David with his a......... 1Sa 17:38
David girded his sword upon his a........ 1Sa 17:39

but he put his a in his tent................. 1Sa 17:54
his head, and stripped off his a........... 1Sa 31:9
they put his a in the house of............. 1Sa 31:10
the young men, and take thee his a..... 2Sa 2:21
bare Joab's a compassed about.......... 2Sa 18:15
of gold, and garments, and a.............. 1Kin 10:25
and they washed his a...................... 1Kin 22:38
all that were able to put on a.............. 2Kin 3:21
horses, a fenced city also, and a......... 2Kin 10:2
and all the house of his a................... 2Kin 20:13
him, they took his head, and his a....... 1Chr 10:9
they put his a in the house of............. 1Chr 10:10
the a of the house of the forest.......... Is 22:8
and all the house of his a................... Is 39:2
them clothed with all sorts of a.......... Eze 38:4
him all his a wherein he trusted.......... Lk 11:22
and let us put on the a of light........... Rom 13:12
by the a of righteousness on the......... 2Cor 6:7
Put on the whole a of God.................. Eph 6:11
take unto you the whole a of God........ Eph 6:13

ARMOURBEARER
hastily unto the young man his a......... Judg 9:54
his a said unto him, Do all that........... 1Sa 14:7
answered Jonathan and his a.............. 1Sa 14:12
And Jonathan said unto his a............. 1Sa 14:12
upon his feet, and his a after him....... 1Sa 14:13
and his a slew after him.................... 1Sa 14:13
his a made, was about twenty men,..... 1Sa 14:14
Jonathan and his a were not there...... 1Sa 14:17
and be became his a........................ 1Sa 16:21
Then said Saul unto his a.................. 1Sa 31:4
But his a would not.......................... 1Sa 31:4
when his a saw that Saul was dead..... 1Sa 31:5
died, and his three sons, and his a..... 1Sa 31:6
a to Joab the son of Zeruiah.............. 2Sa 23:37
Then said Saul to his a, Draw thy....... 1Chr 10:4
But his a would not.......................... 1Chr 10:4
when his a saw that Saul was dead..... 1Chr 10:5
the a of Joab the son of Zeruiah......... 1Chr 11:39

ARMOURY
the a at the turning of the wall........... Neh 3:19
tower of David builded for an a............ Song 4:4
The LORD hath opened his a............... Jer 50:25

ARMS
of his hands were made................... Gen 49:24
underneath are the everlasting a......... Deut 33:27
the cords that were upon his a........... Judg 15:14
them from off his a like a thread......... Judg 16:12
bow of steel is broken by mine a........ 2Sa 22:35
and smote Jehoram between his a....... 2Kin 9:24
the a of the fatherless have been....... Job 22:9
bow of steel is broken by mine a........ Ps 18:34
For the a of the wicked shall be......... Ps 37:17
strength, and strengtheneth her a....... Prov 31:17
it with the strength of his a............... Is 44:12
shall bring thy sons in their a............ Is 49:22
mine a shall judge the people............ Is 51:5
and I will tear them from your a.......... Eze 13:20
of Egypt, and will break his a............ Eze 30:22
I will strengthen the a of the............. Eze 30:24
but I will break Pharaoh's a............... Eze 30:24
the a of the king of Babylon.............. Eze 30:25
the a of Pharaoh shall fall down......... Eze 30:25
his a of silver, his belly and his......... Dan 2:32
eyes as lamps of fire, and his a......... Dan 10:6
the a of the south shall not.............. Dan 11:15
with the a of a flood shall they......... Dan 11:22
a shall stand on his part, and........... Dan 11:31
bound and strengthened their a......... Hos 7:15
to go, taking them by their a............. Hos 11:3
and when he had taken him in his a.... Mk 9:36
And he took them up in his a............ Mk 10:16
Then took he him up in his a............ Lk 2:28

ARMY
the chief captain of his a................... Gen 26:26
and his horsemen, and his a.............. Ex 14:9
what he did unto the a of Egypt......... Deut 11:4
Sisera, the captain of Jabin's a.......... Judg 4:7
we should give bread unto thine a...... Judg 8:6
to Abimelech, Increase thine a.......... Judg 9:29
they slew of the a in the field............ 1Sa 4:2
a man of Benjamin out of the a.......... 1Sa 4:12
I am he that came out of the a........... 1Sa 4:16
and I fled to day out of the a............. 1Sa 4:16
battle in array, a against a............... 1Sa 17:21
battle in array, a against a............... 1Sa 17:21
the carriage, and ran into the a......... 1Sa 17:22
ran toward the a to meet the............. 1Sa 17:48
the a which followed them................ 1Kin 20:19
And number thee an a...................... 1Kin 20:25
like the a that thou hast lost............. 1Kin 20:25
the a of the Chaldees pursued........... 2Kin 25:5
all his a were scattered from him....... 2Kin 25:5
all the a of the Chaldees, that.......... 2Kin 25:10
Joab led forth the power of the a....... 1Chr 20:1
general of the king's a was Joab........ 1Chr 27:34
with an a of valiant men of war.......... 2Chr 13:3
Asa had an a of men that bare.......... 2Chr 14:8
as they went out before the a........... 2Chr 20:21
For the a of the Syrians came........... 2Chr 24:24
let not the a of Israel go with........... 2Chr 25:7
I have given to the a of Israel........... 2Chr 25:9
the a that was come to him out of..... 2Chr 25:10
of the a which Amaziah sent back...... 2Chr 25:13
And under their hand was an a.......... 2Chr 26:13
king had sent captains of the a......... Neh 2:9
the a of Samaria, and said, What....... Neh 4:2
and dwelt as a king in the a.............. Job 29:25

terrible as an a with banners............. Song 6:4
and terrible as an a with banners....... Song 6:10
unto king Hezekiah with a great a....... Is 36:2
forth the chariot and horse, the a...... Is 43:17
of Babylon's a besieged Jerusalem..... Jer 32:2
king of Babylon, and his a................ Jer 34:1
a fought against Jerusalem............... Jer 34:7
hand of the king of Babylon's a......... Jer 34:21
fear of the a of the Chaldeans.......... Jer 35:11
for fear of the a of the Syrians.......... Jer 35:11
Then Pharaoh's a was come forth...... Jer 37:5
Behold, Pharaoh's a, which is............ Jer 37:7
a of the Chaldeans that fight............ Jer 37:10
that when the a of the Chaldeans...... Jer 37:11
Jerusalem for fear of Pharaoh's a....... Jer 37:11
hand of the king of Babylon's a......... Jer 38:3
all his a against Jerusalem, and........ Jer 39:1
Chaldeans' a pursued after them....... Jer 39:5
against the a of Pharaoh-necho......... Jer 46:2
for they shall march with an a........... Jer 46:22
of Babylon came, he and all his a...... Jer 52:4
But the a of the Chaldeans............... Jer 52:8
all his a was scattered from him........ Jer 52:8
all the a of the Chaldeans, that........ Jer 52:14
shall Pharaoh with his mighty a......... Eze 17:17
of Lud and of Phut were in thine a..... Eze 27:10
The men of Arvad with thine a........... Eze 27:11
his a to serve a great service........... Eze 29:18
yet had he no wages, nor his a......... Eze 29:18
it shall be the wages for his a........... Eze 29:19
all his a slain by the sword.............. Eze 32:31
their feet, an exceeding great a........ Eze 37:10
bring thee forth, and all thine a........ Eze 38:4
a great company, and a mighty a....... Eze 38:15
were in his a to bind Shadrach.......... Dan 3:20
to his will in the a of heaven............. Dan 4:35
which shall come with an a............... Dan 11:7
certain years with a great a.............. Dan 11:13
king of the south with a great a......... Dan 11:25
with a very great and mighty a.......... Dan 11:25
him, and his a shall overflow............. Dan 11:26
utter his voice before his a............... Joel 2:11
far off from you the northern a.......... Joel 2:20
my great a which I sent among you.... Joel 2:25
about mine house because of the a.... Zec 9:8
then came I with an a, and rescued.... Acts 23:27
the number of the a of the................ Rev 9:16
on the horse, and against his a.......... Rev 19:19

ARNAN (ar'-nan) Descendants of David.
sons of Rephaiah, the sons of A......... 1Chr 3:21

ARNON (ar'-non) A river in southern Canaan.
and pitched on the other side of A...... Num 21:13
for A is the border of Moab................ Num 21:13
Red sea, and in the brooks of A......... Num 21:14
his land from A unto Jabbok.............. Num 21:24
land out of his hand, even unto A...... Num 21:26
the lords of the high places of A........ Num 21:28
Moab, which is in the border of A....... Num 22:36
journey, and pass over the river A...... Deut 2:24
is by the brink of the river of A.......... Deut 2:36
the river of A unto mount Hermon....... Deut 3:8
Aroer, which is by the river A............ Deut 3:12
unto the river A half the valley.......... Deut 3:16
is by the bank of the river A............. Deut 4:48
from the river A unto mount.............. Josh 12:1
is upon the bank of the river A.......... Josh 12:2
is upon the bank of the river A.......... Josh 13:9
is on the bank of the river A............. Josh 13:16
from A even unto Jabbok, and unto.... Judg 11:13
and pitched on the other side of A..... Judg 11:18
for A was the border of Moab............ Judg 11:18
from A even unto Jabbok, and from.... Judg 11:22
that be along by the coasts of A....... Judg 11:26
Aroer, which is by the river A............ 2Kin 10:33
Moab shalt be at the fords of A......... Is 16:2
tell ye it in A, that Moab is............... Jer 48:20

AROD (a'-rod) See **ARODITES.** A son of Gad.
Of A, the family of the Arodites.......... Num 26:17

ARODI (a'-ro-di) See **ARODITES.** Descendants of
Arod.
Haggi, Shuni, and Ezbon, Eri, and A... Gen 46:16

ARODITES (a'-ro-dites) Same as Arodi.
Of Arod, the family of the A............... Num 26:17

AROER (a-ro'-er)
1. A city in the valley of Jabbok.
Gad built Dibon, and Ataroth, and A... Num 32:34
unto A that is before Rabbah............. Josh 13:25
over Jordan, and pitched in A............ 2Sa 24:5
The cities of A are forsaken.............. Is 17:2
2. An Amorite city.
From A, which is by the brink of........ Deut 2:36
we possessed at that time, from A..... Deut 3:12
From A, which is by the bank of........ Deut 4:48
dwelt in Heshbon, and ruled from A.... Josh 12:2
From A, that is upon the bank of........ Josh 13:9
dwelt in Aroer, even A...................... Josh 13:16
in Heshbon and her towns, and in A... Judg 11:26
And he smote them from A, even....... Judg 11:33
and the Manassites, from A.............. 2Kin 10:33
the son of Joel, who dwelt in A......... 1Chr 5:8
O inhabitant of A, stand by the......... Jer 48:19
3. A city in southern Judah.
And to them which were in A............. 1Sa 30:28

AROERITE (a-o-ur-ite) A native of Aroer.
Jehiel the sons of Hothan the A......... 1Chr 11:44

AROSE
And when the morning a, then the...... Gen 19:15
when she lay down, nor when she a.... Gen 19:33

and the younger *a*, and lay with him . Gen 19:35
when she lay down, nor when she *a* . Gen 19:35
and he *a*, and went to Mesopotamia,. Gen 24:10
Rebekah *a*, and her damsels . Gen 24:61
in the field, and, lo, my sheaf *a* . Gen 37:7
And she *a*, and went away, and laid . Gen 38:19
Now there *a* up a new king over . Ex 1:8
there *a* not a prophet since in . Deut 34:10
So Joshua *a*, and all the people of . Josh 8:3
the ambush *a* quickly out of their . Josh 8:19
And the men *a*, and went away . Josh 18:8
son of Zippor, king of Moab, *a*. Josh 24:9
there *a* another generation after . Judg 2:10
And he *a* out of his seat . Judg 3:20
And Deborah *a*, and went with Barak . Judg 4:9
that time *a* Deborah, a . Judg 4:14
that I *a* a mother in Israel . Judg 5:7
the city *a* early in the morning . Judg 6:28
And Gideon *a*, and slew Zebah and . Judg 8:21
after Abimelech there *a* to defend . Judg 10:1
And after him *a* Jair, a Gileadite, . Judg 10:3
And Manoah *a*, and went after his . Judg 13:11
at midnight, and took the doors . Judg 16:3
And her husband *a*, and went after . Judg 19:3
when they *a* early in the morning, . Judg 19:5
he *a* early in the morning on the . Judg 19:8
And all the people *a* as one man . Judg 20:8
And the children of Israel *a*. Judg 20:18
Then she *a* with her daughters in . Ruth 1:6
And Samuel *a* went to Eli, and . 1Sa 3:6
And he *a* and went to Eli, and said, . 1Sa 3:8
of Ashdod *a* early on the morrow . 1Sa 5:3
when they *a* early on the morrow . 1Sa 5:4
And they *a* early . 1Sa 5:4
And Saul *a*, and they went out both . 1Sa 9:26
And Samuel *a*, and gat him up from . 1Sa 13:15
when he *a* against me, I caught . 1Sa 17:35
to pass, when the Philistine *a*. 1Sa 17:48
the men of Israel and of Judah *a* . 1Sa 17:52
Wherefore David *a* and went, he and. 1Sa 18:27
and Jonathan *a*, and Abner sat by . 1Sa 20:25
So Jonathan *a* from the table . 1Sa 20:34
David *a* out of a place toward the . 1Sa 20:41
And he *a* and departed . 1Sa 20:42
And David *a*, and fled that day for . 1Sa 21:10
which were about six hundred, *a* . 1Sa 23:13
And Jonathan Saul's son *a*, and went . 1Sa 23:16
And they *a*, and went to Ziph before . 1Sa 23:24
Then David *a*, and cut off the . 1Sa 24:4
And David *a* afterward, and went . 1Sa 24:8
And David *a*, and went down to the . 1Sa 25:1
And she *a*, and bowed herself on her . 1Sa 25:41
And Abigail hasted, and *a*, and rode. 1Sa 25:42
Then Saul *a*, and went down to the . 1Sa 26:2
And David *a*, and came to the place . 1Sa 26:5
And David *a*, and he passed over . 1Sa 27:2
So he *a* from the earth, and sat . 1Sa 28:23
All the valiant men *a*, and went . 1Sa 31:12
Then there *a* and went over by . 2Sa 2:15
And David *a*, and went with all the . 2Sa 6:2
that David *a* from off his bed, . 2Sa 11:2
And the elders of his house *a* . 2Sa 12:17
Then David *a* from the earth, and, . 2Sa 12:20
Then all the king's sons *a*. 2Sa 13:29
Then the king *a*, and tare his . 2Sa 13:31
So Joab *a* and went to Geshur, and. 2Sa 14:23
Then Joab *a*, and came to Absalom . 2Sa 14:31
So he *a*, and went to Hebron . 2Sa 15:9
Then David *a*, and all the people . 2Sa 17:22
he saddled his ass, and *a* . 2Sa 17:23
Then the king *a*, and sat in the . 2Sa 19:8
He *a*, and smote the Philistines . 2Sa 21:16
feared because of Solomon, and *a*. 1Kin 1:50
And Shimei *a*, and saddled his ass, . 1Kin 2:40
she *a* at midnight, and took my son . 1Kin 3:20
he *a* from before the altar of the . 1Kin 8:54
they *a* out of Midian, and came to . 1Kin 11:40
And Jeroboam *a*, and fled into Egypt . 1Kin 11:40
And Jeroboam's wife did so, and *a* . 1Kin 14:4
And Jeroboam's wife *a* . 1Kin 14:17
So he *a* and went to Zarephath . 1Kin 17:10
And when he saw that, he *a* . 1Kin 19:3
And he *a*, and did eat and drink, and. 1Kin 19:8
Then he *a*, and went after Elijah, . 1Kin 19:21
And he *a*, and went down with him . 2Kin 1:15
And he *a*, and followed her. . 2Kin 4:30
Wherefore they *a* and fled in the . 2Kin 7:7
the king *a* in the night, and said . 2Kin 7:12
And the woman *a*, and did after the . 2Kin 8:2
And he *a*, and went into the house. . 2Kin 9:6
And he *a* and departed, and came to . 2Kin 10:12
saw that her son was dead, she *a*. 2Kin 11:1
And his servants *a*, and made a . 2Kin 12:20
when they *a* early in the morning, . 2Kin 19:35
neither after him *a* there any . 2Kin 23:25
and the captains of the armies, *a* . 2Kin 25:26
They *a*, all the valiant men, and. . 1Chr 10:12
that there *a* a war at Gezer with . 1Chr 20:4
saw that her son was dead *a*. 2Chr 22:10
Then the Levites *a*, Mahath the . 2Chr 29:12
a and took away the altars . 2Chr 30:14
Then the priests the Levites *a* . 2Chr 30:27
of the LORD *a* against his people . 2Chr 36:16
I *a* up from my heaviness . Ezr 9:5
Then I *a* in the night, I and some few . Neh 2:12
So Esther *a*, and stood before the . Est 8:4
Then Job *a*, and rent his mantle, . Job 1:20
I *a*, and they spake against me . Job 19:18
and the aged *a*, and stood up . Job 29:8
When God *a* to judgment, to save . Ps 76:9

hasteth to his place where he *a* . Eccl 1:5
when they *a* early in the morning, . Is 37:36
Then *a* Ishmael the son of . Jer 41:2
Then I *a*, and went forth into the . Eze 3:23
Then the king *a* very early in the . Dan 6:19
So Jonah *a*, and went unto Nineveh, . Jonah 3:3
he *a* from his throne, and he laid . Jonah 3:6
When he *a*, he took the young . Mt 2:14
And he *a*, and took the young child . Mt 2:21
and she *a*, and ministered unto them . Mt 8:15
there *a* a great tempest in the . Mt 8:24
Then he *a*, and rebuked the winds . Mt 8:26
And he *a*, and departed to his house . Mt 9:7
And he *a*, and followed him . Mt 9:9
And Jesus *a*, and followed him, and . Mt 9:19
her by the hand, and the maid *a*. . Mt 9:25
Then all those virgins *a*, and . Mt 25:7
And the high priest *a*, and said . Mt 26:62
of the saints which slept *a*. . Mt 27:52
And immediately he *a*, took up the . Mk 2:12
And he *a* and followed him . Mk 2:14
there *a* a great storm of wind, and . Mk 4:37
And he *a*, and rebuked the wind, and . Mk 4:39
and straightway the damsel *a* . Mk 5:42
And from thence he *a*, and went into . Mk 7:24
and he *a* . Mk 9:27
he *a* from thence, and cometh into . Mk 10:1
there *a* certain, and bare false. . Mk 14:57
Mary *a* in those days, and went . Lk 1:39
he *a* out of the synagogue, and . Lk 4:38
and immediately she *a* and . Lk 4:39
And he *a* and stood forth . Lk 6:8
and when the flood *a*, the stream . Lk 6:48
Then he *a*, and rebuked the wind, and. Lk 8:24
came again, and she *a* straightway . Lk 8:55
Then there *a* a reasoning among . Lk 9:46
there *a* a mighty famine in that . Lk 15:14
And he *a*, and came to his father. . Lk 15:20
Now when the multitude of them *a* . Lk 23:1
Then *a* Peter, and ran unto the . Lk 24:12
There there *a* a question between . Jn 3:25
the sea *a* by reason of a great . Jn 6:18
she *a* quickly, and came unto him . Jn 11:29
And the young men *a*, wound him up, . Acts 5:6
there *a* a murmuring of the . Acts 6:1
Then there *a* certain of the . Acts 6:9
Till another king *a*, which knew . Acts 7:18
And he *a* and went . Acts 8:27
And Saul *a* from the earth . Acts 9:8
he received sight forthwith, and *a*. Acts 9:18
And he *a* immediately . Acts 9:34
Then Peter *a* and went with them . Acts 9:39
upon the persecution that *a* about . Acts 11:19
the same time there *a* no small . Acts 19:23
there *a* a dissension between the . Acts 23:7
And there *a* a great cry . Acts 23:9
were of the Pharisees' part *a* . Acts 23:9
when there *a* a great dissension, . Acts 23:10
But not long after there *a* . Acts 27:14
there *a* a smoke out of the pit, . Rev 9:2

ARPAD (*ar'pad*) A city near Hamath.
are the gods of Hamath, and A . 2Kin 18:34
king of Hamath, and the king of A . 2Kin 19:13
is not Hamath as A . Is 10:9
Hamath is confounded, and A . Jer 49:23

ARPHAD (*ar'-fad*) See ARPAD. Same as Arpad.
Where are the gods of Hamath and A . Is 36:19
king of Hamath, and the king of A . Is 37:13

ARPHAXAD
Asshur, and A, and Lud . Gen 10:22
And A begat Salah . Gen 10:24
begat A two years after the flood. . Gen 11:10
he begat A five hundred years, . Gen 11:11
A lived five and thirty years, and . Gen 11:12
A lived after he begat Salah . Gen 11:13
Asshur, and A, and Lud . 1Chr 1:17
A begat Shelah, and Shelah begat . 1Chr 1:18
Shem, A, Shelah, . 1Chr 1:24
of Cainan, which was the son of A . Lk 3:36

ARRAY
to fight against them at Gibeah . Judg 20:20
set their battle again in *a* in . Judg 20:22
put themselves in *a* in the first day . Judg 20:22
themselves in *a* against Gibeah . Judg 20:30
put themselves in *a* at Baal-tamar . Judg 20:33
themselves in *a* against Israel . 1Sa 4:2
set the battle in *a* against the . 1Sa 17:2
come out to set your battle in *a* . 1Sa 17:8
had put the battle in *a*, army . 1Sa 17:21
put the battle in *a* at the . 2Sa 10:9
put them in *a* against the Syrians . 2Sa 10:10
that he might put them in *a* . 2Sa 10:10
set themselves in *a* against David . 2Sa 10:17
his servants, Set yourselves in *a* . 1Kin 20:12
themselves in *a* against the city . 1Kin 20:12
put the battle in *a* before the . 1Chr 19:9
put them in *a* against them . 1Chr 19:10
they set themselves in *a* against . 1Chr 19:11
set the battle in *a* against them . 1Chr 19:17
battle in *a* against the Syrians . 1Chr 19:17
Abijah set the battle in *a* with . 2Chr 13:3
a against him with eight hundred . 2Chr 14:10
they set their battle in *a* in the . 2Chr 14:10
that they may *a* themselves in *a* . Job 6:4
do set themselves in *a* against me. . Job 40:10
a thyself with glory and beauty . Job 40:10
set themselves in *a* at the gate. . Is 22:7
set in *a* as men for war against. . Jer 6:23
he shall *a* himself with the land . Jer 43:12

set themselves in *a* against her . Jer 50:9
Put yourselves in *a* against . Jer 50:14
upon horses, every one put in *a* . Jer 50:42
a strong people set in battle *a* . Joel 2:5
or gold, or pearls, or costly *a* . 1Ti 2:9

ARRAYED
a him in vestures of fine linen,. . Gen 41:42
being a in white linen, having . 2Chr 5:12
a them, and shod them, and gave . 2Chr 28:15
a Mordecai, and brought him on . Est 6:11
glory was not *a* like one of these . Mt 6:29
glory was not *a* like one of these . Lk 12:27
a him in a gorgeous robe, and sent . Lk 23:11
a in royal apparel, sat upon . Acts 12:21
these which are *a* in white robes . Rev 7:13
And the woman was *a* in purple . Rev 17:4
she should be *a* in fine linen . Rev 19:8

ARRIVED
they *a* the country of the . Lk 8:26
the next day we *a* at Samos . Acts 20:15

ARROGANCY
let not *a* come out of your mouth . 1Sa 2:3
pride, and *a*, and the evil way, and . Prov 8:13
I will cause the *a* of the proud . Is 13:11
proud his loftiness, and his *a* . Jer 48:29

ARROW
lad ran, he shot an *a* beyond him. . 1Sa 20:36
of the *a* which Jonathan had shot . 1Sa 20:37
and said, Is not the *a* beyond thee. . 1Sa 20:37
the *a* went out at his heart, and . 2Kin 9:24
king of the LORD's deliverance, . 2Kin 13:17
the *a* of deliverance from Syria . 2Kin 13:17
this city, nor shoot an *a* there . 2Kin 19:32
The *a* cannot make him flee . Job 41:28
ready their *a* upon the string. . Ps 11:2
God shall shoot at them with an *a*. . Ps 64:7
nor for the *a* that flieth by day . Ps 91:5
a maul, and a sword, and a sharp *a* . Prov 25:18
this city, nor shoot an *a* there . Is 37:33
Their tongue is as an *a* shot out . Jer 9:8
and set me as a mark for the *a* . Lam 3:12
his *a* shall go forth as the . Zec 9:14

ARROWS
and pierce them through with his *a* . Num 24:8
I will spend mine *a* upon them. . Deut 32:23
will make mine *a* drunk with blood . Deut 32:42
I will shoot three *a* on the side . 1Sa 20:20
a lad, saying, Go, find out the *a* . 1Sa 20:21
the *a* are on this side of thee, . 1Sa 20:21
Behold, the *a* are beyond thee. . 1Sa 20:22
find out now the *a* which I shoot . 1Sa 20:36
Jonathan's lad gathered up the *a* . 1Sa 20:38
And he sent out *a*, and scattered . 2Sa 22:15
said unto him, Take bow and *a* . 2Kin 13:15
And he took unto him bow and *a* . 2Kin 13:15
And he said, Take the *a* . 2Kin 13:18
shooting a out of a bow, even of . 1Chr 12:2
and upon the bulwarks, to shoot *a*. . 2Chr 26:15
For the *a* of the Almighty are . Job 6:4
he ordaineth his *a* against the . Ps 7:13
Yea, he sent out his *a*, and . Ps 18:14
thou shalt make ready thine *a* . Ps 21:12
For thine *a* stick fast in me, and . Ps 38:2
Thine *a* are sharp in the heart of . Ps 45:5
men, whose teeth are spears and *a* . Ps 57:4
he bendeth his bow to shoot his *a*. . Ps 58:7
bend their bows to shoot their *a* . Ps 64:3
There brake he the *a* of the bow . Ps 76:3
thine *a* also went abroad . Ps 77:17
Sharp *a* of the mighty, with coals . Ps 120:4
As *a* are in the hand of a mighty . Ps 127:4
shoot out thine *a*, and destroy . Ps 144:6
mad man who casteth firebrands, *a* . Prov 26:18
Whose *a* are sharp, and all their . Is 5:28
With *a* and with bows shall men . Is 7:24
their *a* shall be as of a mighty . Is 50:9
the bow, shoot at her, spare no *a* . Jer 50:14
Make bright the *a* . Jer 51:11
He hath caused the *a* of his . Lam 3:13
upon them the evil *a* of famine . Eze 5:16
he made his *a* bright, he . Eze 21:21
will cause thine *a* to fall out of . Eze 39:3
the quivers, the bows and the *a* . Eze 39:9
at the light of thine *a* they went . Hab 3:11

ART See PREFACE.

ARTAXERXES (*ar-tax-erx'-ees*) See
ARTAXERXES.
1. A Persian king known as Longimanus.
And in the days of A wrote Bishlam . Ezr 4:7
companions, unto A king of Persia . Ezr 4:7
to A the king in this sort . Ezr 4:7
unto him, even unto A the king . Ezr 4:11

ARTAXERXES' (*ar-tax-erx'-eez*) Refers to
Artaxerxes 1.
Now when the copy of king A . Ezr 4:23

ARTAXERXES (*ar-tax-erx'-ees*)
1. A Persian king known as Longimanus.
And in the days of A . Ezr 4:7
unto A, king of Persia . Ezr 4:7
A the king of this sort . Ezr 4:8
even unto A the king . Ezr 4:11
2. A Persian king known as Cambyses.
and Darius, and A king of Persia . Ezr 6:14
3. A Persian king known as Darius.
in the reign of A king of Persia . Ezr 7:1
in the seventh year of A the king, . Ezr 7:7
king A gave unto Ezra the priest . Ezr 7:11
A, king of kings, unto Ezra the . . Ezr 7:12

ARTEMAS (*ar'-te-mas*) *A companion of Paul.*
When I shall send A unto thee .... Titus 3:12

ARTEMIS See DIANA.

ARTIFICER
an instructer of every a in brass............ Gen 4:22
the counsellor, and the cunning a........ Is 3:3

ARTIFICERS
work to be made by the hands of a...... 1Chr 29:5
Even to the a and builders gave.......... 2Chr 34:11

ARTILLERY
Jonathan gave his a unto his lad.......... 1Sa 20:40

ARTS
a brought their books together .... Acts 19:19

ARUBBOTH See ARUBOTH.

ARUBOTH (*ar'-u-both*) *A district of Solomon's rule.*
The son of Hesed, in A....................... 1Kin 4:10

ARUMAH (*a-ru'-mah*) *A place in Ephraim.*
And Abimelech dwelt at A.................. Judg 9:41

ARVAD (*ar'-vad*) See ARVADITE. *An island near Zidon.*
of Zidon and A were thy mariners...... Eze 27:8
The men of A with thine army were.... Eze 27:11

ARVADITE (*ar'-vad-ite*) *Descendants of Canaan.*
the A, and the Zemarite.................... Gen 10:18
And the A, and the Zemarite, and the 1Chr 1:16

ARVADITES See ARVADITE.

ARZA (*ar'-zah*) *A steward of King Elah of Israel.*
himself drunk in the house of A.......... 1Kin 16:9

AS See PREFACE.

ASA (*a'-sah*) See ASA's.
1. *A king of Judah.*
A his son reigned in his stead 1Kin 15:8
of Israel reigned A over Judah............ 1Kin 15:9
A did that which was right in the........ 1Kin 15:11
A destroyed her idol, and burnt it........ 1Kin 15:13
And there was war between A............ 1Kin 15:16
out or come in to A king of Judah...... 1Kin 15:17
Then A took all the silver and the........ 1Kin 15:18
king A sent them to Ben-hadad,.......... 1Kin 15:18
Ben-hadad hearkened unto king A 1Kin 15:20
Then king A made a proclamation,...... 1Kin 15:22
king A built with them Geba of............ 1Kin 15:22
The rest of all the acts of A................ 1Kin 15:23
A slept with his fathers, and was........ 1Kin 15:24
second year of A king of Judah.......... 1Kin 15:25
Even in the third year of A king........ 1Kin 15:28
And there was war between A............ 1Kin 15:32
In the third year of A king of.............. 1Kin 15:33
sixth year of A king of Judah.............. 1Kin 16:8
seventh year of A king of Judah.......... 1Kin 16:10
seventh year of A king of Judah.......... 1Kin 16:15
first year of A king of Judah................ 1Kin 16:23
eighth year of A king of Judah............ 1Kin 16:29
Jehoshaphat the son of A began to 1Kin 22:41
in all the ways of A his father.............. 1Kin 22:43
in the days of his father A.................. 1Kin 22:46
A his son, Jehoshaphat his son,.......... 1Chr 3:10
A his son reigned in his stead 2Chr 14:1
A did that which was good and.......... 2Chr 14:2
A had an army of men that bare.......... 2Chr 14:8
Then A went out against him, and........ 2Chr 14:10
A cried unto the LORD his God, and.... 2Chr 14:11
smote the Ethiopians before A 2Chr 14:12
A and the people that...................... 2Chr 14:13
And he went out to meet A, and said. 2Chr 15:2
and said unto him, Hear ye me, A 2Chr 15:2
when A heard these words, and the.... 2Chr 15:8
fifteenth year of the reign of A 2Chr 15:10
Maachah the mother of A the king 2Chr 15:16
A cut down her idol, and stamped...... 2Chr 15:16
of A was perfect all his days.............. 2Chr 15:17
thirtieth year of the reign of A 2Chr 15:19
A Baasha king of Israel came up........ 2Chr 16:1
out or come in to A king of Judah...... 2Chr 16:1
Then A brought out silver and gold 2Chr 16:2
Ben-hadad hearkened unto king A 2Chr 16:4
Then A the king took all Judah 2Chr 16:6
the seer came to A king of Judah........ 2Chr 16:7
Then A was wroth with the seer........ 2Chr 16:10
A oppressed some of the people.......... 2Chr 16:10
And, behold, the acts of A.................. 2Chr 16:11
A in the thirty and ninth year of 2Chr 16:12
A slept with his fathers, and died 2Chr 16:13
which A his father had taken 2Chr 17:2
walked in the way of A his father 2Chr 20:32
in the ways of A king of Judah............ 2Chr 21:12
was it which A the king had made ...... Jer 41:9
and Abia begat A .... Mt 1:7
And A begat Josaphat........................ Mt 1:8
2. *Chief of a Levite family.*
and Berechiah the son of A................ 1Chr 9:16

ASAHEL (*as'-a-hel*) *David's sister.*
there, Joab, and Abishai, and A.......... 2Sa 2:18
A was as light of foot as a wild 2Sa 2:18
And A pursued after Abner................ 2Sa 2:19
behind him, and said, Art thou A........ 2Sa 2:20
But A would not turn aside from........ 2Sa 2:21
And Abner said again to A, Turn 2Sa 2:22
to the place where A fell down............ 2Sa 2:23
servants nineteen men and A.............. 2Sa 2:30
And they took up A, and buried him.... 2Sa 2:32
for the blood of A his brother.............. 2Sa 3:27
brother A at Gibeon in the battle 2Sa 3:30
A the brother of Joab was one of 2Sa 23:24
Abishai, and Joab, and A, three.......... 1Chr 11:26
A the brother of Joab, Elhanan 1Chr 11:26
month was A the brother of Joab........ 1Chr 27:7
2. *A Levite teacher.*
and Nethaniah, and Zebadiah, and A.. 2Chr 17:8
3. *A Levite officer.*
and Azaziah, and Nahath, and A 2Chr 31:13
4. *Father of Jonathan.*
Only Jonathan the son of A................ Ezr 10:15

ASAHIAH (*as-a-hi'-ah*) See ASAIAH. *An officer of King Josiah.*
A a servant of the king's, saying.......... 2Kin 22:12
and Achbor, and Shaphan, and A........ 2Kin 22:14

ASAIAH (*as-a'-yah*)
1. *A descendant of Simeon.*
and Jaakobah, and Jeshohaiah, and A 1Chr 4:36
2. *A descendant of Libni.*
son, Haggiah his son, A his son.......... 1Chr 6:30
3. *A Shilonite of Jerusalem.*
A the firstborn, and his sons 1Chr 9:5
4. *A descendant of Merari.*
A the chief, and his brethren two........ 1Chr 15:11
and for the Levites, for Uriel, A 1Chr 15:11
5. *Same as Asahiah.*
A a servant of the king's, saying.......... 2Chr 34:20

ASAPH (*a'-saf*) See ASAPH'S.
1. *Father of Joah.*
and Joah the son of A the recorder 2Kin 18:18
and Joah the son of A the recorder 2Kin 18:37
the scribe, and Joah, the son of A .... Is 36:22
2. *A musician of David and Solomon.*
And his brother A, who stood on........ 1Chr 6:39
even A the son of Berachiah, the........ 1Chr 6:39
brethren, as the son of Berechiah 1Chr 6:39
So the singers, Heman, A, and............ 1Chr 15:19
A the chief, and next to him................ 1Chr 16:5
but A made a sound with cymbals...... 1Chr 16:5
thank the LORD by the hand of A 1Chr 16:7
ark of the covenant of the LORD A...... 1Chr 16:37
to the service of the sons of A 1Chr 25:1
Of the sons of A 1Chr 25:2
of Asaph under the hands of A 1Chr 25:2
to the king's order to A...................... 1Chr 25:2
lot came forth for A to Joseph............ 1Chr 25:9
the singers, all of them of A................ 2Chr 5:12
a Levite of the sons of A.................... 2Chr 20:14
and of the sons of A.......................... 2Chr 29:13
words of David, and of A the seer 2Chr 29:30
the sons of A were in their place........ 2Chr 35:15
commandment of David, and A.......... 2Chr 35:15
the children of A, an hundred .... Ezr 2:41
the sons of A with cymbals................ Ezr 3:10
the children of A, an hundred .... Neh 7:44
the son of Zabdi, the son of A .... Neh 11:17
Of the sons of A, the singers.............. Neh 11:22
the son of Zaccur, the son of A .... Neh 12:35
A of old there were chief of the.......... Neh 12:46
A Psalm of A .... Ps 73:r
Altaschith, A Psalm or Song of A........ Ps 75:r
on Neginoth, A Psalm or Song of A .... Ps 76:r
to Jeduthun, A Psalm of A.................. Ps 77:r
Maschil of A .... Ps 78:r
A Psalm of A .... Ps 79:r
Shoshannim-Eduth, A Psalm of A...... Ps 80:r
upon Gittith, A Psalm of A.................. Ps 81:r
A Psalm of A .... Ps 82:r
A Song or Psalm of A .... Ps 83:r
3. *A Levite family in post-exilic Jerusalem.*
the son of Zichri, the son of A 1Chr 9:15
4. *Descendants of Merari.*
the son of Kore, of the sons of A 1Chr 26:1
5. *A Persian official.*
a letter unto A the keeper of the .... Neh 2:8

ASAPH'S (*a'-safs*) Refers to Asaph 1.
and Joah, A son, the recorder............ Is 36:3

ASAREEL (*a-sar'-e-el*) *A son of Jehaleleel.*
Ziph, and Ziphah, Tiria, and A 1Chr 4:16

ASARELAH (*as-a-re'-lah*) See JESHARELAH. *A son of a musician of David.*
and Joseph, and Nethaniah, and A 1Chr 25:2

ASA'S (*a'-sahz*) Refers to Asa 1.
nevertheless A heart was perfect 1Kin 15:14

ASCEND
the people shall a up every man .... Josh 6:5
Who shall a into the hill of the .... Ps 24:3
He causeth the vapours to a from...... Ps 135:7
If I a up into heaven, thou art............ Ps 139:8
I will a into heaven, I will.................. Is 14:13
I will a above the heights of the.......... Is 14:14
he causeth the vapours to a from........ Jer 10:13

he causeth the vapors to a from........ Jer 51:16
Thou shalt a and come like a storm.... Eze 38:9
of man a up where he was before........ Jn 6:62
I a unto my Father, and your.............. Jn 20:17
heart, Who shall a into heaven.......... Rom 10:6
shall a out of the bottomless pit .... Rev 17:8

ASCENDED
the smoke thereof a as the smoke...... Ex 19:18
they a by the south, and came unto .. Num 13:22
smoke of the city a up to heaven........ Josh 8:20
and that the smoke of the city a .... Josh 8:21
So Joshua a from Gilgal, he, and........ Josh 10:7
a up on the south side unto................ Josh 15:3
LORD a in the flame of the altar .... Judg 13:20
flame of the city a up to heaven........ Judg 20:40
Thou hast a on high, thou hast.......... Ps 68:18
Who hath a up into heaven, or.......... Prov 30:4
no man hath a up to heaven, but........ Jn 3:13
for I am not yet a to my Father .... Jn 20:17
David is not a into the heavens.......... Acts 2:34
after three days he a from.................. Acts 25:1
When he a up on high, he led............ Eph 4:8
(Now that he a, what is it but............ Eph 4:9
that a up far above all heavens.......... Eph 4:10
a up before God out of the................ Rev 8:4
they a up to heaven in a cloud.......... Rev 11:12

ASCENDETH
the beast that a out of the................ Rev 11:7
of their torment a up for ever .... Rev 14:11

ASCENDING
and behold the angels of God a.......... Gen 28:12
I saw gods a out of the earth.............. 1Sa 28:13
he went before, a up to Jerusalem...... Lk 19:28
open, and the angels of God a............ Jn 1:51
saw another angel a from.................. Rev 7:2

ASCENT
the south to the a of Akrabbim.......... Num 34:4
went up by the a of mount Olivet...... 2Sa 15:30
his a by which he went up into.......... 1Kin 10:5
his a by which he went up unto.......... 2Chr 9:4

ASCRIBE
a ye greatness unto our God.............. Deut 32:3
will a righteousness to my Maker ...... Job 36:3
A ye strength unto God...................... Ps 68:34

ASCRIBED
They have a unto David ten................ 1Sa 18:8
to me they have a but thousands........ 1Sa 18:8

ASENATH (*as'-e-nath*) *A great-grandson of Solomon.*
he gave him to wife A........................ Gen 41:45
came, which A the daughter of .... Gen 41:50
Ephraim, which A the daughter of...... Gen 46:20

ASER (*a'-sur*) See ASHER. *Greek form of Asher.*
of Phanuel, of the tribe of A .... Lk 2:36
Of the tribe of A were sealed.............. Rev 7:6

ASH
he planteth an a, and the rain............ Is 44:14

ASHAMED
man and his wife, and were not a...... Gen 2:25
should she not be a seven days.......... Num 12:14
And they tarried till they were a........ Judg 3:25
because the men were greatly a.......... 2Sa 10:5
as people being a steal away when...... 2Sa 19:3
when they urged him till he was a 2Kin 2:17
stedfastly, until he was a.................... 2Kin 8:11
for the men were greatly a................ 1Chr 19:5
the priests and the Levites were a...... 2Chr 30:15
For I was a to require of the .... Ezr 8:22
And said, O my God, I am a................ Ezr 9:6
they came thither, and were a............ Job 6:20
mockest, shall no man make thee a.... Job 11:3
ye are not a that ye make.................. Job 19:3
Let all mine enemies be a.................. Ps 6:10
let them return and be a suddenly .... Ps 6:10
let me not be a, let not mine.............. Ps 25:2
let none that wait on thee be a .... Ps 25:3
let them be a which transgress.......... Ps 25:3
let me not be a.................................. Ps 25:20
let me never be a.............................. Ps 31:1
Let me not be a, O LORD.................... Ps 31:17
let the wicked be a, and let them........ Ps 31:17
and their faces were not a.................. Ps 34:5
Let them be a and brought to.............. Ps 35:26
shall not be a in the evil time............ Ps 37:19
Let them be a and confounded.......... Ps 40:14
God of hosts, be a for my sake .... Ps 69:6
Let them be a and confounded that.... Ps 70:2
O let not the oppressed return a .... Ps 74:21
which hate me may see it, and be a.... Ps 86:17
when they arise, let them be a .... Ps 109:28
Then shall I not be a, when I.............. Ps 119:6
before kings, and will not be a .... Ps 119:46
Let the proud be a............................ Ps 119:78
that I be not a.................................. Ps 119:80
and let me not be a of my hope .... Ps 119:116
they shall not be a, but they.............. Ps 127:5
but she that maketh a is as................ Prov 12:4
For they shall be a of the oaks............ Is 1:29
a of Ethiopia their expectation,.......... Is 20:5
Be thou a, O Zidon............................ Is 23:4
shall be confounded, and the sun a.... Is 24:23
be a for their envy at the people .... Is 26:11
Jacob, Jacob shall not now be a .... Is 29:22
They were all a of a people that .... Is 30:5
Lebanon is a and hewn down............ Is 33:9

ASHAN — column 1 (continued)

incensed against thee shall be a............. Is 41:11
back, they shall be greatly a................ Is 42:17
that they may be a........................... Is 44:9
all his fellows shall be a................... Is 44:11
fear, and they shall be a together........... Is 44:11
They shall be a, and also.................... Is 45:16
ye shall not be a nor confounded............. Is 45:17
incensed against him shall be a.............. Is 45:24
shall not be a that wait for me.............. Is 49:23
and I know that I shall not be a............. Is 50:7
for thou shalt not be a...................... Is 54:4
shall rejoice, but ye shall be a............. Is 65:13
to your joy, and they shall be a............. Is 66:5
As the thief is a when he is................. Jer 2:26
so is the house of Israel a.................. Jer 2:26
thou also shalt be a of Egypt................ Jer 2:36
as thou wast a of Assyria.................... Jer 2:36
forehead, thou refusedst to be a............. Jer 3:3
Were they a when they had.................... Jer 6:15
nay, they were not at all a.................. Jer 6:15
The wise men are a, they are................. Jer 8:9
Were they a when they had.................... Jer 8:12
nay, they were not at all a.................. Jer 8:12
they shall be a of your revenues............ Jer 12:13
they were a and confounded, and............. Jer 14:3
in the earth, the plowmen were a............ Jer 14:4
she hath been a and confounded.............. Jer 15:9
all that forsake thee shall be a............ Jer 17:13
they shall be greatly a..................... Jer 20:11
surely then shalt thou be a................. Jer 22:22
I was a, yea, even confounded............... Jer 31:19
And Moab shall be a of Chemosh.............. Jer 48:13
as the house of Israel was a of............. Jer 48:13
she that bare you shall be a................ Jer 50:12
which are a of thy lewd way................. Eze 16:27
shalt remember thy ways, and be a........... Eze 16:61
terror they are a of their might............ Eze 32:30
be a and confounded for your own............ Eze 36:32
that they may be a of their................. Eze 43:10
if they be a of all that they............... Eze 43:11
they shall be a because of their............ Hos 4:19
Israel shall be a of his own................ Hos 10:6
Be ye a, O ye husbandmen.................... Joel 1:11
and my people shall never be a.............. Joel 2:26
and my people shall never be a.............. Joel 2:27
Then shall the seers be a................... Mic 3:7
thou not be a for all thy doings............ Zeph 3:11
for her expectation shall be a.............. Zec 9:5
be a every one of his vision................ Zec 13:4
therefore shall be a of the................. Mk 8:38
also shall the Son of man be a.............. Mk 8:38
For whosoever shall be a of me.............. Lk 9:26
of him shall the Son of man be a............ Lk 9:26
all his adversaries were a.................. Lk 13:17
to beg I am a............................... Lk 16:3
For I am not a of the gospel of............. Rom 1:16
And hope maketh not a....................... Rom 5:5
those things whereof ye are now a........... Rom 6:21
they shall not be a......................... Rom 9:33
believeth on him shall not be a............. Rom 10:11
thing to him of you, I am not a............. 2Cor 7:14
ye) should be a in this same................ 2Cor 9:4
destruction, I should not be a.............. 2Cor 10:8
that in nothing I shall be a................ Phil 1:20
with him, that he may be a.................. 2Th 3:14
Be not thou therefore a of the............. 2Ti 1:8
nevertheless I am not a..................... 2Ti 1:12
me, and was not a of my chain............... 2Ti 1:16
workman that needeth not to be a........... 2Ti 2:15
he is of the contrary part may be a........ Titus 2:8
he is not a to call them brethren.......... Heb 2:11
wherefore God is not a to be............... Heb 11:16
they may be a that falsely accuse.......... 1Pet 3:16
as a Christian, let him not be a........... 1Pet 4:16
not be a before him at his coming.......... 1Jn 2:28

ASHAN (a'-shan) See COR-ASHAN. A Levitical
   city in Judah.
Libnah, and Ether, and A................... Josh 15:42
Ain, Remmon, and Ether, and A.............. Josh 19:7
and Ain, Rimmon, and Tochen, and A......... 1Chr 4:32
And A with her suburbs..................... 1Chr 6:59

ASHARELAH See ASARELAH.

ASHBEA (ash'-be-ah) Descendants of Shelah.
fine linen, of the house of A.............. 1Chr 4:21

ASHBEL (ash'-bel) See ASHBELITES. A son of
   Benjamin.
were Belah, and Becher, and A.............. Gen 46:21
of A, the family of the.................... Num 26:38
A the second, and Aharah the third......... 1Chr 8:1

ASHBELITES (ash'-bel-ites) Descendants of
   Ashbel.
of Ashbel, the family of the A............. Num 26:38

ASHCHENAZ (ash'-ke-naz) See ASHKENAZ.
   1. A son of Gomer.
A, and Riphath, and Togarmah............... 1Chr 1:6
   2. A tribe near Armenia.
kingdoms of Ararat, Minni, and A........... Jer 51:27

ASHDOD (ash'-dod) See ASHDODITES, AZOTUS.
   A Philistine city.
only in Gaza, in Gath, and in A............ Josh 11:22
unto the sea, all that lay near A.......... Josh 15:46
A with her towns and her villages.......... Josh 15:47
brought it from Eben-ezer unto A........... 1Sa 5:1
when they of A arose early on the.......... 1Sa 5:3
of Dagon in this day....................... 1Sa 5:5
the LORD was heavy upon them of A.......... 1Sa 5:6

ASHDOD — column 2 (continued)

smote them with emerods, even A............ 1Sa 5:6
when the men of A saw that it was.......... 1Sa 5:7
for A one, for Gaza one, for............... 1Sa 6:17
wall of Jabneh, and the wall of A.......... 2Chr 26:6
and built cities about A................... 2Chr 26:6
Jews that had married wives of A........... Neh 13:23
spake half in the speech of A.............. Neh 13:24
the year that Tartan came unto A........... Is 20:1
sent him,) and fought against A............ Is 20:1
and Ekron, and the remnant of A............ Jer 25:20
cut off the inhabitant from A.............. Amos 1:8
Publish in the palaces at A................ Amos 3:9
shall drive out A at the noonday........... Zeph 2:4
And a bastard shall dwell in A............. Zec 9:6

ASHDODITES (ash'-dod-ites) See
   ASHDOTHITES. Inhabitants of Ashdod.
and the Ammonites, and the A............... Neh 4:7

ASHDOTHITES (ash'-doth-ites) See
   ASHDODITES. Same as Ashdodites.
the Gazathites, and the A, the............. Josh 13:3

ASHDOTH-PISGAH (ash''-doth-piz'gah) The
   eastern slope of Mt. Pisgah.
the salt sea, under a eastward............. Deut 3:17
and from the south, under A................ Josh 12:3
And Beth-peor, and A, under................ Josh 13:20

ASHER (ash'-ur) See ASER, ASHERITES.
   1. A son of Jacob by Zilpah.
and she called his name A.................. Gen 30:13
Gad, and A: these are the sons............. Gen 35:26
And the sons of A.......................... Gen 46:17
Out of A his bread shall be fat............ Gen 49:20
Dan, and Naphtali, Gad, and A.............. Ex 1:4
of the daughter of A was Sarah............. Num 26:46
and Benjamin, Naphtali, Gad, and A........ 1Chr 2:2
The sons of A; Imnah, and Isuah........... 1Chr 7:30
All these were the children of A.......... 1Chr 7:40
   2. A tribe descended from Asher 1.
Of A...................................... Num 1:13
Of the children of a, by their............ Num 1:40
of them, even of the tribe of A........... Num 1:41
by him shall be the tribe of A............ Num 1:41
Of A shall be Pagiel the son of........... Num 2:27
prince of the children of A............... Num 7:72
of A was Pagiel the son of Ocran.......... Num 10:26
Of the tribe of A, Sethur the son........ Num 13:13
Of the children of A after their......... Num 26:44
Of A according to those that were........ Num 26:47
of the tribe of the children of A........ Num 34:27
Reuben, Gad, and A, and Zebulun.......... Deut 27:13
of A he said, Let Asher be............... Deut 33:24
of A according to their families......... Josh 19:24
of A according to their families......... Josh 19:31
reacheth to A on the west side........... Josh 19:34
and out of the tribe of A................ Josh 21:6
And out of the tribe of A, Mishal........ Josh 21:30
Neither did A drive out the.............. Judg 1:31
A continued on the sea shore, and........ Judg 5:17
and he sent messengers unto A............ Judg 6:35
out of Naphtali, and out of A............ Judg 7:23
and out of the tribe of A................ 1Chr 6:62
And out of the tribe of A................ 1Chr 6:74
And of A, such as went forth to.......... 1Chr 12:36
Nevertheless divers of A................. 2Chr 30:11
the west side, a portion for A........... Eze 48:2
And by the border of A, from the......... Eze 48:3
one gate of Gad, one gate of A........... Eze 48:34
   3. A town in Manasseh.
Manasseh was from A to Michmethah........ Josh 17:7
met together in A on the north........... Josh 17:10
in A Beth-shean and her towns............ Josh 17:11
Baanah the son of Hushai was in A........ 1Kin 4:16

ASHERITES (ash'-ur-ites) Same as Asher 2.
But the A dwelt among the................ Judg 1:32

ASHES
the Lord, which am but dust and a........ Gen 18:27
you handfuls of a of the furnace......... Ex 9:8
they took a of the furnace, and.......... Ex 9:10
make his pans to receive his a........... Ex 27:3
east part, by the place of the a......... Lev 1:16
where the a are poured out, and.......... Lev 4:12
where the a are poured out, shall........ Lev 4:12
take up the a which the fire hath........ Lev 6:10
carry forth the a without the............ Lev 6:11
take away the a from the altar........... Num 4:13
gather up the a of the heifer............ Num 19:9
the that gathereth the a of the......... Num 19:10
of the a of the burnt heifer of......... Num 19:17
Tamar put a on her head, and rent....... 2Sa 13:19
the a that are upon it shall............ 1Kin 13:3
the a poured out from the altar......... 1Kin 13:5
himself with a upon his face............ 1Kin 20:38
took the a away from his face........... 1Kin 20:41
carried the a of them unto.............. 2Kin 23:4
and put on sackcloth with a............. Est 4:1
and many lay in sackcloth and a......... Est 4:3
and he sat down among the a............. Job 2:8
Your remembrances are like unto a....... Job 13:12
and I am become like dust and a......... Job 30:19
myself, and repent in dust and a....... Job 42:6
For I have eaten a like bread........... Ps 102:9
scattereth the hoar frost like a........ Ps 147:16
He feedeth on a......................... Is 44:20
spread sackcloth and a under him........ Is 58:5
to give unto them beauty for a.......... Is 61:3
sackcloth, and wallow thyself in a...... Jer 6:26
and wallow yourselves in the a.......... Jer 25:34
of the dead bodies, and of the a........ Jer 31:40

ASHES — column 3 (continued)

stones, he hath covered me with a........ Lam 3:16
shall wallow themselves in the a......... Eze 27:30
I will bring thee to a upon the.......... Eze 28:18
with fasting, and sackcloth, and a....... Dan 9:3
him with sackcloth, and sat in a......... Jonah 3:6
for they shall be a under the............ Mal 4:3
long ago in sackcloth and a.............. Mt 11:21
sitting in sackcloth and a............... Lk 10:13
the a of an heifer sprinkling the........ Heb 9:13
Gomorrah into a condemned them........... 2Pet 2:6

ASHHUR See ASHUR.

ASHIMA (ash'-im-ah) An idol of Hamath.
and the men of Hamath made A............. 2Kin 17:30

ASHKELON (ash'-ke-lon) See ASKELON,
   ESHKALONITES. A Philistine city.
upon him, and he went down to A.......... Judg 14:19
the land of the Philistines, and A...... Jer 25:20
A is cut off with the remnant of........ Jer 47:5
hath given it a charge against A........ Jer 47:7
that holdeth the sceptre from A......... Amos 1:8
be forsaken, and A a desolation......... Zeph 2:4
in the houses of A shall they lie....... Zeph 2:7
A shall see it, and fear................ Zec 9:5
Gaza, and A shall not be inhabited...... Zec 9:5

ASHKENAZ (ash'-ke-naz) See ASHCHENAZ. A
   son of Gomer.
A, and Riphath, and Togarmah............. Gen 10:3

ASHNAH (ash'-nah)
   1. A town in Judah near Dan.
valley, Eshtaol, and Zoreah, and A...... Josh 15:33
   2. A town in Judah on the plains.
And Jiphtah, and A, and Nezib,.......... Josh 15:43

ASHPENAZ (ash'-pe-naz) A prince of the
   eunuchs under Nebuchadnezzar.
the king spake unto A the master........ Dan 1:3

ASHRIEL (ash'-re-el) See ASRIEL. A grandson
   of Manasseh.
A, whom she bare........................ 1Chr 7:14

ASHTAROTH (ash'-ta-roth) See
   ASHTERATHITE, ASHTAROTH, ASTORETH,
   ASTAROTH, BEESHTERAH.
   1. A god of the Philistines, Phoenicians, and
      Zidonians.
the LORD, and served Baal and a......... Judg 2:13
the LORD, and served Baalim, and A...... Judg 10:6
A from among you, and prepare your...... 1Sa 7:3
Israel did put away Baalim and A........ 1Sa 7:4
LORD, and have served Baalim and A...... 1Sa 12:10
put his armour in the house of A........ 1Sa 31:10
   2. A city in Bashan.
Og king of Bashan, which was at A....... Josh 9:10
of the giants, that dwelt at A.......... Josh 12:4
Og in Bashan, which reigned in A........ Josh 13:12
And half Gilead, and A, and Edrei....... Josh 13:31
   3. A Levitical city in Manasseh.
suburbs, and A with her suburbs......... 1Chr 6:71

ASHTERATHITE (ash'-ter-a-thite) Family
   name of Uzziah.
Uzzia the A, Shama and Jehiel the....... 1Chr 11:44

ASHTEROTH (ash'-te-roth) A city in Og.
smote the Rephaims in A Karnaim......... Gen 14:5

ASHTEROTH-KARNAIM See ASHTAROTH.

ASHTORETH (ash'-to-reth) See ASHTAROTH.
   Same as Ashtaroth 1.
For Solomon went after A the............ 1Kin 11:5
have worshipped A the goddess of........ 1Kin 11:33
the A the abomination of the............ 2Kin 23:13

ASHUR (ash'-ur) See ASHURITES, ASSHUR,
   ASSUR, ASSYRIA. A son of Hezron.
bare him A the father of Tekoa.......... 1Chr 2:24
A the father of Tekoa had two........... 1Chr 4:5

ASHURBANIPAL See ASNAPPER.

ASHURITES (ash'-ur-ites) See ASSHURIM. A
   tribe in the plain of Esdraelon.
king over Gilead, and over the A........ 2Sa 2:9
the company of the A have made.......... Eze 27:6

ASHVATH (ash'-vath) A descendant of Asher.
Pasach, and Bimhal, and A............... 1Chr 7:33

ASIA (a'-she-ah)
   1. A Roman province.
and Cappadocia, in Pontus, and a........ Acts 2:9
and of them of Cilicia and of A......... Acts 6:9
Ghost to preach the word in A........... Acts 16:6
in A heard the word of the Lord......... Acts 19:10
himself stayed in A for a season........ Acts 19:22
And certain of the chief of A........... Acts 19:31
him into a Sopater of Berea............. Acts 20:4
and of A, Tychicus and Trophimus........ Acts 20:4
he would not spend the time in A........ Acts 20:16
the first day that I came into A........ Acts 20:18
The churches of A salute you............ 1Cor 16:19
our trouble which came to us in A....... 2Cor 1:8
are in A be turned away from me......... 2Ti 1:15
Pontus, Galatia, Cappadocia,............ 1Pet 1:1
the seven churches which are in A....... Rev 1:4
the seven churches which are in A....... Rev 1:11
   2. Another name for Asia Minor.
but almost throughout all A............. Acts 19:26
should be destroyed, whom all A......... Acts 19:27
ended, the Jews which were of A......... Acts 21:27
Whereupon certain Jews from A........... Acts 24:18

to sail by the coasts of A .... Acts 27:2

ASIDE
And Moses said, I will now turn a .... Ex 3:3
LORD saw that he turned a to see .... Ex 3:4
They have turned a quickly out of .... Ex 32:8
unto them, If any man's wife go a .... Num 5:12
if thou hast not gone a to .... Num 5:19
But if thou hast gone a to .... Num 5:20
when a wife goeth a to another .... Num 5:29
the ass turned a out of the way .... Num 22:23
ye shall not turn a to the right .... Deut 5:32
turned a out of the way which I .... Deut 9:12
ye had turned a quickly out of .... Deut 9:16
be not deceived, and ye turn a .... Deut 11:16
but turn a out of the way which I .... Deut 11:28
that he turn not a from the .... Deut 17:20
thou shalt not go a from any of .... Deut 28:14
turn a from the way which I have .... Deut 31:29
that ye turn not a therefrom to .... Josh 23:6
he turned a to see the carcase of .... Judg 14:8
We will not turn a hither into .... Judg 19:12
And they turned a thither, to go .... Judg 19:15
turn a, sit down here .... Ruth 4:1
And he turned a, and sat down .... Ruth 4:1
turned not a to the right hand or 1Sa 6:12
but turned a after lucre, and took 1Sa 8:3
yet turn not a from following the 1Sa 12:21
And turn ye not a 1Sa 12:21
Turn thee a to thy right hand or 2Sa 2:21
not turn a from following of him 2Sa 2:21
Turn thee a from following me 2Sa 2:22
Howbeit he refused to turn a 2Sa 2:23
Joab took him a in the gate to 2Sa 3:27
but David carried it a into the 2Sa 6:10
And the king said unto him, Turn a 2Sa 18:30
And he turned a, and stood still 2Sa 18:30
turned not a from any thing that 1Kin 15:5
and, behold, a man turned 1Kin 20:39
they turned a to fight against 1Kin 22:32
he turned not a from it, doing 2Kin 22:43
thou shalt set a that which is 2Kin 4:4
turned not a to the right hand or 2Kin 22:2
but carried it a into the house 1Chr 13:13
paths of their way are turned a .... Job 6:18
They are all gone a, they are all .... Ps 14:3
proud, nor such as turn a to lies .... Ps 40:4
they were turned a like a .... Ps 78:57
hate the work of them that turn a .... Ps 101:3
As for such as turn a unto their .... Ps 125:5
a by the flocks of thy companions .... Song 1:7
whither is thy beloved turned a .... Song 6:1
To turn a the needy from judgment .... Is 10:2
turn a the just for a thing of .... Is 29:21
turn a out of the path, cause the .... Is 30:11
deceived heart hath turned him a .... Is 44:20
turneth a to tarry for a night .... Jer 14:8
or who shall go a to ask how thou .... Jer 15:5
He hath turned a my ways, and .... Lam 3:11
To turn a the right of a man .... Lam 3:35
turn a the way of the meek .... Amos 2:7
they turn a the poor in the gate .... Amos 5:12
that turn a the stranger from his .... Mal 3:5
he turned a into the parts of .... Mt 2:22
For laying a the commandment of .... Mk 7:8
he took him a from the multitude .... Mk 7:33
went a privately into a desert .... Lk 9:10
supper, and laid a his garments .... Jn 13:4
them to go a out of the council .... Acts 4:15
and went with him a privately .... Acts 23:19
And when they were gone a, they .... Acts 26:31
have turned a unto vain jangling 1Ti 1:6
are already turned a after Satan 1Ti 5:15
let us lay a every weight, and the .... Heb 12:1
Wherefore laying a all malice 1Pet 2:1

ASIEL (a'-se'-el) *Grandfather of Jehu.*
the son of Seraiah, the son of A........ 1Chr 4:35

ASK
it that thou dost a after my name .... Gen 32:29
A me never so much dowry and gift, ... Gen 34:12
who shall a counsel for him after .... Num 27:21
For a now of the days that are .... Deut 4:32
a from the one side of heaven .... Deut 4:32
and make search, and a diligently .... Deut 13:14
a thy father, and he will shew .... Deut 32:7
that when your children a their .... Josh 4:6
When your children shall a their .... Josh 4:21
him to a of her father a field .... Josh 15:18
him to a of her father a field .... Judg 1:14
A counsel, we pray thee, of God, ... Judg 18:5
sins this evil, to a us a king 1Sa 12:19
A thy young men, and they will 1Sa 25:8
Wherefore then dost thou a of me 1Sa 28:16
the thing that I shall a thee 1Sa 14:18
shall surely a counsel at Abel 2Sa 20:18
now I a one petition of thee, ... 1Kin 2:16
said unto her, A me, my mother 1Kin 2:20
why dost thou a Abishag the 1Kin 2:22
a for him the kingdom also 1Kin 2:22
said, A what I shall give thee 1Kin 3:5
to a a thing of thee for her son 1Kin 14:5
A what I shall do for thee, ... 2Kin 2:9
him, A what I shall give thee 2Chr 1:7
together, to a help of the LORD 2Chr 20:4
But a now the beasts, and they .... Job 12:7
A of me, and I shall give thee the .... Ps 2:8
A thee a sign of the LORD thy God .... Is 7:11
a it either in the depth, or in .... Is 7:11
But Ahaz said, I will not a .... Is 7:12
A me of things to come concerning .... Is 45:11

they a of me the ordinances of .... Is 58:2
a for the old paths, where is the .... Jer 6:16
go aside to a how thou doest .... Jer 15:5
A ye now among the heathen, who .... Jer 18:13
or a priest, shall a thee .... Jer 23:33
A ye now, and see whether a man .... Jer 30:6
Jeremiah, I will a thee a thing .... Jer 38:14
a him that fleeth, and her that .... Jer 48:19
They shall a the way to Zion with .... Jer 50:5
the young children a bread .... Lam 4:4
that whosoever shall a a petition .... Dan 6:7
that every man that shall a a .... Dan 6:12
My people a counsel at their .... Hos 4:12
A now the priests concerning the .... Hag 2:11
A ye of the LORD rain in the time .... Zec 10:1
ye have need of, before ye a him .... Mt 6:8
A, and it shall be given you .... Mt 7:7
of you, whom if his son a bread .... Mt 7:9
Or if he a a fish, will he give .... Mt 7:10
good things to them that a him .... Mt 7:11
give her whatsoever she would a .... Mt 14:7
any thing that they shall a .... Mt 18:19
and said, Ye know not what ye a .... Mt 20:22
whatsoever ye shall a in prayer .... Mt 21:22
I also will a you one thing .... Mt 21:24
forth a him any more questions .... Mt 22:46
that they should a Barabbas .... Mt 27:20
A of me whatsoever thou wilt, and .... Mk 6:22
Whatsoever thou shalt a of me .... Mk 6:23
unto her mother, What shall I a .... Mk 6:24
saying, and were afraid to a him .... Mk 9:32
unto them, Ye know not what ye a .... Mk 10:38
I will also a of you one question .... Mk 11:29
that durst a him any question .... Mk 12:34
unto them, I will a you one thing .... Lk 6:9
away thy goods a them not again .... Lk 6:30
they feared to a him of that .... Lk 9:45
And I say unto you, A, and it shall .... Lk 11:9
If a son shall a bread of any of .... Lk 11:11
or if he a a fish, will he for a .... Lk 11:11
Or if he shall a an egg, will he .... Lk 11:12
Holy Spirit to them that a him .... Lk 11:13
much, of him they will a the more .... Lk 12:48
And if any man a you, Why do ye .... Lk 19:31
I will also a you one thing .... Lk 20:3
not a him any question at all .... Lk 20:40
And if I also a you, ye will not .... Lk 22:68
Levites from Jerusalem to a him .... Jn 1:19
a him: he shall speak .... Jn 9:21
He is of age; a him .... Jn 9:23
whatsoever thou wilt a of God, ... Jn 11:22
that he should a who it should be .... Jn 13:24
whatsoever ye shall a in my name .... Jn 14:13
If ye shall a any thing in my .... Jn 14:14
ye shall a what ye will, and it .... Jn 15:7
shall a of the Father in my name .... Jn 15:16
that they were desirous to a him .... Jn 16:19
in that day ye shall a me nothing .... Jn 16:23
Whatsoever ye shall a the Father .... Jn 16:23
a, and ye shall receive, that your .... Jn 16:24
At that day ye shall a in my name .... Jn 16:26
not that any man should a thee .... Jn 16:30
a them which heard me, what I .... Jn 18:21
none of the disciples durst a him .... Jn 21:12
to a alms of them that entered .... Acts 3:2
I a therefore for what intent ye .... Acts 10:29
let them a their husbands at home 1Cor 14:35
above all that we a or think .... Eph 3:20
you lack wisdom, let him a of God .... Jas 1:5
But let him a in faith, nothing .... Jas 1:6
yet ye have not, because ye a not .... Jas 4:2
Ye a, and receive not .... Jas 4:3
because ye a amiss .... Jas 4:3
And whatsoever we a, we receive of 1Jn 3:22
if we a any thing according to 1Jn 5:14
that he hear us, whatsoever we a 1Jn 5:15
is not unto death, he shall a 1Jn 5:16

ASKED
I a her, and said, Whose daughter .... Gen 24:47
of the place a him of his wife .... Gen 26:7
And Jacob a him, and said, Tell me, ... Gen 32:29
and the man a him, saying, What .... Gen 37:15
Then he a the men of that place, ... Gen 38:21
he a Pharaoh's officers that were .... Gen 40:7
The man a us straitly of our .... Gen 43:7
he a them of their welfare, and .... Gen 43:27
My lord a his servants, saying, ... Gen 44:19
they a each other of their .... Ex 18:7
a not counsel at the mouth of the .... Josh 9:14
they gave him the city which he a .... Josh 19:50
the children of Israel a the LORD .... Judg 1:1
He a water, and she gave him milk .... Judg 5:25
And when they enquired and a .... Judg 6:29
but I a him not whence he was, ... Judg 13:6
a counsel of God, and said, Which .... Judg 20:18
a counsel of the Lord, saying, ... Judg 20:23
petition that thou hast a of him 1Sa 1:17
Because I have a him of the LORD 1Sa 1:20
me my petition which I a of him, ... 1Sa 1:27
the people that a of him a king 1Sa 8:10
Saul a counsel of God, Shall I go 1Sa 14:37
and he a and said, Where are Samuel 1Sa 19:22
David earnestly a leave of me 1Sa 20:6
David earnestly a leave of me to 1Sa 20:28
that Solomon had a this thing 1Kin 3:10
Because thou hast a this thing 1Kin 3:11
hast not a for thyself long life 1Kin 3:11
neither hast a riches for thyself 1Kin 3:11
nor hast a the life of thine 1Kin 3:11
but hast a for thyself 1Kin 3:11

thee that which thou hast not a 1Kin 3:13
all her desire, whatsoever she a 1Kin 10:13
he said, Thou hast a a hard thing 2Kin 2:10
And when the king a the woman 2Kin 8:6
heart, and thou hast not a riches 2Chr 1:11
neither yet hast a long life 2Chr 1:11
but hast a wisdom and knowledge 2Chr 1:11
all her desire, whatsoever she a 2Chr 9:12
Then a we those elders, and said .... Ezr 5:9
We a their names also, to certify .... Ezr 5:10
I a them concerning the Jews that .... Neh 1:2
Have ye not a them that go by the .... Job 21:29
He a life of thee, and thou gavest .... Ps 21:4
The people a, and he brought .... Ps 105:40
Egypt, and have a it at my mouth .... Is 30:2
when I a of them, could answer a .... Is 41:28
sought of them that a not for me .... Is 65:1
they a Baruch, saying, Tell us .... Jer 36:17
the king a him secretly in his .... Jer 37:17
princes unto Jeremiah, and a him .... Jer 38:27
that a such things at any .... Dan 2:10
a him the truth of all this .... Dan 7:16
And they a him, saying, Is it .... Mt 12:10
he a his disciples, saying, Whom .... Mt 16:13
And his disciples a him, saying, ... Mt 17:10
is no resurrection, and a him .... Mt 22:23
a him a question, tempting him, ... Mt 22:35
gathered together, Jesus a them .... Mt 22:41
and the governor a him, saying, ... Mt 27:11
the twelve a of him the parable .... Mk 4:10
he a him, What is thy name .... Mk 5:9
with haste unto the king, and a .... Mk 6:25
the Pharisees and scribes a him .... Mk 7:5
his disciples a him concerning .... Mk 7:17
he a them, How many loaves have .... Mk 8:5
him, he a him if he saw ought .... Mk 8:23
and by the way he a his disciples .... Mk 8:27
And they a him, saying, Why say .... Mk 9:11
he a the scribes, What question .... Mk 9:16
he a his father, How long is it .... Mk 9:21
his disciples a him privately .... Mk 9:28
and being in the house he a them .... Mk 9:33
a him, Is it lawful for a man to .... Mk 10:2
in the house his disciples a him .... Mk 10:10
a him, Good Master, what shall I .... Mk 10:17
and they a him, ... Mk 12:18
a him, Which is the first .... Mk 12:28
John and Andrew a him privately, ... Mk 13:3
a Jesus, saying, Answerest thou .... Mk 14:60
Again the high priest a him .... Mk 14:61
And Pilate a him, Art thou the .... Mk 15:2
Pilate a him again, saying, ... Mk 15:4
he a him whether he had been any .... Mk 15:44
he a for a writing table, and .... Lk 1:63
And the people a him, saying, What .... Lk 3:10
And his disciples a him, saying, ... Lk 8:9
And Jesus a him, saying, What is .... Lk 8:30
he a them, saying, Whom say the .... Lk 9:18
a what these things meant .... Lk 15:26
And a certain ruler a him, saying, ... Lk 18:18
pass by, he a what it meant .... Lk 18:36
when he was come near, he a him .... Lk 18:40
And they a him, saying, Master, we .... Lk 20:21
and they a him, ... Lk 20:27
And they a him, saying, Master, ... Lk 21:7
him, saying, Prophesy, who is .... Lk 22:64
And Pilate a him, saying, Art thou .... Lk 23:3
he a whether the man were a .... Lk 23:6
And they a him, What then .... Jn 1:21
And they a him, and said unto him, ... Jn 1:25
thou wouldest have a of him .... Jn 4:10
Then a they him, What man is that .... Jn 5:12
And his disciples a him, saying, ... Jn 9:2
a him how he had received his .... Jn 9:15
And they a them, saying, Is this .... Jn 9:19
Hitherto have ye a nothing in my .... Jn 16:24
Then a he them again, Whom seek .... Jn 18:7
The high priest then a Jesus of .... Jn 18:19
they a of him, saying, Lord, wilt .... Acts 1:6
to go into the temple a an alms .... Acts 3:3
had set them in the midst, they a .... Acts 4:7
and the high priest a them .... Acts 5:27
a whether Simon, which was .... Acts 10:18
a him, What is that thou hast to .... Acts 23:19
he a of what province he was .... Acts 23:34
I a him whether he would go to .... Acts 25:20
unto them that a not after me .... Rom 10:20

ASKELON (as'-ke-lon) See ASHKELON. *A Philistine city.*
A with the coast thereof, and .... Judg 1:18
one, for Gaza one, for A one 1Sa 6:17
it not in the streets of A 2Sa 1:20

ASKEST
Why a thou thus after my name, ... Judg 13:18
a drink of me, which am a woman .... Jn 4:9
Why a thou me? .... Jn 18:21

ASKETH
a thee, saying, Whose art thou .... Gen 32:17
thy son a thee in time to come .... Ex 13:14
when thy son a thee in time to .... Deut 6:20
hands earnestly, the prince a .... Mic 7:3
and the judge a for a reward .... Mic 7:3
Give to him that a thee, and from .... Mt 5:42
For every one that a receiveth .... Mt 7:8
Give to every man that a of thee .... Lk 6:30
For every one that a receiveth .... Lk 11:10
and none of you a me, Whither .... Jn 16:5
an answer to every man that a you 1Pet 3:15

ASKING

of the LORD, in *a* you a king	1Sa 12:17
also for *a* counsel of one that	1Ch 10:13
heart by *a* meat for their lust	Ps 78:18
hearing them, and *a* them questions	Lk 2:46
So when they continued *a* him	Jn 8:7
a no question for conscience sake	1Cor 10:25
a no question for conscience sake	1Cor 10:27

ASLEEP

for he was fast *a* and weary	Judg 4:21
for they were all *a*	1Sa 26:12
lips of those that are *a* to speak	Song 7:9
and he lay, and was fast *a*	Jonah 1:5
but he was *a*	Mt 8:24
the disciples, and findeth them *a*	Mt 26:40
And he came and found them *a* again	Mt 26:43
part of the ship, *a* on a pillow	Mk 4:38
returned, he found them *a* again	Mk 14:40
But as they sailed he fell *a*	Lk 8:23
when he had said this, he fell *a*	Acts 7:60
present, but some are fallen *a*	1Cor 15:6
fallen *a* in Christ are perished	1Cor 15:18
concerning them which are *a*	1Th 4:13
not prevent them which are *a*	1Th 4:15
for since the fathers fell *a*	2Pet 3:4

ASNAH (as'-nah) A family of exiles.

The children of A, the children	Ezr 2:50

ASNAPPER (as-nap'-pur) An Assyrian king.

noble A brought over, and set in	Ezr 4:10

ASP

shall play on the hole of the *a*	Is 11:8

ASPATHA (as'-pa-thah) A son of Haman.

And Parshandatha, and Dalphon, and A.	Est 9:7

ASPS

dragons, and the cruel venom of *a*	Deut 32:33
it is the gall of *a* within him	Job 20:14
He shall suck the poison of *a*	Job 20:16
the poison of *a* is under their	Rom 3:13

ASRIEL (as'-re-el) See ASHRIEL, ASRIELITES. A grandson of Manasseh.

And of A, the family of the	Num 26:31
Helek, and for the children of A	Josh 17:2

ASRIELITES (as'-re-el-ites) Descendants of Asriel.

And of Asriel, the family of the A	Num 26:31

ASS

in the morning, and saddled his *a*	Gen 22:3
men, Abide ye here with the *a*	Gen 22:5
give his *a* provender in the inn	Gen 42:27
clothes, and laded every man his *a*	Gen 44:13
Issachar is a strong *a* couching	Gen 49:14
his sons, and set them upon an *a*	Ex 4:20
every firstling of *a* an thou	Ex 13:13
nor his ox, nor his *a*, nor any	Ex 20:17
an ox or an *a* fall therein	Ex 21:33
alive, whether it be ox, or *a*	Ex 22:4
whether it be for ox, for *a*	Ex 22:9
deliver unto his neighbour an *a*	Ex 22:10
enemy's ox or his *a* going astray	Ex 23:4
If thou see the *a* of him that	Ex 23:5
thine *a* may rest, and the son of	Ex 23:12
But the firstling of an *a* thou	Ex 34:20
I have not taken one *a* from them	Num 16:15
in the morning, and saddled his *a*	Num 22:21
Now he was riding upon his *a*	Num 22:22
the *a* saw the angel of the LORD	Num 22:23
the *a* turned aside out of the way	Num 22:23
and Balaam smote the *a*, to turn	Num 22:23
when the *a* saw the angel of the	Num 22:25
when the *a* saw the angel of the	Num 22:27
and he smote the *a* with a staff	Num 22:27
LORD opened the mouth of the *a*	Num 22:28
And Balaam said unto the *a*	Num 22:29
the *a* said unto Balaam	Num 22:30
Am not I thine *a*	Num 22:30
smitten thine *a* these three times	Num 22:32
the *a* saw me, and turned from me	Num 22:33
nor thine ox, nor thine *a*	Deut 5:14
his maidservant, his ox, or his *a*	Deut 5:21
manner shalt thou do with his *a*	Deut 22:3
shalt not see thy brother's ox or	Deut 22:4
plow with an ox and an *a* together	Deut 22:10
thine *a* shall be violently taken	Deut 28:31
and old, and ox, and sheep, and *a*	Josh 6:21
and she lighted off her *a*	Josh 15:18
and she lighted from off her *a*	Judg 1:14
neither sheep, nor ox, nor *a*	Judg 6:4
sons that rode on thirty *a* colts	Judg 10:4
rode on threescore and ten *a* colts	Judg 12:14
a new jawbone of an *a*	Judg 15:15
said, With the jawbone of an *a*	Judg 15:16
with the jaw of an *a* have I slain	Judg 15:16
the man took her up upon an *a*	Judg 19:28
or whose *a* have I taken	1Sa 12:3
suckling, ox and sheep, camel and *a*	1Sa 15:3
Jesse took an *a* laden with bread	1Sa 16:20
it was so, as she rode on the *a*	1Sa 25:20
she hasted, and lighted off the *a*	1Sa 25:23
and arose, and rode upon an *a*	1Sa 25:42
not followed, he saddled his *a*	1Sa 17:23
said, I will saddle me an *a*	2Sa 19:26
And Shimei arose, and saddled his *a*	1Kin 2:40
unto his sons, Saddle me the *a*	1Kin 13:13
So they saddled him the *a*	1Kin 13:13
that he saddled for him the *a*	1Kin 13:23

the *a* stood by it, the lion also	1Kin 13:24
his sons, saying, Saddle me the *a*	1Kin 13:27
carcase cast in the way, and the *a*	1Kin 13:28
eaten the carcase, nor torn the *a*	1Kin 13:28
man of God, and laid it upon the *a*	1Kin 13:29
Then she saddled an *a*, and said to	2Kin 4:24
Doth the wild *a* bray when he hath	Job 6:5
away the *a* of the fatherless	Job 24:3
Who hath sent out the wild *a* free	Job 39:5
loosed the bands of the wild *a*	Job 39:5
for the horse, a bridle for the *a*	Prov 26:3
owner, and the *a* his master's crib	Is 1:3
the feet of the ox and the *a*	Is 32:20
A wild *a* used to the wilderness	Jer 2:24
be buried with the burial of an *a*	Jer 22:19
a wild *a* alone by himself	Hos 8:9
lowly, and riding upon an *a*	Zec 9:9
and upon a colt the foal of an *a*	Zec 9:9
mule, of the camel, and of the *a*	Zec 14:15
ye shall find an *a* tied, and a	Mt 21:2
thee, meek, and sitting upon an *a*	Mt 21:5
and a colt the foal of an *a*	Mt 21:5
And brought the *a*, and the colt, and	Mt 21:7
his ox or his *a* from the stall	Lk 13:15
an *a* or an ox fallen into a pit	Lk 14:5
when he had found a young *a*	Jn 12:14
the dumb *a* speaking with man's	2Pet 2:16

ASSAULT

and province that would *a* them	Est 8:11
when there was an *a* made both of	Acts 14:5

ASSAULTED

the house of Jason, and sought	Acts 17:5

ASSAY

If we *a* to commune with thee,	Job 4:2

ASSAYED

Or hath God *a* to go and take him a	Deut 4:34
upon his armour, and he *a* to go	1Sa 17:39
he *a* to join himself to the	Acts 9:26
they *a* to go into Bithynia	Acts 16:7

ASSAYING

Egyptians *a* to do were drowned	Heb 11:29

ASSEMBLE

them, all the assembly shall *a*	Num 10:3
A me the men of Judah within	2Sa 20:4
Amasa went to *a* the men of Judah	2Sa 20:5
shall *a* the outcasts of Israel,	Is 11:12
A yourselves and come	Is 45:20
All ye, *a* yourselves, and hear	Is 48:14
A yourselves, and let us go into	Jer 4:5
a yourselves, and let us enter	Jer 8:14
a all the beasts of the field,	Jer 12:9
I will *a* them into the midst of	Jer 21:4
a you out of the countries where,	Eze 11:17
the field, A yourselves, and come	Eze 39:17
shall *a* a multitude of great	Dan 11:10
they *a* themselves for corn and	Hos 7:14
a the elders, gather the children	Joel 2:16
A yourselves, and come, all ye	Joel 3:11
they *a* themselves upon the mountains	Amos 3:9
I will surely *a*, O Jacob, all of	Mic 2:12
will I *a* her that halteth, and I	Mic 4:6
that I may *a* the kingdoms, to	Zeph 3:8

ASSEMBLED

which *a* at the door of the	Ex 38:8
they *a* all the congregation	Num 1:18
of Israel *a* together at Shiloh	Josh 18:1
of Israel *a* themselves together	Judg 10:17
they lay with the women that *a* at	1Sa 2:22
that were with him *a* themselves	1Sa 14:20
Then Solomon *a* the elders of	1Kin 8:1
And all the men of Israel *a*	1Kin 8:2
of Israel, that were *a* unto him	1Kin 8:5
he *a* all the house of Judah, with	1Kin 12:21
David *a* the children of Aaron, and	1Chr 15:4
David *a* all the princes of Israel	1Chr 28:1
Then Solomon *a* the elders of	2Chr 5:2
a themselves unto the king in the	2Chr 5:3
of Israel that were *a* unto him	2Chr 5:6
And on the fourth day they *a*	2Chr 20:26
there *a* at Jerusalem much people	2Chr 30:13
Then were *a* unto me every one	Ezr 9:4
there *a* unto him out of Israel a	Ezr 10:1
of Israel were *a* with fasting	Neh 9:1
the Jews that were at Shushan *a*	Est 9:18
For, lo, the kings were *a*	Ps 48:4
together, and let the people be *a*	Is 43:9
a themselves by troops in the	Jer 5:7
thy company that are *a* unto thee	Eze 38:7
princes *a* together to the king	Dan 6:6
Then these men *a*, and found Daniel	Dan 6:11
Then these men *a* unto the king	Dan 6:15
Then *a* together the chief priests	Mt 26:3
the scribes and the elders were *a*	Mt 26:57
when they were *a* with the elders,	Mt 28:12
with him were *a* the chief	Mk 14:53
were *a* for fear of the Jews	Jn 20:19
being *a* together with them,	Acts 1:4
shaken where they were *a* together,	Acts 4:31
to pass, that a whole year they *a*	Acts 11:26
being *a* with one accord, to send,	Acts 15:25

ASSEMBLIES

the *a* of violent men have sought	Ps 86:14
fastened by the masters of *a*	Eccl 12:11
and sabbaths, the calling of *a*	Is 1:13

of mount Zion, and upon her *a*	Is 4:5
laws and my statutes in all mine *a*	Eze 44:24
I will not smell in your solemn *a*	Amos 5:21

ASSEMBLING

the lookingglasses of the women *a*	Ex 38:8
Not forsaking the *a* of ourselves	Heb 10:25

ASSEMBLY

unto their *a*, mine honour, be not	Gen 49:6
the whole *a* of the congregation	Ex 12:6
to kill this whole *a* with hunger	Ex 16:3
be hid from the eyes of the *a*	Lev 4:13
the *a* was gathered together unto	Lev 8:4
it is a solemn *a*	Lev 23:36
whole *a* of the children of Israel	Num 8:9
use them for the calling of the *a*	Num 10:2
them, all the *a* shall assemble	Num 10:3
the *a* of the congregation of the	Num 14:5
hundred and fifty princes of the *a*	Num 16:2
went from the presence of the *a*	Num 20:6
and gather thou the *a* together	Num 20:8
day ye shall have a solemn *a*	Num 29:35
the LORD spake unto all your *a* in	Deut 5:22
of the fire in the day of the *a*	Deut 9:10
of the fire in the day of the *a*	Deut 10:4
be a solemn *a* to the LORD thy God	Deut 16:8
God in Horeb in the day of the *a*	Deut 18:16
in the *a* of the people of God	Judg 20:2
camp from Jabesh-gilead to the *a*	Judg 21:8
all this *a* shall know that the	Is 17:47
Proclaim a solemn *a* for Baal	2Kin 10:20
eighth day they made a solemn *a*	2Chr 7:9
the whole *a* took counsel to keep	2Chr 30:23
And I set a great *a* against them	Neh 5:7
on the eighth day was a solemn *a*	Neh 8:18
the *a* of the wicked have inclosed	Ps 22:16
be feared in the *a* of the saints	Ps 89:7
praise him in the *a* of the elders	Ps 107:32
in the *a* of the upright, and in	Ps 111:1
midst of the congregation and in	Prov 5:14
upon the *a* of a young men together	Jer 6:11
an *a* of treacherous men	Jer 9:2
I sat not in the *a* of the mockers,	Jer 15:17
spake to all the *a* of the people	Jer 26:17
to come up against Babylon an *a*	Jer 50:9
he hath called an *a* against me to	Lam 1:15
destroyed his places of the *a*	Lam 2:6
not be in the *a* of my people	Eze 13:9
with an *a* of people, which shall	Eze 23:24
ye a fast, call a solemn *a*	Joel 1:14
sanctify a fast, call a solemn *a*	Joel 2:15
are sorrowful for the solemn *a*	Zeph 3:18
for the *a* was confused	Acts 19:32
shall be determined in a lawful *a*	Acts 19:39
thus spoken, he dismissed the *a*	Acts 19:41
To the general *a* and church of the	Heb 12:23
your *a* a man with a gold ring	Jas 2:2

ASSENT

good to the king with one *a*	2Chr 18:12

ASSENTED

And the Jews also *a*, saying that	Acts 24:9

ASSES

had sheep, and oxen, and he *a*	Gen 12:16
and maidservants, and she *a*	Gen 12:16
and maidservants, and camels, and *a*	Gen 24:35
and menservants, and camels, and *a*	Gen 30:43
And I have oxen, and *a*, flocks, and	Gen 32:5
kine, and ten bulls, twenty she *a*	Gen 32:15
sheep, and their oxen, and their *a*	Gen 34:28
as he fed the *a* of Zibeon his	Gen 36:24
they laded their *a* with the corn	Gen 42:26
and take us for bondmen, and our *a*	Gen 43:18
and he gave their *a* provender	Gen 43:24
were sent away, they and their *a*	Gen 44:3
ten *a* laden with the good things	Gen 45:23
ten she *a* laden with corn and	Gen 45:23
cattle of the herds, and for the *a*	Gen 47:17
upon the horses, upon the *a*	Ex 9:3
and of the beeves, and of the *a*	Num 31:28
persons, of the beeves, of the *a*	Num 31:30
And threescore and one thousand *a*	Num 31:34
the *a* were thirty thousand and	Num 31:39
And thirty thousand *a* and five	Num 31:45
daughters, and his oxen, and his *a*	Josh 7:24
and took old sacks upon their *a*	Josh 9:4
Speak, ye that ride on white *a*	Judg 5:10
with him, and a couple of *a*	Judg 19:3
there were with him two *a* saddled	Judg 19:10
both straw and provender for our *a*	Judg 19:19
and gave provender unto the *a*	Judg 19:21
goodliest young men, and your *a*	1Sa 8:16
the *a* of Kish Saul's father were	1Sa 9:3
thee, and arise, go seek the *a*	1Sa 9:3
my father leave caring for the *a*	1Sa 9:5
as for thine *a* that were lost	1Sa 9:20
The *a* which thou wentest to seek	1Sa 10:2
hath left the care of the *a*	1Sa 10:2
And he said, To seek the *a*	1Sa 10:14
us plainly that the *a* were found	1Sa 10:16
and sucklings, and oxen, and *a*	1Sa 22:19
cakes of figs, and laid them on *a*	1Sa 25:18
the sheep, and the oxen, and the *a*	1Sa 27:9
him, with a couple of saddled *a*	2Sa 16:1
The *a* be for the king's household,	2Sa 16:2
of the young men, and one of the *a*	2Kin 4:22
and their horses, and their *a*	2Kin 7:7
a tied, and the tents as they were	2Kin 7:10
of *a* two thousand, and of men an	1Chr 5:21
and Naphtali, brought bread on *a*	1Chr 12:40

over the *a* was Jehdeiah.............. 1Chr 27:30
all the feeble of them upon *a*............ 2Chr 28:15
their *a*, six thousand seven............... Ezr 2:67
seven hundred and twenty *a*............ Neh 7:69
bringing in sheaves, and lading *a*...... Neh 13:15
of oxen, and five hundred she *a*........ Job 1:3
the *a* feeding beside them................. Job 1:14
as wild *a* in the desert, go they......... Job 24:5
yoke of oxen, and a thousand she *a*... Job 42:12
the wild *a* quench their thirst............ Ps 104:11
of horsemen, a chariot of *a*.............. Is 21:7
upon the shoulders of young *a*.......... Is 30:6
the young *a* that ear the ground......... Is 30:24
dens for ever, a joy of wild *a*........... Is 32:14
the wild *a* did stand in the high......... Jer 14:6
whose flesh is as the flesh of *a*......... Eze 23:20
his dwelling was with the wild *a*........ Dan 5:21

ASSHUR (*ash'-ur*) See ASHUR, ASSUR, ASSYRIA.
1. The builder of Nineveh.
Out of that land went forth *A*............ Gen 10:11
2. A son of Shem.
and *A*, and Arphaxad, and Lud.......... Gen 10:22
Elam, and *A*, and Arphaxad, and Lud.. 1Chr 1:17
3. Another name for Assyria.
until *A* shall carry thee away............. Num 24:22
of Chittim, and shall afflict *A*............ Num 24:24
Eden, the merchants of Sheba, *A*...... Eze 27:23
A is there and all her company.......... Eze 32:22
A shall not save us........................... Hos 14:3

ASSHURIM (*ash'-u-rim*) See ASHURITES.
Descendants of Dedan.
And the sons of Dedan were *A*........... Gen 25:3

ASSHURITES See ASHURIM.

ASSIGNED
had a portion *a* them of Pharaoh....... Gen 47:22
they *a* Bezer in the wilderness.......... Josh 20:8
that he *a* Uriah unto a place............. 2Sa 11:16

ASSIR (*as'-sur*)
1. A son of Korah.
A, and Elkanah, and Abiasaph.......... Ex 6:24
son, Korah his son, *A* his son,........... 1Chr 6:22
2. A son of Ebiasaph.
Ebiasaph his son, and *A* his son,....... 1Chr 6:23
The son of Tahath, the son of *A*........ 1Chr 6:37
3. A son of Jeconiah.
A, Salathiel his son,....................... 1Chr 3:17

ASSIST
that ye *a* her in whatsoever.............. Rom 16:2

ASSOCIATE
A yourselves, O ye people, and ye...... Is 8:9

ASSOS (*as'-sos*) *A seaport of Mysia in Asia Minor.*
before to ship, and sailed unto *A*....... Acts 20:13
And when he met with us at *A*........... Acts 20:14

ASS'S
his *a* colt unto the choice vine.......... Gen 49:11
until an *a* head was sold for.............. 2Kin 6:25
man be born like a wild *a* colt........... Job 11:12
King cometh, sitting on an *a* colt........ Jn 12:15

ASSUR (*As'-sur*) See ASSHUR. *Same as Asshur 3.*
the days of Esar-haddon king of *A*..... Ezr 4:2
A also is joined with them................. Ps 83:8

ASSURANCE
and shall have none *a* of thy life....... Deut 28:66
quietness and *a* for ever.................. Is 32:17
he hath given *a* unto all men............ Acts 17:31
of the full *a* of understanding........... Col 2:2
in the Holy Ghost, and in much *a*...... 1Th 1:5
the full *a* of hope unto the end.......... Heb 6:11
a true heart in full *a* of faith............ Heb 10:22

ASSURE
shall *a* our hearts before him............ 1Jn 3:19

ASSURED
unto it, and it shall be *a* to him......... Lev 27:19
give you *a* peace in this place........... Jer 14:13
hast learned and hast been *a* of........ 2Ti 3:14

ASSUREDLY
said unto David, Know thou *a*............ 1Sa 28:1
A Solomon thy son shall reign........... 1Kin 1:13
A Solomon thy son shall reign........... 1Kin 1:17
A Solomon thy son shall reign........... 1Kin 1:30
this land *a* with my whole heart......... Jer 32:41
If thou wilt *a* go forth unto the........... Jer 38:17
drink of the cup have *a* drunken......... Jer 49:12
at the house of Israel know *a*............. Acts 2:36
a gathering that the Lord had........... Acts 16:10

ASSWAGE
of my lips should *a* your grief............ Job 16:5

ASSWAGED
over the earth, and the waters *a*........ Gen 8:1
Though I speak, my grief is not *a*....... Job 16:6

ASSYRIA (*as-sir'-e-ah*) See ASSHUR, ASSYRIAN.
A Mesopotamian empire.
which goeth toward the east of *A*....... Gen 2:14
Egypt, as thou goest toward *A*........... Gen 25:18
Pul the king of *A* came against.......... 2Kin 15:19
silver, to give to the king of *A*........... 2Kin 15:20
So the king of *A* turned back............. 2Kin 15:20
came Tiglath-pileser king of *A*.......... 2Kin 15:29
and carried them captive to *A*........... 2Kin 15:29

to Tiglath-pileser king of *A*.............. 2Kin 16:7
it for a present to the king of *A*......... 2Kin 16:8
the king of *A* hearkened unto him...... 2Kin 16:9
for the king of *A* went up against....... 2Kin 16:9
to meet Tiglath-pileser king of *A*....... 2Kin 16:10
of the LORD for the king of *A*........... 2Kin 16:18
him came up Shalmaneser king of *A*.. 2Kin 17:3
the king of *A* found conspiracy in...... 2Kin 17:4
no present to the king of *A*............... 2Kin 17:4
the king of *A* shut him up................. 2Kin 17:4
Then the king of *A* came up............. 2Kin 17:5
Hoshea the king of *A* took Samaria... 2Kin 17:6
and carried Israel away into *A*.......... 2Kin 17:6
their own land to *A* unto this day....... 2Kin 17:23
the king of *A* brought men from......... 2Kin 17:24
they spake to the king of *A*.............. 2Kin 17:26
Then the king of *A* commanded........ 2Kin 17:27
he rebelled against the king of *A*....... 2Kin 18:7
king of *A* came up against Samaria.... 2Kin 18:9
the king of *A* did carry away............. 2Kin 18:11
did carry away Israel unto *A*............ 2Kin 18:11
did Sennacherib king of *A* come up... 2Kin 18:13
sent to the king of *A* to Lachish........ 2Kin 18:14
the king of *A* appointed unto............ 2Kin 18:14
and gave it to the king of *A*.............. 2Kin 18:15
And the king of *A* sent Tartan.......... 2Kin 18:17
the great king, the king of *A*............. 2Kin 18:19
pledges to my lord the king of *A*........ 2Kin 18:23
of the great king, the king of *A*......... 2Kin 18:28
into the hand of the king of *A*........... 2Kin 18:30
for thus saith the king of *A*.............. 2Kin 18:31
out of the hand of the king of *A*........ 2Kin 18:33
whom the king of *A* his master.......... 2Kin 19:4
the king of *A* have blasphemed me..... 2Kin 19:6
found the king of *A* warring.............. 2Kin 19:8
into the hand of the king of *A*........... 2Kin 19:10
kings of *A* have done to all lands....... 2Kin 19:11
the kings of *A* have destroyed the..... 2Kin 19:17
king of *A* I have heard..................... 2Kin 19:20
So Sennacherib king of *A* departed.... 2Kin 19:36
out of the hand of the king of *A*........ 2Kin 20:6
king of *A* to the river Euphrates........ 2Kin 23:29
king of *A* carried away captive.......... 1Chr 5:6
up the spirit of Pul king of *A*............ 1Chr 5:26
of Tiglath-pilneser king of *A*............ 1Chr 5:26
unto the kings of *A* to help him......... 2Chr 28:16
king of *A* came unto him, and........... 2Chr 28:20
and gave it unto the king of *A*........... 2Chr 28:21
out of the hand of the kings of *A*....... 2Chr 28:21
Sennacherib king of *A* came............. 2Chr 32:1
Why should the kings of *A* come........ 2Chr 32:4
that Sennacherib king of *A*.............. 2Chr 32:9
this did Sennacherib king of *A*.......... 2Chr 32:9
Thus saith Sennacherib king of *A*...... 2Chr 32:10
out of the hand of the king of *A*........ 2Chr 32:11
in the camp of the king of *A*............. 2Chr 32:21
hand of Sennacherib the king of *A*..... 2Chr 32:22
of the host of the king of *A*.............. 2Chr 33:11
heart of the king of *A* unto them....... Ezr 6:22
of the kings of *A* unto this day.......... Neh 9:32
even the king of *A*......................... Is 7:17
the bee that is in the land of *A*.......... Is 7:18
the river, by the king of *A*................ Is 7:20
taken away before the king of *A*........ Is 8:4
and many, even the king of *A*............ Is 8:7
the stout heart of the king of *A*......... Is 10:12
which shall be left, from *A*............... Is 11:11
which shall be left, from *A*............... Is 11:16
be a highway out of Egypt to *A*......... Is 19:23
Egypt, and the Egyptian into *A*.......... Is 19:23
be the third with Egypt and with *A*..... Is 19:24
A the work of my hands, and Israel...... Is 19:25
Sargon the king of *A* sent him.......... Is 20:1
So shall the king of *A* lead away........ Is 20:4
be delivered from the king of *A*......... Is 20:6
ready to perish in the land of *A*......... Is 27:13
king of *A* came up against all the...... Is 36:1
the king of *A* sent Rabshakeh from.... Is 36:2
the great king, the king of *A*............. Is 36:4
thee, to my master the king of *A*....... Is 36:8
of the great king, the king of *A*......... Is 36:13
into the hand of the king of *A*........... Is 36:15
for thus saith the king of *A*.............. Is 36:16
out of the hand of the king of *A*........ Is 36:18
whom the king of *A* his master.......... Is 36:16
the king of *A* have blasphemed me..... Is 37:6
found the king of *A* warring.............. Is 37:8
into the hand of the king of *A*........... Is 37:10
of *A* have done to all lands by........... Is 37:11
the kings of *A* have laid waste.......... Is 37:18
me against Sennacherib king of *A*...... Is 37:21
the LORD concerning the king of *A*.... Is 37:33
So Sennacherib king of *A* departed.... Is 37:37
out of the hand of the king of *A*........ Is 38:6
hast thou to do in the way of *A*.......... Jer 2:18
Egypt, as thou wast ashamed of *A*..... Jer 2:36
the king of *A* hath devoured him........ Jer 50:17
as I have punished the king of *A*....... Jer 50:18
that were the chosen men of *A*.......... Eze 23:7
king of Egypt, they go to *A*.............. Hos 7:11
For they are gone up to *A*................ Hos 8:9
shall eat unclean things in *A*............ Hos 9:3
A for a present to king Jareb............ Hos 10:6
and as a dove out the land of *A*......... Hos 11:11
the land of *A* with the sword............ Mic 5:6
he shall come even from *A*............... Mic 7:12
shepherds slumber, O king of *A*........ Nah 3:18
against the north, and destroy *A*........ Zeph 2:13
of Egypt, and gather them out of *A*.... Zec 10:10

the pride of *A* shall be brought.......... Zec 10:11

ASSYRIAN (*as-sir'-e'-un*) See ASSYRIANS. *An inhabitant of Assyria.*
O *A*, the rod of mine anger, and.......... Is 10:5
in Zion, be not afraid of the *A*........... Is 10:24
I will break the *A* in my land.............. Is 14:25
the *A* shall come into Egypt, and........ Is 19:23
til the *A* founded it for them.............. Is 23:13
LORD shall the *A* be beaten down...... Is 30:31
Then shall the *A* fall with the............ Is 31:8
the *A* oppressed them without........... Is 52:4
the *A* was a cedar in Lebanon with..... Eze 31:3
wound, then went Ephraim to the *A*.... Hos 5:13
this shall be his king,........................ Hos 11:5
when the *A* shall come into our........... Mic 5:5
shall he deliver us from the *A*............ Mic 5:6

ASSYRIANS (*as-sir'-e-uns*)
of the *A* an hundred fourscore........... 2Kin 19:35
Egyptians shall serve with the *A*........ Is 19:23
in the camp of the *A* an hundred........ Is 37:36
to the Egyptians, and to the *A*........... Lam 5:6
played the whore also with the *A*....... Eze 16:28
lovers, on the *A* her neighbours,........ Eze 23:5
lovers, into the hand of the *A*............ Eze 23:9
doted upon the *A* her neighbours....... Eze 23:12
and Koa, and all the *A* with them....... Eze 23:23
do make a covenant with the *A*......... Hos 12:1

ASTAROTH (*as'-ta-roth*) See ASHTAROTH. *A city in Bashan.*
Bashan, which dwelt at *A* in Edrei...... Deut 1:4

ASTONIED
and of my beard, and sat down *a*....... Ezr 9:3
I sat *a* until the evening................... Ezr 9:4
Upright men shall be *a* at this........... Job 17:8
after him shall be *a* at his day........... Job 18:20
As many were *a* at thee................... Is 52:14
Why shouldest thou be as a man *a*..... Jer 14:9
be a one with another, and consume..... Eze 4:17
Nebuchadnezzar the king was *a*........ Dan 3:24
was *a* for one hour, and his.............. Dan 4:19
in him, and his lords were *a*............. Dan 5:9

ASTONISHED
dwell therein shall be *a* at it............. Lev 26:32
one that passeth by it shall be *a*........ 1Kin 9:8
Mark me, and be *a*, and lay your....... Job 21:5
tremble, and are *a* at his reproof....... Job 26:11
Be *a*, O ye heavens, at this, and........ Jer 2:12
and the priests shall be *a*................. Jer 4:9
that passeth thereby shall be *a*......... Jer 18:16
that passeth thereby shall be *a*......... Jer 19:8
one that goeth by it shall be *a*........... Jer 49:17
that goeth by Babylon shall be *a*........ Jer 50:13
remained there *a* among them seven... Eze 3:15
at every moment, and be *a* at thee..... Eze 26:16
of the isles shall be *a* at thee............ Eze 27:35
the people shall be *a* at thee............ Eze 28:19
I was *a* at the vision, but none.......... Dan 8:27
the people were *a* at his doctrine....... Matt 7:28
insomuch that they were *a*............... Mt 13:54
they were *a* at his doctrine.............. Mt 22:33
they were *a* at his doctrine.............. Mk 1:22
And they were *a* with a great............ Mk 5:42
and many hearing him were *a*........... Mk 6:2
And were beyond measure *a*, saying.. Mk 7:37
the disciples were *a* at his words....... Mk 10:24
they were *a* out of measure,............. Mk 10:26
the people was *a* at his doctrine....... Mk 11:18
him were *a* at his understanding....... Lk 2:47
they were *a* at his doctrine.............. Lk 4:32
For he was *a*, and all that were......... Lk 5:9
And her parents were *a*................... Lk 8:56
also of our company made us *a*......... Lk 24:22
a said, Lord, what wilt thou have......... Acts 9:6
which believed were *a*, as many as.... Acts 10:45
the door, and saw him, they were *a*... Acts 12:16
being *a* at the doctrine of the........... Acts 13:12

ASTONISHMENT
and blindness, and *a* of heart........... Deut 28:28
And thou shalt become an *a*............. Deut 28:37
shalt be an *a* to every one that......... 2Chr 7:21
delivered them to trouble, to *a*......... 2Chr 29:8
made us to drink the wine of *a*.......... Ps 60:3
a hath taken hold on me................... Jer 8:21
destroy them, and make them an *a*.... Jer 25:9
shall be a desolation, and an *a*......... Jer 25:11
to make them a desolation, an *a*....... Jer 25:18
the earth, to be a curse, and an *a*...... Jer 25:18
shall be an execration, and an *a*....... Jer 42:18
shall be an execration, and an *a*....... Jer 44:12
your land a desolation, and an *a*....... Jer 44:22
dwelling place for dragons, an *a*....... Jer 51:37
become an *a* among the nations........ Jer 51:41
drink water by measure, and with *a*... Eze 4:16
an *a* unto the nations that are........... Eze 5:15
and drink their water with *a*............. Eze 12:19
and sorrow, with the cup of *a*........... Eze 23:33
I will smite every horse with *a*.......... Zec 12:4
were astonished with a great *a*......... Mk 5:42

ASTRAY
enemy's ox or his ass going *a*........... Ex 23:4
brother's ox or his sheep go *a*........... Deut 22:1
they go *a* as soon as they be born...... Ps 58:3
Before I was afflicted I went *a*.......... Ps 119:67
I have gone *a* like a lost sheep.......... Ps 119:176
of his folly he shall go *a*................... Prov 5:23
her ways, go not *a* in her paths......... Prov 7:25

righteous to go a in an evil way ...... Prov 28:10
All we like sheep have gone a .... Is 53:6
have caused them to go a, they .... Jer 50:6
Israel may go no more a from me ..... Eze 14:11
far from me, when Israel went a ...... Eze 44:10
which went a away from me after ..... Eze 44:10
children of Israel went a from me ..... Eze 44:15
which went not a when the .... Eze 48:11
the children of Israel went a .... Eze 48:11
as the Levites went a .... Eze 48:11
sheep, and one of them be gone a .... Mt 18:12
and seeketh that which is gone a ..... Mt 18:12
ninety and nine which went not a .... Mt 18:13
For ye were as sheep going a 1Pet 2:25
the right way, and are gone a 2Pet 2:15

ASTROLOGER
such things at any magician, or a .... Dan 2:10

ASTROLOGERS
Let now the a, the stargazers, ... Is 47:13
a that were in all his realm .... Dan 1:20
to call the magicians, and the a ..... Dan 2:2
cannot the wise men, the a .... Dan 2:27
Then came in the magicians, the a ... Dan 4:7
cried aloud to bring in the a .... Dan 5:7
made master of the magicians, a ..... Dan 5:11
And now the wise men, the a .... Dan 5:15

ASUNDER
but shall not divide it a .... Lev 1:17
neck, but shall not divide it a .... Lev 5:8
clave a that was under them .... Num 16:31
of fire, and parted them both a 2Kin 2:11
at ease, but he hath broken me a .... Job 16:12
about, he cleaveth my reins a .... Job 16:13
Let us break their bands a .... Ps 2:3
he hath cut a the cords of the ...... Ps 129:4
of the whole earth cut in a .... Jer 50:23
great pain, and No shall be rent a ... Eze 30:16
he beheld, and drove a the nations ... Hab 3:6
staff, even Beauty, and cut it a .... Zec 11:10
Then I cut a mine other staff, ... Zec 11:14
together, let not man put a .... Mt 19:6
And shall cut him a, and appoint .... Mt 24:51
chains had been plucked a by him ... Mk 5:4
together, let not man put a .... Mk 10:9
he burst a in the midst, and all .... Acts 1:18
departed in a one from the other ... Acts 15:39
even to the dividing a of soul and .. Heb 4:12
were stoned, they were sawn a ...... Heb 11:37

ASUPPIM *Storage for temple gods.*
and to his sons the house of A 1Chr 26:15
four a day, and toward A two 1Chr 26:17

ASYNCRITUS (a-sin'-cri-tus) *A Christian
acquaintance of Paul.*
Salute A, Phlegon, Hermas, ... Rom 16:14

AT See PREFACE.

ATAD (a'-tad) *See ABEL-MIZRAIM. A place east
of the Jordan.*
came to the threshingfloor of A .... Gen 50:10
the mourning in the floor of A ...... Gen 50:11

ATARAH (at'-a-rah) *A wife of Jerahmeel.*
another wife, whose name was A 1Chr 2:26

ATAROTH (at'-a-roth) *See ATAROTH-ADAR,
ATROTH.*
1. A city east of the Jordan.
A, and Dibon, and Jazer, and Nimrah, Num 32:3
children of Gad built Dibon, and A .. Num 32:34
2. A city in Ephraim.
unto the borders of Archi to A ...... Josh 16:2
And it went down from Janohah to A Josh 16:7
3. A city in Judah.
and the Netophathites, A, the 1Chr 2:54

ATAROTH-ADAR (at'-a-roth-a'-dar) *See
ATAROTH-ADDAR. A city on the border of
Benjamin.*
and the border descended to A ...... Josh 18:13

ATAROTH-ADDAR (at'-a-roth-ad'-dar) *See
ATAROTH-ADAR. Same as Ataroth-adar.*
on the east side was A, unto .... Josh 16:5

ATE
a the sacrifices of the dead .... Ps 106:28
I a no pleasant bread, neither ...... Dan 10:3
of the angel's hand, and a it up .... Rev 10:10

ATER (a'-tur)
1. An ancestor of an exiled family.
The children of A of Hezekiah ...... Ezr 2:16
The children of A of Hezekiah ...... Neh 7:21
*2. An exiled family who returned under
Zerubbabel.*
of Shallum, the children of A ...... Ezr 2:42
of Shallum, the children of A ...... Neh 7:45
*3. An Israelite who sealed the covenant with
Nehemiah.*
A, Hizkijah, Azzur, ... Neh 10:17

ATHACH (a'-thak) *A city in Judah.*
and to them which were in A 1Sa 30:30

ATHAIAH (ath-a-i'-ah) *A son of Uzziah*
A the son of Uzziah, the son of ..... Neh 11:4

ATHALIAH (ath-a-li'-ah)
1. Daughter of Jezebel.
And his mother's name was A 2Kin 8:26
when A the mother of Ahaziah saw .. 2Kin 11:1

nurse, in the bedchamber from A 2Kin 11:2
A did reign over the land 2Kin 11:3
when A heard the noise of the 2Kin 11:13
A rent her clothes, and cried, ... 2Kin 11:14
they slew A with the sword beside .. 2Kin 11:20
also was A the daughter of Omri 2Chr 22:2
But when A the mother of Ahaziah .. 2Chr 22:10
of Ahaziah), hid him from A 2Chr 22:11
and A reigned over the land 2Chr 22:12
Now when A heard the noise of the . 2Chr 23:12
Then A rent her clothes, and said, .. 2Chr 23:13
they had slain A with the sword 2Chr 23:15
For the sons of A, that wicked 2Chr 24:7
2. A son of Jeroham.
and Shehariah, and 1Chr 8:26
3. Father of Jeshiah.
Jeshaiah the son of A, and with .... Ezr 8:7

ATHENIANS (a-the'-ne-uns) *Citizens of
Athens*
(For all the A and strangers which .. Acts 17:21

ATHENS (ath'-ens) *See ATHENIANS. A city in
Greece.*
conducted Paul brought him unto A. Acts 17:15
while Paul waited for them at A ..... Acts 17:16
Mars' hill, and said, Ye men of A ... Acts 17:22
these things Paul departed from A .. Acts 18:1
it good to be left at A alone 1Th 3:1
Thessalonians was written from A .. 1Th s
Thessalonians was written from A .. 2Th s

ATHIRST
And he was sore a, and called on ... Judg 15:18
and when thou art a, go unto the ... Ruth 2:9
when saw we thee an hungred, or a . Mt 25:44
I will give unto him that is a of ..... Rev 21:6
And let him that is a come .... Rev 22:17

ATHLAI (ath'-lahee) *Married a foreign wife in
exile.*
Jehohanan, Hananiah, Zabbai, and A. Ezr 10:28

ATONEMENT
things wherewith the a was made ... Ex 29:33
bullock for a sin offering for a ..... Ex 29:36
when thou hast made an a for it .... Ex 29:36
shalt make an a for the altar .... Ex 29:37
Aaron shall make an a upon the .... Ex 30:10
he make a upon it throughout your . Ex 30:10
to make an a for your souls .... Ex 30:15
thou shalt take the a money of ..... Ex 30:16
to make an a for your souls .... Ex 30:16
I shall make an a for your sin ..... Ex 32:30
for him to make a for him .... Lev 4:26
priest shall make an a for them .... Lev 4:20
the priest shall make an a for ...... Lev 4:26
priest shall make an a for him ..... Lev 4:31
an a for his sin that he hath .... Lev 4:35
the priest shall make a for him .... Lev 5:6
the priest shall make an a for ...... Lev 5:10
the priest shall make an a for ...... Lev 5:13
the priest shall make an a for ...... Lev 5:16
make an a for him concerning his .. Lev 5:18
make an a for him before the LORD. Lev 6:7
the priest maketh a .... Lev 7:7
to do, to make an a for you .... Lev 8:34
make an a for thyself, and for the .. Lev 9:7
the people, and make an a for them. Lev 9:7
to make a for them before the ..... Lev 10:17
the LORD, and make an a for .... Lev 12:7
priest shall make an a for her ...... Lev 12:8
make an a for him before the LORD. Lev 14:18
make an a for him that is to be .... Lev 14:19
priest shall make an a for him ..... Lev 14:20
to be waved, to make an a for him . Lev 14:21
to make an a for him before the ... Lev 14:29
priest shall make an a for him ..... Lev 14:31
and make an a for the house .... Lev 14:53
the priest shall make an a for ...... Lev 15:15
make an a for himself, and for him. Lev 15:30
make an a for himself, and for the. Lev 16:6
the LORD, to make an a with him ... Lev 16:10
and shall make an a for himself .... Lev 16:11
he shall make an a for the holy .... Lev 16:16
to make an a in the holy place ..... Lev 16:17
and have made an a for himself .... Lev 16:17
the LORD, and make an a for .... Lev 16:18
make an a for himself, and for the. Lev 16:24
in to make a in the holy place ..... Lev 16:27
the priest make a for you .... Lev 16:30
father's stead, shall make the a .... Lev 16:32
he shall make an a for the holy .... Lev 16:33
he shall make an a for the .... Lev 16:33
shall make an a for the priests ..... Lev 16:33
to make an a for the children of ... Lev 16:34
altar to make an a for your souls ... Lev 17:11
that maketh an a for the soul ...... Lev 17:11
the priest shall make an a for ...... Lev 19:22
month there shall be a day of ...... Lev 23:27
for it is a day of a .... Lev 23:28
to make an a for you before the ... Lev 23:28
in the day of a shall ye make the .. Lev 25:9
beside the ram of the a .... Num 5:8
making a shall be made for .... Num 5:8
offering, and make an a for him .... Num 6:11
to make an a for the Levites .... Num 8:12
to make an a for the children of ... Num 8:19
Aaron made an a for them to ...... Num 8:21
the priest shall make an a for ...... Num 15:25
the priest shall make an a for ...... Num 15:28
the LORD, to make an a for .... Num 15:28
and make an a for them .... Num 16:46

and made an a for the people ...... Num 16:47
made an a for the children of ...... Num 25:13
offering, to make an a for you ...... Num 28:22
the goats, to make an a for you .... Num 28:30
offering, to make an a for you ...... Num 29:5
beside the sin offering of a .... Num 29:11
to make an a for our souls before ... Num 31:50
and wherewith shall I make the a ... 2Sa 21:3
holy, and to make an a for Israel ... 1Chr 6:49
to make an a for all Israel 1Chr 6:49
offerings to make an a for Israel ... Neh 10:33
whom we have now received the a .. Rom 5:11

ATONEMENTS
blood of the sin offering of a .... Ex 30:10

ATROTH (a'-troth) *See ATAROTH. A city in
Gad.*
And A, Shophan, and Jaazer, and ..... Num 32:35

ATROTH BETH JOAB See ATROTH.

ATTAI (at'-tahee)
1. A grandson of Sheshan.
and she bare him A 1Chr 2:35
A begat Nathan, and Nathan begat ... 1Chr 2:36
2. A Gadite in David's army.
A the sixth, Eliel the seventh, ... 1Chr 12:11
3. A son of Rehoboam.
which bare him Abijah, and A 2Chr 11:20

ATTAIN
it is high, I cannot a unto it .... Ps 139:6
shall a unto wise counsels .... Prov 1:5
as his hand shall a unto, and an ... Eze 46:7
it be ere they a to innocency ...... Hos 8:5
any means they might a to Phenice. Acts 27:12
If by any means I might a unto ..... Phil 3:11

ATTAINED
have not a unto the days of the .... Gen 47:9
howbeit he a not unto the first 2Sa 23:19
but he a not to the first three 2Sa 23:23
howbeit he a not to the first 1Chr 11:21
but a not to the first three 1Chr 11:25
have a to righteousness, even the ... Rom 9:30
hath not a to the law of .... Rom 9:31
Not as though I had already a ...... Phil 3:12
whereto we have already a .... Phil 3:16
doctrine, whereunto thou hast a 1Ti 4:6

ATTALIA (at-ta-li'-ah) *A seaport near Perga.*
in Perga, they went down into A .... Acts 14:25

ATTEND
he had appointed to a upon her .... Est 4:5
a unto my cry, give ear unto my ... Ps 17:1
A unto me, and hear me .... Ps 55:2
a unto my prayer .... Ps 61:1
and a to the voice of my .... Ps 86:6
A unto my cry .... Ps 142:6
and a to know understanding ...... Prov 4:1
My son, a to my words .... Prov 4:20
a unto my wisdom, and bow thine .. Prov 5:1
a to the words of my mouth .... Prov 7:24
that ye may a upon the Lord 1Cor 7:35

ATTENDANCE
the a of his ministers, and their 1Kin 10:5
the a of his ministers, and their 2Chr 9:4
give a to reading, to exhortation ... 1Ti 4:13
which no man gave a at the altar ... Heb 7:13

ATTENDED
I a unto you, and, behold, there .... Job 32:12
he hath a to the voice of my .... Ps 66:19
that she a unto the things which ... Acts 16:14

ATTENDING
a continually upon this very .... Rom 13:6

ATTENT
let thine ears be a unto the 2Chr 6:40
mine ears a unto the prayer that ... 2Chr 7:15

ATTENTIVE
Let thine ear now be a, and thine .. Neh 1:6
let now thine ear be a to the ...... Neh 1:11
were a unto the book of the law ... Neh 8:3
let thine ears be a to the voice .... Ps 130:2
people were very a to hear him .... Lk 19:48

ATTENTIVELY
Hear ye the noise of his voice, and. Job 37:2

ATTIRE
a woman with the a of an harlot ... Prov 7:10
her ornaments, or a bride her a .... Jer 2:32
in dyed a upon their heads .... Eze 23:15

ATTIRED
the linen mitre shall he be a .... Lev 16:4

AUDIENCE
in the a of the children of Heth .... Gen 23:10
in the a of the people of the land .. Gen 23:13
in the a of the sons of Heth .... Gen 23:16
read in the a of the people .... Ex 24:7
I pray them, speak in thine a 1Sa 25:24
in the a of our God, keep and seek. 1Chr 28:8
of Moses in the a of the people .... Neh 13:1
sayings in the a of the people ..... Lk 7:1
Then in the a of all the people .... Lk 20:45
and ye that fear God, give a .... Acts 13:16
gave a to Barnabas and Paul, ... Acts 15:12
they gave him a unto this word, ... Acts 22:22

AUGMENT

to a yet the fierce anger of the............... Num 32:14

AUGUSTAN See Augustus.

AUGUSTUS (aw-gus'-tus) See Augustus', Caesar. *An emperor of Rome.*

went out a decree from Caesar A............... Lk 2:1
be reserved unto the hearing of A........ Acts 25:21
he himself hath appealed to A............. Acts 25:25

AUGUSTUS' (aw-gus'-tus)

Julius, a centurion of A band............... Acts 27:1

AUL

bore his ear through with an a............... Ex 21:6
Then thou shalt take an a............... Deut 15:17

AUNT

she is thine a............... Lev 18:14

AUSTERE

thee, because thou art an a man............... Lk 19:21
Thou knewest that I was an a man........ Lk 19:22

AUTHOR

For God is not the a of confusion......... 1Cor 14:33
he became the a of eternal............... Heb 5:9
Looking unto Jesus the a and............. Heb 12:2

AUTHORITIES

angels and a and powers being made .. 1Pet 3:22

AUTHORITY

the Jew, wrote with all a............... Est 9:29
When the righteous are in a............... Prov 29:2
he taught them as one having a........... Mt 7:29
For I am a man under a, having........... Mt 8:9
are great exercise a upon them......... Mt 20:25
By what a doest thou these things...... Mt 21:23
and who gave thee this a............... Mt 21:23
you by what a I do these things......... Mt 21:24
I you by what a I do these things........ Mt 21:27
he taught them as one that had a........ Mk 1:27
for with a commandeth he even the..... Mk 1:27
great ones exercise a upon them........ Mk 10:42
By what a doest thou these things...... Mk 11:28
thee this a to do these things........... Mk 11:28
you by what a I do these things......... Mk 11:29
you by what a I do these things......... Mk 11:33
gave a to his servants, and to........... Mk 13:34
for with a and power he commandeth... Lk 4:36
For I also am a man set under a......... Lk 7:8
a over all devils, and to cure............ Lk 9:1
have thou a over ten cities............... Lk 19:17
by what a doest thou these things...... Lk 20:2
who is he that gave thee this a.......... Lk 20:2
I you by what a I do these things....... Lk 20:8
the power and a of the governor......... Lk 20:20
they that exercise a upon them.......... Lk 22:25
hath given him a to execute............. Jn 5:27
an eunuch of great a under............. Acts 8:27
here he hath a from the chief............ Acts 9:14
having received a from the chief........ Acts 26:10
as I went to Damascus with a........... Acts 26:12
have put down all rule and all a........ 1Cor 15:24
boast somewhat more of our a........... 2Cor 10:8
kings, and for all that are in a............ 1Ti 2:2
nor to usurp a over the man............. 1Ti 2:12
and exhort, and rebuke with all a....... Titus 2:15
power, and his seat, and great a......... Rev 13:2

AVA (a'-vah) See Ivah. *An area near Babylon.*

and from Cuthah, and from A............. 2Kin 17:24

AVAILETH

Yet all this a me nothing............... Est 5:13
neither circumcision a any thing......... Gal 5:6
neither circumcision a any thing......... Gal 6:15
prayer of a righteous man a much....... Jas 5:16

AVEN See Beth-aven. *Another name for Heliopolis, in Egypt.*

The young men of A and of............... Eze 30:17
The high places also of A............... Hos 10:8
inhabitant from the plain of A........... Amos 1:5

AVENGE

Thou shalt not a, nor bear any........... Lev 19:18
that shall a the quarrel of my........... Lev 26:25
A the children of Israel of the.......... Num 31:2
and a the Lord of Midian............... Num 31:3
for he will a the blood of his........... Deut 32:43
and thee, and the Lord a me of thee.. 1Sa 24:12
that I may a the blood of my........... 2Kin 9:7
to a themselves on their enemies....... Est 8:13
and a me of mine enemies............... Is 1:24
that he may a him of his............... Jer 46:10
I will a the blood of Jezreel............ Hos 1:4
saying, A me of mine adversary......... Lk 18:3
widow troubleth me, I will a her......... Lk 18:5
And shall not God a his own elect...... Lk 18:7
that he will a them speedily............. Lk 18:8
a not yourselves, but rather give....... Rom 12:19
a our blood on them that dwell on...... Rev 6:10

AVENGED

If Cain shall be a sevenfold............. Gen 4:24
until the people had a themselves...... Josh 10:13
done this, yet will I be a of you......... Judg 15:7
that I may be a at once a of the........ Judg 16:28
that I may be a of mine enemies........ 1Sa 14:24
to be a of the king's enemies........... 1Sa 18:25
or that my lord hath a himself.......... 1Sa 25:31
the Lord hath a my lord the king....... 2Sa 4:8
Lord hath a him of his enemies......... 2Sa 18:19
for the Lord hath a thee this day....... 2Sa 18:31

shall not my soul be a on such a........ Jer 5:9
shall not my soul be a on such a........ Jer 5:29
shall not my soul be a on such a........ Jer 9:9
a him that was oppressed, and.......... Acts 7:24
for God hath a you on her............... Rev 18:20
hath a the blood of his servants........ Rev 19:2

AVENGER

you cities for refuge from the a......... Num 35:12
Lest the a of the blood pursue.......... Deut 19:6
into the hand of the a of blood.......... Deut 19:12
your refuge from the a of blood......... Josh 20:3
if the a of blood pursue after........... Josh 20:5
die by the hand of the a of blood....... Josh 20:9
mightest still the enemy and the a...... Ps 8:2
by reason of the enemy and a........... Ps 44:16
the Lord is the a of all such............ 1Th 4:6

AVENGETH

It is God that a me, and that............ 2Sa 22:48
It is God that a me, and subdueth...... Ps 18:47

AVENGING

ye the Lord for the a of Israel........... Judg 5:2
from a thyself with thine own........... 1Sa 25:26
from a myself with mine own hand..... 1Sa 25:33

AVERSE

by securely as men a from war.......... Mic 2:8

AVIM (a'-vim) See Avims, Avites. *A city near Bethel.*

And A, and Parah, and Ophrah,.......... Josh 18:23

AVIMS (a'-vims) See Avim. *A Canaanite tribe.*

The A which dwelt in Hazerim,.......... Deut 2:23

AVITES (a'-vites) See Avim.
1. *Same as Avims.*
and the Ekronites; also the A........... Josh 13:3
2. *A tribe moved to Samaria.*
The A made Nibhaz and Tartak, and... 2Kin 17:31

AVITH (a'-vith) *Capital of Edom.*

and the name of his city was A.......... Gen 36:35
and the name of his city was A.......... 1Chr 1:46

AVOID

A it, pass not by it, turn from.......... Prov 4:15
and a them............... Rom 16:17
to a fornication, let every man.......... 1Cor 7:2
foolish and unlearned questions a...... 2Ti 2:23
But a foolish questions, and............. Titus 3:9

AVOIDED

David a out of his presence twice...... 1Sa 18:11

AVOIDING

A this, that no man should blame....... 2Cor 8:20
a profane and vain babblings, and...... 1Ti 6:20

AVOUCHED

Thou hast a the Lord this day to....... Deut 26:17
the Lord hath a thee this day to....... Deut 26:18

AVVA See Ava.

AVVIM See Avites.

AWAIT

But their laying a was known of........ Acts 9:24

AWAKE

A, a, Deborah............... Judg 5:12
a, a, utter a song............... Judg 5:12
surely now he would a for thee......... Job 8:6
be no more, they shall not a............. Job 14:12
a for me to the judgment that.......... Ps 7:6
I shall be satisfied, when I a............ Ps 17:15
a to my judgment, even unto my........ Ps 35:23
A, why sleepest thou, O Lord........... Ps 44:23
A up, my glory............... Ps 57:8
a, psaltery and harp............... Ps 57:8
I myself will a early............... Ps 57:8
a to help me, and behold............... Ps 59:4
a to visit all the heathen............... Ps 59:5
a, psaltery and harp............... Ps 108:2
I myself will a early............... Ps 108:2
when I a, I am still with thee........... Ps 139:18
when shall I a............... Prov 23:35
nor a my love, till he please............ Song 2:7
nor a my love, till he please............ Song 3:5
A, O north wind............... Song 4:16
nor a my love, until he please.......... Song 8:4
A and sing, ye that dwell in dust....... Is 26:19
A, a, put on strength, O arm........... Is 51:9
a, as in the ancient days, in............ Is 51:9
A, a, stand up, O Jerusalem,........... Is 51:17
A, a, put on thy strength............... Is 52:1
in that dust of the earth shall a........ Dan 12:2
A, ye drunkards, and weep.............. Joel 1:5
a that shall vex thee, and thou......... Hab 2:7
him that saith to the wood, A........... Hab 2:19
A, O sword, against my shepherd...... Zec 13:7
and they a him, and say unto him,..... Mk 4:38
and when they were a, they saw his.... Lk 9:32
that I may a him out of sleep........... Jn 11:11
it is high time to a out of sleep......... Rom 13:11
A to righteousness, and sin not......... 1Cor 15:34
A thou that sleepest, and arise......... Eph 5:14

AWAKED

Jacob a out of his sleep, and the....... Gen 28:16
he a out of his sleep, and went......... Judg 16:14
saw it, nor knew it, neither a........... 1Sa 26:12
he sleepeth, and must be a............. 1Kin 18:27
him, saying, The child is not a.......... 2Kin 4:31
I a; for the Lord sustained me.......... Ps 3:5

Then the Lord a as one out of.......... Ps 78:65
Upon this I a, and beheld............... Jer 31:26

AWAKEST

so, O Lord, when thou a, thou.......... Ps 73:20
when thou a, it shall talk............... Prov 6:22

AWAKETH

As a dream when one a............... Ps 73:20
but he a, and his soul is empty......... Is 29:8
but he a, and, behold, he is faint....... Is 29:8

AWAKING

of the prison a out of his sleep......... Acts 16:27

AWARE

Or ever I was a, my soul made me..... Song 6:12
O Babylon, and thou wast not a......... Jer 50:24
and in an hour that he is not a of...... Mt 24:50
walk over them are not a of them...... Lk 11:44
and at an hour when he is not a......... Lk 12:46

AWAY See PREFACE.

AWE

Stand in a, and sin not............... Ps 4:4
to the world stand in a of him.......... Ps 33:8
heart standeth in a of thy word......... Ps 119:161

AWOKE

Noah a from his wine, and knew........ Gen 9:24
So Pharaoh a............... Gen 41:4
And Pharaoh a, and, behold, it was.... Gen 41:7
So I a............... Gen 41:21
he a out of his sleep, and said, I...... Judg 16:20
And Solomon a............... 1Kin 3:15
a him, saying, Lord, save us............ Mt 8:25
a him, saying, Master, master, we..... Lk 8:24

AX

by forcing an a against them........... Deut 20:19
share, and his coulter, and his a....... 1Sa 13:20
the a head fell into the water.......... 2Kin 6:5
Shall the a boast itself against........ Is 10:15
hands of the workman, with the a...... Jer 10:3
Thou art my battle a and weapons..... Jer 51:20
now also the a is laid unto the......... Mt 3:10

AXE

with the a to cut down the tree........ Deut 19:5
Abimelech took an a in his hand....... Judg 9:48
there was neither hammer nor a........ 1Kin 6:7
now also the a is laid unto the......... Lk 3:9

AXES

and for the forks, and for the a........ 1Sa 13:21
under a of iron, and made them......... 2Sa 12:31
with harrows of iron, and with a........ 1Chr 20:3
lifted up a upon the thick trees......... Ps 74:5
work thereof at once with a............. Ps 74:6
army, and come against her with a..... Jer 46:22
with his a he shall break down.......... Eze 26:9

AXLETREES

the a of the wheels were joined........ 1Kin 7:32
their a, and their naves, and their...... 1Kin 7:33

AZAL (a'-zal) *A place near Jerusalem.*

the mountains shall reach unto A....... Zec 14:5

AZALIAH (az-a-li'-ah) *Father of Shaphan.*

king sent Shaphan the son of A......... 2Kin 22:3
he sent Shaphan the son of A........... 2Chr 34:8

AZANIAH (az-a-ni'-ah) *Father of Jeshua.*

both Jeshua the son of A, Binnui....... Neh 10:9

AZAREEL (a'zar'-e-el) See Azareel. *A priest from the Immer family.*

and his brethren, Shemaiah, and A..... Neh 12:36

AZAREEL (a'zar'-e-el) See Azareel.
1. *A Korahite in David's army.*
Elkanah, and Jesiah, and A, and........ 1Chr 12:6
2. *A priest during David's time.*
The eleventh to A, he, his sons,....... 1Chr 25:18
3. *A Danite prince during David's time.*
Of Dan, A the son of Jeroham.......... 1Chr 27:22
4. *Married a foreign wife in exile.*
A, and Shelemiah, Shemariah,.......... Ezr 10:41
5. *Same as Azareel.*
and Amashai the son of A, the son.... Neh 11:13

AZAREL See Azareel.

AZARIAH (az-a-ri'-ah) See Ahaziah.
1. *A descendant of Zadok.*
A the son of Zadok the priest,.......... 1Kin 4:2
2. *Captain of Solomon's guard.*
A the son of Nathan was over the...... 1Kin 4:5
3. *A king of Judah.*
And all the people of Judah took A.... 2Kin 14:21
Jeroboam king of Israel began A....... 2Kin 15:1
And the rest of the acts of A........... 2Kin 15:6
So A slept with his fathers............. 2Kin 15:7
eighth year of A king of Judah......... 2Kin 15:8
thirtieth year of A king of Judah....... 2Kin 15:17
In the fiftieth year of A king of........ 2Kin 15:23
fiftieth year of A king of Judah........ 2Kin 15:27
A his son, Jotham his son,............. 1Chr 3:12
4. *A descendant of Judah.*
5. *A descendant of Jerahmeel.*
Obed begat Jehu, and Jehu begat A... 1Chr 2:38
a begat Helez, and Helez begat....... 1Chr 2:39
6. *A son of Ahimaaz.*
And Ahimaaz begat A, and Azariah... 1Chr 6:9
7. *Grandson of Ahimaah.*

And Johanan begat A, (he it is............. 1Chr 6:10
A begat Amariah, and Amariah begat..... 1Chr 6:11
8. A son of Hilkiah.
begat Hilkiah, and Hilkiah begat A........ 1Chr 6:13
A begat Seraiah, and Seraiah begat....... 1Chr 6:14
A the son of Hilkiah, the son of........... 1Chr 9:11
the son of Seraiah, the son of A............ Ezr 7:1
9. A descendant of Kohath.
the son of Joel, the son of A............... 1Chr 6:36
10. A prophet sent to King Asa.
God came upon A the son of Oded........ 2Chr 15:1
11. A son of King Jehoshaphat.
the sons of Jehoshaphat, ... 2Chr 21:2
12. A brother of King Jehoram.
and Jehiel, and Zechariah, and A........ 2Chr 21:2
13. A son of King Jehoram.
A the son of Jehoram king of 2Chr 22:6
14. A conspirator with Joash.
A the son of Jeroham, and Ishmael,..... 2Chr 23:1
15. Another conspirator with Joash.
A the son of Obed, and Maaseiah......... 2Chr 23:1
16. A High Priest.
A the priest went in after him,........... 2Chr 26:17
A the chief priest, and all the............. 2Chr 26:20
17. A chief of Ephraim.
A the son of Johanan, Berechiah 2Chr 28:12
18. Father of Joel.
of Amasai, and Joel the son of A 2Chr 29:12
19. Helped cleanse the Temple.
Abdi, and A the son of Jehalelel:......... 2Chr 29:12
20. A chief priest.
A chief priest of the house 2Chr 31:10
A the ruler of the house of God 2Chr 31:13
21. Great-grandfather of Zadok.
The son of Amariah, the son of .... Ezr 7:3
22. A repairer of the Jerusalem walls.
After him repaired A the son of........... Neh 3:23
from the house of A unto the.............. Neh 3:24
23. An exile with Zerubbabel.
Zerubbabel, Jeshua, Nehemiah, A .... Neh 7:7
24. A priest with Ezra.
Hodijah, Maaseiah, Kelita, A .... Neh 8:7
25. A priest who renewed the covenant.
Seraiah, A, Jeremiah, ... Neh 10:2
26. A prince of Judah.
And A, Ezra, and Meshullam,.............. Neh 12:33
27. The son of Hoshaiah.
Then spake A the son of Hoshaiah,...... Jer 43:2
28. A companion of Daniel.
Daniel, Hananiah, Mishael, and A .... Dan 1:6
and to A, of Abed-nego..................... Dan 1:7
Daniel, Hananiah, Mishael, and A .... Dan 1:11
Daniel, Hananiah, Mishael, and A .... Dan 1:19
known to Hananiah, Mishael, and .... Dan 2:17

AZARYAHU See AZARIAH.

AZAZ (a'-zaz) *Father of Bela.*
And Bela the son of A, the son of 1Chr 5:8

AZAZIAH (az-a-zi'-ah)
1. A Levite who relocated the Ark.
and Obed-edom, and Jeiel, and A 1Chr 15:21
2. Father of Hoshea.
of Ephraim, Hoshea the son of A 1Chr 27:20
3. A Levite during Hezekiah's reign.
And Jehiel, and A, and Nahath, and.. 2Chr 31:13

AZBUK (az'-buk) *Father of Nehemiah.*
repaired Nehemiah the son of A .... Neh 3:16

AZEKAH (a-ze'-kah) *A town in Judah.*
to Beth-horon, and smote them to A ... Josh 10:10
from heaven upon them unto A .... Josh 10:11
Jarmuth, and Adullam, Socoh, and A ... Josh 15:35
and pitched between Shochoh and A 1Sa 17:1
And Adoraim, and Lachish, and 2Chr 11:9
and the fields thereof, at A .... Neh 11:30
in Lachish, and against A .... Jer 34:7

AZEL (a'-zel) See JAAZIEL. *A descendant of King Saul.*
son, Eleasah, A his son 1Chr 8:37
A had six sons, whose names are.......... 1Chr 8:38
All these were the sons of A.............. 1Chr 8:38
son, Eleasah his son, A his son............ 1Chr 9:43
A had six sons, whose names are.......... 1Chr 9:44
these were the sons of A 1Chr 9:44

AZEM (a'-zem) See EZEM. *A city in Judah.*
Baalah, and Iim, and A, ... Josh 15:29
And Hazar-shual, and Balah, and A ...... Josh 19:3

AZGAD (az'-gad)
1. A family of exiles.
The children of A, a thousand two........ Ezr 2:12
The children of A, two thousand......... Neh 7:17
2. An exile with Ezra.
And of the sons of A .... Ezr 8:12
3. A family who sealed the covenant.
Bunni, A, Bebai, ... Neh 10:15

AZIEL (a'-ze-el) *A Levite who relocated the Ark.*
and Zechariah, and A, ... 1Chr 15:20

AZIZA (a-zi'-zah) *Married a foreigner in exile.*
and Jeremoth, and Zabad, and A .... Ezr 10:27

AZMAVETH (az-ma'-veth) See BETH-AZMAVETH.
1. A 'mighty man' of David.
the Arbathite, the Barhumite, ... 2Sa 23:31
the Baharumite, Eliahba the 1Chr 11:33
2. A descendant of Jonathan.

and Jehoadah begat Alemeth, and A 1Chr 8:36
and Jarah begat Alemeth, and A.......... 1Chr 9:42
3. Father of Jeziel and Pelet.
Jeziel, and Pelet, the sons of A 1Chr 12:3
4. A village on the border of Judah.
The children of A, forty and two .... Ezr 2:24
and out of the fields of Geba and A ..... Neh 12:29
5. A treasurer of David.
treasures was A the son of Adiel 1Chr 27:25

AZMON (az'-mon) See HESHMON. *A place in southern Canaan.*
to Hazar-addar, and pass on to A .... Num 34:4
from A unto the river of Egypt .... Num 34:5
From thence it passed toward A .... Josh 15:4

AZNOTH-TABOR (az''-noth-ta'-bor) *Hills on the border of Naphtali.*
the coast turneth westward to A......... Josh 19:34

AZOR (a'-zor) *Great-grandson of Zorobabel.*
and Eliakim begat A .... Mt 1:13
And A begat Sadoc. .... Mt 1:14

AZOTUS (a-zo'-tus) See ASHDOD. *Greek form of Ashdod.*
But Philip was found at A .... Acts 8:40

AZRIEL (az'-re-el)
1. Chief of a family of Manasseh.
Epher, and Ishi, and Eliel, and A, ... 1Chr 5:24
2. Father of Jerimoth
Naphtali, Jerimoth the son of A 1Chr 27:19
3. Father of Seraiah.
and Seraiah the son of A, ... Jer 36:26

AZRIKAM (az'-ri-kam)
1. A son of Neariah.
Elioenai, and Hezekiah, and A 1Chr 3:23
2. A son of Azel.
sons, whose names are these, A 1Chr 8:38
sons, whose names are these, A 1Chr 9:44
3. A descendant of Merari.
the son of Hashub, the son of A 1Chr 9:14
the son of Hashub, the son of A .... Neh 11:15
4. Governor of the house of King Ahaz.
A the governor of the house, and 2Chr 28:7

AZUBAH (a-zu'-bah)
1. Mother of King Jehoshaphat.
his mother's name was A the 1Kin 22:42
his mother's name was A the 2Chr 20:31
2. Wife of Caleb.
begat children of A his wife 1Chr 2:18
when A was dead, Caleb took unto....... 1Chr 2:19

AZUR (a'-zur) See AZZUR.
1. Father of Hananiah.
Hananiah the son of A the prophet ...... Jer 28:1
2. Father of Jaazaniah.
whom I saw Jaazaniah the son of A ...... Eze 11:1

AZZAH (az'-zah) See GAZA. *A Philistine city.*
dwelt in Hazerim, even unto A .... Deut 2:23
the river, from Tiphsah even to A 1Kin 4:24
Philistines, and Ashkelon, and A......... Jer 25:20

AZZAN (az'-zan) *A prince of Issachar.*
of Issachar, Paltiel the son of A .... Num 34:26

AZZUR (az'-zur) *An Israelite who sealed the covenant.*
Ater, Hizkijah, and .... Neh 10:17

B

BAAL (ba'-al) See BAAL-BERITH, BAALE, BAAL-GAD, BAAL-HAMON, BAAL-HANAN, BAAL-HAZOR, BAAL-HERMON, BAALIM, BAAL-MEON, BAAL-PEOR, BAAL-PERAZIM, BAAL-SHALISHA, BAAL-TAMAR.
1. Chief god of the Canaanites.
him up into the high places of .... Num 22:41
forsook the LORD, and served B........... Judg 2:13
altar of B that thy father hath .... Judg 6:25
the altar of B was cast down, and........ Judg 6:28
he hath cast down the altar of B .... Judg 6:30
against him, Will ye plead for B .... Judg 6:31
Let B plead against him, because .... Judg 6:32
Zidonians, and went and served B 1Kin 16:31
altar for B in the house of B.............. 1Kin 16:32
and the prophets of B four hundred 1Kin 18:19
but if B, then follow him 1Kin 18:21
said unto the prophets of B 1Kin 18:25
called on the name of B from 1Kin 18:26
even until noon, saying, O B 1Kin 18:26
unto them, Take the prophets of B 1Kin 18:40
knees which have not bowed unto B 1Kin 19:18
For he served B, and worshipped 1Kin 22:53
of B that his father had made 2Kin 3:2
unto them, Ahab served B a little 2Kin 10:18
unto me all the prophets of B 2Kin 10:19
have a great sacrifice to do to B 2Kin 10:19
destroy the worshippers of B 2Kin 10:19
Proclaim a solemn assembly for B 2Kin 10:20
and all the worshippers of B came 2Kin 10:21
And they came into the house of B 2Kin 10:21
the house of B was full from one 2Kin 10:21
for all the worshippers of B 2Kin 10:22
of Rechab, into the house of B.......... 2Kin 10:23

and said unto the worshippers of B 2Kin 10:23
but the worshippers of B only 2Kin 10:23
to the city of the house of B 2Kin 10:25
the images out of the house of B 2Kin 10:26
brake down the house of B 2Kin 10:27
and brake down the house of B 2Kin 10:27
Jehu destroyed B out of Israel........... 2Kin 10:28
the land went into the house of B 2Kin 11:18
the priest of B before the altars 2Kin 11:18
the host of heaven, and served B 2Kin 17:16
and he reared up altars for B 2Kin 21:3
the vessels that were made for B 2Kin 23:4
also that burned incense unto B 2Kin 23:5
the people went to the house of B....... 2Chr 23:17
the priest of B before the altars 2Chr 23:17
and the prophets prophesied by B .... Jer 2:8
falsely, and burn incense unto B .... Jer 7:9
altars to burn incense unto B .... Jer 11:13
anger in offering incense unto B .... Jer 11:17
taught my people to swear by B .... Jer 12:16
built also the high places of B .... Jer 19:5
fire for burnt offerings unto B .... Jer 19:5
they prophesied in B, and caused .... Jer 23:13
have forgotten my name for B .... Jer 23:27
they have offered incense unto B........ Jer 32:29
they built the high places of B .... Jer 32:35
gold, which they prepared for B .... Hos 2:8
but when he offended in B .... Hos 13:1
the remnant of B from this place........ Zeph 1:4
bowed the knee to the image of B .... Rom 11:4
2. A city in Simeon.
about the same cities, unto B 1Chr 4:33
3. A descendant of Reuben.
son, Reaia his son, B his son, ... 1Chr 5:5
4. A descendant of Benjamin.
son Abdon, and Zur, and Kish, and B .. 1Chr 8:30
Abdon, then Zur, and Kish, and B 1Chr 9:36

BAALAH (ba'-al-ah) See BAALE, BALEH, BILHAH, KIRJATH-BAAL.
1. A city in Judah.
and the border was drawn to B........... Josh 15:9
from B westward unto mount Seir ...... Josh 15:10
B, and Iim, and Azem .... Josh 15:29
went up, and all Israel, to B .... Josh 15:11
2. A hill in Judah.
and passed along to mount B .... Josh 15:11

BAALATH (ba'-al-ath) See BAALATH-BEER. *A town in Dan.*
And Eltekeh, and Gibbethon, and B ..... Josh 19:44
And B, and Tadmor in the wilderness .. 1Kin 9:18
And B, and all the store cities,........... 2Chr 8:6

BAALATH-BEER (ba''-al-ath-be'-ur) *A city in Simeon.*
round about these cities to B .... Josh 19:8

BAAL-BERITH (ba''-al-be'-rith) *An idol.*
after Baalim, and made B their god ..... Judg 8:33
of silver out of the house of B .... Judg 9:4

BAALE (ba'-al-eh) *A form of Baalah.*
were with him from B of Judah 2Sa 6:2

BAALE-JUDAH See BAALE.

BAAL-GAD (ba''-al-gad') *A Canaanite city.*
even unto B in the valley of .... Josh 11:17
from B in the valley of Lebanon .... Josh 12:7
from B under mount Hermon unto ...... Josh 13:5

BAAL-HAMON (ba''-al-ha'-mon) *A place near Samaria.*
Solomon had a vineyard at B .... Song 8:11

BAAL-HANAN (ba'-al-ha'-nan)
1. A king of Edom.
B the son of Achbor reigned in .... Gen 36:38
B the son of Achbor died, and........... Gen 36:39
B the son of Achbor reigned in 1Chr 1:49
when B was dead, Hadad reigned in 1Chr 1:50
2. A superintendent for David.
the low plains was B the Gederite 1Chr 27:28

BAAL-HAZOR (ba''-al-ha'-zor) See HAZOR. *A place near Ephraim.*
Absalom had sheepshearers in B 2Sa 13:23

BAAL-HERMON (ba''-al-her'-mon) *A city near Mt. Hermon.*
from mount B unto the entering in ...... Judg 3:3
they increased from Bashan unto B 1Chr 5:23

BAALI (ba'-al-i) *A rejected title of God.*
and shalt call me no more B .... Hos 2:16

BAALIM (ba'-al-im) See BAAL. *Plural of Baal.*
sight of the LORD, and served B.......... Judg 2:11
the LORD their God, and served B .... Judg 3:7
again, and went a whoring after B .... Judg 8:33
sight of the LORD, and served B.......... Judg 10:6
put away the LORD, and served B .... Judg 10:10
children of Israel did put away B 1Sa 7:4
the LORD, and have served B 1Sa 12:10
the LORD, and thou hast followed B 1Kin 18:18
David, and sought not unto B............ 2Chr 17:3
the LORD they bestow upon B 2Chr 24:7
and made also molten images for B 2Chr 28:2
and he reared up altars for B 2Chr 33:3
the altars of B in his presence........... 2Chr 34:4
polluted, I have not gone after B .... Jer 2:23
of their own heart, and after B .... Jer 9:14
will visit upon her the days of B .... Hos 2:13
the names of B out of her mouth .... Hos 2:17
they sacrificed unto B, and burned...... Hos 11:2

BAALIS (ba'-al-is) A king of the Ammonites.
Dost thou certainly know that B.............. Jer 40:14

BAAL-MEON (ba''-al-me'-on) See BETH-BAAL-
MEON. A Reubenite town.
Nebo, and B, (their names............ Num 32:38
in Aroer, even unto Nebo and B............ 1Chr 5:8
of the country, Beth-jeshimoth, and.. Eze 25:9

BAAL-PEOR (ba''-al-pe'-or) See PEOR. A
Moabite idol.
And Israel joined himself unto B........ Num 25:3
his men that were joined unto B........ Num 25:5
what the LORD did because of B.......... Deut 4:3
for all the men that followed B.......... Deut 4:3
joined themselves also unto B............ Ps 106:28
but they went to B, and separated...... Hos 9:10

BAAL-PERAZIM (ba''-al-per'-a-zim) A place
near the valley of Rephaim.
And David came to B, and David........ 2Sa 5:20
called the name of that place B.......... 2Sa 5:20
So they came up to B...................... 1Chr 14:11
called the name of that place B.......... 1Chr 14:11

BAAL'S (ba'-als)
but B prophets are four hundred........ 1Kin 18:22

BAAL-SHALISHA (ba''-al-shal'-i-shah) A
place in Ephraim
And there came a man from B............ 2Kin 4:42

BAAL-TAMAR (ba''-al-ta'-mar) A place in
Benjamin.
and put themselves in array at B........ Judg 20:33

BAAL-ZEBUB (ba''-al-ze'-bub) See
BEELZEBUB. A Philistine idol.
enquire of B the god of Ekron.......... 2Kin 1:2
to enquire of B the god of Ekron...... 2Kin 1:3
to enquire of B the god of Ekron...... 2Kin 1:6
to enquire of B the god of Ekron...... 2Kin 1:16

BAAL-ZEPHON (ba''-al-ze'-fon) A place near
the Rea Sea crossing.
Migdol and the sea, over against B.... Ex 14:2
sea, beside Pi-hahiroth, before B...... Ex 14:9
Pi-hahiroth, which is before B.......... Num 33:7

BAANA (ba'-an-ah) See BAANAH.
1. An officer in Solomon's army.
B the son of Ahilud........................ 1Kin 4:12
2. Father of Zadok.
them repaired Zadok the son of B...... Neh 3:4

BAANAH (ba'-an-ah) See BAANA.
1. A captain in Ishbosheth's army.
the name of the one was B................ 2Sa 4:2
the Beerothite, Rechab and B............ 2Sa 4:5
Rechab and B his brother escaped...... 2Sa 4:6
B his brother, the sons of Rimmon...... 2Sa 4:9
2. Father of Heleb.
Heleb the son of B, the................... 2Sa 23:29
the son of B the Netophathite.......... 1Chr 11:30
3. An officer in Solomon's army.
B the son of Hushai was in Asher...... 1Kin 4:16
4. An exile who returned with Zerubbabel.
Bilshan, Mizpar, Bigvai, Rehum, B.... Ezr 2:2
Misgereth, Bigvai, Nehum, B............ Neh 7:7
Malluch, Harim, B.......................... Neh 10:27

BAARA (ba'-ar-ah) A wife of Shaharaim.
Hushim and B were his wives............ 1Chr 8:8

BAASEIAH (ba-as-i'-ah) A Gershonite Levite.
The son of Michael, the son of B........ 1Chr 6:40

BAASHA (ba'-ash-ah) A king of Israel.
B king of Israel all their days.......... 1Kin 15:16
B king of Israel went up against........ 1Kin 15:17
thy league with B king of Israel........ 1Kin 15:19
when B heard thereof, that he.......... 1Kin 15:21
thereof, wherewith B had builded...... 1Kin 15:22
B the son of Ahijah, of the house...... 1Kin 15:27
B smote him at Gibbethon, which...... 1Kin 15:27
Asa king of Judah did B slay him...... 1Kin 15:28
B king of Israel all their days.......... 1Kin 15:32
B the son of Ahijah to reign over...... 1Kin 15:33
Jehu the son of Hanani against B...... 1Kin 16:1
will take away the posterity of B...... 1Kin 16:3
Him that dieth of B in the city'........ 1Kin 16:4
Now the rest of the acts of B............ 1Kin 16:5
So B slept with his fathers, and........ 1Kin 16:6
the word of the LORD against B.......... 1Kin 16:7
B to reign over Israel in Tirzah........ 1Kin 16:8
that he slew all the house of B.......... 1Kin 16:11
Zimri destroy all the house of B........ 1Kin 16:11
against B by Jehu the prophet.......... 1Kin 16:12
For all the sins of B, and the............ 1Kin 16:13
the house of B the son of Ahijah........ 1Kin 21:22
the house of B the son of Ahijah........ 2Kin 9:9
year of the reign of Asa B king........ 2Chr 16:1
thy league with B king of Israel........ 2Chr 16:3
when B heard it, that he left off........ 2Chr 16:5
thereof, wherewith B was building.... 2Chr 16:6
made for fear of B king of Israel...... Jer 41:9

BABBLER
and a b is no better....................... Eccl 10:11
some said, What will this b say........ Acts 17:18

BABBLING
who hath b.................................. Prov 23:29

BABBLINGS
trust, avoiding profane and vain b.... 1Ti 6:20
But shun profane and vain b............ 2Ti 2:16

BABE
and, behold, the b wept.................. Ex 2:6
of Mary, the b leaped in her womb.... Lk 1:41
the b leaped in my womb for joy........ Lk 1:44
Ye shall find the b wrapped in.......... Lk 2:12
and the b lying in a manger.............. Lk 2:16
for he is a b................................. Heb 5:13

BABEL (ba'-bel) See BABYLON. A city in the
plain of Shinar.
beginning of his kingdom was B........ Gen 10:10
is the name of it called B................ Gen 11:9

BABES
Out of the mouth of b and.............. Ps 8:2
of their substance to their b............ Ps 17:14
and b shall rule over them.............. Is 3:4
and hast revealed them unto b........ Mt 11:25
never read, Out of the mouth of b.... Mt 21:16
and hast revealed them unto b........ Lk 10:21
of the foolish, a teacher of b............ Rom 2:20
carnal, even as unto b in Christ...... 1Cor 3:1
As newborn b, desire the sincere...... 1Pet 2:2

BABYLON (bab'-il-un) See BABEL,
BABYLONIANS, BABYLONISH, BABYLON'S,
CHALDEA, SHESHACH. Capital of the
Babylonian Empire; located on the Euphrates
River.
of Assyria brought men from B........ 2Kin 17:24
the men of B made Succoth-benoth,.. 2Kin 17:30
the son of Baladan, king of B.......... 2Kin 20:12
from a far country, even from B........ 2Kin 20:14
this day, shall be carried into B........ 2Kin 20:17
in the palace of the king of B.......... 2Kin 20:18
Nebuchadnezzar king of B came up.. 2Kin 24:1
for the king of B had taken from...... 2Kin 24:7
of B came up against Jerusalem...... 2Kin 24:10
king of B came against the city........ 2Kin 24:11
Judah went out to the king of B...... 2Kin 24:12
the king of B took him in.............. 2Kin 24:12
he carried away Jehoiachin to B...... 2Kin 24:15
captivity from Jerusalem to B.......... 2Kin 24:15
of B brought captive to B.............. 2Kin 24:16
the king of B made Mattaniah his.... 2Kin 24:17
rebelled against the king of B.......... 2Kin 24:20
Nebuchadnezzar king of B came...... 2Kin 25:1
him up to the king of B to Riblah.... 2Kin 25:6
of brass, and carried him to B.......... 2Kin 25:7
of king Nebuchadnezzar king of B.... 2Kin 25:8
guard, a servant of the king of B...... 2Kin 25:8
that fell away to the king of B........ 2Kin 25:11
and carried the brass of them to B.... 2Kin 25:13
them to the king of B to Riblah...... 2Kin 25:20
And the king of B smote them........ 2Kin 25:21
Nebuchadnezzar king of B had left.... 2Kin 25:22
heard that the king of B had made.... 2Kin 25:23
the land, and serve the king of B...... 2Kin 25:24
that Evil-merodach king of B in........ 2Kin 25:27
the kings that were with him in B.... 2Kin 25:28
away to B for their transgression...... 1Chr 9:1
ambassadors of the princes of B...... 2Chr 32:31
with fetters, and carried him to B.... 2Chr 33:11
came up Nebuchadnezzar king of B.. 2Chr 36:6
him in fetters, to carry him to B...... 2Chr 36:6
of the house of the LORD to B........ 2Chr 36:7
and put them in his temple at B...... 2Chr 36:7
sent, and brought him to B............ 2Chr 36:10
all these he brought to B................ 2Chr 36:18
the sword carried he away to B........ 2Chr 36:20
brought up from B unto Jerusalem.... Ezr 1:11
B had carried away unto B.............. Ezr 2:1
of Nebuchadnezzar the king of B...... Ezr 5:12
and carried the people away into B.. Ezr 5:12
of B the same king Cyrus made a...... Ezr 5:13
brought them into the temple of B.... Ezr 5:14
king take out of the temple of B...... Ezr 5:14
house, which is there at B.............. Ezr 6:1
the treasures were laid up in B........ Ezr 6:5
at Jerusalem, and brought unto B.... Ezr 6:5
This Ezra went up from B.............. Ezr 7:6
month began he to go up from B...... Ezr 7:9
find in all the province of B............ Ezr 7:16
them that went up with me from B.. Ezr 8:1
the king of B had carried away........ Neh 7:6
king of B came I unto the king........ Neh 13:6
the king of B had carried away........ Est 2:6
Rahab and B to them that know me.. Ps 87:4
By the rivers of B, there we sat........ Ps 137:1
O daughter of B, who art to be........ Ps 137:8
The burden of B, which Isaiah the.... Is 13:1
And B, the glory of kingdoms, the.... Is 13:19
proverb against the king of B.......... Is 14:4
hosts, and cut off from B the name.. Is 14:22
and said, B is fallen, is fallen.......... Is 21:9
the son of Baladan, king of B.......... Is 39:1
far country unto me, even from B...... Is 39:3
this day, shall be carried to B.......... Is 39:6
in the palace of the king of B.......... Is 39:7
For your sake I have sent to B.......... Is 43:14
the dust, O virgin daughter of B...... Is 47:1
he will do his pleasure on B............ Is 48:14
Go ye forth of B, flee ye from.......... Is 48:20
into the hand of the king of B.......... Jer 20:4
shall carry them captive into B........ Jer 20:4
and take them, and carry them to B.. Jer 20:5
this day shall come to B, and there.. Jer 20:6
king of B maketh war against us...... Jer 21:2
ye fight against the king of B.......... Jer 21:4
hand of Nebuchadrezzar king of B.... Jer 21:7
into the hand of the king of B.......... Jer 21:10
hand of Nebuchadrezzar king of B.... Jer 22:25

of B had carried away captive.......... Jer 24:1
and had brought them to B.............. Jer 24:1
year of Nebuchadrezzar king of B.... Jer 25:1
and Nebuchadrezzar the king of B.... Jer 25:9
serve the king of B seventy years.... Jer 25:11
that I will punish the king of B........ Jer 25:12
of Nebuchadnezzar the king of B...... Jer 27:6
same Nebuchadnezzar the king of B.. Jer 27:8
under the yoke of the king of B........ Jer 27:8
Ye shall not serve the king of B...... Jer 27:9
under the yoke of the king of B........ Jer 27:11
under the yoke of the king of B........ Jer 27:12
that will not serve the king of B...... Jer 27:13
Ye shall not serve the king of B...... Jer 27:14
shortly be brought again from B...... Jer 27:16
serve the king of B, and live............ Jer 27:17
and at Jerusalem, go not to B.......... Jer 27:18
Nebuchadnezzar king of B took not.. Jer 27:20
king of Judah from Jerusalem to B.. Jer 27:20
They shall be carried to B.............. Jer 27:22
broken the yoke of the king of B...... Jer 28:2
of B took away from this place........ Jer 28:3
this place, and carried them to B...... Jer 28:3
of Judah, that went into B.............. Jer 28:4
break the yoke of the king of B........ Jer 28:4
captive from B into this place.......... Jer 28:6
of B from the neck of all nations...... Jer 28:11
serve Nebuchadnezzar king of B...... Jer 28:14
away captive from Jerusalem to B.... Jer 29:1
king of Judah sent unto B.............. Jer 29:3
Nebuchadnezzar king of B by saying.. Jer 29:3
away from Jerusalem unto B............ Jer 29:4
at B I will visit you, and perform...... Jer 29:10
hath raised us up prophets in B...... Jer 29:15
I have sent from Jerusalem to B...... Jer 29:20
hand of Nebuchadrezzar king of B.... Jer 29:21
captivity of Judah which are in B...... Jer 29:22
whom the king of B roasted in the.... Jer 29:22
therefore he sent unto us in B.......... Jer 29:28
into the hand of the king of B.......... Jer 32:3
into the hand of the king of B.......... Jer 32:4
And he shall lead Zedekiah to B...... Jer 32:5
hand of Nebuchadnezzar king of B.... Jer 32:28
of the king of B by the sword.......... Jer 32:36
When Nebuchadnezzar king of B...... Jer 34:1
into the hand of the king of B.......... Jer 34:2
behold the eyes of the king of B...... Jer 34:3
to mouth, and thou shalt go to B...... Jer 34:3
king of B came up into the land...... Jer 35:11
The king of B shall certainly.......... Jer 36:29
whom Nebuchadnezzar king of B...... Jer 37:1
into the hand of the king of B.......... Jer 37:17
The king of B shall not come.......... Jer 37:19
by the hand of the king of B............ Jer 38:23
came Nebuchadrezzar king of B...... Jer 39:1
princes of the king of B came in...... Jer 39:3
of the princes in the gate of B........ Jer 39:3
up to Nebuchadnezzar king of B to.. Jer 39:5
Then the king of B slew the sons...... Jer 39:6
also the king of B slew all the........ Jer 39:6
with chains, to carry him to B.......... Jer 39:7
The remnant of the people that........ Jer 39:9
Now Nebuchadrezzar king of B gave.. Jer 39:11
were carried away captive unto B.... Jer 40:1
unto thee to come with me into B.... Jer 40:4
unto thee to come with me into B.... Jer 40:4
whom the king of B hath made........ Jer 40:5
heard that the king of B had made.. Jer 40:7
not carried away captive to B.......... Jer 40:7
the land, and serve the king of B...... Jer 40:9
heard that the king of B had left...... Jer 40:11
whom the king of B had made........ Jer 41:2
whom the king of B made governor.. Jer 41:18
Be not afraid of the king of B.......... Jer 41:18
and carry us away captives into B.... Jer 43:3
take Nebuchadrezzar the king of B.. Jer 43:10
hand of Nebuchadrezzar king of B.... Jer 44:30
of B smote in the fourth year.......... Jer 46:2
king of B should come and smite...... Jer 46:13
king of B shall smite, thus saith...... Jer 49:28
for Nebuchadrezzar king of B hath.... Jer 49:30
that the LORD spake against B.......... Jer 50:1
B is taken, Bel is confounded.......... Jer 50:2
Remove out of the midst of B.......... Jer 50:8
cause to come up against B an.......... Jer 50:9
goeth by B shall be astonished........ Jer 50:13
in array against B round about........ Jer 50:14
Cut off the sower from B, and him.... Jer 50:16
king of B hath broken his bones...... Jer 50:17
I will punish the king of B.............. Jer 50:18
how is B become a desolation.......... Jer 50:23
thee, and thou art also taken, O B.... Jer 50:24
and escape out of the land of B........ Jer 50:28
together the archers against B........ Jer 50:29
and disquiet the inhabitants of B...... Jer 50:34
and upon the inhabitants of B.......... Jer 50:35
against thee, O daughter of B.......... Jer 50:42
The king of B hath heard the.......... Jer 50:43
that he hath taken against B............ Jer 50:45
taking of B the earth is moved........ Jer 50:46
Behold, I will raise up against B...... Jer 51:1
and will send into B fanners............ Jer 51:2
Flee out of the midst of B.............. Jer 51:6
B hath been a golden cup in her...... Jer 51:7
B is suddenly fallen and destroyed.. Jer 51:8
We would have healed B, but she...... Jer 51:9
for his device is against B.............. Jer 51:11
the standard upon the walls of B...... Jer 51:12
against the inhabitants of B............ Jer 51:12

And I will render unto B and to all...... Jer 51:24
LORD shall be performed against B..... Jer 51:29
to make the land of B a.......................... Jer 51:29
The mighty men of B have forborn ...... Jer 51:30
to shew the king of B that his............... Jer 51:31
The daughter of B is like a....................... Jer 51:33
the king of B hath devoured me............. Jer 51:34
to me and to my flesh be upon B.......... Jer 51:35
B shall become heaps, a dwelling......... Jer 51:37
how is B become an astonishment......... Jer 51:41
The sea is come up upon B..................... Jer 51:42
And I will punish Bel in B....................... Jer 51:44
yea, the wall of B shall fall.................... Jer 51:44
upon the graven images of B................. Jer 51:47
that is therein, shall sing for B.............. Jer 51:48
As B hath caused the slain of................ Jer 51:49
so at B shall fall the slain of.................. Jer 51:49
Though B should mount up to.............. Jer 51:53
A sound of a cry cometh from B............ Jer 51:54
Because the LORD hath spoiled B.......... Jer 51:55
is come upon her, even upon B.............. Jer 51:56
The broad walls of B shall be................ Jer 51:58
B in the fourth year of his reign............. Jer 51:59
the evil that should come upon B......... Jer 51:60
words that are written against B............ Jer 51:60
to Seraiah, When thou comest to B...... Jer 51:61
thou shalt say, Thus shall B sink........... Jer 51:64
rebelled against the king of B................ Eze 52:3
Nebuchadrezzar king of B came............ Jer 52:4
To Riblah in the land of Hamath........... Jer 52:9
the king of B slew the sons of............... Jer 52:10
the king of B bound him in chains......... Jer 52:11
and carried him to B.............................. Jer 52:11
year of Nebuchadrezzar king of B......... Jer 52:12
guard, which served the king of B......... Jer 52:12
away, that fell to the king of B............... Jer 52:15
all the brass of them to B....................... Jer 52:17
them to the king of B to Riblah............. Jer 52:26
And the king of B smote them............... Jer 52:27
that Evil-merodach king of B in............ Jer 52:31
the kings that were with him in B.......... Jer 52:32
diet given him of the king of B.............. Jer 52:34
I will bring him to B to the land............ Eze 12:13
Behold, the king of B is come to........... Eze 17:12
and led them with him to B................... Eze 17:12
in the midst of B he shall die................. Eze 17:16
snare, and I will bring him to B............. Eze 17:20
and brought him to the king of B.......... Eze 19:9
sword of the king of B may come.......... Eze 21:19
For the king of B stood at the................. Eze 21:21
the king of B set himself against........... Eze 24:2
Tyrus Nebuchadrezzar king of B............ Eze 26:7
Nebuchadrezzar king of B caused.......... Eze 29:18
unto Nebuchadrezzar king of B............. Eze 29:19
hand of Nebuchadrezzar king of B........ Eze 30:10
the arms of the king of B....................... Eze 30:24
the arms of the king of B....................... Eze 30:25
into the hand of the king of B............... Eze 30:25
king of B shall come upon these............ Eze 32:11
king of B unto Jerusalem, and............... Dan 1:1
to destroy all the wise men of B............ Dan 2:12
forth to slay the wise men of B.............. Dan 2:14
the rest of the wise men of B................. Dan 2:18
to destroy the wise men of B................. Dan 2:24
Destroy not the wise men of B.............. Dan 2:24
over the whole province of B................. Dan 2:48
over all the wise men of B..................... Dan 2:48
the affairs of the province of B.............. Dan 2:49
of Dura, in the province of B................. Dan 3:1
the affairs of the province of B.............. Dan 3:12
Abed-nego, in the province of B............ Dan 3:30
all the wise men of B before me............ Dan 4:6
in the palace of the kingdom of B......... Dan 4:30
and said, Is not this area B.................... Dan 4:30
and said to the wise men of B............... Dan 5:7
king of B Daniel had a dream............... Dan 7:1
field, and thou shalt go even to B......... Mic 4:10
dwellest with the daughter of B............ Zec 2:7
of Jedaiah, which are come from B........ Zec 6:10
time they were carried away to B........... Mt 1:11
And after they were brought to B.......... Mt 1:12
into B are fourteen generations............. Mt 1:17
and I will carry you away beyond B....... Acts 7:43
The church that is at B, elected.............. 1Pet 5:13
B is fallen, is fallen............................... Rev 14:8
great B came in remembrance............... Rev 16:19
B THE GREAT, THE MOTHER OF....... Rev 17:5
B the great is fallen, is fallen................. Rev 18:2
Alas, alas that great city B..................... Rev 18:10
that great city B be thrown down........... Rev 18:21

BABYLONIA See BABYLONISH.

BABYLONIAN See CHALDEANS'.

BABYLONIANS (bab-il-o'-ne-ans) See
CHALDEANS. Inhabitants of Babylonia.
Aphsarites, the Archevites, the B................ Ezr 4:9
the manner of the B of Chaldea............. Eze 23:15
the B came to her into the bed of.......... Eze 23:17
The B, and all the Chaldeans,................ Eze 23:23

BABYLONISH (bab-il-o'-nish) See
BABYLONIANS.
the spoils a goodly B garment.............. Josh 7:21

BABYLON'S (bab'-il-ons)
For then the king of B......................... Jer 32:2
When the king of B army fought........... Jer 34:7
the hand of the king of B army.............. Jer 34:21
the hand of the king of B army.............. Jer 38:3
forth unto the king of B princes............ Jer 38:17

go forth to the king of B princes........... Jer 38:18
forth to the king of B princes................. Jer 38:22
and all the king of B princes................. Jer 39:13

BACA (ba'-cah) A valley near Jerusalem.
the valley of B make it a well................. Ps 84:6

BACHRITES (bak'-rites) Descendants of
Becher.
of Becher, the family of the B................ Num 26:35

BACK
he brought b all the goods, and............ Gen 14:16
And they said, Stand b........................... Gen 19:9
his wife looked b from behind him........ Gen 19:26
to pass, as he drew b his hand.............. Gen 38:29
neither hath he kept b any thing........... Gen 39:9
the LORD caused the sea to go b........... Ex 14:21
wife, after he had sent her b.................. Ex 18:2
surely bring it b to him again................ Ex 23:4
and thou shalt see my b parts............... Ex 33:23
wherefore are ye kept b, that we........... Num 9:7
brought b word unto them..................... Num 13:26
thee, I will get me b again..................... Num 22:34
LORD hath kept thee b from honour..... Num 24:11
dig therewith, and shalt turn b.............. Deut 23:13
turned b upon the pursuers................... Josh 8:20
For Joshua drew not his hand b............ Josh 8:26
And Joshua at that time turned b.......... Josh 11:10
Else if ye do in any wise go b................ Josh 23:12
unto the LORD, and I cannot go b.......... Judg 11:35
turned and went b unto his house......... Judg 18:26
in law a place to lodge her people......... Ruth 1:15
b with Naomi out of the country............ Ruth 2:6
turned his b to go from Samuel............. 1Sa 9:9
for he is turned b from following........... 1Sa 15:11
hath kept me b from hurting thee.......... 1Sa 25:34
the bow of Jonathan turned not b......... 2Sa 1:22
can I bring him b again......................... 2Sa 12:23
thou, and take b thy brethren................ 2Sa 15:20
Carry b there ark of God into the.......... 2Sa 15:25
I will bring b all the people................... 2Sa 17:3
for Joab held b the people..................... 2Sa 18:16
not a word of bringing the king b......... 2Sa 19:10
to bring the king b to his house............. 2Sa 19:11
ye the last to bring b the king............... 2Sa 19:12
turn b again, that I may die in.............. 2Sa 19:37
first had in bringing b our king............. 2Sa 19:43
Bring him b with thee from this............ 1Kin 13:18
So he went b with him, and did eat....... 1Kin 13:19
the prophet that brought him b............. 1Kin 13:20
But camest b, and hast eaten bread...... 1Kin 13:22
the prophet whom he had brought b...... 1Kin 13:23
him b from the way heard thereof......... 1Kin 13:26
it upon the ass, and brought it b............ 1Kin 13:29
and hast cast me behind thy b............... 1Kin 14:9
brought them b into the country............ 1Kin 14:28
hast turned their heart b again............. 1Kin 18:37
And he said unto him, Go b again......... 1Kin 19:15
And he returned b from him.................. 1Kin 19:21
carry him b unto Amon the................... 1Kin 22:26
that they turned b from pursuing.......... 1Kin 22:33
the messengers turned b unto him........ 2Kin 1:5
them, Why are ye now turned b............. 2Kin 1:5
that fell from him, and went b.............. 2Kin 2:13
And he turned b, and looked on them... 2Kin 2:24
king Joram went b to be healed in......... 2Kin 8:29
So the king of Assyria turned b............. 2Kin 15:20
I will turn thee b by the way by............. 2Kin 19:28
ten degrees, or go b ten degrees........... 2Kin 20:9
And Ornan turned b, and saw the......... 1Chr 21:20
And when Judah looked b, behold......... 2Chr 13:14
carry him b to Amon the governor........ 2Chr 18:25
they turned b again from pursuing........ 2Chr 18:32
brought them b unto the LORD God...... 2Chr 19:4
of the army which Amaziah sent b........ 2Chr 25:13
and brought the king word b again....... 2Chr 34:16
and viewed the wall, and turned b........ Neh 2:15
Neither have I gone b from the............. Job 23:12
He holdeth b the face of his.................. Job 26:9
He keepeth b his soul from the............. Job 33:18
To bring b his soul from the pit,............ Job 33:30
because they turned b from him............ Job 34:27
turneth he b from the power of............. Job 39:22
When mine enemies are turned b.......... Ps 9:3
the LORD bringeth b the....................... Ps 14:7
Keep b thy servant also from................. Ps 19:13
shalt thou make them turn their b......... Ps 21:12
let them be turned b and brought......... Ps 35:4
us to turn b from the enemy.................. Ps 44:10
Our heart is not turned b...................... Ps 44:18
Every one of them is gone b.................. Ps 53:3
When God bringeth the captivity........... Ps 53:6
then shall mine enemies turn b............ Ps 56:9
Let them be turned b for a reward......... Ps 70:3
turned n in the day of battle................. Ps 78:9
Yea, they turned b and tempted God ... Ps 78:41
But turned b, and dealt......................... Ps 78:57
So will not we go b from thee................ Ps 80:18
thou hast brought b the captivity.......... Ps 85:1
Jordan was driven b............................. Ps 114:3
Jordan, that thou wast driven b............. Ps 114:5
The plowers plowed upon my b............. Ps 129:3
and turned b that hate Zion................. Ps 129:5
but a rod is for the b of fools................ Prov 10:13
and stripes for the b of fools................ Prov 19:29
ass, and a rod for the fool's b................ Prov 26:3
out, and who shall turn it b.................. Is 14:27
and will not call b his words................. Is 31:2
I will turn thee b by the way by............ Is 37:29
cast all my sins behind thy b................ Is 38:17
They shall be turned b, they................. Is 42:17

and to the south, Keep not b................. Is 43:6
rebellious, neither turned away b.......... Is 50:5
I gave my b to the smiters, and my....... Is 50:6
they have turned their b from me........... Jer 2:27
the LORD is not turned b from us.......... Jer 4:8
neither will I turn b from it................... Jer 4:28
turn b thine hand as a.......................... Jer 6:9
b by a perpetual backsliding................. Jer 8:5
They are turned b to the....................... Jer 11:10
I will shew them the b, and not............. Jer 18:17
I will turn b the weapons of war........... Jer 21:4
And they have turned unto me the b..... Jer 32:33
mire, and they are turned away b.......... Jer 38:22
Now while he was not yet gone b.......... Jer 40:5
Go b also to Gedaliah the son of.......... Jer 40:5
I will keep nothing b from you.............. Jer 42:4
them dismayed and turned away b........ Jer 46:5
and are fled apace, and look not b........ Jer 46:5
for they also are turned b..................... Jer 46:21
not look b to their children for............. Jer 47:3
keepeth b his sword from blood............ Jer 48:10
hath Moab turned the b with shame..... Jer 48:39
Flee ye, turn b, dwell deep, O.............. Jer 49:8
for my feet, he hath turned me b.......... Lam 1:13
he hath drawn b his right hand............. Lam 2:3
me, and cast me behind thy b............... Eze 23:35
I will not go b, neither will I................. Eze 24:14
And I will turn thee b, and put............. Eze 38:4
that is brought b from the sword........... Eze 38:8
And I will turn thee b, and leave.......... Eze 39:2
then he brought me b the way of.......... Eze 44:1
which had upon the b of it four............ Hos 7:6
For Israel slideth b as a....................... Hos 4:16
but none shall look b........................... Nah 2:8
that are turned b from the LORD.......... Zeph 1:6
when I turn b your captivity.................. Zeph 3:20
return b to take his clothes................... Mt 24:18
rolled b the stone from the door........... Mt 28:2
turn b again for to take up his.............. Mk 13:16
they turned b again to Jerusalem,......... Lk 2:45
the ship, and returned b again............. Lk 8:37
hand to the plough, and looking b....... Lk 9:62
saw that he was healed, turned b......... Lk 17:15
let him likewise not return b................. Lk 17:31
time many of his disciples went b........ Jn 6:66
thus said, she turned herself b............. Jn 20:14
kept b part of the price, his.................. Acts 5:2
to keep b part of the price of............... Acts 5:3
hearts turned b again into Egypt.......... Acts 7:39
now I kept b nothing that was.............. Acts 20:20
see, and bow down their b alway......... Rom 11:10
but if any man draw b, my soul........... Heb 10:38
of them who draw b unto perdition...... Heb 10:39
which is of you kept b by fraud............ Jas 5:4

BACKBITERS
B, haters of God, despiteful,................. Rom 1:30

BACKBITETH
He that b not with his tongue,.............. Ps 15:3

BACKBITING
an angry countenance a b tongue......... Prov 25:23

BACKBITINGS
envyings, wraths, strifes, b................... 2Cor 12:20

BACKBONE
shall he take off hard by the b.............. Lev 3:9

BACKS
enemies turn their b unto thee............. Ex 23:27
their b before their enemies.................. Josh 7:8
but turned their b before their.............. Josh 7:12
Therefore they turned their b................ Judg 20:42
of the LORD, and turned their b........... 2Chr 29:6
and cast thy law behind their b............ Neh 9:26
with their b toward the temple of......... Eze 8:16
And their whole body, and their b........ Eze 10:12

BACKSIDE
the flock to the b of the desert............. Ex 3:1
hang over the b of the tabernacle......... Eze 26:12
a book written within and on the b....... Rev 5:1

BACKSLIDER
The b in heart shall be filled................ Prov 14:14

BACKSLIDING
that which b Israel hath done............... Jer 3:6
b Israel committed adultery I had......... Jer 3:8
The b Israel hath justified.................... Jer 3:11
thou b Israel, saith the LORD............... Jer 3:12
O b children, saith the LORD............... Jer 3:14
ye b children, and I will heal............... Jer 3:22
slidden back by a perpetual b.............. Jer 8:5
thou go about, O thou b daughter........ Jer 31:22
thy flowing valley, O b daughter.......... Jer 49:4
Israel slideth back as a b heifer........... Hos 4:16
my people are bent to b from me......... Hos 11:7
I will heal their b, I will love............... Hos 14:4

BACKSLIDINGS
thee, and thy b shall reprove thee,....... Jer 2:19
children, and I will heal your b............ Jer 3:22
many, and their b are increased.......... Jer 5:6
for our b are many........................... Jer 14:7

BACKWARD
both their shoulders, and went b......... Gen 9:23
and their faces were b, and they......... Gen 9:23
so that his rider shall fall b................. Gen 49:17
seat b by the side of the gate............. Isa 4:18
the shadow return b ten degrees......... 2Kin 20:10
brought the shadow ten degrees b....... 2Kin 20:11

and b, but I cannot perceive him ...... Job 23:8
let them be driven b and put to ...... Ps 40:14
let them be turned b, and put to ...... Ps 70:2
unto anger, they are gone away b ...... Is 1:4
that they might go, and fall b ...... Is 28:13
that turneth wise men b, and ...... Is 44:25
And judgment is turned away b ...... Is 59:14
of their evil heart, and went b ...... Jer 7:24
saith the LORD, thou art gone b ...... Jer 15:6
yea, she sigheth, and turneth b ...... Lam 1:8
unto them, I am he, they went b ...... Jn 18:6

BAD

cannot speak unto thee b or good ...... Gen 24:50
not to Jacob either good or b ...... Gen 31:24
not to Jacob either good or b ...... Gen 31:29
good for a b, or a b for a good ...... Lev 27:10
value it, whether it be good or b ...... Lev 27:12
it, whether it be good or b ...... Lev 27:14
search whether it be good or b ...... Lev 27:33
dwell in, whether it be good or b ...... Num 13:19
either good or b of mine own mind ...... Num 24:13
brother Amnon neither good nor b 2Sa 13:22
the king to discern good and b 2Sa 14:17
I may discern between good and b 1Kin 3:9
the b city, and have set up the ...... Ezr 4:12
not be eaten, they were so b ...... Jer 24:2
into vessels, but cast the b away ...... Mt 13:48
all as many as they found, both b ...... Mt 22:10
done, whether it be good or b 2Cor 5:10

BADE

And the man did as Joseph b ...... Gen 43:17
up till the morning, as Moses b ...... Ex 16:24
b stone them with stones ...... Num 14:10
did unto them as the LORD b ...... Josh 11:9
all that her mother in law b her ...... Ruth 3:6
and some b me kill thee 1Sa 24:10
(Also he b them teach the 2Sa 1:18
for thy servant Joab, he b me 2Sa 14:19
on the third day, as the king b 2Chr 10:12
Then Esther b them return ...... Est 4:15
understood they how that the ...... Mt 16:12
And he that b thee and him come and ...... Lk 14:9
that when he that b thee cometh ...... Lk 14:10
said he also to him that b him ...... Lk 14:12
made a great supper, and b many ...... Lk 14:16
the Spirit b me go with them ...... Acts 11:12
But b them farewell, saying, I ...... Acts 18:21
b that he should be examined by ...... Acts 24:24

BADEST

have done according as thou b me ...... Gen 27:19

BADGERS'

b skins, and shittim wood ...... Ex 25:5
and a covering above of b skins ...... Ex 26:14
b skins, and shittim wood ...... Ex 35:7
of rams, and b skins, brought them ...... Ex 35:23
a covering of b skins above that ...... Ex 36:19
red, and the covering of b skins ...... Ex 39:34
thereon the covering of b skins ...... Num 4:6
same with a covering of b skins ...... Num 4:8
within a covering of b skins ...... Num 4:10
it with a covering of b skins ...... Num 4:11
them with a covering of b skins ...... Num 4:12
upon it a covering of b skins ...... Num 4:14
the covering of the b skins that ...... Num 4:25
work, and shod thee with b skin ...... Eze 16:10

BADNESS

in all the land of Egypt for b ...... Gen 41:19

BAG

not have in thy b divers weights ...... Deut 25:13
in a shepherd's b which he had 1Sa 17:40
And David put his hand in his b 1Sa 17:49
transgression is sealed up in a b ...... Job 14:17
He hath taken a b of money with ...... Prov 7:20
the weights of the b are his work ...... Prov 16:11
They lavish gold out of the b ...... Is 46:6
with the b of deceitful weights ...... Mic 6:11
to put it into a b with holes ...... Hag 1:6
he was a thief, and had the b ...... Jn 12:6
thought, because Judas had the b ...... Jn 13:29

BAGS

two talents of silver in two b 2Kin 5:23
came up, and they put up in b 2Kin 12:10
yourselves b which wax not old ...... Lk 12:33

BAHARUMITE (ba-ha'-rum-ite) See
BAHUMITE. Inhabitants of Bahurim.
Azmaveth the B, Eliahba the 1Chr 11:33

BAHURIM (ba-hu'-rim) See BAHARUMITE. A
village near Jerusalem.
her along weeping behind her to B 2Sa 3:16
And when king David came to B 2Sa 16:5
and came to a man's house in B 2Sa 17:18
Gera, a Benjamite, which was of B 2Sa 19:16
the son of Gera, a Benjamite of B 1Kin 2:8

BAJITH (ba'-jith) A temple in Moab.
He is gone up to B, and to Dibon, ... Is 15:2

BAKBAKKAR (bak-bak'-kar) A Levite who
returned from exile.
And B, Heresh, and Galal, and 1Chr 9:15

BAKBUK (bak'-buk) A family which returned
from exile.
The children of B, the children ...... Ezr 2:51
The children of B, the children ...... Neh 7:53

BAKBUKIAH (bak-buk-i'-ah) A Levite exile
who resettled in Jerusalem.
B the second among his brethren, ... Neh 11:17
Also B and Unni, their brethren, ... Neh 12:9
Mattaniah, and B, Obadiah, ... Neh 12:25

BAKE

did b unleavened bread, and they ...... Gen 19:3
b that which ye will b to day, ... Ex 16:23
flour, and b twelve cakes thereof ...... Lev 24:5
ten women shall b your bread in ...... Lev 26:26
did b unleavened bread thereof 1Sa 28:24
in his sight, and did b the cakes 2Sa 13:8
thou shalt b it with dung that ...... Eze 4:12
where they shall b the meat ...... Eze 46:20

BAKED

they b unleavened cakes of the ...... Ex 12:39
b it in pans, and made cakes of it ...... Num 11:8
and for that which is b in the pan 1Chr 23:29
also I have b bread upon the ...... Is 44:19

BAKEMEATS

of all manner of b for Pharaoh ...... Gen 40:17

BAKEN

of a meat offering b in the oven ...... Lev 2:4
be a meat offering b in a pan ...... Lev 2:5
meat offering b in the frying pan ...... Lev 2:7
It shall not be b with leaven ...... Lev 6:17
and when it is b, thou shalt bring ...... Lev 6:21
the b pieces of the meat offering ...... Lev 6:21
offering that is b in the oven, ... Lev 7:9
they shall be b with leaven ...... Lev 23:17
there was a cake b on the coals 1Kin 19:6

BAKER

his b had offended their lord the ...... Gen 40:1
the b of the king of Egypt, which ...... Gen 40:5
When the chief b saw that the ...... Gen 40:16
of the chief b among his servants ...... Gen 40:20
But he hanged the chief b ...... Gen 40:22
house, both me and the chief b ...... Gen 41:10
as an oven heated by the b ...... Hos 7:4
their b sleepeth all the night ...... Hos 7:6

BAKERS

and against the chief of the b ...... Gen 40:2
and to be cooks, and to be b 1Sa 8:13

BAKERS'

of bread out of the b street ...... Jer 37:21

BAKETH

yea, he kindleth it, and b bread ...... Is 44:15

BALAAM (ba'-la-am) See BALAAM'S. Son of
Beor.
unto B the son of Beor to Pethor, ... Num 22:5
and they came unto B, and spake, ... Num 22:7
the princes of Moab abode with B ...... Num 22:8
And God came unto B ...... Num 22:9
B said unto God, Balak the son of ...... Num 22:10
And God said unto B, Thou shalt ...... Num 22:12
B rose up in the morning, and said ...... Num 22:13
B refuseth to come with us ...... Num 22:14
and they came to B ...... Num 22:16
B answered and said unto the ...... Num 22:18
And God came unto B at night ...... Num 22:20
B rose up in the morning, and ...... Num 22:21
B smote the ass, to turn her into ...... Num 22:23
the ass, she fell down under B ...... Num 22:27
B said unto the ass, Because thou ...... Num 22:29
And the ass said unto B, Am not I ...... Num 22:30
the LORD opened the eyes of B ...... Num 22:31
B said unto the angel of the LORD ...... Num 22:34
the angel of the LORD said unto B ...... Num 22:35
So B went with the princes of ...... Num 22:35
when Balak heard that B was come ...... Num 22:36
And Balak said unto B, Did I not ...... Num 22:37
B said unto Balak, Lo, I am come ...... Num 22:38
B went with Balak, and they came ...... Num 22:39
oxen and sheep, and sent to B ...... Num 22:40
on the morrow, that Balak took B ...... Num 22:41
B said unto Balak, Build me here ...... Num 23:1
And Balak did as B had spoken ...... Num 23:2
B offered on every altar a ...... Num 23:2
B said unto Balak, Stand by thy ...... Num 23:3
And God met B ...... Num 23:4
And Balak said unto B, What hast ...... Num 23:11
the LORD met B ...... Num 23:16
B said unto Balak, Neither, ... Num 23:25
And B answered and said unto Balak ...... Num 23:26
And Balak said unto B, Come, I ...... Num 23:27
Balak brought B unto the top of ...... Num 23:28
B said unto Balak, Build me here ...... Num 23:29
And Balak did as B had said ...... Num 23:30
when B saw that it pleased the ...... Num 24:1
B lifted up his eyes, and he saw ...... Num 24:2
the son of Beor hath said, and ...... Num 24:3
anger was kindled against B ...... Num 24:10
And Balak said unto B, I called ...... Num 24:10
B said unto Balak, Spake I not to ...... Num 24:12
the son of Beor hath said, and ...... Num 24:15
B rose up, and went and returned to ...... Num 24:25
B also the son of Beor they slew ...... Num 31:8
Israel, through the counsel of B ...... Num 31:16
B the son of Beor of Pethor of ...... Deut 23:4
thy God would not hearken unto B ...... Deut 23:5
B also the son of Beor, the ...... Josh 13:22
called B the son of Beor to curse ...... Josh 24:9
But I would not hearken unto B ...... Josh 24:10
but hired B against them, that he ...... Neh 13:2

what B the son of Beor answered ...... Mic 6:5
the way of B the son of Bosor 2Pet 2:15
after the error of B for reward ...... Jude 11
them that hold the doctrine of B ...... Rev 2:14

BALAAM'S

crushed B foot against the wall ...... Num 22:25
B anger was kindled, and he smote ...... Num 22:27
And the LORD put a word in B mouth ...... Num 23:5

BALAC (ba'-lak) See BALAK. Greek form of
Balak.
of Balaam, who taught B to cast a ...... Rev 2:14

BALADAN (bal'-adan) See BERODACH-BALADAN,
MERODACH-BALADAN. Father of a Babylonian
king.
Berodach-baladan, the son of B 2Kin 20:12
Merodach-baladan, the son of B ...... Is 39:1

BALAH (ba'-lah) See BAALAH. A city in
Simeon.
And Hazar-shual, and B, and Azem, ... Josh 19:3

BALAK (ba'-lak) See BALAC, BALAK'S. A king of
Moab.
B the son of Zippor saw all that ...... Num 22:2
B the son of Zippor was king of ...... Num 22:4
and spake unto him the words of B ...... Num 22:7
B the son of Zippor, king of Moab ...... Num 22:10
and said unto the princes of B ...... Num 22:13
Moab rose up, and they went unto B ...... Num 22:14
B sent yet again princes, more, ... Num 22:15
Thus saith B the son of Zippor, ... Num 22:16
and said unto the servants of B ...... Num 22:18
If B would give me his house full ...... Num 22:18
Balaam went with the princes of B ...... Num 22:35
B heard that Balaam was come ...... Num 22:36
B said unto Balaam, Did I not ...... Num 22:37
And Balaam said unto B, Lo, I am ...... Num 22:38
And Balaam went with B, and they ...... Num 22:39
B offered oxen and sheep, and sent ...... Num 22:40
that took Balaam, and brought ...... Num 22:41
And Balaam said unto B, Build me ...... Num 23:1
B did as Balaam had spoken ...... Num 23:2
and B and Balaam offered on every ...... Num 23:2
And Balaam said unto B, Stand by ...... Num 23:3
mouth, and said, Return unto B ...... Num 23:5
B the king of Moab hath brought ...... Num 23:7
B said unto Balaam, What hast ...... Num 23:11
B said unto him, Come, I pray ...... Num 23:13
And he said unto B, Stand here by ...... Num 23:15
mouth, and said, Go again unto B ...... Num 23:16
B said unto him, What hath the ...... Num 23:17
his parable, and said, Rise up, B ...... Num 23:18
B said unto Balaam, Neither curse ...... Num 23:25
Balaam answered and said unto B ...... Num 23:26
B said unto Balaam, Come, I pray ...... Num 23:27
B brought Balaam unto the top of ...... Num 23:28
And Balaam said unto B, Build me ...... Num 23:29
B did as Balaam had said, and ...... Num 23:30
B said unto Balaam, I called thee ...... Num 24:10
And Balaam said unto B, Spake I ...... Num 24:12
If B would give me his house full ...... Num 24:13
and B also went his way ...... Num 24:25
Then B the son of Zippor, king of ...... Josh 24:9
better than B the son of Zippor ...... Judg 11:25
remember now what B king of Moab ...... Mic 6:5

BALAK'S

B anger was kindled against ...... Num 24:10

BALANCE

Let me be weighed in an even b ...... Job 31:6
to be laid in the b, they are ...... Ps 62:9
A false b is abomination to the ...... Prov 11:1
A just weight and b are the LORD's ...... Prov 16:11
and a false b is not good ...... Prov 20:23
in scales, and the hills in a b ...... Is 40:12
as the small dust of the b ...... Is 40:15
the bag, and weigh silver in the b ...... Is 46:6

BALANCES

Just b, just weights, a just ...... Lev 19:36
calamity laid in the b together ...... Job 6:2
and weighed him the money in the b ...... Jer 32:10
then take thee b to weigh ...... Eze 5:1
Ye shall have just b, and a just ...... Eze 45:10
Thou art weighed in the b ...... Dan 5:27
the b of deceit are in his hand ...... Hos 12:7
and falsifying the b by deceit ...... Amos 8:5
count them pure with the wicked b ...... Mic 6:11
him had a pair of b in his hand ...... Rev 6:5

BALANCINGS

thou know the b of the clouds ...... Job 37:16

BALD

the b locust after his kind, and ...... Lev 11:22
is fallen off his head, he is b ...... Lev 13:40
toward his face, he is forehead b ...... Lev 13:41
And if there be in the b forehead ...... Lev 13:42
or b forehead, a white reddish ...... Lev 13:42
his b head, or his b forehead ...... Lev 13:42
b head, or in his b forehead ...... Lev 13:43
said unto him, Go up, thou b head 2Kin 2:23
go up, thou b head 2Kin 2:23
or make themselves b for them ...... Jer 16:6
For every head shall be b ...... Jer 48:37
themselves utterly b for thee ...... Eze 27:31
every head was made b, and every ...... Eze 29:18
Make thee b, and poll thee for thy ...... Mic 1:16

BALDNESS

shall not make *b* upon their head	Lev 21:5
nor make any *b* between your eyes	Deut 14:1
and instead of well set hair *b*	Is 3:24
on all their heads shall be *b*	Is 15:2
weeping, and to mourning, and to *b*	Is 22:12
B is come upon Gaza	Jer 47:5
faces, and *b* upon all their heads	Eze 7:18
all loins, and *b* upon every head	Amos 8:10
enlarge thy *b* as the eagle	Mic 1:16

BALL

toss thee like a *b* into a large	Is 22:18

BALM

their camels bearing spicery and *b*	Gen 37:25
the man a present, a little *b*	Gen 43:11
Is there no *b* in Gilead	Jer 8:22
Go up into Gilead, and take *b*	Jer 46:11
take *b* for her pain, if so be she	Jer 51:8
and honey, and oil, and *b*	Eze 27:17

BAMAH (*ba'-mah*) See BAMOTH. *Places where Israel sacrificed to idols.*

thereof is called *B* unto this day	Eze 20:29

BAMOTH (*ba'-moth*) See BAMOTH-BAAL. *A city on the Arnon River.*

and from Nahaliel to *B*	Num 21:19
from *B* in the valley, that is in	Num 21:20

BAMOTH-BAAL (*ba'-moth-ba'-al*) *A Moabite town.*

Dibon, and *B*, and Beth-baal-meon,..	Josh 13:17

BAND

with a *b* round about the hole,	Ex 39:23
and there went with him a *b* of men..	1Sa 10:26
him, and became captain over a *b*	1Kin 11:24
behold, they spied a *b* of men	2Kin 13:21
and made them captains of the *b*	1Chr 12:18
David against the *b* of the rovers	1Chr 12:21
for the *b* of men that came with	2Chr 22:1
of the king a *b* of soldiers	Ezr 8:22
unicorn with his *b* in the furrow	Job 39:10
the earth, even with a *b* of iron	Dan 4:15
the earth, even with a *b* of iron	Dan 4:23
unto him the whole *b* of soldiers	Mt 27:27
and they call together the whole *b*..	Mk 15:16
then, having received a *b* of men	Jn 18:3
Then the *b* and the captain and	Jn 18:12
of the *b* called the Italian *b*	Acts 10:1
unto the chief captain of the *b*,...	Acts 21:31
a centurion of Augustus' *b*	Acts 27:1

BANDED

certain of the Jews *b* together	Acts 23:12

BANDS

herds, and the camels, into two *b*	Gen 32:7
and now I am become two *b*	Gen 32:10
I have broken the *b* of your yoke	Lev 26:13
his *b* loosed from off his hands	Judg 15:14
two men that were captains of *b*	2Sa 4:2
So the *b* of Syria came no more	2Kin 6:23
the *b* of the Moabites invaded the	2Kin 13:20
Pharaoh-nechoh put him in at	2Kin 23:33
against him *b* of the Chaldees	2Kin 24:2
b of the Syrians, and *b* of the	2Kin 24:2
b of the children of Ammon, and	2Kin 24:2
were *b* of soldiers for war, six	1Chr 7:4
b that were ready armed to war	1Chr 12:23
men, that went out to war by *b*	2Chr 26:11
The Chaldeans made out three *b*	Job 1:17
Pleiades, or loose the *b* of Orion	Job 38:31
hath loosed the *b* of the wild ass	Job 39:5
Let us break their *b* asunder	Ps 2:3
For there are no *b* in their death	Ps 73:4
death, and brake their *b* in sunder	Ps 107:14
The *b* of the wicked have robbed	Ps 119:61
go they forth all of them by *b*	Prov 30:27
snares and nets, and her hands as *b*..	Eccl 7:26
lest your *b* be made strong	Is 28:22
thyself from the *b* of thy neck	Is 52:2
to loose the *b* of wickedness, to..	Is 58:6
broken thy yoke, and burst thy *b*..	Jer 2:20
they shall put *b* upon thee	Eze 4:8
behold, I will lay *b* upon thee	Eze 4:8
him to help him, and all his *b*	Eze 12:14
all his *b* shall fall by the sword	Eze 17:21
I have broken the *b* of their yoke	Eze 34:27
Gomer, and all his *b*	Eze 38:6
the north quarters, and all his *b*	Eze 38:6
the land, thou, and all thy *b*	Eze 38:9
will rain upon him, and upon his *b*	Eze 38:22
of Israel, thou, and all thy *b*	Eze 39:4
cords of a man, with *b* of love	Hos 11:4
Beauty, and the other I called *B*.	Zec 11:7
asunder mine other staff, even *B*..	Zec 11:14
and he brake the *b*, and was driven	Lk 8:29
and every one's *b* were loosed	Acts 16:26
Jews, he loosed him from his *b*..	Acts 22:30
the sea, and loosed the rudder *b*	Acts 27:40
b having nourishment ministered,..	Col 2:19

BANI (*ba'-ni*)
  1. A "mighty man" of David.

of Nathan of Zobah, the Gadite,......	2Sa 23:36

  2. A Levite descendant of Merari.

The son of Amzi, the son of	1Chr 6:46

  3. A descendant of Pharez.

the son of Imri, the son of	1Chr 9:4

  4. A family of exiles.

The children of *B*, six hundred	Ezr 2:10

And of the sons of *B*	Ezr 10:29

  5. Father whose sons married foreign wives.

Of the sons of *B*	Ezr 10:34

  6. A Jewish descendant of a foreign woman.

And *B*, and Binnui, Shimei,........	Ezr 10:38

  7. Father of Rehum.

the Levites, Rehum the son of *B*	Neh 3:17
Also Jeshua, and *B*, and Sherebiah,..	Neh 8:7
of the Levites, Jeshua, and *B*	Neh 9:4
Levites, Jeshua, and Kadmiel, *B*	Neh 9:5

  8. A priest who assisted Ezra.

Shebaniah, Bunni, Sherebiah, *B*..	Neh 9:4
Hodijah, *B*, Beninu	Neh 10:13

  9. An Israelite who renewed the covenant under Nehemiah.

Pahath-moab, Elam, Zatthu, *B*	Neh 10:14

  10. A family of exiles.

Jerusalem was Uzzi the son of *B*	Neh 11:22

BANISHED

doth not fetch home again his *b*	2Sa 14:13
that his *b* be not expelled from	2Sa 14:14

BANISHMENT

whether it be unto death, or to *b*	Ezr 7:26
thee false burdens and causes of *b*..	Lam 2:14

BANK

I stood upon the *b* of the river	Gen 41:17
which is by the *b* of the river	Deut 4:48
which is upon the *b* of the river	Josh 12:2
that is upon the *b* of the river	Josh 13:9
that is on the *b* of the river	Josh 13:16
they cast up a *b* against the city	2Sa 20:15
back, and stood by the *b* of Jordan..	2Kin 2:13
shield, nor cast a *b* against it	2Kin 19:32
shields, nor cast a *b* against it	Is 37:33
at the *b* of the river were very....	Eze 47:7
by the river upon the *b* thereof	Eze 47:12
this side of the *b* of the river	Dan 12:5
that side of the *b* of the river	Dan 12:5
not thou my money into the *b*	Lk 19:23

BANKS

all his *b* all the time of harvest	Josh 3:15
place, and flowed over all his *b*	Josh 4:18
when it had overflown all his *b*	1Chr 12:15
channels, and go over all his *b*	Is 8:7
man's voice between the *b* of Ulai..	Dan 8:16

BANNER

Thou hast given a *b* to them that...	Ps 60:4
house, and his *b* over me was love...	Song 2:4
Lift ye up a *b* upon the high	Is 13:2

BANNERS

of our God we will set up our *b*	Ps 20:5
terrible as an army with *b*	Song 6:4
and terrible as an army with *b*	Song 6:10

BANQUET

b that I have prepared for thee	Est 5:4
Haman came to the *b* that Esther	Est 5:5
said unto Esther at the *b* of wine..	Est 5:6
Haman came to the *b* that I shall	Est 5:8
the *b* that she had prepared but...	Est 5:12
merrily with the king unto the *b*	Est 5:14
the *b* that Esther had prepared.....	Est 6:14
Haman came to the *b* with Esther	Est 7:1
the second day at the *b* of wine	Est 7:2
the king arising from the *b* of	Est 7:7
into the place of the *b* of wine	Est 7:8
the companions make a *b* of him	Job 41:6
his lords, came into the *b* house	Dan 5:10
the *b* of them that stretched	Amos 6:7

BANQUETING

He brought me to the *b* house	Song 2:4

BANQUETINGS

excess of wine, revellings, *b*	1Pet 4:3

BAPTISM

and Sadducees come to his *b*	Mt 3:7
the *b* that I am baptized with	Mt 20:22
be baptized with the *b* that I am	Mt 20:22
The *b* of John, whence was it?.....	Mt 21:25
preach the *b* of repentance for	Mk 1:4
be baptized with the *b* that I am	Mk 10:38
with the *b* that I am baptized	Mk 10:39
The *b* of John, was it from heaven..	Mk 11:30
preaching the *b* of repentance for..	Lk 3:3
being baptized with the *b* of John..	Lk 7:29
But I have a *b* to be baptized	Lk 12:50
The *b* of John, was it from heaven..	Lk 20:4
Beginning from the *b* of John	Acts 1:22
after the *b* which John preached....	Acts 10:37
preached before his coming the *b*...	Acts 13:24
Lord, knowing only the *b* of John....	Acts 18:25
they said, Unto John's *b*	Acts 19:3
baptized with the *b* of repentance..	Acts 19:4
buried with him by *b* into death	Rom 6:4
One Lord, one faith, one *b*	Eph 4:5
Buried with him in *b*, wherein......	Col 2:12
b doth also now save us (not the....	1Pet 3:21

BAPTISMS

Of the doctrine of *b*, and of	Heb 6:2

BAPTIST (*bap'-tist*) See BAPTIST'S. *John, the forerunner of Jesus.*

In those days came John the *B*	Mt 3:1
risen a greater than John the *B*	Mt 11:11
from the days of John the *B* until	Mt 11:12
his servants, This is John the *B*	Mt 14:2
Some say that thou art John the *B*	Mt 16:14

---

he spake unto them of John the *B*	Mt 17:13
That John the *B* was risen from	Mk 6:14
she said, The head of John the *B*	Mk 6:24
a charger the head of John the *B*	Mk 6:25
And they answered, John the *B*	Mk 8:28
John *B* hath sent us unto thee,....	Lk 7:20
a greater prophet than John the *B*	Lk 7:28
For John the *B* came neither	Lk 7:33
They answering said, John the *B*	Lk 9:19

BAPTIST'S (*bap'-tists*)

me here John *B* head in a charger..	Mt 14:8

BAPTIZE

I indeed *b* you with water unto	Mt 3:11
he shall *b* you with the Holy	Mt 3:11
John did *b* in the wilderness, and..	Mk 1:4
but he shall *b* you with the Holy	Mk 1:8
I indeed *b* you with water	Lk 3:16
he shall *b* you with the Holy	Lk 3:16
them, saying, I *b* with water	Jn 1:26
he that sent me to *b* with water....	Jn 1:33
For Christ sent me not to *b*	1Cor 1:17

BAPTIZED

And were *b* of him in Jordan,......	Mt 3:6
Jordan unto John, to be *b* of him..	Mt 3:13
I have need to be *b* of thee	Mt 3:14
And Jesus, when he was *b*, went up..	Mt 3:16
b with the baptism that I am *b*	Mt 20:22
b with the baptism that I am *b*	Mt 20:23
were all *b* of him in the river of	Mk 1:5
I indeed have *b* you with water	Mk 1:8
and was *b* of John in Jordan	Mk 1:9
b with the baptism that I am *b*	Mk 10:38
am *b* withal shall ye be *b*	Mk 10:39
believeth and is *b* shall be saved..	Mk 16:16
that came forth to be *b* of him	Lk 3:7
Then came also publicans to be *b*...	Lk 3:12
Now when all the people were *b*	Lk 3:21
to pass, that Jesus also being *b*....	Lk 3:21
being *b* with the baptism of John	Lk 7:29
themselves, being not *b* of him	Lk 7:30
But I have a baptism to be *b* with..	Lk 12:50
there he tarried with them, and *b*	Jn 3:22
and they came, and were *b*	Jn 3:23
b more disciples than John,	Jn 4:1
(Though Jesus himself *b* not	Jn 4:2
the place where John at first *b*......	Jn 10:40
For John truly *b* with water	Acts 1:5
but ye shall be *b* with the Holy	Acts 1:5
be *b* every one of you in the name	Acts 2:38
gladly received his word were *b*....	Acts 2:41
name of Jesus Christ, they were *b*..	Acts 8:16
and when he was *b*, he continued	Acts 8:13
only they were *b* in the name of....	Acts 8:16
what doth hinder me to be *b*	Acts 8:36
and he *b* him	Acts 8:38
forthwith, and arose, and was *b*....	Acts 9:18
water, that these should not be *b*	Acts 10:47
to be *b* in the name of the Lord...	Acts 10:48
he said, John indeed *b* with water..	Acts 11:16
but ye shall be *b* with the Holy	Acts 11:16
And when she was *b*, and her	Acts 16:15
and was *b*, he and all his,.........	Acts 16:33
hearing believed, and were *b*	Acts 18:8
them, Unto what then were ye *b*	Acts 19:3
John verily *b* with the baptism of..	Acts 19:4
they were *b* in the name of the.....	Acts 19:5
arise, and be *b*, and wash away thy..	Acts 22:16
that so many of us as were *b* into	Rom 6:3
Christ were *b* into his death	Rom 6:3
or were ye *b* in the name of Paul....	1Cor 1:13
I thank God that I *b* none of you....	1Cor 1:14
say that I had *b* in mine own name..	1Cor 1:15
I *b* also the household of	1Cor 1:16
I know not whether I *b* any other....	1Cor 1:16
were all *b* unto Moses in the	1Cor 10:2
Spirit are we all *b* into one body....	1Cor 12:13
they do which are *b* for the dead	1Cor 15:29
why are they then *b* for the dead	1Cor 15:29
b into Christ have put on Christ....	Gal 3:27

BAPTIZEST

Why is thou then, if thou be not....	Jn 1:25

BAPTIZETH

is he which is with the Holy Ghost	Jn 1:33
witness, behold, the same *b*	Jn 3:26

BAPTIZING

b them in the name of the Father,..	Mt 28:19
beyond Jordan, where John was *b*	Jn 1:28
therefore am I come *b* with water	Jn 1:31
John also was *b* in Aenon near to	Jn 3:23

BAR

the middle *b* in the midst of the	Ex 26:28
he made the middle *b* to shoot	Ex 36:33
skins, and shall put it upon a *b*	Num 4:10
skins, and shall put them on a *b*	Num 4:12
posts, and went away with them, *b*..	Judg 16:3
then shut the doors, and *b* them.....	Neh 7:3
will break also the *b* of Damascus	Amos 1:5

BARABBAS (*ba-rab'-bas*) *A criminal released instead of Jesus.*

then a notable prisoner, called *B*	Mt 27:16
for, or Jesus which is called *B*	Mt 27:17
multitude that they should ask *B*	Mt 27:20
They said, *B*	Mt 27:21
Then released he *B* unto them	Mt 27:26
And there was one named *B*, which...	Mk 15:7
should rather release *B* unto them	Mk 15:11

BARACHEL (*bar'-ak-el*) *Father of Elihu.*
of Elihu the son of B the Buzite............ Job 32:2
Elihu the son of B the Buzite................. Job 32:6

BARACHIAH See BARACHIAS.

BARACHIAS (*bar'-ak-i'-as*) *Father of Zachariah.*
the blood of Zacharias son of B........... Mt 23:35

BARAK (*ba'rak*) *A captain in Deborah's army.*
called B the son of Abinoam out.......... Judg 4:6
B said unto her, If thou wilt go.............. Judg 4:8
arose, and went with B to Kedesh........ Judg 4:9
B called Zebulun and Naphtali to......... Judg 4:10
they shewed Sisera that B the son....... Judg 4:12
And Deborah said unto B, Up............... Judg 4:14
So B went down from mount Tabor....... Judg 4:14
the edge of the sword before B............ Judg 4:15
But B pursued after the chariots.......... Judg 4:16
as B pursued Sisera, Jael came........... Judg 4:22
B the son of Abinoam on that day......... Judg 5:1
arise, B, and lead thy captivity............. Judg 5:12
even Issachar, and also B.................... Judg 5:15
me to tell of Gedeon, and of B............. Heb 11:32

BARAKEL See BARACHEL.

BARBARIAN
be unto him that speaketh a b............. 1Cor 14:11
speaketh shall be a b unto me............ 1Cor 14:11
nor uncircumcision, B, Scythian......... Col 3:11

BARBARIANS
when the b saw the venomous beast... Acts 28:4
both to the Greeks, and to the............. Rom 1:14

BARBAROUS
the b people shewed us no little.......... Acts 28:2

BARBED
thou fill his skin with b irons............... Job 41:7

BARBER'S
sharp knife, take thee a b razor.......... Eze 5:1

BARE
b Cain, and said, I have gotten a....... Gen 4:1
she again b his brother Abel.............. Gen 4:2
and she conceived, and b Enoch....... Gen 4:17
And Adah b Jabal.............................. Gen 4:20
she also b Tubal-cain, an.................. Gen 4:22
she b a son, and called his name..... Gen 4:25
they b children to them, the same..... Gen 6:4
b up the ark, and it was lift up........... Gen 7:17
Abram's wife b him no children......... Gen 16:1
And Hagar b Abram a son................. Gen 16:15
his son's name, which Hagar b......... Gen 16:15
when Hagar b Ishmael to Abram...... Gen 16:16
And the firstborn b a son, and......... Gen 19:37
And the younger, she also b a son.... Gen 19:38
and they b children.......................... Gen 20:17
b Abraham a son in his old age....... Gen 21:2
unto him, whom Sarah b to him........ Gen 21:3
she b also Tebah, and Gaham, and.. Gen 22:24
of Milcah, which she b unto Nahor.... Gen 22:23
Sarah my master's wife b a son to.... Gen 24:36
son, whom Milcah b unto him........... Gen 24:47
she b him Zimran, and Jokshan, and Gen 25:2
Sarah's handmaid, b unto Abraham.. Gen 25:12
years old when she b them............... Gen 25:26
b a son, and she called his name..... Gen 29:32
she conceived again, and b a son.... Gen 29:33
she conceived again, and b a son.... Gen 29:34
she conceived again, and b a son.... Gen 29:35
saw that she b Jacob no children...... Gen 30:1
conceived, and b Jacob a son.......... Gen 30:5
again, and b Jacob a second son..... Gen 30:7
Zilpah Leah's maid b Jacob a son.... Gen 30:10
Leah's maid b Jacob a second son.. Gen 30:12
and b Jacob the fifth son.................. Gen 30:17
again, and b Jacob the sixth son...... Gen 30:19
and afterwards she b a daughter...... Gen 30:21
And she conceived, and b a son....... Gen 30:23
then all the cattle b speckled............ Gen 31:8
then b all the cattle ringstreaked...... Gen 31:8
1 b the loss of it.............................. Gen 31:39
which she b unto Jacob, went out..... Gen 34:1
And Adah b to Esau Eliphaz............. Gen 36:4
and Bashemath b Reuel.................. Gen 36:4
And Aholibamah b Jeush, and Jaalam, Gen 36:5
and she b to Eliphaz Amalek........... Gen 36:12
she b to Esau Jeush, and Jaalam.... Gen 36:14
And she conceived, and b a son....... Gen 38:3
she conceived again, and b a son.... Gen 38:4
yet again conceived, and b a son..... Gen 38:5
he was at Chezib, when she b him.... Gen 38:5
priest of On b unto him.................... Gen 41:50
know that my wife b me two sons..... Gen 44:27
which she b unto Jacob................... Gen 46:15
these she b unto Jacob, even.......... Gen 46:18
priest of On b unto him.................... Gen 46:20
and she b these unto Jacob............. Gen 46:25
the woman conceived, and b a son.. Ex 2:2
she b him a son, and he called his... Ex 2:22
and she b him Aaron and Moses...... Ex 6:20
she b him Nadab, and Abihu........... Ex 6:23
and she b him Phinehas................. Ex 6:25
how I b you on eagles' wings, and.... Ex 19:4
shall be rent, and his head b........... Lev 13:45

whether it be b within or without....... Lev 13:55
they b it between two upon a............ Num 13:23
whom her mother b to Levi in........... Num 26:59
b unto Amram Aaron and................ Num 26:59
how that the LORD thy God b thee..... Deut 1:31
which b the ark of the covenant........ Deut 31:9
which b the ark of the covenant........ Josh 3:15
as they that b the ark were come...... Josh 3:15
the feet of the priests that b............ Josh 3:17
the priests that b the ark of the........ Josh 3:17
the ark of the covenant stood.......... Josh 4:9
For the priests which b the ark......... Josh 4:10
when the priests that b the ark......... Josh 4:18
which b the ark of the covenant........ Josh 8:33
the people that b the present........... Judg 3:18
she also b him a son, whose name.... Judg 8:31
And Gilead's wife b him sons............ Judg 11:1
and his wife was barren, and b not.... Judg 13:2
And the woman b a son, and called.. Judg 13:24
Pharez, whom Tamar b unto Judah... Ruth 4:12
her conception, and she b a son....... Ruth 4:13
had conceived, that she b a son....... 1Sa 1:20
b three sons and two daughters........ 1Sa 1:4
the young man that b his armour....... 1Sa 14:1
The young man that b the ark of....... 1Sa 14:6
the man that b the shield went......... 1Sa 17:41
that when they that b the ark of........ 2Sa 6:13
became his wife, and b him a son..... 2Sa 11:27
that Uriah's wife b unto David.......... 2Sa 12:15
she b a son, and he called his......... 2Sa 12:24
ten young men that b Joab's............ 2Sa 18:15
whom she b unto Saul, Armoni and... 2Sa 21:8
his mother b him after Absalom........ 1Kin 1:6
and ten thousand that b burdens...... 1Kin 5:15
which b rule over the people that...... 1Kin 9:23
train, with camels that b spices........ 1Kin 10:2
Tahpenes b him Genubath his son... 1Kin 11:20
The LORD, that the guard b them...... 1Kin 14:28
b a son at that season that.............. 2Kin 4:17
and they b them before him............. 2Kin 5:23
she b Zimran, and Jokshan, and...... 1Chr 1:32
his daughter in law b him Pharez...... 1Chr 2:4
And Ephrath b Amasa..................... 1Chr 2:17
unto him Segub, which b him Hur..... 1Chr 2:21
and she b him Segub....................... 1Chr 2:21
then Abiah Hezron's wife b him........ 1Chr 2:24
she b him Ahban, and Molid............. 1Chr 2:29
and she b him Attai......................... 1Chr 2:35
b Haran, and Moza, and Gazez........ 1Chr 2:46
concubine, b Sheber, and Tirhanah.. 1Chr 2:48
She b also Shaaph the father of....... 1Chr 2:49
Naarah b him Ahuzam, and Hepher,.. 1Chr 4:6
Because I b him with sorrow............. 1Chr 4:9
she b Jehizkiah, and Shammai, and.. 1Chr 4:17
his wife Jehudijah b Jered the.......... 1Chr 4:18
Ashriel, whom she b...................... 1Chr 7:14
b Machir the father of Gilead........... 1Chr 7:14
the wife of Machir b a son............... 1Chr 7:16
And his sister Hammoleketh b Ishod.. 1Chr 7:18
b a son, and he called his name...... 1Chr 7:23
children of Judah that b shield........ 1Chr 12:24
b the ark of God upon their............. 1Chr 15:15
God helped the Levites that b the.... 1Chr 15:26
and all the Levites that b the ark...... 1Chr 15:27
that b rule over the people.............. 2Chr 8:10
company, and camels that b spices.. 2Chr 9:1
Which b him children...................... 2Chr 11:19
which b him Abijah, and Attai, and... 2Chr 11:20
had an army of men that b targets.... 2Chr 14:8
that b shields and drew bows, two.... 2Chr 14:8
the wall, and they that b burdens..... Neh 4:17
even their servants b rule over......... Neh 5:15
and bitterness to her that b him........ Prov 17:25
the that b thee shall rejoice............ Prov 23:25
The choice one of her that b her...... Song 6:9
brought thee forth that b thee.......... Song 8:5
and she conceived, and b a son....... Is 8:3
Elam b the quiver with chariots........ Is 22:6
strip you, and make you b............... Is 32:11
make b the leg, uncover the thigh.... Is 47:2
father, and unto Sarah that b you..... Is 51:2
The LORD hath made b his holy arm.. Is 52:10
he b the sin of many, and made....... Is 53:12
he b them, and carried them all....... Is 63:9
discovered, and thy heels made b.... Jer 13:22
their mothers that b them................ Jer 16:3
wherein my mother b me be blessed.. Jer 20:14
out, and thy mother that b thee........ Jer 22:26
But I have made Esau b, I have........ Jer 49:10
she that b you shall be ashamed..... Jer 50:12
I b it upon my shoulder in their........ Eze 12:7
whereas thou wast naked and b...... Eze 16:7
youth, when thou wast naked and b.. Eze 16:22
jewels, and leave thee naked and b.. Eze 16:39
the sceptres of them that b rule...... Eze 19:11
and they were mine, and they b sons. Eze 23:4
and shall leave thee naked and b.... Eze 23:29
their sons, whom they b unto thee.... Eze 23:37
which conceived, and b him a son.... Hos 1:3
conceived again, and b a daughter.. Hos 1:6
she conceived, and b a son............ Hos 1:8
he hath made it clean, and bare...... Joel 1:7
infirmities, and b our sicknesses...... Mt 8:17
For many b false witness against..... Mk 14:56
b false witness against him............. Mk 14:57
all b him witness, and wondered at... Lk 4:22
they that b him stood still................ Lk 7:14
up, and b fruit an hundredfold.......... Lk 8:8
Blessed is the womb that b thee...... Lk 11:27
barren, and the wombs that never b.. Lk 23:29

John b witness of him, and cried....... Jn 1:15
John b record, saying, I saw the....... Jn 1:32
b record that this is the Son of......... Jn 1:34
And they b it.................................. Jn 2:8
he b witness unto the truth.............. Jn 5:33
bag, and b what was put therein....... Jn 12:6
him from the dead, b record............. Jn 12:17
And he that saw it b record............. Jn 19:35
b them witness, giving them the....... Acts 15:8
but b grain, I may chance of............ 1Cor 15:37
Who his own self b our sins in......... 1Pet 2:24
Who b record of the word of God,..... Rev 1:2
which b twelve manner of fruits........ Rev 22:2

BAREFOOT
his head covered, and he went b...... 2Sa 15:30
And he did so, walking naked and b... Is 20:2
b three years for a sign and............. Is 20:3
young and old, naked and b............ Is 20:4

BAREST
because thou b the ark of the.......... 1Kin 2:26
thou never b rule over them............. Is 63:19
Jordan, to whom thou b witness........ Jn 3:26

BARHUMITE (*bar'hu-mite*) See BAHARUMITE.
A form of Baharumite.
the Arbathite, Azmaveth the B.......... 2Sa 23:31

BARIAH (*ba-ri'-ah*) *Grandson of Shechaniah.*
Hattush, and Igeal, and B, and......... 1Chr 3:22

BAR-JESUS (*bar-je'-sus*) See ELYMAS. *Another name of Elymas.*
prophet, a Jew, whose name was B... Acts 13:6

BAR-JONA (*bar-jo'-nah*) See SIMON. *Another name of Simon Peter.*
him, Blessed art thou, Simon B......... Mt 16:17

BAR-JONAH See BAR-JONA.

BARK
are all dumb dogs, they cannot b...... Is 56:10

BARKED
my vine waste, and b my fig tree...... Joel 1:7

BARKOS (*bar'-cos*) *A family who returned from the exile.*
The children of B, the children.......... Ezr 2:53
The children of B, the children.......... Neh 7:55

BARLEY
And the flax and the b was smitten... Ex 9:31
for the b was in the ear, and the....... Ex 9:31
a homer of b seed shall be valued.... Lev 27:16
tenth part of an ephah of b meal....... Num 5:15
A land of wheat, and b, and vines,.... Deut 8:8
a cake of b bread tumbled into......... Judg 7:13
in the beginning of b harvest........... Ruth 1:22
and it was about an ephah of b......... Ruth 2:17
glean unto the end of b harvest....... Ruth 2:23
he winnoweth b to night in the........ Ruth 3:2
it, he measured six measures of b.... Ruth 3:15
six measures of b gave he me......... Ruth 3:17
is near mine, and he hath b there.... 2Sa 14:30
earthen vessels, and wheat, and b... 2Sa 17:28
in the beginning of b harvest........... 2Sa 21:9
B also and straw for the horses and.. 1Kin 4:28
firstfruits, twenty loaves of b.......... 2Kin 4:42
and two measures of b for a shekel.. 2Kin 7:1
and two measures of b for a shekel.. 2Kin 7:16
Two measures of b for a shekel...... 2Kin 7:18
was a parcel of ground full of b....... 1Chr 11:13
and twenty thousand measures of b.. 2Chr 2:10
Now therefore the wheat, and the b.. 2Chr 2:15
of wheat, and ten thousand of b....... 2Chr 27:5
of wheat, and cockle instead of b.... Job 31:40
wheat and the appointed b and the.. Is 28:25
in the field, of wheat, and of b......... Jer 41:8
thou also unto thee wheat, and b..... Eze 4:9
And thou shalt eat it as b cakes....... Eze 4:12
among my people for handfuls of b... Eze 13:19
part of an ephah of an homer of b.... Eze 45:13
of b, and an half homer of b............ Hos 3:2
for the wheat and for the b............. Joel 1:11
here, which hath five b loaves......... Jn 6:9
fragments of the five b loaves......... Jn 6:13
three measures of b for a penny...... Rev 6:6

BARN
thy seed, and gather it into thy b...... Job 39:12
Is the seed yet in the b.................. Hag 2:19
but gather the wheat into my b......... Mt 13:30
neither have storehouse nor b......... Lk 12:24

BARNABAS (*bar'-na-bas*) See JOSES. *A companion of Paul.*
by the apostles was surnamed B...... Acts 4:36
But B took him, and brought him to... Acts 9:27
and they sent forth B, that he......... Acts 11:22
Then departed B to Tarsus............. Acts 11:25
to the elders by the hands of B........ Acts 11:30
And B and Saul returned from......... Acts 12:25
as B, and Simeon that was called..... Acts 13:1
Holy Ghost said, Separate me B...... Acts 13:2
who called for B and Saul, and........ Acts 13:7
proselytes followed Paul and B........ Acts 13:43
B waxed bold, and said, It was....... Acts 13:46
persecution against Paul and B....... Acts 13:50
And they called B, Jupiter............... Acts 14:12
Which when the apostles, B............ Acts 14:14
day be departed with B to Derbe..... Acts 14:20
B had no small dissension and........ Acts 15:2
they determined that Paul and B...... Acts 15:2

B

silence, and gave audience to *B* .... Acts 15:12
to Antioch with Paul and *B* .... Acts 15:22
men unto you with our beloved *B* .... Acts 15:25
B continued in Antioch, teaching ...... Acts 15:35
some days after Paul said unto *B* ...... Acts 15:36
B determined to take with them .... Acts 15:37
so *B* took Mark, and sailed unto .... Acts 15:39
Or I only and *B*, have not we power 1Cor 9:6
went up again to Jerusalem with *B* .... Gal 2:1
B the right hands of fellowship .... Gal 2:9
insomuch that *B* also was carried .... Gal 2:13
you, and Marcus, sister's son to *B* ...... Col 4:10

BARNFLOOR
out of the *b*, or out of the 2Kin 6:27

BARNS
So shall thy *b* be filled with .... Prov 3:10
desolate, the *b* are broken down .... Joel 1:17
do they reap, nor gather into *b* .... Mt 6:26
I will pull down my *b*, and build .... Lk 12:18

BARREL
but an handful of meal in a *b* 1Kin 17:12
The *b* of meal shall not waste, ... 1Kin 17:14
the *b* of meal wasted not, neither 1Kin 17:16

BARRELS
Fill four *b* with water, and pour 1Kin 18:33

BARREN
But Sarai was *b* .... Gen 11:30
for his wife, because she was *b* .... Gen 25:21
but Rachel was *b* .... Gen 29:31
cast their young, nor be *b* .... Ex 23:26
not be male or female *b* among you .... Deut 7:14
and his wife was *b*, and bare not .... Judg 13:2
unto her, Behold now, thou art *b* .... Judg 13:3
so that the *b* hath born seven 1Sa 2:5
water is naught, and the ground *b* 2Kin 2:19
thence any more death or *b* land 2Kin 2:21
entreateth the *b* that beareth not .... Job 24:21
and the *b* land his dwellings .... Job 39:6
He maketh the *b* woman to keep .... Ps 113:9
and the *b* womb .... Prov 30:16
twins, and none is *b* among them .... Song 4:2
and there is not one *b* among them .... Song 6:6
Sing, O *b*, thou that didst not .... Is 54:1
and will drive him into a land *b* .... Joel 2:20
because that Elisabeth was *b* .... Lk 1:7
month with her, who was called *b* ...... Lk 1:36
they shall say, Blessed are the *b* .... Lk 23:29
Rejoice, thou *b* that bearest not .... Gal 4:27
you that ye shall neither be *b* 2Pet 1:8

BARRENNESS
A fruitful land into *b*, for the .... Ps 107:34

BARS
thou shalt make *b* of shittim wood .... Ex 26:26
five *b* for the boards of .... Ex 26:27
five *b* for the boards of the side .... Ex 26:27
of gold for places for the *b* .... Ex 26:29
shalt overlay the *b* with gold .... Ex 26:29
his taches, and his boards, his *b* .... Ex 35:11
he made *b* of shittim wood .... Ex 36:31
five *b* for the boards of the .... Ex 36:31
five *b* for the boards of the .... Ex 36:32
b, and overlaid the *b* with gold .... Ex 36:34
his taches, his boards, his *b* .... Ex 39:33
thereof, and put in the *b* thereof .... Ex 40:18
the *b* thereof, the pillars .... Num 3:36
the *b* thereof, and the pillars .... Num 4:31
with high walls, gates, and *b* .... Deut 3:5
into a town that hath gates and *b* ...... Judg 1:36
cities with walls and brasen *b* 1Kin 4:13
cities, with walls, gates, and *b* 2Chr 8:5
walls, and towers, gates, and *b* 2Chr 14:7
locks thereof, and the *b* thereof .... Neh 3:6
locks thereof, and the *b* thereof .... Neh 3:6
locks thereof, and the *b* thereof .... Neh 3:14
the *b* thereof, and a thousand .... Neh 3:13
locks thereof, and the *b* thereof .... Neh 3:14
the *b* thereof, and the wall of the .... Neh 3:15
shall go down to the *b* of the pit ...... Job 17:16
for it my decreed place, and set *b* ...... Job 38:10
his bones are like *b* of iron .... Job 40:18
cut the *b* of iron in sunder .... Ps 107:16
strengthened the *b* of thy gates .... Ps 147:13
are like the *b* of a castle .... Prov 18:19
and cut in sunder the *b* of iron .... Is 45:2
which have neither gates nor *b* .... Jer 49:31
her *b* are broken .... Jer 51:30
he hath destroyed and broken her *b* .... Lam 2:9
and having neither *b* nor gates .... Eze 38:11
the earth with her *b* was about me .... Jonah 2:6
the fire shall devour thy *b* .... Nah 3:13

BARSABAS (bar'-sab-as) See JOSEPH, JUDAS, JUSTUS.
1. A candidate for apostle.
appointed two, Joseph called *B* .... Acts 1:23
2. A disciple sent to Antioch with Silas.
namely, Judas surnamed *B*, and...... Acts 15:22

BARSABBAS See BARSABAS.

BARTHOLOMEW (bar-thol'-o-mew) See NATHANAEL. *One of Jesus' twelve disciples.*
Philip, and *B*; Thomas, and.............. Mt 10:3
And Andrew, and Philip, and *B*.......... Mk 3:18
James and John, Philip and *B* .... Lk 6:14
and Andrew, Philip, and Thomas, *B*.... Acts 1:13

BARTIMAEUS (bar-ti-me'-us) *A blind beggar, a great number of people, blind B*... Mk 10:46

BARUCH (ba'-rook)
1. A son of Zabbai.
After him *B* the son of Zabbai .... Neh 3:20
2. The scribe of Jeremiah.
Daniel, Ginnethon, *B*, ... Neh 10:6
2. A descendant of Perez.
And Maaseiah the son of *B*, the son.... Neh 11:5
3. The scribe of Jeremiah.
purchase unto *B* the son of .... Jer 32:12
I charged *B* before them, saying,...... Jer 32:13
purchase unto *B* the son of Neriah .... Jer 32:16
called *B* the son of Neriah................ Jer 36:4
B wrote from the mouth of .... Jer 36:4
And Jeremiah commanded *B*, saying,.... Jer 36:5
B the son of Neriah did according...... Jer 36:8
Then read *B* in the book the words .... Jer 36:10
when *B* read the book in the ears ...... Jer 36:13
the son of Cushi, unto *B*.................... Jer 36:14
So *B* the son of Neriah took the........ Jer 36:14
So *B* read it in their ears.................. Jer 36:15
both one and other, and said unto *B*.... Jer 36:16
And they asked *B*, saying, Tell us ...... Jer 36:17
Then *B* answered them, He.............. Jer 36:18
Then said the princes unto *B* .... Jer 36:19
to take *B* the scribe and Jeremiah .... Jer 36:26
the words which *B* wrote at the .... Jer 36:27
roll, and gave it to *B* the scribe........ Jer 36:32
But *B* the son of Neriah setteth .... Jer 43:3
prophet, and *B* the son of Neriah...... Jer 43:6
spake unto *B* the son of Neriah .... Jer 45:1
the God of Israel, unto thee, O *B*...... Jer 45:2

BARZILLAI (bar-zil'-la-i)
1. A friend of David.
B the Gileadite of Rogelim,................ 2Sa 17:27
B the Gileadite came down from 2Sa 19:31
Now *B* was a very aged man, even 2Sa 19:32
And the king said unto *B*, Come 2Sa 19:33
B said unto the king, How long 2Sa 19:34
was come over, the king kissed *B* 2Sa 19:39
unto the sons of *B* the Gileadite........ 1Kin 2:7
of Koz, the children of *B*.................... Ezr 2:61
the daughters of *B* the Gileadite........ Ezr 2:61
of Koz, the children of *B*.................... Neh 7:63
of *B* the Gileadite to wife .... Neh 7:63
2. Husband of Merab.
the son of *B* the Meholathite............ 2Sa 21:8

BASE
will be *b* in mine own sight................ 2Sa 6:22
cubits was the length of one *b* 1Kin 7:27
the ledges there was a above 1Kin 7:29
every *b* had four brasen wheels,........ 1Kin 7:30
was round after the work of the *b* 1Kin 7:31
the wheels were joined to the *b* 1Kin 7:32
to the four corners of one *b* 1Kin 7:34
were of the very *b* itself 1Kin 7:34
in the top of the *b* was there a 1Kin 7:35
on the top of the *b* the ledges 1Kin 7:35
of fools, yea, children of *b* men........ Job 30:8
the *b* against the honourable 1s 3:5
That the kingdom might be *b* .... Eze 17:14
they shall be there a *b* kingdom .... Eze 29:14
and set there upon her own *b* .... Zec 5:11
and *b* before all the people,.............. Mal 2:9
b things of the world, and things...... 1Cor 1:28
who in presence am *b* among you 2Cor 10:1

BASEMATH See BASMATH.

BASER
lewd fellows of the *b* sort.................. Acts 17:5

BASES
And he made ten *b* of brass 1Kin 7:27
the work of the *b* was on this............ 1Kin 7:28
this manner he made the ten *b* 1Kin 7:37
every one of the ten *b* one laver 1Kin 7:38
he put five *b* on the right side........... 1Kin 7:39
ten *b*, and ten lavers on the *b*.......... 1Kin 7:43
Ahaz cut off the borders of the *b* 2Kin 16:17
the house of the LORD, and the *b*...... 2Kin 25:13
the *b* which Solomon had made for 2Kin 25:16
b, and lavers made he upon the.......... 2Chr 4:14
And they set the altar upon his *b*...... Ezr 3:3
the sea, and concerning the *b* .... Jer 27:19
the house of the LORD, and the *b* ...... Jer 52:17
bulls that were under the *b*................ Jer 52:20

BASEST
It shall be the *b* of the kingdoms ...... Eze 29:15
setteth up over it the *b* of men........ Dan 4:17

BASHAN (ba'-shan) See BASHAN-HAVOTH-JAIR.
Kingdom of King Og.
turned and went up by the way of *B* .... Num 21:33
Og the king of *B* went out against .... Num 21:33
and the kingdom of Og king of *B* ...... Num 32:33
in Heshbon, and Og the king of *B* ...... Deut 1:4
turned, and went up the way to *B* ...... Deut 3:1
Og the king of *B* came out against .... Deut 3:1
our hands Og also, the king of *B* ...... Deut 3:3
of Argob, the kingdom of Og in *B* ...... Deut 3:4
plain, and all Gilead, and all *B* .... Deut 3:10
cities of the kingdom of Og in *B* .... Deut 3:10
For only Og king of *B* remained of .... Deut 3:11
And the rest of Gilead, and all *B* .... Deut 3:13
the region of Argob, with all *B* .... Deut 3:13
and Golan in *B*, of the Manasses........ Deut 4:43
land, and the land of Og king of *B* .... Deut 4:47
of Heshbon, and Og the king of *B* ...... Deut 29:7
lambs, and rams of the breed of *B* .... Deut 32:14

he shall leap from *B* .... Deut 33:22
of Heshbon, and Og king of *B* .... Josh 9:10
And the coast of Og king of *B* .... Josh 12:4
Hermon, and in Salcah, and in all *B* .... Josh 12:5
Hermon, and all *B* unto Salcah .... Josh 13:11
All the kingdom of Og in *B* .... Josh 13:12
coast was from Mahanaim, all *B* .... Josh 13:30
all the kingdom of Og king of *B* .... Josh 13:30
the towns of Jair, which are in *B* ...... Josh 13:30
cities of the kingdom of Og in *B* ...... Josh 13:31
war, therefore he had Gilead and *B* .... Josh 17:1
beside the land of Gilead and *B* .... Josh 17:5
Golan in *B* out of the tribe of .... Josh 20:8
the half tribe of Manasseh in *B* .... Josh 21:6
gave Golan in *B* with her suburbs .... Josh 21:27
Moses had given possession in *B* ...... Josh 22:7
region of Argob, which is in *B* 1Kin 4:13
the Amorites, and of Og king of *B* 1Kin 4:19
the river Arnon, even Gilead and *B* 2Kin 10:33
in the land of *B* unto Salchah 1Chr 5:11
next, and Jaanai, and Shaphat in *B* 1Chr 5:12
And they dwelt in Gilead in *B* 1Chr 5:16
increased from *B* unto Baal-hermon 1Chr 5:23
out of the tribe of Manasseh in *B* 1Chr 6:62
Golan in *B* with her suburbs, and 1Chr 6:71
and the land of Og king of *B* .... Neh 9:22
strong bulls of *B* have beset me .... Ps 22:12
hill of God is as the hill of *B* .... Ps 68:15
an high hill as the hill of *B* .... Ps 68:15
said, I will bring again from *B* .... Ps 68:22
of the Amorites, and Og king of *B* .... Ps 135:11
And Og the king of *B* .... Ps 136:20
up, and upon all the oaks of *B* .... Is 2:13
and *B* and Carmel shake off their ...... Is 33:9
and lift up thy voice in *B* .... Jer 22:20
and he shall feed on Carmel and *B* .... Jer 50:19
Of the oaks of *B* have they made ...... Eze 27:6
all of them fatlings of *B* .... Eze 39:18
Hear this word, ye kine of *B* .... Amos 4:1
let them feed in *B* and Gilead, as ...... Mic 7:14
B languisheth, and Carmel, and the .... Nah 1:4
howl, O ye oaks of *B* .... Zec 11:2

BASHAN-HAVOTH-JAIR (ba'''-shan-ha''- voth-ia'-ur) Same as Argob.
called them after his own name, *B*.... Deut 3:14

BASHEMATH (bash'-e-math) See BASMATH.
1. Daughter of Elon the Hittite.
The daughter of Elon the .... Gen 26:34
2. Daughter of Ishmael.
B Ishmael's daughter, sister of .... Gen 36:3
and *B* bare Reuel .... Gen 36:4
the son of *B* the wife of Esau .... Gen 36:10
were the sons of *B* Esau's wife.......... Gen 36:13
are the sons of *B* Esau's wife............ Gen 36:17

BASKET
in the uppermost *b* there was of ...... Gen 40:17
them out of the *b* upon my head........ Gen 40:17
b, and bring them in the *b* .... Ex 29:3
one wafer out of the *b* of the............ Ex 29:23
and the bread that is in the *b*............ Ex 29:32
rams, and a *b* of unleavened bread .... Lev 8:2
out of the *b* of unleavened bread,...... Lev 8:31
that is in the *b* of consecrations .... Lev 8:31
a *b* of unleavened bread, cakes of...... Num 6:15
with the *b* of unleavened bread.......... Num 6:17
one unleavened cake out of the *b*, ... Num 6:19
thee, and shalt put it in a *b* .... Deut 26:2
take the *b* out of thine hand .... Deut 26:4
Blessed shall be thy *b* and thy .... Deut 28:5
Cursed shall be thy *b* and thy .... Deut 28:17
the flesh he put in a *b*, and he .... Judg 6:19
One *b* had very good figs, even.......... Jer 24:2
the other *b* had very naughty figs...... Jer 24:2
behold a *b* of summer fruit................ Amos 8:1
And I said, A *b* of summer fruit.......... Amos 8:2
let him down by the wall in a *b* .... Acts 9:25
through a window in a *b* was I let...... 2Cor 11:33

BASKETS
I had three white *b* on my head .... Gen 40:16
The three *b* are three days;................ Gen 40:18
persons, and put their heads in *b* 2Kin 10:7
as a praegearberthere into the *b*.......... Jer 6:9
two *b* of figs were set before the ...... Jer 24:1
that remained twelve *b* full .... Mt 14:20
meat that was left seven *b* full .... Mt 15:37
and how many *b* ye took up.............. Mt 16:9
and how many *b* ye took up.............. Mt 16:10
they took up twelve *b* full of the ...... Mk 6:43
broken meat that was left seven *b*.... Mk 8:8
how many *b* full of fragments took.... Mk 8:19
how many *b* full of fragments took.... Mk 8:20
that remained to them twelve *b* .... Lk 9:17
and filled twelve *b* with the .... Jn 6:13

BASMATH (bas'-math) See BASHEMATH. *A daughter of Solomon.*
he also took *B* the daughter of 1Kin 4:15

BASON
it in the blood that is in the *b* .... Ex 12:22
with the blood that is in the *b* .... Ex 12:22
poured by weight for every *b* 1Chr 28:17
by weight for every *b* of silver.......... 1Chr 28:17
that he poureth water into a *b* .... Jn 13:5

BASONS
half of the blood, and put it in *b* .... Ex 24:6
ashes, and his shovels, and his *b* ...... Ex 27:3
pots, and the shovels, and the *b* .... Ex 38:3

and the shovels, and the b............ Num 4:14
Brought beds, and b, and earthen 2Sa 17:28
lavers, and the shovels, and the b.... 1Kin 7:40
pots, and the shovels, and the b 1Kin 7:45
bowls, and the snuffers, and the b ... 1Kin 7:50
LORD bowls of silver, snuffers, b..... 2Kin 12:13
for the golden b he gave gold by 1Chr 28:17
And he made an hundred b of gold 2Chr 4:8
pots, and the shovels, and the b...... 2Chr 4:11
And the snuffers, and the b.......... 2Chr 4:22
Thirty b of gold, silver b .... Ezr 1:10
Also twenty b of gold, of a .... Ezr 8:27
a thousand drams of gold, fifty b .... Neh 7:70
And the b, and the firepans, and the .. Jer 52:19

BASTARD
A b shall not enter into the .... Deut 23:2
a b shall dwell in Ashdod, and I .... Zec 9:6

BASTARDS
all are partakers, then are ye b .... Heb 12:8

BAT
kind, and the lapwing, and the b .... Lev 11:19
kind, and the lapwing, and the b .... Deut 14:18

BATH
of vineyard shall yield one b........ Is 5:10
and a just ephah, and a just b ...... Eze 45:10
the b shall be of one measure, ... Eze 45:11
that the b may contain the tenth .... Eze 45:11
the b of oil, ye shall offer the .... Eze 45:14
tenth part of a b out of the cor .... Eze 45:14

BATHE
b himself in water, and be unclean .. Lev 15:5
b himself in water, and be unclean .. Lev 15:6
b himself in water, and be unclean .. Lev 15:7
b himself in water, and be unclean .. Lev 15:8
b himself in water, and be unclean .. Lev 15:10
b himself in water, and be unclean .. Lev 15:11
b his flesh in running water, and .. Lev 15:13
they shall both b themselves in .... Lev 15:18
b himself in water, and be unclean .. Lev 15:21
b himself in water, and be unclean .. Lev 15:22
b himself in water, and be unclean .. Lev 15:27
and b his flesh in water, and ...... Lev 16:26
and b his flesh in water, and ...... Lev 16:28
b himself in water, and be unclean .. Lev 17:15
he wash them, nor b his flesh....... Lev 17:16
he shall b his flesh in water, and.. Num 19:7
b his flesh in water, and shall be.. Num 19:8
b himself in water, and shall be.... Num 19:19

BATHED
For my sword shall be b in heaven .. Is 34:5

BATH-RABBIM (bath-rab'-bim) A gate at Heshbon.
in Heshbon, by the gate of B ...... Song 7:4

BATHS
it contained two thousand b........ 1Kin 7:26
one laver contained forty b........ 1Kin 7:38
and twenty thousand b of wine...... 2Chr 2:10
and twenty thousand b of oil 2Chr 2:10
received and held three thousand b .. 2Chr 4:5
wheat, and to an hundred b of wine .. Ezr 7:22
and to an hundred b of oil .... Ezr 7:22
cor, which is an homer of ten b.... Eze 45:14
for ten b are an homer .... Eze 45:14

BATH-SHEBA (bath'-she-bah) See BATH-SHUA. A wife of David.
And one said, Is not this B........ 2Sa 11:3
And David comforted B his wife 2Sa 12:24
unto B the mother of Solomon 1Kin 1:11
B went in unto the king into the .. 1Kin 1:15
B bowed, and did obeisance unto .. 1Kin 1:16
David answered and said, Call me B .. 1Kin 1:28
Then B bowed with her face to the .. 1Kin 1:31
came to B the mother of Solomon .. 1Kin 2:13
And B said, Well 1Kin 2:18
B therefore went unto king....... 1Kin 2:19
him, after he had gone in to B...... Ps 51:t

BATH-SHUA (bath'-shu-ah) See BATH-SHEBA. A form of Bath-sheba.
of B the daughter of Ammiel 1Chr 3:5

BATS
worship, to the moles and to the b .. Is 2:20

BATTERED
that were with Joab the wall 2Sa 20:15

BATTERING
set b rams against it round about .. Eze 4:2
to appoint b rams against the ...... Eze 21:22

BATTLE
they joined b with them in the .... Gen 14:8
all his people, to the b at Edrei .. Num 21:33
hundreds, which came from the b .. Num 31:14
men of war which went to the b.... Num 31:21
war upon them, who went out to b .. Num 31:27
men of war which went out to b.... Num 31:28
for war, before the LORD to b ..... Num 32:27
over Jordan, every man armed to b .. Num 32:29
neither contend with them in b..... Deut 2:9
it, and contend with him in b ..... Deut 2:24
and all his people, to b at Edrei .. Deut 3:1
out to b against thine enemies .... Deut 20:1
when ye are come nigh unto the b.. Deut 20:3
day unto b against your enemies .. Deut 20:3
his house, lest he die in the b.... Deut 20:5
his house, lest he die in the b.... Deut 20:6

his house, lest he die in the b .... Deut 20:7
came out against us unto b......... Deut 29:7
over before the LORD unto b........ Josh 4:13
city went out against Israel to b.. Josh 8:14
all other they took in b........... Josh 11:19
should come against Israel in b.... Judg 11:20
intend to go up against them in b .. Judg 20:23
from b before the sun was up...... Judg 8:13
to go out to b against the .... Judg 20:14
to the b against the children of .. Judg 20:18
went out to b against Benjamin .... Judg 20:20
set their b again in array in the .. Judg 20:22
Shall I go up again to b against .. Judg 20:23
out to b against the children of .. Judg 20:28
of all Israel, and the b was sore.. Judg 20:34
men of Israel retired in the b .... Judg 20:39
down before us, as in the first b .. Judg 20:39
but the b overtook them .... Judg 20:42
out against the Philistines to b .. 1Sa 4:1
and when they joined b, Israel was .. 1Sa 4:2
drew near to b against Israel...... 1Sa 7:10
it came to pass in the day of b 1Sa 13:22
themselves, and they came to the b .. 1Sa 14:20
followed hard after them in the b .. 1Sa 14:22
the b passed over unto Beth-aven .. 1Sa 14:23
together their armies to b........ 1Sa 17:1
set the b in array against the 1Sa 17:2
come out to set your b in array...... 1Sa 17:8
went and followed Saul to the b .. 1Sa 17:13
the b were Eliab the first born 1Sa 17:13
the fight, and shouted for the b .. 1Sa 17:20
had put the b in array, army 1Sa 17:21
down that thou mightest see the b .. 1Sa 17:28
for the b is the LORD's, and he..... 1Sa 17:47
or he shall descend into b......... 1Sa 26:10
Thou shalt go out with me to b.... 1Sa 28:1
let him not go down with us to b .. 1Sa 29:4
lest in the b he be an adversary.. 1Sa 29:4
shall not go up with us to the b .. 1Sa 29:9
part is that goeth down to the b .. 1Sa 30:24
the b went sore against Saul, and .. 1Sa 31:3
the people are fled from the b..... 2Sa 1:4
fallen in the midst of the b....... 2Sa 1:25
there was a very sore b that day .. 2Sa 2:17
brother Asahel at Gibeon in the b .. 2Sa 3:30
put the b in array at the 2Sa 10:8
of the b was against him before .. 2Sa 10:9
unto the b against the Syrians 2Sa 10:13
the time when kings go forth to b .. 2Sa 11:1
in the forefront of the hottest b .. 2Sa 11:15
make Iy b more strong against 2Sa 11:25
that thou go to b in thine own 2Sa 11:25
the b was in the wood of Ephraim .. 2Sa 18:6
For the b was there scattered 2Sa 18:8
steal away when they flee in b..... 2Sa 19:3
who wandered over us, is dead in b .. 2Sa 19:10
shalt go no more out with us to b .. 2Sa 21:17
that there was again a b with the .. 2Sa 21:18
there was again a b in Gob with .. 2Sa 21:19
And there was yet a b in Gath...... 2Sa 21:20
had girded me with strength to b .. 2Sa 22:40
were there gathered together to b .. 2Sa 23:9
go out to b against their enemy .. 1Kin 8:44
he said, Who shall order the b 1Kin 20:14
the seventh day the b was joined .. 1Kin 20:29
went out into the midst of the b .. 1Kin 20:39
go with me to b to Ramoth-gilead .. 1Kin 22:4
I go against Ramoth-gilead to b .. 1Kin 22:6
we go against Ramoth-gilead to b .. 1Kin 22:15
myself, and enter into the b 1Kin 22:30
himself, and went into the b 1Kin 22:30
And the b increased that day 1Kin 22:35
thou go with me against Moab to b .. 2Kin 3:7
that the b was too sore for him ... 2Kin 3:26
for they cried to God in the b 1Chr 5:20
fit to go out for war and b 1Chr 7:40
to b was twenty and six thousand .. 1Chr 7:40
the b went sore against Saul, and .. 1Chr 10:3
were gathered together to b 1Chr 11:13
and men of war fit for the b...... 1Chr 12:8
the Philistines against Saul to b .. 1Chr 12:19
Zebulun, such as went forth to b .. 1Chr 12:33
of Asher, such as went forth to b .. 1Chr 12:36
of instruments of war for the b .. 1Chr 12:37
that then thou shalt go out to b .. 1Chr 14:15
from their cities, and came to b .. 1Chr 19:7
put the b in array before the...... 1Chr 19:9
the b was set against him before .. 1Chr 19:10
before the Syrians unto b......... 1Chr 19:14
set the b in array against them .. 1Chr 19:17
So when David had put the b in .. 1Chr 19:17
the time that kings go out to b .. 1Chr 20:1
Abijah set the b in array with .. 2Chr 13:3
Jeroboam also set the b in array .. 2Chr 13:3
the b was before and behind 2Chr 13:14
they set the b in array in the .. 2Chr 14:10
Shall we go to Ramoth-gilead to b .. 2Chr 18:5
shall we go to Ramoth-gilead to b .. 2Chr 18:14
myself, and will go to the b 2Chr 18:29
and they went to the b.......... 2Chr 18:29
And the b increased that day 2Chr 18:34
came against Jehoshaphat to b .. 2Chr 20:1
for the b is not yours, but God's .. 2Chr 20:15
shall not need to fight in this b .. 2Chr 20:17
go, do it, be strong for the b 2Chr 25:8
they should not go with him to b .. 2Chr 25:13
him, as a king ready to the b .. Job 15:24
of trouble, against the day of b .. Job 38:23
and he smelleth the b afar off ...... Job 39:25
hand upon him, remember the b .. Job 41:8

me with strength unto the b....... Ps 18:39
and mighty, the LORD mighty in b .. Ps 24:8
from the b that was against me .. Ps 55:18
shield, and the sword, and the b .. Ps 76:3
bows, turned back in the day of b .. Ps 78:9
not made him to stand in the b .. Ps 89:43
covered my head in the day of b .. Ps 140:7
is prepared against the day of b .. Prov 21:31
nor the b to the strong, neither .. Eccl 9:11
For every b of the warrior is ..... Is 9:5
hosts mustereth the host of the b .. Is 13:4
with the sword, nor dead in b .. Is 22:2
briers and thorns against me in b .. Is 27:4
them that turn the b to the gate .. Is 28:6
his anger, and the strength of b .. Is 42:25
as the horse rusheth into the b .. Jer 8:6
men be slain by the sword in b .. Jer 18:21
and shield, and draw near to b .. Jer 46:3
against her, and rise up to the b .. Jer 49:14
A sound of b is in the land, and .. Jer 50:22
put in array, like a man to the b .. Jer 50:42
Thou art my b ax and weapons of .. Jer 51:20
but none goeth to the b .... Eze 7:14
in the b in the day of the LORD .. Eze 13:5
neither in anger, nor in b ...... Dan 11:20
stirred up to b with a very great .. Dan 11:25
by bow, nor by sword, nor by b .. Hos 1:7
the b out of the earth, and will .. Hos 2:18
the b in Gibeah against the ...... Hos 10:9
Beth-arbel in the day of b....... Hos 10:14
as a strong people set in array .. Joel 2:5
with shouting in the day of b .. Amos 1:14
let us rise up against her in b .. Obad 1
the b bow shall be cut off ...... Zec 9:10
them as his goodly horse in the b .. Zec 10:3
the nail, out of him the b bow ..... Zec 10:4
the mire of the streets in the b .. Zec 10:5
nations against Jerusalem to b .. Zec 14:2
as when he fought in the day of b .. Zec 14:3
shall prepare himself to the b .. 1Cor 14:8
like unto horses prepared unto b .. Rev 9:7
of many horses running to b...... Rev 9:9
to gather them to the b of that .. Rev 16:14
to gather them together to b ..... Rev 20:8

BATTLEMENT
thou shalt make a b for thy roof .. Deut 22:8

BATTLEMENTS
take away her b................. Jer 5:10

BATTLES
go out before us, and fight our b .. 1Sa 8:20
for me, and fight the LORD's b 1Sa 18:17
lord fighteth the b of the LORD .. 1Sa 25:28
Out of the spoils won in b did .. 1Chr 26:27
God to help us, and to fight our b .. 2Chr 32:8
in b of shaking will he fight ...... Is 30:32

BAVAI (bav'-a-i) A descendant of Henadad.
B the son of Henadad, the ruler...... Neh 3:18

BAVAI See BAVAI.

BAY
from the b that looketh southward .. Josh 15:2
the b of the sea at the uttermost.. Josh 15:5
b of the salt sea at the south ..... Josh 18:19
himself like a green b tree ...... Ps 37:35
chariot grisled and b horses ...... Zec 6:3
the fourth b horses: and the ...... Zec 6:7

BAZLITH (baz'-lith) See BAZLUTH. A family who returned from exile.
The children of B, the children .. Neh 7:54

BAZLUTH (baz'-luth) See BAZLITH. A form of Bazlith.
The children of B, the children .. Ezr 2:52

BDELLIUM
there is b and the onyx stone...... Gen 2:12
colour thereof as the colour of b...... Num 11:7

BE See PREFACE.

BEACON
till ye be left as a b upon the ...... Is 30:17

BEALIAH (be-a-li'-ah) A warrior in David's army.
Eluzai, and Jerimoth, and B........ 1Chr 12:5

BEALOTH (be'-a-loth) See ALOTH. A city in Judah.
Ziph, and Telem, and B,........... Josh 15:24

BEAM
went away with the pin of the b .. Judg 16:14
his spear was like a weaver's b .. 1Sa 17:7
whose spear was like a weaver's b .. 2Sa 21:19
the thick b were before them 1Kin 7:6
and take thence every man a b 2Kin 6:2
But as one was felling a b 2Kin 6:5
was a spear like a weaver's b 1Chr 11:23
spear staff was like a weaver's b .. 1Chr 20:5
the b out of the timber shall ..... Hab 2:11
but considerest not the b that is .. Mt 7:3
behold, a b is in thine own eye ..... Mt 7:4
first cast out the b out of thine .. Mt 7:5
but perceivest not the b that is .. Lk 6:41
the b that is in thine own eye ..... Lk 6:42
cast out first the b out of thine .. Lk 6:42

BEAMS
that the b should not be fastened .. 1Kin 6:6
and covered the house with b 1Kin 6:9

hewed stone, and a row of cedar b 1Kin 6:36
with cedar b upon the pillars 1Kin 7:2
with cedar above upon the b............ 1Kin 7:3
hewed stones, and a row of cedar b b.. 1Kin 7:12
He overlaid also the house, the b....... 2Chr 3:7
b for the gates of the palace........... Neh 2:8
who also laid the b thereof .... Neh 3:3
they laid the b thereof, and set....... Neh 3:6
Who layeth the b of his chambers...... Ps 104:3
The b of our house are cedar, and..... Song 1:17

BEANS
and flour, and parched corn, and b..... 2Sa 17:28
unto the wheat, and barley, and b..... Eze 4:9

BEAR
is greater than I can b .... Gen 4:13
the land was not able to b them....... Gen 13:6
art with child, and shalt b a son ..... Gen 16:11
that is ninety years old, b............ Gen 17:17
wife shall b thee a son indeed........ Gen 17:19
which Sarah shall b unto thee at ..... Gen 17:21
Shall I of a surety b a child .... Gen 18:13
these eight Milcah did b to Nahor..... Gen 22:23
she shall b upon my knees, that I .... Gen 30:3
them because of their cattle.......... Gen 36:7
then let me b the blame for ever ..... Gen 43:9
then I shall b the blame to my....... Gen 44:32
and bowed his shoulder to b.......... Gen 49:15
they shall b the burden with thee.... Ex 18:22
Thou shalt not b false witness....... Ex 20:16
of the staves to b the table .... Ex 25:27
two sides of the altar, to b it....... Ex 27:7
Aaron shall b their names before..... Ex 28:12
Aaron shall b the names of the ...... Ex 28:29
Aaron shall b the judgment of the... Ex 28:30
that Aaron may b the iniquity of .... Ex 28:38
that they b not iniquity, and die ... Ex 28:43
for the staves to b it withal........ Ex 30:4
sides of the ark, to b the ark....... Ex 37:5
for the staves to b the table........ Ex 37:14
them with gold, to b the table....... Ex 37:15
for the staves to b it withal........ Ex 37:27
of the altar, to b it withal......... Ex 38:7
it, then he shall b his iniquity .... Lev 5:1
guilty, and shall b his iniquity..... Lev 5:17
eateth of it shall b his iniquity ... Lev 7:18
it you to b the iniquity of the .... Lev 10:17
But if she b a maid child, then..... Lev 12:5
the goat shall b upon him all ...... Lev 16:22
then he shall b his iniquity .... Lev 17:16
eateth it shall b his iniquity...... Lev 19:8
nor b any grudge against the .... Lev 19:18
he shall b his iniquity .... Lev 20:17
they shall b their iniquity .... Lev 20:19
they shall b their sin.............. Lev 20:20
they shall b their sin for it, and die... Lev 22:9
Or suffer them to b the iniquity ... Lev 22:16
curseth his God shall b his sin .... Lev 24:15
they shall b the tabernacle, and ... Num 1:50
sons of Kohath shall come to b it... Num 4:15
they shall b the curtains of the.... Num 4:25
this woman shall b her iniquity..... Num 5:31
should b upon their shoulders ...... Num 7:9
season, that man shall b his sin.... Num 9:13
I am not able to b all this .... Num 11:14
they shall b the burden of the ..... Num 11:17
that thou b it not thyself alone.... Num 11:17
How long shall I b with this evil .. Num 14:27
b your whoredoms, until your .... Num 14:33
shall ye b your iniquities, even.... Num 14:34
b the iniquity of the sanctuary..... Num 18:1
thy sons with thee shall b the..... Num 18:1
the congregation, lest they b sin... Num 18:22
they shall b their iniquity .... Num 18:23
ye shall b no sin by reason of it .. Num 18:32
then he shall b their iniquity...... Num 30:15
am not able to b you myself alone... Deut 1:9
I myself alone b your cumbrance .... Deut 1:12
thee, as a man doth b his son...... Deut 1:31
Neither shalt thou b false.......... Deut 5:20
to b the ark of the covenant of ... Deut 10:8
her children which she shall b..... Deut 28:57
that b the ark of the covenant .... Josh 3:3
that b the ark of the LORD .... Josh 3:13
that b the ark of the testimony.... Josh 4:16
seven priests shall b before the .. Josh 6:4
let seven priests b seven .... Josh 6:6
thou shalt conceive, and b a son .. Judg 13:3
thou shalt conceive, and b a son .. Judg 13:5
thou shalt conceive, and b a son .. Judg 13:7
to night, and should also b sons... Ruth 1:12
and there came a lion, and a b.... 1Sa 17:34
slew both the lion and the b...... 1Sa 17:36
lion, and out of the paw of the b... 1Sa 17:37
as a b robbed of her whelps in.... 2Sa 17:8
b the king tidings this day....... 2Sa 18:19
Thou shalt not b tidings this day .. 2Sa 18:20
but thou shalt b tidings another... 2Sa 18:20
this day thou shalt b no tidings... 2Sa 18:20
it was not my son, which I did b... 1Kin 3:21
to b witness against him, saying... 1Kin 21:10
which thou puttest on me will I b .. 2Kin 18:14
root downward, and b fruit upward... 2Kin 19:30
and ten thousand men to b burdens .. 2Chr 2:2
should b rule in his own house..... Est 1:22
I b up the pillars of it .... Ps 75:3
how I do b in my bosom the........ Ps 89:50
They shall b thee up in their ..... Ps 91:12
scornest, thou alone shalt b it.... Prov 9:12

hand of the diligent shall b rule... Prov 12:24
Let a b robbed of her whelps meet ... Prov 17:12
but a wounded spirit who can b...... Prov 18:14
As a roaring lion, and a ranging b... Prov 28:15
and for four which it cannot b...... Prov 30:21
whereof every one b twins............ Song 4:2
I am weary to b them .... Is 1:14
b a son, and shall call his name .... Is 7:14
And the cow and the b shall feed.... Is 11:7
root downward, and b fruit upward... Is 37:31
I have made, and I will b.......... Is 46:4
They b him upon the shoulder,..... Is 46:7
that b the vessels of the LORD.... Is 52:11
for he shall b their iniquities.... Is 53:11
O barren, thou that didst not b.... Is 54:1
the priests b rule by their means... Jer 5:31
this is a grief, and I must b it.... Jer 10:19
b no burden on the sabbath day,.... Jer 17:21
not to b a burden, even entering... Jer 17:27
to husbands, that they may b sons ... Jer 29:6
because I did b the reproach of .... Jer 31:19
that the LORD could no longer b.... Jer 44:22
was unto me as a b bying in wait... Lam 3:10
that he b the yoke in his youth.... Lam 3:27
it thou shalt b their iniquity.... Eze 4:4
so shalt thou b the iniquity of... Eze 4:5
thou shalt b the iniquity of the... Eze 4:6
thou b it upon thy shoulders ...... Eze 12:6
shalt b upon his shoulder in the ... Eze 12:7
they shall b the punishment of.... Eze 14:10
b thine own shame for thy sins .... Eze 16:52
b thy shame, in that thou hast.... Eze 16:52
thou mayest b thine own shame.... Eze 16:54
and that it might b fruit .... Eze 17:8
b fruit, and be a goodly cedar..... Eze 17:23
doth not the son b the iniquity ... Eze 18:19
The son shall not b the iniquity... Eze 18:20
father b the iniquity of the son ... Eze 18:20
therefore b thou also thy.......... Eze 23:35
ye shall b the sins of your idols... Eze 23:49
b their shame with them that go... Eze 32:30
neither b the shame of the......... Eze 34:29
you, they shall b their shame..... Eze 36:7
neither shalt thou b the reproach... Eze 36:15
they shall even b their iniquity ... Eze 44:10
they shall b their iniquity .... Eze 44:12
but they shall b their shame...... Eze 44:13
they shall b them not out into the... Eze 46:20
which shall b rule over all the.... Dan 2:39
beast, a second, like to a b...... Dan 7:5
dried up, they shall b no fruit ... Hos 9:16
I will meet them as a b that is... Hos 13:8
flee from a lion, and a b met him... Amos 5:19
is not able to b all his words..... Amos 7:10
therefore ye shall b the reproach... Mic 6:16
I will b the indignation of the... Mic 7:9
all they that b silver are cut.... Zeph 1:11
If one b holy flesh in the skirt... Hag 2:12
me, Whither do these b the ephah... Zec 5:10
he shall b the glory, and shall ... Zec 6:13
whose shoes I am not worthy to b... Mt 3:11
their hands they shall b thee up... Mt 4:6
Thou shalt not b false witness... Mt 19:18
him they compelled to b his cross... Mt 27:32
Do not b false witness, Defraud... Mk 10:19
and Rufus, to b his cross.......... Mk 15:21
wife Elisabeth shall b thee a son... Lk 1:13
their hands they shall b thee up... Lk 4:11
Truly ye b witness, that ye allow... Lk 11:48
And if it b fruit, well............ Lk 13:9
And whosoever doth not b his cross.. Lk 14:27
though he b long with them .... Lk 18:7
Do not b false witness, Honour..... Lk 18:20
that he might b it after Jesus..... Lk 23:26
to b witness of the Light, that... Jn 1:8
but was sent to b witness of that... Jn 1:8
b unto the governor of the feast... Jn 2:8
Ye yourselves b me witness......... Jn 3:28
If I b witness of myself, my ...... Jn 5:31
b witness of me, that the Father... Jn 5:36
Though I b record of myself, yet... Jn 8:14
I am one that b witness of myself... Jn 8:18
name, they b witness of me .... Jn 10:25
branch cannot b fruit of itself ... Jn 15:4
glorified, that ye b much fruit ... Jn 15:8
And ye also shall b witness....... Jn 15:27
you, but ye cannot b them now..... Jn 16:12
evil, b witness of the evil .... Jn 18:23
that I should b witness unto the... Jn 18:37
to b my name before the Gentiles,... Acts 9:15
our fathers nor we were able to b... Acts 15:10
would that I should b with you .... Acts 18:14
the high priest doth b me witness... Acts 22:5
so must thou b witness also at.... Acts 23:11
could not b up into the wind, we... Acts 27:15
For I b them record that they .... Rom 10:2
Thou shalt not b false witness.... Rom 13:9
to b the infirmities of the weak... Rom 15:1
hitherto ye were not able to b it ... 1Cor 3:2
that ye may be able to b it 1Cor 10:13
we shall also b the image of the... 1Cor 15:49
I b record, yea, and beyond their... 2Cor 8:3
Would to God ye could b with me a... 2Cor 11:1
and indeed b with me.............. 2Cor 11:1
ye might well b with him.......... 2Cor 11:4
if a man b you in bondage, if..... 2Cor 11:20
you shall b his judgment,......... Gal 5:10
B ye one another's burdens, and so.. Gal 6:2
every man shall b his own burden ... Gal 6:5
For I b in my body the marks of... Gal 6:17

For I b him record, for that he hath.. Col 4:13
b children, guide the house, give..... 1Ti 5:14
offered to b the sins of many........ Heb 9:28
my brethren, b olive berries......... Jas 3:12
b witness, and shew unto you that ... 1Jn 1:2
are three that b record in heaven.... 1Jn 5:7
are three that b witness in earth... 1Jn 5:8
yea, and we also b record........... 3Jn 12
how thou canst not b them which.... Rev 2:2
his feet were as the feet of a b.... Rev 13:2

BEARD
a plague upon the head or the b .... Lev 13:29
even a leprosy upon the head or b... Lev 13:30
his hair off his head and his b..... Lev 14:9
thou mar the corners of thy b...... Lev 19:27
shave off the corner of their b.... Lev 21:5
against me, I caught him by his b... 1Sa 17:35
his spittle fall down upon his b.... 1Sa 21:13
his feet, nor trimmed his b........ 2Sa 19:24
by the b with the right hand to ... 2Sa 20:9
the hair of my head and of my b.... Ezr 9:3
upon the b, even Aaron's b........ Ps 133:2
and it shall also consume the b.... Is 7:20
be baldness, and every b cut off ... Is 15:2
shall be bald, and every b clipped... Jer 48:37
upon thine head and upon thy b .... Eze 5:1

BEARDS
off the one half of their b 2Sa 10:4
at Jericho until your b be grown.... 2Sa 10:5
at Jericho until your b be grown.... 1Chr 19:5
men, having their b shaven......... Jer 41:5

BEARERS
of them to be b of burdens 2Chr 2:18
they were over the b of burdens 2Chr 34:13
The strength of the b of burdens... Neh 4:10

BEAREST
now, thou art barren, and b not ... Judg 13:3
that thou b unto thy people....... Ps 106:4
him, Thou b record of thyself..... Jn 8:13
thou b not the root, but the root... Rom 11:18
Rejoice, thou barren that b not ... Gal 4:27

BEARETH
whosoever b ought of the carcase ... Lev 11:25
he that b the carcase of them..... Lev 11:28
he also that b the carcase of it ... Lev 11:40
he that b any of those things..... Lev 15:10
father b the sucking child........ Num 11:12
b shall succeed in the name of.... Deut 25:6
be among you a root that b gall ... Deut 29:18
that it is not sown, nor b........ Deut 29:23
taketh them, b them on her wings... Deut 32:11
up in me b witness to my face..... Job 16:8
entreateth the barren that b not ... Job 24:21
A man that b false witness........ Prov 25:18
but when the wicked b rule........ Prov 29:2
whereof every one b twins......... Song 6:6
spring, for the tree b fruit ...... Joel 2:22
which also b fruit, and bringeth... Mt 13:23
is another that b witness of me ... Jn 5:32
that sent me b witness of me ..... Jn 8:18
Every branch in me that b not .... Jn 15:2
and every branch that b fruit..... Jn 15:2
The Spirit itself b witness with ... Rom 8:16
for he b not the sword in vain.... Rom 13:4
B all things, believeth all........ 1Cor 13:7
But that which b thorns and briers... Heb 6:8
it is the Spirit that b witness... 1Jn 5:6

BEARING
have given you every herb b seed.... Gen 1:29
Lord hath restrained me from b..... Gen 16:2
his name Judah; and left b......... Gen 29:35
When Leah saw that she had left b... Gen 30:9
with their camels b spicery....... Gen 37:25
set forward, b the tabernacle..... Num 10:17
set forward, b the sanctuary...... Num 10:21
and the priests the Levites b it... Josh 3:14
the priests b the ark of the..... Josh 3:14
that the seven priests b the..... Josh 6:8
seven priests b seven trumpets of... Josh 6:13
one b a shield went before him ... 1Sa 17:7
b the ark of the covenant of God... 2Sa 15:24
b precious seed, shall doubtless... Ps 126:6
you a man b a pitcher of water.... Mk 14:13
meet you, b a pitcher of water.... Lk 22:10
he b his cross went forth into a... Jn 19:17
their conscience also b witness... Rom 2:15
my conscience also b me witness... Rom 9:1
Always b about in the body the ... 2Cor 4:10
God also b them witness, both.... Heb 2:4
without the camp, b his reproach... Heb 13:13

BEARS
forth two she b out of the wood ... 2Kin 2:24
We roar all like b, and mourn sore... Is 59:11

BEAST
b of the earth after his kind...... Gen 1:25
God made the b of the earth after... Gen 1:25
to every b of the earth, and to.... Gen 1:30
God formed every b of the field.... Gen 2:19
air, and to every b of the field... Gen 2:20
was more subtil than any b of the ... Gen 3:1
above every b of the field........ Gen 3:14
both man, and b, and the creeping... Gen 6:7
Of every clean b thou shalt take ... Gen 7:2
every b after his kind, and all... Gen 7:14
of fowl, and of cattle, and of b,... Gen 7:21
Every b, every creeping thing, and.. Gen 8:19

and took of every clean b, and of....... Gen 8:20
be upon every b of the earth......... Gen 9:2
hand of every b will I require it......... Gen 9:5
of every b of the earth with you...... Gen 9:10
the ark, to every b of the earth........ Gen 9:10
every b of theirs be ours.......... Gen 34:23
Some evil b hath devoured them...... Gen 37:20
an evil b hath devoured him.......... Gen 37:33
and it became lice in man, and in b ..... Ex 8:17
were lice upon man, and upon b ...... Ex 8:18
with blains upon man, and upon b ..... Ex 9:9
with blains upon man, and upon b ..... Ex 9:10
b which shall be found in the........ Ex 9:19
of Egypt, upon man, and upon b ...... Ex 9:22
was in the field, both man and b ..... Ex 9:25
move his tongue, against man or b ..... Ex 11:7
the land of Egypt, both man and b ..... Ex 12:12
of Israel, both of man and of b .... Ex 13:2
cometh of a b which thou hast....... Ex 13:12
of man, and the firstborn of b .... Ex 13:15
whether it be b or man, it shall....... Ex 19:13
and the dead b shall be his.......... Ex 21:34
be eaten, and shall put in his b .... Ex 22:5
or an ox, or a sheep, or any b .... Ex 22:10
Whosoever lieth with a b shall....... Ex 22:19
the b of the field multiply........... Ex 23:29
it be a carcase of an unclean b .... Lev 5:2
of man, or any unclean b, or any ...... Lev 7:21
the fat of the b that dieth of........ Lev 7:24
whosoever eateth the fat of the b ..... Lev 7:25
whether it be of fowl or of b .... Lev 7:26
The carcases of every b which....... Lev 11:26
And if any b, of which ye may eat, ... Lev 11:39
between the b that may be eaten...... Lev 11:47
the b that may not be eaten......... Lev 11:47
catcheth any b or fowl that may...... Lev 17:13
any b to defile thyself therewith ...... Lev 18:23
before a b to lie down thereto....... Lev 18:23
And if a man lie with a b, he........ Lev 20:15
and ye shall slay the b............ Lev 20:15
And if a woman approach unto any b .. Lev 20:16
shall kill the woman, and the b ...... Lev 20:16
make your souls abominable by b ..... Lev 20:25
he that killeth a b shall make it ...... Lev 24:18
shall make it good; b for b .... Lev 24:18
shall make it good; b for b .... Lev 24:18
And he that killeth a b, he shall...... Lev 24:21
for the b that are in the land........ Lev 25:7
And if it be a b, whereof men........ Lev 27:9
shall at all change b for b .... Lev 27:10
And if it be any unclean b .... Lev 27:11
present the b before the priest....... Lev 27:11
And if it be of an unclean b .... Lev 27:27
that he hath, both of man and b ...... Num 3:13
in Israel, both man and b .... Num 3:13
of Israel are mine, both man and b .... Num 8:17
was taken, both of man and of b ...... Num 31:26
of fifty, both of man and of b .... Num 31:47
The likeness of any b that is on...... Deut 4:17
every b that partaketh the hoof, and .. Deut 14:6
that lieth with any manner of b .... Deut 27:21
the men of every city, as the b .... Judg 20:48
by a wild b that was in Lebanon...... 2Kin 14:9
by a wild b that was in Lebanon...... 2Chr 25:18
neither was there any b with me...... Neh 2:12
save the b that I rode upon......... Neh 2:12
the b that was under me to pass...... Neh 2:14
or that the wild b may break them .... Job 39:15
O LORD, thou preservest man and b .. Ps 36:6
For every b of the forest is mine ..... Ps 50:10
I was as a b before thee............ Ps 73:22
the wild b of the field doth......... Ps 80:13
drink to every b of the field......... Ps 104:11
of Egypt, both of man and b .... Ps 135:8
He giveth to the b his food.......... Ps 147:9
man regardeth the life of his b .... Prov 12:10
man hath no preeminence above a b ... Eccl 3:19
the spirit of the b that goeth....... Eccl 3:21
nor any ravenous b shall go up...... Is 35:9
The b of the field shall honour...... Is 43:20
they are a burden to the weary b ..... Is 46:1
As a b goeth down into the valley..... Is 63:14
this place, upon man, and upon b ..... Jer 7:20
of the heavens and the b are fled..... Jer 9:10
of this city, both man and b .... Jer 21:6
the b that are upon the ground,...... Jer 27:5
of man, and with the seed of b ...... Jer 31:27
It is desolate without man or b ...... Jer 32:43
desolate without man and without b ... Jer 33:10
without inhabitant, and without b .... Jer 33:10
desolate without man and without b ... Jer 33:12
to cease from thence man and b ..... Jer 36:29
they shall depart, both man and b .... Jer 50:3
remain in it, neither man nor b ...... Jer 51:62
and will cut off man and b from it.... Eze 14:13
that I cut off man and b from it...... Eze 14:17
to cut off from it man and b .... Eze 14:19
and the famine, and the noisome b ... Eze 14:21
to cut off from it man and b .... Eze 14:21
and will cut off man and b from it.... Eze 25:13
and cut off man and b out of thee ... Eze 29:8
nor foot of b shall pass through..... Eze 29:11
meat to every b of the field......... Eze 34:8
neither shall the b of the land....... Eze 34:28
I will multiply upon you man and b ... Eze 36:11
to every b of the field, Assemble .... Eze 39:17
or torn, whether it be fowl or b ...... Eze 44:31
And behold another b, a second,..... Dan 7:5
the b had also four heads.......... Dan 7:6
visions, and behold a fourth b .... Dan 7:7

beheld even till the b was slain........ Dan 7:11
know the truth of the fourth b .... Dan 7:19
The fourth b shall be the fourth...... Dan 7:23
the wild b shall tear them........... Hos 13:8
saying, Let neither man nor b .... Jonah 3:7
b be covered with sackcloth, and ..... Jonah 3:8
bind the chariot to the swift b .... Mic 1:13
I will consume man and b .... Zeph 1:3
hire for man, nor any hire for b ...... Zec 8:10
and wine, and set him on his own b ... Lk 10:34
the venomous b hang on his hand ..... Acts 28:4
he shook off the b into the fire...... Acts 28:5
if so much as a b touch the......... Heb 12:20
the first b was like a lion, and....... Rev 4:7
the second b like a calf........... Rev 4:7
the third b had a face as a man,..... Rev 4:7
the fourth b was like a flying....... Rev 4:7
seal, I heard the second b say....... Rev 6:3
seal, I heard the third b say......... Rev 6:5
the voice of the fourth b say......... Rev 6:7
the b that ascendeth out of the ...... Rev 11:7
saw a b rise up out of the sea,...... Rev 13:1
the b which I saw was like unto a .... Rev 13:2
the world wondered after the b ...... Rev 13:3
which gave power unto the b .... Rev 13:4
and they worshipped the b .... Rev 13:4
saying, Who is like unto the b .... Rev 13:4
I beheld another b coming up out .... Rev 13:11
power of the first b before him....... Rev 13:12
therein to worship the first b .... Rev 13:12
power to do in the sight of the b ..... Rev 13:14
should make an image to the b ...... Rev 13:14
give life unto the image of the b ..... Rev 13:15
image of the b should both speak .... Rev 13:15
image of the b should be killed ...... Rev 13:15
the mark, or the name of the b ...... Rev 13:17
count the number of the b .... Rev 13:18
voice, If any man worship the b ..... Rev 14:9
day nor night, who worship the b .... Rev 14:11
had gotten the victory over the b .... Rev 15:2
men which had the mark of the b .... Rev 16:2
his vial upon the seat of the b ...... Rev 16:10
and out of the mouth of the b .... Rev 16:13
sit upon a scarlet coloured b .... Rev 17:3
of the b that carrieth her, which..... Rev 17:7
The b that thou sawest was, and is... Rev 17:8
when they behold the b that was .... Rev 17:8
the b that was, and is not, even ..... Rev 17:11
as kings one hour with the b .... Rev 17:12
power and strength unto the b ...... Rev 17:13
which thou sawest upon the b ...... Rev 17:16
and give their kingdom unto the b ... Rev 17:17
And I saw the b, and the kings of ... Rev 19:19
the b was taken, and with him the ... Rev 19:20
had received the mark of the b ..... Rev 19:20
and which had not worshipped the b .. Rev 20:4
of fire and brimstone, where the b ... Rev 20:10

BEAST'S

let a b heart be given unto him .... Dan 4:16

BEASTS

of b that are not clean by two,....... Gen 7:2
Of clean b, and of b that are........ Gen 7:8
That which was torn of b .... Gen 31:39
and his cattle, and all his b .... Gen 36:6
lade your b, and go, get you unto .... Gen 45:17
and all the firstborn of b .... Ex 11:5
that is torn of b in the field........ Ex 22:31
what they leave the b of the .... Ex 23:11
fat of that which is torn with b ...... Lev 7:24
These are the b which ye shall...... Lev 11:2
all the b that are on the earth....... Lev 11:2
and cheweth the cud, among the b ... Lev 11:3
manner of b that go on all four ..... Lev 11:27
This is the law of the b, and of .... Lev 11:46
or that which was torn with b ...... Lev 17:15
put difference between clean b ..... Lev 20:25
of itself, or is torn with b .... Lev 22:8
I will rid evil b out of the land,..... Lev 26:6
Lord, whether it be of men or b .... Num 18:15
of unclean b shalt thou redeem..... Num 18:15
the congregation and their b drink ... Num 20:8
drank, and their b also........... Num 20:11
all the prey, both of men and of b ... Num 31:11
of the flocks, of all manner of b .... Num 31:30
their goods, and for all their b ...... Num 35:3
lest the b of the field increase...... Deut 7:22
These are the b which ye shall..... Deut 14:4
and cheweth the cud among the b ... Deut 14:6
unto the b of the earth, and no..... Deut 28:26
send the teeth of b upon them..... Deut 32:24
the air, and to the b of the field 1Sa 17:44
to the wild b of the earth......... 1Sa 17:46
nor the b of the field by night...... 2Sa 21:10
he spake also of b, and of fowl,.... 1Kin 4:33
alive, that we lose not all the b 1Kin 18:5
ye, and your cattle, and your b 2Kin 3:17
and stalls for all manner of b 2Chr 32:28
gold, and with goods, and with b.... Ezr 1:4
with gold, with goods, and with b.... Ezr 1:6
be afraid of the b of the earth...... Job 5:22
the b of the field shall be at...... Job 5:23
But ask now the b, and they shall.... Job 12:7
Wherefore are we counted as b ..... Job 18:3
us more than the b of the earth..... Job 35:11
Then the b go into dens, and..... Job 37:8
where all the b of the field play..... Job 40:20
oxen, yea, and the b of the.......... Ps 8:7

he is like the b that perish........... Ps 49:12
not, is like the b that perish......... Ps 49:20
the wild b of the field are mine...... Ps 50:11
saints unto the b of the earth....... Ps 79:2
wherein all the b of the forest...... Ps 104:20
both small and great b .... Ps 104:25
B, and all cattle............... Ps 148:10
She hath killed her b .... Prov 9:2
A lion is strongest among b .... Prov 30:30
see that they themselves are b ..... Eccl 3:18
the sons of men befalleth b .... Eccl 3:19
of rams, and the fat of fed b .... Is 1:11
But wild b of the desert shall....... Is 13:21
the wild b of the islands shall...... Is 13:22
and to the b of the earth.......... Is 18:6
all the b of the earth shall........ Is 18:6
The burden of the b of the south ... Is 30:6
The wild b of the desert shall...... Is 34:14
with the wild b of the island....... Is 34:14
nor the b thereof sufficient for..... Is 40:16
their idols were upon the b .... Is 46:1
All ye b of the field, come to...... Is 56:9
yea, all ye b in the forest........ Is 56:9
and upon mules, and upon swift b ... Is 66:20
heaven, and for the b of the earth ... Jer 7:33
the b are consumed, and the birds .. Jer 12:4
assemble all the b of the field...... Jer 12:9
the b of the earth, to devour and ... Jer 15:3
heaven, and for the b of the earth .. Jer 16:4
heaven, and for the b of the earth .. Jer 19:7
the b of the field have I given...... Jer 27:6
given him the b of the field also.... Jer 28:14
heaven, and to the b of the earth ... Jer 34:20
Therefore the wild b of the........ Jer 50:39
wild b of the islands shall dwell.... Jer 50:39
I send upon you famine and evil b .. Eze 5:17
creeping things, and abominable b .. Eze 8:10
If I cause noisome b to pass...... Eze 14:15
may pass through because of the b .. Eze 14:15
for meat to the b of the field...... Eze 29:5
b of the field bring forth their..... Eze 31:6
all the b of the field shall be...... Eze 31:13
I will fill the b of the whole....... Eze 32:4
I will destroy also all the b .... Eze 32:13
nor the hoofs of b trouble them .... Eze 32:13
I give to the b to be devoured ..... Eze 33:27
meat to all the b of the field...... Eze 34:5
will cause the evil b to cease...... Eze 34:25
the b of the field, and all........ Eze 38:20
to the b of the field to be........ Eze 39:4
the b of the field and the fowls..... Dan 2:38
the b of the field had dominion .... Dan 4:12
let the b get away from under it .... Dan 4:14
the b in the grass of the earth...... Dan 4:15
under which the b of the field...... Dan 4:21
be with the b of the field......... Dan 4:23
shall be with the b of the field..... Dan 4:25
shall be with the b of the field..... Dan 4:32
and his heart was made like the b .. Dan 5:21
four great b came up from the sea ... Dan 7:3
all the b that were before it........ Dan 7:7
As concerning the rest of the b .... Dan 7:12
These great b, which are four,...... Dan 7:17
so that no b might stand before .... Dan 8:4
the b of the field shall eat them .... Hos 2:12
for them with the b of the field .... Hos 2:18
with the b of the field, and with .... Hos 4:3
How do the b groan............ Joel 1:18
The b of the field cry also unto.... Joel 1:20
Be not afraid, ye b of the field..... Joel 2:22
the peace offerings of your fat b ... Amos 5:22
a lion among the b of the forest..... Mic 5:8
cover thee, and the spoil of b ...... Hab 2:17
of her, all the b of the nations..... Zeph 2:14
a place for b to lie down in....... Zeph 2:15
of all the b that shall be in....... Zec 14:15
and was with the wild b .... Mk 1:13
have ye offered to me slain b ..... Acts 7:42
of fourfooted b of the earth....... Acts 10:12
b of the earth, and wild b .... Acts 10:12
b of the earth, and wild b .... Acts 11:6
And provide them b, that they may .. Acts 23:24
man, and to birds, and fourfooted b . Rom 1:23
I have fought with b at Ephesus 1Cor 15:32
flesh of men, another flesh of b 1Cor 15:39
Cretians are alway liars, evil b ..... Titus 1:12
For the bodies of those b .... Heb 13:11
For every kind of b, and of birds,... Jas 3:7
But these, as natural brute b 2Pet 2:12
they know naturally, as brute b .... Jude 10
were four b full of eyes before..... Rev 4:6
the four b had each of them six..... Rev 4:8
And when those b give glory...... Rev 4:9
of the throne and of the four b .... Rev 5:6
he had taken the book, the four b .. Rev 5:8
round about the throne and the b .. Rev 5:11
And the four b said, Amen...... Rev 5:14
thunder, one of the four b saying .. Rev 6:1
in the midst of the four b say..... Rev 6:6
death, and with the b of the earth .. Rev 6:8
and about the elders and the four b. Rev 7:11
the throne, and before the four b .. Rev 14:3
one of the four b gave unto the .... Rev 15:7
of heaven, and fowl, and all b ..... Rev 19:18
elders and the four b fell down and . Rev 19:4

BEAT

thou shalt b some of it very........ Ex 30:36
they did b the gold into thin........ Ex 39:3
or b it in a mortar, and baked it..... Num 11:8
b him above their neighbour....... Deut 25:3

BEATEN

he *b* down the tower of Penuel, and ...... Judg 8:17
b down the city, and sowed it with .... Judg 9:45
b at the door, and spake to the .... Judg 19:22
b out that she had gleaned .... Ruth 2:17
Then did I *b* them as small as the 2Sa 22:43
they *b* down the cities, and on 2Kin 3:25
Three times did Joash *b* him 2Kin 13:25
of the LORD, did the king *b* down 2Kin 23:12
Then did I *b* them small as the .... Ps 18:42
I will *b* down his foes before his .... Ps 89:23
Thou shalt *b* him with the rod, and .... Prov 23:14
they shall *b* their swords into .... Is 2:4
ye that ye *b* my people to pieces .... Is 3:15
that the LORD shall *b* off from .... Is 27:12
b them small, and shalt make the .... Is 41:15
B your plowshares into swords, and .... Joel 3:10
the sun *b* upon the head of Jonah, ... Jonah 4:8
they shall *b* their swords into .... Mic 4:3
thou shalt *b* in pieces many .... Mic 4:13
winds blew, and *b* upon that house .... Mt 7:25
winds blew, and *b* upon that house .... Mt 7:27
b one, and killed another, and .... Mt 21:35
the waves *b* into the ship, so .... Mk 4:37
b him, and sent him away empty .... Mk 12:3
the stream *b* vehemently upon that .... Lk 6:48
which the stream did *b* vehemently .... Lk 6:49
shall begin to *b* the menservants .... Lk 12:45
but the husbandmen *b* him, and .... Lk 20:10
they *b* him also, and entreated him .... Lk 20:11
clothes, and commanded to *b* them .... Acts 16:22
b him before the judgment seat .... Acts 18:17
b in every synagogue them that .... Acts 22:19

BEATEN

had set over them, were *b* .... Ex 5:14
and, behold, thy servants are *b* .... Ex 5:16
of *b* work shalt thou make them, ... Ex 25:18
of *b* work shall the candlestick .... Ex 25:31
shall be one *b* work of pure gold .... Ex 25:36
pure oil olive *b* for the light .... Ex 27:20
fourth part of an hin of *b* oil .... Ex 29:40
b out of one piece made he the .... Ex 37:7
of *b* work made he the candlestick .... Ex 37:17
of it was one *b* work of pure gold .... Ex 37:22
even corn *b* out of full ears .... Lev 2:14
part of the *b* corn thereof, and .... Lev 2:16
full of sweet incense *b* small .... Lev 16:12
pure oil olive *b* for the light .... Lev 24:2
of the candlestick was *b* gold, ... Num 8:4
the flowers thereof, was *b* work .... Num 8:4
fourth part of an hin of *b* oil .... Num 28:5
the wicked man be worthy to be *b* .... Deut 25:2
down, and to be *b* before his face, ... Deut 25:2
as if they were *b* before them .... Josh 8:15
and Abner was *b*, and the men of 2Sa 2:17
two hundred targets of *b* gold 1Kin 10:16
three hundred shields of *b* gold 1Kin 10:17
thousand measures of *b* wheat 2Chr 2:10
two hundred targets of *b* gold 2Chr 9:15
six hundred shekels of *b* gold 2Chr 9:15
hundred shields made he of *b* gold 2Chr 9:16
had *b* the graven images into 2Chr 34:7
they have *b* me, and I felt it not .... Prov 23:35
chalkstones that are *b* in sunder .... Is 27:9
fitches are *b* out with a staff .... Is 28:27
LORD shall the Assyrian be *b* down .... Is 30:31
in the synagogues ye shall be *b* .... Mk 13:9
shall be *b* with many stripes .... Lk 12:47
shall be *b* with few stripes .... Lk 12:48
b them, they commanded that they .... Acts 5:40
They have *b* us openly .... Acts 16:37
Thrice was I *b* with rods 2Cor 11:25

BEATEST

When thou *b* thine olive tree, ... Deut 24:20
for if thou *b* him with the rod, ... Prov 23:13

BEATETH

I, not as one that *b* the air 1Cor 9:26

BEATING

they went on *b* down one another 1Sa 14:16
b some, and killing some .... Mk 12:5
the soldiers, they left *b* of Paul .... Acts 21:32

BEAUTIES

in the *b* of holiness from the .... Ps 110:3

BEAUTIFUL

but Rachel was *b* and well favoured, ... Gen 29:17
among the captives a *b* woman .... Deut 21:11
and withal of a *b* countenance 1Sa 16:12
and of a *b* countenance 1Sa 25:3
the woman was very *b* to look upon 2Sa 11:2
mother, and the maid was fair and *b* ...... Est 2:7
B for situation, the joy of the .... Ps 48:2
made every thing *b* in his time .... Eccl 3:11
Thou art *b*, O my love, as Tirzah .... Song 6:4
How *b* are thy feet with shoes, O .... Song 7:1
shall the branch of the LORD be *b* .... Is 4:2
put on thy *b* garments, O .... Is 52:1
How *b* upon the mountains are the .... Is 52:7
our *b* house, where our fathers .... Is 64:11
that was given thee, thy *b* flock .... Jer 13:20
strong staff broken, and the *b* rod .... Jer 48:17
a *b* crown upon thine head .... Eze 16:12
and thou wast exceeding *b*, and thou ...... Eze 16:13
b crowns upon their heads .... Eze 23:42
which indeed appear *b* outward .... Mt 23:27
of the temple which is called *B* .... Acts 3:2
alms at the *B* gate of the temple .... Acts 3:10

How *b* are the feet of them that .... Rom 10:15

BEAUTIFY

to *b* the house of the LORD which .... Ezr 7:27
he will *b* the meek with salvation .... Ps 149:4
to *b* the place of my sanctuary .... Is 60:13

BEAUTY

thy brother for glory and for *b* .... Ex 28:2
make for them, for glory and for *b* .... Ex 28:40
The *b* of Israel is slain upon thy 2Sa 1:19
much praised as Absalom for his *b* 2Sa 14:25
the LORD in the *b* of holiness 1Chr 16:29
house with precious stones for *b* 2Chr 3:6
should praise the *b* of holiness 2Chr 20:21
the people and the princes her *b* .... Est 1:11
and array thyself with glory and *b* .... Job 40:10
life, to behold the *b* of the LORD .... Ps 27:4
the LORD in the *b* of holiness .... Ps 29:2
thou makest his *b* to consume away .... Ps 39:11
the king greatly desire thy *b* .... Ps 45:11
their *b* shall consume in the .... Ps 49:14
Out of Zion, the perfection of *b* .... Ps 50:2
let the *b* of the LORD our God be .... Ps 90:17
and *b* are in his sanctuary .... Ps 96:6
the LORD in the *b* of holiness .... Ps 96:9
not after her *b* in thine heart .... Prov 6:25
the *b* of old men is the grey head .... Prov 20:29
Favour is deceitful, and *b* is vain, ... Prov 31:30
and burning instead of *b* .... Is 3:24
the *b* of the Chaldees' excellency .... Is 13:19
whose glorious *b* is a fading .... Is 28:1
And the glorious *b*, which is on .... Is 28:4
of glory, and for a diadem of *b* .... Is 28:5
eyes shall see the king in his *b* .... Is 33:17
man, according to the *b* of a man .... Is 44:13
there is no *b* that we should .... Is 53:2
to give unto them *b* for ashes .... Is 61:3
of Zion all her *b* is departed .... Lam 1:6
unto the earth the *b* of Israel .... Lam 2:1
that men call The perfection of *b* .... Lam 2:15
As for the *b* of his ornament, he .... Eze 7:20
forth among the heathen for thy *b* .... Eze 16:14
thou didst trust in thine own *b* .... Eze 16:15
hast made thy *b* to be abhorred, ... Eze 16:25
thou hast said, I am of perfect *b* .... Eze 27:3
thy builders have perfected thy *b* .... Eze 27:4
they have made thy *b* perfect .... Eze 27:11
against the *b* of thy wisdom .... Eze 28:7
full of wisdom, and perfect in *b* .... Eze 28:12
was lifted up because of thy *b* .... Eze 28:17
of God was like unto him in his *b* .... Eze 31:8
Whom dost thou pass in *b* .... Eze 32:19
his *b* shall be as the olive tree, ... Hos 14:6
goodness, and how great is his *b* .... Zec 9:17
the one I called *B*, and the other .... Zec 11:10
And I took my staff, even *B* .... Zec 11:10

BEBAI (beb'-a-i)

1. Father of returned exiles.
The children of *B*, six hundred .... Ezr 2:11
The children of *B*, six hundred .... Neh 7:16
2. Father of returned exiles with Ezra.
And of the sons of *B* .... Ezr 8:11
Zechariah the son of *B*, and with .... Ezr 8:11
Of the sons also of *B* .... Ezr 10:28
3. One who sealed the covenant.
Bunni, Azgad, *B*, ... Neh 10:15

BECAME

and man *b* a living soul .... Gen 2:7
was parted, and *b* into four heads .... Gen 2:10
the same *b* mighty men which were .... Gen 6:4
him, and she *b* a pillar of salt .... Gen 19:26
and she *b* my wife .... Gen 20:12
in the wilderness, and *b* an archer ...... Gen 21:20
took Rebekah, and she *b* his wife .... Gen 24:67
and grew until he *b* very great .... Gen 26:13
For thy servant *b* surety for the .... Gen 44:32
so the land *b* Pharaoh's .... Gen 47:20
only, which *b* not Pharaoh's .... Gen 47:26
bear, and *b* a servant unto tribute ...... Gen 49:15
daughter, and he *b* her son .... Ex 2:10
on the ground, and it *b* a serpent .... Ex 4:3
it, and it *b* a rod in his hand .... Ex 4:4
his servants, and it *b* a serpent .... Ex 7:10
man his rod, and they *b* serpents .... Ex 7:12
it *b* lice in man, and in beast .... Ex 8:17
all the dust of the land *b* lice .... Ex 8:17
it *b* a boil breaking forth with .... Ex 9:10
land of Egypt since it *b* a nation .... Ex 9:24
so it *b* one tabernacle .... Ex 36:13
Miriam *b* leprous, white as snow .... Num 12:10
and they *b* a sign .... Num 26:10
b there a nation, great, mighty, ... Deut 26:5
the people melted, and *b* as water .... Josh 7:5
Hebron therefore *b* the .... Josh 14:14
it *b* the inheritance of the .... Josh 24:32
among them, and *b* tributaries .... Judg 1:30
of Beth-anath *b* tributaries unto .... Judg 1:33
so that they *b* tributaries .... Judg 1:35
which thing *b* a snare unto Gideon .... Judg 8:27
b as flax that was burnt with .... Judg 15:14
one of his sons, who *b* his priest .... Judg 17:5
and the young man *b* his priest .... Judg 17:12
in her bosom, and *b* nurse unto it .... Ruth 4:16
they *b* servants to the 1Sa 10:12
and he *b* his armourbearer 1Sa 16:21
Saul *b* David's enemy continually 1Sa 18:29
and *b* a captain over them 1Sa 22:2
within him, and he *b* as a stone 1Sa 25:37
of David, and *b* his wife 1Sa 25:42

b one troop, and stood on the top 2Sa 2:25
to flee, that he fell, and *b* lame 2Sa 2:23
so the Moabites *b* David's 2Sa 8:2
the Syrians *b* servants to David, ... 2Sa 8:6
they of Edom *b* David's servants 2Sa 8:14
she is his wife, and bare him a son 2Sa 11:27
b captain over a band, when David 1Kin 11:24
And this thing *b* a sin 1Kin 12:30
him again, and *b* as it was before 1Kin 13:6
he *b* one of the priests of the 1Kin 13:33
this thing *b* sin unto the house 1Kin 13:34
Hoshea *b* his servant, and gave him 2Kin 17:3
b vain, and went after the heathen 2Kin 17:15
Jehoiakim *b* his servant three 2Kin 24:1
the Moabites *b* David's servants, ... 1Chr 18:2
the Syrians *b* David's servants, ... 1Chr 18:6
the Edomites *b* David's servants 1Chr 18:13
with David, and *b* his servants 1Chr 19:19
So Jotham *b* mighty, because he 2Chr 27:6
b fat, and delighted themselves in ...... Neh 9:25
of the people of the land *b* Jews .... Est 8:17
and I *b* a proverb to them .... Ps 69:11
they *b* as dung for the earth .... Ps 83:10
I *b* also a reproach unto them .... Ps 109:25
they *b* as women .... Jer 51:30
b a spreading vine of low stature .... Eze 17:6
so it *b* a vine, and brought forth .... Eze 19:11
then a young lion, and it learned .... Eze 19:3
he *b* a young lion, and learned to .... Eze 19:3
and she *b* famous among women .... Eze 23:10
his branches *b* long because of .... Eze 31:5
they *b* meat to all the beasts of .... Eze 34:5
surely because my flock *b* a prey .... Eze 34:8
my flock *b* meat to every beast of .... Eze 34:8
which *b* a prey and derision to the ...... Eze 34:8
b like the chaff of the summer .... Dan 2:35
the image *b* a great mountain .... Dan 2:35
according to his will, and *b* great ...... Dan 8:4
toward the ground, and I *b* dumb .... Dan 10:15
in the day that he *b* a stranger .... Obad 12
did shake, and *b* as dead men .... Mt 28:4
And his raiment *b* shining .... Mk 9:3
he *b* very hungry, and would have .... Acts 10:10
but *b* vain in their imaginations, ... Rom 1:21
to be wise, they *b* fools, ... Rom 1:22
from sin, ye *b* the servants of .... Rom 6:18
And unto the Jews I *b* as a Jew 1Cor 9:20
To the weak *b* I as weak, that I 1Cor 9:22
but when I *b* a man, I put away 1Cor 13:11
yet for your sakes he *b* poor 2Cor 8:9
b obedient unto death, even the .... Phil 2:8
ye *b* followers of us, and of the 1Th 1:6
b followers of the churches of 1Th 2:14
For it *b* him, for whom are all .... Heb 2:10
he *b* the author of eternal .... Heb 5:9
For such an high priest *b* us .... Heb 7:26
whilst ye *b* companions of them .... Heb 10:33
b heir of the righteousness which .... Heb 11:7
the sun *b* black as sackcloth of .... Rev 6:12
of hair, and the moon *b* as blood .... Rev 6:12
toward the ground, and *b* as blood .... Rev 8:8
the third part of the sea *b* blood .... Rev 8:8
part of the waters *b* wormwood .... Rev 8:11
it *b* as the blood of a dead man, ... Rev 16:3
and they *b* blood .... Rev 16:4

BECAMEST

and thou, LORD, *b* their God 1Chr 17:22
the Lord GOD, and *b* mine .... Eze 16:8

BECAUSE See PREFACE.

BECHER (be'-ker) See BACHRITES.

1. A son of Benjamin.
sons of Benjamin were Belah, and *B* ...... Gen 46:21
Bela, and *B*, and Jediael, three 1Chr 7:6
And the sons of *B* 1Chr 7:8
All these are the sons of *B* 1Chr 7:8
2. A son of Ephraim.
of *B*, the family of the Bachrites .... Num 26:35

BECHERITES See BACHRITES.

BECHORATH (be-ko'-rath) An ancestor of King Saul.

the son of Zeror, the son of *B* 1Sa 9:1

BECKONED

for he *b* unto them, and remained .... Lk 1:22
they *b* unto their partners, which .... Lk 5:7
Simon Peter therefore *b* to him .... Jn 13:24
Alexander *b* with the hand, and .... Acts 19:33
b with the hand unto the people .... Acts 21:40
governor had *b* unto him to speak .... Acts 24:10

BECKONING

b unto them with the hand to hold .... Acts 12:17
b with his hand said, Men of .... Acts 13:16

BECOME

the man is *b* as one of us, to .... Gen 3:22
the waters shall no more *b* a .... Gen 9:15
Abraham shall surely *b* a great .... Gen 18:18
and he is *b* great .... Gen 24:35
and now I am *b* two bands .... Gen 32:10
with you, and we will *b* one people ...... Gen 34:16
see what will *b* of his dreams .... Gen 37:20
he also shall *b* a people, and he .... Gen 48:19
he seed shall *b* a multitude of .... Gen 48:19
shall *b* blood upon the dry land .... Ex 4:9
Pharaoh, and it shall *b* a serpent .... Ex 7:9
of water, that they may *b* blood .... Ex 7:19
that it may *b* lice throughout all .... Ex 8:16
it shall *b* small dust in all the .... Ex 9:9
and song, and he is *b* my salvation ...... Ex 15:2

O LORD, is b glorious in power............Ex 15:6
lest the land b desolate, and the........Ex 23:29
we wot not what is b of him.................Ex 32:1
we wot not what is b of him...............Ex 32:23
the land b full of wickedness...............Lev 19:29
shall enter into her, and b bitter.........Num 5:24
b bitter, and her belly shall..............Num 5:27
this day thou art b the people of........Deut 27:9
thou shalt b an astonishment, a........Deut 28:37
our shoes are b old by reason of..........Josh 9:13
go from me, and I shall b weak...........Judg 16:17
from thee, and is b thine enemy.........1Sa 28:16
and thou, LORD, art b their God...........2Sa 7:24
about, and is b my brother's.................1Kin 2:15
thee what shall b of the child............1Kin 14:3
and they shall b a prey and a spoil...2Kin 21:14
that they should b a desolation........2Kin 22:19
did, and what should b of her...............Est 2:11
my skin is broken, and b loathsome......Job 7:5
which are ready to b heaps...............Job 15:28
b old, yea, are mighty in power.........Job 21:7
I am b like dust and ashes...................Job 30:19
Thou art b cruel to me......................Job 30:21
they are all together b filthy...............Ps 14:3
I b like them that go down into..............Ps 28:1
they are altogether b filthy..................Ps 53:3
and b not vain in robbery..................Ps 62:10
I am b a stranger unto my................Ps 69:8
Let their table b a snare before.........Ps 69:22
their welfare, let it b a trap..............Ps 69:22
We are b a reproach to our...............Ps 79:4
and let his prayer b sin....................Ps 109:7
and song, and is b my salvation.......Ps 118:14
heard me, and art b my salvation......Ps 118:21
is b the head stone of the corner......Ps 118:22
For I am b like a bottle in the..........Ps 119:83
have him b his son at the length........Prov 29:21
is the faithful city b an harlot............Is 1:21
Thy silver is b dross, thy wine.............Is 1:22
all the land shall b briers..................Is 7:24
he also is b my salvation.....................Is 12:2
thee, Art thou also b weak as we........Is 14:10
art thou b like unto us......................Is 14:10
of Pharaoh is b brutish......................Is 19:11
The princes of Zoan are b fools...........Is 19:13
the vision of all is b unto you.............Is 29:11
thereof shall b burning pitch.................Is 34:9
the parched ground shall b a pool.........Is 35:7
Their webs shall not b garments..........Is 59:6
A little one shall b a thousand.............Is 60:22
after vanity, and are b vain...................Jer 2:5
b another man's, shall he return...........Jer 3:1
And the prophets shall b wind.............Jer 5:13
therefore they are b great..................Jer 5:27
b a den of robbers in your eyes...........Jer 7:11
For the pastors are b brutish................Jer 10:21
this house shall b a desolation............Jer 22:5
field, and Jerusalem shall b heaps.....Jer 26:18
that Bozrah shall b a desolation..........Jer 49:13
how is Babylon b a desolation...........Jer 50:23
and they shall b as women................Jer 50:37
And Babylon shall b heaps, a..............Jer 51:37
how is Babylon b an astonishment......Jer 51:41
how is she b as a widow....................Lam 1:1
provinces, how is she b tributary.........Lam 1:1
with her, they are b her enemies..........Lam 1:5
her princes are b like harts that.........Lam 1:6
for I am b vile..................................Lam 1:11
How is the gold b dim.......................Lam 4:1
daughter of my people is b cruel.........Lam 4:3
is withered, it is b like a stick............Lam 4:8
Thou art b guilty in thy blood.............Eze 22:4
house of Israel is b to me dross..........Eze 22:18
Because ye are all b dross.................Eze 22:19
it shall b a spoil to the nations............Eze 26:5
is b like the garden of Eden..............Eze 36:35
and ruined cities are b fenced............Eze 36:35
they shall b one in thine hand............Eze 37:17
king, that art grown and b strong........Dan 4:22
thy people are b a reproach to............Dan 9:16
shall b strong with a small................Dan 11:23
And Ephraim said, Yet I am b rich........Hos 12:8
and his spring shall b dry...................Hos 13:15
Samaria shall b desolate...................Hos 13:16
see what would b of the city................Jonah 4:5
field, and Jerusalem shall b heaps......Mic 3:12
their goods shall b a booty.................Zeph 1:13
how is she b a desolation, a...............Zeph 2:15
Zerubbabel thou shalt b a plain............Zec 4:7
b as little children, ye shall................Mt 18:3
the same is b the head of the...........Mt 21:42
will make you to b fishers of men........Mk 1:17
is b the head of the corner...............Mk 12:10
the same is b the head of the.............Lk 20:17
he power to b the sons of God..............Jn 1:12
which is b the head of the corner........Acts 4:11
we wot not what is b of him................Acts 7:40
the soldiers, what was b of Peter........Acts 12:18
they are together b unprofitable..........Rom 3:12
the world may b guilty before God........Rom 3:19
that he might b the father of...............Rom 4:18
b servants to God, ye have your..........Rom 6:22
ye also are b dead to the law by...........Rom 7:4
might b exceeding sinful....................Rom 7:13
in this world, let him b a fool..............1Cor 3:18
let him not b uncircumcised................1Cor 7:18
b a stumblingblock to them that..........1Cor 8:9
I am b as sounding brass, or a............1Cor 13:1
b the firstfruits of them that.............1Cor 15:20
behold, all things are b new...............2Cor 5:17

I am b a fool in glorying...................2Cor 12:11
Am I therefore b your enemy...............Gal 4:16
Christ is b of no effect unto you............Gal 5:4
the things which b sound doctrine........Titus 2:1
b effectual by the acknowledging........Philem 6
are b such as have need of milk..........Heb 5:12
are b judges of evil thoughts................Jas 2:4
thou art b a transgressor of the...........Jas 2:11
are b the kingdoms of our Lord...........Rev 11:15
is b the habitation of devils, and..........Rev 18:2

BECOMETH

holiness b thine house, O LORD...........Ps 93:5
He b poor that dealeth with a.............Prov 10:4
Excellent speech b not a fool.............Prov 17:7
b surety in the presence of his..........Prov 17:18
is born in his kingdom b poor..............Eccl 4:14
for thus it b us to fulfil all..................Mt 3:15
the word, and he b unfruitful..............Mt 13:22
b a tree, so that the birds of..............Mt 13:32
the word, and it b unfruitful..............Mk 4:19
b greater than all herbs, and.............Mk 4:32
once named among you, as b saints......Eph 5:3
be as it b the gospel of Christ...........Phil 1:27
But (which b women professing........1Ti 2:10
be in behaviour as b holiness............Titus 2:3

BECORATH See BECHORATH.

BED

himself, and sat upon the b...............Gen 48:2
thou wentest up to my father's b.........Gen 49:4
gathered up his feet into the b...........Gen 49:33
thy bedchamber, and upon thy b...........Ex 8:3
and he die not, but keepeth his b.........Ex 21:18
Every b, whereon he lieth that............Lev 15:4
his b shall wash his clothes..............Lev 15:5
her b shall wash his clothes.............Lev 15:21
And if it be on her b, or on any..........Lev 15:23
all the b whereon he lieth shall..........Lev 15:24
Every b whereon she lieth all the........Lev 15:26
her as the b of her separation............Lev 15:26
an image, and laid it in the b............1Sa 19:13
Bring him up to me in the b...............1Sa 19:15
there was an image in the b.............1Sa 19:16
from the earth, and sat upon the b.....1Sa 28:23
who lay on a b of noon.....................2Sa 4:5
he lay on his b in his bedchamber........2Sa 4:7
in his own house upon his b................2Sa 4:11
that David arose from off his b............2Sa 11:2
b with the servants of his lord...........2Sa 11:13
unto him, Lay thee down on thy b.........2Sa 13:5
the king bowed himself upon the b.....1Kin 1:47
abode, and laid him upon his own b......1Kin 17:19
And he laid him down upon his b........1Kin 21:4
that b on which thou art gone up.........2Kin 1:4
that b on which thou art gone up.........2Kin 1:6
on that b on which thou art gone up....2Kin 1:16
and let us set for him there a b...........2Kin 4:10
laid him on the b of the man of...........2Kin 4:21
was dead, and laid upon his b............2Kin 4:32
as he defiled his father's.................1Chr 5:1
laid him in the b which was...............2Chr 16:14
the priest, and slew him in his b.........2Chr 24:25
upon the b whereon Esther was...........Est 7:8
My b shall comfort me, my couch.........Job 7:13
I have made my b in the darkness.......Job 17:13
men, in slumberings upon the b..........Job 33:15
also with pain upon his b..................Job 33:19
with your own heart upon your b...........Ps 4:4
all the night make I my b to swim.........Ps 6:6
He deviseth mischief upon his b.........Ps 36:4
him upon the b of languishing............Ps 41:3
make all his b in his sickness.............Ps 41:3
When I remember thee upon my b.........Ps 63:6
of my house, nor go up into my b.........Ps 132:3
if I make my b in hell, behold.............Ps 139:8
I have decked my b with coverings.......Prov 7:16
I have perfumed my b with myrrh.........Prov 7:17
take away thy b from under thee..........Prov 22:27
so doth the slothful upon his b...........Prov 26:14
also our b is green..........................Song 1:16
By night on my b I sought him.............Song 3:1
Behold his b, which is Solomon's.........Song 3:7
His cheeks are as a b of spices..........Song 5:13
For the b is shorter than that a..........Is 28:20
high mountain hast thou set thy b.........Is 57:7
thou hast enlarged thy b, and made......Is 57:8
thou lovedst their b where thou............Is 57:8
came to her into the b of love............Eze 23:17
And satest upon a stately b...............Eze 23:41
They have set her a b in the..............Eze 32:25
visions of thy head upon my b............Dan 2:28
came into thy mind upon thy b...........Dan 2:29
afraid, and the thoughts upon my b.......Dan 4:5
the visions of mine head in my b.........Dan 4:10
the visions of my head upon my b.........Dan 4:13
and visions of his head upon his b........Dan 7:1
in Samaria in the corner of a b...........Amos 3:12
sick of the palsy, lying on a b............Mt 9:2
the palsy, Arise, take up thy b.............Mt 9:6
they let down the b whereon the...........Mk 2:4
to say, Arise, and take up thy b...........Mk 2:9
thee, Arise, and take up thy b...........Mk 2:11
he arose, took up the b, and went.......Mk 2:12
put under a bushel, or under a b..........Mk 4:21
and her daughter laid upon the b.........Mk 7:30
men brought in a b a man which..........Lk 5:18
a vessel, or putteth it under a b..........Lk 8:16
and my children are with me in b.........Lk 11:7
there shall be two men in one b.........Lk 17:34

unto him, Rise, take up thy b................Jn 5:8
was made whole, and took up his b........Jn 5:9
lawful for thee to carry thy b...............Jn 5:10
same said unto me, Take up thy b...........Jn 5:11
said unto thee, Take up thy b...............Jn 5:12
which had kept his b eight years.........Acts 9:33
arise, and make thy b.....................Acts 9:34
in all, and the b undefiled.................Heb 13:4
Behold, I will cast her into a b.............Rev 2:22

BEDAD (be´-dad) Father of Hadad.
died, and Hadad the son of B..............Gen 36:35
was dead, Hadad the son of B..............1Chr 1:46

BEDAN (be´-dan)
1. A judge of Israel.
And the LORD sent Jerubbaal, and B......1Sa 12:11
2. A descendant of Manasseh.
And the sons of Ulam; B....................1Chr 7:17

BEDCHAMBER
into thine house, and into thy b...........Ex 8:3
house, he lay on his bed in his b.........2Sa 4:7
words that thou speakest in thy b........2Kin 6:12
in the b from Athaliah, so that............2Kin 11:2
and put him and his nurse in a b........2Chr 22:11
occupied not the rich in thy b...........Eccl 10:20

BEDEIAH (be-de´-yah) Married a foreign wife
in exile.
Benaiah, B, Cheluh,.........................Ezr 10:35

BED'S
bowed himself upon the b head...........Gen 47:31

BEDS
Brought b, and basons, and earthen.....2Sa 17:28
the b were of gold and silver,................Est 1:6
let them sing aloud upon their b...........Ps 149:5
to lie b of spices, to feed on..............Song 6:2
they shall rest in their b....................Is 57:2
when they howled upon their b...........Hos 7:14
That lie upon b of ivory, and...............Amos 6:4
and work evil upon their b..................Mic 2:1
about in b those that were sick............Mk 6:55
the streets, and laid them on.............Acts 5:15

BEDSTEAD
his b was a b of iron.......................Deut 3:11
for the b that is in the land of...............Is 7:18

BEE
for the b that is in the land of...............Is 7:18

BEELIADA (be-li´-ad-ah) A son of David.
And Elishama, and B, and Eliphalet....1Chr 14:7

BEELZEBUB (be-el´-ze-bub) See BAAL-ZEBUB.
Chief of evil spirits.
called the master of the house B...........Mt 10:25
but by B the prince of the devils..........Mt 12:24
if I by B cast out devils, by...............Mt 12:27
from Jerusalem said, He hath B............Mk 3:22
through B the chief of the devils..........Lk 11:15
that I cast out devils through B............Lk 11:18
if I by B cast out devils, by...............Lk 11:19

BEELZEBULL See BEELZEBUB.

BEEN See PREFACE.

BEER (be´-ur) See BAALATH-BEER, BEER-ELIM,
BEER-LAHAI-ROI, BEER-SHEBA.
1. An Israelite post beyond the Arnon River.
And from thence they went to B............Num 21:16
2. A town in Judah.
ran away, and fled, and went to B..........Judg 9:21

BEERA (be-e´-rah) Son of Zophah.
and Shilshah, and Ithran, and B............1Chr 7:37

BEERAH (be-e´-rah) A Reubenite prince.
B his son, whom Tilgath-pilneser.........1Chr 5:6

BEER-ELIM (be´-ur-e´-lim) A well in Moab.
and the howling thereof unto B............Is 15:8

BEERI (be-e´-ri)
1. Father of Judith.
the daughter of B the Hittite...............Gen 26:34
2. Father of Hosea.
came unto Hosea, the son of B............Hos 1:1

BEER-LAHAI-ROI (be´´´-ur-la´´-hahe-ro´-e) A
well.
Wherefore the well was called B..........Gen 16:14

BEEROTH (be-e´-roth) See BEROTHAH.
1. An Israelite encampment during the
Exodus.
B of the children of Jaakan to..............Deut 10:6
2. A Hivvite city in Canaan.
were Gibeon, and Chephirah, and B......Josh 9:17
Gibeon, and Ramah, and B,..................Josh 18:25
(for B also was reckoned to.................2Sa 4:2
of Kirjath-arim, Chephirah, and B.........Ezr 2:25
Kirjath-jearim, Chephirah, and B..........Neh 7:29

BEEROTHITE (be-er´-o-thite) See
BEEROTHITES, BEROTHITE. An inhabitant of
Beeroth.
Rechab, the sons of Rimmon a B...........2Sa 4:2
And the sons of Rimmon the B.............2Sa 4:5
brother, the sons of Rimmon the B........2Sa 4:9
Zelek the Ammonite, Nahari the B........2Sa 23:37

BEEROTHITES (*be-er'-o-thites*)
The B fled to Gittaim, and were........... 2Sa 4:3

BEER-SHEBA (*be-ur'-she-bah*) A Canaanite city.
wandered in the wilderness of B.......... Gen 21:14
Wherefore he called that place B .... Gen 21:31
Thus they made a covenant at B .... Gen 21:32
And Abraham planted a grove in B .... Gen 21:33
rose up and went together to B .... Gen 22:19
and Abraham dwelt at B.......................... Gen 22:19
And he went up from thence to B ...... Gen 26:23
of the city is B unto this day .... Gen 26:33
Jacob went out from B............................ Gen 28:10
all that he had, and came to B .... Gen 46:1
And Jacob rose up from B...................... Gen 46:5
And Hazar-shual, and B, and .... Josh 15:28
they had in their inheritance B .... Josh 19:2
as one man, from Dan even to B .... Judg 20:1
even to B knew that Samuel was 1Sa 3:20
they were judges in B............................ 1Sa 8:2
and over Judah, from Dan even to B .. 2Sa 3:10
unto thee, from Dan even to B 2Sa 17:11
of Israel, from Dan even to B................ 2Sa 24:2
to the south of Judah, even to B 2Sa 24:7
even to B seventy thousand men 2Sa 24:15
his fig tree, from Dan even to B 1Kin 4:25
went for his life, and came to B.......... 1Kin 19:3
his mother's name was Zibiah of B.... 2Kin 12:1
burned incense, from Geba to B 2Kin 23:8
And they dwelt at B, and Moladah, .. 1Chr 4:28
number Israel from B even to Dan 1Chr 21:2
people from B to mount Ephraim 2Chr 19:4
name also was Zibiah of B...................... 2Chr 24:1
from B even to Dan, that they 2Chr 30:5
And at Hazar-shual, and at B .... Neh 11:27
they dwelt from B unto the valley .... Neh 11:30
into Gilgal, and pass not to B .... Amos 5:5
and, The manner of B liveth .... Amos 8:14

BEES
you, and chased you, as b do................ Deut 1:44
behold, there was a swarm of b.......... Judg 14:8
They compassed me about like b .... Ps 118:12

BE-ESHTARAH See BEESH-TERAH.

BEESH-TERAH (*be-esh'te-rah*) See
ASHTAROTH. A Levitical city in Manasseh,
and B with her suburbs......................... Josh 21:27

BEETLE
the b after his kind, and the................ Lev 11:22

BEEVES
a male without blemish, of the b........ Lev 22:19
a freewill offering in b or sheep........ Lev 22:21
both of the persons, and of the b........ Num 31:28
fifty, of the persons, of the b.............. Num 31:30
threescore and twelve thousand b .... Num 31:33
the b were thirty and six thousand.... Num 31:38
And thirty and six thousand b .... Num 31:44

BEFALL
Lest peradventure mischief b him .... Gen 42:4
if mischief b him by the way in .... Gen 42:38
also from me, and mischief b him...... Gen 44:29
shall b you in the last days.................. Gen 49:1
evils and troubles shall b them.......... Deut 31:17
evil will b you in the latter................ Deut 31:29
There shall no evil b thee...................... Ps 91:10
b thy people in the latter days............ Dan 10:14
the things that shall b me there.......... Acts 20:22

BEFALLEN
and such things have b me.................... Lev 10:19
all the travel that hath b us................ Num 20:14
many evils and troubles are b them.. Deut 31:21
us, why then is all this b us................ Judg 6:13
he thought, Something hath b him.... 1Sa 20:26
every thing that had b him.................... Est 6:13
what was b to the possessed of.......... Mt 8:33

BEFELL
and told him all that b unto them...... Gen 42:29
told him all things that b them............ Josh 2:23
then than all the evil that b.................. 2Sa 19:7
that saw it told them how it b............ Mk 5:16
which b me by the lying in wait.......... Acts 20:19

BEFORE See PREFACE.

BEFOREHAND
take no thought b what ye shall.......... Mk 13:11
make up b your bounty, whereof ye 2Cor 9:5
Some men's sins are open b 1Ti 5:24
good works of some are manifest b.... 1Ti 5:25
signify, when it testified b the............ 1Pet 1:11

BEFORETIME
The Horims also dwelt in Seir b .... Deut 2:12
for Hazor b was the head of all.......... Josh 11:10
unwittingly, and hated him not b........ Josh 20:5
(In Israel, when a man went to 1Sa 9:9
a Prophet was b called a Seer 1Sa 9:9
when all that knew him b saw that.... Isa 10:11
afflict them any more, as b.................... 2Sa 7:10
Israel dwelt in their tents, as b.......... 2Kin 13:5
Now I had not been b sad in his .... Neh 2:1
and b, that we may say, He is.............. Is 41:26
which b in the same city used.............. Acts 8:9

BEG
be continually vagabonds, and b........ Ps 109:10
therefore shall he b in harvest............ Prov 20:4
to b I am ashamed................................ Lk 16:3

BEGAN
then b men to call upon the name...... Gen 4:26
when men b to multiply on the............ Gen 6:1
Noah b to be an husbandman, and .. Gen 9:20
he b to be a mighty one in the............ Gen 10:8
seven years of dearth b to come........ Gen 41:54
b at the eldest, and left at the............ Gen 44:12
the people b to commit whoredom.... Num 25:1
b Moses to declare this law, ... Deut 1:5
the Spirit of the LORD b to move...... Judg 13:25
she b to afflict him, and his................ Judg 16:19
had b to grow again after he was...... Judg 16:22
and when the day b to spring.............. Judg 19:25
they b to smite of the people, and .... Judg 20:31
the battle, Benjamin b to smite.......... Judg 20:39
But when the flame b to arise up...... Judg 20:40
his eyes b to wax dim, that he............ 1Sa 3:2
when he b to reign over Israel............ 2Sa 2:10
years old when he b to reign................ 2Sa 5:4
that he b to build the house of............ 1Kin 6:1
one years old when he b to reign...... 1Kin 14:21
Nadab the son of Jeroboam b to........ 1Kin 15:25
b Baasha the son of Ahijah to............ 1Kin 15:33
b Elah the son of Baasha to reign...... 1Kin 16:8
when he b to reign, as soon as he.... 1Kin 16:11
Judah b Omri to reign over Israel...... 1Kin 16:23
year of Asa king of Judah b Ahab 1Kin 16:29
Asa b to reign over Judah in the........ 1Kin 22:41
five years old when he b to reign...... 1Kin 22:42
Ahaziah the son of Ahab b to.............. 1Kin 22:51
Now Jehoram the son of Ahab b to.... 2Kin 3:1
king of Judah b to reign........................ 2Kin 8:16
old was he when he b to reign............ 2Kin 8:17
was Ahaziah when he b to reign........ 2Kin 8:26
b Ahaziah to reign over Judah............ 2Kin 9:29
the LORD b to cut Israel short............ 2Kin 10:32
was Jehoash when he b to reign........ 2Kin 11:21
year of Jehu Jehoash b to reign.......... 2Kin 12:1
Judah Jehoahaz the son of Jehu b 2Kin 13:1
year of Joash king of Judah b............ 2Kin 13:10
five years old when he b to reign...... 2Kin 14:2
of Israel b to reign in Samaria............ 2Kin 14:23
b Azariah son of Amaziah king of 2Kin 15:1
old was he when he b to reign............ 2Kin 15:2
of Jabesh b to reign in the nine........ 2Kin 15:13
b Menahem the son of Gadi to............ 2Kin 15:17
Pekahiah the son of Menahem b to.. 2Kin 15:22
b to reign over Israel in Samaria........ 2Kin 15:27
b Jotham the son of Uzziah king...... 2Kin 15:32
old was he when he b to reign............ 2Kin 15:33
In those days the LORD b to send...... 2Kin 15:37
Jotham king of Judah b to reign........ 2Kin 16:1
old was Ahaz when he b to reign...... 2Kin 16:2
year of Ahaz king of Judah b.............. 2Kin 17:1
of Ahaz king of Judah b to reign...... 2Kin 18:1
old was he when he b to reign............ 2Kin 18:2
years old when he b to reign................ 2Kin 21:1
two years old when he b to reign...... 2Kin 21:19
years old when he b to reign................ 2Kin 22:1
years old when he b to reign................ 2Kin 23:31
five years old when he b to reign...... 2Kin 23:36
years old when he b to reign................ 2Kin 24:8
one years old when he b to reign...... 2Kin 24:18
b to reign did lift up the head............ 2Kin 25:27
he b to be mighty upon the earth...... 1Chr 1:10
the son of Zeruiah b to number.......... 1Chr 27:24
Then Solomon b to build the house .. 2Chr 3:1
he b to build in the second day.......... 2Chr 3:2
years old when he b to reign................ 2Chr 12:13
year of king Jeroboam b Abijah to.... 2Chr 13:1
And when they b to sing and to........ 2Chr 20:22
five years old when he b to reign...... 2Chr 20:31
two years old when he b to reign...... 2Chr 21:5
old was he when he b to reign............ 2Chr 21:20
was Ahaziah when he b to reign........ 2Chr 22:2
years old when he b to reign................ 2Chr 24:1
five years old when he b to reign...... 2Chr 25:1
old was Uzziah when he b to reign.... 2Chr 26:3
five years old when he b to reign...... 2Chr 27:1
years old when he b to reign................ 2Chr 27:8
years old when he b to reign................ 2Chr 28:1
Hezekiah b to reign when he was...... 2Chr 29:1
Now they b on the first day of............ 2Chr 29:17
And when the burnt offering b............ 2Chr 29:27
the song of the LORD b also............... 2Chr 29:27
In the third month they b to lay........ 2Chr 31:7
Since the people b to bring the.......... 2Chr 31:10
in every work that he b in the............ 2Chr 31:21
years old when he b to reign................ 2Chr 33:1
years old when he b to reign................ 2Chr 33:21
he b to seek after the God of.............. 2Chr 34:3
twelfth year he b to purge Judah........ 2Chr 34:3
years old when he b to reign................ 2Chr 36:2
five years old when he b to reign...... 2Chr 36:5
years old when he b to reign................ 2Chr 36:9
years old when he b to reign................ 2Chr 36:11
b they to offer burnt offerings............ Ezr 3:6
b Zerubbabel the son of Shealtiel...... Ezr 3:8
b to build the house of God which.... Ezr 5:2
month b he to go up from Babylon.... Ezr 7:9
that the breaches b to be stopped...... Neh 4:7
when the gates of Jerusalem b to...... Neh 13:19
years old when he b to reign................ Jer 52:1
Then they b at the ancient men.......... Eze 9:6
Jonah b to enter into the city a .... Jonah 3:4

From that time Jesus b to preach........ Mt 4:17
departed, Jesus b to say unto the...... Mt 11:7
Then b he to upbraid the cities............ Mt 11:20
b to pluck the ears of corn, and.......... Mt 12:1
From that time forth b Jesus to.......... Mt 16:21
to rebuke him, saying, Be it................ Mt 16:22
b every one of them to say unto.......... Mt 26:22
b to be sorrowful and very heavy........ Mt 26:37
Then b he to curse and to swear........ Mt 26:74
as it b to dawn toward the first.......... Mt 28:1
b to publish it much, and to blaze...... Mk 1:45
and his disciples b, as they went........ Mk 2:23
he b again to teach by the sea............ Mk 4:1
they b to pray him to depart out........ Mk 5:17
b to publish in Decapolis how.............. Mk 5:20
he b to teach in the synagogue.......... Mk 6:2
b to send them forth by two and........ Mk 6:7
he b to teach them many things........ Mk 6:34
b to carry about in beds those............ Mk 6:55
b to question with him, seeking.......... Mk 8:11
he b to teach them, that the Son........ Mk 8:31
took him, and b to rebuke him............ Mk 8:32
Then Peter b to say unto him, Lo,...... Mk 10:28
b to tell them what things should...... Mk 10:32
they b to be much displeased with.... Mk 10:41
he b to cry out, and say, Jesus,.......... Mk 10:47
b to cast out them that sold and........ Mk 11:15
he b to speak unto them by................ Mk 12:1
And Jesus answering them b to say.... Mk 13:5
they b to be sorrowful, and to say...... Mk 14:19
b to be sore amazed, and to be.......... Mk 14:33
some b to spit on him, and to............ Mk 14:65
b to say to them that stood by,.......... Mk 14:69
But he b to curse and to swear,.......... Mk 14:71
the multitude crying aloud b to.......... Mk 15:8
b to salute him, Hail, King of............ Mk 15:18
which have been since the world b .... Lk 1:70
Jesus himself b to be about................ Lk 3:23
he b to say unto them, This day........ Lk 4:21
the ships, so that they b to sink........ Lk 5:7
and the Pharisees b to reason............ Lk 5:21
was dead sat up, and b to speak........ Lk 7:15
he b to speak unto the people............ Lk 7:24
b to wash his feet with tears, and...... Lk 7:38
him b to say within themselves.......... Lk 7:49
And when the day b to wear away .... Lk 9:12
he b to say, This is an evil.................. Lk 11:29
the Pharisees b to urge him................ Lk 11:53
he b to say unto his disciples.............. Lk 12:1
with consent b to make excuse .... Lk 14:18
Saying, This man b to build................ Lk 14:30
and he b to be in want........................ Lk 15:14
And they b to be merry........................ Lk 15:24
of the disciples b to rejoice.................. Lk 19:37
b to cast out them that sold................ Lk 19:45
Then b he to speak to the people...... Lk 20:9
And they b to enquire among.............. Lk 22:23
they b to accuse him, saying, We .... Lk 23:2
them the hour when he b to amend .. Jn 4:52
Since the world b was it not................ Jn 9:32
b to wash the disciples' feet, and...... Jn 13:5
of all that Jesus b both to do.............. Acts 1:1
b to speak with other tongues, as .... Acts 2:4
holy prophets since the world b.......... Acts 3:21
b at the same scripture, and................ Acts 8:35
b from Galilee, after the baptism ...... Acts 10:37
as I b to speak, the Holy Ghost.......... Acts 11:15
he b to speak boldly in the.................. Acts 18:26
Tertullus b to accuse him, saying...... Acts 24:2
he had broken it, he b to eat.............. Acts 27:35
was kept secret since the world b...... Rom 16:25
Christ Jesus before the world b.......... 2Ti 1:9
lie, promised before the world b........ Titus 1:2
which at the first b to be spoken........ Heb 2:3

BEGAT
and Irad b Mehujael................................ Gen 4:18
and Mehujael b Methusael.................... Gen 4:18
and Methusael b Lamech........................ Gen 4:18
b a son in his own likeness,................ Gen 5:3
and he b sons and daughters................ Gen 5:4
hundred and five years, and b Enos.... Gen 5:6
after he b Enos eight hundred............ Gen 5:7
years, and b sons and daughters........ Gen 5:7
lived ninety years, and b Cainan........ Gen 5:9
Enos lived after he b Cainan................ Gen 5:10
years, and b sons and daughters........ Gen 5:10
seventy years, and b Mahalaleel.......... Gen 5:12
And Cainan lived after he b.................. Gen 5:13
years, and b sons and daughters........ Gen 5:13
sixty and five years, and b Jared........ Gen 5:15
after he b Jared eight hundred............ Gen 5:16
years, and b sons and daughters........ Gen 5:16
sixty and two years, and he b Enoch .. Gen 5:18
Jared lived after he b Enoch................ Gen 5:19
years, and b sons and daughters........ Gen 5:19
and five years, and b Methuselah........ Gen 5:21
b Methuselah three hundred years,.... Gen 5:22
and b sons and daughters.................... Gen 5:22
and seven years, and b Lamech.......... Gen 5:25
Methuselah lived after he b.................. Gen 5:26
two years, and b sons and daughters .. Gen 5:26
eighty and two years, and b a son .... Gen 5:28
Lamech lived after he b Noah five...... Gen 5:30
years, and b sons and daughters........ Gen 5:30
and b Shem, Ham, and Japheth........ Gen 5:32
Noah b three sons, Shem, Ham, and.. Gen 6:10
And Cush b Nimrod................................ Gen 10:8
Mizraim b Ludim, and............................ Gen 10:13
Canaan b Sidon his firstborn, and...... Gen 10:15
and Arphaxad b Salah............................ Gen 10:24

and Salah *b* Eber .... Gen 10:24
Joktan *b* Almodad, and Sheleph, and .. Gen 10:26
b Arphaxad two years after the .... Gen 11:10
Shem lived after he *b* Arphaxad .... Gen 11:11
years, and *b* sons and daughters .... Gen 11:11
five and thirty years, and *b* Salah ...... Gen 11:12
after he *b* Salah four hundred .... Gen 11:13
years, and *b* sons and daughters .... Gen 11:13
lived thirty years, and *b* Eber .... Gen 11:14
after he *b* Eber four hundred .... Gen 11:15
years, and *b* sons and daughters .... Gen 11:15
four and thirty years, and *b* Peleg ...... Gen 11:16
after he *b* Peleg four hundred .... Gen 11:17
years, and *b* sons and daughters .... Gen 11:17
lived thirty years, and *b* Reu .... Gen 11:18
lived after he *b* Reu two hundred .... Gen 11:19
years, and *b* sons and daughters .... Gen 11:19
two and thirty years, and *b* Serug ...... Gen 11:20
after he *b* Serug two hundred .... Gen 11:21
years, and *b* sons and daughters .... Gen 11:21
lived thirty years, and *b* Nahor .... Gen 11:22
Serug lived after he *b* Nahor two .... Gen 11:23
years, and *b* sons and daughters .... Gen 11:23
nine and twenty years, and *b* Terah .... Gen 11:24
lived after he *b* Terah an hundred ...... Gen 11:25
years, and *b* sons and daughters .... Gen 11:25
and *b* Abram, Nahor, and Haran .... Gen 11:26
Terah *b* Abram, Nahor, and Haran ...... Gen 11:27
and Haran *b* Lot .... Gen 11:27
And Bethuel *b* Rebekah .... Gen 22:23
And Jokshan *b* Sheba, and Dedan ...... Gen 25:3
Abraham *b* Isaac .... Gen 25:19
which they *b* in your land .... Lev 25:45
and Machir *b* Gilead .... Num 26:29
And Kohath *b* Amram .... Num 26:58
Of the Rock that *b* thee thou art........ Deut 32:18
and Gilead *b* Jephthah .... Judg 11:1
Pharez *b* Hezron, ... Ruth 4:18
And Hezron *b* Ram .... Ruth 4:19
and Ram *b* Amminadab...................... Ruth 4:19
And Amminadab *b* Nahshon, and........ Ruth 4:20
Nahshon, and Nahshon *b* Salmon ...... Ruth 4:20
Salmon *b* Boaz, and Boaz *b* Obed...... Ruth 4:21
Obed *b* Jesse .... Ruth 4:22
and Jesse *b* David .... Ruth 4:22
And Cush *b* Nimrod 1Chr 1:10
Mizraim *b* Ludim, and...................... 1Chr 1:11
Canaan *b* Zidon his firstborn, and...... 1Chr 1:13
And Arphaxad *b* Shelah 1Chr 1:18
and Shelah *b* Eber 1Chr 1:18
Joktan *b* Almodad, and Sheleph, and.. 1Chr 1:20
And Abraham *b* Isaac........................ 1Chr 1:34
And Ram *b* Amminadab...................... 1Chr 2:10
and Amminadab *b* Nahshon 1Chr 2:10
And Nahshon *b* Salma 1Chr 2:11
and Salma *b* Boaz 1Chr 2:11
Boaz *b* Obed, and Obed *b* Jesse,...... 1Chr 2:12
Jesse *b* his firstborn Eliab, and 1Chr 2:13
Caleb the son of Hezron *b* 1Chr 2:18
Hur *b* Uri, and Uri *b* Bezaleel 1Chr 2:20
And Segub *b* Jair, who had three and.. 1Chr 2:22
Attai *b* Nathan 1Chr 2:36
and Nathan *b* Zabad 1Chr 2:36
Zabad *b* Ephlal................................ 1Chr 2:37
Ephlal *b* Obed 1Chr 2:37
And Obed *b* Jehu 1Chr 2:38
and Jehu *b* Azariah 1Chr 2:38
And Azariah *b* Helez 1Chr 2:39
and Helez *b* Eleasah 1Chr 2:39
And Eleasah *b* Sisamai 1Chr 2:40
and Sisamai *b* Shallum 1Chr 2:40
Shallum *b* Jekamiah.......................... 1Chr 2:41
and Jekamiah *b* Elishama 1Chr 2:41
And Shema *b* Raham, the father of 1Chr 2:44
and Rekem *b* Shammai...................... 1Chr 2:44
and Haran *b* Gazez 1Chr 2:46
Reaiah the son of Shobal *b* Jahath 1Chr 4:2
and Jahath *b* Ahumai, and Lahad........ 1Chr 4:2
Coz *b* Anub, and Zobebah, and the.... 1Chr 4:8
the brother of Shuah *b* Mehir 1Chr 4:11
Eshton *b* Beth-rapha, and Paseah,...... 1Chr 4:12
And Meonothai *b* Ophrah 1Chr 4:14
and Seraiah *b* Joab, the father of 1Chr 4:14
Eleazar *b* Phinehas 1Chr 6:4
Phinehas *b* Abishua 1Chr 6:4
And Abishua *b* Bukki........................ 1Chr 6:5
and Bukki *b* Uzzi.............................. 1Chr 6:5
And Uzzi *b* Zerahiah........................ 1Chr 6:6
and Zerahiah *b* Meraioth 1Chr 6:6
Meraioth *b* Amariah.......................... 1Chr 6:7
and Amariah *b* Ahitub...................... 1Chr 6:7
And Ahitub *b* Zadok.......................... 1Chr 6:8
and Zadok *b* Ahimaaz 1Chr 6:8
And Ahimaaz *b* Azariah 1Chr 6:9
and Azariah *b* Johanan 1Chr 6:9
And Johanan *b* Azariah, (he it is 1Chr 6:10
And Azariah *b* Amariah 1Chr 6:11
and Amariah *b* Ahitub 1Chr 6:11
And Ahitub *b* Zadok.......................... 1Chr 6:12
and Zadok *b* Shallum........................ 1Chr 6:12
And Shallum *b* Hilkiah...................... 1Chr 6:13
and Hilkiah *b* Azariah 1Chr 6:13
And Azariah *b* Seraiah...................... 1Chr 6:14
and Seraiah *b* Jehozadak 1Chr 6:14
Heber *b* Japhlet, and Shomer, and 1Chr 7:32
Now Benjamin *b* Bela his firstborn 1Chr 8:1
them, and *b* Uzza, and Ahihud............ 1Chr 8:7
Shaharaim *b* children in the 1Chr 8:8
he *b* of Hodesh his wife, Jobab, ... 1Chr 8:9
And of Hushim he *b* Abitub, and 1Chr 8:11

And Mikloth *b* Shimeah 1Chr 8:32
And Ner *b* Kish, and Kish *b* Saul 1Chr 8:33
Saul *b* Jonathan, and Malchi-shua,...... 1Chr 8:33
and Merib-baal *b* Micah.................... 1Chr 8:34
And Ahaz *b* Jehoadah........................ 1Chr 8:36
and Jehoadah *b* Alemeth, and............ 1Chr 8:36
and Zimri *b* Moza,............................ 1Chr 8:36
And Moza *b* Binea 1Chr 8:37
And Mikloth *b* Shimeam 1Chr 9:38
And Ner *b* Kish 1Chr 9:39
and Kish *b* Saul................................ 1Chr 9:39
Saul *b* Jonathan, and Malchi-shua,...... 1Chr 9:39
and Merib-baal *b* Micah.................... 1Chr 9:40
And Ahaz *b* Jarah 1Chr 9:42
Jarah *b* Alemeth, and Azmaveth, and.. 1Chr 9:42
and Zimri *b* Moza 1Chr 9:42
And Moza *b* Binea 1Chr 9:43
David *b* more sons and daughters 1Chr 14:3
b twenty and eight sons, and.............. 2Chr 11:21
b twenty and two sons, and sixteen.... 2Chr 13:21
and he *b* sons and daughters 2Chr 24:3
Jeshua *b* Joiakim .... Neh 12:10
Joiakim also *b* Eliashib...................... Neh 12:10
and Eliashib *b* Joiada........................ Neh 12:10
Joiada *b* Jonathan .... Neh 12:11
and Jonathan *b* Jaddua...................... Neh 12:11
unto thy father that *b* thee................ Prov 23:22
fathers that *b* them in this land.......... Jer 16:3
brought her, and he that *b* her .... Dan 11:6
his mother that *b* him shall say.......... Zec 13:3
his mother that *b* him shall .... Zec 13:3
and Isaac *b* Jacob .... Mt 1:2
and Jacob *b* Judas and his brethren.... Mt 1:2
Judas *b* Phares and Zara of Thamar .... Mt 1:3
and Phares *b* Esrom.......................... Mt 1:3
and Esrom *b* Aram .... Mt 1:3
And Aram *b* Aminadab........................ Mt 1:4
and Aminadab *b* Naasson.................... Mt 1:4
and Naasson *b* Salmon...................... Mt 1:4
and Salmon *b* Booz of Rachab .... Mt 1:5
and Booz *b* Obed of Ruth .... Mt 1:5
and Obed *b* Jesse .... Mt 1:5
And Jesse *b* David the king .... Mt 1:6
David the king *b* Solomon of her .... Mt 1:6
and Solomon *b* Roboam .... Mt 1:7
and Roboam *b* Abia............................ Mt 1:7
and Abia *b* Asaph.............................. Mt 1:7
And Asa *b* Josaphat .... Mt 1:8
and Josaphat *b* Joram........................ Mt 1:8
and Joram *b* Ozias .... Mt 1:8
And Ozias *b* Joatham.......................... Mt 1:9
and Joatham *b* Achaz .... Mt 1:9
and Achaz *b* Ezekias.......................... Mt 1:9
And Ezekias *b* Manasses.................... Mt 1:10
and Manasses *b* Amon........................ Mt 1:10
and Amon *b* Josias .... Mt 1:10
Josias *b* Jechonias and his .... Mt 1:11
to Babylon, Jechonias *b* Salathiel........ Mt 1:12
and Salathiel *b* Zorobabel.................. Mt 1:12
And Zorobabel *b* Abiud...................... Mt 1:13
and Abiud *b* Eliakim.......................... Mt 1:13
and Eliakim *b* Azor............................ Mt 1:13
And Azor *b* Sadoc .... Mt 1:14
and Sadoc *b* Achim............................ Mt 1:14
and Achim *b* Eliud .... Mt 1:14
And Eliud *b* Eleazar .... Mt 1:15
and Eleazar *b* Matthan...................... Mt 1:15
and Matthan *b* Jacob........................ Mt 1:15
Jacob *b* Joseph the husband of .... Mt 1:16
and so Abraham *b* Isaac, and .... Acts 7:8
and Isaac *b* Jacob .... Acts 7:8
Jacob *b* the twelve patriarchs............ Acts 7:8
of Madian, where he *b* two sons .... Acts 7:29
Of his own will *b* he us with the .... Jas 1:18
that loveth him also that is.................. 1Jn 5:1

BEGET

twelve princes shall he *b* .... Gen 17:20
When thou shalt *b* children................ Deut 4:25
Thou shalt *b* sons and daughters,........ Deut 28:41
from thee, which thou shalt *b*.............. 2Kin 20:18
if a man *b* an hundred children,.......... Eccl 6:3
from thee, which thou shalt *b*.............. Is 39:7
ye wives, and *b* sons and daughters .... Jer 29:6
If he *b* a son that is a robber, a.......... Eze 18:10
Now, lo, if he *b* a son, that .... Eze 18:14
which shall *b* children among you ...... Eze 47:22

BEGETTEST

issue, which thou *b* after them .... Gen 48:6
unto his father, What *b* thou.............. Is 45:10

BEGETTETH

He that *b* a fool doeth it to his .... Prov 17:21
he that *b* a wise child shall have .... Prov 23:24
he *b* a son, and there is nothing.......... Eccl 5:14

BEGGAR

lifteth up the *b* from the.................... 1Sa 2:8
was a certain *b* named Lazarus .... Lk 16:20
it came to pass, that the *b* died .... Lk 16:22

BEGGARLY

b elements, whereunto ye desire.......... Gal 4:9

BEGGED

to Pilate, and *b* the body of Jesus...... Mt 27:58
Pilate, and *b* the body of Jesus .... Lk 23:52
Is not this he that sat and *b*.............. Jn 9:8

BEGGING

forsaken, nor his seed *b* bread............ Ps 37:25
sat by the highway side *b* .... Mk 10:46
blind man sat by the way side *b*.......... Lk 18:35

BEGIN

and this they *b* to do........................ Gen 11:6
b to possess it, and contend with........ Deut 2:24
This day will I *b* to put the .... Deut 2:25
b to possess, that thou mayest............ Deut 2:31
b to number the seven weeks from...... Deut 16:9
This day will I *b* to magnify thee .... Josh 3:7
What man is he that will *b* to.............. Judg 10:18
he shall *b* to deliver Israel out .... Judg 13:5
when I *b*, I will also make an end........ 1Sa 3:12
Did I then *b* to enquire of God 1Sa 22:15
Jehoram king of Judah *b* to reign........ 2Kin 8:25
was the principal to *b* the .... Neh 11:17
I *b* to bring evil on the city................ Jer 25:29
and *b* at my sanctuary........................ Eze 9:6
And shall *b* to smite his .... Mt 24:49
b not to say within yourselves,............ Lk 3:8
shall *b* to beat the menservants .... Lk 12:45
ye *b* to stand without, and to.............. Lk 13:25
Then shall ye *b* to say, We have .... Lk 13:26
thou *b* with shame to take the .... Lk 14:9
all that behold it *b* to mock him .... Lk 14:29
these things *b* to come to pass .... Lk 21:28
Then shall they *b* to say to the .... Lk 23:30
Do we *b* again to commend................ 2Cor 3:1
must *b* at the house of God................ 1Pet 4:17
and if it first *b* at us, what.................. 1Pet 4:17
angel, when he shall *b* to sound.......... Rev 10:7

BEGINNEST

weeks from such time as thou *b* to...... Deut 16:9

BEGINNING

In the *b* God created the heaven........ Gen 1:1
the *b* of his kingdom was Babel,.......... Gen 10:10
where his tent had been at the *b* .... Gen 13:3
still *b* favoured, as at the *b*.............. Gen 41:21
the *b* of my strength, the .... Gen 49:3
shall be unto you the *b* of months........ Ex 12:2
from the *b* of the year even unto........ Deut 11:12
for he is the *b* of his strength .... Deut 21:17
from the *b* of revenges upon the........ Deut 32:42
camp in the *b* of the middle watch ...... Judg 7:19
in the *b* of barley harvest .... Ruth 1:22
in the latter end than at the *b*............ Ruth 3:10
in the *b* of barley harvest 2Sa 21:9
from the *b* of harvest until water 2Sa 21:10
so it was at the *b* of their.................. 2Kin 17:25
waste them any more, as at the *b*........ 1Chr 17:9
in the *b* of his reign, wrote they .... Ezr 4:6
Though thy *b* was small, yet thy .... Job 8:7
latter end of Job more than his *b*........ Job 42:12
of the LORD is the *b* of wisdom .... Ps 111:10
Thy word is true from the *b*................ Ps 119:160
of the LORD is the *b* of knowledge ...... Prov 1:7
possessed me in the *b* of his way .... Prov 8:22
up from everlasting, from the *b*.......... Prov 8:23
of the LORD is the *b* of wisdom .... Prov 9:10
The *b* of strife is as when one .... Prov 17:14
may be gotten hastily at the *b* .... Prov 20:21
God maketh from the *b* to the end...... Eccl 3:11
end of a thing than the *b* thereof........ Eccl 7:8
The *b* of the words of his mouth.......... Eccl 10:13
and thy counsellors as at the *b* .... Is 1:26
terrible from their *b* hitherto.............. Is 18:2
terrible from their *b* hitherto .... Is 18:7
it not been told you from the *b*............ Is 40:21
the generations from the *b*.................. Is 41:4
Who hath declared from the *b* .... Is 41:26
Declaring the end from the *b*.............. Is 46:10
the former things from the *b*................ Is 48:3
from the *b* declared it to thee............ Is 48:5
created now, and not from the *b* .... Is 48:7
not spoken in secret from the *b*.......... Is 48:16
For since the *b* of the world men .... Is 64:4
b is the place of our sanctuary............ Jer 17:12
In the *b* of the reign of .... Jer 26:1
In the *b* of the reign of .... Jer 27:1
In the *b* of the reign of Zedekiah........ Jer 28:1
b of the reign of Zedekiah king .... Jer 49:34
in the *b* of the watches pour out .... Lam 2:19
in the *b* of the year, in the................ Eze 40:1
I had seen in the vision at the *b*.......... Dan 9:21
At the *b* of thy supplications the........ Dan 9:23
The *b* of the word of the LORD by ...... Hos 1:2
the *b* of the shooting up of the .... Amos 7:1
she is the *b* of the sin to the .... Mic 1:13
b to sink, he cried, saying, Lord .... Mt 14:30
made them at the *b* made them male.... Mt 19:4
but from the *b* it was not so .... Mt 19:8
b from the last unto the first.............. Mt 20:8
All these are the *b* of sorrows............ Mt 24:8
the *b* of the world to this time .... Mt 24:21
The *b* of the gospel of Jesus.............. Mk 1:1
But from the *b* of the creation .... Mk 10:6
such as was not from the *b* of the...... Mk 13:19
unto us, which from the *b* were .... Lk 1:2
from Galilee to this place .... Lk 23:5
b at Moses and all the prophets,........ Lk 24:27
among all nations, *b* at Jerusalem ...... Lk 24:47
In the *b* was the Word, and the .... Jn 1:1
The same was in the *b* with God.......... Jn 1:2
Every man at the *b* doth set forth........ Jn 2:10
This *b* of miracles did Jesus in .... Jn 2:11
For Jesus knew from the *b* who .... Jn 6:64
b at the eldest, even unto the............ Jn 8:9
that I said unto you from the *b*............ Jn 8:25

He was a murderer from the *b* .... Jn 8:44
ye have been with me from the *b* .... Jn 15:27
I said not unto you at the *b* .... Jn 16:4
B from the baptism of John, unto ...... Acts 1:22
rehearsed the matter from the *b* .... Acts 11:4
fell on them, as on us at the *b* .... Acts 11:15
his works from the *b* of the world ...... Acts 15:18
Which knew me from the *b*, if they ... Acts 26:5
which from the *b* of the world .... Eph 3:9
that in the *b* of the gospel, when ...... Phil 4:15
who is the *b*, the firstborn from ...... Col 1:18
because God hath from the *b* 2Th 2:13
in the *b* hast laid the foundation ...... Heb 1:10
Christ, if we hold the *b* of our .... Heb 3:14
descent, having neither *b* of days ..... Heb 7:3
end is worse with them than the *b* 2Pet 2:20
were from the *b* of the creation 2Pet 3:4
That which was from the *b* 1Jn 1:1
which ye had from the *b* 1Jn 2:7
yet which ye have heard from the *b* 1Jn 2:7
have known him that is from the *b* ... 1Jn 2:13
have known him that is from the *b* ... 1Jn 2:14
which ye have heard from the *b* 1Jn 2:24
from the *b* shall remain in you 1Jn 2:24
for the devil sinneth from the *b* 1Jn 3:8
message that ye heard from the *b* 1Jn 3:11
but that which we had from the *b* 2Jn 5
That, as ye have heard from the *b* 2Jn 6
I am Alpha and Omega, the *b* .... Rev 1:8
the *b* of the creation of God .... Rev 3:14
I am Alpha and Omega, the *b* .... Rev 21:6
I am Alpha and Omega, the *b* .... Rev 22:13

BEGINNINGS
in the *b* of your months, ye shall ...... Num 10:10
in the *b* of your months ye shall ...... Num 28:11
do better unto you that at your *b* ...... Eze 36:11
these are the *b* of sorrows .... Mk 13:8

BEGOTTEN
b Seth were eight hundred years ...... Gen 5:4
b of thy father, she is thy .... Lev 18:11
have I *b* them, that thou .... Num 11:12
The children that are *b* of them ...... Deut 23:8
and ten sons of his body *b* .... Judg 8:30
or who hath *b* the drops of dew .... Job 38:28
this day have I *b* thee .... Ps 2:7
thine heart, Who hath *b* me these ..... Is 49:21
for they have *b* strange children ..... Hos 5:7
as of the only *b* of the Father .... Jn 1:14
the only *b* Son, which is in the ...... Jn 1:18
that he gave his only *b* Son .... Jn 3:16
the name of the only *b* Son of God .... Jn 3:18
my Son, this day have I *b* thee .... Acts 13:33
I have *b* you through the gospel 1Cor 4:15
whom I have *b* in my bonds .... Philem 10
my Son, this day have I *b* thee .... Heb 1:5
art my Son, to day have I *b* thee ..... Heb 5:5
offered up his only *b* son .... Heb 11:17
to his abundant mercy hath *b* us 1Pet 1:3
his only *b* Son into the world 1Jn 4:9
loveth him also that is *b* of him 1Jn 5:1
but he that is *b* of God keepeth 1Jn 5:18
the first *b* of the dead, and the ...... Rev 1:5

BEGUILE
lest any man should *b* you with .... Col 2:4
Let no man *b* you of your reward ...... Col 2:18

BEGUILED
the woman said, The serpent *b* me .... Gen 3:13
wherefore then hast thou *b* me ...... Gen 29:25
wherewith they have *b* you in the ..... Num 25:18
saying, Wherefore have ye *b* us .... Josh 9:22
as the serpent *b* Eve through his 2Cor 11:3

BEGUILING
b unstable souls 2Pet 2:14

BEGUN
the plague is *b* .... Num 16:46
the plague was *b* among the people .... Num 16:47
I have *b* to give Sihon and his ...... Deut 2:31
thou hast *b* to shew thy servant ...... Deut 3:24
before whom thou hast *b* to fall ...... Est 6:13
undertook to do as they had *b* ...... Est 9:23
And when he had *b* to reckon .... Mt 18:24
desired Titus, that as he had *b* 2Cor 8:6
for you, who have *b* before 2Cor 8:10
having *b* in the Spirit, are ye ...... Gal 3:3
that he which hath *b* a good work ...... Phil 1:6
for when they have *b* to wax 1Ti 5:11

BEHALF
the *b* of the children of Israel .... Ex 27:21
sent messengers to David on his *b* 2Sa 3:12
to shew himself strong in the *b* 2Chr 16:9
I have yet to speak on God's *b* ...... Job 36:2
own *b* shall cause the reproach ...... Dan 11:18
I am glad therefore on your *b* ...... Rom 16:19
I thank my God always on your *b* 1Cor 1:4
may be given by many on our *b* 2Cor 1:11
you occasion to glory on our *b* 2Cor 5:12
and of our boasting on your *b* 2Cor 9:3
you should be in vain in this *b* 2Cor 9:3
it is given in the *b* of Christ ...... Phil 1:29
but let him glorify God on this *b* 1Pet 4:16

BEHAVE
should *b* themselves strangely .... Deut 32:27
let us *b* ourselves valiantly for 1Chr 19:13
I will *b* myself wisely in a ...... Ps 101:2
the child shall *b* himself proudly ...... Is 3:5
Doth not *b* itself unseemly, ... 1Cor 13:5

know how thou oughtest to *b* 1Ti 3:15

BEHAVED
sent him, and *b* himself wisely 1Sa 18:5
David *b* himself wisely in all his 1Sa 18:14
saw that he *b* himself very wisely 1Sa 18:15
that David *b* himself more wisely 1Sa 18:30
I *b* myself as though he had been ..... Ps 35:14
Surely I have *b* and quieted myself .... Ps 131:2
as they have *b* themselves ill in ...... Mic 3:4
unblameably we *b* ourselves among 1Th 2:10
for we *b* not ourselves disorderly 2Th 3:7

BEHAVETH
he *b* himself uncomely toward his 1Cor 7:36

BEHAVIOUR
And he changed his *b* before them 1Sa 21:13
he changed his *b* before Abimelech .... Ps 34:t
wife, vigilant, sober, of good *b* 1Ti 3:2
that they be in *b* as becometh ...... Titus 2:3

BEHEADED
heifer that is *b* in the valley ...... Deut 21:6
b him, and took his head, and gat 2Sa 4:7
he sent, and *b* John in the prison ..... Mt 14:10
he said, It is John, whom I *b* .... Mk 6:16
he went and *b* him in the prison, ... Mk 6:27
And Herod said, John have I *b* ...... Lk 9:9
were *b* for the witness of Jesus ...... Rev 20:4

BEHELD
the Egyptians *b* the woman that ...... Gen 12:14
b all the plain of Jordan, that ...... Gen 13:10
all the land of the plain, and *b* ...... Gen 19:28
Jacob *b* the countenance of Laban, ... Gen 31:2
Israel *b* Joseph's sons, and said, ... Gen 48:8
when he *b* the serpent of brass, ... Num 21:9
He hath not *b* iniquity in Jacob, ... Num 23:21
that *b* while Samson made sport ...... Judg 16:27
David *b* the place where Saul lay, ... 1Sa 26:5
as he was destroying, the LORD *b* 1Chr 21:15
I *b* the earth, and, lo, it was ...... Job 31:26
I *b* the transgressors, and was ...... Ps 119:158
I looked on my right hand, and *b* ..... Ps 142:4
b among the simple ones, ... Prov 7:7
Then I *b* all the work of God, ... Eccl 8:17
For I *b*, and there was no man ...... Is 41:28
I *b* the earth, and, lo, it was ...... Jer 4:23
I *b* the mountains, and, lo, they ..... Jer 4:24
b, and, lo, there was no man, and .... Jer 4:25
I *b*, and, lo, the fruitful place, ... Jer 4:26
Upon this I awaked, and *b* .... Jer 31:26
Now as I *b* the living creatures, ... Eze 1:15
Then I *b*, and lo a likeness as the .... Eze 8:2
And when I *b*, lo, the sinews and ..... Eze 37:8
I *b* till the wings thereof were ...... Dan 7:4
After this I *b*, and lo another, ... Dan 7:6
I *b* till the thrones were cast ...... Dan 7:9
I *b* then because of the voice of ..... Dan 7:11
I *b* even till the beast was slain ..... Dan 7:11
b, and the same horn made war ..... Dan 7:21
he *b*, and drove asunder the .... Hab 3:6
But Jesus *b* them, and said unto ..... Mt 19:26
all the people, when they *b* him, ... Mk 9:15
b how the people cast money into .... Mk 12:41
of Joses *b* where he was laid .... Mk 15:47
I *b* Satan as lightning fall from ..... Lk 10:18
he *b* the city, and wept over it, ... Lk 19:41
he *b* them, and said, What is this ...... Lk 20:17
But a certain maid *b* him as he ...... Lk 22:56
b the sepulchre, and how his body .... Lk 23:55
he *b* the linen clothes laid by .... Lk 24:12
we *b* his glory, the glory as of ...... Jn 1:14
And when Jesus *b* him, he said, ... Jn 1:42
spoken these things, while they *b* .... Acts 1:9
b your devotions, I found an .... Acts 17:23
And I *b*, and, lo, in the midst of ..... Rev 5:6
And I *b*, and I heard the voice of .... Rev 5:11
And I *b*, and lo a black horse ...... Rev 6:5
b when he had opened the sixth ..... Rev 6:12
After this I *b*, and lo, a great ...... Rev 7:9
And I *b*, and heard an angel flying, ... Rev 8:13
and their enemies *b* them .... Rev 11:12
I *b* another beast coming up out ..... Rev 13:11

BEHEMOTH
Behold now *b*, which I made with .... Job 40:15

BEHIND
in the tent door, which was *b* him ..... Gen 18:10
look not *b* thee, neither stay ...... Gen 19:17
his wife looked back from *b* him ..... Gen 19:26
behold *b* him a ram caught in a ...... Gen 22:13
and, behold, also he is *b* .... Gen 32:18
Behold, thy servant Jacob is *b* us .... Gen 32:20
there shall not an hoof be left *b* ..... Ex 10:26
maidservant that is *b* the mill .... Ex 11:5
of Israel, removed and went *b* them .... Ex 14:19
their face, and stood *b* them ...... Ex 14:19
If there be yet many years *b* .... Lev 25:51
pitch the tabernacle westward ...... Num 3:23
even all that were feeble *b* these .... Deut 25:18
thee an ambush for the city *b* it, ... Josh 8:2
against the city, even *b* the city, ... Josh 8:4
in ambush against him *b* the city, ... Josh 8:14
when the men of Ai looked *b* them .... Josh 8:20
behold, it is *b* Kirjath-jearim .... Judg 18:12
the Benjamites looked *b* them ...... Judg 20:40
wrapped in a cloth *b* the ephod 1Sa 21:9
And when Saul looked *b* him 1Sa 24:8
those that were left *b* stayed 1Sa 30:9
for two hundred abode *b*, which 1Sa 30:10

And when he looked *b* him, he saw 2Sa 1:7
Then Abner looked *b* him, and said, ... 2Sa 2:20
that the spear came out *b* him 2Sa 2:23
along weeping *b* her to Bahurim 2Sa 3:16
but fetch a compass *b* them 2Sa 5:23
was against him before and *b* 2Sa 10:9
by the way of the hill side *b* him 2Sa 13:34
the top of the throne was round *b* 1Kin 10:19
anger, and hast cast me *b* thy back 1Kin 14:9
sound of his master's feet *b* him 2Kin 6:32
turn thee *b* me 2Kin 9:18
turn thee *b* me 2Kin 9:19
part at the gate *b* the guard 2Kin 11:6
was set against him before and *b* 1Chr 19:10
ambushment to come about *b* them 2Chr 13:13
and the ambushment was *b* them 2Chr 13:13
the battle was before and *b* 2Chr 13:14
I in the lower places *b* the wall ..... Neh 4:13
the rulers were *b* all the house ...... Neh 4:16
and cast thy law *b* their backs ...... Neh 9:26
and castest my words *b* thee .... Ps 50:17
Thou hast beset me *b* and before, ... Ps 139:5
behold, he standeth *b* our wall ...... Song 2:9
before, and the Philistines *b* .... Is 9:12
ears shall hear a word *b* thee .... Is 30:21
hast cast all my sins *b* thy back ..... Is 38:17
B the doors also and the posts .... Is 57:8
gardens *b* one tree in the midst ..... Is 66:17
I heard *b* me a voice of a great ...... Eze 3:12
cast me *b* thy back, therefore ...... Eze 23:35
the separate place which was *b* it ..... Eze 41:15
and *b* them a flame burneth .... Joel 2:3
b them a desolate wilderness .... Joel 2:3
repent, and leave a blessing *b* him .... Joel 2:14
b him were there red horses, ... Zec 1:8
of blood twelve years, came *b* him .... Mt 9:20
and said unto Peter, Get thee *b* me .... Mt 16:23
of Jesus, came in the press *b* .... Mk 5:27
Peter, saying, Get thee *b* me .... Mk 8:33
die, and leave his wife *b* him .... Mk 12:19
Jesus tarried *b* in Jerusalem .... Lk 2:43
and said unto him, Get thee *b* me .... Lk 4:8
stood at his feet *b* him weeping ..... Lk 7:38
Came *b* him, and touched the border .... Lk 8:44
So that ye come *b* in no gift 1Cor 1:7
whit *b* the very chiefest apostles 2Cor 11:5
for in nothing am I *b* the very 2Cor 12:11
those things which are *b*, and ...... Phil 3:13
fill up that which is *b* of the ...... Col 1:24
heard *b* me a great voice, as of a .... Rev 1:10
beasts full of eyes before and *b* ..... Rev 4:6

BEHOLD See PREFACE.
thing that he had made, and *b* .... Gen 1:31
And, *b*, I am with thee, and will ..... Gen 28:15
And the LORD said unto Satan, *B* ..... Job 1:12
And unto man he said, *B*, the fear .... Job 28:28
man may *b* it afar off .... Job 36:25
B, I am vile .... Job 40:4
if I make my bed in hell, *b* .... Ps 139:8
A virgin shall conceive, and .... Is 7:14
B, I and the children whom the ...... Is 8:18
B, God is my salvation .... Is 12:2
the cities of Judah, *B* your God ...... Is 40:9
shall say to Zion, *B*, *b* them .... Is 41:27
b, it is I .... Is 52:6
B me, *b* me, unto a nation .... Is 65:1
B, I am the LORD, the God of all ..... Jer 32:27
b, and see if there be any sorrow .... Lam 1:12
b, thy King cometh unto thee ...... Zec 9:9
B, a virgin shall be with child ..... Mt 1:23
Tell ye the daughter of Sion, *B* ..... Mt 21:5
b the place where they laid him ..... Mk 16:6
And, *b*, thou shalt conceive in thy .... Lk 1:31
for, *b*, I bring you good tidings ...... Lk 2:10
B my hands and my feet, that it is .... Lk 24:39
And, *b*, I send the promise of my .... Lk 24:49
B the Lamb of God, which taketh ..... Jn 1:36
he saith, *B* the Lamb of God .... Jn 1:29
b, thy King cometh, sitting on an .... Jn 12:15
Pilate saith unto them, *B* the man .... Jn 19:5
saith unto the Jews, *B* your King ..... Jn 19:14
unto his mother, Woman, *b* thy son .... Jn 19:26
he to the disciple, *B* thy mother ...... Jn 19:27
And said, *B*, I see the heavens ..... Acts 7:56
for, *b*, he prayeth .... Acts 9:11
b, all things are become new 2Cor 5:17
b, now is the accepted time 2Cor 6:2
b, now is the day of salvation 2Cor 6:2
B, what manner of love the Father 1Jn 3:1
B, I come quickly .... Rev 3:11
B, I stand at the door, and knock .... Rev 3:20
B, I come as a thief .... Rev 16:15
voice out of heaven saying, *B* ...... Rev 21:3
that sat upon the throne said, *B* ..... Rev 21:5
B, I come quickly .... Rev 22:7

BEHOLDEST
for thou *b* mischief and spite, to ..... Ps 10:14
why *b* thou the mote that is in ..... Mt 7:3
why *b* thou the mote that is in ..... Lk 6:41
when thou thyself *b* not the beam .... Lk 6:42

BEHOLDETH
he *b* not the way of the vineyards .... Job 24:18
He *b* all high things .... Job 41:34
he *b* all the sons of men .... Ps 33:13
For he *b* himself, and goeth his ..... Jas 1:24

BEHOLDING
Turn away mine eyes from *b* vanity .... Ps 119:37
place, *b* the evil and the good ...... Prov 15:3

saving the *b* of them with their............ Eccl 5:11
many women were there *b* afar off........ Mt 27:55
Then Jesus *b* him loved him, and.......... Mk 10:21
And the people stood *b*...................... Lk 23:35
b the things which were done,............. Lk 23:48
stood afar off, *b* these things.............. Lk 23:49
b the man which was healed................ Acts 4:14
b the miracles and signs which............ Acts 8:13
who stedfastly *b* him, and.................. Acts 14:9
earnestly *b* the council, said,.............. Acts 23:1
with open face *b* as in a glass............. 2Cor 3:18
b your order, and the stedfastness........ Col 2:5
he is like unto a man *b* his................. Jas 1:23

BEHOVED
thus it *b* Christ to suffer, and to.......... Lk 24:46
Wherefore in all things it *b* him........... Heb 2:17

BEING
have pleasure, my lord *b* old also......... Gen 18:12
the LORD *b* merciful unto him............. Gen 19:16
his son Isaac *b* eight days old.............. Gen 21:4
I *b* in the way, the LORD led me............ Gen 24:27
I *b* few in number, they shall.............. Gen 34:30
his people, *b* old and full of days......... Gen 35:29
b seventeen years old, was................. Gen 37:2
b an hundred and ten years old............ Gen 50:26
their kneadingtroughs *b* bound up........ Ex 12:34
that openeth the matrix, *b* males.......... Ex 13:15
the owner thereof *b* not with it........... Ex 22:14
Foursquare it shall be *b* doubled.......... Ex 28:16
of them that cry for *b* overcome........... Ex 32:18
the breadth thereof, *b* doubled............ Ex 39:9
b a chief man among his people,........... Lev 21:4
b taken from the children of the........... Lev 24:8
princes of Israel, *b* twelve men............ Num 1:44
a wall *b* on this side, and a wall........... Num 22:24
b in her father's house in her.............. Num 30:3
b yet in her youth in her................... Num 30:16
the rest of the prey which the.............. Num 31:32
Baal-meon, (their names *b* changed....... Num 32:38
the kingdom of Og, gave I unto............. Deut 3:13
b matters of controversy within.......... Deut 17:8
she cried not, *b* in the city,............... Deut 22:24
our enemies themselves *b* judges......... Deut 32:31
of you be freed from *b* bondmen.......... Josh 9:23
Aaron, *b* of the families of the........... Josh 21:10
b an hundred and ten years old........... Josh 24:29
b an hundred and ten years old........... Judg 2:8
b threescore and ten persons, upon....... Judg 9:5
b a child, girded with a linen............. 1Sa 2:18
also rejected that from *b* king............ 1Sa 15:23
thee from *b* king over Israel.............. 1Sa 15:26
a great space *b* between them............. 1Sa 26:13
of salt, *b* eighteen thousand men......... 2Sa 8:13
the king's son, lean from *b*............... 2Sa 13:4
b stronger than she, forced her,.......... 2Sa 13:14
as people *b* ashamed steal away........... 2Sa 19:3
he *b* girded with a sword,................. 2Sa 21:16
noise of the city *b* in an uproar.......... 1Kin 1:41
from *b* priest unto the LORD.............. 1Kin 2:27
Hadad *b* yet a little child................. 1Kin 11:17
even her he removed from *b* queen....... 1Kin 15:13
in *b* like the house of Jeroboam.......... 1Kin 16:7
of Israel, *b* seven thousand.............. 1Kin 20:15
Jehoshaphat *b* then king of Judah,........ 2Kin 8:16
b seventy persons, were with the......... 2Kin 10:6
b told, into the hands of them........... 2Kin 12:11
b over the host of the LORD, were........ 1Chr 9:19
household *b* taken for Eleazar............ 1Chr 24:6
b arrayed in white linen, having......... 2Chr 5:12
men, *b* mighty men of valour............. 2Chr 13:3
king, he removed her from *b* queen....... 2Chr 15:16
and departed without *b* desired.......... 2Chr 21:20
in a several house, *b* a leper............. 2Chr 26:21
b set up, let him be hanged.............. Ezr 6:11
b guilty, they offered a ram of.......... Ezr 10:19
b as I am, would go into the............. Neh 6:11
of the provinces, *b* before him........... Est 1:3
(the vessels *b* diverse one from.......... Est 1:7
out, *b* hastened by the king's............ Est 3:15
b hastened and pressed on by the........ Est 8:14
who ever perished, *b* innocent........... Job 4:7
b wholly at ease and quiet.............. Job 21:23
Job died, *b* old and full of days......... Job 42:17
Nevertheless man *b* in honour........... Ps 49:12
b girded with power..................... Ps 65:6
b mine enemies wrongfully, are......... Ps 69:4
b armed, and carrying bows, turned..... Ps 78:9
b full of compassion, forgave.......... Ps 78:38
us cut them off from *b* a nation........ Ps 83:4
to my God while I have my *b*........... Ps 104:33
b bound in affliction and iron......... Ps 107:10
see my substance, yet *b* unperfect...... Ps 139:16
unto my God while I have any *b*........ Ps 146:2
shall keep thy foot from *b* taken....... Prov 3:26
that *b* often reproved hardeneth....... Prov 29:1
all hold swords, *b* expert in war....... Song 3:8
midst thereof *b* paved with love........ Song 3:10
she *b* desolate shall sit upon the...... Is 3:26
is taken away from *b* a city........... Is 17:1
or *b* his counsellor hath taught....... Is 40:13
but the sinner *b* an hundred years..... Is 65:20
Withhold thy foot from *b* unshod...... Jer 2:25
b desolate it mourneth unto me........ Jer 12:11
from *b* a pastor to follow thee........ Jer 17:16
b a nation before me for ever......... Jer 31:36
b an Hebrew or an Hebrewess, go,...... Jer 34:9
when he had taken him *b* bound in..... Jer 40:1
let us cut it off from *b* a nation..... Jer 48:2
be destroyed from *b* a people......... Jer 48:42

b planted, shall it prosper............ Eze 17:10
multitude *b* at ease was with her...... Eze 23:42
which *b* brought forth into the........ Eze 47:8
b in the midst of that which is....... Eze 48:22
b gathered together, saw these........ Dan 3:27
b about threescore and two years...... Dan 5:31
his windows *b* open in his chamber..... Dan 6:10
Now that *b* broken, whereas four....... Dan 8:22
b caused to fly swiftly, touched...... Dan 9:21
b a just man, and not willing to...... Mt 1:19
Then Joseph *b* raised from sleep....... Mt 1:24
b warned of God in a dream that....... Mt 2:12
b warned of God in a dream, he........ Mt 2:22
b evil, know how to give good......... Mt 7:11
b evil, speak good things............. Mt 12:34
b before instructed of her mother..... Mt 14:8
b grieved for the hardness of........ Mk 3:5
b interpreted, Damsel, I say unto..... Mk 5:41
saying the multitude *b* very great..... Mk 8:1
b in the house he asked them,......... Mk 9:33
b in Bethany in the house of......... Mk 14:3
b interpreted, The place of a........ Mk 15:22
b interpreted, My God, my God,....... Mk 15:34
b delivered out of the hand of....... Lk 1:74
espoused wife, *b* great with child..... Lk 2:5
Pontius Pilate *b* governor of......... Lk 3:1
Herod *b* tetrarch of Galilee, and..... Lk 3:1
Caiaphas *b* the high priests, the..... Lk 3:2
b reproved by him for Herodias....... Lk 3:19
past, that Jesus also *b* baptized..... Lk 3:21
b (as was supposed) the son of...... Lk 3:23
Jesus *b* full of the Holy Ghost...... Lk 4:1
b forty days tempted of the devil.... Lk 4:2
synagogues, *b* glorified of all....... Lk 4:15
b baptized with the baptism of...... Lk 7:29
themselves, *b* not baptized of him.... Lk 7:30
they *b* afraid wondered, saying...... Lk 8:25
b evil, know how to give good....... Lk 11:13
a daughter of Abraham, whom.......... Lk 13:16
house *b* angry said to his servant.... Lk 14:21
b in torments, and seeth Abraham.... Lk 16:23
of God, *b* the children of the....... Lk 20:36
b brought before kings and rulers.... Lk 21:12
b of the number of the twelve....... Lk 22:23
b in an agony he prayed more........ Lk 22:44
b interpreted, Master, where........ Jn 1:38
b interpreted, the Christ........... Jn 1:41
b wearied with his journey, sat..... Jn 4:6
b a Jew, askest drink of me,........ Jn 4:9
b a multitude in that place........ Jn 5:13
betray him, *b* one of the twelve.... Jn 6:71
Jesus by night, *b* one of them,).... Jn 7:50
it, *b* convicted by their own....... Jn 8:9
b a man, makest thyself God........ Jn 10:33
the high priest that same year,...... Jn 11:49
but *b* high priest that year, he..... Jn 11:51
And supper *b* ended, the devil...... Jn 13:2
unto you, *b* yet present with you.... Jn 14:25
b his kinsman whose ear Peter cut... Jn 18:26
b a disciple of Jesus, but......... Jn 19:38
b the first day of the week, when... Jn 20:19
then came Jesus, the doors *b* shut.. Jn 20:26
b seen of them forty days, and..... Acts 1:3
b assembled together with them,.... Acts 1:4
b delivered by the determinate..... Acts 2:23
Therefore *b* a prophet, and knowing.. Acts 2:30
Therefore *b* by the right hand of... Acts 2:33
hour of prayer, *b* the ninth hour... Acts 3:1
b grieved that they taught the..... Acts 4:2
b let go, they went to their own... Acts 4:23
b interpreted, The son of......... Acts 4:36
his wife also *b* privy to it....... Acts 5:2
b full of the Holy Ghost, looked... Acts 7:55
b sent forth by the Holy Ghost,.... Acts 13:4
b astonished at the doctrine of... Acts 13:12
b a cripple from his mother's..... Acts 14:8
b brought on their way by the..... Acts 15:3
b read in the synagogues every.... Acts 15:21
b assembled with one accord, to... Acts 15:25
b prophets also themselves,....... Acts 15:32
b recommended by the brethren..... Acts 15:40
b grieved, turned and said to the.. Acts 16:18
b Jews, do exceedingly trouble.... Acts 16:20
neither to observe, *b* Romans..... Acts 16:21
b Romans, and have cast us into... Acts 16:37
we live, and move, and have our *b*.. Acts 17:28
b fervent in the spirit, he spake.. Acts 18:25
there *b* no cause whereby we may... Acts 19:40
b fallen into a deep sleep....... Acts 20:9
b led by the hand of them that... Acts 21:11
b exceedingly mad against them, I. Acts 26:11
of Thessalonica, *b* with us....... Acts 27:2
b exceedingly tossed with a....... Acts 27:18
b understood by the things that.. Rom 1:20
b filled with all unrighteousness. Rom 1:29
b instructed out of the law...... Rom 2:18
b witnessed by the law and the... Rom 3:21
b justified freely by his grace.. Rom 3:24
which he had yet *b* uncircumcised. Rom 4:11
which he had *b* yet uncircumcised. Rom 4:12
And *b* not weak in faith, he...... Rom 4:19
b fully persuaded that, what he... Rom 4:21
Therefore *b* justified by faith,.. Rom 5:1
b now justified by his blood, we. Rom 5:9
b reconciled, we shall be saved.. Rom 5:10
Knowing that Christ *b* raised from. Rom 6:9
B then made free from sin, ye..... Rom 6:18
But now *b* made free from sin, and. Rom 6:22
that *b* dead wherein we were held. Rom 7:6

(For the children *b* not yet born.. Rom 9:11
For they *b* ignorant of God's..... Rom 10:3
b a wild olive tree, wert graffed. Rom 11:17
b many, are one body in Christ,.. Rom 12:5
b sanctified by the Holy Ghost... Rom 15:16
b reviled, we bless.............. 1Cor 4:12
b persecuted, we suffer it....... 1Cor 4:12
b defamed, we intreat............ 1Cor 4:13
Is any man called *b* circumcised.. 1Cor 7:18
Art thou called *b* a servant..... 1Cor 7:21
b a servant, is the Lord's....... 1Cor 7:22
b free, is Christ's servant...... 1Cor 7:22
conscience *b* weak is defiled..... 1Cor 8:7
(*b* not without law to God, but... 1Cor 9:21
For we *b* many are one bread, and. 1Cor 10:17
one body, *b* many, are one body). 1Cor 12:12
If so be that *b* clothed we shall. 2Cor 5:3
tabernacle do groan, *b* burdened.. 2Cor 5:4
but *b* more forward, of his own... 2Cor 8:17
b enriched in every thing to all. 2Cor 9:11
but *b* absent am bold toward you.. 2Cor 10:1
myself from *b* burdensome unto you. 2Cor 11:9
b crafty, I caught you with guile. 2Cor 12:16
b absent now I write to them..... 2Cor 13:2
I write these things *b* absent.... 2Cor 13:10
lest *b* present I should use...... 2Cor 13:10
b more exceedingly zealous of the. Gal 1:14
b a Greek, was compelled to be... Gal 2:3
b a Jew, livest after the manner. Gal 2:14
of the law, *b* made a curse for us. Gal 3:13
b predestinated according to the. Eph 1:11
your understanding *b* enlightened. Eph 1:18
that ye *b* in time past Gentiles.. Eph 2:11
b aliens from the commonwealth of. Eph 2:12
Jesus Christ himself *b* the chief. Eph 2:20
b rooted and grounded in love,... Eph 3:17
b alienated from the life of God. Eph 4:18
Who *b* past feeling have given.... Eph 4:19
B confident of this very thing,... Phil 1:6
B filled with the fruits of....... Phil 1:11
b of one accord, of one mind..... Phil 2:2
b in the form of God, thought it. Phil 2:6
b found in fashion as a man, he.. Phil 2:8
b made conformable unto his death. Phil 3:10
b fruitful in every good work, and. Col 1:10
b knit together in love, and unto. Col 2:2
b dead in your sins and the...... Col 2:13
So *b* affectionately desirous of.. 1Th 2:8
b taken from you for a short time. 1Th 2:17
but the woman *b* deceived was in.. 1Ti 2:14
lest *b* lifted up with pride he... 1Ti 3:6
of a deacon, *b* found blameless... 1Ti 3:10
b mindful of thy tears, that I... 2Ti 1:4
worse, deceiving, and *b* deceived. 2Ti 3:13
b abominable, and disobedient, and. Titus 1:16
That *b* justified by his grace, we. Titus 3:7
sinneth, *b* condemned of himself.. Titus 3:11
b such an one as Paul the aged,.. Philem 9
Who *b* the brightness of his glory. Heb 1:3
b made so much better than the... Heb 1:4
himself hath suffered *b* tempted.. Heb 2:18
a promise *b* left us of entering.. Heb 4:1
not *b* mixed with faith in them... Heb 4:2
b made perfect, he became the.... Heb 5:9
first *b* by interpretation King of. Heb 7:2
For the priesthood *b* changed..... Heb 7:12
But Christ *b* come an high priest. Heb 9:11
by it he *b* dead yet speaketh..... Heb 11:4
b warned of God of things not.... Heb 11:7
b destitute, afflicted, tormented. Heb 11:37
as *b* yourselves also in the body. Heb 13:3
he *b* not a forgetful hearer, but. Jas 1:25
hath not works, is dead, *b* alone. Jas 2:17
b much more precious than of gold. 1Pet 1:7
b born again, not of corruptible. 1Pet 1:23
at the word, *b* disobedient...... 1Pet 2:8
b dead to sins, should live unto. 1Pet 2:24
b in subjection unto their own... 1Pet 3:5
as *b* heirs together of the grace. 1Pet 3:7
b put to death in the flesh, but. 1Pet 3:18
powers *b* made subject unto him.. 1Pet 3:22
Neither as *b* lords over God's.... 1Pet 5:3
but *b* ensamples to the flock..... 1Pet 5:3
b overflowed with water, perished. 2Pet 3:6
wherein the heavens *b* on fire... 2Pet 3:12
b led away with the error of the. 2Pet 3:17
b turned, I saw seven golden..... Rev 1:12
And she *b* with child cried,...... Rev 12:2
b the firstfruits unto God and to. Rev 14:4

BEKAH
A *b* for every man, that is, half. Ex 38:26

BEKERITE See BACHRITES.

BEL (bel) See BAAL. A Babylonian god.
B boweth down, Nebo stoopeth,..... Is 46:1
B is confounded, Merodach is...... Jer 50:2
And I will punish B in Babylon.... Jer 51:44

BELA (bel´-lah) See BELAH, BELAITES.
1. Another name for Zoar.
king of Zeboiim, and the king of B. Gen 14:2
the king of B (the same is Zoar... Gen 14:8
2. An Edomite king.
B the son of Beor reigned in Edom. Gen 36:32
B died, and Jobab the son of Zerah. Gen 36:33
B the son of Beor................. 1Chr 1:43
when B was dead, Jobab the son of. 1Chr 1:44
3. A son of Benjamin.
of B, the family of the Belaites.. Num 26:38
And the sons of B were Ard........ Num 26:40

B, and Becher, and Jediael, three 1Chr 7:6
And the sons of B 1Chr 7:7
Benjamin began B his firstborn 1Chr 8:1
And the sons of B were, Addar, and... 1Chr 8:3
4. A son of Azaz the Reubenite.
B the son of Azaz, the son of 1Chr 5:8

BELAH (be'-lah) See BELA. A form of Bela.
And the sons of Benjamin were B..... Gen 46:21

BELAITES (be'-lah-ites) Descendants of Bela.
of Bela, the family of the B ...... Num 26:38

BELCH
they b out with their mouth ...... Ps 59:7

BELIAL (be'-le-al) A title for a "worthless person."
Certain men, the children of B ...... Deut 13:13
of the city, certain sons of B ...... Judg 19:22
us the men, the children of B ...... Judg 20:13
handmaid for a daughter of B 1Sa 1:16
the sons of Eli were sons of B 1Sa 2:12
But the children of B said 1Sa 10:27
for he is such a son of B...... 1Sa 25:17
I pray thee, regard this man of B...... 1Sa 25:25
all the wicked men and men of B...... 1Sa 30:22
thou bloody man, and thou man of B.. 2Sa 16:7
happened to be there a man of B 2Sa 20:1
But the sons of B shall be all of 2Sa 23:6
And set two men, sons of B 1Kin 21:10
came in two men, children of B...... 1Kin 21:13
the men of B witnessed against...... 1Kin 21:13
him vain men, the children of B...... 2Chr 13:7
what concord hath Christ with B...... 2Cor 6:15

BELIED
They have b the LORD, and said, It...... Jer 5:12

BELIEF
of the Spirit and b of the truth...... 2Th 2:13

BELIEVE
But, behold, they will not b me ...... Ex 4:1
That they may b that the LORD God...... Ex 4:5
to pass, if they will not b thee...... Ex 4:8
that they will b the voice of the...... Ex 4:8
if they will not b also these two...... Ex 4:9
with thee, and b thee for ever ...... Ex 19:9
how long will it be ere they b me ..... Num 14:11
ye did not b the LORD your God ...... Deut 1:32
that did not b in the LORD their 2Kin 17:14
B in the LORD your God, so shall 2Chr 20:20
b his prophets, so shall ye...... 2Chr 20:20
on this manner, neither yet b him 2Chr 32:15
yet would I not b that he had...... Job 9:16
Wilt thou b him, that he will...... Job 39:12
When he speaketh fair, b him not..... Prov 26:25
If ye will not b, surely ye shall...... Is 7:9
b me, and understand that I am he .... Is 43:10
b them not, though they speak ...... Jer 12:6
in your days, which ye will not b...... Hab 1:5
B ye that I am able to do this...... Mt 9:28
these little ones which b in me...... Mt 18:6
us, Why did ye not then b him...... Mt 21:25
afterward, that ye might b him...... Mt 21:32
b it not...... Mt 24:23
b it not...... Mt 24:26
from the cross, and we will b him...... Mt 27:42
repent ye, and b the gospel...... Mk 1:15
synagogue, Be not afraid, only b...... Mk 5:36
said unto him, If thou canst b...... Mk 9:23
and said with tears, Lord, I b...... Mk 9:24
of these little ones that b in me...... Mk 9:42
but shall b that those things...... Mk 11:23
b that ye receive them, and ye...... Mk 11:24
say, Why then did ye not b him......Mk 11:31
b him not...... Mk 13:21
the cross, that we may see and b..... Mk 15:32
signs shall follow them that b...... Mk 16:17
their hearts, lest they should b...... Lk 8:12
have no root, which for a while b...... Lk 8:13
b only, and she shall be made...... Lk 8:50
If I tell you, ye will not b...... Lk 22:67
slow of heart to b all that the ...... Lk 24:25
that all men through him might b...... Jn 1:7
even to them that b on his name ...... Jn 1:12
and ye b not, how shall ye b...... Jn 3:12
b me, the hour cometh, when ye...... Jn 4:21
And said unto the woman, Now we b .. Jn 4:42
signs and wonders, ye will not b...... Jn 4:48
whom he hath sent, him ye b not...... Jn 5:38
How can ye b, which receive...... Jn 5:44
But if ye b not his writings...... Jn 5:47
how shall ye b my words...... Jn 5:47
that ye b on him whom he hath...... Jn 6:29
then, that we may see, and b thee..... Jn 6:30
ye also have seen me, and b not...... Jn 6:36
there are some of you that b not...... Jn 6:64
And we b and are sure that thou art.. Jn 6:69
neither did his brethren b in him...... Jn 7:5
which they that b on him should...... Jn 7:39
for if ye b not that I am he, ye...... Jn 8:24
I tell you the truth, ye b me not...... Jn 8:45
say the truth, why do ye not b me..... Jn 8:46
the Jews did not b concerning him.... Jn 9:18
Dost thou b on the Son of God...... Jn 9:35
he, Lord, that I might b on him...... Jn 9:38
he said, Lord, I b...... Jn 9:38
But ye b not, because ye are not...... Jn 10:26
the works of my Father, b me not...... Jn 10:37
ye b not me, b the works...... Jn 10:38
that ye may know, and b, that the.... Jn 10:38

not there, to the intent ye may b...... Jn 11:15
I b that thou art the Christ, the...... Jn 11:27
thee, that, if thou wouldest b ...... Jn 11:40
that they may b that thou hast...... Jn 11:42
thus alone, all men will b on him...... Jn 11:48
b in the light, that ye may be...... Jn 12:36
Therefore they could not b...... Jn 12:39
words, and b not, I judge him not..... Jn 12:47
to pass, ye may b that I am he ...... Jn 13:19
ye b in God, b also in me...... Jn 14:1
B me that I am in the Father, and..... Jn 14:11
or else b me for the very works'..... Jn 14:11
it is come to pass, ye might b...... Jn 14:29
Of sin, because they b not on me ..... Jn 16:9
by this we b that thou camest...... Jn 16:30
Jesus answered them, Do ye now b..... Jn 16:31
shall b on me through their word...... Jn 17:20
that the world may b that thou...... Jn 17:21
he saith true, that ye might b...... Jn 19:35
hand into his side, I will not b...... Jn 20:25
that ye might b that Jesus is the..... Jn 20:31
I b that Jesus Christ is the Son...... Acts 8:37
by him all that b are justified...... Acts 13:39
work which ye shall in no wise b..... Acts 13:41
hear the word of the gospel, and b.... Acts 15:7
But we b that through the grace...... Acts 15:11
B on the Lord Jesus Christ, and...... Acts 16:31
that they should b on him which...... Acts 19:4
of Jews there are which b...... Acts 21:20
As touching the Gentiles which b..... Acts 21:25
for I b God, that it shall be...... Acts 27:25
For what if some did not b...... Rom 3:3
unto all and upon all them that b..... Rom 3:22
be the father of all them that b...... Rom 4:11
if we b on him that raised up...... Rom 4:24
we b that we shall also live with..... Rom 6:8
shalt b in thine heart that God...... Rom 10:9
how shall they b in him of whom..... Rom 10:14
from them that do not b in Judaea.... Rom 15:31
of preaching to save them that b..... 1Cor 1:21
If any of them that b not bid you..... 1Cor 10:27
and I partly b it...... 1Cor 11:18
for a sign, not to them that b...... 1Cor 14:22
but to them that b not...... 1Cor 14:22
serveth not for them that b...... 1Cor 14:22
but for them which b...... 1Cor 14:22
the minds of them which b not...... 2Cor 4:4
we also b, and therefore speak...... 2Cor 4:13
might be given to them that b...... Gal 3:22
of his power to us-ward who b...... Eph 1:19
of Christ, not only to b on him...... Phil 1:29
to all that b in Macedonia...... 1Th 1:7
ourselves among you that b...... 1Th 2:10
worketh also in you that b...... 1Th 2:13
For if we b that Jesus died and...... 1Th 4:14
b (because our testimony among...... 2Th 1:10
that they should b a lie...... 2Th 2:11
b on him to life everlasting...... 1Ti 1:16
with thanksgiving of them which b.... 1Ti 4:3
men, specially of those that b...... 1Ti 4:10
If we b not, yet he abideth...... 2Ti 2:13
but of them that b to the saving..... Heb 10:39
cometh to God must b that he is..... Heb 11:6
the devils also b, and tremble...... Jas 2:19
Who by him do b in God, that...... 1Pet 1:21
therefore which b he is precious..... 1Pet 2:7
That we should b on the name of..... 1Jn 3:23
b not every spirit, but try the...... 1Jn 4:1
have I written unto you that b on..... 1Jn 5:13
that ye may b on the name of the.... 1Jn 5:13

BELIEVED
And he b in the LORD...... Gen 15:6
heart fainted, for he b them not...... Gen 45:26
And the people b...... Ex 4:31
b the LORD, and his servant Moses... Ex 14:31
and Aaron, Because ye b me not...... Num 20:12
ye b him not, nor hearkened to...... Deut 9:23
And Achish b David, saying, He...... 1Sa 27:12
Howbeit I b not the words, until..... 1Kin 10:7
Howbeit I b not their words,...... 2Chr 9:6
I laughed on them, they b it not..... Job 29:24
unless I had b to see the...... Ps 27:13
Because they b not in God...... Ps 78:22
b not for his wondrous works...... Ps 78:32
Then b they his words...... Ps 106:12
land, they b not his word...... Ps 106:24
I b, therefore have I spoken...... Ps 116:10
for I have b thy commandments...... Ps 119:66
Who hath b our report...... Is 53:1
the son of Ahikam b them not...... Jer 40:14
would not have b that the...... Lam 4:12
upon him, because he b in his God.. Dan 6:23
So the people of Nineveh b God...... Jonah 3:5
and as thou hast b, so be it done...... Matt 8:13
of righteousness, and ye b him not.... Mt 21:32
publicans and the harlots b him...... Mt 21:32
and had been seen of her, b not...... Mk 16:11
neither b they them...... Mk 16:13
because they b not them which had.. Mk 16:14
which are most surely b among us..... Lk 1:1
And blessed is she that b...... Lk 1:45
will say, Why then b ye him not...... Lk 20:5
as idle tales, and they b them not.... Lk 24:11
And while they yet b not for joy..... Lk 24:41
and his disciples b on him...... Jn 2:11
they b the scripture, and the word.... Jn 2:22
many b in his name, when they saw... Jn 2:23
because he hath not b in the name... Jn 3:18
b on him for the saying of the...... Jn 4:41
many more b because of his own..... Jn 4:41

the man b the word that Jesus had .... Jn 4:50
and himself b, and his whole house .... Jn 4:53
b Moses, ye would have b me...... Jn 5:46
who they were that b not, and who.... Jn 6:64
And many of the people b on him..... Jn 7:31
or of the Pharisees b on him...... Jn 7:48
spake these words, many b on him.... Jn 8:30
to those Jews which b on him...... Jn 8:31
them, I told you, and ye b not ...... Jn 10:25
And many b on him there...... Jn 10:42
things which Jesus did, b on him...... Jn 11:45
the Jews went away, and b on Jesus... Jn 12:11
them, yet they b not on him...... Jn 12:37
Lord, who hath b our report...... Jn 12:38
chief rulers also many b on him...... Jn 12:42
have b that I came out from God...... Jn 16:27
they have b that thou didst send...... Jn 17:8
to the sepulchre, and he saw, and b... Jn 20:8
thou hast seen me, thou hast b...... Jn 20:29
that have not seen, and yet have b..... Jn 20:29
all that b were together, and had .... Acts 2:44
of them which heard the word b...... Acts 4:4
of them that b were of one heart..... Acts 4:32
But when they b Philip preaching..... Acts 8:12
Then Simon himself b also...... Acts 8:13
b not that he was a disciple...... Acts 9:26
and many b in the Lord...... Acts 9:42
which b were astonished, as many..... Acts 10:45
who b on the Lord Jesus Christ...... Acts 11:17
and a great number b, and turned..... Acts 11:21
when he saw what was done, b...... Acts 13:12
were ordained to eternal life b...... Acts 13:48
the Jews and also of the Greeks b..... Acts 14:1
them to the Lord, on whom they b..... Acts 14:23
the sect of the Pharisees which b..... Acts 15:5
woman, which was a Jewess, and b.... Acts 16:1
And some of them b, and consorted... Acts 17:4
But the Jews which b not, moved...... Acts 17:5
Therefore many of them b...... Acts 17:12
certain men clave unto him, and b.... Acts 17:34
b on the Lord with all his house...... Acts 18:8
many of the Corinthians hearing b.... Acts 18:8
much which had b through grace..... Acts 18:27
the Holy Ghost since ye b...... Acts 19:2
b not, but spake evil of that way...... Acts 19:9
And many that b came...... Acts 19:18
synagogue them that b on thee...... Acts 22:19
the centurion b the master...... Acts 27:11
some b the things which were...... Acts 28:24
which were spoken, and some b not... Acts 28:24
nations), before him whom he b...... Rom 4:3
Who against hope b in hope...... Rom 4:18
on him in whom they have not b...... Rom 10:14
Lord, who hath b our report...... Rom 10:16
ye in times past have not b God...... Rom 11:30
Even so have these also now not b.... Rom 11:31
salvation nearer than when we b...... Rom 13:11
but ministers by whom ye b...... 1Cor 3:5
you, unless ye have b in vain...... 1Cor 15:2
or they, so we preach, and so ye b.... 1Cor 15:11
according as it is written, I b...... 2Cor 4:13
even we have b in Jesus Christ,...... Gal 2:16
Even as Abraham b God, and it was.. Gal 3:6
in whom also after that ye b...... Eph 1:13
among you was b in that day...... 2Ti 1:10
be damned who b not the truth...... 2Th 2:12
b on in the world, received up...... 1Ti 3:16
for I know whom I have b, and am.... 2Ti 1:12
that they which have b in God...... Titus 3:8
his rest, but to them that b not...... Heb 3:18
For we which have b do enter into... Heb 4:3
perished not with them that b not.... Heb 11:31
which saith, Abraham b God...... Jas 2:23
b the love that God hath to us...... 1Jn 4:16
destroyed them that b not...... Jude 5

BELIEVERS
b were the more added to the Lord... Acts 5:14
but be thou an example of the b...... 1Ti 4:12

BELIEVEST
because thou b not my words...... Lk 1:20
thee under the fig tree, b thou...... Jn 1:50
B thou this...... Jn 11:26
B thou not that I am in the...... Jn 14:10
If thou b with all thine heart,...... Acts 8:37
King Agrippa, b thou the prophets.... Acts 26:27
I know that thou b...... Acts 26:27
Thou b that there is one God...... Jas 2:19

BELIEVETH
He b not that he shall return out..... Job 15:22
neither b he that it is the sound..... Job 39:24
The simple b every word...... Prov 14:15
he that b shall not make haste...... Is 28:16
things are possible to him that b.... Mk 9:23
He that b and is baptized shall be.... Mk 16:16
but he that b not shall be damned... Mk 16:16
That whosoever b in him should...... Jn 3:16
that whosoever b in him should...... Jn 3:16
He that b on him is not condemned.. Jn 3:18
but he that b not is condemned...... Jn 3:18
He that b on the Son hath...... Jn 3:36
he that b not the Son shall not...... Jn 3:36
b on him that sent me, hath...... Jn 5:24
he that b on me hath...... Jn 6:35
to him, may have everlasting...... Jn 6:40
He that b on me hath everlasting.... Jn 6:47
He that b on me, as the scripture .... Jn 7:38
he that b in me, though he were.... Jn 11:25
liveth and b in me shall never die.... Jn 11:26

cried and said, He that *b* on me......... Jn 12:44
b not on me, but on him that sent......... Jn 12:44
that whosoever *b* on me should not ...... Jn 12:46
I say unto you, He that *b* on me .... Jn 14:12
b in him shall receive remission .... Acts 10:43
salvation to every one that *b* .... Rom 1:16
justifier of him which *b* in Jesus .... Rom 3:26
but *b* on him that justifieth the.......... Rom 4:5
whosoever *b* on him shall not be .... Rom 9:33
righteousness to every one that *b*...... Rom 10:4
heart man *b* unto righteousness.......... Rom 10:10
Whosoever *b* on him shall not be........ Rom 10:11
For one *b* that he may eat all............. Rom 14:2
brother hath a wife that *b* not........... 1Cor 7:12
which hath an husband that *b* not ... 1Cor 7:13
b all things, hopeth all things............ 1Cor 13:7
and there come in one that *b* not 1Cor 14:24
hath he that *b* with an infidel 2Cor 6:15
man or woman that *b* have widows...... 1Ti 5:16
he that *b* on him shall not be 1Pet 2:6
Whosoever *b* that Jesus is the............ 1Jn 5:1
but he that *b* that Jesus is the............ 1Jn 5:5
He that *b* on the Son of God hath 1Jn 5:10
he that *b* not God hath made him a 1Jn 5:10
because he *b* not the record that 1Jn 5:10

BELIEVING

ye shall ask in prayer, *b*..................... Mt 21:22
b, and be not faithless, but *b*.............. Jn 20:27
that *b* ye might have life through .... Jn 20:31
b in God with all his house .... Acts 16:34
b all things which are written in ...... Acts 24:14
you with all joy and peace in *b* .... Rom 15:13
And they that have *b* masters............... 1Ti 6:2
though now ye see him not, yet *b*....... 1Pet 1:8

BELL

A golden *b* and a pomegranate............ Ex 28:34
and a pomegranate, a golden *b*............ Ex 28:34
A *b* and a pomegranate, a *b* and a.... Ex 39:26

BELLIES

alway liars, evil beasts, slow *b*........... Titus 1:12

BELLOW

heifer at grass, and *b* as bulls........... Jer 50:11

BELLOWS

The *b* are burned, the lead is............... Jer 6:29

BELLY

b of gold between them round.............. Ex 28:33
they made *b* of pure gold..................... Ex 39:25
and put the *b* between the................... Ex 39:25
there be upon the *b* of the horses....... Zec 14:20

upon thy *b* shalt thou go, and dust...... Gen 3:14
Whatsoever goeth upon the *b*.............. Lev 11:42
thigh to rot, and thy *b* to swell .... Num 5:21
bowels, to make thy *b* to swell............ Num 5:22
her *b* shall swell, and her thigh........... Num 5:27
and the woman through her *b*............. Num 25:8
thigh, and thrust it into his *b* .... Judg 3:21
not draw the dagger out of his *b*........ Judg 3:22
over against the *b* which was by......... 1Kin 7:20
ghost when I came out of the *b* .... Job 3:11
fill his *b* with the east wind............... Job 15:2
and their *b* prepareth deceit............... Job 15:35
God shall cast them out of his *b*......... Job 20:15
shall not feel quietness in his *b* .... Job 20:20
When he is about to fill his *b*............. Job 20:23
my *b* is as wine which hath no .... Job 32:19
force is in the navel of his *b*.............. Job 40:16
whose *b* thou fillest with thy hid .... Ps 17:14
art my God from my mother's *b* .... Ps 22:10
with grief, yea, my soul and my *b*....... Ps 31:9
our *b* cleaveth unto the earth............. Ps 44:25
but the *b* of the wicked shall.............. Prov 13:25
into the innermost parts of the *b* .... Prov 18:8
A man's *b* shall be satisfied with........ Prov 18:20
all the inward parts of the *b*.............. Prov 20:27
stripes the inward parts of the *b*........ Prov 20:30
into the innermost parts of the *b*........ Prov 26:22
his *b* is as bright ivory overlaid......... Song 5:14
thy *b* is like an heap of wheat............. Song 7:2
which are borne by me from the *b*...... Is 46:3
formed thee in the *b* I knew thee .... Jer 1:5
filled his *b* with my delicates .... Jer 51:34
Son of man, cause thy *b* to eat........... Eze 3:3
and his arms of silver, his *b* .... Dan 2:32
Jonah was in the *b* of the fish .... Jonah 1:17
Lord his God out of the fish's *b*......... Jonah 2:1
out of the *b* of hell cried I, and......... Jonah 2:2
When I heard, my *b* trembled .... Hab 3:16
and three nights in the whale's *b* ...... Mt 12:40
in at the mouth goeth into the *b*........ Mt 15:17
into his heart, but into the *b*.............. Mk 7:19
b with the husks that the swine......... Lk 15:16
out of his *b* shall flow rivers of .... Jn 7:38
Jesus Christ, but their own *b* .... Rom 16:18
Meats for the *b*, and the *b* for 1Cor 6:13
destruction, whose God is their *b* ...... Phil 3:19
and it shall make thy *b* bitter .... Rev 10:9
I had eaten it, my *b* was bitter............ Rev 10:10

BELONG

Do not interpretations *b* to God......... Gen 40:8
the possession of the land did *b*......... Lev 27:24
and over all things that *b* to it .... Num 1:50
The secret things *b* unto the LORD..... Deut 29:29
which are revealed *b* unto us............. Deut 29:29
shields of the earth *b* unto God .... Ps 47:9
unto GOD the Lord the issues............... Ps 68:20

These things also *b* to the wise......... Prov 24:23
To the Lord our God *b* mercies.......... Dan 9:9
my name, because ye *b* to Christ........ Mk 9:41
the things which *b* unto thy peace ..... Lk 19:42
for the things that *b* to the Lord........ 1Cor 7:32

BELONGED

on the border of Manasseh *b* to .... Josh 17:8
of the herdmen that *b* to Saul............ 1Sa 21:7
the mighty men which *b* to David 1Kin 1:8
which *b* to the Philistines................... 1Kin 15:27
which *b* to the Philistines................... 1Kin 16:15
which *b* to Judah, for Israel, are 2Kin 14:28
All these *b* to the sons of Machir 1Chr 2:23
which *b* to Judah, to bring up 1Chr 13:6
the burial which *b* to the kings.......... 2Chr 26:23
house which *b* to king Ahasuerus....... Est 1:9
with such things as *b* to her .... Est 2:9
he *b* unto Herod's jurisdiction........... Lk 23:7

BELONGEST

said unto him, To whom *b* thou......... 1Sa 30:13

BELONGETH

This is it that *b* unto the................... Num 8:24
To me is vengeance .... Deut 32:35
by Gibeah, which *b* to Benjamin......... Judg 19:14
into Gibeah that *b* to Benjamin.......... Judg 20:4
which *b* to Judah, and pitched........... 1Sa 17:1
upon the coast which *b* to Judah....... 1Sa 30:14
which *b* to Zidon, and dwell there...... 1Kin 17:9
which *b* to Judah, and left his........... 1Kin 19:3
at Beth-shemesh, which *b* to Judah ... 2Kin 14:11
at Beth-shemesh, which *b* to Judah .. 2Chr 25:21
for this matter *b* unto thee................ Ezr 10:4
Salvation *b* unto the LORD................. Ps 3:8
that power *b* unto God........................ Ps 62:11
Also unto thee, O Lord, *b* mercy........ Ps 62:12
O LORD God, to whom vengeance *b*... Ps 94:1
O God, to whom vengeance *b*.............. Ps 94:1
O Lord, righteousness *b* unto thee...... Dan 9:7
to us *b* confusion of face, to our....... Dan 9:8
But strong meat *b* to them that.......... Heb 5:14
hath said, Vengeance *b* unto me......... Heb 10:30

BELONGING

the service of the sanctuary *b*............ Num 7:9
a part of the field *b* unto Boaz .... Ruth 2:3
Philistines to the five lords................. 1Sa 6:18
meddleth with strife *b* not to him ..... Prov 26:17
b to the city called Bethsaida............ Lk 9:10

BELOVED

If a man have two wives, one............... Deut 21:15
born him children, both the *b*............ Deut 21:15
he may not make the son of the *b* ..... Deut 21:16
The *b* of the LORD shall dwell in .... Deut 33:12
who was *b* of his God, and God made Neh 13:26
That thy *b* may be delivered................ Ps 60:5
That thy *b* may be delivered................ Ps 108:6
for so he giveth his *b* sleep................. Ps 127:2
only *b* in the sight of my mother........ Prov 4:3
My *b* is unto me as a cluster of.......... Song 1:14
Behold, thou art fair, my *b* .... Song 1:16
so is my *b* among the sons................. Song 2:3
The voice of my *b*............................... Song 2:8
My *b* is like a roe or a young............. Song 2:9
My *b* spake, and said unto me, Rise.... Song 2:10
My *b* is mine, and I am his .... Song 2:16
the shadows flee away, turn, my *b*..... Song 2:17
Let my *b* come into his garden, and.... Song 4:16
drink, yea, drink abundantly, O *b*...... Song 5:1
the voice of my *b* that knocketh......... Song 5:2
My *b* put in his hand by the hole .... Song 5:4
I rose up to open to my *b*................... Song 5:5
I opened to my *b*................................ Song 5:6
but my *b* had withdrawn himself........ Song 5:6
of Jerusalem, if ye find my *b*.............. Song 5:8
thy *b* more than another *b*................ Song 5:9
thy *b* more than another *b*................ Song 5:9
My *b* is white and ruddy, the............. Song 5:10
This is my *b*, and this is my............... Song 5:16
Whither is thy *b* gone, O thou........... Song 6:1
whither is thy *b* turned aside............. Song 6:1
My *b* is gone down into his garden..... Song 6:2
am my beloved's, and my *b* is mine.... Song 6:3
mouth like the best wine for my *b* ..... Song 7:9
Come, my *b*, let us go forth into........ Song 7:11
I have laid up for thee, O my *b*.......... Song 7:13
wilderness, leaning upon her *b*.......... Song 8:5
Make haste, my *b*, and be thou like.... Song 8:14
of my *b* touching his vineyard .... Is 5:1
What hath my *b* to do in mine .... Jer 11:15
I have given the dearly *b* of my .... Jer 12:7
for art greatly *b*................................ Dan 9:23
me, O Daniel, a man greatly *b*............ Dan 10:11
And said, O man greatly *b*, fear .... Dan 10:19
love a woman *b* of her friend, yet...... Hos 3:1
even the *b* fruit of their womb.......... Hos 9:16
heaven, saying, This is my *b* Son........ Mt 3:17
my *b*, in whom my soul is well........... Mt 12:18
which said, This is my *b* Son .... Mt 17:5
heaven, saying, Thou art my *b* Son..... Mk 1:11
cloud, saying, This is my *b* Son........... Mk 9:7
which said, Thou art my *b* Son............ Lk 3:22
cloud, saying, This is my *b* Son........... Lk 9:35
I will send my *b* son........................... Lk 20:13
men unto you with our *b* Barnabas.... Acts 15:25
b of God, called to be saints .... Rom 1:7
and her *b*, which was not *b*.............. Rom 9:25
they are *b* for the fathers' sakes........ Rom 11:28
Dearly *b*, avenge not yourselves........ Rom 12:19
Greet Amplias my *b* in the Lord......... Rom 16:8

helper in Christ, and Stachys my *b*..... Rom 16:9
Salute the *b* Persis, which.................. Rom 16:12
but as my *b* sons I warn you.............. 1Cor 4:14
you Timotheus, who is my *b* son 1Cor 4:17
Wherefore, my dearly *b*, flee from 1Cor 10:14
my *b* brethren, be ye stedfast............. 1Cor 15:58
therefore these promises dearly *b*...... 2Cor 7:1
but we do all things, dearly *b*............. 2Cor 12:19
he hath made us accepted in the *b* ..... Eph 1:6
a *b* brother and faithful minister .... Eph 6:21
Wherefore, my *b*, as ye have .... Phil 2:12
Therefore, my brethren dearly *b*......... Phil 4:1
fast in the Lord, my dearly *b*.............. Phil 4:1
as the elect of God, holy and *b*........... Col 3:12
unto you, who is a *b* brother............. Col 4:7
b brother, who is one of you .... Col 4:9
the *b* physician, and Demas, greet...... Col 4:14
Knowing, brethren *b*, your 1Th 1:4
brethren *b* of the Lord, because.......... 2Th 2:13
because they are faithful and *b*........... 1Ti 6:2
To Timothy, my dearly *b* son.............. 2Ti 1:2
unto Philemon our dearly *b*............... Philem 1
And to our *b* Apphia, and Archippus... Philem 2
but above a servant, a brother *b*......... Philem 16
But, *b*, we are persuaded better.......... Heb 6:9
Do not err, my *b* brethren.................. Jas 1:16
my *b* brethren, let every man be .... Jas 1:19
my *b* brethren, Hath not God .... Jas 2:5
Dearly *b*, I beseech you as.................. 1Pet 2:11
b, think it not strange 1Pet 4:12
excellent glory, This is my *b* Son 2Pet 1:17
This second epistle, *b*, I now.............. 2Pet 3:1
But, *b*, be not ignorant of this 2Pet 3:8
Wherefore, *b*, seeing that ye look 2Pet 3:14
even as our *b* brother Paul also.......... 2Pet 3:15
Ye therefore, *b*, seeing ye know 2Pet 3:17
B, now are we the sons of God, and.... 1Jn 3:2
B, if our heart condemn us not.......... 1Jn 3:21
B, believe not every spirit, but........... 1Jn 4:1
B, let us love one another................... 1Jn 4:7
B, if God so loved us, we ought 1Jn 4:11
B, I wish above all things that............ 1Jn 2
B, thou doest faithfully...................... 3Jn 5
B, follow not that which is evil........... 3Jn 11
B, when I gave all diligence to............ Jude 3
But, *b*, remember ye the words........... Jude 17
But ye, *b*, building up yourselves....... Jude 20
the saints about, and the *b* city.......... Rev 20:9

BELOVED'S

I am my *b*, and my beloved is mine..... Song 6:3
I am my *b*, and his desire is .... Song 7:10

BELSHAZZAR (bel-shaz'-ar) A Babylonian
king.
B the king made a great feast to......... Dan 5:1
B, whiles he tasted the wine............... Dan 5:2
Then was king *B* greatly troubled....... Dan 5:9
And thou his son, O *B*, hast not......... Dan 5:22
Then commanded *B*, and they clothed.. Dan 5:29
In that night was *B* the king of.......... Dan 5:30
In the first year of *B* king of.............. Dan 7:1
king *B* a vision appeared unto me...... Dan 8:1

BELTESHAZZAR (bel-te-shaz'-ar) See
DANIEL. The Babylonian name given to
Daniel.
he gave unto Daniel the name of *B*...... Dan 1:7
said to Daniel, whose name was *B*...... Dan 2:26
in before me, whose name was *B*........ Dan 4:8
O *B*, master of the magicians.............. Dan 4:9
Now thou, O *B*, declare the .... Dan 4:18
Then Daniel, whose name was *B*........ Dan 4:19
The king spake, and said, *B*............... Dan 4:19
B answered and said, My lord, the...... Dan 4:19
Daniel, whom the king named *B*........ Dan 5:12
Daniel, whose name was called *B* ...... Dan 10:1

BEMOAN

or who shall *b* thee .... Jer 15:5
neither go to lament nor *b* them......... Jer 16:5
not for the dead, neither *b* him.......... Jer 22:10
All ye that are about him, *b* him .... Jer 48:17
who will *b* her................................... Nah 3:7

BEMOANED

and they *b* him, and comforted him.... Job 42:11

BEMOANING

heard Ephraim *b* himself thus............ Jer 31:18

BEN (ben) A Levite.
the second degree, Zechariah, *B*......... 1Chr 15:18

BENAIAH (ben-ay'-ah)
   I. An officer of David.
B the son of Jehoiada was over 2Sa 8:18
B the son of Jehoiada was over 2Sa 20:23
B the son of Jehoiada, one of 2Sa 23:20
These things did *B* the son of 2Sa 23:22
B the son of Jehoiada, and Nathan..... 1Kin 1:8
But Nathan the prophet, and *B*.......... 1Kin 1:10
B the son of Jehoiada, and thy 1Kin 1:26
prophet, and *B* the son of Jehoiada.... 1Kin 1:32
B the son of Jehoiada answered.......... 1Kin 1:36
B the son of Jehoiada, and the........... 1Kin 1:38
B the son of Jehoiada, and the........... 1Kin 1:44
the hand of *B* the son of Jehoiada...... 1Kin 2:25
Then Solomon sent *B* the son of 1Kin 2:29
B came to the tabernacle of the 1Kin 2:30
B brought the king word again,.......... 1Kin 2:30
So *B* the son of Jehoiada went up,...... 1Kin 2:34
the king put *B* the son of 1Kin 2:35
commanded *B* the son of Jehoiada 1Kin 2:46

B the son of Jehoiada was over............ 1Kin 4:4
B the son of Jehoiada, the son of........ 1Chr 11:22
These things did B the son of............ 1Chr 11:24
B the son of Jehoiada was over............ 1Chr 18:17
month was B the son of Jehoiada........ 1Chr 27:5
This is that B, who was mighty........... 1Chr 27:6
   2. A "mighty man" of David.
B the Pirathonite, Hiddai of the........ 2Sa 23:30
of Benjamin, B the Pirathonite,......... 1Chr 11:31
month was B the Pirathonite............. 1Chr 27:14
   3. A Simeonite family chief.
and Adiel, and Jesimiel, and B........... 1Chr 4:36
   4. A priest of David.
and Jehiel, and Unni, Eliab, and B..... 1Chr 15:18
Eliab, and Maaseiah, and B.............. 1Chr 15:20
and Amasai, and Zechariah, and B..... 1Chr 15:24
and Mattithiah, and Eliab, and B....... 1Chr 16:5
B also and Jahaziel the priests.......... 1Chr 16:6
   5. Father of Jehoiada.
was Jehoiada the son of B................. 1Chr 27:34
   6. Grandfather of Jehaziel.
son of Zechariah, the son of B........... 2Chr 20:14
   7. A Levite during Hezekiah's reign.
and Ismachiah, and Mahath, and B.... 2Chr 31:13
   8. A descendant of Parosh.
and Eleazar, and Malchijah, and B..... Ezr 10:25
   9. A son of Pahath-moab.
Adna, and Chelal, B, Maaseiah,......... Ezr 10:30
   10. A son of Bani.
B, Bedeiah, Chelluh,..................... Ezr 10:35
   11. A son of Nebo.
Zabad, Zebina, Jadau, and Joel, B..... Ezr 10:43
   12. Father of Pelatiah.
of Azur, and Pelatiah the son of B..... Eze 11:1
that Pelatiah the son of B died........... Eze 11:13

BEN-AMMI (ben-am'-mi) A son of Lot.
bare a son, and called his name B....... Gen 19:38

BENCHES
have made thy b of ivory, brought...... Eze 27:6

BEND
For, lo, the wicked b their bow........... Ps 11:2
b their bows to shoot their................ Ps 64:3
they b their tongues like their........... Jer 9:3
Lydians, that handle and b the bow.... Jer 46:9
all ye that b the bow, shoot at............ Jer 50:14
all ye that b the bow, camp............... Jer 50:29
bendeth let the archer b his bow........ Jer 51:3
this vine did b her roots toward......... Eze 17:7

BEN DEKER See DEKAR.

BENDETH
when he b his bow to shoot his.......... Ps 58:7
Against him that b let the archer....... Jer 51:3

BENDING
thee shall come b unto thee.............. Is 60:14

BENEATH
she was buried b Beth-el under an..... Gen 35:8
above, or that is in the earth b........... Ex 20:4
they shall be coupled together b........ Ex 26:24
under the compass of the altar b........ Ex 27:5
b upon the hem of it thou shalt......... Ex 28:33
hands, and brake them b the mount.... Ex 32:19
And they were coupled b, and........... Ex 36:29
thereof b unto the midst of it............ Ex 38:4
that is in the waters b the earth......... Deut 4:18
heaven above, and upon the earth b.... Deut 4:39
above, or that is in the earth b........... Deut 5:8
that is in the waters b the earth......... Deut 5:8
only, and thou shalt not be b............. Deut 28:13
and for the deep that coucheth b........ Deut 33:13
in heaven above, and in earth b......... Josh 2:11
of Midian was b him in the valley....... Judg 7:8
which is by Zartanah b Jezreel........... 1Kin 4:12
the lions and oxen were certain......... 1Kin 7:29
in heaven above, or on earth b........... 1Kin 8:23
His roots shall be dried up b............. Job 18:16
that he may depart from hell b........... Prov 15:24
Hell from b is moved for thee to........ Is 14:9
heavens, and look upon the earth b.... Is 51:6
of the earth searched out b............... Jer 31:37
from above, and his roots from b....... Amos 2:9
as Peter was b in the palace,............. Mk 14:66
he said unto them, Ye are from b....... Jn 8:23
above, and signs in the earth b......... Acts 2:19

BENE BARAK See BENE-BERAK.

BENE-BERAK (be'-ne-be'-rak) A city in Dan.
and B, and Gath-rimmon,................ Josh 19:45

BENEFACTORS
authority upon them are called b....... Lk 22:25

BENEFIT
according to the b done unto him...... 2Chr 32:25
wherewith I said I would b them....... Jer 18:10
that ye might have a second b............ 2Cor 1:15
and beloved, partakers of the b.......... 1Ti 6:2
that thy b should not be as it............. Philem 14

BENEFITS
Lord, who daily loadeth us with b...... Ps 68:19
my soul, and forget not all his b......... Ps 103:2
Lord for all his b toward me.............. Ps 116:12

BENE JAAKAN See BENE-JAAKAN.

BENE-JAAKAN (be'-ne-ja'-a-kan) Namesake
of several wells.
from Moseroth, and pitched in B....... Num 33:31
And they removed from B, and.......... Num 33:32

BENEVOLENCE
render unto the wife due b............... 1Cor 7:3

BEN-HADAD (ben'ha-dad)
   1. A Syrian king, son of Tabrimon.
and king Asa sent them to B............. 1Kin 15:18
So B hearkened unto king Asa, and .. 1Kin 15:20
sent to B king of Syria, that.............. 2Chr 16:2
B hearkened unto king Asa, and........ 2Chr 16:4
   2. A Syrian king during Ahab's reign.
B the king of Syria gathered all......... 1Kin 20:1
and said unto him, Thus saith B......... 1Kin 20:2
again, and said, Thus speaketh B....... 1Kin 20:5
he said unto the messengers of B....... 1Kin 20:9
B sent unto him, and said, The.......... 1Kin 20:10
when B heard this message, as he...... 1Kin 20:12
But B was drinking himself drunk...... 1Kin 20:16
B sent out, and they told him,........... 1Kin 20:17
B the king of Syria escaped on an...... 1Kin 20:20
that B numbered the Syrians, and...... 1Kin 20:26
B fled, and came into the city,........... 1Kin 20:30
and said, Thy servant B saith............ 1Kin 20:32
and they said, Thy brother B............. 1Kin 20:33
Then B came forth to him................. 1Kin 20:33
B said unto him, The cities,.............. 1Kin 20:34
that B king of Syria gathered all........ 2Kin 6:24
B the king of Syria was sick.............. 2Kin 8:7
Thy son B king of Syria hath sent...... 2Kin 8:9
   3. A Syrian king, son of Hazael.
into the hand of B the son of............. 2Kin 13:3
B his son reigned in his stead............ 2Kin 13:24
of B the son of Hazael the cities........ 2Kin 13:25
shall devour the palaces of B............ Amos 1:4
   4. A title for all the Syrian kings.
it shall consume the palaces of B....... Jer 49:27

BEN-HAIL (ben-ha'-il) A prince of Judah.
he sent to his princes, even to B........ 2Chr 17:7

BEN-HANAN (ben-ha'-nan) A son of Shimon.
Shimon were, Amnon, and Rinnah, b.. 1Chr 4:20

BENINU (ben'-i-nu) A Levite who renewed the
covenant.
Hodijah, Bani, B............................ Neh 10:13

BENJAMIN (ben'-ja-min) See BENJAMIN'S,
BENJAMITE.
   1. Youngest son of Jacob.
but his father called him B............... Gen 35:18
Joseph, and B................................ Gen 35:24
But B, Joseph's brother, Jacob.......... Gen 42:4
is not, and ye will take B away.......... Gen 42:36
away your other brother, and B......... Gen 43:14
double money in their hand, and B.... Gen 43:15
And when Joseph saw B with them,... Gen 43:16
up his eyes, and saw his brother B..... Gen 43:29
see, and the eyes of my brother B...... Gen 45:12
and B wept upon his neck................. Gen 45:14
but to B he gave three hundred.......... Gen 45:22
Joseph, and B................................ Gen 46:19
And the sons of B were Belah............ Gen 46:21
Issachar, Zebulun, and B,................. Ex 1:3
Dan, Joseph, and B, Naphtali, Gad,... 1Chr 2:2
The sons of B................................. 1Chr 7:6
Now B begat Bela his firstborn,......... 1Chr 8:1
   2. One of the twelve tribes comprising Israel.
B shall ravin as a wolf:.................... Gen 49:27
Of B... Num 1:11
Of the children of B, by their............ Num 1:36
of them, even of the tribe of B.......... Num 1:37
Then the tribe of B.......................... Num 2:22
Of B shall be Abidan the son of........ Num 2:22
prince of the children of B............... Num 7:60
B was Abidan the son of Gideoni...... Num 10:24
Of the tribe of B, Palti the son.......... Num 13:9
The sons of B after their................. Num 26:38
sons of B after their families............ Num 26:41
Of the tribe of B, Elidad the son........ Num 34:21
and Issachar, and Joseph, and B........ Deut 27:12
Of B he said, The beloved of the....... Deut 33:12
of B came up according to their........ Josh 18:11
inheritance of the children of B........ Josh 18:20
Of B according to their families........ Josh 18:21
of B according to their families......... Josh 18:28
Simeon, and out of the tribe of B...... Josh 21:4
And out of the tribe of B, Gibeon...... Josh 21:17
the children of B did not drive.......... Judg 1:21
of B in Jerusalem unto this day......... Judg 1:21
after thee, B, among thy people......... Judg 5:14
also against Judah, and against B....... Judg 10:9
by Gibeah, which belongeth to B....... Judg 19:14
(Now the children of B heard that..... Judg 20:3
into Gibeah that belongeth to B......... Judg 20:4
do, when they come to Gibeah of B.... Judg 20:10
men through all the tribe of B........... Judg 20:12
But the children of B would not........ Judg 20:13
But the children of B gathered.......... Judg 20:14
the children of B were numbered....... Judg 20:15
And the men of Israel, beside B......... Judg 20:17
battle against the children of B......... Judg 20:18
went out to battle against................ Judg 20:20
the children of B came forth out........ Judg 20:21
the children of B my brother............ Judg 20:23
the children of B the second day....... Judg 20:24
B went forth against them out of....... Judg 20:25
the children of B my brother............ Judg 20:28
children of B on the third day........... Judg 20:30
the children of B went out................ Judg 20:31
And the children of B said................ Judg 20:32
And the LORD smote B before Israel.. Judg 20:35
So the children of B saw that............ Judg 20:36
B began to smite and kill of the........ Judg 20:39

again, the men of B were amazed...... Judg 20:41
there fell of B eighteen thousand...... Judg 20:44
fell that day of B were twenty.......... Judg 20:46
again upon the children of B............ Judg 20:48
give his daughter unto B to wife....... Judg 21:1
repented them for B their brother..... Judg 21:6
to speak to the children of B............ Judg 21:13
B came again at that time................. Judg 21:14
And the people repented them for B... Judg 21:15
the women are destroyed out of B..... Judg 21:16
for them that be escaped of B........... Judg 21:17
be he that giveth a wife to B............. Judg 21:18
they commanded the children of B.... Judg 21:20
of Shiloh, and go to the land of B...... Judg 21:21
And the children of B did so............. Judg 21:23
ran a man of B out of the army......... 1Sa 4:12
Now there was a man of B, whose..... 1Sa 9:1
thee a man out of the land of B......... 1Sa 9:16
the families of the tribe of B............. 1Sa 9:21
in the border of B at Zelzah.............. 1Sa 10:2
near, the tribe of B was taken........... 1Sa 10:20
B to come near by their families....... 1Sa 10:21
were with Jonathan in Gibeah of B.... 1Sa 13:2
up from Gilgal unto Gibeah of B....... 1Sa 13:15
with them, abode in Gibeah of B....... 1Sa 13:16
of Saul in Gibeah of B looked........... 1Sa 14:16
and over Ephraim, and over B.......... 2Sa 2:9
went over by number before B.......... 2Sa 2:15
the children of B gathered............... 2Sa 2:25
of David had smitten of B................ 2Sa 2:31
Abner also spake in the ears of B....... 2Sa 3:19
good to the whole house of B............ 2Sa 3:19
Beerothite, of the children of B........ 2Sa 4:2
Beeroth also was reckoned to B......... 2Sa 4:2
were a thousand men of B with him... 2Sa 19:17
they in the country of B in Zelah....... 2Sa 21:14
of Gibeah of the children of B.......... 2Sa 23:29
Shimei the son of Elah, in B............. 1Kin 4:18
of Judah, with the tribe of B............. 1Kin 12:21
unto all the house of Judah and B...... 1Kin 12:23
Asa built with them Geba of B.......... 1Kin 15:22
And out of the tribe of B.................. 1Chr 6:60
of the tribe of the children of B........ 1Chr 6:65
All these are of the sons of B............ 1Chr 7:10
of Judah, and the children of B......... 1Chr 9:3
And of the sons of B........................ 1Chr 9:7
pertained to the children of B........... 1Chr 11:31
bow, even of Saul's brethren of B....... 1Chr 12:2
there came of the children of B......... 1Chr 12:16
And of the children of B, the............ 1Chr 12:29
B counted he not among them.......... 1Chr 21:6
of B, Jaasiel the son of Abner........... 1Chr 27:21
B an hundred and fourscore............. 2Chr 11:1
and to all Israel in Judah and B......... 2Chr 11:3
in Judah and in B fenced cities......... 2Chr 11:10
having Judah and B on his side......... 2Chr 11:12
all the countries of Judah and B........ 2Chr 11:23
and out of B, that bare shields and.... 2Chr 14:8
ye me, Asa, and all Judah and B........ 2Chr 15:2
out of all the land of Judah and B...... 2Chr 15:8
And he gathered all Judah and B....... 2Chr 15:9
and B... 2Chr 17:17
throughout all Judah and B.............. 2Chr 25:5
the altars out of all Judah and B........ 2Chr 31:1
of Israel, and of all Judah and B........ 2Chr 34:9
in Jerusalem and B to stand to it....... 2Chr 34:32
of the fathers of Judah and B............ Ezr 1:5
B heard that the children of the........ Ezr 4:1
B gathered themselves together........ Ezr 10:9
of Judah, and of the children of B...... Neh 11:4
And these are the sons of B.............. Neh 11:7
The children also of B from Geba...... Neh 11:31
were divisions in Judah, and in B...... Neh 11:36
There is little B with their................ Ps 68:27
Before Ephraim and B and Manasseh.. Ps 80:2
were in Anathoth in the land of B...... Jer 1:1
O ye children of B, gather................ Jer 6:1
Jerusalem, and from the land of B..... Jer 17:26
which is in the country of B.............. Jer 32:8
take witnesses in the land of B.......... Jer 32:44
of the south, and in the land of B....... Jer 33:13
to go into the land of B, to............... Jer 37:12
of Judah and the children of B.......... Eze 48:22
west side, B shall have a portion....... Eze 48:23
And by the border of B, from the...... Eze 48:24
one gate of Joseph, one gate of B...... Eze 48:32
at Beth-aven, after thee, O B............ Hos 5:8
and B shall possess Gilead............... Obad 19
of Cis, a man of the tribe of B........... Acts 13:21
of Abraham, of the tribe of B............ Rom 11:1
of Israel, of the tribe of B................ Phil 3:5
Of the tribe of B were sealed............ Rev 7:8
   3. Great-grandson of Benjamin 1.
Jeush, and B, and Ehud, and............ 1Chr 7:10
   4. A descendant of Harim.
B, Malluch, and Shemariah.............. Ezr 10:32
   5. A repairer of the Jerusalem wall.
After him repaired B and Hashub...... Neh 3:23
   6. Purified the Jerusalem wall.
Judah, and B, and Shemaiah, and...... Neh 12:34
   7. A gate of Jerusalem.
that were in the high gate of B.......... Jer 20:2
And when he was in the gate of B....... Jer 37:13
then sitting in the gate of B.............. Jer 38:7

BENJAMIN'S (ben'-ja-mins)
   1. Refers to Benjamin 1.
but B mess was five times so much.... Gen 43:34
and the cup was found in B sack........ Gen 44:12
he fell upon his brother B neck......... Gen 45:14
   2. Refers to Benjamin 7.

from *B* gate unto the place of the....... Zec 14:10

BENJAMITE (ben'-ja-mite) See BENJAMITES. *A descendant of Benjamin.*
Ehud the son of Gera, a *B*...................... Judg 3:15
Bechorath, the son of Aphiah, a *B*........ 1Sa 9:1
answered and said, Am not I a *B*............ 1Sa 9:21
much more now may this *B* do it............ 2Sa 16:11
And Shimei the son of Gera, a *B*............ 2Sa 19:16
was Sheba, the son of Bichri, a *B*.......... 2Sa 20:1
a *B* of Bahurim, which cursed me............ 1Kin 2:8
of Shimei, the son of Kish, a *B*.............. Est 2:5
the words of Cush the *B*........................ Ps 7:t

BENJAMITES (ben'-ja-mites)
but the men of the place were *B*............ Judg 19:16
of the *B* that day twenty and five........... Judg 20:35
men of Israel gave place to the *B* .... Judg 20:36
the *B* looked behind them, and,............. Judg 20:40
they inclosed the *B* round about .... Judg 20:43
passed through the land of the *B* 1Sa 9:4
stood about him, Hear now, ye *B* 1Sa 22:7
Abiezer the Anetothite, of the *B* 1Chr 27:12

BENO (be'-no) *A descendant of Merari.*
B.. 1Chr 24:26
B, and Shoham, and Zaccur 1Chr 24:27

BEN-ONI (ben-o'-ni) *Rachel's second son.*
died) that she called his name *B*........... Gen 35:18

BENT
he hath *b* his bow, and made it.............. Ps 7:12
have *b* their bow, to cast down.............. Ps 37:14
are sharp, and all their bows *b*............. Is 5:28
drawn sword, and from the *b* bow .... Is 21:15
He hath *b* his bow like an enemy............ Lam 2:4
He hath *b* his bow, and set me as a .... Lam 3:12
my people are *b* to backsliding,............. Hos 11:7
When I have *b* Judah for me,................. Zec 9:13

BEN-ZOHETH (ben-zo'-heth) *A descendant of Caleb.*
sons of Ishi were, Zoheth, and *B*.......... 1Chr 4:20

BEON (be'-on) *A place east of the Jordan River.*
and Shebam, and Nebo, and *B*............... Num 32:3

BEOR (be'-or)
1. Father of Bela.
Bela the son of *B* reigned in Edom......... Gen 36:32
Bela the son of *B*.............................. 1Chr 1:43
2. Father of Balaam.
Balaam also the son of *B* to Pethor ...... Num 22:5
Balaam also the son of *B* said............... Num 24:3
Balaam the son of *B* hath said.............. Num 24:15
Balaam also the son of *B* they .... Num 31:8
son of *B* of Pethor of Mesopotamia....... Deut 23:4
Balaam also the son of *B*, the .... Josh 13:22
Balaam the son of *B* to curse you.......... Josh 24:9
what Balaam the son of *B* answered....... Mic 6:5

BERA (be'-rah) *King of Sodom.*
made war with *B* king of Sodom............. Gen 14:2

BERACAH See BERACHAH.

BERACHAH (ber'-a-kah)
1. A Benjamite warrior in David's army.
and *B*, and Jehu the Antothite,............. 1Chr 12:3
2. A valley in Judah.
themselves in the valley of *B* 2Chr 20:26
place was called, The valley of *B* 2Chr 20:26

BERACHIAH (ber-a-ki'-ah) See BERECHIAH. *Father of Asaph.*
hand, even Asaph the son of *B*............... 1Chr 6:39

BERAIAH (ber-a-i'-ah) *A son of Shimhi.*
and *B*, and Shimrath 1Chr 8:21

BERAKIAH See BERACHIAH.

BEREA (be-re'-a) *A city in Macedonia.*
Paul and Silas by night unto *B*............. Acts 17:10
of God was preached of Paul at *B*.......... Acts 17:13
him into Asia Sopater of *B*................... Acts 20:4

BEREAVE
do I labour, and *b* my soul of good......... Eccl 4:8
I will *b* them of children, I will.............. Jer 15:7
evil beasts, and they shall *b* thee.......... Eze 5:17
no more henceforth *b* them of men........ Eze 36:12
neither *b* thy nations any more,............ Eze 36:14
their children, yet will I *b* them .... Hos 9:12

BEREAVED
Me have ye *b* of my children,................ Gen 42:36
b of my children, I am *b* .... Gen 43:14
wives be *b* of their children .... Jer 18:21
up men, and hast *b* thy nations............. Eze 36:13
as a bear that is *b* of her whelps............ Hos 13:8

BEREAVETH
abroad the sword *b*, at home there .... Lam 1:20

BERECHIAH (ber-e-ki'-ah) See BERACHIAH.
1. A descendant of King Jehoiakim.
And Hashubah, and Ohel, and *B*............ 1Chr 3:20
2. Same as Berachiah.
his brethren, Asaph the son of *B*........... 1Chr 15:17
3. A Levite near Jerusalem.
B the son of Asa, the son of................. 1Chr 9:16
4. A Levite doorkeeper.
And *B* and Elkanah were 1Chr 15:23
5. An Ephraimite.
B the son of Meshillemoth, and............ 2Chr 28:12
6. Father of Meshullam.

repaired Meshullam the son of *B*........... Neh 3:4
son of *B* over against his chamber......... Neh 3:30
of Meshullam the son of *B*................... Neh 6:18
7. Father of Zechariah.
Lord unto Zechariah, the son of *B*......... Zec 1:1
Lord unto Zechariah, the son of *B*......... Zec 1:7

BERED (be'-red)
1. A place in southern Canaan.
behold, it is between Kadesh and *B*....... Gen 16:14
2. An Ephraimite.
B his son, and Tahath his son, and........ 1Chr 7:20

BEREKIAH See BERECHIAH.

BERI (be'-ri) See BERITES. *Son of Zophah.*
and Harnepher, and Shual, and *B*.......... 1Chr 7:36

BERIAH (be-ri'-ah) See BERITES.
1. A son of Asher.
Jimnah, and Ishuah, and Isui, and *B*..... Gen 46:17
and the sons of *B*.............................. Gen 46:17
of *B*, the family of the Beriites.............. Num 26:44
Of the sons of *B*............................... Num 26:45
Imnah, and Isuah, and Ishuai, and *B*..... 1Chr 7:30
And the sons of *B*............................. 1Chr 7:31
2. A son of Ephraim.
a son, and he called his name *B*............ 1Chr 7:23
3. A son of Elpaal.
B also, and Shema, who were heads 1Chr 8:13
and Ispah, and Joha, the sons of *B*........ 1Chr 8:16
4. A Levite.
Jahath, Zina, and Jeush, and *B*............. 1Chr 23:10
but Jeush and *B* had not many sons........ 1Chr 23:11

BERIITES (be-ri'-ites) *Descendants of Beriah 1.*
of Beriah, the family of the *B* .... Num 26:44

BERITES (be'-rites) *Descendants of Beri.*
and to Beth-maachah, and all the *B* 2Sa 20:14

BERITH (be'-rith) See BAAL-BERITH. *Idol at Shechem.*
an hold of the house of the god *B*.......... Judg 9:46

BERNICE (bur-ni'-see) *Daughter of Herod Agrippa.*
B came unto Caesarea to salute............. Acts 25:13
when Agrippa was come, and *B* .... Acts 25:23
rose up, and the governor, and *B*........... Acts 26:30

BERODACH-BALADAN (ber-o'-dak-bal'-a-dan) See MERODACH-BALADAN. *A king of Babylon.*
At that time *B*, the son of.................... 2Kin 20:12

BEROEA See BEREA.

BEROTHAH (be-ro'-thah) See BEROTHAI, BEROTHITE. *A city near Hamath.*
Hamath, *B*, Sibraim, which is .... Eze 47:16

BEROTHAI (be'-ro-thae) See BEROTHAH. *A city of Hadadezer.*
And from Betah, and from *B*, cities 2Sa 8:8

BEROTHITE (be'-ro-thite) See BEEROTHITE. *A native of Beeroth.*
Zelek the Ammonite, Naharai the *B*. 1Chr 11:39

BERRIES
two or three *b* in the top of the .... Is 17:6
tree, my brethren, bear olive *b*............. Jas 3:12

BERYL
And the fourth row a *b*, and an onyx ..... Ex 28:20
And the fourth row, a *b*, an onyx,.......... Ex 39:13
are as gold rings set with the *b*............. Ex 39:13
was like unto the colour of a *b*.............. Eze 1:16
was as the colour of a *b* stone .... Eze 10:9
topaz, and the diamond, the *b*............... Eze 28:13
His body also was like the *b*................. Dan 10:6
the eighth, *b*................................... Rev 21:20

BESAI (be'-sahee) *A family of exiles.*
of Paseah, the children of *B* .... Ezr 2:49
The children of *B*, the children .... Neh 7:52

BESEECH
we *b* thee, three days' journey.............. Ex 3:18
I *b* thee, shew me thy glory .... Ex 33:18
I *b* thee, lay not the sin upon us .... Num 12:11
Heal her now, O God, I *b* thee .... Num 12:13
I *b* thee, let the power of my .... Num 14:17
I *b* thee, the iniquity of this .... Num 14:19
I *b* thee, tell thy servant.................... 1Sa 23:11
I *b* thee, and his servants go with......... 2Sa 13:24
I humbly *b* thee that I may find............. 2Sa 16:4
I *b* thee, O LORD, take away the............. 2Sa 24:10
I *b* thee, save thou us out of his............ 2Kin 19:19
I *b* thee, O LORD, remember now 2Kin 20:3
I *b* thee, do away the iniquity of........... 1Chr 21:8
I *b* thee, thine eyes be open, and.......... 2Chr 6:40
I *b* thee, O LORD God of heaven,............ Neh 1:5
I *b* thee, the word that thou................. Neh 1:8
I *b* thee, let now thine ear be............... Neh 1:11
I *b* thee, that thou hast made me.......... Job 10:9
I *b* thee, and I will speak.................... Job 42:4
we *b* thee, O God of hosts .... Ps 80:14
I *b* thee, deliver my soul .... Ps 116:4
Save now, I *b* thee, O LORD.................. Ps 118:25
I *b* thee, send now prosperity............... Ps 118:25
I *b* thee, the freewill offerings .... Ps 119:108
I *b* thee, how I have walked................. Is 38:3
we *b* thee, we are all thy people .... Is 64:9
We *b* thee, let this man be put to.......... Jer 38:4
I *b* thee, the voice of the LORD,............ Jer 38:20

we *b* thee, our supplication be .... Jer 42:2
thy servants, I *b* thee, ten days .... Dan 1:12
I *b* thee, let thine anger and thy .... Dan 9:16
O Lord God, forgive, I *b* thee .... Amos 7:2
I, O Lord God, cease, I *b* thee............... Amos 7:5
We *b* thee, O Lord, we *b*.................... Jonah 1:14
I *b* thee, my life from me..................... Jonah 4:3
b God that he will be gracious,................ Mal 1:9
they *b* him to put his hand upon .... Mk 7:32
I *b* thee, torment me not.................... Lk 8:28
I *b* thee, look upon my son .... Lk 9:38
I *b* thee, suffer me to speak unto .... Acts 21:39
wherefore I *b* thee to hear me.............. Acts 26:3
I *b* you therefore, brethren, by .... Rom 12:1
Now I *b* you, brethren, for the .... Rom 15:30
Now I *b* you, brethren, mark them......... Rom 16:17
Now I *b* you, brethren, by the 1Cor 1:10
Wherefore I *b* you, be ye 1Cor 4:16
I *b* you, brethren, (ye know the 1Cor 16:15
Wherefore I *b* you that ye would 2Cor 2:8
as though God did *b* you by us,............. 2Cor 5:20
b you also that ye receive not.............. 2Cor 6:1
Now I Paul myself *b* you by the............. 2Cor 10:1
But I *b* you, that I may not be............... 2Cor 10:2
Brethren, I *b* you, be as I am .... Gal 4:12
b you that ye walk worthy of the .... Eph 4:1
I *b* Euodias, and *b* Syntyche,.............. Phil 4:2
b Syntyche, that they be of the............. Phil 4:2
Furthermore then we *b* you 1Th 4:1
but we *b* you, brethren, that ye 1Th 4:10
we *b* you, brethren, to know them 1Th 5:12
Now we *b* you, brethren, by the 2Th 2:1
for love's sake I rather *b* thee .... Philem 9
I *b* thee for my son Onesimus,.............. Philem 10
But I *b* you the rather to do this........... Heb 13:19
I *b* you, brethren, suffer the................ Heb 13:22
I *b* you as strangers and pilgrims,......... 1Pet 2:11
And now I *b* thee, lady, not as.............. 2Jn 5

BESEECHING
came unto him a centurion, *b* him,......... Mt 8:5
b him, and kneeling down to him,.......... Mk 1:40
b him that he would receive and heal..... Lk 7:3

BESET
b the house round about, and beat .... Judg 19:22
b the house round about upon me......... Judg 20:5
bulls of Bashan have *b* me round .... Ps 22:12
Thou hast *b* me behind and before,....... Ps 139:5
own doings have *b* them about.............. Hos 7:2
the sin which doth so easily *b* us........... Heb 12:1

BESIDE
b the first famine that was in .... Gen 26:1
take other wives *b* my daughters .... Gen 31:50
on foot that were men, *b* children .... Ex 12:37
b Pi-hahiroth, before Baal-zephon......... Ex 14:9
pour all the blood *b* the bottom............. Ex 29:12
cast it *b* the altar on the east............... Lev 1:16
and he shall put them *b* the altar.......... Lev 6:10
the *b* burnt sacrifice of the .... Lev 9:17
eat it without leaven *b* the altar........... Lev 10:12
b the other in her life time.................. Lev 18:18
the *b* sabbaths of the LORD, and........... Lev 23:38
b your gifts, and *b* all your .... Lev 23:38
b all your freewill offerings,................ Lev 23:38
the *b* ram of the atonement,................ Num 5:8
lain with thee is *b* thine husband.......... Num 5:20
b that that his hand shall get............... Num 6:21
b this manna, before our eyes.............. Num 11:6
b them that died about the matter........ Num 16:49
and as cedar trees *b* the waters .... Num 24:6
b the continual burnt offering,............. Num 28:10
b the continual burnt offering .... Num 28:15
Ye shall offer these *b* the burnt .... Num 28:23
it shall be offered *b* the..................... Num 28:31
Ye shall offer them *b* the.................... Num 29:6
the *b* burnt offering of the month......... Num 29:6
the *b* sin offering of atonement,........... Num 29:11
the *b* continual burnt offering,............. Num 29:16
the *b* continual burnt offering,............. Num 29:19
the *b* continual burnt offering,............. Num 29:22
the *b* continual burnt offering,............. Num 29:25
the *b* continual burnt offering,............. Num 29:28
the *b* continual burnt offering,............. Num 29:31
the *b* continual burnt offering,............. Num 29:34
the *b* continual burnt offering,............. Num 29:38
b your vows, and your freewill .... Num 29:39
the *b* rest of them that were............... Num 31:8
b unwalled towns a great many .... Deut 3:5
there is none else *b* him.................... Deut 4:35
Gilgal, *b* the plains of Moreh............... Deut 11:30
b that which cometh of the sale .... Deut 18:8
more for thee, *b* these three............... Deut 19:9
the *b* covenant which he made with...... Deut 29:1
the city Adam, that is *b* Zaretan........... Josh 3:16
which is *b* Beth-aven, on the east .... Josh 7:2
king of Ai, which is *b* Beth-el.............. Josh 12:9
and Mearah that is *b* the Sidonians ...... Josh 13:4
the land of Gilead and Bashan,.............. Josh 17:5
in building you an altar *b* the.............. Josh 22:19
b the altar of the LORD our God............ Josh 22:29
and it be dry upon all the earth *b*......... Judg 6:37
pitched *b* the well of Harod................. Judg 7:1
b ornaments, and collars, and............. Judg 8:26
b the chains that were about............... Judg 8:26
b her he had neither son nor .... Judg 11:34
b the inhabitants of Gibeah,............... Judg 20:15
b Benjamin, were numbered four......... Judg 20:17
wait which they had set *b* Gibeah .... Judg 20:36
And she sat *b* the reapers.................. Ruth 2:14
there is none to redeem it *b* thee......... Ruth 4:4

for there is none b thee............... 1Sa 2:2
to battle, and pitched b Eben-ezer .. 1Sa 4:1
stand b my father in the field......... 1Sa 19:3
neither is there any God b thee....... 2Sa 7:22
in Baal-hazor, which is b Ephraim .. 2Sa 13:23
stood b the way of the gate........... 2Sa 15:2
all his servants passed on b him 2Sa 15:18
and took my son from b me............ 1Kin 3:20
sheep, b harts, and roebucks, and .. 1Kin 4:23
B the chief of Solomon's officers 1Kin 5:16
in Ezion-geber, which is b Eloth 1Kin 9:26
b that which Solomon gave her of 1Kin 10:13
B that he had of the merchantmen,.. 1Kin 10:15
and two lions stood b the stays 1Kin 10:19
b the mischief that Hadad did.......... 1Kin 11:25
lay my bones b his bones............... 1Kin 13:31
with the sword b the king's house 2Kin 11:20
set it b the altar, on the right.......... 2Kin 12:9
b his sin wherewith he made Judah .. 2Kin 21:16
the sons of the concubines, and 1Chr 3:9
neither is there any God b them...... 1Chr 17:20
b that which she had brought unto ... 2Chr 9:12
B that which chapmen...................... 2Chr 9:14
b those whom the king put in the 2Chr 17:19
with them other b the Ammonites 2Chr 20:1
LORD, from b the incense altar 2Chr 26:19
B their genealogy of males, from 2Chr 31:16
the freewill offering for the .... Ezr 1:4
b all that was willingly offered .... Ezr 1:6
B their servants and their maids,.... Ezr 2:65
b forty shekels of silver.................. Neh 5:15
b those that came unto us from ...... Neh 5:17
B their manservants and their .... Neh 7:67
b him stood Mattithiah, and Shema, .. Neh 8:4
and the asses feeding b them .... Job 1:14
he leadeth me b the still waters ...... Ps 23:2
upon earth that I desire b thee........ Ps 73:25
feed thy kids b the shepherds'........ Song 1:8
are ye that sow b all waters............ Is 32:20
and b me there is no saviour........... Is 43:11
and b me there is no God................ Is 44:6
Is there a God b me.......................... Is 44:8
none else, there is no God b me...... Is 45:5
the west, that there is none b me .... Is 45:6
and there is no God else b me......... Is 45:21
there is none b me........................... Is 47:8
heart, I am, and none else b me ...... Is 47:8
heart, I am, and none else b me ...... Is 47:10
b those that are gathered unto .... Is 56:8
b thee, what he hath prepared for .... Is 64:4
princes which stood b the king .... Jer 36:21
in, and stood b the brasen altar ..... Eze 9:2
he went in, and stood b the wheels .. Eze 10:6
also turned not from b them............ Eze 10:16
out, the wheels also were b them .... Eze 10:19
their wings, and the wheels b them .. Eze 11:22
thereof from b the great waters ...... Eze 32:13
up, even for others b those............. Hos 13:4
for there is no saviour b me............ Hos 13:4
I am, and there is none b me........... Zeph 2:15
thousand men, b women and children .. Mt 14:21
thousand men, b women and children .. Mt 15:38
I have gained b these five talents.... Mt 25:20
gained two other talents b them...... Mt 25:22
for they said, He is b himself.......... Mk 3:21
b all this, between us and you .... Lk 16:26
b all this, to day is the third............ Lk 24:21
voice, Paul, thou art b thyself......... Acts 26:24
For whether we be b ourselves....... 2Cor 5:13
B those things that are without,...... 2Cor 11:28
b this, giving all diligence, add........ 2Pet 1:5

BESIDES
unto Lot, Hast thou here any b........ Gen 19:12
b Jacob's sons' wives, all the......... Gen 46:26
B the cakes, he shall offer for........ Lev 7:13
not here a prophet of the LORD b 1Kin 22:7
not here a prophet of the LORD b 2Chr 18:6
other lords b these have had........... Is 26:13
there were added b unto them many .. Jer 36:32
b, I know not whether I baptized 1Cor 1:16
unto me even thine own self b........ Philem 19

BESIEGE
thee, then thou shalt b it................. Deut 20:12
When thou shalt b a city a long....... Deut 20:19
he shall b thee in all thy gates,....... Deut 28:52
he shall b thee in all thy gates,....... Deut 28:52
to Keilah, to b David and his men ... 1Sa 23:8
if their enemy is them in the land 1Kin 8:37
city, and his servants did b it.......... 2Kin 24:11
if their enemies b them in the......... 2Chr 6:28
b, O Media..................................... Is 21:2
which b you without the walls, and .. Jer 21:4
to the Chaldeans that b you............ Jer 21:9

BESIEGED
children of Ammon, and b Rabbah ... 2Sa 11:1
b him in Abel of Beth-maachah, and.. 2Sa 20:15
Israel with him, and they b Tirzah ... 1Kin 16:17
b Samaria, and warred against it 1Kin 20:1
host, and went up, and b Samaria.... 2Kin 6:24
and, behold, they b it, until an 2Kin 6:25
and they b Ahaz, but could not....... 2Kin 16:5
to Samaria, and b it three years 2Kin 17:5
came up against Samaria, and b it .. 2Kin 18:9
up all the rivers of the b places...... 2Kin 19:24
Jerusalem, and the city was b 2Kin 24:10
the city was b unto the eleventh..... 2Kin 25:2
of Ammon, and came and b Rabbah .. 2Sa 12:26
b it, and built great bulwarks.......... Eccl 9:14
garden of cucumbers, as a b city .... Is 1:8

up all the rivers of the b places...... Is 37:25
of Babylon's army b Jerusalem ...... Jer 32:2
when the Chaldeans that b............. Jer 37:5
against Jerusalem, and they b it ..... Jer 39:1
So the city was b unto the.............. Jer 52:5
face against it, and it shall be b ..... Eze 4:3
is b shall die by the famine............ Eze 6:12
Babylon on Jerusalem, and it .... Dan 1:1

BESODEIAH (bes-o-di'-ah) A repairer of
Jerusalem's walls.
Paseah, and Meshullam the son of B .. Neh 3:6

BESOM
it with the b of destruction............. Is 14:23

BESOR (be'-sor) A brook in southern Judah.
with him, and came to the brook B .. 1Sa 30:9
could not go over the brook B......... 1Sa 30:10
made also to abide at the brook B .. 1Sa 30:21

BESOUGHT
anguish of his soul, when he b us ... Gen 42:21
Moses b the LORD his God, and said .. Ex 32:11
b the LORD at that time, saying .... Deut 3:23
David therefore b God for the......... 2Sa 12:16
And the man of God b the LORD 1Kin 13:6
b him, and said unto him, O man of .. 1Kin 13:13
And Jehoahaz b the LORD, and the .. 2Kin 13:4
he b the LORD his God, and humbled .. 2Chr 33:12
we fasted and b our God for this .... Ezr 8:23
b him with tears to put away the ..... Est 8:3
b the LORD, and the LORD repeated .. Jer 26:19
So the devils b him, saying, If .... Mt 8:31
b him that he would depart............. Mt 8:34
b him that they might only touch..... Mt 14:36
b him, saying, Send her away .... Mt 15:23
b him, saying, Have patience with .. Mt 18:29
b he him much that he would not..... Mk 5:10
And all the devils b him, saying,...... Mk 5:12
b him greatly, saying, My little .... Mk 5:23
b him that they might touch if it...... Mk 6:56
she b him that he would cast.......... Mk 7:26
unto him, and b him to touch him .... Mk 8:22
and they b him for her..................... Lk 4:38
b him, saying, Lord, if thou wilt...... Lk 5:12
they b him instantly, saying,.......... Lk 7:4
they b him that he would not........... Lk 8:31
they b him that he would suffer ...... Lk 8:32
about b him to depart from them ..... Lk 8:37
b him that he might be with them .... Lk 8:38
b him that he would come into his .. Lk 8:41
I b thy disciples to cast him out...... Lk 9:40
a certain Pharisee b him to dine ..... Lk 11:37
they b him that he would tarry......... Jn 4:40
b him that he would come down, and.. Jn 4:47
b Pilate that their legs might .... Jn 19:31
b Pilate that he might take away..... Jn 19:38
the Gentiles b that these words ..... Acts 13:42
and her household, she b us,........... Acts 16:15
b them, and brought them out, and .. Acts 16:39
b him not to go up to Jerusalem...... Acts 21:12
him against Paul, and b him,........... Acts 25:2
Paul b them all to take meat,.......... Acts 27:33
this thing I b the Lord thrice 2Cor 12:8
As I b thee to abide still at 1Ti 1:3

BEST
take of the b fruits in the land........ Gen 43:11
in the b of the land make thy.......... Gen 47:6
in the b of the land, in the land ...... Gen 47:11
of the b of his own field.................. Ex 22:5
of the b of his own vineyard,.......... Ex 22:5
All the b of the oil.......................... Num 18:12
all the b of the wine, and of the...... Num 18:12
of the LORD, of all the b thereof..... Num 18:29
have received the b thereof from it . Num 18:30
have heaved from it the b of it......... Num 18:32
them marry to whom they think b.... Num 36:6
thy gates, where it liketh him b ...... Deut 23:16
oliveyards, even the b of them 1Sa 8:14
the b of the sheep, and of the......... 1Sa 15:9
people spared the b of the sheep ... 1Sa 15:15
What seemeth you b I will do.......... 2Sa 18:4
and overlaid it with the b gold........ 1Kin 10:18
Look even out the b and meetest of.. 2Kin 10:3
her maids unto the b place of the ... Est 2:9
verily every man at his b state........ Ps 39:5
like the b wine for my beloved,....... Song 7:9
b of Lebanon, all that drink............. Eze 31:16
The b of them is as a brier............. Mic 7:4
servants, Bring forth the b robe ..... Lk 15:22
But covet earnestly the b gifts....... 1Cor 12:31

BESTEAD
shall pass through it, hardly b......... Is 8:21

BESTIR
that then thou shalt b thyself......... 2Sa 5:24

BESTOW
that he may b upon you a blessing.. Ex 32:29
thou shalt b that money for............ Deut 14:26
the LORD did they b upon Baalim 2Chr 24:7
thou shalt have occasion to b......... Ezr 7:20
b it out of the king's treasure......... Ezr 7:20
have no room where to b my fruits... Lk 12:17
there will I b all my fruits and......... Lk 12:18
upon these we b more abundant 1Cor 12:23
though I b all my goods to feed 1Cor 13:3

BESTOWED
whom he b in the cities for.............. 1Kin 10:26
hand, and b them in the house 2Kin 5:24

the money to be b on workmen 2Kin 12:15
b upon him such royal majesty as .. 1Chr 29:25
whom he b in the chariot cities,...... 2Chr 9:25
to all that the LORD hath b on us..... Is 63:7
which he hath b on them according .. Is 63:7
reap that whereon ye b no labour ... Jn 4:38
Mary, who b much labour on us ...... Rom 16:6
his grace which was b upon me was .. 1Cor 15:10
that for the gift b upon us by.......... 2Cor 1:11
b on the churches of Macedonia 2Cor 8:1
lest I have b upon you labour in ..... Gal 4:11
of love the Father hath b upon us ... 1Jn 3:1

BETAH (be'-tah) A city of Hadadezer.
And from B, and from Berothai,...... 2Sa 8:8

BETEN (be'-ten) A city in Asher.
border was Helkath, and Hali, and B. Josh 19:25

BETHABARA (beth-ab'-ar-ah) See
BETHBARAH. A place east of the Jordan River
were done in B beyond Jordan........ Jn 1:28

BETH ACACIA See BETH-SHITTAH.

BETH-ANATH (beth'-a-nath) A city in
Naphtali.
Iron, and Migdal-el, Horem, and B .. Josh 19:38
nor the inhabitants of B.................. Judg 1:33
of B became tributaries unto them .. Judg 1:33

BETH-ANOTH (beth'-a-noth) A city in Judah.
And Maarath, and B, and Eltekon.... Josh 15:59

BETHANY (beth'-a-ny) A village near
Jerusalem.
and went out of the city into B....... Mt 21:17
Now when Jesus was in B, in the .... Mt 26:6
to Jerusalem, unto Bethphage and B .. Mk 11:1
went out unto B with the twelve ..... Mk 11:11
when they were come from B.......... Mk 11:12
being in B in the house of Simon.... Mk 14:3
was come nigh to Bethphage and B .. Lk 19:29
And he led them out as far as to B .. Lk 24:50
man was sick, named Lazarus, of B .. Jn 11:1
Now B was nigh unto Jerusalem,.... Jn 11:18
before the passover came to B........ Jn 12:1

BETH APHRAH See APHRAH.

BETH-ARABAH (beth-ar'-ab-ah) A city of the
Arabah.
passed along by the north of B ...... Josh 15:6
In the wilderness, B, Middin, and .... Josh 15:61
And B, and Zemaraim, and Beth-el, .. Josh 18:22

BETH-ARAM (beth'-a-ram) A city in Gad.
And in the valley, B, and............... Josh 13:27

BETH-ARBEL (beth-ar'-bel) A city destroyed
by the Assyrians.
as Shalman spoiled B in the day .... Hos 10:14

BETH ASHBEA See ASHBEA.

BETH-AVEN (beth-a'-ven) A town in
Benjamin.
Jericho to Ai, which is beside B...... Josh 7:2
were at the wilderness of B............. Josh 18:12
in Michmash, eastward from B 1Sa 13:5
and the battle passed over unto B ... 1Sa 14:23
Gilgal, neither go ye up to B............ Hos 4:15
cry aloud at B, after thee, O........... Hos 5:8
fear because of the calves of B....... Hos 10:5

BETH-AZMAVETH (beth-az'-maveth) See
AZMAVETH. A village in Judah.
The men of B, forty and two............ Neh 7:28

BETH-BAAL-MEON (beth-ba'-al-me'-on) A
Moabite town.
Dibon, and Bamoth-baal, and B ...... Josh 13:17

BETH-BARAH (beth-ba'-rah) See BETHABARA.
A place in Gad.
before them the waters unto B........ Judg 7:24
and took the waters unto B............. Judg 7:24

BETH-BIREI (beth-bir-e-i) See BETH-LEBAOTH.
A town in Simeon.
and Hazar-susim, and at B, and at ... 1Chr 4:31

BETH BIRI See BETH-BIREI.

BETH-CAR (beth'-car) A Philistine stronghold
in Judah.
them, until they came under B 1Sa 7:11

BETH-DAGON (beth-da'-gon)
1. A town in Judah.
And Gederoth, B, and Naamah, and .. Josh 15:41
2. A town in Asher.
turneth toward the sunrising to B .... Josh 19:27

BETH-DIBLATHAIM (beth-dib-lath-a'-im) A
Moabite town.
Dibon, and upon Nebo, and upon B.. Jer 48:22

BETH-EL
unto a mountain on the east of B .... Gen 12:8
having B on the west, and Hai on .... Gen 12:8
journeys from the south even to B ... Gen 13:3
been at the beginning, between B .... Gen 13:3
called the name of that place B ...... Gen 28:19
I am the God of B, where thou......... Gen 31:13
unto Jacob, Arise, go up to B.......... Gen 35:1
And let us arise, and go up to B ...... Gen 35:3
in the land of Canaan, that is, B...... Gen 35:6
was buried beneath B under an oak .. Gen 35:8
place where God spake with him, B . Gen 35:15

And they journeyed from B................ Gen 35:16
Beth-aven, on the east side of B........ Josh 7:2
lie in ambush, and abode between B... Josh 8:9
them to lie in ambush between B........ Josh 8:12
was not a man left in Ai or B............. Josh 8:17
the king of Ai, which is beside B........ Josh 12:9
the king of B, one............................. Josh 12:16
from Jericho throughout mount B....... Josh 16:1
And goeth out from B to Luz.............. Josh 16:2
to the side of Luz, which is B............. Josh 18:13
and Zemaraim, and B........................ Josh 18:22
they also went up against B................ Judg 1:22
house of Joseph sent to descry B........ Judg 1:23
Ramah and B in mount Ephraim........ Judg 4:5
which is on the north side of B.......... Judg 21:19
that goeth up from B to Shechem ...... Judg 21:19
from year to year in circuit to B........ 1Sa 7:16
three men going up to God to B.......... 1Sa 10:3
Saul in Michmash and in mount B...... 1Sa 13:2
To them which were in B, and to........ 1Sa 30:27
And he set the one in B, and the......... 1Kin 12:29
So did he in B, sacrificing unto......... 1Kin 12:32
he placed in B the priests of the........ 1Kin 12:32
the altar which he had made in B....... 1Kin 12:33
by the word of the Lord unto B.......... 1Kin 13:1
had cried against the altar in B.......... 1Kin 13:4
not by the way that he came to B....... 1Kin 13:10
there dwelt an old prophet in B.......... 1Kin 13:11
man of God had done that day in B.... 1Kin 13:11
the Lord against the altar in B........... 1Kin 13:32
for the Lord hath sent me to B........... 2Kin 2:2
So they went down to B..................... 2Kin 2:2
were at B came forth to Elisha 2Kin 2:3
And he went up from thence unto B... 2Kin 2:23
the golden calves that were in B........ 2Kin 10:29
from Samaria came and dwelt in B..... 2Kin 17:28
carried the ashes of them unto B........ 2Kin 23:4
Moreover the altar that was at B........ 2Kin 23:15
hast done against the altar of B......... 2Kin 23:17
the acts that he had done in B............ 2Kin 23:19
and habitations were, B and the......... 1Chr 7:28
B with the towns thereof, and.......... 2Chr 13:19
The men of B and Ai, two hundred.... Ezr 2:28
The men of B and Ai, an hundred...... Neh 7:32
dwelt at Michmash, and Aija, and B.. Neh 11:31
was ashamed of B their confidence.... Jer 48:13
So shall B do unto you because of..... Hos 10:15
he found him in B, and there he .... Hos 12:4
I will also visit the altars of B........... Amos 3:14
Come to B, and transgress................ Amos 4:4
But seek not B, nor enter into............ Amos 5:5
and B shall come to nought............... Amos 5:5
there be none to quench it in B.......... Amos 5:6
Then Amaziah the priest of B sent .... Amos 7:10
prophesy not again any more at B ..... Amos 7:13

BETH-ELITE (beth'-el-ite) A native of Bethel.
days did Hiel the B build Jericho........ 1Kin 16:34

BETH-EMEK (beth-e'-mek) A town in Asher.
toward the north side of B.................. Josh 19:27

BETHER (be'-thur) A district in the Jordan
valley.
hart upon the mountains of B............. Song 2:17

BETHESDA (beth-ez'-dah) A pool in
Jerusalem.
is called in the Hebrew tongue B....... Jn 5:2

BETH-EZEL (beth-e'-zel) A city in Judah.
not forth in the mourning of B.......... Mic 1:11

BETH-GADER (beth-ga'-der) See GEDER. A
descendant of Caleb.
Hareph the father of B....................... 1Chr 2:51

BETH-GAMUL (beth-ga'-mul) A Moabite
town.
And upon Kiriathaim, and upon B..... Jer 48:23

BETH-HACCEREM (beth-hak'-se-rem) A
town in Judah.
of Rechab, the ruler of part of B........ Neh 3:14
and set up a sign of fire in B.............. Jer 6:1

BETH HAKKEREM See BETH-HACCEREM.

BETH-HARAN (beth-ha'-ran) See ELON-BETH-
HARAN. A city in Gad.
And Beth-nimrah, and B, fenced........ Num 32:36

BETH-HOGLA (beth-hog'-lah) See BETH-
HOGLAH. A city in Benjamin.
And the border went up to B............... Josh 15:6

BETH HOGLAH See BETH-HOGLA.

BETH-HOGLAH (beth-hog'-lah) See BETH-
HOGLAH. Same as Beth-hogla.
along to the side of B northward......... Josh 18:19
their families were Jericho, and B....... Josh 18:21

BETH-HORON (beth-ho'-ron) Two cities in
Ephraim, near Benjamin.
along the way that goeth up to B........ Josh 10:10
and were in the going down to B........ Josh 10:11
unto the coast of B the nether............ Josh 16:3
Ataroth-addar, unto B the upper........ Josh 16:5
on the south side of the nether B....... Josh 18:13
that lieth before B southward............. Josh 18:14
suburbs, and B with her suburbs........ Josh 21:22
company turned the way to B............. 1Sa 13:18
built Gezer, and B the nether............. 1Kin 9:17
suburbs, and B with her suburbs........ 1Chr 6:68
who built B the nether, and the.......... 1Chr 7:24
Also he built B the upper................... 2Chr 8:5

B the nether, fenced cities, with........ 2Chr 8:5
Judah, from Samaria even unto B 2Chr 25:13

BETHINK
Yet if they shall b themselves in........ 1Kin 8:47
Yet if they b themselves in the........... 2Chr 6:37

BETH JESHIMOTH See JESIMOTH.

BETH-JESHIMOTH (beth-jesh'-im-oth) See
BETH-JESIMOTH. Same as Beth-jesimoth.
sea on the east, the way to B.............. Josh 12:3
and Ashdoth-pisgah, and B................ Josh 13:20
the glory of the country, B................. Eze 25:9

BETH-JESIMOTH (beth-jes'-im-oth) See
BETH-JESHIMOTH. A Moabite city.
from B even unto Abel-shittim in ...... Num 33:49

BETH-LE-APHRAH See APHRAH.

BETH-LEBAOTH (beth-leb'-a-oth) See BETH-
BISEL. A town in Simeon.
And B, and Sharuhen......................... Josh 19:6

BETH-LEHEM (beth'-le-hem) See BETH-
LEHEMITE, BETH-LEHEM-JUDAH.
1. A city in Judah.
in the way to Ephrath, which is B ...... Gen 35:19
the same is B...................................... Gen 48:7
two went until they came to B............ Ruth 1:19
to pass, when they were come to B..... Ruth 1:19
they came to B in the beginning........ Ruth 1:22
And, behold, Boaz came out of B....... Ruth 2:4
in Ephratah, and be famous in B .... Ruth 4:11
the Lord spake, and came to B........... 1Sa 16:4
to feed his father's sheep at B............ 1Sa 17:15
that he might run to B his city............ 1Sa 20:6
asked leave of me to go to B.............. 1Sa 20:28
his father, which was in B.................. 2Sa 2:32
of the Philistines was then in B.......... 2Sa 23:14
of the water of the well of B............... 2Sa 23:15
drew water out of the well of B.......... 2Sa 23:16
Elhanan the son of Dodo of B............ 2Sa 23:24
garrison was then at B....................... 1Chr 11:16
of the water of the well of B............... 1Chr 11:17
drew water out of the well of B.......... 1Chr 11:18
Elhanan the son of Dodo of B............ 1Chr 11:26
He built even B, and Etam, and......... 2Chr 11:6
The children of B, an hundred............ Ezr 2:21
The men of B and Netophah, an......... Neh 7:26
B Ephratah, though thou be little....... Mic 5:2
2. A town in Zebulun.
and Shimron, and Idalah, and B .... Josh 19:15
3. A town in Ephraim.
him Ibzan of B judged Israel.............. Judg 12:8
died Ibzan, and was buried at B .... Judg 12:10
4. A descendant of Caleb.
Salma the father of B, Hareph the 1Chr 2:51
B, and the Netophathites, Ataroth,..... 1Chr 2:54
of Ephratah, the father of B................ 1Chr 4:4

BETHLEHEM A town in Judea.
of Chimham, which is by B................ Jer 41:17
Now when Jesus was born in B of ..... Mt 2:1
said unto him, In B of Judaea............. Mt 2:5
And thou B, in the land of Juda,........ Mt 2:6
And he sent them to B, and said, Go.. Mt 2:8
all the children that were in B............ Mt 2:16
city of David, which is called B.......... Lk 2:4
Let us now go even unto B................. Lk 2:15
of David, and out of the town of B..... Jn 7:42

BETH-LEHEMITE (beth'-le-hem-ite) A native
of Bethlehem.
I will send thee to Jesse the B............ 1Sa 16:1
I have seen a son of Jesse the B.......... 1Sa 16:18
son of thy servant Jesse the B............ 1Sa 17:58
the son of Jaare-oregim, a B............... 2Sa 21:19

BETH-LEHEM-JUDAH (beth'-le-hem-ju'-
dah) Same as Beth-lehem 1.
out of B of the family of Judah .... Judg 17:7
departed out of the city from B........... Judg 17:8
said unto him, I am a Levite of B .... Judg 17:9
took to him a concubine out of B .... Judg 19:1
him unto her father's house to B .... Judg 19:2
We are passing from B toward the ..... Judg 19:18
and I went to B, but I am now............ Judg 19:18
a certain man of B went to .... Ruth 1:1
and Chilion, Ephrathites of B............. Ruth 1:2
the son of that Ephrathite of B........... 1Sa 17:12

BETH MAACAH

BETH-MAACHAH (beth-ma'-a-kah) See
ABEL-BETH-MAACHAH. A city in Manasseh.
of Israel unto Abel, and to B.............. 2Sa 20:14
came and besieged him in Abel of B... 2Sa 20:15

BETH-MARCABOTH (beth-mar'-cab-oth) A
city in Simeon.
And Ziklag, and B, and Hazar-susah,.. Josh 19:5
And at B, and Hazar-susim, and......... 1Chr 4:31

BETH-MEON (beth-me'-on) See BETH-BAAL-
MEON. A Moabite city.
and upon Beth-gamul, and upon B..... Jer 48:23

BETH-NIMRAH (beth-nim'-rah) See NIMRAH.
A city in Gad.
And B, and Beth-haran, fenced........... Num 32:36
And in the valley, Beth-aram, and B... Josh 13:27

BETH OPHRAH See APHRAH.

BETH-PALET (beth-pa'-let) See BETH-PELET.
A town in Judah.
and Heshmon, and B.......................... Josh 15:27

BETH-PAZZEZ (beth-paz'-zez) A town in
Issachar.
and En-haddah, and B........................ Josh 19:21

BETH PELET See BETH-PALET.

BETH-PEOR (beth-pe'-or) A Moabite city.
in the valley over against B................ Deut 3:29
in the valley over against B................ Deut 4:46
the land of Moab, over against B .... Deut 34:6
And B, and Ashdoth-pisgah, and....... Josh 13:20

BETHPHAGE (beth'-fa-ie) A village near
Jerusalem.
unto Jerusalem, and were come to B.. Mt 21:1
came nigh to Jerusalem, unto B......... Mk 11:1
pass, when he was come nigh to B...... Lk 19:29

BETH-PHELET (beth'-fe-let) See BETH-PALET.
A town in Judah.
at Jeshua, and at Moladah, and at B... Neh 11:26

BETH-RAPHA (beth'-ra-fah) Son of Eshton.
And Eshton begat B, and Paseah, and 1Chr 4:12

BETH-REHOB (beth'-re-hob) A place in
northern Canaan.
was in the valley that lieth by B .... Judg 18:28
sent and hired the Syrians of B.......... 2Sa 10:6

BETHSAIDA (beth-sa'-dah)
1. A city in Galilee.
woe unto thee, B................................ Mt 11:21
to the other side before unto B........... Mk 6:45
woe unto thee, B................................ Lk 10:13
Philip, which was of B of Galilee....... Jn 12:21
2. A place east of Lake Gennesareth.
And he cometh to B............................ Mk 8:22
belonging to the city called B............. Lk 9:10

BETH SHAN See BETH-SHEAN.

BETH-SHAN (beth'-shan) See BETH-SHEAN. A
city in Manasseh.
his body to the wall of B.................... 1Sa 31:10
of his sons from the wall of B............ 1Sa 31:12
stolen them from the street of B......... 2Sa 21:12

BETH-SHEAN (beth-she'-an) See BETH-SHAN.
Same as Beth-shan.
had in Issachar and in Asher B.......... Josh 17:11
of iron, both they who are of B.......... Josh 17:16
drive out the inhabitants of B............. Judg 1:27
Taanach and Megiddo, and all B........ 1Kin 4:12
from B to Abel-meholah, even unto ... 1Kin 4:12
of the children of Manasseh, B.......... 1Chr 7:29

BETH SHEMESH See BETH-SHEMESH.

BETH-SHEMESH (beth'-she-mesh) See BETH-
SHEMITE.
1. A town in Judah.
the north side, and went down to B.... Josh 15:10
suburbs, and B with her suburbs........ Josh 21:16
by the way of his own coast to B........ 1Sa 6:9
the straight way to the way of B......... 1Sa 6:12
after them unto the border of B.......... 1Sa 6:12
they of B were reaping their 1Sa 6:13
the men of B offered burnt 1Sa 6:15
And he smote the men of B, because .. 1Sa 6:19
And the men of B said, Who is able ... 1Sa 6:20
in Makaz, and in Shaalbim, and B 1Kin 4:9
one another in the face at B................ 2Kin 14:11
Jehoash the son of Ahaziah, at B 2Kin 14:13
suburbs, and B with her suburbs........ 1Chr 6:59
he and Amaziah king of Judah, at B... 2Chr 25:21
Joash, the son of Jehoahaz, at B 2Chr 25:23
south of Judah, and had taken B 2Chr 28:18
2. A city in Issachar.
to Tabor, and Shahazimah, and B ...... Josh 19:22
3. A city in Naphtali.
Horem, and Beth-anath, and B........... Josh 19:38
drive out the inhabitants of B............. Judg 1:33
nevertheless the inhabitants of B .... Judg 1:33
4. A temple in Egypt.
shall break also the images of B .... Jer 43:13

BETH-SHEMITE (beth'-shem-ite) An
inhabitant of Beth-shemesh.
into the field of Joshua, a B............... 1Sa 6:14
day in the field of Joshua, the B......... 1Sa 6:18

BETH-SHITTAH (beth-shit'-tah) A place in
the Jordan valley.
and the host fled to B in Zererath ...... Judg 7:22

BETH-TAPPUAH (beth-tap'-pu-ah) A city in
Judah.
And Janum, and B, and Aphekah,...... Josh 15:53

BETHUEL (beth-u'-el) See BETHUL.
1. Son of Nahor.
and Pidash, and Jidlaph, and B .... Gen 22:22
And B begat Rebekah......................... Gen 22:23
came out, who was born to B .... Gen 24:15
daughter of B the son of Milcah......... Gen 24:24
And she said, The daughter of B .... Gen 24:47
B answered and said, The thing......... Gen 24:50
the daughter of B the Syrian of .... Gen 25:20
to the house of B thy mother's........... Gen 28:2
son of B the Syrian, the brother .... Gen 28:5

2. *A town in Simeon.*
And at *B*, and at Hormah, and at...... 1Chr 4:30

BETHUL (*beth'-ul*) See BETHUEL. *A city in Simeon.*
And Eltolad, and *B*, and Hormah, and.. Josh 19:4

BETHZATHA See BETHESDA.

BETHZOR See BETH-ZUR.

BETH-ZUR (*beth'-zur*)
1. *A town in Judah.*
Halhul, *B*, and Gedor,...................... Josh 15:58
And *B*, and Shoco, and Adullam, ... 2Chr 11:7
the ruler of the half part of *B*............ Neh 3:16
2. *A descendant of Caleb.*
and Maon was the father of *B*............. 1Chr 2:45

BETIMES
they rose up *b* in the morning, and ... Gen 26:31
by his messengers, rising up *b* 2Chr 36:15
If thou wouldest seek unto God *b*........ Job 8:5
rising *b* for a prey............................ Job 24:5
that loveth him chasteneth him *b*...... Prov 13:24

BETONIM (*bet'-o-nim*) *A town in Gad.*
unto Ramath-mizpeh, and *B*............... Josh 13:26

BETRAY
be come to *b* me to mine enemies 1Chr 12:17
shall *b* one another, and shall............ Mt 24:10
he sought opportunity to *b* him........... Mt 26:16
you, that one of you shall *b* me.......... Mt 26:21
in the dish, the same shall *b* me......... Mt 26:23
he is at hand that doth *b* me............... Mt 26:46
shall *b* the brother to death................ Mk 13:12
chief priests, to *b* him unto them........ Mk 14:10
how he might conveniently *b* him....... Mk 14:11
which eateth with me shall *b* me........ Mk 14:18
how he might *b* him unto them........... Lk 22:4
sought opportunity to *b* him unto ...... Lk 22:6
believed not, and who should *b* him ... Jn 6:64
for he it was that should *b* him........... Jn 6:71
Simon's son, which should *b* him .... Jn 12:4
Iscariot, Simon's son, to *b* him........... Jn 13:2
For he knew who should *b* him .... Jn 13:11
you, that one of you shall *b* me .... Jn 13:21

BETRAYED
and Judas Iscariot, who also *b* him..... Mt 10:4
shall be *b* into the hands of men .... Mt 17:22
shall be *b* unto the chief priests......... Mt 20:18
Son of man is to be crucified............... Mt 26:2
man by whom the Son of man is *b*...... Mt 26:24
Then Judas, which *b* him, answered.... Mt 26:25
the Son of man is *b* into the.............. Mt 26:45
Now he that *b* him gave them a .... Mt 26:48
that I have *b* the innocent blood......... Mt 27:4
Judas Iscariot, which also *b* him........ Mk 3:19
man by whom the Son of man is *b* ..... Mk 14:21
the Son of man is *b* into the.............. Mk 14:41
he that *b* him had given them a .... Mk 14:44
ye shall be *b* both by parents, and...... Lk 21:16
woe unto that man by whom he is *b* ... Lk 22:22
And Judas also, which *b* him.............. Jn 18:2
And Judas also, which *b* him.............. Jn 18:5
in which he was *b* took bread............ 1Cor 11:23

BETRAYERS
of whom ye have been now the *b* .... Acts 7:52

BETRAYEST
b thou the Son of man with a kiss ...... Lk 22:48

BETRAYETH
Then Judas, which had *b* him............. Mt 27:3
lo, he that *b* me is at hand................. Mk 14:42
the hand of him that *b* me is with ...... Lk 22:21
Lord, which is he that *b* thee.............. Jn 21:20

BETROTH
Thou shalt *b* a wife, and another........ Deut 28:30
I will *b* thee unto me for ever............. Hos 2:19
yea, I will *b* thee unto me in.............. Hos 2:19
I will even *b* thee unto me in .... Hos 2:20

BETROTHED
who hath *b* her to himself, then.......... Ex 21:8
if he have *b* her unto his son,............ Ex 21:9
a man entice a maid that is not *b*....... Ex 22:16
b to an husband, and not at all.......... Lev 19:20
man is there that hath *b* a wife,......... Deut 20:7
is a virgin be *b* unto an husband .... Deut 22:23
than find a *b* damsel in the field........ Deut 22:25
the *b* damsel cried, and there was..... Deut 22:27
that is a virgin, which is not *b*............ Deut 22:28

BETTER
It is *b* that I give her to thee............... Gen 29:19
For it had been *b* for us to serve......... Ex 14:12
were it not *b* for us to return.............. Num 14:3
of the grapes of Ephraim *b* than .... Judg 8:2
of Shechem, Whether is *b* for you ...... Judg 9:2
now art thou any thing *b* than............ Judg 11:25
is it *b* for thee to be a priest............... Judg 18:19
which is *b* to thee than seven............. Ruth 4:15
am not I *b* to thee than ten sons......... 1Sa 1:8
to obey is *b* than sacrifice, and.......... 1Sa 15:22
of thine, that is *b* than thou............... 1Sa 15:28
there is nothing *b* for me than........... 1Sa 27:1
of Hushai the Archite is *b* than 2Sa 17:14
therefore now it is *b* that thou............ 2Sa 18:3
name of Solomon *b* than thy name 1Kin 1:47
b than he, and slew them with the...... 1Kin 2:32
for I am not *b* than my fathers............ 1Kin 19:4
thee for it a *b* vineyard than it 1Kin 21:2

b than all the waters of Israel............. 2Kin 5:12
which were *b* than thyself.................. 2Chr 21:13
unto another that is *b* than she.......... Est 1:19
that a righteous man hath is *b*........... Ps 37:16
thy lovingkindness is *b* than life......... Ps 63:3
b than an ox or bullock that hath .... Ps 69:31
thy courts is *b* than a thousand......... Ps 84:10
It is *b* to trust in the LORD than .... Ps 118:8
It is *b* to trust in the LORD than .... Ps 118:9
The law of thy mouth is *b* unto me .... Ps 119:72
For the merchandise of it is *b* .... Prov 3:14
For wisdom is *b* than rubies.............. Prov 8:11
My fruit is *b* than gold, yea,.............. Prov 8:19
is *b* than he that honoureth............... Prov 12:9
B is little with the fear of the............. Prov 15:16
B is a dinner of herbs where love....... Prov 15:17
B is a little with righteousness .... Prov 16:8
How much *b* is it to get wisdom .... Prov 16:16
B it is to be of an humble spirit .... Prov 16:19
to anger is *b* than the mighty .... Prov 16:32
B is a dry morsel, and quietness .... Prov 17:1
B is the poor that walketh in his........ Prov 19:1
and a poor man is *b* than a liar .... Prov 19:22
It is *b* to dwell in a corner of .... Prov 21:9
It is *b* to dwell in the........................ Prov 21:19
For *b* it is that it be said unto............. Prov 25:7
It is *b* to dwell in the corner of .... Prov 25:24
Open rebuke is *b* than secret love...... Prov 27:5
for *b* is a neighbour that is near .... Prov 27:10
B is the poor that walketh in his........ Prov 28:6
There is nothing *b* for a man .... Eccl 2:24
perceive that there is nothing *b* .... Eccl 3:22
is *b* than both they, which .... Eccl 4:3
B is an handful with quietness, ... Eccl 4:6
Two are *b* than one .... Eccl 4:9
B is a poor and a wise child than .... Eccl 4:13
B is it that thou shouldest not .... Eccl 5:5
an untimely birth is *b* than he .... Eccl 6:3
B is the sight of the eyes than .... Eccl 6:9
vanity, what in man the *b* .... Eccl 6:11
A good name is *b* than precious......... Eccl 7:1
It is *b* to go to the house of .... Eccl 7:2
Sorrow is *b* than laughter .... Eccl 7:3
countenance the heart is made *b* ...... Eccl 7:3
It is *b* to hear the rebuke of the......... Eccl 7:5
B is the end of a thing than the .... Eccl 7:8
is *b* than the proud in spirit............... Eccl 7:8
the former days were *b* than these..... Eccl 7:10
man hath no *b* thing under the sun .... Eccl 8:15
living dog is *b* than a dead lion.......... Eccl 9:4
Wisdom is *b* than strength................ Eccl 9:16
Wisdom is *b* than weapons of war ..... Eccl 9:18
and a babbler is no *b*........................ Eccl 10:11
for thy love is *b* than wine................. Song 1:2
how much is *b* thy love than wine...... Song 4:10
a name *b* than of sons and of .... Is 56:5
be slain with the sword are *b* .... Lam 4:9
will do *b* unto you than at your .... Eze 36:11
times in than all the magicians........... Dan 1:20
for then was it *b* with me .... Hos 2:7
be they *b* than these kingdoms......... Amos 6:2
for it is *b* for me to die than to.......... Jonah 4:3
It is *b* for me to die than to............... Jonah 4:8
Art thou *b* than populous No, that...... Nah 3:8
Are ye not much *b* than they .... Mt 6:26
much then is a man *b* than a sheep.... Mt 12:12
in me, it were *b* for him that a .... Mt 18:6
it is *b* for thee to enter into............... Mt 18:8
it is *b* for thee to enter into............... Mt 18:9
it is *b* for him that a millstone........... Mk 9:42
it is *b* for thee to enter into............... Mk 9:43
it is *b* for thee to enter into............... Mk 9:45
it is *b* for thee to enter into............... Mk 9:47
Sent to him, The old is *b* .... Lk 5:39
much more are ye *b* than the fowls..... Lk 12:24
It were *b* for him that a .... Lk 17:2
are we *b* than they.......................... Rom 3:9
for it is *b* to marry than to burn......... 1Cor 7:9
her not in marriage doeth *b* 1Cor 7:38
neither, if we eat, are we the *b*.......... 1Cor 8:8
for it were *b* for me to die, than......... 1Cor 9:15
ye come together not for the *b*........... 1Cor 11:17
which is far *b* .... Phil 1:23
esteem other *b* than themselves........ Phil 2:3
made so much *b* than the angels....... Heb 1:4
we are persuaded *b* things of you...... Heb 6:9
the less is blessed of the *b* .... Heb 7:7
the bringing in of a *b* hope did.......... Heb 7:19
made a surety of a *b* testament .... Heb 7:22
is the mediator of a *b* covenant .... Heb 8:6
was established upon *b* promises....... Heb 8:6
with *b* sacrifices than these.............. Heb 9:23
that ye have in heaven a *b* .... Heb 10:34
But now they desire a *b* country .... Heb 11:16
might obtain a *b* resurrection .... Heb 11:35
provided some *b* thing for us............. Heb 11:40
that speaketh *b* things than that....... Heb 12:24
For it is *b*, if the will of God................ 1Pet 3:17
For it had been *b* for them not 2Pet 2:21

BETTERED
that she had, and was nothing *b*........ Mk 5:26

BETWEEN
And I will put enmity *b* thee .... Gen 3:15
woman, and *b* thy seed and her seed . Gen 3:15
of the covenant which I make *b* me..... Gen 9:12
be for a token of a covenant *b*............ Gen 9:13
my covenant, which is *b* me .... Gen 9:15
the everlasting covenant *b* God.......... Gen 9:16
which I have established *b* me .... Gen 9:17

And Resen *b* Nineveh and Calah........ Gen 10:12
the beginning, *b* Beth-el and Hai....... Gen 13:3
there was a strife *b* the herdmen....... Gen 13:7
b my herdmen and thy herdmen........ Gen 13:8
lamp that passed *b* those pieces........ Gen 15:17
the LORD judge *b* me and thee........... Gen 16:5
behold, it is *b* Kadesh and Bered ...... Gen 16:14
And I will make my covenant *b* me .... Gen 17:2
I will establish my covenant *b* me ..... Gen 17:7
b me and you and thy seed after .... Gen 17:10
country, and dwelled *b* Kadesh.......... Gen 20:1
and let it be for a witness *b* me......... Gen 31:44
said, This heap is a witness *b* me ...... Gen 31:48
for he said, The LORD watch *b* me ..... Gen 31:49
brought them out from *b* his knees..... Gen 48:12
nor a lawgiver from *b* his feet............ Gen 49:10
ass couching down *b* two burdens..... Gen 49:14
I will put a division *b* my people......... Ex 8:23
sever *b* the cattle of Israel .... Ex 9:4
put a difference *b* the Egyptians .... Ex 11:7
and for a memorial *b* thine eyes......... Ex 13:9
and for frontlets *b* thine eyes............ Ex 13:16
b Migdol and the sea, over against .... Ex 14:2
it came *b* the camp of the................. Ex 14:20
of Sin, which is *b* Elim and Sinai,...... Ex 16:1
and I judge *b* one and another, and I . Ex 18:16
oath of the LORD be *b* them both........ Ex 22:11
from *b* the two cherubims which......... Ex 25:22
divide unto you *b* the holy place........ Ex 26:33
bells of gold *b* them round about .... Ex 28:33
and thou shalt put it *b* the................. Ex 30:18
for it is a sign *b* me and you .... Ex 31:13
It is a sign *b* me and the children....... Ex 31:17
put the bells *b* the pomegranates ...... Ex 39:25
round about *b* the pomegranates ...... Ex 39:25
thou shalt set the laver *b* the .... Ex 40:7
he set the laver *b* the tent of .... Ex 40:30
that ye may put difference *b* holy ...... Lev 10:10
and unholy, and *b* unclean and clean . Lev 10:10
make a difference *b* the unclean .... Lev 11:47
b the beast that may be eaten and..... Lev 11:47
put difference *b* clean beasts............ Lev 20:25
and *b* unclean fowls and clean........... Lev 20:25
laws, which the LORD made *b* him ..... Lev 26:46
from *b* the two cherubims................. Num 7:89
the flesh was yet *b* their teeth,.......... Num 11:33
they bare it *b* two upon a staff .... Num 13:23
And he stood *b* the dead and the .... Num 16:48
of Moab, *b* Moab and the Amorites..... Num 21:13
thereof be divided *b* many .... Num 26:56
b a man and his wife, *b* the............. Num 30:16
b them that took the war upon .... Num 31:27
battle, and *b* all the congregation...... Num 31:27
shall judge *b* the slayer and the .... Num 35:24
b Paran, and Tophel, and Laban, and . Deut 1:1
Hear the causes *b* your brethren........ Deut 1:16
and judge righteously *b* every man .... Deut 1:16
that day had no knowledge *b* good..... Deut 1:39
(I stood *b* the LORD and you at .... Deut 5:5
be as frontlets *b* thine eyes.............. Deut 6:8
may be as frontlets *b* your eyes .... Deut 11:18
nor make any halakase *b* your eyes.... Deut 14:1
b blood and blood, *b* plea and......... Deut 17:8
b stroke and stroke, being matters.... Deut 17:8
b whom the controversy is, shall....... Deut 19:17
If there be a controversy *b* men......... Deut 25:1
that cometh out from *b* her feet......... Deut 28:57
and he shall dwell *b* his shoulders..... Deut 33:12
Yet there shall be a space *b* you........ Josh 3:4
abode *b* Beth-el and Ai, on the.......... Josh 8:9
now there was a valley *b* them .... Josh 8:11
them to lie in ambush *b* Beth-el........ Josh 8:12
forth *b* the children of Judah............. Josh 18:11
hath made Jordan a border *b* us........ Josh 22:25
But that it may be a witness *b* us....... Josh 22:27
but it is a witness *b* us and your .... Josh 22:28
witness is us that the LORD is God ...... Josh 22:34
the LORD, he put darkness *b* you ...... Josh 24:7
the palm tree of Deborah *b* Ramah .... Judg 4:5
for there was peace *b* Jabin the......... Judg 4:17
sent an evil spirit *b* Abimelech.......... Judg 9:23
The LORD be witness *b* us.................. Judg 11:10
this day *b* the children of Israel......... Judg 11:27
times in the camp of Dan *b* Zorah...... Judg 13:25
in the midst *b* two oaks.................... Judg 16:3
and they set him *b* the pillars .... Judg 16:25
him up, and buried him *b* Zorah......... Judg 16:31
sign *b* the men of Israel and the........ Judg 20:38
which dwelleth *b* the cherubims......... 1Sa 4:4
took a stone, and set it *b* Mizpeh 1Sa 7:12
And there was peace *b* Israel 1Sa 7:14
b the passages, by which Jonathan.... 1Sa 14:4
And Saul said, Cast lots *b* me............ 1Sa 14:42
to Judah, and pitched *b* Shochoh 1Sa 17:1
and there was a valley *b* them 1Sa 17:3
a target of brass *b* his shoulders....... 1Sa 17:6
liveth, there is but a step *b* me 1Sa 20:3
of, behold, the LORD be *b* thee 1Sa 20:23
LORD, saying, The LORD be *b* me 1Sa 20:42
saying, The LORD be *b* me and ever.... 1Sa 20:42
The LORD judge *b* me and thee.......... 1Sa 24:12
therefore be judge, and judge *b* me ... 1Sa 24:15
a great space being *b* them............... 1Sa 26:13
was long war *b* the house of Saul....... 2Sa 3:1
there was war *b* the house of Saul..... 2Sa 3:6
that dwelleth *b* the cherubims.......... 2Sa 6:2
and he was taken up *b* the heaven 2Sa 18:9
David sat *b* the two gates................. 2Sa 18:24
and can I discern *b* good and evil 2Sa 19:35
the LORD's oath that was *b* them 2Sa 21:7

b David and Jonathan the son of.......... 2Sa 21:7
people, that I may discern b good.......... 1Kin 3:9
and there was peace b Hiram.......... 1Kin 5:12
and the borders were b the ledges.......... 1Kin 7:28
that were b the ledges were lions.......... 1Kin 7:29
in the clay ground b Succoth.......... 1Kin 7:46
And there was war b Rehoboam.......... 1Kin 14:30
And there was war b Rehoboam.......... 1Kin 15:6
And there was war b Abijam.......... 1Kin 15:7
was war b Asa and Baasha.......... 1Kin 15:16
There is a league b me and thee,.......... 1Kin 15:19
b my father and thy father.......... 1Kin 15:19
was war b Asa and Baasha.......... 1Kin 15:32
So they divided the land b them.......... 1Kin 18:6
How long halt ye b two opinions.......... 1Kin 18:21
and put his face b his knees.......... 1Kin 18:42
three years without war b Syria.......... 1Kin 22:1
smote the king of Israel b the.......... 1Kin 22:34
and made Jehoram b his arms.......... 2Kin 9:24
made a covenant b the LORD.......... 2Kin 11:17
b the king also and the people.......... 2Kin 11:17
from b the altar and the house of.......... 2Kin 16:14
which dwelleth b the cherubims.......... 2Kin 19:15
the way of the gate b two walls.......... 2Kin 25:4
that dwelleth b the cherubims.......... 1Chr 13:6
of the LORD stood b the earth.......... 1Chr 21:16
in the clay ground b Succoth.......... 2Chr 4:17
And there were war b Rehoboam.......... 2Chr 12:15
And there was war b Abijah.......... 2Chr 13:2
There is a league b me and thee,.......... 2Chr 16:3
as there was b my father.......... 2Chr 16:3
smote the king of Israel b the.......... 2Chr 18:33
b blood and blood, b law and.......... 2Chr 19:10
made a covenant b him.......... 2Chr 23:16
b all the people, and b the.......... 2Chr 23:16
b the going up of the corner unto.......... Neh 3:32
that no air can come b them.......... Job 41:16
that dwelleth b the cherubims.......... Ps 80:1
he sitteth b the cherubims.......... Ps 99:1
to cease, and parteth b the mighty.......... Prov 18:18
Ye made also a ditch b the two.......... Is 22:11
that dwelleth b the cherubims.......... Is 37:16
iniquities have separated b you.......... Is 59:2
execute judgment b a man and his.......... Jer 7:5
passed b the parts thereof,.......... Jer 34:18
which passed b the parts of the.......... Jer 34:19
a true and faithful witness b us.......... Jer 42:5
way of the gate b the two walls.......... Jer 52:7
overtook her b the straits.......... Lam 1:3
set it for a wall of iron b thee.......... Eze 4:3
spirit lifted me up b the earth.......... Eze 8:3
b the porch and the altar, were.......... Eze 8:16
Go in b the wheels, even under.......... Eze 10:2
of fire from b the cherubims.......... Eze 10:2
the wheels, from b the cherubims.......... Eze 10:6
b the cherubims unto the fire.......... Eze 10:7
the fire that was b the cherubims.......... Eze 10:7
hath executed true judgment b man.......... Eze 18:8
my sabbaths, to be a sign b me.......... Eze 20:12
and they shall be a sign b me.......... Eze 20:20
have put no difference b the holy.......... Eze 22:26
shewed difference b the unclean.......... Eze 22:26
Behold, I judge b cattle and.......... Eze 34:17
b the rams and the he goats.......... Eze 34:17
will judge b the fat cattle and.......... Eze 34:20
fat cattle and the lean cattle.......... Eze 34:20
and I will judge b cattle and.......... Eze 34:22
b the little chambers were five.......... Eze 40:7
b the chambers was the wideness.......... Eze 41:10
that a palm tree was b a cherub.......... Eze 41:18
make a separation b the sanctuary.......... Eze 42:20
by my costs, and the wall b me.......... Eze 43:8
people the difference b the holy.......... Eze 44:23
them to discern b the unclean.......... Eze 44:23
which is b the border of Damascus.......... Eze 47:16
b the border of Judah and the.......... Eze 48:22
the mouth of it b the teeth of it.......... Dan 7:5
had a notable horn b his eyes.......... Dan 8:5
a man's voice b the banks of Ulai.......... Dan 8:16
the great horn that is b his eyes.......... Dan 8:21
b the seas in the glorious holy.......... Dan 11:45
her adulteries from b her breasts.......... Hos 2:2
weep b the porch and the altar, and.......... Joel 2:17
cannot discern b their right hand.......... Jonah 4:11
lifted up the ephah b the earth.......... Zec 5:9
chariots out from b two mountains.......... Zec 6:1
of peace shall be b them both.......... Zec 6:13
his abominations from b his teeth.......... Zec 9:7
break the brotherhood b Judah.......... Zec 11:14
the LORD hath been witness b thee.......... Mal 2:14
discern b the righteous and.......... Mal 3:18
b him that serveth God and him.......... Mal 3:18
go and tell him his fault b thee.......... Mt 18:15
whom ye slew b the temple.......... Mt 23:35
which perished b the altar.......... Lk 11:51
b us and you there is a great gulf.......... Lk 16:26
they were at enmity b themselves.......... Lk 23:12
b some of John's disciples.......... Jn 3:25
Peter was sleeping b two soldiers.......... Acts 12:6
And put no difference b us.......... Acts 15:9
contention was so sharp b them.......... Acts 15:39
a dissension b the Pharisees.......... Acts 23:7
aside, they talked b themselves.......... Acts 26:31
their own bodies b themselves.......... Rom 1:24
there is no difference b the Jew.......... Rom 10:12
be able to judge b his brethren.......... 1Cor 6:5
There is difference also b a wife.......... 1Cor 7:34
the middle wall of partition b us.......... Eph 2:14
is one God, and one mediator b God.......... 1Ti 2:5

BETWIXT
be a token of the covenant b me.......... Gen 17:11
what is that b me and thee.......... Gen 23:15
now an oath b us, even b us.......... Gen 28:28
set three days' journey b himself.......... Gen 30:36
that they may judge b us both.......... Gen 31:37
see, God is witness b me and thee.......... Gen 31:50
pillar, which I have cast b me.......... Gen 31:51
God of their father, judge b us.......... Gen 31:53
before me, and put a space b drove.......... Gen 32:16
Neither is there any daysman b us.......... Job 9:33
shine by the cloud that cometh b.......... Job 36:32
shall lie all night b my breasts.......... Song 1:13
I pray you, b me and my vineyard.......... Is 5:3
by the gate b the two walls.......... Jer 39:4
For I am in a strait b two.......... Phil 1:23

BEULAH (be-u'-lah) *A name of restored Israel,*
called Hephzi-bah, and thy land B........... Is 62:4

BEWAIL
b the burning when the LORD hath.......... Lev 10:6
b her father and her mother a full.......... Deut 21:13
b my virginity, I and my fellows.......... Judg 11:37
Therefore I will b with me.......... Is 16:9
that I shall b many which have.......... 2Cor 12:21
deliciously with her, shall b her.......... Rev 18:9

BEWAILED
and b her virginity upon the.......... Judg 11:38
And all wept, and b her.......... Lk 8:52
people, and of women, which also b.......... Lk 23:27

BEWAILETH
that b herself, that spreadeth.......... Jer 4:31

BEWARE
B thou than thou bring not my son.......... Gen 24:6
B of him, and obey his voice,.......... Ex 23:21
Then b lest thou forget the LORD,.......... Deut 6:12
B that thou forget not the LORD.......... Deut 8:11
B that there be not a thought in.......... Deut 15:9
Now therefore b, I pray thee, and.......... Judg 13:4
I said unto the woman let her b.......... Judg 13:13
B that thou touch the young man.......... 2Sa 18:12
B that thou pass not such a place.......... 2Kin 6:9
b lest he take thee away with his.......... Job 36:18
a scorner, and the simple will b.......... Prov 19:25
lest Hezekiah persuade you,.......... Is 36:18
B of false prophets, which come.......... Mt 7:15
But b of men.......... Mt 10:17
b of the leaven of the Pharisees.......... Mt 16:6
that ye should b of the leaven of.......... Mt 16:11
then not b of the leaven of bread.......... Mt 16:12
b of the leaven of the Pharisees,.......... Mk 8:15
B of the scribes, which love to.......... Mk 12:38
B ye of the leaven of the.......... Lk 12:1
Take heed, and b of covetousness.......... Lk 12:15
B of the scribes, which desire to.......... Lk 20:46
B therefore, lest that come upon.......... Acts 13:40
B of dogs, b of evil workers.......... Phil 3:2
b of the concision.......... Phil 3:2
B lest any man spoil you through.......... Col 2:8
b lest ye also, being led away.......... 2Pet 3:17

BEWITCHED
b the people of Samaria, giving.......... Acts 8:9
time he had b them with sorceries.......... Acts 8:11
foolish Galatians, who hath you b.......... Gal 3:1

BEWRAY
b not him that wandereth.......... Is 16:3

BEWRAYETH
of his right hand, which b itself.......... Prov 27:16
he heareth cursing, and b it not.......... Prov 29:24
for thy speech b thee.......... Mt 26:73

BEYOND
spread his tent b the tower of.......... Gen 35:21
of Atad, which is b Jordan.......... Gen 50:10
Abel-mizraim, which is b Jordan.......... Gen 50:11
or if it run b the time of her.......... Lev 15:25
I cannot go b the word of the.......... Num 22:18
I cannot go b the commandment of.......... Num 24:13
your God hath given them b Jordan.......... Deut 3:20
the good land that is b Jordan.......... Deut 3:25
Neither is it b the sea, that.......... Deut 30:13
the Amorites, that were b Jordan.......... Josh 9:10
b Jordan eastward, even as Moses.......... Josh 13:8
inheritance b Jordan on the east.......... Josh 18:7
passed b the quarries, and escaped.......... Judg 3:26
Gilead abode b Jordan.......... Judg 5:17
Behold, the arrows are b thee.......... 1Sa 20:22
lad ran, he shot an arrow b him.......... 1Sa 20:36
and said, Is not the arrow b thee.......... 1Sa 20:37
the Syrians that were b the river.......... 2Sa 10:16
unto the place that is b Jordan.......... 1Kin 4:12
and shall scatter them b the river.......... 1Kin 14:15
the Syrians that were b the river.......... 1Chr 19:16
from b the sea on this side Syria.......... 2Chr 20:2
and unto the rest b the river.......... Ezr 4:17
over all countries b the river.......... Ezr 4:20
Tatnai, governor b the river,.......... Ezr 6:6
which are b the river, be ye far.......... Ezr 6:6
even of the tribute b the river.......... Ezr 6:8
treasurers which are b the river.......... Ezr 7:21
the people that are b the river.......... Ezr 7:25
me to the governors b the river.......... Neh 2:7
came to the governors b the river.......... Neh 2:9
from b the tower of the furnaces.......... Neh 12:38
by them is the river, by the king.......... Is 7:20
b Jordan, in Galilee of the.......... Is 9:1
which is b the rivers of Ethiopia.......... Is 18:1

cast forth b the gates of.......... Jer 22:19
of the isles which are b the sea.......... Jer 25:22
to go into captivity b Damascus.......... Amos 5:27
From b the rivers of Ethiopia my.......... Zeph 3:10
b Jordan, Galilee of the Gentiles.......... Mt 4:15
and from Judaea, and from b Jordan.......... Mt 4:25
the coasts of Judaea b Jordan.......... Mt 19:1
and from Idumaea, and from b Jordan.......... Mk 3:8
amazed in themselves b measure.......... Mk 6:51
were b measure astonished, saying.......... Mk 7:37
were done in Bethabara b Jordan.......... Jn 1:28
he that was with thee b Jordan.......... Jn 3:26
went away again b Jordan into the.......... Jn 10:40
I will carry you away b Babylon.......... Acts 7:43
b their power they were willing.......... 2Cor 8:3
not ourselves b our measure.......... 2Cor 10:14
the gospel in the regions b you.......... 2Cor 10:16
how that b measure I persecuted.......... Gal 1:13
That no man go b and defraud his.......... 1Th 4:6

BEZAI (be'-zahee)
I. A family of exiles.
The children of B, three hundred.......... Ezr 2:17
The children of B, three hundred.......... Neh 7:23
2. A family who renewed the covenant.
Hodijah, Hashum, B,.......... Neh 10:18

BEZALEEL (be-zal'-e-el)
I. A craftsman.
called by name B the son of Uri.......... Ex 31:2
called by name B the son of Uri.......... Ex 35:30
Then wrought B and Aholiab, and.......... Ex 36:1
And Moses called B and Aholiab, and.......... Ex 36:2
B made the ark of shittim wood.......... Ex 37:1
B the son of Uri, the son of Hur,.......... Ex 38:22
And Hur begat Uri, and Uri begat B.......... 1Chr 2:20
that B the son of Uri, the son of.......... 2Chr 1:5
2. Married a foreign wife in exile.
Benaiah, Maaseiah, Mattaniah, B,.......... Ezr 10:30

BEZALEEL See BEZALEEL.

BEZEK (be'-zek) See ADONI-BEZEK. *A place in
the Canaan valley.*
of them in B ten thousand men.......... Judg 1:4
And they found Adoni-bezek in B.......... Judg 1:5
And when he numbered them in B.......... 1Sa 11:8

BEZER (be'-zer)
I. A city of refuge.
B in the wilderness, in the plain.......... Deut 4:43
they assigned B in the wilderness.......... Josh 20:8
B with her suburbs, and Jahazah.......... Josh 21:36
B in the wilderness with her.......... 1Chr 6:78
2. A son of Zoph.
B, and Hod, and Shamma.......... 1Chr 7:37

BICHRI (bik'-ri) *Father of Sheba.*
name was Sheba, the son of B.......... 2Sa 20:1
and followed Sheba the son of B.......... 2Sa 20:2
son of B do us more harm than do.......... 2Sa 20:6
pursue after Sheba the son of B.......... 2Sa 20:7
pursued after Sheba the son of B.......... 2Sa 20:10
pursue after Sheba the son of B.......... 2Sa 20:13
Sheba the son of B by name.......... 2Sa 20:21
the head of Sheba the son of B.......... 2Sa 20:22

BICHRITES See BERITES.

BICRI

BID
b them that may make them.......... Num 15:38
until the day I b you shout.......... Josh 6:10
B the servant pass on before us,.......... 1Sa 9:27
ere thou b the people return from.......... 1Sa 25:36
riding for me, except I b thee.......... 2Kin 4:24
if the prophet had b thee do some.......... 2Kin 5:13
will do all that thou shalt b us.......... 2Kin 10:5
it the preaching that I b thee.......... Jonah 3:2
a sacrifice, he hath b his guests.......... Zeph 1:7
b me come unto thee on the water.......... Mt 14:28
ye shall find, b to the marriage.......... Mt 22:9
whatsoever they b you observe.......... Mt 23:3
let me first go b them farewell.......... Lk 9:61
b her therefore that she help me.......... Lk 10:40
lest they also b thee again.......... Lk 14:12
that believe not b you to a feast.......... 1Cor 10:27
house, neither b him God speed.......... 2Jn 10

BIDDEN
and afterwards they eat that be b.......... 1Sa 9:13
place among them that were b.......... 1Sa 9:22
for the LORD hath b him.......... 2Sa 16:11
the angel of the Lord had b him.......... Mt 1:24
them that were b to the wedding.......... Mt 22:3
saying, Tell them which are b.......... Mt 22:4
they which were b were not worthy.......... Mt 22:8
Pharisee which had b him saw it.......... Lk 7:39
a parable to those which were b.......... Lk 14:7
When thou art b of any man to a.......... Lk 14:8
man than thou be of him.......... Lk 14:8
But when thou art b, go and sit.......... Lk 14:10
time to say to them that were b.......... Lk 14:17
were b shall taste of my supper.......... Lk 14:24

BIDDETH
For he that b him God speed is.......... 2Jn 11

BIDDING
son in law, and goeth at thy b.......... 1Sa 22:14

BIDKAR (bid'-kar) *A captain of Jehu.*
Then said Jehu to B his captain.......... 2Kin 9:25

BIER
king David himself followed the b.......... 2Sa 3:31
And he came and touched the b.......... Lk 7:14

BIGTHA (big'-thah) *A servant of Ahasuerus.*
Mehuman, Biztha, Harbona, B............ Est 1:10

BIGTHAN (big'-than) *See BIGTHANA. A conspirator against Ahasuerus.*
two of the king's chamberlains, B....... Est 2:21

BIGTHANA (big'-than-ah) *See BIGTHAN. Same as Bigthan.*
that Mordecai had told of B.................. Est 6:2

BIGVAI (big'-vahee)
1. A family chief with Zerubbabel.
Mordecai, Bilshan, Mizpar, B.............. Ezr 2:2
Mordecai, Bilshan, Mispereth, B......... Neh 7:7
2. A family of exiles with Zerubbabel.
The children of B, two thousand......... Ezr 2:14
The children of B, two thousand......... Neh 7:19
3. A family of exiles with Ezra.
Of the sons also of B.......................... Ezr 8:14
4. A family who renewed the covenant.
Adonijah, B, Adin,.............................. Neh 10:16

BILDAD (bil'-dad) *A friend of Job.*
B the Shuhite, and Zophar the........... Job 2:11
Then answered B the Shuhite.............. Job 8:1
Then answered B the Shuhite.............. Job 18:1
Then answered B the Shuhite.............. Job 25:1
B the Shuhite and Zophar the............. Job 42:9

BILEAM (bil'-e-am) *See IBLEAM. A Levitical city in Manasseh.*
B with her suburbs, for the................ 1Chr 6:70

BILGAH (bil'-gah)
1. A priest during David's time.
The fifteenth to B, the sixteenth........ 1Chr 24:14
2. A priest with Zerubbabel.
Miamin, Maadiah, B,........................... Neh 12:5
Of B, Shammua.................................. Neh 12:18

BILGAI (bil'-gahee) *A priest with Zerubbabel.*
Maaziah, B, Shemaiah........................ Neh 10:8

BILHAH (bil'-hah)
1. Mother of Dan and Naphtali.
B his handmaid to be her maid........... Gen 29:29
And she said, Behold my maid B......... Gen 30:3
she gave him B her handmaid to......... Gen 30:4
B conceived, and bare Jacob a son..... Gen 30:5
B Rachel's maid conceived again,....... Gen 30:7
lay with B his father's concubine........ Gen 35:22
And the sons of B, Rachel's................ Gen 35:25
and the lad was with the sons of B..... Gen 37:2
These are the sons of B, which........... Gen 46:25
Jezer, and Shallum, the sons of B...... 1Chr 7:13
2. A town in Simeon.
And at B, and at Ezem, and at Tolad,.. 1Chr 4:29

BILHAN (bil'-han)
1. Son of Ezer.
B, and Zaavan, and Akan.................... Gen 36:27
B, and Zavan, and Akan,.................... 1Chr 1:42
2. Son of Jediael.
B... 1Chr 7:10
and the sons of B................................ 1Chr 7:10

BILL.
him write her a b of divorcement......... Deut 24:1
write her a b of divorcement, and........ Deut 24:3
Where is the b of your mother's........... Is 50:1
away, and given her a b of divorce....... Jer 3:8
to write a b of divorcement................. Mk 10:4
And he said unto him, Take thy b.......... Lk 16:6
And he said unto him, Take thy b.......... Lk 16:7

BILLOWS
waves and thy b are gone over me....... Ps 42:7
all thy b and thy waves passed............ Jonah 2:3

BILSHAN (bil'-shan) *A Jewish prince with Zerubbabel.*
Seraiah, Reelaiah, Mordecai, B........... Ezr 2:2
Raamiah, Nahamani, Mordecai, B........ Neh 7:7

BIMHAL (bim'-hal) *A son of Japlet.*
Pasach, and B, and Ashvath............... 1Chr 7:33

BIND
they shall b the breastplate by............ Ex 28:28
they did b the breastplate by the......... Ex 39:21
or swear an oath to b his soul............. Num 30:2
b herself by a bond, being in her......... Num 30:3
thou shalt b them for a sign upon........ Deut 6:8
b them for a sign upon your hand,....... Deut 11:18
b up the money in thine hand, and...... Deut 14:25
thou shalt b this line of scarlet........... Josh 2:18
To b Samson are we come up, to do.... Judg 15:10
him, We are come down to b thee........ Judg 15:12
but we will b thee fast, and................ Judg 15:13
that we may b him to afflict him.......... Judg 16:5
If they b me with seven green............ Judg 16:7
If they b me fast with new ropes........ Judg 16:11
and b it as a crown to me................... Job 31:36
Canst thou b the sweet influences...... Job 38:31
Canst thou b the unicorn with his........ Job 39:10
and b their faces in secret.................. Job 40:13
or wilt thou b him for thy..................... Job 41:5
To b his princes at his pleasure.......... Ps 105:22
b the sacrifice with cords, even.......... Ps 118:27
To b their kings with chains, and......... Ps 149:8
b them about thy neck........................ Prov 3:3
B them continually upon thine............ Prov 6:21
B them upon thy fingers, write............ Prov 7:3
B up the testimony, seal the law......... Is 8:16
b them on thee, as a bride doeth......... Is 49:18
he hath sent me to b up the................ Is 61:1
that thou shalt b a stone to it............. Jer 51:63

shall b thee with them, and thou......... Eze 3:25
number, and b them in thy skirts......... Eze 5:3
b the tire of thine head upon............... Eze 24:17
healed, to put a roller to b it............... Eze 30:21
will b up that which was broken........... Eze 34:16
were in his army to b Shadrach........... Dan 3:20
hath smitten, and he will b us up......... Hos 6:1
when they shall b themselves in.......... Hos 10:10
b the chariot to the swift beast........... Mic 1:13
except he first b the strong man......... Mt 12:29
b them in bundles to burn them.......... Mt 13:30
whatsoever thou shalt b on earth........ Mt 16:19
Whatsoever ye shall b on earth........... Mt 18:18
B him hand and foot, and take him..... Mt 22:13
For they b heavy burdens and............. Mt 23:4
he will first b the strong man.............. Mk 3:27
and no man could b him, no, not......... Mk 5:3
to b all that call on thy name.............. Acts 9:14
Gird thyself, and b on thy sandals...... Acts 12:8
So shall the Jews at Jerusalem b........ Acts 21:11

BINDETH
For he maketh sore, and b up............. Job 5:18
He b up the waters in his thick........... Job 26:8
He b the floods from overflowing........ Job 28:11
it b me about as the collar of my........ Job 30:18
they cry not when he b them............... Job 36:13
nor he that b sheaves his bosom........ Ps 129:7
in heart, and b up their wounds.......... Ps 147:3
As he that b a stone in a sling,........... Prov 26:8
in the day that the LORD b up the....... Is 30:26

BINDING
we were b sheaves in the field,........... Gen 37:7
B his foal unto the vine, and his.......... Gen 49:11
it shall have a b of woven work.......... Ex 28:32
every b oath to afflict the soul,.......... Num 30:13
the way unto the death, b.................. Acts 22:4

BINEA (bin'-e-ah) *A son of Moza.*
And Moza begat B............................... 1Chr 8:37
And Moza begat B............................... 1Chr 9:43

BINNUI (bin'-nu-ee)
1. A Levite who returned from exile.
Jeshua, and Noadiah the son of B...... Ezr 8:33
2. A descendant of Pahath-moab.
Mattaniah, Bezaleel, and B,................ Ezr 10:30
3. A descendant of Bani.
And Bani, and B, Shimei,.................... Ezr 10:38
4. A descendant of Henadad.
After him repaired B the son of......... Neh 3:24
B of the sons of Henadad, Kadmiel.... Neh 10:9
5. A family who returned from exile.
The children of B, six hundred........... Neh 7:15
6. A Levite with Zerubbabel.
Jeshua, B, Kadmiel, Sherebiah,......... Neh 12:8

BIRD
his kind, every b of every sort............ Gen 7:14
As for the living b, he shall................ Lev 14:6
the living b in the blood of the.......... Lev 14:6
of the b that was killed over the......... Lev 14:6
shall let the living b loose into........... Lev 14:7
and the scarlet, and the living b......... Lev 14:51
them in the blood of the slain b.......... Lev 14:51
the house with the blood of the b....... Lev 14:52
water, and with the living b................ Lev 14:52
b out of the city into the open............ Lev 14:53
thou play with him as with a b............ Job 41:5
Flee as a b to your mountain.............. Ps 11:1
Our soul is escaped as a b out of....... Ps 124:7
is spread in the sight of any b............ Prov 1:17
as a b from the hand of the............... Prov 6:5
as a b hasteth to the snare, and......... Prov 7:23
the b by wandering, as the................. Prov 26:2
As a b that wandereth from her........... Prov 27:8
for a b of the air shall carry............... Eccl 10:20
rise up at the voice of the b............... Eccl 12:4
as a wandering b cast out of the....... Is 16:2
a ravenous b from the east................ Is 46:11
is unto me as a speckled b................. Jer 12:9
enemies chased me sore, like a b....... Lam 3:52
glory shall fly away like a b................ Hos 9:11
shall tremble as a b out of Egypt........ Hos 11:11
Can a b fall in a snare upon the......... Amos 3:5
of every unclean and hateful b........... Rev 18:2

BIRD'S
If a b nest chance to be before.......... Deut 22:6

BIRDS
but the b divided he not..................... Gen 15:10
the b did eat them out of the............. Gen 40:17
the b shall eat thy flesh from............. Gen 40:19
is to be cleansed two b alive.............. Lev 14:4
shall command that one of the b........ Lev 14:5
take to cleanse the house two b......... Lev 14:49
the b in an earthen vessel over.......... Lev 14:50
Of all clean b ye shall eat.................. Deut 14:11
suffered neither the b of the air......... 2Sa 21:10
Where the b make their nests............. Ps 104:17
as the b that are caught in the.......... Eccl 9:12
time of the singing of b is come........ Song 2:12
As b flying, so will the LORD of.......... Is 31:5
all the b of the heavens were............. Jer 4:25
As a cage is full of b, so are.............. Jer 5:27
the beasts are consumed, and the b.. Jer 12:4
the round about are against her......... Jer 12:9
unto the ravenous b of every sort...... Eze 39:4
their b make their nests..................... Mt 8:20
so that the b of the air come and....... Mt 13:32
holes, and b of the air have nests..... Lk 9:58
like to corruptible man, and to b........ Rom 1:23

of fishes, and another of b................. 1Cor 15:39
For every kind of beasts, and of b...... Jas 3:7

BIRDS'
and his nails like b claws.................. Dan 4:33

BIRSHA (bur'-shah) *A king of Gomorrah.*
with B king of Gomorrah, Shinab....... Gen 14:2

BIRTH
other stone, according to their b........ Ex 28:10
the children are come to the b............ 2Kin 19:3
hidden untimely b I had not been....... Job 3:16
like the untimely b of a woman.......... Ps 58:8
that an untimely b is better than........ Eccl 6:3
of death than the day of one's b........ Eccl 7:1
the children are come to the b............ Is 37:3
Shall I bring to the b, and not............ Is 66:9
Thy b and thy nativity is of the.......... Eze 16:3
fly away like a bird, from the b........... Hos 9:11
Now the b of Jesus Christ was on...... Mt 1:18
and many shall rejoice at his b.......... Lk 1:14
a man which was blind from his b....... Jn 9:1
of whom I travail in b again............... Gal 4:19
with child cried, travailing in b........... Rev 12:2

BIRTHDAY
third day, which was Pharaoh's b...... Gen 40:20
But when Herod's b was kept............. Mt 14:6
that Herod on his b made a supper.... Mk 6:21

BIRTHRIGHT
said, Sell me this day thy b................ Gen 25:31
what profit shall this b do to me........ Gen 25:32
and he sold his b unto Jacob............. Gen 25:33
thus Esau despised his b................... Gen 25:34
he took away my b............................ Gen 27:36
the firstborn according to his b.......... Gen 43:33
his b was given unto the sons of........ 1Chr 5:1
is not to be reckoned after the b........ 1Chr 5:1
but the b was Joseph's...................... 1Chr 5:2
for one morsel of meat sold his b....... Heb 12:16

BIRZAITH *See BIRZAVITH.*

BIRZAVITH (bur'za-vith) *A descendant of Asher.*
Malchiel, who is the father of B......... 1Chr 7:31

BISHLAM (bish'-lam) *A commissioner of Artaxerxes.*
in the days of Artaxerxes wrote B...... Ezr 4:7

BISHOP
If a man desire the office of a b......... 1Ti 3:1
A b then must be blameless, the........ 1Ti 3:2
ordained the first b of the.................. 2Ti 4
For a b must be blameless, as the..... Titus 1:7
ordained the first b of the.................. Titus 4
the shepherd and B of your souls...... 1Pet 2:25

BISHOPRICK
and his b let another take.................. Acts 1:20

BISHOPS
which are at Philippi, with the b......... Phil 1:1

BIT
the people, and they b the people...... Num 21:6
mouth must be held in with b.............. Ps 32:9
on the wall, and a serpent b him........ Amos 5:19

BITE
an hedge, a serpent shall b him......... Eccl 10:8
will b without enchantment................ Eccl 10:11
be charmed, and they shall b you....... Jer 8:17
the serpent, and he shall b them........ Amos 9:3
that b with their teeth, and cry,.......... Mic 3:5
up suddenly that shall b thee............. Hab 2:7
But if ye b and devour one another..... Gal 5:15

BITETH
that b the horse heels, so that............ Gen 49:17
At the last it b like a serpent.............. Prov 23:32

BITHIA *See BITHIAH.*

BITHIAH (bith-i'-ah) *Daughter of Pharaoh.*
these are the sons of B the................ 1Chr 4:18

BITHRON (bith'-ron) *A district in Arabah.*
Jordan, and went through all B............ 2Sa 2:29

BITHYNIA (bith-in'-e-ah) *A Roman province in Asia Minor.*
Mysia, they assayed to go into B........ Acts 16:7
Galatia, Cappadocia, Asia, and B....... 1Pet 1:1

BITS
we put b in the horses' mouths,......... Jas 3:3

BITTEN
To pass, that every one that is b........ Num 21:8
that if a serpent had b any man.......... Num 21:9

BITTER
with a great and exceeding b cry....... Gen 27:34
made their lives b with hard bondage. Ex 1:14
with b herbs they shall eat it............. Ex 12:8
waters of Marah, for they were b....... Ex 15:23
shall have in his hand the b............... Num 5:18
be thou free from this b water........... Num 5:19
blot them out with the b water........... Num 5:23
b water that causeth the curse.......... Num 5:24
shall enter into her, and become b..... Num 5:24
shall enter into her, and become b..... Num 5:27
with unleavened bread and b herbs... Num 9:11
heat, and with b destruction.............. Deut 32:24
of gall, their clusters are b................ Deut 32:32
of Israel, that it was very b................ 2Kin 14:26
and cried with a loud and a b cry...... Est 4:1

and life unto the *b* in soul .... Job 3:20
For thou writest bitter things against ...... Job 13:26
Even to day is my complaint *b*. .... Job 23:2
shoot their arrows, even *b* words .... Ps 64:3
But her end is *b* as wormwood .... Prov 5:4
soul every *b* thing is sweet .... Prov 27:7
I find more *b* than death the .... Eccl 7:26
b* for sweet, and sweet for *b .... Is 5:20
shall be *b* to them that drink it .... Is 24:9
see that it is an evil thing and *b* .... Jer 2:19
thy wickedness, because it is *b* .... Jer 4:18
an only son, most *b* lamentation .... Jer 6:26
Ramah, lamentation, and *b* weeping ...... Jer 31:15
bitterness of heart and *b* wailing .... Eze 27:31
and the end thereof as a *b* day .... Amos 8:10
I raise up the Chaldeans, that *b* .... Hab 1:6
wives, and be not *b* against them .... Col 3:19
the same place sweet water and *b* .... Jas 3:11
But if ye have *b* envying and .... Jas 3:14
waters, because they were made *b* .... Rev 8:11
and it shall make thy belly *b* .... Rev 10:9
as I had eaten it, my belly was *b* .... Rev 10:10

BITTERLY
curse ye *b* the inhabitants .... Judg 5:23
hath dealt very *b* with me .... Ruth 1:20
I will weep *b*, labour not to. .... Is 22:4
ambassadors of peace shall weep *b* .... Is 33:7
against thee, and shall cry *b* .... Eze 27:30
provoked him to anger most *b* .... Hos 12:14
the majesty man shall cry there *b* .... Zeph 1:14
And he went out, and wept *b* .... Mt 26:75
And Peter went out, and wept *b* .... Lk 22:62

BITTERN
make it a possession for the *b* .... Is 14:23
and the *b* shall possess it .... Is 34:11
the *b* shall lodge in the upper .... Zeph 2:14

BITTERNESS
And she was in *b* of soul, and 1Sa 1:10
Surely the *b* of death is past. 1Sa 15:32
it will be *b* in the latter end 2Sa 2:26
will complain in the *b* of my soul .... Job 7:11
my breath; but filleth me with *b* .... Job 9:18
I will speak in the *b* of my soul .... Job 10:1
dieth in the *b* of his soul. .... Job 21:25
The heart knoweth his own *b* .... Prov 14:10
father, and *b* to her that bare him. .... Prov 17:25
all my years in the *b* of my soul .... Is 38:15
Behold, for peace I had great *b* .... Is 38:17
are afflicted, and she is in *b* .... Lam 1:4
He hath filled me with *b*, he hath .... Lam 3:15
and took me away, and I went in *b* .... Eze 3:14
with *b* sigh before their eyes .... Eze 21:6
weep for thee with *b* of heart .... Eze 27:31
son, and shall be in *b* for him .... Zec 12:10
that is in *b* for his firstborn .... Zec 12:10
that thou art in the gall of *b* .... Acts 8:23
mouth is full of cursing and *b* .... Rom 3:14
Let all *b*, and wrath, and anger, and ...... Eph 4:31
lest any root of *b* springing up .... Heb 12:15

BIZJOTHJAH See BIZJOTHJAH.

BIZJOTHJAH (biz-joth'-jah) A town in Judah.
Hazar-shual, and Beer-sheba, and B. ...... Josh 15:28

BIZTHA (biz'-thah) An eunuch of Ahasuerus.
wine, he commanded Mehuman, B. .... Est 1:10

BLACK
and that there is no *b* hair in it. .... Lev 13:31
there is *b* hair grown up .... Lev 13:37
that the heaven was *b* with clouds 1Kin 18:45
of red, and blue, and white, and *b* .... Est 1:6
My skin is *b* upon me, and my bones ..... Job 30:30
in the evening, in the *b* .... Prov 7:9
I am *b*, but comely, O ye .... Song 1:5
Look not upon me, because I am *b* .... Song 1:6
locks are bushy, and *b* as a raven .... Song 5:11
mourn, and the heavens above be *b* .... Jer 4:28
I am *b* .... Jer 8:21
they are *b* unto the ground. .... Jer 14:2
Our skin was *b* like an oven .... Lam 5:10
and in the second chariot *b* horses .... Zec 6:2
The *b* horses which are therein go .... Zec 6:6
not make one hair white or *b* .... Mt 5:36
And I beheld, and lo a *b* horse .... Rev 6:5
the sun became *b* as sackcloth of. .... Rev 6:12

BLACKER
Their visage is *b* than a coal .... Lam 4:8

BLACKISH
Which are *b* by reason of the ice, ... Job 6:16

BLACKNESS
let the *b* of the day terrify it .... Job 3:5
I clothe the heavens with *b* .... Is 50:3
all faces shall gather *b* .... Joel 2:6
and the faces of them all gather *b* .... Nah 2:10
that burned with fire, nor unto *b* .... Heb 12:18
the *b* of darkness for ever .... Jude 13

BLADE
the haft also went in after the *b* .... Judg 3:22
and the fat closed upon the *b* .... Judg 3:22
mine arm fall from my shoulder *b* .... Job 31:22
But when the *b* was sprung up, and ...... Mt 13:26
first the *b*, then the ear, after .... Mk 4:28

BLAINS
breaking forth with *b* upon man .... Ex 9:9
breaking forth with *b* upon man .... Ex 9:10

BLAME
then let me bear the *b* for ever .... Gen 43:9
bear the *b* to my father for ever .... Gen 44:32
that no man should *b* us in this. 2Cor 8:20
without *b* before him in love .... Eph 1:4

BLAMED
thing, that the ministry be not *b* 2Cor 6:3
the face, because he was to be *b* .... Gal 2:11

BLAMELESS
and ye shall be *b*. .... Gen 44:10
We will be *b* of this thine oath. .... Josh 2:17
Now shall I be more *b* than the .... Judg 15:3
profane the sabbath, and are *b* .... Mt 12:5
and ordinances of the Lord *b* .... Lk 1:6
that ye may be *b* in the day of 1Cor 1:8
That ye may be *b* and harmless, the ...... Phil 2:15
which is in the law, *b* .... Phil 3:6
body be preserved *b* unto the 1Th 5:23
A bishop then must be *b*, the 1Ti 3:2
office of a deacon, being found *b* 1Ti 3:10
in charge, that they may be *b* 1Ti 5:7
If any be *b*, the husband of one .... Titus 1:6
For a bishop must be *b*, as the .... Titus 1:7
him in peace, without spot, and *b* 2Pet 3:14

BLASPHEME
to the enemies of the LORD to *b* 2Sa 12:14
him, saying, Thou didst *b* God 1Kin 21:10
people, saying, Naboth did *b* God 1Kin 21:13
shall the enemy *b* thy name for .... Ps 74:10
wherewith soever they shall *b* .... Mk 3:28
But he that shall *b* against the .... Mk 3:29
synagogue, and compelled them to *b* ..... Acts 26:11
that they may learn not to *b* 1Ti 1:20
Do not they *b* that worthy name by ...... Jas 2:7
to *b* his name, and his tabernacle, ... Rev 13:6

BLASPHEMED
son *b* the name of the LORD .... Lev 24:11
of king of Assyria have *b* me 2Kin 19:6
Whom hast thou reproached and *b* 2Kin 19:22
foolish people have *b* thy name .... Ps 74:18
of king of Assyria have *b* me .... Is 37:6
Whom hast thou reproached and *b* ...... Is 37:23
name continually every day is *b* .... Is 52:5
mountains, and *b* me upon the hills ...... Is 65:7
in this your fathers have *b* me. .... Eze 20:27
they opposed themselves, and *b* .... Acts 18:6
For the name of God is *b* among .... Rom 2:24
of God and his doctrine be not *b* 1Ti 6:1
that the word of God be not *b* .... Titus 2:5
the name of God, which hath .... Rev 16:9
***b* the God of heaven because of.** .... Rev 16:11
men *b* God because of the plague. .... Rev 16:21

BLASPHEMER
Who was before a *b*, and a 1Ti 1:13

BLASPHEMERS
nor yet *b* of your goddess. .... Acts 19:37
covetous, boasters, proud, *b* 2Ti 3:2

BLASPHEMEST
and sent into the world, Thou *b* .... Jn 10:36

BLASPHEMETH
he that *b* the name of the LORD, ... Lev 24:16
when he *b* the name of the LORD, ... Lev 24:16
of him that reproacheth and *b* .... Ps 44:16
within themselves, This man *b* .... Mt 9:3
but unto him that *b* against the .... Lk 12:10

BLASPHEMIES
that I have heard all thy *b* which .... Eze 35:12
thefts, false witness, *b* .... Mt 15:19
Why doth this man thus speak *b* .... Mk 2:7
***b* wherewith soever they shall** .... Mk 3:28
Who is this which speaketh *b* .... Lk 5:21
mouth speaking great things and *b* .... Rev 13:5

BLASPHEMING
by Paul, contradicting and *b* .... Acts 13:45

BLASPHEMOUS
him speak *b* words against Moses .... Acts 6:11
***b* words against this holy place** .... Acts 6:13

BLASPHEMOUSLY
many other things *b* spake they .... Lk 22:65

BLASPHEMY
of trouble, and of rebuke, and *b* 2Kin 19:3
out of Judah, and *b* of the .... Is 37:3
***b* shall be forgiven unto men** .... Mt 12:31
but the *b* against the Holy Ghost .... Mt 12:31
clothes, saying, He hath spoken *b* .... Mt 26:65
behold, now ye have heard his *b* .... Mt 26:65
lasciviousness, an evil eye, *b* .... Mk 7:22
Ye have heard the *b* .... Mk 14:64
stone thee not; but for *b* .... Jn 10:33
anger, wrath, malice, *b*, filthy .... Col 3:8
I know the *b* of them which say .... Rev 2:9
and upon his heads the name of *b* .... Rev 13:1
opened his mouth in *b* against God .... Rev 13:6
beast, full of names of *b* .... Rev 17:3

BLAST
with the *b* of thy nostrils the .... Ex 15:8
make a long *b* with the ram's horn .... Josh 6:5
at the *b* of the breath of his 2Sa 22:16
Behold, I will send a *b* upon him 2Kin 19:7
By the *b* of God they perish, and .... Job 4:9
at the *b* of the breath of thy .... Ps 18:15
when the *b* of the terrible ones .... Is 25:4
Behold, I will send a *b* upon him .... Is 37:7

BLASTED
***b* with the east wind sprung up** .... Gen 41:6
***b* with the east wind, sprung up** .... Gen 41:23
the seven empty ears *b* with the .... Gen 41:27
as corn *b* before it be grown up 2Kin 19:26
as corn *b* before it be grown up .... Is 37:27

BLASTING
and with the sword, and with *b* .... Deut 28:22
famine, if there be pestilence, *b* 1Kin 8:37
be pestilence, if there be *b* 2Chr 6:28
I have smitten you with *b* .... Amos 4:9
I smote you with *b* and with mildew.... .. Hag 2:17

BLASTUS (blas'-tus) A servant of Herod Agrippa I.
him, and, having made B the king's... .... Acts 12:20

BLAZE
to *b* abroad the matter, insomuch .... Mk 1:45

BLEATING
What meaneth then this *b* of the 1Sa 15:14

BLEATINGS
to hear the *b* of the flocks .... Judg 5:16

BLEMISH
Your lamb shall be without *b* .... Ex 12:5
bullock, and two rams without *b* .... Ex 29:1
let him offer a male without *b* .... Lev 1:3
shall bring it a male without *b* .... Lev 1:10
it without *b* before the LORD .... Lev 3:1
he shall offer it without *b* .... Lev 3:6
without *b* unto the LORD for a sin .... Lev 4:3
of the goats, a male without *b* .... Lev 4:23
of the goats, a female without *b* .... Lev 4:28
shall bring it a female without *b* .... Lev 4:32
a ram without *b* out of the flocks .... Lev 5:15
a ram without *b* out of the flock .... Lev 5:18
a ram without *b* out of the flock. .... Lev 6:6
for a burnt offering, without *b* .... Lev 9:2
both of the first year, without *b* .... Lev 9:3
shall take two he lambs without *b* .... Lev 14:10
lamb of the first year without *b* .... Lev 14:10
their generations that hath any *b* .... Lev 21:17
man he be that hath a *b*, he shall .... Lev 21:18
or that hath a *b* in his eye .... Lev 21:20
No man that hath a *b* of the seed.... ...... Lev 21:21
he hath a *b* .... Lev 21:21
the altar, because he hath a *b* .... Lev 21:23
at your own will a male without *b* .... Lev 22:19
But whatsoever hath a *b*, that .... Lev 22:20
there shall be no *b* therein .... Lev 22:21
the sheaf an he lamb without *b* of .... Lev 23:12
lambs without *b* of the first year .... Lev 23:18
a man cause a *b* in his neighbour .... Lev 24:19
as he hath caused a *b* in a man .... Lev 24:20
without *b* for a burnt offering. .... Num 6:14
year without *b* for a sin offering. .... Num 6:14
one ram without *b* for peace. .... Num 6:14
without spot, wherein is no *b* .... Num 19:2
they shall be unto you without *b*.... .... Num 28:19
they shall be unto you without *b*.... .... Num 28:31
lambs of the first year without *b*.... .... Num 29:2
they shall be unto you without *b*.... .... Num 29:8
they shall be without *b*. .... Num 29:13
lambs of the first year without *b*.... .... Num 29:20
lambs of the first year without *b*.... .... Num 29:23
lambs of the first year without *b*.... .... Num 29:29
lambs of the first year without *b*.... .... Num 29:32
lambs of the first year without *b*.... .... Num 29:36
And if there be any *b* therein. .... Deut 15:21
lame, or blind, or have any ill *b*.... .... Deut 15:21
bullock, or sheep, wherein is *b*.... .... Deut 17:1
of his head there was no *b* in him. 2Sa 14:25
without *b* for a sin offering .... Eze 43:22
offer a young bullock without *b* .... Eze 43:23
a ram out of the flock without *b* .... Eze 43:23
a ram out of the flock, without *b* .... Eze 43:25
take a young bullock without *b* .... Eze 45:18
seven rams without *b* daily the .... Eze 45:23
day shall he six lambs without *b*.... .... Eze 46:4
b*, and a ram without *b .... Eze 46:4
be a young bullock without *b* .... Eze 46:6
they shall be without *b* .... Eze 46:6
lamb of the first year without *b*.... .... Eze 46:13
Children in whom was no *b*.... .... Dan 1:4
it should be holy and without *b* .... Eph 5:27
of Christ, as of a lamb without *b*.... .... 1Pet 1:19

BLEMISHES
is in them, and *b* be in them .... Lev 22:25
Spots they are and *b*, sporting.... .... 2Pet 2:13

BLESS
a great nation, and I will *b* thee .... Gen 12:2
And I will *b* them that *b* thee .... Gen 12:3
And I will *b* her, and give thee a .... Gen 17:16
yea, I will *b* her, and she shall .... Gen 17:16
That in blessing I will *b* thee .... Gen 22:17
will be with thee, and will *b* thee .... Gen 26:3
I am with thee, and will *b* thee.... .... Gen 26:24
that my soul may *b* thee before I.... .... Gen 27:4
***b* thee before the LORD before my....** .... Gen 27:7
that he may *b* thee before his.... .... Gen 27:10
venison, that thy soul may *b* me.... .... Gen 27:19
venison, that my soul may *b* thee.... ...... Gen 27:25
venison, that thy soul may *b* me.... .... Gen 27:31
B me, even me also, O my father.... .... Gen 27:34
***b* me, even me also, O my father....** .... Gen 27:38
And God Almighty *b* thee, and make.... . Gen 28:3
not let thee go, except thou *b* me.... .... Gen 32:26

thee, unto me, and I will b them...... Gen 48:9
me from all evil, b the lads...... Gen 48:16
saying, In thee shall Israel b...... Gen 48:20
who shall b thee with blessings...... Gen 49:25
and b me also...... Ex 12:32
come unto thee, and I will b thee...... Ex 20:24
he shall b thy bread, and thy...... Ex 23:25
On this wise ye shall b the...... Num 6:23
The LORD b thee, and keep thee...... Num 6:24
and I will b them...... Num 6:27
I have received commandment to b.. Num 23:20
them at all, nor b them at all...... Num 23:25
it pleased the LORD to b Israel...... Num 24:1
b you, as he hath promised you...... Deut 1:11
thee, and b thee, and multiply thee... Deut 7:13
he will also b the fruit of thy...... Deut 7:13
then thou shalt b the LORD thy...... Deut 8:10
to b in his name, unto this day...... Deut 10:8
that the LORD thy God may b thee.. Deut 14:29
for the LORD shall greatly b thee... Deut 15:4
God shall b thee in all thy works... Deut 15:10
the LORD thy God shall b thee in... Deut 15:18
b thee in all thine increase...... Deut 16:15
to b in the name of the LORD...... Deut 21:5
that the LORD thy God may b thee.. Deut 23:20
in his own raiment, and b thee...... Deut 24:13
that the LORD thy God may b thee.. Deut 24:19
b thy people Israel, and the land... Deut 26:15
mount Gerizim to b the people...... Deut 27:12
he shall b thee in the land which... Deut 28:8
to b all the work of thine hand...... Deut 28:12
that he b himself in his heart...... Deut 29:19
the LORD thy God shall b thee in... Deut 30:16
b the LORD, his substance, and accept.. Deut 33:11
that they should b the people of... Josh 8:33
B ye the LORD...... Judg 5:9
answered him, The LORD b thee...... Ruth 2:4
because he doth b the sacrifice...... 1Sa 9:13
David returned to b his household... 2Sa 6:20
to b the house of thy servant...... 2Sa 7:29
to b him, because he had fought... 2Sa 8:10
that ye may b the inheritance of... 2Sa 21:3
came to b our lord king David...... 1Kin 1:47
Oh that thou wouldest b me indeed.. 1Chr 4:10
and David returned to b his house.. 1Chr 16:43
to b the house of thy servant...... 1Chr 17:27
to b in his name for ever...... 1Chr 23:13
Now b the LORD your God...... 1Chr 29:20
b the LORD your God for ever and... Ps 5:12
thou, LORD, wilt b the righteous... Ps 5:12
I will b the LORD, who hath given.. Ps 16:7
congregations will I b the LORD... Ps 26:12
people, and b thine inheritance...... Ps 28:9
people, and b his people with...... Ps 29:11
I will b the LORD at all times...... Ps 34:1
they b with their mouth, but they... Ps 62:4
Thus will I b thee while I live...... Ps 63:4
O b our God, ye people, and make... Ps 66:8
God be merciful unto us, and b us... Ps 67:1
God, even our own God, shall b us... Ps 67:6
God shall b us...... Ps 67:7
B ye God in the congregations...... Ps 68:26
Sing unto the LORD, b his name...... Ps 96:2
thankful unto him, and b his name.. Ps 100:4
B the LORD, O my soul...... Ps 103:1
is within me, b his holy name...... Ps 103:1
B the LORD, O my soul, and forget... Ps 103:2
B the LORD, ye his angels, that...... Ps 103:20
B ye the LORD, all ye his hosts...... Ps 103:21
B the LORD, all his works in all... Ps 103:22
b the LORD, O my soul...... Ps 103:22
B the LORD, O my soul...... Ps 104:1
B thou the LORD, O my soul...... Ps 104:35
Let them curse, but b thou...... Ps 109:28
he will b us...... Ps 115:12
he will b the house of Israel...... Ps 115:12
he will b the house of Aaron...... Ps 115:12
He will b them that fear the LORD.. Ps 115:13
But we will b the LORD from this... Ps 115:18
The LORD shall b thee out of Zion.. Ps 128:5
we b you in the name of the LORD.. Ps 129:8
I will abundantly b her provision... Ps 132:15
b ye the LORD, all ye servants of... Ps 134:1
in the sanctuary, and b the LORD... Ps 134:2
and earth b thee out of Zion...... Ps 134:3
B the LORD, O house of Israel...... Ps 135:19
B the LORD, O house of Aaron...... Ps 135:19
B the LORD, O house of Levi...... Ps 135:20
ye that fear the LORD, b the LORD.. Ps 135:20
I will b thy name for ever and...... Ps 145:1
Every day will I b thee...... Ps 145:2
and thy saints shall b thee...... Ps 145:10
let all flesh b his holy name for... Ps 145:21
and doth not b their mother...... Prov 30:11
for the LORD shall b is...... Is 19:25
himself in the earth shall b...... Is 65:16
nations shall b themselves in him... Jer 4:2
The LORD b thee, O habitation of... Jer 31:23
from this day will I b you...... Hag 2:19
b them that curse you, do good to.. Mt 5:44
B them that curse you, and pray... Lk 6:28
his Son Jesus, sent him to b you... Acts 3:26
B them which persecute you...... Rom 12:14
b, and curse not...... Rom 12:14
being reviled, we b...... 1Cor 4:12
The cup of blessing which we b...... 1Cor 10:16
when thou shalt b with the spirit.. 1Cor 14:16
Surely blessing I will b thee...... Heb 6:14
Therewith we God, even the...... Jas 3:9

BLESSED
God b them, saying, Be fruitful,...... Gen 1:22
God b them, and God said unto them.. Gen 1:28
God b the seventh day,...... Gen 2:3
b them, and called their name Adam.. Gen 5:2
God b Noah and his sons, and said... Gen 9:1
B the LORD God of Shem...... Gen 9:26
all families of the earth be b...... Gen 12:3
he b him, and said...... Gen 14:19
B be Abram of the most high God,... Gen 14:19
b be the most high God, which...... Gen 14:20
Behold, I have b him, and will...... Gen 17:20
of the earth shall be b...... Gen 18:18
all the nations of the earth be b... Gen 22:18
the LORD had b Abraham in all...... Gen 24:1
B be the LORD God of my master....... Gen 24:27
said, Come in, thou b of the LORD.. Gen 24:31
the LORD hath b my master greatly.. Gen 24:35
b the LORD God of my master...... Gen 24:48
they b Rebekah, and said unto her,.. Gen 24:60
Abraham, that God b his son Isaac.. Gen 25:11
all the nations of the earth be b... Gen 26:4
and the LORD b them...... Gen 26:12
thou art now the b of the LORD...... Gen 26:29
so he b him...... Gen 27:23
b him, and said, See, the smell of.. Gen 27:27
of a field which the LORD hath b... Gen 27:27
b be he that blesseth thee...... Gen 27:29
before thou camest, and have b him.. Gen 27:33
yea, and he shall be b...... Gen 27:33
wherewith his father b him...... Gen 27:41
b him, and charged him, and said... Gen 28:1
Esau saw that Isaac had b Jacob...... Gen 28:6
that as he b him he gave him a...... Gen 28:6
the families of the earth be b...... Gen 28:14
for the daughters will call me b... Gen 30:13
the LORD hath b me for thy sake... Gen 30:27
the LORD hath b thee since my...... Gen 30:30
sons and his daughters, and b them.. Gen 31:55
And he b him there...... Gen 32:29
came out of Padan-aram, and b him.. Gen 35:9
that the LORD b the Egyptian's...... Gen 39:5
and Jacob b Pharaoh...... Gen 47:7
Jacob b Pharaoh, and went out from.. Gen 47:10
in the land of Canaan, and b me,... Gen 48:3
he b Joseph, and said, God, before.. Gen 48:15
he b them that day, saying, In...... Gen 48:20
father spake unto them, and b them.. Gen 49:28
to his blessing he b them...... Gen 49:28
B be the LORD, who hath delivered.. Ex 18:10
the LORD b the sabbath day...... Ex 20:11
and Moses b them...... Ex 39:43
B be thou, and came down from...... Lev 9:22
and came out, and b the people...... Lev 9:23
that he whom thou blessest is b... Num 22:6
for they are b...... Num 22:6
thou hast b them altogether...... Num 23:11
and he hath b...... Num 23:20
B is he that blesseth thee, and...... Num 24:9
thou hast altogether b them these.. Num 24:10
For the LORD thy God hath b thee.. Deut 2:7
Thou shalt be b above all people... Deut 7:14
the LORD thy God hath b thee...... Deut 12:7
when the LORD thy God hath b thee.. Deut 14:24
b thee thou shalt give unto him... Deut 15:14
as the LORD thy God hath b thee... Deut 16:10
B shalt thou be in the city, and... Deut 28:3
b shalt thou be in the field...... Deut 28:3
B shall be the fruit of thy body,... Deut 28:4
B shall be thy basket and thy...... Deut 28:5
B shalt thou be when thou comest,.. Deut 28:6
b shalt thou be when thou goest... Deut 28:6
b the children of Israel before...... Deut 33:1
B of the LORD be his land, for...... Deut 33:13
B be he that enlargeth Gad...... Deut 33:20
Let Asher be b with children...... Deut 33:24
And Joshua b him, and gave unto... Josh 14:13
as the LORD hath b me hitherto... Josh 17:14
So Joshua b them, and sent them... Josh 22:6
unto their tents, then he b them... Josh 22:7
and the children of Israel b God... Josh 24:10
therefore he b you still...... Josh 24:10
B above women Jael the wife,...... Judg 5:24
b shall she be above women in the.. Judg 5:24
the child grew, and the LORD b him.. Judg 13:24
B be thou of the LORD, my son...... Judg 17:2
b be he that did take knowledge... Ruth 2:19
B be he of the LORD, who hath not.. Ruth 2:20
B be thou of the LORD, my...... Ruth 3:10
B be the LORD, which hath not...... Ruth 4:14
Eli b Elkanah and his wife, and...... 1Sa 2:20
unto him, B be thou of the LORD... 1Sa 15:13
And Saul said, B be ye of the LORD.. 1Sa 23:21
B be the LORD God of Israel,...... 1Sa 25:32
b be thy advice, and b be...... 1Sa 25:33
B be the LORD, that hath pleaded... 1Sa 25:39
to David, B be thou, my son David.. 1Sa 26:25
B be ye of the LORD, that ye have.. 2Sa 2:5
the LORD b Obed-edom, and all his.. 2Sa 6:11
The LORD hath b the house of...... 2Sa 6:12
he b the people in the name of...... 2Sa 6:18
of thy servant be b for ever...... 2Sa 7:29
he would not go, but b him...... 2Sa 13:25
B be the LORD thy God, which hath.. 2Sa 18:28
king kissed Barzillai, and b him... 2Sa 19:39
and b be my rock...... 2Sa 22:47
B be the LORD God of Israel,...... 1Kin 1:48
And king Solomon shall be b...... 1Kin 2:45
B be the LORD this day, which...... 1Kin 5:7
b all the congregation of Israel... 1Kin 8:14

B be the LORD God of Israel,...... 1Kin 8:15
b all the congregation of Israel... 1Kin 8:55
B be the LORD, that hath given...... 1Kin 8:56
they b the king, and went unto...... 1Kin 8:66
B be the LORD thy God, which...... 1Kin 10:9
the LORD b the house of Obed-edom.. 1Chr 13:14
he b the people in the name of...... 1Chr 16:2
B be the LORD God of Israel for... 1Chr 16:36
O LORD, and it shall be b for ever.. 1Chr 17:27
for God b him...... 1Chr 26:5
Wherefore David b the LORD before.. 1Chr 29:10
B be thou, LORD God of Israel our.. 1Chr 29:10
all the congregation b the LORD,... 1Chr 29:20
B be the LORD God of Israel, that.. 2Chr 2:12
b the whole congregation of...... 2Chr 6:3
B be the LORD God of Israel, who... 2Chr 6:4
B be the LORD God of Israel, which.. 2Chr 9:8
for there they b the LORD...... 2Chr 20:26
the Levites arose and b the people.. 2Chr 30:27
they b the LORD, and his people... 2Chr 31:8
for the LORD hath b his people...... 2Chr 31:10
B be the LORD God of our fathers,.. Ezr 7:27
Ezra b the LORD, the great God...... Neh 8:6
b be thy glorious name, which is... Neh 9:5
the people b all the men, that...... Neh 11:2
thou hast b the work of his hands.. Job 1:10
b be the name of the LORD...... Job 1:21
the ear heard me, then it b me...... Job 29:11
If his loins have not b me...... Job 31:20
So the LORD b the latter end of... Job 42:12
B is the man that walketh not in... Ps 1:1
B are all they that put their...... Ps 2:12
and b be my rock...... Ps 18:46
hast made him most b for ever...... Ps 21:6
B the LORD, because he hath...... Ps 28:6
B the LORD...... Ps 31:21
B is he whose transgression is...... Ps 32:1
B is the man unto whom the LORD... Ps 32:2
B is the nation whose God is the... Ps 33:12
b is the man that trusteth in him... Ps 34:8
For such as be b of him shall...... Ps 37:22
and his seed is b...... Ps 37:26
B is that man that maketh the...... Ps 40:4
B is he that considereth the poor... Ps 41:1
B be b upon the earth...... Ps 41:2
B be the LORD God of Israel from... Ps 41:13
God hath b thee for ever...... Ps 45:2
while he lived he b his soul...... Ps 49:18
B is the man whom thou choosest,... Ps 65:4
B be God, which hath not turned... Ps 66:20
B be the LORD, who daily loadeth... Ps 68:19
B be God...... Ps 68:35
and men shall be b in him...... Ps 72:17
all nations shall call him b...... Ps 72:17
B be the LORD God, the God of...... Ps 72:18
b be his glorious name for ever... Ps 72:19
B are they that dwell in thy...... Ps 84:4
B is the man whose strength is in... Ps 84:5
b is the man that trusteth in...... Ps 84:12
B is the people that know the...... Ps 89:15
B be the LORD for evermore...... Ps 89:52
B is the man whom thou chastenest.. Ps 94:12
B are they that keep judgment, and.. Ps 106:3
B be the LORD God of Israel from... Ps 106:48
B is the man that feareth the...... Ps 112:1
of the upright shall be b...... Ps 112:2
B be the name of the LORD from...... Ps 113:2
Ye are b of the LORD which made... Ps 115:15
B be he that cometh in the name... Ps 118:26
we have b you out of the house of.. Ps 118:26
B are the undefiled in the way,...... Ps 119:1
B are they that keep his...... Ps 119:2
B art thou, O LORD...... Ps 119:12
B be the LORD, who hath not given.. Ps 124:6
B is every one that feareth the...... Ps 128:1
man be b that feareth the LORD...... Ps 128:4
B be the LORD out of Zion, which... Ps 135:21
B be the LORD my strength, which... Ps 144:1
he hath b thy children within...... Ps 147:13
Let thy fountain be b...... Prov 5:18
for b are they that keep my ways... Prov 8:32
B is the man that heareth me,...... Prov 8:34
The memory of the just is b......... Prov 10:7
his children are b after him...... Prov 20:7
the end thereof shall not be b...... Prov 20:21
hath a bountiful eye shall be b...... Prov 22:9
children arise up, and call her b... Prov 31:28
B art thou, O land, when thy king.. Eccl 10:17
The daughters saw her, and b her... Song 6:9
B be Egypt my people, and Assyria.. Is 19:25
b are all they that wait for him... Is 30:18
B are ye that sow beside all...... Is 32:20
alone, and b him, and increased...... Is 51:2
B is the man that doeth this, and... Is 56:2
the seed which the LORD hath b...... Is 61:9
are the seed of the b of the LORD.. Is 65:23
incense, as if he b an idol...... Is 66:3
B is the man that trusteth in the.. Jer 17:7
wherein my mother bare me b...... Jer 20:14
B be the glory of the LORD from... Eze 3:12
Then Daniel b the God of heaven... Dan 2:19
be the name of God for ever and... Dan 2:20
B be the God of Shadrach, Meshach.. Dan 3:28
I b the most High, and I praised... Dan 4:34
B is he that waiteth, and cometh... Dan 12:12
that sell them say, B be the LORD.. Zec 11:5
And all nations shall call you b...... Mal 3:12
B are the poor in spirit...... Mt 5:3
B are they that mourn...... Mt 5:4
B are the meek...... Mt 5:5

B are they which do hunger and ...... Mt 5:6
B are the merciful ...... Mt 5:7
B are the pure in heart ...... Mt 5:8
B are the peacemakers ...... Mt 5:9
B are they which are persecuted ...... Mt 5:10
B are ye, when men shall revile ...... Mt 5:11
b is he, whosoever shall not be ...... Mt 11:6
But b are your eyes, for they see ...... Mt 13:16
and looking up to heaven, he b ...... Mt 14:19
B art thou, Simon Bar-jona ...... Mt 16:17
B is he that cometh in the name ...... Mt 21:9
B is he that cometh in the name ...... Mt 23:39
B is that servant, whom his lord ...... Mt 24:46
ye b of my Father, inherit the ...... Mt 25:34
b it, and gave it to ...... Mt 26:26
he looked up to heaven, and b ...... Mk 6:41
and he b, and commanded to set them ...... Mk 8:7
his hands upon them, and b them ...... Mk 10:16
B is he that cometh in the name ...... Mk 11:9
B be the kingdom of our father ...... Mk 11:10
did eat, Jesus took bread, and b ...... Mk 14:22
thou the Christ, the Son of the B ...... Mk 14:61
b art thou among women ...... Lk 1:28
B art thou among women, and ...... Lk 1:42
b is the fruit of thy womb ...... Lk 1:42
And b is she that believed ...... Lk 1:45
all generations shall call me b ...... Lk 1:48
B be the Lord God of Israel ...... Lk 1:68
in his arms, and b God, and said ...... Lk 2:28
And Simeon b them, and said unto ...... Lk 2:34
disciples, and said, B be ye poor ...... Lk 6:20
B are ye that hunger now ...... Lk 6:21
B are ye that weep now ...... Lk 6:21
B are ye, when men shall hate you ...... Lk 6:22
b is he, whosoever shall not be ...... Lk 7:23
he b them, and brake, and gave to ...... Lk 9:16
B are the eyes which see the ...... Lk 10:23
B is the womb that bare thee, and ...... Lk 11:27
b are they that hear the word of ...... Lk 11:28
B are those servants, whom the ...... Lk 12:37
them so, b are those servants ...... Lk 12:38
B is that servant, whom his lord ...... Lk 12:43
B is he that cometh in the name ...... Lk 13:35
And thou shalt be b ...... Lk 14:14
B is he that shall eat bread in ...... Lk 14:15
B be the King that cometh in the ...... Lk 19:38
B are the barren, and the wombs ...... Lk 23:29
b it, and brake, and gave to them ...... Lk 24:30
he lifted up his hands, and b them ...... Lk 24:50
it came to pass, while he b them ...... Lk 24:51
B is the King of Israel that ...... Jn 12:13
b are they that have not seen, and ...... Jn 20:29
the kindreds of the earth be b ...... Acts 3:25
It is more b to give than to ...... Acts 20:35
the Creator, who is b for ever ...... Rom 1:25
B are they whose iniquities are ...... Rom 4:7
B is the man to whom the Lord ...... Rom 4:8
who is over all, God b for ever ...... Rom 9:5
B be God, even the Father of our 2Cor 1:3
which is b for evermore, knoweth 2Cor 11:31
In thee shall all nations be b ...... Gal 3:8
faith are b with faithful Abraham ...... Gal 3:9
B be the God and Father of our ...... Eph 1:3
who hath b us with all spiritual ...... Eph 1:3
the glorious gospel of the b God 1Ti 1:11
times he shall shew, who is the b 1Ti 6:15
Looking for that b hope, and the ...... Titus 2:13
slaughter of the kings, and b him ...... Heb 7:1
b him that had the promises ...... Heb 7:6
the less is b of the better ...... Heb 7:7
By faith Isaac b Jacob and Esau ...... Heb 11:20
b both the sons of Joseph ...... Heb 11:21
B is the man that endureth ...... Jas 1:12
this man shall be b in his deed ...... Jas 1:25
B be the God and Father of our 1Pet 1:3
B is he that readeth, and they ...... Rev 1:3
B are the dead which die in the ...... Rev 14:13
B is he that watcheth, and keepeth ...... Rev 16:15
B are they which are called unto ...... Rev 19:9
B and holy is he that hath part in ...... Rev 20:6
b is he that keepeth the sayings ...... Rev 22:7
B are they that do his ...... Rev 22:14

BLESSEDNESS
also describeth the b of the man ...... Rom 4:6
Cometh this b then upon the ...... Rom 4:9
Where is then the b ye spake of ...... Gal 4:15

BLESSEST
that he whom thou b is blessed ...... Num 22:6
for thou, O Lord, and it shall 1Chr 17:27
thou b the springing thereof ...... Ps 65:10

BLESSETH
and blessed be he that b thee ...... Gen 27:29
Blessed is he that b thee ...... Num 24:9
For the Lord thy God b thee ...... Deut 15:6
the covetous, whom the Lord ...... Ps 10:3
He b them also, so that they are ...... Ps 107:38
but he b the habitation of the ...... Prov 3:33
He that b his friend with a loud ...... Prov 27:14
That he who b himself in the ...... Is 65:16

BLESSING
and thou shalt be a b ...... Gen 12:2
That in b I will bless thee, and ...... Gen 22:17
bring a curse upon me, and not a b ...... Gen 27:12
Isaac had made an end of b Jacob ...... Gen 27:30
and hath taken away thy b ...... Gen 27:35
now he hath taken away my b ...... Gen 27:36
Hast thou not reserved a b for me ...... Gen 27:36
his father, Hast thou but one b ...... Gen 27:38

b wherewith his father blessed ...... Gen 27:41
And give thee the b of Abraham ...... Gen 28:4
my b that is brought to thee ...... Gen 33:11
the b of the Lord was upon all ...... Gen 39:5
to his b he blessed them ...... Gen 49:28
may bestow upon you a b this day ...... Ex 32:29
Then I will command my b upon you ...... Lev 25:21
I set before you this day a b ...... Deut 11:26
A b, if ye obey the commandments ...... Deut 11:27
put the b upon mount Gerizim ...... Deut 11:29
according to the b of the Lord ...... Deut 12:15
according to the b of the Lord ...... Deut 16:17
the curse into a b unto thee ...... Deut 23:5
The Lord shall command the b upon ...... Deut 28:8
things are come upon thee, the b ...... Deut 30:1
set before you life and death, b ...... Deut 30:19
And this is the b, wherewith Moses ...... Deut 33:1
And this is the b of Judah ...... Deut 33:7
let the b come upon the head of ...... Deut 33:16
and full with the b of the Lord ...... Deut 33:23
Who answered, Give me a b ...... Josh 15:19
And she said unto him, Give me a b ...... Judg 1:15
now this b which thine handmaid 1Sa 25:27
with thy b let the house of thy 2Sa 7:29
thee, take a b of thy servant 2Kin 5:15
which is exalted above all b ...... Neh 9:5
our God turned the curse into a b ...... Neh 13:2
The b of him that was ready to ...... Job 29:13
thy b is upon thy people ...... Ps 3:8
shall receive the b from the Lord ...... Ps 24:5
as he delighted not in b, so let ...... Ps 109:17
The b of the Lord be upon you ...... Ps 129:8
there the Lord commanded the b ...... Ps 133:3
The b of the Lord, it maketh rich ...... Prov 10:22
By the b of the upright the city ...... Prov 11:11
but b shall be upon the head of ...... Prov 11:26
a good b shall come upon them ...... Prov 24:25
even a b in the midst of the land ...... Is 19:24
my b upon thine offspring ...... Is 44:3
for a b is in it ...... Is 65:8
places round about my hill a b ...... Eze 34:26
there shall be showers of b ...... Eze 34:26
that he may cause the b to rest ...... Eze 44:30
repent, and leave a b behind him ...... Joel 2:14
I save you, and ye shall be a b ...... Zec 8:13
of heaven, and pour you out a b ...... Mal 3:10
in the temple, praising and b God ...... Lk 24:53
of the b of the gospel of Christ ...... Rom 15:29
The cup of b which we bless, is 1Cor 10:16
That the b of Abraham might come ...... Gal 3:14
is dressed, receiveth b from God ...... Heb 6:7
Surely b I will bless thee, and ...... Heb 6:14
he would have inherited the b ...... Heb 12:17
of the same mouth proceedeth b ...... Jas 3:10
but contrariwise b 1Pet 3:9
that ye should inherit a b 1Pet 3:9
and honour, and glory, and b ...... Rev 5:12
are in them, heard I saying, B ...... Rev 5:13
B, and glory, and wisdom, and ...... Rev 7:12

BLESSINGS
bless them with b of heaven above ...... Gen 49:25
b of the deep that lieth under ...... Gen 49:25
b of the breasts, and of the womb ...... Gen 49:25
The b of thy father have ...... Gen 49:26
the b of my progenitors unto the ...... Gen 49:26
all these b shall come on thee ...... Deut 28:2
all the words of the law, the b ...... Josh 8:34
him with the b of goodness ...... Ps 21:3
B are upon the head of the just ...... Prov 10:6
faithful man shall abound with b ...... Prov 28:20
upon you, and I will curse your b ...... Mal 2:2
b in heavenly places in Christ ...... Eph 1:3

BLEW
the Lord, and b with the trumpets ...... Josh 6:8
priests that b with the trumpets ...... Josh 6:9
and b with the trumpets ...... Josh 6:13
when the priests b with the ...... Josh 6:16
the priests b with the trumpets ...... Josh 6:20
that he b a trumpet in the ...... Judg 3:27
upon Gideon, and he b a trumpet ...... Judg 6:34
they b the trumpets, and brake the ...... Judg 7:19
three companies b the trumpets ...... Judg 7:20
the three hundred b the trumpets ...... Judg 7:22
Saul b the trumpet throughout all 1Sa 13:3
So Joab b a trumpet, and all the 2Sa 2:28
Joab b the trumpet, and the people 2Sa 18:16
he b a trumpet, and said, We have 2Sa 20:1
he b a trumpet, and they retired 2Sa 20:22
and they b the trumpet 2Kin 9:13
b with trumpets, saying, Jehu is 2Kin 9:13
land rejoiced, and b with trumpets 2Kin 11:14
the floods came, and the winds b ...... Mt 7:25
the floods came, and the winds b ...... Mt 7:27
by reason of a great wind that b ...... Jn 6:18
And when the south wind b softly ...... Acts 27:13
and after one day the south wind b ...... Acts 28:13

BLIND
or deaf, or the seeing, or the b ...... Ex 4:11
put a stumblingblock before the b ...... Lev 19:14
a b man, or a lame, or he that ...... Lev 21:18
B, or broken, or maimed, or ...... Lev 22:22
therein, as if it be lame, or b ...... Deut 15:21
for a gift doth b the eyes of the ...... Deut 16:19
the b to wander out of the way ...... Deut 27:18
as the b gropeth in darkness, and ...... Deut 28:29
bribe to b mine eyes therewith 1Sa 12:3
Except thou take away the b 2Sa 5:6
Jebusites, and the lame and the b 2Sa 5:8
Wherefore they said, The b 2Sa 5:8

I was eyes to the b, and feet was ...... Job 29:15
Lord openeth the eyes of the b ...... Ps 146:8
the eyes of the b shall see out ...... Is 29:18
the eyes of the b shall be opened ...... Is 35:5
To open the b eyes, to bring out ...... Is 42:7
I will bring the b by a way that ...... Is 42:16
and look, ye b, that ye may see ...... Is 42:18
Who is b, but my servant ...... Is 42:19
who is b as he that is perfect, ... Is 42:19
and b as the Lord's servant ...... Is 42:19
Bring forth the b people that ...... Is 43:8
His watchmen are b ...... Is 56:10
We grope for the wall like the b ...... Is 59:10
of the earth, and with them the b ...... Jer 31:8
wandered as b men in the streets ...... Lam 4:14
that they shall walk like b men ...... Zeph 1:17
if ye offer the b for sacrifice ...... Mal 1:8
two b men followed him, crying ...... Mt 9:27
the house, the b men came to him ...... Mt 9:28
The b receive their sight, and the ...... Mt 11:5
him one possessed with a devil, b ...... Mt 12:22
healed him, insomuch that the b ...... Mt 12:22
they be b leaders of the b ...... Mt 15:14
they be b leaders of the b ...... Mt 15:14
if the b lead the b, both ...... Mt 15:14
And if the b lead the b ...... Mt 15:14
with them those that were lame, b ...... Mt 15:30
the lame to walk, and the b to see ...... Mt 15:31
two b men sitting by the way side ...... Mt 20:30
And the b and the lame came to him ...... Mt 21:14
ye b guides, which say, Whosoever ...... Mt 23:16
Ye fools and b ...... Mt 23:17
Ye fools and b ...... Mt 23:19
Ye b guides, which strain at a ...... Mt 23:24
Thou b Pharisee, cleanse first ...... Mt 23:26
and they bring a b man unto him ...... Mk 8:22
he took the b man by the hand, and ...... Mk 8:23
b Bartimaeus, the son of Timaeus, ... Mk 10:46
And they call the b man, saying ...... Mk 10:49
The b man said unto him, Lord, ... Mk 10:51
and recovering of sight to the b ...... Lk 4:18
them, Can the b lead the b ...... Lk 6:39
many that were b he gave sight ...... Lk 7:21
how that the b see, the lame walk ...... Lk 7:22
poor, the maimed, the lame, the b ...... Lk 14:13
the maimed, and the halt, and the b ...... Lk 14:21
a certain b man sat by the way ...... Lk 18:35
multitude of impotent folk, of b ...... Jn 5:3
a man which was b from his birth ...... Jn 9:1
his parents, that he was born b ...... Jn 9:2
eyes of the b man with the clay ...... Jn 9:6
before had seen him that he was b ...... Jn 9:8
him that aforetime was b ...... Jn 9:13
They say unto the b man again ...... Jn 9:17
him, that he had been b, and ...... Jn 9:18
your son, who ye say was born b ...... Jn 9:19
is our son, and that he was born b ...... Jn 9:20
called they the man that was b ...... Jn 9:24
I know, that, whereas I was b ...... Jn 9:25
the eyes of one that was born b ...... Jn 9:32
they which see might be made b ...... Jn 9:39
and said unto him, Are we b also ...... Jn 9:40
said unto them, If ye were b ...... Jn 9:41
a devil open the eyes of the b ...... Jn 10:21
which opened the eyes of the b ...... Jn 11:37
is upon thee, and thou shalt be b ...... Acts 13:11
thou thyself art a guide of the b ...... Rom 2:19
he that lacketh these things is b 2Pet 1:9
and miserable, and poor, and b ...... Rev 3:17

BLINDED
he hath b their eyes, and hardened ...... Jn 12:40
obtained it, and the rest were b ...... Rom 11:7
But their minds were b 2Cor 3:14
b the minds of them which believe 2Cor 4:4
that darkness hath b his eyes 1Jn 2:11

BLINDETH
for the gift b the wise, and ...... Ex 23:8

BLINDFOLDED
And when they had b him, they ...... Lk 22:64

BLINDNESS
at the door of the house with b ...... Gen 19:11
smite them with madness, and b ...... Deut 28:28
this people, I pray thee, with b 2Kin 6:18
he smote them with b according to 2Kin 6:18
every house of the people with b ...... Zec 12:4
that b in part is happened to ...... Rom 11:25
because of the b of their heart ...... Eph 4:18

BLOOD
the voice of thy brother's b ...... Gen 4:10
thy brother's b from thy hand ...... Gen 4:11
thereof, which is the b thereof ...... Gen 9:4
surely your b of your lives will ...... Gen 9:5
Whoso sheddeth man's b ...... Gen 9:6
by man shall his b be shed ...... Gen 9:6
Reuben said unto them, Shed no b ...... Gen 37:22
our brother, and conceal his b ...... Gen 37:26
and dipped the coat in the b ...... Gen 37:31
behold, also his b is required ...... Gen 42:22
and his clothes in the b of grapes ...... Gen 49:11
shall become b upon the dry land ...... Ex 4:9
and they shall be turned to b ...... Ex 7:17
of water, that they may become b ...... Ex 7:19
that there may be b throughout ...... Ex 7:19
in the river were turned to b ...... Ex 7:20
there was b throughout all the ...... Ex 7:21
And they shall take of the b ...... Ex 12:7
the b shall be to you for a token ...... Ex 12:13
and when I see the b, I will pass ...... Ex 12:13

dip it in the *b* that is in the .... Ex 12:22
with the *b* that is in the bason .... Ex 12:22
he seeth the *b* upon the lintel .... Ex 12:23
there shall no *b* be shed for him .... Ex 22:2
there shall be *b* shed for him .... Ex 22:3
Thou shalt not offer the *b* of my .... Ex 23:18
And Moses took half of the *b* .... Ex 24:6
half of the *b* he sprinkled on the .... Ex 24:6
And Moses took the *b*, and sprinkled .... Ex 24:8
Behold the *b* of the covenant .... Ex 24:8
take of the *b* of the bullock .... Ex 29:12
pour all the *b* beside the bottom .... Ex 29:12
the ram, and thou shalt take his *b* .... Ex 29:16
kill the ram, and take of his *b* .... Ex 29:20
sprinkle the *b* upon the altar .... Ex 29:20
of the *b* that is upon the altar .... Ex 29:21
with the *b* of the sin offering of .... Ex 30:10
Thou shalt not offer the *b* of my .... Ex 34:25
Aaron's sons, shall bring the *b* .... Lev 1:5
sprinkle the *b* round about upon .... Lev 1:5
shall sprinkle his *b* round about .... Lev 1:11
the *b* thereof shall be wrung out .... Lev 1:15
the *b* upon the altar round about .... Lev 3:2
b thereof round about upon the .... Lev 3:8
of Aaron shall sprinkle the *b* .... Lev 3:13
that ye eat neither fat nor *b* .... Lev 3:17
shall take of the bullock's *b* .... Lev 4:5
shall dip his finger in the *b* .... Lev 4:6
sprinkle of the *b* seven times .... Lev 4:6
priest shall put some of the *b* .... Lev 4:7
shall pour all the *b* of the .... Lev 4:7
b to the tabernacle of the .... Lev 4:16
dip his finger in some of the *b* .... Lev 4:17
he shall put some of the *b* upon .... Lev 4:18
shall pour out all the *b* at the .... Lev 4:18
b of the sin offering with his .... Lev 4:25
shall pour out his *b* at the .... Lev 4:25
of the *b* thereof with his finger .... Lev 4:30
shall pour out all the *b* thereof .... Lev 4:30
b of the sin offering with his .... Lev 4:34
shall pour out all the *b* thereof .... Lev 4:34
he shall sprinkle of the *b* of the .... Lev 5:9
the rest of the *b* shall be wrung .... Lev 5:9
of the *b* thereof upon any garment .... Lev 6:27
whereof any of the *b* is brought .... Lev 6:30
the *b* thereof shall he sprinkle .... Lev 7:2
the *b* of the peace offerings .... Lev 7:14
ye shall eat no manner of *b* .... Lev 7:26
it be that eateth any manner of *b* .... Lev 7:27
that offereth the *b* of the peace .... Lev 7:33
and Moses took the *b*, and put it .... Lev 8:15
poured the *b* at the bottom of the .... Lev 8:15
Moses sprinkled the *b* upon the .... Lev 8:19
and Moses took of the *b* of it .... Lev 8:23
Moses put of the *b* upon the tip .... Lev 8:24
Moses sprinkled the *b* upon the .... Lev 8:24
of the *b* which was upon the altar .... Lev 8:30
of Aaron brought the *b* unto him .... Lev 9:9
and he dipped his finger in the *b* .... Lev 9:9
poured out the *b* at the bottom of .... Lev 9:9
sons presented unto him the *b* .... Lev 9:12
sons presented unto him the *b* .... Lev 9:18
the *b* of it was not brought in .... Lev 10:18
in the *b* of her purifying three .... Lev 12:4
she shall continue in the *b* of .... Lev 12:5
cleansed from the issue of her *b* .... Lev 12:7
of the living bird in the *b* of .... Lev 14:6
of the *b* of the trespass offering .... Lev 14:14
upon the *b* of the trespass .... Lev 14:17
of the *b* of the trespass offering .... Lev 14:28
upon the place of the *b* of the .... Lev 14:28
dip them in the *b* of the slain .... Lev 14:51
the house with the *b* of the bird .... Lev 14:52
and her issue in her flesh be *b* .... Lev 15:19
b many days out of the time of .... Lev 15:25
take of the *b* of the bullock .... Lev 16:14
the *b* with his finger seven times .... Lev 16:14
bring his *b* within the vail, and .... Lev 16:15
do with that *b* as he did with the .... Lev 16:15
he did with the *b* of the bullock .... Lev 16:15
take of the *b* of the bullock .... Lev 16:18
of the *b* of the goat, and put it .... Lev 16:18
he shall sprinkle of the *b* upon .... Lev 16:19
whose *b* was brought in to make .... Lev 16:27
shall be imputed unto that man .... Lev 17:4
he hath shed *b* .... Lev 17:4
b upon the altar of the LORD at .... Lev 17:6
you, that eateth any manner of *b* .... Lev 17:10
against that soul that eateth *b* .... Lev 17:10
the life of the flesh is in the *b* .... Lev 17:11
for it is the *b* that maketh an .... Lev 17:11
No soul of you shall eat *b* .... Lev 17:12
that sojourneth among you eat *b* .... Lev 17:12
shall even pour out the *b* thereof .... Lev 17:13
the *b* of it is for the life .... Lev 17:14
Ye shall eat the *b* of no manner .... Lev 17:14
of all flesh is the *b* thereof .... Lev 17:14
thou shalt not avenge the *b* of thy .... Lev 19:16
not eat any thing with the *b* .... Lev 19:26
his *b* shall be upon him .... Lev 20:9
their *b* shall be upon them .... Lev 20:11
their *b* shall be upon them .... Lev 20:12
their *b* shall be upon them .... Lev 20:13
their *b* shall be upon them .... Lev 20:16
uncovered the fountain of her *b* .... Lev 20:18
their *b* shall be upon them .... Lev 20:27
sprinkle their *b* upon the altar .... Num 18:17
take of her *b* with his finger .... Num 19:4
sprinkle of her *b* directly before .... Num 19:4
her skin, and her flesh, and her *b* .... Num 19:5

prey, and drink the *b* of the slain .... Num 23:24
The revenger of *b* himself shall .... Num 35:19
the revenger of *b* shall slay the .... Num 35:19
The revenger of *b* according to .... Num 35:24
of the hand of the revenger of *b* .... Num 35:25
the revenger of *b* find him .... Num 35:27
the revenger of *b* kill the slayer .... Num 35:27
shall not be guilty of *b* .... Num 35:27
for *b* it defileth the land .... Num 35:33
of the *b* that is shed therein .... Num 35:33
but by the *b* of him that shed it .... Num 35:33
Only ye shall not eat the *b* .... Deut 12:16
be sure that thou eat not the *b* .... Deut 12:23
for the *b* is the life .... Deut 12:23
offerings, the flesh and the *b* .... Deut 12:27
the *b* of thy sacrifices shall be .... Deut 12:27
thou shalt not eat the *b* thereof .... Deut 15:23
in judgment, between *b* and *b* .... Deut 17:8
of the *b* pursue the slayer .... Deut 19:6
That innocent *b* be not shed in .... Deut 19:10
inheritance, and so *b* be upon thee .... Deut 19:10
into the hand of the avenger of *b* .... Deut 19:10
guilt of innocent *b* from Israel .... Deut 19:13
Our hands have not shed this *b* .... Deut 21:7
lay not innocent *b* unto thy .... Deut 21:8
shall be forgiven them .... Deut 21:8
of innocent *b* from among you .... Deut 21:9
thou bring not *b* upon thine house .... Deut 22:8
drink the pure *b* of the grape .... Deut 32:14
make mine arrows drunk with *b* .... Deut 32:42
and that with the *b* of the slain .... Deut 32:42
will avenge the *b* of his servants .... Deut 32:43
his *b* shall be upon his head, and .... Josh 2:19
his *b* shall be on our head, if .... Josh 2:19
your refuge from the avenger of *b* .... Josh 20:3
the avenger of *b* pursue after him .... Josh 20:5
by the hand of the avenger of *b* .... Josh 20:9
their *b* be laid upon Abimelech .... Judg 9:24
people did eat them with the *b* 1Sa 14:32
LORD, in that they eat with the *b* 1Sa 14:33
the LORD in eating with the *b* 1Sa 14:34
with thou sin against innocent *b* 1Sa 19:5
thee from coming to shed *b* 1Sa 25:26
that thou hast shed *b* causeless 1Sa 25:31
me this day from coming to shed *b* 1Sa 25:33
let not my *b* fall to the earth 1Sa 26:20
unto him, Thy *b* be upon thy head 2Sa 1:16
From the *b* of the slain, from the 2Sa 1:22
for the *b* of Asahel his brother 2Sa 3:27
the *b* of Abner the son of Ner 2Sa 3:28
now require his *b* of your hand 2Sa 4:11
to *b* to destroy any more, lest 2Sa 4:11
all the *b* of the house of Saul 2Sa 16:8
Amasa wallowed in *b* in the midst 2Sa 20:12
is not this the *b* of the men that 2Sa 23:17
shed the *b* of war in peace, and 1Kin 2:5
put the *b* of war upon his girdle 1Kin 2:5
thou down to the grave with *b* 1Kin 2:9
mayest take away the innocent *b* 1Kin 2:31
return his *b* upon his own head 1Kin 2:32
Their *b* shall therefore return 1Kin 2:33
thy *b* shall be upon thine own 1Kin 2:37
till the *b* gushed out upon them 1Kin 18:28
b of Naboth shall dogs lick thy 1Kin 21:19
of Naboth shall dogs lick thy 1Kin 21:19
the turn out of the wound into 1Kin 22:35
and the dogs licked up his *b* 1Kin 22:38
on the other side as red as *b* 2Kin 3:22
And they said, This is *b* 2Kin 3:23
that I may avenge the *b* of my 2Kin 9:7
the *b* of all the servants of the 2Kin 9:7
seen yesterday the *b* of Naboth 2Kin 9:26
the *b* of his sons, saith the LORD 2Kin 9:26
some of her *b* was sprinkled on 2Kin 9:33
sprinkled the *b* of his peace 2Kin 16:13
all the *b* of the burnt offering 2Kin 16:15
all the *b* of the sacrifice 2Kin 16:15
shed innocent *b* very much 2Kin 21:16
for the innocent *b* that he shed 2Kin 24:4
filled Jerusalem with innocent *b* 2Kin 24:4
shall I drink the *b* of these men 1Chr 11:19
Thou hast shed *b* abundantly 1Chr 22:8
much *b* upon the earth in my sight 1Chr 22:8
been a man of war, and hast shed *b* ... 1Chr 28:3
their cities, between *b* and *b* 2Chr 19:10
the *b* of the sons of Jehoiada the 2Chr 24:25
and the priests received the *b* 2Chr 29:22
sprinkled the *b* upon the altar 2Chr 29:22
sprinkled the *b* upon the altar 2Chr 29:22
with their *b* upon the altar 2Chr 29:24
the priests sprinkled the *b* 2Chr 30:16
sprinkled the *b* from their hands 2Chr 35:11
O earth, cover not my *b* .... Job 16:18
Hay young ones also suck up *b* .... Job 39:30
When he maketh inquisition for *b* .... Ps 9:12
offerings of *b* will I not offer .... Ps 16:4
What profit is there in my *b* .... Ps 30:9
of bulls, or drink the *b* of goats .... Ps 50:13
his feet in the *b* of the wicked .... Ps 58:10
dipped in the *b* of thine enemies .... Ps 68:23
shall their *b* be in his sight .... Ps 72:14
And had turned their rivers into *b* .... Ps 78:44
Their *b* have they shed like water .... Ps 79:3
b of thy servants which is shed .... Ps 79:10
and condemn the innocent *b* .... Ps 94:21
He turned their waters into *b* .... Ps 105:29
And shed innocent *b* .... Ps 106:38
even the *b* of their sons and of .... Ps 106:38
and the land was polluted with *b* .... Ps 106:38
with us, let us lay wait for *b* .... Prov 1:11

to evil, and make haste to shed *b* .... Prov 1:16
And they lay wait for their own *b* .... Prov 1:18
and hands that shed innocent *b* .... Prov 6:17
wicked are to lie in wait for *b* .... Prov 12:6
man that doeth violence to the *b* .... Prov 28:17
of the nose bringeth forth *b* .... Prov 30:33
delight not in the *b* of bullocks .... Is 1:11
your hands are full of *b* .... Is 1:15
shall have purged the *b* of .... Is 4:4
noise, and garments rolled in *b* .... Is 9:5
of Dimon shall be full of *b* .... Is 15:9
earth also shall disclose her *b* .... Is 26:21
his ears from hearing of *b* .... Is 33:15
shall be melded with their *b* .... Is 34:3
of the LORD is filled with *b* .... Is 34:6
fatness, and with the *b* of lambs .... Is 34:6
their land shall be soaked with *b* .... Is 34:7
shall be drunken with their own *b* .... Is 49:26
For your hands are defiled with *b* .... Is 59:3
make haste to shed innocent *b* .... Is 59:7
their *b* shall be sprinkled upon .... Is 63:3
as if he offered swine's *b* .... Is 66:3
the *b* of the souls of the poor .... Jer 2:34
shed not innocent *b* in this place .... Jer 7:6
pour out their *b* by the force of .... Jer 18:21
place with the *b* of innocents .... Jer 19:4
shed innocent *b* in this place .... Jer 22:3
and for to shed innocent *b* .... Jer 22:17
bring innocent *b* upon yourselves .... Jer 26:15
and made drunk with their *b* .... Jer 46:10
keepeth back his sword from *b* .... Jer 48:10
my *b* upon the inhabitants of .... Jer 51:35
that have shed the *b* of the just .... Lam 4:13
have polluted themselves with *b* .... Lam 4:14
but his *b* will I require at thine .... Eze 3:18
but his *b* will I require at thine .... Eze 3:20
in shall pass through thee .... Eze 5:17
great, and the land is full of *b* .... Eze 9:9
and pour out my fury upon it in *b* .... Eze 14:19
saw thee polluted in thine own *b* .... Eze 16:6
unto thee when thou wast in thy *b* ..... Eze 16:6
unto thee when thou wast in thy *b* ..... Eze 16:6
washed away thy *b* from thee .... Eze 16:9
bare, and was polluted with thy *b* .... Eze 16:22
by the *b* of thy children, which .... Eze 16:36
wedlock and shed *b* are judged .... Eze 16:38
and I will give thee *b* in fury .... Eze 16:38
that is a robber, a shedder of *b* .... Eze 18:10
his *b* shall be upon him .... Eze 18:13
mother is like a vine in thy *b* .... Eze 19:10
thy *b* shall be in the midst of .... Eze 21:32
The city sheddeth *b* in the midst .... Eze 22:3
in thy *b* that thou hast shed .... Eze 22:4
in thee to their power to shed *b* .... Eze 22:6
men that carry tales to shed *b* .... Eze 22:9
have they taken gifts to shed *b* .... Eze 22:12
at thy *b* which hath been in the .... Eze 22:13
ravening the prey, to shed *b* .... Eze 22:27
b is in their hands, and with .... Eze 23:37
the manner of women that shed *b* ...... Eze 23:45
and *b* is in their hands .... Eze 23:45
For her is in the midst of her .... Eze 24:7
I have set her *b* upon the top of .... Eze 24:8
pestilence, and *b* into her street .... Eze 28:23
I will also water with thy *b* the .... Eze 32:6
his *b* shall be upon his own head .... Eze 33:4
his *b* shall be upon him .... Eze 33:5
but his *b* will I require at the .... Eze 33:6
but his *b* will I require at thine .... Eze 33:8
Ye eat with the *b*, and lift up .... Eze 33:25
eyes toward your idols, and shed *b* ..... Eze 33:25
hast shed the *b* of the children .... Eze 35:5
b, and *b* shall pursue thee .... Eze 35:6
b, even *b* shall pursue thee .... Eze 35:6
my fury upon them for the *b* that ...... Eze 36:18
him with pestilence and with *b* .... Eze 38:22
that ye may eat flesh, and drink *b* ...... Eze 39:17
drink the *b* of the princes of the .... Eze 39:18
drink *b* till ye be drunken, of my .... Eze 39:19
thereon, and to sprinkle *b* thereon ..... Eze 43:18
thou shalt take of the *b* thereof .... Eze 43:20
offer my bread, the fat and the *b* .... Eze 44:7
to offer unto me the fat and the *b* ..... Eze 44:15
take of the *b* of the sin offering .... Eze 45:19
I will avenge the *b* of Jezreel .... Hos 1:4
break out, and *b* toucheth *b* .... Hos 4:2
iniquity, and is polluted with *b* .... Hos 6:8
shall he leave his *b* upon him .... Hos 12:14
in the heavens and in the earth, *b* ...... Joel 2:30
into darkness, and the moon into *b* ..... Joel 2:31
shed innocent *b* in their land .... Joel 3:19
their *b* that I have not cleansed .... Joel 3:21
and lay not upon us innocent *b* .... Jonah 1:14
They build up Zion with *b* .... Mic 3:10
they all lie in wait for *b* .... Mic 7:2
because of men's *b*, and for the .... Hab 2:8
him that buildeth a town with *b* .... Hab 2:12
them afraid, because of men's *b* .... Hab 2:17
their *b* shall be poured out as .... Zeph 1:17
take away his *b* out of his mouth .... Zec 9:7
by the *b* of thy covenant I have .... Zec 9:11
with an issue of *b* twelve years .... Mt 9:20
b hath not revealed it unto thee .... Mt 16:17
them in the *b* of the prophets .... Mt 23:30
righteous *b* shed upon the earth .... Mt 23:35
of righteous Abel unto the *b* .... Mt 23:35
For this is my *b* of the new .... Mt 26:28
I have betrayed the innocent *b* .... Mt 27:4
saith, It is the price of *b* .... Mt 27:6
field was called, The field of *b* .... Mt 27:8

of the b of this just person........ Mt 27:24
His b be on us, and on our........ Mt 27:25
had an issue of b twelve years........ Mk 5:25
fountain of her b was dried up........ Mk 5:29
This is my b of the new testament........ Mk 14:24
having an issue of b twelve years........ Lk 8:43
her issue of b stanched........ Lk 8:44
That the b of all the prophets........ Lk 11:50
From the b of Abel unto the b........ Lk 11:51
whose b Pilate had mingled with........ Lk 13:1
cup is the new testament in my b........ Lk 22:20
of b falling down to the ground........ Lk 22:44
Which were born, not of b........ Jn 1:13
of the Son of man, and drink his b........ Jn 6:53
eateth my flesh, and drinketh my b........ Jn 6:54
indeed, and my b is drink indeed........ Jn 6:55
eateth my flesh, and drinketh my b........ Jn 6:56
and forthwith came there out his........ Jn 19:34
that is to say, The field of b........ Acts 1:19
b, and fire, and vapour of smoke........ Acts 2:19
into darkness, and the moon into b........ Acts 2:20
to bring this man's b upon us........ Acts 5:28
from things strangled, and from b........ Acts 15:20
meats offered to idols, and from b........ Acts 15:29
hath made of one b all nations of........ Acts 17:26
b be upon your own heads........ Acts 18:6
I am pure from the b of all men........ Acts 20:26
he hath purchased with his own b........ Acts 20:28
offered to idols, and from b........ Acts 21:25
when the b of thy martyr Stephen........ Acts 22:20
Their feet are swift to shed b........ Rom 3:15
through faith in his b, to........ Rom 3:25
being now justified by his b........ Rom 5:9
the communion of the b of Christ........ 1Cor 10:16
cup is the new testament in my b........ 1Cor 11:25
of the body and b of the Lord........ 1Cor 11:27
b cannot inherit the kingdom of........ 1Cor 15:50
I conferred not with flesh and b........ Gal 1:16
we have redemption through his b........ Eph 1:7
are made nigh by the b of Christ........ Eph 2:13
we wrestle not against flesh and b........ Eph 6:12
we have redemption through his b........ Col 1:14
peace through the b of his cross........ Col 1:20
are partakers of flesh and b........ Heb 2:14
once every year, not without b........ Heb 9:7
Neither by the b of goats........ Heb 9:12
but by his own b he entered in........ Heb 9:12
For if the b of bulls and of goats........ Heb 9:13
much more shall the b of Christ........ Heb 9:14
testament was dedicated without b........ Heb 9:18
the law, he took the b of calves........ Heb 9:19
This is the b of the testament........ Heb 9:20
with b both the tabernacle........ Heb 9:21
are by the law purged with b........ Heb 9:22
shedding of b is no remission........ Heb 9:22
place every year with b of others........ Heb 9:25
not possible that the b of bulls........ Heb 10:4
the holiest by the b of Jesus........ Heb 10:19
counted the b of the covenant........ Heb 10:29
passover, and the sprinkling of b........ Heb 11:28
Ye have not yet resisted unto b........ Heb 12:4
to the b of sprinkling, that........ Heb 12:24
whose b is brought into the........ Heb 13:11
the people with his own b........ Heb 13:12
through the b of the everlasting........ Heb 13:20
of the b of Jesus Christ........ 1Pet 1:2
But with the precious b of Christ........ 1Pet 1:19
the b of Jesus Christ his Son........ 1Jn 1:7
is he that came by water and b........ 1Jn 5:6
by water only, but by water and b........ 1Jn 5:6
spirit, and the water, and the b........ 1Jn 5:8
us from our sins in his own b........ Rev 1:5
God by thy b out of every kindred........ Rev 5:9
avenge our b on them that dwell........ Rev 6:10
of hair, and the moon became as b........ Rev 6:12
them white in the b of the Lamb........ Rev 7:14
hail and fire mingled with b........ Rev 8:7
third part of the sea became b........ Rev 8:8
over waters to turn them to b........ Rev 11:6
overcame him by the b of the Lamb........ Rev 12:11
b came out of the winepress, even........ Rev 14:20
it became as the b of a dead man........ Rev 16:3
and they became b........ Rev 16:4
they have shed the b of saints........ Rev 16:6
thou hast given them b to drink........ Rev 16:6
drunken with the b of the saints........ Rev 17:6
with the b of the martyrs of........ Rev 17:6
her was found the b of prophets........ Rev 18:24
hath avenged the b of his........ Rev 19:2
with a vesture dipped in b........ Rev 19:13

BLOODGUILTINESS
Deliver me from b, O God, thou........ Ps 51:14

BLOODTHIRSTY
The b hate the upright........ Prov 29:10

BLOODY
Surely a b husband art thou to me........ Ex 4:25
A b husband thou art, because of........ Ex 4:26
Come out, come out, thou b........ 2Sa 16:7
because thou art a b man........ 2Sa 16:8
is for Saul, and for his b house........ 2Sa 21:1
the LORD will abhor the b........ Ps 5:6
sinners, nor my life with b men........ Ps 26:9
b and deceitful men shall not live........ Ps 55:23
iniquity, and save me from b men........ Ps 59:2
from me therefore, ye b men........ Ps 139:19
for the land is full of b crimes........ Eze 7:23
judge, wilt thou judge the b city........ Eze 22:2
Woe to the b city, to the pot........ Eze 24:6
Woe to the b city........ Eze 24:9

Woe to the b city........ Nah 3:1
sick of a fever and of a b flux........ Acts 28:8

BLOOMED
b blossoms, and yielded almonds........ Num 17:8

BLOSSOM
rod, whom I shall choose, shall b........ Num 17:5
their b shall go up as dust........ Is 5:24
Israel shall b and bud, and fill........ Is 27:6
shall rejoice, and b as the rose........ Is 35:1
It shall b abundantly, and rejoice........ Is 35:2
Although the fig tree shall not b........ Hab 3:17

BLOSSOMED
the rod hath b, pride hath budded........ Eze 7:10

BLOSSOMS
it budded, and her b shot forth........ Gen 40:10
brought forth buds, and bloomed b........ Num 17:8

BLOT
b me, I pray thee, out of thy........ Ex 32:32
him will I b out of my book........ Ex 32:33
he shall b them out with the........ Num 5:23
b out their name from under........ Deut 9:14
that thou shalt b out the........ Deut 25:19
the LORD shall b out his name........ Deut 29:20
b out the name of Israel from........ 2Kin 14:27
if any b hath cleaved to mine........ Job 31:7
mercies b out my transgressions........ Ps 51:1
b out all mine iniquities........ Ps 51:9
a wicked man getteth himself a b........ Prov 9:7
neither b out their sin from thy........ Jer 18:23
I will not b out his name out of........ Rev 3:5

BLOTTED
sin be b out from before thee........ Neh 4:5
Let them be b out of the book of........ Ps 69:28
following let their name be b out........ Ps 109:13
the sin of his mother be b out........ Ps 109:14
I have b out, as a thick cloud,........ Is 44:22
that your sins may be b out........ Acts 3:19

BLOTTETH
I, even I, am he that b out thy........ Is 43:25

BLOTTING
B out the handwriting of........ Col 2:14

BLOW
Thou didst b with thy wind, the........ Ex 15:10
And when they shall b with them........ Num 10:3
if they b but with one trumpet,........ Num 10:4
When ye b an alarm, then the........ Num 10:5
When ye b an alarm the second........ Num 10:6
they shall b an alarm for their........ Num 10:6
be gathered together, ye shall b........ Num 10:7
shall b with the trumpets........ Num 10:8
then ye shall b an alarm with the........ Num 10:9
ye shall b with the trumpets over........ Num 10:10
and the trumpets to b in his hand........ Num 31:6
priests shall b with the trumpets........ Josh 6:4
When I b with a trumpet, I and all........ Judg 7:18
then b ye the trumpets also on........ Judg 7:18
in their right hands to b withal........ Judg 7:20
b ye with the trumpet, and say,........ 1Kin 1:34
did b with the trumpets before........ 1Chr 15:24
consumed by the b of thine hand........ Ps 39:10
an east wind to b in the heaven........ Ps 78:26
B up the trumpet in the new moon,........ Ps 81:3
he causeth his wind to b, and the........ Ps 147:18
b upon my garden, that the spices........ Song 4:16
and he shall also b upon them........ Is 40:24
B ye the trumpet in the land........ Jer 4:5
b the trumpet in Tekoa, and set up........ Jer 6:1
breach, with a very grievous b........ Jer 14:17
b the trumpet among the nations,........ Jer 51:27
I will b against them in the fire........ Eze 21:31
to b the fire upon it, to melt it........ Eze 22:20
b upon you in the fire of my........ Eze 22:21
he b the trumpet, and warn the........ Eze 33:3
b not the trumpet, and the people........ Eze 33:6
B ye the cornet in Gibeah, and the........ Hos 5:8
b ye the trumpet in Zion, and........ Joel 2:1
B the trumpet in Zion, sanctify a........ Joel 2:15
brought it home, I did b upon it........ Hag 1:9
the Lord GOD shall b the trumpet........ Zec 9:14
And when ye see the south wind b........ Lk 12:55
wind should not b on the earth........ Rev 7:1

BLOWETH
when he b a trumpet, hear ye........ Is 18:3
the spirit of the LORD b upon it........ Is 40:7
that b the coals in the fire........ Is 54:16
The wind b where it listeth, and........ Jn 3:8

BLOWING
a memorial of b of trumpets........ Lev 23:24
it is a day of b the trumpets........ Num 29:1
going on, and b with the trumpets........ Josh 6:9
going on, and b with the trumpets........ Josh 6:13

BLOWN
a fire not b shall consume him........ Job 20:26
that the great trumpet shall be b........ Is 27:13
They have b the trumpet, even to........ Eze 7:14
Shall a trumpet be b in the city........ Amos 3:6

BLUE
And b, and purple, and scarlet, and........ Ex 25:4
of fine twined linen, and b........ Ex 26:1
of b upon the edge of the one........ Ex 26:4
And thou shalt make a vail of b........ Ex 26:31
for the door of the tent, of b........ Ex 26:36
an hanging of twenty cubits, of b........ Ex 27:16

And they shall take gold, and b........ Ex 28:5
make the ephod of gold, of b........ Ex 28:6
even of gold, of b, and purple, and........ Ex 28:8
of gold, of b, and of purple, and........ Ex 28:15
of the ephod with a lace of b........ Ex 28:28
the robe of the ephod all of b........ Ex 28:31
thou shalt make pomegranates of b........ Ex 28:33
And thou shalt put it on a lace........ Ex 28:37
And b, and purple, and scarlet, and........ Ex 35:6
every man, with whom was found b........ Ex 35:23
which they had spun, both of b........ Ex 35:25
and of the embroiderer, in b........ Ex 35:35
of fine twined linen, and b........ Ex 36:8
he made loops of b on the edge of........ Ex 36:11
And he made a vail of b, and purple........ Ex 36:35
for the tabernacle door of b........ Ex 36:37
of the court was needlework, of b........ Ex 38:18
workman, and an embroiderer in b........ Ex 38:23
And of the b, and purple, and........ Ex 39:1
And he made the ephod of gold, b........ Ex 39:2
into wires, to work it in the b........ Ex 39:3
of gold, b, and purple, and scarlet........ Ex 39:5
of gold, b, and purple, and scarlet........ Ex 39:8
of the ephod with a lace of b........ Ex 39:21
the ephod of woven work, all of b........ Ex 39:22
of the robe pomegranates of b........ Ex 39:24
girdle of fine twined linen, and b........ Ex 39:29
And they tied unto it a lace of b........ Ex 39:31
over it a cloth wholly of b........ Num 4:6
they shall spread a cloth of b........ Num 4:7
And they shall take a cloth of b........ Num 4:9
they shall spread a cloth of b........ Num 4:11
and put them in a cloth of b........ Num 4:12
of the borders a ribband of b........ Num 15:38
and in purple, and crimson, and b........ 2Chr 2:7
and in timber, in purple, in b........ 2Chr 2:14
And he made the vail of b, and........ 2Chr 3:14
Where were white, green, and b........ Est 1:6
upon a pavement of red, and b........ Est 1:6
of the king in royal apparel of b........ Est 8:15
and purple is their clothing........ Jer 10:9
Which were clothed in b........ Eze 23:6
b and purple from the isles of........ Eze 27:7
in b clothes, and broidered work,........ Eze 27:24

BLUENESS
The b of a wound cleanseth away........ Prov 20:30

BLUNT
If the iron be b, and he do not........ Eccl 10:10

BLUSH
to lift up my face to thee, my........ Ezr 9:6
all ashamed, neither could they b........ Jer 6:15
all ashamed, neither could they b........ Jer 8:12

BOANERGES (bo-an-er'-jees) Surname of
James and John, the sons of Zebedee.
and he surnamed them B, which is,........ Mk 3:17

BOAR
The b out of the wood doth waste........ Ps 80:13

BOARD
cubits shall be the length of a b........ Ex 26:16
shall be the breadth of one b........ Ex 26:16
tenons shall there be in one b........ Ex 26:17
under one b for his two tenons........ Ex 26:19
another b for his two tenons........ Ex 26:19
two sockets under one b........ Ex 26:21
and two sockets under another b........ Ex 26:21
two sockets under one b........ Ex 26:25
and two sockets under another b........ Ex 26:25
The length of a b was ten cubits........ Ex 36:21
and the breadth of a bore cubit........ Ex 36:21
One b had two tenons, equally........ Ex 36:22
under one b for his two tenons........ Ex 36:24
another b for his two tenons........ Ex 36:24
two sockets under one b........ Ex 36:26
and two sockets under another b........ Ex 36:26
silver, under every b two sockets........ Ex 36:30

BOARDS
thou shalt make b for the........ Ex 26:15
for all the b of the tabernacle........ Ex 26:17
make the b for the tabernacle........ Ex 26:18
twenty b on the south side........ Ex 26:18
of silver under the twenty b........ Ex 26:19
side there shall be twenty b........ Ex 26:20
westward thou shalt make six b........ Ex 26:22
two b shalt thou make for the........ Ex 26:23
And they shall be eight b, and........ Ex 26:25
five for the b of the one side of........ Ex 26:26
five bars for the b of the other........ Ex 26:27
five bars for the b of the........ Ex 26:27
the b shall reach from end to end........ Ex 26:28
shalt overlay the b with gold........ Ex 26:29
Hollow with b shalt thou make it........ Ex 27:8
covering, his taches, and his b........ Ex 35:11
he made b for the tabernacle........ Ex 36:20
for all the b of the tabernacle........ Ex 36:22
he made b for the tabernacle........ Ex 36:23
twenty b for the south side........ Ex 36:23
silver he made under the twenty b........ Ex 36:24
north corner, he made twenty b........ Ex 36:25
tabernacle westward he made six b........ Ex 36:27
two b made he for the corners of........ Ex 36:28
And there were eight b,........ Ex 36:30
five for the b of the one side of........ Ex 36:31
five bars for the b of the other........ Ex 36:32
five bars for the b of the........ Ex 36:32
b from the one end to the other........ Ex 36:33
And he overlaid the b with gold........ Ex 36:34

B

BOAST

he made the altar hollow with *b*	Ex 38:7
his furniture, his taches, his *b*	Ex 39:33
sockets, and set up the *b* thereof	Ex 40:18
shall be the *b* of the tabernacle	Num 3:36
the *b* of the tabernacle, and the	Num 4:31
house with beams and *b* of cedar	1Kin 6:9
the house within with *b* of cedar	1Kin 6:15
and the walls with *b* of cedar	1Kin 6:16
will inclose her with *b* of cedar	Song 8:9
thy ship *b* of fir trees of Senir	Eze 27:5
And the rest, some on *b*, and some	Acts 27:44

BOAST

b himself as he that putteth it	1Kin 20:11
thine heart lifteth thee up to *b*	2Chr 25:19
soul shall make her *b* in the LORD	Ps 34:2
In God we *b* all the day long, and	Ps 44:8
b themselves in the multitude of	Ps 49:6
workers of iniquity *b* themselves	Ps 94:4
that is themselves of idols	Ps 97:7
b not thyself of to morrow	Prov 27:1
Shall the ax *b* itself against him	Is 10:15
their glory shall ye *b* yourselves	Is 61:6
the law, and makest thy *b* of God	Rom 2:17
Thou that makest thy *b* of the law	Rom 2:23
b not against the branches	Rom 11:18
But if thou *b*, thou bearest not	Rom 11:18
for which I *b* of you to them of	2Cor 9:2
Though I should *b* somewhat	2Cor 10:8
But we will not *b* of things	2Cor 10:13
not to *b* in another man's line of	2Cor 10:16
that I may *b* myself a little	2Cor 11:16
of works, lest any man should *b*	Eph 2:9

BOASTED

your mouth ye have *b* against me	Eze 35:13
For if I have *b* any thing to him	2Cor 7:14

BOASTERS

of God, despiteful, proud, *b*	Rom 1:30
of their own selves, covetous, *b*	2Ti 3:2

BOASTEST

Why *b* thou thyself in mischief, O	Ps 52:1

BOASTETH

For the wicked *b* of his heart's	Ps 10:3
he is gone his way, then he *b*	Prov 20:14
Whoso *b* himself of a false gift	Prov 25:14
little member, and *b* great things	Jas 3:5

BOASTING

Theudas, *b* himself to be somebody	Acts 5:36
Where is *b* then	Rom 3:27
to you in truth, even so our *b*	2Cor 7:14
love, and of our *b* on your behalf	2Cor 8:24
lest our *b* of you should be in	2Cor 9:3
ashamed in this same confident *b*	2Cor 9:4
Not *b* of things without our	2Cor 10:15
this *b* in the regions of Achaia	2Cor 11:10
in this confidence of *b*	2Cor 11:17

BOASTINGS

But now ye rejoice in your *b*	Jas 4:16

BOAT

there went over a ferry *b* to	2Sa 19:18
that there was none other *b* there	Jn 6:22
not with his disciples into the *b*	Jn 6:22
we had much work to come by the *b*	Acts 27:16
had let down the *b* into the sea	Acts 27:30
cut off the ropes of the *b*	Acts 27:32

BOATS

(Howbeit there came other *b* from	Jn 6:23

BOAZ (bo´-az) See Booz.

I. Husband of Ruth.

and his name was *B*	Ruth 2:1
of the field belonging unto *B*	Ruth 2:3
B came from Beth-lehem, and said	Ruth 2:4
Then said *B* unto his servant that	Ruth 2:5
Then said *B* unto Ruth, Hearest	Ruth 2:8
B answered and said unto her, It	Ruth 2:11
B said unto her, At mealtime come	Ruth 2:14
B commanded his young men, saying	Ruth 2:15
with whom I wrought to day is *B*	Ruth 2:19
To glean unto the end of barley	Ruth 2:23
now is not *B* of our kindred, with	Ruth 3:2
when *B* had eaten and drunk, and his	Ruth 3:7
Then went *B* up to the gate, and	Ruth 4:1
kinsman of whom *B* spake came by	Ruth 4:1
Therefore the kinsman said unto *B*	Ruth 4:6
The said *B*, What day thou buyest	Ruth 4:5
Therefore the kinsman said unto *B*	Ruth 4:8
B said unto the elders, and unto	Ruth 4:9
So *B* took Ruth, and she was his	Ruth 4:13
And Salmon begat *B*	Ruth 4:21
And *B* begat Obed	Ruth 4:21
begat Salma, and Salma begat *B*	1Chr 2:11
B begat Obed, and Obed begat Jesse	1Chr 2:12

2. A pillar in Solomon's Temple.

and called the name thereof *B*	1Kin 7:21
and the name of that on the left *B*	2Chr 3:17

BOCHERU (bok´-er-u) A relative of Saul.

whose names are these, Azrikam, *B*	1Chr 8:38
whose names are these, Azrikam, *B*	1Chr 9:44

BOCHIM (bo´-kim) A place near Gilgal.

the LORD came up from Gilgal to *B*	Judg 2:1
called the name of that place *B*	Judg 2:5

BODIES

the sight of my lord, but our *b*	Gen 47:18
the *b* of his sons from the wall	1Sa 31:12
the *b* of his sons, and brought	1Chr 10:12

they were dead *b* fallen to the	2Chr 20:24
both riches with the dead *b*	2Chr 20:25
they have dominion over our *b*	Neh 9:37
ashes, your *b* to *b* of clay	Job 13:12
ashes, your *b* to *b* of clay	Job 13:12
The dead *b* of thy servants have	Ps 79:2
fill the places with the dead *b*	Ps 110:6
And the whole valley of the dead *b*	Jer 31:40
fill them with the dead *b* of men	Jer 33:5
their dead *b* shall be for meat	Jer 34:20
cast all the dead *b* of the men	Jer 41:9
another, and two covered their *b*	Eze 1:11
covered on that side, their *b*	Eze 1:23
upon whose *b* the fire had no	Dan 3:27
king's word, and yielded their *b*	Dan 3:28
be many dead *b* in every place	Amos 8:3
many *b* of the saints which slept	Mt 27:52
that the *b* should not remain upon	Jn 19:31
their own *b* between themselves	Rom 1:24
b by his Spirit that dwelleth in	Rom 8:11
present your *b* a living sacrifice	Rom 12:1
Know ye not that your *b* are the	1Cor 6:15
There are also celestial *b*	1Cor 15:40
and *b* terrestrial	1Cor 15:40
love their wives as their own *b*	Eph 5:28
our *b* washed with pure water	Heb 10:22
For the *b* of those beasts, whose	Heb 13:11
their dead *b* shall lie in the	Rev 11:8
shall see their dead *b* three days	Rev 11:9
their dead *b* to be put in graves	Rev 11:9

BODILY

in a shape like a dove upon him	Lk 3:22
but his *b* presence is weak, and	2Cor 10:10
all the fulness of the Godhead *b*	Col 2:9
For *b* exercise profiteth little	1Ti 4:8

BODY

as it were the *b* of heaven in his	Ex 24:10
shall he go in to uncover her *b*	Lev 21:11
LORD he shall come at no dead *b*	Num 6:6
defiled by the dead *b* of a man	Num 9:6
defiled by the dead *b* of a man	Num 9:7
be unclean by reason of a dead *b*	Num 9:10
He that toucheth the dead *b* of	Num 19:11
dead *b* of any man that is dead	Num 19:13
in the open fields, or a dead *b*	Num 19:16
His *b* shall not remain all night	Deut 21:23
shall be the fruit of thy *b*	Deut 28:4
in goods, in the fruit of thy *b*	Deut 28:11
shall be the fruit of thy *b*	Deut 28:18
eat the fruit of thine own *b*	Deut 28:53
thine hand, in the fruit of thy *b*	Deut 30:9
and ten sons of his *b* begotten	Judg 8:30
they fastened his *b* to the wall	1Sa 31:10
all night, and took the *b* of Saul	1Sa 31:12
he had restored a dead *b* to life	2Kin 8:5
men, and took away the *b* of Saul	1Chr 10:12
the children's sake of mine own *b*	Job 19:17
my skin worms destroy this *b*	Job 19:26
is drawn, and cometh out of the *b*	Job 20:25
Of the fruit of thy *b* will I set	Ps 132:11
thy flesh and thy *b* are consumed	Prov 5:11
fruitful field, both soul and *b*	Is 10:18
with my dead *b* shall they arise	Is 26:19
hast laid thy *b* as the ground	Is 51:23
cast his dead *b* into the graves	Jer 26:23
his dead *b* shall be cast out in	Jer 36:30
were more ruddy in *b* than rubies	Lam 4:7
And their whole *b*, and their backs	Eze 10:12
his *b* was wet with the dew of	Dan 4:33
his *b* was wet with the dew of	Dan 5:21
his *b* destroyed, and given to the	Dan 7:11
in my spirit in the midst of my *b*	Dan 7:15
His *b* also was like the beryl, and	Dan 10:6
the fruit of my *b* for the sin of	Mic 6:7
by a dead *b* touch any of these	Hag 2:13
not that thy whole *b* should be	Mt 5:29
not that thy whole *b* should be	Mt 5:30
The light of the *b* is the eye	Mt 6:22
thy whole *b* shall be full of	Mt 6:22
thy whole *b* shall be full of	Mt 6:23
not yet for your *b*, what ye shall	Mt 6:25
than meat, and the *b* than raiment	Mt 6:25
And fear not them which kill the *b*	Mt 10:28
to destroy both soul and *b* in hell	Mt 10:28
disciples came, and took up the *b*	Mt 14:12
hath poured this ointment on my *b*	Mt 26:12
this is my *b*	Mt 26:26
Pilate, and begged the *b* of Jesus	Mt 27:58
commanded the *b* to be delivered	Mt 27:58
And when Joseph had taken the *b*	Mt 27:59
she felt in her *b* that she was	Mk 5:29
to anoint my *b* to the burying	Mk 14:8
this is my *b*	Mk 14:22
cloth cast about his naked *b*	Mk 14:51
Pilate, and craved the *b* of Jesus	Mk 15:43
he gave the *b* to Joseph	Mk 15:45
The light of the *b* is the eye	Lk 11:34
thy whole *b* also is full of light	Lk 11:34
thy *b* also is full of darkness	Lk 11:34
If thy whole *b* therefore be full	Lk 11:36
afraid of them that kill the *b*	Lk 12:4
neither for the *b*, what ye shall	Lk 12:22
the *b* is more than raiment	Lk 12:23
unto them, Wheresoever the *b* is	Lk 17:37
This is my *b* which is given for	Lk 22:19
Pilate, and begged the *b* of Jesus	Lk 23:52
sepulchre, and how his *b* was laid	Lk 23:55
found not the *b* of the Lord Jesus	Lk 24:3
And when they found not his *b*	Lk 24:23

he spake of the temple of his *b*	Jn 2:21
He might take away the *b* of Jesus	Jn 19:38
therefore, and took the *b* of Jesus	Jn 19:38
Then took they the *b* of Jesus	Jn 19:40
where the *b* of Jesus had lain	Jn 20:12
and turning him to the *b* said	Acts 9:40
So that from his *b* were brought	Acts 19:12
considered not his own *b* now dead	Rom 4:19
that the *b* of sin might be	Rom 6:6
therefore reign in your mortal *b*	Rom 6:12
to the law by the *b* of Christ	Rom 7:4
me from the *b* of this death	Rom 7:24
the *b* is dead because of sin	Rom 8:10
do mortify the deeds of the *b*	Rom 8:13
to wit, the redemption of our *b*	Rom 8:23
as we have many members in one *b*	Rom 12:4
are one *b* in Christ, and every one	Rom 12:5
For I verily, as absent in *b*	1Cor 5:3
Now the *b* is not for fornication	1Cor 6:13
and the Lord for the *b*	1Cor 6:13
is joined to an harlot is one *b*	1Cor 6:16
that a man doeth is without the *b*	1Cor 6:18
sinneth against his own *b*	1Cor 6:18
know ye not that your *b* is the	1Cor 6:19
therefore glorify God in your *b*	1Cor 6:20
wife hath not power of her own *b*	1Cor 7:4
hath not power of his own *b*	1Cor 7:4
that she may be holy both in *b*	1Cor 7:34
But I keep under my *b*, and bring	1Cor 9:27
the communion of the *b* of Christ	1Cor 10:16
many are one bread, and one *b*	1Cor 10:17
this is my *b*, which is broken for	1Cor 11:24
shall be guilty of the *b*	1Cor 11:27
not discerning the Lord's *b*	1Cor 11:29
For as the *b* is one, and hath many	1Cor 12:12
one *b*, being many, are one *b*	1Cor 12:12
are we all baptized into one *b*	1Cor 12:13
For the *b* is not one member, but	1Cor 12:14
not the hand, I am not of the *b*	1Cor 12:15
is it therefore not of the *b*	1Cor 12:15
am not the eye, I am not of the *b*	1Cor 12:16
is it therefore not of the *b*	1Cor 12:16
If the whole *b* were an eye	1Cor 12:17
every one of them in the *b*	1Cor 12:18
all one member, where were the *b*	1Cor 12:19
they many members, yet but one *b*	1Cor 12:20
much more those members of the *b*	1Cor 12:22
And those members of the *b*	1Cor 12:23
God hath tempered the *b* together	1Cor 12:24
should be no schism in the *b*	1Cor 12:25
Now ye are the *b* of Christ	1Cor 12:27
though I give my *b* to be burned	1Cor 13:3
and with what *b* do they come	1Cor 15:35
sowest not that *b* that shall be	1Cor 15:37
But God giveth it a *b* as it hath	1Cor 15:38
him, and to every seed his own *b*	1Cor 15:38
It is sown a natural *b*	1Cor 15:44
is it raised a spiritual *b*	1Cor 15:44
There is a natural *b*	1Cor 15:44
and there is a spiritual *b*	1Cor 15:44
the *b* the dying of the Lord Jesus	2Cor 4:10
might be made manifest in our *b*	2Cor 4:10
whilst we are at home in the *b*	2Cor 5:6
rather to be absent from the *b*	2Cor 5:8
receive the things done in his *b*	2Cor 5:10
years ago, (whether in the *b*	2Cor 12:2
or whether out of the *b*, I cannot	2Cor 12:2
in the *b*, or out of the *b*	2Cor 12:3
for I bear in my *b* the marks of	Gal 6:17
Which is his *b*, the fulness of	Eph 1:23
unto God in one *b* by the cross	Eph 2:16
be fellowheirs, and of the same *b*	Eph 3:6
There is one *b*, and one Spirit	Eph 4:4
the edifying of the *b* of Christ	Eph 4:12
From whom the whole *b* fitly	Eph 4:16
maketh increase of the *b* unto the	Eph 4:16
and he is the saviour of the *b*	Eph 5:23
For we are members of his *b*	Eph 5:30
Christ shall be magnified in my *b*	Phil 1:20
Who shall change our vile *b*	Phil 3:21
like unto his glorious *b*	Phil 3:21
And he is the head of the *b*	Col 1:18
In the *b* of his flesh through	Col 1:22
in putting off the *b* of the sins	Col 2:11
but the *b* is of Christ	Col 2:17
from which all the *b* by joints	Col 2:19
humility, and neglecting of the *b*	Col 2:23
which also ye are called in one *b*	Col 3:15
b be preserved blameless unto the	1Th 5:23
but a *b* hast thou prepared me	Heb 10:5
through the offering of the *b* of	Heb 10:10
as being yourselves also in the *b*	Heb 13:3
things which are needful to the *b*	Jas 2:16
For as the *b* without the spirit	Jas 2:26
able also to bridle the whole *b*	Jas 3:2
and we turn about their whole *b*	Jas 3:3
that it defileth the whole *b*	Jas 3:6
our sins in his own *b* on the tree	1Pet 2:24
he disputed about the *b* of Moses	Jude 9

BODY'S

Christ in my flesh for his *b* sake	Col 1:24

BOHAN (bo´-han) A namesake of a border stone.

the stone of *B* the son of Reuben	Josh 15:6
the stone of *B* the son of Reuben	Josh 18:17

BOIL

shall be a *b* breaking forth with	Ex 9:9
it became a *b* breaking forth with	Ex 9:10
for the *b* was upon the magicians	Ex 9:11

B the flesh at the door of the............... Lev 8:31
even in the skin thereof, was a *b*............ Lev 13:18
in the place of the *b* there be a............... Lev 13:19
of leprosy broken out of the *b*............... Lev 13:20
and spread not, it is a burning *b*........... Lev 13:23
And they took and laid it on the *b*........ 2Kin 20:7
maketh the deep to *b* like a pot............ Job 41:31
lay it for a plaister upon the *b*.............. Is 38:21
the fire causeth the waters to *b*............ Is 64:2
bones under it, and make it *b* well........ Eze 24:5
are the places of them that *b*............... Eze 46:20
are the places of them that *b*............... Eze 46:24
b the sacrifice of the people................. Eze 46:24

BOILED
them, and *b* their flesh with the........... 1Kin 19:21
So we *b* my son, and did eat him........... 2Kin 6:29
My bowels *b*, and rested not................ Job 30:27

BOILING
it was made in *b* places under............... Eze 46:23

BOILS
before Moses because of the *b*............. Ex 9:11
smote Job with sore *b* from the........... Job 2:7

BOISTEROUS
But when he saw the wind *b*................. Mt 14:30

BOKERU See BOCHERU.

BOKIM See BOCHIM.

BOLD
but the righteous are *b* as a lion........... Prov 28:1
Then Paul and Barnabas waxed *b*......... Acts 13:46
But Esaias is very *b*, and saith, I.......... Rom 10:20
but being absent am *b* toward you........ 2Cor 10:1
that I may not be *b* when I am.............. 2Cor 10:2
I think to be *b* against some............... 2Cor 10:2
Howbeit wheresoever any is *b*............. 2Cor 11:21
(I speak foolishly,) I am *b* also............. 2Cor 11:21
are much more *b* to speak the word..... Phil 1:14
we were *b* in our God to speak............. 1Th 2:2
though I might be much *b* in.............. Philem 8

BOLDLY
sword, and came upon the city *b*......... Gen 34:25
went in *b* unto Pilate, and craved......... Mk 15:43
But, lo, he speaketh *b*, and they........... Jn 7:26
how he had preached *b* at Damascus.... Acts 9:27
he spake *b* in the name of the............. Acts 9:29
abode they speaking *b* in the Lord....... Acts 14:3
began to speak *b* in the synagogue...... Acts 18:26
spake *b* for the space of three............. Acts 19:8
the more *b* unto you in some sort........ Rom 15:15
me, that I may open my mouth *b*......... Eph 6:19
that therein I may speak *b*................... Eph 6:20
Let us therefore come *b* unto the......... Heb 4:16
So that we may *b* say, The Lord is........ Heb 13:6

BOLDNESS
the *b* of his face shall be...................... Eccl 8:1
Now when they saw the *b* of Peter....... Acts 4:13
that with all *b* they may speak............ Acts 4:29
they spake the word of God with *b*...... Acts 4:31
Great is my *b* of speech toward............ 2Cor 7:4
In whom we have *b* and access with.... Eph 3:12
be ashamed, but that with all *b*........... Phil 1:20
great *b* in the faith which is in............ 1Ti 3:13
b to enter into the holiest by............... Heb 10:19
that we may have *b* in the day of......... Jn 4:17

BOLLED
was in the ear, and the flax was *b*........ Ex 9:31

BOLSTER
a pillow of goats' hair for his *b*............ 1Sa 19:13
a pillow of goats' hair for his *b*............ 1Sa 19:16
stuck in the ground at his *b*................ 1Sa 26:7
now the spear that is at his *b*.............. 1Sa 26:11
the cruse of water from Saul's *b*.......... 1Sa 26:12
cruse of water that was at his *b*........... 1Sa 26:16

BOLT
from me, and *b* the door after him....... 2Sa 13:17

BOLTED
her out, and *b* the door after her.......... 2Sa 13:18

BOND
an oath to bind his soul with a *b*......... Num 30:3
the LORD, and bind herself by a *b*....... Num 30:3
her *b* wherewith she hath bound......... Num 30:4
every *b* wherewith she hath bound....... Num 30:4
her soul by a *b* with an oath............... Num 30:10
every *b* wherewith she bound her........ Num 30:11
or concerning the *b* of her soul........... Num 30:12
He looseth the *b* of kings................... Job 12:18
you into the *b* of the covenant............ Eze 20:37
from this *b* on the sabbath day........... Lk 13:16
and in the *b* of iniquity..................... Acts 8:23
Gentiles, whether we be *b* or free........ 1Cor 12:13
there is neither *b* nor free................... Gal 3:28
of the Spirit in the *b* of peace............. Eph 4:3
the LORD, whether he be *b* or free....... Eph 6:8
Barbarian, Scythian, *b* nor free........... Col 3:11
which is the *b* of perfectness.............. Col 3:14
and great, rich and poor, free and *b*..... Rev 13:16
flesh of all men, both free and *b*.......... Rev 19:18

BONDAGE
their lives bitter with hard *b*............... Ex 1:14
Israel sighed by reason of the *b*........... Ex 2:23
up unto God by reason of the *b*........... Ex 2:23
whom the Egyptians keep in *b*............ Ex 6:5
and I will rid you out of their *b*........... Ex 6:6

anguish of spirit, and for cruel *b*......... Ex 6:9
from Egypt, out of the house of *b*........ Ex 13:3
from Egypt, from the house of *b*.......... Ex 13:14
of Egypt, out of the house of *b*........... Ex 20:2
of Egypt, from the house of *b*............. Deut 5:6
of Egypt, from the house of *b*............. Deut 6:12
of Egypt, from the house of *b*............. Deut 8:14
you out of the house of *b*.................... Deut 13:5
of Egypt, from the house of *b*............. Deut 13:10
us, and laid upon us hard *b*................. Deut 26:6
of Egypt, from the house of *b*............. Josh 24:17
you forth out of the house of *b*........... Judg 6:8
us a little reviving in our *b*................. Ezr 9:8
God hath not forsaken us in our *b*....... Ezr 9:9
and, lo, we bring into *b* our sons......... Neh 5:5
are brought unto *b* already................. Neh 5:5
because the *b* was heavy upon this...... Neh 5:18
a captain to return to their *b*.............. Neh 9:17
from the hard *b* wherein thou wast..... Is 14:3
and were never in *b* to any man.......... Jn 8:33
they should bring them into *b*............. Acts 7:6
they shall be in *b* will I judge.............. Acts 7:7
the spirit of *b* again to fear................. Rom 8:15
shall be delivered from the *b* of.......... Rom 8:21
is not under *b* in such cases................ 1Cor 7:15
suffer, if a man bring you into *b*.......... 2Cor 11:20
that they might bring us into *b*............ Gal 2:4
were in *b* under the elements of.......... Gal 4:3
ye desire again to be in *b*.................... Gal 4:9
mount Sinai, which gendereth to *b*...... Gal 4:24
is in *b* with her children..................... Gal 4:25
again with the yoke of *b*..................... Gal 5:1
all their lifetime subject to *b*.............. Heb 2:15
of the same is he brought in *b*............. 2Pet 2:19

BONDMAID
with a woman, that is a *b*.................... Lev 19:20
had two sons, the one by a *b*............... Gal 4:22

BONDMAIDS
Both thy bondmen, and thy *b*............. Lev 25:44
of them shall ye buy bondmen and *b*... Lev 25:44

BONDMAN
instead of the lad a *b* to my lord......... Gen 44:33
wast a *b* in the land of Egypt............... Deut 15:15
that thou wast a *b* in Egypt................. Deut 16:12
that thou wast a *b* in Egypt................. Deut 24:18
wast a *b* in the land of Egypt............... Deut 24:22
and the mighty men, and every *b*........ Rev 6:15

BONDMEN
and fall upon us, and take us for *b*....... Gen 43:18
and we also will be my lord's *b*............ Gen 44:9
they shall not be sold as *b*.................. Lev 25:42
Both thy *b*, and thy bondmaids............ Lev 25:44
of them shall ye buy *b* and................. Lev 25:44
they shall be your *b* for ever................ Lev 25:46
that ye should not be their *b*............... Lev 26:13
son, We were Pharaoh's *b* in Egypt...... Deut 6:21
you out of the house of *b*.................... Deut 7:8
be sold unto your enemies for *b*.......... Deut 28:68
none of you be freed from being *b*....... Josh 9:23
of Israel did Solomon make no *b*......... 1Kin 9:22
take unto him my two sons to be *b*...... 2Kin 4:1
of Judah and Jerusalem for *b*.............. 2Chr 28:10
For we were *b*.................................... Ezr 9:9
But if we had been sold for *b*.............. Est 7:4
of Egypt, out of the house of *b*........... Jer 34:13

BONDS
or of her *b* wherewith she hath........... Num 30:5
her *b* wherewith she bound her.......... Num 30:7
all her vows, or all her *b*.................... Num 30:14
thou hast loosed my *b*....................... Ps 116:16
broken the yoke, and burst the *b*......... Jer 5:5
Make thee *b* and yokes, and put them.. Jer 27:2
off thy neck, and will burst thy *b*......... Jer 30:8
and will burst thy *b* in sunder............. Nah 1:13
in every city, saying that *b*................. Acts 20:23
charge worthy of death or of *b*............ Acts 23:29
a certain man left in *b* by Felix............ Acts 25:14
such as I am, except these *b*................ Acts 26:29
nothing worthy of death or of *b*........... Acts 26:31
For which I am an ambassador in *b*...... Eph 6:20
inasmuch as both in my *b*, and in........ Phil 1:7
So that my *b* in Christ are.................. Phil 1:13
Lord, waxing confident by my *b*.......... Phil 1:14
to add affliction to my *b*.................... Phil 1:16
Christ, for which I am also in *b*........... Col 4:3
Remember my *b*................................ Col 4:18
as an evil doer, even unto *b*................ 2Ti 2:9
whom I have begotten in my *b*............ Philem 10
unto me in the *b* of the gospel............ Philem 13
ye had compassion of me in my *b*....... Heb 10:34
and scourgings, yea, moreover of *b*...... Heb 11:36
Remember them that are in *b*.............. Heb 13:3

BONDSERVANT
not compel him to serve as a *b*........... Lev 25:39

BONDSERVICE
levy a tribute of *b* unto this day........... 1Kin 9:21

BONDWOMAN
unto Abraham, Cast out this *b*............ Gen 21:10
for the son of this *b* shall not............. Gen 21:10
of the lad, and because of thy *b*.......... Gen 21:12
son of the *b* will I make a nation......... Gen 21:13
But he who was of the *b* was born........ Gal 4:23
Cast out the *b* and her son................. Gal 4:30
for the son of the *b* shall not be.......... Gal 4:30
we are not children of the *b*................ Gal 4:31

BONDWOMEN
your enemies for bondmen and *b*........ Deut 28:68
for bondmen and *b* unto you............... 2Chr 28:10
we had been sold for bondmen and *b*... Est 7:4

BONE
said, This is now *b* of my bones.......... Gen 2:23
said to him, Surely thou art my *b*........ Gen 29:14
shall ye break a *b* thereof................... Ex 12:46
morning, nor break any *b* of it............ Num 9:12
or a *b* of a man, or a grave................. Num 19:16
and upon him that touched a *b*........... Num 19:18
remember also that I am your *b*........... Judg 9:2
saying, Behold, we are thy *b*............... 2Sa 5:1
ye to Amasa, Art thou not of my *b*....... 2Sa 19:13
saying, Behold, we are thy *b*............... 1Chr 11:1
thine hand now, and touch his *b*......... Job 2:5
My *b* cleaveth to my skin and to my.... Job 19:20
and mine arm be broken from the *b*..... Job 31:22
all mine enemies upon the cheek *b*...... Ps 3:7
a soft tongue breaketh the *b*............... Prov 25:15
came together, *b* to his *b*.................. Eze 37:7
land, when any seeth a man's *b*........... Eze 39:15
A *b* of him shall not be broken............ Jn 19:36

BONES
said, This is now bone of my *b*............ Gen 2:23
ye shall carry up my *b* from hence....... Gen 50:25
Moses took the *b* of Joseph with......... Ex 13:19
carry up my *b* away hence with you..... Ex 13:19
enemies, and shall break their *b*......... Num 24:8
the *b* of Joseph, which the.................. Josh 24:32
divided her, together with her *b*.......... Judg 19:29
And they took their *b*, and buried....... 1Sa 31:13
Ye are my brethren, ye are my *b*.......... 2Sa 19:12
David went and took the *b* of Saul....... 2Sa 21:12
the *b* of Jonathan his son from........... 2Sa 21:12
up from thence the *b* of Saul.............. 2Sa 21:13
the *b* of Jonathan his son.................. 2Sa 21:13
they gathered the *b* of them that........ 2Sa 21:13
the *b* of Saul and Jonathan his son...... 2Sa 21:14
men's *b* shall be burnt upon thee........ 1Kin 13:2
lay my *b* beside his *b*....................... 1Kin 13:31
down, and touched the *b* of Elisha....... 2Kin 13:21
their places with the *b* of men............ 2Kin 23:14
took the *b* out of the sepulchres......... 2Kin 23:16
let no man move his *b*........................ 2Kin 23:18
So they let his *b* alone....................... 2Kin 23:18
with the *b* of the prophet that............ 2Kin 23:18
and burned men's *b* upon them.......... 2Kin 23:20
buried their *b* under the oak in........... 1Chr 10:12
he burnt the *b* of the priests.............. 2Chr 34:5
which made all my *b* to shake............. Job 4:14
flesh, and hast fenced me with *b*......... Job 10:11
His *b* are full of the sin of his............. Job 20:11
his *b* are moistened with marrow........ Job 21:24
my *b* are pierced in me in the............. Job 30:17
my *b* are burned with heat................. Job 30:30
of his *b* with strong pain................... Job 33:19
his *b* that were not seen stick............. Job 33:21
His *b* are as strong pieces of.............. Job 40:18
his *b* are like bars of iron................... Job 40:18
for my *b* are vexed........................... Ps 6:2
all my *b* are out of joint.................... Ps 22:14
I may tell all my *b*............................ Ps 22:17
iniquity, and my *b* are consumed........ Ps 31:10
my *b* waxed old through my roaring..... Ps 32:3
He keepeth all his *b*.......................... Ps 34:20
All my *b* shall say, LORD, who is......... Ps 35:10
rest in my *b* because of my sin........... Ps 38:3
As with a sword in my *b*, mine............ Ps 42:10
that the *b* which thou hast broken....... Ps 51:8
for God hath scattered the *b*............... Ps 53:5
my *b* are burned as an hearth............. Ps 102:3
groaning my *b* cleave to my skin......... Ps 102:5
water, and like oil into his *b*............... Ps 109:18
Our *b* are scattered at the.................. Ps 141:7
to thy navel, and marrow to thy *b*........ Prov 3:8
ashamed is as rottenness in his *b*........ Prov 12:4
but envy the rottenness of the *b*......... Prov 14:30
and a good report maketh the *b* fat...... Prov 15:30
to the soul, and health to the *b*........... Prov 16:24
but a broken spirit drieth the *b*........... Prov 17:22
nor how the *b* do grow in the womb..... Eccl 11:5
a lion, so will he break all my *b*........... Is 38:13
in drought, and make fat thy *b*........... Is 58:11
your *b* shall flourish like an............... Is 66:14
out the *b* of the kings of Judah........... Jer 8:1
the *b* of his princes, and the.............. Jer 8:1
the *b* of the priests, and the.............. Jer 8:1
the *b* of the prophets, and the........... Jer 8:1
the *b* of the inhabitants of................. Jer 8:1
as a burning fire shut up in my *b*........ Jer 20:9
all my *b* shake.................................. Jer 23:9
king of Babylon hath broken his *b*....... Jer 50:17
above hath he sent fire into my *b*........ Lam 1:13
he hath broken my *b*.......................... Lam 3:4
thou didst cleaveth to their *b*............. Lam 4:8
I will scatter your *b* round about......... Eze 6:5
fill it with the choice *b*...................... Eze 24:4
and burn also the *b* under it............... Eze 24:5
them seethe the *b* of it therein............ Eze 24:5
it well, and let the *b* be burned........... Eze 24:10
iniquities shall be upon their *b*.......... Eze 32:27
of the valley which was full of *b*......... Eze 37:1
me, Son of man, can these *b* live......... Eze 37:3
unto me, Prophesy upon these *b*......... Eze 37:4
and say unto them, O ye dry *b*............ Eze 37:4
the Lord GOD unto these *b*................. Eze 37:5
the *b* came together, bone to his......... Eze 37:7
these *b* are the whole house of........... Eze 37:11

B

Our b are dried, and our hope is........ Eze 37:11
brake all their b in pieces on......... Dan 6:24
because he burned the b of............. Amos 2:1
bring out the b out of the house....... Amos 6:10
and their flesh from off their b....... Mic 3:2
and they break their b, and chop....... Mic 3:3
rottenness entered into my b........... Hab 3:16
gnaw out the b till the morrow......... Zeph 3:3
are within full of dead men's b....... Mt 23:27
for a spirit hath not flesh and b..... Lk 24:39
ancle b received strength.............. Acts 3:7
body, of his flesh, and of his b...... Eph 5:30
gave commandment concerning his b Heb 11:22

BONNETS
b shalt thou make for them, for....... Ex 28:40
and his sons, and put the b on them.... Ex 29:9
goodly b of fine linen, and linen..... Ex 39:28
with girdles, and put b upon them..... Lev 8:13
The b, and the ornaments of the....... Is 3:20
have linen b upon their heads......... Eze 44:18

BOOK
This is the b of the generations...... Gen 5:1
Write this for a memorial in a b...... Ex 17:14
he took up the b of the covenant, and Ex 24:7
out of thy b which thou hast.......... Ex 32:32
me, him will I blot out of my b....... Ex 32:33
shall write these curses in a b....... Num 5:23
in the b of the wars of the LORD...... Num 21:14
him a copy of this law in a b out..... Deut 17:18
law that are written in this b....... Deut 28:58
not written in the b of this law..... Deut 28:61
in this b shall lie upon him......... Deut 29:20
are written in this b of the law..... Deut 29:21
curses that are written in this b.... Deut 29:27
are written in this b of the law..... Deut 30:10
the words of this law in a b......... Deut 31:24
Take this b of the law, and put it .. Deut 31:26
This b of the law shall not.......... Josh 1:8
in the b of the law of Moses......... Josh 8:31
is written in the b of the law....... Josh 8:34
this written in the b of Jasher...... Josh 10:13
by cities into seven parts in a b.... Josh 18:9
in the b of the law of Moses......... Josh 23:6
words of the b of the law of God..... Josh 24:26
the kingdom, and wrote it in a b..... 1Sa 10:25
it is written in the b of Jasher..... 2Sa 1:18
in the b of the acts of Solomon...... 1Kin 11:41
they are written in the b of the..... 1Kin 14:19
are they not written in the b of..... 1Kin 14:29
are they not written in the b of..... 1Kin 15:7
are they not written in the b of..... 1Kin 15:23
are they not written in the b of..... 1Kin 15:31
are they not written in the b of..... 1Kin 16:5
are they not written in the b of..... 1Kin 16:14
are they not written in the b of..... 1Kin 16:20
are they not written in the b of..... 1Kin 16:27
are they not written in the b of..... 1Kin 22:39
are they not written in the b of..... 1Kin 22:45
are they not written in the b of..... 2Kin 1:18
are they not written in the b of..... 2Kin 8:23
are they not written in the b of..... 2Kin 10:34
are they not written in the b of..... 2Kin 12:19
are they not written in the b of..... 2Kin 13:8
are they not written in the b of..... 2Kin 13:12
in the b of the law of Moses......... 2Kin 14:6
are they not written in the b of..... 2Kin 14:15
are they not written in the b of..... 2Kin 14:18
are they not written in the b of..... 2Kin 14:28
are they not written in the b of..... 2Kin 15:6
they are written in the b of the..... 2Kin 15:11
they are written in the b of the..... 2Kin 15:15
are they not written in the b of..... 2Kin 15:21
they are written in the b of the..... 2Kin 15:26
they are written in the b of the..... 2Kin 15:31
are they not written in the b of..... 2Kin 15:36
are they not written in the b of..... 2Kin 16:19
are they not written in the b of..... 2Kin 20:20
are they not written in the b of..... 2Kin 21:17
b of the chronicles of the kings..... 2Kin 21:25
I have found the b of the law in.... 2Kin 22:8
And Hilkiah gave the b to Shaphan.... 2Kin 22:8
the priest had delivered me a b..... 2Kin 22:10
the words of the b of the law....... 2Kin 22:11
the words of this b that found...... 2Kin 22:13
unto the words of the b, to do...... 2Kin 22:13
even all the words of the b which... 2Kin 22:16
b of the covenant which was found .. 2Kin 23:2
that were written in this b......... 2Kin 23:3
written in the b of this covenant... 2Kin 23:21
b that Hilkiah the priest found..... 2Kin 23:24
are they not written in the b of.... 2Kin 23:28
are they not written in the b of.... 2Kin 24:5
in the b of the law of Israel....... 1Chr 9:1
in the b of Samuel the seer........ 1Chr 29:29
in the b of Nathan the prophet..... 1Chr 29:29
that are in the b of Gad the seer.. 1Chr 29:29
in the b of Nathan the prophet..... 2Chr 9:29
in the b of Shemaiah the prophet... 2Chr 12:15
in the b of the kings of Judah..... 2Chr 16:11
had the b of the law of the LORD... 2Chr 17:9
are written in the b of Jehu....... 2Chr 20:34
in the b of the kings of Israel.... 2Chr 20:34
the story of the b of the kings.... 2Chr 24:27
in the law in the b of Moses....... 2Chr 25:4
in the b of the kings of Judah..... 2Chr 25:26
in the b of the kings of Judah..... 2Chr 27:7
in the b of the kings of Israel.... 2Chr 28:26
in the b of the kings of Judah and . 2Chr 32:32
in the b of the kings of Israel.... 2Chr 33:18

Hilkiah the priest found a b of..... 2Chr 34:14
I have found the b of the law in.... 2Chr 34:15
delivered the b to Shaphan.......... 2Chr 34:16
Shaphan carried the b to the king... 2Chr 34:16
the priest hath given me a b........ 2Chr 34:18
the words of the b that is found.... 2Chr 34:21
all that is written in this b....... 2Chr 34:21
curses that are written in this b... 2Chr 34:24
b of the covenant that was found.... 2Chr 34:30
which are written in this b......... 2Chr 34:31
it is written in the b of Moses..... 2Chr 35:12
in the b of the kings of Israel..... 2Chr 35:27
b of the records of thy fathers..... Ezr 4:15
thou find in the b of the records... Ezr 4:15
it is written in the b of Moses..... Ezr 6:18
bring the b of the law of Moses..... Neh 8:1
attentive unto the b of the law..... Neh 8:3
Ezra opened the b in the sight of... Neh 8:5
So they read in the b in the........ Neh 8:8
he read in the b of the law of...... Neh 8:18
read in the b of the law of the.... Neh 9:3
in the b of the chronicles......... Neh 12:23
On that day they read in the b of.. Neh 13:1
it was written in the b of the..... Est 2:23
he commanded to bring the b of..... Est 6:1
and it was written in the b........ Est 9:32
are they not written in the b of... Est 10:2
oh that they were printed in a b... Job 19:23
mine adversary had written a b..... Job 31:35
of the b it is written of me....... Ps 40:7
are they not in thy b.............. Ps 56:8
out of the b of the living......... Ps 69:28
in thy b all my members were....... Ps 139:16
the words of a b that is sealed.... Is 29:11
the b is delivered to him that is.. Is 29:12
the deaf hear the words of the b... Is 29:18
and look not in it in a b.......... Is 30:8
Seek ye out of the b of the LORD... Is 34:16
all that is written in this b...... Jer 25:13
I have spoken unto thee in a b..... Jer 30:2
subscribed the b of the purchase... Jer 32:12
Take thee a roll of a b, and write. Jer 36:2
unto him, upon a roll of a b....... Jer 36:4
reading in the b the words of the.. Jer 36:8
Then read Baruch in the b.......... Jer 36:10
had heard out of the b all the..... Jer 36:11
when Baruch read in the b.......... Jer 36:13
and I wrote them with ink in the b. Jer 36:18
in which Jehoiakim king of Judah... Jer 36:32
in a b as the mouth of Jeremiah.... Jer 45:1
So Jeremiah wrote in a b all the... Jer 51:60
made an end of reading this b...... Jer 51:63
and, lo, a roll of a b was therein. Eze 2:9
shall be found written in the b.... Dan 12:1
shut up the words, and seal the b.. Dan 12:4
The b of the vision of Nahum the... Nah 1:1
a b of remembrance was written..... Mal 3:16
The b of the generation of Jesus... Mt 1:1
ye not read in the b of Moses...... Mk 12:26
As it is written in the b of the... Lk 3:4
him the b of the prophet Esaias.... Lk 4:17
And when he had opened the b....... Lk 4:20
And he closed the b, and he gave it Lk 4:20
himself again in the b of Psalms... Lk 20:42
which are not written in this b.... Jn 20:30
it is written in the b of Psalms... Acts 1:20
written in the b of the prophets... Acts 7:42
in the b of the law to do them..... Gal 3:10
whose names are in the b of life... Phil 4:3
hyssop, and sprinkled both the b... Heb 9:19
of the b it is written of me....... Heb 10:7
And, What thou seest, write in a b. Rev 1:11
out his name out of the b of life.. Rev 3:5
on the throne a b written within... Rev 5:1
Who is worthy to open the b........ Rev 5:2
the earth, was able to open the b.. Rev 5:3
worthy to open and to read the b... Rev 5:4
hath prevailed to open the b....... Rev 5:5
took the b out of the right hand... Rev 5:7
And when he had taken the b........ Rev 5:8
Thou art worthy to take the b...... Rev 5:9
had in his hand a little b open.... Rev 10:2
take the little b which is open.... Rev 10:8
unto him, Give me the little b..... Rev 10:9
I took the little b out of the..... Rev 10:10
names are not written in the b of.. Rev 13:8
names were not written in the b.... Rev 17:8
another b was opened.............. Rev 20:12
which is the b of life............ Rev 20:12
was not found written in the b of. Rev 20:15
written in the Lamb's b of life... Rev 21:27
sayings of the prophecy of this b. Rev 22:7
which keep the sayings of this b.. Rev 22:9
sayings of the prophecy of this b. Rev 22:10
words of the prophecy of this b... Rev 22:18
that are written in this b........ Rev 22:18
words of the b of this prophecy... Rev 22:19
his part out of the b of life..... Rev 22:19
which are written in this b....... Rev 22:19

BOOKS
of making many b there is no end... Eccl 12:12
was set, and the b were opened..... Dan 7:10
by the number of the years......... Dan 9:2
the b that should in heaven........ Jn 21:25
arts brought their b together...... Acts 19:19
comest, bring with thee, and the b. 2Ti 4:13
and the b were opened.............. Rev 20:12
which were written in the b........ Rev 20:12

BOOTH
as a b that the keeper maketh...... Job 27:18
the city, and there made him a b... Jonah 4:5

BOOTHS
house, and made b for his cattle... Gen 33:17
Ye shall dwell in b seven days..... Lev 23:42
Israelites born shall dwell in b... Lev 23:42
children of Israel to dwell in b... Neh 8:14
of Israel should dwell in b in..... Neh 8:14
of thick trees, to make b.......... Neh 8:15
them, and made themselves b........ Neh 8:16
made b, and sat under the b........ Neh 8:17

BOOTIES
and thou shalt be for b unto them.. Hab 2:7

BOOTY
And the b, being the rest of the... Num 31:32
And their camels shall be a b...... Jer 49:32
their goods shall become a b....... Zeph 1:13

BOOZ (bo'-oz) See BOAZ. Greek form of Boaz.
And Salmon begat B of Rachab....... Mt 1:5
and B begat Obed of Ruth........... Mt 1:5
of Obed, which was the son of B.... Lk 3:32

BOR-ASHAN See CHOR-ASHAN.

BORDER
the b of the Canaanites was from... Gen 10:19
his b shall be unto Zidon.......... Gen 49:13
the mount, or touch the b of it.... Ex 19:12
thou shalt make unto it a b of an.. Ex 25:25
to the b thereof round about....... Ex 25:25
Over against the b shall the....... Ex 25:27
the breastplate in the b thereof... Ex 28:26
Also he made thereunto a b of an... Ex 37:12
for the b thereof round about...... Ex 37:12
the breastplate in the b thereof... Ex 37:14
Over against the b were the rings.. Ex 37:14
the breastplate, upon the b of it.. Ex 39:19
a city in the uttermost of thy b... Num 20:16
give Israel passage through his b.. Num 20:21
for Arnon is the b of Moab......... Num 21:13
Ar, and lieth upon the b of Moab... Num 21:15
Israel to pass through his b....... Num 21:23
for the b of the children of....... Num 21:24
Moab, which is in the b of Arnon... Num 22:36
in Ije-abarim, in the b of Moab.... Num 33:44
your south b shall be the outmost.. Num 34:3
your b shall turn from the south... Num 34:4
the b shall fetch a compass from... Num 34:5
And as for the western b, ye shall. Num 34:6
even have the great sea for a b.... Num 34:6
this shall be your west b.......... Num 34:6
And this shall be your north b..... Num 34:7
b unto the entrance of Hamath...... Num 34:8
forth of the b shall be to Zedad... Num 34:8
the b shall go on to Ziphron, and . Num 34:9
this shall be your north b......... Num 34:9
east b from Hazar-enan to Shepham.. Num 34:10
the b shall descend, and shall..... Num 34:11
the b shall go down to Jordan, and. Num 34:12
the b of the city of his refuge.... Num 35:26
the b even unto the river Jabbok... Deut 3:16
which is the b of the children of.. Deut 3:16
Lord thy God shall enlarge thy b... Deut 12:20
Gilgal, in the east b of Jericho... Josh 4:19
which is the b of the children of.. Josh 12:5
unto the b of the Geshurites and... Josh 12:5
the b of Sihon king of Heshbon..... Josh 12:5
unto the b of the children of...... Josh 13:10
the b of the Geshurites and........ Josh 13:11
the b of the children of Reuben.... Josh 13:23
was Jordan, and the b thereof...... Josh 13:23
from Mahanaim unto the b of Debir.. Josh 13:26
king of Heshbon, Jordan and his b.. Josh 13:27
even to the b of Edom the.......... Josh 15:1
the b of Edom the................. Josh 15:1
their south b was from the shore... Josh 15:2
the east b was the salt sea........ Josh 15:5
their b in the north quarter was... Josh 15:5
the b went up to Beth-hogla, and... Josh 15:6
the b went up to the stone of...... Josh 15:6
the b went up toward Debir from.... Josh 15:7
the b went up by the valley of..... Josh 15:8
the b went up to the top of the.... Josh 15:8
the b was drawn from the top of.... Josh 15:9
the b was drawn to Baalah, which... Josh 15:9
the b compassed from Baalah........ Josh 15:10
the b went out unto the side of.... Josh 15:11
the b was drawn to Shicron, and.... Josh 15:11
out of the b were at the sea....... Josh 15:11
the west b was to the great sea.... Josh 15:12
the great sea, and the b thereof... Josh 15:12
the b of the children of Ephraim... Josh 16:5
even the b of their inheritance.... Josh 16:5
the b went out toward the sea to... Josh 16:6
the b went about eastward unto..... Josh 16:6
the b went out from Tappuah........ Josh 16:8
the b went along on the right...... Josh 17:7
but Tappuah on the b of Manasseh... Josh 17:8
Manasseh's, and the sea is his b... Josh 17:10
their b on the north side was...... Josh 18:12
the b went up to the side of....... Josh 18:12
the b went over from thence........ Josh 18:13
the b descended to Ataroth-adar.... Josh 18:13
the b was drawn thence, and........ Josh 18:14
the b went out on the west, and.... Josh 18:14
the b came down to the end of the.. Josh 18:16
the b passed along to the side of.. Josh 18:18
the outgoings of the b were at..... Josh 18:19
Jordan was the b of it on the...... Josh 18:20

the *b* of their inheritance was .... Josh 19:10
their *b* went up toward the sea, ... Josh 19:11
unto the *b* of Chisloth-tabor .... Josh 19:12
the *b* compasseth it on the north .... Josh 19:14
their *b* was toward Jezreel, and .... Josh 19:18
of their *b* were at Jordan .... Josh 19:22
their *b* was Helkath, and Hali, and.... Josh 19:25
Rakkon, with the *b* before Japho .... Josh 19:46
hath made Jordan a *b* between us........ Josh 22:25
in the *b* of his inheritance in............... Josh 24:30
in the *b* of his inheritance in............... Judg 2:9
to the *b* of Abel-meholah, unto.......... Judg 7:22
but came not within the *b* of Moab.... Judg 11:18
for Arnon was the *b* of Moab .... Judg 11:18
them unto the *b* of Beth-shemesh...... 1Sa 6:12
in the *b* of Benjamin at Zelzah.......... 1Sa 10:2
turned to the way of the *b* that.......... 1Sa 13:18
his *b* at the river Euphrates 2Sa 8:3
and unto the *b* of Egypt 1Kin 4:21
and upward, and stood in the *b*......... 2Kin 3:21
Philistines, and to the *b* of Egypt....... 2Chr 9:26
them to the *b* of his sanctuary .... Ps 78:54
will establish the *b* of the widow........ Prov 15:25
a pillar at the *b* thereof to the............ Is 19:19
enter into the height of his *b* .... Is 37:24
shall come again to their own *b* .... Jer 31:17
against her from the utmost *b* .... Jer 50:26
will judge you in the *b* of Israel .... Eze 11:10
will judge you in the *b* of Israel .... Eze 11:11
Syene even unto the *b* of Ethiopia..... Eze 29:10
the *b* thereof by the edge thereof........ Eze 43:13
the *b* about it shall be half a .... Eze 43:17
settle, and upon the *b* round about. ... Eze 43:20
the west *b* unto the east *b*................. Eze 45:7
This shall be the *b*, whereby ye .... Eze 47:13
this shall be the *b* of the land............. Eze 47:15
is between the *b* of Damascus .... Eze 47:16
of Damascus and the *b* of Hamath .... Eze 47:16
the *b* from the sea shall be .... Eze 47:17
the *b* of Damascus, and the north...... Eze 47:17
northward, and the *b* of Hamath........ Eze 47:17
from the *b* unto the east sea................ Eze 47:18
shall be the great sea from the *b*......... Eze 47:20
the *b* of Damascus northward, to....... Eze 48:1
And by the *b* of Dan, from the east.... Eze 48:2
by the *b* of Asher, from the east .... Eze 48:3
by the *b* of Naphtali, from the .... Eze 48:4
by the *b* of Manasseh, from the .... Eze 48:5
by the *b* of Ephraim, from the .... Eze 48:6
by the *b* of Reuben, from the east ..... Eze 48:7
by the *b* of Judah, from the east .... Eze 48:8
most holy by the *b* of the Levites ...... Eze 48:12
over against the *b* of the priests........ Eze 48:13
of the oblation toward the east *b*........ Eze 48:21
twenty thousand toward the west *b*.... Eze 48:21
prince's, between the *b* of Judah .... Eze 48:22
the *b* of Benjamin, shall be for .... Eze 48:22
of the Benjamin, from the .... Eze 48:24
by the *b* of Simeon, from the east ..... Eze 48:25
by the *b* of Issachar, from the .... Eze 48:26
by the *b* of Zebulun, from the .... Eze 48:27
And by the *b* of Gad, at the south...... Eze 48:28
the *b* shall be even from Tamar.......... Eze 48:28
remove them far from their *b*............. Joel 3:6
that they might enlarge their *b*........... Amos 1:13
their *b* greater than your *b* .... Amos 6:2
have brought thee even to the *b* .... Obad 7
themselves against their *b* .... Zeph 2:8
And Hamath also shall *b* thereby....... Zec 9:2
The *b* of wickedness, and, The .... Mal 1:4
be magnified from the *b* of Israel....... Mal 1:5
it were but the *b* of his garment .... Mk 6:56
touched the *b* of his garment .... Lk 8:44

BORDERS

were in all the *b* round about............. Gen 23:17
to cities from one end of the *b* .... Gen 47:21
I will smite all thy *b* with frogs........... Ex 8:2
unto the *b* of the land of Canaan....... Ex 16:35
before thee, and enlarge thy *b*............ Ex 34:24
b of their garments throughout.......... Num 15:38
fringe of the *b* a ribband of blue......... Num 15:38
left, until we have passed thy *b*.......... Num 20:17
high way, until we be past thy *b* .... Num 21:22
the *b* of the city of his refuge............. Num 35:27
in the *b* of Dor on the west,............... Josh 11:2
all the *b* of the Philistines, and.......... Josh 13:2
Egypt, even unto the *b* of Ekron .... Josh 13:3
Aphek, to the *b* of the Amorites......... Josh 13:4
unto the *b* of Archi to Ataroth........... Josh 16:2
they came unto the *b* of Jordan.......... Josh 22:10
in the *b* of Jordan, at the.................... Josh 22:11
they had *b*, and the *b* were 1Kin 7:28
on the *b* that were between the 1Kin 7:29
of it were gravings with their *b* 1Kin 7:31
under the *b* were four wheels 1Kin 7:32
the *b* thereof were of the same........... 1Kin 7:35
they had *b*, and the *b* were 1Kin 7:36
Ahaz cut off the *b* of the bases........... 2Kin 16:17
the *b* thereof, from the tower of........ 2Kin 18:8
enter into the lodgings of his *b* 2Kin 19:23
suburbs of Sharon, upon their *b*......... 1Chr 5:16
by the *b* of the children of................. 1Chr 7:29
hast set all the *b* of the earth............. Ps 74:17
He maketh peace in thy *b*, and........... Ps 147:14
We will make thee *b* of gold with ...... Song 1:11
is gone round about the *b* of Moab..... Is 15:8
all thy *b* of pleasant stones .... Is 54:12
nor destruction within thy *b* .... Is 60:18
all thy sins, even in all thy *b* .... Jer 15:13
for sin, throughout all thy *b*............... Jer 17:3

Thy *b* are in the midst of the .... Eze 27:4
in all the *b* thereof round about......... Eze 45:1
and when he treadeth within our *b*.... Mic 5:6
in the *b* of Zabulon and Nephthalim.. Mt 4:13
enlarge the *b* of their garments,......... Mt 23:5
arose, and went into the *b* of Tyre ..... Mk 7:24

BORE

his master shall *b* his ear.................... Ex 21:6
or *b* his jaw through with a thorn .... Job 41:2

BORED

b a hole in the lid of it, and set.......... 2Kin 12:9

BORN

And unto Enoch was *b* Irad................ Gen 4:18
to him also there was *b* a son .... Gen 4:26
and daughters were *b* unto them........ Gen 6:1
them were sons *b* after the flood........ Gen 10:1
even to him were children *b*................ Gen 10:21
And unto Eber were *b* two sons .... Gen 10:25
b in his own house, three hundred..... Gen 14:14
one *b* in my house is mine heir........... Gen 15:3
he that is *b* in the house, or............... Gen 17:12
He that is *b* in thy house, and he .... Gen 17:13
Shall a child be *b* unto him that......... Gen 17:17
and all that were *b* in his house .... Gen 17:23
b in the house, and bought with........ Gen 17:27
of his son that was *b* unto him........... Gen 21:3
when his son Isaac was *b* unto him.... Gen 21:5
for I have *b* him a son in his old .... Gen 21:7
which she had *b* unto Abraham.......... Gen 21:9
she hath also *b* children unto thy...... Gen 22:20
who was *b* to Bethuel, son of............. Gen 24:15
because I have *b* him three sons .... Gen 29:34
me, because I have *b* him six sons...... Gen 30:20
to pass, when Rachel had *b* Joseph.... Gen 30:25
their children which they have *b*........ Gen 31:43
which were *b* to him in Padan-aram... Gen 35:26
which were *b* unto him in the land..... Gen 36:5
unto Joseph were *b* two sons.............. Gen 41:50
the land of Egypt were *b* two............. Gen 46:20
of Rachel, which were *b* to Jacob ...... Gen 46:22
which were *b* him in Egypt, were........ Gen 46:27
which were *b* unto the in the .... Gen 48:5
Every son that is *b* ye shall cast......... Ex 1:22
be a stranger, or *b* in the land .... Ex 12:19
be as one that is *b* in the land .... Ex 12:48
she have *b* him sons or daughters ...... Ex 21:4
conceived seed, and *b* a man child,.... Lev 12:2
that hath *b* a male or a female .... Lev 12:7
mother, whether she be *b* at home...... Lev 18:9
or *b* abroad, even their nakedness ..... Lev 18:9
be unto you as one *b* among you......... Lev 19:34
he that is *b* in his house .... Lev 22:11
b shall dwell in booths .... Lev 23:42
as he that is *b* in the land .... Lev 24:16
and for him that was *b* in the land..... Num 9:14
All that are *b* of the country............... Num 15:13
both for him that is *b* among the,....... Num 15:29
whether he be *b* in the land, or.......... Num 15:30
And unto Aaron was *b* Nadab............ Num 26:60
they have *b* him children, both .... Deut 21:15
but all the people that were *b* in......... Josh 5:5
as he that was *b* among them............. Josh 8:33
do unto the child that shall be *b* .... Judg 13:8
father, who was *b* unto Israel............. Judg 18:29
thee than seven sons, hath *b* him....... Ruth 4:15
saying, There is a son *b* to Naomi....... Ruth 4:17
so that the barren hath *b* seven.......... 1Sa 2:5
for thou hast *b* a son 1Sa 4:20
the battle were Eliab the first *b*.......... 1Sa 17:13
unto David were sons *b* in Hebron 2Sa 3:2
These were *b* to David in Hebron 2Sa 3:5
yet sons and daughters to David 2Sa 5:13
that were *b* unto him in Jerusalem..... 2Sa 5:14
the child also that is *b* unto............... 2Sa 12:14
Absalom there were *b* three sons 2Sa 14:27
he also was *b* to the giant 2Sa 21:20
These four were *b* to the giant in....... 2Sa 21:22
a child shall be *b* unto the house........ 1Kin 13:2
And unto Eber were *b* two sons 1Chr 1:19
which these were *b* unto him of.......... 1Chr 2:3
of Hezron, that were *b* unto him......... 1Chr 2:9
which were *b* unto him in Hebron....... 1Chr 3:1
These six were *b* unto him in.............. 1Chr 3:4
And these were *b* unto him in............. 1Chr 3:5
that were *b* in that land slew.............. 1Chr 7:21
These were *b* unto the giant in 1Chr 20:8
Behold, a son shall be *b* to thee......... 1Chr 22:9
unto Shemaiah his son were sons *b*.... 1Chr 26:6
wives, and such as are *b* of them .... Ezr 10:3
there were *b* unto him seven sons...... Job 1:2
the day perish wherein I was *b*........... Job 3:3
Yet man is *b* unto trouble, as the....... Job 5:7
though man be *b* like a wild ass's ...... Job 11:12
Man that is *b* of a woman is of........... Job 14:1
Art thou the first man that was *b* ...... Job 15:7
and he which is *b* of a woman........... Job 15:14
he be clean that is *b* of a woman....... Job 25:4
thou it, because thou wast then *b* ..... Job 38:21
unto a people that shall be *b* .... Ps 22:31
go astray as soon as they be *b* .... Ps 58:3
the children which should be *b* .... Ps 78:6
this man was *b* there .... Ps 87:4
This and that man was *b* in her.......... Ps 87:5
this man, that this man was *b* there... Ps 87:6
a brother is *b* for adversity .... Prov 17:17
and had servants in my house.............. Eccl 2:7
A time to be *b*, and a time to die........ Eccl 3:2
whereas also he that is *b* in his.......... Eccl 4:14
For unto us a child is *b*, unto us......... Is 9:6

or shall a nation be *b* at once............. Is 66:8
that are *b* in this place, and............... Jer 16:3
Cursed be the day wherein I was *b* .... Jer 20:14
A man child is *b* unto thee.................. Jer 20:15
country, where ye were not *b*.............. Jer 22:26
in the day thou wast *b* they marred... Eze 16:4
in the day that thou wast *b*................ Eze 16:5
you as *b* in the country among the.... Eze 47:22
her as in the day that she was *b*......... Hos 2:3
of Mary, of whom was *b* Jesus............ Mt 1:16
Now when Jesus was *b* in Bethlehem. Mt 2:1
is he that is *b* King of the Jews.......... Mt 2:2
of them where Christ should be *b*....... Mt 2:4
Among them that are *b* of women...... Mt 11:11
which were so *b* from their .... Mt 19:12
for that man if he had not been *b*...... Mt 26:24
that man if he had never been *b*........ Mk 14:21
that holy thing which shall be *b* .... Lk 1:35
For unto you is *b* this day in the........ Lk 2:11
Among those that are *b* of women ..... Lk 7:28
Which were *b*, not of blood, nor .... Jn 1:13
thee, Except a man be *b* again .... Jn 3:3
How can a man be *b* when he is old... Jn 3:4
into his mother's womb, and be *b* ..... Jn 3:4
thee, Except a man be *b* of water...... Jn 3:5
That which is *b* of the flesh is .... Jn 3:6
that which is *b* of the Spirit is........... Jn 3:6
unto thee, Ye must be *b* again............ Jn 3:7
every one that is *b* of the Spirit .... Jn 3:8
We be not *b* of fornication .... Jn 8:41
his parents, that he was *b* blind......... Jn 9:2
your son, who ye say was *b* blind........ Jn 9:19
our son, and that he was *b* blind........ Jn 9:20
the eyes of one that was *b* blind?........ Jn 9:32
Thou wast altogether *b* in sins .... Jn 9:34
that a man is *b* into the world............. Jn 16:21
To this end was I *b*, and for this,........ Jn 18:37
our own tongue, wherein we were *b*.... Acts 2:8
In which time Moses was *b* .... Acts 7:20
b in Pontus, lately come from .... Acts 18:2
b at Alexandria, an eloquent man,..... Acts 18:24
b in Tarsus, a city in Cilicia,............... Acts 22:3
And Paul said, But I was free *b* .... Acts 22:28
(For the children being not yet *b* .... Rom 9:11
as of one *b* out of due time................. 1Cor 15:8
bondwoman was *b* after the flesh....... Gal 4:23
But as then he that was *b* after.......... Gal 4:29
him that was *b* after the Spirit........... Gal 4:29
By faith Moses, when he was *b*........... Heb 11:23
Being *b* again, not of corruptible 1Pet 1:23
doeth righteousness is *b* of him 1Jn 2:29
Whosoever is *b* of God doth not 1Jn 3:9
sin, because he is *b* of God.................. 1Jn 3:9
every one that loveth is *b* of God....... 1Jn 4:7
Jesus is the Christ is *b* of God 1Jn 5:1
For whatsoever is *b* of God................. 1Jn 5:4
whosoever is *b* of God sinneth not..... 1Jn 5:18
her child as soon as it was *b*.............. Rev 12:4

BORNE

that the ark may be *b* with them........ Ex 25:14
that the table may be *b* with them ..... Ex 25:28
stood, and on which it was *b* up .... Judg 16:29
I have *b* chastisement, I will not .... Job 34:31
then I could have *b* it .... Ps 55:12
for thy sake I have *b* reproach............ Ps 69:7
which are *b* by me from the belly........ Is 46:3
Surely he hath *b* our griefs .... Is 53:4
ye shall be *b* upon her sides, and .... Is 66:12
they must needs be *b*, because .... Jer 10:5
She that hath *b* seven languisheth..... Jer 15:9
that thou hast *b* me a man of............. Jer 15:10
because he hath *b* it upon him........... Lam 3:28
we have *b* their iniquities .... Lam 5:7
whom thou hast *b* unto me................. Eze 16:20
Thou hast *b* thy lewdness and thine.. Eze 16:58
yet have they *b* their shame with ...... Eze 32:24
yet have they *b* their shame with ...... Eze 32:25
because ye have *b* the shame of......... Eze 36:6
that they have *b* their shame .... Eze 39:26
But ye have *b* the tabernacle of......... Amos 5:26
unto us, which have *b* the burden...... Mt 20:12
heavy burdens and grievous to be *b*.. Mt 23:4
of the palsy, which was *b* of four .... Mk 2:3
men with burdens grievous to be *b*.... Lk 11:46
sent me, hath *b* witness of me............ Jn 5:37
Sir, if thou have *b* him hence .... Jn 20:15
that he was *b* of the soldiers for......... Acts 21:35
as we have *b* the image of the 1Cor 15:49
Which have *b* witness of thy............... 3Jn 6
And hast *b*, and hast patience, and... Rev 2:3

BORROW

woman shall *b* of her neighbour......... Ex 3:22
let every man *b* of his neighbour........ Ex 11:2
if a man *b* ought of his neighbour ..... Ex 22:14
nations, but thou shalt not *b* .... Deut 15:6
many nations, and thou shalt not *b*... Deut 28:12
b thee vessels abroad of all thy......... 2Kin 4:3
b not a few............ .... 2Kin 4:3
from him that would *b* of thee........... Mt 5:42

BORROWED

they *b* of the Egyptians jewels of....... Ex 12:35
for it was *b*... 2Kin 6:5
We have *b* money for the king's .... Neh 5:4

BORROWER

the *b* is servant to the lender .... Prov 22:7
as with the lender, so with the *b*........ Is 24:2

BORROWETH
The wicked b, and payeth not again...... Ps 37:21

BORSHAN See CHOR-ASHAN.

BOSCATH (bos'-cath) See BOSKETH. *A city in Judah.*
the daughter of Adaiah of B.............. 2Kin 22:1

BOSOM
I have given my maid into thy b........... Gen 16:5
Put now thine hand into thy b............. Ex 4:6
And he put his hand into his b............. Ex 4:6
Put thine hand into thy b again.......... Ex 4:7
he put his hand into his b again......... Ex 4:7
and plucked it out of his b................. Ex 4:7
say unto me, Carry them in thy b....... Num 11:12
daughter, or the wife of thy b........... Deut 13:6
and toward the wife of his b.............. Deut 28:54
evil toward the husband of her b....... Deut 28:56
the child, and laid it in her b............. Ruth 4:16
of his own cup, and lay in his b......... 2Sa 12:3
and thy master's wives unto thy b..... 2Sa 12:8
him, and let her lie in thy b............... 1Kin 1:2
slept, and laid it in her b.................. 1Kin 3:20
and laid her dead child in my b......... 1Kin 3:20
And he took him out of her b............ 1Kin 17:19
by hiding mine iniquity in my b......... Job 31:33
prayer returned into mine own b........ Ps 35:13
pluck it out of thy b......................... Ps 74:11
into their b their reproach................ Ps 79:12
how I do bear in my b the................. Ps 89:50
nor he that bindeth sheaves his b..... Ps 129:7
embrace the b of a stranger.............. Prov 5:20
Can a man take fire in his b.............. Prov 6:27
man taketh a gift out of the b to...... Prov 17:23
man hideth his hand in his b............. Prov 19:24
and a reward in the b strong wrath... Prov 21:14
slothful hideth his hand in the b....... Prov 26:15
anger resteth in the b of fools.......... Eccl 7:9
his arm, and carry them in his b........ Is 40:11
even recompense into their b............ Is 65:6
their former work into their b........... Is 65:7
of the fathers into the b of............... Jer 32:18
poured out into their mothers' b....... Lam 2:12
from her that lieth in thy b............... Mic 7:5
over, shall men give into your b........ Lk 6:38
by the angels into Abraham's b......... Lk 16:22
afar off, and Lazarus in his b............ Lk 16:23
which is in the b of the Father......... Jn 1:18
on Jesus' b one of his disciples........ Jn 13:23

BOSOR (bo'-sor) *Greek form of Besor.*
the way of Balaam the son of B....... 2Pet 2:15

BOSSES
upon the b of his bucklers................ Job 15:26

BOTCH
smite thee with the b of Egypt......... Deut 28:27
with a sore b that cannot be............ Deut 28:35

BOTH See PREFACE.

BOTTLE
a b of water, and gave it unto.......... Gen 21:14
And the water was spent in the b...... Gen 21:15
went, and filled the b with water...... Gen 21:19
And she opened a b of milk............... Judg 4:19
a b of wine, and brought him unto.... 1Sa 1:24
and another carrying a b of wine...... 1Sa 10:3
a b of wine, and a kid, and sent....... 1Sa 16:20
of summer fruits, and a b of wine.... 2Sa 16:1
put thou my tears into thy b............. Ps 56:8
I am become like a b in the smoke... Ps 119:83
Every b shall be filled with wine...... Jer 13:12
every b shall be filled with wine...... Jer 13:12
Go and get a potter's earthen b....... Jer 19:1
Then shalt thou break the b in......... Jer 19:10
drink, that puttest thy b to his........ Hab 2:15

BOTTLES
sacks upon their asses, and wine b... Josh 9:4
these b of wine, which we filled....... Josh 9:13
two b of wine, and five sheep.......... 1Sa 25:18
it is ready to burst like new b......... Job 32:19
or who can stay the b of heaven...... Job 38:37
his vessels, and break their b.......... Jer 48:12
have made him sick with b of wine.. Hos 7:5
do men put new wine into old b....... Mt 9:17
else the b break, and the wine........ Mt 9:17
wine runneth out, and the b perish.. Mt 9:17
but they put new wine into new b.... Mt 9:17
man putteth new wine into old b...... Mk 2:22
the new wine doth burst the b......... Mk 2:22
spilled, and the b will be marred..... Mk 2:22
new wine must be put into new b.... Mk 2:22
man putteth new wine into old b...... Lk 5:37
the new wine will burst the b.......... Lk 5:37
be spilled, and the b shall perish.... Lk 5:37
new wine must be put into new b.... Lk 5:38

BOTTOM
they sank into the b as a stone....... Ex 15:5
blood beside the b of the altar........ Ex 29:12
the b of the altar of the burnt........ Lev 4:7
the b of the altar of the burnt........ Lev 4:18
b of the altar of burnt offering........ Lev 4:25
thereof at the b of the altar........... Lev 4:30
thereof at the b of the altar........... Lev 4:34
wrung out at the b of the altar....... Lev 5:9
the blood at the b of the altar........ Lev 8:15
the blood at the b of the altar........ Lev 9:9
it, and covereth the b of the sea.... Job 36:30
the b thereof of gold, the.............. Song 3:10

even the b shall be a cubit, and....... Eze 43:13
from the b upon the ground even..... Eze 43:14
the b thereof shall be a cubit.......... Eze 43:17
they came at the b of the den......... Dan 6:24
from my sight in the b of the sea.... Amos 9:3
myrtle trees that were in the b........ Zec 1:8
in twain from the top to the b........ Mt 27:51
in twain from the top to the b........ Mk 15:38

BOTTOMLESS
was given the key of the b pit......... Rev 9:1
And he opened the b pit.................. Rev 9:2
which is the angel of the b pit......... Rev 9:11
b pit shall make war against them... Rev 11:7
and shall ascend out of the b pit.... Rev 17:8
having the key of the b pit............. Rev 20:1
And cast him into the b pit............. Rev 20:3

BOTTOMS
down to the b of the mountains...... Jonah 2:6

BOUGH
Joseph is a fruitful b...................... Gen 49:22
even a fruitful b by a well.............. Gen 49:22
cut down a b from the trees, and.... Judg 9:48
likewise.cut down every man his b... Judg 9:49
shall lop the b with terror............... Is 10:33
in the top of the uppermost b......... Is 17:6
strong cities be as a forsaken b...... Is 17:9

BOUGHS
first day the b of goodly trees........ Lev 23:40
the b of thick trees, and willows..... Lev 23:40
shalt not go over the b again......... Deut 24:20
under the thick b of a great oak..... 2Sa 18:9
bring forth b like a plant............... Job 14:9
the b thereof were like the........... Ps 80:10
She sent out her b unto the sea.... Ps 80:11
I will take hold of the b thereof..... Song 7:8
When the b thereof are withered... Is 27:11
and it shall bring forth b............... Eze 17:23
and his top was among the thick b.. Eze 31:3
his b were multiplied, and his........ Eze 31:5
heaven made their nests in his b.... Eze 31:6
the fir trees were not like his b..... Eze 31:8
shot up his top among the thick b.. Eze 31:10
his b are broken by all the............ Eze 31:12
up their top among the thick b...... Eze 31:14
the heaven dwelt in the b thereof.. Dan 4:12

BOUGHT
or b with money of any stranger..... Gen 17:13
he that is b with thy money, must.. Gen 17:13
all that were b with his money,...... Gen 17:23
b with money of the stranger......... Gen 17:27
be b a parcel of a field, where...... Gen 33:19
b him of the hands of the............. Gen 39:1
Joseph b all the land of Egypt........ Gen 47:20
the land of the priests b he not..... Gen 47:22
I have b you this day and your...... Gen 47:23
which Abraham b with the field of.. Gen 49:30
which Abraham b with the field...... Gen 50:13
man's servant that is b for money.. Ex 12:44
b it until the year of jubile........... Lev 25:28
for ever to him that b it............... Lev 25:30
b him from the year that he was... Lev 25:50
of the money that he was b for..... Lev 25:51
the LORD a field which he hath b.. Lev 27:24
return unto him of whom it was b.. Lev 27:24
he thy father that hath b thee....... Deut 32:6
a parcel of ground which Jacob b.. Josh 24:32
that I have b all that was............. Ruth 4:9
little ewe lamb, which he had b.... 2Sa 12:3
So David b the threshingfloor of... 2Sa 24:24
he b the full Samaria of Shemer... 1Kin 16:24
this wall, neither b we any land.... Neh 5:16
Thou hast b me no sweet cane with. Is 43:24
I b the field of Hanameel my........ Jer 32:9
And fields shall be b in this land.. Jer 32:43
So I b her to me for fifteen.......... Hos 3:2
and sold all that he had, and b it.. Mt 13:46
b in the temple, and overthrew the. Mt 21:12
b with them the potter's field,..... Mt 27:7
b in the temple, and overthrew the. Mk 11:15
he b fine linen, and took him down. Mk 15:46
had b sweet spices, that they...... Mk 16:1
I have b a piece of ground, and I.. Lk 14:18
I have b five yoke of oxen, and I.. Lk 14:19
they did eat, they drank, they b... Lk 17:28
that sold therein, and them that b. Lk 19:45
in the sepulchre that Abraham b... Acts 7:16
For ye are b with a price............. 1Cor 6:20
Ye are b with a price.................. 1Cor 7:23
even denying the Lord that b them. 2Pet 2:1

BOUND
b Isaac his son, and laid him on.... Gen 22:9
b upon his hand a scarlet thread,.. Gen 38:28
where the king's prisoners were b.. Gen 39:20
the place where Joseph was b...... Gen 40:3
which were b in the prison........... Gen 40:5
be b in the house of your prison... Gen 42:19
and b him before their eyes......... Gen 42:24
life is b up in the lad's life.......... Gen 44:30
utmost b of the everlasting hills... Gen 49:26
their kneadingthroughs being b up. Ex 12:34
ephod, and b it unto him therewith. Lev 8:7
which hath no covering b upon it... Num 19:15
wherewith she hath b her soul...... Num 30:4
she hath b her soul shall stand..... Num 30:4
wherewith she hath b her soul...... Num 30:5

lips, wherewith she b her soul......... Num 30:6
she b her soul shall stand............. Num 30:7
lips, wherewith she b her soul......... Num 30:8
wherewith they have b their souls... Num 30:9
or b her soul by a bond with a....... Num 30:10
she b her soul shall stand............. Num 30:11
she b the scarlet line in the.......... Josh 2:21
bottles, old, and rent, and b up..... Josh 9:4
they b him with two new cords, and. Judg 15:13
mightest be b to afflict thee.......... Judg 16:6
dried, and she b him with them...... Judg 16:8
wherewith thou mightest be b....... Judg 16:10
b him therewith, and said unto him. Judg 16:12
me wherewith thou mightest be b... Judg 16:13
b him with fetters of brass............ Judg 16:21
the soul of my lord shall be b in.... 1Sa 25:29
Thy hands were not b, nor thy...... 2Sa 3:34
b two talents of silver in two........ 2Kin 5:23
shut him up, and b him in prison... 2Kin 17:4
b him with fetters of brass, and.... 2Kin 25:7
b him with fetters, and carried..... 2Chr 33:11
b him in fetters, to carry him....... 2Chr 36:6
And if they be in fetters............... Job 36:8
take it to the b thereof, and that.. Job 38:20
out those which are b with chains.. Ps 68:6
Thou hast set a b that they may... Ps 104:9
being b in affliction and iron........ Ps 107:10
Foolishness is b in the heart of..... Prov 22:15
who hath b the waters in a........... Prov 30:4
not been closed, neither b up........ Is 1:6
they are b by the archers............. Is 22:3
are found in thee are b together.... Is 22:3
of the prison to them that are b.... Is 61:1
the b of the sea by a perpetual.... Jer 5:22
cause, that thou mayest be b up... Jer 30:13
b him with chains, to carry him.... Jer 39:7
when he had taken him being b in.. Jer 40:1
king of Babylon b him in chains.... Jer 52:11
transgressions is b by his hand..... Lam 1:14
b with cords, and made of cedar,.. Eze 27:24
it shall not be b up to be healed.. Eze 30:21
neither have ye b up that which.... Eze 34:4
these men were b in their coats.... Dan 3:21
fell down b into the midst of the... Dan 3:23
Did not we cast three men b into.. Dan 3:24
The wind hath b her up in her...... Hos 4:19
were like them that remove the b.. Hos 5:10
Though I have b and strengthened. Hos 7:15
The iniquity of Ephraim is b up..... Hos 13:12
her great men were b in chains..... Nah 3:10
b him, and put him in prison for... Mt 14:3
on earth shall be b in heaven....... Mt 16:19
and shall be b in heaven.............. Mt 18:18
And when they had b him, they led. Mt 27:2
he had been often b with fetters... Mk 5:4
b him in prison for Herodias'........ Mk 6:17
b Jesus, and carried him away, and. Mk 15:1
which lay b with them that had.... Mk 15:7
and he was kept b with chains..... Lk 8:29
b up his wounds, pouring in oil..... Lk 10:34
of Abraham, whom Satan hath b... Lk 13:16
b hand and foot with graveclothes. Jn 11:44
his face was b about with a......... Jn 11:44
of the Jews took Jesus, and b him,. Jn 18:12
Now Annas had sent him b unto... Jn 18:24
might bring them b unto Jerusalem. Acts 9:2
them b unto the chief priests...... Acts 9:21
two soldiers, b with two chains.... Acts 12:6
I go b in the spirit unto.............. Acts 20:22
b his own hands and feet, and said. Acts 21:11
for I am ready not to be b only.... Acts 21:13
him to be b with two chains........ Acts 21:33
which were there b unto Jerusalem. Acts 22:5
as they b him with thongs, Paul... Acts 22:25
a Roman, and because he had b him. Acts 22:29
b themselves under a great......... Acts 23:12
We have b ourselves under a great. Acts 23:21
there was a pleasure, left Paul b... Acts 24:27
of Israel I am b with this chain.... Acts 28:20
is b by the law to her husband so. Rom 7:2
Art thou b unto a wife................ 1Cor 7:27
The wife is b by the law as long... 1Cor 7:39
We are to thank God always for... 2Th 1:3
But we are b to give thanks alway. 2Th 2:13
but the word of God is not b........ 2Ti 2:9
that are in bonds, as b with them.. Heb 13:3
b in the great river Euphrates..... Rev 9:14
Satan, and b him a thousand years,. Rev 20:2

BOUNDS
thou shalt set b unto the people.... Ex 19:12
Set b about the mount, and.......... Ex 19:23
I will set thy b from the Red sea.. Ex 23:31
that are a people, and hath b....... Deut 32:8
his b that he cannot pass............ Job 14:5
hath compassed the waters with b.. Job 26:10
have removed the b of the people.. Is 10:13
the b of their habitation............. Acts 17:26

BOUNTIFUL
He that hath a b eye shall be...... Prov 22:9
nor the churl said to be.............. Is 32:5

BOUNTIFULLY
because he hath dealt b with me... Ps 13:6
the LORD hath dealt b with thee... Ps 116:7
Deal b with thy servant, that I.... Ps 119:17
for thou shalt deal b with me...... Ps 142:7
soweth b shall reap also b.......... 2Cor 9:6

BOUNTIFULNESS
enriched in every thing to all b 2Cor 9:11

BOUNTY
Solomon gave her of his royal b 1Kin 10:13
you, and make up beforehand your b 2Cor 9:5
might be ready, as a matter of b 2Cor 9:5

BOW
I do set my b in the cloud, and it .... Gen 9:13
that the b shall be seen in the .... Gen 9:14
the b shall be in the cloud .... Gen 9:16
thy weapons, thy quiver and thy b .... Gen 27:3
thee, and nations b down to thee .... Gen 27:29
thy mother's sons b down to thee .... Gen 27:29
thy brethren indeed come to it .... Gen 37:10
they cried before him, B the knee .... Gen 41:43
with my sword and with my b .... Gen 48:22
children shall b down before thee .... Gen 49:8
But his b abode in strength, and .... Gen 49:24
b down themselves unto me, saying .... Ex 11:8
Thou shalt not b down thyself to .... Ex 20:5
Thou shalt not b down to these .... Ex 23:24
in your land, to b down unto it .... Lev 26:1
Thou shalt not b down thyself .... Deut 5:9
nor b yourselves unto them .... Josh 23:7
with thy sword, nor with thy b .... Josh 24:12
them, and to b down unto them .... Judg 2:19
even to his sword, and to his b 1Sa 18:4
of Judah the use of the b 2Sa 1:18
the b of Jonathan turned not back 2Sa 1:22
so that a b of steel is broken by 2Sa 22:35
certain man drew a b at a venture 1Kin 22:34
I b myself in the house of Rimmon 2Kin 5:18
when I b down myself in the house 2Kin 5:18
with thy sword and with thy b 2Kin 6:22
Jehu drew a b with his full 2Kin 9:24
And Elisha said unto him, Take b 2Kin 13:15
And he took unto him b and arrows 2Kin 13:15
Israel, Put thine hand upon the b 2Kin 13:16
nor b yourselves to them, nor 2Kin 17:35
b down thine ear, and hear 2Kin 19:16
and sword, and to shoot with b 1Chr 5:18
and shooting arrows out of a b 1Chr 12:2
and with him armed men with b 2Chr 17:17
certain man drew a b at a venture 2Chr 18:33
the b of steel shall strike him .... Job 20:24
my b was renewed in my hand .... Job 29:20
let others b down upon her .... Job 31:10
They b themselves, they bring .... Job 39:3
he hath bent his b, and made it .... Ps 7:12
For, lo, the wicked bend their b .... Ps 11:2
so that a b of steel is broken by .... Ps 18:34
to the dust shall b before him .... Ps 22:29
B down thine ear to me .... Ps 31:2
the sword, and have bent their b .... Ps 37:14
For I will not trust in my b .... Ps 44:6
he breaketh the b, and cutteth the .... Ps 46:9
bendeth his b to shoot his arrows .... Ps 58:7
the wilderness shall b before him .... Ps 72:9
brake he the arrows of the b .... Ps 76:3
turned aside like a deceitful b .... Ps 78:57
B down thine ear, O LORD, hear me .... Ps 86:1
O come, let us worship and b down .... Ps 95:6
B thy heavens, O LORD, and come .... Ps 144:5
b thine ear to my understanding .... Prov 5:1
The evil b before the good .... Prov 14:19
B down thine ear, and hear the .... Prov 22:17
the strong men shall b themselves .... Eccl 12:3
Without me they shall b down .... Is 10:4
drawn sword, and from the bent b .... Is 21:15
and as driven stubble to his b .... Is 41:2
That unto me every knee shall b .... Is 45:23
They stoop, they b down together .... Is 46:2
they shall b down to thee with .... Is 49:23
B down, that we may go over .... Is 51:23
is it to b down his head as a .... Is 58:5
they that despised thee shall b .... Is 60:14
ye shall all b down to the .... Is 65:12
Pul, and Lud, that draw the b .... Is 66:19
They shall lay hold on b and spear .... Jer 6:23
tongues like their b for lies .... Jer 9:3
that handle and bend the b .... Jer 46:9
I will break the b of Elam .... Jer 49:35
all ye that bend the b, shoot at .... Jer 50:14
all ye that bend the b, camp .... Jer 50:29
They shall hold the b and the .... Jer 50:42
bendeth let the archer bend his b .... Jer 51:3
He hath bent his b like an enemy .... Lam 2:4
He hath bent his b, and set me as .... Lam 3:12
As the appearance of the b that .... Eze 1:28
I will smite thy b out of thy .... Eze 39:3
that I will break the b of Israel .... Hos 1:5
God, and will not save them by b .... Hos 1:7
and I will break the b of Israel .... Hos 2:18
they are like a deceitful b .... Hos 7:16
he stand that handleth the b .... Amos 2:15
b myself before the high God .... Mic 6:6
the perpetual hills did b .... Hab 3:6
Thy b was made quite naked .... Hab 3:9
the battle b shall be cut off .... Zec 9:10
filled the with Ephraim, and .... Zec 9:13
the nail, out of him the battle b .... Zec 10:4
see, and b down their back alway .... Rom 11:10
Lord, every knee shall b to me .... Rom 14:11
For this cause I b my knees unto .... Eph 3:14
name of Jesus every knee should b .... Phil 2:10
and he that sat on him had a b .... Rev 6:2

BOWED
b himself toward the ground, ... Gen 18:2
he b himself with his face toward .... Gen 19:1

b himself to the people of the .... Gen 23:7
Abraham b down himself before the .... Gen 23:12
the man b down his head, and .... Gen 24:26
I b down my head, and worshipped .... Gen 24:48
b himself to the ground seven .... Gen 33:3
children, and they b themselves .... Gen 33:6
came near, and b themselves .... Gen 33:7
and Rachel, and they b themselves .... Gen 33:7
b down themselves before him with .... Gen 42:6
b themselves to him to the earth .... Gen 43:26
they b down their heads, and made .... Gen 43:28
Israel b himself upon the bed's .... Gen 47:31
he b himself with his face to the .... Gen 48:12
b his shoulder to bear, and became .... Gen 49:15
then they b their heads and .... Ex 4:31
And the people b the head and .... Ex 12:27
b his head toward the earth, and .... Ex 34:8
b down his head, and fell flat .... Num 22:31
did eat, and b down to their gods .... Num 25:2
gods, and b yourselves unto them .... Josh 23:16
b themselves unto them, and .... Judg 2:12
gods, and b themselves unto them .... Judg 2:17
At her feet he b, he fell, he lay .... Judg 5:27
at her feet he b, he fell .... Judg 5:27
where he b, there he fell down .... Judg 5:27
b down upon their knees to drink .... Judg 7:6
he b himself with all his might .... Judg 16:30
b herself to the ground, and said .... Ruth 2:10
she b herself and travailed 1Sa 4:19
ground, and b himself three times 1Sa 20:41
face to the earth, and b himself 1Sa 24:8
face, and b herself to the ground, ... 1Sa 25:23
b herself on her face to 1Sa 25:41
face to the ground, and b himself 1Sa 28:14
b himself, and said, What is 2Sa 9:8
b himself, and thanked the king 2Sa 14:22
b himself on his face to the 2Sa 14:33
Cushi b himself unto Joab, and ran 2Sa 18:21
he b the heart of all the men of 2Sa 19:14
He b the heavens also, and came 2Sa 22:10
b himself before the king on his 2Sa 24:20
And Bath-sheba b, and did obeisance 1Kin 1:16
he b himself before the king with 1Kin 1:23
Then Bath-sheba b with her face 1Kin 1:31
the king b himself upon the bed 1Kin 1:47
b himself to king Solomon 1Kin 1:53
b himself unto her, and sat down, ... 1Kin 2:19
knees which have not b unto Baal 1Kin 19:18
b themselves to the ground before 2Kin 2:15
b herself to the ground, and took, ... 2Kin 4:37
b himself to David with his face 1Chr 21:21
b down their heads, and worshipped 2Chr 20:18
they b themselves with their 2Chr 7:3
Jehoshaphat his head with his face 2Chr 20:18
b down himself before them, and 2Chr 25:14
present with him b themselves 2Chr 29:29
they b their heads and worshipped 2Chr 29:30
they b their heads, and worshipped .... Neh 8:6
that were in the king's gate, b .... Est 3:2
But Mordecai b not, nor did him .... Est 3:2
Haman saw that Mordecai b not .... Est 5:9
He b the heavens also, and came .... Ps 18:9
I b down heavily, as one that .... Ps 35:14
I am b down greatly .... Ps 38:6
For our soul is b down to the .... Ps 44:25
my soul is b down .... Ps 57:6
up all those that be b down .... Ps 145:14
LORD raiseth them that are b down .... Ps 146:8
of men shall be b down, and the, ... Is 2:11
loftiness of man shall be b down .... Is 2:17
I was b down at the hearing of it .... Is 21:3
they b the knee before him, and .... Mt 27:29
was b together, and could in no .... Lk 13:11
b down their faces to the earth, ... Lk 24:5
he b his head, and gave up the .... Jn 19:30
who have not b the knee to the .... Rom 11:4

BOWELS
thine own b shall be thine heir .... Gen 15:4
shall be separated from thy b .... Gen 25:23
for his b did yearn upon his .... Gen 43:30
the curse shall go into thy b .... Num 5:22
which shall proceed out of thy b 2Sa 7:12
my son, which came forth of my b 2Sa 16:11
shed out his b to the ground, and 2Sa 20:10
for her b yearned upon her son, ... 1Kin 3:26
sickness by disease of thy b 2Chr 21:15
until thy b fall out by reason of 2Chr 21:15
his b with an incurable disease 2Chr 21:18
his b fell out by reason of his 2Chr 21:19
b slew him there with the sword 2Chr 32:21
Yet his meat in his b is turned .... Job 20:14
My b boiled, and rested not .... Job 30:27
it is melted in the midst of my b .... Ps 22:14
that took me out of my mother's b .... Ps 71:6
let it come into his b like water .... Ps 109:18
door, and my b were moved for him .... Song 5:4
Wherefore my b shall sound like .... Is 16:11
the offspring of thy b like the .... Is 48:19
from the b of my mother hath he .... Is 49:1
strength, the sounding of thy b .... Is 63:15
My b, my b .... Jer 4:19
therefore my b are troubled for .... Jer 31:20
my b are troubled .... Lam 1:20
my b are troubled, my liver is .... Lam 2:11
fill thy b with this roll that I .... Eze 3:3
their souls, neither fill their b .... Eze 7:19
midst, and all his b is gushed out .... Acts 1:18
ye are straitened in your own b 2Cor 6:12
you all in the b of Jesus Christ, ... Phil 1:8
of the Spirit, if any b and .... Phil 2:1

beloved, b of mercies, kindness, ... Col 3:12
because the b of the saints are .... Philem 7
receive him, that is, mine own b .... Philem 12
refresh my b in the Lord .... Philem 20
shutteth up his b of compassion 1Jn 3:17

BOWETH
likewise every one that b down .... Judg 7:5
And the mean man b down, and the .... Is 2:9
Bel b down, Nebo stoopeth, their .... Is 46:1

BOWING
the LORD, himself to the earth .... Gen 24:52
their eyes b down to the earth .... Ps 17:11
as a b wall shall ye be, and as a .... Ps 62:3
b their knees worshipped him .... Mk 15:19

BOWL
one silver b of seventy shekels, ... Num 7:13
one silver b of seventy shekels, ... Num 7:19
one silver b of seventy shekels, ... Num 7:25
one silver b of seventy shekels, ... Num 7:31
one silver b of seventy shekels, ... Num 7:37
a silver b of seventy shekels, ... Num 7:43
one silver b of seventy shekels, ... Num 7:49
one silver b of seventy shekels, ... Num 7:55
one silver b of seventy shekels, ... Num 7:61
one silver b of seventy shekels, ... Num 7:67
one silver b of seventy shekels, ... Num 7:73
one silver b of seventy shekels, ... Num 7:79
and thirty shekels, each b seventy .... Num 7:85
of the fleece, a b full of water .... Judg 6:38
loosed, or the golden b be broken .... Eccl 12:6
with a b upon the top of it, and .... Zec 4:2
one upon the right side of the b .... Zec 4:3

BOWLS
b thereof, to cover withal .... Ex 25:29
his shaft, and his branches, his b .... Ex 25:31
Three b made like unto almonds, ... Ex 25:33
three b made like almonds in the .... Ex 25:33
be four b made like unto almonds .... Ex 25:34
dishes, and his spoons, and his b .... Ex 37:16
his shaft, and his branch, his b .... Ex 37:17
Three b made after the fashion of .... Ex 37:19
three b made like almonds in .... Ex 37:19
were four b made like almonds .... Ex 37:20
dishes, and the spoons, and the b .... Num 4:7
of silver, twelve silver b, ... Num 7:84
the two b of the chapiters that 1Kin 7:41
to cover the two b of the 1Kin 7:41
to cover the two b of the 1Kin 7:42
And the b, and the snuffers, and the 1Kin 7:50
the house of the LORD of silver 2Kin 12:13
And the firepans, and the b 2Kin 25:15
gold for the fleshhooks, and the b 1Chr 28:17
and the snuffers, and the b .... Jer 52:18
basons, and the firepans, and the b, ... Jer 52:19
That drink wine in b, and anoint .... Amos 6:6
and they shall be filled like b .... Zec 9:15
be like the b before the altar .... Zec 14:20

BOWMEN
the noise of the horsemen and b .... Jer 4:29

BOWS
The b of the mighty men are 1Sa 2:4
They were armed with b, and could 1Chr 12:2
that bare shields and drew b 2Chr 14:8
and helmets, and habergeons, and b 2Chr 26:14
swords, their spears, and their b .... Neh 4:13
the spears, the shields, and the b .... Neh 4:16
heart, and their b shall be broken .... Ps 37:15
bend their b to shoot their .... Ps 64:3
being armed, and carrying b .... Ps 78:9
are sharp, and all their b bent .... Is 5:28
with b shall men come thither .... Is 7:24
Their b also shall dash the young .... Is 13:18
every one of their b is broken .... Jer 51:56
shields and the bucklers, the b .... Eze 39:9

BOWSHOT
a good way off, as it were a b .... Gen 21:16

BOX
take this b of oil in thine hand, ... 2Kin 9:1
Then take the b of oil, and pour 2Kin 9:3
the pine, and the b tree together .... Is 41:19
the b together, to beautify the .... Is 60:13
b of very precious ointment .... Mt 26:7
a woman having an alabaster b of .... Mk 14:3
and she brake the b, and poured it .... Mk 14:3
an alabaster b of ointment .... Lk 7:37

BOY
have given a b for an harlot, and .... Joel 3:3

BOYS
And the b grew .... Gen 25:27
of the city shall be full of b .... Zec 8:5

BOZEZ (bo'-zez) A rock near Michmash.
and the name of the one was B 1Sa 14:4

BOZKATH (boz'-kath) A city in Judah.
Lachish, and Eglon, and .... Josh 15:39

BOZRAH (boz'-rah)
1. The capital city of Edom.
Zerah of B reigned in his stead .... Gen 36:33
Zerah of B reigned in his stead 1Chr 1:44
the LORD hath a sacrifice in B .... Is 34:6
Edom, with dyed garments from B .... Is 63:1
that B shall become a desolation, ... Jer 49:13

eagle, and spread his wings over B......Jer 49:22
shall devour the palaces of B......Amos 1:12
them together as the sheep of B......Mic 2:12
  2. A place in Moab.
And upon Kerioth, and upon B......Jer 48:24

BRACELET
the b that was on his arm, and......2Sa 1:10

BRACELETS
two b for her hands of ten......Gen 24:22
b upon his sister's hands, and......Gen 24:30
her face, and the b upon her hands......Gen 24:47
And she said, Thy signet, and thy b......Gen 38:18
whose are these, the signet, and b......Gen 38:25
willing hearted, and brought b......Ex 35:22
of jewels of gold, chains, and b......Num 31:50
The chains, and the b, and the......Is 3:19
I put b upon thy hands, and a......Eze 16:11
which put b upon their hands, and......Eze 23:42

BRAKE
b every tree of the field......Ex 9:25
all the people b off the golden......Ex 32:3
and b them beneath the mount......Ex 32:19
hands, and b them before your eyes......Deut 9:17
b the pitchers that were in their......Judg 7:19
the pitchers, and held the lamps......Judg 7:20
head, and all to b his skull......Judg 9:53
he b the withs, as a thread of......Judg 16:9
b them from off his arms like......Judg 16:12
side of the gate, and his neck b......1Sa 4:18
the three mighty men b through......2Sa 23:16
they b down the image of Baal, and......2Kin 10:27
b down the house of Baal, and made......2Kin 10:27
the house of Baal, and b it down......2Kin 11:18
his images b they in pieces......2Kin 11:18
b down the wall of Jerusalem from......2Kin 14:13
the images, and cut down the......2Kin 18:4
b in pieces the brasen serpent......2Kin 18:4
he b down the houses of the......2Kin 23:7
b down the high places of the......2Kin 23:8
b them down from thence, and cast......2Kin 23:12
he b in pieces the images, and......2Kin 23:14
altar and the high place he b down......2Kin 23:15
b down the walls of Jerusalem......2Kin 25:10
the three b through the host of......1Chr 11:18
b down the images, and cut down......2Chr 14:3
b into it, and carried away all......2Chr 23:17
b it down, and b his altars and......2Chr 23:17
b down the wall of Jerusalem from......2Chr 25:23
b down the wall of Gath, and the......2Chr 26:6
b the images in pieces, and cut......2Chr 31:1
they b down the altars of Baalim......2Chr 34:4
he b in pieces, and made dust of......2Chr 34:4
b down the wall of Jerusalem, and......2Chr 36:19
I b the jaws of the wicked, and......Job 29:17
the six with doors, when it b forth......Job 38:8
b up for it my decreed place, and......Job 38:10
There b he the arrows of the bow,......Ps 76:3
he b the whole staff of bread......Ps 105:16
b the trees of their coasts......Ps 105:33
the plague b in upon them......Ps 106:29
death, and b their bands in sunder......Ps 107:14
which my covenant they b,......Jer 31:32
b down the walls of Jerusalem......Jer 39:8
b down all the walls of Jerusalem......Jer 52:14
of the LORD, the Chaldeans b......Jer 52:17
despised, and whose covenant he b......Eze 17:16
troubled, and his sleep b from him......Dan 2:1
iron and clay, and b them to pieces......Dan 2:34
that it b in pieces the iron, the......Dan 2:45
b all their bones in pieces or......Dan 7:7
b in pieces, and stamped the......Dan 7:7
b in pieces, and stamped the......Dan 7:19
smote the ram, and had b his two horns......Dan 8:7
up to heaven, he blessed, and b......Mt 14:19
b them, and gave to his disciples,......Mt 15:36
b it, and gave it to the disciples......Mt 26:26
loaves, and gave thanks, and b......Mk 8:6
When I b the five loaves among......Mk 8:19
she b the box, and poured it on......Mk 14:3
b it and gave to them, and said,......Mk 14:22
and their net b......Lk 5:6
he the bands, and was driven of......Lk 8:29
to heaven, he blessed them, and b......Lk 9:16
b it, and gave unto them, saying,......Lk 22:19
took bread, and blessed it, and b......Lk 24:30
b the legs of the first, and of......Jn 19:32
dead already, they b not his legs......Jn 19:33
when he had given thanks, he b it......1Cor 11:24

BRAKEST
in the first tables, which thou b......Ex 34:1
in the first tables that thou b......Deut 10:2
thou b the heads of the dragons......Ps 74:13
Thou b the heads of leviathan in......Ps 74:14
they leaned upon thee, thou b......Eze 29:7

BRAMBLE
said all the trees unto the b......Judg 9:14
the b said unto the trees, If in......Judg 9:15
not, let fire come out of the b......Judg 9:15
nor of a b bush gather they......Lk 6:44

BRAMBLES
b in the fortresses thereof......Is 34:13

BRANCH
with a knob and a flower in one b......Ex 25:33
made like almonds in the other b......Ex 25:33

his shaft, and his b, his bowls,......Ex 37:17
the fashion of almonds in one b......Ex 37:19
made like almonds in another b......Ex 37:19
cut down from thence a b with one......Num 13:23
his b shooteth forth in his......Job 8:16
that the tender b thereof will......Job 14:7
time, and his b shall not be green......Job 15:32
and above shall his b be cut off......Job 18:16
the dew lay all night upon my b......Job 29:19
the b that thou madest strong for......Ps 80:15
righteous shall flourish as a b......Prov 11:28
In that day shall the b of the......Is 4:2
off from Israel head and tail, b,......Is 9:14
a B shall grow out of his roots......Is 11:1
of thy grave like an abominable b......Is 14:19
forsaken bough, and an uppermost b......Is 17:9
head or tail, b or rush, may do......Is 19:15
the b of the terrible ones shall......Is 25:5
the b of my planting, the work of......Is 60:21
raise unto David a righteous B......Jer 23:5
that time, will I cause the B of......Jer 33:15
they put the b to their nose......Eze 8:17
or than a b which is among the......Eze 15:2
took the highest b of the cedar......Eze 17:22
the highest b of the high cedar......Eze 17:22
But out of a b of her roots shall......Dan 11:7
will bring forth my servant the B......Zec 3:8
the man whose name is The B......Zec 6:12
leave them neither root nor b......Mal 4:1
When his b is yet tender, and......Mt 24:32
When her b is yet tender, and......Mk 13:28
Every b in me that beareth not......Jn 15:2
every b that beareth fruit, he......Jn 15:2
As the b cannot bear fruit of......Jn 15:4
in me, he is cast forth as a b......Jn 15:6

BRANCHES
And in the vine were three b......Gen 40:10
The three b are three days......Gen 40:12
whose b run over the wall......Gen 49:22
his shaft, and his b, his bowls,......Ex 25:32
six b shall come out of the sides......Ex 25:32
three b of the candlestick out of......Ex 25:32
three b of the candlestick out of......Ex 25:32
so in the six b that come out of......Ex 25:33
be a knop under two b of the same......Ex 25:35
and a knop under two b of the same......Ex 25:35
and a knop under two b of the same......Ex 25:35
according to the six b that......Ex 25:36
their b shall be of the same......Ex 25:36
six b going out of the sides......Ex 37:18
three b of the candlestick out of......Ex 37:18
three b of the candlestick out of......Ex 37:18
so throughout the six b going out......Ex 37:19
And a knop under two b of the same......Ex 37:21
and a knop under two b of the same......Ex 37:21
and a knop under two b of the same......Ex 37:21
to the six b going out of......Ex 37:21
knops and their b were of the same......Ex 37:22
b of palm trees, and the boughs of......Lev 23:40
fetch olive b, and pine b......Neh 8:15
and myrtle b, and palm b......Neh 8:15
b of thick trees, to make booths,......Neh 8:15
the flame shall dry up his b......Job 15:30
the sea, and her b unto the river......Ps 80:11
which sing among the b......Ps 104:12
her b are stretched out, they are......Is 16:8
in the outmost fruitful b thereof......Is 17:6
and take away and cut down the b......Is 18:5
down, and consume the b thereof......Is 27:10
it, and the b of it are broken......Jer 11:16
whose b turned toward him, and the......Eze 17:6
became a vine, and brought forth b......Eze 17:7
and shot forth her b toward him......Eze 17:7
that it might bring forth b......Eze 17:8
in the shadow of the b thereof......Eze 17:23
full of b by reason of many......Eze 19:10
was exalted among the thick b......Eze 19:11
with the multitude of her b......Eze 19:11
is gone out of a rod of her b......Eze 19:14
a cedar in Lebanon with fair b......Eze 31:3
his b became long because of the......Eze 31:5
under his b did all the beasts of......Eze 31:6
greatness, in the length of his b......Eze 31:7
chestnut trees were not like his b......Eze 31:8
fair by the multitude of his b......Eze 31:9
all the valleys his b are fallen......Eze 31:12
of the field shall be upon his b......Eze 31:13
ye shall shoot forth your b......Eze 36:8
down the tree, and cut off his b......Dan 4:14
under it, and the fowls from his b......Dan 4:14
upon whose b the fowls of the......Dan 4:21
cities, and shall consume his b......Hos 11:6
His b shall spread, and his beauty......Hos 14:6
the b thereof are made white......Joel 1:7
them out, and marred their olive b......Nah 2:2
What be these two olive b which......Zec 4:12
come and lodge in the b thereof......Mt 13:32
others cut down b from the trees......Mt 21:8
herbs, and shooteth out great b......Mk 4:32
others cut down b off the trees......Mk 11:8
of the air lodged in the b of it......Lk 13:19
Took b of palm trees, and went......Jn 12:13
I am the vine, ye are the b......Jn 15:5
if the root be holy, so are the b......Rom 11:16
And if some of the b be broken off......Rom 11:17
Boast not against the b......Rom 11:18
The b were broken off, that I......Rom 11:19
if God spared not the natural b......Rom 11:21
these, which be the natural b......Rom 11:24

BRAND
is not this a b plucked out of......Zec 3:2

BRANDISH
when I shall b my sword before......Eze 32:10

BRANDS
And when he had set the b on fire......Judg 15:5

BRASEN
four b rings in the four corners......Ex 27:4
burnt offering, with his b grate......Ex 35:16
he made for the altar a b grate......Ex 38:4
twenty, and their b sockets twenty......Ex 38:10
the b altar, and the b grate......Ex 38:30
The b altar, and his b grate of......Ex 39:39
and if it be sodden in a b pot......Lev 6:28
the priest took the b censers......Num 16:39
great cities with walls and b bars......1Kin 4:13
And every base had four b wheels......1Kin 7:30
because the b altar that was......1Kin 8:64
made in their stead b shields......1Kin 14:27
And he brought also the b altar......2Kin 16:14
the b altar shall be for me to......2Kin 16:15
off the b oxen that were under it......2Kin 16:17
brake in pieces the b serpent......2Kin 18:4
the b sea that was in the house......2Kin 25:13
wherewith Solomon made the b sea......2Chr 4:16
Moreover the b altar, that......2Chr 1:5
to the b altar before the LORD......2Chr 1:6
For Solomon had made a b scaffold......2Chr 6:13
because the b altar which Solomon......2Chr 7:7
b walls against the whole land,......Jer 1:18
unto this people a fenced b wall......Jer 15:20
the b sea that was in the house......Jer 52:17
twelve b bulls that were under......Jer 52:20
in, and stood beside the b altar......Eze 9:2
and pots, b vessels, and of tables......Mk 7:4

BRASS
of every artificer in b and iron......Gen 4:22
gold, and silver, and b,......Ex 25:3
thou shalt make fifty taches of b......Ex 26:11
cast five sockets of b for them......Ex 26:37
and thou shalt overlay it with b......Ex 27:3
thereof thou shalt make of b......Ex 27:3
for it a grate of network of b......Ex 27:4
wood, and overlay them with b......Ex 27:6
twenty sockets shall be of b......Ex 26:25
and their twenty sockets of b......Ex 27:11
of silver, and their sockets of b......Ex 27:17
linen, and their sockets of b......Ex 27:18
pins of the court, shall be of b......Ex 27:19
Thou shalt also make a laver of b......Ex 30:18
and his foot also of b......Ex 30:18
in gold, and in silver, and in b......Ex 31:4
gold, and silver, and b,......Ex 35:5
b brought the LORD's offering......Ex 35:24
in gold, and in silver and in b......Ex 35:32
he made fifty taches of b......Ex 36:18
but their five sockets were of b......Ex 36:38
and he overlaid it with b......Ex 38:2
the vessels thereof made he of b......Ex 38:3
the four ends of the grate of b......Ex 38:5
wood, and overlaid them with b......Ex 38:6
And he made the laver of b......Ex 38:8
and the foot of it of b......Ex 38:8
and their sockets of b twenty......Ex 38:11
sockets for the pillars were of b......Ex 38:17
four, and their sockets of b four......Ex 38:19
the court round about, were of b......Ex 38:20
the b of the offering was seventy......Ex 38:29
brasen altar, and his grate of b......Ex 39:39
as iron, and your earth is b......Lev 26:19
And Moses made a serpent of b......Num 21:9
when he beheld the serpent of b......Num 21:9
the gold, and the silver, the b......Num 31:22
of whose hills thou mayest dig b......Deut 8:9
that is over thy head shall be b......Deut 28:23
Thy shoes shall be iron and b......Deut 33:25
silver, and gold, and vessels of b......Josh 6:19
the gold, and the vessels of b......Josh 6:24
silver, and with gold, and with b......Josh 22:8
and bound him with fetters of b......Judg 16:21
had an helmet of b upon his head......1Sa 17:5
was five thousand shekels of b......1Sa 17:5
he had greaves of b upon his legs......1Sa 17:6
a target of b between his......1Sa 17:6
put an helmet of b upon his head......1Sa 17:38
king David took exceeding much b......2Sa 8:8
vessels of gold, and vessels of b......2Sa 8:10
hundred shekels of b in weight......2Sa 21:16
was a man of Tyre, a worker in b......1Kin 7:14
and cunning to work all works in b......1Kin 7:14
For he cast two pillars of b......1Kin 7:15
he made two chapiters of molten b......1Kin 7:16
And he made ten bases of b......1Kin 7:27
brasen wheels, and plates of b......1Kin 7:30
Then made he ten lavers of b......1Kin 7:38
of the LORD, were of b bright......1Kin 7:45
and bound him with fetters of b......2Kin 25:7
the pillars of b that were in the......2Kin 25:13
carried the b of them to Babylon......2Kin 25:13
all the vessels of b wherewith......2Kin 25:14
the b of all these vessels was......2Kin 25:16
and the chapiter upon it was b......2Kin 25:17
wreathen work, upon the b......2Kin 25:17
to sound with cymbals of b......1Chr 15:19
brought David very much b......1Chr 18:8
the pillars, and the vessels of b......1Chr 18:8
of vessels of gold and silver and b......1Chr 18:10

b in abundance without weight........ 1Chr 22:3
and of b and iron without weight...... 1Chr 22:14
Of the gold, the silver, and the b..... 1Chr 22:16
and the b for things of b................ 1Chr 29:2
of b eighteen thousand talents........ 1Chr 29:7
in gold, and in silver, and in b......... 2Chr 2:7
work in gold, and in silver, in b....... 2Chr 2:14
Moreover he made an altar of b....... 2Chr 4:1
overlaid the doors of them with b.... 2Chr 4:9
the house of the LORD of both......... 2Chr 4:16
for the weight of the b could not..... 2Chr 4:18
king Rehoboam made shields of b.... 2Chr 12:10
b to mend the house of the LORD..... 2Chr 24:12
or is my flesh of b...................... Job 6:12
b is molten out of the stone.......... Job 28:2
bones are as strong pieces of b....... Job 40:18
as straw, and b as rotten wood....... Job 41:27
For he hath broken the gates of b.... Ps 107:16
break in pieces the gates of b......... Is 45:2
is an iron sinew, and thy brow b...... Is 48:4
For b I will bring gold, and for....... Is 60:17
will bring silver, and for wood b..... Is 60:17
they are b and iron..................... Jer 6:28
Also the pillars of b that were....... Jer 52:17
carried all the b of them to........... Jer 52:17
all the vessels of b wherewith........ Jer 52:18
the b of all these vessels was......... Jer 52:20
And a chapiter of b was upon it...... Jer 52:22
chapiters round about, all of b....... Jer 52:22
like the colour of burnished b........ Eze 1:7
all they are b, and tin, and iron,..... Eze 22:18
As they gather silver, and b.......... Eze 22:20
that the b of it may be hot, and..... Eze 24:11
vessels of b in thy market........... Eze 27:13
was like the appearance of b......... Eze 40:3
his belly and his thighs of b.......... Dan 2:32
was the iron, the clay, the b......... Dan 2:35
and another third kingdom of b..... Dan 2:39
brake in pieces the iron, the b...... Dan 2:45
even with a band of iron and b...... Dan 4:15
even with a band of iron and b...... Dan 4:23
gods of gold, and of silver, of b.... Dan 5:4
the gods of silver, and gold, of b... Dan 5:23
were of iron, and his nails of b..... Dan 7:19
feet like in colour to polished b.... Dan 10:6
iron, and I will make thy hoofs b.. Mic 4:13
the mountains were mountains of b. Zec 6:1
nor silver, nor b in your purses,.... Mt 10:9
I am become as sounding b.......... 1Cor 13:1
And his feet like unto the b......... Rev 1:15
fire, and his feet are like fine b.... Rev 2:18
and idols of gold, and silver, and b Rev 9:20
of most precious wood, and of b.... Rev 18:12

BRAVERY
the b of their tinkling ornaments..... Is 3:18

BRAWLER
but patient, not a b, not.............. 1Ti 3:3

BRAWLERS
speak evil of no man, to be no b..... Titus 3:2

BRAWLING
the housetop, than with a b woman.. Prov 21:9
the housetop, than with a b woman.. Prov 25:24

BRAY
Doth the wild ass b when he hath.... Job 6:5
Though thou shouldest b a fool in.... Prov 27:22

BRAYED
Among the bushes they b............. Job 30:7

BREACH
this b be upon thee.................... Gen 38:29
B for b, eye for eye, tooth............ Lev 24:20
and ye shall know my b of promise.. Num 14:34
made a b in the tribes of Israel..... Judg 21:15
before me, as the b of waters........ 2Sa 5:20
the LORD had made a b upon Uzzah.. 2Sa 6:8
wheresoever any b shall be found.... 2Kin 12:5
the LORD had made a b upon Uzza... 1Chr 13:11
the LORD our God made a b upon us. 1Chr 15:13
that there was no b left therein...... Neh 6:1
He breaketh me with b upon b....... Job 16:14
chosen stood before him in the b.... Ps 106:23
therein is a b in the spirit........... Prov 15:4
let us make a b therein for us,....... Is 7:6
be to you as a b ready to fall........ Is 30:13
bindeth up the b of his people...... Is 30:26
be called, The repairer of the b.... Is 58:12
people is broken with a great b..... Jer 14:17
for thy b is great like the sea....... Lam 2:13
into a city wherein is made a b..... Eze 26:10

BREACHES
the sea shore, and abode in his b.... Judg 5:17
repaired the b of the city of......... 1Kin 11:27
repair the b of the house............. 2Kin 12:5
not repaired the b of the house...... 2Kin 12:6
repair ye not the b of the house..... 2Kin 12:7
deliver it for the b of the house..... 2Kin 12:7
to repair the b of the house.......... 2Kin 12:8
the b of the house of the LORD...... 2Kin 12:12
to repair the b of the house......... 2Kin 22:5
that the b began to be stopped,...... Neh 4:7
heal the b thereof.................... Ps 60:2
also the b of the city of David....... Is 22:9
And ye shall go out at the b......... Amos 4:3
will smite the great house with b.... Amos 6:11
fallen, and close up the b thereof.... Amos 9:11

BREAD
of thy face shalt thou eat b.......... Gen 3:19
king of Salem brought forth b....... Gen 14:18
And I will fetch a morsel of b....... Gen 18:5
a feast, and did bake unleavened b.. Gen 19:3
early in the morning, and took b.... Gen 21:14
Then Jacob gave Esau b and pottage. Gen 25:34
gave the savoury meat and the b.... Gen 27:17
I go, and will give me b to eat...... Gen 28:20
and called his brethren to eat b..... Gen 31:54
and they did eat b, and tarried all... Gen 31:54
And they sat down to eat b.......... Gen 37:25
save the b which he did eat.......... Gen 39:6
all the land of Egypt there was b.... Gen 41:54
the people cried to Pharaoh for b... Gen 41:55
that they should eat b there......... Gen 43:25
himself, and said, Set on b.......... Gen 43:31
might not eat b with the Hebrews... Gen 43:32
she asses laden with corn and b..... Gen 45:23
his father's household, with b....... Gen 47:12
there was no b in all the land....... Gen 47:13
unto Joseph, and said, Give us b.... Gen 47:15
Joseph gave them b in exchange..... Gen 47:17
he fed them with b for all their..... Gen 47:17
buy us and our land for b, and we... Gen 47:19
Out of Asher his b shall be fat...... Gen 49:20
call him, that he may eat b.......... Ex 2:20
roast with fire, and unleavened b... Ex 12:8
days shall ye eat unleavened b...... Ex 12:15
b from the first day until the....... Ex 12:15
observe the feast of unleavened b... Ex 12:17
even, ye shall eat unleavened b..... Ex 12:18
shall ye eat unleavened b............ Ex 12:20
shall no leavened b be eaten........ Ex 13:3
days thou shalt eat unleavened b... Ex 13:6
Unleavened b shall be eaten seven.. Ex 13:7
no leavened b be seen with thee.... Ex 13:7
and when we did eat b to the full... Ex 16:3
I will rain b from heaven for you... Ex 16:4
and in the morning b to the full.... Ex 16:8
morning ye shall be filled with b... Ex 16:12
This is the b which the LORD hath... Ex 16:15
day they gathered twice as much b.. Ex 16:22
the sixth day the b of two days..... Ex 16:29
that they may see the b wherewith.. Ex 16:32
to eat b with Moses' father in...... Ex 18:12
keep the feast of unleavened b..... Ex 23:15
shalt eat unleavened b seven days... Ex 23:15
of my sacrifice with leavened b..... Ex 23:18
your God, and he shall bless thy b.. Ex 23:25
And unleavened b, and cakes........ Ex 29:2
one loaf of b, and one cake of oiled Ex 29:23
b that is before the LORD............ Ex 29:23
the b that is in the basket, by...... Ex 29:32
of the consecrations, or of the b.... Ex 29:34
of unleavened b shalt thou keep.... Ex 34:18
days thou shalt eat unleavened b... Ex 34:18
he did neither eat b, nor drink...... Ex 34:28
he set the b in order upon it........ Ex 40:23
with unleavened b shall it be....... Lev 6:16
leavened b with the sacrifice of.... Lev 7:13
rams, and a basket of unleavened b. Lev 8:2
out of the basket of unleavened b... Lev 8:26
cake, and a cake of oiled b, and.... Lev 8:26
there eat it with the b that is....... Lev 8:31
of the b shall ye burn with fire..... Lev 8:32
the b of their God, they do offer.... Lev 21:6
for he offereth the b of thy God.... Lev 21:8
to offer the b of his God............ Lev 21:17
nigh to offer the b of his God....... Lev 21:21
He shall eat the b of his God........ Lev 21:22
hand shall ye offer the b of your... Lev 22:25
of unleavened b unto the LORD...... Lev 23:6
days ye must eat unleavened b...... Lev 23:14
And ye shall eat neither b........... Lev 23:14
ye shall offer with the b a new..... Lev 23:18
b of the first fruits for a wave...... Lev 23:20
it may be on the b for a memorial.. Lev 24:7
ye shall eat your b to the full...... Lev 26:5
I have broken the staff of your b.... Lev 26:26
shall bake your b in one oven....... Lev 26:26
you your b again by weight......... Lev 26:26
the continual b shall be thereon.... Num 4:7
And a basket of unleavened b....... Num 6:15
of unleavened b anointed with oil.. Num 6:15
with the basket of unleavened b.... Num 6:17
it, and eat it with unleavened b.... Num 9:11
for they are b for us................. Num 14:9
when ye eat of the b of the land.... Num 15:19
for there is no b, neither is......... Num 21:5
and our soul loatheth this light b... Num 21:5
my b for my sacrifices made by..... Num 28:2
days shall unleavened b be eaten... Num 28:17
that man doth not live by b only.... Deut 8:3
shalt eat b without scarceness...... Deut 8:9
neither did eat b nor drink water... Deut 9:9
I did neither eat b, nor drink....... Deut 9:18
shalt eat no leavened b with it...... Deut 16:3
thou eat unleavened b therewith.... Deut 16:3
even the b of affliction.............. Deut 16:3
there shall be no leavened b seen... Deut 16:4
days thou shalt eat unleavened b... Deut 16:8
in the feast of unleavened b......... Deut 16:16
Because they met you not with b.... Deut 23:4
Ye have not eaten b, neither have... Deut 29:6
all the b of their provision was..... Josh 9:5
This our b we took hot for our..... Josh 9:12
a cake of barley b tumbled into..... Judg 7:13
loaves of b unto the people that.... Judg 8:5
we should give b unto thine army... Judg 8:6

that we should give b unto thy...... Judg 8:15
me, I will not eat of thy b.......... Judg 13:16
thine heart with a morsel of b..... Judg 19:5
and there is b and wine also for me. Judg 19:19
his people in giving them b......... Ruth 1:6
come thou hither, and eat of the b.. Ruth 2:14
have hired out themselves for b..... 1Sa 2:5
piece of silver and a morsel of b... 1Sa 2:36
that I may eat a piece of b.......... 1Sa 2:36
for the b is spent in our vessels.... 1Sa 9:7
carrying three loaves of b........... 1Sa 10:3
and give thee two loaves of b....... 1Sa 10:4
And Jesse took an ass laden with b.. 1Sa 16:20
me five loaves of b in mine hand.... 1Sa 21:3
is no common b under mine hand.... 1Sa 21:4
but there is hallowed b.............. 1Sa 21:4
the b is in a manner common, yea,.. 1Sa 21:5
So the priest gave him hallowed b... 1Sa 21:6
for there was no b there but the.... 1Sa 21:6
to put not b in the day when it..... 1Sa 21:6
in that thou hast given him b....... 1Sa 22:13
Shall I then take my b, and my..... 1Sa 25:11
for he had eaten no b all the day... 1Sa 28:20
me set a morsel of b before thee.... 1Sa 28:22
and did bake unleavened b thereof.. 1Sa 28:24
him to David, and gave him b....... 1Sa 30:11
for he had eaten no b, nor drunk... 1Sa 30:12
on the sword, or that lacketh b..... 2Sa 3:29
to me, and more also, if I taste b... 2Sa 3:35
as men, to every one a cake of b.... 2Sa 6:19
thou shalt eat b at my table........ 2Sa 9:7
son shall eat b alway at my table... 2Sa 9:10
neither did he eat b with them..... 2Sa 12:17
they set b before him, and he did... 2Sa 12:20
dead, thou didst rise and eat b..... 2Sa 12:21
upon them two hundred loaves of b. 2Sa 16:1
and the b and summer fruit for the. 2Sa 16:2
neither will I eat b nor drink....... 1Kin 13:8
of the LORD, saying, Eat no b....... 1Kin 13:9
him, Come home with me, and eat b 1Kin 13:15
neither will I eat b nor drink....... 1Kin 13:16
Thou shalt eat no b nor drink....... 1Kin 13:17
thine house, that he may eat b..... 1Kin 13:18
did eat b in his house, and drank... 1Kin 13:19
But camest back, and hast eaten b.. 1Kin 13:22
LORD did say to thee, Eat no b..... 1Kin 13:22
to pass, after he had eaten b....... 1Kin 13:23
And the ravens brought him b...... 1Kin 17:6
and flesh in the morning, and b.... 1Kin 17:6
a morsel of b in thine hand........ 1Kin 17:11
in a cave, and fed them with b..... 1Kin 18:4
in a cave, and fed them with b..... 1Kin 18:13
away his face, and would eat no b.. 1Kin 21:4
so sad, that thou eatest no b....... 1Kin 21:5
arise, and eat b, and let thine...... 1Kin 21:7
and feed him with b of affliction... 1Kin 22:27
and she constrained him to eat b... 2Kin 4:8
by, he turned in thither to eat b.... 2Kin 4:8
man of God b of the firstfruits...... 2Kin 4:42
set b and water before them, that.. 2Kin 6:22
land of corn and wine, a land of b.. 2Kin 18:32
unleavened b among their brethren.. 2Kin 23:9
there was no b for the people of.... 2Kin 25:3
he did eat b continually before..... 2Kin 25:29
brought b on asses, and on camels,.. 1Chr 12:40
woman, to every one a loaf of b.... 1Chr 16:3
even in the feast of unleavened b... 2Chr 8:13
and feed him with b of affliction... 2Chr 18:26
unleavened b in the second month... 2Chr 30:13
kept the feast of unleavened b...... 2Chr 30:21
feast of unleavened b seven days.... 2Chr 35:17
unleavened b seven days with joy.... Ezr 6:22
he came thither, he did eat no b.... Ezr 10:6
not eaten the b of the governor..... Neh 5:14
people, and had taken of them b.... Neh 5:15
not the b of the governor........... Neh 5:18
gavest them b from heaven for...... Neh 9:15
not the children of Israel with b.... Neh 13:2
He wandereth abroad for b.......... Job 15:23
hast withholden b from the hungry. Job 22:7
should be satisfied with b........... Job 27:14
for the earth, out of it cometh b.... Job 28:5
So that his life abhorreth b......... Job 33:20
did eat b with him in his house..... Job 42:11
eat up my people as they eat b..... Ps 14:4
forsaken, nor his seed begging b.... Ps 37:25
I trusted, which did eat of my b.... Ps 41:9
eat up my people as they eat b..... Ps 53:4
can he give b also................... Ps 78:20
feedest them with the b of tears,... Ps 80:5
so that I forgot to eat my b......... Ps 102:4
For I have eaten ashes like b....... Ps 102:9
b which strengtheneth man's heart.. Ps 104:15
he brake the whole staff of b....... Ps 105:16
them with the b of heaven.......... Ps 105:40
let them seek their b also out of.... Ps 109:10
up late, to eat the b of sorrows.... Ps 127:2
I will satisfy her poor with b....... Ps 132:15
For they eat the b of wickedness.... Prov 4:17
a man is brought to a piece of b.... Prov 6:26
Come, eat of my b, and drink of.... Prov 9:5
b eaten in secret is pleasant........ Prov 9:17
honoureth himself, and lacketh b... Prov 12:9
land shall be satisfied with b....... Prov 12:11
and thou shalt be satisfied with b.. Prov 20:13
B of deceit is sweet to a man....... Prov 20:17
he giveth of his b to the poor...... Prov 22:9
Eat thou not the b of him that..... Prov 23:6
be hungry, give him b to eat....... Prov 25:21
his land shall have plenty of b..... Prov 28:19

B

for for a piece of *b* that man .... Prov 28:21
and eateth not the *b* of idleness .... Prov 31:27
eat thy *b* with joy, and drink thy........ Eccl 9:7
strong, neither yet *b* to the wise .... Eccl 9:11
Cast thy *b* upon the waters .... Eccl 11:1
and the staff, the whole stay of *b* .... Is 3:1
house is neither *b* nor clothing .... Is 3:7
saying, We will eat our own *b* .... Is 4:1
with liver *b* him that fled .... Is 21:14
B corn is bruised .... Is 28:28
Lord give you the *b* of adversity .... Is 30:20
b of the increase of the earth,.......... Is 30:23
b shall be given him............................ Is 33:16
land of corn and wine, a land of *b* ...... Is 36:17
yea, he kindleth it, and baketh *b* .... Is 44:15
also I have baked *b* upon the .... Is 44:19
pit, nor that his *b* should fail .... Is 51:14
money for that which is not *b* .... Is 55:2
to the sower, and to the eater .... Is 55:10
not to deal thy *b* to the hungry .... Is 58:7
eat up thine harvest, and thy *b*........... Jer 5:17
of *b* out of the bakers' street........... Jer 37:21
until all the *b* in the city were .... Jer 37:21
there is no more *b* in the city .... Jer 38:9
they did eat *b* together in Mizpah .... Jer 41:1
the trumpet, nor have hunger of *b* ...... Jer 42:14
so that there was no *b* for the............ Jer 52:6
he did continually eat *b* before .... Jer 52:33
All her people sigh, they seek *b*......... Lam 1:11
the young children ask *b*, and no .... Lam 4:4
Assyrians, to be satisfied with *b*........ Lam 5:6
We gat our *b* with the peril of .... Lam 5:9
vessel, and make thee *b* thereof .... Eze 4:9
defiled *b* among the Gentiles .... Eze 4:13
shalt prepare thy *b* therewith .... Eze 4:15
break the staff of *b* in Jerusalem .... Eze 4:16
and they shall eat *b* by weight .... Eze 4:16
That they may want *b* and water, and.. Eze 4:17
and will break your staff of *b*............ Eze 5:16
eat thy *b* with quaking, and drink ...... Eze 12:18
eat their *b* with carefulness .... Eze 12:19
of barley and for pieces of *b* .... Eze 13:19
break the staff of the *b* thereof .... Eze 14:13
sister Sodom, pride, fulness of *b* .... Eze 16:49
hath given his *b* to the hungry............ Eze 18:7
hath given his *b* to the hungry............ Eze 18:16
thy lips, and eat not the *b* of men...... Eze 24:17
your lips, nor eat the *b* of men .... Eze 24:22
in it to eat *b* before the LORD........... Eze 44:3
even my house, when ye offer my *b*...... Eze 44:7
unleavened *b* shall be eaten............... Eze 45:21
I ate no pleasant *b*, neither came...... Dan 10:3
my lovers, that give me my *b* .... Hos 2:5
be unto them as the *b* of mourners..... Hos 9:4
for their *b* for their soul shall .... Hos 9:4
want of *b* in all your places.............. Amos 4:6
the land of Judah, and there eat *b* .... Amos 7:12
in the land, not a famine of *b*........... Amos 8:11
they that eat thy *b* have laid a .... Obad 7
and with his skirt do touch *b* .... Hag 2:12
offer polluted *b* upon mine altar .... Mal 1:7
that these stones be made *b* .... Mt 4:3
Man shall not live by *b* alone .... Mt 4:4
Give us this day our daily *b* .... Mt 6:11
of you, whom if his son ask *b* .... Mt 7:9
not their hands when they eat *b*........ Mt 15:2
not meet to take the children's *b*..... Mt 15:26
have so much *b* in the wilderness ...... Mt 15:33
they had forgotten to take *b*............. Mt 16:5
It is because we have taken no *b* .... Mt 16:7
because ye have brought no *b*............ Mt 16:8
spake it not to you concerning *b*....... Mt 16:11
not beware of the leaven of *b*........... Mt 16:12
b the disciples came to Jesus say....... Mt 26:17
as they were eating, Jesus took *b*..... Mt 26:26
they could not so much eat *b*............. Mk 3:20
no scrip, no *b*, no money in their .... Mk 6:8
the villages, and buy themselves *b*.... Mk 6:36
buy two hundred pennyworth of *b*...... Mk 6:37
his disciples eat *b* with defiled........ Mk 7:2
but eat *b* with unwashen hands........... Mk 7:5
not meet to take the children's *b*..... Mk 7:27
men with *b* here in the wilderness ..... Mk 8:4
disciples had forgotten to take *b* ..... Mk 8:14
It is because we have no *b*................ Mk 8:16
reason ye, because ye have no *b*......... Mk 8:17
the passover, and of unleavened *b* ..... Mk 14:1
And the first day of unleavened *b* ..... Mk 14:12
And as they did eat, Jesus took *b* ..... Mk 14:22
this stone that it be made *b* .... Lk 4:3
man shall not live by *b* alone .... Lk 4:4
eating *b* nor drinking wine .... Lk 7:33
staves, nor scrip, neither *b*............. Lk 9:3
Give us day by day our daily *b*.......... Lk 11:3
If a son shall ask *b* of any of .... Lk 11:11
to eat *b* on the sabbath day .... Lk 14:1
shall eat *b* in the kingdom of God .... Lk 14:15
of my father's have *b* enough .... Lk 15:17
feast of unleavened *b* drew nigh .... Lk 22:1
Then came the day of unleavened *b* ... Lk 22:7
And he took it, and gave thanks, and.. Lk 22:19
sat at meat with them, he took *b*...... Lk 24:30
known of them in breaking of *b* .... Lk 24:35
Philip, Whence shall we buy *b* .... Jn 6:5
Two hundred pennyworth of *b* is......... Jn 6:7
the place where they did eat *b* .... Jn 6:23
He gave them *b* from heaven to eat .... Jn 6:31
gave you *b* but *b* from heaven .... Jn 6:32
giveth you the true *b* from heaven .... Jn 6:32
For the *b* of God is he which............. Jn 6:33

Lord, evermore give us this *b*............ Jn 6:34
unto them, I am the *b* of life .... Jn 6:35
I am the *b* which came down from .... Jn 6:41
I am that *b* of life.......................... Jn 6:48
This is the *b* which cometh down .... Jn 6:50
I am the living *b* which came down .... Jn 6:51
if any man eat of this *b*, he............. Jn 6:51
the *b* that I will give is my.............. Jn 6:51
This is that *b* which came down......... Jn 6:58
of this *b* shall live for ever............. Jn 6:58
He that eateth *b* with me hath.......... Jn 13:18
there, and fish laid thereon, and *b*.... Jn 21:9
Jesus then cometh, and taketh *b*....... Jn 21:13
fellowship, and in breaking of *b*....... Acts 2:42
breaking *b* from house to house,........ Acts 2:46
were the days of unleavened *b*........... Acts 12:3
after the days of unleavened *b*.......... Acts 20:6
came together to break *b*, Paul......... Acts 20:7
come up again, and had broken *b*........ Acts 20:11
he had thus spoken, he took *b*........... Acts 27:35
The unleavened *b* of sincerity 1Cor 5:8
The *b* which we break, is it not 1Cor 10:16
For we being many are one *b* 1Cor 10:17
are all partakers of that one *b*......... 1Cor 10:17
in which he was betrayed took *b* 1Cor 11:23
For as often as ye eat this *b*........... 1Cor 11:26
whosoever shall eat this *b*,.............. 1Cor 11:27
and so let him eat of that *b*............. 1Cor 11:28
both minister *b* for your food........... 2Cor 9:10
did we eat any man's *b* for nought...... 2Th 3:8
they work, and eat their own *b*.......... 2Th 3:12

BREADTH

the *b* of it fifty cubits, and the .... Gen 6:15
length of it and in the *b* of it .... Gen 13:17
a cubit and a half the *b* thereof........ Ex 25:10
a cubit and a half the *b* thereof........ Ex 25:17
thereof, and a cubit the *b* thereof .... Ex 25:23
a border of an hand *b* round about ..... Ex 25:25
the *b* of one curtain four cubits .... Ex 26:2
the *b* of one curtain four cubits .... Ex 26:8
half shall the *b* of one board........... Ex 27:12
the *b* of the court on the .... Ex 27:12
the *b* of the court on the east .... Ex 27:13
the *b* fifty every where, and the....... Ex 27:18
and a span shall be the *b* thereof...... Ex 28:16
thereof, and a cubit the *b* thereof .... Ex 30:2
the *b* of one curtain four cubits .... Ex 36:9
cubits was the *b* of one curtain....... Ex 36:15
the *b* of a board one cubit and a .... Ex 36:21
and a cubit and a half the *b* of it ..... Ex 37:1
one cubit and a half the *b* thereof .... Ex 37:6
thereof, and a cubit the *b* thereof .... Ex 37:10
a cubit, and the *b* of it a cubit......... Ex 37:25
and five cubits the *b* thereof .... Ex 38:1
height in the *b* was five cubits........ Ex 38:18
thereof, and a span the *b* thereof ..... Ex 39:9
and four cubits the *b* of it .... Deut 3:11
could sling stones at an hair *b*......... Judg 20:16
the *b* thereof twenty cubits, and...... 1Kin 6:2
according to the *b* of the house........ 1Kin 6:3
ten cubits was the *b* thereof 1Kin 6:6
in length, and twenty cubits in *b* 1Kin 6:20
the *b* thereof fifty cubits, and......... 1Kin 7:2
the *b* thereof thirty cubits,............. 1Kin 7:6
And it was an hand *b* thick............... 1Kin 7:26
and four cubits the *b* thereof 1Kin 7:27
cubits, and the *b* twenty cubits 2Chr 3:3
according to the *b* of the house........ 2Chr 3:4
according to the *b* of the house........ 2Chr 3:8
the *b* thereof twenty 2Chr 3:8
and twenty cubits the *b* thereof 2Chr 4:1
the *b* thereof threescore cubits .... Ezr 6:3
the *b* of the waters is straitened ..... Job 37:10
thou perceived the *b* of the earth...... Job 38:18
shall fill the *b* of thy land............. Is 8:8
long by the cubit and an hand *b*........ Eze 40:5
he measured the *b* of the building ..... Eze 40:5
he measured the *b* of the entry of ..... Eze 40:11
the *b* was five and twenty cubits,...... Eze 40:13
Then he measured the *b* from the........ Eze 40:20
length thereof, and the *b* thereof ..... Eze 40:21
the *b* five and twenty cubits............. Eze 40:21
the *b* five and twenty cubits............. Eze 40:25
the *b* five and twenty cubits............. Eze 40:36
the *b* of the gate was three............. Eze 40:48
cubits, and the *b* eleven cubits .... Eze 40:49
which was the *b* of the tabernacle..... Eze 41:1
the *b* of the door was ten cubits,...... Eze 41:2
and the *b*, twenty cubits................. Eze 41:4
the *b* of the door, seven cubits........ Eze 41:3
and the *b*, twenty cubits................. Eze 41:4
the *b* of every side chamber, four ..... Eze 41:5
therefore the *b* of the house was...... Eze 41:7
the *b* of the place that was left....... Eze 41:11
Also the *b* of the face of the .... Eze 41:14
door, and the *b* was fifty cubits .... Eze 42:2
was a walk of ten cubits *b* inward ..... Eze 42:4
The cubit is a cubit and an hand *b* .... Eze 43:13
the *b* a cubit, and the border.......... Eze 43:13
be two cubits, and the one cubit........ Eze 43:14
four cubits, and the *b* one cubit .... Eze 43:14
the *b* shall be ten thousand .... Eze 45:1
in length, with five hundred in *b* ..... Eze 45:2
and the *b* of ten thousand............... Eze 45:3
length, and the *b* ten thousand in *b*. Eze 45:5
and twenty thousand reeds in *b* .... Eze 45:6
length, and of ten thousand in *b* ...... Eze 48:9
toward the west ten thousand in *b*..... Eze 48:10
toward the east ten thousand in *b*..... Eze 48:13
in length, and ten thousand in *b*....... Eze 48:13

thousand, and the *b* ten thousand ...... Eze 48:13
that are left in the *b* over............... Eze 48:15
and the *b* thereof six cubits .... Dan 3:1
march through the *b* of the land........ Hab 1:6
to see what is the *b* thereof .... Zec 2:2
and the *b* thereof ten cubits .... Zec 5:2
with all saints what is the *b*,.......... Eph 3:18
went up on the *b* of the earth .... Rev 20:9
the length is as large as the *b*......... Rev 21:16
The length and the *b* and the height.. Rev 21:16

BREAK

Lot, and came near to *b* the door....... Gen 19:9
that thou shalt *b* thy yoke from........ Gen 27:40
neither shall ye *b* a bone thereof...... Ex 12:46
it, then thou shalt *b* his neck......... Ex 13:13
lest they *b* through unto the LORD .... Ex 19:21
lest the LORD *b* forth upon them .... Ex 19:22
the people *b* through to come up........ Ex 19:24
lest he *b* forth upon them .... Ex 19:24
If fire *b* out, and catch in thorns..... Ex 22:6
quite *b* down their images .... Ex 23:24
B off the golden earrings, which .... Ex 32:2
hath any gold, let them *b* it off....... Ex 32:24
b their images, and cut down their .... Ex 34:13
not, then shalt thou *b* his neck........ Ex 34:20
and ye shall *b* it .... Lev 11:33
if a leprosy *b* out abroad in the....... Lev 13:12
b out in the house, after that he ..... Lev 14:43
he shall *b* down the house, the.......... Lev 14:45
but that ye *b* my covenant............... Lev 26:15
I will *b* the pride of your power .... Lev 26:19
to *b* my covenant with them .... Lev 26:44
the morning, nor *b* any bone of it ...... Num 9:12
shall *b* their bones, and pierce......... Num 24:8
he shall not *b* his word, he shall ...... Num 30:2
b down their images, and cut down ..... Deut 7:5
b their pillars, and burn their......... Deut 12:3
b my covenant which I have made .... Deut 31:16
and provoke me, and *b* my covenant ..... Deut 31:20
I will never *b* my covenant with........ Judg 2:1
peace, I will *b* down this tower .... Judg 8:9
many servants now a days that *b*........ 1Sa 25:10
they came to Hebron at *b* of day 2Sa 2:32
b thy league with Baasha king of....... 1Kin 15:19
to *b* through even unto the king......... 2Kin 3:26
did the Chaldees *b* in pieces 2Kin 25:13
b thy league with Baasha king of....... 2Chr 16:3
Should we again *b* thy .... Ezr 9:14
he shall even *b* down their stone....... Neh 4:3
Wilt thou *b* a leaf driven to and .... Job 13:25
b me in pieces with words............... Job 19:2
He shall *b* in pieces mighty men........ Job 34:24
or that the wild beast may *b* them ..... Job 39:15
Let us *b* their bands asunder, and...... Ps 2:3
Thou shalt *b* them with a rod of......... Ps 2:9
B thou the arm of the wicked and ...... Ps 10:15
B their teeth, O God, in their .... Ps 58:6
b out the great teeth of the........... Ps 58:6
shall *b* in pieces the oppressor......... Ps 72:4
But now they *b* down the carved......... Ps 89:31
If they *b* my statutes, and keep........ Ps 89:34
My covenant will I not *b*, nor........... Ps 89:34
They *b* in pieces thy people, O......... Ps 94:5
oil, which shall not *b* my head .... Ps 141:5
a time to *b* down, and a time to......... Eccl 3:3
Until the day *b*, and the shadows....... Song 2:17
Until the day *b*, and the shadows....... Song 4:6
b down the wall thereof, and it .... Is 5:5
they *b* forth into singing............... Is 14:7
That I will *b* the Assyrian in my....... Is 14:25
the clods of his ground .... Is 28:24
nor *b* it with the wheel of his......... Is 28:28
he shall *b* as the breaking of......... Is 30:14
the wilderness shall waters *b* out..... Is 35:6
so will he *b* all my bones............... Is 38:13
A bruised reed shall he not *b*........... Is 42:3
b forth into singing, ye .... Is 44:23
I will *b* in pieces the gates of......... Is 45:2
b forth into singing, O mountains...... Is 49:13
B forth into joy, sing together,....... Is 52:9
b forth into singing, and cry .... Is 54:1
For thou shalt *b* forth on the.......... Is 54:3
the hills shall *b* forth before .... Is 55:12
go free, and that ye *b* every yoke...... Is 58:6
thy light *b* forth as the morning...... Is 58:8
b forth upon all the inhabitants ...... Jer 1:14
B up your fallow ground, and sow....... Jer 4:3
b not thy covenant with us.............. Jer 14:21
Shall iron *b* the northern iron and .... Jer 15:12
Then shalt thou *b* the bottle in .... Jer 19:10
Even so will I *b* this people............ Jer 19:11
for I will *b* the yoke of the king...... Jer 28:4
Even so will I *b* the yoke of .... Jer 28:11
that I will *b* his yoke from off .... Jer 30:8
to *b* down, and to throw down, and..... Jer 31:28
If ye can *b* my covenant of the......... Jer 33:20
He shall *b* also the images of.......... Jer 43:13
which I have built will I *b* down....... Jer 45:4
his vessels, and *b* their bottles....... Jer 48:12
I will *b* the bow of Elam, the.......... Jer 49:35
for with thee will I *b* in pieces ...... Jer 51:20
with thee will I *b* in pieces........... Jer 51:20
the also will I *b* in pieces head ...... Jer 51:21
with thee will I *b* in pieces........... Jer 51:21
with thee will I *b* in pieces........... Jer 51:22
I will also *b* in pieces with thee ..... Jer 51:23
with thee will I *b* in pieces........... Jer 51:23
with thee will I *b* in pieces........... Jer 51:23
I will *b* the staff of bread in .... Eze 4:16

will *b* your staff of bread .... Eze 5:16
So will I *b* down the wall that ye...... Eze 13:14
will *b* the staff of the bread .... Eze 14:13
thee, as women that *b* wedlock .... Eze 16:38
shall *b* down thy high places............ Eze 16:39
or shall he *b* the covenant, and be.... Eze 17:15
thou shalt *b* the sherds thereof,........ Eze 23:34
of Tyrus, and *b* down her towers........ Eze 26:4
axes he shall *b* thy towers .... Eze 26:9
they shall *b* down thy walls, and........ Eze 26:12
of thee by thy hand, thou didst *b*...... Eze 29:7
when I shall *b* there the yokes of...... Eze 30:18
will *b* his arms, the strong, and .... Eze 30:22
but I will *b* Pharaoh's arms, and ...... Eze 30:24
shall it *b* in pieces and bruise .... Dan 2:40
people, but it shall *b* in pieces.......... Dan 2:44
b off thy sins by righteousness.......... Dan 4:27
tread it down, and *b* it in pieces........ Dan 7:23
that I will *b* the bow of Israel .... Hos 1:5
I will *b* the bow and the sword and.... Hos 2:18
committing adultery, they *b* out .... Hos 4:2
he shall *b* down their altars, he .... Hos 10:2
plow, and Jacob shall *b* his clods...... Hos 10:11
b up your fallow ground .... Hos 10:12
and they shall not *b* their ranks........ Joel 2:7
I will *b* also the bar of Damascus...... Amos 1:5
lest he *b* out like fire in the .... Amos 5:6
they *b* their bones, and chop them .... Mic 3:3
For now will I *b* his yoke from .... Nah 1:13
that I might *b* my covenant which .... Zec 11:10
that I might *b* the brotherhood .... Zec 11:14
Whosoever therefore shall *b* one ...... Mt 5:19
and where thieves *b* through .... Mt 6:19
do not *b* through nor steal .... Mt 6:20
else the bottles *b*, and the wine .... Mt 9:17
A bruised reed shall he not *b*,.......... Mt 12:20
came together to *b* bread, Paul .... Acts 20:7
a long while, even till *b* of day........ Acts 20:11
ye to weep and to *b* mine heart........ Acts 21:13
The bread which we *b*, is it not 1Cor 10:16
b forth and cry, thou that .... Gal 4:27

BREAKER

The *b* is come up before them .... Mic 2:13
but if thou be a *b* of the law .... Rom 2:25

BREAKEST

Thou *b* the ships of Tarshish with...... Ps 48:7

BREAKETH

he said, Let me go, for the day *b*...... Gen 32:26
For he *b* me with a tempest, and........ Job 9:17
he *b* down, and it cannot be built .... Job 12:14
He *b* me with breach upon breach,.... Job 16:14
The flood *b* out from the .... Job 28:4
voice of the LORD *b* the cedars .... Ps 29:5
the LORD *b* the cedars of Lebanon .... Ps 29:5
he *b* the bow, and cutteth the .... Ps 46:9
My soul *b* for the longing that it...... Ps 119:20
and a soft tongue *b* the bone .... Prov 25:15
whoso is an hedge, a serpent shall .... Eccl 10:8
is crushed *b* out into a viper .... Is 59:5
as one *b* a potter's vessel, that .... Jer 19:11
hammer that *b* the rock in pieces...... Jer 23:29
bread, and no man *b* it unto them...... Lam 4:4
forasmuch as iron *b* in pieces............ Dan 2:40
and as iron that *b* all these .... Dan 2:40

BREAKING

with him until the *b* of the day........ Gen 32:24
shall be a boil *b* forth with .... Ex 9:9
it became a boil *b* forth with............ Ex 9:10
If a thief be found *b* up, and be........ Ex 22:2
hand like the *b* forth of waters........ 1Chr 14:11
upon me as a wide *b* in of waters.... Job 30:14
that there be no *b* in, nor going........ Ps 144:14
b down the walls, and of crying to.... Is 22:5
whose is cometh suddenly at an .... Is 30:13
he shall break it as the *b* of the........ Is 30:14
the oath in *b* the covenant .... Eze 16:59
the oath by *b* the covenant................ Eze 17:18
of man, with the *b* of thy loins .... Eze 21:6
place of the *b* forth of children........ Hos 13:13
was known of them in *b* of bread .... Lk 24:35
in *b* of bread, and in prayers.............. Acts 2:42
b bread from house to house, did .... Acts 2:46
through *b* the law dishonourest.......... Rom 2:23

BREAKINGS

by reason of *b* they purify................ Job 41:25

BREAST

thou shalt take the *b* of the ram ...... Ex 29:26
the *b* of the wave offering .... Ex 29:27
made by fire, the *b* with the.............. Lev 7:30
that the *b* may be waved for a .... Lev 7:30
but the *b* shall be Aaron's and his.... Lev 7:31
For the wave *b* and the heave .... Lev 7:34
And Moses took the *b*, and waved it.... Lev 8:29
And the wave *b* and heave shoulder ... Lev 10:14
the wave *b* shall they bring with...... Lev 10:15
for the priest, with the wave *b*........ Num 6:20
shall be thine, as the wave *b*............ Num 18:18
pluck the fatherless from the *b*........ Job 24:9
and shalt suck the *b* of kings .... Is 60:16
the sea monsters draw out the *b*...... Lam 4:3
head was of fine gold, his *b*.............. Dan 2:32
unto heaven, but smote upon his *b*.... Lk 18:13
lying on Jesus' *b* saith unto him ...... Jn 13:25
also leaned on his *b* at supper .... Jn 21:20

BREASTPLATE

be set in the ephod, and in the *b*.... Ex 25:7
a *b*, and an ephod, and a robe, and a .. Ex 28:4
thou shalt make the *b* of judgment.... Ex 28:15
thou shalt make upon the *b* chains.... Ex 28:22
make upon the *b* two rings of gold .... Ex 28:23
rings on the two ends of the *b*.......... Ex 28:23
which are on the ends of the *b*.......... Ex 28:24
of the *b* in the border thereof .... Ex 28:26
they shall bind the *b* by the.............. Ex 28:28
that the *b* be not loosed from the .... Ex 28:28
the *b* of judgment upon his heart .... Ex 28:29
put in the *b* of judgment the Urim.... Ex 28:30
the ephod, and the ephod, and the *b*.. Ex 29:5
set for the ephod, and for the *b*........ Ex 35:9
set, for the ephod, and for the *b*...... Ex 35:27
he made the *b* of cunning work,........ Ex 39:8
they made the *b* double .... Ex 39:9
upon the *b* chains at the ends.......... Ex 39:15
rings in the two ends of the *b*.......... Ex 39:16
two rings on the ends of the *b*.......... Ex 39:17
put them on the two ends of the *b*.... Ex 39:19
they did bind the *b* by his rings........ Ex 39:21
that the *b* might not be loosed.......... Ex 39:21
And he put the *b* upon him .... Lev 8:8
also he put in the *b* the Urim .... Lev 8:8
he put on righteousness as a *b*.......... Is 59:17
having on the *b* of righteousness ...... Eph 6:14
sober, putting on the *b* of faith 1Th 5:8

BREASTPLATES

And they had *b*.................................... Rev 9:9
as it were *b* of iron .... Rev 9:9
having *b* of fire, and of jacinth,........ Rev 9:17

BREASTS

lieth under, blessings of the *b* .... Gen 49:25
And they that the fat upon the *b*...... Lev 9:20
And the *b* and the right shoulder ...... Lev 9:21
or why the *b* that I should suck........ Job 3:12
His *b* are full of milk, and his.......... Job 21:24
when I was upon my mother's *b*........ Ps 22:9
let her *b* satisfy thee at all .... Prov 5:19
shall lie all night betwixt my *b*........ Song 1:13
Thy two *b* are like two young roes .... Song 4:5
Thy two *b* are like two young roes .... Song 7:3
thy *b* to clusters of grapes................ Song 7:7
now also thy *b* shall be as................ Song 7:8
that sucked the *b* of my mother........ Song 8:1
a little sister, and she hath no *b*...... Song 8:8
I am a wall, and my *b* like towers.... Song 8:10
the milk, and drawn from the *b*........ Is 28:9
with the *b* of her consolations.......... Is 66:11
thy *b* are fashioned, and thine.......... Eze 16:7
there were their *b* pressed .... Eze 23:3
bruised the *b* of her virginity .... Eze 23:8
thereof, and pluck off thine own *b*.... Eze 23:34
her adulteries from between her *b*.... Hos 2:2
them a miscarrying womb and dry *b*.. Hos 9:14
and those that suck the *b*.................. Joel 2:16
of doves, tabering upon their *b*........ Nah 2:7
which were done, smote their *b*........ Lk 23:48
having their *b* girded with golden .... Rev 15:6

BREATH

into his nostrils the *b* of life............ Gen 2:7
flesh, wherein is the *b* of life............ Gen 6:17
flesh, wherein is the *b* of life............ Gen 7:15
whose nostrils was the *b* of life........ Gen 7:22
blast of the *b* of his nostrils............ 2Sa 22:16
that there was no *b* left in him........ 1Kin 17:17
by the *b* of his nostrils are they...... Job 4:9
will not suffer me to take my *b*........ Job 9:18
thing, and the *b* of all mankind........ Job 12:10
by the *b* of his mouth shall he go .... Job 15:30
My *b* is corrupt, my days are.......... Job 17:1
My *b* is strange to my wife,.............. Job 19:17
All the while my *b* is in me.............. Job 27:3
the *b* of the Almighty hath given...... Job 33:4
unto himself his spirit and his *b*...... Job 34:14
By the *b* of God frost is given.......... Job 37:10
His *b* kindleth coals, and a flame...... Job 41:21
blast of the *b* of thy nostrils .... Ps 18:15
of them by the *b* of his mouth .... Ps 33:6
thou takest away their *b*, they.......... Ps 104:29
is there any *b* in their mouths.......... Ps 135:17
His *b* goeth forth, he returneth........ Ps 146:4
thing that hath *b* praise the LORD .... Ps 150:6
yea, they have all one *b*.................... Eccl 3:19
whose *b* is in his nostrils.................. Is 2:22
with the *b* of his lips shall he.......... Is 11:4
And his *b*, as an overflowing .... Is 30:28
the *b* of the LORD, like a stream ...... Is 30:33
your *b*, as fire, shall devour you ...... Is 33:11
he that giveth *b* unto the people ...... Is 42:5
and there is no *b* in them................ Jer 10:14
and there is no *b* in them................ Jer 51:17
The *b* of our nostrils, the................ Lam 4:20
I will cause *b* to enter into you,........ Eze 37:5
put *b* in you, and ye shall live.......... Eze 37:6
but there was no *b* in them .... Eze 37:8
Come from the four winds, O *b*........ Eze 37:9
the *b* came into them, and they........ Eze 37:10
and the God in whose hand thy *b* is.... Dan 5:23
me, neither is there *b* left in me...... Dan 10:17
there is no *b* at all in the midst ...... Hab 2:19
he giveth to all life, and *b*................ Acts 17:25

BREATHE

there was not any left to *b*................ Josh 11:11
them, neither left they any to *b*........ Josh 11:14
me, and such as *b* out cruelty .... Ps 27:12

b upon these slain, that they may ...... Eze 37:9

BREATHED

b into his nostrils the breath of ...... Gen 2:7
but utterly destroyed all that *b* .... Josh 10:40
left not to Jeroboam any that *b*........ 1Kin 15:29
he, and saith unto them,...................... Jn 20:22

BREATHETH

shalt save alive nothing that *b* .... Deut 20:16

BREATHING

hide not thine ear at my *b*................ Lam 3:56
yet *b* out threatenings and.................. Acts 9:1

BRED

morning, and it *b* worms, and stank .. Ex 16:20

BREECHES

linen *b* to cover their nakedness ...... Ex 28:42
linen *b* of fine twined linen,.............. Ex 39:28
his linen *b* shall he put upon his ...... Lev 6:10
have the linen *b* upon his flesh.......... Lev 16:4
have linen *b* upon their loins............ Eze 44:18

BREED

that they may *b* abundantly in the .... Gen 8:17
lambs, and rams of the *b* of Bashan .. Deut 32:14

BREEDING

even the *b* of nettles, and.................. Zeph 2:9

BRETHEN

There were therefore seven *b* .... Lk 20:29

BRETHREN

father, and told his two *b* without .... Gen 9:22
servants shall he be unto his *b*.......... Gen 9:25
for we be *b* .... Gen 13:8
in the presence of all his *b*................ Gen 16:12
And said, I pray you, *b*, do not so .... Gen 19:7
me to the house of my master's *b*...... Gen 24:27
died in the presence of all his *b*........ Gen 25:18
be lord over thy *b*, and let thy.......... Gen 27:29
all his *b* have I given to him for ...... Gen 27:37
And Jacob said unto them, My *b*........ Gen 29:4
And he took his *b* with him,.............. Gen 31:23
Laban with his *b* pitched in the .... Gen 31:25
before our *b* discern thou what is .... Gen 31:32
here before my *b* and thy *b* .... Gen 31:37
And Jacob said unto his *b*, Gather .... Gen 31:46
called his *b* to eat bread .... Gen 31:54
unto her father and unto her *b*.......... Gen 34:11
Jacob, Simeon and Levi, Dinah's *b* .... Gen 34:25
was feeding the flock with his *b*........ Gen 37:2
when his *b* saw that their father ...... Gen 37:4
loved him more than all his *b* .... Gen 37:4
a dream, and he told it his *b* .... Gen 37:5
his *b* said to him, Shalt thou .... Gen 37:8
another dream, and told it his *b*........ Gen 37:9
it to his father, and to his *b*............ Gen 37:10
thy *b* indeed come to bow down .... Gen 37:10
And his *b* envied him .... Gen 37:11
his *b* went to feed their father's...... Gen 37:12
Do not thy *b* feed the flock in .... Gen 37:13
see whether it be well with thy *b*...... Gen 37:14
And he said, I seek my *b* .... Gen 37:16
And Joseph went after his *b* .... Gen 37:17
when Joseph was come unto his *b*...... Gen 37:23
And Judah said unto his *b*, What...... Gen 37:26
And his *b* were content...................... Gen 37:27
And he returned unto his *b* .... Gen 37:30
that Judah went down from his *b*...... Gen 38:1
he die also, as his *b* did .... Gen 38:11
Joseph's ten *b* went down to buy...... Gen 42:3
Jacob sent not with his *b* .... Gen 42:4
Joseph's *b* came, and bowed .... Gen 42:6
And Joseph saw his *b*, and he knew .. Gen 42:7
And Joseph knew his *b*, but they ...... Gen 42:8
said, Thy servants are twelve *b* .... Gen 42:13
let one of your *b* be bound in the .... Gen 42:19
And he said unto his *b*, My money .... Gen 42:28
We be twelve *b*, sons of our .... Gen 42:32
leave one of your *b* here with me .... Gen 42:33
his *b* came to Joseph's house .... Gen 44:14
and let the lad go up with his *b*........ Gen 44:33
made himself known unto his *b*........ Gen 45:1
And Joseph said unto his *b* .... Gen 45:3
his *b* could not answer him.............. Gen 45:3
And Joseph said unto his *b*................ Gen 45:4
Moreover he kissed all his *b* .... Gen 45:15
after that his *b* talked with him........ Gen 45:15
saying, Joseph's *b* are come.............. Gen 45:16
said unto Joseph, Say unto thy *b*...... Gen 45:17
So he sent his *b* away, and they ...... Gen 45:24
And Joseph said unto his *b*................ Gen 46:31
Pharaoh, and say unto him, My *b*...... Gen 46:31
and said, My father and my *b*............ Gen 47:1
And he took some of his *b*, even ...... Gen 47:2
And Pharaoh said unto his *b* .... Gen 47:3
and thy *b* are come unto thee .... Gen 47:5
make thy father and *b* to dwell .... Gen 47:6
Joseph placed his father and his *b*.... Gen 47:11
nourished his father, and his *b* .... Gen 47:12
of their *b* in their inheritance .... Gen 48:6
to thee one portion above thy *b*........ Gen 48:22
Simeon and Levi are *b* .... Gen 49:5
art he whom thy *b* shall praise .... Gen 49:8
him that was separate from his *b*...... Gen 49:26
all the house of Joseph, and his *b* .... Gen 50:8
returned into Egypt, he, and his *b*.... Gen 50:14
when Joseph's *b* saw that their .... Gen 50:15
the now, the trespass of thy *b* .... Gen 50:17
his *b* also went and fell down............ Gen 50:18

And Joseph said unto his b	Gen 50:24
And Joseph died, and all his b	Ex 1:6
that he went out unto his b	Ex 2:11
smiting an Hebrew, one of his b	Ex 2:11
return unto my b which are in	Ex 4:18
carry your b from before the	Lev 10:4
but let your b, the whole house	Lev 10:6
is the high priest among his b	Lev 21:10
but over your b the children of	Lev 25:46
one of his b may redeem him	Lev 25:48
their b in the tabernacle of the	Num 8:26
all thy b the sons of Levi with	Num 16:10
thy b also of the tribe of Levi,	Num 18:2
I have taken your b the Levites	Num 18:6
when our b died before the LORD	Num 20:3
brought unto his b a Midianitish	Num 25:6
among the b of our father	Num 27:4
among their father's b	Num 27:7
give his inheritance unto his b	Num 27:9
And if he have no b, then ye shall	Num 27:10
inheritance unto his father's b	Num 27:10
And if his father have no b	Num 27:11
of Reuben, Shall your b go to war	Num 32:6
Hear the causes between your b	Deut 1:16
our b have discouraged our heart,	Deut 1:28
of your b the children of Esau	Deut 2:4
from our b the children of Esau	Deut 2:8
your b the children of Israel	Deut 3:18
Lord have given rest unto your b	Deut 3:20
part nor inheritance with his b	Deut 10:9
you a poor man of one of thy b	Deut 15:7
one from among thy b shalt thou	Deut 17:15
be not lifted up above his b	Deut 17:20
have no inheritance among their b	Deut 18:2
as all his b the Levites do,	Deut 18:7
from the midst of thee, of thy b	Deut 18:15
up a Prophet from among their b	Deut 18:18
his b of the children of Israel	Deut 24:7
and needy, whether he be of thy b	Deut 24:14
If b dwell together, and one of	Deut 25:5
neither did he acknowledge his b	Deut 33:9
him that was separated from his b	Deut 33:16
let him be acceptable to his b	Deut 33:24
ye shall pass before your b armed	Josh 1:14
the Lord have given your b rest	Josh 1:15
my father, and my mother, and my b	Josh 2:13
father, and thy mother, and thy b	Josh 2:18
father, and her mother, and her b	Josh 6:23
Nevertheless my b that went up	Josh 14:8
us an inheritance among our b	Josh 17:4
among the b of their father	Josh 17:4
Ye have not left your b these	Josh 22:3
God hath given rest unto your b	Josh 22:4
b on this side Jordan westward	Josh 22:7
spoil of your enemies with your b	Josh 22:8
And he said, They were my b	Judg 8:19
to Shechem unto his mother's b	Judg 9:1
his mother's b spake of him in	Judg 9:3
slew his b the sons of Jerubbaal,	Judg 9:5
aided him in the killing of his b	Judg 9:24
the son of Ebed came with his b	Judg 9:26
Ebed and his b be come to Shechem	Judg 9:31
and Zebul thrust out Gaal and his b	Judg 9:41
father, in slaying his seventy b	Judg 9:56
Then Jephthah fled from his b	Judg 11:3
among the daughters of thy b	Judg 14:3
Then his b and all the house of	Judg 16:31
they came unto their b to Zorah	Judg 18:8
their b said unto them, What say	Judg 18:8
of Laish, and said unto their b	Judg 18:14
and said unto them, My b, my	Judg 18:23
of their b the children of Israel	Judg 20:13
their b come unto us to complain	Judg 21:22
be not cut off from among his b	Ruth 4:10
him in the midst of his b	1Sa 16:13
Take now for thy b an ephah of	1Sa 17:17
and run to the camp to thy b	1Sa 17:17
thousand, and look how thy b fare	1Sa 17:18
army, and came and saluted his b	1Sa 17:22
away, I pray thee, and see my b	1Sa 20:29
and when his b and all his father's	1Sa 22:1
David, Ye shall not do so, my b	1Sa 30:23
return from following their b	2Sa 2:26
of Saul thy father, to his b	2Sa 3:8
return thou, and take back thy b	2Sa 15:20
Ye are my b, ye are my bones and	2Sa 19:12
Why have our b the men of Judah	2Sa 19:41
called all his b the king's sons,	1Kin 1:9
your b the children of Israel	1Kin 12:24
him arise up from among his b	2Kin 9:2
Jehu met with the b of Ahaziah	2Kin 10:13
answered, We are the b of Ahaziah	2Kin 10:13
unleavened bread among their b	2Kin 23:9
was more honourable than his b	1Chr 4:9
but his b had not many children,	1Chr 4:27
For Judah prevailed above his b	1Chr 5:2
his b by their families, when the	1Chr 5:7
their b of the house of their	1Chr 5:13
their b the sons of Merari stood	1Chr 6:44
Their b also the Levites were	1Chr 6:48
their b among all the families of	1Chr 7:5
his b came to comfort him	1Chr 7:22
dwelt with their b in Jerusalem	1Chr 8:32
Jeuel, and their b, six hundred and	1Chr 9:6
And their b, according to their	1Chr 9:9
And their b, heads of the house of	1Chr 9:13
and Talmon, and Ahiman, and their b	1Chr 9:17
the son of Korah, and his b	1Chr 9:19
And their b, which were in their	1Chr 9:25
And other of their b, of the sons	1Chr 9:32
dwelt with their b at Jerusalem	1Chr 9:38
over against their b	1Chr 9:38
bow, even of Saul's b of Benjamin	1Chr 12:2
all their b were at their	1Chr 12:32
for their b had prepared for them	1Chr 12:39
abroad unto our b every where	1Chr 13:2
his b an hundred and twenty	1Chr 15:5
his b two hundred and twenty	1Chr 15:6
his b an hundred and thirty	1Chr 15:7
the chief, and his b two hundred	1Chr 15:8
the chief, and his b fourscore	1Chr 15:9
his b an hundred and twelve	1Chr 15:10
yourselves, both ye and your b	1Chr 15:12
their b to be the singers with	1Chr 15:16
and of his b, Asaph the son of	1Chr 15:17
and of the sons of Merari their b	1Chr 15:17
with them their b of the second	1Chr 15:18
into the hand of Asaph and his b	1Chr 16:7
of the Lord Asaph and his b	1Chr 16:37
And Obed-edom with their b	1Chr 16:38
his b the priests, before the	1Chr 16:39
their b the sons of Kish took	1Chr 23:22
of the sons of Aaron their b	1Chr 23:32
their b the sons of Aaron in the	1Chr 24:31
over against their younger b	1Chr 24:31
with their b that were instructed	1Chr 25:7
to Gedaliah, who with his b	1Chr 25:9
to Zaccur, he, his sons, and his b	1Chr 25:10
to Izri, he, his sons, and his b	1Chr 25:11
Nethaniah, he, his sons, and his b	1Chr 25:12
Bukkiah, he, his sons, and his b	1Chr 25:13
he, his sons, and his b, were	1Chr 25:14
Jeshaiah, he, his sons, and his b	1Chr 25:15
Mattaniah, he, his sons, and his b	1Chr 25:16
to Shimei, he, his sons, and his b	1Chr 25:17
Azareel, he, his sons, and his b	1Chr 25:18
Hashabiah, he, his sons, and his b	1Chr 25:19
Shubael, he, his sons, and his b	1Chr 25:20
he, his sons, and his b, were	1Chr 25:21
Jeremoth, he, his sons, and his b	1Chr 25:22
Hananiah, he, his sons, and his b	1Chr 25:23
he, his sons, and his b, were	1Chr 25:24
to Hanani, he, his sons, and his b	1Chr 25:25
Mallothi, he, his sons, and his b	1Chr 25:26
Eliathah, he, his sons, and his b	1Chr 25:27
to Hothir, he, his sons, and his b	1Chr 25:28
Giddalti, he, his sons, and his b	1Chr 25:29
Mahazioth, he, his sons, and his b	1Chr 25:30
he, his sons, and his b, were	1Chr 25:31
whose b were strong men, Elihu,	1Chr 26:7
they and their sons and their b	1Chr 26:8
And Meshelemiah had sons and b	1Chr 26:9
sons and b of Hosah were thirteen	1Chr 26:11
And his b by Eliezer	1Chr 26:25
his b were over all the treasures	1Chr 26:26
hand of Shelomith, and of his b	1Chr 26:28
Hebronites, Hashabiah and his b	1Chr 26:30
And his b, men of valour, were two	1Chr 26:32
Elihu, one of the b of David	1Chr 27:18
his feet, and said, Hear me, my b	1Chr 28:2
with their sons and their b	2Chr 5:12
go up, nor fight against your b	2Chr 11:4
chief, to be ruler among his b	2Chr 11:22
shall come to you of your b that	2Chr 19:10
come upon you, and upon your b	2Chr 19:10
he had b the sons of Jehoshaphat,	2Chr 21:2
slew all his b with the sword, and	2Chr 21:4
also had slain thy b of the	2Chr 21:13
and the sons of the b of Ahaziah	2Chr 22:8
of their b two hundred thousand	2Chr 28:8
ye have taken captive of your b	2Chr 28:11
city of palm trees, to their b	2Chr 28:15
And they gathered their b, and	2Chr 29:15
wherefore their b the Levites did	2Chr 29:34
like your fathers, and like your b	2Chr 30:7
turn again unto the LORD, your b	2Chr 30:9
to give to their b by courses	2Chr 31:15
the fathers of your b the people	2Chr 35:5
yourselves, and prepare your b	2Chr 35:6
and Shemaiah and Nethaneel, his b	2Chr 35:9
for their b the Levites prepared	2Chr 35:15
his b the priests, and Zerubbabel	Ezr 3:2
the son of Shealtiel, and his b	Ezr 3:2
remnant of their b the priests	Ezr 3:8
Jeshua with his sons and his b	Ezr 3:9
their sons and their b the Levites	Ezr 3:9
for their b the priests, and for	Ezr 6:20
seem good to thee, and to thy b	Ezr 7:18
to his b the Nethinims, and to	Ezr 8:17
Sherebiah, with his sons and his b	Ezr 8:18
of the sons of Merari, his b	Ezr 8:19
and ten of their b with them	Ezr 8:24
the son of Jozadak, and his b	Ezr 10:18
That Hanani, one of my b, came,	Neh 1:2
rose up with his b the priests	Neh 3:1
After him repaired their b	Neh 3:18
And he spake before his b and the	Neh 4:2
and terrible, and fight for your b	Neh 4:14
So neither I, nor my b, nor my	Neh 5:14
wives against their b the Jews	Neh 5:1
flesh is as the flesh of our b	Neh 5:5
have redeemed our b the Jews	Neh 5:8
and will ye even sell your b	Neh 5:8
I likewise, and my b, and my	Neh 5:10
my b have not eaten the bread of	Neh 5:14
And their b, Shebaniah, Hodijah,	Neh 10:10
They clave to their b, their	Neh 10:29
their b that did the work of the	Neh 11:12
And his b, chief of the fathers,	Neh 11:13
And their b, mighty men of valour,	Neh 11:14
Bakbukiah the second among his b	Neh 11:17
their b that kept the gates, were	Neh 11:19
of their b in the days of Jeshua	Neh 12:8
the thanksgiving, he and his b	Neh 12:8
Also Bakbukiah and Unni, their b	Neh 12:9
with their b over against them,	Neh 12:24
And his b, Shemaiah, and Azareel,	Neh 12:36
was to distribute unto their b	Neh 13:13
of the multitude of his b	Est 10:3
My b have dealt deceitfully as a	Job 6:15
He hath put my b far from me	Job 19:13
came there unto him all his b	Job 42:11
them inheritance among their b	Job 42:15
I will declare thy name unto my b	Ps 22:22
I am become a stranger unto my b	Ps 69:8
For my b and companions' sakes, I	Ps 133:1
how pleasant it is for b to dwell	Ps 133:1
and he that soweth discord among b	Prov 6:19
of the inheritance among the b	Prov 17:2
All the b of the poor do hate him,	Prov 19:7
Your b that hated you, that cast	Is 66:5
they shall bring all your b for	Is 66:20
as I have cast out all your b	Jer 7:15
For even thy b, and the house of	Jer 12:6
of your b that are not gone forth	Jer 29:16
the son of Habaziniah, and his b	Jer 35:3
and slew them not among their b	Jer 41:8
his seed is spoiled, and his b	Jer 49:10
of man, thy b, even thy b	Eze 11:15
Say ye unto your b, Ammi	Hos 2:1
Though he be fruitful among his b	Hos 13:15
then the remnant of his b shall	Mic 5:3
and Jacob begat Judas and his b	Mt 1:2
Josias begat Jechonias and his b	Mt 1:11
by the sea of Galilee, saw two b	Mt 4:18
from thence, he saw other two b	Mt 4:21
And if ye salute your b only	Mt 5:47
his b stood without, desiring to	Mt 12:46
thy b stand without, desiring to	Mt 12:47
and who are my b	Mt 12:48
and said, Behold my mother and my b	Mt 12:49
and his b, James, and Joses, and	Mt 13:55
that hath forsaken houses, or b	Mt 19:29
indignation against the two b	Mt 20:24
Now there were with us seven b	Mt 22:25
and all ye are b	Mt 23:8
one of the least of these my b	Mt 25:40
go tell my b that they go into	Mt 28:10
There came then his b and his	Mk 3:31
thy b without seek for thee	Mk 3:32
saying, Who is my mother, or my b	Mk 3:33
and said, Behold my mother and my b	Mk 3:34
no man that hath left house, or b	Mk 10:29
now in this time, houses, and b	Mk 10:30
Now there were seven b	Mk 12:20
came to him his mother and his b	Lk 8:19
thy b stand without, desiring to	Lk 8:20
my b are these which hear the	Lk 8:21
call not thy friends, nor thy b	Lk 14:12
and wife, and children, and b	Lk 14:26
For I have five b	Lk 16:28
hath left house, or parents, or b	Lk 18:29
be betrayed both by parents, and b	Lk 21:16
art converted, strengthen thy b	Lk 22:32
he, and his mother, and his b	Jn 2:12
His b therefore said unto him,	Jn 7:3
neither did his b believe in him	Jn 7:5
But when his b were gone up,	Jn 7:10
but go to my b, and say unto them,	Jn 20:17
this saying abroad among the b	Jn 21:23
mother of Jesus, and with his b	Acts 1:14
Men and b, this scripture must	Acts 1:16
Men and b, let me freely speak	Acts 2:29
rest of the apostles, Men and b	Acts 2:37
And now, b, I wot that through	Acts 3:17
God raise up unto you of your b	Acts 3:22
Wherefore, b, look ye out among	Acts 6:3
And he said, Men, b, and fathers,	Acts 7:2
Joseph was made known to his b	Acts 7:13
his b the children of Israel	Acts 7:23
For he supposed his b would have	Acts 7:25
one again, saying, Sirs, ye are b	Acts 7:26
God raise up unto you of your b	Acts 7:37
Which when the b knew, they	Acts 9:30
certain b from Joppa accompanied	Acts 10:23
b that were in Judaea heard that	Acts 11:1
these six b accompanied me	Acts 11:12
unto the b which dwelt in Judaea	Acts 11:29
things unto James, and to the b	Acts 12:17
unto them, saying, Ye men and b	Acts 13:15
Men and b, children of the stock	Acts 13:26
you therefore, men and b	Acts 13:38
minds evil affected against the b	Acts 14:2
down from Judaea taught the b	Acts 15:1
caused great joy unto all the b	Acts 15:3
up, and said unto them, Men and b	Acts 15:7
James answered, saying, Men and b	Acts 15:13
and Silas, chief men among the b	Acts 15:22
b send greeting unto the b	Acts 15:23
exhorted the b with many words,	Acts 15:32
from the b unto the apostles	Acts 15:33
visit our b in every city where	Acts 15:36
by the b unto the grace of God	Acts 15:40
of by the b that were at Lystra	Acts 16:40
and when they had seen the b	Acts 16:40
certain b sent away Paul	Acts 17:6
the b immediately sent away Paul	Acts 17:10
then immediately the b sent away	Acts 17:14
and then took his leave of the b	Acts 18:18
the b wrote, exhorting the	Acts 18:27

And now, b, I commend you to God, Acts 20:32
to Ptolemais, and saluted the b. Acts 21:7
the b received us gladly Acts 21:17
Men, b, and fathers, hear ye my Acts 22:1
I received letters unto the b. Acts 22:5
the council, said, Men and b Acts 23:1
Then said Paul, I wist not, b Acts 23:5
out in the council, Men and b Acts 23:6
Where we found b, and were desired Acts 28:14
when the b heard of us, they came Acts 28:15
he said unto them, Men and b Acts 28:17
neither any of the b that came Acts 28:21
I would not have you ignorant, b Rom 1:13
Know ye not, b, (for I speak to Rom 7:1
Wherefore, my b, ye also are Rom 7:4
Therefore, b, we are debtors, not Rom 8:12
be the firstborn among many b Rom 8:29
accursed from Christ for my b Rom 9:3
B, my heart's desire and prayer to Rom 10:1
For I would not, b, that ye Rom 11:25
I beseech you therefore, b Rom 12:1
also am persuaded of you, my b Rom 15:14
Nevertheless, b, I have written Rom 15:15
Now I beseech you, b, for the Rom 15:30
the b which are with them Rom 16:14
Now I beseech you, b, mark them Rom 16:17
Now I beseech you, b, by the name 1Cor 1:10
declared unto me of you, my b 1Cor 1:11
For ye see your calling, b 1Cor 1:26
And I, b, when I came to you, came 1Cor 2:1
And I, b, could not speak unto you 1Cor 3:1
And these things, b, I have in a 1Cor 4:6
be able to judge between his b 1Cor 6:5
wrong, and defraud, and that your b 1Cor 6:8
B, let every man, wherein he is 1Cor 7:24
But this I say, b, the time is 1Cor 7:29
But when ye sin so against the b 1Cor 8:12
as the b of the Lord, and Cephas 1Cor 9:5
Moreover, b, I would not that ye 1Cor 10:1
Now I praise you, b, that ye 1Cor 11:2
Wherefore, my b, when ye come 1Cor 11:33
Now concerning spiritual gifts, b 1Cor 12:1
Now, b, if I come unto you 1Cor 14:6
B, be not children in 1Cor 14:20
How is it then, b 1Cor 14:26
Wherefore, b, covet to prophesy 1Cor 14:39
Moreover, b, I declare unto you 1Cor 15:1
of above five hundred b at once 1Cor 15:6
Now this I say, b, that flesh and 1Cor 15:50
Therefore, my beloved b, be ye 1Cor 15:58
for I look for him with the b 1Cor 16:11
him to come unto you with the b 1Cor 16:12
I beseech you, b, (ye know the 1Cor 16:15
All the b greet you 1Cor 16:20
For we would not, b, have you 2Cor 1:8
Moreover, b, we do you to wit of 2Cor 8:1
or our b be enquired of, they are 2Cor 8:23
Yet have I sent the b, lest our 2Cor 9:3
it necessary to exhort the b 2Cor 9:5
the b which came from Macedonia 2Cor 11:9
the sea, in perils among false b 2Cor 11:26
Finally, b, farewell 2Cor 13:11
all the b which are with me, unto Gal 1:2
But I certify you, b, that the Gal 1:11
of false b unawares brought in Gal 2:4
I speak after the manner of Gal 3:15
B, I beseech you, be as I am Gal 4:12
Now we, b, as Isaac was, are the Gal 4:28
So then, b, we are not children Gal 4:31
And I, b, if I yet preach Gal 5:11
For, b, ye have been called unto Gal 5:13
B, if a man be overtaken in a Gal 6:1
B, the grace of our Lord Jesus Gal 6:18
Finally, my b, be strong in the Eph 6:10
Peace be to the b, and love with Eph 6:23
I would ye should understand, b Phil 1:12
And many of the b in the Lord Phil 1:14
Finally, my b, rejoice in the Phil 3:1
B, I count not myself to have Phil 3:13
B, be followers together of me Phil 3:17
my b dearly beloved and longed for Phil 4:1
Finally, b, whatsoever things are Phil 4:8
The b which are with me greet you Phil 4:21
faithful b in Christ which are at Col 1:2
Salute the b which are in Col 4:15
b beloved, your election of God 1Th 1:4
For yourselves, b, know our 1Th 2:1
For ye remember, b, our labour and 1Th 2:9
For ye, b, became followers of 1Th 2:14
But we, b, being taken from you 1Th 2:17
Therefore, b, we were comforted 1Th 3:7
then we beseech you, b, and exhort 1Th 4:1
the b which are in all Macedonia 1Th 4:10
but we beseech you, b, that ye 1Th 4:10
not have you to be ignorant, b 1Th 4:13
of the times and the seasons, b 1Th 5:1
But ye, b, are not in darkness 1Th 5:4
And we beseech you, b, to know 1Th 5:12
Now we exhort you, b, warn them 1Th 5:14
B, pray for us 1Th 5:25
Greet all the b with an holy kiss 1Th 5:26
be read unto all the holy b 1Th 5:27
to thank God always for you, b 2Th 1:3
Now we beseech you, b, by the 2Th 2:1
b beloved of the Lord, because 2Th 2:13
Therefore, b, stand fast, and hold 2Th 2:15
Finally, b, pray for us, that the 2Th 3:1
Now we command you, b, in the 2Th 3:6
But ye, b, be not weary in well 2Th 3:13
If thou put the b in remembrance 1Ti 4:6

and the younger men as b 1Ti 5:1
despise them, because they are b 1Ti 6:2
Linus, and Claudia, and all the b 2Ti 4:21
he is not ashamed to call them b Heb 2:11
I will declare thy name unto my b Heb 2:12
him to be made like unto his b Heb 2:17
Wherefore, holy b, partakers of Heb 3:1
Take heed, b, lest there be in Heb 3:12
to the law, that is, of their b Heb 7:5
Having therefore, b, boldness to Heb 10:19
And I beseech you, b, suffer the Heb 13:22
My b, count it all joy when ye Jas 1:2
Do not err, my beloved b Jas 1:16
Wherefore, my beloved b, let Jas 1:19
My b, have not the faith of our Jas 2:1
Hearken, my beloved b, Hath not Jas 2:5
What doth it profit, my b Jas 2:14
My b, be not many masters Jas 3:1
My b, these things ought not so Jas 3:10
Can the fig tree, my b Jas 3:12
Speak not evil one of another, b Jas 4:11
Be patient therefore, b, unto the Jas 5:7
Grudge not one against another, b Jas 5:9
Take, my b, the prophets, who Jas 5:10
But above all things, my b Jas 5:12
B, if any of you do err from the Jas 5:19
unto unfeigned love of the b 1Pet 1:22
one of another, love as b 1Pet 3:8
in your b that are in the world 1Pet 5:9
Wherefore the rather, b, give 2Pet 1:10
B, I write no new commandment 1Jn 2:7
Marvel not, my b, if the world 1Jn 3:13
unto life, because we love the b 1Jn 3:14
to lay down our lives for the b 1Jn 3:16
rejoiced greatly, when the b came 3Jn 3
whatsoever thou doest to the b 3Jn 5
doth he himself receive the b 3Jn 10
fellowservants also and their b Rev 6:11
the accuser of our b is cast down Rev 12:10
of thy b that have the testimony Rev 19:10
of thy b the prophets, and of Rev 22:9

BRETHREN'S
lest his b heart faint as well as Deut 20:8

BRIBE
b to blind mine eyes therewith 1Sa 12:3
afflict the just, they take a b Amos 5:12

BRIBERY
consume the tabernacles of b Job 15:34

BRIBES
aside after lucre, and took b 1Sa 8:3
and their right hand is full of b Ps 26:10
his hands from holding of b Is 33:15

BRICK
to another, Go to, let us make b Gen 11:3
they had b for stone, and slime Gen 11:3
hard bondage, in morter, and in b Ex 1:14
give the people straw to make b Ex 5:7
task in making b both yesterday Ex 5:14
and they say to us, Make b Ex 5:16
burneth incense upon altars of b Is 65:3

BRICKKILN
and made them pass through the b 2Sa 12:31
and hide them in the clay in the b Jer 43:9
the morter, make strong the b Nah 3:14

BRICKS
And the tale of the b, which they Ex 5:8
shall ye deliver the tale of b Ex 5:18
from your b of your daily task Ex 5:19
The b are fallen down, but we Is 9:10

BRIDE
bind them on thee, as a b doeth Is 49:18
as a b adorneth herself with her Is 61:10
bridegroom rejoiceth over the b Is 62:5
her ornaments, or a b her attire Jer 2:32
bridegroom, and the voice of the b Jer 7:34
bridegroom, and the voice of the b Jer 16:9
bridegroom, and the voice of the b Jer 25:10
bridegroom, and the voice of the b Jer 33:11
and the b out of her closet Joel 2:16
He that hath the b is the Jn 3:29
of the b shall be heard no more Rev 18:23
prepared as a b adorned for her Rev 21:2
hither, I will shew thee the b Rev 21:9
And the Spirit and the b say Rev 22:17

BRIDECHAMBER
Can the children of the b mourn Matt 9:15
Can the children of the b fast Mk 2:19
make the children of the b fast Lk 5:34

BRIDEGROOM
Which is as a b coming out of his Ps 19:5
as a b decketh himself with Is 61:10
as the b rejoiceth over the bride Is 62:5
of gladness, the voice of the b Jer 7:34
of gladness, the voice of the b Jer 16:9
of gladness, the voice of the b Jer 25:10
of gladness, the voice of the b Jer 33:11
let the b go forth of his chamber Joel 2:16
as long as the b is with them Matt 9:15
when the b shall be taken from Matt 9:15
and went forth to meet the b Matt 25:1
While the b tarried, they all Matt 25:5
a cry made, Behold, the b cometh Matt 25:6
they went to buy, the b came Matt 25:10
fast, while the b is with them Mk 2:19
long as they have the b with them Mk 2:19

when the b shall be taken away Mk 2:20
fast, while the b is with them Lk 5:34
when the b shall be taken away Lk 5:35
of the feast called the b Jn 2:9
He that hath the bride is the b Jn 3:29
but the friend of the b, which Jn 3:29
and the voice of the b and of the Rev 18:23

BRIDEGROOM'S
greatly because of the b voice Jn 3:29

BRIDLE
my b in thy lips, and I will turn 2Kin 19:28
also let loose the b before me Job 30:11
can come to him with his double b Job 41:13
must be held in with bit and b Ps 32:9
I will keep my mouth with a b Ps 39:1
a b for the ass, and a rod for the Prov 26:3
there shall be a b in the jaws of Is 30:28
my b in thy lips, and I will turn Is 37:29
able also to b the whole body Jas 3:2

BRIDLES
winepress, even unto the horse b Rev 14:20

BRIDLETH
b not his tongue, but deceiveth Jas 1:26

BRIEFLY
it is b comprehended in this Rom 13:9
as I suppose, I have written b 1Pet 5:12

BRIER
instead of the b shall come up Is 55:13
b unto the house of Israel Eze 28:24
The best of them is as a b Mic 7:4

BRIERS
of the wilderness and with b Judg 8:7
and thorns of the wilderness and b Judg 8:16
but there shall come up b Is 5:6
it shall even be for b and thorns Is 7:23
all the land shall become b Is 7:24
not come thither the fear of b Is 7:25
it shall devour the b and thorns Is 9:18
his thorns and his b in one day Is 10:17
who would set the b and thorns Is 27:4
people shall come up thorns and b Is 32:13
afraid of their words, though b Eze 2:6
b is rejected, and is nigh unto Heb 6:8

BRIGANDINE
that lifteth himself up in his b Jer 51:3

BRIGANDINES
the spears, and put on the b Jer 46:4

BRIGHT
or b spot, and it be in the skin Lev 13:2
If the b spot be white in the Lev 13:4
be a white rising, or a b spot Lev 13:19
But if the b spot stay in his Lev 13:23
that burneth have a white b spot Lev 13:24
if the hair in the b spot be Lev 13:25
be no white hair in the b spot Lev 13:26
if the b spot stay in his place Lev 13:28
b spots, even white b spots Lev 13:38
if the b spots in the skin of Lev 13:39
and for a scab, and for a b spot Lev 14:56
of the Loan, were of b brass 1Kin 7:45
the house of the Loan of b brass 2Chr 4:16
he scattereth his b cloud Job 37:11
now men see not the b light which Job 37:21
his belly is as b ivory overlaid Song 5:14
Make b the arrows Jer 51:11
and the fire was b, and out of the Eze 1:13
it is made b, it is wrapped up Eze 21:15
he made his arrows b, he Eze 21:21
b iron, cassia, and calamus, were Eze 27:19
All the b lights of heaven will I Eze 32:8
lifteth up both the b sword Nah 3:3
so the Loan shall make b clouds Zec 10:1
a b cloud overshadowed them Matt 17:5
as when the b shining of a candle Lk 11:36
man stood before me in b clothing Acts 10:30
the offspring of David, and the b Rev 22:16

BRIGHTNESS
Through the b before him were 2Sa 22:13
shined, or the moon walking in b Job 31:26
At the b that was before him his Ps 18:12
for b, but we walk in darkness Is 59:9
kings to the b of thy rising Is 60:3
neither for b shall the moon give Is 60:19
thereof go forth as b, and the Is 62:1
a b was about it, and out of the Eze 1:4
of fire, and it had b round about Eze 1:27
appearance of the b round about Eze 1:28
upward, as the appearance of b Eze 8:2
full of the b of the Loan's glory Eze 10:4
and they shall defile thy b Eze 28:7
thy wisdom by reason of thy b Eze 28:17
whose b was excellent, stood Dan 2:31
mine honour and b returned unto me Dan 4:36
shine as the b of the firmament Dan 12:3
even very dark, and no b in it Amos 5:20
And his b was as the light Hab 3:4
above the b of the sun, shining Acts 26:13
destroy with the b of his coming 2Th 2:8
Who being the b of his glory Heb 1:3

BRIM
were dipped in the b of the water Josh 3:15
from the one b to the other 1Kin 7:23
under the b of it round about 1Kin 7:24
the b thereof was wrought like 1Kin 7:26

BRIMSTONE (continued)

was wrought like the *b* of a cup..........1Kin 7:26
sea of ten cubits from *b* to *b*..........2Chr 4:2
the *b* of it like the work of the..........2Chr 4:5
like the work of the *b* of a cup..........2Chr 4:5
And they filled them up to the *b*..........Jn 2:7

BRIMSTONE

upon Sodom and upon Gomorrah *b*...Gen 19:24
that the whole land thereof is *b*......Deut 29:23
b shall be scattered upon his............Job 18:15
he shall rain snares, fire and *b*...........Ps 11:6
of the LORD, like a stream of *b*...........Is 30:33
pitch, and the dust thereof into *b*......Is 34:9
and great hailstones, fire, and *b*......Eze 38:22
b from heaven, and destroyed them...Lk 17:29
of fire, and of jacinth, and *b*..........Rev 9:17
mouths issued fire and smoke and *b*...Rev 9:17
and by the smoke, and by the *b*......Rev 9:18
b in the presence of the holy............Rev 14:10
a lake of fire burning with *b*..........Rev 19:20
cast into the lake of fire and *b*......Rev 20:10
lake which burneth with fire and *b*...Rev 21:8

BRING See PREFACE.

sort shall thou *b* into the ark............Gen 6:19
when I *b* a cloud over the earth,........Gen 9:14
with them to *b* them on the way......Gen 18:16
b them out unto us, that we may......Gen 19:5
I shall *b* a curse upon me, and not...Gen 27:12
But *b* your youngest brother unto......Gen 42:34
two sons, if I *b* him not to thee..........Gen 42:37
wives, and *b* your father, and come...Gen 45:19
b them, I pray thee, unto me, and......Gen 48:9
shall *b* thee into the land of the......Ex 13:5
of thy land thou shalt *b* into the......Ex 23:19
to *b* thee into the place which I......Ex 23:20
of a willing heart, let him *b* it..........Ex 35:5
The people *b* much more than......Ex 36:5
then he will *b* us into this land,.......Num 14:8
the LORD was not able to *b* this......Num 14:16
him will I *b* into the land..............Num 14:24
therefore ye shall not *b* this............Num 20:12
b it unto me, and I will hear it..........Deut 1:17
When the LORD thy God shall *b*......Deut 7:1
Then thou shalt *b* her home to......Deut 21:12
b it unto us, that we may hear it......Deut 30:12
Judah, and *b* him unto his people...Deut 33:7
be weaned, and then I will *b* him....1Sa 1:22
if we go, what shall we *b* the man...1Sa 9:7
B the portion which I gave thee,......1Sa 9:23
shouldest thou *b* me to thy father...1Sa 20:8
to *b* about all Israel unto thee..........2Sa 3:12
except thou first *b* Michal Saul's....2Sa 3:13
b him to me, and he shall not............2Sa 14:10
Why are ye the last to *b* the king...2Sa 19:11
to *b* his way upon his head..............1Kin 8:32
B me a new cruse, and put salt..........2Kin 2:20
I will *b* you to the man whom ye......2Kin 6:19
b an offering, and come before him...1Chr 16:29
did not our God *b* all this evil..........Neh 13:18
Did I say, *B* unto me,..................Job 6:22
wilt thou *b* me into dust again..........Job 10:9
Who can *b* a clean thing out of an...Job 14:4
know that thou wilt *b* me to death...Job 30:23
To *b* back his soul from the pit,........Job 33:30
and he shall *b* it to pass..................Ps 37:5
let them *b* me unto thy holy hill,......Ps 43:3
Who will *b* me into the strong............Ps 60:9
shall *b* peace to the people............Ps 72:3
he shall *b* upon them their own......Ps 94:23
Scornful men *b* a city into a......Prov 29:8
for who shall *b* him to see what......Eccl 3:22
God will *b* thee into judgement......Eccl 11:9
For God shall *b* every work into......Eccl 12:14
b thee into my mother's house,......Song 8:2
The LORD shall *b* upon thee..........Is 7:17
them, and *b* them to their place......Is 14:2
fort of thy walls shall he *b* down......Is 25:12
Tell ye, and *b* them near..............Is 45:21
I *b* near my righteousness,..............Is 46:13
Even them will I *b* to my holy..........Is 56:7
that thou *b* the poor that are..........Is 58:7
and for iron I will *b* silver..............Is 60:17
I will *b* forth a seed out of..............Is 65:9
will *b* their fears upon them............Is 66:4
a family, and I will *b* you to Zion......Jer 3:14
lest thou *b* me to nothing..............Jer 10:24
therefore I will *b* upon them all......Jer 11:8
b upon them the day of evil, and......Jer 17:18
I will *b* them from the north..........Jer 31:8
so will I *b* upon them all the..........Jer 32:42
I will *b* it health and cure, and I......Jer 33:6
and of them that shall *b*..............Jer 33:11
I will *b* a fear upon thee, saith......Jer 49:5
will *b* a sword upon you, and I......Eze 6:3
I will *b* you out of the midst..........Eze 11:9
that I would not *b* them into the......Eze 20:15
to *b* them upon the necks of them...Eze 21:29
I will *b* them against thee on..........Eze 23:22
I will *b* them out from the people...Eze 34:13
that I would *b* these against them...Eze 38:17
b her into the wilderness, and......Hos 2:14
which say to their masters, *B*..........Amos 4:1
Yet will I *b* an heir unto thee, O......Mic 1:15
And I will *b* them, and they shall......Zec 8:8
B ye all the tithes into the..............Mal 3:10
she shall *b* forth a son, and thou......Mt 1:21
shall *b* forth a son, and they..........Mt 1:23
be thou there until I *b* the word......Mt 2:13
Therefore if thou *b* thy gift to......Mt 5:23
b him hither to me..................Mt 17:17

loose them, and *b* them unto me........Mt 21:2
they *b* unto him one that was deaf......Mk 7:32
b him unto me................Mk 9:19
loose him, and *b* him..............Mk 11:2
b forth a son, and shalt call his......Lk 1:31
b you good tidings of great joy......Lk 2:10
life, and *b* no fruit to perfection......Lk 8:14
And when they *b* you unto the......Lk 12:11
B forth the best robe, and put it......Lk 15:22
b hither the fatted calf, and kill......Lk 15:23
loose him, and *b* him hither............Lk 19:30
them also I must *b*, and they shall...Jn 10:16
b all things to your remembrance.....Jn 14:26
What accusation *b* ye against this...Jn 18:29
intend to *b* this man's blood upon...Acts 5:28
that they should *b* them unto............Acts 7:6
he might *b* them bound unto............Acts 9:2
to *b* them which were there bound...Acts 22:5
them, and to *b* him into the castle......Acts 23:10
wise, and will *b* to nothing the........1Cor 1:19
who shall *b* you into remembrance...1Cor 4:17
my body, and *b* it into subjection......1Cor 9:27
that ye may *b* me on my journey......1Cor 16:6
if a man *b* you into bondage, if a......2Cor 11:20
schoolmaster to *b* us unto Christ......Gal 3:24
but *b* them up in the nurture and......Eph 6:4
in Jesus will God *b* with him............1Th 4:14
unjust, that he might *b* us to God....1Pet 3:18
b not this doctrine, receive him........2Jn 10
whom if thou *b* forward on their......3Jn 6
of the earth do *b* their glory..........Rev 21:24
And they shall *b* the glory..............Rev 21:26

BRINGERS

the *b* up of the children, sent to......2Kin 10:5

BRINGEST

a valiant man, and *b* good tidings....1Kin 1:42
b me into judgment with thee,..........Job 14:3
that *b* good tidings, get thee up........Is 40:9
that *b* good tidings, lift up thy........Is 40:9
For thou *b* certain strange things...Acts 17:20

BRINGETH

which *b* you out from under the........Ex 6:7
For I am the LORD that *b* you up......Lev 11:45
b it not unto the door of the..........Lev 17:4
b it not unto the door of the..........Lev 17:9
For the LORD thy God *b* thee into......Deut 8:7
that the field *b* forth year by......Deut 14:22
he *b* down to the grave, and..........1Sa 2:6
down to the grave, and *b* up............1Sa 2:6
he *b* low, and lifteth up..............1Sa 2:7
the king said, He also *b* tidings......2Sa 18:26
that *b* down the people under me,...2Sa 22:48
that *b* me forth from mine enemies...2Sa 22:49
into whose hand God *b* abundantly...Job 12:6
b out to light the shadow of............Job 12:22
for wrath *b* the punishments of......Job 19:29
that is hid *b* he forth to light............Job 28:11
that *b* forth his fruit in his............Ps 1:3
when the LORD *b* back the..............Ps 14:7
The LORD *b* the counsel of the..........Ps 33:10
man who *b* wicked devices to pass...Ps 37:7
When God *b* back the captivity of.....Ps 53:6
he *b* out those which are bound........Ps 68:6
he *b* them out of their distresses......Ps 107:28
so he *b* them unto their desired......Ps 107:30
he *b* the wind out of his..............Ps 135:7
mouth of the just *b* forth wisdom...Prov 10:31
moving his lips he *b* evil to pass......Prov 16:30
him, and *b* him before great men......Prov 18:16
that causeth shame, and *b* reproach...Prov 19:26
wicked, and *b* the wheel over them...Prov 20:26
when *b* it with a wicked mind............Prov 21:27
to himself *b* his mother to shame......Prov 29:15
He that delicately *b* up his..............Prov 29:21
The fear of man *b* a snare..............Prov 29:25
churning of milk *b* forth butter......Prov 30:33
of the nose *b* forth blood..............Prov 30:33
forcing of wrath *b* forth strife..........Prov 30:33
she *b* her food from afar..............Prov 31:14
the wood that *b* forth fires............Eccl 2:6
the LORD *b* up upon them the..........Is 8:7
For he *b* down them that dwell on...Is 26:5
he *b* it even to the dust..............Is 26:5
That *b* princes to nothing..............Is 40:23
that *b* out their host by number........Is 40:26
Jerusalem one that *b* good tidings...Is 41:27
Which *b* forth the chariot and..........Is 43:17
feet of him that *b* good tidings........Is 52:7
that *b* good tidings of good, that......Is 52:7
that *b* forth an instrument for..........Is 54:16
For as the earth *b* forth her bud,......Is 61:11
her that *b* forth her first child..........Jer 4:31
b forth the wind out of his............Jer 10:13
b forth the wind out of his............Jer 51:16
which *b* their iniquity to..............Eze 29:16
he *b* forth fruit unto himself............Hos 10:1
feet of him that *b* good tidings........Nah 1:15
that which the ground *b* forth..........Hag 1:11
therefore every tree which *b* not......Mt 3:10
good tree *b* forth good fruit............Mt 7:17
a corrupt tree *b* forth evil fruit........Mt 7:17
Every tree that *b* not forth good......Mt 7:19
of the heart *b* forth good things......Mt 12:35
evil treasure *b* forth evil things......Mt 12:35
b forth, some an hundredfold,..........Mt 13:23
which *b* forth out of his treasure......Mt 13:52
b them up into an high mountain......Mt 17:1
For the earth *b* forth fruit of............Mk 4:28
every tree therefore which *b* not......Lk 3:9

For a good tree *b* not forth..............Lk 6:43
heart *b* forth that which is good......Lk 6:45
heart *b* forth that which is evil........Lk 6:45
if it die, it *b* forth much fruit............Jn 12:24
the same *b* forth much fruit............Jn 15:5
b forth fruit, as it doth also in........Col 1:6
For the grace of God that *b*............Titus 2:11
when he *b* in the firstbegotten..........Heb 1:6
b forth herbs meet for them by........Heb 6:7
hath conceived, it *b* forth sin..........Jas 1:15
it is finished, *b* forth death..........Jas 1:15

BRINGING

b them out from the land of Egypt...Ex 12:42
the people were restrained from *b*...Ex 36:6
b iniquity to remembrance............Num 5:15
by *b* up a slander upon the land,......Num 14:36
ye not a word of *b* the king back......2Sa 19:10
be first had in *b* back our king..........2Sa 19:43
b gold, and silver, ivory, and apes...1Kin 10:22
I am *b* such evil upon Jerusalem......2Kin 21:12
came the ships of Tarshish *b* gold...2Chr 9:21
b in sheaves, and lading asses........Neh 13:15
rejoicing, *b* his sheaves with him......Ps 126:6
b burnt offerings, and sacrifices,......Jer 17:26
b sacrifices of praise, unto the........Jer 17:26
in *b* them forth out of the land..........Eze 20:9
by *b* upon us a great evil..............Dan 9:12
given to a nation *b* forth the............Mt 21:43
b one sick of the palsy, which........Mk 2:3
the spices which they had............Lk 24:1
b sick folks, and them which were...Acts 5:16
b me into captivity to the law of......Rom 7:23
b into captivity every thought to......2Cor 10:5
in *b* many sons unto glory, to..........Heb 2:10
but the *b* in of a better hope did......Heb 7:19
b in the flood upon the world of......2Pet 2:5

BRINK

kine upon the *b* of the river............Gen 41:3
it in the flags by the river's *b*............Ex 2:3
by the river's *b* against he come......Ex 7:15
which is by the *b* of the river of......Deut 2:36
to the *b* of the water of Jordan........Josh 3:8
to return to the *b* of the river..........Eze 47:6

BROAD

cubits long, and five cubits *b*............Ex 27:1
let them make him *b* plates for a......Num 16:38
they were made *b* plates for a..........Num 16:39
chamber was five cubits *b*..............1Kin 6:6
and the middle was six cubits *b*........1Kin 6:6
and the third was seven cubits *b*......1Kin 6:6
cubits long, and five cubits *b*............2Chr 6:13
Jerusalem unto the *b* wall..............Neh 3:8
the furnaces even unto the wall............Neh 12:38
out of the strait into a *b* place..........Job 36:16
thy commandment is exceeding *b*.....Ps 119:96
in the *b* ways I will seek him,..........Song 3:2
he unto us a place of *b* rivers..........Is 33:21
seek in the *b* places thereof, if........Jer 5:1
The *b* walls of Babylon shall be......Jer 51:58
of the gate, which was one need *b*...Eze 40:6
of the gate, which was one need *b*...Eze 40:7
was one reed long, and one reed *b*...Eze 40:7
long, and five and twenty cubits *b*...Eze 40:29
cubits long, and five cubits *b*............Eze 40:30
long, and five and twenty cubits *b*...Eze 40:33
long, and a cubit and an half *b*........Eze 40:42
And within were hooks, an hand *b*...Eze 40:43
long, and an hundred cubits *b*..........Eze 40:47
six cubits on the one side, and..........Eze 41:1
six cubits to on the other side,..........Eze 41:1
the west was seventy cubits *b*..........Eze 41:12
as long as they, and as *b* as they......Eze 41:12
reeds long, and five cubits *b*............Eze 42:20
be twelve cubits long, twelve *b*........Eze 43:16
fourteen *b* in the four squares..........Eze 43:17
of the city five thousand *b*............Eze 45:6
of forty cubits long and thirty *b*......Eze 46:22
one against another in the *b* ways...Nah 2:4
b is the way, that leadeth to..........Mt 7:13
they make *b* their phylacteries,........Mt 23:5

BROADER

than the earth, and *b* than the sea...Job 11:9

BROIDED

not with *b* hair, or gold, or............1Ti 2:9

BROIDERED

a coat, a mitre, and a girdle............Ex 28:4
I clothed thee also with *b* work........Eze 16:10
of fine linen, and silk, and *b* work....Eze 16:13
And lookest thy *b* garments............Eze 16:18
and put off their *b* garments............Eze 26:16
Fine linen with *b* work from Egypt...Eze 27:7
b work, and fine linen, and coral,......Eze 27:16
b work, and in chests of rich............Eze 27:24

BROILED

they gave him a piece of a *b* fish......Lk 24:42

BROKEN

fountains of the great deep *b* up......Gen 7:11
he hath *b* my covenant..............Gen 17:14
she said, How hast thou *b* forth......Gen 38:29
wherein it is sodden shall be *b*..........Lev 6:28
for pots, they shall be *b* down,..........Lev 11:35
of leprosy is out of the boil..............Lev 13:20
it is a leprosy *b* out of the..............Lev 13:25
which hath the issue, shall be *b*........Lev 15:12
or scabbed, or hath his stones *b*......Lev 21:20
Blind, or *b*, or maimed, or having......Lev 22:22

is bruised, or crushed, or b................... Lev 22:24
I have b the bands of your yoke,......... Lev 26:13
when I have b the staff of your..... Lev 26:26
hath b his commandment, that soul... Num 15:31
Then were the horsehoofs b by the..... Judg 5:22
as a thread of tow is b when it...... Judg 16:9
The bows of the mighty men are b........ 1Sa 2:4
of the LORD shall be b to pieces.......... 1Sa 2:10
The LORD hath b forth upon mine..... 2Sa 5:20
a bow of steel is b by mine arms...... 2Sa 22:35
altar of the LORD that was b down... 1Kin 18:30
the ships were b at Ezion-geber....... 1Kin 22:48
the house, that it be not b down...... 2Kin 11:6
And the city was b up, and all the..... 2Kin 25:4
God hath b in upon mine enemies.... 1Chr 14:11
the LORD hath b thy works................ 2Chr 20:37
And the ships were b, that they...... 2Chr 20:37
had b up the house of God............. 2Chr 24:7
that they all were b in pieces............ 2Chr 25:12
built up all the wall that was b....... 2Chr 32:5
Hezekiah his father had b down...... 2Chr 33:3
when he had b down the altars and... 2Chr 34:7
wall of Jerusalem also is b down....... Neh 1:3
of Jerusalem, which is b down.......... Neh 2:13
teeth of the young lions, are b......... Job 4:10
my skin is b, and become loathsome... Job 7:5
at ease, but he hath b me asunder.... Job 16:12
are past, my purposes are b off....... Job 17:11
of the fatherless have been b.......... Job 22:9
wickedness shall be b as a tree........ Job 24:20
mine arm be b from the bone......... Job 31:22
and the high arm shall be b............ Job 38:15
thou hast b the teeth of the............ Ps 3:7
a bow of steel is b by mine arms..... Ps 18:34
I am like a b vessel..................... Ps 31:12
unto them that are of a b heart...... Ps 34:18
not one of them is b................... Ps 34:20
heart, and they bows shall be b....... Ps 37:15
the arms of the wicked shall be b.... Ps 37:17
I am feeble and sore b................. Ps 38:8
Though thou hast sore b us in the... Ps 44:19
which thou hast b may rejoice......... Ps 51:8
sacrifices of God are a b spirit......... Ps 51:17
a b and a contrite heart, O God,...... Ps 51:17
he hath b his covenant................ Ps 55:20
thou hast b it......................... Ps 60:2
Reproach hath b my heart............. Ps 69:20
hast thou then b down her hedges... Ps 80:12
Thou hast b Rahab in pieces, as...... Ps 89:10
Thou hast b down all his hedges...... Ps 89:40
For he hath b the gates of brass,..... Ps 107:16
he might even slay the b in heart..... Ps 109:16
the snare is b, and we are escaped... Ps 124:7
He healeth the b in heart.............. Ps 147:3
his knowledge the depths are b up... Prov 3:20
shall he be b without remedy.......... Prov 6:15
of the heart the spirit is b............. Prov 15:13
but a b spirit drieth the bones........ Prov 17:22
the stone wall thereof was b down... Prov 24:31
time of trouble is like a b tooth....... Prov 25:19
is like a city that is b down........... Prov 25:28
a threefold cord is not quickly b...... Eccl 4:12
loosed, or the golden bowl be b....... Eccl 12:6
the pitcher be b at the fountain....... Eccl 12:6
or the wheel b at the cistern........... Eccl 12:6
the latchet of their shoes be b........ Is 5:27
and five years shall Ephraim be b..... Is 7:8
and ye shall be b in pieces............. Is 8:9
and ye shall be b in pieces............. Is 8:9
and ye shall be b in pieces............. Is 8:9
shall stumble, and fall, and be b...... Is 8:15
For thou hast b the yoke of his....... Is 9:4
The LORD hath b the staff of the...... Is 14:5
rod of him that smote thee is b....... Is 14:29
have b down the principal plants...... Is 16:8
they shall be b in the purposes........ Is 19:10
gods he hath b unto the ground....... Is 21:9
the houses have ye b down to......... Is 22:10
b the everlasting covenant............. Is 24:5
The city of confusion is b down....... Is 24:10
The earth is utterly b down.......... Is 24:19
are withered, they shall be b off...... Is 27:11
go, and fall backward, and be b....... Is 28:13
vessel that is b in pieces.............. Is 30:14
he hath b the covenant, he hath...... Is 33:8
any of the cords thereof be b......... Is 33:20
in the staff of this b reed............. Is 36:6
b cisterns, that can hold no........... Jer 2:13
Tahapanes have b the crown of thy... Jer 2:16
For of old time I have b thy yoke..... Jer 2:20
b down at the presence of the........ Jer 4:26
these have altogether b the yoke...... Jer 5:5
is spoiled, and all my cords are b..... Jer 10:20
the house of Judah have b my......... Jer 11:10
it, and the branches of it are b....... Jer 11:16
people is b with a great breach....... Jer 14:17
this man Coniah a despised b idol..... Jer 22:28
me is b because of the prophets...... Jer 23:9
I have b the yoke of the king of...... Jer 28:2
b the yoke from off the neck of...... Jer 28:11
Thou hast b the yokes of wood....... Jer 28:13
be b with David my servant........... Jer 33:21
b up from Jerusalem for fear of....... Jer 37:11
of the month, the city was b up....... Jer 39:2
say, How is the strong staff b......... Jer 48:17
for it is b down....................... Jer 48:20
Moab is cut off, and his arm is b..... Jer 48:25
for I have b Moab like a vessel....... Jer 48:38
howl, saying, How is it b down........ Jer 48:39
Merodach is b in pieces............... Jer 50:2

her images are b in pieces............. Jer 50:2
king of Babylon hath b his bones...... Jer 50:17
whole earth cut in asunder and b..... Jer 50:23
her bars are b........................ Jer 51:30
every one of their bows is b........... Jer 51:56
of Babylon shall be utterly b........... Jer 51:58
Then the city was b up, and all...... Jer 52:7
he hath destroyed and b her bars..... Lam 2:9
he hath b my bones................... Lam 3:4
He hath also b my teeth within...... Lam 3:16
and your images shall be b............ Eze 6:4
desolate, and your idols may be b..... Eze 6:6
because I am b with their whorish.... Eze 6:9
and my covenant that he hath b...... Eze 17:19
her strong rods were b and............ Eze 19:12
she is b that was the gate of......... Eze 26:2
the east wind hath b thee in the...... Eze 27:26
be b by the seas in the depths of..... Eze 27:34
her foundations shall be b down....... Eze 30:4
I have b the arm of Pharaoh king..... Eze 30:21
the strong, and that which was b..... Eze 30:22
his boughs are b by all the............ Eze 31:12
thou shalt be b in the midst of....... Eze 32:28
have ye bound up that which was b... Eze 34:4
and will bind up that which was b.... Eze 34:16
when I have b the bands of their..... Eze 34:27
they have b my covenant because..... Eze 44:7
to b pieces together, and became..... Dan 2:35
be partly strong, and partly b........ Dan 2:42
was strong, the great horn was b..... Dan 8:8
Now that being b, whereas four...... Dan 8:22
but he shall be b without hand....... Dan 8:25
stand up, his kingdom shall be b...... Dan 11:4
from before him, and shall be b....... Dan 11:22
b in judgment, because he........... Hos 5:11
of Samaria shall be b in pieces....... Hos 8:6
desolate, the barns are b down........ Joel 1:17
so that the ship was like to be b..... Jonah 1:4
they have b up, and have passed..... Mic 2:13
And it was b in that day.............. Zec 11:11
one, nor heal that that is b........... Zec 11:16
they took up of the b meat that..... Matt 15:37
fall on this stone shall be b........... Matt 21:44
suffered his house to be b up.......... Matt 24:43
and when they had b it up, they...... Mark 2:4
him, and the fetters be b in pieces... Mark 5:4
they took up of the b meat that..... Mark 8:8
his house to be b through............ Luke 12:39
fall upon that stone shall be b........ Luke 20:18
he not only had b the sabbath........ John 5:18
the law of Moses should not be b..... John 7:23
and the scripture cannot be b......... John 10:35
Pilate that their legs might be b...... John 19:31
A bone of him shall not be b.......... John 19:36
so many, yet was not the net b....... John 21:11
when the congregation was b up...... Acts 13:43
had b bread, and eaten, and talked... Acts 20:11
and when he had b it, he began to... Acts 27:35
but the hinder part was b with........ Acts 27:41
some on b pieces of the ship.......... Acts 27:44
if some of the branches be b off...... Rom 11:17
say then, The branches were b off..... Rom 11:19
of unbelief they were b off............ Rom 11:20
is my body, which is b for you........ 1Cor 11:24
hath b down the middle wall of....... Eph 2:14
potter shall they be b to shivers...... Rev 2:27

BROKENFOOTED
Or a man that is b, or................ Lev 21:19

BROKENHANDED
a man that is brokenfooted, or b...... Lev 21:19

BROKENHEARTED
he hath sent me to bind up the b..... Is 61:1
he hath sent me to heal the b......... Luke 4:18

BROOD
doth gather her b under her wings... Luke 13:34

BROOK
them, and sent them over the b....... Gen 32:23
thick trees, and willows of the b...... Lev 23:40
And they came unto the b of Eshcol... Num 13:23
The place was called the b Eshcol.... Num 13:24
I, and get you over the b Zered....... Deut 2:13
And we went over the b Zered........ Deut 2:13
we were come over the b Zered....... Deut 2:14
cast the dust thereof into the b....... Deut 9:21
five smooth stones out of the b....... 1Sa 17:40
with him, and came to the b Besor... 1Sa 30:9
could not go over the b Besor......... 1Sa 30:10
made also to abide at the b Besor.... 1Sa 30:21
himself passed over the b Kidron...... 2Sa 15:23
They be gone over the b of water..... 2Sa 17:20
out, and passed over the b Kidron.... 1Kin 2:37
idol, and burnt it by the b Kidron.... 1Kin 15:13
and hide thyself by the b Cherith.... 1Kin 17:3
that thou shalt drink of the b......... 1Kin 17:4
he went and dwelt by the b Cherith... 1Kin 17:5
and he drank of the b................ 1Kin 17:6
a while, that the b dried up.......... 1Kin 17:7
brought them down to the b Kishon... 1Kin 18:40
Jerusalem, unto the b Kidron.......... 2Kin 23:6
and burned it at the b Kidron......... 2Kin 23:6
dust of them into the b Kidron........ 2Kin 23:12
it, and burnt it at the b Kidron....... 2Chr 15:16
them at the end of the b Kidron...... 2Chr 20:16
it out abroad into the b Kidron....... 2Chr 29:16
and cast them into the b Kidron...... 2Chr 30:14
the b that ran through the midst..... 2Chr 32:4
went I up in the night by the b....... Neh 2:15
have dealt deceitfully as a b.......... Job 6:15

of the b compass him about........... Job 40:22
as to Jabin, at the b of Kison......... Ps 83:9
shall drink of the b in the way....... Ps 110:7
of wisdom as a flowing b............. Prov 18:4
away to the b of the willows......... Is 15:7
the fields unto the b of Kidron....... Jer 31:40
his disciples over the b Cedron....... John 18:1

BROOKS
Red sea, and in the b of Arnon,...... Num 21:14
at the stream of the b that goeth.... Num 21:15
a good land, a land of b of water.... Deut 8:7
Hiddai of the b of Gaash............. 2Sa 23:30
fountains of water, and unto all b.... 1Kin 18:5
Hurai of the b of Gaash, Abiel....... 1Chr 11:32
as the stream of b they pass away... Job 6:15
floods, the b of honey and butter.... Job 20:17
of Ophir as the stones of the b....... Job 22:24
hart panteth after the water b........ Ps 42:1
the b of defence shall be emptied.... Is 19:6
the b, by the mouth of the b......... Is 19:7
and every thing sown by the b........ Is 19:7
angle into the b shall lament......... Is 19:8

BROTH
basket, and he put the b in a pot..... Judg 6:19
upon this rock, and pour out the b.... Judg 6:20
b of abominable things is in.......... Is 65:4

BROTHER
And she again bare his b Abel......... Gen 4:2
And Cain talked with Abel his b....... Gen 4:8
Cain rose up against Abel his b....... Gen 4:8
unto Cain, Where is Abel thy b....... Gen 4:9
at the hand of every man's b will.... Gen 9:5
the b of Japheth the elder, even..... Gen 10:21
b of Eshcol, and b of Aner............ Gen 14:13
b of Eshcol, and b of Aner............ Gen 14:13
that his b was taken captive.......... Gen 14:14
and also brought again his b Lot...... Gen 14:16
even she herself said, He is my b..... Gen 20:5
shall come, say of me, He is my b.... Gen 20:13
I have given thy b a thousand........ Gen 20:16
born children unto thy b Nahor....... Gen 22:20
Huz his firstborn, and Buz his b...... Gen 22:21
did bear to Nahor, Abraham's b....... Gen 22:23
the wife of Nahor, Abraham's b....... Gen 24:15
And Rebekah had a b, and his name... Gen 24:29
he gave also to her b and to her..... Gen 24:53
And her b and her mother said, Let... Gen 24:55
And after that came his b out......... Gen 25:26
thy father speak unto Esau thy b..... Gen 27:6
Esau my b is a hairy man, and I am... Gen 27:11
were hairy, as his b Esau's hands.... Gen 27:23
that Esau his b came in from his..... Gen 27:30
Thy b came with subtilty, and hath... Gen 27:35
thou live, and shalt serve thy b...... Gen 27:40
then will I slay my b Jacob........... Gen 27:41
thy b Esau, as touching thee,........ Gen 27:42
flee thou to Laban my b to Haran.... Gen 27:43
Jacob was their mother's b........... Gen 28:2
the b of Rebekah, Jacob's and....... Gen 28:5
daughter of Laban his mother's b..... Gen 29:10
the sheep of Laban his mother's b.... Gen 29:10
the flock of Laban his mother's b..... Gen 29:10
Rachel that he was her father's b..... Gen 29:12
unto Jacob, Because thou art my b.... Gen 29:15
Esau his b unto the land of Seir...... Gen 32:3
saying, We came to thy b Esau....... Gen 32:6
pray thee, from the hand of my b.... Gen 32:11
his hand a present for Esau his b..... Gen 32:13
When Esau my b meeteth thee,....... Gen 32:17
until he came near to his b........... Gen 33:3
And Esau said, I have enough, my b... Gen 33:9
from the face of Esau thy b........... Gen 35:1
he fled from the face of his b......... Gen 35:7
from the face of his b Jacob.......... Gen 36:6
profit is it if we slay our b........... Gen 37:26
for he is our b and our flesh......... Gen 37:27
her, and raise up seed to thy b....... Gen 38:8
that he should give seed to his b..... Gen 38:9
that, behold, his b came out.......... Gen 38:29
And afterward came out his b......... Gen 38:30
But Benjamin, Joseph's b, Jacob...... Gen 42:4
your youngest b come hither.......... Gen 42:15
of you, and let him fetch your b..... Gen 42:16
But bring your youngest b unto me... Gen 42:20
verily guilty concerning our b........ Gen 42:21
And bring your youngest b unto me... Gen 42:34
so will I deliver you your b........... Gen 42:34
for his b is dead, and he is left...... Gen 42:38
face, except your b be with you...... Gen 43:3
If thou wilt send our b with us....... Gen 43:4
face, except your b be with you...... Gen 43:5
the man whether ye had yet a b...... Gen 43:6
have ye another b..................... Gen 43:7
he would say, Bring your b down..... Gen 43:7
Take also your b, and arise, go....... Gen 43:13
he may send away your other b...... Gen 43:14
saw his b Benjamin, his mother's..... Gen 43:29
and said, Is this your younger b...... Gen 43:29
his bowels did yearn upon his b...... Gen 43:30
saying, Have ye a father, or a b...... Gen 44:19
his b is dead, and he alone is........ Gen 44:20
youngest b come down with you...... Gen 44:23
if our youngest b be with us......... Gen 44:26
except our youngest b be with us.... Gen 44:26
And he said, I am Joseph your b...... Gen 45:4
see, and the eyes of my b Benjamin... Gen 45:12
fell upon his b Benjamin's neck...... Gen 45:14
but truly his younger b shall be...... Gen 48:19
Is not Aaron the Levite thy b......... Ex 4:14

B

Aaron thy *b* shall be thy prophet........... Ex 7:1
Aaron thy *b* shall speak unto.............. Ex 7:2
take thou unto thee Aaron thy *b*.......... Ex 28:1
for Aaron thy *b* for glory................. Ex 28:4
holy garments for Aaron thy *b*............ Ex 28:4
shalt put them upon Aaron thy *b*......... Ex 28:41
the camp, and slay every man his *b*...... Ex 32:27
man upon his son, and upon his *b*........ Ex 32:29
Moses, Speak unto Aaron thy *b*........... Lev 16:2
the nakedness of thy father's *b*.......... Lev 18:14
not hate thy *b* in thine heart............ Lev 19:17
and for his daughter, and for his *b*...... Lev 21:2
If thy *b* be waxen poor, and hath........ Lev 25:25
he redeem that which his *b* sold......... Lev 25:25
if thy *b* be waxen poor, and fallen...... Lev 25:35
that thy *b* may live with thee........... Lev 25:36
if thy *b* that dwelleth by thee be....... Lev 25:39
thy *b* that dwelleth by him wax........ Lev 25:47
or for his mother, for his *b*............. Num 6:7
together, thou, and Aaron thy *b*......... Num 20:8
of Edom, Thus saith thy *b* Israel........ Num 20:14
as Aaron thy *b* was gathered............ Num 27:13
our *b* unto his daughters................. Num 36:2
between every man and his *b*............ Deut 1:16
If thy *b*, the son of thy mother,......... Deut 13:6
it of his neighbour, or of his *b*.......... Deut 15:2
thy *b* thine hand shall release.......... Deut 15:3
shut thine hand from thy poor *b*........ Deut 15:7
eye be evil against thy poor *b*.......... Deut 15:9
open thine hand wide unto thy *b*........ Deut 15:11
And if thy *b*, an Hebrew man, or an.... Deut 15:12
over thee, which is not thy *b*........... Deut 17:15
testified falsely against his *b*.......... Deut 19:18
thought to have done unto his *b*........ Deut 19:19
case bring them again unto thy *b*....... Deut 22:1
if thy *b* be not night unto thee,........ Deut 22:2
thee until thy *b* seek after it.......... Deut 22:2
for he is thy *b*......................... Deut 23:7
not lend upon usury to thy *b*........... Deut 23:19
but unto thy *b* thou shalt not........... Deut 23:20
thou dost lend thy *b* any thing......... Deut 24:10
then thy *b* should seem vile unto...... Deut 25:3
her husband's *b* shall go in unto....... Deut 25:5
duty of an husband's *b* unto her....... Deut 25:5
the name of his *b* which is dead........ Deut 25:6
My husband's *b* refuseth to raise...... Deut 25:7
up unto his *b* a name in Israel......... Deut 25:7
the duty of my husband's *b*............. Deut 25:7
eye shall be evil toward her *b*.......... Deut 28:54
as Aaron thy *b* died in mount Hor,..... Deut 32:50
of Kenaz, the *b* of Caleb, took it....... Josh 15:17
And Judah said unto Simeon his *b*...... Judg 1:3
son of Kenaz, Caleb's younger *b*........ Judg 1:13
And Judah went with Simeon his *b*..... Judg 1:17
son of Kenaz, Caleb's younger *b*........ Judg 3:9
for they said, He is our *b*.............. Judg 9:3
of Shechem, because he is your *b*....... Judg 9:18
for fear of Abimelech his *b*............. Judg 9:21
be laid upon Abimelech their *b*......... Judg 9:56
the children of Benjamin my *b*.......... Judg 20:23
the children of Benjamin my *b*.......... Judg 20:28
them for Benjamin their *b*.............. Judg 21:6
land, which was our *b* Elimelech's..... Ruth 4:3
the son of Ahitub, I-chabod's *b*........ 1Sa 14:3
Eliab his eldest *b* heard when he....... 1Sa 17:28
and my *b*, he hath commanded me to... 1Sa 20:29
b to Joab, saying, Who will go......... 1Sa 26:6
for thee, my *b* Jonathan................ 2Sa 1:26
I hold up my face to Joab thy *b*........ 2Sa 2:22
up every one from following his *b*..... 2Sa 2:27
for the blood of Asahel his *b*........... 2Sa 3:27
Joab and Abishai his *b* slew Abner..... 2Sa 3:30
because he had slain their *b*........... 2Sa 3:30
and Rechab and Baanah his escaped..... 2Sa 4:6
answered Rechab and Baanah his *b*..... 2Sa 4:9
into the hand of Abishai his *b*.......... 2Sa 10:10
the son of Shimeah David's *b*........... 2Sa 13:3
love Tamar, my *b* Absalom's sister..... 2Sa 13:4
Go now to thy *b* Amnon's house........ 2Sa 13:8
Tamar went to her *b* Amnon's house.... 2Sa 13:10
into the chamber to Amnon her *b*....... 2Sa 13:10
And she answered him, Nay, my *b*...... 2Sa 13:12
Absalom her *b* said unto her........... 2Sa 13:20
Hath Amnon thy *b* been with thee...... 2Sa 13:20
he is thy *b*............................ 2Sa 13:20
desolate in her *b* Absalom's house..... 2Sa 13:20
Absalom spake unto his *b* Amnon....... 2Sa 13:22
let my *b* Amnon go with us............. 2Sa 13:26
the son of Shimeah David's *b*.......... 2Sa 13:32
Deliver him that smote his *b*.......... 2Sa 14:7
the life of his *b* whom he slew........ 2Sa 14:7
the son of Zeruiah, Joab's *b*........... 2Sa 18:2
Amasa, Art thou in health, my *b*...... 2Sa 20:9
Abishai his *b* pursued after Sheba..... 2Sa 20:10
slew the *b* of Goliath the Gittite...... 2Sa 21:19
Shimeah the *b* of David slew him...... 2Sa 21:21
the *b* of Joab, the son of Zeruiah..... 2Sa 23:18
Asahel the *b* of Joab was one of...... 2Sa 23:24
the mighty men, and Solomon his *b*.... 1Kin 1:10
I feed because of Absalom thy *b*....... 1Kin 2:7
given to Adonijah thy *b* to wife........ 1Kin 2:21
for he is mine elder *b*................. 1Kin 2:22
which thou hast given me, my *b*....... 1Kin 9:13
over him, saying, Alas, my *b*.......... 1Kin 13:30
he is my *b*............................. 1Kin 20:32
and they said, Thy *b* Ben-hadad....... 1Kin 20:33
his father's *b* king in his stead....... 2Kin 24:17
the sons of Jada the *b* of Shammai.... 1Chr 2:32
of Caleb the *b* of Jerahmeel were..... 1Chr 2:42
Chelub the *b* of Shuah begat Mehir.... 1Chr 4:11

his *b* Asaph, who stood on his......... 1Chr 6:39
and the name of his *b* was Sheresh.... 1Chr 7:16
And the sons of his *b* Helem........... 1Chr 7:35
And the sons of Eshek his *b* were...... 1Chr 8:39
And Abishai the *b* of Joab, he was.... 1Chr 11:20
armies were, Asahel the *b* of Joab..... 1Chr 11:26
Joel the *b* of Nathan, Mibhar the..... 1Chr 11:38
the son of Shimri, and Joha his *b*..... 1Chr 11:45
unto the hand of Abishai his *b*........ 1Chr 19:11
fled before Abishai his *b*.............. 1Chr 19:15
the *b* of Goliath the Gittite.......... 1Chr 20:5
son of Shimea David's *b* slew him..... 1Chr 20:7
The *b* of Micah was Ishiah............ 1Chr 24:25
Zetham, and Joel his *b*, which were... 1Chr 26:22
month was Asahel the *b* of Joab....... 1Chr 27:7
Shimei his *b* was the next............ 2Chr 31:12
hand of Cononiah and Shimei his *b*.... 2Chr 31:13
Eliakim his *b* king over Judah......... 2Chr 36:4
And Necho took Jehoahaz his *b*........ 2Chr 36:4
Zedekiah his *b* king over Judah........ 2Chr 36:10
exact usury, every one of his *b*........ Neh 5:7
That I gave my *b* Hanani, and......... Neh 7:2
a pledge from thy *b* for nought........ Job 22:6
I am a *b* to dragons, and.............. Job 30:29
though he had been my friend or *b*.... Ps 35:14
can by any means redeem his *b*........ Ps 49:7
sittest and speakest against thy *b*..... Ps 50:20
a *b* is born for adversity.............. Prov 17:17
to *b* him that is a great waster....... Prov 18:9
A *b* offended is harder to be won...... Prov 18:19
that sticketh closer than a *b*.......... Prov 18:24
that is near than a *b* far off.......... Prov 27:10
yea, he hath neither child nor *b*....... Eccl 4:8
O that thou wert as my *b*, that........ Song 8:1
his *b* the house of his father......... Is 3:6
no man shall spare his *b*.............. Is 9:19
fight every one against his *b*.......... Is 19:2
and every one said to his *b*........... Is 41:6
and trust ye not in any *b*............. Jer 9:4
for every *b* will utterly supplant...... Jer 9:4
lament for him, saying, Ah my *b*....... Jer 22:18
his neighbour, and every one to his *b*.. Jer 31:34
of them, to wit, of a Jew his *b*....... Jer 34:9
ye go every man his *b*, an Hebrew..... Jer 34:14
liberty, every one to his *b*........... Jer 34:17
spoiled his *b* by violence............. Eze 18:18
to another, every one to his *b*........ Eze 33:30
sword shall be against his *b*.......... Eze 38:21
for son, or for daughter, for his *b*... Eze 44:25
He took his *b* by the heel in the...... Hos 12:3
did pursue his *b* with the sword....... Amos 1:11
b Jacob shame shall cover thee........ Obad 10
thy *b* in the day that he became a.... Obad 12
hunt every man his *b* with a.......... Mic 7:2
every one by the sword of his *b*....... Hag 2:22
and compassions every man to his *b*... Zec 7:9
evil against his *b* in your heart....... Zec 7:10
Was not Esau Jacob's *b*............... Mal 1:2
every man against his *b*, by.......... Mal 2:10
called Peter, and Andrew his *b*........ Mt 4:18
the son of Zebedee, and John his *b*.... Mt 4:21
his *b* without a cause shall be in..... Mt 5:22
and whosoever shall say to his *b*...... Mt 5:22
thy *b* hath ought against thee........ Mt 5:23
first be reconciled to thy *b*.......... Mt 5:24
Or how wilt thou say to thy *b*........ Mt 7:4
is called Peter, and Andrew his *b*..... Mt 10:2
the son of Zebedee, and John his *b*.... Mt 10:2
b shall deliver up the *b* to death.... Mt 10:21
is in heaven, the same is my *b*........ Mt 12:50
sake, his *b* Philip's wife............. Mt 14:3
Peter, James, and John his *b*......... Mt 17:1
Moreover if thy *b* shall trespass..... Mt 18:15
hear thee, thou hast gained thy *b*.... Mt 18:15
how oft shall my *b* sin against me.... Mt 18:21
every one his *b* their trespasses...... Mt 18:35
his *b* shall marry his wife............ Mt 22:24
and raise up seed unto his *b*.......... Mt 22:24
issue, left his wife unto his *b*........ Mt 22:25
Andrew his *b* casting a net into...... Mk 1:16
the son of Zebedee, and John his *b*.... Mk 1:19
Zebedee, and John the *b* of James..... Mk 3:17
the will of God, the same is my *b*..... Mk 3:35
and James, and John the *b* of James... Mk 6:3
the *b* of James, and Joses, and of.... Mk 6:3
sake, his *b* Philip's wife............. Mk 6:17
wrote unto us, If a man's *b* die....... Mk 12:19
that his *b* should take his wife,...... Mk 12:19
and raise up seed unto his *b*.......... Mk 12:19
b shall betray the *b* to death....... Mk 13:12
his *b* Philip tetrarch of Iturea....... Lk 3:1
for Herodias his *b* Philip's wife...... Lk 3:19
named Peter,) and Andrew his *b*....... Lk 6:14
And Judas the *b* of James, and Judas.. Lk 6:16
canst thou say to thy *b*, *B*.......... Lk 6:42
unto him, Master, speak to my *b*...... Lk 12:13
he said unto him, Thy *b* is come...... Lk 15:27
for this thy *b* was dead, and is....... Lk 15:32
if thy *b* trespass against thee,........ Lk 17:3
wrote unto us, If any man's *b* die..... Lk 20:28
that his *b* should take his wife,...... Lk 20:28
wife, and raise up seed unto his *b*.... Lk 20:28
him, was Andrew, Simon Peter's *b*.... Jn 1:40
He first findeth his own *b* Simon..... Jn 1:41
Andrew, Simon Peter's *b*, saith....... Jn 6:8
hair, whose *b* Lazarus was sick....... Jn 11:2
comfort them concerning their *b*..... Jn 11:19
been here, my *b* had not died......... Jn 11:21
unto her, Thy *b* shall rise again...... Jn 11:23

been here, my *b* had not died......... Jn 11:32
Zelotes, and Judas the *b* of James..... Acts 1:13
B Saul, the Lord, even Jesus,........... Acts 9:17
he killed James the *b* of John......... Acts 12:2
and said unto him, Thou seest, *b*...... Acts 21:20
B Saul, receive thy sight.............. Acts 22:13
But why dost thou judge thy *b*........ Rom 14:10
why dost thou set at nought thy *b*.... Rom 14:10
But if thy *b* be grieved with thy...... Rom 14:15
any thing whereby thy *b* stumbleth... Rom 14:21
city saluteth you, and Quartus a *b*.... Rom 16:23
will of God, and Sosthenes our *b*...... 1Cor 1:1
is called a *b* be a fornicator......... 1Cor 5:11
But *b* goeth to law with a *b*,........ 1Cor 6:6
If any *b* hath a wife that............. 1Cor 7:12
A *b* or a sister is not under.......... 1Cor 7:15
knowledge shall the weak *b* perish.... 1Cor 8:11
if meat make my *b* to offend.......... 1Cor 8:13
lest I make my *b* to offend........... 1Cor 8:13
As touching our *b* Apollos............ 1Cor 16:12
the will of God, and Timothy our *b*.... 2Cor 1:1
because I found not Titus my *b*....... 2Cor 2:13
And we have sent with him the *b*...... 2Cor 8:18
And we have sent with them our *b*.... 2Cor 8:22
Titus, and with him I sent a *b*........ 2Cor 12:18
I none, save James the Lord's *b*....... Gal 1:19
how I do, Tychicus, a beloved *b*....... Eph 6:21
to send to you Epaphroditus, my *b*.... Phil 2:25
will of God, and Timotheus our *b*...... Col 1:1
unto you, who is a beloved *b*.......... Col 4:7
Onesimus, a faithful and beloved *b*.... Col 4:9
And sent Timotheus, our *b*, and....... 1Th 3:2
defraud his *b* in any matter.......... 1Th 4:6
every *b* that walketh disorderly...... 2Th 3:6
an enemy, but admonish him as a *b*... 2Th 3:15
of Jesus Christ, and Timothy our *b*.... Philem 1
saints are refreshed by thee, *b*....... Philem 7
a *b* beloved, specially to me, but..... Philem 16
Yea, *b*, let me have joy of thee....... Philem 20
his neighbour, and every man his *b*... Heb 8:11
Know ye that our *b* Timothy is set.... Heb 13:23
Let the *b* of low degree rejoice....... Jas 1:9
If a *b* or sister be naked, and........ Jas 2:15
He that speaketh evil of his *b*........ Jas 4:11
of his *b*, and judgeth his *b*......... Jas 4:11
Silvanus, a faithful *b* unto you....... 1Pet 5:12
even as our beloved *b* Paul also....... 2Pet 3:15
is in the light, and hateth his *b*...... 1Jn 2:9
He that loveth his *b* abideth in...... 1Jn 2:10
that hateth his *b* is in darkness...... 1Jn 2:11
neither he that loveth not his *b*...... 1Jn 3:10
of that wicked one, and slew his *b*.... 1Jn 3:12
loveth not his *b* abideth in death..... 1Jn 3:14
hateth his *b* is a murderer............ 1Jn 3:15
good, and seeth his *b* have need...... 1Jn 3:17
say, I love God, and hateth his *b*..... 1Jn 4:20
not his *b* whom he hath seen......... 1Jn 4:20
he who loveth God love his *b* also.... 1Jn 4:21
If any man see his *b* sin a.......... 1Jn 5:16
b of James, to them that are........ Jude 1
I John, who also am your *b*.......... Rev 1:9

BROTHERHOOD

I might break the *b* between Judah ... Zec 11:14
Love the *b*......................... 1Pet 2:17

BROTHERLY

and remembered not the *b* covenant... Amos 1:9
one to another with *b* love.......... Rom 12:10
But as touching *b* love ye need...... 1Th 4:9
Let *b* love continue................. Heb 13:1
And to godliness *b* kindness......... 2Pet 1:7
and to *b* kindness charity........... 2Pet 1:7

BROTHER'S

Am I my *b* keeper................... Gen 4:9
the voice of thy *b* blood crieth...... Gen 4:10
receive thy *b* blood from thy hand... Gen 4:11
And his *b* name was Jubal........... Gen 4:21
and his *b* name was Joktan.......... Gen 10:25
Sarai his wife, and Lot his son...... Gen 12:5
And they took Lot, Abram's *b* son... Gen 14:12
master's *b* daughter unto his son... Gen 24:48
until thy *b* fury turn away......... Gen 27:45
unto Onan, Go in unto thy *b* wife... Gen 38:8
when he went in unto his *b* wife.... Gen 38:9
the nakedness of thy *b* wife........ Lev 18:16
it is thy *b* nakedness.............. Lev 18:16
And if a man shall take his *b* wife... Lev 20:21
he hath uncovered his *b* nakedness.. Lev 20:21
Thou shalt not see thy *b* ox or..... Deut 22:1
and with all lost things of thy *b*... Deut 22:3
Thou shalt not see thy *b* ass or.... Deut 22:4
man like not to take his *b* wife.... Deut 25:7
then let his *b* wife go up to the... Deut 25:7
Then shall his *b* wife come unto.... Deut 25:9
will not build up his *b* house...... Deut 25:9
turned about, and is become thy *b*.. 1Kin 2:15
and his *b* name was Joktan......... 1Chr 1:19
wine in their eldest *b* house....... Job 1:13
wine in their eldest *b* house....... Job 1:18
neither go into thy *b* house in..... Prov 27:10
the mote that is in thy *b* eye...... Mt 7:3
out the mote out of thy *b* eye...... Mt 7:5
for thee to have thy *b* wife........ Mk 6:18
the mote that is in thy *b* eye...... Lk 6:42
out the mote that is in thy *b* eye... Lk 6:42
an occasion to fall in his *b* way.... Rom 14:13
were evil, and his *b* righteous...... 1Jn 3:12

BROTHERS'

unto their father's *b* sons................. Num 36:11

BROUGHT See PREFACE.

BROUGHTEST

which thou *b* out of the land of........... Ex 32:7
(for thou *b* up this people in thy........ Num 14:13
the land whence thou *b* us out say...... Deut 9:28
which thou *b* out by thy mighty.......... Deut 9:29
that leddest out and *b* in Israel.......... 2Sa 5:2
which thou *b* forth out of Egypt,......... 1Kin 8:51
when thou *b* our fathers out of.......... 1Kin 8:53
that leddest out and *b* in Israel.......... 1Chr 11:2
b him forth out of Ur of the................ Neh 9:7
b forth water for them out of the........ Neh 9:15
b them into the land, concerning......... Neh 9:23
Thou *b* us into the net........................ Ps 66:11
but thou *b* us out into a wealthy......... Ps 66:12

BROW

is an iron sinew, and thy *b* brass....... Is 48:4
led him unto the *b* of the hill.............. Lk 4:29

BROWN

all the *b* cattle among the sheep,........ Gen 30:32
b among the sheep, that shall be....... Gen 30:33
all the *b* among the sheep, and.......... Gen 30:35
all the *b* in the flock of Laban............ Gen 30:40

BRUISE

it shall *b* thy head, and thou.............. Gen 3:15
head, and thou shalt *b* his heel......... Gen 3:15
nor *b* it with his horsemen................. Is 28:28
Yet it pleased the LORD to *b* him........ Is 53:10
Thy *b* is incurable, and thy wound...... Jer 30:12
shall it break in pieces and *b*............. Dan 2:40
There is no healing of thy *b*............... Nah 3:19
the God of peace shall *b* Satan......... Rom 16:20

BRUISED

unto the LORD that which is *b*............. Lev 22:24
upon the staff of this *b* reed.............. 2Kin 18:21
Bread corn is *b*................................ Is 28:28
A *b* reed shall he not break, and........ Is 42:3
he was *b* for our iniquities................ Is 53:5
there they *b* the teats of their........... Eze 23:3
they *b* the breasts of her.................. Eze 23:21
A *b* reed shall he not break, and....... Mt 12:20
to set at liberty them that are *b*........ Lk 4:18

BRUISES

but wounds, and, *b*, and putrifying..... Is 1:6

BRUISING

in *b* thy teats by the Egyptians......... Eze 23:21
b him hardly departeth from him........ Lk 9:39

BRUIT

the noise of the *b* is come................ Jer 10:22
all that hear the *b* of thee shall........ Nah 3:19

BRUTE

But these, as natural *b* beasts.......... 2Pet 2:12
as *b* beasts, in those things they...... Jude 10

BRUTISH

the *b* person perish, and leave.......... Ps 49:10
A *b* man knoweth not....................... Ps 92:6
Understand, ye *b* among the people.... Ps 94:8
but he that hateth reproof is *b*.......... Prov 12:1
Surely I am more *b* than any man...... Prov 30:2
of Pharaoh is become *b*.................... Is 19:11
But they are altogether *b*.................. Jer 10:8
Every man is *b* in his knowledge....... Jer 10:14
For the pastors are become *b*........... Jer 10:21
Every man is *b* by his knowledge....... Jer 51:17
thee into the hand of *b* men.............. Eze 21:31

BUCKET

the nations are as a drop of a *b*........ Is 40:15

BUCKETS

shall pour the water out of his *b*........ Num 24:7

BUCKLER

he is a *b* to all them that trust........... 2Sa 22:31
valiant men, men able to bear *b*......... 1Chr 5:18
that could handle shield and *b*........... 1Chr 12:8
my *b*, and the horn of my salvation.... Ps 18:2
he is a *b* to all those that trust.......... Ps 18:30
Take hold of shield and *b*, and.......... Ps 35:2
truth shall be thy shield and *b*........... Ps 91:4
he is a *b* to them that walk............... Prov 2:7
Order ye the *b* and shield, and, draw... Jer 46:3
which shall set against thee *b*........... Eze 23:24
lift up the *b* against thee.................. Eze 26:8

BUCKLERS

captains of hundreds spears, and *b*.... 2Chr 23:9
upon the thick bosses of his *b*........... Job 15:26
whereon there hang a thousand *b*...... Song 4:4
even a great company with *b*............. Eze 38:4
both the shields and the *b*................ Eze 39:9

BUD

the scent of water it will *b*................ Job 14:9
to cause the *b* of the tender herb....... Job 38:27
I make the horn of David to *b*............ Ps 132:17
and the pomegranates *b* forth........... Song 7:12
when the *b* is perfect, and the.......... Is 18:5
Israel shall blossom and *b*............... Is 27:6
and maketh it bring forth and *b*......... Is 55:10
as the earth bringeth forth her *b*........ Is 61:11
to multiply as the *b* of the field......... Eze 16:7
of the house of Israel to *b* forth........ Eze 29:21
the *b* shall yield no meal................. Hos 8:7

BUDDED

and it was as though it *b*, and her..... Gen 40:10
Aaron for the house of Levi was *b*...... Num 17:8
flourished, and the pomegranates *b*.... Song 6:11
rod hath blossomed, pride hath *b*....... Eze 7:10
had manna, and Aaron's rod that *b*..... Heb 9:4

BUDS

was budded, and brought forth *b*........ Num 17:8

BUFFET

to *b* him, and to say unto him,........... Mk 14:65
the messenger of Satan to *b* me........ 2Cor 12:7

BUFFETED

they spit in his face, and *b* him.......... Mt 26:67
and thirst, and are naked, and are *b*... 1Cor 4:11
when ye be *b* for your faults, ye........ 1Pet 2:20

BUILD

let us *b* us a city and a tower,........... Gen 11:4
and they left off to *b* the city............ Gen 11:8
thou shalt not *b* it of hewn stone...... Ex 20:25
B me here seven altars, and.............. Num 23:1
B me here seven altars, and.............. Num 23:29
We will *b* sheepfolds here for our...... Num 32:16
B you cities for your little ones......... Num 32:24
thou shalt *b* bulwarks against the...... Deut 20:20
will not *b* up his brother's house........ Deut 25:9
there shalt thou *b* an altar unto......... Deut 27:5
Thou shalt *b* the altar of the............. Deut 27:6
thou shalt *b* an house, and thou........ Deut 28:30
us now prepare to *b* us an altar........ Josh 22:26
to *b* an altar for burnt offerings........ Josh 22:29
b an altar unto the LORD my God........ Judg 6:26
which two did *b* the house of........... Ruth 4:11
I will *b* him a sure house................. 1Sa 2:35
Shalt thou *b* me an house for me...... 2Sa 7:5
Why *b* ye not me an house of cedar... 2Sa 7:7
He shall *b* an house for my name,...... 2Sa 7:13
saying, I will *b* thee an house.......... 2Sa 7:27
to *b* an altar unto the LORD, that....... 2Sa 24:21
B thee an house in Jerusalem, and..... 1Kin 2:36
an house unto the name of the........... 1Kin 5:3
I purpose to *b* an house unto the...... 1Kin 5:5
he shall *b* an house unto my name..... 1Kin 5:5
timber and stones to *b* the house....... 1Kin 5:18
that he began to *b* the house of........ 1Kin 6:1
tribes of Israel to *b* an house........... 1Kin 8:16
to *b* an house for the name of the..... 1Kin 8:17
heart to *b* an house unto my name..... 1Kin 8:18
thou shalt not *b* the house............... 1Kin 8:19
he shall *b* the house unto my name.... 1Kin 8:19
for to *b* the house of God,................ 1Kin 9:15
Solomon desired to *b* in Jerusalem..... 1Kin 9:19
then did he *b* Millo........................ 1Kin 9:24
Then did Solomon *b* an high place...... 1Kin 11:7
b thee a sure house, as I built.......... 1Kin 11:38
and did the Beth-elite *b* Jericho......... 1Kin 16:34
and carpenters, to *b* him an house..... 1Chr 14:1
Thou shalt not *b* me an house to...... 1Chr 17:4
the LORD will *b* thee an house........... 1Chr 17:10
He shall *b* me an house, and I will..... 1Chr 17:12
that thou wilt *b* him an house........... 1Chr 17:25
that I may *b* an altar therein............ 1Chr 21:22
stones to *b* the house of God........... 1Chr 22:2
charged him to *b* an house for the..... 1Chr 22:6
it was in my mind to *b* an house....... 1Chr 22:7
thou shalt not *b* an house unto my..... 1Chr 22:8
He shall *b* an house for my name...... 1Chr 22:10
b the house of the Lord thy God,....... 1Chr 22:11
b the sanctuary of the LORD............. 1Chr 22:19
I had in mine heart to *b* an house..... 1Chr 28:2
Thou shalt not *b* an house for my...... 1Chr 28:3
thy son, he shall *b* my house.......... 1Chr 28:6
to *b* an house for the sanctuary....... 1Chr 28:10
to *b* thee an house for thine holy...... 1Chr 29:16
to *b* the palace, for the which I........ 1Chr 29:19
Solomon determined to *b* an house.... 2Chr 2:1
didst send him cedars to *b* him an.... 2Chr 2:3
I *b* an house to the name of............. 2Chr 2:4
And the house which I *b* is great...... 2Chr 2:5
But who is able to *b* him an house..... 2Chr 2:6
that I should *b* him an house............ 2Chr 2:6
to *b* shall be wonderful great............ 2Chr 2:9
that might *b* an house for the........... 2Chr 2:12
Then Solomon began to *b* the house... 2Chr 3:1
he began to *b* in the second day....... 2Chr 3:2
tribes of Israel to *b* an house in........ 2Chr 6:5
to *b* an house for the name of the..... 2Chr 6:5
heart to *b* an house for my name...... 2Chr 6:8
thou shalt not *b* the house.............. 2Chr 6:9
he shall *b* the house for my name..... 2Chr 6:9
Solomon desired to *b* in Jerusalem.... 2Chr 8:6
Let us *b* these cities, and make........ 2Chr 14:7
son of David king of Israel did *b*....... 2Chr 35:3
he hath charged me to *b* him an....... 2Chr 36:23
he hath charged me to *b* him an........ Ezr 1:2
b the house of the LORD God of......... Ezr 1:3
to go up to *b* the house of.............. Ezr 1:5
said unto them, Let us *b* with you...... Ezr 4:2
us to *b* an house unto our God......... Ezr 4:3
b unto the LORD God of Israel,.......... Ezr 4:3
began to *b* the house of God which... Ezr 5:2
commanded you to *b* this house........ Ezr 5:3
Who commanded you to *b* this house... Ezr 5:9
b the house that was builded........... Ezr 5:11
a decree to *b* this house of God....... Ezr 5:13
was made of Cyrus the king to *b*...... Ezr 5:17
the elders of the Jews *b* this............ Ezr 6:7
sepulchres, that I may *b* it.............. Neh 2:5
let us *b* up the wall of Jerusalem...... Neh 2:17

And they said, Let us rise up and *b*.... Neh 2:18
we his servants will arise and *b*........ Neh 2:20
gate did the sons of Hassenaah *b*..... Neh 3:3
he *b* it, and set up the doors............ Neh 3:14
he said, Even that which they *b*......... Neh 4:3
we are not able to *b* the wall............ Neh 4:10
destroy them, and not *b* them up....... Ps 28:5
b thou the walls of Jerusalem........... Ps 51:18
will *b* the cities of Judah................. Ps 69:35
ever, and *b* up thy throne to all........ Ps 89:4
When the LORD shall *b* up Zion.......... Ps 102:16
Except the LORD *b* the house,........... Ps 127:1
they labour in vain that *b* it............. Ps 127:1
The LORD doth *b* up Jerusalem.......... Ps 147:2
and afterwards *b* thine house........... Prov 24:27
to break down, and a time to *b* up..... Eccl 3:3
we will *b* upon her a palace of......... Song 8:9
but we will *b* with hewn stones......... Is 9:10
he shall *b* my city, and he shall........ Is 45:13
the shall *b* the old waste places....... Is 58:12
of strangers shall *b* up thy walls...... Is 60:10
they shall *b* the old wastes, they...... Is 61:4
And they shall *b* houses, and........... Is 65:21
They shall not *b*, and another.......... Is 65:22
is the house that ye *b* unto me......... Is 66:1
destroy, and to throw down, to *b*...... Jer 1:10
and concerning a kingdom, to *b*........ Jer 18:9
I will *b* me a wide house and large.... Jer 22:14
and I will *b* them, and not pull.......... Jer 24:6
B ye houses, and dwell in them........ Jer 29:5
b ye houses, and dwell in them........ Jer 29:28
Again I will *b* thee, and thou............ Jer 31:4
so will I watch over them, to *b*......... Jer 31:28
Israel to return, and will *b* them....... Jer 33:7
Neither shall ye *b* house, nor sow..... Jer 35:7
Nor to *b* houses for us to dwell........ Jer 35:9
in this land, them will I *b* you........... Jer 42:10
b a fort against it, and cast a.......... Eze 4:2
let us *b* houses............................. Eze 11:3
to cast a mount, and to *b* a fort....... Eze 21:22
and shall *b* houses, and plant.......... Eze 28:26
I the LORD *b* the ruined places......... Eze 36:36
to *b* Jerusalem unto the Messiah...... Dan 9:25
I will *b* as in the days of old........... Amos 9:11
they shall *b* the waste cities, and..... Amos 9:14
They *b* up Zion with blood, and........ Mic 3:10
they shall also *b* houses, but not...... Zeph 1:13
and bring wood, and *b* the house...... Hag 1:8
To *b* it an house in the land of......... Zec 5:11
he shall *b* the temple of the LORD...... Zec 6:12
Even he shall *b* the temple of the..... Zec 6:13
b in the temple of the LORD, and...... Zec 6:15
Tyrus did *b* herself a strong hold...... Zec 9:3
return and *b* the desolate places...... Mal 1:4
the LORD of hosts, They shall *b*........ Mal 1:4
upon this rock I will *b* my church....... Mt 16:18
because ye *b* the tombs of the......... Mt 23:29
of God, and to *b* it in three days....... Mt 26:61
within three days I will *b*................. Mk 14:58
Woe unto you for ye *b* the.............. Lk 11:47
them, and ye *b* their sepulchres....... Lk 11:48
pull down my barns, and *b* greater.... Lk 12:18
of you, intending to *b* a tower.......... Lk 14:28
Saying, This man began to *b*............ Lk 14:30
what house will ye *b* me................. Acts 7:49
will *b* again the tabernacle of.......... Acts 15:16
I will *b* again the ruins thereof......... Acts 15:16
grace, which is able to *b* you up....... Acts 20:32
lest I should *b* upon another............ Rom 15:20
Now if any man *b* upon this............. 1Cor 3:12
For if I *b* again the things which....... Gal 2:18

BUILDED

he *b* a city, and called the name....... Gen 4:17
Noah *b* an altar unto the LORD.......... Gen 8:20
b Nineveh, and the city Rehoboth,..... Gen 10:11
which the children of men *b*............. Gen 11:5
there *b* he an altar unto the LORD...... Gen 12:7
there *b* he an altar unto the LORD...... Gen 12:8
he *b* an altar there, and called......... Gen 26:25
b an altar under the hill, and........... Ex 24:4
unto the cities which they *b*............. Num 32:38
in that ye have *b* you an altar.......... Josh 22:16
less this house that I have *b*............ 1Kin 8:27
that this house, which I have *b*......... 1Kin 8:43
thereof, wherewith Baasha had *b*...... 1Kin 15:22
b for Ashtoreth the abomination........ 2Kin 23:13
the house that is to be *b* for the....... 1Chr 22:5
b the altar of the God of Israel,........ Ezr 3:2
the children of the captivity *b*........... Ezr 4:1
the king, that, if this city be *b*......... Ezr 4:13
that, if this city be *b* again............. Ezr 4:16
cease, and that this city be not *b*..... Ezr 4:21
which is *b* with great stones, and..... Ezr 5:8
that was *b* these many years ago...... Ezr 5:11
which a great king of Israel *b*.......... Ezr 5:11
house of God be *b* in his place........ Ezr 5:15
at Jerusalem, Let the house be *b*...... Ezr 6:3
And the elders of the Jews *b*........... Ezr 6:14
And they *b*, and finished it,............. Ezr 6:14
priests, and they *b* the sheep gate.... Neh 3:1
next unto him *b* the men of............. Neh 3:2
next to them *b* Zaccur the son of...... Neh 3:2
heard that we *b* the wall, he was...... Neh 4:1
They which *b* on the wall, and they.... Neh 4:17
sword girded by his side, and so *b*.... Neh 4:18
heard that I had *b* the wall.............. Neh 6:1
therein, and the houses were not *b*.... Neh 7:4
for the singers had *b* them.............. Neh 12:29
away an house which he *b* not.......... Job 20:19
Jerusalem is *b* as a city that is....... Ps 122:3

Wisdom hath *b* her house, she hath...... Prov 9:1
Through wisdom is an house *b*........ Prov 24:3
I *b* me houses........... Eccl 2:4
tower of David *b* for an armoury....... Song 4:4
city shall be *b* upon her own heap...... Jer 30:18
He hath *b* against me, and......... Lam 3:5
and the wastes shall be *b*............ Eze 36:10
cities, and the wastes shall be *b*...... Eze 36:33
they sold, they planted, they *b*....... Lk 17:28
In whom ye also are *b* together..... Eph 2:22
inasmuch as he hath *b* the.......... Heb 3:3
For every house is *b* by some man...... Heb 3:4

BUILDEDST
goodly cities, which thou *b* not....... Deut 6:10

BUILDER
which hath foundations, whose *b*..... Heb 11:10

BUILDERS
Solomon's *b* and Hiram's *b*........ 1Kin 5:18
it out to the carpenters and *b*........ 2Chr 34:11
Unto carpenters, and *b*, and masons,.. 2Kin 22:6
b gave they it, to buy hewn stone..... Ezr 3:7
when the *b* laid the foundation of..... Ezr 3:10
thee to anger before the *b*.......... Neh 4:5
For the *b*, every one had his......... Neh 4:18
The stone which the *b* refused is..... Ps 118:22
thy *b* have perfected thy beauty...... Eze 27:4
The stone which the *b* rejected....... Mt 21:42
The stone which the *b* rejected is..... Mk 12:10
The stone which the *b* rejected....... Lk 20:17
which was set at nought of you *b*..... Acts 4:11
the stone which the *b* disallowed..... 1Pet 2:7

BUILDEST
When thou *b* a new house, then...... Deut 22:8
for which cause thou *b* the wall...... Neh 6:6
In that thou *b* thine eminent........ Eze 16:31
b it in three days, save thyself...... Mt 27:40
temple, and *b* it in three days,...... Mk 15:29

BUILDETH
riseth up and *b* this city Jericho..... Josh 6:26
He *b* his house as a moth, and as a.. Job 27:18
Every wise woman *b* her house...... Prov 14:1
Woe unto him that *b* his house by.... Jer 22:13
forgotten his Maker, and *b* temples... Hos 8:14
It is he that *b* his stories in........ Amos 9:6
Woe to him that *b* a town with...... Hab 2:12
foundation, and another *b* thereupon.. 1Cor 3:10
man take heed how he *b* thereupon... 1Cor 3:10

BUILDING
in *b* you an altar beside the........ Josh 22:19
made an end of *b* his own house...... 1Kin 3:1
And the house, when it was in *b*...... 1Kin 6:7
in the house, while it was in *b*...... 1Kin 6:7
this house which thou art in *b*....... 1Kin 6:12
So was he seven years in *b* it........ 1Kin 6:38
But Solomon was *b* his own house..... 1Kin 7:1
the *b* of the house of the LORD....... 1Kin 9:1
that he left off *b* of Ramah.......... 1Kin 15:21
God, and had made ready for the *b*... 1Chr 28:2
for the *b* of the house of God....... 2Chr 3:3
it, that he left off *b* of that........ 2Chr 16:5
thereof, wherewith Baasha was *b*.... 2Chr 16:6
of Judah, and troubled them in *b*..... Ezr 4:4
b the rebellious and the bad city,.... Ezr 4:12
names of the men that make this *b*... Ezr 5:4
even until now hath it been in *b*..... Ezr 5:16
for the *b* of this house of God....... Ezr 6:8
much slothfulness the *b* decayeth.... Eccl 10:18
b forts, to cut off many persons..... Eze 17:17
he measured the breadth of the *b*.... Eze 40:5
Now the *b* that was before the...... Eze 41:12
the wall of the *b* was five cubits,.... Eze 41:9
and the separate place, and the *b*.... Eze 41:13
he measured the length of the *b*..... Eze 41:15
was before the *b* toward the north... Eze 42:1
and than the middlemost of the *b*.... Eze 42:5
therefore the *b* was straitened...... Eze 42:6
place, and over against the *b*....... Eze 42:10
there was a row of *b* round about.... Eze 46:23
and six years was this temple in *b*.... Jn 2:20
God's husbandry, ye are God's *b*..... 1Cor 3:9
dissolved, we have a *b* of God...... 2Cor 5:1
In whom all the *b* fitly framed...... Eph 2:21
that is to say, not of this *b*........ Heb 9:11
b up yourselves on your most holy.... Jude 20
the *b* of the wall of it was of...... Rev 21:18

BUILDINGS
to shew him the *b* of the temple..... Mt 24:1
of stones and what *b* are here....... Mk 13:1
him, Seest thou these great *b*....... Mk 13:2

BUILT
b there an altar unto the LORD....... Gen 13:18
Abraham *b* an altar there, and laid... Gen 22:9
b him an house, and made booths.... Gen 33:17
he *b* there an altar, and called...... Gen 35:7
they *b* for Pharaoh treasure........ Ex 1:11
Moses *b* an altar, and called........ Ex 17:15
saw it, he *b* an altar before it....... Ex 32:5
(Now Hebron was *b* seven years..... Num 13:22
let the city of Sihon be *b*......... Num 21:27
b seven altars, and offered a....... Num 23:14
And the children of Gad *b* Dibon..... Num 32:34
the children of Reuben *b* Heshbon.... Num 32:37
hast *b* goodly houses, and dwelt..... Deut 8:12
it shall not be *b* again........... Deut 13:16
is there that hath *b* a new house..... Deut 20:5
Then Joshua *b* an altar unto the..... Josh 8:30

he *b* the city, and dwelt therein...... Josh 19:50
b there an altar by Jordan........ Josh 22:10
b an altar over against the land..... Josh 22:11
That we have *b* us an altar to....... Josh 22:23
labour, and cities which ye *b* not.... Josh 24:13
b a city, and called the name....... Judg 1:26
Then Gideon *b* an altar there unto.... Judg 6:24
offered upon the altar that was *b*.... Judg 6:28
they *b* a city, and dwelt therein..... Judg 18:28
b there an altar, and offered....... Judg 21:4
there he *b* an altar unto the LORD.... 1Sa 7:17
Saul *b* an altar unto the LORD....... 1Sa 14:35
altar that he *b* unto the LORD....... 1Sa 14:35
David *b* round about from Millo and.. 2Sa 5:9
and they *b* David an house........ 2Sa 5:11
David *b* there an altar unto the...... 2Sa 24:25
house *b* unto the name of the LORD... 1Kin 3:2
which king Solomon *b* for the LORD... 1Kin 6:2
house he *b* chambers round about.... 1Kin 6:5
was *b* of stone made ready before.... 1Kin 6:7
So he *b* the house, and finished it.... 1Kin 6:9
then he *b* chambers against all...... 1Kin 6:10
So Solomon *b* the house, and....... 1Kin 6:14
he *b* the walls of the house........ 1Kin 6:15
he *b* twenty cubits on the sides..... 1Kin 6:16
he even *b* them for it within,....... 1Kin 6:16
he *b* the inner court with three..... 1Kin 6:36
He *b* also the house of the forest.... 1Kin 7:2
I have surely *b* thee an house to.... 1Kin 8:13
have *b* an house for the name of.... 1Kin 8:20
house that I have *b* for thy name.... 1Kin 8:44
house which I have *b* for thy name... 1Kin 8:48
this house, which thou hast *b*....... 1Kin 9:3
when Solomon had *b* the two houses. 1Kin 9:10
And Solomon *b* Gezer............ 1Kin 9:17
house which Solomon had *b* for her... 1Kin 9:24
altar which he *b* unto the LORD...... 1Kin 9:25
and the house that he had *b*........ 1Kin 10:4
Solomon *b* Millo, and repaired the.... 1Kin 11:27
as I *b* for David, and will give...... 1Kin 11:38
Jeroboam *b* Shechem............ 1Kin 12:25
went out from thence, and *b* Penuel.. 1Kin 12:25
For they also *b* them high places,.... 1Kin 14:23
b Ramah, that he might not suffer... 1Kin 15:17
king Asa *b* with them Geba of...... 1Kin 15:22
he did, and the cities which he *b*..... 1Kin 15:23
b on the hill, and called the name... 1Kin 16:24
the name of the city which he *b*..... 1Kin 16:24
Baal, which he had *b* in Samaria..... 1Kin 16:32
with the stones he *b* an altar in..... 1Kin 18:32
made, and all the cities that he *b*.... 1Kin 22:39
He *b* Elath, and restored it to...... 2Kin 14:22
He *b* the higher gate of the house... 2Kin 15:35
Urijah the priest *b* an altar........ 2Kin 16:11
that they had *b* in the house....... 2Kin 16:18
they *b* them high places in all...... 2Kin 17:9
For he *b* up again the high places.... 2Kin 21:3
he *b* altars in the house of........ 2Kin 21:4
he *b* altars for all the host of...... 2Kin 21:5
they *b* forts against it round........ 2Kin 25:1
that Solomon *b* in Jerusalem....... 1Chr 6:10
until Solomon had *b* the house of.... 1Chr 6:32
who *b* Beth-horon the nether, and.... 1Chr 7:24
and Shamed, who *b* Ono.......... 1Chr 8:12
he *b* the city round about, even..... 1Chr 11:8
Why have ye not *b* me an house to... 1Chr 17:6
David *b* there an altar unto the...... 1Chr 21:26
to be *b* to the name of the LORD..... 1Chr 22:19
But I have *b* an house of......... 2Chr 6:2
have *b* the house for the name of.... 2Chr 6:10
less this house which I have *b*...... 2Chr 6:18
I have *b* is called by thy name...... 2Chr 6:33
house which I have *b* for thy name... 2Chr 6:34
house which I have *b* for thy name... 2Chr 6:38
wherein Solomon had *b* the house... 2Chr 8:1
to Solomon, Solomon *b* them........ 2Chr 8:2
he *b* Tadmor in the wilderness, and.. 2Chr 8:4
cities, which he *b* in Hamath....... 2Chr 8:5
Also he *b* Beth-horon the upper,.... 2Chr 8:5
the house that he had *b* for her..... 2Chr 8:11
which he had *b* before the porch,.... 2Chr 8:12
and the house that he had *b*........ 2Chr 9:3
b cities for defence in Judah....... 2Chr 11:5
He *b* even Beth-lehem........... 2Chr 11:6
he *b* fenced cities in Judah........ 2Chr 14:6
So they *b* and prospered.......... 2Chr 14:7
b Ramah, to the intent that he..... 2Chr 16:1
he *b* therewith Geba and Mizpah.... 2Chr 16:6
he *b* in Judah castles, and cities..... 2Chr 17:12
have *b* thee a sanctuary therein..... 2Chr 20:8
He *b* Eloth, and restored it to...... 2Chr 26:2
b cities about Ashdod, and among.... 2Chr 26:6
Moreover Uzziah *b* towers in....... 2Chr 26:9
Also he *b* towers in the desert,...... 2Chr 26:10
He *b* the high gate of the house..... 2Chr 27:3
and on the wall of Ophel he *b* much... 2Chr 27:3
Moreover he *b* cities in the........ 2Chr 27:4
and in the forests he *b* castles...... 2Chr 27:4
b up all the wall that was broken.... 2Chr 32:5
For he *b* again the high places...... 2Chr 33:3
Also he *b* altars in the house of..... 2Chr 33:4
he *b* altars for all the host of...... 2Chr 33:5
Now after this he *b* a wall......... 2Chr 33:14
all the altars that he had *b* in...... 2Chr 33:15
places wherein he *b* high places..... 2Chr 33:19
they *b* it, and set up the doors...... Neh 3:13
he *b* it, and covered it, and set up... Neh 3:15
So *b* we the wall.............. Neh 4:6
came to pass, when the wall was *b*.. Neh 7:1
which *b* desolate places for........ Job 3:14

down, and it cannot be *b* again...... Job 12:14
the Almighty, thou shalt be *b* up..... Job 22:23
he *b* his sanctuary like high....... Ps 78:69
Mercy shall be *b* up for ever....... Ps 89:2
b great bulwarks against it........ Eccl 9:14
b a tower in the midst of it, and..... Is 5:2
it shall never be *b*.............. Is 25:2
cities of Judah, Ye shall be *b*....... Is 44:26
to Jerusalem, Thou shalt be *b*....... Is 44:28
they have *b* the high places of...... Jer 7:31
then shall they be *b* in the midst.... Jer 12:16
They have *b* also the high places.... Jer 19:5
build thee, and thou shalt be *b*...... Jer 31:4
that the city shall be *b* to the...... Jer 31:38
that they *b* it even unto this day.... Jer 32:31
they *b* the high places of Baal,...... Jer 32:35
which I have *b* will I break down..... Jer 45:4
b forts against it round about....... Jer 52:4
one *b* up a wall, and, lo, others..... Eze 13:10
That thou hast also *b* unto thee..... Eze 16:24
Thou hast *b* thy high place at....... Eze 16:25
thou shalt be *b* no more.......... Eze 26:14
that I have *b* for the house of...... Dan 4:30
the street shall be *b* again........ Dan 9:25
ye have *b* houses of hewn stone,.... Amos 5:11
day that thy walls are to be *b*....... Mic 7:11
that the LORD's house should be *b*.... Hag 1:2
my house shall be *b* in it.......... Zec 1:16
laid, that the temple might be *b*..... Zec 8:9
which *b* his house upon a rock...... Mt 7:24
which *b* his house upon the sand.... Mt 7:26
b a tower, and let it out to......... Mt 21:33
b a tower, and let it out to......... Mk 12:1
the hill whereon their city was *b*.... Lk 4:29
He is like a man which *b* an house.... Lk 6:48
b an house upon the earth......... Lk 6:49
and he hath *b* us a synagogue...... Lk 7:5
But Solomon *b* him an house....... Acts 7:47
abide which he hath *b* thereupon.... 1Cor 3:14
are *b* upon the foundation of the..... Eph 2:20
b up in him, and stablished in the... Col 2:7
but he that *b* all things is God...... Heb 3:4
are *b* up a spiritual house, an....... 1Pet 2:5

BUKKI (buk´-ki)
1. A high priest
And Abishua begat B............ 1Chr 6:5
and B begat Uzzi............... 1Chr 6:5
B his son, Uzzi his son, Zerahiah.... 1Chr 6:51
the son of Uzzi, the son of B....... Ezr 7:4
2. A Danite prince
of Dan, B the son of Jogli......... Num 34:22

BUKKIAH (buk-ki´-ah) *A Levite musician.*
B, Mattaniah, Uzziel, Shebuel, and... 1Chr 25:4
The sixth to b, he, his sons, and.... 1Chr 25:13

BUL (bul) *Eighth month of the Hebrew year.*
the eleventh year, in the month B... 1Kin 6:38

BULL
Their *b* gendereth, and faileth not... Job 21:10
the streets, as a wild *b* in a net..... Is 51:20

BULLOCK
Take one young *b*, and two rams..... Ex 29:1
them in the basket, with the *b*...... Ex 29:3
thou shalt cause a *b* to be........ Ex 29:10
hands upon the head of the *b*....... Ex 29:10
shalt kill the *b* before the LORD..... Ex 29:11
shalt take of the blood of the *b*..... Ex 29:12
But the flesh of the *b*, and his...... Ex 29:14
day a *b* for a sin offering for....... Ex 29:36
shall kill the *b* before the LORD..... Lev 1:5
a young *b* without blemish........ Lev 4:3
he shall bring the *b* unto the....... Lev 4:4
kill the *b* before the LORD......... Lev 4:4
b at the bottom of the altar of...... Lev 4:7
fat of the *b* for the sin offering..... Lev 4:8
the *b* of the sacrifice of peace...... Lev 4:10
And the skin of the *b*, and all his.... Lev 4:11
Even the whole *b* shall he carry..... Lev 4:12
shall offer a young *b* for the sin..... Lev 4:14
the head of the *b* before the LORD... Lev 4:15
the *b* shall be killed before the..... Lev 4:15
he shall do with the *b* as he did..... Lev 4:20
did with the *b* for a sin offering..... Lev 4:20
forth the *b* without the camp....... Lev 4:21
burn him as he burned the first *b*.... Lev 4:21
a *b* for the sin offering, and two.... Lev 8:2
he brought the *b* for the sin....... Lev 8:14
the *b* for the sin offering......... Lev 8:14
But the *b*, and his hide, his flesh.... Lev 8:17
Also a *b* and a ram for peace....... Lev 9:4
He slew also the *b* and the ram for... Lev 9:18
And the fat of the *b* and of the ram.. Lev 9:19
with a young *b* for a sin offering..... Lev 16:3
offer his *b* of the sin offering....... Lev 16:6
bring the *b* of the sin offering...... Lev 16:11
shall kill the *b* of the sin......... Lev 16:11
shall take of the blood of the *b*..... Lev 16:14
as he did with the blood of the *b*.... Lev 16:15
shall take of the blood of the *b*..... Lev 16:18
the *b* for the sin offering, and...... Lev 16:27
Either a *b* or a lamb that hath...... Lev 22:23
When a *b*, or a sheep, or a goat,.... Lev 22:27
of the first year, and one young *b*... Lev 23:18
One young *b*, one ram, one lamb of.. Num 7:15
One young *b*, one ram, one lamb of.. Num 7:21
One young *b*, one ram, one lamb of.. Num 7:27
One young *b*, one ram, one lamb of.. Num 7:33
One young *b*, one ram, one lamb of.. Num 7:39
One young *b*, one ram, one lamb of.. Num 7:45

One young *b*, one ram, one lamb of.... Num 7:51
One young *b*, one ram, one lamb of.... Num 7:57
One young *b*, one ram, one lamb of.... Num 7:63
One young *b*, one ram, one lamb of.... Num 7:69
One young *b*, one ram, one lamb of.... Num 7:75
One young *b*, one ram, one lamb of.... Num 7:81
a young *b* with his meat offering........ Num 8:8
another young *b* shalt thou take........ Num 8:8
a *b* for a burnt offering, or for.......... Num 15:8
Then shall he bring with a *b*............. Num 15:9
Thus shall it be done for one *b*......... Num 15:11
one young *b* for a burnt offering....... Num 15:24
Balaam offered on every altar a *b*..... Num 23:2
have offered upon every altar a *b*..... Num 23:4
seven altars, and offered a *b*............. Num 23:14
Balaam had said, and offered a *b*...... Num 23:30
mingled with oil, for one *b*.............. Num 28:12
be half an hin of wine unto a *b*......... Num 28:14
deals shall ye offer for a *b*............... Num 28:20
oil, three tenth deals unto one *b*....... Num 28:28
one young *b*, one ram, seven............. Num 29:2
oil, three tenth deals for a *b*............. Num 29:3
one young *b*, one ram, and seven...... Num 29:8
oil, three tenth deals to a *b*............... Num 29:9
every *b* of the thirteen bullocks........ Num 29:14
one *b*, one ram, seven lambs of........ Num 29:36
their drink offerings for the *b*........... Num 29:37
work with the firstling of thy *b*......... Deut 15:19
unto the LORD thy God any *b*............. Deut 17:1
is like the firstling of his *b*............... Deut 33:17
him, Take thy father's young *b*......... Judg 6:25
even the second *b* of seven years...... Judg 6:25
place, and take the second *b*............. Judg 6:26
the second *b* was offered upon the.... Judg 6:28
And they slew a *b*, and brought the... 1Sa 1:25
then choose one *b* for themselves...... 1Kin 18:23
and I will dress the other *b*............... 1Kin 18:23
Choose you one *b* for yourselves....... 1Kin 18:25
they took the *b* which was given........ 1Kin 18:26
cut the *b* in pieces, and laid him....... 1Kin 18:33
consecrate himself with a young *b*.... 2Chr 13:9
I will take no *b* out of thy house........ Ps 50:9
than an ox or *b* that hath horns......... Ps 69:31
lion shall eat straw like the *b*............ Is 65:25
as a *b* unaccustomed to the yoke....... Jer 31:18
a young *b* for a sin offering.............. Eze 43:19
Thou shalt take the *b* also of the....... Eze 43:21
as they did cleanse it with the *b*........ Eze 43:22
offer a young *b* without blemish........ Eze 43:23
they shall also prepare a young *b*...... Eze 43:25
take a young *b* without blemish......... Eze 45:18
the land a *b* for a sin offering........... Eze 45:22
meat offering of an ephah for a *b*...... Eze 45:24
be a young *b* without blemish........... Eze 46:6
a meat offering, an ephah for a *b*...... Eze 46:7
offering shall be an ephah to a *b*....... Eze 46:11

BULLOCK'S
lay his hand upon the *b* head............. Lev 4:4
shall take of the *b* blood.................... Lev 4:5
b blood to the tabernacle of the........ Lev 4:16

BULLOCKS
the burnt offering were twelve *b*....... Num 7:87
offerings were twenty and four *b*....... Num 7:88
hands upon the heads of the *b*........... Num 8:12
and prepare me here seven *b*............. Num 23:29
two young *b*, and one ram, seven...... Num 28:11
two young *b*, and one ram.................. Num 28:19
one young *b*, one ram, seven lambs.... Num 28:27
thirteen young *b*, two rams, and........ Num 29:13
every bullock of the thirteen *b*.......... Num 29:14
day ye shall offer twelve young *b*..... Num 29:17
their drink offerings for the *b*........... Num 29:18
And on the third day eleven *b*........... Num 29:20
their drink offerings for the *b*........... Num 29:21
And on the fourth day ten *b*.............. Num 29:23
their drink offerings for the *b*........... Num 29:24
And on the fifth day nine *b*............... Num 29:26
their drink offerings for the *b*........... Num 29:27
And on the sixth day eight *b*............. Num 29:29
their drink offerings for the *b*........... Num 29:30
And on the seventh day seven *b*........ Num 29:32
their drink offerings for the *b*........... Num 29:33
him up with her, with three *b*............ 1Sa 1:24
Let them therefore give us two *b*....... 1Kin 18:23
LORD, that they offered seven *b*......... 1Chr 15:26
after that day, even a thousand *b*...... 2Chr 29:21
they brought seven *b*......................... 2Chr 29:21
So they killed the *b*, and the............. 2Chr 29:22
brought, was threescore and ten *b*.... 2Chr 29:32
to the congregation a thousand *b*...... 2Chr 30:24
to the congregation a thousand *b*...... 2Chr 30:24
thousand, and three thousand *b*........ 2Chr 35:7
they have need of, both young *b*........ Ezr 6:9
of this house of God an hundred *b*..... Ezr 6:17
buy speedily with this money *b*......... Ezr 7:17
twelve *b* for all Israel, ninety........... Ezr 8:35
take unto you now seven *b*................ Job 42:8
they offer *b* upon thine altar............. Ps 51:19
I will offer *b* with goats..................... Ps 66:15
I delight not in the blood of *b*........... Is 1:11
them, and the *b* with the bulls........... Is 34:7
in the midst of her like fatted *b*........ Jer 46:21
Slay all her *b*................................... Jer 50:27
rams, of lambs, and of goats, of *b*.... Eze 39:18
offering to the LORD, and even *b*....... Eze 45:23
they sacrifice *b* in Gilgal.................. Hos 12:11

BULLS
their colts, forty kine, and ten *b*........ Gen 32:15
Many *b* have compassed me.............. Ps 22:12

strong *b* of Bashan have beset me..... Ps 22:12
Will I eat the flesh of *b*..................... Ps 50:13
spearmen, the multitude of the *b*...... Ps 68:30
them, and the bullocks with the *b*..... Is 34:7
heifer at grass, and bellow as *b*........ Jer 50:11
twelve brasen *b* that were under....... Jer 52:20
For if the blood of *b* and of goats...... Heb 9:13
not possible that the blood of *b*........ Heb 10:4

BULRUSH
is it to bow down his head as a *b*....... Is 58:5

BULRUSHES
him, she took for him an ark of *b*...... Ex 2:3
in vessels of *b* upon the waters.......... Is 18:2

BULWARKS
thou shalt build *b* against the........... Deut 20:20
to be on the towers and upon the *b*... 2Chr 26:15
Mark ye well her *b*, consider her...... Ps 48:13
it, and built great *b* against it........... Eccl 9:14
will God appoint for walls and a *b*.... Is 26:1

BUNAH (boo'-nah) *Son of Jerahmeel*.
were, Ram the firstborn, and B............ 1Chr 2:25

BUNCH
And ye shall take a *b* of hyssop......... Ex 12:22

BUNCHES
bread, and an hundred *b* of raisins..... 2Sa 16:1
b of raisins, and wine, and oil, and.... 1Chr 12:40
treasures upon the *b* of camels......... Is 30:6

BUNDLE
every man's *b* of money was in his.... Gen 42:35
b of life with the LORD thy God........ 1Sa 25:29
A *b* of myrrh is my wellbeloved......... Song 1:13
Paul had gathered a *b* of sticks......... Acts 28:3

BUNDLES
their father saw the *b* of money......... Gen 42:35
and bind them in *b* to burn them....... Mt 13:30

BUNNI (bun'-ni)
  1. *A Levite with Ezra*.
and Bani, Kadmiel, Shebaniah, B........ Neh 9:4
  2. *Father of Hashabiah*.
son of Hashabiah, the son of B............ Neh 11:15
  3. *A family who renewed the covenant*.
B, Azgad, Bebai,.............................. Neh 10:15

BURDEN
they shall bear the *b* with thee.......... Ex 18:22
hateth the lying under his *b*............... Ex 23:5
These things are the *b* of the............. Num 4:15
one to his service and to his *b*.......... Num 4:19
And this is the charge of their *b*........ Num 4:31
of the charge of their *b*..................... Num 4:32
the service of the *b* in the................. Num 4:47
service, and according to his *b*......... Num 4:49
they shall bear the *b* of all................ Num 11:11
they shall bear the *b* of the............... Num 11:17
bear your cumbrance, and your *b*...... Deut 1:12
then thou shalt be a *b* unto me........... 2Sa 15:33
be yet a *b* unto my lord this day......... 2Sa 19:35
thy servant two mules' *b* of earth...... 2Kin 5:17
of Damascus, forty camels' *b*............ 2Kin 8:9
the LORD laid this *b* upon him........... 2Kin 9:25
it shall not be a *b* upon your............. 2Chr 35:3
that there should no *b* be brought..... Neh 13:19
thee, so that I am a *b* to myself.......... Job 7:20
as an heavy *b* they are too heavy....... Ps 38:4
Cast thy *b* upon the LORD, and he..... Ps 55:22
and the grasshopper shall be a *b*....... Eccl 12:5
hast broken the yoke of his *b*............ Is 9:4
that his *b* shall be taken away.......... Is 10:27
The *b* of Babylon, which Isaiah........ Is 13:1
his *b* depart from off their................. Is 14:25
that king Ahaz died was this *b*.......... Is 14:28
The *b* of Moab................................. Is 15:1
The *b* of Damascus........................... Is 17:1
The *b* of Egypt................................ Is 19:1
The *b* of the desert of the sea........... Is 21:1
The *b* of Dumah............................... Is 21:11
The *b* upon Arabia........................... Is 21:13
The *b* of the valley of vision............. Is 22:1
the *b* that was upon it shall be.......... Is 22:25
The *b* of Tyre.................................. Is 23:1
The *b* of the beasts of the south........ Is 30:6
anger, and the *b* thereof is heavy...... Is 30:27
they are a *b* to the weary beast......... Is 46:1
they could not deliver the *b*.............. Is 46:2
bear no *b* on the sabbath day, nor..... Jer 17:21
Neither carry forth a *b* out of........... Jer 17:22
to bring in no *b* through the.............. Jer 17:24
sabbath day, and not to bear a *b*....... Jer 17:27
saying, What is the *b* of the LORD..... Jer 23:33
shalt then say unto them, What *b*...... Jer 23:33
The *b* of the LORD, I will even.......... Jer 23:33
the *b* of the LORD shall ye............... Jer 23:36
every man's word shall be his *b*........ Jer 23:36
since ye say, The *b* of the LORD........ Jer 23:38
The *b* of the LORD, and I have sent... Jer 23:38
shall not say, The *b* of the LORD....... Jer 23:38
This *b* concerneth the prince in......... Eze 12:10
for the *b* of the king of princes......... Hos 8:10
The *b* of Nineveh............................. Nah 1:1
The *b* which Habakkuk the prophet... Hab 1:1
whom the reproach of it was a *b*....... Zeph 3:18
The *b* of the word of the LORD in...... Zec 9:1
The *b* of the word of the LORD for.... Zec 12:1
all that *b* themselves with it............. Zec 12:3
The *b* of the word of the LORD to..... Mal 1:1

my yoke is easy, and my *b* is light..... Mt 11:30
unto us, which have borne the *b*........ Mt 20:12
to lay upon you no greater *b* than..... Acts 15:28
the ship was to unlade her *b*............. Acts 21:3
But be it so, I did not *b* you.............. 2Cor 12:16
every man shall bear his own *b*......... Gal 6:5
I will put upon you none other *b*....... Rev 2:24

BURDENED
this tabernacle do groan, being *b*...... 2Cor 5:4
that other men be eased, and ye *b*..... 2Cor 8:13

BURDENS
ass couching down between two *b*.... Gen 49:14
to afflict them with their *b*............... Ex 1:11
brethren, and looked on their *b*......... Ex 2:11
get you unto your *b*.......................... Ex 5:4
and ye make them rest from their *b*... Ex 5:5
from under the *b* of the Egyptians..... Ex 6:6
from under the *b* of the Egyptians..... Ex 6:7
Gershonites, to serve, and for *b*........ Num 4:24
the Gershonites, in all their *b*........... Num 4:27
into them in charge all their *b*.......... Num 4:27
and ten thousand that bare *b*............ 1Kin 5:15
and ten thousand men to bear *b*........ 2Chr 2:2
of them to be bearers of *b*................ 2Chr 2:18
greatness of the *b* laid upon him....... 2Chr 24:27
they were over the bearers of *b*........ 2Chr 34:13
of the bearers of *b* is decayed........... Neh 4:10
on the wall, and they that bare *b*...... Neh 4:17
and figs, and all manner of *b*............ Neh 13:15
wickedness, to undo the heavy *b*...... Is 58:6
but have seen for thee false *b*........... Lam 2:14
and ye take from him *b* of wheat....... Amos 5:11
For they bind heavy *b* and grievous... Mt 23:4
men with *b* grievous to be borne....... Lk 11:46
the *b* with one of your fingers.......... Lk 11:46
Bear ye one another's *b*, and so......... Gal 6:2

BURDENSOME
a *b* stone for all people..................... Zec 12:3
kept myself from being *b* unto you.... 2Cor 11:9
be that I myself was not *b* to you....... 2Cor 12:13
and I will not be *b* to you................. 2Cor 12:14
others, when we might have been *b*.. 1Th 2:6

BURIAL
the *b* which belonged to the kings..... 2Chr 26:23
good, and also that he have no *b*....... Eccl 6:3
not be joined with them in *b*............. Is 14:20
be buried with the *b* of an ass.......... Jer 22:19
on my body, she did it for my *b*........ Mt 26:12
men carried Stephen to his *b*............ Acts 8:2

BURIED
thou shalt be *b* in a good old age....... Gen 15:15
Abraham *b* Sarah his wife in the....... Gen 23:19
Ishmael *b* him in the cave of............ Gen 25:9
there was Abraham *b*, and Sarah his.. Gen 25:10
she was *b* beneath Beth-el under....... Gen 35:8
was *b* in the way to Ephrath............. Gen 35:19
and his sons Esau and Jacob *b* him... Gen 35:29
I *b* her there in the way of............... Gen 48:7
There they *b* Abraham and Sarah his.. Gen 49:31
there they *b* Isaac and Rebekah his... Gen 49:31
and there I *b* Leah........................... Gen 49:31
b him in the cave of the field of........ Gen 50:13
father, after he had *b* his father........ Gen 50:14
because there they *b* the people........ Num 11:34
Miriam died there, and was *b* there... Num 20:1
For the Egyptians *b* all their............. Num 33:4
Aaron died, and there he was *b*......... Deut 10:6
he *b* him in a valley in the land........ Deut 34:6
they *b* him in the border of his......... Josh 24:30
b they in Shechem, in a parcel of..... Josh 24:32
they *b* him in a hill that................... Josh 24:33
they *b* him in the border of his......... Judg 2:9
was *b* in the sepulchre of Joash........ Judg 8:32
and died, and was *b* in Shamir......... Judg 10:2
And Jair died, and was *b* in Camon... Judg 10:5
was *b* in one of the cities of............. Judg 12:7
Ibzan, and was *b* at Beth-lehem....... Judg 12:10
was *b* in Aijalon in the country......... Judg 12:12
was *b* in Pirathon in the land of........ Judg 12:15
b him between Zorah and Eshtaol in.. Judg 16:31
will I die, and there will I be *b*......... Ruth 1:17
b him in his house at Ramah............ 1Sa 25:1
b him in Ramah, even in his own...... 1Sa 28:3
and *b* them in a tree at Jabesh, and... 1Sa 31:13
were they that *b* Saul...................... 2Sa 2:4
even unto Saul, and have *b* him........ 2Sa 2:5
b him in the sepulchre of his............ 2Sa 2:32
And they *b* Abner in Hebron............ 2Sa 3:32
b it in the sepulchre of Abner in....... 2Sa 4:12
was *b* in the sepulchre of his............ 2Sa 17:23
be *b* by the grave of my father and... 2Sa 19:37
Jonathan his son *b* they in the.......... 2Sa 21:14
was *b* in the city of David................ 1Kin 2:10
he was *b* in his own house in the...... 1Kin 2:34
was *b* in the city of David his........... 1Kin 11:43
came to pass, after he had *b* him...... 1Kin 13:31
wherein the man of God is *b*............ 1Kin 13:31
And they *b* him............................... 1Kin 14:18
was *b* with his fathers in the............ 1Kin 14:31
they *b* him in the city of David......... 1Kin 15:8
was *b* with his fathers in the............ 1Kin 15:24
his fathers, and was *b* in Tirzah........ 1Kin 16:6
his fathers, and was *b* in Samaria..... 1Kin 16:28
they *b* the king in Samaria.............. 1Kin 22:37
was *b* with his fathers in................. 2Kin 8:24
b him in his sepulchre with his......... 2Kin 9:28
and they *b* him in Samaria.............. 2Kin 10:35

B

they *b* him with his fathers in	2Kin 12:21
and they *b* him in Samaria	2Kin 13:9
Joash was *b* in Samaria with the	2Kin 13:13
And Elisha died, and they *b* him	2Kin 13:20
was *b* in Samaria with the kings	2Kin 13:13
he was *b* at Jerusalem with his	2Kin 14:20
they *b* him with his fathers in	2Kin 15:7
was *b* with his fathers in the	2Kin 15:38
was *b* with his fathers in the	2Kin 16:20
was *b* in the garden of his own	2Kin 21:18
he was *b* in his sepulchre in the	2Kin 21:26
b him in his own sepulchre	2Kin 23:30
b their bones under the oak in	1Chr 10:12
he was *b* in the city of David his	2Chr 9:31
was *b* in the city of David	2Chr 12:16
they *b* him in the city of David	2Chr 14:1
they *b* him in his own sepulchres	2Chr 16:14
was *b* with his fathers in the	2Chr 21:1
Howbeit they *b* him in the city of	2Chr 21:20
they had slain him, they *b* him	2Chr 22:9
they *b* him in the city of David	2Chr 24:16
they *b* him in the city of David	2Chr 24:25
but they *b* him not in the	2Chr 24:25
b him with his fathers in the	2Chr 25:28
they *b* him with his fathers in	2Chr 26:23
they *b* him in the city of David	2Chr 27:9
they *b* him in the city, even in	2Chr 28:27
they *b* him in the chiefest of the	2Chr 32:33
they *b* him in his own house	2Chr 33:20
was *b* in one of the sepulchres of	2Chr 34:24
remain of him shall be *b* in death	Job 27:15
And so I saw the wicked *b*, who had	Eccl 8:10
shall not be gathered, nor be *b*	Jer 8:2
neither shall they be *b*	Jer 16:4
they shall not be *b*, neither	Jer 16:6
shalt die, and shalt be *b* there	Jer 20:6
He shall be *b* with the burial of	Jer 22:19
lamented, neither gathered, nor *b*	Jer 25:33
till the buriers have *b* it in	Eze 39:15
b it, and went and told Jesus	Mt 14:12
the rich man also died, and was *b*	Lk 16:22
David, that he is both dead and *b*	Acts 2:29
up, and carried him out, and *b* him	Acts 5:6
b thy husband are at the door	Acts 5:9
her forth, *b* her by her husband	Acts 5:10
Therefore we are *b* with him by	Rom 6:4
And that he was *b*, and that he rose	1Cor 15:4
B with him in baptism, wherein	Col 2:12

BURIERS

till the *b* have buried it in	Eze 39:15

BURN

make brick, and *b* them throughly	Gen 11:3
thine anger *b* against thy servant	Gen 44:18
the morning ye shall *b* with fire	Ex 12:10
to cause the lamp to *b* always	Ex 27:20
them, and *b* them upon the altar	Ex 29:13
shalt thou *b* with fire without	Ex 29:14
thou shalt *b* the whole ram upon	Ex 29:18
b them upon the altar for a burnt	Ex 29:25
then thou shalt *b* the remainder	Ex 29:34
make an altar to *b* incense upon	Ex 30:1
Aaron shall *b* thereon sweet	Ex 30:7
he shall *b* incense upon it	Ex 30:7
he shall *b* incense upon it, a	Ex 30:8
to *b* offering made by fire unto	Ex 30:20
priest shall *b* all on the altar	Lev 1:9
it all, and *b* it upon the altar	Lev 1:13
his head, and *b* it on the altar	Lev 1:15
the priest shall *b* it upon the	Lev 1:15
the priest shall *b* the memorial	Lev 2:2
shall *b* it upon the altar	Lev 2:9
for ye shall *b* no leaven, nor any	Lev 2:11
the priest shall *b* the memorial	Lev 2:16
Aaron's sons shall *b* it on the	Lev 3:5
the priest shall *b* it upon the	Lev 3:11
the priest shall *b* them upon the	Lev 3:16
the priest shall *b* them upon the	Lev 3:16
b him to the wood with the	Lev 4:12
from him, and *b* it upon the altar	Lev 4:19
b him as he burned the first	Lev 4:21
he shall *b* all his fat upon the	Lev 4:26
the priest shall *b* it upon	Lev 4:31
the priest shall *b* them upon the	Lev 4:35
b it on the altar, according to	Lev 5:12
the priest shall *b* wood on it	Lev 6:12
he shall *b* thereon the fat of the	Lev 6:12
shall *b* it upon the altar for a	Lev 7:5
the priest shall *b* them upon the	Lev 7:5
the priest shall *b* the fat	Lev 7:31
of the bread shall ye *b* with fire	Lev 8:32
He shall therefore *b* that garment	Lev 13:52
thou shalt *b* it in the fire	Lev 13:55
thou shalt *b* that wherein the	Lev 13:57
shall he *b* upon the altar	Lev 16:25
they shall *b* in the fire their	Lev 16:27
b the fat for a sweet savour unto	Lev 17:6
cause the lamps to *b* continually	Lev 24:2
b it upon the altar, and afterward	Num 5:26
shall *b* their fat for an offering	Num 18:17
one shall *b* the heifer in his	Num 19:5
blood, with her dung, shall he *b*	Num 19:5
(for the mountain did *b* with fire	Deut 5:23
b their graven images with fire	Deut 7:5
their gods shall ye *b* with fire	Deut 7:25
and *b* their groves with fire	Deut 12:3
shalt *b* with the city all	Deut 13:16
shall *b* unto the lowest hell, and	Deut 32:22
b their chariots with fire	Josh 11:6
that did Joshua *b*	Josh 11:13

of the tower to *b* it with fire	Judg 9:52
ye will *b* thine house upon thee	Judg 12:1
us the riddle, lest we *b* thee	Judg 14:15
not fail to *b* the part presently	1Sa 2:16
to *b* incense, to wear an ephod	1Sa 2:28
stood by the altar to *b* incense	1Kin 13:1
places that *b* incense upon thee	1Kin 13:2
Upon the great altar *b* the	2Kin 16:15
of Israel did *b* incense to it	2Kin 18:4
b incense in the high places in	2Kin 23:5
to *b* incense before the LORD, to	1Chr 23:13
to *b* before him sweet incense, and	2Chr 2:4
save only to *b* sacrifice before	2Chr 2:6
that they should *b* after the	2Chr 4:20
they *b* unto the LORD every	2Chr 13:11
lamps thereof, to *b* every evening	2Chr 13:11
to *b* incense upon the altar of	2Chr 26:16
to *b* incense unto the LORD, but	2Chr 26:18
that are consecrated to *b* incense	2Chr 26:18
a censer in his hand to *b* incense	2Chr 26:19
to *b* incense unto other gods	2Chr 28:25
minister unto him, and *b* incense	2Chr 29:11
one altar, and *b* incense upon it	2Chr 32:12
to *b* upon the altar of the LORD	Neh 10:34
shall thy jealousy *b* like fire	Ps 79:5
shall thy wrath *b* like fire	Ps 89:46
and they shall both *b* together	Is 1:31
and it shall *b* and devour his	Is 10:17
them, I would *b* them together	Is 27:4
And Lebanon is not sufficient to *b*	Is 40:16
Then shall it be for a man to *b*	Is 44:15
the fire shall *b* them	Is 47:14
b that none can quench it because	Jer 4:4
b incense unto Baal, and walk	Jer 7:9
and it shall *b*, and shall not be	Jer 7:20
Hinnom, to *b* their sons and their	Jer 7:31
even altars to *b* incense unto	Jer 11:13
anger, which shall *b* upon you	Jer 15:14
anger, which shall *b* for ever	Jer 17:4
to *b* their sons with fire for	Jer 19:5
and he shall *b* it with fire	Jer 21:10
b that none can quench it	Jer 21:12
b it with the houses, upon whose	Jer 32:29
and he shall *b* it with fire	Jer 34:2
so shall they *b* odours for thee	Jer 34:5
and and take it, and *b* it with fire	Jer 34:22
king that he would not *b* the roll	Jer 36:25
and take it, and *b* it with fire	Jer 38:23
tent, and *b* this city with fire	Jer 37:10
they shall *b* it with fire, and	Jer 38:18
and he shall *b* them, and carry them	Jer 43:12
Egyptians shall be *b* with fire	Jer 43:13
in that they went to *b* incense	Jer 44:3
to *b* incense unto other gods	Jer 44:5
to *b* incense unto the queen of	Jer 44:17
But since we left off to *b*	Jer 44:18
to *b* incense to the queen of	Jer 44:25
Thou shalt *b* with fire a third	Eze 5:2
the fire, and *b* them in the fire	Eze 5:4
they shall *b* thine houses with	Eze 16:41
b up their houses with fire	Eze 23:47
b also the bones under it, and	Eze 24:5
brass of it may be hot, and may *b*	Eze 24:11
the weapons, both the shields	Eze 39:9
they shall *b* them with fire seven	Eze 39:9
for they shall *b* the weapons with	Eze 39:10
he shall *b* it in the appointed	Eze 43:21
b incense upon the hills, under	Hos 4:13
I will *b* her chariots in the	Nah 2:13
b incense with their drag	Hab 1:16
cometh, that shall *b* as an oven	Mal 4:1
day that cometh shall *b* them up	Mal 4:1
but he will *b* up the chaff with	Mt 3:12
and bind them in bundles to *b* them	Mt 13:30
his lot was to *b* incense when he	Lk 1:9
but the chaff he will *b* with fire	Lk 3:17
Did not our heart *b* within us	Lk 24:32
it is better to marry than to *b*	1Cor 7:9
who is offended, and I *b* not	2Cor 11:29
eat her flesh, and *b* her with fire	Rev 17:16

the gates thereof are *b* with fire	Neh 2:17
heaps of the rubbish which are *b*	Neh 4:2
very wroth, and his anger *b* in him	Est 1:12
hath *b* up the sheep, and the	Job 1:16
me, and my bones are *b* with heat	Job 30:30
while I was musing the fire *b*	Ps 39:3
they have *b* up all the synagogues	Ps 74:8
It is *b* with fire, it is cut down	Ps 80:16
and my bones are *b* as an hearth	Ps 102:3
the flame *b* up the wicked	Ps 106:18
bosom, and his clothes not be *b*	Prov 6:27
hot coals, and his feet not be *b*	Prov 6:28
your cities are *b* with fire	Is 1:7
inhabitants of the earth are *b*	Is 24:6
up shall they be *b* in the fire	Is 33:12
it *b* him, yet he laid it not to	Is 42:25
the fire, thou shalt not be *b*	Is 43:2
I have *b* part of it in the fire	Is 44:19
praised thee, is *b* up with fire	Is 64:11
which have *b* incense upon the	Is 65:7
have *b* incense unto other gods,	Jer 1:16
his cities are *b* without	Jer 2:15
The bellows are *b*, the lead is	Jer 6:29
because they are *b* up, so that	Jer 9:10
is *b* up like a wilderness, that	Jer 9:12
they have *b* incense to vanity, and	Jer 18:15
have *b* incense in it unto other	Jer 19:4
upon whose roofs they have *b*	Jer 19:13
that the king had *b* the roll	Jer 36:27
the king of Judah hath *b*	Jer 36:28
Thou hast *b* this roll, saying,	Jer 36:29
king of Judah had *b* in the fire	Jer 36:32
city shall not be *b* with fire	Jer 38:17
cause this city to be *b* with fire	Jer 38:23
the Chaldeans *b* the king's house	Jer 39:8
had *b* incense unto other gods	Jer 44:15
when we *b* incense to the queen of	Jer 44:19
The incense that ye *b* in the	Jer 44:21
Because ye have *b* incense	Jer 44:23
daughters shall be *b* with fire	Jer 49:2
they have *b* her dwellingplaces	Jer 51:30
the reeds they have *b* with fire	Jer 51:32
high gates shall be *b* with fire	Jer 51:58
b the house of the LORD, and the	Jer 52:13
of the great men, he *b* with fire	Jer 52:13
b against Jacob like a flaming	Lam 2:3
of it, and the midst of it is *b*	Eze 15:4
fire hath devoured it, and it is *b*	Eze 15:5
to the north shall be *b* therein	Eze 20:47
it well, and let the bones be *b*	Eze 24:10
wherein she *b* incense to them,	Hos 2:13
b incense to graven images	Hos 11:2
the flame hath *b* all the trees of	Joel 1:19
because he *b* the bones of the	Amos 2:1
thereof shall be *b* with fire	Mic 1:7
the earth is *b* at his presence,	Nah 1:5
are gathered and *b* in the fire	Mt 13:40
murderers, and *b* up their city	Mt 22:7
them into the fire, and they are *b*	Jn 15:6
and *b* them before all men	Acts 19:19
b in their lust one toward	Rom 1:27
If any man's work shall be *b*	1Cor 3:15
and though I give my body to be *b*	1Cor 13:3
whose end is to be *b*	Heb 6:8
that *b* with fire, nor unto	Heb 12:18
for sin, are *b* without the camp	Heb 13:11
that are therein shall be *b* up	2Pet 3:10
as if they *b* in a furnace	Rev 1:15
she shall be utterly *b* with fire	Rev 18:8

BURNETH

the quick flesh that *b* have a	Lev 13:24
he that *b* them shall wash his	Lev 16:28
he that *b* her shall wash his	Num 19:8
he *b* the chariot in the fire	Ps 46:9
As the fire *b* a wood, and as the	Ps 83:14
b up his enemies round about	Ps 97:3
For wickedness *b* as the fire	Is 9:18
He *b* part thereof in the fire	Is 44:16
thereof as a lamp that *b*	Is 62:1
As when the melting fire *b*	Is 64:2
b incense upon altars of brick	Is 65:3
nose, a fire that *b* all the day	Is 65:5
he that *b* incense, as if he	Is 66:3
him that *b* incense to his gods	Jer 48:35
morning it *b* as a flaming fire	Hos 7:6
and behind them a flame *b*	Joel 2:3
take him up, and he that *b* him	Amos 6:10
in the lake which *b* with fire	Rev 21:8

BURNING

a *b* lamp that passed between	Gen 15:17
B for *b*, wound for wound,	Ex 21:25
B for *b*, wound for wound,	Ex 21:25
because of the *b* upon the altar	Lev 6:9
of the altar shall be *b* in it	Lev 6:9
upon the altar shall be *b* in it	Lev 6:12
shall ever be *b* upon the altar	Lev 6:13
bewail the *b* which the LORD hath	Lev 10:6
and spread not, it is a *b* boil	Lev 13:23
the skin whereof there is a hot *b*	Lev 13:23
is a leprosy broken out of the *b*	Lev 13:25
it is a rising of the *b*, and the	Lev 13:28
it is an inflammation of the *b*	Lev 13:28
of *b* coals of fire off the	Lev 16:12
the *b* a, that shall consume	Num 26:16
take up the censers out of the *b*	Num 16:37
the midst of the *b* of the heifer	Num 19:6
and with an extreme *b*, and	Deut 28:22
is brimstone, and salt, and *b*	Deut 29:23
hunger, and devoured with *b* heat	Deut 32:24

they made a very great *b* for him 2Chr 16:14
And his people made no *b* for him 2Chr 21:19
like the *b* of his fathers 2Chr 21:19
Out of his mouth go *b* lamps ..... Job 41:19
Let *b* coals fall upon them ..... Ps 140:10
in his lips there is as a *b* fire ..... Prov 16:27
As coals are to *b* coals, and wood ..... Prov 26:21
B lips and a wicked heart are like ..... Prov 26:23
and *b* instead of beauty ..... Is 3:24
judgment, and by the spirit of *b* ..... Is 4:4
but this shall be with *b* and fuel ..... Is 9:5
a *b* like the *b* of a fire ..... Is 10:16
a *b* like the *b* of a fire ..... Is 10:16
b with his anger, and the burden ..... Is 30:27
land thereof shall become *b* pitch ..... Is 34:9
as a *b* fire shut up in my bones ..... Jer 20:9
a fire on the hearth *b* before him ..... Jer 36:22
b incense unto other gods in the ..... Jer 44:8
was like *b* coals of fire, and like ..... Eze 1:13
the midst of a *b* fiery furnace ..... Dan 3:6
the midst of a *b* fiery furnace ..... Dan 3:11
the midst of a *b* fiery furnace ..... Dan 3:15
us from the *b* fiery furnace ..... Dan 3:17
them into the *b* fiery furnace ..... Dan 3:20
the midst of the *b* fiery furnace ..... Dan 3:21
the midst of the *b* fiery furnace ..... Dan 3:23
the mouth of the *b* fiery furnace ..... Dan 3:26
flame, and his wheels as *b* fire ..... Dan 7:9
and given to the *b* flame ..... Dan 7:11
a firebrand plucked out of the *b* ..... Amos 4:11
b coals went forth at his feet ..... Hab 3:5
be girded about, and your lights *b* ..... Lk 12:35
He was a *b* and a shining light ..... Jn 5:35
is no sooner risen with a *b* heat ..... Jas 1:11
lamps of fire *b* before the throne ..... Rev 4:5
as it were a great mountain *b* ..... Rev 8:8
b as it were a lamp, and it fell ..... Rev 8:10
they shall see the smoke of her *b* ..... Rev 18:9
when they saw the smoke of her *b* ..... Rev 18:18
a lake of fire *b* with brimstone ..... Rev 19:20

BURNINGS

people shall be as the *b* of lime ..... Is 33:12
us shall dwell with everlasting *b* ..... Is 33:14
with the *b* of thy fathers, the ..... Jer 34:5

BURNISHED

like the colour of *b* brass ..... Eze 1:7

BURNT

offered *b* offerings on the altar ..... Gen 8:20
offer him there for a *b* offering ..... Gen 22:2
clave the wood for the *b* offering ..... Gen 22:3
took the wood of the *b* offering ..... Gen 22:6
is the lamb for a *b* offering ..... Gen 22:7
himself a lamb for a *b* offering ..... Gen 22:8
offered him up for a *b* offering ..... Gen 22:13
Bring her forth, and let her be *b* ..... Gen 38:24
sight, why the bush is not *b* ..... Ex 3:3
and *b* offerings, that we may ..... Ex 10:25
took a *b* offering and sacrifices ..... Ex 18:12
sacrifice thereon thy *b* offerings ..... Ex 20:24
Israel, which offered *b* offerings ..... Ex 24:5
it is a *b* offering unto the LORD ..... Ex 29:18
b offering to the LORD for a *b* offering ..... Ex 29:25
b offering throughout your ..... Ex 29:42
nor *b* sacrifice, nor meat ..... Ex 30:9
the altar of *b* offering with all ..... Ex 30:28
the altar of *b* offering with all ..... Ex 31:9
offered *b* offerings, and brought ..... Ex 32:6
b it in the fire, and ground it to ..... Ex 32:20
The altar of *b* offering, with his ..... Ex 35:16
he made the altar of *b* offering ..... Ex 38:1
b offering before the door of the ..... Ex 40:6
the altar of the *b* offering ..... Ex 40:10
he *b* sweet incense thereon ..... Ex 40:27
he put the altar of *b* offering ..... Ex 40:29
and offered upon it the *b* offering ..... Ex 40:29
If his offering be a *b* sacrifice ..... Lev 1:3
upon the head of the *b* offering ..... Lev 1:4
And he shall flay the *b* offering ..... Lev 1:6
to be a *b* sacrifice, an offering ..... Lev 1:9
of the goats, for a *b* sacrifice ..... Lev 1:10
it is a *b* sacrifice, an offering ..... Lev 1:13
if the *b* sacrifice for his ..... Lev 1:14
it is a *b* sacrifice, an offering ..... Lev 1:17
but they shall not be *b* on the ..... Lev 2:12
on the altar upon the *b* sacrifice ..... Lev 3:5
of the altar of the *b* offering ..... Lev 4:7
upon the altar of the *b* offering ..... Lev 4:10
are poured out shall he be *b* ..... Lev 4:12
of the altar of the *b* offering ..... Lev 4:18
the *b* offering before the LORD ..... Lev 4:24
horns of the altar of *b* offering ..... Lev 4:25
bottom of the altar of *b* offering ..... Lev 4:25
in the place of the *b* offering ..... Lev 4:29
horns of the altar of *b* offering ..... Lev 4:30
where they kill the *b* offering ..... Lev 4:33
horns of the altar of *b* offering ..... Lev 4:34
and the other for a *b* offering ..... Lev 5:7
offer the second for a *b* offering ..... Lev 5:10
This is the law of the *b* offering ..... Lev 6:9
It is the *b* offering, because of ..... Lev 6:9
with the *b* offering on the altar ..... Lev 6:10
lay the *b* offering in order upon ..... Lev 6:12
it shall be wholly *b* ..... Lev 6:22
for the priest shall be wholly *b* ..... Lev 6:23
In the place where the *b* offering ..... Lev 6:25
it shall be *b* in the fire ..... Lev 6:30
b offering shall they kill the ..... Lev 7:2
offereth any man's *b* offering ..... Lev 7:8
b offering which he hath offered ..... Lev 7:8

third day shall be *b* with fire ..... Lev 7:17
it shall be *b* with fire ..... Lev 7:19
This is the law of the *b* offering ..... Lev 7:37
be *b* with fire without the camp ..... Lev 8:17
the ram for the *b* offering ..... Lev 8:18
Moses *b* the head, and the pieces ..... Lev 8:20
Moses *b* the whole ram upon the ..... Lev 8:21
it was a *b* sacrifice for a sweet ..... Lev 8:21
b them on the altar upon the ..... Lev 8:28
on the altar upon the *b* offering ..... Lev 8:28
and a ram for a *b* offering ..... Lev 9:2
without blemish, for a *b* offering ..... Lev 9:3
thy *b* offering, and make an ..... Lev 9:7
sin offering, he *b* upon the altar ..... Lev 9:10
the hide he *b* with fire without ..... Lev 9:11
And he slew the *b* offering ..... Lev 9:12
presented the *b* offering unto him ..... Lev 9:13
and he *b* them upon the altar ..... Lev 9:13
b them upon the *b* offering ..... Lev 9:14
b them upon the *b* offering on ..... Lev 9:14
And he brought the *b* offering ..... Lev 9:16
b it upon the altar ..... Lev 9:17
beside the *b* sacrifice of the ..... Lev 9:17
he *b* the fat upon the altar ..... Lev 9:20
and the *b* offering, and peace ..... Lev 9:22
upon the altar the *b* offering ..... Lev 9:24
offering, and, behold, it was *b* ..... Lev 10:16
their *b* offering before the LORD ..... Lev 10:19
the first year for a *b* offering ..... Lev 12:6
the one for the *b* offering ..... Lev 12:8
it shall be *b* in the fire ..... Lev 13:52
the *b* offering, in the holy place ..... Lev 14:13
he shall kill the *b* offering ..... Lev 14:19
priest shall offer the *b* offering ..... Lev 14:20
and the other a *b* offering ..... Lev 14:31
and the other for a *b* offering ..... Lev 14:31
and the other for a *b* offering ..... Lev 15:15
and the other for a *b* offering ..... Lev 15:30
and a ram for a *b* offering ..... Lev 16:3
and one ram for a *b* offering ..... Lev 16:5
forth, and offer his *b* offering ..... Lev 16:24
the *b* offering of the people, and ..... Lev 16:24
that offereth a *b* offering or ..... Lev 17:8
day, it shall be *b* in the fire ..... Lev 19:6
they shall be *b* with fire ..... Lev 20:14
she shall be *b* with fire ..... Lev 21:9
unto the LORD for a *b* offering ..... Lev 22:18
for a *b* offering unto the LORD ..... Lev 23:12
they shall be for a *b* offering ..... Lev 23:18
a *b* offering, and a meat offering ..... Lev 23:37
and the other for a *b* offering ..... Num 6:11
without blemish for a *b* offering ..... Num 6:14
sin offering, and his *b* offering ..... Num 6:16
the first year, for a *b* offering ..... Num 7:15
the first year, for a *b* offering ..... Num 7:21
the first year, for a *b* offering ..... Num 7:27
the first year, for a *b* offering ..... Num 7:33
the first year, for a *b* offering ..... Num 7:39
the first year, for a *b* offering ..... Num 7:45
the first year, for a *b* offering ..... Num 7:51
the first year, for a *b* offering ..... Num 7:57
the first year, for a *b* offering ..... Num 7:63
the first year, for a *b* offering ..... Num 7:69
the first year, for a *b* offering ..... Num 7:75
the first year, for a *b* offering ..... Num 7:81
All the oxen for the *b* offering ..... Num 7:87
and the other for a *b* offering ..... Num 8:12
trumpets over your *b* offerings ..... Num 10:10
the fire of the LORD *b* among them ..... Num 11:1
the fire of the LORD *b* among them ..... Num 11:3
a *b* offering, or a sacrifice in ..... Num 15:3
with the *b* offering or sacrifice ..... Num 15:5
a bullock for a *b* offering ..... Num 15:8
young bullock for a *b* offering ..... Num 15:24
they that were *b* had offered ..... Num 16:39
b heifer of purification for sin ..... Num 19:17
Balak, Stand by thy *b* offering ..... Num 23:3
lo, he stood by his *b* sacrifice ..... Num 23:6
Stand here by thy *b* offering ..... Num 23:15
he stood by his *b* offering ..... Num 23:17
day, for a continual *b* offering ..... Num 28:3
It is a continual *b* offering ..... Num 28:6
This is the *b* offering of every ..... Num 28:10
beside the continual *b* offering ..... Num 28:10
offer a *b* offering unto the LORD ..... Num 28:11
for a *b* offering of a sweet ..... Num 28:13
This is the *b* offering of every ..... Num 28:14
beside the continual *b* offering ..... Num 28:15
for a *b* offering unto the LORD ..... Num 28:19
the *b* offering in the morning ..... Num 28:23
is for a continual *b* offering ..... Num 28:24
beside the continual *b* offering ..... Num 28:24
But ye shall offer the *b* offering ..... Num 28:27
beside the continual *b* offering ..... Num 28:31
ye shall offer a *b* offering for a ..... Num 29:2
Beside the *b* offering of the ..... Num 29:6
offering, and the daily *b* offering ..... Num 29:6
But ye shall offer a *b* offering ..... Num 29:8
and the continual *b* offering ..... Num 29:11
And ye shall offer a *b* offering ..... Num 29:13
beside the continual *b* offering ..... Num 29:16
beside the continual *b* offering ..... Num 29:19
beside the continual *b* offering ..... Num 29:22
beside the continual *b* offering ..... Num 29:25
beside the continual *b* offering ..... Num 29:28
beside the continual *b* offering ..... Num 29:31
beside the continual *b* offering ..... Num 29:34
But ye shall offer a *b* offering ..... Num 29:36
beside the continual *b* offering ..... Num 29:38
for your *b* offerings, and for your ..... Num 29:39

they *b* all their cities wherein ..... Num 31:10
b it with fire, and stamped it, and ..... Deut 9:21
ye shall bring your *b* offerings ..... Deut 12:6
your *b* offerings, and your ..... Deut 12:11
b offerings in every place that ..... Deut 12:13
thou shalt offer thy *b* offerings ..... Deut 12:14
thou shalt offer thy *b* offerings ..... Deut 12:27
have *b* in the fire to their gods ..... Deut 12:31
thou shalt offer *b* offerings ..... Deut 27:6
They shall be *b* with hunger ..... Deut 32:24
whole *b* sacrifice upon thine ..... Deut 33:10
they *b* the city with fire, and all ..... Josh 6:24
thing shalt be *b* with fire ..... Josh 7:15
And Joshua *b* Ai, and made it an ..... Josh 8:28
they offered thereon *b* offerings ..... Josh 8:31
b their chariots with fire ..... Josh 11:6
and he *b* Hazor with fire ..... Josh 11:11
or if to offer thereon *b* offering ..... Josh 22:23
not for *b* offering, nor for ..... Josh 22:26
before him with our *b* offerings ..... Josh 22:27
not for *b* offerings, nor for ..... Josh 22:28
to build an altar for *b* offering ..... Josh 22:29
offer a *b* sacrifice with the wood ..... Judg 6:26
will offer it up for a *b* offering ..... Judg 11:31
if thou wilt offer a *b* offering ..... Judg 13:16
not have received a *b* offering ..... Judg 13:23
b up both the shocks, and also the ..... Judg 15:5
b her and her father with fire ..... Judg 15:6
as flax that was *b* with fire ..... Judg 15:14
sword, and *b* the city with fire ..... Judg 18:27
offered *b* offerings and peace ..... Judg 20:26
offered *b* offerings and peace ..... Judg 21:4
Also before they *b* the fat 1Sa 2:15
offered the kine a *b* offering 1Sa 6:14
Beth-shemesh offered *b* offerings 1Sa 6:15
offered it for a *b* offering 1Sa 7:9
was offering up the *b* offering 1Sa 7:10
to offer *b* offerings, and to 1Sa 10:8
Bring hither a *b* offering to me 1Sa 13:9
And he offered the *b* offering 1Sa 13:9
an end of offering the *b* offering 1Sa 13:10
and offered a *b* offering 1Sa 13:12
as great delight in *b* offerings 1Sa 15:22
came to Jabesh, and *b* them there 1Sa 31:12
and David offered *b* offerings 2Sa 6:17
an end of offering *b* offerings 2Sa 6:18
here be oxen for *b* sacrifice 2Sa 24:22
neither will I offer *b* offerings 2Sa 24:24
offered *b* offerings and peace 2Sa 24:25
and *b* incense in high places 1Kin 3:3
a thousand *b* offerings did 1Kin 3:4
LORD, and offered up *b* offerings 1Kin 3:15
for there he offered *b* offerings 1Kin 8:64
little to receive the *b* offerings 1Kin 8:64
b it with fire, and slain the 1Kin 9:16
did Solomon offer *b* offerings 1Kin 9:25
he *b* incense upon the altar that 1Kin 9:25
which *b* incense and sacrificed 1Kin 11:8
upon the altar, and *b* incense 1Kin 12:33
men's bones shall be *b* upon thee 1Kin 13:2
idol, and *b* it by the brook Kidron 1Kin 15:13
b the king's house over him with 1Kin 16:18
and pour it on the *b* sacrifice 1Kin 18:33
fell, and consumed the *b* sacrifice 1Kin 18:38
b incense yet in the high places 2Kin 12:43
b up the two captains of the 2Kin 1:14
offered him for a *b* offering upon 2Kin 3:27
b offering nor sacrifice unto 2Kin 5:17
b offerings, Jehu appointed 2Kin 10:24
an end of offering the *b* offering 2Kin 10:25
b incense in the high places 2Kin 12:3
b incense on the high places 2Kin 14:4
b incense on the high 2Kin 15:4
b incense in the high places, and 2Kin 16:4
And he *b* his *b* offering 2Kin 16:13
altar burn the morning *b* offering 2Kin 16:15
and the king's *b* sacrifice 2Kin 16:15
with the *b* offering of all the 2Kin 16:15
all the blood of the *b* offering 2Kin 16:15
there they *b* incense in all the 2Kin 17:11
the Sepharvites *b* their children 2Kin 17:31
he *b* the house of the LORD, and 2Kin 25:9
great man's house he *b* with fire 2Kin 25:9
upon the altar of the *b* offering 1Chr 6:49
and they offered *b* sacrifices 1Chr 16:1
end of offering the *b* offerings 1Chr 16:2
To offer *b* offerings unto the 1Chr 16:40
b offering continually morning 1Chr 16:40
the oxen also for *b* offerings 1Chr 21:23
nor offer *b* offerings without 1Chr 21:24
offered *b* offerings and peace 1Chr 21:26
fire upon the altar of *b* offering 1Chr 21:26
and the altar of the *b* offering 1Chr 21:29
of the *b* offering for Israel 1Chr 21:21
to offer all *b* sacrifices unto 1Chr 23:31
offered *b* offerings unto the LORD 2Chr 1:6
a thousand *b* offerings upon it 2Chr 1:6
for the *b* offerings morning and 2Chr 2:4
b offering they washed in them 2Chr 4:6
and consumed the *b* offering 2Chr 7:1
for there he offered *b* offerings 2Chr 7:7
able to receive the *b* offerings 2Chr 7:7
Then Solomon offered *b* offerings 2Chr 8:12
and every evening *b* sacrifices 2Chr 13:11
it, and *b* it at the brook Kidron 2Chr 15:16
to offer the *b* offerings in the 2Chr 23:18
they offered *b* offerings in the 2Chr 24:14
Moreover he *b* incense in the 2Chr 28:3
b his children in the fire, after 2Chr 28:3
b incense in the high places, and 2Chr 28:4

b offerings in the holy place............2Chr 29:7
LORD, and the altar of *b* offering........2Chr 29:18
commanded that the *b* offering............2Chr 29:24
the *b* offering upon the altar.............2Chr 29:27
when the *b* offering began, the...........2Chr 29:27
until the *b* offering was finished........2Chr 29:28
were of a free heart *b* offerings.........2Chr 29:31
And the number of the *b* offerings........2Chr 29:32
were for a *b* offering to the LORD........2Chr 29:32
not flay all the *b* offerings.............2Chr 29:34
also the *b* offerings were in.............2Chr 29:35
offerings for every *b* offering...........2Chr 29:35
brought in the *b* offerings into..........2Chr 31:2
and Levites for *b* offerings..............2Chr 31:2
his substance for the *b* offerings........2Chr 31:3
evening *b* offering, and the *b*..........2Chr 31:3
he *b* the bones of the priests............2Chr 34:5
And they removed the *b* offerings.........2Chr 35:12
busied in offering of *b* offerings........2Chr 35:14
to offer *b* offerings upon the............2Chr 35:16
they *b* the house of God, and brake.......2Chr 36:19
b all the palaces thereof with...........2Chr 36:19
to offer *b* offering thereon, as..........Ezr 3:2
they offered *b* offerings thereon.........Ezr 3:3
even *b* offerings morning and.............Ezr 3:4
offered the continual *b* offering.........Ezr 3:5
offer *b* offerings unto the LORD..........Ezr 3:6
for the *b* offerings of the God of........Ezr 6:9
offered *b* offerings unto the God.........Ezr 8:35
all this was a *b* offering unto...........Ezr 8:35
and for the continual *b* offering.........Neh 10:33
offered *b* offerings according to.........Job 1:5
up for yourselves a *b* offering...........Job 42:8
and accept thy *b* sacrifice...............Ps 20:3
b offering and sin offering hast.........Ps 40:6
thy sacrifices or thy *b* offerings........Ps 50:8
thou delightest not in *b* offering........Ps 51:16
b offering and whole *b* offering........Ps 51:19
into thy house with *b* offerings..........Ps 66:13
thee *b* sacrifices of fatlings............Ps 66:15
I am full of the *b* offerings of..........Is 1:11
sufficient for a *b* offering..............Is 40:16
small cattle of thy *b* offerings..........Is 43:23
their *b* offerings and their..............Is 56:7
I hate robbery for *b* offering............Is 61:8
your *b* offerings are not.................Jer 6:20
Put your *b* offerings unto your...........Jer 7:21
concerning *b* offerings or................Jer 7:22
and when they offer *b* offering...........Jer 14:12
south, bringing *b* offerings, and.........Jer 17:26
fire for *b* offerings unto Baal...........Jer 19:5
before me to offer *b* offerings...........Jer 33:18
and will make thee a *b* mountain..........Jer 51:25
where they washed the *b* offering.........Eze 40:38
to slay thereon the *b* offering...........Eze 40:39
of hewn stone for the *b* offering.........Eze 40:42
they slew the *b* offering and the.........Eze 40:42
to offer *b* offerings thereon, and........Eze 43:18
up for a *b* offering unto the LORD........Eze 43:24
your *b* offerings upon the altar..........Eze 43:27
they shall slay the *b* offering...........Eze 44:11
for a *b* offering, and for peace..........Eze 45:15
prince's part to give *b* offerings........Eze 45:17
the *b* offering, and the peace............Eze 45:17
prepare a *b* offering to the LORD.........Eze 45:23
according to the *b* offering..............Eze 45:25
shall prepare his *b* offering.............Eze 46:2
the *b* offering that the prince...........Eze 46:4
shall prepare a voluntary *b*..............Eze 46:12
he shall prepare his *b* offering..........Eze 46:12
Thou shalt daily prepare a *b*.............Eze 46:13
for a continual *b* offering...............Eze 46:15
of God more than *b* offerings.............Hos 6:6
Though ye offer me *b* offerings...........Amos 5:22
come before him with *b* offerings.........Mic 6:6
more than all whole *b* offerings..........Mk 12:33
In *b* offerings and sacrifices for........Heb 10:6
b offerings and offering for sin.........Heb 10:8
the third part of trees was *b* up.........Rev 8:7
and all green grass was *b* up.............Rev 8:7

BURST

it is ready to *b* like new bottles........Job 32:19
presses shall *b* out with new wine........Prov 3:10
broken thy yoke, and *b* thy bands.........Jer 2:20
broken the yoke, and *b* the bonds.........Jer 5:5
will *b* thy bonds, and strangers..........Jer 30:8
will *b* thy bonds in sunder...............Nah 1:13
the new wine doth *b* the bottles..........Mk 2:22
the new wine will *b* the bottles..........Lk 5:37
he *b* asunder in the midst, and all.......Acts 1:18

BURSTING

b of it a sherd to take fire from........Is 30:14

BURY

that I may *b* my dead out of my...........Gen 23:4
of our sepulchres is thy dead..............Gen 23:6
but that thou mayest *b* thy dead..........Gen 23:6
should *b* my dead out of my sight.........Gen 23:8
thy dead.....................................Gen 23:11
of me, and I will *b* my dead there........Gen 23:13
b therefore thy dead.....................Gen 23:15
be not, I pray thee, in Egypt..............Gen 47:29
b me in their buryingplace...............Gen 47:30
b me with my fathers in the cave.........Gen 49:29
of Canaan, there shalt thou *b* me.........Gen 50:5
b my father, and I will come again.......Gen 50:5
b thy father, according as he............Gen 50:6
And Joseph went up to *b* his father.......Gen 50:7
went up with him to *b* his father.........Gen 50:14

shalt in any wise *b* him that day.........Deut 21:23
said, and fall upon him, and *b* him.......1Kin 2:31
host was gone up to *b* the slain..........1Kin 11:15
to the city, to mourn and to *b* him.......1Kin 13:29
then *b* me in the sepulchre...............1Kin 13:31
shall mourn for him, and *b* him...........1Kin 14:13
and there shall be none to *b* her.........2Kin 9:10
now this cursed woman, and *b* her.........2Kin 9:34
And they went to *b* her...................2Kin 9:35
and there was none to *b* them.............Ps 79:3
for they shall *b* in Tophet...............Jer 7:32
and they shall have none to *b* them.......Jer 14:16
they shall *b* them in Tophet..............Jer 19:11
till there be no place to *b*..............Jer 19:11
and there shall they *b* Gog...............Eze 39:11
people of the land shall *b* them..........Eze 39:13
passing through the land to *b*............Eze 39:14
them up, Memphis shall *b* them............Hos 9:6
the first to go and *b* my father..........Mt 8:21
and let the dead *b* their dead............Mt 8:22
potter's field, to *b* strangers in........Mt 27:7
me first to go and *b* my father...........Lk 9:59
him, Let the dead *b* their dead...........Lk 9:60
as the manner of the Jews is to *b*........Jn 19:40

BURYING

to pass, as they were *b* a man............2Kin 13:21
the house of Israel be *b* of them.........Eze 39:12
to anoint my body to the *b*...............Mk 14:8
day of my *b* hath she kept this...........Jn 12:7

BURYINGPLACE

me a possession of a *b* with you..........Gen 23:4
a possession of a *b* amongst you..........Gen 23:9
of a *b* by the sons of Heth...............Gen 23:20
of Egypt, and bury me in their *b*.........Gen 47:30
Hittite for a possession of a *b*..........Gen 49:30
of a *b* of Ephron the Hittite.............Gen 50:13
Eshtaol in the *b* of Manoah his...........Judg 16:31

BUSH

of fire out of the midst of a *b*..........Ex 3:2
the *b* burned with fire...................Ex 3:2
and the *b* was not consumed...............Ex 3:2
sight, why the *b* is not burnt............Ex 3:3
him out of the midst of the *b*............Ex 3:4
will of him that dwelt in the *b*..........Deut 33:16
how in the *b* God spake unto him..........Mk 12:26
nor of a bramble *b* gather they...........Lk 6:44
even Moses shewed at the *b*...............Lk 20:37
Lord in a flame of fire in a *b*...........Acts 7:30
which appeared to him in the *b*...........Acts 7:35

BUSHEL

a candle, and put it under a *b*...........Mt 5:15
brought to be put under a *b*..............Mk 4:21
a secret place, neither under a *b*........Lk 11:33

BUSHES

Who cut up mallows by the *b*..............Job 30:4
Among the *b* they brayed..................Job 30:7
and upon all thorns, and upon all *b*......Is 7:19

BUSHY

most fine gold, his locks are *b*..........Song 5:11

BUSIED

b in offering of burnt offerings.........2Chr 35:14

BUSINESS

went unto the house to do his *b*..........Gen 39:11
shall he be charged with any *b*...........Deut 24:5
yours, if ye utter not this our *b*........Josh 2:14
And if thou utter this our *b*.............Josh 2:20
and had no *b* with any man.................Judg 18:7
they had no *b* with any man...............Judg 18:28
thyself when the *b* was in hand...........1Sa 20:19
The king hath commanded me a *b*...........1Sa 21:2
of the *b* whereabout I send thee..........1Sa 21:2
the king's *b* required haste..............1Sa 21:8
for the outward to *b* Israel..............1Chr 26:29
westward in all the *b* of the LORD........1Chr 26:30
and the Levites wait upon their *b*........2Chr 13:10
he had much in the cities of...............2Chr 17:13
Howbeit in the *b* of the..................2Chr 32:31
the outward *b* of the house of God........Neh 11:16
over the *b* of the house of God...........Neh 11:22
the Levites, every one in his *b*..........Neh 13:30
that have the charge of the *b*............Ps 107:23
thou a man diligent in his *b*.............Prov 22:29
cometh through the multitude of *b*........Eccl 5:3
to see the *b* that is done upon...........Eccl 8:16
I rose up, and did the king's *b*..........Dan 8:27
I must be about my Father's *b*............Lk 2:49
whom we may appoint over this *b*..........Acts 6:3
Not slothful in *b*........................Rom 12:11
whatsoever *b* she hath need of you........Rom 16:2
to be quiet, and to do your own *b*........1Th 4:11

BUSY

And as thy servant was *b* here............1Kin 20:40

BUSYBODIES

working not at all, but are *b*............2Th 3:11
only idle, but tattlers also and *b*.......1Ti 5:13

BUSYBODY

or as a *b* in other men's matters.........1Pet 4:15

BUT See PREFACE.

BUTLER

that the *b* of the king of Egypt..........Gen 40:1
of his dream, the *b* and the baker........Gen 40:5
the chief *b* told his dream to............Gen 40:9

manner when thou wast his *b*..............Gen 40:13
lifted up the head of the chief *b*........Gen 40:20
he restored the chief *b* unto his.........Gen 40:21
not the chief *b* remember Joseph..........Gen 40:23
spake the chief *b* unto Pharaoh...........Gen 41:9

BUTLERS

against the chief of the *b*...............Gen 40:2

BUTLERSHIP

the chief butler unto his *b* again........Gen 40:21

BUTTER

And he took *b*, and milk, and the.........Gen 18:8
B of kine, and milk of sheep, with.......Deut 32:14
brought forth in a lordly dish.............Judg 5:25
And honey, and *b*, and cheese, and........2Sa 17:29
floods, the brooks of honey and *b*........Job 20:17
When I washed my steps with *b*............Job 29:6
of his mouth were smoother than *b*........Ps 55:21
churning of milk bringeth forth *b*........Prov 30:33
B and honey shall he eat, that he........Is 7:15
they shall give, he shall eat *b*..........Is 7:22
for *b* and honey shall every one..........Is 7:22

BUTTOCKS

in the middle, even to their *b*...........2Sa 10:4
in the midst hard by their *b*.............1Chr 19:4
even with their *b* uncovered..............Is 20:4

BUY

Egypt to Joseph for to *b* corn............Gen 41:57
thither, and *b* for us from thence........Gen 42:2
went down to *b* corn in Egypt.............Gen 42:3
to *b* corn among those that came..........Gen 42:5
From the land of Canaan to *b* food........Gen 42:7
but to *b* food are thy servants...........Gen 42:10
Go again, *b* us a little food.............Gen 43:2
we will go down and *b* thee food..........Gen 43:4
down at the first time to *b* food.........Gen 43:20
down in our hands to *b* food..............Gen 43:22
Go again, and *b* us a little food.........Gen 44:25
b us and our land for bread, and we......Gen 47:19
If thou *b* an Hebrew servant, six.........Ex 21:2
But if the priest *b* any soul with........Lev 22:11
thou shalt *b* of thy neighbour............Lev 25:15
of them shall ye *b* bondmen...............Lev 25:44
among you, of them shall ye *b*............Lev 25:45
Ye shall *b* meat of them for money........Deut 2:6
ye shall also *b* water of them for........Deut 2:6
and no man shall *b* you...................Deut 28:68
B it before the inhabitants, and.........Ruth 4:4
thou must *b* it also of Ruth the..........Ruth 4:5
said unto Boaz, *B* it for thee............Ruth 4:8
To *b* the threshingfloor of thee..........2Sa 24:21
but I will surely *b* it of thee at........2Sa 24:24
to *b* timber and hewed stone to...........2Kin 12:12
to *b* timber and hewn stone to............2Kin 22:6
but I will verily *b* it for...............1Chr 21:24
to *b* hewn stone, and timber for..........2Chr 34:11
That thou mayest *b* speedily with.........Ezr 7:17
and houses, that we might *b* corn.........Neh 5:3
that we would not *b* it of them on........Neh 10:31
B the truth, and sell it not.............Prov 23:23
come ye, *b*, and eat..................... Is 55:1
b wine and milk without money and........Is 55:1
B thee my field that is in...............Jer 32:7
of redemption is thine to *b* it...........Jer 32:7
B my field, I pray thee, that is.........Jer 32:8
b it for thyself.........................Jer 32:8
B thee the field for money, and..........Jer 32:25
Men shall *b* fields for money, and........Jer 32:44
That we may *b* the poor for silver........Amos 8:6
and *b* themselves victuals................Mt 14:15
that sell, and *b* for yourselves..........Mt 25:9
And while they went to *b*, the............Mt 25:10
villages, and *b* themselves bread.........Mk 6:36
b two hundred pennyworth of bread........Mk 6:37
b meat for all this people...............Lk 9:13
him sell his garment, and *b* one..........Lk 22:36
gone away unto the city to *b* meat........Jn 4:8
Philip, Whence shall we *b* bread..........Jn 6:5
B those things that we have need.........Jn 13:29
and they that *b*, as though they..........1Cor 7:30
and continue there a year, and *b*.........Jas 4:13
I counsel thee to *b* of me gold...........Rev 3:18
And that no man might *b* or sell..........Rev 13:17

BUYER

naught, is naught, saith the *b*..........Prov 20:14
as with the *b*, so with the seller.......Is 24:2
let not the *b* rejoice, nor the..........Eze 7:12

BUYEST

or *b* ought of thy neighbour's...........Lev 25:14
What day thou *b* the field of the........Ruth 4:5

BUYETH

She considereth a field, and *b*..........Prov 31:16
all that he hath, and *b* that field......Mt 13:44
for no man *b* their merchandise..........Rev 18:11

BUZ (*buz*)
1. Son of Nahor.
B his brother, and Kemuel the............Gen 22:21
2. A Gadite.
the son of Jahdo, the son of *B*..........1Chr 5:14
3. A tribe in northern Arabia.
Dedan, and Tema, and *B*, and all that.....Jer 25:23

BUZI (*boo'-zi*) See BUZITE. *Father of Ezekiel.*
Ezekiel the priest, the son of *B*........Eze 1:3

BUZITE (*boo'-zite*) *A member of Buz 3.*
Elihu the son of Barachel the *B*.........Job 32:2
son of Barachel the *B* answered..........Job 32:6

BY See PREFACE.

BYWAYS
the travellers walked through *b* .... Judg 5:6

BYWORD
astonishment, a proverb, and a *b* .... Deut 28:37
a proverb and a *b* among all people..... 1Kin 9:7
proverb and a *b* among all nations....... 2Chr 7:20
made me also a *b* of the people........... Job 17:6
I their song, yea, I am their *b* .... Job 30:9
Thou makest us a *b* among the .... Ps 44:14

C

CAB
the fourth part of a *c* of dove's............ 2Kin 6:25

CABBON (*cab'-bon*) *A town in Judah.*
And C, and Lahmam, and Kithlish..... Josh 15:40

CABINS
into the dungeon, and into the *c*........... Jer 37:16

CABUL (*ca'-bul*) *A town in Asher.*
goeth out to C on the left hand,......... Josh 19:27
them the land of C unto this day 1Kin 9:13

CAESAR (*se'-zur*) *See* CAESAR'S. *Title for the Roman Emperor.*
it lawful to give tribute unto C......... Mt 22:17
Render therefore unto C the............. Mt 22:21
is it lawful to give tribute to C.......... Mk 12:14
Render to C the things that are......... Mk 12:17
went out a decree from C Augustus... Lk 2:1
year of the reign of Tiberius C.......... Lk 3:1
for us to give tribute unto C.............. Lk 20:22
Render therefore unto C the............. Lk 20:25
forbidding to give tribute to C......... Lk 23:2
himself a king speaketh against C..... Jn 19:12
answered, We have no king but C..... Jn 19:15
to pass in the days of Claudius C..... Acts 11:28
do contrary to the decrees of C......... Acts 17:7
the temple, nor yet against C.......... Acts 25:8
I appeal unto C .... Acts 25:11
Hast thou appealed unto C............. Acts 25:12
unto C shalt thou go................... Acts 25:12
kept till I might send him to C......... Acts 25:21
if he had not appealed unto C......... Acts 26:32
thou must be brought before C......... Acts 27:24
was constrained to appeal unto C..... Acts 28:19

CAESAREA (*ses-a-re'-ah*)
1. A town north of Galilee.
into the coasts of C Philippi............ Mt 16:13
into the towns of C Philippi............ Mk 8:27
2. A Judean Mediterranean port.
all the cities, till he came to C......... Acts 8:40
knew, they brought him down to C..... Acts 9:30
certain man in C called Cornelius..... Acts 10:1
morrow after they entered into C..... Acts 10:24
where I was, sent from C unto me..... Acts 11:11
And he went down from Judaea to C... Acts 12:19
And when he had landed at C........... Acts 18:22
company departed, and came unto C... Acts 21:8
certain of the disciples of C............. Acts 21:16
two hundred soldiers to go to C....... Acts 23:23
Who, when they came to C, and........ Acts 23:33
he ascended from C to Jerusalem..... Acts 25:1
that Paul should be kept at C.......... Acts 25:4
ten days, he went down unto C......... Acts 25:6
came unto C to salute Festus........... Acts 25:13

CAESAR'S (*se'-zurs*)
They say unto him, C......................... Mt 22:21
Caesar the things which are C.......... Mt 22:21
And they said unto him, C............... Mk 12:16
to Caesar the things that are C........ Mk 12:17
They answered and said, C.............. Lk 20:24
unto Caesar the things which be C..... Lk 20:25
man go, thou art not C friend .... Jn 19:12
I stand at C judgment seat, where..... Acts 25:10
they that are of C household............ Phil 4:22

CAGE
As a *c* is full of birds, so are......... Jer 5:27
a *c* of every unclean and hateful....... Rev 18:2

CAIAPHAS (*cah'-ya-fus*) *A High Priest during Jesus' time.*
the high priest, who was called C..... Mt 26:3
led him away to C the high priest..... Mt 26:57
C being the high priests, the........... Lk 3:2
And one of them, named C, being..... Jn 11:49
for he was father in law to C.......... Jn 18:13
Now C was he, which gave counsel... Jn 18:14
him bound unto C the high priest..... Jn 18:24
Then led they Jesus from C unto..... Jn 18:28
And Annas the high priest, and C..... Acts 4:6

CAIN
1. Eldest son of Adam and Eve.
and she conceived, and bare C....... Gen 4:1
but C was a tiller of the ground...... Gen 4:2
that C brought of the fruit of......... Gen 4:3
But unto C and to his offering he..... Gen 4:5
And C was very wroth, and his........ Gen 4:5
And the LORD said unto C, Why art... Gen 4:6
C talked with Abel his brother........ Gen 4:8
that C rose up against Abel his........ Gen 4:8

And the LORD said unto C, Where is..... Gen 4:9
And C said unto the LORD, My......... Gen 4:13
Therefore whosoever slayeth C........ Gen 4:15
And the LORD set a mark upon C...... Gen 4:15
C went out from the presence of...... Gen 4:16
And C knew his wife.................... Gen 4:17
If C shall be avenged sevenfold,...... Gen 4:24
seed through of Abel, whom C slew... Gen 6:25
a more excellent sacrifice than C..... Heb 11:4
Not as C, who was of that wicked..... 1Jn 3:12
they have gone in the way of C....... Jude 11
2. A town in Judah.
C, Gibeah, and Timnah............... Josh 15:57

CAINAN (*ca'-nun*) *See* KENAN. *Son of Enos.*
lived ninety years, and begat C....... Gen 5:9
after he begat C eight hundred........ Gen 5:10
C lived seventy years, and begat...... Gen 5:12
C lived after he begat Mahalaleel..... Gen 5:13
all the days of C were nine............ Gen 5:14
Which was the son of C, which was... Lk 3:36
Maleleel, which was the son of C..... Lk 3:37

CAKE
one *c* of oiled bread, and one......... Ex 29:23
LORD, he took one unleavened......... Lev 8:26
a *c* of oiled bread, and one wafer,..... Lev 8:26
two tenth deals shall be in one........ Lev 24:5
one unleavened *c* out of the........... Num 6:19
Ye shall offer up a *c* of the........... Num 15:20
a *c* of barley bread tumbled into..... Judg 7:13
gave him a piece of a *c* of figs....... 1Sa 30:12
as men, to every one a *c* of bread..... 2Sa 6:19
thy God liveth, I have not a *c*........ 1Kin 17:12
make the thereof a little *c* first...... 1Kin 17:13
there was a *c* baken on the coals,..... 1Kin 19:6
Ephraim is a *c* not turned............. Hos 7:8

CAKES
it, and make *c* upon the hearth....... Gen 18:6
they baked unleavened *c* of the...... Ex 12:39
c unleavened tempered with oil,..... Ex 29:2
it shall be unleavened *c* of fine...... Lev 2:4
unleavened *c* mingled with oil....... Lev 7:12
c mingled with oil, of fine flour..... Lev 7:12
Besides the *c*, he shall offer for..... Lev 7:13
flour, and bake twelve *c* thereof..... Lev 24:5
c of fine flour mingled with oil,...... Num 6:15
baked it in pans, and made *c* of it... Num 11:8
after the passover, unleavened *c*..... Josh 5:11
unleavened *c* of an ephah of flour... Judg 6:19
the flesh and the unleavened *c*...... Judg 6:20
the flesh and the unleavened *c*...... Judg 6:21
the flesh and the unleavened *c*...... Judg 6:21
raisins, and two hundred *c* of figs... 1Sa 25:18
make me a couple of *c* in my sight... 2Sa 13:6
made *c* in his sight, and did bake... 2Sa 13:8
in his sight, and did bake the *c*...... 2Sa 13:8
Tamar took the *c* which she had..... 2Sa 13:10
c of figs, and bunches of raisins,..... 1Chr 12:40
offering, and for the shewbread of..... 1Chr 23:29
to make *c* to the queen of heaven,... Jer 7:18
did we make her *c* to worship her... Jer 44:19
And thou shalt eat it as barley *c*..... Eze 4:12

CALAH (*ca'-lah*) *An Assyrian city.*
and the city Rehoboth, and C......... Gen 10:11
And Resen between Nineveh and C... Gen 10:12

CALAMITIES
refuge, until these *c* be overpast..... Ps 57:1
prayer also shall be in their *c*....... Ps 141:5
he that is glad at *c* shall not be..... Prov 17:5

CALAMITY
for the day of their *c* is at hand....... Deut 32:35
prevented me in the day of my *c*..... 2Sa 22:19
my *c* laid in the balances............. Job 6:2
my path, they set forward my *c*...... Job 30:13
prevented me in the day of my *c*..... Ps 18:18
I also will laugh at your *c*............ Prov 1:26
shall his *c* come suddenly........... Prov 6:15
son is the *c* of his father............. Prov 19:13
For their *c* shall rise suddenly...... Prov 24:22
house in the day of thy *c*.............. Prov 27:10
the face, in the day of their *c*....... Jer 18:17
day of their *c* was come upon them... Jer 46:21
The *c* of Moab is near to come, and... Jer 48:16
will bring the *c* of Esau upon him... Jer 49:8
I will bring their *c* from all......... Jer 49:32
the sword in the time of their *c*...... Eze 35:5
my people in the day of their *c*...... Obad 13
affliction in the day of their *c*....... Obad 13
substance in the day of their *c*...... Obad 13

CALAMUS
of sweet *c* two hundred and fifty..... Ex 30:23
c and cinnamon, with all trees of..... Song 4:14
bright iron, cassia, and *c*............. Eze 27:19

CALCOL (*cal'-col*) *See* CHALCOL. *A son of Zerah.*
Zimri, and Ethan, and Heman, and C ... 1Chr 2:6

CALDRON
it into the pan, or kettle, or *c*....... 1Sa 2:14
as out of a seething pot or *c*......... Job 41:20
this city is the *c*, and we be the...... Eze 11:3
the flesh, and this city is the *c*...... Eze 11:7
This city shall not be your *c*......... Eze 11:11
the pot, and flesh within the *c*...... Mic 3:3

CALDRONS
sod they in pots, and in *c*............. 2Chr 35:13
The *c* also, and the shovels, and..... Jer 52:18

firepans, and the bowls, and the *c*..... Jer 52:19

CALEB (*ca'-leb*) *See* CALEB'S, CALEB-EPHRATAH, CHELUBAI.
1. A son of Jephunneh.
of Judah, C the son of Jephunneh..... Num 13:6
C stilled the people before Moses..... Num 13:30
C the son of Jephunneh, and........... Num 14:6
But my servant C, because he had..... Num 14:24
save C the son of Jephunneh, and..... Num 14:30
C the son of Jephunneh, which....... Num 14:38
save C the son of Jephunneh, and..... Num 26:65
Save C the son of Jephunneh the..... Num 32:12
of Judah, C the son of Jephunneh..... Num 34:19
Save C the son of Jephunneh......... Deut 1:36
C the son of Jephunneh the........... Josh 14:6
gave unto C the son of Jephunneh... Josh 14:13
of C the son of Jephunneh unto..... Josh 14:14
unto C the son of Jephunneh for..... Josh 15:13
C drove thence the three sons of..... Josh 15:14
And C said, He that smiteth.......... Josh 15:16
son of Kenaz, the brother of C....... Josh 15:17
C said unto her, What wouldest...... Josh 15:18
gave they to C the son of............. Josh 21:12
And C said, He that smiteth.......... Judg 1:12
C said unto her, What wilt thou..... Judg 1:14
C gave her the upper springs and..... Judg 1:15
And they gave Hebron unto C........ Judg 1:20
and he was of the house of C......... 1Sa 25:3
to Judah, and upon the south of C... 1Sa 30:14
and the daughter of C was Achsa..... 1Chr 2:49
And the sons of C the son of......... 1Chr 4:15
they gave to C the son of............. 1Chr 4:15
2. A son of Hezron.
the sons of Hezron began............ 1Chr 2:18
C took unto him Ephrath, which..... 1Chr 2:19
Now the sons of C the brother of..... 1Chr 2:42
3. A son of Hur.
were the sons of C the son of Hur..... 1Chr 2:50

CALEB-EPHRATAH (*ca'-leb-ef'-ra-tah*) *The place where Hezron died.*
after that Hezron was dead in C..... 1Chr 2:24

CALEB-EPHRATHAH *See* CALEB-EPHRATAH.

CALEB'S (*ca'-lebs*) *Refers to Caleb 1.*
C younger brother, took it............ Judg 1:13
son of Kenaz, C younger brother..... Judg 3:9
C concubine, bare Haran, and Moza,... 1Chr 2:46
C concubine, bare Sheber, and....... 1Chr 2:48

CALF
the herd, and fetch a *c* tender....... Gen 18:7
the *c* which he had dressed, and..... Gen 18:8
after he had made a molten *c*....... Ex 32:4
they have made them a molten *c*..... Ex 32:8
unto the camp, that he saw the *c*... Ex 32:19
he took the *c* which they had made... Ex 32:20
fire, and there came out this *c*...... Ex 32:24
people, because they made the *c*..... Ex 32:35
Take thee a young *c* for a sin....... Lev 9:2
and a *c* and a lamb, both of the..... Lev 9:3
slew the *c* of the sin offering....... Lev 9:8
God, and had made you a molten *c*... Deut 9:16
the *c* which ye had made, and burnt... Deut 9:21
woman had a fat *c* in the house..... 1Sa 28:24
they had made them a molten *c*..... Neh 9:18
cow calveth, and casteth not her *c*... Job 21:10
maketh them also to skip like a *c*... Ps 29:6
They made a *c* in Horeb, and........ Ps 106:19
and the *c* and the young lion and the... Isa 11:6
there shall the *c* feed, and there..... Isa 27:10
me, when they cut the *c* in twain..... Jer 34:18
passed between the parts of the *c*... Jer 34:19
Thy *c*, O Samaria, hath cast thee..... Hos 8:5
but the *c* of Samaria shall be........ Hos 8:6
And bring hither the fatted *c*....... Lk 15:23
father hath killed the fatted *c*....... Lk 15:27
hast killed for him the fatted *c*..... Lk 15:30
they made a *c* in those days, and..... Acts 7:41
and the second beast like a *c*........ Rev 4:7

CALF'S
was like the sole of a *c* foot......... Eze 1:7

CALKERS
men thereof were in thee thy *c*...... Eze 27:9
mariners, and thy pilots, thy *c*...... Eze 27:27

CALL
Adam to see what he would *c* them... Gen 2:19
then began men to *c* upon the name... Gen 4:26
son, and shalt *c* his name Ishmael... Gen 16:11
thou shalt not *c* her name Sarai..... Gen 17:15
thou shalt *c* his name Isaac......... Gen 17:19
We will *c* the damsel, and enquire... Gen 24:57
the daughters will *c* me blessed..... Gen 30:13
to pass, when Pharaoh shall *c* you... Gen 46:33
c to thee a nurse of the Hebrew..... Ex 2:7
c him, that he may eat bread........ Ex 2:20
one *c* thee, and thou eat of his...... Ex 34:15
And Moses sent to *c* Dathan......... Num 16:12
to *c* him, saying, Behold, there..... Num 22:5
him, If the men come to *c* thee...... Num 22:20
send unto thee to *c* thee........... Num 22:37
but the Moabites *c* them Emims..... Deut 2:11
the Ammonites *c* them Zamzummims... Deut 2:20
Hermon the Sidonians *c* Sirion..... Deut 3:9
and the Amorites *c* it Shenir....... Deut 3:9
all things that we *c* upon him for..... Deut 4:7
I *c* heaven and earth to witness..... Deut 4:26
elders of his city shall *c* him........ Deut 25:8
thou shalt *c* them to mind among... Deut 30:1

I c heaven and earth to record...... Deut 30:19
c Joshua, and present yourselves...... Deut 31:14
c heaven and earth to record...... Deut 31:28
They shall c the people unto the...... Deut 33:19
didst not c us to go with thee...... Judg 12:1
C for Samson, that he may make us.. Judg 16:25
and to c peaceably unto them...... Judg 21:13
C me not Naomi, c me Mara...... Ruth 1:20
why then c ye me Naomi, seeing...... Ruth 1:21
for thou didst c me...... 1Sa 3:6
for thou didst c me...... 1Sa 3:8
and it shall be, if he c thee...... 1Sa 3:9
I will c unto the LORD, and he...... 1Sa 12:17
c Jesse to the sacrifice, and I...... 1Sa 16:3
sent to c Ahimelech the priest...... 1Sa 22:11
C now Hushai the Archite also, and.. 2Sa 17:5
I will c on the LORD, who is...... 2Sa 22:4
answered and said, C me Bath-sheba.. 1Kin 1:28
C me Zadok the priest, and Nathan .. 1Kin 1:32
in all that they c for unto thee...... 1Kin 8:52
me to c my sin to remembrance...... 1Kin 17:18
c ye on the name of your gods, and.. 1Kin 18:24
I will c on the name of the LORD...... 1Kin 18:24
c on the name of your gods, but...... 1Kin 18:25
gone to c Micaiah spake unto him...... 1Kin 22:13
his servant, C this Shunammite...... 2Kin 4:12
And he said, C her...... 2Kin 4:15
and said, C this Shunammite...... 2Kin 4:36
c on the name of the LORD his God.. 2Kin 5:11
Now therefore c unto me all the...... 2Kin 10:19
c upon his name, make known his...... 1Chr 16:8
went to c Micaiah spake to him...... 2Chr 18:12
C now, if there be any that will...... Job 5:1
Then c thou, and I will answer...... Job 13:22
Thou shalt c, and I will answer...... Job 14:15
will he always c upon God...... Job 27:10
Hear me when I c, O God of my...... Ps 4:1
LORD will hear when I c unto him...... Ps 4:3
eat bread, and c not upon the LORD.. Ps 14:4
I will c upon the LORD, who is...... Ps 18:3
let the king hear us when we c...... Ps 20:9
they c their lands after their...... Ps 49:11
He shall c to the heavens from...... Ps 50:4
c upon me in the day of trouble...... Ps 50:15
As for me, I will c upon God...... Ps 55:16
all nations shall c him blessed...... Ps 72:17
I c to remembrance my song in the.. Ps 77:6
us, and we will c upon thy name...... Ps 80:18
unto all them that c upon thee...... Ps 86:5
of my trouble I will c upon thee...... Ps 86:7
He shall c upon me, and I will...... Ps 91:15
among them that c upon his name...... Ps 99:6
in the day when I c answer me...... Ps 102:2
c upon his name...... Ps 105:1
therefore will I c upon him as...... Ps 116:2
c upon the name of the LORD...... Ps 116:13
will c upon the name of the LORD.... Ps 116:17
unto all them that c upon him...... Ps 145:18
to all that c upon him in truth...... Ps 145:18
Then shall they c upon me...... Prov 1:28
c understanding thy kinswoman...... Prov 7:4
Unto you, O men, I c...... Prov 8:4
To c passengers who go right on.... Prov 9:15
arise up, and c her blessed...... Prov 31:28
Woe unto them that c evil good...... Is 5:20
shall c his name Immanuel...... Is 7:14
C his name Maher-shalal-hash-baz... Is 8:3
c upon his name, declare his...... Is 12:4
Lord God of hosts c to weeping...... Is 22:12
that I will c my servant Eliakim...... Is 22:20
will not c back his words...... Is 31:2
They shall c the nobles thereof...... Is 34:12
the sun shall he c upon my name...... Is 41:25
another shall c himself by the...... Is 44:5
And who, as I, shall c, and shall .. Is 44:7
which c thee by thy name, am the.. Is 45:3
For they c themselves of the holy.. Is 48:2
when I c unto them, they stand up .. Is 48:13
thou shalt c a nation that thou...... Is 55:5
c ye upon him while he is near...... Is 55:6
wilt thou c this a fast, and an...... Is 58:5
Then shalt thou c, and the LORD...... Is 58:9
c the sabbath a delight, the holy.. Is 58:13
and they shall c thee, The city of.. Is 60:14
but thou shalt c thy walls...... Is 60:18
shall c you the Ministers of our .. Is 61:6
And they shall c them, The holy...... Is 62:12
c his servants by another name...... Is 65:15
come to pass, that before they c...... Is 65:24
I will c all the families of the...... Jer 1:15
At that time they shall c...... Jer 3:17
and I said, Thou shalt c me...... Jer 3:19
Reprobate silver shall men c them.. Jer 6:30
thou shalt also c unto them...... Jer 7:27
c for the mourning women, that...... Jer 9:17
families that c not on thy name...... Jer 10:25
for I will c for a sword upon all.. Jer 25:29
Then shall ye c upon me, and ye...... Jer 29:12
C unto me, and I will answer...... Jer 33:3
C together the archers against...... Jer 50:29
c together against her the...... Jer 51:27
men c The perfection of beauty...... Lam 2:15
but he will c to remembrance the.. Eze 21:23
I will c for the corn, and will...... Eze 36:29
I will c for a sword against him.... Eze 38:21
they shall c it The valley of...... Eze 39:11
king commanded to c the magicians.. Dan 2:2
said unto him, C his name Jezreel.. Hos 1:4
unto him, C her name Lo-ruhamah.... Hos 1:6
Then said God, C his name Lo-ammi.. Hos 1:9

LORD, that thou shalt c me Ishi...... Hos 2:16
and shalt c me no more Baali...... Hos 2:16
they c to Egypt, they go to...... Hos 7:11
c a solemn assembly, gather the...... Joel 1:14
a fast, c a solemn assembly...... Joel 2:15
that whosoever shall c on the...... Joel 2:32
the remnant whom the LORD shall c.. Joel 2:32
they shall c the husbandman to...... Amos 5:16
c upon thy God, if so be that God.. Jonah 1:6
that they may all c upon the name.. Zeph 3:9
hosts, shall ye c every man his...... Zec 3:10
they shall c on my name, and I...... Zec 13:9
and they shall c them, The border.. Mal 1:4
all nations shall c you blessed...... Mal 3:12
And now we c the proud happy...... Mal 3:15
thou shalt c his name JESUS...... Mt 1:21
they shall c his name Emmanuel,...... Mt 1:23
I am not come to c the righteous...... Mt 9:13
they c them of his household...... Mt 10:25
C the labourers, and give them...... Mt 20:8
sent forth his servants to c them.. Mt 22:3
doth David in spirit c him Lord.... Mt 22:43
If David then c him Lord...... Mt 22:45
c no man your father upon the...... Mt 23:9
I came not to c the righteous...... Mk 2:17
they c the blind man, saying unto.. Mk 10:49
whom ye c the King of the Jews...... Mk 15:12
they c together the whole band...... Mk 15:16
thou shalt c his name John...... Lk 1:13
a son, and shalt c his name JESUS.. Lk 1:31
generations shall c me blessed...... Lk 1:48
I came not to c the righteous...... Lk 5:32
why c ye me, Lord, Lord, and do...... Lk 6:46
c not thy friends, nor thy...... Lk 14:12
the poor, the maimed, the lame,...... Lk 14:13
c thy husband, and come hither...... Jn 4:16
Ye c me Master and Lord...... Jn 13:13
Henceforth I c you not servants...... Jn 15:15
that whosoever shall c on the...... Acts 2:21
many as the Lord our God shall c.. Acts 2:39
to bind all that c on thy name...... Acts 9:14
c for one Simon, whose surname is.. Acts 10:5
cleansed, that c not thou common.. Acts 10:15
not c any man common or unclean... Acts 10:28
c hither Simon, whose surname is.. Acts 10:32
cleansed, that c not thou common.. Acts 11:9
for Simon, whose surname is...... Acts 11:13
took upon them to c over them...... Acts 19:13
after the way which they c heresy.. Acts 24:14
season, I will c for thee...... Acts 24:25
I will c them my people, which...... Rom 9:25
is rich unto all that c upon him.. Rom 10:12
For whosoever shall c upon the...... Rom 10:13
How then shall they c on him in...... Rom 10:14
with all that in every place c...... 1Cor 1:2
Moreover I c God for a record...... 2Cor 1:23
When I c to remembrance the...... 2Ti 1:5
with them that c on the Lord out.. 2Ti 2:22
is not ashamed to c them brethren.. Heb 2:11
But c to remembrance the former.... Heb 10:32
let him c for the elders of the...... Jas 5:14
if ye c on the Father, who...... 1Pet 1:17

CALLED See PREFACE.
God c the light Day, and the...... Gen 1:5
Day, and the darkness he c Night... Gen 1:5
God c the firmament Heaven...... Gen 1:8
And God c the dry land...... Gen 1:10
together of the waters c he Seas.. Gen 1:10
whatsoever Adam c every living...... Gen 2:19
she shall be c Woman, because she.. Gen 2:23
c their name Adam, in the day...... Gen 5:2
is the name of it c Babel...... Gen 11:9
thy name any more be c Abram...... Gen 17:5
the angel of the Lord c unto him.. Gen 22:11
shall not be c any more Jacob...... Gen 35:10
and he c his name Israel...... Gen 35:10
but his father c him Benjamin...... Gen 35:18
God c unto him out of the midst... Ex 3:4
Then Pharaoh c for Moses and Aaron.. Ex 8:8
c for Moses and Aaron, and said...... Ex 9:27
the LORD c unto him out of the...... Ex 19:3
Moses c all Israel, and said unto.. Deut 5:1
because it is c the LORD's...... Deut 15:2
art c by the name of the LORD...... Deut 28:10
That the LORD c Samuel...... 1Sa 3:4
for he that is now c a Prophet...... 1Sa 9:9
whose name is c by the name of...... 2Sa 6:2
city, and it be c after my name...... 2Sa 12:28
c all his brethren the king's...... 1Kin 1:9
c on the name of Baal from...... 1Kin 18:26
Jabez c on the God of Israel,...... 1Chr 4:10
offerings, and c upon the LORD...... 1Chr 21:26
which are c by my name, shall...... 2Chr 7:14
her, and that she were c by name.. Est 2:14
the inner court, who is not c...... Est 4:11
I have c upon thee, for thou wilt.. Ps 17:6
they have not c upon God...... Ps 53:4
that have not c upon thy name...... Ps 79:6
I have c daily upon thee, I have.. Ps 88:9
Then c I upon the name of the...... Ps 116:4
and his name shall be c Wonderful.. Is 9:6
it shall be c The way of holiness.. Is 35:8
But thou hast not c upon me...... Is 43:22
which are c by the name of Israel.. Is 48:1
unto me, O Jacob and Israel, my c.. Is 48:12
for mine house shall be c...... Is 56:7
that they might be c trees of...... Is 61:3
bring the day that thou hast c...... Lam 1:21
Thou hast c as in a solemn day my.. Lam 2:22
thereof is c Bamah unto this day.. Eze 20:29

now let Daniel be c, and he will.. Dan 5:12
was born Jesus, who is c Christ... Mt 1:16
and he c his name JESUS...... Mt 1:25
for they shall be c the children.. Mt 5:9
he shall be c the least in the...... Mt 5:19
the same shall be c great in the.. Mt 5:19
is not his mother c Mary...... Mt 13:55
Jesus c a little child unto him,.. Mt 18:2
for many be c, but few chosen...... Mt 20:16
c them, and said, What will ye...... Mt 20:32
My house shall be c the house of.. Mt 21:13
But be not ye c Rabbi...... Mt 23:8
or Jesus which is c Christ...... Mt 27:17
still, and commanded him to be c.. Mk 10:49
Peter c to mind the word that...... Mk 14:72
shall be c the Son of the Highest.. Lk 1:32
of thee shall be c the Son of God.. Lk 1:35
kindred that is c by this name...... Lk 1:61
father, how he would have him c... Lk 1:62
the child, his name was c JESUS... Lk 2:21
am no more worthy to be c thy son.. Lk 15:19
these servants to be c unto him... Lk 19:15
to the place, which is c Calvary.. Lk 23:33
him, Before that Philip c thee...... Jn 1:48
Messias cometh, which is c Christ.. Jn 4:25
A man that is c Jesus made clay,.. Jn 9:11
the street which is c Straight...... Acts 9:11
the disciples were c Christians... Acts 11:26
who c for Barnabas and Saul, and.. Acts 13:7
Gentiles, upon whom my name is c.. Acts 15:17
be c in question for this day's... Acts 19:40
of the dead I am c in question... Acts 23:6
Paul the prisoner c me unto him... Acts 23:18
c to be an apostle, separated...... Rom 1:1
are ye also the c of Jesus Christ.. Rom 1:6
Behold, thou art c a Jew, and...... Rom 2:17
to them who are the c according .. Rom 8:28
there shall they be c the...... Rom 9:26
by whom ye were c unto the...... 1Cor 1:9
But unto them which are c...... 1Cor 1:24
mighty, not many noble, are c...... 1Cor 1:26
if any man that is c a brother be.. 1Cor 5:11
Is any man c being circumcised... 1Cor 7:18
the same calling wherein he was c.. 1Cor 7:20
Art thou c being a servant...... 1Cor 7:21
let every man, wherein he is c...... 1Cor 7:24
c you into the grace of Christ...... Gal 1:6
ye have been c unto liberty...... Gal 5:13
who are c Uncircumcision by that.. Eph 2:11
the vocation wherewith ye are c... Eph 4:1
even as ye are c in one hope of... Eph 4:4
which also ye are c in one body... Col 3:15
himself above all that is c God... 2Th 2:4
Whereunto he c you by our gospel,.. 2Th 2:14
life, whereunto thou art also c... 1Ti 6:12
of science falsely so c...... 1Ti 6:20
daily, while it is c To day...... Heb 3:13
himself, but he that is c of God.. Heb 5:4
they which are c might receive,.. Heb 9:15
is not ashamed to be c their God.. Heb 11:16
refused to be c the son of...... Heb 11:24
worthy name by the which ye are c.. Jas 2:7
he was c the Friend of God...... Jas 2:23
the praises of him who hath c you.. 1Pet 2:9
For even hereunto were ye c...... 1Pet 2:21
knowing that ye are thereunto c... 1Pet 3:9
of him that hath c us to glory...... 2Pet 1:3
we should be c the sons of God...... 1Jn 3:1
preserved in Jesus Christ, and c.. Jude 1
name of the star is c Wormwood...... Rev 8:11
which spiritually is c Sodom...... Rev 11:8
and they that are with him are c.. Rev 17:14
Blessed are they which are c unto.. Rev 19:9

CALLEDST
us thus, that thou c us not...... Judg 8:1
for thou c me...... 1Sa 3:5
Thou c in trouble, and I delivered.. Ps 81:7
Thus thou c to remembrance the... Eze 23:21

CALLEST
said unto him, Why c thou me good.. Mt 19:17
said unto him, Why c thou me good.. Mk 10:18
said unto him, Why c thou me good.. Lk 18:19

CALLETH
that the stranger c to thee for...... 1Kin 8:43
that the stranger c to thee for...... 2Chr 6:33
who c upon God, and he answereth... Job 12:4
Deep c unto deep at the noise of... Ps 42:7
he c them all by their names...... Ps 147:4
and his mouth c for strokes...... Prov 18:6
He c to me out of Seir, Watchman,.. Is 21:11
he c them all by names by the...... Is 40:26
None c for justice, nor any...... Is 59:4
is none that c upon thy name...... Is 64:7
is none among them that c unto me.. Hos 7:7
that c for the waters of the sea,.. Amos 5:8
he that c for the waters of the... Amos 9:6
that, said, This man c for Elias... Mt 27:47
and c unto him whom he would...... Mk 3:13
he c thee...... Mk 10:49
therefore himself c him Lord,...... Mk 12:37
heard it said, Behold, he c Elias.. Mk 15:35
he c together his friends and...... Lk 15:6
it, she c her friends and her...... Lk 15:9
when he c the Lord the God of...... Lk 20:37
David therefore c him Lord...... Lk 20:44
he c his own sheep by name, and... Jn 10:3
The Master is come, and c for thee.. Jn 11:28
c those things which be not as...... Rom 4:17
not of works, but of him that c... Rom 9:11

CALLING

94

CAN

Spirit of God c Jesus accursed _____ 1Cor 12:3
cometh not of him that c you _____ Gal 5:8
Faithful is he that c you _____ 1Th 5:24
which c herself a prophetess, to _____ Rev 2:20

CALLING
them for the c of the assembly _____ Num 10:2
the c of assemblies, I cannot _____ Is 1:13
c the generations from the _____ Is 41:4
C a ravenous bird from the east, _____ Is 46:11
in c to remembrance the days of _____ Eze 23:19
markets, and c unto their fellows, _____ Mt 11:16
without, sent unto him, c him _____ Mk 3:31
Peter c to remembrance saith unto, _____ Mk 11:21
c unto him the centurion, he _____ Mk 15:44
John c unto him two of his _____ Lk 7:19
c one to another, and saying, We _____ Lk 7:32
c upon God, and saying, Lord Jesus _____ Acts 7:59
c on the name of the Lord _____ Acts 22:16
c of God are without repentance _____ Rom 11:29
For ye see your c, brethren, how _____ 1Cor 1:26
the same c wherein he was called _____ 1Cor 7:20
know what is the hope of his c _____ Eph 1:18
are called in one hope of your _____ Eph 4:4
the high c of God in Christ Jesus _____ Phil 3:14
would count you worthy of this c _____ 2Th 1:11
us, and called us with an holy c _____ 2Ti 1:9
partakers of the heavenly c _____ Heb 3:1
Sarah obeyed Abraham, c him lord _____ 1Pet 3:6
give diligence to make your c _____ 2Pet 1:10

CALM
He maketh the storm a c, so that _____ Ps 107:29
that the sea may be c unto us _____ Jonah 1:11
so shall the sea be c unto you _____ Jonah 1:12
and there was a great c _____ Mt 8:26
ceased, and there was a great c _____ Mk 4:39
and they ceased, and there was a c _____ Lk 8:24

CALNEH (cal'-neh) See CALNO, CANNEH. A
center of Babylonian worship
Babel, and Erech, and Accad, and C _____ Gen 10:10
Pass ye unto C, and see _____ Amos 6:2

CALNO (cal'-no) See CALNEH. Same as Calneh.
Is not C as Carchemish _____ Is 10:9

CALVARY
to the place, which is called C _____ Lk 23:33

CALVE
thou mark when the hinds do c _____ Job 39:1
of the LORD maketh the hinds to c _____ Ps 29:9

CALVED
Yea, the hind also c in the field _____ Jer 14:5

CALVES
bring their c home from them _____ 1Sa 6:7
cart, and shut up their c at home _____ 1Sa 6:10
and took sheep, and oxen, and c _____ 1Sa 14:32
counsel, and made two c of gold _____ 1Kin 12:28
unto the c that he had made _____ 1Kin 12:32
the golden c that were in Beth-el _____ 2Kin 10:29
them molten images, even two c _____ 2Kin 17:16
for the c which he had made _____ 2Chr 11:15
and there are with you golden c _____ 2Chr 13:8
with the c of the people, till _____ Ps 68:30
because of the c of Beth-aven _____ Hos 10:5
the men that sacrifice kiss the c _____ Hos 13:2
will we render the c of our lips _____ Hos 14:2
the c out of the midst of the _____ Amos 6:4
offerings, with c of a year old _____ Mic 6:6
grow up as c of the stall _____ Mal 4:2
by the blood of goats and c _____ Heb 9:12
the law, he took the blood of c _____ Heb 9:19

CALVETH
their cow c, and casteth not her _____ Job 21:10

CAME See PREFACE.

CAMEL
saw Isaac, she lighted off the c _____ Gen 24:64
as the c, because he cheweth the _____ Lev 11:4
as the c, and the hare, and the _____ Deut 14:7
and suckling, ox and sheep, c _____ 1Sa 15:3
the horse, of the mule, of the c _____ Zec 14:15
It is easier for a c to go _____ Mt 19:24
strain at a gnat, and swallow a c _____ Mt 23:24
It is easier for a c to go _____ Mk 10:25
For it is easier for a c to go _____ Lk 18:25

CAMEL'S
and put them in the c furniture _____ Gen 31:34
John had his raiment of c hair _____ Mt 3:4
And John was clothed with c hair _____ Mk 1:6

CAMELS
maidservants, and the asses, and c _____ Gen 12:16
ten c of the c of his master _____ Gen 24:10
he made his c to kneel down _____ Gen 24:11
and I will give thy c drink also _____ Gen 24:14
I will draw water for thy c also _____ Gen 24:19
draw water, and drew for all his c _____ Gen 24:20
as the c had done drinking, that _____ Gen 24:22
he stood by the c at the well _____ Gen 24:30
the house, and room for the c _____ Gen 24:31
and the ungirded his c _____ Gen 24:32
gave straw and provender for the c _____ Gen 24:32
and maidservants, and c, and asses _____ Gen 24:35
and I will also draw for thy c _____ Gen 24:44
and I will give thy c drink also _____ Gen 24:46
and she made the c drink also _____ Gen 24:46
damsels, and they rode upon the c _____ Gen 24:61
and, behold, the c were coming _____ Gen 24:63

and menservants, and c, and asses _____ Gen 30:43
set his sons and his wives upon c _____ Gen 31:17
and the flocks, and herds, and the c _____ Gen 32:7
Thirty milch c with their colts _____ Gen 32:15
with their c bearing spicery _____ Gen 37:25
upon the asses, upon the c _____ Ex 9:3
their c were without number _____ Judg 6:5
their c were without number, as _____ Judg 7:12
the oxen, and the asses, and the c _____ 1Sa 27:9
young men, which rode upon c _____ 1Sa 30:17
with c that bare spices, and very _____ 1Kin 10:2
of their c fifty thousand, and c _____ 1Chr 5:21
brought bread on asses, and on c _____ 1Chr 12:40
Over the c also was Obil the _____ 1Chr 27:30
c that bare spices, and gold in _____ 2Chr 9:1
c in abundance, and returned to _____ 2Chr 14:15
Their c, four hundred thirty and _____ Ezr 2:67
Their c, four hundred thirty and _____ Neh 7:69
horseback, and riders on mules, c _____ Est 8:10
c went out, being hastened and _____ Est 8:14
sheep, and three thousand c _____ Job 1:3
three bands, and fell upon the c _____ Job 1:17
thousand sheep, and six thousand c _____ Job 42:12
of asses, and a chariot of c _____ Is 21:7
treasures upon the bunches of c _____ Is 30:6
multitude of c shall cover thee _____ Is 60:6
and all their vessels, and their c _____ Jer 49:29
their c shall be a booty, and the _____ Jer 49:32
I will make Rabbah a stable for c _____ Eze 25:5

CAMELS'
that were on their c necks _____ Judg 8:21
that were about their c necks _____ Judg 8:26
forty c burden, and came and stood _____ 2Kin 8:9

CAMEST
Sarai's maid, whence c thou _____ Gen 16:8
unto the land from whence thou c _____ Gen 24:5
I have eaten of all before thou c _____ Gen 27:33
for in it thou c out from Egypt _____ Ex 23:15
month Abib thou c out from Egypt _____ Ex 34:18
wherefore c thou not unto me _____ Num 22:37
the children of Ammon thou c not _____ Deut 2:37
for thou c forth out of the land _____ Deut 16:3
remember the day when thou c _____ Deut 16:3
that thou c forth out of Egypt _____ Deut 16:6
that thou c not within the days _____ 1Sa 13:11
he said, Why c thou down hither _____ 1Sa 17:28
C thou not from thy journey _____ 2Sa 11:10
Whereas thou c but yesterday, _____ 2Sa 15:20
again by the same way that thou c _____ 1Kin 13:9
the man of God that c from Judah _____ 1Kin 13:14
to go by the way that thou c _____ 1Kin 13:17
But c back, and hast eaten bread _____ 1Kin 13:22
back by the way by which thou c _____ 2Kin 19:28
Thou c down also upon mount Sinai _____ Neh 9:13
back by the way by which thou c _____ Is 37:29
we looked not for, thou c down _____ Is 64:3
before thou c forth out of the _____ Jer 1:5
thou c forth with thy rivers, and _____ Eze 32:2
how c thou in hither not having a _____ Mt 22:12
Rabbi, when c thou hither _____ Jn 6:25
that thou c forth from God _____ Jn 16:30
unto thee in the way as thou c _____ Acts 9:17

CAMON (ca'-mon) A town in Gilead.
And Jair died, and was buried in C _____ Judg 10:5

CAMP
which went before the c of Israel _____ Ex 14:19
between the c of the Egyptians, _____ Ex 14:20
the Egyptians and the c of Israel _____ Ex 14:20
quails came up, and covered the c _____ Ex 16:13
people that was in the c trembled _____ Ex 19:16
out of the c to meet with God _____ Ex 19:17
thou burn with fire without the c _____ Ex 29:14
There is a noise of war in the c _____ Ex 32:17
soon as he came nigh unto the c _____ Ex 32:19
Moses stood in the gate of the c _____ Ex 32:26
gate to gate throughout the c _____ Ex 32:27
the c, afar off from the c _____ Ex 33:7
which was without the c _____ Ex 33:7
And he turned again into the c _____ Ex 33:11
to be proclaimed throughout the c _____ Ex 36:6
without the c unto a clean place _____ Lev 4:12
forth the bullock without the c _____ Lev 4:21
without the c unto a clean place _____ Lev 6:11
he burnt with fire without the c _____ Lev 8:17
he burnt with fire without the c _____ Lev 9:11
before the sanctuary out of the c _____ Lev 10:4
them in their coats out of the c _____ Lev 10:5
without the c shall he _____ Lev 13:46
shall go forth out of the c _____ Lev 14:3
that he shall come into the c _____ Lev 14:8
and afterward come into the c _____ Lev 16:26
one carry forth without the c _____ Lev 16:27
he shall come into the c _____ Lev 16:28
an ox, or lamb, or goat, in the c _____ Lev 17:3
or that killeth it out of the c _____ Lev 17:3
Israel strove together without the c _____ Lev 24:10
that hath caused without the c _____ Lev 24:14
him that had cursed out of the c _____ Lev 24:23
tents, every man by his own c _____ Num 1:52
they of the standard of the c of _____ Num 2:3
in the c of Judah were an hundred _____ Num 2:9
c of Reuben according to their _____ Num 2:10
the c of Reuben were an hundred _____ Num 2:16
shall set forward with the c of _____ Num 2:17
the Levites in the midst of the c _____ Num 2:17
shall be the standard of the c of _____ Num 2:18
the c of Ephraim were an hundred _____ Num 2:24
The standard of the c of Dan _____ Num 2:25

they that were numbered in the c _____ Num 2:31
when the c setteth forward, Aaron _____ Num 4:5
as the c is to set forward _____ Num 4:15
they put out of the c every leper _____ Num 5:2
without the c shall ye put them _____ Num 5:3
so, and put them out without the c _____ Num 5:4
of the c of the children of Judah _____ Num 10:14
the standard of the c of Reuben _____ Num 10:18
the standard of the c of _____ Num 10:22
the standard of the c of the _____ Num 10:25
day, when they went out of the c _____ Num 10:34
in the uttermost parts of the c _____ Num 11:1
dew fell upon the c in the night _____ Num 11:9
remained two of the men in the c _____ Num 11:26
and they prophesied in the c _____ Num 11:26
and Medad so prophesied in the c _____ Num 11:27
And Moses gat him into the c _____ Num 11:30
sea, and let them fall by the c _____ Num 11:31
the other side, round about the c _____ Num 11:31
for themselves round about the c _____ Num 11:32
be shut out from the c seven days _____ Num 12:14
shut out from the c seven days _____ Num 12:15
Moses, departed not out of the c _____ Num 14:44
him with stones without the c _____ Num 15:35
brought him without the c _____ Num 15:36
may bring her forth without the c _____ Num 19:3
he shall come into the c, and his _____ Num 19:7
up without the c in a clean place _____ Num 19:9
unto the c at the plains of Moab, _____ Num 31:12
forth to meet them without the c _____ Num 31:13
ye abide without the c seven days _____ Num 31:19
ye shall come into the c _____ Num 31:24
shall ye go abroad out of the c _____ Deut 23:10
he shall not come within the c _____ Deut 23:10
he shall come into the c again _____ Deut 23:11
have a place also without the c _____ Deut 23:12
God walketh in the midst of thy c _____ Deut 23:14
therefore shall thy c be holy _____ Deut 23:14
and thy stranger that is in thy c _____ Deut 29:11
abode in their places in the c _____ Josh 5:8
into the c, and lodged in the c _____ Josh 6:11
city once, and returned into the c _____ Josh 6:14
make the c of Israel a curse, and _____ Josh 6:18
left them without the c of Israel _____ Josh 6:23
to Joshua unto the c at Gilgal _____ Josh 9:6
unto Joshua to the c to Gilgal _____ Josh 10:6
with him, unto the c to Gilgal _____ Josh 10:15
c to Joshua at Makkedah in peace _____ Josh 10:21
with him, unto the c to Gilgal _____ Josh 10:43
I come to the outside of the c _____ Judg 7:17
also on every side of all the c _____ Judg 7:18
came unto the outside of the c in _____ Judg 7:19
in his place round about the c _____ Judg 7:21
the c of Dan between Zorah _____ Judg 13:25
there came none to the c from _____ Judg 21:8
brought them unto the c to Shiloh _____ Judg 21:12
the people were come into the c _____ 1Sa 4:3
of the LORD came into the c _____ 1Sa 4:5
shout in the c of the Hebrews _____ 1Sa 4:6
of the LORD was come into the c _____ 1Sa 4:7
they said, God is come into the c _____ 1Sa 4:7
the c of the Philistines in three _____ 1Sa 13:17
went up with them into the c from _____ 1Sa 14:21
out of the c of the Philistines _____ 1Sa 14:21
run to the c to thy brethren _____ 1Sa 17:17
go down with me to Saul to the c _____ 1Sa 26:6
a man came out of the c from Saul _____ 2Sa 1:2
Out of the c of Israel am I _____ 2Sa 1:3
over Israel that day in the c _____ 1Kin 16:16
when they came to the c of Israel _____ 2Kin 3:24
and such a place shall be my c _____ 2Kin 6:8
to go unto the c of the Syrians _____ 2Kin 7:5
uttermost part of the c of Syria _____ 2Kin 7:5
even the c as it was, and fled for _____ 2Kin 7:7
to the uttermost part of the c _____ 2Kin 7:8
We came to the c of the Syrians _____ 2Kin 7:10
are they gone out of the c to _____ 2Kin 7:12
smote in the c of the Assyrians _____ 2Kin 19:35
to the c had slain all the eldest _____ 2Chr 22:1
captains in the c of the king of _____ 2Chr 32:21
it fall in the midst of their c _____ Ps 78:28
They envied Moses also in the c _____ Ps 106:16
I will c against thee round about _____ Is 29:3
smote in the c of the Assyrians _____ Is 37:36
the bow, c against it round about _____ Jer 50:29
set the c also against it, and set _____ Eze 4:2
for his c is very great _____ Joel 2:11
which c in the hedges in the cold _____ Nah 3:17
for sin, are burned without the c _____ Heb 13:11
therefore unto him without the c _____ Heb 13:13
compassed the c of the saints _____ Rev 20:9

CAMPED
there Israel c before the mount _____ Ex 19:2

CAMPHIRE
is unto me as a cluster of c in _____ Song 1:14
c, with spikenard _____ Song 4:13

CAMPS
c throughout their hosts were six _____ Num 2:32
that they defile not their c _____ Num 5:3
and for the journeying of the c _____ Num 10:2
then the c that lie on the east _____ Num 10:5
then the c that lie on the south _____ Num 10:6
all the c throughout their hosts _____ Num 10:25
c to come up unto your nostrils _____ Amos 4:10

CAN
is greater than I c bear _____ Gen 4:13
so that if a man c number these _____ Gen 13:16
what c I do this day unto these _____ Gen 31:43

how then c I do this great .... Gen 39:9
there is none that c interpret it .... Gen 41:15
C we find such a one as this is,........ Gen 41:38
food, as much as they c carry .... Gen 44:1
a man as I c certainly divine .... Gen 44:15
I know that he c speak well........... Ex 4:14
get you straw where ye c find it .... Ex 5:11
young pigeons, such as he c get........ Lev 14:30
Who c count the dust of Jacob, and . Num 23:10
How c I myself alone bear your........ Deut 1:12
that c do according to thy works,..... Deut 3:24
how c I dispossess them.............. Deut 7:17
Who c stand before the children ...... Deut 9:2
I c no more go out and come in........ Deut 31:2
any that c deliver out of my hand.... Deut 32:39
if ye c certainly declare it .... Judg 14:12
peradventure he c shew us our way ... 1Sa 9:8
And Samuel said, How c I go........... 1Sa 16:2
no man a man that c play well 1Sa 16:17
what c he have more but the 1Sa 18:8
for who c stretch forth his hand 1Sa 26:9
shalt know what thy servant c do 2Sa 7:20
what c David say more unto thee 2Sa 7:20
Who c tell whether God will be........ 2Sa 12:22
c I bring him back again 2Sa 12:23
none c turn to the right hand or 2Sa 14:19
me every thing that ye c hear.......... 2Sa 15:36
I c discern between good and evil..... 2Sa 19:35
c thy servant taste what I eat or 2Sa 19:35
c I hear any more the voice of......... 2Sa 19:35
c skill to hew timber like unto........ 1Kin 5:6
What c David speak more to thee 1Chr 17:18
for who c judge this thy people,....... 2Chr 1:10
that c skill to grave with the 2Chr 2:7
for I know that thy servants c 2Chr 2:8
For how c I endure to see the .... Est 8:6
or how c I endure to see the............ Est 8:6
when they c find the grave .... Job 3:22
but who c withhold himself from ..... Job 4:2
C that which is unsavoury be .... Job 6:6
The rush grow up without mire........ Job 8:11
the flag grow without water............ Job 8:11
he taketh away, who c hinder him..... Job 9:12
there is none that c deliver out........ Job 10:7
together, then who c hinder him ...... Job 11:10
a man, and there c be no opening...... Job 12:14
Who c bring a clean thing out of ..... Job 14:4
wherewith he c do no good............. Job 15:3
C a man be profitable unto God....... Job 22:2
c he judge through the dark cloud.... Job 22:13
what c the Almighty do for them ..... Job 22:17
is in one mind, and who c turn him... Job 23:13
How then c man be justified with ..... Job 25:4
or how c he be clean that is born...... Job 25:4
of his power who c understand .... Job 26:14
who then c make trouble................ Job 34:29
his face, who then c behold him ...... Job 34:29
or who c say, Thou hast wrought..... Job 36:23
neither c the number of his years ..... Job 36:26
Also c any understand the .... Job 36:29
Who c number the clouds in wisdom . Job 38:37
or who c stay the bottles of............ Job 38:37
thine own right hand c save thee...... Job 40:14
he that made him c make his sword... Job 40:19
he trusteth that he c draw up .... Job 40:23
Who c discover the face of his........ Job 41:13
or who c come to him with his .... Job 41:13
Who c open the doors of his face...... Job 41:14
that no air c come between them....... Job 41:16
that no thought c be withholden ...... Job 42:2
what c the righteous do................. Ps 11:3
Who c understand his errors............ Ps 19:12
none c keep alive his own soul .... Ps 22:29
they are more than I c be numbered... Ps 40:5
None of them c by any means........... Ps 49:7
not fear what flesh c do unto me ...... Ps 56:4
be afraid what man c do unto me ...... Ps 56:11
your pots c feel the thorns............. Ps 58:9
C God furnish a table in the............ Ps 78:19
c he give bread also.................... Ps 78:20
c he provide flesh for his people ...... Ps 78:20
For who in the heaven c be............. Ps 89:6
mighty c be likened unto the LORD ... Ps 89:6
Who c utter the mighty acts of......... Ps 106:2
who c shew forth all his praise......... Ps 106:2
what c man do unto me................. Ps 118:6
who c stand before his cold .... Ps 147:17
C a man take fire in his bosom........ Prov 6:27
C one go upon hot coals, and his ..... Prov 6:28
a wounded spirit who c bear .... Prov 18:14
but a faithful man who c find.......... Prov 20:6
Who c say, I have made my heart ..... Prov 20:9
how c a man then understand his ..... Prov 20:24
seven men that c render a reason...... Prov 26:16
Who c find a virtuous woman......... Prov 31:10
for what c the man do that cometh ... Eccl 2:12
For who c eat, or who else c .... Eccl 2:25
or who else c hasten hereunto,......... Eccl 2:25
so that no man c find out the .... Eccl 3:11
nothing c be put to it, nor any......... Eccl 3:14
but how c one be warm alone........... Eccl 4:11
for who c tell a man what shall........ Eccl 6:12
for who c make that straight,.......... Eccl 7:13
exceeding deep, who c find it out ..... Eccl 7:24
for who c tell him when it shall .... Eccl 8:7
be after him, who c tell him.......... Eccl 10:14
neither c the floods drown it........... Song 8:7
a man c stretch himself on it .... Is 28:20
than that he c wrap himself in it ...... Is 28:20
death c not celebrate thee............. Is 38:18

who among them c declare this........ Is 43:9
there is none that c deliver out......... Is 43:13
yet c he not answer, nor save him ..... Is 46:7
C a woman forget her sucking .... Is 49:15
dogs which c never have enough ...... Is 56:11
cisterns, that c hold no water.......... Jer 2:13
her occasion who c turn her away..... Jer 2:24
if they c save thee in the time.......... Jer 2:28
C a maid forget her ornaments, or.... Jer 2:32
burn that none c quench it .... Jer 4:4
if ye c find a man, if there be .... Jer 5:1
yet c they not prevail.................. Jer 5:22
yet c they not pass over it .... Jer 5:22
so that none c pass through them...... Jer 9:10
neither c men hear the voice of........ Jer 9:10
C the Ethiopian change his skin,....... Jer 13:23
of the Gentiles that c cause rain ...... Jer 14:22
or c the heavens give showers......... Jer 14:22
who c know it?...................... Jer 17:9
and burn that none c quench it .... Jer 21:12
C any hide himself in secret .... Jer 23:24
If heaven above c be measured .... Jer 31:37
if ye c break my covenant of the ...... Jer 33:20
that c do any thing against you........ Jer 38:5
How c it be quiet, seeing the .... Jer 47:7
who c heal thee?.................... Lam 2:13
C thine heart endure, or c............. Eze 22:14
or c thine hands be strong, in .... Eze 22:14
secret that they c hide from thee...... Eze 28:3
c play well on an instrument........... Eze 33:32
Son of man, c these bones live......... Eze 37:3
I shall know that ye c shew me .... Dan 2:9
that c shew the king's matter .... Dan 2:10
If ye c shew it before the king,........ Dan 2:11
that c deliver after this sort .... Dan 3:29
none c stay his hand, or say unto ..... Dan 4:35
For how c the servant of this my...... Dan 10:17
and who c abide it? .... Joel 2:11
C two walk together, except they ..... Amos 3:3
C a bird fall in a snare upon the ...... Amos 3:5
hath spoken, who c but prophesy...... Amos 3:8
Who c tell if God will turn and........ Jonah 3:9
none evil c come upon us .... Mic 3:11
in pieces, and none c deliver .... Mic 5:8
Who c stand before his .... Nah 1:6
who c abide in the fierceness of .... Nah 1:6
No man c serve two masters............ Mt 6:24
c add one cubit unto his stature .... Mt 6:27
neither c a corrupt tree bring .... Mt 7:18
unto them, C the children of the ...... Mt 9:15
Or else how c one enter into a .... Mt 12:29
O generation of vipers, how c ye ..... Mt 12:34
ye c discern the face of the sky........ Mt 16:3
but c ye not discern the signs of....... Mt 16:3
saying, Who then c be saved........... Mt 19:25
how c ye escape the damnation of .... Mt 23:33
your way, make it as sure as ye c ..... Mt 27:65
who c forgive sins but God only ...... Mk 2:7
unto them, C the children of the ...... Mk 2:19
How c Satan cast out Satan............ Mk 3:23
No man c enter into a strong .... Mk 3:27
entering into him c defile him......... Mk 7:15
From whence c a man satisfy these ... Mk 8:4
no fuller on earth c white them .... Mk 9:3
This kind c come forth by nothing..... Mk 9:29
that c lightly speak evil of me .... Mk 9:39
themselves, Who then c be saved...... Mk 10:26
c ye drink of the cup that I .... Mk 10:38
And they said unto him, We c .... Mk 10:39
Who c forgive sins, but God alone.... Lk 5:21
C ye make the children of the .... Lk 5:34
C the blind lead the blind.............. Lk 6:39
that have no more that they c do ...... Lk 12:4
If ye c with taking thought c add..... Lk 12:25
ye c discern the face of the sky .... Lk 12:56
No servant c serve two masters........ Lk 16:13
neither c they pass to us, that .... Lk 16:26
it said, Who then c be saved........... Lk 18:26
Neither c they die any more............ Lk 20:36
C there any good thing come out...... Jn 1:46
for no man c do these miracles .... Jn 3:2
How c a man be born when he is ...... Jn 3:4
c he enter the second time into .... Jn 3:4
unto him, How c these things be ...... Jn 3:9
A man c receive nothing, except ...... Jn 3:27
The Son c do nothing of himself...... Jn 5:19
I c of mine own self do nothing....... Jn 5:30
How c this man give us his flesh ...... Jn 6:52
who c hear it? .... Jn 6:60
that no man c come unto me,.......... Jn 6:65
night cometh, when no man c work... Jn 9:4
How c a man that is a sinner do....... Jn 9:16
C a devil open the eyes of the .... Jn 10:21
and how c we know the way............ Jn 14:5
no more c ye, except ye abide in ...... Jn 15:5
for without me ye c do nothing........ Jn 15:5
And he said, How c I, except some.... Acts 8:31
C any man forbid water, that .... Acts 10:47
Neither c they prove the things .... Acts 24:13
law of God, neither indeed c be .... Rom 8:7
be for us, who c be against us.......... Rom 8:31
neither c he know them, because....... 1Cor 2:14
For other foundation c no man lay.... 1Cor 3:11
that no man c say that Jesus is 1Cor 12:3
For we c do nothing against the 2Cor 13:8
I c do all things through Christ........ Phil 4:13
For what thanks c we render to....... 1Th 3:9
it is certain we c carry nothing 1Ti 6:7

which no man c approach unto........ 1Ti 6:16
whom no man hath seen, nor c see 1Ti 6:16
Who c have compassion on the .... Heb 5:2
c never with those sacrifices........... Heb 10:1
which c never take away sins .... Heb 10:11
c faith save him? .... Jas 2:14
But the tongue c no man tame .... Jas 3:8
C the fig tree, my brethren, bear ...... Jas 3:12
so c no fountain both yield salt .... Jas 3:12
how c he love God whom he hath 1Jn 4:20
an open door, and no man c shut it ... Rev 3:8
which neither c see, nor hear,......... Rev 9:20

CANA (*ca'-nah*) *A village in Galilee.*
was a marriage in C of Galilee.......... Jn 2:1
did Jesus in C of Galilee................ Jn 2:11
came again into C of Galilee........... Jn 4:46
and Nathanael of C in Galilee......... Jn 21:2

CANAAN (*ca'-na-an*) *See* CANAANITE.
  1. Son of Ham.
and Ham is the father of C............. Gen 9:18
And Ham, the father of C, saw the ... Gen 9:22
And he said, Cursed be C............... Gen 9:25
and C shall be his servant.............. Gen 9:26
and C shall be his servant.............. Gen 9:27
Cush, and Mizraim, and Phut, and C. Gen 10:6
C begat Sidon his firstborn, and ...... Gen 10:15
Cush, and Mizraim, Put, and C....... 1Chr 1:8
C begat Zidon his firstborn, and 1Chr 1:13
  2. Place where Canaanites dwelt.
to go into the land of C................ Gen 11:31
forth to go into the land of C .... Gen 12:5
and into the land of C they came...... Gen 12:5
Abram dwelled in the land of C .... Gen 13:12
dwelt ten years in the land of C .... Gen 16:3
art a stranger, all the land of C .... Gen 17:8
same is Hebron in the land of C .... Gen 23:2
same is Hebron in the land of C .... Gen 23:19
take a wife of the daughters of C...... Gen 28:1
take a wife of the daughters of C...... Gen 28:6
of C pleased not Isaac his father ...... Gen 28:8
Isaac his father in the land of C ...... Gen 31:18
which is in the land of C............... Gen 33:18
to Luz, which is in the land of C...... Gen 35:6
his wives of the daughters of C........ Gen 36:2
born unto him in the land of C .... Gen 36:5
which he had got in the land of C .... Gen 36:6
was a stranger, in the land of C .... Gen 37:1
the famine was in the land of C .... Gen 42:5
From the land of C to buy food ...... Gen 42:7
sons of one man in the land of C ..... Gen 42:13
their father unto the land of C .... Gen 42:29
with our father in the land of C ...... Gen 42:32
unto thee out of the land of C .... Gen 44:8
and go, get you unto the land of C ... Gen 45:17
came into the land of C unto .... Gen 45:25
they had gotten in the land of C ..... Gen 46:6
Er and Onan died in the land of C ... Gen 46:12
which were in the land of C .... Gen 46:31
are come out of the land of C .... Gen 47:1
famine is sore in the land of C .... Gen 47:4
all the land of C fainted by .... Gen 47:13
of Egypt, and in the land of C .... Gen 47:14
of Egypt, and in the land of C .... Gen 47:15
unto me at Luz in the land of C ...... Gen 48:3
by me in the land of C in the way .... Gen 48:7
is before Mamre, in the land of C .... Gen 49:30
digged for me in the land of C .... Gen 50:5
carried him into the land of C .... Gen 50:13
them, to give them the land of C ..... Ex 6:4
inhabitants of C shall melt away ..... Ex 15:15
unto the borders of the land of C ..... Lev 14:34
after the doings of the land of C ..... Lev 18:3
Egypt, to give you the land of C ...... Lev 25:38
they may search the land of C .... Num 13:2
them to spy out the land of C .... Num 13:17
Er and Onan died in the land of C ... Num 26:19
among you in the land of C .... Num 32:30
the LORD unto the land of C .... Num 32:32
in the south in the land of C .... Num 33:40
over Jordan into the land of C .... Num 33:51
When ye come into the land of C ..... Num 34:2
even the land of C with the .... Num 34:2
of Israel in the land of C.............. Num 34:29
over Jordan into the land of C .... Num 35:14
shall ye give in the land of C .... Num 35:14
and behold the land of C, which I .... Deut 32:49
fruit of the land of C that year .... Josh 5:12
Israel inherited in the land of C ...... Josh 14:1
them at Shiloh in the land of C .... Josh 21:2
Shiloh, which is in the land of C ..... Josh 22:9
Jordan, that are in the land of C ..... Josh 22:10
altar over against the land of C ...... Josh 22:11
of Gilead, unto the land of C .... Josh 22:32
him throughout all the land of C ..... Josh 24:3
had not known all the wars of C ...... Judg 3:1
into the hand of Jabin king of C ..... Judg 4:2
C before the children of Israel .... Judg 4:23
against Jabin the king of C .... Judg 4:24
had destroyed Jabin king of C .... Judg 4:24
then fought the kings of C in .... Judg 5:19
Shiloh, which is in the land of C ..... Judg 21:12
thee will I give the land of C 1Chr 16:18
thee will I give the land of C .... Ps 105:11
sacrificed unto the idols of C .... Ps 106:38
Bashan, and all the kingdoms of C ... Ps 135:11
of Egypt speak the language of C ..... Is 19:18
thy nativity is of the land of C .... Eze 16:3
in the land of C unto Chaldea......... Eze 16:29

O C, the land of the Philistines, ... Zeph 2:5
a woman of C came out of the same .... Mt 15:22

CANAANITE (ca'-na-an-ite) See CANAANITES,
CANAANITISH, CANAANITISH, ZELOTES.
Descendants of Canaan.
the C was then in the land .... Gen 12:6
and the C and the Perizzite dwelled ..... Gen 13:7
there a daughter of a certain C. .... Gen 38:2
shall drive out the Hivite, the C, ... Ex 23:28
and I will drive out the C. .... Ex 33:2
before the Amorite, and the C. .... Ex 34:11
and when king Arad the C, which ...... Num 21:1
And king Arad the C, which dwelt ..... Num 33:40
Hittite, and the Amorite, the C. .... Josh 9:1
to the C on the east and on the .... Josh 11:3
which is counted to the C. .... Josh 13:3
the C in the house of the LORD of ..... Zec 14:21
Simon the C, and Judas Iscariot, ... Mt 10:4
and Thaddaeus, and Simon the C .... Mk 3:18

CANAANITES (ca'-na-an-ites)
families of the C spread abroad, ... Gen 10:18
borders of the C was from Sidon, ... Gen 10:19
And the Amorites, and the C, ... Gen 15:21
my son of the daughters of the C, ... Gen 24:3
my son of the daughters of the C. ..... Gen 24:37
of the land, among the C and the ...... Gen 34:30
inhabitants of the land, the C, ... Gen 50:11
unto the place of the C, and the ...... Ex 3:8
of Egypt unto the land of the C .... Ex 3:17
bring thee into the land of the C ...... Ex 13:5
bring thee into the land of the C ...... Ex 13:11
and the Perizzites, and the C, ... Ex 23:23
the C dwell by the sea, and by the .... Num 13:29
the C dwelt in the valley, ... Num 14:25
the C are there before you, and ye .... Num 14:43
the C which dwelt in that hill, ... Num 14:45
of Israel, and delivered up the C ...... Num 21:3
sea side, to the land of the C .... Deut 1:7
and the Amorites, and the C, ... Deut 7:1
goeth down, in the land of the C ...... Deut 11:30
Hittites, and the Amorites, the C ...... Deut 20:17
drive out from before you the C .... Josh 3:10
and all the kings of the C .... Josh 5:1
For the C and all the inhabitants, ... Josh 7:9
Hittites, the Amorites, and the C ...... Josh 12:8
the south, all the land of the C .... Josh 13:4
not out the C that dwelt among .... Josh 16:10
but the C dwell among the .... Josh 16:10
but the C would dwell in that .... Josh 17:12
that they put the C to tribute .... Josh 17:13
all the C that dwell in the land .... Josh 17:16
for thou shalt drive out the C .... Josh 17:18
and the Perizzites, and the C .... Josh 24:11
go up for us against the C first .... Judg 1:1
that we may fight against the C .... Judg 1:3
and the Lord delivered the C .... Judg 1:4
against him, and they slew the C ...... Judg 1:5
went down to fight against the C ...... Judg 1:9
the C that dwelt in Hebron .... Judg 1:10
they slew the C that inhabited, ... Judg 1:17
but the C would dwell in that .... Judg 1:27
that they put the C to tribute .... Judg 1:28
but the C that dwelt in Gezer .... Judg 1:29
but the C dwelt in Gezer among ...... Judg 1:29
but the C dwelt among them, and .... Judg 1:30
the Asherites dwelt among the C ..... Judg 1:32
but he dwelt among the C, the .... Judg 1:33
of the Philistines, and all the C ...... Judg 3:3
of Israel dwelt among the C .... Judg 3:5
of the Hivites, and of the C 2Sa 24:7
when the C dwelt in the 1Kin 9:16
their abominations, even of the C ..... Ezr 9:1
him to give the land of the C .... Neh 9:8
inhabitants of the land, the C .... Neh 9:24
shall possess that of the C .... Obad 20

CANAANITESS (ca'-na-an-ite-ess)
him of the daughter of Shua the C ... 1Chr 2:3

CANAANITISH (ca'-na-an-i-tish)
and Shaul the son of a C woman ..... Gen 46:10
and Shaul the son of a C woman ..... Ex 6:15

CANDACE (can'-da-see) *Name for a dynasty
of Ethiopian queens.*
under C queen of the Ethiopians ...... Acts 8:27

CANDLE
his c shall be put out with him .... Job 18:6
How oft is the c of the wicked .... Job 21:17
When his c shined upon my head, ... Job 29:3
For thou wilt light my c .... Ps 18:28
of man is the c of the LORD, ... Prov 20:27
the c of the wicked shall be put ...... Prov 24:20
her c goeth not out by night .... Prov 31:18
millstones, and the light of the c .... Jer 25:10
Neither do men light a c, and put .... Mt 5:15
Is a c brought to be put under a ..... Mk 4:21
No man, when he hath lighted a c .... Lk 8:16
No man, when he hath lighted a c .... Lk 11:33
of a c doth give light, ... Lk 11:36
one piece, doth not light a c, ... Lk 15:8
the light of a c shall shine no .... Rev 18:23
and they need no c, neither light .... Rev 22:5

CANDLES
I will search Jerusalem with c .... Zeph 1:12

CANDLESTICK
thou shalt make a c of pure gold .... Ex 25:31
beaten work shall the c be made ..... Ex 25:31
of the c out of the one side .... Ex 25:32

of the c out of the other side .... Ex 25:32
branches that come out of the c ..... Ex 25:33
in the c shall be four bowls made ... Ex 25:34
that proceed out of the c .... Ex 25:35
the c over against the table on ..... Ex 26:35
and all his vessels, and the c .... Ex 30:27
the pure c with all his furniture .... Ex 31:8
The c also for the light, and his .... Ex 35:14
he made the c of pure gold. .... Ex 37:17
of beaten work made he the c .... Ex 37:17
three branches of the c out of ..... Ex 37:18
three branches of the c out of ..... Ex 37:18
six branches going out of the c ..... Ex 37:19
in the c were four bowls made ..... Ex 37:20
The pure c, with the lamps .... Ex 39:37
and thou shalt bring in the c ...... Ex 40:4
he put the c in the tent of the ..... Ex 40:24
c before the LORD continually ...... Lev 24:4
the ark, and the table, and the c ... Num 3:31
cover the c of the light, and his ... Num 4:9
give light over against the c .... Num 8:2
lamps thereof over against the c ... Num 8:2
this work of the c was of beaten ... Num 8:4
shewed Moses, so he made the c ... Num 8:4
and a table, and a stool, and a c ... 2Kin 4:10
of gold, by weight for every c 1Chr 28:15
silver by weight, both for the c 1Chr 28:15
according to the use of every c 1Chr 28:15
the c of gold with the lamps 2Chr 13:11
wrote over against the c upon the . Dan 5:5
behold a c all of gold, with a ..... Zec 4:2
upon the right side of the c .... Zec 4:11
put it under a bushel, or on a c ... Mt 5:15
and not to be set on a c .... Mk 4:21
but setteth it on a c, that they ... Lk 8:16
under a bushel, but on a c .... Lk 11:33
the first, wherein was the c .... Heb 9:2
will remove thy c out of his ...... Rev 2:5

CANDLESTICKS
the c of pure gold, five on the 1Kin 7:49
Even the weight for the c of gold .. 1Chr 28:15
for the c of silver by weight, ... 1Chr 28:15
he made ten c of gold according ... 2Chr 4:7
Moreover the c with their lamps, .. 2Chr 4:20
bowls, and the caldrons, and the c . Jer 52:19
turned, I saw seven golden c .... Rev 1:12
in the midst of the seven c one .... Rev 1:13
right hand, and the seven golden c . Rev 1:20
the seven c which thou sawest are . Rev 1:20
the midst of the seven golden c ... Rev 2:1
the two c standing before the God . Rev 11:4

CANE
bought me no sweet c with money .. Is 43:24
the sweet c from a far country .... Jer 6:20

CANKER
their word will eat as doth a c 2Ti 2:17

CANKERED
Your gold and silver is c .... Jas 5:3

CANKERWORM
locust hath left hath the c eaten. .. Joel 1:4
that which the c hath left hath .... Joel 1:4
that the locust hath eaten, the c .. Joel 2:25
it shall eat them up like the c ..... Nah 3:15
make thyself many as the c .... Nah 3:15
the c spoileth, and fleeth away .... Nah 3:16

CANNEH (can'-neh) See CALNEH. *A place in
southern Arabia.*
Haran, and C, and Eden, the ...... Eze 27:23

CANNOT
I c escape to the mountain, lest .... Gen 19:19
for I c do any thing till thou be ... Gen 19:22
we c speak unto the bad or good. .. Gen 24:50
And they said, We c, until all the .. Gen 29:8
lord that I c rise up before thee .. Gen 31:35
which c be numbered for multitude. Gen 32:12
We c do this thing, to give our .... Gen 34:14
to Judah, and said, I c find her ... Gen 38:22
we c tell who put our money in .... Gen 43:22
The lad c leave his father .... Gen 44:22
And we said, We c go down .... Gen 44:26
that one c be able to see the ...... Ex 10:5
The people c come up to mount .... Ex 19:23
if he be poor, and c get so much .. Lev 14:21
I c go beyond the word of the .... Num 22:18
and I c reverse it. .... Num 23:20
I c go beyond the commandment of Num 24:13
the land c be cleansed of the ..... Num 35:33
a sore tooth that c be healed. .... Deut 28:35
the people, Ye c serve the LORD. .. Josh 24:19
unto the LORD, and I c go back ... Judg 11:35
But if ye c declare it me, then .... Judg 14:13
I c redeem it for myself, lest I .... Ruth 4:6
for I c redeem it .... Ruth 4:6
which c profit nor deliver 1Sa 12:21
said unto Saul, I c go with these .. 1Sa 17:39
thy soul liveth, O king, I c tell ... 1Sa 17:55
that a man c speak to him 1Sa 25:17
thinking, David c come in 2Sa 5:6
is not gathered up again 2Sa 14:14
because they c be taken with 2Sa 23:6
that c be numbered nor counted .. 1Kin 3:8
heaven of heavens c contain thee . 1Kin 8:27
he c find thee, he shall slay me. .. 1Kin 18:12
heaven of heavens c contain him. . 2Chr 2:6
heaven of heavens c contain thee . 2Chr 6:18
the LORD, that ye c prosper. 2Chr 24:20

for we c stand before thee. .... Ezr 9:15
great work, so that I c come down. . Neh 6:3
so that their hands c perform ...... Job 5:12
c my taste discern perverse .... Job 6:30
he c answer him one of a thousand. Job 9:3
down, and it c be built again ...... Job 12:14
his bounds that he c pass .... Job 14:5
for I c find one wise man among ... Job 17:10
fenced up my way that I c pass. .... Job 19:8
and backward, but I c perceive him Job 23:8
he doth work, but I c behold him. .. Job 23:9
the right hand, that I c see him .... Job 23:9
It c be gotten for gold, neither .... Job 28:15
It c be valued with the gold of .... Job 28:16
gold and the crystal c equal it ..... Job 28:17
we c be satisfied. .... Job 31:31
consumed away, that it c be seen ... Job 33:21
a great ransom c deliver thee ...... Job 36:18
doeth he, which we c comprehend. . Job 37:5
for we c order our speech by ...... Job 37:19
the Almighty, we c find him out ... Job 37:23
together, that they c be sundered. .. Job 41:17
they c be moved. .... Job 41:23
of him that layeth at him c hold. .. Job 41:26
The arrow c make him flee .... Job 41:28
they c be reckoned up in order. .... Ps 40:5
I am so troubled that I c speak. ... Ps 77:4
I am shut up, and I c come forth ... Ps 88:8
is established, that it c be moved. .. Ps 93:1
which c be removed, but abideth .... Ps 125:1
it is high, I c attain unto it. .... Ps 139:6
and for four which it c bear .... Prov 30:21
man c utter it .... Eccl 1:8
is crooked c be made straight ..... Eccl 1:15
which is wanting c be numbered. ... Eccl 1:15
that a man c find out the work .... Eccl 8:17
a man c tell what shall be .... Eccl 10:14
Many waters c quench love .... Song 8:7
of assemblies, I c away with. ...... Is 1:13
and he saith, I c .... Is 29:11
For the grave c praise thee .... Is 38:18
into the pit c hope for thy truth ... Is 38:18
shut their eyes, that they c see .... Is 44:18
hearts, that they c understand ..... Is 44:18
that he c deliver his soul, nor .... Is 44:20
and pray unto a god that c save .... Is 45:20
at all, that it c redeem .... Is 50:2
are all dumb dogs, they c bark. ... Is 56:10
are shepherds that c understand ... Is 56:11
the troubled sea, when it c rest. .. Is 57:20
is not shortened, that it c save .... Is 59:1
have not heard, that it c hear .... Is 59:1
in the street, and equity c enter. . Is 59:14
behold, I c speak. .... Jer 1:6
I c hold my peace, because thou ... Jer 4:19
decree, that it c pass it .... Jer 5:22
uncircumcised, and they c hearken Jer 6:10
in lying words, that c profit ...... Jer 7:8
needs be borne, because they c go . Jer 10:5
for they c do evil, neither also ... Jer 10:5
as a mighty man that c save ...... Jer 14:9
c I do with you as this potter ..... Jer 18:6
that c be made whole again .... Jer 19:11
that c be eaten, they are so evil. .. Jer 24:3
which c be eaten, they are so ..... Jer 24:8
that c be eaten, they are so evil. .. Jer 29:17
the host of heaven c be numbered . Jer 33:22
I c go into the house of the LORD . Jer 36:5
the LORD, though it c be searched . Jer 46:23
it c be quiet .... Jer 49:23
hedged me about, that I c get out. . Lam 3:7
that we c go in our streets ...... Lam 4:18
king hath demanded c the wise men Dan 2:27
which c be measured nor numbered . Hos 1:10
c discern between their right ..... Jonah 4:11
c be satisfied, but gathereth. ..... Hab 2:5
that is set on an hill c be hid. .... Mt 5:14
Ye c serve God and mammon ..... Mt 6:24
A good tree c bring forth evil. .... Mt 7:18
All men c receive this saying, ... Mt 19:11
Jesus, and said, We c tell. .... Mt 21:27
Thinkest thou that I c now pray ... Mt 26:53
himself he c save .... Mt 27:42
bridegroom with them, they c fast . Mk 2:19
itself, that kingdom c stand. ..... Mk 3:24
itself, that house c stand .... Mk 3:25
he c stand, but hath an end ...... Mk 3:26
into the man, it c defile him. .... Mk 7:18
and said unto Jesus, We c tell .... Mk 11:33
himself he c save .... Mk 15:31
I c rise and give thee. .... Lk 11:7
for it c be that a prophet perish .. Lk 13:33
for they c recompense thee .... Lk 14:14
a wife, and therefore I c come .... Lk 14:20
life also, he c be my disciple. .... Lk 14:26
come after me, c be my disciple ... Lk 14:27
that he hath, he c be my disciple. . Lk 14:33
I c dig .... Lk 16:3
Ye c serve God and mammon ..... Lk 16:13
would pass from hence to you c .... Lk 16:26
he c see the kingdom of God. ..... Jn 3:3
he c enter into the kingdom of .... Jn 3:5
The world c hate you .... Jn 7:7
and where I am, thither ye c come . Jn 7:34
and where I am, thither ye c come . Jn 7:36
but ye c tell whence I come, and, . Jn 8:14
whither I go, ye c come .... Jn 8:21
he saith, Whither I go, ye c come . Jn 8:22
even because ye c hear my word. .. Jn 8:43
and the scripture c be broken .... Jn 10:35

C

the Jews, Whither I go, ye c come...... Jn 13:33
Lord, why c I follow thee now .... Jn 13:37
whom the world c receive, because ..... Jn 14:17
As the branch c bear fruit of .... Jn 15:4
unto you, but ye c bear them now ...... Jn 16:12
we c tell what he saith .... Jn 16:18
and we c deny it .... Acts 4:16
For we c but speak the things......... Acts 4:20
it be of God, ye c overthrow it....... Acts 5:39
manner of Moses, ye c be saved........ Acts 15:1
these things c be spoken against ..... Acts 19:36
abide in the ship, ye c be saved...... Acts 27:31
are in the flesh c please God......... Rom 8:8
with groanings which c be uttered..... Rom 8:26
But if they c contain, let them....... 1Cor 7:9
Ye c drink the cup of the Lord,....... 1Cor 10:21
ye c be partakers of the Lord's....... 1Cor 10:21
the eye c say unto the hand, I........ 1Cor 12:21
blood c inherit the kingdom of........ 1Cor 15:50
(whether in the body, I c tell 2Cor 12:2
whether out of the body, I c tell..... 2Cor 12:3
or out of the body, I c tell.......... 2Cor 12:3
c disannul, that it should make....... Gal 3:17
so that ye c do the things that....... Gal 5:17
they that are otherwise c be hid...... 1Ti 5:25
he c deny himself 2Ti 2:13
life, which God, that c lie .... Titus 1:2
Sound speech, that c be condemned..... Titus 2:8
have not an high priest which c ...... Heb 4:15
of which we c now speak............... Heb 9:5
which c be shaken may remain .... Heb 12:27
a kingdom which c be moved............ Heb 12:28
for God c be tempted with evil,....... Jas 1:13
and desire to have, and c obtain...... Jas 4:2
c see afar off, and hath forgotten ... 2Pet 1:9
and that c cease from sin............. 2Pet 2:14
he c sin, because he is born of 1Jn 3:9

CANST

that thou c understand a dream to .... Gen 41:15
he said, Thou c not see my face....... Ex 33:20
whereof thou c not be healed .... Deut 28:27
thou c not stand before this.......... Josh 7:13
How c thou say, I love thee, when .... Judg 16:15
C thou bring me down to this 1Sa 30:15
wheresoever thou c sojourn 2Kin 8:1
gold that thou c find in all the ..... Ezr 7:16
c thou by searching find out God ..... Job 11:7
c thou find out the Almighty unto .... Job 11:7
what c thou do? .... Job 11:8
what c thou know? .... Job 11:8
Or darkness, that thou c not see ..... Job 22:11
If thou c answer me, set thy......... Job 33:5
C thou bind the sweet influences ..... Job 38:31
C thou bring forth Mazzaroth in ...... Job 38:32
or c thou guide Arcturus with his .... Job 38:32
c thou set the dominion thereof ...... Job 38:33
C thou lift up thy voice to the ...... Job 38:34
C thou send lightnings, that they .... Job 38:35
or c thou mark when the hinds do..... Job 39:1
C thou number the months that .... Job 39:2
C thou bind the unicorn with his ..... Job 39:10
C thou make him afraid as a .... Job 39:20
or c thou thunder with a voice ...... Job 40:9
C thou draw out leviathan with an ... Job 41:1
C thou put an hook into his nose..... Job 41:2
C thou fill his skin with barbed..... Job 41:7
I know that thou c do every thing.... Job 42:2
all the things thou c desire are .... Prov 3:15
that thou c not know them .... Prov 5:6
is his son's name, if thou c tell.... Prov 30:4
speech than thou c perceive .... Is 33:19
that thou c not understand .... Is 33:19
How c thou say, I am not polluted ... Jer 2:23
then how c thou contend with .... Jer 12:5
whose words thou c not understand ... Eze 3:6
that thou c make interpretations,.... Dan 5:16
now if thou c read the writing,...... Dan 5:16
evil, and c not look on iniquity..... Hab 1:13
because thou c not make one hair .... Mt 5:36
thou wilt, thou c make me clean ..... Mt 8:2
thou wilt, thou c make me clean ..... Mk 1:40
but if thou c do any thing, have .... Mk 9:22
said unto him, If thou c believe .... Mk 9:23
thou wilt, thou c make me clean ..... Lk 5:12
Either how c thou say to thy .... Lk 6:42
but c not tell whence it cometh...... Jn 3:8
I go, thou c not follow me now ...... Jn 13:36
Who said, C thou speak Greek......... Acts 21:37
how thou c not bear that which ...... Rev 2:2

CAPERNAUM (ca-pur'-na-um) A city in Galilee.

Nazareth, he came and dwelt in C .... Mt 4:13
And when Jesus was entered into C ... Mt 8:5
And thou, C, which art exalted....... Mt 11:23
And when they were come to C .... Mt 17:24
And they went into C .... Mk 1:21
he entered into C after some days ... Mk 2:1
And he came to C .... Mk 9:33
we have heard done in C, do also .... Lk 4:23
And came down to C, a city of .... Lk 4:31
of the people, he entered into C .... Lk 7:1
And thou, C, which art exalted to ... Lk 10:15
After this he went down to C .... Jn 2:12
nobleman, whose son was sick at C ... Jn 4:46
and went over the sea toward C ...... Jn 6:17
also took shipping, and came to C ... Jn 6:24
the synagogue, as he taught in C .... Jn 6:59

CAPHTHORIM (caf'-tho-rim) See CAPHTORIM. People of Caphtor.

whom came the Philistines,) and C ... 1Chr 1:12

CAPHTOR (caf'-tor) See CAPHTORIM. Original land of the Philistines.

which came forth out of C .... Deut 2:23
the remnant of the country of C ..... Jer 47:4
and the Philistines from C........... Amos 9:7

CAPHTORIM (caf'-to-rim) See CAPHTHORIM, CAPHTORIMS. Same as Caphthorim.

out of whom came Philistim,) and C .. Gen 10:14

CAPHTORIMS (caf'-to-rims) See CAPHTORIM.

Hazerim, even unto Azzah, the C...... Deut 2:23

CAPHTORITES See CAPHTORIMS.

CAPPADOCIA (cap-pa-do'-she-ah) A Roman province in Asia Minor.

Mesopotamia, and in Judaea, and C.... Acts 2:9
throughout Pontus, Galatia, C........ 1Pet 1:1

CAPTAIN

Phichol the chief c of his host...... Gen 21:22
Phichol the chief c of his host...... Gen 21:32
Phichol the chief c of his army ..... Gen 26:26
of Pharaoh's, and c of the guard .... Gen 37:36
c of the guard, an Egyptian,......... Gen 39:1
the house of the c of the guard ..... Gen 40:3
the c of the guard charged Joseph ... Gen 40:4
in the c of the guard's house........ Gen 41:10
servant to the c of the guard .... Gen 41:12
be c of the children of Judah .... Num 2:3
the son of Zuar shall be c of the ... Num 2:5
be c of the children of Zebulun ..... Num 2:7
the c of the children of Reuben...... Num 2:10
be c of the children of Simeon ...... Num 2:12
the c of the sons of Gad shall be.... Num 2:14
the c of the sons of Ephraim .... Num 2:18
the c of the children of Manasseh ... Num 2:20
the c of the sons of Benjamin .... Num 2:22
the c of the children of Dan .... Num 2:25
the c of the children of Asher ...... Num 2:27
the c of the children of Naphtali.... Num 2:29
one to another, Let us make a c ..... Num 14:4
but as c of the host of the LORD .... Josh 5:14
the c of the LORD's host said .... Josh 5:15
the c of whose host was Sisera,...... Judg 4:2
c of Jabin's army, with his .... Judg 4:7
unto Jephthah, Come, and be our c ... Judg 11:6
made him head and c over them .... Judg 11:11
him to be c over my people Israel ... 1Sa 9:16
thee to be c over his inheritance ... 1Sa 10:1
c of the host of Hazor, and into 1Sa 12:9
him to be c over his people 1Sa 13:14
the name of the c of his host was ... 1Sa 14:50
unto the c of their thousand 1Sa 17:18
the c of the host, Abner, whose 1Sa 17:55
made him his c over a thousand 1Sa 18:13
and he became a c over them 1Sa 22:2
the son of Ner, the c of his host ... 1Sa 26:5
of Ner, c of Saul's host, took....... 2Sa 2:8
and thou shalt be a c over Israel ... 2Sa 5:2
soul, he shall be chief and c 2Sa 5:8
Shobach the c of the host of 2Sa 10:16
smote Shobach the c of their host ... 2Sa 10:18
Absalom made Amasa c of the host 2Sa 17:25
if thou be not c of the host........ 2Sa 19:13
therefore he was their c............. 2Sa 23:19
said to Joab the c of the host 2Sa 24:2
priest, and Joab the c of the host .. 1Kin 1:19
c of the host of Israel, and Amasa .. 1Kin 2:32
of Jether, c of the host of Judah ... 1Kin 2:32
Joab the c of the host was gone 1Kin 11:15
that Joab the c of the host was 1Kin 11:21
became c over a band, when David ... 1Kin 11:24
c of half his chariots, conspired ... 1Kin 16:9
the c of the host, king over 1Kin 16:16
him a c of fifty with his fifty 2Kin 1:9
and said to the c of fifty.......... 2Kin 1:10
another c of fifty with his fifty .. 2Kin 1:11
he sent again a c of the third 2Kin 1:13
the third c of fifty went up, and .. 2Kin 1:13
the king, or to the c of the host .. 2Kin 4:13
c of the host of the king of 2Kin 5:1
I have an errand to thee, O c 2Kin 9:5
And he said, To thee, O c 2Kin 9:5
Then said Jehu to Bidkar his 2Kin 9:25
a c of his, conspired against him .. 2Kin 15:25
one of the least of my master's.... 2Kin 18:24
tell Hezekiah the c of my people ... 2Kin 20:5
c of the guard, a servant of the ... 2Kin 25:8
that were with the c of the guard .. 2Kin 25:11
did Nebuzar-adan the c of the 2Kin 25:12
But the c of the guard left of 2Kin 25:12
the c of the guard took away 2Kin 25:15
the c of the guard took Seraiah 2Kin 25:18
Nebuzar-adan c of the guard took ... 2Kin 25:20
first shall be chief and c 1Chr 11:6
for he was their c 1Chr 11:21
a c of the Reubenites, and thirty .. 1Chr 11:42
Shophach the c of the host of...... 1Chr 19:16
killed Shophach the c of the host .. 1Chr 19:18
The third c of the host for 1Chr 27:5
The fourth c for the fourth month .. 1Chr 27:7
The fifth c for the fifth month 1Chr 27:8
The sixth c for the sixth month 1Chr 27:9
The seventh c for the seventh 1Chr 27:10
The eighth c for the eighth month .. 1Chr 27:11
The ninth c for the ninth month 1Chr 27:12
The tenth c for the tenth month 1Chr 27:13
The eleventh c for the eleventh 1Chr 27:14
The twelfth c for the twelfth 1Chr 27:15
God himself is with us for our c ... 2Chr 13:12
next to him was Jehohanan the c 2Chr 17:15
a c to return to their bondage..... Neh 9:17

The c of fifty, and the honourable.... Is 3:3
one c of the least of my master's.... Is 36:9
a c of the ward was there, whose..... Jer 37:13
Then Nebuzar-adan the c of the ...... Jer 39:9
But Nebuzar-adan the c of the .... Jer 39:9
Nebuzar-adan the c of the guard...... Jer 39:11
the c of the guard sent, and .... Jer 39:13
the c of the guard had let him go ... Jer 40:1
the c of the guard took Jeremiah,.... Jer 40:2
So the c of the guard gave him ...... Jer 40:5
whom Nebuzar-adan the c of the ...... Jer 41:10
the c of the guard had left .... Jer 43:6
appoint a c against her .... Jer 51:27
c of the guard, which served the .... Jer 52:12
that were with the c of the guard ... Jer 52:14
Then Nebuzar-adan the c of the ...... Jer 52:15
But Nebuzar-adan the c of the .... Jer 52:16
took the c of the guard away .... Jer 52:19
the c of the guard took Seraiah ..... Jer 52:24
So Nebuzar-adan the c of the .... Jer 52:26
the c of the guard carried away ..... Jer 52:30
Arioch the c of the king's guard .... Dan 2:14
and said to Arioch the king's c ..... Dan 2:15
Then the band and the c and .... Jn 18:12
the c of the temple, and the .... Acts 4:1
the c of the temple and the chief ... Acts 5:24
Then went the c with the officers.... Acts 5:26
came unto the chief c of the band ... Acts 21:31
and when they saw the chief c .... Acts 21:32
Then the chief c came near........... Acts 21:33
castle, he said unto the chief c .... Acts 21:37
The chief c commanded him to be ..... Acts 22:24
that, he went and told the chief c .. Acts 22:26
Then the chief c came, and said ..... Acts 22:27
And the chief c answered, With a .... Acts 22:28
the chief c also was afraid,......... Acts 22:29
a great dissension, the chief c ..... Acts 23:10
council signify to the chief c ...... Acts 23:15
this young man unto the chief c ..... Acts 23:17
and brought him to the chief c ...... Acts 23:18
Then the chief c took him by the .... Acts 23:19
So the chief c then let the young ... Acts 23:22
But the chief c Lysias came upon .... Acts 24:7
the chief c shall come down .... Acts 24:22
prisoners to the c of the guard...... Acts 28:16
to make the c of their salvation .... Heb 2:10

CAPTAINS

and c over every one of them .... Ex 14:7
his chosen c also are drowned in .... Ex 15:4
with the c over thousands, and ...... Num 31:14
c over hundreds, which came from .... Num 31:14
the c of thousands, and .... Num 31:48
c of hundreds, came near unto .... Num 31:48
the c of thousands, and the .... Num 31:52
of the c of hundreds, was sixteen ... Num 31:52
the gold of the c of thousands ...... Num 31:54
c over thousands, and c .... Deut 1:15
c over hundreds, and c over .... Deut 1:15
c over fifties, and c over .... Deut 1:15
c over tens, and officers among ..... Deut 1:15
that they shall make c of the .... Deut 20:9
your c of your tribes, your .... Deut 29:10
said unto the c of the men of war ... Josh 10:24
will appoint him c over thousands ... 1Sa 8:12
over thousands, and c over fifties... 1Sa 8:12
and make you all c of thousands 1Sa 22:7
of thousands, and c and hundreds 1Sa 22:7
had two men that were c of bands 2Sa 4:2
set c of thousands and c of 2Sa 18:1
and c of hundreds over them 2Sa 18:1
the c charge concerning Absalom 2Sa 18:5
in the seat, chief among the c 2Sa 23:8
and against the c of the host 2Sa 24:4
the c of the host went out from 2Sa 24:4
the c of the host, and Abiathar 1Kin 1:25
the two c of the hosts of Israel 1Kin 2:5
and his princes, and his c 1Kin 9:22
sent the c of the hosts which he 1Kin 15:20
place, and put c in their rooms 1Kin 20:24
two c that had rule over his 1Kin 22:31
when the c of the chariots saw 1Kin 22:32
when the c of the chariots 1Kin 22:33
burnt up the two c of the former 2Kin 1:14
about, and the c of the chariots 2Kin 8:21
the c of the host were sitting 2Kin 9:5
said to the guard and to the c 2Kin 10:25
the c cast them out, and went to 2Kin 10:25
rulers over hundreds, with the c 2Kin 11:4
the c over the hundreds did 2Kin 11:9
to the c over hundreds did the 2Kin 11:10
commanded the c of the hundreds 2Kin 11:15
rulers over hundreds, and the c 2Kin 11:19
when all the c of the armies,........ 2Kin 25:23
the c of the armies, arose, and 2Kin 25:26
Seir, having for their c Pelatiah ... 1Chr 4:42
a Hachmonite, the chief of the c 1Chr 11:11
Now three of the thirty c went 1Chr 11:15
of the sons of Gad, c of the host ... 1Chr 12:14
Amasai, who was chief of the c 1Chr 12:18
them, and made them c of the band ... 1Chr 12:18
c of the thousands that were of 1Chr 12:20
of valour, and were c in the host ... 1Chr 12:21
father's house twenty and two c 1Chr 12:28
And of Naphtali a thousand c 1Chr 12:34
consulted with the c of thousands ... 1Chr 13:1
the c over thousands, went to 1Chr 15:25
the c of the host separated to 1Chr 26:26
the c over thousands and hundreds ... 1Chr 26:26
the c of the host, had dedicated 1Chr 26:26
c of thousands and hundreds, and 1Chr 27:1

Perez was the chief of all the c 1Chr 27:3
the c of the companies that 1Chr 28:1
the c over the thousands, and 1Chr 28:1
c over the hundreds, and the 1Chr 28:1
the c of thousands and of hundreds 1Chr 29:6
to the c of thousands and of 2Chr 1:2
men of war, and chief of his c 2Chr 8:9
of his chariots and horsemen 2Chr 8:9
put c in them, and store of 2Chr 11:11
sent the c of his armies against 2Chr 16:4
Of Judah, the c of thousands 2Chr 17:14
c of the chariots that were 2Chr 18:30
when the c of the chariots saw 2Chr 18:31
when the c of the chariots 2Chr 18:32
him in, and the c of the chariots 2Chr 21:9
took the c of hundreds, Azariah 2Chr 23:1
to the c of hundreds spears 2Chr 23:9
the priest brought out the c of 2Chr 23:14
And he took the c of hundreds 2Chr 23:20
made them c over thousands, and 2Chr 25:5
c over hundreds, according to the 2Chr 25:5
of Hananiah, one of the king's c 2Chr 26:11
he set c of war over the people, ... 2Chr 32:6
c in the camp of the king of 2Chr 33:11
the c of the host of the king of 2Chr 33:11
put c of war in all the fenced 2Chr 33:14
the king had sent c of the army .... Neh 2:9
afar off, the thunder of the c .... Job 39:25
for thou hast taught them to be c .... Jer 13:21
Now when all the c of the forces .... Jer 40:7
all the c of the forces that were .... Jer 40:13
all the c of the forces that .... Jer 41:11
all the c of the forces that were .... Jer 41:13
all the c of the forces that were .... Jer 41:16
Then all the c of the forces, and .... Jer 42:1
all the c of the forces which .... Jer 42:8
all the c of the forces, and all .... Jer 43:4
all the c of the forces, took all .... Jer 43:5
the will I break in pieces c .... Jer 51:23
the c thereof, and all the rulers .... Jer 51:28
princes, and her wise men, her c .... Jer 51:57
for Jerusalem, to appoint c .... Eze 21:22
Which were clothed with blue, c .... Eze 23:6
the Assyrians her neighbours, c .... Eze 23:12
of them desirable young men, c .... Eze 23:23
princes, the governors, and the c .... Dan 3:2
the princes, the governors, and c .... Dan 3:3
And the princes, governors, and c .... Dan 3:27
the counsellors, and the c .... Dan 6:7
thy c as the great grasshoppers, ... Nah 3:17
a supper to his lords, high c .... Mk 6:21
with the chief priests and c .... Lk 22:4
c of the temple, and the elders, ... Lk 22:52
of hearing, with the chief c .... Acts 25:23
and the rich men, and the chief c .... Rev 6:15
flesh of kings, and the flesh of c .... Rev 19:18

CAPTIVE

that his brother was taken c .... Gen 14:14
ones, and their wives took they c .... Gen 34:29
of the c that was in the dungeon .... Ex 12:29
Asshur shall carry thee away c .... Num 24:22
hands, and thou hast taken them c .... Deut 21:10
Barak, and lead thy captivity c .... Judg 5:12
enemies, which led them away c 1Kin 8:48
before them who carried them c 1Kin 8:50
had brought away c out of the 2Kin 5:2
thou hast taken c with thy sword 2Kin 6:22
and carried them c to Assyria 2Kin 15:29
carried the people of it c to Kir 2Kin 16:9
of Babylon brought c to Babylon 2Kin 24:16
king of Assyria carried away c 1Chr 5:6
land whither they are carried c 2Chr 6:37
children of Judah carry away c 2Chr 25:12
c of their brethren two hundred 2Chr 28:8
ye have taken c of your brethren 2Chr 28:11
before them that lead them c 2Chr 30:9
high, thou hast led captivity c .... Ps 68:18
us away c required of us a song .... Ps 137:3
my children, and am desolate, a c .... Is 49:21
mighty, or the lawful c delivered .... Is 49:24
The c exile hasteneth that he may .... Is 51:14
of thy neck, O c daughter of Zion .... Is 52:2
of Jerusalem c in the fifth month .... Jer 1:3
LORD's flock is carried away c .... Jer 13:17
shall be carried away c all of it .... Jer 13:19
it shall be wholly carried away c .... Jer 13:19
shall carry them c into Babylon .... Jer 20:4
place whither they have led him c .... Jer 22:12
of Babylon had carried away c .... Jer 24:1
that are carried away c of Judah .... Jer 24:5
when he carried away c Jeconiah .... Jer 27:20
and all that is carried away c .... Jer 28:6
away c from Jerusalem to Babylon .... Jer 29:1
I caused you to be carried away c .... Jer 29:14
of the guard carried away c into .... Jer 39:9
were carried away c of Jerusalem .... Jer 40:1
and carried away c unto Babylon .... Jer 40:1
nor carried away c to Babylon .... Jer 40:7
Then Ishmael carried away c all .... Jer 41:10
of Nethaniah carried them away c .... Jer 41:10
away c from Mizpah cast about .... Jer 41:14
of the guard carried away c .... Jer 52:15
away c out of his own land .... Jer 52:27
Nebuchadrezzar carried away c .... Jer 52:28
c from Jerusalem eight hundred .... Jer 52:29
of the guard carried away c .... Jer 52:30
away c the whole captivity .... Amos 1:6
Therefore now shall they go c .... Amos 6:7
c with the first that go c .... Amos 6:7
led away c out of their own land .... Amos 7:11

carried away c his forces .... Obad 11
And Huzzab shall be led away c .... Nah 2:7
be led away c into all nations .... Lk 21:24
up on high, he led captivity c .... Eph 4:8
who are taken c by him at his 2Ti 2:26
lead c silly women laden with 2Ti 3:6

CAPTIVES

as c taken with the sword .... Gen 31:26
took all the women of Midian c .... Num 31:9
And they brought the c, and the .... Num 31:12
your c on the third day, and on .... Num 31:19
seest among the c a beautiful .... Deut 21:11
blood of the slain and of the c .... Deut 32:42
And had taken the women c, that 1Sa 30:2
and their daughters, were taken c 1Sa 30:3
And David's two wives were taken c 1Sa 30:5
away c unto the land of the enemy 1Kin 8:46
land whither they were carried c 1Kin 8:47
land of them that carried them c 1Kin 8:47
of valour, even ten thousand c 2Kin 24:14
they carry them away c unto a 2Chr 6:36
whither they have carried them c 2Chr 6:38
away a great multitude of them c 2Chr 28:5
therefore, and deliver the c again 2Chr 28:11
shall not bring in the c hither 2Chr 28:13
So the armed men left the c 2Chr 28:14
by name rose up, and took the c 2Chr 28:15
smitten Judah, and carried away c 2Chr 28:17
of all those that carried them c .... Ps 106:46
and they shall take them c .... Is 14:2
them c, whose c they were .... Is 14:2
prisoners, and the Ethiopians c .... Is 20:4
my city, and he shall let go my c .... Is 45:13
Even the c of the mighty shall be .... Is 49:25
to proclaim liberty to the c .... Is 61:1
of Judah, with all the c of Judah .... Jer 28:4
elders which were carried away c .... Jer 29:1
unto all that are carried away c .... Jer 29:4
caused you to be carried away c .... Jer 29:7
and carry us away c into Babylon .... Jer 43:3
burn them, and carry them away c .... Jer 43:12
for thy sons are taken c, and thy .... Jer 48:46
c, and thy daughters c .... Jer 48:46
that took them c held them fast .... Jer 50:33
as I was among the c by the river .... Eze 1:1
whither they shall be carried c .... Eze 6:9
of thy c in the midst of them .... Eze 16:53
found a man of the c of Judah .... Dan 2:25
shall also carry c into Egypt .... Dan 11:8
to preach deliverance to the c .... Lk 4:18

CAPTIVITY

into c unto Sihon king of the .... Num 21:29
the raiment of her c from off her .... Deut 21:13
for they shall go into c .... Deut 28:41
the LORD thy God will turn thy c .... Deut 30:3
Barak, and lead thy c captive .... Judg 5:12
the day of the c of the land .... Judg 18:30
those carried he into c from 2Kin 24:15
thirtieth year of the c of 2Kin 25:27
dwelt in their steads until the c 1Chr 5:22
And Jehozadak went into c, when 1Chr 6:15
unto thee in the land of their c 2Chr 6:37
their soul in the land of their c 2Chr 6:38
and our wives are in c for this 2Chr 29:9
the c that were brought up from .... Ezr 1:11
that went up out of the c .... Ezr 2:1
come out of the c went Jerusalem .... Ezr 3:8
the c builded the temple unto the .... Ezr 4:1
the rest of the children of the c .... Ezr 6:16
the children of the c kept the .... Ezr 6:19
for all the children of the c .... Ezr 6:20
which were come again out of c .... Ezr 6:21
which were come out of the c .... Ezr 8:35
of the lands, to the sword, to c .... Ezr 9:7
unto all the children of the c .... Ezr 10:7
And the children of the c did so .... Ezr 10:16
escaped, which were left of the c .... Neh 1:2
c there in the province are in .... Neh 1:3
them for a prey in the land of c .... Neh 4:4
that went up out of the c .... Neh 7:6
again out of the c made booths .... Neh 8:17
the c which had been carried away .... Est 2:6
And the LORD turned the c of Job .... Job 42:10
bringeth back the c of his people .... Ps 14:7
bringeth back the c of his people .... Ps 53:6
on high, thou hast led c captive .... Ps 68:18
And delivered his strength into c .... Ps 78:61
hast brought back the c of Jacob .... Ps 85:1
LORD turned again the c of Zion .... Ps 126:1
Turn again our c, O LORD, as the .... Ps 126:4
my people are gone into c .... Is 5:13
carry thee away with a mighty c .... Is 22:17
but themselves are gone into c .... Is 46:2
are for the c, to the c .... Jer 15:2
in thine house shall go into c .... Jer 20:6
into c, both his princes and his .... Jer 22:22
and I will turn away your c .... Jer 29:14
not gone forth with you into c .... Jer 29:16
word of the LORD, all ye of the c .... Jer 29:20
of Judah which are in Babylon .... Jer 29:22
Babylon, saying, This is long .... Jer 29:28
Send to all them of the c .... Jer 29:31
again the c of my people Israel .... Jer 30:3
thy seed from the land of their c .... Jer 30:10
one of them, shall go into c .... Jer 30:16
again the c of Jacob's tents .... Jer 30:18
when I shall bring again their c .... Jer 31:23
I will cause their c to return .... Jer 32:44
And I will cause the c of Judah .... Jer 33:7

the c of Israel to return, and .... Jer 33:7
cause to return the c of the land .... Jer 33:11
I will cause their c to return .... Jer 33:26
and such as are for c to c .... Jer 43:11
and such as are for c to c .... Jer 43:11
furnish thyself to go into c .... Jer 46:19
thy seed from the land of their c .... Jer 46:27
go forth into c with his priests .... Jer 48:7
neither hath he gone into c .... Jer 48:11
the c of Moab in the latter days .... Jer 48:47
for their king shall go into c .... Jer 49:3
I will bring again the c of the .... Jer 49:6
I will bring again the c of Elam .... Jer 49:39
thirtieth year of the c of .... Jer 52:31
Judah is gone into c because of .... Lam 1:3
are gone into c before the enemy .... Lam 1:5
and my young men are gone into c .... Lam 1:18
iniquity, to turn away thy c .... Lam 2:14
no more carry thee away into c .... Lam 4:22
fifth year of king Jehoiachin's c .... Eze 1:2
And go, get thee to them of the c .... Eze 3:11
came to them of the c at Tel-abib .... Eze 3:15
into Chaldea, to them of the c .... Eze 11:24
c all the things that the LORD .... Eze 11:25
as they that go forth into c .... Eze 12:4
my stuff by day, as stuff for c .... Eze 12:7
they shall remove and go into c .... Eze 12:11
When I shall bring again their c .... Eze 16:53
the c of Sodom and her daughters .... Eze 16:53
the c of Samaria and her daughters .... Eze 16:53
then will I bring again the c of .... Eze 16:53
of Judah, when they went into c .... Eze 25:3
I will bring again the c of Egypt .... Eze 29:14
and these cities shall go into c .... Eze 30:17
and her daughters shall go into c .... Eze 30:18
pass in the twelfth year of our c .... Eze 33:21
went into c for their iniquity .... Eze 39:23
will I bring again the c of Jacob .... Eze 39:25
be led into c among the heathen .... Eze 39:28
five and twentieth year of our c .... Eze 40:1
of the children of the c of Judah .... Dan 5:13
of the children of the c of Judah .... Dan 6:13
by the sword, and by flame, by c .... Dan 11:33
I returned the c of my people .... Hos 6:11
shall bring again the c of Judah .... Joel 3:1
of Syria shall go into c unto Kir .... Amos 1:5
carried away captive the whole c .... Amos 1:6
delivered up the whole c to Edom .... Amos 1:6
And their king shall go into c .... Amos 1:15
for Gilgal shall surely go into c .... Amos 5:5
you to go into c beyond Damascus .... Amos 5:27
go into c forth of his land .... Amos 7:17
though they go into c before .... Amos 9:4
the c of my people Israel .... Amos 9:14
the c of this host of the .... Obad 20
the c of Jerusalem, which is in .... Obad 20
they are gone into c from thee .... Mic 1:16
she carried away, she went into c .... Nah 3:10
shall gather the c as the sand .... Hab 1:9
visit them, and turn away their c .... Zeph 2:7
turn back your c before your eyes .... Zeph 3:20
Take of them of the c, even of .... Zec 6:10
of the city shall go forth into c .... Zec 14:2
bringing me into c to the law of .... Rom 7:23
bringing into c every thought to 2Cor 10:5
he led c captive, and gave gifts .... Eph 4:8
into c shall go into c .... Rev 13:10

CARBUNCLE

be a sardius, a topaz, and a c .... Ex 28:17
was a sardius, a topaz, and a c .... Ex 39:10
sapphire, the emerald, and the c .... Eze 28:13

CARBUNCLES

of agates, and thy gates of c .... Is 54:12

CARCAS (car'-cas) A servant of King Ahasuerus.

Bigtha, and Abagtha, Zethar, and C .... Est 1:10

CARCASE

whether it be a c of an unclean .... Lev 5:2
or a c of unclean cattle, or the .... Lev 5:2
or the c of unclean creeping .... Lev 5:2
their c shall ye not touch .... Lev 11:8
whosoever toucheth the c of them .... Lev 11:24
c of them shall wash his clothes .... Lev 11:25
whoso toucheth their c shall be .... Lev 11:27
he that beareth the c of them .... Lev 11:28
their c falleth shall be unclean .... Lev 11:35
toucheth their c shall be unclean .... Lev 11:36
if any part of their c fall upon .... Lev 11:37
any part of their c fall thereon .... Lev 11:38
he that toucheth the c thereof .... Lev 11:39
he that eateth of the c of it .... Lev 11:40
he also that beareth the c of it .... Lev 11:40
flesh, nor touch their dead c .... Deut 14:8
thy c shall be meat unto all .... Deut 28:26
take his c down from the tree .... Josh 8:29
aside to see the c of the lion .... Judg 14:8
and honey in the c of the lion .... Judg 14:8
honey out of the c of the lion .... Judg 14:9
thy c shall not come unto the 1Kin 13:22
his c was cast in the way, and the 1Kin 13:24
it, the lion also stood by the c 1Kin 13:24
saw the c cast in the way, and 1Kin 13:25
and the lion standing by the c 1Kin 13:25
found his c cast in the way, and 1Kin 13:28
ass and the lion standing by the c 1Kin 13:28
the lion had not eaten the c 1Kin 13:28
took up the c of the man of God 1Kin 13:29
he laid his c in his own grave 1Kin 13:30

the c of Jezebel shall be as dung..... 2Kin 9:37
as a c trodden under feet.................... Isa 14:19
For wheresoever the c is, there............. Mt 24:28

CARCASES

the fowls came down upon the c........ Gen 15:11
shall have their c in abomination........ Lev 11:11
The c of every beast which.................. Lev 11:26
cast your c upon the c of.................... Num 14:26
Your c shall fall in this...................... Num 14:29
But as for you, your c, they............... Num 14:32
until your c be wasted in the.............. Num 14:33
I will give the c of the host of............ Isa 17:46
their c were torn in the midst of.......... Is 5:25
shall come up out of their c............... Is 34:3
look upon the c of the men that.......... Is 66:24
the c of this people shall be................ Jer 7:33
Even the c of men shall fall as............ Jer 9:22
their c shall be meat for the............... Jer 16:4
with the c of their detestable............. Jer 16:18
their c will I give to be meat.............. Jer 19:7
I will lay the dead c of the................. Eze 6:5
nor by the c of their kings in.............. Eze 43:7
the c of their kings, far from me.......... Eze 43:9
of slain, and a great number of c......... Nah 3:3
whose c fell in the wilderness............. Heb 3:17

CARCHEMISH (car'-ke-mish) See
CHARCHEMISH, A city on the Euphrates River.
Is not Calno as to............................. Is 10:9
was by the river Euphrates in C........... Jer 46:2

CARE

hath left the c of the asses................. 1Sa 10:2
flee away, they will not c for us......... 2Sa 18:3
of us die, will they c for us................ 2Sa 18:3
careful for us with all this c............... 2Kin 4:13
nation, than dwelleth without c.......... Jer 49:31
eat bread by weight, and with c.......... Eze 4:16
the c of this world, and the................ Mt 13:22
him to an inn, and took c of him......... Lk 10:34
and said unto him, Take c of him........ Lk 10:35
dost thou not c that my sister............ Lk 10:40
c not for it...................................... 1Cor 7:21
Doth God take c for oxen.................. 1Cor 9:9
have the same c one for another......... 1Cor 12:25
but that our c for you in the............... 2Cor 7:12
which put the same earnest c into........ 2Cor 8:16
the c of all the churches.................... 2Cor 11:28
will naturally c for your state............. Phil 2:20
that now at the last your c of me........ Phil 4:10
how shall he take c of the church........ 1Ti 3:5
Casting all your c upon him............... 1Pet 5:7

CAREAH (ca-re'-ah) See KAREAH. Father of
Johanan.
and Johanan the son of C, and........... 2Kin 25:23

CARED

no man c for my soul........................ Ps 142:4
not that he c for the poor................... Jn 12:6
Gallio c for none of those things......... Acts 18:17

CAREFUL

thou hast been c for us with all........... 2Kin 4:13
shall not be c in the year of................ Jer 17:8
we are not c to answer thee in............ Dan 3:16
her, Martha, Martha, thou art c.......... Lk 10:41
Be c for nothing.............................. Phil 4:6
wherein ye were also c, but ye........... Phil 4:10
might be c to maintain good works...... Titus 3:8

CAREFULLY

Only if thou c hearken unto the.......... Deut 15:5
of Maroth waited c for good............... Mic 1:12
I sent him therefore the more c........... Phil 2:28
though he sought it c with tears.......... Heb 12:17

CAREFULNESS

water with trembling and with c......... Eze 12:18
They shall eat their bread with c......... Eze 12:19
But I would have you without c........... 1Cor 7:32
what c it wrought in you, yea,............ 2Cor 7:11

CARELESS

were therein, how they dwelt c........... Judg 18:7
hear my voice, ye c daughters............. Is 32:9
shall ye be troubled, ye c women......... Is 32:10
be troubled, ye c ones...................... Is 32:11
to make the c Ethiopians afraid........... Eze 30:9

CARELESSLY

to pleasures, that dwellest c............... Is 47:8
them that dwell c in the isles.............. Eze 39:6
the rejoicing city that dwelt c............. Zeph 2:15

CARES

the c of this world, and the................ Mk 4:19
go forth, and are choked with c........... Lk 8:14
c of this life, and so that day.............. Lk 21:34

CAREST

neither c thou for any man................. Mt 22:16
c thou not that we perish................... Mk 4:38
thou art true, and c for no man........... Mk 12:14

CARETH

land which the LORD thy God c for...... Deut 11:12
hireling, and c not for the sheep......... Jn 10:13
He that is unmarried c for The........... 1Cor 7:32
But he that is married c for the........... 1Cor 7:33
The unmarried woman c for the.......... 1Cor 7:34
but she that is married c for the.......... 1Cor 7:34
for he c for you............................... 1Pet 5:7

CARING

my father leave c for the asses............ 1Sa 9:5

CARKAS See CARCAS.

CARMEL (car'-mel) See CARMELITE.
1. A mountain range in Canaan.
the king of Jokneam of C, one............ Josh 12:22
and reacheth to C westward............... Josh 19:26
Samuel, saying, Saul came to C........... 1Sa 15:12
to me all Israel unto mount C.............. 1Kin 18:19
prophets together unto mount C......... 1Kin 18:20
And Elijah went up to the top of C...... 1Kin 18:42
And he went from thence to mount C... 2Kin 2:25
unto the man of God to mount C......... 2Kin 4:25
and into the forest of his C................. 2Kin 19:23
in the mountains, and in C................. 2Chr 26:10
Thine head upon thee is like C............ Song 7:5
and C shake off their fruits................. Is 33:9
unto it, the excellency of C................. Is 35:2
border, and the forest of his C............. Is 37:24
as C by the sea, so shall he come........ Jer 46:18
habitation, and he shall feed on C....... Jer 50:19
the top of C shall wither.................... Amos 1:2
hide themselves in the top of C........... Amos 9:3
in the wood, in the midst of C............. Mic 7:14
Bashan languisheth, and C, and the..... Nah 1:4
2. A town in Judah.
Maon, C, and Ziph, and Juttah,.......... Josh 15:55
Maon, whose possessions were in C..... 1Sa 25:2
and he was shearing his sheep in C...... 1Sa 25:2
the young men, Get you up to C.......... 1Sa 25:5
all the while they were in C................ 1Sa 25:7
David were come to Abigail to C......... 1Sa 25:40

CARMELITE (car'-mel-ite) See CARMELITESS.
An inhabitant of Carmel 2.
Abigail the wife of Nabal the C........... 1Sa 30:5
and Abigail Nabal's wife the C............ 2Sa 2:2
Abigail the wife of Nabal the C........... 2Sa 3:3
Hezrai the C, Paarai the Arbite,.......... 2Sa 23:35
Hezro the C, Naarai the son of........... 1Chr 11:37

CARMELITESS (car'-mel-i-tess)
Jezreelitess, and Abigail the C............ 1Sa 27:3
second Daniel, of Abigail the C........... 1Chr 3:1

CARMI (car'-mi) See CARMITES.
1. Father of Achan.
for Achan, the son of C, the son......... Josh 7:1
and Achan, the son of C, the son........ Josh 7:18
And the sons of C................................ 1Chr 2:7
Pharez, Hezron, and C, and Hur, and.. 1Chr 4:1
2. A son of Reuben.
and Phallu, and Hezron, and C........... Gen 46:9
Hanoch, and Pallu, Hezron, and C...... Ex 6:14
of C, the family of the Carmites......... Num 26:6
Hanoch, and Pallu, Hezron, and C...... 1Chr 5:3

CARMITES (car'-mites) Descendants of Carmi
2.
of Carmi, the family of the C.............. Num 26:6

CARNAL

but I am c, sold under sin.................. Rom 7:14
Because the c mind is enmity............. Rom 8:7
to minister unto them in c things........ Rom 15:27
as unto spiritual, but as unto c............ 1Cor 3:1
For ye are yet c............................... 1Cor 3:3
and divisions, are ye not c................. 1Cor 3:3
are ye not c.................................... 1Cor 3:4
if we shall reap your c things............. 1Cor 9:11
weapons of our warfare are not c........ 2Cor 10:4
after the law of a c commandment...... Heb 7:16
c ordinances, imposed on them.......... Heb 9:10

CARNALLY

lie c with thy neighbour's wife........... Lev 18:20
And whosoever lieth c with a woman... Lev 19:20
And a man lie with her c, and it........ Num 5:13
For to be c minded is death............... Rom 8:6

CARPENTER

So the c encouraged the goldsmith...... Is 41:7
The c stretcheth out his rule............... Is 44:13
Is not this the c, the son of................. Mk 6:3

CARPENTER'S

Is not this the c son......................... Mt 13:55

CARPENTERS

to David, and cedar trees, and c......... 2Sa 5:11
and they laid it out to the c................ 2Kin 12:11
Unto c, and builders, and masons,...... 2Kin 22:6
of cedars, with masons and c............. 1Chr 14:1
c to repair the house of the LORD........ 2Chr 24:12
also unto the masons, and to the c....... Ezra 3:7
the princes of Judah, with the c.......... Jer 24:1
of Judah and Jerusalem, and the c....... Jer 29:2
And the LORD shewed me four c.......... Zec 1:20

CARPUS (car'-pus) A friend of Paul.
cloke that I left at Troas with C.......... 2Ti 4:13

CARRIAGE

the cattle and the c before them......... Judg 18:21
David left his c in the hand of............. 1Sa 17:22
the hand of the keeper of the c........... 1Sa 17:22

CARRIAGES

At Michmash he hath laid up his c...... Is 10:28
your c were heavy loaden.................. Is 46:1
after those days we took up our c........ Acts 21:15

CARRIED

he c away all his cattle, and all.......... Gen 31:18
c away my daughters, as captives,...... Gen 31:26

of Israel c Jacob their father.............. Gen 46:5
For his sons c him into the land.......... Gen 50:13
c them in their coats out of the........... Lev 10:5
c them over with them unto the.......... Josh 4:8
c them up to the top of an hill........... Judg 16:3
of Israel be c about with Gath............ 1Sa 5:8
they c the ark of the God of............... 1Sa 5:8
that, after they had c it about............. 1Sa 5:9
but c them away, and went on their..... 1Sa 30:18
that the Amalekites had c away.......... 1Sa 30:18
but David c it aside into the............... 2Sa 6:10
Abiathar c the ark of God again......... 2Sa 15:29
land whither they were c captives....... 1Kin 8:47
and of them that c them captives........ 1Kin 8:47
before them who c them captive......... 1Kin 8:50
c him up into a loft, where he............ 1Kin 17:19
Then they c him forth out of the......... 1Kin 21:13
c thence silver, and gold, and............ 2Kin 7:8
c thence also, and went and hid it....... 2Kin 7:8
his servants c him in a chariot............ 2Kin 9:28
c them captive to Assyria.................. 2Kin 15:29
c the people of it captive to Kir.......... 2Kin 16:9
c Israel away into Assyria, and.......... 2Kin 17:6
whom the LORD c away before them.... 2Kin 17:11
So was Israel c away out of their........ 2Kin 17:23
they had c away from Samaria came.... 2Kin 17:28
whom they c away from thence........... 2Kin 17:33
this day, shall be c into Babylon.......... 2Kin 20:17
c the ashes of them unto Beth-el......... 2Kin 23:4
his servants c him in a chariot............ 2Kin 23:30
he c out thence all the treasures......... 2Kin 24:13
he c away all Jerusalem, and all........ 2Kin 24:14
he c away Jehoiachin to Babylon........ 2Kin 24:15
those c he into captivity from............. 2Kin 24:15
of brass, and c him to Babylon........... 2Kin 25:7
the brass of them to Babylon.............. 2Kin 25:13
So Judah was c away out of their........ 2Kin 25:21
king of Assyria c away captive........... 1Chr 5:6
and he c them away, even the............. 1Chr 5:26
when the LORD c away Judah.............. 1Chr 6:15
who were c away to Babylon for.......... 1Chr 9:1
they c the ark of God in a new............ 1Chr 13:7
but c it aside into the house of........... 1Chr 13:13
land whither they are c captive........... 2Chr 6:37
whither they have c them captives...... 2Chr 6:38
he c away also the shields of.............. 2Chr 12:9
they c away very much spoil.............. 2Chr 14:13
c away sheep and camels in............... 2Chr 14:15
they c away the droves of Ramah,...... 2Chr 16:6
c away all the substance that was....... 2Chr 21:17
it, and c it to his place again.............. 2Chr 24:11
c away a great multitude of them........ 2Chr 28:5
the children of Israel c away.............. 2Chr 28:5
c all the feeble of them upon............. 2Chr 28:15
smitten Judah, and c away captives..... 2Chr 28:17
with fetters, and c him to Babylon...... 2Chr 33:11
Shaphan c the book to the king,.......... 2Chr 34:16
his brother, and c him to Egypt.......... 2Chr 36:4
Nebuchadnezzar also c of the............. 2Chr 36:7
the sword c he away to Babylon......... 2Chr 36:20
of those which had been c away......... Ezr 2:1
Babylon had c away unto Babylon...... Ezr 2:1
the people away into Babylon............ Ezr 5:12
of those that had been c away............ Ezr 8:35
of those that had been c away............ Ezr 9:4
of them that had been c away............ Ezr 10:6
of those that had been c away............ Ezr 10:8
of those that had been c away............ Neh 7:5
the king of Babylon had c away.......... Neh 7:6
Who had been c away from............... Est 2:6
been c away with Jeconiah king of...... Est 2:6
the king of Babylon had c away.......... Est 2:6
have c them away, yea, and slain....... Job 5:13
of the froward is c headlong.............. Job 5:13
I,should have been c from the............ Job 10:19
though the mountains be c into........... Ps 46:2
of all those that c them captives......... Ps 106:46
For there they that c us away............. Ps 137:3
this day, shall be c to Babylon........... Is 39:6
which are c from the womb................ Is 46:3
shall be c upon their shoulders........... Is 49:22
our griefs, and c our sorrows............. Is 53:4
c them all the days of old.................. Is 63:9
LORD's flock is c away captive........... Jer 13:17
Judah shall be c away captive all........ Jer 13:19
it shall be wholly c away captive........ Jer 13:19
king of Babylon had c away............... Jer 24:1
that are c away captive of Judah......... Jer 24:5
when he c away captive Jeconiah........ Jer 27:20
They shall be c to Babylon,............... Jer 27:22
this place, and c them to Babylon....... Jer 28:3
all that is c away captive, from........... Jer 28:6
elders which were c away captives...... Jer 29:1
c away captive from Jerusalem to....... Jer 29:1
unto all that are c away captives......... Jer 29:4
to be c away from Jerusalem unto...... Jer 29:4
caused you to be c away captives....... Jer 29:4
I caused you to be c away captive....... Jer 29:14
the captain of the guard c away.......... Jer 39:9
were c away captive of Jerusalem....... Jer 40:1
David left his c away captive unto....... Jer 40:1
of them that were not c away............. Jer 40:7
Then Ishmael c away captive all......... Jer 41:10
of Nethaniah c them away captive...... Jer 41:10
c away captive from Mizpah came...... Jer 41:14
c him up unto the king of Babylon...... Jer 52:9
c him to Babylon, and put him in........ Jer 52:11
the captain of the guard c away.......... Jer 52:15
c all the brass of them to.................. Jer 52:17
Thus Judah was c away captive out..... Jer 52:27

Nebuchadrezzar c away captive .... Jer 52:28
year of Nebuchadrezzar he c away ...... Jer 52:29
the captain of the guard c away .... Jer 52:30
whither they shall be c captives .... Eze 6:9
c it into a land of traffick .... Eze 17:4
c me out in the spirit of the .... Eze 37:1
which he c into the land of .... Dan 1:2
the wind c them away, that no .... Dan 2:35
It shall be also c unto Assyria .... Hos 10:6
Assyrians, and oil is c into Egypt .... Hos 12:1
have c into your temples my .... Joel 3:5
because they c away captive the .... Amos 1:6
c away captive his forces .... Obad 11
Yet was she c away, she went into ...... Nah 3:10
time they were c away to Babylon ...... Mt 1:11
c him away, and delivered him to ...... Mk 15:1
there was a dead man c out .... Lk 7:12
died, and was c by the angels into ...... Lk 16:22
from them, and c up into heaven .... Lk 24:51
lame from his mother's womb was c .... Acts 3:2
up, and c him out, and buried him ...... Acts 5:6
were c over into Sychem, and laid ...... Acts 7:16
devout men c Stephen to his .... Acts 8:2
him to be c into the castle .... Acts 21:34
c away unto these dumb idols, ... 1Cor 12:2
c away with their dissimulation .... Gal 2:13
c about with every wind of .... Eph 4:14
Be not c about with divers and .... Heb 13:9
clouds that are c with a tempest 2Pet 2:17
without water, c about of winds .... Jude 12
her to be c away of the flood .... Rev 12:15
So he c me away in the spirit .... Rev 17:3
he c me away in the spirit to a .... Rev 21:10

CARRIEST

Thou c them away as with a flood ...... Ps 90:5

CARRIETH

and as chaff that the storm c away .... Job 21:18
The east wind c him away, and he...... Job 27:21
woman, and of the beast that c her .... Rev 17:7

CARRY

going to c it down to Egypt .... Gen 37:25
c corn for the famine of your .... Gen 42:19
c down the man a present, a .... Gen 43:11
sacks, c it again in your hand .... Gen 43:12
with food, as much as they can c ...... Gen 44:1
which Joseph had sent to c him .... Gen 45:27
which Pharaoh had sent to c him ...... Gen 46:5
thou shalt c me out of Egypt, and .... Gen 47:30
ye shall c up my bones from hence .... Gen 50:25
thou shalt not c forth ought c .... Ex 12:46
ye shall c up my bones away hence .... Ex 13:19
to c us forth out of Egypt .... Ex 14:11
go not with me, c us not up hence .... Ex 33:15
c forth without the camp unto a .... Lev 4:12
he shall c forth the bullock .... Lev 4:21
c forth the ashes without the .... Lev 6:11
c your brethren from before the .... Lev 10:4
he shall c them forth out of the .... Lev 14:45
shall one c forth without the .... Lev 16:27
C them in thy bosom, as a nursing .... Num 11:12
Asshur shall c thee away captive .... Num 24:22
so that thou art not able to c it .... Deut 14:24
Thou shalt c much seed out into .... Deut 28:38
ye shall c them over with you, and .... Josh 4:3
c these ten cheeses unto the 1Sa 17:18
unto him, Go, c them to the city 1Sa 20:40
C back the ark of God into 2Sa 15:25
to c over the king's household 2Sa 19:18
so that they c them away captives 1Kin 8:46
shall c thee whither I know not 1Kin 18:12
then c him out, and slew him 1Kin 21:10
c him back unto Amon the governor.... 1Kin 22:26
hand, and c me out of the host 1Kin 22:34
to c lad, C him to his mother 2Kin 4:19
c him to an inner chamber 2Kin 9:2
C thither one of the priests whom 2Kin 17:27
the king of Assyria did c away 2Kin 18:11
the captain of the guard c away 2Kin 25:11
to c tidings unto their idols, and 1Chr 10:9
None ought to c the ark of God 1Chr 15:2
LORD chosen to c the ark of God 1Chr 15:2
shall no more c the tabernacle 1Chr 23:26
thou shalt c it up to Jerusalem 2Chr 2:16
they c them away captives unto a 2Chr 6:36
c him back to Amon the governor 2Chr 18:25
that thou mayest c me out of the 2Chr 18:33
more than they could c away 2Chr 20:25
children of Judah c away captive 2Chr 25:12
c forth the filthiness out of the 2Chr 29:5
to c it out abroad into the brook 2Chr 29:16
in fetters, to c him to Babylon 2Chr 36:6
c them into the temple that is in .... Ezr 5:15
to c the silver and gold, which .... Ezr 7:15
Why doth thine heart c thee away ...... Job 15:12
he dieth he shall c nothing away .... Ps 49:17
which he may c away in his hand ...... Eccl 5:15
bird of the air shall c the voice .... Eccl 10:20
shall c it away safe, and none .... Is 5:29
shall they c away to the brook of ...... Is 15:7
the LORD will c thee away with a ...... Is 22:17
her own feet shall c her afar off .... Is 23:7
they will c their riches upon the .... Is 30:6
c them in his bosom, and shall .... Is 40:11
and the wind shall c them away .... Is 41:16
even to hoar hairs will I c you .... Is 46:4
even I will c, and will deliver .... Is 46:4
him upon the shoulder, they c him .... Is 46:7
the wind shall c them all away .... Is 57:13
Neither c forth a burden out of .... Jer 17:22

he shall c them captive into .... Jer 20:4
take them, and c them to Babylon .... Jer 20:5
with chains, to c him to Babylon .... Jer 39:7
that he should c him home .... Jer 39:14
c us away captives into Babylon .... Jer 43:3
them, and c them away captives .... Jer 43:12
he will no more c thee away into ...... Lam 4:22
in their sight, and c out thereby .... Eze 12:5
c it forth in the twilight .... Eze 12:6
through the wall to c out thereby ...... Eze 12:12
men that c tales to shed blood .... Eze 22:9
to c away silver and gold, to take ...... Eze 38:13
shall also c captives into Egypt .... Dan 11:8
began to c about in beds those .... Mk 6:55
c any vessel through the temple .... Mk 11:16
C neither purse, nor scrip, nor .... Lk 10:4
not lawful for thee to c thy bed .... Jn 5:10
c thee whither thou wouldest not ...... Jn 21:18
at the door, and shall c thee out .... Acts 5:9
I will c you away beyond Babylon ...... Acts 7:43
is certain we can c nothing out 1Ti 6:7

CARRYING

one c three kids, and another 1Sa 10:3
another c three loaves of bread, ... 1Sa 10:3
another c a bottle of wine 1Sa 10:3
c bows, turned back in the day of ...... Ps 78:9
unto the c away of Jerusalem .... Jer 1:3
from David until the c away into .... Mt 1:17
from the c away into Babylon unto .... Mt 1:17
c her forth, buried her by her .... Acts 5:10

CARSHENA (car-she'-nah) A Persian prince.
And the next unto him was C................ Est 1:14

CART

Now therefore make a new c 1Sa 6:7
no yoke, and tie the kine to the c 1Sa 6:7
of the LORD, and lay it upon the c 1Sa 6:8
milch kine, and tied them to the c 1Sa 6:10
the ark of God upon a new c 1Sa 6:11
the c came into the field of 1Sa 6:14
and they clave the wood of the c 1Sa 6:14
set the ark of God upon a new c 2Sa 6:3
sons of Abinadab, drave the new c 2Sa 6:3
c out of the house of Abinadab 1Chr 13:7
and Uzza and Ahio drave the c 1Chr 13:7
and sin as it were with a c rope.......... Is 5:18
neither is a c wheel turned about........ Is 28:27
break it with the wheel of his c .... Is 28:28
as a c is pressed that is full of .... Amos 2:13

CARVED

house, and fetched the c image .... Judg 18:18
the house within was c with knops 1Kin 6:18
he c all the walls of the house 1Kin 6:29
about with c figures of cherubims 1Kin 6:29
he c upon them carvings of 1Kin 6:32
he c thereon cherubims and palm 1Kin 6:35
with gold fitted upon the c work 1Kin 6:35
And he set a c image, the idol 2Chr 33:7
the c images which Manasseh had 2Chr 33:22
the c images, and the molten 2Chr 34:3
the c images, and the molten 2Chr 34:4
But now they break down the c .... Ps 74:6
with c works, with fine linen of .... Prov 7:16

CARVING

in c of timber, to work in all .... Ex 31:5
in c of wood, to make any manner...... Ex 35:33

CARVINGS

carved upon them c of cherubims...... 1Kin 6:32

CASE

did see that they were in evil c .... Ex 5:19
this is the c of the slayer, ... Deut 19:4
thou shalt in any c bring them .... Deut 22:1
In any c thou shalt deliver him .... Deut 24:13
that people, that is in such a c .... Ps 144:15
ye shall in no c enter into the .... Mt 5:20
If the c of the man be so with............ Mt 19:10
been now a long time in that c .... Jn 5:6

CASEMENT

of my house I looked through my c .... Prov 7:6

CASES

is not under bondage in such c 1Cor 7:15

CASIPHIA (cas-if'-e-ah) A place in Syria.
I do the chief at the place C................ Ezr 8:17
the Nethinims, at the place C............ Ezr 8:17

CASLUHIM (cas'-loo-him) Descendants of
Mizraim.
And Pathrusim, and C, (out of whom Gen 10:14
and C, (of whom came 1Chr 1:12

CASLUHITES See CASLUHIM.

CASSIA

c of five hundred shekels, after .... Ex 30:24
smell of myrrh, and aloes, and c .... Ps 45:8
bright iron, c, and calamus, were ...... Eze 27:19

CAST See PREFACE.

CASTAWAY

to others, I myself should be a c 1Cor 9:27

CASTEDST

thou c them down into destruction. .... Ps 73:18

CASTEST

thou c off fear, and restrainest .... Job 15:4
and c my words behind thee, ... Ps 50:17
LORD, why c thou off my soul .... Ps 88:14

CASTETH

cow calveth, and c not her calf .... Job 21:10
he c the wicked down to the .... Ps 147:6
He c forth his ice like morsels .... Ps 147:17
but he c away the substance of .... Prov 10:3
Slothfulness c into a deep sleep .... Prov 19:15
c down the strength of the .... Prov 21:22
As a mad man who c firebrands .... Prov 26:18
with gold, and c silver chains .... Is 40:19
As a fountain c out her waters, ... Jer 6:7
so she c out her wickedness .... Jer 6:7
He c out devils through the .... Mt 9:34
of the devils c he out devils .... Mk 3:22
He c out devils through Beelzebub .... Lk 11:15
but perfect love c out fear 1Jn 4:18
and c them out of the church 3Jn 10
as a fig tree c her untimely figs.......... Rev 6:13

CASTING

c them down to the ground 2Sa 8:2
all of them had one c, one 1Kin 7:37
c himself down before the house ...... Ezr 10:1
ye see my c down, and are afraid........ Job 6:21
they have defiled by c down the .... Ps 74:7
his crown by c it to the ground .... Ps 89:39
by c up mounts, and building forts .... Eze 17:17
thy c down shall be in the midst .... Mic 6:14
his brother, c a net into the sea .... Mt 4:18
and parted his garments, c lots .... Mt 27:35
his brother c a net into the sea .... Mk 1:16
we saw one c out devils in thy .... Mk 9:38
c away his garment, rose, and came .. Mk 10:50
c lots upon them, what every man .... Mk 15:24
we saw one c out devils in thy .... Lk 9:49
poor widow c in thither two mites .... Lk 21:1
For if the c away of them be the .... Rom 11:15
C down imaginations, and every 2Cor 10:5
C all your care upon him 1Pet 5:7

CASTLE

David took the c of Zion, which 1Chr 11:5
And David dwelt in the c...................... 1Chr 11:7
are like the bars of a c........................ Prov 18:19
him to be carried into the c .... Acts 21:34
as Paul was to be led into the c .... Acts 21:37
him to be brought into the c .... Acts 22:24
them, and to bring him into the c ...... Acts 23:10
he went and entered into the c .... Acts 23:16
go with him, and returned to the c .... Acts 23:32

CASTLES

by their towns, and by their c............ Gen 25:16
they dwelt, and all their goodly c ...... Num 31:10
their c in their coasts, of the 1Chr 6:54
and in the villages, and in the c 1Chr 27:25
and he built in Judah c, and cities 2Chr 17:12
and in the forests he built c 2Chr 27:4

CASTOR (cas'-tor) Patron god of sailors.
in the isle, whose sign was C............ Acts 28:11

CATCH

c in thorns, so that the stacks .... Ex 22:6
c you every man his wife of the .... Judg 21:21
from him, and did hastily c it 1Kin 20:33
we shall c them alive, and get 2Kin 7:12
he lieth in wait to c the poor .... Ps 10:9
he doth c the poor, when he .... Ps 10:9
net that he hath hid c himself .... Ps 35:8
extortioner c all that he hath .... Ps 109:11
they set a trap, they c men .... Jer 5:26
lion, and it neared to c the prey .... Eze 19:3
lion, and learned to c the prey .... Eze 19:6
they c them in their net, and .... Hab 1:15
Herodians, to c him in his words ...... Mk 12:13
from henceforth thou shalt c men ...... Lk 5:10
seeking to c something out of his ...... Lk 11:54

CATCHETH

c any beast or fowl that may be .... Lev 17:13
c away that which was sown in his .... Mt 13:19
and the wolf c them, and scattereth .... Jn 10:12

CATERPILLER

mildew, locust, or if there be c 1Kin 8:37
also their increase unto the c .... Ps 78:46
like the gathering of the c.................. Is 33:4
hath left hath the c eaten.................. Joel 1:4
eaten, the cankerworm, and the c ...... Joel 2:25

CATERPILLERS

or mildew, locusts, or c...................... 2Chr 6:28
spake, and the locusts came, and c .... Ps 105:34
fill thee with men, as with c .... Jer 51:14
horses to come up as the rough c ...... Jer 51:27

CATTLE

living creature after his kind, c .... Gen 1:24
c after their kind, and every .... Gen 1:25
fowl of the air, and over the c............ Gen 1:26
And Adam gave names to all c .... Gen 2:20
this, thou art cursed above all c .... Gen 3:14
in tents, and of such as have c .... Gen 4:20
c after their kind, of every .... Gen 6:20
all the c after their kind, and .... Gen 7:14
the earth, both of fowl, and of c .... Gen 7:21
of the ground, both man, and c .... Gen 7:23
all the c that was with him in .... Gen 8:1
all flesh, both of fowl, and of c .... Gen 8:17
with you, of the fowl, of the c .... Gen 9:10
And Abram was very rich in c .... Gen 13:2
c and the herdmen of Lot's c .... Gen 13:7

the c should be gathered together ____ Gen 29:7
thee, and how thy c was with me ____ Gen 30:29
all the speckled and spotted c ____ Gen 30:32
all the brown c among the sheep, ____ Gen 30:32
and brought forth c ringstraked ____ Gen 30:39
and put them not unto Laban's c ____ Gen 30:40
the stronger c did conceive, ____ Gen 30:41
the eyes of the c in the gutters ____ Gen 30:41
But when the c were feeble ____ Gen 30:42
exceedingly, and had much c ____ Gen 30:43
than all the c bare speckled ____ Gen 31:8
then bare all the c ringstraked ____ Gen 31:8
taken away the c of your father ____ Gen 31:9
at the time that the c conceived ____ Gen 31:10
upon the c were ringstraked ____ Gen 31:10
leap upon the c are ringstraked ____ Gen 31:12
And he carried away all his c ____ Gen 31:18
the c of his getting, which he ____ Gen 31:18
daughters, and six years for thy c ____ Gen 31:41
these c are my c, and all ____ Gen 31:43
according as the c that goeth ____ Gen 33:14
house, and made booths for his c ____ Gen 33:17
sons were with his c in the field ____ Gen 34:5
Shall not their c and their ____ Gen 34:23
persons of his house, and his c ____ Gen 36:6
not bear them because of their c ____ Gen 36:7
And they took their c, and their ____ Gen 46:6
their trade hath been to feed c ____ Gen 46:32
c from our youth even until now ____ Gen 46:34
then make them rulers over my c ____ Gen 47:6
And Joseph said, Give your c ____ Gen 47:16
and I will give you for your c ____ Gen 47:16
they brought their c unto Joseph ____ Gen 47:17
for the c of the herds, and for ____ Gen 47:17
for all their c for that year ____ Gen 47:17
my lord also hath our herds of c ____ Gen 47:18
upon thy c which is in the field ____ Ex 9:3
sever between the c of Israel ____ Ex 9:4
of Israel and the c of Egypt ____ Ex 9:4
and all the c of Egypt died ____ Ex 9:6
but of the c of the children of ____ Ex 9:6
of the c of the Israelites dead ____ Ex 9:7
therefore now, and gather thy c ____ Ex 9:19
his c fee into the houses ____ Ex 9:20
servants and his c in the field ____ Ex 9:21
Our c also shall go with ____ Ex 10:26
and all the firstborn of c ____ Ex 12:29
and herds, even very much c ____ Ex 12:38
our children and our c with thirst ____ Ex 17:3
nor thy maidservant, nor thy c ____ Ex 20:10
and every firstling among thy c ____ Ex 34:19
bring your offering of the c ____ Lev 1:2
beast, or a carcase of unclean c ____ Lev 5:2
Thou shalt not let thy c gender ____ Lev 19:19
And for thy c, and for the beast ____ Lev 25:7
your children, and destroy your c ____ Lev 26:22
the c of the Levites instead of ____ Num 3:41
the c of the children of Israel ____ Num 3:45
the c of the Levites instead of ____ Num 3:45
of the Levites instead of their ____ Num 3:45
that we and our c should die there ____ Num 20:4
my c drink of thy water, then I ____ Num 20:19
and took the spoil of all their c ____ Num 31:9
had a very great multitude of c ____ Num 32:1
the place was a place for c ____ Num 32:1
c, and thy servants have c ____ Num 32:4
build sheepfolds here for our c ____ Num 32:16
wives, our flocks, and all our c ____ Num 32:26
of them shall be for their c ____ Num 35:3
Only the c we took for a prey ____ Deut 2:35
But all the c, and the spoil of ____ Deut 3:7
and your little ones, and your c ____ Deut 3:19
(for I know that ye have much c ____ Deut 3:19
nor thine ass, nor any of thy c ____ Deut 5:14
barren among you, or among your c ____ Deut 7:14
grass in thy fields for thy c ____ Deut 11:15
the c thereof, with the edge of ____ Deut 13:15
and the little ones, and the c ____ Deut 20:14
thy ground, and the fruit of thy c ____ Deut 28:4
body, and in the fruit of thy c ____ Deut 28:11
he shall eat the fruit of thy c ____ Deut 28:51
body, and in the fruit of thy c ____ Deut 30:9
your little ones, and your c ____ Josh 1:14
the c thereof, shall ye take for ____ Josh 8:2
Only the c and the spoil of that ____ Josh 8:27
spoil of these cities, and the c ____ Josh 11:14
with their suburbs for their c ____ Josh 14:4
the suburbs thereof for our c ____ Josh 21:2
your tents, and with very much c ____ Josh 22:8
For they came up with their c ____ Judg 6:5
and put the little ones and the c ____ Judg 18:21
and brought away their c, and ____ 1Sa 23:5
they drave before those other c ____ 1Sa 30:20
fat c by the stone of Zoheleth, ____ 1Kin 1:9
And he hath slain oxen and fat c ____ 1Kin 1:19
day, and hath slain oxen and fat c ____ 1Kin 1:25
for the c that followed them ____ 2Kin 3:9
ye may drink, both ye, and your c ____ 2Kin 3:17
because their c were multiplied ____ 1Chr 5:9
And they took away their c ____ 1Chr 5:21
came down to take away their c ____ 1Chr 7:21
They smote also the tents of c ____ 2Chr 14:15
for he had much c, both in the ____ 2Chr 26:10
thousand and six hundred small c ____ 2Chr 35:8
offerings five thousand small c ____ 2Chr 35:9
over our bodies, and over our c ____ Neh 9:37
of our sons, and of our c, as it ____ Neh 10:36
the c also consuming the vapour ____ Job 36:33
the c upon a thousand hills ____ Ps 50:10
gave up their c also to the hail ____ Ps 78:48

the grass to grow for the c ____ Ps 104:14
suffereth not their c to decrease ____ Ps 107:38
Beasts, and all c ____ Ps 148:10
small c above all that were in ____ Eccl 2:7
and for the treading of lesser c ____ Is 7:25
in that day shall thy c feed in ____ Is 30:23
small c of thy burnt offerings ____ Is 43:23
upon the beasts, and upon the c ____ Is 46:1
can men hear the voice of the c ____ Jer 9:10
the multitude of their c a spoil ____ Jer 49:32
I judge between c and c ____ Eze 34:17
fat c and between the lean c ____ Eze 34:20
I will judge between c and c ____ Eze 34:22
the nations, which have gotten c ____ Eze 38:12
silver and gold, to take away c ____ Eze 38:13
the herds of c are perplexed, ____ Joel 1:18
and also much c ____ Jonah 4:11
forth, and upon men, and upon c ____ Hag 1:11
the multitude of men and c therein ____ Zec 2:4
taught me to keep c from my youth ____ Zec 13:5
a servant plowing or feeding c ____ Lk 17:7
and his children, and his c ____ Jn 4:12

CAUDA See CLAUDA.

CAUGHT
behold behind him a ram c in a ____ Gen 22:13
she c him by his garment, saying, ____ Gen 39:12
c it, and it became a rod in his ____ Ex 4:4
prey which the men of war had c ____ Num 31:32
c him, and cut off his thumbs and ____ Judg 1:6
c a young man of the men of ____ Judg 8:14
c three hundred foxes, and took ____ Judg 15:4
of them that danced, whom they c ____ Judg 21:23
I c him by his beard, and smote ____ 1Sa 17:35
they c every one his fellow by ____ 2Sa 2:16
his head c hold of the oak, and he ____ 2Sa 18:9
c hold on the horns of the altar ____ 1Kin 1:50
he hath c hold on the horns of ____ 1Kin 1:51
c hold on the horns of the altar ____ 1Kin 2:28
Ahijah c the new garment that was ____ 1Kin 11:30
the hill, she c him by the feet ____ 2Kin 4:27
and they c him, (for he was hid in ____ 2Chr 22:9
So she c him, and kissed him, and ____ Prov 7:13
the birds that are c in the snare ____ Eccl 9:12
thou art found, and also c ____ Jer 50:24
c him, and said unto him, O thou ____ Mt 14:31
And they c him, and cast him out of ____ Mt 21:39
And they c him, and beat him, and ____ Mk 12:3
For oftentimes it had c him ____ Lk 8:29
and that night they c nothing ____ Jn 21:3
of the fish which ye have now c ____ Jn 21:10
c him, and brought him to the ____ Acts 6:12
Spirit of the Lord c away Philip ____ Acts 8:39
their gains was gone, they c Paul ____ Acts 16:19
and having c Gaius and Aristarchus, ____ Acts 19:29
the Jews c me in the temple ____ Acts 26:21
And when the ship was c, and could ____ Acts 27:15
such an one c up to the third ____ 2Cor 12:2
How that he was c up into ____ 2Cor 12:4
being crafty, I c you with guile ____ 2Cor 12:16
remain shall be c up together ____ 1Th 4:17
and her child was c up unto God ____ Rev 12:5

CAUL
the c that is above the liver, and ____ Ex 29:13
the c above the liver, and the two ____ Ex 29:22
the c above the liver, with the ____ Lev 3:4
the c above the liver, with the ____ Lev 3:10
the c above the liver, with the ____ Lev 3:15
the c above the liver, ____ Lev 7:4
the c above the liver, and the two ____ Lev 8:16
the c above the liver, and the two ____ Lev 8:25
the c above the liver of the sin ____ Lev 9:10
kidneys, and the c above the liver ____ Lev 9:19
will rend the c of their heart, ____ Hos 13:8

CAULS
about their feet, and their c ____ Is 3:18

CAUSE See PREFACE.

CAUSED
for the LORD God had not c it to ____ Gen 2:5
the LORD God a deep sleep to ____ Gen 2:21
when God c me to wander from my ____ Gen 20:13
For God hath c me to be fruitful ____ Gen 41:52
the LORD c the sea to go back by ____ Ex 14:21
they c it to be proclaimed ____ Ex 36:6
as he hath c a blemish in a man, ____ Lev 24:19
these c the children of Israel, ____ Num 31:16
I have c thee to see it with ____ Deut 34:4
she c him to shave off the seven ____ Judg 16:19
when Samuel had c all the tribes ____ 1Sa 10:20
When he had c the tribe of ____ 1Sa 10:21
Jonathan c David to swear again, ____ 1Sa 20:17
have c thee to rest from all ____ 2Sa 7:11
c Solomon to ride upon king ____ 1Kin 1:38
they have c him to ride upon the ____ 1Kin 1:44
c a seat to be set for the king's ____ 1Kin 2:19
he c him to come up into the ____ 2Kin 9:13
they c their sons and their ____ 2Kin 17:17
the children of Israel to dwell ____ 2Chr 8:2
But Jeroboam c an ambushment to ____ 2Chr 13:13
c the inhabitants of Jerusalem to ____ 2Chr 21:11
he c his children to pass through ____ 2Chr 33:6
he c all that were present in ____ 2Chr 34:32
the God that hath c his name to ____ Ezr 6:12
c the people to understand the ____ Neh 8:7
c them to understand the reading ____ Neh 8:8
the c the gallows to be made ____ Est 5:14
I c the widow's heart to sing for ____ Job 29:13

or have c the eyes of the widow ____ Job 31:16
or have c the owners thereof to ____ Job 31:39
c the light of his cloud to shine ____ Job 37:15
the dayspring to know his place, ____ Job 38:12
Thou hast c men to ride over our ____ Ps 66:12
sea, and c them to pass through ____ Ps 78:13
c waters to run down like rivers ____ Ps 78:16
He c an east wind to blow in the ____ Ps 78:26
upon which thou hast c me to hope ____ Ps 119:49
fair speech she c him to yield ____ Prov 7:21
they have c Egypt to err in every ____ Is 19:14
I have not c thee to serve with ____ Is 43:23
he c the waters to flow out of ____ Is 48:21
Spirit of the LORD c him to rest ____ Is 63:14
c my people Israel to inherit ____ Jer 12:14
so have I c to cleave unto me the ____ Jer 13:11
I have c him to fall upon it ____ Jer 15:8
they have c them to stumble in ____ Jer 18:15
c my people Israel to err ____ Jer 23:13
had c my people to hear my words, ____ Jer 23:22
whom I have c to be carried away ____ Jer 29:4
of the city whither I have c you ____ Jer 29:7
again into the place whence I c ____ Jer 29:14
he c you to trust in a lie ____ Jer 29:31
therefore thou hast c all this ____ Jer 32:23
the servants and the handmaids, ____ Jer 34:11
c every man his servant, and every ____ Jer 34:16
ones have c a cry to be heard ____ Jer 48:4
I have c wine to fail from the ____ Jer 48:33
have c them to go astray, they ____ Jer 50:6
As Babylon hath c the slain of ____ Jer 51:49
the LORD hath c the solemn feasts ____ Lam 2:6
he hath c thine enemy to rejoice ____ Lam 2:17
He hath c the arrows of his ____ Lam 3:13
and he c me to eat that roll ____ Eze 3:2
I have c thee to multiply as the ____ Eze 16:7
Wherefore I c them to go forth ____ Eze 20:10
in that they c to pass through ____ Eze 20:26
thou hast c thy days to draw near ____ Eze 22:4
have also c their sons, whom they ____ Eze 23:37
till I have c my fury to rest ____ Eze 24:13
c his army to serve a great ____ Eze 29:18
down to the grave I c a mourning ____ Eze 31:15
I c Lebanon to mourn for him, and ____ Eze 31:15
which c terror in the land of the ____ Eze 32:23
which c their terror in the land ____ Eze 32:24
though their terror was c in the ____ Eze 32:25
though they c their terror in the ____ Eze 32:30
For I have c my terror in the ____ Eze 32:32
c me to pass by them round about ____ Eze 37:2
which c them to be led into ____ Eze 39:28
the house of Israel to fall ____ Eze 44:12
c me to pass by the four corners ____ Eze 46:21
c me to return to the brink of ____ Eze 47:6
being c to fly swiftly, touched ____ Dan 9:21
of whoredoms hath c them to err ____ Hos 4:12
their lies c them to err, after ____ Amos 2:4
I c it to rain upon one city, and ____ Amos 4:7
c it not to rain upon another ____ Amos 4:7
he c it to be proclaimed and ____ Jonah 3:7
I have c thine iniquity to pass ____ Zec 3:4
ye have c many to stumble at the ____ Mal 2:8
have c that even this man should ____ Jn 11:37
they c great joy unto all the ____ Acts 15:3
But if any have c grief, he hath ____ 2Cor 2:5

CAUSELESS
that thou hast shed blood c ____ 1Sa 25:31
so the curse c shall not come ____ Prov 26:2

CAUSES
thou mayest bring the c unto God ____ Ex 18:19
the hard c they brought unto ____ Ex 18:26
Hear the c between your brethren, ____ Deut 1:16
when for all the c whereby ____ Jer 3:8
false burdens and c of banishment ____ Lam 2:14
hast pleaded the c of my soul ____ Lam 3:58
For these c the Jews caught me in ____ Acts 26:21

CAUSEST
thou c me to ride upon it, and ____ Job 30:22
c to approach unto thee, that he ____ Ps 65:4

CAUSETH
the bitter water that c the curse ____ Num 5:18
bitter water that c the curse ____ Num 5:19
this water that c the curse shall ____ Num 5:22
the bitter water that c the curse ____ Num 5:24
the water that c the curse shall ____ Num 5:27
that the water that c the curse ____ Num 5:27
c them to wander in a wilderness ____ Job 12:24
my understanding c me to answer ____ Job 20:3
He c it to come, whether for ____ Job 37:13
He c the grass to grow for the ____ Ps 104:14
and c them to wander in the ____ Ps 107:40
He c the vapours to ascend from ____ Ps 135:7
he c his wind to blow, and the ____ Ps 147:18
in harvest is a son that c shame ____ Prov 10:5
winketh with the eye c sorrow ____ Prov 10:10
wrath is against him that c strife ____ Prov 15:18
have rule over a son that c shame ____ Prov 17:2
The lot c contentions to cease, ____ Prov 18:18
his mother, is a son that c shame ____ Prov 19:26
that c to err from the words of ____ Prov 19:27
the fire c the waters to boil, to ____ Is 64:2
He c the vapours to ascend from ____ Jer 10:13
he c the vapours to ascend from ____ Jer 51:16
as the sea c his waves to come up ____ Eze 26:3
with any thing that c sweat ____ Eze 44:18
c her to commit adultery ____ Mt 5:32

CAUSEWAY

which always c us to triumph in 2Cor 2:14
which c through us thanksgiving........ 2Cor 9:11
c the earth and them which dwell........ Rev 13:12
he c all, both small and great,........ Rev 13:16

CAUSEWAY

by the c of the going up, ward 1Chr 26:16
At Parbar westward, four at the c...... 1Chr 26:18

CAUSING

c the lips of those that are .... Song 7:9
jaws of the people, c them to err....... Is 30:28
in c you to return to this place .... Jer 30:10
c their flocks to lie down................. Jer 33:12

CAVE

and he dwelt in a c, he and his two..... Gen 19:30
he may give me the c of Machpelah.... Gen 23:9
the c that is therein, I give it .... Gen 23:11
the c which was therein, and all .... Gen 23:17
the c of the field of Machpelah .... Gen 23:19
the c that is therein, were made........ Gen 23:20
buried him in the c of Machpelah ...... Gen 25:9
c that is in the field of Ephron .... Gen 49:29
In the c that is in the field of .... Gen 49:30
of the c that is therein was from....... Gen 49:32
buried him in the c of the field........ Gen 50:13
hid themselves in a c at Makkedah..... Josh 10:16
are found hid in a c at Makkedah ...... Josh 10:17
stones upon the mouth of the c .... Josh 10:18
Joshua, Open the mouth of the c .... Josh 10:22
five kings unto me out of the c .... Josh 10:22
five kings unto him out of the c .... Josh 10:23
cast them into the c wherein they...... Josh 10:27
and escaped to the c of Adullam 1Sa 22:1
by the way, where was a c 1Sa 24:3
remained in the sides of the c 1Sa 24:3
But Saul rose up out of the c 1Sa 24:7
afterward, and went out of the c 1Sa 24:8
to day into mine hand in the c 1Sa 24:10
time unto the c of Adullam 2Sa 23:13
and hid them by fifty in a c 1Kin 18:4
LORD's prophets by fifty in a c 1Kin 18:13
And he came thither unto a c 1Kin 19:9
stood in the entering in of the c 1Kin 19:13
to David, into the c of Adullam......... 1Chr 11:15
when he fled from Saul in the c .... Ps 57:t
A Prayer when he was in the c .... Ps 142:t
It was a c, and a stone lay upon........ Jn 11:38

CAVE'S

laid stones in the c mouth............... Josh 10:27

CAVES

which are in the mountains, and c ..... Judg 6:2
people did hide themselves in c .... Judg 13:6
in c of the earth, and in the............. Job 30:6
into the c of the earth, for fear .... Is 2:19
in the c shall die of the .... Eze 33:27
and in dens and c of the earth .... Heb 11:38

CEASE

and day and night shall not c .... Gen 8:22
and the thunder shall c, neither........ Ex 9:29
shall c waiting upon the service .... Num 8:25
they prophesied, and did not c.......... Num 11:25
I will make to c from me the .... Num 17:5
shall never c out of the land .... Deut 15:11
of them to c from among men.......... Deut 32:26
children c from fearing the Lord .... Josh 22:25
of you, and after that I will c .... Judg 15:7
Benjamin my brother, or shall I c ...... Judg 20:28
C not to cry unto the LORD our 1Sa 7:8
of Ramah, and let his work c 2Chr 16:5
to cause these men to c, and that ..... Ezr 4:21
Jews, and made them to c by force..... Ezr 4:23
they could not cause them to c .... Ezr 5:5
slay them, and cause the work to c .... Neh 4:11
why should the work c, whilst I .... Neh 6:3
There the wicked c from troubling ..... Job 3:17
c then, and let me alone, that I .... Job 10:20
tender branch thereof will not c .... Job 14:7
C from anger, and forsake wrath ...... Ps 37:8
He maketh wars to c unto the end .... Ps 46:9
cause thine anger toward us to c ...... Ps 85:4
Thou hast made his glory to c .... Ps 89:44
The lot causeth contentions to c ...... Prov 18:18
C, my son, to hear the.................. Prov 19:27
honour for a man to c from strife ..... Prov 20:3
yea, strife and reproach shall c .... Prov 22:10
c from thine own wisdom............... Prov 23:4
the grinders c because they are .... Eccl 12:3
c to do evil .... Is 1:16
C ye from man, whose breath is in .... Is 2:22
while, and the indignation shall c ...... Is 10:25
the arrogancy of the proud to c .... Is 13:11
made their vintage shouting to c ...... Is 16:10
also shall c from Ephraim .... Is 17:3
sighing thereof have I made to c ...... Is 21:2
One of Israel to c from before us ...... Is 30:11
when thou shalt c to spoil .... Is 33:1
Then will I cause to c from the .... Jer 7:34
night and day, and let them not c ..... Jer 14:17
I will cause to c out of this............ Jer 16:9
neither shall c from yielding........... Jer 17:8
c from being a nation before me .... Jer 31:36
shall cause to c from thence man...... Jer 36:29
I will cause to c in Moab .... Jer 48:35
let not the apple of thine eye c .... Lam 2:18
and your idols may be broken and c.... Eze 6:6
make the pomp of the strong to c ..... Eze 7:24
I will make this proverb to c .... Eze 12:23
I will cause to c from................... Eze 16:41

make thy lewdness to c from thee..... Eze 23:27
lewdness to c out of the land .... Eze 23:48
cause the noise of thy songs to c ...... Eze 26:13
c by the hand of Nebuchadrezzar ...... Eze 30:10
their images to c out of Noph .... Eze 30:13
her strength shall c in her.............. Eze 30:18
the pomp of her strength shall c ...... Eze 30:18
cause them to c from feeding the ..... Eze 34:10
evil beasts to c out of the land .... Eze 34:25
sacrifice and the oblation to c .... Dan 9:27
the reproach offered by him to c ...... Dan 11:18
will cause to c the kingdom of .... Hos 1:4
also cause all her mirth to c .... Hos 2:11
Then said I, O Lord God, c .... Amos 7:5
wilt thou not c to pervert the.......... Acts 13:10
there be tongues, they shall c 1Cor 13:8
C not to give thanks for you, ... Eph 1:16
do not c to pray for you, and to....... Col 1:9
and that cannot c from sin 2Pet 2:14

CEASED

it to be with Sarah after the .... Gen 18:11
and the thunders and hail c .... Ex 9:33
the hail and the thunders were c...... Ex 9:34
the manna c on the morrow after ..... Josh 5:12
they c not from their own doings, ... Judg 2:19
The inhabitants of the villages c ...... Judg 5:7
they c in Israel, until that I .... Judg 5:7
and they that were hungry c 1Sa 2:5
words in the name of David, and c 1Sa 25:9
Then c the work of the house of ...... Ezr 4:24
So it c unto the second year of .... Ezr 4:24
these three men c to answer Job...... Job 32:1
they did tear me, and c not .... Ps 35:15
sore ran in the night, and c not ...... Ps 77:2
and say, How hath the oppressor c ... Is 14:4
the golden city c .... Is 14:4
The elders have c from the gate ...... Lam 5:14
The joy of our heart is c .... Lam 5:15
the sea c from her raging .... Jonah 1:15
come into the ship, the wind c .... Mt 14:32
And the wind c, and there was a ..... Mk 4:39
and the wind c .... Mk 6:51
in hath not c to kiss my feet .... Lk 7:45
and they c, and there was a calm .... Lk 8:24
in a certain place, when he c .... Lk 11:1
they c not to teach and preach ...... Acts 5:42
And after the uproar was c .... Acts 20:1
I c not to warn every one night ...... Acts 20:31
he would not be persuaded, we c..... Acts 21:14
is the offence of the cross c .... Gal 5:11
he also hath c from his own works.... Heb 4:10
they not have c to be offered .... Heb 10:2
in the flesh hath c from sin........... 1Pet 4:1

CEASETH

for the godly man c .... Ps 12:1
is precious, and it c for ever.......... Ps 49:8
is no talebearer, the strife c .... Prov 26:20
is at an end, the spoiler c .... Is 16:4
The mirth of tabrets c, the noise ..... Is 24:8
endeth, the joy of the harp c.......... Is 24:8
lie waste, the wayfaring man c .... Is 33:8
c not, without any intermission, ... Lam 3:49
who c from raising after he hath ..... Hos 7:4
said, This man c not to speak......... Acts 6:13

CEASING

the LORD in c to pray for you,......... 1Sa 12:23
but prayer was made without c of .... Acts 12:5
that without c I make mention of..... Rom 1:9
without c your work of faith.......... 1Th 1:3
cause also thank we God without c ... 1Th 2:13
Pray without c 1Th 5:17
that without c I have remembrance... 2Ti 1:3

CEDAR

c wood, and scarlet, and hyssop ...... Lev 14:4
the c wood, and the scarlet, and...... Lev 14:6
c wood, and scarlet, and hyssop ...... Lev 14:49
And he shall take the c wood .... Lev 14:51
living bird, and with the c wood....... Lev 14:52
And the priest shall take c wood ...... Num 19:6
as c trees beside the waters........... Num 24:6
c trees, and carpenters, and masons.. 2Sa 5:11
See now, I dwell in an house of c 2Sa 7:2
Why build ye not me an house of c.... 2Sa 7:7
from the c tree that is in 1Kin 4:33
hew me c trees out of Lebanon 1Kin 5:6
thy desire concerning timber of c 1Kin 5:8
So Hiram gave Solomon c trees........ 1Kin 5:10
house with beams and boards of c 1Kin 6:9
on the house with timber of c 1Kin 6:10
the house within with boards of c 1Kin 6:15
and the walls with boards of c 1Kin 6:16
the c of the house within was......... 1Kin 6:18
all was c 1Kin 6:18
covered the altar which was of c 1Kin 6:20
hewed stone, and a row of c beams... 1Kin 6:36
upon four rows of c pillars............. 1Kin 7:2
with c beams upon the pillars 1Kin 7:2
it was covered with c above upon..... 1Kin 7:3
it was covered with c from one 1Kin 7:7
hewed stones, and a row of c beams.. 1Kin 7:12
furnished Solomon with c trees 1Kin 9:11
sent to the c that was in Lebanon 2Kin 14:9
cut down the tall c trees thereof 2Kin 19:23
Also c trees in abundance.............. 1Chr 22:4
Tyre brought much c wood to David... 2Chr 2:3
c trees made he as the sycomore 2Chr 1:15
Send me also c trees, fir trees,....... 2Chr 2:8
c trees made he as the sycomore 2Chr 9:27

sent to the c that was in Lebanon 2Chr 25:18
to bring c trees from Lebanon to...... Ezr 3:7
He moveth his tail like a c .... Job 40:17
he shall grow like a c in Lebanon ..... Ps 92:12
The beams of our house are c .... Song 1:17
will inclose her with boards of c ...... Song 8:9
plant in the wilderness the c .... Is 41:19
and it is cieled with c, and .... Jer 22:14
because thou closest thyself in c ...... Jer 22:15
took the highest branch of the c ...... Eze 17:3
the highest branch of the high c ...... Eze 17:22
and bear fruit, and be a goodly c ..... Eze 17:23
bound with cords, and made of c ...... Eze 27:24
the Assyrian was a c in Lebanon ...... Eze 31:3
for he shall uncover the c work .... Zeph 2:14
for the c is fallen .... Zec 11:2

CEDARS

and devour the c of Lebanon .... Judg 9:15
measures of hewed stones, and c 1Kin 7:11
c made to be as the sycomore 1Kin 10:27
to David, and timber of c, with....... 1Chr 14:1
Lo, I dwell in an house of c 1Chr 17:1
ye not built me an house of c 1Chr 17:6
didst send him c to build him an 2Chr 2:3
voice of the LORD breaketh the c ..... Ps 29:5
LORD breaketh the c of Lebanon ...... Ps 29:5
thereof were like the goodly c .... Ps 80:10
the c of Lebanon, which he hath...... Ps 104:16
fruitful trees, and all c .... Ps 148:9
is as Lebanon, excellent as the c ..... Song 5:15
And upon all the c of Lebanon .... Is 2:13
but we will change them into c .... Is 9:10
the c of Lebanon, saying, Since....... Is 14:8
will cut down the tall c thereof ...... Is 37:24
He heweth him down c, and taketh ... Is 44:14
they shall cut down thy choice .... Jer 22:7
that makest thy nest in the c .... Jer 22:23
they have taken c from Lebanon to ... Eze 27:5
The c in the garden of God could ..... Eze 31:8
was like the height of the c .... Amos 2:9
that the fire may devour thy c .... Zec 11:1

CEDRON (se'-drun) See KIDRON. Same as
Kidron.
his disciples over the brook C............ Jn 18:1

CELEBRATE

even, shall ye c your sabbath .... Lev 23:32
ye shall c it in the seventh .... Lev 23:41
praise thee, death can not c thee...... Is 38:18

CELESTIAL

There are also c bodies, and 1Cor 15:40
but the glory of the c is one........... 1Cor 15:40

CELLARS

wine c was Zabdi the Shiphmite 1Chr 27:27
over the c of oil was Joash 1Chr 27:28

CENCHREA (sen'-kre-ah) Harbor city for
Corinth.
having shorn his head in C.............. Acts 18:18
of the church which is at C .... Rom 16:1
Phebe servant of the church at C ...... Rom s

CENCHREAE See CENCHREA.

CENSER

Aaron, took either of them his c ...... Lev 10:1
he shall take a c full of burning ...... Lev 16:12
And take every man his c, and put .... Num 16:17
before the LORD every man his c ...... Num 16:17
also, and Aaron, each of you his c..... Num 16:17
And they took every man his c........ Num 16:18
Moses said unto Aaron, Take a c ...... Num 16:46
had a c in his hand to burn 2Chr 26:19
with every man his c in his hand ..... Eze 8:11
Which had the golden c, and the ..... Heb 9:4
at the altar, having a golden c .... Rev 8:3
And the angel took the c, and .... Rev 8:5

CENSERS

minister about it, even the c .... Num 4:14
Take you c, Korah, and all his .... Num 16:6
censer, two hundred and fifty c ...... Num 16:17
take up the c out of the burning ..... Num 16:37
The c of these sinners against .... Num 16:38
the priest took the brasen c .... Num 16:39
the spoons, and the c of pure gold ... 1Kin 7:50
basons, and the spoons, and the c 2Chr 4:22

CENTURION

there came unto him a c............... Mt 8:5
The c answered and said, Lord, I ..... Mt 8:8
And Jesus said unto the c, Go thy .... Mt 8:13
Now when the c, and they that were.. Mt 27:54
And when the c, which stood over .... Mk 15:39
and calling unto him the c .... Mk 15:44
And when he knew it of the c .... Mk 15:45
the c sent friends to him, saying ..... Lk 7:6
Now when the c saw what was done,.. Lk 23:47
a c of the band called the .... Acts 10:1
And they said, Cornelius, the c .... Acts 10:22
said unto the c that stood by.......... Acts 22:25
When the c heard that, he went and.. Acts 22:26
And he commanded a c to keep Paul .. Acts 24:23
Julius, a c of Augustus' band .... Acts 27:1
there the c found a ship of .... Acts 27:6
Nevertheless the c believed the ...... Acts 27:11
Paul said to the c and to the .... Acts 27:31
But the c, willing to save Paul,....... Acts 27:43
the c delivered the prisoners to ...... Acts 28:16

C

CENTURION'S
And a certain c servant, who was............ Lk 7:2

CENTURIONS
immediately took soldiers and c............ Acts 21:32
Paul called one of the c unto him............ Acts 23:17
And he called unto them two c............ Acts 23:23

CEPHAS (se´-fas) See PETER. Name given to Simon Peter.
thou shalt be called C, which is............ Jn 1:42
and I of C............ 1Cor 1:12
Whether Paul, or Apollos, or C............ 1Cor 3:22
as the brethren of the Lord, and C............ 1Cor 9:5
And that he was seen of C, then of............ 1Cor 15:5
And when James, C, and John, who............ Gal 2:9

CEREMONIES
and according to all the c thereof........ Num 9:3

CERTAIN
And he lighted upon a c place............ Gen 28:11
a c man found him, and, behold, he........ Gen 37:15
and turned in to a c Adullamite............ Gen 38:1
there a daughter of a c Canaanite............ Gen 38:2
gather a c rate every day, that I............ Ex 16:4
And there were c men, who were............ Num 9:6
with c of the children of Israel............ Num 16:2
C men, the children of Belial............ Deut 13:13
if it be truth, and the thing c............ Deut 13:14
it be true, and the thing c............ Deut 17:4
to his fault, by a c number............ Deut 25:2
a c woman cast a piece of a............ Judg 9:53
there was a c man of Zorah, of............ Judg 13:2
that there was a c Levite............ Judg 19:1
c sons of Belial, beset the house........ Judg 19:22
a c man of Beth-lehem-judah went........ Ruth 1:1
Now there was a c man of............ 1Sa 1:1
Now a c man of the servants of........ 1Sa 21:7
a c man saw it, and told Joab, and........ 2Sa 18:10
thou shalt know for c that thou............ 1Kin 2:37
unto thee, saying, Know for a c........ 1Kin 2:42
oxen were c additions made of............ 1Kin 7:29
c Edomites of his father's............ 1Kin 11:17
a c man of the sons of the............ 1Kin 20:35
a c man drew a bow at a venture, ... 1Kin 22:34
Now there cried a c woman of the ... 2Kin 4:1
appointed unto her a c officer............ 2Kin 8:6
c of them had the charge of the........ 1Chr 9:28
he appointed c of the Levites to........ 1Chr 16:4
Then there went c, and told David........ 1Chr 19:5
Even after a c rate every day, ... 2Chr 8:13
after c years he went down to............ 2Chr 18:2
a c man drew a bow at a venture, ... 2Chr 18:33
Then c of the heads of the............ 2Chr 28:12
with c chief of the fathers, ... Ezr 10:16
came, he and c men of Judah............ Neh 1:2
down and wept, and mourned c days... Neh 1:4
at Jerusalem dwelt c of the............ Neh 11:4
that a c portion should be for............ Neh 11:23
c of the priests' sons with............ Neh 12:35
after c days obtained I leave of............ Neh 13:6
smote c of them, and plucked off........ Neh 13:25
the palace there was a c few............ Est 2:5
There is a c people scattered............ Est 3:8
But know ye for c, that if ye put........ Jer 26:15
Then rose up c of the elders of........ Jer 26:17
c men with him into Egypt............ Jer 26:22
That there came c from Shechem........ Jer 41:5
c of the poor of the people............ Jer 52:15
c of the poor of the land for............ Jer 52:16
The came c of the elders of............ Eze 14:1
that c of the elders of Israel............ Eze 20:1
that he should bring c of the............ Dan 1:3
and the dream is c, and the............ Dan 2:45
that time c Chaldeans came near............ Dan 3:8
There are c Jews whom thou hast........ Dan 3:12
unto that c saint which spake............ Dan 8:13
fainted, and was sick c days............ Dan 8:27
behold a c man clothed in linen,........ Dan 10:5
after c years with a great army........ Dan 11:13
a c scribe came, and said unto him... Mt 8:19
c of the scribes said within............ Mt 9:3
behold, there came a c ruler............ Mt 9:18
Then c of the scribes and of the........ Mt 12:38
there came to him a c man............ Mt 17:14
of heaven likened unto a c king........ Mt 18:23
desiring a c thing of him............ Mt 20:20
A c man had two sons............ Mt 21:28
There was a c householder............ Mt 21:33
of heaven is like unto a c king........ Mt 22:2
But there were c of the scribes............ Mk 2:6
a c woman, which had an issue of........ Mk 5:25
synagogue's house c which said........ Mk 5:35
c of the scribes, which came from... Mk 7:1
For a c woman, whose young............ Mk 7:25
c of them that stood there said............ Mk 11:5
A c man planted a vineyard, and........ Mk 12:1
send unto him c of the Pharisees........ Mk 12:13
And there came a c poor widow............ Mk 12:42
there followed him a c young man........ Mk 14:51
And there arose c, and bare false........ Mk 14:57
a c priest named Zacharias, of............ Lk 1:5
to pass, when he was in a c city............ Lk 5:12
And it came to pass on a c day............ Lk 5:17
c of the Pharisees said unto them... Lk 6:2
a c centurion's servant, who was............ Lk 7:2
There was a c creditor which had........ Lk 7:41
c women, which had been healed of... Lk 8:2
it was told him by c which said............ Lk 8:20
Now it came to pass on a c day............ Lk 8:22
met him out of the city a c man............ Lk 8:27

a c man said unto him, Lord, I............ Lk 9:57
a c lawyer stood up, and tempted............ Lk 10:25
A c man went down from Jerusalem... Lk 10:30
came down a c priest that way............ Lk 10:31
But a c Samaritan, as he............ Lk 10:33
that he entered into a c village............ Lk 10:38
a c woman named Martha received........ Lk 10:38
as he was praying in a c place............ Lk 11:1
a c woman of the company lifted........ Lk 11:27
a c Pharisees besought him to dine... Lk 11:37
The ground of a c rich man............ Lk 12:16
A c man had a fig tree planted in... Lk 13:6
day there came c of the Pharisees... Lk 13:31
there was a c man before him............ Lk 14:2
A c man made a great supper, and........ Lk 14:16
And he said, A c man had two sons... Lk 15:11
a c man was therein, which had an... Lk 16:1
There was a c rich man, which was... Lk 16:19
there was a c beggar named............ Lk 16:20
And as he entered into a c village... Lk 17:12
he spake this parable unto............ Lk 18:9
a c ruler asked him, saying, Good,... Lk 18:18
a c blind man sat by the way side... Lk 18:35
A c nobleman went into a far............ Lk 19:12
A c man planted a vineyard, and........ Lk 20:9
came to him c of the Sadducees............ Lk 20:27
Then c of the scribes answering............ Lk 20:39
he saw also a c poor widow............ Lk 21:2
But a c maid beheld him as he sat... Lk 22:56
(Who for a c sedition made in the... Lk 23:19
prepared, and c others with them........ Lk 24:1
c women also of our company made... Lk 24:22
c of them which were with us went... Lk 24:24
And there was a c nobleman............ Jn 4:46
down at a c season into the pool........ Jn 5:4
a c man was there, which had an........ Jn 5:5
Now a c man was sick, named............ Jn 11:1
there were c Greeks among them............ Jn 12:20
a c man lame from his mother's............ Acts 3:2
But a c man named Ananias, with........ Acts 5:1
privy to it, and brought a c part........ Acts 5:2
there arose c of the synagogue............ Acts 6:9
But there was a c man, called............ Acts 8:9
way, they came unto a c water............ Acts 8:36
there was a c disciple at............ Acts 9:10
Then was Saul c days with the............ Acts 9:19
he found a c man named Aeneas............ Acts 9:33
Joppa a c disciple named Tabitha........ Acts 9:36
There was a c man in Caesarea............ Acts 10:1
a c vessel descending unto him............ Acts 10:11
c brethren from Joppa accompanied... Acts 10:23
prayed they him to tarry c days............ Acts 10:48
A c vessel descend, as it had............ Acts 11:5
his hands to vex c of the church........ Acts 12:1
that was at Antioch c prophets............ Acts 13:1
Paphos, they found a c sorcerer............ Acts 13:6
there sat a c man at Lystra,............ Acts 14:8
came thither c Jews from Antioch........ Acts 15:1
c men which came down from Judaea... Acts 15:1
c other of them, should go up to........ Acts 15:2
But there rose up c of the sect............ Acts 15:5
that c which went out from us............ Acts 15:24
a c disciple was there, named............ Acts 16:1
Timotheus, the son of a c woman........ Acts 16:1
were in that city abiding c days........ Acts 16:12
a c woman named Lydia, a seller........ Acts 16:14
a c damsel possessed with a............ Acts 16:16
took unto them c lewd fellows of... Acts 17:5
c brethren unto the rulers of the... Acts 17:6
Then c philosophers of the............ Acts 17:18
For thou bringest c strange............ Acts 17:20
as c also of your own poets have............ Acts 17:28
Howbeit c men clave unto him, and... Acts 17:34
found a c Jew named Aquila, born........ Acts 18:2
and entered into a c man's house............ Acts 18:7
a c Jew named Apollos, born at............ Acts 18:24
and finding c disciples,............ Acts 19:1
Then c of the vagabond Jews,............ Acts 19:13
For a c man named Demetrius, a............ Acts 19:24
c of the chief of Asia, which............ Acts 19:31
there sat in a window a c young............ Acts 20:9
came down from Judaea a c prophet... Acts 21:10
There went with us also c of the........ Acts 21:16
c of the Jews banded together, and... Acts 23:12
for he hath a c thing to tell him... Acts 23:17
with a c orator named Tertullus,........ Acts 24:1
Whereupon c Jews from Asia found... Acts 24:18
And after c days, when Felix came... Acts 24:24
after c days king Agrippa and............ Acts 25:13
There is a c man left in bonds by... Acts 25:14
But had c questions against him........ Acts 25:19
Of whom I have no c thing to............ Acts 25:26
c other prisoners unto one named........ Acts 27:1
running under a c island which is... Acts 27:16
we must be cast upon a c island............ Acts 27:26
discovered a c creek with a shore... Acts 27:39
Achaia to make a c contribution............ Rom 15:26
have no c dwellingplace place............ 1Cor 4:11
For before that c came from James... Gal 2:12
it is c we can carry nothing out............ 1Ti 6:7
But one in a c place testified,............ Heb 2:6
For he spake in a c place of the............ Heb 4:4
Again, he limiteth a c day............ Heb 4:7
But a c fearful looking for of............ Heb 10:27
For there are c men crept in............ Jude 4

CERTAINLY
I will c return unto thee............ Gen 18:10
We saw c that the LORD was with........ Gen 26:28
could we c know that he would say... Gen 43:7
that such a man as I can c divine... Gen 44:15

will c requite us all the evil............ Gen 50:15
And he said, C I will be with thee... Ex 3:12
If the theft be c found in his............ Ex 22:4
he hath c trespassed against the........ Lev 5:19
congregation shall c stone him............ Lev 24:16
Because it was c told me............ Josh 9:24
if ye can c declare it me within........ Judg 14:12
Thy father c knoweth that I have........ 1Sa 20:3
for if I knew c that evil were............ 1Sa 20:9
thy servant hath c heard that............ 1Sa 23:10
for the LORD will c make my lord........ 1Sa 25:28
even so wilt I c do this day............ 1Kin 1:30
unto him, Thou mayest c recover........ 2Kin 8:10
If thou c return in peace, then............ 2Chr 18:27
for riches c make themselves............ Prov 23:5
Lo, c in vain made he it............ Jer 8:8
Do we not c know that every............ Jer 13:12
Ye shall c drink............ Jer 25:28
The king of Babylon shall c come... Jer 36:29
Dost thou c know that Baalis the........ Jer 40:14
know c that I have admonished you... Jer 42:19
Now therefore know c that ye............ Jer 42:22
But we will c do whatsoever thing... Jer 44:17
c this is the day that we looked........ Lam 2:16
and one shall c come, and overflow,... Dan 11:10
shall c come after certain years........ Dan 11:13
C this was a righteous man............ Lk 23:47

CERTAINTY
Know for a c that the LORD your........ Josh 23:13
and come ye again to me with the c... 1Sa 23:23
know the c of the words of truth........ Prov 22:21
I know of c that ye would gain............ Dar. 2:8
know the c of those things............ Lk 1:4
not know the c for the tumult............ Acts 21:34
c wherefore he was accused of the... Acts 22:30

CERTIFIED
have we sent and c the king............ Ezr 4:14
Esther c the king thereof in............ Est 2:22

CERTIFY
there come word from you to c me... 2Sa 15:28
We c thee king that, if this city........ Ezr 4:16
to c thee, that we might write............ Ezr 5:10
Also we c you, that touching any,... Ezr 7:24
But I c you, brethren, that the............ Gal 1:11

CHAFED
they be c in their minds, as a............ 2Sa 17:8

CHAFF
as c that the storm carrieth away... Job 21:18
but are like the c which the wind........ Ps 1:4
Let them be as c before the wind........ Ps 35:5
and the flame consumeth the c............ Is 5:24
shall be chased as the c of the............ Is 17:13
shall be as c that passeth away............ Is 29:5
Ye shall conceive c, ye shall............ Is 33:11
and shalt make the hills as c............ Is 41:15
What is the c to the wheat............ Jer 23:28
became like the c of the summer............ Dan 2:35
as the c that is driven with the........ Hos 13:3
before the day pass as the c............ Zeph 2:2
up the c with unquenchable fire............ Mt 3:12
but the c he will burn with fire............ Lk 3:17

CHAIN
put a c gold about his neck............ Gen 41:42
work, and wreaths of c work............ 1Kin 7:17
compasseth them about as a c............ Ps 73:6
eyes, with one c of thy neck............ Song 4:9
he hath made my c heavy............ Lam 3:7
Make a c............ Ezr 7:23
thy hands, and a c on thy neck............ Eze 16:11
have a c of gold about his neck,........ Dan 5:7
have a c of gold about thy neck,........ Dan 5:16
put a c of gold about his neck,........ Dan 5:29
of Israel I am bound with this c............ Acts 28:20
me, and was not ashamed of my c............ 2Ti 1:16
pit and a great c in his hand............ Rev 20:1

CHAINS
two c of pure gold at the ends............ Ex 28:14
the wreathen c to the ouches............ Ex 28:14
c at the ends of wreathen work of... Ex 28:22
c of gold in the two rings which........ Ex 28:24
c thou shalt fasten in the two............ Ex 28:25
the breastplate c at the ends............ Ex 39:15
they put the two wreathen c of............ Ex 39:17
two ends of the two wreathen c............ Ex 39:18
hath gotten, of jewels of gold, c,... Num 31:50
beside the c that were about............ Judg 8:26
the c of gold before the oracle............ 1Kin 6:21
and set thereon palm trees and c............ 2Chr 3:5
And he made c, as in the oracle,........ 2Chr 3:16
and put them on the c............ 2Chr 3:16
out those which are bound with c............ Ps 68:6
To bind their kings with c............ Ps 149:8
thy head, and c about thy neck............ Prov 1:9
jewels, thy neck with c of gold............ Song 1:10
The c, and the bracelets, and the... Is 3:19
with gold, and casteth silver c............ Is 40:19
in c they shall come over, and............ Is 45:14
eyes, and bound him with c............ Jer 39:7
in c among all that were carried............ Jer 40:1
the c which were upon thine hand............ Jer 40:4
king of Babylon bound him in c............ Jer 52:11
they brought him with c unto the........ Eze 7:23
And they put him in ward in c............ Eze 19:4
all her great men were bound in c... Nah 3:10
could bind him, no, not with c............ Mk 5:3
often bound with fetters and c............ Mk 5:4

the c had been plucked asunder by .... Mk 5:4
and he was kept bound with c .... Lk 8:29
two soldiers, bound with two c .... Acts 12:6
his c fell off from his hands .... Acts 12:7
him to be bound with two c .... Acts 21:33
delivered them into c of darkness 2Pet 2:4
c under darkness unto the .... Jude 6

CHALCEDONY
the third, a c .... Rev 21:19

CHALCOL (kal'-kol) See CALCOL. *Son of Mahol.*
the Ezrahite, and Heman, and C 1Kin 4:31

CHALDAEANS (kal-de'-uns) See CHALDEANS. *Inhabitants of southern Babylonia.*
came he out of the land of the C .... Acts 7:4

CHALDEA (kal-de'-ah) See BABYLON, CHALDEAN. *Southern portion of Babylonia.*
And C shall be a spoil .... Jer 50:10
to all the inhabitants of C all .... Jer 51:24
blood upon the inhabitants of C .... Jer 51:35
by the Spirit of God into C .... Eze 11:24
in the land of Canaan unto C .... Eze 16:29
manner of the Babylonians in C .... Eze 23:15
sent messengers unto them into C .... Eze 23:16

CHALDEAN (kal-de'-un) See BABYLONIAN, CHALDEANS, CHALDEANS.
the king of Babylon, the C .... Ezr 5:12
any magician, or astrologer, or C .... Dan 2:10

CHALDEANS (kal-de'-uns) See BABYLONIANS, CHALDEANS, CHALDEAN, CHALDEES. *Same as Chaldaeans.*
The C made out three bands, and .... Job 1:17
Behold the land of the C .... Is 23:13
down all their nobles, and the C .... Is 43:14
is no throne, O daughter of the C .... Is 47:1
darkness, O daughter of the C .... Is 47:5
and his arm shall be on the C .... Is 48:14
of Babylon, flee ye from the C .... Is 48:20
king of Babylon, and against the C ...... Jer 21:4
falleth to the C that besiege you .... Jer 21:9
and into the hand of the C .... Jer 22:25
the land of the C for their good .... Jer 24:5
iniquity, and the land of the C .... Jer 25:12
escape out of the hand of the C .... Jer 32:4
though ye fight with the C .... Jer 32:5
is given into the hand of the C .... Jer 32:24
is given into the hand of the C .... Jer 32:25
this city into the hand of the C .... Jer 32:28
And the C, that fight against this .... Jer 32:29
is given into the hand of the C .... Jer 32:43
They come to fight with the C .... Jer 33:5
for fear of the army of the C .... Jer 35:11
and when the C that besieged .... Jer 37:5
The C shall come again, and fight .... Jer 37:8
The C shall surely depart from us .... Jer 37:9
of the C that fight against you .... Jer 37:10
when the army of the C was .... Jer 37:11
Thou fallest away to the C .... Jer 37:13
I fall not away to the C .... Jer 37:14
goeth forth to the C shall live .... Jer 38:2
be given into the hand of the C .... Jer 38:18
the Jews that are fallen to the C .... Jer 38:19
wives and thy children to the C .... Jer 38:23
the C burned the king's house, and ..... Jer 39:8
saying, Fear not to serve the C .... Jer 40:9
dwell at Mizpah to serve the C .... Jer 40:10
the C that were found there, and .... Jer 41:3
Because of the C .... Jer 41:18
deliver us into the hand of the C .... Jer 43:3
of the C by Jeremiah the prophet .... Jer 43:3
go forth out of the land of the C .... Jer 50:8
God of hosts in the land of the C .... Jer 50:25
A sword is upon the C, saith the .... Jer 50:35
against the land of the C .... Jer 50:45
shall fall in the land of the C .... Jer 51:4
from the land of the C .... Jer 51:54
(now the C were by the city round .... Jer 52:7
But the army of the C pursued .... Jer 52:8
And all the army of the C, that .... Jer 52:14
the C brake, and carried all the .... Jer 52:17
in the land of the C by the river .... Eze 1:3
to Babylon to the land of the C .... Eze 12:13
the images of the C portrayed .... Eze 23:14
The Babylonians, and all the C .... Eze 23:23
learning and the tongue of the C .... Dan 1:4
and the sorcerers, and the C .... Dan 2:2
Then spake the C to the king in .... Dan 2:4
king answered and said to the C .... Dan 2:5
The C answered before the king .... Dan 2:10
at that time certain C came near .... Dan 3:8
magicians, the astrologers, the C .... Dan 4:7
bring in the astrologers, the C .... Dan 5:7
of the magicians, astrologers, C .... Dan 5:11
the king of the C slain .... Dan 5:30
made king over the realm of the C ...... Dan 9:1
For, lo, I raise up the C .... Hab 1:6

CHALDEANS' (kal-de'-uns)
But the C army pursued after them ...... Jer 39:5

CHALDEES (kal'-dees) See CHALDEES. *Same as Chaldeans.*
of his nativity, in Ur of the C .... Gen 11:28
forth with them from Ur of the C .... Gen 11:31
brought thee out of Ur of the C .... Gen 15:7
sent against him bands of the C 2Kin 24:2
(now the C were against the city 2Kin 25:4
the army of the C pursued after 2Kin 25:5

And all the army of the C, that 2Kin 25:10
did the C break in pieces, and 2Kin 25:13
not to be the servants of the C 2Kin 25:24
the C that were with him at 2Kin 25:25
for they were afraid of the C 2Kin 25:26
upon them the king of the C 2Chr 36:17
him forth out of Ur of the C .... Neh 9:7

CHALDEES' (kal'-dees) See CHALDEANS.
the beauty of the C excellency .... Is 13:19

CHALKSTONES
as c that are beaten in sunder .... Is 27:9

CHALLENGETH
thing, which another c to be his .... Ex 22:9

CHAMBER
and he entered into his c, and wept .... Gen 43:30
covereth his feet in his summer c .... Judg 3:24
will go in to my wife into the c .... Judg 15:1
wait, abiding with her in the c .... Judg 16:9
liers in wait abiding in the c .... Judg 16:12
Tamar, Bring the meat into the c 2Sa 13:10
into the c to Amnon her brother 2Sa 13:10
and went up to the c over the gate 2Sa 18:33
went in unto the king into the c 1Kin 1:15
The nethermost c was five cubits 1Kin 6:6
The door for the middle c was in 1Kin 6:8
winding stairs into the middle c 1Kin 6:8
them back into the guard c 1Kin 14:28
down out of the c into the house 1Kin 17:23
into the city, into an inner c 1Kin 20:30
into an inner c to hide thyself 1Kin 22:25
his upper c that was in Samaria 2Kin 1:2
Let us make a little c, I pray 2Kin 4:10
thither, and he turned into the c 2Kin 4:11
and carry him to an inner c 2Kin 9:2
by the c of Nathan-melech the 2Kin 23:11
on the top of the upper c of Ahaz 2Kin 23:12
them again into the guard c 2Chr 12:11
into an inner c to hide thyself 2Chr 18:24
went into the c of Johanan the .... Ezr 10:6
of Berechiah over against his c .... Neh 3:30
of the c of the house of our God .... Neh 13:4
he had prepared for him a great c .... Neh 13:5
in preparing him a c in the .... Neh 13:7
stuff of Tobiah out of the c .... Neh 13:8
a bridegroom coming out of his c .... Ps 19:5
into the c of her that conceived .... Song 3:4
into the c of the sons of Hanan .... Jer 35:4
which was by the c of the princes .... Jer 36:4
which was above the c of Maaseiah ..... Jer 35:4
in the c of Gemariah the son of .... Jer 36:10
king's house, into the scribe's c .... Jer 36:12
in the c of Elishama the scribe's .... Jer 36:12
it out of Elishama the scribe's c .... Jer 36:21
every little c was one reed long .... Eze 40:7
little c to the roof of another .... Eze 40:13
And he said unto me, This c .... Eze 40:45
the c whose prospect is toward .... Eze 40:46
and the breadth of every side c .... Eze 41:5
c to the highest by the midst .... Eze 41:7
which was for the side c without .... Eze 41:9
he brought me into the c that was ...... Eze 42:1
open in his c toward Jerusalem .... Dan 6:10
the bridegroom go forth of his c .... Joel 2:16
they laid her in an upper c .... Acts 9:37
they brought him into the upper c ...... Acts 9:39
were many lights in the upper c .... Acts 20:8

CHAMBERING
rioting and drunkenness, not in c .... Rom 13:13

CHAMBERLAIN
chamber of Nathan-melech the c 2Kin 23:11
the custody of Hege the king's c .... Est 2:3
of Shaashgaz, the king's c .... Est 2:14
but what Hegai the king's c .... Est 2:15
Blastus the king's c their friend .... Acts 12:20
Erastus the c of the city .... Rom 16:23

CHAMBERLAINS
the seven c that served in the .... Est 1:10
the king's commandment by his c .... Est 1:12
of the king Ahasuerus by his c .... Est 1:15
king's gate, two of the king's c .... Est 2:21
her c came and told it her .... Est 4:4
for Hatach, one of the king's c .... Est 4:5
and Teresh, two of the king's c .... Est 6:2
with him, came the king's c .... Est 6:14
and Harbonah, one of the c .... Est 7:9

CHAMBERS
the house he built c round about 1Kin 6:5
and he made c round about 1Kin 6:5
then he built c against all the 1Kin 6:10
set office, and were over the c 1Chr 9:26
who remaining in the c were there 1Chr 9:33
LORD, in the courts, and in the c 1Chr 23:28
and of the upper c thereof 1Chr 28:11
of all the c round about, of the 1Chr 28:12
he overlaid the upper c with gold 2Chr 3:9
c in the house of the LORD 2Chr 31:11
in the c of the house of the LORD .... Ezr 8:29
to the c of the house of our God .... Neh 10:37
the house of our God, to the c .... Neh 10:38
new wine, and the oil, unto the c .... Neh 10:39
over the c for the treasures .... Neh 13:9
commanded, and they cleansed the c .. Neh 13:9
Pleiades, and the c of the south .... Job 9:9
the beams of his c in the waters .... Ps 104:3
He watereth the hills from his c .... Ps 104:13
in the c of their kings .... Ps 105:30

going down to the c of death .... Prov 7:27
by knowledge shall the c be .... Prov 24:4
king hath brought me into his c .... Song 1:4
my people, enter thou into thy c .... Is 26:20
and his c by wrong .... Jer 22:13
build me a wide house and large c ...... Jer 22:14
of the LORD, into one of the c .... Jer 35:2
every man in the c of his imagery .... Eze 8:12
which entereth into their privy c .... Eze 21:14
the little c were five cubits .... Eze 40:7
the little c of the gate eastward .... Eze 40:10
c was one cubit on this side .... Eze 40:12
the little c were six cubits on .... Eze 40:12
narrow windows to the little c .... Eze 40:16
court, and, lo, there were c .... Eze 40:17
thirty c were upon the pavement .... Eze 40:17
the little c thereof were three .... Eze 40:21
And the little c thereof, and the .... Eze 40:29
And the little c thereof, and the .... Eze 40:33
The little c thereof, the posts .... Eze 40:36
And the c and the entries thereof .... Eze 40:38
the c of the singers in the inner .... Eze 40:44
the side c were three, one over .... Eze 41:6
house for the side c round about .... Eze 41:6
about still upward to the side c .... Eze 41:7
the foundations of the side c .... Eze 41:8
of the side c that were within .... Eze 41:9
between the c was the wideness of .... Eze 41:10
the doors of the side c were .... Eze 41:11
and upon the side c of the house .... Eze 41:26
before the c was a walk of ten .... Eze 42:4
Now the upper c were shorter .... Eze 42:5
was without over against the c .... Eze 42:7
court on the foreeart of the c .... Eze 42:7
For the length of the c that were .... Eze 42:8
from under these c was the entry .... Eze 42:9
The c were in the thickness of .... Eze 42:10
the c which were toward the north ..... Eze 42:11
according to the doors of the c .... Eze 42:12
Then said he unto me, The north c ..... Eze 42:13
The north c and the south c .... Eze 42:13
separate place, they be holy c .... Eze 42:13
and lay them in the holy c .... Eze 44:19
for a possession for twenty c .... Eze 45:5
into the holy c of the priests, ... Eze 46:19
behold, he is in the secret c .... Mt 24:26

CHAMELEON
And the ferret, and the c, and the ...... Lev 11:30

CHAMOIS
pygarg, and the wild ox, and the c ...... Deut 14:5

CHAMPAIGN
which dwell in the c over against .... Deut 11:30

CHAMPION
there went out a c out of the 1Sa 17:4
them, behold, there came up the c 1Sa 17:23
Philistines saw their c was dead 1Sa 17:51

CHANAAN (ka'-na-un) See CANAAN. *Greek form of Canaan.*
over all the land of Egypt and C, ... Acts 7:11
seven nations in the land of C .... Acts 13:19

CHANCE
If a bird's nest c to be before .... Deut 22:6
it was a c that happened to us 1Sa 6:9
As I happened by c upon mount 2Sa 1:6
time and c happeneth to them all .... Eccl 9:11
by c there came down a certain .... Lk 10:31
it may c of wheat, or of some 1Cor 15:37

CHANCELLOR
Rehum the c and Shimshai the .... Ezr 4:8
Then wrote Rehum the c, and .... Ezr 4:9
king an answer unto Rehum the c .... Ezr 4:17

CHANCETH
uncleanness that c him by night .... Deut 23:10

CHANGE
and be clean, and c your garments ...... Gen 35:2
He shall not alter it, nor c it .... Lev 27:10
he shall at all c beast for beast .... Lev 27:10
or bad, neither shall he c it .... Lev 27:33
if he c it at all, then both it .... Lev 27:33
the c thereof shall be holy .... Lev 27:33
sheets and thirty c of garments .... Judg 14:12
sheets and thirty c of garments .... Judg 14:13
gave c of garments unto them .... Judg 14:19
time will I wait, till my c come .... Job 14:14
They c the night into day .... Job 17:12
as a vesture shalt thou c them .... Ps 102:26
not with them that are given to c ...... Prov 24:21
but we will c them into cedars .... Is 9:10
thou about so much to c thy way .... Jer 2:36
Can the Ethiopian c his skin .... Jer 13:23
most High, and think to c times .... Dan 7:25
therefore will I c their glory .... Hos 4:7
That which they did mind, and he ..... Hab 1:11
clothe thee with c of raiment .... Zec 3:4
For I am the LORD, I c not .... Mal 3:6
shall c the customs which Moses ...... Acts 6:14
for even their women did c the .... Rom 1:26
with you now, and to c my voice .... Gal 4:20
Who shall c our vile body, that .... Phil 3:21
of necessity a c also of the law .... Heb 7:12

CHANGEABLE
The c suits of apparel, and the .... Is 3:22

CHANGED
me, and c my wages ten times .... Gen 31:7
thou hast c my wages ten times .... Gen 31:41

C

c his raiment, and came in unto........ Gen 41:14
be c unto white, he shall come............ Lev 13:16
the plague have not c his colour........ Lev 13:55
Baal-meon, (their names being c........ Num 32:38
he c his behaviour before them, ... 1Sa 21:13
c his apparel, and came into the....... 2Sa 12:20
stead, and c his name to Zedekiah.... 2Kin 24:17
And c his prison garments.............. 2Kin 25:29
of my disease is my garment c........ Job 30:18
when he c his behaviour before....... Ps 34:t
change them, and they shall be c...... Ps 102:26
Thus they c their glory into the....... Ps 106:20
boldness of his face shall be c........ Eccl 8:1
c the ordinance, broken the............ Is 24:5
Hath a nation c their gods............... Jer 2:11
but my people have c their glory...... Jer 2:11
he, and his scent is not c.............. Jer 48:11
And c his prison garments.............. Jer 52:33
how is the most fine gold c........... Lam 4:1
she hath c my judgments into........ Eze 5:6
before me, till the time be c.......... Dan 2:9
his visage was c against Shadrach.. Dan 3:19
neither were their coats c............. Dan 3:27
have c the king's word, and........... Dan 3:28
Let his heart be c from man's........ Dan 4:16
Then the king's countenance was.. Dan 5:6
and his countenance was c in him .. Dan 5:9
nor let thy countenance be c......... Dan 5:10
the writing, that it be not c........... Dan 6:8
the king establisheth may be c...... Dan 6:15
might not be c concerning Daniel.... Dan 6:17
me, and my countenance c in me .... Dan 7:28
he hath c the portion of my........... Mic 2:4
they c their minds, and said that.... Acts 28:6
c the glory of the uncorruptible...... Rom 1:23
Who c the truth of God into a lie .... Rom 1:25
all sleep, but we shall all be c....... 1Cor 15:51
incorruptible, and we shall be c..... 1Cor 15:52
are c into the same image from...... 2Cor 3:18
fold them up, and they shall be c.... Heb 1:12
For the priesthood being c............ Heb 7:12

CHANGERS
doves, and the c of money sitting.... Jn 2:14

CHANGERS'
and poured out the c money............ Jn 2:15

CHANGES
he gave each man c of raiment........ Gen 45:22
of silver, and five c of raiment....... Gen 45:22
of gold, and ten c of raiment.......... 2Kin 5:5
of silver, and two c of garments..... 2Kin 5:23
with two c of garments, and laid..... 2Kin 5:23
c and war are against me............... Job 10:17
Because they have no c, therefore .. Ps 55:19

CHANGEST
thou c his countenance, and.......... Job 14:20

CHANGETH
to his own hurt, and c not.............. Ps 15:4
he c the times and the seasons ..... Dan 2:21

CHANGING
redeeming and concerning c........... Ruth 4:7

CHANNEL
LORD shall beat off from the c of..... Is 27:12

CHANNELS
the c of the sea appeared, the........ 2Sa 22:16
Then the c of waters were seen, ... Ps 18:15
he shall come up over all his c....... Is 8:7

CHANT
That c to the sound of the viol, ... Amos 6:5

CHAPEL
for it is the king's c, and it is........ Amos 7:13

CHAPITER
of the one c was five cubits............ 1Kin 7:16
of the other c was five cubits......... 1Kin 7:16
seven for the one c........................ 1Kin 7:17
and seven for the other c.............. 1Kin 7:17
and so did he for the other c.......... 1Kin 7:18
rows round about upon the other c.. 1Kin 7:18
And the mouth of it within the c 1Kin 7:31
and the c upon it was brass........... 2Kin 25:17
the height of the c three cubits 2Kin 25:17
upon the c round about, all of........ 2Kin 25:17
the c that was on the top of each 2Chr 3:15
And a c of brass was upon it.......... Jer 52:22
height of one c was five cubits....... Jer 52:22

CHAPITERS
and he overlaid their c and their..... Ex 36:38
overlaying of their c of silver......... Ex 38:17
and the overlaying of their c.......... Ex 38:19
the pillars, and overlaid their c...... Ex 38:28
he made two c of molten brass, to .. 1Kin 7:16
for the c which were upon the top ... 1Kin 7:17
to cover the c that were upon the ... 1Kin 7:18
that were upon the top of............... 1Kin 7:19
the c upon the two pillars had........ 1Kin 7:20
the two bowls of the c that were..... 1Kin 7:41
to cover the two bowls of the c....... 1Kin 7:41
the c that were upon the pillars...... 1Kin 7:41
the c which were on the top of........ 2Chr 4:12
c which were on the top of the........ 2Chr 4:12
the c which were upon the pillars.... 2Chr 4:13
upon the c round about, all of........ Jer 52:22

CHAPMEN
Beside that which c and merchants.. 2Chr 9:14

CHAPT
Because the ground is c, for............ Jer 14:4

CHARASHIM (car'-a-shim) Place founded by Joab.
the father of the valley of c............ 1Chr 4:14

CHARCHEMISH (car'-ke-mish) See CARCHEMISH. Same as Carchemish.
to fight against C by Euphrates....... 2Chr 35:20

CHARGE
obeyed my voice, and kept my c...... Gen 26:5
as he blessed him he gave him a c... Gen 28:6
gave them a c unto the children ...... Gen 49:29
c the people, lest they break............ Ex 19:21
keep the c of the LORD, that ye........ Lev 8:35
the Levites shall keep the c of........ Num 1:53
And they shall keep his c, and the .. Num 3:7
the c of the whole congregation ..... Num 3:7
the c of the children of Israel, ... Num 3:8
the c of the sons of Gershon in....... Num 3:25
keeping the c of the sanctuary ...... Num 3:28
their c shall be the ark, and the...... Num 3:31
that keep the c of the sanctuary .... Num 3:32
c of the sons of Merari shall be...... Num 3:36
keeping the c of the sanctuary ...... Num 3:38
the c of the children of Israel .... Num 3:38
unto them in a c all their burdens .. Num 4:27
their c shall be under the hand ...... Num 4:31
this is the c of their burden, ... Num 4:31
of the c of their burden................. Num 4:32
the priest shall c her by an oath ..... Num 5:19
Then the priest shall c the woman .. Num 5:21
the congregation, to keep the c...... Num 8:26
unto the Levites touching their c .... Num 8:26
of Israel kept the c of the LORD, ... Num 9:19
they kept the c of the LORD........... Num 9:23
And they shall keep my c, and the .. Num 18:3
the c of all the tabernacle .... Num 18:3
keep the c of the tabernacle of ..... Num 18:4
shall keep the c of the sanctuary .. Num 18:5
sanctuary, and the c of the altar.... Num 18:5
I also have given thee the c of........ Num 18:8
give him a c in their sight .... Num 27:19
hands upon him, and gave him a c.. Num 27:23
Levites, which keep the c of the .... Num 31:30
Levites, which kept the c of the ..... Num 31:47
men of war which are under our c .. Num 31:49
but Joshua, and encourage him, ... Deut 3:28
the LORD thy God, and keep his c .. Deut 11:1
unto thy people of Israel's c.......... Deut 21:8
that I may give him a c................... Deut 31:14
he gave Joshua the son of Nun a c.. Deut 31:23
but have kept the c of the .... Josh 22:3
I will give c concerning these......... 2Sa 14:8
the captains c concerning Absalom.. 2Sa 18:5
keep the c of the LORD thy God, ... 1Kin 2:3
every man according to his c.......... 1Kin 4:28
all the c of the house of Joseph...... 1Kin 11:28
leaned to have c of the gate........... 2Kin 7:17
because the c was upon them, and.. 1Chr 9:27
certain of them had the c of the 1Chr 9:31
give thee c concerning Israel, ... 1Chr 22:12
the c of the tabernacle of the 1Chr 23:32
the c of the holy place, and the 1Chr 23:32
the c of the sons of Aaron their 1Chr 23:32
for we keep the c of the LORD our .. 2Chr 13:11
therefore the Levites had the c of .. 2Chr 30:17
of the palace, c over Jerusalem...... Neh 7:2
to ourselves yearly with the .... Neh 10:32
that have the c of the business...... Est 3:9
to c her that she should go in......... Est 4:8
hath given him a c over the earth.... Job 34:13
they laid to my c things that I .... Ps 35:11
shall give his angels c over their .... Ps 91:11
I c you, O ye daughters of............... Song 2:7
I c you, O ye daughters of............... Song 3:5
I c you, O daughters of Jerusalem.. Song 5:8
beloved, that thou dost so c us....... Song 5:9
I c you, O daughters of Jerusalem.. Song 8:4
of my wrath will I give him a c........ Is 10:6
king of Babylon gave c concerning.. Jer 39:11
given it a c against Ashkelon........... Jer 47:7
which had the c of the men of war .. Jer 52:25
Cause them that have c over the .... Eze 9:1
the keepers of the c of the house.... Eze 40:46
the keepers of the c of the altar..... Eze 40:46
kept the c of mine holy things........ Eze 44:8
but ye have set keepers of my c...... Eze 44:8
having c at the gates of the .... Eze 44:11
keepers of the c of the house......... Eze 44:14
that kept the c of my sanctuary ..... Eze 44:15
unto me, and they shall keep my c .. Eze 44:16
which have kept my c, which went... Eze 48:11
ways, and if thou wilt keep my c .... Zec 3:7
give his angels c concerning thee... Mt 4:6
I c thee, come out of him, and........ Mk 9:25
shall give his angels c over thee .... Lk 4:10
Lord, lay not this sin to their c .... Acts 7:60
who had the c of all her treasure ... Acts 8:27
Who, having received such a c....... Acts 16:24
his c worthy of death or of bonds ... Acts 23:29
any thing to the c of God's elect..... Rom 8:33
the gospel of Christ without c......... 1Cor 9:18
I c you by the Lord that this 1Th 5:27
that thou mightest c some that 1Ti 1:3
This c I commit unto thee, son........ 1Ti 1:18
And these things give in c............. 1Ti 5:7

I c thee before God, and the Lord.... 1Ti 5:21
I give thee c in the sight of God 1Ti 6:13
C them that are rich in this 1Ti 6:17
I c thee therefore before God, and.. 2Ti 4:1
it may not be laid to their c............ 2Ti 4:16

CHARGEABLE
now go, lest we be c unto thee........ 2Sa 13:25
before me were c unto the people ... Neh 5:15
you, and wanted, I was c to no man.. 2Cor 11:9
we would not be c unto any of you .. 1Th 2:9
we might not be c to any of you....... 2Th 3:8

CHARGED
Abimelech c all his people,............. Gen 26:11
c him, and said unto him, Thou........ Gen 28:1
of the guard c Joseph with them...... Gen 40:4
he c them, and said unto them, I .... Gen 49:29
Pharaoh c all his people, saying, ... Ex 1:22
I c your judges at that time,............ Deut 1:16
shall he be c with any business ..... Deut 24:5
Moses c the people the same day... Deut 27:11
Joshua c them that went to .... Josh 8:8
the servant of the LORD c you .... Josh 22:5
have I not c the young men that ...... Ruth 2:9
father c the people with the oath 1Sa 14:27
Thy father straitly c the people 1Sa 14:28
the messenger, saying, When 1Sa 11:19
in our hearing the king c thee 2Sa 18:12
he c Solomon his son, saying,......... 1Kin 2:1
that I have c thee with 1Kin 2:43
For so was it c me by the word of 1Kin 13:9
whom the LORD had c them, that 2Kin 17:15
c them, saying, Ye shall not fear 2Kin 17:35
c him to build an house for the 1Chr 22:6
judgments which the LORD c Moses.. 1Chr 22:13
he c them, saying, Thus shall ye 2Chr 19:9
he hath c me to build him an 2Chr 36:23
he hath c me to build him an .... Ezr 1:2
that they should not be opened...... Neh 13:19
for Mordecai had c her that she ..... Est 2:10
as Mordecai had c .... Est 2:20
sinned not, nor c God foolishly ...... Job 1:22
and his angels he c with folly .... Job 4:18
c Baruch before them, saying, ... Jer 32:13
father in all that he hath c us......... Jer 35:8
and Jesus straitly c them, saying, .. Mt 9:30
c them that they should not make... Mt 12:16
Then he his disciples that they ...... Mt 16:20
from the mountain, Jesus c them.... Mt 17:9
And he straitly c him, and.............. Mk 1:43
he straitly c them that they .... Mk 3:12
he c them straitly that no man........ Mk 5:43
he c them that they should tell....... Mk 7:36
but the more he c them, so much.... Mk 7:36
he c them, saying, Take heed, ... Mk 8:15
he c them that they should tell....... Mk 8:30
he c them that they should tell....... Mk 9:9
many c him that he should hold ..... Mk 10:48
And he c them to tell no man .... Lk 5:14
but he c them that they should ...... Lk 8:56
And he straitly c them, and............ Lk 9:21
c him, See thou tell no man that ..... Acts 23:22
c every one of you, as a father........ 1Th 2:11
them, and let not the church be c.... 1Ti 5:16

CHARGEDST
for thou c us, saying, Set bounds.... Ex 19:23

CHARGER
And his offering was one silver c .... Num 7:13
for his offering one silver c............ Num 7:19
His offering was one silver c .... Num 7:25
c of the weight of an hundred......... Num 7:31
His offering was one silver c .... Num 7:37
c of the weight of an hundred......... Num 7:43
His offering was one silver c .... Num 7:49
c of the weight of an hundred......... Num 7:55
His offering was one silver c .... Num 7:61
His offering was one silver c .... Num 7:67
His offering was one silver c .... Num 7:73
His offering was one silver c .... Num 7:79
Each c of silver weighing an .... Num 7:85
here John Baptist's head in a c....... Mt 14:8
And his head was brought in a c...... Mt 14:11
by in a c the head of John the......... Mk 6:25
And brought his head in a c............ Mk 6:28

CHARGERS
twelve c of silver, twelve silver...... Num 7:84
thirty c of gold, a thousand............ Ezr 1:9
of gold, a thousand c of silver........ Ezr 1:9

CHARGES
and the Levites to their c............... 2Chr 8:14
c according to their courses 2Chr 31:16
in their c by their courses 2Chr 35:2
And he set the priests in their c 2Chr 35:2
be at c with them, that they may .... Acts 21:24
a warfare any time at his own c 1Cor 9:7

CHARGEST
that thou c me to day with a 2Sa 3:8

CHARGING
the jailer to keep them safely,........ Acts 16:23
c them before the Lord that they..... 2Ti 2:14

CHARIOT
ride in the second c which he had ... Gen 41:43
And Joseph made ready his c .... Gen 46:29
And he made ready his c, and took... Ex 14:6
And took off their c wheels............. Ex 14:25
Sisera lighted down off his c .... Judg 4:15

CHARIOTS (continued)

Why is his c so long in coming...... Judg 5:28
and David houghed all the c horses...... 2Sa 8:4
was like the work of a wheel...... 1Kin 7:33
a c came up and went out of Egypt.. 1Kin 10:29
made speed to get him up to his c...... 1Kin 12:18
up, say unto Ahab, Prepare thy c...... 1Kin 18:44
horse for horse, and c for c...... 1Kin 20:25
horse for horse, and c for c...... 1Kin 20:25
caused him to come up into the c...... 1Kin 20:33
he said unto the driver of his c...... 1Kin 22:34
up in his c against the Syrians...... 1Kin 22:35
he said unto the midst of the c...... 1Kin 22:35
one washed the c in the pool of...... 1Kin 22:38
there appeared a c of fire...... 2Kin 2:11
the c of Israel, and the horsemen...... 2Kin 2:12
with his horses and with his c...... 2Kin 5:9
down from the c to meet him...... 2Kin 5:21
again from his c to meet thee...... 2Kin 5:26
They took therefore two c horses...... 2Kin 7:14
So Jehu rode in a c, and went to...... 2Kin 9:16
And his c was made ready...... 2Kin 9:21
of Judah went out, each in his c...... 2Kin 9:21
heart, and he sunk down in his c...... 2Kin 9:24
and said, Smite him also in the c...... 2Kin 9:27
carried him in a c to Jerusalem...... 2Kin 9:28
he took him up to him into the c...... 2Kin 10:15
So they made him ride in his c...... 2Kin 10:16
the c of Israel, and the horsemen...... 2Kin 13:14
him in a c dead from Megiddo...... 2Kin 23:30
also houghed all the c horses...... 1Chr 18:4
pattern of the c of the cherubims.. 1Chr 28:18
which he placed in the c cities...... 2Chr 1:14
a c for six hundred shekels of...... 2Chr 1:17
Solomon had, and all the c cities...... 2Chr 8:6
whom he bestowed in the c cities...... 2Chr 9:25
made speed to get him up to his c .. 2Chr 10:18
therefore he said to his c man...... 2Chr 18:33
c against the Syrians until the...... 2Chr 18:34
therefore took him out of that c...... 2Chr 35:24
him in the second c that he had...... 2Chr 35:24
he burneth the c in the fire...... Ps 46:9
O God of Jacob, both the c...... Ps 76:6
who maketh the clouds his c...... Ps 104:3
a c of the wood of Lebanon...... Song 3:9
in c with a couple of...... Is 21:7
a c of asses, and a c of...... Is 21:7
behold, here cometh a c of men...... Is 21:9
Which bringeth forth the c...... Is 43:17
thee will I break in pieces the c...... Jer 51:21
bind the c to the swift beast...... Mic 1:13
In the first c were red horses...... Zec 6:2
and in the second c black horses... Zec 6:2
And in the third c white horses...... Zec 6:3
and in the fourth c grisled...... Zec 6:3
I will cut off the c from Ephraim... Zec 9:10
sitting in his c read Esaias the...... Acts 8:28
near, and join thyself to this c...... Acts 8:29
he commanded the c to stand still... Acts 8:38

CHARIOTS

And there went up with him both c.. Gen 50:9
And he took six hundred chosen c.... Ex 14:7
all the c of Egypt, and captains.... Ex 14:7
c of Pharaoh, and his horsemen, and... Ex 14:9
and upon all his host, upon his c.... Ex 14:17
honour upon Pharaoh, upon his c.... Ex 14:18
even all Pharaoh's horses, his c...... Ex 14:23
upon the Egyptians, upon their c.... Ex 14:26
waters returned, and covered the c... Ex 14:28
Pharaoh's c and his host hath he...... Ex 15:4
of Pharaoh went in with his c...... Ex 15:19
unto their horses, and to their c...... Deut 11:4
enemies, and save horses, and c.... Deut 20:1
with horses and a very many...... Josh 11:4
horses, and burn their c with fire... Josh 11:6
and burnt their c with fire...... Josh 11:9
land of the valley have c of iron...... Josh 17:16
though they have iron c, and...... Josh 17:18
pursued after your fathers with c.... Josh 24:6
because they had c of iron...... Judg 1:19
for he had nine hundred c of iron.... Judg 4:3
of Jabin's army, with his c...... Judg 4:7
gathered together all his c...... Judg 4:13
even nine hundred c of iron...... Judg 4:13
discomfited Sisera, and all his c...... Judg 4:15
But Barak pursued after the c...... Judg 4:16
Why tarry the wheels of his c...... Judg 5:28
them for himself, and c...... 1Sa 8:11
and some shall run before his c...... 1Sa 8:11
of war, and instruments of his c...... 1Sa 8:12
with Israel, thirty thousand c...... 1Sa 13:5
and, lo, the c and horsemen...... 2Sa 1:6
David took from him a thousand c..... 2Sa 8:4
reserved of them for an hundred c... 2Sa 8:4
of seven hundred c of the Syrians... 2Sa 10:18
this, that Absalom prepared him c... 2Sa 15:1
and he prepared him c and horsemen... 1Kin 1:5
stalls of horses for his c...... 1Kin 4:26
Solomon had, and cities for his c..... 1Kin 9:19
his captains, and rulers for his c...... 1Kin 9:22
And Solomon gathered together c...... 1Kin 10:26
had a thousand and four hundred c... 1Kin 10:26
he bestowed in the cities for c...... 1Kin 10:26
Zimri, captain of half his c...... 1Kin 16:9
kings with him, and horses, and c.... 1Kin 20:1
out, and smote the horses and c..... 1Kin 20:21
captains that had rule over his c... 1Kin 22:31
captains of the c saw Jehoshaphat... 1Kin 22:32
when the captains of the c...... 1Kin 22:33
sent he thither horses, and c...... 2Kin 6:14
the city both with horses and c...... 2Kin 6:15

c of fire round about Elisha...... 2Kin 6:17
the Syrians to hear a noise of c.... 2Kin 7:6
to Zair, and all the c with him...... 2Kin 8:21
about, and the captains of the c...... 2Kin 8:21
with you, and there are with you c ... 2Kin 10:2
but fifty horsemen, and ten c...... 2Kin 13:7
and put thy trust on Egypt for c...... 2Kin 18:24
With the multitude of my c I am...... 2Kin 19:23
burned the c of the sun with fire... 2Kin 23:11
David took from him a thousand c... 1Chr 18:4
but reserved of them an hundred c... 1Chr 18:4
talents of silver to hire them c...... 1Chr 19:6
hired thirty and two thousand c...... 1Chr 19:7
thousand men which fought in c...... 1Chr 19:18
And Solomon gathered c...... 2Chr 1:14
had a thousand and four hundred c ... 2Chr 1:14
captains, and captains of his c...... 2Chr 8:9
thousand stalls for horses and c...... 2Chr 9:25
With twelve hundred c, and...... 2Chr 12:3
thousand, and three hundred c...... 2Chr 14:9
a huge host, with very many c...... 2Chr 16:8
of the c that were with him...... 2Chr 18:30
captains of the c saw Jehoshaphat... 2Chr 18:31
when the captains of the c...... 2Chr 18:32
princes, and all his c with him...... 2Chr 18:32
him in, and the captains of the c...... 2Chr 21:9
Some trust in c, and some in...... Ps 20:7
The c of God are twenty thousand... Ps 68:17
company of horses in Pharaoh's c... Song 1:9
made me like the c of Ammi-nadib.. Song 6:12
is there any end of their c...... Is 2:7
bare the quiver with c of men...... Is 22:6
valleys shall be full of c...... Is 22:7
there the c of thy glory shall be... Is 22:18
and stay on horses, and trust in...... Is 31:1
and put thy trust on Egypt for c...... Is 36:9
By the multitude of my c am I...... Is 37:24
with his c like a whirlwind, to...... Is 66:15
all nations upon horses, and in c... Is 66:20
his c shall be as a whirlwind...... Jer 4:13
the throne of David, riding in c...... Jer 17:25
the throne of David, riding in c...... Jer 22:4
and rage, ye c...... Jer 46:9
horses, at the rushing of his c...... Jer 47:3
their horses, and upon their c...... Jer 50:37
shall come against thee with c...... Eze 23:24
the north, with horses, and with c.. Eze 26:7
and of the wheels, and of the c...... Eze 26:10
in precious clothes for c...... Eze 27:20
at my table with horses and c...... Eze 39:20
him like a whirlwind, with c...... Dan 11:40
Like the noise of c on the tops...... Joel 2:5
of thee, and I will destroy thy c...... Mic 5:10
shall rage in the flaming...... Nah 2:3
The c shall rage in the streets...... Nah 2:4
and I will burn her c in the smoke... Nah 2:13
horses, and the jumping c...... Nah 3:2
horses and thy c of salvation...... Hab 3:8
that came four c out from...... Zec 6:1
of c of many horses running to...... Rev 9:9
beasts, and sheep, and horses, and c.. Rev 18:13

CHARITABLY

thy meat, now walkest thou not c.... Rom 14:15

CHARITY

puffeth up, but c edifieth...... 1Cor 8:1
men and of angels, and have not c... 1Cor 13:1
remove mountains, and have not c... 1Cor 13:2
body to be burned, and have not c... 1Cor 13:3
C suffereth long, and is kind...... 1Cor 13:4
c envieth not...... 1Cor 13:4
c vaunteth not itself, is not...... 1Cor 13:4
C never faileth...... 1Cor 13:8
And now abideth faith, hope, c...... 1Cor 13:13
but the greatest of these is c...... 1Cor 13:13
Follow after c, and desire...... 1Cor 14:1
all your things be done with c...... 1Cor 16:14
above all these things put on c...... Col 3:14
good tidings of your faith and c...... 1Th 3:6
the c of every one of you all...... 2Th 1:3
is c out of a pure heart, and of a... 1Ti 1:5
if they continue in faith and c...... 1Ti 2:15
in word, in conversation, in c...... 1Ti 4:12
follow righteousness, faith, c...... 2Ti 2:22
purpose, faith, longsuffering, c...... 2Ti 3:10
temperate, sound in faith, in c...... Titus 2:2
have fervent c among yourselves... 1Pet 4:8
for c shall cover the multitude...... 1Pet 4:8
ye one another with a kiss of c...... 1Pet 5:14
and to brotherly kindness c...... 2Pet 1:7
of thy c before the church...... 3Jn 6
are spots in your feasts of c...... Jude 12
I know thy works, and c, and...... Rev 2:19

CHARMED

among you, which will not be c...... Jer 8:17

CHARMER

Or a c, or a consulter with...... Deut 18:11

CHARMERS

hearken to the voice of c...... Ps 58:5
seek to the idols, and to the c...... Is 19:3

CHARMING

of charmers, c never so wisely...... Ps 58:5

CHARRAN (car'-ran) See HARAN. Greek form
of Haran.

Mesopotamia, before he dwelt in C.... Acts 7:2
of the Chaldaeans, and dwelt in C.... Acts 7:4

CHASE

ye shall c your enemies, and they... Lev 26:7
And five of you shall c an hundred... Lev 26:8
of a shaken leaf shall c them...... Lev 26:36
How should one c a thousand...... Deut 32:30
One man of you shall c a thousand... Josh 23:10
let the angel of the LORD c them... Ps 35:5

CHASED

c you, as bees do, and destroyed... Deut 1:44
for they c them before the...... Josh 7:5
wilderness wherein they c them..... Josh 8:24
c them along the way that goeth... Josh 10:10
c them unto great Zidon, and unto.. Josh 11:8
And Abimelech c him, and he fled... Judg 9:40
c them, and trode them down with... Judg 20:43
therefore I c him from me...... Neh 13:28
darkness, and c out of the world... Job 18:18
he shall be c away as a vision of... Job 20:8
And it shall be as the c roe...... Is 13:14
shall be c as the chaff of the...... Is 17:13
Mine enemies c me sore, like a...... Lam 3:52

CHASETH

c away his mother, is a son that... Prov 19:26

CHASING

from c after the Philistines...... 1Sa 17:53

CHASTE

you as a c virgin to Christ...... 2Cor 11:2
To be discreet, c, keepers at...... Titus 2:5
While they behold your c...... 1Pet 3:2

CHASTEN

I will c him with the rod of men,... 2Sa 7:14
anger, neither c me in thy hot...... Ps 6:1
neither c me in thy hot...... Ps 38:1
C thy son while there is hope, and... Prov 19:18
to c thyself before thy God, thy.... Dan 10:12
As many as I love, I rebuke and c... Rev 3:19

CHASTENED

and that, when they have c him..... Deut 21:18
He is c also with pain upon his..... Job 33:19
c my soul with fasting, that was... Ps 69:10
been plagued, and c every morning.. Ps 73:14
The LORD hath c me sore...... Ps 118:18
we are c of the Lord, that we...... 1Cor 11:32
as c, and not killed...... 2Cor 6:9
c us after their own pleasure...... Heb 12:10

CHASTENEST

Blessed is the man whom thou c..... Ps 94:12

CHASTENETH

heart, that, as a man c his son..... Deut 8:5
son, so the LORD thy God c thee... Deut 8:5
he that loveth him c him betimes... Prov 13:24
For whom the Lord loveth he c...... Heb 12:6
son is he whom the father c not..... Heb 12:7

CHASTENING

not thou the c of the Almighty...... Job 5:17
despise not the c of the LORD...... Prov 3:11
a prayer when thy c was upon them.. Is 26:16
not thou the c of the Lord...... Heb 12:5
If ye endure c, God dealeth with... Heb 12:7
Now no c for the present seemeth... Heb 12:11

CHASTISE

will c you seven times for your...... Lev 26:28
city shall take that man and c him... Deut 22:18
but I will c you with scorpions...... 1Kin 12:11
but I will c you with scorpions...... 1Kin 12:14
but I will c you with scorpions...... 2Chr 10:11
but I will c you with scorpions...... 2Chr 10:14
I will c them, as their...... Hos 7:12
in my desire that I should c them.. Hos 10:10
I will therefore c him, and...... Lk 23:16
I will therefore c him, and let...... Lk 23:22

CHASTISED

my father hath c you with whips... 1Kin 12:11
my father also c you with whips.... 1Kin 12:14
my father c you with whips, but I... 2Chr 10:11
my father c you with whips, but I... 2Chr 10:14
hast c me, and I was c...... Jer 31:18

CHASTISEMENT

seen the c of the LORD your God... Deut 11:2
be said unto God, I have borne c... Job 34:31
the c of our peace was upon him... Is 53:5
with the c of a cruel one, for...... Jer 30:14
But if ye be without c, whereof.... Heb 12:8

CHASTISETH

He that c the heathen, shall not..... Ps 94:10

CHATTER

a crane or a swallow, so did I c...... Is 38:14

CHEBAR (ke'-bar) A river in Mesopotamia.

the captives by the river of C...... Eze 1:1
of the Chaldeans by the river C...... Eze 1:3
that dwelt by the river of C...... Eze 3:15
which I saw by the river of C...... Eze 3:23
that I saw by the river of C...... Eze 10:15
God of Israel by the river of C...... Eze 10:20
vision that I saw by the river C.... Eze 43:3

CHECK

I have heard the c of my reproach.. Job 20:3

CHECKER

And nets of c work, and wreaths of.. 1Kin 7:17

CHEDORLAOMER (ke'-dor-la'-o-mer) An
Elamite king.

C king of Elam, and Tidal king of.. Gen 14:1

C

Twelve years they served C .... Gen 14:4
And in the fourteenth year came C ...... Gen 14:5
With C the king of Elam, and with ...... Gen 14:9
return from the slaughter of C .... Gen 14:17

CHEEK
near, and smote Micaiah on the c 1Kin 22:24
near, and smote Micaiah upon the c 2Chr 18:23
he upon the c reproachfully .... Job 16:10
all mine enemies upon the c bone .... Ps 3:7
He giveth his c to him that .... Lam 3:30
he hath the c teeth of a great .... Joel 1:6
of Israel with a rod upon the c .... Mic 5:1
shall smite thee on thy right c .... Mt 5:39
on the one c offer also the other .... Lk 6:29

CHEEKS
priest the shoulder, and the two c ...... Deut 18:3
Thy c are comely with rows of .... Song 1:10
His c are as a bed of spices, as .... Song 5:13
my c to them that plucked off the ...... Is 50:6
night, and her tears are on her c .... Lam 1:2

CHEER
shall c up his wife which he hath ...... Deut 24:5
let thy heart c thee in the days .... Eccl 11:9
Son, be of good c .... Mt 9:2
unto them, saying, Be of good c .... Mt 14:27
and saith unto them, Be of good c ...... Mk 6:50
but be of good c .... Jn 16:33
by him, and said, Be of good c .... Acts 23:11
now I exhort you to be of good c .... Acts 27:22
Wherefore, sirs, be of good c .... Acts 27:25
Then were they all of good c .... Acts 27:36

CHEERETH
I leave my wine, which c God .... Judg 9:13

CHEERFUL
heart maketh a countenance .... Prov 15:13
joy and gladness, and c feasts .... Zec 8:19
corn shall make the young men c .... Zec 9:17
for God loveth a c giver 2Cor 9:7

CHEERFULLY
I do the more c answer for myself ...... Acts 24:10

CHEERFULNESS
he that sheweth mercy, with c .... Rom 12:8

CHEESE
c of kine, for David, and for the 2Sa 17:29
out as milk, and curdled me like c ...... Job 10:10

CHEESES
carry these ten c unto the 1Sa 17:18

CHELAL (ke′-lal) Married a foreign wife in exile.
Adna, and Chelal, Maaseiah, ... Ezr 10:30

CHELLUH (kel′-loo) Married a foreign wife in exile.
Benaiah, Bedeiah, C, ... Ezr 10:35

CHELUB (ke′-lub)
1. A descendant of Caleb.
C the brother of Shuah begat 1Chr 4:11
2. Father of Ezri.
the ground was Ezri the son of C 1Chr 27:26

CHELUBAI (ke-loo′-bahee) Son of Hezron.
Jerahmeel, and Ram, and C, ... 1Chr 2:9

CHELUH See CHELLUH.

CHELUHI See CHELLUH.

CHEMARIMS (kem′-a-rims) Idolatrous priests of Judah.
the name of the C with the .... Zeph 1:4

CHEMOSH (ke′-mosh) A Moabite god.
thou art undone, O people of C .... Num 21:29
not thou possess that which C thy ...... Judg 11:24
Solomon build an high place for C 1Kin 11:7
C the god of the Moabites, and.......... 1Kin 11:33
for C the abomination of the 2Kin 23:13
C shall go forth into captivity .... Jer 48:7
And Moab shall be ashamed of C ...... Jer 48:13
the people of C perisheth.................. Jer 48:46

CHENAANAH (ken-a-a′-nah)
1. Father of Zedekiah.
Zedekiah the son of C made him 1Kin 22:11
Zedekiah the son of C went near 1Kin 22:24
Zedekiah the son of C had made 2Chr 18:10
Zedekiah the son of C came near 2Chr 18:23
2. Brother of Ehud.
Benjamin, and Ehud, and C, ... 1Chr 7:10

CHENANI (ken′-a-ni) A Levite helper of Ezra.
Bunni, Sherebiah, Bani, and C, ... Neh 9:4

CHENANIAH (ken-a-ni′-ah) See CONONIAH.
1. A chief Levite during David's reign.
And C, chief of the Levites, was........ 1Chr 15:22
C the master of the song with the 1Chr 15:27
2. An officer in David's army.
Of the Izharites, C and his sons 1Chr 26:29

CHEPHAR-AMMONI See CHEPHAR-HAAMMONAI.

CHEPHAR-HAAMMONAI (ke′-far-ha-am′-mo-nahee) A town in Benjamin.
And C, and Ophni, and Gaba .... Josh 18:24

CHEPHIRAH (ke-fi′-rah) A Hittite village in Benjamin.
their cities were Gibeon, and C.......... Josh 9:17

And Mizpeh, and C, and Mozah,........ Josh 18:26
The children of Kirjath-arim, C .... Ezr 2:25
The men of Kirjath-jearim, C .... Neh 7:29

CHERAN (ke′-ran) Son of Dishon.
and Eshban, and Ithran, and C .... Gen 36:26
Eshban, and Ithran, and C, ... 1Chr 1:41

CHERETHIMS (ker′-e-thims) See CHERETHITES. A Philistine tribe.
and I will cut off the C, and .... Eze 25:16

CHERETHITES (ker′-e-thites) See CHERETHIMS.
1. Same as Cherethims.
invasion upon the south of the C........ 1Sa 30:14
sea coast, the nation of the C .... Zeph 2:5
2. Executioners and runners in David's army.
of Jehoiada was over both the C 2Sa 8:18
and all the C, and all the 2Sa 15:18
after him Joab's men, and the C 2Sa 20:7
the son of Jehoiada was over the C 2Sa 20:23
the son of Jehoiada, was over the C 1Kin 1:38
the son of Jehoiada was over the 1Kin 1:44
son of Jehoiada was over the C 1Chr 18:17

CHERISH
before the king, and let her c him 1Kin 1:2

CHERISHED
c the king, and ministered to him 1Kin 1:4

CHERISHETH
c it, even as the Lord the church........ Eph 5:29
even as a nurse c her children............ 1Th 2:7

CHERITH (ke′-rith) A brook in Gilead.
and hide thyself by the brook C 1Kin 17:3
he went and dwelt by the brook C 1Kin 17:5

CHERUB (ke′-rub)
1. A winged celestial being.
make one c on the one end, and the .... Ex 25:19
the other c on the other end. .... Ex 25:19
One c on the one end side, and .... Ex 37:8
another c on the other end on............ Ex 37:8
And he rode upon a c, and did fly 2Sa 22:11
cubits was the one wing of the c 1Kin 6:24
cubits the other wing of the c 1Kin 6:24
the other c was ten cubits.................. 1Kin 6:25
of the one c was ten cubits................ 1Kin 6:26
and so was it of the other c 1Kin 6:26
the wing of the other c touched.......... 1Kin 6:27
wing of the one c was five cubits 2Chr 3:11
to the wing of the other c 2Chr 3:12
of the other c was five cubits............ 2Chr 3:12
to the wing of the other c 2Chr 3:12
And he rode upon a c, and did fly ...... Ps 18:10
of Israel was gone up from the c .... Eze 9:3
cherubims, even under the c .... Eze 10:2
the LORD went up from the c .... Eze 10:4
one c stretched forth his hand .... Eze 10:7
the cherubims, one wheel by one c .... Eze 10:9
and another wheel by another c.......... Eze 10:9
first face was the face of a c .... Eze 10:14
art the anointed c that covereth.......... Eze 28:14
I will destroy thee, O covering c .... Eze 28:16
tree was between a c and a .... Eze 41:18
and every c had two faces .... Eze 41:18
2. An exile who returned with Zerubbabel.
up from Tel-melah, Tel-harsa, C .... Ezr 2:59
from Tel-melah, Tel-haresha, C.......... Neh 7:61

CHERUBIM
the east of the garden of Eden C .... Gen 3:24
the c shall stretch forth their .... Ex 25:20

CHERUBIMS
And thou shalt make two c of gold ...... Ex 25:18
the c on the two ends thereof.............. Ex 25:19
seat shall the faces of the c be............ Ex 25:20
from between the two c which are ...... Ex 25:22
with c of cunning work shalt thou ...... Ex 26:1
with c shall it be made...................... Ex 26:31
with c of cunning work made he .... Ex 36:8
with c made he it of cunning work .... Ex 36:35
And he make two c of gold, beaten .... Ex 37:7
he the c on the two ends thereof .... Ex 37:8
the c spread out their wings on.......... Ex 37:9
seatward were the faces of the c .... Ex 37:9
testimony, from between the two c .... Num 7:89
which dwellest between the c 1Sa 4:4
hosts that dwelleth between the c 2Sa 6:2
he made two c of olive tree................ 1Kin 6:23
both the c were of one measure and 1Kin 6:25
he set the c within the inner 1Kin 6:27
forth the wings of the c, so that 1Kin 6:27
And he overlaid the c with gold 1Kin 6:28
about with carved figures of c 1Kin 6:29
he carved upon them carvings of c 1Kin 6:32
gold, and spread gold upon the c 1Kin 6:32
And he carved thereon c and palm 1Kin 6:35
the ledges were lions, oxen, and c 1Kin 7:29
the borders thereof, he graved c 1Kin 7:36
even under the wings of the c 1Kin 8:6
For the c spread forth their two 1Kin 8:7
the c covered the ark and the.............. 1Kin 8:7
which dwellest between the c 2Kin 19:15
LORD, that dwellest between the c 1Chr 13:6
pattern of the chariot of the c 1Chr 28:18
and graved c on the walls 2Chr 3:7
house he made two c of image work .. 2Chr 3:10
the wings of the c were twenty 2Chr 3:11
The wings of these c spread 2Chr 3:13
fine linen, and wrought c thereon 2Chr 3:14
even under the wings of the c 2Chr 5:7

For the c spread forth their 2Chr 5:8
the c covered the ark and the.............. 2Chr 5:8
thou that dwellest between the c .... Ps 80:1
he sitteth between the c .... Ps 99:1
that dwellest between the c .... Is 37:16
c there appeared over them as it .... Eze 10:1
coals of fire from between the c .... Eze 10:2
Now the c stood on the right side ...... Eze 10:3
the wheels, from between the c .... Eze 10:6
c unto the fire that was between .... Eze 10:7
the fire that was between the c .... Eze 10:7
there appeared in the c the form........ Eze 10:8
behold the four wheels by the c .... Eze 10:9
And the c were lifted up.................... Eze 10:15
And when the c went, the wheels...... Eze 10:16
when the c lifted up their wings........ Eze 10:16
of the house, and stood over the c...... Eze 10:18
the c lifted up their wings, and.......... Eze 10:19
and I knew that they were the c .... Eze 10:20
Then did the c lift up their................ Eze 11:22
And it was made with c and palm .... Eze 41:18
ground unto above the door were c .... Eze 41:20
on the doors of the temple, c .... Eze 41:25
over it the c of glory shadowing ...... Heb 9:5

CHERUBIMS'
the sound of the c wings was............ Eze 10:5

CHESALON (kes′-a-lon) A landmark in Judah.
side of mount Jearim, which is C ...... Josh 15:10

CHESED (ke′-sed) A son of Nahor.
And C, and Hazo, and Pildash, and.... Gen 22:22

CHESIL (ke′-sil) A Canaanite town.
And Eltolad, and C, and Hormah, ... Josh 15:30

CHESNUT
poplar, and of the hazel and c tree .... Gen 30:37
the c trees were not like his .... Eze 31:8

CHEST
But Jehoiada the priest took a c 2Kin 12:9
there was much money in the c 2Kin 12:10
king's commandment they made a c.... 2Chr 24:8
and brought in, and cast into the c 2Chr 24:10
that at what time the c was................ 2Chr 24:11
officer came and emptied the c 2Chr 24:11

CHESTS
in c of rich apparel, bound with .... Eze 27:24

CHESULLOTH (ke-sul′-loth) See CHISLOTH-TABOR. A town in Issachar.
border was toward Jezreel, and C ...... Josh 19:18

CHEW
ye not eat of them that c the cud .... Lev 11:4
not eat of them that c the cud .... Deut 14:7
for they c the cud, but divide............ Deut 14:7

CHEWED
between their teeth, ere it was c .... Num 11:33

CHEWETH
the cud, among the beasts, that.......... Lev 11:3
the camel, because he c the cud.......... Lev 11:4
the coney, because he c the cud .... Lev 11:5
And the hare, because he c the cud .... Lev 11:6
yet be c not the cud .... Lev 11:7
nor c the cud, are unclean unto .... Lev 11:26
the cud among the beasts, that.......... Deut 14:6
yet c not the cud, it is unclean .... Deut 14:8

CHEZIB (ke′-zib) See ACHZIB, CHOZEBA. A Canaanite village.
and he was at C, when she bare him.. Gen 38:5

CHICKENS
gathereth her c under her wings .... Mt 23:37

CHIDE
the people did c with Moses .... Ex 17:2
said unto them, Why c ye with me .... Ex 17:2
they did c with him sharply................ Judg 8:1
He will not always c .... Ps 103:9

CHIDING
because of the c of the children .... Ex 17:7

CHIDON (ki′-don) See NACHON. Place where Uzzah died.
came unto the threshingfloor of C...... 1Chr 13:9

CHIEF
Phichol the captain of his host .... Gen 21:22
Phichol the captain of his host .... Gen 26:26
Phichol the captain of his army.......... Gen 26:26
against the c of the butlers, and.......... Gen 40:2
against the c of the bakers.................. Gen 40:2
the c butler told his dream to.............. Gen 40:9
When the c baker saw that the .... Gen 40:16
up the head of the c butler.................. Gen 40:20
of the c baker among his servants...... Gen 40:20
he restored the c butler unto his .... Gen 40:21
the head of the c baker .... Gen 40:22
Yet did not the c butler remember...... Gen 40:23
Then spake the c butler unto .... Gen 41:9
house, both me and the c baker .... Gen 41:10
being a c man among his people, ... Lev 21:4
the c of the house of the father .... Num 3:24
the c of the house of the father .... Num 3:30
the c of the house of the father .... Num 3:32
the c of the house of the Levites .... Num 3:32
the c of the house of the father .... Num 3:35
the c of the congregation .... Num 4:34
the c of Israel numbered, after.......... Num 4:46
the c man of a house among the .... Num 25:14
people, and of a c house in Midian .... Num 25:15
the c fathers of the congregation........ Num 31:26

the c fathers of the tribes of .... Num 32:28
the c fathers of the families of .... Num 36:1
the c fathers of the children of .... Num 36:1
So I took the c of your tribes, ... Deut 1:15
for the c things of the ancient .... Deut 33:15
princes, of each c house a prince .... Josh 22:14
the c of all the people, even of .... Judg 20:2
hither, all the c of the people 1Sa 14:38
the c of the things which should 1Sa 15:21
of David's soul, he shall be c 2Sa 5:8
and David's sons were c rulers 2Sa 8:18
Jairite was a c ruler about David 2Sa 20:26
in the seat, c among the captains 2Sa 23:8
three of the thirty c went down 2Sa 23:13
son of Zeruiah, was c among three 2Sa 23:18
Beside the c of Solomon's 1Kin 5:16
the c of the officers, ... 1Kin 8:1
These were the c of the officers 1Kin 9:23
the hands of the c of the guard 1Kin 14:27
guard took Seraiah the c priest 2Kin 25:18
and of him came the c ruler 1Chr 5:2
was reckoned, were the c, Jeiel, ... 1Chr 5:7
Joel the c, and Shapham the next, ... 1Chr 5:12
c of the house of their fathers 1Chr 5:15
all of them c men, ... 1Chr 7:3
men of valour, c men 1Chr 7:40
by their generations, c men 1Chr 8:28
All these men were c of the 1Chr 9:9
Shallum was the c 1Chr 9:17
these Levites, the four c porters 1Chr 9:26
c of the fathers of the Levites, ... 1Chr 9:33
These c fathers of the Levites. 1Chr 9:34
fathers of the Levites were c 1Chr 9:34
the Jebusites first shall be c 1Chr 11:6
Zeruiah went first up, and was c 1Chr 11:6
These also are the c of the 1Chr 11:10
Hachmonite, the c of the captains 1Chr 11:11
of Joab, the beginning of the three 1Chr 11:20
The c was Ahiezer, then Joash, ... 1Chr 12:3
who was c of the captains, and he 1Chr 12:18
Uriel the c, and his brethren an 1Chr 15:5
Asaiah the c, and his brethren two 1Chr 15:6
Joel the c, and his brethren an 1Chr 15:7
Shemaiah the c, and his brethren 1Chr 15:8
Eliel the c, and his brethren 1Chr 15:9
Amminadab the c, and his brethren 1Chr 15:10
Ye are the c of the fathers of 1Chr 15:12
David spake to the c of the 1Chr 15:16
c of the Levites, was for song 1Chr 15:22
Asaph the c, and next to him 1Chr 16:5
of David were c about the king 1Chr 18:17
the c was Jehiel, and Zetham, and 1Chr 23:8
These were the c of the fathers 1Chr 23:9
And Jahath was the c 1Chr 23:11
of Gershom, Shebuel was the c 1Chr 23:16
of Eliezer were, Rehabiah the c 1Chr 23:17
Shelomith the c 1Chr 23:18
even the c of the fathers, ... 1Chr 23:24
there were more c men found of 1Chr 24:4
c men of the house of their 1Chr 24:4
before the c of the fathers of 1Chr 24:6
the c of the fathers of the 1Chr 24:31
Simri the c, (for though he was 1Chr 26:10
yet his father made him the c 1Chr 26:10
the porters, even among the c men 1Chr 26:12
c fathers, even of Laadan the 1Chr 26:21
the c fathers, the captains over 1Chr 26:26
the Hebronites was Jerijah the c 1Chr 26:31
and seven hundred c fathers 1Chr 26:32
the c fathers and captains of 1Chr 27:1
the children of Perez was the c 1Chr 27:3
the son of Jehoiada, a c priest 1Chr 27:5
Then the c of the fathers and 1Chr 29:6
the LORD to be the c governor 1Chr 29:22
all Israel, the c of the fathers 2Chr 1:2
the c of the fathers of the 2Chr 5:2
c of his captains, and captains of 2Chr 8:9
And these were the c of king 2Chr 8:10
Abijah the son of Maachah the c 2Chr 11:22
the hands of the c of the guard 2Chr 12:10
Adnah the c, and with him mighty 2Chr 17:14
of the c of the fathers of Israel 2Chr 19:8
Amariah the c priest is over you 2Chr 19:11
the c of the fathers of Israel, ... 2Chr 23:2
king called for Jehoiada the c 2Chr 24:6
The whole number of the c of the 2Chr 26:12
And Azariah the c priest, and all 2Chr 26:20
Azariah the c priest of the house 2Chr 31:10
the c of the Levites, gave unto the 2Chr 35:9
Moreover all the c of the priests 2Chr 36:14
Then rose up the c of the fathers .... Ezr 1:5
some of the c of the fathers, ... Ezr 2:68
c of the fathers, who were .... Ezr 3:12
to the c of the fathers, and said .... Ezr 4:2
the rest of the c of the fathers .... Ezr 4:3
the men that were c of them .... Ezr 5:10
the son of Aaron the c priest .... Ezr 7:5
of Israel c men to go up with me .... Ezr 7:28
are now the c of their fathers .... Ezr 8:1
and for Meshullam, c men .... Ezr 8:16
Iddo the c at the place Casiphia .... Ezr 8:17
twelve of the c of the priests .... Ezr 8:24
them before the c of the priests .... Ezr 8:29
c of the fathers of Israel, at .... Ezr 8:29
hath been c in this trespass. .... Ezr 9:2
arose Ezra, and made the c priests .... Ezr 10:5
with certain c of the fathers, ... Ezr 10:16
some of the c of the fathers gave .... Neh 7:70
some of the c of the fathers gave .... Neh 7:71
the c of the fathers of all the .... Neh 8:13

the c of the people .... Neh 10:14
Now these are the c of the .... Neh 11:3
c of the fathers, two hundred .... Neh 11:13
of the c of the Levites, had the .... Neh 11:16
These were the c of the priests .... Neh 12:7
priests, the c of the fathers .... Neh 12:12
were recorded c of the fathers .... Neh 12:22
the c of the fathers, were .... Neh 12:23
And the c of the Levites .... Neh 12:24
old there were c of the singers .... Neh 12:46
the c of the people of the earth .... Job 12:24
I chose out their way, and sat c .... Job 29:25
He is the c of the ways of God .... Job 40:19
To the c Musician on Neginoth, ... Ps 4:t
To the c Musician upon Nehiloth, ... Ps 5:t
To the c Musician on Neginoth .... Ps 6:t
To the c Musician upon Gittith, A .... Ps 8:t
To the c Musician upon .... Ps 9:t
To the c Musician, A Psalm of .... Ps 11:t
To the c Musician upon Sheminith, ... Ps 12:t
To the c Musician, A Psalm of .... Ps 13:t
To the c Musician, A Psalm of .... Ps 14:t
To the c Musician, A Psalm of .... Ps 18:t
To the c Musician, A Psalm of .... Ps 19:t
To the c Musician, A Psalm of .... Ps 20:t
To the c Musician, A Psalm of .... Ps 21:t
To the c Musician upon Aijeleth .... Ps 22:t
To the c Musician, A Psalm of .... Ps 31:t
To the c Musician, A Psalm of .... Ps 36:t
To the c Musician, even to .... Ps 39:t
To the c Musician, A Psalm of .... Ps 40:t
To the c Musician, A Psalm of .... Ps 41:t
To the c Musician, Maschil, for .... Ps 42:t
To the c Musician for the sons of .... Ps 44:t
To the c Musician upon Shoshannim, ... Ps 45:t
To the c Musician for the sons of .... Ps 46:t
To the c Musician, A Psalm for .... Ps 47:t
To the c Musician, A Psalm of .... Ps 49:t
To the c Musician, A Psalm of .... Ps 51:t
To the c Musician, Maschil, A .... Ps 52:t
To the c Musician upon Mahalath, ... Ps 53:t
To the c Musician on Neginoth, ... Ps 54:t
To the c Musician on Neginoth, ... Ps 55:t
To the c Musician upon .... Ps 56:t
To the c Musician, Altaschith, ... Ps 57:t
To the c Musician, Altaschith, ... Ps 58:t
To the c Musician, Altaschith, ... Ps 59:t
To the c Musician upon .... Ps 60:t
To the c Musician upon Neginah, A .... Ps 61:t
To the c Musician, to Jeduthun, A .... Ps 62:t
To the c Musician, A Psalm of .... Ps 64:t
To the c Musician, A Psalm and .... Ps 65:t
To the c Musician, A Song or .... Ps 66:t
To the c Musician on Neginoth, A .... Ps 67:t
To the c Musician, A Psalm or .... Ps 68:t
To the c Musician upon Shoshannim .... Ps 69:t
To the c Musician, A Psalm of .... Ps 70:t
To the c Musician, Altaschith, A .... Ps 75:t
To the c Musician on Neginoth, A .... Ps 76:t
To the c Musician, to Jeduthun, A .... Ps 77:t
the c of their strength in the .... Ps 78:51
To the c Musician upon .... Ps 80:t
To the c Musician upon Gittith, A .... Ps 81:t
To the c Musician upon Gittith, A .... Ps 84:t
To the c Musician, A Psalm for .... Ps 85:t
for the sons of Korah to the c .... Ps 88:t
the c of all their strength. .... Ps 105:36
To the c Musician, A Psalm of .... Ps 109:t
not Jerusalem above my c joy .... Ps 137:6
To the c Musician, A Psalm of .... Ps 139:t
To the c Musician, A Psalm of .... Ps 140:t
She crieth in the c place of .... Prov 1:21
a whisperer separateth c friends .... Prov 16:28
and aloes, with all the c spices .... Song 4:14
even all the c ones of the earth .... Is 14:9
free from the c men thereof .... Is 41:9
to be captains, and as c over these .... Jer 13:21
who was also c governor in the .... Jer 20:1
shout among the c of the nations .... Jer 31:7
bow of Elam, the c of their might .... Jer 49:35
guard took Seraiah the c priest .... Jer 52:24
Her adversaries are the c .... Lam 1:5
in thy fairs with c of all spices .... Eze 27:22
the c prince of Meshech and Tubal, ... Eze 38:2
the c prince of Meshech and Tubal, ... Eze 38:3
the c prince of Meshech and Tubal .... Eze 39:1
c of the governors over all the .... Dan 2:48
to, Michael, one of the c princes .... Dan 10:13
the c of the children of Ammon .... Dan 11:41
which are named c of the nations .... Amos 6:1
themselves with the c ointments. .... Amos 6:6
To the c singer on my stringed .... Hab 3:19
he had gathered all the c priests .... Mt 2:4
c priests and scribes, and he .... Mt 16:21
be betrayed unto the c priests .... Mt 20:18
And whosoever will be c among you. .... Mt 20:27
And when the c priests and scribes .... Mt 21:15
the c priests and the elders of .... Mt 21:23
And when the c priests and .... Mt 21:45
the seats in the synagogues, ... Mt 23:6
Iscariot, went unto the c priests .... Mt 26:14
and staves, from the c priests .... Mt 26:47
Now the c priests, and elders, and .... Mt 26:59
was come, all the c priests .... Mt 27:1
pieces of silver to the c priests .... Mt 27:6
the c priests took the silver .... Mt 27:6
he was accused of the c priests. .... Mt 27:12
But the c priests and elders .... Mt 27:20
Likewise also the c priests .... Mt 27:41

the c priests and Pharisees came .... Mt 27:62
shewed unto the c priests all the .... Mt 28:11
captains, and c estates of Galilee .... Mk 6:21
of the c priests, and scribes, and .... Mk 8:31
be delivered unto the c priests .... Mk 10:33
c priests heard it, and sought how .... Mk 11:18
there come to him the c priests .... Mk 11:27
the c seats in the synagogues, and .... Mk 12:39
the c priests and the scribes .... Mk 14:1
twelve, went unto the c priests .... Mk 14:10
and staves, from the c priest .... Mk 14:43
were assembled all the c priests .... Mk 14:53
the c priests and all the council .... Mk 14:55
the c priests held a consultation .... Mk 15:1
the c priests accused him of many .... Mk 15:3
For he knew that the c priests .... Mk 15:10
But the c priests moved the .... Mk 15:11
Likewise also the c priests .... Mk 15:31
c priests and scribes, and be slain .... Lk 9:22
Beelzebub the c of the devils .... Lk 11:15
into the house of one of the c .... Lk 14:1
how they choose out the c rooms .... Lk 14:7
which was the c among the .... Lk 19:2
But the c priests and the scribes .... Lk 19:47
the c of the people sought to .... Lk 19:47
the c priests and the scribes came .... Lk 20:1
the c priests and the scribes the .... Lk 20:19
and the c rooms at feasts .... Lk 20:46
the c priests and scribes sought .... Lk 22:2
and communed with the c priests .... Lk 22:4
and he that is c, as he that doth .... Lk 22:26
Jesus said unto the c priests .... Lk 22:52
the c priests and the scribes came .... Lk 22:66
Then said Pilate to the c priests .... Lk 23:4
the c priests and scribes stood and .... Lk 23:10
had called together the c priests .... Lk 23:13
of the c priests prevailed. .... Lk 23:23
And how the c priests and our .... Lk 24:20
the c priests sent officers to .... Jn 7:32
the officers to the c priests .... Jn 7:45
Then gathered the c priests .... Jn 11:47
Now both the c priests and the .... Jn 11:57
But the c priests consulted that .... Jn 12:10
Nevertheless among the c rulers .... Jn 12:42
and officers from the c priests .... Jn 18:3
the c priests have delivered thee. .... Jn 18:35
When the c priests therefore and .... Jn 19:6
The c priests answered, We have .... Jn 19:15
Then said the c priests of the .... Jn 19:21
reported all that the c priests .... Acts 4:23
the c priests heard these things, ... Acts 5:24
c priests to bind all that call .... Acts 9:14
them bound unto the c priests .... Acts 9:21
the c men of the city, and raised .... Acts 13:50
because he was the c speaker. .... Acts 14:12
Silas, c men among the brethren .... Acts 15:22
which is the c city of that part, ... Acts 16:12
and of the c women not a few .... Acts 17:4
the c ruler of the synagogue, ... Acts 18:8
the c ruler of the synagogue, and .... Acts 18:17
c of the priests, which did so .... Acts 19:14
And certain of the c of Asia. .... Acts 19:31
unto the c captain of the band .... Acts 21:31
and when they saw the c captain .... Acts 21:32
Then the c captain came near, and .... Acts 21:33
he said unto the c captain .... Acts 21:37
The c captain commanded him to be. .... Acts 22:24
he went and told the c captain .... Acts 22:26
Then the c captain came, and said .... Acts 22:27
the c captain answered, With a .... Acts 22:28
the c captain also was afraid, ... Acts 22:29
bands, and commanded the c priests .... Acts 22:30
the c captain, fearing lest Paul .... Acts 23:10
And they came to the c priests .... Acts 23:14
c captain that he bring him down .... Acts 23:15
this young man unto the c captain .... Acts 23:17
and brought him to the c captain .... Acts 23:18
Then the c captain took him by .... Acts 23:19
So the c captain then let the .... Acts 23:22
But the c captain Lysias came .... Acts 24:7
When Lysias the c captain shall .... Acts 24:22
the c of the Jews informed him .... Acts 25:2
the c priests and the elders of .... Acts 25:15
of hearing, with the c captains .... Acts 25:23
authority from the c priests .... Acts 26:10
and commission from the c priests. .... Acts 26:12
of the c man of the island .... Acts 28:7
called the c of the Jews together .... Acts 28:17
himself being the c corner stone .... Eph 2:20
of whom I am c 1Ti 1:15
I lay in Sion a c corner stone 1Pet 2:6
when the c Shepherd shall appear, ... 1Pet 5:4
the c captains, and the mighty men .... Rev 6:15

CHIEFEST

c of all the offerings of Israel 1Sa 2:29
made them sit in the c place 1Sa 9:22
the c of the herdmen that 1Sa 21:7
they buried him in the c of the 2Chr 32:33
ruddy, the c among ten thousand. .... Song 5:10
And whosoever of you will be the c. .... Mk 10:44
a whit behind the very c apostles 2Cor 11:5
am I behind the very c apostles 2Cor 12:11
the c city of Phrygia Pacatiana. .... 1Ti s

CHIEFLY

c, because that unto them were .... Rom 3:2
c they that are of Caesar's. .... Phil 4:22
But c them that walk after the 2Pet 2:10

CHILD

she had no c .... Gen 11:30
unto her, Behold, thou art with c .... Gen 16:11

C

Every man *c* among you shall be .... Gen 17:10
every man *c* in your generations, ... Gen 17:12
the uncircumcised man *c* whose .... Gen 17:14
Shall a *c* be born unto him that .... Gen 17:17
Shall I of a surety bear a *c* .... Gen 18:13
of Lot with *c* by their father .... Gen 19:36
the *c* grew, and was weaned .... Gen 21:8
it on her shoulder, and the *c* .... Gen 21:14
she cast the *c* under one of the .... Gen 21:15
Let me not see the death of the *c* .... Gen 21:16
brethren, and said, The *c* is not .... Gen 37:30
behold, she is with *c* by whoredom .... Gen 38:24
man, whose these are, am I with *c* .... Gen 38:25
saying, Do not sin against the *c* .... Gen 42:22
a *c* of his old age, a little one .... Gen 44:20
saw him that he was a goodly *c* .... Ex 2:2
with pitch, and put the *c* therein .... Ex 2:3
she had opened it, she saw the *c* .... Ex 2:6
that she may nurse the *c* for thee .... Ex 2:7
said unto her, Take this *c* away .... Ex 2:9
And the woman took the *c*, and .... Ex 2:9
the *c* grew, and she brought him .... Ex 2:10
strive, and hurt a woman with *c* .... Ex 21:22
any widow, or fatherless *c* .... Ex 22:22
conceived seed, and born a man *c* .... Lev 12:2
But if she bear a maid *c*, then .... Lev 12:5
widow, or divorced, and have no *c* .... Lev 22:13
father beareth the sucking *c* .... Num 11:12
and one of them die, and have no *c* ...... Deut 25:5
and she was his only *c* .... Judg 11:34
for the *c* shall be a Nazarite .... Judg 13:5
for the *c* shall be a Nazarite to .... Judg 13:7
do unto the *c* that shall be born .... Judg 13:8
How shall we order the *c*, and how .... Judg 13:12
the *c* grew, and the LORD blessed .... Judg 13:24
And Naomi took the *c*, and laid it .... Ruth 4:16
give unto thine handmaid a man *c* 1Sa 1:11
not go up until the *c* be weaned 1Sa 1:22
and the *c* was young 1Sa 1:24
bullock, and brought the *c* to Eli 1Sa 1:25
For this *c* I prayed 1Sa 1:27
the *c* did minister unto the LORD 1Sa 2:11
before the LORD, being a *c* 1Sa 2:18
the *c* Samuel grew before the LORD 1Sa 2:21
the *c* Samuel grew on, and was in 1Sa 2:26
the *c* Samuel ministered unto the 1Sa 3:1
that the LORD had called the *c* 1Sa 3:8
law, Phinehas' wife, was with *c* 1Sa 4:19
And she named the *c* I-chabod 1Sa 4:21
no *c* unto the day of her death 2Sa 6:23
told David, and said, I am with *c* 2Sa 11:5
the *c* also that is born unto thee 2Sa 12:14
the LORD struck the *c* that 2Sa 12:15
therefore besought God for the *c* 2Sa 12:16
the seventh day, that the *c* died 2Sa 12:18
to tell him that the *c* was dead 2Sa 12:18
while the *c* was yet alive, we 2Sa 12:18
if we tell him that the *c* is dead 2Sa 12:18
perceived that the *c* was dead 2Sa 12:19
unto his servants, Is the *c* dead 2Sa 12:19
thou didst fast and weep for the *c* 2Sa 12:21
but when the *c* was dead, thou 2Sa 12:21
While the *c* was yet alive, I 2Sa 12:22
to me, that the *c* may live 2Sa 12:23
And I am but a little *c* 1Kin 3:7
I was delivered of a *c* with her 1Kin 3:17
this woman's *c* died in the night 1Kin 3:19
and laid her dead *c* in my bosom 1Kin 3:20
in the morning to give my *c* suck 1Kin 3:21
said, Divide the living *c* in two 1Kin 3:25
the living *c* was unto the king 1Kin 3:26
O my lord, give her the living *c* 1Kin 3:26
and said, Give her the living *c* 1Kin 3:27
Hadad being yet a little *c* 1Kin 11:17
a *c* shall be born unto the house 1Kin 13:2
the what shall become of the *c* 1Kin 14:3
into the city, the *c* shall die 1Kin 14:12
threshold of the door, the *c* died 1Kin 14:17
himself upon the *c* three times 1Kin 17:21
the soul of the *c* came into him 1Kin 17:22
And Elijah took the *c*, and brought 1Kin 17:23
answered, Verily she hath no *c* 2Kin 4:14
when the *c* was grown, it fell on 2Kin 4:18
is it well with the *c* 2Kin 4:26
my staff upon the face of the *c* 2Kin 4:29
And the mother of the *c* said 2Kin 4:30
the staff upon the face of the *c* 2Kin 4:31
him, saying, The *c* is not awaked 2Kin 4:31
the *c* was dead, and laid upon his 2Kin 4:32
And he went up, and lay upon the *c* 2Kin 4:34
he stretched himself upon the *c* 2Kin 4:34
and the flesh of the *c* waxed warm 2Kin 4:34
the *c* sneezed seven times 2Kin 4:35
and the *c* opened his eyes 2Kin 4:35
like unto the flesh of a little *c* 2Kin 5:14
and rip up their women with *c* 2Kin 8:12
that were with *c* he ripped up 2Kin 15:16
said, There is a man *c* conceived .... Job 3:3
as a *c* that is weaned of his .... Ps 131:2
my soul is even as a weaned *c* .... Ps 131:2
Even a *c* is known by his doings, ... Prov 20:11
Train up a *c* in the way he should .... Prov 22:6
is bound in the heart of a *c* .... Prov 22:15
not correction from the *c* .... Prov 23:13
a wise *c* shall have joy of him .... Prov 23:24
but a *c* left to himself bringeth .... Prov 29:15
a *c* shall have him become his son .... Prov 29:21
he hath neither *c* nor brother .... Eccl 4:8
a wise *c* than an old and foolish .... Eccl 4:13
with the second *c* that shall .... Eccl 4:15

O land, when thy king is a *c* .... Eccl 10:16
in the womb of her that is with *c* .... Eccl 11:5
the *c* shall behave himself .... Is 3:5
For before the *c* shall know to .... Is 7:16
For before the *c* shall have .... Is 8:4
For unto us a *c* is born, unto us .... Is 9:6
be few, that a *c* may write them, ... Is 10:19
a little *c* shall lead them .... Is 11:6
the sucking *c* shall play on the .... Is 11:8
the weaned *c* shall put his hand .... Is 11:8
Like as a woman with *c*, that .... Is 26:18
We have been with *c*, we have been ..... Is 26:18
Can a woman forget her sucking *c* .... Is 49:15
that didst not travail with *c* .... Is 54:1
for the *c* shall die an hundred .... Is 65:20
she was delivered of a man *c* .... Is 66:7
for I am a *c* .... Jer 1:6
said unto me, Say not, I am a *c* .... Jer 1:7
that bringeth forth her first *c* .... Jer 4:31
A man *c* is born unto thee .... Jer 20:15
whether a man doth travail with *c* .... Jer 30:6
and the lame, the woman with *c* .... Jer 31:8
that travaileth with *c* together .... Jer 31:8
is he a pleasant *c* .... Jer 31:20
cut off from you man and woman, *c* ...... Jer 44:7
The tongue of the sucking *c* .... Lam 4:4
When Israel was a *c*, then I loved .... Hos 11:1
their women with *c* shall be .... Hos 13:16
up the women with *c* of Gilead .... Amos 1:13
found with *c* of the Holy Ghost .... Mt 1:18
Behold, a virgin shall be with *c* .... Mt 1:23
search diligently for the young *c* .... Mt 2:8
stood over where the young *c* was .... Mt 2:9
they saw the young *c* with Mary .... Mt 2:11
Arise, and take the young *c* .... Mt 2:13
seek the young *c* to destroy him .... Mt 2:13
he arose, he took the young *c* .... Mt 2:14
Arise, and take the young *c* .... Mt 2:20
And he arose, and took the young *c* ...... Mt 2:21
to death, and the father the *c* .... Mt 10:21
the *c* was cured from that very .... Mt 17:18
Jesus called a little *c* unto him .... Mt 18:2
humble himself as this little *c* .... Mt 18:4
little *c* in my name receiveth me .... Mt 18:5
the *c* of hell than yourselves .... Mt 23:15
And woe unto them that are with *c* .... Mt 24:19
And he said, Of a *c* .... Mk 9:21
the father of the *c* cried out .... Mk 9:24
And he took a *c*, and set him in the ...... Mk 9:36
the kingdom of God as a little *c* .... Mk 10:15
But woe to them that are with *c* .... Mk 13:17
and they had no *c*, because that .... Lk 1:7
day they came to circumcise the *c* .... Lk 1:59
What manner of *c* shall this be .... Lk 1:66
And thou, *c*, shalt be called the .... Lk 1:76
the *c* grew, and waxed strong in .... Lk 1:80
espoused wife, being great with *c* .... Lk 2:5
was told them concerning this *c* .... Lk 2:17
for the circumcising of the *c* .... Lk 2:21
parents brought in the *c* Jesus .... Lk 2:27
this *c* is set for the fall and .... Lk 2:34
the *c* grew, and waxed strong in .... Lk 2:40
the *c* Jesus tarried behind in .... Lk 2:43
for he is mine only *c* .... Lk 9:38
unclean spirit, and healed the *c* .... Lk 9:42
thought of their heart, took a *c* .... Lk 9:47
this *c* in my name receiveth me .... Lk 9:48
c shall in no wise enter therein .... Lk 18:17
But woe unto them that are with *c* .... Lk 21:23
him, Sir, come down ere my *c* die .... Jn 4:49
as soon as she is delivered of the *c* ...... Jn 16:21
a truth against thy holy *c* Jesus, ... Acts 4:27
by the name of thy holy *c* Jesus .... Acts 4:30
him, when as yet he had no *c* .... Acts 7:5
thou *c* of the devil, thou enemy .... Acts 13:10
I was a *c*, I spake as a *c* 1Cor 13:11
I understood as a *c* 1Cor 13:11
I thought as a *c* 1Cor 13:11
the heir, as long as he is a *c* .... Gal 4:1
as travail upon a woman with *c* 1Th 5:3
that from a *c* thou hast known the 2Ti 3:15
was delivered of a *c* when she was .... Heb 11:11
they saw he was a proper *c* .... Heb 11:23
for devour her *c* as soon as it .... Rev 12:4
And she brought forth a man *c* .... Rev 12:5
her *c* was caught up unto God, and ...... Rev 12:5
which brought forth the man *c* .... Rev 12:13

CHILDBEARING
she shall be saved in *c*, if they 1Ti 2:15

CHILDHOOD
you from my *c* unto this day, ... 1Sa 12:2
for *c* and youth are vanity .... Eccl 11:10

CHILDISH
became a man, I put away *c* things. 1Cor 13:11

CHILDLESS
wilt thou give me, seeing I go *c* .... Gen 15:2
they shall die *c* .... Lev 20:20
they shall die *c* .... Lev 20:21
As thy sword hath made women *c* 1Sa 15:33
shall thy mother be *c* among women 1Sa 15:33
the LORD, Write ye this man *c* .... Jer 22:30
took her to wife, and he died *c* .... Lk 20:30

CHILDREN See PREFACE.

CHILDREN'S
father, that is ours, and our .... Gen 31:16
thy *c* children, and thy flocks, and .... Gen 45:10

of all that is the *c* of Israel .... Ex 9:4
children, and upon the *c* children .... Ex 34:7
c children, and ye shall have .... Deut 4:25
thy *c* for ever, because thou hast .... Josh 14:9
children, and their *c* children 2Kin 17:41
for the *c* sake of mine own body .... Job 19:17
his righteousness unto *c* children .... Ps 103:17
thou shalt see thy *c* children .... Ps 128:6
an inheritance to his *c* children .... Prov 13:22
C children are the crown of old .... Prov 17:6
with your *c* children will I plead .... Jer 2:9
the *c* teeth are set on edge .... Jer 31:29
the *c* teeth are set on edge .... Eze 18:2
their *c* children for ever .... Eze 37:25
is not meet to take the *c* bread .... Mk 15:26
is not meet to take the *c* bread .... Mk 7:27
the table eat of the *c* crumbs .... Mk 7:28

CHILD'S
maid went and called the *c* mother .... Ex 2:8
let this *c* soul come into mine 1Kin 17:21
flesh shall be fresher than a *c* .... Job 33:25
which sought the young *c* life .... Mt 2:20

CHILEAB (kil'-e-ab) See DANIEL. A son of David.
And his second, C, of Abigail the 2Sa 3:3

CHILION (kil'-e-on) See CHILION'S. A son of Elimelech.
name of his two sons Mahlon and C .... Ruth 1:2
and C died also both of them .... Ruth 1:5

CHILION'S (kil'-e-ons)
Elimelech's, and all that was C .... Ruth 4:9

CHILMAD (kil'-mad) An area between Assyria and Arabia.
merchants of Sheba, Asshur, and C .... Eze 27:23

CHIMHAM (kim'-ham) A servant of David.
But behold thy servant C 2Sa 19:37
C shall go over with me, and I 2Sa 19:38
to Gilgal, and C went on with him 2Sa 19:40
and dwelt in the habitation of C .... Jer 41:17

CHIMNEY
and as the smoke out of the *c* .... Hos 13:3

CHINNERETH (kin'-ne-reth) See CHINNEROTH, CINNEROTH, GENNESARET. A district about the Sea of Galilee.
the side of the Sea of C eastward .... Num 34:11
from C even unto the sea of the .... Deut 3:17
sea of C on the other side Jordan .... Josh 13:27
Zer, and Hammath, Rakkath, and C .... Josh 19:35

CHINNEROTH (kin'-ne-roth) See CHINNERETH. Same as CHINNERETH.
and of the plains south of C .... Josh 11:2
plain to the sea of C on the east .... Josh 12:3

CHIOS (ki'-os) An island near Greece.
came the next day over against C .... Acts 20:15

CHISLEU (kis'-lew) Ninth month of the Hebrew year.
And it came to pass in the month C .... Neh 1:1
day of the ninth month, even in C .... Zec 7:1

CHISLEV See CHISLEU.

CHISLON (kis'-lon) Father of Elidad.
of Benjamin, Elidad the son of C .... Num 34:21

CHISLOTH-TABOR (kis'-loth-ta'-bor) See CHESULLOTH. A city in Zebulun.
sunrising unto the border of C .... Josh 19:12

CHITTIM (kit'-tim) See KITTIM. Descendants of Javan.
come come from the coast of C .... Num 24:24
from the land of C it is revealed .... Is 23:1
arise, pass over to C .... Is 23:12
For pass over the isles of C .... Jer 2:10
brought out of the isles of C .... Eze 27:6
For the ships of C shall come .... Dan 11:30

CHIUN (ki'-un) See REMPHAN. Another name for the god Saturn.
C your images, the star of your .... Amos 5:26

CHLOE (clo'-e) A Christian acquaintance of Paul.
them which are of the house of C 1Cor 1:11

CHLOE'S See CHLOE.

CHODE
Jacob was wroth, and c with Laban .... Gen 31:36
And the people c with Moses .... Num 20:3

CHOICE
in the *c* of our sepulchres bury .... Gen 23:6
and his ass's colt into the *c* vine .... Gen 49:11
all your *c* vows which ye vow unto .... Deut 12:11
a *c* young man, and a goodly 1Sa 9:2
chose of all the *c* men of Israel 2Sa 10:9
fenced city, and every *c* city 2Kin 3:19
and the *c* fir trees thereof 2Kin 19:23
heads of their father's house, *c* 1Chr 7:40
chose out of all the *c* of Israel 2Chr 25:5
them three hundred thousand *c* men 2Chr 25:5
daily was one ox and six *c* sheep .... Neh 5:18
and knowledge rather than *c* gold .... Prov 8:10
and my revenue than *c* silver .... Prov 8:19
tongue of the just is as *c* silver .... Prov 10:20
she is the *c* one of her that bare .... Song 6:9
and the *c* fir trees thereof .... Is 37:24

they shall cut down thy c cedars. ..... Jer 22:7
fill it with the c bones .... Eze 24:4
Take the c of the flock, and burn...... Eze 24:5
and all the trees of Eden, the c......... Eze 31:16
while ago God made c among us......... Acts 15:7

CHOICEST
and planted it with the c vine .... Is 5:2
that thy c valleys shall be full .... Is 22:7

CHOKE
c the word, and he becometh .... Mt 13:22
c the word, and it becometh .... Mk 4:19

CHOKED
the thorns sprung up, and c them ...... Mt 13:7
c it, and it yielded no fruit.................. Mk 4:7
and were c in the sea.......................... Mk 5:13
thorns sprang up with it, and c it .... Lk 8:7
are c with cares and riches and.......... Lk 8:14
place into the lake, and were c........... Lk 8:33

CHOLER
he was moved with c against him....... Dan 8:7
the south shall be moved with c......... Dan 11:11

CHOOSE
C us out men, and go out, fight........... Ex 17:9
that the man whom the LORD doth c.... Num 16:7
the man's rod, whom I shall c .... Num 17:5
set his love upon you, nor c you .... Deut 7:7
c out of all your tribes to put............. Deut 12:5
c to cause his name to dwell.............. Deut 12:11
place before it in one of thy tribes..... Deut 12:14
which the LORD thy God shall c .... Deut 12:18
the place which the LORD shall c........ Deut 12:26
shall c to place his name there .... Deut 14:23
God shall c to set his name there .... Deut 14:24
which the LORD thy God shall c.......... Deut 14:25
the place which the LORD shall c........ Deut 15:20
shall c to place his name there .... Deut 16:2
God shall c to place his name in .... Deut 16:6
which the LORD thy God shall c.......... Deut 16:7
the place which the LORD shall c........ Deut 16:15
God in the place which he shall c....... Deut 16:16
which the LORD thy God shall c.......... Deut 17:8
the LORD shall c shall shew thee .... Deut 17:10
whom the LORD thy God shall c......... Deut 17:15
the place which the LORD shall c........ Deut 17:15
he shall c in one of thy gates............. Deut 23:16
shall c to place his name there .... Deut 26:2
therefore c life, that both thou........... Deut 30:19
God in the place which he shall c....... Deut 31:11
in the place which he .... Josh 9:27
c you this day whom ye will serve ...... Josh 24:15
did I c him out of all the tribes........... 1Sa 2:28
c you a man for you, and let him........ 1Sa 17:8
and all the men of Israel..................... 2Sa 16:18
Let me now c out twelve thousand 2Sa 17:1
of Saul, whom the LORD did c............. 2Sa 21:6
c thee one of them, that I may do...... 2Sa 24:12
the city which the LORD did c out....... 1Kin 14:21
let them c one bullock for.................. 1Kin 18:23
C you one bullock for yourselves,....... 1Kin 18:25
c thee one of them, that I may do...... 1Chr 21:10
him, Thus saith the LORD, C thee........ 1Chr 21:11
LORD the God, who didst c Abram ...... Neh 9:7
c out my words to reason with him..... Job 9:14
Let us c to us judgment..................... Job 34:4
thou refuse, or whether thou c .... Job 34:33
teach in the way that he shall c.......... Ps 25:12
He shall c our inheritance for us .... Ps 47:4
did not c the fear of the LORD............ Prov 1:29
oppressor, and c none of his ways ..... Prov 3:31
to refuse the evil, and c the good ...... Is 7:15
c the good, the land that thou........... Is 7:16
on Jacob, and will yet c Israel............ Is 14:1
of Israel, and he shall c thee.............. Is 49:7
c the things that please me, and........ Is 56:4
did c that wherein I delighted............. Is 65:12
I also will c their delusions, and......... Is 66:4
c thou a place, c it at the................... Eze 21:19
c it at the head of the way to............. Eze 21:19
Zion, and shall yet c Jerusalem .... Zec 1:17
land, and shall c Jerusalem again ...... Zec 2:12
yet what I shall c I wot not.................. Phil 1:22

CHOOSEST
thou c the tongue of the crafty........... Job 15:5
Blessed is the man whom thou c......... Ps 65:4

CHOOSETH
So that my soul c strangling............... Job 7:15
c a tree that will not rot...................... Is 40:20
an abomination is he that c you......... Is 41:24

CHOOSING
C rather to suffer affliction.................. Heb 11:25

CHOP
c them in pieces, as for the pot, ... Mic 3:3

CHOR-ASHAN (cor-a′-shan) *A town in Judah,*
and to them which were in C.............. 1Sa 30:30

CHORAZIN (co-ra′-zin) *A city near Capernaum.*
Woe unto thee, C................................ Mt 11:21
Woe unto thee, C................................ Lk 10:13

CHOSE
them wives of all which they c .... Gen 6:2
Then Lot c him all the plain of .... Gen 13:11
Moses c able men out of all............... Ex 18:25
therefore he c their seed after them ... Deut 4:37
he c their seed after them, even .... Deut 10:15

Joshua c out thirty thousand.............. Josh 8:3
They c new gods.................................. Judg 5:8
Saul c three thousand men of............ 1Sa 13:2
c him five smooth stones out of 1Sa 17:40
which c me before thy father, and...... 2Sa 6:21
he c of all the choice men of 2Sa 10:9
I c no city out of all the tribes 1Kin 8:16
but I c David to be over my................. 1Kin 8:16
David my servant's sake, whom I c..... 1Kin 11:34
he c out of all the choice of............... 1Chr 19:10
c me before all the house of my......... 1Chr 28:4
out of the land of Egypt I c to............. 2Chr 6:5
neither c I any man to be a ruler......... 2Chr 6:5
I c out their way, and sat chief,.......... Job 29:25
c not the tribe of Ephraim .... Ps 78:67
But c the tribe of Judah, the.............. Ps 78:68
He c David also his servant, and......... Ps 78:70
c that in which I delighted not............ Is 66:4
In the day when I c Israel................... Eze 20:5
and of them he c twelve, whom also ... Lk 6:13
how they c out the chief rooms .... Lk 14:7
they c Stephen, a man full of .... Acts 6:5
people of Israel c our fathers............. Acts 13:17
Paul c Silas, and departed, being...... Acts 15:40

CHOSEN
And he took six hundred c chariots .... Ex 14:7
his c captains also are drowned.......... Ex 15:4
even him whom he hath c will he........ Num 16:5
the LORD thy God hath c thee to......... Deut 7:6
which the LORD thy God hath c to....... Deut 12:21
the LORD hath c thee to be a .... Deut 14:2
hath c to place his name there .... Deut 16:11
hath c him out of all thy tribes........... Deut 18:5
God hath c to minister unto him......... Deut 21:5
that ye have c you the LORD .... Josh 24:22
cry unto the gods which ye have c...... Judg 10:14
numbered seven hundred c................. Judg 20:15
seven hundred c men lefthanded........ Judg 20:16
thousand c men out of all Israel......... Judg 20:34
king which ye shall have c you............ 1Sa 8:18
See ye him whom the LORD hath c...... 1Sa 10:24
behold the king whom ye have c......... 1Sa 12:13
Neither hath the LORD c this.............. 1Sa 16:8
Neither hath the LORD c this.............. 1Sa 16:9
Jesse, The LORD hath not c these....... 1Sa 16:10
do not I know that thou hast c............ 1Sa 20:30
thousand c men out of all Israel......... 2Sa 24:2
having three thousand c men of......... 2Sa 26:2
together all the c men of Israel 2Sa 6:1
of thy people which thou hast c.......... 1Kin 3:8
toward the city which thou hast c....... 1Kin 8:44
the city which thou hast c................... 1Kin 8:48
Jerusalem's sake which I have c 1Kin 11:13
the city which I have c out of.............. 1Kin 11:32
the city which I have c me to put........ 1Kin 11:36
and fourscore thousand c men............ 1Kin 12:21
which I have c out of all tribes............ 2Kin 21:7
city Jerusalem which I have c.............. 2Kin 23:27
All these which were c to be............... 1Chr 9:22
for them hath the LORD c to carry...... 1Chr 15:2
ye children of Jacob, his c ones........... 1Chr 16:13
Jeduthun, and the rest that were c..... 1Chr 16:41
for he hath c Judah to be the............. 1Chr 28:4
he hath c Solomon my son to sit 1Chr 28:5
for I have c him to be my son, and..... 1Chr 28:6
for the LORD hath c thee to build 1Chr 28:10
my son, whom alone God hath c......... 1Chr 29:1
But I have c Jerusalem, that my.......... 2Chr 6:6
have c David to be over my people..... 2Chr 6:6
this city which thou hast c.................. 2Chr 6:34
toward the city which thou hast c....... 2Chr 6:38
have c this place to myself for............ 2Chr 7:12
For now have I c and sanctified.......... 2Chr 7:16
and fourscore thousand c men............ 2Chr 11:1
the city which the LORD had c out 2Chr 12:13
even four hundred thousand c men..... 2Chr 13:3
with eight hundred thousand c men 2Chr 13:17
five hundred thousand c men 2Chr 13:17
for the LORD hath c you to stand........ 2Chr 29:11
which I have c before all the 2Chr 33:7
I have c to set my name there............ Neh 1:9
for this hast thou c rather than.......... Job 36:21
he hath c for his own inheritance .... Ps 33:12
and smote down the c men of Israel ... Ps 78:31
I have made a covenant with my c ...... Ps 89:3
exalted one c out of the people.......... Ps 89:19
ye children of Jacob his c................... Ps 105:6
and Aaron whom he had c................... Ps 105:26
with joy, and his c with gladness........ Ps 105:43
That I may see the good of thy c........ Ps 106:5
had not Moses his c stood before .... Ps 106:23
I have c the way of truth.................... Ps 119:30
for I have c thy precepts.................... Ps 119:173
For the LORD hath c Zion................... Ps 132:13
For the LORD hath c Jacob unto......... Ps 135:4
rather to be c than silver.................... Prov 16:16
rather to be c than great riches.......... Prov 22:1
for the gardens that ye have c .... Is 1:29
my servant, Jacob whom I have c .... Is 41:8
I have c thee, and not cast thee......... Is 41:9
LORD, and my servant whom I have c .. Is 43:10
to give drink to my people, my c......... Is 43:20
and Israel, whom I have c................... Is 44:1
and thou, Jesurun, whom I have c....... Is 44:2
I have c thee in the furnace of .... Is 48:10
Is it such a fast that I have c.............. Is 58:5
not this the fast that I have c............. Is 58:6
your name for a curse unto my c .... Is 65:15
they have c their own ways, and........ Is 66:3
death shall be c rather than life......... Jer 8:3

families which the LORD hath c .... Jer 33:24
his c young men are gone down to...... Jer 48:15
and who is a c man, that I may .... Jer 49:19
and who is a c man, that I may .... Jer 50:44
that were the c men of Assyria........... Eze 23:7
withstand, neither his c people .... Dan 11:15
for I have c thee, saith the LORD........ Hag 2:23
that hath c Jerusalem rebuke thee ..... Zec 3:2
Behold my servant, whom I have c ..... Mt 12:18
for many be called, but few c .... Mt 20:16
many are called, but few are c........... Mt 22:14
the elect's sake, whom he hath c .... Mk 13:20
Mary hath c that good part, which ..... Lk 10:42
if he be Christ, the c of God............... Lk 23:35
them, Have not I c you twelve............. Jn 6:70
I know whom I have c .... Jn 13:18
not c me, but I have c you................... Jn 15:16
but I have c you out of the world........ Jn 15:19
unto the apostles whom he had c....... Acts 1:2
whether of these two thou hast c .... Acts 1:24
for he is a c vessel unto me, to.......... Acts 9:15
unto witnesses c before of God.......... Acts 10:41
to send c men of their own company... Acts 15:22
to send c men unto you with our........ Acts 15:25
God of our fathers hath c thee........... Acts 22:14
Salute Rufus c in the Lord................... Rom 16:13
But God hath c the foolish things....... 1Cor 1:27
God hath c the weak things of the 1Cor 1:27
which are despised, hath God c 1Cor 1:28
but who was also c of the.................. 2Cor 8:19
According as he hath c us in him........ Eph 1:4
c you to salvation through.................. 2Th 2:13
who hath c him to be a soldier 2Ti 2:4
Hath not God c the poor of this......... Jas 2:5
but c of God, and precious,................ 1Pet 2:4
But ye are a c generation................... 1Pet 2:9
are with him are called, and c............ Rev 17:14

CHOZEBA (ko-ze′-bah) See CHEZIB. *A city in Judah.*
And Jokim, and the men of C.............. 1Chr 4:22

CHRIST (krist) See PREFACE. See also ANTICHRIST, CHRISTIAN, CHRIST'S, CHRIST, JESUS, MESSIAH. *A title of Jesus of Nazareth; Greek for Messiah.*
birth of Jesus C was on this wise .... Mt 1:18
of them where C should be born .... Mt 2:4
answered and said, Thou art the C ..... Mt 16:16
for one is your Master, even C .... Mt 23:8
come in my name, saying, I am C .... Mt 24:5
shall say unto you, Lo, here is C .... Mt 24:23
Saying, Prophesy unto us, thou C....... Mt 26:68
my name, because ye belong to C .... Mk 9:41
Let C the King of Israel descend.......... Mk 15:32
before he had seen the Lord's C .... Lk 2:26
Thou art C the Son of God.................. Lk 4:41
let him save himself, if he be C .... Lk 23:35
on him, saying, If thou be C .... Lk 23:39
Ought not C to have suffered .... Lk 24:26
and thus it behoved C to suffer.......... Lk 24:46
Messias cometh, which is called C...... Jn 4:25
but when C cometh, no man knoweth.. Jn 7:27
Shall C come out of Galilee................ Jn 7:41
That C cometh of the seed of............. Jn 7:42
any man did confess that he was C ..... Jn 9:22
I believe that thou art the C................ Jn 11:27
the law that C abideth for ever........... Jn 12:34
he would raise up C to sit on his........ Acts 2:30
that C should suffer, he hath so......... Acts 3:18
Samaria, and preached C unto them... Acts 8:5
he preached C in the synagogues .... Acts 9:20
that C must needs have suffered,....... Acts 17:3
That C should suffer, and that he....... Acts 26:23
in due time C died for the .... Rom 5:6
were yet sinners, C died for us........... Rom 5:8
that like as C was raised up from....... Rom 6:4
Knowing that C being raised from .... Rom 6:9
dead to the law by the body of C .... Rom 7:4
any man have not the Spirit of C .... Rom 8:9
if C be in you, the body is dead .... Rom 8:10
he that raised up C from the dead...... Rom 8:11
accursed from C for my brethren......... Rom 9:3
as concerning the flesh C came .... Rom 9:5
For C is the end of the law for .... Rom 10:4
to bring C down from above .... Rom 10:6
to bring up C again from the dead...... Rom 10:7
For to this end C both died,................ Rom 14:9
with thy meat, for whom C died .... Rom 14:15
serveth C is acceptable to God .... Rom 14:18
For even C pleased not himself.......... Rom 15:3
as C also received us to the .... Rom 15:7
which C hath not wrought by me......... Rom 15:18
the gospel, not where C was named.... Rom 15:20
the firstfruits of Achaia unto C .... Rom 16:5
But we preach C crucified.................. 1Cor 1:23
C the power of God, and the wisdom... 1Cor 1:24
and C is God's................................... 1Cor 3:23
For even C our passover is................. 1Cor 5:7
and one Lord Jesus C, by whom are ... 1Cor 8:6
brother perish, for whom C died......... 1Cor 8:11
to God, but under the law to C 1Cor 9:21
and that Rock was C.......................... 1Cor 10:4
Neither let us tempt C, as some 1Cor 10:9
how that C died for our sins............... 1Cor 15:3
Now if C be preached that he rose 1Cor 15:12
rise not, then is not C raised.............. 1Cor 15:16
if C be not raised, your faith is 1Cor 15:17
C the firstfruits................................. 1Cor 15:23
have us through C to God-ward.......... 2Cor 3:4
we have known C after the flesh........ 2Cor 5:16

Therefore if any man be in C.............. 2Cor 5:17
To wit, that God was in C................... 2Cor 5:19
what concord hath C with Belial......... 2Cor 6:15
you as a chaste virgin to C................ 2Cor 11:2
law, but by the faith of Jesus C.......... Gal 2:16
even we have believed in Jesus C........ Gal 2:16
be justified by the faith of C............... Gal 2:16
we seek to be justified by C............... Gal 2:17
I am crucified with C........................ Gal 2:20
yet not I, but C liveth in me.............. Gal 2:20
the law, but C is dead in vain............ Gal 2:21
C hath redeemed us from the curse..... Gal 3:13
schoolmaster to bring us unto C......... Gal 3:24
then an heir of God through C............ Gal 4:7
again until C be formed in you............ Gal 4:19
wherewith C hath made us free........... Gal 5:1
C shall profit you nothing.................. Gal 5:2
C is become of no effect unto you........ Gal 5:4
in the cross of our Lord Jesus C.......... Gal 6:14
at that time ye were without C............ Eph 2:12
That C may dwell in your hearts......... Eph 3:17
things, which is the head, even C......... Eph 4:15
But ye have not so learned C.............. Eph 4:20
dead, and C shall give thee light........ Eph 5:14
as the church is subject unto C........... Eph 5:24
even as C also loved the church.......... Eph 5:25
but I speak concerning C and the........ Eph 5:32
of your heart, as unto C.................... Eph 6:5
Some indeed preach C even of envy..... Phil 1:15
The one preach C of contention.......... Phil 1:16
or in truth, C is preached................. Phil 1:18
so now also C shall be magnified......... Phil 1:20
For to me to live is C, and to die........ Phil 1:21
the knowledge of C Jesus my Lord...... Phil 3:8
through C which strengtheneth me...... Phil 4:13
of the world, and not after C.............. Col 2:8
When C, who is our life, shall............ Col 3:4
but C is all, and in all...................... Col 3:11
even as C forgave you, so also do....... Col 3:13
for ye serve the Lord C...................... Col 3:24
the dead in C shall rise first.............. 1Th 4:16
in the name of our Lord Jesus C......... 2Th 3:6
before God, and the Lord Jesus C........ 1Ti 5:21
But C as a son over his own house....... Heb 3:6
So also C glorified not himself............ Heb 5:5
But C being come an high priest......... Heb 9:11
For C is not entered into the.............. Heb 9:24
So C was once offered to bear the....... Heb 9:28
Jesus C the same yesterday, and to..... Heb 13:8
because C also suffered for us............. 1Pet 2:21
Forasmuch then as C hath suffered...... 1Pet 4:1
that denieth that Jesus is the C........... 1Jn 2:22
kingdoms of our Lord, and of his C..... Rev 11:15
of our God, and the power of his C...... Rev 12:10

CHRISTIAN (kris'-tyan) See CHRISTIANS. A
follower of Jesus Christ.
thou persuadest me to be a C.............. Acts 26:28
Yet if any man suffer as a C............... 1Pet 4:16

CHRISTIANS (kris'-tyans)
were called C first in Antioch............. Acts 11:26

CHRIST'S (krists)
for the Lord Jesus C sake.................. Rom 15:30
And ye are C.................................. 1Cor 3:23
We are fools for C sake, but ye.......... 1Cor 4:10
called, being free, is C servant........... 1Cor 7:22
they that are C at his coming............. 1Cor 15:23
came to Troas to preach C gospel....... 2Cor 2:12
we pray you in C stead, be ye............ 2Cor 5:20
man trust to himself that he is C........ 2Cor 10:7
he is C, even so are we C.................. 2Cor 10:7
in distresses for C sake..................... 2Cor 12:10
And if ye be C, then are ye................ Gal 3:29
they that are C have crucified........... Gal 5:24
even as God for C sake hath.............. Eph 4:32
not the things which are Jesus C........ Phil 2:21
ye are partakers of C sufferings......... 1Pet 4:13

CHRISTS (krists)
For there shall arise false C............... Mt 24:24
For false C and false prophets........... Mk 13:22

CHRONICLES
of the c of the kings of Israel............ 1Kin 14:19
of the c of the kings of Judah........... 1Kin 14:29
of the c of the kings of Israel............ 1Kin 15:7
of the c of the kings of Judah........... 1Kin 15:23
of the c of the kings of Israel............ 1Kin 15:31
of the c of the kings of Israel............ 1Kin 16:5
of the c of the kings of Israel............ 1Kin 16:14
of the c of the kings of Israel............ 1Kin 16:20
of the c of the kings of Judah........... 1Kin 16:27
of the c of the kings of Israel............ 1Kin 22:39
of the c of the kings of Judah........... 1Kin 22:45
of the c of the kings of Israel............ 2Kin 1:18
of the c of the kings of Judah........... 2Kin 8:23
of the c of the kings of Israel............ 2Kin 10:34
of the c of the kings of Judah........... 2Kin 12:19
of the c of the kings of Israel............ 2Kin 13:8
of the c of the kings of Judah........... 2Kin 13:12
of the c of the kings of Israel............ 2Kin 14:15
of the c of the kings of Israel............ 2Kin 14:18
of the c of the kings of Israel............ 2Kin 14:28
of the c of the kings of Israel............ 2Kin 15:6
of the c of the kings of Judah........... 2Kin 15:11
of the c of the kings of Judah........... 2Kin 15:15
of the c of the kings of Judah........... 2Kin 15:21
of the c of the kings of Judah........... 2Kin 15:26
of the c of the kings of Judah........... 2Kin 15:36
of the c of the kings of Judah........... 2Kin 16:19

of the c of the kings of Judah........... 2Kin 20:20
of the c of the kings of Judah........... 2Kin 21:17
of the c of the kings of Judah........... 2Kin 21:25
of the c of the kings of Judah........... 2Kin 23:28
of the c of the kings of Judah........... 2Kin 24:5
account of the c of king David.......... 1Chr 27:24
were written in the book of the c....... Neh 12:23
the book of the c before the king....... Est 2:23
the book of records of the c.............. Est 6:1
of the c of the kings of Media........... Est 10:2

CHRYSOLITE
the seventh, a............................... Rev 21:20

CHRYSOPRASUS
the tenth, a c............................... Rev 21:20

CHUB (cub) Allies of Egypt.
and all the mingled people, and C...... Eze 30:5

CHUN (kun) A city in Aran-zobah.
Likewise from Tibhath, and from C..... 1Chr 18:8

CHURCH
upon this rock I will build my c......... Mt 16:18
to hear them, tell it unto the c.......... Mt 18:17
but if he neglect to hear the c.......... Mt 18:17
the Lord added to the c daily............ Acts 2:47
And great fear came upon all the c..... Acts 5:11
is he, that was in the c in the........... Acts 7:38
the c which was at Jerusalem............ Acts 8:1
for Saul, he made havock of the c...... Acts 8:3
of the c which was in Jerusalem........ Acts 11:22
assembled themselves with the c........ Acts 11:26
his hands to vex certain of the c........ Acts 12:1
ceasing of the c unto God for him...... Acts 12:5
Now there were in the c that was....... Acts 13:1
ordained them elders in every c......... Acts 14:23
and had gathered the c together........ Acts 14:27
brought on their way by the c........... Acts 15:3
they were received of the c............... Acts 15:4
and elders, with the whole c............. Acts 15:22
and gone up, and saluted the c......... Acts 18:22
called and the elders of the c............ Acts 20:17
overseers, to feed the c of God.......... Acts 20:28
of the c which is at Cenchrea............ Rom 16:1
Likewise greet the c that is in........... Rom 16:5
mine host, and of the whole c........... Rom 16:23
servant of the c at Cenchrea............. Rom s
Unto the c of God which is at........... 1Cor 1:2
as I teach every where in every c...... 1Cor 4:17
who are least esteemed in the c........ 1Cor 6:4
the Gentiles, nor to the c of God....... 1Cor 10:32
when ye come together in the c......... 1Cor 11:18
or despise ye the c of God............... 1Cor 11:22
And God hath set some in the c........ 1Cor 12:28
that prophesieth edifieth the c.......... 1Cor 14:4
that the c may receive edifying......... 1Cor 14:5
except to the edifying of the c.......... 1Cor 14:12
Yet in the c I had rather speak......... 1Cor 14:19
If therefore the whole c be come....... 1Cor 14:23
let him keep silence in the c............. 1Cor 14:28
shame for women to speak in the c.... 1Cor 14:35
because I persecuted the c of God...... 1Cor 15:9
the c that is in their house............... 1Cor 16:19
unto the c of God which is at........... 2Cor 1:1
measure I persecuted the c of God..... Gal 1:13
the head over all things to the c........ Eph 1:22
the c the manifold wisdom of God...... Eph 3:10
Unto him be glory in the c by.......... Eph 3:21
as Christ is the head of the c............ Eph 5:23
Therefore as the c is subject............. Eph 5:24
even as Christ also loved the c.......... Eph 5:25
it to himself a glorious c.................. Eph 5:27
it, even as the Lord the c................. Eph 5:29
speak concerning Christ and the c...... Eph 5:32
zeal, persecuting the c.................... Phil 3:6
no c communicated with me as......... Phil 4:15
he is the head of the body, the c....... Col 1:18
his body's sake, which is the c.......... Col 1:24
the c which is in his house.............. Col 4:15
also in the c of the Laodiceans.......... Col 4:16
unto the c of the Thessalonians......... 1Th 1:1
unto the c of the Thessalonians......... 2Th 1:1
he take care of the c of God............. 1Ti 3:5
which is the c of the living God........ 1Ti 3:15
them, and let not the c be charged.... 1Ti 5:16
bishop of the c of the Cretians......... Titus s
bishop of the c of the Cretians......... Titus a
and to the c in thy house................ Philem 2
in the midst of the c will I sing......... Heb 2:12
c of the firstborn, which are............ Heb 12:23
him call for the elders of the c.......... Jas 5:14
The c that is at Babylon, elected....... 1Pet 5:13
of thy charity before the c................ 3Jn 6
I wrote unto the c......................... 3Jn 9
and casteth them out of the c........... 3Jn 10
angel of the c of Ephesus write......... Rev 2:1
angel of the c in Smyrna write.......... Rev 2:8
angel of the c in Pergamos write....... Rev 2:12
angel of the c in Thyatira write......... Rev 2:18
angel of the c in Sardis write........... Rev 3:1
And to the angel of the c in............. Rev 3:7
unto the angel of the c of the........... Rev 3:14

CHURCHES
Then had the c rest throughout......... Acts 9:31
and Cilicia, confirming the c............. Acts 15:41
so were the c established in the........ Acts 16:5
which are neither robbers of c........... Acts 19:37
also all the c of the Gentiles............ Rom 16:4
The c of Christ salute you................ Rom 16:16
And so ordain I in all c.................. 1Cor 7:17

such custom, neither the c of God...... 1Cor 11:16
as in all c of the saints................... 1Cor 14:33
your women keep silence in the c...... 1Cor 14:34
given order to the c of Galatia.......... 1Cor 16:1
The c of Asia salute you................. 1Cor 16:19
bestowed on the c of Macedonia........ 2Cor 8:1
the gospel throughout all the c......... 2Cor 8:18
the c to travel with us with this........ 2Cor 8:19
they are the messengers of the c....... 2Cor 8:23
shew ye to them, and before the c..... 2Cor 8:24
I robbed other c, taking wages of...... 2Cor 11:8
me daily, the care of all the c........... 2Cor 11:28
ye were inferior to other c................ 2Cor 12:13
with me, unto the c of Galatia.......... Gal 1:22
was unknown by face unto the c of.... Gal 1:22
became churches of the c of God....... 1Th 2:14
in the c of God for your patience...... 2Th 1:4
to the seven c which are in Asia........ Rev 1:4
the seven c which are in Asia........... Rev 1:11
are the angels of the seven c............ Rev 1:20
which thou sawest are the seven c..... Rev 1:20
what the Spirit saith unto the c......... Rev 2:7
what the Spirit saith unto the c......... Rev 2:11
what the Spirit saith unto the c......... Rev 2:17
all the c shall know that I am he....... Rev 2:23
what the Spirit saith unto the c......... Rev 2:29
what the Spirit saith unto the c......... Rev 3:6
what the Spirit saith unto the c......... Rev 3:13
what the Spirit saith unto the c......... Rev 3:22
unto you these things in the c........... Rev 22:16

CHURL
nor the c said to be bountiful........... Is 32:5
also of the c are evil...................... Is 32:7

CHURLISH
but the man was c and evil in his...... 1Sa 25:3

CHURNING
Surely the c of milk bringeth........... Prov 30:33

CHUSHAN-RISHATHAIM (cu'-shan-rish-a-
tha'-im) A king of Mesopotamia.
the hand of Cushan of Mesopotamia... Judg 3:8
of Israel served C eight years............ Judg 3:8
the Lord delivered C king of............. Judg 3:10
and his hand prevailed against C....... Judg 3:10

CHUZA (cu'-zah) A steward of Herod Antipas.
the wife of C Herod's steward........... Lk 8:3

CIELED
greater house he c with fir tree......... 2Chr 3:5
it is c with cedar, and painted.......... Jer 22:14
c with wood round about, and from.... Eze 41:16
O ye, to dwell in your c houses........ Hag 1:4

CIELING
the house, and the walls of the c...... 1Kin 6:15

CILICIA (sil-ish'-yah) A Roman province in
Asia Minor.
and Alexandrians, and of them of C.... Acts 6:9
Gentiles in Antioch and Syria and C.... Acts 15:23
And he went through Syria and C....... Acts 15:41
am a Jew of Tarsus, a city in............. Acts 21:39
Jew, born in Tarsus, a city in C......... Acts 22:3
he understood that he was of C.......... Acts 23:34
we had sailed over the sea of C......... Acts 27:5
into the regions of Syria and C.......... Gal 1:21

CINNAMON
of sweet c half so much, even two...... Ex 30:23
my bed with myrrh, aloes, and c........ Prov 7:17
calamus and c, with all trees of......... Song 4:14
c, and odours, and ointments............ Rev 18:13

CINNEROTH (sin'-ne-roth) See CHINNEROTH.
Same as Chinneroth.
and Abel-beth-maachah, and all C..... 1Kin 15:20

CIRCLE
sitteth upon the c of the earth.......... Is 40:22

CIRCUIT
from year to year in c to Beth-el....... 1Sa 7:16
and he walketh in the c of heaven..... Job 22:14
his c unto the ends of it.................. Ps 19:6

CIRCUITS
again according to his c................... Eccl 1:6

CIRCUMCISE
ye shall c the flesh of your............... Gen 17:11
C therefore the foreskin of your......... Deut 10:16
LORD thy God will c thine heart........ Deut 30:6
c again the children of Israel............ Josh 5:2
is the cause why Joshua did c........... Josh 5:4
C yourselves to the LORD, and.......... Jer 4:4
day they came to c the child............. Lk 1:59
and ye on the sabbath day c a man.... Jn 7:22
That it was needful to c them........... Acts 15:5
ought not to c their children............ Acts 21:21

CIRCUMCISED
man child among you shall be c......... Gen 17:10
days old shall be c among you........... Gen 17:12
with thy money, must needs be c....... Gen 17:13
flesh of his foreskin is not c............. Gen 17:14
c the flesh of their foreskin in.......... Gen 17:24
when he was c in the flesh of his...... Gen 17:24
when he was c in the flesh of his...... Gen 17:25
In the selfsame day was Abraham c.... Gen 17:26
of the stranger, were c with him....... Gen 17:27
Abraham c his son Isaac being.......... Gen 21:4
be, that every male of you be c......... Gen 34:15
will not hearken unto us, to be c...... Gen 34:15

us be c, as they are c .... Gen 34:22
and every male was c, all that .... Gen 34:24
for money, when thou hast c him ..... Ex 12:44
the LORD, let all his males be c .... Ex 12:48
flesh of his foreskin shall be c .... Lev 12:3
c the children of Israel at the .... Josh 5:3
the people that came out were c .... Josh 5:5
out of Egypt, them they had not c ..... Josh 5:5
up in their stead, them Joshua c ...... Josh 5:7
they had not c them by the way .... Josh 5:7
are c with the uncircumcised .... Jer 9:25
Isaac, and c him the eighth day .... Acts 7:8
Except ye be c after the manner .... Acts 15:1
your souls, saying, Ye must be c ...... Acts 15:24
c him because of the Jews which ...... Acts 16:3
believe, though they be not c .... Rom 4:11
Is any man called being c 1Cor 7:18
let him not be c 1Cor 7:18
a Greek, was compelled to be c .... Gal 2:3
say unto you, that if ye be c .... Gal 5:2
again to every man that is c .... Gal 5:3
flesh, they constrain you to be c ...... Gal 6:12
themselves who are c keep the law ... Gal 6:13
but desire to have you c, that .... Gal 6:13
C the eighth day, of the stock of ...... Phil 3:5
In whom also ye are c with the .... Col 2:11

CIRCUMCISION

they had done c all the people .... Josh 5:8
for the c of the child, his name .... Lk 2:21

CIRCUMCISION

thou art, because of the c .... Ex 4:26
Moses therefore gave unto you c ...... Jn 7:22
man on the sabbath day receive c ..... Jn 7:23
And he gave him the covenant of c .... Acts 7:8
they of the c which believed were ..... Acts 10:45
were of the c contended with him ..... Acts 11:2
For c verily profiteth, if thou .... Rom 2:25
thy c is made uncircumcision .... Rom 2:25
uncircumcision be counted for c ...... Rom 2:26
c dost transgress the law .... Rom 2:27
neither is that c, which is .... Rom 2:28
c is that of the heart, in the .... Rom 2:29
or what profit is there of c .... Rom 3:1
shall justify the c by faith .... Rom 3:30
blessedness then upon the c only ...... Rom 4:9
when he was in c, or in .... Rom 4:10
Not in c, but in uncircumcision .... Rom 4:10
And he received the sign of c .... Rom 4:11
the father of c to them who are .... Rom 4:12
to them who are not of the c only ...... Rom 4:12
of the c for the truth of God .... Rom 15:8
C is nothing, and uncircumcision 1Cor 7:19
gospel of the c was unto Peter .... Gal 2:7
Peter to the apostleship of the c .... Gal 2:8
the heathen, and they unto the c .... Gal 2:9
fearing them which were of the c ...... Gal 2:12
neither c availeth any thing .... Gal 5:6
And I, brethren, if I yet preach c ...... Gal 5:11
neither c availeth any thing .... Gal 6:15
the C in the flesh made by hands ...... Eph 2:11
For we are the c, which worship .... Phil 3:3
with the c made without hands .... Col 2:11
of the flesh by the c of Christ .... Col 2:11
nor uncircumcision, Barbarian, ... Col 3:11
called Justus, who are of the c .... Col 4:11
specially they of the c .... Titus 1:10

CIRCUMSPECT

that I have said unto you be c .... Ex 23:13

CIRCUMSPECTLY

See then that ye walk c, not as .... Eph 5:15

CIS

CIS (sis) See KISH. Father of King Saul.
gave unto them Saul the son of C ...... Acts 13:21

CISTERN

ye every one the waters of his c 2Kin 18:31
Drink waters out of thine own c .... Prov 5:15
or the wheel broken at the c .... Eccl 12:6
every one the waters of his own c ...... Is 36:16

CISTERNS

hewed them out c, broken c .... Jer 2:13

CITIES

Lot dwelled in the c of the plain .... Gen 13:12
And he overthrew those c, and all ..... Gen 19:25
and all the inhabitants of the c .... Gen 19:25
God destroyed the c of the plain .... Gen 19:29
when he overthrew the c in the .... Gen 19:29
the c that were round about them ...... Gen 35:5
and let them keep food in the c .... Gen 41:35
and laid up the food in the c .... Gen 41:48
he removed them to c from one end ... Gen 47:21
they built for Pharaoh treasure c ...... Ex 1:11
the c of the Levites, and the .... Lev 25:32
the houses of the c of their .... Lev 25:32
for the houses of the c of the .... Lev 25:33
of their c may not be sold .... Lev 25:33
gathered together within your c .... Lev 26:25
And I will make your c waste .... Lev 26:31
be desolate, and your c waste .... Lev 26:33
what c they be that they dwell in ...... Num 13:19
the c are walled, and very great .... Num 13:28
I will utterly destroy their c .... Num 21:2
utterly destroyed them and their c .... Num 21:3
And Israel took all these c .... Num 21:25
in all the c of the Amorites .... Num 21:25
all their c wherein they dwelt .... Num 31:10
cattle, and c for our little ones .... Num 32:16
c because of the inhabitants of .... Num 32:17

Build you c for your little ones, ... Num 32:24
shall be there in the c of Gilead .... Num 32:26
with the c thereof in the coasts, ... Num 32:33
even the c of the country round .... Num 32:33
and Berih-haran, fenced c .... Num 32:36
unto the c which they builded, ... Num 32:38
of their possession c to dwell in .... Num 35:2
for the c round about them .... Num 35:2
the c shall they have to dwell in .... Num 35:3
And the suburbs of the c, which ye ... Num 35:4
be to them the suburbs of the c .... Num 35:5
among the c which ye shall give .... Num 35:6
there shall be six c for refuge .... Num 35:6
them ye shall add forty and two c ..... Num 35:6
So all the c which ye shall give .... Num 35:7
Levites shall be forty and eight c ...... Num 35:7
the c which ye shall give shall .... Num 35:8
every one shall give of his c .... Num 35:8
c to be c of refuge for you .... Num 35:11
they shall be unto you c of .... Num 35:12
of these c which ye shall give .... Num 35:13
six c shall ye have for refuge .... Num 35:13
give three c on this side Jordan .... Num 35:14
three c shall ye give in the land .... Num 35:14
which shall be c of refuge .... Num 35:14
These six c shall be a refuge, ... Num 35:15
into what c we shall come .... Deut 1:22
the c are great and walled up to .... Deut 1:28
And we took all his c at that time ..... Deut 2:34
the spoil of the c which we took .... Deut 2:35
nor unto the c in the mountains, ... Deut 2:37
And we took all his c at that time ..... Deut 3:4
took not from them, threescore c ...... Deut 3:4
All these c were fenced with high ..... Deut 3:5
the cattle, and the spoil of the c .... Deut 3:7
All the c of the plain, and all .... Deut 4:43
c of the kingdom of Og in Bashan ..... Deut 3:10
the c thereof, gave I unto the .... Deut 3:12
shall abide in your c which .... Deut 3:19
Then Moses severed three c on .... Deut 4:41
unto one of these c he might live ...... Deut 4:42
to give thee great and goodly c, ... Deut 6:10
c great and fenced up to heaven, ... Deut 9:1
shalt hear say in one of thy c .... Deut 13:12
them, and dwellest in their c .... Deut 19:1
Thou shalt separate three c for .... Deut 19:2
he shall flee unto one of those c .... Deut 19:5
shalt separate three c for thee, ... Deut 19:7
thou add three c more for thee .... Deut 19:9
and fleeth into one of these c .... Deut 19:11
the c which are very far off from, ... Deut 20:15
are not of the c of these nations .... Deut 20:15
But of the c of these people, ... Deut 20:16
they shall measure unto the c .... Deut 21:2
came unto their c on the third .... Josh 9:17
Now their c were Gibeon, and .... Josh 9:17
great city, as one of the royal c .... Josh 10:2
them not to enter into their c .... Josh 10:19
of them entered into fenced c .... Josh 10:20
thereof, and all the c thereof .... Josh 10:37
thereof, and all the c thereof .... Josh 10:39
all the c of those kings, and all .... Josh 11:12
But as for the c that stood still .... Josh 11:13
And all the spoil of these c .... Josh 11:14
them utterly with their c .... Josh 11:21
all the c of Sihon king of the .... Josh 13:10
all her c that are in the plain .... Josh 13:17
All the c of the plain, and all .... Josh 13:21
after their families, the c .... Josh 13:23
all the c of Gilead, and half the .... Josh 13:25
Gad after their families, the c .... Josh 13:28
which are in Bashan, threescore c .... Josh 13:30
c of the kingdom of Og in Bashan, ... Josh 13:31
save c to dwell in, with their .... Josh 14:4
that the c were great and fenced ...... Josh 14:12
went out to the c of mount Ephron .... Josh 15:9
the uttermost c of the tribe of .... Josh 15:21
all the c are twenty and nine, ... Josh 15:32
fourteen c with their villages .... Josh 15:36
sixteen c with their villages .... Josh 15:41
nine c with their villages .... Josh 15:44
eleven c with their villages .... Josh 15:51
nine c with their villages .... Josh 15:54
ten c with their villages .... Josh 15:57
six c with their villages .... Josh 15:59
two c with their villages .... Josh 15:60
six c with their villages .... Josh 15:62
the separate c for the children .... Josh 16:9
all the c with their villages, ... Josh 16:9
these c of Ephraim are among the ..... Josh 17:9
are among the c of Manasseh .... Josh 17:9
out the inhabitants of those c .... Josh 17:12
described it by c into seven .... Josh 18:9
Now the c of the tribe of the .... Josh 18:21
twelve c with their villages .... Josh 18:24
fourteen c with their villages .... Josh 18:28
thirteen c and their villages .... Josh 19:6
four c and their villages .... Josh 19:7
about these c to Baalath-beer .... Josh 19:8
twelve c with their villages .... Josh 19:15
these c with their villages .... Josh 19:16
sixteen c with their villages .... Josh 19:22
to their families, the c and their ...... Josh 19:23
two c with their villages .... Josh 19:30
these c with their villages .... Josh 19:31
And the fenced c are Ziddim .... Josh 19:35
nineteen c with their villages .... Josh 19:38
to their families, the c and their ...... Josh 19:39
these c with their villages .... Josh 19:48
Appoint out for you c of refuge .... Josh 20:2

doth flee unto one of those c .... Josh 20:4
These were the c appointed for .... Josh 20:9
of Moses to give us c to dwell in ...... Josh 21:2
commandment of the LORD, these c ... Josh 21:3
the tribe of Benjamin, thirteen c ..... Josh 21:4
of Moses to give us c to dwell in ...... Josh 21:4
the half tribe of Manasseh, ten c ...... Josh 21:5
of Manasseh in Bashan, thirteen c .... Josh 21:6
of the tribe of Zebulun, twelve c ...... Josh 21:7
these c with their suburbs .... Josh 21:8
these c which are here mentioned ..... Josh 21:9
nine c out of those two tribes .... Josh 21:16
four c .... Josh 21:18
All the c of the children of .... Josh 21:19
were thirteen c with their .... Josh 21:19
even they had the c of their lot .... Josh 21:20
Beth-horon with her suburbs; four c .. Josh 21:22
with her suburbs; four c .... Josh 21:24
with her suburbs; two c .... Josh 21:25
All the c were ten with their .... Josh 21:26
Beesh-terah with her suburbs; two c .. Josh 21:27
En-gannim with her suburbs; four c .. Josh 21:29
Rehob with her suburbs; four c .... Josh 21:31
Kartan with her suburbs; three c ..... Josh 21:32
All the c of the Gershonites .... Josh 21:33
thirteen c with their suburbs .... Josh 21:33
Nahalal with her suburbs; four c ..... Josh 21:35
Mephaath with her suburbs; four c ... Josh 21:37
four c in all .... Josh 21:39
So all the c for the children of .... Josh 21:40
were by their lot twelve c .... Josh 21:40
All the c of the Levites within .... Josh 21:41
eight c with their suburbs .... Josh 21:41
These c were every one with their .... Josh 21:42
thus were all these c .... Josh 21:42
c which ye built not, and ye dwell .... Josh 24:13
ass colts, and they had thirty c .... Judg 10:4
in all the c that be along by the .... Judg 11:26
come to Minnith, even twenty c ...... Judg 11:33
buried in one of the c of Gilead .... Judg 12:7
together out of the c unto Gibeah ..... Judg 20:14
at that time out of the c twenty .... Judg 20:15
them which came out of the c they ... Judg 20:42
fire all the c that they came to .... Judg 20:48
inheritance, and repaired the c ...... Judg 21:23
to the number of all the c of the 1Sa 6:18
the five lords, both of fenced c 1Sa 6:18
the c which the Philistines had 1Sa 7:14
women came out of all c of Israel 1Sa 18:6
in the c of the Jerahmeelites 1Sa 30:29
were in the c of the Kenites 1Sa 30:29
were dead, they forsook the c 1Sa 31:7
go up into any of the c of Judah 2Sa 2:1
and they dwelt in the c of Hebron 2Sa 2:3
c of Hadarezer, king David took 2Sa 8:8
people, and for the c of our God 2Sa 10:12
the c of the children of Ammon 2Sa 12:31
him, lest he get him fenced c 2Sa 20:6
to all the c of the Hivites, and 2Sa 24:7
threescore great c with walls 1Kin 4:13
them in the land of their 1Kin 8:37
twenty c in the land of Galilee 1Kin 9:11
the c which Solomon had given him .. 1Kin 9:12
What c are these which thou hast 1Kin 9:13
all the c of store that Solomon 1Kin 9:19
c for his chariots 1Kin 9:19
c for his horsemen, and that which ... 1Kin 9:19
he bestowed in the c for chariots 1Kin 10:26
which dwelt in the c of Judah 1Kin 12:17
which are in the c of Samaria 1Kin 13:32
he had against the c of Samaria 1Kin 13:32
the c which he built, are they 1Kin 15:23
And Ben-hadad said unto him, The c .. 1Kin 20:34
all the c that he built, are they 1Kin 22:39
And they beat down the c, and on 2Kin 3:25
Ben-hadad the son of Hazael the c 2Kin 13:25
him, and recovered the c of Israel 2Kin 13:25
Gozan, and in the c of the Medes 2Kin 17:6
them high places in all their 2Kin 17:9
placed them in the c of Samaria 2Kin 17:24
and dwelt in the c thereof 2Kin 17:24
and placed in the c of Samaria 2Kin 17:26
in their c wherein they dwelt 2Kin 17:29
Gozan, and in the c of the Medes 2Kin 18:11
against all the fenced c of Judah 2Kin 18:13
waste fenced c into ruinous heaps 2Kin 19:25
the high places in the c of Judah 2Kin 23:5
the priests out of the c of Judah 2Kin 23:8
that were in the c of Samaria 2Kin 23:19
twenty c in the land of Galilee 1Chr 2:22
towns thereof, even threescore c 1Chr 2:23
These were their c unto the reign 1Chr 4:31
and Tochen, and Ashan, five c 1Chr 4:32
that were round about the same c 1Chr 4:33
of Aaron they gave the c of Judah 1Chr 6:57
All their c throughout their 1Chr 6:60
their families were thirteen c 1Chr 6:60
were c given out of the half 1Chr 6:61
tribe of Manasseh, by lot, ten c 1Chr 6:61
of Manasseh in Bashan, thirteen c 1Chr 6:62
of the tribe of Zebulun, twelve c 1Chr 6:63
these c with their suburbs 1Chr 6:64
the children of Benjamin, these c 1Chr 6:65
of the sons of Kohath had c of 1Chr 6:66
of the c of refuge, Shechem in 1Chr 6:67
their possessions in their c were 1Chr 9:2
dead, then they forsook their c 1Chr 10:7
and Levites which are in their c 1Chr 13:2
c of Hadarezer, brought David 1Chr 18:8
themselves together from their c 1Chr 19:7
people, and for the c of our God 1Chr 19:13

C

the c of the children of Ammon 1Chr 20:3
in the fields, in the c, and in............. 1Chr 27:25
which he placed in the chariot c........ 2Chr 1:14
them in the c of their land................. 2Chr 6:28
That the c which Huram had............... 2Chr 8:2
wilderness, and all the store c........... 2Chr 8:5
Beth-horon the nether, fenced c......... 2Chr 8:5
all the store c that Solomon had,....... 2Chr 8:6
and all the chariot c............................ 2Chr 8:6
the c of the horsemen, and all........... 2Chr 8:6
whom he bestowed in the chariot c ... 2Chr 9:25
that dwelt in the c of Judah............... 2Chr 10:17
built c for defence in Judah............... 2Chr 11:5
in Judah and in Benjamin fenced c ... 2Chr 11:10
he took the fenced c which................ 2Chr 12:4
took c from him, Beth-el with the 2Chr 13:19
the c of Judah the high places........... 2Chr 14:5
And he built fenced c in Judah.......... 2Chr 14:6
unto Judah, Let us build these c 2Chr 14:7
smote all the c round about Gerar 2Chr 14:14
and they spoiled all the c.................. 2Chr 14:14
out of the c which he had taken........ 2Chr 15:8
armies against the c of Israel............. 2Chr 16:4
and all the store c of Naphtali........... 2Chr 16:4
in all the fenced c of Judah............... 2Chr 17:2
the c of Ephraim, which Asa 2Chr 17:7
to teach in the c of Judah.................. 2Chr 17:7
throughout all the c of Judah............ 2Chr 17:9
in Judah castles, and c of store 2Chr 17:12
much business in the c of Judah........ 2Chr 17:13
the fenced c throughout all Judah..... 2Chr 17:19
all the fenced c of Judah.................... 2Chr 17:19
brethren that dwell in their c............ 2Chr 19:10
even out of all the c of Judah............ 2Chr 20:4
things, within the c of Judah............. 2Chr 21:3
Levites out of all the c of Judah........ 2Chr 23:2
them, Go out unto the c of Judah...... 2Chr 24:5
battle, fell upon the c of Judah.......... 2Chr 25:13
built c about Ashdod, and among 2Chr 26:6
Moreover he built c in the................. 2Chr 27:4
invaded the c of the low country 2Chr 28:18
went out to the c of Judah................. 2Chr 31:1
his possession, into their own c......... 2Chr 31:1
that dwelt in the c of Judah............... 2Chr 31:6
in the c of the priests, in their........... 2Chr 31:15
fields of the suburbs of their c.......... 2Chr 31:19
and encamped against the fenced c ... 2Chr 32:1
Moreover he provided him c 2Chr 32:29
war in all the fenced c of Judah........ 2Chr 33:14
And so did he in the c of Manasseh .. 2Chr 34:6
the Nethinims, dwelt in their c......... Ezr 2:70
and all Israel in their c...................... Ezr 2:70
children of Israel were in the c .... Ezr 3:1
over, and set in the c of Samaria ...... Ezr 4:10
in our c come at appointed times ..... Ezr 10:14
and all Israel, dwelt in their c .... Neh 7:73
of Israel were in their c..................... Neh 7:73
and proclaim in all their c................. Neh 8:15
And they took strong c, and a fat...... Neh 9:25
in all the c of our tillage .... Neh 10:37
and nine parts to dwell in other c ..... Neh 11:1
but in the c of Judah dwelt every ..... Neh 11:3
one in his possession in their c .... Neh 11:3
were in all the c of Judah.................. Neh 11:20
them out of the fields of the c........... Neh 12:44
themselves together in their c .... Est 9:2
And he dwelleth in desolate c .... Job 15:28
and thou hast destroyed c.................. Ps 9:6
and will build the c of Judah .... Ps 69:35
your c are burned with fire............... Is 1:7
Until the c be wasted without............ Is 6:11
and destroyed the c thereof............... Is 14:17
fill the face of the world with c......... Is 14:21
The c of Aroer are forsaken............... Is 17:2
strong c be as a forsaken bough........ Is 17:9
In that day shall five c in the............ Is 19:18
covenant, he hath despised the c ...... Is 33:8
all the defenced c of Judah .... Is 36:1
defenced c into ruinous heaps........... Is 37:26
say unto the c of Judah, Behold........ Is 40:9
the c thereof lift up their voice......... Is 42:11
to the c of Judah, Ye shall be............ Is 44:26
the desolate c to be inhabited........... Is 54:3
and they shall repair the waste c ...... Is 61:4
Thy holy c are a wilderness, Zion .... Is 64:10
and against all the c of Judah............ Jer 1:15
his c are burned without .... Jer 2:15
the number of thy c are thy gods...... Jer 2:28
and let us go into the defenced c ...... Jer 4:5
thy c shall be laid waste,................... Jer 4:7
voice against the c of Judah.............. Jer 4:16
all the c thereof were broken............ Jer 4:26
leopard shall watch over their c........ Jer 5:6
shall importunely thy fenced c.......... Jer 5:17
what they do in the c of Judah.......... Jer 7:17
to cease from the c of Judah............. Jer 7:34
let us enter into the defenced c .... Jer 8:14
I will make the c of Judah................. Jer 9:11
to make the c of Judah desolate,....... Jer 10:22
all these words in the c of Judah....... Jer 11:6
Then shall the c of Judah .... Jer 11:12
the number of thy c were thy gods ... Jer 11:13
The c of the south shall be shut .... Jer 13:19
shall come from the c of Judah......... Jer 17:26
let that man be as the c which .... Jer 20:16
c which are not inhabited,................. Jer 22:6
the c of Judah, and the kings............ Jer 25:18
and speak unto all the c of Judah..... Jer 26:2
Israel, turn again to these thy c .... Jer 31:21
in the c thereof, when I shall............. Jer 31:23

in all the c thereof together,............. Jer 32:44
the c of Judah............. Jer 32:44
in the c of the mountains.................. Jer 32:44
in the c of the valley......................... Jer 32:44
and in the c of the south................... Jer 32:44
beast, even in the c of Judah............. Jer 33:10
beast, and in all the c thereof............ Jer 33:12
In the c of the mountains.................. Jer 33:13
In the c of the vale............................ Jer 33:13
in the c of the south......................... Jer 33:13
in the c of Judah, shall the............... Jer 33:13
and against all the c thereof.............. Jer 34:1
and against all the c of Judah............ Jer 34:7
remained of the c of Judah............... Jer 34:7
I will make the c of Judah a.............. Jer 34:22
Judah that come out of their c .... Jer 36:6
the c of Judah unto Jerusalem.......... Jer 36:9
made governor over the c of Judah ... Jer 40:5
dwell in your c that ye have.............. Jer 40:10
and upon all the c of Judah .... Jer 44:2
and was kindled in the c of Judah..... Jer 44:6
in the c of Judah, and in the............. Jer 44:17
that ye burned in the c of Judah....... Jer 44:21
for the c thereof shall be................... Jer 48:9
spoiled, and gone up out of her c ..... Jer 48:15
upon all the c of the land of.............. Jer 48:24
that dwell in Moab, leave the c......... Jer 48:28
Gad, and his people dwell in his c .... Jer 48:7
all the c thereof shall be.................... Jer 49:13
and the neighbour c thereof.............. Jer 49:18
and I will kindle a fire in his c .... Jer 50:32
and the neighbour c thereof.............. Jer 50:40
Her c are a desolation, a dry............ Jer 51:43
and the maids in the c of Judah........ Lam 5:11
the c shall be laid waste.................... Eze 6:6
the c that are inhabited shall be........ Eze 12:20
palaces, and he laid waste their c ..... Eze 19:7
open the side of Moab from the c...... Eze 25:9
from his c which are on his .... Eze 25:9
like the c that are not inhabited .... Eze 26:19
her c among the c that are................ Eze 29:12
her c shall be in the midst of............ Eze 30:7
midst of the c that are wasted .... Eze 30:7
these c shall go into captivity........... Eze 30:17
I will lay thy c waste, and thou........ Eze 35:4
and thy c shall not return................. Eze 35:9
to the c that are forsaken, which...... Eze 36:4
the c shall be inhabited, and the....... Eze 36:10
also cause you to dwell in the c .... Eze 36:33
ruined c are become fenced, and...... Eze 36:35
so shall the waste c be filled............. Eze 36:38
they that dwell in the c of .... Eze 39:9
mount, and take the most fenced c ... Dan 11:15
and Judah hath multiplied fenced c .. Hos 8:14
but I will send a fire upon his c .... Hos 8:14
And the sword shall abide on his c ... Hos 11:6
that may save them in all thy c......... Hos 13:10
cleanness of teeth in all your c......... Amos 4:6
So two or three c wandered unto...... Amos 4:8
and they shall build the waste c .... Amos 9:14
shall possess the c of the south......... Obad 20
I will cut off the c of thy land .... Mic 5:11
so will I destroy thy c....................... Mic 5:14
Assyria, and from the fortified c....... Mic 7:12
and alarm against the fenced c .... Zeph 1:16
their c are destroyed, so that............ Zeph 3:6
on the c of Judah, against which....... Zec 1:12
My c through prosperity shall yet..... Zec 1:17
the c thereof round about her,........... Zec 7:7
and the inhabitants of many c .... Zec 8:20
And Jesus went about all the c.......... Mt 9:35
have gone over the c of Israel........... Mt 10:23
to teach and to preach in their c ...... Mt 11:1
the c wherein most of his mighty ..... Mt 11:20
followed him on foot out of the c ..... Mt 14:13
and ran afoot thither out of all c ...... Mk 6:33
he entered, into villages, or c........... Mk 6:56
kingdom of God to other c also .... Lk 4:43
And he went through the c and......... Lk 13:22
have thou authority over ten c .... Lk 19:17
to him, Be thou also over five c........ Lk 19:19
the c round about unto Jerusalem .... Acts 5:16
through he preached in all the c .... Acts 8:40
of Lycaonia, and unto the region ..... Acts 14:6
And as they went through the c .... Acts 16:4
them even unto strange c .... Acts 26:11
And turning the c of Sodom 2Pet 2:6
the c about them in like manner,...... Jude 7
the c of the nations fell .... Rev 16:19

CITIZEN
himself to a c of that country........... Lk 15:15
in Cilicia, a c of no mean city .... Acts 21:39

CITIZENS
But his c hated him, and sent a .... Lk 19:14

CITY See PREFACE.

CLAD
had c himself with a new 1Kin 11:29
was c with zeal as a cloke................. Is 59:17

CLAMOROUS
A foolish woman is c....................... Prov 9:13

CLAMOUR
and wrath, and anger, and c............. Eph 4:31

CLAP
Men shall c their hands at him,........ Job 27:23
O c your hands, all ye people............ Ps 47:1
Let the floods c their hands .... Ps 98:8

of the field shall c their hands.......... Is 55:12
All that pass by c their hands at ...... Lam 2:15
thee shall c the hands over thee....... Nah 3:19

CLAPPED
they c their hands, and said, God..... 2Kin 11:12
Because thou hast c thine hands....... Eze 25:6

CLAPPETH
he c his hands among us, and .... Job 34:37

CLAUDA (claw'-dah) An island near Crete.
certain island which is called C......... Acts 27:16

CLAUDIA (claw'-de-ah) A Roman Christian.
thee, and Pudens, and Linus, and C.. 2Ti 4:21

CLAUDIUS (claw'-de-us)
   1. A Roman emperor.
to pass in the days of C Caesar.......... Acts 11:28
(because that C had commanded all ... Acts 18:2
   2. A Roman officer in Jerusalem.
C Lysias unto the most excellent....... Acts 23:26

CLAVE
c the wood for the burnt offering...... Gen 22:3
his soul c unto Dinah the................. Gen 34:3
that the ground c asunder that .... Num 16:31
But God c an hollow place that .... Judg 15:19
but Ruth c unto her.......................... Ruth 1:14
they c the wood of the cart, and....... 1Sa 6:14
men of Judah c unto their king........ 2Sa 20:2
his hand c unto the sword 2Sa 23:10
Solomon c unto these in love 1Kin 11:2
For he c to the Lord, and departed ... 2Kin 18:6
They c to their brethren, their.......... Neh 10:29
He c the rocks in the wilderness,...... Ps 78:15
he c the rock also, and the waters..... Is 48:21
Howbeit certain men c unto him....... Acts 17:34

CLAWS
and cleaveth the cleft into two c ...... Deut 14:6
and his nails like birds' c.................. Dan 4:33
fat, and tear their c in pieces............ Zec 11:16

CLAY
in the c ground between Succoth 1Kin 7:46
in the c ground between Succoth 2Chr 4:17
in them that dwell in houses of c ..... Job 4:19
that thou hast made me as the c .... Job 10:9
ashes, your bodies to bodies of c ...... Job 13:12
dust, and prepare raiment as the c ... Job 27:16
I also am formed out of the c............ Job 33:6
It is turned as c to the seal .... Job 38:14
horrible pit, out of the miry c........... Ps 40:2
be esteemed as the potter's c............. Is 29:16
and as the potter treadeth c .... Is 41:25
Shall the c say to him that................ Is 45:9
we are the c, and thou our potter ..... Is 64:8
the vessel that he made of c was ...... Jer 18:4
as the c is in the potter's hand,......... Jer 18:6
them in the c in the brickkiln........... Jer 43:9
feet part of iron and part of c .... Dan 2:33
his feet that were of iron and c .... Dan 2:34
Then was the iron, the c, the............ Dan 2:35
feet and toes, part of potters' c .... Dan 2:41
sawest the iron mixed with miry c ... Dan 2:41
were part of iron, and part of c .... Dan 2:42
sawest iron mixed with miry c.......... Dan 2:43
even as iron is not mixed with c .... Dan 2:43
pieces the iron, the brass, the c .... Dan 2:45
go into c, and tread the morter,........ Nah 3:14
that ladeth himself with thick c........ Hab 2:6
made c of the spittle, and he .... Jn 9:6
eyes of the blind man with the c ...... Jn 9:6
A man that is called Jesus made c .... Jn 9:11
sabbath day when Jesus made the c ... Jn 9:14
He put c upon mine eyes, and I .... Jn 9:15
not the potter power over the c .... Rom 9:21

CLEAN
Of every c beast thou shalt take,....... Gen 7:2
of beasts that are not c by two .... Gen 7:2
Of c beasts, and of beasts that .... Gen 7:8
and of beasts that are not c .... Gen 7:8
c beast, and of every c fowl.............. Gen 8:20
gods that are among you, and be c .... Gen 35:2
without the camp unto a c place....... Lev 4:12
without the camp unto a c place....... Lev 6:11
all that be c shall eat thereof............ Lev 7:19
unholy, and between unclean and c .. Lev 10:10
shall ye eat in a c place.................... Lev 11:36
is plenty of water, shall be c .... Lev 11:36
is to be sown, it shall be c................ Lev 11:37
between the unclean and the c.......... Lev 11:47
for her, and she shall be c................. Lev 12:8
the priest shall pronounce him c ...... Lev 13:6
shall wash his clothes, and be c........ Lev 13:6
him c that hath the plague .... Lev 13:13
he is c.. Lev 13:13
him c that hath the plague .... Lev 13:17
he is c.. Lev 13:17
the priest shall pronounce him c ...... Lev 13:23
the priest shall pronounce him c ...... Lev 13:28
shall wash his clothes, and be c........ Lev 13:34
the scall is healed, he is c................. Lev 13:37
the priest shall pronounce him c ...... Lev 13:37
he is c.. Lev 13:39
yet is he c.. Lev 13:40
yet is he c.. Lev 13:41
the second time, and shall be c .... Lev 13:58
thing of skins, to pronounce it c ...... Lev 13:59
be cleansed two birds alive and c ..... Lev 14:4

times, and shall pronounce him c .... Lev 14:7
in water, that he may be c .... Lev 14:8
flesh in water, and shall be c .... Lev 14:9
the priest that maketh him c .... Lev 14:11
the man that is to be made c .... Lev 14:11
for him, and he shall be c .... Lev 14:20
shall pronounce the house c .... Lev 14:48
and it shall be c .... Lev 14:53
it is unclean, and when it is c .... Lev 14:57
the issue spit upon him that is c .... Lev 15:8
in running water, and shall be c .... Lev 15:13
and after that she shall be c .... Lev 15:28
that he may be c from all your .... Lev 16:30
then shall he be c .... Lev 17:15
put difference between c beasts .... Lev 20:25
and between unclean fowls and c .... Lev 20:25
of the holy things, until he be c .... Lev 22:4
the sun is down, he shall be c .... Lev 22:7
thou shalt not make c riddance of .... Lev 23:22
woman be not defiled, but be c .... Num 5:28
clothes, and so make themselves c .... Num 8:7
But the man that is c, and is not .... Num 9:13
every one that is c in thy house .... Num 18:11
every one that is c in thine .... Num 18:13
a man that is c shall gather up .... Num 19:9
up without the camp in a c place .... Num 19:9
on the seventh day he shall be c .... Num 19:12
the seventh day he shall not be c .... Num 19:12
a c person shall take hyssop, and .... Num 19:18
the c person shall sprinkle upon .... Num 19:19
in water, and shall be c at even .... Num 19:19
the fire, and it shall be c .... Num 31:23
the seventh day, and ye shall be c .... Num 31:24
the c may eat thereof, as of the .... Deut 12:15
the c shall eat of them alike .... Deut 12:22
Of all c birds ye shall eat .... Deut 14:11
But of all c fowls ye may eat .... Deut 14:20
the c person shall eat it alike .... Deut 15:22
that is not c by reason of .... Deut 23:10
people were passed c over Jordan .... Josh 3:17
people were c passed over Jordan .... Josh 4:1
all the people were c passed over .... Josh 4:11
hath befallen him, he is not c 1Sa 20:26
surely he is not c 1Sa 20:26
again to thee, and thou shalt be c 2Kin 5:10
may I not wash in them, and be c 2Kin 5:12
he saith to thee, Wash, and be c 2Kin 5:13
of a little child, and he was c 2Kin 5:14
for every one that was not c 2Chr 30:17
and make my hands never so c .... Job 9:30
is pure, and I am c in thine eyes .... Job 11:4
Who can bring a c thing out of an .... Job 14:4
What is man, that he should be c .... Job 15:14
heavens are not c in his sight .... Job 15:15
he that hath c hands shall be .... Job 17:9
or how can he be c that is born .... Job 25:4
I am c without transgression, I .... Job 33:9
The fear of the Lord is c .... Ps 19:9
He that hath c hands, and a pure .... Ps 24:4
me with hyssop, and I shall be c .... Ps 51:7
Create in me a c heart, O God .... Ps 51:10
even to such as are of a c heart .... Ps 73:1
Is his mercy c gone for ever .... Ps 77:8
Where no oxen are, the crib is c .... Prov 14:4
of a man are c in his own eyes .... Prov 16:2
can say, I have made my heart c .... Prov 20:9
to the good and to the c, and to .... Eccl 9:2
Wash you, make you c .... Is 1:16
down, the earth is c dissolved .... Is 24:19
so that there is no place c .... Is 28:8
the ground shall eat c provender .... Is 30:24
be ye c, that bear the vessels of .... Is 52:11
a c vessel into the house of the .... Is 66:20
wilt thou not be made c .... Jer 13:27
between the unclean and the c .... Eze 22:26
will I sprinkle c water upon you .... Eze 36:25
and ye shall be c .... Eze 36:25
between the unclean and the c .... Eze 44:23
he hath made it c bare, and cast .... Joel 1:7
his arm shall be c dried up .... Zec 11:17
thou wilt, thou canst make me c .... Mt 8:2
be thou c .... Mt 8:3
for ye make c the outside of the .... Mt 23:25
the outside of them may be c also .... Mt 23:26
he wrapped it in a c linen cloth .... Mt 27:59
thou wilt, thou canst make me c .... Mk 1:40
be thou c .... Mk 1:41
thou wilt, thou canst make me c .... Lk 5:12
be thou c .... Lk 5:13
make c the outside of the cup .... Lk 11:39
behold, all things are c unto you .... Lk 11:41
his feet, but is c every whit .... Jn 13:10
and ye are c, but not all .... Jn 13:10
said he, Ye are not all c .... Jn 13:11
Now ye are c through the word .... Jn 15:3
I am c .... Acts 18:6
those that were c escaped from 2Pet 2:18
be arrayed in fine linen, c .... Rev 19:8
clothed in fine linen, white and c .... Rev 19:14

CLEANNESS

according to the c of my hands 2Sa 22:21
according to my c in his eye 2Sa 22:25
according to the c of my hands .... Ps 18:20
according to the c of my hands in .... Ps 18:24
I also have given you c of teeth .... Amos 4:6

CLEANSE

and thou shalt c the altar .... Ex 29:36
he shall take to c the house two .... Lev 14:49
he shall c the house with the .... Lev 14:52

c it, and hallow it from the .... Lev 16:19
to c you, that ye may be clean .... Lev 16:30
the children of Israel, and c them .... Num 8:6
thou do unto them, to c them .... Num 8:7
and thou shalt c them, and offer .... Num 8:15
an atonement for them to c them .... Num 8:21
to c the house of the LORD 2Chr 29:15
of the house of the LORD, to c it 2Chr 29:16
that they should c themselves .... Neh 13:22
c thou me from secret faults .... Ps 19:12
iniquity, and c me from my sin .... Ps 51:2
shall a young man c his way .... Ps 119:9
my people, not to fan, nor to c .... Jer 4:11
I will c them from all their .... Jer 33:8
from all your idols, will I c you .... Eze 36:25
they have sinned, and will c them .... Eze 37:23
of them, that they may c the land .... Eze 39:12
the face of the earth, to c it .... Eze 39:14
Thus shall they c the land .... Eze 39:16
thus shalt thou c and purge it .... Eze 43:20
and they shall c the altar .... Eze 43:22
as they did c it with the bullock .... Eze 43:22
blemish, and c the sanctuary .... Eze 45:18
For I will c their blood that I .... Joel 3:21
c the lepers, raise the dead, ... Mt 10:8
c first that which is within the .... Mt 23:26
let us c ourselves from all 2Cor 7:1
c it with the washing of water by .... Eph 5:26
C your hands, ye sinners .... Jas 4:8
to c us from all unrighteousness 1Jn 1:9

CLEANSED

so it shall be c .... Lev 11:32
she shall be c from the issue of .... Lev 12:7
that is to be c two birds alive .... Lev 14:4
be c from the leprosy seven times .... Lev 14:7
he that is to be c shall wash his .... Lev 14:8
right ear of him that is to be c .... Lev 14:14
right ear of him that is to be c .... Lev 14:17
the head of him that is to be c .... Lev 14:18
is to be c from his uncleanness .... Lev 14:19
right ear of him that is to be c .... Lev 14:25
the head of him that is to be c .... Lev 14:28
the head of him that is to be c .... Lev 14:29
that is to be c before the LORD .... Lev 14:31
hath an issue is c of his issue .... Lev 15:13
But if she be c of her issue .... Lev 15:28
the land cannot be c of the blood .... Num 35:33
which we are not c until this day .... Josh 22:17
We have c all the house of the 2Chr 29:18
had not c themselves, yet did 2Chr 30:18
though he be not c according to 2Chr 30:19
altars, and c Judah and Jerusalem 2Chr 34:5
commanded, and they c the chambers .... Neh 13:9
Thus c I them from all strangers .... Neh 13:30
I have, if I be c from my sin .... Job 35:3
Verily I have c my heart in vain, ... Ps 73:13
Thou art the land that is not c .... Eze 22:24
In the day that I shall have c .... Eze 36:33
And after he is c, they shall .... Eze 44:26
then shall the sanctuary be c .... Dan 8:14
their blood that I have not c .... Joel 3:21
And immediately his leprosy was c .... Mt 8:3
the lame walk, the lepers are c .... Mt 11:5
departed from him, and he was c .... Mk 1:42
and none of them was c, saving .... Lk 4:27
the lame walk, the lepers are c .... Lk 7:22
that, as they went, they were c .... Lk 17:14
said, Were there not ten c .... Lk 17:17
the second time, What God hath c .... Acts 10:15
from heaven, What God hath c .... Acts 11:9

CLEANSETH

but the wind passeth, and c them .... Job 37:21
blueness of a wound c away evil .... Prov 20:30
Christ his Son c us from all sin 1Jn 1:7

CLEANSING

been seven of the priest for his c .... Lev 13:7
much in the skin after his c .... Lev 13:35
of the leper in the day of his c .... Lev 14:2
day for his c unto the priest .... Lev 14:23
that which pertaineth to his c .... Lev 14:32
to himself seven days for his c .... Lev 15:13
his head in the day of his c .... Num 6:9
offer for thy c those things .... Eze 43:23
to the priest, and offer for thy c .... Mk 1:44

CLEAR

thou shalt be c from this my oath .... Gen 24:8
shalt thou be c from this my oath .... Gen 24:41
one, thou shalt be c from my oath .... Gen 24:41
or how shall we c ourselves .... Gen 44:16
will by no means c the guilty .... Ex 34:7
the earth by c shining after rain 2Sa 23:4
and be c when thou judgest .... Ps 51:4
c as the sun, and terrible as an .... Song 6:10
place like a c heat upon herbs .... Is 18:4
darken the earth in the c day .... Amos 8:9
that the light shall not be c .... Zec 14:6
yourselves to be c in this matter 2Cor 7:11
like a jasper stone, c as crystal .... Rev 21:11
was pure gold, like unto c glass .... Rev 21:18
c as crystal, proceeding out of .... Rev 22:1

CLEARER

age shall be c than the noonday .... Job 11:17

CLEARING

and by no means c the guilty .... Num 14:18
what c of yourselves, yea, what 2Cor 7:11

CLEARLY

my lips shall utter knowledge c .... Job 33:3
then shalt thou see c to cast out .... Mt 7:5
was restored, and saw every man c .... Mk 8:25
then shalt thou see c to pull out .... Lk 6:42
creation of the world are c seen .... Rom 1:20

CLEARNESS

were the body of heaven in his c .... Ex 24:10

CLEAVE

mother, and shall c unto his wife .... Gen 2:24
he shall c it with the wings .... Lev 1:17
But ye that did c unto the LORD .... Deut 4:4
serve, and to him shalt thou c .... Deut 10:20
in all his ways, and to c unto him .... Deut 11:22
ye shall serve him, and c unto him .... Deut 13:4
there shall c nought of the .... Deut 13:17
make the pestilence c unto thee .... Deut 28:21
and they shall c unto thee .... Deut 28:60
and that thou mayest c unto him .... Deut 30:20
to c unto him, and to serve him .... Josh 22:5
But c unto the LORD your God, as .... Josh 23:8
c unto the remnant of these .... Josh 23:12
of Naaman shall c unto thee 2Kin 5:27
the clods c fast together .... Job 38:38
Thou didst c the fountain and the .... Ps 74:15
it shall not c to me .... Ps 101:3
my groaning my bones c to my skin .... Ps 102:5
let my tongue c to the roof of my .... Ps 137:6
to c unto the house of .... Is 14:1
so have I caused to c unto me the .... Jer 13:11
I will make thy tongue c to the .... Eze 3:26
they shall not c one to another .... Dan 2:43
but many shall c to them with .... Dan 11:34
Thou didst c the earth with .... Hab 3:9
the mount of Olives shall c in .... Zec 14:4
and mother, and shall c to his wife .... Mt 19:5
and mother, and c to his wife .... Mk 10:7
heart they would c unto the Lord .... Acts 11:23
c to that which is good .... Rom 12:9

CLEAVED

Nevertheless he c unto the sins 2Kin 3:3
their tongue c to the roof of .... Job 29:10
if any blot hath c to mine hands .... Job 31:7

CLEAVETH

the cleft into two claws, and .... Deut 14:6
he c my reins asunder, and doth .... Job 16:13
My bone c to my skin and to my .... Job 19:20
and my tongue c to my jaws .... Ps 22:15
say they, c fast unto him .... Ps 41:8
our belly c unto the earth .... Ps 44:25
My soul c unto the dust .... Ps 119:25
cutteth and c wood upon the earth .... Ps 141:7
and he that c wood shall be .... Eccl 10:9
For as the girdle c to the loins .... Jer 13:11
c to the roof of his mouth for .... Lam 4:4
their skin c to their bones .... Lam 4:8
dust of your city, which c on us .... Lk 10:11

CLEFT

cleaveth the c into two claws, and .... Deut 14:6
him, and the valleys shall be c .... Mic 1:4

CLEFTS

that art in the c of the rock .... Song 2:14
To go into the c of the rocks .... Is 2:21
dwellest in the c of the rock .... Jer 49:16
and the little house with c .... Amos 6:11
dwellest in the c of the rock .... Obad 3

CLEMENCY

hear us of thy c a few words .... Acts 24:4

CLEMENT

(clem´-ent) A Companion of Paul.
me in the gospel, with C also .... Phil 4:3

CLEOPAS

(cle´-o-pas) See ALPHAEUS,
CLEOPHAS. A disciple on Emmaus Road.
the one of them, whose name was C .... Lk 24:18

CLEOPHAS

(cle´-o-fas) See CLEOPAS. Husband
of Mary.
sister, Mary the wife of C .... Jn 19:25

CLIFF

they come up by the c of Ziz 2Chr 20:16

CLIFFS

To dwell in the c of the valleys .... Job 30:6

CLIFT

will put thee in a c of the rock .... Ex 33:22

CLIFTS

valleys under the c of the rocks .... Is 57:5

CLIMB

thickets, and they c up upon the rocks .... Jer 4:29
they shall c the wall like men of .... Joel 2:7
they shall c upon the houses .... Joel 2:9
though they c up to heaven, ... Amos 9:2

CLIMBED

Jonathan c up upon his hands and 1Sa 14:13
c up into a sycomore tree to see .... Lk 19:4

CLIMBETH

but c up some other way, the same .... Jn 10:1

CLIPPED

shall be bald, and every beard c .... Jer 48:37

CLODS

clothed with worms and c of dust .... Job 7:5
The c of the valley shall be .... Job 21:33
the c cleave fast together .... Job 38:38

break the c of his ground .... Is 28:24
plow, and Jacob shall break his c .... Hos 10:11
The seed is rotten under their c .... Joel 1:17

CLOKE
and was clad with zeal as a c .... Is 59:17
thy coat, let him have thy c .... Mt 5:40
him that taketh away thy c forbid .... Lk 6:29
now they have no c for their sin .... Jn 15:22
ye know, nor a c of covetousness 1Th 2:5
The c that I left at Troas with 2Ti 4:13
liberty for a c of maliciousness 1Pet 2:16

CLOPAS See CLEOPHAS.

CLOSE
eyes of her husband, and be kept c .... Num 5:13
be afraid out of their c places 2Sa 22:46
while he yet kept himself c 1Chr 12:1
kept c from the fowls of the air .... Job 28:21
shut up together as with a c seal .... Job 41:15
be afraid out of their c places .... Ps 18:45
shall follow c after you there in .... Jer 42:16
And I saw him come c unto the ram .... Dan 8:7
c up the breaches thereof .... Amos 9:11
And they kept it c, and told no man .... Lk 9:36
thence, they sailed c by Crete .... Acts 27:13

CLOSED
c up the flesh instead thereof .... Gen 2:21
For the LORD had fast c up all .... Gen 20:18
the pit, and the earth c upon them .... Num 16:33
the fat c upon the blade, so that .... Judg 3:22
they have not been c, neither .... Is 1:6
deep sleep, and hath c your eyes .... Is 29:10
for the words are c up and sealed .... Dan 12:9
the depth c the round about, the .... Jonah 2:5
and their eyes they have c .... Mt 13:15
he c the book, and he gave it .... Lk 4:20
and their eyes have they c .... Acts 28:27

CLOSER
that sticketh c than a brother .... Prov 18:24

CLOSEST
because thou c thyself in cedar .... Jer 22:15

CLOSET
and the bride out of her c .... Joel 2:16
thou prayest, enter into thy c .... Mt 6:6

CLOSETS
in c shall be proclaimed upon the .... Lk 12:3

CLOTH
spread over it a c wholly of blue .... Num 4:6
they shall spread a c of blue .... Num 4:7
spread upon them a c of scarlet .... Num 4:8
And they shall take a c of blue .... Num 4:9
they shall spread a c of blue .... Num 4:11
and put them in a c of blue .... Num 4:12
and spread a purple c thereon .... Num 4:13
they shall spread the c before .... Deut 22:17
bolster, and covered it with a c 1Sa 19:13
wrapped in a c behind the ephod 1Sa 21:9
cast a c upon him, when he saw 2Sa 20:12
morrow, that he took a thick c 2Kin 8:15
cast them away as a menstruous c .... Is 30:22
of new c unto an old garment .... Mt 9:16
he wrapped it in a clean linen c .... Mt 27:59
piece of new c on an old garment .... Mk 2:21
having a linen c cast about his .... Mk 14:51
And he left the linen c, and fled............... Mk 14:52

CLOTHE
his sons, and c them with coats .... Ex 40:14
and the sent raiment to c Mordecai .... Est 4:4
I will also c her priests with .... Ps 132:16
His enemies will I c with shame .... Ps 132:18
shall c a man with rags .... Prov 23:21
I will c him with thy robe, and .... Is 22:21
thou shalt surely c thee with .... Is 49:18
I c the heavens with blackness, ... Is 50:3
they shall c themselves with .... Eze 26:16
ye c you with the wool, ye kill .... Eze 34:3
ye c you, but there is none warm........... Hag 1:6
I will c thee with change of .... Zec 3:4
if God so c the grass of the .... Mt 6:30
shall he not much more c you .... Mt 6:30
if then God so c the grass .... Lk 12:28
how much more will he c you .... Lk 12:28

CLOTHED
make coats of skins, and c them .... Gen 3:21
c him with the robe, and put the .... Lev 8:7
who c you in scarlet, with other 2Sa 1:24
David was c with a robe of fine 1Chr 15:27
who were c in sackcloth, fell................... 1Chr 21:16
be c with salvation, and let thy 2Chr 6:41
c in their robes, and they sat in 2Chr 18:9
with the spoil c all that were 2Chr 28:15
the king's gate, c with sackcloth............ Est 4:2
My flesh is c with worms and clods ...... Job 7:5
hate thee shall be c with shame .... Job 8:22
Thou hast c me with skin and flesh ...... Job 10:11
put on righteousness, and it c me .... Job 29:14
hast thou c his neck with thunder .... Job 39:19
let them be c with shame and .... Ps 35:26
The pastures are c with flocks .... Ps 65:13
reigneth, he is c with majesty .... Ps 93:1
the LORD is c with majesty, ... Ps 93:1
thou art c with honour and majesty ...... Ps 104:1
As he c himself with cursing shall .... Ps 109:18
mine adversaries be c with shame .... Ps 109:29
priests be c with righteousness .... Ps 132:9

her household are c with scarlet .... Prov 31:21
for he hath c me with the .... Is 61:10
prince shall be c with desolation .... Eze 7:27
man among them was c with linen...... Eze 9:2
he called to the man c with linen........ Eze 9:3
the man c with linen, which had......... Eze 9:11
spake unto the man c with linen......... Eze 10:2
commanded the man c with linen........ Eze 10:6
of him that was c with linen................ Eze 10:7
I c thee also with broidered work....... Eze 16:10
Which were c with blue, captains ...... Eze 23:6
rulers c most gorgeously, ... Eze 23:12
all of them c with all sorts of .... Eze 38:4
they shall be c with linen..................... Eze 44:17
shall be c with scarlet, and have .... Dan 5:7
thou shalt be c with scarlet .... Dan 5:16
they c Daniel with scarlet, and........... Dan 5:29
behold a certain man c in linen .... Dan 10:5
And one said to the man c in linen .... Dan 12:6
And I heard the man c in linen .... Dan 12:7
all such as are c with strange.............. Zeph 1:8
Now Joshua was c with filthy .... Zec 3:3
his head, and c him with garments..... Zec 3:5
or, Wherewithal shall we be c .... Mt 6:31
A man c in soft raiment .... Mt 11:8
Naked, and ye c me........................... Mt 25:36
or naked, and c thee............................ Mt 25:38
naked, and ye c me not........................ Mt 25:43
John was c with camel's hair, and ..... Mk 1:6
and had the legion, sitting, and c .... Mk 5:15
they c him with purple, and................ Mk 15:17
c in a long white garment .... Mk 16:5
A man c in soft raiment .... Lk 7:25
sitting at the feet of Jesus, c .... Lk 8:35
rich man, which was c in purple .... Lk 16:19
earnestly desiring to be c upon........... 2Cor 5:2
If so be that being c we shall.............. 2Cor 5:3
but c upon, that mortality might......... 2Cor 5:4
to another, and be c with humility 1Pet 5:5
c with a garment down to the foot ..... Rev 1:13
same shall be c in white raiment .... Rev 3:5
raiment, that thou mayest be c .... Rev 3:18
sitting, c in white raiment .... Rev 4:4
c with white robes, and palms in ...... Rev 7:9
down from heaven, c with a cloud..... Rev 10:1
threescore days, c in sackcloth.......... Rev 11:3
a woman c with the sun, and the....... Rev 12:1
c in pure and white linen, and........... Rev 15:6
that was c in fine linen, and............... Rev 18:16
he was c with a vesture dipped in ..... Rev 19:13
c in fine linen, white and clean .... Rev 19:14

CLOTHES
and he rent his c .... Gen 37:29
And Jacob rent his c, and put .... Gen 37:34
Then they rent their c, and laded...... Gen 44:13
his c in the blood of grapes............... Gen 49:11
in their c upon their shoulders,......... Ex 12:34
morrow, and let them wash their c .... Ex 19:10
and they washed their c .... Ex 19:14
your heads, neither rend your c .... Lev 10:6
carcase of them shall wash his c ..... Lev 11:25
carcase of them shall wash his c ..... Lev 11:28
carcase of it shall wash his c .... Lev 11:40
carcase of it shall wash his c .... Lev 11:40
and he shall wash his c, and be .... Lev 13:6
and he shall wash his c, and be .... Lev 13:34
his c shall be rent, and his head .... Lev 13:45
to be cleansed shall wash his c .... Lev 14:8
and he shall wash his c, also he ...... Lev 14:9
in the house shall wash his c .... Lev 14:47
in the house shall wash his c .... Lev 14:47
toucheth his bed shall wash his c ... Lev 15:5
hath the issue shall wash his c .... Lev 15:7
hath the issue shall wash his c .... Lev 15:7
then he shall wash his c, and .... Lev 15:8
of those things shall wash his c ...... Lev 15:10
in water, he shall wash his c .... Lev 15:11
for his cleansing, and wash his c .... Lev 15:13
toucheth her bed shall wash his c ... Lev 15:21
she sat upon shall wash his c .... Lev 15:22
be unclean, and shall wash his c .... Lev 15:27
the scapegoat shall wash his c .... Lev 16:26
burneth them shall wash his c .... Lev 16:28
and shall put on the linen c .... Lev 16:32
he shall both wash his c .... Lev 17:15
uncover his head, nor rend his c ..... Lev 21:10
flesh, and let them wash their c ...... Num 8:7
purified, and they washed their c .... Num 8:21
searched the land, rent their c .... Num 14:6
Then the priest shall wash his c ..... Num 19:7
her shall wash his c in water .... Num 19:8
of the heifer shall wash his c .... Num 19:10
purify himself, and wash his c .... Num 19:19
of separation shall wash his c .... Num 19:21
wash your c on the seventh day ..... Num 31:24
your c are not waxen old upon you .. Deut 29:5
And Joshua rent his c, and fell to ... Josh 7:6
he saw her, that he rent his c .... Judg 11:35
the same day with his c rent 1Sa 4:12
And he stript off his c also 1Sa 19:24
camp from Saul with his c rent 2Sa 1:2
Then David took hold on his c 2Sa 1:11
that were with him, Rend your c 2Sa 3:31
stood by with their c 2Sa 13:31
his beard, nor washed his c 2Sa 19:24
and they covered him with c 1Kin 1:1
those words, that he rent his c 1Kin 21:27
and he took hold of his own c 2Kin 2:12
the letter, that he rent his c 2Kin 5:7
the king of Israel rent his c 2Kin 5:8

Wherefore hast thou rent thy c............. 2Kin 5:8
of the woman, that he rent his c 2Kin 6:30
and Athaliah rent her c, and cried,..... 2Kin 11:14
to Hezekiah with their c rent 2Kin 18:37
heard it, that he rent his c 2Kin 19:1
of the law, that he rent his c 2Chr 22:11
and a curse, and hast rent thy c 2Kin 22:19
Then Athaliah rent her c, and said 2Chr 23:13
of the law, that he rent his c 2Chr 34:19
before me, and didst rend thy c 2Chr 34:27
me, none of us put off our c .... Neh 4:23
their c waxed not old, and their .... Neh 9:21
was done, Mordecai rent his c .... Est 4:1
mine own c shall abhor me .... Job 9:31
his bosom, and his c not be burned .... Prov 6:27
to Hezekiah with their c rent .... Is 36:22
heard it, that he rent his c .... Is 37:1
beards shaven, and their c rent .... Jer 41:5
shall strip thee also of thy c .... Eze 16:39
also strip thee out of thy c .... Eze 23:26
in precious c for chariots .... Eze 27:20
in all sorts of things, in blue c .... Eze 27:24
c laid to pledge by every altar .... Amos 2:8
the colt, and put on them their c .... Mt 21:7
field return back to take his c .... Mt 24:18
Then the high priest rent his c .... Mt 26:65
said, If I may touch but his c .... Mk 5:28
press, and said, Who touched my c ... Mk 5:30
Then the high priest rent his c .... Mk 14:63
from him, and put his own c on him ... Mk 15:20
and wrapped him in swaddling c .... Lk 2:7
the babe wrapped in swaddling c ...... Lk 2:12
devils long time, and ware no c .... Lk 8:27
they spread their c in the way .... Lk 19:36
the linen c laid by themselves............ Lk 24:12
it in linen c with the spices................. Jn 19:40
looking in, saw the linen c lying .... Jn 20:5
and seeth the linen c lie .... Jn 20:6
head, not lying with the linen c .... Jn 20:7
their c at a young man's feet............... Acts 7:58
Paul, heard of, they rent their c .... Acts 14:14
the magistrates rent off their c .... Acts 16:22
cried out, and cast off their c .... Acts 22:23

CLOTHEST
Though thou c thyself with .... Jer 4:30

CLOTHING
and stripped the naked of their c .... Job 22:6
the naked to lodge without c .... Job 24:7
cause him to go without c .... Job 24:10
seen any perish for want of c .... Job 31:19
were sick, my c was sackcloth .... Ps 35:13
her c is of wrought gold. .... Ps 45:13
The lambs are for thy c, and the .... Prov 27:26
her c is silk and purple....................... Prov 31:22
Strength and honour are her c .... Prov 31:25
his father, saying, Thou hast c .... Is 3:6
my house is neither bread nor c .... Is 3:7
sufficiently, and for durable c .... Is 23:18
the garments of vengeance for c .... Is 59:17
blue and purple is their c .... Jer 10:9
which come to you in sheep's c .... Mt 7:15
they that wear soft c are in .... Mt 11:8
which love to go in long c .... Mk 12:38
a man stood before me in bright c ... Acts 10:30
to him that weareth the gay c .... Jas 2:3

CLOTHS
the c of service, and the holy .... Ex 31:10
The c of service, to do service .... Ex 35:19
they made c of service, to do .... Ex 39:1
The c of service to do service in....... Ex 39:41

CLOUD
I do set my bow in the c, and it .... Gen 9:13
when I bring a c over the earth.......... Gen 9:14
the bow shall be seen in the c .... Gen 9:16
And the bow shall be in the c .... Gen 9:16
them by day in a pillar of a c .... Ex 13:21
away the pillar of the c by day .... Ex 13:22
the pillar of the c went from.............. Ex 14:19
and it was a c and darkness to them ... Ex 14:20
the pillar of fire and of the c .... Ex 14:24
of the LORD appeared in the c .... Ex 16:10
Lo, I come unto thee in a thick c ...... Ex 19:9
a thick c upon the mount, and the .... Ex 19:16
mount, and a c covered the mount..... Ex 24:15
the c covered it six days.................... Ex 24:16
Moses out of the midst of the c .... Ex 24:16
went into the midst of the c .... Ex 24:18
And the LORD descended in the c ...... Ex 34:5
Then a c covered the tent of the........ Ex 40:34
because the c abode thereon, and ..... Ex 40:35
when the c was taken up from over ... Ex 40:36
But if the c were not taken up, ... Ex 40:37
For the c of the LORD was upon........ Ex 40:38
in the c upon the mercy seat............. Lev 16:2
that the c of the incense may .... Lev 16:13
up the c covered the tabernacle........ Num 9:15
the c covered it by day, and the....... Num 9:16
when the c was taken up from the ... Num 9:17
and in the place where the c abode.... Num 9:17
as long as the c abode upon the....... Num 9:18
when the c tarried long upon the...... Num 9:19
when the c was a few days upon...... Num 9:20
when the c abode from even unto..... Num 9:21
that the c was taken up in the .... Num 9:21
by night that the c was taken up ..... Num 9:21
that the c tarried upon the .... Num 9:22
that the c was taken up from off...... Num 10:11
the c rested in the wilderness of ..... Num 10:12

the c of the LORD was upon them ...... Num 10:34
And the LORD came down in a c............ Num 11:25
came down in the pillar of the c.......... Num 12:5
the c departed from off the .... Num 12:10
that thy c standeth over them, and.... Num 14:14
by daytime in a pillar of a c .... Num 14:14
the c covered it, and the glory of....... Num 16:42
ye should go, and in a c by day.......... Deut 1:33
the midst of the fire, of the c............. Deut 5:22
the tabernacle in a pillar of a c .... Deut 31:15
the pillar of the c stood over............. Deut 31:15
that the c filled the house of 1Kin 8:10
to minister because of the c 1Kin 8:11
ariseth a little c out of the sea.......... 1Kin 18:44
the house was filled with a c............ 2Chr 5:13
to minister by reason of the c.......... 2Chr 5:14
the pillar of the c departed not .... Neh 9:19
let a c dwell upon it .... Job 3:5
As the c is consumed and vanisheth..... Job 7:9
can he judge through the dark c....... Job 22:13
the c is not rent under them.............. Job 26:8
and spreadeth his c upon it .... Job 26:9
and my welfare passeth away as a c... Job 30:15
by the c that cometh betwixt .... Job 36:32
watering he wearieth the thick c........ Job 37:11
he scattereth his bright c .... Job 37:11
the light of his c to shine.................... Job 37:15
When I made the c the garment......... Job 38:9
daytime also he led them with a c ..... Ps 78:14
He spread a c for a covering............ Ps 105:39
is as a c of the latter rain .... Prov 16:15
Zion, and upon her assemblies, a c...... Is 4:5
like a c of dew in the heat of............... Is 18:4
the LORD rideth upon a swift c .... Is 19:1
the heat with the shadow of a c......... Is 25:5
have blotted out, as a thick c........... Is 44:22
thy transgressions, and, as a c .... Is 44:22
Who are these that fly as a c.............. Is 60:8
of Zion with a c in his anger .... Lam 2:1
hast covered thyself with a c .... Lam 3:44
came out of the north, a great c........ Eze 1:4
is in the c in the day of rain .... Eze 1:28
a thick c of incense went up .... Eze 8:11
the c filled the inner court............... Eze 10:3
the house was filled with the c......... Eze 10:4
a c shall cover her, and her .... Eze 30:18
I will cover the sun with a c............. Eze 32:7
be like a c to cover the land .... Eze 38:9
Israel, as a c to cover the land....... Eze 38:16
your goodness is as a morning c....... Hos 6:4
they shall be as the morning c......... Hos 13:3
a bright c overshadowed them.......... Mt 17:5
and behold a voice out of the c......... Mt 17:5
there was a c that overshadowed ..... Mk 9:7
and a voice came out of the c .... Mk 9:7
he thus spake, there came a c .... Lk 9:34
feared as they entered into the c ...... Lk 9:34
there came a voice out of the c......... Lk 9:35
When ye see a c rise out of the .... Lk 12:54
of man coming in a c with power ...... Lk 21:27
a c received him out of their .... Acts 1:9
all our fathers were under the c....... 1Cor 10:1
all baptized unto Moses in the c..... 1Cor 10:2
with so great a c of witnesses .... Heb 12:1
from heaven, clothed with a c........... Rev 10:1
they ascended up to heaven in a c... Rev 11:12
And I looked, and behold a white c... Rev 14:14
upon the c one sat like unto the....... Rev 14:14
voice to him that sat on the c .... Rev 14:16
he that sat on the c thrust 'n........... Rev 14:16

CLOUDS

midst of heaven, with darkness, c....... Deut 4:11
dropped, the c also dropped water ..... Judg 5:4
waters, and thick c of the skies........ 2Sa 22:12
riseth, even a morning without c 2Sa 23:4
that the heaven was black with c...... 1Kin 18:45
and his head reach unto the c .... Job 20:6
Thick c are a covering to him,.......... Job 22:14
up the waters in his thick c .... Job 26:8
behold the c which are higher.......... Job 35:5
Which the c do drop and distil.......... Job 36:28
the spreadings of the c, the............. Job 36:29
With c he covereth the light,............ Job 36:32
thou know the balancings of the c.... Job 37:16
bright light which is in the c............ Job 37:21
thou lift up thy voice to the c .... Job 38:34
Who can number the c in wisdom ..... Job 38:37
waters and thick c of the skies .... Ps 18:11
has before him his thick c passed..... Ps 18:12
faithfulness reacheth unto the c ...... Ps 36:5
heavens, and thy truth unto the c..... Ps 57:10
and his strength is in the c .... Ps 68:34
The c poured out water...................... Ps 77:17
he had commanded the c from above.. Ps 78:23
C and darkness are round about him..... Ps 97:2
who maketh the c his chariot........... Ps 104:3
and thy truth reacheth unto the c..... Ps 108:4
Who covereth the heaven with c ...... Ps 147:8
up, and the c drop down the dew..... Prov 3:20
When he established the c above ...... Prov 8:28
himself of a false gift is like c.......... Prov 25:14
If the c be full of rain, they.............. Eccl 11:3
regardeth the c shall not reap .... Eccl 11:4
nor the c return after the rain .... Eccl 12:2
I will also command the c that .... Is 5:6
ascend above the heights of the c.... Is 14:14
Behold, he shall come up as c .... Jer 4:13
of man came with the c of heaven .... Dan 7:13
and of gloominess, a day of c .... Joel 2:2
the c are the dust of his feet .... Nah 1:3

and gloominess, a day of c.............. Zeph 1:15
so the LORD shall make bright c........ Zec 10:1
in the c of heaven with power........... Mt 24:30
and coming in the c of heaven......... Mt 26:64
coming in the c with great power ..... Mk 13:26
and coming in the c of heaven......... Mk 14:62
up together with them in the c 1Th 4:17
c that are carried with a tempest...... 2Pet 2:17
c they are without water, carried...... Jude 12
Behold, he cometh with c.................. Rev 1:7

CLOUDY

the c pillar descended, and stood ...... Ex 33:9
all the people saw the c pillar .... Ex 33:10
them in the day by a c pillar .... Neh 9:12
spake unto them in the c pillar......... Ps 99:7
day of the LORD is near, a day........... Eze 30:3
they have been scattered in the c .... Eze 34:12

CLOUTED

c upon their feet, and old .... Josh 9:5

CLOUTS

and took thence old cast c................ Jer 38:11
Put now these old cast c .... Jer 38:12

CLOVEN

or of them that divide the c hoof..... Deut 14:7
them c tongues like as of fire............ Acts 2:3

CLOVENFOOTED

parteth the hoof, and is c.................. Lev 11:3
he divide the hoof, and be c .... Lev 11:7
divideth the hoof, and is not c .... Lev 11:26

CLUSTER

a branch with one c of grapes .... Num 13:23
because of the c of grapes which..... Num 13:24
My beloved is unto me as a c of .... Song 1:14
As the new wine is found in the c..... Is 65:8
there is no c to eat............................ Mic 7:1

CLUSTERS

the c thereof brought forth ripe........ Gen 40:10
of gall, their c are bitter .... Deut 32:32
corn, and an hundred c of raisins 1Sa 25:18
cake of figs, and two c of raisins 1Sa 30:12
and thy breasts to c of grapes .... Song 7:7
breasts shall be as c of the vine ...... Song 7:8
gather the c of the vine of the .... Rev 14:18

CNIDUS *(ni '-dus) A port town in southwestern Asia Minor.*

scarce were come over against C........ Acts 27:7

COAL

shall quench my c which is left 2Sa 14:7
me, having a live c in his hand .... Is 6:6
there shall not be a c to warm at ..... Is 47:14
Their visage is blacker than a c .... Lam 4:8

COALS

c of fire from off the altar .... Lev 16:12
c were kindled by it 2Sa 22:9
before him were c of fire kindled....... 2Sa 22:13
there was a cake baken on the c 1Kin 19:6
His breath kindleth c, and a flame .... Job 41:21
c were kindled by it .... Ps 18:8
passed, hail stones and c of fire....... Ps 18:12
hail stones and c of fire..................... Ps 18:13
of the mighty, with c of juniper......... Ps 120:4
Let burning c fall upon them............. Ps 140:10
Can one go upon hot c, and his........ Prov 6:28
For thou shalt heap c of fire .... Prov 25:22
As c are to burning c, and................ Prov 26:21
As c are to burning c......................... Prov 26:21
the c thereof are c of fire................... Song 8:6
the tongs both worketh in the c .... Is 44:12
baked bread upon the c thereof........ Is 44:19
that bloweth the c in the fire............ Is 54:16
was like burning c of fire................... Eze 1:13
fill thine hand with c of fire.............. Eze 10:2
set it empty upon the c thereof........ Eze 24:11
burning c went forth at his feet......... Hab 3:5
there, who had made a fire of c .... Jn 18:18
land, they saw a fire of c there......... Jn 21:9
shalt heap c of fire on his head........ Rom 12:20

COAST

I bring the locusts into thy c............. Ex 10:4
by the sea, and by the c of Jordan ... Num 13:29
by the c of the land of Edom,........... Num 20:23
Arnon, which is in the utmost .... Num 22:36
come come from the c of Chittim...... Num 24:24
of Zin along by the c of Edom........ Num 34:3
c of the salt sea eastward .... Num 34:3
the c shall go down from Shepham ... Num 34:11
Ye are to pass through the c of........ Deut 2:4
Ar, the c of Moab, this day............... Deut 2:18
the c thereof, from Chinnereth......... Deut 3:17
the uttermost sea shall your c be..... Deut 11:24
with thee in all thy c seven days ...... Deut 16:4
If the LORD thy God enlarge thy c..... Deut 19:8
down of the sun, shall be your c....... Josh 1:4
the c of Og king of Bashan, which .... Josh 12:4
The king of Dor in the c of Dor ...... Josh 12:23
their c was from Aroer, that is.......... Josh 13:16
their c was Jazer, and all the .... Josh 13:25
their c was from Mahanaim, all .... Josh 13:30
the uttermost part of the c .... Josh 15:1
out of that c were at the sea............ Josh 15:4
this shall be your south c .... Josh 15:4
the great sea, and the c thereof .... Josh 15:12
This is the c of the children of.......... Josh 15:12
children of Judah toward the c of .... Josh 15:21

westward to the c of Japhleti .... Josh 16:3
unto the c of Beth-horon the .... Josh 16:3
the c of Manasseh was from Asher ... Josh 17:7
the c descended unto the river......... Josh 17:9
the c of Manasseh also was on the ... Josh 17:9
abide in their c on the south............. Josh 18:5
the c of their lot came forth.............. Josh 18:11
this was the south c .... Josh 18:19
the c reacheth to Tabor, and............ Josh 19:22
then the c turneth to Ramah, and..... Josh 19:29
and the c turneth to Hosah.............. Josh 19:29
at the sea from the c to Achzib......... Josh 19:29
their c was from Heleph, from.......... Josh 19:33
then the c turneth westward to .... Josh 19:34
the c of their inheritance was.......... Josh 19:41
the c of the children of Dan went..... Josh 19:47
took Gaza with the c thereof............ Judg 1:18
and Askelon with the c thereof........ Judg 1:18
and Ekron with the c thereof........... Judg 1:18
the c of the Amorites was from......... Judg 1:36
not Israel to pass through his c........ Judg 11:20
way of his own c to Beth-shemesh 1Sa 6:9
came no more into the c of Israel 1Sa 7:13
me any more in any c of Israel.......... 1Sa 27:1
upon the c which belongeth to 1Sa 30:14
He restored the c of Israel from 2Kin 14:25
bless me indeed, and enlarge my c ... 1Chr 4:10
destroy the remnant of the sea c ..... Eze 25:16
which is by the c of Hauran.............. Eze 47:16
to the c of the way of Hethlon.......... Eze 48:1
northward, to the c of Hamath .... Eze 48:1
unto the inhabitants of the sea c...... Zeph 2:5
the sea c shall be dwellings and....... Zeph 2:6
the c shall be for the remnant of...... Zeph 2:7
which is upon the sea c, in the .... Mt 4:13
and from the sea c of Tyre .... Lk 6:17

COASTS

and rested in all the c of Egypt......... Ex 10:14
one locust in all the c of Egypt......... Ex 10:19
out of the c of the Amorites.............. Num 21:13
with the cities thereof in the c .... Num 32:33
land of Canaan with the c thereof.... Num 34:2
with the c thereof round about......... Num 34:12
of Argob unto the c of Geshuri .... Deut 3:14
divide the c of thy land, which.......... Deut 19:3
olive trees throughout all thy c .... Deut 28:40
in all the c of the great sea .... Josh 9:1
abide in their c on the north............. Josh 18:5
by the c thereof round about,........... Josh 18:20
land for inheritance by their c .... Josh 19:49
all the c of the Amorites.................... Judg 11:22
that be along by the c of Arnon........ Judg 11:26
family five men from their c.............. Judg 18:2
sent her into all the c of Israel......... Judg 19:29
even Ashdod and the c thereof......... 1Sa 5:6
the c thereof did Israel deliver 1Sa 7:14
unto all the c of Israel...................... 1Sa 11:3
the c of Israel by the hands of......... 1Sa 11:7
in any of the c of Israel 2Sa 21:5
throughout all the c of Israel............ 1Kin 1:3
smote them in all the c of Israel....... 2Kin 10:32
the c thereof from Tirzah.................. 2Kin 15:16
their castles in their c, of the 1Chr 6:54
c out of the tribe of Ephraim 1Chr 6:66
throughout all the c of Israel............ 1Chr 21:12
to him out of all their c 2Chr 11:13
of flies, and lice in all their c........... Ps 105:31
and brake the trees of their c .... Ps 105:33
raised up from the c of the earth ..... Jer 31:8
them from the c of the earth............ Jer 31:8
raised up from the c of the earth ..... Jer 50:41
of the land take a man of their c ..... Eze 33:2
Zidon, and all the c of Palestine....... Joel 3:4
and in all the c thereof, from .... Mt 2:16
he would depart out of their c .... Mt 8:34
and departed into the c of Tyre......... Mt 15:21
of Canaan came out of the same c.... Mt 15:22
and came into the c of Magdala .... Mt 15:39
into the c of Caesarea Philippi .... Mt 16:13
came into the c of Judaea beyond .... Mt 19:1
pray him to depart out of their c ...... Mk 5:17
departing from the c of Tyre............. Mk 7:31
the midst of the c of Decapolis......... Mk 7:31
cometh into the c of Judaea by......... Mk 10:1
and expelled them out of their c ...... Acts 13:50
the upper c came to Ephesus............ Acts 19:1
and throughout all the c of Judaea ... Acts 26:20
meaning to sail by the c of Asia .... Acts 27:2

COAT

he made him a c of many colours..... Gen 37:3
they stript Joseph out of his c .... Gen 37:23
his c of many colours that was on ... Gen 37:23
And they took Joseph's c, and.......... Gen 37:31
dipped the c in the blood................. Gen 37:31
they sent the c of many colours,...... Gen 37:32
whether it be thy son's c or no........ Gen 37:32
it, and said, It is my son's c .... Gen 37:33
and a robe, and a broidered c .... Ex 28:4
embroider the c of fine linen .... Ex 28:39
garments, and put upon Aaron the c.. Ex 29:5
And he put upon him the c and,....... Lev 8:7
He shall put on the holy linen c ...... Lev 16:4
his mother made him a little c 1Sa 2:19
and he was armed with a c of mail.... 1Sa 17:5
the weight of the c was five 1Sa 17:5
he armed him with a c of mail 1Sa 17:38
came to meet him with his c rent 2Sa 15:32
me about as the collar of my c......... Job 30:18
I have put off my c .... Song 5:3

at the law, and take away thy c .... Mt 5:40
forbid not to take thy c also................ Lk 6:29
and also his c .... Jn 19:23
now the c was without seam, woven....... Jn 19:23
he girt his fisher's c unto him............... Jn 21:7

COATS
did the LORD God make c of skins......... Gen 3:21
Aaron's sons thou shalt make c .... Ex 28:40
his sons, and put c upon them.............. Ex 29:8
they made c of fine linen of............... Ex 39:27
his sons, and clothe them with c.......... Ex 40:14
put c upon them, and girded them .... Lev 8:13
them in their c out of the camp .... Lev 10:5
these men were bound in their c.......... Dan 3:21
neither were their c changed............... Dan 3:27
for your journey, neither two c............ Mt 10:10
and not put on two c .... Mk 6:9
unto them, He that hath two c............. Lk 3:11
neither have two c apiece .... Lk 9:3
by him weeping, and shewing the c...... Acts 9:39

COCK
this night, before the c crow .... Mt 26:34
And immediately the c crew............... Mt 26:74
said unto him, Before the c crow.......... Mt 26:75
night, before the c crow twice.............. Mk 14:30
and the c crew .... Mk 14:68
And the second time the c crew........... Mk 14:72
unto him, Before the c crow twice........ Mk 14:72
the c shall not crow this day,............... Lk 22:34
while he yet spake, the c crew .... Lk 22:60
said unto him, Before the c crow .... Lk 22:61
The c shall not crow, till thou .... Jn 13:38
and immediately the c crew................. Jn 18:27

COCKATRICE
root shall come forth a c .... Is 14:29

COCKATRICE'
shall put his hand on the c den............ Is 11:8
They hatch c eggs, and weave the........ Is 59:5

COCKATRICES
behold, I will send serpents, c............. Jer 8:17

COCKCROWING
even, or at midnight, or at the .... Mk 13:35

COCKLE
of wheat, and c instead of barley......... Job 31:40

COFFER
in a c by the side thereof.................... 1Sa 6:8
the c with the mice of gold and........... 1Sa 6:11
the c that was with it, wherein............ 1Sa 6:15

COFFIN
and he was put in a c in Egypt............. Gen 50:26

COGITATIONS
my c much troubled me, and my.......... Dan 7:28

COLD
seedtime and harvest, and c............... Gen 8:22
they have no covering in the c .... Job 24:7
and c out of the north .... Job 37:9
who can stand before his c................. Ps 147:17
will not plow by reason of the c........... Prov 20:4
As the c of snow in the time of............ Prov 25:13
away a garment in c weather............... Prov 25:20
As c waters to a thirsty soul, so........... Prov 25:25
or shall the c flowing waters .... Jer 18:14
camp in the hedges in th.. c day......... Nah 3:17
of c water only in the name of a.......... Mt 10:42
the love of many shall wax c............... Mt 24:12
for it was c .... Jn 18:18
present rain, and because of the c....... Acts 28:2
thirst, in fastings often, in c............... 2Cor 11:27
that thou art neither c nor hot........... Rev 3:15
I would thou wert c or hot.................. Rev 3:15
lukewarm, and neither c nor hot.......... Rev 3:16

COLHOZEH
repaired Shallum the son of C............. Neh 3:15
the son of Baruch, the son of C........... Neh 11:5

COLLAR
me about as the c of my coat.............. Job 30:18

COLLARS
beside ornaments, and c, and purple .... Judg 8:26

COLLECTION
Judah and out of Jerusalem the c........ 2Chr 24:6
to bring in to the LORD the c............... 2Chr 24:9
concerning the c for the saints........... 1Cor 16:1

COLLEGE
she dwelt in Jerusalem in the c........... 2Kin 22:14
she dwelt in Jerusalem in the c........... 2Chr 34:22

COLLOPS
maketh c of fat on his flanks.............. Job 15:27

COLONY
of that part of Macedonia, and a c....... Acts 16:12

COLORS
I will lay thy stones with fair c............ Is 54:11

COLOSSE (co-los'-see) See COLOSSIANS. A city
in Phrygia.
brethren in Christ which are at C......... Col 1:2

COLOSSIANS (co-los'-yans) Residents of
Colosse.
from Rome to the C by Tychicus.......... Col s

COLOUR
the plague have not changed his c ...... Lev 13:55
the c thereof as the c of............... Num 11:7
when it giveth his c in the cup........... Prov 23:31
midst thereof as the c of amber .... Eze 1:4
like the c of burnished brass.............. Eze 1:7
was like unto the c of a beryl .... Eze 1:16
as the c of the terrible crystal............ Eze 1:22
And I saw as the c of amber............... Eze 1:27
of brightness, as the c of amber .... Eze 8:2
was as the c of a beryl stone.............. Eze 10:9
his feet like in c to polished.............. Dan 10:6
under c as though they would have...... Acts 27:30
arrayed in purple and scarlet c........... Rev 17:4

COLOURED
woman sit upon a scarlet c beast......... Rev 17:3

COLOURS
and he made him a coat of many c ...... Gen 37:3
coat of many c that was on him........... Gen 37:23
And they sent the coat of many c........ Gen 37:32
to Sisera a prey of divers c................ Judg 5:30
a prey of divers of needlework .... Judg 5:30
of divers c of needlework on both .... Judg 5:30
a garment of divers c upon her........... 2Sa 13:18
of divers c that was on her................. 2Sa 13:18
glistering stones, and of divers c 1Chr 29:2
thy high places with divers c.............. Eze 16:16
of feathers, which had divers c........... Eze 17:3

COLT
his ass's c unto the choice vine.......... Gen 49:11
man be born like a wild ass's c .... Job 11:12
upon a c the foal of an ass................. Zec 9:9
find an ass tied, and a c with her........ Mt 21:2
an ass, and a c the foal of an ass........ Mt 21:5
And brought the ass, and the c .... Mt 21:7
into it, ye shall find a c tied .... Mk 11:2
found the c tied by the door .... Mk 11:4
them, What do ye, loosing the c.......... Mk 11:5
And they brought the c to Jesus.......... Mk 11:7
entering ye shall find a c tied............. Lk 19:30
And as they were loosing the c .... Lk 19:33
unto them, Why loose ye the c............ Lk 19:33
cast their garments upon the c .... Lk 19:35
cometh, sitting on an ass's c.............. Jn 12:15

COLTS
Thirty milch camels with their c.......... Gen 32:15
sons that rode on thirty ass c............. Judg 10:4
rode on threescore and ten ass c .... Judg 12:14

COME See PREFACE.

COMELINESS
he hath no form nor c .... Is 53:2
for it was perfect through my c........... Eze 16:14
they set forth thy c......................... Eze 27:10
for my c was turned in me into .... Dan 10:8
parts have more abundant c............... 1Cor 12:23

COMELY
a c person, and the LORD is with.......... 1Sa 16:18
his power, nor his c proportion............ Job 41:12
for praise is c for the upright............. Ps 33:1
and praise is c........................... Ps 147:1
go well, yea, four are c in going.......... Prov 30:29
c for one to eat and to drink, and .... Eccl 5:18
I am black, but c, O ye daughters .... Song 1:5
Thy cheeks are c with rows of .... Song 1:10
voice, and thy countenance is c.......... Song 2:14
of scarlet, and thy speech is c............ Song 4:3
c as Jerusalem, terrible as an............. Song 6:4
c for them that are escaped of .... Is 4:2
the daughter of Zion to a c................ Jer 6:2
upon you, but that which is c 1Cor 7:35
is it c that a woman pray unto............ 1Cor 11:13
For our c parts have no need.............. 1Cor 12:24

COMERS
make the c thereunto perfect............. Heb 10:1

COMEST
as thou c to Gerar, unto Gaza............. Gen 10:19
of Egypt, as thou c unto Zoar .... Gen 13:10
when thou c nigh over against the....... Deut 2:19
When thou c nigh unto a city to.......... Deut 20:10
When thou c into thy neighbour's........ Deut 23:24
When thou c into the standing............ Deut 23:25
shalt thou be when thou c in.............. Deut 28:6
shalt thou be when thou c in.............. Deut 28:19
said unto him, Whence c thou.............. Judg 17:9
that thou c with such a company......... Judg 18:23
and whence c thou.......................... Judg 19:17
from Havilah until thou c to Shur........ 1Sa 15:7
coming, and said, C thou peaceably..... 1Sa 16:4
that thou c to me with staves............. 1Sa 17:43
Thou c to me with a sword, and.......... 1Sa 17:45
said unto him, From whence c thou...... 2Sa 1:3
when thou c to see my face............... 2Sa 3:13
And she said, C thou peaceably........... 1Kin 2:13
and when thou c, anoint Hazael to....... 1Kin 19:15
said unto him, Whence c thou............. 2Kin 5:25
And when thou c thither, look out........ 2Kin 9:2
said unto Satan, Whence c thou.......... Job 1:7
unto Satan, From whence c thou......... Job 2:2
When thou c to Babylon, and shalt...... Jer 51:61
and whence c thou.......................... Jonah 1:8
baptized of thee, and c thou to me...... Mt 3:14
me when thou c into thy kingdom........ Lk 23:42
at Troas with Carpus, when thou c....... 2Ti 4:13

COMETH
the virgin c forth to draw water.......... Gen 24:43
his daughter c with the sheep............ Gen 29:6
And Leah said, A troop c.................... Gen 30:11
also he c to meet thee, and four.......... Gen 32:6
another, Behold, this dreamer c.......... Gen 37:19
thy son Joseph c unto thee................ Gen 48:2
behold, he c forth to meet thee .... Ex 4:14
lo, he c forth to the water.................. Ex 8:20
every firstling that c of a beast........... Ex 13:12
before the LORD, and when he c out ..... Ex 28:35
when he c into the tabernacle of .... Ex 29:30
such water c shall be unclean............. Lev 11:34
the stranger that c nigh shall be......... Num 1:51
the stranger that c nigh shall be......... Num 3:10
the stranger that c nigh shall be......... Num 3:38
the spirit of jealousy c upon him......... Num 5:30
he c out of his mother's womb............ Num 12:12
Whosoever c any thing near unto........ Num 17:13
the stranger that c nigh shall be......... Num 18:7
that c out of the coasts of the .... Num 21:13
of whom c the family of the............... Num 26:5
beside that which c of the sale........... Deut 18:8
it shall be, when evening c on............ Deut 23:11
and cover that which c from thee........ Deut 23:13
that c out from between her feet......... Deut 28:57
that whatsoever c forth of the .... Judg 11:31
of any thing that c of the vine .... Judg 13:14
when it c among us, it may save......... 1Sa 4:3
that he saith c surely to pass............. 1Sa 9:6
Whosoever c not forth after Saul......... 1Sa 11:7
Wherefore c not the son of Jesse 1Sa 20:27
Therefore he c not unto the 1Sa 20:29
whatsoever c to thine hand unto........ 1Sa 25:8
And she said, As old man c up............. 1Sa 28:14
and when thy father c to see thee....... 2Sa 13:5
good man, and c with good tidings....... 2Sa 18:27
but c out of a far country for.............. 1Kin 8:41
the wife of Jeroboam c to ask a.......... 1Kin 14:5
for it shall be, when she c in.............. 1Kin 14:5
and it shall be, when he c to us.......... 1Kin 4:10
look, when the messenger c 2Kin 6:32
came to them, but he c not again........ 2Kin 9:18
even unto them, and c not again......... 2Kin 9:20
as soon as this letter c to you............ 2Kin 10:2
he that c within the ranges, let........... 2Kin 11:8
as he goeth out and as he c in............ 2Kin 11:8
all the money that c into any 2Kin 12:4
on the right side as one c into............ 2Kin 12:9
because he c to judge the earth 1Chr 16:33
thine holy name c of thine hand......... 1Chr 29:16
so that whosoever c to consecrate 2Chr 13:9
There c a great multitude against 2Chr 20:2
If, when evil c upon us, as the............ 2Chr 20:9
great company that c against us.......... 2Chr 20:12
whosoever else c into the house.......... 2Chr 23:7
be ye with the king when he c in........ 2Chr 23:7
long for death, but it c not................ Job 3:21
For my sighing c before I eat.............. Job 3:24
Although affliction c not forth .... Job 5:6
afraid of destruction when it c .... Job 5:21
shock of corn c in in his season.......... Job 5:26
He c forth like a flower, and is............ Job 14:2
the mountain falling c to nought......... Job 14:18
It is drawn, and c out of the body .... Job 20:25
sword c out of his gall .... Job 20:25
how oft c their destruction upon......... Job 21:17
his cry when trouble c upon him......... Job 27:9
for the earth, out of it c bread .... Job 28:5
Whence then c wisdom..................... Job 28:20
shine by the cloud that c betwixt........ Job 36:32
Out of the south c the whirlwind......... Job 37:9
Fair weather c out of the north .... Job 37:22
a night, but joy c in the morning......... Ps 30:5
from him c my salvation.................... Ps 62:1
For promotion c neither from the........ Ps 75:6
that passeth away, and c not again..... Ps 78:39
for he c, for he c to judge................. Ps 96:13
for he c to judge the earth .... Ps 98:9
Blessed be he that c in the name........ Ps 118:26
the hills, from whence c my help......... Ps 121:1
My help c from the LORD, which .... Ps 121:2
I will mock when your fear c .... Prov 1:26
When your fear c as desolation .... Prov 1:27
your destruction c as a whirlwind .... Prov 1:27
distress and anguish c upon you .... Prov 1:27
out of his mouth c knowledge .... Prov 2:6
of the wicked, when it c................... Prov 3:25
When pride c, then c shame.............. Prov 11:2
the wicked c in his stead.................. Prov 11:8
man is loathsome, and c to shame...... Prov 13:5
Only by pride c contention................ Prov 13:10
heart sick, but when the desire c .... Prov 13:12
When the wicked c, then c................ Prov 18:3
but his neighbour c and searcheth...... Prov 18:17
man's judgment c from the LORD .... Prov 29:26
away, and another generation c.......... Eccl 1:4
the man do that c after the king........ Eccl 2:12
For out of prison he c to reign............ Eccl 4:14
For a dream c through the .... Eccl 5:3
For he c in with vanity, and............... Eccl 6:4
All that c is vanity........................... Eccl 11:8
he c leaping upon the mountains,....... Song 2:8
Who is this that c out of the .... Song 3:6
Who is this that c up from the .... Song 8:5
Behold, the day of the LORD c .... Is 13:9
so it c from the desert, from a............ Is 21:1
here c a chariot of men, with a .... Is 21:9
The watchman said, The morning c ..... Is 21:12
he that c up out of the midst of......... Is 24:18

the LORD c out of his place to .... Is 26:21
This also c forth from the LORD .... Is 28:29
whose breaking c suddenly at an .... Is 30:13
the name of the LORD c from far .... Is 30:27
earth, and that which c out of it .... Is 42:5
For as the rain c down, and the. .... Is 55:10
of Zion, Behold, thy salvation c .... Is 62:11
Who is this that c from Edom .... Is 63:1
To what purpose c there to me. .... Jer 6:20
a people c from the north country .... Jer 6:22
and shall not see when good c .... Jer 17:6
and shall not see when heat c .... Jer 17:8
c from the rock of the field. .... Jer 18:14
And when he c, he shall smite the. .... Jer 43:11
Who is this that c up as a flood. .... Jer 46:7
fair hatlet, but destruction c. .... Jer 46:20
it c out of the north .... Jer 46:20
Because of the day that c to .... Jer 47:4
there c up a nation against her. .... Jer 50:3
A sound of a cry c from Babylon .... Jer 51:54
it c to pass, when the Lord .... Lam 3:37
it with dung that c out of man .... Eze 4:12
Destruction c; and they shall seek .... Eze 7:25
his face, and c to the prophet. .... Eze 14:4
c according to the multitude of .... Eze 14:4
c to a prophet to enquire of him .... Eze 14:7
that which c into your mind shall .... Eze 20:32
because it c; and every heart. .... Eze 21:7
behold, it c, and shall be brought .... Eze 21:7
and when this c, ye shall know .... Eze 24:24
for, lo, it c. .... Eze 30:9
word that c forth from the LORD .... Eze 33:30
come unto thee as the people c .... Eze 33:31
And when this c to pass, (lo, it .... Eze 33:33
shall live whither the river c .... Eze 47:9
But he that c against him shall. .... Dan 11:16
c to the thousand three hundred .... Dan 12:12
and the thief c in, and the troop .... Hos 7:1
for the day of the LORD c .... Joel 2:1
the LORD c forth out of his place .... Mic 1:3
when he c into our land, and when .... Mic 5:6
thy watchmen and thy visitation c. .... Mic 7:4
when he c up unto the people, he. .... Hab 3:16
behold, thy King c unto thee .... Zec 9:9
Behold, the day of the LORD c .... Zec 14:1
For, behold, the day c, that .... Mal 4:1
the day that c shall burn them up .... Mal 4:1
but he that c after me is .... Mal 3:11
Then c Jesus from Galilee to .... Mt 3:13
is more than these c of evil .... Mt 5:37
and to another, Come, and he c. .... Mt 8:9
then c the wicked one, and .... Mt 13:19
but that which c out of the mouth .... Mt 15:11
take up the fish that first c up .... Mt 17:27
to that man by whom the offence c. .... Mt 18:7
thy King c unto thee, meek, and. .... Mt 21:5
Blessed is he that c in the name .... Mt 21:9
lord therefore of the vineyard c. .... Mt 21:40
Blessed is he that c in the name .... Mt 23:39
the lightning c out of the east. .... Mt 24:27
as ye think not the Son of man c .... Mt 24:44
when he c shall find so doing .... Mt 24:46
made, Behold, the bridegroom .... Mt 25:6
the hour wherein the Son of man c. .... Mt 25:13
time the lord of those servants c .... Mt 25:19
Then c Jesus with them unto a. .... Mt 26:36
he c unto the disciples, and .... Mt 26:40
Then c he to his disciples, and .... Mt 26:45
There c one mightier than I after .... Mk 1:7
the multitude c together again, ... Mk 3:20
Satan c immediately, and taketh .... Mk 4:15
there c one of the rulers of the .... Mk 5:22
he c to the house of the ruler of .... Mk 5:38
watch of the night he c unto them .... Mk 6:48
That which c out of the man, that. .... Mk 7:20
And he c to Bethsaida .... Mk 8:22
when he c in the glory of his .... Mk 8:38
told them, Elias verily c first. .... Mk 9:12
c into the coasts of Judaea by .... Mk 10:1
Blessed is he that c in the name .... Mk 11:9
that c in the name of the Lord .... Mk 11:10
when the master of the house c .... Mk 13:35
the evening he c with the twelve .... Mk 14:17
And he c, and findeth them sleeping .... Mk 14:37
he c the third time, and saith .... Mk 14:41
c Judas, one of the twelve, and. .... Mk 14:43
there c one of the maids of the .... Mk 14:66
but one mightier than I c. .... Lk 3:16
Whosoever c to me, and heareth my .... Lk 6:47
and to another, Come, and he c. .... Lk 7:8
then c the devil, and taketh away .... Lk 8:12
there c one from the ruler of the .... Lk 8:49
And when he c, he findeth it swept. .... Lk 11:25
that when he c and knocketh, they .... Lk 12:36
when he c shall find watching .... Lk 12:37
for the Son of man c at an hour .... Lk 12:40
when he c shall find so doing .... Lk 12:43
ye say, There c a shower. .... Lk 12:54
and it c to pass .... Lk 12:55
that c in the name of the .... Lk 13:35
that when he had bade thee c. .... Lk 14:10
that c against him with twenty .... Lk 14:31
And when he c home, he calleth. .... Lk 15:6
The kingdom of God c not with. .... Lk 17:20
when the Son of man c, shall he .... Lk 18:8
that c in the name of the Lord .... Lk 19:38
every man that c into the world .... Jn 1:9
He that c after me is preferred. .... Jn 1:15
After me c a man which is .... Jn 1:30
but canst not tell whence it c. .... Jn 3:8

neither c to the light, lest his. .... Jn 3:20
that doeth truth c to the light .... Jn 3:21
He that c from above is above all. .... Jn 3:31
He that c from heaven is above. .... Jn 3:31
Then c he to a city of Samaria. .... Jn 4:5
There c a woman of Samaria to .... Jn 4:7
Woman, believe me, the hour c .... Jn 4:21
But the hour c, and now is, when .... Jn 4:23
unto him, I know that Messias c .... Jn 4:25
four months, and then c harvest. .... Jn 4:35
the honour that c from God only .... Jn 5:44
is he which c down from heaven. .... Jn 6:33
he that c to me shall never .... Jn 6:35
him that c to me I will in no .... Jn 6:37
learned of the Father, c unto me. .... Jn 6:45
bread which c down from heaven .... Jn 6:50
but when Christ c, no man knoweth. .... Jn 7:27
on him, and said, When Christ c .... Jn 7:31
That Christ c of the seed of .... Jn 7:42
the night c, when no man can work. .... Jn 9:4
The thief c not, but for to steal. .... Jn 10:10
in himself c to the grave. .... Jn 11:38
that c in the name of the Lord. .... Jn 12:13
behold, thy King c, sitting on an .... Jn 12:15
Philip c and telleth Andrew .... Jn 12:22
Then c he to Simon Peter. .... Jn 13:6
to man c unto the Father, but by .... Jn 14:6
for the prince of this world c .... Jn 14:30
But this c to pass, that the word .... Jn 15:25
yea, the time c, that whosoever .... Jn 16:2
but the time c, when I shall no. .... Jn 16:25
Behold, the hour c, yea, is now .... Jn 16:32
c thither with learnings and .... Jn 18:3
the week c Mary Magdalene early .... Jn 20:1
c to Simon Peter, and to the other .... Jn 20:2
Then c Simon Peter following him, ... Jn 20:6
Jesus then c, and taketh bread, and. .... Jn 21:13
who, when he c, shall speak unto. .... Acts 13:25
there c one after me, whose shoes .... Acts 13:25
this feast that c in Jerusalem. .... Acts 18:21
C this blessedness then upon the. .... Rom 4:9
So then faith c by hearing .... Rom 10:17
Then c the end, when he shall 1Cor 15:24
For if he that c preacheth 2Cor 11:4
that which c upon me daily, the. 2Cor 11:28
This persuasion c not of him that .... Gal 5:8
c the wrath of God upon the. .... Eph 5:6
things' sake the wrath of God c. .... Col 3:6
Lord so c as a thief in the night. 1Th 5:2
sudden destruction c upon them 1Th 5:3
striffes of words, whereof c envy. 1Ti 6:4
in the rain that c oft upon it. .... Heb 6:7
when he c into the world, he. .... Heb 10:5
for he that c to God must believe. .... Heb 11:6
c down from the Father of lights, ... Jas 1:17
the Lord c with ten thousands of .... Jude 14
Behold, he c with clouds .... Rev 1:7
which c down out of heaven from. .... Rev 3:12
behold, the third woe c quickly. .... Rev 11:14
and when he c, he must continue a. .... Rev 17:10

COMFIRMATION

c of the gospel, ye all are .... Phil 1:7

COMFORT

This same shall c us concerning .... Gen 5:29
of bread, and c ye your hearts .... Gen 18:5
doth c himself, purposing to kill. .... Gen 27:42
his daughters rose up to c him. .... Gen 37:35
C thine heart with a morsel of .... Judg 19:5
C thine heart, I pray thee. .... Judg 19:8
David sent to c him by the hand. 2Sa 10:2
and his brethren came to c him 1Chr 7:22
David sent messengers to c him. 1Chr 19:2
of Ammon to Hanun, to c him 1Chr 19:2
to mourn with him and to c him. .... Job 2:11
Then should I yet have c. .... Job 6:10
When I say, My bed shall c me. .... Job 7:13
all my heaviness, and c myself .... Job 9:27
alone, that I may take c a little .... Job 10:20
How then c ye me in vain, seeing. .... Job 21:34
thy rod and thy staff they c me. .... Ps 23:4
greatness, and c me on every side. .... Ps 71:21
This is my c in my affliction. .... Ps 119:50
thy merciful kindness be for my c. .... Ps 119:76
word, saying, When wilt thou c me. .... Ps 119:82
me with flagons, c me with apples .... Song 2:5
weep bitterly, labour not to c me .... Is 22:4
C ye, c ye my people, saith .... Is 40:1
For the LORD shall c Zion. .... Is 51:3
he will c all her waste places. .... Is 51:3
by whom shall I c thee. .... Is 51:19
Should I receive c in these. .... Is 57:6
to c all that mourn .... Is 61:2
comforteth, so will I c you. .... Is 66:13
When I would c myself against .... Jer 8:18
mourning, to c them for the dead. .... Jer 16:7
mourning into joy, and will c them. .... Jer 31:13
her lovers she hath none to c her. .... Lam 1:2
hands, and there is none to c her. .... Lam 1:17
there is none to c me. .... Lam 1:21
equal to thee, that I may c thee. .... Lam 2:13
And they shall c you, when ye see. .... Eze 14:23
in that thou art a curse then. .... Eze 16:54
and the LORD shall yet c Zion .... Zec 1:17
they c in vain .... Zec 10:2
he said, Daughter, be of good c. .... Mt 9:22
saying unto him, Be of good c. .... Mk 10:49
unto her, Daughter, be of good c. .... Lk 8:48
to c them concerning their. .... Jn 11:19
in the c of the Holy Ghost, were .... Acts 9:31

c of the scriptures might have .... Rom 15:4
edification, and exhortation, and c. 1Cor 14:3
of mercies, and the God of all c. 2Cor 1:3
that we may be able to c them. 2Cor 1:4
by the c wherewith we ourselves. 2Cor 1:4
c him, lest perhaps such a one. 2Cor 2:7
I am filled with c, I am 2Cor 7:4
we were comforted in your c 2Cor 7:13
Be perfect, be of good c, be of 2Cor 13:11
and that he might c your hearts. .... Eph 6:22
Christ, if any c of love, if any .... Phil 2:1
you, that I also may be of good c. .... Phil 2:19
your estate, and c your hearts. .... Col 4:8
God, which have been a c unto me. .... Col 4:11
to c you concerning your faith 1Th 3:2
Wherefore c one another with. 1Th 4:18
Wherefore c yourselves together, ... 1Th 5:11
c the feebleminded, support the. 1Th 5:14
C your hearts, and stablish you in. 2Th 2:17

COMFORTABLE

my lord the king shall now be c 2Sa 14:17
me with good words and c words .... Zec 1:13

COMFORTABLY

speak c unto thy servants 2Sa 19:7
Hezekiah spake c unto all the. 2Chr 30:22
city, and spake c to them, saying. 2Chr 32:6
Speak ye c to Jerusalem, and cry .... Is 40:2
wilderness, and speak c unto her. .... Hos 2:14

COMFORTED

Isaac was c after his mother's. .... Gen 24:67
but he refused to be c .... Gen 37:35
and Judah was c, and went up unto. .... Gen 38:12
he c them, and spake kindly unto. .... Gen 50:21
for that thou hast c me, and for .... Ruth 2:13
David c Bath-sheba his wife, and 2Sa 12:24
for he was c concerning Amnon, ... 2Sa 13:39
c him over all the evil that the. .... Job 42:11
my soul refused to be c .... Ps 77:2
LORD, hast holpen me, and c me. .... Ps 86:17
in their affiiction: for my c is .... Ps 119:50
for the LORD hath c his people .... Is 49:13
for the LORD hath c his people .... Is 52:9
tossed with tempest, and not c .... Is 54:11
ye shall be c in Jerusalem. .... Is 66:13
refused to be c for her children. .... Jer 31:15
to rest upon them, and I will be c. .... Eze 5:13
ye shall be c concerning the evil .... Eze 14:22
shall be c in the nether parts of .... Eze 31:16
shall be c over all his multitude. .... Eze 32:31
her children, and would not be c. .... Mt 2:18
for they shall be c .... Mt 5:4
but now he is c, and thou art. .... Lk 16:25
c her, when they saw Mary, that. .... Jn 11:31
seen the brethren, they c them. .... Acts 16:40
man alive, and were not a little c. .... Acts 20:12
that I may be c together with you. .... Rom 1:12
all may learn, and all may be c. 1Cor 14:31
we ourselves are c of God. 2Cor 1:4
or whether we be c: it is for 2Cor 1:6
c us by the coming of Titus. 2Cor 7:6
wherewith he was c in you. 2Cor 7:7
we were c in your comfort. 2Cor 7:13
That their hearts might be c. .... Col 2:2
As ye know how we exhorted and c. 1Th 2:11
we were c over you in all our. 1Th 3:7

COMFORTEDST

is turned away, and thou c me. .... Is 12:1

COMFORTER

were oppressed, and they had no c. .... Eccl 4:1
but they had no c .... Eccl 4:1
she had no c. .... Lam 1:9
because the c that should relieve. .... Lam 1:16
and he shall give you another C .... Jn 14:16
But the C, which is the Holy .... Jn 14:26
But when the C is come, whom I .... Jn 15:26
the C will not come unto you. .... Jn 16:7

COMFORTERS

that he hath sent c unto thee. 2Sa 10:3
that he hath sent c unto thee. 1Chr 19:3
miserable c are ye all .... Job 16:2
and for c, but I found none. .... Ps 69:20
whence shall I seek c for thee .... Nah 3:7

COMFORTETH

as one that c the mourners. .... Job 29:25
I, even I, am he that c you .... Is 51:12
As one whom his mother c, so will .... Is 66:13
Who c us in all our tribulation, ... 2Cor 1:4
that c those that are cast down,. 2Cor 7:6

COMFORTLESS

I will not leave you c .... Jn 14:18

COMFORTS

within me thy c delight my soul .... Ps 94:19
restore c unto him and to his. .... Is 57:18

COMING

and, behold, the camels were c .... Gen 24:63
LORD hath blessed thee since my c .... Gen 30:30
thee, hinder thee from c unto me. .... Num 22:16
heard of the c of the children of .... Num 33:40
Why is his chariot so long in .... Judg 5:28
meet a company of prophets c down. 1Sa 10:5
of the town trembled at his c. 1Sa 16:4
I saw the son of Jesse c to Nob. 1Sa 22:9
thee from c to shed blood. 1Sa 25:33
me this day from c to shed blood. 1Sa 25:33
thy c in with me in the host is. 1Sa 29:6

of thy c unto me unto this day 1Sa 29:6
to know thy going out and thy c in..... 2Sa 3:25
his servants c on toward him 2Sa 24:20
the son of Rechab c to meet him 2Kin 10:15
the land at the c in of the year.......... 2Kin 13:20
and thy going out, and thy c in........... 2Kin 19:27
Ahaziah was of God by c to Joram 2Chr 22:7
their c unto the house of God at........ Ezr 3:8
a bridegroom c out of his chamber ... Ps 19:5
for he seeth that his day is c .... Ps 37:13
thy c in from this time forth, and...... Ps 121:8
city, at the c in at the doors .... Prov 8:3
for thee to meet thee at thy c .... Is 14:9
shall hail, c down on the forest.......... Is 32:19
and thy going out, and thy c in .... Is 37:28
and the things that are c, and............. Is 44:7
observe the time of their c .... Jer 8:7
an holy one c down from heaven,...... Dan 4:23
According to the days of thy c .... Mic 7:15
he had horns c out of his hand........... Hab 3:4
who may abide the day of his c .... Mal 3:2
prophet before the c of the great ...... Mal 4:5
c out of the tombs, exceeding............. Mt 8:28
the Son of man c in his kingdom........ Mt 16:28
what shall be the sign of thy c .... Mt 24:3
so shall also the c of the Son of .... Mt 24:27
c in the clouds of heaven with........... Mt 24:30
so shall also the c of the Son of .... Mt 24:37
so shall also the c of the Son of .... Mt 24:39
his heart, My lord delayeth his c .... Mt 24:48
then at my c I should have .... Mt 25:27
c in the clouds of heaven..................... Mt 26:64
straightway c up out of the water ..... Mk 1:10
for there were many c and going........ Mk 6:31
shall they see the Son of man c .... Mk 13:26
Lest c suddenly he find you .... Mk 13:36
c in the clouds of heaven..................... Mk 14:62
c out of the country, the father......... Mk 15:21
she c in that instant gave thanks....... Lk 2:38
And as he was yet a c, the devil.......... Lk 9:42
his heart, My lord delayeth his c .... Lk 12:45
by her continual c she weary me .... Lk 18:5
that at my c I might have..................... Lk 19:23
things which are c on the earth .... Lk 21:26
of man c in a cloud with power .... Lk 21:27
c out of the country, and on him .... Lk 23:26
For, behold, the days are c .... Lk 23:29
c to him, and offering him vinegar .... Lk 23:36
who c after me is preferred .... Jn 1:27
day John seeth Jesus c unto him........ Jn 1:29
Jesus saw Nathanael c to him .... Jn 1:47
but while I am c, another..................... Jn 5:7
I say unto you, The hour is c .... Jn 5:25
for the hour is c, in the which........... Jn 5:28
sheep are not, seeth the wolf c .... Jn 10:12
as she heard that Jesus was c .... Jn 11:20
that Jesus was c to Jerusalem............ Jn 12:12
before of the c of the Just One .... Acts 7:52
a vision a man named Ananias c in .... Acts 9:12
And he was with them c in and going Acts 9:28
day an angel of God c in to him .... Acts 10:3
And as Peter was c in, Cornelius........ Acts 10:25
c the baptism of repentance to.......... Acts 13:24
who c thither went into the................ Acts 17:10
And while the day was c on.................. Acts 27:33
been much hindered from c to you.... Rom 15:22
waiting for the c of our Lord 1Cor 1:7
they that are Christ's at his c 1Cor 15:23
I am glad of the c of Stephanas 1Cor 16:17
comforted us by the c of Titus............ 2Cor 7:6
And not by his c only, but by the 2Cor 7:7
is the third time I am c to you 2Cor 13:1
for me by my c to you again............... Phil 1:26
of our Lord Jesus Christ at his c 1Th 2:19
at the c of our Lord Jesus Christ 1Th 3:13
remain unto the c of our Lord 1Th 4:15
the c of our Lord Jesus Christ 1Th 5:23
by the c of our Lord Jesus Christ 2Th 2:1
with the brightness of his c 2Th 2:8
whose c is after the working of......... 2Th 2:9
brethren, unto the c of the Lord .... Jas 5:7
for the c of the Lord draweth .... Jas 5:8
To whom c, as unto a living stone 1Pet 2:4
c of our Lord Jesus Christ, but 2Pet 1:16
Where is the promise of his c 2Pet 3:4
hasting unto the c of the day of......... 2Pet 3:12
be ashamed before him at his c 1Jn 2:28
beast c up out of the earth................. Rev 13:11
c down from God out of heaven,........ Rev 21:2

COMINGS

the c in thereof, and all the .... Eze 43:11

COMMAND

him, that he will c his children .... Gen 18:19
according to that which I c thee .... Gen 27:8
Thy father did c before he died.......... Gen 50:16
shalt speak all that I c thee................. Ex 7:2
our God, as he shall c us .... Ex 8:27
God c thee so, then thou shalt be ..... Ex 18:23
thou shalt c the children of .... Ex 27:20
thou that which I c thee this day ...... Ex 34:11
C Aaron and his sons, saying, This .... Lev 6:9
Then the priest shall c that they .... Lev 13:54
Then shall the priest c to take .... Lev 14:4
the priest shall c that one of .... Lev 14:5
Then the priest shall c that they .... Lev 14:36
Then the priest shall c that they .... Lev 14:40
C the children of Israel, that .... Lev 24:2
Then I will c my blessing upon........... Lev 25:21
C the children of Israel, that .... Num 5:2

the LORD will c concerning you........... Num 9:8
C the children of Israel, and say......... Num 28:2
C the children of Israel, and say......... Num 34:2
C the children of Israel, that .... Num 35:2
c concerning the daughters of .... Num 36:6
c thou the people, saying, Ye are....... Deut 2:4
add unto the word which I c you .... Deut 4:2
the LORD your God which I c you .... Deut 4:2
which I c thee this day, that it .... Deut 4:40
his commandments, which I c thee.... Deut 6:2
which I c thee this day, shall be .... Deut 6:6
which I c thee this day, to do .... Deut 7:11
All the commandments which I c....... Deut 8:1
statutes, which I c thee this day .... Deut 8:11
which I c thee this day for thy .... Deut 10:13
which I c you this day, that ye........... Deut 11:8
which I c you this day, to love............ Deut 11:13
these commandments which I c you . Deut 11:22
your God, which I c you this day .... Deut 11:27
of the way which I c you this day ..... Deut 11:28
shall ye bring all that I c you............. Deut 12:11
thou shalt do all that I c thee............. Deut 12:14
all these words which I c thee............ Deut 12:28
What thing soever I c you .... Deut 12:32
which I c thee this day, to do............. Deut 13:18
which I c thee this day .... Deut 15:5
therefore I c thee, saying, Thou .... Deut 15:11
therefore I c thee this thing to.......... Deut 15:15
unto them all that I shall c him.......... Deut 18:18
Wherefore I c thee, saying, Thou ...... Deut 19:7
which I c thee this day, to love.......... Deut 19:9
therefore I c thee to do this .... Deut 24:18
therefore I c thee to do this .... Deut 24:22
which I c you this day .... Deut 27:1
which I c you this day, in mount....... Deut 27:4
statutes, which I c thee this day .... Deut 27:10
which I c thee this day, that the........ Deut 28:1
The LORD shall c the blessing............. Deut 28:8
which I c thee this day, to .... Deut 28:13
the words which I c thee this day ..... Deut 28:14
statutes which I c thee this day .... Deut 28:15
to all that I c thee this day................. Deut 30:2
which I c thee this day .... Deut 30:8
which I c thee this day, it is............... Deut 30:11
In that I c thee this day to love .... Deut 30:16
which ye shall c your children to....... Deut 32:46
c the people, saying, Prepare you ..... Josh 1:11
thou shalt c the priests that.............. Josh 3:8
c ye them, saying, Take you hence .... Josh 4:3
C the priests that bear the ark .... Josh 4:16
servant, so did Moses c Joshua .... Josh 11:15
Let our lord now c thy servants 1Sa 16:16
Now therefore c thou that they 1Kin 5:6
hearken unto all that I c thee 1Kin 11:38
or if I c the locusts to devour 2Chr 7:13
Doth the eagle mount up at thy c ..... Job 39:27
Yet the LORD will c his .... Ps 42:8
c deliverances for Jacob....................... Ps 44:4
I will also c the clouds that................ Is 5:6
the work of my hands c ye me .... Is 45:11
whatsoever I c thee thou shalt .... Jer 1:7
speak unto them all that I c thee ...... Jer 1:17
according to all which I c you .... Jer 11:4
all the words that I c thee to.............. Jer 26:2
c them to say unto their masters....... Jer 27:4
Behold, I will c, saith the LORD,......... Jer 34:22
whom thou didst c that they .... Lam 1:10
sea, thence will I c the serpent.......... Amos 9:3
thence will I c the sword..................... Amos 9:4
For, lo, I will c, and I will sift............. Amos 9:9
c that these stones be made bread ... Mt 4:3
Why did Moses then c to give a .... Mt 19:7
C therefore that the sepulchre be .... Mt 27:64
unto them, What did Moses c you ..... Mk 10:3
c this stone that it be made................ Lk 4:3
c them to go out into the deep .... Lk 8:31
wilt thou that we c fire to come .... Lk 9:54
if ye do whatsoever I c you .... Jn 15:14
These things I c you, that ye.............. Jn 15:17
Did not we straitly c you that ye....... Acts 5:28
to c them to keep the law of.............. Acts 15:5
I c thee in the name of Jesus.............. Acts 16:18
And unto the married I c, yet not...... 1Cor 7:10
will do the things which we c you...... 2Th 3:4
Now we c you, brethren, in the 2Th 3:6
Now them that are such we c 2Th 3:12
These things c and teach...................... 1Ti 4:11

COMMANDED

And the LORD God c the man .... Gen 2:16
whereof I c thee that thou .... Gen 3:11
of the tree, of which I c thee .... Gen 3:17
according to all that God c him.......... Gen 6:22
unto all that the LORD c him .... Gen 7:5
and the female, as God had c Noah... Gen 7:9
of all flesh, as God had c him .... Gen 7:16
Pharaoh c his men concerning him ... Gen 12:20
eight days old, as God had c him .... Gen 21:4
he c them, saying, Thus shall ye .... Gen 32:4
he c the foremost, saying, When ...... Gen 32:17
he c the second, and the third,.......... Gen 32:19
Then Joseph c to fill their sacks .... Gen 42:25
he c the steward of his house,........... Gen 44:1
Now thou art c, this do ye .... Gen 45:19
land of Rameses, as Pharaoh had c.... Gen 47:11
Joseph c his servants.......................... Gen 50:2
unto him according as he c them ...... Gen 50:12
not as the king of Egypt c them .... Ex 1:17
all the signs which he had c him........ Ex 4:28
Pharaoh c the same day the............... Ex 5:6
and Aaron did as the LORD c them ..... Ex 7:6

and they did so as the LORD had c...... Ex 7:10
and Aaron did so, as the LORD c......... Ex 7:20
and did as the LORD had c Moses .... Ex 12:28
as the LORD c Moses and Aaron, so.... Ex 12:50
the thing which the LORD had c......... Ex 16:16
As the LORD c Moses, so Aaron .... Ex 16:34
these words which the LORD c him.... Ex 19:7
bread seven days, as I c thee .... Ex 23:15
to all things which I have c thee .... Ex 29:35
may make all that I have c thee .... Ex 31:6
that I have c thee shall they do......... Ex 31:11
out of the way which I c them........... Ex 32:8
Sinai, as the LORD had c him............... Ex 34:4
eat unleavened bread, as I c thee ...... Ex 34:18
of Israel that which he was c .... Ex 34:34
the words which the LORD hath c ...... Ex 35:1
is the thing which the LORD c .... Ex 35:4
and make all that the LORD hath c..... Ex 35:10
which the LORD had c to be made ..... Ex 35:29
to all that the LORD had c.................... Ex 36:1
work, which the LORD c to make........ Ex 36:5
made all that the LORD c Moses......... Ex 39:1
as the LORD c Moses............................ Ex 39:1
as the LORD c Moses............................ Ex 39:5
as the LORD c Moses............................ Ex 39:7
as the LORD c Moses............................ Ex 39:21
as the LORD c Moses............................ Ex 39:26
as the LORD c Moses............................ Ex 39:29
as the LORD c Moses............................ Ex 39:31
to all that the LORD c Moses............... Ex 39:32
to all that the LORD c Moses............... Ex 39:42
had done it as the LORD had c............ Ex 39:43
to all that the LORD c him................... Ex 40:16
as the LORD c Moses............................ Ex 40:19
as the LORD c him................................ Ex 40:21
as the LORD had c Moses..................... Ex 40:23
as the LORD c Moses............................ Ex 40:25
as the LORD c Moses............................ Ex 40:27
as the LORD c Moses............................ Ex 40:29
as the LORD c Moses............................ Ex 40:32
Which the LORD c to be given them.... Lev 7:36
Which the LORD c Moses in mount .... Lev 7:38
in the day that he c the children........ Lev 7:38
And Moses did as the LORD c him....... Lev 8:4
thing which the LORD c to be done .... Lev 8:5
as the LORD c Moses............................ Lev 8:9
as the LORD c.. Lev 8:13
as the LORD c Moses............................ Lev 8:17
as the LORD c Moses............................ Lev 8:21
as the LORD c Moses............................ Lev 8:29
basket of consecrations, as I c .... Lev 8:31
day, so the LORD hath c to do .... Lev 8:34
for so I am c.. Lev 8:35
the LORD c by the hand of Moses ...... Lev 8:36
c before the tabernacle of the........... Lev 9:5
the LORD c that ye should do .... Lev 9:6
as the LORD c.. Lev 9:7
as the LORD c.. Lev 9:10
before the LORD; as Moses c .... Lev 9:21
the LORD, which he c them not.......... Lev 10:1
for so I am c.. Lev 10:13
as the LORD hath c.............................. Lev 10:15
it in the holy place, as I c .... Lev 10:18
And he did as the LORD c Moses......... Lev 16:34
the thing which the LORD hath c .... Lev 17:2
of Israel did as the LORD c Moses ..... Lev 24:23
which the LORD c Moses for the .... Num 27:34
As the LORD c Moses, so he................ Num 1:19
to all that the LORD c Moses............... Num 1:54
as the LORD c Moses............................ Num 2:33
to all that the LORD c Moses............... Num 2:34
the word of the LORD, as he was c .... Num 3:16
Moses numbered, as the LORD c him. Num 3:42
of the LORD, as the LORD c Moses ..... Num 3:51
of him, as the LORD c Moses.............. Num 4:49
candlestick, as the LORD c Moses ...... Num 8:3
unto all that the LORD c Moses........... Num 8:20
as the LORD had c Moses..................... Num 8:22
to all that the LORD c Moses............... Num 9:5
hath c you by the hand of Moses....... Num 15:23
the day that the LORD c Moses........... Num 15:23
as the LORD c Moses............................ Num 15:36
And Aaron took as Moses c, and ran. Num 16:47
as the LORD c him, so did he .... Num 17:11
of the law which the LORD hath c ..... Num 19:2
from before the LORD, as he c him .... Num 20:9
And Moses did as the LORD c .... Num 20:27
as the LORD c Moses and the............. Num 26:4
of judgment, as the LORD c Moses .... Num 27:11
and Moses did as the LORD c him...... Num 27:22
as the LORD c by the hand of .... Num 27:23
to all that the LORD c Moses............... Num 29:40
the thing which the LORD hath c .... Num 30:1
statutes, which the LORD c Moses .... Num 30:16
Midianites, as the LORD c Moses .... Num 31:7
of the law which the LORD c Moses .. Num 31:21
priest did as the LORD c Moses......... Num 31:31
the priest, as the LORD c Moses .... Num 31:41
as the LORD c Moses............................ Num 31:47
them Moses c Eleazar the priest........ Num 32:28
Moses c the children of Israel .... Num 34:13
which the LORD c to give unto the .... Num 34:13
These are they whom the LORD c to . Num 34:29
The LORD c my lord to give the .... Num 36:2
my lord was c by the LORD to give.... Num 36:2
unto Moses according as he c them... Num 36:5
Even as the LORD c Moses, so did..... Num 36:10
which the LORD c by the hand of...... Num 36:13
I c you at that time all the .... Deut 1:18
as the LORD our God c us..................... Deut 1:19

to all that the LORD our God c us......... Deut 1:41
I c you at that time, saying, The............ Deut 3:18
I c Joshua at that time, saying,............. Deut 3:21
even as the LORD my God c me................. Deut 4:5
which he c you to perform, even............. Deut 4:13
the LORD c me at that time to............... Deut 4:14
as the LORD thy God hath c thee............. Deut 5:12
therefore the LORD thy God c thee........... Deut 5:15
as the LORD thy God hath c thee............. Deut 5:16
as the LORD your God hath c you............. Deut 5:32
the LORD your God hath c you................ Deut 5:33
the LORD your God c to teach you........... Deut 6:1
statutes, which he hath c thee.............. Deut 6:17
which the LORD our God hath c you........... Deut 6:20
the LORD c us to do all these............... Deut 6:24
the LORD our God, as he hath c us........... Deut 6:25
out of the way which I c them............... Deut 9:12
the way which the LORD had c you............ Deut 9:16
there they be, as the LORD c me............. Deut 10:5
hath given thee, as I have c thee......... Deut 12:21
LORD thy God c thee to walk in.............. Deut 13:5
of heaven, which I have not c.............. Deut 17:3
which I have not c him to speak............ Deut 18:20
as the LORD thy God hath c thee............ Deut 20:17
as I c them, so ye shall observe........... Deut 24:8
which thou hast c me........................ Deut 26:13
to all that thou hast c me................. Deut 26:14
hath c thee to do these statutes.......... Deut 26:16
the elders of Israel c the people.......... Deut 27:1
and his statutes which he c thee........... Deut 28:45
which the LORD c Moses to make............. Deut 29:1
commandments which I have c you........... Deut 31:5
And Moses c them, saying, At the.......... Deut 31:10
That Moses c the Levites, which........... Deut 31:25
from the way which I have c you........... Deut 31:29
Moses c us a law, even the................ Deut 33:4
him, and did as the LORD c Moses.......... Deut 34:9
which Moses my servant c thee.............. Josh 1:7
Have not I c thee........................... Josh 1:9
Then Joshua c the officers of the......... Josh 1:10
the servant of the LORD c you.............. Josh 1:13
they c the people, saying, When........... Josh 3:3
of Israel did so as Joshua c.............. Josh 4:8
was finished that the LORD c.............. Josh 4:10
to all that Moses c Joshua................. Josh 4:10
Joshua therefore c the priests............ Josh 4:17
And Joshua had c the people............... Josh 6:10
my covenant which I c them................ Josh 7:11
he c them, saying, Behold, ye............. Josh 8:4
See, I have c you.......................... Josh 8:8
of the LORD which he c Joshua............. Josh 8:27
Joshua c that they should take............ Josh 8:29
the children of Israel.................... Josh 8:31
servant of the LORD had c before.......... Josh 8:33
not a word of all that Moses c........... Josh 8:35
how that the LORD thy God c his.......... Josh 9:24
down of the sun, that Joshua c........... Josh 10:27
as the LORD God of Israel c............... Josh 10:40
Moses the servant of the LORD c.......... Josh 11:12
As the LORD c Moses his servant........... Josh 11:15
of all that the LORD c Moses.............. Josh 11:15
destroy them, as the LORD c Moses......... Josh 11:20
an inheritance, as I have c thee.......... Josh 13:6
as the LORD c by the hand of............. Josh 14:2
As the LORD c Moses, so the............... Josh 14:5
The LORD c Moses to give us an............ Josh 17:4
The LORD c by the hand of Moses........... Josh 21:2
as the LORD c by the hand of.............. Josh 21:8
the servant of the LORD c you............. Josh 22:2
my voice in all that I c you.............. Josh 22:22
covenant of the LORD your God, which he c you... Josh 23:16
covenant which I c their fathers.......... Judg 2:20
which he c their fathers by the........... Judg 3:4
Hath not the LORD God of Israel c......... Judg 4:6
all that I c her let her observe.......... Judg 13:14
c them, saying, Go and smite the.......... Judg 21:10
Therefore they c the children of......... Judg 21:20
Boaz c his young men, saying, Let......... Ruth 2:15
which I have c in my habitation........... 1Sa 2:29
the LORD thy God, which he c thee......... 1Sa 13:13
the LORD hath c him to be captain......... 1Sa 13:14
kept that which the LORD c thee........... 1Sa 13:14
took, and went, as Jesse had c him....... 1Sa 17:20
Saul c his servants, saying,.............. 1Sa 18:22
brother, he hath c me to be there........ 1Sa 20:29
The king hath c me a business............ 1Sa 21:2
send thee, and what I have c thee......... 1Sa 21:2
David c his young men, and they.......... 2Sa 4:12
did so, as the LORD had c him............. 2Sa 5:25
whom I c to feed my people Israel......... 2Sa 7:7
as since the time that I c judges........ 2Sa 7:11
lord the king hath c his servant......... 2Sa 9:11
Now Absalom had c his servants........... 2Sa 13:28
have not I c you........................... 2Sa 13:28
did unto Amnon as Absalom had c.......... 2Sa 13:29
And the king c Joab and Abishai and...... 2Sa 18:5
performed all that the king c............ 2Sa 21:14
of Gad, went up as the LORD c............ 2Sa 24:19
So the king c Benaiah the son of......... 1Kin 2:46
And the king c, and they brought......... 1Kin 5:17
judgments, which he c our fathers........ 1Kin 8:58
to all that I have c thee................. 1Kin 9:4
had c him concerning this thing.......... 1Kin 11:10
he kept not that which the LORD c........ 1Kin 11:10
my statutes, which I have c thee......... 1Kin 11:11
which the LORD thy God c thee............ 1Kin 13:21
he c him all the days of his life........ 1Kin 15:5
I have c the ravens to feed thee......... 1Kin 17:4
I have c a widow woman there to.......... 1Kin 17:9
the king of Syria c his thirty........... 1Kin 22:31

he c them, saying, This is the............ 2Kin 11:5
things that Jehoiada the priest c........ 2Kin 11:9
But Jehoiada the priest c the............. 2Kin 11:15
law of Moses, wherein the LORD c......... 2Kin 14:6
king Ahaz c Urijah the priest............ 2Kin 16:15
according to all that king Ahaz c........ 2Kin 16:16
the law which I c your fathers........... 2Kin 17:13
Then the king of Assyria c................ 2Kin 17:27
the LORD c the children of Jacob......... 2Kin 17:34
which the LORD c Moses..................... 2Kin 18:6
Moses the servant of the LORD c.......... 2Kin 18:12
to all that I have c them................. 2Kin 21:8
law that my servant Moses c them......... 2Kin 21:8
the king c Hilkiah the priest, and....... 2Kin 22:12
the king c Hilkiah the high.............. 2Kin 23:4
the king c all the people, saying........ 2Kin 23:21
Moses the servant of God had c........... 1Chr 6:49
David therefore did as God c him......... 1Chr 14:16
as Moses c according to the word......... 1Chr 15:15
the word which he c to a thousand........ 1Chr 16:15
of the LORD, which he c Israel........... 1Chr 16:40
whom I c to feed my people,.............. 1Chr 17:6
since the time that I c judges to........ 1Chr 17:10
Is it not I that c the people to......... 1Chr 21:17
of the LORD c Gad to say to David........ 1Chr 21:18
And the LORD c the angel................. 1Chr 21:27
David c to gather together the........... 1Chr 22:2
David also c all the princes of.......... 1Chr 22:17
to the order c unto them,................ 1Chr 23:31
the LORD God of Israel had c him......... 1Chr 24:19
to all that I have c thee................ 2Chr 7:17
for so had David the man of God c........ 2Chr 8:14
c Judah to seek the LORD God of.......... 2Chr 14:4
Now the king of Syria had c thee......... 2Chr 18:30
that Jehoiada the priest had c........... 2Chr 23:8
book of Moses, where the LORD c.......... 2Chr 25:4
he c the priests the sons of............. 2Chr 29:21
for the king c that the burnt........... 2Chr 29:24
Hezekiah c to offer the burnt............ 2Chr 29:27
the princes c the Levites to sing........ 2Chr 29:30
Moreover he c the people that........... 2Chr 31:4
Then Hezekiah c to prepare............... 2Chr 31:11
c Judah and Jerusalem, saying, Ye....... 2Chr 32:12
heed to do all that I have c them........ 2Chr 33:8
c Judah to serve the LORD God of........ 2Chr 33:16
And the king c Hilkiah, and Ahikam....... 2Chr 34:20
for God c me to make haste............... 2Chr 35:21
the king of Persia hath c us............. Ezr 4:3
And I c, and search hath been made,...... Ezr 4:19
Who hath c you to build this............ Ezr 5:3
Who c you to build this house, and....... Ezr 5:9
Whatsoever is c by the God of........... Ezr 7:23
Which thou hast c by thy servants........ Ezr 9:11
which the LORD had c to Israel........... Neh 8:1
law which the LORD had c by Moses........ Neh 8:14
which was c to be given to the........... Neh 13:5
Then I c, and they cleansed the.......... Neh 13:9
I c that the gates should be shut........ Neh 13:19
I c the Levites that they should........ Neh 13:22
he c Mehuman, Biztha, Harbona,........... Est 1:10
The king Ahasuerus c Vashti the.......... Est 1:17
the king had so c concerning him......... Est 3:2
had c unto the king's lieutenants........ Est 3:12
Then Mordecai c to answer Esther,........ Est 4:13
to all that Esther had c him............. Est 4:17
he c to bring the book of records........ Est 6:1
all that Mordecai c unto the Jews........ Est 8:9
the king c it so to be done.............. Est 9:14
he c by letters that his wicked.......... Est 9:25
Hast thou c the morning since thy....... Job 38:12
did according as the LORD c them........ Job 42:9
to the judgment that thou hast c......... Ps 7:6
he c, and it stood fast.................. Ps 33:9
Thy God hath c thy strength.............. Ps 68:28
which he c our fathers, that they........ Ps 78:5
Though he had c the clouds from.......... Ps 78:23
the word which he c to a thousand........ Ps 105:8
concerning whom the LORD c them.......... Ps 106:34
he hath c his covenant for ever.......... Ps 111:9
Thou hast c us to keep thy............... Ps 119:4
that thou hast c are righteous.......... Ps 119:138
for there the LORD c the blessing........ Ps 133:3
for he c, and they were created.......... Ps 148:5
I have c my sanctified ones, I........... Is 13:3
for my mouth it hath c, and his......... Is 34:16
and all their host have I c.............. Is 45:12
and my molten image, hath c them........ Is 48:5
nor c them in the day that I............. Jer 7:22
But this thing c I them, saying,......... Jer 7:23
in all the ways that I have c you........ Jer 7:23
which I c them not, neither came......... Jer 7:31
Which I c your fathers in the day........ Jer 11:4
covenant, which I c them to do........... Jer 11:8
it by Euphrates, as the LORD c me........ Jer 13:5
which I c thee to hide there............. Jer 13:6
them not, neither have I c them.......... Jer 14:14
sabbath day, as I c your fathers......... Jer 17:22
unto Baal, which I c not, nor............ Jer 19:5
yet I sent them not, nor c them.......... Jer 23:32
had c him to speak unto all the.......... Jer 26:8
my name, which I have not c them......... Jer 29:23
which I c them not, neither came......... Jer 32:35
the son of Rechab our father c us........ Jer 35:6
all that Jonadab our father c us......... Jer 35:10
that he c his sons not to drink.......... Jer 35:14
of their father, which he c them......... Jer 35:16
unto all that he hath c you.............. Jer 35:18
And Jeremiah c Baruch, saying, I......... Jer 36:5
that Jeremiah the prophet c them......... Jer 36:8
But the king c Jerahmeel the son......... Jer 36:26

Then Zedekiah the king c that............ Jer 37:21
Then the king c Ebed-melech the......... Jer 38:10
these words that the king had c.......... Jer 38:27
to all that I have c thee................ Jer 50:21
c Seraiah the son of Neriah.............. Jer 51:59
the LORD hath c concerning Jacob,....... Lam 1:17
that he had c in the days of old........ Lam 2:17
I have done as thou hast c me............ Eze 9:11
that when he had c the man............... Eze 10:6
And I did so as I was c.................. Eze 12:7
I did in the morning as I was c......... Eze 24:18
So I prophesied as I was c............... Eze 37:7
So I prophesied as he c me............... Eze 37:10
Then the king c to call the............. Dan 2:2
c to destroy all the wise men of........ Dan 2:12
c that they should offer an............. Dan 2:46
cried aloud, To you it is c.............. Dan 3:4
fury c to bring Shadrach, Meshach....... Dan 3:13
c that they should heat the............. Dan 3:19
he c the most mighty men that........... Dan 3:20
whereas they c to leave the stump....... Dan 4:26
c to bring the golden and silver........ Dan 5:2
Then c Belshazzar, and they.............. Dan 5:29
Then the king c, and they brought....... Dan 6:16
c that they should take Daniel up....... Dan 6:23
And the king c, and they brought........ Dan 6:24
c the prophets, saying, Prophesy........ Amos 2:12
which I c my servants the............... Zec 1:6
which I c unto him in Horeb for......... Mal 4:4
and offer the gift that Moses c......... Mt 8:4
c them, saying, Go not into the......... Mt 10:5
at meat, he c it to be given her........ Mt 14:9
he c the multitude to sit down on....... Mt 14:19
For God c, saying, Honour thy........... Mt 15:4
he c the multitude to sit down on....... Mt 15:35
his lord c him to be sold, and his...... Mt 18:25
went, and did as Jesus c them........... Mt 21:6
Then Pilate c the body to be............ Mt 27:58
things whatsoever I have c you.......... Mt 28:20
those things which Moses c.............. Mk 1:44
c that something should be given........ Mk 5:43
c them that they should take............ Mk 6:8
and c his head to be brought............ Mk 6:27
he c them to make all sit down by....... Mk 6:39
he c the people to sit down on.......... Mk 8:6
c to set them also before them.......... Mk 8:7
still, and c him to be called........... Mk 10:49
unto them even as Jesus had c........... Mk 11:6
work, and c the porter to watch......... Mk 13:34
cleansing, according as Moses c......... Lk 5:14
(For he had c the unclean spirit........ Lk 8:29
and he c to give her meat............... Lk 8:55
c them to tell no man that thing........ Lk 9:21
Lord, it is done as thou hast c......... Lk 14:22
he did the things that were c him....... Lk 17:9
all those things which are c you........ Lk 17:10
c him to be brought unto him............ Lk 18:40
then he c these servants to be......... Lk 19:15
Now Moses in the law c us................ Jn 8:5
c them that they should not............. Acts 1:4
But when they had c them to go.......... Acts 4:15
c them not to speak at all nor......... Acts 4:18
c to put the apostles forth in.......... Acts 5:34
they c that they should not speak....... Acts 5:40
he c the chariot to stand still......... Acts 8:38
all things that are c thee of God....... Acts 10:33
he c us to preach unto the people....... Acts 10:42
he c them to be baptized in the......... Acts 10:48
c that they should be put to............ Acts 12:19
For so hath the Lord c us................ Acts 13:47
their clothes, and c to beat them....... Acts 16:22
(because that Claudius had c all........ Acts 18:2
c him to be bound with two chains....... Acts 21:33
he c him to be carried into the......... Acts 21:34
The chief captain c him to be........... Acts 22:24
c the chief priests and all their....... Acts 22:30
the high priest Ananias c them.......... Acts 23:2
c the soldiers to go down, and to....... Acts 23:10
the soldiers, as it was c them,......... Acts 23:31
he c him to be kept in Herod's.......... Acts 23:35
he c a centurion to keep Paul, and...... Acts 24:23
seat c Paul to be brought............... Acts 25:6
c the man to be brought forth........... Acts 25:17
I c him to be kept till I might......... Acts 25:21
c that they which could swim............ Acts 27:43
but they are c to be under............. 1Cor 14:34
who c the light to shine out of........ 2Cor 4:6
with your own hands, as we c you........ 1Th 4:11
we were with you, this we c you......... 2Th 3:10
could not endure that which was c....... Heb 12:20
it was c them that they should......... Rev 9:4

COMMANDEDST

which thou c thy servant Moses.......... Neh 1:7
that thou c thy servant Moses........... Neh 1:8
c them precepts, statutes, and......... Neh 9:14
of all that thou c them to do........... Jer 32:23

COMMANDER

a leader and c to the people............ Is 55:4

COMMANDEST

All that thou c us we will do........... Josh 1:16
thy words in all that thou c him........ Josh 1:18
c me to be smitten contrary to......... Acts 23:3

COMMANDETH

is the thing which the LORD c.......... Ex 16:32
Thy servants will do as my lord c...... Num 32:25
Which c the sun, and it riseth not..... Job 9:7
c that they return from iniquity....... Job 36:10
c it not to shine by the cloud......... Job 36:32

that they may do whatsoever he c........ Job 37:12
For he c, and raiseth the stormy........ Ps 107:25
to pass, when the Lord c it not .... Lam 3:37
For, behold, the Lord c, and he.......... Amos 6:11
for with authority c he even the........... Mk 1:27
power he c the unclean spirits,.......... Lk 4:36
for he c even the winds and water,..... Lk 8:25
but now c all men every where to...... Acts 17:30

COMMANDING

had made an end of c his sons........ Gen 49:33
an end of c his twelve disciples........ Mt 11:1
C his accusers to come unto thee...... Acts 24:8
c to abstain from meats, which 1Ti 4:3

COMMANDMENT

according to the c of Pharaoh........... Gen 45:21
according to the c of the Lord.......... Ex 17:1
which I will give thee in c unto .... Ex 25:22
he gave them in c all that the.......... Ex 34:32
And Moses gave c, and they caused..... Ex 36:6
according to the c of Moses.......... Ex 38:21
numbered at the c of the Lord.......... Num 3:39
the c of the Lord by the hand of....... Num 4:37
according to the c of the Lord.......... Num 4:41
According to the c of the Lord.......... Num 4:49
At the c of the Lord the children........ Num 9:18
at the c of the Lord they pitched....... Num 9:18
according to the c of the Lord.......... Num 9:20
according to the c of the Lord.......... Num 9:20
At the c of the Lord they rested....... Num 9:23
at the c of the Lord they.......... Num 9:23
at the c of the Lord by the hand....... Num 9:23
the c of the Lord by the hand of....... Num 10:13
Moses by the c of the Lord.......... Num 13:3
ye transgress the c of the Lord........ Num 14:41
of the Lord, and hath broken his c..... Num 15:31
I have received c to bless.......... Num 23:20
go beyond the c of the Lord.......... Num 24:13
against my c in the desert of Zin....... Num 27:14
journeys by the c of the Lord.......... Num 33:2
mount Hor at the c of the Lord........ Num 33:38
Lord had given him in c unto them .... Deut 1:3
the c of the Lord your God.......... Deut 1:26
against the c of the Lord.......... Deut 1:43
the c of the Lord your God.......... Deut 9:23
that he turn not aside from the c ...... Deut 17:20
For this c which I command thee...... Deut 30:11
be that doth rebel against thy c .... Josh 1:18
according to the c of the Lord.......... Josh 8:8
according to the c of the Lord to....... Josh 15:13
Therefore according to the c of .... Josh 17:4
at the c of the Lord, these.......... Josh 21:3
of the c of the Lord your God.......... Josh 22:3
take diligent heed to do the c .... Josh 22:5
not rebel against the c of the.......... 1Sa 12:14
rebel against the c of the Lord 1Sa 12:15
kept the c of the Lord thy God......... 1Sa 13:13
have performed the c of the Lord...... 1Sa 15:13
transgressed the c of the Lord 1Sa 15:24
thou despised the c of the Lord 2Sa 12:9
the c that I have charged thee.......... 1Kin 2:43
hast not kept the c which the.......... 1Kin 13:21
c which the Lord commanded thee..... 2Kin 17:34
ordinances, and the law, and the c 2Kin 17:37
for the king's c was, saying,.......... 2Kin 18:36
according to the c of Pharaoh.......... 2Kin 23:35
Surely at the c of the Lord came...... 2Kin 24:3
their brethren were at their c 1Chr 12:32
their gods there, David gave a c 1Chr 14:12
people will be wholly at thy c 1Chr 28:21
according to the c of Moses.......... 2Chr 8:13
they departed not from the c of 2Chr 8:15
and to do the law and the c.......... 2Chr 14:4
blood and blood, between law and c... 2Chr 19:10
according to the c of Moses the....... 2Chr 24:6
at the king's c they made a chest...... 2Chr 24:8
stoned him with stones at the c 2Chr 24:21
according to the c of the king.......... 2Chr 29:15
according to the c of David.......... 2Chr 29:25
for so was the c of the Lord by........ 2Chr 29:25
and according to the c of the king..... 2Chr 30:6
one heart to do the c of the king 2Chr 30:12
And as soon as the c came abroad..... 2Chr 31:5
at the c of Hezekiah the king, and..... 2Chr 31:13
according to the king's c.......... 2Chr 35:10
according to the c of David.......... 2Chr 35:15
according to the c of king Josiah...... 2Chr 35:16
Give ye now c to cause these men..... Ezr 4:21
until another c shall be given .... Ezr 4:21
according to the c of the God of....... Ezr 6:14
and according to the c of Cyrus....... Ezr 6:14
I sent them with c unto Iddo the...... Ezr 8:17
that tremble at the c of our God....... Ezr 10:3
was the king's c concerning them...... Neh 11:23
according to the c of David the........ Neh 12:24
according to the c of David.......... Neh 12:45
the king's c by his chamberlains....... Est 1:12
she hath not performed the c of........ Est 1:15
let there go a royal c from him........ Est 1:19
came to pass, when the king's c .... Est 2:8
for Esther did the c of Mordecai...... Est 2:20
transgressest thou the king's c .... Est 3:3
a c to be given in every province....... Est 3:14
being hastened by the king's c .... Est 3:15
whithersoever the king's c.......... Est 4:3
gave him a c to Mordecai, to know.... Est 4:5
and gave him c unto Mordecai........ Est 4:10
a c to be given in every province....... Est 8:13
and pressed on by the king's c.......... Est 8:14
city, whithersoever the king's c........ Est 8:17

COMMANDMENTS

my voice, and kept my charge, my c... Gen 26:5
sight, and will give ear to his c .... Ex 15:26
How long refuse ye to keep my c ...... Ex 16:28
them that love me, and keep my c ..... Ex 20:6
a law, and c which I have written....... Ex 24:12
words of the covenant, the ten c .... Ex 34:28
ignorance against any of the c of .... Lev 4:13
somewhat against any of the c of ...... Lev 4:13
ignorance against any of the c of .... Lev 4:22
somewhat against any of the c of ...... Lev 4:27
to be done by the c of the Lord........ Lev 5:17
Therefore shall ye keep my c.......... Lev 22:31
walk in my statutes, and keep my c.... Lev 26:3
me, and will not do all these c .... Lev 26:14
so that ye will not do all my c.......... Lev 26:15
These are the c, which the Lord........ Lev 27:34
and not observed all these c.......... Num 15:22
and remember all the c of the Lord... Num 15:39
ye may remember, and do all my c..... Num 15:40
These are the c and the judgments,.... Num 36:13
that ye may keep the c of the.......... Deut 4:2
you to perform, even ten c.......... Deut 4:13
therefore his statutes, and his c .... Deut 4:40
of them that love me and keep my c.. Deut 5:10
fear me, and keep all my c always...... Deut 5:29
I will speak unto thee all the c .... Deut 5:31
Now these are the c, the statutes ...... Deut 6:1

to keep all his statutes and his c .... Deut 6:2
keep the c of the Lord your God........ Deut 6:17
these c before the Lord our God........ Deut 6:25
him and keep his c to a thousand....... Deut 7:9
Thou shalt therefore keep the c .... Deut 7:11
All the c which I command thee,........ Deut 8:1
whether thou wouldest keep his c ...... Deut 8:2
keep the c of the Lord thy God.......... Deut 8:6
thy God, in not keeping his c.......... Deut 8:11
to the first writing, the ten c.......... Deut 10:4
To keep the c of the Lord.......... Deut 10:13
and his judgments, and his c.......... Deut 11:1
c which I command you this day........ Deut 11:8
hearken diligently unto my c.......... Deut 11:13
all these c which I command you....... Deut 11:22
if ye obey the c of the Lord your....... Deut 11:27
obey the c of the Lord your God........ Deut 11:28
God, and fear him, and keep his c ...... Deut 13:4
to keep all his c which I command .... Deut 13:18
to observe to do all these c.......... Deut 15:5
shalt keep all these c to do them....... Deut 19:9
according to all thy c which thou...... Deut 26:13
I have not transgressed thy c .... Deut 26:13
and to keep his statutes, and his c...... Deut 26:17
thou shouldest keep all his c.......... Deut 26:18
Keep all the c which I command....... Deut 27:1
of the Lord thy God, and do his c...... Deut 27:10
to do all his c which I command....... Deut 28:1
keep the c of the Lord thy God.......... Deut 28:9
unto the c of the Lord thy God.......... Deut 28:13
God, to observe to do all his c.......... Deut 28:15
the Lord thy God, to keep his c......... Deut 28:45
do all his c which I command thee..... Deut 30:8
the Lord thy God, to keep his c......... Deut 30:16
in his ways, and to keep his c .... Deut 30:16
the c which I have commanded you.... Deut 31:5
in all his ways, and to keep his c .... Josh 22:5
in, obeying the c of the Lord.......... Judg 2:17
hearken unto the c of the Lord.......... Judg 3:4
me, and hath not performed my c....... 1Sa 15:11
to keep his statutes, and his c.......... 1Kin 2:3
ways, to keep my statutes and my c ... 1Kin 3:14
keep all my c to walk in them.......... 1Kin 6:12
in all his ways, and to keep his c 1Kin 8:58
in his statutes, and to keep his c........ 1Kin 8:61
children, and will not keep my c........ 1Kin 9:6
I chose, because he kept my c.......... 1Kin 11:34
to keep my statutes and my c 1Kin 11:38
my servant David, who kept my c....... 1Kin 14:8
have forsaken the c of the Lord......... 1Kin 18:18
from your evil ways, and keep my c.... 2Kin 17:13
they left all the c of the Lord.......... 2Kin 17:16
not the c of the Lord thee.......... 2Kin 17:19
following him, but kept his c.......... 2Kin 18:6
after the Lord, and to keep his c........ 2Kin 23:3
if he be constant to do my c.......... 1Chr 28:7
seek for all the c of the Lord.......... 1Chr 28:8
a perfect heart, to keep thy c.......... 1Chr 29:19
and forsake my statutes and my c...... 2Chr 7:19
of his father, and walked in his c....... 2Chr 17:4
transgress ye the c of the Lord......... 2Chr 24:20
God, and in the law, and in the c 2Chr 31:21
after the Lord, and to keep his c........ 2Chr 34:31
of the words of the c of the Lord....... Ezr 7:11
for we have forsaken thy c.......... Ezr 9:10
Should we again break thy c.......... Ezr 9:14
that love him and observe his c .... Neh 1:5
thee, and have not kept the c.......... Neh 1:7
if ye turn unto me, and keep my c...... Neh 1:9
and true laws, good statutes and c ..... Neh 9:13
necks, and hearkened not to thy c...... Neh 9:16
and hearkened not unto thy c.......... Neh 9:29
thy law, nor hearkened unto thy c...... Neh 9:34
do all the c of the Lord our Lord....... Neh 10:29
the words of God, but keep his c .... Ps 78:7
my statutes, and keep not my c.......... Ps 89:31
that remember his c to do them........ Ps 103:18
excel in strength, that do his c.......... Ps 103:20
all his c are sure.......... Ps 111:7
have all they that do his c.......... Ps 111:10
that delighteth greatly in his c.......... Ps 112:1
I have respect unto all thy c.......... Ps 119:6
O let me not wander from thy c .... Ps 119:10
hide not thy c from me.......... Ps 119:19
cursed, which do err from thy c........ Ps 119:21
I will run the way of thy c.......... Ps 119:32
me to go in the path of thy c.......... Ps 119:35
And I will delight myself in thy c .... Ps 119:47
also will I lift up unto thy c.......... Ps 119:48
and delayed not to keep thy c.......... Ps 119:60
for I have believed thy c.......... Ps 119:66
that I may learn thy c.......... Ps 119:73
All thy c are faithful.......... Ps 119:86
Thou through thy c hast made me...... Ps 119:98
for I will keep the c of my God......... Ps 119:115
Therefore I love thy c above gold ...... Ps 119:127
for I longed for thy c.......... Ps 119:131
yet thy c are my delights.......... Ps 119:143
and all thy c are truth.......... Ps 119:151
for thy salvation, and done thy c........ Ps 119:166
for all thy c are righteousness.......... Ps 119:172
for I do not forget thy c.......... Ps 119:176
my words, and hide my c with thee.... Prov 2:1
but let thine heart keep my c.......... Prov 3:1
keep my c, and live.......... Prov 4:4
words, and lay up my c with thee....... Prov 7:1
Keep my c, and live.......... Prov 7:2
The wise in heart will receive c .... Prov 10:8
Fear God, and keep his c.......... Eccl 12:13
that thou hadst hearkened to my c ..... Is 48:18

him, and to them that keep his c .... Dan 9:4
the Lord, and have not kept his c .... Amos 2:4
shall break one of these least c .... Mt 5:19
for doctrines the c of men .... Mt 15:9
wilt enter into life, keep the c .... Mt 19:17
On these two c hang all the law .... Mt 22:40
for doctrines the c of men .... Mk 7:7
Thou knowest the c, Do not commit .. Mk 10:19
him, The first of all the c is .... Mk 12:29
before God, walking in all the c .... Lk 1:6
Thou knowest the c, Do not commit .. Lk 18:20
If ye love me, keep my c .... Jn 14:15
He that hath my c, and keepeth .... Jn 14:21
If ye keep my c, ye shall abide .... Jn 15:10
even as I have kept my Father's c .... Jn 15:10
the Holy Ghost had given c unto .... Acts 1:2
but the keeping of the c of God 1Cor 7:19
unto you are the c of the Lord 1Cor 14:37
even the law of c contained in .... Eph 2:15
after the c and doctrines of men .... Col 2:22
(touching whom ye received c .... Col 4:10
For ye know what c we gave you by 1Th 4:2
c of men, that turn from the .... Titus 1:14
we know him, if we keep his c 1Jn 2:3
I know him, and keepeth not his c 1Jn 2:4
of him, because we keep his c 1Jn 3:22
keepeth his c dwelleth in him 1Jn 3:24
when we love God, and keep his c 1Jn 5:2
love of God, that we keep his c 1Jn 5:3
and his c are not grievous 1Jn 5:3
is love, that we walk after his c 2Jn 6
her seed, which keep the c of God .... Rev 12:17
are they that keep the c of God .... Rev 14:12
Blessed are they that do his c .... Rev 22:14

COMMEND

into thy hands I c my spirit .... Lk 23:46
I c you to God, and to the word of .... Acts 20:32
c the righteousness of God .... Rom 3:5
I c unto you Phebe our sister .... Rom 16:1
Do we begin again to c ourselves 2Cor 3:1
For we c not ourselves again unto 2Cor 5:12
with some that c themselves 2Cor 10:12

COMMENDATION

some others, epistles of c to you 2Cor 3:1
to you, or letters of c from you 2Cor 3:1

COMMENDED

saw her, and c her before Pharaoh .... Gen 12:15
A man shall be c according to his .... Prov 12:8
Then I c mirth, because a man .... Eccl 8:15
the lord c the unjust steward .... Lk 16:8
they c them to the Lord, on whom .. Acts 14:23
for I ought to have been c of you 2Cor 12:11

COMMENDETH

But God c his love toward us, in .... Rom 5:8
But meat c us not to God 1Cor 8:8
For not he that c himself is 2Cor 10:18
is approved, but whom the Lord c 2Cor 10:18

COMMENDING

truth c ourselves to every man's 2Cor 4:2

COMMISSION

c from the chief priests, ... Acts 26:12

COMMISSIONS

they delivered the king's c unto .... Ezr 8:36

COMMIT

Thou shalt not c adultery .... Ex 20:14
If a soul c a trespass, and sin .... Lev 5:15
c any of these things which are .... Lev 5:17
c a trespass against the Lord, and .... Lev 6:2
and shall not c any of these .... Lev 18:26
For whosoever shall c any of .... Lev 18:29
even the souls that c them shall .... Lev 18:29
that ye c not any one of these .... Lev 18:30
to whoredom with Molech, from .... Lev 20:5
When a man or woman shall c .... Num 5:6
any sin that men c, to do .... Num 5:6
c a trespass against him, ... Num 5:12
the people began to c whoredom .... Num 25:1
to c trespass against the Lord in .... Num 31:16
Neither shalt thou c adultery .... Deut 5:18
shall henceforth c no more any .... Deut 19:20
c a trespass in the accursed .... Josh 7:14
If he c iniquity, I will chasten 2Sa 7:14
of Jerusalem to c fornication 2Chr 21:11
and unto God would I c my cause .... Job 5:8
that he should c iniquity, ... Job 34:10
Into thine hand I c my spirit .... Ps 31:5
C thy way unto the Lord .... Ps 37:5
C thy works unto the Lord, and thy .. Prov 16:3
to kings to c wickedness .... Prov 16:12
I will c thy government into his .... Is 22:21
shall c fornication with all the .... Is 23:17
c adultery, and swear falsely, and .. Jer 7:9
and weary themselves to c iniquity .... Jer 9:5
they c adultery, and walk in lies. .... Jer 23:14
c Jeremiah into the court of the .... Jer 37:21
Wherefore c ye this great evil .... Jer 44:7
and c iniquity, and I lay a .... Eze 3:20
the abominations which they c .... Eze 8:17
didst c whoredom with them, ... Eze 16:17
followeth thee to c whoredoms .... Eze 16:34
thou shalt not c this lewdness .... Eze 16:43
c ye whoredom after their .... Eze 20:30
the midst of them they c lewdness .... Eze 22:9
Will they now c whoredoms with .... Eze 23:43
and c iniquity, all his .... Eze 33:13
they shall c whoredom, and shall .. Hos 4:10

your daughters shall c whoredom .... Hos 4:13
and your spouses shall c adultery .... Hos 4:13
daughters when they c whoredom .... Hos 4:14
your spouses when they c adultery .. Hos 4:14
for they c lewdness. .... Hos 6:9
for they c falsehood. .... Hos 7:1
time, Thou shalt not c adultery .... Mt 5:27
causeth her to c adultery: .... Mt 5:32
which is put away doth c adultery .... Mt 19:9
murder, Thou shalt not c adultery .... Mt 19:18
Do not c adultery, Do not kill, ... Mk 10:19
did c things worthy of stripes, ... Lk 12:48
who will c to your trust the true .... Lk 16:11
Do not c adultery, Do not kill, ... Lk 18:20
Jesus did not c himself unto them. .... Jn 2:24
that they which c such things are .... Rom 1:32
against them which c such things.... Rom 2:2
a man should not c adultery .... Rom 2:22
dost thou c adultery .... Rom 2:22
idols, dost thou c sacrilege .... Rom 2:22
this, Thou shalt not c adultery. .... Rom 13:9
Neither let us c fornication 1Cor 10:8
This charge I c unto thee 1Ti 1:18
the same c thou to faithful men, ... 2Ti 2:2
ye c sin, and are convinced of the .... Jas 2:9
Do not c adultery, said also, Do .... Jas 2:11
Now if thou c no adultery .... Jas 2:11
according to the will of God c 1Pet 4:19
is born of God doth not c sin. 1Jn 3:9
unto idols, and to c fornication .... Rev 2:14
my servants to c fornication .... Rev 2:20
them that c adultery with her .... Rev 2:22

COMMITTED

he hath c all that he hath to my .... Gen 39:8
prison c to Joseph's hand all the .... Gen 39:22
for his sin that he hath c .... Lev 4:35
for his trespass, which he hath c .... Lev 5:7
customs, which were c before you.... Lev 18:30
of them have c an abomination .... Lev 20:13
for they c all these things, and .... Lev 20:23
if ought be c by ignorance. .... Num 15:24
which have c that wicked thing, ... Deut 17:5
if a man have c a sin worthy of .... Deut 21:22
c a trespass in the accursed .... Josh 7:1
have c against the God of Israel .... Josh 22:16
because ye have not c this .... Josh 22:31
for they have c lewdness and folly .. Judg 20:6
perversely, we have c wickedness 1Kin 8:47
with their sins which they had c 1Kin 14:22
c them unto the hands of the. 1Kin 14:27
which he c against the Lord. 1Chr 10:13
c them to the hands of the chief 2Chr 12:10
All that was c to thy servants, ... 2Chr 34:16
we have c iniquity, we have done .... Ps 106:6
For my people have c two evils .... Jer 2:13
whereby backsliding Israel c .... Jer 3:8
c adultery with stones and with .... Jer 3:9
to the full, they then c adultery .... Jer 5:7
horrible thing is c in the land. .... Jer 5:30
when they had c abomination. .... Jer 6:15
when they had c abomination .... Jer 8:12
have c against the Lord our God.... Jer 16:10
they have c villany in Israel .... Jer 29:23
have c adultery with their .... Jer 29:23
c him unto Gedaliah the son of .... Jer 39:14
had c unto him men, and women, and.. Jer 40:7
the captain of the guard had c to.... Jer 41:10
have c to provoke me to anger .... Jer 44:3
which they have c in the land of .... Jer 44:9
the abominations which ye have c .... Jer 44:22
have c in all their abominations .... Eze 6:9
because they have c a trespass .... Eze 15:8
Thou hast also c fornication with .... Eze 16:26
and c abomination before me. .... Eze 16:50
hath Samaria c half of thy sins. .... Eze 16:51
hast c more abominable than they .... Eze 16:52
to the idols, hath c abomination, ... Eze 18:12
from all his sins that he hath c .... Eze 18:21
his transgressions that he hath c .... Eze 18:22
his wickedness that he hath c .... Eze 18:24
his transgressions that he hath c .... Eze 18:28
in that they have c a trespass .... Eze 20:27
for all your evils that ye have c.... Eze 20:43
one hath c abomination with his .... Eze 22:11
they c whoredoms in Egypt .... Eze 23:3
they c whoredoms in their youth .... Eze 23:3
Thus she c her whoredoms with.... Eze 23:7
That they have c adultery .... Eze 23:37
their idols have they c adultery .... Eze 23:37
for his iniquity that he hath c .... Eze 33:13
c shall be mentioned unto him. .... Eze 33:16
abominations which they have c .... Eze 33:29
abominations that they have c .... Eze 43:8
the abominations which they have c .. Eze 44:13
have c iniquity, and have done .... Dan 9:5
the land hath c great whoredom.... Hos 1:2
they have c whoredom continually .... Hos 4:18
and an abomination is c in Israel.... Mal 2:11
c adultery with her already in .... Mt 5:28
with him, who had c murder in the .. Mk 15:7
and to whom men have c much .... Lk 12:48
but hath c all judgment unto the .... Jn 5:22
men and women c them to prison.... Acts 8:3
or have c any thing worthy of .... Acts 25:11
he had c nothing worthy of death.... Acts 25:25
they c themselves unto the sea,.... Acts 27:40
though I have c nothing against.... Acts 28:17
them were c the oracles of God. .... Rom 3:2
of the gospel is c unto me 1Cor 9:17
fornication, as some of them c 1Cor 10:8

hath c unto us the word of 2Cor 5:19
Have I c an offence in abasing 2Cor 11:7
lasciviousness which they have c 2Cor 12:21
the uncircumcision was c unto me .... Gal 2:7
God, which was c to my trust. 1Ti 1:11
keep that which is c to thy trust.... 1Ti 6:20
have c unto him against that day 2Ti 1:12
That good thing which was c unto.. 2Ti 1:14
which is c unto me according to .... Titus 1:3
and if he have c sins, they shall .... Jas 5:15
but c himself to him that judgeth 1Pet 2:23
deeds which they have ungodly c .... Jude 15
of the earth have c fornication. .... Rev 17:2
earth have c fornication with her .... Rev 18:3
who have c fornication and lived. .... Rev 18:9

COMMITTEST

thou c whoredom, and Israel is .... Hos 5:3

COMMITTETH

the man that c adultery with .... Lev 20:10
even he that c adultery with his. .... Lev 20:10
the poor c himself unto thee. .... Ps 10:14
But whoso c adultery with a woman.. Prov 6:32
that the house of Israel c here. .... Eze 8:6
But as a wife that c adultery .... Eze 16:32
c iniquity, and doeth according to .... Eze 18:24
c iniquity, and dieth in them .... Eze 18:26
c iniquity, he shall even die .... Eze 18:28
her that is divorced c adultery .... Mt 5:32
shall marry another, c adultery .... Mt 19:9
another, c adultery against her .... Mk 10:11
to another, she c adultery .... Mk 10:12
and marrieth another, c adultery.... Lk 16:18
away from her husband c adultery .... Lk 16:18
Whosoever c sin is the servant of .... Jn 8:34
but he that c fornication sinneth 1Cor 6:18
Whosoever c sin transgresseth.... 1Jn 3:4
He that c sin is of the devil 1Jn 3:8

COMMITTING

of life, without c iniquity .... Eze 33:15
c adultery, they break out, and .... Hos 4:2

COMMODIOUS

the haven was not c to winter in.... Acts 27:12

COMMON

if any one of the c people sin .... Lev 4:27
men die the c death of all men .... Num 16:29
There is no c bread under mine. 1Sa 21:4
and the bread is in a manner c 1Sa 21:5
the sun, and it is c among men .... Eccl 6:1
into the graves of the c people. .... Jer 26:23
and shall eat them as c things. .... Jer 31:5
with the men of the c sort were .... Eze 23:42
took Jesus into the c hall. .... Mt 27:27
the c people heard him gladly. .... Mk 12:37
together, and had all things c .... Acts 2:44
but they had all things c .... Acts 4:32
and put them in the c prison .... Acts 5:18
any thing that is c or unclean .... Acts 10:14
cleansed, that call not thou c .... Acts 10:15
not call any man c or unclean .... Acts 10:28
for nothing c or unclean hath at .... Acts 11:8
cleansed, that call not thou c .... Acts 11:9
taken you but such as is c to man.... 1Cor 10:13
mine own son after the c faith .... Titus 1:4
write unto you of the c salvation .... Jude 3

COMMONLY

this saying is c reported among .... Mt 28:15
It is reported c that there is 1Cor 5:1

COMMONWEALTH

being aliens from the c of Israel .... Eph 2:12

COMMOTION

a great c out of the north .... Jer 10:22

COMMOTIONS

when ye shall hear of wars and c .... Lk 21:9

COMMUNE

went out unto Jacob to c with him .... Gen 34:6
I will c with thee from above the .... Ex 25:22
C with David secretly, and say, ... 1Sa 18:22
I will c with my father of thee 1Sa 19:3
If we assay to c with thee .... Job 4:2
c with your own heart upon your .... Ps 4:4
they c of laying snares privily .... Ps 64:5
I c with mine own heart .... Ps 77:6

COMMUNED

he c with them, saying, If it be .... Gen 23:8
Hamor c with them, saying, The .... Gen 34:8
c with the men of their city, ... Gen 34:20
c with them, and took from them .... Gen 42:24
they c with him at the door of .... Gen 43:19
c with them, and will at the .... Judg 9:1
Samuel c with Saul upon the top 1Sa 9:25
c with Abigail, to take her to 1Sa 25:39
she c with him of all that was in 1Kin 10:2
and they c with her 2Kin 22:14
she c with him of all that was in 2Chr 9:1
I c with mine own heart, saying, ... Eccl 1:16
And the king c with them .... Dan 1:19
So the angel that c with me said. .... Zec 1:14
c one with another what they .... Lk 6:11
c with the chief priests and .... Lk 22:4
pass, that, while they c together .... Lk 24:15
him the oftener, and c with him .... Acts 24:26

COMMUNICATE

c unto him that teacheth in all .... Gal 6:6
that ye did c with my affliction .... Phil 4:14

ready to distribute, willing to c........... 1Ti 6:18
But to do good and not to c forget not .... Heb 13:16

COMMUNICATED
c unto them that gospel which I .... Gal 2:2
no church c with me as concerning....... Phil 4:15

COMMUNICATION
Abner had c with the elders of.......... 2Sa 3:17
them, Ye know the man, and his c........ 2Kin 9:11
But let your c be, Yea, yea.............. Mt 5:37
Let no corrupt c proceed out of......... Eph 4:29
filthy c out of your mouth................ Col 3:8
That the c of thy faith may........... Philem 6

COMMUNICATIONS
What manner of c are these that....... Lk 24:17
evil c corrupt good manners........... 1Cor 15:33

COMMUNING
as he had left c with Abraham........... Gen 18:33
of c with him upon mount Sinai.......... Ex 31:18

COMMUNION
is it not the c of the blood of............ 1Cor 10:16
is it not the c of the body of............. 1Cor 10:16
what c hath light with darkness........ 2Cor 6:14
the c of the Holy Ghost, be with....... 2Cor 13:14

COMPACT
as a city that is c together.............. Ps 122:3

COMPACTED
c by that which every joint.............. Eph 4:16

COMPANIED
of these men which have c with us...... Acts 1:21

COMPANIES
three hundred men into three c .... Judg 7:16
the three c blew the trumpets, and...... Judg 7:20
wait against Shechem in four c......... Judg 9:34
and divided them into three c........... Judg 9:43
the two other c ran upon all the .... Judg 9:44
Saul put the people in three c......... 1Sa 11:11
of the Philistines in three c............. 1Sa 13:17
And the Syrians had gone out by c...... 2Kin 5:2
in the c of the children of Levi......... 1Chr 9:18
the captains of the c that............... 1Chr 28:1
appointed two great c of them......... Neh 12:31
So stood the two c of them that........ Neh 12:40
the c of Sheba waited for them......... Job 6:19
O ye travelling c of Dedanim.......... Is 21:13
criest, let thy c deliver thee............ Is 57:13
chariots, and with horsemen, and c..... Eze 26:7
down by c upon the green grass......... Mk 6:39

COMPANION
his brother, and every man his c....... Ex 32:27
Samson's wife was given to his c....... Judg 14:20
therefore I gave her to thy c............ Judg 15:2
his wife, and given her to his c......... Judg 15:6
the Archite was the king's c............ 1Chr 27:33
to dragons, and a c to owls............. Job 30:29
I am a c of all them that fear.......... Ps 119:63
but a c of fools shall be................. Prov 13:20
but he that is a c of riotous men...... Prov 28:7
the same is the c of a destroyer....... Prov 28:24
yet is she thy c, and the wife of....... Mal 2:14
c in labour, and fellow soldier,........ Phil 2:25
c in tribulation, and in the............. Rev 1:9

COMPANIONS
and she went with her c, and.......... Judg 11:38
brought thirty c to be with him........ Judg 14:11
Tabeel, and the rest of their c......... Ezr 4:7
scribe, and the rest of their c......... Ezr 4:9
to the rest of their c that dwell....... Ezr 4:17
Shimshai the scribe, and their c....... Ezr 4:23
and Shethar-boznai, and their c........ Ezr 5:3
your c the Apharsachites, which....... Ezr 6:6
river, Shethar-boznai, and their c..... Ezr 6:13
answer thee, and thy c with thee...... Job 35:4
Shall the c make a banquet of him..... Job 41:6
the virgins her c that follow her...... Ps 45:14
aside by the flocks of thy c............ Song 1:7
the c hearken to thy voice............. Song 8:13
are rebellious, and c of thieves....... Is 1:23
for the children of Israel his c........ Eze 37:16
for all the house of Israel his c...... Eze 37:16
Mishael, and Azariah, his c............ Dan 2:17
Paul's c in travel, they rushed........ Acts 19:29
whilst ye became c of them that...... Heb 10:33

COMPANIONS'
c sakes, I will now say, Peace be..... Ps 122:8

COMPANY
said, If Esau come to the one c........ Gen 32:8
then the other c which is left.......... Gen 32:8
lodged that night in the c............. Gen 32:21
a c of nations shall be of thee,....... Gen 35:11
a c of Ishmeelites came from.......... Gen 37:25
and it was a very great c.............. Gen 50:9
they spake unto all the c of the...... Num 14:7
unto Korah and unto all his c......... Num 16:5
you censers, Korah, and all his c..... Num 16:6
all thy c are gathered together...... Num 16:11
all thy c before the LORD, thou,..... Num 16:16
he be not as Korah, and as his c..... Num 16:40
Now shall this c lick up all that .... Num 22:4
against Aaron in the c of Korah..... Num 26:9
with Korah, when that c died........ Num 26:10
he was not in the c of them that.... Num 27:3
the LORD in the c of Korah......... Num 27:3

another c come along by the plain..... Judg 9:37
the c that was with him, rushed...... Judg 9:44
that thou comest with such a c....... Judg 18:23
that thou shalt meet a c of........... 1Sa 10:5
behold, a c of prophets met him...... 1Sa 10:10
one c turned unto the way that....... 1Sa 13:17
another c turned the way to.......... 1Sa 13:18
another c turned to the way of....... 1Sa 13:18
when they saw the c of the.......... 1Sa 19:20
thou bring me down to this c......... 1Sa 30:15
I will bring thee down to this c..... 1Sa 30:15
delivered the c that came against.... 1Sa 30:23
the man of God, he and all his c..... 2Kin 5:15
he spied the c of Jehu as he came... 2Kin 9:17
and said, I see a c.................. 2Kin 9:17
at Jerusalem, with a very great c.... 2Chr 9:1
great c that cometh against us....... 2Chr 20:12
came with a small c of men......... 2Chr 24:24
the other c of them that gave....... Neh 12:38
thou hast made desolate all my c.... Job 16:7
Which goeth in c with the workers... Job 34:8
walked unto the house of God in..... Ps 55:14
great was the c of those that....... Ps 68:11
Rebuke the c of spearmen, the...... Ps 68:30
and covered the c of Abiram........ Ps 106:17
And a fire was kindled in their c.... Ps 106:18
but he that keepeth c with......... Prov 29:3
to a c of horses in Pharaoh's...... Song 1:9
As it were the c of two armies..... Song 6:13
a great c shall return thither...... Jer 31:8
also bring up a c against thee..... Eze 16:40
great c make for him in the war.... Eze 17:17
I will bring up a c upon them...... Eze 23:46
the c shall stone them with....... Eze 23:47
the c of the Ashurites have made... Eze 27:6
in all thy c which is in the......... Eze 27:27
all thy c in the midst of thee...... Eze 27:34
over thee with a c of many people.. Eze 32:3
Asshur is there and all her c...... Eze 32:22
is round about her grave........... Eze 32:23
even a great c with bucklers and... Eze 38:4
all thy c that are assembled....... Eze 38:7
gathered thy c to take a prey...... Eze 38:13
riding upon horses, a great c...... Eze 38:15
so the c of priests murder in the.. Hos 6:9
him to have been in the c......... Lk 2:44
there was a great c of publicans... Lk 5:29
the c of his disciples, and a........ Lk 6:17
shall separate you from their c.... Lk 6:22
them sit down by fifties in a c..... Lk 9:14
behold, a man of the c cried out... Lk 9:38
of the c lifted up her voice........ Lk 11:27
one of the c said unto him......... Lk 12:13
followed him a great c of people... Lk 23:27
also of our c made us astonished... Lk 24:22
saw a great c come unto him, he.. Jn 6:5
let go, they went to their own c... Acts 4:23
a great c of the priests were...... Acts 6:7
for a man that is a Jew to keep c.. Acts 10:28
his c loosed from Paphos, they.... Acts 13:13
their own c from Antioch with Paul.. Acts 15:22
the base sort, and gathered a c.... Acts 17:5
we that were of Paul's departed... Acts 21:8
I be somewhat filled with your c... Rom 15:24
epistle not to c with fornicators... 1Cor 5:9
written unto you not to keep c..... 1Cor 5:11
have no c with him, that he may... 2Th 3:14
and to an innumerable c of angels. Heb 12:22
all the c in ships, and sailors,..... Rev 18:17

COMPARABLE
c to fine gold, how are they........ Lam 4:2

COMPARE
what likeness will ye c unto him.... Is 40:18
c me, that we may be like......... Is 46:5
what comparison shall we c it..... Mk 4:30
or c ourselves with some that...... 2Cor 10:12

COMPARED
the heaven can be c unto the LORD.. Ps 89:6
desire are not to be c unto her.... Prov 3:15
be desired are not to be c to it.... Prov 8:11
I have c thee, O my love, to a..... Song 1:9
time are not worthy to be c with... Rom 8:18

COMPARING
c spiritual things with spiritual.... 1Cor 2:13
c themselves among themselves,.... 2Cor 10:12

COMPARISON
What have I done now in c of you... Judg 8:2
what was I able to do in c of you... Judg 8:3
your eyes in c of it as nothing...... Hag 2:3
or with what c shall we compare... Mk 4:30

COMPASS
under the c of the altar beneath.... Ex 27:5
grate of network under the c....... Ex 38:4
a round about by the way of Edom.. Num 21:4
the border shall fetch a c from.... Num 34:5
And ye shall c the city, all ye..... Josh 6:3
ye shall c the city seven times.... Josh 6:4
c the city, and let him that is..... Josh 6:7
to Adar, and fetched a c to Karkaa. Josh 15:3
but fetch a c behind them......... 2Sa 5:23
cubits did c either of them about... 1Kin 7:15
cubits did c it round about........ 1Kin 7:23
a round c of half a cubit high...... 1Kin 7:35
they fetched a c of seven days'.... 2Kin 3:9
ye shall c the king round about,... 2Kin 11:8
from brim to brim, round in c...... 2Chr 4:2
cubits did it round about.......... 2Chr 4:2

which did c it round about........ 2Chr 4:3
the Levites shall c the king....... 2Chr 23:7
His archers c me round about, he.. Job 16:13
willows of the brook c him about... Job 40:22
wilt thou c him as with a shield.... Ps 5:12
of the people c thee about......... Ps 7:7
my deadly enemies, who c me about. Ps 17:9
so will I c thine altar, O LORD..... Ps 26:6
thou shalt c me about with songs... Ps 32:7
the LORD, mercy shall c him about... Ps 32:10
of my heels shall c me about...... Ps 49:5
the head of those that c me about.. Ps 140:9
the righteous shall c me about...... Ps 142:7
when he set a c upon the face of... Prov 8:27
and he marketh it out with the c.. Is 44:13
that c yourselves about with...... Is 50:11
the earth, A woman shall c a man... Jer 31:22
Gareb, and shall c about to Goath... Jer 31:39
fillet of twelve cubits did c it.... Jer 52:21
wicked doth c about the righteous.. Hab 1:4
for ye c sea and land to make one.. Mt 23:15
c thee round, and keep thee in on.. Lk 19:43
And from thence we fetched a c..... Acts 28:13

COMPASSED
c the house round, both old and.... Gen 19:4
we c mount Seir many days......... Deut 2:1
Ye have c this mountain long...... Deut 2:3
So the ark of the LORD c the city... Josh 6:11
second day they c the city once.... Josh 6:14
c the city after the same manner... Josh 6:15
day they c the city seven times.... Josh 6:15
the border c from Baalah westward.. Josh 15:10
c the corner of the sea southward.. Josh 18:14
c the land of Edom, and the land... Judg 11:18
they c him in, and laid wait for.... Judg 16:2
for Saul and his men c David....... 1Sa 23:26
that bare Joab's armour c about.... 2Sa 18:15
When the waves of death c me...... 2Sa 22:5
The sorrows of hell c me about.... 2Sa 22:6
by night, and c the city about...... 2Kin 6:14
an host c the city both with....... 2Kin 6:15
the Edomites which c him about.... 2Kin 8:21
Therefore they c about him to...... 2Chr 18:31
smote the Edomites which c him in.. 2Chr 21:9
c about Ophel, and raised it up a... 2Chr 33:14
me, and hath c me with his net..... Job 19:6
He hath c the waters with bounds,.. Job 26:10
They have now c us in our steps.... Ps 17:11
The sorrows of death c me......... Ps 18:4
The sorrows of hell c me about.... Ps 18:5
Many bulls have c me.............. Ps 22:12
For dogs have c me................ Ps 22:16
innumerable evils have c me about.. Ps 40:12
they c me about together......... Ps 88:17
They c me about also with words.... Ps 109:3
The sorrows of death c me........ Ps 116:3
All nations c me about............ Ps 118:10
They c me about.................. Ps 118:11
yea, they c me about.............. Ps 118:11
They c me about like bees........ Ps 118:12
me, and c me with gall and travel.. Lam 3:5
and the floods c me about......... Jonah 2:3
The waters c me about, even to.... Jonah 2:5
shall see Jerusalem c with armies.. Lk 21:20
himself also is c with infirmity.... Heb 5:2
after they were c about seven..... Heb 11:30
Wherefore seeing we also are c.... Heb 12:1
c the camp of the saints about,.... Rev 20:9

COMPASSEST
Thou c my path and my lying down,.. Ps 139:3

COMPASSETH
that is it which c the whole land.. Gen 2:11
the same is it that c the whole.... Gen 2:13
the border c it on the north side.. Josh 19:14
Therefore pride c them about as a.. Ps 73:6
Ephraim c me about with lies, and.. Hos 11:12

COMPASSING
round about there were knops c it.. 1Kin 7:24
in a cubit, c the sea round about... 1Kin 7:24
in a cubit, the sea round about..... 2Chr 4:3

COMPASSION
And she had c on him, and said,..... Ex 2:6
have c upon thee, and multiply..... Deut 13:17
have c upon thee, and will return... Deut 30:3
for ye have c on me............... 1Sa 23:21
give them c before them who....... 1Kin 8:50
that they may have c on them...... 1Kin 8:50
had c on them, and had respect..... 2Kin 13:23
your children shall find c before... 2Chr 30:9
because he had c on his people..... 2Chr 36:15
no c upon young man or maiden..... 2Chr 36:17
But he, being full of c, forgave..... Ps 78:38
thou, O Lord, art a God full of c.... Ps 86:15
the LORD is gracious and full of c.. Ps 111:4
he is gracious, and full of c....... Ps 112:4
LORD is gracious, and full of c..... Ps 145:8
not have c on the son of her womb.. Is 49:15
have c on them, and will bring..... Jer 12:15
yet will he have c according to..... Lam 3:32
unto thee, to have c upon thee..... Eze 16:5
again, he will have c upon us...... Mic 7:19
he was moved with c on them...... Mt 9:36
and was moved with c toward them.. Mt 14:14
I have c on the multitude,......... Mt 15:32
of that servant was moved with c.. Mt 18:27
have had c on thy fellowservant.... Mt 18:33
So Jesus had c on them, and....... Mt 20:34
And Jesus, moved with c, put forth.. Mk 1:41

for thee, and hath had c on thee .... Mk 5:19
and was moved with c toward them...... Mk 6:34
I have c on the multitude, ... Mk 8:2
thing, have c on us, and help us .... Mk 9:22
the Lord saw her, he had c on her............ Lk 7:13
when he saw him, he had c on him........ Lk 10:33
off, his father saw him, and had c........ Lk 15:20
have c on whom I will have c.................. Rom 9:15
Who can have c on the ignorant,.............. Heb 5:2
For ye had c of me in my bonds, ... Heb 10:34
having c one of another, love as............ 1Pet 3:8
up his bowels of c from him 1Jn 3:17
And of some have c, making a.................. Jude 22

COMPASSIONS
consumed, because his c fail not...... Lam 3:22
c every man to his brother .... Zec 7:9

COMPEL
thou shalt not c him to serve as............ Lev 25:39
none did c.. Est 1:8
whosoever shall c thee to go a............ Mt 5:41
they c one Simon a Cyrenian, who ...... Mk 15:21
c them to come in, that my house........ Lk 14:23

COMPELLED
together with the woman, c him 1Sa 28:23
fornication, and a Judah thereto 2Chr 21:11
him they c to bear his cross.................. Mt 27:32
synagogue, and c them to blaspheme Acts 26:11
ye have c me 2Cor 12:11
a Greek, was c to be circumcised.......... Gal 2:3

COMPELLEST
why c thou the Gentiles to live........ Gal 2:14

COMPLAIN
their brethren come unto us to c .... Judg 21:22
I will c in the bitterness of my................ Job 7:11
the furrows likewise thereof c............ Job 31:38
Wherefore doth a living man c............ Lam 3:39

COMPLAINED
And when the people c, it...................... Num 11:1
I c, and my spirit was overwhelmed ...... Ps 77:3

COMPLAINERS
These are murmurers, c, walking .... Jude 16

COMPLAINING
that there be no c in our streets .... Ps 144:14

COMPLAINT
for out of the abundance of my c........ 1Sa 1:16
me, my couch shall ease my c.............. Job 7:13
If I say, I will forget my c .... Job 9:27
I will leave my c upon myself .... Job 10:1
As for me, is my c to man...................... Job 21:4
Even to day is my c bitter...................... Job 23:2
I mourn in my c, and make a noise ...... Ps 55:2
poureth out his c before the Lord........ Ps 102:t
I poured out my c before him................ Ps 142:2

COMPLAINTS
grievous c against Paul, which.............. Acts 25:7

COMPLETE
seven sabbaths shall be c .... Lev 23:15
And ye are c in him, which is the........ Col 2:10
and c in all the will of God.................... Col 4:12

COMPOSITION
other like it, after the c of it................ Ex 30:32
according to the c thereof........................ Ex 30:37

COMPOUND
an ointment c after the art of .... Ex 30:25

COMPOUNDETH
Whosoever c any like it, or.................... Ex 30:33

COMPREHEND
doeth he, which we cannot c.................. Job 37:5
May be able to c with all saints .... Eph 3:18

COMPREHENDED
c the dust of the earth in a.................... Is 40:12
and the darkness c it not............................ Jn 1:5
it is briefly c in this saying,.................. Rom 13:9

CONANIAH (co-na-ni'-ah) See CONONIAH. A
chief Levite during Josiah's time.
C also, and Shemaiah and Nethaneel,.. 2Chr 35:9

CONCEAL
Say our brother, and c his blood........ Gen 37:26
spare, neither shalt thou c him............ Deut 13:8
is with the Almighty will I not c .... Job 27:11
I will not c his parts, nor his.............. Job 41:12
is the glory of God to c a thing .... Prov 25:2
publish, and c not...................................... Jer 50:2

CONCEALED
for I have not c the words of the .... Job 6:10
I have not c thy lovingkindness,.......... Ps 40:10

CONCEALETH
of a faithful spirit c the matter............ Prov 11:13
A prudent man c knowledge .... Prov 12:23

CONCEIT
and as an high wall in his own c.......... Prov 18:11
lest he be wise in his own c.................. Prov 26:5
thou a man wise in his own c................ Prov 26:12
sluggard is wiser in his own c .... Prov 26:16
The rich man is wise in his own c........ Prov 28:11

CONCEITS
ye should be wise in your own c........ Rom 11:25
Be not wise in your own c.................... Rom 12:16

CONCEIVE
that they should c when they came ... Gen 30:38
the stronger cattle did c...................... Gen 30:41
that they might c among the rods ...... Gen 30:41
shall be free, and shall c seed.............. Num 5:28
but thou shalt c, and bear a son.......... Judg 13:3
For, lo, thou shalt c, and bear a.......... Judg 13:5
unto me, Behold, thou shalt c.............. Judg 13:7
They c mischief, and bring forth.......... Job 15:35
and in sin did my mother c me .... Ps 51:5
Behold, a virgin shall c, and bear...... Is 7:14
Ye shall c chaff, ye shall bring .... Is 33:11
they c mischief, and bring forth.......... Is 59:4
thou shalt c in thy womb, and.............. Lk 1:31
received strength to c seed.................... Heb 11:11

CONCEIVED
and she c, and bare Cain, and said,...... Gen 4:1
and she c, and bare Enoch.................... Gen 4:17
he went in unto Hagar, and she c ...... Gen 16:4
and when she saw that she had c .... Gen 16:4
and when she saw that she had c .... Gen 16:5
For Sarah c, and bare Abraham a........ Gen 21:2
of him, and Rebekah his wife c............ Gen 25:21
And Leah c, and bare a son, and she.. Gen 29:32
she c again, and bare a son .... Gen 29:33
she c again, and bare a son .... Gen 29:34
she c again, and bare a son .... Gen 29:35
And Bilhah c, and bare Jacob a son.... Gen 30:5
And Bilhah Rachel's maid c again...... Gen 30:7
God hearkened unto Leah, and she c.. Gen 30:17
Leah c again, and bare Jacob the........ Gen 30:19
And she c, and bare a son .... Gen 30:23
the flocks c before the rods, and........ Gen 30:39
at the time that the cattle c.................. Gen 31:10
And she c, and bare a son .... Gen 38:3
she c again, and bare a son .... Gen 38:4
And she yet again c, and bare a son.... Gen 38:5
came in unto her, and she c by him.... Gen 38:18
And the woman c, and bare a .... Ex 2:2
saying, If a woman have c seed............ Lev 12:2
Have I c all this people.......................... Num 11:12
was come about after Hannah had c.... 1Sa 1:20
visited Hannah, so that she c 1Sa 2:21
And the woman c, and sent and told .. 1Sa 4:19
And the woman c, and bare a son at .. 2Kin 4:17
he went in to his wife, and she c 1Chr 7:23
was said, There is a man child c.......... Job 3:3
hath c mischief, and brought forth .... Ps 7:14
into the chamber of her that c me ...... Song 3:4
and she c, and bare a son .... Is 8:3
hath c a purpose against you .... Jer 49:30
which c, and bare him a son.................. Hos 1:3
she c again, and bare a daughter........ Hos 1:6
she had weaned Lo-ruhamah, she c .... Hos 1:8
she that c them hath done .... Hos 2:5
for that which is in her is c of.............. Mt 1:20
those days his wife Elisabeth c .... Lk 1:24
she hath also c a son in her old............ Lk 1:36
angel before he was c in the womb...... Lk 2:21
why hast thou c this thing in .... Acts 5:4
when Rebecca also had c by one........ Rom 9:10
Then when lust hath c, it........................ Jas 1:15

CONCEIVING
speaking oppression and revolt, c........ Is 59:13

CONCEPTION
multiply thy sorrow and thy c .... Gen 3:16
in unto her, the Lord gave her c .... Ruth 4:13
and from the womb, and from the c.... Hos 9:11

CONCERN
which c the Lord Jesus Christ .... Acts 28:31
things which c mine infirmities 2Cor 11:30

CONCERNETH
Lord will perfect that which c me ...... Ps 138:8
This burden c the prince in.................... Eze 12:10

CONCERNING
same shall comfort us c our work........ Gen 5:29
Pharaoh commanded his men c him.... Gen 12:20
accepted thee c this thing also.............. Gen 19:21
and sware to him c that matter............ Gen 24:9
told him c the well which they .... Gen 26:32
are verily guilty c our brother.............. Gen 42:21
c the which I did swear to give .... Ex 6:8
made with you c all these words.......... Ex 24:8
c things which ought not to be .... Lev 4:2
c things which should not be done ...... Lev 4:13
of the Lord his God c things................ Lev 4:22
an atonement for him c his sin............ Lev 4:26
c things which ought not to be .... Lev 4:27
an atonement for him c his sin............ Lev 5:6
c his ignorance wherein he erred .... Lev 5:18
which was lost, and lieth c it................ Lev 6:3
for ever in your generations c.............. Lev 6:18
C the beasts of the Lord, which .... Lev 23:2
c the tithe of the herd, or c.................. Lev 27:32
commanded Moses c the Levites.......... Num 8:20
had commanded Moses c the Levites.. Num 8:22
what the Lord will command c you .... Num 9:8
Lord hath spoken good c Israel........ Num 10:29
c which I sware to make you dwell .... Num 14:30
tribes c the children of Israel .... Num 36:1
out of her lips c her vows...................... Num 30:12
or c the bond of her soul, shall............ Num 30:12
c them Moses commanded...................... Num 32:28
c the daughters of Zelophehad.............. Num 36:6
unto Moses the man of God c me .... Josh 14:6

the Lord your God spake c you .... Josh 23:14
And Samson said c them, Now shall.... Judg 15:3
c him that came not up to the............ Judg 21:5
former time in Israel c redeeming...... Ruth 4:7
c changing, for to confirm all.............. Ruth 4:7
which I have spoken c his house 1Sa 3:11
good that he hath spoken c thee........ 1Sa 25:30
to day with a fault c this woman 2Sa 3:8
thou hast spoken c thy servant 2Sa 7:25
c his house, establish it for.................. 2Sa 7:25
David all the things c the war.............. 2Sa 11:18
for he was comforted c Amnon............ 2Sa 13:39
and I will give charge c thee................ 2Sa 14:8
all the captains charge c Absalom...... 2Sa 18:5
his word which he spake c me.............. 1Kin 2:4
which he spake c the house of Eli 1Kin 2:27
all thy desire c timber of cedar............ 1Kin 5:8
and c timber of fir 1Kin 5:8
C this house which thou art in 1Kin 6:12
Moreover c a stranger, that is.............. 1Kin 8:41
of Solomon c the name of the Lord.... 1Kin 10:1
Of the nations c which the Lord........ 1Kin 11:2
had commanded him c this.................... 1Kin 11:10
he doth not prophesy good c me.......... 1Kin 22:8
he would prophesy no good c me........ 1Kin 22:18
Lord hath spoken evil c thee.............. 1Kin 22:23
Lord spake c the house of Ahab.......... 2Kin 10:10
c whom the Lord had charged.............. 2Kin 17:15
that the Lord hath spoken c him........ 2Kin 19:21
the Lord c the king of Assyria............ 2Kin 19:32
c the words of this book that is............ 2Kin 22:13
all that which is written c us................ 2Kin 22:13
to the word of the Lord c Israel 1Chr 11:10
thou hast spoken c thy servant 1Chr 17:23
c his house be established for.............. 1Chr 17:23
to comfort him c his father.................. 1Chr 19:2
and give thee charge c Israel.............. 1Chr 22:12
Lord charged Moses with c Israel...... 1Chr 23:14
Now c Moses the man of God, his...... 1Chr 23:14
C Kehabiah 1Chr 24:21
C Kish.. 1Chr 24:29
C the divisions of the porters.............. 1Chr 26:1
As c the sons of Laadan........................ 1Chr 26:21
Moreover c the treasurer, which is 2Chr 8:12
c any matter, or c the treasures.......... 2Chr 8:15
and of Iddo the seer c genealogies 2Chr 12:15
also c Maachah the mother of Asa...... 2Chr 15:16
Now c his sons, and the greatness...... 2Chr 24:27
c the children of Israel and Judah 2Chr 31:6
and the Levites c the heaps.................. 2Chr 31:9
c the words of the book that is............ 2Chr 34:21
saith the Lord God of Israel c 2Chr 34:26
answer by letter c this matter .... Ezr 5:5
his pleasure to us c this matter .... Ezr 5:17
Cyrus the king made a decree c.......... Ezr 6:3
counsellors, to enquire c Judah.......... Ezr 7:14
is hope in Israel c this thing .... Ezr 10:2
I asked them c the Jews that had........ Neh 1:2
of the captivity, and c Jerusalem........ Neh 1:2
c which thou hadst promised to.......... Neh 9:23
was the king's commandment c them Neh 11:23
hand in all matters c the people.......... Neh 11:24
c this, and wipe not out my good........ Neh 13:14
my God, c this also, and spare me ...... Neh 13:22
the king had so commanded c him...... Est 3:2
which they had seen c this matter ...... Est 9:26
The noise thereof sheweth c it .... Job 36:33
it, the cattle also c the vapour............ Job 36:33
c the words of Cush the Benjamite .... Ps 7:t
C the works of men, by the word........ Ps 17:4
and speak wickedly c oppression .... Ps 73:8
let it repent thee c thy servants.......... Ps 90:13
c whom the Lord commanded them .... Ps 106:34
precepts c all things to be right.......... Ps 119:128
C thy testimonies, I have known........ Ps 119:152
repent himself c his servants .... Ps 135:14
search out by wisdom c all things...... Eccl 1:13
I said in mine heart c the estate.......... Eccl 3:18
dost not enquire wisely c this .... Eccl 7:10
son of Amoz, which he saw c Judah .... Is 1:1
the son of Amoz saw c Judah .... Is 2:1
man's pen c Maher-shalal-hash-baz...... Is 8:1
spoken c Moab since that time............ Is 16:13
As at the report c Egypt, so.................. Is 23:5
c the house of Jacob, Jacob shall........ Is 29:22
c whom the Lord commanded them.... Is 36:t
he heard say c Tirhakah king of.......... Is 37:9
which the Lord hath spoken c him...... Is 37:22
the Lord c the king of Assyria............ Is 37:33
me of things to come c my sons.......... Is 45:11
c the work of my hands command ye .. Is 45:11
c burnt offerings or sacrifices............ Jer 7:22
came to Jeremiah c the dearth............ Jer 14:1
c the prophets that prophesy in.......... Jer 14:15
thus saith the Lord c the sons............ Jer 16:3
c the daughters that are born in.......... Jer 16:3
c their mothers that bare them,.......... Jer 16:3
c their fathers that begat them............ Jer 16:3
instant I shall speak c a nation.......... Jer 18:7
c a kingdom, to pluck up, and to........ Jer 18:7
instant I shall speak c a nation.......... Jer 18:9
c a kingdom, to build and to plant .... Jer 18:9
c Jehoiakim the son of Josiah............ Jer 22:18
the Lord of hosts c the prophets........ Jer 23:15
c all the people of Judah in the.......... Jer 25:1
the Lord of hosts c the pillars............ Jer 27:19
c the sea, and c the bases...................... Jer 27:19
c the residue of the vessels that .... Jer 27:19
c the vessels that remain in the.......... Jer 27:21

Thus saith the LORD c Shemaiah .... Jer 29:31
c Israel and c Judah .... Jer 30:4
c this city, whereof ye say, It .... Jer 32:36
c the houses of this city, and .... Jer 33:4
c the houses of the kings of......... Jer 33:4
king of Babylon gave charge c......... Jer 39:11
The LORD hath said c you, O ye......... Jer 42:19
The word that came to Jeremiah c .... Jer 44:1
C The Ammonites, thus saith the......... Jer 49:1
C Edom, thus saith the LORD of......... Jer 49:7
C Damascus .... Jer 49:23
C Kedar, and c the kingdoms......... Jer 49:28
c the pillars, the height of one......... Jer 52:21
the LORD hath commanded c Jacob ... Lam 1:17
Israel which prophesy c Jerusalem ... Eze 13:16
a prophet to enquire of him c me......... Eze 14:7
ye shall be comforted c the evil......... Eze 14:22
even c all that I have brought......... Eze 14:22
this proverb c the land of Israel......... Eze 18:2
the Lord GOD c the Ammonites......... Eze 21:28
and c their reproach......... Eze 21:28
therefore c the land of Israel......... Eze 36:6
ears all that I say unto thee c......... Eze 44:5
C the ordinance of oil, the bath......... Eze 45:14
c the which I lifted up mine hand... Eze 47:14
the God of heaven c this secret......... Dan 2:18
and made a proclamation c him......... Dan 5:29
against Daniel c the kingdom......... Dan 6:4
against him c the law of his God......... Dan 6:5
the king c the king's decree......... Dan 6:12
might not be changed c Daniel......... Dan 6:17
As c the rest of the beasts, they......... Dan 7:12
the vision c the daily sacrifice......... Dan 8:13
which he saw c Israel in the days ... Amos 1:1
Thus saith the LORD GOD c Edom......... Obad 1
of Judah, which he saw c Samaria ... Mic 1:1
Thus saith the LORD c the......... Mic 3:5
hath given a commandment c thee ... Nah 1:14
Ask now the priests c the law......... Hag 2:11
give his angels charge c thee......... Mt 4:6
to say unto the multitudes of John... Mt 11:7
I spake it not to you c bread......... Mt 16:11
the devil, and also c the swine......... Mk 5:16
disciples asked him c the parable...... Mk 7:17
which was told them c this child...... Lk 2:17
to speak unto the people c John......... Lk 7:24
c the Son of man shall be......... Lk 18:31
for the things c me have an end......... Lk 22:37
C Jesus of Nazareth, which was a ... Lk 24:19
scriptures the things c himself......... Lk 24:27
prophets, and in the psalms, c me... Lk 24:44
murmuring among the people c him... Jn 7:12
people murmured such things c him... Jn 7:32
the Jews did not believe c him......... Jn 9:18
to comfort them c their brother......... Jn 11:19
of David spake before c Judas......... Acts 1:16
For David speaketh c him, I......... Acts 2:25
the things c the kingdom of God...... Acts 8:12
as c that he raised him up from......... Acts 13:34
the things c the kingdom of God...... Acts 19:8
enquire any thing c other matters...... Acts 19:39
whereof they were informed c thee... Acts 21:24
not receive thy testimony c me......... Acts 22:18
something more perfectly c him......... Acts 23:15
heard him c the faith in Christ......... Acts 24:24
c the crime laid against him......... Acts 25:16
letters out of Judaea c thee......... Acts 28:21
for as c this sect, we know that...... Acts 28:22
of God, persuading them c Jesus...... Acts 28:23
C his Son Jesus Christ our Lord,...... Rom 1:3
of whom as c the flesh Christ......... Rom 9:5
Esaias also crieth c Israel......... Rom 9:27
As c the gospel, they are enemies... Rom 11:28
which is good, and simple c evil...... Rom 16:19
c him that hath so done this deed ... 1Cor 5:3
Now c the things whereof ye wrote ... 1Cor 7:1
Now c virgins I have no......... 1Cor 7:25
As c therefore the eating of......... 1Cor 8:4
Now c spiritual gifts, brethren,...... 1Cor 12:1
Now c the collection for the......... 1Cor 16:1
my partner and fellowhelper c you... 2Cor 8:23
I speak as c reproach, as though...... 2Cor 11:21
That ye put off c the former......... Eph 4:22
but I speak c Christ and the......... Eph 5:32
C zeal, persecuting the church......... Phil 3:6
communicated with me as c giving...... Phil 4:15
and to comfort you c your faith...... 1Th 3:2
c them which are asleep, that ye...... 1Th 4:13
will of God in Christ Jesus c you...... 1Th 5:18
away c faith have made shipwreck... 1Ti 1:19
professing have erred c the faith...... 1Ti 6:21
Who c the truth have erred,......... 2Ti 2:18
minds, reprobate c the faith......... 2Ti 3:8
Moses spake nothing c priesthood ... Heb 7:14
Jacob and Esau c things to come ... Heb 11:20
and gave commandment c his bones... Heb 11:22
think it not strange c the fiery......... 1Pet 4:12
Lord is not slack c his promise......... 2Pet 3:9
unto you c them that seduce you...... 1Jn 2:26

CONCISION
of evil workers, beware of the c......... Phil 3:2

CONCLUDE
Therefore we c that a man is......... Rom 3:28

CONCLUDED
c that they observe no such thing... Acts 21:25
For God hath c them all in......... Rom 11:32
scripture hath c all under sin......... Gal 3:22

CONCLUSION
Let us hear the c of the whole......... Eccl 12:13

CONCORD
what c hath Christ with Belial......... 2Cor 6:15

CONCOURSE
crieth in the chief place of c......... Prov 1:21
we may give an account of this c... Acts 19:40

CONCUBINE
And his c, whose name was Reumah... Gen 22:24
and lay with Bilhah his father's c...... Gen 35:22
Timna was c to Eliphaz Esau's son... Gen 36:12
his c that was in Shechem, she......... Judg 8:31
who took to him a c out of......... Judg 19:1
his c played the whore against......... Judg 19:2
rose up to depart, he, and his c...... Judg 19:9
saddled, his c also was with him...... Judg 19:10
is my daughter a maiden, and his c... Judg 19:24
so the man took his c, and brought... Judg 19:25
the woman his c was fallen down... Judg 19:26
a knife, and laid hold on his c...... Judg 19:29
belongeth to Benjamin, I and my c... Judg 20:4
my c have they forced, that she...... Judg 20:5
And I took my c, and cut her in...... Judg 20:6
And Saul had a c, whose name was... 2Sa 3:7
thou gone in unto my father's c...... 2Sa 3:7
of Aiah, the c of Saul, had done...... 2Sa 21:11
the sons of Keturah, Abraham's c...... 1Chr 1:32
And Ephah, Caleb's c, bare Haran,... 1Chr 2:46
Maachah, Caleb's c, bare Sheber,...... 1Chr 2:48
(but his c the Aramitess bare......... 1Chr 7:14

CONCUBINES
But unto the sons of the c......... Gen 25:6
And David took him more c and wives... 2Sa 5:13
king left ten women, which were c... 2Sa 15:16
Go in unto thy father's c......... 2Sa 16:21
went in unto his father's c in......... 2Sa 16:22
thy wives, and the lives of thy c...... 2Sa 19:5
the king took the ten women his c... 2Sa 20:3
princesses, and three hundred c...... 1Kin 11:3
David, beside the sons of the c......... 1Chr 3:9
above all his wives and his c......... 2Chr 11:21
threescore wives, and threescore c... 2Chr 11:21
chamberlain, which kept the c......... Est 2:14
threescore queens, and fourscore c... Song 6:8
yea, the queens and the c, and they... Song 6:9
his princes, his wives, and his c...... Dan 5:2
his princes, his wives, and his c...... Dan 5:3
and thy lords, thy wives, and thy c... Dan 5:23

CONCUPISCENCE
wrought in me all manner of c......... Rom 7:8
inordinate affection, evil c......... Col 3:5
Not in the lust of c, even as the...... 1Th 4:5

CONDEMN
and whom the judges shall c......... Ex 22:9
the righteous, and c the wicked...... Deut 25:1
myself, mine own mouth shall c me... Job 9:20
I will say unto God, Do not c me...... Job 10:2
wilt thou c him that is most just...... Job 34:17
wilt thou c me, that thou mayest...... Job 40:8
nor c him when he is judged......... Ps 37:33
and c the innocent blood......... Ps 94:21
him from those that c his soul......... Ps 109:31
a man of wicked devices will he c... Prov 12:2
who is he that shall c me......... Is 50:9
thee in judgment thou shalt c......... Is 54:17
this generation, and shall c it......... Mt 12:41
this generation, and shall c it......... Mt 12:42
they shall c him to death,......... Mt 20:18
they shall c him to death, and......... Mk 10:33
c not, and ye shall not be......... Lk 6:37
men of this generation, and c them... Lk 11:31
this generation, and shall c it......... Lk 11:32
Son into the world to c the world... Jn 3:17
unto her, Neither do I c thee......... Jn 8:11
I speak not this to c you......... 2Cor 7:3
For if our heart c us, God is......... 1Jn 3:20
Beloved, if our heart c us not......... 1Jn 3:21

CONDEMNATION
seeing thou art in the same c......... Lk 23:40
And this is the c, that light is......... Jn 3:19
life, and shall not come into c......... Jn 5:24
for the judgment was by one to c...... Rom 5:16
judgment came upon all men to c...... Rom 5:18
There is therefore now no c to......... Rom 8:1
that ye come not together unto c...... 1Cor 11:34
if the ministration of c be glory...... 2Cor 3:9
he fall into the c of the devil......... 1Ti 3:6
we shall receive the greater c......... Jas 3:1
lest ye fall into c......... Jas 5:12
before c old ordained to this c...... Jude 4

CONDEMNED
c the land in an hundred talents...... 2Chr 36:3
found no answer, and yet had c Job... Job 32:3
he shall be judged, let him be c...... Ps 109:7
the c in the house of their god......... Amos 2:8
ye would not have c the guiltless... Mt 12:7
and by thy words thou shalt be c... Mt 12:37
him, when he saw that he was c...... Mt 27:3
they all c him to be guilty of......... Mk 14:64
condemn not, and ye shall not be c... Lk 6:37
delivered him to be c to death......... Lk 24:20
He that believeth on him is not c... Jn 3:18
that believeth not is c already......... Jn 3:18
hath no man c thee......... Jn 8:10
and for sin, c sin in the flesh......... Rom 8:3
we should not be c with the world... 1Cor 11:32

Sound speech, that cannot be c......... Titus 2:8
and sinneth, being c of himself......... Titus 3:11
by the which he c the world......... Heb 11:7
Ye have c and killed the just......... Jas 5:6
another, brethren, lest ye be c......... Jas 5:9
Gomorrah into ashes c them with...... 2Pet 2:6

CONDEMNEST
judgest another, thou c thyself......... Rom 2:1

CONDEMNETH
Thine own mouth c thee, and not I... Job 15:6
he that c the just, even they......... Prov 17:15
Who is he that c......... Rom 8:34
Happy is he that c not himself in... Rom 14:22

CONDEMNING
c the wicked, to bring his way......... 1Kin 8:32
they have fulfilled them in c him... Acts 13:27

CONDESCEND
but c to men of low estate......... Rom 12:16

CONDITION
On this c will I make a covenant...... 1Sa 11:2

CONDITIONS
ambassage, and desireth c of peace... Lk 14:32

CONDUCT
to c the king over Jordan......... 2Sa 19:15
the king, to c him over Jordan......... 2Sa 19:31
but c him forth in peace, that he... 1Cor 16:11

CONDUCTED
the people of Judah c the king,...... 2Sa 19:40
they that c Paul brought him unto ... Acts 17:15

CONDUIT
stood by the c of the upper pool,... 2Kin 18:17
and how he made a pool, and a c... 2Kin 20:20
at the end of the c of the upper...... Is 7:3
he stood by the c of the upper......... Is 36:2

CONEY
And the c, because he cheweth the... Lev 11:5
the camel, and the hare, and the c... Deut 14:7

CONFECTION
perfume, a c after the art of the......... Ex 30:35

CONFECTIONARIES
will take your daughters to be c......... 1Sa 8:13

CONFEDERACY
Say ye not, A c, to all them to......... Is 8:12
whom this people shall say, A c......... Is 8:12
All the men of thy c have brought... Obad 7

CONFEDERATE
and these were c with Abram......... Gen 14:13
they are c against thee......... Ps 83:5
saying, Syria is c with Ephraim...... Is 7:2

CONFERENCE
somewhat in c added nothing to me... Gal 2:6

CONFERRED
he c with Joab the son of Zeruiah... 1Kin 1:7
council, they c among themselves,... Acts 4:15
when he had c with the council,...... Acts 25:12
immediately I c not with flesh and... Gal 1:16

CONFESS
that he shall c that he hath......... Lev 5:5
c over him all the iniquities of...... Lev 16:21
If they shall c their iniquity,......... Lev 26:40
Then they shall c their sin which... Num 5:7
c thy name, and pray, and make...... 1Kin 8:33
c thy name, and turn from their...... 1Kin 8:35
c thy name, and pray and make...... 2Chr 6:24
c thy name, and turn from their...... 2Chr 6:26
c the sins of the children of......... Neh 1:6
Then will I also c unto thee that...... Job 40:14
I will c my transgressions unto......... Ps 32:5
therefore shall c me before men...... Mt 10:32
him will I c also before my......... Mt 10:32
Whosoever shall c me before men...... Lk 12:8
also c before the angels of God......... Lk 12:8
any man did c that he was Christ ... Jn 9:22
the Pharisees they did not c him... Jn 12:42
but the Pharisees c both......... Acts 23:8
But this I c unto thee, that......... Acts 24:14
That if thou shalt c with thy......... Rom 10:9
and every tongue shall c to God...... Rom 14:11
For this cause I will c to thee......... Rom 15:9
that every tongue should c that......... Phil 2:11
C your faults one to another, and...... Jas 5:16
If we c our sins, he is faithful......... 1Jn 1:9
Whosoever shall c that Jesus is......... 1Jn 4:15
who c not that Jesus Christ is......... 2Jn 7
but I will c his name before my......... Rev 3:5

CONFESSED
Ezra had prayed, and when he had c... Ezr 10:1
c their sins, and the iniquities......... Neh 9:2
and another fourth part they c......... Neh 9:3
And he c, and denied not......... Jn 1:20
but c, I am not the Christ......... Jn 1:20
And many that believed came, and c... Acts 19:18
c that they were strangers and......... Heb 11:13

CONFESSETH
but whoso c and forsaketh them...... Prov 28:13
Every spirit that c that Jesus......... 1Jn 4:2
every spirit that c not that......... 1Jn 4:3

CONFESSING

c my sin and the sin of my people	Dan 9:20
of him in Jordan, c their sins	Mt 3:6
the river of Jordan, c their sins	Mk 1:5

CONFESSION

God of Israel, and make c unto him	Josh 7:19
making a c to the LORD God of their	2Chr 30:22
Now therefore make c unto the	Ezr 10:11
the LORD my God, and made my c	Dan 9:4
with the mouth c is made unto	Rom 10:10
Pontius Pilate witnessed a good c	1Ti 6:13

CONFIDENCE

men of Shechem put their c in him	Judg 9:26
What c is this wherein thou	2Kin 18:19
is not this thy fear, thy c	Job 4:6
His c shall be rooted out of his	Job 18:14
to the fine gold, Thou art my c	Job 31:24
who art the c of all the ends of	Ps 65:5
in the LORD than to put c in man	Ps 118:8
the LORD than to put c in princes	Ps 118:9
For the LORD shall be thy c	Prov 3:26
the fear of the LORD is strong c	Prov 14:26
the strength of the c thereof	Prov 21:22
C in an unfaithful man in time of	Prov 25:19
in c shall be your strength	Is 30:15
What c is this wherein thou	Is 36:4
was ashamed of Beth-el their c	Jer 48:13
yea, they shall dwell with c	Eze 28:26
more the c of the house of Israel	Eze 29:16
a friend, put ye not c in a guide	Mic 7:5
the Lord Jesus Christ, with all c	Acts 28:31
in this c I was minded to come	2Cor 1:15
having c in you all, that my joy	2Cor 2:3
I have c in you in all things	2Cor 7:16
upon the great c which I have in	2Cor 8:22
when I am present with that c	2Cor 10:2
foolishly, in this c of boasting	2Cor 11:17
I have c in you through the Lord,	Gal 5:10
access with c by the faith of him.	Eph 3:12
And having this c, I know that I	Phil 1:25
Jesus, and have no c in the flesh	Phil 3:3
I might also have c in the flesh	Phil 3:4
we have c in the Lord touching	2Th 3:4
Having c in thy obedience I wrote	Philem 21
are we, if we hold fast the c	Heb 3:6
of our c stedfast unto the end	Heb 3:14
Cast not away therefore your c	Heb 10:35
he shall appear, we may have c	1Jn 2:28
us not, then have we c toward God	1Jn 3:21
this is the c that we have in him	1Jn 5:14

CONFIDENCES

for the LORD hath rejected thy c	Jer 2:37

CONFIDENT

against me, in this will I be c	Ps 27:3
but the fool rageth, and is c	Prov 14:16
art c that thou thyself art a	Rom 2:19
Therefore we are always c	2Cor 5:6
We are c, I say, and willing	2Cor 5:8
ashamed in this same c boasting	2Cor 9:4
Being c of this very thing, that	Phil 1:6
waxing c by my bonds, are much	Phil 1:14

CONFIDENTLY

one hour after another c affirmed	Lk 22:59

CONFIRM

changing, for to c all things	Ruth 4:7
in after thee, and c thy words	1Kin 1:14
him to c the kingdom in his hand	2Kin 15:19
to c this second letter of Purim	Est 9:29
To c these days of Purim in their	Est 9:31
thou didst c thine inheritance	Ps 68:9
weak hands, and c the feeble knees	Is 35:3
hope that they would c the word	Eze 13:6
he shall c the covenant with many	Dan 9:27
the Mede, even I, stood to c	Dan 11:1
to c the promises made unto the	Rom 15:8
Who shall also c you unto the end	1Cor 1:8
ye would c your love toward him	2Cor 2:8

CONFIRMATION

an oath for c is to them an end	Heb 6:16

CONFIRMED

For thou hast c to thyself thy	2Sa 7:24
as the kingdom was c in his hand	2Kin 14:5
Lord had c him king over Israel	1Chr 14:2
hath c the same to Jacob for a	1Chr 16:17
the decree of Esther c these	Est 9:32
c the same unto Jacob for a law,	Ps 105:10
he hath c his words, which he	Dan 9:12
with many words, and c them	Acts 15:32
testimony of Christ was c in you	1Cor 1:6
a man's covenant, yet if it be c	Gal 3:15
that was c before of God in	Gal 3:17
was c unto us by them that heard	Heb 2:3
of his counsel, c it by an oath	Heb 6:17

CONFIRMETH

he c them, because he held his	Num 30:14
Cursed be he that c not all the	Deut 27:26
That c the word of his servant	Is 44:26

CONFIRMING

c the word with signs following	Mk 16:20
C the souls of the disciples, and	Acts 14:22
Syria and Cilicia, c the churches	Acts 15:41

CONFISCATION

or to c of goods, or to	Ezr 7:26

CONFLICT

Having the same c which ye saw in	Phil 1:30
knew what great c I have for you	Col 2:1

CONFORMABLE

being made c unto his death	Phil 3:10

CONFORMED

to be c to the image of his Son	Rom 8:29
And be not c to this world	Rom 12:2

CONFOUND

there c their language, that they	Gen 11:7
because the LORD did there c the	Gen 11:9
lest I c thee before them	Jer 1:17
things of the world to c the wise	1Cor 1:27
to c the things which are mighty	1Cor 1:27

CONFOUNDED

power, they were dismayed and c	2Kin 19:26
trusted in thee, and were not c	Job 6:20
Let them be c and put to shame	Ps 22:5
c together that seek after my	Ps 35:4
that seek thee for for my sake	Ps 40:14
c that seek after my soul	Ps 69:6
Let them be c and consumed that	Ps 70:2
for they are c, for they are	Ps 71:13
Let them be c and troubled for	Ps 71:24
C be all they that serve graven	Ps 83:17
Let them all be c and turned back	Ps 97:7
ye shall be c for the gardens	Ps 129:5
that weave networks, shall be c	Is 1:29
Then the moon shall be c, and the	Is 19:9
power, they were dismayed and c	Is 24:23
thee shall be ashamed and c	Is 37:27
They shall be ashamed, and also c	Is 41:11
ashamed nor c world without end	Is 45:16
therefore shall I not be c	Is 45:17
neither be thou c	Is 50:7
we are greatly c, because we have	Is 54:4
every founder is c by the graven	Jer 8:9
they were ashamed and c, and	Jer 10:14
she hath been ashamed and c	Jer 14:3
Let them be c that persecute me,	Jer 17:18
but let not me be c	Jer 17:18
and c for all thy wickedness	Jer 22:22
I was ashamed, yea, even c	Jer 31:19
The daughter of Egypt shall be c	Jer 46:24
Kiriathaim is c and taken	Jer 48:1
Misgab is c and dismayed	Jer 48:1
Moab is c	Jer 48:20
Hamath is c, and Arpad	Jer 49:23
say, Babylon is taken, Bel is c	Jer 50:2
her idols are c, her images are	Jer 50:2
Your mother shall be sore c	Jer 50:12
every founder is c by the graven	Jer 51:17
and her whole land shall be c	Jer 51:47
We are c, because we have heard	Jer 51:51
yea, be thou c also, and bear thy	Eze 16:52
mayest be c in all that thou hast	Eze 16:54
thou mayest remember, and be c	Eze 16:63
c for your own ways, O house of	Eze 36:32
be ashamed, and the diviners c	Mic 3:7
the riders on horses shall be c	Zec 10:5
came together, and were c, because	Acts 2:6
c the Jews which dwelt at	Acts 9:22
believeth on him shall not be c	1Pet 2:6

CONFUSED

of the warrior is with c noise	Is 9:5
for the assembly was c	Acts 19:32

CONFUSION

it is c	Lev 18:23
they have wrought c	Lev 20:12
the son of Jesse to thine own c	1Sa 20:30
unto the c of thy mother's	1Sa 20:30
to c of face, as it is this day	Ezr 9:7
I am full of c	Job 10:15
brought to c that devise my hurt	Ps 35:4
brought to c together that	Ps 35:26
My c is continually before me, and	Ps 44:15
be turned backward, and put to c	Ps 70:2
let me never be put to c	Ps 71:1
cover themselves with their own c	Ps 109:29
The city of c is broken down	Is 24:10
in the shadow of Egypt your c	Is 30:3
stretch out upon it the line of c	Is 34:11
their molten images are wind and c	Is 41:29
they shall go to c together that	Is 45:16
for c they shall rejoice in their	Is 61:7
our shame, and our c covereth us	Jer 3:25
to the c of their own faces	Jer 7:19
their everlasting c shall never	Jer 20:11
unto thee, but unto us c of faces	Dan 9:7
O Lord, to us belongeth c of face	Dan 9:8
the whole city was filled with c	Acts 19:29
For God is not the author of c	1Cor 14:33
envying and strife, is there is c	Jas 3:16

CONGEALED

the depths were c in the heart of	Ex 15:8

CONGRATULATE

to c him, because he had fought	1Chr 18:10

CONGREGATION

Speak ye unto all the c of Israel	Ex 12:3
the whole assembly of the c of	Ex 12:6
be cut off from the c of Israel	Ex 12:19

All the c of Israel shall keep it	Ex 12:47
all the c of the children of	Ex 16:1
the whole c of the children of	Ex 16:2
Say unto all the c of the	Ex 16:9
whole c of the children of Israel	Ex 16:10
and all the rulers of the c came	Ex 16:22
all the c of the children of	Ex 17:1
the c without the vail	Ex 27:21
in unto the tabernacle of the c	Ex 28:43
door of the tabernacle of the c	Ex 29:4
before the tabernacle of the c	Ex 29:10
door of the tabernacle of the c	Ex 29:11
into the tabernacle of the c to	Ex 29:30
door of the tabernacle of the c	Ex 29:32
of the c before the LORD	Ex 29:42
sanctify the tabernacle of the c	Ex 29:44
of the tabernacle of the c	Ex 30:16
between the tabernacle of the c	Ex 30:18
go into the tabernacle of the c	Ex 30:20
the tabernacle of the c therewith	Ex 30:26
in the tabernacle of the c	Ex 30:36
The tabernacle of the c, and the	Ex 31:7
called it the Tabernacle of the c	Ex 33:7
out unto the tabernacle of the c	Ex 33:7
rulers of the c returned unto him	Ex 34:31
Moses gathered all the c of the	Ex 35:1
Moses spake unto all the c of the	Ex 35:4
all the c of the children of	Ex 35:20
work of the tabernacle of the c	Ex 35:21
door of the tabernacle of the c	Ex 38:8
of the c was an hundred talents	Ex 38:25
door of the tabernacle of the c	Ex 38:30
of the tent of the c finished	Ex 39:32
tabernacle, for the tent of the c	Ex 39:32
tabernacle of the tent of the c	Ex 40:2
tabernacle of the tent of the c	Ex 40:6
laver between the tent of the c	Ex 40:7
door of the tabernacle of the c	Ex 40:12
the table in the tent of the c	Ex 40:22
candlestick in the tent of the c	Ex 40:24
the tent of the c before the vail	Ex 40:26
tabernacle of the tent of the c	Ex 40:29
laver between the tent of the c	Ex 40:30
went into the tent of the c	Ex 40:32
a cloud covered the tent of the c	Ex 40:34
to enter into the tent of the c	Ex 40:35
out of the tabernacle of the c	Lev 1:1
of the c before the LORD	Lev 1:3
door of the tabernacle of the c	Lev 1:5
door of the tabernacle of the c	Lev 3:2
it before the tabernacle of the c	Lev 3:8
it before the tabernacle of the c	Lev 3:13
of the c before the LORD	Lev 4:4
it to the tabernacle of the c	Lev 4:5
is in the tabernacle of the c	Lev 4:7
door of the tabernacle of the c	Lev 4:7
if the whole c of Israel sin	Lev 4:13
then the c shall offer a young	Lev 4:14
before the tabernacle of the c	Lev 4:14
the elders of the c shall lay	Lev 4:15
blood to the tabernacle of the c	Lev 4:16
is in the tabernacle of the c	Lev 4:18
door of the tabernacle of the c	Lev 4:18
it is a sin offering for the c	Lev 4:21
of the c they shall eat it	Lev 6:16
court of the tabernacle of the c	Lev 6:26
into the tabernacle of the c to	Lev 6:30
gather thou all the c together	Lev 8:3
door of the tabernacle of the c	Lev 8:3
door of the tabernacle of the c	Lev 8:4
And Moses said unto the c, This is	Lev 8:5
door of the tabernacle of the c	Lev 8:31
tabernacle of the c in seven days	Lev 8:33
of the tabernacle of the c day	Lev 8:35
before the tabernacle of the c	Lev 9:5
all the c drew near and stood	Lev 9:5
went into the tabernacle of the c	Lev 9:23
door of the tabernacle of the c	Lev 10:7
go into the tabernacle of the c	Lev 10:9
you to bear the iniquity of the c	Lev 10:17
door of the tabernacle of the c	Lev 12:6
door of the tabernacle of the c	Lev 14:11
door of the tabernacle of the c	Lev 14:23
door of the tabernacle of the c	Lev 15:14
door of the tabernacle of the c	Lev 15:29
he shall take of the c of the	Lev 16:5
door of the tabernacle of the c	Lev 16:7
he do for the tabernacle of the c	Lev 16:16
the c when he goeth in to make an	Lev 16:17
and for all the c of Israel	Lev 16:17
place, and the tabernacle of the c	Lev 16:20
come into the tabernacle of the c	Lev 16:23
for the tabernacle of the c	Lev 16:33
and for all the people of the c	Lev 16:33
door of the tabernacle of the c	Lev 17:4
door of the tabernacle of the c	Lev 17:5
door of the tabernacle of the c	Lev 17:6
door of the tabernacle of the c	Lev 17:9
Speak unto all the c of the	Lev 19:2
door of the tabernacle of the c	Lev 19:21
in the tabernacle of the c	Lev 24:3
head, and let all the c stone him	Lev 24:14
all the c shall certainly stone	Lev 24:14
Sinai, in the tabernacle of the c	Num 1:1
tabernacle of the c, the	Num 1:16
These were the renowned of the c	Num 1:16
they assembled all the c together	Num 1:18
the c of the children of Israel	Num 1:53
of the c shall they pitch	Num 2:2
Then the tabernacle of the c	Num 2:17

the charge of the whole c before .... Num 3:7
before the tabernacle of the c .... Num 3:7
of the tabernacle of the c .... Num 3:8
of the c shall be the tabernacle .... Num 3:25
door of the tabernacle of the c .... Num 3:25
the tabernacle of the c eastward........ Num 3:38
work in the tabernacle of the c .... Num 4:3
Kohath in the tabernacle of the .... Num 4:4
Kohath in the tabernacle of the c...... Num 4:15
work in the tabernacle of the c .... Num 4:23
and the tabernacle of the c .... Num 4:25
door of the tabernacle of the c.......... Num 4:28
in the tabernacle of the c .... Num 4:28
work of the tabernacle of the c .... Num 4:30
in the tabernacle of the c .... Num 4:31
in the tabernacle of the c .... Num 4:33
the chief of the c numbered the .... Num 4:34
work in the tabernacle of the .... Num 4:37
in the tabernacle of the c .... Num 4:37
work in the tabernacle of the c .... Num 4:39
in the tabernacle of the c .... Num 4:41
work in the tabernacle of the c .... Num 4:43
burden in the tabernacle of the c...... Num 4:47
door of the tabernacle of the c.......... Num 6:10
door of the tabernacle of the c.......... Num 6:13
door of the tabernacle of the c.......... Num 6:18
of the tabernacle of the c .... Num 7:5
of the c to speak with him .... Num 7:89
before the tabernacle of the c .... Num 8:9
of the tabernacle of the c .... Num 8:15
Israel in the tabernacle of the c........ Num 8:19
all the c of the children of .... Num 8:20
tabernacle of the c before Aaron ...... Num 8:22
of the tabernacle of the c .... Num 8:24
door of the tabernacle of the c.......... Num 8:26
But when the c is to be gathered....... Num 10:7
them unto the tabernacle of the c..... Num 11:16
unto the tabernacle of the c .... Num 12:4
to all the c of the children of .... Num 13:26
word unto them, and unto all the c ... Num 13:26
all the c lifted up their voice,........... Num 14:1
the whole c said unto them, Would ... Num 14:2
the c of the children of Israel .... Num 14:5
But all the c bade stone them........... Num 14:10
in the tabernacle of the c before ...... Num 14:10
shall I bear with this evil c .... Num 14:27
surely do it unto all this evil c......... Num 14:35
made all the c to murmur against ..... Num 14:36
shall be both for you of the c .... Num 15:15
without the knowledge of the c .... Num 15:24
that all the c shall offer one............. Num 15:24
the c of the children of Israel .... Num 15:25
the c of the children of Israel .... Num 15:26
Moses and Aaron, and unto all the c . Num 15:33
all the c shall stone him with............ Num 15:35
all the c brought him without the ..... Num 15:36
of the assembly, famous in the c....... Num 16:2
you, seeing all the c are holy .... Num 16:3
above the c of the LORD .... Num 16:3
you from the c of Israel .... Num 16:9
to stand before the c to minister...... Num 16:9
tabernacle of the c with Moses......... Num 16:18
Korah gathered all the c against ...... Num 16:19
door of the tabernacle of the c......... Num 16:19
the tabernacle of the c .... Num 16:19
the LORD appeared unto all the c ...... Num 16:19
yourselves from among this c .... Num 16:21
wilt thou be wroth with all the c...... Num 16:22
Speak unto the c, saying, Get you..... Num 16:24
And he spake unto the c, saying,...... Num 16:26
and they perished from among the c . Num 16:33
the c of the children of Israel .... Num 16:41
when the c was gathered against ...... Num 16:42
toward the tabernacle of the c .... Num 16:42
before the tabernacle of the c .... Num 16:43
Get you up from among this c .... Num 16:45
incense, and go quickly unto the c.... Num 16:46
and ran into the midst of the c........ Num 16:47
door of the tabernacle of the c......... Num 16:50
of the c before the testimony .... Num 17:4
charge of the tabernacle of the c...... Num 18:4
of the tabernacle of the .... Num 18:4
of the tabernacle of the c .... Num 18:21
come nigh the tabernacle of the c..... Num 18:22
of the tabernacle of the c .... Num 18:31
in the tabernacle of the c .... Num 18:31
tabernacle of the c seven times........ Num 19:4
it shall be kept for the c of the........ Num 19:9
shall be cut off from among the c..... Num 19:20
of Israel, even the whole c .... Num 20:1
And there was no water for the c...... Num 20:2
up the c of the LORD into this.......... Num 20:4
door of the tabernacle of the c......... Num 20:6
so thou shalt give the c and their .... Num 20:8
Aaron gathered the c together .... Num 20:10
the c drank, and their beasts also .... Num 20:11
ye shall not bring this c into............ Num 20:12
of Israel, even the whole c .... Num 20:22
Hor in the sight of all the c .... Num 20:27
when all the c saw that Aaron was.... Num 20:29
in the sight of all the c of the .... Num 25:6
door of the tabernacle of the c......... Num 25:6
it, he rose up from among the c ...... Num 25:7
Take the sum of all the c of the........ Num 26:2
which were famous in the c.............. Num 26:9
before the princes and all the c .... Num 27:2
door of the tabernacle of the c......... Num 27:2
of Zin, in the strife of the c .... Num 27:14
all flesh, set a man over the c .... Num 27:16
that the c of the LORD be not as....... Num 27:17

the priest, and before all the c .... Num 27:19
that all the c of the children of .... Num 27:20
Israel with him, even all the c .... Num 27:21
the priest, and before all the c .... Num 27:22
unto the c of the children of .... Num 31:12
and all the princes of the c.............. Num 31:13
a plague among the c of the LORD..... Num 31:16
and the chief fathers of the c........... Num 31:26
to battle, and between all the c .... Num 31:27
the c was three hundred thousand.... Num 31:43
into the tabernacle of the c .... Num 31:54
and unto the princes of the c .... Num 32:2
LORD smote before the c of Israel...... Num 32:4
he stand before the c in judgment.... Num 35:12
Then the c shall judge between .... Num 35:24
the c shall deliver the slayer .... Num 35:25
the c shall restore him to the.......... Num 35:25
not enter into the c of the LORD .... Deut 23:1
not enter into the c of the LORD .... Deut 23:2
not enter into the c of the LORD .... Deut 23:2
not enter into the c of the LORD .... Deut 23:3
into the c of the LORD for ever .... Deut 23:3
the c of the LORD in their third .... Deut 23:8
in the tabernacle of the c .... Deut 31:14
in the tabernacle of the c .... Deut 31:14
the c of Israel the words of this....... Deut 31:30
the inheritance of the c of Jacob...... Deut 33:4
not before all the c of Israel .... Josh 8:35
princes of the c sware unto them ..... Josh 9:15
because the princes of the c had....... Josh 9:18
all the c murmured against the .... Josh 9:18
the princes said unto all the c .... Josh 9:19
drawers of water unto all the c........ Josh 9:21
and drawers of water for the c .... Josh 9:27
the whole c of the children of .... Josh 18:1
up the tabernacle of the c there....... Josh 18:1
door of the tabernacle of the c......... Josh 19:51
stand before the c for judgment ...... Josh 20:6
until he stood before the c .... Josh 20:9
the whole c of the children of .... Josh 22:12
saith the whole c of the LORD .... Josh 22:16
was a plague in the c of the LORD .... Josh 22:17
wroth with the whole c of Israel ...... Josh 22:18
wrath fell on all the c of Israel......... Josh 22:20
priest, and the princes of the c........ Josh 22:30
the c was gathered together as......... Judg 20:1
not up with the c unto the LORD ...... Judg 21:5
the c sent thither twelve .... Judg 21:10
the whole c sent one to speak to,.... Judg 21:13
Then the elders of the c said........... Judg 21:16
door of the tabernacle of the 1Sa 2:22
LORD, and the tabernacle of the c..... 1Kin 8:4
all the c of Israel, that were 1Kin 8:5
and blessed all the c of Israel.......... 1Kin 8:14
the c of Israel stood 1Kin 8:14
presence of all the c of Israel 1Kin 8:22
blessed all the c of Israel with 1Kin 8:55
and all Israel with him, a great c 1Kin 8:65
the c of Israel came, and 1Kin 12:3
sent and called him unto the c 1Kin 12:20
tabernacle of the c with singing 1Chr 9:21
door of the tabernacle of the c......... 1Chr 9:21
said unto all the c of Israel.............. 1Chr 13:2
and the c said that they would do..... 1Chr 13:4
charge of the tabernacle of the c 1Chr 23:32
of all Israel the c of the LORD........... 1Chr 28:8
the king said unto all the c 1Chr 29:1
blessed the LORD before all the c...... 1Chr 29:10
And David said to all the c 1Chr 29:20
all the c blessed the LORD God of...... 1Chr 29:20
all the c with him, went to the........ 2Chr 1:3
the tabernacle of the c of God......... 2Chr 1:3
Solomon and the c sought unto it 2Chr 1:5
was at the tabernacle of the c 2Chr 1:6
before the tabernacle of the c 2Chr 1:13
ark, and the tabernacle of the c....... 2Chr 5:5
all the c of Israel that were 2Chr 5:6
and blessed the whole c of Israel...... 2Chr 6:3
all the c of Israel stood................... 2Chr 6:3
presence of all the c of Israel 2Chr 6:12
knees before all the c of Israel 2Chr 6:13
Israel with him, a very great c 2Chr 7:8
stood in the c of Judah and............. 2Chr 20:5
of the LORD in the midst of the c...... 2Chr 20:14
all the c made a covenant with........ 2Chr 23:3
of the c of Israel, for the 2Chr 24:6
before the princes and all the c 2Chr 28:14
offering before the king and the c.... 2Chr 29:23
all the c worshipped, and the 2Chr 29:28
the c brought in sacrifices and........ 2Chr 29:31
offerings, which the c brought......... 2Chr 29:32
all the c in Jerusalem, to keep......... 2Chr 30:2
pleased the king and all the c 2Chr 30:4
the second month, a very great c 2Chr 30:13
in the c that were not sanctified 2Chr 30:17
give to the c a thousand bullocks..... 2Chr 30:24
gave to the c a thousand bullocks.... 2Chr 30:24
all the c of Judah, with the 2Chr 30:25
all the c that came out of Israel...... 2Chr 30:25
daughters, through all the c 2Chr 31:18
thy together was forty and.............. Ezr 2:64
of Israel a very great c of men .... Ezr 10:1
himself separated from the c of........ Ezr 10:8
Then all the c answered and said .... Ezr 10:12
now our rulers of all the c stand..... Ezr 10:14
And all the c said, Amen, and.......... Neh 5:13
The whole c together was forty and . Neh 7:66
the law before the c both of men..... Neh 8:2
all the c of them that were come .... Neh 8:17
come into the c of God for ever ...... Neh 13:1

For the c of hypocrites shall be........ Job 15:34
I stood up, and I cried in the c .... Job 30:28
sinners in the c of the righteous ...... Ps 1:5
So shall the c of the people............. Ps 7:7
midst of the c will I praise thee ...... Ps 22:22
shall be of thee in the great c .... Ps 22:25
I have hated the c of evildoers......... Ps 26:5
give thee thanks in the great c .... Ps 35:18
righteousness in the great c............ Ps 40:9
and thy truth from the great c......... Ps 40:10
indeed speak righteousness, O c ...... Ps 58:1
Thy c hath dwelt therein .... Ps 68:10
Remember thy c, which thou hast .... Ps 74:2
forget not the c of thy poor for....... Ps 74:19
the c I will judge uprightly .... Ps 75:2
standeth in the c of the mighty .... Ps 82:1
also in the c of the saints................ Ps 89:5
him also in the c of the people .... Ps 107:32
of the upright, and in the c .... Ps 111:1
and his praise in the c of saints....... Ps 149:1
in all evil in the midst of the c .... Prov 5:14
shall remain in the c of the dead..... Prov 21:16
be shewed before the whole c .... Prov 26:26
sit also upon the mount of the c...... Is 14:13
hear, ye nations, and know, O c ...... Jer 6:18
their c shall be established .... Jer 30:20
they should not enter into the c ...... Lam 1:10
them, as their c hath heard .... Hos 7:12
Gather the people, sanctify the c..... Joel 2:16
cord by lot in the c of the LORD....... Mic 2:5
Now when the c was broken up,....... Acts 13:43

CONGREGATIONS
in the c will I bless the c................. Ps 26:12
Bless ye God in the c, even the .... Ps 68:26
roar in the midst of thy c .... Ps 74:4

CONIAH (co-ni´-ah) See JEHOIACHIN. Another
name for Jehoiachin.
though C the son of Jehoiakim .... Jer 22:24
Is this man C a despised broken....... Jer 22:28
instead of C the son of Jehoiakim..... Jer 37:1

CONIES
and the rocks for the c .... Num 10:18
The c are but a feeble folk, yet .... Prov 30:26

CONONIAH (co-no-ni´-ah) See CONANIAH. A
Levite during Hezekiah's time.
over which C the Levite was ruler..... 2Chr 31:12
overseers under the hand of C.......... 2Chr 31:13

CONQUER
he went forth conquering, and to c.. Rev 6:2

CONQUERING
and he went forth, c, and to conquer .. Rev 6:2

CONQUERORS
than c through him that loved us...... Rom 8:37

CONSCIENCE
being convicted by their own c......... Jn 8:9
I have lived in all good c before........ Acts 23:1
to have always a c void of................ Acts 24:16
their c also bearing witness, and...... Rom 2:15
my c also bearing me witness in....... Rom 9:1
for wrath, but also for c sake.......... Rom 13:5
for some with c of the idol unto....... 1Cor 8:7
their c being weak is defiled............ 1Cor 8:7
shall not the c of him which is 1Cor 8:10
brethren, and wound their weak c.... 1Cor 8:12
asking no question for c sake 1Cor 10:25
asking no question for c sake 1Cor 10:27
that shewed it, and for c sake......... 1Cor 10:28
C, I say, not thine own, but............. 1Cor 10:29
liberty judged of another man's c.... 1Cor 10:29
is this, the testimony of our c 2Cor 1:12
every man's c in the sight of God..... 2Cor 4:2
of a pure heart, and of a good c 1Ti 1:5
Holding faith, and a good c 1Ti 1:19
mystery of the faith in a pure c....... 1Ti 3:9
having their c seared with a hot...... 1Ti 4:2
from my forefathers with pure c 2Ti 1:3
even their mind and c is defiled....... Titus 1:15
perfect, as pertaining to the c .... Heb 9:9
purge your c from dead works to..... Heb 9:14
should have had no more c of sins... Heb 10:2
hearts sprinkled from an evil c .... Heb 10:22
for we trust we have a good c......... Heb 13:18
if a man for c toward God endure ... 1Pet 2:19
Having a good c 1Pet 3:16
the answer of a good c toward God... 1Pet 3:21

CONSCIENCES
also are made manifest in your c 2Cor 5:11

CONSECRATE
make Aaron's garments to c him ...... Ex 28:3
c them, and sanctify them, that ...... Ex 28:41
and thou shalt c Aaron and his sons.. Ex 29:9
the atonement was made, to c......... Ex 29:33
seven days shalt thou c .... Ex 29:35
c them, that they may minister .... Ex 30:30
C yourselves to day to the LORD,...... Ex 32:29
for seven days shall he c you .... Lev 8:33
whom he shall c to minister in .... Lev 16:32
he shall c unto the LORD the days .... Num 6:12
who then is willing to c his............. 1Chr 29:5
so that whosoever cometh to c 2Chr 13:9
and they shall c themselves............. Eze 43:26
I will c their gain unto the LORD....... Mic 4:13

C (margin letter)

CONSECRATED

therein, and to be c in them .... Ex 29:29
that is c to put on the garments,....... Lev 21:10
whom he c to minister in the .... Num 3:3
and iron, are c unto the LORD .... Josh 6:19
c one of his sons, who became his..... Judg 17:5
And Micah c the Levite .... Judg 17:12
he c him, and he became one of the .. 1Kin 13:33
that are c to burn incense. 2Chr 26:18
Now ye have c yourselves unto the ... 2Chr 29:31
the c things were six hundred 2Chr 29:33
were c unto the LORD their God. 2Chr 31:6
feasts of the LORD that were c .... Ezr 3:5
the Son, who is c for evermore........ Heb 7:28
way, which he hath c for us. .... Heb 10:20

CONSECRATION

for it is a ram of c .... Ex 29:22
breast of the ram of Aaron's c......... Ex 29:26
is heaved up, of the ram of the c ..... Ex 29:27
thou shalt take the ram of the c....... Ex 29:31
the other ram, the ram of c .... Lev 8:22
for of the ram of c it was Moses' ..... Lev 8:29
the days of your c be at an end........ Lev 8:33
because the c of his God is upon...... Num 6:7
he hath defiled the head of his c...... Num 6:9

CONSECRATIONS

And if ought of the flesh of the c..... Ex 29:34
trespass offering, and of the c......... Lev 7:37
they were c for a sweet savour........ Lev 8:28
bread that is in the basket of the c.... Lev 8:31

CONSENT

But in this will we c unto you. .... Gen 34:15
Only herein will the men c unto .... Gen 34:22
only let us c unto them, and they ..... Gen 34:23
Thou shalt not c unto him. .... Deut 13:8
he not would not do c................... Judg 11:17
and they came out with one c 1Sa 11:7
him, Hearken unto him, nor c 1Kin 20:8
consulted together with one c .... Ps 83:5
sinners entice thee, c thou not........ Prov 1:10
of priests murder in the way by c...... Hos 6:9
the LORD, to serve him with one c .... Zeph 3:9
they all with one c began to make .... Lk 14:18
I c unto the law that it is good. .... Rom 7:16
except it be with c for a time. 1Cor 7:5
c not to wholesome words, even 1Ti 6:3

CONSENTED

the priests c to receive no more 2Kin 12:8
So he c to them in this matter,........ Dan 1:14
The same had not c to the counsel.... Lk 23:51
longer time with them, he c not....... Acts 18:20

CONSENTEDST

a thief, then thou c with him. .... Ps 50:18

CONSENTING

Saul was c unto his death.............. Acts 8:1
c unto his death, and kept the .... Acts 22:20

CONSIDER

c that this nation is thy people........ Ex 33:13
Then the priest shall c .... Lev 13:13
c it in thine heart, that the .... Deut 4:39
Thou shalt also c in thine heart....... Deut 8:5
c the years of many generations ...... Deut 32:7
that they would c their latter .... Deut 32:29
now therefore c what ye have to ...... Judg 18:14
c of it, take advice, and speak........ Judg 19:30
for c how great things he hath 1Sa 12:24
know and c what thou wilt do 1Sa 25:17
wherefore c, I pray you, and see 2Kin 5:7
will he not then c it .... Job 11:11
when I c, I am afraid of him........... Job 23:15
would not c any of his ways........... Job 34:27
c the wondrous works of God......... Job 37:14
my meditation .... Ps 5:1
When I c thy heavens, the work of ... Ps 8:3
c my trouble which I suffer of......... Ps 9:13
C and hear me, O LORD my God .... Ps 13:3
C mine enemies .... Ps 25:19
thou shalt diligently c his place ...... Ps 37:10
Hearken, O daughter, and c .... Ps 45:10
well her bulwarks, c her palaces ...... Ps 48:13
Now c this, ye that forget God, ... Ps 50:22
they shall wisely c of his doing .... Ps 64:9
but I will c thy testimonies. .... Ps 119:95
C mine affliction, and deliver me .... Ps 119:153
C how I love thy precepts .... Ps 119:159
c her ways, and be wise. .... Prov 6:6
c diligently what is before thee. ...... Prov 23:1
he that pondereth the heart c it ...... Prov 24:12
for they c not that they do evil .... Eccl 5:1
C the work of God .... Eccl 7:13
but in the day of adversity c .... Eccl 7:14
not know, my people doth not c...... Is 1:3
neither c the operation of his......... Is 5:12
c thee, saying, Is this the man .... Is 14:16
I will c in my dwelling place. .... Is 18:4
That they may see, and know, and c .. Is 41:20
what they be, that we may c them .... Is 41:22
neither c the things of old............ Is 43:18
they had not heard shall they c .... Is 52:15
c diligently, and see if there be ...... Jer 2:10
C ye, and call for the mourning ...... Jer 9:17
days ye shall c it perfectly........... Jer 23:20
in the latter days ye shall c it .... Jer 30:24
see, O LORD, and c .... Lam 1:11
c to whom thou hast done this ...... Lam 2:20
c, and behold our reproach........... Lam 5:1

it may be they will c, though .... Eze 12:3
the matter, and c the vision .... Dan 9:23
they c not in their hearts that I ...... Hos 7:2
C your ways. .... Hag 1:5
C your ways. .... Hag 1:7
c from this day and upward, from .... Hag 2:15
C now from this day and upward, ... Hag 2:18
the LORD's temple was laid, c in ..... Hag 2:18
C the lilies of the field, how .... Mt 6:28
C the ravens .... Lk 12:24
how they they grow .... Lk 12:27
Nor c that it is expedient for us...... Jn 11:50
together for to c of this matter ...... Acts 15:6
C what I say .... Acts 15:6
c the Apostle and High Priest of ..... Heb 3:1
Now c how great this man was, ... Heb 7:4
let us c one another to provoke ...... Heb 10:24
For c him that endured such .... Heb 12:3

CONSIDERED

but when I had c it in the 1Kin 3:21
I have c the things which thou....... 1Kin 5:8
Hast thou c my servant Job, that ..... Job 1:8
Hast thou c my servant Job, that ..... Job 2:3
for thou hast c my trouble............ Ps 31:7
I have c the days of old, the .... Ps 77:5
Then I saw, and I c it well .... Prov 24:32
c all the oppressions that are .... Eccl 4:1
I c all travail, and every right .... Eccl 4:4
I c the living which walk .... Eccl 4:15
For all this I c in my heart even ...... Eccl 9:1
I c the horns, and, behold, there ..... Dan 7:8
For they c not the miracle of the .... Mk 6:52
I had fastened mine eyes, I c .... Acts 11:6
And when he had c the thing .... Acts 12:12
he c not his own body now dead,..... Rom 4:19

CONSIDEREST

C thou not what this people have .... Jer 33:24
but c not the beam that is in .... Mt 7:3

CONSIDERETH

he c all their works .... Ps 33:15
Blessed is he that c the poor.......... Ps 41:1
wisely c the house of the wicked ..... Prov 21:12
c not that poverty shall come .... Prov 28:22
The righteous c the cause of the ..... Prov 29:7
She c a field, and buyeth it .... Prov 31:16
none c in his heart, neither is........ Is 44:19
sins which he hath done, and c ...... Eze 18:14
Because he c, and turneth away...... Eze 18:28

CONSIDERING

none c that the righteous is .... Is 57:1
And as I was c, behold, an he goat... Dan 8:5
c thyself, lest thou also be.......... Gal 6:1
c the end of their conversation ...... Heb 13:7

CONSIST

things, and by him all things c .... Col 1:17

CONSISTETH

for a man's life c not in the.......... Lk 12:15

CONSOLATION

of c to drink for their father or ...... Jer 16:7
waiting for the c of Israel .... Lk 2:25
for ye have received your c .... Lk 6:24
being interpreted, The son of c ...... Acts 4:36
had read, they rejoiced for the c ..... Acts 15:31
c grant you to be likeminded one .... Rom 15:5
so our c also aboundeth by Christ ... 2Cor 1:5
we be afflicted, it is for your c 2Cor 1:6
we be comforted, it is for your c 2Cor 1:6
so shall ye be also of the c 2Cor 1:7
but by the c wherewith he was 2Cor 7:7
be therefore any c in Christ.......... Phil 2:1
and hath given us everlasting c 2Th 2:16
c in thy love, because the bowels ... Philem 7
to lie, we might have a strong c ..... Heb 6:18

CONSOLATIONS

Are the c of God small with thee ..... Job 15:11
my speech, and let this be your c .... Job 21:2
with the breasts of her c .... Is 66:11

CONSORTED

believed, and c with Paul and Silas .. Acts 17:4

CONSPIRACY

And the c was strong 2Sa 15:12
his servants arose, and made a c 2Kin 12:20
Now they made a c against him in 2Kin 14:19
his c which he made, behold, they ... 2Kin 15:15
made a c against Pekah the son of ... 2Kin 15:30
king of Assyria found c in Hoshea ... 2Kin 17:4
made a c against him in Jerusalem... 2Chr 25:27
A c is found among the men of ...... Jer 11:9
There is a c of her prophets in ...... Eze 22:25
than forty which had made this c .... Acts 23:13

CONSPIRATORS

is among the c with Absalom. 2Sa 15:31

CONSPIRED

they c against him to slay him........ Gen 37:18
That all of you have c against me..... 1Sa 22:8
him, Why have ye c against me....... 1Sa 22:13
house of Issachar, c against him 1Kin 15:27
c against him, as he was in........... 1Kin 16:9
encamped heard say, Zimri hath c ... 1Kin 16:16
the son of Nimshi c against Joram ... 2Kin 9:14
I c against my master, and slew 2Kin 10:9
the son of Jabesh c against him 2Kin 15:10
c against him, and smote him in 2Kin 15:25
servants of Amon c against him...... 2Kin 21:23

them that had c against king Amon.. 2Kin 21:24
they c against him, and stoned him . 2Chr 24:21
his own servants c against him....... 2Chr 24:25
these are they that c against him 2Chr 33:24
And his servants c against him....... 2Chr 33:24
them that had c against king Amon.. 2Chr 33:25
c all of them together to come and... Neh 4:8
Amos hath c against thee in the...... Amos 7:10

CONSTANT

if he be c to do my commandments ... 1Chr 28:7

CONSTANTLY

the man that heareth speaketh c ..... Prov 21:28
But she c affirmed that it was .... Acts 12:15
things I will that thou affirm c....... Titus 3:8

CONSTELLATIONS

the c thereof shall not give .... Is 13:10

CONSTRAIN

they c you to be circumcised. .... Gal 6:12

CONSTRAINED

and she c him to eat bread 2Kin 4:8
straightway Jesus c his disciples ..... Mt 14:22
straightway he c his disciples to ..... Mk 6:45
But they c him, saying, Abide .... Lk 24:29
And us, and c us .... Acts 16:15
I was c to appeal unto Caesar. .... Acts 28:19

CONSTRAINETH

the spirit within me c me .... Job 32:18
For the love of Christ c us............ 2Cor 5:14

CONSTRAINT

the oversight thereof, not by c 1Pet 5:2

CONSULT

They only c to cast him down from ... Ps 62:4

CONSULTATION

priests held a c with the elders....... Mk 15:1

CONSULTED

king Rehoboam c with the old men,.. 1Kin 12:6
c with the young men that were 1Kin 12:8
David c with the captains of 1Chr 13:1
when he had c with the people, he ... 2Chr 20:21
Then I c with myself, and I .... Neh 5:7
c against thy hidden ones........... Ps 83:3
For they have c together with one ... Ps 83:5
he c with images, he looked in ...... Eze 21:21
have c together to establish a........ Dan 6:7
now what Balak king of Moab c ...... Mic 6:5
Thou hast c shame to thy house by... Hab 2:10
c that they might take Jesus by....... Mt 26:4
But the chief priests c that they ..... Jn 12:10

CONSULTER

or a c with familiar spirits, or .... Deut 18:11

CONSULTETH

c whether he be able with ten .... Lk 14:31

CONSUME

and the famine shall c the land. ..... Gen 41:30
them, and that I may c them .... Ex 32:10
to c them from the face of the .... Ex 32:12
lest I c thee in the way............... Ex 33:3
of thee in a moment, and c thee ..... Ex 33:5
ague, that shall c the eyes .... Lev 26:16
that I may c them in a moment...... Num 16:21
that I may c them as in a moment ... Num 16:45
for this great fire will c us .... Deut 5:25
thou shalt c all the people which.... Deut 7:16
thou mayest not c them at once..... Deut 7:22
for the locust shall c it. .... Deut 28:38
of thy land shall the locust c .... Deut 28:42
shall c the earth with her .... Deut 32:22
c you, after that he hath done........ Josh 24:20
altar, shall he to c thine eyes........ 1Sa 2:33
heaven, and c thee and thy fifty...... 2Kin 1:10
heaven, and c thee and thy fifty...... 2Kin 1:12
thou didst not utterly c them .... Neh 9:31
to c them, and to destroy them ...... Est 9:24
fire shall c the tabernacles of........ Job 15:34
a fire not blown shall c him.......... Job 20:26
Drought and heat c the snow waters .. Job 24:19
they shall c .... Ps 37:20
into smoke shall they c away .... Ps 37:20
his beauty to c away like a moth ..... Ps 39:11
their beauty shall c in the grave...... Ps 49:14
C them in wrath, c them, ... Ps 59:13
their days did he c in vanity.......... Ps 78:33
and it shall also c the beard......... Is 7:20
shall c the glory of his forest, ... Is 10:18
down, and c the branches thereof ... Is 27:10
I will surely c them, saith the ...... Jer 8:13
but I will c them by the sword, ... Jer 14:12
it shall c the palaces of .... Jer 49:27
c away for their iniquity............. Eze 4:17
hailstones in my fury to c it .... Eze 13:13
them in the wilderness, to c them .. Eze 20:13
to c because of the glittering........ Eze 21:28
wilt c thy filthiness out of thee ..... Eze 22:15
the c flesh, and spice it well, and ... Eze 24:10
desolate, they are given us to c ..... Eze 35:12
c all these kingdoms, and it shall ... Dan 2:44
take away his dominion, to c .... Dan 7:26
shall c his branches, and devour .... Hos 11:6
I will utterly c all things from ...... Zeph 1:2
I will c man and beast .... Zeph 1:3
I will c the fowls of the heaven,..... Zeph 1:3
shall c it with the timber............. Zec 5:4
Their flesh shall c away while .... Zec 14:12

CONSUMED

their eyes shall c away in their .... Zec 14:12
their tongue shall c away in .... Zec 14:12
c them, even as Elias did .... Lk 9:54
whom the Lord shall c with the 2Th 2:8
that ye may c it upon your lusts .... Jas 4:3

CONSUMED

lest thou be c in the iniquity of .... Gen 19:15
to the mountain, lest thou be c .... Gen 19:17
in the day the drought c me .... Gen 31:40
with fire, and the bush was not c .... Ex 3:2
wrath, which c them as stubble .... Ex 15:7
or the field, be c therewith .... Ex 22:6
the ashes which the fire hath c .... Lev 6:10
c upon the altar the burnt .... Lev 9:24
c them that were in the uttermost ...... Num 11:1
half c when he cometh out of his .... Num 12:12
this wilderness they shall be c .... Num 14:35
lest ye be c in all their sins .... Num 16:26
c the two hundred and fifty men .... Num 16:35
shall we be c with dying .... Num 17:13
it hath c Ar of Moab, and the .... Num 21:28
that I c not the children of .... Num 25:11
in the sight of the LORD, was c .... Num 32:13
among the host, until they were c ...... Deut 2:15
when all the men of war were c .... Deut 2:16
until he have c thee from off the .... Deut 28:21
which came out of Egypt, were c .... Josh 5:6
of the sword, until they were c .... Josh 8:24
great slaughter, till they were c .... Josh 10:20
c the flesh and the unleavened .... Judg 6:21
still do wickedly, ye shall be c 1Sa 12:25
against them until they be c 1Sa 15:18
the king, The man that c us 2Sa 21:5
not again until I had c them 2Sa 22:38
I have c them, and wounded 2Sa 22:39
c the burnt sacrifice, and the 1Kin 18:38
Syrians, until thou have c them 1Kin 22:11
heaven, and c him and his fifty 2Kin 1:10
heaven, and c him and his fifty 2Kin 1:12
of the Israelites that are c 2Kin 7:13
in Aphek, till thou have c them 2Kin 13:17
Syria till thou hadst c it 2Kin 13:19
c the burnt offering and the 2Chr 7:1
whom the children of Israel c not 2Chr 8:8
shalt push Syria until they be c 2Chr 18:10
with us till thou hadst c us .... Ezr 9:14
the gates thereof are c with fire .... Neh 2:3
gates thereof were c with fire .... Neh 2:13
sheep, and the servants, and c them .. Job 1:16
breath of his nostrils are they c .... Job 4:9
they are c out of their place .... Job 6:17
As the cloud is c and vanisheth .... Job 7:9
though my reins be c within me .... Job 19:27
His flesh is c away, that it .... Job 33:21
Mine eye is c because of grief .... Ps 6:7
did I turn again till they were c ...... Ps 18:37
mine eye is c with grief, yea, my ..... Ps 31:9
mine iniquity, and my bones are c ... Ps 31:10
I am c by the blow of thine hand ..... Ps 39:10
c that are adversaries to my soul..... Ps 71:13
they are utterly c with terrors .... Ps 73:19
The fire c their young men.............. Ps 78:63
For we are c by thine anger, and ... Ps 90:7
For my days are c like smoke........ Ps 102:3
the sinners be c out of the earth...... Ps 104:35
They had almost c me upon earth..... Ps 119:87
My zeal hath c me, because mine... Ps 119:139
when thy flesh and thy body are c ... Prov 5:11
that forsake the LORD shall be c ...... Is 1:28
oppressors are c out of the land....... Is 16:4
to nought, and the extorter is c .... Is 16:4
thy face from us, and hast c us .... Is 64:7
and the mouse, shall be c together .. Is 66:17
thou hast c them, but they have ...... Jer 5:3
burned, the lead is of the fire .... Jer 6:29
after them, till I have c them .... Jer 9:16
him, and c him, and have made his .. Jer 10:25
the beasts are c, and the birds .... Jer 12:4
famine shall those prophets be c .... Jer 14:15
and they shall be c by the sword..... Jer 16:4
my days should be c with shame..... Jer 20:18
till they be c from off the land....... Jer 24:10
until I have c them by his hand...... Jer 27:8
until all the roll was c in the .... Jer 36:23
there, and they shall all be c .... Jer 44:12
they shall even be c by the sword... Jer 44:12
have been c by the sword and by ... Jer 44:18
of Egypt shall be c by the sword ... Jer 44:27
after them, till I have c them .... Jer 49:37
and brought up hath mine enemy c .. Lam 2:22
LORD's mercies that we are not c ..... Lam 3:22
they be c in the midst of thee .... Eze 5:12
ye shall be c in the midst .... Eze 13:14
the fire c them .... Eze 19:12
I have c them with the fire of my ... Eze 22:31
it, that the scum of it may be c....... Eze 24:11
they shall be no more c with........ Eze 34:29
wherefore I have c them in mine .... Eze 43:8
shall the fruit thereof be c .... Eze 47:12
which by his hand shall be c .... Dan 11:16
ye sons of Jacob are not c .... Mal 3:6
that ye be not c one of another ...... Gal 5:15

CONSUMETH

And he, as a rotten thing, c .... Job 13:28
the remnant of them the fire c .... Job 22:20
is a fire that c to destruction .... Job 31:12
stubble, and the flame of the chaff . Is 5:24

CONSUMING

For the LORD thy God is a c fire .... Deut 4:24
as a c fire he shall destroy them .... Deut 9:3

For our God is a c fire .... Heb 12:29

CONSUMMATION

it desolate, even until the c........... Dan 9:27

CONSUMPTION

even appoint over you terror, c ...... Lev 26:16
LORD shall smite thee with a c .... Deut 28:22
the c decreed shall overflow with ... Is 10:22
Lord GOD of hosts shall make a c .. Is 10:23
from the Lord GOD of hosts a c ...... Is 28:22

CONTAIN

heaven of heavens cannot c thee.... 1Kin 8:27
as great as would c two measures ... 1Kin 18:32
and heaven of heavens cannot c him.. 2Chr 2:6
heaven of heavens cannot c thee 2Chr 6:18
that the bath may c the tenth......... Eze 45:11
not c the books that should be....... Jn 21:25
But if they cannot c, let them 1Cor 7:9

CONTAINED

it c two thousand baths 1Kin 7:26
one laver c forty baths 1Kin 7:38
by nature the things c in the law .... Rom 2:14
of commandments c in ordinances .. Eph 2:15
also it is c in the scripture 1Pet 2:6

CONTAINING

it c much .... Eze 23:32

CONTAINING

c two or three firkins apiece .... Jn 2:6

CONTEMN

Wherefore doth the wicked c God .... Ps 10:13
what if the sword c even the rod ..... Eze 21:13

CONTEMNED

In whose eyes a vile person is c ...... Ps 15:4
the counsel of the most High c ...... Ps 107:11
for love, it would utterly be c .... Song 8:7
and the glory of Moab shall be c .... Is 16:14

CONTEMNETH

it c the rod of my son, as every ..... Eze 21:10

CONTEMPT

Thus shall there arise too much c .... Est 1:18
He poureth c upon princes, and ...... Job 12:21
or did the c of families terrify .... Job 31:34
He poureth c upon princes, and ..... Ps 107:40
Remove from me reproach and c .... Ps 119:22
we are exceedingly filled with c .... Ps 123:3
ease, and with the c of the proud.... Ps 123:4
wicked cometh, then cometh also c .. Prov 18:3
glory, and to bring into c all the..... Is 23:9
and some to shame and everlasting c.. Dan 12:2

CONTEMPTIBLE

say, The table of the LORD is c ...... Mal 1:7
thereof, even his meat, is c .... Mal 1:12
Therefore have I also made you c ... Mal 2:9
presence is weak, and his speech c .. 2Cor 10:10

CONTEMPTUOUSLY

c against the righteous .... Ps 31:18

CONTENDED

neither c with them in battle .... Deut 2:9
it, and c with him in battle .... Deut 2:24
If he will c with him, he cannot ..... Job 9:3
will ye c for God .... Job 13:8
such as keep the law c with them.... Prov 28:4
neither may he c with him that is ... Eccl 6:10
for I will c with him that .... Is 49:25
who will c with me .... Is 50:8
For I will not c for ever .... Is 57:16
then how canst thou c with horses .. Jer 12:5
the voice of them that c with me .... Jer 18:19
the Lord GOD called to c by fire .... Amos 7:4
c thou before the mountains, and ... Mic 6:1
c for the faith which was once .... Jude 3

CONTENDED

Then c I with the rulers, and .... Neh 13:11
Then I c with the nobles of Judah ... Neh 13:17
I c with them, and cursed them, and .. Neh 13:25
maidservant, when they c with me ... Job 31:13
them, even them that c with him .... Is 41:12
of the circumcision c with him .... Acts 11:2

CONTENDEST

shew me wherefore thou c with me .. Job 10:2

CONTENDETH

Shall he that c with the Almighty ... Job 40:2
If a wise man c with a foolish .... Prov 29:9
contend with him that c with .... Is 49:25

CONTENDING

when c with the devil he disputed ... Jude 9

CONTENT

And his brethren were c .... Gen 37:27
Moses was c to dwell with the man . Ex 2:21
when Moses heard that, he was c .... Lev 10:20
would to God we had been c .... Josh 7:7
the Levite was c to dwell with ...... Judg 17:11
had said unto the man, Be c........... Judg 19:6
And Naaman said, Be c, take two ... 2Kin 5:23
he said, Be c, I pray thee, ... 2Kin 6:3
Now therefore be c, look upon me ... Job 6:28
neither will he rest, though .... Prov 6:35
Pilate, willing to c the people .... Mk 15:15
and be c with your wages.............. Lk 3:14
state I am, therewith to be c .... Phil 4:11
and raiment let us be therewith c ... 1Ti 6:8
be c with such things as ye have..... Heb 13:5

not c therewith, neither doth he 3Jn 10

CONTENTION

Only by pride cometh c .... Prov 13:10
therefore leave off c, before it .... Prov 17:14
A fool's lips enter into c .... Prov 18:6
the scorner, and c shall go out .... Prov 22:10
a man of c to the whole earth........ Jer 15:10
are that raise up strife and c .... Hab 1:3
the c was so sharp between them, ... Acts 15:39
The one preach Christ of c .... Phil 1:16
you the gospel of God with much c .. 1Th 2:2

CONTENTIONS

The lot causeth c to cease .... Prov 18:18
their c are like the bars of a .... Prov 18:19
the c of a wife are a continual ...... Prov 19:13
who hath c .... Prov 23:29
Chloe, that there are c among you ... 1Cor 1:11
questions, and genealogies, and c .... Titus 3:9

CONTENTIOUS

in the wilderness, than with a c ...... Prov 21:19
so is a c man to kindle strife .... Prov 26:21
rainy day and a c woman are alike ... Prov 27:15
But unto them that are c, and do..... Rom 2:8
But if any man seem to be c 1Cor 11:16

CONTENTMENT

godliness with c is great gain 1Ti 6:6

CONTINUAL

This shall be a c burnt offering....... Ex 29:42
the c bread shall be thereon.......... Num 4:7
for day, for a c burnt offering........ Num 28:3
It is a c burnt offering, which .... Num 28:6
beside the c burnt offering, and..... Num 28:10
beside the c burnt offering, and..... Num 28:15
which is for a c burnt offering....... Num 28:23
beside the c burnt offering........... Num 28:24
them beside the c burnt offering.... Num 28:31
the c burnt offering, and the meat .. Num 29:11
beside the c burnt offering, his..... Num 29:16
beside the c burnt offering, and..... Num 29:19
beside the c burnt offering, and..... Num 29:22
beside the c burnt offering, his..... Num 29:25
beside the c burnt offering, and..... Num 29:28
beside the c burnt offering, his..... Num 29:31
beside the c burnt offering, and..... Num 29:34
beside the c burnt offering, his..... Num 29:38
his allowance was a c allowance 2Kin 25:30
for the c shewbread, and for the 2Chr 2:4
offered the c burnt offering .... Ezr 3:5
for the c meat offering, and for-.... Neh 10:33
for the c burnt offering, of the ...... Neh 10:33
of a merry heart hath a c feast ...... Prov 15:15
of a wife are a c dropping .... Prov 19:13
A c dropping in a very rainy day ... Prov 27:15
people in wrath with a c stroke...... Is 14:6
of Luhith c weeping shall go up ..... Jer 48:5
there was a c diet given him of ..... Jer 52:34
sever out men of c employment ..... Eze 39:14
morning for a c burnt offering....... Eze 46:15
lest by her c coming she weary me . Lk 18:5
heaviness and sorrow in my heart .. Rom 9:2

CONTINUALLY

of his heart was only evil c............ Gen 6:5
returned from off the earth c .... Gen 8:3
the waters decreased c until the.... Gen 8:5
for a memorial before the LORD c ... Ex 28:29
upon his heart before the LORD c ... Ex 28:30
of the first year day for day c........ Ex 29:38
to cause the lamps to burn c......... Lev 24:2
before the LORD c .... Lev 24:3
candlestick before the LORD c ...... Lev 24:4
set it in order before the LORD c ... Lev 24:8
that are of the LORD went on c...... Josh 6:13
and Saul became David's enemy c .. 1Sa 18:29
shalt eat bread at my table 2Sa 9:7
for he did eat c at the king's 2Sa 9:13
people increased c with Absalom ... 2Sa 15:12
before me c in the room of Joab.... 2Sa 19:13
which stand c before the 1Kin 10:8
man of God, which passeth by us c .. 2Kin 4:9
he did eat bread c before him all ... 2Kin 25:29
the priests with trumpets c 1Chr 16:6
and his strength, seek his face c 1Chr 16:11
to minister before the ark c 1Chr 16:37
of the burnt offering c morning..... 1Chr 16:40
unto them, c before the LORD 1Chr 23:31
which stand c before the 2Chr 9:7
between Rehoboam and Jeroboam c .. 2Chr 12:15
LORD c all the days of Jehoiada..... 2Chr 24:14
Thus did Job c .... Job 1:5
his praise shall c be in my mouth ... Ps 34:1
yea, let them say c, Let the LORD .. Ps 35:27
me; thy loving-kindness .... Ps 38:17
and thy truth c preserve me .... Ps 40:11
such as love thy salvation say c..... Ps 40:16
while they c say unto me, Where.... Ps 42:3
My confusion is c before me .... Ps 44:15
to have been c before me .... Ps 50:8
God of my salvation c .... Ps 52:1
melt away as waters which run c.... Ps 58:7
and make their loins c to shake..... Ps 69:23
such as love thy salvation say ...... Ps 70:4
whereunto I may c resort .... Ps 71:3
my praise shall be c of thee .... Ps 71:6
But I will hope c, and will yet .... Ps 71:14
also shall be made for him c .... Ps 72:15
Nevertheless I am c with thee........ Ps 73:23
rise up against thee increaseth c .... Ps 74:23
Let his children be c vagabonds ..... Ps 109:10

Let them be before the Lord c........ Ps 109:15
a girdle wherewith he is girded c...... Ps 109:19
that I keep thy law c for ever.......... Ps 119:44
have respect unto thy statutes c...... Ps 119:117
c are they gathered together for...... Ps 140:2
his heart, he deviseth mischief c..... Prov 6:14
Bind them c upon thine heart, and... Prov 6:21
it whirleth about c, and the wind..... Eccl 1:6
I stand c upon the watchtower in..... Is 21:8
thy walls are c before me............... Is 49:16
hast feared c every day because...... Is 51:13
my name c every day is blasphemed.. Is 52:5
And the Lord shall guide thee c........ Is 58:11
thy gates shall be open c................ Is 60:11
me to anger c to my face................. Is 65:3
before me c is grief and wounds...... Jer 6:7
offerings, and to do sacrifice c........ Jer 33:18
he did c eat bread before him all..... Jer 52:33
a meat offering c by a perpetual...... Eze 46:14
Thy God whom thou servest c.......... Dan 6:16
is thy God, whom thou servest c...... Dan 6:20
they have committed whoredom c...... Hos 4:18
and judgment, and wait on thy God c.. Hos 12:6
so shall all the heathen drink c........ Obad 16
hath not thy wickedness passed c..... Nah 3:19
not spare c to slay the nations........ Hab 1:17
were c in the temple, praising and... Lk 24:53
will give ourselves c to prayer........ Acts 6:4
of them that waited on him c........... Acts 10:7
attending c upon this very thing...... Rom 13:6
abideth a priest c........................ Heb 7:3
year c make the comers thereunto... Heb 10:1
the sacrifice of praise to God c....... Heb 13:15

CONTINUANCE
even great plagues, and of long c..... Deut 28:59
and sore sicknesses, and of long c... Deut 28:59
which in c were fashioned, when...... Ps 139:16
in those is c, and we shall be........... Is 64:5
To them who by patient c in well...... Rom 2:7

CONTINUE
if he c a day or two, he shall............ Ex 21:21
she shall then c in the blood of........ Lev 12:4
she shall c in the blood of her......... Lev 12:5
you c following the Lord your God.... 1Sa 12:14
But now thy kingdom shall not c...... 1Sa 13:14
that it may c for ever before.......... 2Sa 7:29
That the Lord may c his word......... 1Kin 2:4
neither shall his substance c........... Job 15:29
doth not mine eye c in their............ Job 17:2
O c thy lovingkindness unto them..... Ps 36:10
their houses shall c for ever............ Ps 49:11
children of thy servants shall c........ Ps 102:28
They c this day according to........... Ps 119:91
that c until night, till wine............. Is 5:11
vessel, that they may c many days.... Jer 32:14
he shall c more years than the......... Dan 11:8
because they c with me now three.... Mt 15:32
If ye c in my word, then are ye........ Jn 8:31
c ye in my love............................ Jn 15:9
persuaded them to c in the grace..... Acts 13:43
exhorting them to c in the faith....... Acts 14:22
I c unto this day, witnessing........... Acts 26:22
Shall we c in sin, that grace may...... Rom 6:1
if thou c in his goodness................ Rom 11:22
of the gospel might c with you........ Gal 2:5
abide and c with you all for your...... Phil 1:25
If ye c in the faith grounded and..... Col 1:23
C in prayer, and watch in the same... Col 4:2
if they c in faith and charity and..... 1Ti 2:15
c in them.................................. 1Ti 4:16
But c thou in the things which......... 2Ti 3:14
suffered to c by reason of death...... Heb 7:23
Let brotherly love c...................... Heb 13:1
c there a year, and buy and sell........ Jas 4:13
all things c as they were from......... 2Pet 3:4
you, ye also shall c in the Son......... 1Jn 2:24
was given unto him to c forty.......... Rev 13:5
cometh, he must c a short space...... Rev 17:10

CONTINUED
and they c a season in ward............ Gen 40:4
Asher c on the sea shore, and......... Judg 5:17
the country of Moab, and c there...... Ruth 1:2
hath c even from the morning.......... Ruth 2:7
as she c praying before the Lord...... 1Sa 1:12
the ark of the Lord c in the............ 2Sa 6:11
they c three years without war........ 1Kin 22:1
all this c until the burnt................ 2Chr 29:28
also I c in the work of this wall....... Neh 5:16
Moreover Job c his parable............. Job 27:1
Moreover Job c his parable............. Job 29:1
his name shall be c as long as......... Ps 72:17
Daniel c even unto the first year...... Dan 1:21
c all night in prayer to God............ Lk 6:12
Ye are they which have c with me.... Lk 22:28
they c there not many days............. Jn 2:12
So when they c asking him.............. Jn 8:7
there c with his disciples............... Jn 11:54
These all c with one accord in......... Acts 1:14
And they c stedfastly in the............ Acts 2:42
that c with Philip, and wondered,.... Acts 8:13
But Peter c knocking.................... Acts 12:16
Barnabas c in Antioch, teaching...... Acts 15:35
he c there a year and six months,..... Acts 18:11
this c by the space of two years....... Acts 19:10
c his speech until midnight............. Acts 20:7
c fasting, having taken nothing....... Acts 27:33
because they c not in my covenant... Heb 8:9
would no doubt have c with us......... 1Jn 2:19

CONTINUETH
fleeth also as a shadow, and c not.... Job 14:2
Cursed is every one that c not in...... Gal 3:10
c in supplications and prayers......... 1Ti 5:5
But this man, because he c ever....... Heb 7:24
c therein, he being not a............... Jas 1:25

CONTINUING
forth with fury, a c whirlwind......... Jer 30:23
c daily with one accord in the......... Acts 2:46
c instant in prayer....................... Rom 12:12
For here have we no c city.............. Heb 13:14

CONTRADICTING
which were spoken by Paul, c.......... Acts 13:45

CONTRADICTION
without all c the less is blessed....... Heb 7:7
such c of sinners against himself..... Heb 12:3

CONTRARIWISE
So that c ye ought rather to............ 2Cor 2:7
But c, when they saw that the......... Gal 2:7
but c blessing............................ 1Pet 3:9

CONTRARY
And if ye walk c unto me, and will.... Lev 26:21
things, but will walk c unto me........ Lev 26:23
Then will I also walk c unto you....... Lev 26:24
unto me, but walk c unto me........... Lev 26:27
Then I will walk c unto you also....... Lev 26:28
also they have walked c unto me...... Lev 26:40
I also have walked c unto them........ Lev 26:41
(though it was turned to the c......... Est 9:1
the c is in free from other women.... Eze 16:34
unto thee, therefore thou art c........ Eze 16:34
for the wind was c........................ Mt 14:24
for the wind was c unto them.......... Mk 6:48
these all do c to the decrees of....... Acts 17:7
men to worship God c to the law...... Acts 18:13
me to be smitten c to the law.......... Acts 23:3
things c to the name of Jesus of...... Acts 26:9
Cyprus, because the winds were c..... Acts 27:4
wert grafted c to nature into a........ Rom 11:24
offences c to the doctrine which...... Rom 16:17
these are c the one to the other....... Gal 5:17
was against us, which was c to us..... Col 2:14
not God, and are c to all men.......... 1Th 2:15
thing that is c to sound doctrine...... 1Ti 1:10
is of the c part may be ashamed...... Titus 2:8

CONTRIBUTION
Achaia to make a certain c for......... Rom 15:26

CONTRITE
saveth such as be of a c spirit......... Ps 34:18
a c heart, O God, thou wilt not........ Ps 51:17
with him also that is of a c............. Is 57:15
to revive the heart of the c ones...... Is 57:15
of a c spirit, and trembleth at my.... Is 66:2

CONTROVERSIES
judgment of the Lord, and for c....... 2Chr 19:8

CONTROVERSY
matters of c within thy gates.......... Deut 17:8
the men, between whom the c is....... Deut 19:17
and by their word shall every c........ Deut 21:5
If there be a c between men........... Deut 25:1
that when any man that had a c........ 2Sa 15:2
of recompences for the c of Zion..... Is 34:8
Lord hath a c with the nations......... Jer 25:31
in c they shall stand in judgment..... Eze 44:24
for the Lord hath a c with the......... Hos 4:1
The Lord hath also a c with Judah.... Hos 12:2
ye, O mountains, the Lord's c.......... Mic 6:2
the Lord hath a c with his people..... Mic 6:2
without c great is the mystery of..... 1Ti 3:16

CONVENIENT
feed me with food c for me............. Prov 30:8
c for thee to go, thither go............. Jer 40:4
it seemeth c unto thee to go........... Jer 40:5
when a c day was come, that Herod.. Mk 6:21
when I have a c season, I will.......... Acts 24:25
do those things which are not c....... Rom 1:28
come when he shall have c time....... 1Cor 16:12
nor jesting, which are not c............ Eph 5:4
to enjoin thee that which is c.......... Philem 8

CONVENIENTLY
sought how he might c betray him.... Mk 14:11

CONVERSANT
strangers that were c among them.... Josh 8:35
as long as we were c with them....... 1Sa 25:15

CONVERSATION
to slay such as be of upright c......... Ps 37:14
his c aright will I shew the.............. Ps 50:23
we have had our c in the world........ 2Cor 1:12
For ye have heard of my c in time.... Gal 1:13
c in times past in the lusts of......... Eph 2:3
the former c the old man, which...... Eph 4:22
Only let your c be as it becometh.... Phil 1:27
For our c is in heaven.................... Phil 3:20
of the believers, in word, in c......... 1Ti 4:12
Let your c be without.................... Heb 13:5
considering the end of their c.......... Heb 13:7
good c his works with meekness of... Jas 3:13
so be ye holy in all manner of c....... 1Pet 1:15
from your vain c received by........... 1Pet 1:18
Having your c honest among the...... 1Pet 2:12
word be won by the c of the wives.... 1Pet 3:1
your chaste c coupled with fear....... 1Pet 3:2
accuse your good c in Christ........... 1Pet 3:16

COPY
that he shall write him a c............. Deut 17:18
stones a c of the law of Moses........ Josh 8:32
This is the c of the letter that......... Ezr 4:11
Now when the c of king................. Ezr 4:23
The c of the letter that Tatnai,....... Ezr 5:6
Now this is the c of the letter........ Ezr 7:11
The c of the writing for a............... Est 3:14
Also he gave him the c of the......... Est 4:8
The c of the writing for a............... Est 8:13

with the filthy c of the wicked........ 2Pet 2:7
ought ye to be in all holy c............. 2Pet 3:11

CONVERSION
declaring the c of the Gentiles........ Acts 15:3

CONVERT
understand with their heart, and c.... Is 6:10
err from the truth, and one c him..... Jas 5:19

CONVERTED
and sinners shall be c unto thee...... Ps 51:13
of the sea shall be c unto thee......... Is 60:5
with their heart, and should be c...... Mt 13:15
I say unto you, Except ye be c......... Mt 18:3
lest at any time they should be c...... Mk 4:12
and when thou art c, strengthen...... Lk 22:32
with their heart, and be c.............. Jn 12:40
Repent ye therefore, and be c......... Acts 3:19
with their heart, and should be c...... Acts 28:27

CONVERTETH
that he which c the sinner from....... Jas 5:20

CONVERTING
the Lord is perfect, c the soul......... Ps 19:7

CONVERTS
and her c with righteousness........... Is 1:27

CONVEY
I will c them by sea in floats........... 1Kin 5:9
that they may c me over till I.......... Neh 2:7

CONVEYED
for Jesus had c himself away.......... Jn 5:13

CONVICTED
being c by their own conscience,..... Jn 8:9

CONVINCE
to exhort and to c the gainsayers..... Titus 1:9
to c all that are ungodly among....... Jude 15

CONVINCED
there was none of you that c Job..... Job 32:12
For he mightily c the Jews.............. Acts 18:28
he is c of all, he is judged of.......... 1Cor 14:24
are c of the law as transgressors..... Jas 2:9

CONVINCETH
Which of you c me of sin................ Jn 8:46

CONVOCATION
day there shall be an holy c............ Ex 12:16
there shall be an holy c to you......... Ex 12:16
is the sabbath of rest, an holy c...... Lev 23:3
first day ye shall have an holy c....... Lev 23:7
in the seventh day is an holy c........ Lev 23:8
that it may be an holy c unto you..... Lev 23:21
of blowing of trumpets, an holy c.... Lev 23:24
it shall be an holy c unto you.......... Lev 23:27
the first day shall be an holy c........ Lev 23:35
day shall be an holy c unto you....... Lev 23:36
the first day shall be an holy c........ Num 28:18
day ye shall have an holy c............. Num 28:25
be out, ye shall have an holy c........ Num 28:26
month, ye shall have an holy c......... Num 29:1
of this seventh month an holy c....... Num 29:7

CONVOCATIONS
ye shall proclaim to be holy c......... Lev 23:2
feasts of the Lord, even holy c........ Lev 23:4
ye shall proclaim to be holy c......... Lev 23:37

COOK
And Samuel said unto the c............ 1Sa 9:23
the c took up the shoulder, and....... 1Sa 9:24

COOKS
to be confectionaries, and to be c.... 1Sa 8:13

COOL
in the garden in the c of the day...... Gen 3:8
finger in water, and c my tongue...... Lk 16:24

COOS (co'-os) An island near Cnidus.
with a straight course unto C.......... Acts 21:1

COPIED
of Hezekiah king of Judah c out....... Prov 25:1

COPING
from the foundation unto the c........ 1Kin 7:9

COPPER
and two vessels of fine c,............... Ezr 8:27

COPPERSMITH
Alexander the c did me much evil..... 2Ti 4:14

COPULATION
man's seed of c go out from him...... Lev 15:16
skin, whereon is the seed of c......... Lev 15:17
whom man shall lie with seed of c.... Lev 15:18

COR
tenth part of a bath out of the c .... Eze 45:14

CORAL
No mention shall be made of c .... Job 28:18
work, and fine linen, and c .... Eze 27:16

CORBAN (cor´-ban) A sacred gift.
to his father or mother, It is C .... Mk 7:11

CORD
down by a c through the window .... Josh 2:15
Because he hath loosed my c .... Job 30:11
or his tongue with a c which thou .... Job 41:1
a threefold c is not quickly .... Eccl 4:12
Or ever the silver c be loosed .... Eccl 12:6
have none that shall cast a by .... Mic 2:5

CORDS
the pins of the court, and their c .... Ex 35:18
hanging for the court gate, his c .... Ex 39:40
the c of it for all the service .... Num 3:26
and their pins, and their c .... Num 3:37
the altar round about, and their c ...... Num 4:26
and their pins, and their c .... Num 4:32
bound him with two new c .... Judg 15:13
the c that were upon his arms .... Judg 15:14
fastened with c of fine linen .... Est 1:6
be holden in c of affliction .... Job 36:8
and cast away their c from us .... Ps 2:3
bind the sacrifice with c .... Ps 118:27
cut asunder the c of the wicked .... Ps 129:4
have hid a snare for me, and c .... Ps 140:5
be holden with the c of his sins .... Prov 5:22
draw iniquity with c of vanity .... Is 5:18
any of the c thereof be broken .... Is 33:20
spare not, lengthen thy c .... Is 54:2
spoiled, and all my c are broken .... Jer 10:20
and they let down Jeremiah with c ... Jer 38:6
let them down by c into the .... Jer 38:11
under thine armholes under the c ...... Jer 38:12
So they drew up Jeremiah with c ...... Jer 38:13
of rich apparel, bound with c .... Eze 27:24
I drew them with c of a man .... Hos 11:4
he had made a scourge of small c ..... Jn 2:15

CORE (co´-ree) See KORAH. Greek form of
Korah.
perished in the gainsaying of C .... Jude 11

CORIANDER
and it was like a c seed, white .... Ex 16:31
And the manna was as c seed .... Num 11:7

CORINTH (cor´-inth) See CORINTHIANS,
CORINTHUS. Capital of Achaia.
from Athens, and came to C .... Acts 18:1
that, while Apollos was at C .... Acts 19:1
the church of God which is at C 1Cor 1:2
the church of God which is at C 2Cor 1:1
you I came not as yet unto C 2Cor 1:23
Erastus abode at C 2Ti 4:20

CORINTHIANS (co-rin´-the-uns) Residents of
Corinth.
many of the C hearing believed, ... Acts 18:8
The first epistle to the C was .... 1Cor s
O ye C, our mouth is open unto 2Cor 6:11
the C was written from Philippi .... 2Cor s

CORINTHUS (co-rin´-thus) See CORINTH.
Same as Corinth.
Written to the Romans from C .... Rom s

CORMORANT
And the little owl, and the c .... Lev 11:17
and the gier eagle, and the c .... Deut 14:17
But the c and the bittern shall .... Is 34:11
both the c and the bittern shall .... Zeph 2:14

CORN
of the earth, and plenty of c .... Gen 27:28
and with c and wine have I .... Gen 27:37
seven ears of c came up upon one ..... Gen 41:5
lay up c under the hand of .... Gen 41:35
Joseph gathered c as the sand of .... Gen 41:49
into Egypt for Joseph for to buy c ...... Gen 41:57
saw that there was c in Egypt .... Gen 42:1
heard that there is c in Egypt .... Gen 42:2
went down to buy c in Egypt .... Gen 42:3
to buy c among those that came .... Gen 42:5
carry c for the famine of your .... Gen 42:19
to fill their sacks with c .... Gen 42:25
they laded their asses with the c .... Gen 42:26
when they had eaten up the c .... Gen 43:2
of the youngest, and his c money ...... Gen 44:2
and ten she asses laden with c .... Gen 45:23
for the c which they bought .... Gen 47:14
thorns, so that the stacks of c .... Ex 22:6
or the standing c, or the field .... Ex 22:6
green ears of c dried by the fire .... Lev 2:14
even c beaten out of full ears .... Lev 2:14
it, part of the beaten c thereof .... Lev 2:16
eat neither bread, nor parched c .... Lev 23:14
were the c of the threshingfloor .... Num 18:27
and the fruit of thy land, thy c .... Deut 7:13
that thou mayest gather in thy c .... Deut 11:14
thy gates the tithe of thy c .... Deut 12:17
name there, the tithe of thy c .... Deut 12:17
to put the sickle to the c .... Deut 16:9
that thou hast gathered in thy c .... Deut 16:13
The firstfruit also of thy c .... Deut 18:4
the standing c of thy neighbour .... Deut 23:25
unto thy neighbour's standing c .... Deut 23:25
the ox when he treadeth out the c ...... Deut 25:4

shall not leave thee either c .... Deut 28:51
Jacob shall be upon a land of c .... Deut 33:28
they did eat of the old c of the .... Josh 5:11
parched c in the selfsame day .... Josh 5:11
eaten of the old c of the land .... Josh 5:12
the standing c of the Philistines .... Judg 15:5
shocks, and also the standing c .... Judg 15:5
glean ears of c after him in .... Ruth 2:2
and he reached her parched c .... Ruth 2:14
down at the end of the heap of c ...... Ruth 3:7
an ephah of this parched c 1Sa 17:17
and five measures of parched c 1Sa 25:18
mouth, and spread ground c thereon . 2Sa 17:19
and barley, and flour, and parched c . 2Sa 17:28
full ears of c in the husk 2Kin 4:42
like your own land, a land of c 2Kin 18:32
as c blasted before it be grown 2Kin 19:26
in abundance the firstfruits of c 2Chr 31:5
also for the increase of c 2Chr 32:28
therefore we take up c for them .... Neh 5:2
and houses, that we might buy c .... Neh 5:3
might exact of them money and c ...... Neh 5:10
part of the money, and of the c .... Neh 5:11
shall bring the offering of the c .... Neh 10:39
vessels, and the tithe of the c .... Neh 13:5
all Judah the tithe of the c .... Neh 13:12
like as a shock of c cometh in .... Job 5:26
reap every one his c in the field .... Job 24:6
off as the tops of the ears of c .... Job 24:24
good liking, they grow up with c .... Job 39:4
than in the time that their c .... Ps 4:7
thou preparest them c, when thou ..... Ps 65:9
also are covered over with c .... Ps 65:13
of c in the earth upon the top of .... Ps 72:16
had given them of the c of heaven ..... Ps 78:24
He that withholdeth c, the people ..... Prov 11:26
the harvestman gathereth the c .... Is 17:5
threshing, and the c of my floor .... Is 21:10
Bread c is bruised .... Is 28:28
like your own land, a land of c .... Is 36:17
as c blasted before it be grown .... Is 37:27
c to be meat for thine enemies .... Is 62:8
say to their mothers, Where is c .... Lam 2:12
and I will call for the c, and will .... Eze 36:29
did not know that I gave her c .... Hos 2:8
take away my c in the time .... Hos 2:9
And the earth shall hear the c .... Hos 2:22
they assemble themselves for c .... Hos 7:14
and loveth to tread out the c .... Hos 10:11
they shall revive as the c .... Hos 14:7
for the c is wasted .... Joel 1:10
for the c is withered .... Joel 1:17
people, Behold, I will send you c .... Joel 2:19
moon be gone, that we may sell c ...... Amos 8:5
like as c is sifted in a sieve, ... Amos 9:9
upon the mountains, and upon the c . Hag 1:11
c shall make the young men .... Zec 9:17
on the sabbath day through the c ..... Mt 12:1
and began to pluck the ears of c .... Mt 12:1
that he went through the c fields ...... Mk 2:23
they went, to pluck the ears of c .... Mk 2:23
after that the full e in the ear .... Mk 4:28
that he went through the c fields ...... Lk 6:1
disciples plucked the ears of c .... Lk 6:1
Except a c of wheat fall into the .... Jn 12:24
heard that there was c in Egypt .... Acts 7:12
of the ox that treadeth out the c 1Cor 9:9
the ox that treadeth out the c 1Ti 5:18

CORNELIUS (cor-ne´-le-us) A Roman
centurion converted by Peter.
certain man in Caesarea called C ...... Acts 10:1
in to him, and saying unto him, C ..... Acts 10:3
which spake unto C was departed ..... Acts 10:7
C had made enquiry for Simon's .... Acts 10:17
which were sent unto him from C ...... Acts 10:21
C the centurion, a just man, and ...... Acts 10:22
C waited for them, and had called .... Acts 10:24
C met him, and fell down at his .... Acts 10:25
C said, Four days ago I was .... Acts 10:30
And said, C, thy prayer is heard, ... Acts 10:31

CORNER
which is toward the north c .... Ex 36:25
shave off the c of their beard .... Lev 21:5
compassed the c of the sea .... Josh 18:14
from the right c of the temple to 2Kin 11:11
to the left c of the temple 2Kin 11:11
gate of Ephraim unto the c gate 2Kin 14:13
the gate of Ephraim to the c gate 2Chr 25:23
towers in Jerusalem at the c gate 2Chr 26:9
altars in every c of Jerusalem 2Chr 28:24
of the wall, even unto the c .... Neh 3:24
and to the going up of the c .... Neh 3:31
between the going up of the c .... Neh 3:32
or who laid the c stone thereof .... Job 38:6
is become the head stone of the c ..... Ps 118:22
our daughters may be as c stones ..... Ps 144:12
through the street near her c .... Prov 7:8
and lieth in wait at every c .... Prov 7:12
to dwell in a c of the housetop .... Prov 21:9
to dwell in the c of the housetop ...... Prov 25:24
a tried stone, a precious c stone ...... Is 28:16
be removed into a c any more .... Is 30:20
Hananeel unto the gate of the .... Jer 31:38
unto the c of the horse gate .... Jer 31:40
and shall devour the c of Moab .... Jer 48:45
not take of thee a stone for a c .... Jer 51:26
in every c of the court there was ...... Eze 46:21
in Samaria in the c of a bed .... Amos 3:12
the ox hath come forth the c .... Zec 10:4

the first gate, unto the c gate .... Zec 14:10
same is become the head of the c .... Mt 21:42
is become the head of the c .... Mk 12:10
same is become the head of the c .... Lk 20:17
which is become the head of the c .... Acts 4:11
this thing was not done in a c .... Acts 26:26
himself being the chief c stone .... Eph 2:20
I lay in Sion a chief c stone 1Pet 2:6
same is made the head of the c 1Pet 2:7

CORNERS
and put them in the four c thereof .... Ex 25:12
four c that are on the four feet .... Ex 25:26
c of the tabernacle in the two .... Ex 26:23
they shall be for the two .... Ex 26:24
of it upon the four c thereof .... Ex 27:2
rings in the four c thereof .... Ex 27:4
crown of it, by the two c thereof ...... Ex 30:4
two boards made he for the c of ...... Ex 36:28
did to both of them in both the c .... Ex 36:29
to be set by the four c of it .... Ex 37:3
four c that were in the four feet ...... Ex 37:13
crown thereof, by the two c of it ...... Ex 37:27
horns thereof on the four c of it ...... Ex 38:2
wholly reap the c of thy field............ Lev 19:9
not round the c of your heads .... Lev 19:27
shalt thou mar the c of thy beard .... Lev 19:27
c of thy field when thou reapest .... Lev 23:22
and shall smite the c of Moab .... Num 24:17
said, I would scatter them into c ...... Deut 32:26
and the four c thereof had 1Kin 7:30
to the four c of one base 1Kin 7:34
and didst divide them into c .... Neh 9:22
and smote the four c of the house ... Job 1:19
from the four c of the earth............. Is 11:12
and all that are in the utmost c ...... Jer 9:26
and all that are in the utmost c ...... Jer 25:23
them that are in the utmost c .... Jer 49:32
come upon the four c of the land .... Eze 7:2
the c thereof, and the length .... Eze 41:22
on the four c of the settle, and .... Eze 43:20
upon the four c of the settle of .... Eze 45:19
pass by the four c of the court .... Eze 46:21
In the four c of the court there ...... Eze 46:22
these four c were of one measure .... Eze 46:22
bowls, and as the c of the altar ...... Zec 9:15
in the c of the streets, that .... Mt 6:5
a great sheet knit at the four c ...... Acts 10:11
let down from heaven by four c ...... Acts 11:5
on the four c of the earth .... Rev 7:1

CORNET
shouting, and with sound of the c 1Chr 15:28
sound of c make a joyful noise .... Ps 98:6
time ye hear the sound of the c .... Dan 3:5
people heard the sound of the c ...... Dan 3:7
shall hear the sound of the c .... Dan 3:10
time ye hear the sound of the c .... Dan 3:15
Blow ye the c in Gibeah, and the .... Hos 5:8

CORNETS
and on timbrels, and on c, and on ... 2Sa 6:5
and with trumpets, and with c 2Chr 15:14

CORNFLOOR
hast loved a reward upon every c ..... Hos 9:1

CORPSE
of it, they came and took up his c..... Mk 6:29

CORPSES
behold, they were all dead c 2Kin 19:35
behold, they were all dead c .... Is 37:36
and there is none end of their c ...... Nah 3:3
they stumble upon their c .... Nah 3:3

CORRECT
rebukes doct c man for iniquity ...... Ps 39:11
the heathen, shall not he c .... Ps 94:10
C thy son, and he shall give thee .... Prov 29:17
Thine own wickedness shall c thee... Jer 2:19
O LORD, c me, but with judgment .... Jer 10:24
but I will c thee in measure, and .... Jer 30:11
of thee, but c thee in measure, ... Jer 46:28

CORRECTED
A servant will not be c by words....... Prov 29:19
fathers of our flesh which c us .... Heb 12:9

CORRECTETH
happy is the man whom God c .... Job 5:17
For whom the LORD loveth he c .... Prov 3:12

CORRECTION
causeth it to come, whether for c .... Job 37:13
neither be weary of his c .... Prov 3:11
as a fool to the c of the stocks........ Prov 7:22
C is grievous unto him that .... Prov 15:10
but the rod of c shall drive it .... Prov 22:15
Withhold not c from the child......... Prov 23:13
they received no c .... Jer 2:30
they have refused to receive c .... Jer 5:3
LORD their God, nor receiveth c ..... Jer 7:28
thou hast established them for c ..... Hab 1:12
the received not c .... Zeph 3:2
for doctrine, for reproof, for c 2Ti 3:16

CORRUPT
The earth also was c before God...... Gen 6:11
the earth, and, behold, it was c ...... Gen 6:12
Lest ye c yourselves, and make you.. Deut 4:16
shall c yourselves, and make a .... Deut 4:25
ye will utterly c yourselves............. Deut 31:29
My breath is c, my days are .... Job 17:1
They are c, they have done.............. Ps 14:1

CORRUPTED

are c because of my foolishness	Ps 38:5
C are they, and have done	Ps 53:1
They are c, and speak wickedly	Ps 73:8
troubled fountain, and a c spring	Prov 25:26
nor according to your c doings	Eze 20:44
she was more c in her inordinate	Eze 23:11
c words to speak before me, till	Dan 2:9
covenant shall he c by flatteries	Dan 11:32
unto the Lord a c thing	Mal 1:14
I will c your seed, and spread	Mal 2:3
earth, where moth and rust doth c	Mt 6:19
neither moth nor rust doth c	Mt 6:20
but a c tree bringeth forth evil	Mt 7:17
neither can a c tree bring forth	Mt 7:18
the tree c, and his fruit c	Mt 12:33
tree bringeth not forth c fruit	Lk 6:43
neither doth a c tree bring forth	Lk 6:43
communications c good manners	1Cor 15:33
as many, which c the word of God	2Cor 2:17
which is c according to the	Eph 4:22
Let no c communication proceed	Eph 4:29
disputings of men of c minds	1Ti 6:5
men of c minds, reprobate	2Ti 3:8
in those things they c themselves	Jude 10
which did c the earth with her	Rev 19:2

CORRUPTED

for all flesh had c his way upon	Gen 6:12
the land was c by reason of the	Ex 8:24
land of Egypt, and c themselves	Ex 32:7
out of Egypt have c themselves	Deut 9:12
They have c themselves, their	Deut 32:5
c themselves more than their	Judg 2:19
thou wast c more than they in all	Eze 16:47
thou hast c thy wisdom by reason	Eze 28:17
They have deeply c themselves	Hos 9:9
rose early, and c all their doings	Zeph 3:7
ye have c the covenant of Levi	Mal 2:8
wronged no man, we have c no man	2Cor 7:2
so your minds should be c from	2Cor 11:3
Your riches are c, and your	Jas 5:2

CORRUPTERS

of evildoers, children that are c	Is 1:4
they are all c	Jer 6:28

CORRUPTETH

thief approacheth, neither moth c	Lk 12:33

CORRUPTIBLE

into an image made like to c man	Rom 1:23
they do it to obtain a c crown	1Cor 9:25
For this c must put on	1Cor 15:53
So when this c shall have put on	1Cor 15:54
were not redeemed with c things	1Pet 1:18
Being born again, not of c seed	1Pet 1:23
the heart, in that which is not c	1Pet 3:4

CORRUPTING

him the daughter of women, c her	Dan 11:17

CORRUPTION

because their c is in them	Lev 22:25
the right hand of the mount of c	2Kin 23:13
I have said to c, Thou art my	Job 17:14
suffer thine Holy One to see c	Ps 16:10
still live for ever, and not see c	Ps 49:9
delivered it from the pit of c	Is 38:17
was turned in me into c, and I	Dan 10:8
thou broughtest up my life from	Jonah 2:6
suffer thine Holy One to see c	Acts 2:27
hell, neither his flesh did see c	Acts 2:31
dead, now no more to return to c	Acts 13:34
suffer thine Holy One to see c	Acts 13:35
laid unto his fathers, and saw c	Acts 13:36
whom God raised again, saw no c	Acts 13:37
of c into the glorious liberty of	Rom 8:21
It is sown in c	1Cor 15:42
neither doth c inherit	1Cor 15:50
flesh shall of the flesh reap c	Gal 6:8
having escaped the c that is in	2Pet 1:4
utterly perish in their own c	2Pet 2:12
themselves are the servants of c	2Pet 2:19

CORRUPTLY

And the people did yet c	2Chr 27:2
We have dealt very c against thee	Neh 1:7

COSAM (co'-sam) Son of Elmodam; ancestor of Jesus

of Addi, which was the son of C	Lk 3:28

COST

we eaten at all of the king's c	2Sa 19:42
of that which doth c me nothing	2Sa 24:24
offer burnt offerings without c	1Chr 21:24
not down first, and counteth the c	Lk 14:28

COSTLINESS

in the sea by reason of her c	Rev 18:19

COSTLY

c stones, and hewed stones, to lay	1Kin 5:17
All these were of c stones	1Kin 7:9
And the foundation was of c stones	1Kin 7:10
And above were c stones, after the	1Kin 7:11
of ointment of spikenard, very c	Jn 12:3
or gold, or pearls, or c array	1Ti 2:9

COTES

manner of beasts, and c for flocks	2Chr 32:28

COTTAGE

Zion is left as a c in a vineyard	Is 1:8
and shall be removed like a c	Is 24:20

COTTAGES

c for shepherds, and folds for	Zeph 2:6

COUCH

he went up to my c	Gen 49:4
my c shall ease my complaint	Job 7:13
When they c in their dens, and	Job 38:40
I water my c with my tears	Ps 6:6
of a bed, and in Damascus in a c	Amos 3:12
his c into the midst before Jesus	Lk 5:19
thee, Arise, and take up thy c	Lk 5:24

COUCHED

he c as a lion, and as an old lion	Gen 49:9
He c, he lay down as a lion, and	Num 24:9

COUCHES

stretch themselves upon their c	Amos 6:4
and laid them on beds and c	Acts 5:15

COUCHETH

and for the deep that c beneath	Deut 33:13

COUCHING

ass c down between two burdens	Gen 49:14

COUCHINGPLACE

and the Ammonites a c for flocks	Eze 25:5

COULD

so that they c not dwell together	Gen 13:6
were dim, so that he c not see	Gen 27:1
wherein they were strangers c not	Gen 36:7
c not speak peaceably unto him	Gen 37:4
but there was none that c	Gen 41:8
it c not be known that they had	Gen 41:21
was none that c declare it to me	Gen 41:24
c we certainly know that he would	Gen 43:7
Then Joseph c not refrain himself	Gen 45:1
his brethren c not answer him	Gen 45:3
dim for age, so that he c not see	Gen 48:10
when she c not longer hide him	Ex 2:3
the Egyptians c not drink of the	Ex 7:21
for they c not drink of the water	Ex 7:24
bring forth lice, but they c not	Ex 8:18
the magicians c not stand before	Ex 9:11
c not tarry, neither had they	Ex 12:39
they c not drink of the waters of	Ex 15:23
that they c not keep the passover	Num 9:6
the children of Israel c not	Josh 7:12
of Judah c not drive them out	Josh 15:63
Yet the children of Manasseh c	Josh 17:12
but c not drive out the	Judg 1:19
so that they c not any longer	Judg 2:14
so that he c not draw the dagger	Judg 3:22
that he c not do it by day, that	Judg 6:27
for he c not frame to pronounce	Judg 12:6
they c not in three days expound	Judg 14:14
sojourn where he c find a place	Judg 17:8
every one c sling stones at an	Judg 20:16
rose up before one c know another	Ruth 3:14
to wax dim, that he c not see	1Sa 3:2
eyes were dim, that he c not see	1Sa 4:15
sought him, he c not be found	1Sa 10:21
and went whithersoever they c go	1Sa 23:13
c not go over the brook Besor	1Sa 30:10
that they c not follow David	1Sa 30:21
he c not live after that he was	2Sa 1:10
he c not answer Abner a word	2Sa 3:11
c not find them, they returned to	2Sa 17:20
them, that they c not arise	2Sa 22:39
how that David my father c not	1Kin 5:3
that c not be told nor numbered	1Kin 8:5
So that the priests c not stand	1Kin 8:11
so that he c not pull it in again	1Kin 13:4
But Ahijah c not see	1Kin 14:4
king of Edom: but they c not	2Kin 3:26
And they c not eat thereof	2Kin 4:40
Ahaz, but c not overcome him	2Kin 16:5
c use both the right hand and the	1Chr 12:2
that c handle shield and buckler	1Chr 12:8
fifty thousand, which c keep rank	1Chr 12:33
that c keep rank, came with a	1Chr 12:38
But David c not go before it to	1Chr 21:30
of the brass c not be found out	2Chr 4:18
which c not be told nor numbered	2Chr 5:6
So that the priests c not stand	2Chr 5:14
the priests c enter into the	2Chr 7:2
and c not withstand them	2Chr 13:7
that they c not recover	2Chr 14:13
more than they c carry away	2Chr 20:25
that c handle spear and shield	2Chr 25:5
which c not deliver their own	2Chr 25:15
so that they c not flay all the	2Chr 29:34
For they c not keep it at that	2Chr 30:3
that c deliver his people out of	2Chr 32:14
all that c skill of instruments	2Chr 34:12
but they c not shew their	Ezr 2:59
So that the people c not discern	Ezr 3:13
that they c not cause them to	Ezr 6:20
but they c not shew their	Neh 7:61
and women, and all that c hear with	Neh 8:2
women, and those that c understand	Neh 8:3
c not speak in the Jews' language	Neh 13:24
On that night c not the king	Est 6:1
tongue, although the enemy c not	Est 7:4
and no man c withstand them	Est 9:2
but I c not discern the form	Job 4:16
I also c speak as ye do	Job 16:4
c heap up words against you, and	Job 16:4
of his highness I c not endure	Job 31:23
sought him, but he c not be found	Ps 37:36
then I c have borne it	Ps 55:12

COULD

they have more than heart c wish	Ps 73:7
floods, that they c not drink	Ps 78:44
sought him, but I c not find him	Song 3:1
What c have been done more to my	Is 5:4
but c not prevail against it	Is 7:1
a people that c not profit them	Is 30:5
they c not well strengthen their	Is 33:23
they c not spread the sail	Is 33:23
I asked of them, c answer a word	Is 41:28
they c not deliver the burden	Is 46:2
all ashamed, neither c they blush	Jer 6:15
all ashamed, neither c they blush	Jer 8:12
yet my mind c not be toward this	Jer 15:1
with forbearing, and I c not stay	Jer 20:9
which c not be eaten, they were	Jer 24:2
So that the LORD c no longer bear	Jer 44:22
so that men c not touch their	Lam 4:14
for a nation that c not save us	Lam 4:17
the garden of God c not hide him	Eze 31:8
a river that I c not pass over	Eze 47:5
a river that c not be passed over	Eze 47:5
but they c not read the writing	Dan 5:8
but they c not shew the	Dan 5:15
but they c find none occasion nor	Dan 6:4
that c deliver out of his hand	Dan 8:4
there was none that c deliver the	Dan 8:7
yet c he not heal you, nor cure	Hos 5:13
but they c not	Jonah 1:13
disciples, and they c not cure him	Mt 17:16
Why c not we cast him out	Mt 17:19
c ye not watch with me one hour	Mt 26:40
saw that he c prevail nothing	Mt 27:24
insomuch that Jesus c no more	Mk 1:45
when they c not come nigh unto	Mk 2:4
so that they c not so much as eat	Mk 3:20
no man c bind him, no, not with	Mk 5:3
neither c any man tame him	Mk 5:4
he c there do no mighty work	Mk 6:5
but she c not	Mk 6:19
but he c not be hid	Mk 7:24
and they c not	Mk 9:18
Why c not we cast him out	Mk 9:28
She hath done what she c	Mk 14:8
out, he c not speak unto them	Lk 1:22
when they c not find by what way	Lk 5:19
that house, and c not shake it	Lk 6:48
c not come at him for the press	Lk 8:19
neither c be healed of any	Lk 8:43
and they c not	Lk 9:40
c in no wise lift up herself	Lk 13:11
they c not answer him again to	Lk 14:6
c not for the press, because he	Lk 19:3
c not find what they might do	Lk 19:48
that they c not tell whence it	Lk 20:7
they c not take hold of his words	Lk 20:26
were not of God, he c do nothing	Jn 9:33
C not this man, which opened the	Jn 11:37
Therefore they c not believe	Jn 12:39
c not contain the books that	Jn 21:25
they c say nothing against it	Acts 4:14
was I, that I c withstand God	Acts 11:17
from which ye c not be justified	Acts 13:39
when he c not know the certainty	Acts 21:34
when I c not see for the glory of	Acts 22:11
Paul, which they c not prove	Acts 25:7
c not bear up into the wind, we	Acts 27:15
commanded that they which c swim	Acts 27:43
For what the law c not do	Rom 8:3
For I c wish that myself were	Rom 9:3
c not speak unto you as unto	1Cor 3:1
so that I c remove mountains, and	1Cor 13:2
c not stedfastly behold the face	2Cor 3:7
that the children of Israel c not	2Cor 3:13
Would to God ye c bear with a	2Cor 11:1
law given which c have given life	Gal 3:21
when we c no longer forbear	1Th 3:1
when I c no longer forbear, I	1Th 3:5
So we see that they c not enter	Heb 3:19
because he c swear by no greater	Heb 6:13
that c not make him that did the	Heb 9:9
(For they c not endure that which	Heb 12:20
multitude, which no man c number	Rev 7:9
no man c learn that song but the	Rev 14:3

COULDEST

and done evil things as thou c	Jer 3:5
them, and yet c not be satisfied	Eze 16:28
c not thou watch one hour	Mk 14:37
Thou c have no power at all	Jn 19:11

COULDST

seeing thou c reveal this secret	Dan 2:47

COULTER

every man his share, and his c	1Sa 13:20

COULTERS

for the mattocks, and for the c	1Sa 13:21

COUNCIL

the princes of Judah and their c	Ps 68:27
Raca, shall be in danger of the c	Mt 5:22
held a c against him, how they	Mt 12:14
priests, and elders, and all the c	Mt 26:59
all the c sought for witness	Mk 14:55
elders and scribes and the whole c	Mk 15:1
together, and led him into their c	Lk 22:66
priests and the Pharisees a c	Jn 11:47
them to go aside out of the c	Acts 4:15
him, and called the c together	Acts 5:21
them, they set them before the c	Acts 5:27
Then stood them up one in the c	Acts 5:34
from the presence of the c	Acts 5:41

him, and brought him to the c............ Acts 6:12
And all that sat in the c, looking...... Acts 6:15
priests and all their c to appear....... Acts 22:30
Paul, earnestly beholding the c......... Acts 23:1
Pharisees, he cried out in the c........ Acts 23:6
Now therefore ye with the c............. Acts 23:15
down Paul to morrow into the c.......... Acts 23:20
I brought him forth into their c........ Acts 23:28
in me, while I stood before the c....... Acts 24:20
when he had conferred with the c........ Acts 25:12

COUNCILS
they will deliver you up to the c....... Mt 10:17
they shall deliver you up to c.......... Mk 13:9

COUNSEL
unto my voice, I will give thee c....... Ex 18:19
who shall ask c for him after the....... Num 27:21
Israel, through the c of Balaam......... Num 31:16
For they are a nation void of c......... Deut 32:28
asked not c at the mouth of the......... Josh 9:14
And they said unto him, Ask c........... Judg 18:5
give here your advice and c............. Judg 20:7
asked c of God, and said, Which of...... Judg 20:18
asked c of the LORD, saying............. Judg 20:23
And Saul asked c of God, Shall I........ 1Sa 14:37
turn the c of Ahithophel into........... 2Sa 15:31
for me defeat the c of Ahithophel....... 2Sa 15:34
Give c among you what we shall do....... 2Sa 16:20
the c of Ahithophel, which he........... 2Sa 16:23
so was all the c of Ahithophel.......... 2Sa 16:23
The c that Ahithophel hath given........ 2Sa 17:7
Therefore I c that all Israel be........ 2Sa 17:11
The c of Hushai the Archite is.......... 2Sa 17:14
better than the c of Ahithophel......... 2Sa 17:14
defeat the good c of Ahithophel......... 2Sa 17:14
and thus did Ahithophel c Absalom....... 2Sa 17:15
saw that his c was not followed......... 2Sa 17:23
They shall surely ask c at Abel......... 2Sa 20:18
let me, I pray thee, give thee c........ 1Kin 1:12
he forsook the c of the old men......... 1Kin 12:8
What c give ye that we may answer....... 1Kin 12:9
old men's c that they gave him.......... 1Kin 12:13
them after the c of the young men....... 1Kin 12:14
Whereupon the king took................. 1Kin 12:28
took c with his servants, saying........ 2Kin 6:8
are but vain words; I have c............ 2Kin 18:20
also for asking c of one that had....... 1Chr 10:13
king Rehoboam took c with the old....... 2Chr 10:6
What c give ye me to return............. 2Chr 10:6
But he forsook the c which the.......... 2Chr 10:8
took c with the young men that.......... 2Chr 10:8
forsook the c of the old men............ 2Chr 10:13
He walked also after their c............ 2Chr 22:5
Art thou made of the king's c........... 2Chr 25:16
and hast not hearkened unto my c........ 2Chr 25:16
For the king had taken c, and his....... 2Chr 30:2
the whole assembly took c to keep....... 2Chr 30:23
He took c with his princes and his...... 2Chr 32:3
according to the c of my lord........... Ezr 10:3
according to the c of the princes....... Ezr 10:8
God had brought their c to nought....... Neh 4:15
and let us take c together.............. Neh 6:7
the c of the froward is carried........ Job 5:13
and shine upon the c of the wicked...... Job 10:3
is wisdom and strength, he hath c....... Job 12:13
his own c shall cast him down........... Job 18:7
the c of the wicked is far from......... Job 21:16
but the c of the wicked is far.......... Job 22:18
waited, and kept silence at my c........ Job 29:21
c by words without knowledge............ Job 38:2
that hideth c without knowledge......... Job 42:3
not in the c of the ungodly............ Ps 1:1
and the rulers take c together.......... Ps 2:2
long shall I take c in my soul.......... Ps 13:2
Ye have shamed the c of the poor........ Ps 14:6
the LORD, who hath given me c........... Ps 16:7
own heart, and fulfil all thy c......... Ps 20:4
while they took c together............. Ps 31:13
The LORD bringeth the c of the.......... Ps 33:10
The c of the LORD standeth for.......... Ps 33:11
We took sweet c together, and.......... Ps 55:14
from the secret c of the wicked........ Ps 64:2
wait for my soul take c together....... Ps 71:10
Thou shalt guide me with thy c......... Ps 73:24
taken crafty c against thy people...... Ps 83:3
they waited not for his c.............. Ps 106:13
they provoked him with their c......... Ps 106:43
contemned the c of the most High....... Ps 107:11
ye have set at nought all my c......... Prov 1:25
They would none of my c................ Prov 1:30
C is mine, and sound wisdom............ Prov 8:14
Where no c is, the people fall......... Prov 11:14
he that hearkeneth unto c is wise...... Prov 12:15
Without c purposes are................. Prov 15:22
Hear c, and receive instruction,...... Prov 19:20
nevertheless the c of the LORD......... Prov 19:21
C in the heart of man is like.......... Prov 20:5
Every purpose is established by c...... Prov 20:18
nor c against the LORD................. Prov 21:30
For by wise c thou shalt make thy...... Prov 24:6
of a man's friend by hearty c.......... Prov 27:9
I c thee to keep the king's............ Eccl 8:2
let the c of the Holy One of........... Is 5:19
have taken evil c against thee......... Is 7:5
Take c together, and it shall come..... Is 8:10
and understanding, the c of the........ Is 11:2
Take c, execute judgment............... Is 16:3
and I will destroy thy c thereof....... Is 19:3
the c of the wise counsellors of....... Is 19:11
because of the c of the LORD of........ Is 19:17

hath taken this c against Tyre......... Is 23:8
of hosts, which is wonderful in c...... Is 28:29
to hide their c from the LORD.......... Is 29:15
saith the LORD, that take c............ Is 30:1
they are but vain words) I have c...... Is 36:5
With whom took he c, and who........... Is 40:14
And performeth the c of his............ Is 44:26
yea, let them take c together.......... Is 45:21
My c shall stand, and I will do........ Is 46:10
executeth my c from a far country...... Is 46:11
nor c from the wise, nor the word...... Jer 18:18
all their c against me to slay me...... Jer 18:23
I will make void the c of Judah........ Jer 19:7
hath stood in the c of the LORD........ Jer 23:18
But if they had stood in my c.......... Jer 23:22
Great in c, and mighty in work......... Jer 32:19
and if I give thee c, wilt thou........ Jer 38:15
is c perished from the prudent......... Jer 49:7
Therefore hear the c of the LORD....... Jer 49:20
Babylon hath taken c against you....... Jer 49:30
hear ye the c of the LORD.............. Jer 50:45
priest, and c from the ancients....... Eze 7:26
give wicked c in this city............. Eze 11:2
Then Daniel answered with c............ Dan 2:14
let my c be acceptable unto thee,...... Dan 4:27
My people ask c at their stocks........ Hos 4:12
shall be ashamed of his own c.......... Hos 10:6
neither understand they his c.......... Mic 4:12
the c of peace shall be between........ Zec 6:13
took c how they might entangle......... Mt 22:15
elders of the people took c............ Mt 27:1
And they took c, and bought with....... Mt 27:7
with the elders, and had taken c....... Mt 28:12
straightway took c with the............ Mk 3:6
lawyers rejected the c of God.......... Lk 7:30
same had not consented to the c........ Lk 23:51
took c together for to put him to...... Jn 11:53
which gave c to the Jews, that it...... Jn 18:14
delivered by the determinate c......... Acts 2:23
by c determined before to be........... Acts 4:28
the heart, and took c to slay them..... Acts 5:33
for if this c or this work be of....... Acts 5:38
the Jews took c to kill him............ Acts 9:23
declare unto you all the c of God...... Acts 20:27
the soldiers' c was to kill the........ Acts 27:42
after the c of his own will............ Eph 1:11
promise the immutability of his c...... Heb 6:17
took c to buy of my gold tried......... Rev 3:18

COUNSELED
How hast thou c him that hath no....... Job 26:3

COUNSELLED
which he c in those days, was as....... 2Sa 16:23
and thus and thus have I c............. 2Sa 17:11
hath Ahithophel c against you.......... 2Sa 17:21

COUNSELLOR
the Gilonite, David's c, from his...... 2Sa 15:12
for Zechariah his son, a wise c........ 1Chr 26:14
Jonathan David's uncle was a c......... 1Chr 27:32
And Ahithophel was the king's c........ 1Chr 27:33
mother was his c to do wickedly........ 2Chr 22:3
and the honourable man, and the c...... Is 3:3
name shall be called Wonderful, C...... Is 9:6
or being his c hath taught him......... Is 40:13
among them, and there was no c......... Is 41:28
is thy c perished?..................... Mic 4:9
evil against the LORD, a wicked c...... Nah 1:11
of Arimathaea, an honourable c......... Mk 15:43
there was a man named Joseph, a c...... Lk 23:50
or who hath been his c................. Rom 11:34

COUNSELLORS
for they were his c after the.......... 2Chr 22:4
And hired c against them, to........... Ezr 4:5
of the king, and of his seven c........ Ezr 7:14
his c have freely offered unto......... Ezr 7:15
unto me before the king, and his c..... Ezr 7:28
our God, which the king, and his c..... Ezr 7:28
c of the earth, which built............ Job 3:14
He leadeth c away spoiled, and......... Job 12:17
also are my delight, and my c.......... Ps 119:24
multitude of c there is safety......... Prov 11:14
but to the c of peace is joy........... Prov 12:20
of c they are established.............. Prov 15:22
in multitude of c there is safety...... Prov 24:6
thy c as at the beginning.............. Is 1:26
the counsel of the wise c.............. Is 19:11
the judges, the treasurers, the c...... Dan 3:2
the judges, the treasurers, the c...... Dan 3:3
and spake, and said unto his c......... Dan 3:24
and captains, and the king's c......... Dan 3:27
and my c and my lords sought unto...... Dan 4:36
governors, and the princes, the c...... Dan 6:7

COUNSELS
it is turned round about by his c...... Job 37:12
let them fall by their own c........... Ps 5:10
and they walked in their own c......... Ps 81:12
shalt attain unto wise c............... Prov 1:5
but the c of the wicked are............ Prov 12:5
to thee excellent things in c.......... Prov 22:20
thy c of old are faithfulness and...... Is 25:1
wearied in the multitude of thy c...... Jer 7:24
their ear, but walked in the c......... Jer 7:24
them, because of their own c........... Hos 11:6
of Ahab, and ye walk in their c........ Mic 6:16
make manifest the c of the hearts..... 1Cor 4:5

COUNT
shall make your c for the lamb......... Ex 12:4
then ye shall c the fruit thereof...... Lev 19:23

ye shall c unto you from the........... Lev 23:15
Then let him c the years of the....... Lev 25:27
jubile, then he shall c with him....... Lev 25:52
Who can c the dust of Jacob, and....... Num 23:10
C not thine handmaid for a............. 1Sa 1:16
and my maids, c me for a stranger...... Job 19:15
he see my ways, and c all my steps..... Job 31:4
The LORD shall c, when he writeth...... Ps 87:6
If I should c them, they are more...... Ps 139:18
I c them mine enemies.................. Ps 139:22
Shall I c them pure with the........... Mic 6:11
neither c I my life dear unto.......... Acts 20:24
I c all things but loss for the........ Phil 3:8
do c them but dung, that I may......... Phil 3:8
Brethren, I c not myself to have....... Phil 3:13
that our God would c you worthy........ 2Th 1:11
Yet c him not as an enemy, but......... 2Th 3:15
servants as are under the yoke c....... 1Ti 6:1
If thou c me therefore a partner,..... Philem 1:17
c it all joy when ye fall into......... Jas 1:2
we c them happy which endure.......... Jas 5:11
as they that c it pleasure to......... 2Pet 2:13
promise, as some men c slackness...... 2Pet 3:9
the c the number of the beast......... Rev 13:18

COUNTED
he c it to him for righteousness...... Gen 15:6
that shall be c stolen with me........ Gen 30:33
were c of my son's strangers.......... Gen 31:15
of testimony, as it was c............. Ex 38:21
as far as the fields of the country... Lev 25:31
then it shall be c unto the........... Num 18:30
which is c to the Canaanite........... Josh 13:3
son Solomon shall be c offenders...... 1Kin 1:21
be numbered nor c for multitude....... 1Kin 3:8
Benjamin c he not among them.......... 1Chr 21:6
as they were c by number of names..... 1Chr 23:24
for they were c faithful, and......... Neh 13:13
Wherefore are we c as beasts.......... Job 18:3
Darts are c as stubble................ Job 41:29
we are c as sheep for the............. Ps 44:22
I am c with them that go down......... Ps 88:4
And that was c unto him for........... Ps 106:31
he holdeth his peace, is c wise....... Prov 17:28
it shall be c a curse to him.......... Prov 27:14
hoofs shall be c like flint........... Is 5:28
fruitful field be c for a forest...... Is 32:15
where is he that c the towers......... Is 33:18
are c to him as the small dust of..... Is 40:15
they are c to him less than........... Is 40:17
but they were c as a strange.......... Hos 8:12
because they c him as a prophet....... Mt 14:5
for all men c John, that he was a..... Mk 11:32
rejoicing that they were c worthy..... Acts 5:41
they c the price of them, and......... Acts 19:19
be c for circumcision................. Rom 2:26
God, and it was c unto him for........ Rom 4:3
his faith is c for righteousness...... Rom 4:5
of the promise are c for the seed..... Rom 9:8
those I c loss for Christ............. Phil 3:7
that ye may be c worthy of the........ 2Th 1:5
me, for that he c me faithful......... 1Ti 1:12
well be c worthy of double honour..... 1Ti 5:17
For this man was c worthy of more..... Heb 3:3
But he whose descent is not........... Heb 7:6
hath c the blood of the covenant,.... Heb 10:29

COUNTENANCE
was very wroth, and his c fell........ Gen 4:5
and why is thy c fallen............... Gen 4:6
And Jacob beheld the c of Laban....... Gen 31:2
unto them, I see your father's c...... Gen 31:5
Neither shalt thou c a poor man....... Ex 23:3
The LORD lift up his c upon thee...... Num 6:26
A nation of fierce c, which shall..... Deut 28:50
his c was like the c of............... Judg 13:6
did eat, and her c was no more sad.... 1Sa 1:18
unto Samuel, Look not on his c........ 1Sa 16:7
ruddy, and withal of a beautiful c.... 1Sa 16:12
a youth, and ruddy, and of a fair c... 1Sa 17:42
and of a beautiful c................. 1Sa 25:3
she was a woman of a fair c........... 2Sa 14:27
And he settled his c stedfastly....... 2Kin 8:11
said unto me, Why is thy c sad........ Neh 2:2
why should not my c be sad............ Neh 2:3
thou changest his c, and sendest...... Job 14:20
the light of my c they cast not....... Job 29:24
up the light of thy c upon us......... Ps 4:6
through the pride of his c............ Ps 10:4
for his c doth behold the upright..... Ps 11:7
him exceeding glad with thy c......... Ps 21:6
praise him for the help of his c...... Ps 42:5
him, who is the health of my c....... Ps 42:11
him, who is the health of my c....... Ps 43:5
thine arm, and the light of thy c..... Ps 44:3
perish at the rebuke of thy c......... Ps 80:16
O LORD, in the light of thy c......... Ps 89:15
secret sins in the light of thy c..... Ps 90:8
A merry heart maketh a cheerful c..... Prov 15:13
the light of the king's c is life..... Prov 16:15
so doth an angry c a backbiting....... Prov 25:23
sharpeneth the c of his friend........ Prov 27:17
of the c the heart is made better..... Eccl 7:3
of the stairs, let me see thy c....... Song 2:14
thy voice, and thy c is comely........ Song 2:14
his c is as Lebanon, excellent as..... Song 5:15
The shew of their c doth witness...... Is 3:9
they shall be troubled in their c..... Eze 27:35
the c of the children that eat of..... Dan 1:13
Then the king's c was changed......... Dan 5:6
his c was changed in him, and his..... Dan 5:9

thee, nor let thy c be changed .... Dan 5:10
me, and my c changed in me .... Dan 7:28
to the full, a king of fierce c .... Dan 8:23
as the hypocrites, of a sad c .... Mt 6:16
His c was like lightning, and his ...... Mt 28:3
the fashion of his c was altered .... Lk 9:29
make me full of joy with thy c .... Acts 2:28
of Moses for the glory of his c 2Cor 3:7
his c was as the sun shineth in .... Rev 1:16

COUNTENANCES
Then let our c be looked upon .... Dan 1:13
ten days their c appeared fairer .... Dan 1:15

COUNTERVAIL
could not c the king's damage .... Est 7:4

COUNTETH
he c me unto him as one of his .... Job 19:11
me, he c me for his enemy,.............. Job 33:10
c the cost, whether he have .... Lk 14:28

COUNTING
c one by one, to find out the .... Eccl 7:27

COUNTRIES
after their tongues, in their c .... Gen 10:20
thy seed, I will give all these c .... Gen 26:3
give unto thy seed all these c .... Gen 26:4
all c came into Egypt to Joseph .... Gen 41:57
These are the c which Moses did ...... Josh 13:32
these are the c which the .... Josh 14:1
and her towns, even three c .... Josh 17:11
they among all the gods of the c 2Kin 18:35
fame and of glory throughout all c 1Chr 22:5
and over all the kingdoms of the c 1Chr 29:30
throughout all the c of Judah 2Chr 11:23
service of the kingdoms of the c 2Chr 12:8
upon all the inhabitants of the c 2Chr 15:5
on all the kingdoms of those c 2Chr 20:29
c that pertained to the children 2Chr 34:33
because of the people of those c .... Ezr 3:3
ruled over all c beyond the river ...... Ezr 4:20
shall wound the heads over many c ... Ps 110:6
and give ear, all ye of far c .... Is 8:9
waste all the nations, and their c ...... Is 37:18
all c whither I have driven them .... Jer 23:3
from all c whither I had driven......... Jer 23:8
prophesied both against many c .... Jer 28:8
I will gather them out of all c .... Jer 32:37
Edom, and that were in all the c .... Jer 40:11
c that are round about her .... Eze 5:5
the c that are round about her .... Eze 5:6
shall be scattered through the c .... Eze 6:8
I have scattered them among the c .... Eze 11:16
in the c where they shall come......... Eze 11:16
assemble you out of the c where .... Eze 11:17
and disperse them in the c .... Eze 12:15
and disperse them through the c ...... Eze 20:23
heathen, as the families of the c ...... Eze 20:32
of the c wherein ye are scattered ...... Eze 20:34
gather you out of the c wherein........ Eze 20:41
heathen, and a mocking to all c .... Eze 22:4
and disperse thee in the c .... Eze 22:15
cause thee to perish out of the c ...... Eze 25:7
midst of the c that are desolate .... Eze 29:12
will disperse them through the c ...... Eze 29:12
midst of the c that are desolate .... Eze 30:7
will disperse them through the c ...... Eze 30:23
and disperse them among the c .... Eze 30:26
into the c which thou hast not .... Eze 32:9
people, and gather them from the c ... Eze 34:13
these two c shall be mine, and we .... Eze 35:10
they were dispersed through the c ..... Eze 36:19
and gather you out of all c .... Eze 36:24
through all the c whither thou .... Dan 9:7
and he shall enter into the c .... Dan 11:40
many c shall be overthrown .... Dan 11:41
forth his hand also upon the c .... Dan 11:42
they shall remember me in far c .... Zec 10:9
that are in the c enter thereinto........ Lk 21:21

COUNTRY
unto Abram, Get thee out of thy c ..... Gen 12:1
smote all the c of the Amalekites...... Gen 14:7
the smoke of the c went up as the .... Gen 19:28
from thence toward the south c .... Gen 20:1
But thou shalt go unto my c .... Gen 24:4
for he dwelt in the south c .... Gen 24:62
lived, eastward, unto the east c .... Gen 25:6
It must not be so done in our c .... Gen 29:26
unto mine own place, and to my ...... Gen 30:25
the land of Seir, the c of Edom .... Gen 32:3
saidst unto me, Return unto thy c ..... Gen 32:9
Hamor the Hivite, prince of the c ...... Gen 34:2
went into the c from the face of .... Gen 36:6
us, and took us for spies of the c ...... Gen 42:30
And the man, the lord of the c .... Gen 42:33
land of Egypt, in the c of Goshen ..... Gen 47:27
whether it be one of your own c .... Lev 16:29
whether it be one of your own c .... Lev 17:15
as for one of your own c .... Lev 24:22
be counted as the fields of the c ...... Lev 25:31
All that are born of the c shall .... Num 15:13
pass, I pray thee, through thy c .... Num 20:17
valley, that is in the c of Moab .... Num 21:20
Even the c which the LORD smote...... Num 32:4
the cities of the c round about .... Num 32:33
the c of Argob unto the coasts of ..... Deut 3:14
in the wilderness, in the plain c ...... Deut 4:43
that I am come unto the c which ...... Deut 26:3
of Israel to search out the c .... Josh 2:2

be come to search out all the c .... Josh 2:3
of the c do faint because of us .... Josh 2:24
two men that had spied out the c ..... Josh 6:22
was noised throughout all the c .... Josh 6:27
them, saying, Go up and view the c ... Josh 7:2
Israel, We be come from a far c .... Josh 9:6
From a very far c thy servants.......... Josh 9:9
inhabitants of our c spake to us .... Josh 9:11
smote all the c of the hills .... Josh 10:40
all the c of Goshen, even unto .... Josh 10:41
the hills, and all the south c .... Josh 11:16
the kings of the c which Joshua .... Josh 12:7
the wilderness, and in the south c .... Josh 12:8
of the hill c from Lebanon unto........ Josh 13:6
dukes of Sihon, dwelling in the c ..... Josh 13:21
then get thee up to the wood c .... Josh 17:15
made an end of dividing the c .... Josh 19:51
is Hebron, in the hill c of Judah ...... Josh 21:11
to go unto the c of Gilead .... Josh 22:9
the c was in quietness forty............. Judg 8:28
the inhabitants of that c .... Judg 11:21
in Ajalon in the c of Zebulun.......... Judg 12:12
enemy, and the destroyer of our c ..... Judg 16:24
went to spy out the c of Laish .... Judg 18:14
sent her throughout all the c of .... Judg 20:6
went to sojourn in the c of Moab ...... Ruth 1:1
And they came into the c of Moab ..... Ruth 1:2
might return from the c of Moab .... Ruth 1:6
for she had heard in the c of .... Ruth 1:6
returned out of the c of Moab .... Ruth 1:22
with Naomi out of the c of Moab ...... Ruth 2:6
come again out of the c of Moab ...... Ruth 4:3
the ark of the LORD was in the c 1Sa 6:1
of c villages, even unto the 1Sa 6:18
the camp from the c round about 1Sa 14:21
me a place in some town in the c 1Sa 27:5
time that David dwelt in the c of 1Sa 27:7
in the c of the Philistines 1Sa 27:11
all the c wept with a loud voice,....... 2Sa 15:23
over the face of all the c 2Sa 18:8
in the c of Benjamin in Zelah.......... 2Sa 21:14
son of Uri was in the c of Gilead...... 1Kin 4:19
in the c of Sihon king of the 1Kin 4:19
of all the children of the east c 1Kin 4:30
of a far c for thy name's sake 1Kin 8:41
she turned and went to her own c 1Kin 10:13
and of the governors of the c 1Kin 10:15
that I may go to mine own c 1Kin 11:21
thou seekest to go to thine own c 1Kin 11:22
but the Syrians filled the c 1Kin 20:27
city, and every man to his own c 1Kin 22:36
the c was filled with water.............. 2Kin 3:20
the Moabites, even in their c 2Kin 3:24
their c out of mine hand, that 2Kin 18:35
said, They are come from a far c 2Kin 20:14
begat children in the c of Moab 1Chr 8:8
wasted the c of the children of 1Chr 20:1
but is come from a far c for thy 2Chr 6:32
governors of the c brought gold........ 2Chr 9:14
much cattle, both in the low c 2Chr 26:10
invaded the cities of the low c 2Chr 28:18
to city through the c of Ephraim....... 2Chr 30:10
the plain c round about Jerusalem .... Neh 12:28
so is good news from a far c .... Prov 25:25
Your c is desolate, your cities .... Is 1:7
They come from a far c, from the ..... Is 13:5
thee like a ball into a large c .... Is 22:18
are come from a far c unto the .... Is 39:3
executeth my counsel from a far c .... Is 46:11
I brought you into a plentiful c .... Jer 2:7
that watchers come from a far c .... Jer 4:16
and the sweet cane from a far c .... Jer 6:20
a people cometh from the north c ..... Jer 6:22
of them that dwell in a far c .... Jer 8:19
commotion out of the north c .... Jer 10:22
no more, nor see his native c .... Jer 22:10
that bare thee, into another c .... Jer 22:26
of Israel out of the north c .... Jer 31:8
will bring them from the north c ...... Jer 31:8
which is in the c of Benjamin .... Jer 32:8
in the c of Pathros, saying,............. Jer 44:1
north c by the river Euphrates......... Jer 46:10
the remnant of the c of Caphtor ...... Jer 47:4
judgment is come upon the plain c ... Jer 48:21
of great nations from the north .... Jer 50:9
us go every one into his own c .... Jer 50:16
out of the c where they sojourn .... Eze 20:38
into the c for the which I lifted .... Eze 20:42
his frontiers, the glory of the c .... Eze 25:9
the c shall be destitute of that .... Eze 32:15
all the inhabited places of the c ...... Eze 34:13
issue out toward the east c .... Eze 47:8
be unto you as born in the c .... Eze 47:22
And Jacob fled into the c of Syria ..... Hos 12:12
what is thy c? .... Jonah 1:8
my saying, when I was yet in my c .... Jonah 4:2
therein go forth into the north c ...... Zec 6:6
go forth toward the south c .... Zec 6:6
c have quieted my spirit in the .... Zec 6:8
quieted my spirit in the north c .... Zec 6:8
east c, and from the west c .... Zec 8:7
into their own c another way,........... Mt 2:12
side into the c of the Gergesenes..... Mt 8:28
abroad his fame in all that c .... Mt 9:31
when he was come into his own c ..... Mt 13:54
without honour, save in his own c .... Mt 13:57
out into all that c round about .... Mt 14:35
husbandmen, and went into a far c ... Mt 21:33
as a man travelling into a far c .... Mt 25:14

into the c of the Gadarenes............. Mk 5:1
not send them away out of the c ...... Mk 5:10
told it in the city, and in the c .... Mk 5:14
thence, and came into his own c ...... Mk 6:1
without honour, but in his own c ..... Mk 6:4
may go into the c round about......... Mk 6:36
into villages, or cities, or c .... Mk 6:56
husbandmen, and went into a far c ... Mk 12:1
passed by, coming out of the c .... Mk 15:21
they walked, and went into the c ...... Mk 16:12
went into the hill c with haste......... Lk 1:39
all the hill c of Judaea................... Lk 1:65
And there were in the same c .... Lk 2:8
came into all the c about Jordan...... Lk 3:3
Capernaum, do also here in thy c ..... Lk 4:23
prophet is accepted in his own c ...... Lk 4:24
every place of the c round about ...... Lk 4:37
arrived at the c of the Gadarenes ..... Lk 8:26
told it in the city and in the c .... Lk 8:34
c of the Gadarenes round about .... Lk 8:37
c round about, and lodge, and get .... Lk 9:12
and took his journey into a far c ...... Lk 15:13
himself to a citizen of that c .... Lk 15:15
a far c to receive for himself a .... Lk 19:12
went into a far c for a long time....... Lk 20:9
a Cyrenian, coming out of the c .... Lk 23:26
hath no honour in his own c .... Jn 4:44
unto a c near to the wilderness........ Jn 11:54
many went out of the c up to .... Jn 11:55
a Levite, and of the c of Cyprus .... Acts 4:36
unto him, Get thee out of thy c........ Acts 7:3
because their c was nourished by ..... Acts 12:20
was nourished by the king's c .... Acts 12:20
was with the deputy of the c .... Acts 13:7
and went over all the c of Galatia ..... Acts 18:23
that they drew near to some c .... Acts 27:27
of promise, as in a strange c .... Heb 11:9
plainly that they seek a c .... Heb 11:14
that c from whence they came out .... Heb 11:15
But now they desire a better c .... Heb 11:16

COUNTRYMEN
robbers, in perils by mine own c 2Cor 11:26
like things of your own c 1Th 2:14

COUPLE
c the curtains together with the .... Ex 26:6
thou shalt c five curtains by,........... Ex 26:9
c the tent together, that it may .... Ex 26:11
of brass to c the tent together .... Ex 36:18
for it, to c it together .... Ex 39:4
servant with her, and a c of .... Jdg 19:10
make me a c of cakes in my sight,.... 2Sa 13:6
with a c of asses saddled, and 2Sa 16:1
a chariot with a c of horsemen .... Is 21:7
of men, with a c of horsemen .... Is 21:9

COUPLED
be c together one to another........... Ex 26:3
shall be c one to another............... Ex 26:3
they shall be c together beneath,..... Ex 26:24
they shall be c together above .... Ex 26:24
he c the five curtains one unto....... Ex 36:10
curtains he c one unto another....... Ex 36:10
the c curtains one unto another...... Ex 36:13
he c five curtains by themselves,.... Ex 36:16
And they were c beneath, and .... Ex 36:29
c together at the head thereof,........ Ex 36:29
the two edges was it c together ...... Ex 39:4
chaste conversation c with fear 1Pet 3:2

COUPLETH
of the curtain which c the second ... Ex 26:10
of the curtain which c the second ... Ex 36:17

COUPLING
from the selvedge in the c .... Ex 26:4
curtain, in the c of the second....... Ex 26:4
that is in the c of the second........ Ex 26:5
curtain that is outmost in the c ..... Ex 26:10
over against the other c thereof ...... Ex 28:27
from the selvedge in the c .... Ex 36:11
curtain, in the c of the second....... Ex 36:11
which was in the c of the second.... Ex 36:12
edge of the curtain in the c .... Ex 36:17
over against the other c thereof ...... Ex 39:20

COUPLINGS
buy them stone, and timber for c 2Chr 34:11

COURAGE
And be ye of good c, and bring of ... Num 13:20
Be strong and of a good c, fear ...... Deut 31:6
Israel, Be strong and of a good c ..... Deut 31:7
and said, Be strong and of a good c .. Deut 31:23
Be strong and of a good c............. Josh 1:6
Be strong and of a good c............. Josh 1:9
only be strong and of a good c .... Josh 1:18
remain any more c in any man ...... Josh 2:11
dismayed, be strong and of good c .. Josh 10:25
Be of good c, and let us play the 2Sa 10:12
Be of good c, and let us behave..... 1Chr 19:13
be strong, and of good c............... 1Chr 22:13
his son, Be strong and of good c 1Chr 28:20
of Oded the prophet, he took c....... 2Chr 15:8
be of good c, and do it .... Ezr 10:4
be of good c, and he shall............ Ps 27:14
Be of good c, and he shall............ Ps 31:24
said to his brother, Be of good c ..... Is 41:6
his c against the king of the .... Dan 11:25
saw, he thanked God, and took c ..... Acts 28:15

COURAGEOUS
Only be thou strong and very c .... Josh 1:7
Be ye therefore very c to keep .... Josh 23:6
be c, and be valiant 2Sa 13:28
Be strong and c, be not afraid nor 2Chr 32:7
he that is c among the mighty .... Amos 2:16

COURAGEOUSLY
Deal c, and the LORD shall be with 2Chr 19:11

COURSE
of every c were twenty and four 1Chr 27:1
Over the first c for the first 1Chr 27:2
in his c were twenty and four 1Chr 27:4
over the c of the second month 1Chr 27:4
of his c was Mikloth also the 1Chr 27:4
in his c likewise were twenty and 1Chr 27:4
in his c were twenty and four 1Chr 27:5
in his c was Ammizabad his son 1Chr 27:6
in his c were twenty and 1Chr 27:7
in his c were twenty and four 1Chr 27:7
in his c were twenty and 1Chr 27:8
in his c were twenty and 1Chr 27:9
that ministered to the king by c 1Chr 28:1
and did not then wait by c 1Chr 5:11
sang together by c in praising .... Ezr 3:11
of the earth are out of c .... Ps 82:5
every one turned to his c .... Jer 8:6
their c is evil, and their force .... Jer 23:10
named Zacharias, of the c of Abia .... Lk 1:5
before God in the order of his c .... Lk 1:8
And as John fulfilled his c .... Acts 13:25
with a straight c to Samothracia .... Acts 16:11
that I might finish my c with joy .... Acts 20:24
came with a straight c unto Coos .... Acts 21:1
we had finished our c from Tyre .... Acts 21:7
the most by three, and that by c 1Cor 14:27
according to the c of this world .... Eph 2:2
word of the Lord may have free c 2Th 3:1
good fight, I have finished my c 2Ti 4:7
setteth on fire the c of nature .... Jas 3:6

COURSES
the stars in their c fought .... Judg 5:20
ten thousand a month by c 1Kin 5:14
into c among the sons of Levi 1Chr 23:6
the king in any matter of the c 1Chr 27:1
Also for the c of the priests and 1Chr 28:13
the c of the priests and the 1Chr 28:21
the c of the priests to their 2Chr 8:14
also by their c at every gate 2Chr 8:14
the priest dismissed not the c 2Chr 23:8
appointed the c of the priests 2Chr 31:2
and the Levites after their c 2Chr 31:2
to give to their brethren by c 2Chr 31:15
charges according to their c 2Chr 31:16
in their charges by their c 2Chr 31:17
of your fathers, after your c 2Chr 35:4
place, and the Levites in their c 2Chr 35:10
and the Levites in their c .... Ezr 6:18
grass, as willows by the water c .... Is 44:4

COURT
make the c of the tabernacle .... Ex 27:9
the c of fine twined linen of an .... Ex 27:9
for the breadth of the c on the .... Ex 27:12
the breadth of the c on the east .... Ex 27:13
for the gate of the c shall be an .... Ex 27:16
c shall be filleted with silver .... Ex 27:17
The length of the c shall be an .... Ex 27:18
thereof, and all the pins of the c .... Ex 27:19
The hangings of the c, his .... Ex 35:17
the hanging for the door of the c .... Ex 35:17
tabernacle, and the pins of the c .... Ex 35:18
And he made the c .... Ex 38:9
the c were of fine twined linen .... Ex 38:9
for the other side of the c gate .... Ex 38:15
All the hangings of the c round .... Ex 38:16
all the pillars of the c were .... Ex 38:17
the gate of the c was needlework .... Ex 38:18
to the hangings of the c .... Ex 38:18
of the c round about, were of .... Ex 38:20
the sockets of the c round about .... Ex 38:31
and the sockets of the c round about .... Ex 38:31
all the pins of the c round about .... Ex 38:31
The hangings of the c, his .... Ex 39:40
and the hanging for the c gate .... Ex 39:40
shalt set up the c round about .... Ex 40:8
hang up the hanging at the c gate .... Ex 40:8
he reared up the c round about .... Ex 40:33
set up the hanging of the c gate .... Ex 40:33
in the c of the tabernacle of the .... Lev 6:16
in the c of the tabernacle of the .... Lev 6:26
And the hangings of the c, and the .... Num 3:26
the curtain for the door of the c .... Num 3:26
the pillars of the c round about .... Num 3:37
And the hangings of the c, and the .... Num 4:26
for the door of the gate of the c .... Num 4:26
the pillars of the c round about .... Num 4:32
which had a well in his c 2Sa 17:18
he built the inner c with three 1Kin 6:36
had another c within the porch 1Kin 7:8
on the outside toward the great c 1Kin 7:9
the great c round about was with 1Kin 7:12
both for the inner c of the house 1Kin 7:12
c that was before the house of 1Kin 8:64
was gone out into the middle c 2Kin 20:4

he made the c of the priests 2Chr 4:9
great c, and doors for the c 2Chr 4:9
had set it in the midst of the c 2Chr 6:13
hallowed the middle of the c that 2Chr 7:7
of the LORD, before the new c 2Chr 20:5
in the c of the house of the LORD 2Chr 24:21
the c of the house of the LORD 2Chr 29:16
that was by the c of the prison .... Neh 3:25
in the c of the garden of the .... Est 1:5
before the c of the women's house .... Est 2:11
unto the king into the inner c .... Est 4:11
stood in the inner c of the .... Est 5:1
the queen standing in the c .... Est 5:2
And the king said, Who is in the c .... Est 6:4
the outward c of the king's house .... Est 6:4
Behold, Haman standeth in the c .... Est 6:5
of dragons, and a c for owls .... Is 34:13
he stood in the c of the prison's .... Jer 19:14
Stand in the c of the LORD's .... Jer 26:2
shut up in the c of the prison .... Jer 32:2
uncle's son came to me in the c .... Jer 32:8
that sat in the c of the prison .... Jer 32:12
shut up in the c of the prison .... Jer 33:1
the scribe, in the c of the .... Jer 36:10
went in to the king into the c .... Jer 36:20
Jeremiah into the c of the prison .... Jer 37:21
remained in the c of the prison .... Jer 37:21
that was in the c of the prison .... Jer 38:6
remained in the c of the prison .... Jer 38:13
So Jeremiah abode in the c of the .... Jer 38:28
out of the c of the prison .... Jer 39:14
shut up in the c of the prison .... Jer 39:15
brought me to the door of the c .... Eze 8:7
the inner c of the LORD's house .... Eze 8:16
and the cloud filled the inner c .... Eze 10:3
the c was full of the brightness .... Eze 10:4
was heard even to the outer c .... Eze 10:5
of the c round about the gate .... Eze 40:14
brought he me into the outward c .... Eze 40:17
made for the c round about .... Eze 40:17
forefront of the inner c without .... Eze 40:19
the gate of the outward c that .... Eze 40:20
the gate of the inner c was over .... Eze 40:23
in the inner c toward the south .... Eze 40:27
to the inner c by the south gate .... Eze 40:28
thereof were toward the utter c .... Eze 40:31
into the inner c toward the east .... Eze 40:32
thereof were toward the outward c .... Eze 40:34
thereof were toward the utter c .... Eze 40:37
of the singers in the inner c .... Eze 40:44
So he measured the c, an hundred .... Eze 40:47
temple, and the porches of the c .... Eze 41:15
brought me forth into the utter c .... Eze 42:1
cubits which were for the inner c .... Eze 42:3
which was for the utter c .... Eze 42:3
toward the utter c on the .... Eze 42:7
in the utter c was fifty cubits .... Eze 42:8
goeth into them from the utter c .... Eze 42:9
the wall of the c toward the east .... Eze 42:10
the holy place into the utter c .... Eze 42:14
and brought me into the inner c .... Eze 43:5
in at the gates of the inner c .... Eze 44:17
in the gates of the inner c .... Eze 44:17
they go forth into the utter c .... Eze 44:19
into the utter c to the people .... Eze 44:19
when they enter into the inner c .... Eze 44:21
the sanctuary, unto the inner c .... Eze 44:27
posts of the gate of the inner c .... Eze 45:19
The gate of the inner c that .... Eze 46:1
them not out into the utter c .... Eze 46:20
brought me forth into the utter c .... Eze 46:21
pass by the four corners of the c .... Eze 46:21
corner of the c there was a c .... Eze 46:21
In the four corners of the c .... Eze 46:22
chapel, and it is the king's c .... Amos 7:13
But the c which is without the .... Rev 11:2

COURTEOUS
as brethren, be pitiful, be c 1Pet 3:8

COURTEOUSLY
Julius c entreated Paul, and gave .... Acts 27:3
us, and lodged us three days c .... Acts 28:7

COURTS
two c of the house of the LORD 2Kin 21:5
two c of the house of the LORD 2Kin 23:12
the house of the LORD, in the c 1Chr 23:28
he shall build my house and my c 1Chr 28:6
of the c of the house of the LORD 1Chr 28:12
in the c of the house of 2Chr 23:5
two c of the house of the LORD 2Chr 33:5
roof of his house, and in the c .... Neh 8:16
in the c of the house of God, and .... Neh 8:16
in the c of the house of God .... Neh 13:7
thee, that he may dwell in thy c .... Ps 65:4
fainteth for the c of the LORD .... Ps 84:2
For a day in thy c is better than .... Ps 84:10
flourish in the c of our God .... Ps 92:13
an offering, and come into his c .... Ps 96:8
and into his c with praise .... Ps 100:4
In the c of the LORD's house .... Ps 116:19
in the c of the house of our God .... Ps 135:2
this at your hand, to tread my c .... Is 1:12
drink it in the c of my holiness .... Is 62:9
fill the c with the slain .... Eze 9:7
pillars as the pillars of the c .... Eze 42:6
c joined of forty cubits long .... Eze 46:22
my house, and shalt also keep my c .... Zec 3:7
live delicately, are in kings' c .... Lk 7:25

COUSIN
thy c Elisabeth, she hath also .... Lk 1:36

COUSINS
her c heard how the Lord had .... Lk 1:58

COVENANT
with thee will I establish my c .... Gen 6:18
behold, I establish my c with you .... Gen 9:9
And I will establish my c with you .... Gen 9:11
of the c which I make between me .... Gen 9:12
be for a token of a c between me .... Gen 9:13
And I will remember my c, which is .... Gen 9:15
the everlasting c between God .... Gen 9:16
Noah, This is the token of the c .... Gen 9:17
day the LORD made a c with Abram .... Gen 15:18
And I will make my c between me .... Gen 17:2
my c is with thee, and thou shalt .... Gen 17:4
I will establish my c between me .... Gen 17:7
generations for an everlasting c .... Gen 17:7
Thou shalt keep my c therefore .... Gen 17:9
This is my c, which ye shall keep .... Gen 17:10
be a token of the c betwixt me .... Gen 17:11
my c shall be in your flesh for .... Gen 17:13
your flesh for an everlasting c .... Gen 17:13
he hath broken my c .... Gen 17:14
I will establish my c with him .... Gen 17:19
with him for an everlasting c .... Gen 17:19
But my c will I establish with .... Gen 17:21
and both of them made a c .... Gen 21:27
Thus they made a c at Beer-sheba .... Gen 21:32
and let us make a c with thee .... Gen 26:28
come thou, let us make a c .... Gen 31:44
God remembered his c with Abraham .... Ex 2:24
also established my c with them .... Ex 6:4
and I have remembered my c .... Ex 6:5
my voice indeed, and keep my c .... Ex 19:5
Thou shalt make no c with them .... Ex 23:32
And he took the book of the c .... Ex 24:7
said, Behold the blood of the c .... Ex 24:8
generations, for a perpetual c .... Ex 31:16
And he said, Behold, I make a c .... Ex 34:10
lest thou make a c with the .... Ex 34:12
Lest thou make a c with the .... Ex 34:15
words I have made a c with thee .... Ex 34:27
the tables the words of the c .... Ex 34:28
thou suffer the salt of the c of .... Lev 2:13
of Israel by an everlasting c .... Lev 24:8
you, and establish my c with you .... Lev 26:9
but that ye break my c .... Lev 26:15
shall avenge the quarrel of my c .... Lev 26:25
will I remember my c with Jacob .... Lev 26:42
also my c with Isaac .... Lev 26:42
also my c with Abraham will I .... Lev 26:42
and to break my c with them .... Lev 26:44
remember the c of their ancestors .... Lev 26:45
the ark of the c of the LORD went .... Num 10:33
the ark of the c of the LORD .... Num 14:44
it is a c of salt for ever before .... Num 18:19
I give unto him my c of peace .... Num 25:12
even the c of an everlasting .... Num 25:13
And he declared unto you his c .... Deut 4:13
lest ye forget the c of the LORD .... Deut 4:23
nor forget the c of thy fathers .... Deut 4:31
our God made a c with us in Horeb .... Deut 5:2
made not this c with our fathers .... Deut 5:3
thou shalt make no c with them .... Deut 7:2
the faithful God, which keepeth c .... Deut 7:9
God shall keep unto thee the c .... Deut 7:12
that he may establish his c which .... Deut 8:18
even the tables of the c which .... Deut 9:9
stone, even the tables of the c .... Deut 9:11
of the c were in my two hands .... Deut 9:15
bear the ark of the c of the LORD .... Deut 10:8
thy God, in transgressing his c .... Deut 17:2
These are the words of the c .... Deut 29:1
beside the c which he made with .... Deut 29:1
therefore the words of this c .... Deut 29:9
into c with the LORD thy God .... Deut 29:12
with you only do I make this c .... Deut 29:14
to all the curses of the c that .... Deut 29:21
the c of the LORD God of their .... Deut 29:25
bare the ark of the c of the LORD .... Deut 31:9
break my c which I have made with .... Deut 31:16
and provoke me, and break my c .... Deut 31:20
bare the ark of the c of the LORD .... Deut 31:25
ark of the c of the LORD your God .... Deut 31:26
observed thy word, and kept thy c .... Deut 33:9
ark of the c of the LORD your God .... Josh 3:3
saying, Take up the ark of the c .... Josh 3:6
And they took up the ark of the c .... Josh 3:6
that bear the ark of the c .... Josh 3:6
the ark of the c of the Lord of .... Josh 3:11
ark of the c before the people .... Josh 3:14
that bare the ark of the c the .... Josh 3:17
the ark of the c of the Lord .... Josh 4:7
which bare the ark of the c stood .... Josh 4:9
that bare the ark of the c .... Josh 4:18
them, Take up the ark of the c .... Josh 6:6
the ark of the c of the LORD .... Josh 6:8
my c which I commanded them .... Josh 7:11
transgressed the c of the LORD .... Josh 7:15
bare the ark of the c of the LORD .... Josh 8:33
the c of the LORD your God .... Josh 23:16
So Joshua made a c with the .... Josh 24:25
I will never break my c with you .... Judg 2:1
people hath transgressed my c .... Judg 2:20
(for the ark of the c of God was .... Judg 20:27
Let us fetch the ark of the c 1Sa 4:3
ark of the c of the LORD of hosts 1Sa 4:4
with the ark of the c of God 1Sa 4:4

when the ark of the c of the LORD.............1Sa 4:5
Make a c with us, and we will 1Sa 11:1
will I make a c with thee, that I.................1Sa 11:2
Then Jonathan and David made a c 1Sa 18:3
into a c of the LORD with thee......................1Sa 20:8
So Jonathan made a c with the......................1Sa 20:16
they two made a c before the LORD............1Sa 23:18
bearing the ark of the c of God..................2Sa 15:24
made with me an everlasting c...................2Sa 23:5
the ark of the c of the LORD........................1Kin 3:15
the ark of the c of the LORD........................1Kin 6:19
might bring up the ark of the c 1Kin 8:1
brought in the ark of the c of 1Kin 8:6
when the LORD made a c with the 1Kin 8:9
ark, wherein is the c of the LORD...............1Kin 8:21
on earth beneath, who keepest c.................1Kin 8:23
thee, and thou hast not kept my c.............1Kin 11:11
of Israel have forsaken thy c.......................1Kin 19:10
of Israel have forsaken thy c.......................1Kin 19:14
I will send thee away with this c................1Kin 20:34
So he made a c with him, and sent...........1Kin 20:34
made a c with them, and took an 2Kin 11:4
Jehoiada made a c between the 2Kin 11:17
because of his c with Abraham...................2Kin 13:23
his c that he made with their.....................2Kin 17:15
With whom the LORD had made a c...........2Kin 17:35
the c that I have made with you................2Kin 17:38
their God, but transgressed his c...............2Kin 18:12
the words of the book of the c 2Kin 22:2
made a c before the LORD, to walk 2Kin 23:3
to perform the words of this c 2Kin 23:3
And all the people stood to the c..............2Kin 23:3
is written in the book of this c 2Kin 23:21
David made a c with them in 1Chr 11:3
c of the LORD out of the house of 1Chr 15:25
bare the ark of the c of the LORD.............1Chr 15:26
the c of the LORD with shouting 1Chr 15:28
as the ark of the c of the LORD..................1Chr 15:29
before the ark of the c of God...................1Chr 16:6
Be ye mindful always of his c....................1Chr 16:15
Even of the c which he made with...........1Chr 16:16
and to Israel for an everlasting c 1Chr 16:17
ark of the c of the LORD Asaph.................1Chr 16:37
but the ark of the c of the LORD.................1Chr 17:1
the ark of the c of the LORD......................1Chr 22:19
for the ark of the c of the LORD...............1Chr 28:2
the ark of the c of the LORD......................1Chr 28:18
to bring up the ark of the c of...................2Chr 5:2
brought in the ark of the c of.....................2Chr 5:7
when the LORD made a c with the 2Chr 5:10
ark, wherein is the c of the LORD.............2Chr 6:11
which keepest c, and shewest mercy 2Chr 6:14
him and to his sons by a c of salt 2Chr 13:5
they entered into a c to seek the 2Chr 15:12
because of the c that he had made...........2Chr 21:7
son of Zichri, into c with him.....................2Chr 23:1
all the congregation made a c.....................2Chr 23:3
And Jehoiada made a c between him 2Chr 23:16
a c with the LORD God of Israel..................2Chr 29:10
the words of the book of the c 2Chr 34:30
made a c before the LORD, to walk...........2Chr 34:31
to perform the words of the c.....................2Chr 34:31
did according to the c of God....................2Chr 34:32
Now therefore let us make a c ....Ezr 10:3
and terrible God, that keepeth c................Neh 1:5
madest a c with him to give the................Neh 9:8
the terrible God, and keepest c..................Neh 9:32
of all this we make a sure c........................Neh 9:38
the c of the priesthood, and of...................Neh 13:29
I made a c with mine eyes............................Job 31:1
Will he make a c with thee..........................Job 41:4
and truth unto such as keep his c.............Ps 25:10
and he will shew them his c.........................Ps 25:14
have we dealt falsely in thy c......................Ps 44:17
made a c with me by sacrifice.......................Ps 50:5
shouldest take my c in thy mouth..............Ps 50:16
he hath broken his c......................................Ps 55:20
Have respect unto the c...............................Ps 74:20
They kept not the c of God.........................Ps 78:10
were they stedfast in his c...........................Ps 78:37
I have made a c with my chosen, I............Ps 89:3
my c shall stand fast with him ....Ps 89:28
My c will I not break, nor alter...................Ps 89:34
made void the c of thy servant...................Ps 89:39
To such as keep his c, and to ....Ps 103:18
He hath remembered his c for ever............Ps 105:8
Which c he made with Abraham, and ....Ps 105:9
and to Israel for an everlasting c...............Ps 105:10
And he remembered for them his c............Ps 106:45
he will ever be mindful of his c.................Ps 111:5
he hath commanded his c for ever.............Ps 111:9
If thy children will keep my c....................Ps 132:12
and forgettest the c of her God.................Prov 2:17
broken the everlasting c...............................Is 24:5
said, We have made a c with death............Is 28:15
your c with death shall be..........................Is 28:18
he hath broken the c, he hath.....................Is 33:8
give thee for a c of the people.....................Is 42:6
give thee for a c of the people.....................Is 49:8
neither shall the c of my peace...................Is 54:10
make an everlasting c with you..................Is 55:3
please me, and take hold of my c..............Is 56:4
it, and taketh hold of my c..........................Is 56:6
bed, and made thee a c with them...........Is 57:8
As for me, this is my c with them.............Is 59:21
make an everlasting c with them...............Is 61:8
The ark of the c of the LORD......................Jer 3:16
Hear ye the words of this c.........................Jer 11:2
obeyeth not the words of this c..................Jer 11:3
Hear ye the words of this c.........................Jer 11:6

upon them all the words of this c.............Jer 11:8
house of Judah have broken my c.............Jer 11:10
remember, break not thy c with us...........Jer 14:21
the c of the LORD their God.........................Jer 22:9
that I will make a new c with the..............Jer 31:31
Not according to the c that I ....Jer 31:32
which my c they brake, although I............Jer 31:32
But this shall be the c that I......................Jer 31:33
make an everlasting c with them...............Jer 32:40
If ye can break my c of the day.................Jer 33:20
my c of the night, and that there..............Jer 33:20
Then may also my c be broken with ....Jer 33:21
If my c be not with day and night,...........Jer 33:25
the king Zedekiah had made a c................Jer 34:8
which had entered into the c......................Jer 34:10
I made a c with your fathers in..................Jer 34:13
ye had made a c before me in the.............Jer 34:15
men that have transgressed my c..............Jer 34:18
c which they had made before me.............Jer 34:18
to the Lord in a perpetual c that..............Jer 50:5
and entered into a c with thee...................Eze 16:8
the oath in breaking the c..........................Eze 16:59
my c with thee in the days of thy............Eze 16:60
unto thee an everlasting c..........................Eze 16:60
for daughters, but not by thy c.................Eze 16:61
I will establish my c with thee..................Eze 16:62
made a c with him, and hath taken..........Eze 17:13
keeping of his c it might stand ....Eze 17:14
or shall he break the c, and be ....Eze 17:15
whose c he brake, even with him..............Eze 17:16
the oath by breaking the c..........................Eze 17:18
my c that he hath broken, even it............Eze 17:19
bring you into the bond of the c...............Eze 20:37
will make with them a c of peace.............Eze 34:25
will make a c of peace with them.............Eze 37:26
be an everlasting c with them....................Eze 37:26
broken my c because of all your................Eze 44:7
and dreadful God, keeping the c................Dan 9:4
he shall confirm the c with many..............Dan 9:27
yea, also the prince of the c......................Dan 11:22
heart shall be against the holy c...............Dan 11:28
indignation against the holy c....................Dan 11:30
with them that forsake the holy c.............Dan 11:30
c shall he corrupt by flatteries..................Dan 11:32
in that day will I make a c for...................Hos 2:18
like men have transgressed the c..............Hos 6:7
they have transgressed my c.......................Hos 8:1
swearing falsely in making a c...................Hos 10:4
they do make a c with the...........................Hos 12:1
and remembered not the brotherly c.........Amos 1:9
by the blood of thy c I have sent..............Zec 9:11
that I might break my c which I................Zec 11:10
that my c might be with Levi......................Mal 2:4
My c was with him of life and....................Mal 2:5
ye have corrupted the c of Levi.................Mal 2:8
by profaning the c of our fathers...............Mal 2:10
companion, and the wife of thy c.............Mal 2:14
even the messenger of the c.......................Mal 3:1
and to remember his holy c........................Lk 1:72
of the c which God made with our............Acts 3:25
he gave him the c of circumcision............Acts 7:8
For this is my c unto them.........................Rom 11:27
Though it be but a man's c........................Gal 3:15
And this I say, that the c...........................Gal 3:17
he is the mediator of a better c................Heb 8:6
For if that first c had been.........................Heb 8:7
when I will make a new c with the...........Heb 8:8
Not according to the c that I ....Heb 8:9
they continued not in my c.........................Heb 8:9
For this is the c that I will........................Heb 8:10
In that he saith, A new c...........................Heb 8:13
Then verily the first c had also.................Heb 9:1
the ark of the c overlaid round..................Heb 9:4
budded, and the tables of the c................Heb 9:4
This is the c that I will make.....................Heb 10:16
hath counted the blood of the c...............Heb 10:29
Jesus the mediator of the new c...............Heb 12:24
the blood of the everlasting c...................Heb 13:20

COVENANTBREAKERS

Without understanding, c, without ....Rom 1:31

COVENANTED

according as I have c with David...............2Chr 7:18
I c with you when ye came out of..............Hag 2:5
they c with him for thirty pieces ....Mt 26:15
were glad, and c to give him money..........Lk 22:5

COVENANTS

adoption, and the glory, and the c...........Rom 9:4
for these are the two c................................Gal 4:24
strangers from the c of promise ....Eph 2:12

COVER

they shall c the face of the.........................Ex 10:5
man shall dig a pit, and not c it................Ex 21:33
and bowls thereof, to c withal ....Ex 25:29
side and on that side, to c it.......................Ex 26:13
breeches to c their nakedness.....................Ex 28:42
will c thee with my hand while I ....Ex 33:22
bowls, and his covers to c withal ....Ex 37:16
and c the ark with the vail.........................Ex 40:3
the leprosy c all the skin of him...............Lev 13:12
the cloud of the incense may c..................Lev 16:13
blood thereof, and c it with dust..............Lev 17:13
c the ark of testimony with it....................Num 4:5
the bowls, and covers to c withal..............Num 4:7
c the same with a covering of....................Num 4:8
the candlestick of the light,.......................Num 4:9
c it with a covering of badgers'.................Num 4:11
c them with a covering of...........................Num 4:12
they c the face of the earth, and...............Num 22:5

c that which cometh from thee.................Deut 23:13
the LORD shall c him all the day...............Deut 33:12
and Saul went in to c his feet 1Sa 24:3
to c the chapiters that were upon.............1Kin 7:18
to c the two bowls of the 1Kin 7:41
to c the two bowls of the............................1Kin 7:42
the two wreaths to c the two......................2Chr 4:12
to c the two pommels of the 2Chr 4:13
c not their iniquity, and let not.................Neh 4:5
c not thou my blood, and let my..............Job 16:18
dust, and the worms shall c them ....Job 21:26
and abundance of waters c thee................Job 22:11
abundance of waters may c thee................Job 38:34
The shady trees c him with their ....Job 40:22
He shall c thee with his feathers...............Ps 91:4
turn not again to c the earth......................Ps 104:9
let them c themselves with their ....Ps 109:29
Surely the darkness shall c me...................Ps 139:11
mischief of their own lips c them..............Ps 140:9
the LORD, as the waters c the sea.............Is 11:9
under thee, and the worms c thee.............Is 14:11
captivity, and will surely c thee................Is 22:17
and shall no more c her slain......................Is 26:21
that c with a covering, not.........................Is 30:1
seest the naked, that thou c him...............Is 58:7
neither shall they c themselves...................Is 59:6
the darkness shall c the earth.....................Is 60:2
multitude of camels shall c thee................Is 60:6
I will go up, and will c the earth...............Jer 46:8
sackcloth, and horror shall c them............Eze 7:18
thou shalt c thy face, that thou................Eze 12:6
he shall c his face, that he see..................Eze 12:12
the ground, to c it with dust.....................Eze 24:7
c not thy lips, and eat not the..................Eze 24:17
ye shall not c your lips, nor eat................Eze 24:22
horses their dust shall c thee.....................Eze 26:10
and great waters shall c thee.....................Eze 26:19
as for her, a cloud shall c her....................Eze 30:18
I will c the heaven, and make the.............Eze 32:7
I will c the sun with a cloud, and.............Eze 32:7
c you with skin, and put breath in............Eze 37:6
be like a cloud to c the land......................Eze 38:9
Israel, as a cloud to c the land..................Eze 38:16
my flax given to c her nakedness..............Hos 2:9
shall say to the mountains, C us................Hos 10:8
brother Jacob shame shall c thee...............Obad 10
yea, they shall all c their lips.....................Mic 3:7
shame shall c her which said unto............Mic 7:10
the LORD, as the waters c the sea.............Hab 2:14
violence of Lebanon shall c thee...............Hab 2:17
to c his face, and to buffet him,...............Mk 14:65
and to the hills, C us.................................Lk 23:30
indeed ought not to c his head.................1Cor 11:7
for charity shall c the multitude...............1Pet 4:8

COVERED

under the whole heaven, were c.................Gen 7:19
and the mountains were c...........................Gen 7:20
c the nakedness of their father...................Gen 9:23
she took a vail, and c herself......................Gen 24:65
c her with a vail, and wrapped...................Gen 38:14
because she had c her face..........................Gen 38:15
came up, and c the land of Egypt.............Ex 8:6
For they c the face of the whole...............Ex 10:15
c the chariots, and the horsemen,.............Ex 14:28
The depths have c them..............................Ex 15:5
with thy wind, the sea c them....................Ex 15:10
the quails came up, and c the camp.........Ex 16:13
the mount, and a cloud c the mount........Ex 24:15
Sinai, and the cloud c it six days..............Ex 24:16
c with their wings over the mercy.............Ex 37:9
c the ark of the testimony...........................Ex 40:21
Then a cloud c the tent of the ....Ex 40:34
the leprosy have c all his flesh...................Lev 13:13
to see when the holy things are c..............Num 4:20
six c wagons, and twelve oxen...................Num 7:3
up the cloud c the tabernacle.....................Num 9:16
the cloud c it by day, and the....................Num 9:16
and, behold, the cloud c it ....Num 16:42
thick, thou art c with fatness.....................Deut 32:15
the sea upon them, and c them..................Josh 24:7
the tent, she c him with a mantle.............Judg 4:18
milk, and gave him drink, and c him........Judg 4:19
his bolster, and c it with a cloth...............1Sa 19:13
and he is c with a mantle...........................1Sa 28:14
as he went up, and had his head c............2Sa 15:30
was with him c every man his head..........2Sa 15:30
But the king c his face, and the................2Sa 19:4
they c him with clothes, but he..................1Kin 1:1
c the house with beams and boards..........1Kin 6:9
he c them on the inside with wood...........1Kin 6:15
the floor of the house with.........................1Kin 6:15
so c the altar which was of cedar.............1Kin 6:20
c them with gold fitted upon the.............1Kin 6:35
it was c with cedar above upon.................1Kin 7:3
it was c with cedar from one side.............1Kin 7:7
ark, and the cherubims c the ark..............1Kin 8:7
c himself with sackcloth, and went..........2Kin 19:1
c with sackcloth, to Isaiah the..................2Kin 19:2
the ark of the covenant of the....................1Chr 28:18
ark, and the cherubims c the ark..............2Chr 5:8
c it, and set up the doors thereof..............Neh 3:15
mourning, and having his head c..............Est 6:12
king's mouth, they c Haman's face...........Est 7:8
neither hath he c the darkness...................Job 23:17
If I c my transgressions as Adam,..............Job 31:33
is forgiven, whose sin is c..........................Ps 32:1
and the shame of my face hath c me........Ps 44:15
c us with the shadow of death...................Ps 44:19
valleys also are c over with corn...............Ps 65:13
the wings of a dove c with silver...............Ps 68:13

shame hath c my face .... Ps 69:7
let them be c with reproach and .... Ps 71:13
The hills were c with the shadow .... Ps 80:10
thou hast c all their sin .... Ps 85:2
thou hast c him with shame .... Ps 89:45
the waters c their enemies .... Ps 106:11
and c the company of Abiram .... Ps 106:17
thou hast c me in my mother's ...... Ps 139:13
thou hast c my head in the day of ... Ps 140:7
nettles had c the face thereof .... Prov 24:31
a potsherd c with silver dross .... Prov 26:23
Whose hatred is c by deceit .... Prov 26:26
his name shall be c with darkness .... Eccl 6:4
with twain he c his feet .... Is 6:2
and with twain he c his feet .... Is 6:2
your rulers, the seers hath he c ..... Is 29:10
c himself with sackcloth, and went ... Is 37:1
of the priests c with sackcloth ...... Is 37:2
I have c thee in the shadow of ...... Is 51:16
he hath c me with the robe of ...... Is 61:10
and confounded, and c their heads .... Jer 14:3
were ashamed, they c their heads .... Jer 14:4
she is c with the multitude of ...... Jer 51:42
shame hath c our faces .... Jer 51:51
How hath the Lord c the daughter .... Lam 2:1
stones, he hath c me with ashes ..... Lam 3:16
Thou hast c with anger, and .... Lam 3:43
Thou hast c thyself with a cloud, ... Lam 3:44
to another, and two c their bodies ... Eze 1:11
which c on this side, and every ..... Eze 1:23
which c on that side, their .... Eze 1:23
over thee, and c thy nakedness ...... Eze 16:8
fine linen, and I c thee with silk .... Eze 16:10
hath c the naked with a garment .... Eze 18:7
hath c the naked with a garment, ... Eze 18:16
a rock, that it should not be c ..... Eze 24:8
of Elishah was that which c thee .... Eze 27:7
I c the deep for him, and I .... Eze 31:15
them, and the skin c them above .... Eze 37:8
windows, and the windows were c ... Eze 41:16
c him with sackcloth, and sat in .... Jonah 3:6
beast be c with sackcloth, and cry ... Jonah 3:8
His glory c the heavens, and the .... Hab 3:3
the ship was c with the waves ..... Mt 8:24
for there is nothing c, that .... Mt 10:26
For there is nothing c, that .... Lk 12:2
are forgiven, and whose sins are c ... Rom 4:7
or prophesying, having his head c 1Cor 11:4
For if the woman be not c 1Cor 11:6
be shorn or shaven, let her be c 1Cor 11:6

COVEREDST
Thou c it with the deep as with a ... Ps 104:6
thy broidered garments, and c them ... Eze 16:18

COVEREST
vesture, wherewith thou c thyself .... Deut 22:12
Who c thyself with light as with .... Ps 104:2

COVERETH
all the fat that c the inwards ...... Ex 29:13
and the fat that c the inwards ..... Ex 29:22
the fat that c the inwards .... Lev 3:3
and the fat that c the inwards ..... Lev 3:14
the fat that c the inwards .... Lev 4:8
and the fat that c the inwards ..... Lev 7:3
that which c the inwards, and the ... Lev 9:19
which c the face of the earth ..... Num 22:11
Surely he c his feet in his .... Judg 3:24
he c the faces of the judges ...... Job 9:24
Because he c his face with his .... Job 15:27
it, and c the bottom of the sea ... Job 36:30
With clouds he c the light .... Job 36:32
violence c them as a garment ...... Ps 73:6
him as the garment which c him .... Ps 109:19
Who c the heaven with clouds, who... Ps 147:8
but violence c the mouth of the .... Prov 10:6
but violence c the mouth of the .... Prov 10:11
but love c all sins .... Prov 10:12
but a prudent man c shame .... Prov 12:16
He that c a transgression seeketh ... Prov 17:9
He that c his sins shall not .... Prov 28:13
our shame, and our confusion c us ... Jer 3:25
art the anointed cherub that c ..... Eze 28:14
for one c violence with his .... Mal 2:16
c it with a vessel, or putteth it ... Lk 8:16

COVERING
and Noah removed the c of the ark ... Gen 8:13
he is to thee a c of the eyes ...... Gen 20:16
For that is his c only, it is his .... Ex 22:27
c the mercy seat with their wings ... Ex 25:20
to be a c upon the tabernacle ..... Ex 26:7
thou shalt make a c for the tent ... Ex 26:14
a c above of badgers' skins .... Ex 26:14
tabernacle, his tent, and his c .... Ex 35:11
mercy seat, and the vail of the c ... Ex 35:12
he made a c for the tent of rams' ... Ex 36:19
a c of badgers' skins above that ... Ex 36:19
the c of rams' skins dyed red, and ... Ex 39:34
the c of badgers' skins .... Ex 39:34
and the vail of the c .... Ex 39:34
put the c of the tent above upon ... Ex 40:19
and set up the vail of the c ...... Ex 40:21
he shall put a c upon his upper .... Num 3:25
the c thereof, and the hanging for ... Num 3:25
they shall take down the c vail .... Num 4:5
thereon the c of badgers' skins .... Num 4:6
same with a c of badgers' skins .... Num 4:8
within a c of badgers' skins ...... Num 4:10
cover it with a c of badgers' skins ... Num 4:11

them with a c of badgers' skins .... Num 4:12
upon it a c of badgers' skins ...... Num 4:14
made an end of the sanctuary ...... Num 4:15
of the congregation, his c .... Num 4:25
the c of the badgers' skins that ... Num 4:25
broad plates for a c of the altar ... Num 16:38
broad plates for a c of the altar ... Num 16:39
which hath no c bound upon it .... Num 19:15
spread a c over the well's mouth, ... 2Sa 17:19
Thick clouds are a c to him .... Job 22:14
that they have no c in the cold ... Job 24:7
him, and destruction hath no c .... Job 26:6
clothing, or any poor without c ... Job 31:19
He spread a cloud for a c .... Ps 105:39
the c of it of purple, the midst ... Song 3:10
And he discovered the c of Judah ... Is 22:8
of the c cast over all people ...... Is 25:7
the c narrower than that he can ... Is 28:20
and that cover with a c, but not ... Is 30:1
Ye shall defile also the c of thy ... Is 30:22
and I make sackcloth their c ...... Is 50:3
every precious stone was thy c .... Eze 28:13
O c cherub, from the midst of the ... Eze 28:16
the altar of the LORD with .... Mal 2:13
for her hair is given her for a c ... 1Cor 11:15

COVERINGS
decked my bed with c of tapestry ... Prov 7:16
She maketh herself c of tapestry ... Prov 31:22

COVERS
c thereof, and bowls thereof, the ... Ex 25:29
his c to cover withal, of pure ..... Ex 37:16
the bowls, and c to cover withal ... Num 4:7

COVERT
came down by the c of the hill 1Sa 25:20
the c for the sabbath that they ... 2Kin 16:18
abide in the c to lie in wait ...... Job 38:40
in the c of the reed, and fens .... Job 40:21
will trust in the c of thy wings ... Ps 61:4
for a c from storm and from rain ... Is 4:6
be thou a c to them from the face ... Is 16:4
the wind, and a c from the tempest ... Is 32:2
He hath forsaken his c, as the .... Jer 25:38

COVET
Thou shalt not c thy neighbour's ... Ex 20:17
thou shalt not c thy neighbour's ... Deut 5:21
wife, neither shalt thou c thy ..... Deut 5:21
they c fields, and take them by ... Mic 2:2
law had said, Thou shalt not c ... Rom 7:7
false witness, Thou shalt not c ... Rom 13:9
But c earnestly the best gifts 1Cor 12:31
c to prophesy, and forbid not to ... 1Cor 14:39

COVETED
shekels weight, then I c them .... Josh 7:21
I have c no man's silver, or gold ... Acts 20:33
of this world, so they c 1Ti 6:10

COVETETH
He c greedily all the day long .... Prov 21:26
Woe to him that c an evil .... Hab 2:9

COVETOUS
heart's desire, and blesseth the c ... Ps 10:3
And the Pharisees also, who were c ... Lk 16:14
of this world, or with the c 1Cor 5:10
a brother be a fornicator, or c 1Cor 5:11
Nor thieves, nor c, nor drunkards ... 1Cor 6:10
nor unclean person, nor c man .... Eph 5:5
but patient, not a brawler, not c ... 1Ti 3:3
be lovers of their own selves, c ... 2Ti 3:2
have exercised with c practices 2Pet 2:14

COVETOUSNESS
fear God, men of truth, hating c ... Ex 18:21
unto thy testimonies, and not to c ... Ps 119:36
but he that hateth c shall .... Prov 28:16
The iniquity of his c was I wroth ... Is 57:17
of them every one is given to c ... Jer 6:13
the greatest is given to c .... Jer 8:10
thine heart are not but for thy c ... Jer 22:17
is come, and the measure of thy c ... Jer 51:13
their heart goeth after their c .... Eze 33:31
coveteth an evil c to his house ... Hab 2:9
Thefts, covetousness, wickedness, deceit, ... Mk 7:22
them, Take heed, and beware of c ... Lk 12:15
fornication, wickedness, c .... Rom 1:29
matter of bounty, and not as of c ... 2Cor 9:5
and all uncleanness, or c .... Eph 5:3
evil concupiscence, and c .... Col 3:5
as ye know, nor a cloke of c 1Th 2:5
your conversation be without c ... Heb 13:5
through c shall they with feigned ... 2Pet 2:3

COVOCATION
month ye shall have an holy c .... Num 29:12

COW
And whether it be c or ewe .... Lev 22:28
But the firstling of a c, or the ... Num 18:17
their c calveth, and casteth not ... Job 21:10
a man shall nourish a young c .... Is 7:21
And the c and the bear shall feed ... Is 11:7
every c at that which is before ... Amos 4:3

COW'S
I have given thee c dung for ..... Eze 4:15

COZ (coz) *A descendant of Caleb.*
C begat Anub, and Zobebah, and the ... 1Chr 4:8

COZBI (coz'-bi) *A Midianite woman.*
woman that was slain was c ...... Num 25:15
of Peor, and in the matter of c ... Num 25:18

COZEBA See CHOZEBA.

CRACKLING
For as the c of thorns under a .... Eccl 7:6

CRACKNELS
take with thee ten loaves, and c ... 1Kin 14:3

CRAFT
cause to prosper in his hand ..... Dan 8:25
how they might take him by c ..... Mk 14:1
And because he was of the same c ... Acts 18:3
that by this c we have our wealth ... Acts 19:25
our c is in danger to be set at ... Acts 19:27
craftsman, of whatsoever craft he be ... Rev 18:22

CRAFTINESS
He taketh the wise in their own c ... Job 5:13
But he perceived their c, and said ... Lk 20:23
He taketh the wise in their own c ... 1Cor 3:19
of dishonesty, not walking in c ... 2Cor 4:2
the sleight of men, and cunning c ... Eph 4:14

CRAFTSMAN
the work of the hands of the c ... Deut 27:15
and no c, of whatsoever craft he ... Rev 18:22

CRAFTSMEN
thousand captives, and all the c ... 2Kin 24:14
might, even seven thousand, and c ... 2Kin 24:16
for they were c 1Chr 4:14
Lod, and Ono, the valley of c .... Neh 11:35
all of it the work of the c ...... Hos 13:2
brought no small gain unto the c ... Acts 19:24
the c which are with him, have a ... Acts 19:38

CRAFTY
The devices of the c, so that .... Job 5:12
thou choosest the tongue of the c ... Job 15:5
They have taken c counsel against ... Ps 83:3
nevertheless, being c, I caught ... 2Cor 12:16

CRAG
upon the c of the rock, and the ... Job 39:28

CRANE
Like a c or a swallow, so did I ... Is 38:14
and the turtle and the c and the ... Jer 8:7

CRASHING
and a great c from the hills ..... Zeph 1:10

CRAVED
Pilate, and the body of Jesus ..... Mk 15:43

CRAVETH
for his mouth c it of him .... Prov 16:26

CREATE
C in me a clean heart, O God ..... Ps 51:10
the LORD will c upon every .... Is 4:5
I form the light, and c darkness ... Is 45:7
I make peace, and c evil .... Is 45:7
I c the fruit of the lips .... Is 57:19
I c new heavens and a new earth ... Is 65:17
for ever in that which I c .... Is 65:18
I c Jerusalem a rejoicing, and her ... Is 65:18

CREATED
In the beginning God c the heaven ... Gen 1:1
God c great whales, and every .... Gen 1:21
So God c man in his own image ... Gen 1:27
in the image of God c he him .... Gen 1:27
male and female c he them .... Gen 1:27
from all his work which God c .... Gen 2:3
and of the earth when they were c ... Gen 2:4
In the day that God c man .... Gen 5:1
Male and female c he them .... Gen 5:2
Adam, in the day they were c .... Gen 5:2
have c from the face of the earth ... Gen 6:7
day that God c man upon the earth ... Deut 4:32
and the south thou hast c them ... Ps 89:12
shall be c shall praise the LORD ... Ps 102:18
forth thy spirit, they are c ...... Ps 104:30
for he commanded, and they were c ... Ps 148:5
and behold who hath c these things ... Is 40:26
the Holy One of Israel hath c it ... Is 41:20
he that c the heavens, and ...... Is 42:5
thus saith the LORD that c thee, ... Is 43:1
for I have c him for my glory, I ... Is 43:7
I the LORD have c it .... Is 45:8
made the earth, and c man upon it ... Is 45:12
saith the LORD that c the heavens ... Is 45:18
he c it not in vain, he formed it ... Is 45:18
They are c now, and not from the ... Is 48:7
I have c the smith that bloweth ... Is 54:16
I have c the waster to destroy ... Is 54:16
for the LORD hath c a new thing ... Jer 31:22
in the place where thou wast c ... Eze 21:30
thee in the day that thou wast c ... Eze 28:13
from the day that thou wast c .... Eze 28:15
hath not one God c us .... Mal 2:10
which God c unto this man .... Mk 13:19
was the man c for the woman 1Cor 11:9
in Christ Jesus unto good works ... Eph 2:10
who c all things by Jesus Christ ... Eph 3:9
after God is c in righteousness ... Eph 4:24
For by him were all things c ..... Col 1:16
all things were c by him, and for ... Col 1:16
after the image of him that c him ... Col 3:10
which God hath c to be received ... 1Ti 4:3
for thou hast c all things .... Rev 4:11
thy pleasure they are and were c ... Rev 4:11
who c heaven, and the things that ... Rev 10:6

CREATETH
c the wind, and declareth unto man ... Amos 4:13

CREATION
of the c God made them male ..... Mk 10:6
the c which God created unto this ... Mk 13:19

things of him from the c of the .... Rom 1:20
we know that the whole c groaneth.... Rom 8:22
were from the beginning of the c 2Pet 3:4
the beginning of the c of God............ Rev 3:14

CREATOR

Remember now thy C in the days of.... Eccl 12:1
the C of the ends of the earth,............ Is 40:28
of Israel, thy King............................... Is 43:15
the creature more than the C............. Rom 1:25
well doing, as unto a faithful C........... 1Pet 4:19

CREATURE

the moving c that hath life................ Gen 1:20
and every living c that moveth........... Gen 1:21
forth the living c after his kind........... Gen 1:24
Adam called every living c................. Gen 2:19
every living c that is with you,........... Gen 9:10
every living c that is with you,........... Gen 9:12
and every living c of all flesh............ Gen 9:15
every living c of all flesh that............ Gen 9:16
of every living c that moveth in......... Lev 11:46
of every c that creepeth upon the...... Lev 11:46
of the living c was in the wheels........ Eze 1:20
of the living c was in the wheels........ Eze 1:21
living c was as the colour of the........ Eze 1:22
This is the living c that I saw............. Eze 10:15
of the living c was in them................ Eze 10:17
This is the living c that I saw............. Eze 10:20
and preach the gospel to every c....... Mk 16:15
served the c more than the................ Rom 1:25
c waiteth for the manifestation........... Rom 8:19
For the c was made subject to........... Rom 8:20
Because the c itself also shall........... Rom 8:21
nor depth, nor any other c.................. Rom 8:39
man be in Christ, he is a new c......... 2Cor 5:17
nor circumcision, but a new c............ Gal 6:15
God, the firstborn of every c.............. Col 1:15
to every c which is under heaven...... Col 1:23
For every c of God is good, and........ 1Ti 4:4
Neither is there any c that is............. Heb 4:13
every c which is in heaven, and on.... Rev 5:13

CREATURES

houses shall be full of doleful c......... Is 13:21
the likeness of four living c............... Eze 1:5
for the likeness of the living c........... Eze 1:13
up and down among the living c........ Eze 1:13
And the living c ran and returned....... Eze 1:14
Now as I beheld the living c.............. Eze 1:15
upon the earth by the living c............ Eze 1:15
And when the living c went................ Eze 1:19
when the living c were lifted up.......... Eze 1:19
living c that touched one another....... Eze 3:13
be a kind of firstfruits of his c........... Jas 1:18
of the c which were in the sea........... Rev 8:9

CREDITOR

Every c that lendeth ought unto......... Deut 15:2
the c is come to take unto him my...... 2Kin 4:1
There was a certain c which had........ Lk 7:41

CREDITORS

or which of my c is it to whom I......... Is 50:1

CREEK

a certain c with a shore, into.............. Acts 27:39

CREEP

All fowls that c, going upon all........... Lev 11:20
things that c upon the earth............... Lev 11:29
unclean to you among all that c......... Lev 11:31
things that c upon the earth............... Lev 11:42
beasts of the forest do c forth........... Ps 104:20
things that c upon the earth............... Eze 38:20
sort are they which c move................ 2Ti 3:6

CREEPETH

every thing that c upon the earth....... Gen 1:25
thing that c upon the earth................ Gen 1:28
every thing that c upon the earth....... Gen 1:30
every thing that c upon the earth....... Gen 7:8
every creeping thing that c upon....... Gen 7:14
thing that c upon the earth................ Gen 7:21
thing that c upon the earth................ Gen 8:17
whatsoever c upon the earth,............. Gen 8:19
every creeping thing that c upon....... Lev 11:41
with any creeping thing that c........... Lev 11:43
thing that c upon the earth................ Lev 11:44
creature that c upon the earth,.......... Lev 11:46
living thing that c on the ground........ Lev 20:25
of any thing that c on the ground...... Deut 4:18

CREEPING

c thing, and beast of the earth........... Gen 1:24
over every c thing that creepeth........ Gen 1:26
the c thing, and the fowls of the........ Gen 6:7
of every c thing of the earth.............. Gen 6:20
every c thing that creepeth upon....... Gen 7:14
of every c thing that creepeth........... Gen 7:21
the c things, and the fowl of the........ Gen 7:23
of every c thing that creepeth........... Gen 8:17
Every beast, every c thing................. Gen 8:19
the carcase of unclean c things........ Lev 5:2
may ye eat of every flying c.............. Lev 11:21
But all other flying c things............... Lev 11:23
the c things that creep upon the........ Lev 11:29
every c thing that creepeth upon....... Lev 11:41
hath more feet among all c things..... Lev 11:42
with any c thing that creepeth........... Lev 11:43
of c thing that creepeth upon the...... Lev 11:44
Or whosoever toucheth any c thing... Lev 22:5
every c thing that flieth is................. Deut 14:19
of c things, and of fishes.................. 1Kin 4:33

wherein are things c innumerable ..... Ps 104:25
c things, and flying fowl.................... Ps 148:10
and behold every form of c things..... Eze 8:10
all c things that creep upon the........ Eze 38:20
with the c things of the ground......... Hos 2:18
of the sea, as the c things................ Hab 1:14
c things, and fowls of the air............ Acts 10:12
c things, and fowls of the air............ Acts 11:6
and fourfooted beasts, and c things.. Rom 1:23

CREPT

are certain men c in unawares......... Jude 4

CRESCENS (cres'-sens) A companion of Paul.

C to Galatia, Titus unto Dalmatia...... 2Ti 4:10

CRETE (creet) See CRETES. An island south of Greece.

suffering us, we sailed under C......... Acts 27:7
which is an haven of C, and lieth...... Acts 27:12
thence, they sailed close by C.......... Acts 27:13
me, and not have loosed from C....... Acts 27:21
For this cause left I thee in C........... Titus 1:5

CRETES (creets) See CRETIANS. Inhabitants of Crete.

C and Arabians, we do hear them..... Acts 2:11

CRETIANS (cre'-shuns) See CRETES. Same as Cretes.

The C are alway liars, evil............... Titus 1:12
bishop of the church of the C........... Titus s

CREW

And immediately the cock c.............. Mt 26:74
and the cock c................................ Mk 14:68
And the second time the cock c........ Mk 14:72
while he yet spake, the cock c.......... Lk 22:60
and immediately the cock c.............. Jn 18:27

CRIB

to serve thee, or abide by thy c........ Job 39:9
Where no oxen are, the c is clean..... Prov 14:4
owner, and the ass his master's c..... Is 1:3

CRIED

he c with a great and exceeding....... Gen 27:34
with me, and I c with a loud voice..... Gen 39:14
that I lifted up my voice and c........... Gen 39:15
as I lifted up my voice and c............. Gen 39:18
they c before him, Bow the knee....... Gen 41:43
the people c to Pharaoh for bread.... Gen 41:55
and he c, Cause every man to go..... Gen 45:1
reason of the bondage, and they c.... Ex 2:23
c unto Pharaoh, saying, Wherefore... Ex 5:15
the c unto the LORD because of........ Ex 8:12
of Israel c out unto the LORD............ Ex 14:10
And he c unto the LORD.................... Ex 15:25
Moses c unto the LORD, saying,....... Ex 17:4
And the people c unto Moses........... Num 11:2
Moses c unto the LORD, saying,....... Num 12:13
lifted up their voice, and c................ Num 14:1
the damsel, because she c not.......... Deut 22:24
field, and the betrothed damsel c...... Deut 22:27
when we c unto the LORD God of...... Deut 26:7
when they c unto the LORD, he put... Josh 24:7
of Israel c unto the LORD................. Judg 3:9
of Israel c unto the LORD................. Judg 3:15
of Israel c unto the LORD................. Judg 4:3
c through the lattice, Why is his....... Judg 5:28
of Israel c unto the LORD................. Judg 6:6
when the children of Israel c............ Judg 6:7
and they c, The sword of the LORD,.. Judg 7:20
and all the host ran, and c............... Judg 7:21
and lifted up his voice, and c........... Judg 9:7
of Israel c unto the LORD................. Judg 10:10
ye c to me, and I delivered you......... Judg 10:12
they c unto the children of Dan........ Judg 18:23
and told it, all the city c out............. Judg 18:25
Ekron, that the Ekronites c out......... 1Sa 5:10
Samuel c unto the LORD for Israel.... 1Sa 7:9
your fathers c unto the LORD,........... 1Sa 12:8
they c unto the LORD, and said, We.. 1Sa 12:10
he c unto the LORD all night............. 1Sa 15:11
c unto the armies of Israel, and....... 1Sa 17:8
Jonathan c after the lad, and said..... 1Sa 20:37
Jonathan c after the lad, Make......... 1Sa 20:38
c after Saul, saying, My lord the....... 1Sa 24:8
David c to the people, and to........... 1Sa 26:14
Samuel, she c with a loud voice....... 1Sa 28:12
and the watchman c, and told the..... 2Sa 18:25
the king c with a loud voice, O........ 2Sa 19:4
Then c a wise woman out of the....... 2Sa 20:16
upon the LORD, and c to my God...... 2Sa 22:7
he c against the altar in the............ 1Kin 13:2
which had c against the altar in....... 1Kin 13:4
he c unto the man of God that......... 1Kin 13:21
For the saying which he c by the...... 1Kin 13:32
he c unto the LORD, and said, O...... 1Kin 17:20
c unto the LORD, and said, O LORD.. 1Kin 17:21
they c aloud, and cut themselves..... 1Kin 18:28
passed by, he c unto the king.......... 1Kin 20:39
and Jehoshaphat c out..................... 1Kin 22:32
And Elisha saw it, and he c.............. 2Kin 2:12
Now there c a certain woman of....... 2Kin 4:1
of the pottage, that they c out.......... 2Kin 4:40
and he c, and said, Alas, master...... 2Kin 6:5
there c a woman unto him, saying,... 2Kin 6:26
c to the king for her house and........ 2Kin 8:5
Athaliah rent her clothes, and c....... 2Kin 11:14
c with a loud voice in the Jews'........ 2Kin 18:28
the prophet c unto the LORD............ 2Kin 20:11
for they c to God in the battle,......... 1Chr 5:20

they c unto the LORD, and the......... 2Chr 13:14
Asa c unto the LORD his God, and... 2Chr 14:11
but Jehoshaphat c out, and the........ 2Chr 18:31
Then they c with a loud voice in...... 2Chr 32:18
of Amoz, prayed and c to heaven.... 2Chr 32:20
c with a loud voice unto the LORD.... Neh 9:4
trouble, when they c unto thee......... Neh 9:27
c unto thee, thou heardest them....... Neh 9:28
c with a loud and a bitter cry........... Est 4:1
I delivered the poor that c................ Job 29:12
(they c after them as after a........... Job 30:5
up, and I c in the congregation........ Job 30:28
I c unto the LORD with my voice,...... Ps 3:4
upon the LORD, and c unto my God... Ps 18:6
They c, but there was none to.......... Ps 18:41
They c unto thee, and were............. Ps 22:5
but when he c unto him, he heard.... Ps 22:24
I c unto thee, and thou hast............. Ps 30:2
I c to thee, O LORD........................ Ps 30:8
supplications when I c unto thee....... Ps 31:22
This poor man c, and the LORD........ Ps 34:6
I c unto him with my mouth, and he.. Ps 66:17
I c unto God with my voice, even..... Ps 77:1
God of my salvation, I have c day..... Ps 88:1
But unto thee have I c, O LORD........ Ps 88:13
Then they c unto the LORD in.......... Ps 107:6
Then they c unto the LORD in.......... Ps 107:13
I c with my whole heart.................. Ps 119:145
I c unto thee................................. Ps 119:146
the dawning of the morning, and c... Ps 119:147
In my distress I c unto the LORD,..... Ps 120:1
of the depths have I c unto thee....... Ps 130:1
In the day when I c thou................. Ps 138:3
I c unto the LORD with my voice...... Ps 142:1
I c unto thee, O LORD.................... Ps 142:5
one c unto another, and said, Holy... Is 6:3
moved at the voice of him that c...... Is 6:4
And he c, A lion............................ Is 21:8
have I c concerning this, Their........ Is 30:7
c with a loud voice in the Jews'....... Is 36:13
Destruction upon destruction is c..... Jer 4:20
I c out, I c violence and................. Jer 20:8
c out, I c violence and spoil............ Jer 20:8
Their heart c unto the Lord, O......... Lam 2:18
They c unto them, Depart ye........... Lam 4:15
He c also in mine ears with a......... Eze 9:1
that I fell upon my face, and c........ Eze 9:8
it was c unto them in my hearing,.... Eze 10:13
c with a loud voice, and said, Ah.... Eze 11:13
Then an herald c aloud, To you it.... Dan 3:4
He c aloud, and said this, Hew....... Dan 4:14
The king c aloud to bring in the...... Dan 5:7
he c with a lamentable voice unto... Dan 6:20
they have not c unto me with.......... Hos 7:14
c every man unto his god, and cast.. Jonah 1:5
Wherefore they c unto the LORD...... Jonah 1:14
I c by reason of mine affliction........ Jonah 2:2
out of the belly of hell c I............... Jonah 2:2
the city a day's journey, and he c.... Jonah 3:4
whom the former prophets have c.... Zec 1:4
Then c he upon me, and spake unto. Zec 6:8
hath c by the former prophets......... Zec 7:7
it is come to pass, that as he c....... Zec 7:13
so they c, and I would not hear,...... Zec 7:13
And, behold, they c out, saying,...... Mt 8:29
and they c out for fear.................... Mt 14:26
and beginning to sink, he c............ Mt 14:30
c unto him, saying, Have mercy on.. Mt 15:22
c out, saying, Have mercy on us,..... Mt 20:30
but they c the more, saying, Have... Mt 20:31
went before, and that followed, c..... Mt 21:9
But they c out the more, saying,...... Mt 27:23
hour Jesus c with a loud voice........ Mt 27:46
when he had c again with a loud..... Mt 27:50
an unclean spirit, and he c out........ Mk 1:23
c with a loud voice, he came out..... Mk 1:26
him, fell down before him, and c...... Mk 3:11
c with a loud voice, and said,......... Mk 5:7
it had been a spirit, and c out......... Mk 6:49
the father of the child c out............ Mk 9:24
And the spirit c, and rent him sore... Mk 9:26
but he c the more a great deal,....... Mk 10:48
before, and they that followed, c..... Mk 11:9
they c out again, Crucify him.......... Mk 15:13
they c out the more exceedingly,..... Mk 15:14
hour Jesus c with a loud voice........ Mk 15:34
Jesus c with a loud voice, and........ Mk 15:37
against him, saw that he so c out.... Mk 15:39
and c out with a loud voice,............ Lk 4:33
he had said these things, he c........ Lk 8:8
he c out, and fell down before him... Lk 8:28
a man of the company c out............ Lk 9:38
And he c and said, Father Abraham. Lk 16:24
And he c, saying, Jesus, thou son... Lk 18:38
but he c so much the more, Thou.... Lk 18:39
they c out all at once, saying,......... Lk 23:18
But they c, saying, Crucify him,...... Lk 23:21
when Jesus had c with a loud......... Lk 23:46
John bare witness of him, and c...... Jn 1:15
Then c Jesus in the temple as he.... Jn 7:28
of the feast, Jesus stood and c....... Jn 7:37
he c with a loud voice, Lazarus...... Jn 11:43
and went forth to meet him, and c... Jn 12:13
Jesus c and said, He that.............. Jn 12:44
Then c they all again, saying,......... Jn 18:40
and officers saw him, they c out..... Jn 19:6
but the Jews c out, saying, If......... Jn 19:12
But they c out, Away with him,....... Jn 19:15
Then they c out with a loud voice ... Acts 7:57
c with a loud voice, Lord, lay.......... Acts 7:60

CRIES

same followed Paul and us, and c........... Acts 16:17
But Paul c with a loud voice,.............. Acts 16:28
c out, saying, Great is Diana of........... Acts 19:28
Some therefore c one thing,................ Acts 19:32
the space of two hours c out,............. Acts 19:34
some c one thing, some another,........... Acts 21:34
And as they c out, and cast off........... Acts 22:23
wherefore they c so against him........... Acts 23:6
he c out in the council, Men and.......... Acts 23:6
that I c standing among them,............. Acts 24:21
they c with a loud voice, saying,......... Rev 6:10
he c with a loud voice to the............. Rev 7:2
c with a loud voice, saying,.............. Rev 7:10
c with a loud voice, as when a............ Rev 10:3
and when he had c, seven thunders......... Rev 10:3
And she being with child c................ Rev 12:2
c with a loud cry to him that had......... Rev 14:18
he c mightily with a strong voice,........ Rev 18:2
c when they saw the smoke of her.......... Rev 18:18
cast dust on their heads, and c........... Rev 18:19
he c with a loud voice, saying to......... Rev 19:17

CRIES

the c of them which have reaped........... Jas 5:4

CREST

Moses, Wherefore c thou unto me........... Ex 14:15
Who art thou that c to the king........... 1Sa 26:14
if thou c after knowledge, and............ Prov 2:3
When thou c//let thy companies............ Is 57:13
Why c thou for thine affliction........... Jer 30:15

CRIETH

blood c unto me from the ground........... Gen 4:10
come to pass, when he c unto me........... Ex 22:27
and the soul of the wounded c out......... Job 24:12
shall deliver the needy when he c......... Ps 72:12
my flesh c out for the living God......... Ps 84:2
Wisdom c without.......................... Prov 1:20
She c in the chief place of............... Prov 1:21
She c at the gates, at the entry.......... Prov 8:3
she c upon the highest places of.......... Prov 9:3
is in pain, and c out in her pangs........ Is 26:17
of him that c in the wilderness........... Is 40:3
it c out against me....................... Jer 12:8
The LORD's voice c unto the city.......... Mic 6:9
for she c after us........................ Mt 15:23
taketh him, and he suddenly c out......... Lk 9:39
Esaias also c concerning Israel,.......... Rom 9:27
is of you kept back by fraud, c........... Jas 5:4

CRIME

For this is an heinous c.................. Job 31:11
concerning the c laid against him......... Acts 25:16

CRIMES

for the land is full of bloody c.......... Eze 7:23
to signify the c laid against him......... Acts 25:27

CRIMSON

and in iron, and in purple, and c......... 2Chr 2:7
blue, and in fine linen, and in c......... 2Chr 2:14
the vail of blue, and purple, and c....... 2Chr 3:14
though they be red like c................. Is 1:18
thou clothest thyself with c.............. Jer 4:30

CRIPPLE

being a c from his mother's womb,......... Acts 14:8

CRISPING

and the wimples, and the c pins,.......... Is 3:22

CRISPUS (cris'-pus) A convert of Paul.

And C, the chief ruler of the............. Acts 18:8
I baptized none of you, but C............. 1Cor 1:14

CROOKBACKT

Or c, or a dwarf, or that hath a.......... Lev 21:20

CROOKED

are a perverse and c generation.......... Deut 32:5
hand hath formed the c serpent........... Job 26:13
as turn aside unto their c ways.......... Ps 125:5
Whose ways are c, and they froward....... Prov 2:15
That which is c cannot be made........... Eccl 1:15
straight, which he hath made c........... Eccl 7:13
even leviathan that c serpent............ Is 27:1
the c shall be made straight, and........ Is 40:4
before them, and c things straight....... Is 42:16
make the c places straight............... Is 45:2
they have made them c paths.............. Is 59:8
stone, he hath made my paths c........... Lam 3:9
the c shall be made straight, and........ Lk 3:5
rebuke, in the midst of a c.............. Phil 2:15

CROP

away his c with his feathers............. Lev 1:16
I will c off from the top of his......... Eze 17:22

CROPPED

He c off the top of his young............ Eze 17:4

CROSS

And he that taketh not his c............. Mt 10:38
deny himself, and take up his c.......... Mt 16:24
him they compelled to bear his c......... Mt 27:32
Son of God, come down from the c......... Mt 27:40
let him now come down from the c......... Mt 27:42
deny himself, and take up his c.......... Mk 8:34
and come, take up the c, and follow...... Mk 10:21
Alexander and Rufus, to bear his c....... Mk 15:21
thyself, and come down from the c........ Mk 15:30
of Israel descend now from the c......... Mk 15:32
himself, and take up his c daily......... Lk 9:23
And whosoever doth not bear his c........ Lk 14:27

and on him they laid the c............... Lk 23:26
he bearing his c went forth into......... Jn 19:17
wrote a title, and put it on the c....... Jn 19:19
by the c of Jesus his mother............. Jn 19:25
upon the c on the sabbath day............ Jn 19:31
lest the c of Christ should be........... 1Cor 1:17
of the c is to them that perish......... 1Cor 1:18
the offence of the c ceased.............. Gal 5:11
persecution for the c of Christ.......... Gal 6:12
save in the c of our Lord Jesus.......... Gal 6:14
unto God in one body by the c............ Eph 2:16
death, even the death of the c........... Phil 2:8
the enemies of the c of Christ........... Phil 3:18
peace through the blood of his c......... Col 1:20
of the way, nailing it to his c.......... Col 2:14
was set before him endured the c......... Heb 12:2

CROSSWAY

thou have stood in the c, to cut......... Obad 14

CROUCH

c to him for a piece of silver and....... 1Sa 2:36

CROUCHETH

He c, and humbleth himself, that......... Ps 10:10

CROW

this night, before the cock c............ Mt 26:34
said unto him, Before the cock c......... Mt 26:75
night, before the cock c twice........... Mk 14:30
said unto him, Before the cock c......... Mk 14:72
the cock shall not c this day............ Lk 22:34
said unto him, Before the cock c......... Lk 22:61
unto thee, The cock shall not c.......... Jn 13:38

CROWN

on the c of the head of him that......... Gen 49:26
upon it a c of gold round about.......... Ex 25:11
make thereto a c of gold round........... Ex 25:24
thou shalt make a golden c to the........ Ex 25:25
put the holy c upon the mitre............ Ex 29:6
unto it a c of gold round about.......... Ex 30:3
thou make to it under the c of it........ Ex 30:4
made a c of gold to it round............. Ex 37:2
made thereunto a c of gold round......... Ex 37:11
made a c of gold for the border.......... Ex 37:12
unto it a c of gold round about.......... Ex 37:26
gold for it under the c thereof.......... Ex 37:27
plate of the holy c of pure gold......... Ex 39:30
put the golden plate, the holy c......... Lev 8:9
for the c of the anointing oil of........ Lev 21:12
the arm with the c of the head........... Deut 33:20
I took the c that was upon his........... 2Sa 1:10
their king's c from off his head......... 2Sa 12:30
to the c of his head there was no........ 2Sa 14:25
put the c upon him, and gave him......... 2Kin 11:12
David took the c of their king........... 1Chr 20:2
king's son, and put upon him the c....... 2Chr 23:11
before the king with the c royal......... Est 1:11
he set the royal c upon her head......... Est 2:17
the c royal which is set upon his........ Est 6:8
white, and with a great c of gold........ Est 8:15
the sole of his foot unto his c.......... Job 2:7
and taken the c from my head............. Job 19:9
shoulder, and bind it as a c to me....... Job 31:36
thou settest a c of pure gold on......... Ps 21:3
thou hast profaned his c by.............. Ps 89:39
upon himself shall his c flourish........ Ps 132:18
a c of glory shall she deliver to........ Prov 4:9
woman is a c to her husband.............. Prov 12:4
The c of the wise is their riches........ Prov 14:24
The hoary head is a c of glory........... Prov 16:31
children are the c of old men............ Prov 17:6
doth the c endure to every............... Prov 27:24
c wherewith his mother crowned........... Song 3:11
c of the head of the daughters of........ Is 3:17
Woe to the c of pride, to the............ Is 28:1
The c of pride, the drunkards of......... Is 28:3
Loap of hosts be for a c of glory........ Is 28:5
Thou shalt also be a c of glory.......... Is 62:3
have broken the c of thy head............ Jer 2:16
down, even the c of your glory........... Jer 13:18
Moab, and the c of the head of the....... Jer 48:45
the c is fallen from our head............ Lam 5:16
a beautiful c upon thine head............ Eze 16:12
the diadem, and take off the c........... Eze 21:26
shall be as the stones of a c............ Zec 9:16
they had plaited a c of thorns........... Mt 27:29
purple, and platted a c of thorns....... Mk 15:17
soldiers platted a c of thorns........... Jn 19:2
forth, wearing the c of thorns.......... Jn 19:5
do it to obtain a corruptible c......... 1Cor 9:25
and longed for, my joy and c............ Phil 4:1
hope, or joy, or c of rejoicing......... 1Th 2:19
up for me a c of righteousness.......... 2Ti 4:8
ye shall receive a c of glory........... 1Pet 5:4
and I will give thee a c of life........ Rev 2:10
thou hast, that no man take thy c....... Rev 3:11
and a c was given unto him.............. Rev 6:2
upon her head a c of twelve stars....... Rev 12:1
having on his head a golden c........... Rev 14:14

CROWNED

hast c him with glory and honour........ Ps 8:5
the prudent are c with knowledge........ Prov 14:18
the crown wherewith his mother c........ Song 3:11
Thy c are as the locusts, and thy....... Nah 3:17
for masteries, yet is he not c.......... 2Ti 2:5
of death, c with glory and honour....... Heb 2:9

CROWNEDST

thou c him with glory and honour,....... Heb 2:7

CROWNEST

Thou c the year with thy goodness....... Ps 65:11

CROWNETH

who c thee with lovingkindness and...... Ps 103:4

CROWNING

the c, whose merchants are.............. Is 23:8

CROWNS

beautiful c upon their heads............ Eze 23:42
take silver and gold, and make c........ Zec 6:11
the c shall be to Helem, and to......... Zec 6:14
they had on their heads c of gold....... Rev 4:4
cast their c before the throne,......... Rev 4:10
heads were as it were c like gold....... Rev 9:7
horns, and seven c upon his heads....... Rev 12:3
horns, and upon his horns ten c......... Rev 13:1
fire, and on his head were many c....... Rev 19:12

CRUCIFIED

Son of man is betrayed to be c.......... Mt 26:2
all say unto him, Let him be c.......... Mt 27:22
the more, saying, Let him be c.......... Mt 27:23
Jesus, he delivered him to be c......... Mt 27:26
And they c him, and parted his.......... Mt 27:35
were there two thieves c with him....... Mt 27:38
also, which were c with him............. Mt 27:44
that ye seek Jesus, which was c......... Mt 28:5
when he had scourged him, to be c....... Mk 15:15
And when they had c him, they........... Mk 15:24
was the third hour, and they c him...... Mk 15:25
they that were c with him reviled....... Mk 15:32
Jesus of Nazareth, which was c.......... Mk 16:6
requiring that he might be c............ Lk 23:23
called Calvary, there they c him........ Lk 23:33
the hands of sinful men, and be c....... Lk 24:7
condemned to death, and have c him...... Lk 24:20
him therefore unto them to be c......... Jn 19:16
Where they c him, and two others........ Jn 19:18
Jesus was c was nigh to the city........ Jn 19:20
soldiers, when they had c Jesus......... Jn 19:23
of the other which was c with him....... Jn 19:32
where he was c there was a garden....... Jn 19:41
taken, and by wicked hands have c....... Acts 2:23
that same Jesus, whom ye have c......... Acts 2:36
Christ of Nazareth, whom ye c........... Acts 4:10
that our old man is c with him.......... Rom 6:6
But we preach Christ c, unto the........ 1Cor 1:23
Jesus, save Jesus Christ, and him c..... 1Cor 2:2
not have c the Lord of glory............ 1Cor 2:8
though he was c through weakness........ 2Cor 13:4
I am c with Christ...................... Gal 2:20
evidently set forth, c among you........ Gal 3:1
they that are Christ's have c the....... Gal 5:24
by whom the world is c unto me.......... Gal 6:14
Egypt, where also our Lord was c........ Rev 11:8

CRUCIFY

mock, and to scourge, and to c him...... Mt 20:19
some of them ye shall kill and c........ Mt 23:34
on him, and led him away to c him....... Mt 27:31
And they cried out again, C him......... Mk 15:13
out the more exceedingly, C him......... Mk 15:14
on him, and led him out to c him........ Mk 15:20
And with him they c two thieves......... Mk 15:27
cried, saying, C him, c him............. Lk 23:21
out, saying, C him, c him............... Jn 19:6
unto them, Take ye him, and c him....... Jn 19:6
not that I have power to c thee......... Jn 19:10
with him, away with him, c him.......... Jn 19:15
unto them, Shall I c your King.......... Jn 19:15
seeing they c to themselves the......... Heb 6:6

CRUEL

and their wrath, for it was c........... Gen 49:7
of spirit, and for c bondage............ Ex 6:9
dragons, and the c venom of asps........ Deut 32:33
Thou art become c to me................. Job 30:21
and they hate me with c hatred.......... Ps 25:19
hand of the uprightness of a man........ Ps 71:4
others, and thy years unto the c........ Prov 5:9
but he that is c troubleth his.......... Prov 11:17
mercies of the wicked are c............. Prov 12:10
therefore a c messenger shall be........ Prov 17:11
Wrath is c, and anger is................ Prov 27:4
jealousy is c as the grave.............. Song 8:6
c both with wrath and fierce anger...... Is 13:9
over into the hand of a c lord.......... Is 19:4
they are c, and have no mercy........... Jer 6:23
with the chastisement of a c one........ Jer 30:14
they are c, and will not shew........... Jer 50:42
daughter of my people is become c....... Lam 4:3
And others had trial of c mockings...... Heb 11:36

CRUELLY

father, because he c oppressed.......... Eze 18:18

CRUELTY

instruments of c are in their........... Gen 49:5
That the c done to the threescore....... Judg 9:24
me, and such as breathe out c........... Ps 27:12
are full of the habitations of c........ Ps 74:20
with c have ye ruled them............... Eze 34:4

CRUMBS

yet the dogs eat of the c which......... Mt 15:27
the table eat of the children's c....... Mk 7:28
desiring to be fed with the c........... Lk 16:21

CRUSE
the c of water, and let us go............... 1Sa 26:11
the c of water from Saul's.................... 1Sa 26:12
the c of water that was at his............... 1Sa 26:16
a c of honey, and go to him................. 1Kin 14:3
a barrel, and a little oil in a c............. 1Kin 17:12
neither shall the c of oil fail............... 1Kin 17:14
neither did the c of oil fail................ 1Kin 17:16
and a c of water at his head............... 1Kin 19:6
And he said, Bring me a new c........... 2Kin 2:20

CRUSH
that the foot may c them, or that........ Job 39:15
against me to c my young men............ Lam 1:15
To c under his feet all the.................. Lam 3:34
which c the needy, which say to.......... Amos 4:1

CRUSHED
LORD that which is bruised, or c......... Lev 22:24
c Balaam's foot against the wall.......... Num 22:25
be only oppressed and c alway........... Deut 28:33
which are c before the moth.............. Job 4:19
they are c in the gate, neither............ Job 5:4
that which is c breaketh out into........ Is 59:5
hath devoured me, he hath c me......... Jer 51:34

CRY
LORD said, Because the c of Sodom..... Gen 18:20
according to the c of it, which............ Gen 18:21
because the c of them is waxen.......... Gen 19:13
a great and exceeding bitter c............ Gen 27:34
their c came up unto God by.............. Ex 2:23
have heard their c by reason of.......... Ex 3:7
the c of the children of Israel............. Ex 3:9
therefore they c, saying, Let us.......... Ex 5:8
And there shall be a great c.............. Ex 11:6
and there was a great c in Egypt......... Ex 12:30
they c at all unto me........................ Ex 22:23
I will surely hear their c................... Ex 22:23
of them that c for being overcome...... Ex 32:18
upon his upper lip, and shall c........... Lev 13:45
about them fled at the c of them......... Num 16:34
he c unto the LORD against thee......... Deut 15:9
lest he c against thee unto the........... Deut 24:15
c unto the gods which have to........... Judg 10:14
the c of the city went up to............... 1Sa 5:12
Cease not to c unto the LORD our....... 1Sa 7:8
ye shall c out in that day................... 1Sa 8:18
because their c is come unto me......... 1Sa 9:16
I yet to c any more unto the king........ 2Sa 19:28
my c did enter into his ears............... 2Sa 22:7
my God, to hearken unto the c........... 1Kin 8:28
mocked them, and said, C aloud......... 1Kin 18:27
she went forth to c unto the king........ 2Kin 8:3
my God, to hearken unto the c........... 2Chr 6:19
trumpets to c alarm against you.......... 2Chr 13:12
c unto thee in our affliction................ 2Chr 20:9
there was a great c of the people........ Neh 5:1
very angry when I heard their c.......... Neh 5:6
heardest their c by the Red sea.......... Neh 9:9
cried with a loud and a bitter c........... Est 4:1
of the fastings and their c................. Est 9:31
blood, and let my c have no place....... Job 16:18
I c out of wrong, but I am not............ Job 19:7
I c aloud, but there is no................... Job 19:7
Will God hear his c when trouble........ Job 27:9
I c unto thee, and thou dost not......... Job 30:20
though they c in his destruction......... Job 30:24
If my land c against me, or that.......... Job 31:38
So that they cause the c of the........... Job 34:28
he heareth the c of the afflicted......... Job 34:28
they make the oppressed to c............ Job 35:9
they c out by reason of the arm.......... Job 35:9
There they c, but none giveth............. Job 35:12
they c not when he bindeth them....... Job 36:13
when his young ones c unto God........ Job 38:41
Hearken unto the voice of my c.......... Ps 5:2
not the c of the humble.................... Ps 9:12
right, O LORD, attend unto my c......... Ps 17:1
my c came before him, even into........ Ps 18:6
I c in the daytime, but thou............... Ps 22:2
O LORD, when I c with my voice......... Ps 27:7
Unto thee will I c, O LORD my........... Ps 28:1
when I c unto thee, when I lift........... Ps 28:2
and his ears are open unto their c....... Ps 34:15
The righteous c, and the LORD........... Ps 34:17
O LORD, and give ear unto my c......... Ps 39:12
inclined unto me, and heard my c....... Ps 40:1
at noon, will I pray, and c aloud......... Ps 55:17
When I c unto thee, then shall........... Ps 56:9
I will c unto God most high............... Ps 57:2
Hear my c, O God.......................... Ps 61:1
of the earth will I c unto thee............ Ps 61:2
for I c unto thee daily...................... Ps 86:3
incline thine ear unto my c............... Ps 88:2
He shall c unto me, Thou art my......... Ps 89:26
LORD, and let my c come unto thee..... Ps 102:1
affliction, when he heard their c......... Ps 106:44
Then they c unto the LORD in............ Ps 107:19
Then they c unto the LORD in............ Ps 107:28
Let my c come near before thee, O..... Ps 119:169
Lord, I c unto thee......................... Ps 141:1
unto my voice, when I c unto thee...... Ps 141:1
Attend unto my c........................... Ps 142:6
he also will hear their c................... Ps 145:19
and to the young ravens which c........ Ps 147:9
Doth not wisdom c......................... Prov 8:1
his ears at the c of the poor............. Prov 21:13
he also shall c himself.................... Prov 21:13
heard in quiet more than the c of....... Eccl 9:17
for righteousness, but behold a c........ Is 5:7
child shall have knowledge to c......... Is 8:4
C out and shout, thou inhabitant....... Is 12:6
shall c in their desolate houses.......... Is 13:22
c, O city... Is 14:31
And Heshbon shall c, and Elealeh...... Is 15:4
soldiers of Moab shall c out.............. Is 15:4
My heart shall c out for Moab............ Is 15:5
shall raise up a c of destruction......... Is 15:5
For the c is gone round about the....... Is 15:8
for they shall c unto the LORD........... Is 19:20
they shall c aloud from the sea.......... Is 24:14
c ye out, and................................... Is 29:9
unto thee at the voice of thy c........... Is 30:19
valiant ones shall c without............... Is 33:7
the satyr shall c to his fellow............. Is 34:14
c unto her, that her warfare is........... Is 40:2
The voice said, C............................. Is 40:6
And he said, What shall I c................ Is 40:6
He shall not c, nor lift up, nor............ Is 42:2
he shall c, yea, roar......................... Is 42:13
now will I c like a travailing.............. Is 42:14
whose c is in the ships..................... Is 43:14
yea, one shall c unto him................. Is 46:7
c aloud, thou that didst not............... Is 54:1
C aloud, spare not, lift up thy............ Is 58:1
thou shalt c, and he shall say............ Is 58:9
but ye shall c for sorrow of.............. Is 65:14
c in the ears of Jerusalem................. Jer 2:2
thou not from this time c unto me...... Jer 3:4
c, gather together, and say............... Jer 4:5
neither lift up c nor prayer for.......... Jer 7:16
Behold the voice of the c of the......... Jer 8:19
and though they shall c unto me........ Jer 11:11
c unto the gods unto whom they........ Jer 11:12
neither lift up a c or prayer for.......... Jer 11:14
they c unto me for their trouble......... Jer 11:14
the c of Jerusalem is gone up............ Jer 14:2
fast, I will not hear their c................ Jer 14:12
Let a c be heard from their................ Jer 18:22
let him hear the c in the morning....... Jer 20:16
Go up to Lebanon, and c.................. Jer 22:20
in Bashan, and c from the passages.... Jer 22:20
Howl, ye shepherds, and c................ Jer 25:34
A voice of the c of the shepherds....... Jer 25:36
upon the mount Ephraim shall c......... Jer 31:6
thy c hath filled the land.................. Jer 46:12
They did c there, Pharaoh king of....... Jer 46:17
then the men shall c, and all the........ Jer 47:2
ones have caused a c to be heard....... Jer 48:4
have heard a c of destruction............ Jer 48:5
howl and c; tell ye it in Arnon........... Jer 48:20
I will c out for all Moab.................... Jer 48:31
From the c of Heshbon even unto....... Jer 48:34
c, ye daughters of Rabbah, gird......... Jer 49:3
at the c the noise thereof was............ Jer 49:21
and they shall c unto them.............. Jer 49:29
the c is heard among the nations....... Jer 50:46
A sound of a c cometh from.............. Jer 51:54
Arise, c out in the night................... Lam 2:19
Also when I c and shout, he............. Lam 3:8
eat at my breathing, at my c............. Lam 3:56
though they c in mine ears with a....... Eze 8:18
that c for all the abominations.......... Eze 9:4
C and howl, son of man.................... Eze 21:12
Forbear to c, make no mourning........ Eze 24:17
of thy fall, when the wounded........... Eze 26:15
the sound of the c of thy pilots.......... Eze 27:28
shall c bitterly, and shall cast............ Eze 27:30
c aloud at Beth-aven, after the.......... Hos 5:8
Israel shall c unto me, My God.......... Hos 8:2
your God, and c unto the LORD......... Joel 1:14
O LORD, to thee will I c................... Joel 1:19
of the field c also unto thee.............. Joel 1:20
a young lion c out of his den............. Amos 3:4
that great city, and c against it.......... Jonah 1:2
sackcloth, and c mightily unto God..... Jonah 3:8
Then shall they c unto the LORD........ Mic 3:4
that bite with their teeth, and c......... Mic 3:5
Now why dost thou c out aloud.......... Mic 4:9
Stand, stand, shall they c................. Nah 2:8
O LORD, how long shall I c............... Hab 1:2
even c out unto thee of violence........ Hab 1:2
the stone shall c out of the wall......... Hab 2:11
noise of a c from the fish gate........... Zeph 1:10
mighty man shall c there bitterly........ Zeph 1:14
C thou, saying, Thus saith the........... Zec 1:14
C yet, saying, Thus saith the............. Zec 1:17
He shall not strive, nor c................. Mt 12:19
And at midnight there was a c made.... Mt 25:6
of Nazareth, he began to c out.......... Mk 10:47
avenge his own elect, which c day...... Lk 18:7
stones would immediately c out......... Lk 19:40
And there arose a great c................. Acts 23:9
Spirit of adoption, whereby we c........ Rom 8:15
break forth and c, thou that.............. Gal 4:27
cried with a loud c to him that.......... Rev 14:18

CRYING
when Eli heard the noise of the c....... 1Sa 4:14
hand on her head, and went on c....... 2Sa 13:19
regardeth he the c of the driver......... Job 39:7
I am weary of my c......................... Ps 69:3
let not thy soul spare for his c........... Prov 19:18
horseleach hath two daughters, c....... Prov 30:15
walls, and of c to the mountains........ Is 22:5
There is a c for wine in the............... Is 24:11
heard in her, nor the voice of c......... Is 65:19
A voice of c shall be from................ Jer 48:3
thereof with shoutings, c................. Jer 48:33
with weeping, and with c out............ Mal 2:13
The voice of one c in the................. Mt 3:3
two blind men followed him, c......... Mt 9:27
the children c in the temple, and....... Mt 21:15
The voice of one c in the.................. Mk 1:3
the mountains, and in the tombs, c.... Mk 5:5
the multitude c aloud began to.......... Mk 15:8
The voice of one c in the.................. Lk 3:4
c out, and saying, Thou art Christ...... Lk 4:41
voice of one c in the wilderness........ Jn 1:23
c with loud voice, came out of.......... Acts 8:7
ran in among the people, c out.......... Acts 14:14
unto the rulers of the city, c............. Acts 17:6
C out, Men of Israel, help................. Acts 21:28
of the people followed after, c.......... Acts 21:36
c that he ought not to live any.......... Acts 25:24
of his Son into your hearts, c............ Gal 4:6
and supplications with strong c......... Heb 5:7
c with a loud voice to him that......... Rev 14:15
more death, neither sorrow, nor c...... Rev 21:4

CRYSTAL
The gold and the c cannot equal it..... Job 28:17
as the colour of the terrible c............ Eze 1:22
was a sea of glass like unto c............ Rev 4:6
like a jasper stone, clear as c............ Rev 21:11
of water of life, clear as c................ Rev 22:1

CUBIT
in a c shalt thou finish it above......... Gen 6:16
be the length thereof, and a c............ Ex 25:10
half the breadth thereof, and a c........ Ex 25:10
be the length thereof, and a c............ Ex 25:17
c the breadth thereof, and a.............. Ex 25:23
a c on the one side, and a................. Ex 26:13
be the length of a board, and a c........ Ex 26:16
A c shall be the length thereof........... Ex 30:2
and a c the breadth thereof............... Ex 30:2
and the breadth of a board one c....... Ex 36:21
half was the length of it, and a c........ Ex 37:1
a half the breadth of it, and a c......... Ex 37:1
was the length thereof, and one c....... Ex 37:6
c the breadth thereof, and a.............. Ex 37:10
a c, and the breadth of it a c............. Ex 37:25
of it, after the c of a man................. Deut 3:11
had two edges, of a c length............. Judg 3:16
knops compassing it, ten in a c.......... 1Kin 7:24
the chapiter and above was a c.......... 1Kin 7:31
after the work of the base, a c........... 1Kin 7:31
a wheel was a c and half a c............. 1Kin 7:32
a round compass of half a c high....... 1Kin 7:35
ten in a c, compassing the sea.......... 2Chr 4:3
reed of six cubits long by the c.......... Eze 40:5
chambers was one c on this side........ Eze 40:12
the space was one c on that side........ Eze 40:12
a c and an half long, and a c............ Eze 40:42
and an half broad, and one c high...... Eze 40:42
breadth inward, a way of one c.......... Eze 42:4
The c is a c and an hand................. Eze 43:13
The c is a c and an hand................. Eze 43:13
be a c, and the breadth a c.............. Eze 43:14
two cubits, and the breadth one c...... Eze 43:14
four cubits, and the breadth one c..... Eze 43:14
border about it shall be half a c......... Eze 43:17
bottom thereof shall be a about......... Eze 43:17
can add one c unto his stature.......... Mt 6:27
can add to his stature one c............. Lk 12:25

CUBITS
the ark shall be three hundred c........ Gen 6:15
c, the breadth of it fifty c................. Gen 6:15
c the length of it thirty c.................. Gen 6:15
Fifteen c upward did the waters......... Gen 7:20
two c and a half shall be the............ Ex 25:10
two c and a half shall be the............ Ex 25:17
two c shall be the length thereof........ Ex 25:23
shall be eight and twenty c............... Ex 26:2
the breadth of one curtain four c........ Ex 26:2
of one curtain shall be thirty c........... Ex 26:8
the breadth of one curtain four c........ Ex 26:8
Ten c shall be the length of a............ Ex 26:16
five c long, and five c broad............. Ex 27:1
height thereof shall be three c........... Ex 27:1
of an hundred c long for one side....... Ex 27:9
be hangings of an hundred c long...... Ex 27:11
side shall be hangings of fifty c......... Ex 27:12
side eastward shall be fifty c............ Ex 27:13
of the gate shall be fifteen c............. Ex 27:14
side shall be hangings fifteen c......... Ex 27:15
shall be an hanging of twenty c......... Ex 27:16
the court shall be an hundred c......... Ex 27:18
the height five c of fine twined.......... Ex 27:18
two c shall be the height thereof........ Ex 30:2
one curtain was twenty and eight c..... Ex 36:9
the breadth of one curtain four c........ Ex 36:9
four c was the breadth of one........... Ex 36:15
The length of a board was ten c......... Ex 36:21
two c and a half was the length of a... Ex 37:6
two c and a half was the length......... Ex 37:6
two c was the length thereof, and...... Ex 37:10
two c was the height of it................. Ex 37:25
five c was the length thereof, and...... Ex 38:1
five c the breadth thereof................. Ex 38:1
three c the height thereof................. Ex 38:1
fine twined linen, an hundred c......... Ex 38:9
the hangings were an hundred c........ Ex 38:11
side were hangings of fifty c............. Ex 38:12
the east side eastward fifty c............ Ex 38:13
side of the gate were fifteen c........... Ex 38:14
hand, were hangings of fifteen c........ Ex 38:15
the breadth of the court was fifty c..... Ex 38:18
height in the breadth was five c......... Ex 38:18
as it were two c high upon the.......... Num 11:31
outward a thousand c round about..... Num 35:4

C

on the east side two thousand c......	Num 35:5
on the south side two thousand c......	Num 35:5
on the west side two thousand c......	Num 35:5
on the north side two thousand c......	Num 35:5
nine c was the length thereof, and.	Deut 3:11
four c the breadth of it, after........	Deut 3:11
about two thousand c by measure.....	Josh 3:4
of Gath, whose height was six c......	1Sa 17:4
length thereof was threescore c........	1Kin 6:2
and the breadth thereof twenty c.....	1Kin 6:2
and the height thereof thirty c........	1Kin 6:2
twenty c was the length thereof,......	1Kin 6:3
ten c was the breadth thereof.........	1Kin 6:3
chamber was five c broad..............	1Kin 6:6
and the middle was six c broad........	1Kin 6:6
and the third was seven c broad......	1Kin 6:6
all the house, five c high.............	1Kin 6:10
he built twenty c on the sides of....	1Kin 6:16
before it, was forty c long.............	1Kin 6:17
forepart was twenty c in length......	1Kin 6:20
twenty c in breadth.....................	1Kin 6:20
twenty c in the height thereof........	1Kin 6:20
of olive tree, each ten c high.........	1Kin 6:23
five c was the one wing of the.......	1Kin 6:24
five c the other wing of the..........	1Kin 6:24
part of the other were ten c..........	1Kin 6:24
And the other cherub was ten c......	1Kin 6:25
of the one cherub was ten c..........	1Kin 6:26
length thereof was an hundred c......	1Kin 7:2
and the breadth thereof fifty c.......	1Kin 7:2
and the height thereof thirty c........	1Kin 7:2
the length thereof was fifty c.........	1Kin 7:6
and the breadth thereof thirty c......	1Kin 7:6
ten c, and stones of eight c..........	1Kin 7:10
brass, of eighteen c high apiece......	1Kin 7:15
a line of twelve c did compass.......	1Kin 7:15
of the one chapter was five c........	1Kin 7:16
of the other chapter was five c......	1Kin 7:16
of lily work in the porch, four c......	1Kin 7:19
ten c from the one brim to the.......	1Kin 7:23
about, and his height was five c......	1Kin 7:23
a line of thirty c did compass it.....	1Kin 7:23
four c was the length of one base...	1Kin 7:27
the breadth thereof, and.........	1Kin 7:27
and three c the height of it..........	1Kin 7:27
and every laver was four c...........	1Kin 7:38
the corner gate, four hundred c......	2Kin 14:13
of the one pillar was eighteen c.....	2Kin 25:17
height of the chapiter three c........	2Kin 25:17
man of great stature, five c high....	1Chr 11:23
The length by c after the first......	2Chr 3:3
first measure was threescore c.......	2Chr 3:3
c, and the breadth twenty c.........	2Chr 3:3
breadth of the house, twenty c......	2Chr 3:4
breadth of the house, twenty c......	2Chr 3:8
and the breadth thereof twenty c....	2Chr 3:8
the cherubims were twenty c long..	2Chr 3:11
wing of the one cherub was five c...	2Chr 3:11
other wing was likewise five c.......	2Chr 3:11
of the other cherub was five c.......	2Chr 3:12
and the other wing was five c also..	2Chr 3:12
spread themselves forth twenty c....	2Chr 3:13
pillars of thirty and five c high......	2Chr 3:15
top of each of them was five c......	2Chr 3:15
twenty c the length thereof, and....	2Chr 4:1
twenty c the breadth thereof, and...	2Chr 4:1
and ten c the height thereof.........	2Chr 4:1
sea of ten c from brim to brim......	2Chr 4:2
five c the height thereof..............	2Chr 4:2
a line of thirty c did compass it.....	2Chr 4:2
a brasen scaffold, of five c long.....	2Chr 6:13
five c broad, and three c.............	2Chr 6:13
the corner gate, four hundred c......	2Chr 25:23
the height thereof threescore c......	Ezr 6:3
the breadth thereof threescore c....	Ezr 6:3
a thousand c on the wall unto the..	Neh 3:13
a gallows be made of fifty c high....	Est 5:14
also, the gallows fifty c high........	Est 7:9
of one pillar was eighteen c.........	Jer 52:21
fillet of twelve c did compass it.....	Jer 52:21
height of one chapiter was five c....	Jer 52:22
reed of six c long by the cubit......	Eze 40:5
the little chambers were five c......	Eze 40:7
the porch of the gate, eight c.......	Eze 40:9
and the posts thereof, two c.........	Eze 40:9
of the entry of the gate, ten c......	Eze 40:11
length of the gate, thirteen c.......	Eze 40:11
chambers were six c on this side....	Eze 40:12
and six c on that side................	Eze 40:12
the breadth was five and twenty c..	Eze 40:13
made also posts of threescore c.....	Eze 40:14
of the inner gate were fifty c........	Eze 40:15
without, an hundred c eastward......	Eze 40:19
the length thereof was fifty c........	Eze 40:21
and the breadth five and twenty c..	Eze 40:21
from gate to gate an hundred c.....	Eze 40:23
the length was fifty c.................	Eze 40:25
and the breadth five and twenty c..	Eze 40:25
toward the south an hundred c......	Eze 40:27
it was fifty c long.....................	Eze 40:29
and five and twenty c broad..........	Eze 40:29
about were five and twenty c long..	Eze 40:30
and five c broad.......................	Eze 40:30
it was fifty c long.....................	Eze 40:33
and five and twenty c broad..........	Eze 40:33
the length was fifty c, and the......	Eze 40:36
and the breadth five and twenty c..	Eze 40:36
the court, an hundred c long.........	Eze 40:47
and an hundred c broad...............	Eze 40:47
five c on this side.....................	Eze 40:48

and five c on that side................	Eze 40:48
the gate was three c on this side...	Eze 40:48
and three c on that side..............	Eze 40:48
length of the porch was twenty c...	Eze 40:49
and the breadth eleven c.............	Eze 40:49
six c broad on the one side, and....	Eze 41:1
six c broad on the other side........	Eze 41:1
the breadth of the door was ten c..	Eze 41:2
door were five c on the one side....	Eze 41:2
and five c on the other side..........	Eze 41:2
the length thereof, forty c...........	Eze 41:2
and the breadth, twenty c............	Eze 41:2
the post of the door, two c...........	Eze 41:3
and the door, six c....................	Eze 41:3
the breadth of the door, seven c....	Eze 41:3
the length thereof, twenty c..........	Eze 41:4
and the breadth, twenty c, before...	Eze 41:4
the wall of the house, six c..........	Eze 41:5
of every side chamber, four..........	Eze 41:5
were a full reed of six great.........	Eze 41:8
side chamber without, was five c....	Eze 41:9
was the wideness of twenty c........	Eze 41:10
was left was five c round about.....	Eze 41:11
the west was seventy c broad........	Eze 41:12
was five c thick round about.........	Eze 41:12
and the length thereof ninety c......	Eze 41:12
the house, an hundred c long........	Eze 41:13
walls thereof, an hundred c..........	Eze 41:13
toward the east, an hundred c.......	Eze 41:14
on the other side, an hundred c.....	Eze 41:15
altar of wood was three c high......	Eze 41:22
and the length thereof two c.........	Eze 41:22
an hundred c was the north door....	Eze 42:2
and the breadth was fifty c..........	Eze 42:2
Over against the twenty c which....	Eze 42:3
a walk of ten c breadth inward......	Eze 42:4
the length thereof was fifty c........	Eze 42:7
in the utter court was fifty c........	Eze 42:8
the temple were an hundred c.......	Eze 42:8
measures of the altar after the c....	Eze 43:13
the lower settle shall be two c......	Eze 43:14
greater settle shall be four c........	Eze 43:14
So the altar shall be four c..........	Eze 43:15
the altar shall be twelve c long......	Eze 43:16
settle shall be fourteen c long......	Eze 43:17
fifty c round about for the..........	Eze 45:2
courts joined of forty c long.........	Eze 46:22
he measured a thousand c...........	Eze 47:3
whose height was threescore c.......	Dan 3:1
and the breadth thereof six c........	Dan 3:1
the length thereof is twenty c.......	Zec 5:2
and the breadth thereof ten c.......	Zec 5:2
but as it were two hundred c........	Jn 21:8
an hundred and forty and four c.....	Rev 21:17

CUCKOW

owl, and the night hawk, and the c...	Lev 11:16
owl, and the night hawk, and the c...	Deut 14:15

CUCUMBERS

the c, and the melons, and the......	Num 11:5
as a lodge in a garden of c...........	Is 1:8

CUD

is clovenfooted, and cheweth the c..	Lev 11:3
not eat of them that chew the c.....	Lev 11:4
camel, because he cheweth the c.....	Lev 11:4
coney, because he cheweth the c.....	Lev 11:5
hare, because he cheweth the c......	Lev 11:6
yet he cheweth not the c.............	Lev 11:7
clovenfooted, nor cheweth the c.....	Lev 11:26
cheweth the c among the beasts,....	Deut 14:6
not eat of them that chew the c.....	Deut 14:7
for they chew the c, but divide......	Deut 14:8
the hoof, yet cheweth not the c......	Deut 14:8

CUMBERED

But Martha was c about much.......	Lk 10:40

CUMBERETH

why c it the ground...................	Lk 13:7

CUMBRANCE

can I myself alone bear your c.......	Deut 1:12

CUMI

hand, and said unto her, Talitha c...	Mk 5:41

CUMMIN

the fitches, and scatter the c........	Is 28:25
wheel turned about upon the c.......	Is 28:27
with a staff, and the c with a rod...	Is 28:27
pay tithe of mint and anise and c...	Mt 23:23

CUN See Chun.

CUNNING

and Esau was a c hunter, a man of..	Gen 25:27
with cherubims of c work shalt.......	Ex 26:1
and fine twined linen of c work......	Ex 26:31
and fine twined linen, with c work..	Ex 28:6
of judgment with c work.............	Ex 28:15
To devise c works, to work in.......	Ex 31:4
to make any manner of c work......	Ex 35:33
of the c workman, and of the.......	Ex 35:35
and of those that devise c work.....	Ex 35:35
cherubims of c work made he them..	Ex 36:8
cherubims made he it of c work.....	Ex 36:35
a c workman, and an embroiderer in.	Ex 38:23
and in the fine linen, with c work...	Ex 39:3
he made the breastplate of c work..	Ex 39:8
who is a c player on an harp.........	1Sa 16:16
that is c in playing, and a mighty...	1Sa 16:18
c to work all works in brass.........	1Kin 7:14
all manner of c men for every......	1Chr 22:15

of the Lord, even all that were c....	1Chr 25:7
therefore a man c to work in gold...	2Chr 2:7
can skill to grave with the c men....	2Chr 2:7
And now I have sent a c man........	2Chr 2:13
be put to him, with thy c men.......	2Chr 2:14
with the c men of my lord David....	2Chr 2:14
engines, invented by c men..........	2Chr 26:15
let my right hand forget her c.......	Ps 137:5
work of the hands of a c workman..	Song 7:1
the c artificer, and the eloquent....	Is 3:3
he seeketh unto him a c workman...	Is 40:20
and send for c women, that they....	Jer 9:17
they are all the work of c men......	Jer 10:9
c in knowledge, and understanding..	Dan 1:4
c craftiness, whereby they lie in....	Eph 4:14

CUNNINGLY

not followed c devised fables........	2Pet 1:16

CUP

Pharaoh's c was in my hand.........	Gen 40:11
and pressed them into Pharaoh's c..	Gen 40:11
I gave the c into Pharaoh's hand...	Gen 40:11
deliver Pharaoh's c into his hand...	Gen 40:13
he gave the c into Pharaoh's hand..	Gen 40:21
And put my c, the silver c..........	Gen 44:2
the c was found in Benjamin's......	Gen 44:12
he also with whom the c is found..	Gen 44:16
man in whose hand the c is found..	Gen 44:17
own meat, and drank of his own c..	2Sa 12:3
was wrought like the brim of a c...	1Kin 7:26
like the work of the brim of a c....	2Chr 4:5
shall be the portion of their c.......	Ps 11:6
of mine inheritance and of my c.....	Ps 16:5
my c runneth over....................	Ps 23:5
waters of a full c are wrung out....	Ps 73:10
the hand of the Lord there is a c...	Ps 75:8
I will take the c of salvation.........	Ps 116:13
it giveth his colour in the c.........	Prov 23:31
of the Lord the c of his fury........	Is 51:17
the dregs of the c of trembling......	Is 51:17
of thine hand the c of trembling....	Is 51:22
the dregs of the c of my fury.......	Is 51:22
the c of consolation to drink for....	Jer 16:7
Take the wine c of this fury at......	Jer 25:15
Then took I the c at the Lord's.....	Jer 25:17
take the c at thine hand to drink....	Jer 25:28
of the c have assuredly drunken....	Jer 49:12
a golden c in the Lord's hand.......	Jer 51:7
the c also shall pass through.......	Lam 4:21
will I give her c into thine hand....	Eze 23:31
drink of thy sister's deep...........	Eze 23:32
with the c of astonishment and.....	Eze 23:33
with the c of thy sister Samaria.....	Eze 23:33
the c of the Lord's right hand......	Hab 2:16
I will make Jerusalem a c of........	Zec 12:2
c of cold water only in the name....	Mt 10:42
of the c that I shall drink of........	Mt 20:22
Ye shall drink indeed of my c.......	Mt 20:23
make clean the outside of the c.....	Mt 23:25
first that which is within the c......	Mt 23:26
And he took the c, and gave thanks..	Mt 26:27
possible, let this c pass from me....	Mt 26:39
if this c may not pass away from...	Mt 26:42
a c of water to drink in my name...	Mk 9:41
ye drink of the c that I drink of....	Mk 10:38
drink of the c that I drink of.......	Mk 10:39
And he took the c, and when he had..	Mk 14:23
take away this c from me............	Mk 14:36
make clean the outside of the c.....	Lk 11:39
And he took the c, and gave thanks,.	Lk 22:17
Likewise also the c after supper.....	Lk 22:20
This is the new testament in my.....	Lk 22:20
be willing, remove this c from me...	Lk 22:42
the c which my Father hath given...	Jn 18:11
The c of blessing which we bless,...	1Cor 10:16
Ye cannot drink the c of the Lord...	1Cor 10:21
and the c of devils..................	1Cor 10:21
same manner also he took the c.....	1Cor 11:25
This c is the new testament in my...	1Cor 11:25
eat this bread, and drink this c.....	1Cor 11:26
drink this c of the Lord.............	1Cor 11:27
of that bread, and drink of that c...	1Cor 11:28
into the c of his indignation........	Rev 14:10
to give unto her the c of the.......	Rev 16:19
having a golden c in her hand.......	Rev 17:4
in the c which she hath filled.......	Rev 18:6

CUPBEARER

For I was the king's c................	Neh 1:11

CUPBEARERS

and their apparel, and his c..........	1Kin 10:5
his c also, and their apparel.........	2Chr 9:4

CUPS

and the bowls, and the c............	1Chr 28:17
quantity, from the vessels of c......	Is 22:24
pots full of wine, and c, and I......	Jer 35:5
and the spoons, and the c...........	Jer 52:19
to hold, as the washing of c........	Mk 7:4
men, as the washing of pots and c..	Mk 7:8

CURDLED

out as milk, and c me like cheese...	Job 10:10

CURE

health and, c and, I will c them.....	Jer 33:6
heal you, nor c you of your wound..	Hos 5:13
and they could not c him............	Mt 17:16
over all devils, and to c diseases....	Lk 9:1

CURED

for thou shalt not be c	Jer 46:11
the child was c from that very	Mt 17:18
in that same hour he c many of	Lk 7:21
said unto him that was c, It is	Jn 5:10

CURES

I do c to day and to morrow, and	Lk 13:32

CURIOUS

the c girdle of the ephod, which	Ex 28:8
above the c girdle of the ephod	Ex 28:27
above the c girdle of the ephod	Ex 28:28
gird him with the c girdle of the	Ex 29:5
And to devise c works, to work in	Ex 35:32
the c girdle of his ephod, that	Ex 39:5
above the c girdle of the ephod	Ex 39:20
above the c girdle of the ephod	Ex 39:21
with the c girdle of the ephod	Lev 8:7
used c arts brought their books	Acts 19:19

CURIOUSLY

c wrought in the lowest parts of	Ps 139:15

CURRENT

c money with the merchant	Gen 23:16

CURSE

I will not again c the ground any	Gen 8:21
thee, and c him that curseth thee	Gen 12:3
and I shall bring a c upon me	Gen 27:12
said unto him, Upon me be thy c	Gen 27:13
nor c the ruler of thy people	Ex 22:28
Thou shalt not c the deaf	Lev 19:14
bitter water that causeth the c	Num 5:18
bitter water that causeth the c	Num 5:19
the woman, The LORD make thee a c	Num 5:21
the c shall go into thy bowels	Num 5:22
bitter water that causeth the c	Num 5:24
the c shall enter into her	Num 5:24
the c shall enter into her	Num 5:27
shall be a c among her people	Num 5:27
I pray thee, c me this people	Num 22:6
come now, c me them	Num 22:11
thou shalt not c the people	Num 22:12
I pray thee, c me this people	Num 22:17
c me Jacob, and come, defy Israel	Num 23:7
How shall I c, whom God hath not	Num 23:8
I took thee to c mine enemies	Num 23:11
and c me them from thence	Num 23:13
Neither c them at all, nor bless	Num 23:25
thou mayest c me them from thence	Num 23:27
I called thee to c mine enemies	Num 24:10
you this day a blessing and a c	Deut 11:26
And a c, if ye will not obey the	Deut 11:28
Gerizim, and the c upon mount Ebal	Deut 11:29
Pethor of Mesopotamia, to c thee	Deut 23:4
the c into a blessing unto thee	Deut 23:5
shall stand upon mount Ebal to c	Deut 27:13
he hearteth the words of this c	Deut 29:19
upon thee, the blessing and the c	Deut 30:1
and make the camp of Israel a c	Josh 6:18
Balaam the son of Beor to c you	Josh 24:9
C ye Meroz, said the angel of the	Judg 5:23
c ye bitterly the inhabitants	Judg 5:23
upon them came the c of Jotham	Judg 9:57
this dead dog c my lord the king	2Sa 16:9
so let him c, because the LORD	2Sa 16:10
LORD hath said unto him, C David	2Sa 16:10
let him alone, and let him c	2Sa 16:11
c in the day when I went to	1Kin 2:8
should become a desolation and a c	2Kin 22:19
their nobles, and entered into a c	Neh 10:29
them, that he should c them	Neh 13:2
God turned the c into a blessing	Neh 13:2
he will c thee to thy face	Job 1:11
he will c thee to thy face	Job 2:5
c God, and die	Job 2:9
Let them c it	Job 3:8
that c the day, who are ready	Job 3:8
to sin by wishing a c to his soul	Job 31:30
their mouth, but they c inwardly	Ps 62:4
Let them c, but bless thou	Ps 109:28
The c of the LORD is in the house	Prov 3:33
corn, the people shall c him	Prov 11:26
him shall the people c, nations	Prov 24:24
so the c causeless shall not come	Prov 26:2
it shall be counted a c to him	Prov 27:14
his eyes shall have many a c	Prov 28:27
unto his master, lest he c thee	Prov 30:10
lest thou hear thy servant c thee	Eccl 7:21
C not the king, do not sin in thy	Eccl 10:20
c not the rich in thy bedchamber	Eccl 10:20
c their king and their God, and	Is 8:21
hath the c devoured the earth	Is 24:6
and upon the people of my c	Is 34:5
and have given Jacob to the c	Is 43:28
your name for a c unto my chosen	Is 65:15
yet every one of them doth c me	Jer 15:10
and a proverb, a taunt and a c	Jer 24:9
astonishment, an hissing, and a c	Jer 25:18
will make this city a c to all	Jer 26:6
kingdoms of the earth, to be a c	Jer 29:18
of them shall be taken up a c by	Jer 29:22
and an astonishment, and a c	Jer 42:18
off, and that ye might be a c	Jer 44:8
and an astonishment, and a c	Jer 44:12
and an astonishment, and a c	Jer 44:22
a reproach, a waste, and a c	Jer 49:13
sorrow of heart, thy c unto them	Lam 3:65
therefore the c is poured upon us	Dan 9:11
This is the c that goeth forth	Zec 5:3
as ye were a c among the heathen	Zec 8:13

I will even send a c upon you	Mal 2:2
and I will c your blessings	Mal 2:2
Ye are cursed with a c	Mal 3:9
come and smite the earth with a c	Mal 4:6
enemies, bless them that c you	Mt 5:44
Then began he to c and to swear	Mt 26:74
But he began to c and to swear	Mk 14:71
Bless them that c you, and pray	Lk 6:28
and bound themselves under a c	Acts 23:12
bound ourselves under a great c	Acts 23:14
bless, and c not	Rom 12:14
works of the law are under the c	Gal 3:10
redeemed us from the c of the law	Gal 3:13
being made a c for us	Gal 3:13
and therewith c we men, which are	Jas 3:9
And there shall be no more c	Rev 22:3

CURSED

thou art c above all cattle, and	Gen 3:14
c is the ground for thy sake	Gen 3:17
now art thou c from the earth	Gen 4:11
the ground which the LORD hath c	Gen 5:29
And he said, C be Canaan	Gen 9:25
c be every one that curseth thee	Gen 27:29
C be their anger, for it was	Gen 49:7
he hath c his father or his	Lev 20:9
the name of the LORD, and c	Lev 24:11
him that hath c without the camp	Lev 24:14
him that had c out of the camp	Lev 24:23
and he whom thou cursest is c	Num 22:6
I curse, whom God hath not c	Num 23:8
c is he that curseth thee	Num 24:9
lest thou be a c thing like it	Deut 7:26
for it is a c thing	Deut 7:26
of the c thing to thine hand	Deut 13:17
C be the man that maketh any	Deut 27:15
C be he that setteth light by his	Deut 27:16
C be he that removeth his	Deut 27:17
C be he that maketh the blind to	Deut 27:18
C be he that perverteth the	Deut 27:19
C be he that lieth with his	Deut 27:20
C be he that lieth with any	Deut 27:21
C be he that lieth with his	Deut 27:22
C be he that lieth with his	Deut 27:23
C be he that smiteth his	Deut 27:24
C be he that taketh reward to	Deut 27:25
C be he that confirmeth not all	Deut 27:26
C shalt thou be in the city, and	Deut 28:16
c shalt thou be in the field	Deut 28:16
C shall be thy basket and thy	Deut 28:17
C shall be the fruit of thy body	Deut 28:18
C shalt thou be when thou comest	Deut 28:19
c shalt thou be when thou goest	Deut 28:19
C be the man before the LORD	Josh 6:26
Now therefore ye are c, and there	Josh 9:23
did eat and drink, and c Abimelech	Judg 9:27
C be the man that giveth a wife to	Judg 21:18
C be the man that eateth any food	1Sa 14:24
C be the man that eateth any food	1Sa 14:28
the Philistine c David by his	1Sa 17:43
c be they before the LORD	1Sa 26:19
came forth, and c still as he came	2Sa 16:5
And thus said Shimei when he c	2Sa 16:7
c as he went, and threw stones at	2Sa 16:13
because he c the LORD's anointed	2Sa 19:21
which c me with a grievous curse	1Kin 2:8
c them in the name of the LORD	2Kin 2:24
and said, Go, see now this woman c	2Kin 9:34
c them, and smote certain of them	Neh 13:25
sinned, and c God in their hearts	Job 1:5
Job his mouth, and c his day	Job 3:1
but suddenly I c his habitation	Job 5:3
their portion is c in the earth	Job 24:18
they that be c of him shall be	Ps 37:22
I have rebuked the proud that are c	Ps 119:21
thyself likewise hast c others	Eccl 7:22
C be the man that obeyeth not the	Jer 11:3
C be the man that trusteth in man	Jer 17:5
C be the day wherein I was born	Jer 20:14
C be the man who brought tidings	Jer 20:15
C be he that doeth the work of	Jer 48:10
c be he that keepeth back his	Jer 48:10
thyself likewise hast c others	Eccl 7:22
left hand, Depart from me, ye c	Mt 25:41
who knoweth not the law are c	Jn 7:49
C is every one that continueth	Gal 3:10
C is every one that hangeth on a	Gal 3:13
with covetous practices; c children	2Pet 2:14

CURSEDST

from thee, about which thou c	Judg 17:2
which thou c is withered away	Mk 11:21

CURSES

shall write these c in a book	Num 5:23
that all these c shall come upon	Deut 28:15
Moreover all these c shall come	Deut 28:45
all the c that are written in	Deut 29:20
according to all the c of the	Deut 29:27
to bring upon it all the c that	Deut 29:27
all these c upon thine enemies	Deut 30:7
even all the c that are written	2Chr 34:24

CURSEST

and he whom thou c is cursed	Num 22:6

CURSETH

thee, and curse him that c thee	Gen 12:3
cursed be every one that c thee	Gen 27:29
he that c his father, or his	Ex 21:17
For every one that c his father	Lev 20:9

Whosoever c his God shall bear	Lev 24:15
thee, and cursed is he that c thee	Num 24:9
Whoso c his father or his mother,	Prov 20:20
a generation that c their father	Prov 30:11
He that c father or mother, let	Mt 15:4
Whoso c father or mother, let him	Mk 7:10

CURSING

the woman with an oath of c	Num 5:21
The LORD shall send upon thee c	Deut 28:20
you life and death, blessing and c	Deut 30:19
me good for his c this day	Ps 109:17
His mouth is full of c and deceit	Ps 10:7
and for c and lying which they	Ps 59:12
As he loved c, so let it come	Ps 109:17
with c like as with his garment	Ps 109:18
he heareth c, and bewrayeth it not	Prov 29:24
Whose mouth is full of c and	Rom 3:14
is rejected, and is nigh unto c	Heb 6:8
mouth proceedeth blessing and c	Jas 3:10

CURSINGS

of the law, the blessings and c	Josh 8:34

CURTAIN

length of one c shall be eight	Ex 26:2
the breadth of one c four cubits	Ex 26:2
one c from the selvedge in the	Ex 26:4
the uttermost edge of another c	Ex 26:4
shalt thou make in the one c	Ex 26:5
thou make in the edge of the c	Ex 26:5
The length of one c shall be	Ex 26:8
the breadth of one c four cubits	Ex 26:8
shalt double the sixth c in the	Ex 26:9
loops on the edge of the one c	Ex 26:10
the c which coupleth the second	Ex 26:10
the half c that remaineth, shall	Ex 26:12
The length of one c was twenty	Ex 36:9
the breadth of one c four cubits	Ex 36:9
of one c from the selvedge in the	Ex 36:11
the uttermost side of another c	Ex 36:11
Fifty loops made he in one c	Ex 36:12
made he in the edge of the c	Ex 36:12
the loops held one c to another	Ex 36:12
length of one c was thirty cubits	Ex 36:15
cubits was the breadth of one c	Ex 36:15
edge of the c in the coupling	Ex 36:17
the c which coupleth the second	Ex 36:17
the c for the door of the court,	Num 3:26
out the heavens like a c	Ps 104:2
stretcheth out the heavens as a c	Is 40:22

CURTAINS

with ten c of fine twined linen	Ex 26:1
every one of the c shall have one	Ex 26:2
The five c shall be coupled	Ex 26:3
other five c shall be coupled one	Ex 26:3
couple the c together with the	Ex 26:6
thou shalt make c of goats' hair	Ex 26:7
eleven c shalt thou make	Ex 26:7
the eleven c shall be all of one	Ex 26:8
shalt couple five c by themselves	Ex 26:9
six c by themselves, and shalt	Ex 26:9
remaineth of the c of the tent	Ex 26:12
the length of the c of the tent	Ex 26:13
made ten c of fine twined linen	Ex 36:8
the c were all of one size	Ex 36:9
the five c one unto another	Ex 36:10
the other five c he coupled one	Ex 36:10
coupled the c one unto another	Ex 36:13
he made c of goats' hair for the	Ex 36:14
c he made them	Ex 36:14
the eleven c were of one size	Ex 36:15
he coupled five c by themselves	Ex 36:16
and six c by themselves	Ex 36:16
bear the c of the tabernacle	Num 4:25
the ark of God dwelleth within c	2Sa 7:2
of the LORD remaineth under c	1Chr 17:1
of Kedar, as the c of Solomon	Song 1:5
forth the c of thine habitations	Is 54:2
spoiled, and my c in a moment	Jer 4:20
tent any more, and to set up my c	Jer 10:20
shalt take to themselves their c	Jer 49:29
the c of the land of Midian did	Hab 3:7

CUSH (*cush*) See ETHIOPIA.

1. A son of Ham.

C, and Mizraim, and Phut	Gen 10:6
the sons of C, Seba, and Havilah	Gen 10:7
And C begat Nimrod	Gen 10:8
C, and Mizraim, Put, and Canaan	1Chr 1:8
the sons of C, Seba, and Havilah	1Chr 1:9
And C begat Nimrod	1Chr 1:10

2. A Benjamite.

the words of C the Benjamite	Ps 7:t

3. Land of descendants of Cush.

Egypt, and from Pathros, and from C	Is 11:11

CUSHAN (*cu'-shan*) See CUSHAN-RISHATHAIM.

Same as Chushan-rishathaim.

saw the tents of C in affliction	Hab 3:7

CUSHAN-RISHATHAIM

CUSHI (*cu'-shi*)

1. Messenger of David.

Then said Joab to C, Go tell the	2Sa 18:21
C bowed himself unto Joab, and ran	2Sa 18:21
would run after C, and run after C	2Sa 18:22
way of the plain, and overran C	2Sa 18:23
And, behold, C came	2Sa 18:31
C said, Tidings, my lord the king	2Sa 18:31
And the king said unto C, Is the	2Sa 18:32
C answered, The enemies of my	2Sa 18:32

2. *Ancestor of Jehudi.*
son of Shelemiah, son of C .... Jer 36:14
   3. *Father of Zephaniah.*
came unto Zephaniah the son of C .... Zeph 1:1

CUSTODY
And under the c and charge of the ...... Num 3:36
unto the c of Hege the king's .... Est 2:3
to the c of Hegai, that Esther .... Est 2:8
to the c of Hegai, keeper of the .... Est 2:8
to the c of Shaashgaz, the king's ...... Est 2:14

CUSTOM
for the c of women is upon me .... Gen 31:35
And it was a c in Israel, ... Judg 11:39
the priest's c with the people 1Sa 2:13
by number, according to the c .... Ezr 3:4
they not pay toll, tribute, and c .... Ezr 4:13
and toll, tribute, and c, was paid .... Ezr 4:20
to impose toll, tribute, or c .... Ezr 7:24
sealed according to the law and c .... Jer 32:11
sitting at the receipt of c .... Mt 9:9
of the earth take c or tribute .... Mt 17:25
sitting at the receipt of c .... Mk 2:14
According to the c of the .... Lk 1:9
do for him after the c of the law .... Lk 2:27
after the c of the feast .... Lk 2:42
and, as his c was, he went into .... Lk 4:16
Levi, sitting at the receipt of c .... Lk 5:27
But ye have a c, that I should .... Jn 18:39
c to whom c; fear to whom fear .... Rom 13:7
be contentious, we have no such c 1Cor 11:16

CUSTOMS
not any one of these abominable c .... Lev 18:30
For the c of the people are vain ...... Jer 10:3
shall change the c which Moses .... Acts 6:14
And teach c, which are not lawful .... Acts 16:21
neither to walk after the c .... Acts 21:21
I know thee to be expert in all c .... Acts 26:3
or c of our fathers, yet was I .... Acts 28:17

CUT
neither shall all flesh be c off .... Gen 9:11
that soul shall be c off from his .... Gen 17:14
c off the foreskin of her son, and .... Ex 4:25
thou shalt be c off from the. .... Ex 9:15
soul shall be c off from Israel .... Ex 12:15
even that soul shall be c off .... Ex 12:19
and I will c them off .... Ex 23:23
thou shalt c the ram in pieces, ... Ex 29:17
shall even be c off from his .... Ex 30:33
shall even be c off from his .... Ex 30:38
that soul shall be c off from .... Ex 31:14
images, and c down their groves .... Ex 34:13
c it into wires, to work it in .... Ex 39:3
offering, and c it into his pieces .... Lev 1:6
he shall c it into his pieces, ... Lev 1:12
shall be c off from his people .... Lev 7:20
shall be c off from his people .... Lev 7:21
it shall be c off from his people .... Lev 7:25
shall be c off from his people .... Lev 7:27
And he c the ram into pieces .... Lev 8:20
that man shall be c off from .... Lev 17:4
even that man shall be c off from ...... Lev 17:9
will c him off from among his .... Lev 17:10
eateth it shall be c off .... Lev 17:14
be c off from among their people ...... Lev 18:29
that soul shall be c off from .... Lev 19:8
will c him off from among his .... Lev 20:3
will c him off, and all that go a .... Lev 20:5
will c him off from among his .... Lev 20:6
they shall be c off in the sight .... Lev 20:17
both of them shall be c off from ...... Lev 20:18
that soul shall be c off from my ...... Lev 22:3
or crushed, or broken, or c .... Lev 22:24
he shall be c off from among his ...... Lev 23:29
c down your images, and cast your .... Lev 26:30
C ye not off the tribe of the .... Num 4:18
be c off from among his people ...... Num 9:13
c down from thence a branch with .... Num 13:23
of Israel c down from thence .... Num 13:24
that soul shall be c off .... Num 15:30
that soul shall utterly be c off .... Num 15:31
soul shall be c off from Israel .... Num 19:13
that soul shall be c off from .... Num 19:20
c down their groves, and burn .... Deut 7:5
c off the nations from before ...... Deut 12:29
ye shall not c yourselves .... Deut 14:1
thy God hath c off the nations ...... Deut 19:1
with the axe to c down the tree ...... Deut 19:5
thou shalt c them down (for ...... Deut 20:19
thou shalt destroy and c them down .. Deut 20:20
or hath his privy member c off ...... Deut 23:1
Then thou shalt c off her hand ...... Deut 25:12
c off from the waters that come ...... Josh 3:13
salt was, failed, and were c off .... Josh 3:16
were c off before the ark of the ...... Josh 4:7
the waters of Jordan were c off ...... Josh 4:7
c off our name from the earth ...... Josh 7:9
c off the Anakims from the .... Josh 11:21
c down for thyself there in the ...... Josh 17:15
a wood, and thou shalt c it down ...... Josh 17:18
all the nations that I have c off ...... Josh 23:4
c off his thumbs and his great .... Judg 1:6
thumbs and their great toes c off ...... Judg 1:7
c down the grove that is by it .... Judg 6:25
the grove which thou shalt c down ...... Judg 6:26
the grove was c down that was by .... Judg 6:28
because he hath c down the grove .... Judg 6:30
c down a bough from the trees, and ... Judg 9:48
all the people likewise c down .... Judg 9:49

c her in pieces, and sent her .... Judg 20:6
There is one tribe c off from .... Judg 21:6
c off from among his brethren .... Ruth 4:10
that I will c off thine arm, and 1Sa 2:31
whom I shall not c off from mine 1Sa 2:33
were c off upon the threshold 1Sa 5:4
him, and c off his head therewith 1Sa 17:51
But also thou shalt not c off thy 1Sa 20:15
not when the LORD hath c off the 1Sa 20:15
c off the skirt of Saul's robe 1Sa 24:4
because he had c off Saul's skirt 1Sa 24:5
for in that I c off the skirt of 1Sa 24:11
that thou wilt not c off my seed 1Sa 24:21
how he hath c off those that have 1Sa 28:9
they c off his head, and stripped 1Sa 31:9
c off their hands and their feet 2Sa 4:12
have c off all thine enemies out 2Sa 7:9
c off their garments in the 2Sa 10:4
they c off the head of Sheba the 2Sa 20:22
Then will I c off Israel out of 1Kin 9:7
until he had c off every male in 1Kin 11:16
of Jeroboam, even to c it off 1Kin 13:34
will c off from Jeroboam him that 1Kin 14:10
who shall c off the house of 1Kin 14:14
when Jezebel c off the prophets 1Kin 18:4
c it in pieces, and lay it on wood 1Kin 18:23
c themselves after their manner 1Kin 18:28
c the bullock in pieces, and laid 1Kin 18:33
will c off from Ahab him that 1Kin 21:21
came to Jordan, they c down wood 2Kin 6:4
he c down a stick, and cast it in 2Kin 6:6
will c off from Ahab him that 2Kin 9:8
the LORD began to c Israel short 2Kin 10:32
king Ahaz c off the borders of 2Kin 16:17
c down the groves, and brake in 2Kin 18:4
At that time did Hezekiah c off 2Kin 18:16
will c down the tall cedar trees 2Kin 19:23
c down the groves, and brake in 2Kin 23:14
c in pieces all the vessels of 2Kin 24:13
have c off all thine enemies from 1Chr 17:8
c off their garments in the midst. ... 1Chr 19:4
c them with saws, and with harrows .. 1Chr 20:3
can skill to c timber in Lebanon. 2Chr 2:8
the hewers that c timber 2Chr 2:10
we will c wood out of Lebanon, as 2Chr 2:16
the images, and c down the groves .. 2Chr 14:3
Asa c down her idol, and stamped 2Chr 15:16
to c off the house of Ahab 2Chr 22:7
for he was c off from the house 2Chr 26:21
c in pieces the vessels of the 2Chr 28:24
c down the groves, and threw down ... 2Chr 31:1
which c off all the mighty men of 2Chr 32:21
on high above them, he c down 2Chr 34:4
c down all the idols throughout 2Chr 34:7
or where were the righteous c off ...... Job 4:7
let loose his hand, and c me off ...... Job 6:9
not c down it, withereth before ...... Job 8:12
Whose hope shall be c off, ... Job 8:14
If he c off, and shut up, or .... Job 11:10
forth like a flower, and is c down ...... Job 14:2
hope of a tree, if it be c down ...... Job 14:7
above shall his branch be c off ...... Job 18:16
his months is c off in the midst ...... Job 21:21
Which were c down out of time, ... Job 22:16
our substance is not c down ...... Job 22:20
Because I was not c off before ...... Job 23:17
c off as the tops of the ears of ...... Job 24:24
Who c up mallows by the bushes, ... Job 30:4
when people are c off in their. ...... Job 36:20
The LORD shall c off .... Ps 12:3
I am c off from before thine eyes ...... Ps 31:22
to c off the remembrance of them. .. Ps 34:16
soon be c down like the grass ...... Ps 37:2
For evildoers shall be c off ...... Ps 37:9
be cursed of him shall be c off ...... Ps 37:22
seed of the wicked shall be c off ...... Ps 37:28
when the wicked are c off .... Ps 37:34
end of the wicked shall be c off ...... Ps 37:38
c them off in thy truth .... Ps 54:5
let them be as c in pieces. ...... Ps 58:7
the wicked also will I c off .... Ps 75:10
He shall c off the spirit of .... Ps 76:12
is burned with fire, it is c down ...... Ps 80:16
let us c them off from being a ...... Ps 83:4
they are c off from thy hand. ...... Ps 88:5
thy terrors have c me off .... Ps 88:16
in the evening it is c down .... Ps 90:6
for it is soon c off, and we fly. ...... Ps 90:10
shall c them off in their own. ...... Ps 94:23
the LORD our God shall c them off ...... Ps 94:23
his neighbour, him will I c off ...... Ps 101:5
that I may c off all wicked doers ...... Ps 101:8
c the bars of iron in sunder ...... Ps 107:16
Let his posterity be c off .... Ps 109:13
that he may c off the memory of ...... Ps 109:15
he hath c asunder the cords of ...... Ps 129:4
of thy mercy c off mine enemies, ... Ps 143:12
so shalt c off from earth ...... Prov 2:22
the froward tongue shall be c out ...... Prov 10:31
expectation shall not be c off ...... Prov 23:18
expectation shall not be c off ...... Prov 24:14
the sycomores are c down, but we ...... Is 9:10
LORD will c off from Israel head ...... Is 9:14
and c off nations not a few ...... Is 10:7
he shall c down the thickets of ...... Is 10:34
of Judah shall be c off. ...... Is 11:13
how art thou c down to the ground .. Is 14:12
c off from Babylon the name, and ...... Is 14:22
be baldness, and every beard c off ...... Is 15:2
he shall both c off the sprigs ...... Is 18:5

take away and c down the branches ...... Is 18:5
be removed, and be c down, and fall .. Is 22:25
that was upon it shall be c off ...... Is 22:25
that watch for iniquity are c off ...... Is 29:20
as thorns c up shall they be .... Is 33:12
I will c down the tall cedars ...... Is 37:24
I have c off like a weaver my ...... Is 38:12
he will c me off with pining .... Is 38:12
c in sunder the bars of iron. ...... Is 45:2
for thee, that I c thee not off. ...... Is 48:9
c off not destroyed from before ...... Is 48:19
Art thou not it that hath c Rahab. .... Is 51:9
for he was c off out of the land ...... Is 53:8
sign that shall not be c off ...... Is 55:13
name, that shall not be c off ...... Is 56:5
as if he c off a dog's neck. ...... Is 66:3
is c off from their mouth .... Jer 7:28
C off thine hair, O Jerusalem, and .. Jer 7:29
to c off the children from ...... Jer 9:21
let us c him off from the land of ...... Jer 11:19
nor c themselves, nor make. ...... Jer 16:6
they shall c down thy choice ...... Jer 22:7
are c down because of the fierce ...... Jer 25:37
when they c the calf in twain, and .. Jer 34:18
he c it with the penknife, and ...... Jer 36:23
having c themselves, with. ...... Jer 41:5
to c off from you man and woman, .. Jer 44:7
that ye might c yourselves off, ... Jer 44:8
for evil, and to c off all Judah ...... Jer 44:11
They shall c down her fruits, ... Jer 46:23
to c off from Tyrus and Zidon. ...... Jer 47:4
Ashkelon is c off with the .... Jer 47:5
how long wilt thou c thyself. ...... Jer 47:5
let us c it off from being a. ...... Jer 48:2
Also thou shalt be c down. ...... Jer 48:2
The horn of Moab is c off ...... Jer 48:25
of war shall be c off in that day ...... Jer 49:26
C off the sower from Babylon, and ... Jer 50:16
of the whole earth c in asunder. ...... Jer 50:23
of war shall be c off in that day ...... Jer 50:30
be not c off in her iniquity. ...... Jer 51:6
to c it off, that none shall. ...... Jer 51:62
He hath c off in his fierce anger. .... Lam 2:3
They have c off my life in the ...... Lam 3:53
then I said, I am c off. ...... Lam 3:54
and your images may be c down. .... Eze 6:6
I will c him off from the midst. ...... Eze 14:8
will c off man and beast from it ...... Eze 14:13
so that I c off man and beast from .. Eze 14:17
to c off from it man and beast ...... Eze 14:19
to c off from it man and beast ...... Eze 14:21
wast born thy navel was not c ...... Eze 16:4
c off the fruit thereof, that it ...... Eze 17:9
forts, to c off many persons. ...... Eze 17:17
and will c off from thee the ...... Eze 21:3
Seeing then that I will c off ...... Eze 21:4
I will c thee off from the people ...... Eze 25:7
will c off man and beast from it ...... Eze 25:13
I will c off the Cherethims, and ...... Eze 25:16
c off man and beast out of thee. .... Eze 29:8
for the multitude of No. ...... Eze 30:15
have c him off, and have left him ...... Eze 31:12
c off from it him that passeth ...... Eze 35:7
we are c off for our parts. ...... Eze 37:11
neither c down any out of the ...... Eze 39:10
thereof, ye shall be c in pieces. .... Dan 2:5
a stone was c out without hands ...... Dan 2:34
was c out of the mountain without ... Dan 2:45
shall be c in pieces, and their ...... Dan 3:29
c off his branches, shake off his. .... Dan 4:14
two weeks shall Messiah be c off ...... Dan 9:26
idols, that they may be c off ...... Hos 8:4
her king is c off as the foam ...... Hos 10:7
king of Israel utterly be c off ...... Hos 10:15
for it is c off from your mouth ...... Joel 1:5
the drink offering is c off from ...... Joel 1:9
Is not the meat c off before our ...... Joel 1:16
c off the inhabitant from the ...... Amos 1:5
I will c off the inhabitant from ...... Amos 1:8
I will c off the judge from the ...... Amos 2:3
horns of the altar shall be c off ...... Amos 3:14
c them in the head, all of them ...... Amos 9:1
by night, (how art thou c off ...... Obad 5
of Esau may be c by slaughter. ...... Obad 9
and thou shalt be c off for ever ...... Obad 10
to c off those of his that did ...... Obad 14
all thine enemies shall be c off. .... Mic 5:9
that I will c off thy horses out. .... Mic 5:10
I will c off the cities of thy ...... Mic 5:11
I will c off witchcrafts out of ...... Mic 5:12
graven images also will I c off ...... Mic 5:13
yet thus shall they be c down. ...... Nah 1:12
will I c off the graven image. ...... Nah 1:14
he is utterly c off. ...... Nah 1:15
I will c off thy prey from the. ...... Nah 2:13
the sword shall c thee off ...... Nah 3:15
that shall c off man from the fold ...... Hab 3:17
I will c off man from off the ...... Zeph 1:3
I will c off the remnant of Baal. .... Zeph 1:4
the merchant people are c down ...... Zeph 1:11
they that bear silver are c off ...... Zeph 1:11
I have c off the nations. ...... Zeph 3:6
dwelling should not be c off. ...... Zeph 3:7
one that sweareth shall be c off ...... Zec 5:3
one that sweareth shall be c off ...... Zec 5:3
I will c off the pride of the ...... Zec 9:6
I will c off the chariot from ...... Zec 9:10
and the battle bow shall be c off ...... Zec 9:10
also I c off in one month ...... Zec 11:8
is to be c off, let it be c off. ...... Zec 11:9

c it asunder, that I might break .... Zec 11:10
Then I c asunder mine other staff .... Zec 11:14
not visit those that be c off .... Zec 11:16
with it shall be c in pieces .... Zec 12:3
that I will c off the names of .... Zec 13:2
two parts therein shall be c off .... Zec 13:8
shall not be c off from the city .... Zec 14:2
The Lord will c off the man that .... Mal 2:12
c it off, and cast it from thee .... Mt 5:30
c them off, and cast them from .... Mt 18:8
others c down branches from them .... Mt 21:8
shall c him asunder, and appoint .... Mt 24:51
if thy hand offend thee, c it off .... Mk 9:43
if thy foot offend thee, c it off .... Mk 9:45
others c down branches off the .... Mk 11:8
the high priest, and c off his ear .... Mk 14:47
will c him in sunder, and will .... Lk 12:46
c it down .... Lk 13:7
after that thou shalt c it down .... Lk 13:9
priest, and c off his right ear .... Lk 22:50
servant, and c off his right ear .... Jn 18:10
his kinsman whose ear Peter c off .... Jn 18:26
they were c to the heart, and took .... Acts 5:33
they were c to the heart, and they .... Acts 7:54
Then the soldiers c off the ropes .... Acts 27:32
c it short in righteousness .... Rom 9:28
thou also shalt be c off .... Rom 11:22
For if thou wert c out of the .... Rom 11:24
that I may c off occasion from 2Cor 11:12
were even c off which trouble you .... Gal 5:12

CUTH (cuth) See Cuthah. *A Babylonian city.*
the men of C made Nergal, and the.. 2Kin 17:30

CUTHAH (cu´-thah) See Cuth. *Same as Cuth.*
men from Babylon, and from C 2Kin 17:24

CUTTEST
When thou c down thine harvest in . Deut 24:19

CUTTETH
He c out rivers among the rocks .... Job 28:10
the bow, and c the spear in .... Ps 46:9
the grave's mouth, as when one c .... Ps 141:7
the hand of a fool c off the feet .... Prov 26:6
He that c a tree out of the .... Jer 10:3
chambers, and c him out windows .... Jer 22:14

CUTTING
in c of stones, to set them, and .... Ex 31:5
in the c of stones, to set them .... Ex 35:33
I said in the c off of my days, I .... Is 38:10
to thy house by c off many people .... Hab 2:10
crying, and c himself with stones .... Mk 5:5

CUTTINGS
Ye shall not make any c in your .... Lev 19:28
nor make any c in their flesh .... Lev 21:5
upon all the hands shall be c .... Jer 48:37

CUZA See Chuza.

CYMBAL
sounding brass, or a tinkling 1Cor 13:1

CYMBALS
timbrels, and on cornets, and on c 2Sa 6:5
and with timbrels, and with c 1Chr 13:8
musick, psalteries and harps and c 1Chr 15:16
to sound with c of brass 1Chr 15:19
and with trumpets, and with c 1Chr 15:28
but Asaph made a sound with c 1Chr 16:5
c for those that should make a 1Chr 16:42
harps, with psalteries, and with c 1Chr 25:1
in the house of the Lord, with c 1Chr 25:6
arrayed in white linen, having c 2Chr 5:12
voice with the trumpets and c 2Chr 5:13
in the house of the Lord with c 2Chr 29:25
Levites the sons of Asaph with c .... Ezr 3:10
and with singing, with c, ... Neh 12:27
Praise him upon the loud c .... Ps 150:5
him upon the high sounding c .... Ps 150:5

CYPRESS
him down cedars, and taketh the c .... Is 44:14

CYPRUS (si´-prus) *An island off the Syrian coast.*
a Levite, and the country of C .... Acts 4:36
travelled as far as Phenice, and .... Acts 11:19
And some of them were men of C .... Acts 11:20
and from thence they sailed to C .... Acts 13:4
took Mark, and sailed unto C .... Acts 15:39
Now when we had discovered C .... Acts 21:3
brought with them one Mnason of C .. Acts 21:16
from thence, we sailed under C .... Acts 27:4

CYRENE (si-re´-ne) See Cyrenian. *A Libyan city.*
came out, they found a man of C .... Mt 27:32
and in the parts of Libya about C .... Acts 2:10
of them were men of Cyprus and C .. Acts 11:20
was called Niger, and Lucius of C .... Acts 13:1

CYRENIAN (si-re´-he-an) See Cyrenians. *A native of Cyrene.*
And they compel one Simon a C .... Mk 15:21
laid hold upon one Simon, a C .... Lk 23:26

CYRENIANS (si-re´-ne-ans)
synagogue of the Libertines, and C...... Acts 6:9

CYRENIUS (si-re´-ne-us) *A Roman governor of Syria.*
made when C was governor of Syria .. Lk 2:2

CYRUS (si´-rus) *Founder of the Persian Empire.*
first year of C king of Persia 2Chr 36:22
up the spirit of C king of Persia 2Chr 36:22
Thus saith C king of Persia, All 2Chr 36:23
first year of C king of Persia .... Ezr 1:1
up the spirit of C king of Persia .... Ezr 1:1
Thus saith C king of Persia, The .... Ezr 1:2
Also C the king brought forth the .... Ezr 1:7
Even those did C king of Persia .... Ezr 1:8
that they had of C king of Persia .... Ezr 3:7
as king C the king of Persia hath .... Ezr 4:3
all the days of C king of Persia .... Ezr 4:5
But in the first year of C the .... Ezr 5:13
C made a decree to build this .... Ezr 5:13
those did C the king take out of .... Ezr 5:14
that a decree was made of C the .... Ezr 5:17
In the first year of C the king .... Ezr 6:3
the same C the king made a decree .. Ezr 6:3
according to the commandment of C.. Ezr 6:14
That saith of C, He is my .... Is 44:28
the Lord to his anointed, to C .... Is 45:1
unto the first year of C king .... Dan 1:21
and in the reign of C the Persian .... Dan 6:28
In the third year of C king of .... Dan 10:1

D

DABAREH (dab´-a-reh) See Daberath. *A Levitical city in Issachar.*
her suburbs, D with her suburbs, ... Josh 21:28

DABBASHETH (dab´-ba-sheth) *A border city of Issachar.*
sea, and Maralah, and reached to D... Josh 19:11

DABBESHETH See Dabbasheth.

DABERATH (dab´-e-rath) See Dabareh. *Same as Dabareh.*
and then goeth out to D, and goeth .. Josh 19:12
her suburbs, D with her suburbs, ... 1Chr 6:72

DAGGER
made him a d which had two edges .... Judg 3:16
took the d from his right thigh, ... Judg 3:21
nor draw the d out of his belly .... Judg 3:22

DAGON See Beth-dagon, Dagon's. *A Philistine god.*
great sacrifice unto D their god .... Judg 16:23
house of D, and set it by 1Sa 5:2
D was fallen upon his face to the 1Sa 5:3
And they took D, and set him in his .. 1Sa 5:3
D was fallen upon his face to the 1Sa 5:4
and the head of D and both the 1Sa 5:4
the stump of D was left to him 1Sa 5:4
neither the priests of D, nor any 1Sa 5:5
of D in Ashdod unto this day 1Sa 5:5
sore upon us, and upon D our god 1Sa 5:7
his head in the temple of D 1Chr 10:10

DAGON'S
nor any that come into D house. 1Sa 5:5

DAILY
your d tasks, as when there was .... Ex 5:13
from your bricks of your d task .... Ex 5:19
be twice as much as they gather d ...... Ex 16:5
the d meat offering, and the .... Num 4:16
this manner ye shall offer d .... Num 28:24
the d burnt offering, and his meat .... Num 28:24
she pressed him d with her words... Judg 16:16
a d rate for every day, all the 2Kin 25:30
his d portion for their services 2Chr 31:16
offered the d burnt offerings by ...... Ezr 3:4
was prepared for me d was one ox ...... Neh 5:18
pass, when they spake d unto him ...... Est 3:4
soul, having sorrow in my heart d ...... Ps 13:2
while they say d unto me, Where ...... Ps 42:10
he fighting d oppresseth me .... Ps 56:1
enemies would d swallow me up ...... Ps 56:2
that I may d perform my vows .... Ps 61:8
who d loadeth us with benefits, ... Ps 68:19
and d shall he be praised .... Ps 72:15
foolish man reproacheth thee d .... Ps 74:22
for I cry unto thee d .... Ps 86:3
Lord, I have called d upon thee. .... Ps 88:9
came round about me d like water ...... Ps 88:17
I was d his delight, rejoicing .... Prov 8:30
watching d at my gates, waiting .... Prov 8:34
Yet they seek me d, and delight to ...... Is 58:2
d rising up early and sending them. .... Jer 7:25
I am in derision d, every one, ... Jer 20:7
unto me, and a derision d .... Jer 20:8
that they should give him d a .... Jer 37:21
and Noph shall have distresses d ...... Eze 30:16
without blemish d the seven days ...... Eze 45:23
of the goats d for a sin offering .... Eze 45:23
Thou shalt d prepare a burnt .... Eze 46:13
the king appointed them a d .... Dan 1:5
by him the d sacrifice was taken ...... Dan 8:11
the d sacrifice by reason of .... Dan 8:12
vision concerning the d sacrifice ...... Dan 8:13
shalt take away the d sacrifice .... Dan 11:31
And from the time that the d .... Dan 12:11
he d increaseth lies and .... Hos 12:1
Give us this day our d bread, ... Mt 6:11
I sat d with you teaching in the .... Mt 26:55
I was d with you in the temple .... Mk 14:49

himself, and take up his cross d .... Lk 9:23
Give us day by day our d bread .... Lk 11:3
he taught d in the temple .... Lk 19:47
When I was d with you in the .... Lk 22:53
continuing d with one accord in ...... Acts 2:46
church d such as should be saved ...... Acts 2:47
whom they laid d at the gate of ...... Acts 3:2
d in the temple, and in every .... Acts 5:42
neglected in the d ministration ...... Acts 6:1
faith, and increased in number d ...... Acts 16:5
and searched the scriptures d .... Acts 17:11
in the market d with them that ...... Acts 17:17
disputing d in the school of one...... Acts 19:9
in Christ Jesus our Lord, I die d 1Cor 15:31
that which cometh upon me d 2Cor 11:28
But exhort one another d, while .... Heb 3:13
Who needeth not d, as those high ...... Heb 7:27
priest standeth d ministering .... Heb 10:11
be naked, and destitute of d food..... Jas 2:15

DAINTIES
be fat, and he shall yield royal d ...... Gen 49:20
and let me not eat of their d .... Ps 141:4
Be not desirous of his d .... Prov 23:3

DAINTY
bread, and his soul d meat .... Job 33:20
neither desire thou his d meats........ Prov 23:6
thee, and all things which were d ...... Rev 18:14

DALAIAH (dal-a-i´-ah) See Delaiah. *A descendant of Judah.*
and Akkub, and Johanan, and D....... 1Chr 3:24

DALE
of Shaveh, which is the king's d ...... Gen 14:17
pillar, which is in the king's d 2Sa 18:18

DALMANUTHA (dal-ma-nu´-thah) *A village in Galilee.*
and came into the parts of D .... Mk 8:10

DALMATIA (dal-ma´-she-ah) *A Roman province west of Macedonia.*
Crescens to Galatia, Titus unto D 2Ti 4:10

DALPHON (dal´-fon) *A son of Haman.*
And Parshandatha, and D, and Aspatha . Est 9:7

DAM
seven days it shall be with his d ...... Ex 22:30
shall be seven days under the d ...... Lev 22:27
the d sitting upon the young, or ...... Deut 22:6
not take the d with the young .... Deut 22:6
shalt in any wise let the d go .... Deut 22:7

DAMAGE
why should d grow to the hurt of ...... Ezr 4:22
not countervail the king's d .... Est 7:4
off the feet, and drinketh d .... Prov 26:6
and the king should have no d .... Dan 6:2
will be with hurt and much d .... Acts 27:10
might receive d by us in nothing 2Cor 7:9

DAMARIS (dam´-a-ris) *An Athenian convert of Paul.*
Areopagite, and a woman named D..... Acts 17:34

DAMASCENES (dam-as-senes´) *Inhabitants of Damascus.*
the city of the D with a garrison...... 2Cor 11:32

DAMASCUS (da-mas´-cus) See Damascenes, Syria-Damascus. *A city in Syria.*
which is on the left hand of D .... Gen 14:15
of my house is this Eliezer of D ...... Gen 15:2
when the Syrians of D came to 2Sa 8:5
David put garrisons in Syria of D. 2Sa 8:6
and they went to D, and dwelt 1Kin 11:24
and dwelt therein, and reigned in D. .. 1Kin 11:24
king of Syria, that dwelt at D 1Kin 15:18
on thy way to the wilderness of D... 1Kin 19:15
shalt make streets for thee in D 1Kin 20:34
not Abana and Pharpar, rivers of D... 2Kin 5:12
And Elisha came to D 2Kin 8:7
even of every good thing of D 2Kin 8:9
he warred, and how he recovered D... 2Kin 14:28
king of Assyria went up against D 2Kin 16:9
king Ahaz went to D to meet 2Kin 16:10
and saw an altar that was at D 2Kin 16:10
that king Ahaz had sent from D 2Kin 16:11
it against king Ahaz came from D 2Kin 16:11
the king was come from D 2Kin 16:12
when the Syrians of D came to 1Chr 18:5
king of Syria, that dwelt at D 2Chr 16:2
spoil of them unto the king of D 2Chr 24:23
captives, and brought them to D 2Chr 28:5
he sacrificed unto the gods of D 2Chr 28:23
of Lebanon which looketh toward D... Song 7:4
For the head of Syria is D .... Is 7:8
and the head of D is Rezin .... Is 7:8
and my mother, the riches of D ...... Is 8:4
is not Samaria as D .... Is 10:9
The burden of D .... Is 17:1
D is taken away from being a city..... Is 17:1
Ephraim, and the kingdom from D ...... Is 17:3
Concerning D, Hamath is confounded... Jer 49:23
D is waxed feeble, and turneth ...... Jer 49:24
kindle a fire in the wall of D .... Jer 49:27
D was thy merchant in the .... Eze 27:18
which is between the border of D...... Eze 47:16
be Hazar-enan, the border of D......... Eze 47:17
measure from Hauran, and from D...... Eze 47:18
the border of D northward.............. Eze 48:1
For three transgressions of D .... Amos 1:3

I will break also the bar of *D* ...... Amos 1:5
of a bed, and in *D* in a couch .... Amos 3:12
you to go into captivity beyond *D* ... Amos 5:27
D shall be the rest thereof .... Zec 9:1
letters to *D* to the synagogues .... Acts 9:2
as he journeyed, he came near *D* ..... Acts 9:3
the hand, and brought him into *D* ..... Acts 9:8
there was a certain disciple at *D* ..... Acts 9:10
the disciples which were at *D* .... Acts 9:19
the Jews which dwelt at *D* .... Acts 9:22
boldly at *D* in the name of Jesus ..... Acts 9:27
unto the brethren, and went to *D* ..... Acts 22:5
was come nigh unto *D* about noon ... Acts 22:6
said unto me, Arise, and go into *D* ... Acts 22:10
that were with me, I came into *D* ..... Acts 22:11
as I went to *D* with authority .... Acts 26:12
But shewed first unto them of *D* ...... Acts 26:20
In *D* the governor under Aretas 2Cor 11:32
Arabia, and returned again unto *D* ... Gal 1:17

DAMNABLE

privily shall bring in d heresies 2Pet 2:1

DAMNATION

ye shall receive the greater *d* .... Mt 23:14
how can ye escape the *d* of hell .... Mt 23:33
but is in danger of eternal *d* .... Mk 3:29
these shall receive greater *d* .... Mk 12:40
the same shall receive greater *d* ...... Lk 20:47
evil, unto the resurrection of *d* .... Jn 5:29
whose *d* is just .... Rom 3:8
shall receive to themselves *d* .... Rom 13:2
drinketh to himself, not 1Cor 11:29
Having *d*, because they have cast 1Ti 5:12
not, and their *d* slumbereth not 2Pet 2:3

DAMNED

he that believeth not shall be *d* .... Mk 16:16
he that doubteth is *d* if he eat .... Rom 14:23
That they all might be *d* who 2Th 2:12

DAMSEL

that the *d* to whom I shall say, ... Gen 24:14
the *d* was very fair to look upon, ... Gen 24:16
And the *d* ran, and told them of her... Gen 24:28
Let the *d* abide with us a few .... Gen 24:55
And they said, We will call the *d* ...... Gen 24:57
of Jacob, and he loved the *d* .... Gen 34:3
and spake kindly unto the *d* .... Gen 34:3
saying, Get me this *d* to wife............. Gen 34:4
but give me the *d* to wife .... Gen 34:12
Then shall the father of the *d* .... Deut 22:15
them unto the father of the *d* .... Deut 22:19
virginity be not found for the *d* .... Deut 22:20
the *d* to the door of her father's .... Deut 22:21
If a *d* that is a virgin be .... Deut 22:23
the *d*, because she cried not, ... Deut 22:24
find a betrothed *d* in the field .... Deut 22:27
But unto the *d* thou shalt do .... Deut 22:26
there is in the *d* no sin worthy .... Deut 22:26
field, and the betrothed *d* cried .... Deut 22:27
If a man find a *d* that is a .... Deut 22:28
to every man a *d* or two .... Judg 5:30
when the father of the *d* saw him .... Judg 19:3
over the reapers, Whose *d* is this..... Ruth 2:5
It is the Moabitish *d* that came .... Ruth 2:6
So they sought for a fair *d* 1Kin 1:3
the *d* was very fair, and cherished 1Kin 1:4
in a charger, and given to the *d* .... Mt 14:11
a *d* came unto him, saying, Thou ..... Mt 26:69
the *d* is not dead, but sleepeth .... Mk 5:39
the father and the mother of the *d* ... Mk 5:40
entereth in where the *d* was lying...... Mk 5:40
And he took the *d* by the hand .... Mk 5:41
which is, being interpreted, *D* .... Mk 5:41
And straightway the *d* arose .... Mk 5:42
him, the king said unto the *d* .... Mk 6:22
in a charger, and gave it to the *d* ..... Mk 6:28
the *d* gave it to her mother .... Mk 6:28
Then saith the *d* that kept the .... Jn 18:17
a *d* came to hearken, named Rhoda... Acts 12:13
a certain *d* possessed with a .... Acts 16:16

DAMSEL'S

d virginity unto the elders of .... Deut 22:15
the *d* father shall say unto the .... Deut 22:16
with her shall give unto the *d* .... Deut 22:29
the *d* father, retained him .... Judg 19:4
the *d* father said unto his son in ...... Judg 19:5
for the *d* father had said unto .... Judg 19:8
the *d* father said, Comfort thine .... Judg 19:8
the *d* father, said unto him, ... Judg 19:9

DAMSELS

And Rebekah arose, and her *d* .... Gen 24:61
with five *d* of hers that went 1Sa 25:42
among them were the *d* playing .... Ps 68:25

DAN (dan) *See* DANITES, DAN-JAAN, LAISH, MAHANEH-DAN.

1. *A son of Jacob.*

therefore called she his name *D* .... Gen 30:6
D, and Naphtali .... Gen 35:25
And the sons of *D* .... Gen 46:23
D shall judge his people, as one....... Gen 49:16
D shall be a serpent by the way, ... Gen 49:17
D, and Naphtali, Gad, and Asher ...... Ex 1:4
therein, and called Leshem, *D* .... Josh 19:47
after the name of *D* their father .... Josh 19:47
after the name of *D* their father .... Judg 18:29
D, Joseph, and Benjamin, Naphtali,... 1Chr 2:2
D also and Javan going to and fro..... Eze 27:19

2. *A city and tribal territory in northern Canaan.*

eighteen, and pursued them unto *D* .. Gen 14:14
all the land of Gilead, unto *D* .... Deut 34:1
called the name of the city *D* .... Judg 18:29
from *D* even to Beer-sheba, with...... Judg 20:1
all Israel from *D* even to 1Sa 3:20
from *D* even to Beer-sheba 2Sa 3:10
from *D* even to Beer-sheba, as the... 2Sa 17:11
from *D* even to Beer-sheba 2Sa 24:2
from *D* even to Beer-sheba seventy... 2Sa 24:15
from *D* even to Beer-sheba, all......... 1Kin 4:25
Beth-el, and the other put he in *D* 1Kin 12:29
before the one, even unto *D* 1Kin 12:30
of Israel, and smote Ijon, and *D* 1Kin 15:20
in Beth-el, and that were in *D* 2Kin 10:29
Israel from Beer-sheba even to *D* 1Chr 21:2
and they smote Ijon, and *D*, and 2Chr 16:4
Israel, from Beer-sheba even to *D* 2Chr 30:5
For a voice declareth from *D* .... Jer 4:15
of his horses was heard from *D* .... Jer 8:16
a portion for *D* .... Eze 48:1
And by the border of *D*, from the ..... Eze 48:2
gate of Benjamin, one gate of *D* ...... Eze 48:32
of Samaria, and say, Thy god, O *D* ... Amos 8:14

3. *Tribe descended from Dan 1.*

of Ahisamach, of the tribe of *D* .... Ex 31:6
of Ahisamach, of the tribe of *D* .... Ex 35:34
of Ahisamach, of the tribe of *D* .... Ex 38:23
of Dibri, of the tribe of *D* .... Lev 24:11
Of *D*; Ahiezer the son .... Num 1:12
Of the children of *D*, by their .... Num 1:38
of them, even of the tribe of *D* .... Num 1:39
The standard of the camp of *D* .... Num 2:25
of *D* shall be Ahiezer the son of ...... Num 2:25
of *D* were an hundred thousand .... Num 2:31
prince of the children of *D* .... Num 7:66
of the children of *D* set forward........ Num 10:25
of the tribe of *D*, Ammiel the son ..... Num 13:12
sons of *D* after their families............ Num 26:42
of *D* after their families .... Num 26:42
of the tribe of the children of *D* .... Num 34:22
Gad, and Asher, and Zebulun, *D*....... Deut 27:13
Dan he said, *D* is a lion's whelp .... Deut 33:22
of *D* according to their families .... Josh 19:40
of *D* went out too little for them .... Josh 19:47
therefore the children of *D* went .... Josh 19:47
of *D* according to their families .... Josh 19:48
Ephraim, and out of the tribe of *D*..... Josh 21:5
And out of the tribe of *D*, Eltekeh .... Josh 21:23
children of *D* into the mountain......... Judg 1:34
why did *D* remain in ships .... Judg 5:17
in the camp of *D* between Zorah ...... Judg 13:25
the children of *D* sent of their .... Judg 18:2
which were the children of *D* .... Judg 18:16
and overtook the children of *D* .... Judg 18:22
they cried unto the children of *D* ...... Judg 18:23
the children of *D* said unto him, ... Judg 18:25
the children of *D* went their way .... Judg 18:26
the children of *D* set up the .... Judg 18:30
were priests to the tribe of *D* .... Judg 18:30
of *D*, Azareel the son of Jeroham..... 1Chr 27:22
of a woman of the daughters of *D* 2Chr 2:14

DANCE

of Shiloh come out to *d* in dances .... Judg 21:21
like a flock, and their children *d* .... Job 21:11
Let them praise his name in the *d* .... Ps 149:3
Praise him with the timbrel and *d* ..... Ps 150:4
a time to mourn, and a time to *d* ...... Eccl 3:4
earth, and their years shall *d* there .... Is 13:21
shall the virgin rejoice in the *d* .... Jer 31:13
our *d* is turned into mourning .... Lam 5:15

DANCED

to their number, of them that *d* .... Judg 21:23
David *d* before the LORD with all 2Sa 6:14
piped unto you, and ye have not *d*.... Mt 11:17
of Herodias *d* before them, ... Mt 14:6
the said Herodias came in, and *d*..... Mk 6:22
piped unto you, and ye have not *d*.... Lk 7:32

DANCES

after her with timbrels and with *d*..... Ex 15:20
meet him with timbrels and with *d* .... Judg 11:34
of Shiloh come out to dance in *d*...... Judg 21:21
sing one to another of him in *d* 1Sa 21:11
they sang one to another in *d* 1Sa 29:5
shalt go forth in the *d* of them, ... Jer 31:4

DANCING

that he saw the calf, and the *d* .... Ex 32:19
cities of Israel, singing and *d* 1Sa 18:6
leaping and *d* before the LORD 2Sa 6:16
out at a window saw king David *d* 1Chr 15:29
turned for my mourning into *d* .... Ps 30:11
the house, he heard musick and *d*.... Lk 15:25

DANDLED

her sides, and be *d* upon her knees... Is 66:12

DANGER

shall be in *d* of the judgment........... Mt 5:21
shall be in *d* of the judgment........... Mt 5:22
shall be in *d* of the council .... Mt 5:22
shall be in *d* of hell fire .... Mt 5:22
but is in *d* of eternal damnation .... Mk 3:29
craft is in *d* to be set at nought .... Acts 19:27
For we are in *d* to be called in .... Acts 19:40

DANGEROUS

spent, and when sailing was now *d*.... Acts 27:9

DANIEL *See* BELTESHAZZAR.

1. *A son of David.*

the second *D*, of Abigail the 1Chr 3:1

2. *An Israelite who renewed the covenant.*

of the sons of Ithamar; *D* .... Ezr 8:2
D, Ginnethon, Baruch, ... Neh 10:6

3. *A major prophet.*

Though these three men, Noah, *D* ..... Eze 14:14
Though Noah, *D*, and Job, were in ..... Eze 14:20
Behold, thou art wiser than *D* .... Eze 28:3
were of the children of Judah, *D* ...... Dan 1:6
for he gave unto *D* the name of .... Dan 1:7
But *D* purposed in his heart that .... Dan 1:8
Now God had brought *D* into favour... Dan 1:9
prince of the eunuchs said unto *D* .... Dan 1:10
Then said *D* to Melzar, whom the ..... Dan 1:11
of the eunuchs had set over *D* .... Dan 1:11
D had understanding in all .... Dan 1:17
them all was found none like *D* .... Dan 1:19
D continued even unto the first......... Dan 1:21
and they sought *D* and his fellows..... Dan 2:13
Then *D* answered with counsel and... Dan 2:14
Arioch made the thing known to *D* .... Dan 2:15
Then *D* went in, and desired of the... Dan 2:16
Then *D* went to his house, and made.. Dan 2:17
that *D* and his fellows should not ..... Dan 2:18
revealed unto *D* in a night vision...... Dan 2:19
Then *D* blessed the God of heaven ... Dan 2:19
D answered and said, Blessed be ...... Dan 2:20
Therefore *D* went in unto Arioch, ... Dan 2:24
Then Arioch brought in *D* before ...... Dan 2:25
The king answered and said to *D*...... Dan 2:26
D answered in the presence of the.... Dan 2:27
upon his face, and worshipped *D* ..... Dan 2:46
The king answered unto *D*, and said... Dan 2:47
Then the king made *D* a great man.... Dan 2:48
Then *D* requested of the king, and..... Dan 2:49
but *D* sat in the gate of the king ...... Dan 2:49
But at the last *D* came in before ...... Dan 4:8
Then *D*, whose name was .... Dan 4:19
doubts, were found in the same *D* .... Dan 5:12
now let *D* be called, and he will .... Dan 5:12
Then was *D* brought in before the .... Dan 5:13
said unto Daniel, Art thou that *D* ..... Dan 5:13
Then *D* answered and said before .... Dan 5:17
and they clothed *D* with scarlet .... Dan 5:29
of whom *D* was first .... Dan 6:2
Then this *D* was preferred above ...... Dan 6:3
against *D* concerning the kingdom .... Dan 6:4
find any occasion against this *D* .... Dan 6:5
Now when *D* knew that the writing.... Dan 6:10
found *D* praying and making .... Dan 6:11
and said before the king, That *D* ...... Dan 6:13
set his heart on *D* to deliver him...... Dan 6:14
king commanded, and they brought *D*.. Dan 6:16
Now the king spake and said unto *D*.. Dan 6:16
might not be changed concerning *D*... Dan 6:17
with a lamentable voice unto *D* .... Dan 6:20
king spake and said to Daniel, O *D* ... Dan 6:20
Then said *D* unto the king, O king.... Dan 6:21
should take *D* up out of the den .... Dan 6:23
So *D* was taken up out of the den,.... Dan 6:23
those men which had accused *D* ...... Dan 6:24
and fear before the God of *D* .... Dan 6:26
who hath delivered *D* from the .... Dan 6:27
So this *D* prospered in the reign ...... Dan 6:28
king of Babylon *D* had a dream........ Dan 7:1
D spake and said, I saw in my .... Dan 7:2
I *D* was grieved in my spirit in .... Dan 7:15
As for me *D*, my cogitations much.... Dan 7:28
appeared unto me, even unto me *D* ... Dan 8:1
it came to pass, when I, even I *D* ..... Dan 8:15
I *D* fainted, and was sick certain ...... Dan 8:27
the first year of his reign I *D* .... Dan 9:2
and talked with me, and said, O *D*.... Dan 9:22
a thing was revealed unto *D* .... Dan 10:1
In those days I *D* was mourning .... Dan 10:2
And I *D* alone saw the vision .... Dan 10:7
And he said unto me, O *D*, a man .... Dan 10:11
Then said he unto me, Fear not, *D*.... Dan 10:12
But thou, O *D*, shut up the words,..... Dan 12:4
Then I *D* looked, and, behold, ... Dan 12:5
And he said, Go thy way, *D* .... Dan 12:9
spoken of by *D* the prophet .... Mt 24:15
spoken of by *D* the prophet .... Mk 13:14

DANITES (*dan'-ites*) *Descendants of Dan 1.*

of Zorah, of the family of the *D* .... Judg 13:2
D sought them an inheritance to .... Judg 18:1
thence of the family of the *D* .... Judg 18:11
of the *D* expert in war twenty and 1Chr 12:35

DAN-JAAN (*dan-ja'-an*) *A place between Gilead and Zidon.*

and they came to *D*, and about to 2Sa 24:6

DANNAH (*dan'-nah*) *A city in Judah.*

And *D*, and Kirjath-sannah, which is ... Josh 15:49

DARA (*da'-rah*) *See* DARDA. *A son of Zerah.*

Ethan, and Heman, and Calcol, and *D*.. 1Chr 2:6

DARDA (*dar'-dah*) *See* DARDA. *A wise man.* and Heman, and Chalcol, and *D*......... 1Kin 4:31

DARE

is so fierce that *d* stir him up .... Job 41:10
good man some would even *d* to die... Rom 5:7
For I will not *d* to speak of any .... Rom 15:18
D any of you, having a matter 1Cor 6:1

For we d not make ourselves of 2Cor 10:12

DARIUS (da-rī'-us)
  I. Darius Hystaspes, king of Persia.
the reign of D king of Persia .... Ezr 4:5
of the reign of D king of Persia .... Ezr 4:24
cease, till the matter came to D .... Ezr 5:5
the river, sent unto D the king .... Ezr 5:6
Unto D the king, all peace .... Ezr 5:7
Then D the king made a decree, and .... Ezr 6:1
I D have made a decree .... Ezr 6:12
to that which D the king had sent ...... Ezr 6:13
to the commandment of Cyrus, and D.. Ezr 6:14
year of the reign of D the king .... Ezr 6:15
In the second year of D the king .... Hag 1:1
in the second year of D the king .... Hag 1:15
month, in the second year of D .... Hag 2:10
month, in the second year of D .... Zec 1:1
Sebat, in the second year of D .... Zec 1:7
pass in the fourth year of king D .... Zec 7:1
  2. Darius Nothus, king of Persia.
to the reign of D the Persian .... Neh 12:22
  3. Cyaxares, king of Media.
D the Median took the kingdom, ... Dan 5:31
It pleased D to set over the .... Dan 6:1
and said thus unto him, King D .... Dan 6:6
Wherefore king D signed the .... Dan 6:9
Then king D wrote unto all people .... Dan 6:25
prospered in the reign of D................. Dan 6:28
year of D the son of Ahasuerus .... Dan 9:1
I in the first year of D the Mede .... Dan 11:1

DARK
the sun went down, and it was d .... Gen 15:17
of the plague be somewhat d .... Lev 13:6
than the skin, but be somewhat d ...... Lev 13:21
the other skin, but be somewhat d .... Lev 13:26
in the skin, but it be somewhat d ...... Lev 13:28
the plague be somewhat d after .... Lev 13:56
apparently, and not in d speeches ...... Num 12:8
of the gate, when it was d .... Josh 2:5
d waters, and thick clouds of the 2Sa 22:12
began to be d before the sabbath ...... Neh 13:19
of the twilight thereof be d .... Job 3:9
They grope in the d without light ...... Job 12:25
shall be d in his tabernacle. .... Job 18:6
can he judge through the d cloud ...... Job 22:13
In the d they dig through houses, ... Job 24:16
round about him were d waters .... Ps 18:11
Let their way be d and slippery.......... Ps 35:6
I will open my d saying upon the ...... Ps 49:4
for the d places of the earth are .... Ps 74:20
I will utter d sayings of old .... Ps 78:2
thy wonders be known in the d .... Ps 88:12
He sent darkness, and made it d .... Ps 105:28
of the wise, and their d sayings .... Prov 1:6
evening, in the black and d night ...... Prov 7:9
Lord, that their works are in the d ...... Is 29:15
in a d place of the earth. .... Is 45:19
feet stumble upon the mountains ...... Jer 13:16
He hath set me in d places, ... Lam 3:6
the house of Israel do in the d .... Eze 8:12
and make the stars thereof d .... Eze 32:7
of heaven will I make d over thee ...... Eze 32:8
scattered in the cloudy and d day ...... Eze 34:12
and understanding of sentences .... Dan 8:23
the sun and the moon shall be d .... Joel 2:10
and maketh the day of wrath, ... Amos 5:8
even very d, and no brightness in ...... Amos 5:20
and it shall be d unto you. .... Mic 3:6
and the day shall be d over them........ Mic 3:6
light shall not be clear, nor d .... Zec 14:6
full of light, having no part d .... Lk 11:36
And it was now d, and Jesus was not .. Jn 6:17
early, when it was yet d, unto............ Jn 20:1
a light that shineth in a d place 2Pet 1:19

DARKEN
I will d the earth in the clear .... Amos 8:9

DARKENED
earth, so that the land was d .... Ex 10:15
Let their eyes be d, that they .... Ps 69:23
the moon, or the stars, be not d .... Eccl 12:2
that took out of the windows be d .... Eccl 12:3
the light is d in the heavens .... Is 5:30
the Lord of hosts is the land d .... Is 9:19
the sun shall be d in his going .... Is 13:10
all joy is d, the mirth of the .... Is 24:11
also the day shall be d, when .... Eze 30:18
The sun and the moon shall be d ...... Joel 3:15
his right eye shall be utterly d .... Zec 11:17
of those days shall the sun be d .... Mt 24:29
tribulation, the sun shall be d .... Mk 13:24
And the sun was d, and the veil of .... Lk 23:45
and their foolish heart was d .... Rom 1:21
Let their eyes be d, that they .... Rom 11:10
Having the understanding d .... Eph 4:18
as the third part of them was d .... Rev 8:12
the air were d by reason of the .... Rev 9:2

DARKENETH
Who is this that d counsel by .... Job 38:2

DARKISH
skin of their flesh be d white. .... Lev 13:39

DARKLY
For now we see through a glass, d 1Cor 13:12

DARKNESS
d was upon the face of the deep .... Gen 1:2
God divided the light from the d .... Gen 1:4
Day, and the d he called Night .... Gen 1:5

and to divide the light from the d ...... Gen 1:18
horror of great d fell upon him .... Gen 15:12
that there may be d over the land ...... Ex 10:21
Egypt, even d which may be felt .... Ex 10:21
there was a thick d in all the .... Ex 10:22
d to them, but it gave light by .... Ex 14:20
unto the thick d where God was, ... Ex 20:21
with d, clouds, and thick d................ Deut 4:11
of the cloud, and the thick d .... Deut 5:22
voice out of the midst of the d .... Deut 5:23
as the blind gropeth in .... Deut 28:29
he put d between you and the............ Josh 24:7
the wicked shall be silent in d 1Sa 2:9
and d was under his feet 2Sa 22:10
he made d pavilions round about 2Sa 22:12
and the Lord will lighten my d 2Sa 22:29
he would dwell in the thick d 1Kin 8:12
he would dwell in the thick d 2Chr 6:1
Let that day be d .... Job 3:4
Let d and the shadow of death .... Job 3:5
that night, let d seize upon it .... Job 3:6
They meet with d in the daytime ...... Job 5:14
not return, even to the land of d .... Job 10:21
A land of d, as d itself .... Job 10:22
order, and where the light is as d ...... Job 10:22
discovereth deep things out of d .... Job 12:22
not that he shall return out of d .... Job 15:22
the day of d is ready at his hand ...... Job 15:23
He shall not depart out of d .... Job 15:30
the light is short because of d............ Job 17:12
I have made my bed in the d .... Job 17:13
shall be driven from light into d .... Job 18:18
and he hath set d in my paths. .... Job 19:8
All d shall be hid in his secret .... Job 20:26
Or d, that thou canst not see. .... Job 22:11
I was not cut off before the d .... Job 23:17
he covered the d from my face .... Job 23:17
He setteth an end to d, and .... Job 28:3
the stones of d, and the shadow of .... Job 28:3
by his light I walked through d .... Job 29:3
I waited for light, there came d .... Job 30:26
There is no d, nor shadow of .... Job 34:22
order our speech by reason of d .... Job 37:19
thick d a swaddlingband for it, ... Job 38:9
and as for d, where is the place .... Job 38:19
and d was under his feet .... Ps 18:9
He made d his secret place. .... Ps 18:11
Lord my God will enlighten my d ...... Ps 18:28
they walk on in d .... Ps 82:5
laid me in the lowest pit, in d .... Ps 88:6
me, and mine acquaintance into d .... Ps 88:18
the pestilence that walketh in d .... Ps 91:6
Clouds and d are round about him. .... Ps 97:2
Thou makest d, and it is night .... Ps 104:20
He sent d, and made it dark. .... Ps 105:28
Such as sit in d and in the shadow .... Ps 107:10
He brought them out of d and the .... Ps 107:14
there ariseth light in the d .... Ps 112:4
Surely the d shall cover me. .... Ps 139:11
the d hideth not from thee .... Ps 139:12
the d and the light are both alike....... Ps 139:12
he hath made me to dwell in d. .... Ps 143:3
to walk in the ways of d .... Prov 2:13
The way of the wicked is as d .... Prov 4:19
shall be put out in obscure d .... Prov 20:20
as far as light exceedeth d. .... Eccl 2:13
but the fool walketh in d .... Eccl 2:14
All his days also he eateth in d .... Eccl 5:17
in with vanity, and departeth in d .... Eccl 6:4
his name shall be covered with d ...... Eccl 6:4
let him remember the days of d .... Eccl 11:8
that put d for light, and light............ Is 5:20
for light, and light for d .... Is 5:20
one look unto the land, behold d ...... Is 5:30
and behold trouble and d, dimness .... Is 8:22
and they shall be driven to d .... Is 8:22
in d have seen a great light. .... Is 9:2
see out of obscurity, and out of d ...... Is 29:18
them that sit in d out of the .... Is 42:7
I will make d before them, ... Is 42:16
will give thee the treasures of d .... Is 45:3
I form the light, and create d .... Is 45:7
thou silent, and get thee into d .... Is 47:5
to them that are in d, Shew .... Is 49:9
of his servant, that walketh in d .... Is 50:10
and thy d be as the noonday .... Is 58:10
for brightness, but we walk in d .... Is 59:9
the d shall cover the earth, and .... Is 60:2
the earth, and gross of the people .... Is 60:2
a land of d? .... Jer 2:31
Lord your God, before he cause d ...... Jer 13:16
of death, and make it gross d .... Jer 13:16
them as slippery ways in the d .... Jer 23:12
hath led me, and brought me into d .. Lam 3:2
set d upon thy land, saith the .... Eze 32:8
he knoweth what is in the d .... Dan 2:22
A day of d and of gloominess, a .... Joel 2:2
a day of clouds and thick d .... Joel 2:2
The sun shall be turned into d .... Joel 2:31
that maketh the morning d .... Amos 4:13
the day of the Lord be d, and not...... Amos 5:18
not the day of the Lord be d.............. Amos 5:20
when I sit in d, the Lord shall .... Mic 7:8
d shall pursue his enemies .... Nah 1:8
and desolation, and a day of d .... Zeph 1:15
which sat in d saw a great light. .... Mt 4:16
thy whole body shall be full of d ...... Mt 6:23
be d, how great is that d .... Mt 6:23
shall be cast out into outer d .... Mt 8:12

What I tell you in d, that speak .... Mt 10:27
away, and cast him into outer d .... Mt 22:13
unprofitable servant into outer d ...... Mt 25:30
was d over all the land unto the .... Mt 27:45
there was d over the whole land .... Mk 15:33
give light to them that sit in d .... Lk 1:79
evil, thy body also is full of d .... Lk 11:34
light which is in thee be not d .... Lk 11:35
in d shall be heard in the light.......... Lk 12:3
is your hour, and the power of d .... Lk 22:53
there was a d over all the earth .... Lk 23:44
And the light shineth in d .... Jn 1:5
the d comprehended it not .... Jn 1:5
men loved d rather than light, ... Jn 3:19
followeth me shall not walk in d .... Jn 8:12
the light, lest d come upon you. .... Jn 12:35
for he that walketh in d knoweth ...... Jn 12:35
on me should not abide in d .... Jn 12:46
The sun shall be turned into d .... Acts 2:20
there fell on him a mist and a d. .... Acts 13:11
and to turn them from d to light........ Acts 26:18
a light of them which are in d .... Rom 2:19
therefore cast off the works of d .... Rom 13:12
to light the hidden things of d 1Cor 4:5
the light to shine out of d 2Cor 4:6
what communion hath light with d 2Cor 6:14
For ye were sometimes d, but now .... Eph 5:8
with the unfruitful works of d .... Eph 5:11
the rulers of the d of this world .... Eph 6:12
delivered us from the power of d .... Col 1:13
But ye, brethren, are not in d 1Th 5:4
we are not of the night, nor of d 1Th 5:5
fire, nor unto blackness, and d .... Heb 12:18
of d into his marvellous light 1Pet 2:9
delivered them into chains of d 2Pet 2:4
to whom the mist of d is reserved 2Pet 2:17
light, and in him is no d at all 1Jn 1:5
fellowship with him, and walk in d 1Jn 1:6
because the d is past, and the, ... 1Jn 2:8
brother, is in d even until now 1Jn 2:9
is in d, and walketh in d 1Jn 2:11
because that d hath blinded his 1Jn 2:11
in everlasting chains under d.............. Jude 6
the blackness of d for ever................ Jude 13
and his kingdom was full of d .... Rev 16:10

DARKON (dar'-kon) *A family of exiles.*
of Jaalah, the children of D................ Ezr 2:56
of Jaala, the children of D.................. Neh 7:58

DARLING
my d from the power of the dog.......... Ps 22:20
destructions, my d from the lions........ Ps 35:17

DART
the spear, the d, nor the.................... Job 41:26
Till a d strike through his liver .... Prov 7:23
or thrust through with a d .... Heb 12:20

DARTS
And he took three d in his hand........ 2Sa 18:14
in the city of David, and made d 2Chr 32:5
D are counted as stubble.................. Job 41:29
all the fiery d of the wicked .... Eph 6:16

DASH
wilt d their children, and rip up 2Kin 8:12
thou shalt d them in pieces like .... Ps 2:9
lest thou d thy foot against a .... Ps 91:12
Their bows also shall d the young...... Is 13:18
I will d them one against another ...... Jer 13:14
lest at any time thou d thy foot .... Mt 4:6
lest at any time thou d thy foot .... Lk 4:11

DASHED
hath d in pieces the enemy................ Ex 15:6
be d to pieces before their eyes .... Is 13:16
the mother was d in pieces .... Hos 10:14
infants shall be d in pieces................ Hos 13:16
their young children also were d in .... Nah 3:10

DASHETH
d thy little ones against the .... Ps 137:9
He that d in pieces is come up .... Nah 2:1

DATHAN (da'-than) *A conspirator against Moses.*
of Kohath, the son of Levi, and D...... Num 16:1
And Moses sent to call D.................... Num 16:12
about the tabernacle of Korah, D ...... Num 16:24
rose up and went unto D .... Num 16:25
from the tabernacle of Korah, D .... Num 16:27
and D and Abiram came out................ Num 16:27
Nemuel, and D, and Abiram.............. Num 26:9
This is that D and Abiram.................. Num 26:9
And what he did unto D and Abiram, .. Deut 11:6
earth opened and swallowed up D .... Ps 106:17

DAUB
Say unto them which d it with.......... Eze 13:11

DAUBED
d it with slime and with pitch, and.... Ex 2:3
others d it with untempered.............. Eze 13:10
daubing wherewith ye have d it .... Eze 13:12
ye have d with untempered morter .... Eze 13:14
upon them that have d it with .... Eze 13:14
no more, neither they that d it .... Eze 13:15
her prophets have d them with .... Eze 22:28

DAUBING
Where is the d wherewith ye have .... Eze 13:12

DAUGHTER
the d of Haran, the father of .... Gen 11:29
son's son, and Sarai his d in law........ Gen 11:31

she is the d of my father, but............ Gen 20:12
but not the d of my mother............... Gen 20:12
And said, Whose d art thou............... Gen 24:23
I am the d of Bethuel the son of........ Gen 24:24
her, and said, Whose d art thou......... Gen 24:47
The d of Bethuel, Nahor's son........... Gen 24:47
master's brother's d unto his son...... Gen 24:48
the d of Bethuel the Syrian of.......... Gen 25:20
Judith the d of Beeri the Hittite....... Gen 26:34
Bashemath the d of Elon the............. Gen 26:34
the d of Ishmael Abraham's son......... Gen 28:9
Rachel his d cometh with the............ Gen 29:6
when Jacob saw Rachel the d of......... Gen 29:10
years for Rachel thy younger d......... Gen 29:18
evening, that he took Leah his d........ Gen 29:23
Laban gave unto his d Leah Zilpah...... Gen 29:24
him Rachel his d to wife also........... Gen 29:28
Laban gave to Rachel his d Bilhah...... Gen 29:29
And afterwards she bare a d............. Gen 30:21
And Dinah the d of Leah, which she..... Gen 34:1
clave unto Dinah the d of Jacob........ Gen 34:3
that he had defiled Dinah his d........ Gen 34:5
in Israel in lying with Jacob's d...... Gen 34:7
my son Shechem longeth for your d...... Gen 34:8
then will we take our d, and we........ Gen 34:17
he had delight in Jacob's d............. Gen 34:19
Adah the d of Elon the Hittite......... Gen 36:2
Aholibamah the d of Anah the........... Gen 36:2
Anah the d of Zibeon the Hivite........ Gen 36:2
And Bashemath Ishmael's d, sister...... Gen 36:3
d of Anah the d of Zibeon.............. Gen 36:14
came of Aholibamah the d of Anah...... Gen 36:18
and Aholibamah the d of Anah.......... Gen 36:25
the d of Matred, the d of.............. Gen 36:39
Judah saw there a d of a certain...... Gen 38:2
said Judah to Tamar his d in law...... Gen 38:11
in process of time the d of Shuah..... Gen 38:12
not that she was his d in law......... Gen 38:16
Tamar thy d in law hath played........ Gen 38:24
the d of Poti-pherah priest of On..... Gen 41:45
came, which Asenath the d of.......... Gen 41:50
in Padan-aram, with his d Dinah....... Gen 46:15
whom Laban gave to Leah his d......... Gen 46:18
Ephraim, which Asenath the d of....... Gen 46:20
Laban gave unto Rachel his d.......... Gen 46:25
but if it be a d, then she shall...... Ex 1:16
every d ye shall save alive........... Ex 1:22
Levi, and took to wife a d of Levi.... Ex 2:1
the d of Pharaoh came down to......... Ex 2:5
said his sister to Pharaoh's d........ Ex 2:7
Pharaoh's d said to her, Go........... Ex 2:8
Pharaoh's d said unto her, Take....... Ex 2:9
she brought him unto Pharaoh's d...... Ex 2:10
and he gave Moses Zipporah his d...... Ex 2:21
of Amminadab, sister of Naashon....... Ex 6:23
thou, nor thy son, nor thy d.......... Ex 20:10
if a man sell his d to be a........... Ex 21:7
gored a son, or have gored a d........ Ex 21:31
fulfilled, for a son, or for a d...... Lev 12:6
the d of thy father, or d............. Lev 18:9
d, or of thy daughter's d............. Lev 18:10
of thy father's wife's d.............. Lev 18:11
the nakedness of thy d in law......... Lev 18:15
the nakedness of a woman and her d.... Lev 18:17
son's d, or her daughter's d.......... Lev 18:17
Do not prostitute thy d, to cause..... Lev 19:29
And if a man lie with his d in law.... Lev 20:12
father's d, or his mother's d......... Lev 20:17
and for his son, and for his d........ Lev 21:2
the d of any priest, if she........... Lev 21:9
If the priest's d also be married..... Lev 22:12
But if the priest's d be a widow...... Lev 22:13
the d of Dibri, of the tribe of...... Lev 24:11
was slain was Cozbi, the d of Zur..... Num 25:15
the d of a prince of Midian.......... Num 25:18
the name of the d of Asher was....... Num 26:46
the d of Levi, whom her mother....... Num 26:59
inheritance to pass unto his d....... Num 27:8
And if he have no d, then ye shall.... Num 27:9
wife, between the father and his d.... Num 30:16
And every d, that possesseth an...... Num 36:8
thou, nor thy son, nor thy d......... Deut 5:14
thy d thou shalt not give unto....... Deut 7:3
nor his d shalt thou take unto....... Deut 7:3
thou, and thy son, and thy d......... Deut 12:18
thy mother, or thy son, or thy d..... Deut 13:6
God, thou, and thy son, and thy d.... Deut 16:11
feast, thou, and thy son, and thy d.. Deut 16:14
or his d to pass through the fire.... Deut 18:10
I gave my d unto this man to wife.... Deut 22:16
saying, I found not thy d a maid..... Deut 22:17
the d of his father, or the......... Deut 27:22
father, or the d of his mother...... Deut 27:22
toward her son, and toward her d.... Deut 28:56
will I give Achsah my d to wife..... Josh 15:16
he gave him Achsah his d to wife.... Josh 15:17
will I give Achsah my d to wife..... Judg 1:12
he gave him Achsah his d to wife.... Judg 1:13
his d came out to meet him with.... Judg 11:34
her he had neither son nor d....... Judg 11:34
his clothes, and said, Alas, my d.. Judg 11:35
went yearly to lament the d of..... Judg 11:40
Behold, here is my d a maiden...... Judg 19:24
give his d unto Benjamin to wife... Judg 21:1
her d in law, with her, which...... Ruth 1:22
And she said unto her, Go, my d.... Ruth 2:2
unto Ruth, Hearest thou not, my d.. Ruth 2:8
And Naomi said unto her d in law... Ruth 2:22
d in law, It is good, my d......... Ruth 2:22
mother in law said unto her, My d.. Ruth 3:1

Blessed be thou of the LORD, my d... Ruth 3:10
And now, my d, fear not............. Ruth 3:11
law, she said, Who art thou, my d... Ruth 3:16
Then said she, Sit still, my d...... Ruth 3:18
for thy d in law, which loveth...... Ruth 4:15
thine handmaid for a d of Belial.... 1Sa 1:16
his d in law, Phinehas' wife, was... 1Sa 4:19
was Ahinoam, the d of Ahimaaz....... 1Sa 14:50
riches, and will give him his d..... 1Sa 17:25
to David, Behold my elder d Merab... 1Sa 18:17
at the time when Merab Saul's d..... 1Sa 18:19
And Michal Saul's d loved David..... 1Sa 18:20
gave him Michal his d to wife....... 1Sa 18:27
and that Michal Saul's d loved him.. 1Sa 18:28
But Saul had given Michal his d..... 1Sa 25:44
the d of Talmai king of Geshur...... 2Sa 3:3
name was Rizpah, the d of Aiah...... 2Sa 3:7
thou first bring Michal Saul's d.... 2Sa 3:13
Michal Saul's d looked through a.... 2Sa 6:16
Michal the d of Saul came out to.... 2Sa 6:20
Therefore Michal the d of Saul...... 2Sa 6:23
the d of Eliam, the wife of Uriah... 2Sa 11:3
his bosom, and was unto him as a d.. 2Sa 12:3
were born three sons, and one d..... 2Sa 14:27
in to Abigail the d of Nahash....... 2Sa 17:25
two sons of Rizpah the d of Aiah.... 2Sa 21:8
five sons of Michal the d of Saul... 2Sa 21:8
Rizpah the d of Aiah took........... 2Sa 21:10
David what Rizpah the d of Aiah..... 2Sa 21:11
of Egypt, and took Pharaoh's d...... 1Kin 3:1
Taphath the d of Solomon to wife.... 1Kin 4:11
Basmath the d of Solomon to wife.... 1Kin 4:15
also an house for Pharaoh's d....... 1Kin 7:8
given it for a present unto his d... 1Kin 9:16
But Pharaoh's d came up out of...... 1Kin 9:24
together with the d of Pharaoh...... 1Kin 11:1
was Maachah, the d of Abishalom..... 1Kin 15:2
was Maachah, the d of Abishalom..... 1Kin 15:10
the d of Ethbaal king of the........ 1Kin 16:31
name was Azubah the d of Shilhi..... 1Kin 22:42
for the d of Ahab was his wife...... 2Kin 8:18
the d of Omri king of Israel........ 2Kin 8:26
for she is a king's d.............. 2Kin 9:34
the d of king Joram, sister of..... 2Kin 11:2
Give thy d to my son to wife....... 2Kin 14:9
name was Jerusha, the d of Zadok... 2Kin 15:33
also was Abi, the d of Zachariah... 2Kin 18:2
The virgin the d of Zion hath...... 2Kin 19:21
the d of Jerusalem hath shaken..... 2Kin 19:21
the d of Haruz of Jotbah........... 2Kin 21:19
the d of Adaiah of Boscath......... 2Kin 22:1
his d to pass through the fire to.. 2Kin 23:10
the d of Jeremiah of Libnah........ 2Kin 23:31
the d of Pedaiah of Rumah.......... 2Kin 23:36
the d of Elnathan of Jerusalem..... 2Kin 24:8
the d of Jeremiah of Libnah........ 2Kin 24:18
the d of Matred, the d of.......... 1Chr 1:50
of the d of Shua the Canaanitess... 1Chr 2:3
Tamar his d in law bare him........ 1Chr 2:4
d of Machir the father of Gilead... 1Chr 2:21
Sheshan gave his d to Jarha his.... 1Chr 2:35
the d of Caleb was Achsa........... 1Chr 2:49
the d of Talmai king of Geshur..... 1Chr 3:2
of Bath-shua the d of Ammiel....... 1Chr 3:5
sons of Bithiah the d of Pharaoh... 1Chr 4:18
his d was Sherah, who built........ 1Chr 7:24
that Michal the d of Saul looking.. 1Chr 15:29
Solomon brought up the d of........ 2Chr 8:11
Rehoboam took him Mahalath the d... 2Chr 11:18
Abihail the d of Eliab the son of.. 2Chr 11:18
he took Maachah the d of Absalom... 2Chr 11:20
Rehoboam loved Maachah the d of.... 2Chr 11:21
Michaiah the d of Uriel of Gibeah.. 2Chr 13:2
name was Azubah the d of Shilhi.... 2Chr 20:31
for he had the d of Ahab to wife... 2Chr 21:6
also was Athaliah the d of Omri.... 2Chr 22:2
the d of the king, took Joash the.. 2Chr 22:11
the d of king Jehoram, the wife.... 2Chr 22:11
Give thy d to my son to wife....... 2Chr 25:18
also was Jerushah, the d of Zadok.. 2Chr 27:1
was Abijah, the d of Zechariah..... 2Chr 29:1
the d of Meshullam the son of...... Neh 6:18
that is, Esther, his uncle's d..... Est 2:7
were dead, took for his own d...... Est 2:7
the d of Abihail the uncle of...... Est 2:15
who had taken her for his d........ Est 2:15
the d of Abihail, and Mordecai the. Est 9:29
in the gates of the d of Zion...... Ps 9:14
Hearken, O d, and consider, and.... Ps 45:10
the d of Tyre shall be there with.. Ps 45:12
The king's d is all glorious....... Ps 45:13
O d of Babylon, who art to be...... Ps 137:8
thy feet with shoes, O prince's d.. Song 7:1
the d of Zion is left as a......... Is 1:8
Lift up thy voice, O d of Gallim... Is 10:30
the mount of the d of Zion......... Is 10:32
unto the mount of the d of Zion.... Is 16:1
spoiling of the d of my people..... Is 22:4
land as a river, O d of Tarshish... Is 23:10
thou oppressed virgin, d of Zidon.. Is 23:12
the d of Zion, hath despised thee.. Is 37:22
the d of Jerusalem hath shaken..... Is 37:22
O virgin d of Babylon, sit on the.. Is 47:1
no throne, O d of the Chaldeans.... Is 47:1
darkness, O d of the Chaldeans..... Is 47:5
of thy neck, O captive d of Zion... Is 52:2
world, Say ye to the d of Zion..... Is 62:11
toward the d of my people.......... Jer 4:11
child, the voice of the d of Zion.. Jer 4:31
I have likened the d of Zion to a.. Jer 6:2

of the d of my people slightly...... Jer 6:14
for war against thee, O d of Zion... Jer 6:23
O d of my people, gird thee with.... Jer 6:26
of the d of my people slightly...... Jer 8:11
the voice of the cry of the d of.... Jer 8:19
For the hurt of the d of my......... Jer 8:21
of the d of my people recovered..... Jer 8:22
the slain of the d of my people..... Jer 9:1
shall I do for the d of my people... Jer 9:7
for the virgin d of my people is.... Jer 14:17
go about, O thou backsliding d...... Jer 31:22
balm, O virgin, the d of Egypt...... Jer 46:11
O thou d dwelling in Egypt,......... Jer 46:19
The d of Egypt shall be............. Jer 46:24
Thou d that dost inhabit Dibon,..... Jer 48:18
flowing valley, O backsliding d..... Jer 49:4
against thee, O d of Babylon........ Jer 50:42
The d of Babylon is like a.......... Jer 51:33
the d of Jeremiah of Libnah......... Jer 52:1
from the d of Zion all her beauty... Lam 1:6
the d of Judah, as in a winepress... Lam 1:15
the d of Zion with a cloud in his... Lam 2:1
strong holds of the d of Judah...... Lam 2:2
the tabernacle of the d of Zion..... Lam 2:4
in the d of Judah mourning.......... Lam 2:5
destroy the wall of the d of Zion... Lam 2:8
The elders of the d of Zion sit..... Lam 2:10
destruction of the d of my people... Lam 2:11
I liken to thee, O d of Jerusalem... Lam 2:13
comfort thee, O virgin d of Zion.... Lam 2:13
their head at the d of Jerusalem.... Lam 2:15
the Lord, O wall of the d of Zion... Lam 2:18
destruction of the d of my people... Lam 3:48
the d of my people is become........ Lam 4:3
of the iniquity of the d of my...... Lam 4:6
destruction of the d of my people... Lam 4:10
O d of Edom, that dwellest in the... Lam 4:21
is accomplished, O d of Zion........ Lam 4:22
visit thine iniquity, O d of Edom... Lam 4:22
shall deliver neither son nor d..... Eze 14:20
As is the mother, so is her d....... Eze 16:44
Thou art thy mother's d, that....... Eze 16:45
hath lewdly defiled his d in law.... Eze 22:11
his sister, his father's d.......... Eze 22:11
for mother, or for son, or for d.... Eze 44:25
for the king's d of the south....... Dan 11:6
he shall give him the d of woman.... Dan 11:17
and took Gomer the d of Diblaim..... Hos 1:3
she conceived again, and bare a d... Hos 1:6
of the sin to the d of Zion......... Mic 1:13
the strong hold of the d of Zion.... Mic 4:8
shall come to the d of Jerusalem.... Mic 4:8
O d of Zion, like a woman in........ Mic 4:10
Arise and thresh, O d of Zion....... Mic 4:13
thyself in troops, O d of troops.... Mic 5:1
the d riseth up against her......... Mic 7:6
the d in law against her mother..... Mic 7:6
even the d of my dispersed, shall... Zeph 3:10
Sing, O d of Zion.................. Zeph 3:14
all the heart, O d of Jerusalem.... Zeph 3:14
dwellest with the d of Babylon..... Zec 2:7
Sing and rejoice, O d of Zion...... Zec 2:10
Rejoice greatly, O d of Zion....... Zec 9:9
shout, O d of Jerusalem............ Zec 9:9
married the d of a strange god..... Mal 2:11
saying, My d is even now dead...... Mt 9:18
and when he saw her, he said, d.... Mt 9:22
the d against her mother, and the.. Mt 10:35
the d in law against her mother.... Mt 10:35
he that loveth son or d more than.. Mt 10:37
the d of Herodias danced before.... Mt 14:6
my d is grievously vexed with a.... Mt 15:22
her d was made whole from that..... Mt 15:28
Tell ye the d of Sion, Behold,..... Mt 21:5
My little d lieth at the point of.. Mk 5:23
And he said unto her, D, thy faith.. Mk 5:34
certain which said, Thy d is dead... Mk 5:35
when the d of the said Herodias.... Mk 6:22
whose young d had an unclean....... Mk 7:25
cast forth the devil out of her d.. Mk 7:26
the devil is gone out of thy d..... Mk 7:29
out, and her d laid upon the bed... Mk 7:30
the d of Phanuel, of the tribe of.. Lk 2:36
For he had one only d, about....... Lk 8:42
And he said unto her, D, be of..... Lk 8:48
saying to him, Thy d is dead....... Lk 8:49
the mother against the d........... Lk 12:53
and the d against the mother....... Lk 12:53
in law against her d in law........ Lk 12:53
the d in law against her mother.... Lk 12:53
being a d of Abraham, whom Satan... Lk 13:16
Fear not, d of Sion................ Jn 12:15
Pharaoh's d took him up, and....... Acts 7:21
be called the son of Pharaoh's d... Heb 11:24

DAUGHTER'S
daughter, or of thy d daughter....... Lev 18:10
or her d daughter, to uncover her... Lev 18:17
are the tokens of my d virginity.... Deut 22:17

DAUGHTERS
and he begat sons and d.............. Gen 5:4
seven years, and begat sons and d... Gen 5:7
fifteen years, and begat sons and d. Gen 5:10
forty years, and begat sons and d... Gen 5:13
thirty years, and begat sons and d.. Gen 5:16
hundred years, and begat sons and d. Gen 5:19
hundred years, and begat sons and d. Gen 5:22
and two years, and begat sons and d. Gen 5:26
and five years, and begat sons and d Gen 5:30
earth, and d were born unto them,... Gen 6:1

the d of men that they were fair....... Gen 6:2
of God came in unto the d of men........ Gen 6:4
hundred years, and begat sons and d.... Gen 11:11
three years, and begat sons and d....... Gen 11:13
three years, and begat sons and d....... Gen 11:15
thirty years, and begat sons and d....... Gen 11:17
and nine years, and begat sons and d .. Gen 11:19
seven years, and begat sons and d....... Gen 11:21
hundred years, and begat sons and d.... Gen 11:23
years, and begat sons and d.............. Gen 11:25
I have two d which have not known..... Gen 19:8
son in law, and thy two d................. Gen 19:12
sons in law, which married his d......... Gen 19:14
take thy wife, and thy two d............... Gen 19:15
and upon the hand of his two d........... Gen 19:16
mountain, and his two d with him....... Gen 19:30
dwelt in a cave, he and his two d......... Gen 19:30
Thus were both the d of Lot with....... Gen 19:36
my son of the d of the Canaanites....... Gen 24:3
the d of the men of the city come........ Gen 24:13
my son of the d of the Canaanites....... Gen 24:37
my life because of the d of Heth......... Gen 27:46
take a wife of the d of Heth.............. Gen 27:46
which are of the d of the land............ Gen 27:46
take a wife of the d of the Canaan...... Gen 28:1
d of Laban thy mother's brother......... Gen 28:2
take a wife of the d of Canaan........... Gen 28:6
Esau seeing then that the d of Canaan.. Gen 28:8
And Laban had two d..................... Gen 29:16
for the d will call me blessed............ Gen 30:13
to me, and carried away my d............. Gen 31:26
me to kiss my sons and my d............. Gen 31:28
take by force thy d from me.............. Gen 31:31
thee fourteen years for thy two d....... Gen 31:41
These d are my d, and................... Gen 31:43
Jacob, These d are my d................. Gen 31:43
can I do this day unto these my d....... Gen 31:43
If thou shalt afflict my d................ Gen 31:50
take other wives beside my d............ Gen 31:50
up, and kissed his sons and his d......... Gen 31:55
went out to see the d of the land........ Gen 34:1
with us, and give your d unto us.......... Gen 34:9
unto us, and take our d unto you......... Gen 34:9
Then will we give our d unto you......... Gen 34:16
and we will take your d unto us.......... Gen 34:16
us take their d to us for wives........... Gen 34:16
and let us give them our d................ Gen 34:21
took his wives of the d of Canaan....... Gen 36:2
his wives, and his sons, and his d......... Gen 36:6
all his d rose up to comfort him......... Gen 37:35
his d, and his sons' d................... Gen 46:7
his d were thirty and three.............. Gen 46:15
the priest of Midian had seven d........ Ex 2:16
And he said unto his d, And where...... Ex 2:20
upon your sons, and upon your d........ Ex 3:22
one of the d of Putiel to wife........... Ex 6:25
old, with our sons and with our d........ Ex 10:9
and she have born him sons or d......... Ex 21:4
with her after the manner of d.......... Ex 21:9
wives, of your sons, and of your d....... Ex 32:2
take of their d unto thy sons............ Ex 34:16
their d go a whoring after their......... Ex 34:16
and thy sons, and thy d with thee....... Lev 10:14
the flesh of your d shall ye eat........... Lev 26:29
to thy d with thee, by a statute......... Num 18:11
thy d with thee, by a statute for........ Num 18:19
his sons that escaped, and his d......... Num 21:29
whoredom with the d of Moab.......... Num 25:1
son of Hepher had no sons, but d........ Num 26:33
the names of the d of Zelophehad....... Num 26:33
Then came the d of Zelophehad......... Num 27:1
and these are the names of his d......... Num 27:1
The d of Zelophehad speak right....... Num 27:7
Zelophehad our brother unto his d...... Num 36:2
concerning the d of Zelophehad......... Num 36:6
so did the d of Zelophehad............. Num 36:10
the d of Zelophehad, were married...... Num 36:11
God, ye, and your sons, and your d...... Deut 12:12
their d they have burnt in the.......... Deut 12:31
be no more of the d of Israel........... Deut 23:17
thy d shall be given unto another....... Deut 28:32
Thou shalt beget sons and d............. Deut 28:41
the flesh of thy sons and of thy d....... Deut 28:53
of his sons, and of his d............... Deut 32:19
of gold, and his sons, and his d.......... Josh 7:24
of Manasseh, had no sons, but d......... Josh 17:3
and these are the names of his d......... Josh 17:3
Because the d of Manasseh had an...... Josh 17:6
they took their d to be their........... Judg 3:6
gave their d to their sons, and.......... Judg 3:6
That the d of Israel went yearly........ Judg 11:40
he had thirty sons, and thirty d......... Judg 12:9
took in thirty d from abroad for........ Judg 12:9
of the d of the Philistines.............. Judg 14:1
of the d of the Philistines.............. Judg 14:2
woman among the d of thy brethren.... Judg 14:3
not give them of our d to wives......... Judg 21:7
may not give them wives of our d....... Judg 21:18
if the d of Shiloh come out to.......... Judg 21:21
man his wife of the d of Shiloh......... Judg 21:21
Then she arose with her d in law........ Ruth 1:6
her two d in law with her.............. Ruth 1:7
Naomi said unto her two d in law...... Ruth 1:8
And Naomi said, Turn again, my d....... Ruth 1:11
Turn again, my d, go your way.......... Ruth 1:12
nay, my d.............................. Ruth 1:13
wife, and to all her sons and her d....... 1Sa 1:4
and bare three sons and two d........... 1Sa 2:21
he will take your d to be.............. 1Sa 8:13
the names of his two d were 1Sa 14:49

wives, and their sons, and their d........ 1Sa 30:3
man for his sons and for his d............ 1Sa 30:6
nor great, neither sons nor d............. 1Sa 30:19
lest the d of the Philistines............. 2Sa 1:20
lest the d of the uncircumcised......... 2Sa 1:20
Ye d of Israel, weep over Saul........... 2Sa 1:24
were yet sons and d born to David...... 2Sa 5:13
d that were virgins apparelled.......... 2Sa 13:18
the lives of thy sons and of thy d........ 2Sa 19:5
their d to pass through the fire,......... 2Kin 17:17
No Shechan had no sons, but d.......... 1Chr 2:34
Shimei had sixteen sons and six d....... 1Chr 4:27
and Zelophehad had d.................. 1Chr 7:15
and David begat more sons and d....... 1Chr 14:3
died, and had no sons, but d............. 1Chr 23:22
to Heman fourteen sons and three d.... 1Chr 25:5
son of a woman of the d of Dan......... 2Chr 2:14
and eight sons, and threescore d........ 2Chr 11:21
twenty and two sons, and sixteen d..... 2Chr 13:21
and he begat sons and d................ 2Chr 24:3
thousand, women, sons, and d........... 2Chr 28:8
the sword, and our sons and our d....... 2Chr 29:9
wives, and their sons, and their d........ 2Chr 31:18
which took a wife of the d of.......... Ezr 2:61
taken of their d for themselves......... Ezr 9:12
give not your d unto their sons......... Ezr 9:12
take thou d unto your sons............. Ezr 9:12
part of Jerusalem, he and his d......... Neh 3:12
brethren, your sons, and your d......... Neh 4:14
that said, We, our sons, and our d....... Neh 5:2
our d to be servants................... Neh 5:5
some of our d are brought unto......... Neh 5:5
which took one of the d of............. Neh 7:63
wives, their sons, and their d........... Neh 10:28
that we would not give our d unto...... Neh 10:30
nor take their d for our sons........... Neh 10:30
not give your d unto their sons......... Neh 13:25
nor take their d unto your sons......... Neh 13:25
unto him seven sons and three d........ Job 1:2
his d were eating and drinking.......... Job 1:13
thy d were eating and drinking.......... Job 1:18
He had also seven sons and three d..... Job 42:13
found so fair as the d of Job........... Job 42:15
Kings' d were among thy.............. Ps 45:9
let the d of Judah be glad.............. Ps 48:11
the d of Judah rejoiced because........ Ps 97:8
sons and their d unto devils,........... Ps 106:37
blood of their sons and of their d....... Ps 106:38
that our d may be as corner............ Ps 144:12
The horseleach hath two d............. Prov 30:15
Many d have done virtuously, but....... Prov 31:29
all the d of musick shall be............ Eccl 12:4
O ye d of Jerusalem, as the tents....... Song 1:5
thorns, so is my love among the d....... Song 2:2
O ye d of Jerusalem, by the roes,....... Song 2:7
O ye d of Jerusalem, by the roes,....... Song 3:5
with love, for the d of Jerusalem....... Song 3:10
O ye d of Zion, and behold king....... Song 3:11
O ye d of Jerusalem, if ye find my...... Song 5:8
is my friend, O d of Jerusalem......... Song 5:16
The d saw her, and blessed her......... Song 6:9
O d of Jerusalem, that ye stir.......... Song 8:4
Because the d of Zion are haughty...... Is 3:16
of the head of the d of Zion............ Is 3:17
away the filth of the d of Zion.......... Is 4:4
so the d of Moab shall be at the........ Is 16:2
hear my voice, ye careless d............ Is 32:9
my d from the ends of the earth........ Is 43:6
thy d shall be carried upon their........ Is 49:22
name better than of sons and of d...... Is 56:5
thy d shall be nursed at thy side........ Is 60:4
herds, their sons and their d............ Jer 3:24
thy sons and thy d should eat........... Jer 5:17
their sons and their d in the fire........ Jer 7:31
mouth, and teach your d wailing........ Jer 9:20
their d shall die by famine............. Jer 11:22
nor their sons, nor their d............. Jer 14:16
thou have sons or d in this place,....... Jer 16:2
concerning the d that are born in....... Jer 16:3
sons and the flesh of their d............ Jer 19:9
Take ye wives, and beget sons and d.... Jer 29:6
give your d to husbands................ Jer 29:6
that they may bear sons and d.......... Jer 29:6
their d to pass through the fire......... Jer 32:35
our wives, our sons, nor our d.......... Jer 35:8
were in Mizpah, even the king's d...... Jer 41:10
and children, and the king's d.......... Jer 43:6
taken captives, and thy d captives....... Jer 48:46
her d shall be burned with fire......... Jer 49:2
ye d of Rabbah, gird you with.......... Jer 49:3
because of all the d of my city.......... Lam 3:51
face against the d of thy people........ Eze 13:17
shall deliver neither sons nor d......... Eze 14:16
shall deliver neither sons nor d......... Eze 14:18
be brought forth, both sons and d....... Eze 14:22
thou hast taken thy sons and thy d...... Eze 16:20
the d of the Philistines, which,......... Eze 16:27
her d that dwell at thy left hand....... Eze 16:46
thy right hand, is Sodom and her d..... Eze 16:46
hath not done, she nor her d........... Eze 16:48
as thou hast done, thou and thy d....... Eze 16:48
idleness was in her and in her d......... Eze 16:49
the captivity of Sodom and her d....... Eze 16:53
the captivity of Samaria and her d..... Eze 16:53
When thy sisters, Sodom and her d..... Eze 16:55
her d shall return to their............. Eze 16:55
thy d shall return to your former....... Eze 16:55
of thy reproach of the d of Syria....... Eze 16:57
the d of the Philistines, which,......... Eze 16:57
I will give them unto thee for d......... Eze 16:61

two women, the d of one mother........ Eze 23:2
were mine, and they bare sons and d.... Eze 23:4
they took her sons and her d........... Eze 23:10
they shall take thy sons and thy d....... Eze 23:25
shall slay their sons and their d......... Eze 23:47
your d whom ye have left shall......... Eze 24:21
minds, their sons and their d........... Eze 24:25
her d which are in the field............. Eze 26:6
with the sword thy d in the field........ Eze 26:8
her d shall go into captivity............ Eze 30:18
the d of the nations shall lament....... Eze 32:16
the d of the famous nations, unto....... Eze 32:18
therefore your d shall commit.......... Hos 4:13
I will not punish your d when.......... Hos 4:14
your d shall prophesy, your old......... Joel 2:28
your d into the hand of the........... Joel 3:8
thy d shall fall by the sword, and....... Amos 7:17
and his wife was of the d of Aaron...... Lk 1:5
D of Jerusalem, weep not for me........ Lk 23:28
your d shall prophesy, and your....... Acts 2:17
And the same man had four d............ Acts 21:9
you, and ye shall be my sons and d...... 2Cor 6:18
whose d ye are, as long as ye do........ 1Pet 3:6

DAVID See PREFACE. See also David's.
Second king of Israel.
begat Jesse, and Jesse begat D.......... Ruth 4:22
came upon D from that day forward.... 1Sa 16:13
that D took an harp, and played......... 1Sa 16:23
a covenant with the house of D......... 1Sa 20:16
So D reigned over all Israel, and........ 1Chr 18:14
he broken with D my servant........... Jer 33:21
multiply the seed of D my servant...... Jer 33:22
D my servant, so that I will not......... Jer 33:26
crying, and saying, Thou son of D...... Mt 9:27
and said, Is not this the son of D....... Mt 12:23
saying, Hosanna to the son of D........ Mt 21:9
more a great deal, Thou son of D....... Mk 10:48
was of the house and lineage of D...... Lk 2:4
Christ cometh of the seed of D......... Jn 7:42
For D speaketh concerning him, I....... Acts 2:25
of D was raised from the dead.......... 2Ti 2:8
am the root and the offspring of D..... Rev 22:16

DAVID'S
Saul became D enemy continually...... 1Sa 18:29
also sent messengers unto D house..... 1Sa 19:11
Michal D wife told him, saying,........ 1Sa 19:11
it at the hand of D enemies............ 1Sa 20:16
Saul's side, and D place was empty..... 1Sa 20:25
the month, that D place was empty 1Sa 20:27
D men said unto him, Behold, we....... 1Sa 24:4
that D heart smote him, because........ 1Sa 24:5
when D young men came, they spake... 1Sa 25:9
And Nabal answered D servants......... 1Sa 25:10
So D young men turned their way,...... 1Sa 25:12
D wife, to Phalti the son of............ 1Sa 25:44
And Saul knew D voice, and said, Is.... 1Sa 26:17
D two wives were taken captives,....... 1Sa 30:5
cattle, and said, This is D spoil......... 1Sa 30:20
there lacked of D servants............. 2Sa 2:30
sixth, Ithream, by Eglah D wife......... 2Sa 3:5
blind, that are hated of D soul......... 2Sa 5:8
so the Moabites became D servants..... 2Sa 8:2
they of Edom became D servants....... 2Sa 8:14
and D sons were chief rulers........... 2Sa 8:18
D servants came into the land of....... 2Sa 10:2
Wherefore Hanun took D servants...... 2Sa 10:4
D anger was greatly kindled............ 2Sa 12:5
and it was set on D head.............. 2Sa 12:30
the son of Shimeah D brother.......... 2Sa 13:3
the son of Shimeah D brother.......... 2Sa 13:32
D counsellor, from his city, even....... 2Sa 15:12
So Hushai D friend came into the....... 2Sa 15:37
D friend, was come unto Absalom,..... 2Sa 16:16
all D men with him, over Jordan........ 2Sa 17:22
D heart smote him after that he........ 2Sa 24:10
the prophet Gad, D seer, saying,........ 2Sa 24:11
Solomon to ride upon king D mule..... 1Kin 1:38
one tribe for my servant D sake........ 1Kin 11:32
Nevertheless for D sake did the........ 1Kin 15:4
did the priest give king D spears........ 2Kin 11:10
sake, and for my servant D sake........ 2Kin 19:34
sake, and for my servant D sake........ 2Kin 20:6
and the Moabites became D servants... 1Chr 18:2
and the Syrians became D servants..... 1Chr 18:6
the Edomites became D servants....... 1Chr 18:13
Wherefore Hanun took D servants...... 1Chr 19:4
and it was set upon D head............ 1Chr 20:2
son of Shimea D brother slew him...... 1Chr 20:7
spake unto Gad, D seer, saying,........ 1Chr 21:9
of the substance which was king D..... 1Chr 27:31
Also Jonathan D uncle was a........... 1Chr 27:32
and shields, that had been king D...... 2Chr 23:9
For thy servant D sake turn not........ Ps 132:10
D psalm of praise....................... Ps 145:1
sake, and for my servant D sake........ Is 37:35
the kings that sit upon D throne........ Jer 13:13
How say they that Christ is D son...... Lk 20:41

DAWN
as it began to d toward the first......... Mt 28:1
in a dark place, until the day d.......... 2Pet 1:19

DAWNING
rose early about the d of the day........ Josh 6:15
the woman in the d of the day.......... Judg 19:26
let it see the d of the day.............. Job 3:9
to and fro unto the d of the day........ Job 7:4
I prevented the d of the morning....... Ps 119:147

DAY

DAY See PREFACE.

And God called the light *D*	Gen 1:5
and the morning were the first *d*	Gen 1:5
and the morning were the second *d*	Gen 1:8
and the morning were the third *d*	Gen 1:13
to divide the *d* from the night	Gen 1:14
the greater light to rule the *d*	Gen 1:16
And to rule over the *d* and over the	Gen 1:18
and the morning were the fourth *d*	Gen 1:19
and the morning were the fifth *d*	Gen 1:23
and the morning were the sixth *d*	Gen 1:31
on the seventh *d* God ended his	Gen 2:2
he rested on the seventh *d* from	Gen 2:2
And God blessed the seventh *d*	Gen 2:3
in the *d* that the LORD God made	Gen 2:4
Remember the sabbath *d*, to keep	Ex 20:8
Keep the sabbath *d* to sanctify it	Deut 5:12
For a *d* in thy courts is better	Ps 84:10
not what a *d* may bring forth	Prov 27:1
Behold the *d*, behold, it is come	Eze 7:10
in that *d* when I make up my	Mal 3:17
Give us this *d* our daily bread	Mt 6:11
and be raised again the third *d*	Mt 16:21
the third *d* he shall be raised	Mt 17:23
the third *d* he shall rise again	Mt 20:19
But of that *d* and hour knoweth no	Mt 24:36
for ye know neither the *d* nor the	Mt 25:13
killed, he shall rise the third *d*	Mk 9:31
the third *d* he shall rise again	Mk 10:34
But of that *d* and that hour	Mk 13:32
For unto you is born this *d* in	Lk 2:11
the third *d* he shall rise again	Lk 18:33
This *d* is salvation come to this	Lk 19:9
so that *d* come upon you unawares	Lk 21:34
and the third *d* rise again	Lk 24:7
to rise from the dead the third *d*	Lk 24:46
raise it up again at the last *d*	Jn 6:39
I will raise him up at the last *d*	Jn 6:40
At that *d* ye shall know that I am	Jn 14:20
Him God raised up the third *d*	Acts 10:40
In the *d* when God shall judge the	Rom 2:16
sake we are killed all the *d* long	Rom 8:36
d according to the scriptures	1Cor 15:4
now is the *d* of salvation	2Cor 6:2
know perfectly that the *d* of the	1Th 5:2
To *d* if ye will hear his voice	Heb 3:7
that one *d* is with the Lord as a	2Pet 3:8
and a thousand years as one *d*	2Pet 3:8
But the *d* of the Lord will come	2Pet 3:10

DAY'S

as it were a *d* journey on this	Num 11:31
as it were a *d* journey on this	Num 11:31
But he himself went a *d* journey	1Kin 19:4
as every *d* work required	1Chr 16:37
also according unto this *d* decree	Est 9:13
enter into the city a *d* journey	Jonah 3:4
in the company, went a *d* journey	Lk 2:44
Jerusalem a sabbath *d* journey	Acts 1:12
in question for this *d* uproar	Acts 19:40

DAYS See PREFACE.

DAYS'

he set three *d* journey betwixt	Gen 30:36
pursued after them seven *d* journey	Gen 31:23
thee, three *d* journey into the	Ex 3:18
three *d* journey into the desert	Ex 5:3
We will go three *d* journey into	Ex 8:27
mount of the LORD three *d* journey	Num 10:33
them in the three *d* journey	Num 10:33
went three *d* journey in the	Num 33:8
(There are eleven *d* journey from	Deut 1:2
unto him, Give us seven *d* respite	1Sa 11:3
be three *d* pestilence in thy land	2Sa 24:13
a compass of seven *d* journey	2Kin 3:9
great city of three *d* journey	Jonah 3:3

DAYSMAN

Neither is there any *d* betwixt us	Job 9:33

DAYSPRING

caused the *d* to know his place	Job 38:12
whereby the *d* from on high hath	Lk 1:78

DAYTIME

by *d* in a pillar of a cloud, and	Num 14:14
They meet with darkness in the *d*	Job 5:14
marked for themselves in the *d*	Job 24:16
O my God, I cry in the *d*, but	Ps 22:2
his lovingkindness in the *d*	Ps 42:8
In the *d* also he led them with a	Ps 78:14
a shadow in the *d* from the heat	Is 4:6
upon the watchtower in the *d*	Is 21:8
it pleasure to riot in the *d*	2Pet 2:13

DEACON

let them use the office of a *d*	1Ti 3:10
a *d* well purchase to themselves a	1Ti 3:13

DEACONS

Philippi, with the bishops and *d*	Phil 1:1
Likewise must the *d* be grave	1Ti 3:8
Let the *d* be the husbands of one	1Ti 3:12

DEAD

him, Behold, thou art but a *d* man	Gen 20:3
stood up from before his *d*	Gen 23:3
I may bury my *d* out of my sight	Gen 23:4
of our sepulchres bury thy *d*	Gen 23:6
but that thou mayest bury thy *d*	Gen 23:6
should bury my *d* out of my sight	Gen 23:8
bury thy *d*	Gen 23:11
of me, I will bury my *d* there	Gen 23:13

bury therefore thy *d*	Gen 23:15
for his brother is *d*, and he is	Gen 42:38
and his brother is *d*, and he be alone	Gen 44:20
saw that their father was *d*	Gen 50:15
for all the men are *d* which	Ex 4:19
of the cattle of the Israelites *d*	Ex 9:7
a house where there was not one *d*	Ex 12:30
for they said, We be all *d* men	Ex 12:33
Egyptians *d* upon the sea shore	Ex 14:30
and the *d* beast shall be his	Ex 21:34
the *d* ox also they shall divide	Ex 21:35
and the *d* shall be his own	Ex 21:35
doth touch them, when they be *d*	Lev 11:31
any of them, when they are *d*	Lev 11:32
cuttings in your flesh for the *d*	Lev 19:28
for the *d* among his people	Lev 21:1
shall he go in to any *d* body	Lev 21:11
thing that is unclean by the *d*	Lev 22:4
and whosoever is defiled by the *d*	Num 5:2
LORD he shall come at no *d* body	Num 6:6
him, for that he sinned by the *d*	Num 6:11
defiled by the *d* body of a man	Num 9:6
defiled by the *d* body of a man	Num 9:7
be unclean by reason of a *d* body	Num 9:10
Let her not be as one *d*, of whom	Num 12:12
And he stood between the *d*	Num 16:48
He that toucheth the body of the *d*	Num 19:11
Whosoever toucheth the *d* body of	Num 19:13
d body of any man that is *d*	Num 19:13
in the open fields, or a *d* body	Num 19:16
a bone, or one slain, or one *d*	Num 19:16
congregation saw that Aaron was *d*	Num 20:29
and *d* from among the people	Deut 2:16
between your eyes for the *d*	Deut 14:1
flesh, nor touch their *d* carcase	Deut 14:8
the wife of the *d* shall not marry	Deut 25:5
name of his brother which is *d*	Deut 25:6
nor given ought thereof for the *d*	Deut 26:14
Moses my servant is *d*	Josh 1:2
to pass, when the judge was *d*	Judg 2:19
was fallen down on the earth *d*	Judg 3:25
of the LORD, when Ehud was *d*	Judg 4:1
her tent, behold, Sisera lay *d*	Judg 4:22
he bowed, there he fell down *d*	Judg 5:27
to pass, as soon as Gideon was *d*	Judg 8:33
Israel saw that Abimelech was *d*	Judg 9:55
So the *d* which he slew at his	Judg 16:30
have they forced, that she is *d*	Judg 20:5
you, as ye have dealt with the *d*	Ruth 1:8
to the living and to the *d*	Ruth 2:20
the Moabitess, the wife of the *d*	Ruth 4:5
of the *d* upon his inheritance	Ruth 4:5
of the *d* upon his inheritance	Ruth 4:10
that the name of the *d* be not cut	Ruth 4:10
also, Hophni and Phinehas, are *d*	1Sa 4:17
in law and her husband were *d*	1Sa 4:19
saw their champion was *d*, they	1Sa 17:51
after a *d* dog, after a flea	1Sa 24:14
when David heard that Nabal was *d*	1Sa 25:39
Now Samuel was *d*, and all Israel	1Sa 28:3
armourbearer saw that Saul was *d*	1Sa 31:5
and that Saul and his sons were *d*	1Sa 31:7
the people also are fallen and *d*	2Sa 1:4
and Jonathan his son are *d* also	2Sa 1:4
Saul and Jonathan his son be *d*	2Sa 1:5
for your master Saul is *d*	2Sa 2:7
heard that Abner was in Hebron	2Sa 4:1
me, saying, Behold, Saul is *d*	2Sa 4:10
look upon such a *d* dog as I am	2Sa 9:8
Uriah the Hittite is *d* also	2Sa 11:21
some of the king's servants be *d*	2Sa 11:24
Uriah the Hittite is *d* also	2Sa 11:24
that Uriah her husband was *d*	2Sa 11:26
to tell him that the child was *d*	2Sa 12:18
we tell him that the child is *d*	2Sa 12:18
perceived that the child was *d*	2Sa 12:19
unto his servants, Is the child *d*	2Sa 12:19
And they said, He is *d*	2Sa 12:19
but when the child was *d*, thou	2Sa 12:21
But now he is *d*, wherefore should	2Sa 12:23
for Amnon only is *d*	2Sa 13:32
that all the king's sons are *d*	2Sa 13:33
for Amnon only is *d*	2Sa 13:33
concerning Amnon, seeing he was *d*	2Sa 14:2
had a long time mourned for the *d*	2Sa 14:2
widow woman, and mine husband is *d*	2Sa 14:5
Why should this *d* dog curse my	2Sa 16:9
because the king's son is *d*	2Sa 18:20
anointed over us, is *d* in battle	2Sa 19:10
but *d* men before my lord the king	2Sa 19:28
laid her *d* child in my bosom	1Kin 3:20
my child suck, behold, it was *d*	1Kin 3:21
is my son, and the *d* is thy son	1Kin 3:22
but the *d* is thy son, and the	1Kin 3:22
that liveth, and thy son is the *d*	1Kin 3:23
but thy son is the *d*, and my son	1Kin 3:23
the captain of the host was *d*	1Kin 11:21
to his sons, saying, When I am *d*	1Kin 13:31
saying, Naboth is stoned, and is *d*	1Kin 21:14
that Naboth was stoned, and was *d*	1Kin 21:15
for Naboth is not alive, but *d*	1Kin 21:15
heard that Naboth was *d*	1Kin 21:16
it came to pass, when Ahab was *d*	2Kin 3:5
Thy servant my husband is *d*	2Kin 4:1
house, behold, the child was *d*	2Kin 4:32
he had restored a *d* body to life	2Kin 8:5
of Ahaziah saw that her son was *d*	2Kin 11:1
behold, they were all *d* corpses	2Kin 19:35
him in a chariot from Megiddo	2Kin 23:30
And when Bela was *d*, Jobab the son	1Chr 1:44

And when Jobab was *d*, Husham of	1Chr 1:45
And when Husham was *d*, Hadad the	1Chr 1:47
And when Hadad was *d*, Samlah of	1Chr 1:47
And when Samlah was *d*, Shaul of	1Chr 1:48
And when Shaul was *d*, Baal-hanan	1Chr 1:49
And when Baal-hanan was *d*, Hadad	1Chr 1:50
And when Azubah was *d*, Caleb took	1Chr 2:19
Hezron was *d* in Caleb-ephratah	1Chr 2:24
armourbearer saw that Saul was *d*	1Chr 10:5
and that Saul and his sons were *d*	1Chr 10:7
they were *d* bodies fallen to the	2Chr 20:24
both riches with the *d* bodies	2Chr 20:25
of Ahaziah saw that her son was *d*	2Chr 22:10
when her father and mother were *d*	Est 2:7
upon the young men, and they are *d*	Job 1:19
D things are formed from under	Job 26:5
forgotten as a *d* man out of mind	Ps 31:12
and horse are cast into a *d* sleep	Ps 76:6
The *d* bodies of thy servants have	Ps 79:2
Free among the *d*, like the slain	Ps 88:5
Wilt thou shew wonders to the *d*	Ps 88:10
shalt the *d* arise and praise thee	Ps 88:10
and ate the sacrifices of the *d*	Ps 106:28
fill the places with the *d* bodies	Ps 110:6
The *d* praise not the LORD	Ps 115:17
as those that have been long *d*	Ps 143:3
death, and her paths unto the *d*	Prov 2:18
knoweth not that the *d* are there	Prov 9:18
in the congregation of the *d*	Prov 21:16
Wherefore 1 praised the *d* which	Eccl 4:2
the *d* which are already *d* more	Eccl 4:2
and after that they go to the *d*	Eccl 9:3
dog is better than a *d* lion	Eccl 9:4
but the *d* know not any thing	Eccl 9:5
D flies cause the ointment of the	Eccl 10:1
for the living to the *d*	Is 8:19
it stirreth up the *d* for thee	Is 14:9
with the sword, nor *d* in battle	Is 22:2
They are *d*, they shall not live	Is 26:14
Thy *d* men shall live, together	Is 26:19
together with my *d* body shall	Is 26:19
and the earth shall cast out the *d*	Is 26:19
behold, they were all *d* corpses	Is 37:36
are in desolate places as *d* men	Is 59:10
to comfort them for the *d*	Jer 16:7
Weep ye not for the *d*, neither	Jer 22:10
cast his *d* body into the graves	Jer 26:23
the whole valley of the *d* bodies	Jer 31:40
them with the *d* bodies of men	Jer 33:5
their *d* bodies shall be for meat	Jer 34:20
his *d* body shall be cast out in	Jer 36:30
cast all the *d* bodies of the men	Jer 41:9
places, as they that be *d* of old	Lam 3:6
I will lay the *d* carcases of the	Eze 6:5
cry, make no mourning for the *d*	Eze 24:17
they shall come at no *d* person to	Eze 44:25
of any thing that is *d* of itself	Eze 44:31
there shall be many *d* bodies in	Amos 8:3
by a *d* body touch any of these	Hag 2:13
But when Herod was *d*, behold, an	Mt 2:19
for they are *d* which sought the	Mt 2:20
and let the *d* bury their *d*	Mt 8:22
saying, My daughter is even now *d*	Mt 9:18
for the maid is not *d*, but	Mt 9:24
cleanse the lepers, raise the *d*	Mt 10:8
the *d* are raised up, and the poor	Mt 11:5
he is risen from the *d*	Mt 14:2
of man be risen again from the *d*	Mt 17:9
the resurrection of the *d*	Mt 22:31
God is not the God of the *d*	Mt 22:32
are within full of *d* men's bones	Mt 23:27
people, He is risen from the *d*	Mt 27:64
did shake, and became as *d* men	Mt 28:4
that he is risen from the *d*	Mt 28:7
which said, Thy daughter is *d*	Mk 5:35
the damsel is not *d*, but sleepeth	Mk 5:39
the Baptist was risen from the *d*	Mk 6:14
he is risen from the *d*	Mk 6:16
Son of man were risen from the *d*	Mk 9:9
the rising from the *d* should mean	Mk 9:10
and he was as one *d*	Mk 9:26
insomuch that many said, He is *d*	Mk 9:26
when they shall rise from the *d*	Mk 12:25
And as touching the *d*, that they	Mk 12:26
He is not the God of the *d*	Mk 12:27
marvelled if he were already *d*	Mk 15:44
whether he had been any while *d*	Mk 15:44
there was a *d* man carried out	Lk 7:12
And he that was *d* sat up, and began	Lk 7:15
the *d* are raised, to the poor	Lk 7:22
saying to him, Thy daughter is *d*	Lk 8:49
she is not *d*, but sleepeth	Lk 8:52
to scorn, knowing that she was *d*	Lk 8:53
that John was risen from the *d*	Lk 9:7
Let the *d* bury their *d*	Lk 9:60
and departed, leaving him half *d*	Lk 10:30
For this my son was *d*, and is	Lk 15:24
for this thy brother was *d*	Lk 15:32
if one went unto them from the *d*	Lk 16:30
though one rose from the *d*	Lk 16:31
and the resurrection from the *d*	Lk 20:35
Now that the *d* are raised	Lk 20:37
For he is not a God of the *d*	Lk 20:38
seek ye the living among the *d*	Lk 24:5
to rise from of the third day	Lk 24:46
therefore he was risen from the *d*	Jn 2:22
as the Father raiseth up the *d*	Jn 5:21
when the *d* shall hear the voice	Jn 5:25
manna in the wilderness, and are *d*	Jn 6:49
fathers did eat manna, and are *d*	Jn 6:58

Abraham is *d*, and the prophets .... Jn 8:52
our father Abraham, which is *d* .... Jn 8:53
and the prophets are *d* .... Jn 8:53
unto them plainly, Lazarus is *d* .... Jn 11:14
believeth in me, though he were *d* .... Jn 11:25
the sister of him that was *d* .... Jn 11:39
for he hath been *d* four days .... Jn 11:39
the place where the *d* was laid .... Jn 11:41
thence, when his father was *d* .... Jn 11:44
And he that was *d* came forth .... Jn 11:44
Lazarus was which had been *d* .... Jn 12:1
d, whom he raised from the *d* .... Jn 12:1
whom he had raised from the *d* .... Jn 12:9
grave, and raised him from the *d* .... Jn 12:17
and saw that he was *d* already .... Jn 19:33
he must rise again from the *d* .... Jn 20:9
that he was risen from the *d* .... Jn 21:14
David, that he is both *d* and .... Acts 2:29
whom God had raised from the *d* .... Acts 3:15
Jesus the resurrection from the *d* .... Acts 4:2
whom God raised from the *d* .... Acts 4:10
young men came in, and found her *d* .... Acts 5:10
thence, when his father was *d* .... Acts 7:4
with him after he rose from the *d* .... Acts 10:41
God to be the Judge of quick and *d* .... Acts 10:42
But God raised him from the *d* .... Acts 13:30
that he raised him up from the *d* .... Acts 13:34
the city, supposing he had been *d* .... Acts 14:19
and risen again from the *d* .... Acts 17:3
he hath raised him from the *d* .... Acts 17:31
of the resurrection of the *d* .... Acts 17:32
the third left, and was taken up *d* .... Acts 20:9
resurrection of the *d* I am called .... Acts 23:6
shall be a resurrection of the *d* .... Acts 24:15
the resurrection of the *d* I am .... Acts 24:21
and of one Jesus, which was *d* .... Acts 25:19
you, that God should raise the *d* .... Acts 26:8
first that should rise from the *d* .... Acts 26:23
or fallen down *d* suddenly .... Acts 28:6
by the resurrection from the *d* .... Rom 1:4
even God, who quickeneth the *d* .... Rom 4:17
considered not his own body now *d* .... Rom 4:19
up Jesus our Lord from the *d* .... Rom 4:24
the offence of one many be *d* .... Rom 5:15
How shall we, that are *d* to sin .... Rom 6:2
the *d* by the glory of the Father .... Rom 6:4
For he that is *d* is freed from .... Rom 6:7
Now if we be *d* with Christ .... Rom 6:8
raised from the *d* dieth no more .... Rom 6:9
to be *d* indeed unto sin, but .... Rom 6:11
those that are alive from the *d* .... Rom 6:13
but if the husband be *d*, she is .... Rom 7:2
but if her husband be *d*, she is .... Rom 7:3
ye also are become *d* to the law .... Rom 7:4
to him who is raised from the *d* .... Rom 7:4
that being *d* wherein we were held .... Rom 7:6
For without the law sin was *d* .... Rom 7:8
the body is because of sin .... Rom 8:10
up Jesus from the *d* dwell in you .... Rom 8:11
d shall also quicken your mortal .... Rom 8:11
bring up Christ again from the *d* .... Rom 10:7
God hath raised him from the *d* .... Rom 10:9
of them be, but life from the *d* .... Rom 11:15
he might be Lord both of the *d* .... Rom 14:9
but if her husband be *d*, she is 1Cor 7:39
preached that he rose from the *d* 1Cor 15:12
there is no resurrection of the *d* 1Cor 15:12
there be no resurrection of the *d* 1Cor 15:13
up, if so be that the *d* rise not 1Cor 15:15
For if the *d* rise not, then is 1Cor 15:16
now is Christ risen from the *d* 1Cor 15:20
also the resurrection of the *d* 1Cor 15:21
do which are baptized for the *d* 1Cor 15:29
if the *d* rise not at all 1Cor 15:29
are they then baptized for the *d* 1Cor 15:29
it me, if the *d* rise not 1Cor 15:32
will say, How are the *d* raised up 1Cor 15:35
also is the resurrection of the *d* 1Cor 15:42
sound, and the *d* shall be raised 1Cor 15:52
but in God which raiseth the *d* 2Cor 1:9
one died for all, then were all *d* 2Cor 5:14
Father, who raised him from the *d* .... Gal 1:1
I through the law am *d* to the law .... Gal 2:19
the law, when Christ is *d* in vain .... Gal 2:21
when he raised him from the *d* .... Eph 1:20
who were *d* in trespasses and sins .... Eph 2:1
Even when we were *d* in sins .... Eph 2:5
sleepest, and arise from the *d* .... Eph 5:14
unto the resurrection of the *d* .... Phil 3:11
the firstborn from the *d* .... Col 1:18
who hath raised him from the *d* .... Col 2:12
being *d* in your sins and the .... Col 2:13
Wherefore if ye be *d* with Christ .... Col 2:20
For ye are *d*, and your life is hid .... Col 3:3
heaven, whom he raised from the *d* 1Th 1:10
the *d* in Christ shall rise first 1Th 4:16
in pleasure is *d* while she liveth 1Ti 5:6
from the *d* according to my gospel 2Ti 2:8
For if we be *d* with him, we shall 2Ti 2:11
the *d* at his appearing and his 2Ti 4:1
of repentance from *d* works .... Heb 6:1
and of resurrection of the *d* .... Heb 6:2
purge your conscience from *d* .... Heb 9:14
is of force after men are *d* .... Heb 9:17
and by it he being *d* yet speaketh .... Heb 11:4
even of one, and him as good as *d* .... Heb 11:12
to raise him up, even from the *d* .... Heb 11:19
their *d* raised to life again .... Heb 11:35
again from the *d* our Lord Jesus .... Heb 13:20
faith, if it hath no works, is *d* .... Jas 2:17
that faith without works is *d* .... Jas 2:20

the body without the spirit is *d* .... Jas 2:26
so faith without works is *d* also .... Jas 2:26
of Jesus Christ from the *d* 1Pet 1:3
that raised him up from the *d* 1Pet 1:21
being *d* to sins, should live unto 1Pet 2:24
ready to judge the quick and the *d* 1Pet 4:5
preached also to them that are *d* 1Pet 4:6
withereth, without fruit, twice *d* .... Jude 12
and the first begotten of the *d* .... Rev 1:5
saw him, I fell at his feet as *d* .... Rev 1:17
I am he that liveth, and was *d* .... Rev 1:18
first and the last, which was *d* .... Rev 2:8
a name that thou livest, and art *d* .... Rev 3:1
their *d* bodies shall lie in the .... Rev 11:8
see their *d* bodies three days .... Rev 11:9
shall not suffer their *d* bodies .... Rev 11:9
is come, and the time of the *d* .... Rev 11:18
Blessed are the *d* which die in .... Rev 14:13
it became as the blood of a *d* man .... Rev 16:3
But the rest of the *d* lived not .... Rev 20:5
And I saw the *d*, small and great .... Rev 20:12
the *d* were judged out of those .... Rev 20:12
gave up the *d* which were in it .... Rev 20:13
up the *d* which were in them .... Rev 20:13

DEADLY

for there was a *d* destruction 1Sa 5:11
oppress me, from my *d* enemies .... Ps 17:9
the groanings of a *d* wounded man .... Eze 30:24
and if they drink any of thing .... Mk 16:18
an unruly evil, full of *d* poison .... Jas 3:8
and his *d* wound was healed .... Rev 13:3
beast, whose *d* wound was healed .... Rev 13:12

DEADNESS

neither yet the *d* of Sarah's womb .... Rom 4:19

DEAF

or who maketh the dumb, or *d* .... Ex 4:11
Thou shalt not curse the *d* .... Lev 19:14
But I, as a *d* man, heard not .... Ps 38:13
they are like the *d* adder that .... Ps 58:4
in that day shall the *d* hear the .... Is 29:18
the ears of the *d* shall be .... Is 35:5
Hear, ye *d* .... Is 42:18
or *d*, as my messenger that I sent .... Is 42:19
eyes, and the *d* that have ears .... Is 43:8
mouth, their ears shall be *d* .... Mic 7:16
the *d* hear, the dead are raised .... Mt 11:5
bring unto him one that was *d* .... Mk 7:32
he maketh both the *d* to hear .... Mk 7:37
d spirit, I charge thee, come out .... Mk 9:25
the *d* hear, the dead are raised .... Lk 7:22

DEAL

now will we *d* worse with thee, ... Gen 19:9
thou wilt not *d* falsely with me .... Gen 21:23
And now if ye will *d* kindly .... Gen 24:49
and I will *d* well with thee .... Gen 32:9
Should he *d* with our sister as .... Gen 34:31
of kindly and truly with me .... Gen 47:29
let us *d* wisely with them .... Ex 1:10
but let not Pharaoh *d* deceitfully .... Ex 8:29
he shall *d* with her after the .... Ex 21:9
thou shalt *d* with thy vineyard .... Ex 23:11
tenth of *d* flour mingled with the .... Ex 29:40
one tenth *d* of fine flour mingled .... Lev 14:21
not steal, neither *d* falsely .... Lev 19:11
if thou *d* thus with me, kill me .... Num 11:15
tenth *d* of flour mingled with the .... Num 15:4
a several tenth *d* of flour .... Num 28:13
A several tenth *d* shalt thou .... Num 28:20
A several tenth *d* unto one lamb .... Num 28:29
one tenth *d* for one lamb .... Num 29:4
A several tenth *d* for one lamb .... Num 29:10
a several tenth *d* to each lamb of .... Num 29:15
But thus shalt ye *d* with them .... Deut 7:5
the land, that we will *d* kindly .... Josh 2:14
Therefore thou shalt *d* kindly .... Ruth 1:8
deceitfully, and will *d* kindly .... Isa 20:8
D gently for my sake with the 2Sa 18:5
As thou didst *d* with David my 2Chr 2:3
dwell therein, even so *d* with me 2Chr 2:3
D courageously, and the Lord shall 2Chr 19:11
lest I *d* with you after your .... Job 42:8
unto the fools, D not foolishly .... Ps 75:4
to *d* subtilly with his servants .... Ps 105:25
D bountifully with thy servant .... Ps 119:17
for thou shalt *d* bountifully with .... Ps 142:7
but they that *d* truly are his .... Prov 12:22
of uprightness shall he *d* unjustly .... Is 26:10
make an end to *d* treacherously .... Is 33:1
they shall *d* treacherously with .... Is 33:1
wouldest yet *d* treacherously .... Is 48:8
my servant shall *d* prudently .... Is 52:13
Is it not to *d* thy bread to the .... Is 58:7
happy that *d* very treacherously .... Jer 12:1
d thus with them in the time of .... Jer 18:23
if so be that the Lord will *d* .... Jer 21:2
Therefore will I also *d* in fury .... Eze 8:18
I will even *d* with thee as thou .... Eze 16:59
kept my judgments, to *d* truly .... Eze 18:9
the days that I shall *d* with thee .... Eze 22:14
they shall *d* furiously with thee .... Eze 23:25
they shall *d* with thee hatefully .... Eze 23:29
he shall surely *d* with him .... Eze 31:11
thou seest, *d* with thy servants .... Dan 1:13
shall *d* against them, and shall .... Dan 11:7
upon them that *d* treacherously .... Hab 1:13
why do we *d* treacherously every .... Mal 2:10
let none *d* treacherously against .... Mal 2:15

that ye *d* not treacherously .... Mal 2:16
more a great *d* they published it .... Mk 7:36
but he cried the more a great *d* .... Mk 10:48

DEALER

the treacherous *d* dealeth .... Is 21:2

DEALERS

the treacherous *d* have dealt .... Is 24:16
the treacherous *d* have dealt very .... Is 24:16

DEALEST

Wherefore *d* thou thus with thy .... Ex 5:15
d treacherously, and they dealt .... Is 33:1

DEALETH

thus *d* Micah with me, and hath .... Judg 18:4
told me that he *d* very subtilly 1Sa 23:22
poor that *d* with a slack hand .... Prov 10:4
prudent man *d* with knowledge .... Prov 13:16
He that is soon angry *d* foolishly .... Prov 14:17
is his name, who *d* in proud wrath .... Prov 21:24
dealer *d* treacherously, and the .... Is 21:2
the priest every one of falsely .... Jer 6:13
the priest every one *d* falsely .... Jer 8:10
God *d* with you as with sons .... Heb 12:7

DEALING

his violent *d* shall come down .... Ps 7:16

DEALINGS

of your evil *d* by all this people 1Sa 2:23
have no *d* with the Samaritans .... Jn 4:9

DEALS

three tenth *d* of fine flour for a .... Lev 14:10
thereof shall be two tenth *d* of .... Lev 23:13
two waue loaves of two tenth *d* .... Lev 23:17
two tenth *d* shall be in one cake .... Lev 24:5
for a meat offering two tenth *d* .... Num 15:6
of *d* flour mingled with half an .... Num 15:9
two tenth *d* of flour for a meat .... Num 28:9
three tenth *d* of flour for a meat .... Num 28:12
two tenth *d* of flour for a meat .... Num 28:12
three tenth *d* shall ye offer for .... Num 28:20
bullock, and two tenth *d* for a ram .... Num 28:20
three tenth *d* unto one bullock, ... Num 28:28
two tenth *d* unto one ram, ... Num 28:28
three tenth *d* for a bullock .... Num 29:3
and two tenth *d* for a ram .... Num 29:3
three tenth *d* to a bullock .... Num 29:9
and two tenth *d* to one ram, ... Num 29:9
three tenth *d* unto every bullock .... Num 29:14
two tenth *d* to each ram of the .... Num 29:14

DEALT

when Sarai *d* hardly with her, she .... Gen 16:6
because God hath *d* graciously .... Gen 33:11
Wherefore *d* ye so ill with me, as .... Gen 43:6
Therefore God *d* well with the .... Ex 1:20
hast thou *d* thus with us, to .... Ex 14:11
they *d* proudly he was above them .... Ex 18:11
seeing he hath *d* deceitfully with .... Ex 21:8
if ye have *d* well with Jerubbaal .... Judg 9:16
If ye then have *d* truly and .... Judg 9:19
and the men of Shechem *d* .... Judg 9:23
as ye have *d* with the dead, and .... Ruth 1:8
hath *d* very bitterly with me .... Ruth 1:20
how that thou hast *d* well with me 1Sa 24:18
shall have *d* well with my lord 1Sa 25:31
he *d* among all the people, even 2Sa 6:19
for they *d* faithfully 2Kin 12:15
d with familiar spirits and 2Kin 21:6
hand, because they *d* faithfully 2Kin 22:7
he *d* to every one of Israel, both 1Chr 16:3
Even so *d* David with all the 1Chr 20:3
done amiss, and have *d* wickedly 2Chr 6:37
he *d* wisely, and dispersed of all 2Chr 11:23
d with a familiar spirit, and with 2Chr 33:6
We have *d* very corruptly against .... Neh 1:7
that they *d* proudly against them .... Neh 9:10
But they and our fathers *d* proudly .... Neh 9:16
yet they *d* proudly, and hearkened .... Neh 9:29
My brethren have *d* deceitfully as .... Job 6:15
because he hath *d* bountifully .... Ps 13:6
neither have we *d* falsely in thy .... Ps 44:17
d unfaithfully like their fathers .... Ps 78:57
He hath not *d* with us after our .... Ps 103:10
for the Lord hath *d* bountifully .... Ps 116:7
Thou hast *d* well with thy servant .... Ps 119:65
for they *d* perversely with me .... Ps 119:78
He hath not *d* so with any nation .... Ps 147:20
dealers have *d* treacherously .... Is 24:16
dealers have *d* very treacherously .... Is 24:16
they *d* not treacherously with .... Is 33:1
so have ye *d* treacherously with .... Jer 3:20
the house of Judah have *d* very .... Jer 5:11
even they have *d* treacherously .... Jer 12:6
all her friends have *d* .... Lam 1:2
in the midst of thee have they *d* .... Eze 22:7
Because that Edom hath *d* against .... Eze 25:12
the Philistines have *d* by revenge .... Eze 25:15
They have *d* treacherously against .... Hos 5:7
there have they *d* treacherously .... Hos 6:7
that hath *d* wondrously with you .... Joel 2:26
our doings, so hath he *d* with us .... Zec 1:6
Judah hath *d* treacherously, and an .... Mal 2:11
whom thou hast *d* treacherously .... Mal 2:14
Thus hath the Lord *d* with me in .... Lk 1:25
Son, why hast thou thus *d* with us .... Lk 2:48
The same *d* subtilly with our .... Acts 7:19
of the Jews have *d* with me .... Acts 25:24
according as God hath *d* to every .... Rom 12:3

DEAR

Is Ephraim my d son .... Jer 31:20
who was d unto him, was sick, and........ Lk 7:2
count I my life unto myself................ Acts 20:24
followers of God, as d children .... Eph 5:1
of Epaphras our d fellowservant .... Col 1:7
us into the kingdom of his d Son .... Col 1:13
souls, because ye were d unto us........... 1Th 2:8

DEARLY

I have given the d beloved of my .... Jer 12:7
D beloved, avenge not yourselves,....... Rom 12:19
my d beloved, flee from idolatry........ 1Cor 10:14
these promises d beloved, let us 2Cor 7:1
d beloved, for your edifying.............. 2Cor 12:19
Therefore, my brethren d beloved .... Phil 4:1
fast in the Lord, my d beloved........... Phil 4:1
To Timothy, my d beloved son 2Ti 1:2
unto Philemon our d beloved .... Philem 1
D beloved, I beseech you as.............. 1Pet 2:11

DEATH

seven years of d began to come........ Gen 41:54
and the d was in all lands................ Gen 41:54
and there was a d in the land............... 2Kin 4:38
If there be in the land of Abraham...... 2Chr 6:28
might bury corn, because of the d......... Neh 5:3
came to Jeremiah concerning the d..... Jer 14:1
Now there came a d over all the.......... Acts 7:11
great d throughout all the world......... Acts 11:28

DEATH

Let me not see the d of the child .... Gen 21:16
comforted after his mother's d .... Gen 24:67
to pass after the d of Abraham .... Gen 25:11
his wife shall surely be put to d.......... Gen 26:11
them after the d of Abraham........... Gen 26:18
old, I know not the day of my d........... Gen 27:2
thee before the LORD before my d........ Gen 27:7
he may bless thee before his d.......... Gen 27:10
may take away from me this d only... Ex 10:17
mount shall be surely put to d......... Ex 19:12
he die, shall be surely put to d............ Ex 21:12
mother, shall be surely put to d........... Ex 21:15
hand, he shall surely be put to d........... Ex 21:16
mother, shall surely be put to d........... Ex 21:17
his owner also shall be put to d........... Ex 21:29
a beast shall surely be put to d........... Ex 22:19
it shall surely be put to d................. Ex 31:14
day, he shall surely be put to d........... Ex 31:15
work therein shall be put to d .... Ex 35:2
the d of the two sons of Aaron .... Lev 16:1
they shall not be put to d................ Lev 19:20
he shall surely be put to d............... Lev 20:2
mother shall be surely put to d.......... Lev 20:9
shall surely be put to d................... Lev 20:10
of them shall surely be put to d......... Lev 20:11
of them shall surely be put to d......... Lev 20:12
they shall surely be put to d............ Lev 20:13
he shall surely be put to d............... Lev 20:15
they shall surely be put to d............ Lev 20:16
wizard, shall surely be put to d......... Lev 20:27
LORD, he shall surely be put to d......... Lev 24:16
of the LORD, shall be put to d............. Lev 24:16
any man shall surely be put to d........ Lev 24:17
a man, he shall be put to d................. Lev 24:21
but shall surely be put to d............... Lev 27:29
cometh nigh shall be put to d .... Num 1:51
cometh nigh shall be put to d .... Num 3:10
cometh nigh shall be put to d .... Num 3:38
The man shall be surely put to d........ Num 15:35
men die the common d of all men ...... Num 16:29
cometh nigh shall be put to d .... Num 18:7
Let me die the d of the righteous .... Num 23:10
murderer shall surely be put to d....... Num 35:16
murderer shall surely be put to d....... Num 35:17
murderer shall surely be put to d....... Num 35:18
him shall surely be put to d............... Num 35:21
it unto the d of the high priest........... Num 35:25
until the d of the high priest............. Num 35:28
but after the d of the high.............. Num 35:28
to d by the mouth of witnesses.......... Num 35:30
a murderer, which is guilty of d......... Num 35:31
but he shall be surely put to d........... Num 35:31
until the d of the priest................. Num 35:32
of dreams, shall be put to d.............. Deut 13:5
be first upon him to put him to d....... Deut 17:6
is worthy of d be put to d................. Deut 17:6
witness he shall not be put to d......... Deut 17:6
be first upon him to put him to d........ Deut 17:7
whereas he was not worthy of d.......... Deut 19:6
have committed a sin worthy of d....... Deut 21:22
and he be to be put to d.................. Deut 21:22
in the damsel no matter worthy of d.... Deut 22:26
not be put to d for the children.......... Deut 24:16
be put to d for the fathers............... Deut 24:16
shall be put to d for his own sin .... Deut 24:16
thee this day life and good, and.......... Deut 30:15
I have set before you life and d.......... Deut 30:19
and how much more after my d........... Deut 31:27
my d ye will utterly corrupt.............. Deut 31:29
children of Israel before his d.......... Deut 33:1
Now after the d of Moses the .... Josh 1:1
him, he shall be put to d.................. Josh 1:18
have, and deliver our lives from d....... Josh 2:13
until the d of the high priest........... Josh 20:6
Now after the d of Joshua it came ...... Judg 1:1
jeoparded their lives unto the d.......... Judg 5:18
let him be put to d whilst it is............ Judg 6:31
from the womb to the day of his d....... Judg 13:7
so that his soul was vexed unto d........ Judg 16:16
d were more than they which he .... Judg 16:30

Gibeah, that we may put them to d..... Judg 20:13
He shall surely be put to d .... Judg 21:5
also, if ought but d part the............ Ruth 1:17
law since the d of thine husband........ Ruth 2:11
about the time of her d the women...... 1Sa 4:20
men, that we may put them to d......... 1Sa 11:12
not a man be put to d this day 1Sa 11:13
the bitterness of d is past................ 1Sa 15:32
see Saul until the day of his d............ 1Sa 15:35
is but a step between me and d........... 1Sa 20:3
I have occasioned the d of all 1Sa 22:22
came to pass after the d of Saul.......... 2Sa 1:1
in their d they were not divided.......... 2Sa 1:23
no child unto the day of her d........... 2Sa 6:23
two lines measured he to put to d........ 2Sa 8:2
shall be, whether in d or life............ 2Sa 15:21
not Shimei be put to d for this........... 2Sa 19:21
be put to d this day in Israel............. 2Sa 19:22
shut up unto the day of their d.......... 2Sa 20:3
were put to d in the days of............. 2Sa 21:9
When the waves of d compassed me..... 2Sa 22:5
the snares of d prevented me.......... 2Sa 22:6
not put thee to d with the sword 1Kin 2:8
shall be put to d this day................ 1Kin 2:24
for thou art worthy of d................ 1Kin 2:26
not at this time put thee to d 1Kin 2:26
in Egypt until the d of Solomon 1Kin 11:40
Israel after the d of Ahab................. 2Kin 1:1
thence any more d or barren land........ 2Kin 2:21
man of God, there is d in the pot........ 2Kin 4:40
not be put to d for the children 2Kin 14:6
be put to d for the fathers............... 2Kin 14:6
shall be put to d for his own sin 2Kin 14:6
king of Judah lived after the d.......... 2Kin 14:17
was a leper unto the day of his d......... 2Kin 15:5
days was Hezekiah sick unto d........... 2Kin 20:1
prepared abundantly before his d....... 1Chr 22:5
God of Israel should be put to d.......... 2Chr 15:13
after the d of his father to his........... 2Chr 24:4
the house, he shall be put to d 2Chr 23:7
Now after the d of Jehoiada came 2Chr 24:17
d of Joash son of Jehoahaz king.......... 2Chr 25:25
was a leper unto the day of his d......... 2Chr 26:21
days Hezekiah was sick to the d.......... 2Chr 32:24
Jerusalem did him honour at his d....... 2Chr 32:33
upon him, whether in be unto d........... Ezr 7:26
is one law of his to put him to d.......... Est 4:11
and the shadow of d stain it............. Job 3:5
Which long for d, but it cometh .... Job 3:21
he shall redeem thee from d.............. Job 5:20
and d rather than my life................. Job 7:15
of darkness and the shadow of............ Job 10:21
and of the shadow of d, without.......... Job 10:22
out to light the shadow of d .... Job 12:22
on my eyelids is the shadow of d......... Job 16:16
even the firstborn of d shall............. Job 18:13
to them even as the shadow of d........ Job 24:17
in the terrors of the shadow of d......... Job 24:17
of him shall be buried in d............... Job 27:15
of darkness, and the shadow of........... Job 28:3
d way, We have heard the fame........... Job 28:22
know that thou wilt bring me to d........ Job 30:23
is no darkness, nor shadow of d.......... Job 34:22
Have the gates of d been opened......... Job 38:17
seen the doors of the shadow of d........ Job 38:17
For in d there is no remembrance .... Ps 6:5
for him the instruments of d............. Ps 7:13
liftest me up from the gates of d......... Ps 9:13
eyes, lest I sleep the sleep of d............ Ps 13:3
The sorrows of d compassed me.......... Ps 18:4
the snares of d prevented me............ Ps 18:5
brought me into the dust of d............ Ps 22:15
the valley of the shadow of d............ Ps 23:4
To deliver their soul from d.............. Ps 33:19
covered us with the shadow of d......... Ps 44:19
he will be our guide even unto d......... Ps 48:14
d shall feed on them..................... Ps 49:14
the terrors of a fallen upon............. Ps 55:4
Let d seize upon them, and let........... Ps 55:15
hast delivered my soul from d............ Ps 56:13
the Lord being the issues from d......... Ps 68:20
For there are no bands in their d.......... Ps 73:4
he spared not their soul from d.......... Ps 78:50
that liveth, and shall not see d........... Ps 89:48
those that are appointed to d............ Ps 102:20
in darkness and in the shadow of d...... Ps 107:10
of darkness and the shadow of d......... Ps 107:14
draw near unto the gates of d........... Ps 107:18
The sorrows of d compassed me.......... Ps 116:3
hast delivered my soul from d............ Ps 116:8
the LORD is the d of his saints............ Ps 116:15
he hath not given me over unto d........ Ps 118:18
For her house inclineth unto d............ Prov 2:18
Her feet go down to d.................... Prov 5:5
going down to the chambers of d......... Prov 7:27
all they that hate me love d.............. Prov 8:36
righteousness delivereth from d......... Prov 10:2
righteousness delivereth from d......... Prov 11:4
evil pursueth it to his own d............. Prov 11:19
the pathway thereof there is no d........ Prov 12:28
to depart from the snares of d........... Prov 13:14
the end thereof are the ways of d........ Prov 14:12
to depart from the snares of d........... Prov 14:27
the righteous hath hope in his d......... Prov 14:32
of a king is as messengers of d.......... Prov 16:14
the end thereof are the ways of d........ Prov 16:25
D and life are in the power of the........ Prov 18:21
to and fro of them that seek d............ Prov 21:6
them that are drawn unto d.............. Prov 24:11
casteth firebrands, arrows, and......... Prov 26:18

the day of d than the day of............ Eccl 7:1
find more bitter than d the woman....... Eccl 7:26
hath he power in the day of d .... Eccl 8:8
for love is strong as d.................... Song 8:6
in the land of the shadow of .... Is 9:2
He will swallow up d in victory........... Is 25:8
We have made a covenant with d......... Is 28:15
your covenant with d shall be............ Is 28:18
days was Hezekiah sick unto d........... Is 38:1
thee, d can not celebrate thee........... Is 38:18
wicked, and with the rich in his d........ Is 53:9
hath poured out his soul unto d.......... Is 53:12
of drought, and of the shadow of d...... Jer 2:6
d shall be chosen rather than............ Jer 8:3
For d is come up into our windows....... Jer 9:21
he turn it into the shadow of d .... Jer 13:16
Such as are for d, to d.................... Jer 15:2
Such as are for d, to d.................... Jer 15:2
and let their men be put to d .... Jer 18:21
the way of life, and the way of d......... Jer 21:8
certain, that if ye put me to d............ Jer 26:15
and all Judah put him at all to d .... Jer 26:19
the king sought to put him to d.......... Jer 26:21
of the people to put him to d .... Jer 26:24
thee, let this man be put to d............. Jer 38:4
with thou not surely put me to d......... Jer 38:15
soul, I will not put thee to d .... Jer 38:16
us, and we will not put thee to d .... Jer 38:25
that they might put us to d .... Jer 43:3
such as are for d to d..................... Jer 43:11
in prison till the day of his d .... Jer 52:11
put them to d in Riblah in the .... Jer 52:27
a portion until the day of his d .... Jer 52:34
bereaveth, at home there is as d .... Lam 1:20
in the d of him that dieth................ Eze 18:32
for they are all delivered unto d .... Eze 31:14
pleasure in the d of the wicked........... Eze 33:11
I will redeem them from d................ Hos 13:14
O d, I will be thy plagues................. Hos 13:14
the shadow of d into the morning....... Amos 5:8
do well to be angry, even unto d .... Jonah 4:9
his desire as hell, and is as d.............. Hab 2:5
And was there until the d of Herod...... Mt 2:15
shadow of d light is sprung up............ Mt 4:16
shall deliver up the brother to d......... Mt 10:21
and cause them to be put to d............ Mt 10:21
when he would have put him to d......... Mt 14:5
or mother, let him die the d.............. Mt 15:4
here, which shall not taste of d........... Mt 16:28
and they shall condemn him to d .... Mt 20:18
exceeding sorrowful, even unto d ...... Mt 26:38
against Jesus, to put him to d............ Mt 26:59
and said, He is guilty of d................ Mt 26:66
against Jesus to put him to d............. Mt 27:1
daughter lieth at the point of d.......... Mk 5:23
or mother, let him die the d.............. Mk 7:10
here, which shall not taste of d........... Mk 9:1
and they shall condemn him to d .... Mk 10:33
shall betray the brother to d............. Mk 13:12
shall cause them to be put to d.......... Mk 13:12
him by craft, and put him to d........... Mk 14:1
is exceeding sorrowful unto d .... Mk 14:34
against Jesus to put him to d............. Mk 14:55
condemned him to be guilty of d........ Mk 14:64
in darkness and in the shadow of d..... Lk 1:79
Ghost, that he should not see d.......... Lk 2:26
here, which shall not taste of d........... Lk 9:27
scourge him, and put him to d .... Lk 18:33
shall they cause to be put to d .... Lk 21:16
thee, both into prison, and to d........... Lk 22:33
worthy of d is done unto him .... Lk 23:15
I have found no cause of d in him........ Lk 23:22
led with him to be put to d.............. Lk 23:32
him to be condemned to d, and have... Lk 24:20
for he was at the point of d............... Jn 4:47
but is passed from d unto life............ Jn 5:24
my saying, he shall never see d........... Jn 8:51
saying, he shall never taste of d.......... Jn 8:52
said, This sickness is not unto d.......... Jn 11:4
Howbeit Jesus spake of his d............. Jn 11:13
together for to put him to d.............. Jn 11:53
they might put Lazarus also to d......... Jn 12:10
signifying what d he should die .... Jn 12:33
lawful for us to put any man to d......... Jn 18:31
signifying what d he should die .... Jn 18:32
signifying by what d he should.......... Jn 21:19
up, having loosed the pains of d.......... Acts 2:24
And Saul was consenting unto his d..... Acts 8:1
that they should be put to d .... Acts 12:19
they found no cause of d in him.......... Acts 13:28
I persecuted this way unto the d......... Acts 22:4
by, and consenting unto his d............ Acts 22:20
charge worthy of d or of bonds.......... Acts 23:29
committed any thing worthy of d........ Acts 25:11
had committed nothing worthy of d..... Acts 25:25
and when they were put to d .... Acts 26:10
nothing worthy of d or of bonds......... Acts 26:31
there was no cause of d in me............ Acts 28:18
such things are worthy of d.............. Rom 1:32
to God by the d of his Son................ Rom 5:10
into the world, and d by sin.............. Rom 5:12
so d passed upon all men, for............ Rom 5:12
Nevertheless d reigned from Adam...... Rom 5:14
man's offence d reigned by one.......... Rom 5:17
That as sin hath reigned unto d.......... Rom 5:21
Christ were baptized into his d .... Rom 6:3
buried with him by baptism into d...... Rom 6:4
together in the likeness of his d .... Rom 6:5
d hath no more dominion over him...... Rom 6:9
whether of sin unto d, or of.............. Rom 6:16

for the end of those things is d .... Rom 6:21
For the wages of sin is d .... Rom 6:23
to bring forth fruit unto d .... Rom 7:5
to life, I found to be unto d .... Rom 7:10
that which is good made d unto me ... Rom 7:13
working d in me by that which is ...... Rom 7:13
me from the body of this d .... Rom 7:24
me free from the law of sin and d ..... Rom 8:2
For to be carnally minded is d .... Rom 8:6
I am persuaded, that neither d .... Rom 8:38
or the world, or life, or d 1Cor 3:22
last, as it were appointed to d 1Cor 4:9
do shew the Lord's d till he come 1Cor 11:26
For since by man came d, by man 1Cor 15:21
that shall be destroyed is d 1Cor 15:26
D is swallowed up in victory 1Cor 15:54
O d, where is thy sting 1Cor 15:55
The sting of d is sin 1Cor 15:56
the sentence of d in ourselves 2Cor 1:9
delivered us from so great a d 2Cor 1:10
we are the savour of d unto d 2Cor 2:16
we are the savour of d unto d 2Cor 2:16
But if the ministration of d 2Cor 3:7
delivered unto d for Jesus' sake......... 2Cor 4:11
So then d worketh in us, but life....... 2Cor 4:12
the sorrow of the world worketh d 2Cor 7:10
whether it be by life, or by d .... Phil 1:20
and became obedient unto d .... Phil 2:8
even the d of the cross..................... Phil 2:8
indeed he was sick nigh unto d .... Phil 2:27
work of Christ he was nigh unto d .... Phil 2:30
being made conformable unto his d ... Phil 3:10
the body of his flesh through d .... Col 1:22
Christ, who hath abolished d............. 2Ti 1:10
the angels for the suffering of d......... Heb 2:9
God should taste for every man .... Heb 2:9
that through d he might destroy .... Heb 2:14
him that had the power of d .... Heb 2:14
them who through fear of d were ...... Heb 2:15
that was able to save him from d ...... Heb 5:7
to continue by reason of d .... Heb 7:23
new testament, that by means of d .... Heb 9:15
be the d of the testator .... Heb 9:16
that he should not see d .... Heb 11:5
it is finished, bringeth forth d .... Jas 1:15
his way shall save a soul from d .... Jas 5:20
God, being put to d in the flesh......... 1Pet 3:18
we have passed from d unto life 1Jn 3:14
not his brother abideth in d 1Jn 3:14
sin a sin which is not unto d 1Jn 5:16
life for them that sin not unto d 1Jn 5:16
There is a sin unto d 1Jn 5:16
and there is a sin not unto d 1Jn 5:17
and have the keys of hell and of d ..... Rev 1:18
be thou faithful unto d, and I .... Rev 2:10
shall not be hurt of the second d .... Rev 2:11
I will kill her children with d .... Rev 2:23
and his name that sat on him was D ... Rev 6:8
sword, and with hunger, and with d ... Rev 6:8
And in those days shall men seek d .... Rev 9:6
to die, and d shall flee from them ...... Rev 9:6
loved not their lives unto the d .... Rev 12:11
his heads as it were wounded to d ..... Rev 13:3
her plagues come in one day, d .... Rev 18:8
such the second d hath no power ...... Rev 20:6
and d and hell delivered up the .... Rev 20:13
And d and hell were cast into the ...... Rev 20:14
This is the second d .... Rev 20:14
and there shall be no more d .... Rev 21:4
which is the second d .... Rev 21:8

DEATHS
They shall die of grievous d .... Jer 16:4
thou shalt die the d of them that .... Eze 28:8
Thou shalt die the d of the .... Eze 28:10
prisons more frequent, in oft 2Cor 11:23

DEBASE
didst d thyself even unto hell .... Is 57:9

DEBATE
D thy cause with thy neighbour......... Prov 25:9
forth, thou wilt d with it .... Is 27:8
Behold, ye fast for strife and d .... Is 58:4
full of envy, murder, d, deceit, ... Rom 1:29

DEBATES
lest there be d, envyings, wraths....... 2Cor 12:20

DEBIR (de´-bur) See KIRJATH-SANNAH,
KIRJATH-SEPHER.
1. An Amorite king.
unto D king of Eglon, saying,............ Josh 10:3
2. A city in Judah.
and all Israel with him, to D .... Josh 10:38
done to Hebron, so he did to D .... Josh 10:39
mountains, from Hebron, from D .... Josh 11:21
The king of D, one .... Josh 12:13
toward D from the valley of Achor .... Josh 15:7
up thence to the inhabitants of D ...... Josh 15:15
and the name of D before was .... Josh 15:15
and Kirjath-sannah, which is D .... Josh 15:49
suburbs, and D with her suburbs, ... Josh 21:15
went against the inhabitants of D .... Judg 1:11
and the name of D before was .... Judg 1:11
her suburbs, D with her suburbs, ... 1Chr 6:58
3. The boundary of God.
Mahanaim unto the border of D .... Josh 13:26

DEBORAH (deb´-o-rah)
1. Rebekah's nurse.
But D Rebekah's nurse died, and .... Gen 35:8
2. A judge of Israel.

And D, a prophetess, the wife of .... Judg 4:4
the palm tree of D between Ramah .... Judg 4:5
D arose, and went with Barak to .... Judg 4:9
and D went up with him .... Judg 4:10
And D said unto Barak, Up .... Judg 4:14
Then sang D and Barak the son of ..... Judg 5:1
in Israel, until that I D arose .... Judg 5:7
Awake, awake, D .... Judg 5:12
princes of Issachar were with D......... Judg 5:15

DEBT
and every one that was in d 1Sa 22:2
Go, sell the oil, and pay thy d 2Kin 4:7
year, and the exaction of every d .... Neh 10:31
loosed him, and forgave him the d ..... Mt 18:27
prison, till he should pay the d .... Mt 18:30
I forgave thee all that d .... Mt 18:32
not reckoned of grace, but of d .... Rom 4:4

DEBTOR
hath restored to the d his pledge........ Eze 18:7
the gold of the temple, he is a d .... Mt 23:16
I am a d both to the Greeks, and to ... Rom 1:14
that he is a d to do the whole .... Gal 5:3

DEBTORS
us our debts, as we forgive our d........ Mt 6:12
certain creditor which had two d .... Lk 7:41
one of his lord's d unto him .... Lk 16:5
Therefore, brethren, we are d .... Rom 8:12
and their d they are .... Rom 15:27

DEBTS
of them that are sureties for d .... Prov 22:26
And forgive us our d, as we .... Mt 6:12

DECAPOLIS (de-cap´-o-lis) A district east of
the Jordan River.
of people from Galilee, and from D.... Mt 4:25
began to publish in D how great........ Mk 5:20
the midst of the coasts of D............... Mk 7:31

DECAY
poor, and fallen in d with thee.......... Lev 25:35

DECAYED
of the bearers of burdens is d .... Neh 4:10
raise up the d places thereof.............. Is 44:26

DECAYETH
fail from the sea, and the flood d....... Job 14:11
much slothfulness the building d .... Eccl 10:18
Now that which d and waxeth old is... Heb 8:13

DECEASE
spake of his d which he should .... Lk 9:31
that ye may be able after my d to 2Pet 1:15

DECEASED
they are d, they shall not rise............ Is 26:14
when he had married a wife, d........... Mt 22:25

DECEIT
and their belly prepareth d .... Job 15:35
wickedness, nor my tongue utter d ..... Job 27:4
or if my foot hath hasted to d .... Job 31:5
His mouth is full of cursing and d ..... Ps 10:7
of his mouth are iniquity and d.......... Ps 36:3
to evil, and thy tongue frameth d .... Ps 50:19
d and guile depart not from her......... Ps 55:11
He shall redeem their soul from d ...... Ps 72:14
He that worketh d shall not dwell...... Ps 101:7
for their d is falsehood .... Ps 119:118
the counsels of the wicked are d .... Prov 12:5
but a false witness d .... Prov 12:17
D is in the heart of them that .... Prov 12:20
but the folly of fools is d .... Prov 14:8
Bread of d is sweet to a man .... Prov 20:17
lips, and layeth up d within him........ Prov 26:24
Whose hatred is covered by d .... Prov 26:26
neither was any d in his mouth .... Is 53:9
so are their houses full of d .... Jer 5:27
they hold fast d, they refuse to .... Jer 8:5
habitation is in the midst of d .... Jer 9:6
through d they refuse to know me, ... Jer 9:6
it speaketh d .... Jer 9:8
nought, and the d of their heart .... Jer 14:14
of the d of their own heart .... Jer 23:26
and the house of Israel with d............ Hos 11:12
the balances of d are in his hand........ Hos 12:7
and falsifying the balances by d .... Amos 8:5
houses with violence and d .... Zeph 1:9
covetousness, wickedness, d .... Mk 7:22
full of envy, murder, debate, d .... Rom 1:29
their tongues they have used d........... Rom 3:13
you through philosophy and vain d .... Col 2:8
For our exhortation was not of d 1Th 2:3

DECEITFUL
will abhor the bloody and d man........ Ps 5:6
but they devise d matters against .... Ps 35:20
O deliver me from the d and unjust ... Ps 43:1
devouring words, O thou d tongue..... Ps 52:4
d men shall not live out half .... Ps 55:23
were turned aside like a d bow .... Ps 78:57
the mouth of the d are opened........... Ps 109:2
lying lips, and from a d tongue .... Ps 120:2
The wicked worketh a d work .... Prov 11:18
but a d witness speaketh lies .... Prov 14:25
for they are d meat .... Prov 23:3
but the kisses of an enemy are d .... Prov 27:6
poor and the d man meet together ..... Prov 29:13
Favour is d, and beauty is vain.......... Prov 31:30
The heart is d above all things,.......... Jer 17:9
they are like a d bow .... Hos 7:16
and with the bag of d weights .... Mic 6:11

---

their tongue is d in their mouth .... Mic 6:12
neither shall a d tongue be found....... Zeph 3:13
apostles, d workers, transforming 2Cor 11:13
corrupt according to the d lusts......... Eph 4:22

DECEITFULLY
Shechem and Hamor his father d........ Gen 34:13
but let not Pharaoh deal d any .... Ex 8:29
the thing which he hath d gotten .... Lev 6:4
brethren have dealt d as a brook........ Job 6:15
and talk d for him .... Job 13:7
his soul unto vanity, nor sworn d....... Ps 24:4
like a sharp razor, working d .... Ps 52:2
that doeth the work of the LORD d ..... Jer 48:10
made with him he shall work d .... Dan 11:23
nor handling the word of God d 2Cor 4:2

DECEITFULNESS
the d of riches, choke the word,......... Mt 13:22
the d of riches, and the lusts of .... Mk 4:19
be hardened through the d of sin .... Heb 3:13

DECEITS
imagine d all the day long .... Ps 38:12
unto us smooth things, prophesy d ..... Is 30:10

DECEIVABLENESS
with all d of unrighteousness in 2Th 2:10

DECEIVE
of Ner, that he came to d thee............ 2Sa 3:25
did I not say, Do not d me................. 2Kin 4:28
the king, Let not Hezekiah d you 2Kin 18:29
God in whom thou trustest d thee 2Kin 19:10
therefore let not Hezekiah d you 2Chr 32:15
and d not with thy lips..................... Prov 24:28
the king, Let not Hezekiah d you .... Is 36:14
d thee, saying, Jerusalem shall .... Is 37:10
they will d every one his .... Jer 9:5
d you, neither hearken to your .... Jer 29:8
D not yourselves, saying, The .... Jer 37:9
they wear a rough garment to d .... Zec 13:4
them, Take heed that no man d you.... Mt 24:4
and shall d many............................ Mt 24:5
shall rise, and shall d many............... Mt 24:11
they shall d the very elect................. Mt 24:24
say, Take heed lest any man d you..... Mk 13:5
and shall d many............................ Mk 13:6
fair speeches d the hearts of the........ Rom 16:18
Let no man d himself....................... 1Cor 3:18
whereby they lie in wait to d .... Eph 4:14
Let no man d you with vain words .... Eph 5:6
Let no man d you by any means 2Th 2:3
we d ourselves, and the truth is......... 1Jn 1:8
Little children, let no man d you........ 1Jn 3:7
that he should d the nations no .... Rev 20:3
shall go out to d the nations .... Rev 20:8

DECEIVED
And your father hath d me, and........ Gen 31:7
violence, or hath d this neighbour...... Lev 6:2
that your heart be not d .... Deut 11:16
Michal, Why hast thou d me so......... 1Sa 19:17
Saul, saying, Why hast thou d me 1Sa 28:12
My lord, O king, my servant d me 2Sa 19:26
the d and the deceiver are his .... Job 12:16
not him that is d trust in vanity .... Job 15:31
mine heart have been d by a woman... Job 31:9
whosoever is d thereby is not............ Prov 20:1
fools, the princes of Noph are d .... Is 19:13
a d heart hath turned him aside,........ Is 44:20
thou hast greatly d this people .... Jer 4:10
O LORD, thou hast d me, and I was ... Jer 20:7
thou hast d me, and I was d .... Jer 20:7
Thy terribleness hath d thee.............. Jer 49:16
for my lovers, but they d me .... Lam 1:19
if the prophet be d when he hath .... Eze 14:9
I the LORD have d that prophet .... Eze 14:9
pride of thine heart hath d thee .... Obad 3
at peace with thee have d thee........... Obad 7
said, Take heed that ye be not d .... Lk 21:8
them the Pharisees, Are ye also d ...... Jn 7:47
d me, and by it slew me.................... Rom 7:11
Be not d: neither fornicators 1Cor 6:9
Be not d: evil communications 1Cor 15:33
Be not d; God is not......................... Gal 6:7
And Adam was not d, but the woman .. 1Ti 2:14
but the woman being d was in the 1Ti 2:14
and worse, deceiving, and being d 2Ti 3:13
sometimes foolish, disobedient, d....... Titus 3:3
thy sorceries were all nations d .... Rev 18:23
with which he d them that had.......... Rev 19:20
the devil that d them was cast .... Rev 20:10

DECEIVER
me, and I shall seem to him as a d ..... Gen 27:12
the deceived and the d are his........... Job 12:16
But cursed be the d, which hath......... Mal 1:14
Sir, we remember that that d said ...... Mt 27:63
This is a d and an antichrist.............. 2Jn 7

DECEIVERS
as d, and yet true 2Cor 6:8
many unruly and vain talkers and d ... Titus 1:10
For many d are entered into the......... 2Jn 7

DECEIVETH
is the man that d his neighbour......... Prov 26:19
but he d the people .... Jn 7:12
when he is nothing, he d himself........ Gal 6:3
but d his own heart, this man's .... Jas 1:26
and Satan, which d the whole world ... Rev 12:9
d them that dwell on the earth by...... Rev 13:14

DECEIVING

shall wax worse and worse, d	2Ti 3:13
hearers only, d your own selves	Jas 1:22

DECEIVINGS

own d while they feast with you	2Pet 2:13

DECENTLY

Let all things be done d and in	1Cor 14:40

DECIDED

thyself hast it	1Kin 20:40

DECISION

multitudes in the valley of d	Joel 3:14
LORD is near in the valley of d	Joel 3:14

DECK

D thyself now with majesty and	Job 40:10
They d it with silver and with	Jer 10:4

DECKED

I have d my bed with coverings of	Prov 7:16
I d thee also with ornaments, and	Eze 16:11
Thus wast thou d with gold	Eze 16:13
she d herself with her earrings	Hos 2:13
d with gold and precious stones and	Rev 17:4
d with gold, and precious stones,	Rev 18:16

DECKEDST

d thy high places with divers	Eze 16:16
d thyself with ornaments,	Eze 23:40

DECKEST

though thou d thee with ornaments	Jer 4:30

DECKETH

as a bridegroom d himself with	Is 61:10

DECLARATION

the d of the greatness of	Est 10:2
my speech, and my d with your ears	Job 13:17
d of those things which are most	Lk 1:1
Lord, and of your ready mind	2Cor 8:19

DECLARE

was none that could d it to me	Gen 41:24
Moab, began Moses to d this law	Deut 1:5
shall d his cause in the ears of	Josh 20:4
if ye can certainly d it me	Judg 14:12
But if ye cannot d it me, then	Judg 14:13
that he may d unto us the riddle	Judg 14:15
the words of the prophets d good	1Kin 22:13
D his glory among the heathen	1Chr 16:24
d good to the king with one	2Chr 18:12
to d it unto her, and to charge	Est 4:8
of the sea shall d unto thee	Job 12:8
that which I have seen I will d	Job 15:17
Who shall d his way to his face	Job 21:31
Then did he see it, and d it	Job 28:27
I would d unto him the number of	Job 31:37
d, if thou hast understanding	Job 38:4
if thou knowest it all	Job 38:18
demand of thee, and d thou unto me	Job 40:7
demand of thee, and d thou unto me	Job 42:4
I will d the decree	Ps 2:7
d among the people his doings	Ps 9:11
The heavens d the glory of God	Ps 19:1
I will d thy name unto my	Ps 22:22
shall d his righteousness unto a	Ps 22:31
shall it d thy truth	Ps 30:9
For I will d mine iniquity	Ps 38:18
if I would d and speak of them,	Ps 40:5
heavens shall d his righteousness	Ps 50:6
hast thou to do to d my statutes	Ps 50:16
fear, and shall d the work of God	Ps 64:9
I will d what he hath done for my	Ps 66:16
that I may d all thy works	Ps 73:28
name is near thy wondrous works d	Ps 75:1
But I will d for ever	Ps 75:9
arise and d them to their children	Ps 78:6
D his glory among the heathen,	Ps 96:3
The heavens d his righteousness,	Ps 97:6
To d the name of the LORD in Zion	Ps 102:21
d his works with rejoicing	Ps 107:22
live, and d the works of the LORD	Ps 118:17
and shall d thy mighty acts	Ps 145:4
and I will d thy greatness	Ps 145:6
in heart even to d all this	Eccl 9:1
they d their sin as Sodom, they	Is 3:9
d his doings among the people,	Is 12:4
watchman, let him d what he seeth	Is 21:6
or d us things for to come	Is 41:22
to pass, and new things do I d	Is 42:9
d his praise in the islands	Is 42:12
who among them can d this	Is 43:9
d thou, that thou mayest be	Is 43:26
as I, shall call, and shall d it	Is 44:7
I d things that are right	Is 45:19
and will not ye d it	Is 48:6
with a voice of singing d ye	Is 48:20
who shall d his generation	Is 53:8
I will d thy righteousness, and	Is 57:12
they shall d my glory among the	Is 66:19
D ye in Judah, and publish in	Jer 4:5
D this in the house of Jacob, and	Jer 5:20
hath spoken, that he may d it	Jer 9:12
d it in the isles afar off, and	Jer 31:10
If I d it unto thee, wilt thou	Jer 38:15
D unto us now what thou hast said	Jer 38:25
answer you, I will d it unto you	Jer 42:4
so d unto us, and we will do it	Jer 42:20
D ye in Egypt, and publish in	Jer 46:14
D ye among the nations, and	Jer 50:2
to d in Zion the vengeance of the	Jer 50:28
let us d in Zion the work of the	Jer 51:10
that they may d all their	Eze 12:16
d unto them their abominations	Eze 23:36
d all that thou seest to the	Eze 40:4
d the interpretation thereof,	Dan 4:18
D ye it not at Gath, weep ye not	Mic 1:10
to d unto Jacob his transgression	Mic 3:8
even to day do I d that I will	Zec 9:12
D unto us the parable of the	Mt 13:36
unto him, D unto us this parable	Mt 15:15
unto them thy name, and will d it	Jn 17:26
who shall d his generation	Acts 8:33
we d unto you glad tidings, how	Acts 13:32
though a man d it unto you	Acts 13:41
worship, him d I unto you	Acts 17:23
For I have not shunned to d unto	Acts 20:27
to d his righteousness for the	Rom 3:25
To d, I say, at this time his	Rom 3:26
for the day shall d it, because	1Cor 3:13
Now in this that I d unto you I	1Cor 11:17
I d unto you the gospel which I	1Cor 15:1
state shall Tychicus d unto you	Col 4:7
I will d thy name unto my	Heb 2:12
things d plainly that they seek a	Heb 11:14
heard of we unto you, that ye also	1Jn 1:3
d unto you, that God is light, and	1Jn 1:5

DECLARED

that my name may be d throughout	Ex 9:16
Moses d unto the children of	Lev 23:44
they d their pedigrees after	Num 1:18
because it was not d what should	Num 15:34
he d unto you his covenant, which	Deut 4:13
For thou hast d this day that	2Sa 19:6
the words that were d unto them	Neh 8:12
plentifully of the thing as it is	Job 26:3
I have d thy faithfulness and thy	Ps 40:10
hitherto have I d thy wondrous	Ps 71:17
thou hast d thy strength among	Ps 77:14
lovingkindness be d in the grave	Ps 88:11
With my lips have I d all the	Ps 119:13
I have d my ways, and thou	Ps 119:26
A grievous vision is d unto me	Is 21:2
God of Israel, have I d it	Is 21:10
Who hath d from the beginning,	Is 41:26
I have d, and have saved, and I	Is 43:12
thee from that time, and have d it	Is 44:8
who hath d this from ancient time	Is 45:21
I have d the former things from	Is 48:3
from the beginning d it to thee	Is 48:5
among them hath d these things	Is 48:14
Then Michaiah d unto them all the	Jer 36:13
now I have this day d it to you	Jer 42:21
she d unto him before all the	Lk 8:47
of the Father, he hath d him	Jn 1:18
I have d unto them thy name, and	Jn 17:26
d unto them how he had seen the	Acts 9:27
when he had d all these things	Acts 10:8
d unto them how the Lord had	Acts 12:17
they d all things that God had	Acts 15:4
Simeon hath d how God at the	Acts 15:14
he d particularly what things God	Acts 21:19
Festus d Paul's cause unto the	Acts 25:14
d to be the Son of God with power	Rom 1:4
thee, and that my name might be d	Rom 9:17
For it hath been d unto me of you	1Cor 1:11
d to be the epistle of Christ,	2Cor 3:3
Who also d unto us your love in	Col 1:8
as he hath d to his servants the	Rev 10:7

DECLARETH

yea, there is none that d	Is 41:26
For a voice d from Dan, and	Jer 4:15
and their staff d unto them	Hos 4:12
d unto man what is his thought,	Amos 4:13

DECLARING

D the end from the beginning, and	Is 46:10
d the conversion of the Gentiles	Acts 15:3
d what miracles and wonders God	Acts 15:12
d unto you the testimony of God	1Cor 2:1

DECLINE

to d after many to wrest judgment	Ex 23:2
thou shalt not d from the	Deut 17:11
yet do I not d from thy	Ps 119:157
neither d from the words of my	Prov 4:5
Let not thine heart d to her ways	Prov 7:25

DECLINED

d neither to the right hand, nor	2Chr 34:2
his way have I kept, and not d	Job 23:11
have our steps d from thy way	Ps 44:18
yet have I not d from thy law	Ps 119:51

DECLINETH

My days are like a shadow that d	Ps 102:11
am gone like the shadow when it d	Ps 109:23

DECREASE

suffereth not their cattle to d	Ps 107:38
He must increase, but I must d	Jn 3:30

DECREASED

the waters d continually until	Gen 8:5

DECREE

So they established a d for	2Chr 30:5
a d to build this house of God	Ezr 5:13
that a d was made of Cyrus the	Ezr 5:17
Then Darius the king made a d,	Ezr 6:1
d concerning the house of God at	Ezr 6:3
Moreover I make a d what ye shall	Ezr 6:8
Also I have made a d, that	Ezr 6:11

I Darius have made a d	Ezr 6:12
I make a d, that all they of the	Ezr 7:13
do make a d to all the treasurers	Ezr 7:21
when the king's d which he shall	Est 1:20
his d was heard, and when many	Est 2:8
the d was given in Shushan the	Est 3:15
his d came, there was great	Est 4:3
d that was given at Shushan to	Est 4:8
the d was given at Shushan the	Est 8:14
his d came, the Jews had joy and	Est 8:17
his d drew near to be put in	Est 9:1
also according unto this day's d	Est 9:13
d was given in Shushan	Est 9:14
the d of Esther confirmed these	Est 9:32
Thou shalt also d a thing	Job 22:28
When he made a d for the rain	Job 28:26
I will declare the d	Ps 2:7
he hath made a d which shall not	Ps 148:6
kings reign, and princes d justice	Prov 8:15
When he gave to the sea his d	Prov 8:29
Woe unto them that d unrighteous	Is 10:1
bound of the sea by a perpetual d	Jer 5:22
dream, there is but one d for you	Dan 2:9
the d went forth that the wise	Dan 2:13
Why is the d so hasty from the	Dan 2:15
Thou, O king, hast made a d	Dan 3:10
Therefore I make a d, That every	Dan 3:29
Therefore make I a d to bring in	Dan 4:6
is by the d of the watchers	Dan 4:17
this is the d of the most High,	Dan 4:24
statute, and to make a firm d	Dan 6:7
Now, O king, establish the d	Dan 6:8
signed the writing and the d	Dan 6:9
the king concerning the king's d	Dan 6:12
Hast thou not signed a d, that	Dan 6:12
nor the d that thou hast signed,	Dan 6:13
That no d nor statute which the	Dan 6:15
I make a d, That in every	Dan 6:26
Nineveh by the d of the king and	Jonah 3:7
day shall the d be far removed	Mic 7:11
Before the d bring forth, before	Zeph 2:2
went out a d from Caesar Augustus	Lk 2:1

DECREED

done, and what was d against her	Est 2:1
as they had d for themselves and	Est 9:31
And brake up for it my d place	Job 38:10
the consumption d shall overflow	Is 10:22
hath so d in his heart that he	1Cor 7:37

DECREES

them that decree unrighteous d	Is 10:1
delivered them the d for to keep	Acts 16:4
do contrary to the d of Caesar	Acts 17:7

DEDAN (de'-dan) See DEDANIM.
1. A grandson of Cush.

sons of Raamah; Sheba, and D	Gen 10:7
sons of Raamah; Sheba, and D	1Chr 1:9

2. A son of Jokshan.

And Jokshan begat Sheba, and D	Gen 25:3
the sons of D were Asshurim, and	Gen 25:3
sons of Jokshan; Sheba, and D	1Chr 1:32

3. A district between Sela and the Salt Sea.

D, and Tema, and Buz, and all that	Jer 25:23
dwell deep, O inhabitants of D	Jer 49:8
they of D shall fall by the sword	Jer 49:8
The men of D were thy merchants	Eze 27:15
D was thy merchant in precious	Eze 27:20
Sheba, and D, and the merchants of	Eze 38:13

DEDANIM (ded'-a-nim) See DODANIM.
Descendants of Raamah.

O ye travelling companies of D	Is 21:13

DEDANITES See DEDANIM.

DEDICATE

the battle, and another man d it	Deut 20:5
king David did d unto the LORD	2Sa 8:11
d to maintain the house of the	1Chr 26:27
to d it to him, and to burn before	2Chr 2:4

DEDICATED

a new house, and hath not d it	Deut 20:5
I had wholly d the silver unto	Judg 17:3
gold that he had d of all nations	2Sa 8:11
which David his father had d	1Kin 7:51
of Israel d the house of the LORD	1Kin 8:63
the things which his father had d	1Kin 15:15
and the things which himself had d	1Kin 15:15
All the money of the d things	2Kin 12:4
fathers, kings of Judah, had d	2Kin 12:18
also king David d unto the LORD	1Chr 18:11
the treasures of the d things	1Chr 26:20
all the treasures of the d things	1Chr 26:26
the captains of the host, had d	1Chr 26:26
and Joab the son of Zeruiah, had d	1Chr 26:28
and whosoever had d any thing	1Chr 26:28
of the treasuries of the d things	1Chr 28:12
that David his father had d	2Chr 5:1
all the people of the house of	2Chr 15:18
the things that his father had d	2Chr 15:18
and that he himself had d	2Chr 15:18
also all the things of the	2Chr 24:7
tithes and the d things faithfully	2Chr 31:12
every d thing in Israel shall be	Eze 44:29
testament was d without blood	Heb 9:18

DEDICATING

the princes offered for d of the	Num 7:10
his day, for the d of the altar	Num 7:84

DEDICATION
This was the *d* of the altar .... Num 7:84
This was the *d* of the altar .... Num 7:88
for they kept the *d* of the altar.............. 2Chr 7:9
kept the *d* of this house of God .... Ezr 6:16
offered at the *d* of this house of .... Ezr 6:17
at the *d* of the wall of Jerusalem.............. Neh 12:27
to keep the *d* with gladness, both .... Neh 12:27
Song at the *d* of the house of................ Ps 30:t
to come to the *d* of the image............... Dan 3:2
unto the *d* of the image that .... Dan 3:3
at Jerusalem the feast of the *d*.............. Jn 10:22

DEED
What *d* is this that ye have done .... Gen 44:15
in very *d* for this cause have I .... Ex 9:16
There was no such *d* done nor seen .... Judg 19:30
For in very *d*, as the LORD God of....... 1Sa 25:34
that Saul was come in very *d*............... 1Sa 26:4
because by this *d* thou hast given 2Sa 12:14
But will God in very *d* dwell with......... 2Chr 6:18
For this *d* of the queen shall .... Est 1:17
have heard of the *d* of the queen........... Est 1:18
to the counsel and *d* of them .... Lk 23:51
which was a prophet mighty in *d* .... Lk 24:19
good *d* done to the impotent man .... Acts 4:9
Gentiles obedient, by word and *d*........ Rom 15:18
that he that hath done this *d* 1Cor 5:2
him that hath so done this *d* 1Cor 5:3
be also in *d* when we are present........ 2Cor 10:11
And whatsoever ye do in word or *d*...... Col 3:17
man shall be blessed in his *d* .... Jas 1:25
but in *d* and in truth 1Jn 3:18

DEEDS
thou hast done *d* unto me that .... Gen 20:9
make known his *d* among the people 1Chr 16:8
And his *d*, first and last, behold,......... 2Chr 35:27
is come upon us for our evil *d* .... Ezr 9:13
reported his good *d* before me............ Neh 6:19
wipe not out my good *d* that I............. Neh 13:14
Give them according to their *d*............. Ps 28:4
make known his *d* among the people...... Ps 105:1
According to their *d*, accordingly.......... Is 59:18
they overpass the *d* of the wicked .... Jer 5:28
them according to their *d*.................. Jer 25:14
ye allow the *d* of your fathers.............. Lk 11:48
receive the due reward of our *d* .... Lk 23:41
light, because their *d* were evil............ Jn 3:19
lest his *d* should be reproved............... Jn 3:20
that his *d* may be made manifest,......... Jn 3:21
Ye do the *d* of your father .... Jn 8:41
and was mighty in words and in *d*......... Acts 7:22
and confessed, and shewed their *d* ...... Acts 19:18
that very worthy *d* are done unto........ Acts 24:2
to every man according to his *d*............ Rom 2:6
Therefore by the *d* of the law .... Rom 3:20
by faith without the *d* of the law.......... Rom 3:28
do mortify the *d* of the body.............. Rom 8:13
in signs, and wonders, and mighty *d*..... 2Cor 12:12
put off the old man with his *d* .... Col 3:9
day to day with their unlawful *d*.......... 2Pet 2:8
speed is partaker of his evil *d* 2Jn 11
remember his *d* which he doeth............ 3Jn 10
ungodly of which they have ungodly....... Jude 15
hatest the *d* of the Nicolaitanes........... Rev 2:6
except they repent of their *d* .... Rev 2:22
sores, and repented not of their *d*......... Rev 16:11

DEEMED
about midnight the shipmen *d* that..... Acts 27:27

DEEP
was upon the face of the *d* .... Gen 1:2
the LORD God caused a *d* sleep to........ Gen 2:21
of the great *d* broken up, and the .... Gen 7:11
The fountains also of the *d*................ Gen 8:2
a *d* sleep fell upon Abram................ Gen 15:12
of the *d* that lieth under .... Gen 49:25
for the *d* that coucheth beneath,......... Deut 33:13
because a *d* sleep from the LORD.......... 1Sa 26:12
when *d* sleep falleth on men,.............. Job 4:13
He discovereth *d* things out of............ Job 12:22
when *d* sleep falleth upon men, in........ Job 33:15
and the face of the *d* is frozen............ Job 38:30
He maketh the *d* to boil like a .... Job 41:31
one would think the *d* to be hoary........ Job 41:32
thy judgments are a great *d* .... Ps 36:6
D calleth unto *d* at the noise............ Ps 42:7
D calleth unto *d* at the noise............ Ps 42:7
one of them, and the heart, is *d*........... Ps 64:6
I sink in *d* mire, where there is........... Ps 69:2
I am come into *d* waters, where .... Ps 69:2
hate me, and out of the *d* waters.......... Ps 69:14
neither let the *d* swallow me up........... Ps 69:15
and didst cause it to take *d* root.......... Ps 80:9
and thy thoughts are very *d* .... Ps 92:5
are the *d* places of the earth.............. Ps 95:4
it with the *d* as with a garment.......... Ps 104:6
the LORD, and his wonders in the *d* ...... Ps 107:24
in the seas, and all *d* places.............. Ps 135:6
into *d* pits, that they rise not............. Ps 140:10
the fountains of the *d* .... Prov 8:28
of a man's mouth are as *d* waters........ Prov 18:4
casteth into a *d* sleep.................... Prov 19:15
the heart of man is like *d* water......... Prov 20:5
mouth of strange women is a *d* pit...... Prov 22:14
For a whore is a *d* ditch................. Prov 23:27
which is far off, and exceeding *d*........ Eccl 7:24
upon you the spirit of *d* sleep............. Is 29:10
Woe unto them that seek *d* to hide....... Is 29:15
he hath made it *d* and large.............. Is 30:33

That saith to the *d*, Be dry, and I .... Is 44:27
sea, the waters of the great *d* .... Is 51:10
That led them through the *d* .... Is 63:13
Flee ye, turn back, dwell *d* .... Jer 49:8
Flee, get you far back, dwell *d* .... Jer 49:30
shalt drink of thy sister's cup *d* .... Eze 23:32
I shall bring up the *d* upon these........ Eze 26:19
the *d* set him up on high with her....... Eze 31:4
I covered the *d* for him, and I........... Eze 31:15
Then will I make their waters *d* .... Eze 32:14
and to have drunk of the *d* waters .... Eze 34:18
He revealeth the *d* and the secret .... Dan 2:22
I was in a *d* sleep on my face............. Dan 8:18
then was I in a *d* sleep on my .... Dan 10:9
fire, and it devoured the great *d* .... Amos 7:4
For thou hadst cast me into the *d* .... Jonah 2:3
the *d* uttered his voice, and .... Hab 3:10
unto Simon, Launch out into the *d* .... Lk 5:4
which built an house, and digged *d*....... Lk 6:48
command them to go out into the *d* ...... Lk 8:31
to draw with, and the well is *d* .... Jn 4:11
being fallen into a *d* sleep .... Acts 20:9
Or, Who shall descend into the *d* .... Rom 10:7
things, yea, the *d* things of God 1Cor 2:10
their *d* poverty abounded unto the....... 2Cor 8:2
and a day I have been in the *d* 2Cor 11:25

DEEPER
the plague in sight be *d* than the .... Lev 13:3
in sight be not *d* than the skin .... Lev 13:4
and it be in sight *d* than the skin .... Lev 13:25
if it be in sight *d* than the skin .... Lev 13:30
be not in sight *d* than the skin .... Lev 13:31
be not in sight *d* than the skin .... Lev 13:32
nor be in sight *d* than the skin .... Lev 13:34
d than hell; what canst thou know? .... Job 11:8
a people of a *d* speech than thou.......... Is 33:19

DEEPLY
of Israel have *d* revolted................... Is 31:6
They have *d* corrupted themselves,....... Hos 9:9
he sighed *d* in his spirit, and............. Mk 8:12

DEEPNESS
because they had no *d* of earth............ Mt 13:5

DEEPS
thou threwest into the *d*, as a .... Neh 9:11
lowest pit, in darkness, in the *d* .... Ps 88:6
the earth, ye dragons, and all *d*.......... Ps 148:7
all the *d* of the river shall dry .... Zec 10:11

DEER
and the roebuck, and the fallow *d*....... Deut 14:5

DEFAMED
Being *d*, we intreat...................... 1Cor 4:13

DEFAMING
For I heard the *d* of many................. Jer 20:10

DEFEAT
then mayest thou for me the *d* 2Sa 15:34
For the LORD had appointed to *d* 2Sa 17:14

DEFENCE
their *d* is departed from them, and....... Num 14:9
and built cities for *d* in Judah 2Chr 11:5
Yea, the Almighty shall be thy *d* .... Job 22:25
My *d* is of God, which saveth the........ Ps 7:10
for an house of *d* to save me .... Ps 31:2
for God is my *d* .... Ps 59:9
for thou hast been my *d* and refuge ...... Ps 59:16
for God is my *d*, and the God of my ..... Ps 59:17
he is my *d* .... Ps 62:2
he is my *d* .... Ps 62:6
For the LORD is our *d* .... Ps 89:18
But the LORD is my *d* .... Ps 94:22
For wisdom is a *d* .... Eccl 7:12
and money is a *d* .... Eccl 7:12
upon all the glory shall be a *d* .... Is 4:5
the brooks of *d* shall be emptied.......... Is 19:6
his place of *d* shall be the .... Is 33:16
and the *d* shall be prepared.............. Nah 2:5
have made his *d* unto the people .... Acts 19:33
hear ye my *d* which I make now.......... Acts 22:1
as both in my bonds, and in the *d*........ Phil 1:7
I am set for the *d* of the gospel........... Phil 1:17

DEFENCED
of a *d* city a ruin...................... Is 25:2
Yet the *d* city shall be desolate,.......... Is 27:10
against all the *d* cities of Judah.......... 2Ki 18:13
waste *d* cities into ruinous heaps......... Is 37:26
have made thee this day a *d* city.......... Jer 1:18
and let us go into the *d* cities............ Jer 4:5
and let us enter into the *d* cities......... Jer 8:14
for these *d* cities remained of .... Jer 34:7
and to Judah in Jerusalem the *d* .... Eze 21:20

DEFEND
to *d* Israel Tola the son of Puah .... Judg 10:1
For I will *d* this city, to save 2Kin 19:34
I will *d* this city for mine own 2Kin 20:6
name of the God of Jacob *d* thee .... Ps 20:1
d me from them that rise up............... Ps 59:1
D the poor and fatherless .... Ps 82:3
the LORD of hosts *d* Jerusalem .... Is 31:5
For I will *d* this city to save it............ Is 37:35
and I will *d* this city..................... Is 38:6
The LORD of hosts shall *d* them .... Zec 9:15
In that day shall the LORD *d* the .... Zec 12:8

DEFENDED
of it, and slew the Philistines.............. 2Sa 23:12
he *d* him, and avenged that was........ Acts 7:24

DEFENDEST
for joy, because thou *d* them.............. Ps 5:11

DEFENDING
d also he will deliver it .... Is 31:5

DEFER
a vow unto God, *d* not to pay it .... Eccl 5:4
name's sake will I *d* mine anger.......... Is 48:9
d not, for thine own sake, O my.......... Dan 9:19

DEFERRED
the young man *d* not to do the............ Gen 34:19
Hope *d* maketh the heart sick, but .... Prov 13:12
he *d* them, and said, When Lysias........ Acts 24:22

DEFERRETH
discretion of a man *d* his anger .... Prov 19:11

DEFIED
I defy, whom the LORD hath not *d* ...... Num 23:8
seeing he hath *d* the armies of 1Sa 17:36
of Israel, whom thou hast *d*.............. 1Sa 17:45
And when he *d* Israel, Jonathan the..... 2Sa 21:21
when they *d* the Philistines that......... 2Sa 23:9
But when he *d* Israel, Jonathan 1Chr 20:7

DEFILE
neither shall ye *d* yourselves............. Lev 11:44
when they *d* my tabernacle that is .... Lev 15:31
wife, to *d* thyself with her................ Lev 18:20
any beast to *d* thyself therewith.......... Lev 18:23
D not ye yourselves in any of............... Lev 18:24
not you out also, when ye *d* it .... Lev 18:28
that ye *d* not yourselves therein.......... Lev 18:30
to *d* my sanctuary, and to profane........ Lev 20:3
But he shall not *d* himself .... Lev 21:4
nor *d* himself for his father, or........... Lev 21:11
not eat to *d* himself therewith .... Lev 22:8
that they *d* not their camps, in........... Num 5:3
D not therefore the land which ye .... Num 35:34
children of Ammon, did the king *d*...... 2Kin 23:13
how shall I *d* them?..................... Song 5:3
Ye shall *d* also the covering of........... Is 30:22
is called by my name, to *d* it .... Jer 32:34
shalt enter into it, and *d* it .... Eze 7:22
D the house, and fill the courts .... Eze 9:7
d not yourselves with the idols .... Eze 20:7
nor *d* yourselves with their idols .... Eze 20:18
against herself to *d* herself .... Eze 22:3
they shall *d* thy brightness............... Eze 28:7
ye *d* every one his neighbour's .... Eze 33:26
Neither shall they *d* themselves.......... Eze 37:23
the house of Israel no more *d* .... Eze 43:7
at no dead person to *d* themselves....... Eze 44:25
no husband, they may *d* themselves...... Eze 44:25
in his heart that he would not *d* .... Dan 1:8
that he might not *d* himself .... Dan 1:8
and they *d* the man....................... Mt 15:18
are the things which *d* a man............ Mt 15:20
that entering into him can *d* him......... Mk 7:15
those are they that *d* the man............ Mk 7:15
into the man, it cannot *d* him............. Mk 7:18
come from within, and *d* the man......... Mk 7:23
If any man *d* the temple of God,......... 1Cor 3:17
for them that *d* themselves with.......... 1Ti 1:10
these filthy dreamers *d* the flesh......... Jude 8

DEFILED
her, and lay with her, and *d* her .... Gen 34:2
that he had *d* Dinah his daughter .... Gen 34:5
because he had *d* Dinah their........... Gen 34:13
because they had *d* their sister .... Gen 34:27
be that a man shall be *d* withal.......... Lev 5:3
them, that ye should be *d* thereby .... Lev 11:43
shall be in him he shall be *d*............. Lev 13:46
goeth from him, and is *d* therewith...... Lev 15:32
are *d* which I cast out before you........ Lev 18:24
And the land is *d* .... Lev 18:25
were before you, and the land is *d* ...... Lev 18:27
after wizards, to be *d* by them........... Lev 19:31
There shall none be *d* for the............ Lev 21:1
for her may he be *d*..................... Lev 21:3
and whosoever is *d* by the dead......... Num 5:2
and be kept close, and she be *d*.......... Num 5:13
jealous of his wife, and she be *d* .... Num 5:14
of his wife, and she be not *d*............. Num 5:14
of thy husband, and if thou be *d* .... Num 5:20
come to pass, that, if she be *d* .... Num 5:27
And if the woman be not *d*, but be...... Num 5:28
instead of her husband, and is *d* .... Num 6:9
he hath of the head of his............... Num 6:9
because his separation was *d*............. Num 6:12
who were *d* by the dead body of a ...... Num 9:6
We are *d* by the dead body of a .... Num 9:7
because he hath of the sanctuary .... Num 19:20
that thy land be not *d*, which .... Deut 21:23
the fruit of thy vineyard, be *d* .... Deut 22:9
be his wife, after that she is *d*........... Deut 24:4
at the high places where the.............. 2Kin 23:8
he *d* Topheth, which is in the 2Kin 23:10
forasmuch as he *d* his father's.......... 1Chr 5:1
they have *d* the priesthood .... Neh 13:29
my skin, and *d* my horn in the dust..... Job 16:15
they have *d* by casting down the........ Ps 74:7
thy holy temple have they *d* .... Ps 79:1
Thus were they *d* with their own .... Ps 106:39
The earth also is *d* under the........... Is 24:5
For your hands are with blood .... Is 59:3
ye *d* my land, and made mine .... Jer 2:7
her whoredom, that she *d* the land...... Jer 3:9
because they have *d* my land .... Jer 16:18
shall be *d* as the place of Tophet........ Jer 19:13

their *d* bread among the Gentiles........... Eze 4:13
because thou hast *d* my sanctuary .... Eze 5:11
and their holy places shall be *d* .... Eze 7:24
neither hath *d* his neighbour's .... Eze 18:6
and *d* his neighbour's wife,................... Eze 18:11
hath not *d* his neighbour's wife, ... Eze 18:15
doings, wherein ye have been *d*............ Eze 20:43
hast *d* thyself in thine idols................... Eze 22:4
hath lewdly *d* his daughter in law........ Eze 22:11
all their idols she *d* herself .... Eze 23:7
Then I saw that she was *d* .... Eze 23:13
they *d* her with their whoredom, ... Eze 23:17
they have *d* my sanctuary in the .... Eze 23:38
Thou hast *d* thy sanctuaries by .... Eze 28:18
they *d* it by their own way and by .... Eze 36:17
they have even *d* my holy name by ...... Eze 43:8
whoredom, and Israel is *d* .... Hos 5:3
whoredom of Ephraim, Israel is *d* .... Hos 6:10
thee, that say, Let her be *d* .... Mic 4:11
of his disciples eat bread with *d* .... Mk 7:2
hall, lest they should be *d* .... Jn 18:28
their conscience being weak is *d* 1Cor 8:7
but unto them that are *d* and .... Titus 1:15
their mind and conscience is *d* .... Titus 1:15
trouble you, and thereby many be *d*..... Heb 12:15
which have not *d* their garments........... Rev 3:4
they which were not *d* with women ...... Rev 14:4

DEFILEDST
then *d* thou it .... Gen 49:4

DEFILETH
every one that *d* it shall surely .... Ex 31:14
of the tabernacle of the LORD................... Num 19:13
for blood it *d* the land........................... Num 35:33
goeth into the mouth *d* a man............... Mt 15:11
out of the mouth, this *d* a man.............. Mt 15:11
with unwashen hands *d* not a man....... Mt 15:20
out of the man, that *d* the man............. Mk 7:20
that it *d* the whole body, and .... Jas 3:6
enter into it any thing that *d* .... Rev 21:27

DEFRAUD
Thou shalt not *d* thy neighbour............. Lev 19:13
D not, Honour thy father and................ Mk 10:19
Nay, ye do wrong, and *d*, and that 1Cor 6:8
D ye not one the other, except it 1Cor 7:5
of his brother in any matter 1Th 4:6

DEFRAUDED
or whom have I *d*?.................................. 1Sa 12:3
And they said, Thou hast not *d* us........ 1Sa 12:4
rather suffer yourselves to be *d*............ 1Cor 6:7
no man, we have *d* no man................... 2Cor 7:2

DEFY
curse me Jacob, and come, *d* Israel...... Num 23:7
or how shall I *d*, whom the LORD .... Num 23:8
I *d* the armies of Israel this day............. 1Sa 17:10
surely to *d* Israel is he come up............ 1Sa 17:25
that he should *d* the armies of 1Sa 17:26

DEGENERATE
then art thou turned into the *d* .... Jer 2:21

DEGREE
their brethren of the second *d* 1Chr 15:18
to the estate of a man of high *d*........... 1Chr 17:17
Surely men of low *d* are vanity............. Ps 62:9
and men of high *d* are a lie .... Ps 62:9
seats, and exalted them of low *d* .... Lk 1:52
purchase to themselves a good *d*......... 1Ti 3:13
Let the brother of low *d* rejoice .... Jas 1:9

DEGREES
shall the shadow go forward ten *d*....... 2Kin 20:9
or go back ten *d* 2Kin 20:9
for the shadow to go down ten *d* 2Kin 20:10
the shadow return backward ten *d* 2Kin 20:10
brought the shadow ten *d* backward.... 2Kin 20:11
A Song of *d* .... Ps 120:1
A Song of *d* .... Ps 121:1
A Song of *d* of David............................ Ps 122:1
A Song of *d* .... Ps 123:1
A Song of *d* of David............................ Ps 124:1
A Song of *d* .... Ps 125:1
A Song of *d* .... Ps 126:1
A Song of *d* for Solomon...................... Ps 127:1
A Song of *d* .... Ps 128:1
A Song of *d* .... Ps 129:1
A Song of *d* .... Ps 130:1
A Song of *d* .... Ps 131:1
A Song of *d* of David............................ Ps 132:1
A Song of *d* of David............................ Ps 133:1
A Song of *d* .... Ps 134:1
bring again the shadow of the *d* .... Is 38:8
sun dial of Ahaz, ten *d* backward......... Is 38:8
So the sun returned ten *d* .... Is 38:8
by which *d* it was gone down................ Is 38:8

DEHAVITES (de-ha'-vites) *Foreign settlers in*
Samaria.
the Susanchites, the *D*, and the .... Ezr 4:9

DEKAR (de'-kar) *Father of an officer of*
Solomon.
The son of *D*, in Makaz, and in 1Kin 4:9

DELAIAH (del-a-i'-ah) See DALAIAH.
1. A priest of David.
The three and twentieth to *D* 1Chr 24:18
2. A family with a lost genealogy.
The children of *D*, the children............. Ezr 2:60
The children of *D*, the children............. Neh 7:62
3. An opponent of Nehemiah.

son of *D* the son of Mehetabeel............ Neh 6:10
4. A prince of Judah.
D the son of Shemaiah, and.................. Jer 36:12
Nevertheless Elnathan and *D*............... Jer 36:25

DELAY
Thou shalt not *d* to offer the................. Ex 22:29
he would not *d* to come to them .... Acts 9:38
without any *d* on the morrow I sat....... Acts 25:17

DELAYED
d to come down out of the mount......... Ex 32:1
d not to keep thy commandments .... Ps 119:60

DELAYETH
his heart, My lord *d* his coming .... Mt 24:48
his heart, My lord *d* his coming .... Lk 12:45

DELECTABLE
their *d* things shall not profit................. Is 44:9

DELICACIES
through the abundance of her *d*............ Rev 18:3

DELICATE
is tender among you, and very *d*........... Deut 28:54
d woman among you, which would .... Deut 28:56
no more be called tender and *d*............. Is 47:1
of Zion to a comely and *d* woman......... Jer 6:2
and poll thee for thy *d* children.............. Mic 1:16

DELICATELY
And Agag came unto him *d*................... 1Sa 15:32
He that *d* bringeth up his servant......... Prov 29:21
They that did feed *d* are desolate.......... Lam 4:5
gorgeously apparelled, and live *d* .... Lk 7:25

DELICATENESS
of her foot upon the ground for *d* .... Deut 28:56

DELICATES
hath filled his belly with my *d* .... Jer 51:34

DELICIOUSLY
glorified herself, and lived *d*................. Rev 18:7
lived *d* with her, shall bewail .... Rev 18:9

DELIGHT
because he had *d* in Jacob's.................. Gen 34:19
If the LORD *d* in us, then he will .... Num 14:8
Only the LORD had a *d* in thy .... Deut 10:15
be, if thou have no *d* in her .... Deut 21:14
as great *d* in burnt offerings 1Sa 15:22
Behold, the king hath *d* in thee............. 1Sa 18:22
he thus say, I have no *d* in thee............. 2Sa 15:26
my lord the king *d* in this thing............. 2Sa 24:3
To whom would the king *d* to do .... Est 6:6
thou have thy *d* in the Almighty............ Job 22:26
Will he *d* himself in the Almighty .... Job 27:10
that he should *d* himself with God........ Job 34:9
But his *d* is in the law of the .... Ps 1:2
excellent, in whom is all my *d* .... Ps 16:3
D thyself also in the LORD .... Ps 37:4
shall *d* themselves in the .... Ps 37:11
I *d* to do thy will, O my God .... Ps 40:8
but in *d* in lies .... Ps 62:4
thou the people that *d* in war................ Ps 68:30
for in whom they *d* .... Ps 68:30
within my comforts *d* my soul .... Ps 94:19
I will *d* myself in thy statutes................ Ps 119:16
Thy testimonies also are my *d* .... Ps 119:24
for therein do I *d* .... Ps 119:35
And I will *d* myself in thy....................... Ps 119:47
but I *d* in thy law .... Ps 119:70
for thy law is my *d* .... Ps 119:77
and thy law is my *d* .... Ps 119:174
the scorners *d* in their scorning........... Prov 1:22
d in the frowardness of the .... Prov 2:14
and I was daily his *d*, rejoicing .... Prov 8:30
but a just weight is his *d* .... Prov 11:1
upright in their way are his *d*................ Prov 11:20
they that deal truly are his *d*................. Prov 12:22
prayer of the upright is his *d* .... Prov 15:8
Righteous lips are the *d* of kings .... Prov 16:13
A fool hath no *d* in understanding .... Prov 18:2
D is not seemly for a fool....................... Prov 19:10
them that rebuke him shall be *d* .... Prov 24:25
he shall give *d* unto thy soul................. Prov 29:17
under his shadow with great *d* .... Song 2:3
I *d* not in the blood of bullocks............. Is 1:11
for gold, they shall not *d* in it................ Is 13:17
let your soul *d* itself in fatness .... Is 55:2
to know my ways, as a nation .... Is 58:2
they take *d* in approaching to God .... Is 58:2
and call the sabbath a *d*, the holy........ Is 58:13
Then shalt thou *d* thyself in the............ Is 58:14
they have no *d* in it .... Jer 6:10
for in these things I *d*, saith .... Jer 9:24
of the covenant, whom ye *d* in.............. Mal 3:1
For I *d* in the law of God after............... Rom 7:22

DELIGHTED
Saul's son *d* much in David 1Sa 19:2
delivered me, because he *d* in me 2Sa 22:20
which *d* in thee, to set thee on 1Kin 10:9
which *d* in thee to set thee on 2Chr 9:8
d themselves in thy great...................... Neh 9:25
no more, except the king *d* in her......... Est 2:14
delivered me, because he *d* in me .... Ps 18:19
when seeing me *d* in him .... Ps 22:8
as he *d* not in blessing, so let .... Ps 109:17
did choose that wherein I *d* not............ Is 65:12
and chose that in which I *d* not............. Is 66:4
be *d* with the abundance of her .... Is 66:11

DELIGHTEST
thou *d* not in burnt offering .... Ps 51:16

DELIGHTETH
the man whom the king *d* to honour ... Est 6:6
the man whom the king *d* to honour ... Est 6:7
withal whom the king *d* to honour .... Est 6:7
the man whom the king *d* to honour ... Est 6:9
the man whom the king *d* to honour ... Est 6:11
and he *d* in his way................................ Ps 37:23
the LORD, that greatly in his................... Ps 112:1
He *d* not in the strength of the .... Ps 147:10
as a father the son in whom he *d*......... Prov 3:12
mine elect, in whom my soul *d* .... Is 42:1
for the LORD *d* in thee, and thy .... Is 62:4
ways, and their soul *d* in their.............. Is 66:3
for ever, because he *d* in mercy .... Mic 7:18
of the LORD, and he *d* in them .... Mal 2:17

DELIGHTS
you in scarlet, with other *d*.................... 2Sa 1:24
Unless thy law had been my *d* .... Ps 119:92
yet thy commandments are my *d* .... Ps 119:143
my *d* were with the sons of men .... Prov 8:31
the *d* of the sons of men, as................. Eccl 2:8
pleasant art thou, O love, for *d* .... Song 7:6

DELIGHTSOME
for ye shall be a *d* land, saith................ Mal 3:12

DELILAH (de-li'-lah) *Woman who betrayed*
Samson.
valley of Sorek, whose name was *D*..... Judg 16:4
D said to Samson, Tell me, I pray......... Judg 16:6
D said unto Samson, Behold, thou....... Judg 16:10
D therefore took new ropes, and.......... Judg 16:12
D said unto Samson, Hitherto thou ..... Judg 16:13
when *D* saw that he had told her .... Judg 16:18

DELIVER
D me, I pray thee, from the hand .... Gen 32:11
to *d* him to his father again .... Gen 37:22
thou shalt of Pharaoh's cup into............ Gen 40:13
so will I *d* you your brother, and.......... Gen 42:34
d him into my hand, and I will............. Gen 42:37
I am come down to *d* them out of .... Ex 3:8
yet shall ye *d* the tale of bricks .... Ex 5:18
but God *d* him into his hand .... Ex 21:13
If a man shall *d* unto his....................... Ex 22:7
If a man *d* unto his neighbour an .... Ex 22:10
thou shalt *d* it unto him by that........... Ex 22:26
for I will *d* the inhabitants of............... Ex 23:31
they shall *d* you your bread again .... Lev 26:26
If thou wilt indeed *d* this people .... Num 21:2
the congregation shall of the.................. Num 35:25
to *d* us into the hand of the .... Deut 1:27
that he might *d* him into thy hand........ Deut 2:30
for I will *d* him, and all his .... Deut 7:2
thy God shall *d* them before thee .... Deut 7:23
the LORD thy God shall *d* them .... Deut 7:24
thy God shall *d* them unto thee............ Deut 7:23
he shall *d* their kings into thine .... Deut 7:24
d him into the hand of the .... Deut 19:12
to *d* thee, and to give up thine .... Deut 23:14
Thou shalt not *d* unto his master .... Deut 23:15
In any case thou shalt *d* him the.......... Deut 24:13
d her husband out of the hand of........ Deut 25:11
any that can *d* out of my hand............. Deut 32:39
have, and *d* our lives from death......... Josh 2:13
to *d* us into the hand of the .... Josh 7:7
your God will *d* it into your hand .... Josh 8:7
morrow about this time I will *d*............ Josh 11:6
then they shall not *d* the slayer .... Josh 20:5
I will *d* him into thine hand................... Judg 4:7
the Midianites into thine hand .... Judg 7:7
Israel, Did not I *d* you from the .... Judg 10:11
wherefore I will *d* you no more .... Judg 10:13
let them *d* you in the time of .... Judg 10:14
d us only, we pray thee, this day......... Judg 10:15
the LORD *d* them before me, shall...... Judg 11:9
If thou shalt without fail *d* the .... Judg 11:30
he shall begin to *d* Israel out of.......... Judg 13:5
that we may *d* thee into the hand........ Judg 15:12
fast, and *d* thee into their hand .... Judg 15:13
Now therefore *d* us the men................. Judg 20:28
I will *d* them into thine hand............... Judg 20:28
who shall *d* us out of the hand of 1Sa 4:8
he will *d* you out of the hand of 1Sa 7:3
Israel *d* out of the hands of the 1Sa 7:14
but now *d* us out of the hand of.......... 1Sa 12:10
things, which cannot profit nor *d*......... 1Sa 12:21
wilt thou *d* them into the hand of 1Sa 14:37
he will *d* me out of the hand of........... 1Sa 17:37
the LORD *d* them into thine hand........ 1Sa 17:46
for I will *d* the Philistines into............. 1Sa 23:4
of Keilah *d* me up into his hand 1Sa 23:11
Will the men of Keilah *d* me 1Sa 23:12
Lord said, They will *d* thee up.............. 1Sa 23:12
our part shall be to *d* him into 1Sa 23:20
I will *d* thine enemy into thine 1Sa 24:4
cause, and *d* me out of thine hand 1Sa 24:15
Lord, and let him out of all 2Sa 14:16
Moreover the LORD will also *d*............ 2Sa 18:19
the LORD also shall of thee 2Sa 18:19
nor *d* me into the hands of my 2Sa 20:15
D me my wife Michal, which I 2Sa 3:14
wilt thou *d* them into mine hand 2Sa 5:19
for I will doubtless *d* the 2Sa 5:19
D him that smote his brother............... 2Sa 14:7
to *d* his handmaid out of the hand...... 2Sa 14:16
d him only, and I will depart from....... 2Sa 20:21
d them to the enemy, so that they 1Kin 8:46
that thou wouldest *d* thy servant........ 1Kin 18:9

Thou shalt d me thy silver, and ... 1Kin 20:5
I will d it into thine hand this ... 1Kin 20:13
therefore will I d all this great ... 1Kin 20:28
for the Lord shall d it into the ... 1Kin 22:6
for the Lord shall d it into the ... 1Kin 22:12
for the Lord shall d it into the ... 1Kin 22:15
to d them into the hand of Moab ... 2Kin 3:10
to d them into the hand of Moab ... 2Kin 3:13
he will d the Moabites also into... 2Kin 3:18
but d it for the breaches of the ... 2Kin 12:7
he shall d you out of the hand of ... 2Kin 17:39
I will d thee two thousand horses... 2Kin 18:23
be able to d you out of his hand... 2Kin 18:29
saying, The Lord will surely d us... 2Kin 18:30
you, saying, The Lord will d us... 2Kin 18:32
that the Lord should d Jerusalem... 2Kin 18:35
and I will d thee and this city out... 2Kin 20:6
d them into the hand of their... 2Kin 21:14
let them d it into the hand of... 2Kin 22:5
wilt thou d them into mine hand ... 1Chr 14:10
for I will d them into thine hand ... 1Chr 14:10
d us from the heathen, that we ... 1Chr 16:35
d them over before their enemies... 2Chr 6:36
for God will d it into the king's... 2Chr 18:5
for the Lord shall d it into the ... 2Chr 18:11
which could not d their own... 2Chr 25:15
that he might d them into the ... 2Chr 25:20
d the captives again, which ye... 2Chr 28:11
The Lord our God shall d us out ... 2Chr 32:11
to d their lands out of mine hand... 2Chr 32:13
that could d his people out of ... 2Chr 32:14
be able to d you out of mine hand... 2Chr 32:14
to d his people out of mine hand ... 2Chr 32:15
your God d you out of mine hand ... 2Chr 32:15
d his people out of mine hand ... 2Chr 32:17
those d thou before the God of ... Ezr 7:19
many times didst thou d them ... Neh 9:28
neither is there any to d them ... Job 5:4
He shall d thee in six troubles ... Job 5:19
D me from the enemy's hand ... Job 6:23
none that can d out of thine hand ... Job 10:7
He shall d the island of the ... Job 22:30
D him from going down to the pit... Job 33:24
He will d his soul from going... Job 33:28
then a great ransom cannot d thee... Job 36:18
Return, O Lord, d my soul... Ps 6:4
them that persecute me, and d me... Ps 7:1
pieces, while there is none to d ... Ps 7:2
d my soul from the wicked, which ... Ps 17:13
trusted, and thou didst d them... Ps 22:4
on the Lord that he would d him... Ps 22:8
let him d him, seeing he... Ps 22:8
D my soul from the sword... Ps 22:20
O keep my soul, and d me... Ps 25:20
D me not over unto the will of ... Ps 27:12
d me in thy righteousness... Ps 31:1
d me speedily... Ps 31:2
d me from the hand of mine... Ps 31:15
neither shall he d any by his... Ps 33:17
To d their soul from death, and to ... Ps 33:19
Lord shall help them, and d them... Ps 37:40
he shall d them from the wicked, ... Ps 37:40
D me from all my transgressions... Ps 39:8
Be pleased, O Lord, to d me... Ps 40:13
the Lord will d him in time of ... Ps 41:1
thou wilt not d him unto the will... Ps 41:2
O d me from the deceitful and ... Ps 43:1
I will d thee, and thou shalt... Ps 50:15
in pieces, and there be none to d ... Ps 50:22
D me from bloodguiltiness, O God,... Ps 51:14
wilt not thou d my feet from... Ps 56:13
D me from mine enemies, O my God ... Ps 59:1
D me from the workers of iniquity ... Ps 59:2
D me out of the mire, and let me ... Ps 69:14
d me because of mine enemies... Ps 69:18
Make haste, O God, to d me... Ps 70:1
D me in thy righteousness, and... Ps 71:2
D me, O my God, out of the hand ... Ps 71:4
for there is none to d him... Ps 71:11
For he shall d the needy when he ... Ps 72:12
O d not the soul of thy... Ps 74:19
d us, and purge away our sins, for ... Ps 79:9
D the poor and needy... Ps 82:4
shall he d his soul from the hand ... Ps 89:48
Surely he shall d thee from the ... Ps 91:3
upon me, therefore will I d him ... Ps 91:14
I will d him, and honour him... Ps 91:15
Many times did he d them... Ps 106:43
the mercy is good, d thou me... Ps 109:21
O Lord, I beseech thee, d my soul ... Ps 116:4
D me from the oppression of man... Ps 119:134
Consider mine affliction, and d me... Ps 119:153
Plead my cause, and d me... Ps 119:154
d me according to thy word... Ps 119:170
D my soul, O Lord, from lying... Ps 120:2
D me, O Lord, from the evil man... Ps 140:1
D me from my persecutors... Ps 142:6
D me, O Lord, from mine enemies... Ps 143:9
d me out of great waters, from ... Ps 144:7
d me from the hand of strange... Ps 144:11
To d thee from the way of the ... Prov 2:12
To d thee from the strange woman,... Prov 2:16
of glory shall she d to thee ... Prov 4:9
d thyself, when thou art come... Prov 6:3
D thyself as a roe from the hand... Prov 6:5
of the upright shall d them... Prov 11:6
mouth of the upright shall d them... Prov 12:6
for if thou d him, yet thou must... Prov 19:19
shalt d his soul from hell... Prov 23:14
If thou forbear to d them that ... Prov 24:11

neither shall wickedness d those... Eccl 8:8
it away safe, and none shall d it ... Is 5:29
a great one, and he shall d them ... Is 19:20
which men d to one that is... Is 29:11
defending also he will d it... Is 31:5
for he shall not be able to d you ... Is 36:14
saying, The Lord will surely d us ... Is 36:15
you, saying, The Lord will d us... Is 36:18
that the Lord should d Jerusalem... Is 36:20
And I will d thee and this city out... Is 38:6
is none that can d out of my hand... Is 43:13
prayeth unto it, and saith, D me... Is 44:17
aside, that he cannot d his soul... Is 44:20
they could not d the burden... Is 46:2
even I will carry, and will d you... Is 46:4
they shall not d themselves from... Is 47:14
or have I no power to d... Is 50:2
criest, let thy companies d thee... Is 57:13
for I am with thee to d thee... Jer 1:8
thee, saith the Lord, to d thee... Jer 1:19
I d to the sword before their... Jer 15:9
to d thee, saith the Lord... Jer 15:20
I will d thee out of the hand of... Jer 15:21
Therefore d up their children to ... Jer 18:21
Moreover I will d all the... Jer 20:5
I will d Zedekiah king of Judah,... Jer 21:7
d him that is spoiled out of the ... Jer 21:12
d the spoiled out of the hand of ... Jer 22:3
I will d them to be removed into... Jer 24:9
will d them to be removed to all ... Jer 29:18
I will d them into the hand of ... Jer 29:21
lest they d me into their hand,... Jer 38:19
said, They shall not d thee... Jer 38:20
But I will d thee in that day,... Jer 39:17
For I will surely d thee, and thou... Jer 39:18
you, and to d you from his hand... Jer 42:11
for to d us into the hand of the ... Jer 43:11
d such as are for death to death... Jer 43:11
I will d them into the hand of ... Jer 46:26
Babylon, and d every man his soul... Jer 51:6
d ye every man his soul from the... Jer 51:45
that doth d us out of their hand ... Lam 5:8
d them in the day of the wrath of ... Eze 7:19
d you into the hands of strangers... Eze 11:9
d my people out of your hand, ... Eze 13:21
for I will d my people out of... Eze 13:23
they should d but their own souls... Eze 14:14
they shall d neither sons nor... Eze 14:16
they shall d neither sons nor... Eze 14:18
they shall d neither son nor ... Eze 14:20
they shall but d their own souls... Eze 14:20
d thee into the hand of brutish... Eze 21:31
I will d thee into the hand of... Eze 23:28
therefore I will d thee to the... Eze 25:4
will d thee for a spoil to the... Eze 25:7
taketh warning shall d his soul... Eze 33:5
shall not d him in the day of his... Eze 33:12
for I will d my flock from their... Eze 34:10
will d them out of all places... Eze 34:12
that shall d you out of my hands... Dan 3:15
to d us from the burning fiery... Dan 3:17
he will d us out of thine hand, O... Dan 3:17
God that can d after this sort... Dan 3:29
set his heart on Daniel to d him... Dan 6:14
going down of the sun to d him... Dan 6:14
continually, he will d thee... Dan 6:16
able to d thee from the lions... Dan 6:20
any that could d out of his hand... Dan 8:4
could d the ram out of his hand... Dan 8:7
none shall d her out of mine hand... Hos 2:10
how shall I d thee, Israel... Hos 11:8
captivity, to d them up to Edom... Amos 1:6
shall the mighty d himself... Amos 2:14
swift of foot shall not d himself ... Amos 2:15
that rideth the horse d himself... Amos 2:15
therefore will I d up the city... Amos 6:8
his head, to d him from his grief... Jonah 4:6
thus shall he d us from the... Mic 5:6
teareth in pieces, and none can d ... Mic 5:8
shalt take hold, but shalt not d ... Mic 6:14
d them in the day of the Lord's... Zeph 1:18
D thyself, O Zion, that dwellest... Zec 2:7
I will d the men every one into ... Zec 11:6
of their hand I will not d them... Zec 11:6
the adversary d thee to the judge... Mt 5:25
the judge d thee to the officer,... Mt 5:25
temptation, but d us from evil... Mt 6:13
for they will d you up to the... Mt 10:17
But when they d you up, take no... Mt 10:19
the brother shall d up the... Mt 10:21
shall d him to the Gentiles to... Mt 20:19
Then shall they d you up to be... Mt 24:9
give me, and I will d him unto you... Mt 26:15
let him d him now, if he will... Mt 27:43
shall d him to the Gentiles... Mk 10:33
for they shall d you up to... Mk 13:9
d you up, take no thought... Mk 13:11
but d us from evil... Lk 11:4
the judge d thee to the officer,... Lk 12:58
shall d thee into the power... Lk 20:20
that God by his hand would d them ... Acts 7:25
and am come down to d them... Acts 7:34
shall d him into the hands of the... Acts 21:11
no man may d me unto them... Acts 25:11
of the Romans to d any man to die ... Acts 25:16
who shall d me from the body of ... Rom 7:24
To d such a one unto Satan for... 1Cor 5:5
from so great a death, and doth d ... 2Cor 1:10
we trust that he will yet d us... 2Cor 1:10
that he might d us from this... Gal 1:4

the Lord shall d me from every ... 2Ti 4:18
d them who through fear of death... Heb 2:15
The Lord knoweth how to d ... 2Pet 2:9

DELIVERANCE

to save your lives by a great d... Gen 45:7
Thou hast given this great d into... Judg 15:18
the Lord had given d unto Syria... 2Kin 5:1
said, The arrow of the Lord's d... 2Kin 13:17
and the arrow of d from Syria... 2Kin 13:17
the Lord saved them by a great d... 1Chr 11:14
but I will grant them some d... 2Chr 12:7
and hast given us such d as this... Ezr 9:13
d arise to the Jews from another ... Est 4:14
Great d giveth he to his king... Ps 18:50
compass me about with songs of d ... Ps 32:7
not wrought any d in the earth... Is 26:18
Zion and in Jerusalem shall be d... Joel 2:32
But upon mount Zion shall be d... Obad 17
to preach d to the captives, and... Lk 4:18
were tortured, not accepting d... Heb 11:35

DELIVERANCES

command d for Jacob... Ps 44:4

DELIVERED

into your hand are they d... Gen 9:2
which hath d thine enemies into ... Gen 14:20
her days to be d were fulfilled... Gen 25:24
he d them into the hand of his... Gen 32:16
he d him out of their hands... Gen 37:21
are d ere the midwives come in... Ex 1:19
An Egyptian d us out of the hand ... Ex 2:19
hast thou d thy people at all... Ex 5:23
the Egyptians, and d our houses... Ex 12:27
d me from the sword of Pharaoh... Ex 18:4
the way, and how the Lord d them... Ex 18:8
whom he had d out of the hand of ... Ex 18:9
who hath d you out of the hand of... Ex 18:10
who hath d the people from under... Ex 18:10
in that which was d him to keep... Lev 6:2
or that which was d him to keep ... Lev 6:4
ye shall be d into the hand of ... Lev 26:25
of Israel, and d up the Canaanites... Num 21:3
for I have d him into thy hand... Num 21:34
So there were d out of the... Num 31:5
the Lord our God d him before us... Deut 2:33
the Lord our God d all unto us... Deut 2:36
So the Lord our God d into our... Deut 3:3
of stone, and d them unto me... Deut 5:22
the Lord d unto me two tables of ... Deut 9:10
God hath d it into thine hands... Deut 20:13
God hath d them into thine hands ... Deut 21:10
d it unto the priests the sons of ... Deut 31:9
Truly the Lord hath d into our... Josh 2:24
d them out of the hand of the... Josh 9:26
for I have d them into thine hand... Josh 10:8
Lord d up the Amorites before the ... Josh 10:12
God hath d them into your hand... Josh 10:19
And the Lord d it also, and the ... Josh 10:30
the Lord d Lachish into the hand... Josh 10:32
the Lord d them into the hand of ... Josh 11:8
the Lord d all their enemies into ... Josh 21:44
now ye have d the children of ... Josh 22:31
so I d you out of their hand... Josh 24:10
and I d them into your hand... Josh 24:11
I have d the land into his hand... Judg 1:2
the Lord d the Canaanites and the ... Judg 1:4
he d them into the hands of... Judg 2:14
which d them out of the hand of ... Judg 2:16
d them out of the hand of their... Judg 2:18
neither d he them into the hand... Judg 2:23
who d them, even Othniel the son ... Judg 3:9
the Lord d Chushan-rishathaim,... Judg 3:10
for the Lord hath d your enemies... Judg 3:28
and he also d Israel... Judg 3:31
hath d Sisera into thine hand... Judg 4:14
They that are d from the noise of ... Judg 5:11
the Lord d them into the hand of ... Judg 6:1
I d you out of the hand of the... Judg 6:9
d us into the hands of Midian... Judg 6:13
for I have d it into thine hand ... Judg 7:9
into his hand God d Midian... Judg 7:14
For the Lord hath d into your... Judg 7:15
God hath d into your hands the... Judg 8:3
when the Lord hath d Zebah... Judg 8:7
for thou hast d us from the hand... Judg 8:22
who had d them out of the hands... Judg 8:34
d you out of the hand of Midian... Judg 9:17
I d you out of the Egyptians... Judg 10:11
And the Lord God of Israel d Sihon... Judg 11:21
the Lord d them into his hands... Judg 11:32
ye d me not out of their hands... Judg 12:2
And when I saw that ye d me not... Judg 12:3
the Lord d them into my hand... Judg 13:1
the Lord d them into the hand of ... Judg 13:1
Our god hath d Samson our enemy... Judg 16:23
Our god hath d into our hands our... Judg 16:24
was with child, near to be d... 1Sa 4:19
d you out of the hand of the... 1Sa 10:18
d you out of the hand of your ... 1Sa 12:11
for the Lord hath d them into our ... 1Sa 14:10
for the Lord hath d them into the ... 1Sa 14:12
of Israel out of the hands of them... 1Sa 14:48
him, and d it out of his mouth... 1Sa 17:35
The Lord that d me out of the paw ... 1Sa 17:37
God hath d him into mine hand... 1Sa 23:7
but God d him not into his hand... 1Sa 23:14
d thee to day into mine hand in ... 1Sa 24:10
the Lord had d thee into mine ... 1Sa 24:18
God hath d thine enemy into thine... 1Sa 26:8
for the Lord d thee into my hand... 1Sa 26:23

d the company that came against ... 1Sa 30:23
have not d thee into the hand of 2Sa 3:8
the rest of the people he d into 2Sa 10:10
I d thee out of the hand of Saul 2Sa 12:7
the LORD hath d the kingdom into 2Sa 16:8
which hath d up the men that 2Sa 18:28
he d us out of the hand of the 2Sa 19:9
men of his sons be d unto us 2Sa 21:6
he d them into the hands of the 2Sa 21:9
in the day that the LORD had d 2Sa 22:1
He d me from my strong enemy, and... 2Sa 22:18
he d me, because he delighted in 2Sa 22:20
Thou also hast d me from the 2Sa 22:44
thou hast d me from the violent 2Sa 22:49
I was d of a child with her in 1Kin 3:17
the third day after that I was d 1Kin 3:18
that this woman was d also 1Kin 3:18
the LORD hath d into mine hand the lion ... 1Kin 13:26
d them into the hand of his 1Kin 15:18
house, and d him unto his mother ... 1Kin 17:23
into whose hand they d the money .. 2Kin 12:15
he d them into the hand of Hazael ... 2Kin 13:3
d them into the hand of spoilers, ... 2Kin 17:20
this city shall not be d into the 2Kin 18:30
any of the gods of the nations d ... 2Kin 18:33
have they d Samaria out of mine ... 2Kin 18:34
that have d their country out of ... 2Kin 18:35
Jerusalem shall not be d into the ... 2Kin 19:10
and shalt thou be d 2Kin 19:11
d them which my fathers have 2Kin 19:12
money that was d into their hand ... 2Kin 22:7
have d it into the hand of them ... 2Kin 22:9
d them out of the hand of those ... 2Kin 22:10
Hagarites were d into their hand 1Chr 5:20
d it, and slew the Philistines 1Chr 11:14
Then on that day David d first 1Chr 16:7
the rest of the people he d unto 1Chr 16:43
God d them into their hand 1Chr 13:16
he d them into their hand 2Chr 16:8
they shall be d into your hand 2Chr 18:14
d to the captains of hundreds 2Chr 23:9
the LORD d a very great host into ... 2Chr 24:24
Wherefore the LORD his God d him ... 2Chr 28:5
he was also d into the hand of 2Chr 28:5
he hath d them into your hand, and .. 2Chr 28:9
he hath d them to trouble, to 2Chr 29:8
d their people out of mine hand 2Chr 32:17
they d the money that was brought... 2Chr 34:9
Hilkiah of the book to Shaphan 2Chr 34:15
have d it into the hand of the 2Chr 34:17
Babylon, and they were d unto one .... Ezr 5:14
he d us from the hand of the .... Ezr 8:31
they d the king's commissions............. Ezr 8:36
been d into the hand of the kings ..... Ezr 9:7
horse be d to the hand of one of .... Est 6:9
God hath d me to the ungodly, and.. Job 16:11
it is d by the pureness of thine...... Job 22:30
so should I be d for ever from my...... Job 23:7
Because I d the poor that cried,........ Job 29:12
I have d him that without cause ...... Ps 7:4
d him from the hand of all his......... Ps 18:1
He d me from my strong enemy, and... Ps 18:17
he d me, because he delighted in ...... Ps 18:19
Thou hast d me from the strivings... Ps 18:43
thou hast d me from the violent........ Ps 18:48
They cried unto thee, and were d....... Ps 22:5
man is not d by much strength......... Ps 33:16
me, and d me from all my fears......... Ps 34:4
For he hath d me out of all............. Ps 54:7
He hath d my soul in peace from...... Ps 55:18
For thou hast d my soul from.......... Ps 56:13
That thy beloved may be d............. Ps 60:5
let me be d from them that hate....... Ps 69:14
day when he d them from the enemy... Ps 78:42
d his strength into captivity, and...... Ps 78:61
his hands were d from the pots........ Ps 81:6
calledst in trouble, and I d thee...... Ps 81:7
thou hast d my soul from the........... Ps 86:13
he d them out of their distresses...... Ps 107:6
d them from their destructions......... Ps 107:20
That thy beloved may be d............. Ps 108:6
For thou hast d my soul from.......... Ps 116:8
The righteous is d out of trouble...... Prov 11:8
knowledge shall the just be d.......... Prov 11:9
seed of the righteous shall be d...... Prov 11:21
walketh wisely, he shall be d......... Prov 28:26
and he by his wisdom d the city...... Eccl 9:15
to be d from the king of Assyria...... Is 20:6
the book is d to him that is not...... Is 29:12
he hath d them to the slaughter........ Is 34:2
this city shall not be d into the...... Is 36:15
any of the gods of the nations d..... Is 36:18
have they d Samaria out of my....... Is 36:19
that have d their land out of my...... Is 36:20
and shalt thou be d....................... Is 37:11
d them which my fathers have......... Is 37:12
hast in love to my soul d it........... Is 38:17
mighty, or the lawful captive d...... Is 49:24
prey of the terrible shall be d........ Is 49:25
came, she was d of a man child....... Is 66:7
and say, We are d to do all these.... Jer 7:10
for he hath d the soul of the.......... Jer 20:13
but shall surely be d into the......... Jer 32:4
Now when I had d the evidence of.... Jer 32:16
It shall be d into the hand of......... Jer 32:36
be taken, and d into his hand......... Jer 34:3
thou shalt be d into the hand of...... Jer 37:17
she shall be d into the hand of........ Jer 46:24
the Lord hath d me into their......... Lam 1:14
but thou hast d thy soul................. Eze 3:19

also thou hast d thy soul................. Eze 3:21
they only shall be d, but the......... Eze 14:16
they only shall be d themselves...... Eze 14:18
d them to cause them to pass........ Eze 16:21
d thee unto the will of them that...... Eze 16:27
he break the covenant, and be d...... Eze 17:15
Wherefore I have d her into the...... Eze 23:9
I have therefore d him into the...... Eze 31:11
for they are all d unto death......... Eze 31:14
she is d to the sword.................... Eze 32:20
but thou hast d thy soul............... Eze 33:9
d them out of the hand of those...... Eze 34:27
of his servants that trusted in...... Dan 3:28
who hath d Daniel from the power... Dan 6:27
that time thy people shall be d...... Dan 12:1
the name of the LORD shall be d..... Joel 2:32
because they d up the whole......... Amos 1:9
escapeth of them shall not be d...... Amos 9:1
neither shouldest thou have d up...... Obad 14
there shalt thou be d.................... Mic 4:10
that he may be d from the power..... Hab 2:9
they that tempt God are even d....... Mal 3:15
All things are d unto me of my...... Mt 11:27
d him to the tormentors, till he...... Mt 18:34
and d unto them his goods............. Mt 25:14
d him to Pontius Pilate the.......... Mt 27:2
knew that for envy they had d him... Mt 27:18
Jesus, he d him to be crucified...... Mt 27:26
Pilate commanded the body to be d... Mt 27:58
your tradition, which ye have d...... Mk 7:13
The Son of man is d into the........ Mk 9:31
shall be d unto the chief priests.... Mk 10:33
him away, and d him to Pilate....... Mk 15:1
chief priests had d him for envy...... Mk 15:10
d Jesus, when he had scourged him... Mk 15:15
Even as they d them unto us.......... Lk 1:2
time came that she should be d...... Lk 1:57
being d out of the hand of our....... Lk 1:74
accomplished that she should be d.... Lk 2:6
for that is d unto me..................... Lk 4:6
there was d unto him the book of... Lk 4:17
And he d him to his mother........... Lk 7:15
d him again to his father.............. Lk 9:42
shall be d into the hands of men...... Lk 9:44
All things are d to me of my......... Lk 10:22
that thou mayest be d from him...... Lk 12:58
For he shall be d unto the............ Lk 18:32
d them ten pounds, and said unto... Lk 19:13
but he d Jesus to their will........... Lk 23:25
The Son of man must be d into the... Lk 24:7
Our Sisters of him to be condemned... Lk 24:20
as soon as she is d of the child...... Jn 16:21
would not have d him up unto thee... Jn 18:30
chief priests have d thee unto me.... Jn 18:35
I should not be d to the Jews......... Jn 18:36
therefore he that d me unto thee..... Jn 19:11
Then d he him therefore unto them... Jn 19:16
being d by the determinate.......... Acts 2:23
whom ye d up, and denied him in.... Acts 3:13
the customs which Moses d us........ Acts 6:14
d him out of all his afflictions,...... Acts 7:10
d him to four quaternions of......... Acts 12:4
hath d me out of the hand of........ Acts 12:11
together, they d the epistle........... Acts 15:30
they d them the decrees to.......... Acts 16:4
d the epistle to the governor,....... Acts 23:33
sail into Italy, they d Paul.......... Acts 27:1
the centurion of the prisoners to.... Acts 28:16
yet was I d prisoner from........... Acts 28:17
Who was d for our offences, and..... Rom 4:25
form of doctrine which was d you... Rom 6:17
But now we are d from the law...... Rom 7:6
creature itself also shall be d......... Rom 8:21
but d him up for us all, how.......... Rom 8:32
That I may be d from them that do.. Rom 15:31
ordinances, as I d them to you...... 1Cor 11:2
Lord that which also I d unto you... 1Cor 11:23
For I d unto you first of all......... 1Cor 15:3
when he shall have d up the......... 1Cor 15:24
Who d us from so great a death,..... 2Cor 1:10
d unto death for Jesus' sake......... 2Cor 4:11
Who hath d us from the power of.... Col 1:13
which d us from the wrath to come... 1Th 1:10
And that we may be d from........... 2Th 3:2
whom I have d unto Satan, that...... 1Ti 1:20
but out of them all the Lord d me.... 2Ti 3:11
I was d out of the mouth of the...... 2Ti 4:17
was d of a child when she was...... Heb 11:11
d them into chains of darkness,..... 2Pet 2:4
d just Lot, vexed with the filthy..... 2Pet 2:7
the holy commandment d unto them ... 2Pet 2:21
which was once d unto the saints.... Jude 3
in birth, and pained to be d.......... Rev 12:2
the woman which was ready to be d.. Rev 12:4
hell d up the dead which were in..... Rev 20:13

DELIVEREDST

Therefore thou d them into the...... Neh 9:27
thou d unto me five talents.......... Mt 25:20
thou d unto me two talents.......... Mt 25:22

DELIVERER

the LORD raised up a d to the........ Judg 3:9
LORD, the LORD raised them up a d ... Judg 3:15
And there was no d, because it was.. Judg 18:28
my rock, and my fortress, and my d... 2Sa 22:2
my rock, and my fortress, and my d.. Ps 18:2
thou art my help and my d........... Ps 40:17
thou art my help and my d........... Ps 70:5
my high tower, and my d............. Ps 144:2
a d by the hand of the angel........ Acts 7:35

shall come out of Sion the D......... Rom 11:26

DELIVEREST

which d the poor from him that is ..... Ps 35:10
that which thou d will I give up ...... Mic 6:14

DELIVERETH

He d the poor in his affliction,........ Job 36:15
He d me from mine enemies............ Ps 18:48
them that fear him, and d them....... Ps 34:7
d them out of all their troubles....... Ps 34:17
but the LORD d him out of them....... Ps 34:19
he d them out of the hand of the..... Ps 97:10
who d David his servant from the..... Ps 144:10
but righteousness d from death...... Prov 10:2
but righteousness d from death...... Prov 11:4
A true witness d souls.................. Prov 14:25
d girdles unto the merchant.......... Prov 31:24
they are for a prey, and none d....... Is 42:22
He d and rescueth, and he worketh... Dan 6:27

DELIVERING

d you up to the synagogues, and..... Lk 21:12
d into prisons both men and women... Acts 22:4
D thee from the people, and from.... Acts 26:17

DELIVERY

draweth near the time of her d....... Is 26:17

DELUSION

God shall send them strong d........ 2Th 2:11

DELUSIONS

I also will choose their d.............. Is 66:4

DEMAND

for I will d of thee, and answer....... Job 38:3
I will d of thee, and declare thou..... Job 40:7
I will d of thee, and declare thou..... Job 42:4
the d by the word of the holy........ Dan 4:17

DEMANDED

set over them, were beaten, and d.... Ex 5:14
David d of him how Joab did, and 2Sa 11:7
For D hath forsaken me, having ...... Dan 2:27
he d of them where Christ should..... Mt 2:4
And the soldiers likewise d of him... Lk 3:14
when he was d of the Pharisees,...... Lk 17:20
d who he was, and what he........... Acts 21:33

DEMAS (de'-mas) *A companion of Paul.*
Luke, the beloved physician, and D ... Col 4:14
Marcus, Aristarchus, D, Lucas, my ... Philem 24

DEMETRIUS (de-me'-tre-us)
   1. An opponent of Paul.
For a certain man named D........... Acts 19:24
Wherefore if D, and the craftsmen... Acts 19:38
   2. Disciple commended by John.
D hath good report of all men, and... 3Jn 12

DEMONSTRATION

but in d of the Spirit and of........ 1Cor 2:4

DEN

wait secretly as a lion in his d...... Ps 10:9
put his hand on the cockatrice' d.... Is 11:8
become a d of robbers in your....... Jer 7:11
heaps, and a d of dragons............ Jer 9:11
Judah desolate, and a d of dragons... Jer 10:22
shall be cast into d of lions........... Dan 6:7
shall be cast into the d of lions...... Dan 6:12
and cast him into the d of lions...... Dan 6:16
and laid upon the mouth of the d.... Dan 6:17
went in haste unto the d of lions.... Dan 6:19
And when he came to the d, he...... Dan 6:20
take Daniel up out of the d.......... Dan 6:23
Daniel was taken up out of the d.... Dan 6:23
cast them into the d of lions........ Dan 6:24
they came at the bottom of the d.... Dan 6:24
a young lion cry out of his d........ Amos 3:4
ye have made it a d of thieves...... Mt 21:13
ye have made it a d of thieves...... Mk 11:17
ye have made it a d of thieves...... Lk 19:46

DENIED

Then Sarah d, saying, I laughed...... Gen 18:15
and I d him not.......................... 1Kin 20:7
for I should have d the God that..... Job 31:28
But he d before them all, saying,.... Mt 26:70
again he d it with an oath, I do not.. Mt 26:72
But he d, saying, I know not,........ Mk 14:68
And he d it again...................... Mk 14:70
When all d, Peter and they that..... Lk 8:45
be d before the angels of God....... Lk 12:9
he d him, saying, Woman, I know.... Lk 22:57
And he confessed, and d not......... Jn 1:20
crow, till thou hast d me thrice...... Jn 13:38
He d it, and said, I am not.......... Jn 18:25
Peter then d again...................... Jn 18:27
d him in the presence of Pilate,..... Acts 3:13
But ye d the Holy One and the Just... Acts 3:14
he hath d the faith, and is worse.... 1Ti 5:8
my name, and hast not d my faith... Rev 2:13
my word, and hast not d my name... Rev 3:8

DENIETH

But he that d me before men shall ... Lk 12:9
that d that Jesus is the Christ........ 1Jn 2:22
that d the Father and the Son........ 1Jn 2:22
Whosoever d the Son, the same...... 1Jn 2:23

DENOUNCE
I d unto you this day, that ye............ Deut 30:18

DENS
of Israel made them the d which............ Judg 6:2
Then the beasts go into d............ Job 37:8
When they couch in their d............ Job 38:40
and lay them down in their d............ Ps 104:22
and Hermon, from the lions' d............ Song 4:8
and towers shall be for d for ever............ Is 32:14
with prey, and his d with ravin............ Nah 2:12
deserts, and in mountains, and in d .... Heb 11:38
free man, hid themselves in the d............ Rev 6:15

DENY
unto you, lest ye d your God............ Josh 24:27
one petition of thee, d me not............ 1Kin 2:16
his place, then it shall d him............ Job 8:18
d me them not before I die............ Prov 30:7
d thee, and say, Who is the LORD?...... Prov 30:9
whosoever shall d me before men...... Mt 10:33
him will I also d before my............ Mt 10:33
came after me, let him d himself............ Mt 16:24
cock crow, thou shalt d me thrice...... Mt 26:34
with thee, yet will I not d thee............ Mt 26:35
cock crow, thou shalt d me thrice...... Mt 26:75
come after me, let him d himself............ Mk 8:34
twice, thou shalt d me thrice............ Mk 14:30
I will not d thee in any wise............ Mk 14:31
twice, thou shalt d me thrice............ Mk 14:72
come after me, let him d himself......... Lk 9:23
which d that there is any............ Lk 20:27
thrice d that thou knowest me......... Lk 22:34
cock crow, thou shalt d me thrice ...... Lk 22:61
and we cannot d it............ Acts 4:16
if we d him, he also will d us............ 2Ti 2:12
if we d him, he also will d us............ 2Ti 2:12
he cannot d himself............ 2Ti 2:13
but in works they d him, being......... Titus 1:16

DENYING
but d the power thereof............ 2Ti 3:5
d ungodliness and worldly lusts,......... Titus 2:12
even d the Lord that bought them,...... 2Pet 2:1
d the only Lord God, and our Lord........ Jude 4

DEPART
or if thou d to the right hand,............ Gen 13:9
sceptre shall not d from Judah............ Gen 49:10
And the frogs shall d from thee............ Ex 8:11
of flies may d from Pharaoh............ Ex 8:29
And Moses let his father in law d ...... Ex 18:27
so that her fruit d from her............ Ex 21:22
And the LORD said unto Moses, D ...... Ex 33:1
And then shall he d from thee............ Lev 25:41
but I will d to mine own land, and..... Num 10:30
unto the congregation, saying, D....... Num 16:26
lest they d from thy heart all............ Deut 4:9
didst d out of the land of Egypt............ Deut 9:7
law shall not d out of thy mouth......... Josh 1:8
So Joshua let the people d............ Josh 24:28
D not hence, I pray thee, until I......... Judg 6:18
d early from mount Gilead............ Judg 7:3
the morning, that he rose up to d...... Judg 19:5
And when the man rose up to d......... Judg 19:7
the morning on the fifth day to d...... Judg 19:8
And when the man rose up to d......... Judg 19:9
Saul said unto the Kenites, Go, d...... 1Sa 15:6
d, and get thee into the land of......... 1Sa 22:5
in the morning, and have light, d...... 1Sa 29:10
rose up early to d in the morning...... 1Sa 29:11
they may lead them away, and d......... 1Sa 30:22
mercy shall not d away from him....... 2Sa 7:15
and to morrow I will let thee d............ 1Sa 11:12
shall never d from thine house............ 2Sa 12:10
make speed to d, lest he overtake..... 2Sa 15:14
only, and I will d from the city............ 2Sa 20:21
statutes, I did not d from them............ 2Sa 22:23
Hadad said to Pharaoh, Let me d..... 1Kin 11:21
D yet for three days, then come......... 1Kin 12:5
of the LORD, and returned to d............ 1Kin 12:24
of Israel, that he may d from me......... 1Kin 15:19
of Israel, that he may d from me......... 2Chr 16:3
and God moved them to d from him . 2Chr 18:31
they might not d from their............ 2Chr 35:15
How long wilt thou not d from me..... Job 7:19
He shall not d out of darkness............ Job 15:30
The increase of his house shall d....... Job 20:28
the say unto God, D from us............ Job 21:14
Which said unto God, D from us......... Job 22:17
to d from evil is understanding............ Job 28:28
D from me, all ye workers of............ Ps 6:8
D from evil, and do good............ Ps 34:14
D from evil, and do good............ Ps 37:27
guile d not from her streets............ Ps 55:11
A froward heart shall d from me......... Ps 101:4
D from me, ye evildoers............ Ps 119:115
d from me therefore, ye bloody............ Ps 139:19
fear the LORD, and d from evil............ Prov 3:7
let not them d from thine eyes............ Prov 4:21
Let them not d from thine eyes............ Prov 4:21
d not from the words of my mouth..... Prov 5:7
to d from the snares of death............ Prov 13:14
to fools to d from evil............ Prov 13:19
to d from the snares of death............ Prov 15:24
that he may d from hell beneath......... Prov 15:24
fear of the LORD men d from evil....... Prov 16:6
of the upright is to d from evil............ Prov 16:17
evil shall not d from his house............ Prov 17:13
he is old, he will not d from it............ Prov 22:6
not his foolishness d from him............ Prov 27:22
The envy also of Ephraim shall d....... Is 11:13

shall his yoke d from off them............ Is 14:25
his burden d from off their............ Is 14:25
D ye, d ye, go ye out from............ Is 52:11
ye, d ye, go ye out from thence,......... Is 52:11
For the mountains shall d............ Is 54:10
my kindness shall not d from thee..... Is 54:10
shall not d out of thy mouth, nor....... Is 59:21
lest my soul d from thee............ Jer 6:8
they that d from me shall be............ Jer 17:13
those ordinances d from before me.... Jer 31:36
that they shall not d from me............ Jer 32:40
Chaldeans shall surely d from us....... Jer 37:9
for they shall not d............ Jer 37:9
they shall remove, they shall d............ Jer 50:3
They cried unto them, D ye............ Lam 4:15
d, d, touch not............ Lam 4:15
d, d, touch not............ Lam 4:15
and my jealousy shall d from thee..... Eze 16:42
also to them when I d from them......... Hos 9:12
Arise ye, and d............ Mic 2:10
the sceptre of Egypt shall d away....... Zec 10:11
d from me, ye that work iniquity......... Mt 7:23
to d unto the other side............ Mt 8:18
he would d out of their coasts............ Mt 8:34
when ye d out of that house or......... Mt 10:14
said unto them, They need not d......... Mt 14:16
D from me, ye cursed, into............ Mt 25:41
pray him to d out of their coasts...... Mk 5:17
abide till ye d from that place............ Mk 6:10
nor hear you, when ye d thence......... Mk 6:11
thou thy servant d in peace............ Lk 2:29
that he should not d from them......... Lk 4:42
Jesus' knees, saying, D from me......... Lk 5:8
about beseught him to d from them.... Lk 8:37
into, there abide, and thence d............ Lk 9:4
thee, thou shalt not d thence............ Lk 12:59
d from me, all ye workers of............ Lk 13:27
him, Get thee out, and d hence......... Lk 13:31
are in the midst of it d out............ Lk 21:21
D hence, and go into Judaea, that..... Jn 7:3
d out of this world unto the............ Jn 13:1
but if I d, I will send him unto............ Jn 16:7
they should not d from Jerusalem..... Acts 1:4
now therefore d, and go in peace...... Acts 16:36
desired them to d out of the city........ Acts 16:39
commanded all Jews to d from Rome. Acts 18:2
them, ready to d on the morrow........ Acts 20:7
And he said unto me, D............ Acts 22:21
captain then let the young man d..... Acts 23:22
himself would d shortly thither............ Acts 25:4
part advised to d thence also............ Acts 27:12
not the wife d from her husband......... 1Cor 7:10
But and if she d, let her remain......... 1Cor 7:11
But if the unbelieving d, let him........ 1Cor 7:15
the unbelieving d, let him d............ 1Cor 7:15
thrice, that it might d from me............ 2Cor 12:8
betwixt two, having a desire to d....... Phil 1:23
times some shall d from the faith...... 1Ti 4:1
name of Christ d from iniquity............ 2Ti 2:19
D in peace, be ye warmed and............ Jas 2:16

DEPARTED
So Abram d, as the LORD had............ Gen 12:4
years old when he d out of Haran...... Gen 12:4
in Sodom, and his goods, and d......... Gen 14:12
and she d, and wandered in the......... Gen 21:14
of the camels of his master, and d..... Gen 24:10
Isaac d thence, and pitched his......... Gen 26:17
away, and they d from him in peace.. Gen 26:31
my sleep d from mine eyes............ Gen 31:40
and Laban d, and returned unto his.. Gen 31:55
And the man said, They are a hence . Gen 37:17
asses with the corn, and d thence..... Gen 42:26
sent his brethren away, and they d.... Gen 45:24
For they were d from Rephidim............ Ex 19:2
d not out of the tabernacle............ Ex 33:11
of the children of Israel d from............ Ex 35:20
if the plague be d from them............ Lev 13:58
they d from the mount of the LORD.. Num 10:33
kindled against them; and he d......... Num 12:9
And the cloud d from off the............ Num 12:10
their defence is d from them............ Num 14:9
and Moses, d not out of the camp..... Num 14:44
the elders of Midian d with the......... Num 22:7
they d from Rameses in the first...... Num 33:3
they d from Succoth, and pitched..... Num 33:6
they d from before Pi-hahiroth,......... Num 33:8
they d from Dophkah............ Num 33:13
they d from Rephidim, and pitched... Num 33:15
they d from Kibroth-hattaavah, and . Num 33:17
they d from Hazeroth, and pitched.... Num 33:18
they d from Rithmah, and pitched..... Num 33:19
they d from Rimmon-parez, and......... Num 33:20
they d from Tahath, and pitched at ... Num 33:27
they d from Hashmonah, and............ Num 33:30
they d from Moseroth, and pitched... Num 33:31
they d from Ebronah, and encamped Num 33:35
they d from mount Hor, and pitched Num 33:41
they d from Zalmonah, and pitched.. Num 33:42
they d from Punon, and pitched in... Num 33:43
they d from Oboth, and pitched in... Num 33:44
they d from Iim, and pitched in......... Num 33:45
they d from the mountains of............ Num 33:48
when we d from Horeb, we went....... Deut 1:19
when she is d out of his house,......... Deut 24:2
And she sent them away, and they d . Josh 2:21
d from the children of Israel out...... Josh 8:29
of the LORD d not from his sight....... Judg 6:21
they d every man unto his place........ Judg 9:55
not that the LORD was d from him..... Judg 16:20
the man d out of the city from......... Judg 17:8

Then the five men d, and came to...... Judg 18:7
So they turned and d, and put the..... Judg 18:21
that night, but he rose up and d....... Judg 19:10
of Israel d thence at that time............ Judg 21:24
The glory is d from Israel............ 1Sa 4:21
said, The glory is d from Israel............ 1Sa 4:22
not let the people go, and they d...... 1Sa 6:6
When thou art d from me to day,...... 1Sa 10:2
So the Kenites d from among the...... 1Sa 15:6
Spirit of the LORD d from Saul............ 1Sa 16:14
and the evil spirit d from him............ 1Sa 16:23
was with him, and was d from Saul... 1Sa 18:12
And he arose and d............ 1Sa 20:42
David therefore d thence, and............ 1Sa 22:1
Then David d, and came into the...... 1Sa 22:5
arose and d out of Keilah, and went. 1Sa 23:13
God is d from me, and answereth me. 1Sa 28:15
seeing the LORD is d from thee............ 1Sa 28:16
So all the people d every one to......... 2Sa 6:19
Uriah d out of the king's house,......... 2Sa 11:8
And Nathan d unto his house............ 2Sa 12:15
came to pass, after they were d......... 2Sa 17:21
from the day the king d until the...... 2Sa 19:24
have not wickedly d from my God..... 2Sa 22:22
And the people d............ 1Kin 12:5
So Israel d unto their tents............ 1Kin 12:16
And Jeroboam's wife arose, and d.... 1Kin 14:17
So he d thence, and found Elisha..... 1Kin 19:19
And the messengers d, and brought. 1Kin 20:9
as soon as thou art d from me............ 1Kin 20:36
And as soon as he was d from him.... 1Kin 20:36
So the prophet d, and waited for...... 1Kin 20:38
And Elijah d............ 2Kin 1:4
he d not therefrom............ 2Kin 3:3
they d from him, and returned to...... 2Kin 3:27
And he d, and took with him ten...... 2Kin 5:5
So he d from him a little way............ 2Kin 5:19
and he let the men go, and they d..... 2Kin 5:24
So he d from Elisha, and came to...... 2Kin 8:14
And he arose and d, and came to...... 2Kin 10:12
And when he was d thence, he............ 2Kin 10:15
Jehu d not from after them, to......... 2Kin 10:29
for he d not from the sins of............ 2Kin 10:31
he d not therefrom............ 2Kin 13:2
Nevertheless they d not from the...... 2Kin 13:6
he d not from all the sins of............ 2Kin 13:11
he d not from all the sins of............ 2Kin 14:24
he d not from the sins of............ 2Kin 15:9
he d not all his days from the............ 2Kin 15:18
he d not from the sins of............ 2Kin 15:24
he d not from the sins of............ 2Kin 15:28
they d not from them............ 2Kin 17:22
d not from following him, but............ 2Kin 18:6
heard that he was d from Lachish..... 2Kin 19:8
So Sennacherib king of Assyria d.... 2Kin 19:36
all the people d every man to his..... 1Chr 16:43
Wherefore Joab d, and went............ 1Chr 21:4
they d not from the commandment... 2Chr 8:15
And the people d............ 2Chr 10:5
d not from it, doing that which............ 2Chr 20:32
years, and d without being desired... 2Chr 21:20
And when they were d from him......... 2Chr 24:25
all his days they d not from............ 2Chr 34:33
Then we d from the river of Ahava... Ezr 8:31
the cloud d not from them by day..... Neh 9:19
have not wickedly d from my God.... Ps 18:21
who drove him away, and he d............ Ps 34:1
Egypt was glad when they d............ Ps 105:38
I have not d from thy judgments...... Ps 119:102
the day that Ephraim d from Judah... Is 7:17
heard that he was d from Lachish..... Is 37:8
So Sennacherib king of Assyria d.... Is 37:37
Mine age is d, and is removed from.. Is 38:12
the smiths, were d from Jerusalem... Jer 29:2
of them, they d from Jerusalem......... Jer 37:5
d to go over to the Ammonites............ Jer 41:10
And they d, and dwelt in the............ Jer 41:17
of Zion all her beauty is d............ Lam 1:6
heart, which hath d from me............ Eze 6:9
Then the glory of the LORD d from.... Eze 10:18
The kingdom is d from thee............ Dan 4:31
thereof, because it is d from it............ Hos 10:5
But ye are d out of the way............ Mal 2:8
they had heard the king, they d......... Mt 2:9
they d into their own country............ Mt 2:12
And when they were d, behold, the... Mt 2:13
mother by night, and d into Egypt.... Mt 2:14
into prison, he d into Galilee............ Mt 4:12
And he arose, and d to his house...... Mt 9:7
And when Jesus d thence, two blind. Mt 9:27
But they, when they were d............ Mt 9:31
he d thence to teach and to preach.. Mt 11:1
And as they d, Jesus began to say.... Mt 11:7
And when he was d thence, he went.. Mt 12:9
these parables, he d thence............ Mt 13:53
he d thence by ship into a desert..... Mt 14:13
And when he had sent the............ Mt 15:21
Jesus d from thence, and came nigh. Mt 15:29
And he left them, and d............ Mt 16:4
and he d out of him............ Mt 17:18
he d from Galilee, and came into..... Mt 19:1
his hands on them, and d thence...... Mt 19:15
as they d from Jericho, a great......... Mt 20:29
went out, and d from the temple...... Mt 24:1
of silver in the temple, and d............ Mt 27:5
the door of the sepulchre, and d...... Mt 27:60
they d quickly from the sepulchre..... Mt 28:8
d into a solitary place, and there...... Mk 1:35
the leprosy d from him, and he was.. Mk 1:42
And he d, and began to publish in... Mk 5:20

they *d* into a desert place by.................. Mk 6:32
he *d* into a mountain to pray.................. Mk 6:46
ship again *d* to the other side.............. Mk 8:13
they *d* thence, and passed through......... Mk 9:30
he *d* to his own house............................ Lk 1:23
And the angel *d* from her..................... Lk 1:38
which *d* not from the temple, but........... Lk 2:37
he *d* from him for a season.................... Lk 4:13
And when it was day, he *d* and went..... Lk 4:42
the leprosy *d* from him.......................... Lk 5:13
d to his own house, glorifying............... Lk 5:25
the messengers of John were *d* .... Lk 7:24
out of whom the devils were *d* .... Lk 8:38
d besought him that he might be........... Lk 8:38
And they *d*, and went through the......... Lk 9:6
as they *d* from him, Peter said............. Lk 9:33
his raiment, and wounded him, and *d*... Lk 10:30
And on the morrow when he *d* .... Lk 10:35
clothes laid by themselves, and *d*......... Lk 24:12
Judaea, and *d* again into Galilee........... Jn 4:3
Now after two days *he d* thence............ Jn 4:43
The man *d*, and told the Jews that....... Jn 5:15
he *d* again into a mountain................... Jn 6:15
These things spake Jesus, and *d* .... Jn 12:36
they *d* from the presence of the........... Acts 5:41
which spake unto Cornelius was *d*......... Acts 10:7
Then *d* Barnabas to Tarsus, for to....... Acts 11:25
and forthwith the angel *d* from him..... Acts 12:10
And he *d*, and went into another........... Acts 12:17
the Holy Ghost, *d* unto Seleucia............ Acts 13:4
But when they *d* from Perga.................. Acts 13:14
the next day he *d* with Barnabas.......... Acts 14:20
who *d* from them from Pamphylia,......... Acts 15:38
that they *d* in asunder one from............ Acts 15:39
And Paul chose Silas, and *d* .... Acts 15:40
they comforted them, and *d* .... Acts 16:40
to him with all speed, they *d* .... Acts 17:15
So Paul *d* from among them.................... Acts 17:33
these things Paul *d* from Athens............ Acts 18:1
he *d* thence, and entered into a............. Acts 18:7
had spent some time there, he *d*........... Acts 18:23
he *d* from them, and separated the...... Acts 19:9
and the diseases *d* from them.................. Acts 19:12
d for to go into Macedonia...................... Acts 20:1
even till break of day, so he *d*............... Acts 20:11
had accomplished those days, we *d*....... Acts 21:5
we that were of Paul's company *d*........ Acts 21:8
Then straightway they *d* from him........ Acts 22:29
and when we *d*, they laded us with...... Acts 28:10
after three months we *d* in a ship......... Acts 28:11
not among themselves, they *d*............... Acts 28:25
had said these words, the Jews *d*........... Acts 28:29
when I *d* from Macedonia, no................. Phil 4:15
world, and is *d* unto Thessalonica......... 2Ti 4:10
he therefore *d* for a season.................... Philem 15
the heaven *d* as a scroll when it.......... Rev 6:14
soul lusted after are *d* from thee.......... Rev 18:14
dainty and goodly are *d* from thee....... Rev 18:14

DEPARTETH

wind carrieth him away, and he *d*......... Job 27:21
wise man feareth, and *d* from evil........ Prov 14:16
d in darkness, and his name shall......... Eccl 6:4
he that *d* from evil maketh.................... Is 59:15
treacherously *d* from her husband........ Jer 3:20
whose heart *d* from the LORD................. Jer 17:5
the prey *d* not...................................... Nah 3:1
and bruising him hardly *d* from him...... Lk 9:39

DEPARTING

to pass, as her soul was in *d* .... Gen 35:18
their *d* out of the land of Egypt............. Ex 16:1
d away from our God, speaking.............. Is 59:13
even by *d* from thy precepts and........... Dan 9:5
transgressed thy law, even by *d*........... Dan 9:11
great whoredom, *d* from the LORD.......... Hos 1:2
And the people saw them *d*, and many.. Mk 6:33
d from the coasts of Tyre and............... Mk 7:31
John *d* from them returned to................ Acts 13:13
that after my *d* shall grievous.............. Acts 20:29
in *d* from the living God........................ Heb 3:12
made mention of the *d* of the............... Heb 11:22

DEPARTURE

sea shall be troubled at thy *d*............... Eze 26:18
and the time of my *d* is at hand............ 2Ti 4:6

DEPOSED

he was *d* from his kingly throne,........... Dan 5:20

DEPRIVED

why should I be *d* also of you................ Gen 27:45
Because God hath *d* her of wisdom......... Job 39:17
I am *d* of the residue of my years........... Is 38:10

DEPTH

The *d* saith, It is not in me.................... Job 28:14
walked in the search of the *d* .... Job 38:16
he layeth up the *d* in storehouses........ Ps 33:7
a compass upon the face of the *d*.......... Prov 8:27
for height, and the earth for *d*............. Prov 25:3
ask it either in the *d*, or in the............ Is 7:11
the *d* closed me round about, the........... Jonah 2:5
were drowned in the *d* of the sea.......... Mt 18:6
up, because it had no *d* of earth............ Mk 4:5
Nor height, nor *d*, nor any other........... Rom 8:39
O the *d* of the riches both of the.......... Rom 11:33
is the breadth, and length, and *d*......... Eph 3:18

DEPTHS

The *d* have covered them...................... Ex 15:5
the *d* were congealed in the heart......... Ex 15:8
d that spring out of valleys and........... Deut 8:7

again from the *d* of the sea.................. Ps 68:22
up again from the *d* of the earth........... Ps 71:20
the *d* also were troubled........................ Ps 77:16
them drink as out of the great *d*........... Ps 78:15
so he led them through the *d* .... Ps 106:9
they go down again to the *d*.................. Ps 107:26
Out of the *d* have I cried unto............... Ps 130:1
his knowledge the *d* are broken up....... Prov 3:20
When there were no *d*, I was................. Prov 8:24
her guests are in the *d* of hell.............. Prov 9:18
that hath made the *d* of the sea a........ Is 51:10
be broken by the seas in the *d* of......... Eze 27:34
their sins into the *d* of the sea............. Mic 7:19
have not known the *d* of Satan............. Rev 2:24

DEPUTED

but there is no man of the king.............. 2Sa 15:3

DEPUTIES

and to the lieutenants, and the *d*......... Est 8:9
and the lieutenants, and the *d*............. Est 9:3
the law is open, and there are *d*.......... Acts 19:38

DEPUTY

a *d* was king...................................... 1Kin 22:47
was with the *d* of the country............... Acts 13:7
to turn away the *d* from the faith........ Acts 13:8
Then the *d*, when he saw what was..... Acts 13:12
when Gallio was the *d* of Achaia........... Acts 18:12

DERBE

(dêr'-by) A south Galatian town.
of it, and fled unto Lystra and *D* .... Acts 14:6
he departed with Barnabas to *D* .... Acts 14:20
Then came he to *D* and Lystra............... Acts 16:1
and Gaius of *D*, and Timotheus............ Acts 20:4

DERIDE

they shall *d* every strong hold.............. Hab 1:10

DERIDED

and they *d* him...................................... Lk 16:14
the rulers also with them *d* him........... Lk 23:35

DERISION

are younger than I have me in *d*.......... Job 30:1
The Lord shall have them in *d*.............. Ps 2:4
a *d* to them that are round about......... Ps 44:13
shalt have all the heathen in *d*............. Ps 59:8
d to them that are round about us......... Ps 79:4
proud have had me greatly in *d*............. Ps 119:51
I am in *d* daily, every one...................... Jer 20:7
made a reproach unto me, and a *d*........ Jer 20:8
vomit, and he also shall be in *d* .... Jer 48:26
For was not Israel a *d* unto thee.......... Jer 48:27
so shall Moab be a *d* and a.................... Jer 48:39
I was a *d* to all my people.................... Lam 3:14
be laughed to scorn and had in *d*......... Eze 23:32
d to the residue of the heathen............ Eze 36:4
this shall be their *d* in the land............ Hos 7:16

DESCEND

and the border shall *d*, and shall......... Num 34:11
or shall *d* into battle............................ 1Sa 26:10
his glory shall not *d* after him.............. Ps 49:17
that rejoiceth, shall *d* into it................. Is 5:14
with them that *d* into the pit................ Eze 26:20
with them that *d* into the pit................. Eze 31:16
of Israel our love from the cross............. Mk 15:32
saw a vision, A certain vessel *d* .... Acts 11:5
Who shall *d* into the deep...................... Rom 10:7
shall *d* from heaven with a shout......... 1Th 4:16

DESCENDED

the LORD *d* upon it in fire...................... Ex 19:18
tabernacle, the cloudy pillar *d*............. Ex 33:9
the LORD in the cloud, and stood........... Ex 34:5
the brook that *d* out of the mount....... Deut 9:21
d from the mountain, and passed......... Josh 2:23
the coast of unto the river Kanah,......... Josh 17:9
the border *d* to Ataroth-adar,.............. Josh 18:13
d to the valley of Hinnom, to the......... Josh 18:16
on the south, and *d* to En-rogel,........... Josh 18:16
d to :he stone of Bohan the son........... Josh 18:17
as the dew that *d* upon the................... Ps 133:3
ascended up into heaven, or *d* .... Prov 30:4
And the rain *d*, and the floods came.... Mt 7:25
And the rain *d*, and the floods came.... Mt 7:27
angel of the Lord *d* from heaven.......... Mt 28:2
the Holy Ghost *d* in a bodily................. Lk 3:22
the high priest *d* with the elders.......... Acts 24:1
what is it but that he also *d*................. Eph 4:9
He that *d* is the same also that............ Eph 4:10

DESCENDETH

This wisdom *d* not from above, but...... Jas 3:15

DESCENDING

of God ascending and *d* on it............... Gen 28:12
the Spirit of God like a dove *d*............. Mt 3:16
the Spirit like a dove *d* upon him......... Mk 1:10
I saw the Spirit from heaven.................. Jn 1:32
whom thou shalt see the Spirit *d*......... Jn 1:33
and *d* upon the Son of man.................. Jn 1:51
and a certain vessel *d* unto him........... Acts 10:11
d out of heaven from God,..................... Rev 21:10

DESCENT

even now in the *d* of the mount of....... Lk 19:37
father, without mother, without *d*....... Heb 7:3
But he whose *d* is not counted.............. Heb 7:6

DESCRIBE

d it according to the inheritance......... Josh 18:4
Ye shall therefore *d* the land............... Josh 18:6
them that went to *d* the land.............. Josh 18:8
d it, and come again to me, that I........ Josh 18:8

DESCRIBED

d it by cities into seven parts............... Josh 18:9
he *d* unto him the princes of............... Judg 8:14

DESCRIBETH

Even as David also *d* the...................... Rom 4:6
For Moses *d* the righteousness............. Rom 10:5

DESCRIPTION

bring the *d* hither to me, that I........... Josh 18:6

DESCRY

house of Joseph sent to *d* Beth-el....... Judg 1:23

DESERT

flock to the backside of the *d*.............. Ex 3:1
three days' journey into the *d*.............. Ex 5:3
and were come to the *d* of Sinai.......... Ex 19:2
from the *d* unto the river...................... Ex 23:31
into the *d* of Zin in the first................. Num 20:1
my commandment in the *d* of Zin........ Num 27:14
they removed from the *d* of Sinai......... Num 33:16
He found him in a *d* land, and in........ Deut 32:10
Also he built towers in the *d* 2Chr 26:10
Behold, as wild asses in the *d*............. Job 24:5
render to them their *d* .... Ps 28:4
and grieve him in the *d*....................... Ps 78:40
I am like an owl of the *d*..................... Ps 102:6
and tempted God in the *d*.................... Ps 106:14
her *d* like the garden of the LORD......... Is 51:3
shall be like the heath in the *d*........... Jer 17:6
people that dwell in the *d*.................... Jer 25:24
a wilderness, a dry land, and a *d*......... Jer 50:12
the wild beasts of the *d* with.............. Jer 50:39
country, and go down into the *d*.......... Eze 47:8
by ship into a *d* place apart................. Mt 14:13
to him, saying, This is a *d* place.......... Mt 14:15
unto you, Behold, he is in the *d*........... Mt 24:26
city, but was without in *d* places......... Mk 1:45
yourselves apart into a *d* place............ Mk 6:31
they departed into a *d* place by........... Mk 6:32
him, and said, This is a *d* place........... Mk 8:5
departed and went into a *d* place........ Lk 4:42
a *d* place belonging to the city............ Lk 9:10
for we are here in a *d* place................. Lk 9:12
fathers did eat manna in the *d*........... Jn 6:31
Jerusalem unto Gaza, which is *d*......... Acts 8:26

DESERTS

when he led them through the *d*.......... Is 48:21
wilderness, through a land of *d* .... Jer 2:6
to their *d* will I judge them.................. Jer 7:3
are like the foxes in the *d* .... Eze 13:4
was in the *d* till the day of his............ Lk 1:80
they wandered in *d*, and in.................. Heb 11:38

DESERVE

us less than our iniquities *d*................ Ezr 9:13

DESERVETH

thee less than thine iniquity *d*............. Job 11:6

DESERVING

according to the *d* of his hands............ Judg 9:16

DESIRABLE

rulers, all of them *d* young men............ Eze 23:6
horses, all of them *d* young men.......... Eze 23:12
all of them *d* young men, captains........ Eze 23:23

DESIRE

thy *d* shall be to thy husband, and....... Gen 3:16
And unto thee shall be his *d*................. Gen 4:7
for that ye did *d*................................. Ex 10:11
neither shalt any man *d* thy land......... Ex 34:24
Neither shalt thou *d* thy........................ Deut 5:21
thou shalt not *d* the silver or.............. Deut 7:25
come with all the *d* of his mind............ Deut 18:6
hast *d* unto her, that thou.................... Deut 21:11
I would *d* a request of you, that........... Judg 8:24
And on whom is all the *d* of Israel....... 1Sa 9:20
the *d* of thy soul to come down............ 2Sa 3:21
is all my salvation, and all my *d* 2Sa 23:5
I *d* one small petition of thee............... 1Kin 2:20
I will do all thy *d* concerning............... 1Kin 5:8
and thou shalt accomplish my *d*........... 1Kin 5:9
fir trees according to all his *d*............. 1Kin 5:10
all Solomon's *d* which he was............... 1Kin 9:1
with gold, according to all his *d* 1Kin 9:11
unto the queen of Sheba all her *d*....... 1Kin 10:13
said, Did I *d* a son of my lord............... 2Kin 4:28
to the queen of Sheba all her *d*........... 2Chr 9:12
and sought him with their whole *d*...... 2Chr 15:15
servants, who to fear thy name............. Neh 1:11
and I *d* to reason with God.................... Job 13:3
thou wilt have a *d* to the work of......... Job 14:15
for we *d* not the knowledge of thy....... Job 21:14
withhold the poor from their *d*............ Job 31:16
behold, my *d* is, that the...................... Job 31:35
speak, for I *d* to justify thee................ Job 33:32
My *d* is that Job may be tried.............. Job 34:36
D not the night, when people are......... Job 36:20
wicked boasteth of his heart's *d*......... Ps 10:3
hast heard the *d* of the humble........... Ps 10:17
Thou hast given him his heart's *d*....... Ps 21:2

Lord, all my *d* is before thee .... Ps 38:9
and offering thou didst not *d* .... Ps 40:6
the king greatly *d* thy beauty .... Ps 45:11
hath seen his *d* upon mine enemies .... Ps 54:7
let me see my *d* upon mine enemies .... Ps 59:10
put to confusion, that *d* my hurt .... Ps 70:2
upon earth that I *d* beside thee .... Ps 73:25
for he gave them their own *d* .... Ps 78:29
shall see my *d* on mine enemies .... Ps 92:11
mine ears shall hear my *d* of the .... Ps 92:11
he see his *d* upon his enemies .... Ps 112:8
the *d* of the wicked shall perish .... Ps 112:10
I see my *d* upon them that hate me .... Ps 118:7
satisfiest the *d* of every living .... Ps 145:16
He will fulfil the *d* of them that .... Ps 145:19
all the things thou canst *d* are .... Prov 3:15
but the *d* of the righteous shall .... Prov 10:24
The *d* of the righteous is only .... Prov 11:23
heart sick, but when the *d* cometh .... Prov 13:12
The *d* accomplished is sweet to .... Prov 13:19
Through a man, having separated .... Prov 18:1
The *d* of a man is his kindness .... Prov 19:22
The *d* of the slothful killeth him .... Prov 21:25
neither *d* thou his dainty meats .... Prov 23:6
neither *d* to be with them .... Prov 24:1
eyes than the wandering of the *d* .... Eccl 6:9
be a burden, and *d* shall fail .... Eccl 12:5
beloved's, and his *d* is toward me .... Song 7:10
the *d* of our soul is to thy name .... Is 26:8
is no beauty that we should *d* him .... Is 53:2
land whereunto they *d* to return .... Jer 22:27
in the place whither ye *d* to go .... Jer 42:22
have a *d* to return to dwell there .... Jer 44:14
I take away from the *d* of .... Eze 24:16
the *d* of your eyes, and that which .... Eze 24:21
the *d* of their eyes, and that .... Eze 24:25
That they would *d* mercies of the .... Dan 2:18
nor the *d* of women, nor regard .... Dan 11:37
It is in my *d* that I should .... Hos 10:10
Woe unto you that *d* the day of .... Amos 5:18
he uttereth his mischievous *d* .... Mic 7:3
home, who enlargeth his *d* as hell .... Hab 2:5
the *d* of all nations shall come .... Hag 2:7
If any man *d* to be first, the .... Mk 9:35
do for us whatsoever we shall *d* .... Mk 10:35
unto you, What things soever ye *d* .... Mk 11:24
d him to do as he had ever done .... Mk 15:8
when ye shall *d* to see one of the .... Lk 17:22
which *d* to walk in long robes, and .... Lk 20:46
With *d* I have desired to eat this .... Lk 22:15
The Jews have agreed to thee .... Acts 23:20
But we *d* to hear of thee what .... Acts 28:22
Brethren, my heart's *d* and prayer .... Rom 10:1
having a great *d* these many years .... Rom 15:23
d spiritual gifts, but rather 1Cor 14:1
when he told us your earnest *d* 2Cor 7:7
what fear, yea, what vehement *d* 2Cor 7:11
from them which *d* occasion 2Cor 11:12
For though I would *d* to glory 2Cor 12:6
whereunto ye *d* again to be in .... Gal 4:9
I *d* to be present with you now .... Gal 4:20
ye that *d* to be under the law, do .... Gal 4:21
As many as *d* to make a fair shew .... Gal 6:12
but *d* to have you circumcised .... Gal 6:13
Wherefore I *d* that ye faint not .... Eph 3:13
having a *d* to depart, and to be .... Phil 1:23
Not because I *d* a gift .... Phil 4:17
but I *d* fruit that may abound to .... Phil 4:17
to *d* that ye might be filled with .... Col 1:9
to see your face with great *d* 1Th 2:17
If a man of the office of a bishop 1Ti 3:1
we *d* that every one of you do .... Heb 6:11
But now they *d* a better country, ... Heb 11:16
d to have, and cannot obtain .... Jas 4:2
things the angels *d* to look into 1Pet 1:12
d the sincere milk of the word, ... 1Pet 2:2
shall *d* to die, and death shall .... Rev 9:6

DESIRED

a tree to be *d* to make one wise, ... Gen 3:6
ye have chosen, and whom ye have *d* 1Sa 12:13
that which Solomon *d* to build in 1Kin 9:19
all that Solomon *d* to build in 2Chr 8:6
And he *d* many wives 2Chr 11:23
and departed without being *d* 2Chr 21:20
whatsoever she *d* was given her to .... Est 2:13
shall not save of that which he *d* .... Job 20:20
More to be *d* are they than gold, ... Ps 19:10
One thing have I *d* of the LORD .... Ps 27:4
bringeth them unto their *d* haven .... Ps 107:30
he hath a *d* for his habitation .... Ps 132:13
for I have *d* it .... Ps 132:14
all the things that may be *d* are .... Prov 8:11
There is treasure to be *d* .... Prov 21:20
mine eyes of I kept not from them .... Eccl 2:10
of the oaks which ye have *d* .... Is 1:29
soul have I *d* thee in the night .... Is 26:9
neither have I *d* the woeful day .... Jer 17:16
d of the king that he would give .... Dan 2:16
unto me now what we *d* of thee .... Dan 2:23
For I *d* mercy, and not sacrifice .... Hos 6:6
my soul of the firstripe fruit .... Mic 7:1
gather together, O nation not *d* .... Zeph 2:1
righteous men have *d* to see those .... Mt 13:17
tempting *d* him that he would shew .... Mt 16:1
one prisoner, whomsoever they *d* .... Mt 27:15
one of the Pharisees *d* him that .... Lk 7:36
And he *d* to see him .... Lk 9:9
kings have *d* to see those things .... Lk 10:24
With desire I have *d* to eat this, ... Lk 22:15
Satan hath *d* to have you, that he .... Lk 22:31

---

cast into prison, whom they had *d* .... Lk 23:25
d him, saying, Sir, we would see .... Jn 12:21
a murderer to be granted unto .... Acts 3:14
d to find a tabernacle for the .... Acts 7:46
he *d* Philip that he would come up .... Acts 8:31
d of him letters to Damascus to .... Acts 9:2
chamberlain their friend, *d* peace .... Acts 12:20
d to hear the word of God .... Acts 13:7
And afterward they *d* a king .... Acts 13:21
yet *d* they Pilate that he should .... Acts 13:28
d them to depart out of the city .... Acts 16:39
When they *d* him to tarry longer .... Acts 18:20
d favour against him, that he .... Acts 25:3
were *d* to tarry with them seven .... Acts 28:14
I greatly *d* him to come unto you 1Cor 16:12
Insomuch that we *d* Titus, that as 2Cor 8:6
I *d* Titus, and with him I sent a 2Cor 12:18
the petitions that we *d* of him 1Jn 5:15

DESIREDST

According to all that thou *d* of .... Deut 18:16
all that debt, because thou *d* me, ... Mt 18:32

DESIRES

give thee the *d* of thine heart .... Ps 37:4
not, O LORD, the *d* of the wicked .... Ps 140:8
fulfilling the *d* of the flesh .... Eph 2:3

DESIREST

thou *d* truth in the inward parts .... Ps 51:6
For thou *d* not sacrifice .... Ps 51:16

DESIRETH

or for whatsoever thy soul *d* .... Deut 14:26
then take as much as thy soul *d* 1Sa 2:16
The king of not any dowry, but as 1Sa 18:25
unto David, Whatsoever thy soul *d* 1Sa 20:4
reign over all that thine heart *d* 2Sa 3:21
according to all that thy soul *d* 1Kin 11:37
a servant earnestly *d* the shadow .... Job 7:2
And what his soul *d*, even that he .... Job 23:13
What man is he that *d* life .... Ps 34:12
the hill which God *d* to dwell in .... Ps 68:16
The wicked *d* the net of evil men .... Prov 12:12
The soul of the sluggard *d* .... Prov 13:4
The soul of the wicked *d* evil .... Prov 21:10
for his soul of all that he *d* .... Eccl 6:2
drunk old wine straightway *d* new .... Lk 5:39
and *d* conditions of peace .... Lk 14:32
of a bishop, he *d* a good work 1Ti 3:1

DESIRING

without, *d* to speak with him .... Mt 12:46
without, *d* to speak with him .... Mt 12:47
him, and *d* a certain thing of him .... Mt 20:20
stand without, *d* to see thee .... Lk 8:20
d to be fed with the crumbs which .... Lk 16:21
d him that he would not delay to .... Acts 9:38
d him that he would not adventure .... Acts 19:31
d to have judgment against him .... Acts 25:15
earnestly *d* to be clothed upon 2Cor 5:2
d greatly to see us, as we also 1Th 3:6
d to be something, being 1Ti 1:7
Greatly *d* to see thee, being 2Ti 1:4

DESIROUS

Be not *d* of his dainties .... Prov 23:3
for he was *d* to see him of a long .... Lk 23:8
knew that they were *d* to ask him .... Jn 16:19
a garrison, *d* to apprehend me 2Cor 11:32
Let us not be *d* of vain glory .... Gal 5:26
So being affectionately *d* of you, ... 1Th 2:8

DESOLATE

not die, that the land be not *d* .... Gen 47:19
lest the land become *d*, and the .... Ex 23:29
and your high ways shall be *d* .... Lev 26:22
and your land shall be *d*, and your .... Lev 26:33
sabbaths, as long as it lieth *d* .... Lev 26:34
long as it lieth *d* it shall rest .... Lev 26:35
while she lieth *d* without them .... Lev 26:43
So Tamar remained *d* in her 2Sa 13:20
as she lay *d* she kept sabbath 2Chr 36:21
earth, which built *d* places for .... Job 3:14
And he dwelleth in *d* cities .... Job 15:28
of hypocrites shall be *d*, and fire .... Job 15:34
thou hast made *d* all my company .... Job 16:7
the wilderness in former time *d* .... Job 30:3
To satisfy the *d* and waste ground .... Job 38:27
for I am *d* and afflicted .... Ps 25:16
hate the righteous shall be *d* .... Ps 34:21
them that trust in him shall be *d* .... Ps 34:22
Let them be *d* for a reward of .... Ps 40:15
Let their habitation be *d* .... Ps 69:25
bread also out of their *d* places .... Ps 109:10
my heart within me is *d* .... Ps 143:4
Your country is *d*, your cities, ... Is 1:7
it in your presence, and it is *d* .... Is 1:7
she being *d* shall sit upon the .... Is 3:26
Of a truth many houses shall be *d* .... Is 5:9
man, and the land be utterly *d* .... Is 6:11
rest all of them in the *d* valleys .... Is 7:19
fierce anger, to lay the land *d* .... Is 13:9
shall cry in their *d* houses .... Is 13:22
the waters of Nimrim shall be *d* .... Is 15:6
and they that dwell therein are *d* .... Is 24:6
Yet the defenced city shall be *d* .... Is 27:10
cause to inherit the *d* heritages .... Is 49:8
thy *d* places, and the land of thy .... Is 49:19
I have lost my children, and am *d* .... Is 49:21
of the *d* than the children of the .... Is 54:1
make the *d* cities to be inhabited .... Is 54:3
we are in *d* places as dead men .... Is 59:10

---

thy land any more be termed *D* .... Is 62:4
be horribly afraid, be ye very *d* .... Jer 2:12
from his place to make thy land *d* .... Jer 4:7
said, The whole land shall be *d* .... Jer 4:27
lest I make thee *d*, a land not .... Jer 6:8
for the land shall be *d* .... Jer 7:34
I will make the cities of Judah *d* .... Jer 9:11
to make the cities of Judah *d* .... Jer 10:22
and have made his habitation *d* .... Jer 10:25
pleasant portion a *d* wilderness .... Jer 12:10
They have made it *d* .... Jer 12:11
being *d* it mourneth unto me .... Jer 12:11
the whole land is made *d*, because .... Jer 12:11
To make their land *d*, and a .... Jer 18:16
And I will make this city *d* .... Jer 19:8
for their land is *d* because of .... Jer 25:38
this city shall be *d* without an .... Jer 26:9
It is *d* without man or beast .... Jer 32:43
ye say shall be *d* without man .... Jer 33:10
streets of Jerusalem, that are *d* .... Jer 33:10
which is *d* without man and without .... Jer 33:12
and they are wasted and *d*, as at .... Jer 44:6
waste and *d* without an inhabitant ... Jer 46:19
for the cities thereof shall be *d* .... Jer 48:9
waters also of Nimrim shall be *d* .... Jer 48:34
and it shall be a *d* heap, and her .... Jer 49:2
their habitations *d* with them .... Jer 49:20
her, which shall make her land *d* .... Jer 50:3
but it shall be wholly *d* .... Jer 50:13
make their habitation *d* with them .... Jer 50:45
but thou shalt be *d* for ever .... Jer 51:26
but that it shall be *d* for ever .... Jer 51:62
all her gates are *d* .... Lam 1:4
he hath made me *d* and faint all .... Lam 1:13
my children are *d*, because the .... Lam 1:16
he hath made me *d* .... Lam 3:11
delicately are *d* in the streets .... Lam 4:5
the mountain of Zion, which is *d* .... Lam 5:18
And your altars shall be *d* .... Eze 6:4
and the high places shall be *d* .... Eze 6:6
may be laid waste and made *d* .... Eze 6:6
upon them, and make the land *d* .... Eze 6:14
more *d* than the wilderness toward .... Eze 6:14
that her land may be *d* from all .... Eze 12:19
waste, and the land shall be *d* .... Eze 12:20
and they spoil it, so that it be *d* .... Eze 14:15
but the land shall be *d* .... Eze 14:16
And I will make the land *d* .... Eze 15:8
And he knew their *d* palaces .... Eze 19:7
and the land was *d*, and the fulness .... Eze 19:7
womb, that I might make them *d* .... Eze 20:26
the land of Teman, when it was *d* .... Eze 25:3
and I will make it *d* from Teman .... Eze 25:13
When I shall make thee a *d* city .... Eze 26:19
of the earth, in places of old .... Eze 26:20
And the land of Egypt shall be *d* .... Eze 29:9
land of Egypt utterly waste and *d* .... Eze 29:10
d in the midst of the countries .... Eze 29:12
midst of the countries that are *d* .... Eze 29:12
laid waste shall be of forty years .... Eze 29:12
they shall be *d* in the midst of .... Eze 30:7
midst of the countries that are *d* .... Eze 30:7
And I will make Pathros *d*, and will ... Eze 30:14
I shall make the land of Egypt *d* .... Eze 32:15
For I will lay the land most *d* .... Eze 32:28
mountains of Israel shall be *d* .... Eze 33:28
land most *d* because of all their .... Eze 33:29
thee, and I will make thee most *d* ...... Eze 35:3
cities waste, and thou shalt be *d* .... Eze 35:4
will I make mount Seir most *d* .... Eze 35:7
Israel, saying, They are laid *d* .... Eze 35:12
rejoiceth, I will make thee *d* .... Eze 35:14
house of Israel, because it was *d* .... Eze 35:15
thou shalt be *d*, O mount Seir, and ... Eze 35:15
Because they have made you *d* .... Eze 36:3
to the valleys, to the *d* wastes .... Eze 36:4
the *d* land shall be tilled, ... Eze 36:34
whereas it lay *d* in the sight of .... Eze 36:34
This land that was *d* is become .... Eze 36:35
and the waste and *d* ruined .... Eze 36:35
places, and plant that which was *d* ... Eze 36:36
to turn thine hand upon the *d* .... Eze 38:12
upon thy sanctuary that is *d* .... Dan 9:17
abominations he shall make it *d* .... Dan 9:27
shall be poured upon the *d* .... Dan 9:27
the abomination that maketh *d* .... Dan 11:31
abomination that maketh *d* set up ... Dan 12:11
Ephraim shall be *d* in the day of .... Hos 5:9
Samaria shall become *d* .... Hos 13:16
clods, the garners are laid *d* .... Joel 1:17
the flocks of sheep are made *d* .... Joel 1:18
and behind them a *d* wilderness .... Joel 2:3
drive him into a land barren and *d* .... Joel 2:20
and Edom shall be a *d* wilderness ...... Joel 3:19
high places of Isaac shall be *d* .... Amos 7:9
the idols thereof will I lay *d* .... Mic 1:7
in making thee *d* because of thy .... Mic 6:13
the land shall be *d* because of .... Mic 7:13
their towers are *d* .... Zeph 3:6
Thus the land was *d* after them, ... Zec 7:14
for they laid the pleasant land *d* .... Zec 7:14
will return and build the *d* places .... Mal 1:4
your house is left unto you *d* .... Mt 23:38
your house is left unto you *d* .... Lk 13:35
Psalms, Let his habitation be *d* .... Acts 1:20
for the *d* hath many more children .... Gal 4:27
she that is a widow indeed, and *d* 1Ti 5:5
the whore, and shall make her *d* .... Rev 17:16
for in one hour is she made *d* .... Rev 18:19

DESOLATION

and bring your sanctuaries unto d.....	Lev 26:31
And I will bring the land into d......	Lev 26:32
for ever, even a d unto this day.......	Josh 8:28
that they should become a d........	2Kin 22:19
who therefore gave them up to d......	2Chr 30:7
in the d they rolled themselves........	Job 30:14
How are they brought into d............	Ps 73:19
When your fear cometh as d...........	Prov 1:27
neither of the d of the wicked.........	Prov 3:25
in the d which shall come from........	Is 10:3
and there shall be a........................	Is 17:9
In the city is left d, and the...........	Is 24:12
d shall come upon them suddenly,.....	Is 47:11
d, and destruction, and the famine,....	Is 51:19
is a wilderness, Jerusalem a d.........	Is 64:10
that this house shall become a d.......	Jer 22:5
And this whole land shall be a d.......	Jer 25:11
princes thereof, to make them a d.....	Jer 25:18
Judah a d without an inhabitant........	Jer 34:22
and, behold, this day they are a d......	Jer 44:2
therefore is your land a d...............	Jer 44:22
that Bozrah shall become a d...........	Jer 49:13
Also Edom shall be a d..................	Jer 49:17
for dragons, and a d for ever...........	Jer 49:33
become a d among the nations.........	Jer 50:23
Babylon a d without an inhabitant.....	Jer 51:29
Her cities are a d, a dry land,..........	Jer 51:43
and a snare is come upon us, d.........	Lam 3:47
prince shall be clothed with d.........	Eze 7:27
with the cup of astonishment and d...	Eze 23:33
and the transgression of d..............	Dan 8:13
the daily increaseth lies and d.........	Hos 12:1
Egypt shall be a d, and Edom shall....	Joel 3:19
that I should make thee a d.............	Mic 6:16
a booty, and their houses a d...........	Zeph 1:13
distress, a day of wasteness and d....	Zeph 1:15
be forsaken, and Ashkelon a d........	Zeph 2:4
and saltpits, and a perpetual d.........	Zeph 2:9
and will make Nineveh a d, and dry..	Zeph 2:13
d shall be in the thresholds............	Zeph 2:14
how is she become a d, a place........	Zeph 2:15
against itself is brought to d...........	Mt 12:25
shall see the abomination of d.........	Mt 24:15
ye shall see the abomination of d.....	Mk 13:14
against itself is brought to d...........	Lk 11:17
know that the d thereof is nigh........	Lk 21:20

DESOLATIONS

God, and to repair the d thereof.......	Ezr 9:9
what d he hath made in the earth.......	Ps 46:8
up thy feet unto the perpetual d.......	Ps 74:3
they shall raise up the former d........	Is 61:4
the d of many generations..............	Is 61:4
and hissing, and perpetual d...........	Jer 25:9
and will make it perpetual d............	Jer 25:12
I will make thee perpetual d............	Eze 35:9
years in the d of Jerusalem.............	Dan 9:2
open thine eyes, and behold our d....	Dan 9:18
end of the war d are determined.......	Dan 9:26

DESPAIR

and Saul shall d of me, to seek me....	1Sa 27:1
d of all the labour which I took........	Eccl 2:20
we are perplexed, but not in d..........	2Cor 4:8

DESPAIRED

insomuch that we d even of life........	2Cor 1:8

DESPERATE

and the speeches of one that is d......	Job 6:26
the day of grief and of d sorrow.......	Is 17:11

DESPERATELY

above all things, and d wicked.........	Jer 17:9

DESPISE

And if ye shall d my statutes...........	Lev 26:15
they that d me shall be lightly..........	1Sa 2:30
why then did ye d us, that our..........	2Sa 19:43
so that they shall d their................	Est 1:17
therefore d not thou the.................	Job 5:17
I would d my life......................	Job 9:21
that thou shouldest d the work of......	Job 10:3
If I did d the cause of my...............	Job 31:13
heart, O God, thou wilt not d...........	Ps 51:17
awakest, thou shalt d their image.....	Ps 73:20
destitute, and not d their prayer.......	Ps 102:17
but fools d wisdom and instruction...	Prov 1:7
d not the chastening of the LORD......	Prov 3:11
Men do not d a thief, if he steal.......	Prov 6:30
for he will d the wisdom of thy........	Prov 23:9
d not thy mother when she is old......	Prov 23:22
of Israel, Because ye d this word......	Is 30:12
thy lovers will d thee, they will........	Jer 4:30
say still unto them that d me...........	Jer 23:17
all that honoured her d her..............	Lam 1:8
which d thee round about...............	Eze 16:57
that d them round about the...........	Eze 28:26
I d your feast days, and I will..........	Amos 5:21
you, O priests, that d my name........	Mal 1:6
hold to the one, and d the other.......	Mt 6:24
Take heed that ye d not one of........	Mt 18:10
hold to the one, and d the other.......	Lk 16:13
that eateth d him that eateth not......	Rom 14:3
or d ye the church of God, and.........	1Cor 11:22
Let no man therefore d him.............	1Cor 16:11
D not prophesyings....................	1Th 5:20
Let no man d thy youth..................	1Ti 4:12
masters, let them not d them............	1Ti 6:2
Let no man d thee.......................	Titus 2:15
d not thou the chastening of the.......	Heb 12:5
of uncleanness, and d government.....	2Pet 2:10

d dominion, and speak evil of...........	Jude 8

DESPISED

her mistress was d in her eyes.........	Gen 16:4
conceived, I was d in her eyes.........	Gen 16:5
thus Esau d his birthright...............	Gen 25:34
even because they d my judgments,...	Lev 26:43
because that ye have d the LORD.......	Num 11:20
know the land which ye have d.........	Num 14:31
Because he hath d the word of the....	Num 15:31
this the people that thou hast d........	Judg 9:38
And they d him, and brought him no..	1Sa 10:27
and she d him in her heart...............	2Sa 6:16
Wherefore hast thou d the...............	2Sa 12:9
because thou hast d me, and hast......	2Sa 12:10
the daughter of Zion hath d thee......	2Kin 19:21
and she d him in her heart...............	1Chr 15:29
d his words, and misused his...........	2Chr 36:16
d us, and said, What is this thing......	Neh 2:19
for we are d...........................	Neh 4:4
d in the thought of him that is.........	Job 12:5
Yea, young children d me...............	Job 19:18
of men, and d of the people............	Ps 22:6
For he hath not d nor abhorred........	Ps 22:24
to shame, because God hath d them...	Ps 53:5
they d the pleasant land, they.........	Ps 106:24
I am small and d.......................	Ps 119:141
they d all my reproof....................	Prov 1:30
and my heart d reproof..................	Prov 5:12
is of a perverse heart shall be d.......	Prov 12:8
He that is d, and hath a servant,.......	Prov 12:9
the poor man's wisdom is d.............	Eccl 9:16
yea, I should not be d....................	Song 8:1
d the word of the Holy One of.........	Is 5:24
he hath d the cities, he.................	Is 33:8
the daughter of Zion, hath d thee......	Is 37:22
He is d and rejected of men.............	Is 53:3
he was d, and we esteemed him not..	Is 53:3
all they that d thee shall bow..........	Is 60:14
this man Coniah a d broken idol........	Jer 22:28
thus they have d my people.............	Jer 33:24
and d among men.......................	Jer 49:15
hath d in the indignation of his........	Lam 2:6
which hast d the oath in breaking.....	Eze 16:59
made him king, whose oath he d........	Eze 17:16
Seeing he d the oath by breaking.....	Eze 17:18
surely mine oath that he hath d........	Eze 17:19
they d my judgments, which if a.......	Eze 20:13
Because they d my judgments..........	Eze 20:16
but had d my statutes, and had........	Eze 20:24
Thou hast d mine holy things, and....	Eze 22:8
are round about them, that d them....	Eze 28:24
because they have d the law of........	Amos 2:4
thou art greatly d......................	Obad 2
For who hath d the day of small.......	Zec 4:10
say, Wherein have we d thy name.....	Mal 1:6
they were righteous, and d others.....	Lk 18:9
great goddess Diana should be d.......	Acts 19:27
the world, and things which are d......	1Cor 1:28
ye are honourable, but we are d........	1Cor 4:10
which was in my flesh ye d not........	Gal 4:14
He that d Moses' law died without....	Heb 10:28
But ye have d the poor.................	Jas 2:6

DESPISERS

Behold, ye d, and wonder, and.........	Acts 13:41
of those that are good,..................	2Ti 3:3

DESPISEST

Or d thou the riches of his..............	Rom 2:4

DESPISETH

God is mighty, and d not any...........	Job 36:5
the poor, and d not his prisoners......	Ps 69:33
is void of wisdom d his neighbour....	Prov 11:12
Whoso d the word shall be.............	Prov 13:13
is perverse in his ways d him..........	Prov 14:2
He that d his neighbour sinneth........	Prov 14:21
A fool d his father's instruction........	Prov 15:5
but a foolish man d his mother.........	Prov 15:20
instruction d his own soul..............	Prov 15:32
but he that d his ways shall die........	Prov 19:16
d to obey his mother, the ravens......	Prov 30:17
the that d the gain of oppressions.....	Is 33:15
his Holy One, to him whom man d.....	Is 49:7
he that d you d me......................	Lk 10:16
d me d him that sent me.................	Lk 10:16
He therefore that d, d not man.........	1Th 4:8

DESPISING

of the shame, and is set down at.......	Heb 12:2

DESPITE

thy d against the land of Israel.........	Eze 25:6
hath done d unto the Spirit of..........	Heb 10:29

DESPITEFUL

taken vengeance with a d heart........	Eze 25:15
with d minds, to cast it out for........	Eze 36:5
Backbiters, haters of God, d............	Rom 1:30

DESPITEFULLY

and pray for them which d use you....	Mt 5:44
and pray for them which d use you....	Lk 6:28
with their rulers, to use them d........	Acts 14:5

DESTITUTE

who hath not left d my master of......	Gen 24:27
will regard the prayer of the d.........	Ps 102:17
leave not my soul d.....................	Ps 141:8
is joy to him that is d of wisdom......	Prov 15:21
the country shall be d of that..........	Eze 32:15
d of the truth, supposing that..........	1Ti 6:5
being d, afflicted, tormented..........	Heb 11:37

be naked, and d of daily food,.........	Jas 2:15

DESTROY

I will d man whom I have created......	Gen 6:7
I will d them with the earth.............	Gen 6:13
to d all flesh, wherein is the...........	Gen 6:17
that I have made will I d from..........	Gen 7:4
more be a flood to d the earth.........	Gen 9:11
become a flood to d all flesh...........	Gen 9:15
Wilt thou also d the righteous.........	Gen 18:23
wilt thou also d and not spare the.....	Gen 18:24
wilt thou d all the city for lack........	Gen 18:28
forty and five, I will not d it...........	Gen 18:28
I will not d it for twenty's sake.......	Gen 18:31
I will not d it for ten's sake...........	Gen 18:32
For we will d this place, because......	Gen 19:13
and the LORD hath sent us to d it......	Gen 19:13
for the LORD will d this city............	Gen 19:14
to d the frogs from thee and thy.......	Ex 8:9
shalt not be upon you to d you........	Ex 12:13
my sword, my hand shall d them.......	Ex 15:9
will d all the people to whom..........	Ex 23:27
But ye shall d their altars..............	Ex 34:13
the same soul will I d from among.....	Lev 23:30
d your cattle, and make you few in....	Lev 26:22
I will d your high places, and cut.....	Lev 26:30
to d them utterly, and to break my....	Lev 26:44
I will utterly d their cities.............	Num 21:2
d all the children of Sheth.............	Num 24:17
shall d him that remaineth of the......	Num 24:19
ye shall d all this people...............	Num 32:15
d all their pictures, and d.............	Num 33:52
the hand of the Amorites, to d us.....	Deut 1:27
to d them from among the host,.......	Deut 2:15
not forsake thee, neither d thee.......	Deut 4:31
d thee from off the face of the.........	Deut 6:15
smite them, and utterly d them........	Deut 7:2
against you, and d them suddenly.....	Deut 7:4
ye shall d their altars, and break......	Deut 7:5
hate him to their face, to d them......	Deut 7:10
shall d them with a mighty.............	Deut 7:23
thou shalt d their name from...........	Deut 7:24
a consuming fire he shall d them......	Deut 9:3
d them quickly, as the LORD hath.....	Deut 9:3
Let me alone, that I may d them.......	Deut 9:14
was wroth against you to d you........	Deut 9:19
the LORD had said he would d you....	Deut 9:25
d not thy people and thine..............	Deut 9:26
and the LORD would not d thee........	Deut 10:10
Ye shall utterly d all the places.......	Deut 12:2
d the names of them out of that........	Deut 12:3
But thou shalt utterly d them..........	Deut 20:17
thou shalt not d the trees..............	Deut 20:19
not trees for meat, thou shalt d........	Deut 20:20
will rejoice over you to d you..........	Deut 28:63
he will d these nations from...........	Deut 31:3
shall d both the young man and the...	Deut 32:25
and shall say, D them..................	Deut 33:27
the hand of the Amorites, to d us.....	Josh 7:7
except ye d the accursed from.........	Josh 7:12
to d all the inhabitants of..............	Josh 9:24
that he might d them utterly...........	Josh 11:20
favour, but that he might d them......	Josh 11:20
to d the land wherein the..............	Josh 22:33
entered into the land to d it............	Judg 6:5
do, Ye shall utterly d every male......	Judg 21:11
utterly d all that they have, and.......	1Sa 15:3
lest I d you with them..................	1Sa 15:6
good, and would not utterly d them...	1Sa 15:9
utterly d the sinners the...............	1Sa 15:18
to d the city for my sake...............	1Sa 23:10
that thou wilt not d my name out......	1Sa 24:21
David said to Abishai, D him not......	1Sa 26:9
people in to d the king thy lord.......	1Sa 26:15
hand to d the LORD's anointed.........	2Sa 1:14
and we will d the heir also.............	2Sa 14:7
revengers of blood to d any more.....	2Sa 14:11
lest they d my son....................	2Sa 14:11
hand of the man that would d me......	2Sa 14:16
thou seekest to d a city and a.........	2Sa 20:19
me, that I should swallow up or d.....	2Sa 20:20
that I might d them that hate me......	2Sa 22:41
his hand upon Jerusalem to d it........	2Sa 24:16
also were not able utterly to d.........	1Kin 9:21
to d it from off the face of the........	1Kin 13:34
Thus did Zimri d all the house of......	1Kin 16:12
Yet the LORD would not d Judah......	2Kin 8:19
might d the worshippers of Baal.......	2Kin 10:19
and Jacob, and would not d them......	2Kin 13:23
to d it, as the LORD......................	2Kin 18:25
LORD against this place to d it........	2Kin 18:25
Go up against this land, and d it.......	2Kin 18:25
sent them against Judah to d it........	2Kin 24:2
an angel unto Jerusalem to d it........	1Chr 21:15
therefore I will not d them.............	2Chr 12:7
he would not d him altogether.........	2Chr 12:12
Seir, utterly to slay and d them........	2Chr 20:23
every one helped to d another.........	2Chr 20:23
would not of the house of David.......	2Chr 21:7
Joash had determined to d thee.......	2Chr 25:16
is with me, that he d thee not..........	2Chr 35:21
name to dwell there d all kings........	Ezr 6:12
to d this house of God which is........	Ezr 6:12
to d all the Jews that were.............	Est 3:6
for the Jews, to d them.................	Est 4:7
was given at Shushan to d them.......	Est 4:8
which he wrote to d the Jews..........	Est 8:5
and to stand for their life, to d........	Est 8:11
against the Jews to d them.............	Est 9:24
to consume them, and to d them.......	Est 9:24
him, to d him without cause...........	Job 2:3

that it would please God to *d* me .... Job 6:9
If he *d* him from his place, then .... Job 8:18
.... Job 10:8
after my skin worms *d* this body .... Job 19:26
Thou shalt *d* them that speak .... Ps 5:6
D thou them, O God .... Ps 5:10
that I might *d* them that hate me .... Ps 18:40
fruit shalt thou *d* from the earth .... Ps 21:10
of his hands, he shall *d* them .... Ps 28:5
that seek after my soul to *d* it .... Ps 40:14
shall likewise *d* thee for ever .... Ps 52:5
D, O Lord, and divide their .... Ps 55:9
those that seek my soul, to *d* it .... Ps 63:9
they that would *d* me, being mine .... Ps 69:4
hearts, Let us *d* them together .... Ps 74:8
I will early *d* all the wicked of .... Ps 101:8
he said that he would *d* them .... Ps 106:23
his wrath, lest he should *d* them .... Ps 106:23
They did not *d* the nations .... Ps 106:34
name of the Lord I will *d* them .... Ps 118:10
name of the Lord I will *d* them .... Ps 118:11
name of the Lord I will *d* them .... Ps 118:12
wicked have waited for me to *d* me .... Ps 119:95
d all them that afflict my soul .... Ps 143:12
shoot out thine arrows, and *d* them .... Ps 144:6
but all the wicked will he *d* .... Ps 145:20
prosperity of fools shall *d* them .... Prov 1:32
of transgressors shall *d* them .... Prov 11:3
The Lord will *d* the house of the .... Prov 15:25
of the wicked shall *d* them .... Prov 21:7
d the work of thine hands .... Eccl 5:6
why shouldest thou *d* thyself .... Eccl 7:16
to err, and *d* the way of thy paths .... Is 3:12
but it is in his heart to *d* .... Is 10:7
nor *d* in all my holy mountain .... Is 11:9
the Lord shall utterly *d* the .... Is 11:15
indignation, to *d* the whole land .... Is 13:5
he shall *d* the sinners thereof .... Is 13:9
I will *d* the counsel thereof .... Is 19:3
to *d* the strong holds thereof .... Is 23:11
he will *d* in this mountain the .... Is 25:7
to *d* the poor with lying words .... Is 32:7
Gold against this land to *d* it .... Is 36:10
Go up against this land, and *d* it .... Is 36:10
I will *d* and devour at once .... Is 42:14
as if he were ready to *d* .... Is 51:13
and I have created the waster to *d* .... Is 54:16
cluster, and one saith, *D* it not .... Is 65:8
sakes, that I may not *d* them all .... Is 65:8
nor *d* in all my holy mountain .... Is 65:25
out, and to pull down, and to *d* .... Jer 1:10
Go ye up upon her walls, and *d* .... Jer 5:10
by night, and let us *d* her palaces .... Jer 6:5
Let us *d* the tree with the fruit .... Jer 11:19
d that nation, saith the Lord .... Jer 12:17
spare, nor have mercy, but *d* them .... Jer 13:14
of the earth, to devour and *d* .... Jer 15:3
my hand against thee, and *d* thee .... Jer 15:6
I will *d* my people, since they .... Jer 15:7
d them with double destruction .... Jer 17:18
up, and to pull down, and to *d* .... Jer 18:7
Woe be unto the pastors that *d* .... Jer 23:1
about, and will utterly *d* them .... Jer 25:9
down, and to throw down, and to *d* .... Jer 31:28
d this land, and shall cause to .... Jer 36:29
I will *d* the city and the .... Jer 46:8
he shall *d* thy strong holds .... Jer 48:18
they will *d* till they have enough .... Jer 49:9
will *d* from thence the king and .... Jer 49:38
utterly *d* after them, saith the .... Jer 50:21
her up as heaps, and *d* her utterly .... Jer 50:26
d ye utterly all her host .... Jer 51:3
is against Babylon, to *d* it .... Jer 51:11
and with thee will I *d* kingdoms .... Jer 51:20
The Lord hath purposed to *d* the .... Lam 2:8
d them in anger from under the .... Lam 3:66
and which I will send to *d* you .... Eze 5:16
I will *d* your high places .... Eze 6:3
wilt thou *d* all the residue of .... Eze 9:8
will *d* him from the midst of my .... Eze 14:9
of brutish men, and skilful to *d* .... Eze 21:31
to *d* souls, to get dishonest gain .... Eze 22:27
the land, that I should not *d* it .... Eze 22:30
I will *d* thee .... Eze 25:7
to *d* it for the old hatred .... Eze 25:15
the remnant of the sea coast .... Eze 25:16
they shall *d* the walls of Tyrus .... Eze 26:4
walls, and *d* thy pleasant houses .... Eze 26:12
and I will *d* thee, O covering .... Eze 28:16
shall be brought to *d* the land .... Eze 30:11
I will also *d* the idols, and I .... Eze 30:13
I will *d* also all the beasts .... Eze 32:13
but I will *d* the fat and the .... Eze 34:16
I saw when I came to *d* the city .... Eze 43:3
commanded to *d* all the wise men .... Dan 2:24
to *d* the wise men of Babylon .... Dan 2:24
D not the wise men of Babylon .... Dan 2:24
Hew the tree down, and *d* it .... Dan 4:23
consume and to *d* it unto the end .... Dan 7:26
he shall *d* wonderfully, and shall .... Dan 8:24
shall *d* the mighty and the holy .... Dan 8:24
heart, and by peace shall *d* many .... Dan 8:25
that shall come shall *d* the city .... Dan 9:26
portion of his meat shall *d* him .... Dan 11:26
go forth with great fury to *d* .... Dan 11:44
I will *d* her vines and her fig .... Hos 2:12
the night, and I will *d* thy mother .... Hos 4:5
I will not return to *d* Ephraim .... Hos 11:9
I will *d* it from off the face of .... Amos 9:8
not utterly *d* the house of Jacob .... Amos 9:8

even the wise men out of Edom, ... Obad 8
it is polluted, it shall *d* you .... Mic 2:10
of thee, and I will *d* thy chariots .... Mic 5:10
so will I *d* thy cities .... Mic 5:14
Philistines, I will even *d* thee .... Zeph 2:5
against the north, and *d* Assyria .... Zeph 2:13
I will *d* the strength of the .... Hag 2:22
that I will seek to *d* all the .... Zec 12:9
he shall not *d* the fruits of your .... Mal 3:11
seek the young child to *d* him .... Mt 2:13
not that I am come to *d* the law .... Mt 5:17
I am not come to *d*, but to fulfil .... Mt 5:17
him which is able to *d* both soul .... Mt 10:28
against him, how they might *d* him .... Mt 12:14
will miserably *d* those wicked men .... Mt 21:41
I am able to *d* the temple of God .... Mt 26:61
should ask Barabbas, and *d* Jesus .... Mt 27:20
art thou come to *d* us .... Mk 1:24
against him, how they might *d* him .... Mk 3:6
and into the waters, to *d* him .... Mk 9:22
and sought how they might *d* him .... Mk 11:18
the husbandmen, and *d* the .... Mk 12:9
I will *d* this temple that is made .... Mk 14:58
art thou come to *d* us .... Lk 4:34
to save life, or to *d* it .... Lk 6:9
man is not come to *d* men's lives .... Lk 9:56
of the people sought to *d* him .... Lk 19:47
d these husbandmen, and shall give .... Lk 20:16
D this temple, and in three days I .... Jn 2:19
for to steal, and to kill, and to *d* .... Jn 10:10
of Nazareth shall *d* this place .... Acts 6:14
D not him with thy meat, for whom .... Rom 14:15
For meat *d* not the work of God .... Rom 14:20
I will *d* the wisdom of the wise 1Cor 1:19
temple of God, him shall God *d* 1Cor 3:17
but God shall *d* both it and them 1Cor 6:13
shall *d* with the brightness of 2Th 2:8
that through death he might *d* him .... Heb 2:14
who is able to save and to *d* .... Jas 4:12
that he might *d* the works of the 1Jn 3:8
d them which *d* the earth .... Rev 11:18

DESTROYED

every living substance was *d* .... Gen 7:23
they were *d* from the earth .... Gen 7:23
where, before the Lord *d* Sodom .... Gen 13:10
when God *d* the cities of the .... Gen 19:29
and I shall be *d*, I and my house .... Gen 34:30
thou not yet that Egypt is *d* .... Ex 10:7
Lord only, he shall be utterly *d* .... Ex 22:20
and they utterly *d* them and their .... Num 21:3
d you in Seir, even unto Hormah .... Deut 1:44
when they had *d* them from before .... Deut 2:12
but the Lord *d* them before them .... Deut 2:21
when he *d* the Horims from before .... Deut 2:22
d them, and dwelt in their stead .... Deut 2:23
that time, and utterly *d* the men .... Deut 2:34
And we utterly *d* them, as we did .... Deut 3:6
God hath *d* them from among you .... Deut 4:3
upon it, but shall utterly be *d* .... Deut 4:26
hide themselves from thee, be *d* .... Deut 7:20
destruction, until they be *d* .... Deut 7:23
thee, until thou have *d* them .... Deut 7:24
was angry with you to have *d* you .... Deut 9:8
angry with Aaron to have *d* him .... Deut 9:20
how the Lord hath *d* them unto .... Deut 11:4
that they be *d* from before thee .... Deut 12:30
unto for to do, until thou be *d* .... Deut 28:20
down upon thee, until thou be *d* .... Deut 28:24
and overtake thee, till thou be *d* .... Deut 28:45
thy neck, until he have *d* thee .... Deut 28:48
of thy land, until thou be *d* .... Deut 28:51
thy sheep, until he have *d* thee .... Deut 28:51
bring upon thee, until thou be *d* .... Deut 28:61
unto the land of them, whom he *d* .... Deut 31:4
Sihon and Og, whom ye utterly *d* .... Josh 2:10
they utterly *d* all that was in .... Josh 6:21
until he had utterly *d* all the .... Josh 8:26
had taken Ai, and had utterly *d* it .... Josh 10:1
and the king thereof he utterly *d* .... Josh 10:28
therein he utterly *d* that day .... Josh 10:35
but *d* it utterly, and all the .... Josh 10:37
utterly *d* all the souls there .... Josh 10:39
but utterly *d* all that breathed .... Josh 10:40
the sword, and he utterly *d* them .... Josh 11:12
the sword, until they had *d* them .... Josh 11:14
Joshua them utterly with their .... Josh 11:21
until he have *d* you from off this .... Josh 23:15
and I *d* them from before you .... Josh 24:8
Zephath, and utterly *d* it .... Judg 1:17
until they had *d* Jabin king of .... Judg 4:24
the increase of the earth, till .... Judg 6:4
d down to the ground of the .... Judg 20:21
d down to the ground of the .... Judg 20:25
the children of Israel *d* of the .... Judg 20:35
they *d* in the midst of them .... Judg 20:42
the women are *d* out of Benjamin .... Judg 21:16
a tribe be not *d* out of Israel .... Judg 21:17
he *d* them, and smote them with 1Sa 5:6
utterly *d* all the people with the 1Sa 15:8
and refuse, that they *d* utterly 1Sa 15:9
and the rest we have utterly *d* 1Sa 15:15
have utterly *d* the Amalekites 1Sa 15:20
which should have been utterly *d* 1Sa 15:21
they of the children of Ammon, and 2Sa 11:1
be *d* from remaining in any of the 2Sa 21:5
pursued mine enemies, and *d* them 2Sa 22:38
to the angel that *d* the people 2Sa 24:16
Asa *d* her idol, and burnt it by 1Kin 15:13
that breathed, until he had *d* him 1Kin 15:29
in Samaria, till he had *d* him 2Kin 10:17

Thus Jehu *d* Baal out of Israel 2Kin 10:28
she arose and *d* all the seed royal 2Kin 11:1
for the king of Syria had *d* them 2Kin 13:7
them which my fathers have *d* 2Kin 19:12
of Assyria have *d* the nations 2Kin 19:17
therefore they have *d* them 2Kin 19:18
which Hezekiah his father had *d* 2Kin 21:3
before the children of Israel 2Kin 21:9
d them utterly unto this day, and 1Chr 4:41
the land, whom God *d* before them 1Chr 5:25
and Joab *d* all the country of 1Chr 20:1
months to be *d* before thy foes 1Chr 21:12
evil, and said to the angel that *d* 1Chr 21:15
for they were *d* before the Lord 2Chr 14:13
And nation was *d* of nation 2Chr 15:6
turned from them, and *d* them not 2Chr 20:10
d all the seed royal of the house 2Chr 22:10
d all the princes of the people 2Chr 24:23
until they had utterly *d* them all 2Chr 31:1
nations that my fathers utterly *d* 2Chr 32:14
whom the Lord had *d* before the 2Chr 33:9
which the kings of Judah had *d* 2Chr 34:11
d all the goodly vessels thereof 2Chr 36:19
for which cause was this city *d* .... Ezr 4:15
who *d* this house, and carried the .... Ezr 5:12
it be written that they may be *d* .... Est 3:9
and thy father's house shall be *d* .... Est 4:14
are sold, I and my people, to be *d* .... Est 7:4
Jews slew and *d* five hundred men .... Est 9:6
d five hundred men in Shushan the .... Est 9:12
They are *d* from morning to .... Job 4:20
He hath *d* me on every side, and I .... Job 19:10
in the night, so that they are *d* .... Job 34:25
thou hast *d* the wicked, thou hast .... Ps 9:5
and thou hast *d* cities .... Ps 9:6
If the foundations be *d*, what can .... Ps 11:3
transgressors shall be *d* together .... Ps 37:38
thou hast *d* all them that go a .... Ps 73:27
their iniquity, and *d* them not .... Ps 78:38
and frogs, which *d* them .... Ps 78:45
He of their vines with hail, and .... Ps 78:47
is that they shall be *d* for ever .... Ps 92:7
of Babylon, who art to be *d* .... Ps 137:8
despiseth the word shall be *d* .... Prov 13:13
a companion of fools shall be *d* .... Prov 13:20
is that is *d* for want of judgment .... Prov 13:23
his neck, shall suddenly be *d* .... Prov 29:1
they that are led of them are *d* .... Is 9:16
the yoke shall be *d* because of .... Is 10:27
and *d* the cities thereof .... Is 14:17
because thou hast *d* thy land .... Is 14:20
d them, and made all their memory .... Is 26:14
he hath utterly *d* them, he hath .... Is 34:2
them which my fathers have *d* .... Is 37:12
therefore they have *d* them .... Is 37:19
been cut off nor *d* from before me .... Is 48:19
Many castors have *d* my vineyard .... Jer 12:10
for all thy lovers are *d* .... Jer 22:20
Moab is *d* .... Jer 48:4
perish, and the plain shall be *d* .... Jer 48:8
Moab shall be *d* from being a .... Jer 48:42
Babylon is suddenly fallen and *d* .... Jer 51:8
Yet *d* I the Amorite before them .... Amos 2:9
yet I *d* his fruit from above, and .... Amos 2:9
their cities are *d*, so that there .... Zeph 3:6
of those murderers, and burned up .... Mt 22:7
and the flood came, and *d* them all .... Lk 17:27
from heaven, and *d* them all .... Lk 17:29
shall be *d* from among the people .... Acts 3:23
Is not this he that *d* them which .... Acts 9:21
when he had *d* seven nations in .... Acts 13:19
and her magnificence should be *d* .... Acts 19:27
that the body of sin might be *d* .... Rom 6:6
tempted, and were *d* of serpents 1Cor 10:9
and were *d* of the destroyer 1Cor 10:10
enemy that shall be *d* is death 1Cor 15:26
cast down, but not *d* 2Cor 4:9
the faith which once he *d* .... Gal 1:23
build again the things which I *d* .... Gal 2:18
lest he that *d* the firstborn .... Heb 11:28
beasts, made to be taken and *d* 2Pet 2:12
afterward *d* them that believed .... Jude 5
third part of the ships were *d* .... Rev 8:9

DESTROYER

will not suffer the *d* to come in .... Ex 12:23
the *d* of our country, which slew .... Judg 16:24
in prosperity the *d* shall come .... Job 15:21
kept me from the paths of the *d* .... Ps 17:4
the same is the companion of a *d* .... Prov 28:24
the *d* of the Gentiles is on his .... Jer 4:7
and were destroyed of the *d* 1Cor 10:10

DESTROYERS

the grave, and his life to the *d* .... Job 33:22
thy *d* and they that made thee .... Is 49:17

DESTROYEST

And I will prepare d against thee.......... Jer 22:7
O ye d of mine heritage, because .... Jer 50:11

DESTROYED

and thou of the hope of man .... Job 14:19
the LORD, which d all the earth .... Jer 51:25
Thou that d the temple, and .... Mt 27:40
thou that d the temple, and .... Mk 15:29

DESTROYETH

which the LORD d before your face ...... Deut 8:20
He d the perfect and the wicked........... Job 9:22
increaseth the nations, and d them ..... Job 12:23
he that doeth it d his own soul............. Prov 6:32
with his mouth d his neighbour.......... Prov 11:9
thy ways to that which d kings............ Prov 31:3
and a gift d the heart .... Eccl 7:7
but one sinner d much good.................. Eccl 9:18

DESTROYING

of Heshbon, utterly d the men............. Deut 3:6
d it utterly, and all that is .... Deut 13:15
edge of the sword, utterly d them .... Josh 11:11
to all lands, by d them utterly 2Kin 19:11
land, and the angel of the LORD d 1Chr 21:12
and as he was d, the LORD beheld,...... 1Chr 21:15
a d atorm, as a flood of mighty .... Is 28:2
to all lands by d them utterly .... Is 37:11
your prophets, like a lion .... Jer 2:30
that rise up against me, a d wind....... Jer 51:1
O d mountain, saith the LORD,............ Jer 51:25
not withdrawn his hand from d .... Lam 2:8
man with his d weapon in his hand .... Eze 9:1
mine eye spared them from d of them.. Eze 20:17

DESTRUCTION

destroy them with a mighty d .... Deut 7:23
burning heat, and with bitter d .... Deut 32:24
the city with a very great d 1Sa 5:9
for there was a deadly d 1Sa 5:11
a man whom I appointed to utter d 1Kin 20:42
the death of his father to his d 2Chr 22:4
the d of Ahaziah was of God by........... 2Chr 22:7
his heart was lifted up to his d 2Chr 26:16
endure to see the d of my kindred...... Est 8:6
of the sword, and slaughter, and d ..... Est 9:5
be afraid of d when it cometh .... Job 5:21
At d and famine thou shalt laugh....... Job 5:22
d shall be ready at his side .... Job 18:12
how oft cometh their d upon them ..... Job 21:17
His eyes shall see his d, and he.......... Job 21:20
is reserved to the day of d .... Job 21:30
before him, and d hath no covering..... Job 26:6
D and death say, We have heard the... Job 28:22
up against me the ways of their d ...... Job 30:12
grave, though they cry in his d .... Job 30:24
Is not d to the wicked .... Job 31:3
it is a fire that consumeth to d .... Job 31:12
For d from God was a terror to me...... Job 31:23
at the d of him that hated me............. Job 31:29
Let d come upon him at unawares...... Ps 35:8
into that very d let him fall.................. Ps 35:8
bring them down into the pit of d ...... Ps 55:23
thou castedst them down into d .... Ps 73:18
or thy faithfulness in d........................ Ps 88:11
Thou turnest man to d .... Ps 90:3
nor for the d that wasteth at............... Ps 91:6
Who redeemeth thy life from d .... Ps 103:4
your d cometh as a whirlwind............. Prov 1:27
mouth of the foolish is near d .... Prov 10:14
the d of the poor is their .... Prov 10:15
but d shall be to the workers of .... Prov 10:29
wide his lips shall have d .... Prov 13:3
of people is the d of the prince .... Prov 14:28
Hell and d are before the LORD........... Prov 15:11
Pride goeth before d, and an .... Prov 16:18
that exalteth his gate seeketh d .... Prov 17:19
A fool's mouth is his d, and his.......... Prov 18:7
Before the heart of man is .... Prov 18:12
but d shall be to the workers of .... Prov 21:15
For their heart studieth d .... Prov 24:2
Hell and d are never full .... Prov 27:20
of all such as are appointed to d......... Prov 31:8
the d of the transgressors and of .... Is 1:28
cease, and mine anger in their d .... Is 10:25
come as a d from the Almighty .... Is 13:6
will sweep it with the besom of d .... Is 14:23
they shall raise up a cry of d .... Is 15:5
shall be called, The city of d .... Is 19:18
and the gate is smitten with d .... Is 24:12
places, and the land of thy d .... Is 49:19
desolation, and d, and the famine,..... Is 51:19
wasting and d are in their paths......... Is 59:7
wasting nor d within thy borders .... Is 60:18
evil from the north, and a great d....... Jer 4:6
D upon d is cried .... Jer 4:20
out of the north, and great d............... Jer 6:1
and destroy them with double d .... Jer 17:18
a very fair heifer, but d cometh .... Jer 46:20
Horonaim, spoiling and great d.......... Jer 48:3
the enemies have heard a cry of d ...... Jer 48:5
is in the land, and of great d .... Jer 50:22
great d from the land of the .... Jer 51:54
for the d of the daughter of my .... Lam 2:11
is come upon us, desolation and d ...... Lam 3:47
d of the daughter of my people........... Lam 3:48
they were their meat in the d of .... Lam 4:10
which shall be for their d .... Eze 5:16
D cometh; and they shall seek............ Eze 7:25
bring thy d among the nations .... Eze 32:9
fled from me: d unto them.................. Hos 7:13
lo, they are gone because of d .... Hos 9:6
O grave, I will be thy d .... Hos 13:14

as a d from the Almighty shall it......... Joel 1:15
of Judah in the day of their d.............. Obad 12
destroy you, even with a sore d .... Mic 2:10
and there shall be no more utter d ..... Zec 14:11
is the way, that leadeth to d................ Mt 7:13
D and misery are in their ways........... Rom 3:16
the vessels of wrath fitted to d .... Rom 9:22
unto Satan for the d of the flesh......... 1Cor 5:5
edification, and not for your d 2Cor 10:8
me to edification, and not to d............ 2Cor 13:10
Whose end is d, whose God is............. Phil 3:19
then sudden d cometh upon them,..... 1Th 5:3
be punished with everlasting d 2Th 1:9
lusts, which drown men in d 1Ti 6:9
and bring upon themselves swift d..... 2Pet 2:1
scriptures, unto their own d 2Pet 3:16

DESTRUCTIONS

d are come to a perpetual end.............. Ps 9:6
rescue my soul from their d .... Ps 35:17
and delivered them from their d .... Ps 107:20

DETAIN

LORD, I pray thee, let us d thee .... Judg 13:15
unto Manoah, Though thou d me....... Judg 13:16

DETAINED

there that day, d before the LORD 1Sa 21:7

DETERMINATE

being delivered by the d counsel......... Acts 2:23

DETERMINATION

for my d is to gather the nations .... Zeph 3:8

DETERMINE

and he shall pay as the judges d .... Ex 21:22

DETERMINED

be sure that evil is d by him 1Sa 20:7
d by my father to come upon thee....... 1Sa 20:9
Jonathan knew that it was d of 1Sa 20:33
for evil is d against our master,.......... 1Sa 25:17
of Absalom this hath been d from....... 2Sa 13:32
Solomon d to build an house for 2Chr 2:1
that God hath d to destroy thee.......... 2Chr 25:16
evil d against him by the king .... Est 7:7
Seeing his days are d, the number ..... Job 14:5
shalt make a consumption, even d ..... Is 10:23
hosts, which he hath d against it........ Is 28:22
even d upon the whole earth.............. Is 28:22
weeks are d upon thy people.............. Dan 9:24
end of the war desolations are d .... Dan 9:26
that d shall be poured upon the .... Dan 9:27
for that that is d shall be done........... Dan 11:36
the Son of man goeth, as it was d ...... Lk 22:22
when he was d to let him go .... Acts 3:13
thy counsel d before to be done.......... Acts 4:28
d to send relief unto the .... Acts 11:29
they d that Paul and Barnabas, and... Acts 15:2
Barnabas d to take with them John.... Acts 15:37
hath d the times before appointed..... Acts 17:26
it shall be d in a lawful...................... Acts 19:39
For Paul had d to sail by Ephesus....... Acts 20:16
to Augustus, I have d to send him...... Acts 25:25
when it was d that we should sail....... Acts 27:1
For I d not to know any thing 1Cor 2:2
But I d this with myself, that I............ 2Cor 2:1
for I have d there to winter .... Titus 3:12

DETEST

but thou shalt utterly d it .... Deut 7:26

DETESTABLE

with the carcases of their d .... Jer 16:18
sanctuary with all thy d things........... Eze 5:11
of their d things therein...................... Eze 7:20
away all the d things thereof.............. Eze 11:18
after the heart of their d things.......... Eze 11:21
idols, nor with their d things............. Eze 37:23

DEUEL (de-oo'-el) See REUEL, *Father of
Eliasaph.*

Eliasaph the son of D........................... Num 1:14
sixth day Eliasaph the son of D........... Num 7:42
offering of Eliasaph the son of D .... Num 7:47
of Gad was Eliasaph the son of D .... Num 10:20

DEVICE

to find out every d which shall 2Chr 2:14
his d that he had devised against .... Est 8:3
by letters that his wicked d .... Est 9:25
they imagined a mischievous d .... Ps 21:11
further not his wicked d .... Ps 140:8
for there is no work, nor d .... Eccl 9:10
you, and devise a d against you.......... Jer 18:11
for his d is against Babylon, to........... Jer 51:11
Lament after the manner of the.......... Lam 3:62
stone, graven by art and man's d .... Acts 17:29

DEVICES

disappointeth the d of the crafty .... Job 5:12
the d which ye wrongfully imagine..... Job 21:27
in the d that they have imagined....... Ps 10:2
the hearts of d of the people .... Ps 33:10
man who bringeth wicked d to pass ... Ps 37:7
and be filled with their own d .... Prov 1:31
a man of wicked d will he condemn.... Prov 12:2
and a man of wicked d is hated .... Prov 14:17
There are many d in a man's heart..... Prov 19:21
he deviseth wicked d to destroy .... Is 32:7
they had devised d against me .... Jer 18:18
but we will walk after our own d .... Jer 18:12
let us devise d against Jeremiah........ Jer 18:18
he shall forecast his d against .... Dan 11:24
they shall forecast d against him....... Dan 11:25
for we are not ignorant of his d.......... 2Cor 2:11

DEVIL

wilderness to be tempted of the d .... Mt 4:1
Then the d taketh him up into the ...... Mt 4:5
the d taketh him up into an .... Mt 4:8
Then the d leaveth him, and,.............. Mt 4:11
him a dumb man possessed with a d .. Mt 9:32
when the d was cast out, the dumb .... Mt 9:33
and they say, He hath a d .... Mt 11:18
unto him one possessed with a d .... Mt 12:22
enemy that sowed them is the d .... Mt 13:39
is grievously vexed with a d................ Mt 15:22
And Jesus rebuked the d...................... Mt 17:18
fire, prepared for the d and his .... Mt 25:41
him that was possessed with the d ..... Mk 5:15
him that was possessed with the d ..... Mk 5:16
the d prayed him that he might be...... Mk 5:18
forth the d out of her daughter .... Mk 7:26
the d is gone out of thy daughter .... Mk 7:29
house, she found the d gone out .... Mk 7:30
Being forty days tempted of the d ...... Lk 4:2
the d said unto him, If thou be........... Lk 4:3
And the d, taking him up into an .... Lk 4:5
the d said unto him, All this,.............. Lk 4:6
when the d had ended all his .... Lk 4:13
had a spirit of an unclean d............... Lk 4:33
when the d had thrown him in the..... Lk 4:35
and ye say, He hath a d .... Lk 7:33
then cometh the d, and taketh away .. Lk 8:12
was driven of the d into the .... Lk 8:29
the d threw him down, and tare him.. Lk 9:42
And he was casting out a d .... Lk 11:14
when the d was gone out, the dumb... Lk 11:14
you twelve, and one of you is a d .... Jn 6:70
answered and said, Thou hast a d ...... Jn 7:20
Ye are of your father the d .... Jn 8:44
thou art a Samaritan, and hast a d .... Jn 8:48
Jesus answered, I have not a d .... Jn 8:49
Now we know that thou hast a d .... Jn 8:52
And many of them said, He hath a d... Jn 10:20
the words of him that hath a d .... Jn 10:21
Can a d open the eyes of the............... Jn 10:21
the d having now put into the............. Jn 13:2
all that were oppressed of the d .... Acts 10:38
all mischief, thou child of the d .... Acts 13:10
Neither give place to the d .... Eph 4:27
stand against the wiles of the d .... Eph 6:11
into the condemnation of the d 1Ti 3:6
reproach and the snare of the d.......... 1Ti 3:7
out of the snare of the d 2Ti 2:26
power of death, that is, the d .... Heb 2:14
Resist the d, and he will flee............... Jas 4:7
because your adversary the d 1Pet 5:8
that committeth sin is of the d 1Jn 3:8
for the d sinneth from the 1Jn 3:8
might destroy the works of the d 1Jn 3:8
and the children of the d 1Jn 3:10
when contending with the d he .... Jude 9
the d shall cast some of you into .... Rev 2:10
that old serpent, called the D.............. Rev 12:9
for the d is come down unto you,........ Rev 12:12
that old serpent, which is the D.......... Rev 20:2
the d that deceived them was cast ...... Rev 20:10

DEVILISH

above, but is earthly, sensual, d......... Jas 3:15

DEVILS

offer their sacrifices unto d .... Lev 17:7
They sacrificed unto d, not to............. Deut 32:17
for the high places, and for the d 2Chr 11:15
sons and their daughters unto d .... Ps 106:37
those which were possessed with d ..... Mt 4:24
and in thy name have cast out d .... Mt 7:22
many that were possessed with d .... Mt 8:16
met him was possessed with d .... Mt 8:28
So the d besought him, saying, If .... Mt 8:31
to the possessed of the d .... Mt 8:33
He casteth out d through the .... Mt 9:34
through the prince of the d .... Mt 9:34
raise the dead, cast out d .... Mt 10:8
This fellow doth not cast out d .... Mt 12:24
by Beelzebub the prince of the d .... Mt 12:24
And if I by Beelzebub cast out d .... Mt 12:27
But if I cast out d by the Spirit........... Mt 12:28
them that were possessed with d .... Mk 1:32
diseases, and cast out many d .... Mk 1:34
and suffered not the d to speak.......... Mk 1:34
all Galilee, and cast out d .... Mk 1:39
heal sicknesses, and to cast out d ...... Mk 3:15
of the d casteth he out d .... Mk 3:22
all the d besought him, saying,........... Mk 5:12
And they cast out many d, and........... Mk 6:13
saw one casting out d in thy name ..... Mk 9:38
out of whom he had cast seven d .... Mk 16:9
In my name shall they cast out d........ Mk 16:17
d also came out of many, crying......... Lk 4:41
out of whom went seven d .... Lk 8:2
man, which had d long time................ Lk 8:27
because many d were entered into ..... Lk 8:30
Then went the d out of the man,........ Lk 8:33
out of whom the d were departed,...... Lk 8:35
was possessed of the d was healed ..... Lk 8:36
Now the man out of whom the d .... Lk 8:38
power and authority over all d............ Lk 9:1
saw one casting out d in thy name ..... Lk 9:49
even the d are subject unto us............ Lk 10:17
said, He casteth out d through .... Lk 11:15
Beelzebub the chief of the d .... Lk 11:15
I cast out d through Beelzebub .... Lk 11:19
And if I by Beelzebub cast out d .... Lk 11:19
with the finger of God cast out d........ Lk 11:20
that fox, Behold, I cast out d.............. Lk 13:32

sacrifice, they sacrifice to *d* 1Cor 10:20
ye should have fellowship with *d* 1Cor 10:20
cup of the Lord, and the cup of *d* 1Cor 10:21
table, and of the table of *d* 1Cor 10:21
spirits, and doctrines of *d* 1Ti 4:1
that also believe, and tremble .... Jas 2:19
that they should not worship *d* .... Rev 9:20
For they are the spirits of *d* .... Rev 16:14
and is become the habitation of *d* ...... Rev 18:2

DEVISE

To *d* cunning works, to work in .... Ex 31:4
to *d* curious works, to work in .... Ex 35:32
and of those that *d* cunning work .... Ex 35:35
yet doth he *d* means, that his 2Sa 14:14
to confusion that *d* my hurt .... Ps 35:4
but they *d* deceitful matters .... Ps 35:20
against me do they *d* my hurt .... Ps 41:7
D not evil against thy neighbour .... Prov 3:29
Do they not err that *d* evil .... Prov 14:22
shall he to them that *d* good .... Prov 14:22
his eyes to *d* froward things .... Prov 16:30
you, and a device against you .... Jer 18:11
let us *d* devices against Jeremiah .... Jer 18:18
these are the men that *d* mischief .... Eze 11:2
Woe to them that *d* iniquity .... Mic 2:1
this family do I *d* an evil .... Mic 2:3

DEVISED

that *d* against us that we should 2Sa 21:5
which he had *d* of his own heart 1Kin 12:33
had *d* against the Jews .... Est 8:3
d by Haman the son of Hammedatha .... Est 8:5
had *d* against the Jews, to destroy .... Est 9:24
which he *d* against the Jews .... Est 9:25
they *d* to take away my life .... Ps 31:13
they had *d* devices against me .... Jer 11:19
they have *d* evil against it .... Jer 48:2
for the Lord hath both *d* and done .... Jer 51:12
hath done that which he had *d* .... Lam 2:17
not followed cunningly *d* fables 2Pet 1:16

DEVISETH

He *d* mischief upon his bed .... Ps 36:4
Thy tongue *d* mischiefs .... Ps 52:2
he *d* mischief continually .... Prov 6:14
An heart that *d* wicked .... Prov 6:18
A man's heart *d* his way .... Prov 16:9
He that *d* to do evil shall be .... Prov 24:8
he *d* wicked devices to destroy .... Is 32:7
But the liberal *d* liberal things .... Is 32:8

DEVOTE

that a man shall *d* unto the Lord .... Lev 27:28

DEVOTED

holy unto the Lord, as a field *d* .... Lev 27:21
Notwithstanding no *d* thing .... Lev 27:28
every *d* thing is most holy unto .... Lev 27:28
None *d*, which shall be .... Lev 27:29
which shall be *d* of men .... Lev 27:29
Every thing *d* in Israel shall be .... Num 18:14
thy servant, who is *d* to thy fear .... Ps 119:38

DEVOTIONS

as I passed by, and beheld your *d* .... Acts 17:23

DEVOUR

the morning he shall *d* the prey .... Gen 49:27
blood, and my sword shall *d* flesh .... Deut 32:42
and of the cedars of Lebanon .... Judg 9:15
d the men of Shechem, and the .... Judg 9:20
house of Millo, and *d* Abimelech .... Judg 9:20
said, Shall the sword *d* for ever 2Sa 2:26
command the locusts to *d* the land 2Chr 7:13
It shall *d* the strength of his .... Job 18:13
of death shall *d* his strength .... Job 18:13
wrath, and the fire shall *d* them .... Ps 21:9
a fire shall *d* before him .... Ps 50:3
wild beast of the field doth *d* it .... Ps 80:13
to *d* the poor from off the earth .... Prov 30:14
strangers *d* it in your presence .... Is 1:7
they shall *d* Israel with open .... Is 9:12
it shall *d* the briers and thorns .... Is 9:18
d his thorns and his briers in one .... Is 10:17
of thine enemies shall *d* them .... Is 26:11
not of a mean man, shall *d* him .... Is 31:8
your breath, as fire, shall *d* you .... Is 33:11
I will destroy and *d* at once .... Is 42:14
ye beasts of the field, come to *d* .... Is 56:9
all that *d* him shall offend .... Jer 2:3
people wood, and it shall *d* them .... Jer 5:14
beasts of the field, come to *d* .... Jer 12:9
d from the one end of the land .... Jer 12:12
and the beasts of the earth, to *d* .... Jer 15:3
it shall *d* the palaces of .... Jer 17:27
it shall *d* all things round about .... Jer 21:14
that *d* thee shall be devoured .... Jer 30:16
and the sword shall *d*, and it shall ...... Jer 46:10
sword shall *d* round about the .... Jer 46:14
shall *d* the corner of Moab, and .... Jer 48:45
it shall *d* all round about him .... Jer 50:32
famine and pestilence shall *d* him .... Eze 7:15
and another fire shall *d* them .... Eze 15:7
it shall *d* every green tree in .... Eze 20:47
them through the fire, to *d* them .... Eze 23:37
midst of thee, it shall *d* thee .... Eze 28:18
the beast of the land *d* them .... Eze 34:28
thou shalt *d* men no more, neither ...... Eze 36:14
thus unto it, Arise, *d* much flesh .... Dan 7:5
shall *d* the whole earth, and shall .... Dan 7:23
now shall a month *d* them with .... Hos 5:7
it shall *d* the palaces thereof .... Hos 8:14

d them, because of their own .... Hos 11:6
there will I *d* them like a lion .... Hos 13:8
which shall *d* the palaces of .... Amos 1:4
which shall *d* the palaces thereof .... Amos 1:7
which shall *d* the palaces thereof .... Amos 1:10
which shall *d* the palaces of .... Amos 1:12
it shall *d* the palaces thereof .... Amos 1:14
it shall *d* the palaces of Kirioth .... Amos 2:2
it shall *d* the palaces of .... Amos 2:5
d it, and there be none to quench .... Amos 5:6
shall kindle in them, and *d* them .... Obad 18
the sword shall *d* thy young lions .... Nah 2:13
the fire shall *d* thy bars .... Nah 3:13
There shall the fire *d* thee .... Nah 3:15
was as to *d* the poor secretly .... Hab 3:14
and they shall *d*, and subdue with .... Zec 9:15
that the fire may *d* thy cedars .... Zec 11:1
they shall *d* all the people round .... Zec 12:6
for ye *d* widows' houses, and for a .... Mt 23:14
Which *d* widows' houses, and for a .... Mk 12:40
Which *d* widows' houses, and for a .... Lk 20:47
you into bondage, if a man *d* you 2Cor 11:20
d one another, take heed that ye .... Gal 5:15
which shall *d* the adversaries .... Heb 10:27
about, seeking whom he may *d* 1Pet 5:8
for to *d* her child as soon as it .... Rev 12:4

DEVOURED

hath quite *d* also our money .... Gen 31:15
say, Some evil beast hath *d* him .... Gen 37:20
an evil beast hath *d* him .... Gen 37:33
seven thin ears of the seven rank .... Gen 41:7
the thin ears of the seven good .... Gen 41:24
of them, and they died before the .... Lev 10:2
what time the fire *d* two hundred .... Num 26:10
from them, and they shall be *d* .... Deut 31:17
d with burning heat, and with .... Deut 32:24
the wood *d* more people that day 2Sa 18:8
people that day than the sword *d* 2Sa 18:8
and fire out *d* his mouth 2Sa 22:9
and fire out of his mouth .... Ps 18:8
of flies among them, which *d* them ...... Ps 78:45
For they have *d* Jacob, and laid .... Ps 79:7
d the fruit of their ground .... Ps 105:35
ye shall be *d* with the sword .... Is 1:20
hath the curse of the earth .... Is 24:6
own sword hath *d* your prophets .... Jer 2:30
For shame hath *d* the labour of .... Jer 3:24
have *d* the land, and all that is .... Jer 8:16
d him, and consumed him, and have .... Jer 10:25
they that devour thee shall be .... Jer 30:16
All that found them have *d* them .... Jer 50:7
the king of Assyria hath *d* him .... Jer 50:17
the king of Babylon hath *d* me .... Jer 51:34
it hath *d* the foundations thereof .... Lam 4:11
any work, when the fire hath *d* it .... Eze 15:5
thou sacrificed unto them to be *d* .... Eze 16:20
to catch the prey; it *d* men .... Eze 19:3
to catch the prey, and *d* men .... Eze 19:6
branches, which hath *d* her fruit .... Eze 19:14
they have *d* souls .... Eze 22:25
residue shall be *d* by the fire .... Eze 23:25
will I give to the beasts to be *d* .... Eze 33:27
the beasts of the field to be *d* .... Eze 39:4
it *d* and brake in pieces, and .... Dan 7:7
which *d*, brake in pieces, and .... Dan 7:19
an oven, and have *d* their judges .... Hos 7:7
Strangers have *d* his strength .... Hos 7:9
for the fire hath *d* the pastures .... Joel 1:19
the fire hath *d* the pastures of .... Joel 1:20
increased, the palmerworm *d* them ...... Amos 4:9
it the great deep, and did eat .... Amos 7:4
they shall be *d* as stubble fully .... Nah 1:10
be *d* by the fire of his jealousy .... Zeph 1:18
for all the earth shall be *d* with .... Zeph 3:8
and she shall be *d* with fire .... Zec 9:4
and the fowls came and *d* them up ...... Mt 13:4
fowls of the air came and *d* it up .... Mk 4:4
and the fowls of the air *d* it .... Lk 8:5
which hath *d* thy living with .... Lk 15:30
from God out of heaven, and *d* them .... Rev 20:9

DEVOURER

will rebuke the *d* for your sakes .... Mal 3:11

DEVOUREST

say unto you, Thou land *d* up men ...... Eze 36:13

DEVOURETH

for the sword of one as well as 2Sa 11:25
mouth of the wicked iniquity .... Prov 19:28
the man who *d* that which is holy .... Prov 20:25
as the fire *d* the stubble .... Is 5:24
flaming fire, which *d* round about .... Lam 2:3
the fire *d* both the ends of it, ... Eze 15:4
A fire *d* before them .... Joel 2:3
flame of fire that *d* the stubble .... Joel 2:5
thy tongue when the wicked *d* thee ...... Hab 1:13
their mouth, and *d* their enemies .... Rev 11:5

DEVOURING

the glory of the Lord was like a *d* .... Ex 24:17
Thou lovest all *d* words, O thou .... Ps 52:4
tempest, and the flame of *d* fire .... Is 29:6
and his tongue as a *d* fire .... Is 30:27
and with the flame of a *d* fire .... Is 30:30
us shall dwell with the *d* fire .... Is 33:14

DEVOUT

and the same man was just and .... Lk 2:25
d men, out of every nation under .... Acts 2:5
d men carried Stephen to his .... Acts 8:2
A man, and one that feared God .... Acts 10:2

DEW

God give thee of the *d* of heaven .... Gen 27:28
of the *d* of heaven from above .... Gen 27:39
in the morning the *d* lay round .... Ex 16:13
when the *d* that lay was gone up, ... Ex 16:14
when the *d* fell upon the camp in .... Num 11:9
my speech shall distil as the *d* .... Deut 32:2
things of heaven, for the *d* .... Deut 33:13
his heavens shall drop down *d* .... Deut 33:28
if the *d* be on the fleece only, ... Judg 6:37
wringed the *d* out of the fleece, ... Judg 6:38
all the ground let there be *d* .... Judg 6:39
there was *d* on all the ground .... Judg 6:40
of Gilboa, let there be no *d* 2Sa 1:21
as the *d* falleth on the ground 2Sa 17:12
there shall not be *d* nor rain 1Kin 17:1
the *d* lay all night upon my .... Job 29:19
who hath begotten the drops of *d* .... Job 38:28
thou hast the *d* of thy youth .... Ps 110:3
As the *d* of Hermon, and as the *d* ...... Ps 133:3
up, and the clouds drop down the *d* .... Prov 3:20
his favour is as *d* upon the grass .... Prov 19:12
for my head is filled with *d* .... Song 5:2
like a cloud of *d* in the heat of .... Is 18:4
for thy *d* is as the *d* of herbs, ... Is 26:19
it be wet with the *d* of heaven .... Dan 4:15
it be wet with the *d* of heaven .... Dan 4:23
wet thee with the *d* of heaven .... Dan 4:25
body was wet with the *d* of heaven ...... Dan 4:33
body was wet with the *d* of heaven ...... Dan 5:21
as the early *d* it goeth away .... Hos 6:4
as the early *d* that passeth away, ... Hos 13:3
I will be as the *d* unto Israel .... Hos 14:5
many people as a *d* from the Lord .... Mic 5:7
heaven over you is stayed from *d* .... Hag 1:10
and the heavens shall give their *d* .... Zec 8:12

DIADEM

my judgment was as a robe and a *d* .... Job 29:14
for a *d* of beauty, unto the .... Is 28:5
a royal *d* in the hand of thy God .... Is 62:3
thine head, and take off the .... Eze 21:26

DIAL

it had gone down in the *d* of Ahaz 2Kin 20:11
is gone down in the sun of Ahaz .... Is 38:8

DIAMOND

be an emerald, a sapphire, and a *d* ...... Ex 28:18
an emerald, a sapphire, and a *d*, ... Ex 39:11
of iron, and with the point of a *d* .... Jer 17:1
the sardius, topaz, and the *d* .... Eze 28:13

DIANA (di-an'-ah) A Greek goddess.

which made silver shrines for *D* .... Acts 19:24
goddess *D* should be despised .... Acts 19:27
Great is *D* of the Ephesians .... Acts 19:28
Great is *D* of the Ephesians .... Acts 19:34
worshipper of the great goddess *D* ...... Acts 19:35

DIBLAH See Diblath.

DIBLAIM (dib'-la-im) *Father of Gomer.*
and took Gomer the daughter of *D* ...... Hos 1:3

DIBLATH (dib'-lath) *A place in northern Canaan.*
than the wilderness toward *D* .... Eze 6:14

DIBON (di'-bon) See Dibon-gad, Dimon.
   1. *A Moabite city.*
Heshbon is perished even unto *D* .... Num 21:30
Ataroth, and *D*, and Jazer, and .... Num 32:3
And the children of Gad built *D* .... Num 32:34
He is gone up to Bajith, and to *D* .... Is 15:2
   2. *An undefined city.*
and all the plain of Medeba unto *D* ...... Josh 13:9
D, and Bamoth-baal, and .... Josh 13:17
Thou daughter that dost inhabit *D* .... Jer 48:18
And upon *D*, and upon Nebo .... Jer 48:22
   3. *A town in Judah.*
in the villages thereof, and at *D* .... Neh 11:25

DIBON-GAD (di'-bon-gad') *An encampment during the Exodus.*
from Iim, and pitched in *D* .... Num 33:45
And they removed from *D*, and .... Num 33:46

DIBRI (dib'-ri) *Father of Shelomith.*
was Shelomith, the daughter of *D* .... Lev 24:11

DID See Preface.

DIDDEST

as thou *d* the Egyptian yesterday .... Acts 7:28

DIDST

why *d* thou not tell me that she .... Gen 12:18
but thou *d* laugh .... Gen 18:15
I know that thou *d* this in the .... Gen 20:6
neither *d* thou tell me, neither .... Gen 21:26
Wherefore *d* thou flee away .... Gen 31:27
d not tell me, that I might have .... Gen 31:27
of my hand *d* thou require it, ... Gen 31:39
Thou *d* blow with thy wind, the .... Ex 15:10
as thou *d* anoint their father, ... Ex 40:15
thou shalt do to him as thou *d* .... Num 21:34
thou shalt do unto him as thou *d* .... Deut 3:2
from the day that thou *d* depart .... Deut 9:7
thou *d* drink the pure blood of .... Deut 32:14
whom thou *d* prove at Massah, and ...... Deut 33:8

with whom thou d strive at the........Deut 33:8
which thou d let us down by............Josh 2:18
her king as thou d unto Jericho........Josh 8:2
d not call us to go with thee..........Judg 12:1
thou d send come again unto us.........Judg 13:8
for thou d call me......................1Sa 3:6
for thou d call me......................1Sa 3:8
Wherefore then d thou not obey..........1Sa 15:19
but d fly upon the spoil, and...........1Sa 15:19
d evil in the sight of the LORD.........1Sa 15:19
thou sawest it, and d rejoice...........1Sa 19:5
come to the place where thou d..........1Sa 20:19
men of my lord, whom thou d send........1Sa 25:25
why then d thou not go down unto........2Sa 11:10
For thou d it secretly..................2Sa 12:12
thou d fast and weep for the child......2Sa 12:21
the child was dead, thou d rise.........2Sa 12:21
the other that thou d unto me...........2Sa 13:16
why d thou not smite him there to.......2Sa 18:11
yet d thou set thy servant among........2Sa 19:28
D not thou, my lord, O king.............1Kin 1:13
that thou d to David my father..........1Kin 2:44
thou d well that it was in thine........1Kin 8:18
For thou d separate them from...........1Kin 8:53
All that thou d send for to thy.........1Kin 20:9
Thou d blaspheme God and the king.......1Kin 21:10
For thy people Israel d thou make.......1Chr 17:22
As thou d deal with David my............2Chr 2:3
d send him cedars to build him an.......2Chr 2:3
thou d well in that it was in...........2Chr 6:8
because thou d rely on the LORD,........2Chr 16:8
who d drive out the inhabitants.........2Chr 20:7
thou d humble thyself before God,.......2Chr 34:27
d rend thy clothes, and weep............2Chr 34:27
who d choose Abram, and broughtest......Neh 9:7
d see the affliction of our.............Neh 9:9
So d thou get thee a name, as it........Neh 9:10
thou d divide the sea before them.......Neh 9:11
wonders that thou d among them..........Neh 9:17
forty years d thou sustain them.........Neh 9:21
d divide them into corners..............Neh 9:22
many times d thou deliver them..........Neh 9:28
Yet many years d thou forbear...........Neh 9:30
thou d not utterly consume them.........Neh 9:31
wherewith thou d testify against........Neh 9:34
trusted, and thou d deliver them........Ps 22:4
thou d make me hope when I was..........Ps 22:9
thou d hide thy face, and I was.........Ps 30:7
because thou d it........................Ps 39:9
and offering thou d not desire..........Ps 40:6
what work thou d in their days..........Ps 44:1
How thou d drive out the heathen........Ps 44:2
how thou d afflict the people, and......Ps 44:2
which d not go out with our.............Ps 60:10
when thou d march through the...........Ps 68:7
d send a plentiful rain.................Ps 68:9
whereby thou d confirm thine............Ps 68:9
Surely thou d set them in...............Ps 73:18
Thou d divide the sea by thy............Ps 74:13
Thou d cleave the fountain and the......Ps 74:15
Thou d cause judgment to be heard.......Ps 76:8
d cause it to take deep root, and.......Ps 80:9
which d weaken the nations..............Is 14:12
thou d look in that day to the..........Is 22:8
thou d shew them no mercy...............Is 47:6
so that thou d not lay these............Is 47:7
neither d remember the latter end.......Is 47:7
things, and thou d not know them........Is 48:6
O barren, thou that d not bear..........Is 54:1
thou that d not travail with............Is 54:1
d increase thy perfumes, and d..........Is 57:9
d debase thyself even unto hell.........Is 57:9
so d thou lead thy people, to...........Is 63:14
When thou d terrible things which.......Is 64:3
which thou d swear to their.............Jer 32:22
How d thou write all these words........Jer 36:17
Thou d say, Woe is me now...............Jer 45:3
whom thou d command that they...........Lam 1:10
thou d eat fine flour, and honey,.......Eze 16:13
thou d prosper into a kingdom...........Eze 16:13
But thou d trust in thine own...........Eze 16:15
And of thy garments thou d take.........Eze 16:16
d commit whoredom with them,............Eze 16:17
which thou d give unto them.............Eze 16:36
for whom thou d wash thyself............Eze 23:40
thou d enrich the kings of the..........Eze 27:33
thou d break, and rend all their........Eze 29:7
As thou d rejoice at the................Eze 35:15
from the first day that thou d..........Dan 10:12
because thou d trust in thy way,........Hos 10:13
that thou d ride upon thine.............Hab 3:8
Thou d cleave the earth with............Hab 3:9
Thou d march through the land in........Hab 3:12
thou d thresh the heathen in............Hab 3:12
Thou d strike through with his..........Hab 3:14
Thou d walk through the sea with........Hab 3:15
d not thou sow good seed in thy.........Mt 13:27
faith, wherefore d thou doubt...........Mt 14:31
d not thou agree with me for a..........Mt 20:13
head with oil thou d not anoint.........Lk 7:46
and reapest that thou d not sow.........Lk 19:21
have believed that thou d send me.......Jn 17:8
uncircumcised, and d eat with them......Acts 11:3
hast thou that thou d not receive.......1Cor 4:7
now if thou d receive it, why...........1Cor 4:7
d set him over the works of thy.........Heb 2:7
unto me, Wherefore d thou marvel........Rev 17:7

DIDYMUS (did'-i-mus) See THOMAS. *Another
name for Thomas the apostle.*
said Thomas, which is called D.........Jn 11:16

one of the twelve, called D............Jn 20:24
Simon Peter, and Thomas called D.......Jn 21:2

DIE

thereof thou shalt surely d............Gen 2:17
shall ye touch it, lest ye d...........Gen 3:3
the woman, Ye shall not surely d.......Gen 3:4
that is in the earth shall d...........Gen 6:17
lest some evil take me, and I d........Gen 19:19
thou that thou shalt surely d..........Gen 20:7
Behold, I am at the point to d.........Gen 25:32
Because I said, Lest I d for her.......Gen 26:9
my soul may bless thee before I d......Gen 27:4
Give me children, or else I d..........Gen 30:1
one day, all the flock will d..........Gen 33:13
said, Lest peradventure he d also......Gen 38:11
that we may live, and not d............Gen 42:2
be verified, and ye shall not d........Gen 42:20
that we may live, and not d............Gen 43:8
it be found, both let him d............Gen 44:9
his father, his father would d.........Gen 44:22
is not with us, that he will d.........Gen 44:31
I will go and see him before I d.......Gen 45:28
said unto Joseph, Now let me d.........Gen 46:30
why should we d in thy presence........Gen 47:15
shall we d before thine eyes...........Gen 47:19
seed, that we may live, and not d......Gen 47:19
time drew nigh that Israel must d......Gen 47:29
said unto Joseph, Behold, I d..........Gen 48:21
made me swear, saying, Lo, I d.........Gen 50:5
said unto his brethren, I d............Gen 50:24
fish that is in the river shall d......Ex 7:18
there shall nothing d of all that......Ex 9:4
down upon them, and they shall d.......Ex 9:19
thou seest my face thou shalt d........Ex 10:28
in the land of Egypt shall d...........Ex 11:5
us away to d in the wilderness.........Ex 14:11
we should d in the wilderness..........Ex 14:12
not God speak with us, lest we d.......Ex 20:19
that smiteth a man, so that he d.......Ex 21:12
from mine altar, that he may d.........Ex 21:14
he d not, but keepeth his bed..........Ex 21:18
a rod, and he d under his hand.........Ex 21:20
a man or a woman, that they d..........Ex 21:28
ox hurt another's, that he d...........Ex 21:35
up, and be smitten that he d...........Ex 22:2
and it d, or be hurt, or driven........Ex 22:10
neighbour, and it be hurt, or d........Ex 22:14
when he cometh out, that he d not......Ex 28:35
that they bear not iniquity, and d.....Ex 28:43
wash with water, that they d not.......Ex 30:20
and their feet, that they d not........Ex 30:21
charge of the LORD, that ye d not......Lev 8:35
lest ye d, and lest wrath come.........Lev 10:6
of the congregation, lest ye d.........Lev 10:7
of the congregation, lest ye d.........Lev 10:9
any beast, of which ye may eat, d......Lev 11:39
that they d not in their...............Lev 15:31
that he d not.........................Lev 16:2
upon the testimony, that he d..........Lev 16:13
they shall d childless.................Lev 20:20
d therefore, if they profane it........Lev 22:9
touch any holy thing, lest they d......Num 4:15
that they may live, and not d..........Num 4:19
things are covered, lest they d........Num 4:20
or for his sister, when they d.........Num 6:7
if any man d very suddenly by him......Num 6:9
consumed, and there they shall d.......Num 11:33
If these men d the common death........Num 16:29
from me, that they d not...............Num 17:10
unto Moses, saying, Behold, we d.......Num 17:12
tabernacle of the LORD shall d.........Num 17:13
that neither they, nor ye also, d......Num 18:22
lest they bear sin, and d..............Num 18:32
the children of Israel, lest ye d......Num 18:32
we and our cattle should d there.......Num 20:4
unto his people, and shall d there.....Num 20:26
of Egypt to d in the wilderness........Num 21:5
Let me d the death of the..............Num 23:10
shall surely d in the wilderness.......Num 26:65
of Israel, saying, If a man d..........Num 27:8
that the manslayer d not, until........Num 35:12
instrument of iron, so that he d.......Num 35:16
wherewith he may d, and he d...........Num 35:17
wherewith he may d, and he d...........Num 35:18
him by laying of wait, that he d.......Num 35:20
him with his hand, that he d...........Num 35:21
any stone, wherewith a man may d.......Num 35:23
and cast it upon him, that he d........Num 35:23
any person to cause him to d...........Num 35:30
But I must d in this land, I must......Deut 4:22
Now therefore why should we d..........Deut 5:25
our God any more, then we shall d......Deut 5:25
stone him with stones, that he d.......Deut 13:10
them with stones, till they d..........Deut 17:5
the judge, even that man shall d.......Deut 17:12
great fire any more, that I d not......Deut 18:16
gods, even that prophet shall d........Deut 18:20
upon his neighbour, that he d..........Deut 19:5
and smite him mortally that he d.......Deut 19:11
avenger of blood, that he may d........Deut 19:12
lest he d in the battle, and...........Deut 20:5
lest he d in the battle, and...........Deut 20:6
lest he d in the battle, and...........Deut 20:7
stone him with stones, that he d.......Deut 21:21
stone her with stones that she d.......Deut 22:21
then they shall both of them d.........Deut 22:22
them with stones that they d...........Deut 22:24
only that lay with her shall d.........Deut 22:25
or if the latter husband d.............Deut 24:3
then that thief shall d................Deut 24:7

dwell together, and one of them d......Deut 25:5
days approach that thou must d.........Deut 31:14
d in the mount whither thou goest......Deut 32:50
Let Reuben live, and not d.............Deut 33:6
not d by the hand of the avenger.......Josh 20:9
thou shalt not d.......................Judg 6:23
Bring out thy son, that he may d.......Judg 6:30
with his wife, We shall surely d.......Judg 13:22
and now shall I d for thirst...........Judg 15:18
Let me d with the Philistines..........Judg 16:30
Where thou diest, will I d.............Ruth 1:17
d in the flower of their age...........1Sa 2:33
one day they shall d both of them......1Sa 2:34
the LORD thy God, that we d not........1Sa 12:19
my son, he shall surely d..............1Sa 14:39
in mine hand, and, lo, I must d........1Sa 14:43
for thou shalt surely d, Jonathan......1Sa 14:44
said unto Saul, Shall Jonathan d.......1Sa 14:45
thou shalt not d.......................1Sa 20:2
of the LORD, that I d not..............1Sa 20:14
unto me, for he shall surely d.........1Sa 22:16
king said, Thou shalt surely d.........1Sa 22:16
or his day shall come to d.............1Sa 26:10
LORD liveth, ye are worthy to d........1Sa 26:16
for my life, to cause me to d..........1Sa 28:9
him, that he may be smitten, and d.....2Sa 11:15
done this thing shall surely d.........2Sa 12:5
thou shalt not d.......................2Sa 12:13
is born unto thee shall surely d.......2Sa 12:14
For we must needs d, and are as........2Sa 14:14
neither if half of us d, will..........2Sa 18:3
unto Shimei, Thou shalt not d..........2Sa 19:23
that I may d in mine own city, and.....2Sa 19:37
shall be found in him, he shall d......1Kin 1:52
David drew nigh that he should d.......1Kin 2:1
but I will d here.......................1Kin 2:30
certain that thou shalt surely d.......1Kin 2:37
whither, that thou shalt surely d......1Kin 2:42
into the city, the child shall d.......1Kin 14:12
my son, that we may eat it, and d......1Kin 17:12
for himself that he might d............1Kin 19:4
out, and stone him, that he may d......1Kin 21:10
art gone up, but shalt surely d........2Kin 1:4
art gone up, but shalt surely d........2Kin 1:6
art gone up, but shalt surely d........2Kin 1:16
Why sit we here until we d.............2Kin 7:3
in the city, and we shall d there......2Kin 7:4
if we sit still here, we d also........2Kin 7:4
if they kill us, we shall but d........2Kin 7:4
thou shalt surely d, and shalt d.......2Kin 8:10
honey, that ye may live, and not d.....2Kin 18:32
for thou shalt d, and not live.........2Kin 20:1
shalt not d for the children...........2Chr 25:4
the children d for the fathers.........2Chr 25:4
every man shall d for his own sin......2Chr 25:4
over yourselves to d by famine.........2Chr 32:11
curse God, and d......................Job 2:9
shall d even in without wisdom.........Job 4:21
and wisdom shall d with you............Job 12:2
the stock thereof d in the ground......Job 14:8
If a man d, shall he live again........Job 14:14
till I d I will not remove mine........Job 27:5
I shall d in my nest, and I shall......Job 29:18
In a moment shall they d, and the......Job 34:20
they shall d without knowledge.........Job 36:12
They d in youth, and their life is.....Job 36:14
speak evil of me, When shall he d......Ps 41:5
For he seeth that wise men d...........Ps 49:10
those that are appointed to d..........Ps 79:11
But ye shall d like men, and fall......Ps 82:7
ready to d from my youth up............Ps 88:15
takest away their breath, they d.......Ps 104:29
I shall not d, but live, and...........Ps 118:17
He shall d without instruction.........Prov 5:23
but fools d for want of wisdom.........Prov 10:21
and he that hateth reproof shall d.....Prov 15:10
that despiseth his ways shall d........Prov 19:16
him with the rod, he shall not d.......Prov 23:13
deny me them not before I d............Prov 30:7
A time to be born, and a time to d.....Eccl 3:2
the living know that they shall d......Eccl 9:5
for to morrow we shall d...............Is 22:13
not be purged from you till ye d.......Is 22:14
there shalt thou d, and there the......Is 22:18
for thou shalt d, and not live.........Is 38:1
therein shall d in like manner.........Is 51:6
be afraid of a man that shall d........Is 51:12
that the should not d in the pit.......Is 51:14
for the child shall d an hundred.......Is 65:20
for their worm shall not d.............Is 66:24
that thou d not by our hand............Jer 11:21
young men shall d by the sword.........Jer 11:22
their daughters shall d by famine......Jer 11:22
They shall d of grievous deaths........Jer 16:4
and the small shall d in this land.....Jer 16:6
to Babylon, and there thou shalt d.....Jer 20:6
the land d of a great.................Jer 21:6
in this city shall d by the sword......Jer 21:9
But he shall d in the place............Jer 22:12
and there shall ye d..................Jer 22:26
him, saying, Thou shalt surely d.......Jer 26:8
saying, This man is worthy to d........Jer 26:11
This man is not worthy to d............Jer 26:16
Why will ye d, thou and thy people.....Jer 27:13
this year thou shalt d, because.......Jer 28:16
But every one shall d for his own......Jer 31:30
Thou shalt not d by the sword..........Jer 34:4
But thou shalt d in peace..............Jer 34:5
the scribe, lest I d there.............Jer 37:20

in this city shall *d* by the sword .... Jer 38:2
he is like to *d* for hunger in the............... Jer 38:9
out of the dungeon, before he *d* .... Jer 38:10
these words, and thou shalt not *d* .... Jer 38:24
to Jonathan's house, to *d* there............... Jer 38:26
and there ye shall *d* .... Jer 42:16
they shall *d* by the sword, by the .... Jer 42:17
that ye shall *d* by the sword................... Jer 42:22
they shall *d*, from the least even .... Jer 44:12
the wicked, Thou shalt surely *d* .... Eze 3:18
man shall *d* in his iniquity .... Eze 3:18
he shall *d* in his iniquity .... Eze 3:19
before him, he shall *d* .... Eze 3:20
he shall *d* in his sin, and his .... Eze 3:20
thee shall *d* with the pestilence .... Eze 6:12
far off shall *d* of the pestilence .... Eze 6:12
is besieged shall *d* by the famine .... Eze 6:12
the field shall *d* with the sword .... Eze 7:15
see it, though he shall *d* there.............. Eze 12:13
slay the souls that should not *d* .... Eze 13:19
midst of Babylon he shall *d* .... Eze 17:16
the soul that sinneth, it shall *d* .... Eze 18:4
he shall surely *d* .... Eze 18:13
he shall not *d* for the iniquity .... Eze 18:17
even he shall *d* in his iniquity .... Eze 18:18
The soul that sinneth, it shall *d* .... Eze 18:20
shall surely live, he shall not *d* .... Eze 18:21
at all that the wicked should *d* .... Eze 18:23
hath sinned, in them shall he *d* .... Eze 18:24
that he hath done shall he *d* .... Eze 18:26
shall surely live, he shall not *d* .... Eze 18:28
for why will ye *d*, O house of .... Eze 18:31
thou shalt *d* the deaths of them .... Eze 28:8
Thou shalt *d* the deaths of the .... Eze 28:10
O wicked man, thou shalt surely *d* .... Eze 33:8
man shall *d* in his iniquity .... Eze 33:8
he shall *d* in his iniquity .... Eze 33:9
for why will ye *d*, O house of .... Eze 33:11
hath committed, he shall *d* for it .... Eze 33:13
the wicked, Thou shalt surely *d* .... Eze 33:14
shall surely live, he shall not *d* .... Eze 33:15
iniquity, he shall even of thereby .... Eze 33:18
caves shall *d* of the pestilence .... Eze 33:27
Moab shall *d* with tumult, with .... Amos 2:2
in one house, that they shall *d* .... Amos 6:9
Jeroboam shall *d* by the sword .... Amos 7:11
thou shalt *d* in a polluted land .... Amos 7:17
of my people shall *d* by the sword .... Amos 9:10
better for me to *d* than to live.............. Jonah 4:3
and wished in himself to *d* .... Jonah 4:8
better for me to *d* than to live.............. Jonah 4:8
we shall not *d* .... Hab 1:12
that that dieth, let it *d* .... Zec 11:9
therein shall be cut off and *d* .... Zec 13:8
or mother, let him *d* the death .... Mt 15:4
Master, Moses said, If a man *d*............... Mt 22:24
him, Though I should *d* with thee............ Mt 26:35
or mother, let him *d* the death .... Mk 7:10
unto us, If a man's brother *d* .... Mk 12:19
If I should *d* with thee, I will.............. Mk 14:31
unto him, was sick, and ready to *d*.......... Lk 7:2
unto us, If any man's brother *d*............. Lk 20:28
he *d* without children, that his .... Lk 20:28
Neither can they *d* any more .... Lk 20:36
Sir, come down ere my child *d* .... Jn 4:49
a man may eat thereof, and not *d* .... Jn 6:50
seek me, and shall *d* in your sins........... Jn 8:21
you, that ye shall *d* in your sins........... Jn 8:24
I am he, ye shall *d* in your sins............ Jn 8:24
also go, that we may *d* with him............. Jn 11:16
and believeth in me shall never *d* .... Jn 11:26
one man should *d* for the people .... Jn 11:50
Jesus should *d* for that nation .... Jn 11:51
wheat fall into the ground and *d* .... Jn 12:24
but if it *d*, it bringeth forth .... Jn 12:24
signifying what death he should *d* .... Jn 12:33
one man should *d* for the people .... Jn 18:14
signifying what death he should *d* .... Jn 18:32
law, and by our law he ought to *d* .... Jn 19:7
that that disciple should not *d* .... Jn 21:23
said not unto him, He shall not *d* .... Jn 21:23
but also to *d* at Jerusalem for the .... Acts 21:13
of death, I refuse not to *d* .... Acts 25:11
Romans to deliver any man to *d* .... Acts 25:16
for a righteous man will one *d* .... Rom 5:7
man some would even dare to *d* .... Rom 5:7
live after the flesh, ye shall *d* .... Rom 8:13
we *d*, we *d* unto the Lord .... Rom 14:8
whether we live therefore, or *d* .... Rom 14:8
for it were better for me to *d* 1Cor 9:15
For as in Adam all *d*, even so in 1Cor 15:22
Christ Jesus our Lord, I *d* daily 1Cor 15:31
for to morrow we *d* 1Cor 15:32
is not quickened, except it *d* 1Cor 15:36
that ye are in our hearts to *d* 2Cor 7:3
live is Christ, and to *d* is gain .... Phil 1:21
here men that *d* receive tithes .... Heb 7:8
is appointed unto men once to *d* .... Heb 9:27
which remain, that are ready to *d* .... Rev 3:2
and shall desire to *d*, and death .... Rev 9:6
Blessed are the dead which *d* in .... Rev 14:13

DIED

and thirty years: and he *d*.................. Gen 5:5
and twelve years: and he *d*................. Gen 5:8
and five years: and he *d*................... Gen 5:11
and ten years: and he *d*.................... Gen 5:14
and five years: and he *d*................... Gen 5:17
and *d* .... Gen 5:20
and nine years: and he *d*................... Gen 5:27
and seven years: and he *d*.................. Gen 5:31

all flesh *d* that moved upon the.............. Gen 7:21
all that was in the dry land, *d* .... Gen 7:22
and fifty years: and he *d* .... Gen 9:29
Haran *d* before his father Terah .... Gen 11:28
and Terah *d* in Haran .... Gen 11:32
And Sarah *d* in Kirjath-arba .... Gen 23:2
d in a good old age, an old man.............. Gen 25:8
and he gave up the ghost and *d* .... Gen 25:17
he *d* in the presence of all his .... Gen 25:18
But Deborah Rebekah's nurse *d* .... Gen 35:8
(for she *d*) that she called his.............. Gen 35:18
And Rachel *d*, and was buried in the .... Gen 35:19
And Isaac gave up the ghost, and *d*.......... Gen 35:29
And Bela *d*, and Jobab the son of .... Gen 36:33
And Jobab *d*, and Husham .... Gen 36:34
And Husham *d*, and Hadad .... Gen 36:35
And Hadad *d*, and Samlah .... Gen 36:36
And Samlah *d*, and Saul of Rehoboth .... Gen 36:37
And Saul *d*, and Baal-hanan the son .... Gen 36:38
And Baal-hanan the son of Achbor *d*.......... Gen 36:39
daughter of Shuah Judah's wife *d* .... Gen 38:12
Onan *d* in the land of Canaan................ Gen 46:12
Rachel *d* by me in the land of .... Gen 48:7
father did command before he *d* .... Gen 50:16
So Joseph *d*, being an hundred and .... Gen 50:26
And Joseph *d*, and all his brethren,.......... Ex 1:6
of time, that the king of Egypt *d* .... Ex 2:23
the fish that was in the river *d* .... Ex 7:21
the frogs *d* of the houses, ... Ex 8:13
and all the cattle of Egypt *d* .... Ex 9:6
the children of Israel *d* not one .... Ex 9:6
Would to God we had *d* by the hand........... Ex 16:3
them, and they *d* before the LORD .... Lev 10:2
offered before the LORD, and *d* .... Lev 16:1
eateth that which *d* of itself .... Lev 17:15
Abihu before the LORD, when................... Num 3:4
we had *d* in the land of Egypt .... Num 14:2
God we had *d* in this wilderness .... Num 14:2
d by the plague before the LORD .... Num 14:37
stoned him with stones, and he *d* .... Num 15:36
Now they that *d* in the plague................ Num 16:49
beside them that *d* about the................. Num 16:49
and Miriam *d* there, and was buried........... Num 20:1
Would God that we had *d* when our .... Num 20:3
our brethren *d* before the LORD .... Num 20:3
Aaron of there in the top of the .... Num 20:28
and much people of Israel *d* .... Num 21:6
those that *d* in the plague were .... Num 25:9
with Korah, when that company *d*.............. Num 26:10
the children of Korah *d* not.................. Num 26:11
Onan *d* in the land of Canaan................ Num 26:19
and Nadab and Abihu *d*, when they............ Num 26:61
Our father *d* in the wilderness,.............. Num 27:3
but *d* in his own sin, and had no............. Num 27:3
d there, in the fortieth year .... Num 33:38
years old when he *d* in mount Hor .... Num 33:39
there Aaron *d*, and there he was.............. Deut 10:6
Aaron thy brother *d* in mount Hor .... Deut 32:50
LORD *d* there in the land of Moab .... Deut 34:5
and twenty years old when he *d* .... Deut 34:7
d in the wilderness by the way,............. Josh 5:4
upon them unto Azekah, and they *d*........... Josh 10:11
they were more which *d* with............. Josh 10:11
Nun, the servant of the LORD, *d*............. Josh 24:29
And Eleazar the son of Aaron *d* .... Josh 24:33
him to Jerusalem, and there he *d*............ Judg 1:7
Nun, the servant of the LORD, *d*............. Judg 2:8
which Joshua left when he *d* .... Judg 2:21
And Othniel the son of Kenaz *d*.............. Judg 3:11
asleep and weary. So he *d* .... Judg 4:21
son of Joash *d* in a good old age .... Judg 8:32
of the tower of Shechem *d* also.............. Judg 9:49
man thrust him through, and he *d*............ Judg 9:54
twenty and three years, and *d* .... Judg 10:2
And Jair *d*, and was buried in Camon......... Judg 10:5
Then Jephthah the Gileadite, and .... Judg 12:7
Then *d* Ibzan, and was buried at............. Judg 12:10
And Elon the Zebulonite *d*, and was.......... Judg 12:12
son of Hillel the Pirathonite *d* .... Judg 12:15
And Elimelech Naomi's husband *d* .... Ruth 1:3
Chilion *d* also both of them.................. Ruth 1:5
gate, and his neck brake, and he *d*.......... 1Sa 4:18
the men that *d* not were smitten 1Sa 5:12
rescued Jonathan, that he *d* not.............. 1Sa 14:45
And Samuel *d*; and all the Israelites........ 1Sa 25:1
that his heart *d* within him.................. 1Sa 25:37
the LORD smote Nabal, that he *d*............. 1Sa 25:38
upon his sword, and *d* with him.............. 1Sa 31:5
So Saul *d*, and his three sons, and.......... 1Sa 31:6
And he smote him that he *d*.................. 2Sa 1:15
there, and *d* in the same place 2Sa 2:23
Asahel fell down and *d* stood still 2Sa 2:23
three hundred and threescore men *d*.......... 2Sa 2:31
under the fifth rib, that he *d* 2Sa 3:27
and said, *d* Abner as a fool dieth........... 2Sa 3:33
there he *d* by the ark of God................ 2Sa 6:7
king of the children of Ammon *d*............. 2Sa 10:1
of their host, who of there................... 2Sa 11:17
and Uriah the Hittite *d* also................ 2Sa 11:17
the wall, that he *d* in Thebez............... 2Sa 11:21
the seventh day, that the child *d*........... 2Sa 12:18
in order, and hanged himself, and *d*......... 2Sa 17:23
would God I had *d* for thee 2Sa 18:33
lived, and all we had *d* this day............ 2Sa 19:6
him not again; and he *d* 2Sa 20:10
there *d* of the people from Dan.............. 2Sa 24:15
and he fell upon him that he *d* 1Kin 2:25
out, and fell upon him, that he *d*........... 1Kin 2:46
this woman's child *d* in the night........... 1Kin 3:19
stoned him with stones, that he *d* 1Kin 12:18

of the door, the child *d* 1Kin 14:17
house over him with fire, and *d* 1Kin 16:18
so Tibni *d*, and Omri reigned................ 1Kin 16:22
stoned him with stones, that he *d*........... 1Kin 21:13
against the Syrians, and *d* at even.......... 1Kin 22:35
So the king *d*, and was brought to........... 1Kin 22:37
So he *d* according to the word of............ 2Kin 1:17
on her knees till noon, and then *d*.......... 2Kin 4:20
upon him in the gate, and he *d* 2Kin 7:17
gate, and *d*, as the man of God 2Kin 7:20
it on his face, so that he *d* 2Kin 8:15
And he fled to Megiddo, and *d* there......... 2Kin 9:27
his servants, smote him, and he *d* 2Kin 12:21
sick of his sickness whereof he *d*........... 2Kin 13:14
And Elisha *d*, and they buried him 2Kin 13:20
So Hazael king of Syria *d* 2Kin 13:24
and he came to Egypt, and *d* there........... 2Kin 23:34
him, and smote Gedaliah, that he *d*.......... 2Kin 25:25
Hadad *d* also. And the dukes 1Chr 1:51
but Seled *d* without children 1Chr 2:30
Jether *d* without children. 1Chr 2:32
fell likewise on the sword, and *d* 1Chr 10:5
So Saul *d*, and his three sons 1Chr 10:6
and all his house *d* together 1Chr 10:6
So Saul *d* for his transgression 1Chr 10:13
and there he *d* before God................... 1Chr 13:10
king of the children of Ammon *d*............. 1Chr 19:1
And Eleazar *d*, and had no sons, but......... 1Chr 23:22
Abihu *d* before their father,................ 1Chr 24:2
he *d* in a good old age, full of 1Chr 29:28
stoned him with stones, that he *d*........... 2Chr 10:18
and the LORD struck him, and he *d* 2Chr 13:20
d in the one and fortieth year of 2Chr 16:13
time of the sun going down he *d* 2Chr 18:34
so he *d* of sore diseases 2Chr 21:19
and was full of days when he *d* 2Chr 24:15
thirty years old was he when he *d*........... 2Chr 24:15
And when he *d*, he said, The LORD 2Chr 24:22
and slew him on his bed, and he *d*........... 2Chr 24:25
brought him to Jerusalem, and he *d*.......... 2Chr 35:24
Why *d* I not from the womb................... Job 3:11
So Job *d*, being old and full of .... Job 42:17
d I saw also the Lord sitting .... Is 6:1
that king Ahaz *d* was this burden............ Is 14:28
So Hananiah the prophet *d* the............... Jer 28:17
Pelatiah the son of Benaiah *d* .... Eze 11:13
and at even my wife *d* .... Eze 24:18
when he offended in Baal, he *d* .... Hos 13:1
And last of all the woman *d* also............ Mt 22:27
And the second took her, and *d*.............. Mk 12:21
last of all the woman *d* also................ Mk 12:22
came to pass, that the beggar *d* .... Lk 16:22
the rich man also *d*, and was .... Lk 16:22
a wife, and *d* without children .... Lk 20:29
her to wife, and he *d* childless .... Lk 20:30
and they left no children, and *d*............ Lk 20:31
Last of all the woman *d* also................ Lk 20:32
been here, my brother had not *d* .... Jn 11:21
been here, my brother had not *d* .... Jn 11:32
even this man should not have *d* .... Jn 11:37
Jacob went down into Egypt, and *d*........... Acts 7:15
days, that she was sick, and *d* .... Acts 9:37
due time Christ *d* for the ungodly........... Rom 5:6
were yet sinners, Christ *d* for us........... Rom 5:8
that he *d*, he *d* unto sin once .... Rom 6:10
came, sin revived, and I *d* .... Rom 7:9
It is Christ that *d*, yea rather,............ Rom 8:34
For to this end Christ both *d* .... Rom 14:9
with thy meat, for whom Christ *d*............ Rom 14:15
brother perish, for whom Christ *d*........... 1Cor 8:11
how that Christ *d* for our sins 1Cor 15:3
thus judge, that if one *d* for all 2Cor 5:14
And that he *d* for all, that they 2Cor 5:15
but unto him which *d* for them 2Cor 5:15
For if we believe that Jesus *d* 1Th 4:14
Who *d* for us, that, whether we 1Th 5:10
law of without mercy under two or .... Heb 10:28
These all *d* in faith, not having .... Heb 11:13
By faith Joseph, when he *d* .... Heb 11:22
were in the sea, and had life, *d* .... Rev 8:9
many men *d* of the waters, because .... Rev 8:11
and every living soul *d* in the sea .... Rev 16:3

DIEST

Where thou *d*, will I die, and.............. Ruth 1:17

DIET

And for his *d*, there was a .... Jer 52:34
there was a continual given him.............. Jer 52:34

DIETH

fat of the beast that *d* of itself .... Lev 7:24
That which *d* of itself, or is............... Lev 22:8
the law, when a man *d* in a tent .... Num 19:14
eat of any thing that *d* of itself .... Deut 14:21
and said, Died Abner as a fool *d*............ 2Sa 3:33
Him that *d* of Jeroboam in the 1Kin 14:11
him that *d* in the field shall the 1Kin 14:11
Him that *d* of Baasha in the city 1Kin 16:4
him that *d* of his in the fields 1Kin 16:4
Him that *d* of Ahab in the city 1Kin 21:24
him that *d* in the field shall the 1Kin 21:24
But man *d*, and wasteth away .... Job 14:10
One *d* in his full strength, being .... Job 21:23
another *d* in the bitterness of .... Job 21:25
For when he *d* he shall carry .... Ps 49:17
When a wicked man *d*, his .... Prov 11:7
And how of the wise man .... Eccl 2:16
as the one *d*, so of the other .... Eccl 3:19
is no water, and *d* for thirst .... Is 50:2
he that eateth of their eggs *d*............. Is 59:5
eaten of that which *d* of itself .... Eze 4:14

D

committeth iniquity, and d in them..... Eze 18:26
in the death of him that d..................... Eze 18:32
that that d, let it die.......................... Zec 11:9
Where their worm d not, and the........ Mk 9:44
Where their worm d not, and the........ Mk 9:46
Where their worm d not, and the........ Mk 9:48
raised from the dead d no more......... Rom 6:9
himself, and no man d to himself........ Rom 14:7

DIFFER
who maketh thee to d from another.... 1Cor 4:7

DIFFERENCE
put a d between the Egyptians............ Ex 11:7
And that ye may put d between holy... Lev 10:10
To make a d between the unclean........ Lev 11:47
put d between clean beasts................. Lev 20:25
have put no d between the holy.......... Eze 22:26
they shewed d between the unclean.... Eze 22:26
my people the d between the holy....... Eze 44:23
put no d between us and them,........... Acts 15:9
for there is no d................................. Rom 3:22
For there is no d between the Jew...... Rom 10:12
There is also between a wife and....... 1Cor 7:34
some have compassion, making a d..... Jude 22

DIFFERENCES
there are of d administrations,........... 1Cor 12:5

DIFFERETH
for one star d from another star........ 1Cor 15:41
d nothing from a servant, though........ Gal 4:1

DIFFERING
Having then gifts d according to......... Rom 12:6

DIG
a pit, or if a man shall d a pit.............. Ex 21:33
whose hills thou mayest d brass......... Deut 8:9
abroad, thou shalt d therewith.......... Deut 23:13
d for it more than for hid................... Job 3:21
ye d a pit for your friend.................... Job 6:27
yea, thou shalt d about thee............... Job 11:18
In the dark they d through houses..... Job 24:16
me, Son of man, d now in the wall...... Eze 8:8
D thou through the wall in their......... Eze 12:5
they shall d through the wall to......... Eze 12:7
Though they d into hell, thence.......... Amos 9:2
also, till I shall d about it.................. Lk 13:8
I cannot d....................................... Lk 16:3

DIGGED
unto me, that I have d this well......... Gen 21:30
had d in the days of Abraham his....... Gen 26:15
Isaac d again the wells of water......... Gen 26:18
Isaac's servants d in the valley.......... Gen 26:19
they d another well, and strove.......... Gen 26:21
from thence, and d another well........ Gen 26:22
there Isaac's servants d a well........... Gen 26:25
the well which they had..................... Gen 26:32
their selfwill they d down a wall........ Gen 49:6
in my grave which I have d for me..... Gen 50:5
all the Egyptians d round about.......... Ex 7:24
The princes of the well....................... Num 21:18
the nobles of the people d it............... Num 21:18
thou filledst not, and wells d.............. Deut 6:11
I have d and drunk strange waters,.... 2Kin 19:24
in the desert, and d many wells.......... 2Chr 26:10
houses full of all goods, wells d.......... Neh 9:25
d it, and is fallen into the ditch.......... Ps 7:15
cause they have d for my soul............ Ps 35:7
they have d a pit before me, into........ Ps 57:6
until the pit be d for the wicked........ Ps 94:13
The proud have d pits for me............. Ps 119:85
it shall not be pruned, nor d.............. Is 5:6
that shall be d with the mattock........ Is 7:25
I have d, and drunk water................. Is 37:25
hole of the pit whence ye are d.......... Is 51:1
Then I went to Euphrates, and d........ Jer 13:7
for they have d a pit for my soul........ Jer 18:20
for they have d a pit to take me,........ Jer 18:22
when I had d in the wall, behold......... Eze 8:8
in the even I d through the wall......... Eze 12:7
d a winepress in it, and built a.......... Mt 21:33
d in the earth, and hid his lord's....... Mt 25:18
a place for the winefat, and............... Mk 12:1
d deep, and laid the foundation on..... Lk 6:48
prophets, and d down thine altars...... Rom 11:3

DIGGEDST
and wells digged, which thou d not.... Deut 6:11

DIGGETH
An ungodly man d up evil................... Prov 16:27
Whoso d a pit shall fall therein.......... Prov 26:27
He that d a pit shall fall into.............. Eccl 10:8

DIGNITIES
are not afraid to speak evil of............. 2Pet 2:10
dominion, and speak evil of d.............. Jude 8

DIGNITY
my strength, the excellency of d......... Gen 49:3
d hath been done to Mordecai for...... Esth 6:3
Folly is set in great d, and the........... Eccl 10:6
and their d shall proceed of.............. Hab 1:7

DIKLAH (dik'-lah) A son of Joktan.
And Hadoram, and Uzal, and D........... Gen 10:27
Hadoram also, and Uzal, and D.......... 1Chr 1:21

DILEAN (dil'-e-an) A city in Judah.
And D, and Mizpeh, and Joktheel,..... Josh 15:38

DILIGENCE
Keep thy heart with all d.................... Prov 4:23
give d that thou mayest be................. Lk 12:58
he that ruleth, with d......................... Rom 12:8
and knowledge, and in all d................ 2Cor 8:7
Do thy d to come shortly unto me...... 2Ti 4:9
Do thy d to come before winter......... 2Ti 4:21
one of you do shew the same d to...... Heb 6:11
And beside this, giving all d............... 2Pet 1:5
give d to make your calling and......... 2Pet 1:10
when I gave all d to write unto.......... Jude 3

DILIGENT
judges shall make d inquisition.......... Deut 19:18
But take d heed to do the.................. Josh 22:5
they accomplish a d search................ Ps 64:6
and my spirit made d search.............. Ps 77:6
The hand of the d maketh rich.......... Prov 10:4
The hand of the d shall bear rule...... Prov 12:24
substance of a d man is precious....... Prov 12:27
soul of the d shall be made fat.......... Prov 13:4
The thoughts of the d tend only........ Prov 21:5
thou a man d in his business............. Prov 22:29
Be thou d to know the state of.......... Prov 27:23
proved d in many things.................... 2Cor 8:22
but now much more d......................... 2Cor 8:22
be d to come unto me to Nicopolis..... Titus 3:12
be d that ye may be found of him...... 2Pet 3:14

DILIGENTLY
If thou wilt d hearken to the............. Ex 15:26
Moses d sought the goat of the.......... Lev 10:16
to thyself, and keep thy soul d........... Deut 4:9
teach them d unto thy children......... Deut 6:7
Ye shall d keep the commandments.... Deut 6:17
if ye shall hearken d unto my............ Deut 11:13
For if ye shall d keep all these.......... Deut 11:22
enquire, and make search, and ask d.. Deut 13:14
hast heard of it, and enquired d......... Deut 17:4
of leprosy, that thou observe d.......... Deut 24:8
if thou shalt hearken d unto the........ Deut 28:1
Now the men did d observe whether... 1Kin 20:33
let it be d done for the house of........ Ezr 7:23
Hear d my speech, and my................ Job 13:17
Hear d my speech, and let this be..... Job 21:2
thou shalt d consider his place,......... Ps 37:10
us to keep thy precepts d................... Ps 119:4
d to seek thy face, and I have........... Prov 7:15
He that d seeketh good procureth...... Prov 11:27
consider d what is before thee........... Prov 23:1
he hearkened d with much heed......... Is 21:7
hearken d unto me, and eat ye that... Is 55:2
and send unto Kedar, and consider d. Jer 2:10
if they will d learn the ways of......... Jer 12:16
if ye d hearken unto me, saith.......... Jer 17:24
if ye will d obey the voice of............. Zec 6:15
enquired them d what time the.......... Mt 2:7
search d for the young child............... Mt 2:8
he had enquired of the wise men....... Mt 2:16
house, and seek d till she find it....... Lk 15:8
taught of the things of the Lord,....... Acts 18:25
if she have d followed every good...... 1Ti 5:10
in Rome, he sought me out very d...... 2Ti 1:17
and Apollos on their journey d.......... Titus 3:13
rewarder of them that d seek him...... Heb 11:6
Looking d lest any man fail of............ Heb 12:15
he enquired and searched d............... 1Pet 1:10

DIM
Isaac was old, and his eyes were d..... Gen 27:1
the eyes of Israel were d for age........ Gen 48:10
his eye was not d, nor his.................. Deut 34:7
place, and his eyes began to wax d.... 1Sa 3:2
and his eyes were d, that he could..... 1Sa 4:15
Mine eye also is d by reason of......... Job 17:7
of them that see shall not be d.......... Is 32:3
How is the gold become d.................. Lam 4:1
for these things our eyes are d........... Lam 5:17

DIMINISH
ye shall not d ought thereof.............. Ex 5:8
duty of marriage, shall he not d........ Ex 21:10
thou shalt d the price of it................ Lev 25:16
neither shall ye d ought from it........ Deut 4:2
not add thereto, nor d from it............ Deut 12:32
d not a word.. Jer 26:2
therefore will I also d thee................ Eze 5:11
for I will d them, that they............... Eze 29:15

DIMINISHED
not ought of your work shall be d...... Ex 5:11
gotten by vanity shall be d................ Prov 13:11
the children of Kedar, shall be d........ Is 21:17
may be increased there, and not d..... Jer 29:6
have d thine ordinary food, and........ Eze 16:27

DIMINISHING
the d of them the riches of the.......... Rom 11:12

DIMNAH (dim'-nah) A Levitical city in Zebulun.
D with her suburbs, Nahalal with...... Josh 21:35

DIMNESS
trouble and darkness, d of anguish..... Is 8:22
Nevertheless the d shall not be.......... Is 9:1

DIMON (di'-mon) See DIBON, DIMONAH. A Moabite city.
For the waters of D shall be full......... Is 15:9
For I will bring more upon D.............. Is 15:9

DIMONAH (di-mo'-nah) See DIMON. A city in Judah.
And Kinah, and D, and Adadah,......... Josh 15:22

DINAH See DINAH'S. A daughter of Jacob.
a daughter, and called her name D...... Gen 30:21
D the daughter of Leah, which she..... Gen 34:1
his soul clave unto D the................... Gen 34:3
he had defiled D his daughter........... Gen 34:5
he had defiled D their sister.............. Gen 34:13
took D out of Shechem's house, and.. Gen 34:26
Padan-aram, with his daughter D...... Gen 46:15

DINAH'S
D brethren, took each man his........... Gen 34:25

DINAITES (di'-na-ites) Foreign settlers in Samaria.
the D, the Apharsathchites, the......... Ezr 4:9

DINE
these men shall d with me at noon..... Gen 43:16
besought him to d with him............... Lk 11:37
Jesus saith unto them, Come and d.... Jn 21:12

DINED
So when they had d, Jesus saith......... Jn 21:15

DINHABAH (din'-ha-bah) Capital of Edom.
and the name of his city was D.......... Gen 36:32
and the name of his city was D.......... 1Chr 1:43

DINNER
Better is a d of herbs where love....... Prov 15:17
Behold, I have prepared my d............ Mt 22:4
he had not first washed before d....... Lk 11:38
When thou makest a d or a supper..... Lk 14:12

DIONYSIUS (di-on-ish'-yus) An Athenian convert of Paul.
the which was D the Areopagite......... Acts 17:34

DIOTREPHES (di-ot'-re-feez) A believer condemned by John.
but D, who loveth to have the............ 3Jn 9

DIP
d it in the blood that is in the............ Ex 12:22
the priest shall d his finger in........... Lev 4:6
the priest shall d his finger in........... Lev 4:17
and the hyssop, and shall d them...... Lev 14:6
the priest shall d his right................ Lev 14:16
d them in the blood of the slain........ Lev 14:51
d it in the water, and sprinkle it....... Num 19:18
let him d his foot in oil..................... Deut 33:24
of thy morsel in the vinegar............. Ruth 2:14
that he may d the tip of his.............. Lk 16:24

DIPPED
goats, and d the coat in the blood...... Gen 37:31
and d his finger in the blood, and...... Lev 9:9
were d in the brim of the water........ Josh 3:15
d it in an honeycomb, and put his..... 1Sa 14:27
d himself seven times in Jordan,....... 2Kin 5:14
d it in water, and spread it on........... 2Kin 8:15
That thy foot may be d in the........... Ps 68:23
give a sop, when I have d it.............. Jn 13:26
And when he had d the sop, he gave.. Jn 13:26
clothed with a vesture d in blood...... Rev 19:13

DIPPETH
He that d his hand with me in the..... Mt 26:23
that d with me in the dish................. Mk 14:20

DIRECT
to d his face unto Goshen.................. Gen 46:28
will I d my prayer unto thee............. Ps 5:3
him, and he shall d thy paths........... Prov 3:6
of the perfect shall d his way........... Prov 11:5
but wisdom is profitable to d............. Eccl 10:10
and I will d all his ways.................... Is 45:13
I will d their work in truth, and....... Is 61:8
man that walketh to d his steps....... Jer 10:23
Jesus Christ, d our way unto you...... 1Th 3:11
the Lord d your hearts into the......... 2Th 3:5

DIRECTED
Now he hath not d his words............. Job 32:14
O that my ways were d to keep thy... Ps 119:5
Who hath d the Spirit of the LORD.... Is 40:13

DIRECTETH
He d it under the whole heaven,........ Job 37:3
but the LORD d his steps................... Prov 16:9
as for the upright, he d his way........ Prov 21:29

DIRECTION
by the d of the lawgiver, with........... Num 21:18

DIRECTLY
sprinkle of her blood d before........... Num 19:4
even the way d before the wall......... Eze 42:12

DIRT
and the d came out............................ Judg 3:22
them out as the d in the streets........ Ps 18:42
whose waters cast up mire and d....... Is 57:20

DISALLOW
But if her father d her in the............ Num 30:5

DISALLOWED
her, because her father d her............ Num 30:5
But if her husband d her on the........ Num 30:8
his peace at her, and d her not.......... Num 30:11
of indeed of men, but chosen of........ 1Pet 2:4
the stone which the builders d........... 1Pet 2:7

DISANNUL

Wilt thou also *d* my judgment .... Job 40:8
hath purposed, and who shall *d* it ...... Is 14:27
and thirty years after, cannot *d* .... Gal 3:17

DISANNULLED

covenant with death shall be *d* .... Is 28:18

DISANNULLETH

yet if it be confirmed, no man *d* .... Gal 3:15

DISANNULLING

For there is verily a *d* of the .... Heb 7:18

DISAPPOINT

O LORD, *d* him, cast him down .... Ps 17:13

DISAPPOINTED

Without counsel purposes are *d* .... Prov 15:22

DISAPPOINTETH

He *d* the devices of the crafty, ... Job 5:12

DISCERN

before our brethren *d* thou what .... Gen 31:32
and she said, *D*, I pray thee, ... Gen 38:25
so is my lord the king to *d* good 2Sa 14:17
can I *d* between good and evil 2Sa 19:35
that I may *d* between good and bad..... 1Kin 3:9
understanding to *d* judgment 1Kin 3:11
So that the people could not *d* .... Ezr 3:13
but I could not *d* the form .... Job 4:16
cannot my taste *d* perverse things ..... Job 6:30
cause them to *d* between the .... Eze 44:23
cannot *d* between their right hand ...... Jonah 4:11
d between the righteous and the .... Mal 3:18
ye can *d* the face of the sky .... Mt 16:3
but can ye not *d* the signs of the .... Mt 16:3
ye can *d* the face of the sky and .... Lk 12:56
is it that ye do not *d* this time .... Lk 12:56
senses exercised to *d* both good........ Heb 5:14

DISCERNED

he *d* him not, because his hands......... Gen 27:23
the king of Israel *d* him that he 1Kin 20:41
I *d* among the youths, a young man .... Prov 7:7
because they are spiritually 1Cor 2:14

DISCERNER

is a *d* of the thoughts and intents ...... Heb 4:12

DISCERNETH

and a wise man's heart *d* both time .... Eccl 8:5

DISCERNING

to himself, not of the Lord's body 1Cor 11:29
to another *d* of spirits......................... 1Cor 12:10

DISCHARGE

and there is no *d* in that war .... Eccl 8:8

DISCHARGED

and will cause them to be *d* there....... 1Kin 5:9

DISCIPLE

The *d* is not above his master .... Mt 10:24
It is enough for the *d* that he be .... Mt 10:25
water only in the name of a *d* .... Mt 10:42
who also himself was Jesus' .... Mt 27:57
The *d* is not above his master .... Lk 6:40
own life also, he cannot be my *d* .... Lk 14:26
and come after me, cannot be my *d* ... Lk 14:27
that he hath, he cannot be my *d* .... Lk 14:33
him, and said, Thou art his *d* .... Jn 9:28
Jesus, and so did another *d* .... Jn 18:15
that *d* was known unto the high .... Jn 18:16
Then went out that other *d* .... Jn 18:16
the *d* standing by, whom he loved,..... Jn 19:26
Then saith he to the *d*, Behold .... Jn 19:27
from that hour that *d* took her .... Jn 19:27
being a *d* of Jesus, but secretly .... Jn 19:38
to Simon Peter, and to the other *d* ... Jn 20:2
went forth, and that other *d* .... Jn 20:3
the other *d* did outrun Peter, and...... Jn 20:4
Then went in also that other *d* .... Jn 20:8
Therefore that *d* whom Jesus loved ... Jn 21:7
seeth the *d* whom Jesus loved .... Jn 21:20
that that *d* should not die................... Jn 21:23
This is the *d* which testifieth of .... Jn 21:24
there was a certain *d* at Damascus ..... Acts 9:10
and believed not that he was a *d* .... Acts 9:26
Joppa a certain *d* named Tabitha........ Acts 9:36
and, behold, a certain *d* was there...... Acts 16:1
one Mnason of Cyprus, an old *d* .... Acts 21:16

DISCIPLES

seal the law among my *d* .... Is 8:16
he was set, his *d* came unto him......... Mt 5:1
And another of his *d* said unto him..... Mt 8:21
into a ship, his *d* followed him .... Mt 8:23
his *d* came to him, and awoke him, ... Mt 8:25
and sat down with him and his *d* .... Mt 9:10
saw it, they said unto his *d* .... Mt 9:11
Then came to him the *d* of John .... Mt 9:14
fast oft, but thy *d* fast not................. Mt 9:14
and followed him, and so his *d* .... Mt 9:19
Then saith he unto his *d*, The............ Mt 9:37
had called unto him his twelve *d* .... Mt 10:1
an end of commanding his twelve *d* ... Mt 11:1
of Christ, he sent two of his *d* .... Mt 11:2
his *d* were an hungred, and began...... Mt 12:1
thy *d* do that which is not lawful .... Mt 12:2
forth his hand toward his *d* .... Mt 12:49
the *d* came, and said unto him, Why .. Mt 13:10
his *d* came unto him, saying, ... Mt 13:36
his *d* came, and took up the body, ... Mt 14:12
his *d* came to him, saying, This........... Mt 14:15

and gave the loaves to his *d* .... Mt 14:19
and the *d* to the multitude.................. Mt 14:19
his *d* to get into a ship, and to .... Mt 14:22
when the *d* saw him walking on the .... Mt 14:26
Why do thy *d* transgress the .... Mt 15:2
Then came his *d*, and said unto him, .. Mt 15:12
his *d* came and besought him, ... Mt 15:23
Then Jesus called his *d* unto him........ Mt 15:32
his *d* say unto him, Whence should .... Mt 15:33
and brake them, and gave to his *d* ..... Mt 15:36
and the *d* to the multitude................. Mt 15:36
when his *d* were come to the other ... Mt 16:5
Caesarea Philippi, he asked his *d* .... Mt 16:13
Then charged he his *d* that they .... Mt 16:20
began Jesus to shew unto his *d* .... Mt 16:21
Then said Jesus unto his *d* .... Mt 16:24
And when the *d* heard it, they fell...... Mt 17:6
his *d* asked him, saying, Why then ..... Mt 17:10
Then the *d* understood that he .... Mt 17:13
And I brought him to thy *d* .... Mt 17:16
Then came the *d* to Jesus apart,......... Mt 17:19
same time came the *d* unto Jesus ...... Mt 18:1
His *d* say unto him, If the case .... Mt 19:10
and the *d* rebuked them..................... Mt 19:13
Then said Jesus unto his *d* .... Mt 19:23
When his *d* heard it, they were .... Mt 19:25
the twelve *d* apart in the way .... Mt 20:17
of Olives, then sent Jesus two *d* .... Mt 21:1
the *d* went, and did as Jesus .... Mt 21:6
And when the *d* saw it, they .... Mt 21:20
him their *d* with the Herodians .... Mt 22:16
to the multitude, and to his *d* .... Mt 23:1
his *d* came to him for to shew him ..... Mt 24:1
the *d* came unto him privately,........... Mt 24:3
these sayings, he said unto his *d* .... Mt 26:1
But when his *d* saw it, they had .... Mt 26:8
bread the *d* came to Jesus .... Mt 26:17
passover at thy house with my *d* .... Mt 26:18
the *d* did as Jesus had appointed ...... Mt 26:19
and brake it, and gave it to the *d* ...... Mt 26:26
Likewise also said all the *d* .... Mt 26:35
Gethsemane, and saith unto the *d* ..... Mt 26:36
And he cometh unto the *d*, and .... Mt 26:40
Then cometh he to his *d*, and saith .... Mt 26:45
Then all the *d* forsook him................. Mt 26:56
lest his *d* come by night, and............. Mt 27:64
tell his *d* that he is risen from .... Mt 28:7
and did run to bring his *d* word.......... Mt 28:8
And as they went to tell his *d* .... Mt 28:9
His *d* came by night, and stole him..... Mt 28:13
Then the eleven *d* went away into ...... Mt 28:16
also together with Jesus and his *d* ..... Mk 2:15
and sinners, they said unto his *d* .... Mk 2:16
the *d* of John and of the Pharisees ..... Mk 2:18
unto him, Why do the *d* of John......... Mk 2:18
fast, but thy *d* fast not...................... Mk 2:18
his *d* began, as they went, to............ Mk 2:23
himself with his *d* to the sea .... Mk 3:7
And he spake to his *d*, that .... Mk 3:9
he expounded all things to his *d* .... Mk 4:34
his *d* said unto him, Thou seest .... Mk 5:31
and his *d* follow him .... Mk 6:1
when his *d* heard of it, they came...... Mk 6:29
his *d* came unto him, and said, ... Mk 6:35
gave them to his *d* to set before .... Mk 6:41
his *d* to get into the ship, unto .... Mk 6:45
of his *d* eat bread with defiled .... Mk 7:2
Why walk not thy *d* according to .... Mk 7:5
his *d* asked him concerning the .... Mk 7:17
eat, Jesus called his *d* unto him .... Mk 8:1
his *d* answered him, From whence ..... Mk 8:4
gave to his *d* to set before them........ Mk 8:6
he entered into a ship with his *d* .... Mk 8:10
Now the *d* had forgotten to take ...... Mk 8:14
And Jesus went out, and his *d* .... Mk 8:27
and by the way he asked his *d* .... Mk 8:27
turned about and looked on his *d* ...... Mk 8:33
people unto him with his *d* also .... Mk 8:34
And when he came to his *d*, he saw ... Mk 9:14
I spake to thy *d* that they should ...... Mk 9:18
his *d* asked him privately, Why .... Mk 9:28
For he taught his *d*, and said unto ..... Mk 9:31
in the house his *d* asked him .... Mk 10:10
his *d* rebuked those that brought ...... Mk 10:13
round about, and saith unto his *d* ...... Mk 10:23
the *d* were astonished at his .... Mk 10:24
he went out of Jericho with his *d* ...... Mk 10:46
he sendeth forth two of his *d* .... Mk 11:1
And his *d* heard it .... Mk 11:14
And he called unto him his *d* .... Mk 12:43
one of his *d* saith unto him, ... Mk 13:1
his *d* said unto him, Where wilt .... Mk 14:12
And he sendeth forth two of his *d* ..... Mk 14:13
shall eat the passover with my *d* .... Mk 14:14
his *d* went forth, and came into .... Mk 14:16
and he saith to his *d*, Sit ye here .... Mk 14:32
But go your way, tell his *d* .... Mk 16:7
Pharisees murmured against his *d* ...... Lk 5:30
Why do the *d* of John fast often,....... Lk 5:33
likewise the *d* of the Pharisees .... Lk 5:33
his *d* plucked the ears of corn, ... Lk 6:1
was day, he called unto him his *d* ...... Lk 6:13
plain, and the company of his *d* .... Lk 6:17
And he lifted up his eyes on his *d* ...... Lk 6:20
many of his *d* went with him, and ...... Lk 7:11
the *d* of John shewed him of all .... Lk 7:18
two of his *d* sent them to Jesus .... Lk 7:19
his *d* asked him, saying, What .... Lk 8:9
he went into a ship with his *d* .... Lk 8:22
he called his twelve *d* together .... Lk 9:1

And he said to his *d*, Make them .... Lk 9:14
gave to the *d* to set before the .... Lk 9:16
praying, his *d* were with him .... Lk 9:18
I besought thy *d* to cast him out .... Lk 9:40
Jesus did, he said unto his *d* .... Lk 9:43
And when his *d* James and John saw .. Lk 9:54
And he turned him unto his *d* .... Lk 10:23
one of his *d* said unto him, Lord, ... Lk 11:1
pray, as John also taught his *d* .... Lk 11:1
to say unto his *d* first of all .... Lk 12:1
he said unto his *d*, Therefore .... Lk 12:22
And he said also unto his *d* .... Lk 16:1
Then said he unto the *d*, It is .... Lk 17:1
And he said unto the *d*, The days ...... Lk 17:22
but when his *d* saw it, they .... Lk 18:15
of Olives, he sent two of his *d* .... Lk 19:29
of the *d* began to rejoice .... Lk 19:37
unto him, Master, rebuke thy *d* .... Lk 19:39
all the people he said unto his *d* .... Lk 20:45
shall eat the passover with my *d* .... Lk 22:11
and his *d* also followed him .... Lk 22:39
from prayer, and was come to his *d* ... Lk 22:45
after John stood, and two of his *d* ..... Jn 1:35
the two *d* heard him speak, and .... Jn 1:37
both Jesus was called, and his *d* .... Jn 2:2
and his *d* believed on him .... Jn 2:11
mother, and his brethren, and his *d* ... Jn 2:12
his *d* remembered that he was .... Jn 2:17
his *d* remembered that he had said .... Jn 2:22
his *d* into the land of Judaea .... Jn 3:22
question between some of John's *d* ... Jn 3:25
made and baptized more *d* than John . Jn 4:1
himself baptized not, but his *d* .... Jn 4:2
(For his *d* were gone away unto .... Jn 4:8
And upon this came his *d*, and .... Jn 4:27
the mean while his *d* prayed him........ Jn 4:31
said the *d* one to another.................. Jn 4:33
and there he sat with his *d* .... Jn 6:3
One of his *d*, Andrew, Simon .... Jn 6:8
thanks, he distributed to the *d* .... Jn 6:11
the *d* to them that were set down ...... Jn 6:11
were filled, he said unto his *d* .... Jn 6:12
his *d* went down unto the sea, ... Jn 6:16
one wherefore his *d* were entered ..... Jn 6:22
went not with his *d* into the boat ...... Jn 6:22
but that his *d* were gone away .... Jn 6:22
was not there, neither his *d* .... Jn 6:24
Many therefore of his *d*, when .... Jn 6:60
himself that his *d* murmured at it ...... Jn 6:61
that time many of his *d* went back ..... Jn 6:66
that thy *d* also may see the works ..... Jn 7:3
my word, then are ye my *d* indeed..... Jn 8:31
his *d* asked him, saying, Master, ... Jn 9:2
will ye also be his *d* .... Jn 9:27
but we are Moses' *d* .... Jn 9:28
Then after that saith he to his *d* .... Jn 11:7
His *d* say unto him, Master, the .... Jn 11:8
Then said his *d*, Lord, if he .... Jn 11:12
and there continued with his *d* .... Jn 11:54
his *d*, Judas .... Jn 12:4
understood not his *d* at the first .... Jn 12:16
Then the *d* looked one on another,.... Jn 13:22
on Jesus' bosom one of his *d* .... Jn 13:23
all men know that ye are my *d* .... Jn 13:35
so shall ye be my *d* .... Jn 15:8
some of his *d* among themselves........ Jn 16:17
His *d* said unto him, Lo, now, ... Jn 16:29
the which he entered, and his *d* .... Jn 18:1
resorted thither with his *d* .... Jn 18:2
not thou also one of this man's *d* ...... Jn 18:17
priest then asked Jesus of his *d* .... Jn 18:19
Art not thou also one of his *d* .... Jn 18:25
Then the *d* went away again unto ...... Jn 20:10
told the *d* that she had seen the .... Jn 20:18
the doors were shut where the *d* ...... Jn 20:19
Then were the *d* glad, when they ...... Jn 20:20
The other *d* therefore said unto .... Jn 20:25
days again his *d* were within .... Jn 20:26
Jesus in the presence of his *d* .... Jn 20:30
to the *d* at the sea of Tiberias .... Jn 21:1
of Zebedee, and two other of his *d* ... Jn 21:2
but the *d* knew not that it was .... Jn 21:4
the other *d* came in a little ship .... Jn 21:8
none of the *d* durst ask him, Who ...... Jn 21:12
Jesus shewed himself to his *d* .... Jn 21:14
stood up in the midst of the *d* .... Acts 1:15
number of the *d* was multiplied .... Acts 6:1
the multitude of the *d* unto them .... Acts 6:2
the number of the *d* multiplied in .... Acts 6:7
against the *d* of the Lord .... Acts 9:1
with the *d* which were at Damascus ... Acts 9:19
Then the *d* took him by night, and ..... Acts 9:25
assayed to join himself to the *d* .... Acts 9:26
had heard that Peter was .... Acts 9:38
the *d* were called Christians............... Acts 11:26
Then the *d*, every man according ...... Acts 11:29
the *d* were filled with joy, and........... Acts 13:52
as the *d* stood round about him, ... Acts 14:20
Confirming the souls of the *d* .... Acts 14:22
they abode long time with the *d* .... Acts 14:28
put a yoke upon the neck of the *d* .... Acts 15:10
in order, strengthening all the *d* .... Acts 18:23
exhorting the *d* to receive him .... Acts 19:30
and finding certain *d* .... Acts 19:1
from them, and separated the *d* .... Acts 19:9
people, the *d* suffered him not .... Acts 19:30
Paul called unto him the *d* .... Acts 20:1
when the *d* came together to break ... Acts 20:7
things, to draw away *d* after them ..... Acts 20:30

And finding *d*, we tarried there .... Acts 21:4
also certain of the *d* of Caesarea .... Acts 21:16

DISCIPLES'
and began to wash the *d* feet .... Jn 13:5

DISCIPLINE
He openeth also their ear to *d* .... Job 36:10

DISCLOSE
the earth also shall *d* her blood .... Is 26:21

DISCOMFITED
And Joshua of Amalek and his people .... Ex 17:13
d them, even unto Hormah .... Num 14:45
the Lord *d* them before Israel, and .... Josh 10:10
And the Lord *d* Sisera, and all his .... Judg 4:15
and Zalmunna, and *d* all the host .... Judg 8:12
upon the Philistines, and *d* them 1Sa 7:10
lightning, and *d* them 2Sa 22:15
he shot out lightnings, and *d* them .... Ps 18:14
and his young men shall be *d* .... Is 31:8

DISCOMFITURE
and there was a very great *d* 1Sa 14:20

DISCONTENTED
in debt, and every one that was *d* 1Sa 22:2

DISCONTINUE
shalt *d* from thine heritage that .... Jer 17:4

DISCORD
he soweth *d* .... Prov 6:14
he that soweth *d* among brethren .... Prov 6:19

DISCOURAGE
wherefore *d* ye the heart of the .... Num 32:7

DISCOURAGED
was much *d* because of the way .... Num 21:4
they *d* the heart of the children .... Num 32:9
fear not, neither be *d* .... Deut 1:21
our brethren have *d* our heart .... Deut 1:28
He shall not fail nor be *d* .... Is 42:4
children to anger, lest they be *d* .... Col 3:21

DISCOVER
wife, nor *d* his father's skirt .... Deut 22:30
we will *d* ourselves unto them 1Sa 14:8
Who can *d* the face of his garment .... Job 41:13
but that his heart may *d* itself .... Prov 18:2
d not a secret to another .... Prov 25:9
the Lord will *d* their secret .... Is 3:17
Therefore will I *d* thy skirts .... Jer 13:26
he will *d* thy sins .... Lam 4:22
will *d* thy nakedness unto them, ... Eze 16:37
now will I *d* her lewdness in the .... Hos 2:10
I will *d* the foundations thereof .... Mic 1:6
I will *d* thy skirts upon thy face .... Nah 3:5

DISCOVERED
thy nakedness be not *d* therefore .... Ex 20:26
the hatch *d* her fountain, and she .... Lev 20:18
both of them *d* themselves unto 1Sa 14:11
When Saul heard that David was *d* 1Sa 22:6
foundations of the world were *d* 2Sa 22:16
of the world were *d* at thy rebuke. .... Ps 18:15
he *d* the covering of Judah, and .... Is 22:8
for thou hast *d* thyself to .... Is 57:8
thine iniquity are thy skirts *d* .... Jer 13:22
they have not *d* thine iniquity, ... Lam 2:14
the foundation thereof shall be *d* .... Eze 13:14
thy nakedness *d* through thy .... Eze 16:36
Before thy wickedness was *d* .... Eze 16:57
in that your transgressions are *d* .... Eze 21:24
In thee have they *d* their .... Eze 22:10
These *d* her nakedness. .... Eze 23:10
So she *d* her whoredoms, and .... Eze 23:18
her whoredoms, and *d* her nakedness. .... Eze 23:18
of thy whoredoms shall be *d* .... Eze 23:29
the iniquity of Ephraim was *d* .... Hos 7:1
Now when we had *d* Cyprus, we left... .... Acts 21:3
that a certain creek with a *d* .... Acts 27:39

DISCOVERETH
He *d* deep things out of darkness, ... Job 12:22
hinds to calve, and the forests *d* .... Ps 29:9

DISCOVERING
by *d* the foundation unto the neck .... Hab 3:13

DISCREET
let Pharaoh look out a man *d* .... Gen 41:33
thee all this, there is none so *d* .... Gen 41:39
To be *d*, chaste, keepers at home, ... Titus 2:5

DISCREETLY
when Jesus saw that he answered *d* .... Mk 12:34

DISCRETION
he will guide his affairs with *d* .... Ps 112:5
to the young man knowledge and *d* .... Prov 1:4
d shall preserve thee, ... Prov 2:11
keep sound wisdom and *d* .... Prov 3:21
That thou mayest regard *d* .... Prov 5:2
a fair woman which is without *d* .... Prov 11:22
The *d* of a man deferreth his. .... Prov 19:11
his God doth instruct him to *d* .... Is 28:26
out the heavens by his *d* .... Jer 10:12

DISDAINED
about, and saw David, he *d* him 1Sa 17:42
whose fathers I would have to *d* .... Job 30:1

DISEASE
whether I shall recover of this *d* 2Kin 1:2
saying, Shall I recover of this *d* 2Kin 8:8
saying, Shall I recover of this *d* 2Kin 8:9

until his *d* was exceeding great 2Chr 16:12
yet in his *d* he sought not to the 2Chr 16:12
great sickness by *d* of thy bowels 2Chr 21:15
in his bowels with an incurable *d* 2Chr 21:18
of my *d* is my garment changed .... Job 30:18
are filled with a loathsome *d* .... Ps 38:7
An evil *d*, say they, cleaveth .... Ps 41:8
is vanity, and it is an evil *d* .... Eccl 6:2
all manner of *d* among the people. .... Mt 4:23
and every *d* among the people .... Mt 9:35
of sickness and all manner of *d* .... Mt 10:1
made whole of whatsoever *d* he had .... Jn 5:4

DISEASED
his old age he was *d* in his feet. 1Kin 15:23
of his reign was *d* in his feet 2Chr 16:12
The *d* have ye not strengthened, ... Eze 34:4
pushed all the *d* with your horns, ... Eze 34:21
which was *d* with an issue of .... Mt 9:20
brought unto him all that were *d* .... Mt 14:35
brought unto him all that were *d* .... Mk 1:32
which he did on them that were *d* .... Jn 6:2

DISEASES
put none of these *d* upon thee. .... Ex 15:26
put none of the evil of Egypt upon .... Deut 7:15
upon thee all the *d* of Egypt .... Deut 28:60
so he died of sore *d* 2Chr 21:19
(for they left him in great *d* 2Chr 24:25
who healeth all thy *d* .... Ps 103:3
that were taken with divers *d* .... Mt 4:24
many that were sick of divers *d* .... Mk 1:34
divers *d* brought them unto him .... Lk 4:40
him, and to be healed of their *d* .... Lk 6:17
over all devils, and to cure *d* .... Lk 9:1
the *d* departed from them, and the ... . Acts 19:12
which had *d* in the island, came, ... Acts 28:9

DISFIGURE
for they *d* their faces, that they .... Mt 6:16

DISGRACE
do not *d* the throne of thy glory .... Jer 14:21

DISGUISE
d thyself, that thou be not known 1Kin 14:2
unto Jehoshaphat, I will *d* myself 1Kin 22:30
unto Jehoshaphat, I will *d* myself 2Chr 18:29

DISGUISED
Saul *d* himself, and put on other 1Sa 28:8
d himself with ashes upon his... .... 1Kin 20:38
And the king of Israel *d* himself 1Kin 22:30
So the king of Israel *d* himself 2Chr 18:29
but *d* himself, that he might 2Chr 35:22

DISGUISETH
and *d* his face .... Job 24:15

DISH
forth butter in a lordly *d* .... Judg 5:25
Jerusalem as a man wipeth a *d* 2Kin 21:13
dippeth his hand with me in the *d* ... . Mt 26:23
that dippeth with me in the *d* .... Mk 14:20

DISHAN (di'-shan) See DISHON. A son of Seir.
And Dishon, and Ezer, and D .... Gen 36:21
The children of D are these .... Gen 36:28
Duke Dishon, duke Ezer, duke D .... Gen 36:30
and Dishon, and Ezer, and D 1Chr 1:38
The sons of D 1Chr 1:42

DISHES
And thou shalt make the *d* thereof ... . Ex 25:29
which were upon the table, his *d* ... . Ex 37:16
of blue, and put thereon the *d* .... Num 4:7

DISHON (di'-shon) See DISHAN.
 1. A son of Seir.
And D, and Ezer, and Dishan .... Gen 36:21
And these are the children of D .... Gen 36:26
Duke D, duke Ezer, duke Dishan .... Gen 36:30
Shobal, and Zibeon, and Anah, and D 1Chr 1:38
 2. A son of Anah.
D, and Aholibamah the daughter of ... Gen 36:25
The sons of Anah; D 1Chr 1:41
And the sons of D 1Chr 1:41

DISHONEST
thy *d* gain which thou hast made ... . Eze 22:13
to destroy souls, to get *d* gain .... Eze 22:27

DISHONESTY
renounced the hidden things of *d* 2Cor 4:2

DISHONOUR
meet for us to see the king's *d* .... Ezr 4:14
d that magnify themselves against... .... Ps 35:26
my reproach, and my shame, and my *d* Ps 69:19
reproach and *d* that seek my hurt.... .... Ps 71:13
A wound and *d* shall he get .... Prov 6:33
I honour my Father, and ye *d* me.... .... Jn 8:49
to *d* their own bodies between .... Rom 1:24
unto honour, and another unto *d* ...... Rom 9:21
It is sown in *d* 1Cor 15:43
By honour and *d*, by evil report and .. 2Cor 6:8
and some to honour, and some to *d* ... 2Ti 2:20

DISHONOUREST
breaking the law of thou God .... Rom 2:23

DISHONOURETH
For the son of the father, the .... Mic 7:6
his head covered, *d* his head.......... 1Cor 11:4
her head uncovered *d* her head 1Cor 11:5

DISINHERIT
d them, and will make of thee a .... Num 14:12

DISMAYED
fear not, neither be *d* .... Deut 31:8
be not afraid, neither be thou *d* ...... Josh 1:9
Fear not, neither be thou *d* .... Josh 8:1
unto them, Fear not, nor be *d* .... Josh 10:25
of the Philistine, they were *d* 1Sa 17:11
of small power, they were *d* 2Kin 19:26
dread not, nor be *d* 1Chr 22:13
fear not, nor be *d* 1Chr 28:20
Be not afraid nor *d* by reason of 2Chr 20:15
fear not, nor be *d* 2Chr 20:17
be not afraid nor *d* for the king 2Chr 32:7
I was *d* at the seeing of it .... Is 21:3
were of small power, they were *d* .... Is 37:27
be not *d* .... Is 41:10
or do evil, that we may be *d* .... Is 41:23
be not *d* at their faces, lest I .... Jer 1:17
wise men are ashamed, they are *d* ... Jer 8:9
be not *d* at the signs of heaven ...... Jer 10:2
for the heathen are *d* at them .... Jer 10:2
be *d*, but let not me be *d* .... Jer 17:18
they shall fear no more, nor be *d* .... Jer 23:4
neither be *d*, O Israel .... Jer 30:10
Wherefore have I seen them *d* .... Jer 46:5
O my servant Jacob, and be not *d* .... Jer 46:27
Misgab is confounded and *d* .... Jer 48:1
Elam to be before their enemies, ... Jer 49:37
and they shall be *d* .... Jer 50:36
nor be *d* at their looks, though .... Eze 2:6
neither be *d* at their looks, ... Eze 3:9
mighty men, O Teman, shall be *d* ...... Obad 9

DISMAYING
a *d* to all them about him .... Jer 48:39

DISMISSED
the priest *d* not the courses 2Chr 23:8
So when they were *d*, they came to... Acts 15:30
thus spoken, he *d* the assembly ...... Acts 19:41

DISOBEDIENCE
For as by one man's *d* many were .... Rom 5:19
in a readiness to revenge all *d* 2Cor 10:6
now worketh in the children of *d* .... Eph 2:2
of God upon the children of *d* .... Eph 5:6
God cometh on the children of *d* ...... Col 3:6
d received a just recompence of ...... Heb 2:2

DISOBEDIENT
who was *d* unto the word of the 1Kin 13:26
Nevertheless they were *d*, and .... Neh 9:26
the *d* to the wisdom of the just .... Lk 1:17
I was not *d* unto the heavenly .... Acts 26:19
of evil things, *d* to parents, ... Rom 1:30
stretched forth my hands unto a *d* ... Rom 10:21
man, but for the lawless and *d* 1Ti 1:9
d to parents, unthankful, unholy, ... 2Ti 3:2
deny him, being abominable, and *d* ... Titus 1:16
also were sometimes foolish, *d* .... Titus 3:3
but unto them which be *d*, the 1Pet 2:7
stumble at the word, being *d* 1Pet 2:8
Which sometime were *d*, when once ... 1Pet 3:20

DISOBEYED
thou hast *d* the mouth of the LORD ... 1Kin 13:21

DISORDERLY
from every brother that walketh *d* ... 2Th 3:6
behaved not ourselves among you 2Th 3:7
are some which walk among you *d* ... 2Th 3:11

DISPATCH
and *d* them with their swords .... Eze 23:47

DISPENSATION
a *d* of the gospel is committed 1Cor 9:17
That in the *d* of the fulness of .... Eph 1:10
If ye have heard of the *d* of the ...... Eph 3:2
according to the *d* of God which ...... Col 1:25

DISPERSE
D yourselves among the people, and ... 1Sa 14:34
The lips of the wise *d* knowledge .... Prov 15:7
and *d* them in the countries .... Eze 12:15
them through the countries .... Eze 20:23
d thee in the countries, and will .... Eze 22:15
will *d* them through the countries .... Eze 29:12
will *d* them through the countries .... Eze 30:23
d them among the countries. .... Eze 30:26

DISPERSED
d of all his children throughout. 2Chr 11:23
d among the people in all the .... Est 3:8
He hath *d*, he hath given to the ...... Ps 112:9
Let thy fountains be *d* abroad .... Prov 5:16
gather together the *d* of Judah .... Is 11:12
they were *d* through the countries .... Eze 36:19
even the daughter of my *d* .... Zeph 3:10
go unto the *d* among the Gentiles .... Jn 7:35
as many as obeyed him, were *d* .... Acts 5:37
it is written, He hath *d* abroad 2Cor 9:9

DISPERSIONS
of your *d* are accomplished .... Jer 25:34

DISPLAYED
that it may be *d* because of the .... Ps 60:4

DISPLEASE
Let it not *d* my lord that I .... Gen 31:35
now therefore, if it *d* thee .... Num 22:34
that thou *d* not the lords of the 1Sa 29:7
Joab, Let not this thing *d* thee 2Sa 11:25
it *d* him, and he turn away his .... Prov 24:18

DISPLEASED

the thing which he did d the LORD ..... Gen 38:10
the head of Ephraim, it d him .... Gen 48:17
people complained, it d the LORD ...... Num 11:1
Moses also was d. .... Num 11:10
But the thing of Samuel, when they 1Sa 8:6
very wroth, and the saying d him 1Sa 18:8
And David was d, because the LORD 2Sa 6:8
that David had done d the LORD 2Sa 11:27
his father had not d him at any 1Kin 1:6
went to his house heavy and d 1Kin 20:43
d because of the word which 1Kin 21:4
And David was d, because the LORD 1Chr 13:11
God was d with this thing 1Chr 21:7
scattered us, thou hast been d. .... Ps 60:1
it d him that there was no .... Is 59:15
was sore d with himself, and set. .... Dan 6:14
But it d Jonah exceedingly, and he ..... Jonah 4:1
Was the LORD d against the rivers....... Hab 3:8
been sore d with your fathers............ Zec 1:2
I am very sore d with the heathen ..... Zec 1:15
for I was but a little d, and they .... Zec 1:15
they were sore d, ... Mt 21:15
when Jesus saw it, he was much d. ..... Mk 10:14
began to be much d with James .... Mk 10:41
Herod was highly d with them of .... Acts 12:20

DISPLEASURE

was afraid of the anger and hot d. ...... Deut 9:19
Philistines, though I do them a d .... Judg 15:3
wrath, and vex them in his sore d ...... Ps 2:5
neither chasten me in thy hot d. .... Ps 6:1
neither chasten me in thy hot d. .... Ps 38:1

DISPOSED

Or who hath d the whole world. .... Job 34:13
Dost thou know when God d them. ..... Job 37:15
when he was d to pass into Achaia..... Acts 18:27
you to a feast, and ye be d to go. 1Cor 10:27

DISPOSING

but the whole d thereof is of the........ Prov 16:33

DISPOSITION

the law by the d of angels................... Acts 7:53

DISPOSSESS

ye shall d the inhabitants of the......... Num 33:53
how can I d them .... Deut 7:17

DISPOSSESSED

d the Amorite which was in it .... Num 32:39
the Amorites from before his............. Judg 11:23

DISPUTATION

d with them, they determined that ..... Acts 15:2

DISPUTATIONS

receive ye, but not to doubtful d......... Rom 14:1

DISPUTE

the righteous might d with him .... Job 23:7

DISPUTED

What was it that ye d among .... Mk 9:33
way they had d among themselves ..... Mk 9:34
Jesus, and d against the Grecians....... Acts 9:29
Therefore d he in the synagogue .... Acts 17:17
he d about the body of Moses............. Jude 9

DISPUTER

where is the d of this world................ 1Cor 1:20

DISPUTING

and of Asia, d with Stephen .... Acts 6:9
And when there had been much d ...... Acts 15:7
for the space of three months, d .... Acts 19:8
d daily in the school of one .... Acts 19:9
me in the temple with any man .... Acts 24:12

DISPUTINGS

things without murmurings and d...... Phil 2:14
Perverse d of men of corrupt 1Ti 6:5

DISQUIET

the inhabitants of Babylon .... Jer 50:34

DISQUIETED

said to Saul, Why hast thou d me 1Sa 28:15
surely they are d in vain .... Ps 39:6
and why art thou d in me................... Ps 42:5
and why art thou d within me .... Ps 42:11
and why art thou d within me .... Ps 43:5
For three things the earth is d .... Prov 30:21

DISQUIETNESS

by reason of the d of my heart. .... Ps 38:8

DISSEMBLED

d also, and they have put it even........ Josh 7:11
For ye d in your hearts, when ye .... Jer 42:20
the other Jews d likewise with .... Gal 2:13

DISSEMBLERS

neither will I go in with d.................. Ps 26:4

DISSEMBLETH

He that hateth d with his lips .... Prov 26:24

DISSENSION

Paul and Barnabas had no small ...... Acts 15:2
there arose a d between the .... Acts 23:7
And when there arose a great d .... Acts 23:10

DISSIMULATION

Let love be without d......................... Rom 12:9
was carried away with their d .... Gal 2:13

DISSOLVE

make interpretations, and d doubts ..... Dan 5:16

DISSOLVED

all the inhabitants thereof are d......... Ps 75:3
thou, whole Palestina, art d .... Is 14:31
broken down, the earth is clean d ..... Is 24:19
all the host of heaven shall be d .... Is 34:4
opened, and the palace shall be d ...... Nah 2:6
house of this tabernacle were d 2Cor 5:1
that all these things shall be d 2Pet 3:11
heavens being on fire shall be d 2Pet 3:12

DISSOLVEST

ride upon it, and d my substance....... Job 30:22

DISSOLVING

of doubts, were found in the. .... Dan 5:12

DISTAFF

spindle, and her hands hold the d ..... Prov 31:19

DISTANT

equally d one from another .... Ex 36:22

DISTIL

my speech shall d as the dew .... Deut 32:2
do drop and d upon man abundantly ... Job 36:28

DISTINCTION

they give a d in the sounds................ 1Cor 14:7

DISTINCTLY

in the book in the law of God d.......... Neh 8:8

DISTRACTED

while I suffer thy terrors I am d .... Ps 88:15

DISTRACTION

attend upon the Lord without d 1Cor 7:35

DISTRESS

answered me in the day of my d .... Gen 35:3
therefore is this d come upon us .... Gen 42:21
D not the Moabites, neither............... Deut 2:9
d them not, nor meddle with them..... Deut 2:19
thine enemies shall d thee .... Deut 28:53
shall d thee in all thy gates .... Deut 28:55
enemy shall d thee in thy gates. .... Deut 28:57
come unto me now when ye are in d. ... Judg 11:7
And every one that was in d 1Sa 22:2
In my d I called upon the LORD,......... 2Sa 22:7
redeemed my soul out of all d. 1Kin 1:29
in the time of his d did he 2Chr 28:22
Ye see the d that we are in, how......... Neh 2:17
pleasure, and we are in great d. .... Neh 9:37
hast enlarged me when I was in d ...... Ps 4:1
In my d I called upon the LORD,......... Ps 18:6
I called upon the LORD in d. .... Ps 118:5
In my d I cried unto the LORD, and.... Ps 120:1
when d and anguish cometh............... Prov 1:27
a strength to the needy in his d .... Is 25:4
Yet I will d Ariel, and there .... Is 29:2
and her munition, and that d her ...... Is 29:7
land at this once, and will d them...... Jer 10:18
for I am in d. .... Lam 1:20
spoken proudly in the day of d .... Obad 12
that did remain in the day of d .... Obad 14
of wrath, a day of trouble and d .... Zeph 1:15
And I will bring d upon men. .... Zeph 1:17
shall be great d in the land .... Lk 21:23
and upon the earth d of nations......... Lk 21:25
shall tribulation, or d, or.................... Rom 8:35
this is good for the present d 1Cor 7:26
our affliction and d by your faith....... 1Th 3:7

DISTRESSED

Jacob was greatly afraid and d .... Gen 32:7
Moab was d because of the .... Num 22:3
and they were greatly d. .... Judg 2:15
so that Israel was sore d .... Judg 10:9
a strait, (for the people were d. 1Sa 13:6
the men of Israel were d that day 1Sa 14:24
And Saul answered, I am sore d. 1Sa 28:15
And David was greatly d. 1Sa 30:6
I am d for thee, my brother................ 2Sa 1:26
d him, but strengthened him not 2Chr 28:20
troubled on every side, yet not d. 2Cor 4:8

DISTRESSES

O bring thou me out of my d. .... Ps 25:17
he delivered them out of their d......... Ps 107:6
and he saved them out of their d .... Ps 107:13
and he saveth them out of their d ...... Ps 107:19
he bringeth them out of their d .... Ps 107:28
and Noph shall have d daily .... Eze 30:16
afflictions, in necessities, in d........... 2Cor 6:4
For Christ's sake 2Cor 12:10

DISTRIBUTE

d for inheritance in the plains .... Josh 13:32
to d the oblations of the LORD,.......... 2Chr 31:14
was to d unto their brethren .... Neh 13:13
d unto the poor, and thou shalt......... Lk 18:22
be rich in good works, ready to d 1Ti 6:18

DISTRIBUTED

d for inheritance to them.................. Josh 14:1
offered, of them, both Zadok d 1Chr 24:3
whom David had d in the house of 2Chr 23:18
he d to the disciples, and the .... Jn 6:11
But as God hath d to every man 1Cor 7:17
the rule which God hath d to us 2Cor 10:13

DISTRIBUTETH

God sorrows in his anger................... Job 21:17

DISTRIBUTING

D to the necessity of saints .... Rom 12:13

DISTRIBUTION

d was made unto every man .... Acts 4:35
and for your liberal d unto them........ 2Cor 9:13

DITCH

Yet shalt thou plunge me in the d ...... Job 9:31
fallen into the d which he made .... Ps 7:15
For a whore is a deep d..................... Prov 23:27
Ye made also a d between the two ..... Is 22:11
blind, both shall fall into the d .... Mt 15:14
they not both fall into the .... Lk 6:39

DITCHES

LORD, Make this valley full of d......... 2Kin 3:16

DIVERS

not sow thy vineyard with d seeds...... Deut 22:9
not wear a garment of d sorts .... Deut 22:11
not have in thy bag d weights............ Deut 25:13
have in thine house d measures......... Deut 25:14
to Sisera a prey of d colours.............. Judg 5:30
a prey of d colours of needlework...... Judg 5:30
of d colours of needlework on .... Judg 5:30
a garment of d colours upon her 2Sa 13:18
rent her garment of d colours 2Sa 13:19
of d colours, and all manner of 1Chr 29:2
of kinds of spices prepared by the..... 2Chr 16:14
d also of the princes of Israel............. 2Chr 21:4
Nevertheless d of Asher and 2Chr 30:11
He sent d sorts of flies among .... Ps 78:45
there came d sorts of flies, and .... Ps 105:31
D weights, and d measures, ... Prov 20:10
D weights are an abomination unto .. Prov 20:23
words there are also d vanities .... Eccl 5:7
thy high places with d colours .... Eze 16:16
of feathers, which had d colours .... Eze 17:3
that were taken with d diseases......... Mt 4:24
and earthquakes, in d places............. Mt 24:7
many that were sick of d diseases ..... Mk 1:34
for d of them came from far .... Mk 8:3
shall be earthquakes in d places........ Mk 13:8
d diseases brought them unto him..... Lk 4:40
earthquakes shall be in d places........ Lk 21:11
But when d were hardened, and......... Acts 19:9
to another d kinds of tongues............ 1Cor 12:10
with sins, led away with d lusts.......... 2Ti 3:6
deceived, serving d lusts .... Titus 3:3
in d manners spake in time past........ Heb 1:1
with d miracles, and gifts of the .... Heb 2:4
d washings, and carnal ordinances.... Heb 9:10
Be not carried about with d .... Heb 13:9
when ye fall into d temptations.......... Jas 1:2

DIVERSE

thy cattle gender with a d kind........... Lev 19:19
vessels being d one from another ...... Est 1:7
their laws are d from all people .... Est 3:8
from the sea, d one from another....... Dan 7:3
it was d from all the beasts that......... Dan 7:7
which was d from all the others, ... Dan 7:19
which shall be d from all................... Dan 7:23
he shall be d from the first, and......... Dan 7:24

DIVERSITIES

Now there are d of gifts, but the........ 1Cor 12:4
there are d of operations, but it......... 1Cor 12:6
helps, governments, d of tongues...... 1Cor 12:28

DIVIDE

let it d the waters from the................ Gen 1:6
to d the day from the night .... Gen 1:14
to d the light from the darkness........ Gen 1:18
I will d them in Jacob, and .... Gen 49:7
and at night he shall d the spoil......... Gen 49:27
thine hand over the sea, and d it .... Ex 14:16
will overtake, I will d the spoil .... Ex 15:9
the live ox, and d the money of it...... Ex 21:35
and the dead ox also they shall d....... Ex 21:35
the vail shall d unto you between....... Ex 26:33
but shall not d it asunder .... Lev 1:17
neck, but shall not d it asunder .... Lev 5:8
cud, or of them that d the hoof .... Lev 11:4
the swine, though he d the hoof .... Lev 11:7
of the prey into two parts .... Num 31:27
ye shall d the land by lot for an .... Num 33:54
which shall d the land unto you......... Num 34:17
to d the land by inheritance .... Num 34:18
for d the inheritance among .... Num 34:29
or of them that d the cloven hoof ...... Deut 14:7
chew the cud, but d not the hoof ...... Deut 14:7
d the coasts of thy land, which .... Deut 19:3
d for an inheritance the land .... Josh 1:6
only d thou it by lot unto the .... Josh 13:6
Now therefore d this land for an .... Josh 13:7
they shall d it into seven parts.......... Josh 18:5
the spoil of your enemies with.......... Josh 22:8
Said, Thou and Ziba d the land .... Josh 19:29
D the living child in two, and............ 1Kin 3:25
neither mine nor thine, but d it 1Kin 3:26
thou didst d the sea before the .... Neh 9:11
didst d them into corners.................. Neh 9:22
the innocent shall d the silver .... Job 27:17
O Lord, and d their tongues............... Ps 55:9
I will d Shechem, and mete out the .. Ps 60:6
Thou didst d the sea by thy .... Ps 74:13
I will d Shechem, and mete out the .. Ps 108:7
than to d the spoil with the .... Prov 16:19
men rejoice when they d the spoil..... Is 9:3

D

DIVIDED

Therefore will I d him a portion	Is 53:12
he shall d the spoil with the	Is 53:12
balances to weigh, and the hair	Eze 5:1
when ye shall d by lot the land	Eze 45:1
So shall ye d this land unto you	Eze 47:21
that ye shall d it by lot for an	Eze 47:22
shall d by lot unto the tribes of	Eze 48:29
shall d the land for gain	Dan 11:39
that he d the inheritance with me	Lk 12:13
this, and d it among yourselves	Lk 22:17

DIVIDETH

God d the light from the darkness	Gen 1:4
d the waters which were under the	Gen 1:7
of the Gentiles in their lands	Gen 10:5
for in his days was the earth d	Gen 10:25
by these were the nations d in	Gen 10:32
he d himself against them, he and	Gen 14:15
d them in the midst, and laid each	Gen 15:10
but the birds d he not	Gen 15:10
he d the people that was with him	Gen 32:7
he d the children unto Leah, and	Gen 33:1
dry land, and the waters were d	Ex 14:21
Unto these the land shall be d	Num 26:53
the land shall be d by	Num 26:55
thereof be d between many	Num 26:56
which Moses d from the men that	Num 31:42
hath d unto all nations under the	Deut 4:19
When the Most High d to the	Deut 32:8
of Israel did, and they d the land	Josh 14:5
there Joshua d the land unto the	Josh 18:10
d for an inheritance by lot in	Josh 18:51
I have d unto you by lot these	Josh 23:4
have they not d the prey	Judg 5:30
he d the three hundred men into	Judg 7:16
d them into three companies, and	Judg 9:43
d her, together with her bones	Judg 19:29
and in their death they were not d	2Sa 1:23
people of Israel d into two parts	1Kin 16:21
So they d the land between them	1Kin 18:6
the waters, and they were d hither	2Kin 2:8
in his days the earth was d	1Chr 1:19
David d them into courses among	1Chr 23:6
and thus were they d	1Chr 24:4
Thus were they d by lot, one sort	1Chr 24:5
d them speedily among all the	2Chr 35:13
Who hath d a watercourse for the	Job 38:25
that tarried at home of the spoil	Ps 68:12
He d the sea, and caused them to	Ps 78:13
d them an inheritance by line, and	Ps 78:55
To him which d the Red sea into	Ps 136:13
is the prey of a great spoil d	Is 33:23
his hand hath d it unto them by	Is 34:17
that d the sea, whose waves	Is 51:15
The anger of the Lord hath d them	Lam 4:16
neither shall they be d into two	Eze 37:22
of iron, the kingdom shall be d	Dan 2:41
Thy kingdom is d, and given to the	Dan 5:28
shall be d toward the four winds	Dan 11:4
Their heart is d	Hos 10:2
and thy land shall be d by line	Amos 7:17
turning away by hath d our fields	Mic 2:4
thy spoil shall be d in the midst	Zec 14:1
Every kingdom d against itself is	Mt 12:25
every city or house d against	Mt 12:25
Satan, he is d against himself	Mt 12:26
if a kingdom be d against itself	Mk 3:24
if a house be d against itself	Mk 3:25
rise up against himself, and be d	Mk 3:26
the two fishes d he among them	Mk 6:41
Every kingdom d against itself is	Lk 11:17
a house d against a house falleth	Lk 11:17
Satan also be d against himself	Lk 11:18
shall be five in one house d	Lk 12:52
father shall be d against the son	Lk 12:53
he d unto them his living	Lk 15:12
he d their land to them by lot	Acts 13:19
the multitude of the city was d	Acts 14:4
and the multitude was d	Acts 23:7
Is Christ d?	1Cor 1:13
great city was d into three parts	Rev 16:19

DIVIDER

made me a judge or a d over you	Lk 12:14

DIVIDETH

the cud, but d not the hoof	Lev 11:4
the cud, but d not the hoof	Lev 11:5
the cud, but d not the hoof	Lev 11:6
of every beast which d the hoof	Lev 11:26
the swine, because it d the hoof	Deut 14:8
He d the sea with his power, and	Job 26:12
of the Lord d the flames of fire	Ps 29:7
as a shepherd d his sheep from	Mt 25:32
he trusted, and d his spoils	Lk 11:22

DIVIDING

of d the land for inheritance by	Josh 19:49
they made an end of d the country	Josh 19:51
d the water before them, to make	Is 63:12
a time and times and d of time	Dan 7:25
d to every man severally as he	1Cor 12:11
rightly d the word of truth	2Ti 2:15
even to the d asunder of soul	Heb 4:12

DIVINATION

the rewards of d in their hand	Num 22:7
is there any d against Israel	Num 23:23
through the fire, or that useth d	Deut 18:10
pass through the fire, and used d	2Kin 17:17
unto you a false vision and d	Jer 14:14
d within the house of Israel	Eze 12:24

They have seen vanity and lying d	Eze 13:6
and have ye not spoken a lying d	Eze 13:7
head of the two ways, to use d	Eze 21:21
hand was the d for Jerusalem	Eze 21:22
them as a false d in their sight	Eze 21:23
with a spirit of d met us	Acts 16:16

DIVINATIONS

see no more vanity, nor divine d	Eze 13:23

DIVINE

such a man as I can certainly d	Gen 44:15
d unto me by the familiar spirit	1Sa 28:8
A d sentence is in the lips of	Prov 16:10
that see vanity, and that d lies	Eze 13:9
no more vanity, nor d divinations	Eze 13:23
whiles they d a lie unto thee, to	Eze 22:28
unto you, that ye shall not d	Mic 3:6
the prophets thereof d for money	Mic 3:11
had also ordinances of d service	Heb 9:1
According as his d power hath	2Pet 1:3
be partakers of the d nature	2Pet 1:4

DIVINERS

observers of times, and unto d	Deut 18:14
called for the priests and the d	1Sa 6:2
of the liars, and maketh d mad	Is 44:25
to your prophets, nor to your d	Jer 27:9
Let not your prophets and your d	Jer 29:8
be ashamed, and the d confounded	Mic 3:7
the d have seen a lie, and have	Zec 10:2

DIVINETH

drinketh, and whereby indeed he d	Gen 44:5

DIVINING

d lies unto them, saying, Thus	Eze 22:28

DIVISION

I will put a d between my people	Ex 8:23
after the d of the families of	2Chr 35:5
you, Nay; but rather d	Lk 12:51
So there was a d among the people	Jn 7:43
And there was a d among them	Jn 9:16
There was a d therefore again	Jn 10:19

DIVISIONS

to their d by their tribes	Josh 11:23
a possession according to their d	Josh 12:7
of Israel according to their d	Josh 18:10
For the d of Reuben there were	Judg 5:15
For the d of Reuben there were	Judg 5:16
Now these are the d of the sons	1Chr 24:1
Concerning the d of the porters	1Chr 26:1
For the d of the porters	1Chr 26:12
These are the d of the porters	1Chr 26:19
d of the families of the fathers	1Chr 26:26
might give according to the d of	2Chr 35:12
they set the priests in their d	Ezr 6:18
And of the Levites were d in Judah	Neh 11:36
brethren, mark them which cause d	Rom 16:17
and that there be no d among you	1Cor 1:10
you envying, and strife, and d	1Cor 3:3
I hear that there be d among you	1Cor 11:18

DIVORCE

away, and given her a bill of d	Jer 3:8

DIVORCED

or a d woman, or profane, or an	Lev 21:14
daughter be a widow, or d	Lev 22:13
of a widow, and her that is d	Num 30:9
her that is d committeth adultery	Mt 5:32

DIVORCEMENT

let him write her a bill of d	Deut 24:1
her, and write her a bill of d	Deut 24:3
is the bill of your mother's d	Is 50:1
let him give her a writing of d	Mt 5:31
command to give a writing of d	Mt 19:7
suffered to write a bill of d	Mk 10:4

DIZAHAB (diz'-a-hab) A place in the Sinai wilderness.

and Laban, and Hazeroth, and D	Deut 1:1

DO SEE PREFACE.

DOCTOR

a d of the law, had in reputation	Acts 5:34

DOCTORS

sitting in the midst of the d	Lk 2:46
d of the law sitting by, which	Lk 5:17

DOCTRINE

My d shall drop as the rain, my	Deut 32:2
My d is pure, and I am clean in	Job 11:4
For I give you good d, forsake ye	Prov 4:2
shall he make to understand d	Is 28:9
they that murmured shall learn d	Is 29:24
the stock is a d of vanities	Jer 10:8
people were astonished at his d	Mt 7:28
but of the d of the Pharisees and	Mt 16:12
they were astonished at his d	Mt 22:33
And they were astonished at his d	Mk 1:22
what new d is this	Mk 1:27
and said unto them in his d	Mk 4:2
people was astonished at his d	Mk 11:18
And he said unto them in his d	Mk 12:38
And they were astonished at his d	Lk 4:32
My d is not mine, but his that	Jn 7:16
his will, he shall know of the d	Jn 7:17
of his disciples, and of his d	Jn 18:19
stedfastly in the apostles' d and	Acts 2:42
have filled Jerusalem with your d	Acts 5:28
astonished at the d of the Lord	Acts 13:12

May we know what this new d	Acts 17:19
form of d which was delivered you	Rom 6:17
to the d which ye have learned	Rom 16:17
by prophesying, or by d	1Cor 14:6
one of you hath a psalm, hath a d	1Cor 14:26
about with every wind of d	Eph 4:14
some that they teach no other d	1Ti 1:3
thing that is contrary to sound d	1Ti 1:10
the words of faith and of good d	1Ti 4:6
to reading, to exhortation, to d	1Ti 4:13
heed unto thyself, and unto the d	1Ti 4:16
they who labour in the word and d	1Ti 5:17
of God and his d be not blasphemed	1Ti 6:1
of the d is according to	1Ti 6:3
But thou hast fully known my d	2Ti 3:10
of God, and is profitable for d	2Ti 3:16
with all longsuffering and d	2Ti 4:2
when they will not endure sound d	2Ti 4:3
be able by sound d both to exhort	Titus 1:9
the things which become sound d	Titus 2:1
in d shewing uncorruptness	Titus 2:7
that they may adorn the d of God	Titus 2:10
the principles of the d of Christ	Heb 6:1
Of the d of baptisms, and of	Heb 6:2
and abideth not in the d of Christ	2Jn 9
that abideth in the d of Christ	2Jn 9
any unto you, and bring not this d	2Jn 10
them that hold the d of Balaam	Rev 2:14
hold the d of the Nicolaitanes	Rev 2:15
as many as have not this d	Rev 2:24

DOCTRINES

teaching for d the commandments	Mt 15:9
teaching for d the commandments	Mk 7:7
the commandments and d of men	Col 2:22
seducing spirits, and d of devils	1Ti 4:1
about with divers and strange d	Heb 13:9

DODAI (do'-dahee) See Dodo. A captain in David's army.

the second month was D an Ahohite..	1Chr 27:4

DODANIM (do'-da-nim) See Rodanim. Descendants of Javan.

and Tarshish, Kittim, and D	Gen 10:4
and Tarshish, Kittim, and D	1Chr 1:7

DODAVAH (do'-da-vah) Father of Eliezer.

Then Eliezer the son of D of	2Chr 20:37

DODAVAHU See Dodavah.

DODO (do'-do) See Dodai.

1. Grandfather of Tola.

the son of Puah, the son of D	Judg 10:1

2. Father of Eleazar.

Eleazar the son of D the Ahohite	2Sa 23:9
him was Eleazar the son of D	1Chr 11:12

3. Father of Elhanan.

the son of D of Beth-lehem	2Sa 23:24
the son of D of Beth-lehem	1Chr 11:26

DOEG (do'-eg) Chief herdsman of King Saul.

and his name was D, an Edomite	1Sa 21:7
Then answered D the Edomite	1Sa 22:9
And the king said to D, Turn thou	1Sa 22:18
D the Edomite turned, and he fell	1Sa 22:18
when D the Edomite was there	1Sa 22:22
when D the Edomite came and told	Ps 52:t

DOER

did there, he was the d of it	Gen 39:22
the d of evil according to his	2Sa 3:39
plentifully rewardeth the proud d	Ps 31:23
A wicked d giveth heed to false	Prov 17:4
I suffer trouble, as an evil d	2Ti 2:9
a hearer of the word, and not a d	Jas 1:23
but a d of the work, this man	Jas 1:25
law, thou art not a d of the law	Jas 4:11

DOERS

the hand of the d of the work	2Kin 22:5
let them give it to the d of the	2Kin 22:5
neither will he help the evil d	Job 8:20
d from the city of the Lord	Ps 101:8
But be ye d of the word, and not	Jas 1:22

DOEST

If thou d well, shalt thou not be	Gen 4:7
If thou d not well, sin lieth at	Gen 4:7
is with thee in all that thou d	Gen 21:22
thing that thou d to the people	Ex 18:14
The thing that thou d is not good	Ex 18:17
when thou d that which is good and	Deut 12:28
work of thine hand which thou d	Deut 14:29
bless thee in all that thou d	Deut 15:18
but thou d me wrong to war	Judg 11:27
in, and to know all that thou d	2Sa 3:25
mayest prosper in all that thou d	1Kin 2:3
him, What d thou here, Elijah	1Kin 19:9
and said, What d thou here, Elijah	1Kin 19:13
and mark, and see what thou d	1Kin 20:22
will say unto him, What d thou	Job 9:12
sinnest, what d thou against him	Job 35:6
multiplied, what d thou unto him	Job 35:6
when thou d well to thyself	Ps 49:18
Thou art the God that d wonders	Ps 77:14
art great, and d wondrous things	Ps 86:10
Thou art good, and d good	Ps 119:68
who may say unto him, What d thou	Eccl 8:4
when thou d evil, then thou	Jer 11:15
shalt go aside to ask how thou d	Jer 15:5
said unto thee, What d thou	Eze 12:9
seeing thou d all these things	Eze 16:30

things are to us, that thou d so .... Eze 24:19
or say unto him, What d thou.......... Dan 4:35
the LORD, D thou well to be angry ..... Jonah 4:4
D thou well to be angry for the........ Jonah 4:9
Therefore when thou d thine alms........ Mt 6:2
But when thou d alms, let not thy...... Mt 6:3
authority d thou these things.......... Mt 21:23
authority d thou these things.......... Mk 11:28
authority d thou these things.......... Lk 20:2
seeing that thou d these things........ Jn 2:18
can do these miracles that thou d...... Jn 3:2
may see the works that thou d.......... Jn 7:3
said Jesus unto him, That thou d....... Jn 13:27
saying, Take heed what thou d.......... Acts 22:26
that judgest of the same things........ Rom 2:1
d the same, that thou shalt............ Rom 2:3
there is one God; thou d well.......... Jas 2:19
thou d faithfully whatsoever thou...... 3Jn 5
whatsoever thou d to the brethren...... 3Jn 5

DOETH

seen all that Laban d unto thee........ Gen 31:12
for whosoever d any work therein,...... Ex 31:14
whosoever d any work in the............ Ex 31:15
whosoever d work therein shall be...... Ex 35:2
while he d somewhat against any........ Lev 4:27
in any of all these that a man d....... Lev 6:3
that d any work in that same day....... Lev 23:30
But the soul that d ought.............. Num 15:30
who shall live when God d this......... Num 24:23
Which d great things and............... Job 5:9
Which d great things past finding...... Job 9:10
his soul desireth, even that he d...... Job 23:13
and d not good to the widow............ Job 24:21
great things d he, which we............ Job 37:5
and whatsoever he d shall prosper...... Ps 1:3
works, there is none that d good....... Ps 14:1
there is none that d good.............. Ps 14:3
nor d evil to his neighbour, nor....... Ps 15:3
He that d these things shall........... Ps 15:5
there is none that d good.............. Ps 53:1
there is none that d good.............. Ps 53:3
who only d wondrous things............. Ps 72:18
he that d righteousness at all......... Ps 106:3
hand of the LORD d valiantly........... Ps 118:15
hand of the LORD d valiantly........... Ps 118:16
To him who alone d great wonders....... Ps 136:4
he that d it destroyeth his own........ Prov 6:32
The merciful man d good to his......... Prov 11:17
the heart of the foolish d not so..... Prov 15:7
a fool d it to his sorrow.............. Prov 17:21
A merry heart d good like a............ Prov 17:22
A man that d violence to the........... Prov 28:17
and of mirth, What d it................ Eccl 2:2
I know that, whatsoever God d.......... Eccl 3:14
and God d it, that men should fear..... Eccl 3:14
just man upon earth, that d............ Eccl 7:20
for he d whatsoever pleaseth him....... Eccl 8:3
bind them on thee, as a bride d........ Is 49:18
Blessed is the man that d this......... Is 56:2
Wherefore the LORD our God d........... Jer 5:19
Cursed be he that d the work of........ Jer 48:10
he escape that d such things........... Eze 17:15
that d the like to any one of.......... Eze 18:10
that d not any of those duties,........ Eze 18:11
considereth, and d not such like,...... Eze 18:14
and d according to all the............. Eze 18:24
that the wicked man d, shall he........ Eze 18:24
d that which is lawful and right,...... Eze 18:27
he d according to his will in the...... Dan 4:35
in all his works what d he............. Dan 9:14
name, saith the LORD that d this....... Amos 9:12
will cut off the man that d this....... Mal 2:12
Every one that d evil is good in....... Mal 2:17
hand know what thy right hand d........ Mt 6:3
but he that d the will of my........... Mt 7:21
d them, I will liken him unto a........ Mt 7:24
of them not, shall be likened unto..... Mt 7:26
my servant, Do this, and he d it....... Mt 8:9
d them, I will shew you to whom........ Lk 6:47
d not, is like a man that without...... Lk 6:49
my servant, Do this, and he d.......... Lk 7:8
For every one that d evil hateth....... Jn 3:20
But he that d truth cometh to the...... Jn 3:21
for what things soever he d............ Jn 5:19
these also of the Son likewise......... Jn 5:19
him all things that himself d.......... Jn 5:20
no man that d any thing in secret...... Jn 7:4
it hear him, and know what he d........ Jn 9:31
of his will, him he heareth............ Jn 9:31
for this man d many miracles........... Jn 11:47
dwelleth in me, he d the works......... Jn 14:10
knoweth not what his lord d............ Jn 15:15
will think that he d God service....... Jn 16:2
the Lord, who d all these things....... Acts 15:17
This man d nothing worthy of........... Acts 26:31
every soul of man that d evil.......... Rom 2:9
there is none that d good.............. Rom 3:12
That the man which d these things...... Rom 10:5
wrath upon him that d evil............. Rom 13:4
that a man d is without the body....... 1Cor 6:18
he will keep his virgin, d well........ 1Cor 7:37
giveth her in marriage d well.......... 1Cor 7:38
her not in marriage d better........... 1Cor 7:38
d he it by the works of the law........ Gal 3:5
The man that d them shall live in...... Gal 3:12
whatsoever good thing any man d........ Eph 6:8
But he that d wrong shall receive...... Col 3:25
d it not, to him it is sin............. Jas 4:17
but he that d the will of God.......... 1Jn 2:17
ye know that every one that d.......... 1Jn 2:29

he that d righteousness is............. 1Jn 3:7
whosoever d not righteousness is....... 1Jn 3:10
remember his deeds which he d.......... 3Jn 10
He that d good is of God............... 3Jn 11
but he that d evil hath not seen....... 3Jn 11
he d great wonders, so that he......... Rev 13:13

DOG

shall not a d move his tongue.......... Ex 11:7
of a whore, or the price of a d........ Deut 23:18
as a d lappeth, him shalt thou......... Judg 7:5
said unto David, Am I a d.............. 1Sa 17:43
after a dead d, after a flea........... 1Sa 24:14
look upon such a dead d as I am........ 2Sa 9:8
Why should this dead d curse my........ 2Sa 16:9
But what, is thy servant a d........... 2Kin 8:13
darling from the power of the d........ Ps 22:20
they make a noise like a............... Ps 59:6
and let them make a noise like a d..... Ps 59:14
As a d returneth to his vomit, so,..... Prov 26:11
one that taketh a d by the ears........ Prov 26:17
for a living d is better than a........ Eccl 9:4
The d is turned to his own vomit....... 2Pet 2:22

DOG'S

and saith, Am I a d head, which........ 2Sa 3:8
a lamb, as if he cut off a d neck...... Is 66:3

DOGS

ye shall cast it to the d.............. Ex 22:31
in the city shall the d eat............ 1Kin 14:11
in the city shall the d eat............ 1Kin 16:4
In the place where d licked the........ 1Kin 21:19
of Naboth shall d lick thy blood...... 1Kin 21:19
The d shall eat Jezebel by the......... 1Kin 21:23
Ahab in the city the d shall eat....... 1Kin 21:24
the d licked up his blood.............. 1Kin 22:38
the d shall eat Jezebel in the......... 2Kin 9:10
shall d eat the flesh of Jezebel...... 2Kin 9:36
have set with the d of my flock....... Job 30:1
For d have compassed me................ Ps 22:16
the tongue of thy d in the same........ Ps 68:23
all ignorant, they are all dumb d...... Is 56:10
they are greedy d which can never...... Is 56:11
the d to tear, and the fowls of....... Jer 15:3
not that which is holy unto the d...... Mt 7:6
bread, and to cast it to d............. Mt 15:26
yet the d eat of the crumbs which..... Mt 15:27
bread, and to cast it unto d........... Mk 7:27
yet the d under the table eat of...... Mk 7:28
moreover the d came and licked his..... Lk 16:21
Beware of d, beware of evil............ Phil 3:2
For without are d, and sorcerers,..... Rev 22:15

DOING

hast now done foolishly in so d........ Gen 31:28
ye have done evil in so d.............. Gen 44:5
fearful in praises, d wonders.......... Ex 15:11
without d any thing else, go........... Num 20:19
in d wickedly in the sight of the..... Deut 9:18
So Hiram made an end of d all the..... 1Kin 7:40
d evil in the sight of the LORD....... 1Kin 16:19
d that which was right in the......... 1Kin 22:43
in d that which was evil in the....... 2Kin 21:16
Arise therefore, and be d, and the.... 1Chr 22:16
d that which was right in the......... 2Chr 20:32
d according to their abominations..... Ezr 9:1
I am d a great work, so that I........ Neh 6:3
in so d my maker would soon take...... Job 32:22
shall wisely consider of his d........ Ps 64:9
he is terrible in his d toward........ Ps 66:5
This is the LORD's d................... Ps 118:23
keepeth his hand from d any evil...... Is 56:2
from d thy pleasure on my holy........ Is 58:13
not d thine own ways, nor finding..... Is 58:13
this is the Lord's d, and it is....... Mt 21:42
when he cometh shall find so d........ Mt 24:46
This was the Lord's d, and it is...... Mk 12:11
when he cometh shall find so d........ Lk 12:43
who went about d good, and healing.... Acts 10:38
they have found any evil d in me...... Acts 24:20
in well d seek for glory and.......... Rom 2:7
for in so d thou shalt heap coals..... Rom 12:20
Now therefore perform the d of it..... 2Cor 8:11
And let us not be weary in well d..... Gal 6:9
d the will of God from the heart...... Eph 6:6
With good will d service, as to....... Eph 6:7
brethren, be not weary in well d...... 2Th 3:13
for in d this thou shalt do........... 1Ti 4:16
another, d nothing by partiality...... 1Ti 5:21
that with well d ye may put to........ 1Pet 2:15
be so, that ye suffer for well d...... 1Pet 3:17
for well d, than for evil d........... 1Pet 3:17
of their souls to him in well d....... 1Pet 4:19

DOINGS

After the d of the land of Egypt,..... Lev 18:3
after the d of the land of Canaan..... Lev 18:3
of the wickedness of thy d............ Deut 28:20
they ceased not from their own d...... Judg 2:19
man was churlish and evil in his d.... 1Sa 25:3
and not after the d of Israel......... 2Chr 17:4
declare among the people his d........ Ps 9:11
of all thy work, and talk of thy d.... Ps 77:12
Even a child is known by his d........ Prov 20:11
of your d from before mine eyes....... Is 1:16
thy d are against the LORD, to........ Is 3:8
shalt can the fruit of their d........ Is 3:10
declare his d among the people,...... Is 12:4
it because of the evil of your d...... Jer 4:4
thy d have procured these things..... Jer 4:18
Israel, Amend your ways and your d.... Jer 7:3
amend your ways and your d............ Jer 7:5

then thou shewedst me their d......... Jer 11:18
according to the fruit of his d....... Jer 17:10
and make your ways and your d good.... Jer 18:11
it, because of the evil of your d..... Jer 21:12
according to the fruit of your d...... Jer 21:14
visit upon you the evil of your d..... Jer 23:2
way, and from the evil of their d..... Jer 23:22
way, and from the evil of their d..... Jer 25:5
because of the evil of their d........ Jer 26:3
now amend your ways and your d........ Jer 26:13
according to the fruit of his d....... Jer 32:19
his evil way, and amend your d........ Jer 35:15
because of the evil of your d......... Jer 44:22
ye shall see their way and their d.... Eze 14:22
when ye see their ways and their d.... Eze 14:23
remember your ways, and all your d.... Eze 20:43
nor according to your corrupt d....... Eze 20:44
in all your d your sins do appear..... Eze 21:24
thy ways, and according to thy d...... Eze 24:14
it by their own way and by their d.... Eze 36:17
to their d I judged them.............. Eze 36:19
that your d were not good, and....... Eze 36:31
ways, and reward them their d......... Hos 4:9
their d to turn unto their God....... Hos 5:4
now their own d have beset them...... Hos 7:2
for the wickedness of their d I...... Hos 9:15
according to his d will he........... Hos 12:2
are these his d..................... Mic 2:7
behaved themselves ill in their d.... Mic 3:4
therein, for the fruit of their d.... Mic 7:13
early, and corrupted all their d..... Zeph 3:7
thou not be ashamed for all thy d.... Zeph 3:11
evil ways, and from your evil d...... Zec 1:4
our ways, and according to our d..... Zec 1:6

DOLEFUL

shall be full of d creatures......... Is 13:21
and lament with a d lamentation...... Mic 2:4

DOMINION

let them have d over the fish of..... Gen 1:26
have d over the fish of the sea,..... Gen 1:28
pass when thou shalt have d........... Gen 27:40
shalt thou indeed have d over us..... Gen 37:8
shall come he that shall have d...... Num 24:19
have d over the nobles among the..... Judg 5:13
made me have d over the mighty....... Judg 5:13
the Philistines had d over Israel.... Judg 14:4
For he had d over all the region..... 1Kin 4:24
and in all the land of his d......... 1Kin 9:19
in his house, nor in all his d....... 2Kin 20:13
and Saraph, who had the d in Moab.... 1Chr 4:22
his d by the river Euphrates......... 1Chr 18:3
throughout all the land of his d.... 2Chr 8:6
from under the d of Judah............ 2Chr 21:8
so that they had the d over them..... Neh 9:28
also they have d over our bodies,.... Neh 9:37
D and fear are with him.............. Job 25:2
canst thou set the d of thereof in... Job 38:33
Thou madest him to have d over....... Ps 8:6
let them not have d over me.......... Ps 19:13
the upright shall have d over........ Ps 49:14
He shall have d also from sea to..... Ps 72:8
his works in all places of his d..... Ps 103:22
his sanctuary, and Israel his d...... Ps 114:2
not any iniquity have d over me...... Ps 119:133
thy d endureth throughout all........ Ps 145:13
besides thee have had d over us...... Is 26:13
in his house, nor in all his d....... Is 39:2
kingdoms of the earth of his d....... Jer 34:1
thereof, and all the land of his d... Jer 51:28
his d is from generation to.......... Dan 4:3
thy d to the end of the earth........ Dan 4:22
whose d is an everlasting d.......... Dan 4:34
That in every d of my kingdom men.... Dan 6:26
his d shall be even unto the end..... Dan 6:26
and d was given to it................ Dan 7:6
they had their d taken away.......... Dan 7:12
And there was given him d, and....... Dan 7:14
his d is an everlasting d............ Dan 7:14
and they shall take away his d....... Dan 7:26
And the kingdom and d, and the....... Dan 7:27
up, that shall rule with great d..... Dan 8:11
according to his d which he ruled.... Dan 11:3
be strong above him, and his d....... Dan 11:5
that he shall be a great d........... Dan 11:5
shall it come, even the first d..... Mic 4:8
and it shall be from sea even to..... Zec 9:10
the Gentiles exercise d over them.... Mt 20:25
death hath no more d over him....... Rom 6:9
For sin shall not have d over you.... Rom 6:14
how that the law hath d over a...... Rom 7:1
that we have d over your faith...... 2Cor 1:24
and power, and might, and d......... Eph 1:21
be praise and d for ever and ever... 1Pet 4:11
be glory and d for ever and ever.... 1Pet 5:11
defile the flesh, despise d......... Jude 8
Saviour, be glory and majesty, d... Jude 25
be glory and d for ever and ever.... Rev 1:6

DOMINIONS

of all shall serve and obey him...... Dan 7:27
whether they be thrones, or d........ Col 1:16

DONE See PREFACE.

DOOR

not well, sin lieth at the d.......... Gen 4:7
work of the ark shalt thou set....... Gen 6:16
he sat in the tent d in the heat..... Gen 18:1
ran to meet them from the tent d..... Gen 18:2
And Sarah heard in the tent d........ Gen 18:10
Lot went out at the d unto them...... Gen 19:6

and shut the *d* after him......................... Gen 19:6
Lot, and came near to break the *d*.......... Gen 19:9
house to them, and shut to the *d*.......... Gen 19:10
the *d* of the house with blindness......... Gen 19:11
wearied themselves to find the *d*.......... Gen 19:11
with him at the *d* of the house................ Gen 43:19
on the upper *d* post of the houses........ Ex 12:7
d of his house until the morning............ Ex 12:22
the LORD will pass over the *d*............... Ex 12:23
he shall also bring him to the *d*............ Ex 21:6
or unto the *d* post.................................... Ex 21:6
an hanging for the *d* of the tent........... Ex 26:36
the *d* of the tabernacle of the.............. Ex 29:4
by the *d* of the tabernacle of................ Ex 29:11
by the *d* of the tabernacle of the......... Ex 29:32
your generations at the *d* of the.......... Ex 29:42
and stood every man at his tent *d*........ Ex 33:8
stood at the *d* of the tabernacle, *d*.... Ex 33:9
pillar stand at the tabernacle *d*............. Ex 33:10
every man in his tent *d*........................... Ex 33:10
the hanging for the *d* at the.................. Ex 35:15
hanging for the *d* of the court............... Ex 35:17
for the tabernacle *d* of blue.................. Ex 36:37
which assembled at the *d* of the........... Ex 38:8
to the *d* of the tabernacle of the......... Ex 38:30
the hanging for the tabernacle *d*......... Ex 39:38
of the *d* of the tabernacle.................... Ex 40:5
to the *d* of the tabernacle of the......... Ex 40:6
his sons unto the *d* of the..................... Ex 40:12
at the *d* of the tabernacle.................... Ex 40:28
d of the tabernacle of the..................... Ex 40:29
at the *d* of the tabernacle of............... Lev 1:3
by the *d* of the tabernacle of................ Lev 1:5
and kill it at the *d* of the...................... Lev 3:2
which is at the *d* of the.......................... Lev 4:7
which is at the *d* of the.......................... Lev 4:18
the *d* of the tabernacle of the.............. Lev 8:3
of the *d* of the tabernacle of................ Lev 8:4
Boil the flesh at the *d* of the................. Lev 8:31
of the *d* of the tabernacle of................ Lev 8:33
at the *d* of the tabernacle of................ Lev 8:35
the *d* of the tabernacle of.................... Lev 10:7
unto the *d* of the tabernacle of........... Lev 12:6
at the *d* of the tabernacle of................ Lev 14:11
unto the *d* of the tabernacle of........... Lev 14:23
the house to the *d* of the house.......... Lev 14:38
the *d* of the tabernacle of the.............. Lev 15:14
to the *d* of the tabernacle of................ Lev 15:29
at the *d* of the tabernacle of................ Lev 17:4
the *d* of the tabernacle of the.............. Lev 17:4
unto the *d* of the tabernacle of........... Lev 17:5
at the *d* of the tabernacle of................ Lev 17:6
the *d* of the tabernacle of the.............. Lev 17:9
the *d* of the tabernacle of.................... Lev 19:21
the hanging for the *d* of the................. Num 3:25
curtain for the *d* of the court................ Num 3:26
the hanging for the *d* of the................. Num 3:26
the hanging for the *d* of the gate........ Num 4:25
to the *d* of the tabernacle of the......... Num 6:10
the *d* of the tabernacle of.................... Num 6:13
at the *d* of the tabernacle.................... Num 6:18
at the *d* of the tabernacle of............... Num 10:3
every man in the *d* of his tent.............. Num 11:10
stood in the *d* of the tabernacle,........ Num 12:5
stood in the *d* of the tabernacle.......... Num 16:18
against them unto the *d* of the............. Num 16:19
stood in the *d* of their tents, and........ Num 16:27
the *d* of the tabernacle of.................... Num 16:50
the *d* of the tabernacle of.................... Num 20:6
by the *d* of the tabernacle of the......... Num 25:6
upon the *d* posts of thine house.......... Num 27:2
it through his ear unto the *d*................. Deut 11:30
to the *d* of our father's house.............. Deut 15:17
over the *d* of the tabernacle................ Deut 22:21
at the *d* of the tabernacle of the......... Deut 31:15
her, Stand in the *d* of the tent of the.. Josh 19:51
went hard unto the *d* of the tower...... Judg 2:4
round about, and beat at the *d*............ Judg 9:52
fell down at the *d* of the man's............ Judg 19:22
fallen down at the *d* of the house........ Judg 19:26
at the *d* of the tabernacle of the......... Judg 19:27
But Uriah slept at the *d* of the.............. 1Sa 5:22
from me, and bolt the *d* after her......... 2Sa 11:9
out, and bolted the *d* after her............. 2Sa 13:17
The *d* for the middle chamber was...... 2Sa 13:18
So also made he for the *d* of the.......... 1Kin 6:8
leaves of the one *d* were folding.......... 1Kin 6:34
of the other *d* were folding................... 1Kin 6:34
her feet, as she came in at the *d*......... 1Kin 14:6
came to the threshold of the *d*............ 1Kin 14:17
which kept the *d* of the king's.............. 1Kin 14:27
thou shalt shut the *d* upon thee.......... 2Kin 4:4
from him, and shut the *d* upon her...... 2Kin 4:5
called her, she stood in the *d*............... 2Kin 4:15
of God, and shut the *d* upon him......... 2Kin 4:21
shut the *d* upon them twain, and......... 2Kin 4:33
stood at the *d* of the house of............. 2Kin 5:9
d, and hold him fast at the *d*............. 2Kin 6:32
Then open the *d*, and flee, and........... 2Kin 9:3
And he opened the *d*, and fled............ 2Kin 9:10
the priests that kept the *d* put............ 2Kin 12:9
which the keepers of the *d* have......... 2Kin 22:4
order, and the keepers of the *d*............ 2Kin 25:18
and the three keepers of the *d*............ 2Kin 25:18
of the *d* of the tabernacle of the......... 1Chr 9:21
d of the house of Eliashib the............. Neh 3:20
from the *d* of the house of.................... Neh 3:21
Teresh, of those which kept the *d*....... Est 2:21

the keepers of the *d*, who sought........ Est 6:2
laid wait at my neighbour's *d*............... Job 31:9
silence, and went not out of the *d*...... Job 31:34
Keep the *d* of my lips............................. Ps 141:3
come not nigh the *d* of her house........ Prov 5:8
she sitteth at the *d* of her house......... Prov 9:14
As a turneth upon his hinges, so........... Prov 26:14
in his hand by the hole of the *d*.......... Song 5:4
and if she be a *d*, we will inclose........ Song 8:9
the posts of the *d* moved at the......... Is 6:4
of Shallum, the keeper of the *d*........... Jer 35:4
and the three keepers of the *d*............ Jer 52:24
to the *d* of the inner gate, that............ Eze 8:3
brought me to the *d* of the court.......... Eze 8:7
digged in the wall, behold a *d*.............. Eze 8:8
Then he brought me to the *d* of.......... Eze 8:14
at the *d* of the temple of the............... Eze 8:16
every one stood at the *d* of the............ Eze 10:19
behold at the *d* of the gate five.......... Eze 11:1
and twenty cubits, *d* against *d*.......... Eze 40:13
breadth of the *d* was ten cubits........... Eze 41:2
the sides of the *d* were five.................. Eze 41:3
and measured the post of the *d*........... Eze 41:3
and the *d*, six cubits.............................. Eze 41:3
and the breadth of the *d*, seven.......... Eze 41:3
one *d* toward the north, and................ Eze 41:11
another *d* toward the south................. Eze 41:11
The *d* posts, and the narrow................. Eze 41:16
frame stories, over against the *d*........ Eze 41:16
To that above the *d*, even unto............ Eze 41:17
unto above the *d* were cherubims....... Eze 41:18
two leaves for the one *d*....................... Eze 41:24
and two leaves for the other *d*............ Eze 41:24
an hundred cubits was the north *d*...... Eze 42:12
was a *d* in the head of the way............ Eze 46:3
the land shall worship at the *d*............ Eze 46:3
the again unto the *d* of the house....... Eze 47:1
valley of Achor for a *d* of hope............ Hos 2:15
said, Smite the lintel of the *d*.............. Amos 9:1
and when thou hast shut thy *d*............ Mt 6:6
and the *d* was shut............................... Mt 25:10
stone to the *d* of the sepulchre........... Mt 27:60
rolled back the stone from the *d*.......... Mt 28:2
was gathered together at the *d*........... Mk 1:33
no, not so much as about the *d*........... Mk 2:2
found the colt tied by the *d*................. Mk 11:4
stone unto the *d* of the sepulchre....... Mk 15:46
stone from the *d* of the sepulchre....... Mk 16:3
the *d* is now shut, and my children...... Lk 11:7
risen up, and hath shut to the *d*.......... Lk 13:25
without, and to knock at the *d*............. Lk 13:25
not by the *d* into the sheepfold........... Jn 10:1
d is the shepherd of the sheep............ Jn 10:2
unto you, I am the *d* of the sheep........ Jn 10:7
I am the *d*... Jn 10:9
But Peter stood at the *d* without......... Jn 18:16
and spake unto her that kept the *d*..... Jn 18:16
damsel that kept the *d* unto Peter...... Jn 18:17
buried thy husband are at the *d*........... Acts 5:9
before the *d* kept the prison................ Acts 12:6
knocked at the *d* of the gate............... Acts 12:13
and when they had opened the *d*......... Acts 12:16
how he had opened the *d* of faith........ Acts 14:27
For a great *d* and effectual is.............. 1Cor 16:9
a *d* was opened unto me of the........... 2Cor 2:12
open unto us a *d* of utterance............. Col 4:3
the judge standeth before the *d*.......... Jas 5:9
I have set before thee an open *d*......... Rev 3:8
Behold, I stand at the *d*, and............... Rev 3:20
man hear my voice, and open the *d*..... Rev 3:20
behold, a *d* was opened in heaven...... Rev 4:1

DOORKEEPER

I had rather be a *d* in the house......... Ps 84:10

DOORKEEPERS

and Elkanah were *d* for the ark........... 1Chr 15:23
and Jehiah were *d* for the ark............. 1Chr 15:24

DOORS

of thy house into the street................... Josh 2:19
shut the *d* of the parlour upon............. Judg 3:23
the *d* of the parlour were locked,........ Judg 3:24
opened not the *d* of the parlour.......... Judg 3:25
of the *d* of my house to meet me......... Judg 11:31
took the *d* of the gate of the............... Judg 16:3
opened the *d* of the house, and.......... Judg 19:27
opened the *d* of the house of the......... 1Sa 3:15
and scrabbled on the *d* of the gate...... 1Sa 21:13
oracle he made *d* of olive tree............ 1Kin 6:31
The two *d* also were of olive tree........ 1Kin 6:32
the two *d* were *d* of fir tree............... 1Kin 6:34
And all the *d* and posts were square.... 1Kin 7:5
both for the *d* of the inner house........ 1Kin 7:50
for the *d* of the house, to wit,............. 1Kin 7:50
the *d* of the temple of the LORD........... 2Kin 18:16
the nails for the *d* of the gates............ 1Chr 22:3
and the *d* thereof, with gold................. 2Chr 3:7
great court, and *d* for the court.......... 2Chr 4:9
overlaid the *d* of them with brass........ 2Chr 4:9
the inner *d* thereof for the most......... 2Chr 4:22
the *d* of the house of the temple......... 2Chr 4:22
shall be porters of the *d*...................... 2Chr 23:4
shut up the *d* of the house of the........ 2Chr 28:24
opened the *d* of the house of the........ 2Chr 29:3
have shut up the *d* of the porch........... 2Chr 29:7
the *d* had gathered of the hand of....... 2Chr 34:9
it, and set up the *d* of............................ Neh 3:1
thereof, and set up the *d* thereof........ Neh 3:3
thereof, and set up the *d* thereof........ Neh 3:6
built it, and set up the *d* thereof......... Neh 3:13
built it, and set up the *d* thereof......... Neh 3:14

it, and set up the *d* thereof.................. Neh 3:15
not set up the *d* upon the gates.......... Neh 6:1
let us shut the *d* of the temple............ Neh 6:10
was built, and I had set up the *d*......... Neh 7:1
stand by, let them shut the *d*.............. Neh 7:3
not up the *d* of my mother's womb...... Job 3:10
but I opened my *d* to the....................... Job 31:32
Or who shut up the sea with *d*............. Job 38:8
decreed place, and set bars and *d*....... Job 38:10
or hast thou seen the *d* of the............ Job 38:17
Who can open the *d* of his face........... Job 41:14
he ye lifted up, ye everlasting *d*.......... Ps 24:7
lift them up, ye everlasting *d*.............. Ps 24:9
above, and opened the *d* of heaven.... Ps 78:23
city, at the coming in at the *d*............. Prov 8:3
waiting at the posts of my *d*................ Prov 8:34
the *d* shall be shut in the..................... Eccl 12:4
and shut thy *d* about thee.................... Is 26:20
Behind the *d* also and the posts......... Is 57:8
in the *d* of the houses, and speak....... Eze 33:30
the *d* of the side chambers were......... Eze 41:11
temple and the sanctuary had two *d*... Eze 41:23
the *d* had two leaves apiece, two........ Eze 41:24
on the *d* of the temple, cherubims...... Eze 41:25
and their *d* toward the north............... Eze 42:4
fashions, and according to their *d*....... Eze 42:11
according to the *d* of the...................... Eze 42:12
keep the *d* of thy mouth from her........ Mic 7:5
Open thy *d*, O Lebanon, that the......... Zec 11:1
that would shut the *d* for nought......... Mal 1:10
that it is near, even at the *d*................ Mt 24:33
that it is nigh, even at the *d*................ Mk 13:29
when the *d* were shut where the.......... Jn 20:19
the *d* being shut, and stood in the...... Jn 20:26
Lord by night opened the prison *d*....... Acts 5:19
standing without before the *d*............. Acts 5:23
immediately all the *d* were opened...... Acts 16:26
and seeing the prison *d* open............... Acts 16:27
and forthwith the *d* were shut............. Acts 21:30

DOPHKAH (*dof'-kah*) An encampment during
 the Exodus.
of Sin, and encamped in *D*.................... Num 33:12
And they departed from *D*, and............ Num 33:13

DOR (*dor*) See EN-DOR. *A Canaanite city.*
in the borders of *D* on the west............ Josh 11:2
The king of *D* in the coast of *D*............ Josh 12:23
towns, and the inhabitants of *D*............ Josh 17:11
towns, nor the inhabitants of *D*............ Judg 1:27
Abinadab, in all the region of *D*............ 1Kin 4:11
towns, Megiddo and her towns, *D*......... 1Chr 7:29

DORCAS (*dor'-cas*) See TABITHA. *Disciple
 raised from the dead by Peter.*
by interpretation is called *D*................ Acts 9:36
coats and garments which *D* made....... Acts 9:39

DOST

it that thou *d* ask after my name.......... Gen 32:29
when thou *d* overtake them, say........... Gen 44:4
d thou go to possess their land............ Deut 9:5
When thou *d* lend thy brother any........ Deut 24:10
the man to whom thou *d* lend shall...... Deut 24:11
Thou *d* hate me, and lovest me............ Judg 14:16
after whom *d* thou pursue..................... 1Sa 24:14
Wherefore then *d* thou ask of me........ 1Sa 28:16
why *d* thou ask Abishag the................. 1Kin 2:22
D thou now govern the kingdom of...... 1Kin 21:7
Now on whom *d* thou trust, that.......... 2Kin 18:20
sin, when thou *d* afflict them............... 2Chr 6:26
For what *d* thou make request............. Neh 2:4
D thou still retain thine........................ Job 2:9
And why *d* thou not pardon my............ Job 7:21
yet thou *d* destroy me........................... Job 10:8
if thou open thine eyes upon such......... Job 14:3
thou *d* not watch over my sin.............. Job 14:16
d thou restrain wisdom to thyself........ Job 15:8
unto thee, and thou *d* not hear me....... Job 30:20
Why *d* thou strive against him.............. Job 33:13
D thou know when God disposed........... Job 37:15
D thou know the balancings of the...... Job 37:16
When thou with rebukes *d* correct....... Ps 39:11
why *d* thou cast me off.......................... Ps 43:2
d not increase thy wealth by................ Ps 44:12
thou *d* establish equity, thou............... Ps 99:4
honour, when thou *d* embrace her........ Prov 4:8
For thou *d* not enquire wisely.............. Eccl 7:10
beloved, that thou *d* so charge us........ Song 5:9
d weigh the path of the just................. Is 26:7
now on whom *d* thou trust, that.......... Is 36:5
Wherefore *d* thou prophesy, and say... Jer 32:3
D thou certainly know that Baalis......... Jer 40:14
daughter that *d* inhabit Dibon.............. Jer 48:18
Wherefore *d* thou forget us for............. Lam 5:20
thou *d* dwell among scorpions............. Eze 2:6
Whom *d* thou pass in beauty................. Eze 32:19
if thou *d* not speak to warn the........... Eze 33:8
Now why *d* thou cry out aloud.............. Mic 4:9
Why *d* thou shew me iniquity, and....... Hab 1:3
thou *d* not care that my sister.............. Lk 10:40
thou *d* fear God, seeing thou............... Lk 23:40
what *d* thou work?................................. Jn 6:30
born in sins, and *d* thou teach us......... Jn 9:34
D thou believe on the Son of God......... Jn 9:35
thou *d* make us to doubt....................... Jn 10:24
him, Lord, *d* thou wash my feet........... Jn 13:6
should not steal, *d* thou steal.............. Rom 2:21
adultery, *d* thou commit adultery........ Rom 2:22
idols, *d* thou commit sacrilege............ Rom 2:22
circumcision *d* transgress the law....... Rom 2:27
But why *d* thou judge thy brother........ Rom 14:10

or why d thou set at nought thou........ Rom 14:10
why d thou glory, as if thou.......... 1Cor 4:7
d thou not judge and avenge our....... Rev 6:10

DOTE
and they shall d: a sword is .... Jer 50:36

DOTED
she d on her lovers, on the .... Eze 23:5
and with all on whom she d .... Eze 23:7
of the Assyrians, upon whom she d.... Eze 23:7
She d upon the Assyrians her .... Eze 23:12
eyes, she d upon them, and sent ..... Eze 23:16
For she d upon their paramours ...... Eze 23:20

DOTH
For God d know that in the day ye.... Gen 3:5
d comfort himself, purposing to...... Gen 27:42
d my father yet live .... Gen 45:3
d put a difference between the ...... Ex 11:7
I am the LORD that d sanctify you..... Ex 31:13
why d thy wrath wax hot against...... Ex 32:11
whosoever d touch them, when they ... Lev 11:31
d fall, it shall be unclean .... Lev 11:32
of the fruits d he sell unto thee ... Lev 25:16
when the LORD d make thy thigh to.... Num 5:21
the man whom the LORD d choose ...... Num 16:7
the LORD d command concerning the.... Num 36:6
the LORD our God d give unto us ..... Deut 1:20
which the LORD our God d give us..... Deut 1:25
as a man d bear his son, in all ..... Deut 1:31
this day that God d talk with man ... Deut 5:24
that man d not live by bread only ... Deut 8:3
the mouth of the LORD d man live .... Deut 8:3
of these nations the LORD d drive ... Deut 9:4
these nations the LORD thy God d..... Deut 9:5
what d the LORD thy God require...... Deut 10:12
He d execute the judgement of the ... Deut 10:18
for a gift d blind the eyes of ...... Deut 16:19
abominations the LORD thy God d ..... Deut 18:12
which the LORD thy God d give .... Deut 20:16
God, he it is that d go with thee ... Deut 31:6
he it is that d go before thee...... Deut 31:8
Whosoever he be that d flee .... Josh 1:18
when he that d flee unto one of .... Josh 20:4
it shall be, when any man d come .... Judg 4:20
d know that thou art a righteous ... Ruth 3:11
because he d bless the sacrifice 1Sa 9:13
D not David hide himself with us 1Sa 23:19
D not David hide himself in the..... 1Sa 26:1
Wherefore my lord thus pursue 1Sa 26:18
as when one d hunt a partridge in ... 1Sa 26:20
that David d honour thy father 2Sa 10:3
for the king d speak this thing 2Sa 14:13
in that the king d not fetch home ... 2Sa 14:13
neither d God respect any person 2Sa 14:14
yet d he devise means, that his..... 2Sa 14:14
the king d sit in the gate 2Sa 19:8
For thy servant d know that I 2Sa 19:20
but why d my lord the king.......... 2Sa 24:3
of that which d cost me nothing 2Sa 24:24
the son of Haggith d reign 1Kin 1:11
when then d Adonijah reign 1Kin 1:13
for he d not prophesy good 1Kin 22:8
spirit of Elijah d rest on Elisha ... 2Kin 2:15
that this man d send unto me to 2Kin 5:7
that David d honour thy father 1Chr 19:3
why then d my lord require this..... 1Chr 21:3
as d thy people Israel, and thou 2Chr 6:33
D not Hezekiah persuade you to 2Chr 32:11
D Job fear God for nought .... Job 1:9
D not their excellency which is ..... Job 4:21
neither d trouble spring out of ..... Job 5:6
The wild ass bray when he hath ...... Job 6:5
but what d your arguing reprove ..... Job 6:25
D God pervert judgment .... Job 8:3
or d the Almighty pervert justice ... Job 8:3
D not the ear try words............. Job 12:11
Why d thine heart carry thee away ... Job 15:12
my reins asunder, and d not spare ... Job 16:13
d not mine eye continue in their ... Job 17:2
And thou sayest, How d God know ..... Job 22:13
On the left hand, where he d work ... Job 23:9
so d the grave those which have .... Job 24:19
upon whom d not his light arise .... Job 25:3
D not he see my ways, and count .... Job 31:4
Therefore d Job open his mouth in ... Job 35:16
he d establish them for ever, and ... Job 36:7
the hawk fly by thy wisdom, and ..... Job 39:26
the eagle mount up at thy .... Job 39:27
By his reasings a light of shine .... Job 41:18
in his law d he meditate day and ... Ps 1:2
in his pride d persecute the poor ... Ps 10:2
in the secret places d he murder ... Ps 10:8
he d catch the poor, when he .... Ps 10:9
Wherefore d the wicked contemn ..... Ps 10:13
his countenance d behold the....... Ps 11:7
in his temple d every one speak .... Ps 29:9
because mine enemy d not triumph ... Ps 41:11
D not David hide himself with us .... Ps 54:1
for who, say they, d hear .... Ps 59:7
he d send out his voice, and that ... Ps 68:33
And they say, How d God know........ Ps 73:11
why d thine anger smoke against..... Ps 74:1
his promise fail for evermore....... Ps 77:8
boar out of the wood d waste it..... Ps 80:13
beast of the field d devour it ..... Ps 80:13
neither d God understand this ...... Ps 92:6
therefore d my soul keep them ...... Ps 119:129
wait for the LORD, my soul d wait ... Ps 130:5
The LORD d build up Jerusalem ...... Ps 147:2
These six things d the LORD hate .... Prov 6:16

D not wisdom cry? .... Prov 8:1
a stranger d not intermeddle with ... Prov 14:10
he that d keep his soul shall be .... Prov 22:5
d not he that pondereth the heart ... Prov 24:12
thy soul, d not he know it.......... Prov 24:12
so d an angry countenance a......... Prov 25:23
so d the slothful upon his bed...... Prov 26:14
so d the sweetness of a man's ...... Prov 27:9
d the crown endure to every .... Prov 27:24
but the righteous d sing and .... Prov 29:6
and d not bless their mother .... Prov 30:11
her husband d safely trust in her ... Prov 31:11
so d a little folly him that is .... Eccl 10:1
and his right hand d embrace me ..... Song 2:6
but Israel d not know .... Is 1:3
my people d not consider .... Is 1:3
neither d the cause of the widow .... Is 1:23
d take away from Jerusalem and ..... Is 3:1
d witness against them .... Is 3:13
neither d his heart think so........ Is 10:7
D the plowman plough all day to sow . Is 28:24
d he open and break the clods of ... Is 28:24
d he not cast abroad the fitches ... Is 28:25
For his God d instruct him to ...... Is 28:26
him to discretion, and d teach him .. Is 28:26
stream of brimstone, d kindle it ... Is 30:33
the villages that Kedar d inhabit ... Is 42:11
an ash, and the rain d nourish it ... Is 44:14
day that I am he that d appoint..... Is 52:6
neither d justice overtake us ...... Is 59:9
glory for that which d not profit ... Jer 2:11
for to thee d it appertain .... Jer 10:7
Wherefore d the way of the wicked ... Jer 12:1
the LORD d not accept them .... Jer 14:10
yet every one of them d curse me.... Jer 15:10
that none d return from his .... Jer 23:14
see whether a man d travail with .... Jer 30:6
him, as a shepherd d his flock ..... Jer 31:10
why then d their king inherit Gad ... Jer 49:1
neither d any son of man pass ...... Jer 51:43
How d the city sit solitary, that ... Lam 1:1
For he d not afflict willingly...... Lam 3:33
Wherefore d a living man complain ... Lam 3:39
there is none that d deliver us .... Lam 5:8
When a righteous man d turn from .... Eze 3:20
he d not sin, he shall surely ...... Eze 3:21
d not the son bear the iniquity .... Eze 3:21
of me, D he not speak parables ..... Eze 20:49
that d not understand shall .... Hos 4:14
of Israel d testify to his face .... Hos 5:5
what d the LORD require of thee,.... Mic 6:8
judgment d never go forth .... Hab 1:4
for the wicked d compass about ..... Hab 1:4
every morning d he bring his .... Zeph 3:5
rust d corrupt, and where thieves ... Mt 6:19
neither moth nor rust d corrupt ... Mt 6:20
This fellow d not cast out devils ... Mt 12:24
D not your master pay tribute ...... Mt 17:24
d he not leave the ninety and nine .. Mt 18:12
is put away d commit adultery ...... Mt 19:9
How then d David in spirit call ..... Mt 22:43
not what hour your Lord d come ..... Mt 24:42
he is at hand that d betray me ..... Mt 26:46
Why d this man thus speak .... Mk 2:7
the new wine d burst the bottles ... Mk 2:22
Why d this generation seek after ... Mk 8:12
My soul d magnify the Lord .... Lk 1:46
neither d a corrupt tree bring ..... Lk 6:43
of a candle d give thee light ...... Lk 11:36
d not each one of you on the .... Lk 13:15
as a hen d gather her brood under ... Lk 13:34
whosoever d not bear his cross ..... Lk 14:27
d not leave the ninety and nine in .. Lk 15:4
d not light a candle, and sweep .... Lk 15:8
D he thank that servant because .... Lk 17:9
that is chief, as he that d serve ... Lk 22:26
beginning d set forth good wine .... Jn 2:10
said unto them, D this offend you ... Jn 6:61
D our law judge any man, before .... Jn 7:51
how then d he now see .... Jn 9:19
Therefore d my Father love me ..... Jn 10:17
even by him d this man stand here ... Acts 4:10
what d hinder me to be baptized .... Acts 8:36
the high priest d bear me witness ... Acts 22:5
much learning d make thee mad ...... Acts 26:24
man seeth, why d he yet hope for.... Rom 8:24
unto me, Why d he yet find fault ... Rom 9:19
to the Lord he d not regard it ..... Rom 14:6
D God take care for oxen 1Cor 9:9
d not even nature itself teach 1Cor 11:14
D not behave itself unseemly 1Cor 13:5
neither d corruption inherit 1Cor 15:50
so great a death, and d deliver 2Cor 1:10
much more d the ministration of 2Cor 3:9
for whatsoever d make manifest is ... Eph 5:13
as it d also in you, since the ..... Col 1:6
as a father d his children 1Th 2:11
of iniquity d already work 2Th 2:7
their word will eat as d a canker ... 2Ti 2:17
all shall wax old as d a garment ... Heb 1:11
the sin which d so easily beset .... Heb 12:1
What d it profit, my brethren ...... Jas 2:14
to the body; what d it profit? ..... Jas 2:16
D a fountain send forth at the ..... Jas 3:11
and he d not resist you .... Jas 5:6
d also now save us (not the 1Pet 3:21
and so d Marcus my son 1Pet 5:13
it d not yet appear what we shall ... 1Jn 3:2
is born of God d not commit sin 1Jn 3:9
neither d he himself receive the ... 3Jn 10

and in righteousness he d judge..... Rev 19:11

DOTHAN (do´-than) A city in Manasseh.
I heard them say, Let us go to D ..... Gen 37:17
his brethren, and found them in D.... Gen 37:17
him, saying, Behold, he is in D...... 2Kin 6:13

DOTING
but d about questions and strifes ... 1Ti 6:4

DOUBLE
take d money in your hand .... Gen 43:12
they took d money in their hand..... Gen 43:15
he shall restore d .... Ex 22:4
the thief be found, let him pay d ... Ex 22:7
he shall pay d unto his neighbour ... Ex 22:9
shalt of the sixth curtain in the ... Ex 26:9
they made the breastplate d .... Ex 39:9
worth a d hired servant to thee .... Deut 15:18
by giving him a d portion of all .... Deut 21:17
let a d portion of thy spirit be 2Kin 2:9
they were not of d heart 1Chr 12:33
that they are d to that which is .... Job 11:6
can come to him with his d bridle ... Job 41:13
with a d heart do they speak .... Ps 12:2
LORD's hand d for all her sins ..... Is 40:2
For your shame ye shall have d ..... Is 61:7
land they shall possess the d ...... Is 61:7
their iniquity and their sin d ..... Jer 16:18
destroy them with d destruction .... Jer 17:18
that I will render d unto thee ..... Zec 9:12
be counted worthy of d honour 1Ti 5:17
A d minded man is unstable in all ... Jas 1:8
purify your hearts, ye d minded .... Jas 4:8
unto her d according to .... Rev 18:6
hath filled fill to her d .... Rev 18:6

DOUBLED
dream was d unto Pharaoh twice ..... Gen 41:32
Foursquare it shall be being d ..... Ex 28:16
span the breadth thereof, being d ... Ex 39:9
let the sword be d the third time ... Eze 21:14

DOUBLETONGUED
must the deacons be grave, not d 1Ti 3:8

DOUBT
is without d rent in pieces .... Gen 37:33
life shall hang in d before thee .... Deut 28:66
No d but ye are the people, and .... Job 12:2
faith, wherefore didst thou d ...... Mt 14:31
d not, ye shall not only do this .... Mt 21:21
shalt not d in his heart, but ...... Mk 11:23
no d the kingdom of God is come ..... Lk 11:20
How long dost thou make us to d ..... Jn 10:24
were all amazed, and were in d ..... Acts 2:12
No d this man is a murderer, whom ... Acts 28:4
For our sakes, no d, this is 1Cor 9:10
for I stand in d of you .... Gal 4:20
they would no d have continued 1Jn 2:19

DOUBTED
but some d .... Mt 28:17
they d of them whereunto this ...... Acts 5:24
Now while Peter d in himself what ... Acts 10:17
because I d of such manner of ...... Acts 25:20

DOUBTETH
he that d is damned if he eat ...... Rom 14:23

DOUBTFUL
drink, neither be ye of d mind ..... Lk 12:29
but not to d disputations .... Rom 14:1

DOUBTING
on another, of d whom he spake ..... Jn 13:22
down, and go with them, d nothing... Acts 10:20
bade me go with them, nothing d .... Acts 11:12
up holy hands, without wrath and d .. 1Ti 2:8

DOUBTLESS
D ye shall not come into the land ... Num 14:30
for I will d deliver the 2Sa 5:19
shall d come again with rejoicing ... Ps 126:6
D thou art our father, though ..... Is 63:16
unto others, yet d I am to you 1Cor 9:2
not expedient for me d to glory 2Cor 12:1
Yea d, and I count all things but ... Phil 3:8

DOUBTS
sentences, and dissolving of d ..... Dan 5:12
interpretations, and dissolve d .... Dan 5:16

DOUGH
the people took their d before it ... Ex 12:34
baked unleavened cakes of the d ..... Ex 12:39
of your d for an heave offering ..... Num 15:20
Of the first of your d ye shall..... Num 15:21
bring the firstfruits of our d ..... Neh 10:37
and the women kneaded their d ...... Jer 7:18
the priest the first of your d ..... Eze 44:30
after he hath kneaded the d .... Hos 7:4

DOVE
Also he sent forth a d from him .... Gen 8:8
But the d found no rest for the .... Gen 8:9
sent forth the d out of the ark .... Gen 8:10
the d came in to him in the .... Gen 8:11
and sent forth the d .... Gen 8:12
O that I had wings like a d .... Ps 55:6
wings of a d covered with silver ... Ps 68:13
O my d, that art in the clefts of ... Song 2:14
to me, my sister, my love, my d .... Song 5:2
My d, my undefiled is but one ...... Song 6:9
I did mourn as a d .... Is 38:14
be like the d that maketh her ..... Jer 48:28
is like a silly d without heart .... Hos 7:11

DOVE'S
as a d out of the land of Assyria...... Hos 11:11
Spirit of God descending like a d...... Mt 3:16
the Spirit like a d descending...... Mk 1:10
a bodily shape like a d upon him...... Lk 3:22
descending from heaven like a d...... Jn 1:32

DOVE'S
the fourth part of a cab of d...... 2Kin 6:25

DOVES
eyes of thy by the rivers of waters...... Song 5:12
like bears, and mourn sore like d...... Is 59:11
as the d to their windows...... Is 60:8
mountains like d of the valleys...... Eze 7:16
lead her as with the voice of d...... Nah 2:7
as serpents, and harmless as d...... Mt 10:16
and the seats of them that sold d...... Mt 21:12
and the seats of them that sold d...... Mk 11:15
that sold oxen and sheep and d...... Jn 2:14
And said unto them that sold d...... Jn 2:16

DOVE'S
thou art fair; thou hast d eyes...... Song 1:15
thou hast d eyes within thy locks...... Song 4:1

DOWN See PREFACE.

DOWNSITTING
Thou knowest my d and mine...... Ps 139:2

DOWNWARD
Judah shall yet again take root d...... 2Kin 19:30
beast that goeth d to the earth...... Eccl 3:21
of Judah shall again take root d...... Is 37:31
appearance of his loins even d...... Eze 1:27
appearance of his loins even d...... Eze 8:2

DOWRY
God hath endued me with a good d...... Gen 30:20
Ask me never so much d and gift,...... Gen 34:12
according to the d of virgins...... Ex 22:17
The king desireth not any d...... 1Sa 18:25

DRAG
net, and gather them in their d...... Hab 1:15
net, and burn incense unto their d...... Hab 1:16

DRAGGING
cubits,) d the net with fishes...... Jn 21:8

DRAGON
valley, even before the d well...... Neh 2:13
the d shalt thou trample under...... Ps 91:13
he shall slay the d that is in...... Is 27:1
hath cut Rahab, and wounded the d...... Is 51:9
he hath swallowed me up like a d...... Jer 51:34
the great d that lieth in the...... Eze 29:3
and behold a great red d, having...... Rev 12:3
the d stood before the woman...... Rev 12:4
his angels fought against the d...... Rev 12:7
the d fought and his angels,...... Rev 12:7
the great d was cast out, that...... Rev 12:9
when the d saw that he was cast...... Rev 12:13
which the d cast out of his mouth...... Rev 12:16
the d was wroth with the woman,...... Rev 12:17
the d gave him his power, and his...... Rev 13:2
they worshipped the d which gave...... Rev 13:4
like a lamb, and he spake as a d...... Rev 13:11
come out of the mouth of the d,...... Rev 16:13
And he laid hold on the d, that...... Rev 20:2

DRAGONS
Their wine is the poison of d...... Deut 32:33
I am a brother to d, and a...... Job 30:29
sore broken us in the place of d...... Ps 44:19
the heads of the d in the waters...... Ps 74:13
the LORD from the earth, ye d...... Ps 148:7
d in their pleasant palaces...... Is 13:22
and it shall be an habitation of d...... Is 34:13
in the habitation of d, where...... Is 35:7
the field shall honour me, the d...... Is 43:20
Jerusalem heaps, and a den of d...... Jer 9:11
of Judah desolate, and a den of d...... Jer 10:22
they snuffed up the wind like d...... Jer 14:6
Hazor shall be a dwelling for d...... Jer 49:33
heaps, a dwelling place for d...... Jer 51:37
I will make a wailing like the d...... Mic 1:8
waste for the d of the wilderness...... Mal 1:3

DRAMS
talents and ten thousand d...... 1Chr 29:7
and one thousand of gold...... Ezr 2:69
basons of gold, of a thousand d...... Ezr 8:27
the treasure a thousand d of gold...... Neh 7:70
work twenty thousand d of gold...... Neh 7:71
was twenty thousand d of gold...... Neh 7:72

DRANK
he d of the wine, and was drunken...... Gen 9:21
so I d, and she made the camels...... Gen 24:46
and he brought him wine, and he d...... Gen 27:25
they d, and were merry...... Gen 43:34
abundantly, and the congregation d...... Num 20:11
d the wine of their drink...... Deut 32:38
d of his own cup, and lay in his...... 2Sa 12:3
bread in his house, and d water...... 1Kin 13:19
and he d of the brook...... 1Kin 17:6
meat, and of the wine which he d...... Dan 1:5
nor with the wine which he d...... Dan 1:8
d wine before the thousand...... Dan 5:1
and his concubines, d in them...... Dan 5:3
They d wine, and praised the gods...... Dan 5:4
and they all d of it...... Mk 14:23
They did eat, they d, they...... Lk 17:27
they did eat, they d, they bought...... Lk 17:28
d thereof himself, and his...... Jn 4:12

for they d of that spiritual Rock...... 1Cor 10:4

DRAUGHT
made it a d house unto this day...... 2Kin 10:27
belly, and is cast out into the d...... Mt 15:17
belly, and goeth out into the d...... Mk 7:19
and let down your nets for a d...... Lk 5:4
at the d of the fishes which they...... Lk 5:9

DRAVE
wheels, that they d them heavily...... Ex 14:25
they d not out the Canaanites...... Josh 16:10
which d them out from before you,...... Josh 24:12
the LORD d out from before us all...... Josh 24:18
he d out the inhabitants of the...... Judg 1:19
d them out from before you, and...... Judg 6:9
which they d before those other...... 1Sa 30:20
sons of Abinadab, d the new cart...... 2Sa 6:3
Syria, and the Jews from Elath...... 2Kin 16:6
Jeroboam d Israel from following...... 2Kin 17:21
and Uzza and Ahio of the cart...... 1Chr 13:7
whom God d out before the face of...... Acts 7:45
he d them from the judgment seat...... Acts 18:16

DRAW
time that women go out to d water...... Gen 24:11
of the city come out to d water...... Gen 24:13
I will d water for thy camels...... Gen 24:19
again unto the well to d water...... Gen 24:20
virgin cometh forth to d water...... Gen 24:43
I will also d for thy camels...... Gen 24:44
And he said, D not nigh hither...... Ex 3:5
them, D out and take you a lamb...... Ex 12:21
I will d my sword, my hand shall...... Ex 15:9
will d out a sword after you...... Lev 26:33
so that he could not d the dagger...... Judg 3:22
d toward mount Tabor, and take...... Judg 4:6
I will d unto thee to the river...... Judg 4:7
D thy sword, and slay me, that men...... Judg 9:54
let us d near to one of these...... Judg 19:13
d them from the city unto the...... Judg 20:32
maidens going out to d water...... 1Sa 9:11
Let us d near hither unto God...... 1Sa 14:36
D ye near hither, all the chief...... 1Sa 14:38
D thy sword, and thrust me through...... 1Sa 31:4
we will d it into the river...... 2Sa 17:13
D thy sword, and thrust me through...... 1Chr 10:4
and every man shall d after him...... Job 21:33
he trusteth that he can d up...... Job 40:23
Canst thou d out leviathan with...... Job 41:1
D me not away with the wicked, and...... Ps 28:3
D out also the spear, and stop the...... Ps 35:3
D nigh unto my soul, and redeem it...... Ps 69:18
is good for me to d near to God...... Ps 73:28
with thou d out thine anger to...... Ps 85:5
they d near unto the gates of...... Ps 107:18
They d nigh that follow after......... Ps 119:150
of understanding will d it out,...... Prov 20:5
come not, nor the years of haps...... Eccl 12:1
D me, we will run after thee...... Song 1:4
Woe unto them that d iniquity...... Is 5:18
of the Holy One of Israel d nigh...... Is 5:19
ye d water out of the wells of...... Is 12:3
people d near me with their mouth...... Is 29:13
d near together, ye that are...... Is 45:20
But d near hither, ye sons of the...... Is 57:3
a wide mouth, and d out the tongue...... Is 57:4
if thou d out thy soul to the...... Is 58:10
that d the bow, to Tubal, and...... Is 66:19
and I will cause him to d near...... Jer 30:21
and shield, and d near to battle...... Jer 46:3
of the flock shall d them out...... Jer 49:20
the flock shall d them out...... Jer 50:45
the sea monsters d out the breast...... Lam 4:3
I will d out a sword after them...... Eze 5:2
I will d out a sword after them...... Eze 5:12
charge over the city to d near...... Eze 9:1
I will d out the sword after them...... Eze 12:14
will d forth my sword out of his...... Eze 21:3
hast caused thy days to d near,...... Eze 22:4
they shall d their swords against...... Eze 28:7
they shall d their swords against...... Eze 30:11
d her and all her multitudes...... Eze 32:20
let all the men of war d near...... Joel 3:9
D these waters for the siege...... Nah 3:14
to d out fifty vessels out of the...... Hag 2:16
D out now, and bear unto the...... Jn 2:8
a woman of Samaria to d water...... Jn 4:7
Sir, thou hast nothing to d with...... Jn 4:11
not, neither come hither to d...... Jn 4:15
Father which hath sent me d him...... Jn 6:44
the earth, will d all men unto me...... Jn 12:32
now they were not able to d it...... Jn 21:6
to d away disciples after them...... Acts 20:30
by the which we d nigh unto God...... Heb 7:19
Let us d near with a true heart...... Heb 10:22
but if any man d back, my soul...... Heb 10:38
of them who d back unto perdition...... Heb 10:39
of you before the judgment seats...... Jas 2:6
D nigh to God, and he will d...... Jas 4:8

DRAWER
thy wood unto the d of thy water...... Deut 29:11

DRAWERS
wood and d of water unto all the...... Josh 9:21
for the house of my...... Josh 9:23
d of water for the congregation,...... Josh 9:27

DRAWETH
The wife of the one d near for to...... Deut 25:11
now the day d toward evening, I...... Judg 19:9
He d also the mighty with his...... Job 24:22

his soul d near unto the grave,...... Job 33:22
when he d him into his net...... Ps 10:9
my life d nigh unto the grave...... Ps 88:3
that d near the time of her...... Is 26:17
The time is come, the day d near...... Eze 7:12
This people d nigh unto me with...... Mt 15:8
and the time of near...... Lk 21:8
for your redemption d nigh...... Lk 21:28
for the coming of the Lord d nigh...... Jas 5:8

DRAWING
archers in the places of d water...... Judg 5:11
the sea, and d nigh unto the ship...... Jn 6:19

DRAWN
way, and his sword in his hand...... Num 22:23
way, and his sword d in his hand...... Num 22:31
and which hath not d in the yoke...... Deut 21:3
not hear, but shalt be d away...... Deut 30:17
him with his sword d in his hand...... Josh 5:13
till we have d them from the city...... Josh 8:6
were d away from the city...... Josh 8:16
the border was d from the top of...... Josh 15:9
and the border was d to Baalah...... Josh 15:9
and the border was d to Shicron...... Josh 15:11
And the border was d thence...... Josh 18:14
was d from the north, and went...... Josh 18:17
were d away from the city...... Judg 20:31
that which the young men have d...... Ruth 2:9
having a d sword in his hand...... 1Chr 21:16
Is is d, and cometh out of the...... Job 20:25
The wicked have d out the sword...... Ps 37:14
than oil, yet were they d swords...... Ps 55:21
them that are d unto death...... Prov 24:11
from the swords, from the d sword...... Is 21:15
the milk, and d from the breasts...... Is 28:9
with the burial of an ass, d...... Jer 22:19
with lovingkindness have I d thee...... Jer 31:3
he hath d back his right hand...... Lam 2:3
have d forth my sword out of his...... Eze 21:5
thou, The sword, the sword is d...... Eze 21:28
all were d up again into heaven...... Acts 11:10
when he is d away of his own lust...... Jas 1:14

DREAD
the d of you shall be upon every...... Gen 9:2
Fear and d shall fall upon them...... Ex 15:16
D not, neither be afraid of them...... Deut 1:29
will I begin to put the d of thee...... Deut 2:25
the d of you upon all the land...... Deut 11:25
d not, nor be dismayed...... 1Chr 22:13
and his d fall upon you...... Job 13:11
let not thy d make me afraid...... Job 13:21
your fear, and let him be your d...... Is 8:13

DREADFUL
and said, How d is this place...... Gen 28:17
A d sound is in his ears...... Job 15:21
were so high that they were d...... Eze 1:18
and behold a fourth beast,...... Dan 7:7
from all the others, exceeding d...... Dan 7:19
d God, keeping the covenant and...... Dan 9:4
They are terrible and d...... Hab 1:7
my name is dreadful among the heathen...... Mal 1:14
of the great and d day of the LORD...... Mal 4:5

DREAM
came to Abimelech in a d by night...... Gen 20:3
And God said unto him in a d...... Gen 20:6
up mine eyes, and saw in a d...... Gen 31:10
angel of God spake unto me in a d...... Gen 31:11
Laban the Syrian in a d by night...... Gen 31:24
And Joseph dreamed a d, and he told...... Gen 37:5
this d which I have dreamed...... Gen 37:6
And he dreamed yet another d...... Gen 37:9
Behold, I have dreamed a d more...... Gen 37:9
What is this d that thou hast...... Gen 37:10
And they dreamed a d both of them...... Gen 40:5
each man his d in one night...... Gen 40:5
to the interpretation of his d...... Gen 40:5
unto him, We have dreamed a d...... Gen 40:8
chief butler told his d to Joseph...... Gen 40:9
and said to him, In my d...... Gen 40:9
unto Joseph, I also was in my d...... Gen 40:16
awoke, and, behold, it was a d...... Gen 41:7
and Pharaoh told them his d...... Gen 41:8
And we dreamed a d in one night...... Gen 41:11
to the interpretation of his d...... Gen 41:11
to his d he did interpret...... Gen 41:12
unto Joseph, I have dreamed a d...... Gen 41:15
understand a d to interpret it...... Gen 41:15
Pharaoh said unto Joseph, In my d...... Gen 41:17
And I saw in my d, and, behold,...... Gen 41:22
Pharaoh, The d of Pharaoh is one...... Gen 41:25
are seven years: the d is one...... Gen 41:26
for that the d was doubled unto...... Gen 41:32
and will speak unto him in a d...... Num 12:6
man that told a d unto his fellow...... Judg 7:13
and said, Behold, I dreamed a d...... Judg 7:13
Gideon heard the telling of the d...... Judg 7:15
to Solomon in a d by night...... 1Kin 3:5
and, behold, it was a d...... 1Kin 3:15
He shall fly away as a d, and...... Job 20:8
In a d, in a vision of the night,...... Job 33:15
As a d when one awaketh...... Ps 73:20
of Zion, we were like them that d...... Ps 126:1
For a d cometh through the...... Eccl 5:3
shall be as a d of a night vision...... Is 29:7
hath a d, let him tell a d...... Jer 23:28
unto them, I have dreamed a d...... Dan 2:3
spirit was troubled to know the d...... Dan 2:3
tell my servants the d, and we...... Dan 2:4
will not make known unto me the d...... Dan 2:5

But if ye shew the *d*, and the .... Dan 2:6
therefore shew me the *d*, and the .... Dan 2:6
the king tell his servants the *d* .... Dan 2:7
will not make known unto me the *d* .... Dan 2:9
therefore tell me the *d*, and I .... Dan 2:9
unto me the *d* which I have seen .... Dan 2:26
Thy *d*, and the visions of thy head .... Dan 2:28
This is the *d*; and we will .... Dan 2:36
and the *d* is certain, and the .... Dan 2:45
I saw a *d* which made me afraid, ... Dan 4:5
me the interpretation of the *d* .... Dan 4:6
and I told the *d* before them .... Dan 4:7
and before him I told the *d* .... Dan 4:8
visions of my *d* that I have seen .... Dan 4:9
This *d* I king Nebuchadnezzar have .... Dan 4:18
said, Belteshazzar, let not the *d* .... Dan 4:19
the *d* be to them that hate thee, ... Dan 4:19
king of Babylon Daniel had a *d* .... Dan 7:1
then he wrote the *d*, and told the .... Dan 7:1
your old men shall *dreams* .... Joel 2:28
The Lord appeared unto him in a *d* .... Mt 1:20
being warned of God in a *d* that .... Mt 2:12
Lord appeareth to Joseph in a *d* .... Mt 2:13
in a *d* to Joseph in Egypt .... Mt 2:19
being warned of God in a *d* .... Mt 2:22
this day in a *d* because of him .... Mt 27:19
and your old men shall *d dreams* .... Acts 2:17

DREAMED

And he *d*, and behold a ladder set .... Gen 28:12
Joseph *d* a dream, and he told it .... Gen 37:5
you, this dream which I have *d* .... Gen 37:6
he *d* yet another dream, and told .... Gen 37:9
Behold, I have *d* a dream more .... Gen 37:9
is this dream that thou hast *d* .... Gen 37:10
they *d* a dream both of them, each .... Gen 40:5
said unto him, We have *d* a dream .... Gen 40:8
of two full years, that Pharaoh *d* .... Gen 41:1
And he slept and *d* the second time .... Gen 41:5
we *d* a dream in one night, I and .... Gen 41:11
we *d* each man according to the .... Gen 41:11
I have *d* a dream, and there is .... Gen 41:15
the dreams which he *d* of them .... Gen 42:9
I *d* a dream, and, lo, a cake of .... Judg 7:13
saying, I have *d*, I have *d* .... Jer 23:25
dreams which ye cause to be *d* .... Jer 29:8
Nebuchadnezzar *d* dreams, ... Dan 2:1
I have *d* a dream, and my spirit .... Dan 2:3

DREAMER

to another, Behold, this *d* cometh .... Gen 37:19
or a *d* of dreams, and giveth thee .... Deut 13:1
that prophet, or that *d* of dreams .... Deut 13:3
or that *d* of dreams, shall be put .... Deut 13:5

DREAMERS

to your diviners, nor to your *d* .... Jer 27:9
these filthy *d* defile the flesh .... Jude 8

DREAMETH

even be as when an hungry man *d* .... Is 29:8
or as when a thirsty man *d* .... Is 29:8

DREAMS

hated him yet the more for his *d* .... Gen 37:8
see what will become of his *d* .... Gen 37:20
and he interpreted to us our *d* .... Gen 41:12
Joseph remembered the *d* which he .... Gen 42:9
you a prophet, or a dreamer of *d* .... Deut 13:1
prophet, or that dreamer of *d* .... Deut 13:3
prophet, or that dreamer of *d* .... Deut 13:5
answered him not, neither by *d* 1Sa 28:6
neither by prophets, nor by *d* 1Sa 28:15
Then thou scarest me with *d* .... Job 7:14
For in the multitude of *d* .... Eccl 5:7
to forget my name by their *d* .... Jer 23:27
them that prophesy false *d* .... Jer 23:32
neither hearken to your *d* which .... Jer 29:8
understanding in all visions and *d* .... Dan 1:17
Nebuchadnezzar dreamed *d* .... Dan 2:1
for to shew the king his *d* .... Dan 2:2
understanding, interpreting of *d* .... Dan 5:12
your old men shall dream *d* .... Joel 2:28
seen a lie, and have told false *d* .... Zec 10:2
and your old men shall dream *d* .... Acts 2:17

DREGS

but the *d* thereof, all the wicked .... Ps 75:8
thou hast drunken the *d* of the .... Is 51:17
even the *d* of the cup of my fury .... Is 51:22

DRESS

into the garden of Eden to *d* it .... Gen 2:15
and he hasted to *d* it .... Gen 18:7
d them, but shalt neither drink .... Deut 28:39
to *d* for the wayfaring man that 2Sa 12:4
d the meat in my sight, that I 2Sa 13:5
Amnon's house, and *d* him meat 2Sa 13:7
d it for me and my son, that we 1Kin 17:12
I will *d* the other bullock, and 1Kin 18:23
for yourselves, and *d* it first 1Kin 18:25

DRESSED

milk, and the calf which he had *d* .... Gen 18:8
all that is *d* in the fryingpan, ... Lev 7:9
of wine, and five sheep ready *d* 1Sa 25:18
d it for the man that was come to 2Sa 12:4
king, and had neither *d* his feet 2Sa 19:24
was given them, and they *d* it 1Kin 18:26
meet for them by whom it is *d* .... Heb 6:7

DRESSER

he unto the *d* of his vineyard .... Lk 13:7

DRESSERS

vine *d* in the mountains, and in 2Chr 26:10

DRESSETH

when he *d* the lamps, he shall .... Ex 30:7

DREW

And Abraham *d* near, and said, Wilt .... Gen 18:23
water, and *d* for all his camels .... Gen 24:20
down unto the well, and *d* water .... Gen 24:45
and they *d* and lifted up Joseph out .... Gen 37:28
as he *d* back his hand, that, ... Gen 38:29
the time of high that Israel must .... Gen 47:29
Because I *d* him out of the water .... Ex 2:10
of water, and filled the troughs to .... Ex 2:16
also *d* water enough for us, and .... Ex 2:19
And when Pharaoh *d* nigh, the .... Ex 14:10
Moses *d* near unto the thick .... Ex 20:21
and all the congregation *d* near .... Lev 9:5
d nigh, and came before the city, ... Josh 8:11
For Joshua *d* not his hand back, ... Josh 8:26
twenty thousand men that *d* sword .... Judg 8:10
But the youth *d* not his sword .... Judg 8:20
thousand footmen that *d* sword .... Judg 20:2
and six thousand men that *d* sword .... Judg 20:15
hundred thousand men that *d* sword .... Judg 20:17
all these *d* the sword .... Judg 20:25
all these *d* the sword .... Judg 20:35
liers in wait *d* themselves along .... Judg 20:37
thousand men that *d* the sword .... Judg 20:46
So he *d* off his shoe .... Ruth 4:8
of water, and poured it out before 1Sa 7:6
the Philistines *d* near to battle 1Sa 7:10
Then Saul *d* near to Samuel in the 1Sa 9:18
And the Philistine *d* near morning 1Sa 17:16
he *d* near to the Philistine 1Sa 17:40
came on and *d* near unto David 1Sa 17:41
d nigh to meet David, that David 1Sa 17:48
d it out of the sheath thereof, ... 1Sa 17:51
And Joab *d* nigh, and the people 2Sa 10:13
And he came apace, and *d* near 2Sa 18:25
he *d* me out of many waters 2Sa 22:17
of water out of the well of 2Sa 23:16
valiant men that *d* sword 2Sa 24:9
Now the days of David *d* nigh that 1Kin 2:1
they *d* out the staves, that the 1Kin 8:8
a certain man *d* a bow at a 1Kin 22:34
seven hundred men that *d* swords 2Kin 3:26
Jehu *d* a bow with his full 2Kin 9:24
d water out of the well of 1Chr 11:18
d nigh before the Syrians unto 1Chr 19:14
of forth the Syrians that were, ... 1Chr 19:16
hundred thousand men that *d* sword 1Chr 21:5
and ten thousand men that *d* sword 1Chr 21:5
they *d* out the staves of the ark, ... 2Chr 5:9
of bows, two hundred and fourscore 2Chr 14:8
a certain man *d* a bow at a 2Chr 18:33
So Esther *d* near, and touched the .... Est 5:2
his decree *d* near to be put in .... Est 9:1
he *d* me out of many waters .... Ps 18:16
were afraid, *d* near, and came .... Is 41:5
So they *d* up Jeremiah with cords, ... Jer 38:13
I *d* them with cords of a man, ... Hos 11:4
she *d* not near to her God .... Zeph 3:2
they *d* to shore, and sat down, and .... Mt 13:48
when they *d* nigh unto Jerusalem, ... Mt 21:1
when the time of the *d* near .... Mt 21:34
of his sword, and struck a servant .... Mt 26:51
of Gennesaret, and *d* to the shore .... Mk 6:53
of them that stood by *d* a sword .... Mk 14:47
Then *d* near unto him all the .... Lk 15:1
d nigh to the house, he heard .... Lk 15:25
feast of unleavened bread *d* nigh .... Lk 22:1
d near unto Jesus to kiss him .... Lk 22:47
preparation, and the sabbath *d* on .... Lk 23:54
and reasoned, Jesus himself *d* near .... Lk 24:15
they *d* nigh unto the village, ... Lk 24:28
servants which *d* the water knew .... Jn 2:9
Simon Peter having a sword *d* it .... Jn 18:10
of the net to land full of great .... Jn 21:11
d away much people after him .... Acts 5:37
the time of the promise *d* nigh .... Acts 7:17
as he *d* near to behold it, the .... Acts 7:31
d nigh unto the city, Peter went .... Acts 10:9
of him out of the city, supposing .... Acts 14:19
of them into the marketplace unto .... Acts 16:19
he *d* out his sword, and would have .... Acts 16:27
they *d* Jason and certain brethren .... Acts 17:6
they of Alexander out of the .... Acts 19:33
Paul, and *d* him out of the temple .... Acts 21:30
that they *d* near to some country .... Acts 27:27
his tail the third part of the .... Rev 12:4

DREWEST

Thou *d* near in the day that I .... Lam 3:57

DRIED

were *d* up from off the earth .... Gen 8:7
the waters were *d* up from off the .... Gen 8:13
day of the month, was the earth *d* .... Gen 8:14
green ears of corn *d* by the fire .... Lev 2:14
nor eat moist grapes, or *d* .... Num 6:3
But now our soul is *d* away .... Num 11:6
For we have heard how the LORD *d* .... Josh 2:10
For the LORD your God *d* up the .... Josh 4:23
which he *d* up from before us, ... Josh 4:23
heard that the LORD had *d* up the .... Josh 5:1
green withs that were never *d* .... Judg 16:7
green withs with which had not been *d* .... Judg 16:8
d up, so that he could not pull 1Kin 13:4

a while, that the brook *d* up 1Kin 17:7
I *d* up all the rivers of besieged 2Kin 19:24
His roots shall be *d* up beneath, ... Job 18:16
they are *d* up, they are gone away .... Job 28:4
My strength is *d* up like a .... Ps 22:15
my throat is *d* .... Ps 69:3
the Red sea also, and it was *d* up .... Ps 106:9
their multitude *d* up with thirst .... Is 5:13
the river shall be wasted and *d* up .... Is 19:5
defence shall be emptied and *d* up .... Is 19:6
have I *d* up all the rivers of the .... Is 37:25
thou not it which hath *d* the sea, ... Is 51:10
places of the wilderness are *d* up .... Jer 23:10
and they shall be *d* up .... Jer 50:38
have *d* up the green tree, and have .... Eze 17:24
and the east wind *d* up her fruit .... Eze 19:12
behold, they say, Our bones are *d* .... Eze 37:11
is smitten, their root is *d* up .... Hos 9:16
and his fountain shall be *d* up .... Hos 13:15
the new wine is *d* up, the oil .... Joel 1:10
The vine is *d* up, and the fig tree .... Joel 1:12
for the rivers of waters are *d* up .... Joel 1:20
his arm shall be clean *d* up .... Zec 11:17
fountain of her blood was *d* up .... Mk 5:29
the fig tree *d* up from the roots .... Mk 11:20
and the water thereof was *d* up .... Rev 16:12

DRIEDST

thou *d* up mighty rivers .... Ps 74:15

DRIETH

and the flood decayeth, and *d* up .... Job 14:11
but a broken spirit *d* the bones .... Prov 17:22
a river, and *d* up all the rivers. .... Nah 1:4

DRINK

let us make our father *d* wine .... Gen 19:32
their father *d* wine that night, ... Gen 19:33
let us make him *d* wine this night .... Gen 19:34
father *d* wine that night also .... Gen 19:35
with water, and gave the lad *d* .... Gen 21:19
I pray thee, that I may *d* .... Gen 24:14
and she shall say, *D*, ... Gen 24:14
and I will give thy camels *d* also .... Gen 24:14
of a little water of thy pitcher .... Gen 24:17
And she said, *D*, my lord .... Gen 24:18
upon her hand, and gave him *d* .... Gen 24:18
And when she had done giving him *d* .... Gen 24:19
little water of thy pitcher to *d* .... Gen 24:43
And she say to me, Both of thou .... Gen 24:44
and I said unto her, Let me *d* .... Gen 24:45
from her shoulder, and said, *D* .... Gen 24:46
and I will give thy camels *d* also .... Gen 24:46
and she made the camels *d* also .... Gen 24:46
And they did eat and *d*, he and the .... Gen 24:54
and he did eat and *d*, and rose up, ... Gen 25:34
a feast, and they did eat and *d* .... Gen 26:30
troughs when the flocks came to *d* .... Gen 30:38
conceive when they came to *d* .... Gen 30:38
he poured a *d* offering thereon, ... Gen 35:14
to *d* of the water of the river .... Ex 7:18
the Egyptians could not *d* of the .... Ex 7:21
about the river for water to *d* .... Ex 7:24
for they could not *d* of the water .... Ex 7:24
they could not *d* of the waters of .... Ex 15:23
Moses, saying, What shall we *d* .... Ex 15:24
was no water for the people to *d* .... Ex 17:1
said, Give us water that we may *d* .... Ex 17:2
out of it, that the people may *d* .... Ex 17:6
they saw God, and did eat and *d* .... Ex 24:11
an hin of wine for a *d* offering .... Ex 29:40
to the *d* offering thereof .... Ex 29:41
shalt ye pour *d* offering thereon .... Ex 30:9
people sat down to eat and to *d* .... Ex 32:6
the children of Israel of it .... Ex 32:20
neither eat bread, nor *d* water .... Ex 34:28
Do not *d* wine nor strong *d*, ... Lev 10:9
Do not *d* wine nor strong *d* .... Lev 10:9
all *d* that may be drunk in every .... Lev 11:34
the *d* offering thereof shall be .... Lev 23:13
their *d* offerings, even an .... Lev 23:18
of offerings, every thing upon his, ... Lev 23:37
he shall cause the woman to *d* the .... Num 5:24
cause the woman to *d* the water .... Num 5:26
he hath made her to *d* the water .... Num 5:27
himself from wine and strong *d* .... Num 6:3
shall *d* no vinegar of wine, or .... Num 6:3
of wine, or vinegar of strong *d* .... Num 6:3
neither shall he *d* any liquor of .... Num 6:3
offering, and their *d* offerings .... Num 6:15
meat offering, and his *d* offering .... Num 6:17
that the Nazarite may *d* wine .... Num 6:20
a *d* offering that thou preparest .... Num 15:5
for a *d* offering thou shalt offer .... Num 15:7
thou shalt bring for a *d* offering .... Num 15:10
his *d* offering, according to the .... Num 15:24
neither is there any water to *d* .... Num 20:5
congregation and their beasts *d* .... Num 20:8
neither will we *d* of the water of .... Num 20:17
my cattle *d* of thy water, then I .... Num 20:19
we will not *d* of the waters of .... Num 21:22
prey, and *d* the blood of the slain .... Num 23:24
the *d* offering thereof shall be, ... Num 28:7
unto the LORD for a *d* offering .... Num 28:7
as the *d* offering thereof, thou .... Num 28:7
oil, and the *d* offerings thereof .... Num 28:9
burnt offering, and his *d* offering .... Num 28:10
their *d* offerings shall be half .... Num 28:14
burnt offering, and his *d* offering .... Num 28:24
burnt offering, and his *d* offering .... Num 28:24
blemish) and their *d* offerings .... Num 28:31
their *d* offerings, according unto .... Num 29:6

of it, and their d offerings...... Num 29:11
meat offering, and his d offering...... Num 29:16
their d offerings for the...... Num 29:16
thereof, and their d...... Num 29:19
their d offerings for the...... Num 29:21
meat offering, and his d offering...... Num 29:22
their d offerings for the...... Num 29:24
meat offering, and his d...... Num 29:25
their d offerings for the...... Num 29:28
meat offering, and his d offering...... Num 29:30
their d offerings for the...... Num 29:31
meat offering, and his d offering...... Num 29:33
their d offerings for the...... Num 29:34
meat offering, and the bullock...... Num 29:37
meat offering, and his d...... Num 29:38
for your d offerings, and for your...... Num 29:39
was no water for the people to d...... Num 33:14
of them for money, that ye may d...... Deut 2:6
me water for money, that I may d...... Deut 2:28
neither did eat bread nor d water...... Deut 9:9
nor d water, because of all your...... Deut 9:18
or for wine, or for strong d...... Deut 14:26
but shalt neither d of the wine...... Deut 28:39
have ye drunk wine or strong d...... Deut 29:6
thou didst d the pure blood of...... Deut 32:14
the wine of their d offerings...... Deut 32:38
I pray thee, a little water to d...... Judg 4:19
a bottle of milk, and gave him d...... Judg 4:19
boweth down upon his knees to d...... Judg 7:5
down upon their knees to d water...... Judg 7:6
of their god, and did eat and d...... Judg 9:27
d not wine nor strong d...... Judg 13:4
and d not wine nor strong d...... Judg 13:7
now d no wine nor strong...... Judg 13:7
no wine nor strong d...... Judg 13:7
neither let her d wine or strong...... Judg 13:14
let her d wine or strong d...... Judg 13:14
so they did eat and d, and lodged...... Judg 19:4
eat and d both of them together...... Judg 19:6
their feet, and did eat and d...... Judg 19:21
d of that which the young men...... Ruth 2:9
drunken neither wine nor strong d...... 1Sa 1:15
and they made him d water...... 1Sa 30:11
into mine house, to eat and to d...... 2Sa 11:11
him, he did eat and d before him...... 2Sa 11:13
be faint in the wilderness may d...... 2Sa 16:2
taste what I eat or what I d...... 2Sa 19:35
Oh that one would give me d of...... 2Sa 23:15
he would not d thereof, but...... 2Sa 23:16
therefore he would not d it...... 2Sa 23:17
d before him, and say, God save...... 1Kin 1:25
bread nor d water in this place...... 1Kin 13:8
nor d water, nor turn again by...... 1Kin 13:9
neither will I eat bread nor d...... 1Kin 13:16
eat no bread nor d water there...... 1Kin 13:17
that he may eat bread and d water...... 1Kin 13:18
thee, Eat no bread, and d no water...... 1Kin 13:22
that thou shalt d of the brook...... 1Kin 17:4
water in a vessel, that I may d...... 1Kin 17:10
unto Ahab, Get thee up, eat and d...... 1Kin 18:41
So Ahab went up to eat and to d...... 1Kin 18:42
And he did eat and d, and laid him...... 1Kin 19:6
And he arose, and did eat and d...... 1Kin 19:8
filled with water, that ye may d...... 2Kin 3:17
them, that they may eat and d...... 2Kin 6:22
into one tent, and did eat and d...... 2Kin 7:8
he was come in, he did eat and d...... 2Kin 9:34
and poured his d offerings...... 2Kin 16:13
offering, and their d offerings...... 2Kin 16:15
of their own piss with you...... 2Kin 18:27
d ye every one the waters of his...... 2Kin 18:31
Oh that one would give me d of...... 1Chr 11:17
but David would not d of it...... 1Chr 11:18
shall I d the blood of these men...... 1Chr 11:19
Therefore he would not d it...... 1Chr 11:19
lambs, with their d offerings...... 1Chr 29:21
d before the Lord on that day...... 1Chr 29:22
them, and gave them to eat and to d...... 2Chr 28:15
the d offerings for every burnt...... 2Chr 29:35
and meat, and d, and oil, unto them...... Ezr 3:7
their d offerings, and other them...... Ezr 7:17
he did eat no bread, nor d water...... Ezr 10:6
d the sweet, and send portions...... Neh 8:10
went their way to eat, and to d...... Neh 8:12
they gave them d in vessels of...... Est 1:7
the king and Haman sat down to d...... Est 3:15
and neither eat nor d three days...... Est 4:16
sisters to eat and to d with them...... Job 1:4
he shall d of the wrath of the...... Job 21:20
not given water to the weary to d...... Job 22:7
their d offerings of blood will I...... Ps 16:4
thou shalt make them d of the...... Ps 36:8
of bulls, or d the blood of goats...... Ps 50:13
thou hast made us to d the wine...... Ps 60:3
thirst they gave me vinegar to d...... Ps 69:21
shall wring them out, and d them...... Ps 75:8
gave them d as out of the great...... Ps 78:15
floods, that they could not d...... Ps 78:44
them tears to d in great measure...... Ps 80:5
mingled my d with weeping...... Ps 102:9
They give d to every beast of the...... Ps 104:11
He shall d of the brook in the...... Ps 110:7
and d the wine of violence...... Prov 4:17
D waters out of thine own cistern...... Prov 5:15
d of the wine which I have...... Prov 9:5
is a mocker, strong d is raging...... Prov 20:1
Eat and d, saith he to thee...... Prov 23:7
be thirsty, give him water to d...... Prov 25:21
it is not for kings to d wine...... Prov 31:4

nor for princes strong d...... Prov 31:4
Lest they d, and forget the law,...... Prov 31:5
Give strong d unto him that is...... Prov 31:6
Let him d, and forget his poverty,...... Prov 31:7
man, than that he should eat and d...... Eccl 2:24
that every man should eat and d...... Eccl 3:13
and comely for one to eat and to d...... Eccl 5:18
the sun, than to eat, and to d...... Eccl 8:15
d thy wine with a merry heart...... Eccl 9:7
d, yea, d abundantly, O...... Song 5:1
yea, d abundantly, O beloved...... Song 5:1
I would cause thee to d of spiced...... Song 8:2
that they may follow strong d...... Is 5:11
them that are mighty to d wine,...... Is 5:22
of strength to mingle strong d...... Is 5:22
watch in the watchtower, eat, d...... Is 21:5
let us eat and d...... Is 22:13
They shall not d wine with a song...... Is 24:9
strong d shall be bitter to them...... Is 24:9
shall be bitter to them that d it...... Is 24:9
through strong d are out of the...... Is 28:7
have erred through strong d...... Is 28:7
out of the way through strong d...... Is 28:7
stagger, but not with strong d...... Is 29:9
he will cause the d of the...... Is 32:6
d their own piss with you...... Is 36:12
d ye every one the waters of his...... Is 36:16
to give d to my people, my chosen...... Is 43:20
thou shalt no more d it again...... Is 51:22
will fill ourselves with strong d...... Is 56:12
hast thou poured a d offering...... Is 57:6
the stranger shall not d thy wine...... Is 62:8
have brought it together shall d...... Is 62:9
that furnish the d offering unto...... Is 65:11
behold, my servants shall d...... Is 65:13
Egypt, to d the waters of Sihor...... Jer 2:18
to d the waters of the river...... Jer 2:18
to pour out d offerings unto...... Jer 7:18
and given us water of gall to d...... Jer 8:14
and give them water of gall to d...... Jer 9:15
d for their father or for their...... Jer 16:7
to sit with them to eat and to d...... Jer 16:8
have poured out d offerings unto...... Jer 19:13
did not thy father eat and d...... Jer 22:15
make them d the water of gall...... Jer 23:15
to whom I send thee, to d it...... Jer 25:15
And they shall d, and be moved, and...... Jer 25:16
and made all the nations to d...... Jer 25:17
of Sheshach shall d after them...... Jer 25:26
D ye, and be drunken, and spue, and...... Jer 25:27
take the cup at thine hand to d...... Jer 25:28
Ye shall certainly d...... Jer 25:28
pour out d offerings unto other...... Jer 32:29
chambers, and give them wine to d...... Jer 35:2
and I said unto them, D ye wine...... Jer 35:5
But they said, We will d no wine....... Jer 35:6
us, saying, Ye shall d no wine...... Jer 35:6
to d no wine all our days,...... Jer 35:8
commanded his sons not to d wine...... Jer 35:14
for unto this day they d none...... Jer 35:14
to pour out d offerings unto her,...... Jer 44:17
to pour out d offerings unto her...... Jer 44:18
poured out d offerings unto her,...... Jer 44:19
pour out d offerings unto her,...... Jer 44:19
pour out d offerings unto her,...... Jer 44:19
to d of the cup have assuredly...... Jer 49:12
but thou shalt surely d of it...... Jer 49:12
Thou shalt d also water by...... Eze 4:11
from time to time shalt thou d...... Eze 4:11
they shall d water by measure, and...... Eze 4:16
d thy water with trembling and...... Eze 12:18
d their water with astonishment,...... Eze 12:19
out there their d offerings...... Eze 20:28
Thou shalt d of thy sister's cup...... Eze 23:32
Thou shalt even d it and suck it...... Eze 23:34
fruit, and they shall d thy milk...... Eze 25:4
their height, all that d water...... Eze 31:14
best of Lebanon, and that d water...... Eze 31:16
they d that which ye have fouled...... Eze 34:19
vineyards, and of the wine thereof...... Eze 39:17
of the blood of the princes of the...... Eze 39:18
d blood till ye be drunken, of my...... Eze 39:19
Neither shall any priest d wine...... Eze 44:21
d offerings, in the feasts, and in...... Eze 45:17
appointed your meat and your d...... Dan 1:10
us pulse to eat, and water to d...... Dan 1:12
and the wine that they should d...... Dan 1:16
his concubines, might d therein...... Dan 5:2
wool and my flax, mine oil and my d...... Hos 2:5
Their d is sour...... Hos 4:18
the d offering is cut off from...... Joel 1:9
the d offering is withholden from...... Joel 1:13
a d offering unto the LORD your...... Joel 2:14
girl for wine, that they might d...... Joel 3:3
they d the wine of the condemned...... Amos 2:8
ye gave the Nazarites wine to d...... Amos 2:12
their masters, Bring, and let us d...... Amos 4:1
unto one city, to d water...... Amos 4:8
but ye shall not d wine of them...... Amos 5:11
That d wine in bowls, and anoint...... Amos 6:6
continually, yea, they shall d...... Obad 16
let them not feed, nor d water...... Jonah 3:7
unto thee of wine and of strong d...... Mic 2:11
meat, and he shall not d wine...... Mic 6:15
him that giveth his neighbour d...... Hab 2:15
d thou also, and let thy foreskin...... Hab 2:16
but not of the wine thereof...... Zeph 1:13
ye d, but ye are not filled with d...... Hag 1:6
but ye are not filled with d...... Hag 1:6

when ye did eat, and when ye did d...... Zec 7:6
yourselves, and d for yourselves,...... Zec 7:6
and they shall d, and make a noise...... Zec 9:15
ye shall eat, or what ye shall d...... Mt 6:25
or, What shall we d...... Mt 6:31
whosoever shall give to d unto...... Mt 10:42
d of the cup that I shall d...... Mt 20:22
Ye shall d indeed of my cup, and...... Mt 20:23
and to eat and d with the drunken...... Mt 24:49
I was thirsty, and ye gave me d...... Mt 25:35
or thirsty, and gave thee d...... Mt 25:37
I was thirsty, and ye gave me no d...... Mt 25:42
to them, saying, D ye all of it...... Mt 26:27
I will not d henceforth of this...... Mt 26:29
until that day when I d it new...... Mt 26:29
pass away from me, except I d it...... Mt 26:42
vinegar to d mingled with gall...... Mt 27:34
tasted thereof, he would not d...... Mt 27:34
it on a reed, and gave him to d...... Mt 27:48
a cup of water to d in my name...... Mk 9:41
can ye d of the cup that I d...... Mk 10:38
d of the cup that I d of...... Mk 10:38
I will d no more of the fruit of...... Mk 14:25
until that day that I d it new in...... Mk 14:25
they gave him to d wine mingled...... Mk 15:23
it on a reed, and gave him to d...... Mk 15:36
if they d any deadly thing, it...... Mk 16:18
shall d neither wine nor strong...... Lk 1:15
neither wine nor strong d...... Lk 1:15
d with publicans and sinners....... Lk 5:30
but thine eat and d...... Lk 5:33
take thine ease, eat, and be...... Lk 12:19
ye shall eat, or what ye shall d...... Lk 12:29
and maidens, and to eat and...... Lk 12:45
and afterward thou shalt eat and d...... Lk 17:8
I will not d of the fruit of the...... Lk 22:18
d at my table in my kingdom, and...... Lk 22:30
saith unto her, Give me to d...... Jn 4:7
thou, being a Jew, askest d of me...... Jn 4:9
that saith to thee, Give me to d...... Jn 4:10
d his blood, ye have no life in...... Jn 6:53
indeed, and my blood is d indeed...... Jn 6:55
let him come unto me, and d...... Jn 7:37
hath given me, shall I not d it...... Jn 18:11
sight, and neither did eat nor d...... Acts 9:9
d with him after he rose from the...... Acts 10:41
nor d till they had killed Paul...... Acts 23:12
nor d till they have killed him...... Acts 23:21
if he thirst, give him d...... Rom 12:20
kingdom of God is not meat and d...... Rom 14:17
to eat flesh, nor to d wine...... Rom 14:21
Have we not power to eat and to d...... 1Cor 9:4
all d the same spiritual d...... 1Cor 10:4
all the same spiritual d...... 1Cor 10:4
The people sat down to eat and d...... 1Cor 10:7
Ye cannot d the cup of the Lord,...... 1Cor 10:21
Whether therefore ye eat, or d...... 1Cor 10:31
ye not house to eat and to d in...... 1Cor 11:22
this do ye, as oft as ye d it...... 1Cor 11:25
d this cup, ye do shew the Lord's...... 1Cor 11:26
bread, and d this cup of the Lord,...... 1Cor 11:27
of that bread, and d of that cup...... 1Cor 11:28
all made to d into one Spirit...... 1Cor 12:13
let us eat and d...... 1Cor 15:32
judge you in meat, or in d...... Col 2:16
D no longer water, but use a...... 1Ti 5:23
because she made all nations d of...... Rev 14:8
The same shall d of the wine of...... Rev 14:10
thou hast given them blood to d...... Rev 16:6

DRINKERS
all ye d of wine, because of the...... Joel 1:5

DRINKETH
Is not this it in which my lord d...... Gen 44:5
d water of the rain of heaven...... Deut 11:11
the poison whereof d up my spirit...... Job 6:4
which d iniquity like water...... Job 15:16
who d up scorning like water...... Job 34:7
he d up a river, and hasteth not...... Job 40:23
cutteth off the feet, and d damage...... Prov 26:6
man dreameth, and, behold, he d...... Is 29:8
he d no water, and is faint...... Is 44:12
d with publicans and sinners...... Mk 2:16
Whosoever d of this water shall...... Jn 4:13
But whosoever d of the water that...... Jn 4:14
of my blood, hath eternal life...... Jn 6:54
d my blood, dwelleth in me, and I...... Jn 6:56
d unworthily, eateth and d...... 1Cor 11:29
For the earth which d in the rain...... Heb 6:7

DRINKING
also, until they have done d...... Gen 24:19
to pass, as the camels had done d...... Gen 24:22
he shall have done eating and d...... Ruth 3:3
upon all the earth, eating and d...... 1Sa 30:16
the sea in multitude, eating and d...... 1Kin 4:20
all king Solomon's d vessels were...... 1Kin 10:21
of himself drunk in the house of...... 1Kin 16:9
heard this message, as he was d...... 1Kin 20:12
But Ben-hadad was d himself drunk...... 1Kin 20:16
David three days, eating and d...... 1Chr 12:39
all the d vessels of king Solomon...... 2Chr 9:20
the d was according to the law...... Est 1:8
d wine in their eldest brother's...... Job 1:13
d wine in their eldest brother's...... Job 1:18
sheep, eating flesh, and d wine...... Is 22:13
John came neither eating nor d...... Mt 11:18
The Son of man came eating and d...... Mt 11:19
the flood they were eating and d...... Mt 24:38
neither eating bread nor d wine...... Lk 7:33
Son of man is come eating and d...... Lk 7:34

d such things as they give .... Lk 10:7
DRINKS
Which stood only in meats and d .... Heb 9:10
DRIVE
shall he d them out of his land .... Ex 6:1
which shall d out the Hivite, the .... Ex 23:28
I will not d them out from before .... Ex 23:29
little I will d them out from .... Ex 23:30
thou shalt d them out before thee .... Ex 23:31
I will d out the Canaanite, the .... Ex 33:2
I d out before thee the Amorite, ... Ex 34:11
that I may d them out of the land .... Num 22:6
to overcome them, and d them out ...... Num 22:11
Then ye shall d out all the .... Num 33:52
But if ye will not d out the .... Num 33:55
To d out nations from before thee .... Deut 4:38
so shalt thou d them out, ... Deut 9:3
doth d them out from before thee .... Deut 9:4
doth d them out from before thee .... Deut 9:5
Then will the LORD d out all .... Deut 11:23
the LORD thy God doth d them out ..... Deut 18:12
fail d out from before you the .... Josh 3:10
them will I d out from before the .... Josh 13:6
he be able to d them out .... Josh 14:12
could not d them out .... Josh 15:63
d out the inhabitants of those .... Josh 17:12
but did not utterly d them out .... Josh 17:13
for thou shalt d out the .... Josh 17:18
d them from out of your sight .... Josh 23:5
d out any of these nations from .... Josh 23:13
but could not d out the .... Judg 1:19
did not d out the Jebusites that .... Judg 1:21
Neither did Manasseh d out the .... Judg 1:27
and did not utterly d them out .... Judg 1:28
Neither did Ephraim d out the .... Judg 1:29
Neither did Zebulun d out the .... Judg 1:30
Neither did Asher d out the .... Judg 1:31
for they did not d them out .... Judg 1:32
Neither did Naphtali d out the .... Judg 1:33
I will not d them out from before .... Judg 2:3
I also will not henceforth d out .... Judg 2:21
God shall d out from before us .... Judg 11:24
an ass, and said to her servant, D 2Kin 4:24
who didst d out the inhabitants 2Chr 20:7
side, and shall d him to his feet .... Job 18:11
They d away the ass of the .... Job 24:3
How thou didst d out the heathen .... Ps 44:2
is driven away, so d them away .... Ps 68:2
shall d it far from him .... Prov 22:15
I will d thee from thy station, ... Is 22:19
all places whither I shall d them .... Jer 27:10
and that I should d you out .... Jer 27:10
that I might d you out, and that .... Jer 27:15
not, because the LORD did d them .... Jer 46:15
Gentiles, whither I will d them .... Eze 4:13
That they shall d thee from them, ... Dan 4:25
they shall d thee from men, and .... Dan 4:32
I will d them out of mine house .... Hos 9:15
will d him into a land barren and .... Joel 2:20
they shall d out Ashdod at the .... Zeph 2:4
up into the wind, we let her d .... Acts 27:15

DRIVEN
thou hast d me out this day from .... Gen 4:14
they were d out from Pharaoh's .... Ex 10:11
or d away, no man seeing it .... Ex 22:10
until he hath d out his enemies .... Num 32:21
shouldest be d to worship them, ... Deut 4:19
the LORD thy God hath d thee .... Deut 30:1
If any of thine be d out unto the .... Deut 30:4
For the LORD hath d out from .... Josh 23:9
for they have d me out this day 1Sa 26:19
is wisdom d quite from me .... Job 6:13
Wilt thou break a leaf d to .... Job 13:25
He shall be d from light into .... Job 18:18
They were d forth from among men, ... Job 30:5
let them be d backward and put to ...... Ps 40:14
As smoke is d away, so drive them .... Ps 68:2
Jordan was d back .... Ps 114:3
Jordan, that thou wast d back .... Ps 114:5
The wicked is d away in his .... Prov 14:32
and they shall be d to darkness .... Is 8:22
wither, be d away, and be no more .... Is 19:7
sword, and as d stubble to his bow .... Is 41:2
the places whither I have d them .... Jer 8:3
the lands whither he had d them .... Jer 16:15
d them away, and have not visited .... Jer 23:2
countries whither I have d them .... Jer 23:3
countries whither I had d them .... Jer 23:8
they shall be d on, and fall .... Jer 23:12
the places whither I have d you .... Jer 29:14
the nations whither I have d them .... Jer 29:18
whither I have d them in mine .... Jer 32:37
of all places whither they were d .... Jer 40:12
nations, whither they had been d .... Jer 43:5
the nations whither I have d them .... Jer 46:28
ye shall be d out every man right .... Jer 49:5
the lions have d him away .... Jer 50:17
I have d him out for his .... Eze 31:11
again that which was d away .... Eze 34:4
bring again that which was d away ..... Eze 34:16
he was d from men, and did eat .... Dan 4:33
he was d from the sons of men .... Dan 5:21
whither thou hast d them, because .... Dan 9:7
as the chaff that is d with the .... Hos 13:3
I will gather her that is d out .... Mic 4:6
and gather her that was d out .... Zeph 3:19
was d of the devil into the .... Lk 8:29
strake sail, and so were d .... Acts 27:17
night was come, as we were d up .... Acts 27:27

a wave of the sea d with the wind .... Jas 1:6
are d of fierce winds, yet are .... Jas 3:4
DRIVER
he said unto the d of his chariot 1Kin 22:34
regardeth he the crying of the d .... Job 39:7
DRIVETH
for he d furiously 2Kin 9:20
the chaff which the wind d away .... Ps 1:4
The north wind d away rain .... Prov 25:23
immediately the spirit d him into .... Mk 1:12
DRIVING
without d them out hastily .... Judg 2:23
the d is like the d of Jehu 2Kin 9:20
the d is like the d of Jehu 2Kin 9:20
by d out nations from before thy 1Chr 17:21
DROMEDARIES
d brought they unto the place 1Kin 4:28
on mules, camels, and young d .... Est 8:10
thee, the d of Midian and Ephah .... Is 60:6
DROMEDARY
thou art a swift d traversing her .... Jer 2:23

DROP
My doctrine shall d as the rain .... Deut 32:2
also his heavens shall d down dew ..... Deut 33:28
Which the clouds do d and distil .... Job 36:28
and thy paths d fatness .... Ps 65:11
They d upon the pastures of the .... Ps 65:12
the clouds d down the dew .... Prov 3:20
a strange woman d as an honeycomb .... Prov 5:3
O my spouse, d as the honeycomb ..... Song 4:11
nations are as a d of a bucket .... Is 40:15
D down, ye heavens, from above .... Is 45:8
d thy word toward the south, and ...... Eze 20:46
d thy word toward the holy places ...... Eze 21:2
mountains shall d down new wine .... Joel 3:18
d not thy word against the house .... Amos 7:16
the mountains shall d sweet wine .... Amos 9:13
DROPPED
earth trembled, and the heavens d .... Judg 5:4
the clouds also d water .... Judg 5:4
the wood, behold, the honey d 1Sa 14:26
of harvest until water d upon 2Sa 21:10
and my speech d upon them .... Job 29:22
the heavens also d at the .... Ps 68:8
my hands d with myrrh, and my .... Song 5:5
DROPPETH
of the hands the house d through .... Eccl 10:18
DROPPING
of a wife are a continual d .... Prov 19:13
A continual d in a very rainy day .... Prov 27:15
lilies, d sweet smelling myrrh .... Song 5:13
DROPS
he maketh small the d of water .... Job 36:27
or who hath begotten the d of dew ...... Job 38:28
my locks with the d of the night .... Song 5:2
d of blood falling down to the .... Lk 22:44
DROPSY
man before him which had the d .... Lk 14:2
DROSS
The wicked of the earth like d .... Ps 119:119
Take away the d from the silver, ... Prov 25:4
a potsherd covered with silver d .... Prov 26:23
Thy silver is become d, thy wine .... Is 1:22
thee, and purely purge away thy d .... Is 1:25
the house of Israel is to me become d .... Eze 22:18
they are even the d of silver .... Eze 22:18
Because ye are all become d .... Eze 22:19
DROUGHT
in the day d consumed me .... Gen 31:40
serpents, and scorpions, and d .... Deut 8:15
D and heat consume the snow waters .... Job 24:19
is turned into the d of summer .... Ps 32:4
and satisfy thy soul in d .... Is 58:11
and of pits, through a land of d .... Jer 2:6
not be careful in the year of d .... Jer 17:8
A d is upon her waters .... Jer 50:38
in the land of great d .... Hos 13:5
And I called for a d upon the land .... Hag 1:11

DROVE
So he d out the man .... Gen 3:24
the carcases, Abram d them away .... Gen 15:11
servants, every d by themselves .... Gen 32:16
me, and put a space betwixt d .... Gen 32:16
and put a space betwixt d and .... Gen 32:16
thou by all this d which I met .... Gen 33:8
the shepherds came and d them away ... Ex 2:17
d out the Amorites that were .... Num 21:32
Caleb d thence the three sons of .... Josh 15:14
who d away the inhabitants of 1Chr 8:13
who d him away, and he departed .... Ps 34:t
beheld, and d asunder the nations .... Hab 3:6
he d them all out of the temple, ... Jn 2:15
DROVES
third, and that followed the d .... Gen 32:19

DROWN
love, neither can the floods d it .... Song 8:7
which d men in destruction and 1Ti 6:9
DROWNED
also are d in the Red sea .... Ex 15:4
and it shall be cast out and d .... Amos 8:8
and shall be d, as by the flood of .... Amos 9:5

that he were d in the depth of .... Mt 18:6
Egyptians assaying to do were d .... Heb 11:29
DROWSINESS
d shall clothe a man with rags .... Prov 23:21
DRUNK
all drink that may be d in every .... Lev 11:34
neither have ye d wine or strong .... Deut 29:6
when he had d, his spirit came .... Judg 15:19
And when Boaz had eaten and d .... Ruth 3:7
in Shiloh, and after they had d 1Sa 1:9
nor d any water, three days and 1Sa 30:12
and he made him d 2Sa 11:13
d water in the place, of the 1Kin 13:22
eaten bread, and after he had d 1Kin 13:23
drinking himself d in the house 1Kin 16:9
himself d in the pavilions 1Kin 20:16
and when they had eaten and d 2Kin 6:23
of strange waters, and have d the 2Kin 19:24
I have d my wine with my milk .... Song 5:1
I have digged, and d water .... Is 37:25
which hast d at the hand of the .... Is 51:17
make them d in my fury, and I will .... Is 63:6
and made d with their blood .... Jer 46:10
And I will make d her princes .... Jer 51:57
to have d of the deep waters, but .... Eze 34:18
concubines, have d wine in them .... Dan 5:23
For as ye have d upon my holy .... Obad 16
No man also having d old wine .... Lk 5:39
d in thy presence, and thou hast .... Lk 13:26
and when men have well d, then .... Jn 2:10
be not d with wine, wherein is .... Eph 5:18
been made d with the wine of her .... Rev 17:2
For all nations have d of the .... Rev 18:3

DRUNKARD
he is a glutton, and a d .... Deut 21:20
For the d and the glutton shall .... Prov 23:21
goeth up into the hand of a d .... Prov 26:9
shall reel to and fro like a d .... Is 24:20
an idolater, or a railer, or a d 1Cor 5:11

DRUNKARDS
and I was the song of the d .... Ps 69:12
to the d of Ephraim, whose .... Is 28:1
the d of Ephraim, shall be .... Is 28:3
Awake, ye d, and weep .... Joel 1:5
and while they are drunken as d .... Nah 1:10
Nor thieves, nor covetous, nor d 1Cor 6:10

DRUNKEN
And he drank of the wine, and was d .... Gen 9:21
Eli thought she had been d 1Sa 1:13
unto her, How long wilt thou be d 1Sa 1:14
I have d neither wine nor strong 1Sa 1:15
them to stagger like a d man .... Is 24:26
and fro, and stagger like a d man .... Ps 107:27
as a d man staggereth in his .... Is 19:14
they are d, but not with wine .... Is 29:9
they shall be d with their own .... Is 49:26
thou hast d the dregs of the cup .... Is 51:17
now this, thou afflicted, and d .... Is 51:21
I am like a d man, and like a man .... Jer 23:9
Drink ye, and be d, and spue, and .... Jer 25:27
Make ye him d for he magnified .... Jer 48:26
drink of the cup have assuredly d .... Jer 49:12
hand, that made all the earth d .... Jer 51:7
the nations have d of her wine .... Jer 51:7
feasts, and I will make them d .... Jer 51:39
he hath made me d with wormwood ... Lam 3:15
thou shalt be d, and shalt make .... Lam 4:21
We have d our water for money .... Lam 5:4
full, and drink blood till ye be d .... Eze 39:19
and while they are d as drunkards ...... Nah 1:10
Thou also shalt be d .... Nah 3:11
to him, and makest him d also, ... Hab 2:15
and to eat and drink with the d .... Mt 24:49
and to eat and drink, and to be d .... Lk 12:45
serve me, till I have eaten and d .... Lk 17:8
For these are not d, as ye .... Acts 2:15
and one is hungry, and another is d 1Cor 11:21
be d are in the night 1Th 5:7
I saw the woman d with the blood .... Rev 17:6

DRUNKENNESS
of mine heart, to add to thirst .... Deut 29:19
for strength, and not for d .... Eccl 10:17
inhabitants of Jerusalem, with d .... Jer 13:13
Thou shalt be filled with d .... Eze 23:33
overcharged with surfeiting, and d .... Lk 21:34
not in rioting and d, not in .... Rom 13:13
Envyings, murders, d, revellings, ... Gal 5:21

DRUSILLA (dru-sil'-lah) Wife of Felix.
when Felix came with his wife d .... Acts 24:24

DRY
place, and let the d land appear .... Gen 1:9
And God called the d land Earth .... Gen 1:10
of all that was in the d land .... Gen 7:22
the face of the ground was d .... Gen 8:13
river, and pour it upon the d land .... Ex 4:9
become blood upon the d land .... Ex 4:9
children of Israel shall go on d .... Ex 14:16
night, and made the sea d land .... Ex 14:21
of the sea upon the d ground .... Ex 14:22
children of Israel walked upon d .... Ex 14:29
on d land in the midst of the sea .... Ex 15:19
offering, mingled with oil, and d .... Lev 7:10
it is a d scall, even a leprosy .... Lev 13:30
of the LORD stood firm on d .... Josh 3:17

passed over on d ground, until .... Josh 3:17
were lifted up unto the d land .... Josh 4:18
came over this Jordan on d land .... Josh 4:22
bread of their provision was d .... Josh 9:5
but now, behold, it is d, and it .... Josh 9:12
it be d upon all the earth beside .... Judg 6:37
let it now be d only upon the .... Judg 6:39
for it was d upon the fleece only .... Judg 6:40
they two went over on d ground 2Kin 2:8
midst of the sea on the d land .... Neh 9:11
the waters, and they d up .... Job 12:15
and wilt thou pursue the d stubble .... Job 13:25
the flame shall d up his branches .... Job 15:30
my flesh longeth for thee in a d .... Ps 63:1
He turned the sea into d land .... Ps 66:6
the rebellious dwell in a d land .... Ps 68:6
and his hands formed the d land .... Ps 95:5
they ran in the d places like a .... Ps 105:41
and the watersprings into d ground .... Ps 107:33
d ground into watersprings .... Ps 107:35
Better is a d morsel, and .... Prov 17:1
as the heat in a d place .... Is 25:5
as rivers of water in a d place .... Is 32:2
the d land springs of water .... Is 35:7
and hills, and d up all their herbs ...... Is 42:15
islands, and I will d up the pools .... Is 42:15
and floods upon the d ground .... Is 44:3
That saith to the deep, Be d .... Is 44:27
and I will d up thy rivers .... Is 44:27
at my rebuke I d up the sea .... Is 50:2
and as a root out of a d ground .... Is 53:2
eunuch say, Behold, I am a d tree .... Is 56:3
A d wind of the high places in .... Jer 4:11
wilderness, a d land, and a desert .... Jer 50:12
I will d up her sea .... Jer 50:38
and make her springs d .... Jer 51:36
a d land, and a wilderness, a land .... Jer 51:43
have made the d tree to flourish .... Eze 17:24
planted in the wilderness, in a d .... Eze 19:13
tree in thee, and every d tree .... Eze 20:47
And I will make the rivers d .... Eze 30:12
and, lo, they were very d .... Eze 37:2
O ye d bones, hear the word of .... Eze 37:4
and set her like a d land .... Hos 2:3
a miscarrying womb and d breasts .... Hos 9:14
and his spring shall become d .... Hos 13:15
hath made the sea and the d land .... Jonah 1:9
vomited out Jonah upon the d land .... Jonah 2:10
rebuketh the sea, and maketh it d .... Nah 1:4
be devoured as stubble fully d .... Nah 1:10
and d like a wilderness .... Zeph 2:13
earth, and the sea, and the d land .... Hag 2:6
the deeps of the river shall d up .... Zec 10:11
man, he walketh through d places .... Mt 12:43
man, he walketh through d places .... Lk 11:24
tree, what shall be done in the d .... Lk 23:31
through the Red sea as by d land .... Heb 11:29

DRYSHOD

streams, and make men go over d .... Is 11:15

DUE

it is thy d, and thy sons' d .... Lev 10:13
they be thy d, and thy sons' d .... Lev 10:14
I will give you rain in d season .... Lev 26:4
offer unto me in their d season .... Num 28:2
rain of your land in his d season .... Deut 11:14
be the priest's d from the people .... Deut 18:3
their foot shall slide in d time .... Deut 32:35
sought him not after the d order 1Chr 15:13
LORD the glory d unto his name 1Chr 16:29
for the singers, d for every day .... Neh 11:23
LORD the glory d unto his name .... Ps 29:2
LORD the glory d unto his name .... Ps 96:8
give them their meat in d season .... Ps 104:27
them their meat in d season .... Ps 145:15
good from them to whom it is d .... Prov 3:27
and a word spoken in d season .... Prov 15:23
and thy princes eat in d season .... Eccl 10:17
pay all that was d unto him .... Mt 18:34
to give them meat in d season .... Mt 24:45
their portion of meat in d season .... Lk 12:42
for we receive the d reward of .... Lk 23:41
in d time Christ died for the .... Rom 5:6
tribute to whom tribute is d .... Rom 13:7
unto the wife d benevolence 1Cor 7:3
as of one born out of d time 1Cor 15:8
for in d season we shall reap, if .... Gal 6:9
all, to be testified in d time 1Ti 2:6
But hath in d times manifested .... Titus 1:3
that he may exalt you in d time 1Pet 5:6

DUES

Render therefore to all their d .... Rom 13:7

DUKE

firstborn son of Esau; d Teman .... Gen 36:15
d Omar, d Zepho, d Kenaz, ... Gen 36:15
D Korah, d Gatam, and d .... Gen 36:16
D Korah, d Gatam, and d Amalek .... Gen 36:16
d Nahath, d Zerah .... Gen 36:17
d Shammah, d .... Gen 36:17
d Jeush, d Jaalam, d Korah .... Gen 36:18
came of the Horites; d Lotan .... Gen 36:29
d Shobal, d Zibeon, d Anah, ... Gen 36:29
D Dishon, d Ezer, d Dishan .... Gen 36:30
by their names; d Timnah .... Gen 36:40
d Alvah, d Jetheth .... Gen 36:40
D Aholibamah, d Elah, d Pinon, ... Gen 36:41
d Kenaz, d Teman, d Mibzar, ... Gen 36:42
D Magdiel, d Iram .... Gen 36:43
of Edom were; d Timnah 1Chr 1:51

d Aliah, d Jetheth 1Chr 1:51
D Aholibamah, d Elah, d Pinon 1Chr 1:52
D Kenaz, d Teman, d Mibzar, ... 1Chr 1:53
D Magdiel, d Iram 1Chr 1:54

DUKES

These were d the sons of Esau .... Gen 36:15
these are the d that came of .... Gen 36:15
these are the d that came of .... Gen 36:16
these were the d that came of .... Gen 36:18
who is Edom, and these are their d ...... Gen 36:19
these are the d of the Horites, ... Gen 36:21
These are the d that came of the .... Gen 36:29
these are the d that came of Hori .... Gen 36:30
among their d in the land of Seir .... Gen 36:30
names of the d that came of Esau .... Gen 36:40
these be the d of Edom, according .... Gen 36:43
Then the d of Edom shall be .... Ex 15:15
and Reba, which were d of Sihon .... Josh 13:21
And the d of Edom were 1Chr 1:51
These are the d of Edom 1Chr 1:54

DULCIMER

flute, harp, sackbut, psaltery, d .... Dan 3:5
harp, sackbut, psaltery, and d .... Dan 3:10
harp, sackbut, psaltery, and d .... Dan 3:15

DULL

and their ears are d of hearing .... Mt 13:15
and their ears are d of hearing .... Acts 28:27
seeing ye are d of hearing .... Heb 5:11

DUMAH (doo′-mah)
1. Son of Ishmael.
And Mishma, and D, and Massa, ... Gen 25:14
Mishma, and D, Massa, Hadad, and, ... 1Chr 1:30
2. A city in Judah.
Arab, and D, and Eshean, ... Josh 15:52
3. An undetermined city.
The burden of D. He calleth to .... Is 21:11

DUMB

or who maketh the d, or deaf, or .... Ex 4:11
I was as a man that openeth not .... Ps 38:13
I was d with silence, I held my .... Ps 39:2
I was d, I opened not my mouth .... Ps 39:9
Open thy mouth for the d in the .... Prov 31:8
hart, and the tongue of the d sing ...... Is 35:6
a sheep before her shearers is d .... Is 53:7
all ignorant, they are all d dogs .... Is 56:10
thy mouth, that thou shalt be d .... Eze 3:26
thou shalt speak, and be no more d, ... Eze 24:27
was opened, and I was no more d .... Eze 33:22
toward the ground, and I became d .... Dan 10:15
trusteth therein, to make d idols .... Hab 2:18
to the d stone, Arise, it shall .... Hab 2:19
they brought to him a d man .... Mt 9:32
devil was cast out, the d spake .... Mt 9:33
the blind and d both spake and saw ...... Mt 12:22
those that were lame, blind, d .... Mt 15:30
when they saw the d to speak .... Mt 15:31
deaf to hear, and the d to speak .... Mk 7:37
my son, which hath a d spirit .... Mk 9:17
spirit, saying unto him, Thou d .... Mk 9:25
And, behold, thou shalt be d .... Lk 1:20
casting out a devil, and it was d .... Lk 11:14
devil was gone out, the d spake .... Lk 11:14
like a lamb d before his shearer, ... Acts 8:32
carried away unto these d idols 1Cor 12:2
the d ass speaking with man's 2Pet 2:16

DUNG

bullock, and his skin, and his d .... Ex 29:14
legs, and his inwards, and his d .... Lev 4:11
and his hide, his flesh, and his d ...... Lev 8:17
skins, and their flesh, and their d ..... Lev 16:27
flesh, and her blood, with her d .... Num 19:5
Jeroboam, as a man taketh away d 1Kin 14:10
d for five pieces of silver 2Kin 6:25
d upon the face of the field in 2Kin 9:37
that they may eat their own d 2Kin 18:27
the dragon well, and to the d port ...... Neh 2:13
on the wall unto the d gate .... Neh 3:13
But the d gate repaired Malchiah .... Neh 3:14
upon the wall toward the d gate .... Neh 12:31
perish for ever like his own d .... Job 20:7
they became as d for the earth .... Ps 83:10
that they may eat their own d .... Is 36:12
they shall be d upon the face .... Jer 8:2
fall as d upon the open field .... Jer 9:22
but they shall be as d upon the .... Jer 16:4
they shall be d upon the ground, ... Jer 25:33
it with d that cometh out of man .... Eze 4:12
given thee cow's d for man's d .... Eze 4:15
given thee cow's d for man's d .... Eze 4:15
as dust, and their flesh as the d .... Zeph 1:17
spread d upon your faces .... Mal 2:3
even the d of your solemn feasts .... Mal 2:3
I shall dig about it, and d it .... Lk 13:8
things, and do count them but d .... Phil 3:8

DUNGEON

they should put me into the d .... Gen 40:15
brought him hastily out of the d .... Gen 41:14
of the captive that was in the d .... Ex 12:29
Jeremiah was entered into the d .... Jer 37:16
cast him into the d of Malchiah .... Jer 38:6
in the d there was no water, but .... Jer 38:6
they had put Jeremiah in the d .... Jer 38:7
whom they have cast into the d .... Jer 38:9
Jeremiah the prophet out of the d .... Jer 38:10
by cords into the d to Jeremiah .... Jer 38:11

and took him up out of the d .... Jer 38:13
have cut off my life in the d .... Lam 3:53
name, O LORD, out of the low d .... Lam 3:55

DUNGHILL

lifteth up the beggar from the d 1Sa 2:8
his house be made a d for this .... Ezr 6:11
and lifteth the needy out of the d ...... Ps 113:7
straw is trodden down for the d .... Is 25:10
and your houses shall be made a d .... Dan 2:5
and their houses shall be made a d ...... Dan 3:29
for the land, nor yet for the d .... Lk 14:35

DUNGHILLS

brought up in scarlet embrace d .... Lam 4:5

DURA (doo′-rah) A plain in Babylonia.
he set it up in the plain of D .... Dan 3:1

DURABLE

d riches and righteousness .... Prov 8:18
sufficiently, and for d clothing .... Is 23:18

DURETH

in himself, but d for a while .... Mt 13:21

DURST

that d presume in his heart to do. ...... Est 7:5
d not shew you mine opinion .... Job 32:6
neither d any man from that day .... Mt 22:46
no man after that d ask him any .... Mk 12:34
after that they d not ask him any .... Lk 20:40
none of the disciples d ask him .... John 21:12
of the rest of no man join himself ..... Acts 5:13
Moses trembled, and d not behold. ...... Acts 7:32
d not bring against him a railing .... Jude 9

DUST

formed man of the d of the ground .... Gen 2:7
d shalt thou eat all the days of .... Gen 3:14
for d thou art, and unto d .... Gen 3:19
thy seed as the d of the earth .... Gen 13:16
man can number the d of the earth. ..... Gen 13:16
unto the Lord, which am but d .... Gen 18:27
shalt be as the d of the earth .... Gen 28:14
smite the d of the land, that it .... Ex 8:16
smote the d of the earth, and it .... Ex 8:17
all the d of the land became lice ...... Ex 8:17
it shall become small d in all .... Ex 9:9
they shall pour out the d thereof ...... Lev 14:41
blood thereof, and cover it with d ..... Lev 17:13
of the d that is in the floor of .... Num 5:17
Who can count the d of Jacob .... Num 23:10
even until it was as small as d .... Deut 9:21
I cast the d thereof into the .... Deut 9:21
the rain of thy land powder and d ...... Deut 28:24
the poison of serpents of the d .... Deut 32:24
Israel, and put d upon their heads. .... Josh 7:6
raiseth up the poor out of the d 1Sa 2:8
and threw stones at him, and cast d 2Sa 16:13
as small as the d of the earth 2Sa 22:43
as I exalted thee out of the d 1Kin 16:2
the wood, and the stones, and the d 1Kin 18:38
if the d of Samaria shall suffice. 1Kin 20:10
made them like the d by threshing 2Kin 13:7
cast the d of them into the brook 2Kin 23:12
the d of the earth in multitude 2Chr 1:9
made d of them, and strowed it 2Chr 34:4
sprinkled d upon their heads .... Job 2:12
whose foundation is in the d .... Job 4:19
cometh not forth of the d .... Job 5:6
clothed with worms and clods of d ...... Job 7:5
for now shall I sleep in the d .... Job 7:21
wilt thou bring me into d again .... Job 10:9
grow out of the d of the earth .... Job 14:19
skin, and defiled my horn in the d ..... Job 16:15
our rest together is in the d .... Job 17:16
shall lie down with him in the d .... Job 20:11
shall lie down alike in the d .... Job 21:26
Then shalt thou lay up gold as d .... Job 22:24
Though he heap up silver as the d ...... Job 27:16
and it hath d of gold .... Job 28:6
the mire, and I am become like d .... Job 30:19
and man shall turn again unto d .... Job 34:15
When the d groweth into hardness, ... Job 38:38
earth, and warmeth them in the d .... Job 39:14
Hide them in the d together .... Job 40:13
I abhor myself, and repent in d .... Job 42:6
and lay mine honour in the d .... Ps 7:5
small as the d before the wind .... Ps 18:42
brought me into the d of death .... Ps 22:15
to the d shall bow before him .... Ps 22:29
shall the d praise thee .... Ps 30:9
our soul is bowed down to the d .... Ps 44:25
and his enemies shall lick the d .... Ps 72:9
rained flesh also upon them as d .... Ps 78:27
stones, and favour the d thereof .... Ps 102:14
He remembereth that we are d .... Ps 103:14
they die, and return to their d .... Ps 104:29
to the d, and dost thou .... Ps 119:25
My soul cleaveth unto the d .... Ps 119:25
part of the d of the world .... Prov 8:26
the d, and all turn to d again .... Eccl 3:20
Then shall the d return to the .... Eccl 12:7
the rock, and hide thee in the d .... Is 2:10
and their blossom shall go up as d ..... Is 5:24
to the ground, even to the d .... Is 25:12
he bringeth it even to the d .... Is 26:5
Awake and sing, ye that dwell in d. .... Is 26:19
speech shall be low out of the d .... Is 29:4
speech shall whisper out of the d ...... Is 29:4
strangers shall be like small d .... Is 29:5
their d made fat with fatness. .... Is 34:7

the *d* thereof into brimstone, and ...... Is 34:9
comprehended the *d* of the earth ...... Is 40:12
as the small *d* of the balance ...... Is 40:15
gave them as the *d* to his sword ...... Is 41:2
Come down, and sit in the *d* ...... Is 47:1
and lick up the *d* of thy feet ...... Is 49:23
Shake thyself from the *d* ...... Is 52:2
d shall be the serpent's meat ...... Is 65:25
have cast up *d* upon their heads ...... Lam 2:10
He putteth his mouth into the *d* ...... Lam 3:29
the ground, to cover it with *d* ...... Eze 24:7
I will also scrape her *d* from her ...... Eze 26:4
horses their *d* shall cover thee ...... Eze 26:10
thy *d* in the midst of the water ...... Eze 26:12
shall cast up *d* upon their heads, ... Eze 27:30
in the *d* of the earth shall awake ...... Dan 12:2
That pant after the *d* of the ...... Amos 2:7
of Aphrah roll thyself in the *d* ...... Mic 1:10
shall lick the *d* like a serpent ...... Mic 7:17
the clouds are the *d* of his feet ...... Nah 1:3
thy nobles shall dwell in the *d* ...... Nah 3:18
for they shall heap *d*, and take it ...... Hab 1:10
blood shall be poured out as *d* ...... Zeph 1:17
and heaped up silver as the *d* ...... Zec 9:3
shake off the *d* of your feet, ... Mt 10:14
shake off the *d* under your feet, ... Mk 6:11
shake off the very of them ...... Lk 9:5
Even the very *d* of your city ...... Lk 10:11
But they shook off the *d* of their ...... Acts 13:51
clothes, and threw *d* into the air, ... Acts 22:23
they cast *d* on their heads, and ...... Rev 18:19

DUTIES

And that doeth not any of those *d* ...... Eze 18:11

DUTY

her *d* of marriage, shall he not ...... Ex 21:10
perform the *d* of an husband's ...... Deut 25:5
the *d* of my husband's brother ...... Deut 25:7
as the *d* of every day required 2Chr 8:14
as the *d* of every day required ...... Ezr 3:4
for this is the whole *d* of man ...... Eccl 12:13
done that which was our *d* to do ...... Lk 17:10
their *d* is also to minister unto. ...... Rom 15:27

DWARF

Or crookback, or a *d*, or that ...... Lev 21:20

DWELL

the father of such as *d* in tents. ...... Gen 4:20
he shall *d* in the tents of Shem ...... Gen 9:27
them, that they might *d* together ...... Gen 13:6
so that they could not *d* together ...... Gen 13:6
he shall *d* in the presence of all ...... Gen 16:12
for he feared to *d* in Zoar ...... Gen 19:30
d where it pleaseth thee. ...... Gen 20:15
of the Canaanites, among whom I *d* ...... Gen 24:37
the Canaanites, in whose land I *d* ...... Gen 24:37
d in the land which I shall tell ...... Gen 26:2
now will my husband *d* with me ...... Gen 30:20
And ye shall *d* with us ...... Gen 34:10
and trade ye therein, and get you. ...... Gen 34:10
we will *d* with you, and we will ...... Gen 34:16
therefore let them *d* in the land. ...... Gen 34:21
consent unto us for to *d* with us ...... Gen 34:22
unto them, and they will *d* with us. ...... Gen 34:23
go up to Beth-el, and there ...... Gen 35:1
than that they might *d* together. ...... Gen 36:7
thou shalt *d* in the land of ...... Gen 45:10
that ye may *d* in the land of ...... Gen 46:34
let thy servants *d* in the land of ...... Gen 47:4
make thy father and brethren to *d* ...... Gen 47:6
in the land of Goshen let them *d* ...... Gen 47:6
Zebulun shall *d* at the haven of ...... Gen 49:13
was content to *d* with the man ...... Ex 2:21
of Goshen, in which my people *d* ...... Ex 8:22
thou hast made for thee to *d* in ...... Ex 15:17
They shall out *d* in thy land ...... Ex 23:33
that I may *d* among them ...... Ex 25:8
I will *d* among the children of ...... Ex 29:45
of Egypt, that I may *d* among them. ...... Ex 29:46
he shall *d* alone. ...... Lev 13:46
whither I bring you to *d* therein ...... Lev 20:22
Ye shall *d* in booths seven days ...... Lev 23:42
Israelites born shall *d* in booths. ...... Lev 23:42
children of Israel to *d* in booths. ...... Lev 23:43
ye shall *d* in the land in safety ...... Lev 25:18
your fill, and *d* therein in safety ...... Lev 25:19
full, and *d* in your land safely ...... Lev 26:5
your enemies which *d* therein. ...... Lev 26:32
camps, in the midst whereof I *d* ...... Num 5:3
what the land is that they *d* in ...... Num 13:19
cities they be that they *d* in ...... Num 13:19
be strong that *d* in the land ...... Num 13:28
The Amalekites *d* in the land of ...... Num 13:29
the Amorites, in the mountains ...... Num 13:29
and the Canaanites *d* by the sea ...... Num 13:29
I sware to make you *d* therein ...... Num 14:30
lo, the people shall *d* alone ...... Num 23:9
our little ones shall *d* in ...... Num 32:17
of the land, and *d* therein ...... Num 33:53
vex you in the land wherein ye *d* ...... Num 33:55
their possession cities to *d* ...... Num 35:2
cities shall they have to *d* in ...... Num 35:3
come again to *d* in the land. ...... Num 35:32
ye shall inhabit, wherein I *d* ...... Num 35:34
for I the LORD *d* among the ...... Num 35:34
children of Esau, which *d* in Seir ...... Deut 2:4
children of Esau, which *d* in Seir ...... Deut 2:29
and the Moabites which *d* in Ar ...... Deut 2:29
which *d* in the champaign over ...... Deut 11:30
ye shall possess it, and *d* therein. ...... Deut 11:31

d in the land which the LORD your ...... Deut 12:10
about, so that ye *d* in safety. ...... Deut 12:10
to cause his name to *d* there ...... Deut 12:11
God hath given thee to *d* there ...... Deut 13:12
shalt *d* therein, and shalt say, I ...... Deut 17:14
He shall *d* with thee, even among ...... Deut 23:16
If brethren *d* together, and one of ...... Deut 25:5
and thou shalt not *d* therein ...... Deut 28:30
that thou mayest *d* in the land ...... Deut 30:20
the LORD shall *d* in safety by him ...... Deut 33:12
he shall *d* between his shoulders ...... Deut 33:12
then shall *d* in safety alone ...... Deut 33:28
Peradventure ye *d* among us ...... Josh 9:7
when ye *d* among us ...... Josh 9:22
d in the mountains are gathered ...... Josh 10:6
the Maachathites *d* among the ...... Josh 13:13
in the land, save cities to *d* in ...... Josh 14:4
but the Jebusites *d* with the ...... Josh 15:63
but the Canaanites *d* among the ...... Josh 16:10
Canaanites would *d* in that land. ...... Josh 17:12
all the Canaanites that *d* in the ...... Josh 17:16
a place, that he may *d* among them ...... Josh 20:4
he shall *d* in that city, until he ...... Josh 20:6
Moses to give us cities to *d* in ...... Josh 21:2
ye built not, and ye *d* in them ...... Josh 24:13
the Amorites, in whose land ye *d* ...... Josh 24:15
the Jebusites *d* with the ...... Judg 1:21
Canaanites would *d* in that land ...... Judg 1:27
But the Amorites would *d* in mount ...... Judg 1:35
the Amorites, in whose land ye *d* ...... Judg 6:10
that they should not *d* in Shechem ...... Judg 9:41
D with me, and be unto me a father ...... Judg 17:10
was content to *d* with the man ...... Judg 17:11
them an inheritance to *d* in ...... Judg 18:1
made them *d* in this place ...... Judg 18:28
the country, that I may *d* there 1Sa 27:5
for why should thy servant *d* in 1Sa 27:5
I *d* in an house of cedar, but the 2Sa 7:2
build me an house for me to *d* in 2Sa 7:5
that they may *d* in a place of 2Sa 7:10
of there, and go not forth thence. 1Kin 2:36
this woman *d* in one house 1Kin 3:17
I will *d* among the children of 1Kin 6:13
he would *d* in the thick darkness 1Kin 8:12
built thee an house to *d* in 1Kin 8:13
will God indeed *d* on the earth 1Kin 8:27
belongeth to Zidon, and *d* there 1Kin 17:9
I *d* among mine own people 2Kin 4:13
the place where we *d* with thee is 2Kin 6:1
us a place there, where we may *d* 2Kin 6:2
d there, and let him teach them 2Kin 17:27
in the land, and serve the king 2Kin 25:24
I *d* in an house of cedars, but 1Chr 17:1
not build me an house to *d* in 1Chr 17:4
they shall *d* in their place, and 1Chr 17:9
that they may *d* in Jerusalem for 1Chr 23:25
build him an house to *d* therein 2Chr 2:3
he would *d* in the thick darkness 2Chr 6:1
very deed *d* with men on the earth 2Chr 6:18
the children of Israel to *d* there 2Chr 8:2
My wife shall not *d* in the house 2Chr 8:11
brethren that *d* in their cities 2Chr 19:10
companions that *d* in Samaria ...... Ezr 4:17
name to *d* there destroy all kings ...... Ezr 6:12
d in booths in the feast of the ...... Neh 8:14
to bring one of ten to *d* in ...... Neh 11:1
nine parts to *d* in other cities ...... Neh 11:1
themselves to *d* at Jerusalem ...... Neh 11:2
let a cloud upon it ...... Job 3:5
in them that *d* in houses of clay ...... Job 4:19
wickedness *d* in thy tabernacles ...... Job 11:14
It shall *d* in his tabernacle, ... Job 18:15
They that *d* in mine house, and my ...... Job 19:15
To *d* in the cliffs of the valleys ...... Job 30:6
LORD, only makest me *d* in safety ...... Ps 4:8
neither shall evil *d* with thee ...... Ps 5:4
who shall *d* in thy holy hill ...... Ps 15:1
I will *d* in the house of the LORD ...... Ps 23:6
the world, and they that *d* therein ...... Ps 24:1
His soul shall *d* at ease ...... Ps 25:13
that I may *d* in the house of the ...... Ps 27:4
so shalt thou *d* in the land ...... Ps 37:3
and *d* for evermore ...... Ps 37:27
the land, and therein for ever ...... Ps 37:29
that he may *d* in thy courts ...... Ps 65:4
They also that *d* in the uttermost ...... Ps 65:8
the rebellious *d* in a dry land ...... Ps 68:6
hill which God desireth to *d* in ...... Ps 68:16
the LORD will *d* in it for ever ...... Ps 68:16
the LORD God might *d* among them. ...... Ps 68:18
let none *d* in their tents ...... Ps 69:25
that they may *d* there, and have it ...... Ps 69:35
love his name shall *d* therein ...... Ps 69:36
They that *d* in the wilderness ...... Ps 72:9
of Israel to *d* in their tents ...... Ps 78:55
are they that *d* in thy house ...... Ps 84:4
than to *d* in the tents of ...... Ps 84:10
that glory may *d* in our land ...... Ps 85:9
the world, and they that *d* therein ...... Ps 98:7
shall not *d* within my house ...... Ps 101:6
they found no city to *d* in ...... Ps 107:4
wickedness of them that *d* therein ...... Ps 107:34
there he maketh the hungry to *d* ...... Ps 107:36
that I *d* in the tents of Kedar ...... Ps 120:5
here will I *d*; for I have ...... Ps 132:14
brethren to *d* together in unity ...... Ps 133:1
d in the uttermost parts of the ...... Ps 139:9
upright shall *d* in thy presence ...... Ps 140:13
he hath made me to *d* in darkness ...... Ps 143:3

hearkeneth unto me shall *d* safely ...... Prov 1:33
the upright shall *d* in the land. ...... Prov 2:21
I wisdom *d* with prudence, and find ...... Prov 8:12
It is better to *d* in a corner of ...... Prov 21:9
It is better to *d* in the ...... Prov 21:19
It is better to *d* in the corner ...... Prov 25:24
I *d* in the midst of a people of ...... Is 6:5
that that *d* in the land of the ...... Is 9:2
wolf also shall *d* with the lamb ...... Is 11:6
and owls shall *d* there, and satyrs ...... Is 13:21
Let mine outcasts *d* with thee ...... Is 16:4
for them that *d* in the wilderness ...... Is 23:13
for them that *d* before the LORD ...... Is 23:18
they that *d* therein are desolate. ...... Is 24:6
bringeth down them that *d* on high ...... Is 26:5
Awake and sing, ye that *d* in dust ...... Is 26:19
shall *d* in Zion at Jerusalem ...... Is 30:19
shall *d* in the wilderness ...... Is 32:16
my people shall *d* in a peaceable ...... Is 32:18
Who among us shall *d* with the ...... Is 33:14
who among us shall *d* with ...... Is 33:14
He shall *d* on high ...... Is 33:16
the people that *d* therein shall ...... Is 33:24
also and the raven shall *d* in it ...... Is 34:11
generation shall they *d* therein, ... Is 34:17
them out as a tent to *d* in ...... Is 40:22
give place to me that I may *d* ...... Is 49:20
that that *d* therein shall die in ...... Is 51:6
I *d* in the high and holy place. ...... Is 57:15
The restorer of paths to *d* in. ...... Is 58:12
it, and my servants shall *d* there ...... Is 65:9
forsaken, and not a man *d* therein ...... Jer 4:29
will cause you to *d* in this place ...... Jer 7:3
I cause you to *d* in this place ...... Jer 7:7
the city, and those that *d* therein ...... Jer 8:16
of them that *d* in a far country ...... Jer 8:19
corners, that *d* in the wilderness ...... Jer 9:26
wickedness of them that *d* therein. ...... Jer 12:4
all that *d* in thine house shall ...... Jer 20:6
saved, and Israel shall *d* safely ...... Jer 23:6
they shall *d* in their own land ...... Jer 23:8
them that *d* in the land of Egypt ...... Jer 24:8
d in the land that the LORD hath ...... Jer 25:5
people that *d* in the desert ...... Jer 25:24
they shall tilt it, and *d* therein ...... Jer 27:11
Build ye houses, and *d* in them ...... Jer 29:5
build ye houses, and *d* in them ...... Jer 29:28
have a man to *d* among this people ...... Jer 29:32
there shall *d* in Judah itself, and ...... Jer 31:24
and I will cause them to *d* safely ...... Jer 32:37
and Jerusalem shall *d* safely ...... Jer 33:16
all your days ye shall *d* in tents ...... Jer 35:7
to build houses for us to *d* in ...... Jer 35:9
so we *d* at Jerusalem ...... Jer 35:11
ye shall *d* in the land which I ...... Jer 35:15
d with him among the people ...... Jer 40:5
d in the land, and serve the king ...... Jer 40:9
I will *d* at Mizpah to serve the ...... Jer 40:10
d in your cities that ye have ...... Jer 40:10
We will not *d* in this land, ... Jer 42:13
and there will we *d* ...... Jer 42:14
to *d* in the land of Judah ...... Jer 42:15
to *d* in the land of Judah ...... Jer 43:5
Jews which *d* in the land of Egypt ...... Jer 44:1
at Migdol, and at ...... Jer 44:1
of Egypt, whither ye be gone to *d* ...... Jer 44:8
them that *d* in the land of Egypt ...... Jer 44:13
a desire to return to *d* there ...... Jer 44:14
all Judah that *d* in the land of ...... Jer 44:26
the city, and them that *d* therein ...... Jer 47:2
without any to *d* therein. ...... Jer 48:9
O ye that *d* in Moab, leave the ...... Jer 48:28
d in the rock, and be like the ...... Jer 48:28
his people *d* in his cities ...... Jer 49:31
d deep, O inhabitants of Dedan ...... Jer 49:8
shall a son of man *d* in it. ...... Jer 49:18
d deep, O ye inhabitants of Hazor ...... Jer 49:30
gates nor bars, which *d* alone ...... Jer 49:31
there, nor any son of man *d* in it ...... Jer 49:33
desolate, and none shall *d* therein ...... Jer 50:3
of the islands shall *d* there ...... Jer 50:39
and the owls shall *d* therein. ...... Jer 50:39
shall any son of man *d* therein. ...... Jer 50:40
against them that *d* in the midst ...... Jer 51:1
thou dost *d* among scorpions ...... Eze 2:6
of all them that *d* there ...... Eze 12:19
daughters that *d* at thy left hand ...... Eze 16:46
under it shall *d* all fowl of ...... Eze 17:23
the branches thereof shall they *d* ...... Eze 17:23
then shall they *d* in their land ...... Eze 28:25
they shall *d* safely therein, and ...... Eze 28:26
they shall *d* with confidence, ... Eze 28:26
smite all them that *d* therein ...... Eze 32:15
they shall *d* safely in the ...... Eze 34:25
but they shall *d* safely, and none ...... Eze 34:28
ye shall *d* in the land that I ...... Eze 36:28
also cause you to *d* in the cities ...... Eze 36:33
they shall *d* in the land that I ...... Eze 37:25
and they shall *d* therein, even ...... Eze 37:25
they shall *d* safely all of them ...... Eze 38:8
that *d* safely, all of them ...... Eze 38:8
that *d* in the midst of the land ...... Eze 38:12
among them that *d* carelessly in ...... Eze 39:6
that that *d* in the cities of ...... Eze 39:9
where I will *d* in the midst of ...... Eze 43:7
I will *d* in the midst of them for ...... Eze 43:9
wheresoever the children of men *d* ...... Dan 2:38
that *d* in all the earth ...... Dan 4:1
that *d* in all the earth ...... Dan 6:25
They shall not *d* in the LORD's ...... Hos 9:3

yet make thee to d in tabernacles .... Hos 12:9
They that d under his shadow .... Hos 14:7
But Judah shall d for ever .... Joel 3:20
of Israel be taken out that d in .... Amos 3:12
stone, but ye shall not d in them .... Amos 5:11
all that d therein shall mourn.............. Amos 9:5
thou shalt d in the field, and............... Mic 4:10
because of them that d therein .... Mic 7:13
which d solitarily in the wood, ... Mic 7:14
the world, and all that d therein.......... Nah 1:5
he noble, and all in the dust .... Nah 3:18
city, and of all that d therein............... Hab 2:8
city, and of all that d therein............... Hab 2:17
of all them that d in the land .... Zeph 1:18
to d in your cieled houses, and............ Hag 1:4
I will d in the midst of thee, ... Zec 2:10
I will d in the midst of thee, and......... Zec 2:11
will d in the midst of Jerusalem .... Zec 8:3
old women d in the streets of .... Zec 8:4
they shall d in the midst of................. Zec 8:8
And a bastard shall d in Ashdod .... Zec 9:6
And men shall d in it, and there .... Zec 14:11
and they enter in and d there .... Mt 12:45
and they enter in, and d there .... Lk 11:26
d on the face of the whole earth.......... Lk 21:35
desolate, and let no man d therein ...... Acts 1:20
all ye that d at Jerusalem, be.............. Acts 2:14
to all them that d in Jerusalem .... Acts 4:16
into this land, wherein ye now d .... Acts 7:4
For they that d at Jerusalem .... Acts 13:27
to d on all the face of the earth........... Acts 17:26
but Paul was suffered to d by............. Acts 28:16
that the Spirit of God d in you .... Rom 8:9
up Jesus from the dead d in you .... Rom 8:11
and she be pleased to d with him.......... 1Cor 7:12
and if he be pleased to d with her......... 1Cor 7:13
I will d in them, and walk in them 2Cor 6:16
That Christ may d in your hearts .... Eph 3:17
that in him should all fulness d .... Col 1:19
Let the word of Christ d in you .... Col 3:16
d with them according to.................... 1Pet 3:7
Hereby know we that we d in him........ 1Jn 4:13
to try them that d upon the earth......... Rev 3:10
blood on them that d on the earth......... Rev 6:10
on the throne shall among them .... Rev 7:15
they that d upon the earth shall .... Rev 11:10
ye heavens, and ye that d in them .... Rev 12:12
and them that d in heaven................... Rev 13:6
all that d upon the earth shall .... Rev 13:8
them which d therein to worship.......... Rev 13:12
deceiveth them that d on the................ Rev 13:14
to them that d on the earth .... Rev 13:14
unto them that d on the earth.............. Rev 14:6
they that d on the earth shall .... Rev 17:8
he will d with them, and they.............. Rev 21:3

DWELLED

the Perizzite d then in the land .... Gen 13:7
Abram d in the land of Canaan, and..... Gen 13:12
Lot d in the cities of the plain,............ Gen 13:12
d between Kadesh and Shur, and.......... Gen 20:1
they d there about ten years................ Ruth 1:4
on every side, and ye d safe................. 1Sa 12:11

DWELLERS

d on the earth, see ye, when he........... Is 18:3
known unto all the d at Jerusalem....... Acts 1:19
the d in Mesopotamia, and in.............. Acts 2:9

DWELLEST

them, and d in their land .... Deut 12:29
in their cities, and in their .... Deut 19:1
and possessest it, and d therein........... Deut 26:1
which d between the cherubims, ... 2Kin 19:15
thou that d between the cherubims ...... Ps 80:1
O thou that d in the heavens............... Ps 123:1
Thou that d in the gardens, the .... Song 8:13
hosts, O my people that d in Zion .... Is 10:24
that d between the cherubims,............. Is 37:16
that carelessly, that sayest in .... Is 47:8
O thou that d in the clefts of .... Jer 49:16
O thou that d upon many waters, ... Jer 51:13
of Edom, that d in the land of Uz .... Lam 4:21
thee, O thou that d in the land............. Eze 7:7
of man, thou d in the midst of a.......... Eze 12:2
thou that d in the clefts of the .... Obad 3
that d with the daughter of................. Zec 2:7
Master,) where d thou........................ Jn 1:38
I know thy works, and where thou d.... Rev 2:13

DWELLETH

But the stranger that d with you.......... Lev 19:34
if thy brother that d by thee be............ Lev 25:39
brother that d by him wax poor .... Lev 25:47
and the people that d therein.............. Num 13:18
he d as a lion, and teareth the............. Deut 33:20
she d in Israel even unto this.............. Josh 6:25
wherein the LORD's tabernacle d......... Josh 22:19
which d between the cherubims 1Sa 4:4
while he d in the country of the 1Sa 27:11
that d between the cherubims.............. 2Sa 6:2
the ark of God d within curtains 2Sa 7:2
that d between the cherubims,............. 1Chr 13:6
he d in desolate cities, and in .... Job 15:28
Where is the way where light d .... Job 38:19
She d and abideth on the rock,............ Job 39:28
to the LORD, which d in Zion.............. Ps 9:11
and the place where thine honour d..... Ps 26:8
He that d in the secret place of .... Ps 91:1
the LORD our God, who d on high,....... Ps 113:5
out of Zion, which d at Jerusalem...... Ps 135:21
seeing he d securely for him............... Prov 3:29

of hosts, which d in mount Zion......... Is 8:18
for he d on high................................ Is 33:16
the people that d in this city .... Jer 29:16
desolation, and no man d therein,........ Jer 44:2
that d without care, saith the.............. Jer 49:31
a land wherein no man d, neither .... Jer 51:43
she d among the heathen, she............. Lam 1:3
that d at thy right hand, is.................. Eze 16:46
the king d that made him king........... Eze 17:16
when my people of Israel d safely....... Eze 38:14
darkness, and the light d with him ..... Dan 2:22
every one that d therein shall............. Hos 4:3
for the LORD is in Zion....................... Joel 3:21
and every one mourn that d therein..... Amos 8:8
by it, and by him that d therein .... Mt 23:21
my blood, d in me, and I in him.......... Jn 6:56
but the Father that d in me .... Jn 14:10
for he d with you, and shall be in .... Jn 14:17
Howbeit the most High d not in .... Acts 7:48
d not in temples made with hands....... Acts 17:24
that do it, but sin that d in me............ Rom 7:17
is, in my flesh,) d no good thing .... Rom 7:18
that do it, but sin that d in me .... Rom 7:20
by his Spirit that d in you.................. Rom 8:11
that the Spirit of God d in you 1Cor 3:16
For in him d all the fulness of............ Col 2:9
by the Holy Ghost which d in us 2Ti 1:14
The spirit that d in us lusteth .... Jas 4:5
earth, wherein d righteousness........... 2Pet 3:13
how d the love of God in him............. 1Jn 3:17
keepeth his commandments d in him... 1Jn 3:24
God d in us, and his love is 1Jn 4:12
God d in him, and he in God.............. 1Jn 4:15
he that d in love d in God.................. 1Jn 4:16
the truth's sake, which d in us............ 2Jn 2
slain among you, where Satan d......... Rev 2:13

DWELLING

their d was from Mesha, as thou......... Gen 10:30
Jacob was a plain man, d in tents .... Gen 25:27
thy d shall be the fatness of the.......... Gen 27:39
if a man sell a d house in a .... Lev 25:29
that goeth down to the d of Ar............ Num 21:15
dukes of Sihon, d in the country .... Num 13:21
hear thou in heaven thy d place 1Kin 8:30
hear thou in heaven thy d place 1Kin 8:39
Hear thou in heaven thy d place 1Kin 8:43
in heaven thy d place, and 1Kin 8:49
were in his city, of whom Naboth 1Kin 21:8
at the beginning of their d there 2Kin 17:25
they ministered before the d 1Chr 6:32
Now these are their d places............. 1Chr 6:54
and a place for thy d for ever 2Chr 6:2
hear thou from thy d place 2Chr 6:21
hear thou from heaven thy d place 2Chr 6:30
heavens, even from thy d place.......... 2Chr 6:33
heavens, even from thy d place.......... 2Chr 6:39
came up to his holy d place 2Chr 30:27
on his people, and on his d place 2Chr 36:15
the d place of the wicked shall........... Job 8:22
where are the d places of the .... Job 21:28
their d places to all generations......... Ps 49:11
consume in the grave from their d ..... Ps 49:14
and pluck thee out of thy d place,....... Ps 52:5
defiled by casting down the d .... Ps 74:7
and his d place in Zion...................... Ps 76:2
Jacob, and laid waste his d place in .... Ps 79:7
thou hast been our d place in all .... Ps 90:1
shall any plague come nigh thy d .... Ps 91:10
and oil in the d of the wise .... Prov 21:20
against the d of the righteous .... Prov 24:15
upon every d place of mount Zion ..... Is 4:5
I will consider in my d place.............. Is 18:4
O thou daughter d in Egypt,............... Jer 46:19
And Hazor shall be a d for dragons .... Jer 49:33
a d place for dragons, an................... Jer 51:37
all of them d without walls, and......... Eze 38:11
profane place for the city, for d.......... Eze 48:15
whose d is not with flesh,.................. Dan 2:11
thy d shall be with the beasts of .... Dan 4:25
thy d shall be with the beasts of .... Dan 4:32
his d was with the wild asses............ Dan 5:21
I am the LORD your God d in Zion...... Joel 3:17
Where is the d of the lions................. Nah 2:11
so their d should not be cut off,.......... Zeph 3:7
Who had his d among the tombs .... Mk 5:3
there were d at Jerusalem Jews,......... Acts 2:5
Jews and Greeks also d at Ephesus..... Acts 19:17
d in the light which no man can 1Ti 6:16
d in tabernacles with Isaac and.......... Heb 11:9
that righteous man d among them 2Pet 2:8

DWELLINGPLACE

parable, and said, Strong is thy d....... Num 24:21
and have no certain d place................ 1Cor 4:11

DWELLINGPLACES

tents, and have mercy on his d........... Jer 30:18
they have burned her d...................... Jer 51:30
In all your d the cities shall be .... Eze 6:6
will save them out of all their d .... Eze 37:23
to possess the d that are not.............. Hab 1:6

DWELLINGS

of Israel had light in their d .... Ex 10:23
generations throughout all your d....... Lev 3:17
or of beast, in any of your d............... Lev 7:26
sabbath of the LORD in all your d .... Lev 23:3
your generations in all your d............ Lev 23:14
d throughout your generations............ Lev 23:21
your generations in all your d............ Lev 23:31
your generations in all your d .... Num 35:29

nor any remaining in his d................. Job 18:19
such are the d of the wicked .... Job 18:21
and the barren land his d .... Job 39:6
for wickedness is in their d .... Ps 55:15
Zion more than all the d of Jacob....... Ps 87:2
habitation, and in sure d, and in .... Is 32:18
because our d have cast us out............ Jer 9:19
in thee, and make their d in thee .... Eze 25:4
And the sea coast shall be d .... Zeph 2:6

DWELT

d in the land of Nod, on the east......... Gen 4:16
and they d there .... Gen 11:2
they came unto Haran, and d there...... Gen 11:31
d in the plain of Mamre, which is....... Gen 13:18
Amorites, that d in Hazezon-tamar..... Gen 14:7
who d in Sodom, and his goods, and... Gen 14:12
for he d in the plain of Mamre .... Gen 14:13
after Abram had d ten years in........... Gen 16:3
the cities in the which Lot d.............. Gen 19:29
d in the mountain, and his two .... Gen 19:30
he d in a cave, he and his two .... Gen 19:30
d in the wilderness, and became an.... Gen 21:20
he d in the wilderness of Paran .... Gen 21:21
and Abraham d at Beer-sheba............ Gen 22:19
Ephron among the children of............ Gen 23:10
for he d in the south country .... Gen 24:62
Isaac d by the well Lahai-roi............. Gen 25:11
they d from Havilah unto Shur.......... Gen 25:18
And Isaac d in Gerar........................ Gen 26:6
the valley of Gerar, and d there.......... Gen 26:17
when Israel d in that land, that .... Gen 35:22
Thus d Esau in mount Seir .... Gen 36:8
Jacob d in the land wherein his......... Gen 37:1
went and d in her father's house........ Gen 38:11
Israel d in the land of Egypt, in......... Gen 47:27
Joseph d in Egypt, he, and his.......... Gen 50:22
and d in the land of Midian .... Ex 2:15
who d in Egypt, was four hundred .... Ex 12:40
the land of Egypt, wherein ye d .... Lev 18:3
your sabbaths, when ye d upon it ...... Lev 26:35
and the Canaanites in the valley ...... Num 14:25
Canaanites which d in that hill .... Num 14:45
we have d in Egypt a long time .... Num 20:15
which d in the south, heard tell .... Num 21:1
Israel d in all the cities of the.......... Num 21:25
Thus Israel d in the land of the........ Num 21:31
the Amorites, which d at Heshbon ... Num 21:34
all their cities wherein they d .... Num 31:10
and he d therein .... Num 32:40
which d in the south in the land ...... Num 33:40
which d in Heshbon, and Og the....... Deut 1:4
which d at Astaroth in Edrei............ Deut 1:4
Ye have d long enough in this.......... Deut 1:6
which d in that mountain, came .... Deut 1:44
which d in Seir, through the way ...... Deut 2:8
The Emims d there in times past ..... Deut 2:10
The Horims also d in Seir .... Deut 2:12
before them, and d in their stead....... Deut 2:12
giants d therein in old time.............. Deut 2:20
them, and d in their stead................ Deut 2:21
of Esau, which d in Seir, when he ..... Deut 2:22
d in their stead even unto this.......... Deut 2:22
And the Avims which d in Hazerim ... Deut 2:23
them, and d in their stead................ Deut 2:23
the Amorites, which d at Heshbon ..... Deut 3:2
who d at Heshbon, whom Moses and ... Deut 4:46
built goodly houses, and d therein...... Deut 8:12
we have d in the land of Egypt .... Deut 29:16
will of him that d in the bush............ Deut 33:16
town wall, and she d upon the wall .... Josh 2:15
d on the other side Jordan .... Josh 7:7
and that they d among them .... Josh 9:16
who d in Heshbon, and ruled from ..... Josh 12:2
that d at Ashtaroth and at Edrei,........ Josh 12:4
the Canaanites that d in Gezer .... Josh 16:10
d therein, and called Leshem, Dan,.... Josh 19:47
he built the city, and d therein .... Josh 19:50
they possessed it, and d therein......... Josh 21:43
the children of Reuben and Gad,........ Josh 22:33
Your fathers d on the other side......... Josh 24:2
ye d in the wilderness a long .... Josh 24:7
which d on the other side Jordan....... Josh 24:8
the Amorites which d in the land ...... Josh 24:18
that d in the mountain, and in the ..... Judg 1:9
the Canaanites that d in Hebron......... Judg 1:10
the Canaanites that d among the people ... Judg 1:16
the Canaanites that d in Gezer .... Judg 1:29
but the Canaanites d in Gezer .... Judg 1:29
the Canaanites d among them............ Judg 1:30
but d among the Canaanites,.............. Judg 1:33
Hivites that d in mount Lebanon .... Judg 3:3
of Israel d among the Canaanites....... Judg 3:5
which d in Harosheth of the.............. Judg 4:2
she d under the palm tree of .... Judg 4:5
d in tents on the east of Nobah .... Judg 8:11
Joash went and d in his own house .... Judg 8:29
d there, for fear of Abimelech........... Judg 9:21
And Abimelech d at Arumah .... Judg 9:41
and Jephthah d in mount Ephraim ..... Judg 10:1
brethren, and d in the land of Tob...... Judg 11:3
While Israel d in Heshbon................ Judg 11:26
d in the top of the rock Etam .... Judg 15:8
were therein, how they d careless...... Judg 18:7
they built a city, and d therein .... Judg 18:28
repaired the cities, and d in them ...... Judg 21:23
and d with her mother in law .... Ruth 2:23
he and Samuel went and d in Naioth .. 1Sa 19:18
they d with him all the while 1Sa 22:4
d in strong holds in En-gedi............. 1Sa 23:29

David *d* with Achish at Gath, he...... 1Sa 27:3
the time that David *d* in the............... 1Sa 27:7
the Philistines came and *d* in them.... 1Sa 31:7
they *d* in the cities of Hebron............ 2Sa 2:3
So David *d* in the fort, and called...... 2Sa 5:9
Whereas I have not *d* in any house.... 2Sa 7:6
all that *d* in the house of Ziba.......... 2Sa 9:12
So Mephibosheth *d* in Jerusalem....... 2Sa 9:13
So Absalom *d* two full years in......... 2Sa 14:28
Shimei in Jerusalem many days......... 1Kin 2:38
And Judah and Israel *d* safely.......... 1Kin 4:25
his house where he *d* had another...... 1Kin 7:8
the Cananaites that *d* in the city........ 1Kin 9:16
d therein, and reigned in Damascus .. 1Kin 11:24
Solomon, and Jeroboam *d* in Egypt.... 1Kin 12:2
which *d* in the cities of Judah............ 1Kin 12:17
in mount Ephraim, and therein............ 1Kin 12:25
Now there *d* an old prophet in.......... 1Kin 13:11
the city where the old prophet *d*........ 1Kin 13:25
that *d* at Damascus, saying.............. 1Kin 15:18
building of Ramah, and *d* in Tirzah.... 1Kin 15:21
d by the brook Cherith, that is.......... 1Kin 17:5
of Israel *d* in their tents.................. 2Kin 13:5
death, and *d* in a several house......... 2Kin 15:5
Elath, and *d* there unto this day........ 2Kin 16:6
and *d* in the cities thereof................ 1Chr 17:24
d in Beth-el, and taught them how..... 1Chr 17:28
in their cities wherein they *d*............. 2Kin 17:29
returned, and *d* at Nineveh.............. 2Kin 19:36
(now she *d* in Jerusalem in the.......... 2Kin 22:14
of the scribes which *d* at Jabez.......... 1Chr 2:55
those that *d* among plants and.......... 1Chr 4:23
there they *d* with the king for........... 1Chr 4:23
they *d* at Beer-sheba, and Moladah,... 1Chr 4:28
they of Ham had *d* there of old.......... 1Chr 4:40
this day, and *d* in their rooms........... 1Chr 4:41
escaped, and *d* there unto this day..... 1Chr 4:43
who *d* in Aroer, even unto Nebo and... 1Chr 5:8
they *d* in their tents throughout......... 1Chr 5:10
of Gad *d* over against them.............. 1Chr 5:11
they *d* in Gilead in Bashan, and in..... 1Chr 5:16
they *d* in their steads until the.......... 1Chr 5:22
tribe of Manasseh *d* in the land......... 1Chr 5:23
In these *d* the children of Joseph....... 1Chr 7:29
These *d* in Jerusalem...................... 1Chr 8:28
at Gibeon *d* the father of Gibeon....... 1Chr 8:29
these also *d* with their brethren......... 1Chr 8:32
d in their possessions in their........... 1Chr 9:2
in Jerusalem *d* of the children of....... 1Chr 9:3
that *d* in the villages of the.............. 1Chr 9:16
these *d* at Jerusalem...................... 1Chr 9:34
in Gibeon *d* the father of Gibeon,...... 1Chr 9:35
they also *d* with their brethren........... 1Chr 9:38
the Philistines came and *d* in them.... 1Chr 10:7
And David *d* in the castle................. 1Chr 11:7
For I have not *d* in an house............ 1Chr 17:5
that *d* in the cities of Judah.............. 2Chr 11:5
Rehoboam *d* in Jerusalem, and built.. 2Chr 11:5
that *d* at Damascus, saying.............. 2Chr 16:2
Jehoshaphat *d* at Jerusalem............. 2Chr 19:4
they *d* therein, and have built........... 2Chr 20:8
the Arabians that *d* in Gur-baal........ 2Chr 26:7
d in a several house, being a............ 2Chr 26:21
and they *d* there.......................... 2Chr 28:18
that *d* in Judah, rejoiced................. 2Chr 30:25
that *d* in Jerusalem to give the.......... 2Chr 31:4
that *d* in the cities of Judah.............. 2Chr 31:6
(now she *d* in Jerusalem in the.......... 2Chr 34:22
d in their cities, and all Israel........... Ezr 2:70
Moreover the Nethinims *d* in Ophel.... Neh 3:26
the Jews which *d* by them came........ Neh 4:12
and all Israel, *d* in their cities........... Neh 7:73
of the people *d* at Jerusalem............ Neh 11:1
the province that *d* in Jerusalem....... Neh 11:3
but in the cities of Judah *d*.............. Neh 11:3
at Jerusalem *d* certain of the............ Neh 11:4
All the sons of Perez that *d* at.......... Neh 11:6
But the Nethinims *d* in Ophel........... Neh 11:21
of Judah *d* at Kirjath-arba............... Neh 11:25
they *d* from Beer-sheba unto the....... Neh 11:30
Benjamin from Geba *d* at Michmash.. Neh 11:31
There *d* men of Tyre also therein....... Neh 13:16
that *d* in the unwalled towns,........... Est 9:19
and the honourable man *d* in it......... Job 22:8
d as a king in the army, as one......... Job 29:25
Thy congregation hath *d* therein....... Ps 68:10
mount Zion, wherein thou hast *d*....... Ps 74:2
my soul had almost *d* in silence........ Ps 94:17
My soul hath long *d* with him that..... Ps 120:6
neither shall it be *d* in from.............. Is 13:20
to Ariel, the city where David *d*......... Is 29:1
went and returned, and *d* at Nineveh. Is 37:37
passed through, and where no man *d*.. Jer 2:6
But we have *d* in tents, and have...... Jer 35:10
so he *d* among the people................ Jer 39:14
d with him among the people that...... Jer 40:6
d in the habitation of Chimham,........ Jer 41:17
that *d* in the land of Egypt............... Jer 44:15
neither shall it be *d* in from.............. Jer 50:39
that *d* by the river of Chebar, and..... Eze 3:15
under his shadow *d* all great............ Eze 31:6
that *d* under his shadow in the.......... Eze 31:17
of Israel *d* in their own land............. Eze 36:17
wherein your fathers have *d*............. Eze 37:25
when they *d* safely in their land,....... Eze 39:26
heaven *d* in the boughs thereof......... Dan 4:12
which the beasts of the field *d*........... Dan 4:21
rejoicing city that *d* carelessly.......... Zeph 2:15
d in a city called Nazareth............... Mt 2:23
d in Capernaum, which is upon the.... Mt 4:13

on all that *d* round about them.......... Lk 1:65
above all men that *d* in Jerusalem..... Lk 13:4
of among us, (and we beheld his........ Jn 1:14
They came and saw where he *d*......... Jn 1:39
before he *d* in Charran.................... Acts 7:2
the Chaldaeans, and *d* in Charran..... Acts 7:4
the Jews which *d* at Damascus......... Acts 9:22
to the saints which *d* at Lydda.......... Acts 9:32
And all that *d* at Lydda and Saron..... Acts 9:35
the brethren which *d* in Judaea......... Acts 11:29
d as strangers in the land of............. Acts 13:17
so that all they which *d* in Asia......... Acts 19:10
of all the Jews which *d* there............ Acts 22:12
Paul *d* two whole years in his own..... Acts 28:30
which *d* first in thy grandmother....... 2Ti 1:5
them that *d* on the earth.................. Rev 11:10

DYED

And rams' skins *d* red, and badgers'... Ex 25:5
for the tent of rams' skins *d* red........ Ex 26:14
And rams' skins *d* red, and badgers'... Ex 35:7
for the tent of rams' skins *d* red........ Ex 36:19
the covering of rams' skins *d* red....... Ex 39:34
with *d* garments from Bozrah............ Is 63:1
exceeding in *d* attire upon their......... Eze 23:15

DYING

shall we be consumed with *d*............ Num 17:13
took a wife, and *d* left no seed.......... Mk 12:20
years of age, and she lay a *d*............. Lk 8:42
the body the *d* of the Lord Jesus....... 2Cor 4:10
as *d*, and, behold, we live................ 2Cor 6:9
By faith Jacob, when he was a *d*....... Heb 11:21

E

EACH

laid *e* piece one against another........ Gen 15:10
took *e* man his sword, and came....... Gen 34:25
e man his dream in one night........... Gen 40:5
e man according to the interpretation. Gen 40:5
we dreamed *e* man according to the .. Gen 41:11
to *e* man according to his dream....... Gen 41:12
he gave *e* man changes of raiment.... Gen 45:22
they asked *e* other of their............... Ex 18:7
of *e* shall there be a like weight......... Ex 30:34
put pure frankincense upon *e* row..... Lev 24:7
e one was for the house of his.......... Num 1:44
the princes, and for *e* one an ox....... Num 7:3
e prince on his day, for the.............. Num 7:11
E charger of silver weighing an........ Num 7:85
and thirty shekels, *e* bowl seventy..... Num 7:85
e day for a year, shall ye bear.......... Num 14:34
and Aaron, *e* of you his censer......... Num 16:17
for *e* prince one, according to........... Num 17:6
two tenth deals to *e* ram of the........ Num 29:14
a several tenth deal to *e* lamb of....... Num 29:15
among you three men for *e* tribe....... Josh 18:4
of *e* chief house a prince................. Josh 22:14
e one was an head of the house of.... Josh 22:14
e one resembled the children of a..... Judg 8:18
not to *e* man his wife in the war........ Judg 21:22
return *e* to her mother's house......... Ruth 1:8
e of you in the house of her............. Ruth 1:9
e man his month in a year made....... 1Kin 4:7
of olive tree, *e* ten cubits high.......... 1Kin 6:23
king of Judah sat *e* on his throne...... 2Chr 18:9
e in his chariot, and they went......... 2Kin 9:21
of *e* man fifty shekels of silver,......... 2Kin 15:20
on *e* hand, and six on *e* foot.......... 1Chr 20:6
top of *e* of them was five cubits........ 2Chr 3:15
rows of pomegranates on *e* wreath.... 2Chr 4:13
stays on *e* side of the sitting............. 2Chr 9:18
to the language of *e* people.............. Neh 13:24
and peace have kissed *e* other......... Ps 85:10
which they made *e* one for himself.... Is 2:20
e one had six wings....................... Is 6:2
of dragons, where *e* lay, shall be...... Is 35:7
e one walking in his uprightness....... Is 57:2
appointed thee *e* day for a year........ Eze 4:6
upon *e* post were palm trees............ Eze 40:16
measured *e* post of the porch........... Eze 40:48
doth not *e* one of you on the............. Lk 13:15
of fire, and it sat upon *e* of them...... Acts 2:3
let *e* esteem other better than........... Phil 2:3
you all toward *e* other aboundeth...... 2Th 1:3
the four beasts had *e* of them six...... Rev 4:8

EAGLE

the *e*, and the ossifrage, and the....... Lev 11:13
and the pelican, and the gier *e*......... Lev 11:18
the *e*, and the ossifrage, and the....... Deut 14:12
And the pelican, and the gier *e*......... Deut 14:17
earth, as swift as the *e* flieth............ Deut 28:49
As an *e* stirreth up her nest,............. Deut 32:11
as the *e* that hasteth to the prey....... Job 9:26
Doth the *e* mount up at thy.............. Job 39:27
fly away as an *e* toward heaven........ Prov 23:5
The way of an *e* in the air................ Prov 30:19
Behold, he shall fly as an *e*.............. Jer 48:40
make thy nest as high as the *e*......... Jer 49:16
he shall come up and fly as the *e*...... Jer 49:22
four also had the face of an *e*........... Eze 1:10
and the fourth the face of an *e*......... Eze 10:14
A great *e* with great wings............... Eze 17:3
another great *e* with great wings....... Eze 17:7
He shall come as an *e* against the..... Hos 8:1

thou exalt thyself as the *e*............... Obad 4
enlarge thy baldness as the *e*.......... Mic 1:16
fly as the *e* that hasteth to eat.......... Hab 1:8
fourth beast was like a flying *e*......... Rev 4:7
were given two wings of a great *e* ..... Rev 12:14

EAGLE'S

thy youth is renewed like the *e*......... Ps 103:5
was like a lion, and had *e* wings....... Dan 7:4

EAGLES

they were swifter than *e*, they.......... 2Sa 1:23
out, and the young *e* shall eat it....... Prov 30:17
shall mount up with wings as *e*......... Is 40:31
his horses are swifter than *e*............ Jer 4:13
swifter than the *e* of the heaven....... Lam 4:19
there will the *e* be gathered............. Mt 24:28
thither will the *e* be gathered........... Lk 17:37

EAGLES'

and how I bare you on *e* wings......... Ex 19:4
hairs were grown like *e* feathers....... Dan 4:33

EAR

for the barley was in the *e*............... Ex 9:31
wilt give *e* to his commandments,..... Ex 15:26
bore his *e* through with an aul.......... Ex 21:6
the tip of the right *e* of Aaron.......... Ex 29:20
tip of the right *e* of his son............. Ex 29:20
upon the tip of Aaron's right *e*......... Lev 8:23
upon the tip of their right *e*............. Lev 8:24
it upon the tip of the right *e* of........ Lev 14:14
e of him that is to be cleansed......... Lev 14:17
it upon the tip of the right *e* of........ Lev 14:25
e of him that is to be cleansed......... Lev 14:28
your voice, nor give *e* unto you........ Deut 1:45
it through his *e* unto the door.......... Deut 15:17
Give *e*, O ye heavens, and I will....... Deut 32:1
give *e*, O ye princes....................... Judg 5:3
and will set them to *e* his ground...... 1Sa 8:12
in his *e* a day before Saul came....... 1Sa 9:15
LORD, bow down thine *e*, and hear ... 2Kin 19:16
but they would not give *e*................ 2Chr 24:19
Let mine *e* now be attentive, and..... Neh 1:6
let now thine *e* be attentive to......... Neh 1:11
yet would they not give *e*................. Neh 9:30
mine *e* received a little thereof......... Job 4:12
Doth not the *e* try words................. Job 12:11
mine *e* hath heard and understood.... Job 13:1
When the *e* heard me, then it........... Job 29:11
Unto me men gave *e*, and waited, and Job 29:21
I gave *e* to your reasons, whilst........ Job 32:11
give *e* unto me, ye that have........... Job 34:2
For the *e* trieth words, as the.......... Job 34:3
also their *e* to discipline.................. Job 36:10
of thee by the hearing of the *e*........ Job 42:5
Give *e* to my words, O LORD............ Ps 5:1
thou wilt cause thine *e* to hear......... Ps 10:17
give *e* unto my prayer, that goeth..... Ps 17:1
incline thine *e* unto me, and hear..... Ps 17:6
Bow down thine *e* to me................. Ps 31:2
O LORD, and give *e* unto my cry....... Ps 39:12
and consider, and incline thine *e*...... Ps 45:10
give *e*, all ye inhabitants of the........ Ps 49:1
will incline mine *e* to a parable........ Ps 49:4
give *e* to the words of my mouth...... Ps 54:2
Give *e* to my prayer, O God............ Ps 55:1
deaf adder that stoppeth her *e*........ Ps 58:4
incline thine *e* unto me, and save..... Ps 71:2
and he gave *e* unto me.................. Ps 77:1
Give *e*, O my people, to my law....... Ps 78:1
Give *e*, O Shepherd of Israel,.......... Ps 80:1
give *e*, O God of Jacob................... Ps 84:8
Bow down thine *e*, O LORD, hear me. Ps 86:1
Give *e*, O LORD, unto my prayer...... Ps 86:6
incline thine *e* unto my cry.............. Ps 88:2
He that planted the *e*, shall he......... Ps 94:9
incline thine *e* unto the.................. Ps 102:2
he hath inclined his *e* unto me........ Ps 116:2
give *e* unto my voice, when I cry...... Ps 141:1
give *e* to my supplications.............. Ps 143:1
thou incline thine *e* unto wisdom..... Prov 2:2
incline thine *e* unto my sayings....... Prov 4:20
bow thine *e* to my understanding..... Prov 5:1
nor inclined mine *e* to them that...... Prov 5:13
The *e* that heareth the reproof of..... Prov 15:31
a liar giveth *e* to a naughty............. Prov 17:4
the *e* of the wise seeketh............... Prov 18:15
The hearing *e*, and the seeing *e*.... Prov 20:12
Bow down thine *e*, and hear the...... Prov 22:17
wise reprover upon an obedient *e*.... Prov 25:12
away his *e* from hearing the law...... Prov 28:9
nor the *e* filled with hearing........... Eccl 1:8
Hear, O heavens, and give *e*.......... Is 1:2
give *e* unto the law of our God,....... Is 1:10
and give *e*, all ye of far.................. Is 8:9
Give ye *e*, and hear my voice......... Is 28:23
the young asses that *e* the ground... Is 30:24
give *e* unto my speech................... Is 32:9
Incline thine *e*, O LORD, and hear... Is 37:17
Who among you will give *e* to this.... Is 42:23
time that thine *e* was not opened..... Is 48:8
he waketh mine *e* to hear as the..... Is 50:4
The Lord GOD hath opened mine *e*.. Is 50:5
give *e* unto me, O my nation.......... Is 51:4
Incline your *e*, and come unto me.... Is 55:3
neither his *e* heavy, that it.............. Is 59:1
not heard, nor perceived by the *e*.... Is 64:4
their *e* is uncircumcised, and they.... Jer 6:10
not, nor inclined their *e*................. Jer 7:24
not unto me, nor inclined their *e*..... Jer 7:26
let your *e* receive the word of.......... Jer 9:20

obeyed not, nor inclined their *e* .... Jer 11:8
Hear ye, and give *e* .... Jer 13:15
not, neither inclined their *e* .... Jer 17:23
nor inclined your *e* to hear .... Jer 25:4
unto me, neither inclined their *e* .... Jer 34:14
but ye have not inclined your *e* .... Jer 35:15
nor inclined their *e* to turn from .... Jer 44:5
hide not thine *e* at my breathing, ... Lam 3:56
O my God, incline thine *e* .... Dan 9:18
and give ye *e*, O house of the king .... Hos 5:1
Hear this, ye old men, and give *e* .... Joel 1:2
lion two legs, or a piece of an *e* .... Amos 3:12
and what ye hear in the *e*, that .... Mt 10:27
high priest's, and smote off his *e* .... Mt 26:51
first the blade, then the *e*, ... Mk 4:28
after that the full corn in the *e* .... Mk 4:28
the high priest, and cut off his *e* .... Mk 14:47
which ye have spoken in the *e* in .... Lk 12:3
priest, and cut off his right *e* .... Lk 22:50
And he touched his *e*, and healed .... Lk 22:51
servant, and cut off his right *e* .... Jn 18:10
his kinsman whose *e* Peter cut off .... Jn 18:26
nor *e* heard, neither have entered 1Cor 2:9
if the *e* shall say, Because I am 1Cor 12:16
He that hath an *e*, let him hear .... Rev 2:7
He that hath an *e*, let him hear .... Rev 2:11
He that hath an *e*, let him hear .... Rev 2:17
He that hath an *e*, let him hear .... Rev 2:29
He that hath an *e*, let him hear .... Rev 3:6
He that hath an *e*, let him hear .... Rev 3:13
He that hath an *e*, let him hear .... Rev 3:22
If any man have an *e*, let him hear .... Rev 13:9

EARED
which is neither *e* nor sown .... Deut 21:4

EARING
shall neither be *e* nor harvest .... Gen 45:6
in *e* time and in harvest thou .... Ex 34:21

EARLY
your feet, and ye shall rise up *e* .... Gen 19:2
Abraham gat up *e* in the morning, ... Gen 19:27
Abimelech rose *e* in the morning .... Gen 20:8
Abraham rose up *e* in the morning, ... Gen 21:14
Abraham rose up *e* in the morning, ... Gen 22:3
Jacob rose up *e* in the morning, ... Gen 28:18
e in the morning Laban rose up, ... Gen 31:55
Rise up *e* in the morning, and, ... Ex 8:20
Rise up *e* in the morning, and .... Ex 9:13
rose up *e* in the morning, and .... Ex 24:4
they rose up *e* on the morrow, and .... Ex 32:6
Moses rose up *e* in the morning, ... Ex 34:4
they rose up *e* in the morning, and .... Num 14:40
Joshua rose *e* in the morning .... Josh 3:1
Joshua rose *e* in the morning, and .... Josh 6:12
that they rose *e* about the .... Josh 6:15
Joshua rose up *e* in the morning .... Josh 7:16
Joshua rose up *e* in the morning .... Josh 8:10
it, that they hasted and rose up *e* .... Josh 8:14
the city arose *e* in the morning .... Judg 6:28
for he rose up *e* on the morrow .... Judg 6:38
that were with him, rose up *e* .... Judg 7:1
depart *e* from mount Gilead .... Judg 7:3
the sun is up, thou shalt rise *e* .... Judg 9:33
when they arose *e* in the morning .... Judg 19:5
he arose *e* in the morning on the .... Judg 19:8
to morrow get you *e* on your way .... Judg 19:9
morrow, that the people rose *e* .... Judg 21:4
And they rose up in the morning *e* 1Sa 1:19
of Ashdod arose *e* on the morrow 1Sa 5:3
when they arose *e* on the morrow 1Sa 5:4
And they arose *e* 1Sa 9:26
when Samuel rose *e* to meet Saul 1Sa 15:12
David rose up *e* in the morning, ... 1Sa 17:20
Wherefore now rise up *e* in the 1Sa 29:10
soon as ye be up *e* in the morning, ... 1Sa 29:10
his men rose up *e* to depart in 1Sa 29:11
And Absalom rose up *e*, and stood 2Sa 15:2
they rose up *e* in the morning, and 2Kin 3:22
of the man of God was risen *e* 2Kin 6:15
when they arose *e* in the morning 2Kin 19:35
they rose *e* in the morning, and 2Chr 20:20
Then Hezekiah the king rose *e* 2Chr 29:20
rose up *e* in the morning, and .... Job 1:5
shall help her, and that right *e* .... Ps 46:5
I myself will awake *e* .... Ps 57:8
e will I seek thee. .... Ps 63:1
returned and enquired *e* after God. .... Ps 78:34
O satisfy us *e* with thy mercy; .... Ps 90:14
I will *e* destroy all the wicked .... Ps 101:8
I myself will awake *e* .... Ps 108:2
It is vain for you to rise up *e* .... Ps 127:2
they shall seek me *e*, but they .... Prov 1:28
that seek me *e* shall find me. .... Prov 8:17
rising *e* in the morning, it shall .... Prov 27:14
Let us get up *e* to the vineyards .... Song 7:12
that rise up *e* in the morning .... Is 5:11
within me will I seek thee *e* .... Is 26:9
when they arose *e* in the morning .... Is 37:36
and I spake unto you, rising up *e* .... Jer 7:13
the prophets, daily rising up *e* .... Jer 7:25
even unto this day, rising *e* .... Jer 11:7
I have spoken unto you, rising *e* .... Jer 25:3
servants the prophets, rising *e* .... Jer 25:4
I sent unto you, both rising up *e* .... Jer 26:5
the prophets, rising up *e* .... Jer 29:19
though I taught them, rising up *e* .... Jer 32:33
I have spoken unto you, rising *e* .... Jer 35:14
the prophets, rising up *e* .... Jer 35:15
servants the prophets, rising *e* .... Jer 44:4
king arose very *e* in the morning .... Dan 6:19

affliction they will seek me *e* .... Hos 5:15
as the *e* dew it goeth away, ... Hos 6:4
as the *e* dew that passeth away, ... Hos 13:3
but they rose *e*, and corrupted all .... Zeph 3:7
which went out *e* in the morning .... Mt 20:1
very *e* in the morning the first .... Mk 16:2
Now when Jesus was risen *e* the .... Mk 16:9
all the people came *e* in the .... Lk 21:38
very *e* in the morning, they came .... Lk 24:1
which were *e* at the sepulchre. .... Lk 24:22
And And *e* in the morning he came .... Jn 8:1
e in the morning he came again .... Jn 8:2
of judgment: and it was *e* .... Jn 18:28
the week cometh Mary Magdalene .... Jn 20:1
into the temple *e* in the morning .... Acts 5:21
for it, until he receive the *e* .... Jas 5:7

EARNEST
For the *e* expectation of the .... Rom 8:19
given the *e* of the Spirit in our 2Cor 1:22
given unto us the *e* of the Spirit 2Cor 5:5
when he told us your *e* desire 2Cor 7:7
which put the same *e* care into 2Cor 8:16
Which is the *e* of our inheritance .... Eph 1:14
According to my *e* expectation .... Phil 1:20
we ought to give the more *e* heed........... Heb 2:1

EARNESTLY
Did I not *e* send unto thee to .... Num 22:37
David *e* asked leave of me that he.......... 1Sa 20:6
David *e* asked leave of me to go............. 1Sa 20:28
Zabbai *e* repaired the other piece .... Neh 3:20
As a servant *e* desireth the .... Job 7:2
For I *e* protested unto your .... Jer 11:7
I do *e* remember him still .... Jer 31:20
may do evil with both hands *e* .... Mic 7:3
in an agony he prayed more *e* .... Lk 22:44
e looked upon him, and said, This .... Lk 22:56
or why look ye so *e* on us .... Acts 3:12
e beholding the council, said, ... Acts 23:1
But covet *e* the best gifts 1Cor 12:31
e desiring to be clothed upon 2Cor 5:2
he prayed *e* that it might not .... Jas 5:17
exhort you that ye should *e* .... Jude 3

EARNETH
he that *e* wages *e* wages to .... Hag 1:6

EARRING
golden *e* of half a shekel weight .... Gen 24:22
came to pass, when he saw the *e* .... Gen 24:30
I put the *e* upon her face, and the........... Gen 24:47
money, and every one an *e* of gold .... Job 42:11
As an *e* of gold, and an ornament, ... Prov 25:12

EARRINGS
all their *e* which were in their .... Gen 35:4
unto them, Break off the golden *e* .... Ex 32:2
golden *e* which were in their ears .... Ex 32:3
and brought bracelets, and *e* .... Ex 35:22
chains, and bracelets, rings, *e* .... Num 31:50
me every man the *e* of his prey .... Judg 8:24
(For they had golden *e*, because .... Judg 8:24
every man the *e* of his prey .... Judg 8:25
golden *e* that he requested was a .... Judg 8:26
and the tablets, and the *e* .... Is 3:20
in thine ears, and a beautiful .... Eze 16:12
and she decked herself with her *e*. .... Hos 2:13

EARS
told all these things in their *e* .... Gen 20:8
earrings which were in their *e* .... Gen 35:4
seven *e* of corn came up upon one......... Gen 41:5
And, behold, seven thin *e* and .... Gen 41:6
the seven thin *e* devoured the .... Gen 41:7
devoured the seven rank and full *e* .... Gen 41:7
seven *e* came up in one stalk, ... Gen 41:22
And, behold, seven *e*, withered, ... Gen 41:23
e devoured the seven good *e* .... Gen 41:24
the seven good *e* are seven years .... Gen 41:26
the seven empty *e* blasted with .... Gen 41:27
thee, speak a word in my lord's *e*, ... Gen 44:18
in the *e* of Pharaoh, saying, ... Gen 50:4
mayest tell in the *e* of thy son .... Ex 10:2
Speak now in the *e* of the people .... Ex 11:2
and rehearse it in the *e* of Joshua .... Ex 17:14
which are in the *e* of your wives. .... Ex 32:2
earrings which were in their *e* .... Ex 32:3
of thy firstfruits green *e* of .... Lev 2:14
even corn beaten out of full *e* .... Lev 2:14
nor parched corn, nor green *e* .... Lev 23:14
ye have wept in the *e* of the LORD .... Num 11:18
LORD, as ye have spoken in mine *e* .... Num 14:28
which I speak in your *e* this day .... Deut 5:1
pluck the *e* with thine hand .... Deut 23:25
see, and *e* to hear, unto this day .... Deut 29:4
may speak these words in their *e* .... Deut 31:28
Moses spake in the *e* of all the .... Deut 31:30
this song in the *e* of the people .... Deut 32:44
the *e* of the elders of that city .... Josh 20:4
proclaim in the *e* of the people .... Judg 7:3
in the *e* of all the men of .... Judg 9:2
brethren spake of him in the *e* of .... Judg 9:3
and speakest of alas in mine *e* .... Judg 17:2
glean *e* of corn after him in .... Ruth 2:2
at which both the *e* of every one 1Sa 3:11
them in the *e* of the LORD 1Sa 8:21
tidings in the *e* of the people 1Sa 11:4
bleating of the sheep in mine *e* 1Sa 15:14
those words in the *e* of David 1Sa 18:23
also spake in the *e* of Benjamin. 2Sa 3:19
the *e* of David in Hebron all that 2Sa 3:19
all that we have heard with our *e* 2Sa 7:22

and my cry did enter into his *e* 2Sa 22:7
full *e* of corn in the husk. 2Kin 4:42
e of the people that are on the 2Kin 18:26
thy tumult is come up into mine *e* 2Kin 19:28
of it, both his *e* shall tingle. 2Kin 21:12
he read in their *e* all the words, ... 2Kin 23:2
all that we have heard with our *e* 1Chr 17:20
let thine *e* be attent unto the 2Chr 6:40
mine *e* attent unto the prayer 2Chr 7:15
he read in their *e* all the words 2Chr 34:30
the *e* of all the people were, ... Neh 8:3
and my declaration with your *e* .... Job 13:17
A dreadful sound is in his *e* .... Job 15:21
off as the tops of the *e* of corn .... Job 24:24
heard the fame thereof with our *e* .... Job 28:22
Then he openeth the *e* of men .... Job 33:16
and openeth their *e* in oppression .... Job 36:15
came before him, even into his *e* .... Ps 18:6
his *e* are open unto their cry .... Ps 34:15
mine *e* hast thou opened. .... Ps 40:6
We have heard with our *e*, O God, ... Ps 44:1
incline your *e* to the words of my .... Ps 78:1
mine *e* shalt hear my desire of. .... Ps 92:11
They have *e*, but they hear not. .... Ps 115:6
let thine *e* be attentive to the .... Ps 130:2
They have *e*, but they hear not. .... Ps 135:17
Whoso stoppeth his *e* at the cry .... Prov 21:13
Speak not in the *e* of a fool .... Prov 23:9
thine *e* to the words of knowledge .... Prov 23:12
one that taketh a dog by the *e* .... Prov 26:17
In mine *e* said the LORD of hosts .... Is 5:9
people fat, and make their *e* heavy .... Is 6:10
their eyes, and hear with their *e* .... Is 6:10
after the hearing of his *e* .... Is 11:3
reapeth the *e* with his arm .... Is 17:5
e in the valley of Rephaim .... Is 17:5
in mine *e* by the LORD of hosts .... Is 22:14
thine *e* shall hear a word behind .... Is 30:21
the *e* of them that hear shall .... Is 32:3
that stoppeth his *e* from hearing .... Is 33:15
the *e* of the deaf shall be .... Is 35:5
the *e* of the people that are .... Is 36:11
tumult, is come up into mine *e* .... Is 37:29
opening the *e*, but he heareth not .... Is 42:20
eyes, and the deaf that have *e* .... Is 43:8
other, shall say again in thine *e* .... Is 49:20
cry in the *e* of Jerusalem, saying .... Jer 2:2
which have *e*, and hear not .... Jer 5:21
heareth, his *e* shall tingle. .... Jer 19:3
as ye have heard with your *e* .... Jer 26:11
speak all these words in your *e* .... Jer 26:15
this word that I speak in thine *e* .... Jer 28:7
in the *e* of all the people .... Jer 28:7
in the *e* of Jeremiah the prophet .... Jer 29:29
the *e* of the people in the LORD's .... Jer 36:6
thou shalt read them in the *e* of .... Jer 36:6
in the *e* of all the people .... Jer 36:10
the book in the *e* of the people .... Jer 36:13
hast read in the *e* of the people .... Jer 36:14
Sit down now, and read it in our *e* .... Jer 36:15
So Baruch read it in their *e* .... Jer 36:15
the words in the *e* of the king .... Jer 36:20
read it in the *e* of the king, ... Jer 36:21
in the *e* of all the princes which .... Jer 36:21
thine heart, and hear with thine *e* .... Eze 3:10
cry in mine *e* with a loud voice .... Eze 8:18
also in mine *e* with a loud voice .... Eze 9:1
they have *e* to hear, and hear not .... Eze 12:2
forehead, and earrings in thine *e* .... Eze 16:12
take away thy nose and thine *e* .... Eze 23:25
thee to hear it with thine *e* .... Eze 24:26
thine eyes, and hear with thine *e* .... Eze 40:4
hear with thine *e* all that I say .... Eze 44:5
mouth, their *e* shall be deaf .... Mic 7:16
the shoulder, and stopped their *e* .... Zec 7:11
He that hath *e* to hear, let him .... Mt 11:15
and began to pluck the *e* of corn. .... Mt 12:1
Who hath *e* to hear, let him hear. .... Mt 13:9
their *e* are dull of hearing, and .... Mt 13:15
their eyes, and hear with their *e* .... Mt 13:16
and your *e*, for they hear. .... Mt 13:16
Who hath *e* to hear, let him hear. .... Mt 13:43
if this come to the governor's *e* .... Mt 28:14
they went, to pluck the *e* of corn .... Mk 2:23
unto them, He that hath *e* to hear .... Mk 4:9
If any man have *e* to hear .... Mk 4:23
If any man have *e* to hear .... Mk 7:16
and put his fingers into his *e* .... Mk 7:33
And straightway his *e* were opened, ... Mk 7:35
and having *e*, hear ye not .... Mk 8:18
thy salutation sounded in mine *e* .... Lk 1:44
scripture fulfilled in your *e* .... Lk 4:21
disciples plucked the *e* of corn .... Lk 6:1
he cried, He that hath *e* to hear .... Lk 8:8
sayings sink down into your *e* .... Lk 9:44
He that hath *e* to hear, let him .... Lk 14:35
and uncircumcised in heart and *e* .... Acts 7:51
a loud voice, and stopped their *e* .... Acts 7:57
the *e* of the church which was in .... Acts 11:22
certain strange things to our *e* .... Acts 17:20
their *e* are dull of hearing, and .... Acts 28:27
their eyes, and hear with their *e* .... Acts 28:27
e that they should not hear .... Rom 11:8
teachers, having itching *e* 2Ti 4:3
turn away their *e* from the truth 2Ti 4:4
into the *e* of the Lord of Sabaoth. .... Jas 5:4
his *e* are open unto their prayers 1Pet 3:12

EARTH See PREFACE.
God created the heaven and the *e* .... Gen 1:1
the *e* were finished, and all .... Gen 2:1

And God looked upon the e, and,........ Gen 6:12
for the e is filled with violence.......... Gen 6:13
I will destroy them with the e.......... Gen 6:13
of a covenant between me and the e.... Gen 9:13
the nations of the e be blessed.......... Gen 22:18
the nations of the e be blessed.......... Gen 26:4
Then the e shook and trembled.......... 2Sa 22:8
From going to and fro in the e.......... Job 1:7
an appointed time to man upon e........ Job 7:1
is thy name in all the e .... Ps 8:1
The e is the LORD's, and .... Ps 24:1
But the meek shall inherit the e........ Ps 37:11
All the e shall worship thee, and ...... Ps 66:4
fear before him, all the e .... Ps 96:9
but the e abideth for ever .... Eccl 1:4
The e is utterly broken down .... Is 24:19
the e is clean dissolved, the.......... Is 24:19
ye saved, all the ends of the e........ Is 45:22
for they shall inherit the e............ Mt 5:5
Ye are the salt of the e .... Mt 5:13
Thy will be done in e, as it is........ Mt 6:10
e shall pass away, but my words ...... Mt 24:35
Heaven and e shall pass away .... Mk 13:31
on e peace, good will toward men .... Lk 2:14
The first man is of the e 1Cor 15:47
into the lower parts of the e .... Eph 4:9
things in heaven, and things in e...... Phil 2:10
strangers and pilgrims on the e........ Heb 11:13
he was cast out into the e .... Rev 12:9
And I saw a new heaven and a new e.. Rev 21:1

EARTHEN

But the e vessel wherein it is .... Lev 6:28
every e vessel, whereinto any of ...... Lev 11:33
in an e vessel over running water...... Lev 14:5
in an e vessel over running water...... Lev 14:50
take holy water in an e vessel .... Num 5:17
e vessels, and wheat, and barley,...... 2Sa 17:28
Go and get a potter's e bottle.......... Jer 19:1
and put them in an e vessel .... Jer 32:14
are they esteemed as e pitchers ...... Lam 4:2
have this treasure in e vessels........ 2Cor 4:7

EARTHLY

If I have told you e things .... Jn 3:12
he that is of the earth is e .... Jn 3:31
For we know that if our e house........ 2Cor 5:1
in their shame, who mind e things.... Phil 3:19
not from above, but is e, sensual...... Jas 3:15

EARTHQUAKE

and after the wind an e 1Kin 19:11
but the LORD was not in the e 1Kin 19:11
And after the e a fire................ 1Kin 19:12
of hosts with thunder, and with e...... Is 29:6
of Israel, two years before the e ...... Amos 1:1
e in the days of Uzziah king of........ Zec 14:5
him, watching Jesus, saw the e .... Mt 27:54
And, behold, there was a great e ...... Mt 28:2
And suddenly there was a great e...... Acts 16:26
seal, and, lo, there was a great e...... Rev 6:12
and lightnings, and an e .... Rev 8:5
the same hour was there a great e .... Rev 11:13
in the e were slain of men seven ...... Rev 11:13
voices, and thunderings, and an e .... Rev 11:19
and there was a great e, such as...... Rev 16:18
upon the earth, so mighty an e ...... Rev 16:18

EARTHQUAKES

be famines, and pestilences, and e .... Mt 24:7
there shall be e in divers places........ Mk 13:8
great e shall be in divers places........ Lk 21:11

EARTHY

The first man is of the earth, e........ 1Cor 15:47
As is the e, such are they also 1Cor 15:48
such are they also that are e 1Cor 15:48
we have borne the image of the e 1Cor 15:49

EASE

when thou wilt e thyself abroad ...... Deut 23:13
nations shalt thou find no e .... Deut 28:65
trode them down with e over.......... Judg 20:43
now therefore e thou somewhat the .. 2Chr 10:4
E somewhat the yoke that thy 2Chr 10:9
me, my couch shall e my complaint .. Job 7:13
the thought of him that is at e........ Job 12:5
I was at e, but he hath broken me.... Job 16:12
full strength, being wholly at e ...... Job 21:23
His soul shall dwell at e .... Ps 25:13
scorning of those that are at e .... Ps 123:4
I will e me of mine adversaries,...... Is 1:24
Rise up, ye women that are at e ...... Is 32:9
Tremble, ye women that are at e ...... Is 32:11
return, and be in rest and at e .... Jer 46:27
hath been at e from his youth........ Jer 48:11
multitude being at e was with her .... Eze 23:42
Woe to them that are at e in Zion .... Amos 6:1
with the heathen that are at e .... Zec 1:15
take thine e, eat, drink, and be........ Lk 12:19

EASED

and though I forbear, what am I e...... Job 16:6
I mean not that other men be e........ 2Cor 8:13

EASIER

so shall it be for e thyself.............. Ex 18:22
For whether is e, to say, Thy .... Mt 9:5
It is e for a camel to go through........ Mt 19:24
Whether is it e to say to the.......... Mk 2:9
It is e for a camel to go through........ Mk 10:25
Whether is it e, to say, Thy sins be.... Lk 5:23
it is e for heaven and earth to .... Lk 16:17
For it is e for a camel to go.......... Lk 18:25

is not e provoked, thinketh no........ 1Cor 13:5
the sin which doth so e beset us........ Heb 12:1

EAST

goeth toward the e of Assyria .... Gen 2:14
he placed at the e of the garden........ Gen 3:24
the land of Nod, on the e of Eden...... Gen 4:16
unto Sephar a mount of the e .... Gen 10:30
as they journeyed from the e .... Gen 11:2
a mountain on the e of Beth-el .... Gen 12:8
on the west, and Hai on the e.......... Gen 12:8
and Lot journeyed e .... Gen 13:11
eastward, unto e a country .... Gen 25:6
abroad to the west, and to the e...... Gen 28:14
the land of the people of the e........ Gen 29:1
blasted with the e wind sprung up.... Gen 41:6
thin, and blasted with the e wind.... Gen 41:23
empty ears blasted with the e .... Gen 41:27
the LORD brought an e wind upon...... Ex 10:13
the e wind brought the locusts........ Ex 10:13
by a strong e wind all that night...... Ex 14:21
e side eastward shall be fifty .... Ex 27:13
for the e side eastward fifty .... Ex 38:13
it beside the altar on the e part ...... Lev 1:16
on the e side toward the rising........ Num 2:3
the tabernacle toward the e............ Num 3:38
on the e parts shall go forward ...... Num 10:5
out of the mountains of the e .... Num 23:7
ye shall point out your e border...... Num 34:10
to Riblah, on the e side of Ain........ Num 34:11
on the e side two thousand cubits .... Num 35:5
in the e border of Jericho .... Josh 4:19
on the e side of Beth-el, and.......... Josh 7:2
And to the Canaanite on the e........ Josh 11:3
Hermon, and all the plain on the e .... Josh 12:1
to the sea of Chinnereth on the e...... Josh 12:3
plain, even the salt sea on the e........ Josh 12:3
the e border was the salt sea,.......... Josh 15:5
the water of Jericho on the e .... Josh 16:1
on the e side was Ataroth-addar........ Josh 16:5
passed by it on the e to Janohah...... Josh 16:6
north, and in Issachar on the e .... Josh 17:10
beyond Jordan on the e, which........ Josh 18:7
the border of it on the e side.......... Josh 18:20
along on the e to Gittah-hepher........ Josh 19:13
and the children of the e.............. Judg 6:3
the children of the e were.............. Judg 6:33
all the children of the e lay .... Judg 7:12
hosts of the children of the e.......... Judg 8:10
dwelt in tents on the e of Nobah...... Judg 8:11
came by the e side of the land of .... Judg 11:18
on the e side of the highway toward .. Judg 21:19
all the children of the e country 1Kin 4:30
and three looking east on the e........ 1Kin 7:25
even unto the e side of the 1Chr 4:39
all the e land of Gilead 1Chr 5:10
on the e side of Jordan, were........ 1Chr 6:78
were the porters, toward the e 1Chr 9:24
of the valleys, both toward the e 1Chr 12:15
and three looking toward the e........ 2Chr 4:4
on the right side of the e end........ 2Chr 5:12
stood at the e end of the altar,........ 2Chr 5:12
them together into the e street........ 2Chr 29:4
Levite, the porter toward the e........ 2Chr 31:14
the water gate toward the e .... Neh 3:26
the keeper of the e gate .... Neh 3:29
greatest of all the men of the e ...... Job 1:3
and fill his belly with the e wind .... Job 15:2
The e wind carrieth him away, and .. Job 27:21
the e wind upon the earth............ Job 38:24
ships of Tarshish with an e wind...... Ps 48:7
cometh neither from the e............ Ps 75:6
He caused an e wind to blow in...... Ps 78:26
As far as the e is from the west,...... Ps 103:12
them out of the lands, from the e...... Ps 107:3
they be replenished from the e........ Is 2:6
spoil them of the e together.......... Is 11:14
wind in the day of the e wind........ Is 27:8
up the righteous man from the e...... Is 41:2
I will bring thy seed from the e ...... Is 43:5
a ravenous bird from the e .... Is 46:11
with an e wind before the enemy .... Jer 18:17
is by the entry of the e gate .... Jer 19:2
of the horse gate toward the e........ Jer 31:40
Kedar, and spoil the men of the e .... Jer 49:28
Loko, and their faces toward the e .. Eze 8:16
worshipped the sun toward the e .... Eze 8:16
of the e gate of the LORD's house .... Eze 10:19
brought me unto the e gate of the.... Eze 11:1
is on the e side of the city .... Eze 11:23
when the e wind toucheth it .... Eze 17:10
the e wind dried up her fruit .... Eze 19:12
the men of the e for a possession.... Eze 25:4
men of the e with the Ammonites...... Eze 25:10
the e wind hath broken thee in ...... Eze 27:26
passengers on the e of the sea........ Eze 39:11
gate which looketh toward the e...... Eze 40:6
gate that looketh toward the e........ Eze 40:22
toward the north, and toward the e .. Eze 40:23
into the inner court toward the e...... Eze 40:32
one at the side of the e gate............ Eze 41:11
the separate place toward the e........ Eze 41:14
was the entry on the e side.......... Eze 42:9
wall of the court toward the e .... Eze 42:10
before the wall toward the e .... Eze 42:12
whose prospect is toward the e ...... Eze 42:15
He measured the e side with the...... Eze 42:16
gate that looketh toward the e........ Eze 43:1
Israel came from the way of the e.... Eze 43:2
whose prospect is toward the e ...... Eze 43:4

stairs shall look toward the e............ Eze 43:17
which looketh toward the e.............. Eze 44:1
and from the e side eastward.......... Eze 45:7
the west border unto the e border...... Eze 45:7
e shall be shut the six working.......... Eze 46:1
gate that looketh toward the e .... Eze 46:12
of the house stood toward the e........ Eze 47:1
issue out toward the e country .... Eze 47:8
the e side ye shall measure from...... Eze 47:18
from the border unto the e sea........ Eze 47:18
And this is the e side .... Eze 47:18
for these are his sides .... Eze 48:1
from the e side unto the west .... Eze 48:2
from the e side even unto the .... Eze 48:3
from the e side unto the west .... Eze 48:4
from the e side unto the west .... Eze 48:5
from the e side unto the west .... Eze 48:6
from the e side unto the west .... Eze 48:7
from the e side unto the west .... Eze 48:8
from the e side unto the west .... Eze 48:8
toward the e ten thousand in .... Eze 48:10
on the e side four thousand and ...... Eze 48:16
toward the e two hundred and fifty.... Eze 48:17
the oblation toward the e border...... Eze 48:21
from the e side unto the west .... Eze 48:23
from the e side toward the .... Eze 48:24
from the e side unto the west .... Eze 48:25
from the e side unto the west .... Eze 48:26
from the e side unto the west .... Eze 48:27
at the e side four thousand and ...... Eze 48:32
toward the south, and toward the e .. Dan 8:9
But tidings out of the e and out ...... Dan 11:44
and followeth after the e wind .... Hos 12:1
an e wind shall come, the wind of .... Hos 13:15
with his face toward the e sea.......... Joel 2:20
and from the north even to the e...... Amos 8:12
sat on the e side of the city, and...... Jonah 4:5
God prepared a vehement e wind .... Jonah 4:8
faces shall sup up as the e wind ...... Hab 1:9
save my people from the e country .. Zec 8:7
is before Jerusalem on the e .... Zec 14:4
in the midst thereof toward the e .... Zec 14:4
wise men from the e to Jerusalem .... Mt 2:1
we have seen his star in the e .... Mt 2:2
the star, which they saw in the e...... Mt 2:9
That many shall come from the e...... Mt 8:11
the lightning cometh out of the e...... Mt 24:27
And they shall come from the e ...... Lk 13:29
angel ascending from the e .... Rev 7:2
kings of the e might be prepared...... Rev 16:12
On the e three gates.................. Rev 21:13

EASTER Passover.

intending after E to bring him.......... Acts 12:4

EASTWARD

God planted a garden e in Eden ...... Gen 2:8
art northward, and southward, and e.. Gen 13:14
his son, while he yet lived, e.......... Gen 25:6
east side e shall be fifty cubits........ Ex 27:13
for the east side e fifty cubits.......... Ex 38:13
his finger upon the mercy seat e ...... Lev 16:14
tabernacle of the congregation e ...... Num 3:38
to us on this side Jordan e .... Num 32:19
outmost coast of the salt sea e........ Num 34:3
side of the sea of Chinnereth e........ Num 34:11
this side Jordan near Jericho e........ Num 34:15
salt sea, under Ashdoth-pisgah e...... Deut 3:17
and northward, and southward, and e Deut 3:27
the plain on this side Jordan e........ Deut 4:49
and unto the valley of Mizpeh e...... Josh 11:8
Moses gave them, beyond Jordan e .. Josh 13:8
on the other side Jordan e .... Josh 13:27
other side Jordan, by Jericho, e...... Josh 13:32
went about e unto Taanath-shiloh .... Josh 16:6
turned from Sarid e toward the ...... Josh 19:12
other side Jordan by Jericho e........ Josh 20:8
in Michmash, e from Beth-aven 1Sa 13:5
house e over against the south........ 1Chr 7:39
Get thee hence, and turn thee e 1Kin 17:3
From Jordan e, all the land of........ 2Kin 10:33
And he said, Open the window e...... 2Kin 13:17
e he inhabited unto the entering...... 1Chr 5:9
e Naaran, and westward Gezer, with .. 1Chr 7:28
waited in the king's gate e............ 1Chr 9:18
the lot e fell to Shelemiah.............. 1Chr 26:14
E were six Levites, northward 1Chr 26:17
David, even unto the water gate e.... Neh 12:37
the LORD's house, which looketh e.... Eze 11:1
gate e were three on this side........ Eze 40:10
without, an hundred cubits e.......... Eze 40:19
westward, and from the east side e .. Eze 45:7
the threshold of the house e .... Eze 47:1
gate by the way that looketh e........ Eze 47:2
the line in his hand went forth e...... Eze 47:3
portion shall be ten thousand e...... Eze 48:18

EASY

but knowledge is e unto him that...... Prov 14:6
For my yoke is e, and my burden is.... Mt 11:30
tongue words e to be understood...... 1Cor 14:9
e to be intreated, full of mercy ...... Jas 3:17

EAT See PREFACE.

the garden thou mayest freely e ...... Gen 2:16
and evil, thou shalt not e of it........ Gen 2:17
Ye shall not e of every tree of........ Gen 3:1
of the fruit thereof, and did e .... Gen 3:6
and he did e .... Gen 3:6
Ye shall not e any thing with the .... Lev 10:26
Only ye shall not e the blood........ Deut 12:16
him, and said unto him, Arise and e.. 1Kin 19:5

E

thy son, that we may e him to day......2Kin 6:28
Give thy son, that we may e him..........2Kin 6:29
up corn for them, that we may e...........Neh 5:2
The meek shall e and be satisfied..........Ps 22:26
Man did e angels' food........................Ps 78:25
ye shall e the good of the land..............Is 1:19
come ye, buy, and e............................Is 55:1
For they shall e, and not have................Hos 4:10
Thou shalt e, but not be.......................Mic 6:14
ye e, but ye have not enough.................Hag 1:6
for your life, what ye shall e.................Mt 6:25
not their hands when they e bread..........Mt 15:2
but to e with unwashen hands...............Mt 15:20
the disciples, and said, Take, e..............Mt 26:26
And as they did e, Jesus took................Mk 14:22
and gave to them, and said, Take, e.......Mk 14:22
e such things as are set before...............Lk 10:8
take thine ease, e, drink, and be............Lk 12:19
Except ye e the flesh of the Son............Jn 6:53
Rise, Peter; kill, and e.........................Acts 10:13
Arise, Peter; slay and e.......................Acts 11:7
that he may e all things........................Rom 14:2
Whether therefore ye e, or drink.........1Cor 10:31
he brake it, and said, Take, e..............1Cor 11:24
I give to e of the tree of life.................Rev 2:7

EATEN

Hast thou e of the tree, whereof..........Gen 3:11
hast e of the tree, of which I.................Gen 3:17
unto thee of all food that is e...............Gen 6:21
that which the young men have e............Gen 14:24
I have e of all before thou...................Gen 27:33
rams of thy flock have I not e...............Gen 31:38
And when they had e them up...............Gen 41:21
not be known that they had e them........Gen 41:21
when they had e up the corn which.........Gen 43:2
in one house shall I be e.......................Ex 12:46
shall no leavened bread be e................Ex 13:3
bread shall be e seven days..................Ex 13:7
and his flesh shall not be e..................Ex 21:28
cause a field or vineyard to be e............Ex 22:5
it shall not be e, because it is................Ex 29:34
shall it be e in the holy place................Lev 6:16
it shall not be e..................................Lev 6:23
in the holy place shall it be e...............Lev 6:26
in the holy place, shall it be e..............Lev 6:30
it shall be e in the holy place...............Lev 7:6
for thanksgiving shall be e the..............Lev 7:15
it shall be e the same day that..............Lev 7:16
the remainder of it shall be e...............Lev 7:16
be e at all on the third day...................Lev 7:18
any unclean thing shall not be e...........Lev 7:19
Wherefore have ye not e the sin............Lev 10:17
have e it in the holy place...................Lev 10:18
if I had e the sin offering to................Lev 10:19
they shall not be e, they are an.............Lev 11:34
Of all meat which may be e..................Lev 11:34
it shall not be e.................................Lev 11:41
between the beast that may be e............Lev 11:47
and the beast that may not be e............Lev 11:47
any beast or fowl that may be e............Lev 17:13
It shall be e the same day ye................Lev 19:6
if it be e at all on the third.................Lev 19:7
it shall not be e of............................Lev 19:23
On the same day it shall be e up...........Num 28:17
days shall unleavened bread be e...........Num 28:17
when thou shalt have e and be full.........Deut 6:11
When thou hast e and art full...............Deut 8:10
Lest when thou hast e and art full.........Deut 8:12
as the roebuck and the hart is e............Deut 12:22
they shall not be e..............................Deut 14:19
vineyard, and hath not yet e of it..........Deut 20:6
I have not e thereof in my...................Deut 26:14
Ye have not e bread, neither have..........Deut 29:6
and they shall have e and filled.............Deut 31:20
had e of the old corn of the land..........Josh 5:12
And when Boaz had e and drunk, and.....Ruth 3:7
up after they had e in Shiloh................1Sa 1:9
if haply the people had e freely............1Sa 14:30
for he had e no bread all the day..........1Sa 28:20
and when he had e, his spirit came........1Sa 30:12
for he had e no bread, nor drunk..........1Sa 30:12
have we e at all of the king's.................2Sa 19:42
hast e bread and drunk water in...........1Kin 13:22
to pass, after he had e bread................1Kin 13:23
the lion had e of the carcase................1Kin 13:28
and when they had e and drunk, he.......2Kin 6:23
my brethren have not e the bread..........Neh 5:14
is unsavoury be e without salt..............Job 6:6
as a garment that is moth e.................Job 13:28
Or have e my morsel myself alone,........Job 31:17
the fatherless hath not e thereof..........Job 31:17
If I have e the fruits thereof................Job 31:39
zeal of thine house hath e me up..........Ps 69:9
For I have e ashes like bread, and.........Ps 102:9
bread e in secret is pleasant.................Prov 9:17
thou hast e shalt thou vomit up............Prov 23:8
I have e my honeycomb with my.............Song 5:1
for ye have e up the vineyard...............Is 3:14
thereof, and it shall be e up...................Is 5:5
and it shall return, and shall be e...........Is 6:13
I have roasted flesh, and e...................Is 44:19
for they have e up Jacob, and................Jer 10:25
figs, which could not be e....................Jer 24:2
evil, very evil, that cannot be e.............Jer 24:3
the evil figs, which cannot be e.............Jer 24:8
like vile figs, that cannot be e..............Jer 29:17
The fathers have e a sour grape............Jer 31:29
up even till now have I not e of.............Eze 4:14
The fathers have e sour grapes.............Eze 18:2
hath not e upon the mountains,............Eze 18:6

duties, but even hath e upon.................Eze 18:11
That hath not e upon the.....................Eze 18:15
you to have e up the good pasture.........Eze 34:18
because they had e the.........................Eze 45:21
ye have e the fruit of lies.....................Hos 10:13
hath left with the locust......................Joel 1:4
hath left hath the cankerworm e............Joel 1:4
hath left hath the caterpiller e..............Joel 1:4
the years that the locust hath e.............Joel 2:25
they that had e were about five.............Mt 14:21
they that had e were about four.............Mk 8:9
shall ye begin to say, We have e............Lk 13:26
and serve me, till I have e....................Lk 17:8
zeal of thine house hath e me up..........Jn 2:17
and above unto them that had e............Jn 6:13
very hungry, and would have e..............Acts 10:10
for I have never e any thing that...........Acts 10:14
he was e of worms, and gave up the......Acts 12:23
again, and had broken bread, and e.......Acts 20:11
And when they had e enough.................Acts 27:38
and as soon as I had e it, my................Rev 10:10

EATER

Out of the e came forth meat, and.........Judg 14:14
to the sower, and bread to the e............Is 55:10
even fall into the mouth of the e...........Nah 3:12

EATERS

among riotous e of flesh.......................Prov 23:20

EATEST

for in the day that thou e.....................Gen 2:17
and why e thou not..............................1Sa 1:8
so sad, that thou e no bread.................1Kin 21:5

EATETH

for whosoever e leavened bread............Ex 12:15
for whosoever e that which is...............Ex 12:19
the soul that e of it shall bear..............Lev 7:18
But the soul that e of the flesh............Lev 7:20
For whosoever e the fat of the.............Lev 7:25
even the soul that e it shall be.............Lev 7:25
it be that e any manner of blood...........Lev 7:27
he that e of the carcase of it................Lev 11:40
he that e in the house shall wash..........Lev 14:47
that e any manner of blood..................Lev 17:10
against that soul that e blood................Lev 17:10
whosoever e it shall be cut off..............Lev 17:14
every soul that e that which died..........Lev 17:15
Therefore every one that e it.................Lev 19:8
it, is a land that e up the......................Num 13:32
man that e any food until evening..........1Sa 14:24
the man that e any food this day...........1Sa 14:28
Whose harvest the hungry e up.............Job 5:5
soul, and never e with pleasure.............Job 21:25
he e grass as an ox...............................Job 40:15
similitude of an ox that e grass.............Ps 106:20
The righteous e to the satisfying...........Prov 13:25
she e, and wipeth her mouth, and..........Prov 30:20
e not the bread of idleness....................Prov 31:27
together, and e his own flesh................Eccl 4:5
his days also he e in darkness..............Eccl 5:17
eat thereof, but a stranger e it.............Eccl 6:2
it is yet in his hand he e it up...............Is 28:4
man dreameth, and, behold, he e..........Is 29:8
with part thereof he e flesh..................Is 44:16
he that e of their eggs dieth, and..........Is 59:5
every man that e the sour grape...........Jer 31:30
Why e your Master with publicans..........Mt 9:11
disciples, How is it that he e................Mk 2:16
One of you which e with me shall..........Mk 14:18
receiveth sinners, and e with them........Lk 15:2
Whoso e my flesh, and drinketh my.......Jn 6:56
He that e my flesh, and drinketh............Jn 6:56
so he that e me, even he shall...............Jn 6:57
he that e of this bread shall................Jn 6:58
He that e bread with me hath...............Jn 13:18
another, who is weak, e herbs..............Rom 14:2
e despise him that e not......................Rom 14:3
which e not judge him that e...............Rom 14:3
He that e, e to the Lord,.....................Rom 14:6
e not, to the Lord e not......................Rom 14:6
for that man who e with offence...........Rom 14:20
because he e not of faith.....................Rom 14:23
e not of the fruit thereof....................1Cor 9:7
e not of the milk of the flock...............1Cor 9:7
e and drinketh unworthily, e................1Cor 11:29

EATING

every man according to his e................Ex 12:4
it every man according to his e.............Ex 16:16
every man according to his e................Ex 16:18
every man according to his e................Ex 16:21
in his hands, and went on e..................Judg 14:9
man, until he shall have done e............Ruth 3:3
the LORD in e with the blood.................1Sa 14:34
abroad upon all the earth,....................1Sa 30:16
it as they had made an end of e............1Kin 1:41
is by the sea in multitude,....................1Kin 4:20
as they were e of the pottage...............2Kin 4:40
were with David three days, e...............1Chr 12:39
his sons and his daughters were e.........Job 1:13
Thy sons and thy daughters were e........Job 1:18
rain it upon him while he is e...............Job 20:23
e flesh, and drinking wine....................Is 22:13
midst, e swine's flesh, and the.............Is 66:17
an end of e the grass of the land..........Amos 7:2
John came neither e nor drinking..........Mt 11:18
The Son of man came e and drinking....Mt 11:19
were before the flood they were e.........Mt 24:38
And as they were e, Jesus took............Mt 26:26
neither e bread nor drinking wine..........Lk 7:33
The Son of man is come e and..............Lk 7:34

And in the same house remain, e..........Lk 10:7
the e of those things that are...............1Cor 8:4
For in e every one taketh before...........1Cor 11:21

EBAL (e'-bal) Son of Shobal.
Manahath, and E, Shepho,...................Gen 36:23
and the curse upon mount E..................Deut 11:29
command you this day, in mount E.........Deut 27:4
shalt stand upon mount E to curse........Deut 27:13
the LORD God of Israel in mount E..........Josh 8:30
half of them over against mount E.........Josh 8:33
And E, and Abimael, and Sheba,............1Chr 1:22
Alian, and Manahath, and E, Shephi,.....1Chr 1:40

EBED (e'-bed) See EBED-MELECH.
1. Father of Gaal.
Gaal the son of E came with his.............Judg 9:26
And Gaal the son of E said....................Judg 9:28
the words of Gaal the son of E..............Judg 9:30
saying, Behold, Gaal the son of E..........Judg 9:31
And Gaal the son of E went out.............Judg 9:35
2. A family of exiles.
E the son of Jonathan, and with............Ezr 8:6

EBED-MELECH (e'-bed-me'-lek) An Ethiopian eunuch.
Now when E the Ethiopian, one of.........Jer 38:7
E went forth out of the king's...............Jer 38:8
king commanded E the Ethiopian...........Jer 38:10
So E took the men with him, and...........Jer 38:11
E the Ethiopian said unto.....................Jer 38:12
speak to E the Ethiopian, saying,..........Jer 39:16

EBEN-EZER
to battle, and pitched beside E..............1Sa 4:1
and brought it from E unto Ashdod........1Sa 5:1
Shen, and called the name of it E..........1Sa 7:12

EBER (e'-bur) See HEBER.
1. A great-grandson of Shem.
father of all the children of E...............Gen 10:21
and Salah begat E..............................Gen 10:24
unto E were born two sons....................Gen 10:25
lived thirty years, and begat E.............1Chr 1:14
after he begat E four hundred...............Gen 11:15
E lived four and thirty years, and..........Gen 11:16
E lived after he begat Peleg four...........Gen 11:17
begat Shelah, and Shelah begat E.........1Chr 1:18
unto E were born two sons...................1Chr 1:19
E, Peleg, Reu,...................................1Chr 1:25
2. Descendants of Eber I.
Asshur, and shall afflict E...................Num 24:24
3. Son of Elpaal.
E, and Misham, and Shamed, who,.......1Chr 8:12
4. A priest of the Amok family.
Kallai; of Amok, E..............................Neh 12:20

EBEZ See ABEZ.

EBIASAPH (e-bi'-a-saf) See ABIASAPH. A great-grandson of Korah.
E his son, and Assir his son,................1Chr 6:23
the son of Assir, the son of E...............1Chr 6:37
the son of Kore, the son of E...............1Chr 9:19

EBONY
for present horns of ivory and e............Eze 27:15

EBRONAH (eb-ro'-nah) An encampment during the Exodus.
from Jotbathah, and encamped at E.......Num 33:34
And they departed from E, and.............Num 33:35

ECBATANA See ACHMETHA.

ED (ed) Name of an altar.
of Gad called the altar E......................Josh 22:34

EDAR (e'-dar) See EDER. A name of a watchtower.
his tent beyond the tower of E..............Gen 35:21

EDEN (e'-dun)
1. Original land of Adam and Eve.
planted a garden eastward in E..............Gen 2:8
went out of E to water the garden..........Gen 2:10
into the garden of E to dress it..............Gen 2:15
him forth from the garden of E..............Gen 3:23
east of the garden of E Cherubim..........Gen 3:24
the land of Nod, on the east of E...........Gen 4:16
will make her wilderness like E.............Is 51:3
hast been in E the garden of God..........Eze 28:13
so that all the trees of E......................Eze 31:9
and all the trees of E, the choice..........Eze 31:16
in greatness among the trees of E.........Eze 31:18
of E unto the nether parts of the..........Eze 31:18
is become like the garden of E.............Eze 36:35
is as the garden of E before them.........Joel 2:3
2. An undetermined place.
the children of E which were in............2Kin 19:12
the children of E which were in............Is 37:12
Haran, and Canneh, and E, the.............Eze 27:23
the sceptre from the house of E............Amos 1:5
3. A Levite during Hezekiah's time.
of Zimmah, and E the son of Joah.........2Chr 29:12
and E, and Miniamin,.........................2Chr 31:15

EDER (e'-dur) See EDAR. A city in southern Judah.
were Kabzeel, and E............................Josh 15:21
2. A grandson of Merari.
Mahli, and E, and Jeremoth, three.......1Chr 23:23
Mahli, and E, and Jerimoth..................1Chr 24:30

EDGE

his son with the *e* of the sword .... Gen 34:26
in the *e* of the wilderness .... Ex 13:20
people with the *e* of the sword .... Ex 17:13
the *e* of the one curtain from the .... Ex 26:4
uttermost *e* of another curtain .... Ex 26:4
loops shalt thou make in the *e* of .... Ex 26:5
the *e* of the one curtain that is .... Ex 26:10
fifty loops in the *e* of the .... Ex 26:10
on the *e* of one curtain from the .... Ex 36:11
fifty loops made he in the *e* of .... Ex 36:12
e of the curtain in the coupling .... Ex 36:17
fifty loops made he upon the *e* of .... Ex 36:17
smote him with the *e* of the sword .... Num 21:24
Etham, which is in the *e* of the .... Num 33:6
in the *e* of the land of Edom .... Num 33:37
that city with the *e* of the sword .... Deut 13:15
thereof, with the *e* of the sword .... Deut 13:15
thereof with the *e* of the sword .... Deut 20:13
and ass, with the *e* of the sword .... Josh 6:21
all fallen on the *e* of the sword .... Josh 8:24
smote it with the *e* of the sword .... Josh 8:24
smote it with the *e* of the sword .... Josh 10:28
smote it with the *e* of the sword .... Josh 10:30
smote it with the *e* of the sword .... Josh 10:32
smote it with the *e* of the sword .... Josh 10:35
smote it with the *e* of the sword .... Josh 10:37
them with the *e* of the sword .... Josh 10:39
therein with the *e* of the sword .... Josh 11:11
them with the *e* of the sword .... Josh 11:12
smote with the *e* of the sword .... Josh 11:14
even unto the *e* of the sea of .... Josh 15:4
smote it with the *e* of the sword .... Josh 19:47
it with the *e* of the sword .... Judg 1:8
the city with the *e* of the sword .... Judg 1:25
with the *e* of the sword before .... Judg 4:15
fell upon the *e* of the sword .... Judg 4:16
them with the *e* of the sword .... Judg 18:27
the city with the *e* of the sword .... Judg 20:37
them with the *e* of the sword .... Judg 20:48
with the *e* of the sword, with the...... Judg 21:10
people with the *e* of the sword 1Sa 15:8
smote he with the *e* of the sword 1Sa 22:19
and sheep, with the *e* of the sword..... 1Sa 22:19
the city with the *e* of the sword 2Kin 10:25
them with the *e* of the sword .... Job 1:15
servants with the *e* of the sword .... Job 1:16
servants with the *e* of the sword .... Job 1:17
also turned the *e* of his sword .... Ps 89:43
be blunt, and he do not whet the *e* .... Eccl 10:10
them with the *e* of the sword .... Jer 21:7
the children's teeth are set on *e* .... Jer 31:29
his teeth shall be set on *e* .... Jer 31:30
the children's teeth are set on *e* .... Eze 18:2
the border thereof by the *e* .... Eze 43:13
shall fall by the *e* of the sword .... Lk 21:24
escaped the *e* of the sword, out .... Heb 11:34

EDGES

joined at the two *e* thereof .... Ex 28:7
by the two *e* was it coupled .... Ex 39:4
made him a dagger which had two *e*.. Judg 3:16
hath the sharp sword with two *e*......... Rev 2:12

EDIFICATION

his neighbour for his good to *e*............ Rom 15:2
speaketh unto him to *e*, and................. 1Cor 14:3
the Lord hath given us for *e*................. 2Cor 10:8
which the Lord hath given me to *e* 2Cor 13:10

EDIFIED

and Galilee and Samaria, and were *e*.. Acts 9:31
well, but the other is not *e*................... 1Cor 14:17

EDIFIETH

puffeth up, but charity *e*....................... 1Cor 8:1
in an unknown tongue *e* himself 1Cor 14:4
he that prophesieth *e* the church 1Cor 14:4

EDIFY

wherewith one may *e* another .... Rom 14:19
for me, but all things *e* not 1Cor 10:23
e one another, even as also ye do........ 1Th 5:11

EDIFYING

that the church may receive *e* 1Cor 14:5
may excel to the *e* of the church 1Cor 14:12
Let all things be done unto *e* 1Cor 14:26
dearly beloved, for your *e* 2Cor 12:19
for the *e* of the body of Christ .... Eph 4:12
body unto the *e* of itself in love......... Eph 4:16
which is good to the use of *e*............... Eph 4:29
than godly *e* which is in faith 1Ti 1:4

EDOM (*e'-dum*) See EDOMITES, ESAU, IDUMEA, OBED-EDOM.

Another name for Esau.

children of Seir in the land of E............. Gen 36:21
that reigned in the land of E.................. Gen 36:31
Bela the son of Beor reigned in E.......... Gen 36:32
these be the dukes of E........................... Gen 36:43
the dukes of E shall be amazed .... Ex 15:15
from Kadesh unto the king of E .... Num 20:14
E said unto him, Thou shalt not............. Num 20:18
E came out against him with much .... Num 20:20
Thus E refused to give Israel.................. Num 20:21
by the coast of the land of E.................. Num 21:4
Red sea, to compass the land of E......... Num 21:4
E shall be a possession, Seir .... Num 24:18
Hor, in the edge of the land of E .... Num 33:37
of Zin along by the coast of E .... Num 34:3
even to the border of E the..................... Josh 15:1
coast of E southward were Kabzeel ...... Josh 15:21

EDOMITE (*e'-dum-ite*) See EDOMITES. A *descendant of Esau.*

Thou shalt not abhor an E .... Deut 23:7
and his name was Doeg, an E.................. 1Sa 21:7
Then answered Doeg the E, which 1Sa 22:9
And Doeg the E turned, and he fell........ 1Sa 22:18
day, when Doeg the E was there 1Sa 22:22
unto Solomon, Hadad the E 1Kin 11:14
of David, then Doeg the E came............. Ps 52:t

EDOMITES (*e'-dum-ites*)

the father of the E in mount Seir........... Gen 36:9
he is Esau the father of the E.................. Gen 36:43
of the Moabites, Ammonites, ... 1Kin 11:1
certain E of his father's........................... 1Kin 11:17
smote the E which compassed him........ 2Kin 8:21
the son Zeruiah slew of the E in 1Chr 18:12
all the E became David's servants 1Chr 18:13
In his days the E revolted from.............. 2Chr 21:8
smote the E which compassed him........ 2Chr 21:9
So the E revolted from under the 2Chr 21:10
come from the slaughter of the E........... 2Chr 25:14
Lo, thou hast smitten the E 2Chr 25:19
For again the E had come and................ 2Chr 28:17

EDREI (*ed'-re-i*)

1. A city in Bashan.

his people, to the battle at E................... Num 21:33
which dwelt at Astaroth in E.................. Deut 1:4
and all his people, to battle at E .... Deut 3:1
and all Bashan, unto Salchah and E ...... Deut 3:10
that dwelt at Astaroth and at E.............. Josh 12:4
reigned in Ashtaroth and in E................ Josh 13:12
half Gilead, and Ashtaroth, and E......... Josh 13:31

2. A city in Naphtali.

And Kedesh, and E, and En-hazor,........ Josh 19:37

EFFECT

she bound her soul, of none *e* .... Num 30:8
and they spake to her to that *e* 2Chr 34:22

devices of the people of none *e* .... Ps 33:10
the *e* of righteousness quietness .... Is 32:17
his lies shall not so *e* .... Jer 48:30
at hand, and the *e* of every vision........ Eze 12:23
God of none *e* by your tradition........... Mt 15:6
of none *e* through your tradition .... Mk 7:13
make the faith of God without *e*.......... Rom 3:3
and the promise made of none *e* .... Rom 4:14
the word of God hath taken none *e* ..... Rom 9:6
Christ should be made of none *e*........... 1Cor 1:17
should make the promise of none *e*...... Gal 3:17
Christ is become of no *e* unto you .... Gal 5:4

EFFECTED

his own house, he prosperously *e* 2Chr 7:11

EFFECTUAL

e is opened unto me, and there are 1Cor 16:9
which is *e* in the enduring of the 2Cor 1:6
me by the *e* working of his power........ Eph 3:7
according to the *e* working in the........ Eph 4:16
of thy faith may become *e* by the........ Philem 6
The *e* fervent prayer of a .... Jas 5:16

EFFECTUALLY

(For he that wrought *e* in Peter........... Gal 2:8
which *e* worketh also in you that......... 1Th 2:13

EFFEMINATE

idolaters, nor adulterers, nor *e* 1Cor 6:9

EGG

any taste in the white of an *e* .... Job 6:6
Or if he shall ask an *e*, will he .... Lk 11:12

EGGS

whether they be young ones, or *e* .... Deut 22:6
upon the young, or upon the *e* .... Deut 22:6
Which leaveth her *e* in the earth........... Job 39:14
as one gathereth *e* that are left .... Is 10:14
They hatch cockatrice' *e*, and .... Is 59:5
he that eateth of their *e* dieth .... Is 59:5
As the partridge sitteth on *e* .... Jer 17:11

EGLAH (*eg'-lah*) See MICHAL. *A wife of David.*

sixth, Ithream, by E David's wife............ 2Sa 3:5
the sixth, Ithream by E his wife.............. 1Chr 3:3

EGLAIM (*eg'-la-im*) See EN-EGLAIM. *A Moabite city.*

the howling thereof unto E...................... Is 15:8

EGLON (*eg'-lon*)

1. An Amorite city.

Lachish, and unto Debir king of E .... Josh 10:3
king of Lachish, the king of E .... Josh 10:5
king of Lachish, and the king of E......... Josh 10:23
from Lachish Joshua passed unto E........ Josh 10:34
And Joshua went up from E, and all...... Josh 10:36
to all that he had done to E .... Josh 10:37
The king of E, one .... Josh 12:12
Lachish, and Bozkath, and E................... Josh 15:39

2. A Moabite king.

the LORD strengthened E the king......... Judg 3:12
the children of Israel served E................. Judg 3:14
a present unto E the king of Moab.......... Judg 3:15
the present unto E king of Moab............. Judg 3:17
and E was a very fat man......................... Judg 3:17

EGYPT (*e'-ipt*) See PREFACE. SEE ALSO EGYPTIAN, MIZRAIM. *Kingdom in northeast Africa.*

went down into E to sojourn there......... Gen 12:10
sold him into E unto Potiphar .... Gen 37:36
your brother, whom ye sold into E .... Gen 45:4
land of Canaan, and came into E .... Gen 46:6
the children of Israel out of E .... Ex 3:10
of the land of E by their armies .... Ex 12:51
day, in which ye came out from E........... Ex 13:3
there is a people come forth out of E ..... Num 22:5
Thou hast brought a vine out of E.......... Ps 80:8
The burden of E... Is 19:1
be a highway out of E to Assyria .... Is 19:23
E is like a very fair heifer, but .... Jer 46:20
And they committed whoredoms in E.... Eze 23:3
and they shall spoil the pomp of E......... Eze 32:12
and his mother, and flee into E................ Mt 2:13
By faith he forsook E, not....................... Heb 11:27

EGYPTIAN (*e-jip'-shun*) See EGYPTIAN's, EGYPTIANS.

1. An inhabitant of Egypt.

and she had an handmaid, an E .... Gen 16:1
wife took Hagar her maid the E .... Gen 16:3
Sarah saw the son of Hagar the E........... Gen 21:9
Abraham's son, whom Hagar the E......... Gen 25:12
captain of the guard, an E....................... Gen 39:1
in the house of his master the E.............. Gen 39:2
women are not as the E women............... Ex 1:19
he spied an E smiting an Hebrew............ Ex 2:11
there was no man, he slew the E .... Ex 2:12
kill me, as thou killedst the E .... Ex 2:14
An E delivered us out of the hand........... Ex 2:19
woman, whose father was an E................ Lev 24:10
thou shalt not abhor an E .... Deut 23:7
And they found an E in the field 1Sa 30:11
And he slew an E, a goodly man............. 2Sa 23:21
the E had a spear in his hand 2Sa 23:21
And Sheshan had a servant, an E............ 1Chr 2:34
And he slew an E, a man of great 1Chr 11:23
the E into Assyria, and the .... Is 19:23
was oppressed, and smote the E .... Acts 7:24
as thou diddest the E yesterday .... Acts 7:28
Art not thou that E, which before .... Acts 21:38

2. The Red Sea.

destroy the tongue of the E sea .... Is 11:15

EGYPTIAN'S (e-jip'-shuns)
the E house for Joseph's sake .... Gen 39:5
the spear out of the E hand 2Sa 23:21
in the E hand was a spear like a 1Chr 11:23
the spear out of the E hand 1Chr 11:23

EGYPTIANS (e-jip'-shuns)
when the E shall see thee, that .... Gen 12:12
the E beheld the woman that she .... Gen 12:14
and Pharaoh said unto all the E .... Gen 41:55
storehouses, and sold unto the E .... Gen 41:56
them by themselves, and for the E ..... Gen 43:32
because the E might not eat bread ..... Gen 43:32
that is an abomination unto the E ...... Gen 43:32
and the E and the house of Pharaoh ... Gen 45:2
is an abomination unto the E .... Gen 46:34
all the E came unto Joseph, and .... Gen 47:15
for the E sold every man his .... Gen 47:20
the E mourned for him threescore ...... Gen 50:3
is a grievous mourning to the E .... Gen 50:11
the E made the children of Israel .... Ex 1:13
them out of the hand of the E .... Ex 3:8
wherewith the E oppress them .... Ex 3:9
favour in the sight of the E .... Ex 3:21
and ye shall spoil the E .... Ex 3:22
whom the E keep in bondage .... Ex 6:5
from under the burdens of the E .... Ex 6:6
from under the burdens of the E .... Ex 6:7
the E shall know that I am the .... Ex 7:5
the E shall toibe to drink of the .... Ex 7:18
the E could not drink of the .... Ex 7:21
all the E digged round about the .... Ex 7:24
the houses of the E shall be full .... Ex 8:21
of the E to the LORD our God .... Ex 8:26
of the E before their eyes .... Ex 8:26
the magicians, and upon all the E ...... Ex 9:11
and the houses of all the E .... Ex 10:6
favour in the sight of the E .... Ex 11:3
put a difference between the E .... Ex 11:7
will pass through to smite the E .... Ex 12:23
in Egypt, when he smote the E .... Ex 12:27
and all his servants, and all the E ...... Ex 12:30
the E were urgent upon the people ..... Ex 12:33
the E jewels of silver .... Ex 12:35
favour in the sight of the E .... Ex 12:36
And they spoiled the E .... Ex 12:36
that the E may know that I am the ...... Ex 14:4
But the E pursued after them, all .... Ex 14:9
behold, the E marched after them ...... Ex 14:10
us alone, that we may serve the E ...... Ex 14:12
been better for us to serve the E .... Ex 14:12
for the E whom ye have seen to .... Ex 14:13
I will harden the hearts of the E .... Ex 14:17
the E shall know that I am the .... Ex 14:18
it came between the camp of the E ..... Ex 14:20
the E pursued, and went in after .... Ex 14:23
the E through the pillar of fire .... Ex 14:24
and troubled the host of the E .... Ex 14:24
so that the E said, Let us .... Ex 14:25
fighteth for them against the E .... Ex 14:25
waters may come again upon the E ..... Ex 14:26
and the E fled against it .... Ex 14:27
the LORD overthrew the E in the .... Ex 14:27
that day out of the hand of the E .... Ex 14:30
Israel saw the E dead upon the .... Ex 14:30
which the LORD did upon the E .... Ex 14:31
which I have brought upon the E .... Ex 15:26
to the E for Israel's sake, and .... Ex 18:8
out of the hand of the E .... Ex 18:9
you out of the hand of the E .... Ex 18:10
from under the hand of the E .... Ex 18:10
have seen what I did unto the E .... Ex 19:4
Wherefore should the E speak .... Ex 32:12
Then the E shall hear it, (for .... Num 14:13
the E vexed us, and our fathers .... Num 20:15
hand in the sight of all the E .... Num 33:3
For the E buried all their .... Num 33:4
the E evil entreated us, and .... Deut 26:6
the E pursued after your fathers .... Josh 24:6
put darkness between you and the E ... Josh 24:7
you out of the hand of the E .... Judg 6:9
Did not I deliver you from the E .... Judg 10:11
the E with all the plagues in the 1Sa 4:8
ye harden your hearts, as the E 1Sa 6:6
you out of the hand of the E 1Sa 10:18
Hittites, and the kings of the E 2Kin 7:6
Ammonites, the Moabites, the E .... Ezr 9:1
set the E against the E .... Is 19:2
the E will I give over into the .... Is 19:4
the E shall know the LORD in that ...... Is 19:21
the E shall serve with .... Is 19:23
Assyria lead away the E prisoners ...... Is 20:4
For the E shall help in vain, and .... Is 30:7
Now the E are men, and not God .... Is 31:3
of the E shall he burn with fire .... Jer 43:13
We have given the hand to the E .... Lam 5:6
with the E thy neighbours .... Eze 16:26
the E for the paps of thy youth .... Eze 23:21
scatter the E among the nations .... Eze 29:12
E from the people whither they .... Eze 29:13
scatter the E among the nations .... Eze 30:23
scatter the E among the nations .... Eze 30:26
in all the wisdom of the E .... Acts 7:22
which the E assaying to do were .... Heb 11:29

EHI (e'-hi) See AHARAH. A son of Benjamin.
and Ashbel, Gera, and Naaman, & ...... Gen 46:21

EHUD (e'-hud)
1. A son of Gera.
E the son of Gera, a Benjamite, a ...... Judg 3:15
But E made him a dagger which had ... Judg 3:16
And E came unto him .... Judg 3:20

E said, I have a message from God ...... Judg 3:20
E put forth his left hand, and .... Judg 3:21
Then E went forth through the .... Judg 3:23
E escaped while they tarried, and ...... Judg 3:26
of the LORD, when E was dead .... Judg 4:1
  2. A great-grandson of Benjamin.
Jeush, and Benjamin, and E, and 1Chr 7:10
And these are the sons of E 1Chr 8:6

EIGHT
Seth were a hundred and .... Gen 5:4
after he begat Enos a hundred .... Gen 5:7
after he begat Cainan a hundred .... Gen 5:10
he begat Mahalaleel a hundred .... Gen 5:13
after he begat Jared a hundred .... Gen 5:16
he begat Enoch a hundred years .... Gen 5:19
he that is a days old shall be .... Gen 17:12
his son Isaac being a days old .... Gen 21:4
these a Micah did bear to Nahor .... Gen 22:23
length of one curtain shall be .... Ex 26:2
And they shall be a boards .... Ex 26:25
a cubits, and the breadth of one .... Ex 36:9
And there were a boards .... Ex 36:30
a thousand and a hundred, ... Num 2:24
were a thousand and six hundred ...... Num 3:28
were a thousand and five hundred ..... Num 4:48
a oxen he gave unto the sons of .... Num 7:8
And on the sixth day a bullocks .... Num 29:29
shall be forty and a cities .... Num 35:7
Zered, was thirty and a years .... Deut 2:14
a cities with their suburbs .... Josh 21:41
served Chushan-rishathaim a years .... Judg 3:8
and he judged Israel a years .... Judg 12:14
Now Eli was ninety and a years old 1Sa 4:15
and he had a sons 1Sa 17:12
up his spear against a hundred 2Sa 23:8
there were in Israel a hundred 2Sa 24:9
ten cubits, and stones of a cubits 1Kin 7:10
he reigned a years in Jerusalem 2Kin 8:17
in Samaria was twenty and a years ... 2Kin 10:36
Josiah was a years old when he 2Kin 22:1
a hundred, ready armed to the war 1Chr 12:24
a hundred, mighty men of valour, ... 1Chr 12:30
and threescore and six hundred 1Chr 12:35
their brethren, threescore and a 1Chr 16:38
by man, was thirty and a thousand 1Chr 23:3
a among the sons of Ithamar 1Chr 24:4
was two hundred fourscore and a 1Chr 25:7
a sons, and threescore daughters 2Chr 11:21
in array against him with a 2Chr 13:3
he reigned a years in Jerusalem 2Chr 21:20
he reigned in Jerusalem a 2Chr 21:20
house of the LORD in a days 2Chr 29:17
Josiah was a years old when he 2Chr 34:1
Jehoiachin was a years old when 2Chr 36:9
and Joab, two thousand a hundred .... Ezr 2:6
of Ater of Hezekiah, ninety and a ...... Ezr 2:16
Anathoth, an hundred twenty and a ... Ezr 2:23
of Asaph, an hundred twenty and a ... Ezr 2:41
and with him twenty and a males ...... Ezr 8:11
thousand and a hundred and eighteen . Neh 7:11
of Zattu, a hundred forty and five ..... Neh 7:15
of Binnui, six hundred forty and a ..... Neh 7:15
of Bebai, six hundred twenty and a ... Neh 7:16
of Ater of Hezekiah, ninety and a ...... Neh 7:21
Hashum, three hundred twenty and a . Neh 7:22
an hundred fourscore and a .... Neh 7:26
Anathoth, an hundred twenty and a ... Neh 7:27
of Asaph, an hundred forty and a ...... Neh 7:44
of Shobai, an hundred thirty and a .... Neh 7:45
threescore and a valiant men .... Neh 11:6
Sallai, nine hundred twenty and a ..... Neh 11:8
the house were a hundred twenty ...... Neh 11:12
of valour, an hundred twenty and a ... Neh 11:14
a portion to seven, and also to a .... Eccl 11:2
escaped from Johanan with a men ..... Jer 41:15
from Jerusalem a hundred thirty .... Jer 52:29
a gate the cubits .... Eze 40:9
and the going up to a had a steps ...... Eze 40:31
and the going up to it had a steps ..... Eze 40:34
and the going up to it had a steps ..... Eze 40:37
a tables, whereupon they slew .... Eze 40:41
shepherds, and a principal men .... Mic 5:5
when a days were accomplished for ... Lk 2:21
an a days after these sayings .... Lk 9:28
an infirmity thirty and a years .... Jn 5:5
after a days again his disciples .... Jn 20:26
which had kept his bed a years .... Acts 9:33
a souls were saved by water 1Pet 3:20

EIGHTEEN
his own house, three hundred and a ... Gen 14:14
Eglon the king of Moab a years, ... Judg 3:14
a years, all the children of .... Judg 10:8
of Israel again a thousand men .... Judg 20:25
fell of Benjamin a thousand men .... Judg 20:44
of salt, being a thousand men 2Sa 8:13
of brass, of a cubits high apiece 1Kin 7:15
Jehoiachin was a years old when 2Kin 24:8
of the one pillar was a cubits 2Kin 25:17
half tribe of Manasseh a thousand, ... 1Chr 12:31
in the valley of salt a thousand 1Chr 18:12
sons and brethren, strong men, a 1Chr 26:9
of brass a thousand talents, and 2Chr 29:7
(for he took a wives, and 2Chr 11:21
with him two hundred and a males .... Ezr 8:9
with his sons and his brethren, a ...... Ezr 8:18
thousand and eight hundred and a .... Neh 7:15
height of one pillar was a cubits .... Jer 52:21
round about a thousand measures ..... Eze 48:35
Or those a, upon whom the tower ..... Lk 13:4

---

had a spirit of infirmity a years .... Lk 13:11
hath bound, lo, these a years .... Lk 13:16

EIGHTEENTH
Now in the a year of king 1Kin 15:1
over Israel in Samaria the a year 2Kin 3:1
pass in the a year of king Josiah, ... 2Kin 22:3
But in the a year of king Josiah, ... 2Kin 23:23
to Hezir, the a to Aphses, ... 1Chr 24:15
The a to Hanani, he, his sons, and 1Chr 25:25
Now in the a year of king 2Chr 13:1
Now in the a year of his reign, ... 2Chr 34:8
In the a year of the reign of 2Chr 35:19
of Judah, which was the a year of ..... Jer 32:1
In the a year of Nebuchadrezzar ...... Jer 52:29

EIGHTH
on the a day thou shalt give it .... Ex 22:30
And it came to pass on the a day ...... Lev 9:1
in the a day the flesh of his .... Lev 12:3
on the a day he shall take two he ...... Lev 14:10
he shall bring them on the a day ...... Lev 14:23
on the a day he shall take to him ...... Lev 15:14
on the a day she shall take unto .... Lev 15:29
and from the a day and thenceforth ... Lev 22:27
on the a day shall be an holy .... Lev 23:36
on the a day shall be a sabbath .... Lev 23:39
And ye shall sow the a year .... Lev 25:22
on the a day he shall bring two .... Num 6:10
On the a day offered Gamaliel the ..... Num 7:54
On the a day ye shall have a .... Num 29:35
month Bul, which is the a month 1Kin 6:38
On the a day he sent the people 1Kin 8:66
ordained a feast in the a month 1Kin 12:32
the fifteenth day of the a month 1Kin 12:33
a year of Asa king of Judah began 1Kin 16:29
a year of Azariah king of Judah 2Kin 15:8
him in the a year of his reign 2Kin 24:12
Johanan the a, Elzabad the ninth, ... 1Chr 12:12
to Hakkoz, the a to Abijah, ... 1Chr 24:10
The a to Jeshaiah, he, his sons, ... 1Chr 25:15
the seventh, Peulthai the a 1Chr 26:5
a captain for the a month 1Chr 27:11
in the a day they made a solemn 2Chr 7:9
on the a day of the month came 2Chr 29:17
For in the a year of his reign, ... 2Chr 34:3
on the a day was a solemn .... Neh 8:18
it shall be, that upon the a day .... Eze 43:27
In the a month, in the second .... Zec 1:1
that on the a day they came to .... Lk 1:59
and circumcised him the a day .... Acts 7:8
Circumcised the a day, of the .... Phil 3:5
but saved Noah the a person 2Pet 2:5
was, and is not, even he is the a ...... Rev 17:11
the a, beryl .... Rev 21:20

EIGHTIETH
a year after the children of 1Kin 6:1

EIGHTY
And Methuselah lived an hundred a ... Gen 5:25
he begat Lamech seven hundred a ..... Gen 5:26
And Lamech lived an hundred a .... Gen 5:30

EITHER
speak not to Jacob a good or bad ...... Gen 31:24
speak not to Jacob a good or bad ...... Gen 31:29
took a of them his censer, and put .... Lev 10:1
e in the warp, or in the woof, or .... Lev 13:48
e in the warp, or in the woof .... Lev 13:51
e in the warp, or in the woof, or .... Lev 13:53
e in the warp, or in the woof .... Lev 13:57
e warp, or woof, or whatsoever .... Lev 13:58
e in the warp, or woof, or any .... Lev 13:59
a bullock or a lamb that hath .... Lev 22:23
E his uncle, or his uncle's son, ... Lev 25:49
When e man or woman shall .... Num 6:2
where was no way to turn e to the .... Num 22:26
to do e good or bad of mine own ...... Num 24:13
a the sun, or moon, or any of the ..... Deut 17:3
also shall not leave thee e corn .... Deut 28:51
e that all the sons of Jerubbaal .... Judg 9:2
will do nothing e great or small 1Sa 20:2
e that thou hast shed blood 1Sa 25:31
e great or small, but carried 1Sa 30:2
did compass e of them about 1Kin 7:15
there were stays on e side on the 1Kin 10:19
e he is talking, or he is 1Kin 18:27
E three years' famine 1Chr 21:12
Judah sat e of them on his throne 2Chr 18:9
no man knoweth e love or hatred ..... Eccl 9:1
e this or that, or whether they .... Eccl 11:6
ask it e in the depth, or in the .... Is 7:11
e the graves, or the images .... Is 17:8
e on the right hand, or on the .... Eze 21:16
for e he will hate the one, and .... Mt 6:24
E make the tree good, and his .... Mt 12:33
for how canst thou say to thy .... Lk 6:42
E what woman having ten pieces of ... Lk 15:8
for e he will hate the one, and .... Lk 16:13
on e side one, and Jesus in the .... Jn 19:18
but e to tell, or to hear some .... Acts 17:21
speak to you e by revelation 1Cor 14:6
attained, e were already perfect ...... Phil 3:12
e a vine, figs .... Jas 3:12
on e side of the river, was there ...... Rev 22:2

EKER (e'-ker) Descendant of Judah.
were, Maaz, and Jamin, and E 1Chr 2:27

EKRON (ec'-ron) See EKRONITES. A Philistine
city.
unto the borders of E northward ...... Josh 13:3
out unto the side of E northward ...... Josh 15:11

E, with her towns and her villages ...... Josh 15:45
From E even unto the sea, all............ Josh 15:46
And Elon, and Thimnathah, and E....... Josh 19:43
and E with the coast thereof............. Judg 1:18
they sent the ark of God to E........... 1Sa 5:10
pass, as the ark of God came to E...... 1Sa 5:10
they returned to E the same day...... 1Sa 6:16
one, for Gath one, for E one............ 1Sa 6:17
to Israel, from E even unto Gath 1Sa 7:14
the valley, and to the gates of E........ 1Sa 17:52
even unto Gath, and unto E............. 1Sa 17:52
of Baal-zebub the god of E............... 2Kin 1:2
of Baal-zebub the god of E............... 2Kin 1:3
of Baal-zebub the god of E............... 2Kin 1:6
of Baal-zebub the god of E............... 2Kin 1:16
and Ashkelon, and Azzah, and E....... Jer 25:20
I will turn mine hand against E......... Amos 1:8
noonday, and E shall be rooted up..... Zeph 2:4
it, and be very sorrowful, and E........ Zec 9:5
in Judah, and E as a Jebusite............ Zec 9:7

EKRONITES (ek'-ron-ites) Inhabitants of Ekron.
the Gittites, and the E.................... Josh 13:3
that the E cried out, saying............. 1Sa 5:10

ELADAH (el'-a-dah) A descendant of Ephraim.
E his son, and Tahath his son........... 1Chr 7:20

ELAH (e'-lah)
1. An Edomite prince.
Duke Aholibamah, duke E, duke ...... Gen 36:41
Duke Aholibamah, duke E, duke 1Chr 1:52
2. A valley in Judah.
and pitched by the valley of E.......... 1Sa 17:2
Israel, were in the valley of E........... 1Sa 17:19
thou slewest in the valley of E.......... 1Sa 21:9
3. Father of Shimei.
Shimei the son of E, in Benjamin..... 1Kin 4:18
4. Son of King Baasha of Israel.
E his son reigned in his stead............ 1Kin 16:6
E the son of Baasha to reign over...... 1Kin 16:8
Baasha, and the sins of E his son...... 1Kin 16:13
Now the rest of the acts of E........... 1Kin 16:14
5. Father of King Hoshea of Israel.
Hoshea the son of E made a............. 2Kin 15:30
Judah began Hoshea the son of E...... 2Kin 17:1
of Hoshea son of E king of Israel...... 2Kin 18:1
of Hoshea son of E king of Israel...... 2Kin 18:9
6. A son of Caleb.
of Jephunneh; Iru, E....................... 1Chr 4:15
and the sons of E, even Kenaz 1Chr 4:15
7. A Benjamite.
E the son of Uzzi, the son of 1Chr 9:8

ELAM (e'-lam) See ELAMITES, PERSIA.
1. A son of Shem.
E, and Asshur, and Arphaxad........... Gen 10:22
E, and Asshur, and Arphaxad........... 1Chr 1:17
2. Land of the Elamites.
Ellasar, Chedorlaomer king of E....... Gen 14:1
With Chedorlaomer the king of E...... Gen 14:9
Pathros, and from Cush, and from E... Is 11:11
Go up, O E...................................... Is 21:2
E bare the quiver with chariots .... Is 22:6
of Zimri, and all the kings of E......... Jer 25:25
E in the beginning of the reign......... Jer 49:34
Behold, I will break the bow of E..... Jer 49:35
upon E will I bring the four.............. Jer 49:36
the outcasts of E shall not come....... Jer 49:36
For I will cause E to be dismayed...... Jer 49:37
And I will set my throne in E............ Jer 49:38
bring again the captivity of E............ Jer 49:39
There is E and all her multitude........ Eze 32:24
which is in the province of E............. Dan 8:2
3. Son of Shashak.
And Hananiah, and E....................... 1Chr 8:24
4. A son of Meshelemiah.
E the fifth, Jehohanan the sixth........ 1Chr 26:3
5. A family of exiles with Zerubbabel.
The children of E, a thousand two..... Ezr 2:7
The children of E, a thousand two..... Neh 7:12
6. A family of exiles with Zerubbabel.
The children of the other E.............. Ezr 2:31
The children of the other E.............. Neh 7:34
7. A family of exiles with Ezra.
And of the sons of E....................... Ezr 8:7
8. An ancestor of Shechaniah.
of Jehiel, one of the sons of E.......... Ezr 10:2
And of the sons of E....................... Ezr 10:26
9. A chief who renewed the covenant.
Parosh, Pahath-moab, E, Zatthu...... Neh 10:14
10. A priest who purified the wall.
and Malchijah, and E...................... Neh 12:42

ELAMITES (e'-lam-ites) See PERSIANS. Foreign
settlers in Samaria.
the Dehavites, and the E.................. Ezr 4:9
Parthians, and Medes, and E............ Acts 2:9

ELASAH (el'-a-sah) See ELEASA.
1. Married a foreign wife.
Ishmael, Nethaneel, Jozabad, and E... Ezr 10:22
2. An ambassador of Hezekiah.
By the hand of E the son of .... Jer 29:3

ELATH (e'-lath) See ELOTH. An Elamite town.
the way of the plain from E............. Deut 2:8
He built E, and restored it to........... 2Kin 14:22
of Syria recovered E to Syria............ 2Kin 16:6
and drave the Jews from E............... 2Kin 16:6
and the Syrians came to E, and......... 2Kin 16:6

EL-BERITH See BERITH.

EL-BETH-EL
an altar, and called the place E......... Gen 35:7

ELDAD (el'-da-dah) A son of Midian.
Hanoch, and Abidah, and E.............. Gen 25:4
Epher, and Henoch, and Abida, and E... 1Chr 1:33

ELDAD (el'-dad) An elder and prophet with
Moses.
camp, the name of the one was E...... Num 11:26
man, and told Moses, and said, E...... Num 11:27

ELDER
the brother of Japheth the .... Gen 10:21
the e shall serve the younger............ Gen 25:23
these words of Esau her e son........... Gen 27:42
the name of the e was Leah.............. Gen 29:16
Behold my e daughter Merab, her..... 1Sa 18:17
for he is mine e brother.................... 1Kin 2:22
aged men, much e than thy father..... Job 15:10
because they were e than he............. Job 32:4
thine e sister is Samaria, she and...... Eze 16:46
receive thy sisters, thine e.............. Eze 16:61
names of them were Aholah the e..... Eze 23:4
Now his e son was in the field.......... Lk 15:25
The e shall serve the younger........... Rom 9:12
Rebuke not an e, but intreat him...... 1Ti 5:1
The e women as mothers.................. 1Ti 5:2
Against an e receive not an............... 1Ti 5:19
you I exhort, who am also an e.......... 1Pet 5:1
submit yourselves unto the e............ 1Pet 5:5
The e unto the elect lady and her...... 2Jn 1
The e unto the wellbeloved Gaius..... 3Jn 1

ELDERS
of Pharaoh, the e of his house........... Gen 50:7
all the e of the land of Egypt............ Gen 50:7
gather the e of Israel together.......... Ex 3:16
the e of Israel, unto the king of....... Ex 3:18
the e of the children of Israel........... Ex 4:29
called for all the e of Israel.............. Ex 12:21
take with thee of the e of Israel........ Ex 17:5
in the sight of the e of Israel............ Ex 17:6
all the e of Israel, to eat bread......... Ex 18:12
and called for the e of the people..... Ex 19:7
and seventy of the e of Israel........... Ex 24:1
and seventy of the e of Israel........... Ex 24:9
And he said unto the e, Tarry ye...... Ex 24:14
the e of the congregation shall......... Lev 4:15
and his sons, and the e of Israel....... Lev 9:1
the seventy men of the e of Israel..... Num 11:16
knewest to be the e of the people..... Num 11:16
men of the e of the people............... Num 11:24
and gave it unto the seventy e.......... Num 11:25
the camp, he and the e of Israel........ Num 16:25
the e of Israel followed him............. Num 16:25
And Moab said unto the e of Midian... Num 22:4
e of Moab and the e of Midian......... Num 22:7
heads of your tribes, and your e........ Deut 5:23
Then the e of his city shall send....... Deut 19:12
Then thy e and thy judges shall........ Deut 21:2
even the e of that city shall.............. Deut 21:3
the e of that city shall bring............. Deut 21:4
all the e of that city, that are............ Deut 21:6
him out unto the e of his city........... Deut 21:19
shall say unto the e of his city.......... Deut 21:20
the e of the city in the gate.............. Deut 22:15
father shall say unto the e............... Deut 22:16
cloth before the e of the city............ Deut 22:17
the e of that city shall take............... Deut 22:18
wife go up to the gate unto the e...... Deut 25:7
Then the e of his city shall call......... Deut 25:8
unto him in the presence of the e..... Deut 25:9
Moses with the e of Israel................ Deut 27:1
captains of your tribes, your e.......... Deut 29:10
Loro, and unto all the e of Israel....... Deut 31:9
unto me all the e of your tribes......... Deut 31:28
thy e, and they will tell thee............. Deut 32:7
the e of Israel, and put upon............ Josh 7:6
the e of Israel, before the .... Josh 8:10
And all Israel, and their e.................. Josh 8:33
Wherefore our e and all the............. Josh 9:11
in the ears of the e of that city........ Josh 20:4
for all Israel, and for their e............. Josh 23:2
and called for the e of Israel............. Josh 24:1, 31
all the days of the e that................. Josh 24:31
the e thereof, even threescore and... Judg 8:14
And he took the e of the city........... Judg 8:16
the e of Gilead went to fetch........... Judg 11:5
said unto the e of Gilead.................. Judg 11:7
the e of Gilead said unto.................. Judg 11:8
said unto the e of Gilead.................. Judg 11:9
the e of Gilead said unto.................. Judg 11:10
went with the e of Gilead................. Judg 11:11
Then the e of the congregation........ Judg 21:16
took ten men of the e of the city...... Ruth 4:2
before the e of my people................ Ruth 4:4
And Boaz said unto the e, and unto... Ruth 4:9
that were in the gate, and the e........ Ruth 4:11
the e of Israel said, Wherefore......... 1Sa 4:3
Then all the e of Israel gathered....... 1Sa 8:4
the e of Jabesh said unto him........... 1Sa 11:3
before the e of my people, and......... 1Sa 15:30
the e of the town trembled at his...... 1Sa 16:4
of the spoil unto the e of Judah........ 1Sa 30:26
with the e of Israel, saying, Ye......... 2Sa 3:17
So all the e of Israel came to........... 2Sa 5:3
the e of his house arose, and went.... 2Sa 12:17
well, and all the e of Israel............... 2Sa 17:4
Absalom, and the e of Israel............. 2Sa 17:15

saying, Speak unto the e of Judah..... 2Sa 19:11
Solomon assembled the e of Israel..... 1Kin 8:1
all the e of Israel came, and the........ 1Kin 8:3
called all the e of the people............ 1Kin 20:7
And all the e and all the people........ 1Kin 20:8
and sent the letters unto the e.......... 1Kin 21:8
the men of his city, even the e.......... 1Kin 21:11
his house, and the e sat with him...... 2Kin 6:32
came to him, he said to the e............ 2Kin 6:32
the rulers of Jezreel, to the e............ 2Kin 10:1
the e also, and the bringers up of..... 2Kin 10:5
the e of the priests, covered............. 2Kin 19:2
unto him all the e of Judah.............. 2Kin 23:1
Therefore came all the e of.............. 1Chr 11:3
the e of Israel, and the captains........ 1Chr 15:25
the e of Israel, who were clothed...... 1Chr 21:16
Solomon assembled the e of Israel..... 2Chr 5:2
And all the e of Israel came.............. 2Chr 5:4
together all the e of Judah............... 2Chr 34:29
God was upon the e of the Jews........ Ezr 5:5
Then asked we those e, and said....... Ezr 5:9
the e of the Jews build this............... Ezr 6:7
e of these Jews for the building......... Ezr 6:8
the e of the Jews builded, and.......... Ezr 6:14
counsel of the princes and the e........ Ezr 10:8
and with them the e of every city...... Ezr 10:14
him in the assembly of the .... Ps 107:32
sitteth among the e of the land......... Prov 31:23
the e of the priests covered with....... Is 37:2
up certain of the e of the land.......... Jer 26:17
of the e which were carried away...... Jer 29:1
mine e gave up the ghost in the........ Lam 1:19
The e of the daughter of Zion sit...... Lam 2:10
priests, they favoured not the e........ Lam 4:16
the faces of e were not honoured..... Lam 5:12
The e have ceased from the gate...... Lam 5:14
the e of Judah sat before me............ Eze 8:1
of the e of Israel unto me................ Eze 14:1
that certain of the e of Israel............ Eze 20:1
man, speak unto the e of Israel......... Eze 20:3
a solemn assembly, gather the e....... Joel 1:14
the congregation, assemble the e...... Joel 2:16
transgress the tradition of the e....... Mt 15:2
and suffer many things of the e........ Mt 16:21
the e of the people came unto him.... Mt 21:23
the e of the people, unto the............ Mt 26:3
chief priests and e of the people....... Mt 26:47
scribes and the e were assembled..... Mt 26:57
Now the chief priests, and e............. Mt 26:59
e of the people took counsel............ Mt 27:1
silver to the chief priests and e......... Mt 27:3
accused of the chief priests and........ Mt 27:12
e persuaded the multitude that......... Mt 27:20
him, with the scribes and e.............. Mt 27:41
they were assembled with the.......... Mt 28:12
holding the tradition of the e........... Mk 7:3
to the tradition of the e................... Mk 7:5
things, and be rejected of the e........ Mk 8:31
priests, and the scribes, and the e..... Mk 11:27
priest and the scribes and the e........ Mk 14:43
all the chief priests and the e........... Mk 14:53
held a consultation with the e.......... Mk 15:1
sent unto him the e of the Jews........ Lk 7:3
things, and be rejected of the e........ Lk 9:22
scribes came upon him with the e..... Lk 20:1
captains of the temple, and the e...... Lk 22:52
the e of the people and the chief...... Lk 22:66
morrow, that their rulers, and e........ Acts 4:5
of the people, and e of Israel........... Acts 4:8
priests and e had said unto them...... Acts 4:23
stirred up the people, and the e........ Acts 6:12
sent it to the e by the hands of........ Acts 11:30
ordained them e in every church...... Acts 14:23
apostles and e about this question.... Acts 15:2
church, and of the apostles and e..... Acts 15:4
e came together for to consider....... Acts 15:6
Then pleased it the apostles and e.... Acts 15:22
The apostles and e and brethren....... Acts 15:23
e which were at Jerusalem................ Acts 16:4
called the e of the church................ Acts 20:17
and all the e were present................ Acts 21:18
and all the estate of the e................ Acts 22:5
came to the chief priests and e......... Acts 23:14
high priest descended with the e...... Acts 24:1
the e of the Jews informed me......... Acts 25:15
Let the e that rule well be............... 1Ti 5:17
ordain e in every city, as I had......... Titus 1:5
For by it the e obtained a good........ Heb 11:2
him call for the e of the church........ Jas 5:14
The e which are among you I........... 1Pet 5:1
twenty e sitting, clothed in............. Rev 4:4
twenty e fall down before him......... Rev 4:10
one of the e saith unto me, Weep..... Rev 5:5
beasts, and in the midst of the e...... Rev 5:6
twenty e fell down before the.......... Rev 5:8
the throne and the beasts and the e... Rev 5:11
twenty e fell down and worshipped... Rev 5:14
about the throne, and about the e.... Rev 7:11
And one of the e answered, saying.... Rev 7:13
And the four and twenty e, which..... Rev 11:16
before the four beasts, and the .... Rev 14:3
And the four and twenty e and the... Rev 19:4

ELDEST
unto his e servant of his house......... Gen 24:2
not see, he called Esau his e son........ Gen 27:1
goodly raiment of her e son Esau...... Gen 27:15
And he searched, and began at the e... Gen 44:12
of Reuben, Israel's e son.................. Num 1:20
Reuben, the e son of Israel............... Num 26:5
the three sons of Jesse went and....... 1Sa 17:13

the three *e* followed Saul.............. 1Sa 17:14
Eliab his *e* brother heard when he..... 1Sa 17:28
Then he took his *e* son that............. 2Kin 3:27
to the camp had slain all the *e*........ 2Chr 22:1
wine in their *e* brother's house......... Job 1:13
wine in their *e* brother's house......... Job 1:18
one by one, beginning at the *e*......... Jn 8:9

ELEAD (*e'-le-ad*) A descendant of Ephraim.
  Shuthelah his son, and Ezer, and E... 1Chr 7:21

ELEADAH See ELADAH.

ELEALEH (*el-e-a'-leh*) An Amorite village.
  and Nimrah, and Heshbon, and E....... Num 32:3
  of Reuben built Heshbon, and E....... Num 32:37
  And Heshbon shall cry, and E........... Is 15:4
  with my tears, O Heshbon, and E....... Is 16:9
  the cry of Heshbon even unto E....... Jer 48:34

ELEASAH (*ele-'-a-sah*) See ELASAH.
  1. A son of Helez.
  begat Helez, and Helez begat E........ 1Chr 2:39
  E begat Sisamai, and Sisamai begat ... 1Chr 2:40
  2. A descendant of King Saul.
  his son, E his son, Azel his son........ 1Chr 8:37
  his son, E his son, Azel his son........ 1Chr 9:43

ELEAZAR (*ele-a'-zar*)
  1. A son of Aaron.
  she bare him Nadab, and Abihu, E...... Ex 6:23
  E Aaron's son took him one of the...... Ex 6:25
  even Aaron, Nadab and Abihu, E....... Ex 28:1
  Moses said unto Aaron, and unto E.... Lev 10:6
  Moses spake unto Aaron, and unto E.. Lev 10:12
  and he was angry with E................... Lev 10:16
  Nadab the firstborn, and Abihu, E..... Num 3:2
  and E and Ithamar ministered in the .. Num 3:4
  E the son of Aaron the priest........... Num 3:32
  to the office of E the son of............ Num 4:16
  Speak unto E the son of Aaron the.... Num 16:37
  E the priest took the brasen............ Num 16:39
  shall give her unto E the priest......... Num 19:3
  E the priest shall take of her........... Num 19:4
  E his son, and bring them up unto...... Num 20:25
  and put them upon E his son............ Num 20:26
  and put them upon E his son............ Num 20:28
  E came down from the mount........... Num 20:28
  And when Phinehas, the son of E...... Num 25:7
  Phinehas, the son of E, the son........ Num 25:11
  unto E the son of Aaron the............ Num 26:1
  E the priest spake with them in........ Num 26:3
  was born Nadab, and Abihu, E......... Num 26:60
  E the priest, who numbered the........ Num 26:63
  before E the priest, and before........ Num 27:2
  And set him before E the priest........ Num 27:19
  shall stand before E the priest......... Num 27:21
  and set him before E the priest......... Num 27:22
  Phinehas the son of E the priest....... Num 31:6
  E the priest, and unto the.............. Num 31:12
  E the priest, and all the princes....... Num 31:13
  E the priest said unto the men of...... Num 31:21
  E the priest, and the chief............. Num 31:26
  and give it unto E the priest........... Num 31:29
  E the priest did as the LORD........... Num 31:31
  unto E the priest, as the LORD........ Num 31:41
  E the priest took the gold of........... Num 31:51
  E the priest took the gold of........... Num 31:54
  to E the priest, and unto the.......... Num 32:2
  Moses commanded E the............... Num 32:28
  E the priest, and Joshua the son...... Num 34:17
  E his son ministered in the............. Num 20:28
  which E the priest, and Joshua the ... Josh 14:1
  came near before E the priest......... Josh 17:4
  which E the priest, and Joshua the ... Josh 19:51
  of the Levites unto E the priest........ Josh 21:1
  Phinehas the son of E the priest....... Josh 22:13
  Phinehas the son of E the priest....... Josh 22:31
  Phinehas the son of E the priest....... Josh 22:32
  And E the son of Aaron died........... Josh 24:33
  and Phinehas, the son of E............. Judg 20:28
  Nadab, and Abihu, E, and Ithamar ... 1Chr 6:3
  E begat Phinehas, Phinehas begat 1Chr 6:4
  E his son, Phinehas his son............. 1Chr 6:50
  Phinehas the son of E was the......... 1Chr 9:20
  Nadab, and Abihu, E, and Ithamar ... 1Chr 24:1
  therefore E and Ithamar executed...... 1Chr 24:2
  them, both Zadok of the sons of E.... 1Chr 24:3
  of E than of the sons of Ithamar....... 1Chr 24:4
  Among the sons of E there were....... 1Chr 24:4
  of God, were of the sons of E......... 1Chr 24:5
  household being taken for E........... 1Chr 24:6
  the son of Phinehas, the son of E..... Ezr 7:5
  2. Son of Abinadab.
  sanctified E his son to keep the....... 1Sa 7:1
  3. Son of Dodo.
  after him was E the son of Dodo...... 2Sa 23:9
  after him was E the son of Dodo...... 1Chr 11:12
  4. Son of Mahli.
  The sons of Mahli; E, and Kish........ 1Chr 23:21
  E died, and had no sons, but........... 1Chr 23:22
  Of Mahli came E, who had no sons... 1Chr 24:28
  5. Son of Phinehas.
  with him was E the son of............. Ezr 8:33
  6. Married a foreign wife.
  and Malchiah, and Miamin, and E..... Ezr 10:25
  7. A priest in Nehemiah's time.
  And Maaseiah, and Shemaiah, and E. Neh 12:42
  8. Son of Eliud; ancestor of Jesus.
  And Eliud begat E......................... Mt 1:15
  and E begat Matthan..................... Mt 1:15

ELECT
  mine *e*, in whom my soul............... Is 42:1
  servant's sake, and Israel mine *e*..... Is 45:4
  mine *e* shall inherit it, and my......... Is 65:9
  mine *e* shall long enjoy the work...... Is 65:22
  they shall deceive the very *e*.......... Mt 24:24
  his *e* from the four winds............... Mt 24:31
  if it were possible, even the *e*......... Mk 13:22
  his *e* from the four winds............... Mk 13:27
  And shall not God avenge his own *e* ... Lk 18:7
  thing to the charge of God's *e*........ Rom 8:33
  Put on therefore, as the *e* of God.... Col 3:12
  the *e* angels, that thou observe....... 1Ti 5:21
  according to the faith of God's *e*..... Titus 1:1
  E according to the foreknowledge..... 1Pet 1:2
  in Sion a chief corner stone, *e*........ 1Pet 2:6
  The elder unto the *e*................... 2Jn 1
  of thy *e* sister greet thee.............. 2Jn 13

ELECTED
  e together with you, saluteth you..... 1Pet 5:13

ELECTION
  of God according to *e* might stand.... Rom 9:11
  according to the *e* of grace........... Rom 11:5
  but the *e* hath obtained it, and....... Rom 11:7
  but as touching the *e*, they are....... Rom 11:28
  brethren beloved, your *e* of God..... 1Th 1:4
  to make your calling and *e* sure...... 2Pet 1:10

ELECT'S
  but for the *e* sake those days......... Mt 24:22
  but for the *e* sake, whom he hath.... Mk 13:20
  endure all things for the *e* sakes..... 2Ti 2:10

EL-ELOHE-ISRAEL (*el-el-o'-he-iz'-rah-el*) An
altar of Jacob near Shechem.
  there an altar, and called it E.......... Gen 33:20

ELEMENTS
  bondage under the *e* of the world.... Gal 4:3
  again to the weak and beggarly *e*..... Gal 4:9
  the *e* shall melt with fervent......... 2Pet 3:10
  the *e* shall melt with fervent......... 2Pet 3:12

ELEPH (*e'-lef*) A town in Benjamin.
  And Zelah, E, and Jebusi, which is..... Josh 18:28

ELEVEN
  his *e* sons, and passed over the...... Gen 32:22
  made *e* stars obeisance to me........ Gen 37:9
  e curtains shalt thou make........... Ex 26:7
  the curtains shall be all of.............. Ex 26:8
  e curtains he made..................... Ex 36:14
  the curtains were of one size.......... Ex 36:15
  And on the third day *e* bullocks...... Num 29:20
  (There are *e* days' journey from...... Deut 1:2
  e cities with their villages............. Josh 15:51
  of us *e* hundred pieces of silver...... Judg 16:5
  The *e* hundred shekels of silver...... Judg 17:2
  when he had restored the *e*.......... Judg 17:3
  he reigned *e* years in Jerusalem...... 2Kin 23:36
  he reigned *e* years in Jerusalem...... 2Kin 24:18
  reigned *e* years in Jerusalem......... 2Chr 36:5
  reigned *e* years in Jerusalem......... 2Chr 36:11
  he reigned *e* years in Jerusalem...... Jer 52:1
  cubits, and the breadth *e* cubits..... Eze 40:49
  Then the *e* disciples went away...... Mt 28:16
  unto the *e* as they sat at meat...... Mk 16:14
  told all these things unto the *e*....... Lk 24:9
  found the *e* gathered together, and.. Lk 24:33
  was numbered with the *e* apostles... Acts 1:26
  But Peter, standing up with the *e*.... Acts 2:14

ELEVENTH
  On the *e* day Pagiel the son of........ Num 7:72
  the fortieth year, in the *e* month..... Deut 1:3
  And in the *e* year, in the month....... 1Kin 6:38
  in the *e* year of Joram the son of..... 2Kin 9:29
  unto the *e* year of king Zedekiah..... 2Kin 25:2
  the tenth, Machbanai the *e*........... 1Chr 12:13
  The *e* to Eliashib, the twelfth to..... 1Chr 24:12
  The *e* to Azareel, he, his sons....... 1Chr 25:18
  The *e* captain for the *e*.............. 1Chr 27:14
  unto the end of the *e* year of......... Jer 1:3
  in the *e* year of Zedekiah, in the..... Jer 39:2
  unto the *e* year of king Zedekiah..... Jer 52:5
  And it came to pass in the *e* year.... Eze 26:1
  And it came to pass in the *e* year.... Eze 30:20
  And it came to pass in the *e* year.... Eze 31:1
  and twentieth day of the *e* month.... Zec 1:7
  about the *e* hour he went out, and... Mt 20:6
  that were hired about the *e* hour..... Mt 20:9
  the *e*, a jacinth......................... Rev 21:20

ELHANAN (*el-ha'-nan*)
  1. Son of Jair.
  where E the son of Jaare-oregim,..... 2Sa 21:19
  E the son of Jair slew Lahmi the....... 1Chr 20:5
  2. One of David's mighty men.
  E the son of Dodo of Beth-lehem,.... 2Sa 23:24
  E the son of Dodo of Beth-lehem,.... 1Chr 11:26

ELI (*e'-li*) See ELI'S, ELOI.
  1. A High Priest of Israel.
  And the twin sons of E Hophni and.... 1Sa 1:3
  Now E the priest sat upon a seat...... 1Sa 1:9
  the LORD, that E marked her mouth... 1Sa 1:12
  therefore E thought she had been..... 1Sa 1:13
  E said unto her, How long wilt........ 1Sa 1:14
  Then E answered and said, Go in...... 1Sa 1:17
  and brought the child to E............. 1Sa 1:25
  unto the LORD before E the priest.... 1Sa 2:11
  Now the sons of E were sons of....... 1Sa 2:12
  E blessed Elkanah and his wife, and... 1Sa 2:20

Now E was very old, and heard all ... 1Sa 2:22
And there came a man of God unto E.. 1Sa 2:27
ministered unto the LORD before E 1Sa 3:1
when E was laid down in his place...... 1Sa 3:2
And he ran unto E, and said, Here...... 1Sa 3:5
And Samuel arose and went to E........ 1Sa 3:6
And he arose and went to E, and said .. 1Sa 3:8
E perceived that the LORD had......... 1Sa 3:8
Therefore E said unto Samuel, Go,..... 1Sa 3:9
E all things which I have spoken........ 1Sa 3:12
I have sworn unto the house of E...... 1Sa 3:14
feared to shew E the vision............. 1Sa 3:15
Then E called Samuel, and said,........ 1Sa 3:16
and the two sons of E, Hophni and..... 1Sa 4:4
and the two sons of E, Hophni and..... 1Sa 4:11
E sat upon a seat by the wayside...... 1Sa 4:13
when E heard the noise of the.......... 1Sa 4:14
man came in hastily, and told E......... 1Sa 4:14
Now E was ninety and eight years..... 1Sa 4:15
And the man said unto E, I am he...... 1Sa 4:16
the son of Phinehas, the son of E....... 1Sa 14:3
the house of E in Shiloh.................. 1Kin 2:27
2. An Aramaic term for God.
with a loud voice, saying, Eli, E......... Mt 27:46

ELIAB (*e'-le-ab*) See ELIAB'S, ELIEL.
  1. Son of Helon.
  E the son of Helon......................... Num 1:9
  E the son of Helon shall be............. Num 2:7
  the third day E the son of Helon....... Num 7:24
  offering of E the son of Helon.......... Num 7:29
  of Zebulun was E the son of Helon.... Num 10:16
  2. Father of Dathan.
  Dathan and Abiram, the sons of E..... Num 16:1
  Dathan and Abiram, the sons of E..... Num 16:12
  the sons of Pallu; E....................... Num 26:8
  And the sons of E......................... Num 26:9
  Dathan and Abiram, the sons of E..... Deut 11:6
  3. A son of Jesse.
  were come, that he looked on E....... 1Sa 16:6
  the battle were E the first born........ 1Sa 17:13
  E his eldest brother heard when....... 1Sa 17:28
  And Jesse begat his firstborn E......... 1Chr 2:13
  daughter of E the son of Jesse......... 2Chr 11:18
  4. A Levite ancestor of Samuel.
  E his son, Jeroham his son.............. 1Chr 6:27
  5. A leader in David's army.
  Obadiah the second, E the third,....... 1Chr 12:9
  6. A Levite in David's time.
  and Jehiel, and Unni, E, and........... 1Chr 15:18
  and Jehiel, and Unni, and E............ 1Chr 15:20
  and Jehiel, and Mattithiah, and E...... 1Chr 16:5

ELIAB'S (*e'-le-abs*)
  E anger was kindled against David...... 1Sa 17:28

ELIADA (*e-li'-a-dah*) See ELIADAH.
  1. A son of David.
  And Elishama, and E, and Eliphalet.... 2Sa 5:16
  And Elishama, and E, and Eliphelet,... 1Chr 3:8
  E a mighty man of valour, and with ... 2Chr 17:17

ELIADAH (*e-li'-a-dah*) See ELIADA. An
opponent of King David.
  adversary, Rezon the son of E.......... 1Kin 11:23

ELIAH (*e-li'-ah*) See ELIJAH. A son of Jeroham.
  And Jaresiah, and E, and Zichri, the... 1Chr 8:27
  and Abdi, and Jeremoth, and E......... Ezr 10:26

ELIAHBA (*e-li'-ah-bah*) A 'mighty man' of
David.
  the Shaalbonite, of the sons of......... 2Sa 23:32
  Baharumite, E the Shaalbonite,......... 1Chr 11:33

ELIAKIM (*e-li'-a-kim*) See JEHOIAKIM.
  1. A son of Hilkiah.
  out to them E the son of Hilkiah....... 2Kin 18:18
  Then said E the son of Hilkiah......... 2Kin 18:26
  Then came E the son of Hilkiah,....... 2Kin 18:37
  And he sent E, which was over the 2Kin 19:2
  my servant E the son of Hilkiah........ Is 22:20
  Then came forth unto him E............ Is 36:3
  Then said E and Shebna and Joah..... Is 36:11
  Then came E, the son of Hilkiah,...... Is 36:22
  And he sent E, who was over the ...... Is 37:2
  2. Original name of Jehoiakim.
  Pharaoh-nechoh made E the son of ... 2Kin 23:34
  the king of Egypt made E his.......... 2Chr 36:4
  3. A priest who dedicated the wall.
  E, Maaseiah, Miniamin, Michaiah,...... Neh 12:41
  4. Son of Abiud; ancestor of Jesus.
  and Abiud begat E........................ Mt 1:13
  and E begat Azor......................... Mt 1:13
  of Jonan, which was the son of E...... Lk 3:30

ELIAM (*e'-le-am*)
  1. Father of Bathsheba.
  Bath-sheba, the daughter of E.......... 2Sa 11:3
  2. A mighty man of David.
  E the son of Ahithophel the............ 2Sa 23:34

ELIAS (*e-li'-as*) See ELIJAH. Greek form of
Elijah.
  if ye will receive it, this is E........... Mt 11:14
  some, E; and others, Jeremias......... Mt 16:14
  then Moses and E talking with him.... Mt 17:3
  and one for Moses, and one for E...... Mt 17:4
  scribes that E must first come......... Mt 17:10
  E truly shall first come.................. Mt 17:11
  That E is come already, and they...... Mt 17:12
  said, This man calleth for E............ Mt 27:47
  let us see whether E will come to..... Mt 27:49

Others said, That it is E............................. Mk 6:15
but some say, E... Mk 8:28
appeared unto them E with Moses............ Mk 9:4
and one for Moses, and one for E............ Mk 9:5
scribes that E must first come.................. Mk 9:11
E verily cometh first, and........................ Mk 9:12
That E is indeed come, and they............. Mk 9:13
it said, Behold, he calleth E..................... Mk 15:35
let us see whether E will come to............ Mk 15:36
him in the spirit and power of E.............. Lk 1:17
were in Israel in the days of E.................. Lk 4:25
But unto none of them was E sent........... Lk 4:26
And of some, that E had appeared........... Lk 9:8
but some say E... Lk 9:19
two men, which were Moses and E.......... Lk 9:30
and one for Moses, and one for E............ Lk 9:33
and consume them, even as E did............ Lk 9:54
Art thou E?... Jn 1:21
if thou be not that Christ, nor E............... Jn 1:25
not what the scripture saith of E.............. Rom 11:2
E was a man subject to like..................... Jas 5:17

ELIASAPH (e-li'-a-saf)
   1. A chief of Gad.
E the son of Deuel................................... Num 1:14
Gad shall be E the son of Reuel.............. Num 2:14
the sixth day E the son of Deuel.............. Num 7:42
offering of E the son of Deuel.................. Num 7:47
of Gad was E the son of Deuel................. Num 10:20
   2. A Gershonite leader.
shall be E the son of Lael....................... Num 3:24

ELIASHIB (e-li'-a-shib)
   1. A descendant of Judah.
of Elioenai were, Hodaiah, and E............ 1Chr 3:24
   2. A priest in David's time.
The eleventh to E, the twelfth to.............. 1Chr 24:12
   3. Son of Joiakim.
chamber of Johanan the son of E............. Ezr 10:6
Joiakim, Joiakim also begat E.................. Neh 12:10
and E begat Jaiada.................................. Neh 12:10
The Levites in the days of E..................... Neh 12:22
the days of Johanan the son of E.............. Neh 12:23
   4. Married a foreign wife.
E.. Ezr 10:24
   5. Son of Zotta.
Elioenai, E, Mattaniah, and..................... Ezr 10:27
   6. Son of Bani.
Vaniah, Meremoth, E................................ Ezr 10:36
   7. High Priest during Nehemiah's time.
Then E the high priest rose up................. Neh 3:1
of the house of E the high priest.............. Neh 3:20
from the door of the house of E............... Neh 3:21
even to the end of the house of E............ Neh 3:21
this, E the priest, having the.................... Neh 13:4
of the evil that E did for Tobiah............... Neh 13:7
the son of E the high priest, was............. Neh 13:28

ELIATHAH (e-li'-a-thah) *A son of Heman.*
and Jerimoth, Hananiah, Hanani, E......... 1Chr 25:4
The twentieth to E, he, his sons,............. 1Chr 25:27

ELIDAD (e-li'-dad) *Son of Chislon.*
of Benjamin, E the son of Chislon......... Num 34:21

ELIEHOENAI See Elihoenai.

ELIEL (e-li'-el) *See Eliah.*
   1. Head of the house of Manasseh.
even Epher, and Ishi, and E..................... 1Chr 5:24
   2. Son of Jeroham.
the son of Jeroham, the son of E.............. 1Chr 6:34
   3. A son of Shashak.
And Elienai, and Zilthai, and E................ 1Chr 8:20
   4. A son of Shashak.
And Ishpan, and Heber, and E................. 1Chr 8:22
   5. A captain in David's army.
E the Mahavite, and Jeribai, and............ 1Chr 11:46
   6. A 'mighty man' of David.
E, and Obed, and Jasiel the..................... 1Chr 11:47
   7. A Gadite ally of David.
Attai the sixth, E the seventh,.................. 1Chr 12:11
   8. A chief of Judah.
E the chief, and his brethren.................... 1Chr 15:9
   9. A chief Levite.
Asaiah, and Joel, Shemaiah, and E......... 1Chr 15:11
   10. A Levite in Hezekiah's time.
and Jerimoth, and Jozabad, and E.......... 2Chr 31:13

ELIENAI (e-li-e'-nahee) *A son of Shimhi.*
And E, and Zilthai, and Eliel,.................. 1Chr 8:20

ELIEZER
of my house is this E of Damascus.......... Gen 15:2
And the name of the other was E.............. Ex 18:4
Zemira, and Joash, and E, and................ 1Chr 7:8
and Zechariah, and Benaiah, and E........ 1Chr 15:24
sons of Moses were, Gershom, and E....... 1Chr 23:15
And the sons of E were, Rehabiah........... 1Chr 23:17
And E had none other sons...................... 1Chr 23:17
And his brethren by E............................... 1Chr 26:25
was E the son of Zichri............................. 1Chr 27:16
Then E the son of Dodavah of................. 2Chr 20:37
Then sent I for E, for Ariel, for................ Ezr 8:16
Maaseiah, and E, and Jarib, and............. Ezr 10:18
Kelita,) Pethahiah, Judah, and E............ Ezr 10:23
E, Ishjiah, Malchiah, Shemaiah,.............. Ezr 10:31
of Jose, which was the son of E.............. Lk 3:29

ELIHOENAI (e-li-ho-e'-nahee) *See Elioenai. A family of exiles.*
E the son of Zerahiah, and with.............. Ezr 8:4

ELIHOREPH (e-li-ho'-ref) *A scribe of Solomon.*
and Ahiah, the sons of Shisha,................ 1Kin 4:3

ELIHU (e-li'-hew)
   1. Great-grandfather of Samuel.
the son of Jeroham, the son of E.............. 1Sa 1:1
   2. A soldier of David.
and Michael, and Jozabad, and E.......... 1Chr 12:20
   3. A Tabernacle servant.
whose brethren were strong men, E........ 1Chr 26:7
   4. Brother of David.
Of Judah, E, one of the brethren.............. 1Chr 27:18
   5. A friend of Job.
Then was kindled the wrath of E.............. Job 32:2
Now E had waited till Job had.................. Job 32:4
When E saw that there was no.................. Job 32:5
E the son of Barachel the Buzite.............. Job 32:6
Furthermore E answered and said,......... Job 34:1
E spake moreover, and said,.................... Job 35:1
E also proceeded, and said,..................... Job 36:1

ELIJAH (e-li'-jah) *See Eliah, Elias.*
   1. The prophet.
E the Tishbite, who was of the................. 1Kin 17:1
E said unto her, Fear not.......................... 1Kin 17:13
did according to the saying of E.............. 1Kin 17:15
of the Lord, which he spake by E............. 1Kin 17:16
And she said unto E, What have I........... 1Kin 17:18
E said unto her, Give me thy.................... 1Kin 17:19
And the Lord heard the voice of E........... 1Kin 17:22
E took the child, and brought him........... 1Kin 17:23
E said, See, thy son liveth........................ 1Kin 17:23
And the woman said to E, Now by............ 1Kin 17:24
Lord came to E in the third year.............. 1Kin 18:1
E went to shew himself unto Ahab.......... 1Kin 18:2
was in the way, behold, E met him.......... 1Kin 18:7
and said, Art thou thou my lord E............ 1Kin 18:7
tell thy lord, Behold, E is here.................. 1Kin 18:8
tell thy lord, Behold, E is here.................. 1Kin 18:11
tell thy lord, Behold, E is here.................. 1Kin 18:14
E said, As the Lord of hosts.................... 1Kin 18:15
and Ahab went to meet E......................... 1Kin 18:16
it came to pass, when Ahab saw E........... 1Kin 18:17
E came unto all the people, and.............. 1Kin 18:21
Then said E unto the people, I................. 1Kin 18:22
E said unto the prophets of Baal............. 1Kin 18:25
that E mocked them, and said, Cry.......... 1Kin 18:27
E said unto all the people, Come............. 1Kin 18:30
E took twelve stones, according.............. 1Kin 18:31
that E the prophet came near, and.......... 1Kin 18:36
E said unto them, Take the...................... 1Kin 18:40
E brought them down to the brook........... 1Kin 18:40
E said unto Ahab, Get thee up,................ 1Kin 18:41
E went up to the top of Carmel................ 1Kin 18:42
And the hand of the Lord was on E.......... 1Kin 18:46
told Jezebel all that E had done.............. 1Kin 19:1
Jezebel sent a messenger unto E............ 1Kin 19:2
unto him, What doest thou here, E........... 1Kin 19:9
when E heard it, that he wrapped........... 1Kin 19:13
and said, What doest thou here, E........... 1Kin 19:13
E passed by him, and cast his.................. 1Kin 19:19
he left the oxen, and ran after E.............. 1Kin 19:20
Then he arose, and went after E.............. 1Kin 19:21
the Lord came to E the Tishbite.............. 1Kin 21:17
And Ahab said to E, Hast thou................. 1Kin 21:20
the Lord came to E the Tishbite.............. 2Kin 1:3
E departed... 2Kin 1:4
And he said, It is E the Tishbite.............. 2Kin 1:8
E answered and said to the captain........ 2Kin 1:10
E answered and said unto them, If.......... 2Kin 1:12
and fell on his knees before E.................. 2Kin 1:13
the angel of the Lord said unto E............ 2Kin 1:15
of the Lord which E had spoken.............. 2Kin 1:17
up E into heaven by a whirlwind.............. 2Kin 2:1
that E went with Elisha from.................... 2Kin 2:1
E said unto Elisha, Tarry here,................ 2Kin 2:2
E said unto him, Elisha, tarry................... 2Kin 2:4
E said unto him, Tarry, I pray.................. 2Kin 2:6
E took his mantle, and wrapped it........... 2Kin 2:8
that E said unto Elisha, Ask what............ 2Kin 2:9
E went up by a whirlwind into.................. 2Kin 2:11
mantle of E that fell from him.................. 2Kin 2:13
mantle of E that fell from him.................. 2Kin 2:14
said, Where is the Lord God of E............. 2Kin 2:14
The spirit of E doth rest on....................... 2Kin 2:15
poured water on the hands of E............... 2Kin 3:11
by his servant E the Tishbite.................... 2Kin 9:36
which he spake by his servant E.............. 2Kin 10:10
of the Lord, which he spake to E............. 2Kin 10:17
writing to him from E the prophet............ 2Chr 21:12
I will send you E the prophet................... Mal 4:5
   2. Married a foreign wife.
Maaseiah, and E, and Shemaiah, and..... Ezr 10:21

ELIKA (e-li'-kah) *A guard of David.*
the Harodite, E the Harodite,................... 2Sa 23:25

ELIM (e-lim) *See Beer-elim. An encampment during the Exodus.*
And they came to E, where were.............. Ex 15:27
And they took their journey from E.......... Ex 16:1
of Sin, which is between E....................... Ex 16:1
from Marah, and came unto E.................. Num 33:9
in E were twelve fountains of................... Num 33:9
And they removed from E, and................. Num 33:10

ELIMELECH (e-lim'-e-lek) *See Elimelech's. Husband of Naomi.*
And the name of the man was E.............. Ruth 1:2
And E Naomi's husband died................... Ruth 1:3
man of wealth, of the family of E............ Ruth 2:1
Boaz, who was of the kindred of E.......... Ruth 2:3

ELIMELECH'S
of land, which was our brother E............. Ruth 4:3
that I have bought all that was E............. Ruth 4:9

ELIOENAI (e-li-o-e'-nahee) *See Elihoenai.*
   1. A son of Neariah.
E, and Hezekiah, and Azrikam, three..... 1Chr 3:23
And the sons of E were, Hodaiah,........... 1Chr 3:24
   2. A Simeonite prince.
And E, and Jaakobah............................... 1Chr 4:36
   3. A son of Becher.
and Joash, and Eliezer, and E................. 1Chr 7:8
   4. A Temple servant.
the sixth, E the seventh........................... 1Chr 26:3
   5. Married a foreign wife.
E, Maaseiah, Ishmael, Nethaneel,........... Ezr 10:22
   6. A son of Zattu.
E, Eliashib, Mattaniah, and..................... Ezr 10:27
   7. A priest during Nehemiah's time.
Maaseiah, Miniamin, Michaiah, E........... Neh 12:41

ELIPHAL (el'-i-fal) *A captain in David's army.*
the Hararite, E the son of Ur,................... 1Chr 11:35

ELIPHALET (e-lif'-a-let) *See Eliphelet.*
   Elpalet. *A son of David.*
And Elishama, and Eliada, and E............ 2Sa 5:16
And Elishama, and Beeliada, and E........ 1Chr 14:7

ELIPHAZ (el'-if-az)
   1. A son of Esau.
And Adah bare to Esau E........................ Gen 36:4
E the son of Adah the wife of.................. Gen 36:10
And the sons of E were Teman,............... Gen 36:11
was concubine to E Esau's son............... Gen 36:12
and she bare to E Amalek....................... Gen 36:12
the sons of E the firstborn son................ Gen 36:15
came of E in the land of Edom................ Gen 36:16
E, Reuel, and Jeush, and Jaalam, and.... 1Chr 1:35
The sons of E; Teman, and...................... 1Chr 1:36
   2. A friend of Job.
E the Temanite, and Bildad the.............. Job 2:11
Then E the Temanite answered and........ Job 4:1
Then answered E the Temanite................ Job 15:1
Then E the Temanite answered and........ Job 22:1
the Lord said to E the Temanite.............. Job 42:7
So E the Temanite and Bildad the.......... Job 42:9

ELIPHELEH (e-lif'-e-leh) *A Levite singer.*
and Mattithiah, and E.............................. 1Chr 15:18
and E, and Mikneiah,............................... 1Chr 15:21

ELIPHELEHU See Elipheleh.

ELIPHELET (e-lif'-e-let) *See Eliphalet.*
   1. A 'mighty man' of David.
E the son of Ahasbai, the son of............. 2Sa 23:34
   2. A son of David.
Ibhar also, and Elishama, and E............. 1Chr 3:6
   3. Same as Eliphat.
And Elishama, and Eliada, and E............ 1Chr 3:8
   4. A descendant of King Saul.
Jehush the second, and E the third......... 1Chr 8:39
   5. A family of exiles.
whose names are these, E........................ Ezr 8:13
   6. A son of Hashum.
Mattenai, Mattathah, Zabad, E................ Ezr 10:33

ELIS (e-'lize) *Refers to Eli 1.*
that the iniquity of E house..................... 1Sa 3:14

ELISABETH (e-liz'-a-beth) *See Elisabeth's. Mother of John the Baptist.*
of Aaron, and her name was E.................. Lk 1:5
child, because that E was barren.............. Lk 1:7
thy wife E shall bear thee a son,............. Lk 1:13
those days his wife E conceived.............. Lk 1:24
And, behold, thy cousin E, she............... Lk 1:36
house of Zacharias, and saluted E.......... Lk 1:40
when E heard the salutation of................. Lk 1:41
E was filled with the Holy Ghost............. Lk 1:41

ELISABETH'S (e-liz'-a-beths)
Now E full time came that she................. Lk 1:57

ELISEUS (el-i-se'-us) *See Elisha. Greek form of Elisha.*
in the time of E the prophet..................... Lk 4:27

ELISHA (e-li'-shah) *See Eliseus. A prophet.*
and E the son of Shaphat of.................... 1Kin 19:16
the sword of Jehu shall E slay................. 1Kin 19:17
found E the son of Shaphat, who............ 1Kin 19:19
Elijah went with E from Gilgal................ 2Kin 2:1
And Elijah said unto E, Tarry here.......... 2Kin 2:2
E said unto him, As the Lord................... 2Kin 2:2
were at Beth-el came forth to E............... 2Kin 2:3
And Elijah said unto him, E.................... 2Kin 2:4
that were at Jericho came to E................. 2Kin 2:5
over, that Elijah said unto E.................... 2Kin 2:9
E said, I pray thee, let a double.............. 2Kin 2:9
E saw it, and he cried, My father,........... 2Kin 2:12
and thither: and E went over.................... 2Kin 2:14
spirit of Elijah doth rest on E.................. 2Kin 2:15
the men of the city said unto E................ 2Kin 2:19
to the saying of E which he spake........... 2Kin 2:22
Here is E the son of Shaphat,.................. 2Kin 3:11
E said unto the king of Israel,................. 2Kin 3:13
E said, As the Lord of hosts.................... 2Kin 3:14
the sons of the prophets unto E............... 2Kin 4:1
E said unto her, What shall I do............. 2Kin 4:2
that it passed to Shunem, where............. 2Kin 4:8
season that E had said unto her.............. 2Kin 4:17
and came into the house,........................ 2Kin 4:32
And E came again to Gilgal.................... 2Kin 4:38
when E the man of God had heard.......... 2Kin 5:8

at the door of the house of *E* 2Kin 5:9
E sent a messenger unto him, ... 2Kin 5:10
the servant of the man of God 2Kin 5:20
E said unto him, Whence comest 2Kin 5:25
sons of the prophets said unto *E* 2Kin 6:1
but *E*, the prophet that is in 2Kin 6:12
I prayed, and said, LORD, I pray 2Kin 6:17
and chariots of fire round about *E* 2Kin 6:17
E prayed unto the LORD, and said, ... 2Kin 6:18
according to the word of *E* 2Kin 6:18
E said unto them, This is not the 2Kin 6:19
come into Samaria, that *E* said 2Kin 6:20
And the king of Israel said unto *E*, ... 2Kin 6:21
if the head of *E* the son of 2Kin 6:31
But *E* sat in his house, and the 2Kin 6:32
Then *E* said, Hear ye the word of 2Kin 7:1
Then spake *E* unto the woman, ... 2Kin 8:1
the great things that *E* hath done 2Kin 8:4
her son, whom *E* restored to life 2Kin 8:5
And *E* came to Damascus 2Kin 8:7
E said unto him, Go, say unto him 2Kin 8:10
E answered, The LORD hath shewed ... 2Kin 8:13
So he departed from *E*, and came to ... 2Kin 8:14
said to him, What said *E* to thee 2Kin 8:14
E the prophet called one of the 2Kin 9:1
Now *E* was fallen sick of his 2Kin 13:14
E said unto him, Take bow and 2Kin 13:15
E put his hands upon the king's 2Kin 13:16
Then *E* said, Shoot 2Kin 13:17
E died, and they buried him. 2Kin 13:20
the man into the sepulchre of *E* 2Kin 13:21
down, and touched the bones of *E*. 2Kin 13:21

ELISHAH (e-li'-shah) *A son of Javan.*
E, and Tarshish, Kittim, and .... Gen 10:4
E, and Tarshish, Kittim, and 1Chr 1:7
purple from the isles of *E* was .... Eze 27:7

ELISHAMA (e-lish'-a-mah) *See* ELISHUA.
  1. Grandfather of Joshua.
E the son of Ammihud .... Num 1:10
shall be *E* the son of Ammihud .... Num 2:18
seventh day *E* the son of Ammihud ..... Num 7:48
offering of *E* the son of Ammihud .... Num 7:53
over his host was *E* the son of .... Num 10:22
son, Ammihud his son, *E* his son, ... 1Chr 7:26
  2. A son of David.
E, and Eliada, and Eliphalet 2Sa 5:16
Ibhar also, and *E*, and Eliphelet, ... 1Chr 3:6
And *E*, and Eliada, and Eliphelet, ... 1Chr 3:8
And *E*, and Beeliada, and Eliphalet 1Chr 14:7
  3. A descendant of Judah.
the son of Nethaniah the son of .... Jer 41:1
  4. Son of Jekamiah.
Jekamiah, and Jekamiah begat *E*. 1Chr 2:41
  5. Same as Elishua.
son of Nethaniah, the son of *E* 2Kin 25:25
  6. A priest who taught the law.
with them *E* and Jehoram, ... 2Chr 17:8
  7. A scribe of Jehoiakim.
even *E* the scribe, and Delaiah the ...... Jer 36:12
in the chamber of *E* the scribe. .... Jer 36:20
he took it out of *E* the scribe's. .... Jer 36:21

ELISHAPHAT (e-lish'-a-fat) *Assisted in
  making Joash king.*
E the son of Zichri, into 2Chr 23:1

ELISHEBA (e-lish'-e-bah) *Daughter of
  Amminadab.*
And Aaron took him *E*, daughter of ..... Ex 6:23

ELISHUA (e-lish'-oo-ah) *See* ELISHAMA. *A son
  of David.*
Ibhar also, and *E*, and Nepheg, and 2Sa 5:15
And Ibhar, and *E*, and Elpalet, ... 1Chr 14:5

ELIUD (e-li'-ud) *Son of Achis; ancestor of Jesus.*
and Achim begat *E*. .... Mt 1:14
And *E* begat Eleazar .... Mt 1:15

ELIZABETH *See* ELISABETH.

ELIZAPHAN (e-liz'-a-fan) *See* ELZAPHAN.
  1. Son of Uzziel.
shall be *E* the son of Uzziel .... Num 3:30
Of the sons of *E*. 1Chr 15:8
  2. Son of Parnach.
of Zebulun, *E* the son of Parnach .... Num 34:25
  3. A family of Levites.
And of the sons of *E* 2Chr 29:13

ELIZUR (e-li'-zur) *Son of Shedeur.*
E the son of Shedeur .... Num 1:5
shall be *E* the son of Shedeur .... Num 2:10
On the fourth day *E* the son of .... Num 7:30
offering of *E* the son of Shedeur .... Num 7:35
over his host was *E* the son of .... Num 10:18

ELKANAH (el-ka'-nah)
  1. A grandson of Korah.
Assir, and *E*, and Abiasaph .... Ex 6:24
E his son, and Ebiasaph his son, ... 1Chr 6:23
  2. Father of Samuel.
mount Ephraim, and his name was *E*..... 1Sa 1:1
when the time was that *E* offered 1Sa 1:4
Then said *E* her husband to her, ... 1Sa 1:8
and *E* knew Hannah his wife 1Sa 1:19
And the man *E*, and all his house, ... 1Sa 1:21
E her husband said unto her, Do 1Sa 1:23
E went to Ramah to his house. 1Sa 2:11
And Eli blessed *E* and his wife, and 1Sa 2:20
son, Jeroham, his son, *E* his son, ... 1Chr 6:27
The son of *E*, the son of Jeroham, ... 1Chr 6:34
  3. A Levite.

the sons of *E*; Amasai, and 1Chr 6:25
The son of *E*, the son of Joel, ... 1Chr 6:36
  4. A descendant of Kohath.
the sons of *E* 1Chr 6:25
The son of Zuph, the son of *E*. 1Chr 6:35
  5. Father of Asa.
the son of Asa, the son of *E* 1Chr 9:16
  6. A soldier in David's army.
E, and Jesiah, and Azareel, and 1Chr 12:6
  7. A Levite doorkeeper.
E were doorkeepers for the ark 1Chr 15:23
  8. An officer of King Ahaz.
E that was next to the king 2Chr 28:7

ELKOSH *See* ELKOSHITE.

ELKOSHITE
book of the vision of Nahum the *E* ...... Nah 1:1

ELLASAR (el'-la-sar) *A Babylonian city.*
king of Shinar, Arioch king of *E* .... Gen 14:1
of Shinar, and Arioch king of *E* .... Gen 14:9

ELMODAM (el-mo'-dam) *Son of Er.*
of Cosam, which was the son of *E* .... Lk 3:28

ELMS
hills, under oaks and poplars and *e* ...... Hos 4:13

ELNAAM (el-na'-am) *Father of two of David's
  'mighty men.*
and Joshaviah, the sons of *E*. 1Chr 11:46

ELNATHAN (el-na'-than)
  1. Father of Nehushta.
the daughter of *E* of Jerusalem, ... 2Kin 24:8
E the son of Achbor, and certain .... Jer 26:22
E the son of Achbor, and Gemariah .... Jer 36:12
Nevertheless *E* and Delaiah and .... Jer 36:25
  2. Name of three Levites during Ezra's time.
for Ariel, for Shemaiah, and for *E* .... Ezr 8:16
for Jarib, and for *E* .... Ezr 8:16
also for Joiarib, and for *E* .... Ezr 8:16

ELOI (e-lo'-ee) *See* ELI. *Same as Eli 2.*
a loud voice, saying, *E*, *E* .... Mk 15:34

ELON (e'-lon) *See* ELONITES.
  1. Esau's father-in-law.
the daughter of *E* the Hittite .... Gen 26:34
the daughter of *E* the Hittite .... Gen 36:2
  2. A son of Zebulun.
Sered, and *E*, and Jahleel .... Gen 46:14
of *E*, the family of the Elonites. .... Num 26:26
  3. Danite town.
And *E*, and Thimnathah, and Ekron, ... Josh 19:43
  4. A Judge of Israel.
After him *E*, a Zebulonite, ... Judg 12:11
E the Zebulonite died, and was .... Judg 12:12

ELON-BETH-HANAN (e'-lon-beth-ha'-nan) *A
  Danite town.*
Shaalbim, and Beth-shemesh, and *E*.... 1Kin 4:9

ELONITES (e'-lon-ites) *Descendants of Elon 2.*
of Elon, the family of the *E*. .... Num 26:26

ELOQUENT
the LORD, O my Lord, I am not *e*........ Ex 4:10
artificer, and the *e* orator .... Is 3:3
an *e* man, and mighty in the. .... Acts 18:24

ELOTH (e'-loth) *See* ELATH. *Same as Elath.*
in Ezion-geber, which is beside *E*. 1Kin 9:26
Solomon to Ezion-geber, and to *E* 2Chr 8:17
He built *E*, and restored it to 2Chr 26:2

ELPAAL (el-pa'-al) *A son of Shaharaim.*
of Hushim he begat Abitub, and *E* 1Chr 8:11
The sons of *E*; Eber, and Misham 1Chr 8:12
Jeziah, and Jobab, the sons of *E* 1Chr 8:18

ELPALET (el-pa'-let) *See* ELIPHALET. *A son of
  David.*
And Ibhar, and Elishua, and *E* 1Chr 14:5

EL-PARAN (el-pa'-ran) *A place in southern
  Canaan.*
in their mount Seir, unto *E* .... Gen 14:6

ELPELET *See* ELPALET.

ELSE
Give me children, or *e* I die .... Gen 30:1
or *e* by the life of Pharaoh .... Gen 42:16
E, if thou wilt not let my people .... Ex 8:21
E, if thou refuse to let my .... Ex 10:4
only, without doing any thing *e* .... Num 20:19
there is some *e* beside him .... Deut 4:35
the earth beneath: there is none *e* ...... Deut 4:39
E if ye do in any wise go back, ... Josh 23:12
This is nothing *e* save the sword .... Judg 7:14
if I taste bread, or ought *e* 2Sa 3:35
for we shall not *e* escape from 2Sa 15:14
is God, and that there is none *e* 1Kin 8:60
or *e* thou shalt pay a talent of 1Kin 20:39
or *e*, if it please thee, I will 1Kin 21:6
or *e* three days the sword of 1Chr 21:12
whosoever *e* cometh into the house 2Chr 23:7
this is nothing *e* but sorrow of .... Neh 2:2
I would I give it .... Ps 51:16
or who *e* can hasten hereunto, ... Eccl 2:25
I am the LORD, and there is none *e* ..... Is 45:5
I am the LORD, and there is none *e*. .... Is 45:6
and there is none *e*, there is no. .... Is 45:18
and there is none *e* .... Is 45:18
and there is no God *e* beside me. .... Is 45:21
for I am God, and there is none *e* .... Is 45:22

for I am God, and there is none *e* .... Is 46:9
heart, I am, and none *e* beside me ...... Is 47:8
heart, I am, and none *e* beside me ...... Is 47:10
I am the LORD your God, and none *e* ... Joel 2:27
or *e* he will hold to the one, and .... Mt 6:24
e the bottles break, and the wine .... Mt 9:17
Or *e* how can one enter into a .... Mt 12:29
or *e* make the tree corrupt, and .... Mt 12:33
the new piece that filled it up .... Mk 2:21
the new wine doth burst the .... Mk 2:22
or *e* the new wine will burst the .... Lk 5:37
Or *e*, while the other is yet a .... Lk 14:32
or *e* he will hold to the one, and .... Lk 16:13
or *e* believe me for the very. .... Jn 14:11
spent their time in nothing *e* .... Acts 17:21
Or *e* let these same here say, if. .... Acts 24:20
or *e* excusing one another. .... Rom 2:15
or *e* were your children unclean 1Cor 7:14
E when thou shalt bless with the 1Cor 14:16
E what shall they do which are 1Cor 15:29
or *e* be absent, I may hear of. .... Phil 1:27
or *e* I will come unto thee .... Rev 2:5
or *e* I will come unto thee .... Rev 2:16

ELTEKE *See* ELTEKEH.

ELTEKEH (el-te-keh) *A Danite city.*
And *E*, and Gibbethon, and Baalath,.... Josh 19:44
E with her suburbs, Gibbethon, ... Josh 21:23

ELTEKON (el-te-kon) *A city in Judah.*
And Maarath, and Beth-anoth, and *E* ... Josh 15:59

ELTOLAD (el-to'-lad) *A city in Judah.*
And *E*, and Chesil, and Hormah, ... Josh 15:30
And *E*, and Bethul, and Hormah, ... Josh 19:4

ELUL (e'-lul) *Sixth month of the Hebrew year.*
and fifth day of the month *E* .... Neh 6:15

ELUZAI (e-loo'-zahee) *A soldier in David's
  army.*
E, and Jerimoth, and Bealiah, and 1Chr 12:5

ELYMAS (el'-i-mas) *See* BAR-JESUS. *A sorcerer.*
But *E* the sorcerer (for so is his .... Acts 13:8

ELZABAD (el'-za-bad)
  1. A soldier in David's army.
Johanan the eighth, *E* the ninth,......... 1Chr 12:12
  2. Son of Shemaiah.
Othni, and Rephael, and Obed, *E* 1Chr 26:7

ELZAPHAN (el'-za-fan) *See* ELIZAPHAN. *A son
  of Uzziel.*
Mishael, and *E*, and Zithri,.............. Ex 6:22
And Moses called Mishael and *E* .... Lev 10:4

EMBALM
the physicians to his father .... Gen 50:2

EMBALMED
and the physicians *e* Israel. .... Gen 50:2
the days of those which are *e* .... Gen 50:3
and they *e* him, and he was put in a ... Gen 50:26

EMBOLDENED
of him which is weak be *e* to eat 1Cor 8:10

EMBOLDENETH
or what *e* thee that thou .... Job 16:3

EMBRACE
time of life, thou shalt *e* a son 2Kin 4:16
to honour, when thou dost *e* her ...... Job 24:8
e the bosom of a stranger .... Prov 4:8
a time to *e*, and a time to refrain ...... Eccl 3:5
head, and his right hand doth *e* me .... Song 2:6
and his right hand should *e* me. .... Song 8:3
brought up in scarlet *e* dunghills ...... Lam 4:5

EMBRACED
e him, and kissed him, and brought.... Gen 29:13
e him, and fell on his neck, and .... Gen 33:4
and he kissed them, and *e* them .... Gen 48:10
e them, and departed for to go .... Acts 20:1
e them, and confessed that they .... Heb 11:13

EMBRACING
and a time to refrain from *e*. .... Eccl 3:5
him, and him said, Trouble not .... Acts 20:10

EMBROIDER
thou shalt *e* the coat of fine .... Ex 28:39

EMBROIDERER
the cunning workman, and of the *e* .... Ex 35:35
an *e* in blue, and in purple, and in. ..... Ex 38:23

EMEK KEZIZ *See* KEZIZ.

EMERALD
And the second row shall be an *e* .... Ex 28:18
And the second row, an *e*, a .... Ex 39:11
the jasper, the sapphire, the *e*......... Eze 28:13
throne, in sight like unto an *e* .... Rev 4:3
a chalcedony; the fourth, an *e* .... Rev 21:19

EMERALDS
they occupied in thy fairs with *e*........ Eze 27:16

EMERODS
the botch of Egypt, and with the *e*. ... Deut 28:27
them, and smote them with *e* 1Sa 5:6
they had *e* in their secret parts. 1Sa 5:9
died not were smitten with the *e* 1Sa 5:12
They answered, Five golden *e* 1Sa 6:4
ye shall make images of your *e* 1Sa 6:5
of gold and the images of their *e* 1Sa 6:11

the golden *e* which the 1Sa 6:17

EMIM See EMIMS.

EMIMS (*e'-mims*) *A race of giants.*
the *E* in Shaveh Kiriathaim,............ Gen 14:5
The *E* dwelt therein in times past........ Deut 2:10
but the Moabites call them *E*.......... Deut 2:11

EMINENT
also built unto thee an *e* place.............. Eze 16:24
In that thou buildest thine *e* .... Eze 16:31
shall throw down thine *e* place.......... Eze 16:39
it upon an high mountain and *e* .... Eze 17:22

EMITES See EMIMS.

EMMANUEL (*em-man'-uel*) See IMMANUEL. *A Messianic name.*
and they shall call his name *E*........... Mt 1:23

EMMAUS (*em'-ma-us*) *A village near Jerusalem.*
same day to a village called *E*........... Lk 24:13

EMMOR (*em'-mor*) See HAMOR. *Father of Sychem.*
sons of *E* the father of Sychem........... Acts 7:16

EMPIRE
be published throughout all his *e*........ Est 1:20

EMPLOY
life) to *e* them in the siege............. Deut 20:19

EMPLOYED
for they were in *e* that work day...... 1Chr 9:33
Tikvah were *e* about this matter......... Ezr 10:15

EMPLOYMENT
sever out men of continual *e*............ Eze 39:14

EMPTIED
e her pitcher into the trough, and..... Gen 24:20
to pass as they *e* their sacks............ Gen 42:35
e the chest, and took it, and......... 2Chr 24:11
even thus be he shaken out, and *e*..... Neh 5:13
the brooks of defence shall be *e*........ Is 19:6
The land shall be utterly *e*.............. Is 24:3
hath not been *e* from vessel to........ Jer 48:11
for the emptiers have *e* them out....... Nah 2:2

EMPTIERS
for the *e* have emptied them out,........ Nah 2:2

EMPTINESS
of confusion, and the stones of *e*...... Is 34:11

EMPTY
thou hadst sent me away now *e*....... Gen 31:42
and the pit was *e*, there was no...... Gen 37:24
the seven *e* ears blasted with the..... Gen 41:27
when ye go, ye shall not go *e* .... Ex 3:21
and none shall appear before me *e*..... Ex 23:15
And none shall appear before me *e*..... Ex 34:20
command that they *e* the house........ Lev 14:36
thou shalt not let him go away *e*..... Deut 15:13
not appear before the LORD *e* .... Deut 16:16
with *e* pitchers, and lamps within...... Judg 7:16
LORD hath brought me home again *e*.... Ruth 1:21
Go not *e* unto thy mother in law...... Ruth 3:17
the God of Israel, send it not *e*........ 1Sa 6:3
because thy seat will be *e* 1Sa 20:18
side, and David's place was *e* 1Sa 20:25
month, that David's place was *e*....... 1Sa 20:27
the sword of Saul returned not *e*...... 2Sa 1:22
thy neighbours, even *e* vessels......... 2Kin 4:3
Thou hast sent widows away *e*......... Job 22:9
out the north over the *e* place.......... Job 26:7
they *e* themselves upon the earth..... Eccl 11:3
the Lord maketh the earth *e*.......... Is 24:1
but he awaketh, and his soul is *e*...... Is 29:8
to make *e* the soul of the hungry,..... Is 32:6
returned with thirr vessels *e*.......... Jer 14:3
shall *e* his vessels, and break.......... Jer 48:12
fan her, and shall *e* her land........... Jer 51:2
me, he hath made me an *e* vessel..... Jer 51:34
Then set it *e* upon the coals........... Eze 24:11
Israel is an *e* vine, he bringeth....... Hos 10:1
She is *e*, and void, and waste......... Nah 2:10
Shall they therefore *e* their net....... Hab 1:17
pipes *e* the golden oil out of.......... Zec 4:12
when he is come, he findeth it *e*....... Mt 12:44
and beat him, and sent him away *e*..... Mk 12:3
and the rich he hath sent *e* away..... Lk 1:53
beat him, and sent him away *e*........ Lk 20:10
shamefully, and sent him away *e*....... Lk 20:11

EMULATION
to *e* them which are my flesh............ Rom 11:14

EMULATIONS
witchcraft, hatred, variance, *e*.......... Gal 5:20

EN-MISHPAT
And they returned, and came to *E*...... Gen 14:7

ENABLED
Jesus our Lord, who hath *e* me........ 1Ti 1:12

ENAIM

ENAM (*e'-nam*) *A city in Judah.*
and En-gannim, Tappuah, and *E*........ Josh 15:34

ENAN (*e'-nan*) See HAZAR-ENAN. *Father of Ahira.*
Ahira the son of *E* .... Num 1:15
shall be Ahira the son of *E*............ Num 2:29
twelfth day Ahira the son of *E*......... Num 7:78

offering of Ahira the son of *E*......... Num 7:83
Naphtali was Ahira the son of *E*...... Num 10:27

ENCAMP
e before Pi-hahiroth, between.......... Ex 14:2
before it shall ye *e* by the sea........ Ex 14:2
it, and shall *e* round about the........ Num 1:50
as they *e*, so shall they set........... Num 2:17
those that *e* by him shall be the..... Num 2:27
But those that *e* before the........... Num 3:38
how we are to *e* in the wilderness..... Num 10:31
e against the city, and take it......... 2Sa 12:28
e round about my tabernacle.......... Job 19:12
an host should *e* against me.......... Ps 27:3
I will *e* about mine house because..... Zec 9:8

ENCAMPED
e in Etham, in the edge of the........ Ex 13:20
they *e* there by the waters............. Ex 15:27
where he *e* at the mount of God...... Ex 18:5
from Elim, and *e* by the Red sea...... Num 33:10
e in the wilderness of Sin............. Num 33:11
of Sin, and *e* in Dophkah............. Num 33:12
from Dophkah, and *e* in Alush........ Num 33:13
e at Rephidim, where was no water.... Num 33:14
and *e* at Hazeroth....................... Num 33:17
mount Shapher, and *e* in Haradah..... Num 33:24
from Makheloth, and *e* at Tahath..... Num 33:26
and *e* at Moseroth....................... Num 33:30
Bene-jaakan, and *e* at Hor-hagidgad.. Num 33:32
from Jotbathah, and *e* at Ebronah.... Num 33:34
from Ebronah, and *e* at Ezion-gaber.. Num 33:35
and *e* in Abron-abhlathaam............ Num 33:46
e in Gilgal, in the east border......... Josh 4:19
children of Israel *e* in Gilgal.......... Josh 5:10
e before Gibeon, and make war........ Josh 10:5
e against it, and fought against...... Josh 10:31
they *e* against it, and fought.......... Josh 10:34
they *e* against them, and destroyed.... Judg 6:4
against Thebez, and took it............. Judg 9:50
gathered together, and *e* in Gilead.... Judg 10:17
together, and *e* in Mizpeh............. Judg 10:17
the morning, and *e* against Gibeah.... Judg 20:19
up, and *e* against Jabesh-gilead...... 1Sa 11:1
but the Philistines *e* in Michmash..... 1Sa 13:16
my lord, are *e* in the open fields...... 2Sa 11:11
the people were *e* against............. 1Kin 16:15
the people that were *e* heard say..... 1Kin 16:16
e in the valley of Rephaim............ 1Chr 11:15
e against the fenced cities, and....... 2Chr 32:1

ENCAMPETH
The angel of the LORD *e* round........ Ps 34:7
bones of him that *e* against thee...... Ps 53:5

ENCAMPING
and overtook them *e* by the sea...... Ex 14:9

ENCHANTER
an observer of times, or an *e*......... Deut 18:10

ENCHANTERS
to your dreamers, nor to your *e*....... Jer 27:9

ENCHANTMENT
neither shall ye use *e*, nor............ Lev 19:26
there is no *e* against Jacob........... Num 23:23
the serpent will bite without *e*........ Eccl 10:11

ENCHANTMENTS
did in like manner with their *e*......... Ex 7:11
of Egypt did so with their *e*........... Ex 7:22
the magicians did so with their *e*..... Ex 8:7
with their *e* to bring forth lice........ Ex 8:18
as at other times, to seek for *e*...... Num 24:1
the fire, and used divination and *e*.... 2Kin 17:17
and observed times, and used *e* 2Kin 21:6
also he observed times, and used *e*.... 2Chr 33:6
the great abundance of thine *e*....... Is 47:9
Stand now with thine *e*, and with..... Is 47:12

ENCOUNTERED
and of the Stoicks, *e* him............. Acts 17:18

ENCOURAGE
e him: for he shall cause.............. Deut 1:38
and *e* him, and strengthen him........ Deut 3:28
overthrow it: and *e* thou him.......... 2Sa 11:25
They *e* themselves in an evil........... Ps 64:5

ENCOURAGED
the men of Israel *e* themselves....... Judg 20:22
but David *e* himself in the LORD....... 1Sa 30:6
that they might be *e* in the law....... 2Chr 31:4
e them to the service of the........... 2Chr 35:2
So the carpenter *e* the goldsmith..... Is 41:7

END
The *e* of all flesh is come before....... Gen 6:13
after the *e* of the hundred and........ Gen 8:3
to pass at the *e* of forty days......... Gen 8:6
which is in the *e* of his field.......... Gen 23:9
had made an *e* of blessing Jacob...... Gen 27:30
pass at the *e* of two full years........ Gen 41:1
e of the borders of Egypt even to..... Gen 47:21
Egypt even to the other *e* thereof..... Gen 47:21
made an *e* of commanding his sons.... Gen 49:33
to the *e* thou mayest know that I..... Ex 8:22
pass at the *e* of four hundred......... Ex 12:41
which is in the *e* of the year.......... Ex 23:16
And make one cherub on the one *e*.... Ex 25:19
the other cherub on the other *e*....... Ex 25:19
boards shall reach from *e* to *e*...... Ex 26:28
Moses, when he had made an *e* of..... Ex 31:18
of ingathering at the year's *e*......... Ex 34:22
from the one to the other............... Ex 36:33

One cherub on the *e* on this side...... Ex 37:8
on the other *e* on that side........... Ex 37:8
of your consecration be at an *e*....... Lev 8:33
when he hath made an *e* of........... Lev 16:20
To the *e* that the children of.......... Lev 17:5
his sons have made an *e* of........... Num 4:15
as he had made an *e* of speaking..... Num 16:31
and let my last *e* be like his.......... Num 23:10
but his latter *e* shall be that he...... Num 24:20
to do thee good at thy latter *e*....... Deut 8:16
to pass at the *e* of forty days......... Deut 9:11
year even unto the *e* of the year...... Deut 11:12
from the one *e* of the earth even..... Deut 13:7
unto the other *e* of the earth......... Deut 13:7
At the *e* of three years thou.......... Deut 14:28
At the *e* of every seven years.......... Deut 15:1
to the *e* that he should multiply...... Deut 17:16
to the *e* that he may prolong his...... Deut 17:20
an *e* of speaking unto the people..... Deut 20:9
When thou hast made an *e* of......... Deut 26:12
from the *e* of the earth, as swift..... Deut 28:49
from the one *e* of the earth even..... Deut 28:64
At the *e* of every seven years, in..... Deut 31:10
when Moses had made an *e* of........ Deut 31:24
I will see what their *e* shall be....... Deut 32:20
would consider their latter *e* .... Deut 32:29
Moses made an *e* of speaking all..... Deut 32:45
when Israel had made an *e* of......... Josh 8:24
it came to pass at the *e* of three..... Josh 9:16
an *e* of slaying them with a very..... Josh 10:20
sea, even unto the *e* of Jordan....... Josh 15:5
which is at the *e* of the valley........ Josh 15:8
was from the *e* of Kirjath-jearim..... Josh 18:15
the *e* of the mountain that lieth...... Josh 18:16
salt sea at the south *e* of Jordan..... Josh 18:19
When they had made an *e* of.......... Josh 19:49
So they made an *e* of dividing the..... Josh 19:51
when he had made an *e* to offer...... Judg 3:18
e of the staff that was in his.......... Judg 6:21
to pass at the *e* of two months....... Judg 11:39
when he had made an *e* of speaking.. Judg 15:17
behold, the day groweth to an *e*...... Judg 19:9
unto the *e* of barley harvest.......... Ruth 2:23
down at the *e* of the heap of corn.... Ruth 3:7
latter *e* than at the beginning......... Ruth 3:10
I begin, I will also make an *e*......... 1Sa 3:12
going down to the *e* of the city....... 1Sa 9:27
he had made an *e* of prophesying..... 1Sa 10:13
of offering the burnt offering.......... 1Sa 13:10
wherefore he put forth the *e* of...... 1Sa 14:27
the *e* of the rod that was in mine..... 1Sa 14:43
when he had made an *e* of speaking.. 1Sa 18:1
when David had made an *e* of......... 1Sa 24:16
e of the spear smote him under....... 2Sa 2:23
be bitterness in the latter *e*.......... 2Sa 2:26
an *e* of offering burnt offerings....... 2Sa 6:18
When thou hast made an *e* of......... 2Sa 7:11
as he had made an *e* of speaking..... 2Sa 13:36
every year's *e* that he polled it....... 2Sa 14:26
Jerusalem at the *e* of nine months.... 2Sa 24:8
as they had made an *e* of eating..... 1Kin 1:41
to pass at the *e* of three years....... 1Kin 2:39
until he had made an *e* of............ 1Kin 3:1
So Hiram made an *e* of doing all..... 1Kin 7:40
an *e* of praying all this prayer........ 1Kin 8:54
to pass at the *e* of twenty years..... 1Kin 9:10
to pass at the seven years' *e*......... 2Kin 8:3
was full from one *e* to another....... 2Kin 10:21
as soon as he had made an *e* of...... 2Kin 10:25
at the *e* of three years they took..... 2Kin 18:10
Jerusalem from one *e* to another...... 2Kin 21:16
when David had made an *e* of......... 1Chr 16:2
on the right side of the east.......... 2Chr 4:10
stood at the east *e* of the altar...... 2Chr 5:12
Solomon had made an *e* of praying.... 2Chr 7:1
to pass at the *e* of twenty years..... 2Chr 8:1
find them at the *e* of the brook...... 2Chr 20:16
when they had made an *e* of.......... 2Chr 20:23
after the *e* of two years, his.......... 2Chr 21:19
chest, until they had made an *e*...... 2Chr 24:10
came to pass at the *e* of the year.... 2Chr 24:23
of the first month they made an *e*.... 2Chr 29:17
they had made an *e* of offering....... 2Chr 29:29
from one *e* to another with their..... Ezr 9:11
they made an *e* with all the men..... Ezr 10:17
to the *e* of the house of Eliashib..... Neh 3:21
will they make an *e* in a day......... Neh 4:2
and what is mine *e*, that I should.... Job 6:11
yet thy latter *e* should greatly....... Job 8:7
Shall vain words have an *e*........... Job 16:3
it be ere ye make an *e* of words...... Job 18:2
the day and night come to an *e*...... Job 26:10
He setteth an *e* to darkness........... Job 28:3
that Job may be tried unto the *e*..... Job 34:36
e of Job more than his beginning..... Job 42:12
of the wicked come to an *e*........... Ps 7:9
are come to a perpetual *e*............ Ps 9:6
their words to the *e* of the world..... Ps 19:4
forth is from the *e* of the heaven..... Ps 19:6
from the *e* that my glory may sing.... Ps 30:12
for the *e* of that man is peace........ Ps 37:37
the *e* of the wicked shall be cut...... Ps 37:38
LORD, make me to know mine *e*........ Ps 39:4
to cease unto the *e* of the earth...... Ps 46:9
From the *e* of the earth will I........ Ps 61:2
then understood I their *e*............. Ps 73:17
and thy years shall have no *e*......... Ps 102:27
man, and are at their wit's *e*......... Ps 107:27
and I shall keep it unto the *e*........ Ps 119:33
I have seen an *e* of all............... Ps 119:96

E

statutes alway, even unto the e	Ps 119:112
But her e is bitter as wormwood,	Prov 5:4
but the e thereof are the ways of	Prov 14:12
the e of that mirth is heaviness	Prov 14:13
but the e thereof are the ways of	Prov 16:25
be wise in thy latter e	Prov 19:20
but the e thereof shall not be	Prov 20:21
For surely there is an e	Prov 23:18
not what to do in the e thereof	Prov 25:8
from the beginning to the e	Eccl 3:11
yet is there no e of all his	Eccl 4:8
There is no e of all the people,	Eccl 4:16
for that is the e of all men	Eccl 7:2
Better is the e of a thing than	Eccl 7:8
to the e than the beginning	Eccl 7:8
to the e than that should find	Eccl 7:14
the e of his talk is mischievous	Eccl 10:13
making many books there is no e	Eccl 12:12
is there any e of their treasures	Is 2:7
is there any e of their chariots	Is 2:7
unto them from the e of the earth	Is 5:26
at the e of the conduit of the	Is 7:3
and peace there shall be no e	Is 9:7
from the e of heaven, even the	Is 13:5
for the extortioner is at an e	Is 16:4
after the e of seventy years	Is 23:15
pass after the e of seventy years	Is 23:17
make an e to deal treacherously,	Is 33:1
night wilt thou make an e of me	Is 38:12
night wilt thou make an e of me	Is 38:13
and know the latter e of them	Is 41:22
praise from the e of the earth	Is 42:10
nor confounded world without e	Is 45:17
Declaring the e from the	Is 46:10
didst remember the latter e of it	Is 47:7
it even to the e of the earth	Is 48:20
salvation unto the e of the earth	Is 49:6
unto the e of the world, Say ye	Is 62:11
unto the e of the eleventh year	Jer 1:3
will he keep it to the e	Jer 3:5
yet will I not make a full e	Jer 4:27
but make not a full e	Jer 5:10
I will not make a full e with you	Jer 5:18
will ye do in the e thereof V	Jer 5:31
said, He shall not see our last e	Jer 12:4
e of the land even to the other	Jer 12:12
even to the other e of the land	Jer 12:12
days, and at his e shall be a fool	Jer 17:11
one e of the earth even unto the	Jer 25:33
unto the other e of the earth	Jer 25:33
when Jeremiah had made an e of	Jer 26:8
evil, to give you an expected e	Jer 29:11
though I make a full e of all	Jer 30:11
will I not make a full e of thee	Jer 30:11
And there is hope in thine e	Jer 31:17
At the e of seven years let ye go	Jer 34:14
that when Jeremiah had made an e	Jer 43:1
until there be an e of them	Jer 44:27
for I will make a full e of all	Jer 46:28
I will not make a full e of thee	Jer 46:28
thine e is come, and the measure	Jer 51:13
that his city is taken at one e	Jer 51:31
made an e of reading this book	Jer 51:63
she remembereth not her last e	Lam 1:9
our e is near, our days are	Lam 4:18
for our e is come	Lam 4:18
to pass at the e of seven days	Eze 3:16
An e, the e is come upon	Eze 7:2
Now is the e come upon thee, and I	Eze 7:3
An e is come, the e is come	Eze 7:6
wilt thou make a full e of the	Eze 11:13
neither did I make an e of them	Eze 20:17
to the e that they might know	Eze 20:26
when iniquity shall have an e	Eze 21:25
their iniquity shall have an e	Eze 21:29
At the e of forty years will I	Eze 29:13
To the e that none of all the	Eze 31:14
time that their iniquity had an e	Eze 35:5
after the e of seven months shall	Eze 39:14
the separate place at the e	Eze 41:12
Now when he had made an e of	Eze 42:15
hast made an e of cleansing it	Eze 43:23
From the north e to the coast of	Eze 48:1
that at the e thereof they might	Dan 1:5
at the e of ten days then	Dan 1:15
Now at the e of the days that the	Dan 1:18
thereof to the e of all the earth	Dan 4:11
dominion to the e of the earth	Dan 4:22
At the e of twelve months	Dan 4:29
And at the e of the days I	Dan 4:34
dominion shall be even unto the e	Dan 6:26
and to destroy it unto the e	Dan 7:26
Hitherto is the e of the matter	Dan 7:28
time of the e shall be the vision	Dan 8:17
in the last e of the indignation	Dan 8:19
the time appointed the e shall be	Dan 8:19
and to make an e of sins, and to	Dan 9:24
the e thereof shall be with a	Dan 9:26
unto the e of the war desolations	Dan 9:26
in the e of years they shall join	Dan 11:6
for yet the e shall be at the	Dan 11:27
white, even to the time of the e	Dan 11:35
at the time of the e shall the	Dan 11:40
yet he shall come to his e	Dan 11:45
book, even to the time of the e	Dan 12:4
it be to the e of these wonders	Dan 12:6
shall be the e of these things	Dan 12:8
and sealed till the time of the e	Dan 12:9
But go thou thy way till the e be	Dan 12:13
in thy lot at the e of the days	Dan 12:13
the great houses shall have an e	Amos 3:15

to what e is it for you	Amos 5:18
The e is come upon my people of	Amos 7:2
The e is come upon my people of	Amos 8:2
the e thereof as a bitter day	Amos 8:10
to the e that every one of the	Obad 9
an utter e of the place thereof	Nah 1:8
he will make an utter e	Nah 1:9
for there is none e of the store	Nah 2:9
there is none e of their corpses	Nah 3:3
but at the e it shall speak, and,	Hab 2:3
endureth to the e shall be saved	Mt 10:22
when Jesus had made an e of	Mt 11:1
the harvest is the e of the world	Mt 13:39
it be in the e of this world	Mt 13:40
shall it be at the e of the world	Mt 13:49
coming, and of the e of the world	Mt 24:3
to pass, but the e is not yet	Mt 24:6
he that shall endure unto the e	Mt 24:13
and then shall the e come	Mt 24:14
from one e of heaven to the other	Mt 24:31
with the servants, to see the e	Mt 26:58
In the e of the sabbath, as it	Mt 28:1
even unto the e of the world	Mt 28:20
he cannot stand, but hath an e	Mk 3:26
but the e shall not be yet	Mk 13:7
he that shall endure unto the e	Mk 13:13
his kingdom there shall be no e	Lk 1:33
a parable unto them to this e	Lk 18:1
but the e is not by and by	Lk 21:9
things concerning me have an e	Lk 22:37
world, he loved them unto the e	Jn 13:1
To this e was I born, and for this	Jn 18:37
to the e they might not live	Acts 7:19
to the e ye may be established	Rom 1:11
to the e the promise might be	Rom 4:16
for the e of those things is	Rom 6:21
and the e everlasting life	Rom 6:22
For Christ is the e of the law	Rom 10:4
For to this e Christ both died,	Rom 14:9
shall also confirm you unto the e	1Cor 1:8
Then cometh the e, when he shall	1Cor 15:24
shall acknowledge even to the e	2Cor 1:13
For to this e also did I write,	2Cor 2:9
the e of that which is abolished	2Cor 3:13
whose e shall be according to	2Cor 11:15
all ages, world without e	Eph 3:21
Whose e is destruction, whose God	Phil 3:19
To the e he may stablish your	1Th 3:13
Now the e of the commandment is	1Ti 1:5
of the hope firm unto the e	Heb 3:6
confidence stedfast unto the e	Heb 3:14
whose e is to be burned	Heb 6:8
full assurance of hope unto the e	Heb 6:11
is to them an e of all strife	Heb 6:16
beginning of days, nor e of life	Heb 7:3
but now once in the e of the	Heb 9:26
considering the e of their	Heb 13:7
and have seen the e of the Lord	Jas 5:11
Receiving the e of your faith	1Pet 1:9
hope to the e for the grace that	1Pet 1:13
But the e of all things is at	1Pet 4:7
what shall the e be of them that	1Pet 4:17
the latter e is worse with them	2Pet 2:20
and keepeth my works unto the e	Rev 2:26
and Omega, the beginning and the e	Rev 21:6
and Omega, the beginning and the e	Rev 22:13

ENDAMAGE

so thou shalt e the revenue of	Ezr 4:13

ENDANGER

ye make me e my head to the king	Dan 1:10

ENDANGERED

cleaveth wood shall be e thereby	Eccl 10:9

ENDEAVOUR

Moreover I will e that you may be	2Pet 1:15

ENDEAVOURED

immediately we e to go into	Acts 16:10
e the more abundantly to see your	1Th 2:17

ENDEAVOURING

to keep the unity of the Spirit	Eph 4:3

ENDEAVOURS

to the wickedness of their e	Ps 28:4

ENDED

on the seventh day God e his work	Gen 2:2
was in the land of Egypt, were e	Gen 41:53
When that year was e, they came	Gen 47:18
of this song, until they were e	Deut 31:30
and mourning for Moses were e	Deut 34:8
until they have e all my harvest	Ruth 2:21
and so they e the matter	2Sa 20:18
So was e all the work that king	1Kin 7:51
help them, till the work was e	2Chr 29:34
The words of Job are e	Job 31:40
of David the son of Jesse are e	Ps 72:20
days of thy mourning shall be e	Is 60:20
harvest is past, the summer is e	Jer 8:20
till thou hast e the days of thy	Eze 4:8
when Jesus had e these sayings	Mt 7:28
and when they were e, he afterward	Lk 4:2
devil had e all the temptation	Lk 4:13
Now when he had e all his sayings	Lk 7:1
and supper being e, the devil	Jn 13:2
After these things were e	Acts 19:21
when the seven days were almost e	Acts 21:27

ENDETH

the noise of them that rejoice e	Is 24:8

ENDING

and Omega, the beginning and the e	Rev 1:8

ENDLESS

e genealogies, which minister	1Ti 1:4
but after the power of an e life	Heb 7:16

EN-DOR (en'-dor) A village near Mt. Tabor.

towns, and the inhabitants of E	Josh 17:11
that hath a familiar spirit at E	1Sa 28:7
Which perished at E: they became	Ps 83:10

ENDOW

he shall surely e her to be his	Ex 22:16

ENDS

in the two e of the mercy seat	Ex 25:18
cherubims on the two e thereof	Ex 25:19
two chains of pure gold at the e	Ex 28:14
e of wreathen work of pure gold	Ex 28:22
on the two e of the breastplate	Ex 28:23
are on the e of the breastplate	Ex 28:24
the other two e of the two	Ex 28:25
two e of the breastplate in the	Ex 28:26
on the two e of the mercy seat	Ex 37:7
cherubims on the two e thereof	Ex 37:8
the four e of the grate of brass	Ex 38:5
the breastplate chains at the e	Ex 39:15
in the two e of the breastplate	Ex 39:16
rings on the e of the breastplate	Ex 39:17
the two e of the two wreathen	Ex 39:18
on the two e of the breastplate	Ex 39:19
together to the e of the earth	Deut 33:17
shall judge the e of the earth	1Sa 2:10
that the e of the staves were	1Kin 8:8
that the e of the staves were	2Chr 5:9
he looketh to the e of the earth	Job 28:24
lightning unto the e of the earth	Job 37:3
take hold of the e of the earth	Job 38:13
and his circuit unto the e of it	Ps 19:6
All the e of the world shall	Ps 22:27
praise unto the e of the earth	Ps 48:10
in Jacob unto the e of the earth	Ps 59:13
of all the e of the earth	Ps 65:5
all the e of the earth shall fear	Ps 67:7
the river unto the e of the earth	Ps 72:8
all the e of the earth have seen	Ps 98:3
to ascend from the e of the earth	Ps 135:7
a fool are in the e of the earth	Prov 17:24
all the e of the earth	Prov 30:4
far unto all the e of the earth	Is 26:15
the Creator of the e of the earth	Is 40:28
the e of the earth were afraid,	Is 41:5
taken from the e of the earth	Is 41:9
daughters from the e of the earth	Is 43:6
ye saved, all the e of the earth	Is 45:22
all the e of the earth shall see	Is 52:10
to ascend from the e of the earth	Jer 10:13
unto thee from the e of the earth	Jer 16:19
come even to the e of the earth	Jer 25:31
to ascend from the e of the earth	Jer 51:16
fire devoureth both the e of it	Eze 15:4
be great unto the e of the earth	Mic 5:4
river even to the e of the earth	Zec 9:10
salvation unto the e of the earth	Acts 13:47
words unto the e of the world	Rom 10:18
upon whom the e of the world are	1Cor 10:11

ENDUED

God hath e me with a good dowry	Gen 30:20
e with prudence and understanding,	2Chr 2:12
e with understanding, of Huram my	2Chr 2:13
until ye be e with power from on	Lk 24:49
e with knowledge among you	Jas 3:13

ENDURE

me and the children be able to e	Gen 33:14
so, then thou shalt be able to e	Ex 18:23
For how can I e to see the evil	Est 8:6
or how can I e to see the	Est 8:6
hold it fast, but it shall not e	Job 8:15
of his highness I could not e	Job 31:23
But the LORD shall e for ever	Ps 9:7
weeping may e for a night,	Ps 30:5
thee as long as the sun and moon e	Ps 72:5
His name shall e for ever	Ps 72:17
also will I make to e for ever	Ps 89:29
His seed shall e for ever	Ps 89:36
thou, O LORD, shalt e for ever	Ps 102:12
shall perish, but thou shalt e	Ps 102:26
of the LORD shall e for ever	Ps 104:31
doth the crown e to every	Prov 27:24
Can thine heart e, or can thine	Eze 22:14
But he that shall e unto the end	Mt 24:13
and so e but for a time	Mk 4:17
but he that shall e unto the end	Mk 13:13
and tribulations that ye e	2Th 1:4
Thou therefore e hardness	2Ti 2:3
Therefore I e all things for the	2Ti 2:10
they will not e sound doctrine	2Ti 4:3
e afflictions, do the work of	2Ti 4:5
If ye e chastening, God dealeth	Heb 12:7
(For they could not e that which	Heb 12:20
we count them happy which e	Jas 5:11
for conscience toward God e grief	1Pet 2:19

ENDURED

their time should have e for ever	Ps 81:15
e with much longsuffering the	Rom 9:22
what persecutions I e	2Ti 3:11
And so, after he had patiently e	Heb 6:15

ENDURETH

ye e a great fight of afflictions	Heb 10:32
for he e, as seeing him who is	Heb 11:27
was set before him e the cross	Heb 12:2
For consider him that e such	Heb 12:3

ENDURETH

for his mercy e for ever	1Chr 16:34
because his mercy e for ever	1Chr 16:41
for his mercy e for ever	2Chr 5:13
for his mercy e for ever	2Chr 7:3
because his mercy e for ever	2Chr 7:6
for his mercy e for ever	2Chr 20:21
for his mercy e for ever toward	Ezr 3:11
For his anger e but a moment	Ps 30:5
the goodness of God e continually	Ps 52:1
of peace so long as the moon e	Ps 72:7
his truth e to all generations	Ps 100:5
for his mercy e for ever	Ps 106:1
for his mercy e for ever	Ps 107:1
and his righteousness e for ever	Ps 111:3
his praise e for ever	Ps 111:10
and his righteousness e for ever	Ps 112:3
his righteousness e for ever	Ps 112:9
the truth of the LORD e for ever	Ps 117:2
because his mercy e for ever	Ps 118:1
say, that his mercy e for ever	Ps 118:2
say, that his mercy e for ever	Ps 118:3
say, that his mercy e for ever	Ps 118:4
for his mercy e for ever	Ps 118:29
righteous judgments e for ever	Ps 119:160
Thy name, O LORD, e for ever	Ps 135:13
for his mercy e for ever	Ps 136:1
for his mercy e for ever	Ps 136:2
for his mercy e for ever	Ps 136:3
for his mercy e for ever	Ps 136:4
for his mercy e for ever	Ps 136:5
for his mercy e for ever	Ps 136:6
for his mercy e for ever	Ps 136:7
for his mercy e for ever	Ps 136:8
for his mercy e for ever	Ps 136:9
for his mercy e for ever	Ps 136:10
for his mercy e for ever	Ps 136:11
for his mercy e for ever	Ps 136:12
for his mercy e for ever	Ps 136:13
for his mercy e for ever	Ps 136:14
for his mercy e for ever	Ps 136:15
for his mercy e for ever	Ps 136:16
for his mercy e for ever	Ps 136:17
for his mercy e for ever	Ps 136:18
for his mercy e for ever	Ps 136:19
for his mercy e for ever	Ps 136:20
for his mercy e for ever	Ps 136:21
for his mercy e for ever	Ps 136:22
for his mercy e for ever	Ps 136:23
for his mercy e for ever	Ps 136:24
for his mercy e for ever	Ps 136:25
thy mercy, O LORD, e for ever	Ps 138:8
thy dominion e throughout all	Ps 145:13
but he that e to the end shall be	Jer 33:11
which e unto everlasting life	Mt 10:22
hopeth all things, e all things	Jn 6:27
is the man that e temptation	1Cor 13:7
the word of the Lord e for ever	Jas 1:12
	1Pet 1:25

ENDURING

of the LORD is clean, e for ever	Ps 19:9
which is effectual in the e	2Cor 1:6
heaven a better and an e substance	Heb 10:34

EN-EGLAIM (en-eg'-la-im) A place near the Salt Sea.

upon it from En-gedi even unto E.	Eze 47:10

ENEMIES

delivered thine e into thy hand	Gen 14:20
shall possess the gate of his e	Gen 22:17
shall be in the neck of thine e	Gen 49:8
war, they join also unto our e	Ex 1:10
I will be an enemy unto thine e	Ex 23:22
I will make all thine e turn	Ex 23:27
unto their shame among their e	Ex 32:25
And ye shall chase your e, and they	Lev 26:7
your e shall fall before you by	Lev 26:8
in vain, for your e shall eat it	Lev 26:16
ye shall be slain before your e	Lev 26:17
your e which dwell therein shall	Lev 26:32
hearts in the lands of their e	Lev 26:36
no power to stand before your e	Lev 26:37
land of your e shall eat you up	Lev 26:38
them into the land of their e	Lev 26:41
they be in the land of their e	Lev 26:44
and ye shall be saved from your e	Num 10:9
LORD, and let thine e be scattered	Num 10:35
ye be not smitten before your e	Num 14:42
I took thee to curse mine e	Num 23:11
he shall eat up the nations his e	Num 24:8
I called thee to curse mine e	Num 24:10
shall be a possession for his e	Num 24:18
driven out his e from before him	Num 32:21
lest ye be smitten before your e	Deut 1:42
out all thine e from before thee	Deut 6:19
rest from all your e round about	Deut 12:10
out to battle against thine e	Deut 20:1
day unto battle against your e	Deut 20:3
to fight for you against your e	Deut 20:4
shalt eat the spoil of thine e	Deut 20:14
forth to war against thine e	Deut 21:10
host goeth forth against thine e	Deut 23:9
and to give up thine e before thee	Deut 23:14
rest from all thine e round about	Deut 25:19

The LORD shall cause thine e that	Deut 28:7
thee to be smitten before thine e	Deut 28:25
sheep shall be given unto thine e	Deut 28:31
shalt thou serve thine e which	Deut 28:48
wherewith thine e shall distress	Deut 28:53
wherewith thine e shall distress	Deut 28:55
be sold unto your e for bondmen	Deut 28:68
put all these curses upon thine e	Deut 30:7
even our e themselves being	Deut 32:31
I will render vengeance to mine e	Deut 32:41
be thou an help to him from his e	Deut 33:7
thine e shall be found liars unto	Deut 33:29
their backs before their e	Josh 7:8
could not stand before their e	Josh 7:12
turned their backs before their e	Josh 7:12
canst not stand before thine e	Josh 7:13
avenged themselves upon their e	Josh 10:13
ye not, but pursue after your e	Josh 10:19
all your e against whom ye fight	Josh 10:25
a man of all their e before them	Josh 21:44
all their e into their hand	Josh 21:44
of your e with your brethren	Josh 22:8
from all their e round about	Josh 23:1
the hands of their e round about	Judg 2:14
any longer stand before their e	Judg 2:14
their e all the days of the judge	Judg 2:18
the Moabites into your hand	Judg 3:28
So let all thine e perish	Judg 5:31
of all their e on every side	Judg 8:34
vengeance for them of thine e	Judg 11:36
my mouth is enlarged over mine e	1Sa 2:1
save us out of the hand of our e	1Sa 4:3
us out of the hand of our e	1Sa 12:10
the hand of your e on every side	1Sa 12:11
that I may be avenged on mine e	1Sa 14:24
spoil of their e which they found	1Sa 14:30
against all his e on every side	1Sa 14:47
to be avenged of the king's e	1Sa 18:25
the e of David every one from the	1Sa 20:15
it at the hand of David's e	1Sa 20:16
also do God unto the e of David	1Sa 25:22
thine own hand, now let thine e	1Sa 25:26
and the souls of thine e, them	1Sa 25:29
against the e of my lord the king	1Sa 29:8
of the spoil of the e of the LORD	1Sa 30:26
and out of the hand of all their e	2Sa 3:18
forth upon mine e before me	2Sa 5:20
rest round about from all his e	2Sa 7:1
off all thine e out of thy sight	2Sa 7:9
thee to rest from all thine e	2Sa 7:11
to the e of the LORD to blaspheme	2Sa 12:14
LORD hath avenged him of his e	2Sa 18:19
The e of my lord the king, and all	2Sa 18:32
In that thou lovest thine e	2Sa 19:6
saved us out of the hand of our e	2Sa 19:9
him out of the hand of all his e	2Sa 22:1
so shall I be saved from mine e	2Sa 22:4
I have pursued mine e, and	2Sa 22:38
also given me the necks of mine e	2Sa 22:41
bringeth me forth from mine e	2Sa 22:49
flee three months before thine e	2Sa 24:13
hast asked the life of thine e	1Kin 3:11
soul, in the land of their e	1Kin 8:48
you out of the hand of all your e	2Kin 17:39
them into the hand of their e	2Kin 21:14
a prey and a spoil to all their e	2Kin 21:14
ye be come to betray me to mine e	1Chr 12:17
God hath broken in upon mine e	1Chr 14:11
off all thine e from before thee	1Chr 17:8
I will subdue all thine e	1Chr 17:10
sword of thine e overtaketh thee	1Chr 21:12
rest from all his e round about	1Chr 22:9
honour, nor the life of thine e	2Chr 1:11
if their e besiege them in the	2Chr 6:28
go out to war against their e by	2Chr 6:34
deliver them over before their e	2Chr 6:36
made them to rejoice over their e	2Chr 20:27
fought against the e of Israel	2Chr 20:29
them into the hand of their e	2Chr 25:20
when our e heard that it was	Neh 4:15
the reproach of the heathen our e	Neh 5:9
the Arabian, and the rest of our e	Neh 6:1
that when all our e heard thereof	Neh 6:16
them into the hand of their e	Neh 9:27
them out of the hand of their e	Neh 9:27
thou them in the hand of their e	Neh 9:28
to avenge themselves on their e	Est 8:13
in the day that the e of the Jews	Est 9:1
e with the stroke of the sword	Est 9:5
lives, and had rest from their e	Est 9:16
the Jews rested from their e	Est 9:22
me unto him as one of his e	Job 19:11
all mine e upon the cheek bone	Ps 3:7
righteousness because of mine e	Ps 5:8
waxeth old because of all mine e	Ps 6:7
Let all mine e be ashamed	Ps 6:10
because of the rage of mine e	Ps 7:6
strength because of thine e	Ps 8:2
When mine e are turned back, they	Ps 9:3
as for all his e, he puffeth at	Ps 10:5
that oppress me, from my deadly e	Ps 17:9
him from the hand of all his e	Ps 18:v
so shall I be saved from mine e	Ps 18:3
I have pursued mine e, and	Ps 18:37
also given me the necks of mine e	Ps 18:40
He delivereth me from mine	Ps 18:48
hand shall find out all thine e	Ps 21:8
me in the presence of mine e	Ps 23:5
let not mine e triumph over me	Ps 25:2
Consider mine e; for they are	Ps 25:19

When the wicked, even mine e	Ps 27:2
up above mine e round about me	Ps 27:6
a plain path, because of mine e	Ps 27:11
not over unto the will of mine e	Ps 27:12
I was a reproach among all mine e	Ps 31:11
me from the hand of mine e	Ps 31:15
mine e wrongfully rejoice over me	Ps 35:19
the e of the LORD shall be as the	Ps 37:20
But mine e are lively, and they	Ps 38:19
him unto the will of his e	Ps 41:2
Mine e speak evil of me, When	Ps 41:5
in my bones, mine e reproach me	Ps 42:10
thee will we push down our e	Ps 44:5
But thou hast saved us from our e	Ps 44:7
in the heart of the king's e	Ps 45:5
He shall reward evil unto mine e	Ps 54:5
hath seen his desire upon mine e	Ps 54:7
Mine e would daily swallow me up	Ps 56:2
thee, then shall mine e turn back	Ps 56:9
Deliver me from mine e, O my God	Ps 59:1
let me see my desire upon mine e	Ps 59:10
it is that shall tread down our e	Ps 60:12
of thy power shalt thine e submit	Ps 66:3
God arise, let his e be scattered	Ps 68:1
God shall wound the head of his e	Ps 68:21
be dipped in the blood of thine e	Ps 68:23
me, being mine e wrongfully	Ps 69:4
deliver me because of mine e	Ps 69:18
For mine e speak against me	Ps 71:10
his e shall lick the dust	Ps 72:9
Thine e roar in the midst of thy	Ps 74:4
Forget not the voice of thine e	Ps 74:23
but the sea overwhelmed their e	Ps 78:53
he smote his e in the hinder	Ps 78:66
our e laugh among themselves	Ps 80:6
should soon have subdued their e	Ps 81:14
For, lo, thine e make a tumult	Ps 83:2
thine e with thy strong arm	Ps 89:10
hast made all his e to rejoice	Ps 89:42
Wherewith thine e have reproached	Ps 89:51
For, lo, thine e, O LORD, for, lo	Ps 92:9
for, lo, thine e shall perish	Ps 92:9
shall see my desire on mine e	Ps 92:11
and burneth up his e round about	Ps 97:3
Mine e reproach me all the day	Ps 102:8
made them stronger than their e	Ps 105:24
And the waters covered their e	Ps 106:11
Their e also oppressed them, and	Ps 106:42
it is that shall tread down our e	Ps 108:13
I make thine e thy footstool	Ps 110:1
rule thou in the midst of thine e	Ps 110:2
he see his desire upon his e	Ps 112:8
hast made me wiser than mine e	Ps 119:98
because mine e have forgotten thy	Ps 119:139
Many are my persecutors and mine e	Ps 119:157
speak with the e in the gate	Ps 127:5
His e will I clothe with shame	Ps 132:18
And hath redeemed us from our e	Ps 136:24
hand against the wrath of mine e	Ps 138:7
thine e take thy name in vain	Ps 139:20
I count them mine e	Ps 139:22
Deliver me, O LORD, from mine e	Ps 143:9
And of thy mercy cut off mine e	Ps 143:12
he maketh even his e to be at	Prov 16:7
and avenge me of mine e	Is 1:24
him, and join his e together	Is 9:11
fire of thine e shall devour them	Is 26:11
he shall prevail against his e	Is 42:13
adversaries, recompence to his e	Is 59:18
thy corn to be meat for thine e	Is 62:8
rendereth recompence to his e	Is 66:6
and his indignation toward his e	Is 66:14
of my soul into the hand of her e	Jer 12:7
to the sword before their e	Jer 15:9
make thee to pass with thine e	Jer 15:14
e in the land which thou knowest	Jer 17:4
fall by the sword before their e	Jer 19:7
and straitness, wherewith their e	Jer 19:9
fall by the sword of their e	Jer 20:4
I give into the hand of their e	Jer 20:5
and into the hand of their e	Jer 21:7
them into the hand of their e	Jer 34:20
I give into the hand of their e	Jer 34:21
of Egypt into the hand of his e	Jer 44:30
the going down of Horonaim the e	Jer 48:5
to be dismayed before their e	Jer 49:37
with her, they are become her e	Lam 1:2
are the chief, her e prosper	Lam 1:5
all mine e have heard of my	Lam 1:21
All thine e have opened their	Lam 2:16
All our e have opened their	Lam 3:46
Mine e chased me sore, like a	Lam 3:52
them into the hand of their e	Eze 39:23
interpretation thereof to thine e	Dan 4:19
go into captivity before their e	Amos 9:4
free from the hand of thine e	Mic 4:10
all thine e shall be cut off	Mic 5:9
a man's e are the men of his own	Mic 7:6
and he reserveth wrath for his e	Nah 1:2
and darkness shall pursue his e	Nah 1:8
be set wide open unto thine e	Nah 3:13
which tread down their e in the	Zec 10:5
But I say unto you, Love your e	Mt 5:44
till I make thine e thy footstool	Mt 22:44
till I make thine e thy footstool	Mk 12:36
we should be saved from our e	Lk 1:71
out of the hand of our e might	Lk 1:74
unto you which hear, Love your e	Lk 6:27
But love ye your e, and do good	Lk 6:35
But those mine e, which would not	Lk 19:27

that thine e shall cast a trench......... Lk 19:43
Till I make thine e thy footstool......... Lk 20:43
For if, when we were e, we were ...... Rom 5:10
they are e for your sakes.................. Rom 11:28
he hath put all e under his feet 1Cor 15:25
that they are the e of the cross.......... Phil 3:18
e in your mind by wicked works,...... Col 1:21
I make thine e thy footstool............. Heb 1:13
till his e be made his footstool.......... Heb 10:13
their mouth, and devoureth their e .... Rev 11:5
and their e beheld them .... Rev 11:12

ENEMIES'
desolate, and ye be in your e land.... Lev 26:34
in their iniquity in your e lands......... Lev 26:39
them out of their e lands.................. Eze 39:27

ENEMY
LORD, hath dashed in pieces the e.... Ex 15:6
The e said, I will pursue, I will.......... Ex 15:9
then I will be an e unto thine .... Ex 23:22
delivered into the hand of the e .... Lev 26:25
against the e that oppresseth you,..... Num 10:9
that he die, and was not his e............ Num 35:23
wherewith thine e shall distress......... Deut 28:57
that I feared the wrath of the e .... Deut 32:27
beginning of revenges upon the e ..... Deut 32:42
thrust out the e from before thee....... Deut 33:27
Samson our e into our hand.............. Judg 16:23
delivered into our hands our e .... Judg 16:24
shalt see an e in my habitation 1Sa 2:32
Saul became David's e continually.... 1Sa 18:29
me so, and sent away mine e 1Sa 19:17
deliver thine e into thine hand.......... 1Sa 24:4
For if a man find his e, will he 1Sa 24:19
thine e into thine hand this day 1Sa 26:8
from thee, and is become thine e 1Sa 28:16
the son of Saul thine e, which............ 2Sa 4:8
He delivered me from my strong e 2Sa 22:18
be smitten down before the e............ 1Kin 8:33
if their e besiege them in the............. 1Kin 8:37
go out to battle against their e 1Kin 8:44
them, and deliver them to the e 1Kin 8:46
captives unto the land of the e 1Kin 8:46
Hast thou found me, O mine e 1Kin 21:20
be put to the worse before the e 2Chr 6:24
shall make thee fall before the e 2Chr 25:8
to help the king against the e 2Chr 26:13
help us against the e in the way .... Ezr 8:22
us from the hand of the e .... Ezr 8:31
the Agagite, the Jews' e .... Est 3:10
tongue, although the e could not........ Est 7:4
and e is this wicked Haman .... Est 7:6
the Jews' e unto Esther the queen...... Est 8:1
the e of the Jews, slew they............... Est 9:10
the e of all the Jews, had .... Est 9:24
face, and holdest me for thine e......... Job 13:24
mine e sharpeneth his eyes upon...... Job 16:9
Let mine e be as the wicked, and...... Job 27:7
me, he counteth me for his e .... Job 33:10
him that without cause is mine e .... Ps 7:4
Let the e persecute my soul, and...... Ps 7:5
that thou mightest still the e .... Ps 8:2
O thou e, destructions are come ...... Ps 9:6
shall mine e be exalted over me......... Ps 13:2
Lest mine e say, I have prevailed ...... Ps 13:4
He delivered me from my strong e .... Ps 18:17
shut me up into the hand of the e...... Ps 31:8
because mine e doth not triumph...... Ps 41:11
the oppression of the e .... Ps 42:9
of the oppression of the e .... Ps 43:2
makest us to turn back from the e ..... Ps 44:10
by reason of the e and avenger.......... Ps 44:16
Because of the voice of the e............ Ps 55:3
For it was not an e that.................... Ps 55:12
me, and a strong tower from the e..... Ps 61:3
my life from fear of the e .... Ps 64:1
even all that the e hath done............ Ps 74:3
shall the e blaspheme thy name......... Ps 74:10
that the e hath reproached, O .... Ps 74:18
when he delivered them from the e ... Ps 78:42
The e shall not exact upon him .... Ps 89:22
them from the hand of the e .... Ps 106:10
redeemed from the hand of the e ...... Ps 107:2
For the e hath persecuted my soul ... Ps 143:3
Rejoice not when thine e falleth .... Prov 24:17
If thine e be hungry, give him .... Prov 25:21
the kisses of an e are deceitful.......... Prov 27:6
When the e shall come in like a .... Is 59:19
he was turned to be their e .... Is 63:10
for the sword of the e and fear is...... Jer 6:25
verily I will cause the e to................. Jer 15:11
as with an east wind before the e ...... Jer 18:17
thee with the wound of an e .... Jer 30:14
come again from the land of the e .... Jer 31:16
king of Babylon, his e, and that........ Jer 44:30
gone into captivity before the e .... Lam 1:5
fell into the hand of the e .... Lam 1:7
for the e hath magnified himself .... Lam 1:9
desolate, because the e prevailed ..... Lam 1:16
his right hand from before the e .... Lam 2:3
He hath bent his bow like an e .... Lam 2:4
The Lord was as an e .... Lam 2:5
of the e the walls of her palaces .... Lam 2:7
thine e to rejoice over thee .... Lam 2:17
brought up hath mine e consumed,... Lam 2:22
the e should have entered into.......... Lam 4:12
Because the e hath said against......... Eze 36:2
the e shall pursue him .... Hos 8:3
my people is risen up as an e .... Mic 2:8
Rejoice not against me, O mine e ..... Mic 7:8

she that is mine e shall see it .... Mic 7:10
seek strength because of the e........... Nah 3:11
he hath cast out thine e .... Zeph 3:15
thy neighbour, and hate thine e........ Mt 5:43
his e came and sowed tares among.... Mt 13:25
unto them, An e hath done this......... Mt 13:28
The e that sowed them is the............ Mt 13:39
and over all the power of the e .... Lk 10:19
thou e of all righteousness, wilt........ Acts 13:10
Therefore if thine e hunger.............. Rom 12:20
The last e that shall be 1Cor 15:26
Am I therefore become your e .... Gal 4:16
Yet count him not as an e 2Th 3:15
of the world is the e of God.............. Jas 4:4

ENEMY'S
If thou meet thine e ox or his............ Ex 23:4
Or, Deliver me from the e hand .... Job 8:23
and his glory into the e hand............. Ps 78:61

ENFLAMING
E yourselves with idols under............ Is 57:5

ENGAGED
for who is this that e his heart,.......... Jer 30:21

EN-GANNIM (en-gan´-nim)
 1. A city in Judah.
and E, Tappuah, and Enam .... Josh 15:34
 2. A city in Issachar.
and E, and En-haddah, and............... Josh 19:21
her suburbs, E and her suburbs......... Josh 21:29

EN-GEDI (en-ghe´-di) See HAZAZON-TAMAR. A
 town on the Salt Sea.
and the city of Salt, and E .... Josh 15:62
and dwelt in strong holds at E 1Sa 23:29
David is in the wilderness of E 1Sa 24:1
be in Hazazon-tamar, which is E 2Chr 20:2
of camphire in the vineyards of E...... Song 1:14
it from E even unto En-eglaim........... Eze 47:10

ENGINES
And he made in Jerusalem 2Chr 26:15
he shall set e of war against thy........ Eze 26:9

ENGRAFTED
receive with meekness the e word..... Jas 1:21

ENGRAVE
shalt thou e the two stones with........ Ex 28:11
I will e the graving thereof,............... Zec 3:9

ENGRAVEN
e in stones, was glorious, so 2Cor 3:7

ENGRAVER
With the work of an e in stone .... Ex 28:11
work all manner of work, of the e ..... Ex 35:35
of the tribe of Dan, an e .... Ex 38:23

ENGRAVINGS
like the e of a signet, shalt................ Ex 28:11
names, like the e of a signet.............. Ex 28:21
like the e of a signet, HOLINESS...... Ex 28:36
like the e of a signet, every one .... Ex 39:14
like to the e of a signet..................... Ex 39:30

EN-HADDAH (en-had´-dah) A city in Issachar.
And Remeth, and En-gannim, and E . Josh 19:21

EN-HAKKORE (en-hak´-ko-re) A spring.
he called the name thereof E .... Judg 15:19

EN-HAZOR (en-ha´-zor) A city in Naphtali.
And Kedesh, and Edrei, and E .... Josh 19:37

ENJOIN
e thee that which is convenient.......... Philem 8

ENJOINED
and Esther the queen had e them...... Est 9:31
Who hath e him his way .... Job 36:23
which God hath unto you .... Heb 9:20

ENJOY
shall the land e her sabbaths............. Lev 26:34
the land rest, and e her sabbaths....... Lev 26:34
shall e her sabbaths, while she.......... Lev 26:43
e every man the inheritance of.......... Num 36:8
but thou shalt not e them.................. Deut 28:41
e it, which Moses the LORD's........... Josh 1:15
with mirth, therefore e pleasure .... Eccl 2:1
his soul e good in his labour............. Eccl 2:24
e the good of all his labour, it........... Eccl 3:13
to e the good of all his labour .... Eccl 5:18
mine elect shall long e the work........ Is 65:22
that by thee we e great quietness,..... Acts 24:2
giveth us richly all things to e 1Ti 6:17
than to e the pleasures of sin .... Heb 11:25

ENJOYED
until the land had e her sabbaths....... 2Chr 36:21

ENLARGE
God shall e Japheth, and he shall..... Gen 9:27
the LORD thy God shall e thy borders. Ex 34:24
Lord thy God shall e thy border........ Deut 12:20
if the LORD thy God e thy coast .... Deut 19:8
e my coast, and that thine hand 1Chr 4:10
when thou shalt e my heart.............. Ps 119:32
The place of thy tent, and let............ Is 54:2
that they might e their border .... Amos 1:13
e thy baldness as the eagle............... Mic 1:16
the borders of their garments,.......... Mt 23:5

ENLARGED
My mouth is over mine enemies,....... 1Sa 2:1
Thou hast e my steps under me......... 2Sa 22:37

thou hast e me when I was in............ Ps 4:1
Thou hast e my steps under me,........ Ps 18:36
The troubles of my heart are e........... Ps 25:17
Therefore hath hell e herself............. Is 5:14
thou hast e thy bed, and made thee .. Is 57:8
thine heart shall fear, and be e .... Is 60:5
is open unto you, our heart is e 2Cor 6:11
unto my children,) be ye also e 2Cor 6:13
that we shall be e by you 2Cor 10:15

ENLARGEMENT
at this time, then shall there e .... Est 4:14

ENLARGETH
he said, Blessed be he that e Gad...... Deut 33:20
he e the nations, and straiteneth .... Job 12:23
who e his desire as hell, and is.......... Hab 2:5

ENLARGING
And there was an e, and a winding ... Eze 41:7

ENLIGHTEN
LORD my God will e my darkness..... Ps 18:28

ENLIGHTENED
and his eyes were e 1Sa 14:27
you, how mine eyes have been e 1Sa 14:29
to be e with the light of the............... Job 33:30
His lightnings e the world .... Ps 97:4
of your understanding being e .... Eph 1:18
for those who were once e .... Heb 6:4

ENLIGHTENING
of the LORD is pure, e the eyes........ Ps 19:8

ENMITY
I will put e between thee and the...... Gen 3:15
Or in e smite him with his hand,...... Num 35:21
he thrust him suddenly without e ...... Num 35:22
they were at e between themselves.... Lk 23:12
the carnal mind is e against God....... Rom 8:7
abolished in his flesh the e .... Eph 2:15
cross, having slain the e thereby .... Eph 2:16
of the world is e with God................ Jas 4:4

ENOCH (e´-nok) See HENOCH.
 1. Son of Cain.
and she conceived, and bare E.......... Gen 4:17
And unto E was born Irad .... Gen 4:18
 2. A city built by Cain.
after the name of his son, E.............. Gen 4:17
 3. A son of Jared.
sixty and two years, and he begat E... Gen 5:18
he begat E eight hundred years......... Gen 5:19
E lived sixty and five years, and........ Gen 5:21
E walked with God after he begat ..... Gen 5:22
all the days of E were three .... Gen 5:23
And E walked with God .... Gen 5:24
Mathusala, which was the son of E... Lk 3:37
By faith E was translated that he .... Heb 11:5
E also, the seventh from Adam,........ Jude 14

ENOS (e´-nos) See ENOSH. Son of Seth.
and he called his name E .... Gen 4:26
hundred and five years, and begat E.. Gen 5:6
after he begat E eight hundred.......... Gen 5:7
E lived ninety years, and begat......... Gen 5:9
E lived after he begat Cainan............ Gen 5:10
all the days of E were nine .... Gen 5:11
Which was the son of E, which was... Lk 3:38

ENOSH (e´-nosh) See ENOS. Same as Enos.
Adam, Sheth, E,............................. 1Chr 1:1

ENOUGH
We have both straw and provender e . Gen 24:25
And Esau said, I have e, my .... Gen 33:11
with me, and because I have e .... Gen 33:9
behold, it is large e for them .... Gen 34:21
And Israel said, It is e .... Gen 45:28
and also drew water e for us .... Ex 2:19
Intreat the LORD (for it is e) .... Ex 9:28
e for the service of the work .... Ex 36:5
have dwelt long e in this mount .... Deut 1:6
compassed this mountain long e .... Deut 2:3
said, The hill is not e for us.............. Josh 17:16
destroyed the people, It is e 2Sa 24:16
and said, It is e 1Kin 19:4
the angel that destroyed, It is e 1Chr 21:15
of the LORD, we have had e to eat.... 2Chr 31:10
have goats' milk e for thy food.......... Prov 27:27
vain persons shall have poverty e ...... Prov 28:19
yea, four things say not, It is e .... Prov 30:15
the fire that saith not, It is e .... Prov 30:16
dogs which can never have e .... Is 56:11
will destroy till they have e .... Jer 49:9
For they shall eat, and not have e...... Hos 4:10
not have stolen till they had e .... Obad 5
tear in pieces e for his whelps.......... Nah 2:12
ye eat, but ye have not e .... Hag 1:6
shall not be room e to receive it .... Mal 3:10
It is e for the disciple that he............ Mt 10:25
lest there be not e for us .... Mt 25:9
it is e, the hour is come .... Mk 14:41
of my father's have bread e .... Lk 15:17
And he said unto them, It is e .... Lk 22:38
And when they had eaten, they .... Acts 27:38

ENQUIRE
the damsel, and e at her mouth........ Gen 24:57
And she went to e of the LORD........ Gen 25:22
people come unto me to e .... Ex 18:15
that thou e not after their gods,........ Deut 12:30
Then shalt thou e, and make search.. Deut 13:14
that shall be in those days, and......... Deut 17:9
e of thee, and say, Is there any .... Judg 4:20

when a man went to e of God 1Sa 9:9
E thou whose son the stripling is 1Sa 17:56
I then begin to e of God for him 1Sa 22:15
that I may go to her, and of her 1Sa 28:7
said unto the king of Israel, E. 1Kin 22:5
besides, that we might e of him 1Kin 22:7
by whom we may e of the LORD 1Kin 22:8
e of Baal-zebub the god of Ekron 2Kin 1:2
that ye go to e of Baal-zebub the 2Kin 1:3
that thou sendest to e of 2Kin 1:6
e of Baal-zebub the god of Ekron 2Kin 1:16
no God in Israel to e of his word 2Kin 1:16
that we may e of the LORD by him 2Kin 3:11
e of the LORD by him, saying 2Kin 8:8
altar shall be for me to e by 2Kin 16:15
e of the LORD for me, and for the 2Kin 22:13
which sent you to e of the LORD 2Kin 22:18
had a familiar spirit, to e of it 1Chr 10:13
to e of his welfare, and to 1Chr 18:10
not go before it to e of God 1Chr 21:30
said unto the king of Israel, E 2Chr 18:6
besides, that we might e of him 2Chr 18:6
man, by whom we may e of the LORD 2Chr 18:7
who sent unto him to e of the 2Chr 32:31
e of the LORD for me, and for them 2Chr 34:21
who sent you to e of the LORD 2Chr 34:26
to e concerning Judah and .... Ezr 7:14
For e, I pray thee, of the former ...... Job 8:8
the LORD, and to e in his temple .... Ps 27:4
for thou dost not e wisely .... Eccl 7:10
also the night: if ye will e .... Is 21:12
e ye: return, come .... Is 21:12
E, I pray thee, of the LORD for .... Jer 21:2
that sent you unto me to e of me .... Jer 37:7
prophet to e of him concerning me ..... Eze 14:7
of Israel came to e of the LORD .... Eze 20:1
Are ye come to e of me .... Eze 20:3
enter, e who in it is worthy .... Mt 10:11
they began to e among themselves, ... Lk 22:23
Do ye e among yourselves of that, ... Jn 16:19
e in the house of Judas for one .... Acts 9:11
But if ye e any thing concerning .... Acts 19:39
as though ye would e something .... Acts 23:15
as though they would e somewhat .... Acts 23:20
Whether any do e of Titus 2Cor 8:23

ENQUIRED
e diligently, and, behold, it be .... Deut 17:4
And when they e and asked, they .... Judg 6:29
the men of Succoth, and e of him .... Judg 8:14
children of Israel e of the LORD .... Judg 20:27
Therefore they e of the LORD 1Sa 10:22
the e of the LORD for him, and gave 1Sa 22:10
hast e of God for him, that he 1Sa 22:13
Therefore David e of the LORD 1Sa 23:2
Then David e of the LORD 1Sa 23:4
when Saul e of the LORD, the LORD 1Sa 23:8
David e at the LORD, saying 1Sa 30:8
that David e of the LORD, saying 2Sa 2:1
David e of the LORD, saying 2Sa 5:19
when David e of the LORD, he said 2Sa 5:23
David sent and e after the woman 2Sa 11:3
was as if a man had e at the 2Sa 16:23
and David e of the LORD 2Sa 21:1
And e not of the LORD 1Chr 10:14
for we e not at it in the days of 1Chr 13:3
David e of God, saying, Shall I 1Chr 14:10
Therefore David e again of God 1Chr 14:14
returned and e early after God .... Ps 78:34
should I be e of at all by them .... Eze 14:3
Gop, I will not be e of by you .... Eze 20:3
and shall I be e of by you .... Eze 20:31
Gop, I will not be e of by you .... Eze 20:31
I will yet for this be e of by .... Eze 36:37
that the king e of them, he .... Dan 1:20
sought the LORD, nor for him .... Zeph 1:6
e of them diligently what time .... Mt 2:7
had diligently e of the wise men ...... Mt 2:16
Then e he of them the hour when .... Jn 4:52
or our brethren be e of, they are ...... Acts 4:9
salvation the prophets have e 1Pet 1:10

ENQUIREST
That thou e after mine iniquity, ... Job 10:6

ENQUIRY
is holy, and, after vows to make e .... Prov 20:25
had made e for Simon's house .... Acts 10:17

ENRICH
the king will e him with great 1Sa 17:25
thou didst e the kings of the .... Eze 27:33

ENRICHED
in every thing ye are e by him 1Cor 1:5
Being e in every thing to all 2Cor 9:11

ENRICHEST
thou greatly e it with the river ...... Ps 65:9

EN-RIMMON (en-rim'-mon) See AIN, RIMMON.
A city in Judah.
And at E, and at Zareah, and at .... Neh 11:29

EN-ROGEL (en-ro'-ghel) A fountain near
Jerusalem.
the goings out thereof were at E ...... Josh 15:7
on the south, and descended to E ...... Josh 18:16
Jonathan and Ahimaaz stayed by E 2Sa 17:17
stone of Zoheleth, which is by E 1Kin 1:9

ENSAMPLE
walk so as ye have us for an e .... Phil 3:17
an e unto us to follow us 2Th 3:9

making them an e unto those that 2Pet 2:6

ENSAMPLES
things happened unto them for e 1Cor 10:11
So that we were e to all that 1Th 1:7
but being e to the flock 1Pet 5:3

EN-SHEMESH (en-she'-mesh) A spring.
passed toward the waters of E .... Josh 15:7
the north, and went forth to E .... Josh 18:17

ENSIGN
with the e of their father's........... Num 2:2
he will lift up an e to the .... Is 5:26
stand for an e of the people .... Is 11:10
shall set up an e for the nations ..... Is 11:12
lifteth up an e on the mountains ...... Is 18:3
a mountain, and as an e on an hill .... Is 30:17
princes shall be afraid of the e ...... Is 31:9
lifted up as an e upon his land .... Zec 9:16

ENSIGNS
they set up their e for signs .... Ps 74:4

ENSNARED
reign not, lest the people be e .... Job 34:30

ENSUE
let him seek peace, and e it 1Pet 3:11

ENTANGLE
how they might e him in his talk ...... Mt 22:15

ENTANGLED
They are e in the land, the .... Ex 14:3
be not e again with the yoke of ...... Gal 5:1
Christ, they are again e therein 2Pet 2:20

ENTANGLETH
No man that warreth e himself 2Ti 2:4

EN-TAPPUAH (en-tap'-poo-ah) A town in
Manasseh.
hand unto the inhabitants of E .... Josh 17:7

ENTER
he was come near to e into Egypt ...... Gen 12:11
able to e into the tent of the .... Ex 40:35
all that e into the host, to do .... Num 4:3
all that e in to perform the .... Num 4:23
the curse shall e into her .... Num 5:24
the curse shall e into her .... Num 5:27
for he shall not e into the land ...... Num 20:24
shall not e into the congregation ..... Deut 23:1
A bastard shall not e into the .... Deut 23:2
e into the congregation of the .... Deut 23:2
e into the congregation of the .... Deut 23:3
e into the congregation of the .... Deut 23:3
e into the congregation of the .... Deut 23:8
That thou shouldest e into .... Deut 29:12
them not to e into their cities .... Josh 10:19
go, and to e to possess the land ...... Judg 18:9
my cry did e into his ears 2Sa 22:7
and when thy feet e into the city 1Kin 14:12
myself, and e into the battle 1Kin 22:30
We will e into the city, then the 2Kin 7:4
A third part of you that e in on 2Kin 11:5
I will e into the lodgings of his 2Kin 19:23
the priests could not e into the 2Chr 7:2
unclean in any thing should e in 2Chr 23:19
e into his sanctuary, which he 2Chr 30:8
for the house that I shall e into ..... Neh 2:8
for none might e into the king's ...... Est 4:2
will he e with thee into judgment ..... Job 22:4
that he should e into judgment .... Job 34:23
Their sword shall e into their .... Ps 37:15
they shall e into the king's .... Ps 45:15
they should not e into my rest .... Ps 95:11
E into his gates with .... Ps 100:4
into which the righteous shall e ...... Ps 118:20
e not into judgment with thy .... Ps 143:2
E not into the path of the wicked ..... Prov 4:14
A fool's lips e into contention, ... Prov 18:6
e not into the fields of the .... Prov 23:10
E into the rock, and hide thee in ..... Is 2:10
The LORD will e into judgment .... Is 3:14
which keepeth the truth may e in ...... Is 26:2
e thou into thy chambers, and shut ... Is 26:20
I will e into the height of his ...... Is 37:24
He shall e into peace: .... Is 57:2
in the street, and equity cannot e ... Is 59:14
that e in at these gates to .... Jer 7:2
let us e into the defenced cities .... Jer 8:14
if I e into the city, then behold .... Jer 14:18
E not into the house of mourning, ... Jer 16:5
that e in by these gates .... Jer 17:20
Then shall there e into the gates .... Jer 17:25
or who shall e into our .... Jer 21:13
thy people that e in by these .... Jer 22:2
then shall there e in by the .... Jer 22:4
Bethlehem, to e into Egypt, ... Jer 41:17
set your faces to e into Egypt .... Jer 42:15
you, when ye shall e into Egypt ...... Jer 42:18
not e into thy congregation .... Lam 1:10
of his savior to e into my reins ..... Lam 3:13
for the robbers shall e into it ...... Eze 7:22
neither shall they e into the .... Eze 13:9
they shall not e into the land of ... Eze 20:38
when he shall e into thy gates, ... Eze 26:10
as men e into a city wherein is ..... Eze 26:10
I will cause breath to e into you ... Eze 37:5
When the priests e therein .... Eze 42:14
and no man shall e in by it .... Eze 44:2
he shall e by the way of the .... Eze 44:3
shall e into my sanctuary, of any ... Eze 44:9

They shall e into my sanctuary, ... Eze 44:16
that when they e in at the gates ..... Eze 44:17
when they e into the inner court ..... Eze 44:21
the prince shall e by the way of ..... Eze 46:2
And when the prince shall e .... Eze 46:8
shall e into the fortress of the .... Dan 11:7
He shall also set his face to e ..... Dan 11:17
He shall e peaceably even upon ...... Dan 11:24
he shall e into the countries, and .. Dan 11:40
He shall e also into the glorious ... Dan 11:41
I will not e into the city .... Hos 11:9
they shall e in at the windows ...... Joel 2:9
nor e into Gilgal, and pass not to .. Amos 5:5
Jonah began to e into the city a .... Jonah 3:4
it shall e into the house of the ... Zec 5:4
ye shall in no case e into the ..... Mt 5:20
e into thy closet, and when thou ... Mt 6:6
E ye in at the strait gate .... Mt 7:13
shall e into the kingdom of .... Mt 7:21
city of the Samaritans e ye not .... Mt 10:5
city or town ye shall e, enquire ... Mt 10:11
Or else how can one e into a .... Mt 12:29
wicked than himself, and they e in . Mt 12:45
ye shall not e into the kingdom .... Mt 18:3
to e into life halt or maimed ...... Mt 18:8
thee to e into life with one eye ... Mt 18:9
but if thou wilt e into life .... Mt 19:17
e into the kingdom of heaven .... Mt 19:23
than for a rich man to e into the .. Mt 19:24
e thou into the joy of thy lord .... Mt 25:21
e thou into the joy of thy lord .... Mt 25:23
that ye e not into temptation ..... Mt 26:41
no more openly e into the city .... Mk 1:45
No man can e into a strong man's .. Mk 3:27
swine, that we may e into them .... Mk 5:12
place soever ye e into a house .... Mk 6:10
out of him, and e no more into him . Mk 9:25
for thee to e into life maimed .... Mk 9:43
for thee to e halt into life ...... Mk 9:45
it is better for thee to e into ... Mk 9:47
child, he shall not e therein ..... Mk 10:15
riches e into the kingdom of God .. Mk 10:23
to e into the kingdom of God ...... Mk 10:24
than for a rich man to e into the . Mk 10:25
into the house, neither e therein . Mk 13:15
lest ye e into temptation .... Mk 14:38
thou shouldest e under my roof .... Lk 7:6
that they which e in may see the .. Lk 8:16
would suffer them to e into them .. Lk 8:32
And whatsoever house ye e into .... Lk 9:4
And into whatsoever house ye e .... Lk 10:5
And into whatsoever city ye e ..... Lk 10:8
But into whatsoever city ye e ..... Lk 10:10
and they e in, and dwell there: ... Lk 11:26
Strive to e in at the strait gate . Lk 13:24
I say unto you, will seek to e in . Lk 13:24
child shall in no wise e therein .. Lk 18:17
riches e into the kingdom of God .. Lk 18:24
than for a rich man to e into the . Lk 18:25
are in the countries e thereinto .. Lk 21:21
them, Pray that ye e not into ..... Lk 22:40
lest ye e into temptation .... Lk 22:46
things, and to e into his glory ... Lk 24:26
can he e the second time into his . Jn 3:4
he cannot e into the kingdom of ... Jn 3:5
by me if any man e in, he shall ... Jn 10:9
e into the kingdom of God .... Acts 14:22
grievous wolves e in among you .... Acts 20:29
They shall not e into my rest ..... Heb 3:11
they should not e into his rest ... Heb 3:18
not e in because of unbelief ...... Heb 3:19
have believed do e into rest ...... Heb 4:3
if they shall e into my rest ...... Heb 4:3
If they shall e into my rest ...... Heb 4:5
that some must e therein, and they . Heb 4:6
therefore to e into that rest ..... Heb 4:11
boldness to e into the holiest by . Heb 10:19
man was able to e into the temple . Rev 15:8
there shall in no wise e into it .. Rev 21:27
may e in through the gates into ... Rev 22:14

ENTERED
In the selfsame day e Noah .... Gen 7:13
in unto him, and e into his house.. Gen 19:3
the earth when Lot e into Zoar .... Gen 19:23
tent, and e into Rachel's tent .... Gen 31:33
he e into his chamber, and wept ... Gen 43:30
as Moses e into the tabernacle, ... Ex 33:9
which are e into those houses ..... Josh 2:3
they e into the city, and took it, . Josh 8:19
of them e into fenced cities. ..... Josh 10:20
they e into the land to destroy ... Judg 6:5
they e into an hold of the house .. Judg 9:46
Abishai, and e into the city 2Sa 10:14
e into another tent, and carried .. 2Kin 7:8
as Jehu e in at the gate, she 2Kin 9:31
his brother, and e into the city .. 1Chr 19:15
when the king e into the house of . 2Chr 12:11
they e into a covenant to seek 2Chr 15:12
howbeit he e not into the temple .. 2Chr 27:2
e into Judah, and encamped against . 2Chr 32:1
e by the gate of the valley, and .. Neh 2:15
e into a curse, and into an oath, . Neh 10:29
Hast thou e into the springs of ... Job 38:16
Hast thou e into the treasures of . Job 38:22
but when ye e, ye defiled my land . Jer 2:7
is e into our palaces, to cut off . Jer 9:21
which had e into the covenant, ... Jer 34:10
Jeremiah was e into the dungeon, .. Jer 37:16
the heathen e into her sanctuary, . Lam 1:10
the enemy should have e into the .. Lam 4:12

the spirit *e* into me when he .... Eze 2:2
Then the spirit *e* into me...................... Eze 3:24
e into a covenant with thee........................ Eze 36:20
when they *e* unto the heathen,................. Eze 36:20
they *e* into the wall which was of .... Eze 41:6
hath *e* in by it, therefore it .... Eze 44:2
foreigners *e* into his gates, and .... Obad 11
Thou shouldest not have *e* into .... Obad 13
rottenness *e* into my bones, and I .... Hab 3:16
when Jesus was *e* into Capernaum .... Mt 8:5
And when he was *e* into a ship............... Mt 8:23
he *e* into a ship, and passed over,............. Mt 9:1
How he *e* into the house of God,.............. Mt 12:4
the day that Noe *e* into the ark................ Mt 24:38
day he *e* into the synagogue..................... Mk 1:21
they *e* into the house of Simon and......... Mk 1:29
again he *e* into Capernaum after............. Mk 2:1
he *e* again into the synagogue.................. Mk 3:1
so that he *e* into a ship, and sat............... Mk 4:1
went out, and *e* into the swine................ Mk 5:13
And whithersoever he *e*, into................... Mk 6:56
when he was *e* into the house from.......... Mk 7:17
he *e* into an house, and would have no..... Mk 7:24
straightway he *e* into a ship with............ Mk 8:10
and as soon as ye be *e* into it .... Mk 11:2
Jesus *e* into Jerusalem, and into .... Mk 11:11
e into the house of Zacharias, and .... Lk 1:40
and *e* into Simon's house .... Lk 4:38
he *e* into one of the ships, which .... Lk 5:3
that he *e* into the synagogue and .... Lk 6:6
the people, he *e* into Capernaum .... Lk 7:1
I *e* into thine house, thou gavest............. Lk 7:44
many devils were *e* into him .... Lk 8:30
of the man, and *e* into the swine .... Lk 8:33
feared as they *e* into the cloud .... Lk 9:34
went, and *e* into a village of the .... Lk 9:52
that he *e* into a certain village................ Lk 10:38
ye *e* not in yourselves, and them .... Lk 11:52
as he *e* into a certain village,.................. Lk 17:12
the day that Noe *e* into the ark............... Lk 17:27
And Jesus *e* and passed through .... Lk 19:1
Then *e* Satan into Judas surnamed .... Lk 22:3
when ye are *e* into the city,..................... Lk 22:10
And they *e* in, and found not the .... Lk 24:3
ye are *e* into their labours .... Jn 4:38
e into a ship, and went over the .... Jn 6:17
whereinto his disciples were *e* .... Jn 6:22
And after the sop Satan *e* into him .... Jn 13:27
was a garden, into the which he *e* .... Jn 18:1
Then Pilate *e* into the judgment .... Jn 18:33
e into a ship immediately.......................... Jn 21:3
of them that *e* into the temple .... Acts 3:2
e with them into the temple,.................... Acts 3:8
they *e* into the temple early in .... Acts 5:21
went his way, and *e* into the house .... Acts 9:17
morrow after they *e* into Caesarea........... Acts 10:24
hath at any time *e* into my mouth .... Acts 11:8
we *e* into the man's house,........................ Acts 11:12
e into the house of Lydia.......................... Acts 16:40
into a certain man's house,........................... Acts 18:7
but he himself *e* into .... Acts 18:19
would have *e* in unto the people............. Acts 19:30
we *e* into the house of Philip the............ Acts 21:8
with them *e* into the temple .... Acts 21:26
e into the castle, and told Paul .... Acts 23:16
was *e* into the place of hearing,............... Acts 25:23
to whom Paul *e* in, and prayed, and .... Acts 28:8
by one man sin *e* into the world.............. Rom 5:12
Moreover the law *e*, that the.................... Rom 5:20
neither have *e* into the heart of 1Cor 2:9
e not in because of unbelief..................... Heb 4:6
For he that is *e* into his rest .... Heb 4:10
the forerunner is for us *e*,........................ Heb 6:20
but by his own blood *e* in once .... Heb 9:12
For Christ is not *e* into the holy............. Heb 9:24
e into the ears of the Lord of .... Jas 5:4
deceivers are *e* into the world.................. 2Jn 7
of life from God *e* into them .... Rev 11:11

ENTERETH

every one that *e* into the service .... Num 4:30
every one that *e* into the service .... Num 4:35
every one that *e* into the service .... Num 4:39
every one that *e* into the service .... Num 4:43
even unto every one that *e* into............... 2Chr 31:16
When wisdom *e* into thine heart,............. Prov 2:10
A reproof *e* more into a wise man .... Prov 17:10
which *e* into their privy chambers .... Eze 21:14
the east, as one *e* into .... Eze 42:12
he that *e* in by the way of the .... Eze 46:9
he that *e* by the way of the south............ Eze 46:9
that whatsoever *e* in at the mouth........... Mt 15:17
e in where the damsel was lying............... Mk 5:40
thing from without *e* into the man .... Mk 7:18
Because it *e* not into his heart,................. Mk 7:19
him into the house where he *e* .... Lk 22:10
He that *e* not by the door into................. Jn 10:1
But he that *e* in by the door is................. Jn 10:2
which *e* into that within the veil............. Heb 6:19
as the high priest which *e* .... Heb 9:25

ENTERING

at the *e* in of the tabernacle...................... Ex 35:15
cast it at the *e* of the gate....................... Josh 8:29
Hermon unto the *e* into Hamath .... Josh 13:5
at the *e* of the gate of the city .... Josh 20:4
unto the *e* in of Hamath.......................... Judg 3:3
stood in the *e* of the gate of the .... Judg 9:35
even unto the *e* of the gate .... Judg 9:40
stood in the *e* of the gate of the .... Judg 9:44
Dan, stood by the *e* of the gate .... Judg 18:16

the priest stood in the *e* of the .... Judg 18:17
by *e* into a town that hath gates.............. 1Sa 13:17
in array at the *e* in of the gate................ 2Sa 10:8
then even unto the *e* of the gate.............. 2Sa 11:23
for the *e* of the oracle he made................ 1Kin 6:31
from the *e* in of Hamath unto the........... 1Kin 8:65
stood in the *e* in of the cave.................... 1Kin 19:13
men at the *e* in of the gate 2Kin 7:3
at the *e* in of the gate until the 2Kin 10:8
the coast of Israel from the *e* of............. 2Kin 14:25
e in of the gate of Joshua the................... 2Kin 23:8
at the *e* in of the house of the 2Kin 23:11
e in of the wilderness from the 1Chr 5:9
Egypt even unto the *e* of Hemath 1Chr 13:5
from the *e* in of Hamath unto the........... 2Chr 7:8
the *e* in of the gate of Samaria................ 2Chr 18:9
part of you *e* on the sabbath.................... 2Chr 23:4
stood at his pillar at the *e* in 2Chr 23:13
when she was come to the *e* of the 2Chr 23:15
abroad even to the *e* in of Egypt........... 2Chr 26:8
even to the *e* in at the fish gate............... 2Chr 33:14
that there is no house, no *e* in .... Is 23:1
the *e* of the gates of Jerusalem .... Jer 1:15
even *e* in at the gates of .... Jer 17:27
mark well the *e* in of the house,............. Eze 8:5
e in of Hemath unto the river of .... Amos 6:14
ye them that are *e* to go in .... Mt 23:13
and the lusts of other things *e* in............ Mk 4:19
that *e* into him can defile him.................. Mk 7:15
e into the ship again departed to .... Mk 8:13
e into the sepulchre, they saw a.............. Mk 16:5
them that were *e* in ye hindered.............. Lk 11:52
to them at your *e* shall............................ Lk 19:30
e into every house, and haling men......... Acts 8:3
e into a ship of Adramyttium, we............ Acts 27:2
manner of *e* in we had unto you.............. 1Th 1:9
being left us of *e* into his rest................. Heb 4:1

ENTERPRISE

hands cannot perform their *e* .... Job 5:12

ENTERTAIN

Be not forgetful to *e* strangers .... Heb 13:2

ENTERTAINED

some have *e* angels unawares................... Heb 13:2

ENTICE

if a man *e* a maid that is not .... Ex 22:16
e thee secretly, saying, Let us.................. Deut 13:6
E thy husband, that he may .... Judg 14:15
E him, and see wherein his great............. Judg 16:5
Who shall *e* Ahab king of Israel,............. 2Chr 18:19
the LORD, and said, I will *e* him.............. 2Chr 18:20
the LORD said, Thou shalt *e* him............. 2Chr 18:21
My son, if sinners *e* thee......................... Prov 1:10

ENTICED

And my heart hath been secretly *e*.......... Job 31:27
saying, Peradventure he will be *e*............ Jer 20:10
drawn away of his own lust, and *e*........... Jas 1:14

ENTICETH

A violent man *e* his neighbour................. Prov 16:29

ENTICING

not with *e* words of man's wisdom.......... 1Cor 2:4
should beguile you with *e* words .... Col 2:4

ENTIRE

work, that ye may be perfect and *e*.......... Jas 1:4

ENTRANCE

your border unto the *e* of Hamath .... Num 34:8
the *e* into the city, and we will................ Judg 1:24
shewed them the *e* into the city............... Judg 1:25
before Ahab to the *e* of Jezreel 1Kin 18:46
in the *e* of the gate of Samaria 1Kin 22:10
And they went to the *e* of Gedor 1Chr 4:39
that kept the *e* of the king's.................... 2Chr 12:10
The *e* of thy words giveth light............... Ps 119:130
the face of the gate of the *e* .... Eze 40:15
know our *e* in unto you, that it............... 1Th 2:1
For so an *e* shall be ministered................ 2Pet 1:11

ENTRANCES

instead of Nimrod in the *e* thereof.......... Mic 5:6

ENTREAT

I will cause the enemy to *e* thee .... Jer 15:11
e them evil four hundred years .... Acts 7:6

ENTREATED

he *e* Abram well for her sake.................. Gen 12:16
hast thou so evil *e* this people .... Ex 5:22
And the Egyptians evil *e* us..................... Deut 26:6
e them spitefully, and slew them............. Mt 22:6
shall be mocked, and spitefully *e*............ Lk 18:32
e him shamefully, and sent him............... Lk 20:11
evil *e* our fathers, so that they .... Acts 7:19
And Julius courteously *e* Paul .... Acts 27:3
before, and were shamefully *e*................. 1Th 2:2

ENTREATETH

He evil *e* the barren that beareth .... Job 24:21

ENTRIES

the *e* thereof were by the posts............... Eze 40:38

ENTRY

house, and the king's was without.............. 2Kin 16:18
the LORD, were keepers of the *e*............. 1Chr 9:19
for the *e* of the house, the inner 2Chr 4:22
at the *e* of the city, at the .... Prov 8:3
which is by the *e* of the new................... Jer 19:2
sat down in the *e* of the new gate........... Jer 26:10
at the *e* of the new gate of the .... Jer 36:10

e that is in the house of the.................... Jer 38:14
which is at the *e* of Pharaoh's................. Jer 43:9
this image of jealousy in the *e* .... Eze 8:5
art situate at the *e* of the sea .... Eze 27:3
the breadth of the *e* of the gate.............. Eze 40:11
up to the *e* of the north gate .... Eze 40:40
was the *e* on the east side........................ Eze 42:9
After he brought me through the *e* .... Eze 46:19

ENVIED

and the Philistines *e* him .... Gen 26:14
no children, Rachel *e* her sister............... Gen 30:1
And his brethren *e* him .... Gen 37:11
They *e* Moses also in the camp, and........ Ps 106:16
this a man is *e* of his neighbour .... Eccl 4:4
were in the garden of God, *e* him .... Eze 31:9

ENVIES

all guile, and hypocrisies, and *e*.............. 1Pet 2:1

ENVIEST

said unto him, *E* thou for my sake .... Num 11:29

ENVIETH

charity *e* not 1Cor 13:4

ENVIOUS

neither be thou *e* against the.................... Ps 37:1
For I was *e* at the foolish, when.............. Ps 73:3
Be not thou *e* against evil men,............... Prov 24:1
neither be thou *e* at the wicked.............. Prov 24:19

ENVIRON

shall *e* us round, and cut off our .... Josh 7:9

ENVY

man, and *e* slayeth the silly one .... Job 5:2
E thou not the oppressor, and................. Prov 3:31
but *e* the rottenness of the bones............ Prov 14:30
Let not thine heart *e* sinners .... Prov 23:17
but who is able to stand before *e* .... Prov 27:4
love, and their hatred, and their *e* .... Eccl 9:6
The *e* also of Ephraim shall..................... Is 11:13
Ephraim shall not *e* Judah....................... Is 11:13
ashamed for their *e* at the people............. Is 26:11
according to thine *e* which thou .... Eze 35:11
For he knew that for *e* they had.............. Mt 27:18
priests had delivered him for *e* .... Mk 15:10
And the patriarchs, moved with *e*........... Acts 7:9
they were filled with *e*, and.................... Acts 13:45
which believed not, moved with *e*........... Acts 17:5
full of *e*, murder, debate, deceit.............. Rom 1:29
indeed preach Christ even of *e*................. Phil 1:15
of words, whereof cometh *e* 1Ti 6:4
pleasures, living in malice and *e* .... Titus 3:3
that dwelleth in us lusteth to *e* .... Jas 4:5

ENVYING

and wantonness, not in strife and *e*......... Rom 13:13
for whereas there is among you *e* 1Cor 3:3
one another, *e* one another....................... Gal 5:26
But if ye have bitter *e* and strife............. Jas 3:14
For where *e* and strife is, there............... Jas 3:16

ENVYINGS

lest there be debates, *e*, wraths,.............. 2Cor 12:20
E, murders, drunkenness,.......................... Gal 5:21

EPAENETUS (ep-en'-e-tus) *A Christian acquaintance of Paul.*
Salute my wellbeloved *E*, who is .... Rom 16:5

EPAPHRAS (ep'-a-fras) *A Christian acquaintance of Paul.*
As ye also learned of *E* our dear .... Col 1:7
E, who is one of you, a servant................ Col 4:12
There salute thee *E*, my............................ Philem 23

EPAPHRODITUS (e-paf-ro-di'-tus) *A fellow-worker with Paul.*
it necessary to send to you *E*.................... Phil 2:25
having received of *E* the things................ Phil 4:18
to the Philippians from Rome by *E*.......... Phil s

EPENETUS See EPAENETUS.

EPHAH (e'-fah)
1. A son of Midian; grandson of Abraham.
E, and Epher, and Hanoch .... Gen 25:4
E, and Epher, and Hanoch 1Chr 1:33
the dromedaries of Midian and *E* .... Is 60:6
2. A concubine of Caleb.
And *E*, Caleb's concubine, bare 1Chr 2:46
3. A son of Jahdai.
Geshem, and Pelet, and *E* 1Chr 2:47
4. A grain measure.
an omer is the tenth part of an *e* .... Ex 16:36
of an *e* of fine flour for a sin .... Lev 5:11
the tenth part of an *e* of fine................... Lev 6:20
balances, just weights, a just *e* .... Lev 19:36
tenth part of an *e* of barley meal .... Num 5:15
a tenth part of an *e* of flour for .... Num 28:5
unleavened cakes of an *e* of flour .... Judg 6:19
and it was about an *e* of barley................ Ruth 2:17
one *e* of flour, and a bottle of................. 1Sa 1:24
an *e* of this parched corn 1Sa 17:17
seed of an homer shall yield an *e* .... Is 5:10
have just balances, and a just *e* .... Eze 45:10
The *e* and the bath shall be of one .... Eze 45:10
the *e* the tenth part of an homer............. Eze 45:11
part of an *e* of an homer of wheat.......... Eze 45:13
of an *e* of an homer of barley................. Eze 45:13
offering of an *e* for a bullock .... Eze 45:24
an *e* for a ram, and an hin of oil............. Eze 45:24
a ram, and an hin of oil for an *e* .... Eze 45:24
offering shall be an *e* for a ram,.............. Eze 46:5
to give, and an hin of oil to an *e* .... Eze 46:5

an *e* for a bullock, and .... Eze 46:7
an *e* for a ram, and for the lambs .... Eze 46:7
unto, and an hin of oil to an *e* .... Eze 46:7
shall be an *e* to a bullock .... Eze 46:11
an *e* to a ram, and to the lambs as .... Eze 46:11
to give, and an hin of oil to an *e* .... Eze 46:11
morning, the sixth part of an *e* .... Eze 46:14
forth wheat, making the *e* small .... Amos 8:5
This is an *e* that goeth forth .... Zec 5:6
sitteth in the midst of the *e* .... Zec 5:7
cast it into the midst of the *e* .... Zec 5:8
lifted up the *e* between the earth .... Zec 5:9
me, Whither do these bear the *e* .... Zec 5:10

EPHAI (e'-fahee) Family who remained in
    Jerusalem during captivity.
the sons of E the Netophathite, ... Jer 40:8

EPHER (e'-fur)
    1. A son of Midian; grandson of Abraham.
E, and Hanoch, and Abidah .... Gen 25:4
E, and Hanoch, and Abida, ... 1Chr 1:33
    2. A descendant of Judah.
Ezra were, Jether, and Mered, and E. .. 1Chr 4:17
    3. A chief of Manasseh.
house of their fathers, even E. 1Chr 5:24

EPHES-DAMMIM
    between Shochoh and Azekah, in E. 1Sa 17:1

EPHESIAN (e-fe'-zhun) See EPHESIANS. *A*
    resident of Ephesus.
him in the city Trophimus an E .... Acts 21:29

EPHESIANS (e-fe'-zhuns)
saying, Great is Diana of the E .... Acts 19:28
out, Great is Diana of the E .... Acts 19:34
E is a worshipper of the great .... Acts 19:35
from Rome unto the E by Tychicus .... Eph *s*
bishop of the church of the E .... 2Ti *s*

EPHESUS (ef'-e-sus) See EPHESIAN. *Capital of*
    Roman province of Asia.
And he came to E, and left them .... Acts 18:19
And he sailed from E .... Acts 18:21
in the scriptures, came to E .... Acts 18:24
the upper coasts came to E .... Acts 19:1
Jews and Greeks also dwelling at E .... Acts 19:17
see and hear, that not alone at E .... Acts 19:26
the people, he said, Ye men of E .... Acts 19:35
Paul had determined to sail by E .... Acts 20:16
And from Miletus he sent to E .... Acts 20:17
I have fought with beasts at E 1Cor 15:32
I will tarry at E until Pentecost 1Cor 16:8
God, to the saints which are at E .... Eph 1:1
besought thee to abide still at E 1Ti 1:3
things he ministered unto me at E 2Ti 1:18
And Tychicus have I sent to E 2Ti 4:12
unto E, and unto Smyrna, and unto .... Rev 1:11
angel of the church of E write .... Rev 2:1

EPHLAL (ef'-lal) *A descendant of Pharez.*
And Zabad begat E, and E begat 1Chr 2:37
begat E, and E begat Obed, ... 1Chr 2:37

EPHOD (e'-fod)
    1. Father of Hanniel.
of Manasseh, Hanniel the son of E... .... Num 34:23
    2. A priestly garment.
and stones to be set in the e .... Ex 25:7
a breastplate, and an e, and a .... Ex 28:4
And they shall make the e of gold. .... Ex 28:6
And the curious girdle of the e .... Ex 28:8
upon the shoulders of the e for .... Ex 28:12
work of the e thou shalt make it .... Ex 28:15
shoulderpieces of the e before it .... Ex 28:25
is in the side of the e inward .... Ex 28:26
the two sides of the e underneath .... Ex 28:27
above the curious girdle of the e .... Ex 28:27
of the e with a lace of blue, ... Ex 28:28
above the curious girdle of the e .... Ex 28:28
be not loosed from the e .... Ex 28:28
the robe of the e all of blue .... Ex 28:31
the coat, and the robe of the e .... Ex 29:5
and the e, and the breastplate, ... Ex 29:5
with the curious girdle of the e .... Ex 29:5
and stones to be set for the e .... Ex 35:9
and stones to be set, for the e .... Ex 35:27
And he made the e of gold, blue, ... Ex 39:2
And the curious girdle of his e .... Ex 39:5
them on the shoulders of the e .... Ex 39:7
work, like the work of the e .... Ex 39:8
on the shoulderpieces of the e .... Ex 39:18
was on the side of the e inward .... Ex 39:19
the two sides of the e underneath .... Ex 39:20
above the curious girdle of the e .... Ex 39:20
of the e with a lace of blue .... Ex 39:21
above the curious girdle of the e .... Ex 39:21
might not be loosed from the e .... Ex 39:21
the robe of the e of woven work .... Ex 39:22
put the e upon him, and he girded .... Lev 8:7
with the curious girdle of the e .... Lev 8:7
And Gideon made an e thereof .... Judg 8:27
an house of gods, and made an e .... Judg 17:5
there is in these houses an e .... Judg 18:14
took the graven image, and the e .... Judg 18:17
fetched the carved image, the e .... Judg 18:18
heart was glad, and he took the e .... Judg 18:20
a child, girded with a linen e 1Sa 2:18
incense, to wear an e before me 1Sa 2:28
priest in Shiloh, wearing an e 1Sa 14:3
wrapped in a cloth behind the e 1Sa 21:9
persons that did wear a linen e 1Sa 22:18
came down with an e in his hand 1Sa 23:6

the priest, Bring hither the e 1Sa 23:9
pray thee, bring me hither the e............ 1Sa 30:7
brought thither the e to David 1Sa 30:7
David was girded with a linen e 2Sa 6:14
also had upon him an e of linen 1Chr 15:27
without an image, and without an e .... Hos 3:4

EPHPHATHA
he sighed, and saith unto him, ... Mk 7:34

EPHRAIM (e'-fra-im) See EPHRAIMITE,
    EPHRAIM'S, EPHRAIN.
    1. A son of Joseph.
name of the second called he E .... Gen 41:52
of Egypt were born Manasseh and E.. ...... Gen 46:20
him his two sons, Manasseh and E .... Gen 48:1
And now thy two sons, E .... Gen 48:5
E in his right hand toward .... Gen 48:13
his right hand upon the head of E .... Gen 48:17
bless, saying, God make thee as E .... Gen 48:20
and he set E before Manasseh .... Gen 48:20
their families were Manasseh and .... Num 26:28
And the sons of E 1Chr 7:20
E their father mourned many days,.......... 1Chr 7:22
    2. One of the twelve tribes comprising Israel.
children of Joseph: of E .... Num 1:10
namely, of the children of E .... Num 1:32
of them, even of the tribe of E .... Num 1:33
of E according to their armies .... Num 2:18
the captain of the sons of E .... Num 2:18
of E were an hundred thousand .... Num 2:19
prince of the children of E.................... Num 7:48
E set forward according to their .... Num 10:22
Of the tribe of E, Oshea the son............. Num 13:8
sons of E after their families .... Num 26:35
of E according to those that were .... Num 26:37
of the tribe of the children of E .... Num 34:24
they are the ten thousands of E .... Deut 33:17
And all Naphtali, and the land of E......... Deut 34:2
were two tribes, Manasseh and E............ Josh 14:4
children of Joseph, Manasseh and E .... Josh 16:4
the border of the children of E .... Josh 16:5
children of E by their families .... Josh 16:5
cities for the children of E were .... Josh 16:9
belonged to the children of E .... Josh 17:8
these cities of E are among them. .... Josh 17:9
the house of Joseph, even to E .... Josh 17:17
of the families of the tribe of E .... Josh 21:5
their lot out of the tribe of E .... Josh 21:20
Neither did E drive out the .... Judg 1:29
Out of E was there a root of them, ... Judg 5:14
Then all the men of E gathered .... Judg 7:24
the men of E said unto him, Why .... Judg 8:1
of E better than the vintage of .... Judg 8:2
and against the house of E .... Judg 10:9
the men of E gathered themselves .... Judg 12:1
men of Gilead, and fought with E .... Judg 12:4
and the men of Gilead smote E .... Judg 12:4
of E among the Ephraimites................... Judg 12:4
in Pirathon in the land of E .... Judg 12:15
and over Jezreel, and over E 2Sa 2:9
coasts out of the tribe of E 1Chr 6:66
Benjamin, and of the children of E.......... 1Chr 9:3
the children of E twenty thousand, ... 1Chr 12:30
Pelonite, of the children of E 1Chr 27:10
Pirathonite, of the children of E 1Chr 27:14
Of the children of E, Hoshea the 1Chr 27:20
the strangers with them out of E 2Chr 15:9
of Judah, and in the cities of E 2Chr 17:2
wit, with all the children of E 2Chr 25:7
that was come to him out of E 2Chr 25:10
And Zichri, a mighty man of E 2Chr 28:7
of the heads of the children of E 2Chr 28:12
Judah, and wrote letters also to E 2Chr 30:1
to city through the country of E 2Chr 30:10
of the people, even many of E 2Chr 30:18
in E also and Manasseh, until they 2Chr 31:1
in the cities of Manasseh, and E 2Chr 34:6
of the hand of Manasseh and E 2Chr 34:9
E also is the strength of mine .... Ps 60:7
The children of E, being armed, ... Ps 78:9
and chose not the tribe of E .... Ps 78:67
Before E and Benjamin and Manasseh ...... Ps 80:2
E also is the strength of mine .... Ps 108:8
Syria is confederate with E .... Is 7:2
Because Syria, E, and the son of .... Is 7:5
and five years shall E be broken, ... Is 7:8
And the head of E is Samaria, ... Is 7:9
from the day that E departed from .... Is 7:17
all the people shall know, even E .... Is 9:9
Manasseh, E .... Is 9:21
and E, Manasseh .... Is 9:21
The envy also of E shall depart.............. Is 11:13
E shall not envy Judah .... Is 11:13
and Judah shall not vex E .... Is 11:13
fortress also shall cease from E .... Is 17:3
of pride, to the drunkards of E .... Is 28:1
of pride, the drunkards of E .... Is 28:3
even the whole seed of E .... Jer 7:15
to Israel, and E is my firstborn .... Jer 31:9
I have surely heard E bemoaning............ Jer 31:18
Is E my dear son .... Jer 31:20
it, For Joseph, the stick of E .... Eze 37:16
Joseph, which is in the hand of E .... Eze 37:19
the west side, a portion for E .... Eze 48:5
And by the border of E, from the .... Eze 48:6
E is joined to idols .... Hos 4:17
I know E, and Israel is not hid .... Hos 5:3
for now, O E, thou committest .... Hos 5:3
and E fall in their iniquity .... Hos 5:5
E shall be desolate in the day of .... Hos 5:9

E is oppressed and broken in .... Hos 5:11
will I be unto E as a moth .... Hos 5:12
When E saw his sickness, and Judah........ Hos 5:13
then went E to the Assyrian, and .... Hos 5:13
For I will be unto E as a lion .... Hos 5:14
O E, what shall I do unto thee .... Hos 6:4
there is the whoredom of E .... Hos 6:10
the iniquity of E was discovered .... Hos 7:1
E, he hath mixed himself among .... Hos 7:8
E is a cake not turned .... Hos 7:8
E also is like a silly dove .... Hos 7:11
E hath hired lovers .... Hos 8:9
Because E hath made many altars, ... Hos 8:11
but E shall return to Egypt, and .... Hos 9:3
The watchman of E was with my God ..... Hos 9:8
As for E, their glory shall fly .... Hos 9:11
E, as I saw Tyrus, is planted in .... Hos 9:13
but E shall bring forth his .... Hos 9:13
E is smitten, their root is dried .... Hos 9:16
E shall receive shame, and Israel .... Hos 10:6
E is as an heifer that is taught, ... Hos 10:11
I will make E to ride .... Hos 10:11
I taught E also to go, taking .... Hos 11:3
How shall I give thee up, E .... Hos 11:8
I will not return to destroy .... Hos 11:9
E compasseth me about with lies, ... Hos 11:12
E feedeth on wind, and followeth .... Hos 12:1
E said, Yet I am become rich, I .... Hos 12:8
E provoked him to anger most .... Hos 12:14
When E spake trembling, he .... Hos 13:1
The iniquity of E is bound up .... Hos 13:12
E shall say, What have I to do .... Hos 14:8
shall possess the fields of E .... Obad 19
I will cut off the chariot from E .... Zec 9:10
for me, filled the bow with E .... Zec 9:13
they of E shall be like a mighty............. Zec 10:7
    3. Mountains in Samaria.
if mount E be too narrow for thee .... Josh 17:15
even Timnath-serah in mount E .... Josh 19:50
Naphtali, and Shechem in mount E .... Josh 20:7
with her suburbs in mount E .... Josh 21:21
which is in mount E, on the .... Josh 24:30
which was given him in mount E .... Josh 24:33
Timnath-heres, in the mount of E .... Judg 2:9
a trumpet in the mountain of E .... Judg 3:27
Ramah and Beth-el in mount E .... Judg 4:5
messengers throughout all mount E .... Judg 7:24
and he dwelt in Shamir in mount E .... Judg 10:1
And there was a man of mount E .... Judg 17:1
he came to mount E in the house........... Judg 17:8
who when they came to mount E .... Judg 18:2
they passed thence unto mount E .... Judg 18:13
sojourning on the side of mount E .... Judg 19:1
even, which was also of mount E .... Judg 19:16
toward the side of mount E .... Judg 19:18
of Ramathaim-zophim, of mount E 1Sa 1:1
And he passed through mount E 1Sa 9:4
had hid themselves in mount E 1Sa 14:22
but a man of mount E, Sheba the 2Sa 20:21
The son of Hur, in mount E.................. 1Kin 4:8
Jeroboam built Shechem in mount E 1Kin 12:25
E two young men of the sons of 2Kin 5:22
in mount E with her suburbs 2Chr 6:57
Zemaraim, which is in mount E 2Chr 13:4
which he had taken from mount E 2Chr 15:8
people from Beer-sheba to mount E 2Chr 19:4
affliction from mount E .... Jer 4:15
upon the mount E shall cry .... Jer 31:6
shall be satisfied upon mount E .... Jer 50:19
    4. A town near Absalom's farm.
in Baal-hazor, which is beside E 2Sa 13:23
    5. Battle site between David's and Absalom's
    armies.
the battle was in the wood of E 2Sa 18:6
    6. A northern gate at Jerusalem.
gate of E unto the corner gate............... 2Kin 14:13
the gate of E to the corner gate............. 2Chr 25:23
and in the street of the gate of E .... Neh 8:16
And from above the gate of E .... Neh 12:39
    7. A city near Jerusalem.
wilderness, into a city called E .... Jn 11:54

EPHRAIMITE (e'-fra-im-ite) See EPHRAIMITES.
    A descendant of Ephraim.
said unto him, Art thou an E .... Judg 12:5

EPHRAIMITES (e'-fra-im-ites)
dwell among the E unto this day .... Josh 16:10
fugitives of Ephraim among the E .... Judg 12:4
passages of Jordan before the E .... Judg 12:5
that when those E which were .... Judg 12:5
fell at that time of the E forty .... Judg 12:6

EPHRAIM'S (e'-fra-ims)
    1. Refers to Ephraim 1.
hand, and laid it upon E head .... Gen 48:14
to remove it from E head unto .... Gen 48:17
Joseph saw E children of the .... Gen 50:23
    2. Refers to Ephraim 2.
Southward it was E, and northward .. .. Josh 16:5

EPHRAIN (e'-fra-in) See EPHRAIM, EPHRON. *A*
    city in Benjamin.
and E with the towns thereof................ 2Chr 13:19

EPHRATAH (ef'-rat-ah) See BETHLEHEM,
    CALEB-EPHRATAH, EPHRATH, EPHRATHITE.
    1. Another name for Bethlehem-judah.
and do thou worthily in E, and be .... Ruth 4:11
Lo, we heard of it at E .... Ps 132:6
But thou, Beth-lehem E, though............. Mic 5:2
    2. A wife of Caleb.
son of Hur, the firstborn of E 1Chr 2:50

sons of Hur, the firstborn of E............ 1Chr 4:4

EPHRATH (e'-frath) See EPHRATAH.
   1. A city in Judah.
was but a little way to come to E......... Gen 35:16
and was buried in the way to E............ Gen 35:19
but a little way to come unto E............ Gen 48:7
buried her there in the way of E.......... Gen 48:7
   2. Same as Ephratah 2.
was dead, Caleb took unto him E........ 1Chr 2:19

EPHRATHAH See EPHRATAH.

EPHRATHITE (ef'-rath-ite) See EPHRATHITES.
   An inhabitant of Bethlehem Judah.
of Tohu, the son of Zuph, an E........... 1Sa 1:1
son of that E of Beth-lehem-judah...... 1Sa 17:12
an E of Zereda, Solomon's servant 1Kin 11:26

EPHRATHITES (ef'-rath-ites)
and Chilion, E of Beth-lehem-judah....... Ruth 1:2

EPHRON (e'-fron) See EPHRAIM, EPHRAIN.
   1. Son of Zohar.
for me to E the son of Zohar.............. Gen 23:8
E dwelt among the children of........... Gen 23:10
E the Hittite answered Abraham in...... Gen 23:10
he spake unto E in the audience .... Gen 23:13
E answered Abraham, saying unto ...... Gen 23:14
And Abraham hearkened unto E........... Gen 23:16
Abraham weighed to E the silver .... Gen 23:16
And the field of E, which was in......... Gen 23:17
in the field of E the son of............... Gen 25:9
is in the field of E the Hittite............ Gen 49:29
bought with the field of E the .... Gen 49:30
a buryingplace of E the Hittite.......... Gen 50:13
   2. A mountain between Judah and Benjamin.
went out to the cities of mount E....... Josh 15:9

EPICUREANS (ep-i-cu-re'-ans) Followers of
   the philosopher Epicurus.
certain philosophers of the E............. Acts 17:18

EPISTLE
together, they delivered the e............ Acts 15:30
delivered the e to the governor,......... Acts 23:33
I Tertius, who wrote this e................ Rom 16:22
I wrote unto you in an e not to.......... 1Cor 5:9
The first e to the Corinthians .... 1Cor s
Ye are our e written in our............... 2Cor 3:2
the e of Christ ministered by us.......... 2Cor 3:3
the same e hath made you sorry.......... 2Cor 7:8
The second e to the Corinthians.......... 2Cor s
when this e is read among you,........... Col 4:16
likewise read the e from Laodicea ...... Col 4:16
this e be read unto all the holy 1Th 5:27
The first e unto the........................ 1Th s
taught, whether by word, or our e...... 2Th 2:15
man obey not our word by this e........ 2Th 3:14
which is the token in every e............. 2Th 3:17
The second e to the Thessalonians ...... 2Th s
The second e unto Timotheus,........... 2Ti s
This second e, beloved, I now............ 2Pet 3:1

EPISTLES
e of commendation to you, or........... 2Cor 3:1
As also in all his e, speaking in 2Pet 3:16

EQUAL
gold and the crystal cannot e it.......... Job 28:17
topaz of Ethiopia shall not e it.......... Job 28:19
eyes behold the things that are e....... Ps 17:2
But it was thou, a man mine e........... Ps 55:13
The legs of the lame are not e........... Prov 26:7
will ye liken me, or shall I be e......... Is 40:25
will ye liken me, and make me e .... Is 46:5
what shall I e to thee, that I............. Lam 2:13
say, The way of the Lord is not e....... Eze 18:25
Is not my way e............................ Eze 18:25
The way of the Lord is not e............. Eze 18:29
of Israel, are not my ways e.............. Eze 18:29
say, The way of the Lord is not e....... Eze 33:17
as for them, their way is not e.......... Eze 33:17
say, The way of the Lord is not e....... Eze 33:20
and thou hast made them e unto us .... Mt 20:12
for they are e unto the angels........... Lk 20:36
Father, making himself e with God..... Jn 5:18
it not robbery to be e with God......... Phil 2:6
servants that which is just and e........ Col 4:1
breadth and the height of it are e....... Rev 21:16

EQUALITY
But by an e, that now at this 2Cor 8:14
that there may be e......................... 2Cor 8:14

EQUALLY
e distant one from another................ Ex 36:22

EQUALS
many my e in mine own nation........... Gal 1:14

EQUITY
the world, and the people with e .... Ps 98:9
thou dost establish e, thou............... Ps 99:4
justice, and judgment, and e.............. Prov 1:3
righteousness, and judgment, and e .... Prov 2:9
good, nor to strike princes for e......... Prov 17:26
wisdom, and in knowledge, and in e ... Eccl 2:21
reprove with e for the meek of .... Is 11:4
turn, and no man saw it, in e............ Is 59:14
abhor judgment, and pervert all e ...... Mic 3:9
he walked with me in peace and e....... Mal 2:6

ER (ur)
   1. A son of Judah.
and he called his name E.................. Gen 38:3
took a wife for E his firstborn........... Gen 38:6

And E, Judah's firstborn, was............ Gen 38:7
E, and Onan, and Shelah.................. Gen 46:12
but E and Onan died in the land of .... Gen 46:12
The sons of Judah were E and Onan .. Num 26:19
and E and Onan died in the land of ... Num 26:19
E, and Onan, and Shelah.................. 1Chr 2:3
And E, the firstborn of Judah, was..... 1Chr 2:3
   2. A son of Shelah.
E the father of Lecah, and Laadah 1Chr 4:21
   3. Father of Elmodan; ancestor of Jesus.
Elmodam, which was the son of .... Lk 3:28

ERAN (e'-ran) See ERANITES. *A son of Shath-*
   elah.
of E, the family of the Eranites.......... Num 26:36

ERANITES (e'-ran-ites) *Descendants of Eran.*
of Eran, the family of the E.............. Num 26:36

ERASTUS (e-ras'-tus)
   1. A fellow-worker with Paul.
unto him, Timotheus and E................ Acts 19:22
E abode at Corinth......................... 2Ti 4:20
   2. A Corinthian city official.
E the chamberlain of the city............ Rom 16:23

ERE
are delivered e the midwives come...... Ex 1:19
e it was chewed, the wrath of the ...... Num 11:33
long will it be e they believe me........ Num 14:11
e the lamp of God went out in the..... 1Sa 3:3
e thou bid the people return from...... 2Sa 2:26
but e the messenger came to him,....... 2Kin 6:32
How long will it be e ye make an...... Job 18:2
long will it be e thou be quiet........... Jer 47:6
how long will it be e they attain........ Hos 8:5
Sir, come down e my child die........... Jn 4:49

ERECH (e'-rek) See ARCHEVITES. *A city in*
   Shinar.
of his kingdom was Babel, and E........ Gen 10:10

ERECTED
he e there an altar, and called it........ Gen 33:20

ERI (e'-ri) See ERITES. *A son of Gad.*
and Haggi, Shuni, and Ezbon, E......... Gen 46:16
of E, the family of the Erites............. Num 26:16

ERITES (e'-rites) *Descendants of Eri.*
of Eri, the family of the E................ Num 26:16

ERR
the inhabitants of Jerusalem to e........ 2Chr 33:9
a people that do e in their heart........ Ps 95:10
which do e from thy commandments.... Ps 119:21
all them that e from thy statutes........ Ps 119:118
Do they not e that devise evil............ Prov 14:22
to e from the words of knowledge ...... Prov 19:27
which lead thee cause thee to e.......... Is 3:12
of this people cause them to e........... Is 9:16
Egypt to e in every work thereof .... Is 19:14
they e in vision, they stumble in........ Is 28:7
of the people, causing them to e........ Is 30:28
though fools, shall not e therein......... Is 35:8
thou made us to e from thy ways...... Is 63:17
and caused my people Israel to e....... Jer 23:13
my people to e by their lies.............. Jer 23:32
whoredoms hath caused them to e...... Hos 4:12
and their lies caused them to e......... Amos 2:4
prophets that make my people e........ Mic 3:5
and said unto them, Ye do e............ Mt 22:29
unto them, Do ye not therefore e...... Mk 12:24
ye therefore do greatly e................. Mk 12:27
They do alway e in their heart.......... Heb 3:10
Do not e, my beloved brethren......... Jas 1:16
if any of you do e from the truth...... Jas 5:19

ERRAND
not eat, until I have told mine e........ Gen 24:33
said, I have a secret e unto thee........ Judg 3:19
and he said, I have an e to thee........ 2Kin 9:5

ERRED
his ignorance wherein he e............... Lev 5:18
And if ye have e, and not observed.... Num 15:22
the fool, and have e exceedingly........ 1Sa 26:21
me to understand wherein I have e ..... Job 6:24
And be it indeed that I have e........... Job 19:4
yet I e not from thy precepts........... Ps 119:110
But they also have e through mine ..... Is 28:7
the prophet have e through strong..... Is 28:7
They also that e in spirit shall......... Is 29:24
they have e from the faith, and........ 1Ti 6:10
have e concerning the faith............. 1Ti 6:21
Who concerning the truth have e....... 2Ti 2:18

ERROR
and God smote him there for his e 2Sa 6:7
mine e remaineth with myself........... Job 19:4
the angel, that it was an e............... Eccl 5:6
as an e which proceedeth from the..... Eccl 10:5
to utter e against the LORD, to........ Is 32:6
them any e or fault found in him...... Dan 6:4
so the last e shall be worse than....... Mt 27:64
of their e which was meant............. Rom 1:27
e of his way shall save a soul.......... Jas 5:20
escaped from them who live in........ 2Pet 2:18
led away with the e of the wicked..... 2Pet 3:17
of truth, and the spirit of.............. 1Jn 4:6
after the e of Balaam for reward...... Jude 11

ERRORS
Who can understand his e................. Ps 19:12
They are vanity, and the work of e .... Jer 10:15
They are vanity, the work of e.......... Jer 51:18
and for the e of the people.............. Heb 9:7

ESAIAS (e-sah'-yas) See ISAIAH. *Greek form of*
   Isaiah.
was spoken of by the prophet E......... Mt 3:3
which was spoken by E the prophet.... Mt 4:14
which was spoken by E the prophet.... Mt 8:17
which was spoken by E the prophet.... Mt 12:17
is fulfilled the prophecy of E............ Mt 13:14
well did E prophesy of you,.............. Mt 15:7
Well hath E prophesied of you.......... Mk 7:6
of the words of E the prophet........... Lk 3:4
him the book of the prophet E.......... Lk 4:17
the Lord, as said the prophet E......... Jn 1:23
That the saying of E which.............. Jn 12:38
because that E said again................ Jn 12:39
These things said E, when he saw ...... Jn 12:41
in his chariot read E the prophet ...... Acts 8:28
and heard him read the prophet E ..... Acts 8:30
by E the prophet unto our fathers...... Acts 28:25
E also crieth concerning Israel,......... Rom 9:27
as E said before, Except the Lord...... Rom 9:29
For E saith, Lord, who hath............. Rom 10:16
But E is very bold, and saith, I......... Rom 10:20
E saith, There shall be a root of....... Rom 15:12

ESAR-HADDON (e'-zar-had'-dun) *An*
   Assyrian king.
E his son reigned in his stead............ 2Kin 19:37
since the days of E king of Assur....... Ezr 4:2
E his son reigned in his stead............ Is 37:38

ESAU (e'-saw)
   1. A son of Isaac.
and they called his name E............... Gen 25:25
E was a cunning hunter, a man of ..... Gen 25:27
And Isaac loved E, because he did ..... Gen 25:28
E came from the field, and he was .... Gen 25:29
E said to Jacob, Feed me, I pray....... Gen 25:30
E said, Behold, I am at the point....... Gen 25:32
Then Jacob gave E bread and........... Gen 25:34
thus E despised his birthright........... Gen 25:34
E was forty years old when he.......... Gen 26:34
he called E his eldest son, and.......... Gen 27:1
when Isaac spake to E his son.......... Gen 27:5
E went to the field to hunt for........ Gen 27:5
father speak unto E thy brother........ Gen 27:6
E my brother is a hairy man, and I ... Gen 27:11
raiment of her eldest son E.............. Gen 27:15
his father, I am E thy firstborn........ Gen 27:19
thou be my very son E or not......... Gen 27:21
but the hands are the hands of E...... Gen 27:22
he said, Art thou my very son E....... Gen 27:24
that E his brother came in from....... Gen 27:30
I am thy son, thy firstborn E........... Gen 27:32
when E heard the words of his......... Gen 27:34
And Isaac answered and said unto E .. Gen 27:37
E said unto his father, Hast thou...... Gen 27:38
E lifted up his voice, and wept......... Gen 27:38
E hated Jacob because of the.......... Gen 27:41
E said in his heart, The days of....... Gen 27:41
these words of E her elder son........ Gen 27:42
unto him, Behold, thy brother E...... Gen 27:42
When E saw that Isaac had blessed ... Gen 28:6
E seeing that the daughters of......... Gen 28:8
Then went E unto Ishmael, and took.. Gen 28:9
to E his brother unto the land of..... Gen 32:3
shall ye speak unto my lord E......... Gen 32:4
saying, We came to thy brother E..... Gen 32:6
If E come to the one company, and .. Gen 32:8
of my brother, from the hand of E ... Gen 32:11
hand a present for E his brother...... Gen 32:13
When E my brother meeteth thee,..... Gen 32:17
is a present sent unto my lord E...... Gen 32:18
this manner shall ye speak unto E.... Gen 32:19
E came, and with him four hundred .. Gen 33:1
E ran to meet him, and embraced..... Gen 33:4
E said, I have enough, my brother.... Gen 33:9
E said, Let me now leave with......... Gen 33:15
So E returned that day on his way ... Gen 33:16
from the face of E thy brother........ Gen 35:1
and his sons E and Jacob buried him.. Gen 35:29
these are the generations of E......... Gen 36:1
E took his wives of the daughters..... Gen 36:2
And Adah bare to E Eliphaz............ Gen 36:4
these are the sons of E, which......... Gen 36:5
E took his wives, and his sons, and .. Gen 36:6
it in mount Seir: E is Edom............ Gen 36:8
these are the generations of E......... Gen 36:9
the son of Adah the wife of E......... Gen 36:10
son of Bashemath the wife of E....... Gen 36:10
and she bare to E Jeush, and Jaalam .. Gen 36:14
These were dukes of the sons of E .... Gen 36:15
of Eliphaz the firstborn son of E...... Gen 36:15
These are the sons of E, who is....... Gen 36:19
names of the dukes that came of E ... Gen 36:40
he is E the father of the................ Gen 36:43
And I gave unto Isaac Jacob and E ... Josh 24:4
and I gave unto E mount Seir.......... Josh 24:4
sons of Isaac, E and Israel............. 1Chr 1:34
Was not E Jacob's brother............. Mal 1:2
And I hated E, and laid his............. Mal 1:3
or profane person, as E, who for...... Heb 12:16
   2. Descendants of Esau.
your brethren the children of E........ Deut 2:4
Seir unto E for a possession........... Deut 2:5
our brethren the children of E......... Deut 2:8
the children of E succeeded them ..... Deut 2:12

As he did to the children of E............. Deut 2:22
children of E which dwell in Seir......... Deut 2:29
The sons of E.................................... 1Chr 1:35
bring the calamity of E upon him......... Jer 49:8
But I have made E bare, I have............ Jer 49:10
are the things of E searched out........... Obad 6
and the house of E for stubble.............. Obad 18
any remaining of the house of E........... Obad 18
have I loved, but E have I hated........... Rom 9:13
E concerning things to come................ Heb 11:20

3. A mountain.

out of the mount of E............................ Obad 8
of E may be cut off by slaughter........... Obad 9
shall possess the mount of E................. Obad 19
Zion to judge the mount of E................ Obad 21

ESAU'S (e'-saws) Refers to Esau 1.

and his hand took hold on E heel......... Gen 25:26
hairy, as his brother E hands................ Gen 27:23
of Rebekah, Jacob's and E mother........ Gen 28:5
These are the names of E sons.............. Gen 36:10
was concubine to Eliphaz E son............ Gen 36:12
were the sons of Adah E wife............... Gen 36:12
were the sons of Bashemath E wife....... Gen 36:13
the daughter of Zibeon, E wife............. Gen 36:14
these are the sons of Reuel E son......... Gen 36:17
are the sons of Bashemath E wife......... Gen 36:17
are the sons of Aholibamah E wife....... Gen 36:18
the daughter of Anah, E wife............... Gen 36:18

ESCAPE

that he said, E for thy life.................... Gen 19:17
e to the mountain, lest thou be............. Gen 19:17
I cannot e to the mountain, lest........... Gen 19:19
let me e thither, (is it a................. Gen 19:20
Haste thee, e thither........................... Gen 19:22
company which he left shall e............... Gen 32:8
they let none of them remain or e......... Josh 8:22
speedily e into the land of the.............. 1Sa 27:1
so shall I e out of his hand.................. 1Sa 27:1
we shall not else e from Absalom.......... 2Sa 15:14
he get him fenced cities, and e us......... 2Sa 20:6
let not one of them e......................... 1Kin 18:40
then let none go forth nor e out............ 2Kin 9:15
have brought into your hands e............ 2Kin 10:24
they that e out of mount Zion.............. 2Kin 19:31
God, to leave us a remnant to e............ Ezr 9:8
thou shalt e in the king's house........... Est 4:13
shall fail, and they shall not e.............. Job 11:20
I would hasten my e from the............... Ps 55:8
Shall they e by iniquity...................... Ps 56:7
righteousness, and cause me to e.......... Ps 71:2
own nets, whilst that I withal e............ Ps 141:10
he that speaketh lies shall not e........... Prov 19:5
pleaseth God shall e from her............... Eccl 7:26
and how shall we e............................. Is 20:6
they that e out of mount Zion.............. Is 37:32
I will send those that e of them............ Is 66:19
which they shall not be able to e........... Jer 11:11
the principal of the flock to e............... Jer 25:35
not e out of the hand of the................. Jer 32:4
thou shalt not e out of his hand........... Jer 34:3
thou shalt not e out of their................ Jer 38:18
thou shalt not e out of their................ Jer 38:23
none of them shall remain or e............. Jer 42:17
shall e or remain, that they................. Jer 44:14
shall return but such as shall e............. Jer 44:14
Yet a small number that e the.............. Jer 44:28
flee away, nor the mighty man e........... Jer 46:6
every city, and no city shall e.............. Jer 48:8
e out of the land of Babylon, to........... Jer 50:28
let none thereof e.............................. Jer 50:29
e the sword among the nations............. Eze 6:8
they that e of you shall remember......... Eze 6:9
But they that e of them shall............... Eze 7:16
shall e, and shall be on the.................. Eze 17:15
he that doeth such things shall e........... Eze 17:15
all these things, he shall not e.............. Eze 17:18
but these shall e of them hand............. Dan 11:41
and the land of Egypt shall not e.......... Dan 11:42
yea, and nothing shall e them.............. Joel 2:3
cut off those of his that did e.............. Obad 14
how can ye e the damnation of............. Mt 23:33
to all these things that shall................ Lk 21:36
any of them should swim out, and e...... Acts 27:42
that thou shalt e the judgment of......... Rom 2:3
temptation also make a way to e.......... 1Cor 10:13
and they shall not e............................ 1Th 5:3
How shall we e, if we neglect so........... Heb 2:3
earth, much more shall not we e........... Heb 12:25

ESCAPED

And there came one that had e............. Gen 14:13
the residue of that which is e............... Gen 32:8
he hath given his sons that e............... Num 21:29
is e from his master unto thee.............. Deut 23:15
Ehud which they had tarried, and......... Judg 3:26
the quarries, and e unto Seirath.......... Judg 3:26
and there e not a man........................ Judg 3:29
Ephraimites which were e said............. Judg 12:5
for them that be e of Benjamin............ Judg 21:17
but the people e................................ 1Sa 14:41
and David fled, and that night............. 1Sa 19:10
and he went, and fled, and e............... 1Sa 19:12
away mine enemy, that he is e............. 1Sa 19:17
So David fled, and e, and came to......... 1Sa 19:18
thence, and e to the cave Adullam........ 1Sa 22:1
son of Ahitub, named Abiathar, e......... 1Sa 22:20
Saul that David was e from Keilah........ 1Sa 23:13
there e not a man of them, save............ 1Sa 30:17
Out of the camp of Israel am I e........... 2Sa 1:3
and Rechab and Baanah his brother e.... 2Sa 4:6

Ben-hadad the king of Syria e on......... 1Kin 20:20
the remnant that is e of the................. 2Kin 19:30
they e into the land of Armenia............ 2Kin 19:37
of the Amalekites that were e............... 1Chr 4:43
king of Syria e out of thine hand.......... 2Chr 16:7
fallen to the earth, and none e............. 2Chr 20:24
that are e out of the hand of the........... 2Chr 30:6
them that had e from the sword............ 2Chr 36:20
for we remain yet e, as it is.................. Ezr 9:15
concerning the Jews that had e............. Ezr 9:15
I only am e alone to tell thee............... Job 1:15
I only am e alone to tell thee............... Job 1:16
I only am e alone to tell thee............... Job 1:17
I only am e alone to tell thee............... Job 1:19
I am e with the skin of my teeth.......... Job 19:20
Our soul is e as a bird out of............... Ps 124:7
the snare is broken, and we are e.......... Ps 124:7
for them that are e of Israel................. Is 4:2
such as are e of the house of............... Is 10:20
the remnant that is e of the................. Is 37:31
they e into the land of Armenia............ Is 37:38
ye that are e of the nations.................. Is 45:20
e from Johanan with eight men............ Jer 41:15
Ye that have e the sword, go away........ Jer 51:50
Lord's anger none e nor remained......... Lam 2:22
mouth be opened to him which is e....... Eze 24:27
that one that had e out of................... Eze 33:21
evening, afore he that was e came........ Eze 33:22
but he e out of their hand................... Acts 19:16
that they e all safe to land................... Acts 27:44
And when they were e, then they.......... Acts 28:1
whom, though he hath e the sea.......... Acts 28:4
down by the wall, and e his hands........ 2Cor 11:33
the edge of the sword, out of............... Heb 11:34
For if they e not who refused him......... Heb 12:25
having e the corruption that is............. 2Pet 1:4
those that were clean e from them........ 2Pet 2:18
For if after they have e the................. 2Pet 2:20

ESCAPETH

that him that e the sword escape.......... 1Kin 19:17
him that e from the sword of Jehu........ 1Kin 19:17
lions upon him that e of Moab............. Is 15:9
him that fleeth, and her that e............. Jer 48:19
That he that e in that day shall........... Eze 24:26
he that e of them shall not be.............. Amos 9:1

ESCAPING

there should be no remnant nor e......... Ezr 9:14

ESCHEW

Let him e evil, and do good................. 1Pet 3:11

ESCHEWED

and one that feared God, and e evil....... Job 1:1

ESCHEWETH

one that feareth God, and e evil........... Job 1:8
one that feareth God, and e evil........... Job 2:3

ESEK (e'-sek) A well in the valley of Gerar.

he called the name of the well E........... Gen 26:20

ESHAN See Eshean.

ESH-BAAL (esh'-ba-al) Another name for ISH-BOSHETH. A son of King Saul.

and Abinadab, and E........................... 1Chr 8:33
and Abinadab, and E........................... 1Chr 9:39

ESHBAN

Hemdan, and E, and Ithran, and......... Gen 36:26
E, and Ithran, and Cheran................... 1Chr 1:41

ESHCOL (esh'-col)

1. Brother of Mamre and Aner.

Mamre the Amorite, brother of E.......... Gen 14:13
men which went with me, Aner, E........ Gen 14:24

2. A valley or brook in Hebron.

And they came unto the brook of E....... Num 13:23
The place was called the brook E.......... Num 13:24
they went up unto the valley of E......... Num 32:9
and came unto the valley of E.............. Deut 1:24

ESHEAN (e'-e-an) A city in Judea.

Arab, and Dumah, and E..................... Josh 15:52

ESHEK (e'-shek) A descendant of King Saul.

the sons of E his brother were,............. 1Chr 8:39

ESHKALONITES (esh'-ka-lon-ites) Inhabitants of Ashkelon.

and the Ashdothites, the E................... Josh 13:3

ESHTAOL (esh'-ta-ol) See Eshtaulites. A town in Judah.

in the valley, E, and Zoreah,............... Josh 15:33
their inheritance was Zorah, and E....... Josh 19:41
camp of Dan between Zorah and E........ Judg 13:25
E in the buryingplace of Manoah.......... Judg 16:31
of valour, from Zorah, and from E........ Judg 18:2
unto their brethren to Zorah and E....... Judg 18:8
Danites, out of Zorah and out of E........ Judg 18:11

ESHTAULITES See Eshtaulites.

ESHTAULITES (esh'-ta-u-lites) Inhabitants of Eshtaol.

came the Zareathites, and the E............ 1Chr 2:53

ESHTEMOA (esh-te-mo'-ah) See Eshtemoh.

1. A Levitical town in Judah.

suburbs, and E with her suburbs,......... Josh 21:14
and to them which were in E................. Josh 28:28
with her suburbs, and Jattir, and E....... 1Chr 6:57

2. A descendant of Ezra.

and Ishbah the father of E................... 1Chr 4:17
the Garmite, and E the Maachathite...... 1Chr 4:19

ESHTEMOH (esh'-te-moh) See Eshtemoa.

Same as Eshtemoa 1.
And Anab, and E, and Anim,............... Josh 15:50

ESHTON (esh'-ton) Grandson of Chelub.

Mehir, which was the father of E.......... 1Chr 4:11
E begat Beth-rapha, and Paseah, and.... 1Chr 4:12

ESLI (es'-li) Father of Naum; ancestor of Jesus.

of Naum, which was the son of E.......... Lk 3:25

ESPECIALLY

but e among my neighbours, and a....... Ps 31:11
E because I know thee to be.................. Acts 26:3
e unto them who are of the.................. Gal 6:10
e they who labour in the word and....... 1Ti 5:17
the books, but e the parchments........... 2Ti 4:13

ESPIED

in the inn, he e his money.................... Gen 42:27
into a land that I had e for them........... Eze 20:6

ESPOUSALS

crowned him in the day of his e............ Song 3:11
of thy youth, the love of thine e........... Jer 2:2

ESPOUSED

which I e to me for an hundred............. 2Sa 3:14
his mother Mary was e to Joseph.......... Mt 1:18
To a virgin e to a man whose name....... Lk 1:27
To be taxed with Mary his e wife......... Lk 2:5
having e you to one husband,............... 2Cor 11:2

ESPY

Kadesh-barnea to e out the land.......... Josh 14:7
of Aroer, stand by the way, and e......... Jer 48:19

ESROM (es'-rom) See Hezron. Son of Phares; ancestor of Jesus.

and Phares begat E............................ Mt 1:3
and E begat Aram.............................. Mt 1:3
of Aram, which was the son of E.......... Lk 3:33

ESTABLISH

with thee will I my my covenant........... Gen 6:18
I e my covenant with you, and with...... Gen 9:9
I will e my covenant with you.............. Gen 9:11
I will e my covenant between me.......... Gen 17:7
I will e my covenant with him for......... Gen 17:19
my covenant will I e with Isaac............ Gen 17:21
you, and e my covenant with you......... Lev 26:9
the soul, her husband may e it............. Num 30:13
that he may e his covenant which........ Deut 8:18
The LORD shall e thee an holy............. Deut 28:9
That he may e thee to day for a........... Deut 29:13
only the LORD e his word.................... 1Sa 1:23
bowels, and I will e his kingdom.......... 2Sa 7:12
e it for ever, and do as thou hast......... 2Sa 7:25
Then I will e the throne of thy............. 1Kin 9:5
son after him, and to e Jerusalem........ 1Kin 15:4
and I will e his kingdom..................... 1Chr 17:11
I will e the throne of his..................... 1Chr 22:10
Moreover I will e his kingdom for........ 1Chr 28:7
to e them for ever, therefore................ 2Chr 9:8
he doth e them for ever, and they........ Job 36:7
but e the just: for the righteous........... Ps 7:9
God will e it for ever.......................... Ps 48:8
the highest himself shall e her............. Ps 87:5
shalt thou e in the very heavens........... Ps 89:2
Thy seed will I e for ever.................... Ps 89:4
e thou the work of our hands upon....... Ps 90:17
the work of our hands e thou it............ Ps 90:17
thou dost e equity, thou....................... Ps 99:4
but he will e the border of the............. Prov 15:25
to e it with judgment and with............ Is 9:7
to e the earth, to cause to.................... Is 49:8
And give him no rest, till he e.............. Is 62:7
the LORD that formed it, to e it........... Jer 33:2
I will e unto them an everlasting.......... Eze 16:60
I will e my covenant with thee............. Eze 16:62
together to e a royal statute................. Dan 6:7
e the decree, and sign the writing........ Dan 6:8
exalt themselves to e the vision........... Dan 11:14
good, and e judgment in the gate......... Amos 5:15
yea, we e the law.............................. Rom 3:31
going about to e their own.................. Rom 10:3
to e you, and to comfort you............... 1Th 3:2
first, that he may e the second............ Heb 10:9

ESTABLISHED

which I have e between me.................. Gen 9:17
is because the thing is e by God........... Gen 41:32
I have also e my covenant with............ Ex 6:4
O Lord, which thy hands have e........... Ex 15:17
e for ever to him that bought it........... Lev 25:30
witnesses, shall the matter be e............ Deut 19:15
Hath he not made thee, and e.............. Deut 32:6
was e to be a prophet of the LORD....... 1Sa 3:20
e thy kingdom upon Israel for............. 1Sa 13:13
the ground, thou shalt not be e............ 1Sa 20:31
Israel shall be e in thine hand............. 1Sa 24:20
LORD had e him king over Israel......... 2Sa 5:12
shall be e for ever before the............... 2Sa 7:16
thy throne shall be e for ever............... 2Sa 7:16
servant David be e before thee............. 2Sa 7:26
and his kingdom was e greatly............. 1Kin 2:12
the LORD liveth, which hath e............. 1Kin 2:24
be e before the LORD for ever............. 1Kin 2:45
the kingdom was e in the hand of........ 1Kin 2:46
throne shall be e for evermore............. 1Chr 17:14
his house be e for ever, and do as........ 1Chr 17:23
Let it even be e, that thy name............ 1Chr 17:24
thy servant be e before thee................. 1Chr 17:24
promise unto David my father be e....... 2Chr 1:9
when Rehoboam had e the kingdom..... 2Chr 12:1

ESTABLISHETH

Lord your God, so shall ye be e.	2Chr 20:20
when the kingdom was e to him.	2Chr 25:3
So they e a decree to make.	2Chr 30:5
Their seed is in their sight.	Job 21:8
thing, and it shall be e unto thee.	Job 22:28
the seas, and it e upon the floods.	Ps 24:2
feet upon a rock, and e my goings.	Ps 40:2
For he e a testimony in Jacob, and.	Ps 78:69
earth which he hath e for ever.	Ps 78:69
With whom my hand shall be e.	Ps 89:21
It shall be e for ever as the.	Ps 89:37
Thy throne is e of old.	Ps 93:2
the world also shall be e that it.	Ps 96:10
their seed shall be e before thee.	Ps 102:28
His heart is e, he shall not be.	Ps 112:8
thou hast e the earth, and it.	Ps 119:90
an evil speaker be e in the earth.	Ps 140:11
hath he e the heavens.	Prov 3:19
feet, and let all thy ways be e.	Prov 4:26
When he e the clouds above.	Prov 8:28
man shall not be e by wickedness.	Prov 12:3
lip of truth shall be e for ever.	Prov 12:19
of counsellors they are e.	Prov 15:22
Lord, and thy thoughts shall be e.	Prov 16:3
the throne is e by righteousness.	Prov 16:12
Every purpose is e by counsel.	Prov 20:18
and by understanding it is e.	Prov 24:3
shall be e in righteousness.	Prov 25:5
his throne shall be e for ever.	Prov 29:14
who hath e all the ends of the.	Prov 30:4
be e in the top of the mountains.	Is 2:2
believe, surely ye shall not be e.	Is 7:9
And in mercy shall the throne be e.	Is 16:5
he hath e it, he created it not.	Is 45:18
In righteousness shalt thou be e.	Is 54:14
he hath e the world by his wisdom.	Jer 10:12
congregation shall be e before me.	Jer 30:20
he hath e the world by his wisdom.	Jer 51:15
I was e in my kingdom, and.	Dan 4:36
be e in the top of the mountains.	Mic 4:1
thou hast e them for correction.	Hab 1:12
and it shall be e, and set there.	Zec 5:11
witnesses every word may be e.	Mt 18:16
were the churches e in the faith.	Acts 16:5
gift, to the end ye may be e.	Rom 1:11
witnesses shall every word be e.	2Cor 13:1
that ye might be e.	Heb 8:6
that the heart be e with grace.	Heb 13:9
be e in the present truth.	2Pet 1:12

ESTABLISHMENT

then he e all her vows, or all.	Num 30:14
The king by judgment e the land.	Prov 29:4
which the king e may be changed.	Dan 6:15

ESTABLISHMENT

the e thereof, Sennacherib king.	2Chr 32:1

ESTATE

to the e of a man of high degree.	1Chr 17:17
e unto another that is better.	Est 1:19
Who remembered us in our low e.	Ps 136:23
saying, Lo, I am come to great e.	Eccl 1:16
the e of the sons of men, that.	Eccl 3:18
shall return to their former e.	Eze 16:55
shalt return to their former e.	Eze 16:55
they return to your former estate.	Eze 16:55
roots shall one stand up in his e.	Dan 11:7
Then shall stand up in his e a.	Dan 11:20
in his e shall stand up a vile.	Dan 11:21
But in his e shall he honour the.	Dan 11:38
the low e of his handmaiden.	Lk 1:48
and all the e of the elders.	Acts 22:5
but condescend to men of low e.	Rom 12:16
that he might know your e.	Col 4:8
which kept not their first e.	Jude 6

ESTATES

will settle you after your old e.	Eze 36:11
captains, and chief of Galilee.	Mk 6:21

ESTEEM

Will he e thy riches.	Job 36:19
Therefore I e all thy precepts.	Ps 119:128
yet we did e him stricken.	Is 53:4
e other better than themselves.	Phil 2:3
to e them very highly in love for.	1Th 5:13

ESTEEMED

lightly the Rock of his.	Deut 32:15
despise me shall be lightly e.	1Sa 2:30
I am a poor man, and lightly e.	1Sa 18:23
I have e the words of his mouth.	Job 23:12
lips is e a man of understanding.	Prov 17:28
shall be e as the potter's clay.	Is 29:16
field shall be e as a forest.	Is 29:17
he was despised, and we e him not.	Is 53:3
how are they e as earthen.	Lam 4:2
for that which is highly e among.	Lk 16:15
who are least in the church.	1Cor 6:4

ESTEEMETH

He e iron as straw, and brass as.	Job 41:27
One man e one day above another.	Rom 14:5
another e every day alike.	Rom 14:5
but to him that e any thing to be.	Rom 14:14

ESTEEMING

E the reproach of Christ greater.	Heb 11:26

ESTHER (est'-thur) See ESTHER'S, HADASSAH.

A Jewish queen.

brought up Hadassah, that is, E.	Est 2:7
that E was brought also unto the.	Est 2:8

E had not shewed her people nor.	Est 2:10
women's house, to know how E did.	Est 2:11
Now when the turn of E, the.	Est 2:15
E obtained favour in the sight of.	Est 2:15
So E was taken unto king.	Est 2:16
the king loved E above all the.	Est 2:17
E had not yet shewed her kindred.	Est 2:20
for E did the commandment of.	Est 2:20
who told it unto E the queen.	Est 2:22
E certified the king thereof in.	Est 2:22
Then called E for Hatach, one of.	Est 4:5
destroy them, to shew it unto E.	Est 4:8
told E the words of Mordecai.	Est 4:9
Again E spake unto Hatach, and.	Est 4:10
Mordecai commanded to tell E.	Est 4:13
Then E bade them return Mordecai.	Est 4:15
to all that E had commanded him.	Est 4:17
that E put on her royal apparel.	Est 5:1
when the king saw E the queen.	Est 5:2
the king held out to E the golden.	Est 5:2
So E drew near, and touched the.	Est 5:2
unto her, What wilt thou, queen E.	Est 5:3
E answered, If it seem good unto.	Est 5:4
that he may do as E hath said.	Est 5:5
the banquet that E had prepared.	Est 5:5
the king said unto E at the.	Est 5:6
Then answered E, and said, My.	Est 5:7
E the queen did let no man come.	Est 5:12
the banquet that E had prepared.	Est 6:14
came to banquet with E the queen.	Est 7:1
unto E on the second day at the.	Est 7:2
What is thy petition, queen E.	Est 7:2
Then E the queen answered and said.	Est 7:3
answered and said unto E the queen.	Est 7:5
E said, The adversary and enemy is.	Est 7:6
for his life to E the queen.	Est 7:7
fallen upon the bed whereon E was.	Est 7:8
the Jews' enemy unto E the queen.	Est 8:1
for E had told what he was unto.	Est 8:1
E set Mordecai over the house of.	Est 8:2
E spake yet again before the king.	Est 8:3
out the golden sceptre toward E.	Est 8:4
So E arose, and stood before the.	Est 8:4
Ahasuerus said unto E the queen.	Est 8:7
I have given E the house of Haman.	Est 8:7
And the king said unto E, The.	Est 9:12
Then said E, If it please the.	Est 9:13
But when E came before the king.	Est 9:25
Then E the queen, the daughter of.	Est 9:29
E the queen had enjoined them, and.	Est 9:31
the decree of E confirmed these.	Est 9:32

ESTHER'S (es'-thurs)

and his servants, even E feast.	Est 2:18
So E maids and her chamberlains.	Est 4:4
And they told to Mordecai E words.	Est 4:12

ESTIMATE

Lord, then the priest shall e it.	Lev 27:14
as the priest shall e it, so.	Lev 27:14

ESTIMATION

with thy e by shekels of silver.	Lev 5:15
out of the flock, with thy e.	Lev 5:18
out of the flock, with thy e.	Lev 6:6
shall be for the Lord by thy e.	Lev 27:2
thy e shall be of the male from.	Lev 27:3
even thy e shall be fifty shekels.	Lev 27:3
then thy e shall be thirty.	Lev 27:4
then thy e shall be of the male.	Lev 27:5
then thy e shall be of the male.	Lev 27:6
for the female thy e shall be.	Lev 27:6
then thy e shall be fifteen.	Lev 27:7
But if he be poorer than thy e.	Lev 27:8
a fifth part thereof unto thy e.	Lev 27:13
of the money of thy e unto it.	Lev 27:15
then thy e shall be according to.	Lev 27:16
according to thy e it shall stand.	Lev 27:17
and it shall be abated from thy e.	Lev 27:18
of the money of thy e unto it.	Lev 27:19
unto him the worth of thy e.	Lev 27:23
he shall give thine e in that day.	Lev 27:23
redeem it according to thine e.	Lev 27:27
shall be sold according to thy e.	Lev 27:27
thou redeem, according to thine e.	Num 18:16

ESTIMATIONS

all thy e shall be according to.	Lev 27:25

ESTRANGED

acquaintance are verily e from me.	Job 19:13
The wicked are e from the womb.	Ps 58:3
They were not e from their lust.	Ps 78:30
have e this place, and have burned.	Jer 19:4
because they are e from me.	Eze 14:5

ETAM (e'-tam)

1. An area in western Judah.

and dwelt in the top of the rock E.	Judg 15:8
went to the top of the rock E.	Judg 15:11

2. A descendant of Judah.

And these were of the father of E.	1Chr 4:3

3. A village in Simeon.

And their villages were, E.	1Chr 4:32

4. A town in Judah.

He built even Beth-lehem, and E.	2Chr 11:6

ETERNAL

The e God is thy refuge, and.	Deut 33:27
I will make thee an e excellency.	Is 60:15
but the righteous into life e.	Mt 19:16
but is in danger of e damnation.	Mk 3:29

I do that I may inherit e life.	Mk 10:17
and in the world to come e life.	Mk 10:30
what shall I do to inherit e life.	Lk 10:25
what shall I do to inherit e life.	Lk 18:18
not perish, but have e life.	Jn 3:15
and gathereth fruit unto life e.	Jn 4:36
in them ye think ye have e life.	Jn 5:39
and drinketh my blood, hath e life.	Jn 6:54
thou hast the words of e life.	Jn 6:68
And I give unto them e life.	Jn 10:28
world shall keep it unto life e.	Jn 12:25
that he should give e life to as.	Jn 17:2
And this is life e, that they.	Jn 17:3
were ordained to e life believed.	Acts 13:48
that are made, even his e power.	Rom 1:20
and honour and immortality, e life.	Rom 2:7
through righteousness unto e life.	Rom 5:21
but the gift of God is e life.	Rom 6:23
exceeding and e weight of glory.	2Cor 4:17
things which are not seen are e.	2Cor 4:18
made with hands, e in the heavens.	2Cor 5:1
According to the e purpose which.	Eph 3:11
Now unto the King e, immortal.	1Ti 1:17
of faith, lay hold on e life.	1Ti 6:12
that they may lay hold on e life.	1Ti 6:19
is in Christ Jesus with e glory.	2Ti 2:10
In hope of e life, which God.	Titus 1:2
according to the hope of e life.	Titus 3:7
he became the author of e.	Heb 5:9
of the dead, and of e judgment.	Heb 6:2
having obtained e redemption for.	Heb 9:12
who through the e Spirit offered.	Heb 9:14
the promise of e inheritance.	Heb 9:15
unto his e glory by Christ Jesus.	1Pet 5:10
and shew unto you that e life.	1Jn 1:2
he hath promised us, even e life.	1Jn 2:25
hath e life abiding in him.	1Jn 3:15
that God hath given to us e life.	1Jn 5:11
ye may know that ye have e life.	1Jn 5:13
This is the true God, and e life.	1Jn 5:20
suffering the vengeance of e fire.	Jude 7
our Lord Jesus Christ unto e life.	Jude 21

ETERNITY

and lofty One that inhabiteth e.	Is 57:15

ETHAM (e'-tham) An encampment during the Exodus.

from Succoth, and encamped in E.	Ex 13:20
from Succoth, and pitched in E.	Num 33:6
And they removed from E.	Num 33:7
journey in the wilderness of E.	Num 33:8

ETHAN (e'-than)

1. A wise man in Solomon's time.

than E the Ezrahite, and Heman, and.	1Kin 4:31
Maschil of E the Ezrahite.	Ps 89:t

2. A son of Zerah.

Zimri, and E, and Heman, and Calcol.	1Chr 2:6
And the sons of E.	1Chr 2:8

3. A descendant of Gershon.

The son of E, the son of Zimmah.	1Chr 6:42

4. A descendant of Merari.

E the son of Kishi, the son of.	1Chr 6:44
brethren, E the son of Kushaiah.	1Chr 15:17
the singers, Heman, Asaph, and E.	1Chr 15:19

ETHANIM (eth'-a-nim) Seventh month of the Hebrew year.

at the feast in the month E.	1Kin 8:2

ETHBAAL (eth'-ba-al) Father of Jezebel.

of E king of the Zidonians.	1Kin 16:31

ETHER (e'-ther) A city in Judah.

Libnah, and E, and Ashan.	Josh 15:42
Ain, Remmon, and E, and Ashan.	Josh 19:7

ETHIOPIA (e-tho-o'-pe-ah) See CUSH, ETHIOPIAN.

1. The land south of Egypt.

compasseth the whole land of E.	Gen 2:13
reigned from India even unto E.	Est 1:1
which are from India unto E.	Est 8:9
The topaz of E shall not equal it.	Job 28:19
behold Philistia, and Tyre, with E.	Ps 87:4
which is beyond the rivers of E.	Is 18:1
Syene even unto the border of E.	Eze 29:10
the rivers of E may suppliants.	Zeph 3:10
and, behold, a man of E, an eunuch.	Acts 8:27

2. Inhabitants of Ethiopia.

heard say of Tirhakah king of E.	2Kin 19:9
E shall soon stretch out her.	Ps 68:31
and wonder upon Egypt and upon E.	Is 20:3
ashamed of E their expectation.	Is 20:5
say concerning Tirhakah king of E.	Is 37:9
I gave Egypt for thy ransom, E.	Is 43:3
of Egypt, and merchandise of E.	Is 45:14
and great pain shall be in E.	Eze 30:4
E, and Libya, and Lydia, and all the.	Eze 30:5
Persia, E, and Libya with them.	Eze 38:5
E and Egypt were her strength, and.	Nah 3:9

ETHIOPIAN

the E woman whom he had married.	Num 12:1
for he had married an E woman.	Num 12:1
the E with an host of a thousand.	2Chr 14:9
Can the E change his skin, or the.	Jer 13:23
Now when Ebed-melech the E.	Jer 38:7
king commanded Ebed-melech the E.	Jer 38:10
Ebed-melech the E said unto.	Jer 38:12
Go and speak to Ebed-melech the E.	Jer 39:16

ETHIOPIANS *Inhabitants of Ethiopia.*
the tubim, the Sukkiims, and the E...	2Chr 12:3
the Lord smote the E before Asa ...	2Chr 14:12
before Judah; and the E fled	2Chr 14:12
the E were overthrown, that they ...	2Chr 14:13
Were not the E and the Lubims a	2Chr 16:8
Arabians, that were near the E.........	2Chr 21:16
The E captives, young and old, ...	Is 20:4
the E and the Libyans, that handle.....	Jer 46:9
to make the careless E afraid............	Eze 30:9
the E shall be at his steps................	Dan 11:43
not as children of the E unto me.........	Amos 9:7
Ye E also, ye shall be slain by...........	Zeph 2:12
under Candace queen of the E	Acts 8:27

ETH-KAZIN

ETHNAN *(eth'-nan) Grandson of Ashur.*
were, Zereth, and Jezoar, and E............	1Chr 4:7

ETHNI *(eth'-ni) See Jeaterai. Ancestor of Asaph.*
The son of E, the son of Zerah, ...	1Chr 6:41

EUBULUS *(yu-bu'-lus) A Christian acquaintance of Paul.*
E greeteth thee, and Pudens, and.........	2Ti 4:21

EUNICE *(yu-ni'-see) Mother of Timothy.*
grandmother Lois, and thy mother E	2Ti 1:5

EUNUCH
neither let the e say, Behold, I	Is 56:3
He took also out of the city an e.........	Jer 52:25
an e of great authority under	Acts 8:27
the e answered Philip, and said, I.......	Acts 8:34
the e said, See, here is water..............	Acts 8:36
the water, both Philip and the e	Acts 8:38
that the e saw him no more................	Acts 8:39

EUNUCHS
looked out to him two or three e	2Kin 9:32
they shall be e in the palace of	2Kin 20:18
they shall be e in the palace of	Is 39:7
unto the e that keep my sabbaths........	Is 56:4
the king, and the queen, and the e	Jer 29:2
the princes of Jerusalem, the e	Jer 34:19
one of the e which was in the	Jer 38:7
women, and the children, and the e ...	Jer 41:16
unto Ashpenaz the master of his e	Dan 1:3
the prince of the e gave names..........	Dan 1:7
of the e that he might not defile	Dan 1:8
love with the prince of the e	Dan 1:9
prince of the e said unto Daniel	Dan 1:10
of the e had set over Daniel	Dan 1:11
of the e brought them in before	Dan 1:18
For there are some e, which were	Mt 19:12
and there are some e, which were	Mt 19:12
e, which were made e of men............	Mt 19:12
and there be e, which have made	Mt 19:12
which have made themselves e for	Mt 19:12

EUODIAS *(yu-o'-de-as) A Christian at Philippi.*
I beseech E, and beseech Syntyche,......	Phil 4:2

EUPHRATES *(yu-fra'-teze) A river in Mesopotamia.*
And the fourth river is E	Gen 2:14
unto the great river, the river E	Gen 15:18
unto the great river, the river E	Deut 1:7
from the river, the river E	Deut 11:24
unto the great river, the river E..........	Josh 1:4
recover his border at the river E	2Sa 8:3
king of Assyria to the river E	2Kin 23:29
river of Egypt unto the river E	2Kin 24:7
the wilderness from the river E	1Chr 5:9
his dominion by the river E	1Chr 18:3
to fight against Charchemish by E	2Chr 35:20
upon thy loins, and arise, go to E.......	Jer 13:4
So I went, and hid it by E	Jer 13:5
Lord said unto me, Arise, go to E	Jer 13:6
Then I went to E, and digged, and......	Jer 13:7
was by the river E in Carchemish	Jer 46:2
toward the north by the river E	Jer 46:6
the north country by the river E	Jer 46:10
and cast it into the midst of E	Jer 51:63
are bound in the great river E	Rev 9:14
his vial upon the great river E	Rev 16:12

EURAQUILO See Euroclydon.

EUROCLYDON *(yu-roc'-lid-on) A Mediterranean wind.*
it a tempestuous wind, called E	Acts 27:14

EUTYCHUS *(yu'-tik-us) Youth restored to life.*
a certain young man named E..............	Acts 20:9

EVANGELIST
into the house of Philip the e	Acts 21:8
afflictions, do the work of an e	2Ti 4:5

EVANGELISTS
and some, e; and some, pastors..........	Eph 4:11

EVE *(eev) Wife of Adam.*
And Adam called his wife's name E......	Gen 3:20
And Adam knew E his wife	Gen 4:1
beguiled E through his subtilty	2Cor 11:3
For Adam was first formed, then E	1Ti 2:13

EVEN See PREFACE.

EVENING
And the e and the morning were the	Gen 1:5
And the e and the morning were the	Gen 1:8
And the e and the morning were the	Gen 1:13
And the e and the morning were the	Gen 1:19

And the e and the morning were the ...	Gen 1:23
And the e and the morning were the ...	Gen 1:31
the dove came in to him in the e	Gen 8:11
of water at the time of the e	Gen 24:11
And it came to pass in the e	Gen 29:23
came out of the field in the e	Gen 30:16
of Israel shall kill it in the e	Ex 12:6
give you in the e flesh to eat.............	Ex 16:8
Moses from the morning unto the e	Ex 18:13
from e to morning before the Lord......	Ex 27:21
the e unto the morning before the	Lev 24:3
when e cometh on, he shall wash........	Deut 23:11
upon the trees until the e	Josh 10:26
now the day draweth toward e	Judg 19:9
man that eateth any food until e.........	1Sa 14:24
Philistine drew near morning and e	1Sa 17:16
even unto the e of the next day	1Sa 30:17
and bread and flesh in the e	1Kin 17:6
the offering of the e sacrifice.............	1Kin 18:29
the offering of the e sacrifice.............	1Kin 18:36
the e meat offering, and the	2Kin 16:15
offering continually morning and e	1Chr 16:40
the burnt offerings morning and e	2Chr 2:4
every e burnt sacrifices and sweet......	2Chr 13:11
lamps thereof, to burn every e	2Chr 13:11
e burnt offerings, and the burnt	2Chr 31:3
even burnt offerings morning and e	Ezr 3:3
astonied until the e sacrifice..............	Ezr 9:4
at the e sacrifice I arose up...............	Ezr 9:5
In the e she went, and on the	Est 2:14
are destroyed from morning to e	Job 4:20
And at morning, and at noon, will I	Ps 55:17
They return at e: they make a	Ps 59:6
And at e let them return....................	Ps 59:14
of the morning and to rejoice	Ps 65:8
in the e it is cut down, and...............	Ps 90:6
work and to his labour until the e	Ps 104:23
up of my hands as the e sacrifice	Ps 141:2
In the twilight, in the e	Prov 7:9
in the e withhold not thine hand	Eccl 11:6
of the e are stretched out.................	Jer 6:4
of the Lord was upon me till the e	Eze 33:22
shall not be shut until the e	Eze 46:2
And the vision of the e and the	Dan 8:26
about the time of the e oblation	Dan 9:21
are more fierce than the e wolves......	Hab 1:8
shall they lie down in the e	Zeph 2:7
her judges are e wolves....................	Zeph 3:3
that at e time it shall be light............	Zec 14:7
And when it was e, his disciples	Mt 14:15
and when the e was come, he was	Mt 14:23
and said unto them, When it is e	Mt 16:2
in the e he cometh with the..............	Mk 14:17
for it is toward e, and the day is	Lk 24:29
Then the same day at e, being the	Jn 20:19
the prophets, from morning till e	Acts 28:23

EVENINGS
a wolf of the e shall spoil them,........	Jer 5:6

EVENINGTIDE
And it came to pass in an e	2Sa 11:2
And behold at e trouble	Is 17:14

EVENT
that one e happeneth to them all........	Eccl 2:14
there is one e to the righteous,..........	Eccl 9:2
sun, that there is one e unto all..........	Eccl 9:3

EVENTIDE
to meditate in the field at the	Gen 24:63
the ark of the Lord until the e	Josh 7:6
of Ai he hanged on a tree until e........	Josh 8:29
now the e was come, he went out	Mk 11:11
for it was now e	Acts 4:3

EVER
of life, and eat, and live for...............	Gen 3:22
I give it, and to thy seed for you........	Gen 13:15
then let me bear the blame for e	Gen 43:9
bear the blame to my father for e	Gen 44:32
this is my name for e, and this is	Ex 3:15
it a feast by an ordinance for e	Ex 12:14
generations by an ordinance for e	Ex 12:17
to thee and to thy sons for e.............	Ex 12:24
see them again no more for e	Ex 14:13
The Lord shall reign for e	Ex 15:18
Lord shall reign for e and	Ex 15:18
unto thee, and believe thee for e	Ex 19:9
and he shall serve him for e..............	Ex 21:6
it shall be a statute for e unto	Ex 27:21
it shall be a statute for unto him	Ex 28:43
his sons' by a statute for from............	Ex 29:28
shall be a statute for e to them	Ex 30:21
and the children of Israel for e...........	Ex 31:17
and they shall inherit it for e	Ex 32:13
it shall be a burning upon	Lev 6:13
it shall be a statute for e in	Lev 6:18
is a statute for e unto the Lord..........	Lev 6:22
for e from among the children of	Lev 7:34
by a statute for e throughout.............	Lev 7:36
it shall be a statute for e	Lev 10:9
with thee, by a statute for e	Lev 10:15
shall be a statute for e unto you	Lev 16:29
your souls, by a statute for e	Lev 16:31
for e unto them throughout their	Lev 17:7
it shall be a statute for e	Lev 23:14
in all your dwellings........................	Lev 23:21
it shall be a statute for e	Lev 23:31
statute for e in your generations,.......	Lev 23:41
statute for e in your generations........	Lev 24:3
The land shall not be sold for e..........	Lev 25:23
for e to him that bought it................	Lev 25:30

they shall be your bondmen for e.......	Lev 25:46
for e throughout your generations	Num 10:8
an ordinance for e in your.................	Num 15:15
thy sons, by an ordinance for e	Num 18:8
with thee, by a statute for e..............	Num 18:11
with thee, by a statute for e..............	Num 18:19
for e before the Lord unto thee..........	Num 18:19
it shall be a statute for e	Num 18:23
among them, for a statute for e	Num 19:10
upon which thou hast ridden e...........	Num 22:30
was I e wont to do so unto thee.........	Num 22:30
end shall be that he perish for e.........	Num 24:20
and he also shall perish for e	Num 24:24
Did e people hear the voice of	Deut 4:33
Lord thy God giveth thee, for e	Deut 4:40
and with their children for e	Deut 5:29
thy children after thee for e	Deut 12:28
and it shall be an heap for e	Deut 13:16
and he shall be thy servant for e	Deut 15:17
the Lord, him and his sons for e	Deut 18:5
thy God, and to walk in all his ways....	Deut 19:9
congregation of the Lord for e	Deut 23:3
prosperity all thy days for e	Deut 23:6
a wonder, and upon thy seed for e......	Deut 28:46
unto us and to our children for e	Deut 29:29
to heaven, and say, I live for e	Deut 32:40
unto the children of Israel for e	Josh 4:7
fear the Lord your God for e	Josh 4:24
Ai, and made it an heap for e	Josh 8:28
and thy children's for e, because	Josh 14:9
did he e strive against Israel,.............	Judg 11:25
or did he e fight against them,...........	Judg 11:25
the Lord, and there abide for e	1Sa 1:22
should walk before me for e	1Sa 2:30
an old man in thine house for e	1Sa 2:32
walk before mine anointed for e.........	1Sa 2:35
for e for the iniquity which he	1Sa 3:13
with sacrifice nor offering for e	1Sa 3:14
thy kingdom upon Israel for e	1Sa 13:13
thy kindness from my house for e.......	1Sa 20:15
Lord be between thee and me for e	1Sa 20:23
between my seed and thy seed for e ...	1Sa 20:42
he shall be my servant for e	1Sa 27:12
thee keeper of mine head for e..........	1Sa 28:2
Shall the sword devour for e	2Sa 2:26
guiltless before the Lord for e	2Sa 3:28
the throne of his kingdom for e	2Sa 7:13
he established for e before thee..........	2Sa 7:16
throne shall be established for e	2Sa 7:16
to be a people unto thee for e	2Sa 7:24
his house, establish it for e	2Sa 7:25
let thy name be magnified for e.........	2Sa 7:26
it may continue for e before thee	2Sa 7:29
of thy servant be blessed for e	2Sa 7:29
Let my lord king David live for e	1Kin 1:31
upon the head of his seed for e..........	1Kin 2:33
be peace for e from the Lord	1Kin 2:33
established before the Lord for e........	1Kin 2:45
for Hiram was e a lover of David........	1Kin 5:1
place for thee to abide in for e	1Kin 8:13
built, to put my name there for e	1Kin 9:3
of thy kingdom upon Israel for e	1Kin 9:5
the Lord loved Israel for e	1Kin 10:9
the seed of David, but not for e.........	1Kin 11:39
they will be thy servants for e	1Kin 12:7
unto thee, and unto thy seed for e	2Kin 5:27
Israel, will I put my name for e..........	2Kin 21:7
and to minister unto him for e	1Chr 15:2
for his mercy endureth for e	1Chr 16:34
be the Lord God of Israel for e	1Chr 16:36
Lord God of Israel for e and	1Chr 16:36
because his mercy endureth for e	1Chr 16:41
I will stablish his throne for e	1Chr 17:12
thou make thine own people for e	1Chr 17:22
his house be established for e	1Chr 17:23
thy name may be magnified for e	1Chr 17:24
that it may be before thee for e.........	1Chr 17:27
and it shall be blessed for e	1Chr 17:27
of his kingdom over Israel for e	1Chr 22:10
holy things, he and his sons for e	1Chr 23:13
and to bless in his name for e	1Chr 23:13
they may dwell in Jerusalem for e	1Chr 23:25
to be king over Israel for e	1Chr 28:4
will establish his kingdom for e	1Chr 28:7
for your children after you for e	1Chr 28:8
him, he will cast thee off for e	1Chr 28:9
Israel our father, for e and e	1Chr 29:10
fathers, keep this for e in the	1Chr 29:18
is an ordinance for e to Israel............	2Chr 2:4
for his mercy endureth for e	2Chr 5:13
and a place for thy dwelling for e.......	2Chr 6:2
for his mercy endureth for e	2Chr 7:3
because his mercy endureth for e	2Chr 7:6
that my name may be there for e	2Chr 7:16
Israel, to establish them for e	2Chr 9:8
they will be thy servants for e	2Chr 10:7
over Israel to David for e	2Chr 13:5
seed of Abraham thy friend for e	2Chr 20:7
for his mercy endureth for e	2Chr 20:21
light to him and to his sons for e	2Chr 21:7
which he hath sanctified for e	2Chr 30:8
Jerusalem shall my name be there	2Chr 33:4
Israel, will I put my name for e..........	2Chr 33:7
endureth for e toward Israel..............	Ezr 3:11
to prepare their heart for wealth for e .	Ezr 9:12
to your children for e	Ezr 9:12
the king, Let the king live for e	Neh 2:3
the Lord your God for e and e	Neh 9:5
the congregation of God for e............	Neh 13:1

who e perished, being innocent .... Job 4:7
they perish for e without any .... Job 4:20
Thou prevailest for e against him .... Job 14:20
pen and lead in the rock for e .... Job 19:24
perish for e like his own dung .... Job 20:7
be delivered for e from my judge .... Job 23:7
yea, he doth establish them for e .... Job 36:7
thou take him for a servant for e .... Job 41:4
let them e shout for joy, because .... Ps 5:11
hast put out their name for e .... Ps 9:5
put out their name for e and e .... Ps 9:5
But the LORD shall endure for e .... Ps 9:7
the poor shall not perish for e .... Ps 9:18
The LORD is King for e and e .... Ps 10:16
The LORD is King for e and e .... Ps 10:16
them from this generation for e .... Ps 12:7
forget me, O LORD, for e? .... Ps 13:1
the LORD is clean, enduring for e .... Ps 19:9
it him, even length of days for e .... Ps 21:4
even length of days for e and e .... Ps 21:4
hast made him most blessed for e .... Ps 21:6
your heart shall live for e .... Ps 22:26
in the house of the LORD for e .... Ps 23:6
for they have been e of old .... Ps 25:6
Mine eyes are e toward the LORD .... Ps 25:15
them also, and lift them up for e .... Ps 28:9
yea, the LORD sitteth King for e .... Ps 29:10
will give thanks unto thee for e .... Ps 30:12
of the LORD standeth for e .... Ps 33:11
their inheritance shall be for e .... Ps 37:18
He is e merciful, and lendeth .... Ps 37:26
they are preserved for e .... Ps 37:28
the land, and dwell therein for e .... Ps 37:29
settest me before thy face for e .... Ps 41:12
long, and praise thy name for e .... Ps 44:8
arise, cast us not off for e .... Ps 44:23
God hath blessed thee for e .... Ps 45:2
Thy throne, O God, is for e .... Ps 45:6
throne, O God, is for e and e .... Ps 45:6
the people praise thee for e .... Ps 45:17
people praise thee for e and e .... Ps 45:17
God will establish it for e .... Ps 48:8
For this God is our God for e .... Ps 48:14
this God is our God for e and e .... Ps 48:14
is precious, and it ceaseth for e .... Ps 49:8
that he should still live for e .... Ps 49:9
their houses shall continue for e .... Ps 49:11
and my sin is e before me .... Ps 51:3
shall likewise destroy thee for e .... Ps 52:5
I trust in the mercy of God for e .... Ps 52:8
in the mercy of God for e and e .... Ps 52:8
I will praise thee for e, because .... Ps 52:9
abide in thy tabernacle for e .... Ps 61:4
He shall abide before God for e .... Ps 61:7
I sing praise unto thy name for e .... Ps 61:8
he ruleth by his power for e .... Ps 66:7
the LORD will dwell in it for e .... Ps 68:16
His name shall endure for e .... Ps 72:17
be his glorious name for e .... Ps 72:19
of my heart, and my portion for e .... Ps 73:26
why hast thou cast us off for e .... Ps 74:1
enemy blaspheme thy name for e .... Ps 74:10
congregation of thy poor for e .... Ps 74:19
But I will declare for e .... Ps 75:9
Will the LORD cast off for e .... Ps 77:7
Is his mercy clean gone for e .... Ps 77:8
which he hath established for e .... Ps 78:69
wilt thou be angry for e .... Ps 79:13
will give thee thanks for e .... Ps 79:13
time should have endured for e .... Ps 81:15
be confounded and troubled for e .... Ps 83:17
Wilt thou be angry with us for e .... Ps 85:5
of the mercies of the LORD for e .... Ps 89:1
Mercy shall be built up for e .... Ps 89:2
Thy seed will I establish for e .... Ps 89:4
also will I make to endure for e .... Ps 89:29
His seed shall endure for e .... Ps 89:36
be established for e as the moon .... Ps 89:37
wilt thou hide thyself for e .... Ps 89:46
or e thou hadst formed the earth .... Ps 90:2
they shall be destroyed for e .... Ps 92:7
thine house, O LORD, for e .... Ps 93:5
thou, O LORD, shalt endure for e .... Ps 102:12
will he keep his anger for e .... Ps 103:9
it should not be removed for e .... Ps 104:5
of the LORD shall endure for e .... Ps 104:31
remembered his covenant for e .... Ps 105:8
for his mercy endureth for e .... Ps 106:1
for his mercy endureth for e .... Ps 107:1
Thou art a priest for e after the .... Ps 110:4
his righteousness endureth for e .... Ps 111:3
he will e be mindful of his .... Ps 111:5
They stand fast for e and e, and .... Ps 111:8
They stand fast for e and e .... Ps 111:8
hath commanded his covenant for e ..... Ps 111:9
his praise endureth for e .... Ps 111:10
his righteousness endureth for e .... Ps 112:3
he shall not be moved for e .... Ps 112:6
his righteousness endureth for e .... Ps 112:9
truth of the LORD endureth for e .... Ps 117:2
because his mercy endureth for e .... Ps 118:1
that his mercy endureth for e .... Ps 118:2
that his mercy endureth for e .... Ps 118:3
that his mercy endureth for e .... Ps 118:4
for his mercy endureth for e .... Ps 118:29
I keep thy law continually for e .... Ps 119:44
thy law continually for e and e .... Ps 119:44
For e, O LORD, thy word is .... Ps 119:89
for they are e with me .... Ps 119:98
have I taken as an heritage for e .... Ps 119:111

that thou hast founded them for e .... Ps 119:152
judgments endureth for e .... Ps 119:160
be removed, but abideth for e .... Ps 125:1
people from henceforth even for e .... Ps 125:2
the LORD from henceforth and for e ...... Ps 131:3
This is my rest for e .... Ps 132:14
Thy name, O LORD, endureth for e .... Ps 135:13
for his mercy endureth for e .... Ps 136:1
for his mercy endureth for e .... Ps 136:2
for his mercy endureth for e .... Ps 136:3
for his mercy endureth for e .... Ps 136:4
for his mercy endureth for e .... Ps 136:5
for his mercy endureth for e .... Ps 136:6
for his mercy endureth for e .... Ps 136:7
for his mercy endureth for e .... Ps 136:8
for his mercy endureth for e .... Ps 136:9
for his mercy endureth for e .... Ps 136:10
for his mercy endureth for e .... Ps 136:11
for his mercy endureth for e .... Ps 136:12
for his mercy endureth for e .... Ps 136:13
for his mercy endureth for e .... Ps 136:14
for his mercy endureth for e .... Ps 136:15
for his mercy endureth for e .... Ps 136:16
for his mercy endureth for e .... Ps 136:17
for his mercy endureth for e .... Ps 136:18
for his mercy endureth for e .... Ps 136:19
for his mercy endureth for e .... Ps 136:20
for his mercy endureth for e .... Ps 136:21
for his mercy endureth for e .... Ps 136:22
for his mercy endureth for e .... Ps 136:23
for his mercy endureth for e .... Ps 136:24
for his mercy endureth for e .... Ps 136:25
for his mercy endureth for e .... Ps 136:26
thy mercy, O LORD, endureth for e .... Ps 138:8
and I will bless thy name for e .... Ps 145:1
will bless thy name for e and e .... Ps 145:1
and I will praise thy name for e .... Ps 145:2
praise thy name for e and e .... Ps 145:2
flesh bless his holy name for e .... Ps 145:21
bless his holy name for e and e .... Ps 145:21
which keepeth truth for e .... Ps 146:6
The LORD shall reign for e .... Ps 146:10
hath also stablished them for e .... Ps 148:6
stablished them for e and e .... Ps 148:6
the beginning, or e the earth was .... Prov 8:23
truth shall be established for e .... Prov 12:19
For riches are not for e .... Prov 27:24
throne shall be established for e .... Prov 29:14
but the earth abideth for e .... Eccl 1:4
wise more than of the fool for e .... Eccl 2:16
God doeth, it shall be for e .... Eccl 3:14
they any more a portion for e in .... Eccl 9:6
O e the silver cord be loosed .... Eccl 12:6
Or e I was aware, my soul made me ...... Song 6:12
from henceforth even for e .... Is 9:7
Trust ye in the LORD for e .... Is 26:4
he will not e be threshing .... Is 28:28
may be for the time to come for e .... Is 30:8
the time to come for e and e .... Is 30:8
and towers shall be for dens for e .... Is 32:14
quietness and assurance for e .... Is 32:17
stakes thereof shall be removed .... Is 33:20
smoke thereof shall go up for e .... Is 34:10
none shall pass through it for e .... Is 34:10
pass through it for e and e .... Is 34:10
they shall possess it for e .... Is 34:17
word of our God shall stand for e .... Is 40:8
saidst, I shall be a lady for e .... Is 47:7
but my salvation shall be for e .... Is 51:6
my righteousness shall be for e .... Is 51:8
For I will not contend for e .... Is 57:16
LORD, from henceforth and for e .... Is 59:21
they shall inherit the land for e .... Is 60:21
neither remember iniquity for e .... Is 64:9
rejoice for e in that which I .... Is 65:18
Will he reserve his anger for e .... Jer 3:5
and I will not keep anger for e .... Jer 3:12
to your fathers, for e and e .... Jer 7:7
anger, which shall burn for e .... Jer 17:4
and this city shall remain for e .... Jer 17:25
and to your fathers for e and e .... Jer 25:5
being a nation before me for e .... Jer 31:36
nor thrown down any more for e .... Jer 31:40
way, that they may fear me for e .... Jer 32:39
for his mercy endureth for e .... Jer 33:11
neither ye, nor your sons for e .... Jer 35:6
a man to stand before me for e .... Jer 35:19
dragons, and a desolation for e .... Jer 49:33
shall be no more inhabited for e .... Jer 50:39
but thou shalt be desolate for e .... Jer 51:26
that it shall be desolate for e .... Jer 51:62
the Lord will not cast off for e .... Lam 3:31
Thou, O LORD, remainest for e .... Lam 5:19
dost thou forget us for e .... Lam 5:20
their children's children for e .... Eze 37:25
David shall be their prince for e .... Eze 37:25
of the children of Israel for e .... Eze 43:7
dwell in the midst of them for e .... Eze 43:9
in Syriack, O king, live for e .... Dan 2:4
Blessed be the name of God for e .... Dan 2:20
be the name of God for e and e .... Dan 2:20
kingdoms, and it shall stand for e .... Dan 2:44
O king, live for e .... Dan 3:9
and honoured him than live for e .... Dan 4:34
spake and said, O king, live for e .... Dan 5:10
unto him, King Darius, live for e .... Dan 6:6
unto the king, O king, live for e .... Dan 6:21
all their bones in pieces or e .... Dan 6:24
the living God, and stedfast for e .... Dan 6:26
the kingdom for e, even for e .... Dan 7:18

for e, even for e and e .... Dan 7:18
righteousness as the stars for e .... Dan 12:3
as the stars for e and e .... Dan 12:3
for e that it shall be for a time .... Dan 12:7
I will betroth thee unto me for e .... Hos 2:19
there hath not been e the like .... Joel 2:2
But Judah shall dwell for e .... Joel 3:20
and he kept his wrath for e .... Amos 1:11
and thou shalt be cut off for e .... Obad 10
with her bars was about me for e .... Jonah 2:6
have ye taken away my glory for e .... Mic 2:9
name of the LORD our God for e .... Mic 4:5
of the LORD our God for e and e .... Mic 4:5
Zion from henceforth, even for e .... Mic 4:7
he retaineth not his anger for e .... Mic 7:18
the prophets, do they live for e .... Zec 1:5
the LORD hath indignation for e .... Mal 1:4
and the power, and the glory, for e ...... Mt 6:13
grow on thee henceforward for e .... Mt 21:19
to this time, no, nor e shall be .... Mt 24:21
eat fruit of thee hereafter for e .... Mk 11:14
to do as he had e done unto them .... Mk 15:8
over the house of Jacob for e .... Lk 1:33
to Abraham, and to his seed for e .... Lk 1:55
unto him, Son, thou art e with me .... Lk 15:31
told me all things that e I did .... Jn 4:29
He told me all that e I did .... Jn 4:39
this bread, he shall live for e .... Jn 6:51
of this bread shall live for e .... Jn 6:58
abideth not in the house for e .... Jn 8:35
but the Son abideth .... Jn 8:35
All that e came before me are .... Jn 10:8
the law that Christ abideth for e .... Jn 12:34
that he may abide with you for e .... Jn 14:16
I e taught in the synagogue, and .... Jn 18:20
or e he come near, are ready to .... Acts 23:15
the Creator, who is blessed for e .... Rom 1:25
is over all, God blessed for e .... Rom 9:5
to whom be glory for e .... Rom 11:36
glory through Jesus Christ for e .... Rom 16:27
his righteousness remaineth for e 2Cor 9:9
To whom be glory for e and e .... Gal 1:5
For no man e yet hated his own .... Eph 5:29
our Father be glory for e and e .... Phil 4:20
so shall we e be with the Lord 1Th 4:17
but e follow that which is good, ... 1Th 5:15
be honour and glory for e and e 1Ti 1:17
E learning, and never able to come 2Ti 3:7
to whom be glory for e and e 2Ti 4:18
thou shouldest receive him for e .... Philem 15
throne, O God, is for e and e .... Heb 1:8
Thou art a priest for e after the .... Heb 5:6
made an high priest for e after .... Heb 6:20
Thou art a priest for e after the .... Heb 7:17
Thou art a priest for e after the .... Heb 7:21
this man, because he continueth e ...... Heb 7:24
seeing he e liveth to make .... Heb 7:25
one sacrifice for sins for e .... Heb 10:12
for e them that are sanctified .... Heb 10:14
yesterday, and to day, and for e .... Heb 13:8
to whom be glory for e and e .... Heb 13:21
which liveth and abideth for e 1Pet 1:23
word of the Lord endureth for e 1Pet 1:25
praise and dominion for e and e 1Pet 5:11
glory and dominion for e and e 1Pet 5:11
of darkness is reserved for e 2Pet 2:17
To him be glory both now and for e 2Pet 3:18
the will of God abideth for e 1Jn 2:17
in us, and shall be with us for e 2Jn 2
the blackness of darkness for e .... Jude 13
dominion and power, both now and e ... Jude 25
glory and dominion for e and e .... Rev 1:6
throne, who liveth for e and e .... Rev 4:9
him that liveth for e and e .... Rev 4:10
and unto the Lamb for e and e .... Rev 5:13
him that liveth for e and e .... Rev 5:14
be unto our God for e and e .... Rev 7:12
by him that liveth for e and e .... Rev 10:6
and he shall reign for e and e .... Rev 11:15
ascendeth up for e and e .... Rev 14:11
of God, who liveth for e and e .... Rev 15:7
her smoke rose up for e and e .... Rev 19:3
day and night for e and e .... Rev 20:10
and they shall reign for e and e .... Rev 22:5

EVERLASTING

the e covenant between God .... Gen 9:16
generations for an e covenant .... Gen 17:7
of Canaan, for an e possession .... Gen 17:8
in your flesh for an e covenant .... Gen 17:13
with him for an e covenant .... Gen 17:19
the name of the LORD, the e God .... Gen 21:33
after thee for an e possession .... Gen 48:4
the utmost bound of the e hills .... Gen 49:26
an e priesthood throughout their .... Ex 40:15
shall be an e statute unto you .... Lev 16:34
of Israel by an e covenant .... Lev 24:8
the covenant of an e priesthood .... Num 25:13
and underneath are the e arms .... Deut 33:27
hath made with me an e covenant 2Sa 23:5
and to Israel for an e covenant 1Chr 16:17
and be ye lifted up, ye e doors .... Ps 24:7
even lift them up, ye e doors .... Ps 24:9
Israel from e, and to e .... Ps 41:13
world, even from e to e .... Ps 90:2
thou art from e .... Ps 93:2
his mercy is e .... Ps 100:5
e to e upon them that .... Ps 103:17
and to Israel for an e covenant .... Ps 105:10
of Israel from e to e .... Ps 106:48
shall be in e remembrance .... Ps 112:6

is an e righteousness, and thy law...... Ps 119:142
of thy testimonies is e .... Ps 119:144
in me, and lead me in the way e .... Ps 139:24
Thy kingdom is an e kingdom............ Ps 145:13
I was set up from e, from the............. Prov 8:23
the righteous is an e foundation .... Prov 10:25
The e Father, The Prince of Peace ...... Is 9:6
ordinance, broken the e covenant........ Is 24:5
in the LORD JEHOVAH is e strength ...... Is 26:4
us shall dwell with e burnings............ Is 33:14
songs and e joy upon their heads........ Is 35:10
thou not heard, that the e God............ Is 40:28
in the LORD with an e salvation .... Is 45:17
e joy shall be upon their head............. Is 51:11
but with e kindness will I have............ Is 54:8
I will make an e covenant with............ Is 55:3
for an e sign that shall not be .... Is 55:13
I will give them an e name .... Is 56:5
shall be unto thee an e light .... Is 60:19
the LORD shall be thine e light .... Is 60:20
e joy shall be unto them.................... Is 61:7
I will make an e covenant with .... Is 61:8
them, to make himself an e name .... Is 63:12
thy name is from e .... Is 63:16
is the living God, and an e king .... Jer 10:10
their e confusion shall never be......... Jer 20:11
I will bring an e reproach upon .... Jer 23:40
I have loved thee with an e love......... Jer 31:3
I will make an e covenant with .... Jer 32:40
establish unto thee an e covenant ...... Eze 16:60
it shall be an e covenant with............ Eze 37:26
his kingdom is an e kingdom .... Dan 4:3
whose dominion is an e dominion........ Dan 4:34
his dominion is an e dominion .... Dan 7:14
whose kingdom is an e kingdom .... Dan 7:27
to bring in e righteousness, and.......... Dan 9:24
earth shall awake, some to e life .... Dan 12:2
and some to shame and e contempt .... Dan 12:2
have been from of old, from e............ Mic 5:2
Art thou not from e, O LORD my .... Hab 1:12
the e mountains were scattered.......... Hab 3:6
his ways are e .... Hab 3:6
two feet to be cast into e fire .... Mt 18:8
and shall inherit e life..................... Mt 19:29
from me, ye cursed, into e fire........... Mt 25:41
shall go away into e punishment .... Mt 25:46
receive you into e habitations .... Lk 16:9
and in the world to come life .... Lk 18:30
not perish, but have e life.................. Jn 3:16
believeth on the Son hath e life .... Jn 3:36
of water springing up into e life.......... Jn 4:14
on him that sent me, hath e life .... Jn 5:24
meat which endureth unto e life......... Jn 6:27
believeth on him, may have e life .... Jn 6:40
that believeth on me hath e life .... Jn 6:47
that his commandment is life e........... Jn 12:50
yourselves unworthy of e life .... Acts 13:46
unto holiness, and the end e life......... Rom 6:22
to the commandment of the e God ...... Rom 16:26
shall of the Spirit reap life e.............. Gal 6:8
Who shall be punished with e............. 2Th 1:9
and hath given us a consolation........... 2Th 2:16
believe on him to life e 1Ti 1:16
to whom be honour and power e 1Ti 6:16
the blood of the e covenant............... Heb 13:20
into the e kingdom of our Lord............ 2Pet 1:11
he hath reserved in e chains.............. Jude 6
having the e gospel to preach .... Rev 14:6

EVERMORE

be only oppressed and spoiled e .... Deut 28:29
unto David, and to his seed for e 2Sa 22:51
you, ye shall observe to do for e 2Kin 17:37
throne shall be established for e 1Chr 17:14
hand there are pleasures for e........... Ps 16:11
to David, and to his seed for e .... Ps 18:50
and dwell for e .... Ps 37:27
doth his promise fail for e.................. Ps 77:8
and I will glorify thy name for e .... Ps 86:12
mercy will I keep for him for e .... Ps 89:28
Blessed be the LORD for e .... Ps 89:52
thou, LORD, art most high for e........... Ps 92:8
seek his face e .... Ps 105:4
unto all generations for e .... Ps 106:31
from this time forth and for e .... Ps 113:2
from this time forth and for e .... Ps 115:18
this time forth, and even for e............ Ps 121:8
also sit upon thy throne for e .... Ps 132:12
the blessing, even life for e .... Ps 133:3
in the midst of them for e .... Eze 37:26
be in the midst of them for e .... Eze 37:28
him, Lord, e give us this bread .... Jn 6:34
Christ, which is blessed for e.............. 2Cor 11:31
Rejoice e 1Th 5:16
the Son, who is consecrated for e .... Heb 7:28
and, behold, I am alive for e .... Rev 1:18

EVERY See PREFACE.

EVI (e'-vi) A Midian prince.
namely, e, and Rekem, and Zur, and.... Num 31:8
with the princes of Midian, E............ Josh 13:21

EVIDENCE

And I subscribed the e, and sealed...... Jer 32:10
So I took the e of the purchase........... Jer 32:11
I gave the e of the purchase unto .... Jer 32:12
this e of the purchase, both .... Jer 32:14
sealed, and this e which is open .... Jer 32:14
Now when I had delivered the e of ...... Jer 32:16
for, the e of things not seen .... Heb 11:1

EVIDENCES

Take these e, this evidence of .... Jer 32:14
fields for money, and subscribe e .... Jer 32:44

EVIDENT

for it is e unto you if I lie .... Job 6:28
law in the sight of God, it is e .... Gal 3:11
to them an e token of perdition .... Phil 1:28
For it is e that our Lord sprang .... Heb 7:14
And it is yet far more e .... Heb 7:15

EVIDENTLY

He saw in a vision e about the .... Acts 10:3
Christ hath been e set forth............... Gal 3:1

EVIL See PREFACE.

be as gods, knowing good and e .... Gen 3:5
his heart was only e continually .... Gen 6:5
they brought up an e report of .... Num 13:32
LORD shall separate him unto e .... Deut 29:21
day life and good, and death and e ...... Deut 30:15
e will befall you in the latter............. Deut 31:29
because ye will do e in the sight .... Deut 31:29
if it seem e unto you to serve .... Josh 24:15
an e spirit from God troubleth 1Sa 16:15
when the e spirit from God was 1Sa 16:23
the e spirit departed from him 1Sa 16:23
that the e spirit from God came 1Sa 18:10
the e spirit from the LORD was 1Sa 19:9
than feareth God, and escheweth e ..... Job 1:8
shadow of death, I will fear no e .... Ps 23:4
Keep thy tongue from e, and .... Ps 34:13
There shall no e befall thee .... Ps 91:10
To that love the LORD, hate e.............. Ps 97:10
For their feet run to e, and make .... Prov 1:16
and go not in the way of e men .... Prov 4:14
in every place, beholding the e .... Prov 15:3
while the e days come not, nor .... Eccl 12:1
that call e good, and good e .... Is 5:20
that he may know to refuse the e .... Is 7:15
and turn every man from his e way ..... Jer 26:3
set my face against you for e .... Jer 44:11
An e, an only e, behold, is.................. Eze 7:5
turn ye, turn ye from your e ways .... Eze 33:11
Seek good, and not e, that ye may...... Amos 5:14
Hate the e, and love the good, and...... Amos 5:15
that they turned from their e way .... Jonah 3:10
Who hate the good, and love the e ...... Mic 3:2
maketh his sun to rise on the e .... Mt 5:45
temptation, but deliver us from e .... Mt 6:13
unto the day is the e thereof .... Mt 6:34
think ye e in your hearts .... Mt 9:4
said, Why, what e hath he done .... Mt 27:23
that can lightly speak e of me............ Mk 9:39
an e man out of the e treasure .... Lk 6:45
but deliver us from e .... Lk 11:4
light, because their deeds were e .... Jn 3:19
one that doeth e hateth the light......... Jn 3:20
the e spirit answered and said............ Acts 19:15
but the e which I would not, that......... Rom 7:19
do good, e is present with me .... Rom 7:21
Abhor that which is e .... Rom 12:9
Recompense to no man e for e .... Rom 12:17
Be not overcome of e .... Rom 12:21
but overcome e with good .... Rom 12:21
not then your good be e spoken of ...... Rom 14:16
easily provoked, thinketh no e 1Cor 13:5
the time, because the days are e .... Eph 5:16
See that none render e for e.............. 1Th 5:15
Abstain from all appearance of e 1Th 5:22
of money is the root of all e 1Ti 6:10
To speak of no man, to be no .... Titus 3:2
follow not that which is e 3Jn 11
he that doeth e hath not seen God 3Jn 11

EVILDOER

every one is an hypocrite and an e ...... Is 9:17
or as a thief, or as an e 1Pet 4:15

EVILDOERS

have hated the congregation of e .... Ps 26:5
Fret not thyself because of e .... Ps 37:1
For e shall be cut off........................ Ps 37:9
will rise up for me against the e .... Ps 94:16
Depart from me, ye e .... Ps 119:115
laden with iniquity, a seed of e .... Is 1:4
the seed of e shall never be.............. Is 14:20
arise against the house of the e .... Is 31:2
of the poor from the hand of e .... Jer 20:13
strengthen also the hands of e .... Jer 23:14
they speak against you as e 1Pet 2:12
by him for the punishment of e 1Pet 2:14
they speak evil of you, as of e 1Pet 3:16

EVILFAVOUREDNESS

wherein is blemish, or any e .... Deut 17:1

EVIL-MERODACH (e'-vil-mer'-o-dak) Son of
Nebuchadnezzar.
that E king of Babylon in the 2Kin 25:27
that E king of Babylon in the .... Jer 52:31

EVILS

they shall be devoured, and many e ..... Deut 31:17
day, Are not these e come upon us...... Deut 31:17
e which they shall have wrought......... Deut 31:18
shall come to pass, when many e .... Deut 31:21
For innumerable e have compassed ..... Ps 40:12
my people have committed two e .... Jer 2:13
e which they have committed in .... Eze 6:9
all your e that ye have committed........ Eze 20:43
for all the e which Herod had .... Lk 3:19

Abraham set seven e lambs of the ...... Gen 21:28
What mean these seven e lambs .... Gen 21:29
For these seven e lambs shalt .... Gen 21:30
one e lamb of the first year .... Lev 14:10
And whether it be cow or e .... Lev 22:28
one e lamb of the first year .... Num 6:14
nothing, save one little e lamb 2Sa 12:3

EWES

thy e and thy she goats have not .... Gen 31:38
and twenty he goats, two hundred e .... Gen 32:14
From following thee e great with .... Ps 78:71

EXACT

he shall not e it of his...................... Deut 15:2
foreigner thou mayest e it again......... Deut 15:3
Ye e usury, every one of his............... Neh 5:7
might e of them money and corn........ Neh 5:10
and the oil, that ye e of them............. Neh 5:11
The enemy shall not e upon him .... Ps 89:22
pleasure, and e all your labours .... Is 58:3
E no more than that which is .... Lk 3:13

EXACTED

Menahem e the money of Israel,........ 2Kin 15:20
he e the silver and the gold of 2Kin 23:35

EXACTETH

God e of thee less than thine............. Job 11:6

EXACTION

year, and the e of every debt............. Neh 10:31

EXACTIONS

take away your e from my people .... Eze 45:9

EXACTORS

peace, and thine e righteousness......... Is 60:17

EXALT

my father's God, and I will e him .... Ex 15:2
e the horn of his anointed................. 1Sa 2:10
therefore shalt thou not e them.......... Job 17:4
let us e his name together .... Ps 34:3
he shall e thee to inherit the............. Ps 37:34
not the rebellious e themselves .... Ps 66:7
But my horn shalt thou e like the .... Ps 92:10
E ye the LORD our God, and worship ..... Ps 99:5
E the LORD our God, and worship at..... Ps 99:9
Let them e him also in the .... Ps 107:32
thou art my God, I will e thee............ Ps 118:28
lest they e themselves .... Ps 140:8
E thee, and shall promote thee .... Prov 4:8
e the voice unto them, shake the........ Is 13:2
I will e my throne above the.............. Is 14:13
I will e thee, I will praise thy............. Is 25:1
e him that is low, and abase him .... Eze 21:26
neither shall it e itself any .... Eze 29:15
e themselves for their height .... Eze 31:14
e themselves to establish the............ Dan 11:14
and the small e himself, and magnify .. Dan 11:36
High, none at all would e him............ Hos 11:7
Though thou e thyself as the .... Obad 4
whosoever shall e himself shall .... Mt 23:12
take of you, if a man e himself 2Cor 11:20
that he may e you in due time 1Pet 5:6

EXALTED

Agag, and his kingdom shall be e .... Num 24:7
LORD, mine horn is e in the LORD......... 1Sa 2:1
that he had e his kingdom for his 2Sa 5:12
e be the God of the rock of my 2Sa 22:47
the son of Haggith e himself 1Kin 1:5
Forasmuch as I e thee from among 1Kin 14:7
Forasmuch as I e thee out of the 1Kin 16:2
whom hast thou e thy voice.............. 2Kin 19:22
thou art e as head above all 1Chr 29:11
which is e above all blessing and........ Neh 9:5
which mourn may be e to safety .... Job 5:11
They are e for a little while............... Job 24:24
them for ever, and they are e .... Job 36:7
side, when the vilest men are e .... Ps 12:8
shall mine enemy be e over me .... Ps 13:2
let the God of my salvation be e .... Ps 18:46
Be thou e, LORD, in thine own .... Ps 21:13
I will be among the heathen .... Ps 46:10
I will be e in the earth..................... Ps 46:10
he is greatly e .... Ps 47:9
Be thou e, O God, above the.............. Ps 57:5
Be thou e, O God, above the.............. Ps 57:11
horns of the righteous shall be e........ Ps 75:10
thy righteousness shall they be e........ Ps 89:16
in thy favour our horn shall be e .... Ps 89:17
I have e one chosen out of the........... Ps 89:19
and ...in my name shall his horn be e.. Ps 89:24
thou art e far above all gods............. Ps 97:9
Be thou e, O God, above the.............. Ps 108:5
his horn shall be e with honour .... Ps 112:9
The right hand of the LORD is e .... Ps 118:16
of the upright the city is e .... Prov 11:11
shall be e above the hills.................. Is 2:2
Lord alone shall be e in that day .... Is 2:11
LORD alone shall be e in that day........ Is 2:17
of hosts shall be e in judgment.......... Is 5:16
make mention that his name is e .... Is 12:4
you, and therefore will he be e .... Is 30:18
The LORD is e .... Is 33:5
now will I be e .... Is 33:10
whom hast thou e thy voice.............. Is 37:23
Every valley shall be e, and every .... Is 40:4
a way, and my highways shall be e ...... Is 49:11
deal prudently, he shall be e .... Is 52:13
have e the low tree, have dried.......... Eze 17:24

E

her stature was e among the thick....... Eze 19:11
Therefore his height was e above....... Eze 31:5
trembling, he e himself in Israel....... Hos 13:1
were filled, and their heart was e....... Hos 13:6
it shall be e above the hills....... Mic 4:1
which art e unto heaven, shalt be....... Mt 11:23
shall humble himself shall be e....... Mt 23:12
seats, and e them of low degree....... Lk 1:52
Capernaum, which art e to heaven....... Lk 10:15
that humbleth himself shall be e....... Lk 14:11
that humbleth himself shall be e....... Lk 18:14
being by the right hand of God e....... Acts 2:33
Him hath God e with his right....... Acts 5:31
e the people when they dwelt as....... Acts 13:17
abasing myself that ye might be e....... 2Cor 11:7
lest I should be e above measure....... 2Cor 12:7
lest I should be e above measure....... 2Cor 12:7
God also hath highly e him....... Phil 2:9
degree rejoice in that he is e....... Jas 1:9

EXALTEST
As yet a thou thyself against my....... Ex 9:17

EXALTETH
Behold, God e by his power....... Job 36:22
He is the horn of his people....... Ps 148:14
that is hasty of spirit e....... Prov 14:29
Righteousness e a nation....... Prov 14:34
he that e his gate seeketh....... Prov 17:19
For whosoever e himself shall be....... Lk 14:11
for every one that e himself....... Lk 18:14
every high thing that e itself....... 2Cor 10:5
e himself above all that is....... 2Th 2:4

EXAMINATION
O king Agrippa, that, after e had....... Acts 25:26

EXAMINE
the tenth month to e the matter....... Ezr 10:16
he, O LORD, and prove me....... Ps 26:2
to them that do e me is this....... 1Cor 9:3
But let a man e himself, and so....... 1Cor 11:28
E yourselves, whether ye be in....... 2Cor 13:5

EXAMINED
having e him before you, have....... Lk 23:14
If we this day be e of the good....... Acts 4:9
he e the keepers, and commanded....... Acts 12:19
that he should be e by scourging....... Acts 22:24
from him which should have e him....... Acts 22:29
Who, when they had e me, would....... Acts 28:18

EXAMINING
by e of whom thyself mayest take....... Acts 24:8

EXAMPLE
willing to make her a publick e....... Mt 1:19
For I have given you an e....... Jn 13:15
but be thou an e of the believers....... 1Ti 4:12
fall after the same e of unbelief....... Heb 4:11
Who serve unto the e and shadow of....... Heb 8:5
for an e of suffering affliction....... Jas 5:10
suffered for us, leaving us an e....... 1Pet 2:21
flesh, are set forth for an e....... Jude 7

EXAMPLES
Now these things were our e....... 1Cor 10:6

EXCEED
stripes he may give him, and not e....... Deut 25:3
lest, if he should e, and beat him....... Deut 25:3
shall e the righteousness of the....... Mt 5:20
of righteousness e in glory....... 2Cor 3:9

EXCEEDED
one with another, until David e....... 1Sa 20:41
So king Solomon e all the kings....... 1Kin 10:23
transgressions that they have e....... Job 36:9

EXCEEDEST
for thou e the fame that I heard....... 2Chr 9:6

EXCEEDETH
prosperity e the fame which I....... 1Kin 10:7

EXCEEDING
thy shield, and thy e great reward....... Gen 15:1
And I will make thee e fruitful....... Gen 17:6
e bitter cry, and said unto his....... Gen 27:34
and multiplied, and waxed e mighty....... Ex 1:7
the voice of the trumpet e loud....... Ex 19:16
to search it, is an e good land....... Num 14:7
Talk no more so e proudly....... 1Sa 2:3
king David took e much brass....... 2Sa 8:8
The rich man had e many flocks....... 2Sa 12:2
wisdom and understanding e much....... 1Kin 4:29
because they were e many....... 1Kin 7:47
he brought also e much spoil out....... 1Chr 20:2
for the LORD must be e magnifical....... 1Chr 22:5
and spears, and made them e strong....... 2Chr 11:12
for there was e much spoil in....... 2Chr 14:14
until his disease was e great....... 2Chr 16:12
And Hezekiah had e much riches....... 2Chr 32:27
thou hast made him e glad with....... Ps 21:6
altar of God, unto God my e joy....... Ps 43:4
but thy commandment is e broad....... Ps 119:96
the earth, but they are e wise....... Prov 30:24
e deep, who can find it out....... Eccl 7:24
(he is e proud) his loftiness, and....... Jer 48:29
of Israel and Judah is e great....... Eze 9:9
and thou wast e beautiful, and thou....... Eze 16:13
e in dyed attire upon their heads....... Eze 23:15
upon their feet, an e great army....... Eze 37:10
the fish of the great sea, e many....... Eze 47:10
was urgent, and the furnace e hot....... Dan 3:22
Then was the king e glad for him....... Dan 6:23

e dreadful, whose teeth were of....... Dan 7:19
little horn, which waxed e great....... Dan 8:9
Now Nineveh was an e great city....... Jonah 3:3
So Jonah was e glad of the gourd....... Jonah 4:6
they rejoiced with e great joy....... Mt 2:10
was e wroth, and sent forth, and....... Mt 2:16
him up into an e high mountain....... Mt 4:8
Rejoice, and be e glad....... Mt 5:12
e fierce, so that no man might....... Mt 8:28
And they were e sorry....... Mt 17:23
And they were e sorrowful, and....... Mt 26:22
unto them, My soul is e sorrowful....... Mt 26:38
And the king was e sorry....... Mk 6:26
became shining, e white as snow....... Mk 9:3
My soul is e sorrowful unto death....... Mk 14:34
Herod saw Jesus, he was e glad....... Lk 23:8
was e fair, and nourished up in....... Acts 7:20
commandment might become e sinful....... Rom 7:13
worketh for us a far more e....... 2Cor 4:17
comfort, I am e joyful in all our....... 2Cor 7:4
you for the e grace of God in you....... 2Cor 9:14
what is the e greatness of his....... Eph 1:19
the e riches of his grace in his....... Eph 2:7
do e abundantly above all that we....... Eph 3:20
Lord was e abundant with faith....... 1Ti 1:14
ye may be glad also with e joy....... 1Pet 4:13
Whereby are given unto us e great....... 2Pet 1:4
presence of his glory with e joy....... Jude 24
the plague thereof was e great....... Rev 16:21

EXCEEDINGLY
waters prevailed e upon the earth....... Gen 7:19
and sinners before the LORD e....... Gen 13:13
her, I will multiply thy seed e....... Gen 16:10
and thee, and will multiply thee e....... Gen 17:2
fruitful, and will multiply him e....... Gen 17:20
And Isaac trembled very e, and said....... Gen 27:33
And the man increased e, and had....... Gen 30:43
therein, and grew, and multiplied e....... Gen 47:27
played the fool, and have erred e....... 1Sa 26:21
Then Amnon hated her e....... 2Sa 13:15
But they were e afraid, and said....... Mk 4:41
in the sight of all Israel....... 1Chr 29:25
was with him, and magnified him e....... 2Chr 1:1
And Jehoshaphat waxed great e....... 2Chr 17:12
for he strengthened himself e....... 2Chr 26:8
it grieved them e that there was....... Neh 2:10
Then was the queen e grieved....... Est 4:4
Which rejoice e, and are glad....... Job 3:22
yea, let them e rejoice....... Ps 68:3
But lusted e in the wilderness....... Ps 106:14
and I love them e....... Ps 119:167
for we are e filled with contempt....... Ps 123:3
Our soul is e filled with the....... Ps 123:4
dissolved, the earth is moved e....... Is 24:19
dreadful and terrible, and strong e....... Dan 7:7
Then were the men e afraid....... Jonah 1:10
men that they feared the LORD e....... Jonah 1:16
But it displeased Jonah e....... Jonah 4:1
heard it, they were e amazed....... Mt 19:25
And they feared e, and said one to....... Mk 4:41
And they cried out the more e....... Mk 15:14
Jews, do e trouble our city....... Acts 16:20
being e mad against them, I....... Acts 26:11
we being e tossed with a tempest....... Acts 27:18
the more joyed we for the joy....... 2Cor 7:13
being more e zealous of the....... Gal 1:14
day praying e that we might see....... 1Th 3:10
because that your faith groweth e....... 2Th 1:3
Moses said, I fear and quake....... Heb 12:21

EXCEL
as water, thou shalt not e....... Gen 49:4
with harps on the Sheminith to e....... 1Chr 15:21
that e in strength, that do his....... Ps 103:20
images did e them in Jerusalem....... Is 10:10
seek that ye may e to the....... 1Cor 14:12

EXCELLED
Solomon's wisdom e the wisdom of....... 1Kin 4:30

EXCELLENCY
of dignity, and the e of power....... Gen 49:3
in the greatness of thine e thou....... Ex 15:7
thy help, and in his e on the sky....... Deut 33:26
and who is the sword of thy e....... Deut 33:29
Doth not their e which is in them....... Job 4:21
Shall not his e make you afraid....... Job 13:11
Though his e mount up to the....... Job 20:6
with the voice of his e....... Job 37:4
thyself now with majesty and e....... Job 40:10
the e of Jacob whom he loved....... Ps 47:4
to cast him down from his e....... Ps 62:4
his e is over Israel, and his....... Ps 68:34
but the e of knowledge is, that....... Eccl 7:12
the beauty of the Chaldees'....... Is 13:19
of the Carmel and Sharon, they....... Is 35:2
of the LORD, and the e of our God....... Is 35:2
I will make thee an eternal e....... Is 60:15
the e of your strength, the....... Eze 24:21
of hosts, I abhor the e of Jacob....... Amos 6:8
LORD hath sworn by the e of Jacob....... Amos 8:7
hath turned away the e of Jacob....... Nah 2:2
of Jacob, as the e of Israel....... Nah 2:2
came not with e of speech or of....... 1Cor 2:1
that the e of the power may be of....... 2Cor 4:7
the e of the knowledge of Christ....... Phil 3:8

EXCELLENT
honour of his e majesty many days....... Est 1:4
he is e in power, and in judgment....... Job 37:23
how e is thy name in all the....... Ps 8:1
how e is thy name in all the....... Ps 8:9

are in the earth, to his e....... Ps 16:3
How e is thy lovingkindness, O....... Ps 36:7
e than the mountains of prey....... Ps 76:4
it shall be an e oil, which shall....... Ps 141:5
for his name alone is e....... Ps 148:13
him according to his e greatness....... Ps 150:2
for I will speak of e things....... Prov 8:6
is more e than his neighbour....... Prov 12:26
E speech becometh not a fool....... Prov 17:7
understanding is of an e spirit....... Prov 17:27
to thee e things in counsels....... Prov 22:20
is as Lebanon, e as the cedars....... Song 5:15
the fruit of the earth shall be e....... Is 4:2
for he hath done e things....... Is 12:5
in counsel, and e in working....... Is 28:29
and thou art come to e ornaments....... Eze 16:7
image, whose brightness was e....... Dan 2:31
e majesty was added unto me....... Dan 4:36
Forasmuch as an e spirit, and....... Dan 5:12
e wisdom is found in thee....... Dan 5:14
because an e spirit was in him....... Dan 6:3
thee in order, most e Theophilus....... Lk 1:3
Claudius Lysias unto the most e....... Acts 23:26
the things that are more e....... Rom 2:18
yet shew I unto you a more e way....... 1Cor 12:31
ye may approve things that are e....... Phil 1:10
obtained a more e name than they....... Heb 1:4
he obtained a more e ministry....... Heb 8:6
God a more e sacrifice than Cain....... Heb 11:4
a voice to him from the e glory....... 2Pet 1:17

EXCELLEST
virtuously, but thou e them all....... Prov 31:29

EXCELLETH
Then I saw that wisdom e folly....... Eccl 2:13
as far as light e darkness....... Eccl 2:13
by reason of the glory that e....... 2Cor 3:10

EXCEPT
E the God of my father, the God....... Gen 31:42
not let thee go, e thou bless me....... Gen 32:26
e your youngest brother come....... Gen 42:15
e your brother be with you....... Gen 43:3
e your brother be with you....... Gen 43:5
For e we had lingered, surely now....... Gen 43:10
E your youngest brother come down....... Gen 44:23
e our youngest brother be with us....... Gen 44:26
e the land of the priests only....... Gen 47:26
e thou make thyself altogether a....... Num 16:13
e their Rock had sold them, and....... Deut 32:30
e ye destroy the accursed from....... Josh 7:12
e thou hadst hasted and come to....... 1Sa 25:34
to do God to Abner, and more also....... 2Sa 3:9
e thou first bring Michal Saul's....... 2Sa 3:13
E thou take away the blind and the....... 2Sa 5:6
thy riding for me, e I bid thee....... 2Kin 4:24
the king delighted in her, and....... Est 2:14
e such to whom the king shall....... Est 4:11
E the LORD build the house, they....... Ps 127:1
e the LORD keep the city, the....... Ps 127:1
e they have done mischief....... Prov 4:16
E the LORD of hosts had left unto....... Is 1:9
e the gods, whose dwelling is not....... Dan 2:11
worship any god, e their own God....... Dan 3:28
Daniel, e we find it against him....... Dan 6:5
walk together, e they be agreed....... Amos 3:3
That e your righteousness shall....... Mt 5:20
e he first bind the strong man....... Mt 12:29
E ye be converted, and become as....... Mt 18:3
e it be for fornication, and shall....... Mt 19:9
e those days should be shortened....... Mt 24:22
e I drink it, thy will be done....... Mt 26:42
e he first bind the strong....... Mk 3:27
e they wash their hands oft, eat....... Mk 7:3
e they wash, they eat not....... Mk 7:4
e that the Lord had shortened....... Mk 13:20
e we should go and buy meat for....... Lk 9:13
e ye repent, ye shall all....... Lk 13:3
e ye repent, ye shall all....... Lk 13:5
thou doest, e God be with him....... Jn 3:2
E a man be born again, he cannot....... Jn 3:3
E a man be born of water and of....... Jn 3:5
e ye be given him from heaven....... Jn 3:27
E ye see signs and wonders, ye....... Jn 4:48
e the Father which hath sent me....... Jn 6:44
E ye eat the flesh of the Son of....... Jn 6:53
e it were given unto him of my....... Jn 6:65
E a corn of wheat fall into the....... Jn 12:24
of itself, e it abide in the vine....... Jn 15:4
no more can ye, e ye abide in me....... Jn 15:4
e it were given them from above....... Jn 19:11
E I shall see in his hands the....... Jn 20:25
Judaea and Samaria, e the apostles....... Acts 8:1
e some man should guide me....... Acts 8:31
E ye be circumcised after the....... Acts 15:1
E it be for this one voice, that....... Acts 24:21
such as I am, e these bonds....... Acts 26:29
E these abide in the ship, ye....... Acts 27:31
the law had said, Thou shalt....... Rom 7:7
E the Lord of Sabaoth had left us....... Rom 9:29
shall they preach, e they be sent....... Rom 10:15
e it be with consent for a time....... 1Cor 7:5
e he interpret, that the church....... 1Cor 14:5
e I shall speak to you either by....... 1Cor 14:6
e they give a distinction in the....... 1Cor 14:7
e ye utter by the tongue words....... 1Cor 14:9
sowest is not quickened, e it die....... 1Cor 15:36
e it be that I myself was not....... 2Cor 12:13
is in you, e ye be reprobates....... 2Cor 13:5
e there come a falling away first....... 2Th 2:3
not crowned, e he strive lawfully....... 2Ti 2:5

out of his place, e thou repent .... Rev 2:5
e they repent of their deeds .... Rev 2:22

EXCEPTED
him, it is manifest that he is e 1Cor 15:27

EXCESS
they are full of extortion and e .... Mt 23:25
not drunk with wine, wherein is e .... Eph 5:18
lusts, of wine, revellings, ... 1Pet 4:3
with them to the same e of riot 1Pet 4:4

EXCHANGE
gave them bread in e for horses .... Gen 47:17
the e thereof shall be holy .... Lev 27:10
the e of it shall not be for .... Job 28:17
shall not sell of it, neither e .... Eze 48:14
a man give in e for his soul .... Mt 16:26
a man give in e for his soul .... Mk 8:37

EXCHANGERS
to have put my money to the e .... Mt 25:27

EXCLUDE
yea, they would e you, that ye .... Gal 4:17

EXCLUDED
is boasting then? It is e .... Rom 3:27

EXCUSE
with one consent began to make e .... Lk 14:18
so that they are without e .... Rom 1:20
think ye that we e ourselves unto 2Cor 12:19

EXCUSED
I pray thee have me e .... Lk 14:18
I pray thee have me e .... Lk 14:19

EXCUSING
accusing or else e one another .... Rom 2:15

EXECRATION
and ye shall be an e, and an .... Jer 42:18
and they shall be an e, and an .... Jer 44:12

EXECUTE
gods of Egypt I will e judgment .... Ex 12:12
the priest shall e upon her all .... Num 5:30
that they may e the service of .... Num 8:11
He doth e the judgment of the .... Deut 10:18
e my judgments, and keep all my 1Kin 6:12
shall e judgment upon them .... Ps 119:84
To e vengeance upon the heathen, ... Ps 149:7
To e upon them the judgment .... Ps 149:9
Take counsel, e judgment .... Is 16:3
if ye throughly e judgment .... Jer 7:5
E judgment in the morning, and .... Jer 21:12
E ye judgment and righteousness, ... Jer 22:3
shall e judgment and justice in .... Jer 23:5
and he shall e judgment and .... Jer 33:15
will e judgments in the midst of .... Eze 5:8
I will e judgments in thee, and .... Eze 5:10
when I shall e judgments in thee .... Eze 5:15
will e judgments among you .... Eze 11:9
e judgments upon thee in the .... Eze 16:41
I will e judgments upon Moab .... Eze 25:11
I will e great vengeance upon .... Eze 25:17
Zoan, and will e judgments in No .... Eze 30:14
Thus will I e judgments in Egypt .... Eze 30:19
e judgment and justice, take away .... Eze 45:9
I will not e the fierceness of .... Hos 11:9
I will e vengeance in anger and .... Mic 5:15
my cause, and judgment for me .... Mic 7:9
E true judgment, and shew mercy and .... Zec 7:9
e the judgment of truth and peace .... Zec 8:16
him authority to e judgment also .... Jn 5:27
a revenger to e wrath upon him .... Rom 13:4
To e judgment upon all, and to .... Jude 15

EXECUTED
gods also the LORD e judgments .... Num 33:4
he e the justice of the LORD, and .... Deut 33:21
David e judgment and justice unto 2Sa 8:15
(he it is that e the priest's 1Chr 6:10
e judgment and justice among all 1Chr 18:14
Ithamar e the priest's office 1Chr 24:2
So they e judgment against Joash 2Chr 24:24
let judgment be e speedily upon .... Ezr 7:26
stood up Phinehas, and e judgment .... Ps 106:30
an evil work is not e speedily .... Eccl 8:11
shall not return, until he have e .... Jer 23:20
neither e my judgments, but have .... Eze 11:12
hath e true judgment between man .... Eze 18:8
hath e my judgments, hath walked .... Eze 18:17
they had not e my judgments .... Eze 20:24
for they had e judgment upon her .... Eze 23:10
I shall have e judgments in her .... Eze 28:22
when I have e judgments upon all .... Eze 28:26
see my judgment that I have e .... Eze 39:21
that while he e the priest's .... Lk 1:8

EXECUTEDST
nor e his fierce wrath upon 1Sa 28:18

EXECUTEST
thou e judgment and righteousness .... Ps 99:4

EXECUTETH
known by the judgment which he e .... Ps 9:16
The LORD e righteousness and .... Ps 103:6
Which e judgment for the .... Ps 146:7
the man that e my counsel from a .... Is 46:11
if there be any that e judgment .... Jer 5:1
for he is strong that e his word .... Joel 2:11

EXECUTING
in e that which is right in mine 2Kin 10:30
e the priest's office unto the 2Chr 11:14
when Jehu was e judgment upon the 2Chr 22:8

EXECUTION
decree drew near to be put in e .... Est 9:1

EXECUTIONER
And immediately the king sent an e .... Mk 6:27

EXEMPTED
throughout all Judah; none was e 1Kin 15:22

EXERCISE
neither do I e myself in great .... Ps 131:1
the LORD which e lovingkindness .... Jer 9:24
the Gentiles e dominion over them .... Mt 20:25
are great e authority upon them .... Mt 20:25
the Gentiles e lordship over them .... Mk 10:42
their great ones e authority upon .... Mk 10:42
the Gentiles e lordship over them .... Lk 22:25
they that e authority upon them .... Lk 22:25
And herein do I e myself, to have .... Acts 24:16
e thyself rather unto godliness 1Ti 4:7
For bodily e profiteth little 1Ti 4:8

EXERCISED
the sons of man to be e therewith .... Eccl 1:13
to the sons of men to be e in it .... Eccl 3:10
e robbery, and have vexed the poor .... Eze 22:29
senses e to discern both good .... Heb 5:14
unto them which are e thereby .... Heb 12:11
an heart they have e with 2Pet 2:14

EXERCISETH
he e all the power of the first .... Rev 13:12

EXHORT
other words did he testify and e .... Acts 2:40
now I e you to be of good cheer .... Acts 27:22
it necessary to e the brethren 2Cor 9:5
e you by the Lord Jesus, that as 1Th 4:1
Now we e you, brethren, warn them 1Th 5:14
e by our Lord Jesus Christ, that 2Th 3:12
I e therefore, that, first of all 1Ti 2:1
These things teach and e 1Ti 6:2
e with all longsuffering and 2Ti 4:2
able by sound doctrine both to e .... Titus 1:9
men likewise e to be sober minded .... Titus 2:6
E servants to be obedient unto .... Titus 2:9
These things speak, and e, and .... Titus 2:15
But e one another daily, while it .... Heb 3:13
elders which are among you I e 1Pet 5:1
e you that ye should earnestly .... Jude 3

EXHORTATION
many other things in his e .... Lk 3:18
have any word of e for the people .... Acts 13:15
parts, and had given them much e .... Acts 20:2
Or he that exhorteth, on e .... Rom 12:8
unto men to edification, and e 1Cor 14:3
For indeed he accepted the e 2Cor 8:17
For our e was not of deceit, nor 1Th 2:3
give attendance to reading, to e 1Ti 4:13
ye have forgotten the e which .... Heb 12:5
brethren, suffer the word of e .... Heb 13:22

EXHORTED
e them all, that with purpose of .... Acts 11:23
e the brethren with many words, ... Acts 15:32
As ye know how we e and comforted .. 1Th 2:11

EXHORTETH
Or he that e, on exhortation .... Rom 12:8

EXHORTING
e them to continue in the faith, ... Acts 14:22
e the disciples to receive him, ... Acts 18:27
but e one another .... Heb 10:25
I have written briefly, e 1Pet 5:12

EXILE
thou art a stranger, and also an e 2Sa 15:19
The captive e hasteneth that he .... Is 51:14

EXORCISTS
certain of the vagabond Jews, e .... Acts 19:13

EXPECTATION
the e of the poor shall not .... Ps 9:18
for my e is from him .... Ps 62:5
but the e of the wicked shall .... Prov 10:28
man dieth, his e shall perish .... Prov 11:7
but the e of the wicked is wrath .... Prov 11:23
thine e shall not be cut off .... Prov 23:18
thy e shall not be cut off .... Prov 24:14
and ashamed of Ethiopia their e .... Is 20:5
that day, Behold, such is our e .... Is 20:6
for her e shall be ashamed .... Zec 9:5
And as the people were in e .... Lk 3:15
from all the e of the people of .... Acts 12:11
For the earnest e of the creature .... Rom 8:19
According to my earnest e .... Phil 1:20

EXPECTED
not of evil, to give you an e end .... Jer 29:11

EXPECTING
e receive something of them .... Acts 3:5
From henceforth e till his .... Heb 10:13

EXPEDIENT
Nor consider that it is e for us .... Jn 11:50
It is e for you that I go away .... Jn 16:7
that it was e that one man should .... Jn 18:14
unto me, but all things are not e 1Cor 6:12
for me, but all things are not e 1Cor 10:23

for this is e for you, who have 2Cor 8:10
It is not e for me doubtless to 2Cor 12:1

EXPEL
he shall e them from before you, ... Josh 23:5
e me out of my father's house .... Judg 11:7

EXPELLED
of Israel e not the Geshurites .... Josh 13:13
he e thence the three sons of .... Judg 1:20
his banished be expelled from him 2Sa 14:14
e them out of their coasts .... Acts 13:50

EXPENCES
let the e be given out of the .... Ezr 6:4
forthwith e be given unto these .... Ezr 6:8

EXPERIENCE
for I have learned by e that he .... Gen 30:27
my heart had great e of wisdom .... Eccl 1:16
And patience, e .... Rom 5:4
and e, hope .... Rom 5:4

EXPERIMENT
Whiles by the e of this 2Cor 9:13

EXPERT
e in war, with all instruments of 1Chr 12:33
And of the Danites e in war twenty .. 1Chr 12:35
e in war, and e in war, forty thousand 1Chr 12:36
all bold swords, being e in war .... Song 3:8
shall be as of a mighty e man .... Jer 50:9
know thee to be e in all customs .... Acts 26:3

EXPIRED
and the days were not e 1Sa 18:26
to pass, after the year was e 2Sa 11:1
when thy days be e that thou must .. 1Chr 17:11
pass, that after the year was e 1Chr 20:1
And when the year was e, king 2Chr 36:10
And when these days were e .... Est 1:5
And when these days are e, it .... Eze 43:27
And when forty years were e .... Acts 7:30
And when the thousand years are e .... Rev 20:7

EXPLOITS
and he shall do e, and return to .... Dan 11:28
God shall be strong, and do e .... Dan 11:32

EXPOUND
not in three days e the riddle .... Judg 14:14

EXPOUNDED
unto them which e the riddle .... Judg 14:19
he e all things to his disciples .... Mk 4:34
he e unto them in all the .... Lk 24:27
e it by order unto them, saying, ... Acts 11:4
e unto him the way of God more .... Acts 18:26
to whom he e and testified the .... Acts 28:23

EXPRESS
the e image of his person, and .... Heb 1:3

EXPRESSED
men which are e by their names .... Num 1:17
thousand, which were e by name 1Chr 12:31
were chosen, who were e by name 1Chr 16:41
men which were e by name rose up .. 2Chr 28:15
city, the men that were e by name .. 2Chr 31:19
all of them were e by name .... Ezr 8:20

EXPRESSLY
If I e say unto the lad, Behold, ... 1Sa 20:21
came e unto Ezekiel the priest .... Eze 1:3
Now the Spirit speaketh e 1Ti 4:1

EXTEND
there be none to e mercy unto him .... Ps 109:12
I will e peace to her like a .... Is 66:12

EXTENDED
hath e mercy unto me before the .... Ezr 7:28
but hath e mercy unto us in the .... Ezr 9:9

EXTENDETH
my goodness e not to thee .... Ps 16:2

EXTINCT
breath is corrupt, my days are e .... Job 17:1
they are e, they are quenched as .... Is 43:17

EXTOL
I will e thee, O LORD .... Ps 30:1
e him that rideth upon the .... Ps 68:4
I will e thee, my God, O king .... Ps 145:1
Now I Nebuchadnezzar praise and e .... Dan 4:37

EXTOLLED
mouth, and he was e with my tongue .... Ps 66:17
shall be exalted and e .... Is 52:13

EXTORTION
gained of thy neighbours by e .... Eze 22:12
but within they are full of e .... Mt 23:25

EXTORTIONER
Let the e catch all that he hath .... Ps 109:11
for the e is at an end, the .... Is 16:4
a railer, or a drunkard, or an e 1Cor 5:11

EXTORTIONERS
that I am not as other men are, e .... Lk 18:11
world, or with the covetous, or e 1Cor 5:10
drunkards, nor revilers, nor e 1Cor 6:10

EXTREME
and with an e burning, and with. Deut 28:22

EXTREMITY
yet he knoweth it not in great e. Job 35:15

EYE
E for e, tooth for tooth, hand. Ex 21:24
a man smite the e of his servant. Ex 21:26
or the e of his maid, that it. Ex 21:26
or that hath a blemish in his e. Lev 21:20
e for e, tooth for tooth. Lev 24:20
thine e shall have no pity upon. Deut 7:16
neither shall thine e pity him. Deut 13:8
thine e be evil against thy poor. Deut 15:9
Thine e shall not pity him, but. Deut 19:13
And thine e shall not pity. Deut 19:21
e for e, tooth for tooth, hand. Deut 19:21
thine e shall not pity her. Deut 25:12
his e shall be evil toward his. Deut 28:54
her e shall be evil toward the. Deut 28:56
he kept him as the apple of his e. Deut 32:10
his e was not dim, nor his. Deut 34:7
but mine e spared thee. 1Sa 24:10
to my cleanness in his e sight. 2Sa 22:25
But the e of their God was upon. Ezr 5:5
mine e shall no more see good. Job 7:7
The e of him that hath seen me. Job 7:8
up the ghost, and no e had seen me. Job 10:18
mine e hath seen all this, mine. Job 13:1
but mine e poureth out tears unto. Job 16:20
doth not mine e continue in their. Job 17:2
Mine e also is dim by reason of. Job 17:7
The e also which saw him shall. Job 20:9
The e also of the adulterer. Job 24:15
saying, No e shall see me. Job 24:15
the vulture's e hath not seen. Job 28:7
his e seeth every precious thing. Job 28:10
and when the e saw me, it gave. Job 29:11
but now mine e seeth thee. Job 42:5
Mine e is consumed because of. Ps 6:7
Keep me as the apple of the e. Ps 17:8
mine e is consumed with grief. Ps 31:9
I will guide thee with mine e. Ps 32:8
the e of the Lord is upon them. Ps 33:18
e that hate me without a cause. Ps 35:19
Aha, aha, our e hath seen it. Ps 35:21
mine e hath seen his desire upon. Ps 54:7
Mine e mourneth by reason of. Ps 88:9
Mine e also shall see my desire. Ps 92:11
he that formed the e, shall he. Ps 94:9
and my law as the apple of thine e. Prov 7:2
winketh with the e causeth sorrow. Prov 10:10
The hearing ear, and the seeing e. Prov 20:12
a bountiful e shall be blessed. Prov 22:9
bread of him that hath an evil e. Prov 23:6
hasteth to be rich hath an evil e. Prov 28:22
The e that mocketh at his father. Prov 30:17
the e is not satisfied with. Eccl 1:8
neither is his e satisfied with. Eccl 4:8
their e shall not spare children. Is 13:18
for they shall see e to e. Is 52:8
the ear, neither hath the e seen. Is 64:4
mine e shall weep sore, and run. Jer 13:17
mine e, mine e runneth down. Lam 1:16
to the e in the tabernacle of the. Lam 2:4
not the apple of thine e cease. Lam 2:18
Mine e runneth down with rivers. Lam 3:48
Mine e trickleth down, and ceaseth. Lam 3:49
Mine e affecteth mine heart. Lam 3:51
neither shall mine e spare. Eze 5:11
mine e shall not spare thee. Eze 7:4
mine e shall not spare, neither. Eze 7:9
mine e shall not spare, neither. Eze 8:18
let not your e spare, neither. Eze 9:5
mine e shall not spare, neither. Eze 9:10
Now e pitied thee, to do any of. Eze 16:5
Nevertheless mine e spared them. Eze 20:17
and let our e look upon Zion. Mic 4:11
you toucheth the apple of his e. Zec 2:8
upon his arm, and upon his right e. Zec 11:17
his right e shall be utterly. Zec 11:17
And if thy right e offend thee. Mt 5:29
hath been said, An e for an e. Mt 5:38
The light of the body is the e. Mt 6:22
if therefore thine e be single. Mt 6:22
But if thine e be evil, thy whole. Mt 6:23
mote that is in thy brother's e. Mt 7:3
the beam that is in thine own e. Mt 7:3
pull out the mote out of thine e. Mt 7:4
behold, a beam is in thine own e. Mt 7:4
out the beam out of thine own e. Mt 7:5
the mote out of thy brother's e. Mt 7:5
if thine e offend thee, pluck it. Mt 18:9
to enter into life with one e. Mt 18:9
to go through the e of a needle. Mt 19:24
Is thine e evil, because I am. Mt 20:15
deceit, lasciviousness, an evil e. Mk 7:22
if thine e offend thee, pluck it. Mk 9:47
the kingdom of God with one e. Mk 9:47
to go through the e of a needle. Mk 10:25
mote that is in thy brother's e. Lk 6:41
the beam that is in thine own e. Lk 6:41
out the mote that is in thine e. Lk 6:41
the beam that is in thine own e. Lk 6:42
first the beam out of thine own e. Lk 6:42
mote that is in thy brother's e. Lk 6:42
The light of the body is the e. Lk 11:34
therefore when thine e is single. Lk 11:34
but when thine e is evil, thy. Lk 11:34
camel to go through a needle's e. Lk 18:25

E hath not seen, nor ear heard. 1Cor 2:9
shall say, Because I am not the e. 1Cor 12:16
If the whole body were an e. 1Cor 12:17
the e cannot say unto the hand, I. 1Cor 12:21
moment, in the twinkling of an e. 1Cor 15:52
every e shall see him, and they. Rev 1:7

EYEBROWS
his head and his beard and his e. Lev 14:9

EYED
Leah was tender e. Gen 29:17
Saul e David from that day and. 1Sa 18:9

EYELIDS
on my e is the shadow of death. Job 16:16
are like the e of the morning. Job 41:18
his eyes behold, his e try. Ps 11:4
mine eyes, or slumber to mine e. Ps 132:4
let thine e look straight before. Prov 4:25
eyes, nor slumber to thine e. Prov 6:4
let her take thee with her e. Prov 6:25
and their e are lifted up. Prov 30:13
our e gush out with waters. Jer 9:18

EYE'S
let him go free for his e sake. Ex 21:26

EYES
then your e shall be opened, and. Gen 3:5
and that it was pleasant to the e. Gen 3:6
the e of them both were opened. Gen 3:7
found grace in the e of the Lord. Gen 6:8
And Lot lifted up his e, and beheld. Gen 13:10
from him, Lift up now thine e. Gen 13:14
mistress was despised in her e. Gen 16:5
I was despised in her e. Gen 16:5
And he lift up his e and looked, and. Gen 18:2
ye to them as is good in your e. Gen 19:8
he is to thee a covering of the e. Gen 20:16
And God opened her e. Gen 21:19
third day Abraham lifted up his e. Gen 22:4
And Abraham lifted up his e. Gen 22:13
and he lifted up his e, and saw, and. Gen 24:63
And Rebekah lifted up her e. Gen 24:64
when Jacob was old, and his e. Gen 27:1
if I have found favour in thine e. Gen 30:27
e of the cattle in the gutters. Gen 30:41
that I lifted up mine e, and saw. Gen 31:10
And he said, Lift up now thine e. Gen 31:12
and my sheep departed from mine e. Gen 31:40
And Jacob lifted up his e, and. Gen 33:1
And he lifted up his e, and saw the. Gen 33:5
Let me find grace in your e. Gen 34:11
and they lifted up their e. Gen 37:25
wife cast her e upon Joseph. Gen 39:7
was good in the e of Pharaoh. Gen 41:37
in the e of all his servants. Gen 41:37
and bound him before their e. Gen 42:24
And he lifted up his e, and saw. Gen 43:29
that I may see e upon him. Gen 44:21
And, behold, your e see, and the. Gen 45:12
the e of my brother Benjamin. Gen 45:12
shall put his hand upon thine e. Gen 46:4
shall we die before thine e. Gen 47:19
Now the e of Israel were dim for. Gen 48:10
His e shall be red with wine, and. Gen 49:12
now I have found grace in your e. Gen 50:4
be abhorred in the e of Pharaoh. Ex 5:21
in the e of his servants, to put. Ex 5:21
of the Egyptians before their e. Ex 8:26
and for a memorial between thine e. Ex 13:9
and for frontlets between thine e. Ex 13:16
of Israel lifted up their e. Ex 14:10
the e of the children of Israel. Ex 24:17
be hid from the e of the assembly. Lev 4:13
ways hide their e from the man. Lev 20:4
ague, that shall consume the e. Lev 26:16
be hid from the e of her husband. Num 5:13
thou mayest be to us instead of e. Num 10:31
beside this manna, before our e. Num 11:6
your own heart and your own e. Num 15:39
thou put out the e of these men. Num 16:14
ye unto the rock before their e. Num 20:8
to sanctify me in the e of the. Num 20:12
The Lord opened the e of Balaam. Num 22:31
And Balaam lifted up his e. Num 24:2
the man whose e are open hath. Num 24:3
a trance, but having his e open. Num 24:4
the man whose e are open hath. Num 24:15
a trance, but having his e open. Num 24:16
me at the water before their e. Num 27:14
of them shall be pricks in your e. Num 33:55
for you in Egypt before your e. Deut 1:30
Thine e have seen all that the. Deut 3:21
and lift up thine e westward. Deut 3:27
and behold it with thine e. Deut 3:27
Your e have seen what the Lord. Deut 4:3
things which thine e have seen. Deut 4:9
thou lift up thine e unto heaven. Deut 4:19
for you in Egypt before your e. Deut 4:34
be as frontlets between thine e. Deut 6:8
all his household, before our e. Deut 6:22
temptations which thine e saw. Deut 7:19
and brake them before your e. Deut 9:17
things, which thine e have seen. Deut 10:21
But your e have seen all the. Deut 11:7
ear of the Lord thy God are. Deut 11:12
be as frontlets between your e. Deut 11:18
whatsoever is right in his own e. Deut 12:8
in the e of the Lord thy God. Deut 13:18
between your e for the dead. Deut 14:1
gift doth blind the e of the wise. Deut 16:19

blood, neither have our e seen it. Deut 21:7
that she find no favour in his e. Deut 24:1
ox shall be slain before thine e. Deut 28:31
thine e shall look, and fail with. Deut 28:32
of thine e which thou shalt see. Deut 28:34
trembling heart, and failing of e. Deut 28:65
of thine e which thou shalt see. Deut 28:67
your e in the land of Egypt unto. Deut 29:2
which thine e have seen, the. Deut 29:3
e to see, and ears to hear, unto. Deut 29:4
thee to see it with thine e. Deut 34:4
Jericho, that he lifted up his e. Josh 5:13
your sides, and thorns in your e. Josh 23:13
your e have seen what I have done. Judg 2:7
took him, and put out his e. Judg 16:21
of the Philistines for my two e. Judg 16:28
that which was right in his own e. Judg 17:6
And when he had lifted up his e. Judg 19:17
that which was right in his own e. Judg 21:25
Let thine e be on the field that. Ruth 2:9
Why have I found grace in thine e. Ruth 2:10
shall be to consume thine e. 1Sa 2:33
his e began to wax dim, that he. 1Sa 3:2
his e were dim, that he could not. 1Sa 4:15
and they lifted up their e. 1Sa 6:13
I may thrust out all your right e. 1Sa 11:2
bribe to blind mine e therewith. 1Sa 12:3
the Lord will do before your e. 1Sa 12:16
and his e were enlightened. 1Sa 14:27
how mine e have been enlightened. 1Sa 14:29
I have found grace in thine e. 1Sa 20:3
if I have found favour in thine e. 1Sa 20:29
this day thine e have seen how. 1Sa 24:10
young men find favour in thine e. 1Sa 25:8
was precious in thine e this day. 1Sa 26:21
much set by this day in mine e. 1Sa 26:24
much set by in the e of the Lord. 1Sa 26:24
I have now found grace in thine e. 2Sa 16:4
to day in the e of the handmaids. 2Sa 6:20
take thy wives before thine e. 2Sa 12:11
kept the watch lifted up his e. 2Sa 13:34
find favour in the e of the Lord. 2Sa 15:25
unto the wall, and lifted up his e. 2Sa 18:24
therefore what is good in thine e. 2Sa 19:27
but thine e are upon the haughty. 2Sa 22:28
that the e of my lord the king. 2Sa 24:3
the e of all Israel are upon thee. 1Kin 1:20
this day, mine e even seeing it. 1Kin 1:48
That thine e may be open toward. 1Kin 8:29
That thine e may be open unto the. 1Kin 8:52
which thine e may be open unto the. 1Kin 8:52
I came, and mine e had seen it. 1Kin 10:7
do that which is right in mine e. 1Kin 11:33
for his e were set by reason of. 1Kin 14:4
only which was right in mine e. 1Kin 14:8
was right in the e of the Lord. 1Kin 15:5
was right in the e of the Lord. 1Kin 15:11
wrought evil in the e of the Lord. 1Kin 16:25
whatsoever is pleasant in thine e. 1Kin 20:6
was right in the e of the Lord. 1Kin 22:43
his e upon his e, and his hands. 2Kin 4:34
times, and the child opened his e. 2Kin 4:35
Lord, I pray thee, open his e. 2Kin 6:17
opened the e of the young man. 2Kin 6:17
open the e of these men, that. 2Kin 6:20
And the Lord opened their e. 2Kin 6:20
thou shalt see it with thine e. 2Kin 7:2
thou shalt see it with thine e. 2Kin 7:19
that which is right in thine e. 2Kin 10:5
was right in his sight in mine e. 2Kin 10:30
then, Lord, thine e, and see. 2Kin 19:16
and lifted up thine e on high. 2Kin 19:22
thine e shall not see all the. 2Kin 22:20
the sons of Zedekiah before his e. 2Kin 25:7
and put out the e of Zedekiah. 2Kin 25:7
right in the e of all the people. 1Chr 13:4
this was a small thing in thine e. 1Chr 17:17
And David lifted up his e, and saw. 1Chr 21:16
do that which is good in his e. 1Chr 21:23
That thine e may be open upon. 2Chr 6:20
thine e be open, and let thine. 2Chr 6:40
Now mine e shall be open, and. 2Chr 7:15
and mine e and mine heart shall be. 2Chr 7:16
I came, and mine e had seen it. 2Chr 9:6
right in the e of the Lord his. 2Chr 14:2
For the e of the Lord run to and. 2Chr 16:9
but our e are upon thee. 2Chr 20:12
was evil in the e of the Lord our. 2Chr 21:6
evil in the e of the Lord our God. 2Chr 29:6
to hissing, as ye see with your e. 2Chr 29:8
neither shall thine e see all the. 2Chr 34:28
house was laid before thine e. Ezr 3:12
that our God may lighten our e. Ezr 9:8
now be attentive, and thine e open. Neh 1:6
much cast down in their own e. Neh 6:16
despise their husbands in their e. Est 1:17
king, and I be pleasing in his e. Est 8:5
they lifted up their e afar off. Job 2:12
womb, nor hid sorrow from mine e. Job 3:10
an image was before mine e. Job 4:16
e are upon me, and I am not. Job 7:8
Hast thou e of flesh. Job 10:4
is pure, and I am clean in thine e. Job 11:4
But the e of the wicked shall. Job 11:20
open thine e upon such an one. Job 14:3
his e seem as we with your e. Job 15:12
enemy sharpeneth his e upon me. Job 16:9
even the e of his children shall. Job 17:5
mine e shall behold, and not. Job 19:27
and their offspring before their e. Job 21:8

His *e* shall see his destruction, ... Job 21:20
yet his *e* are upon their ways .... Job 24:23
he openeth his *e*, and he is not. .... Job 27:19
is hid from the *e* of all living. .... Job 28:21
I was *e* to the blind, and feet was .... Job 29:15
I made a covenant with mine *e* .... Job 31:1
and mine heart walked after mine *e* .... Job 31:7
or have caused the *e* of the widow .... Job 31:16
he was righteous in his own *e* .... Job 32:1
For his *e* are upon the ways of .... Job 34:21
not his *e* from the righteous .... Job 36:7
prey, and her *e* behold afar off .... Job 39:29
He taketh it with his *e* .... Job 40:24
his *e* are like the eyelids of the .... Job 41:18
his *e* are privily set against the .... Ps 10:8
his *e* behold, his eyelids try, ... Ps 11:4
lighten mine *e*, lest I sleep the .... Ps 13:3
In whose *e* a vile person is .... Ps 15:4
let thine *e* behold the things .... Ps 17:2
they have set their *e* bowing down, ... Ps 17:11
LORD is pure, enlightening the *e* .... Ps 19:8
Mine *e* are ever toward the LORD .... Ps 25:15
lovingkindness is before mine *e* .... Ps 26:3
I am cut off from before thine *e* .... Ps 31:22
The *e* of the LORD are upon the .... Ps 34:15
is no fear of God before his *e* .... Ps 36:1
flattereth himself in his own *e* .... Ps 36:2
as for the light of mine *e* .... Ps 38:10
set them in order before thine *e* .... Ps 50:21
his *e* behold the nations .... Ps 66:7
mine *e* fail while I wait for my, ... Ps 69:3
Let their *e* be darkened, that .... Ps 69:23
Their *e* stand out with fatness. .... Ps 73:7
Thou holdest mine *e* waking. .... Ps 77:4
Only with thine *e* shalt thou. .... Ps 91:8
set no wicked thing before mine *e* .... Ps 101:3
Mine *e* shall be upon the faithful .... Ps 101:6
e have they, but they see not .... Ps 115:5
mine *e* from tears, and my feet .... Ps 116:8
it is marvellous in our *e* .... Ps 118:23
Open thou mine *e*, that I may .... Ps 119:18
Turn away mine *e* from beholding .... Ps 119:37
Mine *e* fail for thy word, saying, ... Ps 119:82
Mine *e* fail for thy salvation, and .... Ps 119:123
Rivers of waters run down mine *e* .... Ps 119:136
Mine *e* prevent the night watches, ... Ps 119:148
lift up mine *e* unto the hills. .... Ps 121:1
Unto thee lift I up mine *e* .... Ps 123:1
as the *e* of servants look unto .... Ps 123:2
as the *e* of a maiden unto the .... Ps 123:2
so our *e* wait upon the LORD our .... Ps 123:2
is not haughty, nor mine *e* lofty .... Ps 131:1
I will not give sleep to mine *e* .... Ps 132:4
e have they, but they see not. .... Ps 135:16
Thine *e* did see my substance, yet. .... Ps 139:16
But mine *e* are unto thee, O God .... Ps 141:8
The *e* of all wait upon thee. .... Ps 145:15
LORD openeth the *e* of the blind. .... Ps 146:8
Be not wise in thine own *e* .... Prov 3:7
let not them depart from thine *e* .... Prov 3:21
Let them not depart from thine *e* .... Prov 4:21
Let thine *e* look right on, and let .... Prov 4:25
man are before the *e* of the LORD .... Prov 5:21
Give not sleep to thine *e* .... Prov 6:4
He winketh with his *e*, he .... Prov 6:13
the teeth, and as smoke to the *e* .... Prov 10:26
of a fool is right in his own *e* .... Prov 12:15
The *e* of the LORD are in every .... Prov 15:3
The light of the *e* rejoiceth the, ... Prov 15:30
of a man are clean in his own *e*. .... Prov 16:2
He shutteth his *e* to devise .... Prov 16:30
in the *e* of him that hath it .... Prov 17:8
but the *e* of a fool are in the .... Prov 17:24
away all evil with his *e* .... Prov 20:8
open thine *e*, and thou shalt be .... Prov 20:13
of a man is right in his own *e* .... Prov 21:2
findeth no favour in his *e* .... Prov 21:10
The *e* of the LORD preserve. .... Prov 22:12
Wilt thou set thine *e* upon that .... Prov 23:5
let thine *e* observe my ways .... Prov 23:26
who hath redness of *e* .... Prov 23:29
Thine *e* shall behold strange. .... Prov 23:33
the prince whom thine *e* have seen. .... Prov 25:7
so the *e* of man are never .... Prov 27:20
but he that hideth his *e* shall. .... Prov 28:27
the LORD lighteneth both their *e* .... Prov 29:13
that are pure in their own *e* .... Prov 30:12
O how lofty are their *e* .... Prov 30:13
whatsoever mine *e* desired I kept .... Eccl 2:10
The wise man's *e* are in his head .... Eccl 2:14
beholding of them with their *e* .... Eccl 5:11
the *e* than the wandering of the .... Eccl 6:9
nor night seeth sleep with his *e* .... Eccl 8:16
it is for the *e* to behold the sun .... Eccl 11:7
heart, and in the sight of thine *e* .... Eccl 11:9
thou hast doves', ... Song 1:15
hast doves' within thy locks .... Song 4:1
my heart with one of thine *e* .... Song 4:9
His *e* are as the *e* of doves by .... Song 5:12
Turn away thine *e* from me .... Song 6:5
thine *e* like the fishpools in .... Song 7:4
then was I in his *e* as one that .... Song 8:10
I will hide mine *e* from you .... Is 1:15
of your doings from before mine *e* .... Is 1:16
to provoke the *e* of his glory .... Is 3:8
stretched forth necks and wanton *e* .... Is 3:16
the *e* of the lofty shall be .... Is 5:15
them that are wise in their own *e* .... Is 5:21
for mine *e* have seen the King, ... Is 6:5
their ears heavy, and shut their *e* .... Is 6:10

lest they see with their *e* .... Is 6:10
Judge after the sight of his *e* .... Is 11:3
dashed to pieces before their *e* .... Is 13:16
his *e* shall have respect to the .... Is 17:7
deep sleep, and hath closed your *e*. .... Is 29:10
the *e* of the blind shall see out. .... Is 29:18
but thine *e* shall see thy. .... Is 30:20
the *e* of them that see shall not. .... Is 32:3
shutteth his *e* from seeing evil. .... Is 33:15
Thine *e* shall see the king in his. .... Is 33:17
thine *e* shall see Jerusalem a. .... Is 33:20
Then the *e* of the blind shall be .... Is 35:5
open thine *e*, O LORD, and see .... Is 37:17
and lifted up thine *e* on high .... Is 37:23
mine *e* fail with looking upward .... Is 38:14
Lift up your *e* on high, and behold .... Is 40:26
To open the blind *e*, to bring out. .... Is 42:7
the blind people that have *e* .... Is 43:8
for he hath shut their *e*, that .... Is 44:18
be glorious in the *e* of the LORD .... Is 49:5
Lift up thine *e* round about .... Is 49:18
Lift up your *e* to the heavens, and .... Is 51:6
arm in the *e* of all the nations. .... Is 52:10
and we grope as if we had no *e*. .... Is 59:10
Lift up thine *e* round about. .... Is 60:4
but did evil before mine *e* .... Is 65:12
because they are hid from mine *e* .... Is 65:16
but they did evil before mine *e* .... Is 66:4
Lift up thine *e* unto the high .... Jer 3:2
are not thine *e* upon the truth .... Jer 5:3
which have *e*, and see not .... Jer 5:21
become a den of robbers in your *e* .... Jer 7:11
mine *e* a fountain of tears, that .... Jer 9:1
that our *e* run down with .... Jer 9:18
Lift up your *e*, and behold them. .... Jer 13:20
their *e* did fail, because there .... Jer 14:6
Let mine *e* run down with tears .... Jer 14:17
cease out of this place in your *e*. .... Jer 16:9
For mine *e* are upon all their. .... Jer 16:17
is their iniquity hid from mine *e* .... Jer 16:17
and thine *e* shall behold it. .... Jer 20:4
But thine *e* and thine heart are. .... Jer 22:17
set mine *e* upon them for good .... Jer 24:6
he shall slay them before your *e* .... Jer 29:21
weeping, and thine *e* from tears. .... Jer 31:16
his *e* shall behold his .... Jer 32:4
for thine *e* are open upon all the. .... Jer 32:19
thine *e* shall behold the *e* of .... Jer 34:3
the *e* of the king of Babylon .... Jer 34:3
Zedekiah in Riblah before his *e* .... Jer 39:6
Moreover he put out Zedekiah's *e* .... Jer 39:7
of many, as thine *e* do behold us. .... Jer 42:2
was evil in the *e* of the LORD. .... Jer 52:2
the sons of Zedekiah before his .... Jer 52:10
Then he put out the *e* of Zedekiah .... Jer 52:11
Mine *e* do fail with tears, my .... Lam 2:11
our *e* as yet failed for our vain .... Lam 4:17
for these things our *e* are dim .... Lam 5:17
full of *e* round about them four .... Eze 1:18
departed from me, and with their *e* .... Eze 6:9
lift up thine *e* now the way .... Eze 8:5
So I lifted up mine *e* the way .... Eze 8:5
were full of *e* round about. .... Eze 10:12
house, which have *e* to see .... Eze 12:2
he see not the ground with his *e* .... Eze 12:12
neither hath lifted up his *e* to .... Eze 18:6
hath lifted up his *e* to the idols .... Eze 18:12
neither hath lifted up his *e* to .... Eze 18:15
man the abominations of his *e* .... Eze 20:7
away the abominations of their *e* .... Eze 20:8
their *e* were after their fathers' .... Eze 20:24
have hid their *e* from my sabbaths .... Eze 22:26
soon as she saw them with her *e* .... Eze 23:16
not lift up thine *e* unto thine .... Eze 23:27
wash thyself, paintedst thy *e* .... Eze 23:40
desire of thine *e* with a stroke .... Eze 24:16
strength, the desire of your *e* .... Eze 24:21
glory, the desire of their *e* .... Eze 24:25
lift up your *e* toward your idols, ... Eze 33:25
sanctified in you before their *e* .... Eze 36:23
be in thine hand before their *e* .... Eze 37:20
in thee, O Gog, before their *e* .... Eze 38:16
be known in the *e* of many nations .... Eze 38:23
Son of man, behold with thine *e* .... Eze 40:4
mark well, and behold with thine *e* .... Eze 44:5
lifted up mine *e* unto heaven. .... Dan 4:34
in this horn were *e* like the *e* .... Dan 7:8
horn were *e* like the *e* of man .... Dan 7:8
even of that horn that had *e* .... Dan 7:20
Then I lifted up mine *e*, and saw, ... Dan 8:3
had a notable horn between his *e* .... Dan 8:5
between his *e* is the first king. .... Dan 8:21
open thine *e*, and behold our .... Dan 9:18
Then I lifted up mine *e*, and .... Dan 10:5
his *e* as lamps of fire, and his .... Dan 10:6
shall be hid from mine *e* .... Hos 13:14
not the meat cut off before our *e* .... Joel 1:16
I will set mine *e* upon them for .... Amos 9:4
the *e* of the LORD God are upon .... Amos 9:8
mine *e* shall behold her .... Mic 7:10
Thou art of purer *e* than to .... Hab 1:13
back your captivity before your *e* .... Zeph 3:20
is it not in your *e* in comparison .... Hag 2:3
Then I lifted up mine *e*, and saw, ... Zec 1:18
I lifted up mine *e* again, and .... Zec 2:1
upon one stone shall be seven *e* .... Zec 3:9
they are the *e* of the LORD .... Zec 4:10
I turned, and lifted up mine *e* .... Zec 5:1
said unto me, Lift up now thine *e* .... Zec 5:5

Then lifted I up mine *e*, and .... Zec 5:9
And I turned, and lifted up mine *e* .... Zec 6:1
If it be marvellous in the *e* of .... Zec 8:6
it also be marvellous in mine *e* .... Zec 8:6
when the *e* of man, as of all the .... Zec 9:1
for now have I seen with mine *e* .... Zec 9:8
I will open mine *e* upon the house .... Zec 12:4
their *e* shall consume away in .... Zec 14:12
your *e* shall see, and ye shall say .... Mal 1:5
Then touched he their *e*, saying, ... Mt 9:29
And their *e* were opened. .... Mt 9:30
and their *e* they have closed .... Mt 13:15
time they should see with their *e* .... Mt 13:15
But blessed are your *e*, for they .... Mt 13:16
when they had lifted up their *e* .... Mt 17:8
rather than having two *e* to be .... Mt 18:9
Lord, that our *e* may be opened .... Mt 20:33
on them, and touched their *e* .... Mt 20:34
their *e* received sight, and they .... Mt 20:34
and it is marvellous in our *e* .... Mt 21:42
for their *e* were heavy .... Mt 26:43
Having *e*, see ye not .... Mk 8:18
and when he had spit on his *e* .... Mk 8:23
he put his hands again upon his *e* .... Mk 8:25
than having two *e* to be cast into. .... Mk 9:47
and it is marvellous in our *e* .... Mk 12:11
again, (for their *e* were heavy, ... Mk 14:40
For mine *e* have seen thy .... Lk 2:30
the *e* of all them that were in .... Lk 4:20
lifted up his *e* on his disciples .... Lk 6:20
Blessed are the *e* which see the .... Lk 10:23
And in hell he lift up his *e* .... Lk 16:23
up so much as his *e* unto heaven. .... Lk 18:13
but now they are hid from thine *e* .... Lk 19:42
But their *e* were holden that they .... Lk 24:16
their *e* were opened, and they knew .... Lk 24:31
I say unto you, Lift up your *e* .... Jn 4:35
When Jesus then lifted up his *e* .... Jn 6:5
he anointed the *e* of the blind .... Jn 9:6
unto him, How were thine *e* opened .... Jn 9:10
made clay, and anointed mine *e* .... Jn 9:11
made the clay, and opened mine *e* .... Jn 9:14
them, He put clay upon mine *e* .... Jn 9:15
him, that he hath opened thine *e* .... Jn 9:17
or who hath opened his *e*, we know .... Jn 9:21
how opened he thine *e* .... Jn 9:26
is, and yet he hath opened mine *e* .... Jn 9:30
the *e* of one that was born blind. .... Jn 9:32
a devil open the *e* of the blind .... Jn 10:21
which opened the *e* of the blind .... Jn 11:37
And Jesus lifted up his *e*, and said .... Jn 11:41
He hath blinded their *e*, and .... Jn 12:40
they should not see with their *e* .... Jn 12:40
and lifted up his *e* to heaven .... Jn 17:1
fastening his *e* upon him with .... Acts 3:4
when his *e* were opened, he saw no .... Acts 9:8
from his *e* as it had been scales. .... Acts 9:18
And she opened her *e* .... Acts 9:40
which when I had fastened mine *e* .... Acts 11:6
the Holy Ghost, set his *e* on him .... Acts 13:9
To open their *e*, and to turn them .... Acts 26:18
and their *e* have they closed .... Acts 28:27
lest they should see with their *e* .... Acts 28:27
is no fear of God before their *e* .... Rom 3:18
e that they should not see, and .... Rom 11:8
Let their *e* be darkened, that .... Rom 11:10
before whose *e* Jesus Christ hath .... Gal 3:1
would have plucked out your own *e* .... Gal 4:15
The *e* of your understanding being .... Eph 1:18
opened unto the *e* of him with .... Heb 4:13
For the *e* of the Lord are over 1Pet 3:12
Having *e* full of adultery, and 2Pet 2:14
which we have seen with our *e* 1Jn 1:1
that darkness hath blinded his *e* 1Jn 2:11
the flesh, and the lust of the *e* 1Jn 2:16
his *e* were as a flame of fire .... Rev 1:14
who hath his *e* like unto a flame .... Rev 2:18
anoint thine *e* with eyesalve, ... Rev 3:18
were four beasts full of *e* before .... Rev 4:6
and they were full of *e* within .... Rev 4:8
having seven horns and seven *e* .... Rev 5:6
wipe away all tears from their *e* .... Rev 7:17
His *e* were as a flame of fire, and .... Rev 19:12
wipe away all tears from their *e* .... Rev 21:4

EYESALVE
and anoint thine eyes with *e* .... Rev 3:18

EYESERVICE
not with *e*, as menpleasers .... Eph 6:6
Not with *e*, as menpleasers .... Col 3:22

EYESIGHT
clearness of thy hands in his *e* .... Ps 18:24

EYEWITNESSES
which from the beginning were *e* .... Lk 1:2
but were *e* of his majesty 2Pet 1:16

EZAR (*e'-zar*) See EZER. *A son of Seir.*
Zibeon, and Anah, and Dishon, and *E* 1Chr 1:38

EZBAI (*ez'-bahee*) *Father of Naarai.*
Carmelite, Naarai the son of *E* 1Chr 11:37

EZBON (*ez'-bon*)
1. *Son of Gad.*
Ziphion, and Haggi, Shuni, and *E* .... Gen 46:16
2. *Son of Bela.*
E, and Uzzi, and Uzziel, and 1Chr 7:7

EZEKIAS (*ez-e-ki'-as*) See HEZEKIAH. *Greek form of Hezekiah.*
and Achaz begat *E* .... Mt 1:9

And E begat Manasses .... Mt 1:10

EZEKIEL
came expressly unto E the priest ...... Eze 1:3
Thus E is unto you a sign .... Eze 24:24

EZEL
and shalt remain by the stone E....... 1Sa 20:19

EZEM
And at Bilhah, and at E, and at......... 1Chr 4:29

EZER
  1. Son of Seir the Horite.
And Dishon, and E, and Dishan....... Gen 36:21
The children of E are these.......... Gen 36:27
Duke Dishon, duke E, duke Dishan.... Gen 36:30
The sons of E; Bilhan................ 1Chr 1:42
  2. A descendant of Judah.
Gedor, and E the father of Hushah 1Chr 4:4
  3. A son of Ephraim.
son, and Shuthelah his son, and E..... 1Chr 7:21
  4. A Gadite who fought for David.
E the first, Obadiah the second...... 1Chr 12:9
  5. A Levite who repaired the Jerusalem wall.
him repaired E the son of Jeshua .... Neh 3:19
  6. A priest in the time of Nehemiah.
and Malchijah, and Elam, and E....... Neh 12:42

EZION-GABER
from Ebronah, and encamped at E..... Num 33:35
And they removed from E, and .... Num 33:36
the plain from Elath, and from E ..... Deut 2:8
and they made the ships in E......... 2Chr 20:36

EZION-GEBER (e´-ze-on-ghe´-bur) *See* EZION-
GABER. *An Israelite seaport.*
Solomon made a navy of ships in E.... 1Kin 9:26
for the ships were broken at E....... 1Kin 22:48
Then went Solomon to E, and to 2Chr 8:17

EZNITE (ez´-nite) *Descendant of Adino.*
the same was Adino the E............ 2Sa 23:8

EZRA (ez´-rah) *See* AZARIAH, EZRAHITE.
  1. A descendant of Judah.
And the sons of E were, Jether, and .. 1Chr 4:17
  2. Priest who led exiles back to Jerusalem.
E the son of Seraiah, the son of ..... Ezr 7:1
This E went up from Babylon......... Ezr 7:6
For E had prepared his heart to ..... Ezr 7:10
Artaxerxes gave unto E the priest... Ezr 7:11
unto E the priest, a scribe of ...... Ezr 7:12
that whatsoever E the priest........ Ezr 7:21
And thou, E, after the wisdom of .... Ezr 7:25
Now when E had prayed, and when he . Ezr 10:1
of Elam, answered and said unto E.... Ezr 10:2
Then arose E, and made the chief .... Ezr 10:5
Then E rose up from before the...... Ezr 10:6
E the priest stood up, and said...... Ezr 10:10
the priest, with certain chief ...... Ezr 10:16
they spake unto E the scribe to..... Neh 8:1
E the priest brought the law........ Neh 8:2
E the scribe stood upon a pulpit..... Neh 8:4
E opened the book in the sight of.... Neh 8:5
E blessed the LORD, the great God.... Neh 8:6
E the priest the scribe, and the .... Neh 8:9
unto E the scribe, even to.......... Neh 8:13
Of E, Meshullam.................... Neh 12:13
of E the priest, the scribe......... Neh 12:26
And Azariah, E, and Meshullam,...... Neh 12:33
God, and E the scribe before them.... Neh 12:36
  3. A priest who returned from exile.
Seraiah, Jeremiah, E,.............. Neh 12:1

EZRAH

EZRAHITE (ez´-rah-hite)
than Ethan the E, and Heman, and ... 1Kin 4:31
Leannoth, Maschil of Heman the E.... Ps 88:t
Maschil of Ethan the E............. Ps 89:t

EZRI (ez´-ri) *A superintendent of David.*
ground was E the son of Chelub....... 1Chr 27:26

F

FABLES
Neither give heed to f and endless... 1Ti 1:4
refuse profane and old wives' f...... 1Ti 4:7
truth, and shall be turned unto f 2Ti 4:4
Not giving heed to Jewish f.......... Titus 1:14
not followed cunningly devised f 2Pet 1:16

FACE
was upon the f of the deep.......... Gen 1:2
moved upon the f of the waters...... Gen 1:2
is upon the f of all the earth....... Gen 1:29
watered the whole f of the ground... Gen 2:6
In the sweat of thy f shalt thou..... Gen 3:19
this day from the f of the earth..... Gen 4:14
from thy f shall I be hid............ Gen 4:14
to multiply on the f of the earth.... Gen 6:1
created from the f of the earth...... Gen 6:7
alive upon the f of all the earth.... Gen 7:3
from off the f of the earth.......... Gen 7:4
ark went upon the f of the waters ... Gen 7:18
was upon the f of the ground........ Gen 7:23
from off the f of the ground......... Gen 8:8
were on the f of the whole earth..... Gen 8:9
the f of the ground was dry......... Gen 8:13

upon the f of the whole earth .... Gen 11:4
upon the f of all the earth.......... Gen 11:9
upon the f of all the earth.......... Gen 11:9
with her, she fled from her f........ Gen 16:6
I flee from the f of my mistress..... Gen 16:8
And Abram fell on his f............. Gen 17:3
Then Abraham fell upon his f........ Gen 17:17
with his f toward the ground........ Gen 19:1
great before the f of the LORD....... Gen 19:13
and I put the earring upon her f..... Gen 24:47
come for my hire before thy f....... Gen 30:33
set his f toward the mount Gilead ... Gen 31:21
me, and afterward I will see his f.... Gen 32:20
for I have seen God f............... Gen 32:30
for therefore I have seen thy f...... Gen 33:10
as though I had seen the f of God.... Gen 33:10
from the f of Esau thy brother....... Gen 35:1
he fled from the f of his brother.... Gen 35:7
from the f of his brother Jacob...... Gen 36:6
because she had covered her f....... Gen 38:15
was over all the f of the earth...... Gen 41:56
us, saying, Ye shall not see my f.... Gen 43:3
unto us, Ye shall not see my f ...... Gen 43:5
And he washed his f, and went out,... Gen 43:31
you, ye shall see my f no more...... Gen 44:23
for we may not see the man's f...... Gen 44:26
to direct his f unto Goshen......... Gen 46:28
me die, since I have seen thy f...... Gen 46:30
I had not thought to see thy f....... Gen 48:11
himself with his f to the earth..... Gen 48:12
Joseph fell upon his father's f..... Gen 50:1
went and fell down before his f..... Gen 50:18
Moses fled from the f of Pharaoh.... Ex 2:15
And Moses hid his f................ Ex 3:6
shall cover the f of the earth...... Ex 10:5
covered the f of the whole earth.... Ex 10:15
heed to thyself, see my f no more... Ex 10:28
thou seest my f thou shalt die...... Ex 10:28
I will see thy f again no more....... Ex 10:29
cloud went from before their f...... Ex 14:19
Let us flee from the f of Israel..... Ex 14:25
upon the f of the wilderness........ Ex 16:14
them from the f of the earth........ Ex 23:12
LORD spake unto Moses f to f........ Ex 33:11
that are upon the f of the earth.... Ex 33:16
he said, Thou canst not see my f.... Ex 33:20
but my f shall not be seen......... Ex 33:23
wist not that the skin of his f..... Ex 34:29
behold, the skin of his f shone...... Ex 34:30
with them, he put a vail on his f ... Ex 34:33
the skin of Moses' f shone.......... Ex 34:35
of Israel saw the f of Moses........ Ex 34:35
that the skin of Moses' f shone..... Ex 34:35
put the vail upon his f again....... Ex 34:35
the part of his head toward his f ... Lev 13:41
I will even set my f against that ... Lev 17:10
honour the f of the old man, and ... Lev 19:32
I will set my f against that man ... Lev 20:3
I will set my f against that man ... Lev 20:5
even set my f against that soul .... Lev 20:6
And I will set my f against you .... Lev 26:17
LORD make his f shine upon thee ... Num 6:25
high upon the f of the earth ...... Num 11:31
were upon the f of the earth ...... Num 12:3
her father had but spit in her f ... Num 12:14
that thou LORD art seen f to f..... Num 14:14
heard it, he fell upon his f....... Num 16:4
one shall slay her before his f.... Num 19:3
they cover the f of the earth...... Num 22:5
which covereth the f of the earth.. Num 22:11
his head, and fell flat on his f.... Num 22:31
but he set his f toward the....... Num 24:1
not be afraid of the f of man..... Deut 1:17
LORD talked with you f to f....... Deut 5:4
thee from off the f of the earth... Deut 6:15
that are upon the f of the earth... Deut 7:6
them that hate him to their f..... Deut 7:10
him, he will repay him to his f... Deut 7:10
the LORD destroyeth before your f . Deut 8:20
bring them down before thy f...... Deut 9:3
and to be beaten before thy f...... Deut 25:2
off his foot, and spit in his f..... Deut 25:9
thee to be smitten before thy f.... Deut 28:7
taken away from before thy f...... Deut 28:31
shall give them up before your f .. Deut 31:5
and I will hide my f from them..... Deut 31:17
I will surely hide my f in that.... Deut 31:18
said, I will hide my f from them... Deut 32:20
whom the LORD knew f to f........ Deut 34:10
Joshua fell on his f to the earth .. Josh 5:14
his f before the ark of the LORD... Josh 7:6
liest thou thus upon thy f........ Josh 7:10
an angel of the LORD f to f....... Judg 6:22
Then she fell on her f, and bowed.. Ruth 2:10
Dagon was fallen upon his f to ... 1Sa 5:3
Dagon was fallen upon his f to ... 1Sa 5:4
he fell upon his f to the earth ... 1Sa 17:49
every one from the f of the earth.. 1Sa 20:15
fell on his f to the ground, and... 1Sa 20:41
stooped with his f to the earth... 1Sa 24:8
and fell before David on her f.... 1Sa 25:23
herself on her f to the earth..... 1Sa 25:41
earth before the f of the LORD.... 1Sa 26:20
stooped with his f to the ground.. 1Sa 28:14
hold up my f to Joab thy brother.. 2Sa 2:22
that is, Thou shalt not see my f.. 2Sa 3:13
when thou comest to see my f..... 2Sa 3:13
come unto David, he fell on his f . 2Sa 9:6
she fell on her f to the ground... 2Sa 14:4
Joab fell to the ground on his f .. 2Sa 14:22
house, and let him not see my f... 2Sa 14:24

house, and saw not the king's f..... 2Sa 14:24
and saw not the king's f........... 2Sa 14:28
therefore let me see the king's f... 2Sa 14:32
bowed himself on his f to the...... 2Sa 14:33
over the f of all the country...... 2Sa 18:8
earth upon his f before the king... 2Sa 18:28
But the king covered his f......... 2Sa 19:4
the king on his f upon the ground .. 2Sa 24:20
the king with his f to the ground.. 1Kin 1:23
bowed with her f to the earth...... 1Kin 1:31
And the king turned his f about.... 1Kin 8:14
Intreat now the f of the LORD thy .. 1Kin 13:6
it from off the f of the earth..... 1Kin 13:34
and he knew him, and fell on his f . 1Kin 18:7
put his f between his knees........ 1Kin 18:42
he wrapped his f in his mantle..... 1Kin 19:13
himself with ashes upon his f 1Kin 20:38
and took the ashes away from his f.. 1Kin 20:41
his bed, and turned away his f..... 1Kin 21:4
my staff upon the f of the child... 2Kin 4:29
the staff upon the f of the child... 2Kin 4:31
in water, and spread it on his f.... 2Kin 8:15
and she painted her f, and tired... 2Kin 9:30
he lifted up his f to the window... 2Kin 9:32
shall be as dung upon the f of the.. 2Kin 9:37
Hazael set his f to go up to....... 2Kin 12:17
down unto him, and wept over his f. 2Kin 13:14
let us look one another in the f... 2Kin 14:8
another in the f at Beth-shemesh.. 2Kin 14:11
then wilt thou turn away the f of .. 2Kin 18:24
Then he turned his f to the wall... 2Kin 20:2
strength, seek his f continually... 1Chr 16:11
to David with his f to the ground.. 1Chr 21:21
And the king turned his f, and 2Chr 6:3
not away the f of thine anointed .. 2Chr 6:42
themselves, and pray, and seek my f. 2Chr 7:14
his head with his f to the ground.. 2Chr 20:18
let us see one another in the f 2Chr 25:21
and they saw one another in the f.. 2Chr 25:21
will not turn away his f from you... 2Chr 30:9
with shame of f to his own land.... 2Chr 32:21
would not turn his f from him...... 2Chr 35:22
and blush to lift up my f to thee... Ezr 9:6
to a spoil, and to confusion of f... Ezr 9:7
and Media, which saw the king's f.. Est 1:14
mouth, they covered Haman's f..... Est 7:8
and he will curse thee to thy f .... Job 1:11
and he will curse thee to thy f .... Job 2:5
Then a spirit passed before my f... Job 4:15
thou lift up thy f without spot.... Job 11:15
Wherefore hidest thou thy f....... Job 13:24
covereth his f with his fatness.... Job 15:27
up in the beareth witness to my f.. Job 16:8
My f is foul with weeping, and on.. Job 16:16
shall declare his way to his f..... Job 21:31
and shalt lift up thy f unto God... Job 22:26
he covered the darkness from my f . Job 23:17
and disguiseth his f.............. Job 24:15
holdeth back the f of his throne... Job 26:9
me, and spare not to spit in my f.. Job 30:10
and he shall see his f with joy.... Job 33:26
and when he hideth his f, who then. Job 34:29
the f of the world in the earth.... Job 37:12
the f of the deep is frozen........ Job 38:30
can discover the f of his garment.. Job 41:13
Who can open the doors of his f.... Job 41:14
make thy way straight before my f.. Ps 5:8
he hideth his f.................. Ps 10:11
long wilt thou hide thy f from me.. Ps 13:1
behold thy f in righteousness..... Ps 17:15
thy strings against the f of them.. Ps 21:12
hath he hid his f from them....... Ps 22:24
that seek him, that seek thy f..... Ps 24:6
When thou saidst, Seek ye my f.... Ps 27:8
my heart said unto thee, Thy f..... Ps 27:8
Hide not thy f far from me......... Ps 27:9
thou didst hide thy f, and I was... Ps 30:7
Make thy f to shine upon thy...... Ps 31:16
The f of the LORD is against them.. Ps 34:16
settest me before thy f for ever... Ps 41:12
the shame of my f hath covered me. Ps 44:15
Wherefore hidest thou thy f....... Ps 44:24
Hide thy f from my sins, and blot.. Ps 51:9
cause his f to shine upon us....... Ps 67:1
shame hath covered my f.......... Ps 69:7
hide not thy f from thy servant... Ps 69:17
O God, and cause thy f to shine.... Ps 80:3
of hosts, and cause thy f to shine.. Ps 80:7
of hosts, cause thy f to shine..... Ps 80:19
look upon the f of thine anointed.. Ps 84:9
why hidest thou thy f from me..... Ps 88:14
and truth shall go before thy f.... Ps 89:14
beat down his foes before his f.... Ps 89:23
Hide not thy f from me in the day.. Ps 102:2
and oil to make his f shine....... Ps 104:15
Thou hidest thy f, they are....... Ps 104:29
thou renewest the f of the earth... Ps 104:30
seek his f evermore.............. Ps 105:4
Make thy f to shine upon thy...... Ps 119:135
not away the f of thine anointed .. Ps 132:10
hide not thy f from me, lest I be... Ps 143:7
with an impudent f said unto him... Prov 7:13
thee, diligently seek my f......... Prov 7:15
a compass upon the f of the deep... Prov 8:27
A wicked man hardeneth his f...... Prov 21:29
nettles had covered the f thereof.. Prov 24:31
As in water f answereth to f....... Prov 27:19
wisdom maketh his f to shine...... Eccl 8:1
of his f shall be changed.......... Eccl 8:1
with twain he covered his f....... Is 6:2

that hideth his f from the house........Is 8:17
nor fill the f of the world with........Is 14:21
to them from the f of the spoiler........Is 16:4
the world upon the f of the earth........Is 23:17
destroy in this mountain the f of........Is 25:7
fill the f of the world with........Is 27:6
he hath made plain the f thereof........Is 28:25
neither shall his f now wax pale........Is 29:22
then wilt thou turn away the f of........Is 36:9
turned his f toward the wall........Is 38:2
with their f toward the earth........Is 49:23
I hid not my f from shame........Is 50:6
have I set my f like a flint........Is 50:7
I hid my f from thee for a moment........Is 54:8
your sins have hid his f from you........Is 59:2
for thou hast hid thy f from us........Is 64:7
me to anger continually to my f........Is 65:3
the f thereof is toward the north........Jer 1:13
back unto me, and not their f........Jer 2:27
thou rentest thy f with painting........Jer 4:30
for dung upon the f of the earth........Jer 8:2
I discover thy skirts upon thy........Jer 13:26
as dung upon the f of the earth........Jer 16:4
they are not hid from my f........Jer 16:17
shew them the back, and not the f........Jer 18:17
For I have set my f against this........Jer 21:10
hand of them whose f thou fearest........Jer 22:25
which are upon the f of the earth........Jer 25:26
then from off the f of the earth........Jer 28:16
should remove it from before my f........Jer 32:31
unto me the back, and not the f........Jer 32:33
I have hid my f from this city........Jer 33:5
I will set my f against you for........Jer 44:11
water before the f of the Lord........Lam 2:19
man before the f of the most High........Lam 3:35
they four had the f of a man........Eze 1:10
the f of a lion, on the right........Eze 1:10
they four had the f of an ox on........Eze 1:10
four also had the f of an eagle........Eze 1:10
when I saw it, I fell upon my f........Eze 1:28
I have made thy f strong against........Eze 3:8
and I fell on my f........Eze 3:23
set thy f against it, and it shall........Eze 4:3
Therefore thou shalt set thy f........Eze 4:7
set thy f toward the mountains of........Eze 6:2
My f will I turn also from them........Eze 7:22
I was left, that I fell upon my f........Eze 9:8
first f was the f of a cherub........Eze 10:14
second f was the f of a man........Eze 10:14
and the third the f of a lion........Eze 10:14
and the fourth the f of an eagle........Eze 10:14
Then fell I down upon my f........Eze 11:13
thou shalt cover thy f, that thou........Eze 12:6
he shall cover his f, that he see........Eze 12:12
set thy f against the daughters........Eze 13:17
of their iniquity before their f........Eze 14:3
of his iniquity before his f........Eze 14:4
of his iniquity before his f........Eze 14:7
I will set my f against that man,........Eze 14:8
And I will set my f against them........Eze 15:7
when I set my f against them........Eze 15:7
will I plead with you to f........Eze 20:35
will I plead with you to f........Eze 20:35
set thy f toward the south, and........Eze 20:46
set thy f toward Jerusalem, and........Eze 21:2
left, whithersoever thy f is set........Eze 21:16
set thy f against the Ammonites........Eze 25:2
set thy f against Zidon, and........Eze 28:21
set thy f against Pharaoh king of........Eze 29:2
upon all the f of the earth........Eze 34:6
set thy f against mount Seir, and........Eze 35:2
set thy f against Gog, the land........Eze 38:2
my fury shall come up in my f........Eze 38:18
that are upon the f of the earth........Eze 38:20
remain upon the f of the earth........Eze 38:20
therefore hid I my f from them........Eze 39:23
unto them, and hid my f from them........Eze 39:24
I hide my f any more from them........Eze 39:29
from the f of the gate of the........Eze 40:15
gate of the entrance unto the f........Eze 40:15
the breadth of the f of the house........Eze 41:14
So that the f of a man was toward........Eze 41:19
the f of a young lion toward the........Eze 41:19
and the f of the sanctuary........Eze 41:21
upon the f of the porch without........Eze 41:25
and I fell upon my f........Eze 43:3
and I fell upon my f........Eze 44:4
Nebuchadnezzar fell upon his f........Dan 2:46
west on the f of the whole earth........Dan 8:5
I was afraid, and fell upon my f........Dan 8:17
sleep on my f toward the ground........Dan 8:18
I set my f unto the Lord God, to........Dan 9:3
to us belongeth confusion of f........Dan 9:8
cause thy f to shine upon thy........Dan 9:17
his f as the appearance of........Dan 10:6
was I in a deep sleep on my f........Dan 10:9
and my f toward the ground........Dan 10:9
I set my f toward the ground, and........Dan 10:15
He shall also set his f to enter........Dan 11:17
he turn his f unto the isles........Dan 11:18
he shall turn his f toward........Dan 11:19
of Israel doth testify to his f........Hos 5:5
their offence, and seek my f........Hos 5:15
they are before my f........Hos 7:2
of Israel testifieth to his f........Hos 7:10
Before their f the people shall........Joel 2:6
with his f toward the east sea,........Joel 2:20
them out upon the f of the earth........Amos 5:8
them out upon the f of the earth........Amos 9:6
it from off the f of the earth........Amos 9:8

he will even hide his f from them........Mic 3:4
in pieces is come up before thy f........Nah 2:1
discover thy skirts upon thy f........Nah 3:5
over the f of the whole earth........Zec 5:3
anoint thine head, and wash thy f........Mt 6:17
I send my messenger before thy f........Mt 11:10
ye can discern the f of the sky........Mt 16:3
his f did shine as the sun, and........Mt 17:2
heard it, they fell on their f........Mt 17:6
angels do always behold the f of........Mt 18:10
little farther, and fell on his f........Mt 26:39
Then did they spit in his f........Mt 26:67
I send my messenger before thy f........Mk 1:2
to spit on him, and to cover his f........Mk 14:65
for thou shalt go before the f of........Lk 1:76
before the f of all people........Lk 2:31
who seeing Jesus fell on his f........Lk 5:12
I send my messenger before thy f........Lk 7:27
set his f to go to Jerusalem........Lk 9:51
And sent messengers before his f........Lk 9:52
because his f was as though he........Lk 9:53
two before his f into every city........Lk 10:1
ye can discern the f of the sky........Lk 12:56
And fell down on his f at his feet........Lk 17:16
dwell on the f of the whole earth........Lk 21:35
him, they struck him on the f........Lk 22:64
his f was bound about with a........Jn 11:44
the Lord always before my f........Acts 2:25
saw his f as it had been the........Acts 6:15
out before the f of our fathers........Acts 7:45
dwell on all the f of the earth........Acts 17:26
of God, shall see my f no more........Acts 20:25
they should see his f no more........Acts 20:38
have the accusers f to f........Acts 25:16
but then f to f........1Cor 13:12
down on his f he will worship God........1Cor 14:25
of Moses for the glory of his........2Cor 3:7
which put a vail over his f........2Cor 3:13
with open f beholding as in a........2Cor 3:18
of God in the f of Jesus Christ........2Cor 4:6
if a man smite you on the f........2Cor 11:20
was unknown by f unto the........Gal 1:22
Antioch, I withstood him to the f........Gal 2:11
have not seen my f in the flesh........1Th 2:17
to see your f with great desire........1Th 2:17
that we might see your f, and........1Th 3:10
his natural f in a glass........Jas 1:23
but the f of the Lord is against........1Pet 3:12
speak f to f, that our joy may........2Jn 12
come unto you, and speak f to f........2Jn 12
thee, and we shall speak f to f........3Jn 14
thee, and we shall speak f to f........3Jn 14
the third beast had a f as a man........Rev 4:7
hide us from the f of him that........Rev 6:16
his f was as it were the sun, and........Rev 10:1
from the f of the serpent........Rev 12:14
sat on it, from whose f the earth........Rev 20:11
And they shall see his f........Rev 22:4

FACES

their f were backward, and they........Gen 9:23
men turned their f from thence........Gen 18:22
set the f of the flocks toward........Gen 30:40
him with their f to the earth........Gen 42:6
laid before their f all these........Ex 19:7
his fear may be before your f........Ex 20:20
their f shall look one to another........Ex 25:20
shall the f of the cherubims be........Ex 25:20
with their f one to another........Ex 37:9
were the f of the cherubims........Ex 37:9
they shouted, and fell on their f........Lev 9:24
Aaron fell on their f before all........Num 14:5
And they fell upon their f........Num 16:22
And they fell upon their f........Num 16:45
and they fell upon their f........Num 20:6
and fell on their f to the ground........Judg 13:20
And they turned their f, and said........Judg 18:23
day the f of all thy servants........2Sa 19:5
that all Israel set their f on me........1Kin 2:15
saw it, they fell on their f........1Kin 18:39
f were like the f of lions........1Chr 12:8
in sackcloth, and upon their f........1Chr 21:16
feet, and their f were inward........2Chr 3:13
bowed themselves with their f to........2Chr 7:3
have turned away their f from the........2Chr 29:6
Lord with their f to the ground........Neh 8:6
he covereth the f of the judges........Job 9:24
and bind their f in secret........Job 40:13
and their f were not ashamed........Ps 34:5
Fill their f with shame........Ps 83:16
and grind the f of the poor........Is 3:15
their f shall as flames........Is 13:8
wipe away tears from off all f........Is 25:8
we hid as it were our f from him........Is 53:3
Be not afraid of their f........Jer 1:8
be not dismayed at their f........Jer 1:17
made their f harder than a rock........Jer 5:3
to the confusion of their own f........Jer 7:19
all f are turned into paleness........Jer 30:6
set your f to enter into Egypt........Jer 42:15
to go into Egypt to sojourn........Jer 42:17
that have set their f to go into........Jer 44:12
to Zion with their f thitherward........Jer 50:5
shame hath covered our f........Jer 51:51
of f of elders were not honoured........Lam 5:12
And every one had four f, and every........Eze 1:6
and they four had their f and their........Eze 1:8
As for the likeness of their f........Eze 1:10
Thus were their f........Eze 1:11
living creatures, his four f........Eze 1:15
thy face strong against their........Eze 3:8

and shame shall be upon all f........Eze 7:18
Lord, and their f toward the east........Eze 8:16
And every one had four f........Eze 10:14
Every one had four f........Eze 10:21
the likeness of their f was the........Eze 10:22
of which I saw by the river of........Eze 10:22
turn away your f from all your........Eze 14:6
all f from the south to the north........Eze 20:47
and every cherub had two f........Eze 41:18
for why should he see your f........Dan 1:10
thee, but unto us confusion of f........Dan 9:7
all f shall gather blackness........Joel 2:6
and the f of them all gather........Nah 2:10
their f shall sup as the east........Hab 1:9
seed, and spread dung upon your f........Mal 2:3
for they disfigure their f........Mt 6:16
bowed down their f to the earth........Lk 24:5
fell before the throne on their f........Rev 7:11
their f were as the f of men........Rev 9:7
their seats, fell upon their f........Rev 11:16

FADE

Strangers shall f away, and they........2Sa 22:46
The strangers shall f........Ps 18:45
and we all do f as a leaf........Is 64:6
the fig tree, and the leaf shall f........Jer 8:13
for meat, whose leaf shall not f........Eze 47:12
the rich man f away in his ways........Jas 1:11

FADETH

shall be as an oak whose leaf f........Is 1:30
f away, the world languisheth and........Is 24:4
f away, the haughty people of the........Is 24:4
The grass withereth, the flower f........Is 40:7
The grass withereth, the flower f........Is 40:8
that f not away, reserved in........1Pet 1:4
a crown of glory that f not away........1Pet 5:4

FADING

glorious beauty is a f flower........Is 28:1
fat valley, shall be a f flower........Is 28:4

FAIL

you for your cattle, if money f........Gen 47:16
f with longing for them all the........Deut 28:32
he will not f thee, nor forsake........Deut 31:6
be with thee, he will not f thee........Deut 31:8
I will not f thee, nor forsake........Josh 1:5
that he will without f drive out........Josh 3:10
If thou shalt without f deliver........Judg 11:30
Let them not f to burn the fat........1Sa 2:16
no man's heart f because of him........1Sa 17:32
I should not f to sit with the........1Sa 20:5
them, and without f recover all........1Sa 30:8
let there not f from the house of........2Sa 3:29
there shall not f thee (said he).........1Kin 2:4
There shall not f thee a man in........1Kin 8:25
There shall not f thee a man upon........1Kin 9:5
neither shall the cruse of oil f........1Kin 17:14
neither did the cruse of oil f........1Kin 17:16
he will not f thee, nor forsake........1Chr 28:20
There shall not f thee a man in........2Chr 6:16
There shall not f thee a man to........2Chr 7:18
heed now that ye f not to do this........Ezr 4:22
given them day by day without f........Ezr 6:9
let nothing f of all that thou........Est 6:10
unto them, so as it should not f........Est 9:27
should not f from among the Jews........Est 9:28
the eyes of the wicked shall f........Job 11:20
As the waters f from the sea........Job 14:11
the eyes of his children shall f........Job 17:5
caused the eyes of the widow to f........Job 31:16
for the faithful f from among the........Ps 12:1
mine eyes f while I wait for my........Ps 69:3
doth his promise f for evermore........Ps 77:8
nor suffer my faithfulness to f........Ps 89:33
Mine eyes f for thy word, saying........Ps 119:82
Mine eyes f for thy salvation, and........Ps 119:123
and the rod of his anger shall f........Prov 22:8
be a burden, and desire shall f........Eccl 12:5
shall f in the midst thereof........Is 19:3
the waters shall f from the sea........Is 19:5
and all the glory of Kedar shall f........Is 21:16
the day shall all f together........Is 31:3
the drink of the thirsty to f........Is 32:6
for the vintage shall f, the........Is 32:10
no one of these shall f, none........Is 34:16
mine eyes f with looking upward........Is 38:14
He shall not f nor be discouraged........Is 42:4
pit, nor that his bread should f........Is 51:14
for the spirit should f before me........Is 57:16
of water, whose waters f not........Is 58:11
their eyes did f, because there........Is 58:11
me as a liar, and as waters that f........Jer 15:18
when .o f from the winepresses........Jer 48:33
Mine eyes do f with tears........Lam 2:11
because his compassions f not........Lam 3:22
and the new wine shall f in her........Hos 9:2
to make the poor of the land to f........Amos 8:4
the labour of the olive shall f........Hab 3:17
that, when ye f, they may receive........Lk 16:9
than one tittle of the law to f........Lk 16:17
there be prophecies, they shall f........1Cor 13:8
same, and thy years shall not f........Heb 1:12
for the time would f me to tell........Heb 11:32
any man f of the grace of God........Heb 12:15

FAILED

and their f heart them, and they........Gen 42:28
when money f in the land of Egypt........Gen 47:15
the plain, even the salt sea, f........Josh 3:16
There f not ought of any good........Josh 21:45

that not one thing hath *f* of all .... Josh 23:14
and not one thing hath *f* thereof .... Josh 23:14
there hath not *f* one word of all 1Kin 8:56
My kinsfolk have *f*, and my .... Job 19:14
refuge *f* me; no man cared .... Ps 142:4
my soul *f* when he spake .... Song 5:6
their might hath *f* .... Jer 51:30
our eyes as yet *f* for our vain .... Lam 4:17

FAILETH

for the money *f* .... Gen 47:15
Their bull gendereth, and *f* not .... Job 21:10
my strength *f* because of mine .... Ps 31:10
heart panteth, my strength *f* me .... Ps 38:10
therefore my heart *f* me .... Ps 40:12
forsake me not when my strength *f* .... Ps 71:9
My flesh and my heart *f* .... Ps 73:26
and my flesh *f* of fatness .... Ps 109:24
my spirit *f* .... Ps 143:7
by the way, his wisdom *f* him .... Eccl 10:3
hay is withered away, the grass *f* .... Is 15:6
strong in power; not one *f* .... Is 40:26
and their tongue *f* for thirst .... Is 41:17
he is hungry, and his strength *f* .... Is 44:12
Yea, truth *f* .... Is 59:15
are prolonged, and every vision *f* .... Eze 12:22
his judgment to light, he *f* not .... Zeph 3:5
in the heavens that *f* not .... Lk 12:33
Charity never *f* 1Cor 13:8

FAILING

f of eyes, and sorrow of mind .... Deut 28:65
Men's hearts *f* them for fear, and .... Lk 21:26

FAIN

he would *f* flee out of his hand .... Job 27:22
he would *f* have filled his belly .... Lk 15:16

FAINT

came from the field, and he was *f* .... Gen 25:29
red pottage; for I am *f* .... Gen 25:30
let not your hearts *f*, fear not, ... Deut 20:3
heart *f* as well as his heart .... Deut 20:8
behind thee, when thou wast *f* .... Deut 25:18
of the land *f* because of you .... Josh 2:9
of the country do *f* because of us .... Josh 2:24
hundred men that were with him, *f* .... Judg 8:4
for they be *f*, and I am pursuing .... Judg 8:5
And the people were *f* 1Sa 14:28
and the people were very *f* 1Sa 14:31
which were so *f* that they could 1Sa 30:10
which were so *f* that they could 1Sa 30:21
wine, that such as be *f* in the 2Sa 16:2
and David waxed *f* 2Sa 21:15
If thou *f* in the day of adversity .... Prov 24:10
is sick, and the whole heart *f* .... Is 1:5
Therefore shall all hands be *f* .... Is 13:7
he awaketh, and, behold, he is *f* .... Is 29:8
He giveth power to the *f* .... Is 40:29
Even the youths shall *f* and be .... Is 40:30
and they shall walk, and not *f* .... Is 40:31
he drinketh no water, and is *f* .... Is 44:12
sorrow, my heart is *f* in me .... Jer 8:18
And lest your heart *f*, and ye fear .... Jer 51:46
made me desolate and *f* all the day .... Lam 1:13
sighs are many, and my heart is *f* .... Lam 1:22
that *f* for hunger in the top of .... Lam 2:19
For this our heart is *f* .... Lam 5:17
feeble, and every spirit shall *f* .... Eze 21:7
gates, that their heart may *f* .... Eze 21:15
virgins and young men *f* for thirst .... Amos 8:13
fasting, lest they *f* in the way .... Mt 15:32
houses, they will *f* by the way .... Mk 8:3
ought always to pray, and not to *f* .... Lk 18:1
we have received mercy, we *f* not 2Cor 4:1
For which cause we *f* not 2Cor 4:16
season we shall reap, if we *f* not .... Gal 6:9
Wherefore I desire that ye *f* not .... Eph 3:13
ye be wearied and *f* in your minds .... Heb 12:3
nor *f* when thou art rebuked of .... Heb 12:5

FAINTED

And Jacob's heart *f*, for he .... Gen 45:26
all the land of Canaan *f* by .... Gen 47:13
I had *f*, unless I had believed to .... Ps 27:13
and thirsty, their soul *f* in them .... Ps 107:5
Thy sons have *f*, they lie at the .... Is 51:20
I *f* in my sighing, and I find no .... Jer 45:3
the trees of the field *f* for him .... Eze 31:15
And I Daniel *f*, and was sick .... Dan 8:27
When my soul *f* within me I .... Jonah 2:7
upon the head of Jonah, that he *f* .... Jonah 4:8
on them, because they *f*, and were .... Mt 9:36
sake hast laboured, and hast not *f* .... Rev 2:3

FAINTEST

it is come upon thee, and thou *f* .... Job 4:5

FAINTETH

even for the courts of the LORD .... Ps 84:2
My soul *f* for thy salvation .... Ps 119:81
he as when a standard-bearer *f* .... Is 10:18
earth, *f* not, neither is weary .... Is 40:28

FAINTHEARTED

man is there that is fearful and *f* .... Deut 20:8
neither be *f* for the two tails of .... Is 7:4
they are *f* .... Jer 49:23

FAINTNESS

f into their hearts in the lands .... Lev 26:36

FAIR

daughters of men that they were *f* .... Gen 6:2
thou art a *f* woman to look upon .... Gen 12:11

the woman that she was very *f* .... Gen 12:14
damsel was very *f* to look upon .... Gen 24:16
because she was *f* to look upon .... Gen 26:7
and ruddy, and of a *f* countenance 1Sa 17:42
the son of David had a *f* sister 2Sa 13:1
was a woman of a *f* countenance 2Sa 14:27
So they sought for a *f* damsel 1Kin 1:3
And the damsel was very *f*, and 1Kin 1:4
for she was *f* to look on .... Est 1:11
Let there be *f* young virgins .... Est 2:2
may gather together all the *f* .... Est 2:3
nor mother, and the maid was *f* .... Est 2:7
f weather cometh out of the north .... Job 37:22
so *f* as the daughters of Job .... Job 42:15
With her much *f* speech she caused .... Prov 7:21
so is a *f* woman which is without .... Prov 11:22
When he speaketh *f*, believe him .... Prov 26:25
Behold, thou art *f*, my love .... Song 1:15
behold, thou art *f* .... Song 1:15
Behold, thou art *f*, my beloved, ... Song 1:16
my love, my *f* one, and come away .... Song 2:10
my love, my *f* one, and come away .... Song 2:13
Behold, thou art *f*, my love .... Song 4:1
behold, thou art *f* .... Song 4:1
Thou art all *f*, my love .... Song 4:7
How *f* is thy love, my sister, my .... Song 4:10
f as the moon, clear as the sun, ... Song 6:10
How *f* and how pleasant art thou, O .... Song 7:6
be desolate, even great and *f* .... Is 5:9
will lay thy stones with *f* colors .... Is 54:11
in vain shalt thou make thyself *f* .... Jer 4:30
the name, A green olive tree, *f* .... Jer 11:16
they speak *f* words unto thee .... Jer 12:6
Egypt is like a very *f* heifer .... Jer 46:20
taken thy *f* jewels of my gold .... Eze 16:17
and shalt take thy *f* jewels .... Eze 16:39
and take away thy *f* jewels .... Eze 23:26
cedar in Lebanon with *f* branches. .... Eze 31:3
Thus was he *f* in his greatness, ... Eze 31:7
I have made him *f* by the .... Eze 31:9
The leaves thereof were *f* .... Dan 4:12
Whose leaves were *f*, and the fruit, ... Dan 4:21
but I passed over upon her *f* neck .... Hos 10:11
In that day shall the *f* virgins .... Amos 8:13
Let them set a *f* mitre upon his .... Zec 3:5
So they set a *f* mitre upon his. .... Zec 3:5
ye say, It will be *f* weather .... Mt 16:2
was born, and was exceeding *f* .... Acts 7:20
which is called The *f* havens .... Acts 27:8
f speeches deceive the hearts of .... Rom 16:18
to make a *f* shew in the flesh .... Gal 6:12

FAIRER

not her younger sister *f* than she .... Judg 15:2
Thou art *f* than the children of .... Ps 45:2
their countenances appeared *f* .... Dan 1:15

FAIREST

O thou *f* among women, go thy way .... Song 1:8
beloved, O thou *f* among women .... Song 5:9
gone, O thou *f* among women. .... Song 6:1

FAIRS

and lead, they traded in thy *f* .... Eze 27:12
traded in thy *f* with horses .... Eze 27:14
occupied in thy *f* with emeralds .... Eze 27:16
going to and fro occupied in thy *f* .... Eze 27:19
they occupied in thy *f* with chief .... Eze 27:27
Thy riches, and thy *f*, thy .... Eze 27:27

FAITH

children in whom is no *f* .... Deut 32:20
but the just shall live by his *f* .... Hab 2:4
more clothe you, O ye of little *f* .... Mt 6:30
you, I have not found so great *f* .... Mt 8:10
are ye fearful, O ye of little *f* .... Mt 8:26
Jesus seeing their *f* said unto. .... Mt 9:2
thy *f* hath made thee whole. .... Mt 9:22
to your *f* be it unto you .... Mt 9:29
said unto him, O thou of little *f* .... Mt 14:31
unto her, O woman, great is thy *f* .... Mt 15:28
said unto them, O ye of little *f* .... Mt 16:8
If ye have *f* as a grain of .... Mt 17:20
I say unto you, If ye have *f* .... Mt 21:21
of the law, judgment, mercy, and *f* .... Mt 23:23
thy *f* hath made thee whole .... Mk 5:34
how is it that ye have no *f* .... Mk 4:40
thy *f* hath made thee whole .... Mk 5:34
thy *f* hath made thee whole .... Mk 10:52
saith unto them, Have *f* in God .... Mk 11:22
And when he saw their *f*, he said .... Lk 5:20
you, I have not found so great *f* .... Lk 7:9
the woman, Thy *f* hath saved thee .... Lk 7:50
said unto them, Where is your *f* .... Lk 8:25
thy *f* hath made thee whole .... Lk 8:48
he clothe you, O ye of little *f* .... Lk 12:28
unto the Lord, Increase our *f* .... Lk 17:5
If ye had *f* as a grain of mustard .... Lk 17:6
thy *f* hath made thee whole .... Lk 17:19
shall he find *f* on the earth .... Lk 18:8
thy *f* hath saved thee .... Lk 18:42
for thee, that thy *f* fail not .... Lk 22:32
his name through *f* in his name .... Acts 3:16
the *f* which is by him hath given.. .... Acts 3:16
chose Stephen, a man full of *f* .... Acts 6:5
priests were obedient to the *f* .... Acts 6:7
And Stephen, full of *f* and power, ... Acts 6:8
and full of the Holy Ghost and of *f*... .... Acts 11:24
turn away the deputy from the *f* .... Acts 13:8
that he had *f* to be healed .... Acts 14:9
them to continue in the *f* .... Acts 14:22
the door of *f* unto the Gentiles. .... Acts 14:27

them, purifying their hearts by *f*.. .... Acts 15:9
the churches established in the *f*..... .... Acts 16:5
f toward our Lord Jesus Christ .... Acts 20:21
him concerning the *f* in Christ .... Acts 24:24
are sanctified by *f* that is in me .... Acts 26:18
to the *f* among all nations .... Rom 1:5
you all, that your *f* is spoken of .... Rom 1:8
you by the mutual *f* both of you .... Rom 1:12
of God revealed from *f* to *f* .... Rom 1:17
written, The just shall live by *f* .... Rom 1:17
make the *f* of God without effect... .... Rom 3:3
of God which is by *f* of Jesus .... Rom 3:22
through *f* in his blood, to .... Rom 3:25
but by the law of *f* .... Rom 3:27
that a man is justified by *f* .... Rom 3:28
justify the circumcision by *f* .... Rom 3:30
and uncircumcision through *f* .... Rom 3:30
then make void the law through *f* .... Rom 3:31
the ungodly, his *f* is counted for... .... Rom 4:5
for we say that *f* was reckoned to .... Rom 4:9
of the *f* which he had yet being .... Rom 4:11
of that *f* of our father Abraham .... Rom 4:12
through the righteousness of *f* .... Rom 4:13
f is made void, and the promise .... Rom 4:14
Therefore it is of *f*, that it .... Rom 4:16
also which is of the *f* of Abraham .... Rom 4:16
And being not weak in *f*, he .... Rom 4:19
but was strong in *f*, giving glory .... Rom 4:20
Therefore being justified by *f* .... Rom 5:1
by *f* into this grace wherein we .... Rom 5:2
the righteousness which is of *f* .... Rom 9:30
Because they sought it not by *f* .... Rom 9:32
is of *f* speaketh on this wise .... Rom 10:6
that is, the word of *f*, which we .... Rom 10:8
So then *f* cometh by hearing, and.. .... Rom 10:17
broken off, and thou standest by *f* .... Rom 11:20
to every man the measure of *f* .... Rom 12:3
according to the proportion of *f* .... Rom 12:6
that is weak in the *f* receive ye .... Rom 14:1
Hast thou *f* .... Rom 14:22
eat, because he eateth not of *f* .... Rom 14:23
for whatsoever is not of *f* is sin .... Rom 14:23
nations for the obedience of *f* .... Rom 16:26
That your *f* should not stand in 1Cor 2:5
To another *f* by the same Spirit 1Cor 12:9
and though I have all *f*, so that I 1Cor 13:2
And now abideth *f*, hope, charity, ... 1Cor 13:13
vain, and your *f* is also vain 1Cor 15:14
be not raised, your *f* is vain 1Cor 15:17
Watch ye, stand fast in the *f* 1Cor 16:13
that we have dominion over your *f* 2Cor 1:24
for by *f* ye stand 2Cor 1:24
We having the same spirit of *f* 2Cor 4:13
(For we walk by *f*, not by sight 2Cor 5:7
as ye abound in every thing, in *f* 2Cor 8:7
when your *f* is increased, that we 2Cor 10:15
whether ye be in the *f* 2Cor 13:5
the *f* which once be destroyed .... Gal 1:23
but by the *f* of Jesus Christ, ... Gal 2:16
be justified by the *f* of Christ .... Gal 2:16
I live by the *f* of the Son of God .... Gal 2:20
the law, or by the hearing of *f* .... Gal 3:2
the law, or by the hearing of *f* .... Gal 3:5
that they which are of *f*, the. .... Gal 3:7
justify the heathen through *f* .... Gal 3:8
So then they which be of *f* are .... Gal 3:9
for, The just shall live by *f* .... Gal 3:11
And the law is not of *f* .... Gal 3:12
promise of the Spirit through *f* .... Gal 3:14
that the promise by *f* of Jesus .... Gal 3:22
But before *f* came, we were kept .... Gal 3:23
shut up unto the *f* which should .... Gal 3:23
that we might be justified by *f* .... Gal 3:24
But after that *f* is come, we are .... Gal 3:25
of God by *f* in Christ Jesus .... Gal 3:26
the hope of righteousness by *f* .... Gal 5:5
but *f* which worketh by love .... Gal 5:6
gentleness, goodness, *f* .... Gal 5:22
who are of the household of *f* .... Gal 6:10
heard of your *f* in the Lord Jesus .... Eph 1:15
by grace are ye saved through *f* .... Eph 2:8
with confidence by the *f* of him .... Eph 3:12
may dwell in your hearts by *f* .... Eph 3:17
One Lord, one *f*, one baptism, ... Eph 4:5
we all come in the unity of the *f* .... Eph 4:13
Above all, taking the shield of *f* .... Eph 6:16
to the brethren, and love with *f* .... Eph 6:23
for your furtherance and joy of *f* .... Phil 1:25
together for the *f* of the gospel .... Phil 1:27
sacrifice and service of your *f* .... Phil 2:17
which is through the *f* of Christ .... Phil 3:9
which is of God by *f* .... Phil 3:9
heard of your *f* in Christ Jesus .... Col 1:4
If ye continue in the *f* grounded .... Col 1:23
stedfastness of your *f* in Christ .... Col 2:5
up in him, and stablished in the *f* .... Col 2:7
the *f* of the operation of God .... Col 2:12
without ceasing your work of *f* 1Th 1:3
of *f* to God-ward is spread abroad 1Th 1:8
to comfort you concerning your *f* 1Th 3:2
forbear, I sent to know your *f* 1Th 3:5
brought us good tidings of your *f* 1Th 3:6
affliction and distress by your *f* 1Th 3:7
that which is lacking in your *f* 1Th 3:10
putting on the breastplate of *f* 1Th 5:8
because that your *f* groweth 2Th 1:3
f in all your persecutions and 2Th 1:4
and the work of *f* with power 2Th 1:11
for all men have not *f* 2Th 3:2
Unto Timothy, my own son in the *f* 1Ti 1:2

than godly edifying which is in *f*. 1Ti 1:4
conscience, and of *f* unfeigned..............1Ti 1:5
was exceeding abundant with *f*..............1Ti 1:14
Holding *f*, and a good conscience...............1Ti 1:19
concerning *f* have made shipwreck...........1Ti 1:19
a teacher of the Gentiles in *f*...............1Ti 2:7
if they continue in *f* and charity..............1Ti 2:15
of the *f* in a pure conscience.............1Ti 3:9
great boldness in the *f* which is............1Ti 3:13
some shall depart from the *f*..............1Ti 4:1
nourished up in the words of *f*............1Ti 4:6
in charity, in spirit, in *f*..............1Ti 4:12
own house, he hath denied the *f*...........1Ti 5:8
they have cast off their first *f*..............1Ti 5:12
after, they have erred from the *f*............1Ti 6:10
after righteousness, godliness, *f*...........1Ti 6:11
Fight the good fight of *f*..............1Ti 6:12
have erred concerning the *f*..............1Ti 6:21
the unfeigned *f* that is in thee............2Ti 1:5
which thou hast heard of me, in *f*...........2Ti 1:13
and overthrow the *f* of some..............2Ti 2:18
but follow righteousness, *f*...........2Ti 2:22
minds, reprobate concerning the *f*..........2Ti 3:8
manner of life, purpose, *f*..............2Ti 3:10
f which is in Christ Jesus...........2Ti 3:15
my course, I have kept the *f*..............2Ti 4:7
according to the *f* of God's elect..........Titus 1:1
mine own son after the common *f*..........Titus 1:4
that they may be sound in the *f*............Titus 1:13
grave, temperate, sound in *f*..............Titus 2:2
Greet them that love us in the *f*............Titus 3:15
Hearing of thy love and *f*, which..........Philem 5
thy *f* may become effectual by the.........Philem 6
not being mixed with *f* in them............Heb 4:2
dead works, and of *f* toward God............Heb 6:1
followers of them who through *f*............Heb 6:12
true heart in full assurance of *f*...........Heb 10:22
of our *f* without wavering..............Heb 10:23
Now the just shall live by *f*..............Heb 10:38
Now *f* is the substance of things...........Heb 11:1
Through *f* we understand that the..........Heb 11:3
By *f* Abel offered unto God a more..........Heb 11:4
By *f* Enoch was translated that he..........Heb 11:5
But without *f* it is impossible to...........Heb 11:6
By *f* Noah, being warned of God of..........Heb 11:7
the righteousness which is by *f*............Heb 11:7
By *f* Abraham, when he was called...........Heb 11:8
By *f* he sojourned in the land of...........Heb 11:9
Through *f* also Sara herself..............Heb 11:11
These all died in *f*, not having............Heb 11:13
By *f* Abraham, when he was tried...........Heb 11:17
By *f* Isaac blessed Jacob and Esau..........Heb 11:20
By *f* Jacob, when he was a dying...........Heb 11:21
By *f* Joseph, when he died, made...........Heb 11:22
By *f* Moses, when he was born, was.........Heb 11:23
By *f* Moses, when he was come to...........Heb 11:24
By *f* he forsook Egypt, not..............Heb 11:27
Through *f* he kept the passover...........Heb 11:28
By *f* they passed through the Red..........Heb 11:29
By *f* the walls of Jericho fell............Heb 11:30
By *f* the harlot Rahab perished...........Heb 11:31
Who through *f* subdued kingdoms,..........Heb 11:33
obtained a good report through *f*..........Heb 11:39
the author and finisher of our *f*...........Heb 12:2
whose *f* follow, considering the...........Heb 13:7
trying of your *f* worketh patience..........Jas 1:3
But let him ask in *f*, nothing............Jas 1:6
have not the *f* of our Lord Jesus...........Jas 2:1
the poor of this world rich in *f*...........Jas 2:5
though a man say he hath *f*..............Jas 2:14
can *f* save him?..............Jas 2:14
Even so *f*, if it hath not works,...........Jas 2:17
Yea, a man may say, Thou hast *f*..........Jas 2:18
shew me thy *f* without thy works,.........Jas 2:18
I will shew thee my *f* by my works.........Jas 2:18
that *f* without works is dead............Jas 2:20
Seest thou how *f* wrought with his..........Jas 2:22
and by works was *f* made perfect..........Jas 2:22
is justified, and not by *f* only...........Jas 2:24
so *f* without works is dead also...........Jas 2:26
the prayer of *f* shall save the...........Jas 5:15
f unto salvation ought to be............1Pet 1:5
That the trial of your *f*, being...........1Pet 1:7
Receiving the end of your *f*..............1Pet 1:9
that your *f* and hope might be in..........1Pet 1:21
Whom resist stedfast in the *f*............1Pet 5:9
precious *f* with us through the...........2Pet 1:1
diligence, add to your *f* virtue..........2Pet 1:5
overcometh the world, even our *f*..........1Jn 5:4
earnestly contend for the *f* which..........Jude 3
up yourselves on your most holy *f*..........Jude 20
my name, and hast not denied my *f*.........Rev 2:13
and charity, and service, and *f*...........Rev 2:19
patience and the *f* of the saints..........Rev 13:10
of God, and the *f* of Jesus..............Rev 14:12

FAITHFUL

who is *f* in all mine house..............Num 12:7
thy God, he is God, the *f* God............Deut 7:9
And I will raise me up a *f* priest..........1Sa 2:35
who is so *f* among all thy............1Sa 22:14
that are peaceable and *f* in Israel.........2Sa 20:19
for he was a *f* man, and feared God.........Neh 7:2
foundest his heart *f* before thee..........Neh 9:8
for they were counted *f*, and their.........Neh 13:13
for the *f* fail from among the............Ps 12:1
for the LORD preserveth the *f*............Ps 31:23
moon, and as a *f* witness in heaven.........Ps 89:37
shall be upon the *f* of the land...........Ps 101:6
All thy commandments are *f*..............Ps 119:86
commanded are righteous and very *f*........Ps 119:138

but he that is of a *f* spirit............Prov 11:13
but a *f* ambassador is health............Prov 13:17
A *f* witness will not lie............Prov 14:5
but a *f* man who can find............Prov 20:6
so is a *f* messenger to them that..........Prov 25:13
F are the wounds of a friend...........Prov 27:6
A *f* man shall abound with............Prov 28:20
How is the *f* city become an............Is 1:21
city of righteousness, the *f* city.........Is 1:26
I took unto me *f* witnesses to..........Is 8:2
because of the LORD that is *f*...........Is 49:7
f witness between us, if we do..........Jer 42:5
forasmuch as he was *f*, neither..........Dan 6:4
with God, and is *f* with the saints........Hos 11:12
Who then is a *f* and wise servant,.........Mt 24:45
Well done, thou good and *f* servant........Mt 25:21
thou hast been *f* over a few..........Mt 25:21
him, Well done, good and *f* servant........Mt 25:23
thou hast been *f* over a few..........Mt 25:23
the Lord said, Who then is that *f*..........Lk 12:42
He that is *f* in that which is..........Lk 16:10
which is least is *f* also in much..........Lk 16:10
been *f* in the unrighteous mammon.........Lk 16:11
if ye have not been *f* in that...........Lk 16:12
thou hast been *f* in a very little.........Lk 19:17
judged me to be *f* to the Lord...........Acts 16:15
God is *f*, by whom ye were called..........1Cor 1:9
stewards, that a man be found *f*..........1Cor 4:2
f in the Lord, who shall bring..........1Cor 4:17
mercy of the Lord to be *f*...........1Cor 7:25
but God is *f*, who will not suffer.........1Cor 10:13
faith are blessed with *f* Abraham..........Gal 3:9
and to the *f* in Christ Jesus............Eph 1:1
f minister in the Lord, shall...........Eph 6:21
f brethren in Christ which are at.........Col 1:2
who is for you a *f* minister of...........Col 1:7
a *f* minister and fellowservant in.........Col 4:7
With Onesimus, a *f* and beloved..........Col 4:9
F is that calleth you, who...........1Th 5:24
But the Lord is *f*, who shall...........2Th 3:3
me, for that he counted me *f*...........1Ti 1:12
This is a *f* saying, and worthy of.........1Ti 1:15
sober, *f* in all things............1Ti 3:11
This is a *f* saying, and worthy of.........1Ti 4:9
them service, because they are *f*..........1Ti 6:2
the same commit thou to *f* men..........2Ti 2:2
This is a *f* saying.............2Ti 2:11
we believe not, yet he abideth *f*..........2Ti 2:13
having *f* children not accused or..........Titus 1:6
Holding fast the *f* word as he...........Titus 1:9
This is a *f* saying, and these............Titus 3:8
and *f* high priest in things............Heb 2:17
Who was *f* to him that appointed..........Heb 3:2
also Moses was *f* in all his house.........Heb 3:2
verily was *f* in all his house...........Heb 3:5
(for he is *f* that promised...........Heb 10:23
she judged him *f* who had promised.........Heb 11:11
well doing, as unto a *f* Creator..........1Pet 4:19
a *f* brother unto you, as I...........1Pet 5:12
If we confess our sins, he is *f*..........1Jn 1:9
Christ, who is the *f* witness............Rev 1:5
be thou *f* unto death, and I will..........Rev 2:10
wherein Antipas was my *f* martyr..........Rev 2:13
things saith the Amen, the *f*...........Rev 3:14
him are called, and chosen, and *f*.........Rev 17:14
he that sat upon him was called *F*.........Rev 19:11
for these words are true and *f*...........Rev 21:5
said unto me, These sayings are *f*.........Rev 22:6

FAITHFULLY

for they dealt *f*..............2Kin 12:15
their hand, because they dealt *f*..........2Kin 22:7
ye do in the fear of the LORD, *f*..........2Chr 19:9
tithes and the dedicated things *f*.........2Chr 31:12
And the men did the work *f*............2Chr 34:12
The king that *f* judgeth the poor,.........Prov 29:14
my word, let him speak my word *f*.........Jer 23:28
thou doest *f* whatsoever thou............3Jn 5

FAITHFULNESS

man his righteousness and his *f*..........1Sa 26:23
For there is no *f* in their mouth..........Ps 5:9
thy *f* reacheth unto the clouds...........Ps 36:5
I have declared thy *f* and thy...........Ps 40:10
or thy *f* in destruction............Ps 88:11
known thy *f* to all generations...........Ps 89:1
thy *f* shalt thou establish in the.........Ps 89:2
thy *f* also in the congregation of.........Ps 89:5
or to thy *f* round about thee...........Ps 89:8
But my *f* and my mercy shall be...........Ps 89:24
from him, nor suffer my *f* to fail.........Ps 89:33
morning, and thy *f* every night,..........Ps 92:2
that thou in *f* hast afflicted me.........Ps 119:75
Thy *f* is unto all generations..........Ps 119:90
in thy *f* answer me, and in thy..........Ps 143:1
the girdle of his reins............Is 11:5
thy counsels of old are *f*...........Is 25:1
great is thy *f*...........Lam 3:23
even betroth thee unto me in *f*..........Hos 2:20

FAITHLESS

Then Jesus answered and said, O *f*..........Mt 17:17
O *f* generation, how long shall I..........Mk 9:19
And Jesus answering said, O *f*............Lk 9:41
and be not *f*, but believing..............Jn 20:27

FALL

a deep sleep to *upon Adam*..............Gen 2:21
f upon us, and take us for bondmen.........Gen 43:18
See that ye *f* not out by the way..........Gen 45:24
that his rider shall *f* backward...........Gen 49:17
lest he *f* upon us with pestilence..........Ex 5:3

Fear and dread shall *f* upon them..........Ex 15:16
it, and an ox or an ass *f* therein..........Ex 21:33
them, when they are dead, doth *f*..........Lev 11:32
if any part of their carcase *f*...........Lev 11:37
part of their carcase *f* thereon..........Lev 11:38
lest the land *f* to whoredom..............Lev 19:29
they shall *f* before you by the...........Lev 26:7
your enemies shall *f* before you,..........Lev 26:8
they shall *f* when none pursueth...........Lev 26:36
they shall *f* one upon another, as.........Lev 26:37
let them *f* by the camp, as it..........Num 11:31
to *f* by the sword, that our wives.........Num 14:3
shall *f* in this wilderness..............Num 14:29
they shall *f* in this wilderness..........Num 14:32
you, and ye shall *f* by the sword..........Num 14:43
f unto you for an inheritance...........Num 34:2
ass or his ox *f* down by the way..........Deut 22:4
house, if any man *f* from thence..........Deut 22:8
of the city shall *f* down flat...........Josh 6:5
said, Rise thou, and *f* upon us...........Judg 8:21
that ye will not *f* upon me..............Judg 15:12
thirst, and *f* into the hand of the........Judg 15:18
let *f* also some of the handfuls..........Ruth 2:16
thou know how the matter will *f*..........Ruth 3:18
none of his words *f* to the ground.........1Sa 3:19
hair of his head *f* to the ground..........1Sa 14:45
f by the hand of the Philistines,.........1Sa 18:25
let his spittle *f* down upon his..........1Sa 21:13
not put forth their hand to *f*............1Sa 22:17
Turn thou, and *f* upon the priests.........1Sa 22:18
let not my blood *f* to the earth..........1Sa 26:20
and said, Go near, and *f* upon him.........2Sa 1:15
hair of thy son *f* to the earth...........2Sa 14:11
let us *f* now into the hand of the.........2Sa 24:14
let me not *f* into the hand of man.........2Sa 24:14
not an hair of him *f* to the earth.........1Kin 1:52
Jehoiada, saying, Go, *f* upon him.........1Kin 2:29
said, and *f* upon him, and bury him........1Kin 2:31
may go up and *f* at Ramoth-gilead.........1Kin 22:20
let us *f* unto the host of the...........2Kin 7:4
Know now that there shall *f* unto.........2Kin 10:10
thy hurt, that thou shouldest *f*..........2Kin 14:10
I will cause him to *f* by the...........2Kin 19:7
He will *f* to his master Saul to..........1Chr 12:19
let me *f* now into the hand of the.........1Chr 21:13
but let me not *f* into the hand of.........1Chr 21:13
may go up and *f* at Ramoth-gilead.........2Chr 18:19
until thy bowels *f* out by reason.........2Chr 21:15
make thee *f* before the enemy..........2Chr 25:8
thine hurt, that thou shouldest *f*.........2Chr 25:19
before whom thou hast begun to *f*..........Est 6:13
but shalt surely *f* before him............Est 6:13
and his dread *f* upon you............Job 13:11
Then let mine arm *f* from my...........Job 31:22
let them *f* by their own counsels..........Ps 5:10
are turned back, they shall *f*............Ps 9:3
that the poor may *f* by his strong.........Ps 10:10
that very destruction let him *f*...........Ps 35:8
Though he *f*, he shall not be..............Ps 37:24
whereby the people *f* under thee...........Ps 45:5
They shall *f* by the sword............Ps 63:10
own tongue to *f* upon themselves..........Ps 64:8
all kings shall *f* down before him.........Ps 72:11
he let it *f* in the midst of their.........Ps 78:28
f like one of the princes..............Ps 82:7
A thousand shall *f* at thy side...........Ps 91:7
thrust sore at me that I might *f*..........Ps 118:13
Let burning coals *f* upon them............Ps 140:10
Let the wicked *f* into their own...........Ps 141:10
The LORD upholdeth all that *f*............Ps 145:14
away, unless they cause some to *f*.........Prov 4:16
but a prating fool shall *f*............Prov 10:8
but a prating fool shall *f*............Prov 10:10
but the wicked shall *f* by his own.........Prov 11:5
Where no counsel is, the people *f*.........Prov 11:14
trusteth in his riches shall *f*...........Prov 11:28
and an haughty spirit before a *f*.........Prov 16:18
of the LORD shall *f* therein............Prov 22:14
the wicked shall *f* into mischief.........Prov 24:16
diggeth a pit shall *f* therein............Prov 26:27
he shall himself into his own............Prov 28:10
his heart shall *f* into mischief.........Prov 28:14
in his ways shall *f* at once...........Prov 28:18
the righteous shall see their *f*..........Prov 29:16
For if they *f*, the one will lift.........Eccl 4:10
diggeth a pit shall *f* into it............Eccl 10:8
if the tree *f* toward the south,..........Eccl 11:3
Thy men shall *f* by the sword............Is 3:25
among them shall stumble, and *f*..........Is 8:15
they shall *f* under the slain............Is 10:4
Lebanon shall *f* by a mighty one.........Is 10:34
unto them shall *f* by the sword...........Is 13:15
be removed, and be cut down, and *f*........Is 22:25
of the fear shall *f* into the pit.........Is 24:18
and it shall *f*, and not rise again........Is 24:20
f backward, and be broken, and..........Is 28:13
be to you as a breach ready to *f*.........Is 30:13
slaughter, when the towers *f*...........Is 30:25
both he that helpeth shall *f*...........Is 31:3
and he that is holpen shall *f* down........Is 31:3
the Assyrian *f* with the sword..........Is 31:8
and all their host shall *f* down..........Is 34:4
I will cause him to *f* by the............Is 37:7
and the young men shall utterly *f*........Is 40:30
shall I bow down to the stock of a.........Is 44:19
they shall *f* down unto thee, they........Is 45:14
they *f* down, yea, they worship..........Is 46:6
and mischief shall *f* upon thee..........Is 47:11
against thee shall *f* for thy sake.........Is 54:15
cause mine anger to *f* upon you..........Jer 3:12

they shall f among them that f...... Jer 6:15
sons together shall f upon them........ Jer 6:21
Shall they f, and not arise.............. Jer 8:4
shall they f among them that f........ Jer 8:12
f as dung upon the open field............ Jer 9:22
caused him to f upon it suddenly...... Jer 15:8
I will cause them to f by the........... Jer 19:7
they shall f by the sword................ Jer 20:4
shall be driven on, and f therein...... Jer 23:12
it shall f grievously upon the.......... Jer 23:19
ye, and be drunken, and spue, and f.. Jer 25:27
ye shall f like a pleasant vessel........ Jer 25:34
it shall f with pain upon the............ Jer 30:23
I f not away to the Chaldeans........... Jer 37:14
and thou shalt not f by the sword...... Jer 39:18
and f in the land of Egypt................ Jer 44:12
f toward the north by the river......... Jer 46:6
He made many to f, yea, one fell...... Jer 46:16
the fear shall f into the pit............. Jer 48:44
is moved at the noise of their f........ Jer 49:21
young men shall f in her streets........ Jer 49:26
her young men f in the streets.......... Jer 50:30
the most proud shall stumble and f.... Jer 50:32
Thus the slain shall f in the............ Jer 51:4
yea, the wall of Babylon shall f........ Jer 51:44
slain shall f in the midst of her........ Jer 51:47
caused the slain of Israel to f........... Jer 51:49
so at Babylon shall f the slain.......... Jer 51:49
he hath made my strength to f.......... Lam 1:14
a third part shall f by the sword........ Eze 5:12
the slain shall f in the midst of........ Eze 6:7
for they shall f by the sword............ Eze 6:11
that is near shall f by the sword........ Eze 6:12
Ye shall f by the sword.................. Eze 11:10
morter, that it shall f.................... Eze 13:11
ye, O great hailstones, shall f.......... Eze 13:11
be discovered, and it shall f............ Eze 13:14
his bands shall f by the sword.......... Eze 17:21
thy remnant shall f by the sword...... Eze 23:25
let no lot f upon it...................... Eze 24:6
ye have left shall f by the sword....... Eze 24:21
of Dedan shall f by the sword.......... Eze 25:13
isles shake at the sound of thy f........ Eze 26:15
isle tremble in the day of thy f......... Eze 26:18
shall f into the midst of the............. Eze 27:27
in the midst of thee shall f............. Eze 27:34
thou shalt f upon the open fields....... Eze 29:5
when the slain shall f in Egypt......... Eze 30:4
shall f with them by the sword......... Eze 30:5
also that uphold Egypt shall f.......... Eze 30:6
shall they f in it by the sword.......... Eze 30:6
of Pi-beseth shall f by the sword....... Eze 30:17
the sword to f out of his hand.......... Eze 30:22
the arms of Pharaoh shall f down..... Eze 30:25
to shake at the sound of his f........... Eze 31:16
his own life, in the day of thy f......... Eze 32:10
will I cause thy multitude to f.......... Eze 32:12
They shall f in the midst of them...... Eze 32:20
he shall not f thereby in the day....... Eze 33:12
the wastes shall f by the sword........ Eze 33:27
shall they f that are slain with......... Eze 35:8
cause thy nations to f any more........ Eze 36:15
down, and the steep places shall f..... Eze 38:20
every wall shall f to the ground........ Eze 38:20
arrows to f out of thy right hand....... Eze 39:3
Thou shalt f upon the mountains....... Eze 39:4
Thou shalt f upon the open field....... Eze 39:5
of Israel to f into iniquity............... Eze 44:12
this land shall f unto you for........... Eze 47:14
ye f down and worship the golden..... Dan 3:5
all kinds of musick, shall f down...... Dan 3:10
ye f down and worship the image...... Dan 3:15
but they shall f......................... Dan 11:14
but he shall stumble and f.............. Dan 11:19
and many shall f down slain............ Dan 11:26
yet they shall f by the sword........... Dan 11:33
Now when they shall f, they shall..... Dan 11:34
of them of understanding shall f....... Dan 11:35
Therefore shall thou f in the day...... Hos 4:5
shall f with thee in the night........... Hos 4:5
that doth not understand shall f........ Hos 4:14
Ephraim f in their iniquity.............. Hos 5:5
Judah also shall f with them........... Hos 5:5
their princes shall f by the.............. Hos 7:16
and to the hills, F on us................. Hos 10:8
they shall f by the sword................ Hos 13:16
the transgressors shall f therein....... Hos 14:9
when they f upon the sword, they..... Joel 2:8
Can a bird f in a snare upon the........ Amos 3:5
be cut off, and f to the ground.......... Amos 3:14
daughters shall f by the sword.......... Amos 7:17
even they shall f, and never rise....... Amos 8:14
the least grain f upon the earth......... Amos 9:9
when I f, I shall arise.................... Mic 7:8
they shall even f into the mouth........ Nah 3:12
I give thee, if thou wilt f down......... Mt 4:9
and great was the f of it................. Mt 7:27
one of them shall not f on the........... Mt 10:29
if it f into a pit on the sabbath.......... Mt 12:11
both shall f into the ditch............... Mt 15:14
which f from their masters' table....... Mt 15:27
whosoever shall f on this stone......... Mt 21:44

F

but on whomsoever it shall f........... Lk 20:18
they shall f by the edge of the.......... Lk 21:24
to say to the mountains, F on us....... Lk 23:30
a corn of wheat f into the ground...... Jn 12:24
they should f into the quicksands..... Acts 27:17
of the boat, and let her f off............ Acts 27:32
f from the head of any of you........... Acts 27:34
they stumbled that they should f...... Rom 11:11
but rather through their f............... Rom 11:11
Now if the f of them be the............. Rom 11:12
or an occasion to f in his................ Rom 14:13
the standeth take heed lest he f......... 1Cor 10:12
he f into the condemnation of the..... 1Ti 3:6
lest he f into reproach and the.......... 1Ti 3:7
will be rich f into temptation........... 1Ti 6:9
lest any man f after the same........... Heb 4:11
If they shall f away, to renew.......... Heb 6:6
It is a fearful thing to f into............ Heb 10:31
when ye f into divers temptations..... Jas 1:2
lest ye f into condemnation............. Jas 5:12
do these things, ye shall never f........ 2Pet 1:10
f from your own stedfastness........... 2Pet 3:17
twenty elders f down before him...... Rev 4:10
F on us, and hide us from the face..... Rev 6:16
I saw a star f from heaven unto......... Rev 9:1

FALLEN

and why is thy countenance f........... Gen 4:6
man whose hair is f off his head....... Lev 13:40
he that hath his hair f off from......... Lev 13:41
poor, and f in decay with thee.......... Lev 25:35
is f to us on this side Jordan............ Num 32:19
and that your terror is f upon us....... Josh 2:9
when they were all f on the edge...... Josh 8:24
their lord was f down dead on the..... Judg 3:25
f unto them among the tribes of........ Judg 18:1
the woman was concubine was f....... Judg 19:27
Dagon was f upon his face to the...... 1Sa 5:3
Dagon was f upon his face to the...... 1Sa 5:4
from the LORD was f upon them....... 1Sa 26:12
his three sons f in mount Gilboa....... 1Sa 31:8
and many of the people also are f...... 2Sa 1:4
not live after that he was f.............. 2Sa 1:10
because they were f by the sword..... 2Sa 1:12
how are the mighty f..................... 2Sa 1:19
How are the mighty f in the midst..... 2Sa 1:25
How are the mighty f, and the......... 2Sa 1:27
a great man f this day in Israel......... 2Sa 3:38
yea, they are f under my feet.......... 2Sa 22:39
Now Elisha was f sick of his........... 2Kin 13:14
his sons f in mount Gilboa.............. 1Chr 10:8
were dead bodies f to the earth........ 2Chr 20:24
our fathers have f by the sword........ 2Chr 29:9
Haman was f upon the bed whereon... Est 7:8
The fire of God is f from heaven....... Job 1:16
is f into the ditch which he made...... Ps 7:15
The lines are f unto me in.............. Ps 16:6
they are f under my feet................. Ps 18:38
They are brought down and f........... Ps 20:8
are the workers of iniquity f........... Ps 36:12
terrors of death are f upon me.......... Ps 55:4
whereof they are f themselves......... Ps 57:6
reproached thee are f upon me......... Ps 69:9
is ruined, and Judah is f................. Is 3:8
The bricks are f down, but we.......... Is 9:10
How art thou f from heaven............ Is 14:12
fruits and for thy harvest is f........... Is 16:9
he answered and said, Babylon is f.... Is 21:9
and said, Babylon is f, is f.............. Is 21:9
the inhabitants of the world f........... Is 26:18
for truth is f in the street, and......... Is 59:14
down to the Chaldeans.................. Jer 38:19
and they are f both together............ Jer 46:12
the spoiler is f upon thy summer...... Jer 48:32
her foundations are f, her walls........ Jer 50:15
Babylon is suddenly f and.............. Jer 51:8
my young men are f by the sword..... Lam 2:21
The crown is f from our head........... Lam 5:16
Lo, when the wall is f, shall it......... Eze 13:12
the valleys his branches are f........... Eze 31:12
all of them slain, f by the sword....... Eze 32:22
f by the sword, which caused........... Eze 32:23
f by the sword, which are gone........ Eze 32:24
that are f of the uncircumcised......... Eze 32:27
all their kings are f...................... Hos 7:7
for thou hast f by thine iniquity....... Hos 14:1
The virgin of Israel is f................. Amos 5:2
the tabernacle of David that is f....... Amos 9:11
for the cedar is f........................ Zec 11:2
have an ass or an ox f into a pit....... Lk 14:5
as yet he was f upon none of them.... Acts 8:16
of David, which is f down.............. Acts 15:16
being f into a deep sleep................ Acts 20:9
when we were all f to the earth........ Acts 26:14
last we should have f upon rocks...... Acts 27:29
swollen, or f down dead suddenly..... Acts 28:6
present, but some are f asleep.......... 1Cor 15:6
Then they also which are f asleep..... 1Cor 15:18
ye are f from grace...................... Gal 5:4
which happened unto me have f out... Phil 1:12
therefore from whence thou art f...... Rev 2:5
saying, Babylon is, is f................. Rev 14:8
five are f, and one is, and the.......... Rev 17:10
Babylon the great is f, is f............. Rev 18:2

FALLEST

Thou f away to the Chaldeans......... Jer 37:13

FALLETH

when there f out any war, they......... Ex 1:10
vessel, whereinto any of them f........ Lev 11:33
their carcase f shall be unclean........ Lev 11:35

be in the place where his lot f.......... Num 33:54
or that f on the sword, or that.......... 2Sa 3:29
as a man f before wicked men, so..... 2Sa 3:34
him as the dew f on the ground........ 2Sa 17:12
night, when deep sleep f on men...... Job 4:13
night, when deep sleep f upon men... Job 33:15
wicked messenger f into mischief..... Prov 13:17
a perverse tongue f into mischief..... Prov 17:20
For a just man f seven times............ Prov 24:16
Rejoice not when thine enemy f....... Prov 24:17
to him that is alone when he f.......... Eccl 4:10
when it f suddenly upon them.......... Eccl 9:12
in the place where the tree f............ Eccl 11:3
as the leaf f off from the vine.......... Is 34:4
a graven image, and f down thereto... Is 44:15
he f down unto it, and worshippeth... Is 44:17
f to the Chaldeans that besiege........ Jer 21:9
whoso f not down and worshippeth... Dan 3:6
whoso f not down and worshippeth... Dan 3:11
for ofttimes he f into the fire.......... Mt 17:15
a house divided against a house f...... Lk 11:17
the portion of goods that f to me...... Lk 15:12
his own master he standeth or f....... Rom 14:4
grass, and the flower thereof f......... Jas 1:11
and the flower thereof f away......... 1Pet 1:24

FALLING

f into a trance, but having his.......... Num 24:4
f into a trance, but having his.......... Num 24:16
have upholden him that was f.......... Job 4:4
the mountain f cometh to nought...... Job 14:18
not thou deliver my feet from f........ Ps 56:13
from tears, and my feet from f......... Ps 116:8
A righteous man f down before the.... Prov 25:26
as a f fig from the fig tree.............. Is 34:4
f down before him, she declared....... Lk 8:47
of blood f down to the ground......... Lk 22:44
f headlong, he burst asunder in........ Acts 1:18
f into a place where two seas met..... Acts 27:41
so f down on his face he will........... 1Cor 14:25
except there come a f away first....... 2Th 2:3
that is able to keep you from f.......... Jude 24

FALLOW

the f deer, and the wild goat, and..... Deut 14:5
Jerusalem, Break up your f ground... Jer 4:3
break up your f ground.................. Hos 10:12

FALLOWDEER

beside harts, and roebucks, and f...... 1Kin 4:23

FALSE

Thou shalt not bear f witness.......... Ex 20:16
Thou shalt not raise a f report......... Ex 23:1
Keep thee far from a f matter.......... Ex 23:7
Neither shalt thou bear f witness...... Deut 5:20
If a f witness rise up against............ Deut 19:16
if the witness be a f witness............ Deut 19:18
And they said, It is f.................... 2Kin 9:12
For truly my words shall not be f...... Job 36:4
for f witnesses are risen up............. Ps 27:12
F witnesses did rise up.................. Ps 35:11
therefore I hate every f way............ Ps 119:104
and I hate every f way................... Ps 119:128
be done unto thee, thou f tongue...... Ps 120:3
A f witness that speaketh lies,......... Prov 6:19
A f balance is abomination to the...... Prov 11:1
but a f witness deceit.................... Prov 12:17
but a f witness will utter lies........... Prov 14:5
wicked doer giveth heed to f lips...... Prov 17:4
A f witness shall not be................. Prov 19:5
A f witness shall not be................. Prov 19:9
and a f balance is not good............. Prov 20:23
A f witness shall perish................. Prov 21:28
of a f gift is like clouds................ Prov 25:14
A man that beareth f witness.......... Prov 25:18
they prophesy unto you a f vision..... Jer 14:14
them that prophesy f dreams.......... Jer 23:32
Then said Jeremiah, It is f............. Jer 37:14
but have seen for thee f burdens...... Lam 2:14
as a f divination in their sight......... Eze 21:23
and love no f oath....................... Zec 8:17
seen a lie, and have told f dreams..... Zec 10:2
against f swearers, and against........ Mal 3:5
Beware of f prophets, which come.... Mt 7:15
thefts, f witness, blasphemies......... Mt 15:19
Thou shalt not bear f witness.......... Mt 19:18
many f prophets shall rise, and........ Mt 24:11
For there shall arise f Christs.......... Mt 24:24
f prophets, and shall shew great....... Mt 24:24
sought f witness against Jesus......... Mt 26:59
though many f witnesses came, yet... Mt 26:60
At the last came two f witnesses...... Mt 26:60
not steal, Do not bear f witness....... Mk 10:19
For f Christs and f prophets........... Mk 13:22
For many bare f witness against....... Mk 14:56
bare f witness against him.............. Mk 14:57
their fathers to the f prophets......... Lk 6:26
not steal, Do not bear f witness....... Lk 18:20
from any man by f accusation.......... Lk 19:8
set up f witnesses, which said,........ Acts 6:13
a f prophet, a Jew, whose name....... Acts 13:6
Thou shalt not bear f witness.......... Rom 13:9
we are found f witnesses of God...... 1Cor 15:15
For such are f apostles.................. 2Cor 11:13
sea, in perils among f brethren........ 2Cor 11:26
that because of f brethren.............. Gal 2:4
f accusers, incontinent, fierce,........ 2Ti 3:3
not f accusers, not given to much.... Titus 2:3
But there were f prophets also........ 2Pet 2:1
shall be f teachers among you......... 2Pet 2:1
because many f prophets are gone.... 1Jn 4:1

out of the mouth of the f prophet........ Rev 16:13
with him the f prophet that .... Rev 19:20
the f prophet are, and shall be.......... Rev 20:10

FALSEHOOD
wrought f against mine own life......... 2Sa 18:13
in your answers there remaineth f....... Job 21:34
mischief, and brought forth f........... Ps 7:14
for their deceit is f .... Ps 119:118
right hand is a right hand of f......... Ps 144:8
right hand is a right hand of f......... Ps 144:11
under f have we hid ourselves........... Is 28:15
of transgression, a seed of f .... Is 57:4
from the heart words of f .... Is 59:13
for his molten image is f .... Jer 10:14
forgotten me, and trusted in f .... Jer 13:25
for his molten image is f .... Jer 51:17
for they commit f; and the thief....... Hos 7:1
f do lie, saying, I will prophesy....... Mic 2:11

FALSELY
that thou wilt not deal f with me....... Gen 21:23
concerning it, and sweareth f .... Lev 6:3
that about which he hath sworn f .... Lev 6:5
shall not steal, neither deal f .... Lev 19:11
ye shall not swear by my name f .... Lev 19:12
hath testified f against his .... Deut 19:18
have we dealt f in thy covenant......... Ps 44:17
surely they swear f .... Jer 5:2
The prophets prophesy f, and the........ Jer 5:31
the priest every one dealeth f.......... Jer 6:13
and commit adultery, and swear f........ Jer 7:9
the priest every one dealeth f.......... Jer 8:10
For they prophesy f unto you in......... Jer 29:9
for thou speakest f of Ishmael.......... Jer 40:16
unto Jeremiah, Thou speakest f.......... Jer 43:2
swearing f in making a covenant......... Hos 10:4
of him that sweareth f by my name....... Zec 5:4
all manner of evil against you f........ Mt 5:11
to no man, neither accuse any f......... Lk 3:14
of science f so called 1Ti 6:20
they may be ashamed that f accuse....... 1Pet 3:16

FALSIFYING
and f the balances by deceit .... Amos 8:5

FAME
the f thereof was heard in.............. Gen 45:16
heard the f of thee will speak.......... Num 14:15
his f was noised throughout all .... Josh 6:27
for we have heard the f of him .... Josh 9:9
his f was in all nations round.......... 1Kin 4:31
f of Solomon concerning the name........ 1Kin 10:1
exceedeth the f which I heard........... 1Kin 10:7
the f of David went out into all........ 1Chr 14:17
be exceeding magnifical, of f 1Chr 22:5
Sheba heard of the f of Solomon......... 2Chr 9:1
thou exceedest the f that I heard 2Chr 9:6
his f went out throughout all the....... Est 9:4
We have heard the f thereof with........ Job 28:22
off, that have not heard my f .... Is 66:19
We have heard the f thereof............. Jer 6:24
f in every land where they have......... Zeph 3:19
his f went throughout all Syria......... Mt 4:24
the f hereof went abroad into all....... Mt 9:26
spread abroad his f in all that......... Mt 9:31
tetrarch heard of the f of Jesus........ Mt 14:1
immediately his f spread abroad......... Mk 1:28
there went out a f of him through ...... Lk 4:14
the f of him went out into every....... Lk 4:37
more went there a f abroad of him ...... Lk 5:15

FAMILIAR
not them that have f spirits........... Lev 19:31
after such as have f spirits........... Lev 20:6
or woman that hath a f spirit.......... Lev 20:27
or a consulter with f spirits.......... Deut 18:11
put away those that had f spirits...... 1Sa 28:3
me a woman that hath a f spirit........ 1Sa 28:7
that hath a f spirit at En-dor......... 1Sa 28:7
divine unto me by the f spirit......... 1Sa 28:8
cut off those that have f spirits...... 1Sa 28:9
and dealt with f spirits and........... 2Kin 21:6
the workers with f spirits............. 2Kin 23:24
of one that had a f spirit............. 1Chr 10:13
and dealt with a f spirit.............. 2Chr 33:6
my f friends have forgotten me .... Job 19:14
Yea, mine own f friend, in whom I ..... Ps 41:9
unto them that have f spirits.......... Is 8:19
and to them that have f spirits........ Is 19:3
as of one that hath a f spirit......... Is 29:4

FAMILIARS
All my f watched for my halting,....... Jer 20:10

FAMILIES
after his tongue, after their f........ Gen 10:5
afterward were the f of the............ Gen 10:18
the sons of Ham, after their f......... Gen 10:20
the sons of Shem, after their f .... Gen 10:31
These are the f of the sons of......... Gen 10:32
in thee shall all f of the earth....... Gen 12:3
all the f of the earth be blessed...... Gen 28:14
of Esau, according to their f .... Gen 36:40
with bread, according to their f....... Gen 47:12
these be the f of Reuben............... Ex 6:14
these are the f of Simeon.............. Ex 6:15
and Shimi, according to their f........ Ex 6:17
these are the f of the Levi according.. Ex 6:19
these are the f of the Korhites........ Ex 6:24
the Levites according to their f....... Ex 6:25
you a lamb according to your f......... Ex 12:21
of their f that are with you,.......... Lev 25:45

children of Israel, after their f ..... Num 1:2
their pedigrees after their f.......... Num 1:18
their generations, after their f....... Num 1:20
their generations, after their f....... Num 1:22
their generations, after their f....... Num 1:24
their generations, after their f....... Num 1:26
their generations, after their f....... Num 1:28
their generations, after their f....... Num 1:30
their generations, after their f....... Num 1:32
their generations, after their f....... Num 1:34
their generations, after their f....... Num 1:36
their generations, after their f....... Num 1:38
their generations, after their f....... Num 1:40
their generations, after their f....... Num 1:42
forward, every one after their f....... Num 2:34
of their fathers, by their f........... Num 3:15
of the sons of Gershon by their f...... Num 3:18
And the sons of Kohath by their f...... Num 3:19
And the sons of Merari by their f...... Num 3:20
These are the f of the Levites......... Num 3:20
these are the f of the .... Num 3:21
The f of the Gershonites shall......... Num 3:23
these are the f of the Kohathites...... Num 3:27
The f of the sons of Kohath shall ..... Num 3:29
the f of the Kohathites shall be....... Num 3:30
these are the f of Merari.............. Num 3:33
the house of the father of their f..... Num 3:35
of the LORD, throughout their f........ Num 3:39
the sons of Levi, after their f........ Num 4:2
of the Kohathites from among .... Num 4:18
their fathers, by their f.............. Num 4:22
of the f of the Gershonites............ Num 4:24
This is the service of the f of........ Num 4:24
shall number them after their f........ Num 4:29
of the f of the sons of Merari......... Num 4:33
of the Kohathites after their f........ Num 4:34
were numbered of them by their f....... Num 4:36
of the f of the Kohathites............. Num 4:37
of Gershon, throughout their f......... Num 4:38
of them, throughout their f............ Num 4:40
of the f of the sons of Gershon........ Num 4:41
of the f of the sons of Merari......... Num 4:42
throughout their f, by the house....... Num 4:42
numbered of them after their f......... Num 4:44
of the f of the sons of Merari......... Num 4:45
of Israel numbered, after their f...... Num 4:46
people weep throughout their f......... Num 11:10
These are the f of the Reubenites...... Num 26:7
The sons of Simeon after their f....... Num 26:12
These are the f of the Simeonites...... Num 26:14
The children of Gad after their f...... Num 26:15
These are the f of the children .... Num 26:18
sons of Judah after their f were....... Num 26:20
These are the f of Judah .... Num 26:22
sons of Issachar after their f......... Num 26:23
These are the f of Issachar............ Num 26:25
the sons of Zebulun after their f...... Num 26:26
These are the f of the .... Num 26:27
after their f were Manasseh............ Num 26:28
These are the f of Manasseh............ Num 26:34
the sons of Ephraim after their f...... Num 26:35
These are the f of the sons of......... Num 26:37
the sons of Joseph after their f....... Num 26:37
sons of Benjamin after their f......... Num 26:38
These are the f of the sons of......... Num 26:41
are the sons of Dan after their f...... Num 26:42
These are the f of Dan after........... Num 26:42
the f of Dan after..................... Num 26:42
All the f of the Shuhamites,........... Num 26:43
children of Asher after their f .... Num 26:44
These are the f of the sons of......... Num 26:47
sons of Naphtali after their f......... Num 26:48
These are the f of Naphtali............ Num 26:50
of Naphtali according to their f....... Num 26:50
of the Levites after their f........... Num 26:57
These are the f of the Levites......... Num 26:58
of the f of Manasseh the son of........ Num 27:1
for an inheritance among your f........ Num 33:54
their fathers of the f of the.......... Num 36:1
of the f of the sons of Joseph,........ Num 36:1
they were married into the f of........ Num 36:6
come according to the f thereof........ Josh 7:14
inheritance according to their f....... Josh 13:15
children of Reuben after their f....... Josh 13:23
children of Gad according their f ..... Josh 13:24
the children of Gad after their f...... Josh 13:28
children of Manasseh by their f .... Josh 13:29
the children of Machir by their f...... Josh 13:31
the children of Judah by their f....... Josh 15:1
round about according to their f....... Josh 15:12
of Judah according to their f.......... Josh 15:20
according to their f was thus.......... Josh 16:5
children of Ephraim by their f......... Josh 16:8
children of Manasseh by their f .... Josh 17:2
the son of Joseph by their f........... Josh 17:2
came up according to their f........... Josh 18:11
round about, according to their f ..... Josh 18:20
according to their f were Jericho...... Josh 18:21
of Benjamin according to their f....... Josh 18:28
of Simeon according to their f......... Josh 19:1
of Simeon according to their f......... Josh 19:8
of Zebulun according to their f........ Josh 19:10
of Zebulun according to their f........ Josh 19:16
of Issachar according to their f....... Josh 19:17
of Issachar according to their f....... Josh 19:23
of Asher according to their f.......... Josh 19:24
of Asher according to their f.......... Josh 19:31
of Naphtali according to their f....... Josh 19:32
of Naphtali according to their f....... Josh 19:39
of Dan according to their f............ Josh 19:40

of Dan according to their f............ Josh 19:48
out for the f of the Kohathites........ Josh 21:4
of the f of the tribe of Ephraim....... Josh 21:5
of the f of the tribe of Issachar...... Josh 21:6
f had out of the tribe of Reuben....... Josh 21:7
being of the f of the Kohathites,...... Josh 21:10
the f of the children of Kohath,....... Josh 21:20
f of the children of Kohath that....... Josh 21:26
of the f of the Levites, out of........ Josh 21:27
Gershonites according to their f....... Josh 21:33
unto the f of the children of.......... Josh 21:34
the children of Merari by their f...... Josh 21:40
remaining of the f of the Levites...... Josh 21:40
the f of the tribe of Benjamin......... 1Sa 9:21
Benjamin to come near by their f....... 1Sa 10:21
And the f of Kirjath-jearim............ 1Chr 2:53
the f of the scribes which dwelt....... 1Chr 2:55
These are the f of the Zorathites...... 1Chr 4:2
the f of Aharhel the son of Harum 1Chr 4:8
the f of the house of them that 1Chr 4:21
names were princes in their f.......... 1Chr 4:38
And his brethren by their f............ 1Chr 5:7
these are the f of the Levites......... 1Chr 6:19
of the f of the Kohathites............. 1Chr 6:54
their f were thirteen cities........... 1Chr 6:60
of Gershom throughout their f out...... 1Chr 6:62
given by lot, throughout their f....... 1Chr 6:63
the residue of the f of the sons....... 1Chr 6:66
their brethren among all the f of...... 1Chr 7:5
to the divisions of the f of........... 2Chr 35:5
division of the f of the Levites....... 2Chr 35:5
divisions of the f of the people 2Chr 35:12
after their f with their swords........ Neh 4:13
did the contempt of f terrify me ...... Job 31:34
God setteth the solitary in f.......... Ps 68:6
maketh him f like a flock.............. Ps 107:41
I will call all the f of the........... Jer 1:15
all the f of the house of Israel....... Jer 2:4
upon the f that call not on thy .... Jer 10:25
and take all the f of the north........ Jer 25:9
be the God of all the f of Israel...... Jer 31:1
The two f which the LORD hath.......... Jer 33:24
as the f of the countries, to......... Eze 20:32
I known of all the f of the earth...... Amos 3:2
f through her witchcrafts.............. Nah 3:4
All the f that remain, every .... Zec 12:14
will not come up of all the f of ...... Zec 14:17

FAMILY
that man, and against his f............ Lev 20:5
shall return every man unto his f ..... Lev 25:10
and shall return unto his own f........ Lev 25:41
to the stock of the stranger's f....... Lev 25:47
unto him of his f may redeem him ...... Lev 25:49
Gershon was the f of the Libnites ..... Num 3:21
and the f of the Shimites.............. Num 3:21
Kohath was the f of the Amramites..... Num 3:27
the f of the Izeharites, and the....... Num 3:27
the f of the Hebronites, and the....... Num 3:27
and the f of the Uzzielites............ Num 3:27
Merari was the f of the Mahlites....... Num 3:33
and the f of the Mushites.............. Num 3:33
cometh the f of the Hanochites......... Num 26:5
of Pallu, the f of the Palluites....... Num 26:5
Hezron, the f of the Hezronites........ Num 26:6
of Carmi, the f of the Carmites........ Num 26:6
Nemuel, the f of the Nemuelites........ Num 26:12
of Jamin, the f of the Jaminites....... Num 26:12
Jachin, the f of the Jachinites........ Num 26:12
Of Zerah, the f of the Zarhites........ Num 26:13
of Shaul, the f of the Shaulites....... Num 26:13
Zephon, the f of the Zephonites........ Num 26:15
of Haggi, the f of the Haggites........ Num 26:15
of Shuni, the f of the Shunites........ Num 26:15
Of Ozni, the f of the Oznites.......... Num 26:16
of Eri, the f of the Erites............ Num 26:16
Of Arod, the f of the Arodites......... Num 26:17
of Areli, the f of the Arelites........ Num 26:17
Shelah, the f of the Shelanites........ Num 26:20
of Pharez, the f of the Pharzites ..... Num 26:20
of Zerah, the f of the Zarhites........ Num 26:20
Hezron, the f of the Hezronites........ Num 26:21
of Hamul, the f of the Hamulites....... Num 26:21
of Tola, the f of the Tolaites......... Num 26:23
of Pua, the f of the Punites........... Num 26:23
Jashub, the f of the Jashubites........ Num 26:24
Shimron, the f of the Shimronites ..... Num 26:24
of Sered, the f of the Sardites........ Num 26:26
of Elon, the f of the Elonites......... Num 26:26
Jahleel, the f of the Jahleelites...... Num 26:26
Machir, the f of the Machirites........ Num 26:29
come the f of the Gileadites........... Num 26:29
Jeezer, the f of the Jeezerites........ Num 26:30
of Helek, the f of the Helekites....... Num 26:30
Asriel, the f of the Asrielites........ Num 26:31
Shechem, the f of the Shechemites ..... Num 26:31
Shemida, the f of the Shemidaites ..... Num 26:32
Hepher, the f of the Hepherites........ Num 26:32
the f of the Shuthalhites.............. Num 26:35
of Becher, the f of the Bachrites ..... Num 26:35
of Tahan, the f of the Tahanites....... Num 26:35
of Eran, the f of the Eranites......... Num 26:36
of Bela, the f of the Belaites......... Num 26:38
Ashbel, the f of the Ashbelites........ Num 26:38
Ahiram, the f of the Ahiramites........ Num 26:38
Shupham, the f of the Shuphamites ..... Num 26:39
Hupham, the f of the Huphamites........ Num 26:39
of Ard, the f of the Ardites........... Num 26:40
of Naaman, the f of the Naamites....... Num 26:40
Shuham, the f of the Shuhamites........ Num 26:42
of Jimna, the f of the Jimnites........ Num 26:44

F

of Jesui, the _f_ of the Jesuites .... Num 26:44
of Beriah, the _f_ of the Berites .... Num 26:44
of Heber, the _f_ of the Heberites......... Num 26:45
the _f_ of the Malchielites .... Num 26:45
Jahzeel, the _f_ of the Jahzeelites .... Num 26:48
of Guni, the _f_ of the Gunites............ Num 26:48
of Jezer, the _f_ of the Jezerites.......... Num 26:49
Shillem, the _f_ of the Shillemites .... Num 26:49
Gershon, the _f_ of the Gershonites....... Num 26:57
Kohath, the _f_ of the Kohathites......... Num 26:57
of Merari, the _f_ of the Merarites........ Num 26:57
the _f_ of the Libnites........................ Num 26:58
the _f_ of the Hebronites.................... Num 26:58
the _f_ of the Mahlites....................... Num 26:58
the _f_ of the Mushites....................... Num 26:58
Mushites, the _f_ of the Korathites .... Num 26:58
be done away from among his _f_........... Num 27:4
that is next to him of his _f_................. Num 27:11
only to the _f_ of the tribe of .... Num 36:6
the _f_ of the tribe of her father........... Num 36:8
tribe of the _f_ of their father .... Num 36:12
be among you man, or woman, or _f_..... Deut 29:18
the _f_ which The LORD shall take .... Josh 7:14
And he brought the _f_ of Judah............ Josh 7:17
he took the _f_ of the Zarhites .... Josh 7:17
he brought the _f_ of the Zarhites .... Josh 7:17
they let go the man and all his _f_ .... Judg 1:25
my _f_ is poor in Manasseh, and I am ... Judg 6:15
with all the _f_ of the house of............. Judg 9:1
of the _f_ of the Danites, whose............ Judg 13:2
of the _f_ of Judah, who was a............. Judg 17:7
_f_ five men from their coasts .... Judg 18:2
thence of the _f_ of the Danites........... Judg 18:11
unto a tribe and a _f_ in Israel .... Judg 18:19
man to his tribe and to his _f_............. Judg 21:24
of wealth, of the _f_ of Elimelech......... Ruth 2:1
my _f_ the least of all the.................. 1Sa 9:21
the _f_ of Matri was taken, and Saul 1Sa 10:21
life, or my father's _f_ in Israel............ 1Sa 18:18
sacrifice there for all the 1Sa 20:6
for our _f_ hath a sacrifice in the 1Sa 20:6
the whole _f_ is risen against 2Sa 14:7
man of the _f_ of the house of Saul 2Sa 16:5
neither did all their _f_ multiply........... 1Chr 4:27
the _f_ of that tribe.......................... 1Chr 6:61
for the _f_ of the remnant of the.......... 1Chr 6:70
_f_ of the half tribe of Manasseh.......... 1Chr 6:71
ark of God remained with the _f_ of..... 1Chr 13:14
every generation, every _f_................. Est 9:28
you one of a city, and two of a _f_ .... Jer 3:14
them that remain of this evil _f_.......... Jer 8:3
against the whole _f_ which I............... Amos 3:1
against this _f_ do I devise an............. Mic 2:3
land shall mourn, every _f_ apart .... Zec 12:12
the _f_ of the house of David apart....... Zec 12:12
the _f_ of the house of Nathan............. Zec 12:12
The _f_ of the house of Levi apart........ Zec 12:13
the _f_ of Shimei apart, and their......... Zec 12:13
that remain, every _f_ apart .... Zec 12:14
if the _f_ of Egypt go not up, and....... Zec 14:18
Of whom the whole _f_ in heaven........ Eph 3:15

FAMINE

And there was a _f_ in the land............ Gen 12:10
for the _f_ was grievous in the .... Gen 12:10
And there was a _f_ that was in............ Gen 26:1
beside the first _f_ that was in............. Gen 26:1
wind shall be seven years of _f_ .... Gen 41:27
arise after them seven years of _f_ .... Gen 41:30
the _f_ shall consume the land .... Gen 41:30
by reason of that _f_ following............. Gen 41:31
land against the seven years of _f_ .... Gen 41:36
the land perish not through the _f_....... Gen 41:36
sons before the years of _f_ came......... Gen 41:50
the _f_ was over all the face of............ Gen 41:56
the _f_ waxed sore in the land of......... Gen 41:56
because that the _f_ was so sore in .... Gen 41:57
for the _f_ was in the land of .... Gen 42:5
corn for the _f_ of your houses............ Gen 42:19
take food for the _f_ of your.............. Gen 42:33
the _f_ was sore in the land................ Gen 43:1
years hath the _f_ been in the land....... Gen 45:6
for yet there are five years of _f_ .... Gen 45:11
for the _f_ is sore in the land of.......... Gen 47:4
for the _f_ was very sore, so that .... Gen 47:13
Canaan fainted by reason of the _f_ ..... Gen 47:13
because the _f_ prevailed over them ..... Gen 47:20
that there was a _f_ in the land............ Ruth 1:1
Then there was a _f_ in the days of 2Sa 21:1
Shall seven years of _f_ come unto 2Sa 24:13
If there be in the land _f_ 1Kin 8:37
And there was a sore _f_ in Samaria..... 1Kin 18:2
And there was a great _f_ in Samaria 2Kin 6:25
then the _f_ is in the city, and we 2Kin 7:4
for the LORD hath called for a _f_ 2Kin 8:1
month the _f_ prevailed in the city....... 2Kin 25:3
Either three years _f_......................... 1Chr 21:12
judgment, or pestilence, or _f_............ 2Chr 20:9
give over yourselves to die by _f_......... 2Chr 32:11
In _f_ he shall redeem thee from .... Job 5:20
destruction and _f_ thou shalt laugh..... Job 5:22
For want and _f_ they were solitary...... Job 30:3
death, and to keep them alive in _f_ .... Ps 33:19
in the days of _f_ they shall be............ Ps 37:19
he called for a _f_ upon the land.......... Ps 105:16
and I will kill thy root with _f_ .... Is 14:30
and destruction, and the _f_................ Is 51:19
neither shall we sword nor _f_ .... Jer 5:12
and their daughters shall die by _f_ ...... Jer 11:22
them by the sword, and by the _f_ .... Jer 14:12
sword, neither shall ye have _f_........... Jer 14:13

_f_ shall not be in this land................. Jer 14:15
_f_ shall those prophets be.................. Jer 14:15
of Jerusalem because of the _f_............ Jer 14:16
behold them that are sick with _f_ .... Jer 14:18
as are for the _f_, to the _f_ .... Jer 15:2
be consumed by the sword, and by _f_ .. Jer 16:4
up their children to the _f_ .... Jer 18:21
from the sword, and from the _f_......... Jer 21:7
die by the sword, and by the _f_ .... Jer 21:9
And I will send the sword, the _f_ .... Jer 24:10
with the sword, and with the _f_ .... Jer 27:8
people, by the sword, by the _f_ .... Jer 27:13
send upon them the sword, the _f_....... Jer 29:17
them with the sword, with the _f_........ Jer 29:18
because of the sword, and of the _f_..... Jer 32:24
Babylon by the sword, and by the _f_ ... Jer 32:36
to the pestilence, and to the _f_........... Jer 34:17
shall die by the sword, by the _f_ .... Jer 38:2
in the land of Egypt, and the _f_ .... Jer 42:16
shall die by the sword, by the _f_ .... Jer 42:17
shall die by the sword, by the _f_ .... Jer 42:22
consumed by the sword and by the _f_ .. Jer 44:12
by the sword and by the _f_................ Jer 44:12
Jerusalem, by the sword, by the _f_ ..... Jer 44:13
consumed by the sword and by the _f_ .. Jer 44:18
consumed by the sword and by the _f_ .. Jer 44:27
the _f_ was sore in the city, so............ Jer 52:6
an oven because of the terrible _f_ .... Lam 5:10
with _f_ shall they be consumed in ...... Eze 5:12
upon them the evil arrows of _f_ .... Eze 5:16
and I will increase the _f_ upon you ..... Eze 5:16
So will I send upon you _f_ .... Eze 5:17
shall fall by the sword, by the _f_ .... Eze 6:11
and is besieged shall die by the _f_ ...... Eze 6:12
and the pestilence and the _f_ within .... Eze 7:15
and he that is in the city, _f_ .... Eze 7:15
them from the sword, from the _f_ .... Eze 12:16
thereof, and will send _f_ upon it .... Eze 14:13
Jerusalem, the sword, and the _f_ .... Eze 14:21
increase it, and lay no _f_ upon you ..... Eze 36:29
reproach of _f_ among the heathen....... Eze 36:30
that I will send a _f_ in the land .... Amos 8:11
not a _f_ of bread, nor a thirst............ Amos 8:11
when great _f_ was throughout all........ Lk 4:25
space a mighty _f_ in that land .... Lk 15:14
or distress, or persecution, or _f_......... Rom 8:35
one day, death, and mourning, and _f_ .. Rev 18:8

FAMINES

and there shall be _f_, and................. Mt 24:7
places, and there shall be _f_ .... Mk 13:8
shall be in divers places, and _f_ .... Lk 21:11

FAMISH

The soul of the righteous to _f_ .... Prov 10:3
for he will _f_ all the gods of the .... Zeph 2:11

FAMISHED

when all the land of Egypt was _f_ ...... Gen 41:55
and their honourable men are _f_ .... Is 5:13

FAMOUS

_f_ in the congregation, men of .... Num 16:2
which were _f_ in the congregation...... Num 26:9
Ephratah, and be _f_ in Beth-lehem ..... Ruth 4:11
that his name may be _f_ in Israel........ Ruth 4:14
_f_ men, and heads of the house of 1Chr 5:24
_f_ throughout the house of their......... 1Chr 12:30
A man was _f_ according as he had ...... Ps 74:5
And slew _f_ kings .... Ps 136:18
and slew became _f_ among women...... Eze 23:10
and the daughters of _f_ nations.......... Eze 32:18

FAN

with the shovel and with the _f_.......... Is 30:24
Thou shalt _f_ them, and the wind .... Is 41:16
daughter of my people, not to _f_ .... Jer 4:11
I will _f_ them with a _f_ in the .... Jer 15:7
Babylon fanners, that shall _f_ her .... Jer 51:2
Whose _f_ is in his hand, and he .... Mt 3:12
Whose _f_ is in his hand, and he .... Lk 3:17

FANNERS

And will send unto Babylon _f_ .... Jer 51:2

FAR

That be _f_ from thee to do after .... Gen 18:25
the wicked, that be _f_ from thee......... Gen 18:25
out of the city, and not yet _f_ off........ Gen 44:4
only ye shall not go very _f_ away........ Ex 8:28
Keep thee _f_ from a false matter .... Ex 23:7
_f_ off about the tabernacle of the........ Num 2:2
his name there be too _f_ from thee ..... Deut 12:21
or _f_ off from thee, from the one .... Deut 13:7
if the place be too _f_ from thee .... Deut 14:24
which are very _f_ off from thee.......... Deut 20:15
a nation against thee from _f_ .... Deut 28:49
that shall come from a _f_ land........... Deut 29:22
from thee, neither is it _f_ off............. Deut 30:11
an heap very _f_ from the city Adam ... Josh 3:16
go not very _f_ from the city, but .... Josh 8:4
We be come from a _f_ country .... Josh 9:6
From a very _f_ country they.............. Josh 9:9
saying, We are very _f_ from you......... Josh 9:22
for you, and adventured his life _f_ ...... Judg 9:17
they were _f_ from the Zidonians......... Judg 18:7
because it was _f_ from Zidon............. Judg 18:28
by Jebus, the day was _f_ spent .... Judg 19:11
The LORD saith, Be it _f_ from me........ 1Sa 2:30
Jonathan said, _f_ be it from thee 1Sa 20:9
be it _f_ from me.............................. 1Sa 22:15
tarried in a place that was _f_ off 2Sa 15:17
_f_ be it, _f_ be it from thee 2Sa 20:20

_f_ be it from me, that I should 2Sa 20:20
Be it _f_ from me, O LORD, that I......... 2Sa 23:17
but cometh out of a _f_ country for 1Kin 8:41
the land of the enemy, _f_ or near....... 1Kin 8:46
They are come from a _f_ country 2Kin 20:14
but is come from a _f_ country for 2Chr 6:32
unto a land _f_ off or near.................. 2Chr 6:36
And his name spread _f_ abroad 2Chr 26:15
the river, be ye _f_ from thence........... Ezr 6:6
upon the wall, one _f_ from another..... Neh 4:19
king Ahasuerus, both nigh and _f_ .... Est 9:20
His children are _f_ from safety............ Job 5:4
be in thine hand, put it _f_ away.......... Job 11:14
Withdraw thine hand _f_ from me .... Job 13:21
He hath put my brethren _f_ from me ... Job 19:13
of the wicked is _f_ from me............... Job 21:16
of the wicked is _f_ from me............... Job 22:18
iniquity _f_ from thy tabernacles.......... Job 22:23
abhor me, they flee _f_ from me .... Job 30:10
_f_ be it from God, that he should........ Job 34:10
thy judgments are _f_ above out of ...... Ps 10:5
why art thou so _f_ from helping me .... Ps 22:1
Be not _f_ from me............................ Ps 22:11
But be not thou _f_ from me............... Ps 22:19
Hide not thy face _f_ from me............. Ps 27:9
O Lord, be not _f_ from me................. Ps 35:22
O my God, be not _f_ from me .... Ps 38:21
Lo, then would I wander _f_ off .... Ps 55:7
O God, be not _f_ from me .... Ps 71:12
they that are _f_ from thee shall.......... Ps 73:27
away mine acquaintance _f_ from me .... Ps 88:8
and friend hast thou put _f_ from me .... Ps 88:18
thou art exalted _f_ above all gods....... Ps 97:9
As _f_ as the east is from the west....... Ps 103:12
so _f_ hath he removed our .... Ps 103:12
blessing, so let it be _f_ from him......... Ps 109:17
they are _f_ from thy law .... Ps 119:150
Salvation is _f_ from the wicked .... Ps 119:155
and perverse lips put _f_ from thee ...... Prov 4:24
Remove thy way _f_ from her .... Prov 5:8
The LORD is _f_ from the wicked.......... Prov 15:29
more do his friends go _f_ from him ..... Prov 19:7
his soul shall be _f_ from them............ Prov 22:5
shall drive it _f_ from him .... Prov 22:15
so is good news from a _f_ country ...... Prov 25:25
that is near than a brother _f_ off......... Prov 27:10
Remove _f_ from me vanity and lies..... Prov 30:8
for her price is _f_ above rubies........... Prov 31:10
as _f_ as light excelleth darkness......... Eccl 2:13
but it was _f_ from me....................... Eccl 7:23
That which is _f_ off, and exceeding..... Eccl 7:24
an ensign to the nations from _f_ .... Is 5:26
the LORD have removed men _f_ away ... Is 6:12
give ear, all ye of _f_ countries .... Is 8:9
which shall come from _f_ .... Is 10:3
They come from a _f_ country .... Is 13:5
them, and they shall flee _f_ off .... Is 17:13
they shall turn the rivers _f_ away........ Is 19:6
together, which have fled from _f_ .... Is 22:3
thou hadst removed it _f_ unto all........ Is 26:15
removed their heart _f_ from me .... Is 29:13
name of the LORD cometh from _f_ ...... Is 30:27
Hear, ye that are _f_ off, what I .... Is 33:13
the land that is very _f_ off .... Is 33:17
are come from a _f_ country unto me .... Is 39:3
bring my sons from _f_, and my .... Is 43:6
my counsel from a _f_ country .... Is 46:11
that are _f_ from righteousness............ Is 46:12
it shall not be _f_ off, and my .... Is 46:13
and hearken, ye people, from _f_ .... Is 49:1
Behold, these shall come from _f_........ Is 49:12
swallowed thee up shall be _f_ away ..... Is 49:19
thou shalt be _f_ from oppression .... Is 54:14
didst send thy messengers _f_ off......... Is 57:9
Peace, peace to him that is _f_ off .... Is 57:19
Therefore is judgment _f_ from us .... Is 59:9
but it is _f_ off from us...................... Is 59:11
thy sons shall come from _f_ .... Is 60:4
first, to bring thy sons from _f_ .... Is 60:9
me, that they are gone _f_ from me ...... Jer 2:5
watchers come from a _f_ country........ Jer 4:16
bring a nation upon you from _f_......... Jer 5:15
the sweet came from a _f_ country....... Jer 6:20
of them that dwell in a _f_ country ...... Jer 8:19
mouth, and _f_ from their reins........... Jer 12:2
And all the kings of the north, _f_ .... Jer 25:26
to remove you _f_ from your land .... Jer 27:10
of the land of Moab, _f_ or near.......... Jer 48:24
Thus _f_ is the judgment of Moab .... Jer 48:47
Flee, get you _f_ off, dwell deep.......... Jer 49:30
Thus _f_ are the words of Jeremiah...... Jer 51:64
relieve my soul is _f_ from me .... Lam 1:16
removed my soul _f_ off from peace..... Lam 3:17
He that is _f_ off shall die of the .... Eze 6:12
have I set it _f_ from them.................. Eze 7:20
that I should go _f_ off from my .... Eze 8:6
Said, Get you _f_ from the LORD.......... Eze 11:15
cast them _f_ off among the heathen .... Eze 11:16
of the times that are _f_ off .... Eze 12:27
and those that be _f_ from thee .... Eze 22:5
have sent for men to come from _f_ ..... Eze 23:40
_f_ from me, and I will dwell in the ..... Eze 43:9
that are gone away _f_ from me .... Eze 44:10
that are near, and that are _f_ off .... Dan 9:7
the fourth shall be _f_ richer than........ Dan 11:2
But I will remove _f_ off from you .... Joel 2:20
remove them _f_ from their border ...... Joel 3:6
to the Sabeans, to a people _f_ off....... Joel 3:8
Ye that put _f_ away the evil day,........ Amos 6:3
her that was cast _f_ off and a strong ... Mic 4:7

day shall the decree be f removed .... Mic 7:11
their horsemen shall come from f .... Hab 1:8
they that are f off shall come and .... Zec 6:15
shall remember me in f countries .... Zec 10:9
but their heart is f from me .... Mt 15:8
saying, Be it f from thee, Lord .... Mt 16:22
and went into a f country .... Mt 21:33
a man travelling into a f country .... Mt 25:14
And when the day was now f spent .... Mk 6:35
and now the time is f passed .... Mk 6:35
but their heart is f from me .... Mk 7:6
for divers of them came from f .... Mk 8:3
and went into a f country .... Mk 12:1
Thou art not f from the kingdom .... Mk 12:34
is as a man taking a f journey .... Mk 13:34
he was now not f from the house .... Lk 7:6
took his journey into a f country .... Lk 15:13
f country to receive for himself .... Lk 19:12
went into a f country for a long .... Lk 20:9
and said, Suffer ye thus f .... Lk 22:51
evening, and the day is f spent .... Lk 24:29
led them out as f as to Bethany .... Lk 24:50
(for they were not f from land .... Jn 21:8
Stephen travelled as f as Phenice .... Acts 11:19
that he should go as f as Antioch .... Acts 11:22
though he be not f from every one .... Acts 17:27
for I will send thee f hence unto .... Acts 22:21
to meet us as f as Appii Forum .... Acts 28:15
The night is f spent, the day is .... Rom 13:12
worketh for us a f more exceeding 2Cor 4:17
for we are come as f as to you 2Cor 10:14
f above all principality, and .... Eph 1:21
Jesus ye who sometimes were f off .... Eph 2:13
ascended up f above all heavens .... Eph 4:10
be with Christ; which is f better .... Phil 1:23
And it is yet f more evident .... Heb 7:15

FARE

and look how thy brethren f 1Sa 17:18
so he paid the f thereof, and went .... Jonah 1:3
shall do well. F ye well .... Acts 15:29

FARED

linen, and f sumptuously every day .... Lk 16:19

FAREWELL

but let me first go bid them f .... Lk 9:61
But bade them f, saying, I must .... Acts 18:21
what they had against him. F .... Acts 23:30
Finally, brethren, f 2Cor 13:11

FARM

and went their ways, one to his f .... Mt 22:5

FARTHER

And he went a little f, and fell on .... Mt 26:39
he had gone a little f thence .... Mk 1:19
of Judaea by the f side of Jordan .... Mk 10:1

FARTHING

thou hast paid the uttermost f .... Mt 5:26
Are not two sparrows sold for a f .... Mt 10:29
in two mites, which make a f .... Mk 12:42

FARTHINGS

not five sparrows sold for two f .... Lk 12:6

FASHION

this is the f which thou shalt .... Gen 6:15
f thereof which was shewed thee .... Ex 26:30
the f of almonds in one branch .... Ex 37:19
and according to all the f of it 1Kin 6:38
the priest the f of the altar 2Kin 16:10
did not one f us in the womb .... Job 31:15
the f thereof, and the goings out .... Eze 43:11
saying, We never saw it on this f .... Mk 2:12
the f of his countenance was .... Lk 9:29
to the f that he had seen .... Acts 7:44
for the f of this world passeth 1Cor 7:31
And being found in f as a man .... Phil 2:8
grace of the f of it perisheth .... Jas 1:11

FASHIONED

f it with a graving tool, after .... Ex 32:4
f me together round about .... Job 10:8
Thy hands have made me and f me .... Ps 119:73
which in continuance were f .... Ps 139:16
unto him that I it long ago .... Is 22:11
thy breasts are f, and thine hair .... Eze 16:7
that it may be f like unto his .... Phil 3:21

FASHIONETH

He f their hearts alike .... Ps 33:15
f it with hammers, and worketh it .... Is 44:12
the clay say to him that f it .... Is 45:9

FASHIONING

not f yourselves according to the 1Pet 1:14

FASHIONS

were both according to their f .... Eze 42:11

FAST

For the Lord had f closed up all .... Gen 20:18
for he was f asleep and weary .... Judg 4:21
but we will bind thee f, and .... Judg 15:13
If they bind me f with new ropes .... Judg 16:11
but abide here f by my maidens .... Ruth 2:8
Thou shalt keep f by my young men .... Ruth 2:21
So she kept f by the maidens of .... Ruth 2:23
thou didst f and weep for the 2Sa 12:21
he is dead, wherefore should I f 2Sa 12:23
the letters, saying, Proclaim a f 1Kin 21:9
They proclaimed a f, and set 1Kin 21:12
door, and hold him f at the door 2Kin 6:32
proclaimed a f throughout all 2Chr 20:3

walls, and this work goeth f on .... Ezr 5:8
Then I proclaimed a f there .... Ezr 8:21
f ye for me, and neither eat nor .... Est 4:16
and my maidens will f likewise .... Est 4:16
still he holdeth f his integrity .... Job 2:3
he shall hold it f, but it shall .... Job 8:15
My righteousness I hold f .... Job 27:6
and the clods cleave f together .... Job 38:38
he commanded, and it stood f .... Ps 33:9
For thine arrows stick f in me .... Ps 38:2
say they, cleaveth f unto him .... Ps 41:8
When they f, I will not hear .... Jer 14:12
that they proclaimed a f before .... Jer 36:9
say ye, Stand f, and prepare thee .... Jer 46:14
come, and his affliction hasteth f .... Jer 48:16
took them captives held them f .... Jer 50:33
Sanctify ye a f, call a solemn .... Joel 1:14
the trumpet in Zion, sanctify a f .... Joel 2:15
and he lay, and was f asleep .... Jonah 1:5
believed God, and proclaimed a f .... Jonah 3:5
years, did ye at all f unto me .... Zec 7:5
The f of the fourth month, and the .... Zec 8:19
the f of the fifth .... Zec 8:19
the f of the seventh .... Zec 8:19
and the f of .... Zec 8:19
Moreover when ye f, be not, as .... Mt 6:16
they may appear unto men to f .... Mt 6:16
thou appear not unto men to f .... Mt 6:18
Why do we and the Pharisees oft .... Mt 9:14
f oft, but thy disciples f not .... Mt 9:14
from them, and then shall they f .... Mt 9:15
hold him f .... Mt 26:48
and of the Pharisees used to f .... Mk 2:18
of John and of the Pharisees .... Mk 2:18
but thy disciples f not .... Mk 2:18
children of the bridechamber f .... Mk 2:19
with them, they cannot f .... Mk 2:19
then shall they f in those days .... Mk 2:20
do the disciples of John f often .... Mk 5:33
children of the bridechamber .... Lk 5:34
then shall they f in those days .... Lk 5:35
I twice in the week, I give .... Lk 18:12
made their feet f in the stocks .... Acts 16:24
because the f was now already .... Acts 27:9
and the forepart stuck f, and .... Acts 27:41
stand f in the faith, quit you 1Cor 16:13
Stand f therefore in the liberty .... Gal 5:1
that ye stand f in one spirit .... Phil 1:27
so stand f in the Lord, my dearly .... Phil 4:1
live, if ye stand f in the Lord 1Th 3:8
hold f that which is good 1Th 5:21
Therefore, brethren, stand f 2Th 2:15
Hold f the form of sound words 2Ti 1:13
Holding f the faithful word as he .... Titus 1:9
if we hold f the confidence and .... Heb 3:6
let us hold f our profession .... Heb 4:14
Let us hold f the profession of .... Heb 10:23
and thou holdest f my name .... Rev 2:13
have already hold f till I come .... Rev 2:25
hast received and heard, and hold f .... Rev 3:3
hold that f which thou hast, that .... Rev 3:11

FASTED

f that day until even, and offered .... Judg 20:26
f on that day, and said there, We 1Sa 7:6
a tree at Jabesh, and f seven days 1Sa 31:13
f until even, for Saul, and for 2Sa 1:12
and David f, and went in, and lay 2Sa 12:16
the child was yet alive, I f 2Sa 12:22
sackcloth upon his flesh, and f 1Kin 21:27
oak in Jabesh, and f seven days 1Chr 10:12
So we f and besought our God for .... Ezr 8:23
and mourned certain days, and f .... Neh 1:4
Wherefore have we f, say they, and .... Is 58:3
to the priests, saying, When ye f .... Zec 7:5
And when he had f forty days .... Mt 4:2
they ministered to the Lord, and f .... Acts 13:2
And when they had f and prayed, and .... Acts 13:3

FASTEN

f the wreathen chains to the .... Ex 28:14
thou shalt f in the two ouches .... Ex 28:25
to f it on high upon the mitre .... Ex 39:31
I will f him as a nail in a sure .... Is 22:23
they f it with nails and with .... Jer 10:4

FASTENED

chains f in the two ouches .... Ex 39:18
f his sockets, and set up the .... Ex 40:18
temples, and f it into the ground .... Judg 4:21
she f it with the pin, and said .... Judg 16:14
they f his body to the wall of 1Sa 31:10
f upon his loins in the sheath 2Sa 20:8
be f in the walls of the house 1Kin 6:10
f his head in the temple of Dagon 1Chr 10:10
which were f to the throne, and 2Chr 9:18
f with cords of fine linen and .... Est 1:6
are the foundations thereof f .... Job 38:6
as nails f by the masters of .... Eccl 12:11
shall the nail that is f in the .... Is 22:25
he f it with nails, that it .... Is 41:7

an hand broad, f round about .... Eze 40:43
in the synagogue were f on him .... Lk 4:20
the which when I had f mine eyes .... Acts 11:6
out of the heat, and f on his hand .... Acts 28:3

FASTENING

f his eyes upon him with John, ... Acts 3:4

FASTEST

But thou, when thou f, anoint .... Mt 6:17

FASTING

of Israel were assembled with f .... Neh 9:1
mourning among the Jews, and f .... Est 4:3
I humbled my soul with f .... Ps 35:13
wept, and chastened my soul with f .... Ps 69:10
My knees are weak through f .... Ps 109:24
the Lord's house upon the f day .... Jer 36:6
his palace, and passed the night f .... Dan 6:18
prayer and supplications, with f .... Dan 9:3
me with all your heart, and with f .... Joel 2:12
and I will not send them away f .... Mt 15:32
goeth not out but by prayer and f .... Mt 17:21
them away f to their own houses .... Mk 8:3
by nothing, but by prayer and f .... Mk 9:29
days ago I was f until this hour .... Acts 10:30
church, and had prayed with f .... Acts 14:23
ye have tarried and continued f .... Acts 27:33
that ye may give yourselves to f 1Cor 7:5

FASTINGS

their seed, the matters of the f .... Est 9:31
the temple, but served God with f .... Lk 2:37
in labours, in watchings, in f 2Cor 6:5
in f often, in cold and nakedness 2Cor 11:27

FAT

of his flock and of the f thereof .... Gen 4:4
the seven well favoured and f kine .... Gen 41:4
did eat up the first seven f kine .... Gen 41:20
and ye shall eat the f of the land .... Gen 45:18
Out of Asher his bread shall be f .... Gen 49:20
neither shall the f of my .... Ex 23:18
thou shalt take all the f that .... Ex 29:13
the f that is upon them, and burn .... Ex 29:13
thou shalt take of the ram the f .... Ex 29:22
the f that covereth the inwards, ... Ex 29:22
the f that is upon them, and burn .... Ex 29:22
lay the parts, the head, and the f .... Lev 1:8
pieces, with his head and his f .... Lev 1:12
the f that covereth the inwards, ... Lev 3:3
all the f that is upon the .... Lev 3:3
the f that is on them, which is .... Lev 3:4
the f thereof, and the whole rump, ... Lev 3:9
the f that covereth the inwards .... Lev 3:9
all the f that is upon the .... Lev 3:9
the f that is upon them, which is .... Lev 3:10
the f that covereth the inwards, ... Lev 3:14
all the f that is upon the .... Lev 3:14
the f that is upon them, which is .... Lev 3:15
all the f is the Lord's .... Lev 3:16
that ye eat neither f nor blood .... Lev 3:17
the f of the bullock for the sin .... Lev 4:8
the f that covereth the inwards, ... Lev 4:8
all the f that was upon the .... Lev 4:8
the f that is upon them, which is .... Lev 4:9
he shall take all his f from him .... Lev 4:19
burn all his f upon the altar .... Lev 4:26
as the f of the sacrifice of .... Lev 4:26
shall take away all the f thereof .... Lev 4:31
as the f is taken away from off .... Lev 4:31
shall take away all the f thereof .... Lev 4:35
as the f of the lamb is taken .... Lev 4:35
the f of the peace offerings .... Lev 6:12
offer it all the f thereof .... Lev 7:3
the f that covereth the inwards, ... Lev 7:3
the f that is on them, which is .... Lev 7:4
Ye shall eat no manner of f .... Lev 7:23
the f of the beast that dieth of .... Lev 7:24
the f of that which is torn with .... Lev 7:24
eateth the f of the beast .... Lev 7:25
the f with the breast, it shall .... Lev 7:30
shall burn the f upon the altar .... Lev 7:31
the f of the peace offerings, and .... Lev 7:33
he took all the f that was upon .... Lev 8:16
and the two kidneys, and their f .... Lev 8:16
the head, and the pieces, and the f .... Lev 8:20
And he took the f, and the rump, and .... Lev 8:25
all the f that was upon the .... Lev 8:25
and the two kidneys, and their f .... Lev 8:25
one wafer, and put them on the f .... Lev 8:26
But the f, and the kidneys, and the .... Lev 9:10
the f of the bullock and of the .... Lev 9:19
they put the f upon the breasts, ... Lev 9:20
he burnt the f upon the altar .... Lev 9:20
altar the burnt offering and the f .... Lev 9:24
offerings made by fire of the f .... Lev 10:15
the f of the sin offering shall .... Lev 16:25
burn the f for a sweet savour .... Lev 17:6
land is, whether it be f or lean .... Num 13:20
shalt burn their f at .... Num 18:17
and filled themselves, and waxen f .... Deut 31:20
with f of lambs, and rams of the .... Deut 32:14
with the f of kidneys of wheat .... Deut 32:14
But Jeshurun waxed f, and kicked .... Deut 32:15
thou art waxen f, thou art grown .... Deut 32:15
Which did eat the f thereof .... Deut 32:38
again the f was a very f man .... Judg 3:17
the f closed upon the blade, so .... Judg 3:22
Also before they buried the f 1Sa 2:15
not fail to burn the f presently 1Sa 2:16
to make yourselves f with the 1Sa 2:29
and to hearken than the f of rams 1Sa 15:22

the woman had a *f* calf in the 1Sa 28:24
from the *f* of the mighty, the bow 2Sa 1:22
f cattle by the store of Zoheleth 1Kin 1:9
f cattle and sheep in abundance, ... 1Kin 1:19
f cattle and sheep in abundance, ... 1Kin 1:25
Ten *f* oxen, and twenty oxen out of ... 1Kin 4:23
the *f* of the peace offerings............... 1Kin 8:64
the *f* of the peace offerings............... 1Kin 8:64
And they found *f* pasture and good, ... 1Chr 4:40
the *f* of the peace offerings,............... 2Chr 7:7
and the meat offerings, and the *f* 2Chr 7:7
with the *f* of the peace offerings 2Chr 29:35
offerings and the *f* until night. 2Chr 35:14
unto them, Go your way, eat the *f* ... Neh 8:10
a *f* land, and possessed houses........... Neh 9:25
eat, and were filled, and became *f* ..... Neh 9:25
f land which thou gavest before.......... Neh 9:35
maketh collops of *f* on his flanks......... Job 15:27
They are inclosed in their own *f* .... Ps 17:10
All they that be *f* upon earth .... Ps 22:29
LORD shall be as the *f* of lambs .... Ps 37:20
they shall be *f* and flourishing .... Ps 92:14
Their heart is as *f* as grease .... Ps 119:70
The liberal soul shall be made *f* .... Prov 11:25
of the diligent shall be made *f* .... Prov 13:4
a good report maketh the bones *f* ...... Prov 15:30
trust in the LORD shall be made *f* ...... Prov 28:25
of rams, and the *f* of fed beasts .... Is 1:11
the waste places of the *f* .... Is 5:17
Make the heart of this people *f* .... Is 6:10
send among his *f* ones leanness .... Is 10:16
all people a feast of *f* things, ... Is 25:6
of *f* things full of marrow, of .... Is 25:6
of the *f* valleys of them that are .... Is 28:1
is on the head of the *f* valley .... Is 28:4
of the earth, and it shall be *f* .... Is 30:23
it is made *f* with fatness, and .... Is 34:6
with the *f* of the kidneys of rams .... Is 34:6
and their dust made *f* with fatness ..... Is 34:7
me with the *f* of thy sacrifices .... Is 43:24
in drought, and make *f* thy bones .... Is 58:11
They are waxen *f*, they shine .... Jer 5:28
because ye are grown *f* as the .... Jer 50:11
Ye eat the *f*, and ye clothe you .... Eze 34:3
in a *f* pasture shall they feed .... Eze 34:14
but I will destroy the *f* and the .... Eze 34:16
will judge between the *f* cattle .... Eze 34:20
ye shall eat *f* till ye be full, ... Eze 39:19
when ye offer my bread, the *f*, ... Eze 44:7
before me to offer unto me the *f* .... Eze 44:15
out of the *f* pastures of Israel. .... Eze 45:15
peace offerings of your *f* beasts .... Amos 5:22
by them their portion is *f* .... Hab 1:16
he shall eat the flesh of the *f* .... Zec 11:16

FATFLESHED
seven well favoured kine and *f* .... Gen 41:2
up out of the river seven kine, *f* .... Gen 41:18

FATHER See PREFACE.

Therefore shall a man leave his *f* ...... Gen 2:24
thou shalt be a *f* of many nations ...... Gen 17:4
said, I am God, the God of thy *f*......... Gen 46:3
Honour thy *f* and thy mother .... Ex 20:12
Honour thy *f* and thy mother, as .... Deut 5:16
be my son, and I will be his *f*. 1Chr 22:10
I was a *f* to the poor .... Job 29:16
A *f* of the fatherless, and a judge ..... Ps 68:5
Like as a *f* pitieth his children,.......... Ps 103:13
A wise son maketh a glad *f* .... Prov 10:1
A foolish son is a grief to his *f* .... Prov 17:25
son is the calamity of his *f* .... Prov 19:13
The mighty God, The everlasting *f* ... Is 9:6
Have we not all one *f*....................... Mal 2:10
glorify your *F* which is in heaven....... Mt 5:16
thy *F* which seeth in secret .... Mt 6:4
for your *F* knoweth what things ye ... Mt 6:8
Our *F* which art in heaven,............... Mt 6:9
will of my *F* which is in heaven .... Mt 7:21
before my *F* which is in heaven .... Mt 10:32
before my *F* which is in heaven .... Mt 10:33
He that loveth *f* or mother more .... Mt 10:37
will of my *F* which is in heaven .... Mt 12:50
commanded, saying, Honour thy *F* ... Mt 15:4
this cause shall a man leave *f*............ Mt 19:5
Honour thy *f* and thy mother............ Mt 19:19
or brethren, or sisters, or *f*............... Mt 19:29
call no man your *f* upon the earth ..... Mt 23:9
hand, Come, ye blessed of my *F*....... Mt 25:34
face, and prayed, saying, O my *F*...... Mt 26:39
them in the name of the *F* .... Mt 28:19
For Moses said, Honour thy *f* .... Mk 7:10
cause shall a man leave his *f* .... Mk 10:7
me first to go and bury my *f*. .... Lk 9:59
knoweth who the Son is, but the *F* ... Lk 10:22
Our *F* which art in heaven,.............. Lk 11:2
I will arise and go to my *f*,............... Lk 15:18
bear false witness, Honour thy *f* ...... Lk 18:20
Then said Jesus, *F*, forgive .... Lk 23:34
My *F* worketh hitherto, and I work ... Jn 5:17
Not that any man hath seen the *F* ..... Jn 6:46
it were given unto him of my *F* .... Jn 6:65
they unto him, Where is thy *F* .... Jn 8:19
Ye neither know me, nor my *F* .... Jn 8:19
ye should have known my *F* also ...... Jn 8:19
that he spake to them of the *F* .... Jn 8:27
but as my *F* hath taught me, I .... Jn 8:28
the *F* hath not left me alone.............. Jn 8:29
we have one *F*, even God .... Jn 8:41
As the *F* knoweth me, even so know ... Jn 10:15
I and my *F* are one .... Jn 10:30

and believe, that the *F* is in me .... Jn 10:38
no man cometh unto the *F*, but by ..... Jn 14:6
ye should have known my *F* also .... Jn 14:7
unto him, Lord, shew us the *F* .... Jn 14:8
am in the *F*, and the *F* in me............ Jn 14:11
ye shall know that I am in my *F* .... Jn 14:20
vine, and my *F* is the husbandman..... Jn 15:1
up his eyes to heaven, and said, *F* .... Jn 17:1
Holy *F*, keep through thine own.......... Jn 17:11
as my *F* hath sent me, even so .... Jn 20:21
made thee a *f* of many nations .... Rom 4:17
adoption, whereby we cry, Abba, *F*.... Rom 8:15
to us there is but one God, the *F* 1Cor 8:6
F of our Lord Jesus Christ, which...... 2Cor 11:31
F of all, who is above all, and .... Eph 4:6
Lord, to the glory of God the *F*.......... Phil 2:11
And again, I will be to him a *F*........... Heb 1:5
cometh down from the *F* of lights ..... Jas 1:17
love the *F* hath bestowed upon us 1Jn 3:1
that bear record in heaven, the *F* 1Jn 5:7
set down with my *F* in his throne ...... Rev 3:21

FATHERLESS
not afflict any widow, or *f* child .... Ex 22:22
be widows, and your children *f* .... Ex 22:24
execute the judgment of the *f* .... Deut 10:18
thee), and the stranger, and the *f* ...... Deut 14:29
gates, and the stranger, and the *f* ...... Deut 16:11
Levite, the stranger, and the *f* .... Deut 16:14
of the stranger, nor of the *f* .... Deut 24:17
be for the stranger, for the *f* .... Deut 24:19
be for the stranger, for the *f* .... Deut 24:20
be for the stranger, for the *f* .... Deut 24:21
the Levite, the stranger, the *f* .... Deut 26:12
and unto the stranger, to the *f* .... Deut 26:13
the judgment of the stranger, *f* .... Deut 27:19
Yea, ye overwhelm the *f*, and ye....... Job 6:27
the arms of the *f* have been .... Job 22:9
They drive away the ass of the *f* .... Job 24:3
They pluck the *f* from the breast,....... Job 24:9
the poor that cried, and the *f* .... Job 29:12
the *f* hath not eaten thereof .... Job 31:17
lifted up my hand against the *f* .... Job 31:21
thou art the helper of the *f* .... Ps 10:14
To judge the *f* and the oppressed, ... Ps 10:18
A father of the *f*, and a judge of .... Ps 68:5
Defend the poor and *f* .... Ps 82:3
and the stranger, and murder the *f* .... Ps 94:6
Let his children be *f*, and his .... Ps 109:9
be any to favour his *f* children .... Ps 109:12
he relieveth the *f* and widow .... Ps 146:9
not into the fields of the *f* .... Prov 23:10
the oppressed, judge the *f* .... Is 1:17
they judge not the *f*, neither .... Is 1:23
shall have mercy on their *f* .... Is 9:17
prey, and that they may rob the *f* ..... Is 10:2
not the cause, the cause of the *f* ...... Jer 5:28
oppress the stranger, the *f* .... Jer 7:6
violence to the stranger, the *f* .... Jer 22:3
Leave thy *f* children, I will .... Jer 49:11
We are orphans and *f*, our mothers ... Lam 5:3
in thee have they vexed the *f* .... Eze 22:7
for in thee the *f* findeth mercy .... Hos 14:3
oppress not the widow, nor the *f* ..... Zec 7:10
in his wages, the widow, and the *f* ... Mal 3:5
Father is this, To visit the *f* .... Jas 1:27

FATHER'S
and they saw not their *f* nakedness .... Gen 9:23
thy kindred, and from thy *f* house .... Gen 12:1
me to wander from my *f* house .... Gen 20:13
which took me from my *f* house .... Gen 24:7
is there room in thy *f* house for .... Gen 24:23
But thou shalt go unto my *f* house .... Gen 24:38
of my kindred, and of my *f* house ..... Gen 24:40
For all the wells which his *f* .... Gen 26:15
come again to my *f* house in peace ... Gen 28:21
Rachel came with her *f* sheep .... Gen 29:9
Rachel that he was her *f* brother .... Gen 29:12
taken away all that was our *f* .... Gen 31:1
of that which was our *f* hath he......... Gen 31:1
I see your *f* countenance, that it .... Gen 31:5
inheritance for us in our *f* house .... Gen 31:14
stolen the images that were her *f* ...... Gen 31:19
sore longedst after thy *f* house .... Gen 31:30
lay with Bilhah his *f* concubine .... Gen 35:22
the sons of Zilpah, his *f* wives.......... Gen 37:2
to feed their *f* flock in Shechem .... Gen 37:12
Remain a widow at thy *f* house......... Gen 38:11
went and dwelt in her *f* house .... Gen 38:11
all my toil, and all my *f* house. .... Gen 41:51
his brethren, and unto his *f* house ..... Gen 46:31
my *f* house, which were in the .... Gen 46:31
all his *f* household, with bread, ... Gen 47:12
and he held up his *f* hand, to .... Gen 48:17
thou wentest up to thy *f* bed; .... Gen 49:4
thy *f* children shall bow down......... Gen 49:8
And Joseph fell upon his *f* face......... Gen 50:1
and his brethren, and his *f* house ...... Gen 50:8
in Egypt, he, and his *f* house .... Gen 50:22
troughs to water their *f* flock. .... Ex 2:16
him Jochebed his *f* sister to wife...... Ex 6:20
my God, and I will exalt him. .... Ex 15:2
priest's office in his *f* stead. .... Lev 16:32
The nakedness of thy *f* wife shalt ..... Lev 18:8
it is thy *f* nakedness .... Lev 18:8
of thy *f* wife's daughter, ... Lev 18:11
the nakedness of thy *f* sister .... Lev 18:12
she is thy *f* near kinswoman .... Lev 18:12
the nakedness of thy *f* brother .... Lev 18:14
his *f* wife hath uncovered his .... Lev 20:11

hath uncovered his *f* nakedness .... Lev 20:11
his *f* daughter, or his mother's.......... Lev 20:17
sister, nor of thy *f* sister .... Lev 20:19
and a returned unto her *f* house, ... Lev 22:13
she shall eat of her *f* meat .... Lev 22:13
with the ensign of their *f* house .... Num 2:2
thy *f* house with their shall bear ...... Num 18:1
among their *f* brethren .... Num 27:7
inheritance unto his *f* brethren .... Num 27:10
being in her *f* house in her youth ..... Num 30:3
yet in her youth in her *f* house .... Num 30:16
unto their *f* brothers' sons .... Num 36:11
damsel to the door of her *f* house, ... Deut 22:21
to play the whore in her *f* house .... Deut 22:21
A man shall not take his *f* wife .... Deut 22:30
nor discover his *f* skirt. .... Deut 22:30
be he that lieth with his *f* wife .... Deut 27:20
because he uncovereth his *f* skirt...... Deut 27:20
shew kindness unto my *f* house, ... Josh 2:12
all thy *f* household, home unto.......... Josh 2:18
her *f* household, and all that she .... Josh 6:25
and I am the least in my *f* house .... Judg 6:15
Take thy *f* young bullock, even .... Judg 6:25
because he feared his *f* household ..... Judg 6:27
went unto his *f* house at Ophrah .... Judg 9:5
up against my *f* house this day .... Judg 9:18
shalt not inherit in our *f* house .... Judg 11:2
me, and expel me out of my *f* house .. Judg 11:7
thee and thy *f* house with fire .... Judg 14:15
and he went up to his *f* house .... Judg 14:19
her *f* house to Beth-lehem-judah. ..... Judg 19:2
she brought him into her *f* house ...... Judg 19:3
arm, and the arm of thy *f* house 1Sa 2:31
on thee, and on all thy *f* house 1Sa 9:20
to feed his *f* sheep at Beth-lehem 1Sa 17:15
make his *f* house free in Israel.......... 1Sa 17:25
Thy servant kept his *f* sheep 1Sa 17:34
go no more home to his *f* house 1Sa 18:2
or my *f* family in Israel, that I 1Sa 18:18
all his *f* house heard it, they 1Sa 22:1
son of Ahitub, and all his *f* house 1Sa 22:11
thou, and all thy *f* house 1Sa 22:16
of all the persons of thy *f* house 1Sa 22:22
destroy my name out of my *f* house .. 1Sa 24:21
thou gone in unto my *f* concubine..... 2Sa 3:7
of Joab, and on all his *f* house 2Sa 3:29
kindness for Jonathan thy *f* sake 2Sa 9:7
be on me, and on my *f* house 2Sa 14:9
have been thy *f* servant hitherto 2Sa 15:34
I have served in thy *f* presence. 2Sa 16:19
Go in unto thy *f* concubines. 2Sa 16:21
Absalom went in unto his *f* 2Sa 16:22
For all of my *f* house were but 2Sa 19:28
against me, and against my *f* house ... 2Sa 24:17
not do it for David thy *f* sake 1Kin 11:12
of his *f* servants with him 1Kin 11:17
shalt be thicker than my *f* loins 1Kin 12:10
thy *f* house, in that ye have 1Kin 18:18
sons, and set him on his *f* throne 2Kin 10:3
and made him king in his *f* stead 2Kin 23:30
his *f* brother king in his stead 2Kin 24:17
forasmuch as he defiled his *f* bed 1Chr 5:1
Shemuel, heads of their *f* house 1Chr 7:2
of Asher, heads of their *f* house 1Chr 7:40
of his *f* house twenty and two 1Chr 12:28
God, be on me, and on my *f* house 1Chr 21:17
according to their *f* house 1Chr 23:11
with understanding, of Huram thy *f* .. 2Chr 2:13
shall be thicker than my *f* loins........ 2Chr 10:10
slain thy brethren of thy *f* house 2Chr 21:13
king in his *f* stead in Jerusalem 2Chr 36:1
they could not shew their *f* house ..... Ezr 2:59
both I and my *f* house have sinned .... Neh 1:6
they could not shew their *f* house ..... Neh 7:61
thy *f* house shall be destroyed .... Est 4:14
thine own people, and thy *f* house ..... Ps 45:10
For I was my *f* son, tender and .... Prov 4:3
keep thy *f* commandment, and .... Prov 6:20
on heareth his *f* instruction .... Prov 13:1
fool despiseth his *f* instruction .... Prov 15:5
thy *f* friend, forsake not .... Prov 27:10
the people, and upon thy *f* house ...... Is 7:17
a glorious throne to his *f* house .... Is 22:23
him all the glory of his *f* house .... Is 22:24
but obey their *f* commandment .... Jer 35:14
that seeth all his *f* sins which. .... Eze 18:14
his sister, his *f* daughter .... Eze 22:11
it new with you in my *F* kingdom ..... Mt 26:29
I must be about my *F* business.......... Lk 2:49
in his own glory, and in his *F* .... Lk 9:26
for it is your *F* good pleasure to .... Lk 12:32
of my *f* have bread enough .... Lk 15:17
wouldest send him to my *f* house ..... Lk 16:27
make not my *F* house an house of .... Jn 2:16
I am come in my *F* name, and ye ...... Jn 5:43
this is the *F* will which hath .... Jn 6:39
the works that I do in my *F* name ..... Jn 10:25
to pluck them out of my *F* hand .... Jn 10:29
In my *F* house are many mansions ... Jn 14:2
not mine, but the *F* which sent me .... Jn 14:24
as I have kept my *F* commandments .. Jn 15:10
up in his *f* house three months .... Acts 7:20
that one should have his *f* wife 1Cor 5:1
having his *f* name written in. .... Rev 14:1

FATHERS See PREFACE.

FATHERS'
be the heads of their *f* houses. .... Ex 6:14
nor thy *f* fathers have seen, ... Ex 10:6
one, according to their *f* houses........ Num 17:6

F

upward, throughout their f house........ Num 26:2
ye are risen up in your f stead......... Num 32:14
the place of my f sepulchres........... Neh 2:3
unto the city of my f sepulchres....... Neh 2:5
eyes were after their f idols.......... Eze 20:24
they discovered their f nakedness...... Eze 22:10
have not done, nor his f fathers....... Dan 11:24
they are beloved for the f sakes....... Rom 11:28

FATHOMS
And sounded, and found it twenty f.. Acts 27:28
again, and found it fifteen f......... Acts 27:28

FATLING
The young lion and the f together... Is 11:6

FATLINGS
and of the oxen, and of the f......... 1Sa 15:9
paces, he sacrificed oxen and f....... 2Sa 6:13
unto the burnt sacrifices of f........ Ps 66:15
bullocks, all of them f of Bashan.... Eze 39:18
my f are killed, and all things...... Mt 22:4

FATNESS
the f of the earth, and plenty of... Gen 27:28
shall be the f of the earth.......... Gen 27:39
thick, thou art covered with f....... Deut 32:15
unto them, Should I leave my f....... Judg 9:9
he covereth his face with his f...... Job 15:27
on thy table should be full of f.... Job 36:16
satisfied with the f of thy house.... Ps 36:8
be satisfied as with marrow and f.... Ps 63:5
and thy paths drop f................. Ps 65:11
Their eyes stand out with f.......... Ps 73:7
and my flesh faileth of f............ Ps 109:24
the f of his flesh shall wax lean.... Is 17:4
with blood, it is made fat with f.... Is 34:6
and their dust made fat with f....... Is 34:7
let your soul delight itself in f.... Is 55:2
the soul of the priests with f....... Jer 31:14
the root and f of the olive tree..... Rom 11:17

FATS
the f shall overflow with wine and.. Joel 2:24
the press is full, the f overflow.... Joel 3:13

FATTED
and fallowdeer, and f fowl............ 1Kin 4:23
the midst of her like f bullocks..... Jer 46:21
And bring hither the f calf.......... Lk 15:23
thy father hath killed the f calf.... Lk 15:27
hast killed for him the f calf....... Lk 15:30

FATTER
f in flesh than all the children..... Dan 1:15

FATTEST
upon them, and slew the f of them.... Ps 78:31
upon the f places of the province.... Dan 11:24

FAULT
but the f is in thine own people..... Ex 5:16
his face, according to his f......... Deut 25:2
I have found no f in him since he.... 1Sa 29:3
with a f concerning this woman....... 2Sa 3:8
prepare themselves without my f...... Ps 59:4
could find none occasion nor f....... Dan 6:4
there any error or f found in him.... Dan 6:4
go and tell him his f between thee... Mt 18:15
unwashen, hands, they found f........ Mk 7:2
people, I find no f in this man...... Lk 23:4
have found no f in this man.......... Lk 23:14
them, I find in him no f at all...... Jn 18:38
may know that I find no f in him..... Jn 19:4
for I find no f in him............... Jn 19:6
unto me, Why doth he yet find f...... Rom 9:19
there is utterly a f among you....... 1Cor 6:7
if a man be overtaken in a f......... Gal 6:1
For finding f with them, he saith.... Heb 8:8
for they are without f before the... Rev 14:5

FAULTLESS
if that first covenant had been f.... Heb 8:7
to present you f before the.......... Jude 24

FAULTS
I do remember my f this day.......... Gen 41:9
cleanse thou me from secret f........ Ps 19:12
Confess your f one to another, and... Jas 5:16
when ye be buffeted for your f....... 1Pet 2:20

FAULTY
this thing as one which is f......... 2Sa 14:13
now shall they be found f............ Hos 10:2

FAVOUR
now I have found f in thy sight...... Gen 18:3
if I have found f in thine eyes...... Gen 30:27
gave him f in the sight of the....... Gen 39:21
I will give this people f in the.... Ex 3:21
the LORD gave the people f in the.... Ex 11:3
the LORD gave the people f in the.... Ex 12:36
have I not found f in thy sight...... Num 11:11
if I have found f in thy sight....... Num 11:15
that she find no f in his eyes....... Deut 24:1
the old, nor shew f to the young..... Deut 28:50
O Naphtali, satisfied with f......... Deut 33:23
and that they might have no f........ Josh 11:20
Let me find f in thy sight, my....... Ruth 2:13
was in f both with the LORD, and.... 1Sa 2:26
for he hath found f in my sight..... 1Sa 16:22
if I have found f in thine eyes..... 1Sa 20:29
young men find f in thine eyes...... 1Sa 25:8
nevertheless the lords f thee not... 1Sa 29:6
if I shall find f in the eyes of.... 2Sa 15:25
Hadad found great f in the sight... 1Kin 11:19

servant have found f in thy sight.... Neh 2:5
Esther obtained f in the sight of.... Est 2:15
if in his sight more than all the.... Est 2:17
that she obtained f in his sight..... Est 5:2
If I have found f in the sight of.... Est 5:8
If I have found f in thy sight....... Est 7:3
and if I have found f in his sight... Est 8:5
Thou hast granted me life and f...... Job 10:12
with f wilt thou compass him as..... Ps 5:12
in his f is life...................... Ps 30:5
by thy f thou hast made my.......... Ps 30:7
that f my righteous cause............ Ps 35:27
because thou hadst a f unto them.... Ps 44:3
the people shall intreat thy f...... Ps 45:12
in thy f our horn shall be.......... Ps 89:17
for the time to f her, yea, the..... Ps 102:13
her stones, and f the dust thereof.. Ps 102:14
with the f that thou bearest unto... Ps 106:4
any to f his fatherless children.... Ps 109:12
A good man sheweth f, and lendeth... Ps 112:5
I intreated thy f with my whole.... Ps 119:58
So shalt thou find f and good....... Prov 3:4
and shall obtain f of the LORD...... Prov 8:35
seeketh good procureth f............ Prov 11:27
good man obtaineth f of the LORD.... Prov 12:2
Good understanding giveth f......... Prov 13:15
among the righteous there is f...... Prov 14:9
The king's f is toward a wise....... Prov 14:35
his f is as a cloud of the latter.. Prov 16:15
thing, and obtaineth f of the LORD.. Prov 18:22
will intreat the f of the prince... Prov 19:6
but his f is as dew upon the....... Prov 19:12
findeth no f in his eyes........... Prov 21:10
loving f rather than silver and.... Prov 22:1
f than he that flattereth with.... Prov 28:23
Many seek the ruler's f............ Prov 29:26
F is deceitful, and beauty is vain.. Prov 31:30
nor yet f to men of skill.......... Eccl 9:11
I in his eyes as one that found f.. Song 8:10
Let f be shewed to the wicked,.... Is 26:10
formed them will shew them no f... Is 27:11
but in my f have I had mercy on... Is 60:10
where I will not shew you f....... Jer 16:13
Now God had brought Daniel into f.. Dan 1:9
for thou hast found f with God.... Lk 1:30
stature, and in f with God and man.. Lk 2:52
having f with all the people...... Acts 2:47
his afflictions, and gave him f... Acts 7:10
Who found f before God, and....... Acts 7:46
desired f against him, that he.... Acts 25:3

FAVOURABLE
Be f unto them for our sakes....... Judg 21:22
God, and he will be f unto him..... Job 33:26
and will he be f no more........... Ps 77:7
thou hast been f unto thy land..... Ps 85:1

FAVOURED
Rachel was beautiful and well f.... Gen 29:17
was a goodly person, and well f.... Gen 39:6
of the river seven well f kine..... Gen 41:2
them out of the river, ill f....... Gen 41:3
And the ill f and leanfleshed kine.. Gen 41:4
kine did eat up the seven well f... Gen 41:4
seven kine, fatfleshed and well f.. Gen 41:18
up after them, poor and very ill f.. Gen 41:19
the ill f kine did eat up the...... Gen 41:20
but they were still ill f.......... Gen 41:27
ill f kine that came up after..... Gen 41:27
priests, they f not the elders.... Lam 4:16
whom was no blemish, but well f.... Dan 1:4
Hail, thou that art highly f...... Lk 1:28

FAVOUREST
By this I know that thou f me...... Ps 41:11

FAVOURETH
by him, and said, He that f Joab... 2Sa 20:11

FEAR
the f of you and the dread of you.. Gen 9:2
in a vision, saying, F not, Abram... Gen 15:1
Surely the f of God is not in...... Gen 20:11
f not; for God hath heard......... Gen 21:17
f not, for I am with thee, and.... Gen 26:24
the f of Isaac, had been with me... Gen 31:42
Jacob sware by the f of his....... Gen 31:53
for I f him, lest he will come and.. Gen 32:11
the midwife said unto her, F not... Gen 35:17
for I f God........................ Gen 42:18
he said, Peace be to you, f not.... Gen 43:23
f not to go down into Egypt....... Gen 46:3
And Joseph said unto them, F not... Gen 50:19
Now therefore f not................ Gen 50:21
ye will not yet f the LORD......... Ex 9:30
F ye not, stand still, and see the.. Ex 14:13
F and dread shall fall upon them.. Ex 15:16
people able men, such as f God.... Ex 18:21
Moses said unto the people, F not.. Ex 20:20
that his f may be before your..... Ex 20:20
I will send my f before thee...... Ex 23:27
Ye shall f every man his mother... Lev 19:3
the blind, but shalt f thy God.... Lev 19:14
face of the old man, and f thy God.. Lev 19:32
thou shalt f thy God............... Lev 25:17
but f thy God...................... Lev 25:36
but shalt f thy God................ Lev 25:43
neither f ye the people of the.... Num 14:9
saith unto us: f them not.......... Num 14:9
LORD said unto Moses, F him not.... Num 21:34
f not, neither be discouraged..... Deut 1:21
the f thee upon the nations....... Deut 2:25
The LORD said unto me, F him not... Deut 3:2

Ye shall not f them................ Deut 3:22
that they may learn to f me all.... Deut 4:10
in them, that they would f me...... Deut 5:29
thou mightest f the LORD thy God... Deut 6:2
Thou shalt f the LORD thy God, and.. Deut 6:13
to f the LORD our God, for our..... Deut 6:24
to walk in his ways, and to f him.. Deut 8:6
but to f the LORD thy God, to...... Deut 10:12
Thou shalt f the LORD thy God...... Deut 10:20
your God shall lay the f of you.... Deut 11:25
f him, and keep his commandments,.. Deut 13:4
And all Israel shall hear, and f... Deut 13:11
to f the LORD thy God always....... Deut 14:23
all the people shall hear, and f... Deut 17:13
may learn to f the LORD his God.... Deut 17:19
which remain shall hear, and f..... Deut 19:20
f not, and do not tremble, neither.. Deut 20:3
and all Israel shall hear, and f... Deut 21:21
that thou mayest f this glorious... Deut 28:58
and thou shalt f day and night, and.. Deut 28:66
for the f of thine heart.......... Deut 28:67
heart wherewith thou shalt f...... Deut 28:67
f not, nor be afraid of them...... Deut 31:6
f not, neither be dismayed........ Deut 31:8
f the LORD your God, and observe... Deut 31:12
learn to f the LORD your God, as.. Deut 31:13
that ye might f the LORD your God.. Josh 4:24
f not, neither be thou dismayed... Josh 8:1
LORD said unto Joshua, F them not.. Josh 10:8
f not, nor be dismayed, be strong.. Josh 10:25
done it for f of this thing....... Josh 22:24
Now therefore f the LORD, and..... Josh 24:14
turn in to me; f not.............. Judg 4:18
f not the gods of the Amorites,... Judg 6:10
f not; thou shalt not die......... Judg 6:23
But if thou f to go down, go thou.. Judg 7:10
for f of Abimelech his brother.... Judg 9:21
And now, my daughter, f not....... Ruth 3:11
stood by her said unto her, F not.. 1Sa 4:20
the f of the LORD fell on the..... 1Sa 11:7
If ye will f the LORD, and serve... 1Sa 12:14
said unto the people, F not....... 1Sa 12:20
Only f the LORD, and serve him in.. 1Sa 12:24
and find that day for f of Saul... 1Sa 23:26
Abide thou with me, f not......... 1Sa 23:23
And he said unto him, F not....... 1Sa 23:17
haste to get away for f of Saul... 1Sa 23:26
And David said unto him, F not.... 2Sa 9:7
then kill him, f not.............. 2Sa 13:28
be just, ruling in the f of God... 2Sa 23:3
That they may f thee all the days.. 1Kin 8:40
to f thee, as do thy people....... 1Kin 8:43
And Elijah said unto her, F not... 1Kin 17:13
but I thy servant f the LORD from.. 1Kin 18:12
that thy servant did f the LORD... 2Kin 4:1
And he answered, F not............ 2Kin 6:16
them how they should f the LORD... 2Kin 17:28
they f not the LORD, neither do... 2Kin 17:34
saying, Ye shall not f other gods.. 2Kin 17:35
stretched out arm, him shall ye f.. 2Kin 17:36
and ye shall not f other gods..... 2Kin 17:37
neither shall ye f other gods..... 2Kin 17:38
But the LORD your God ye shall f... 2Kin 17:39
F not to be the servants of the... 2Kin 25:24
the LORD brought the f of him..... 1Chr 14:17
f before him, all the earth....... 1Chr 16:30
f not, nor be dismayed............ 1Chr 28:20
That they may f thee, to walk in a.. 2Chr 6:31
f thee, as doth thy people Israel.. 2Chr 6:33
for the f of the LORD came upon... 2Chr 14:14
the f of the LORD fell upon all... 2Chr 17:10
Wherefore now let the f of the.... 2Chr 19:7
shall ye do in the f of the LORD... 2Chr 19:9
f not, nor be dismayed............ 2Chr 20:17
the f of God was on all the....... 2Chr 20:29
for I was upon them because of... Ezr 3:3
who desire to f thy name.......... Neh 1:11
the f of our God because of the... Neh 5:9
not I, because of the f of God.... Neh 5:15
that would have put me in f....... Neh 6:14
sent letters to put me in f....... Neh 6:19
for the f of the Jews fell upon... Est 8:17
for the f of them fell upon all... Est 9:2
because the f of Mordecai fell.... Est 9:3
Doth Job f God for nought......... Job 1:9
Is not this thy f, thy confidence.. Job 4:6
F came upon me, and trembling,.... Job 4:14
forsaketh the f of the Almighty... Job 6:14
me, and let not his f terrify me... Job 9:34
Then would I speak, and not f him.. Job 9:35
shalt be stedfast, and shalt not f.. Job 11:15
Yea, thou castest off f, and...... Job 15:4
Their houses are safe from f...... Job 21:9
he reprove thee for f of thee..... Job 22:4
thee, and sudden f troubleth thee.. Job 22:10
Dominion and f are with him....... Job 25:2
the f of the LORD, that is wisdom.. Job 28:28
Did I f a great multitude, or did.. Job 31:34
Men do therefore f him............ Job 37:24
her labour is in vain without f... Job 39:16
He mocketh at f, and is not....... Job 39:22
his like, who is made without f... Job 41:33
Serve the LORD with f, and rejoice.. Ps 2:11
in thy f will I worship toward.... Ps 5:7
Put them in f, O LORD............. Ps 9:20
There were they in great f........ Ps 14:5
he honoureth them that f the LORD.. Ps 15:4
The f of the LORD is clean........ Ps 19:9
Ye that f the LORD, praise him.... Ps 22:23
f him, all ye the seed of Israel.. Ps 22:23

my vows before them that *f* him .... Ps 22:25
shadow of death, I will *f* no evil.......... Ps 23:4
the LORD is with them that *f* him.......... Ps 25:14
whom shall I *f*? .... Ps 27:1
against me, my heart shall not *f* .... Ps 27:3
and a *f* to mine acquaintance .... Ps 31:11
f was on every side.......... Ps 31:13
hast laid up for them that *f* thee .... Ps 31:19
Let all the earth *f* the LORD .... Ps 33:8
the LORD is upon them that *f* him.......... Ps 33:18
round about them that *f* him.......... Ps 34:7
O *f* the LORD, ye his saints .... Ps 34:9
is no want to them that *f* him .... Ps 34:9
will teach you the *f* of the LORD .... Ps 34:11
that there is no *f* of God before .... Ps 36:1
many shall see it, and *f*, and shall .... Ps 40:3
Therefore will not we *f*, though .... Ps 46:2
f took hold upon them there, and.......... Ps 48:6
Wherefore should I *f* in the days .... Ps 49:5
righteous also shall see, and *f* .... Ps 52:6
There were they in great *f* .... Ps 53:5
in great *f*, where no *f* was .... Ps 53:5
changes, therefore they *f* not God.......... Ps 55:19
I will not *f* what flesh can do .... Ps 56:4
a banner to them that *f* thee .... Ps 60:4
heritage of those that *f* thy name.......... Ps 61:5
my life from *f* of the enemy .... Ps 64:1
do they shoot at him, and *f* not .... Ps 64:4
And all men shall *f*, and shall .... Ps 64:9
Come and hear, all ye that *f* God .... Ps 66:16
the ends of the earth shall *f* him.......... Ps 67:7
They shall *f* thee as long as the .... Ps 72:5
salvation is nigh them that *f* him.......... Ps 85:9
unite my heart to *f* thy name.......... Ps 86:11
even according to thy *f*, so is.......... Ps 90:11
f before him, all the earth.......... Ps 96:9
shall *f* the name of the LORD .... Ps 102:15
his mercy toward them that *f* him .... Ps 103:11
the LORD pitieth them that *f* him.......... Ps 103:13
everlasting upon them that *f* him.......... Ps 103:17
for the *f* of them fell upon them .... Ps 105:38
given meat unto them that *f* him .... Ps 111:5
The *f* of the LORD is the.......... Ps 111:10
Ye that *f* the LORD, trust in the.......... Ps 115:11
will bless them that *f* the LORD.......... Ps 115:13
Let them now that *f* the LORD say .... Ps 118:4
I will not *f* .... Ps 118:6
servant, who is devoted to thy *f*.......... Ps 119:38
Turn away my reproach which I *f* .... Ps 119:39
companion of all them that *f* thee.......... Ps 119:63
They that *f* thee will be glad .... Ps 119:74
Let those that *f* thee turn unto.......... Ps 119:79
My flesh trembleth for *f* of thee.......... Ps 119:120
ye that *f* the LORD, bless the.......... Ps 135:20
the desire of them that *f* him .... Ps 145:19
pleasure in them that *f* him .... Ps 147:11
The *f* of the LORD is the.......... Prov 1:7
I will mock when your *f* cometh.......... Prov 1:26
When your *f* cometh as desolation,.......... Prov 1:27
did not choose the *f* of the LORD .... Prov 1:29
and shall be quiet from *f* of evil.......... Prov 1:33
thou understand the *f* of the LORD .... Prov 2:5
f the LORD, and depart from evil .... Prov 3:7
Be not afraid of sudden .... Prov 3:25
The *f* of the LORD is to hate evil.......... Prov 8:13
The *f* of the LORD is the.......... Prov 9:10
The *f* of the wicked, it shall .... Prov 10:24
The *f* of the LORD prolongeth days .... Prov 10:27
in the *f* of the LORD is strong.......... Prov 14:26
The *f* of the LORD is a fountain.......... Prov 14:27
Better is little with the *f* of.......... Prov 15:16
The *f* of the LORD is the.......... Prov 15:33
by the *f* of the LORD men depart.......... Prov 16:6
The *f* of the LORD tendeth to life.......... Prov 19:23
The *f* of a king is as the roaring.......... Prov 20:2
the *f* of the LORD are riches, and.......... Prov 22:4
but be thou in the *f* of the LORD .... Prov 23:17
f thou the LORD and the king.......... Prov 24:21
The *f* of man bringeth a snare .... Prov 29:25
it, that men should *f* before him.......... Eccl 3:14
but *f* thou God.......... Eccl 5:7
be well with them that *f* God.......... Eccl 8:12
God, which *f* before him .... Eccl 8:12
f God, and keep his commandments. Eccl 12:13
thigh because of *f* in the night.......... Song 3:8
for *f* of the LORD, and for the.......... Is 2:10
for *f* of the LORD, and for the.......... Is 2:19
for *f* of the LORD, and for the.......... Is 2:21
f not, neither be fainthearted .... Is 7:4
not come thither the *f* of briers .... Is 7:25
neither *f* ye their *f*, nor be.......... Is 8:12
neither *f* ye their *f*, nor be.......... Is 8:12
and let him be your *f*, and let him.......... Is 8:13
knowledge and of the *f* of the LORD .... Is 11:2
in the *f* of the LORD .... Is 11:3
from thy sorrow, and from thy *f*.......... Is 14:3
f because of the shaking, at the .... Is 19:16
hath he turned into *f* unto me.......... Is 21:4
f, and the pit, and the snare, are.......... Is 24:17
of the *f* shall fall into the pit.......... Is 24:18
the terrible nations shall *f* thee.......... Is 25:3
their *f* toward me is taught by .... Is 29:13
shall *f* the God of Israel.......... Is 29:23
over to his strong hold for *f*.......... Is 31:9
because of the *f* of the LORD is treasure.......... Is 33:6
a fearful heart, Be strong, *f* not .... Is 35:4
f thou not; for I am .... Is 41:10
hand, saying unto thee, *f* not .... Is 41:13
f not, thou worm Jacob, and ye men.. Is 41:14
that formed thee, O Israel, *f* not.......... Is 43:1

f not: for I am with thee.......... Is 43:5
f not, O Jacob, my servant.......... Is 44:2
f ye not, neither be afraid .... Is 44:8
yet they shall *f*, and they shall .... Is 44:11
f ye not the reproach of men,.......... Is 51:7
f not; for thou shalt not be ashamed.. Is 54:4
for thou shalt not *f* .... Is 54:14
So shall they *f* the name of the .... Is 59:19
together, and thine heart shall *f* .... Is 60:5
and hardened our heart from thy *f* ... Is 63:17
that my *f* is not in thee, saith.......... Jer 2:19
f ye not me? saith the LORD .... Jer 5:22
Let us now *f* the LORD our God, ... Jer 5:24
the enemy and *f* is on every side .... Jer 6:25
Who would not *f* thee, O King of .... Jer 10:7
defaming of many, *f* on every side.... Jer 20:10
and they shall *f* no more, nor be .... Jer 23:4
did he not *f* the LORD, and.......... Jer 26:19
heard a voice of trembling, of *f* .... Jer 30:5
Therefore *f* thou not, O my.......... Jer 30:10
way, that they may *f* me for ever .... Jer 32:39
I will put my *f* in their hearts,.......... Jer 32:40
and they shall *f* and tremble for .... Jer 33:9
let us go to Jerusalem for *f* of.......... Jer 35:11
for *f* of the army of the Syrians.......... Jer 35:11
Jerusalem for *f* of Pharaoh's army .... Jer 37:11
f not to serve the Chaldeans.......... Jer 40:9
for *f* of Baasha king of Israel.......... Jer 41:9
f not round about, saith the .... Jer 46:27
But *f* not thou, O my servant.......... Jer 46:27
f thou not, O Jacob my servant,.......... Jer 46:28
f, and the pit, and the snare,.......... Jer 48:43
the *f* shall fall into the pit .... Jer 48:44
I will bring a *f* upon thee .... Jer 49:5
to flee, and *f* hath seized on her.......... Jer 49:24
cry unto them, *f* is on every side.......... Jer 49:29
for *f* of the oppressing sword .... Jer 50:16
for the rumour that shall be .... Jer 51:46
f and a snare is come upon us,.......... Lam 3:47
thou saidst, *f* not.......... Lam 3:57
f them not, neither be dismayed.......... Eze 3:9
I will put a *f* in the land of .... Eze 30:13
f my lord the king, who hath .... Dan 1:10
f before the God of Daniel .... Dan 6:26
said he unto me, *f* not, Daniel .... Dan 10:12
O man greatly beloved, *f* not.......... Dan 10:19
shall *f* the LORD and his goodness .... Hos 3:5
f because of the calves of .... Hos 10:5
f not, O land.......... Joel 2:21
lion hath roared, who will not *f* ... Amos 3:8
I *f* the LORD, the God of heaven,.......... Jonah 1:9
God, and shall *f* because of thee .... Mic 7:17
the people did *f* before the LORD ..... Hag 1:12
remaineth among you: *f* ye not .... Hag 2:5
f not, but let your hands be.......... Zec 8:13
to the house of Judah: *f* ye not .... Zec 8:15
Ashkelon shall see it, and *f* .... Zec 9:5
if I be a master, where is my *f*.......... Mal 1:6
for the *f* wherewith he feared me.......... Mal 2:5
f not me, saith the LORD of hosts,.......... Mal 3:5
But unto you that *f* my name shall.......... Mal 4:2
f not to take unto thee Mary thy ... Mt 1:20
f them not therefore .... Mt 10:26
f not them which kill the body,.......... Mt 10:28
but rather *f* him which is able to .... Mt 10:28
f ye not therefore, ye are of .... Mt 10:31
and they cried out for *f* .... Mt 14:26
we *f* the people.......... Mt 21:26
for *f* of him the keepers did .... Mt 28:4
and said unto the women, *f* not ye ... Mt 28:5
quickly from the sepulchre with *f* ... Mt 28:8
was troubled, and *f* fell upon him ... Lk 1:12
said unto him, *f* not, Zacharias.......... Lk 1:13
angel said unto her, *f* not, Mary.......... Lk 1:30
that *f* him from generation to.......... Lk 1:50
f came on all that dwelt round.......... Lk 1:65
enemies might serve him without *f* .. Lk 1:74
the angel said unto them, *f* not .... Lk 2:10
And Jesus said unto Simon, *f* not .... Lk 5:10
God, and were filled with *f* .... Lk 7:16
And there came a *f* on all .... Lk 7:16
for they were taken with great *f* .... Lk 8:37
he answered him, saying, *f* not .... Lk 8:50
will forewarn you whom ye shall *f* ... Lk 12:5
f him, which after he hath killed.......... Lk 12:5
yea, I say unto you, *f* him.......... Lk 12:5
f not, little flock.......... Lk 12:27
f not, little flock,.......... Lk 12:32
himself, Though I *f* not God.......... Lk 18:4
Men's hearts failing them for *f* .... Lk 21:26
him, saying, Dost not thou *f* God .... Lk 23:40
openly of him for *f* of the Jews.......... Jn 7:13
f not, daughter of Sion .... Jn 12:15
but secretly for *f* of the Jews.......... Jn 19:38
were assembled for *f* of the Jews.......... Jn 20:19
And *f* came upon every soul.......... Acts 2:43
great *f* came on all them that .... Acts 5:5
great *f* came upon all the church,.......... Acts 5:11
and walking in the *f* of the Lord.......... Acts 9:31
Men of Israel, and ye that *f* God .... Acts 13:16
I fell on them all, and the name .... Acts 19:17
Saying, *f* not, Paul.......... Acts 27:24
himself for *f* of God before their.......... Rom 3:18
the spirit of bondage again to *f* .... Rom 8:15
Be not highminded, but *f* .... Rom 11:20
to whom custom; *f* to whom .... Rom 13:7
to whom *f*; honour to whom .... Rom 13:7
was with you in weakness, and in *f* .. 1Cor 2:3

that he may be with you without *f* ... 1Cor 16:10
holiness in the *f* of God 2Cor 7:1
what indignation, yea, what *f* 2Cor 7:11
obedience of you all, how with *f* 2Cor 7:15
But I *f*, lest by any means, as.......... 2Cor 11:3
For I *f*, lest, when I come, I 2Cor 12:20
one to another in the *f* of God .... Eph 5:21
according to the flesh, with *f* .... Eph 6:5
bold to speak the word without *f* .... Phil 1:14
out your own salvation with *f* .... Phil 2:12
all, that others also may *f* 1Ti 5:20
hath not given us the spirit of *f* 2Ti 1:7
through *f* of death were all their .... Heb 2:15
us therefore, *f*, lest, a.......... Heb 4:1
not seen as yet, moved with *f* .... Heb 11:7
that Moses said, I exceedingly *f* .... Heb 12:21
with reverence and godly *f* .... Heb 12:28
I will not *f* what man shall do .... Heb 13:6
time of your sojourning here in *f* ... 1Pet 1:17
f God. Honour the king 1Pet 2:17
to your masters with all *f* 1Pet 2:18
conversation coupled with *f* 1Pet 3:2
that is in you with meekness and *f* .. 1Pet 3:15
There is no *f* in love.......... 1Jn 4:18
but perfect love casteth out *f* 1Jn 4:18
because *f* hath torment 1Jn 4:18
you, feeding themselves without *f* ... Jude 12
And others save with *f*, pulling .... Jude 23
upon me, saying unto me, *f* not .... Rev 1:17
f none of those things which thou ... Rev 2:10
great *f* fell upon them which saw .... Rev 11:11
saints, and them that *f* thy name .... Rev 11:18
f God, and give glory to him.......... Rev 14:7
Who shall not *f* thee, O Lord, and ... Rev 15:4
afar off for the *f* of her torment .... Rev 18:10
afar off for the *f* of her torment .... Rev 18:15
ye his servants, and ye that *f* him ... Rev 19:5

FEARED

for he *f* to dwell in Zoar .... Gen 19:30
for he *f* to say, She is my wife.......... Gen 26:7
But the midwives *f* God, and did.......... Ex 1:17
pass, because the midwives *f* God .... Ex 1:21
And Moses *f*, and said, Surely this.... Ex 2:14
He that *f* the word of the LORD .... Ex 9:20
and the people *f* the LORD, and.......... Ex 14:31
and he *f* not God.......... Deut 25:18
newly up, whom your fathers *f* not .... Deut 32:17
Were it not that I *f* the wrath of .... Deut 32:27
and they *f* him, as they *f* .... Josh 4:14
That they *f* greatly, because .... Josh 10:2
because he *f* his father's.......... Judg 6:27
for he, because he was yet a *f* .... Judg 8:20
Samuel *f* to shew Eli the vision 1Sa 3:15
all the people greatly *f* the LORD 1Sa 12:18
for the people *f* the oath.......... 1Sa 14:26
because I *f* the people, and obeyed ... 1Sa 15:24
a word again, because he *f* him 2Sa 3:11
So the Syrians *f* to help the.......... 2Sa 10:19
the servants of David *f* to tell 2Sa 12:18
Adonijah *f* because of Solomon, and ... 1Kin 1:50
and they *f* the king 1Kin 3:28
(Now Obadiah *f* the LORD greatly 1Kin 18:3
of Egypt, and had *f* other gods,.......... 2Kin 17:7
there, that they *f* not the LORD 2Kin 17:25
So they *f* the LORD, and made unto ... 2Kin 17:32
They *f* the LORD, and served their ... 2Kin 17:33
So these nations *f* the LORD, and 2Kin 17:41
he also is to be *f* above all gods ... 1Chr 16:25
And Jehoshaphat *f*, and set himself.... 2Chr 20:3
faithful man, and *f* God above many ... Neh 7:2
and upright, and one that *f* God .... Job 1:1
which I greatly *f* is come upon me ... Job 3:25
Thou, even thou, art to be *f* .... Ps 76:7
the earth *f*, and was still.......... Ps 76:8
unto him that ought to be *f* .... Ps 76:11
on safely, so that they *f* not.......... Ps 78:53
God is greatly to be *f* in the.......... Ps 89:7
he is to be *f* above all gods .... Ps 96:4
with thee, that thou mayest be *f* .... Ps 130:4
The isles saw it, and *f* .... Is 41:5
hast *f* continually every day .... Is 51:13
whom hast thou been afraid or *f* .... Is 57:11
treacherous sister Judah *f* not.......... Jer 3:8
pass, that the sword, which ye *f* .... Jer 42:16
this day, neither have they *f* .... Jer 44:10
Ye have *f* the sword.......... Eze 11:8
trembled and *f* before him.......... Dan 5:19
because we *f* not the LORD.......... Hos 10:3
Then the men *f* the LORD.......... Jonah 1:16
for the fear wherewith he *f* me.......... Mal 2:5
Then they that *f* the LORD spake.......... Mal 3:16
him for them that *f* the LORD.......... Mal 3:16
he *f* the multitude, because they .... Mt 14:5
they *f* the multitude, because.......... Mt 21:46
they greatly, saying, Truly .... Mt 27:54
they *f* exceedingly, and said one ...... Mk 4:41
For Herod *f* John, knowing that he ... Mk 6:20
for they *f* him, because all the.......... Mk 11:18
they *f* the people .... Mk 11:32
lay hold on him, but *f* the people.......... Mk 12:12
they *f* as they entered into the .... Lk 9:34
they *f* to ask him of that saying........ Lk 9:45
which *f* not God, neither regarded .... Lk 18:2
For I *f* thee, because thou art an .... Lk 19:21
they *f* the people .... Lk 20:19
for they *f* the people .... Lk 22:2
parents, because they *f* the Jews.......... Jn 9:22
for they *f* the people, lest they .... Acts 5:26
one that *f* God with all his house ... Acts 10:2
and they *f*, when they heard that .... Acts 16:38

death, and was heard in that he f .... Heb 5:7

FEAREST
for now I know that thou f God .... Gen 22:12
even of old, and thou f me not........... Is 57:11
hand of them whose face thou f.......... Jer 22:25

FEARETH
Behold, Adonijah f king Solomon ... 1Kin 1:51
and an upright man, one that f God....... Job 1:8
and an upright man, one that f God....... Job 2:3
What man is he that f the LORD........... Ps 25:12
is the man that f the LORD .... Ps 112:1
is every one that f the Lord .... Ps 128:1
man be blessed that f the LORD........... Ps 128:4
but he that f the commandment .... Prov 13:13
in his uprightness f the Lord .... Prov 14:2
A wise man f, and departeth from ..... Prov 14:16
Happy is the man that f alway .... Prov 28:14
but a woman that f the LORD............. Prov 31:30
for he that f God shall come............... Eccl 7:18
because he f not before God............... Eccl 8:13
sweareth, as he that f an oath............. Eccl 9:2
Who is among you that f the LORD ...... Is 50:10
a just man, and one that f God........... Acts 10:22
But in every nation he that f him....... Acts 10:35
and whosoever among you f God......... Acts 13:26
He that f is not made perfect in......... 1Jn 4:18

FEARFUL
f in praises, doing wonders................ Ex 15:11
say, What man is there that is.......... Deut 20:8
and f name, THE LORD THY GOD.. Deut 28:58
people, saying, Whosoever is f .... Judg 7:3
Say to them that are of a f heart .... Is 35:4
he saith unto them, Why are ye f .... Mt 8:26
said unto them, Why are ye so f .... Mk 4:40
f sights and great signs shall............. Lk 21:11
But a certain f looking for of.............. Heb 10:27
It is a f thing to fall into the............. Heb 10:31
But the f, and unbelieving, and the .... Rev 21:8

FEARFULLY
for I am f and wonderfully made......... Ps 139:14

FEARFULNESS
F and trembling are come upon me,..... Ps 55:5
My heart panted, f affrighted me........ Is 21:4
f hath surprised the hypocrites .... Is 33:14

FEARING
children cease from f the LORD.......... Josh 22:25
But the woman f and trembling,......... Mk 5:33
f lest Paul should have been.............. Acts 23:10
f lest they should fall into the............. Acts 27:17
Then f lest we should have fallen....... Acts 27:29
himself, f them which were of the ...... Gal 2:12
but in singleness of heart, f God......... Col 3:22
not f the wrath of the king................ Heb 11:27

FEARS
me, and delivered me from all my f ..... Ps 34:4
f shall be in the way, and the............ Eccl 12:5
and will bring their f upon them .... Is 66:4
were fightings, within were f 2Cor 7:5

FEAST
and he made them a f, and did bake .... Gen 19:3
Abraham made a great f the same....... Gen 21:8
And he made them a f, and they did ... Gen 26:30
the men of the place, and made a f...... Gen 29:22
that he made a f unto all his .... Gen 40:20
that they may hold a f unto me in ...... Ex 5:1
we must hold a f unto the LORD .... Ex 10:9
ye shall keep it a f to the LORD......... Ex 12:14
ye shall keep it a f by an................... Ex 12:14
observe the f of unleavened bread....... Ex 12:17
day shall be a f to the LORD.............. Ex 13:6
keep a f unto me in the year .... Ex 23:14
keep the f of unleavened bread .... Ex 23:15
the f of harvest, the firstfruits .... Ex 23:16
the f of ingathering, which is in .... Ex 23:16
To morrow is a f to the LORD............ Ex 32:5
The f of unleavened bread shalt......... Ex 34:18
thou shalt observe the f of weeks....... Ex 34:22
the f of ingathering at the .... Ex 34:22
shall the sacrifice of the f .... Ex 34:25
f of unleavened bread unto the .... Lev 23:6
of tabernacles for seven days............. Lev 23:34
ye shall keep a f unto the LORD......... Lev 23:39
ye shall keep it a f unto the .... Lev 23:41
day of this month is the f .... Num 28:17
ye shall keep a f unto the LORD......... Num 29:12
thou shalt keep the f of weeks........... Deut 16:10
Thou shalt observe the f of................ Deut 16:13
And thou shalt rejoice in thy f.......... Deut 16:14
f unto the LORD thy God in the .... Deut 16:15
in the f of unleavened bread, and ...... Deut 16:16
bread, and in the f of weeks.............. Deut 16:16
and in the f of tabernacles................. Deut 16:16
release, in the f of tabernacles,......... Deut 31:10
and Samson made there a f .... Judg 14:10
me within the seven days of the f ...... Judg 14:12
seven days, while their f lasted.......... Judg 14:17
there is a f of the LORD in .... Judg 21:19
he held a f in his house, like............. 1Sa 25:36
his house, like the f of a king............ 1Sa 25:36
and the men that were with him a f.... 2Sa 3:20
made a f to all his servants............... 1Kin 3:15
at the f in the month Ethanim.......... 1Kin 8:2
And at that time Solomon held a f 1Kin 8:65
ordained a f in the eighth month 1Kin 12:32
like unto the f that is in Judah,......... 1Kin 12:32
ordained a f unto the children of 1Kin 12:33

f which was in the seventh month 2Chr 5:3
Solomon kept the f seven days........... 2Chr 7:8
seven days, and the f seven days........ 2Chr 7:9
even in the f of unleavened bread 2Chr 8:13
bread, and in the f of weeks.............. 2Chr 8:13
and in the f of tabernacles................. 2Chr 8:13
much people to keep the f of............. 2Chr 30:13
present at Jerusalem kept the f 2Chr 30:21
eat throughout the f seven days......... 2Chr 30:22
the f of unleavened bread seven 2Chr 35:17
kept also the f of tabernacles .... Ezr 3:4
kept the f of unleavened bread .... Ezr 6:22
in the f of the seventh month .... Neh 8:14
And they kept the f seven days.......... Neh 8:18
he made a f unto all his princes......... Est 1:3
the king made a f unto all the .... Est 1:5
a f for the women in the royal .... Est 1:9
a great f unto all his princes............. Est 2:18
and his servants, even Esther's f .... Est 2:18
the Jews had joy and gladness, a f ..... Est 8:17
appointed, on our solemn f day.......... Ps 81:3
a merry heart hath a continual f......... Prov 15:15
A f is made for laughter, and wine .... Eccl 10:19
unto all people a f of fat things .... Is 25:6
a f of wines on the lees, of fat........... Is 25:6
LORD, as in the day of a solemn f ..... Lam 2:7
the passover, a f of seven days........... Eze 45:21
seven days of the f he shall .... Eze 45:23
like in the f of the seven days........... Eze 45:25
the king made a great f to a.............. Dan 5:1
her f days, her new moons, and her ... Hos 2:11
in the day of the f of the LORD.......... Hos 9:5
as in the days of the solemn f .... Hos 12:9
I hate, I despise your f days .... Amos 5:21
to keep the f of tabernacles............... Zec 14:16
up to keep the f of tabernacles.......... Zec 14:18
up to keep the f of tabernacles.......... Zec 14:19
two days is the f of the passover .... Mt 26:2
But they said, Not on the f day......... Mt 26:5
of the f of unleavened bread the........ Mt 26:17
Now at that f the governor was......... Mt 27:15
days was the f of the passover........... Mk 14:1
But they said, Not on the f day......... Mk 14:2
Now at that f he released unto .... Mk 15:6
year at the f of the passover............. Lk 2:41
after the custom of the f .... Lk 2:42
him a great f in his own house.......... Lk 5:29
But when thou makest a f, call .... Lk 14:13
Now the f of unleavened bread .... Lk 22:1
release one unto them at the f .... Lk 23:17
bear unto the governor of the f .... Jn 2:8
When the ruler of the f had.............. Jn 2:9
the governor of the f called the .... Jn 2:9
at the passover, in the f day .... Jn 2:23
that he did at Jerusalem at the f .... Jn 4:45
for they also went unto the f .... Jn 4:45
this there was a f of the Jews............ Jn 5:1
a f of the Jews, was nigh.................. Jn 6:4
Now the Jews' f of tabernacles .... Jn 7:8
Go ye up unto this f .... Jn 7:8
I go not up yet unto this f .... Jn 7:8
then went he also up unto the f .... Jn 7:10
Then the Jews sought him at the f ..... Jn 7:11
Now about the midst of the f .... Jn 7:14
last day, that great day of the f .... Jn 7:37
Jerusalem the f of the dedication .... Jn 10:22
that he will not come to the f .... Jn 11:56
people that were come to the f .... Jn 12:12
that came up to worship at the f .... Jn 12:20
Now before the f of the passover,....... Jn 13:1
we have need of against the f .... Jn 13:29
this f that cometh in Jerusalem .... Acts 18:21
Therefore let us keep the f 1Cor 5:8
that believe not bid you to a f 1Cor 10:27
deceivings while they f with you........ 2Pet 2:13
of charity, when they f with you........ Jude 12

FEASTED
f in their houses, every one his.......... Job 1:4

FEASTING
they, and made it a day of f .... Est 9:17
rested, and made it a day of f .... Est 9:18
month Adar a day of gladness and f ... Est 9:19
they should make them days of f .... Est 9:22
days of their f were gone about......... Job 1:5
than to go to the house of f.............. Eccl 7:2
not also go into the house of f .... Jer 16:8

FEASTS
Concerning the f of the LORD........... Lev 23:2
convocations, even these are my f ...... Lev 23:2
These are the f of the LORD.............. Lev 23:4
These are the f of the LORD.............. Lev 23:37
of Israel the f of the LORD............... Lev 23:44
offering, or in your solemn f .... Num 15:3
do unto the LORD in your set f .... Num 29:39
in the new moons, and on the set f 1Chr 23:31
on the solemn f of the LORD our....... 2Chr 2:4
the new moons, and on the solemn f .. 2Chr 8:13
the new moons, and for the set f 2Chr 31:3
of all the set f of the LORD that....... Neh 10:33
of the new moons, for the set f .... Neh 10:33
With hypocritical mockers in f .... Ps 35:16
your appointed f my soul hateth .... Is 1:14
and pipe, and wine, are in their f...... Is 5:12
In their heat I will make their f .... Jer 51:39
because none come to the solemn f .... Lam 1:4
the LORD hath caused the solemn f ... Lam 2:6
of Jerusalem in her solemn f .... Eze 36:38
and drink offerings, in the f .... Eze 45:17
before the LORD in the solemn f ...... Eze 46:9

And in the f and in the solemnities ... Eze 46:11
her sabbaths, and all her solemn f ..... Hos 2:11
I will turn your f into mourning .... Amos 8:10
O Judah, keep thy solemn f .... Nah 1:15
joy and gladness, and cheerful f........ Zec 8:19
the dung of your solemn f .... Mal 2:3
And love the uppermost rooms at f .... Mt 23:6
and the uppermost rooms at f .... Mk 12:39
and the chief rooms at f .... Lk 20:46
are spots in your f of charity............ Jude 12

FEATHERED
f fowls like as the sand of the .... Ps 78:27
Speak unto every f fowl, and to......... Eze 39:17

FEATHERS
pluck away his crop with his f .... Lev 1:16
or wings and f unto the ostrich .... Job 39:13
silver, and her f with yellow gold ...... Ps 68:13
He shall cover thee with his f .... Ps 91:4
wings, longwinged, full of f .... Eze 17:3
eagle with great wings and many f .... Eze 17:7
hairs were grown like eagles' f .... Dan 4:33

FED
Jacob f the rest of Laban's................ Gen 30:36
as he f the asses of Zibeon his .... Gen 36:24
and they f in a meadow................... Gen 41:2
and they f in a meadow................... Gen 41:18
he f them with bread for all............. Gen 47:17
the God which f me all my life .... Gen 48:15
I have f you in the wilderness........... Ex 16:32
f thee with manna, which thou......... Deut 8:3
Who f thee in the wilderness with,.... Deut 8:16
f them, but went not in unto them ... 2Sa 20:3
f them with bread and water............ 1Kin 18:4
f them with bread and water............ 1Kin 18:13
over the herds that f in Sharon......... 1Chr 27:29
land, and verily thou shalt be f .... Ps 37:3
So he f them according to the........... Ps 78:72
He should have f them also with....... Ps 81:16
of rams, and the fat of f beasts......... Is 1:11
when I had f them to the full,.......... Jer 5:7
They were as f horses in the............ Jer 5:8
oil, and honey, wherewith I f thee..... Eze 16:19
the wool, ye kill them that are f .... Eze 34:3
f themselves, and f not my flock........ Eze 34:8
thereof, and all flesh was f of it .... Dan 4:12
they f him with grass like oxen,........ Dan 5:21
and I f the flock.............................. Zec 11:7
saw we thee an hungred, and f thee... Mt 25:37
they that f the swine fled, and .... Mk 5:14
When they that f them saw what....... Lk 8:34
desiring to be f with the crumbs ...... Lk 16:21
I have f you with milk, and not 1Cor 3:2

FEEBLE
But when the cattle were f .... Gen 30:42
even all that were f behind thee .... Deut 25:18
hath many children is waxed f 1Sa 2:5
dead in Hebron, his hands were f 2Sa 4:1
carried all the f of them upon........... 2Chr 28:15
and said, What do these f Jews.......... Neh 4:2
hast strengthened the f knees .... Job 4:4
I am f and sore broken.................... Ps 38:8
there was not one f person among..... Ps 105:37
The conies are but a f folk............... Prov 30:26
remnant shall be very small and f ..... Is 16:14
hands, and confirm the f knees .... Is 35:3
our hands wax f.............................. Jer 6:24
Damascus is waxed f, and turneth..... Jer 49:24
of them, and his hands waxed f .... Jer 50:43
All hands shall be f, and all .... Eze 7:17
melt, and all hands shall be f .... Eze 21:7
he that is f among them at that........ Eze 21:12
the body, which seem to be more f 1Cor 12:22
which hang down, and the f knees .... Heb 12:12

FEEBLEMINDED
that are unruly, comfort the f 1Th 5:14

FEEBLENESS
to their children for fear of hands...... Jer 47:3

FEEBLER
so the f were Laban's, and the.......... Gen 30:42

FEED
F me, I pray thee, with that same...... Gen 25:30
ye the sheep, and go and f them........ Gen 29:7
this thing for me, I will again f .... Gen 30:31
his brethren went to f their .... Gen 37:12
Do not thy brethren f the flock .... Gen 37:13
where they f their flocks .... Gen 37:16
their trade hath been to f cattle .... Gen 46:32
shall f in another man's field .... Ex 22:5
nor herds f before that mount .... Ex 34:3
Saul to f his father's sheep at........... 1Sa 17:15
Thou shalt f my people Israel, and 2Sa 5:2
I commanded to f my people Israel ... 2Sa 7:7
me, and I will f thee with me in 2Sa 19:33
the ravens to f thee there................. 1Kin 17:4
him with bread of affliction and....... 1Kin 22:27
Thou shalt f my people Israel, and 1Chr 11:2
whom I commanded to f my people... 1Chr 17:6
f him with bread of affliction and 2Chr 18:26
take away flocks, and f thereof......... Job 24:2
the worm shall f sweetly on him ...... Job 24:20
f them also, and lift them up for....... Ps 28:9
death shall f on them...................... Ps 49:14
brought him to f Jacob his people .... Ps 78:71
The lips of the righteous f many ...... Prov 10:21
f me with food convenient for me,..... Prov 30:8
f thy kids beside the shepherds'......... Song 1:8

twins, which *f* among the lilies .... Song 4:5
to *f* in the gardens, and to gather .... Song 6:2
the lambs *f* after their manner .... Is 5:17
And the cow and the bear shall *f* .... Is 11:7
the firstborn of the poor shall *f* .... Is 14:30
there shall the calf *f*, and there .... Is 27:10
thy cattle *f* in large pastures .... Is 30:23
He shall *f* his flock like a .... Is 40:11
They shall *f* in the ways, and .... Is 49:9
I will *f* them that oppress thee .... Is 49:26
f thee with the heritage of Jacob .... Is 58:14
f your flocks, and the sons of the .... Is 61:5
wolf and the lamb shall *f* together .... Is 65:25
which shall *f* you with knowledge .... Jer 3:15
they shall *f* every one in his .... Jer 6:3
Behold, I will *f* them, even this .... Jer 9:15
the pastors that *f* my people .... Jer 23:2
over them which shall *f* them .... Jer 23:4
I will *f* them with wormwood, and .... Jer 23:15
he shall *f* on Carmel and Bashan, ... Jer 50:19
They that did *f* delicately are .... Lam 4:5
of Israel that do *f* themselves .... Eze 34:2
not the shepherds *f* the flocks .... Eze 34:2
but ye *f* not the flock .... Eze 34:3
shepherds *f* themselves any more .... Eze 34:10
f them upon the mountains of .... Eze 34:13
I will *f* them in a good pasture .... Eze 34:14
in a fat pasture shall they *f* .... Eze 34:14
I will *f* my flock, and I will .... Eze 34:15
I will *f* them with judgment .... Eze 34:16
over them, and he shall *f* them .... Eze 34:23
he shall *f* them, and he shall be .... Eze 34:23
they that *f* of the portion of his .... Dan 11:26
now the LORD will *f* them as a .... Hos 4:16
and the winepress shall not *f* them .... Hos 9:2
let them not *f*, nor drink water .... Jonah 3:7
f in the strength of the LORD, in .... Mic 5:4
f thy people with thy rod, the .... Mic 7:14
let them *f* in Bashan and Gilead, ... Mic 7:14
they shall *f* thereupon .... Zeph 2:7
for they shall *f* and lie down, and .... Zeph 3:13
f the flock of the slaughter .... Zec 11:4
I will *f* the flock of slaughter, ... Zec 11:7
Then said I, I will not *f* you .... Zec 11:9
nor *f* that that standeth still .... Zec 11:16
him into his fields to *f* swine .... Lk 15:15
He saith unto him, F my lambs .... Jn 21:15
He saith unto him, F my sheep .... Jn 21:16
Jesus saith unto him, F my sheep .... Jn 21:17
to *f* the church of God, which he .... Acts 20:28
if thine enemy hunger, *f* him .... Rom 12:20
bestow all my goods to *f* the poor 1Cor 13:3
F the flock of God which is among 1Pet 5:2
midst of the throne shall *f* them .... Rev 7:17
that they should *f* her there a .... Rev 12:6

FEEDEST
Thou *f* them with the bread of .... Ps 80:5
whom my soul loveth, where thou *f* .... Song 1:7

FEEDETH
mouth of fools *f* on foolishness .... Prov 15:14
he *f* among the lilies .... Song 2:16
he *f* among the lilies .... Song 6:3
He *f* on ashes .... Is 44:20
Ephraim *f* on wind, and followeth .... Hos 12:1
yet your heavenly Father *f* them .... Mt 6:26
and God *f* them .... Lk 12:24
or who *f* a flock, and eateth not 1Cor 9:7

FEEDING
was *f* the flock with his brethren .... Gen 37:2
and the asses *f* beside them .... Job 1:14
them to cease from *f* the flock .... Eze 34:10
the *f* place of the young lions, ... Nah 2:11
from them an herd of many swine *f* .... Mt 8:30
mountains a great herd of swine *f* .... Mk 5:11
of many swine *f* on the mountain .... Lk 8:32
a servant plowing or *f* cattle .... Lk 17:7
f themselves without fear .... Jude 12

FEEL
My father peradventure will *f* me .... Gen 27:12
I pray thee, that I may *f* thee .... Gen 27:21
Suffer me that I may *f* the .... Judg 16:26
Surely he shall not *f* quietness .... Job 20:20
Before your pots can *f* the thorns .... Ps 58:9
commandment shall *f* no evil thing .... Eccl 8:5
if haply they might *f* after him .... Acts 17:27

FEELING
Who being past *f* have given .... Eph 4:19
with the *f* of our infirmities .... Heb 4:15

FEET
you, be fetched, and wash your *f* .... Gen 18:4
tarry all night, and wash your *f* .... Gen 19:2
camels, and water to wash his *f* .... Gen 24:32
the men's *f* that were with him .... Gen 24:32
water, and they washed their *f* .... Gen 43:24
nor a lawgiver from between his *f* .... Gen 49:10
he gathered up his *f* into the bed .... Gen 49:33
put off thy shoes from off thy *f* .... Ex 3:5
of her son, and cast it at his *f* .... Ex 4:25
girded, your shoes on your *f* .... Ex 12:11
there was under his *f* as it were .... Ex 24:10
that are on the four *f* thereof .... Ex 25:26
their hands and their *f* thereat .... Ex 30:19
shall wash their hands and their *f* .... Ex 30:21
that were in the four *f* thereof .... Ex 37:13
their hands and their *f* thereat .... Ex 40:31
the great toes of their right *f* .... Lev 8:24
which have legs above their *f* .... Lev 11:21

things, which have four *f* .... Lev 11:23
or whatsoever hath more *f* among .... Lev 11:42
thing else, go through on my *f* .... Num 20:19
only I will pass through on my *f* .... Deut 2:28
your *f* shall tread shall be yours .... Deut 11:24
cometh out from between her *f* .... Deut 28:57
and they sat down at thy *f* .... Deut 33:3
as soon as the soles of the *f* of .... Josh 3:13
the *f* of the priests that bare .... Josh 3:15
where the priests' *f* stood firm .... Josh 4:3
in the place where the *f* of the .... Josh 4:9
the soles of the priests' *f* were .... Josh 4:18
old shoes and clouted upon their *f* .... Josh 9:5
put your *f* upon the necks of .... Josh 10:24
put their *f* upon the necks of .... Josh 10:24
thy *f* have trodden shall be thine .... Josh 14:9
his *f* in his summer chamber .... Judg 3:24
up with ten thousand men at his *f* .... Judg 4:10
chariot, and fled away on his *f* .... Judg 4:15
f to the tent of Jael the wife of .... Judg 4:17
At her *f* he bowed, he fell, he .... Judg 5:27
at her *f* he bowed, he fell .... Judg 5:27
and they washed their *f*, and did .... Judg 19:21
shalt go in, and uncover his *f* .... Ruth 3:4
came softly, and uncovered his *f* .... Ruth 3:7
and, behold, a woman lay at his *f* .... Ruth 3:8
she lay at his *f* until the .... Ruth 3:14
He will keep the *f* of his saints 1Sa 2:9
up upon his hands and upon his *f* 1Sa 14:13
and Saul went in to cover his *f* 1Sa 24:3
And fell at his *f*, and said, Upon 1Sa 25:24
be a servant to wash the *f* of the 1Sa 25:41
nor thy *f* put into fetters 2Sa 3:34
had a son that was lame in his *f* 2Sa 4:4
and cut off their hands and their *f* 2Sa 4:12
yet a son, which is lame on his *f* 2Sa 9:3
and was lame on both his *f* 2Sa 9:13
down to thy house, and wash thy *f* 2Sa 11:8
and had neither dressed his *f* 2Sa 19:24
and darkness was under his *f* 2Sa 22:10
He maketh my *f* like hinds' 2Sa 22:34
so that my *f* did not slip 2Sa 22:37
yea, they are fallen under my *f* 2Sa 22:39
in his shoes that were on his *f* 1Kin 2:5
put them under the soles of his *f* 1Kin 5:3
Ahijah heard the sound of her *f* 1Kin 14:6
when thy *f* enter into the city, ... 1Kin 14:12
old age he was diseased in his *f* 1Kin 15:23
the hill, she caught him by the *f* 2Kin 4:27
she went in, and fell at his *f* 2Kin 4:37
of his master's *f* behind him 2Kin 6:32
of her than the skull, and the *f* 2Kin 9:35
he revived, and stood up on his *f* 2Kin 13:21
with the sole of my *f* have I 2Kin 19:24
Neither will I make the *f* of 2Kin 21:8
the king stood up upon his *f* 1Chr 28:2
and they stood on their *f*, and 2Chr 3:13
his reign was diseased in his *f* 2Chr 16:12
not old, and their *f* swelled not .... Neh 9:21
the king, and fell down at his *f* .... Est 8:3
f is as a lamp despised in the .... Job 12:5
Thou puttest my *f* also in the .... Job 13:27
a print upon the heels of my *f* .... Job 13:27
is cast into a net by his own *f* .... Job 18:8
side, and shall drive him to his *f* .... Job 18:11
the blind, and I was I to the lame .... Job 29:15
they push away my *f*, and they .... Job 30:12
He putteth my *f* in the stocks .... Job 33:11
hast put all things under their *f* .... Ps 8:6
and darkness was under his *f* .... Ps 18:9
He maketh my *f* like hinds' *f* .... Ps 18:33
under me, that my *f* did not slip .... Ps 18:36
they are fallen under my *f* .... Ps 18:38
they pierced my hands and my *f* .... Ps 22:16
shall pluck my *f* out of the net .... Ps 25:15
hast set my *f* in a large room .... Ps 31:8
clay, and set my *f* upon a rock, and .... Ps 40:2
us, and the nations under our *f* .... Ps 47:3
thou deliver my *f* from falling .... Ps 56:13
he shall wash his *f* in the blood .... Ps 58:10
suffereth not our *f* to be moved .... Ps 66:9
as for me, my *f* were almost gone .... Ps 73:2
Lift up thy *f* unto the perpetual .... Ps 74:3
dragon shalt thou trample under *f* .... Ps 91:13
Whose *f* they hurt with fetters .... Ps 105:18
f have they, but they walk not .... Ps 115:7
from tears, and my *f* from falling .... Ps 116:8
turned my *f* unto thy testimonies .... Ps 119:59
my *f* from every evil way, that I .... Ps 119:101
The word is a lamp unto my *f* .... Ps 119:105
Our *f* shall stand within thy .... Ps 122:2
For their *f* run to evil, and make .... Prov 1:16
Ponder the path of thy *f*, and let .... Prov 4:26
Her *f* go down to death .... Prov 5:5
his eyes, he speaketh with his *f* .... Prov 6:13
f that be swift in running to .... Prov 6:18
hot coals, and his *f* not be burned .... Prov 6:28
her *f* abide not in her house .... Prov 7:11
that hasteth with his *f* sinneth .... Prov 19:2
hand of a fool cutteth off the *f* .... Prov 26:6
spreadeth a net for his *f* .... Prov 29:5
I have washed my *f* .... Song 5:3
beautiful are thy *f* with shoes .... Song 7:1
and making a tinkling with their *f* .... Is 3:16
tinkling ornaments about their *f* .... Is 3:18
and with twain he covered his *f* .... Is 6:2
the head, and the hair of the *f* .... Is 7:20
as a carcase trodden under *f* .... Is 14:19
her own *f* shall carry her afar .... Is 23:7
even the *f* of the poor, and the .... Is 26:6

Ephraim, shall be trodden under *f* .... Is 28:3
forth thither the *f* of the ox .... Is 32:20
with the sole of my *f* have I .... Is 37:25
that he had not gone while his *f* .... Is 41:3
and lick up the dust of thy *f* .... Is 49:23
the *f* of him that bringeth good .... Is 52:7
Their *f* run to evil, and they make .... Is 59:7
make the place of my *f* glorious .... Is 60:13
down at the soles of thy *f* .... Is 60:14
before your *f* stumble upon the .... Jer 13:16
they have not refrained their *f* .... Jer 14:10
take me, and hid snares for my *f* .... Jer 18:22
thy *f* are sunk in the mire, and .... Jer 38:22
he hath spread a net for my *f* .... Lam 1:13
To crush under his *f* all the .... Lam 3:34
And their *f* were straight *f* .... Eze 1:7
the sole of their *f* was like the .... Eze 1:7
me, Son of man, stand upon thy *f* .... Eze 2:1
unto me, and set me upon my *f* .... Eze 2:2
into me, and set me upon my *f* .... Eze 3:24
hast opened thy *f* to every one .... Eze 16:25
and put on thy shoes upon thy *f* .... Eze 24:17
heads, and your shoes upon your *f* .... Eze 24:23
hands, and stamped with thy *f* .... Eze 25:6
troubledst the waters with thy *f* .... Eze 32:2
the *f* residue of your pastures .... Eze 34:18
must foul the residue with your *f* .... Eze 34:18
which ye have trodden with your *f* .... Eze 34:19
which ye have fouled with your *f* .... Eze 34:19
lived, and stood up upon their *f* .... Eze 37:10
and the place of the soles of my *f* .... Eze 43:7
his *f* part of iron and part of .... Dan 2:33
upon his *f* that were of iron .... Dan 2:34
And whereas thou sawest the *f* .... Dan 2:41
toes of the *f* were part of iron .... Dan 2:42
and made stand upon the *f* as a man .... Dan 7:4
the residue with the *f* of it .... Dan 7:7
and stamped the residue with his *f* .... Dan 7:19
his *f* like in colour to polished .... Dan 10:6
the clouds are the dust of his *f* .... Nah 1:3
the *f* of him that bringeth good .... Nah 1:15
burning coals went forth at his *f* .... Hab 3:5
will make my *f* like hinds' .... Hab 3:19
his *f* shall stand in that day .... Zec 14:4
while they stand upon their *f* .... Zec 14:12
ashes under the soles of your *f* .... Mal 4:3
Their *f* are swift to shed blood .... Rom 3:15
shake off the dust of your *f* .... Mt 10:14
and cast them down at Jesus' *f* .... Mt 15:30
two *f* to be cast into everlasting .... Mt 18:8
fellowservant fell down at his *f* .... Mt 18:29
And they came and held him by the *f* .... Mt 28:9
when he saw him, he fell at his *f* .... Mk 5:22
f for a testimony against them .... Mk 6:11
of him, and came and fell at his *f* .... Mk 7:25
than having two *f* to be cast into .... Mk 9:45
to guide our *f* into the way of .... Lk 1:79
stood at his *f* behind him weeping, ... Lk 7:38
and began to wash his *f* with tears .... Lk 7:38
of her head, and kissed his *f* .... Lk 7:38
thou gavest me no water for my *f* .... Lk 7:44
she hath washed my *f* with tears .... Lk 7:44
hath not ceased to kiss my *f* .... Lk 7:45
hath anointed my *f* with ointment .... Lk 7:46
sitting at the *f* of Jesus .... Lk 8:35
clothed, and sitting at the *f* of .... Lk 8:35
off the very dust from your *f* for .... Lk 9:5
Mary, which also sat at Jesus' *f* .... Lk 10:39
on his hand, and shoes on his *f* .... Lk 15:22
And fell down on his face at his *f* .... Lk 17:16
Behold my hands and my *f*, that it .... Lk 24:39
he shewed them his hands and his *f* .... Lk 24:40
wiped his *f* with her hair, whose .... Jn 11:2
saw him, she fell down at his *f* .... Jn 11:32
and anointed the *f* of Jesus .... Jn 12:3
wiped his *f* with her hair .... Jn 12:3
and began to wash the disciples' *f* .... Jn 13:5
him, Lord, dost thou wash my *f* .... Jn 13:6
him, Thou shalt never wash my *f* .... Jn 13:8
unto him, Lord, not my *f* only .... Jn 13:9
needeth not save to wash his *f* .... Jn 13:10
So after he had washed their *f* .... Jn 13:12
and Master, have washed your *f* .... Jn 13:14
ought to wash one another's *f* .... Jn 13:14
the head, and the other at the *f* .... Jn 20:12
and immediately his *f* and ancle .... Acts 3:7
laid them down at the apostles' *f* .... Acts 4:35
laid them down at the apostles' *f* .... Acts 4:37
and laid it at the apostles' *f* .... Acts 5:2
of them which have buried .... Acts 5:9
she down straightway at his *f* .... Acts 5:10
him, Put off thy shoes from thy *f* .... Acts 7:33
their clothes at a young man's *f* .... Acts 7:58
met him, and fell down at his *f* .... Acts 10:25
whose shoes of his *f* I am not .... Acts 13:25
the dust of their *f* against them .... Acts 13:51
man at Lystra, impotent in his *f* .... Acts 14:8
voice, Stand upright on thy *f* .... Acts 14:10
made their *f* fast in the stocks .... Acts 16:24
and bound his own hands and *f* .... Acts 21:11
in this city at the *f* of Gamaliel .... Acts 22:3
But rise, and stand upon thy *f* .... Acts 26:16
Their *f* are swift to shed blood .... Rom 3:15
How beautiful are the *f* of them .... Rom 10:15
bruise Satan under your *f* shortly .... Rom 16:20
put again the head to the *f* 1Cor 12:21
hath put all enemies under his *f* 1Cor 15:25
hath put all things under his *f* 1Cor 15:27
put all things under his *f* .... Eph 1:22
your *f* shod with the preparation .... Eph 6:15

F

if she have washed the saints' *f*................ 1Ti 5:10
things in subjection under his *f*................. Heb 2:8
And make straight paths for your *f*... Heb 12:13
his *f* like unto fine brass, as if................ Rev 1:15
saw him, I fell at his *f* as dead............... Rev 1:17
his *f* are like the brass......................... Rev 2:18
to come and worship before thy *f*.......... Rev 3:9
sun, and his *f* as pillars of fire................ Rev 10:1
them, and they stood upon their *f*......... Rev 11:11
the sun, and the moon under her *f*......... Rev 12:1
his *f* were as the *f* of a bear.................. Rev 13:2
I fell at his *f* to worship him.................. Rev 19:10
f of the angel which shewed me............. Rev 22:8

FEIGN

f thyself to be a mourner, and put......... 2Sa 14:2
that she shall *f* herself to be................... 1Kin 14:5
which should *f* themselves just............... Lk 20:20

FEIGNED

f himself mad in their hands, and......... 1Sa 21:13
that goeth not out of *f* lips...................... Ps 17:1
covetousness shall they with *f*.................. 2Pet 2:3

FEIGNEDLY

me with her whole heart, but *f*................ Jer 3:10

FEIGNEST

why *f* thou thyself to be another............ 1Kin 14:6
but thou *f* them out of thine own........... Neh 6:8

FELIX' (fe'-lix) See FELIX. A Roman procurator of Judea.

him safe unto *F* the governor.................. Acts 23:24
governor *F* sendeth greeting.................... Acts 23:26
and in all places, most noble *F*............... Acts 24:3
when *F* heard these things, having........ Acts 24:22
when *F* came with his wife...................... Acts 24:24
I trembled, and answered, Go thy............ Acts 24:25
and *F*, willing to shew the Jews a.......... Acts 24:27
a certain man left in bonds by *F*............ Acts 25:14

FELIX' (fe'-lix)

Porcius Festus came into *F* room............ Acts 24:27

FELL

very wroth, and his countenance *f*......... Gen 4:5
and Gomorrah fled, and *f* there............. Gen 14:10
down, a deep sleep *f* upon Abram.......... Gen 15:12
of great darkness *f* upon him................. Gen 15:12
for his *f* upon his face............................ Gen 17:3
Then Abraham *f* upon his face, and...... Gen 17:17
f on his neck, and kissed him................ Gen 33:4
they *f* before him on the ground............ Gen 44:14
he *f* upon his brother Benjamin's.......... Gen 45:14
he *f* on his neck, and wept on his.......... Gen 46:29
Joseph *f* upon his father's face,............. Gen 50:1
went and *f* down before his face............ Gen 50:18
there *f* of the people that day................. Ex 32:28
they shouted, and *f* on their faces......... Lev 9:24
goat upon which the LORD's lot *f*........... Lev 16:9
on which the lot *f* to be the.................... Lev 16:10
that was among them *f* a lusting........... Num 11:4
when the dew *f* upon the camp in.......... Num 11:9
in the night, the manna *f* upon it........... Num 11:9
Aaron *f* on their faces before all.......... Num 14:5
heard it, he *f* upon his face..................... Num 14:5
they *f* upon their faces, and said,......... Num 16:4
And they *f* upon their faces.................... Num 16:45
and they *f* upon their faces..................... Num 20:6
the LORD, she *f* down under Balaam..... Num 22:27
his head, and *f* flat on his face.............. Num 22:31
f down before the LORD, as at............... Deut 9:18
Thus I *f* down before the LORD................ Deut 9:25
nights, as I *f* down at the first............... Deut 9:25
Joshua *f* on his face to the earth........... Josh 5:14
shout, that the wall *f* down flat.............. Josh 6:20
f to the earth upon his face.................... Josh 7:6
it was, that all that *f* that day................ Josh 8:25
and they *f* upon them............................. Josh 11:7
Joseph *f* from Jordan by Jericho............ Josh 16:1
there *f* ten portions to Manasseh,......... Josh 17:5
wrath *f* on all the congregation............. Josh 22:20
all the host of Sisera *f* upon the........... Judg 4:16
At her feet he bowed, he *f*..................... Judg 5:27
at her feet he bowed, he *f*...................... Judg 5:27
he bowed, there he *f* down dead,.......... Judg 5:27
a tent, and smote it that it *f*................... Judg 7:13
for there *f* an hundred and twenty......... Judg 8:10
there *f* at that time of the...................... Judg 12:6
f on their faces to the ground................. Judg 13:20
the house *f* upon the lords, and............. Judg 16:30
f down at the door of the man's............. Judg 19:26
there *f* of Benjamin eighteen.................. Judg 20:44
So that all which *f* that day of............... Judg 20:46
Then she *f* on her face, and bowed....... Ruth 2:10
for there *f* of Israel thirty...................... 1Sa 4:10
that he *f* from off the seat....................... 1Sa 4:18
fear of the LORD *f* on the people........... 1Sa 11:7
and I *f* before Jonathan.......................... 1Sa 14:13
he *f* upon his face to the earth.............. 1Sa 17:49
f down by the way to Shaaraim............. 1Sa 17:52
f on his face to the ground, and............ 1Sa 20:41
he *f* upon the priests, and slew on........ 1Sa 22:18
before David fell on her face, and.......... 1Sa 25:23
f at his feet, and said, Upon me,............ 1Sa 25:24
Then Saul *f* straightway all along......... 1Sa 28:20
since he *f* unto me unto this day........... 1Sa 29:3
because three days agone I *f* sick.......... 1Sa 30:13
f down slain in mount Gilboa................. 1Sa 31:1
Saul took a sword, and *f* upon it........... 1Sa 31:4
he likewise upon his sword, and.............. 1Sa 31:5
that he *f* to the earth, and did............... 2Sa 1:2

so they *f* down together.......................... 2Sa 2:16
he *f* down there, and died in the............ 2Sa 2:23
to the place where Asahel *f* down.......... 2Sa 2:23
she made haste to flee, that he *f*........... 2Sa 4:4
David, he *f* on his face, and did............ 2Sa 9:6
there *f* some of the people of the......... 2Sa 11:17
that he *f* sick for his sister..................... 2Sa 13:2
she *f* on her face to the ground,............ 2Sa 14:4
Joab *f* to the ground on his face,........... 2Sa 14:22
he *f* down to the earth upon his............ 2Sa 18:28
of Gera *f* down before the king.............. 2Sa 19:18
and as he went forth it *f* out.................. 2Sa 20:8
they *f* all seven together, and............... 2Sa 21:9
f by the hand of David, and by the....... 2Sa 21:22
he *f* upon him that he died..................... 1Kin 2:25
who *f* upon two men more righteous..... 1Kin 2:32
up, and *f* upon him, and slew him........ 1Kin 2:34
out, and *f* upon him, that he died......... 1Kin 2:46
Abijah the son of Jeroboam *f* sick........ 1Kin 14:1
the mistress of the house, *f* sick........... 1Kin 17:17
f on his face, and said, Art thou........... 1Kin 18:7
Then the fire of the LORD *f*.................... 1Kin 18:38
saw it, they *f* on their faces.................. 1Kin 18:39
and there a wall *f* upon twenty............. 1Kin 20:30
Ahaziah *f* down through a lattice.......... 2Kin 1:2
f on his knees before Elijah, and.......... 2Kin 1:13
mantle of Elijah that *f* from him........... 2Kin 2:13
mantle of Elijah that *f* from him........... 2Kin 2:14
shall *f* every good tree, and stop........... 2Kin 3:19
it *f* on a day, that Elisha passed........... 2Kin 4:8
it *f* on a day, that he came.................... 2Kin 4:11
it *f* on a day, that he went out.............. 2Kin 4:18
at his feet, and bowed herself................. 2Kin 4:37
the ax head *f* into the water.................. 2Kin 6:5
the man of God said, Where *f* it........... 2Kin 6:6
And so it *f* out unto him......................... 2Kin 7:20
the fugitives that *f* away to the............ 2Kin 25:11
Hagarites, who *f* by their hand............. 1Chr 5:10
For there *f* down many slain,................ 1Chr 5:22
f down slain in mount Gilboa................. 1Chr 10:1
Saul took a sword, and *f* upon it........... 1Chr 10:4
he likewise on the sword, and................. 1Chr 10:5
there *f* some of Manasseh to David...... 1Chr 12:19
there *f* to him of Manasseh, Adnah...... 1Chr 12:20
they *f* by the hand of David, and.......... 1Chr 20:8
there *f* of Israel seventy....................... 1Chr 21:14
in sackcloth, *f* upon their faces............ 1Chr 21:16
the lot eastward *f* to Shelemiah............ 1Chr 26:14
because there *f* wrath for it................... 1Chr 27:24
so there *f* down slain of Israel.............. 2Chr 13:17
for they *f* to him out of Israel.............. 2Chr 15:9
the fear of the LORD *f* upon all............. 2Chr 17:10
of Jerusalem *f* before the LORD............. 2Chr 20:18
his bowels *f* out by reason of his.......... 2Chr 21:19
f upon the cities of Judah, from........... 2Chr 25:13
I *f* upon my knees, and spread out........ Ezr 9:5
f down at his feet, and besought........... Est 8:3
the fear of the Jews *f* upon them.......... Est 8:17
fear of them *f* upon all the.................... Est 9:2
the fear of Mordecai *f* upon them........ Est 9:3
And the Sabeans *f* upon them............... Job 1:15
f upon the camels, and have................. Job 1:17
it *f* upon the young men, and they....... Job 1:19
f down upon the ground, and................ Job 1:20
up my flesh, they stumbled and *f*......... Ps 27:2
Their priests *f* by the sword................... Ps 78:64
for the fear of them *f* upon them........... Ps 105:38
they *f* down, and there was none to....... Ps 107:12
in the city, and those that *f* away.......... Jer 39:9
that *f* to him, with the rest of.............. Jer 39:9
to fall, yea, one *f* upon another............ Jer 46:16
in the city, and those that *f* away......... Jer 52:15
that *f* to the king of Babylon, and......... Jer 52:15
when her people *f* into the hand.......... Lam 1:7
the children *f* under the wood............... Lam 5:13
I *f* upon my face, and I heard a............. Eze 1:28
and I *f* on my face................................. Eze 3:23
of the LORD GOD *f* there upon me.......... Eze 8:1
that I *f* upon my face, and cried,......... Eze 9:8
the Spirit of the LORD *f* upon me......... Eze 11:5
Then I *f* down upon my face, and.......... Eze 39:23
so I they all by the sword....................... Eze 43:3
and I *f* upon my face.............................. Eze 44:4
Nebuchadnezzar *f* upon his face........... Dan 2:46
f down and worshipped the golden....... Dan 3:7
f down bound into the midst of............. Dan 3:23
there *f* a voice from heaven,................. Dan 4:31
came up, and before whom three *f*....... Dan 7:20
I was afraid, and *f* upon my face.......... Dan 8:17
but a great quaking *f* upon them.......... Dan 10:7
lots, and the lot *f* upon Jonah.............. Jonah 1:7
f down, and worshipped him................. Mt 2:11
and it *f* not: for it was founded........... Mt 7:25
and it *f*: and great was the fall............ Mt 7:27
some seeds *f* by the way side, and....... Mt 13:4
Some *f* upon stony places, where........ Mt 13:5
And some *f* among thorns...................... Mt 13:7
But other *f* into good ground, and......... Mt 13:8
they *f* on their face, and were............... Mt 17:6
The servant therefore *f* down................ Mt 18:26
fellowservant *f* down at his feet........... Mt 18:29
f on his face, and prayed, saying,........ Mt 26:39
f down before him, and cried,.............. Mk 3:11
some *f* by the way side, and the........... Mk 4:4
some *f* on stony ground, where it.......... Mk 4:5
some *f* among thorns, and the.............. Mk 4:7
other *f* on good ground, and did........... Mk 4:8
he saw him, he *f* at his feet,................ Mk 5:22
f down before him, and told him.......... Mk 5:33

of him, and came and *f* at his feet........ Mk 7:25
he *f* on the ground, and wallowed........ Mk 9:20
f on the ground, and prayed that,........ Mk 14:35
was troubled, and fear *f* upon him....... Lk 1:12
he *f* down at Jesus' knees, saying........ Lk 5:8
who seeing Jesus *f* on his face............. Lk 5:12
vehemently, and immediately it *f*........ Lk 6:49
he sowed, some *f* by the way side........ Lk 8:5
And some *f* upon a rock.......................... Lk 8:6
And some *f* among thorns....................... Lk 8:7
other *f* on good ground, and sprang...... Lk 8:8
that which *f* among thorns are.............. Lk 8:14
But as they sailed he *f* asleep................ Lk 8:23
f down before him, and with a loud...... Lk 8:28
he *f* down at Jesus' feet, and................ Lk 8:41
f among thieves, which stripped............ Lk 10:30
unto him that *f* among the thieves....... Lk 10:36
upon whom the tower in Siloam *f*........ Lk 13:4
f on his neck, and kissed him............... Lk 15:20
which *f* from the rich man's table........ Lk 16:21
f down on his face at his feet................ Lk 17:16
she *f* down at his feet, saying.............. Jn 11:32
went backward, and *f* to the ground..... Jn 18:6
which Judas by transgression *f*............. Acts 1:25
and the lot *f* upon Matthias.................. Acts 1:26
hearing these words *f* down.................. Acts 5:5
Then *f* she down straightway at........... Acts 5:10
he had said this, he *f* asleep................ Acts 7:60
he *f* to the earth, and heard a.............. Acts 9:4
immediately there *f* from his eyes........ Acts 9:18
made ready, he *f* into a trance,............ Acts 10:10
f down at his feet, and worshipped....... Acts 10:25
the Holy Ghost *f* on all them................ Acts 10:44
speak, the Holy Ghost *f* on them......... Acts 11:15
his chains *f* off from his hands............ Acts 12:7
immediately there *f* on him a mist...... Acts 13:11
f on sleep, and was laid unto his......... Acts 13:36
f down before Paul and Silas,............... Acts 16:29
fear *f* on them all, and the name......... Acts 19:17
image which *f* down from Jupiter........ Acts 19:35
f down from the third loft, and............ Acts 20:9
f on him, and embracing him said....... Acts 20:10
on Paul's neck, and kissed him,............ Acts 20:37
I *f* unto the ground, and heard a......... Acts 22:7
on them which *f*, severity..................... Rom 11:22
them that reproached thee *f* on me...... Rom 15:3
f in one day three and twenty.............. 1Cor 10:8
sinned, whose carcases *f* in the............ Heb 3:17
faith the walls of Jericho *f* down.......... Heb 11:30
for since the fathers *f* asleep................ 2Pet 3:4
saw him, I *f* at his feet as dead............ Rev 1:17
twenty elders *f* down before the........... Rev 5:8
the four and twenty elders *f* down........ Rev 5:14
stars of heaven *f* unto the earth........... Rev 6:13
f before the throne on their................. Rev 7:11
there *f* a great star from heaven,......... Rev 8:10
it *f* upon the third part of the.............. Rev 8:10
great fear *f* upon them which saw........ Rev 11:11
and the tenth part of the city *f*............ Rev 11:13
f upon their faces, and worshipped....... Rev 11:16
there *f* a noisome and grievous............ Rev 16:2
and the cities of the nations *f*.............. Rev 16:19
there *f* upon men a great hail out........ Rev 16:21
elders and the four beasts *f* down....... Rev 19:4
I *f* at his feet to worship him............... Rev 19:10
I *f* down to worship before the............. Rev 22:8

FELLED

of water, and *f* all the good trees......... 2Kin 3:25

FELLER

no *f* is come up against us...................... Is 14:8

FELLEST

before wicked men, so *f* thou................ 2Sa 3:34

FELLING

But as one was *f* a beam, the ax........... 2Kin 6:5

FELLOES

and their naves, and their *f*................... 1Kin 7:33

FELLOW

This one *f* came in to sojourn, and....... Gen 19:9
Wherefore smitest thou thy *f*................. Ex 2:13
man that told a dream unto his *f*.......... Judg 7:13
his *f* answered and said, This is........... Judg 7:14
every man's sword against his *f*............ Judg 7:22
man's sword was against his *f*.............. 1Sa 14:20
this *f* to play the mad man in my......... 1Sa 21:15
shall this *f* come into my house............ 1Sa 21:15
this *f* hath in the wilderness................. 1Sa 25:21
said unto him, Make this *f* return......... 1Sa 29:4
every one his *f* by the head.................. 2Sa 2:16
Put this *f* in the prison, and feed......... 1Kin 22:27
wherefore came this mad *f* to thee....... 2Kin 9:11
Put this *f* in the prison, and feed......... 2Chr 18:26
fall, the one will lift up his *f*............... Eccl 4:10
and the satyr shall cry to his *f*............ Is 34:14
And they said every one to his *f*......... Jonah 1:7
and against the man that is my *f*......... Zec 13:7
This *f* doth not cast out devils,............ Mt 12:24
And said, This I said, I am able.............. Mt 26:61
This *f* was also with Jesus of.............. Mt 26:71
Of a truth this *f* also was with,........... Lk 22:59
We found this *f* perverting the............. Lk 23:2
as for this *f*, we know not from............ Jn 9:29
This *f* persuadeth men to worship........ Acts 18:13
Away with such a *f* from the earth....... Acts 22:22
have found this man a pestilent *f*........ Acts 24:5
f soldier, but your messenger, and...... Phil 2:25
These only are my *f* workers unto....... Col 4:11

FELLOWCITIZENS
but f with the saints, and of the ...... Eph 2:19

FELLOWDISCIPLES
is called Didymus, unto his f............ Jn 11:16

FELLOWHEIRS
That the Gentiles should be f........... Eph 3:6

FELLOWHELPER
is my partner and f concerning you ... 2Cor 8:23

FELLOWHELPERS
that we might be f to the truth........... 3Jn 8

FELLOWLABOURER
our f in the gospel of Christ, to....... 1Th 3:2
Philemon our dearly beloved, and f ... Philem 1

FELLOWLABOURERS
Clement also, and with other my f ..... Phil 4:3
Aristarchus, Demas, Lucas, my f ..... Philem 24

FELLOWPRISONER
Aristarchus my f saluteth you......... Col 4:10
Epaphras, my f in Christ Jesus, ... Philem 23

FELLOWPRISONERS
and Junia, my kinsmen, and my f ...... Rom 16:7

FELLOW'S
and thrust my sword in his f side 2Sa 2:16

FELLOWS
and bewail my virginity, I and my f ... Judg 11:37
lest angry f run upon thee, and....... Judg 18:25
as one of the vain f shamelessly...... 2Sa 6:20
the oil of gladness above thy f......... Ps 45:7
all his f shall be ashamed .... Is 44:11
and the tribes of Israel his f.......... Eze 37:19
Daniel and his f to be slain .... Dan 2:13
his f should not perish with the .... Dan 2:18
look was more stout than his f......... Dan 7:20
thy f that sit before thee.............. Zec 3:8
markets, and calling unto their f ...... Mt 11:16
certain lewd f of the baser sort........ Acts 17:5
the oil of gladness above thy f......... Heb 1:9

FELLOWSERVANT
his f fell down at his feet, and......... Mt 18:29
also have had compassion on thy f ... Mt 18:33
learned of Epaphras our dear f .... Col 1:7
minister and f in the Lord............. Col 4:7
I am thy f, and of thy brethren .... Rev 19:10
for I am thy f, and of thy............. Rev 22:9

FELLOWSERVANTS
went out, and found one of his f ...... Mt 18:28
So when his f saw what was done, ... Mt 18:31
And shall begin to smite his f......... Mt 24:49
little season, until their f also........ Rev 6:11

FELLOWSHIP
delivered him to keep, or in f.......... Lev 6:2
of iniquity have f with thee............ Ps 94:20
in the apostles' doctrine and f .... Acts 2:42
the f of his Son Jesus Christ our 1Cor 1:9
that ye should have f with devils 1Cor 10:20
for what f hath righteousness.......... 2Cor 6:14
take upon us the f of the............. 2Cor 8:4
and Barnabas the right hands of f .... Gal 2:9
see what is the f of the mystery....... Eph 3:9
have no f with the unfruitful........... Eph 5:11
For your f in the gospel from the ..... Phil 1:5
if any f of the Spirit, if any.......... Phil 2:1
the f of his sufferings, being......... Phil 3:10
that ye also may have f with us 1Jn 1:3
truly our f is with the Father,......... 1Jn 1:3
If we say that we have f with him...... 1Jn 1:6
we have f one with another, and 1Jn 1:7

FELLOWSOLDIER
Apphia, and Archippus our f .... Philem 2

FELT
he f him, and said, The voice is ..... Gen 27:22
even darkness which may be f......... Ex 10:21
have beaten me, and I f it not........ Prov 23:35
she f in her body that she was .... Mk 5:29
beast into the fire, and f no harm..... Acts 28:5

FEMALE
male and f created he them............ Gen 1:27
Male and f created he them........... Gen 5:2
they shall be male and f .... Gen 6:19
thee by sevens, the male and his f ... Gen 7:2
clean by two, the male and his f ...... Gen 7:2
air by sevens, the male and f .... Gen 7:3
into the ark, the male and the f....... Gen 7:9
of all flesh, as God had............. Gen 7:16
whether it be a male or............. Lev 3:1
male or f, he shall offer it........... Lev 3:6
offering for it, a female; for his sin .. Lev 4:28
bring it a f without blemish.......... Lev 4:32
a f from the flock, a lamb or a ...... Lev 5:6
her that hath born a male or a f ..... Lev 12:7
And if it be a f, then thy........... Lev 27:4
shekels, and for the f ten shekels.... Lev 27:5
for the f thy estimation shall be ..... Lev 27:6
shekels, and for the f ten shekels.... Lev 27:7
f shall ye put out, without the....... Num 5:3
figure, the likeness of male or f ..... Deut 4:16
not be male or f barren among you ... Deut 7:14
the beginning made them male and f .. Mk 10:6
creation God made them male and f .. Mk 10:6
free, there is neither male nor f ..... Gal 3:28

FENCE
shall ye be, and as a tottering f....... Ps 62:3

FENCED
in the f cities because of the .... Num 32:17
and Beth-haran, f cities............. Num 32:36
cities were f with high walls......... Deut 3:5
cities great and f up to heaven,..... Deut 9:1
f walls come down, wherein thou .... Deut 28:52
of them entered into f cities......... Josh 10:20
that the cities were great and f ..... Josh 14:12
the f cities are Ziddim, Zer, and.... Josh 19:35
the five locks, both of f cities...... 1Sa 6:18
him, lest he get him f cities......... 2Sa 20:6
touch them must be f with iron...... 2Sa 23:7
And ye shall smite every f city 2Kin 3:19
horses, a f city also, and armour 2Kin 10:2
the watchmen to the f city 2Kin 17:9
of the watchmen to the f city 2Kin 18:8
against all the f cities of Judah...... 2Kin 18:13
waste f cities into ruinous heaps 2Kin 19:25
f cities, with walls, gates, and...... 2Chr 8:5
in Judah and in Benjamin f cities ... 2Chr 11:10
and Benjamin, unto every f city 2Chr 11:23
he took the f cities which 2Chr 12:4
he built f cities in Judah........... 2Chr 14:6
in all the f cities of Judah......... 2Chr 17:2
the f cities throughout all Judah 2Chr 17:19
all the f cities of Judah............ 2Chr 19:5
things, with f cities in Judah....... 2Chr 21:3
and encamped against the f cities.... 2Chr 32:1
war in all the f cities of Judah...... 2Chr 33:14
hast f me with bones and sinews..... Job 10:11
He hath f up my way that I cannot ... Job 19:8
high tower, and upon every f wall ... Is 2:15
And he f it, and gathered out the ... Is 5:2
shall impoverish thy f cities........ Jer 5:17
unto this people a f brasen wall..... Jer 15:20
and ruined cities are become f ...... Eze 36:35
mount, and take the most f cities ... Dan 11:15
and Judah hath multiplied f cities ... Hos 8:14
and alarm against the f cities....... Zeph 1:16

FENS
in the covert of the reed, and ...... Job 40:21

FERRET
And the f, and the chameleon, and... Lev 11:30

FERRY
there went over a f boat to carry 2Sa 19:18

FERVENT
being f in the spirit, he spake ...... Acts 18:25
f in spirit; serving the Lord......... Rom 12:11
mourning, your f mind toward me..... 2Cor 7:7
The effectual f prayer of a......... Jas 5:16
above all things have f charity 1Pet 4:8
elements shall melt with f heat 2Pet 3:10
elements shall melt with f heat 2Pet 3:12

FERVENTLY
always labouring f for you in .... Col 4:12
one another with a pure heart f 1Pet 1:22

FESTUS (fes'-tus) See YESTUS'. A Roman
procurator of Judea.
Porcius F came into Felix' room ...... Acts 24:27
Now when F was come into the ...... Acts 25:1
But F answered, that Paul should .... Acts 25:4
But F, willing to do the Jews a ...... Acts 25:9
Then F, when he had conferred...... Acts 25:12
came unto Caesarea to salute F ..... Acts 25:13
F declared Paul's cause unto the .... Acts 25:14
Then Agrippa said unto F, I would ... Acts 25:22
said, King Agrippa, and all men ..... Acts 25:24
F said with a loud voice, Paul,...... Acts 26:24
said, I am not mad, most noble F .... Acts 26:25
Then said Agrippa unto F, This,..... Acts 26:32

FESTUS' (fes'-tus)
at F commandment Paul was .... Acts 25:23

FETCH
I will f a morsel of bread, and ...... Gen 18:5
f me from thence two good kids of ... Gen 27:9
obey my voice, and go f me them .... Gen 27:13
will send, and f thee from thence..... Gen 27:45
let him f your brother, and ye....... Gen 42:16
flags, she sent her maid to f it ...... Ex 2:5
must we f you water out of this ..... Num 20:10
the border shall f a compass from ... Num 34:5
f him thence, and deliver him into ... Deut 19:12
go into his house to f his pledge .... Deut 24:10
thou shalt not go again to f it ...... Deut 24:19
and from thence will he f thee...... Deut 30:4
the elders of Gilead went to f ...... Judg 11:5
to f virtual for the people, that..... Judg 20:10
Let us f the ark of the covenant 1Sa 4:3
come ye down, and f it up to you 1Sa 6:21
said unto Jesse, Send and f him 1Sa 16:11
f him unto me, for he shall 1Sa 20:31
the young men come over and f it ... 1Sa 26:22
but f a compass behind them, and ... 2Sa 5:23
not f home again his banished...... 2Sa 14:13
To f about this form of speech...... 2Sa 14:20
F me, I pray thee, a little water 1Kin 17:10
And as she was going to f it 1Kin 17:11
he is, that I may send and f him 2Kin 6:13
F quickly Micaiah the son of Imla.... 2Chr 18:8
f olive branches, and pine .... Neh 8:15
I will f my knowledge from afar,.... Job 36:3
Come ye, say they, I will f wine .... Is 56:12
king sent Jehudi to f the roll ...... Jer 36:21

FETCHED
a little water, I pray you, be f....... Gen 18:4
he went, and f, and brought .... Gen 27:14
to Adar, and f a compass to Karkaa ... Josh 15:3
f the carved image, the ephod, and .. Judg 18:18
And they ran and f them thence..... 1Sa 10:23
as though they would have f wheat ... 2Sa 4:6
f him out of the house of Machir, ... 2Sa 9:5
f her to his house, and she became .. 2Sa 11:27
f thence a wise woman, and said..... 2Sa 14:2
sent and f Hiram out of Tyre 1Kin 7:13
f from thence gold, four hundred 1Kin 9:28
they f a compass of seven days'..... 2Kin 3:9
f the rulers over hundreds, with 2Kin 11:4
And they f up, and brought forth 2Chr 1:17
f them, and brought them again 2Chr 12:11
they f forth Urijah out of Egypt,..... Jer 26:23
And from thence we f a compass ..... Acts 28:13

FETCHETH
his hand f a stroke with the axe..... Deut 19:5

FETCHT
f a calf tender and good, and gave.... Gen 18:7

FETTERS
and bound him with f of brass....... Judg 16:21
bound, nor thy feet put into f....... 2Sa 3:34
and bound him with f of brass....... 2Kin 25:7
the thorns, and bound him with f 2Chr 33:11
of Babylon, and bound him in f...... 2Chr 36:6
And if they be bound in f, and be.... Job 36:8
Whose feet they hurt with f........ Ps 105:18
and their nobles with f of iron ...... Ps 149:8
he had been often bound with f ..... Mk 5:4
by him, and the f broken in pieces ... Mk 5:4
kept bound with chains and in f ..... Lk 8:29

FEVER
with a consumption, and with a f .... Deut 28:22
mother laid, and sick of a f......... Mt 8:14
her hand, and the f left her......... Mt 8:15
wife's mother lay sick of a f........ Mk 1:30
and immediately the f left her ...... Mk 1:31
mother was taken with a great f ..... Lk 4:38
stood over her, and rebuked the f ... Lk 4:39
the seventh hour the f left him ..... Jn 4:52
father of Publius lay sick of a f ..... Acts 28:8

FEW
the damsel abide with us a f days ... Gen 24:55
And tarry with him a f days......... Gen 27:44
they seemed unto him but a f days ... Gen 29:20
I being f in number, they shall...... Gen 34:30
f and evil have the days of the ..... Gen 47:9
if there remain but f years unto .... Lev 25:52
cattle, and make thou f in number ... Lev 26:22
when the cloud was a f days upon ... Num 9:20
they be strong or weak, f or many ... Num 13:18
to f thou shalt give the less........ Num 26:54
be divided between many and f ..... Num 26:56
that have f ye shall give .... Num 33:54
that have f ye shall give f......... Num 35:8
ye shall be left f in number .... Deut 4:27
and sojourned there with a f ...... Deut 26:5
And ye shall be left f in number .... Deut 28:62
and let not his men be f .... Deut 33:6
for they are but f .... Josh 7:3
the Lord to save by many or by f ... 1Sa 14:6
those f sheep in the wilderness 1Sa 17:28
empty vessels; borrow not a f 2Kin 4:3
When ye were but f, even a f 1Chr 16:19
When ye were but f, even a f 1Chr 16:19
But the priests were too f 2Chr 29:34
night, I and some f men with me..... Neh 2:12
but the people were f therein ...... Neh 7:4
Are not my days f .... Job 10:20
is born of a woman is of f days...... Job 14:1
When a f years are come, then I .... Job 16:22
they were but a f men in number .... Ps 105:12
yea, very f, and strangers in it ..... Ps 105:12
Let his days be f .... Ps 109:8
therefore let thy words be f........ Eccl 5:2
a little city, and f men within it .... Eccl 9:14
grinders cease because they are f ... Eccl 12:3
and cut off nations not a f .... Is 10:7
trees of his forest shall be f....... Is 10:19
earth are burned, and f men left..... Is 24:6
them, and they shall not be f....... Jer 30:19
(for we are left but a f number) .... Jer 42:2
also take thereof a f in number ..... Eze 5:3
But I will leave a f men of them .... Eze 12:16
but within f days he shall be....... Dan 11:20
life, and f there be that find it .... Mt 7:14
but the labourers are f .... Mt 9:37
said, Seven, and a little fishes ..... Mt 15:34
for many be called, but f chosen .... Mt 20:16
many are called, but f are chosen ... Mt 22:14
been faithful over a f things ...... Mt 25:21
been faithful over a f things ...... Mt 25:23
laid his hands upon a f sick folk .... Mk 6:5
they had a f small fishes .... Mk 8:7
is great, but the labourers are f ... Lk 10:2
shall be beaten with f stripes ..... Lk 12:48
are there f that be saved......... Lk 13:23
and of the chief women not a f ..... Acts 17:4
were Greeks, and of men, not a f ... Acts 17:12
hear us of thy clemency a f words ... Acts 24:4
(as I wrote afore in f words .... Eph 3:3
For they verily for a f days........ Heb 12:10
a letter unto you in f words .... Heb 13:22

FEWER

ark was a preparing, wherein *f*............ 1Pet 3:20
But I have a *f* things against .... Rev 2:14
I have a *f* things against thee .... Rev 2:20
Thou hast a *f* names even in .... Rev 3:4

FEWER

to the *f* ye shall give the less .... Num 33:54

FEWEST

for ye were the *f* of all people .... Deut 7:7

FEWNESS

according to the *f* of years thou .... Lev 25:16

FIDELITY

but shewing all good *f*.......................... Titus 2:10

FIELD

every plant of the *f* before it .... Gen 2:5
herb of the *f* before it grew................. Gen 2:5
God formed every beast of the *f*......... Gen 2:19
air, and to every beast of the *f*............ Gen 2:20
the *f* which the Lord God had made..... Gen 3:1
and above every beast of the *f*............ Gen 3:14
thou shalt eat the herb of the *f*........... Gen 3:18
to pass, when they were in the *f*.......... Gen 4:8
which is in the end of his *f*................... Gen 23:9
the *f* give I thee, and the cave .... Gen 23:11
I will give thee money for the *f*............. Gen 23:13
the *f* of Ephron, which was in.............. Gen 23:17
which was before Mamre, the *f*........... Gen 23:17
all the trees that were in the *f*.............. Gen 23:17
the *f* of Machpelah before Mamre....... Gen 23:19
And the *f*, and the cave that is .... Gen 23:20
meditate in the *f* at the eventide......... Gen 24:63
that walketh in the *f* to meet us........... Gen 24:65
in the *f* of Ephron the son of.............. Gen 25:10
The *f* which Abraham purchased of .... Gen 25:10
a cunning hunter, a man of the *f*......... Gen 25:27
and Esau came from the *f*, and he ...... Gen 25:29
and thy bow, and go out to the *f*......... Gen 27:3
Esau went to the *f* to hunt for............. Gen 27:5
a *f* which the Lord hath blessed.......... Gen 27:27
looked, and behold a well in the *f*........ Gen 29:2
and found mandrakes in the *f*.............. Gen 30:14
came out of the *f* in the evening......... Gen 30:16
Leah to the *f* unto his flock................. Gen 31:4
And he bought a parcel of a *f*............. Gen 33:19
were with his cattle in the *f*................. Gen 34:5
out of the *f* when they heard it............ Gen 34:7
city, and that which was in the *f*.......... Gen 34:28
who smote Midian in the *f* of Moab..... Gen 36:35
we were binding sheaves in the *f*........ Gen 37:7
behold, he was wandering in the *f*....... Gen 37:15
he had in the house, and in the *f*......... Gen 39:5
the food of the *f*, which was............... Gen 41:48
Egyptians sold every man his *f*........... Gen 47:20
be your own, for seed of the *f*............. Gen 47:24
is in the *f* of Ephron the Hittite .... Gen 49:29
that is in the *f* of Machpelah............... Gen 49:30
the *f* of Ephron the Hittite for a .... Gen 49:30
The Purchase of the *f* and of the .... Gen 49:32
in the cave of the *f* of Machpelah........ Gen 50:13
with the *f* for a possession of a........... Gen 50:13
in all manner of service in the *f* .... Ex 1:14
upon thy cattle which is in the *f*.......... Ex 9:3
and all that thou hast in the *f*.............. Ex 9:19
which shall be found in the *f*............... Ex 9:19
servants and his cattle in the *f*............ Ex 9:21
and upon every herb of the *f*.............. Ex 9:22
of Egypt all that was in the *f*............... Ex 9:25
hail smote every herb of the *f*............. Ex 9:25
and brake every tree of the *f*.............. Ex 9:25
groweth for you out of the *f*................ Ex 10:5
trees, or in the herbs of the *f*............. Ex 10:15
day ye shall not find it in the *f*............. Ex 16:25
If a man shall cause a *f* or .... Ex 22:5
and shall feed in another man's *f*........ Ex 22:5
of the best of his own *f*, and of .... Ex 22:5
or the standing corn, or the *f*.............. Ex 22:6
that is torn of beasts in the *f*.............. Ex 22:31
the beasts of the *f* shall eat .... Ex 23:11
which thou hast sown in the *f*.............. Ex 23:16
in thy labours out of the *f*................... Ex 23:16
the beast of the *f* multiply .... Ex 23:29
living bird loose into the open *f*........... Lev 14:7
which they offer in the open *f*............. Lev 17:5
wholly reap the corners of thy *f*.......... Lev 19:9
not sow thy *f* with mingled seed......... Lev 19:19
of thy *f* when thou reapest.................. Lev 23:22
Six years thou shalt sow thy *f*............. Lev 25:3
thou shalt neither sow thy *f*................ Lev 25:4
the increase thereof out of the *f*......... Lev 25:12
But the *f* of the suburbs of their .... Lev 25:34
the trees of the *f* shall yield............... Lev 26:4
part of a *f* of his possession .... Lev 27:16
If he sanctify his *f* from the .... Lev 27:17
sanctify his *f* after the jubile .... Lev 27:18
if he that sanctified the *f* will .... Lev 27:19
And if he will not redeem the *f*............ Lev 27:20
he have sold the *f* to another man...... Lev 27:20
But the *f*, when it goeth out in .... Lev 27:21
unto the Lord, as a *f* devoted............. Lev 27:21
the Lord as the *f* which he hath bought ... Lev 27:22
of the *f* of his possession, shall .... Lev 27:28
ox licketh up the grass of the *f* .... Num 22:4
of the way, and went into the *f*........... Num 22:23
brought him into the *f* of Zophim .... Num 23:14
thy neighbour's house, his *f* .... Deut 5:21
of the *f* increase upon thee .... Deut 7:22
that *f* bringeth forth year by .... Deut 14:22
f is man's life) to employ them........... Deut 20:19

to possess it, lying in the *f*................. Deut 21:1
find a betrothed damsel in the *f*.......... Deut 22:25
For he found her in the *f*..................... Deut 22:27
down thine harvest in thy *f*................. Deut 24:19
and hast forgot a sheaf in the *f*.......... Deut 24:19
and blessed shalt thou be in the *f*...... Deut 28:3
and cursed shalt thou be in the *f*....... Deut 28:16
carry much seed out into the *f*........... Deut 28:38
the inhabitants of Ai in the *f*............... Josh 8:24
him to ask of her father a *f*................. Josh 15:18
him to ask of her father a *f*................. Judg 1:14
marchedst out of the *f* of Edom.......... Judg 5:4
death in the high places of the *f*......... Judg 5:18
thee, and lie in wait in the *f*................ Judg 9:32
the people went out into the *f*............. Judg 9:42
companies, and laid wait in the *f*......... Judg 9:43
the woman as she sat in the *f*............. Judg 13:9
his work out of the *f* at even.............. Judg 19:16
and the other to Gibeah in the *f*......... Judg 20:31
Naomi, Let me now go to the *f* .... Ruth 2:2
gleaned in the *f* after the .... Ruth 2:3
part of the *f* belonging unto Boaz ...... Ruth 2:3
Go not to glean in another *f*............... Ruth 2:8
be on the *f* that they do reap............. Ruth 2:9
she gleaned in the *f* until even............ Ruth 2:17
they meet thee not in any other *f*....... Ruth 2:22
buyest the *f* of the hand of Naomi...... Ruth 4:5
in the *f* about four thousand men....... 1Sa 4:2
cart came into the *f* of Joshua 1Sa 6:14
unto this day in the *f* of Joshua.......... 1Sa 6:18
came after the herd out of the *f*......... 1Sa 11:5
trembling in the host, in the *f*............. 1Sa 14:15
air, and to the beasts of the *f* 1Sa 17:44
my father in the *f* where thou art 1Sa 19:3
the *f* unto the third day at even.......... 1Sa 20:5
Come, and let us go out into the *f*...... 1Sa 20:11
went out both of them into the *f*......... 1Sa 20:11
So David hid himself in the *f* 1Sa 20:24
the *f* at the time appointed with......... 1Sa 20:35
they found an Egyptian in the *f*.......... 1Sa 30:11
were by themselves in the *f*................ 2Sa 10:8
and came out unto us into the *f*.......... 2Sa 11:23
they two strove together in the *f* 2Sa 14:6
Joab's *f* is near mine, and he hath 2Sa 14:30
servants set the *f* on fire..................... 2Sa 14:30
thy servants set my *f* on fire 2Sa 14:31
robbed of her whelps in the *f*............. 2Sa 17:8
out into the *f* against Israel................. 2Sa 18:6
out of the highway into the *f*.............. 2Sa 20:12
nor the beasts of the *f* by night 2Sa 21:10
and they two were alone in the *f*........ 1Kin 11:29
him that dieth in the *f* shall the 1Kin 14:11
him that dieth in the *f* shall the 1Kin 21:24
out into the *f* to gather herbs............. 2Kin 4:39
camp to hide themselves in the *f*........ 2Kin 7:12
all the fruits of the *f* since the 2Kin 8:6
of the *f* of Naboth the Jezreelite......... 2Kin 9:25
the *f* in the portion of Jezreel 2Kin 9:37
in the highway of the fuller's *f*............ 2Kin 18:17
they were as the grass of the *f*........... 2Kin 19:26
smote Midian in the *f* of Moab............ 1Chr 1:46
come were by themselves in the *f*...... 1Chr 19:9
f for tillage of the ground was............ 1Chr 27:26
him with his fathers in the *f* of 2Chr 26:23
and of all the increase of the *f*........... 2Chr 31:5
were fled every one to his *f* .... Neh 13:10
league with the stones of the *f*........... Job 5:23
the beasts of the *f* shall be at .... Job 5:23
reap every one his corn in the *f*......... Job 24:6
all the beasts of the *f* play.................. Job 40:20
oxen, yea, and the beasts of the *f*...... Ps 8:7
the wild beasts of the *f* are mine........ Ps 50:11
land of Egypt, in the *f* of Zoan........... Ps 78:12
and his wonders in the *f* of Zoan........ Ps 78:43
beast of the *f* doth devour it............... Ps 80:13
Let the *f* be joyful, and all that........... Ps 96:12
as a flower of the *f*, so he................... Ps 103:15
drink to every beast of the *f*............... Ps 104:11
make it fit for thyself in the *f*.............. Prov 24:27
I went by the *f* of the slothful............. Prov 24:30
the goats are the price of the *f*........... Prov 27:26
She considereth a *f*, and buyeth it ...... Prov 31:16
king himself is served by the *f*............ Eccl 5:9
roes, and by the hinds of the *f*........... Song 2:7
roes, and by the hinds of the *f*........... Song 3:5
let us go forth into the *f*..................... Song 7:11
to house, that lay *f* to .... Is 5:8
to house, that lay *f* to .... Is 5:8
in the highway of the fuller's *f*............ Is 7:3
his forest, and of his fruitful *f*............. Is 10:18
and joy out of the plentiful *f*.............. Is 16:10
shall be turned into a fruitful *f* .... Is 29:17
the fruitful *f* shall be esteemed .... Is 29:17
and the wilderness be a fruitful *f*........ Is 32:15
the fruitful *f* be counted for a .... Is 32:15
remain in the fruitful *f*......................... Is 32:16
in the highway of the fuller's *f*............ Is 36:2
they were as the grass of the *f*........... Is 37:27
thereof is as the flower of the *f*.......... Is 40:6
beast of the *f* shall honour me .... Is 43:20
all the trees of the *f* shall clap........... Is 55:12
All ye beasts of the *f*, come to .... Is 56:9
As keepers of a *f*, are they .... Jer 4:17
Go not forth into the *f*, nor walk......... Jer 6:25
beast, and upon the trees of the *f*...... Jer 7:20
fall as dung upon the open *f*............... Jer 9:22
and the herbs of every *f* wither .... Jer 12:4
assemble all the beasts of the *f*......... Jer 12:9
the hind also calved in the *f*............... Jer 14:5
If I go forth into the *f*, then .... Jer 14:18

O my mountain in the *f*, I will.............. Jer 17:3
cometh from the rock of the *f* .... Jer 18:14
Zion shall be plowed like a *f*............... Jer 26:18
the beasts of the *f* have I given......... Jer 27:6
him the beasts of the *f* also............... Jer 28:14
Buy thee my *f* that is in Anathoth....... Jer 32:7
Lord, and said unto me, Buy my *f*....... Jer 32:8
I bought the *f* of Hanameel my........... Jer 32:9
God, Buy thee the *f* for money........... Jer 32:25
neither have we vineyard, nor *f* .... Jer 35:9
for we have treasures in the *f*............. Jer 41:8
is taken from the plentiful *f*................. Jer 48:33
for want of the fruits of the *f* .... Lam 4:9
he that is in the *f* shall die.................. Eze 7:15
thou wast cast out in the open *f*......... Eze 16:5
to multiply as the bud of the *f*............ Eze 16:7
and planted it in a fruitful *f*................. Eze 17:5
all the trees of the *f* shall know.......... Eze 17:24
against the forest of the south *f*.......... Eze 20:46
the *f* shall be slain by the sword......... Eze 26:6
the sword thy daughters in the *f*......... Eze 26:8
for meat to the beasts of the *f*........... Eze 29:5
unto all the trees of the *f*................... Eze 31:4
above all the trees of the *f*................. Eze 31:5
of the *f* bring forth their young.......... Eze 31:6
all the beasts of the *f* shall be .... Eze 31:13
trees of the *f* fainted for him.............. Eze 31:15
cast thee forth upon the open *f*.......... Eze 32:4
him that is in the open *f* will I............. Eze 33:27
meat to all the beasts of the *f*............ Eze 34:5
meat to every beast of the *f*............... Eze 34:8
the tree of the *f* shall yield her .... Eze 34:27
tree, and the increase of the *f*........... Eze 36:30
heaven, and the beasts of the *f*.......... Eze 38:20
beasts of the *f* to be devoured........... Eze 39:4
Thou shalt fall upon the open *f*........... Eze 39:5
shall take no wood out of the *f* .... Eze 39:10
fowl, and to every beast of the *f*........ Eze 39:17
of men dwell, the beasts of the *f* .... Dan 2:38
the beasts of the *f* had shadow.......... Dan 4:12
in the tender grass of the *f*................. Dan 4:15
which the beasts of the *f* dwelt.......... Dan 4:21
in the tender grass of the *f*................. Dan 4:23
be with the beasts of the *f*................. Dan 4:23
shall be with the beasts of the *f* .... Dan 4:25
shall be with the beasts of the *f* .... Dan 4:32
beasts of the *f* shall eat them .... Hos 2:12
for them with the beasts of the *f* .... Hos 2:18
with the beasts of the *f*...................... Hos 4:3
hemlock in the furrows of the *f*.......... Hos 10:4
The *f* is wasted, the land.................... Joel 1:10
the harvest of the *f* is perished.......... Joel 1:11
tree, even all the trees of the *f*.......... Joel 1:12
burned all the trees of the *f*............... Joel 1:19
The beasts of the *f* cry also unto....... Joel 1:20
Be not afraid, ye beasts of the *f*......... Joel 2:22
make Samaria as an heap of the *f*...... Mic 1:6
for your sake be plowed as a *f*........... Mic 3:12
and thou shalt dwell in the *f*.............. Mic 4:10
rain, to every one grass in the *f*........ Zec 10:1
fruit before the time in the *f*.............. Mal 3:11
Consider the lilies of the *f*.................. Mt 6:28
God so clothe the grass of the *f*......... Mt 6:30
which sowed good seed in his *f*.......... Mt 13:24
not thou sow good seed in thy *f*......... Mt 13:27
a man took, and sowed in his *f*.......... Mt 13:31
the parable of the tares of the *f*.......... Mt 13:36
The *f* is the world .... Mt 13:38
is like unto treasure hid in a *f*............. Mt 13:44
that he hath, and buyeth that *f*........... Mt 13:44
return back to take his clothes.............. Mt 24:18
Then shall two be in the *f*................... Mt 24:40
bought with them the potter's *f*.......... Mt 27:7
Wherefore that *f* was called................ Mt 27:8
The *f* of blood, unto this day .... Mt 27:8
And gave them for the potter's *f*......... Mt 27:10
let him that is in the *f* not turn........... Mk 13:16
shepherds abiding in the *f*.................. Lk 2:8
grass, which is to day in the *f*............. Lk 12:28
Now his elder son was in the *f*........... Lk 15:25
and by, when he is come from the *f*.... Lk 17:7
and he that is in the *f*, let him .... Lk 17:31
Two men shall be in the *f* .... Lk 17:36
Now this man purchased a *f* with .... Acts 1:18
insomuch as that *f* is called in .... Acts 1:19
that is to say, The *f* of blood............. Acts 1:19

FIELDS

of the villages, and out of the *f*.......... Ex 8:13
out of the city into the open *f*............ Lev 14:53
counted as the *f* of the country .... Lev 25:31
is not of the *f* of his possession .... Lev 27:22
or given us inheritance of *f*................. Num 16:14
slain with a sword in the open *f* .... Num 19:16
we will not pass through the *f*............. Num 20:17
we will not turn into the *f*................... Num 21:22
grass in thy *f* for thy cattle .... Deut 11:15
might eat the increase of the *f*........... Deut 32:13
of Sodom, and of the *f* of Gomorrah.... Deut 32:32
But the *f* of the city, and the .... Josh 21:12
And they went out into the *f*.............. Judg 9:27
all the people that were in the *f*.......... Judg 9:44
And he will take your *f*, and he 1Sa 8:14
of Jesse give every one of you *f*......... 1Sa 22:7
with them, when we were in the *f* 1Sa 25:15
upon you, nor *f* of offerings 2Sa 1:21
lord, are encamped in the open *f*........ 2Sa 11:11
to Anathoth, unto thine own *f* 1Kin 2:26
him that dieth of his in the *f*.............. 1Kin 16:4
Jerusalem in the *f* of Kidron.............. 2Kin 23:4
But the *f* of the city, and the 1Chr 6:56

let the f rejoice, and all that is 1Chr 16:32
and over the storehouses in the f 1Chr 27:25
which were in the f of the 2Chr 31:19
And for the villages, with their f .... Neh 11:25
the f thereof, at Azekah, and in .... Neh 11:30
Gilgal, and out of the f of Geba .... Neh 12:29
f of the cities the portions of .... Neh 12:44
and sendeth waters upon the f .... Job 5:10
And sow the f, and plant vineyards, .. Ps 107:37
we found it in the f of the wood .... Ps 132:6
had not made the earth, nor the f ...... Prov 8:26
not into the f of the fatherless .... Prov 23:10
For the f of Heshbon languish, and .... Is 16:8
for the teats, for the pleasant f .... Is 32:12
turned unto others, with their f .... Jer 6:12
their f to them that shall .... Jer 8:10
on the hills in the f .... Jer 13:27
all the f unto the brook of .... Jer 31:40
Houses and f and vineyards shall be .. Jer 32:15
I shall be bought in this land, ... Jer 32:43
Men shall buy f for money.................. Jer 32:44
vineyards and f at the same time ...... Jer 39:10
of the forces which were in the f ...... Jer 40:7
of the forces that were in the f .... Jer 40:13
thou shalt fall upon the open f .... Eze 29:5
as heaps in the furrows of the f .... Hos 12:11
shall possess the f of Ephraim .... Obad 19
of Ephraim, and the f of Samaria ...... Obad 19
And they covet f, and take them by .. Mic 2:2
away he hath divided our f .... Mic 2:4
the f shall yield no meat .... Hab 3:17
the corn f on the sabbath day .... Mk 2:23
that he went through the corn f .... Lk 6:1
sent him into his f to feed swine .... Lk 15:15
up your eyes, and look on the f .... Jn 4:35
who have reaped down your f .... Jas 5:4

FIERCE
be their anger, for it was f .... Gen 49:7
Turn from thy f wrath, and repent ...... Ex 32:12
that the f anger of the LORD may .... Num 25:4
to augment yet the f anger of the ...... Num 32:14
A nation of f countenance .... Deut 28:50
arose from the table in f anger 1Sa 20:34
his f wrath upon Amalek 1Sa 28:18
for the f wrath of the LORD is 2Chr 28:11
there is f wrath against Israel 2Chr 28:13
that his f wrath may turn away 2Chr 29:10
until the f wrath of our God for .... Ezr 10:14
lion, and the voice of the f lion .... Job 4:10
Thou huntest me as a f lion .... Job 10:16
nor the f lion passed by it .... Job 28:8
None is so f that dare stir him .... Job 41:10
Thy f wrath goeth over me .... Ps 88:16
for the f anger of Rezin with .... Is 7:4
f anger, to lay the land desolate .... Is 13:9
and in the day of his f anger .... Is 13:13
a f king shall rule over them, ... Is 19:4
Thou shalt not see a f people .... Is 33:19
for the f anger of the LORD is .... Jer 4:8
of the LORD, and by his f anger .... Jer 4:26
of the f anger of the LORD .... Jer 12:13
of the f anger of the LORD .... Jer 25:37
and because of his f anger .... Jer 25:38
The f anger of the LORD shall not ...... Jer 30:24
evil upon them, even my f anger .... Jer 49:37
soul from the f anger of the LORD ...... Jer 51:45
me in the day of his f anger .... Lam 1:12
He hath cut off in his f anger .... Lam 2:3
he hath poured out his f anger .... Lam 4:11
a king of f countenance, and .... Dan 8:23
and turn away from his f anger .... Jonah 3:9
are more f than the evening .... Hab 1:8
before the f anger of the LORD .... Zeph 2:2
indignation, even all my f anger .... Zeph 3:8
out of the tombs, exceeding f .... Mt 8:28
And they were the more f, saying, ... Lk 23:5
false accusers, incontinent, f 2Ti 3:3
great, and are driven of f winds .... Jas 3:4

FIERCENESS
may turn from the f of his anger ...... Deut 13:17
turned from the f of his anger .... Josh 7:26
not from the f of his great wrath 2Kin 23:26
that the f of his wrath may turn 2Chr 30:8
He swalloweth the ground with f ...... Job 39:24
cast upon them the f of his anger .... Ps 78:49
thyself from the f of thine anger ...... Ps 85:3
because of the f of the oppressor .... Jer 25:38
not execute the f of mine anger ...... Hos 11:9
can abide in the f of his anger .... Nah 1:6
of the wine of the f of his wrath ...... Rev 16:19
treadeth the winepress of the f .... Rev 19:15

FIERCER
f than the words of the men of 2Sa 19:43

FIERY
the LORD sent f serpents among ...... Num 21:6
unto Moses, Make thee a f serpent .. Num 21:8
wherein were f serpents, and .... Deut 8:15
right hand went a f law for them...... Deut 33:2
Thou shalt make them as a f oven .... Ps 21:9
fruit shall be a f flying serpent .... Is 14:29
f flying serpent, they will carry .... Is 30:6
the midst of a burning f furnace ...... Dan 3:6
the midst of a burning f furnace ...... Dan 3:11
the midst of a burning f furnace ...... Dan 3:15
us from the burning f furnace .... Dan 3:17
them into the burning f furnace .... Dan 3:20
midst of the burning f furnace .... Dan 3:21
midst of the burning f furnace .... Dan 3:23

mouth of the burning f furnace........ Dan 3:26
his throne was like the f flame .... Dan 7:9
A f stream issued and came forth ...... Dan 7:10
all the f darts of the wicked.............. Eph 6:16
f indignation, which shall devour ...... Heb 10:27
the f trial which is to try you 1Pet 4:12

FIFTEEN
f years, and begat sons and .... Gen 5:10
F cubits upward did the waters .... Gen 7:20
an hundred threescore and f years.... Gen 25:7
of the gate shall be f cubits .... Ex 27:14
side shall be hangings f cubits .... Ex 27:15
side of the gate were f cubits .... Ex 38:14
hand, were hangings of f cubits .... Ex 38:15
f shekels after the shekel of .... Ex 38:25
thy estimation shall be f shekels ...... Lev 27:7
six hundred and threescore and f .... Num 31:37
about f thousand men, all that .... Judg 8:10
Now Ziba had f sons and twenty 2Sa 9:10
his f sons and his twenty servants 2Sa 19:17
on forty five pillars, f in a row 1Kin 7:3
Jehoahaz king of Israel f years 2Kin 14:17
I will add unto thy days f years 2Kin 20:6
Jehoahaz king of Israel f years.......... 2Chr 25:25
I will add unto thy days f years .... Is 38:5
f shekels, shall be your maneh .... Eze 45:12
her to me for f pieces of silver .... Hos 3:2
Jerusalem, about f furlongs off .... Jn 11:18
kindred, threescore and f souls .... Acts 7:14
again, and found it f fathoms .... Acts 27:28
Peter, and abode with him f days ...... Gal 1:18

FIFTEENTH
on the f day of the second month...... Ex 16:1
on the f day of the same month is .... Lev 23:6
The f day of this seventh month .... Lev 23:34
Also in the f day of the seventh .... Lev 23:39
in the f day of this month is in .... Num 28:17
on the f day of the seventh month .... Num 29:12
on the f day of the first month .... Num 33:3
on the f day of the month, like.......... 1Kin 12:32
the f day of the eighth month............ 1Kin 12:33
In the f year of Amaziah the son 2Kin 14:23
The f day, the sixteenth to 1Chr 24:14
The f to Jeremoth, he, his sons, ... 1Chr 25:22
in the f year of the reign of Asa 2Chr 15:10
on the f day of the same they .... Est 9:18
the f day of the same, yearly.............. Est 9:21
in the f day of the month, that .... Eze 32:17
in the f day of the month, shall .... Eze 45:25
Now in the f year of the reign of ...... Lk 3:1

FIFTH
and the morning were the f day .... Gen 1:23
and bare Jacob the f son .... Gen 30:17
take up the f part of the land of .... Gen 41:34
give the f part unto Pharaoh .... Gen 47:24
Pharaoh should have the f part .... Gen 47:26
and shall add the f part thereto.......... Lev 5:16
shall add the f part more thereto ...... Lev 6:5
in the f year shall ye eat of it .... Lev 19:25
put the f part thereof unto it .... Lev 22:14
then he shall add a f part .... Lev 27:13
then he shall add the f part of .... Lev 27:15
then he shall add the f part of .... Lev 27:19
shall add a f part of it thereto............ Lev 27:27
add thereto the f part thereof .... Lev 27:31
and add unto it the f part thereof...... Num 5:7
On the f day Shelumiel the son of .... Num 7:36
on the f day nine bullocks, two, ... Num 29:26
in the first day of the f month .... Num 33:38
the f lot came out for the tribe .... Josh 19:24
morning on the f day to depart .... Judg 19:8
spear smote him under the f rib 2Sa 2:23
and the f, Shephatiah the son of........ 2Sa 3:4
smote him there under the f rib 2Sa 3:27
and they smote him under the f rib .. 2Sa 4:6
smote him therewith in the f rib 2Sa 20:10
posts were a f part of the wall............ 1Kin 6:31
in the f year of king Rehoboam.......... 1Kin 14:25
in the f year of Joram the son of 2Kin 8:16
And in the f month, on the seventh .. 2Kin 25:8
the fourth, Raddai the f........................ 1Chr 2:14
The f, Shephatiah of Abital 1Chr 3:3
Nohah the fourth, and Rapha the f 1Chr 8:2
the fourth, Jeremiah the f 1Chr 12:10
The f to Malchijah, the sixth to 1Chr 24:9
The f to Nethaniah, he, his sons, ... 1Chr 25:12
Elam the f, Jehohanan the sixth, ... 1Chr 26:3
the fourth, and Nethaneel the f 1Chr 26:4
The f captain for the f month.............. 1Chr 27:8
that in the f year of king 2Chr 12:2
came to Jerusalem in the f month...... Ezr 7:8
on the first day of the f month............ Ezr 7:9
unto me in like manner the f time...... Neh 6:5
f day of the month Elul, in fifty .... Neh 6:15
Jerusalem captive in the f month ...... Jer 1:3
fourth year, and in the f month.......... Jer 28:1
it came to pass in the f year of .... Jer 36:9
Now in the f month, in the tenth ...... Jer 52:12
in the f day of the month, as I .... Eze 1:1
In the f day of the month .... Eze 1:2
which was the f year of king .... Eze 1:2
in the f day of the month, as I .... Eze 8:1
the seventh year, in the f month ...... Eze 20:1
in the f day of the month, that .... Eze 33:21
Should I weep in the f month .... Zec 7:3
ye fasted and mourned in the f .... Zec 7:5
month, and the fast of the f .... Zec 8:19
And when he had opened the f seal .. Rev 6:9
the f angel sounded, and I saw a ...... Rev 9:1

the f angel poured out his vial .... Rev 16:10
The f, sardonyx; the sixth .... Rev 21:20

FIFTIES
rulers of hundreds, rulers of f .... Ex 18:21
rulers of hundreds, rulers of f .... Ex 18:25
over hundreds, and captains over f .... Deut 1:15
thousands, and captains over f 1Sa 8:12
the former f with their f 2Kin 1:14
in ranks, by hundreds, and by f .... Mk 6:40
them sit down by f in a company ...... Lk 9:14

FIFTIETH
And ye shall hallow the f year............ Lev 25:10
shall that f year be unto you.............. Lev 25:11
In the f year of Azariah king of 2Kin 15:23
f year of Azariah king of Judah 2Kin 15:27

FIFTY
the breadth of it f cubits .... Gen 6:15
the earth an hundred and f days .... Gen 7:24
f days the waters were abated .... Gen 8:3
flood three hundred and f years.......... Gen 9:28
Noah were nine hundred and f years.. Gen 9:29
Peradventure there be f righteous...... Gen 18:24
the f righteous that are therein .... Gen 18:24
If I find in Sodom f righteous .... Gen 18:26
lack five of the f righteous .... Gen 18:28
f loops shalt thou make in the............ Ex 26:5
f loops shalt thou make in the............ Ex 26:10
thou shalt make f taches of gold........ Ex 26:6
thou shalt make f loops on the .... Ex 26:10
f loops in the edge of the .... Ex 26:10
thou shalt make f taches of brass ...... Ex 26:11
shall be hangings of f cubits.............. Ex 27:12
side eastward shall be f cubits .... Ex 27:13
and the breadth f every where .... Ex 27:18
f shekels, and of sweet calamus .... Ex 30:23
calamus two hundred and f shekels, .. Ex 30:23
f loops made in one curtain, ... Ex 36:12
f loops made he in the edge of .... Ex 36:12
he made f taches of gold, and............ Ex 36:13
And he made f loops upon the .... Ex 36:17
f loops made he upon the edge of .... Ex 36:17
he made f taches of brass to .... Ex 36:18
side were hangings of f cubits............ Ex 38:12
the east side eastward f cubits .... Ex 38:13
thousand and five hundred and f ...... Ex 38:26
sabbath shall ye number f days .... Lev 23:16
shall be f shekels of silver .... Lev 27:3
be valued at f shekels of silver.......... Num 1:23
of the tribe of Simeon, were f .... Num 1:23
and five thousand six hundred and f .. Num 1:25
of the tribe of Issachar, were f .... Num 1:29
of the tribe of Zebulun, were f .... Num 1:31
of the tribe of Naphtali, were f .... Num 1:43
thousand and five hundred and f ...... Num 1:46
were numbered thereof, were f .... Num 2:6
were numbered thereof, were f .... Num 2:8
were numbered of them, were f .... Num 2:13
five thousand and six hundred and f .. Num 2:15
were an hundred thousand and f ...... Num 2:16
one thousand and four hundred and f .. Num 2:23
were numbered of them, were f .... Num 2:30
Dan were an hundred thousand and f .. Num 2:31
thousand and five hundred and f ...... Num 2:32
and upward even until f years old .... Num 4:3
upward until f years old shall .... Num 4:23
upward even into f years old.............. Num 4:30
and upward even unto f years old .... Num 4:35
two thousand seven hundred and f .. Num 4:36
and upward even unto f years old .... Num 4:39
and upward even unto f years old .... Num 4:43
and upward even unto f years old .... Num 4:47
from the age of f years they .... Num 8:25
f princes of the assembly, famous .... Num 16:2
censer, two hundred and f censers .... Num 16:35
f men that offered incense .... Num 16:35
devoured two hundred and f men...... Num 16:49
that were numbered of them, f.......... Num 26:34
who were f and three thousand and .. Num 26:47
thou shalt take one portion of f.......... Num 31:30
half, Moses took one portion of f ...... Num 31:47
seven hundred and f shekels .... Num 31:52
father f shekels of silver .... Deut 22:29
wedge of gold of f shekels weight .... Josh 7:21
he smote of the people f thousand 1Sa 6:19
and f men to run before him 2Sa 15:1
the oxen for f shekels of silver 2Sa 24:24
and f men to run before him 1Kin 1:5
and the breadth thereof f cubits 1Kin 7:2
the length thereof was f cubits 1Kin 7:6
Solomon's work, five hundred and f .. 1Kin 9:23
and an horse for an hundred and f 1Kin 10:29
and hid them by f in a cave................ 1Kin 18:4
LORD's prophets by f in a cave.......... 1Kin 18:13
of Baal four hundred and f 1Kin 18:19
are four hundred and f men 1Kin 18:22
him a captain of f with his f 2Kin 1:9
and said to the captain of f................ 2Kin 1:10
heaven, and consume thee and thy f .. 2Kin 1:10
heaven, and consumed him and his f .. 2Kin 1:10
captain of f with his f 2Kin 1:11
heaven, and consume thee and thy f .. 2Kin 1:12
heaven, and consumed him and his f .. 2Kin 1:12
of the third f with his f 2Kin 1:13
And the third captain of f went up 2Kin 1:13
the life of these f thy servants............ 2Kin 1:13
f men of the sons of the prophets 2Kin 2:7
be with thirty servants' strong men.... 2Kin 2:16
They sent therefore f men 2Kin 2:17
people to Jehoahaz but f horsemen .. 2Kin 13:7

two and *f* years in Jerusalem 2Kin 15:2
of each man *f* shekels of silver, ... 2Kin 15:20
with him *f* men of the Gileadites. 2Kin 15:25
he began to reign, and reigned *f* 2Kin 21:1
of their camels *f* thousand 1Chr 5:21
f thousand, and of asses two 1Chr 6:21
and sons' sons, an hundred and *f* 1Chr 8:40
generations, nine hundred and *f* 1Chr 9:9
f thousand, which could keep rank 1Chr 12:33
and an horse for an hundred and *f* 2Chr 1:17
f thousand and three thousand and 2Chr 2:17
the nails was *f* shekels of gold. 2Chr 3:9
officers, even two hundred and *f* 2Chr 8:10
of talents of gold, and brought 2Chr 8:18
began to reign, and he reigned *f* 2Chr 26:3
began to reign, and he reigned *f* 2Chr 33:1
of Elam, a thousand two hundred *f* ..... Ezr 2:7
of Bigvai, two thousand *f* .... Ezr 2:14
children of Adin, four hundred *f* .... Ezr 2:15
The men of Netophah, *f* and six .... Ezr 2:22
The children of Nebo, *f* and two .... Ezr 2:29
children of Magbish, an hundred *f* .... Ezr 2:30
Elam, a thousand two hundred *f* .... Ezr 2:31
children of Immer, a thousand *f* .... Ezr 2:37
children of Nekoda, six hundred *f* .... Ezr 2:60
of the males an hundred and *f* .... Ezr 8:3
of Jonathan, and with him *f* males. ..... Ezr 8:6
f talents of silver, and silver........... Ezr 8:26
f of the Jews and rulers, beside. .... Neh 5:17
fifth day of the month Elul, in *f*......... Neh 6:15
children of Arah, six hundred *f* .... Neh 7:10
of Elam, a thousand two hundred *f* ...... Neh 7:12
children of Adin, six hundred *f* .... Neh 7:20
The men of the other Nebo, *f* .... Neh 7:33
Elam, a thousand two hundred *f* .... Neh 7:34
children of Immer, a thousand *f* .... Neh 7:40
of Jonathan, and with him *f* .... Neh 7:70
gallows be made of *f* cubits high. .... Est 5:14
also, the gallows *f* cubits high........... Est 7:9
The Captain of *f*, and the .... Is 3:3
of the inner gate were *f* cubits. .... Eze 40:15
the length thereof was *f* cubits. .... Eze 40:21
the length was *f* cubits, and the .... Eze 40:25
it was *f* cubits long, and five and .... Eze 40:29
it was *f* cubits long, and five and .... Eze 40:33
it was *f* cubits, and the .... Eze 40:36
door, and the breadth was *f* cubits ...... Eze 42:2
the length thereof was *f* cubits. .... Eze 42:7
in the utter court was *f* cubits .... Eze 42:8
f cubits round about for the .... Eze 45:2
toward the north two hundred and *f*..... Eze 48:17
toward the south two hundred and *f*..... Eze 48:17
toward the east two hundred and *f* ...... Eze 48:17
toward the west two hundred and *f* ...... Eze 48:17
out *f* vessels out of the press........... Hag 2:16
hundred pence, and the other *f* .... Lk 7:41
and sit down quickly, and write *f* .... Lk 16:6
him, Thou art not yet *f* years old .... Jn 8:57
of great fishes, an hundred and *f* .... Jn 21:11
f years, until Samuel the prophet .... Acts 13:20
found it *f* thousand pieces of .... Acts 19:19

FIG

they sawed *f* leaves together, and........ Gen 3:7
and *f* trees, and pomegranates, ... Deut 8:8
And the trees said to the *f* tree,........ Judg 9:10
But the *f* tree said unto them, ... Judg 9:11
his vine and under his *f* tree........... 1Kin 4:25
vine, and every one of his *f* tree....... 2Kin 18:31
their vines also and their *f* trees...... Ps 105:33
Whoso keepeth the *f* tree shall. .... Prov 27:18
The *f* tree putteth forth her .... Song 2:13
as a falling *f* from the *f* tree. .... Is 34:4
vine, and every one of his *f* tree....... Is 36:16
eat up thy vines and thy *f* trees. .... Jer 5:17
the vine, nor figs on the *f* tree........ Jer 8:13
her *f* trees, whereof she hath .... Hos 2:12
in the *f* tree at her first time......... Hos 9:10
vine waste, and barked my *f* tree........ Joel 1:7
up, and the *f* tree languisheth .... Joel 1:12
the *f* tree and the vine do yield. .... Joel 2:22
your *f* trees and your olive trees. ...... Amos 4:9
his vine and under his *f* tree........... Mic 4:4
f trees with the firstripe figs. .... Nah 3:12
Although the *f* tree shall not. .... Hab 3:17
the *f* tree, and the pomegranate, ... Hag 2:19
the vine and under the *f* tree. .... Zec 3:10
when he saw a *f* tree in the way, ... Mt 21:19
presently the *f* tree withered .... Mt 21:19
How soon is the *f* tree withered. .... Mt 21:20
this which is done to the *f* tree........ Mt 21:21
Now learn a parable of the *f* tree....... Mt 24:32
seeing a *f* tree afar off having......... Mk 11:13
they saw the *f* tree dried up from....... Mk 11:20
the *f* tree which thou cursedst is....... Mk 11:21
Now learn a parable of the *f* tree....... Mk 13:28
A certain man had a *f* tree .... Lk 13:6
come seeking fruit on this *f* tree....... Lk 13:6
Behold the *f* tree, and all the .... Lk 21:29
when thou wast under the *f* tree......... Jn 1:48
thee, I saw thee under the *f* tree....... Jn 1:50
Can the *f* tree, my brethren, bear ...... Jas 3:12
even as a *f* tree casteth her.......... Rev 6:13

FIGHT

f against us, and so get them up........ Ex 1:10
The LORD shall *f* for you, and ye........ Ex 14:14
out men, and go out, *f* with Amalek ..... Ex 17:9
before you, he shall *f* for you........ Deut 1:30
the LORD, we will go up and *f* .... Deut 1:41
unto them, Go not up, neither *f* .... Deut 1:42

and all his people, to *f* at Jahaz........ Deut 2:32
LORD your God he shall *f* for you........ Deut 3:22
to *f* for you against your enemies........ Deut 20:4
nigh unto a city to *f* against it........ Deut 20:10
to *f* with Joshua and with Israel,....... Josh 9:2
your enemies against whom ye *f* .... Josh 10:25
of Merom, to *f* against Israel .... Josh 11:5
Dan went up to *f* against Leshem .... Josh 19:47
first, to *f* against them .... Judg 1:1
that we may *f* against the.............. Judg 1:3
down to *f* against the Canaanites....... Judg 1:9
wentest to *f* with the Midianites .... Judg 8:1
out, I pray now, and *f* with them....... Judg 9:38
Jordan to *f* also against Judah .... Judg 10:9
man is he that will begin to *f* .... Judg 10:18
that we may *f* with the children........ Judg 11:6
against the children of Ammon, ... Judg 11:9
If ye bring me home again to *f* .... Judg 11:9
come against me to *f* in my land. .... Judg 11:12
or did he ever *f* against them .... Judg 11:25
of Ammon to *f* against them .... Judg 11:32
f against the children of Ammon .... Judg 12:1
unto me this day, to *f* against me ...... Judg 12:3
array to *f* against them at Gibeah ...... Judg 20:20
quit yourselves like men, and *f* 1Sa 4:9
out before us, and *f* our battles........ 1Sa 8:20
together to *f* with Israel 1Sa 13:5
f against them until they be 1Sa 15:18
If he be able to *f* with me 1Sa 17:9
me a man, that we may *f* together 1Sa 17:10
the host was going forth to the *f* 1Sa 17:20
will go and *f* with this Philistine...... 1Sa 17:32
this Philistine to *f* with him.......... 1Sa 17:33
for me, and I will *f* the LORD's battles . 1Sa 18:17
the Philistines *f* against Keilah 1Sa 23:1
for warfare, to *f* with Israel 1Sa 28:1
that I may not go *f* against the 1Sa 29:8
nigh unto the city when ye did *f* 2Sa 11:20
to *f* against the house of Israel,....... 1Kin 12:21
nor *f* against your brethren the 1Kin 12:24
but let us *f* against them in the 1Kin 20:23
we will *f* against them in the.......... 1Kin 20:25
up to Aphek, to *f* against Israel........ 1Kin 20:26
f neither with small nor great,......... 1Kin 22:31
turned aside to *f* against him.......... 1Kin 22:32
were come up to *f* against them......... 2Kin 3:21
f for your master's house 2Kin 10:3
he is come out to *f* against thee 2Kin 19:9
to *f* against Israel, that he 2Chr 11:1
nor *f* against your brethren........... 2Chr 11:4
f ye not against the LORD God of 2Chr 13:12
f ye not with small or great,.......... 2Chr 18:30
they compassed about him to *f* 2Chr 18:31
not need to *f* in this battle 2Chr 20:17
purposed to *f* against Jerusalem........ 2Chr 32:2
to help us, and to *f* our battles 2Chr 32:8
up to *f* against Charchemish by 2Chr 35:20
himself, that he might *f* with him 2Chr 35:22
came to *f* in the valley of 2Chr 35:22
to *f* against Jerusalem, and to .... Neh 4:8
for your brethren, your sons, ... Neh 4:14
our God shall *f* for us. .... Neh 4:20
f against them that *f* against......... Ps 35:1
they be many that *f* against me......... Ps 56:2
hands to war, and my fingers to *f* ...... Ps 144:1
they shall *f* every one against .... Is 19:2
the nations that *f* against Ariel .... Is 29:7
even all that *f* against her .... Is 29:7
that *f* against mount Zion. .... Is 29:8
of shaking will he *f* with it. .... Is 30:32
come down to *f* for mount Zion .... Is 31:4
they shall *f* against thee. .... Jer 1:19
they shall *f* against thee, but .... Jer 15:20
wherewith ye *f* against the king .... Jer 21:4
I myself will *f* against you with .... Jer 21:5
though ye *f* with the Chaldeans, ... Jer 32:5
that *f* against it, because of the....... Jer 32:24
that *f* against this city, shall......... Jer 32:29
They come to *f* with the Chaldeans...... Jer 33:5
and they shall *f* against it .... Jer 34:22
f against this city, and take it, ... Jer 37:8
the Chaldeans that *f* against you........ Jer 37:10
went to *f* with Ishmael the son of ...... Jer 41:12
men of Babylon have forborn to *f* .... Jer 51:30
now will I return to *f* with the .... Dan 10:20
f with him, even with the king of ...... Dan 11:11
and they shall *f*, because the LORD ..... Zec 10:5
f against those nations, as when .... Zec 14:3
Judah also shall *f* at Jerusalem........ Zec 14:14
world, then would my servants .... Jn 18:36
ye be found even to *f* against God ...... Acts 5:39
to him, let us not *f* against God .... Acts 23:9
so *f* I, not as one that beateth 1Cor 9:26
f the good *f* of faith. 1Ti 6:12
I have fought a good *f*, I have 2Ti 4:7
endured a great *f* of afflictions .... Heb 10:32
made strong, waxed valiant in *f*........ Heb 11:34
ye *f* and war, yet ye have not .... Jas 4:2
will *f* against them with the .... Rev 2:16

FIGHTETH

for the LORD *f* for them against......... Ex 14:25
your God, he it is that *f* for you....... Josh 23:10
because my lord *f* the battles of 1Sa 25:28

FIGHTING

of Elah, *f* with the Philistines 1Sa 17:19
Uzziah had an host of men............... 2Chr 26:11
he *f* daily oppresseth me .... Ps 56:1

FIGHTINGS

without were *f*, within were fears....... 2Cor 7:5
whence come wars and *f* among you....... Jas 4:1

FIGS

of the pomegranates, and of the *f*....... Num 13:23
it is no place of seed, or of *f*......... Num 20:5
and two hundred cakes of *f*. 1Sa 25:18
gave him a piece of a cake of *f*. 1Sa 30:12
And Isaiah said, Take a lump of *f* 2Kin 20:7
oxen, and meat, meal, cakes of *f*. 1Chr 12:40
as also wine, grapes, and *f* .... Neh 13:15
tree putteth forth her green *f*......... Song 2:13
said, Let them take a lump of *f*. .... Is 38:21
nor *f* on the fig tree, and the. .... Jer 8:13
two baskets of *f* were set before. ...... Jer 24:1
One basket had very good *f* .... Jer 24:2
even like the *f* that are first......... Jer 24:2
other basket had very naughty *f*........ Jer 24:2
And I said, F................ .... Jer 24:3
the good *f*, very good .... Jer 24:3
Like these good *f*, so will I .... Jer 24:5
And as the evil *f*, which cannot be ..... Jer 24:8
and will make them like the vile *f*..... Jer 29:17
fig trees with the firstripe *f*. .... Nah 3:12
of thorns, or *f* of thistles........... Mt 7:16
for the time of *f* was not yet.......... Mk 11:13
For of thorns men do not gather *f* ...... Lk 6:44
either a vine, *f*....................... Jas 3:12
a fig tree casteth her untimely *f* ...... Rev 6:13

FIGURE

image, the similitude of any *f* .... Deut 4:16
and maketh it after the *f* of a man ..... Is 44:13
who is the *f* of him that was to .... Rom 5:14
I have in a *f* transferred to........... 1Cor 4:6
Which was a *f* for the time then. .... Heb 9:9
also he received him in a *f* .... Heb 11:19
The like *f* whereunto even baptism...... 1Pet 3:21

FIGURES

about with carved *f* of cherubims........ 1Kin 6:29
f which ye made to worship them. .... Acts 7:43
which are the *f* of the true. .... Heb 9:24

FILE

Yet they had a *f* for the mattocks....... 1Sa 13:21

FILL

the waters in the seas, and *f*.......... Gen 1:22
to *f* their sacks with corn .... Gen 42:25
f the men's sacks with food, as........ Gen 44:1
And they shall *f* thy houses. .... Ex 10:6
f an omer of it to be kept for .... Ex 16:32
her fruit, and ye shall eat your *f* ..... Lev 25:19
thy *f* at thine own pleasure .... Deut 23:24
f thine horn with oil, and go, I 1Sa 16:1
f four barrels with water, and 1Kin 18:33
Till he *f* thy mouth with laughing ...... Job 8:21
f his belly with the east wind .... Job 15:2
When he is about to *f* his belly........ Job 20:23
f my mouth with arguments. .... Job 23:4
or *f* the appetite of the young .... Job 38:39
Canst thou *f* his skin with barbed ...... Job 41:7
thy mouth wide, and I will *f* it........ Ps 81:10
f their faces with shame. .... Ps 83:16
he shall *f* the places with the .... Ps 110:6
we shall *f* our houses with spoil .... Prov 1:13
let us take our *f* of love until .... Prov 7:18
and I will *f* their treasures .... Prov 8:21
out of his wings shall *f*. .... Is 8:8
nor *f* the face of the world with .... Is 14:21
f the face of the world with .... Is 27:6
we will *f* ourselves with strong .... Is 56:12
I will *f* the inhabitants of .... Jer 13:13
Do not I *f* heaven and earth........... Jer 23:24
but it is to *f* them with the dead ...... Jer 33:5
Surely I will *f* thee with men.......... Jer 51:14
f thy bowels with this roll that .... Eze 3:3
souls, neither *f* their bowels.......... Eze 7:19
the courts with the slain .... Eze 9:7
f thine hand with coals of fire. .... Eze 10:2
f it with the choice bones. .... Eze 24:4
the land with the slain .... Eze 30:11
I will *f* the beasts of the whole .... Eze 32:4
the valleys with thy height .... Eze 32:5
I will *f* his mountains with his .... Eze 35:8
which *f* their masters' houses.......... Zeph 1:9
I will *f* this house with glory .... Hag 2:7
for that which is put in to *f* it .... Mt 9:16
as to *f* so great a multitude.......... Mt 15:33
f ye up then the measure of your .... Mt 23:32
f the waterpots with water. .... Jn 2:7
God of hope *f* you with all joy .... Rom 15:13
that he might *f* all things........... Eph 4:10
f up that which is behind of the ...... Col 1:24
saved, to *f* up their sins alway 1Th 2:16
she hath filled *f* to her double. .... Rev 18:6

FILLED

and the earth was *f* with violence....... Gen 6:11
for the earth is *f* with violence....... Gen 6:13
of the bottle with water, and gave. ...... Gen 21:19
f her pitcher, and came up........... Gen 24:16
them, and *f* them with water. .... Gen 26:15
and the land was *f* with them .... Ex 1:7
f the troughs to water their. .... Ex 2:16
morning ye shall be *f* with bread .... Ex 16:12
whom I have *f* with the spirit of .... Ex 28:3
f them with the spirit of .... Ex 31:3
he hath *f* him with the spirit of .... Ex 35:31
Them hath he *f* with wisdom of .... Ex 35:35
of the tabernacle, and the *f*.......... Ex 40:34
of the LORD *f* the tabernacle. .... Ex 40:35
all the earth shall be *f* with the ...... Num 14:21
may eat within thy gates, and be *f* ..... Deut 26:12
f themselves, and waxen fat............ Deut 31:20
these bottles of wine, which we *f*....... Josh 9:13

and he was f with wisdom, and......... 1Kin 7:14
that the cloud f the house of the 1Kin 8:10
LORD had f the house of the LORD 1Kin 8:11
he f the trench also with water 1Kin 18:35
but the Syrians f the country............ 1Kin 20:27
that valley shall be f with water 2Kin 3:17
and the country was f with water...... 2Kin 3:20
cast every man his stone, and f it 2Kin 3:25
till he had f Jerusalem from one....... 2Kin 21:16
f their places with the bones of 2Kin 23:14
for he f Jerusalem with innocent 2Kin 24:4
then the house was f with a cloud 2Chr 5:13
the LORD had f the house of God...... 2Chr 5:14
the glory of the LORD f the house 2Chr 7:1
the LORD had f the LORD's house 2Chr 7:2
bed which was f with sweet odours ... 2Chr 16:14
which have f it from one end to .... Ezr 9:11
so they did eat, and were f............... Neh 9:25
who f their houses with silver .... Job 3:15
thou hast f me with wrinkles, ... Job 16:8
Yet he f their houses with good .... Job 22:18
For my loins are f with .... Ps 38:7
Let my mouth be f with thy praise .... Ps 71:8
whole earth be f with his glory .... Ps 72:19
So they did eat, and were well f........ Ps 78:29
take deep root, and it f the .... Ps 80:9
thine hand, they are f with good ...... Ps 104:28
are exceedingly f with contempt........ Ps 123:3
Our soul is exceedingly f with .... Ps 123:4
was our mouth f with laughter .... Ps 126:2
be f with their own devices .... Prov 1:31
shall thy barns be f with plenty......... Prov 3:10
strangers be f with thy wealth .... Prov 5:10
wicked shall be f with mischief .... Prov 12:21
shall be f with his own ways .... Prov 14:14
of his lips shall he be f..................... Prov 18:20
his mouth shall be f with gravel........ Prov 20:17
chambers be f with all precious .... Prov 24:4
thee, lest thou be f therewith .... Prov 25:16
earth that is not f with water........... Prov 30:16
and a fool when he is f with meat .... Prov 30:22
nor the ear f with hearing .... Eccl 1:8
and his soul be not f with good .... Eccl 6:3
and yet the appetite is not f............. Eccl 6:7
for my head is f with dew .... Song 5:2
up, and his train f the temple .... Is 6:1
and the house was f with smoke........ Is 6:4
are my loins f with pain..................... Is 21:3
he hath f Zion with judgment and..... Is 33:5
placed in the f house also he .... Is 34:6
neither hast thou f me with the .... Is 43:24
old man that hath not f his days....... Is 65:20
Every bottle shall be f with wine....... Jer 13:12
every bottle shall be f with wine....... Jer 13:12
for thou hast f me with..................... Jer 15:17
they have f mine inheritance with .... Jer 16:18
have f this place with the blood .... Jer 19:4
f it with them that were slain .... Jer 41:9
shame, and thy city hath f the land... Jer 46:12
though their land was f with sin .... Jer 51:5
he hath f his belly with my............... Jer 51:34
He hath f me with bitterness, he ...... Lam 3:15
he is f full with reproach.................. Lam 3:30
for they have f the land with .... Eze 8:17
the cloud f the inner court............... Eze 10:3
The house was f with the cloud,........ Eze 10:4
ye have f the streets thereof............. Eze 11:6
Thou shalt be f with drunkenness .... Eze 23:33
of thy merchandise they have f......... Eze 28:16
cities be f with flocks of men............ Eze 36:38
Thus ye shall be f at my table........... Eze 39:20
the glory of the LORD f the house...... Eze 43:5
the LORD f the house of the LORD ...... Eze 44:4
mountain, and f the whole earth....... Dan 2:35
to their pasture, so were they f......... Hos 13:6
they were f, and their heart was........ Hos 13:6
f his holes with prey, and his........... Nah 2:12
For the earth shall be f with the ...... Hab 2:14
Thou art f with shame for glory .... Hab 2:16
but ye are not f with drink .... Hag 1:6
the bow with Ephraim, and raised .... Zec 9:13
and they shall be f like bowls,.......... Zec 9:15
for they shall be f.......................... Mt 5:6
And they did all eat, and were f........ Mt 14:20
And they did all eat, and were f........ Mt 15:37
f it with vinegar, and put it on a...... Mt 27:48
else the new piece that f it up .... Mk 2:21
And they did all eat, and were f........ Mk 6:42
her, Let the children first be f............ Mk 7:27
So they did eat, and were f .... Mk 8:8
f a sponge full of vinegar, and......... Mk 15:36
he shall be f with the Holy Ghost...... Lk 1:15
Elisabeth was f with the Holy .... Lk 1:41
He hath f the hungry with good........ Lk 1:53
was f with the Holy Ghost................. Lk 1:67
strong in spirit, f with wisdom.......... Lk 2:40
Every valley shall be f, and every ..... Lk 3:5
these things, were f with wrath,........ Lk 4:28
f both the ships, so that they .... Lk 5:7
were f with fear, saying, We have ..... Lk 5:26
And they were f with madness.......... Lk 6:11
for ye shall be f............................... Lk 6:21
they were f with water, and were ..... Lk 8:23
And they did eat, and were all f........ Lk 9:17
come in, that my house may be f ...... Lk 14:23
he would fain have f his belly .... Lk 15:16
they f them up to the brim .... Jn 2:7
When they were f, he said unto........ Jn 6:12
f twelve baskets with the .... Jn 6:13
did eat of the loaves, and were f ...... Jn 6:26

the house was f with the odour of .... Jn 12:3
you, sorrow hath f your heart .... Jn 16:6
they f a spunge with vinegar, and .... Jn 19:29
it f all the house where they............ Acts 2:2
they were all f with the Holy........... Acts 2:4
they were f with wonder and .... Acts 3:10
f with the Holy Ghost, and said .... Acts 4:8
they were all f with the Holy........... Acts 4:31
why hath Satan f thine heart to ...... Acts 5:3
and were f with indignation,............. Acts 5:17
ye have f Jerusalem with your.......... Acts 5:28
and be f with the Holy Ghost .... Acts 9:17
f with the Holy Ghost, set his .... Acts 13:9
multitudes, they were f with envy..... Acts 13:45
And the disciples were f with joy...... Acts 13:52
whole city was f with confusion .... Acts 19:29
Being f with all unrighteousness,...... Rom 1:29
f with all knowledge, able also......... Rom 15:14
I be somewhat f with your company.. Rom 15:24
I am f with comfort, I am 2Cor 7:4
that ye might be f with all the .... Eph 3:19
but be f with the Spirit..................... Eph 5:18
Being f with the fruits of .... Phil 1:11
to desire that ye might be f with...... Col 1:9
tears, that I may be f with joy.......... 2Ti 1:4
in peace, be ye warmed and f .... Jas 2:16
f it with fire of the altar, and .... Rev 8:5
for in them is f up the wrath of....... Rev 15:1
the temple was f with smoke from.... Rev 15:8
the hath f fill to her double............. Rev 18:6
the fowls were f with their flesh ...... Rev 19:21

FILLEDST

all good things, which thou f not...... Deut 6:11
of the seas, thou f many people........ Eze 27:33

FILLEST

whose belly thou f with thy hid....... Ps 17:14

FILLET

a f of twelve cubits did compass...... Jer 52:21

FILLETED

the court shall be f with silver.......... Ex 27:17
of the court were f with silver.......... Ex 38:17
their chapters, and f them................ Ex 38:28

FILLETH

breath, but f me with bitterness .... Job 9:18
the rain also f the pools................... Ps 84:6
f the hungry soul with goodness ...... Ps 107:9
the mower f not his hand................. Ps 129:7
f thee with the finest of the .... Ps 147:14
fulness of him that f all in all .... Eph 1:23

FILLETS

their f shall be of silver.................... Ex 27:11
the pillars and their f of silver......... Ex 27:11
chapters and their f with gold.......... Ex 36:38
pillars and their f were of silver .... Ex 38:10
the pillars and their f of silver......... Ex 38:11
the pillars and their f of silver......... Ex 38:12
the pillars and their f of silver......... Ex 38:12
chapters and their f of silver .... Ex 38:19

FILLING

f our hearts with food and .... Acts 14:17

FILTH

the f of the daughters of Zion.......... Is 4:4
will cast abominable f upon thee...... Nah 3:6
are made as the f of the world......... 1Cor 4:13
away of the f of the flesh................. 1Pet 3:21

FILTHINESS

carry forth the f out of the holy....... 2Chr 29:5
the f of the heathen of the land....... Ezr 6:21
the f of the people of the lands .... Ezr 9:11
and yet is not washed from own f .... Prov 30:12
all tables are full of vomit and f....... Is 28:8
Her f is in her skirts........................ Lam 1:9
Because thy f was poured out, and... Eze 16:36
and will consume thy f out of the .... Eze 22:15
that the f of it may be molten in...... Eze 24:11
In thy f is lewdness........................ Eze 24:13
not be purged from thy f any more... Eze 24:13
from all your f, and from all your .... Eze 36:25
ourselves from all f of the flesh....... 2Cor 7:1
Neither f, nor foolish talking,........... Eph 5:4
Wherefore lay apart all f.................. Jas 1:21
and by the overflowing of f 1Pet 2:7

FILTHY

f is man, which drinketh iniquity ..... Job 15:16
they are all together become f .... Ps 14:3
they are altogether become f .... Ps 53:3
our righteousnesses are as f rags...... Is 64:6
Woe to her that is f and polluted,.... Zeph 3:1
was clothed with f garments............ Zec 3:3
Take away the f garments from him... Zec 3:4
f communication out of your mouth .. Col 3:8
no striker, not greedy of f lucre 1Ti 3:3
much wine, not greedy of f lucre...... 1Ti 3:8
no striker, not given to f lucre .... Titus 1:7
ought not, for f lucre's sake............. Titus 1:11
not for f lucre, but of a ready 1Pet 5:2
vexed with the f conversation of 2Pet 2:7
Likewise also these f dreamers......... Jude 8
and he which is f, let him be........... Rev 22:11
let him be f still .... Rev 22:11

FINALLY

F, brethren, farewell........................ 2Cor 13:11
F, my brethren, be strong in the ...... Eph 6:10
F, my brethren, rejoice in the .... Phil 3:1

F, brethren, whatsoever things.......... Phil 4:8
F, brethren, pray for us, that 2Th 3:1
F, be ye all of one mind, having....... 1Pet 3:8

FIND

If I in Sodom fifty righteous .... Gen 18:26
If I f there forty and five, I .... Gen 18:28
not do it, if I f thirty there.............. Gen 18:30
weaned themselves to f the door ...... Gen 19:11
that I may f grace in thy sight......... Gen 32:5
ye speak unto Esau, when ye f him... Gen 32:19
These are to f grace in the sight ...... Gen 33:8
let me f grace in the sight of my ..... Gen 33:15
Let me f grace in your eyes, and ..... Gen 34:11
to Judah, and said, I cannot f her ... Gen 38:22
Can we f such a one as this is, a .... Gen 41:38
let us f grace in the sight of my ..... Gen 47:25
get you straw where ye can f it....... Ex 5:11
ye shall not f it in the field .... Ex 16:25
that I may f grace in the field .... Ex 33:13
be sure your sin will f you out........ Num 32:23
the revenger of blood f him............ Num 35:27
LORD thy God, thou shalt f him........ Deut 4:29
a man f her in the city, and lie........ Deut 22:23
But if a man f a betrothed damsel ... Deut 22:25
If a man f a damsel that is a .... Deut 22:28
that she f no favour in his eyes....... Deut 24:1
nations shalt thou f no ease............ Deut 28:65
to them as thou shalt f occasion..... Judg 9:33
if it out, then I will give you .... Judg 14:12
sojourn where he could f a place..... Judg 17:8
to sojourn where I may f a place ..... Judg 17:9
LORD grant you that ye may f rest ... Ruth 1:9
in whose sight I shall f grace.......... Ruth 2:2
Let me f favour in thy sight, my...... Ruth 2:13
handmaid f grace in thy sight 1Sa 1:18
city, ye shall straightway f him........ 1Sa 9:13
about this time ye shall f him 1Sa 9:13
then thou shalt f two men by.......... 1Sa 10:2
lad, saying, Go, f out the arrows 1Sa 20:21
f out now the arrows which I 1Sa 20:36
Saul my father shall not f thee 1Sa 23:17
For if a man f his enemy, will he 1Sa 24:19
young men f favour in thine eyes 1Sa 25:8
if I shall f favour in the eyes 2Sa 15:25
that I may f grace in thy sight........ 2Sa 16:4
had sought and could not f them 2Sa 17:20
peradventure we may f grass to 1Kin 18:5
and tell Ahab, and he cannot f thee.. 1Kin 18:12
to f out every device which shall 2Chr 2:14
ye shall f them at the end of the 2Chr 20:16
your children shall f compassion...... 2Chr 30:9
of Assyria come, and f much water... 2Chr 32:4
so shalt thou f the book of .... Ezr 4:15
gold that thou canst f in all the...... Ezr 7:16
glad, when they can f the grave ...... Job 3:22
Canst thou by searching f out God... Job 11:7
canst thou f out the Almighty......... Job 11:7
for I cannot f one wise man among.. Job 19:10
that I knew where I might f him ...... Job 23:3
cause every man to f according to ... Job 34:11
the Almighty, we cannot f him out... Job 37:23
his wickedness till thou f none .... Ps 10:15
hast tried me, and shalt f nothing ... Ps 17:3
Thine hand shall f out all thine .... Ps 21:8
thy right hand shall f out those ...... Ps 21:8
Until I f out a place for the .... Ps 132:5
We shall f all precious substance..... Prov 1:13
me early, but they shall not f me ..... Prov 1:28
LORD, and the knowledge of God...... Prov 2:5
So shalt thou f favour and good...... Prov 3:4
are life unto those that f them .... Prov 4:22
and right to them that f knowledge.. Prov 8:9
and f out knowledge of witty .... Prov 8:12
that seek me early shall f me.......... Prov 8:17
a matter wisely shall f good............ Prov 16:20
understanding shall f good............... Prov 19:8
but a faithful man who can f.......... Prov 20:6
shall f more favour than he that ..... Prov 28:23
Who can f a virtuous woman........... Prov 31:10
so that no man can f out the work .. Eccl 3:11
man should f nothing after him....... Eccl 7:14
exceeding deep, who can f it out ..... Eccl 7:24
I f more bitter than death the .... Eccl 7:26
one by one, to f out the account..... Eccl 7:27
yet my soul seeketh, but I f not...... Eccl 7:28
that a man cannot f out the work ... Eccl 8:17
it out, yet he shall not f it.............. Eccl 8:17
yet shall he not be able to f it .... Eccl 8:17
for thou shalt f it after many .... Eccl 11:1
sought to f out acceptable words .... Eccl 12:10
sought him, but I could not f him ... Song 5:6
if ye f my beloved, that ye tell........ Song 5:8
when I should f thee without........... Song 8:1
f for herself a place of rest .... Is 34:14
seek them, and shalt not f them ..... Is 41:12
day of your fast ye f pleasure.......... Is 58:3
in her month they shall f her.......... Jer 2:24
place thereof, if ye can f a man ...... Jer 5:1
ye shall f rest for your souls........... Jer 6:16
them, that they may f it so .... Jer 10:18
f me, when ye shall search for me ... Jer 29:13
in my sighing, and I f no rest.......... Jer 45:3
like harts that f no pasture .... Lam 1:6
her prophets also f no vision........... Lam 2:9
princes sought to f occasion............ Dan 6:4
except we f it against him............... Dan 6:5
that she shall not f her paths.......... Hos 2:6
seek them, but shall not f them....... Hos 2:7

but they shall not f him .... Hos 5:6
in all my labours they shall f .... Hos 12:8
of the LORD, and shall not f it .... Amos 8:12
seek, and ye shall f .... Mt 7:7
life, and few there be that f it .... Mt 7:14
his life for my sake shall f it .... Mt 10:39
ye shall f rest unto your souls .... Mt 11:29
his life for my sake shall f it .... Mt 16:25
thou shalt f a piece of money .... Mt 17:27
And if so be that he f it, verily .... Mt 18:13
ye shall f an ass tied, and a colt .... Mt 21:2
and as many as ye shall f .... Mt 22:9
when he cometh shall f so doing .... Mt 24:46
ye shall f a colt tied, whereon .... Mk 11:2
he might f any thing thereon .... Mk 11:13
coming suddenly he f you sleeping ... Mk 13:36
Ye shall f the babe wrapped in .... Lk 2:12
when they could not f by what way ... Lk 5:19
that they might f an accusation .... Lk 6:7
seek, and ye shall f .... Lk 11:9
when he cometh shall f watching ...... Lk 12:37
f them so, blessed are those .... Lk 12:38
when he cometh shall f so doing .... Lk 12:43
fruit on this fig tree, and f none .... Lk 13:7
that which is lost, until he f it .... Lk 15:4
and seek diligently till she f it .... Lk 15:8
shall he f faith on the earth .... Lk 18:8
entering ye shall f a colt tied .... Lk 19:30
could not f what they might do .... Lk 23:4
people, I f no fault in this man .... Lk 23:4
shall seek me, and shall not f me ...... Jn 7:34
he go, that we shall not f him .... Jn 7:35
shall seek me, and shall not f me ...... Jn 7:36
shall go in and out, and f pasture ..... Jn 10:9
I f in him no fault at all .... Jn 18:38
may know that I f no fault in him ..... Jn 19:4
for I f no fault in him .... Jn 19:6
side of the ship, and ye shall f .... Jn 21:6
desired to f a tabernacle for the .... Acts 7:46
f him, though he be not far from .... Acts 17:27
saying, We f no evil in this man .... Acts 23:9
that which is good f not .... Rom 7:18
I f then a law, that, when I .... Rom 7:21
unto me, Why doth he yet f fault ...... Rom 9:19
you unprepared, we (that we say 2Cor 9:4
I shall not f you such as I would 2Cor 12:20
f mercy of the Lord in that day 2Ti 1:18
f grace to help in time of need .... Heb 4:16
men seek death, and shall not f it ..... Rev 9:6
thou shalt f them no more at all .... Rev 18:14

FINDEST

With whomsoever thou f thy gods ..... Gen 31:32
me, Son of man, eat that thou f .... Eze 3:1

FINDETH

every one that f me shall slay me ...... Gen 4:14
he f occasions against me, he .... Job 33:10
word, as one that f great spoil .... Ps 119:162
Happy is the man that f wisdom .... Prov 3:13
For whoso f me f life .... Prov 8:35
seeketh wisdom, and f it not .... Prov 14:6
hath a froward heart f no good .... Prov 17:20
Whoso f a wife f a good .... Prov 18:22
his neighbour f no favour in his .... Prov 21:10
righteousness and mercy f life .... Prov 21:21
Whatsoever thy hand f to do .... Eccl 9:10
among the heathen, she f no rest ...... Lam 1:3
in thee the fatherless f mercy .... Hos 14:3
and he that seeketh f .... Mt 7:8
He that f his life shall lose it .... Mt 10:39
places, seeking rest, and f none .... Mt 12:43
is come, he f it empty, swept, and ..... Mt 12:44
f them asleep, and saith unto .... Mt 26:40
them sleeping, and saith unto .... Mk 14:37
and he that seeketh f .... Lk 11:10
he f it swept and garnished .... Lk 11:25
He first f his own brother Simon, ... Jn 1:41
f Philip, and saith unto him, ... Jn 1:43
Philip f Nathanael, and saith unto ... Jn 1:45
Afterward Jesus f him in the .... Jn 5:14

FINDING

lest any f him should kill him .... Gen 4:15
doeth great things past f out .... Job 9:10
nor f thine own pleasure, nor .... Is 58:13
f none, he saith, I will return .... Lk 11:24
f nothing how they might punish ...... Acts 4:21
and f certain disciples, ... Acts 19:1
f a ship sailing over unto .... Acts 21:2
disciples, we tarried there .... Acts 21:4
judgments, and his ways past f out ... Rom 11:33
For f fault with them, he saith, ... Heb 8:8

FINE

quickly three measures of f meal ...... Gen 18:6
him in vestures of f linen .... Gen 41:42
and f linen, and goats' hair, ... Ex 25:4
ten curtains of f twined linen .... Ex 26:1
f twined linen of cunning work, ... Ex 26:31
f twined linen, wrought with .... Ex 26:36
of f twined linen of an hundred .... Ex 27:9
f twined linen, wrought with .... Ex 27:16
five cubits of f twined linen .... Ex 27:18
and purple, and scarlet, and f linen, . Ex 28:5
f twined linen, with cunning work .... Ex 28:6
and scarlet, and f twined linen .... Ex 28:8
of f twined linen, shalt thou............... Ex 28:15
embroider the coat of f linen, ... Ex 28:39
shalt make the mitre of f linen, ... Ex 28:39
and f linen, and goats' hair, ... Ex 35:6
f linen, and goats' hair, and red .... Ex 35:23

and of scarlet, and of f linen .... Ex 35:25
in f linen, and of the weaver, ... Ex 35:35
ten curtains of f twined linen .... Ex 36:8
and scarlet, and f twined linen .... Ex 36:8
f twined linen, of needlework .... Ex 36:37
the court were of f twined linen. .... Ex 38:9
about were of f twined linen .... Ex 38:16
and scarlet, and f twined linen .... Ex 38:18
purple, and in scarlet, and f linen ..... Ex 38:23
and scarlet, and f twined linen .... Ex 39:2
in the scarlet, and in the f linen .... Ex 39:3
and scarlet, and f linen .... Ex 39:5
and scarlet, and f twined linen .... Ex 39:8
they made coats of f linen of .... Ex 39:27
And a mitre of f linen, ... Ex 39:28
and goodly bonnets of f linen .... Ex 39:28
linen breeches of f twined linen .... Ex 39:28
a girdle of f twined linen, and .... Ex 39:29
his offering shall be of f flour .... Lev 2:1
cakes of f flour mingled with oil .... Lev 2:4
it shall be of f flour unleavened .... Lev 2:5
shall be made of f flour with oil .... Lev 2:7
of f flour for a sin offering, ... Lev 5:11
of f flour for a meat offering .... Lev 6:20
with oil, of f flour, fried .... Lev 7:12
three tenth deals of f flour for .... Lev 14:10
one tenth deal of f flour mingled ...... Lev 14:21
deals of f flour mingled with oil, ... Lev 23:13
they shall be of f flour .... Lev 23:17
And thou shalt take f flour .... Lev 24:5
cakes of f flour mingled with oil .... Num 6:15
both of them were full of f flour .... Num 7:13
both of them full of f flour .... Num 7:19
both of them full of f flour .... Num 7:25
both of them full of f flour .... Num 7:31
both of them full of f flour .... Num 7:37
both of them full of f flour .... Num 7:43
both of them full of f flour .... Num 7:55
both of them full of f flour .... Num 7:61
both of them full of f flour .... Num 7:67
both of them full of f flour .... Num 7:73
both of them full of f flour .... Num 7:79
even f flour mingled with oil, and. .... Num 8:8
was thirty measures of f flour 1Kin 4:22
of f flour be sold for a shekel 2Kin 7:1
So a measure of f flour was sold 2Kin 7:16
a measure of f flour for a shekel 2Kin 7:18
of them that wrought f linen 1Chr 4:21
the f flour, and the wine, and the 1Chr 9:29
clothed with a robe of f linen 1Chr 15:27
for the f flour for meat offering........ 1Chr 23:29
in f linen, and in crimson 2Chr 3:14
which he overlaid with f gold 2Chr 3:5
and he overlaid it with f gold 2Chr 3:8
f linen, and wrought cherubims 2Chr 3:14
and two vessels of f copper .... Ezr 8:27
fastened with cords of f linen .... Est 1:6
and with a garment of f linen .... Est 8:15
a place for gold where they f it .... Job 28:1
shall not be for jewels of f gold .... Job 28:17
hope, or have said to the f gold .... Job 31:24
than gold, yea, than much f gold .... Ps 19:10
yea, above f gold .... Ps 119:127
and the gain thereof than f gold........ Prov 3:14
works, with f linen of Egypt .... Prov 7:16
than gold, yea, than f gold .... Prov 8:19
of gold, and an ornament of f gold ... Prov 25:12
She maketh f linen, and selleth it ..... Prov 31:24
His head is as the most f gold .... Song 5:11
set upon sockets of f gold .... Song 5:15
the f linen, and the hoods, and the ... Is 3:23
a man more precious than f gold .... Is 13:12
Moreover they that work in f flax ..... Is 19:9
how is the most f gold changed .... Lam 4:1
of Zion, comparable to f gold .... Lam 4:2
I girded thee about with f linen .... Eze 16:10
and thy raiment was of f linen .... Eze 16:13
thou didst eat f flour, and honey, ... Eze 16:13
f flour, and oil, and honey, ... Eze 16:19
f linen with broidered work from ..... Eze 27:7
f linen, and coral, and agate .... Eze 27:16
oil, to temper with the f flour .... Eze 46:14
This image's head was of f gold. .... Dan 2:32
were girded with f gold of Uphaz ..... Dan 10:5
f gold as the mire of the streets........ Zec 9:3
And he bought f linen, and took him . Mk 15:46
f linen, and fared sumptuously .... Lk 16:19
And his feet like unto f brass .... Rev 1:15
and his feet are like f brass .... Rev 2:18
f linen, and purple, and silk, and ...... Rev 18:12
f flour, and wheat, and beasts, and ... Rev 18:13
city, that was clothed in f linen .... Rev 18:16
she should be arrayed in f linen .... Rev 19:8
for the f linen is the .... Rev 19:8
white horses, clothed in f linen .... Rev 19:14

FINER

come forth a vessel for the f .... Prov 25:4

FINEST

them also with the f of the wheat ...... Ps 81:16
with the f of the wheat .... Ps 147:14

FINGER

Pharaoh, This is the f of God .... Ex 8:19
the horns of the altar with thy f .... Ex 29:12
stone, written with the f of God, ... Ex 31:18
shall dip his f in the blood, ... Lev 4:6
dip his f in some of the blood, ... Lev 4:17
of the sin offering with his f .... Lev 4:25
of the blood thereof with his f .... Lev 4:30

of the sin offering with his f .... Lev 4:34
the altar round about with his f .... Lev 8:15
and he dipped his f in the blood .... Lev 9:9
f in the oil that is in his left .... Lev 14:16
his f seven times before the LORD ... Lev 14:16
shall sprinkle with his right f .... Lev 14:27
sprinkle it with his f upon the .... Lev 16:14
the blood with his f seven times, ... Lev 16:14
upon it with his f seven times, ... Lev 16:19
take of her blood with his f .... Num 19:4
stone written with the f of God .... Deut 9:10
My little f shall be thicker than. 1Kin 12:10
My little f shall be thicker than, ... 2Chr 10:10
yoke, the putting forth of the f .... Is 58:9
But if I with the f of God cast .... Lk 11:20
may dip the tip of his f in water .... Lk 16:24
with his f wrote on the ground, ... Jn 8:6
put my f into the print of the .... Jn 20:25
he to Thomas, Reach hither thy f ...... Jn 20:27

FINGERS

that had on every hand six f 2Sa 21:20
a man of great stature, whose f 1Chr 20:6
thy heavens, the work of thy f .... Ps 8:3
my hands to war, and my f to fight ... Ps 144:1
his feet, he teacheth with his f .... Prov 6:13
Bind them upon thy f, write them ..... Prov 7:3
my f with sweet smelling myrrh, ... Song 5:5
that which their own f have made. ..... Is 2:8
that which his f have made .... Is 17:8
blood, and your f with iniquity .... Is 59:3
the thickness thereof was four f .... Jer 52:21
four came forth of a man's hand .... Dan 5:5
not move them with one of their f .... Mt 23:4
put his f into his ears, and he .... Mk 7:33
the burdens with one of your f .... Lk 11:46

FINING

The f pot is for silver, and the........... Prov 17:3
As the f pot for silver, and the.......... Prov 27:21

FINISH

in a cubit shalt thou f it above .... Gen 6:16
to f the transgression, and to .... Dan 9:24
his hands shall also f it .... Zec 4:9
he have sufficient to f it .... Lk 14:28
and is not able to f it, all that .... Lk 14:29
to build, and was not able to f .... Lk 14:30
that sent me, and to f his work, ... Jn 4:34
the Father hath given me to f .... Jn 5:36
so that I might f my course with .... Acts 20:24
f the work, and cut it .... Rom 9:28
so he would also f in you the 2Cor 8:6

FINISHED

the heavens and the earth were f .... Gen 2:1
of the tent of the congregation f .... Ex 39:32
So Moses f the work .... Ex 40:33
law in a book, until they were f .... Deut 31:24
until every thing was f that the .... Josh 4:10
until he have f the thing this. .... Ruth 3:18
So he built the house, and f it, ... 1Kin 6:9
Solomon built the house, and f it, ... 1Kin 6:14
until he had f all the house 1Kin 6:22
was the house f throughout all. 1Kin 6:38
years, and he f all his house 1Kin 7:1
so was the work of the pillars f 1Kin 7:22
when Solomon had f the building 1Kin 9:1
So he f the house 1Kin 9:25
began to number, but he f not 1Chr 27:24
until thou hast f all the work............ 1Chr 28:20
Huram f the work that he was to 2Chr 4:11
for the house of the LORD was f 2Chr 5:1
Thus Solomon f the house of the 2Chr 7:11
of the LORD, and until it was f 2Chr 8:16
And when they had f it, they 2Chr 24:14
until the burnt offering was f 2Chr 29:28
Now when all this was f, all. 2Chr 31:1
f them in the seventh month 2Chr 31:7
in building, and yet it is not f .... Ezr 5:16
and f it, according to the .... Ezr 6:14
this house was f on the third day ..... Ezr 6:15
So the wall was f in the twenty .... Neh 6:15
numbered thy kingdom, and f it .... Dan 5:26
all these things shall be f .... Dan 12:7
when Jesus had f these parables .... Mt 13:53
when Jesus had f these sayings .... Mt 19:1
when Jesus had f these sayings .... Mt 26:1
I have f the work which thou .... Jn 17:4
the vinegar, he said, It is f .... Jn 19:30
when we had f our course from .... Acts 21:7
I have f my course, I have kept 2Ti 4:7
although the works were f from .... Heb 4:3
and sin, when it is f, bringeth .... Jas 1:15
the mystery of God should be f .... Rev 10:7
they shall have f their testimony ...... Rev 11:7
until the thousand years were f .... Rev 20:5

FINISHER

the author and f of our faith .... Heb 12:2

FINS

whatsoever hath f and scales in .... Lev 11:9
And all that have not f and scales ..... Lev 11:10
Whatsoever hath no f nor scales, ... Lev 11:12
all that have f and scales shall .... Deut 14:9
And whatsoever hath not f and .... Deut 14:10

FIR

of instruments made of f wood 2Sa 6:5
cedar, and concerning timber of f 1Kin 5:8
f trees according to all his 1Kin 5:10
the house with planks of f 1Kin 6:15

And the two doors were of f tree...... 1Kin 6:34
f trees, and with gold, according...... 1Kin 9:11
the choice f trees thereof...... 2Kin 19:23
f trees, and algum trees, out of...... 2Chr 2:8
house he cieled with f tree...... 2Chr 3:5
the f trees are her house...... Ps 104:17
are cedar, and our rafters of f...... Song 1:17
the f trees rejoice at thee, and...... Is 14:8
the choice f trees thereof...... Is 37:24
will set in the desert the f tree...... Is 41:19
thorn shall come up the f tree...... Is 55:13
the f tree, the pine tree, and the...... Is 60:13
ship boards of f trees of Senir...... Eze 27:5
the f trees were not like his...... Eze 31:8
I am like a green f tree...... Hos 14:8
the f trees shall be terribly...... Nah 2:3
Howl, f tree...... Zec 11:2

FIRE

f from the LORD out of heaven...... Gen 19:24
and he took the f in his hand...... Gen 22:6
And he said, Behold the f and the...... Gen 22:7
of f out of the midst of a bush...... Ex 3:2
behold, the bush burned with f...... Ex 3:2
the f ran along upon the ground...... Ex 9:23
f mingled with the hail, very...... Ex 9:24
flesh in that night, roast with f...... Ex 12:8
all with water, but roast with f...... Ex 12:9
the morning ye shall burn with f...... Ex 12:10
and by night in a pillar of f...... Ex 13:21
day, nor the pillar of f by night...... Ex 13:22
Egyptians through the pillar of f...... Ex 14:24
the LORD descended upon it in f...... Ex 19:18
If f break out, and catch in...... Ex 22:6
he that kindled the f shall...... Ex 22:6
f on the top of the mount in the...... Ex 24:17
thou burn with f without the camp...... Ex 29:14
offering made by f unto the LORD...... Ex 29:18
offering made by f unto the LORD...... Ex 29:25
shalt burn the remainder with f...... Ex 29:34
offering made by f unto the LORD...... Ex 29:41
offering made by f unto the LORD...... Ex 30:20
had made, and burnt it in the f...... Ex 32:20
then I cast it into the f...... Ex 32:24
Ye shall kindle no f throughout...... Ex 35:3
f was on it by night, in the...... Ex 40:38
priest shall put f upon the altar...... Lev 1:7
lay the wood in order upon the f...... Lev 1:7
on the f which is upon the altar...... Lev 1:8
sacrifice, an offering made by f...... Lev 1:9
on the f which is upon the altar...... Lev 1:12
sacrifice, an offering made by f...... Lev 1:13
upon the wood that is upon the f...... Lev 1:17
sacrifice, an offering made by f...... Lev 1:17
to be an offering made by f...... Lev 2:2
offerings of the LORD made by f...... Lev 2:3
it is an offering made by f...... Lev 2:9
offerings of the LORD made by f...... Lev 2:10
offering of the LORD made by f...... Lev 2:11
green ears of corn dried by the f...... Lev 2:14
offering made by f unto the LORD...... Lev 2:16
offering made by f unto the LORD...... Lev 3:3
is upon the wood that is on the f...... Lev 3:5
it is an offering made by f...... Lev 3:5
offering made by f unto the LORD...... Lev 3:9
offering made by f unto the LORD...... Lev 3:11
offering made by f unto the LORD...... Lev 3:14
made by f for a sweet savour...... Lev 3:16
and burn him on the wood with f...... Lev 4:12
offerings made by f unto the LORD...... Lev 4:35
offerings made by f unto the LORD...... Lev 5:12
the f of the altar shall be...... Lev 6:9
take up the ashes which the f...... Lev 6:10
the f upon the altar shall be...... Lev 6:12
The f shall ever be burning upon...... Lev 6:13
portion of my offerings made by f...... Lev 6:17
offerings of the LORD made by f...... Lev 6:18
it shall be burnt in the f...... Lev 6:30
offering made by f unto the LORD...... Lev 7:5
third day shall be burnt with f...... Lev 7:17
it shall be burnt with f...... Lev 7:19
offering made by f unto the LORD...... Lev 7:25
offerings of the LORD made by f...... Lev 7:30
offerings of the LORD made by f...... Lev 7:35
he burnt with f without the camp...... Lev 8:17
offering made by f unto the LORD...... Lev 8:21
offering made by f unto the LORD...... Lev 8:28
of the bread shall ye burn with f...... Lev 8:32
he burnt with f without the camp...... Lev 9:11
there came a f out from before...... Lev 9:24
put f therein, and put incense...... Lev 10:1
offered strange f before the LORD...... Lev 10:1
And there went out f from the LORD...... Lev 10:2
offerings of the LORD made by f...... Lev 10:12
sacrifices of the LORD made by f...... Lev 10:13
offerings made by f of the fat...... Lev 10:15
it shall be burnt in the f...... Lev 13:52
thou shalt burn it in the f...... Lev 13:55
that wherein the plague is with f...... Lev 13:57
f from off the altar before the...... Lev 16:12
upon the f before the LORD...... Lev 16:13
shall burn in the f their skins...... Lev 16:27
seed pass through the f to Molech...... Lev 18:21
day, it shall be burnt in the f...... Lev 19:6
they shall be burnt with f...... Lev 20:14
offerings of the LORD made by f...... Lev 21:6
she shall be burnt with f...... Lev 21:9
offerings of the LORD made by f...... Lev 21:21
nor make an offering by f of them...... Lev 22:22
offering made by f unto the LORD...... Lev 22:27
by f unto the LORD seven days...... Lev 23:8

an offering made by f unto the...... Lev 23:13
even an offering made by f...... Lev 23:18
offering made by f unto the LORD...... Lev 23:25
offering made by f unto the LORD...... Lev 23:27
offering made by f unto the LORD...... Lev 23:36
offering made by f unto the LORD...... Lev 23:36
offering made by f unto the LORD...... Lev 23:37
offering made by f unto the LORD...... Lev 24:7
made by f by a perpetual statute...... Lev 24:9
offered strange f before the LORD...... Num 3:4
put it in the f which is under...... Num 6:18
as it were the appearance of f...... Num 9:15
and the appearance of f by night...... Num 9:16
the f of the LORD burnt among...... Num 11:1
unto the LORD, the f was quenched...... Num 11:2
because the f of the LORD burnt...... Num 11:3
and in a pillar of f by night...... Num 14:14
an offering by f unto the LORD...... Num 15:3
wine, for an offering made by f...... Num 15:10
in offering an offering made by f...... Num 15:13
will offer an offering made by f...... Num 15:14
sacrifice made by f unto the LORD...... Num 15:25
put f therein, and put incense in...... Num 16:7
put f in them, and laid incense...... Num 16:18
there came out a f from the LORD...... Num 16:35
and scatter thou the f yonder...... Num 16:37
put f therein from off the altar...... Num 16:46
holy things, reserved from the f...... Num 18:9
fat for an offering made by f...... Num 18:17
For there is a f gone out of...... Num 21:28
what time the f devoured two...... Num 26:10
offered strange f before the LORD...... Num 26:61
bread for my sacrifices made by f...... Num 28:2
This is the offering made by f...... Num 28:3
sacrifice made by f unto the LORD...... Num 28:6
offer it, a sacrifice made by f...... Num 28:8
for a burnt offering made by f...... Num 28:19
meat of the sacrifice made by f...... Num 28:24
sacrifice made by f unto the LORD...... Num 28:19
offering, a sacrifice made by f...... Num 29:13
offering, a sacrifice made by f...... Num 29:36
all their goodly castles, with f...... Num 31:10
Every thing that may abide the f...... Num 31:23
ye shall make it go through the f...... Num 31:23
all that abideth not the f...... Num 31:23
in f by night, to shew you by...... Deut 1:33
with f unto the midst of heaven...... Deut 4:11
you out of the midst of the f...... Deut 4:12
Horeb out of the midst of the f...... Deut 4:15
the LORD thy God is a consuming f...... Deut 4:24
out of the midst of the f...... Deut 4:33
earth he shewed thee his great f...... Deut 4:36
words out of the midst of the f...... Deut 4:36
mount out of the midst of the f...... Deut 5:4
ye were afraid by reason of the f...... Deut 5:5
mount out of the midst of the f...... Deut 5:22
(for the mountain did burn with f...... Deut 5:23
voice out of the midst of the f...... Deut 5:24
for this great f will consume us...... Deut 5:25
out of the midst of the f...... Deut 5:26
burn their graven images with f...... Deut 7:5
their gods shall ye burn with f...... Deut 7:25
as a consuming f he shall destroy...... Deut 9:3
the f in the day of the assembly...... Deut 9:10
mount, and the mount burned with f...... Deut 9:15
ye had made, and burnt it with f...... Deut 9:21
the f in the day of the assembly...... Deut 10:4
and burn their groves with f...... Deut 12:3
have burnt in the f to their gods...... Deut 12:31
and shalt burn with f the city...... Deut 13:16
offerings of the LORD made by f...... Deut 18:1
daughter to pass through the f...... Deut 18:10
let me see this great f any more...... Deut 18:16
For a f is kindled in mine anger...... Deut 32:22
set on f the foundations of the...... Deut 32:22
And they burnt the city with f...... Josh 6:24
thing shalt be burnt with f...... Josh 7:15
stones, and burned them with f...... Josh 7:25
that ye shall set the city on f...... Josh 8:8
and hasted and set the city on f...... Josh 8:19
and burn their chariots with f...... Josh 11:6
and burnt their chariots with f...... Josh 11:9
and he burnt Hazor with f...... Josh 11:11
made by f are their inheritance...... Josh 13:14
the sword, and set the city on f...... Judg 1:8
there rose up f out of the rock,...... Judg 6:21
let f come out of the bramble, and...... Judg 9:15
let f come out from Abimelech, and...... Judg 9:20
let f come out from the men of...... Judg 9:20
and set the hold on f upon them...... Judg 9:49
of the tower to burn it with f...... Judg 9:52
burn thine house upon thee with f...... Judg 12:1
thee and thy father's house with f...... Judg 14:15
when he had set the brands on f...... Judg 15:5
and burnt her and her father with f...... Judg 15:6
as flax that was burnt with f...... Judg 15:14
is broken when it toucheth the f...... Judg 16:9
sword, and burnt the city with f...... Judg 18:27
also they set on f all the cities...... Judg 20:48
by f of the children of Israel...... 1Sa 2:28
Ziklag, and burned it with f...... 1Sa 30:1
and, behold, it was burned with f...... 1Sa 30:3
and we burned Ziklag with f...... 1Sa 30:14
go and set it on f...... 2Sa 14:30
servants set the field on f...... 2Sa 14:30
thy servants set my field on f...... 2Sa 14:31
f out of his mouth devoured...... 2Sa 22:9
him were coals of f kindled...... 2Sa 22:13
burned with f in the same place...... 2Sa 23:7

taken Gezer, and burnt it with f...... 1Kin 9:16
the king's house over him with f...... 1Kin 16:18
lay it on wood, and put no f under...... 1Kin 18:23
lay it on wood, and put no f under...... 1Kin 18:23
and the God that answereth by f...... 1Kin 18:24
of your gods, but put no f under...... 1Kin 18:25
Then the f of the LORD fell, and...... 1Kin 18:38
And after the earthquake a f...... 1Kin 19:12
but the LORD was not in the f...... 1Kin 19:12
after the f a still small voice...... 1Kin 19:12
then let f come down from heaven,...... 2Kin 1:10
And there came down f from heaven...... 2Kin 1:10
let f come down from heaven, and...... 2Kin 1:12
the f of God came down from...... 2Kin 1:12
there came f down from heaven, and...... 2Kin 1:14
a chariot of f, and horses of f...... 2Kin 2:11
chariots of f round about Elisha...... 2Kin 6:17
strong holds wilt thou set on f...... 2Kin 8:12
his son to pass through the f...... 2Kin 16:3
daughters to pass through the f...... 2Kin 17:17
children in f to Adrammelech...... 2Kin 17:31
have cast their gods into the f...... 2Kin 19:18
made his son pass through the f...... 2Kin 21:6
to pass through the f to Molech...... 2Kin 23:10
the chariots of the sun with f...... 2Kin 23:11
great man's house burnt he with f...... 2Kin 25:9
and they were burned with f...... 1Chr 14:12
by f upon the altar of burnt...... 1Chr 21:26
the f came down from heaven, and...... 2Chr 7:1
of Israel saw how the f came down...... 2Chr 7:3
and burnt his children in the f...... 2Chr 28:3
the f in the valley of the son of...... 2Chr 33:6
with f according to the ordinance...... 2Chr 35:13
all the palaces thereof with f...... 2Chr 36:19
gates thereof are burned with f...... Neh 1:3
gates thereof are consumed with f...... Neh 2:3
thereof were consumed with f...... Neh 2:13
gates thereof are burned with f...... Neh 2:17
and in the night by a pillar of f...... Neh 9:12
neither the pillar of f by night...... Neh 9:19
The f of God is fallen from...... Job 1:16
f shall consume the tabernacles...... Job 15:34
spark of his f shall not shine...... Job 18:5
a f not blown shall consume him...... Job 20:26
remnant of them the f consumeth...... Job 22:20
it is turned up as it were f...... Job 28:5
For it is a f that consumeth to...... Job 31:12
lamps, and sparks of f leap out...... Job 41:19
wicked he shall rain snares, f...... Ps 11:6
f out of his mouth devoured...... Ps 18:8
passed, hail stones and coals of f...... Ps 18:12
hail stones and coals of f...... Ps 18:13
wrath, and the f shall devour them...... Ps 21:9
the LORD divideth the flames of f...... Ps 29:7
while I was musing the f burned...... Ps 39:3
he burneth the chariot in the f...... Ps 46:9
a f shall devour before him, and...... Ps 50:3
even among them that are set on f...... Ps 57:4
we went through f and through...... Ps 66:12
as wax melteth before the f...... Ps 68:2
They have cast f into thy...... Ps 74:7
all the night with a light of f...... Ps 78:14
so a f was kindled against Jacob,...... Ps 78:21
The f consumed their young men...... Ps 78:63
shall thy jealousy burn like f...... Ps 79:5
It is burned with f, it is cut...... Ps 80:16
As the f burneth a wood, and as...... Ps 83:14
flame setteth the mountains on f...... Ps 83:14
shall thy wrath burn like f...... Ps 89:46
A f goeth before him, and burneth...... Ps 97:3
his ministers a flaming f...... Ps 104:4
rain, and flaming f in their land...... Ps 105:32
f to give light in the night...... Ps 105:39
a f was kindled in their company...... Ps 106:18
are quenched as the f of thorns...... Ps 118:12
let them be cast into the f...... Ps 140:10
f, and hail; snow, and...... Ps 148:8
Can a man take f in his bosom...... Prov 6:27
his lips there is as a burning f...... Prov 16:27
heap coals of f upon his head...... Prov 25:22
no wood is, there the f goeth out...... Prov 26:20
to burning coals, and wood to f...... Prov 26:21
the f that saith not, It is...... Prov 30:16
the coals thereof are coals of f...... Song 8:6
your cities are burned with f...... Is 1:7
shining of a flaming f by night...... Is 4:5
Therefore as the f devoureth the...... Is 5:24
be with burning and fuel of f...... Is 9:5
For wickedness burneth as the f...... Is 9:18
shall be as the fuel of the f...... Is 9:19
a burning like the burning of a f...... Is 10:16
light of Israel shall be for a f...... Is 10:17
the f of thine enemies shall...... Is 26:11
the women come, and set them on f...... Is 27:11
and the flame of devouring f...... Is 29:6
a sherd to take f from the hearth...... Is 30:14
and his tongue as a devouring f...... Is 30:27
with the flame of a devouring f...... Is 30:30
for Tophet is ordained... f and much...... Is 30:33
whose f is in Zion, and his...... Is 31:9
your breath, as f, shall devour...... Is 33:11
up shall they be burned in the f...... Is 33:12
have cast their gods into the f...... Is 37:19
it hath set him on f round about...... Is 42:25
when thou walkest through the f...... Is 43:2
the burning hath passed over the f...... Is 44:16
Aha, I am warm, I have seen the f...... Is 44:16
I have burned part of it in the f...... Is 44:19
the f shall burn them...... Is 47:14

warm, nor f to sit before it	Is 47:14
Behold, all ye that kindle a f	Is 50:11
walk in the light of your f	Is 50:11
that bloweth the coals in the f	Is 54:16
As when the melting f burneth	Is 64:2
the f causeth the waters to boil,	Is 64:2
praised thee, is burned up with f	Is 64:11
a f that burneth all the day	Is 65:5
behold, the LORD will come with f	Is 66:15
and his rebuke with flames of f	Is 66:15
For by f and by his sword will the	Is 66:16
neither shall their f be quenched	Is 66:24
lest my fury come forth like f	Jer 4:4
will make my words in thy mouth f	Jer 5:14
up a sign of f in Beth-haccerem	Jer 6:1
the lead is consumed of the f	Jer 6:29
wood, and the fathers kindle the f	Jer 7:18
sons and their daughters in the f	Jer 7:31
tumult he hath kindled f upon it	Jer 11:16
for a f is kindled in mine anger,	Jer 15:14
ye have kindled a f in mine anger	Jer 17:4
I kindle a f in the gates thereof	Jer 17:27
to burn their sons with f for	Jer 19:5
a burning f shut up in my bones	Jer 20:9
and he shall burn it with f	Jer 21:10
lest my fury go out like f	Jer 21:12
I will kindle a f in the forest	Jer 21:14
cedars, and cast them into the f	Jer 22:7
Is not my word like as a f	Jer 23:29
king of Babylon roasted in the f	Jer 29:22
set f on this city, and burn it	Jer 32:29
to pass through the f unto Molech	Jer 32:35
and he shall burn it with f	Jer 34:2
and and take it, and burn it with f	Jer 34:22
there was a f on the hearth	Jer 36:22
cast it into the f that was on	Jer 36:23
in the f that was on the hearth	Jer 36:23
king of Judah had burned in the f	Jer 36:32
and take it, and burn it with f	Jer 37:8
tent, and burn this city with f	Jer 37:10
city shall not be burned with f	Jer 38:17
and they shall burn it with f	Jer 38:18
this city to be burned with f	Jer 38:23
the houses of the people, with f	Jer 39:8
I will kindle a f in the houses	Jer 43:12
Egyptians shall burn with f	Jer 43:13
but a f shall come forth out of	Jer 48:45
daughters shall be burned with f	Jer 49:2
I will kindle a f in the wall of	Jer 49:27
I will kindle a f in his cities	Jer 50:32
the reeds they have burned with f	Jer 51:32
high gates shall be burned with f	Jer 51:58
in vain, and the folk in the f	Jer 51:58
the great men, burned he with f	Jer 52:13
hath he sent f into my bones	Lam 1:13
against Jacob like a flaming f	Lam 2:3
he poured out his fury like f	Lam 2:4
and hath kindled a f in Zion	Lam 4:11
a f infolding itself, and a	Eze 1:4
amber, out of the midst of the f	Eze 1:4
was like burning coals of f	Eze 1:13
living creatures, and the f was bright	Eze 1:13
out of the f went forth lightning	Eze 1:13
as the appearance of f round	Eze 1:27
as it were the appearance of f	Eze 1:27
Thou shalt burn with f a third	Eze 5:2
cast them into the midst of the f	Eze 5:4
and burn them in the f	Eze 5:4
for thereof shall a f come forth	Eze 5:4
a likeness as the appearance of f	Eze 8:2
of his loins even downward, f	Eze 8:2
of f from between the cherubims	Eze 10:2
Take f from between the wheels,	Eze 10:6
f that was between the cherubims	Eze 10:7
it is cast into the f for fuel	Eze 15:4
the f devoureth both the ends of	Eze 15:4
when the f hath devoured it, and	Eze 15:5
I have given to the f for fuel	Eze 15:6
they shall go out from one f	Eze 15:7
another f shall devour them	Eze 15:7
to pass through the f for them	Eze 16:21
shall burn thine houses with f	Eze 16:41
the f consumed them	Eze 19:12
f is gone out of a rod of her	Eze 19:14
the f that openeth the womb	Eze 20:26
your sons to pass through the f	Eze 20:31
Behold, I will kindle a f in thee	Eze 20:47
against thee in the f of my wrath	Eze 21:31
Thou shalt be for fuel to the f	Eze 21:32
furnace, to blow the f upon it	Eze 22:20
upon you in the f of my wrath	Eze 22:21
them with the f of my wrath	Eze 22:31
shall be devoured by the f	Eze 23:25
to pass through the f through the	Eze 23:37
and burn up their houses with f	Eze 23:47
even make the pile for great	Eze 24:9
Heap on wood, kindle the f	Eze 24:10
her scum shall be in the f	Eze 24:12
in the midst of the stones of f	Eze 28:14
from the midst of the stones of f	Eze 28:16
forth a f from the midst of thee	Eze 28:18
when I have set a f in Egypt	Eze 30:8
desolate, and will set f in Zoan	Eze 30:14
And I will set f in Egypt	Eze 30:16
Surely in the f of my jealousy	Eze 36:5
in the f of my wrath have I	Eze 38:19
rain, and great hailstones,	Eze 38:22
And I will send a f on Magog	Eze 39:6
shall go forth, and shall set on f	Eze 39:9
burn them with f seven years	Eze 39:9
shall burn the weapons with f	Eze 39:10
the flame of the f slew those men	Dan 3:22
men bound into the midst of the f	Dan 3:24
walking in the midst of the f	Dan 3:25
came forth of the midst of the f	Dan 3:26
whose bodies the f had no power	Dan 3:27
nor the smell of f had passed on	Dan 3:27
flame, and his wheels as burning f	Dan 7:9
his eyes as lamps of f	Dan 10:6
morning it burneth as a flaming f	Hos 7:6
I will send a f upon his cities	Hos 8:14
for the f hath devoured the	Joel 1:19
the f hath devoured the pastures	Joel 1:20
A f devoureth before them	Joel 2:3
of f that devoureth the stubble	Joel 2:5
and in the earth, blood, and f	Joel 2:30
But I will send a f into the	Amos 1:4
But I will send a f on the wall	Amos 1:7
But I will send a f upon Teman	Amos 1:12
But I will kindle a f in the wall	Amos 1:14
But I will send a f upon Moab	Amos 2:2
But I will send a f upon Judah	Amos 2:5
out like f in the house of Joseph	Amos 5:6
Lord GOD called to contend by f	Amos 7:4
the house of Jacob shall be a	Obad 18
be cleft, as wax before the f	Mic 1:4
shall be burned with the f	Mic 1:7
his fury is poured out like f	Nah 1:6
the f shall devour thy bars	Nah 3:13
There shall the f devour thee	Nah 3:15
people shall labour in the very f	Hab 2:13
devoured by the f of his jealousy	Zeph 1:18
with the f of my jealousy	Zeph 3:8
unto her a wall of f round about	Zec 2:5
this a brand plucked out of the f	Zec 3:2
and she shall be devoured with f	Zec 9:4
that the f may devour thy cedars	Zec 11:1
an hearth of f among the wood	Zec 12:6
and like a torch of f in a sheaf	Zec 12:6
the third part through the f	Zec 13:9
neither do ye kindle f on mine	Mal 1:10
for he is like a refiner's f	Mal 3:2
is hewn down, and cast into the f	Mt 3:10
with the Holy Ghost, and with f	Mt 3:11
up the chaff with unquenchable f	Mt 3:12
shall be in danger of hell f	Mt 5:22
is hewn down, and cast into the f	Mt 7:19
are gathered and burned in the f	Mt 13:40
cast them into a furnace of f	Mt 13:42
cast them into the furnace of f	Mt 13:50
ofttimes he falleth into the f	Mt 17:15
to be cast into everlasting f	Mt 18:8
two eyes to be cast into hell f	Mt 18:9
me, ye cursed, into everlasting f	Mt 25:41
it hath cast him into the f	Mk 9:22
into the f that never shall be	Mk 9:43
not, and the f is not quenched	Mk 9:44
into the f that never shall be	Mk 9:45
not, and the f is not quenched	Mk 9:46
two eyes to be cast into hell f	Mk 9:47
not, and the f is not quenched	Mk 9:48
every one shall be salted with f	Mk 9:49
and warmed himself at the f	Mk 14:54
is hewn down, and cast into the f	Lk 3:9
you with the Holy Ghost and with f	Lk 3:16
he will burn with f unquenchable	Lk 3:17
f to come down from heaven	Lk 9:54
I am come to send f on the earth	Lk 12:49
Lot went out of Sodom it rained f	Lk 17:29
when they had kindled a f in the	Lk 22:55
beheld him as he sat by the f	Lk 22:56
them, and cast them into the f	Jn 15:6
there, who had made a f of coals	Jn 18:18
they saw a f of coals there, and	Jn 21:9
them cloven tongues like as of f	Acts 2:3
blood, and f, and vapour of smoke	Acts 2:19
Lord in a flame of f in a bush	Acts 7:30
for they kindled a f, and received	Acts 28:2
of sticks, and laid them on the f	Acts 28:3
he shook off the beast into the f	Acts 28:5
shall heap coals of f on his head	Rom 12:20
because it shall be revealed by f	1Cor 3:13
the f shall try every man's work	1Cor 3:13
yet so as by f	1Cor 3:15
In flaming f taking vengeance on	2Th 1:8
and his ministers a flame of f	Heb 1:7
Quenched the violence of f	Heb 11:34
be touched, and that burned with f	Heb 12:18
For our God is a consuming f	Heb 12:29
a matter a little f kindleth	Jas 3:5
And the tongue is a f, a world of	Jas 3:6
setteth on f the course of nature	Jas 3:6
and it is set on f of hell	Jas 3:6
shall eat your flesh as it were f	Jas 5:3
though it be tried with f	1Pet 1:7
reserved unto f against the day	2Pet 3:7
being on f shall be dissolved	2Pet 3:12
the vengeance of eternal f	Jude 7
fear, pulling them out of the f	Jude 23
and his eyes were as a flame of f	Rev 1:14
his eyes like unto a flame of f	Rev 2:18
to buy of me gold tried in the f	Rev 3:18
of f burning before the throne	Rev 4:5
and filled it with f of the altar	Rev 8:5
f mingled with blood, and they	Rev 8:7
with f was cast into the sea	Rev 8:8
on them, having breastplates of f	Rev 9:17
and out of their mouths issued f	Rev 9:17
part of men killed, by the f	Rev 9:18
sun, and his feet as pillars of f	Rev 10:1
f proceedeth out of their mouth,	Rev 11:5
so that he maketh f come down	Rev 13:13
and he shall be tormented with f	Rev 14:10
the altar, which had power over f	Rev 14:18
a sea of glass mingled with f	Rev 15:2
unto him to scorch men with f	Rev 16:8
eat her flesh, and burn her with f	Rev 17:16
shall be utterly burned with f	Rev 18:8
His eyes were as a flame of f	Rev 19:12
lake of f burning with brimstone	Rev 19:20
f came down from God out of	Rev 20:9
them was cast into the lake of f	Rev 20:10
hell were cast into the lake of f	Rev 20:14
life was cast into the lake of f	Rev 20:15
in the lake which burneth with f	Rev 21:8

FIREBRAND

put a f in the midst between two	Judg 15:4
ye were as a f plucked out of the	Amos 4:11

FIREBRANDS

three hundred foxes, and took f	Judg 15:4
As a mad man who casteth f	Prov 26:18
the two tails of these smoking f	Is 7:4

FIREPANS

and his fleshhooks, and his f	Ex 27:3
and the fleshhooks, and the f	Ex 38:3
And the f, and the bowls, and such	2Kin 25:15
the basons, and the f, and the	Jer 52:19

FIRES

glorify ye the LORD in the f	Is 24:15

FIRKINS

containing two or three f apiece	Jn 2:6

FIRM

f on dry ground in the midst of	Josh 3:17
where the priests' feet stood f	Josh 4:3
they are f in themselves	Job 41:23
His heart is as f as a stone	Job 41:24
but their strength is f	Ps 73:4
statute, and to make a f decree	Dan 6:7
of the hope f unto the end	Heb 3:6

FIRMAMENT

Let there be a f in the midst of	Gen 1:6
And God made the f, and divided the	Gen 1:7
the f from the waters which were	Gen 1:7
the waters which were above the f	Gen 1:7
And God called the f Heaven	Gen 1:8
Let there be lights in the f of	Gen 1:14
the f of the heaven to give light	Gen 1:15
God set them in the f	Gen 1:17
the earth in the open f of heaven	Gen 1:20
the f sheweth his handywork	Ps 19:1
praise him in the f of his power	Ps 150:1
is the likeness of the f upon the	Eze 1:22
under the f were their wings	Eze 1:23
the f that was over their heads	Eze 1:25
above the f that was over their	Eze 1:26
in the f that was above the head	Eze 10:1
shine as the brightness of the f	Dan 12:3

FIRST

and the morning were the f day	Gen 1:5
The name of the f is Pison	Gen 2:11
on the f day of the month, were	Gen 8:5
and f year, in the month	Gen 8:13
the f day of the month, the	Gen 8:13
which he had made there at the f	Gen 13:4
the f came out red, all over like	Gen 25:25
beside the f famine that was in	Gen 26:1
that city was called Luz at the f	Gen 28:19
thread, saying, This came out f	Gen 38:28
did eat up the f seven fat kine	Gen 41:20
at the f time are we brought in	Gen 43:18
down at the f time to buy food	Gen 43:20
to the voice of the f sign	Ex 4:8
it shall be the f month of the	Ex 12:2
blemish, a male of the f year	Ex 12:5
even the f day ye shall put away	Ex 12:15
the f day until the seventh day	Ex 12:15
in the f day there shall be an	Ex 12:16
In the f month, on the fourteenth	Ex 12:18
to offer the f of thy ripe fruits	Ex 22:29
The f of the firstfruits of thy	Ex 23:19
the f row shall be a sardius, a	Ex 28:17
this shall be the f row	Ex 28:17
two lambs of the f year day by	Ex 29:38
tables of stone like unto the f	Ex 34:1
words that were in the f tables	Ex 34:4
tables of stone like unto the f	Ex 34:4
The f of the firstfruits of thy	Ex 34:26
the f row was a sardius, a topaz,	Ex 39:10
this was the f row	Ex 39:10
On the f day of the f month	Ex 40:2
On the f day of the f month	Ex 40:2
it came to pass in the f month	Ex 40:17
on the f day of the month, that	Ex 40:17
him as he burned the f bullock	Lev 4:21
which is for the sin offering f	Lev 5:8
and a lamb, both of the f year	Lev 9:3
and offered it for sin, as the f	Lev 9:15
the f year for a burnt offering	Lev 12:6
one ewe lamb of the f year	Lev 14:10
the f month at even is the LORD's	Lev 23:5
In the f day ye shall have an	Lev 23:7
f year for a burnt offering unto	Lev 23:12
without blemish of the f year	Lev 23:18
two lambs of the f year	Lev 23:19
the fruits for a wave offering	Lev 23:20

in the f day of the month, shall....... Lev 23:24
On the f day shall be an holy.......... Lev 23:35
On the f day shall be a sabbath,...... Lev 23:39
ye shall take you on the f day .... Lev 23:40
on the f day of the second month ..... Num 1:18
on the f day of the second month ..... Num 1:18
These shall f set forth .... Num 2:9
shall bring a lamb of the f year .... Num 6:12
one he lamb of the f year without ..... Num 6:14
one ewe lamb of the f year............. Num 6:14
the f day was Nahshon the son of..... Num 7:12
one ram, one lamb of the f year....... Num 7:15
goats, five lambs of the f year.......... Num 7:17
one ram, one lamb of the f year....... Num 7:21
goats, five lambs of the f year.......... Num 7:23
one ram, one lamb of the f year....... Num 7:27
goats, five lambs of the f year.......... Num 7:29
one ram, one lamb of the f year....... Num 7:33
goats, five lambs of the f year.......... Num 7:35
one ram, one lamb of the f year....... Num 7:39
goats, five lambs of the f year.......... Num 7:41
one ram, one lamb of the f year....... Num 7:45
goats, five lambs of the f year.......... Num 7:47
one ram, one lamb of the f year....... Num 7:51
goats, five lambs of the f year.......... Num 7:53
one ram, one lamb of the f year....... Num 7:57
goats, five lambs of the f year.......... Num 7:59
one ram, one lamb of the f year....... Num 7:63
goats, five lambs of the f year.......... Num 7:65
one ram, one lamb of the f year....... Num 7:69
goats, five lambs of the f year.......... Num 7:71
one ram, one lamb of the f year....... Num 7:75
goats, five lambs of the f year.......... Num 7:77
one ram, one lamb of the f year....... Num 7:81
goats, five lambs of the f year.......... Num 7:83
the lambs of the f year twelve.......... Num 7:87
the lambs of the f year sixty............. Num 7:88
in the f month of the second year ..... Num 9:1
on the fourteenth day of the f .... Num 9:5
they f took their journey................. Num 10:13
In the f place went the standard...... Num 10:14
the f of your dough for an heave...... Num 15:20
Of the f of your dough ye shall......... Num 15:21
of the f year for a sin offering .... Num 15:27
whatsoever is f ripe in the land,....... Num 18:13
the desert of Zin in the f month .... Num 20:1
Amalek was the f of the nations....... Num 24:20
two lambs of the f year without .... Num 28:3
lambs of the f year without spot ...... Num 28:9
lambs of the f year without spot,...... Num 28:11
f month is the passover of the......... Num 28:16
In the f day shall be an holy............ Num 28:18
ram, and seven lambs of the f year .. Num 28:19
seven lambs of the f year................ Num 28:27
on the f day of the month, ye.......... Num 29:1
seven lambs of the f year without .... Num 29:2
ram, and seven lambs of the f .... Num 29:8
and fourteen lambs of the f year ..... Num 29:13
lambs of the f year without spot ...... Num 29:17
of the f year without blemish .... Num 29:20
of the f year without blemish .... Num 29:23
lambs of the f year without spot ...... Num 29:26
of the f year without blemish .... Num 29:29
of the f year without blemish .... Num 29:32
seven lambs of the f year without .... Num 29:36
from Rameses in the f month........... Num 33:3
the fifteenth day of the f month ...... Num 33:3
in the f day of the fifth month.......... Num 33:38
on the f day of the month, that....... Deut 1:3
down before the LORD, as at the f.... Deut 9:18
nights, as I fell down at the f .... Deut 9:25
tables of stone like unto the f.......... Deut 10:1
the f tables which thou brakest........ Deut 10:2
tables of stone like unto the f.......... Deut 10:3
according to the f writing................ Deut 10:4
mount, according to the f................ Deut 10:10
the f rain and the latter rain,.......... Deut 11:14
thine hand shall be f upon him to .... Deut 13:9
sacrificedst the f day at even.......... Deut 16:4
be f upon him to put him to death ... Deut 17:7
the f of the fleece of thy sheep,...... Deut 18:4
That thou shalt take of the f of....... Deut 26:2
he provided the f part for .... Deut 33:21
on the tenth day of the f month ...... Josh 4:19
come out against us, as at the f...... Josh 8:5
They fee before us, as at the f .... Josh 8:6
for theirs was the f lot.................... Josh 21:10
for us against the Canaanites .... Judg 1:1
of the city was Laish at the f .... Judg 18:29
Which of us shall go up f to the .... Judg 20:18
LORD said, Judah shall go up f .... Judg 20:18
put themselves in array the f day .... Judg 20:22
down before us, as at the f .... Judg 20:32
before us, as in the f battle .... Judg 20:39
that f slaughter, which Jonathan 1Sa 14:14
the same was the f altar that he...... 1Sa 14:35
the battle were filled the f born....... 1Sa 17:13
except thou f bring Michal Saul's 2Sa 3:13
of them be overthrown at the f 2Sa 17:9
I am come the f this day of all......... 2Sa 19:20
f had in bringing back our king........ 2Sa 19:43
days of harvest, in the f days.......... 2Sa 21:9
he attained not unto the f three...... 2Sa 23:19
he attained not to the f three......... 2Sa 23:23
f year of Asa king of Judah began ... 1Kin 16:23
make me thereof a little cake f 1Kin 17:13
for yourselves, and dress it f 1Kin 18:25
to thy servant at the f I will do....... 1Kin 20:9
of the provinces went out f 1Kin 20:17
Now the f inhabitants that dwelt...... 1Chr 9:2

the Jebusites f shall be chief 1Chr 11:6
Joab the son of Zeruiah went f up ... 1Chr 11:6
he attained not to the f three......... 1Chr 11:21
but attained not to the f three........ 1Chr 11:25
Ezer the f, Obadiah the second,...... 1Chr 12:9
went over Jordan in the f month..... 1Chr 12:15
because ye did it not at the f 1Chr 15:13
on that day David delivered f 1Chr 16:7
Jeriah the f, Amariah the second,.... 1Chr 23:19
Micah the f, and Jesiah the second .. 1Chr 23:20
Now the f lot came forth to 1Chr 24:7
of Rehabiah, the f was Isshiah 1Chr 24:21
Jeriah the f, Amariah the second,.... 1Chr 24:23
Now the f lot came forth for 1Chr 25:9
Over the f course for the f 1Chr 27:2
of the host for the f month............. 1Chr 27:3
Now the acts of David the king, f.... 1Chr 29:29
f measure was threescore cubits 2Chr 3:3
rest of the acts of Solomon, f......... 2Chr 9:29
Now the acts of Rehoboam, f 2Chr 12:15
And, behold, the acts of Asa, f....... 2Chr 16:11
in the f ways of his father David 2Chr 17:3
of the acts of Jehoshaphat, f 2Chr 20:34
rest of the acts of Amaziah, f 2Chr 25:26
the rest of the acts of Uzziah, f 2Chr 26:22
of his acts and of all his ways, f..... 2Chr 28:26
He in the f year of his reign, in 2Chr 29:3
year of his reign, in the f month..... 2Chr 29:3
Now they began on the f day of 2Chr 29:17
day of the f month to sanctify 2Chr 29:17
of the f month they made an end ... 2Chr 29:17
the fourteenth day of the f month .. 2Chr 35:1
And his deeds, f and last, behold,... 2Chr 35:27
Now in the f year of Cyrus king 2Chr 36:22
Now in the f year of Cyrus king ...... Ezr 1:1
From the f day of the seventh......... Ezr 3:6
men, that had seen the f house...... Ezr 3:12
But in the f year of Cyrus the .... Ezr 5:13
In the f year of Cyrus the king .... Ezr 6:3
the fourteenth day of the f .... Ezr 6:19
For upon the f day of the .... Ezr 7:9
f month began he to go up from .... Ezr 7:9
on the f day of the fifth month ...... Ezr 7:9
on the twelfth day of the f .... Ezr 8:31
sat down in the f day of .... Ezr 10:16
by the f day of the f month .... Ezr 10:17
by the f day of the f month .... Ezr 10:17
of them which came up at the f..... Neh 7:5
upon the f day of the seventh....... Neh 8:2
from the f day unto the last day,.... Neh 8:18
which sat the f in the kingdom....... Est 1:14
In the f month, that is, the.......... Est 3:7
the thirteenth day of the f month .. Est 3:12
Art thou the f man that was born... Job 15:7
And he called the name of the f .... Job 42:14
He that is f in his own cause......... Prov 18:17
restore thy judges as at the f ...... Is 1:26
when at the f he lightly .... Is 9:1
the LORD, the f, and with the .... Is 41:4
The f shall say to Zion, Behold,..... Is 41:27
Thy f father hath sinned, and thy .. Is 43:27
I am the f, and I am the last .... Is 44:6
I am the f, I also am the last .... Is 48:12
me, and the ships of Tarshish f ..... Is 60:9
that bringeth forth her f child....... Jer 4:31
where I set my name at the f .... Jer 7:12
I will recompense their .... Jer 16:18
like the figs that are f ripe .... Jer 24:2
of Judah, that was the f year of... Jer 25:1
and will build them, as at the f.... Jer 33:7
of the land, as at the f, saith....... Jer 33:11
words that were in the f roll......... Jer 36:28
the f king of Assyria hath .... Jer 50:17
king of Babylon in the f year of.... Jer 52:31
the f face was the face of a .... Eze 10:14
in the f day of the month, that..... Eze 26:1
and twentieth year, in the f month.. Eze 29:17
in the f day of the month, the....... Eze 29:17
the eleventh year, in the f month .. Eze 30:20
in the f day of the month, that..... Eze 31:1
year, in the f day of the f month .. Eze 32:1
after the measure of the f gate .... Eze 40:21
the f of all the firstfruits of .... Eze 44:30
the priest the f of your dough ...... Eze 44:30
In the f month, in the .... Eze 45:18
in the f day of the month, thou..... Eze 45:18
In the f month, in the fourteenth... Eze 45:21
of the f year without blemish........ Dan 11:21
unto the f year of king Cyrus .... Dan 1:21
of whom Daniel was f .... Dan 6:2
In the f year of Belshazzar king ... Dan 7:1
The f was like a lion, and had...... Dan 7:4
whom there were three of the f.... Dan 7:8
and he shall be diverse from the f.. Dan 7:24
which appeared unto me at the f .. Dan 8:1
is between his eyes is the f king... Dan 8:21
In the f year of Darius the son ..... Dan 9:1
In the f year of his reign I........... Dan 9:2
and twentieth day of the f month .. Dan 10:4
for from the f day that thou......... Dan 10:12
Also I in the f year of Darius .... Dan 11:1
will go and return to my f husband .. Hos 2:7
in the f fig tree at her f time........ Hos 9:10
and the latter rain in the f month .. Joel 2:23
with the f that go captive .... Amos 6:7
it come, even the f dominion........ Mic 4:8
in the f day of the month, came.... Hag 1:1
saw this house in her f glory........ Hag 2:3
In the f chariot were red horses.... Zec 6:2
shall save the tents of Judah f ..... Zec 12:7

gate unto the place of the f gate ... Zec 14:10
be reconciled to thy brother,......... Mt 5:24
But seek ye f the kingdom of God,.. Mt 6:33
f cast out the beam out of thine .... Mt 7:5
unto him, Lord, suffer me f to go.... Mt 8:21
The f, Simon, who is called Peter.... Mt 10:2
except he f bind the strong man..... Mt 12:29
of that man is worse than the f...... Mt 12:45
Gather ye together f the tares........ Mt 13:30
scribes that Elias must f come,....... Mt 17:10
them, Elias truly shall f come......... Mt 17:11
take up the fish that f cometh up... Mt 17:27
But many that are f shall be last .... Mt 19:30
and the last shall be f .... Mt 19:30
from the last unto the f .... Mt 20:8
But when the f came, they .... Mt 20:10
shall be f, and the f last .... Mt 20:16
and he came to the f, and said, Son .. Mt 21:28
They say unto him, The f .... Mt 21:31
other servants more than the f ..... Mt 21:36
and the f, when he had married a .. Mt 22:25 [F]
This is the f and great .... Mt 22:38
cleanse f that which is within .... Mt 23:26
Now the f day of the feast of .... Mt 26:17
error shall be worse than the f...... Mt 27:64
dawn toward the f day of the week .. Mt 28:1
except he will f bind the strong .... Mk 3:27
f the blade, then the ear, after..... Mk 4:28
her, Let the children f be filled ..... Mk 7:27
scribes that Elias must f come....... Mk 9:11
told them, Elias verily cometh f ..... Mk 9:12
them, If any man desire to be f ..... Mk 9:35
But many that are f shall be last ... Mk 10:31
and the last f .... Mk 10:31
the f took a wife, and dying left ..... Mk 12:20
Which is the f commandment of all .. Mk 12:28
The f of all the commandments is,.. Mk 12:29
this is the f commandment .... Mk 12:30
the gospel must f be published ...... Mk 13:10
the f day of unleavened bread,....... Mk 14:12
the morning the f day of the week .. Mk 16:9
risen early the f day of the week ... Mk 16:9
he appeared f to Mary Magdalene,.. Mk 16:9
of all things from the very f.......... Lk 1:3
this taxing was f made when .... Lk 2:2
on the second sabbath after the f .. Lk 6:1
cast out f the beam out of thine ... Lk 6:42
he said, Lord, suffer me f to go..... Lk 9:59
but let me f go bid them farewell... Lk 9:61
f say, Peace be to this house........ Lk 10:5
of that man is worse than the f..... Lk 11:26
he had not f washed before dinner .. Lk 11:38
say unto his disciples f of all........ Lk 12:1
there are last which shall be f ...... Lk 13:30
there are f which shall be last ...... Lk 13:30
The f said unto him, I have .... Lk 14:18
build a tower, sitteth not down f .... Lk 14:28
another king, sitteth not down f .... Lk 14:31
unto him, and said unto the f .... Lk 16:5
But f must he suffer many things,... Lk 17:25
Then came the f, saying, Lord,...... Lk 19:16
the f took a wife, and died............ Lk 20:29
these things must f come to pass... Lk 21:9
Now upon the f day of the week,.... Lk 24:1
He findeth his own brother .... Jn 1:41
whosoever then f after the .... Jn 5:4
let him f cast a stone at her.......... Jn 8:7
place where John at f baptized...... Jn 10:40
not his disciples at the f .... Jn 12:16
And led him away to Annas f........ Jn 18:13
and brake the legs of the f .... Jn 19:32
which at the f came to Jesus by.... Jn 19:39
The f day of the week cometh Mary .. Jn 20:1
Peter, and came f to the sepulchre.. Jn 20:4
which came f to the sepulchre, and .. Jn 20:8
being the f day of the week, when... Jn 20:19
Unto you f God, having raised up ... Acts 3:26
Egypt, he sent out our fathers f..... Acts 7:12
called Christians f in Antioch .... Acts 11:26
When they were past the f............ Acts 12:10
When John had f preached before .. Acts 13:24
should f have been spoken to you... Acts 13:46
at the f did visit the Gentiles .... Acts 15:14
upon the f day of the week, when... Acts 20:7
from the f day that I came into..... Acts 20:18
which was at the f among mine own .. Acts 26:4
But shewed f unto them of .... Acts 26:20
that he should be the f that........ Acts 26:23
cast themselves f into the sea...... Acts 27:43
f, I thank my God through Jesus ... Rom 1:8
to the Jew f, and also to the........ Rom 1:16
man that doeth evil, of the Jew f .. Rom 2:9
that worketh good, to the Jew f .... Rom 2:10
f Moses saith, I will provoke you ... Rom 10:19
Or who hath f given to him, and it.. Rom 11:35
if f I be somewhat filled with........ Rom 15:24
for I am of the f fruits of 1Cor 1:18
f apostles, secondarily prophets,.... 1Cor 12:28
by, let the f hold his peace........... 1Cor 14:30
you f of all that which I also........ 1Cor 15:3
The f man Adam was made a living .. 1Cor 15:45
that was not f which is spiritual 1Cor 15:46
The f man is of the earth, earthy .. 1Cor 15:47
Upon the f day of the week let..... 1Cor 16:2
The f epistle to the Corinthians .... 1Cor *
but f gave their own selves to...... 2Cor 8:5
For if there be f a willing mind,..... 2Cor 8:12
the gospel unto you at the f .... Gal 4:13
glory, who f trusted in Christ .... Eph 1:12
f into the lower parts of the .... Eph 4:9

which is the *f* commandment with........ Eph 6:2
gospel from the *f* day until now.............. Phil 1:5
the dead in Christ shall rise *f*............ 1Th 4:16
The *f* epistle unto the .... 1Th s
there come a falling away *f*................. 2Th 2:3
that in me *f* Jesus Christ might 1Ti 1:16
of all, supplications, prayers,................ 1Ti 2:1
For Adam was *f* formed, then Eve.......... 1Ti 2:13
And let these also *f* be proved............. 1Ti 3:10
let them learn *f* to shew piety at.......... 1Ti 5:4
they have cast off their *f* faith............ 1Ti 5:12
The *f* to Timothy was written from...... 1Ti s
which dwelt *f* in thy grandmother........ 2Ti 1:5
must be *f* partaker of the fruits............ 2Ti 2:6
At my *f* answer no man stood with......... 2Ti 4:16
ordained the *f* bishop of the .... 2Ti s
that is an heretick after the *f*............. Titus 3:10
ordained the *f* bishop of the .... Titus s
which at the *f* began to be spoken........ Heb 2:3
they to whom it was *f* preached........... Heb 4:6
f principles of the oracles of............... Heb 5:12
being by interpretation King of.......... Heb 7:2
f for his own sins, and then for............ Heb 7:27
For if that *f* covenant had been .... Heb 8:7
covenant, he hath made the *f* old......... Heb 8:13
Then verily the *f* covenant had............ Heb 9:1
the *f*, wherein was the....................... Heb 9:2
went always into the *f* tabernacle........ Heb 9:6
while as the *f* tabernacle was yet.......... Heb 9:8
that were under the *f* testament.......... Heb 9:15
Whereupon neither the *f* testament..... Heb 9:18
He taketh away the *f*, that he may........ Heb 10:9
that is from above is *f* pure................. Jas 3:17
if it *f* begin at us, what shall 1Pet 4:17
Knowing this *f*, that no prophecy........ 2Pet 1:20
Knowing this *f*, that there shall 2Pet 3:3
love him, because he *f* loved us 1Jn 4:19
which kept not their *f* estate............... Jude 6
the *f* begotten of the dead, and .... Rev 1:5
I am Alpha and Omega, the *f*............... Rev 1:11
I am the *f* and the last........................ Rev 1:17
because thou hast left thy *f* love .... Rev 2:4
and repent, and do the *f* works............ Rev 2:5
These things saith the *f* and the.......... Rev 2:8
and the last to be more than the *f*....... Rev 2:19
the *f* voice which I heard was as.......... Rev 4:1
there was like a lion, and...................... Rev 4:7
The *f* angel sounded, and there........... Rev 8:7
power of the *f* beast before him........... Rev 13:12
therein to worship the *f* beast .... Rev 13:12
the *f* went, and poured out his............ Rev 16:2
This is the *f* resurrection..................... Rev 20:5
hath part in the *f* resurrection............ Rev 20:6
f heaven and the *f* earth................... Rev 21:1
The *f* foundation was jasper................ Rev 21:19
the beginning and the end, the *f*........ Rev 22:13

FIRSTBEGOTTEN

bringeth in the *f* into the world.......... Heb 1:6

FIRSTBORN

And Canaan begat Sidon his *f*............. Gen 10:15
the *f* said unto the younger, Our......... Gen 19:31
the *f* went in, and lay with her............ Gen 19:33
that the *f* said unto the younger,......... Gen 19:34
the *f* bare a son, and called his........... Gen 19:37
Huz his *f*, and Buz his brother, and..... Gen 22:21
the *f* of Ishmael, Nebajoth .... Gen 25:13
unto his father, I am Esau thy *f*.......... Gen 27:19
he said, I am thy son, thy *f* Esau......... Gen 27:32
to give the younger before the *f*......... Gen 29:26
Reuben, Jacob's *f*, and Simeon, and.... Gen 35:23
sons of Eliphaz the *f* son of Esau......... Gen 36:15
And Judah took a wife for Er his *f*...... Gen 38:6
And Er, Judah's *f*, was wicked in......... Gen 38:7
called the name of the *f* Manasseh...... Gen 41:51
the *f* according to his birthright......... Gen 43:33
Reuben, Jacob's *f* .... Gen 46:8
for Manasseh was the *f*..................... Gen 48:14
for this is the *f*................................. Gen 48:18
Reuben, thou art my *f*, my might,....... Gen 49:3
LORD, Israel is my son, even my *f*........ Ex 4:22
I will slay thy son, even thy *f*.............. Ex 4:23
sons of Reuben the *f* of Israel............. Ex 6:14
all the *f* in the land of Egypt.............. Ex 11:5
from the *f* of Pharaoh that .... Ex 11:5
throne, even unto the *f* of the............ Ex 11:5
and all the *f* of beasts........................ Ex 11:5
will smite all the *f* in the land............ Ex 12:12
all the *f* in the land of Egypt.............. Ex 12:29
from the *f* of Pharaoh that sat on....... Ex 12:29
the *f* of the captive that was in the..... Ex 12:29
and all the *f* of cattle......................... Ex 12:29
Sanctify unto me all the *f*.................. Ex 13:2
all the *f* of man among thy................. Ex 13:13
all the *f* in the land of Egypt.............. Ex 13:15
land of Egypt, both the *f* of man......... Ex 13:15
of man, and the *f* of beast.................. Ex 13:15
but all the *f* of my children I.............. Ex 13:15
the *f* of thy sons shall thou give.......... Ex 22:29
All the *f* of thy sons thou shalt .... Ex 34:20
Nadab the *f*, and Abihu, Eleazar,........ Num 3:2
of Israel instead of all the *f* .... Num 3:12
Because all the *f* are mine.................. Num 3:13
f in the land of Egypt I hallowed........ Num 3:13
unto me all the *f* in Israel .... Num 3:13
Number all the *f* of the males of......... Num 3:40
f among the children of Israel .... Num 3:41
all the *f* among the children of........... Num 3:42
all the *f* males by the number of .... Num 3:43
f among the children of Israel .... Num 3:45

thirteen of the *f* of the children.......... Num 3:46
Of the *f* of the children of.................. Num 3:50
even instead of the *f* of all the........... Num 8:16
For all the *f* of the children of............ Num 8:17
every *f* in the land of Egypt I............. Num 8:17
the *f* of the children of Israel............. Num 8:17
nevertheless the *f* of man shalt .... Num 18:15
the Egyptians buried all their *f*.......... Num 33:4
if the *f* son be hers that was.............. Deut 21:15
f before the son of the hated .... Deut 21:16
which is indeed the *f*........................ Deut 21:16
the son of the hated for the *f*............. Deut 21:17
the right of the *f* is his .... Deut 21:17
that the *f* which she beareth.............. Deut 25:6
the foundation thereof in his *f*........... Josh 6:26
for he was the *f* of Joseph .... Josh 17:1
wit, for Machir the *f* of Manasseh...... Josh 17:1
And he said unto Jether his *f*............. Judg 8:20
Now the name of his *f* was Joel.......... 1Sa 8:2
the name of the *f* Merab, and the...... 1Sa 14:49
that was Ammon, of Ahinoam the 2Sa 3:2
thereof in Abiram his *f*, and set 1Kin 16:34
And Canaan begat Zidon his *f*........... 1Chr 1:13
The *f* of Ishmael, Nebaioth................ 1Chr 1:29
the *f* of Judah, was evil in the............ 1Chr 2:3
And Jesse begat his *f* Eliab................. 1Chr 2:13
of Jerahmeel the *f* of Hezron were..... 1Chr 2:25
Ram the *f*, and Bunah....................... 1Chr 2:25
of Ram the *f* of Jerahmeel were......... 1Chr 2:27
of Jerahmeel were, Mesha his *f*......... 1Chr 2:42
the son of Hur, the *f* of Ephratah....... 1Chr 2:50
the *f* of Ammon, of Ahinoam the....... 1Chr 3:1
the *f* Johanan, the second................. 1Chr 3:15
the *f* of Ephratah, the father of 1Chr 4:4
sons of Reuben the *f* of Israel............. 1Chr 5:1
(for he was the *f*.............................. 1Chr 5:1
of Reuben the *f* of Israel were,.......... 1Chr 5:3
of Vashni, and Abiah 1Chr 6:28
his *f* Bashan were his 1Chr 8:1
his *f* son Abdon, and Zur, and Kish,... 1Chr 8:30
his brother were, Ulam his *f*.............. 1Chr 8:39
Asaiah the *f*, and his sons................. 1Chr 9:5
who was the *f* of Shallum the 1Chr 9:31
his *f* son Abdon, then Zur, and......... 1Chr 9:36
Meshelemiah were, Zechariah the *f*... 1Chr 26:2
of Obed-edom were, Shemaiah the *f*... 1Chr 26:4
(for though he was not the *f*.............. 1Chr 26:10
because he was the *f*......................... 2Chr 21:3
Also the *f* of our sons, and of our....... Neh 10:36
even the *f* of death shall devour......... Job 18:13
And smote all the *f* in Egypt............. Ps 78:51
Also I will make him my *f*................. Ps 89:27
also all the *f* in their land .... Ps 105:36
Who smote the *f* of Egypt, both of..... Ps 135:8
him that smote Egypt in their *f*......... Ps 136:10
the *f* of the poor shall feed, and........ Is 14:30
to Israel, and Ephraim is my *f*........... Jer 31:9
shall I give my *f* for my .... Mic 6:7
that is in bitterness for his *f*............. Zec 12:10
she had brought forth her *f* son .... Mt 1:25
And she brought forth her *f* son......... Lk 2:7
be the *f* among many brethren.......... Rom 8:29
God, the *f* of every creature............... Col 1:15
beginning, the *f* from the dead .... Col 1:18
destroyed the *f* should touch them.... Heb 11:28
assembly and church of the *f*............ Heb 12:23

FIRSTFRUIT

The *f* also of thy corn, of thine.......... Deut 18:4
For if the *f* be holy, the lump is.......... Rom 11:16

FIRSTFRUITS

the *f* of thy labours, which thou .... Ex 23:16
The first of the *f* of thy land.............. Ex 23:19
of the *f* wheat harvest, and the .... Ex 34:22
The first of the *f* of thy land.............. Ex 34:26
As for the oblation of the *f*................ Lev 2:12
offering of thy *f* unto the LORD......... Lev 2:14
for the meat offering of the *f*............. Lev 2:14
ye shall bring a sheaf of the *f*............ Lev 23:10
they are the *f* unto the LORD,............ Lev 23:17
the *f* of them which they shall.......... Num 18:12
Also in the day of the *f*, when ye .... Num 28:26
I have brought the *f* of the land........ Deut 26:10
the man of God bread of the *f*........... 2Kin 4:42
in abundance the *f* of corn.............. 2Chr 31:5
to bring the *f* of our ground, and...... Neh 10:35
the *f* of all fruit of all trees,............. Neh 10:35
should bring the *f* of our dough........ Neh 10:37
for the offerings, for the..................... Neh 12:44
at times appointed, and for the .... Neh 13:31
with the *f* of all thine increase......... Prov 3:9
LORD, and the *f* of his increase......... Jer 2:3
the *f* of your oblations, with all........ Eze 20:40
first of all the *f* of all things.............. Eze 44:30
nor alienate the *f* of the land............ Eze 48:14
which have the *f* of the Spirit............ Rom 8:23
who is the *f* of Achaia unto.............. Rom 16:5
become the *f* of them that slept........ 1Cor 15:20
Christ the *f*.................................... 1Cor 15:23
that it is the *f* of Achaia................... 1Cor 16:15
be a kind of *f* of his creatures........... Jas 1:18
among men, being the *f* unto God..... Rev 14:4

FIRSTLING

every *f* that cometh of a beast............ Ex 13:12
every *f* of an ass thou shalt .... Ex 13:13
every *f* among thy cattle, whether..... Ex 34:19
But the *f* of an ass thou shalt .... Ex 34:20
Only the *f* of the beasts, which.......... Lev 27:26
which should be the LORD's *f*............ Lev 27:26
the *f* of unclean beasts shalt............. Num 18:15

f of a cow, or the *f*......................... Num 18:17
or the *f* of a goat, thou shalt .... Num 18:17
All the *f* males that come of thy......... Deut 15:19
to work with the *f* of thy bullock....... Deut 15:19
nor shear the *f* of thy sheep.............. Deut 15:19
is like the *f* of his bullock.................. Deut 33:17

FIRSTLINGS

brought of the *f* of his flock............... Gen 4:4
all the *f* among the cattle of the......... Num 3:41
the *f* of your herds and of your.......... Deut 12:6
or the *f* of thy herds or of thy............ Deut 12:17
the *f* of thy herds and of thy............. Deut 14:23
the *f* of our herds and of our............. Neh 10:36

FIRSTRIPE

time was the time of the *f* grapes....... Num 13:20
I saw your fathers as the *f* in .... Hos 9:10
my soul desired the *f* fruit .... Mic 7:1
be like fig trees with the *f* figs........... Nah 3:12

FISH

dominion over the *f* of the sea............ Gen 1:26
dominion over the *f* of the sea............ Gen 1:28
the *f* that is in the river shall .... Ex 7:18
the *f* that was in the river died........... Ex 7:21
We remember the *f*, which we did...... Num 11:5
or shall all the *f* of the sea be............ Num 11:22
the likeness of any *f* that is in .... Deut 4:18
to the entering in at the *f* gate.......... 2Chr 33:14
But the *f* gate did the sons of............ Neh 3:3
the old gate, and above the *f* gate..... Neh 12:39
also therein, which brought *f* .... Neh 13:16
or his head with *f* spears.................. Job 41:7
into blood, and slew their *f* .... Ps 105:29
that make sluices and ponds for *f*...... Is 19:10
their *f* stinketh, because there........... Is 50:2
the LORD, and they shall *f* them....... Jer 16:16
I will cause the *f* of thy rivers............ Eze 29:4
all the *f* of thy rivers shall................ Eze 29:4
thee and all the *f* of thy rivers........... Eze 29:5
be a very great multitude of *f*............ Eze 47:9
their *f* shall be according to.............. Eze 47:10
as the *f* of the great sea,................... Eze 47:10
a great *f* to swallow up Jonah .... Jonah 1:17
in the belly of the *f* three days........... Jonah 1:17
And the LORD spake unto the *f*.......... Jonah 2:10
noise of a cry from the *f* gate............ Zeph 1:10
Or if he ask a *f*, will he give............... Mt 7:10
take up the *f* that first cometh.......... Mt 17:27
or if he ask a *f*................................ Lk 11:11
will he for a *f* give him a .... Lk 11:11
gave him a piece of a broiled *f*.......... Lk 24:42
and *f* laid thereon, and bread........... Jn 21:9
Bring of the *f* which ye have now...... Jn 21:10
and giveth them, and likewise............ Jn 21:13

FISHERMEN

but the *f* were gone out of them,........ Lk 5:2

FISHER'S

he girt his *f* coat unto him, (for .... Jn 21:7

FISHERS

The *f* also shall mourn, and all.......... Is 19:8
Behold, I will send for many *f*............ Jer 16:16
that the *f* shall stand upon it............ Eze 47:10
for they were *f*................................ Mt 4:18
me, and I will make you *f* of men....... Mt 4:19
for they were *f*................................ Mk 1:16
will make you to become *f* of men..... Mk 1:17

FISHES

and upon all the *f* of the sea............. Gen 9:2
and of creeping things, and of *f*......... 1Kin 4:33
the *f* of the sea shall declare............. Job 12:8
as the *f* that are taken in an.............. Eccl 9:12
So that the *f* of the sea, and.............. Eze 38:20
the *f* of the sea also shall be.............. Hos 4:3
And makest men as the *f* of the sea.... Hab 1:14
and the *f* of the sea, and the............. Zeph 1:3
here but five loaves, and two *f*.......... Mt 14:17
the five loaves, and the two *f* .... Mt 14:19
said, Seven, and a few little *f*........... Mt 15:34
he took the seven loaves and the *f*.... Mt 15:36
knew, they say, Five, and two *f*......... Mk 6:38
the five loaves and the two *f*............. Mk 6:41
the two *f* divided he among them...... Mk 6:41
of the fragments, and of the *f*........... Mk 6:43
And they had a few small *f*............... Mk 8:7
inclosed a great multitude of *f*.......... Lk 5:6
of the *f* which they had taken .... Lk 5:9
no more but five loaves and two *f*...... Lk 9:13
took the five loaves and the two *f*..... Lk 9:16
barley loaves, and two small *f*.......... Jn 6:9
likewise of the *f* as much as they ...... Jn 6:11
to draw it for the multitude of *f*........ Jn 21:6
cubits), dragging the net with *f* .... Jn 21:8
the net to land full of great *f* .... Jn 21:11
flesh of beasts, another of *f* 1Cor 15:39

FISHHOOKS

hooks, and your posterity with *f* .... Amos 4:2

FISHING

Peter saith unto them, I go a *f*........... Jn 21:3

FISHPOOLS

thine eyes like the *f* in Heshbon....... Song 7:4

FISH'S

LORD his God out of the *f* belly......... Jonah 2:1

FIST

with a stone, or with his *f*................. Ex 21:18
to smite with the *f* of wickedness...... Is 58:4

FISTS
hath gathered the wind in his f .... Prov 30:4

FIT
of a f man into the wilderness .... Lev 16:21
f to go out for war and battle 1Chr 7:11
men of war f for the battle, that 1Chr 12:8
is it f to say to a king, Thou .... Job 34:18
make it f for thyself in the .... Prov 24:27
is f for the kingdom of God .... Lk 9:62
It is neither f for the land .... Lk 14:35
for it is not f that he should .... Acts 22:22
husbands, as it is f in the Lord .... Col 3:18

FITCHES
doth he not cast abroad the f .... Is 28:25
For the f are not threshed with a .... Is 28:27
but the f are beaten out with a .... Is 28:27
and lentiles, and millet, and f .... Eze 4:9

FITLY
A word f spoken is like apples of .... Prov 25:11
washed with milk, and f set .... Song 5:12
In whom all the building f framed .... Eph 2:21
the whole body f joined together .... Eph 4:16

FITTED
with gold f upon the carved work 1Kin 6:35
shall withal be f in thy lips .... Prov 22:18
vessels of wrath f to destruction .... Rom 9:22

FITTETH
he f it with planes, and he .... Is 44:13

FIVE
hundred and f, and begat Enos .... Gen 5:6
Enos were nine hundred and f years .... Gen 5:11
sixty and f years, and begat Jared .... Gen 5:15
eight hundred ninety and f years .... Gen 5:17
f years, and begat Methuselah .... Gen 5:21
three hundred sixty and f years .... Gen 5:23
he begat Noah f hundred ninety .... Gen 5:30
f years, and begat sons and .... Gen 5:30
Noah was f hundred years old .... Gen 5:32
he begat Arphaxad f hundred years .... Gen 11:11
And Arphaxad lived f and thirty .... Gen 11:12
Terah were two hundred and f years .... Gen 11:32
f years old when he departed out .... Gen 12:4
Eliasar; four kings with f .... Gen 14:9
lack f of the fifty righteous .... Gen 18:28
all the city for lack of f .... Gen 18:28
said, If I find there forty and f .... Gen 18:28
but Benjamin's mess was f times .... Gen 45:6
and yet there are f years, in the .... Gen 45:6
yet there are f years of famine .... Gen 45:11
silver, and f changes of raiment .... Gen 45:22
some of his brethren, even f .... Gen 47:2
he shall restore f oxen for an ox .... Ex 22:1
The f curtains shall be coupled .... Ex 26:3
other f curtains shall be coupled .... Ex 26:3
thou shalt couple f curtains by .... Ex 26:9
f for the boards of the one side .... Ex 26:26
f bars for the boards of the .... Ex 26:26
f bars for the boards of the side .... Ex 26:27
hanging f pillars of shittim wood .... Ex 26:37
thou shalt cast f sockets of .... Ex 26:37
f cubits long, and f cubits .... Ex 27:1
the height f cubits of the .... Ex 27:18
of pure myrrh f hundred shekels .... Ex 30:23
of cassia f hundred shekels .... Ex 30:24
he coupled the f curtains one .... Ex 36:10
the other f curtains he coupled .... Ex 36:10
And he coupled f curtains by .... Ex 36:16
f for the boards of the one side .... Ex 36:31
f bars for the boards of the .... Ex 36:32
f bars for the boards of the .... Ex 36:32
the f pillars of it with their .... Ex 36:38
but their f sockets were of brass .... Ex 36:38
cubits was the length thereof .... Ex 38:1
f cubits the breadth thereof .... Ex 38:1
in the breadth was f cubits .... Ex 38:18
and f hundred and fifty men .... Ex 38:26
shekels he made hooks for the .... Ex 38:28
of you shall chase an hundred .... Lev 26:8
if it be from f years old even .... Lev 27:5
a month old even unto f years old .... Lev 27:6
of the male f shekels of silver .... Lev 27:6
and six thousand and f hundred .... Num 1:21
f thousand six hundred and fifty .... Num 1:23
forty thousand and f hundred .... Num 1:33
f thousand and four hundred .... Num 1:37
and one thousand and f hundred .... Num 1:41
thousand and f hundred and fifty .... Num 1:46
and six thousand and f hundred .... Num 2:11
f thousand and six hundred and .... Num 2:15
were forty thousand and f hundred .... Num 2:19
f thousand and four hundred .... Num 2:23
and one thousand and f hundred .... Num 2:28
thousand and f hundred and fifty .... Num 2:32
were seven thousand and f hundred .... Num 3:34
Thou shalt even take f shekels .... Num 3:47
f shekels, after the shekel of .... Num 3:50
and f hundred and fourscore .... Num 4:48
f rams, f he goats, f lambs .... Num 7:17
f rams, f he goats, f lambs .... Num 7:23
f rams, f he goats, f lambs .... Num 7:29
f rams, f he goats, f lambs .... Num 7:35
f rams, f he goats, f lambs .... Num 7:41
f rams, f he goats, f lambs .... Num 7:47
f rams, f he goats, f lambs .... Num 7:53
f rams, f he goats, f lambs .... Num 7:59
f rams, f he goats, f lambs .... Num 7:65
f rams, f he goats, f lambs .... Num 7:71
the f goats, f lambs of the .... Num 7:71

f rams, f he goats, f lambs .... Num 7:77
f rams, f he goats, f lambs .... Num 7:83
f years old and upward they shall .... Num 8:24
nor f days, neither ten days, nor .... Num 11:19
for the money of f shekels .... Num 18:16
them, forty thousand and f hundred .... Num 26:18
and sixteen thousand and f hundred .... Num 26:22
threescore thousand and f hundred .... Num 26:27
and two thousand and f hundred .... Num 26:37
f thousand and six hundred .... Num 26:41
f thousand and four hundred .... Num 26:50
Hur, and Reba, f kings of Midian .... Num 31:8
one soul of f hundred, both of .... Num 31:28
thousand and f thousand sheep .... Num 31:32
thousand and f hundred sheep .... Num 31:36
were thirty thousand and f hundred .... Num 31:39
thousand and f hundred sheep .... Num 31:43
thousand asses and f hundred .... Num 31:45
And he took f thousand men .... Josh 8:12
Therefore the f kings of the .... Josh 10:5
But these f kings fled, and hid .... Josh 10:16
The f kings are found hid in a .... Josh 10:17
bring out those f kings unto me .... Josh 10:22
brought forth those f kings unto .... Josh 10:23
them, and hanged them on f trees .... Josh 10:26
f lords of the Philistines .... Josh 13:3
f years, even since the LORD .... Josh 14:10
this day fourscore and f years old .... Josh 14:10
f lords of the Philistines, and .... Judg 3:3
family f men from their coasts .... Judg 18:2
Then the f men departed, and came .... Judg 18:7
Then answered the f men that went .... Judg 18:14
the f men that went to spy out .... Judg 18:17
f thousand and an hundred men .... Judg 20:35
in the highways f thousand men .... Judg 20:45
f thousand men that drew the .... Judg 20:46
f golden emerods, and f golden 1Sa 6:4
f golden mice, according to the 1Sa 6:4
And when the f lords of the 1Sa 6:16
belonging to the f lords, both of 1Sa 6:18
was f thousand shekels of brass 1Sa 17:5
chose him f smooth stones out of 1Sa 17:40
give me f loaves of bread in mine 1Sa 21:3
f persons that did wear a linen 1Sa 22:18
f sheep ready dressed, and 1Sa 25:18
f measures of parched corn, and an 1Sa 25:18
with f damsels of hers that went 1Sa 25:42
He was f years old when the 2Sa 4:4
the f sons of Michal the daughter 2Sa 21:8
Judah were f hundred thousand men 2Sa 24:9
and his songs were a thousand and f 1Kin 4:32
chamber was f cubits broad 1Kin 6:6
all the house, f cubits high 1Kin 6:10
f cubits was the one wing of the 1Kin 6:24
f cubits the other wing of the 1Kin 6:24
that lay on forty f pillars 1Kin 7:3
of one other chapter was f cubits 1Kin 7:16
the other chapter was f cubits 1Kin 7:16
about, and his height was f cubits 1Kin 7:23
he put f bases on the right side 1Kin 7:39
f on the left side of the house 1Kin 7:39
f on the right side, and f 1Kin 7:49
on the left, before the oracle 1Kin 7:49
f hundred and fifty, which bare 1Kin 9:23
f years old when he began to 1Kin 22:42
twenty and f years in Jerusalem 1Kin 22:42
dung for f pieces of silver 2Kin 6:25
f of the horses that remain 2Kin 7:13
have smitten f or six times 2Kin 13:19
f years old when he began to 2Kin 14:2
And twenty years old was he when 2Kin 15:33
f years old was he when he began 2Kin 19:35
hundred fourscore and f thousand 2Kin 19:35
fifty and f years in Jerusalem 2Kin 21:1
f years old when he began to 2Kin 23:36
men of them that were in the 2Kin 25:19
All the sons of Judah were f 1Chr 2:4
of them in all 1Chr 2:6
and Hasadiah, Jushab-hesed, f 1Chr 3:20
and Tochen, and Ashan, f cities 1Chr 4:32
f hundred men, went to mount Seir 1Chr 4:42
and Obadiah, and Joel, Ishiah, f 1Chr 7:3
and Uzziel, and Jerimoth, and Iri, f 1Chr 7:7
of great stature, f cubits high 1Chr 11:23
of God of gold f thousand talents 1Chr 29:7
of the one chapter was f cubits 2Chr 3:11
other wing was likewise f cubits 2Chr 3:11
of the other cherub was f cubits 2Chr 3:12
the other wing was f cubits also 2Chr 3:12
f cubits high, and the chapter 2Chr 3:15
top of each of them was f cubits 2Chr 3:15
f cubits the height thereof 2Chr 4:2
put f on the right hand, and 2Chr 4:6
f on the left, to wash in them 2Chr 4:6
f on the right hand, and f on 2Chr 4:7
f on the right side, and f on 2Chr 4:8
of f cubits long, and f cubits 2Chr 6:13
f hundred thousand chosen men 2Chr 13:17
there was no more war unto the f 2Chr 15:19
f years old when he began to 2Chr 20:31
twenty and f years in Jerusalem 2Chr 20:31
f years old when he began to 2Chr 25:1
f hundred, that made war with 2Chr 25:5
f years old when he began to 2Chr 27:1
He was f and twenty years old when 2Chr 27:8
began to reign when he was f 2Chr 29:1
fifty and f years in Jerusalem 2Chr 33:1
offerings f thousand small cattle 2Chr 35:9
small cattle, and f hundred oxen 2Chr 35:9
f years old when he began to 2Chr 36:5

gold and of silver were f thousand .... Ezr 1:11
Arah, seven hundred seventy and f .... Ezr 2:5
of Zattu, nine hundred forty and f .... Ezr 2:8
children of Gibbar, ninety and f .... Ezr 2:20
and Ono, seven hundred twenty and f .... Ezr 2:33
Jericho, three hundred forty and f .... Ezr 2:34
mules, two hundred forty and f .... Ezr 2:66
camels, four hundred thirty and f .... Ezr 2:67
f thousand pound of silver, and .... Ezr 2:69
Zattu, eight hundred forty and f .... Neh 7:13
of Adin, six hundred fifty and f .... Neh 7:20
children of Gibeon, ninety and f .... Neh 7:25
Jericho, three hundred forty and f .... Neh 7:36
f singing men and singing women .... Neh 7:67
mules, two hundred forty and f .... Neh 7:68
camels, four hundred thirty and f .... Neh 7:69
f hundred and thirty priests' .... Neh 7:70
slew and destroyed f hundred men .... Est 9:6
destroyed f hundred men in .... Est 9:12
f thousand, but they laid not .... Est 9:16
f hundred yoke of oxen, and f .... Job 1:3
f hundred she asses, and a very .... Job 1:3
f years shall Ephraim be broken .... Is 7:8
four or f in the outmost fruitful .... Is 17:6
In that day shall f cities in the .... Is 19:18
at the rebuke of f shall ye flee .... Is 30:17
and fourscore and f thousand .... Is 37:36
of one chapter was f cubits .... Jer 52:22
seven hundred forty and f persons .... Jer 52:30
in the twelfth month, in the f .... Jer 52:31
porch and the altar, were about f .... Eze 8:16
behold at the door of the gate f .... Eze 11:1
In the f and twentieth year of our .... Eze 40:1
the little chambers were f cubits .... Eze 40:7
the breadth was f and twenty .... Eze 40:13
fifty cubits, and the breadth f .... Eze 40:21
fifty cubits, and the breadth f .... Eze 40:25
it was fifty cubits long, and f .... Eze 40:29
And the arches round about were f .... Eze 40:30
cubits long, and f cubits broad .... Eze 40:30
it was fifty cubits long, and f .... Eze 40:33
fifty cubits, and the breadth f .... Eze 40:36
f cubits on this side .... Eze 40:48
and f cubits on that side .... Eze 40:48
were f cubits on the one side .... Eze 41:2
f cubits on the other side .... Eze 41:2
chamber without, was f cubits .... Eze 41:9
was left was f cubits round about .... Eze 41:11
was f cubits thick round about .... Eze 41:12
f hundred reeds, with the .... Eze 42:16
f hundred reeds, with the .... Eze 42:17
f hundred reeds, with the .... Eze 42:18
measured f hundred reeds with the .... Eze 42:19
f hundred reeds long, and .... Eze 42:20
f hundred broad, to make a .... Eze 42:20
length shall be the length of f .... Eze 45:1
the sanctuary f hundred in length .... Eze 45:2
with f hundred in breadth, square .... Eze 45:2
thou measure the length of f .... Eze 45:3
And the f and twenty thousand of .... Eze 45:5
city f thousand broad, and f .... Eze 45:6
twenty shekels, f and twenty .... Eze 45:12
which ye shall offer of .... Eze 48:8
offer unto the LORD shall be of f .... Eze 48:9
toward the north f and twenty .... Eze 48:10
in breadth, and toward the south f .... Eze 48:10
priests the Levites shall have f .... Eze 48:13
all the length shall be f .... Eze 48:13
the f thousand, that are left in .... Eze 48:15
in the breadth over against the f .... Eze 48:16
f hundred, and the south side four .... Eze 48:16
f hundred, and on the east side .... Eze 48:16
f hundred, and the west side four .... Eze 48:16
side four thousand and f hundred .... Eze 48:17
be f and twenty thousand by f .... Eze 48:20
of the city, over against the f .... Eze 48:21
and westward over against the f .... Eze 48:21
thousand and f hundred measures .... Eze 48:30
side four thousand and f hundred .... Eze 48:32
thousand and f hundred measures .... Eze 48:33
f hundred, with their three gates .... Eze 48:34
the thousand three hundred and f .... Dan 12:12
him, We have here but f loaves .... Mt 14:17
the grass, and took the f loaves .... Mt 14:19
eaten were about f thousand men .... Mt 14:21
neither remember the f loaves of .... Mt 16:9
the f thousand, and how many baskets .... Mt 16:9
of them were wise, and f were .... Mt 25:2
And unto one he gave f talents .... Mt 25:15
had received the f talents went .... Mt 25:16
and made them other f talents .... Mt 25:16
that had received f talents came .... Mt 25:20
came and brought other f talents .... Mt 25:20
deliveredst unto me f talents .... Mt 25:20
gained beside them f talents more .... Mt 25:20
And when they knew, they say, F .... Mk 6:38
And when he had taken the f loaves .... Mk 6:41
loaves were about f thousand men .... Mk 6:44
When I brake the f loaves among .... Mk 8:19
f thousand, how many baskets .... Mk 8:19
and his herself f months, saying .... Lk 1:24
the one owed f hundred pence, and .... Lk 7:41
We have no more but f loaves .... Lk 9:13
they were about f thousand men .... Lk 9:14
Then he took the f loaves .... Lk 9:16
Are not f sparrows sold for two .... Lk 12:6
shall be f in one house divided .... Lk 12:52
I have bought f yoke of oxen .... Lk 14:19
For I have f brethren .... Lk 16:28
thy pound hath gained f pounds .... Lk 19:18

him, Be thou also over f cities .... Lk 19:19
For thou hast had f husbands .... Jn 4:18
tongue Bethesda, having f porches .... Jn 5:2
which hath f barley loaves, and .... Jn 6:9
down, in number about f thousand .... Jn 6:10
fragments of the f barley loaves .... Jn 6:13
So when they had rowed about f .... Jn 6:19
of the men was about f thousand .... Acts 4:4
came unto them to Troas in f days .... Acts 20:6
after f days Ananias the high .... Acts 24:1
f words with my understanding 1Cor 14:19
he was seen of above f hundred 1Cor 15:6
Of the Jews f times received I 2Cor 11:24
they should be tormented f months ...... Rev 9:5
power was to hurt men f months .... Rev 9:10
f are fallen, and one is, and the .... Rev 17:10

FIXED
My heart is f, O God, my heart is .... Ps 57:7
is f, O God, my heart is f .... Ps 57:7
O God, my heart is f .... Ps 108:1
his heart is f, trusting in the .... Ps 112:7
us and you there is a great gulf f .... Lk 16:26

FLAG
can the f grow without water .... Job 8:11

FLAGON
piece of flesh, and a f of wine 2Sa 6:19
piece of flesh, and a f of wine 1Chr 16:3

FLAGONS
Stay me with f, comfort me with .... Song 2:5
even to all the vessels of f .... Is 22:24
to other gods, and love f of wine .... Hos 3:1

FLAGS
she laid it in the f by the .... Ex 2:3
when she saw the ark among the f .... Ex 2:5
the reeds and f shall wither .... Is 19:6

FLAKES
The f of his flesh are joined .... Job 41:23

FLAME
a f of fire out of the midst of a .... Ex 3:2
a f from the city of Sihon .... Num 21:28
when the f went up toward heaven .... Judg 13:20
ascended in the f of the altar .... Judg 13:20
f with smoke rise up out of the .... Judg 20:38
But when the f began to arise up .... Judg 20:40
the f of the city ascended up to .... Judg 20:40
the f shall dry up his branches .... Job 15:30
a f goeth out of his mouth .... Job 41:21
as the f setteth the mountains on .... Ps 83:14
the f burned up the wicked .... Ps 106:18
which hath a most vehement f .... Song 8:6
the f consumeth the chaff, so .... Is 5:24
a fire, and his Holy One for a f .... Is 10:17
and the f of devouring fire .... Is 29:6
with the f of a devouring fire .... Is 30:30
shall the f kindle upon thee .... Is 43:2
from the power of the f .... Is 47:14
a f from the midst of Sihon, and .... Jer 48:45
the flaming f shall not be .... Eze 20:47
the f of the fire slew those men .... Dan 3:22
his throne was like the fiery f .... Dan 7:9
and given to the burning f .... Dan 7:11
shall fall by the sword, and by f .... Dan 11:33
hath burned all the trees .... Joel 1:19
and behind them a f burneth .... Joel 2:3
like the noise of a f of fire .... Joel 2:5
fire, and the house of Joseph a f .... Obad 18
for I am tormented in this f .... Lk 16:24
the Lord in a f of fire in a bush .... Acts 7:30
and his ministers a f of fire .... Heb 1:7
and his eyes were as a f of fire .... Rev 1:14
his eyes like unto a f of fire .... Rev 2:18
His eyes were as a f of fire .... Rev 19:12

FLAMES
the Lord divideth the f of fire .... Ps 29:7
their faces shall be as f .... Is 13:8
and his rebuke with f of fire .... Is 66:15

FLAMING
a f sword which turned every way, ... Gen 3:24
his ministers a f fire .... Ps 104:4
for rain, and f fire in their land .... Ps 105:32
the shining of a f fire by night .... Is 4:5
against Jacob like a f fire .... Lam 2:3
the f flame shall not be quenched ...... Eze 20:47
morning it burneth as a f fire .... Hos 7:6
with f torches in the day of his .... Nah 2:3
In f fire taking vengeance on 2Th 1:8

FLANKS
is on them, which is by the f .... Lev 3:4
is upon them, which is by the f .... Lev 3:10
is upon them, which is by the f .... Lev 3:15
is upon them, which is by the f .... Lev 4:9
is on them, which is by the f .... Lev 7:4
and maketh collops of fat on his f ...... Job 15:27

FLASH
appearance of a f of lightning .... Eze 1:14

FLAT
a lame, or he that hath a f nose .... Lev 21:18
his head, and fell f on his face .... Num 22:31
of the city shall fall down f .... Josh 6:5
shout, that the wall fell down f .... Josh 6:20

FLATTER
they f with their tongue .... Ps 5:9
they did f him with their mouth .... Ps 78:36

FLATTERETH
For he f himself in his own eyes, ... Ps 36:2
stranger which f with her words .... Prov 2:16
stranger which f with her words .... Prov 7:5
not with him that f with his lips .... Prov 20:19
than he that f with the tongue .... Prov 28:23
A man that f his neighbour .... Prov 29:5

FLATTERIES
and obtain the kingdom by f .... Dan 11:21
covenant and the corrupt by f .... Dan 11:32
many shall cleave to them with f .... Dan 11:34

FLATTERING
let me give f titles unto man .... Job 32:21
For I know not to give f titles .... Job 32:22
with f lips and with a double .... Ps 12:2
The Lord shall cut off all f lips .... Ps 12:3
with the f of her lips she forced .... Prov 7:21
and a f mouth worketh ruin .... Prov 26:28
f divination within the house of .... Eze 12:24
at any time used we f words 1Th 2:5

FLATTERY
He that speaketh f to his friends .... Job 17:5
from the f of the tongue of a .... Prov 6:24

FLAX
And the f and the barley was .... Ex 9:31
in the ear, and the f was bolled .... Ex 9:31
and hid them with the stalks of f .... Josh 2:6
as f that was burnt with fire .... Judg 15:14
She seeketh wool, and f, and .... Prov 31:13
Moreover they that work in fine f ...... Is 19:9
the smoking f shall he not quench ..... Is 42:3
with a line of f in his hand .... Eze 40:3
and my water, my wool and my f .... Hos 2:5
my f given to cover her nakedness ...... Hos 2:9
smoking f shall he not quench, ... Mt 12:20

FLAY
he shall f the burnt offering, and .... Lev 1:6
so that they could not f all the 2Chr 29:34
their skin from off them .... Mic 3:3

FLAYED
hands, and the Levites f them 2Chr 35:11

FLEA
after a dead dog, after a f 1Sa 24:14
of Israel is come out to seek a f 1Sa 26:20

FLED
the kings of Sodom and Gomorrah f .... Gen 14:10
that remained f to the mountain .... Gen 14:10
with her, she f from her face .... Gen 16:6
in that he told him not that he f .... Gen 31:20
So he f with all that he had .... Gen 31:21
on the third day that Jacob was f .... Gen 31:22
when he f from the face of his .... Gen 35:7
his garment in her hand, and f .... Gen 39:12
in her hand, and was f forth, ... Gen 39:13
he left his garment with me, and f ...... Gen 39:15
his garment with me, and f out .... Gen 39:18
but Moses f from the face of .... Ex 2:15
and Moses f from before it .... Ex 4:3
king of Egypt that the people f .... Ex 14:5
and the Egyptians f against it .... Ex 14:27
about them f at the cry of them .... Num 16:34
of his refuge, whither he was f .... Num 35:25
of his refuge, whither he was f .... Num 35:26
is f to the city of his refuge .... Num 35:32
they f before the men of Ai .... Josh 7:4
f by the way of the wilderness .... Josh 8:15
and the people that f to the .... Josh 8:20
as they f from before Israel, and .... Josh 10:11
But these five kings f, and hid, ... Josh 10:16
unto the city from whence he f .... Josh 20:6
But Adoni-bezek f .... Judg 1:6
chariot, and f away on his feet .... Judg 4:15
Howbeit Sisera f away on his feet ..... Judg 4:17
all the host ran, and cried, and f ...... Judg 7:21
the host f to Beth-shittah in .... Judg 7:22
And when Zebah and Zalmunna f ...... Judg 8:12
And Jotham ran away, and f .... Judg 9:21
he f before him, and many were .... Judg 9:40
thither f all the men and women, ... Judg 9:51
Then Jephthah f from before him ...... Judg 11:3
f toward the wilderness unto the .... Judg 20:45
to the wilderness unto the rock .... Judg 20:47
they f every man into his tent 1Sa 4:10
I f to day out of the army 1Sa 4:16
and said, Israel is f before the 1Sa 4:17
they heard that the Philistines f 1Sa 14:22
f from him, and were sore afraid 1Sa 17:24
their champion was dead, they f 1Sa 17:51
and they f from him 1Sa 19:8
and David f, and escaped that night ... 1Sa 19:10
and he went, and f, and escaped 1Sa 19:12
So David f, and escaped, and came 1Sa 19:18
David f from Naioth in Ramah, and 1Sa 20:1
f that day for fear of Saul, and 1Sa 21:10
and because they knew when he f 1Sa 22:17
escaped, and f after David 1Sa 22:20
of Ahimelech f to David to Keilah 1Sa 23:6
Saul that David was f to Gath 1Sa 27:4
men, which rode upon camels, and f ... 1Sa 30:17
the men of Israel f before 1Sa 31:7
saw that the men of Israel f 1Sa 31:7
they forsook the cities, and f 1Sa 31:7
the people are f from the battle 2Sa 1:4
And the Beerothites f to Gittaim 2Sa 4:3
and his nurse took him up, and f 2Sa 4:4
and they f before him 2Sa 10:13

Ammon saw that the Syrians were f 2Sa 10:14
then f they also before Abishai, ... 2Sa 10:14
the Syrians f before Israel 2Sa 10:18
gat him up upon his mule, and f 2Sa 13:29
But Absalom f. And the young man 2Sa 13:34
But Absalom f, and went to Talmai 2Sa 13:37
So Absalom f, and went to Geshur 2Sa 13:38
all Israel f every one to his 2Sa 18:17
for Israel had f every man to his 2Sa 19:8
now he is f out of the land for 2Sa 19:9
the people f from the Philistines 2Sa 23:11
for so they came to me when I f 1Kin 2:7
Joab f unto the tabernacle of the 1Kin 2:28
f unto the tabernacle of the Lord 1Kin 2:29
That Hadad f, he and certain 1Kin 11:17
which f from his lord Hadadezer 1Kin 11:23
f into Egypt, unto Shishak king 1Kin 11:40
(for he was f from the presence 1Kin 12:2
and the Syrians f 1Kin 20:20
But the rest f to Aphek, into the 1Kin 20:30
And Ben-hadad f, and came into the .. 1Kin 20:30
so that they f before them 2Kin 3:24
f in the twilight, and left their 2Kin 7:7
as it was, and f for their life 2Kin 7:7
the people f into their tents 2Kin 8:21
And he opened the door, and f 2Kin 9:10
And Joram turned his hands, and f 2Kin 9:23
he f by the way of the garden 2Kin 9:27
he f to Megiddo, and died there 2Kin 9:27
they f every man to their tents 2Kin 14:12
and he f to Lachish 2Kin 14:19
all the men of war f by night by 2Kin 25:4
the men of Israel f from before 1Chr 10:1
in the valley saw that they f 1Chr 10:7
they forsook their cities, and f 1Chr 10:7
the people f before him 1Chr 11:13
and they f before him 1Chr 19:14
Ammon saw that the Syrians were f ... 1Chr 19:15
they likewise f before Abishai 1Chr 19:15
But the Syrians f before Israel 1Chr 19:18
whither he had f from the 2Chr 10:2
children of Israel f before Judah 2Chr 13:16
and the Ethiopians f 2Chr 14:12
they f every man to his tent 2Chr 25:22
and he f to Lachish 2Chr 25:27
were f every one to his field .... Neh 13:10
when he f from Absalom his son .... Ps 3:t
that did see me without f from me ..... Ps 31:11
when he f from Saul in the cave .... Ps 57:t
At thy rebuke they f .... Ps 104:7
The sea saw it, and f .... Ps 114:3
Gibeah of Saul is f .... Is 10:29
with their bread him that f .... Is 21:14
they f from the swords, from .... Is 21:15
All thy rulers are f together .... Is 22:3
together, which have f from far .... Is 22:3
noise of the tumult the people f ...... Is 33:3
the birds of the heavens were f .... Jer 4:25
of the heavens and the beast are f .... Jer 9:10
heard it, he was afraid, and f .... Jer 26:21
of the men of war, then they f .... Jer 39:4
are f apace, and look not back .... Jer 46:5
back, and are f away together .... Jer 46:21
They that f stood under the .... Jer 48:45
up, and all the men of war f .... Jer 52:7
when they f away and wandered, ... Lam 4:15
so that they f to hide themselves ..... Dan 10:7
for they have f from me .... Hos 7:13
Jacob f into the country of Syria ...... Hos 12:12
For the men knew that he f from ...... Jonah 1:10
Therefore I f before unto .... Jonah 4:2
like as ye f from before the .... Zec 14:5
And they that kept them f, and went .. Mt 8:33
the disciples forsook him, and f .... Mt 26:56
And they that fed the swine f .... Mk 5:14
And they all forsook him, and f .... Mk 14:50
linen cloth, and f from them naked .. Mk 14:52
quickly, and f from the sepulchre .... Mk 16:8
them saw what was done, they f ...... Lk 8:34
Then f Moses at this saying, and ...... Acts 7:29
unto Lystra and Derbe, cities of ...... Acts 14:6
that the prisoners had been f .... Acts 16:27
so that they f out of that house .... Acts 19:16
who have f for refuge to lay hold ..... Heb 6:18
the woman f into the wilderness, ... Rev 12:6
And every island f away, and the ..... Rev 16:20
the earth and the heaven f away ...... Rev 20:11

FLEDDEST
thou f from the face of Esau thy .... Gen 35:1
thee, O thou sea, that thou f .... Ps 114:5

FLEE
I f from the face of my mistress .... Gen 16:8
now, this city is near to f unto .... Gen 19:20
thou to Laban my brother to .... Gen 27:43
didst thou f away secretly .... Gen 31:27
his cattle f into the houses .... Ex 9:20
Let us f from the face of Israel .... Ex 14:25
thee a place whither he shall f .... Ex 21:13
ye shall f when none pursueth you ... Lev 26:17
and they shall f, as fleeing from ..... Lev 26:36
then that hate thee f before thee, ... Num 10:35
Therefore now f thou to thy place .... Num 24:11
manslayer, that he may f thither ...... Num 35:6
that the slayer may f thither .... Num 35:11
any person unawares may f thither ... Num 35:15
That the slayer might f thither .... Deut 4:42
that every slayer may f thither .... Deut 19:3
the slayer, which shall f thither ...... Deut 19:4
he shall f unto one of those .... Deut 19:5

way, and f before thee seven ways..... Deut 28:7
them, and f seven ways before them Deut 28:25
first, that we will f before them......... Josh 8:5
They f before us, as at the first.......... Josh 8:6
therefore we will f before them.......... Josh 8:6
power to f this way or that way.......... Josh 8:20
and unwittingly may f thither.............. Josh 20:3
when he that doth f unto one of....... Josh 20:9
at unawares might f thither............... Josh 20:9
children of Israel said, Let us f........ Judg 20:32
to pass, as she made haste to f......... 2Sa 4:4
at Jerusalem, Arise, and let us f....... 2Sa 15:14
people that are with him shall f......... 2Sa 15:14
for if we f away, they will not.......... 2Sa 18:3
steal away when they f in battle...... 2Sa 19:3
or wilt thou f three months............... 2Sa 24:13
to his chariot, to f to Jerusalem....... 1Kin 12:18
Then open the door, and f, and........ 2Kin 9:3
to his chariot, to f to Jerusalem....... 2Chr 10:18
I said, Should such a man as I f........ Neh 6:11
they f away, they see no good.......... Job 9:25
He shall f from the iron weapon,...... Job 20:24
he would fain f out of his hand......... Job 27:22
they f far from me, and spare not..... Job 30:10
The arrow cannot make him f........... Job 41:28
F as a bird to your mountain............ Ps 11:1
all that see them shall f away........... Ps 64:8
also that hate him f before him......... Ps 68:1
Kings of armies did f apace.............. Ps 68:12
shall I f from thy presence................ Ps 139:7
I f unto thee to hide me.................... Ps 143:9
The wicked f when no man pursueth. Prov 28:1
of any person shall f to the pit......... Prov 28:17
day break, and the shadows f away.. Song 2:17
day break, and the shadows f away.. Song 4:6
to whom will ye f for help................ Is 10:3
of Gebim gather themselves to f....... Is 10:31
f every one into his own land........... Is 13:14
his fugitives shall f unto Zoar.......... Is 15:5
them, and they shall f far off............ Is 17:13
whither we f for help to be.............. Is 20:6
for we will f upon horses.................. Is 30:16
therefore shall ye f........................... Is 30:16
One thousand shall f at the.............. Is 30:17
at the rebuke of five shall ye f........ Is 30:17
but he shall f from the sword, and... Is 31:8
and sorrow and sighing shall f away. Is 35:10
f ye from the Chaldeans, with a....... Is 48:20
sorrow and mourning shall f away... Is 51:11
The whole city shall f for the........... Jer 4:29
gather yourselves to f out of the..... Jer 6:1
shepherds shall have no way to f..... Jer 25:35
Let not the swift f away, nor the..... Jer 46:6
F, save your lives, and be like.......... Jer 48:6
wings unto Moab, that it may f........ Jer 48:9
F ye, turn back, dwell deep, O......... Jer 49:8
feeble, and turneth herself to f........ Jer 49:24
F, get you far off, dwell deep, O...... Jer 49:30
they shall f every one to his own..... Jer 50:16
The voice of them that f and............ Jer 50:28
F out of the midst of Babylon, and.. Jer 51:6
shall f away naked in that day......... Amos 2:16
As if a man did f from a lion............ Amos 5:19
f thee away into the land of............. Amos 7:12
fleeth of them shall not f away........ Amos 9:1
But Jonah rose up to f unto............. Jonah 1:3
yet they shall f away........................ Nah 2:8
look upon thee shall f from thee...... Nah 3:7
thee when he shall f when they f away.. Nah 3:17
f from the land of the north............. Zec 2:6
ye shall f to the valley of................. Zec 14:5
yea, ye shall f, like as ye fled.......... Zec 14:5
f into Egypt, and be thou there........ Mt 2:13
you to f from the wrath to come...... Mt 3:7
in this city, f ye into another........... Mt 10:23
be in Judaea f into the mountains.... Mt 24:16
be in Judaea f to the mountains....... Mk 13:14
you to f from the wrath to come...... Lk 3:7
are in Judaea f to the mountains...... Lk 21:21
not follow, but will f from him........ Jn 10:5
were about to f out of the ship........ Acts 27:30
F fornication..................................... 1Cor 6:18
dearly beloved, f from idolatry........ 1Cor 10:14
O man of God, f these things........... 1Ti 6:11
F also youthful lusts......................... 2Ti 2:22
the devil, and he will f from you...... Jas 4:7
die, and death shall f from them...... Rev 9:6

FLEECE
the first of the f of thy sheep........... Deut 18:4
I will put a f of wool in the............. Judg 6:37
and if the dew be on the f only........ Judg 6:37
morrow, and thrust the f together..... Judg 6:38
and wringed the dew out of the f..... Judg 6:38
thee, but this once with the f........... Judg 6:39
let it now be dry only upon the f..... Judg 6:39
for it was dry upon the f only.......... Judg 6:40
not warmed with the f of my sheep. Job 31:20

FLEEING
shall flee, as f from a sword............. Lev 26:36
that f unto one of these cities.......... Deut 4:42
f into the wilderness in former......... Job 30:3

FLEETH
f into one of these cities.................... Deut 19:11
he f also as a shadow, and............... Job 14:2
that he who f from the battle........... Is 24:18
ask him that f, and her that.............. Jer 48:19
the fear f from the fear shall........... Jer 48:44
he that f of them shall not flee........ Amos 9:1
cankerworm spoileth, and f away..... Nah 3:16

and leaveth the sheep, and f............. Jn 10:12
The hireling f, because he is an........ Jn 10:13

FLESH
closed up the f instead thereof......... Gen 2:21
of my bones, and f of my f.............. Gen 2:23
and they shall be one f..................... Gen 2:24
with man, for that he also is f.......... Gen 6:3
for all f had corrupted his way........ Gen 6:12
The end of all f is come before....... Gen 6:13
upon the earth, to destroy all f........ Gen 6:17
And of every living thing of all f.... Gen 6:19
into the ark, two and two of all f..... Gen 7:15
went in male and female of all f..... Gen 7:16
all f died that moved upon the........ Gen 7:21
thing that is with thee, of all f........ Gen 8:17
But f with the life thereof,.............. Gen 9:4
neither shall all f be cut off............. Gen 9:11
and every living creature of all f..... Gen 9:15
become a flood to destroy all f........ Gen 9:15
all f that is upon the earth................ Gen 9:16
circumcise the f of your foreskin..... Gen 17:11
f for an everlasting covenant........... Gen 17:13
whose f of his foreskin is not.......... Gen 17:14
circumcised the f of their................. Gen 17:23
in the f of his foreskin...................... Gen 17:24
in the f of his foreskin...................... Gen 17:25
Surely thou art my bone and my f... Gen 29:14
for he is our brother and our f......... Gen 37:27
shall eat thy f from off thee............. Gen 40:19
was turned again as his other f........ Ex 4:7
shall eat the f in that night.............. Ex 12:8
of the f abroad out of the house...... Ex 12:46
Egypt, when we sat by the f pots..... Ex 16:3
give you in the evening f to eat...... Ex 16:8
saying, At even ye shall eat f.......... Ex 16:12
and his f shall not be eaten............. Ex 21:28
neither shall ye eat any f that.......... Ex 22:31
But the f of the bullock, and his..... Ex 29:14
seethe his f in the holy place.......... Ex 29:31
sons shall eat the f of the ram......... Ex 29:32
And if ought of the f of the............ Ex 29:34
Upon man's f shall it not be........... Ex 30:32
with the bullock, and all his f.......... Lev 4:11
breeches shall he put upon his f...... Lev 6:10
touch the f thereof shall be holy..... Lev 6:27
the f of the sacrifice of his............. Lev 7:15
But the remainder of the f of the.... Lev 7:17
if any of the f of the sacrifice......... Lev 7:18
the f that toucheth any unclean....... Lev 7:19
and as for the f, all that be.............. Lev 7:19
the f of the sacrifice of peace......... Lev 7:20
eat of the f of the sacrifice of......... Lev 7:21
the bullock, and his hide, his f........ Lev 8:17
Boil the f at the door of the............ Lev 8:31
And that which remaineth of the f... Lev 8:32
And the f and the hide he burnt...... Lev 9:11
Of their f shall ye not eat, and....... Lev 11:8
ye shall not eat of their f................. Lev 11:11
in the eighth day the f of his.......... Lev 12:3
in the skin of his f a rising.............. Lev 13:2
it be in the skin of his f like........... Lev 13:2
the plague in the skin of the........... Lev 13:3
be deeper than the skin of his......... Lev 13:3
be white in the skin of his f............ Lev 13:4
be quick raw f in the rising............ Lev 13:10
old leprosy in the skin of his f........ Lev 13:11
leprosy have covered all his f.......... Lev 13:13
But when raw f appeareth in him,... Lev 13:14
And the priest shall see the raw f.... Lev 13:15
for the raw f is unclean................... Lev 13:15
Or if the raw f turn again................ Lev 13:16
The f also, in which, even in the..... Lev 13:18
Or if there be any f, in the skin...... Lev 13:24
the quick f that burneth have a....... Lev 13:24
the skin of their f bright spots........ Lev 13:38
skin of their f be darkish white...... Lev 13:39
appeareth in the skin of their f........ Lev 13:43
also he shall wash his f in water..... Lev 14:9
hath a running issue out of his f..... Lev 15:2
whether his f run with his issue,..... Lev 15:3
or his f be stopped from his............ Lev 15:3
he that toucheth the f of him.......... Lev 15:7
bathe his f in running water, and.... Lev 15:13
he shall wash all his f in water....... Lev 15:16
and her issue in her f be blood....... Lev 15:19
the linen breeches upon his f.......... Lev 16:4
shall he wash his f in water............ Lev 16:4
he shall wash his f with water in.... Lev 16:24
clothes, and bathe his f in water..... Lev 16:26
the fire their skins, and their f........ Lev 16:27
clothes, and bathe his f in water..... Lev 16:28
the life of the f is in the blood....... Lev 17:11
For it is the life of all f.................. Lev 17:14
eat the blood of no manner of f...... Lev 17:14
for the life of all f is the................ Lev 17:14
he wash them not, nor bathe his f... Lev 17:16
cuttings in your f for the dead......... Lev 19:28
nor make any cuttings in their f...... Lev 21:5
unless he wash his f with water...... Lev 22:6
ye shall eat the f of your sons......... Lev 26:29
the f of your daughters shall ye...... Lev 26:29
and let them shave all their f........... Num 8:7
said, Who shall give us f to eat...... Num 11:4
Whence should I have f to give....... Num 11:13
weep unto me, saying, Give us f..... Num 11:13
to morrow, and ye shall eat f.......... Num 11:18
Who shall give us f to eat............... Num 11:18
the LORD will give you f, and ye.... Num 11:18
hast said, I will give them f............ Num 11:21

while the f was yet between their.... Num 11:33
of whom the f is half consumed...... Num 12:12
the God of the spirits of all f......... Num 16:22
that openeth the matrix in all f........ Num 18:15
the f of them shall be thine, as....... Num 18:18
her skin, and her f, and her blood,... Num 19:5
and he shall bathe his f in water..... Num 19:7
in water, and bathe his f in water... Num 19:8
the God of the spirits of all f......... Num 27:16
For who is there of all f.................. Deut 5:26
kill and eat f in all thy gates,......... Deut 12:15
and thou shalt say, I will eat f........ Deut 12:20
because thy soul longeth to eat f..... Deut 12:20
thou mayest eat f, whatsoever thy... Deut 12:20
not eat the life with the f................ Deut 12:23
offer thy burnt offerings, the f........ Deut 12:27
thy God, and thou shalt eat the f.... Deut 12:27
ye shall not eat of their f................ Deut 14:8
shall there any thing of the f........... Deut 16:4
the f of thy sons and of thy............ Deut 28:53
f of his children whom he shall...... Deut 28:55
blood, and my sword shall devour f. Deut 32:42
the f be put in a basket, and he...... Judg 6:19
of God said unto him, Take the f..... Judg 6:20
was in his hand, and touched the f... Judg 6:21
of the rock, and consumed the f...... Judg 6:21
then I will tear your f with the....... Judg 8:7
that I am your bone and your f........ Judg 9:2
while the f was in seething, with.... 1Sa 2:13
Give f to roast for the priest........... 1Sa 2:15
he will not have sodden f of thee.... 1Sa 2:15
I will give thy f unto the fowls........ 1Sa 17:44
my f that I have killed for my......... 1Sa 25:11
Behold, we are thy bone and thy f... 2Sa 5:1
of bread, and a good piece of f....... 2Sa 6:19
brethren, ye are my bones and my f. 2Sa 19:12
thou not of my bone, and of my f... 2Sa 19:13
f in the morning, and bread and...... 1Kin 17:6
and bread and f in the evening....... 1Kin 17:6
them, and boiled their f with the.... 1Kin 19:21
and put sackcloth upon his f............ 1Kin 21:27
the f of the child waxed warm........ 2Kin 4:34
thy f shall come again to thee,....... 2Kin 5:10
his f came again like unto the......... 2Kin 5:14
like unto the f of a little child........ 2Kin 5:14
had sackcloth within upon his f....... 2Kin 6:30
shall dogs eat the f of Jezebel........ 2Kin 9:36
Behold, we are thy bone and thy f... 1Chr 11:1
of bread, and a good piece of f....... 1Chr 16:3
With his is an arm of f.................... 2Chr 32:8
f is as the f of our brethren............. Neh 5:5
now, and touch his bone and his f... Job 2:5
the hair of my f stood up................ Job 4:15
or is my f of brass.......................... Job 6:12
My f is clothed with worms and..... Job 7:5
Hast thou eyes of f......................... Job 10:4
hast clothed me with skin and f...... Job 10:11
do I take my f in my teeth.............. Job 13:14
But his f upon him shall have.......... Job 14:22
cleaveth to my skin and to my f..... Job 19:20
and are not satisfied with my f....... Job 19:22
yet in my f shall I see God............. Job 19:26
and trembling taketh hold on my f.. Job 21:6
said not, Oh that we had of his f..... Job 31:31
His f is consumed away, that it...... Job 33:21
His f shall be fresher than a............ Job 33:25
All f shall perish together, and....... Job 34:15
The flakes of his f are joined.......... Job 41:23
my f also shall rest in hope............ Ps 16:9
foes, came upon me to eat up my f. Ps 27:2
in my f because of thine anger........ Ps 38:3
and there is no soundness in my f... Ps 38:7
Will I eat the f of bulls................... Ps 50:13
not fear what f can do unto me....... Ps 56:4
my f longeth for thee in a dry and.. Ps 63:1
unto thee shall all f come................ Ps 65:2
My f and my heart faileth............... Ps 73:26
can he provide f for his people....... Ps 78:20
He rained f also upon them as........ Ps 78:27
remembered that they were but f.... Ps 78:39
the f of thy saints unto the............. Ps 79:2
my f crieth out for the living.......... Ps 84:2
and my f faileth of fatness.............. Ps 109:24
My f trembleth for fear of thee...... Ps 119:120
Who giveth food to all f................. Ps 136:25
let all f bless his holy name for...... Ps 145:21
them, and health to all their f......... Prov 4:22
mourn at the last, when thy f.......... Prov 5:11
that is cruel troubleth his own f...... Prov 11:17
sound heart is the life of the........... Prov 14:30
among riotous eaters of f................ Prov 23:20
together, and eateth his own f......... Eccl 4:5
thy mouth to cause thy f to sin....... Eccl 5:6
and put away evil from thy f........... Eccl 11:10
study is a weariness of the f............ Eccl 12:12
every man the f of his own arm...... Is 9:20
fatness of his f shall wax lean........ Is 17:4
eating, and killing sheep, eating f... Is 22:13
and their horses f, and not spirit..... Is 31:3
all f shall see it together................. Is 40:5
All f is grass, and all the................ Is 40:6
and part thereof he eateth f............. Is 44:16
I have roasted f, and eaten it.......... Is 44:19
oppress thee with their own f.......... Is 49:26
all f shall know that I the LORD..... Is 49:26
hide not thyself from thine own f.... Is 58:7
monuments, which eat swine's f...... Is 65:4
will the LORD plead with all f........ Is 66:16
eating swine's f............................... Is 66:17
shall all f come to worship............. Is 66:23

shall be an abhorring unto all f	Is 66:24
unto your sacrifices, and eat f	Jer 7:21
the holy f is passed from thee	Jer 11:15
no f shall have peace	Jer 12:12
maketh f his arm, and whose heart	Jer 17:5
them to eat the f of their sons	Jer 19:9
the f of their daughters, and they	Jer 19:9
the f of his friend in the siege	Jer 19:9
nations, he will plead with all f	Jer 25:31
I am the LORD, the God of all f	Jer 32:27
I will bring evil upon all f	Jer 45:5
to my f be upon Babylon, shall	Jer 51:35
My f and my skin hath he made old	Lam 3:4
there abominable f into my mouth	Eze 4:14
is the caldron, and we be the f	Eze 11:3
the midst of it, they are the f	Eze 11:7
ye be the f in the midst thereof	Eze 11:11
the stony heart out of their f	Eze 11:19
and will give them an heart of f	Eze 11:19
thy neighbours, great of f	Eze 16:26
all f shall see that I the LORD	Eze 20:48
all f from the south to the north	Eze 21:4
That all f may know that I the	Eze 21:5
whose f is as the f of asses	Eze 23:20
kindle the fire, consume the f	Eze 24:10
I will lay thy f upon the	Eze 32:5
the stony heart out of your f	Eze 36:26
and I will give you an heart of f	Eze 36:26
you, and will bring up f upon you	Eze 37:6
the f came up upon them, and the	Eze 37:8
of Israel, that ye may eat f	Eze 39:17
Ye shall eat the f of the mighty	Eze 39:18
tables was the f of the offering	Eze 40:43
in heart, and uncircumcised in f	Eze 44:7
in heart, nor uncircumcised in f	Eze 44:9
fatter in f than all the children	Dan 1:15
whose dwelling is not with f	Dan 2:11
thereof, and all f was fed of it	Dan 4:12
unto it, Arise, devour much f	Dan 7:5
neither came f nor wine in my	Dan 10:3
They sacrifice f for the	Hos 8:13
pour out my spirit upon all f	Joel 2:28
their f from off their bones	Mic 3:2
Who also eat the f of my people	Mic 3:3
pot, and as f within the caldron	Mic 3:3
as dust, and their f as the dung	Zeph 1:17
If one bear holy f in the skirt	Hag 2:12
Be silent, O all f, before the	Zec 2:13
eat every one the f of another	Zec 11:9
but he shall eat the f of the fat	Zec 11:16
Their f shall consume away while	Zec 14:12
for f and blood hath not revealed	Mt 16:17
and they twain shall be one f	Mt 19:5
they are no more twain, but one f	Mt 19:6
there should no f be saved	Mt 24:22
is willing, but the f is weak	Mt 26:41
And they twain shall be one f	Mk 10:8
they are no more twain, but one f	Mk 10:8
those days, no f should be saved	Mk 13:20
truly is ready, but the f is weak	Mk 14:38
all f shall see the salvation of	Lk 3:6
for a spirit hath not f and bones	Lk 24:39
blood, nor of the will of the f	Jn 1:13
And the Word was made f, and dwelt	Jn 1:14
which is born of the f is	Jn 3:6
which is born of the f is	Jn 3:6
bread that I will give is my f	Jn 6:51
can this man give us his f to eat	Jn 6:52
ye eat the f of the Son of man	Jn 6:53
Whoso eateth my f, and drinketh my	Jn 6:54
For my f is meat indeed, and my	Jn 6:55
He that eateth my f, and drinketh	Jn 6:56
the f profiteth nothing	Jn 6:63
Ye judge after the f	Jn 8:15
hast given him power over all f	Jn 17:2
pour out of my Spirit upon all f	Acts 2:17
moreover also my f shall rest in	Acts 2:26
of his loins, according to the f	Acts 2:30
neither his f did see corruption	Acts 2:31
seed of David according to the f	Rom 1:3
which is outward in the f	Rom 2:28
no f be justified in his sight	Rom 3:20
father, as pertaining to the f	Rom 4:1
of the infirmity of your f	Rom 6:19
For when we were in the f	Rom 7:5
know that in me (that is, in my f	Rom 7:18
but with the f the law of sin	Rom 7:25
Jesus, who walk not after the f	Rom 8:1
in that it was weak through the f	Rom 8:3
Son in the likeness of sinful f	Rom 8:3
for sin, condemned sin in the f	Rom 8:3
in us, who walk not after the f	Rom 8:4
f do mind the things of the f	Rom 8:5
are in the f cannot please God	Rom 8:8
But ye are not in the f, but in	Rom 8:9
to the f, to live after the f	Rom 8:12
For if ye live after the f	Rom 8:13
my kinsmen according to the f	Rom 9:3
as concerning the f Christ came	Rom 9:5
which are the children of the f	Rom 9:8
to emulation them which are my f	Rom 11:14
and make not provision for the f	Rom 13:14
It is good neither to eat f	Rom 14:21
not many wise men after the f	1Cor 1:26
That no f should glory in his	1Cor 1:29
for the destruction of the f	1Cor 5:5
for two, saith he, shall be one f	1Cor 6:16
such shall have trouble in the f	1Cor 7:28
I will eat no f while the world	1Cor 8:13
Behold Israel after the f	1Cor 10:18
All f is not the same f	1Cor 15:39
but there is one kind of f of men	1Cor 15:39
another f of beasts, another of	1Cor 15:39
Now this I say, brethren, that f	1Cor 15:50
do I purpose according to the f	2Cor 1:17
be made manifest in our mortal f	2Cor 4:11
know we no man after the f	2Cor 5:16
we have known Christ after the f	2Cor 5:16
from all filthiness of the f	2Cor 7:1
our f had no rest, but we were	2Cor 7:5
if we walked according to the f	2Cor 10:2
For though we walk in the f	2Cor 10:3
we do not war after the f	2Cor 10:3
that many glory after the f	2Cor 11:18
was given to me a thorn in the f	2Cor 12:7
I conferred not with f and blood	Gal 1:16
the law shall no f be justified	Gal 2:16
life which I now live in the f	Gal 2:20
are ye now made perfect by the f	Gal 3:3
how through infirmity of the f	Gal 4:13
which was in my f ye despised not	Gal 4:14
bondwoman was born after the f	Gal 4:23
f persecuted him that was born	Gal 4:29
liberty for an occasion to the f	Gal 5:13
not fulfil the lust of the f	Gal 5:16
For the f lusteth against the	Gal 5:17
and the Spirit against the f	Gal 5:17
the works of the f are manifest	Gal 5:19
the f with the affections	Gal 5:24
to his f shall of the f reap	Gal 6:8
to make a fair shew in the f	Gal 6:12
that they may glory in your f	Gal 6:13
times past in the lusts of our f	Eph 2:3
fulfilling the desires of the f	Eph 2:3
in time past Gentiles in the f	Eph 2:11
in the f made by hands	Eph 2:11
abolished in his f the enmity	Eph 2:15
no man ever yet hated his own f	Eph 5:29
are members of his body, of his f	Eph 5:30
wife, and they two shall be one f	Eph 5:31
your masters according to the f	Eph 6:5
For we wrestle not against f	Eph 6:12
But if I live in the f, this is	Phil 1:22
in the f is more needful for you	Phil 1:24
and have no confidence in the f	Phil 3:3
also have confidence in the f	Phil 3:4
whereof he might trust in the f	Phil 3:4
the body of his f through death	Col 1:22
in my f for his body's sake	Col 1:24
as have not seen my face in the f	Col 2:1
For though I be absent in the f	Col 2:5
f by the circumcision of Christ	Col 2:11
and the uncircumcision of your f	Col 2:13
honour to the satisfying of the f	Col 2:23
your masters according to the f	Col 3:22
God was manifest in the f	1Ti 3:16
more unto thee, both in the f	Philem 16
the children are partakers of f	Heb 2:14
Who in the days of his f, when he	Heb 5:7
to the purifying of the f	Heb 9:13
the veil, that is to say, his f	Heb 10:20
of our f which corrected us	Heb 12:9
shall eat your f as it were fire	Jas 5:3
For all f is as grass, and all the	1Pet 1:24
God, being put to death in the f	1Pet 3:18
away of the filth of the f	1Pet 3:21
hath suffered for us in the f	1Pet 4:1
in the f hath ceased from sin	1Pet 4:1
in the f to the lusts of men	1Pet 4:2
judged according to men in the f	1Pet 4:6
them that walk after the f in the	2Pet 2:10
allure through the lusts of the f	2Pet 2:18
in the world, the lust of the f	1Jn 2:16
Christ is come in the f is of God	1Jn 4:2
is come in the f is not of God	1Jn 4:3
Jesus Christ is come in the f	2Jn 7
and going after strange f	Jude 7
filthy dreamers defile the f	Jude 8
even the garment spotted by the f	Jude 23
That ye may eat the f of kings	Rev 19:18
the f of captains, and the f	Rev 19:18
the f of mighty men	Rev 19:18
the f of horses, and of them that	Rev 19:18
the f of all men, both free and	Rev 19:18
fowls were filled with their f	Rev 19:21

FLESHHOOK

with a f of three teeth in his	1Sa 2:13
all that the f brought up in the	1Sa 2:14

FLESHHOOKS

shovels, and his basons, and his f	Ex 27:3
shovels, and the basons, and the f	Ex 38:3
about it, even the censers, the f	Num 4:14
Also pure gold for the f, and the	1Chr 28:17
also, and the shovels, and the f	2Chr 4:16

FLESHLY

sincerity, not with f wisdom	2Cor 1:12
vainly puffed up by his f mind	Col 2:18
and pilgrims, abstain from f lusts	1Pet 2:11

FLESHY

but in f tables of the heart	2Cor 3:3

FLEW

the people f upon the spoil, and	1Sa 14:32
Then f one of the seraphims unto	Is 6:6

FLIES

I will send swarms of f upon thee	Ex 8:21
shall be full of swarms of f	Ex 8:21
no swarms of f shall be there	Ex 8:22
of f into the house of Pharaoh	Ex 8:24
by reason of the swarm of f	Ex 8:24
of f may depart from Pharaoh	Ex 8:29
the swarms of f from Pharaoh	Ex 8:31
sent divers sorts of f among them	Ps 78:45
and there came divers sorts of f	Ps 105:31
Dead f cause the ointment of the	Eccl 10:1

FLIETH

any winged fowl that f in the air	Deut 4:17
thing that f is unclean unto you	Deut 14:19
earth, as swift as the eagle f	Deut 28:49
nor for the arrow that f by day	Ps 91:5

FLIGHT

you shall put ten thousand to f	Lev 26:8
and two put ten thousand to f	Deut 32:30
they put to f all them of the	1Chr 12:15
go out with haste, nor go by f	Is 52:12
Therefore the f shall perish from	Amos 2:14
that your f be not in the winter	Mt 24:20
pray ye that your f be not in the	Mk 13:18
turned to f the armies of the	Heb 11:34

FLINT

forth water out of the rock of f	Deut 8:15
the f into a fountain of waters	Ps 114:8
hoofs shall be counted like f	Is 5:28
have I set my face like a f	Is 50:7
than f have I made thy forehead	Eze 3:9

FLINTY

rock, and oil out of the f rock	Deut 32:13

FLOATS

I will convey them by sea in f	1Kin 5:9

FLOCK

of the firstlings of his f	Gen 4:4
ewe lambs of the f by themselves	Gen 21:28
Go now to the f, and fetch me from	Gen 27:9
watered the f of Laban his	Gen 29:10
I will again feed and keep thy f	Gen 30:31
pass through all thy f to day	Gen 30:32
all the brown in the f of Laban	Gen 30:40
and Leah to the field unto his f	Gen 31:4
the rams of thy f have I not	Gen 31:38
them one day, all the f will die	Gen 33:13
was feeding the f with his	Gen 37:2
feed their father's f in Shechem	Gen 37:12
brethren feed the f in Shechem	Gen 37:13
I will send these a kid from the f	Gen 38:17
troughs to water their father's f	Ex 2:16
helped them, and watered their f	Ex 2:17
enough for us, and watered the f	Ex 2:19
Now Moses kept the f of Jethro	Ex 3:1
he led the f to the backside of	Ex 3:1
even of the herd, and of the f	Lev 1:2
unto the Lord of the f	Lev 3:6
hath sinned, a female from the f	Lev 5:6
ram without blemish out of the f	Lev 5:18
ram without blemish out of the f	Lev 6:6
tithe of the herd, or of the f	Lev 27:32
LORD, of the herd, or of the f	Num 15:3
of thy herds or of thy f, nor any	Deut 12:17
kill of thy herd and of thy f	Deut 12:21
him liberally out of thy f	Deut 15:14
of thy f thou shalt sanctify unto	Deut 15:19
unto the LORD thy God, of the f	Deut 16:2
bear, and took a lamb out of the f	1Sa 17:34
and he spared to take of his own f	2Sa 12:4
gave to the people, of the f	2Chr 35:7
a ram of the f for their trespass	Ezr 10:19
forth their little ones like a f	Job 21:11
to have set with the dogs of my f	Job 30:1
like a f by the hand of Moses	Ps 77:20
them in the wilderness like a f	Ps 78:52
thou that leadest Joseph like a f	Ps 80:1
and maketh him families like a f	Ps 107:41
thou makest thy f to rest at noon	Song 1:7
forth by the footsteps of the f	Song 1:8
thy hair is as a f of goats	Song 4:1
Thy teeth are like a f of sheep	Song 4:2
thy hair is as a f of goats that	Song 6:5
Thy teeth are as a f of sheep	Song 6:6
shall feed his f like a shepherd	Is 40:11
sea with the shepherd of his f	Is 63:11
because the LORD's f is carried	Jer 13:17
where is the f that was given	Jer 13:20
was given thee, thy beautiful f	Jer 13:20
Ye have scattered my f, and driven	Jer 23:2
f out of all countries whither I	Jer 23:3
the ashes, ye principal of the f	Jer 25:34
the principal of the f to escape	Jer 25:35
howling of the principal of the f	Jer 25:36
him, as a shepherd doth his f	Jer 31:10
oil, and for the young of the f	Jer 31:12
of the f shall draw them out	Jer 49:20
of the f shall draw them out	Jer 50:45
where shepherd and his f	Jer 51:23
Take the choice of the f, and burn	Eze 24:5
but ye feed not the f	Eze 34:3
my f was scattered upon all the	Eze 34:6
surely because my f became a prey	Eze 34:8
my f became meat to every beast	Eze 34:8
did my shepherds search for my f	Eze 34:8
fed themselves, and fed not my f	Eze 34:8
I will require my f at their hand	Eze 34:10
them to cease from feeding the f	Eze 34:10
deliver my f from their mouth	Eze 34:10
As a shepherd seeketh out his f	Eze 34:12
I will feed my f, and I will cause	Eze 34:15

F

And as for you, O my f, thus saith.......... Eze 34:17
And as for my f, they eat that .... Eze 34:19
Therefore will I save my f .... Eze 34:22
And ye my f, the f of my.......................... Eze 34:31
the f of my pasture, are men, and............ Eze 34:31
increase them with men like a f .... Eze 36:37
As the holy f, as the f of........................... Eze 36:38
ram out of the f without blemish .... Eze 43:23
bullock, and a ram out of the f .... Eze 43:25
And one lamb out of the f, out of .... Eze 45:15
and eat the lambs out of the f................. Amos 6:4
LORD took me as I followed the f............ Amos 7:15
neither man nor beast, herd nor f .... Jonah 3:7
as the f in the midst of their .... Mic 2:12
And thou, O tower of the f........................ Mic 4:8
the f of thine heritage, which .... Mic 7:14
the f shall be cut off from the .... Hab 3:17
that day as the f of his people .... Zec 9:16
they went their way as a f .... Zec 10:2
visited his f the house of Judah .... Zec 10:3
Feed the f of the slaughter .... Zec 11:4
And I will feed the f of slaughter .... Zec 11:7
even you, O poor of the f .... Zec 11:7
and I fed the f .... Zec 11:7
so the poor of the f that waited............... Zec 11:11
idol shepherd that leaveth the f.............. Zec 11:17
which hath in his f a male......................... Mal 1:14
the sheep of the f shall be .... Mt 26:31
watch over their f by night .... Lk 2:8
Fear not, little f .... Lk 12:32
unto yourselves, and to all the f .... Acts 20:28
in among you, not sparing the f .... Acts 20:29
or who feedeth a f, and eateth not 1Cor 9:7
eateth not of the milk of the f 1Cor 9:7
Feed the f of God which is among 1Pet 5:2
but being ensamples to the f 1Pet 5:3

FLOCKS

which went with Abram, had f............... Gen 13:5
and he hath given him f, and herds,...... Gen 24:35
For he had possession of f .... Gen 26:14
there were three of sheep lying.............. Gen 29:2
of that well they watered the f .... Gen 29:2
thither were all the f gathered .... Gen 29:3
until all the f be gathered........................ Gen 29:8
Jacob fed the rest of Laban's f................ Gen 30:36
f in the gutters in the watering .... Gen 30:38
troughs when the f came to drink .... Gen 30:38
the f conceived before the rods,............. Gen 30:39
set the faces of the f toward the .... Gen 30:40
and he put his own f by themselves....... Gen 30:40
And I have oxen, and asses, f................... Gen 32:5
that was with him, and the f.................... Gen 32:7
the children are tender, and the f.......... Gen 33:13
thy brethren, and well with the f........... Gen 37:14
thee, where they feed their f .... Gen 37:16
thy children's children, and thy f .... Gen 45:10
and they have brought their f .... Gen 46:32
father and my brethren, and their f ...... Gen 47:1
have no pasture for their f .... Gen 47:4
exchange for horses, and for the f .... Gen 47:17
their little ones, and their f .... Gen 50:8
and with our daughters, with our f....... Ex 10:9
only let your f and your herds be .... Ex 10:24
Also take your f and your herds,............ Ex 12:32
and f, and herds, even very much.......... Ex 12:38
neither let the f nor herds feed.............. Ex 34:3
And if his offering be of the f.................. Lev 1:10
ram without blemish out of the f........... Lev 5:15
Shall the f and the herds be slain .... Num 11:22
all their cattle, and all their f .... Num 31:9
beeves, of the asses, and of the f............ Num 31:30
Our little ones, our wives, our f .... Num 32:26
the f of thy sheep, in the land .... Deut 7:13
thy f multiply, and thy silver and .... Deut 8:13
of your herds and of your f .... Deut 12:6
of thy herds and of thy f........................... Deut 14:23
thy kine, and the f of thy sheep............. Deut 28:4
thy kine, and the f of thy sheep.............. Deut 28:18
or f of thy sheep, until he have............... Deut 28:51
to hear the bleatings of the f .... Judg 5:16
And David took all the f and the 1Sa 30:20
The rich man had exceeding many f...... 2Sa 12:2
them like two little f of kids 1Kin 20:27
to seek pasture for their f 1Chr 4:39
was pasture there for their f 1Chr 4:41
over the f was Jaziz the Hagerite 1Chr 27:31
and the Arabians brought him f.............. 2Chr 17:11
manner of beasts, and cotes for f........... 2Chr 32:28
him cities, and possessions of f 2Chr 32:29
of our herds and of our f, to .... Neh 10:36
they violently take away .... Job 24:2
The pastures are clothed with f .... Ps 65:13
their f to hot thunderbolts....................... Ps 78:48
to know the state of thy f .... Prov 27:23
aside by the f of thy companions............ Song 1:7
they shall be for f, which shall .... Is 17:2
joy of wild asses, a pasture of f.............. Is 32:14
All the f of Kedar shall be .... Is 60:7
shall stand and feed your .... Is 61:5
And Sharon shall be a fold of f............... Is 65:10
their f and their herds, their .... Jer 3:24
they shall eat up thy f and thine .... Jer 5:17
with their f shall come unto her............. Jer 6:3
all their f shall be scattered .... Jer 10:21
and they that go forth with f .... Jer 31:24
causing their f to lie down........................ Jer 33:12
shall the f pass again under the.............. Jer 33:13
their f shall they take away..................... Jer 49:29
be as the he goats before the f .... Jer 50:8
Ammonites a couchingplace for f .... Eze 25:5

not the shepherds feed the f .... Eze 34:2
cities be filled with f of men.................... Eze 36:38
They shall go with their f .... Hos 5:6
the f of sheep are made desolate .... Joel 1:18
a young lion among the f of sheep .... Mic 5:8
for shepherds, and folds for f .... Zeph 2:6
shall lie down in the midst of .... Zeph 2:14

FLOOD

do bring a f of waters upon the .... Gen 6:17
of waters was upon the earth .... Gen 7:6
because of the waters of the f .... Gen 7:7
of the f were upon the earth .... Gen 7:10
the f was forty days upon the .... Gen 7:17
off any more by the waters of a f............ Gen 9:11
more be a f to destroy the earth............. Gen 9:11
become a f to destroy all flesh .... Gen 9:15
lived after the f three hundred .... Gen 9:28
them were sons born after the f .... Gen 10:1
divided in the earth after the f .... Gen 10:32
Arphaxad two years after the f............... Gen 11:10
other side of the f in old time.................. Josh 24:2
from the other side of the f .... Josh 24:3
served on the other side of the f............. Josh 24:14
were on the other side of the f................ Josh 24:15
the f decayeth and drieth up .... Job 14:11
foundation was overflown with a f .... Job 22:16
The f breaketh out from the .... Job 28:4
The LORD sitteth upon the f .... Ps 29:10
they went through the f on foot .... Ps 66:6
cleave fountain and the f .... Ps 74:15
carriest them away as with a f .... Ps 90:5
storm, as a f of mighty waters .... Is 28:2
the enemy shall come in like a f .... Is 59:19
Who is this that cometh up as a f .... Jer 46:7
Egypt riseth up like a f, and his............. Jer 46:8
and shall be an overflowing f.................. Jer 47:2
the end thereof shall be with a .... Dan 9:26
with the arms of a f shall they .... Dan 11:22
and it shall rise up wholly as a f .... Amos 8:8
and drowned, as by the f of Egypt......... Amos 8:8
it shall rise up wholly like a f................. Amos 9:5
be drowned, as by the f of Egypt .... Amos 9:5
But with an overrunning f he will......... Nah 1:8
before the f they were eating .... Mt 24:38
And knew not until the f came................ Mt 24:39
and when the f arose, the stream .... Lk 6:48
the f came, and destroyed them all ...... Lk 17:27
bringing in the f upon the world........... 2Pet 2:5
water as a f after the woman .... Rev 12:15
her to be carried away of the f .... Rev 12:15
swallowed up the f which the.................. Rev 12:16

FLOODS

the f stood upright as an heap,.............. Ex 15:8
the f of ungodly men made me 2Sa 22:5
shall not see the rivers, the f .... Job 20:17
He bindeth the f from overflowing........ Job 28:11
the f of ungodly men made me .... Ps 18:4
and established it upon the f .... Ps 24:2
surely in the f of great waters .... Ps 32:6
waters, where the f overflow me .... Ps 69:2
and their f, that they could not.............. Ps 78:44
The f have lifted up, O LORD, the .... Ps 93:3
the f have lifted up their voice............... Ps 93:3
the f lift up their waves .... Ps 93:3
Let the f clap their hands .... Ps 98:8
love, neither can the f drown it.............. Song 8:7
thirsty, and f upon the dry ground .... Is 44:3
and I restrained the f thereof................. Eze 31:15
and the f compassed me about................ Jonah 2:3
the f came, and the winds blew, and .... Mt 7:25
the f came, and the winds blew, and .... Mt 7:27

FLOOR

saw the mourning in the f of Atad........ Gen 50:11
of the dust that is in the f of.................... Num 5:17
out of thy flock, and out of thy f .... Deut 15:14
put a fleece of wool in the f .... Judg 6:37
thee, and get thee down to the f .... Ruth 3:3
And she went down unto the f .... Ruth 3:6
that a woman came into the f .... Ruth 3:14
both the f of the house, and the 1Kin 6:15
covered the f of the house with 1Kin 6:15
sides of the house, both the f 1Kin 6:16
the f of the house he overlaid 1Kin 6:30
one side of the f to the other 1Kin 7:7
to f the houses which the kings 2Chr 34:11
my threshing, and the corn of my f ...... Is 21:10
The f and the winepress shall not......... Hos 9:2
with the whirlwind out of the f.............. Hos 13:3
them as the sheaves into the f................. Mic 4:12
and he will throughly purge his f.......... Mt 3:12
and he will throughly purge his f.......... Lk 3:17

FLOORS

the f shall be full of wheat, and .... Joel 2:24

FLOTES

it to thee in f by sea to Joppa.................. 2Chr 2:16

FLOUR

of wheaten f shalt thou make them ...... Ex 29:2
the one lamb a tenth deal of f .... Ex 29:40
his offering shall be of fine f .... Lev 2:1
his handful of the f thereof .... Lev 2:2
cakes of fine f mingled with oil .... Lev 2:4
it shall be of fine f unleavened............... Lev 2:5
shall be made of fine f with oil .... Lev 2:7
of fine f for a sin offering........................ Lev 5:11
of the f of the meat offering, and .... Lev 6:15
f for a meat offering perpetual............... Lev 6:20
cakes mingled with oil, of fine f .... Lev 7:12

of fine f for a meat offering .... Lev 14:10
one tenth deal of fine f mingled .... Lev 14:21
deals of fine f mingled with oil .... Lev 23:13
they shall be of fine f .... Lev 23:17
And thou shalt take fine f......................... Lev 24:5
cakes of fine f mingled with oil,............. Num 6:15
f mingled with oil for a meat .... Num 7:13
both of them full of fine f .... Num 7:19
both of them full of fine f .... Num 7:25
both of them full of fine f .... Num 7:31
both of them full of fine f .... Num 7:37
both of them full of fine f .... Num 7:43
both of them full of fine f .... Num 7:49
both of them full of fine f .... Num 7:55
both of them full of fine f .... Num 7:61
both of them full of fine f .... Num 7:67
both of them full of fine f .... Num 7:73
both of them full of fine f .... Num 7:79
even fine f mingled with oil, and .... Num 8:8
offering of a tenth deal of f .... Num 15:4
offering two tenth deals of f .... Num 15:6
of three tenth deals of f mingled........... Num 15:9
an ephah of f for a meat offering............ Num 28:5
two tenth deals of f for a meat............... Num 28:9
deals of f for a meat offering .... Num 28:12
two tenth deals of f for a meat................ Num 28:12
a several tenth deal of f mingled............ Num 28:13
shall be of f mingled with oil .... Num 28:20
offering of f mingled with oil .... Num 28:28
shall be of f mingled with oil .... Num 29:3
shall be of f mingled with oil .... Num 29:9
shall be of f mingled with oil .... Num 29:14
unleavened cakes of an ephah of f......... Judg 6:19
three bullocks, and one ephah of f......... 1Sa 1:24
hasted, and killed it, and took f 1Sa 28:24
And she took f, and kneaded it, and...... 2Sa 13:8
and wheat, and barley, and f................... 1Kin 4:22
day was thirty measures of fine f 1Kin 4:22
of fine f be sold for a shekel 2Kin 7:1
So a measure of fine f was sold 2Kin 7:16
a measure of fine f for a shekel.............. 2Kin 7:18
of the sanctuary, and the fine f 1Chr 9:29
for the fine f for meat offering,.............. 1Chr 23:29
thou didst eat fine f, and honey,........... Eze 16:13
also which I gave thee, fine f .... Eze 16:19
of oil, to temper with the fine f.............. Eze 46:14
and wine, and oil, and fine f .... Rev 18:13

FLOURISH

In his days shall the righteous f............. Ps 72:7
they of the city shall f like .... Ps 72:16
all the workers of iniquity do f............... Ps 92:7
shall f like the palm tree......................... Ps 92:12
the righteous shall f as a branch .... Prov 11:28
tabernacle of the upright shall f............ Prov 14:11
way, and the almond tree shall f............ Eccl 12:5
let us see if the vine f, whether .... Song 7:12
shalt thou make thy seed to f .... Is 17:11
your bones shall f like an herb............... Is 66:14
and have made the dry tree to f.............. Eze 17:24

FLOURISHED

and to see whether the vine f.................. Song 6:11
last your care of me hath f again .... Phil 4:10

FLOURISHETH

In the morning it f, and groweth .... Ps 90:6
as a flower of the field, so he f............... Ps 103:15

FLOURISHING

they shall be fat and.................................. Ps 92:14
in mine house, and f in my palace......... Dan 4:4

FLOW

his goods shall f away in the day .... Job 20:28
his wind to blow, and the waters f .... Ps 147:18
that the spices thereof may f out........... Song 4:16
and all nations shall f unto it .... Is 2:2
he caused the waters to f out of............. Is 48:21
might f down at thy presence.................. Is 64:1
shall f together to the goodness .... Jer 31:12
the nations shall not f together .... Jer 51:44
and the hills shall f with milk................ Joel 3:18
of Judah shall f with waters................... Joel 3:18
and people shall f unto it .... Mic 4:1
shall f rivers of living water .... Jn 7:38

FLOWED

f over all his banks, as they did .... Josh 4:18
the mountains f down at thy................... Is 64:3
Waters f over mine head.......................... Lam 3:54

FLOWER

with a knop and a f in one branch......... Ex 25:33
other branch, with a knop and a f.......... Ex 25:33
in one branch, a knop and a f .... Ex 37:19
in another branch, a knop and a f .... Ex 37:19
shall die in the f of their age................... Isa 2:33
He cometh forth like a f, and is .... Job 14:2
shall cast off his f as the olive................ Job 15:33
as a f of the field, so he........................... Ps 103:15
sour grape is ripening in the f................ Is 18:5
glorious beauty is a fading f .... Is 28:1
fat valley, shall be a fading f .... Is 28:4
thereof is as the f of the field .... Is 40:6
The grass withereth, the f fadeth.......... Is 40:7
The grass withereth, the f fadeth.......... Is 40:8
the f of Lebanon languisheth.................. Nah 1:4
if she pass the f of her age...................... 1Cor 7:36
because as the f of the grass he.............. Jas 1:10

the f thereof falleth, and the .... Jas 1:11
glory of man as the f of grass 1Pet 1:24
the f thereof falleth away 1Pet 1:24

FLOWERS
his bowls, his knops, and his f .... Ex 25:31
with their knops and their f .... Ex 25:34
his bowls, his knops, and his f .... Ex 37:17
like almonds, his knops, and his f .... Ex 37:20
her f be upon him, he shall be .... Lev 15:24
And of her that is sick of her f .... Lev 15:33
shaft thereof, unto the f thereof .... Num 8:4
was carved with knops and open f 1Kin 6:18
cherubims and palm trees and open f 1Kin 6:29
cherubims and palm trees and open f 1Kin 6:32
cherubims and palm trees and open f 1Kin 6:35
brim of a cup, with f of lilies 1Kin 7:26
before the oracle, with the f 1Kin 7:49
brim of a cup, with f of lilies 2Chr 4:5
And the f, and the lamps, and the 2Chr 4:21
The f appear on the earth .... Song 2:12
as a bed of spices, as sweet f .... Song 5:13

FLOWETH
it, a land that f with milk .... Lev 20:24
us, and surely it f with milk .... Num 13:27
a land which f with milk and honey .... Num 14:8
up out of a land that f with milk .... Num 16:13
us into a land that f with milk .... Num 16:14
in the land that f with .... Deut 6:3
seed, a land that f with milk .... Deut 11:9
even a land that f with milk .... Deut 26:9
fathers, a land that f with milk .... Deut 26:15
thee, a land that f with milk .... Deut 27:3
that f with milk and honey .... Deut 31:20
give us, a land that f with milk .... Josh 5:6

FLOWING
a large, unto a land f with milk .... Ex 3:8
unto a land f with milk and honey .... Ex 3:17
a land f with milk and honey, that .... Ex 13:5
Unto a land f with milk and honey .... Ex 33:3
wellspring of wisdom as a f brook .... Prov 18:4
of the Gentiles like a f stream .... Is 66:12
to give them a land f with milk .... Jer 11:5
or shall the cold f waters that .... Jer 18:14
a land f with milk and honey .... Jer 32:22
thy f valley, O backsliding .... Jer 49:4
f with milk and honey, which is .... Eze 20:6
f with milk and honey, which is .... Eze 20:15

FLUTE
hear the sound of the cornet, f .... Dan 3:5
heard the sound of the cornet, f .... Dan 3:7
hear the sound of the cornet, f .... Dan 3:10
hear the sound of the cornet, f .... Dan 3:15

FLUTTERETH
f over her young, spreadeth .... Deut 32:11

FLUX
sick of a fever and of a bloody f .... Acts 28:8

FLY
fowl that may f above the earth .... Gen 1:20
but didst f upon the spoil, and 1Sa 15:19
he rode upon a cherub, and did f 2Sa 22:11
trouble, as the sparks f upward .... Job 5:7
He shall f away as a dream, and .... Job 20:8
Doth the hawk f by thy wisdom .... Job 39:26
he rode upon a cherub, and did f .... Ps 18:10
he did f upon the wings of the .... Ps 18:10
for then would f away, and be at .... Ps 55:6
it is soon cut off, and we f away .... Ps 90:10
they f away as an eagle toward .... Prov 23:5
his feet, and with f he did fly .... Is 6:2
the Lord shall hiss for the f .... Is 7:18
But they shall f upon the .... Is 11:14
Who are these that f as a cloud .... Is 60:8
he shall f as an eagle, and shall .... Jer 48:40
f as the eagle, and spread his .... Jer 49:22
hunt the souls to make them f .... Eze 13:20
souls that ye hunt to make them f .... Eze 13:20
being caused to f swiftly .... Dan 9:21
glory shall f away like a bird .... Hos 9:11
they shall f as the eagle that .... Hab 1:8
that she might f into the .... Rev 12:14
I saw another angel f in the .... Rev 14:6
that f in the midst of heaven .... Rev 19:17

FLYING
Yet these may ye eat of every f .... Lev 11:21
But all other f creeping things, ... Lev 11:23
creeping things, and f fowl .... Ps 148:10
by wandering, as the swallow by f .... Prov 26:2
fruit shall be a fiery f serpent .... Is 14:29
fiery f serpent, they will carry .... Is 30:6
As birds f, so will the Lord of .... Is 31:5
and looked, and behold a f roll .... Zec 5:1
And I answered, I see a f roll .... Zec 5:2
fourth beast was like a f eagle .... Rev 4:7
heard an angel f through the .... Rev 8:13

FOAL
Binding his f unto the vine, and .... Gen 49:11
and upon a colt the f of an ass .... Zec 9:9
an ass, and a colt the f of an ass .... Mt 21:5

FOALS
bulls, twenty she asses, and ten f .... Gen 32:15

FOAM
cut off as the f upon the water .... Hos 10:7

FOAMETH
and he f, and gnasheth with his .... Mk 9:18
and it teareth him that he f again .... Lk 9:39

FOAMING
fell on the ground, and wallowed f .... Mk 9:20
of the sea, f out their own shame .... Jude 13

FODDER
or loweth the ox over his f .... Job 6:5

FOES
to be destroyed before thy f 1Chr 21:12
and slew of their f seventy .... Est 9:16
wicked, even mine enemies and my f .... Ps 27:2
hast not made any f to rejoice .... Ps 30:1
beat down his f before his face .... Ps 89:23
a man's f shall be they of his .... Mt 10:36
Until I make thy f footstool .... Acts 2:35

FOLD
the shepherds make their f there .... Is 13:20
And Sharon shall be a f of flocks .... Is 65:10
of Israel shall their f be .... Eze 34:14
there shall they lie in a good f .... Eze 34:14
the flock in the midst of their f .... Mic 2:12
flock shall be cut off from the f .... Hab 3:17
I have, which are not of this f .... Jn 10:16
and there shall be one f, and one .... Jn 10:16
as a vesture shalt thou f them up .... Heb 1:12

FOLDEN
For while they be f together as .... Nah 1:10

FOLDETH
The fool f his hands together, and .... Eccl 4:5

FOLDING
two leaves of the one door were f 1Kin 6:34
leaves of the other door were f 1Kin 6:34
a little f of the hands to sleep .... Prov 6:10
a little f of the hands to sleep .... Prov 24:33

FOLDS
little ones, and f for your sheep .... Num 32:24
and f of sheep .... Num 32:36
house, nor be goats out of thy f .... Ps 50:9
will bring them again to their f .... Jer 23:3
for shepherds, and f for flocks .... Zeph 2:6

FOLK
some of the f that are with me .... Gen 33:15
The conies are but a feeble f .... Prov 30:26
the f in the fire, and they shall .... Jer 51:58
laid his hands upon a few sick f .... Mk 6:5
a great multitude of impotent f .... Jn 5:3

FOLKS
unto Jerusalem, bringing sick f .... Acts 5:16

FOLLOW
be willing to f me unto this land .... Gen 24:5
will not be willing to f me .... Gen 24:8
the woman will not f me .... Gen 24:39
his steward, Up, f after the men .... Gen 44:4
and all the people that f thee .... Ex 11:8
heart, that he shall f after them .... Ex 14:4
Egyptians, and they shall f them .... Ex 14:17
from her, and yet no mischief f .... Ex 21:22
And if any mischief f, then thou .... Ex 21:23
Thou shalt not f a multitude to .... Ex 23:2
is altogether just shalt thou f .... Deut 16:20
of the Lord, if the thing f not .... Deut 18:22
And he said unto them, f after me .... Judg 3:28
bread unto the people that f me .... Judg 8:5
hearts inclined to f Abimelech .... Judg 9:3
unto the young men that f my lord 1Sa 25:27
faint that they could not f David 1Sa 30:21
among the people that f Absalom 2Sa 17:9
if the Lord be God, f him 1Kin 18:21
but if Baal, then f him 1Kin 18:21
my mother, and then I will f thee 1Kin 19:20
for all the people that f me 1Kin 20:10
f me, and I will bring you to the 2Kin 6:19
mercy shall f me all the days of .... Ps 23:6
because I f the thing that good .... Ps 38:20
f her shall be brought unto thee .... Ps 45:14
the upright in heart shall f it .... Ps 94:15
draw nigh that f after mischief .... Ps 119:150
that they may f strong drink .... Is 5:11
ye that f after righteousness, ye .... Is 51:1
from being a pastor to f thee .... Jer 17:16
that f close after thee, there in .... Jer 42:16
that f their own spirit, and have .... Eze 13:3
she shall f after her lovers, but .... Hos 2:7
if we f on to know the Lord .... Hos 6:3
f me, and I will make you fishers .... Mt 4:19
I will f thee whithersoever thou .... Mt 8:19
But Jesus said unto him, F me .... Mt 8:22
and he saith unto him, F me .... Mt 9:9
and take up his cross, and f me .... Mt 16:24
and come and f me .... Mt 19:21
of custom, and said unto him, f me .... Mk 2:14
And he suffered no man to f him .... Mk 5:37
and his disciples f him .... Mk 6:1
and take up his cross, and f me .... Mk 8:34
come, take up the cross, and f me .... Mk 10:21
bearing a pitcher of water; f him .... Mk 14:13
signs shall f them that believe .... Mk 16:17
and he said unto him, F me .... Lk 5:27
take up his cross daily, and f me .... Lk 9:23
I will f thee whithersoever thou .... Lk 9:57
And he said unto another, F me .... Lk 9:59
also said, Lord, I will f thee .... Lk 9:61
go not after them, nor f them .... Lk 17:23
in heaven: and come, f me .... Lk 18:22
f him into the house where he .... Lk 22:10
were about him saw what would f .... Lk 22:49
Philip, and saith unto him, F me .... Jn 1:43
before them, and the sheep f him .... Jn 10:4

And a stranger will they not f .... Jn 10:5
and I know them, and they f me .... Jn 10:27
If any man serve me, let him f me .... Jn 12:26
I go, thou canst not f me now .... Jn 13:36
but thou shalt f me afterwards .... Jn 13:36
Lord, why cannot I f thee now .... Jn 13:37
this, he saith unto him, F me .... Jn 21:19
is that to thee? f thou me .... Jn 21:22
from Samuel and those that f after .... Acts 3:24
thy garment about thee, and f me .... Acts 12:8
Let us therefore f after the .... Rom 14:19
F after charity, and desire 1Cor 14:1
but I f after, if that I may .... Phil 3:12
but ever f that which is good, ... 1Th 5:15
know how ye ought to f us 2Th 3:7
an ensample unto you to f us 2Th 3:9
and some men they f after 1Ti 5:24
f after righteousness, godliness, ... 1Ti 6:11
but f righteousness, faith 2Ti 2:22
F peace with all men, and holiness .... Heb 12:14
whose faith f, considering the .... Heb 13:7
and the glory that should f 1Pet 1:11
that ye should f his steps 1Pet 2:21
many shall f their pernicious 2Pet 2:2
f not that which is evil, but 3Jn 11
These are they which f the Lamb .... Rev 14:4
and their works do f them .... Rev 14:13

FOLLOWED
upon the camels, and the man .... Gen 24:61
all that f the droves, saying, On .... Gen 32:19
hath f me fully, him will I bring .... Num 14:24
and the elders of Israel f him .... Num 16:25
because they have not wholly f me .... Num 32:11
for they have wholly f the Lord .... Num 32:12
because he hath wholly f the Lord .... Deut 1:36
for all the men that f Baal-peor .... Deut 4:3
the covenant of the Lord f them .... Josh 6:8
but I wholly f the Lord my God .... Josh 14:8
hast wholly f the Lord my God .... Josh 14:9
wholly f the Lord God of Israel .... Josh 14:14
f other gods, of the gods of the .... Judg 2:12
and light persons, which f him .... Judg 9:4
f Abimelech, and put them to the .... Judg 9:49
and all the people f him trembling 1Sa 13:7
even they also f hard after them 1Sa 14:22
went and f Saul to the battle 1Sa 17:13
and the three eldest f Saul 1Sa 17:14
the Philistines f hard upon Saul 1Sa 31:2
horsemen f hard after him 2Sa 1:6
But the house of Judah f David 2Sa 2:10
And king David himself f the bier 2Sa 3:31
there f him a mess of meat from 2Sa 11:8
saw that his counsel was not f 2Sa 17:23
f Sheba the son of Bichri 2Sa 20:2
none that f the house of David 1Kin 12:20
who f me with all his heart, to 1Kin 14:8
half of the people f Tibni the 1Kin 16:21
and half f Omri 1Kin 16:21
But the people that f Omri 1Kin 16:22
that f Tibni the son of Ginath 1Kin 16:22
the Lord, and thou hast f Baalim 1Kin 18:18
city, and the army which f them 1Kin 20:19
and for the cattle that f them 2Kin 3:9
And he arose, and f her 2Kin 4:30
So Gehazi f after Naaman 2Kin 5:21
Jehu f after him, and said, Smite 2Kin 9:27
f the sins of Jeroboam the son of 2Kin 13:2
they f vanity, and became vain, and 2Kin 17:15
The Philistines f hard after Saul 1Chr 10:2
the men of the guard which f me .... Neh 4:23
players on instruments f after .... Ps 68:25
whither the beast looked they f it .... Eze 10:11
the Lord took me as I f the flock .... Amos 7:15
left their nets, and f him .... Mt 4:20
ship and their father, and f him .... Mt 4:22
there f him great multitudes of .... Mt 4:25
mountain, great multitudes f him .... Mt 8:1
marvelled, and said to them that f .... Mt 8:10
into a ship, his disciples f him .... Mt 8:23
And he arose, and f him .... Mt 9:9
f him, and so did his disciples .... Mt 9:19
thence, two blind men f him .... Mt 9:27
and great multitudes f him .... Mt 12:15
they f him on foot out of the .... Mt 14:13
And great multitudes f him .... Mt 19:2
we have forsaken all, and f thee .... Mt 19:27
unto you, That ye which have f me .... Mt 19:28
Jericho, a great multitude f him .... Mt 20:29
received sight, and they f him .... Mt 20:34
that went before, and that f .... Mt 21:9
But Peter f him afar off unto the .... Mt 26:58
which f Jesus from Galilee, ... Mt 27:55
that f the day of the preparation .... Mt 27:62
they forsook their nets, and f him .... Mk 1:18
that were with him f after him .... Mk 1:36
And he arose and f him .... Mk 2:14
there were many, and they f him .... Mk 2:15
multitude from Galilee f him .... Mk 3:7
and much people f him, and thronged .... Mk 5:24
we have left all, and have f thee .... Mk 10:28
and as they f, they were afraid .... Mk 10:32
his sight, and f Jesus in the way .... Mk 10:52
that went before, and they that f .... Mk 11:9
there f him a certain young man, ... Mk 14:51
Peter f him afar off, even into .... Mk 14:54
f him, and ministered unto him .... Mk 15:41
they forsook all, and f him .... Lk 5:11
And he left all, rose up, and f him .... Lk 5:28
said unto the people that f him .... Lk 7:9
people, they knew it, f him .... Lk 9:11

F

Lo, we have left all, and f thee .... Lk 18:28
sight, and f him, glorifying God .... Lk 18:43
and his disciples also f him .... Lk 22:39
And Peter f afar off .... Lk 22:54
there f him a great company of .... Lk 23:27
the women that f him from Galilee .... Lk 23:49
f after, and beheld the sepulchre, ... Lk 23:55
heard him speak, and they f Jesus .... Jn 1:37
f him, was Andrew, Simon Peter's .... Jn 1:40
And a great multitude f him .... Jn 6:2
f her, saying, She goeth unto the .... Jn 11:31
And Simon Peter f Jesus, and so did .... Jn 18:15
And he went out, and f him .... Acts 12:9
and religious proselytes f Paul .... Acts 13:43
The same f Paul and us, and cried, ... Acts 16:17
multitude of the people f after .... Acts 21:36
which f not after righteousness, ... Rom 9:30
Israel, which f after the law of .... Rom 9:31
that spiritual Rock that f them 1Cor 10:4
have diligently f every good work 1Ti 5:10
For we have not f cunningly 2Pet 1:16
him was Death, and Hell f with him .... Rev 6:8
angel sounded, and there f hail .... Rev 8:7
there f another angel, saying, ... Rev 14:8
And the third angel f them .... Rev 14:9
in heaven f him upon white horses. .... Rev 19:14

FOLLOWEDST
inasmuch as thou f not young men .... Ruth 3:10

FOLLOWERS
I beseech you, be ye f of me 1Cor 4:16
Be ye f of me, even as I also am 1Cor 11:1
Be ye therefore f of God, as dear .... Eph 5:1
be f together of me, and mark them .... Phil 3:17
And ye became f of us, and of the 1Th 1:6
became f of the churches of God 1Th 2:14
but f of them who through faith .... Heb 6:12
if ye be f of that which is good 1Pet 3:13

FOLLOWETH
him that f her kill with the 2Kin 11:15
and whoso f her, let him be slain 2Chr 23:14
My soul f hard after thee .... Ps 63:8
but he that f vain persons is .... Prov 12:11
him that f after righteousness. .... Prov 15:9
He that f after righteousness and .... Prov 21:21
but he that f after vain persons .... Prov 28:19
loveth gifts, and f after rewards. .... Is 1:23
whereas none f thee to commit .... Eze 16:34
on wind, and f after the east wind .... Hos 12:1
f after me, is not worthy of me .... Mt 10:38
in thy name, and he f not us .... Mk 9:38
forbad him, because he f not us. .... Mk 9:38
him, because he f not with us. .... Lk 9:49
he that f me shall not walk in .... Jn 8:12

FOLLOWING
land by reason of that famine f .... Gen 41:31
will turn away thy son from me .... Deut 7:4
that thou be not snared by f them .... Deut 12:30
away this day from f the LORD .... Josh 22:16
away this day from f the LORD .... Josh 22:18
an altar to turn from f the LORD .... Josh 22:23
and turn this day from f the LORD .... Josh 22:29
in f other gods to serve them, and .... Judg 2:19
or to return from f after thee .... Ruth 1:16
you continue f the LORD your God 1Sa 12:14
turn not aside from f the LORD 1Sa 12:20
went up from f the Philistines 1Sa 14:46
for he is turned back from f me 1Sa 15:11
returned from f the Philistines 1Sa 24:1
hand nor to the left from f Abner 2Sa 2:19
not turn aside from f of him 2Sa 2:21
Asahel, Turn thee aside from f me 2Sa 2:22
return from f their brethren 2Sa 2:26
up every one from f his brother. 2Sa 2:27
And Joab returned from f Abner 2Sa 2:30
from f the sheep, to be ruler 2Sa 7:8
they f Adonijah helped him 1Kin 1:7
if ye shall at all turn from f me 1Kin 9:6
he did very abominably in f idols 1Kin 21:26
drave Israel from f the LORD 2Kin 17:21
LORD, and departed not from f him 2Kin 18:6
sheepcote, even from f the sheep 1Chr 17:7
f the LORD they made a conspiracy: 2Chr 25:27
they departed not from f the LORD 2Chr 34:33
may tell it to the generation f .... Ps 48:13
From f the ewes great with young .... Ps 78:71
in the generation f let them .... Ps 109:13
confirming the word with signs f .... Mk 16:20
day, and to morrow, and the day f .... Lk 13:33
Then Jesus turned, and saw them f .... Jn 1:38
The day f Jesus would go forth .... Jn 1:43
The day f, when the people which .... Jn 6:22
Then cometh Simon Peter f .... Jn 20:6
the disciple whom Jesus loved f .... Jn 21:20
the day f unto Rhodes, and from .... Acts 21:1
the day f Paul went in with us. .... Acts 21:18
the night f the Lord stood by him. .... Acts 23:11
the way of Balaam the son of 2Pet 2:15

FOLLY
because he had wrought f in .... Gen 34:7
she hath wrought f in Israel .... Deut 22:21
he hath wrought f in Israel .... Josh 7:15
into mine house, do not this f .... Judg 19:23
committed lewdness and f in Israel .... Judg 20:6
according to all the f that they .... Judg 20:10
is his name, and f is with him 1Sa 25:25
do not thou this f 2Sa 13:12
and his angels he charged with f .... Job 4:18
yet God layeth not f to them .... Job 24:12

lest I deal with you after your f .... Job 42:8
This their way is their f .... Ps 49:13
but let them not turn again to f .... Ps 85:8
of his f he shall go astray .... Prov 5:23
but a fool layeth open his f .... Prov 13:16
but the f of fools is deceit .... Prov 14:8
The simple inherit f .... Prov 14:18
but the foolishness of fools is f .... Prov 14:24
is hasty of spirit exalteth f .... Prov 14:29
F is joy to him that is destitute .... Prov 15:21
but the instruction of fools is f .... Prov 16:22
man, rather than a fool in his f .... Prov 17:12
before he heareth it, it is f .... Prov 18:13
not a fool according to his f .... Prov 26:4
Answer a fool according to his f .... Prov 26:5
so a fool returneth to his f .... Prov 26:11
wisdom, and to know madness and f .... Eccl 1:17
and to lay hold on f, till I might .... Eccl 2:3
behold wisdom, and madness, and f .... Eccl 2:12
I saw that wisdom excelleth f .... Eccl 2:13
and to know the wickedness of f .... Eccl 7:25
so doth a little f him that is in .... Eccl 10:1
F is set in great dignity, and the .... Eccl 10:6
and every mouth speaketh f .... Is 9:17
I have seen f in the prophets of .... Jer 23:13
bear with me a little in my f 2Cor 11:1
for their f shall be manifest 2Ti 3:9

FOOD
to the sight, and good for f .... Gen 2:9
saw that the tree was good for f .... Gen 3:6
unto thee of all f that is eaten .... Gen 6:21
and it shall be for f for thee. .... Gen 6:21
let them gather all the f of .... Gen 41:35
and let them keep f in the cities .... Gen 41:35
that f shall be for store to the .... Gen 41:36
up all the f of the seven years, ... Gen 41:48
laid up the f in the cities .... Gen 41:48
the f of the field, which was .... Gen 41:48
From the land of Canaan to buy f .... Gen 42:7
but to buy f are thy servants. .... Gen 42:10
take f for the famine of your .... Gen 42:33
them, Go again, buy us a little f .... Gen 43:2
us, we will go down and buy thee f .... Gen 43:4
down at the first time to buy f. .... Gen 43:20
down in our hands to buy f .... Gen 43:22
Fill the men's sacks with f .... Gen 44:1
Go again, and buy us a little f .... Gen 44:25
seed of the field, and for your f .... Gen 47:24
for f for your little ones .... Gen 47:24
her f, her raiment, and her duty .... Ex 21:10
it is the f of the offering made .... Lev 3:11
it is the f of the offering made .... Lev 3:16
planted all manner of trees for f .... Lev 19:23
because it is his f .... Lev 22:7
the stranger, in giving him f .... Deut 10:18
that eateth any f until evening 1Sa 14:24
none of the people tasted any f 1Sa 14:24
man that eateth any f this day 1Sa 14:28
master's son may have f to eat 2Sa 9:10
in giving f for my household 1Kin 5:9
of wheat for f to his household 1Kin 5:11
mouth more than my necessary f .... Job 23:12
wilderness yieldeth f for them. .... Job 24:5
Who provideth for the raven his f .... Job 38:41
the mountains bring him forth f .... Job 40:20
Man did eat angels' f .... Ps 78:25
bring forth f out of the earth. .... Ps 104:14
Who giveth f to all flesh .... Ps 136:25
which giveth f to the hungry .... Ps 146:7
He giveth to the beast his f .... Ps 147:9
gathereth her f in the harvest. .... Prov 6:8
Much f is in the tillage of the .... Prov 13:23
have goats' milk enough for thy f .... Prov 27:27
for the f of thy household, and .... Prov 27:27
sweeping rain which leaveth no f .... Prov 28:3
feed me with f convenient for me .... Prov 30:8
she bringeth her f from afar .... Prov 31:14
have diminished thine ordinary f .... Eze 16:27
f unto them that serve the city, ... Eze 48:18
filling our hearts with f .... Acts 14:17
both minister bread for your f 2Cor 9:10
And having f and raiment let us be 1Ti 6:8
be naked, and destitute of daily f .... Jas 2:15

FOOL
behold, I have played the f 1Sa 26:21
and said, Died Abner as a f dieth 2Sa 3:33
The f hath said in his heart, ... Ps 14:1
that wise men die, likewise the f .... Ps 49:10
The f hath said in his heart, ... Ps 53:1
neither doth a f understand this .... Ps 92:6
or as a f to the correction of .... Prov 7:22
but a prating f shall fall .... Prov 10:8
but a prating f shall fall .... Prov 10:10
that uttereth a slander, is a f .... Prov 10:18
is as sport to a f to do mischief .... Prov 10:23
the f shall be servant to the .... Prov 11:29
The way of a f is right in his .... Prov 12:15
but a f layeth open his folly. .... Prov 13:16
but every f will be meddling. .... Prov 14:16
A f despiseth his father's .... Prov 15:5
Excellent speech becometh not a f .... Prov 17:7
than an hundred stripes into a f .... Prov 17:10
man, rather than a f in his folly .... Prov 17:12
in the hand of a f to get wisdom .... Prov 17:16
He that begetteth a f doeth it to .... Prov 17:21
and the father of a f hath no joy .... Prov 17:21
the eyes of a f are in the .... Prov 17:24
Even a f, when he holdeth his .... Prov 17:28
A f hath no delight in .... Prov 18:2

perverse in his lips, and is a f .... Prov 19:1
Delight is not seemly for a f .... Prov 19:10
but every f will be meddling. .... Prov 20:3
Speak not in the ears of a f .... Prov 23:9
Wisdom is too high for a f .... Prov 24:7
so honour is not seemly for a f .... Prov 26:1
Answer not a f according to his .... Prov 26:4
Answer a f according to his folly .... Prov 26:5
hand of a f cutteth off the feet .... Prov 26:6
is he that giveth honour to a f .... Prov 26:8
all things both rewardeth the f .... Prov 26:10
so a f returneth to his folly .... Prov 26:11
is more hope of a f than of him .... Prov 26:12
Though thou shouldest bray a f in .... Prov 27:22
but a fool trusteth in his own .... Prov 28:26
A f uttereth all his mind .... Prov 29:11
is more hope of a f than of him .... Prov 29:20
a f when he is filled with meat .... Prov 30:22
but the f walketh in darkness .... Eccl 2:14
heart, As it happeneth to the f .... Eccl 2:15
wise more than of the f for ever .... Eccl 2:16
the wise man? as the f .... Eccl 2:16
he shall be a wise man or a f .... Eccl 2:19
The f foldeth his hands together, ... Eccl 4:5
hath the wise more than the f .... Eccl 6:8
pot, so is the laughter of the f .... Eccl 7:6
when he that is a f walketh by .... Eccl 10:3
saith to every one that he is a f .... Eccl 10:3
but the lips of a f will swallow. .... Eccl 10:12
A f also is full of words. .... Eccl 10:14
days, and at his end shall be a f .... Jer 17:11
the prophet is a f, the spiritual .... Hos 9:7
but whosoever shall say, Thou .... Mt 5:22
But God said unto him, Thou f .... Lk 12:20
in this world, let him become a f 1Cor 3:18
Thou f, that which thou sowest is 1Cor 15:36
fool, yet as a f receive me, that 2Cor 11:16
yet as a f receive me, that I may 2Cor 11:16
(I speak as a f) I am more 2Cor 11:23
to glory, I shall not be a f 2Cor 12:6
I am become a f in glorying 2Cor 12:11

FOOLISH
the LORD, O f people and unwise .... Deut 32:6
them to anger with a f nation .... Deut 32:21
as one of the f women speaketh .... Job 2:10
For wrath killeth the f man .... Job 5:2
I have seen the f taking root .... Job 5:3
The f shall not stand in thy .... Ps 5:5
make me not the reproach of the f .... Ps 39:8
For I was envious at the f .... Ps 73:3
So f was I, and ignorant .... Ps 73:22
that the f people have blasphemed. .... Ps 74:18
remember how the f man .... Ps 74:22
Forsake the f, and live .... Prov 9:6
A f woman is clamorous .... Prov 9:13
but a f son is the heaviness of .... Prov 10:1
of the f is near destruction. .... Prov 10:14
but the f plucketh it down with .... Prov 14:1
mouth of the f is a rod of pride .... Prov 14:3
Go from the presence of a f man .... Prov 14:7
the heart of the f doeth not so. .... Prov 15:7
but a f man despiseth his mother. .... Prov 15:20
A f son is a grief to his father, ... Prov 17:25
A f son is the calamity of his .... Prov 19:13
but a f man spendeth it up .... Prov 21:20
wise man contendeth with a f man .... Prov 29:9
f king, who will no more be .... Eccl 4:13
much wicked, neither be thou f .... Eccl 7:17
The labour of the f wearieth .... Eccl 10:15
and maketh their knowledge f .... Is 44:25
For my people is f, they have not .... Jer 4:22
these are poor; they are f .... Jer 5:4
now this, O f people, and without .... Jer 5:21
they are altogether brutish and f .... Jer 10:8
seen vain and f things for thee .... Lam 2:14
Woe unto the f prophets, that .... Eze 13:3
the instruments of a f shepherd .... Zec 11:15
shall be likened unto a f man .... Mt 7:26
of them were wise, and five were f .... Mt 25:2
They that were f took their lamps .... Mt 25:3
the f said unto the wise, Give us .... Mt 25:8
their f heart was darkened. .... Rom 1:21
An instructor of the f, a teacher .... Rom 2:20
by a f nation I will anger you. .... Rom 10:19
hath not God made f the wisdom of 1Cor 1:20
But God hath chosen the f things, ... 1Cor 1:27
O f Galatians, who hath bewitched .... Gal 3:1
Are ye so f? .... Gal 3:3
nor f talking, nor jesting, which .... Eph 5:4
and a snare, and into many f 1Ti 6:9
But f and unlearned questions 2Ti 2:23
ourselves also were sometimes f .... Titus 3:3
But avoid f questions, and .... Titus 3:9
to silence the ignorance of f men 1Pet 2:15

FOOLISHLY
thou hast now done f in so doing .... Gen 31:28
upon us, wherein we have done f .... Num 12:11
said to Saul, Thou hast done f 1Sa 13:13
for I have done very f 2Sa 24:10
for I have done very f 1Chr 21:8
Herein thou hast done f 2Chr 16:9
Job sinned not, nor charged God f .... Job 1:22
I said unto the fools, Deal not f .... Ps 75:4
He that is soon angry dealeth f .... Prov 14:17
If thou hast done f in lifting up .... Prov 30:32
after the Lord, but as it were f 2Cor 11:17
any is bold, (I speak f,) I am 2Cor 11:21

FOOLISHNESS
the counsel of Ahithophel into f 2Sa 15:31
and are corrupt because of my f .... Ps 38:5

O God, thou knowest my f....................... Ps 69:5
the heart of fools proclaimeth f .... Prov 12:23
but the f of fools is folly .... Prov 14:24
the mouth of fools poureth out f .... Prov 15:2
the mouth of fools feedeth on f .... Prov 15:14
The f of man perverteth his way .... Prov 19:3
F is bound in the heart of a .... Prov 22:15
The thought of f is sin .... Prov 24:9
will not his f depart from him .... Prov 27:22
wickedness of folly, even of f .... Eccl 7:25
of the words of his mouth is f .... Eccl 10:13
an evil eye, blasphemy, pride, f .... Mk 7:22
cross is to them that perish f 1Cor 1:18
it pleased God by the f of 1Cor 1:21
and unto the Greeks f 1Cor 1:23
Because the f of God is wiser 1Cor 1:25
for they are f unto him 1Cor 2:14
of this world is f with God 1Cor 3:19

FOOL'S

A f wrath is presently known .... Prov 12:16
A f lips enter into contention .... Prov 18:6
A f mouth is his destruction, and ...... Prov 18:7
the ass, and a rod for the f back .... Prov 26:3
but a f wrath is heavier than .... Prov 27:3
a f voice is known by multitude .... Eccl 5:3
but a f heart at his left .... Eccl 10:2

FOOLS

be as one of the f in Israel 2Sa 13:13
spoiled, and maketh the judges f .... Job 12:17
They were children of f, yea, ... Job 30:8
I said unto the f, Deal not .... Ps 75:4
and ye f, when will ye be wise .... Ps 94:8
F, because of their transgression ...... Ps 107:17
but f despise wisdom and .... Prov 1:7
scorning, and f hate knowledge .... Prov 1:22
the prosperity of f shall destroy .... Prov 1:32
shame shall be the promotion of f ...... Prov 3:35
and, ye f, be ye of an .... Prov 8:5
but f die for want of wisdom .... Prov 10:21
but the heart of fools proclaimeth ...... Prov 12:23
to f to depart from evil .... Prov 13:19
companion of f shall be destroyed ...... Prov 13:20
but the folly of f is deceit .... Prov 14:8
F make a mock at sin .... Prov 14:9
but the foolishness of f is folly .... Prov 14:24
in the midst of f is made known .... Prov 14:33
but the mouth of f poureth out .... Prov 15:2
but the mouth of f feedeth on .... Prov 15:14
but the instruction of f is folly .... Prov 16:22
and stripes for the back of f .... Prov 19:29
so is a parable in the mouth of f .... Prov 26:7
so is a parable in the mouth of f .... Prov 26:9
than to give the sacrifice of f .... Eccl 5:1
for he hath no pleasure in f .... Eccl 5:4
but the heart of f is in the .... Eccl 7:4
for a man to hear the song of f .... Eccl 7:5
anger resteth in the bosom of f .... Eccl 7:9
cry of him that ruleth among f .... Eccl 9:17
Surely the princes of Zoan are f .... Is 19:11
The princes of Zoan are become f ...... Is 19:13
the wayfaring men, though f .... Is 35:8
Ye f and blind .... Mt 23:17
Ye f and blind .... Mt 23:19
Ye f, did not he that made that .... Lk 11:40
Then he said unto them, O f .... Lk 24:25
to be wise, they became f .... Rom 1:22
We are f for Christ's sake, but 1Cor 4:10
For ye suffer f gladly, seeing ye 2Cor 11:19
ye walk circumspectly, not as f .... Eph 5:15

FOOT

no rest for the sole of her f .... Gen 8:9
or f in all the land of Egypt .... Gen 41:44
thousand on f that were men .... Ex 12:37
tooth, hand for hand, f for f .... Ex 21:24
the great toe of their right f .... Ex 29:20
his f also of brass, to wash .... Ex 30:18
vessels, and the laver and his f .... Ex 30:28
furniture, and the laver and his f .... Ex 31:9
his vessels, the laver and his f .... Ex 35:16
the f of it of brass, of the .... Ex 38:8
his vessels, the laver and his f .... Ex 39:39
shalt anoint the laver and his f .... Ex 40:11
vessels, both the laver and his f .... Lev 8:11
upon the great toe of his right f .... Lev 8:23
from his head even to his f .... Lev 13:12
upon the great toe of his right f .... Lev 14:14
upon the great toe of his right f .... Lev 14:17
upon the great toe of his right f .... Lev 14:25
upon the great toe of his right f .... Lev 14:28
Balaam's f against the wall .... Num 22:25
thee, neither did thy f swell .... Deut 8:4
seed, and wateredst it with thy f .... Deut 11:10
tooth, hand for hand, f for f .... Deut 19:21
and loose his shoe from off his f .... Deut 25:9
from the sole of thy f unto the .... Deut 28:35
sole of her f upon the ground for .... Deut 28:56
shall the sole of thy f have rest .... Deut 28:65
shoe is not waxen old upon thy f .... Deut 29:5
their f shall slide in due time .... Deut 32:35
and let him dip his f in oil .... Deut 33:24
sole of your f shall tread upon .... Josh 1:3
Loose thy shoe from off thy f .... Josh 5:15
he was sent on f into the valley .... Judg 5:15
was as light of f as a wild roe 2Sa 2:18
from the sole of his f even to 2Sa 14:25
fingers, and on every f six toes 2Sa 21:20
and he trode her under f 2Kin 9:33
on each hand, and six on each f 1Chr 20:6
will I any more remove the f of 2Chr 33:8

the sole of his f unto his crown .... Job 2:7
My f hath held his steps, his way .... Job 23:11
the waters forgotten of the f .... Job 28:4
or if my f hath hasted to deceit .... Job 31:5
that the f may crush them .... Job 39:15
they hid is their own f taken .... Ps 9:15
My f standeth in an even place .... Ps 26:12
Let not the f of pride come .... Ps 36:11
when my f slippeth, they magnify ...... Ps 38:16
they went through the flood on f .... Ps 66:6
That thy f may be dipped in the .... Ps 68:23
thou dash thy f against a stone .... Ps 91:12
When I said, My f slippeth .... Ps 94:18
will not suffer thy f to be moved .... Ps 121:3
refrain thy f from their path .... Prov 1:15
and thy f shall not stumble .... Prov 3:23
shall keep thy f from being taken ...... Prov 3:26
remove thy f from evil .... Prov 4:27
Withdraw thy f from thy .... Prov 25:17
broken tooth, and a f out of joint ...... Prov 25:19
Keep thy f when thou goest to the ..... Eccl 5:1
From the sole of the f even unto .... Is 1:6
my mountains tread him under f .... Is 14:25
meted out and trodden under f .... Is 18:7
and put off thy shoe from thy f .... Is 20:2
The f shall tread it down, even .... Is 26:6
the east, called him to his f .... Is 41:2
turn away thy f from the sabbath ...... Is 58:13
Withhold thy f from being unshod,..... Jer 2:25
have trodden my portion under f .... Jer 12:10
The Lord hath trodden under f all ..... Lam 1:15
was like the sole of a calf's f .... Eze 1:7
thine hand, and stamp with thy f ...... Eze 6:11
No f of man shall pass through it ...... Eze 29:11
nor f of beast shall pass through ...... Eze 29:11
neither shall the f of man .... Eze 32:13
and the foot to be trodden under f .... Dan 8:13
he that is swift of f shall not .... Amos 2:15
thou dash thy f against a stone .... Mt 4:6
and to be trodden under f of .... Mt 5:13
him on f out of the cities .... Mt 14:13
if thy hand or thy f offend thee .... Mt 18:8
the servants, Bind him hand and f .... Mt 22:13
if thy f offend thee, cut it off .... Mk 9:45
thou dash thy f against a stone .... Lk 4:11
bound hand and f with graveclothes . Jn 11:44
not so much as to set his f on .... Acts 7:5
If the f shall say, Because I am 1Cor 12:15
trodden under f the Son of God .... Heb 10:29
with a garment down to the f .... Rev 1:13
he set his right f upon the sea .... Rev 10:2
and his left f on the earth .... Rev 10:2
shall they tread under f forty .... Rev 11:2

FOOTBREADTH

land, no, not so much as a f .... Deut 2:5

FOOTMEN

i am, are six hundred thousand f...... Num 11:21
thousand f that drew sword .... Judg 20:2
fell of Israel thirty thousand f 1Sa 4:10
in Telaim, two hundred thousand f ... 1Sa 15:4
unto the f that stood about him 1Sa 22:17
horsemen, and twenty thousand f 2Sa 8:4
of Zoba, twenty thousand f 2Sa 10:6
an hundred thousand f in one day 1Kin 20:29
ten chariots, and ten thousand f 2Kin 13:7
horsemen, and twenty thousand f 1Chr 18:4
in chariots, and forty thousand f 1Chr 19:18
If thou hast run with the f 1Chr 19:18

FOOTSTEPS

in thy paths, that my f slip not .... Ps 17:5
waters, and thy f are not known .... Ps 77:19
the f of thine anointed .... Ps 89:51
way forth by the f of the flock .... Song 1:8

FOOTSTOOL

for the f of our God, and had made.... 1Chr 28:2
with a f of gold, which were 2Chr 9:18
Lord our God, and worship at his f .... Ps 99:5
until I make thine enemies thy f .... Ps 110:1
we will worship at his f .... Ps 132:7
my throne, and the earth is my f .... Is 66:1
remembered not his f in the day .... Lam 2:1
for it is his f .... Mt 5:35
till I make thine enemies thy f .... Mt 22:44
till I make thine enemies thy f .... Mk 12:36
Till I make thine enemies thy f .... Lk 20:43
Until I make thy foes thy f .... Acts 2:35
is my throne, and earth is my f .... Acts 7:49
until I make thine enemies thy f .... Heb 1:13
till his enemies be made his f .... Heb 10:13
there, or sit here under my f .... Jas 2:3

FOR See PREFACE.

FORASMUCH

F as God hath shewed thee all .... Gen 41:39
f as thou knowest how we are to .... Num 10:31
f as he hath no part nor .... Deut 12:12
f as the Lord hath said unto you, ... Deut 17:16
f as the Lord hath blessed me .... Josh 17:14
f as the Lord hath taken .... Judg 11:36
f as we have sworn both of us in 1Sa 20:42
f as when the Lord had delivered 1Sa 24:18
f as my lord the king is come 2Sa 19:30
f as this is done of thee, and 1Kin 11:11
f as thou hast disobeyed the 1Kin 13:21
f as I exalted thee from among, ... 1Kin 14:7
f as I exalted thee out of the 1Kin 16:2
f as thou hast sent messengers to 2Kin 1:16
f as he defiled his father's bed, ... 1Chr 5:1

F as it was in thine heart to............... 2Chr 6:8
F as thou art sent of the king. .... Ezr 7:14
F as this people refuseth the .... Is 8:6
F as this people draw near me .... Is 29:13
F as there is none like unto thee........ Jer 10:6
F as among all the wise men of .... Jer 10:7
F as iron breaketh in pieces and .... Dan 2:40
F as thou sawest the iron mixed .... Dan 2:41
F as thou sawest that the stone .... Dan 2:45
F as all the wise men of my .... Dan 4:18
F as an excellent spirit, and .... Dan 5:12
F as he was faithful, neither was....... Dan 6:4
f as before him innocency was .... Dan 6:22
F therefore as your treading is. .... Amos 5:11
But f as he had not to pay, his .... Mt 18:25
F as many have taken in hand to ...... Lk 1:1
f as Lydda was nigh to Joppa, and..... Acts 9:38
F then as God gave them the like ...... Acts 11:17
F as we have heard, that certain....... Acts 15:24
F then as we are the offspring of....... Acts 17:29
F as I know that thou hast been .... Acts 24:10
f as he is the image and glory of 1Cor 11:7
F as ye are zealous of spiritual 1Cor 14:12
f as ye know that your labour is 1Cor 15:58
F as ye are manifestly declared 2Cor 3:3
F then as the children are .... Heb 2:14
F as ye know that ye were not........... 1Pet 1:18
F then as Christ hath suffered 1Pet 4:1

FORBAD

whatsoever the Lord our God f .... Deut 2:37
But John f him, saying, I have .... Mt 3:14
we f him, because he followeth .... Mk 9:38
we f him, because he followeth .... Lk 9:49
f the madness of the prophet 2Pet 2:16

FORBARE

and he f to go forth 1Sa 23:13
Then the prophet f, and said, I 2Chr 25:16
So he f, and slew them not among ..... Jer 41:8

FORBEAR

wouldest f to help him, thou .... Ex 23:5
But if thou shalt f to vow .... Deut 23:22
to battle, or shall I f 1Kin 22:6
to battle, or shall I f 1Kin 22:15
to battle, or shall f 2Chr 18:5
to battle, or shall f 2Chr 18:14
f, why shouldest thou be smitten...... 2Chr 25:16
f thee from meddling with God, ... 2Chr 35:21
Yet many years didst thou f them..... Neh 9:30
and though I f, what am I eased .... Job 16:6
If thou f to deliver them that .... Prov 24:11
to come with me into Babylon, ... Jer 40:4
will hear, or whether they will f .... Eze 2:5
will hear, or whether they will f .... Eze 2:7
will hear, or whether they will f .... Eze 3:11
and he that forbeareth, let him .... Eze 3:27
F to cry, make no mourning for .... Eze 24:17
my price; and if not, f .... Zec 11:12
have not we power to f working......... 1Cor 9:6
but now I f, lest any man should 2Cor 12:6
when we could no longer f 1Th 3:1
cause, when I could no longer f 1Th 3:5

FORBEARANCE

the riches of his goodness and f .... Rom 2:4
are past, through the f of God .... Rom 3:25

FORBEARETH

f to keep the passover, even the .... Num 9:13
and he that f, let him forbear........... Eze 3:27

FORBEARING

By long f is a prince persuaded, ... Prov 25:15
my bones, and I was weary with f..... Jer 20:9
f one another in love .... Eph 4:2
things unto them, f threatening........ Eph 6:9
F one another, and forgiving one ...... Col 3:13

FORBID

God that thy servants should do .... Gen 44:7
God f that I should do so .... Gen 44:17
and said, My lord Moses, f them .... Num 11:28
God f that we should rebel .... Josh 22:29
God f that we should forsake the ...... Josh 24:16
God f that I should sin against 1Sa 12:23
God f as the Lord liveth 1Sa 14:45
And he said unto him, God f 1Sa 20:2
The Lord f that I should do this 1Sa 24:6
The Lord f that I should stretch 1Sa 26:11
said to Abab, The Lord f it me. 1Kin 21:3
And said, My God f it me, that I 1Chr 11:19
God f that I should justify you. .... Job 27:5
f them not, to come unto me .... Mt 19:14
But Jesus said, F him not. .... Mk 9:39
to come unto me, and f them not. ..... Mk 10:14
cloke f not to take thy coat also .... Lk 6:29
And Jesus said unto him, F him not. . Lk 9:50
to come unto me, and f them not, ... Lk 18:16
they heard it, they said, God f. .... Lk 20:16
Can any man f water, that these....... Acts 10:47
that he should f none of his............. Acts 24:23
God f: yea, let God be true .... Rom 3:4
God f: for then how shall God .... Rom 3:6
God f: yea, we establish the law ...... Rom 3:31
God f. How shall we .... Rom 6:2
but under grace? God f .... Rom 6:15
Is the law sin? God f .... Rom 7:7
good made death unto me? God f ..... Rom 7:13
unrighteousness with God? God f ..... Rom 9:14
God cast away his people? God f ...... Rom 11:1
that they should fall? God f .... Rom 11:11

FORBIDDEN
members of an harlot? God f............1Cor 6:15
f not to speak with tongues............1Cor 14:39
the minister of sin? God f............Gal 2:17
the promises of God? God f............Gal 3:21
But God that I should glory............Gal 6:14

FORBIDDETH
f them that would, and casteth............3Jn 10

FORBIDDING
f to give tribute to Caesar............Lk 23:2
with all confidence, no man f him......Acts 28:31
f us to speak to the Gentiles..........1Th 2:16
f to marry, and commanding to..........1Ti 4:3

FORBORN
men of Babylon have f to fight.........Jer 51:30

FORCE
take by f thy daughters from me........Gen 31:31
in the field, and the man f her........Deut 22:25
not dim, nor his natural f abated......Deut 34:7
and if not, I will take it by f........Judg 2:16
him, Nay, my brother, do not f me......2Sa 13:12
Jews, and made them to cease by f......Ezr 4:23
Will he f the queen also before........Est 7:8
By the great f of my disease is........Job 30:18
his f is in the navel of his..........Job 40:16
their blood by the f of the sword......Jer 18:21
is evil, and their f is not right......Jer 23:10
of Heshbon because of the f............Jer 48:45
but with f and with cruelty have.......Eze 34:4
the f of the sword in the time of......Eze 35:5
strong shall not strengthen his.......Amos 2:14
and the violent take it by f...........Mt 11:12
they would come and take him by f......Jn 6:15
to take him by f from among them,......Acts 23:10
is of f after men are dead.............Heb 9:17

FORCED
the Amorites the children of...........Judg 1:34
and my concubine have they f...........Judg 20:5
I f myself therefore, and offered......1Sa 13:12
than she, f her, and lay with her......2Sa 13:14
because he had f his sister Tamar......2Sa 13:32
day that he f his sister Tamar.........2Sa 13:22
flattering of her lips she f him.......Prov 7:21

FORCES
he placed f in all the fenced..........2Chr 17:2
gold, nor all the f of strength........Job 36:19
the f of the Gentiles shall come.......Is 60:5
unto thee the f of the Gentiles........Is 60:11
of the f which were in the fields......Jer 40:7
of the f that were with him............Jer 40:13
of the f that were with him............Jer 41:11
of the f that were with him............Jer 41:13
of the f that were with him............Jer 41:13
Then all the captains of the f.........Jer 42:1
of the f which were with him...........Jer 42:8
and all the captains of the f..........Jer 43:4
and all the captains of the f..........Jer 43:5
assemble a multitude of great f........Dan 11:10
shall he honour the God of f...........Dan 11:38
carried away captive his f.............Obad 11

FORCIBLE
How f are right words.................Job 6:25

FORCING
thereof by f an ax against them........Deut 20:19
so the f of wrath bringeth forth......Prov 30:33

FORD
sons, and passed over the f Jabbok.....Gen 32:22

FORDS
them the way to Jordan unto the f......Josh 2:7
took the f of Jordan toward Moab,......Judg 3:28
Moab shall be at the f of Arnon........Is 16:2

FORECAST
he shall f his devices against.........Dan 11:24
for they shall f devices against......Dan 11:25

FOREFATHERS
back to the iniquities of their f......Jer 11:10
from my f with pure conscience.........2Ti 1:3

FOREFRONT
in the f of the tabernacle.............Ex 26:9
upon the f of the mitre it shall.......Ex 28:37
upon the mitre, even upon his f........Lev 8:9
The f of the one was situate...........1Sa 14:5
Set ye Uriah in the f of the...........2Sa 11:15
from the f of the house, from..........2Kin 16:14
and Jehoshaphat in the f of the........2Chr 20:27
the f of the lower gate unto the.......Eze 40:19
the f of the inner court without......Eze 40:19
for the f of the house stood...........Eze 47:1

FOREHEAD
And it shall be upon Aaron's f.........Ex 28:38
and it shall be always upon his f......Ex 28:38
toward his face, he is f bald..........Lev 13:41
be in the bald head, or bald f.........Lev 13:42
in his bald head, or his bald f........Lev 13:42
his bald head, or in bald head.........Lev 13:43
and smote the Philistine in his f......1Sa 17:49
that the stone sunk into his f.........1Sa 17:49
f before the priests in the house......2Chr 26:19
behold, he was leprous in his f........2Chr 26:20

and thou hadst a whore's f.............Jer 3:3
thy f strong against thee.............Eze 3:8
than flint have I made thy f..........Eze 3:9
And I put a jewel on thy f............Eze 16:12
and receive his mark in his f..........Rev 14:9
upon her f was a name written,........Rev 17:5

FOREHEADS
forehead strong against their f........Eze 3:8
set a mark upon the f of the men......Eze 9:4
servants of our God in their f.........Rev 7:3
not the seal of God in their f.........Rev 9:4
their right hand, or in their f........Rev 13:16
Father's name written in their f......Rev 14:1
received his mark upon their f.........Rev 20:4
his name shall be in their f...........Rev 22:4

FOREIGNER
A f and an hired servant shall not.....Ex 12:45
Of a f thou mayest exact it again......Deut 15:3

FOREIGNERS
f entered into his gates, and cast......Obad 11
ye are no more strangers and f.........Eph 2:19

FOREKNEW
cast away his people which he f........Rom 11:2

FOREKNOW
For whom he did f, he also did.........Rom 8:29

FOREKNOWLEDGE
of God, ye have taken, and by..........Acts 2:23
the f of God the Father...............1Pet 1:2

FOREMOST
And he commanded the f, saying,........Gen 32:17
the handmaids and their children f.....Gen 33:2
f is like the running of Ahimaaz......2Sa 18:27

FOREORDAINED
Who verily was f before the............1Pet 1:20

FOREPART
underneath, toward the f thereof......Ex 28:27
underneath, toward the f of it.........Ex 39:20
the oracle in the f was twenty.........1Kin 6:20
court on the f of the chambers.........Eze 42:7
the f stuck fast, and remained........Acts 27:41

FORERUNNER
Whither the f is for us entered,......Heb 6:20

FORESAW
I f the Lord always before my..........Acts 2:25

FORESEEING
f that God would justify the...........Gal 3:8

FORESEETH
A prudent man f the evil, and.........Prov 22:3
A prudent man f the evil, and.........Prov 27:12

FORESHIP
have cast anchors out of the f.........Acts 27:30

FORESKIN
circumcise the flesh of your f........Gen 17:11
flesh of his f is not circumcised......Gen 17:14
of the f in the selfsame day..........Gen 17:23
circumcised in the flesh of his f.....Gen 17:24
circumcised in the flesh of his f.....Gen 17:25
and cut off the f of her son..........Ex 4:25
of his f shall be circumcised.........Lev 12:3
therefore the f of your heart.........Deut 10:16
also, and let thy f be uncovered.......Hab 2:16

FORESKINS
of Israel at the hill of the f........Josh 5:3
dowry, but an hundred f of the.........1Sa 18:25
and David brought their f, and they....1Sa 18:27
an hundred f of the Philistines........2Sa 3:14
and take away the f of your heart......Jer 4:4

FOREST
and came into the f of Hareth.........1Sa 22:5
the house of the f of Lebanon..........1Kin 7:2
in the house of the f of Lebanon......1Kin 10:17
f of Lebanon were of pure gold.........1Kin 10:21
and into the f his Carmel..............2Kin 19:23
in the house of the f of Lebanon......2Chr 9:16
of Lebanon were of pure gold...........2Chr 9:20
Asaph the keeper of the king's f.......Neh 2:8
For every beast of the f is mine......Ps 50:10
beasts of the f do creep forth........Ps 104:20
kindle in the thickets of the f.......Is 9:18
shall consume the glory of his f......Is 10:18
the trees of his f shall be few.......Is 10:19
the thickets of the f with iron.......Is 10:34
In the f in Arabia shall ye lodge......Is 21:13
the armour of the house of the f......Is 22:8
field shall be esteemed as a f........Is 29:17
fruitful field be counted for a f.....Is 32:15
shall hail, coming down on the f.......Is 32:19
border, and the f of his Carmel.......Is 37:24
himself among the trees of the f......Is 44:14
into singing, ye mountains, O f........Is 44:23
yea, all ye beasts in the f...........Is 56:9
lion out of the f shall slay them.....Jer 5:6
one cutteth a tree out of the f.......Jer 10:3
is unto me as a lion in the f.........Jer 12:8
house as the high places of a f.......Jer 26:18
They shall cut down her f.............Jer 46:23
which is among the trees of the f.....Eze 15:2
tree among the trees of the f.........Eze 15:6
against the f of the south field......Eze 20:46
say to the f of the south, Hear.......Eze 20:47

and I will make them a f, and the.....Hos 2:12
Will a lion roar in the f.............Amos 3:4
house as the high places of the f.....Mic 3:12
a lion among the beasts of the f......Mic 5:8
for the f of the vintage is come......Zec 11:2

FORESTS
in the f he built castles and.........2Chr 27:4
to calve, and discovereth the f.......Ps 29:9
neither cut down any out of the f......Eze 39:10

FORETELL
f you, as if I were present, the.......2Cor 13:2

FORETOLD
behold, I have f you all things........Mk 13:23
have likewise f of these days.........Acts 3:24

FOREWARN
But I will f you whom ye shall.........Lk 12:5

FOREWARNED
all such, as we also have f you.......1Th 4:6

FORFEITED
all his substance should be f.........Ezr 10:8

FORGAT
butler remember Joseph, but f him......Gen 40:23
f the Lord their God, and served......Judg 3:7
when they f the Lord their God........1Sa 12:9
f his works, and his wonders that......Ps 78:11
They soon f his works...............Ps 106:13
They f God their saviour, which......Ps 106:21
I f prosperity.......................Lam 3:17
lovers, and f me, saith the Lord......Hos 2:13

FORGAVE
f their iniquity, and destroyed......Ps 78:38
and loosed him, and f him the debt....Mt 18:27
I f thee all that debt, because......Mt 18:32
to pay, he frankly f them both........Lk 7:42
that he, to whom he f most............Lk 7:43
f any thing, to whom I f it...........2Cor 2:10
for your sakes f I it in the..........2Cor 2:10
even as Christ f you, so also do......Col 3:13

FORGAVEST
thou f the iniquity of my sin.........Ps 32:5
thou wast a God that f them...........Ps 99:8

FORGED
The proud have f a lie against me......Ps 119:69

FORGERS
But ye are f of lies, ye are all......Job 13:4

FORGET
he f that which thou hast done to......Gen 27:45
he, hath made me f all my toil........Gen 41:51
lest thou f the things which..........Deut 4:9
lest ye f the covenant of the.........Deut 4:23
nor f the covenant of thy fathers.....Deut 4:31
Then beware lest thou f the Lord......Deut 6:12
Beware that thou f not the Lord.......Deut 8:11
thou f the Lord thy God, which........Deut 8:14
thou do at all f the Lord thy God.....Deut 8:19
f not, how thou provokedst the........Deut 9:7
thou shalt not f it.................Deut 25:19
not f thine handmaid, but wilt........1Sa 1:11
have made with you ye shall not f.....2Kin 17:38
are the paths of all that f God.......Job 8:13
I will f my complaint, I will.........Job 9:27
Because thou shalt f thy misery.......Job 11:16
The womb shall f him................Job 24:20
and all the nations that f God........Ps 9:17
f not the humble.....................Ps 10:12
How long wilt thou f me, O Lord.......Ps 13:1
f also thine own people, and thy......Ps 45:10
Now consider this, ye that f God......Ps 50:22
Slay them not, lest my people f......Ps 59:11
f not the congregation of thy.........Ps 74:19
f not the voice of thine enemies......Ps 74:23
not f the works of God, but keep......Ps 78:7
so that I f to eat my bread...........Ps 102:4
soul, and f not all his benefits......Ps 103:2
I will not f thy word...............Ps 119:16
yet do I not f thy statutes..........Ps 119:83
I will never f thy precepts..........Ps 119:93
yet do I not f thy law..............Ps 119:109
yet do not f I thy precepts..........Ps 119:141
for I do not f thy law..............Ps 119:153
for I do not f thy commandments......Ps 119:176
If I f thee, O Jerusalem.............Ps 137:5
let my right hand f her cunning......Ps 137:5
My son, f not my law.................Prov 3:1
get understanding: f it not..........Prov 4:5
the law, and pervert the.............Prov 31:5
f his poverty, and remember his......Prov 31:7
Can a woman f her sucking child,......Is 49:15
yea, they may f, yet will I not......Is 49:15
may f, yet will I not f thee.........Is 49:15
for thou shalt f the shame of thy.....Is 54:4
the holy mountain, that............Is 65:11
Can a maid f her ornaments, or a......Jer 2:32
think to cause my people to f my......Jer 23:27
I, even I, will utterly f you.........Jer 23:39
Wherefore dost thou f us for ever.....Lam 5:20
I will also f thy children...........Hos 4:6
I will never f any of their works.....Amos 8:7
is not unrighteous to f your works....Heb 6:10
do good and to communicate f not......Heb 13:16

FORGETFUL
Be not f to entertain strangers.......Heb 13:2
therein, he being not a f hearer......Jas 1:25

FORGETFULNESS
righteousness in the land of *f* .... Ps 88:12

FORGETTEST
face, and *f* our affliction and our .... Ps 44:24
f the LORD thy maker, that hath .... Is 51:13

FORGETTETH
f that the foot may crush them, ... Job 39:15
he *f* not the cry of the humble .... Ps 9:12
f the covenant of her God, ... Prov 2:17
straightway *f* what manner of man... Jas 1:24

FORGETTING
f those things which are behind, ... Phil 3:13

FORGIVE
So shall ye say unto Joseph, F .... Gen 50:17
f the trespass of the servants of .... Gen 50:17
Now therefore *f*, I pray thee, my .... Ex 10:17
Yet now, if thou wilt *f* their sin...... Ex 32:32
and the LORD shall *f* her, because .... Num 30:5
and the LORD shall *f* her. .... Num 30:8
and the LORD shall *f* her. .... Num 30:12
he will not *f* your transgressions .... Josh 24:19
f the trespass of thine handmaid 1Sa 25:28
and when thou hearest, *f* 1Kin 8:30
the sin of thy people Israel, ... 1Kin 8:34
the sin of thy servants, and of 1Kin 8:36
heaven thy dwelling place, and *f* 1Kin 8:39
f thy people that have sinned 1Kin 8:50
and when thou hearest, *f* 2Chr 6:21
the sin of thy people Israel, ... 2Chr 6:25
the sin of thy servants, and of 2Chr 6:27
heaven thy dwelling place, and *f* 2Chr 6:30
thy people which have sinned 2Chr 6:39
will *f* their sin, and will heal 2Chr 7:14
and *f* all my sins. .... Ps 25:18
Lord, art good, and ready to *f* .... Ps 86:5
therefore *f* them not .... Is 2:9
f not their iniquity, neither .... Jer 18:23
for I will *f* their iniquity, and I .... Jer 31:34
that I may *f* their iniquity and... Jer 36:3
O Lord, hear; O Lord, *f* .... Dan 9:19
land, then I said, O Lord God, *f*... Amos 7:2
f us our debts, as we *f* our........ Mt 6:12
For if ye *f* men their trespasses, ... Mt 6:14
heavenly Father will also *f* you......... Mt 6:14
But if ye *f* not men their .... Mt 6:15
your Father *f* your trespasses......... Mt 6:15
man hath power on earth to *f*... Mt 9:6
sin against me, and I *f* him? .... Mt 18:21
if ye from your hearts *f* not......... Mt 18:35
who can *f* sins but God only......... Mk 2:7
man hath power on earth to *f* sins... Mk 2:10
And when ye stand praying, *f*... Mk 11:25
heaven may *f* you your trespasses... Mk 11:25
But if ye do not *f*, neither will... Mk 11:26
is in heaven *f* your trespasses. .... Mk 11:26
Who can *f* sins, but God alone......... Lk 5:21
hath power upon earth to *f* sins... Lk 5:24
f, and ye shall be forgiven. .... Lk 6:37
And *f* us our sins. .... Lk 11:4
for we also *f* every one that is......... Lk 11:4
and if he repent, *f* him............... Lk 17:3
thou shalt *f* him. .... Lk 17:4
Then said Jesus, Father, *f* them...... Lk 23:34
ye ought rather to *f* him, and......... 2Cor 2:7
ye *f* any thing, I also 2Cor 2:10
f me this wrong 2Cor 12:13
just to *f* us our sins, and to......... 1Jn 1:9

FORGIVEN
for them, and it shall be *f* them .... Lev 4:20
his sin, and it shall be *f* him............ Lev 4:26
for him, and it shall be *f* him......... Lev 4:31
committed, and it shall be *f*......... Lev 4:35
hath sinned, and it shall be *f* him...... Lev 5:10
of these, and it shall be *f* him......... Lev 5:13
offering, and it shall be *f* him......... Lev 5:16
wist it not, and it shall be *f* him...... Lev 5:18
it shall be *f* him for any thing......... Lev 6:7
which he hath done shall be *f* him ... Lev 19:22
and as thou hast *f* this people......... Num 14:19
of Israel, and it shall be *f* them... Num 15:25
And it shall be *f* all the......... Num 15:26
and it shall be *f* him......... Num 15:28
And the blood shall be *f* them......... Deut 21:8
is he whose transgression is *f*......... Ps 32:1
Thou hast *f* the iniquity of thy......... Ps 85:2
therein shall be their iniquity......... Is 33:24
thy sins be *f* thee .... Mt 9:2
to say, Thy sins be *f* thee......... Mt 9:5
and blasphemy shall be *f* unto men ... Mt 12:31
Ghost shall not be *f* unto men......... Mt 12:31
the Son of man, it shall be *f* him... Mt 12:32
Holy Ghost, it shall not be *f* him... Mt 12:32
palsy, Son, thy sins be *f*......... Mk 2:5
of the palsy, Thy sins be *f* thee... Mk 2:9
All sins shall be *f* unto the sons... Mk 3:28
and their sins should be *f* them... Mk 4:12
him, Man, thy sins are *f* thee......... Lk 5:20
to say, Thy sins be *f* thee......... Lk 5:23
forgive, and ye shall be *f*......... Lk 6:37
Her sins, which are many, are *f*... Lk 7:47
but to whom little is *f*, the same...... Lk 7:47
he said unto her, Thy sins are *f*... Lk 7:48
the Son of man, it shall be *f* him... Lk 12:10
the Holy Ghost it shall not be *f*... Lk 12:10
of thine heart may be *f* thee......... Acts 8:22
are they whose iniquities are *f*... Rom 4:7
God for Christ's sake hath *f* you... Eph 4:32
having *f* you all trespasses......... Col 2:13

sins, they shall be *f* him......... Jas 5:15
because your sins are *f* you for......... 1Jn 2:12

FORGIVENESS
But there is *f* with thee, that......... Ps 130:4
the Holy Ghost hath never *f*......... Mk 3:29
to Israel, and *f* of sins. .... Acts 5:31
preached unto you the *f* of sins... Acts 13:38
that they may receive *f* of sins...... Acts 26:18
the *f* of sins, according to the......... Eph 1:7
his blood, even the *f* of sins......... Col 1:14

FORGIVENESSES
Lord our God belong mercies and *f*...... Dan 9:9

FORGIVETH
Who *f* all thine iniquities......... Ps 103:3
Who is this that *f* sins also......... Lk 7:49

FORGIVING
f iniquity and transgression and......... Ex 34:7
f iniquity and transgression, and... Num 14:18
f one another, even as God for......... Eph 4:32
f one another, if any man have a...... Col 3:13

FORGOT
hast *f* a sheaf in the field, thou ...... Deut 24:19

FORGOTTEN
shall be *f* in the land of Egypt......... Gen 41:30
neither have I *f* them. .... Deut 26:13
for it shall not be *f* out of the......... Deut 31:21
hast *f* God that formed thee......... Deut 32:18
and my familiar friends have *f* me ...... Job 19:14
even the waters *f* of the foot......... Job 28:4
the needy shall not alway be *f*......... Ps 9:18
said in his heart, God hath *f*......... Ps 10:11
I am *f* as a dead man out of mind......... Ps 31:12
God my rock, Why hast thou *f* me...... Ps 42:9
yet have we not *f* thee, neither......... Ps 44:17
If we have *f* the name of our God...... Ps 44:20
Hath God *f* to be gracious......... Ps 77:9
but I have not *f* thy law......... Ps 119:61
mine enemies have *f* thy words......... Ps 119:139
the days to come shall all be *f*...... Eccl 2:16
they were *f* in the city where......... Eccl 8:10
for the memory of them is *f*......... Eccl 9:5
Because thou hast *f* the God of......... Is 17:10
Tyre shall be *f* seventy years......... Is 23:15
thou hast not that been *f*......... Is 23:16
Israel, thou shalt not be *f* of me...... Is 44:21
forsaken me, and my Lord hath *f* me... Is 49:14
because the former troubles are *f*... Is 65:16
yet my people have *f* me days......... Jer 2:32
they have *f* the LORD their God......... Jer 3:21
because thou hast *f* me, and......... Jer 13:25
Because my people hath *f* me......... Jer 18:15
confusion shall never be *f*......... Jer 20:11
fathers have *f* my name for Baal......... Jer 23:27
shame, which shall not be *f*......... Jer 23:40
All thy lovers have *f* thee......... Jer 30:14
Have ye *f* the wickedness of your...... Jer 44:9
covenant that shall not be *f*......... Jer 50:5
they have *f* their restingplace......... Jer 50:6
and sabbaths to be *f* in Zion......... Lam 2:6
by extortion, and hast *f* me......... Eze 22:12
Because thou hast *f* me, and cast...... Eze 23:35
seeing thou hast *f* the law of thy...... Hos 4:6
For Israel hath *f* his Maker......... Hos 8:14
therefore have they *f* me......... Hos 13:6
side, they had *f* to take bread......... Mt 16:5
the disciples had *f* to take bread... Mk 8:14
not one of them is *f* before God...... Lk 12:6
ye have *f* the exhortation which......... Heb 12:5
hath *f* that he was purged from......... 2Pet 1:9

FORKS
and for the coulters, and for the *f*...... 1Sa 13:21

FORM
And the earth was without *f*......... Gen 1:2
he said unto her, What *f* is he of......... 1Sa 28:14
To fetch about this *f* of speech......... 2Sa 14:20
of gold according to their *f*......... 2Chr 4:7
I could not discern the *f* thereof...... Job 4:16
if *f* the light, and create darkness... Is 45:7
his *f* more than the sons of men...... Is 52:14
he hath no *f* nor comeliness......... Is 53:2
earth, and, lo, it was without *f*......... Jer 4:23
And he put forth the *f* of an hand... Eze 8:3
behold every *f* of creeping things... Eze 8:10
the *f* of a man's hand under their... Eze 10:8
shew them the *f* of the house......... Eze 43:11
they may keep the whole *f* thereof... Eze 43:11
the *f* thereof was terrible......... Dan 2:31
the *f* of his visage was changed... Dan 3:19
the *f* of the fourth is like the......... Dan 3:25
in another *f* unto two of them......... Mk 16:12
which hast the *f* of knowledge......... Rom 2:20
of doctrine which was delivered......... Rom 6:17
Who, being in the *f* of God......... Phil 2:6
took upon him the *f* of a servant...... Phil 2:7
Hold fast the *f* of sound words......... 2Ti 1:13
Having a *f* of godliness, but......... 2Ti 3:5

FORMED
the LORD God *f* man of the dust of...... Gen 2:7
he put the man whom he had *f*......... Gen 2:8
God *f* every beast of the field......... Gen 2:19
and hast forgotten God that *f* thee... Deut 32:18
of ancient times that I have *f* it...... 2Kin 19:25
Dead things are *f* from under the... Job 26:5
his hand hath *f* the crooked......... Job 26:13
I also am *f* out of the clay......... Job 33:6

or ever thou hadst *f* the earth......... Ps 90:2
he that *f* the eye, shall he not......... Ps 94:9
and his hands *f* the dry land......... Ps 95:5
The great God that *f* all things......... Prov 26:10
he that *f* them will shew them no ...... Is 27:11
ancient times, that I have *f* it......... Is 37:26
thee, O Jacob, and he that *f* thee...... Is 43:1
him for my glory, I have *f* him......... Is 43:7
before me there was no God *f*......... Is 43:10
This people have I *f* for myself......... Is 43:21
f thee from the womb, which will...... Is 44:2
Who hath *f* a god, or molten a......... Is 44:10
I have *f* thee .... Is 44:21
he that *f* thee from the womb, I... Is 44:24
God himself that *f* the earth......... Is 45:18
in vain, he *f* it to be inhabited......... Is 45:18
saith the LORD that *f* me from the...... Is 49:5
No weapon that is *f* against thee...... Is 54:17
Before I *f* thee in the belly I......... Jer 1:5
maker thereof, that he *f* it......... Jer 33:2
behold, he *f* grasshoppers in the...... Amos 7:1
Shall the thing *f* say to him that...... Rom 9:20
thing *f* say to him that *f* it......... Rom 9:20
again until Christ be *f* in you......... Gal 4:19
For Adam was first *f*, then Eve......... 1Ti 2:13

FORMER
after the *f* manner when thou wast...... Gen 40:13
fought against the *f* king of Moab... Num 21:26
Her *f* husband, which sent her......... Deut 24:4
in *f* time in Israel concerning......... Ruth 4:7
him again after the *f* manner......... 1Sa 17:30
the *f* fifties with their fifties......... 2Kin 1:14
day they do after the *f* manners...... 2Kin 17:34
but they did after their *f* manner... 2Kin 17:40
But the *f* governors that had been... Neh 5:15
I pray thee, of the *f* age......... Job 8:8
the wilderness in *f* time desolate...... Job 30:3
not against us *f* iniquities......... Ps 79:8
where are thy *f* lovingkindnesses, ... Ps 89:49
is no remembrance of *f* things......... Eccl 1:11
What is the cause that the *f* days... Eccl 7:10
let them shew the *f* things......... Is 41:22
the *f* things are come to pass, and...... Is 42:9
declare this, and shew us *f* things... Is 43:9
Remember ye not the *f* things......... Is 43:18
Remember the *f* things of old......... Is 46:9
I have declared the *f* things from...... Is 48:3
shall raise up the *f* desolations...... Is 61:4
their *f* work into their bosom......... Is 65:7
because the *f* troubles are......... Is 65:16
the *f* shall not be remembered......... Is 65:17
God, that giveth rain, both the *f*... Jer 5:24
for he is the *f* of all things......... Jer 10:16
the *f* kings which were before......... Jer 34:5
write in it all the *f* words that...... Jer 36:28
for he is the *f* of all things......... Jer 51:19
shall return to their *f* estate......... Eze 16:55
shall return to their *f* estate......... Eze 16:55
shall return to your *f* estate......... Eze 16:55
a multitude greater than the *f*......... Dan 11:13
but it shall not be as the *f*......... Dan 11:29
latter and *f* rain upon the earth...... Hos 6:3
given you the *f* rain moderately...... Joel 2:23
the *f* rain, and the latter rain in... Joel 2:23
shall be greater than of the *f*......... Hag 2:9
unto whom the *f* prophets have......... Zec 1:4
LORD hath cried by the *f* prophets... Zec 7:7
in his spirit by the *f* prophets......... Zec 7:12
of this people as in the *f* days......... Zec 8:11
half of them toward the *f* sea......... Zec 14:8
the days of old, and as in *f* years... Mal 3:4
that *f* treatise have I made, O......... Acts 1:1
the *f* conversation the old man......... Eph 4:22
call to remembrance the *f* days......... Heb 10:32
to the *f* lusts in your ignorance...... 1Pet 1:14
for the *f* things are passed away... Rev 21:4

FORMETH
he that *f* the mountains, and......... Amos 4:13
f the spirit of man within him......... Zec 12:1

FORMS
in thereof, and all the *f* thereof......... Eze 43:11
thereof, and all the *f* thereof......... Eze 43:11

FORNICATION
of Jerusalem to commit *f*, and......... 2Chr 21:11
shall commit *f* with all the......... Is 23:17
f with the Egyptians thy......... Eze 16:26
thy *f* in the land of Canaan unto... Eze 16:29
wife, saving for the cause of *f*...... Mt 5:32
away his wife, except it be for *f*... Mt 19:9
they to him, We be not born of *f*... Jn 8:41
pollutions of idols, and from *f*...... Acts 15:20
from things strangled, and from *f*... Acts 15:29
and from strangled, and from *f*...... Acts 21:25
with all unrighteousness, *f*......... Rom 1:29
that there is *f* among you......... 1Cor 5:1
such *f* as is not so much as named... 1Cor 5:1
Now the body is not for *f*......... 1Cor 6:13
Flee *f*. Every sin that......... 1Cor 6:18
but he that committeth *f* sinneth... 1Cor 6:18
Nevertheless, to avoid *f*, let......... 1Cor 7:2
Neither let us commit *f*, as some... 1Cor 10:8
repented of the uncleanness and *f*... 2Cor 12:21
Adultery, *f*, uncleanness......... Gal 5:19
But all and uncleanness, or......... Eph 5:3
f, uncleanness, inordinate......... Col 3:5
that ye should abstain from *f*......... 1Th 4:3
giving themselves over to *f*......... Jude 7
unto idols, and to commit *f*......... Rev 2:14

to seduce my servants to commit f....... Rev 2:20
gave her space to repent of her f....... Rev 2:21
their sorceries, nor of their f........... Rev 9:21
of the wine of the wrath of her f......... Rev 14:8
of the earth have committed f........... Rev 17:2
made drunk with the wine of her f....... Rev 17:2
and filthiness of her f.................... Rev 17:4
of the wine of the wrath of her f......... Rev 18:3
earth have committed f with her......... Rev 18:3
the earth, who have committed f......... Rev 18:9
did corrupt the earth with her f.......... Rev 19:2

FORNICATIONS
pouredst out thy f on every one........ Eze 16:15
thoughts, murders, adulteries, f........ Mt 15:19
evil thoughts, adulteries, f............... Mk 7:21

FORNICATOR
that is called a brother be a f............ 1Cor 5:11
Lest there be any f, or profane......... Heb 12:16

FORNICATORS
an epistle not to company with f....... 1Cor 5:9
with the f of this world, or with......... 1Cor 5:10
neither f, nor idolaters, nor............. 1Cor 6:9

FORSAKE
he will not f thee, neither................ Deut 4:31
f not the Levite as long as thou........ Deut 12:19
thou shalt not f him.................... Deut 14:27
he will not fail thee, nor f thee......... Deut 31:6
not fail thee, neither f thee............ Deut 31:8
go to be among them, and will f me.... Deut 31:16
in that day, and I will f them........... Deut 31:17
I will not fail thee, nor f thee.......... Josh 1:5
forbid that we should f the LORD....... Josh 24:16
If ye f the LORD, and serve............. Josh 24:20
Should I f my sweetness, and my...... Judg 9:11
For the LORD will not f his.............. 1Sa 12:22
will not f my people Israel.............. 1Kin 6:13
let him not leave us, nor f us.......... 1Kin 8:57
I will f the remnant of mine........... 2Kin 21:14
but if thou f him, he will cast......... 1Chr 28:9
nor f thee, until thou hast........... 1Chr 28:20
f my statutes and my................. 2Chr 7:19
if ye f him, he will f you............... 2Chr 15:2
is against all them that f him......... Ezr 8:22
utterly consume them, nor f them..... Neh 9:31
we will not f the house of our......... Neh 10:39
if not, but keep it still............... Job 20:13
leave me not, neither f me............ Ps 27:9
When my father and my mother f me... Ps 27:10
Cease from anger, and f wrath........ Ps 37:8
f me not, O God....................... Ps 38:21
f me not when my strength faileth.... Ps 71:9
and greyheaded, O God, f me not..... Ps 71:18
If his children f my law, and walk..... Ps 89:30
neither will he f his inheritance...... Ps 94:14
O f me not utterly..................... Ps 119:8
of the wicked that f thy law........... Ps 119:53
f not the works of thine own.......... Ps 138:8
f not the law of thy mother........... Prov 1:8
Let not mercy and truth f thee....... Prov 3:3
good doctrine, f ye not my law........ Prov 4:2
f her not, and she shall preserve..... Prov 4:6
f not the law of thy mother........... Prov 6:20
F the foolish, and live................ Prov 9:6
and thy father's friend, f not......... Prov 27:10
They that f the law praise the........ Prov 28:4
they that f the LORD shall be......... Is 1:28
the God of Israel will not f them...... Is 41:17
I do unto them, and not f them....... Is 42:16
Let the wicked f his way, and the.... Is 55:7
But ye are they that f the LORD...... Is 65:11
all that f thee shall be ashamed..... Jer 17:13
I will even f you, saith the LORD..... Jer 23:33
forget you, and I will f you........... Jer 23:39
f her, and let us go every one........ Jer 51:9
us for ever, and f us so long time.... Lam 5:20
neither did they f the idols of........ Eze 20:8
them that f the holy covenant....... Dan 11:30
lying vanities f their own mercy...... Jonah 2:8
are among the Gentiles to f Moses.... Acts 21:21
will never leave thee, nor f thee...... Heb 13:5

FORSAKEN
doings, whereby thou hast f me....... Deut 28:20
Because they have f the covenant.... Deut 29:25
but now the LORD hath f us........... Judg 6:13
both because we have f our God...... Judg 10:10
Yet ye have f me, and served other... Judg 10:13
day, wherewith they have f me........ 1Sa 8:8
because we have f the LORD.......... 1Sa 12:10
Because that they have f me.......... 1Kin 11:33
house, in that ye have f the......... 1Kin 18:18
of Israel have f thy covenant........ 1Kin 19:10
of Israel have f thy covenant........ 1Kin 19:14
Because they have f me, and have... 2Kin 22:17
Thus saith the LORD, Ye have f me... 2Chr 12:5
is our God, and we have not f him.... 2Chr 13:10
but ye have f him..................... 2Chr 13:11
because he had f the LORD God of.... 2Chr 21:10
because ye have f the LORD.......... 2Chr 24:20
he hath also f you.................... 2Chr 24:20
because they had f the LORD God.... 2Chr 24:24
because they had f the LORD God.... 2Chr 28:6
the LORD our God, and have f him.... 2Chr 29:6
Because they have f me, and have.... 2Chr 34:25
God hath not f us in our bondage..... Ezr 9:9
for we have f thy commandments..... Ezr 9:10
said, Why is the house of God f...... Neh 13:11
shall the earth be f for thee.......... Job 18:4
hath oppressed and hath f the poor.. Job 20:19

hast not f them that seek thee........ Ps 9:10
God, my God, why hast thou f me..... Ps 22:1
have I not seen the righteous f....... Ps 37:25
Saying, God hath f him............... Ps 71:11
they have f the LORD, they have..... Is 1:4
Therefore hast thy people............ Is 2:6
shall be f of both her kings........... Is 7:16
The cities of Aroer are f.............. Is 17:2
his strong cities be as a f bough..... Is 17:9
be desolate, and the habitation f.... Is 27:10
Because the palaces shall be f....... Is 32:14
But Zion said, The LORD hath f me... Is 49:14
hath called thee as a woman f....... Is 54:6
For a small moment have I f thee.... Is 54:7
Whereas thou hast been f and hated. Is 60:15
Thou shalt no more be termed F...... Is 62:4
called, Sought out, A city not f...... Is 62:12
their wickedness, who have f me..... Jer 1:16
they have f me the fountain of....... Jer 2:13
that thou hast f the LORD thy God... Jer 2:17
that thou hast f the LORD thy God... Jer 2:19
every city shall be f, and not a....... Jer 4:29
thy children have f me, and sworn.... Jer 5:7
answer them, Like as ye have f me... Jer 5:19
f the generation of his wrath........ Jer 7:29
Because they have f my law which.... Jer 9:13
because we have f the land.......... Jer 9:19
I have f mine house, I have left...... Jer 12:7
Thou hast f me, saith the LORD...... Jer 15:6
Because your fathers have f me...... Jer 16:11
worshipped them, and have f me..... Jer 16:11
because they have f the LORD........ Jer 17:13
that come from another place be f... Jer 18:14
Because they have f me, and have... Jer 19:4
Because they have f the covenant... Jer 22:9
He hath f his covert, as the lion..... Jer 25:38
For Israel hath not been f........... Jer 51:5
the LORD hath f the earth........... Eze 8:12
say, The LORD hath f the earth...... Eze 9:9
and to the cities that are f.......... Eze 36:4
she is f upon her land............... Amos 5:2
For Gaza shall be f, and Ashkelon.... Zeph 2:4
unto him, Behold, we have f all...... Mt 19:27
And every one that hath f houses.... Mt 19:29
God, my God, why hast thou f me..... Mt 27:46
God, my God, why hast thou f me..... Mk 15:34
Persecuted, but not f................ 2Cor 4:9
For Demas hath f me, having loved... 2Ti 4:10
Which have f the right way, and..... 2Pet 2:15

FORSAKETH
but he f the fear of the Almighty..... Job 6:14
judgment, and f not his saints....... Ps 37:28
Which f the guide of her youth....... Prov 2:17
grievous unto him that f the way.... Prov 15:10
and f them shall have mercy........ Prov 28:13
you that f not all that he hath....... Lk 14:33

FORSAKING
there be a great f in the midst....... Is 6:12
Not f the assembling of ourselves... Heb 10:25

FORSOMUCH
f as he also is a son of Abraham..... Lk 19:9

FORSOOK
then he f God which made him, and. Deut 32:15
they f the LORD God of their......... Judg 2:12
they f the LORD, and served Baal.... Judg 2:13
f the LORD, and served not him...... Judg 10:6
they f the cities, and fled........... 1Sa 31:7
Because they f the LORD their God... 1Kin 9:9
But he f the counsel of the old...... 1Kin 12:8
f the old men's counsel that they... 1Kin 12:13
he f the LORD God of his fathers..... 2Kin 21:22
then they f their cities, and fled.... 1Chr 10:7
Because they f the LORD God of...... 2Chr 7:22
But he f the counsel which the...... 2Chr 10:8
king Rehoboam f the counsel of...... 2Chr 10:13
he f the law of the LORD, and all.... 2Chr 12:1
So that he f the tabernacle of...... Ps 78:60
but I f not thy precepts............ Ps 119:87
f not the ordinance of their God.... Is 58:2
f it, because there was no grass.... Jer 14:5
Then all the disciples f him........ Mt 26:56
And straightway they f their nets... Mk 1:18
And they all f him, and fled........ Mk 14:50
their ships to land, they f all...... Lk 5:11
stood with me, but all men f me..... 2Ti 4:16
By faith he f Egypt, not fearing..... Heb 11:27

FORSOOKEST
of great kindness, and f them not... Neh 9:17
f them not in the wilderness........ Neh 9:19

FORSWEAR
time, Thou shalt not f thyself....... Mt 5:33

FORT
So David dwelt in the f, and......... 2Sa 5:9
the fortress of the high f of thy..... Is 25:12
build a f against it, and cast a...... Eze 4:2
to cast a mount, and to build a f.... Eze 17:17
and he shall make a f against thee.. Eze 26:8
face toward the f of thine own land. Dan 11:19

FORTH See PREFACE.

FORTHWITH
f expences be given unto these...... Ezr 6:8
f they sprung up, because they...... Mt 13:5
f he came to Jesus, and said, Hail... Mt 26:49
f, when they were come out of the... Mk 1:29
charged him, and f sent him away... Mk 1:43

And f Jesus gave them leave......... Mk 5:13
f came there out blood and water... Jn 19:34
and he received sight f, and arose,.. Acts 9:18
f the angel departed from him....... Acts 12:10
and f the doors were shut........... Acts 21:30

FORTIETH
in the f year after the children...... Num 33:38
And it came to pass in the f year... Deut 1:3
In the f year of the reign of........ 1Chr 26:31
in one one and f year of his reign.... 2Chr 16:13

FORTIFIED
he f the strong holds, and put....... 2Chr 11:11
turning of the wall, and f them...... 2Chr 26:9
they f Jerusalem unto the broad..... Neh 3:8
Assyria, and from the f cities....... Mic 7:12

FORTIFY
they f the city against thee......... Judg 9:31
will they f themselves.............. Neh 4:2
have ye broken down to f the wall... Is 22:10
though she should f the height of... Jer 51:53
strong, f thy power mightily........ Nah 2:1
for the siege, f thy strong holds.... Nah 3:14

FORTRESS
The LORD is my rock, and my f....... 2Sa 22:2
The LORD is my rock, and my f....... Ps 18:2
For thou art my rock and my f....... Ps 31:3
me, for thou art my rock and my f... Ps 71:3
the LORD, He is my refuge and my f.. Ps 91:2
My goodness, and my f.............. Ps 144:2
The f also shall cease from......... Is 17:3
the f of the high fort of thy......... Is 25:12
a f among my people, that thou..... Jer 6:27
the land, O inhabitant of the f..... Jer 10:17
O LORD, my strength, and my f...... Jer 16:19
shalt enter into the f of the....... Dan 11:7
and be stirred up, even to his f...... Dan 11:10
spoiled shall come against the f.... Amos 5:9
from the f even to the river, and.... Mic 7:12

FORTRESSES
and brambles in the f thereof....... Is 34:13
all thy f shall be spoiled, as....... Hos 10:14

FORTS
they built f against it round....... 2Kin 25:1
and I will raise f against thee...... Is 29:3
the f and towers shall be forts..... Is 32:14
built f against it round about...... Eze 21:22
casting up mounts, and building f... Eze 17:17
and they that be in the f........... Eze 33:27

FORTUNATUS (for-chu-na'-tus) A Christian
acquaintance of Paul.
of the coming of Stephanas and F.... 1Cor 16:17
from Philippi by Stephanas, and F.... 1Cor s

FORTY
f years, and begat sons and........ Gen 5:13
it to rain upon the earth f days..... Gen 7:4
the earth f days and f nights....... Gen 7:4
the earth f days of nights.......... Gen 7:12
the flood was f days upon the...... Gen 7:17
came to pass at the end of f days... Gen 8:6
And he said, If I find there f....... Gen 18:28
there shall be f found there....... Gen 18:29
Isaac was f years old when he...... Gen 25:20
Esau was f years old when he took... Gen 26:34
f kine, and ten bulls, twenty she... Gen 32:15
age of Jacob was an hundred f...... Gen 47:28
f days were fulfilled for him....... Gen 50:3
of Israel did eat manna f years.... Ex 16:35
the mount f days and f nights..... Ex 24:18
thou shalt make f sockets of...... Ex 26:19
their f sockets of silver........... Ex 26:21
the LORD f days and f nights...... Ex 34:28
f sockets of silver he made under.. Ex 36:24
their f sockets of silver.......... Ex 36:26
of years shall be unto thee f...... Lev 25:8
of the tribe of Reuben, were f..... Num 1:21
even of the tribe of Gad, were f.... Num 1:25
were f thousand and five hundred.. Num 1:33
of the tribe of Asher, were f...... Num 1:41
were numbered thereof, were f.... Num 2:11
were numbered of them, were f.... Num 2:15
were f thousand and five hundred.. Num 2:19
were numbered of them, were f.... Num 2:28
of the land after f days.......... Num 13:25
wander in the wilderness f years.. Num 14:33
ye searched the land, even f days.. Num 14:34
even f years, and ye shall know my. Num 14:34
that were numbered of them were f. Num 26:7
f thousand and five hundred...... Num 26:18
that were numbered of them were f. Num 26:41
that were numbered of them were f. Num 26:50
wander in the wilderness f years... Num 32:13
and to them ye shall add f........ Num 35:6
give to the Levites shall be f..... Num 35:7
these f years the LORD thy God.... Deut 2:7
these f years in the wilderness.... Deut 8:2
did thy foot swell, these f years... Deut 8:4
then I abode in the mount f days... Deut 9:9
f nights, I neither did eat bread... Deut 9:9
came to pass at the end of f days... Deut 9:11
f nights, that the LORD gave me.... Deut 9:11
the first, f days and f nights...... Deut 9:18
fell down before the LORD f days... Deut 9:25
f nights, as I fell down at the..... Deut 9:25
time, f days and f nights.......... Deut 10:10
If stripes he may give him, and not. Deut 25:3
I have led you f years in the....... Deut 29:5

About f thousand prepared for war...... Josh 4:13
walked f years in the wilderness...... Josh 5:6
F years old was I when Moses the ...... Josh 14:7
me alive, as he said, these f ...... Josh 14:10
of the children of Israel were f...... Josh 21:41
And the land had rest f years ...... Judg 3:11
seen among f thousand in Israel ...... Judg 5:8
And the land had rest f years ...... Judg 5:31
f years in the days of Gideon ...... Judg 8:28
at that time of the Ephraimites f...... Judg 12:6
And he had f sons and thirty ...... Judg 12:14
hand of the Philistines f years...... Judg 13:1
And he had judged Israel f years 1Sa 4:18
and presented himself f days 1Sa 17:16
was f years old when he began to...... 2Sa 2:10
to reign, and he reigned f years...... 2Sa 5:4
f thousand horsemen, and smote...... 2Sa 10:18
And it came to pass after f years 2Sa 15:7
reigned over Israel were f years 1Kin 2:11
Solomon had f thousand stalls of 1Kin 4:26
before it, was f cubits long 1Kin 6:17
that lay on f five pillars...... 1Kin 7:3
one laver contained f baths 1Kin 7:38
over all Israel was f years...... 1Kin 11:42
Rehoboam was f and one years old...... 1Kin 14:21
And f and one years reigned he in...... 1Kin 15:10
the strength of that meat f days...... 1Kin 19:8
f nights unto Horeb the mount of 1Kin 19:8
bears out of the wood, and tare...... 2Kin 2:24
f camels' burden, and came and 2Kin 8:9
shearing house, even two and f men 2Kin 10:14
f years reigned he in Jerusalem...... 2Kin 12:1
to reign in Samaria, and reigned f...... 2Kin 14:23
f thousand seven hundred and 1Chr 5:18
battle, expert in war, f thousand...... 1Chr 12:36
f thousand footmen, and killed...... 1Chr 19:18
reigned over Israel was f years...... 1Chr 29:27
Jerusalem over all Israel f years...... 2Chr 9:30
f years old when he began to...... 2Chr 12:13
F and two years old was Ahaziah...... 2Chr 22:2
he reigned f years in Jerusalem...... 2Chr 24:1
children of Zattu, nine hundred f ...... Ezr 2:8
children of Bani, six hundred f ...... Ezr 2:10
The children of Azmaveth, f...... Ezr 2:24
and Beeroth, seven hundred and f ...... Ezr 2:25
of Jericho, three hundred f ...... Ezr 2:34
Pashur, a thousand two hundred f ...... Ezr 2:38
whole congregation together was f...... Ezr 2:64
their mules, two hundred f ...... Ezr 2:66
beside f shekels of silver...... Neh 5:15
of Zattu, eight hundred f...... Neh 7:13
children of Binnui, six hundred f ...... Neh 7:15
The men of Beth-azmaveth, f...... Neh 7:28
and Beeroth, seven hundred f ...... Neh 7:29
of Jericho, three hundred f ...... Neh 7:36
Pashur, a thousand two hundred f ...... Neh 7:41
children of Asaph, an hundred f...... Neh 7:44
children of Nekoda, six hundred f...... Neh 7:62
whole congregation together was f...... Neh 7:66
and they had two hundred f ...... Neh 7:67
their mules, two hundred f ...... Neh 7:68
f years didst thou sustain them ...... Neh 9:21
of the fathers, two hundred f ...... Neh 11:13
f years, and saw his sons and his...... Job 42:16
F years and I grieved with...... Ps 95:10
of the Jews seven hundred f...... Jer 52:30
of the house of Judah f days...... Eze 4:6
shall it be inhabited f years...... Eze 29:11
waste shall be desolate f years...... Eze 29:12
At the end of f years will I ...... Eze 29:13
the length thereof, f cubits ...... Eze 41:2
courts joined of f cubits long...... Eze 46:22
led you f years through the ...... Amos 2:10
in the wilderness f years ...... Amos 5:25
Yet f days, and Nineveh shall be ...... Jonah 3:4
And when he had fasted f days...... Mt 4:2
f nights, he was afterward an ...... Mt 4:2
there in the wilderness f days...... Mk 1:13
Being f days tempted of the devil ...... Lk 4:2
Then said the Jews, F and six...... Jn 2:20
proofs, being seen of them f days...... Acts 1:3
For the man was above f years old...... Acts 4:22
And when he was full f years old...... Acts 7:23
when f years were expired, there...... Acts 7:30
sea, and in the wilderness f years...... Acts 7:36
of f years in the wilderness ...... Acts 7:42
about the time of f years...... Acts 13:18
Benjamin, by the space of f years...... Acts 13:21
they were more than f which had ...... Acts 23:13
for him of them more than f men ...... Acts 23:21
received I f stripes save one...... 2Cor 11:24
me, and saw my works f years...... Heb 3:9
with whom was he grieved f years...... Heb 3:17
there were sealed an hundred and f...... Rev 7:4
shall they tread under foot f...... Rev 11:2
was given unto him to continue f...... Rev 13:5
Sion, and with him an hundred f...... Rev 14:1
that song but the hundred and f...... Rev 14:3
the wall thereof, an hundred and f...... Rev 21:17

FORTY'S
said, I will not do it for f sake...... Gen 18:29

FORUM
came to meet us as far as Appii f...... Acts 28:15

FORWARD
man waxed great, and went f...... Gen 26:13
of Israel, that they go f...... Ex 14:15
And when the tabernacle setteth f...... Num 1:51
of the congregation shall set f...... Num 2:17
they encamp, so shall they set f...... Num 2:17

they shall go f in the third rank...... Num 2:24
their standards, and so they set f...... Num 2:34
And when the camp setteth f ...... Num 4:5
as the camp is to set f...... Num 4:15
lie on the east parts shall go f ...... Num 10:5
And the sons of Merari set f...... Num 10:17
set f according to their armies...... Num 10:18
And the Kohathites set f, bearing...... Num 10:21
set f according to their armies...... Num 10:22
camp of the children of Dan set f...... Num 10:25
to their armies, when they set f...... Num 10:28
came to pass, when the ark set f ...... Num 10:35
And the children of Israel set f ...... Num 21:10
And the children of Israel set f ...... Num 22:1
them on yonder side Jordan, or f...... Num 32:19
that was with him, rushed f...... Judg 9:44
shalt thou go on f from thence...... 1Sa 10:3
came upon David from that day f...... 1Sa 16:13
eyed David from that day and f...... 1Sa 18:9
And it was so from that day f...... 1Sa 30:25
but they went f smiting the 2Kin 3:24
to her servant, Drive, and go f...... 2Kin 4:24
shall the shadow go f ten degrees...... 2Kin 20:9
four thousand were to set f the...... 1Chr 23:4
of the Kohathites, to set it f...... 2Chr 34:12
to set f the work of the house of...... Ezr 3:8
to set f the workmen in the house...... Ezr 3:9
Behold, I go f, but he is not...... Job 23:8
they set f my calamity, they have...... Job 30:13
heart, and went backward, and not f...... Jer 7:24
they went every one straight f...... Eze 1:9
And they went every one straight f...... Eze 1:12
they went every one straight f...... Eze 10:22
Lord their God from that day and f...... Eze 39:22
that upon the eighth day, and so f...... Eze 43:27
they helped f the affliction ...... Zec 1:15
he went f a little, and fell on...... Mk 14:35
multitude, the Jews putting him f ...... Acts 19:33
do, but also to be f a year ago 2Cor 8:10
but being more f of his own 2Cor 8:17
the same which I also was f to do ...... Gal 2:10
whom if thou bring f on their...... 3Jn 6

FORWARDNESS
by occasion of the f of others 2Cor 8:8
For I know the f of your mind 2Cor 9:2

FOUGHT
f with Israel in Rephidim ...... Ex 17:8
had said to him, and f with Amalek ...... Ex 17:10
then he f against Israel, and took...... Num 21:1
to Jahaz, and f against Israel...... Num 21:23
who had f against the former king...... Num 21:26
for the LORD for Israel...... Josh 10:14
unto Libnah, and f against Libnah...... Josh 10:31
against it, and f against it ...... Josh 10:31
against it, and f against it ...... Josh 10:34
to Debir, and f against it...... Josh 10:38
Lord God of Israel f for Israel ...... Josh 10:42
God is he that hath f for you...... Josh 23:3
and they f with you ...... Josh 24:8
the men of Jericho f against you...... Josh 24:11
they f against him, and they slew ...... Judg 1:5
of Judah f against Jerusalem...... Judg 1:8
The kings came and f...... Judg 5:19
then f the kings of Canaan in ...... Judg 5:19
They f from heaven...... Judg 5:20
in their courses f against Sisera...... Judg 5:20
(For my father f for you, and...... Judg 9:17
of Shechem, and f with Abimelech...... Judg 9:39
Abimelech f against the city all ...... Judg 9:45
f against it, and went hard unto...... Judg 9:52
in Jahaz, and f against Israel ...... Judg 11:20
men of Gilead, and f with Ephraim ...... Judg 12:4
And the Philistines f, and Israel...... 1Sa 4:10
of Moab, and they f against them...... 1Sa 14:47
f against all his enemies on 1Sa 14:47
f with the Philistines, and slew 1Sa 19:8
f with the Philistines, and...... 1Sa 23:5
the Philistines f against Israel 1Sa 31:1
no more, neither f they any more 2Sa 2:28
him, because he had f against 2Sa 8:10
against David, and f with him...... 2Sa 10:17
the city went out, and f with Joab...... 2Sa 11:17
Joab f against Rabbah of the 2Sa 12:26
f against Rabbah, and have 2Sa 12:27
and f against it, and took it 2Sa 12:29
f against the Philistines...... 2Sa 21:15
when he f against Hazael king of...... 2Kin 8:29
when he f with Hazael king of 2Kin 9:15
f against Gath, and took it 2Kin 12:17
his might wherewith he f against...... 2Kin 13:12
how he f with Amaziah king of...... 2Kin 14:15
the Philistines f against Israel 1Chr 10:1
him, because he had f against 1Chr 18:10
the Syrians, they f with him...... 1Chr 19:17
thousand men which f in chariots 1Chr 19:18
they had heard that the LoRD f 2Chr 20:29
when he f with Hazael king of 2Chr 22:6
He f also with the king of the 2Chr 27:5
f against me without a cause...... Ps 109:3
f against Ashdod, and took in ...... Is 20:1
their enemy, and he f against them ...... Is 63:10
f against Jerusalem, and against...... Jer 34:1
f against Jerusalem, and ...... Jer 34:7
as when he f in the day of battle ...... Zec 14:3
that have f against Jerusalem ...... Zec 14:12
I have f with beasts at Ephesus...... 1Cor 15:32
I have f a good fight, I have...... 2Ti 4:7
his angels f against the dragon...... Rev 12:7

and the dragon f and his angels,...... Rev 12:7

FOUL
My face is f with weeping, and on ...... Job 16:16
but ye must f the residue with...... Eze 34:18
It will be f weather to day...... Mt 16:3
together, he rebuked the f spirit ...... Mk 9:25
and the hold of every f spirit ...... Rev 18:2

FOULED
which ye have f with your feet...... Eze 34:19

FOULEDST
with thy feet, and f their rivers ...... Eze 32:2

FOUND
was not f an help meet for him ...... Gen 2:20
But Noah f grace in the eyes of ...... Gen 6:8
But the dove f no rest for the ...... Gen 8:9
that they f a plain in the land ...... Gen 11:2
the angel of the LORD f her by a...... Gen 16:7
if now I have f favour in thy...... Gen 18:3
there shall be forty f there ...... Gen 18:29
there shall thirty be f there...... Gen 18:30
there shall be twenty f there...... Gen 18:31
Peradventure ten shall be f there ...... Gen 18:32
thy servant hath f grace in thy...... Gen 19:19
f there a well of springing water ...... Gen 26:19
and said unto him, We have f water ...... Gen 26:32
it that thou hast f it so quickly...... Gen 27:20
f mandrakes in the field, and...... Gen 30:14
if I have f favour in thine eyes,...... Gen 30:27
but he f them not ...... Gen 31:33
all the tent, but f them not...... Gen 31:34
he searched, but f not the images ...... Gen 31:35
what hast thou f of all thy...... Gen 31:37
if now I have f grace in thy ...... Gen 33:10
this was that Anah that f the...... Gen 36:24
And a certain man f him, and...... Gen 37:15
his brethren, and f them in Dothan...... Gen 37:17
and said, This have we f ...... Gen 37:32
but he f her not...... Gen 38:20
this kid, and thou hast not f her ...... Gen 38:23
Joseph f grace in his sight, and ...... Gen 39:4
which we f in our sacks' mouths,...... Gen 44:8
of thy servants it be f, both let...... Gen 44:9
he with whom it is f shall be my ...... Gen 44:10
the cup was f in Benjamin's sack...... Gen 44:12
God hath f out the iniquity of...... Gen 44:16
and he also with whom the cup is f...... Gen 44:16
man in whose hand the cup is f...... Gen 44:17
that was f in the land of Egypt...... Gen 47:14
If now I have f grace in thy...... Gen 47:29
if now I have f grace in your...... Gen 50:4
which shall be f in the field...... Ex 19:19
be no leaven f in your houses...... Ex 12:19
in the wilderness, and f no water...... Ex 15:22
day for to gather, and they f none...... Ex 16:27
him, or if he be f in his hand ...... Ex 21:16
If a thief be f breaking up...... Ex 22:2
be certainly f in his hand alive...... Ex 22:4
if the thief be f, let him pay...... Ex 22:7
If the thief be not f, then the ...... Ex 22:8
thou hast also f grace in my ...... Ex 33:12
if I have f grace in thy sight,...... Ex 33:13
thy people have f grace in thy ...... Ex 33:16
for thou hast f grace in my sight ...... Ex 33:17
If now I have f grace in thy...... Ex 34:9
every man, with whom was f blue...... Ex 35:23
with whom was f shittim wood for ...... Ex 35:24
Or have f that which was lost, and...... Lev 6:3
or the lost thing which he f ...... Lev 6:4
have I not f favour in thy sight...... Num 11:11
if I have f favour in thy sight...... Num 11:15
they f a man that gathered sticks...... Num 15:32
they that f him gathering sticks...... Num 15:33
if we have f grace in thy sight,...... Num 32:5
If there be f among you, within...... Deut 17:2
There shall not be f among you...... Deut 18:10
that all the people that is f...... Deut 20:11
If one be f slain in the land...... Deut 21:1
he hath lost, and thou hast f ...... Deut 22:3
I came to her, I f her not a maid...... Deut 22:14
I f not thy daughter a maid ...... Deut 22:17
virginity be not f for the damsel...... Deut 22:20
If a man be f lying with a woman...... Deut 22:22
For he f her in the field, and the...... Deut 22:27
and lie with her, and they be f...... Deut 22:28
his eyes, because he hath f some ...... Deut 24:1
if a man be f stealing any of his ...... Deut 24:7
He f him in a desert land, and in ...... Deut 32:10
shall be f liars unto thee ...... Deut 33:29
all the way, but f them not...... Josh 2:22
The five kings are f hid in a ...... Josh 10:17
they f Adoni-bezek in Bezek...... Judg 1:5
If now I have f grace in thy...... Judg 6:17
ye had not f out my riddle...... Judg 14:18
he f a new jawbone of an ass, and ...... Judg 15:15
they f among the inhabitants of...... Judg 21:12
Why have I f grace in thine eyes,...... Ruth 2:10
of Shalisha, but they f them not...... 1Sa 9:4
Benjamites, but they f them not...... 1Sa 9:4
they f young maidens going out to 1Sa 9:11
for they are f...... 1Sa 9:20
which thou wentest to seek are f 1Sa 10:16
us plainly that the asses were f...... 1Sa 10:16
sought him, he could not be f 1Sa 10:21
ye have not f ought in my hand...... 1Sa 12:5
Now there was no smith f...... 1Sa 13:19
spear f in the hand of any of the 1Sa 13:22
with Jonathan his son was there f 1Sa 13:22
of their enemies which they f...... 1Sa 14:30

for he hath *f* favour in my sight 1Sa 16:22
that I have *f* grace in thine eyes 1Sa 20:3
if I have *f* favour in thine eyes, ... 1Sa 20:29
evil hath not been *f* in thee all 1Sa 25:28
If I have now *f* grace in thine 1Sa 27:5
I have *f* no fault in him since he 1Sa 29:3
for I have not *f* evil in thee 1Sa 29:6
what hast thou *f* in thy servant 1Sa 29:8
they *f* an Egyptian in the field, ... 1Sa 30:11
strip the slain, that they *f* Saul 1Sa 31:8
f in his heart to pray this 2Sa 7:27
that I have *f* grace in thy sight 2Sa 14:22
in some place where he shall be *f* 2Sa 17:12
be not one small stone *f* there 2Sa 17:13
f Abishag a Shunammite, and 1Kin 1:3
if wickedness shall be *f* in him 1Kin 1:52
was the weight of the brass *f* out 1Kin 7:47
Hadad *f* great favour in the sight 1Kin 11:19
the Shilonite *f* him in the way 1Kin 11:29
f him sitting under an oak 1Kin 13:14
f his carcase cast in the way, and 1Kin 13:24
because in him there is *f* some 1Kin 14:13
and nation, that they *f* thee not 1Kin 18:10
f Elisha the son of Shaphat, who 1Kin 19:19
departed from him, a lion *f* him 1Kin 20:36
Then he *f* another man, and said, ... 1Kin 20:37
said to Elijah, Hast thou *f* me 1Kin 21:20
And he answered, I have *f* thee 1Kin 21:20
sought three days, but *f* him not 2Kin 2:17
a wild vine, and gathered 2Kin 4:39
but they *f* no more of her than 2Kin 9:35
wheresoever any breach shall be *f* 2Kin 12:5
told the money that was *f* in the 2Kin 12:10
all the gold that was *f* in the 2Kin 12:18
were *f* in the house of the LORD 2Kin 14:14
gold that was *f* in the house of 2Kin 16:8
the king of Assyria *f* conspiracy 2Kin 17:4
was *f* in the house of the LORD 2Kin 18:15
the king of Assyria warring 2Kin 19:8
all that was *f* in his treasures 2Kin 20:13
I have *f* the book of the law in 2Kin 22:8
the money that was *f* in the house 2Kin 22:9
the words of this book that is *f* 2Kin 22:13
was *f* in the house of the LORD 2Kin 23:2
priest *f* in the house of the LORD 2Kin 23:24
which were *f* in the city, and the 2Kin 25:19
the land that were *f* in the city, ... 2Kin 25:19
they *f* fat pasture and good, and 1Chr 4:40
the habitations that were *f* there 1Chr 4:41
strip the slain, that they *f* Saul 1Chr 10:8
therefore thy servant hath *f* in 1Chr 17:25
f it to weigh a talent of gold, ... 1Chr 20:2
there were more chief men *f* 1Chr 24:4
there were *f* among them mighty 1Chr 26:31
seek him, he will be *f* of thee 1Chr 28:9
f gave them to the treasure of 1Chr 29:8
they were *f* an hundred and fifty 2Chr 2:17
of the brass could not be *f* out 2Chr 4:18
ye seek him, he will be *f* of you 2Chr 15:2
and sought him, he was *f* of them 2Chr 15:4
and he was *f* of them 2Chr 15:15
there are good things *f* in thee 2Chr 19:3
they *f* among them in abundance 2Chr 20:25
that was *f* in the king's house 2Chr 21:17
the princes of Judah, and the 2Chr 22:8
f them three hundred thousand 2Chr 25:5
were *f* in the house of God with 2Chr 29:16
all the uncleanness that they *f* 2Chr 29:16
Hilkiah the priest *f* a book of 2Chr 34:14
I have *f* the book of the law in 2Chr 34:15
was *f* in the house of the LORD 2Chr 34:17
the words of the book that is *f* 2Chr 34:21
was *f* in the house of the LORD 2Chr 34:30
did, and that which was *f* in him 2Chr 36:8
by genealogy, but they were not *f* .... Ezr 2:62
it is *f* that this city of old .... Ezr 4:19
there was *f* at Achmetha, in the .... Ezr 6:2
f there none of the sons of Levi .... Ezr 8:15
f that had taken strange wives .... Ezr 10:18
have *f* favour in thy sight .... Neh 2:5
peace, and *f* nothing to answer .... Neh 5:8
If a register of the genealogy .... Neh 7:5
the first, and *f* written therein, ... Neh 7:5
by genealogy, but it was not *f* .... Neh 7:64
they *f* written in the law which .... Neh 8:14
and therein was *f* written, that .... Neh 13:1
made of the matter, it was *f* out .... Est 2:23
If I have *f* favour in the sight .... Est 5:8
it was *f* written, that Mordecai .... Est 6:2
If I have *f* favour in thy sight, ... Est 7:3
if I have *f* favour in his sight, ... Est 8:5
the root of the matter is *f* in me .... Job 19:28
as a dream, and shall not be *f* .... Job 20:8
But where shall wisdom be *f* .... Job 28:12
neither is it *f* in the land of .... Job 28:13
lifted up myself when evil *f* him .... Job 31:29
because they had *f* no answer .... Job 32:3
should say, We have *f* out wisdom .... Job 32:13
I have *f* a ransom .... Job 33:24
in all the land were no women *f* .... Job 42:15
in a time when thou mayest be *f* .... Ps 32:6
his iniquity be *f* to be hateful .... Ps 36:2
sought him, but he could not be *f* .... Ps 37:36
and for comforters, but I *f* none .... Ps 69:20
men of might have *f* their hands .... Ps 76:5
Yea, the sparrow hath *f* an house .... Ps 84:3
I have *f* David my servant .... Ps 89:20
they *f* no city to dwell in .... Ps 107:4
I *f* trouble and sorrow .... Ps 116:3
we *f* it in the fields of the wood .... Ps 132:6

But if he be *f*, he shall restore .... Prov 6:31
seek thy face, and I have *f* thee .... Prov 7:15
hath understanding wisdom is *f* .... Prov 10:13
glory, if it be *f* in the way of .... Prov 16:31
when thou hast *f* it, then there .... Prov 24:14
Hast thou *f* honey .... Prov 25:16
reprove thee, and thou be *f* a liar .... Prov 30:6
curse thee, and thou be *f* guilty .... Prov 30:10
Behold, this have I *f*, saith the .... Eccl 7:27
one man among a thousand have I *f* .... Eccl 7:28
among all those have I not *f* .... Eccl 7:28
Lo, this only have I *f*, that God .... Eccl 7:29
Now there was *f* in it a poor wise .... Eccl 9:15
I sought him, but I *f* him not .... Song 3:1
I sought him, but I *f* him not .... Song 3:2
that go about the city *f* me .... Song 3:3
but I *f* him whom my soul loveth .... Song 3:4
that went about the city *f* me .... Song 5:7
in his eyes as one that *f* favour .... Song 8:10
As my hand hath *f* the kingdoms of .... Is 10:10
my hand hath *f* as a nest the .... Is 10:14
Every one that is *f* shall be .... Is 13:15
all that are *f* in thee are bound .... Is 22:3
so that there shall not be *f* in, ... Is 30:14
thereon, it shall not be *f* there .... Is 35:9
the king of Assyria warring .... Is 37:8
all that was *f* in his treasures .... Is 39:2
and gladness shall be *f* therein, ... Is 51:3
ye the LORD while he may be *f* .... Is 55:6
thou hast *f* the life of thine .... Is 57:10
I am *f* of them that sought me not .... Is 65:1
the new wine is *f* in the cluster .... Is 65:8
have your fathers *f* in me .... Jer 2:5
the thief is ashamed when he is *f* .... Jer 2:26
Also in thy skirts is *f* the blood .... Jer 2:34
I have not *f* it by secret search, ... Jer 2:34
among my people are *f* wicked men .... Jer 5:26
A conspiracy is *f* among the men .... Jer 11:9
came to the pits, and *f* no water .... Jer 14:3
Thy words were *f*, and I did eat .... Jer 15:16
house have I *f* their wickedness .... Jer 23:11
And I will be *f* of you, saith the .... Jer 29:14
sword *f* grace in the wilderness .... Jer 31:2
the Chaldeans that were *f* there .... Jer 41:3
But ten men were *f* among them .... Jer 41:8
f him by the great waters that .... Jer 41:12
was *f* among thieves .... Jer 48:27
All that *f* them have devoured .... Jer 50:7
of Judah, and they shall not be *f* .... Jer 50:20
thou art *f*, and also caught, ... Jer 50:24
person, which were *f* in the city, ... Jer 52:25
that were *f* in the midst of the .... Jer 52:25
we have *f*, we have seen it .... Lam 2:16
not destroy it: but I *f* none .... Eze 22:30
till iniquity was *f* in thee .... Eze 28:15
them all was *f* none like Daniel .... Dan 1:19
he *f* them ten times better than .... Dan 1:20
I have *f* a man of the captives of .... Dan 2:25
that no place was *f* for them .... Dan 2:35
wisdom of the gods, was *f* in him .... Dan 5:11
were *f* in the same Daniel, whom .... Dan 5:12
and excellent wisdom is *f* in thee .... Dan 5:14
in the balances, and art *f* wanting .... Dan 5:27
there any error or fault *f* in him .... Dan 6:4
f Daniel praying and making, ... Dan 6:11
before him innocency was *f* in me .... Dan 6:22
no manner of hurt was *f* upon him .... Dan 6:23
stumble and fall, and not be *f* .... Dan 11:19
shall be *f* written in the book, ... Dan 12:1
I *f* Israel like grapes in the .... Hos 9:10
now shall they be *f* faulty .... Hos 10:2
f him in Beth-el, and there he .... Hos 12:4
I have *f* me out substance .... Hos 12:8
From me is thy fruit *f* .... Hos 14:8
he *f* a ship going to Tarshish .... Jonah 1:3
of Israel were *f* in thee .... Mic 1:13
tongue be *f* in their mouth .... Zeph 3:13
and place shall not be *f* for them .... Zec 10:10
and iniquity was not *f* in his lips .... Mal 2:6
she was *f* with child of the Holy .... Mt 1:18
and when ye have *f* him, bring me .... Mt 2:8
I have not *f* so great faith, no, ... Mt 8:10
the which when a man hath *f* .... Mt 13:44
when he had *f* one pearl of great .... Mt 13:46
f one of his fellowservants, ... Mt 18:28
f others standing idle, and saith .... Mt 20:6
f nothing thereon, but leaves .... Mt 21:19
together all as many as they *f* .... Mt 22:10
And he came and *f* them asleep again .... Mt 26:40
But *f* none: yea, though .... Mt 26:60
witnesses came, yet *f* they none .... Mt 26:60
they *f* a man of Cyrene, Simon by .... Mt 27:32
And when they had *f* him, they said .... Mk 1:37
unwashen, hands, they *f* fault .... Mk 7:2
she *f* the devil gone out, and her .... Mk 7:30
the colt tied by the door .... Mk 11:4
to it, he *f* nothing but leaves .... Mk 11:13
f as he had said unto them .... Mk 11:4
he *f* them asleep again, (for .... Mk 14:40
and *f* none .... Mk 14:55
for thou hast *f* favour with God .... Lk 1:30
f Mary, and Joseph, and the babe .... Lk 2:16
And when they *f* him not, they .... Lk 2:45
days they *f* him in the temple .... Lk 2:46
the which when a man hath *f* .... Lk 4:17
I have not *f* so great faith, no, ... Lk 7:9
the servant whole that had been .... Lk 7:10
f the man, out of whom the devils .... Lk 8:35
voice was past, Jesus was *f* alone .... Lk 9:36

sought fruit thereon, and *f* none .... Lk 13:6
And when he hath *f* it, he layeth .... Lk 15:5
for I have *f* my sheep which was .... Lk 15:6
And when she hath *f* it, she .... Lk 15:9
for I have *f* the piece which I .... Lk 15:9
he was lost, and is *f* .... Lk 15:24
and was lost, and is *f* .... Lk 15:32
There are not *f* that returned to .... Lk 17:18
f even as he had said unto them .... Lk 19:32
f as he had said unto them .... Lk 22:13
he *f* them sleeping for sorrow, ... Lk 22:45
We *f* this fellow perverting the .... Lk 23:2
have *f* no fault in this man .... Lk 23:14
I have *f* no cause of death in him .... Lk 23:22
they *f* the stone rolled away from .... Lk 24:2
f not the body of the Lord Jesus .... Lk 24:3
when they *f* not his body, they .... Lk 24:23
it even so as the women had .... Lk 24:24
the eleven gathered together .... Lk 24:33
We have *f* the Messias, which is, ... Jn 1:41
and saith unto him, We have *f* him .... Jn 1:45
f in the temple those that sold .... Jn 2:14
when they had *f* him on the other .... Jn 6:25
and when he had *f* him, he said .... Jn 9:35
he *f* that he had lain in the .... Jn 11:17
Jesus, when he had *f* a young ass .... Jn 12:14
f her dead, and, carrying her .... Acts 5:10
f them not in the prison, they .... Acts 5:22
The prison truly *f* we shut with .... Acts 5:23
we had opened, we *f* no man within .... Acts 5:23
lest haply ye be *f* even to fight .... Acts 5:39
our fathers *f* no sustenance .... Acts 7:11
Who *f* favour before God, and .... Acts 7:46
But Philip was *f* at Azotus .... Acts 8:40
that if he *f* any of this way .... Acts 9:2
there he *f* a certain man named .... Acts 9:33
many that were come together .... Acts 10:27
And when he had *f* him, he brought .... Acts 11:26
f him not, he examined the .... Acts 12:19
they *f* a certain sorcerer, a .... Acts 13:6
I have *f* David the son of Jesse, ... Acts 13:22
though they *f* no cause of death .... Acts 13:28
And when they *f* them not, they .... Acts 17:6
devotions, I *f* an altar with this .... Acts 17:23
f a certain Jew named Aquila, ... Acts 18:2
f it fifty thousand pieces of .... Acts 19:19
For we have *f* this man a .... Acts 24:5
they neither *f* me in the temple .... Acts 24:12
certain Jews from Asia *f* me .... Acts 24:18
if they have *f* any evil doing in .... Acts 24:20
But when I *f* that he had .... Acts 25:25
there the centurion *f* a ship of .... Acts 27:6
sounded, and *f* it twenty fathoms .... Acts 27:28
again, and *f* it fifteen fathoms .... Acts 27:28
Where we *f* brethren, and were .... Acts 28:14
pertaining to the flesh, hath *f* .... Rom 4:1
to life, I *f* to be unto death .... Rom 7:10
I was *f* of them that sought me .... Rom 10:20
that a man be *f* faithful 1Cor 4:2
we are *f* false witnesses of God 1Cor 15:15
because I *f* not Titus my brother 2Cor 2:13
clothed we shall not be *f* naked 2Cor 5:3
I made before Titus, is *f* a truth 2Cor 7:14
glory, they may be *f* even as we 2Cor 9:4
that I shall be *f* unto you such 2Cor 12:20
we ourselves also are *f* sinners .... Gal 2:17
being *f* in fashion as a man, he .... Phil 2:8
be *f* in him, not having mine own .... Phil 3:9
of a deacon, being *f* blameless 1Ti 3:10
me out very diligently, and *f* me 2Ti 1:17
and was not *f*, because God had .... Heb 11:5
he *f* no place of repentance, ... Heb 12:17
might be *f* unto praise and honour 1Pet 1:7
neither was guile *f* in his mouth 1Pet 2:22
that ye may be *f* of him in peace 2Pet 3:14
I rejoiced greatly that I *f* of 2Jn 4
and are not, and hast *f* them liars .... Rev 2:2
for I have not *f* thy works .... Rev 3:2
no man was *f* worthy to open .... Rev 5:4
their place *f* any more in heaven .... Rev 12:8
And in their mouth was *f* no guile .... Rev 14:5
away, and the mountains were not *f* .... Rev 16:20
shall be *f* no more at all .... Rev 18:21
shall be *f* any more in thee .... Rev 18:21
in her was *f* the blood of .... Rev 18:24
there was *f* no place for them .... Rev 20:11
whosoever was not *f* written in .... Rev 20:15

FOUNDATION

the *f* thereof even until now .... Ex 9:18
he shall lay the *f* thereof in his .... Josh 6:26
to lay the *f* of the house 1Kin 5:17
In the fourth year was the *f* of 1Kin 6:37
even from the *f* unto the coping, ... 1Kin 7:9
the *f* was of costly stones, even 1Kin 7:10
he laid the *f* thereof in Abiram 1Kin 16:34
of the *f* of the house of the LORD 2Chr 8:16
a third part at the gate of the *f* 2Chr 23:5
began to lay the *f* of the heaps 2Chr 31:7
But the *f* of the temple of the .... Ezr 3:6
the *f* of the temple of the LORD .... Ezr 3:10
because the *f* of the house of the .... Ezr 3:11
when the *f* of this house was laid .... Ezr 3:12
laid the *f* of the house of God .... Ezr 5:16
whose is in the dust, which are .... Job 4:19
whose *f* was overflown with a .... Job 22:16
His *f* is in the holy mountains .... Ps 87:1
hast thou laid the *f* of the earth .... Ps 102:25
rase it, even to the *f* thereof .... Ps 137:7
the righteous is an everlasting *f* .... Prov 10:25
I lay in Zion for a *f* a stone .... Is 28:16

a precious corner stone, a sure *f*............... Is 28:16
the temple, Thy *f* shall be laid.................. Is 44:28
also hath laid the *f* of the earth.............. Is 48:13
so that the *f* thereof shall be................... Eze 13:14
discovering the *f* unto the neck................ Hab 3:13
even from the day that the *f* of.............. Hag 2:18
have laid the *f* of this house................... Zec 4:9
the *f* of the house of the LORD of............ Zec 8:9
layeth the *f* of the earth, and................. Zec 12:1
secret from the *f* of the world............... Mt 13:35
for you from the *f* of the world............... Mt 25:34
deep, and laid the *f* on a rock................ Lk 6:48
is like a man that without a *f*................... Lk 6:49
was shed from the *f* of the world.......... Lk 11:50
haply, after he hath laid the *f*................. Lk 14:29
me before the *f* of the world.................. Jn 17:24
should build upon another man's *f*...... Rom 15:20
masterbuilder, I have laid the *f*............. 1Cor 3:10
For other *f* can no man lay than.......... 1Cor 3:11
if any man build upon this *f* gold......... 1Cor 3:12
in him before the *f* of the world........... Eph 1:4
built upon the *f* of the apostles............ Eph 2:20
a good *f* against the time to come......... 1Ti 6:19
Nevertheless the *f* of God.................... 2Ti 2:19
hast laid the *f* of the earth................... Heb 1:10
finished from the *f* of the world............ Heb 4:3
not laying again the *f* of......................... Heb 6:1
suffered since the *f* of the world.......... Heb 9:26
before the *f* of the world...................... 1Pet 1:20
slain from the *f* of the world................. Rev 13:8
of life from the *f* of the world............... Rev 17:8
The first *f* was jasper............................. Rev 21:19

FOUNDATIONS

and set on fire the *f* of the.................... Deut 32:22
the *f* of heaven moved and shook,........ 2Sa 22:8
appeared, the *f* of the world were........ 2Sa 22:16
walls thereof, and joined the *f*............... Ezr 4:12
let the *f* thereof be strongly................... Ezr 6:3
when I laid the *f* of the earth................ Job 38:4
are the *f* thereof fastened..................... Job 38:6
If the *f* be destroyed, what can............ Ps 11:3
the *f* also of the hills moved and......... Ps 18:7
seen, and the *f* of the world were........ Ps 18:15
all the *f* of the earth are out of............ Ps 82:5
Who laid the *f* of the earth................... Ps 104:5
he appointed the *f* of the earth............ Prov 8:29
for the *f* of Kir-hareseth shall................ Is 16:7
the *f* of the earth do shake.................... Is 24:18
from the *f* of the earth........................... Is 40:21
and laid the *f* of the earth..................... Is 51:13
lay the *f* of the earth, and say.............. Is 51:16
and lay thy *f* with sapphires.................. Is 54:11
up the *f* of many generations................ Is 58:12
the *f* of the earth searched out............ Jer 31:37
her *f* are fallen, her walls are................ Jer 50:15
for a corner, nor a stone for *f*............... Jer 51:26
and it hath devoured the *f* thereof....... Lam 4:11
her *f* shall be broken down................... Eze 30:4
the *f* of the side chambers were a........ Eze 41:8
and I will discover the *f* thereof............ Mic 1:6
and ye strong *f* of the earth.................. Mic 6:2
so that the *f* of the prison were........... Acts 16:26
he looked for a city which hath *f*.......... Heb 11:10
the wall of the city had twelve *f*............ Rev 21:14
the *f* of the wall of the city.................... Rev 21:19

FOUNDED

For he hath *f* it upon the seas............... Ps 24:2
fulness thereof, thou hast *f* them.......... Ps 89:11
place which thou hast *f* for them........... Ps 104:8
that thou hast *f* them for ever.............. Ps 119:152
LORD by wisdom hath *f* the earth......... Prov 3:19
That the LORD hath *f* Zion...................... Is 14:32
til the Assyrian *f* it for them.................. Is 23:13
hath *f* his troop in the earth................. Amos 9:6
for it was *f* upon a rock......................... Mt 7:25
for it was *f* upon a rock......................... Lk 6:48

FOUNDER

of silver, and gave them to the *f*........... Judg 17:4
the *f* melteth in vain.............................. Jer 6:29
workman, and of the hands of the *f*...... Jer 10:9
every *f* is confounded by the................ Jer 10:14
every *f* is confounded by the................ Jer 51:17

FOUNDEST

f his heart faithful before thee,............. Neh 9:8

FOUNTAIN

by a *f* of water in the wilderness.......... Gen 16:7
by the *f* in the way to Shur................... Gen 16:7
Nevertheless a *f* or pit, wherein........... Lev 11:36
he hath discovered her *f*, and she........ Lev 20:18
hath uncovered the *f* her blood............ Lev 20:18
the *f* of Jacob shall be upon a.............. Deut 33:28
the *f* of the water of Nephtoah............. Josh 15:9
by a *f* which is in Jezreel...................... 1Sa 29:1
I went on to the gate of the *f*................ Neh 2:14
came to the *f* and the king.................... Neh 3:15
And at the *f* gate, which was over........ Neh 12:37
For with thee is the *f* of life.................. Ps 36:9
the Lord, from the *f* of Israel................ Ps 68:26
Thou didst cleave the *f* and the........... Ps 74:15
the flint into a *f* of waters.................... Ps 114:8
Let thy *f* be blessed.............................. Prov 5:18
law of the wise is a *f* of life................. Prov 13:14
the fear of the LORD is a *f* of life......... Prov 14:27
the wicked is as a troubled *f*................. Prov 25:26
or the pitcher be broken at the *f*........... Eccl 12:6
a spring shut up, a *f* sealed.................. Song 4:12
A *f* of gardens, a well of living.............. Song 4:15
me the *f* of living waters....................... Jer 2:13

As a *f* casteth out her waters, so......... Jer 6:7
waters, and mine eyes a *f* of tears....... Jer 9:1
the LORD, the *f* of living waters............ Jer 17:13
dry, and his *f* shall be dried up............ Hos 13:15
a *f* shall come forth of the house........ Joel 3:18
a *f* opened to the house of David......... Zec 13:1
straightway the *f* of her blood.............. Mk 5:29
Doth a *f* send forth at the same........... Jas 3:11
so can no *f* both yield salt water.......... Jas 3:12
the *f* of the water of life freely.............. Rev 21:6

FOUNTAINS

the same day were all the *f* of............... Gen 7:11
The *f* also of the deep and the.............. Gen 8:2
and in Elim were twelve *f* of water....... Num 33:9
a land of brooks of water, of *f*.............. Deut 8:7
the land, unto all *f* of water.................. 1Kin 18:5
the *f* which were without the city......... 2Chr 32:3
together, who stopped all the *f*............. 2Chr 32:4
Let thy *f* be dispersed abroad, and...... Prov 5:16
when there were no *f* abounding.......... Prov 8:24
he strengthened the *f* of the deep....... Prov 8:28
f in the midst of the valleys.................. Is 41:18
lead them unto living *f* of waters.......... Rev 7:17
rivers, and upon the *f* of waters........... Rev 8:10
and the sea, and the *f* of waters.......... Rev 14:7
upon the rivers and *f* of waters............ Rev 16:4

FOUR

parted, and became into *f* heads.......... Gen 2:10
after he begat Salah *f* hundred............ Gen 11:13
after he begat Eber *f* hundred.............. Gen 11:15
And Eber lived *f* and thirty years,........ Gen 11:16
after he begat Peleg *f* hundred............ Gen 11:17
f kings with five......................................Gen 14:9
afflict them *f* hundred years................. Gen 15:13
the land is worth *f* hundred.................. Gen 23:15
f hundred shekels of silver.................... Gen 23:16
thee, and *f* hundred men with him....... Gen 32:6
came, and with him *f* hundred men...... Gen 33:1
f parts shall be your own, for............... Gen 47:24
was *f* hundred and thirty years............ Ex 12:40
pass at the end of the *f* hundred.......... Ex 12:41
for an ox, and *f* sheep for a sheep....... Ex 22:1
thou shalt cast *f* rings of gold............... Ex 25:12
put them in the *f* corners thereof......... Ex 25:12
shalt make for it *f* rings of gold............ Ex 25:26
put the rings in the *f* corners............... Ex 25:26
that are on the *f* feet thereof............... Ex 25:26
in the candlestick shall be *f*................. Ex 25:34
breadth of one curtain *f* cubits............. Ex 26:2
breadth of one curtain *f* cubits............. Ex 26:8
it upon *f* pillars of shittim wood............ Ex 26:32
upon the *f* sockets of silver................... Ex 26:32
of it upon the *f* corners thereof............ Ex 27:2
make *f* brasen rings in the *f*................ Ex 27:4
shall be *f*, and their sockets *f*............. Ex 27:16
of stones, even *f* rows of stones.......... Ex 28:17
breadth of one curtain *f* cubits............. Ex 36:9
f cubits was the breadth of one........... Ex 36:15
he made thereunto *f* pillars of.............. Ex 36:36
he cast for them *f* sockets of................ Ex 36:36
And he cast for it *f* rings of gold.......... Ex 37:3
to be set by the *f* corners of it.............. Ex 37:3
And he cast for it *f* rings of gold.......... Ex 37:13
put the rings upon the *f* corners.......... Ex 37:13
that were in the *f* feet thereof.............. Ex 37:13
were *f* bowls made like almonds.......... Ex 37:20
thereof on the *f* corners of it................ Ex 38:2
he cast *f* rings for the *f* ends............. Ex 38:5
And their pillars were *f*.......................... Ex 38:19
and their sockets of brass *f*.................. Ex 38:19
two thousand and *f* hundred shekels.... Ex 38:29
they set in it *f* rows of stones.............. Ex 39:10
that creep, going upon all *f*.................. Lev 11:20
thing that goeth upon all *f*.................... Lev 11:21
things, which have *f* feet...................... Lev 11:23
manner of beasts that go on all *f*......... Lev 11:27
and whatsoever goeth upon all *f*.......... Lev 11:42
and *f* thousand and *f* hundred........... Num 1:29
and seven thousand and *f* hundred..... Num 1:31
and five thousand and *f* hundred......... Num 1:37
and three thousand and *f* hundred...... Num 1:43
and *f* thousand and *f* hundred........... Num 2:6
and seven thousand and *f* hundred..... Num 2:8
f hundred, throughout their................. Num 2:9
f hundred and fifty, throughout........... Num 2:16
and five thousand and *f* hundred......... Num 2:23
and three thousand and *f* hundred...... Num 2:30
oxen he gave unto the sons of................ Num 7:7
f wagons and eight oxen he gave......... Num 7:8
f hundred shekels, after the................ Num 7:85
of bullocks, the rams sixty, the.............. Num 7:88
plague were twenty and *f*..................... Num 25:9
f thousand and three hundred............. Num 26:25
and *f* thousand and *f* hundred........... Num 26:43
and three thousand and *f* hundred...... Num 26:47
and *f* thousand and *f* hundred........... Num 26:50
f cubits the breadth of it, after........... Deut 3:11
the *f* quarters of thy vesture................ Deut 22:12
f cities and their villages..................... Josh 19:7
Almon with her suburbs; *f* cities.......... Josh 21:18
Beth-horon with her suburbs; *f* cities.. Josh 21:22
with her suburbs; *f* cities..................... Josh 21:24
with her suburbs; *f* cities..................... Josh 21:29
Rehob with her suburbs; *f* cities.......... Josh 21:31
with her suburbs; *f* cities..................... Josh 21:35
with her suburbs; *f* cities..................... Josh 21:37
Jazer with her suburbs; *f* cities............ Josh 21:39
against Shechem in *f* companies.......... Judg 9:34
the Gileadite *f* days in a year.............. Judg 11:40

and was there *f* whole months............. Judg 19:2
f hundred thousand footmen that....... Judg 20:2
were numbered *f* hundred thousand.... Judg 20:17
abode in the rock Rimmon *f* months.... Judg 20:47
f hundred young virgins, that had....... Judg 21:12
in the field about *f* thousand men........ 1Sa 4:2
were with him about *f* hundred men..... 1Sa 22:2
after David about *f* hundred men.......... 1Sa 25:13
was a full year and *f* months................ 1Sa 27:7
pursued, he and *f* hundred men........... 1Sa 30:10
save *f* hundred young men, which......... 1Sa 30:17
and on every foot six toes, *f*................ 2Sa 21:20
These *f* were born to the giant in........ 2Sa 21:22
it came to pass in the *f* hundred.......... 1Kin 6:1
upon *f* rows of cedar pillars,................. 1Kin 7:2
lily work in the porch, *f* cubits............. 1Kin 7:19
f cubits was the length of one.............. 1Kin 7:27
f cubits the breadth thereof, and......... 1Kin 7:27
And every base had *f* brasen wheels.... 1Kin 7:30
the *f* corners thereof had..................... 1Kin 7:30
under the borders were *f* wheels......... 1Kin 7:32
there were *f* undersetters to the......... 1Kin 7:34
to the *f* corners of one base................. 1Kin 7:34
and every laver was *f* cubits................ 1Kin 7:38
f hundred pomegranates for the.......... 1Kin 7:42
f hundred and twenty talents, and....... 1Kin 9:28
f hundred chariots, and twelve............ 1Kin 10:26
in Tirzah, twenty and *f* years.............. 1Kin 15:33
and the prophets of Baal *f* hundred..... 1Kin 18:19
prophets of the groves *f* hundred......... 1Kin 18:19
but Baal's prophets are *f* hundred....... 1Kin 18:22
Fill *f* barrels with water, and................ 1Kin 18:33
about *f* hundred men, and said unto.... 1Kin 22:6
there were *f* leprous men at the.......... 2Kin 7:3
the corner gate, *f* hundred cubits........ 2Kin 14:13
Shobab, and Nathan, and Solomon, *f*.... 1Chr 3:5
bow, and skilful in war, were *f*............. 1Chr 7:40
and Puah, Jashub, and Shimron, *f*........ 1Chr 7:1
and two thousand and thirty and *f*....... 1Chr 7:7
In *f* quarters were the porters,............ 1Chr 9:24
of the chief porters, were in................... 1Chr 9:26
the children of Levi *f* thousand............ 1Chr 12:26
whose fingers and toes were *f*............. 1Chr 20:6
Judah was *f* hundred threescore and... 1Chr 21:5
and his *f* sons with him had................. 1Chr 21:20
f thousand were to set forward............ 1Chr 23:4
Moreover *f* thousand were porters....... 1Chr 23:5
f thousand praised the LORD with........ 1Chr 23:5
These *f* were the sons of Shimei.......... 1Chr 23:10
Izhar, Hebron, and Uzziel, *f*................. 1Chr 23:12
and twentieth to Delaiah, the *f*............ 1Chr 24:18
The *f* and twentieth to........................ 1Chr 25:31
f a day, southward *f* a day................. 1Chr 26:17
at the causeway, and two at................... 1Chr 26:18
course were twenty and *f* thousand.... 1Chr 27:1
course were twenty and *f* thousand.... 1Chr 27:2
were twenty and *f* thousand................ 1Chr 27:4
course were twenty and *f* thousand.... 1Chr 27:5
course were twenty and *f* thousand.... 1Chr 27:7
course were twenty and *f* thousand.... 1Chr 27:8
course were twenty and *f* thousand.... 1Chr 27:9
course were twenty and *f* thousand.... 1Chr 27:10
course were twenty and *f* thousand.... 1Chr 27:11
course were twenty and *f* thousand.... 1Chr 27:12
course were twenty and *f* thousand.... 1Chr 27:13
course were twenty and *f* thousand.... 1Chr 27:14
course were twenty and *f* thousand.... 1Chr 27:15
f hundred chariots, and twelve............ 2Chr 1:14
f hundred pomegranates on the two.... 2Chr 4:13
Ophir, and took thence *f* hundred........ 2Chr 8:18
Solomon had *f* thousand stalls for....... 2Chr 9:25
even *f* hundred thousand chosen........ 2Chr 13:3
of prophets *f* hundred men................. 2Chr 18:5
the corner gate, *f* hundred cubits........ 2Chr 25:23
basons of a second sort *f* hundred...... Ezr 1:10
were five thousand and *f* hundred....... Ezr 1:11
a thousand two hundred fifty and *f*...... Ezr 2:7
of Adin, *f* hundred fifty and *f*............. Ezr 2:15
a thousand two hundred fifty and *f*...... Ezr 2:31
of Hodaviah, seventy and *f*................... Ezr 2:40
hundred thirty and *f*, the...................... Ezr 2:64
two hundred rams, *f* hundred lambs..... Ezr 6:17
unto me *f* times after this sort............. Neh 6:4
a thousand two hundred fifty and *f*...... Neh 7:12
Bezai, three hundred twenty and *f*....... Neh 7:23
a thousand two hundred fifty and *f*...... Neh 7:34
children of Hodevah, seventy and *f*...... Neh 7:43
camels, *f* hundred thirty and five........ Neh 7:69
were *f* hundred threescore.................... Neh 11:18
were two hundred fourscore and *f*....... Neh 11:46
smote the *f* corners of the house,........ Job 1:19
sons' sons, even *f* generations............ Job 42:16
f things say not, it is enough................ Prov 30:15
for me, yea, *f* which I know not........... Prov 30:18
for *f* which it cannot bear.................... Prov 30:21
There be *f* things which are................. Prov 30:24
well, yea, *f* are comely in going........... Prov 30:29
from the *f* corners of the earth............ Is 11:12
of five in the outmost fruitful................ Is 17:6
I will appoint over them *f* kinds........... Jer 15:3
Jehudi had read three or *f* leaves........ Jer 36:23
upon Elam will I bring the *f*................. Jer 49:36
from the *f* quarters of heaven.............. Jer 49:36
thickness thereof was *f* fingers............ Jer 52:21
all the persons were *f* thousand.......... Jer 52:30
likeness of *f* living creatures............... Eze 1:5
And every one had *f* faces.................... Eze 1:6
and every one had *f* wings................... Eze 1:6
their wings on their *f* sides.................. Eze 1:8
they *f* had their faces and their........... Eze 1:8

F

they *f* had the face of a man, and...... Eze 1:10
they *f* had the face of an ox on .... Eze 1:10
they *f* also had the face of an .... Eze 1:10
creatures, with his *f* faces .... Eze 1:15
and they *f* had one likeness............ Eze 1:16
they went upon their *f* sides .... Eze 1:17
full of eyes round about them *f* .... Eze 1:18
upon the *f* corners of the land .... Eze 7:2
behold the *f* wheels by the .... Eze 10:9
they *f* had one likeness, as if a .... Eze 10:10
they went upon their *f* sides........... Eze 10:11
even the wheels that they *f* had .... Eze 10:12
And every one had *f* faces .... Eze 10:14
Every one had *f* faces apiece........... Eze 10:21
and every one *f* wings................. Eze 10:21
How much more when I send my *f* .... Eze 14:21
Come from the *f* winds, O breath,...... Eze 37:9
F tables were on this side, and......... Eze 40:41
f tables on that side, by the......... Eze 40:41
the *f* tables were of hewn stone .... Eze 40:42
f cubits, round about the house .... Eze 40:43
He measured it by the *f* sides .... Eze 42:20
greater settle shall be *f* cubits...... Eze 43:14
So the altar shall be *f* cubits........ Eze 43:15
altar and upward shall be *f* horns ..... Eze 43:15
square in the *f* squares thereof .... Eze 43:16
broad in the *f* squares thereof .... Eze 43:17
and put it on the *f* horns of it .... Eze 43:20
on the *f* corners of the settle,....... Eze 43:20
upon the *f* corners of the settle ...... Eze 43:20
by the *f* corners of the court .... Eze 46:21
In the *f* corners of the court......... Eze 46:22
these *f* corners were of one .... Eze 46:22
about in them, round about them *f* ..... Eze 46:23
the north side *f* thousand............. Eze 48:16
and the south side *f* thousand......... Eze 48:16
and on the east side *f* thousand .... Eze 48:16
and the west side *f* thousand.......... Eze 48:16
f thousand and five hundred........... Eze 48:30
And at the east side *f* thousand .... Eze 48:32
And at the south side *f* thousand ...... Eze 48:33
At the west side *f* thousand........... Eze 48:34
As for these *f* children, God gave..... Dan 1:17
I see *f* men loose, walking in the ..... Dan 3:25
the *f* winds of the heaven strove...... Dan 7:2
f great beasts came up from the....... Dan 7:3
the back of it *f* wings of a fowl ...... Dan 7:6
the beast had also *f* heads............ Dan 7:6
These great beasts, which are *f* .... Dan 7:17
are *f* kings, which shall arise .... Dan 7:17
for it came up *f* notable ones .... Dan 8:8
ones toward the *f* winds of heaven ..... Dan 8:8
whereas *f* stood up for it .... Dan 8:22
f kingdoms shall stand up out of...... Dan 8:22
And in the *f* and twentieth day of ..... Dan 10:4
toward the *f* winds of heaven .... Dan 11:4
of Damascus, and for *f*, I will not.... Amos 1:3
transgressions of Gaza, and for *f* ..... Amos 1:6
transgressions of Tyrus, and for *f* .... Amos 1:9
transgressions of Edom, and for *f* ..... Amos 1:11
the children of Ammon, and for *f* ...... Amos 1:13
transgressions of Moab, and for *f* ..... Amos 2:1
transgressions of Judah, and for *f* .... Amos 2:4
of Israel, and for *f*, I will not...... Amos 2:6
In the *f* and twentieth day of the..... Hag 1:15
In the *f* and twentieth day of the..... Hag 2:10
this day and upward, from the *f* .... Hag 2:18
LORD came unto Haggai in the *f* .... Hag 2:20
Upon the *f* and twentieth day of .... Zec 1:7
eyes, and saw, and behold *f* horns ..... Zec 1:18
the LORD shewed me *f* carpenters .... Zec 1:20
as the *f* winds of the heaven.......... Zec 2:6
there came *f* chariots out from........ Zec 6:1
These are the *f* spirits of the........ Zec 6:5
that did eat were *f* thousand men ...... Mt 15:38
seven loaves of the *f* thousand........ Mt 16:10
his elect from the *f* winds............ Mt 24:31
the palsy, which was borne of *f* .... Mk 2:3
had eaten were about *f* thousand .... Mk 8:9
when the seven among *f* thousand .... Mk 8:20
his elect from the *f* winds............ Mk 13:27
f years, which departed not from ...... Lk 2:37
not ye, There are yet *f* months........ Jn 4:35
lain in the grave *f* days already ..... Jn 11:17
for he hath been dead *f* days.......... Jn 11:39
made *f* parts, to every soldier a ...... Jn 19:23
of men, about *f* hundred, joined .... Acts 5:36
entreat them evil *f* hundred years ..... Acts 7:6
great sheet knit at the *f* corners ..... Acts 10:11
F days ago I was fasting until.......... Acts 10:30
let down from heaven by *f* corners ..... Acts 11:5
delivered him to *f* quaternions of ..... Acts 12:4
about the space of *f* hundred .... Acts 13:20
And the same man had *f* daughters ...... Acts 21:9
We have *f* men which have .... Acts 21:23
f thousand men that were.............. Acts 21:38
they cast *f* anchors out of the .... Acts 27:29
the law, which was *f* thousand......... Acts 3:17
And round about the throne were *f* ..... Rev 4:4
and upon the seats I saw *f* .... Rev 4:4
were *f* beasts full of eyes before..... Rev 4:6
the *f* beasts had each of them six..... Rev 4:8
The *f* and twenty elders fall down..... Rev 4:10
of the throne and of the *f* beasts .... Rev 5:6
the *f* beasts and *f* and twenty ...... Rev 5:8
And the *f* and twenty elders fell ..... Rev 5:14
one of the *f* beasts saying, Come ..... Rev 6:1
in the midst of the *f* beasts say ..... Rev 6:6
after these things I saw *f* angels .... Rev 7:1

on the *f* corners of the earth......... Rev 7:1
holding the *f* winds of the earth,..... Rev 7:1
with a loud voice to the *f* angels ..... Rev 7:2
f thousand of all the tribes of....... Rev 7:4
the *f* beasts, and fell before the ..... Rev 7:11
I heard a voice from the *f* horns ...... Rev 9:13
Loose the *f* angels which are .... Rev 9:14
the *f* angels were loosed, which .... Rev 9:15
And the *f* and twenty elders, which..... Rev 11:16
f thousand, having his Father's....... Rev 14:1
throne, and before the *f* beasts,...... Rev 14:3
f thousand, which were redeemed....... Rev 14:3
one of the *f* beasts gave unto the ..... Rev 15:7
And the *f* and twenty elders and the ... Rev 19:4
the *f* beasts fell down and........... Rev 19:4
in the *f* quarters of the city......... Rev 20:8
f cubits, according to the........... Rev 21:17

FOURFOLD
And he shall restore the lamb *f* 2Sa 12:6
false accusation, I restore him *f* ..... Lk 19:8

FOURFOOTED
manner of *f* beasts of the earth,...... Acts 10:12
saw *f* beasts of the earth, and........ Acts 11:6
f beasts, and creeping things .... Rom 1:23

FOURSCORE
And Abram was *f* and six years old,.... Gen 16:16
Isaac were an hundred and *f* years..... Gen 35:28
and Moses was *f* years old, and .... Ex 7:7
f years old, and Aaron *f* .... Ex 7:7
f thousand and six thousand and....... Num 2:9
thousand and five hundred and *f* ...... Num 4:48
and now, lo, I am this day *f* .... Josh 14:10
And the land had rest *f* years......... Judg 3:30
priests, and slew on that day *f* ...... Sa 22:18
a very aged man, even *f* years old..... 2Sa 19:32
I am this day *f* years old............ 2Sa 19:35
and *f* thousand hewers in the......... 1Kin 5:15
f thousand chosen men, which were..... 1Kin 12:21
was sold for *f* pieces of silver 2Kin 6:25
Jehu appointed *f* men without......... 2Kin 10:24
of the Assyrians an hundred *f* 2Kin 19:35
in all by their genealogies *f* 1Chr 7:5
the chief, and his brethren *f* 1Chr 15:9
were cunning, was two hundred *f* 1Chr 25:7
f thousand to hew in the mountain 2Chr 2:2
f thousand to be hewers in the 2Chr 2:18
f thousand chosen men, which were..... 2Chr 11:1
bows, two hundred and *f* thousand 2Chr 14:8
him two hundred and *f* thousand 2Chr 17:15
f thousand ready prepared for the 2Chr 17:18
with him *f* priests of the LORD,....... 2Chr 26:17
of Michael, and with him *f* males ..... Ezr 8:8
and Netophah, an hundred *f* .... Neh 7:26
the holy city were two hundred *f* ..... Neh 11:18
days, even an hundred and *f* days ..... Est 1:4
of strength they be *f* years.......... Ps 90:10
f concubines, and virgins without .... Song 6:8
of the Assyrians an hundred and *f* .... Is 37:36
and from Samaria, even *f* men .... Jer 41:5
And she was a widow of about *f* .... Lk 2:37
him, Take thy bill, and write *f* ...... Lk 16:7

FOURSQUARE
the altar shall be *f*................. Ex 27:1
It shall be being doubled.............. Ex 28:16
breadth thereof; *f* shall it be .... Ex 30:2
of it a cubit; it was *f* .... Ex 37:25
the breadth thereof; it was *f* .... Ex 38:1
It was *f*; they made the .... Ex 39:9
gravings with their borders, *f* 1Kin 7:31
and an hundred cubits broad, *f* ...... Eze 40:47
shall offer the holy oblation *f* ..... Eze 48:20
And the city lieth *f*, and the .... Rev 21:16

FOURTEEN
I served thee *f* years for thy two .... Gen 31:41
all the souls were *f* .... Gen 46:22
f thousand and six hundred .... Num 1:27
f thousand and six hundred .... Num 2:24
in the plague were *f* thousand....... Num 16:49
f lambs of the first year .... Num 29:13
deal to each lamb of the *f* lambs .... Num 29:15
f lambs of the first year without ... Num 29:17
f lambs of the first year without ... Num 29:20
f lambs of the first year without ... Num 29:23
f lambs of the first year without ... Num 29:26
f lambs of the first year without ... Num 29:29
f lambs of the first year without ... Num 29:32
f cities with their villages .... Josh 15:36
f cities with their villages .... Josh 18:28
days and seven days, even *f* days 1Kin 8:65
And God gave to Heman *f* sons......... 1Chr 25:5
waxed mighty, and married *f* wives 2Chr 13:21
for he had *f* thousand sheep, and ..... Job 42:12
the settle shall be *f* cubits long .... Eze 43:17
f broad in the four squares .... Eze 43:17
to David are *f* generations .... Mt 1:17
into Babylon are *f* generations ...... Mt 1:17
unto Christ are *f* generations....... Mt 1:17
a man in Christ above *f* years ago 2Cor 12:2
Then *f* years after I went up......... Gal 2:1

FOURTEENTH
in the *f* year came Chedorlaomer,..... Gen 14:5
until the *f* day of the same month ... Ex 12:6
on the *f* day of the month at even ... Ex 12:18
In the *f* day of the first month..... Num 9:5
In the *f* day of this month, at ..... Num 9:3
they kept the passover on the *f* ..... Num 9:5
the *f* day of the second month at ... Num 9:11

in the *f* day of the first month...... Num 28:16
kept the passover on the *f* day .... Josh 5:10
Now in the *f* year of king............ 2Kin 18:13
to Huppah, the *f* to Jeshebeab,....... 1Chr 24:13
The *f* to Mattithiah, he, his sons 1Chr 25:21
on the *f* day of the second month..... 2Chr 30:15
on the *f* day of the first month...... 2Chr 35:1
upon the *f* day of the first month .... Ezr 6:19
the *f* day also of the month Adar ..... Est 9:15
on the *f* day of the same month .... Est 9:17
day thereof, and on the *f* thereof .... Est 9:18
made the *f* day of the month Adar ..... Est 9:19
keep the *f* day of the month Adar ..... Est 9:21
in the *f* year of king Hezekiah....... Is 36:1
in the *f* year after that the city .... Eze 40:1
in the *f* day of the month, ye .... Eze 45:21
But when the *f* night was come, as,... Acts 27:27
This day is the *f* day that ye .... Acts 27:33

FOURTH
and the morning were the *f* day .... Gen 1:19
And the *f* river is Euphrates .... Gen 2:14
But in the *f* generation they......... Gen 15:16
f generation of them that hate me .... Ex 20:5
the *f* row a beryl, an onyx, and...... Ex 28:20
f part of an hin of beaten oil....... Ex 29:40
the *f* part of an hin of wine for..... Ex 29:40
the third and to the *f* generation ... Ex 34:7
And the *f* row, a beryl, an onyx,.... Ex 39:13
But in the *f* year all the fruit..... Lev 19:24
be of wine, the *f* part of a hin .... Lev 23:13
On the *f* day Elizur the son of ..... Num 7:30
unto the third and *f* generation .... Num 14:18
with the *f* part of an hin of oil.... Num 15:4
the *f* part of an hin of wine for ... Num 15:5
number of the *f* part of Israel..... Num 23:10
mingled with the *f* part of an hin .. Num 28:5
offering thereof shall be the *f* .... Num 28:7
a part of an hin unto a lamb .... Num 28:14
on the *f* day ten bullocks, two...... Num 29:23
f generation of them that hate me .. Deut 5:9
the *f* lot came out to Issachar...... Josh 19:17
And it came to pass on the *f* day ... Judg 19:5
I have here at hand the *f* part of .. 1Sa 9:8
And the *f*, Adonijah the son of 2Sa 3:4
in the *f* year of Solomon's reign ... 1Kin 6:1
olive tree, a *f* part of the wall ... 1Kin 6:33
In the *f* year was the foundation .. 1Kin 6:37
to reign over Judah in the *f* year . 1Kin 22:41
the *f* part of a cab of dove's...... 2Kin 6:25
thy children of the *f* generation .. 2Kin 10:30
of Israel unto the *f* generation ... 2Kin 15:12
in the *f* year of king Hezekiah 2Kin 18:9
on the ninth day of the *f* month ... 2Kin 25:3
Nethaneel the *f*, Raddai the fifth .. 1Chr 2:14
the *f*, Adonijah the son of 1Chr 3:2
the third Zedekiah, the *f* Shallum . 1Chr 3:15
Nohah the *f*, and Rapha the fifth .. 1Chr 8:2
Mishmannah the *f*, Jeremiah the 1Chr 12:10
the third, and Jekameam the *f* 1Chr 23:19
third to Harim, the *f* to Seorim,.. 1Chr 24:8
the third, Jekameam the *f* 1Chr 24:23
The *f* to Izri, he, his sons, and .. 1Chr 25:11
the third, Jathniel the *f* 1Chr 26:2
Joah the third, and Sacar the *f* ... 1Chr 26:4
the third, Zechariah the *f* 1Chr 26:11
The *f* captain for the *f* 1Chr 27:7
The *f* captain for the *f* 1Chr 27:7
in the *f* year of his reign 2Chr 3:2
on the *f* day they assembled 2Chr 20:26
Now on the *f* day was the silver ... Ezr 8:33
f day of this month the children .. Neh 9:1
their God one *f* part of the day ... Neh 9:3
another *f* part they confessed, and . Neh 9:3
in the *f* year of Jehoiakim the son of . Jer 25:1
king of Judah, in the *f* year ...... Jer 36:1
it came to pass in the *f* year of .. Jer 36:1
year of Zedekiah, in the *f* month .. Jer 39:2
in the *f* year of Jehoiakim the .... Jer 46:1
f year of Jehoiakim the son of .... Jer 46:2
in the *f* year of his reign .... Jer 51:59
And in the *f* month, in the ninth .. Jer 52:6
thirtieth year, in the *f* month .... Eze 1:1
the *f* the face of an eagle .... Eze 10:14
the *f* kingdom shall be strong as .. Dan 2:40
the form of the *f* is like the Son . Dan 3:25
visions, and behold a *f* beast ..... Dan 7:7
know the truth of the *f* beast ..... Dan 7:19
The *f* beast shall be the *f* ...... Dan 7:23
The *f* shall be far richer than .... Dan 11:2
in the *f* chariot grisled and bay .. Zec 6:3
pass in the *f* year of king Darius . Zec 7:1
in the *f* day of the ninth month ... Zec 7:1
The Fast of the *f*, and the Fast ... Zec 8:19
in the *f* watch of the night Jesus . Mt 14:25
about the *f* watch of the night he . Mk 6:48
the *f* beast was like a flying ..... Rev 4:7
And when he had opened the *f* seal .. Rev 6:7
the voice of the *f* beast say ...... Rev 6:7
them over the *f* part of the earth .. Rev 6:8
the *f* angel sounded, and the third . Rev 8:12
the *f* angel poured out his vial .... Rev 16:8
the *f*, an emerald.................. Rev 21:19

FOWL
f that may fly above the earth in ... Gen 1:20
every winged *f* after his kind ...... Gen 1:21
let *f* multiply in the earth .... Gen 1:22
over the *f* of the air, and over .... Gen 1:26
over the *f* of the air, and over .... Gen 1:28
to every *f* of the air, and to ...... Gen 1:30

FOWLER 248 FRIEND

the field, and every f of the air .... Gen 2:19
to the f of the air, and to every .... Gen 2:20
every f after his kind, every.............. Gen 7:14
moved upon the earth, both of f........... Gen 7:21
things, and the f of the heaven............ Gen 7:23
thee, of all flesh, both of f............... Gen 8:17
every creeping thing, and every f......... Gen 8:19
clean beast, and of every clean f.......... Gen 8:20
earth, and upon every f of the air .... Gen 9:2
that is with you, of the f .... Gen 9:10
whether it be of f or of beast .... Lev 7:26
law of the beasts, and of the f............ Lev 11:46
any beast or f that may be eaten .... Lev 17:13
abominable by beast, or by f .... Lev 20:25
winged f that flieth in the air .... Deut 4:17
and fallowdeer, and fatted f.............. 1Kin 4:23
he spake also of beasts, and of f.......... 1Kin 4:33
is a path which no f knoweth............. Job 28:7
The f of the air, and the fish of .... Ps 8:8
creeping things, and flying f .... Ps 148:10
both the f of the heavens and the .... Jer 9:10
shall dwell all f of every wing .... Eze 17:23
Speak unto every feathered f .... Eze 39:17
or torn, whether it be f or beast .... Eze 44:31
the back of it four wings of a .... Dan 7:6

FOWLER

thee from the snare of the f.............. Ps 91:3
as a bird from the hand of the f........... Prov 6:5
is a snare of a f in all his ways........... Hos 9:8

FOWLERS

a bird out of the snare of the f........... Ps 124:7

FOWLS

thing, and the f of the air................ Gen 6:7
Of f after their kind, and of .... Gen 6:20
Of f also of the air by sevens............. Gen 7:3
that are not clean, and of f............... Gen 7:8
when the f came down upon the.......... Gen 15:11
his offering to the LORD be of f .... Lev 1:14
have in abomination among the f .... Lev 11:13
All f that creep, going upon all........... Lev 11:20
and unclean, and between unclean f...... Lev 20:25
But of all clean f ye may eat.............. Deut 14:20
be meat unto all f of the air .... Deut 28:26
thy flesh unto the f of the air 1Sa 17:44
this day unto the f of the air 1Sa 17:46
field shall the f of the air eat 1Kin 14:11
fields shall the f of the air eat 1Kin 16:4
field shall the f of the air eat 1Kin 21:24
also f were prepared for me, and .... Neh 5:18
kept close from the f of the air .... Job 12:7
us wiser than the f of heaven............. Job 35:11
I know all the f of the mountains......... Ps 50:11
feathered f like as the sand of .... Ps 78:27
be meat unto the f of the heaven......... Ps 79:2
By them shall the f of the heaven........ Ps 104:12
unto the f of the mountains.............. Is 18:6
the f shall summer upon them, and ...... Is 18:6
be meat for the f of the heaven .... Jer 7:33
the f of the heaven, and the .... Jer 15:3
shall be meat for the f of the heaven..... Jer 16:4
be meat for the f of the heaven .... Jer 19:7
for meat unto the f of the heaven........ Jer 34:20
field and to the f of the heaven.......... Eze 29:5
All the f of heaven made their............ Eze 31:6
all the f of the heaven remain............ Eze 31:13
will cause all the f .... Eze 32:4
the f of the heaven, and the .... Eze 38:20
the f of the heaven hath he given........ Dan 2:38
the f of the heaven dwelt in the .... Dan 4:12
it, and the f from his branches........... Dan 4:14
the f of the heaven had their .... Dan 4:21
with the f of heaven, and with the....... Hos 2:18
field, and with the f of heaven........... Hos 4:3
them down as the f of the heaven........ Hos 7:12
will consume the f of the heaven......... Zeph 1:3
Behold the f of the air .... Mt 6:26
the f came and devoured them up........ Mt 13:4
the f of the air came and devoured...... Mk 4:4
so that the f of the air may .... Mk 4:32
the f of the air devoured it .... Lk 8:5
more are ye better than the f............ Lk 12:24
the f of the air lodged in the............. Lk 13:19
creeping things, and f of the air......... Acts 10:12
creeping things, and f of the air......... Acts 11:6
saying to all the f that fly in............. Rev 19:17
all the f were filled with their .... Rev 19:21

FOX

if a f go up, he shall even break .... Neh 4:3
unto them, Go ye, and tell that f .... Lk 13:32

FOXES

went and caught three hundred f........ Judg 15:4
they shall be a portion for f.............. Ps 63:10
Take us the f, the little f................ Song 2:15
Take us the f, the little f................ Song 2:15
is desolate, the f walk upon it .... Lam 5:18
are like the f in the deserts .... Eze 13:4
The f have holes, and the birds of .... Mt 8:20
F have holes, and birds of the air .... Lk 9:58

FRAGMENTS

they took up of the f that .... Mt 14:20
up twelve baskets full of the f........... Mk 6:43
many baskets full of took ye up......... Mk 8:19
many baskets full of took ye up......... Mk 8:20
there was taken up of f that .... Lk 9:17
Gather up the f that remain .... Jn 6:12
up of the five barley loaves.............. Jn 6:13

FRAIL

that I may know how f I am............... Ps 39:4

FRAME

for he could not f to pronounce .... Judg 12:6
For he knoweth our f .... Ps 103:14
I f evil against you, and devise a......... Jer 18:11
by which was as the f of a city .... Eze 40:2
They will not f their doings to........... Hos 5:4

FRAMED

or shall the thing f say of him........... Is 29:16
thing f say of him that f it .... Is 29:16
f together groweth unto an holy .... Eph 2:21
worlds were f by the word of God .... Heb 11:3

FRAMETH

to evil, and thy tongue f deceit.......... Ps 50:19
which f mischief by a law................ Ps 94:20

FRANKINCENSE

these sweet spices with pure f........... Ex 30:34
oil upon it, and put f thereon............ Lev 2:1
thereof, with all the f thereof........... Lev 2:2
put oil upon it, and lay f thereon .... Lev 2:15
thereof, with all the f thereof........... Lev 2:16
shall he put any f thereon............... Lev 5:11
all the f which is upon the meat......... Lev 6:15
shalt put pure f upon each row .... Lev 24:7
no oil upon it, nor put f thereon......... Num 5:15
and the wine, and the oil, and the f..... 1Chr 9:29
laid the meat offering, and the f........ Neh 13:5
with the meat offering and the f........ Neh 13:9
smoke, perfumed with myrrh and f..... Song 3:6
of myrrh, and to the hill of f .... Song 4:6
and cinnamon, with all trees of f .... Song 4:14
gold, and f, and myrrh.................. Mt 2:11
and odours, and ointments, and f....... Rev 18:13

FRANKLY

to pay, he f forgave them both........... Lk 7:42

FRAUD

is full of cursing and deceit and f........ Ps 10:7
which is of you kept back by f........... Jas 5:4

FRAY

and no man shall f them away .... Deut 28:26
and none shall f them away .... Jer 7:33
but these are come to f them............ Zec 1:21

FRECKLED

it is a f spot that groweth in .... Lev 13:39

FREE

he shall go out f for nothing .... Ex 21:2
I will not go out f .... Ex 21:5
shall she go out f without money........ Ex 21:11
let him go f for his eye's sake........... Ex 21:26
he shall let him go f for his .... Ex 21:27
him f offerings every morning .... Ex 36:3
to death, because she was not f .... Lev 19:20
be thou f from this bitter water .... Num 5:19
then she shall be f, and shall............ Num 5:28
thou shalt let him go f from thee........ Deut 15:12
thou sendest him out f from thee .... Deut 15:13
thou sendest him away f from thee..... Deut 15:18
but he shall be f at home one............ Deut 24:5
his father's house f in Israel 1Sa 17:25
remaining in the chambers were f 1Chr 9:33
as many as were of a f heart............ 2Chr 29:31
the servant is f from his master .... Job 3:19
Who hath sent out the wild ass f .... Job 39:5
and uphold me with thy f spirit......... Ps 51:12
f among the dead, like the slain .... Ps 88:5
of the people, and let him go f .... Ps 105:20
and to let the oppressed go f .... Is 58:6
an Hebrew or an Hebrewess, go f .... Jer 34:9
every one his maidservant, go f .... Jer 34:10
handmaids, whom they had let go f..... Jer 34:11
thou shalt let him go f from thee .... Jer 34:14
and publish the f offerings .... Amos 4:5
or his mother, he shall be f .... Mt 15:6
unto him, Then are the children f ...... Mt 17:26
he shall be f .... Mk 7:11
and the truth shall make you f.......... Jn 8:32
sayest thou, Ye shall be made f .... Jn 8:33
Son therefore shall make you f.......... Jn 8:36
ye shall be f indeed .... Jn 8:36
And Paul said, But I was f born .... Acts 22:28
offence, so also is the f gift............. Rom 5:15
but the f gift is of many .... Rom 5:16
the f gift came upon all men unto ...... Rom 5:18
Being then made f from sin .... Rom 6:18
ye were f from righteousness .... Rom 6:20
But now being made f from .... Rom 6:22
be dead, she is f from that law .... Rom 7:3
made me f from the law of sin .... Rom 8:2
but if thou mayest be made f 1Cor 7:21
also he that is called, being f 1Cor 7:22
am I not f? 1Cor 9:1
For though I be f from all men......... 1Cor 9:19
Gentiles, whether we be bond or f..... 1Cor 12:13
there is neither bond nor f .... Gal 3:28
But Jerusalem which is above is f ..... Gal 4:26
heir with the son of the f woman ...... Gal 4:30
of the bondwoman, but of the f........ Gal 4:31
wherewith Christ hath made us f ...... Gal 5:1
the Lord, whether he be bond or f ..... Eph 6:8
Barbarian, Scythian, bond nor f ...... Col 3:11
for of the Lord may have f course...... Th 3:1
As f, and not using your liberty....... 1Pet 2:16
and every bondman, and every f man .. Rev 6:15
small and great, rich and poor, f....... Rev 13:16

and the flesh of all men, both f .... Rev 19:18

FREED

of you be f from being bondmen .... Josh 9:23
For he that is dead is f from sin .... Rom 6:7

FREEDMEN See LIBERTINES.

FREEDOM

at all redeemed, nor f given her .... Lev 19:20
a great sum obtained I this f .... Acts 22:28

FREELY

of the garden thou mayest f eat .... Gen 2:16
fish, which we did eat in Egypt f .... Num 11:5
f to day of the spoil of their............ 1Sa 14:30
offered f for the house of God to .... Ezr 2:68
his counsellors have f offered .... Ezr 7:15
I will f sacrifice unto thee .... Ps 54:6
backsliding, I will love them f .... Hos 14:4
f ye have received, f give .... Mt 10:8
f ye have received, f give .... Mt 10:8
let me f speak unto you of the.......... Acts 2:29
before whom also I speak f .... Acts 26:26
Being justified f by his grace........... Rom 3:24
him also f give us all things .... Rom 8:32
that are f given to us of God............ 1Cor 2:12
to you the gospel of God f 2Cor 11:7
fountain of the water of life f........... Rev 21:6
let him take the water of life f .... Rev 22:17

FREEMAN

being a servant, is the Lord's f 1Cor 7:22

FREEWILL

vows, and for all his f offerings......... Lev 22:18
or a f offering in beeves or.............. Lev 22:21
thou offer for a f offering.............. Lev 22:23
and beside all your f offerings.......... Lev 23:38
or in a f offering, or in your .... Num 15:3
your f offerings, for your burnt .... Num 29:39
vows, and your f offerings, and the.... Deut 12:6
nor thy f offerings, or heave .... Deut 12:17
of a f offering of thine hand .... Deut 16:10
even a f offering, according as........ Deut 23:23
was over the f offerings of God........ 2Chr 31:14
beside the f offering for the........... Ezr 1:4
a f offering unto the LORD .... Ezr 3:5
their own f to go up to Jerusalem ..... Ezr 7:13
with the f offering of the people ...... Ezr 7:16
the gold are a f offering unto.......... Ezr 8:28
the f offerings of my mouth, O........ Ps 119:108

FREEWOMAN

by a bondmaid, the other by a f .... Gal 4:22
but he of the f was by promise .... Gal 4:23

FREQUENT

above measure, in prisons more f....... 2Cor 11:23

FRESH

of it was as the taste of f oil .... Num 11:8
My glory was f in me, and my bow ...... Job 29:20
I shall be anointed with f oil............ Ps 92:10
both yield salt water and f .... Jas 3:12

FRESHER

flesh shall be f than a child's .... Job 33:25

FRET

it is f inward, whether it be .... Lev 13:55
her sore, for to make her f.............. 1Sa 1:6
F not thyself because of .... Ps 37:1
f not thyself because of him who .... Ps 37:7
f not thyself in any wise to do.......... Ps 37:8
F not thyself because of evil men ...... Prov 24:19
hungry, they shall f themselves........ Is 8:21

FRETTED

but hast f me in all these things....... Eze 16:43

FRETTETH

his heart f against the LORD .... Prov 19:3

FRETTING

the plague is a f leprosy .... Lev 13:51
for it is a f leprosy...................... Lev 13:52
it is a f leprosy in the house .... Lev 14:44

FRIED

with oil, or fine flour, f................. Lev 7:12
the pan, and for that which is f......... 1Chr 23:29

FRIEND

his f Hirah the Adullamite............. Gen 38:12
the hand of his f the Adullamite....... Gen 38:20
as a man speaketh unto his f .... Ex 33:11
the wife of thy bosom, or thy f......... Deut 13:6
whom he had used as his f.............. Judg 14:20
But Amnon had a f, whose name was... 2Sa 13:3
So Hushai David's f came into the 2Sa 15:37
Hushai the Archite, David's f.......... 2Sa 16:16
Is this thy kindness to thy f........... 2Sa 16:17
why wentest thou not with thy f 2Sa 16:17
officer, and the king's f................ 1Kin 4:5
seed of Abraham thy f for ever......... 2Chr 20:7
pity should be shewed from his f....... Job 6:14
and ye dig a pit for your f.............. Job 6:27
he had been my f or brother........... Ps 35:14
Yea, mine own familiar f, in whom..... Ps 41:9
f hast thou put far from me, and....... Ps 88:18
son, if thou be surety for thy f .... Prov 6:1
art come into the hand of thy f......... Prov 6:3
thyself, and make sure thy f........... Prov 6:3
A f loveth at all times, and a .... Prov 17:17
surety in the presence of his f .... Prov 17:18
there is a f that sticketh closer .... Prov 18:24

FRIENDLY

every man is a f to him that	Prov 19:6
his lips the king shall be his f	Prov 22:11
Faithful are the wounds of a f	Prov 27:6
of a man's f by hearty counsel	Prov 27:9
Thine own f, and thy father's	Prov 27:10
own f, and thy father's	Prov 27:10
blesseth his f with a loud voice	Prov 27:14
the countenance of his f	Prov 27:17
is my beloved, and this is my f	Song 5:16
chosen, the seed of Abraham my f	Is 41:8
neighbour and his f shall perish	Jer 6:21
the flesh of his f in the siege	Jer 19:9
love a woman beloved of her f	Hos 3:1
Trust ye not in a f, put ye not	Mic 7:5
of publicans and sinners	Mt 11:19
answered one of them, and said, F	Mt 20:13
And he saith unto him, F, how	Mt 22:12
And Jesus said unto him, F	Mt 26:50
a f of publicans and sinners	Lk 7:34
them, Which of you shall have a f	Lk 11:5
at midnight, and say unto him, F	Lk 11:5
For a f of mine in his journey is	Lk 11:6
and give him, because he is his f	Lk 11:8
cometh, he may say unto thee, F	Lk 14:10
but the f of the bridegroom,	Jn 3:29
unto them, Our f Lazarus sleepeth	Jn 11:11
man go, thou art not Caesar's f	Jn 19:12
the king's chamberlain their f	Acts 12:20
and he was called the F of God	Jas 2:23
a f of the world is the enemy of	Jas 4:4

FRIENDLY

after her, to speak f unto her	Judg 19:3
hast spoken f unto thine handmaid	Ruth 2:13
hath friends must shew himself f	Prov 18:24

FRIENDS

Gerar, and Ahuzzath one of his f	Gen 26:26
elders of Judah, even to his f	1Sa 30:26
to his brethren, and to his f	2Sa 3:8
thine enemies, and hatest thy f	2Sa 19:6
of his kinsfolks, nor of his f	1Kin 16:11
home, he sent and called for his f	Est 5:10
unto him, Let a gallows	Est 5:14
all his f every thing that had	Est 6:13
Now when Job's three f heard of	Job 2:11
My f scorn me	Job 16:20
that speaketh flattery to his f	Job 17:5
my familiar f have forgotten me	Job 19:14
All my inward f abhorred me	Job 19:19
me, have pity upon me, O ye my f	Job 19:21
his three f was his wrath kindled	Job 32:3
thee, and against thy two f	Job 42:7
of Job, when he prayed for his f	Job 42:10
my f stand aloof from my sore	Ps 38:11
but the rich hath many f	Prov 14:20
and a whisperer separateth chief f	Prov 16:28
a matter separateth very f	Prov 17:9
A man that hath f must shew	Prov 18:24
Wealth maketh many f	Prov 19:4
more do his f go far from him	Prov 19:7
eat, O f; drink, yea,	Song 5:1
to thyself, and to all thy f	Jer 20:4
buried there, thou, and all thy f	Jer 20:6
Thy f have set thee on, and have	Jer 38:22
all her f have dealt	Lam 1:2
was wounded in the house of my f	Zec 13:6
when his f heard of it, they went	Mk 3:21
saith unto him, Go home to thy f	Mk 5:19
the centurion sent f to him	Lk 7:6
And I say unto you my f, Be not	Lk 12:4
or a supper, call not thy f	Lk 14:12
home, he calleth together his f	Lk 15:6
hath found it, she calleth her f	Lk 15:9
that I might make merry with my f	Lk 15:29
to yourselves f of the mammon of	Lk 16:9
and brethren, and kinsfolks, and f	Lk 21:16
and Herod were made f together	Lk 23:12
a man lay down his life for his f	Jn 15:13
Ye are my f, if ye do whatsoever	Jn 15:14
but I have called you f	Jn 15:15
together his kinsmen and near f	Acts 10:24
chief of Asia, which were his f	Acts 19:31
go unto his f to refresh himself	Acts 27:3
Our f salute thee	3Jn 14
Greet thee by name	3Jn 14

FRIENDSHIP

Make no f with an angry man	Prov 22:24
know ye not that the f of the	Jas 4:4

FRINGE

that they put upon the f of the	Num 15:38
And it shall be unto you for a f	Num 15:39

FRINGES

them f in the borders of their	Num 15:38
Thou shalt make thee f upon the	Deut 22:12

FRO

a raven, which went forth to and f	Gen 8:7
and walked in the house to and f	2Kin 4:35
throughout the whole earth, to	2Chr 16:9
f in the earth, and from walking	Job 1:7
f in the earth, and from walking	Job 2:2
unto the dawning of the day	Job 7:4
thou break a leaf driven to and f	Job 13:25
They reel to and f, and stagger	Ps 107:27
of them that seek death	Prov 21:6
f like a drunkard, and shall be	Is 24:20
of locusts shall he run upon	Is 33:4
a captive, and removing to and f	Is 49:21
ye to and f through the streets of	Jer 5:1

and run to and f by the hedges	Jer 49:3
to and f occupied in thy fairs	Eze 27:19
many shall run to and f, and	Dan 12:4
shall run to and f in the city	Joel 2:9
f to seek the word of the LORD	Amos 8:12
to walk to and f through the earth	Zec 1:10
f through the earth, and, behold,	Zec 1:11
f through the whole earth	Zec 4:10
walk to and f through the earth	Zec 6:7
to walk to and f through the earth	Zec 6:7
walked to and f through the earth	Zec 6:7
no more children, tossed to and f	Eph 4:14

FROGS

will smite all thy borders with f	Ex 8:2
shall bring forth f abundantly	Ex 8:3
the f shall come up both on thee,	Ex 8:3
cause f to come up upon the land	Ex 8:5
the f came up, and covered the	Ex 8:6
brought up f upon the land of	Ex 8:7
he may take away the f from me	Ex 8:8
to destroy the f from thee	Ex 8:9
the f shall depart from thee, and,	Ex 8:11
f which he had brought against	Ex 8:12
the f died out of the houses, out	Ex 8:13
and f, which destroyed them	Ps 78:45
land brought forth f in abundance	Ps 105:30
f come out of the mouth of the	Rev 16:13

FROM See PREFACE.

FRONT

When Joab saw that the f of the	2Sa 10:9
that was in the f of the house	2Chr 3:4

FRONTIERS

his cities which are on his f	Eze 25:9

FRONTLETS

hand, and for f between thine eyes	Ex 13:16
they shall be as f between thine	Deut 6:8
may be as f between your eyes	Deut 11:18

FROST

consumed me, and the f by night	Gen 31:40
small as the hoar f on the ground	Ex 16:14
By the breath of God is given	Job 37:10
and the hoary f of heaven, who,	Job 38:29
and their sycomore trees with f	Ps 78:47
scattereth the hoar f like ashes	Ps 147:16
heat, and in the night to the f	Jer 36:30

FROWARD

for they are a very f generation	Deut 32:20
with the f thou wilt shew thyself	2Sa 22:27
the counsel of the f is carried	Job 5:13
thyself pure; and with the f	Ps 18:26
thou wilt shew thyself f	Ps 18:26
A f heart shall depart from me	Ps 101:4
the man that speaketh f things	Prov 2:12
crooked, and they f in their paths	Prov 2:15
For the f is abomination to the	Prov 3:32
Put away from thee a f mouth	Prov 4:24
man, walketh with a f mouth	Prov 6:12
there is nothing f or perverse in	Prov 8:8
way, and the f mouth, do I hate	Prov 8:13
but the f tongue shall be cut out	Prov 10:31
They that are of a f heart are	Prov 11:20
A f man soweth strife	Prov 16:28
his eyes to devise f things	Prov 16:30
He that hath a f heart findeth no	Prov 17:20
The way of man is f and strange	Prov 21:8
and snares are in the way of the f	Prov 22:5
good and gentle, but also to the f	1Pet 2:18

FROWARDLY

he went on f in the way of his	Is 57:17

FROWARDNESS

and delight in the f of the wicked	Prov 2:14
F is in his heart, he deviseth	Prov 6:14
mouth of the wicked speaketh f	Prov 10:32

FROZEN

and the face of the deep is f	Job 38:30

FRUIT

the f tree yielding f after	Gen 1:11
his kind, and the tree yielding f	Gen 1:12
in the which is the f of a tree	Gen 1:29
We may eat of the f of the trees	Gen 3:2
But of the f of the tree which is	Gen 3:3
wise, she took of the f thereof	Gen 3:6
that Cain brought of the f of the	Gen 4:3
from these the f of the womb	Gen 30:2
all the f of the trees which he	Ex 10:15
so that her f depart from her, and	Ex 21:22
then ye shall count the f thereof	Lev 19:23
But in the fourth year all the f	Lev 19:24
shall ye eat of the f thereof	Lev 19:25
gathered in the f of the land	Lev 23:39
and gather in the f thereof	Lev 25:3
And the land shall yield her f	Lev 25:19
bring forth f for three years	Lev 25:21
eat yet of old f until the ninth	Lev 25:22
of the field shall yield their f	Lev 26:4
or of the f of the tree, is the	Lev 27:30
and bring of the f of the land	Num 13:20
and shewed them the f of the land	Num 13:26
and this is the f of it	Num 13:27
they took of the f of the land in	Deut 1:25
will also bless the f of thy womb	Deut 7:13
the f of thy land, thy corn, and	Deut 7:13
and that the land yield not her f	Deut 11:17
lest the f of thy seed which thou	Deut 11:19

the f of thy vineyard, be defiled	Deut 22:9
first of all the f of the earth	Deut 26:2
shall be the f of thy body	Deut 28:4
the f of thy ground, and the f	Deut 28:4
the f of thy cattle, the increase	Deut 28:4
in the f of thy body, and in the	Deut 28:11
in the f of thy cattle, and in the	Deut 28:11
in the f of thy ground, in the	Deut 28:11
Cursed shall be the f of thy body	Deut 28:18
the f of thy land, the increase	Deut 28:18
The f of thy land, and all thy	Deut 28:33
for thine olive shall cast his f	Deut 28:40
of thy land shall the locust	Deut 28:42
he shall eat the f of thy cattle	Deut 28:51
the f of thy land, until thou be	Deut 28:51
shalt eat the f of thine own body	Deut 28:53
in the f of thy body	Deut 30:9
in the f of thy cattle	Deut 30:9
in the f of thy land, for good	Deut 30:9
but they did eat of the f of the	Josh 5:12
my sweetness, and my good f	Judg 9:11
summer f for the young men to eat	2Sa 16:2
root downward, and bear f upward	2Kin 19:30
and f trees in abundance	Neh 9:25
our fathers to eat the f thereof	Neh 9:36
firstfruits of all f of all trees	Neh 10:35
the f of all manner of trees, of	Neh 10:37
forth his f in his season	Ps 1:3
Their f shalt thou destroy from	Ps 21:10
the f thereof shall shake like	Ps 72:16
still bring forth f in old age	Ps 92:14
satisfied with the f of thy works	Ps 104:13
devoured the f of their ground	Ps 105:35
the f of the womb is his reward	Ps 127:3
Of the f of thy body will I set	Ps 132:11
eat of the f of their own way	Prov 1:31
My f is better than gold, yea,	Prov 8:19
the f of the wicked to sin	Prov 10:16
The f of the righteous is a tree	Prov 11:30
root of the righteous yieldeth f	Prov 12:12
with good by the f of his mouth	Prov 12:14
eat good by the f of his mouth	Prov 13:2
satisfied with the f of his mouth	Prov 18:20
love it shall eat the f thereof	Prov 18:21
fig tree shall eat the f thereof	Prov 27:18
with the f of her hands she	Prov 31:16
Give her of the f of her hands	Prov 31:31
his f was sweet to my taste	Song 2:3
every one for the f thereof was	Song 8:11
keep the f thereof two hundred	Song 8:12
shall eat the f of their doings	Is 3:10
the f of the earth shall be	Is 4:2
I will punish the f of the stout	Is 10:12
have no pity on the f of the womb	Is 13:18
his f shall be a fiery flying	Is 14:29
fill the face of the world with f	Is 27:6
this is all the f to take away	Is 27:9
as the hasty f before the summer	Is 28:4
vineyards, and eat the f thereof	Is 37:30
root downward, and bear f upward	Is 37:31
I create the f of the lips	Is 57:19
vineyards, and eat the f of them	Is 65:21
country, to eat the f thereof	Jer 2:7
even the f of their thoughts,	Jer 6:19
and upon the f of the ground	Jer 7:20
olive tree, fair, and of goodly f	Jer 11:16
the tree with the f thereof	Jer 11:19
grow, yea, they bring forth f	Jer 12:2
shall cease from yielding f	Jer 17:10
according to the f of his doings	Jer 17:10
according to the f of your doings	Jer 21:14
gardens, and eat the f of them	Jer 29:5
gardens, and eat the f of them	Jer 29:28
according to the f of his doings	Jer 32:19
Shall the women eat their f	Lam 2:20
branches, and that it might bear f	Eze 17:8
thereof, and cut off the f thereof	Eze 17:9
bring forth boughs, and bear f	Eze 17:23
and the east wind dried up her f	Eze 19:12
which hath devoured her f	Eze 19:14
they shall eat thy f, and they	Eze 25:4
of the field shall yield her f	Eze 34:27
yield your f to my people of	Eze 36:8
and they shall increase and bring f	Eze 36:11
I will multiply the f of the tree	Eze 36:30
neither shall the f thereof be	Eze 47:12
new f according to his months	Eze 47:12
the f thereof shall be for meat,	Eze 47:12
the f thereof much, and in it was	Dan 4:12
off his leaves, and scatter his f	Dan 4:14
the f thereof much, and in it was	Dan 4:21
is dried up, they shall bear no f	Hos 9:16
even the beloved f of their womb	Hos 9:16
he bringeth forth f unto himself	Hos 10:1
to the multitude of his f he hath	Hos 10:1
ye have eaten the f of lies	Hos 10:13
From me is thy f found	Hos 14:8
for the tree beareth her f	Joel 2:22
yet I destroyed his f from above	Amos 2:9
the f of righteousness into	Amos 6:12
and a gatherer of sycomore f	Amos 7:14
and behold a basket of summer f	Amos 8:1
And I said, A basket of summer f	Amos 8:2
gardens, and eat the f of them	Amos 9:14
the f of my body for the sin of	Mic 6:7
my soul desired the firstripe f	Mic 7:1
for the f of their doings	Mic 7:13
neither shall f be in the vines	Hab 3:17
and the earth is stayed from her f	Hag 1:10
the vine shall give her f	Zec 8:12

F

the *f* thereof, even his meat, is .... Mal 1:12
shall your vine cast her *f* before .... Mal 3:11
not forth good *f* is hewn down .... Mt 3:10
good tree bringeth forth good *f* .... Mt 7:17
tree bringeth forth evil *f* .... Mt 7:17
tree cannot bring forth evil *f* .... Mt 7:18
a corrupt tree bring forth good *f* .... Mt 7:18
not forth good *f* is hewn down .... Mt 7:19
make the tree good, and his *f* good .... Mt 12:33
tree corrupt, and his *f* corrupt .... Mt 12:33
for the tree is known by his *f* .... Mt 12:33
good ground, and brought forth *f* .... Mt 13:8
which also beareth *f*, and bringeth .... Mt 13:23
was sprung up, and brought forth *f* .... Mt 13:26
unto it, Let no *f* grow on thee .... Mt 21:19
when the time of the *f* drew near .... Mt 21:34
henceforth of this *f* of the vine .... Mt 26:29
and choked it, and it yielded no *f* .... Mk 4:7
did yield *f* that sprang up and .... Mk 4:8
and receive it, and bring forth *f* .... Mk 4:20
earth bringeth forth *f* of herself .... Mk 4:28
But when the *f* is brought forth, ... Mk 4:29
No man eat *f* of thee hereafter .... Mk 11:14
of the *f* of the vineyard .... Mk 12:2
no more of the *f* of the vine .... Mk 14:25
and blessed is the *f* of thy womb .... Lk 1:42
not forth good *f* is hewn down .... Lk 3:9
tree bringeth not forth corrupt *f* .... Lk 6:43
a corrupt tree bring forth good *f* .... Lk 6:43
every tree is known by his own *f* .... Lk 6:44
up, and bare *f* an hundredfold .... Lk 8:8
life, and bring no *f* to perfection .... Lk 8:14
bring forth *f* with patience .... Lk 8:15
sought *f* thereon, and found none .... Lk 13:6
I come seeking *f* on this fig tree .... Lk 13:7
And if it bear *f*, well .... Lk 13:9
give him of the *f* of the vineyard .... Lk 20:10
not drink of the *f* of the vine .... Lk 22:18
gathereth *f* unto life eternal .... Jn 4:36
it die, it bringeth forth much *f* .... Jn 12:24
that beareth not *f* he taketh away .... Jn 15:2
and every branch that beareth *f* .... Jn 15:2
that it may bring forth more *f* .... Jn 15:2
branch cannot bear *f* of itself .... Jn 15:4
the same bringeth forth much *f* .... Jn 15:5
glorified, that ye bear much *f* .... Jn 15:8
ye should go and bring forth *f* .... Jn 15:16
that your *f* should remain .... Jn 15:16
that of the *f* of his loins .... Acts 2:30
might have some *f* among you also .... Rom 1:13
What *f* had ye then in those .... Rom 6:21
ye have your *f* unto holiness, and .... Rom 6:22
we should bring forth *f* unto God .... Rom 7:4
to bring forth *f* unto death .... Rom 7:5
and have sealed to them this *f* .... Rom 15:28
and eateth not of the *f* thereof 1Cor 9:7
But the *f* of the Spirit is love, ... Gal 5:22
(For the *f* of the Spirit is in .... Eph 5:9
this is the *f* of my labour .... Phil 1:22
but I desire *f* that may abound to .... Phil 4:17
and bringeth forth *f*, as it doth .... Col 1:6
it yieldeth the peaceable *f* of .... Heb 12:11
the *f* of our lips giving thanks .... Heb 13:15
the *f* of righteousness is sown in .... Jas 3:18
for the precious *f* of the earth .... Jas 5:7
and the earth brought forth her *f* .... Jas 5:18
trees whose *f* withereth, without .... Jude 12
whose *f* withereth, without .... Jude 12
and yielded her *f* every month .... Rev 22:2

FRUITFUL

And God blessed them, saying, Be *f* .... Gen 1:22
them, and God said unto them, Be *f* .... Gen 1:28
abundantly in the earth, and be *f* .... Gen 8:17
his sons, and said unto them, Be *f* .... Gen 9:1
And you, be ye *f*, and multiply .... Gen 9:7
And I will make thee exceeding *f* .... Gen 17:6
blessed him, and will make him *f* .... Gen 17:20
us, and we shall be *f* in the land .... Gen 26:22
bless thee, and make thee *f* .... Gen 28:3
be *f* and multiply .... Gen 35:11
be *f* in the land of my affliction .... Gen 41:52
me, Behold, I will make thee *f* .... Gen 48:4
Joseph is a *f* bough .... Gen 49:22
even a *f* bough by a well .... Gen 49:22
And the children of Israel were *f* .... Ex 1:7
respect unto you, and make you *f* .... Lev 26:9
A *f* land into barrenness, for the .... Ps 107:34
Thy wife shall be as a *f* vine by .... Ps 128:3
f trees, and all cedars .... Ps 148:9
hath a vineyard in a very *f* hill .... Is 5:1
of his forest, and of his *f* field .... Is 10:18
in the outmost *f* branches thereof .... Is 17:6
shall be turned into a *f* field, ... Is 29:17
the *f* field shall be esteemed as .... Is 29:17
pleasant fields, for the *f* vine .... Is 32:12
and the wilderness be a *f* field .... Is 32:15
the *f* field be counted for a .... Is 32:15
remain in the *f* field .... Is 32:16
the *f* place was a wilderness, and .... Jer 4:26
and they shall be *f* and increase .... Jer 23:3
land, and planted it in a *f* field .... Eze 17:5
she was *f* and full of branches by .... Eze 19:10
Though he be *f* among his brethren .... Hos 13:15
f seasons, filling our hearts .... Acts 14:17
being *f* in every good work, and .... Col 1:10

FRUITS

take of the best *f* in the land in .... Gen 43:11
to offer the first of thy ripe *f* .... Ex 22:29
and shalt gather in thy *f* thereof .... Ex 23:10

---

with the bread of the first *f* for .... Lev 23:20
of the *f* he shall sell unto thee .... Lev 25:15
of the *f* doth he sell unto thee .... Lev 25:16
until her *f* come in ye shall eat .... Lev 25:22
trees of the land yield their *f* .... Lev 26:20
for the precious *f* brought forth .... Deut 33:14
him, and thou shalt bring in the *f* 2Sa 9:10
and an hundred of summer *f* 2Sa 16:1
all the *f* of the field since the 2Kin 8:6
vineyards, and eat the *f* thereof 2Kin 19:29
If I have eaten the *f* thereof .... Job 31:39
which may yield *f* of increase .... Ps 107:37
trees in them of all kind of *f* .... Eccl 2:5
of pomegranates, with pleasant *f* .... Song 4:13
his garden, and eat his pleasant *f* .... Song 4:16
nuts to see the *f* of the valley .... Song 6:11
are all manner of pleasant *f* .... Song 7:13
for the shouting for thy summer *f* .... Is 16:9
and Carmel shake off their *f* .... Is 33:9
ye, gather ye wine, and summer *f* .... Jer 40:10
wine and summer *f* very much .... Jer 40:12
is fallen upon thy summer *f* .... Jer 48:32
for want of the *f* of the field .... Lam 4:9
they have gathered the summer *f* .... Mic 7:1
not destroy the *f* of your ground .... Mal 3:11
therefore *f* meet for repentance .... Mt 3:8
Ye shall know them by their *f* .... Mt 7:16
by their *f* ye shall know them .... Mt 7:20
they might receive the *f* of it .... Mt 21:34
render him the *f* in their seasons .... Mt 21:41
bringing forth the *f* thereof .... Mt 21:43
therefore *f* worthy of repentance .... Lk 3:8
have no room where to bestow my *f* .... Lk 12:17
and there will I bestow all my *f* .... Lk 12:18
sown, and increase the *f* of your 2Cor 9:10
with the *f* of righteousness .... Phil 1:11
must be first partaker of the *f* 2Ti 2:6
full of mercy and good *f*, without .... Jas 3:17
the *f* that thy soul lusted after .... Rev 18:14
which bare twelve manner of *f* .... Rev 22:2

FRUSTRATE

to *f* their purpose, all the days .... Ezr 4:5
I do not *f* the grace of God .... Gal 2:21

FRUSTRATETH

That *f* the tokens of the liars, ... Is 44:25

FRYING

meat offering baken in the *f* pan .... Lev 2:7

FRYINGPAN

and all that is dressed in the *f* .... Lev 7:9

FUEL

be with burning and *f* of fire .... Is 9:5
shall be as the *f* of the fire .... Is 9:19
it is cast into the fire for *f* .... Eze 15:4
I have given to the fire for *f* .... Eze 15:6
Thou shalt be for *f* to the fire .... Eze 21:32

FUGITIVE

a *f* and a vagabond shalt thou be .... Gen 4:12
and I shall be a *f* and a vagabond .... Gen 4:14

FUGITIVES

Ye Gileadites are *f* of Ephraim .... Judg 12:4
that fell away to the king 2Kin 25:11
his *f* shall flee unto Zoar, an .... Is 15:5
all his *f* with all his bands .... Eze 17:21

FULFIL

f her week, and we will give thee .... Gen 29:27
f your wishes, your daily tasks, ... Ex 5:13
the number of thy days I will *f* .... Ex 23:26
that he might *f* the word of the 1Kin 2:27
takest heed to *f* the statutes 1Chr 22:13
To *f* the word of the LORD by the 2Chr 36:21
of *f* threescore and ten years 2Chr 36:21
number the months that they *f* .... Job 39:2
own heart, and *f* all thy counsel .... Ps 20:4
the LORD *f* all thy petitions .... Ps 20:5
He will *f* the desire of them that .... Ps 145:19
us to *f* all righteousness .... Mt 3:15
am not come to destroy, but to *f* .... Mt 5:17
heart, which shall *f* all my will .... Acts 13:22
if it *f* the law, Judge thee, who .... Rom 2:27
the flesh, to *f* the lusts thereof .... Rom 13:14
ye shall not *f* the lust of the .... Gal 5:16
and so *f* the law of Christ .... Gal 6:2
f ye my joy, that ye be .... Phil 2:2
me for you, to *f* the word of God .... Col 1:25
in the Lord, that thou *f* it .... Col 4:17
f all the good pleasure of his 2Th 1:11
If ye *f* the royal law according .... Jas 2:8
put in their hearts to *f* his will .... Rev 17:17

FULFILLED

her days to be delivered were *f* .... Gen 25:24
me my wife, for my days are *f* .... Gen 29:21
And Jacob did so, and *f* her week .... Gen 29:28
And forty days were *f* for him .... Gen 50:3
for so are *f* the days of those .... Gen 50:3
Wherefore have ye not *f* your task .... Ex 5:14
And seven days were *f*, after that .... Ex 7:25
the days of her purifying be *f* .... Lev 12:4
the days of her purifying are *f* .... Lev 12:6
until the days be *f*, in the which .... Num 6:5
the days of his separation are *f* .... Num 6:13
And when thy days be *f*, and thou 2Sa 7:12
in that the king hath *f* the 2Sa 14:22
and hath with his hand *f* it 1Kin 8:15
hast *f* it with thine hand, as it 1Kin 8:24
who hath with his hands *f* that 2Chr 6:4

---

hast *f* it with thine hand, as it 2Chr 6:15
the mouth of Jeremiah might be *f* .... Ezr 1:1
But thou hast *f* the judgment of .... Job 36:17
f with your hand, saying, We will .... Jer 44:25
he hath *f* his word that he had .... Lam 2:17
our end is near, our days are *f* .... Lam 4:18
when the days of the siege are *f* .... Eze 5:2
the thing *f* upon Nebuchadnezzar .... Dan 4:33
till three whole weeks were *f* .... Dan 10:3
that it might be *f* which was .... Mt 1:22
that it might be *f* which was .... Mt 2:15
Then was *f* that which was spoken .... Mt 2:17
that it might be *f* which was .... Mt 2:23
That it might be *f* which was .... Mt 4:14
pass from the law, till all be *f* .... Mt 5:18
That it might be *f* which was .... Mt 8:17
That it might be *f* which was .... Mt 12:17
in them is *f* the prophecy of .... Mt 13:14
That it might be *f* which was .... Mt 13:35
that it might be *f* which was .... Mt 21:4
pass, till all these things be *f* .... Mt 24:34
then shall the scriptures be *f* .... Mt 26:54
of the prophets might be *f* .... Mt 26:56
Then was *f* that which was spoken .... Mt 27:9
that it might be *f* which was .... Mt 27:35
And saying, The time is *f*, and the .... Mk 1:15
when all these things shall be *f* .... Mk 13:4
but the scriptures must be *f* .... Mk 14:49
And the scripture was *f*, which .... Mk 15:28
which shall be *f* in their season .... Lk 1:20
And when they had *f* the days .... Lk 2:43
is this scripture *f* in your ears .... Lk 4:21
things which are written may be *f* .... Lk 21:22
the times of the Gentiles be *f* .... Lk 21:24
not pass away, till all be *f* .... Lk 21:32
until it be *f* in the kingdom of .... Lk 22:16
you, that all things must be *f* .... Lk 24:44
this my joy therefore is *f* .... Jn 3:29
that Esaias the prophet might be *f* .... Jn 12:38
but that the scripture may be *f* .... Jn 13:18
that the word might be *f* that is .... Jn 15:25
that the scripture might be *f* .... Jn 17:12
might have my joy *f* in themselves .... Jn 17:13
That the saying might be *f*, ... Jn 18:9
that the scripture might be *f* .... Jn 18:32
that the scripture might be *f* .... Jn 19:24
that the scripture might be *f* .... Jn 19:28
that the scripture should be *f* .... Jn 19:36
scripture must needs have been *f* .... Acts 1:16
should suffer, he hath so *f* .... Acts 3:18
And after that many days were *f* .... Acts 9:23
when they had *f* their ministry, ... Acts 12:25
as John *f* his course, he said, ... Acts 13:25
they have *f* them in condemning .... Acts 13:27
when they had *f* all that was .... Acts 13:29
God hath *f* the same unto us their .... Acts 13:33
of God for the work which they *f* .... Acts 14:26
of the law might be *f* in us .... Rom 8:4
loveth another hath *f* the law .... Rom 13:8
when your obedience is *f* 2Cor 10:6
For all the law is *f* in one word, ... Gal 5:14
the scripture was *f* which saith .... Jas 2:23
killed as they were, should be *f* .... Rev 6:11
of the seven angels were *f* .... Rev 15:8
until the words of God shall be *f* .... Rev 17:17
the thousand years should be *f* .... Rev 20:3

FULFILLING

stormy wind *f* his word .... Ps 148:8
love is the *f* of the law .... Rom 13:10
f the desires of the flesh and of .... Eph 2:3

FULL

vale of Siddim was *f* of slimepits .... Gen 14:10
of the Amorites is not yet *f* .... Gen 15:16
age, an old man, and *f* of years .... Gen 25:8
people, being old and *f* of days .... Gen 35:29
to pass at the end of two *f* years .... Gen 41:1
devoured the seven rank and *f* ears .... Gen 41:7
ears came up in one stalk, *f* .... Gen 41:22
his sack, our money in *f* weight .... Gen 43:21
shall be *f* of swarms of flies .... Ex 8:21
and when we did eat bread to the *f* .... Ex 16:3
and in the morning bread to the *f* .... Ex 16:8
put an omer *f* of manna therein, ... Ex 16:33
for he should make *f* restitution .... Ex 22:3
even corn beaten out of *f* ears .... Lev 2:14
he shall take a censer *f* of .... Lev 16:12
his hands *f* of sweet incense .... Lev 16:12
perfumes, *f* of incense for .... Lev 16:12
within a *f* year may he redeem it .... Lev 25:29
within the space of a *f* year .... Lev 25:30
ye shall eat your bread to the *f* .... Lev 26:5
both of them were *f* of fine flour .... Num 7:13
ten shekels of gold, *f* of incense .... Num 7:14
both of them *f* of fine flour .... Num 7:19
gold of ten shekels, *f* of incense .... Num 7:20
both of them *f* of fine flour .... Num 7:25
of ten shekels, *f* of incense .... Num 7:26
both of them *f* of fine flour .... Num 7:31
of ten shekels, *f* of incense .... Num 7:32
both of them *f* of fine flour .... Num 7:37
of ten shekels, *f* of incense .... Num 7:38
both of them *f* of fine flour .... Num 7:43
of ten shekels, *f* of incense .... Num 7:44
both of them *f* of fine flour .... Num 7:49
of ten shekels, *f* of incense .... Num 7:50
both of them *f* of fine flour .... Num 7:55
of ten shekels, *f* of incense .... Num 7:56
both of them *f* of fine flour .... Num 7:61
of ten shekels, *f* of incense .... Num 7:62

both of them f of fine flour...............Num 7:67
of ten shekels, f of incense................Num 7:68
both of them f of fine flour................Num 7:73
of ten shekels, f of incense................Num 7:74
both of them f of fine flour................Num 7:79
of ten shekels, f of incense................Num 7:80
f of incense, weighing ten..................Num 7:86
give me his house f of silver...............Num 22:18
give me his house f of silver...............Num 24:13
houses f of all good things,................Deut 6:11
thou shalt have eaten and be f..............Deut 6:11
When thou hast eaten and art f..............Deut 8:10
when thou hast eaten and art f..............Deut 8:12
that thou mayest eat and be f...............Deut 11:15
father and her mother a f full..............Deut 22:17
f with the blessing of the Lord,...........Deut 33:23
Nun was f of the spirit of wisdom...........Deut 34:9
of the fleece, a bowl f of water............Judg 6:38
Now the house was f of men..................Judg 16:27
I went out f, and the Lord hath.............Ruth 1:21
a f reward be given thee of the.............Ruth 2:12
They that were f have hired out.............1Sa 2:5
gave them in f tale to the king.............1Sa 18:27
of the Philistines was a f year.............1Sa 18:27
with one f line to keep alive...............2Sa 8:2
it came to pass after two f years...........2Sa 13:23
dwelt two f years in Jerusalem..............2Sa 14:28
a piece of ground f of lentiles.............2Sa 23:11
Make this valley f of ditches...............2Kin 3:16
shalt set aside that which is f.............2Kin 4:4
to pass, when the vessels were f............2Kin 4:6
thereof wild gourds his lap f...............2Kin 4:39
f ears of corn in the husk..................2Kin 4:42
the mountain was f of horses................2Kin 6:17
lo, all the way was f of garments...........2Kin 7:15
drew a bow with his f strength..............2Kin 9:24
the house of Baal was f from one............2Kin 10:21
he reigned a f month in Samaria.............2Kin 15:13
a parcel of ground f of barley..............1Chr 11:13
shalt grant it me for the price f...........1Chr 21:22
verily buy it for the f price...............1Chr 21:24
f of days, he made Solomon his..............1Chr 23:1
f of days, riches, and honour...............1Chr 29:28
was f of days when he died..................2Chr 24:15
possessed houses f of all goods.............Neh 9:25
then was Haman f of wrath...................Est 3:5
of indignation against.................Est 5:9
come to thy grave in a f age................Job 5:26
I am f of tossings to and fro unto..........Job 7:4
I am f of confusion.........................Job 10:15
should a man f of talk be...................Job 11:2
is of few days, and f of trouble............Job 14:1
His bones are f of the sin of his..........Job 20:11
One dieth in his f strength.................Job 21:23
His breasts are f of milk...................Job 21:24
For I am f of matter........................Job 32:18
thy table should be f of fatness............Job 36:16
Job died, being old and f days..............Job 42:17
His mouth is f of cursing...................Ps 10:7
they are f of children, and leave...........Ps 17:14
their right hand is f of bribes.............Ps 26:10
voice of the Lord is f of majesty...........Ps 29:4
the earth is f of the goodness of...........Ps 33:5
right hand is f of righteousness............Ps 48:10
river of God, which is f of water...........Ps 65:9
and I am f of heaviness.....................Ps 69:20
waters of a f cup are wrung out.............Ps 73:10
dark places of the earth are f of..........Ps 74:20
it is f of mixture..........................Ps 75:8
he sent them meat to the f..................Ps 78:25
being f of compassion, forgave.............Ps 78:38
art a God f of compassion, and..............Ps 86:15
For my soul is f of troubles................Ps 88:3
trees of the Lord are f of sap..............Ps 104:16
the earth is f of thy riches................Ps 104:24
is gracious and f of compassion.............Ps 111:4
f of compassion, and righteous..............Ps 112:4
earth, O Lord, is f of thy mercy............Ps 119:64
that hath his quiver f of them..............Ps 127:5
That our garners may be f...................Ps 144:13
is gracious, and f of compassion............Ps 145:8
than an house f of sacrifices...............Prov 17:1
The f soul loatheth an honeycomb............Prov 27:7
Hell and destruction are never f...........Prov 27:20
Lest I be f, and deny thee, and say.........Prov 30:9
yet the sea is not f........................Eccl 1:7
All things are f of labour..................Eccl 1:8
both the hands f with travail...............Eccl 4:6
of the sons of men is f of evil.............Eccl 9:3
A fool also is f of words...................Eccl 10:14
If the clouds be f of rain..................Eccl 11:3
I am f of the burnt offerings of............Is 1:11
your hands are f of blood...................Is 1:15
it was f of judgment........................Is 1:21
Their land also is f of silver..............Is 2:7
their land is also f of horses..............Is 2:7
Their land also is f of idols...............Is 2:8
the whole earth is f of his glory...........Is 6:3
for the earth shall be f of the.............Is 11:9
shall be f of doleful creatures.............Is 13:21
of Dimon shall be f of blood................Is 15:9
Thou that art f of stirs, a.................Is 22:2
valleys shall be f of chariots..............Is 22:7
lees, of fat things f of marrow.............Is 25:6
For all tables are f of vomit...............Is 28:8
his lips are f of indignation, and..........Is 30:27
they are f of the fury of the...............Is 51:20
Even a f wind from those places.............Jer 4:12
yet will I not make a f end.................Jer 4:27
when I had fed them to the f................Jer 5:7

but make not a f end........................Jer 5:10
I will not make a f end with you............Jer 5:18
As a cage is f of birds, so are.............Jer 5:27
so are their houses f of deceit.............Jer 5:27
Therefore I am f of the fury of............Jer 6:11
aged with him that is f of days.............Jer 6:11
For the land is f of adulterers.............Jer 23:10
Within two f years will I bring.............Jer 28:3
within the space of two f years.............Jer 28:11
though I make a f end of all................Jer 30:11
will I not make a f end of thee.............Jer 30:11
of the Rechabites pots f of wine............Jer 35:5
for I will make a f end of all..............Jer 46:28
I will not make a f end of thee.............Jer 46:28
solitary, that was f of people..............Lam 1:1
he is filled f with reproach................Lam 3:30
their rings were f of eyes round............Eze 1:18
the land is f of bloody.....................Eze 7:23
and the city is f of violence...............Eze 7:23
great, and the land is f of blood...........Eze 9:9
the city f of perverseness..................Eze 9:9
the court was f of the brightness...........Eze 10:4
were f of eyes round about, even...........Eze 10:12
with thou make a f end of the...............Eze 11:13
of feathers, which had divers...............Eze 17:3
But truly I am f of power by the............Mic 3:8
men thereof are f of violence...............Mic 6:12
it is all f of lies and robbery.............Nah 3:1
and the earth was f of his praise...........Hab 3:3
of the city shall be f of boys..............Zec 8:5
whole body shall be f of light..............Mt 6:22
whole body shall be f of darkness...........Mt 6:23
Which, when it was f, they drew.............Mt 13:48
that remained twelve baskets f..............Mt 14:20
that was left seven baskets f...............Mt 15:37
within they are f of extortion..............Mt 23:25
but are within f of dead men's..............Mt 23:27
but within ye are f of hypocrisy............Mt 23:28
after that the f corn in the ear...........Mk 4:28
the ship, so that it was now f.............Mk 4:37
twelve baskets f of the fragments..........Mk 6:43
f well ye reject the commandment............Mk 7:9
how many baskets f of fragments.............Mk 8:19
how many baskets f of fragments.............Mk 8:20
and filled a spunge f of vinegar...........Mk 15:36
Now Elisabeth's f time came that...........Lk 1:57
Jesus being f of the Holy Ghost.............Lk 4:1
city, behold a man f of leprosy.............Lk 5:12
Woe unto you that are f.....................Lk 6:25
thy whole body also is f of light..........Lk 11:34
thy body also is f of darkness..............Lk 11:34
body therefore be f of light...............Lk 11:36
the whole shall be f of light..............Lk 11:36
your inward part is f of ravening...........Lk 11:39
was laid at his gate, f of sores...........Lk 16:20
the Father,) f of grace and truth..........Jn 1:14
for my time is not yet f come...............Jn 7:8
you, and that your joy might be f...........Jn 15:11
receive, that your joy may be f.............Jn 16:24
we set a vessel f of vinegar................Jn 19:29
the net to land f of great fishes..........Jn 21:11
said, These men are f of new wine...........Acts 2:13
thou shalt make me f of joy with...........Acts 2:28
f of the Holy Ghost and wisdom,.............Acts 6:3
a man f of faith and of the Holy............Acts 6:5
f of faith and power, did great............Acts 6:8
man f of faith forty years old, it.........Acts 7:23
being f of the Holy Ghost, looked...........Acts 7:55
this woman was f of good works..............Acts 9:36
f of the Holy Ghost and of faith............Acts 11:24
O f of all subtilty and all.................Acts 13:10
sayings, they were f of wrath...............Acts 19:28
of envy, murder, debate, deceit............Rom 1:29
Whose mouth is f of cursing.................Rom 3:14
that ye also are f of goodness..............Rom 15:14
Now ye are f, now ye are rich, ye..........1Cor 4:8
was of heaviness, because that.............Phil 2:26
I am instructed both to be f................Phil 4:12
I am f, having received of..................Phil 4:18
love, and unto all riches of the...........Col 2:2
make f proof of thy ministry................2Ti 4:5
to them that are of f age...................Heb 5:14
f assurance of hope unto the end............Heb 6:11
heart in f assurance of faith...............Heb 10:22
unruly evil, f of deadly poison.............Jas 3:8
of mercy and good fruits,...................Jas 3:17
joy unspeakable and f of glory..............1Pet 1:8
Having eyes f of adultery...................2Pet 2:14
but that we receive a f reward..............2Jn 8
to face, that our joy may be f..............2Jn 12
were four beasts f of eyes before...........Rev 4:6
they were f of eyes within..................Rev 4:8
and golden vials f of odours................Rev 5:8
vials f of the wrath of God.................Rev 15:7
and his kingdom was f of darkness...........Rev 16:10
f of names of blasphemy, having............Rev 17:3

cup in her hand f of abominations...........Rev 17:4
vials f of the seven last plagues...........Rev 21:9

FULLER
so as no f on earth can white...............Mk 9:3

FULLER'S
is in the highway of the f field............2Kin 18:17
in the highway of the f field...............Is 7:3
in the highway of the f field...............Is 36:2

FULLERS'
a refiner's fire, and like f sope...........Mal 3:2

FULLY
Moses had f set up the tabernacle...........Num 7:1
with him, and hath followed me f............Num 14:24
It hath f been shewed me, all...............Ruth 2:11
went not f after the Lord, as did...........1Kin 11:6
men is f set in them to do evil.............Eccl 8:11
be devoured as stubble f dry................Nah 1:10
the day of Pentecost was f come.............Acts 2:1
being f persuaded that, what he.............Rom 4:21
Let every man be f persuaded in.............Rom 14:5
I have f preached the gospel of.............Rom 15:19
But thou hast f known my doctrine...........2Ti 3:10
me the preaching might be f known...........2Ti 4:17
for her grapes are f ripe...................Rev 14:18

FULNESS
as the f of the winepress...................Num 18:27
f thereof, and for the good will............Deut 33:16
the sea roar, and the f thereof.............1Chr 16:32
In the f of his sufficiency he..............Job 20:22
in thy presence is f of joy.................Ps 16:11
is the Lord's, and the f thereof............Ps 24:1
world is mine, and the f thereof............Ps 50:12
the f thereof, thou hast founded............Ps 89:11
the sea roar, and the f thereof.............Ps 96:11
the sea roar, and the f thereof.............Ps 98:7
f of bread, and abundance of................Eze 16:49
the f thereof, by the noise of..............Eze 19:7
of his f have all we received, and..........Jn 1:16
how much more their f........................Rom 11:12
until the f of the Gentiles be..............Rom 11:25
I shall come in the f of the................Rom 15:29
is the Lord's, and the f thereof............1Cor 10:26
the f thereof, and the f thereof............1Cor 10:28
But when the f of the time was..............Gal 4:4
of the f of times he might gather...........Eph 1:10
of him that filleth all in..................Eph 1:23
be filled with all the f of God.............Eph 3:19
of the stature of the f of Christ...........Eph 4:13
that in him should all f dwell..............Col 1:19
all the f of the Godhead bodily.............Col 2:9

FURBISH
f the spears, and put on the................Jer 46:4

FURBISHED
a sword is sharpened, and also f............Eze 21:9
it is f that it may glitter.................Eze 21:10
And he hath given it to be f................Eze 21:11
sword is sharpened, and it is f.............Eze 21:11
for the slaughter it is f...................Eze 21:28

FURIOUS
with a f man thou shalt not go..............Prov 22:24
strife, and a f man aboundeth in............Prov 29:22
anger and in fury and in f rebukes..........Eze 5:15
upon them with f rebukes....................Eze 25:17
the king was angry and very f...............Dan 2:12
the Lord revengeth, and is f................Nah 1:2

FURIOUSLY
for he driveth f.............................2Kin 9:20
and they shall deal f with thee.............Eze 23:25

FURLONGS
from Jerusalem about threescore f...........Lk 24:13
about five and twenty or thirty f...........Jn 6:19
Jerusalem, about fifteen f off..............Jn 11:18
of a thousand and six hundred f.............Rev 14:20
with the reed, twelve thousand f............Rev 21:16

FURNACE
it was dark, behold a smoking f.............Gen 15:17
went up as the smoke of a f.................Gen 19:28
to you handfuls of ashes of the f...........Ex 9:8
And they took ashes of the f................Ex 9:10
ascended as the smoke of a f................Ex 19:18
you forth out of the iron f.................Deut 4:20
from the midst of the f of iron.............1Kin 8:51
as silver tried in a f of earth............Ps 12:6
is for silver, and the f for gold...........Prov 17:3
pot for silver, and the f for gold..........Prov 27:21
is in Zion, and his f in Jerusalem..........Is 31:9
thee in the f of affliction.................Is 48:10
land of Egypt, from the iron f..............Jer 11:4
and lead, in the midst of the f.............Eze 22:18
and tin, into the midst of the f............Eze 22:20
is melted in the midst of the f.............Eze 22:22
the midst of a burning fiery................Dan 3:6
the midst of a burning fiery................Dan 3:11
the midst of a burning fiery................Dan 3:15
us from the burning fiery f.................Dan 3:17
that they should heat the f one.............Dan 3:19
them into the burning fiery f...............Dan 3:20
the midst of the burning fiery f............Dan 3:21
f exceeding hot, the flame of...............Dan 3:22
the midst of the burning fiery f............Dan 3:23
the mouth of the burning fiery f............Dan 3:26
shall cast them into a f of fire............Mt 13:42
cast them into the f of fire................Mt 13:50
brass, as if they burned in a f.............Rev 1:15

pit, as the smoke of a great f.................. Rev 9:2

FURNACES
piece, and the tower of the f................ Neh 3:11
of the f even unto the broad wall....... Neh 12:38

FURNISH
Thou shalt f him liberally out of.... Deut 15:14
said, Can God f a table in the.............. Ps 78:19
that f the drink offering unto.............. Is 65:11
f thyself to go into captivity............. Jer 46:19

FURNISHED
had f Solomon with cedar trees........ 1Kin 9:11
she hath also f her table...................... Prov 9:2
and the wedding was f with guests.... Mt 22:10
shew you a large upper room f.......... Mk 14:15
shew you a large upper room f.......... Lk 22:12
throughly f unto all good works.......... 2Ti 3:17

FURNITURE
and put them in the camel's f........ Gen 31:34
all the f of the tabernacle,................. Ex 31:7
And the table and his f, and the.......... Ex 31:8
pure candlestick with all his f............. Ex 31:8
of burnt offering with all his f............ Ex 31:9
also for the light, and his f................ Ex 35:14
Moses, the tent, and all his f............. Ex 39:33
glory out of all the pleasant f............. Nah 2:9

FURROW
unicorn with his band in the f.......... Job 39:10

FURROWS
or that the f likewise thereof............ Job 31:38
thou settlest the f thereof................... Ps 65:10
they made long their f...................... Ps 129:3
it by the f of her plantation................ Eze 17:7
it with a f where it grew................. Eze 17:10
as hemlock in the f of the field........ Hos 10:4
bind themselves in their two f......... Hos 10:10
as heaps in the f of the fields......... Hos 12:11

FURTHER
And the angel of the LORD went f..... Num 22:26
shall speak f unto the people........... Deut 20:8
they enquired of the LORD f............ 1Sa 10:22
or what is thy request f...................... Est 9:12
shalt thou come, but no f................... Job 38:11
but I will proceed no f......................... Job 40:5
f not his wicked device....................... Ps 140:8
yea f; though a wise man think to...... Eccl 8:17
And f, by these, my son, be............ Eccl 12:12
what f need have we of witnesses...... Mt 26:65
troublest thou the Master any f........ Mk 5:35
What need we any f witnesses.......... Mk 14:63
said, What need we any f witness..... Lk 22:71
as though he would have gone f....... Lk 24:28
it spread no f among the people...... Acts 4:17
when they had f threatened them..... Acts 4:21
he proceeded f to take Peter also..... Acts 12:3
f brought Greeks also into the.......... Acts 21:28
that I be not f tedious unto thee....... Acts 24:4
and when they had gone a little f...... Acts 27:28
But they shall proceed no f............... 2Ti 3:9
what f need was there that............... Heb 7:11

FURTHERANCE
rather unto the f of the gospel........ Phil 1:12
continue with you all for your f........ Phil 1:25

FURTHERED
they f the people, and the house....... Ezr 8:36

FURTHERMORE
And the LORD said f unto him............ Ex 4:6
The LORD was angry with me for...... Deut 4:21
F the LORD spake unto me, saying..... Deut 9:13
David said f, As the LORD liveth,...... 1Sa 26:10
F I tell thee that the LORD will........ 1Chr 17:10
F over the tribes of Israel.................. 1Chr 27:16
F David the king said unto all......... 1Chr 29:1
F he made the court of the............... 2Chr 4:9
F Elihu answered and said,............... Job 34:1
He said f unto me, Son of man,......... Eze 8:6
And f, that ye have sent for men...... Eze 23:40
F, when I came to Troas to preach 2Cor 2:12
F then we beseech you, brethren,...... 1Th 4:1
F we have had fathers of our............. Heb 12:9

FURY
until thy brother's f turn away.......... Gen 27:44
walk contrary unto you also in f......... Lev 26:28
God shall cast the f of his wrath........ Job 20:23
F is not in me... Is 27:4
his f upon all their armies.................. Is 34:2
upon him the f of his anger............... Is 42:25
because of the f of the oppressor...... Is 51:13
where is the f of the oppressor.......... Is 51:13
hand of the LORD the cup of his f....... Is 51:17
are full of the f of the LORD.............. Is 51:20
even the dregs of the cup of my f...... Is 51:22
f over the tribes of Israel................... Is 59:18
anger, and trample them in my f......... Is 63:3
and my f, it upheld me........................ Is 63:5
anger, and make them drunk in my f.... Is 63:6
to render his anger with f.................. Is 66:15
lest my f come forth like fire,........... Jer 4:4
I am full of the f of the LORD............. Jer 6:11
my f shall be poured out upon........... Jer 7:20
Pour out thy f upon the heathen....... Jer 10:25
arm, even in anger, and in f................ Jer 21:5
lest my f go out like fire, and........... Jer 21:12
of the LORD is gone forth in f............. Jer 23:19
the wine cup of this f at my hand..... Jer 25:15

of the LORD goeth forth with f........... Jer 30:23
of my f from the day that they........... Jer 32:31
them in mine anger, and in my f........ Jer 32:37
slain in mine anger and in my f......... Jer 33:5
anger and the f that the LORD hath..... Jer 36:7
my f hath been poured forth upon...... Jer 42:18
so shall my f be poured forth............ Jer 42:18
Wherefore my f and mine anger was ... Jer 44:6
he poured out his f like fire.............. Lam 2:4
The LORD hath accomplished his f...... Lam 4:11
I will cause my f to rest upon............ Eze 5:13
I have accomplished my f in them.... Eze 5:13
in thee in anger and in f and in........ Eze 5:15
will I accomplish my f upon them...... Eze 6:12
I shortly pour out my f upon thee...... Eze 7:8
Therefore will I also deal in f.......... Eze 8:18
out of thy f upon Jerusalem............. Eze 9:8
it with a stormy wind in my f........... Eze 13:13
hailstones in my f to consume it...... Eze 13:13
pour out my f upon it in blood,........ Eze 14:19
and I will give thee blood in f........... Eze 16:38
So will I make my f toward thee...... Eze 16:42
But she was plucked up in f............ Eze 19:12
I will pour out my f upon them......... Eze 20:8
I would pour out my f upon them...... Eze 20:13
I would pour out my f upon them...... Eze 20:21
with f poured out, will I rule............ Eze 20:33
out arm, and with f poured out......... Eze 20:34
and I will cause my f to rest........... Eze 21:17
you in mine anger and in my f........... Eze 22:20
have poured out my f upon you........ Eze 22:22
That it might cause f to come up...... Eze 24:8
caused my f to rest upon them......... Eze 24:13
mine anger and according to my f...... Eze 25:14
And I will pour my f upon Sin............ Eze 30:15
spoken in my jealousy and in my f..... Eze 36:6
Wherefore I poured my f upon them... Eze 36:18
that my f shall come up in my........... Eze 38:18
f commanded to bring Shadrach,....... Dan 3:13
Then was Nebuchadnezzar full of f.... Dan 3:19
unto him in the f of his power.......... Dan 8:6
thy f be turned away from the.......... Dan 9:16
go forth with great f to destroy........ Dan 11:44
f upon the heathen, such as they...... Mic 5:15
his f is poured out like fire, and....... Nah 1:6
was jealous for her with great f........ Zec 8:2

G

GAAL (ga'-al) A son of Ebed
G the son of Ebed came with his........ Judg 9:26
G the son of Ebed said, Who is.......... Judg 9:28
the words of G the son of Ebed......... Judg 9:30
G the son of Ebed and his brethren... Judg 9:31
G the son of Ebed went out, and....... Judg 9:35
when G saw the people, he said to..... Judg 9:36
G spake again and said, See there..... Judg 9:37
G went out before the men of............ Judg 9:39
and Zebul thrust out G and his.......... Judg 9:41

GAASH (ga'-ash) A mountain near Mt. Ephraim.
the north side of the hill of G.......... Josh 24:30
on the north side of the hill of G....... Judg 2:9
Hiddai of the brooks of G.................. 2Sa 23:30
Hurai of the brooks of G, Abiel........ 1Chr 11:32

GABA (ga'-bah) See GEBA. A Levitical city in Benjamin.
and Ophni, and G,.............................. Josh 18:24
The children of Ramah and G............ Ezr 2:26
The men of Ramah and G, six............ Neh 7:30

GABBAI (gab'-bahee) A family of exiles.
And after him G, Sallai, nine............ Neh 11:8

GABBATHA (gab'-ba-thah) Place where Pilate judged.
Pavement, but in the Hebrew, G,...... Jn 19:13

GABRIEL (ga'-bre-el) An angel.
of Ulai, which called, and said, G...... Dan 8:16
in prayer, even the man G................... Dan 9:21
answering said unto him, I am G....... Lk 1:19
in the sixth month the angel G.......... Lk 1:26

GAD (gad)
1. A son of Jacob.
and she called his name G................. Gen 30:11
Leah's handmaid, G, and Asher........ Gen 35:26
And the sons of G................................ Gen 46:16
G, a troop shall overcome him......... Gen 49:19
Dan, and Naphtali, G, and Asher...... Ex 1:4
the children of G dwelt over.............. 1Chr 5:11
2. The tribe descended from Gad I.
Of G; Eliasaph the son of................. Num 1:14
Of the children of G, by their........... Num 1:24
of them, even of the tribe of G.......... Num 1:25
Then the tribe of G............................. Num 1:25
the captain of the sons of G............. Num 2:14
prince of the children of G................ Num 7:42
G was Eliasaph the son of Deuel....... Num 10:20
Of the tribe of G, Geuel the son....... Num 13:15
The children of G after their............ Num 26:15
of G according to those that were..... Num 26:18
the children of G had a very............ Num 32:1
The children of G and the children.... Num 32:2
Moses said unto the children of G..... Num 32:6

And the children of G and the........... Num 32:25
unto them, If the children of G.......... Num 32:29
And the children of G and the........... Num 32:31
them, even to the children of G......... Num 32:33
And the children of G built Dibon...... Num 32:34
the tribe of the children of G............ Num 34:14
Reuben, G, and Asher, and Zebulun.... Deut 27:13
of G he said, Blessed be he that...... Deut 33:20
Blessed be he that enlargeth G........ Deut 33:20
of Reuben, and the children of G...... Josh 4:12
inheritance unto the tribe of G......... Josh 13:24
of G according their families............ Josh 13:24
Of G after their families................... Josh 13:28
and G, and Reuben, and half the....... Josh 18:7
in Gilead out of the tribe of G.......... Josh 20:8
Reuben, and out of the tribe of G...... Josh 21:7
And out of the tribe of G, Ramoth..... Josh 21:38
of Reuben and the children of G........ Josh 22:9
of Reuben and the children of G........ Josh 22:10
Reuben, and to the children of G....... Josh 22:11
Reuben, and to the children of G....... Josh 22:13
Reuben, and to the children of G....... Josh 22:15
of Reuben and children of G............. Josh 22:25
of Reuben and the children of G........ Josh 22:30
Reuben, and to the children of G....... Josh 22:31
Reuben, and from the children of G ... Josh 22:32
the children of Reuben and G dwelt.... Josh 22:33
the children of G called the.............. Josh 22:34
went over Jordan to the land of G..... 1Sa 13:7
in the midst of the river of G.......... 2Sa 24:5
Joseph, and Benjamin, Naphtali, G.... 1Chr 2:2
and out of the tribe of G................... 1Chr 6:63
And out of the tribe of G................... 1Chr 6:80
These were of the sons of G............. 1Chr 12:14
then doth their king inherit G........... Jer 49:1
unto the west side, G a portion........ Eze 48:27
And by the border of G, at the......... Eze 48:28
one gate of G, one gate of Asher,..... Eze 48:34
Of the tribe of G were sealed........... Rev 7:5
3. A prophet who assisted David
the prophet G said unto David,......... 1Sa 22:5
the LORD came unto the prophet G.... 2Sa 24:11
So G came to David, and told him,.... 2Sa 24:13
And David said unto G, I am in a...... 2Sa 24:14
G came that day to David, and said ... 2Sa 24:18
according to the saying of G............. 2Sa 24:19
and the LORD spake unto G, David's... 1Chr 21:9
So G came to David, and said unto ... 1Chr 21:11
And David said unto G, I am in a...... 1Chr 21:13
LORD commanded G to say to David.... 1Chr 21:18
David went up at the saying of G...... 1Chr 21:19
and in the book of G the seer............ 1Chr 29:29
of G the king's seer, and Nathan 2Chr 29:25

GADARENES (gad-a-renes') Inhabitants of Gadara.
sea, into the country of the G........... Mk 5:1
arrived at the country of the G......... Lk 8:26
the G round about besought him to.... Lk 8:37

GADDEST
Why g thou about so much to........... Jer 2:36

GADDI (gad'-di) One of the twelve spies.
of Manasseh, G the son of Susi......... Num 13:11

GADDIEL (gad'-de-el) One of the twelve spies.
of Zebulun, G the son of Sodi........... Num 13:10

GADI (ga'-di) Father of Menahem.
the son of G went up from Tirzah..... 2Kin 15:14
the son of G to reign over Israel...... 2Kin 15:17

GADITE (gad'-ite) See GADITES. A member of the tribe of Dan.
of Nathan of Zobah, Bani the G......... 2Sa 23:36

GADITES (gad'-ites)
I unto the Reubenites and to the G.... Deut 3:12
unto the G I gave from Gilead.......... Deut 3:16
and Ramoth in Gilead, of the G......... Deut 4:43
unto the Reubenites, and to the G..... Deut 29:8
And to the Reubenites, and to the G ... Josh 1:12
unto the Reubenites, and the G......... Josh 12:6
the G have received their.................. Josh 13:8
called the Reubenites and the G....... Josh 22:1
in the land of Gilead, the G.............. 2Kin 10:33
even the Reubenites, and the G......... 1Chr 5:26
And of the G there separated............ 1Chr 12:8
of the Reubenites, and the G............ 1Chr 12:37
rulers over the Reubenites, the G..... 1Chr 26:32

GAHAM (ga'-ham) A son of Nahor.
Reumah, she bare also Tebah, and G .. Gen 22:24

GAHAR (ga'-har) A family of exiles.
of Giddel, the children of G.............. Ezr 2:47
of Giddel, the children of G.............. Neh 7:49

GAHER
they took no g of money................... Judg 5:19
or is it g to him, that thou.............. Job 22:3
of every one that is greedy of g........ Prov 1:19
the g thereof than fine gold.............. Prov 3:14
He that is greedy of g troubleth........ Prov 15:27
unjust g increaseth his substance..... Prov 28:8
despiseth the g of oppressions......... Is 33:15
own way, every one for his g............ Is 56:11
dishonest g which thou hast made..... Eze 22:13
destroy souls, to get dishonest g...... Eze 22:27
that ye would g the time, because ..... Dan 2:8

GAINED

and shall divide the land for g .... Dan 11:39
consecrate their g unto the LORD........ Mic 4:13
if he shall g the whole world, and .... Mt 16:26
if he shall g the whole world, and......... Mk 8:36
if he g the whole world, and lose .... Lk 9:25
her masters much g by soothsaying... Acts 16:16
brought no small g unto the .... Acts 19:24
unto all, that I might g the more 1Cor 9:19
as a Jew, that I might g the Jews 1Cor 9:20
that I might g them that are 1Cor 9:20
that I might g them that are 1Cor 9:21
as weak, that I might g the weak 1Cor 9:22
Did I make a g of you by any of 2Cor 12:17
Did Titus make a g of you 2Cor 12:18
to live is Christ, and to die is g........ Phil 1:21
But what things were g to me......... Phil 3:7
supposing that g is godliness 1Ti 6:5
with contentment is great g 1Ti 6:6
a year, and buy and sell, and get g ... Jas 4:13

GAINED

the hypocrite, though he hath g .... Job 27:8
thou hast greedily g of thy............. Eze 22:12
thee, thou hast g thy brother............. Mt 18:15
received two, he also g other two....... Mt 25:17
I have g beside them five talents .... Mt 25:20
I have g two other talents beside .... Mt 25:22
much every man had g by trading....... Lk 19:15
Lord, thy pound hath g ten pounds ... Lk 19:16
thy pound hath g five pounds .... Lk 19:18
to have g this harm and loss............. Acts 27:21

GAINS

that the hope of their g was gone ... Acts 16:19

GAINSAY

shall not be able to g nor resist .... Lk 21:15

GAINSAYERS

to exhort and to convince the g......... Titus 1:9

GAINSAYING

came I unto you without g .... Acts 10:29
unto a disobedient and g people......... Rom 10:21
and perished in the g of Core .... Jude 11

GAIUS (gah´-yus)
1. A native of Macedonia.
and having caught G .... Acts 19:29
2. A native of Derbe.
and G of Derbe, and Timotheus .... Acts 20:4
3. A native of Corinth.
G mine host, and of the whole......... Rom 16:23
none of you, but Crispus and G......... 1Cor 1:14
4. Addressee of John's third epistle.
The elder unto the wellbeloved G.......... 3Jn 1

GALAL (ga´-lal)
1. Son of Jeduthun.
And Bakbakkar, Heresh, and G......... 1Chr 9:15
2. A Levite exile.
the son of Shemaiah, the son of G 1Chr 9:16
the son of Shammua, the son of G .... Neh 11:17

GALATIA (ga-la´-she-ah) See GALATIANS. A
Roman province in Asia Minor.
Phrygia and the region of G............. Acts 16:6
and went over all the country of G ... Acts 18:23
given order to the churches of G 1Cor 16:1
with me, unto the churches of G......... Gal 1:2
Crescens to G, Titus unto 2Ti 4:10
scattered throughout Pontus, G......... 1Pet 1:1

GALATIANS (ga-la´-she-uns) Inhabitants of
Galatia.
O foolish G, who hath bewitched .... Gal 3:1
Unto the G written from Rome........... Gal s

GALBANUM
spices, stacte, and onycha, and g .... Ex 30:34

GALEED (ga´-le-ed) See JAGAR-SAHADUTHA. A
memorial mound of stones.
but Jacob called it G .... Gen 31:47
was the name of it called G .... Gen 31:48

GALILAEAN (gal-i-le´-un) See GALILAEANS. An
inhabitant of Galilee.
for thou art a G, and thy speech .... Mk 14:70
for he is a G............. Lk 22:59
he asked whether the man were a G ... Lk 23:6

GALILAEANS (gal-i-le-uns)
some that told him of the G .... Lk 13:1
Suppose ye that these G were .... Lk 13:2
were sinners above all the G .... Lk 13:2
the G received him, having seen......... Jn 4:45
are not all these which speak G......... Acts 2:7

GALILEE (gal´-i-lee) See GALILAEAN. A district
north of Samaria.
Kedesh in G in mount Naphtali............. Josh 20:7
Kedesh in G with her suburbs, to....... Josh 21:32
twenty cities in the land of G............. 1Kin 9:11
Hazor, and Gilead, and G............. 2Kin 15:29
Kedesh in G with her suburbs, and ... 1Chr 6:76
Jordan, in G of the nations .... Is 9:1
turned aside into the parts of G .... Mt 2:22
Jesus from G to Jordan unto John....... Mt 3:13
into prison, he departed into G .... Mt 4:12
beyond Jordan, G of the Gentiles .... Mt 4:15
And Jesus, walking by the sea of G ... Mt 4:18
And Jesus went about all G .... Mt 4:23
great multitudes of people from G ...... Mt 4:25
and came nigh unto the sea of G ...... Mt 15:29
And while they abode in G, Jesus........ Mt 17:22
these things, he departed from G......... Mt 19:1

---

the prophet of Nazareth of G .... Mt 21:11
I will go before you into G............. Mt 26:32
Thou also wast with Jesus of G......... Mt 26:69
off, which followed Jesus from G .... Mt 27:55
he goeth before you into G............. Mt 28:7
my brethren that they go into G .... Mt 28:10
eleven disciples went away into G......... Mt 28:16
came from Nazareth of G............. Mk 1:9
put in prison, Jesus came into G......... Mk 1:14
Now as he walked by the sea of G....... Mk 1:16
all the region round about G .... Mk 1:28
their synagogues throughout all G .... Mk 1:39
multitude from G followed him............. Mk 3:7
captains, and chief estates of G......... Mk 6:21
Sidon, he came unto the sea of G....... Mk 7:31
thence, and passed through G .... Mk 9:30
I will go before you into G .... Mk 14:28
(Who also, when he was in G......... Mk 15:41
that he goeth before you into G......... Mk 16:7
sent from God unto a city of G............. Lk 1:26
And Joseph also went up from G......... Lk 2:4
of the Lord, they returned into G .... Lk 2:39
and Herod being tetrarch of G............. Lk 3:1
in the power of the Spirit into G......... Lk 4:14
down to Capernaum, a city of G......... Lk 4:31
preached in the synagogues of G .... Lk 4:44
were come out of every town of G ...... Lk 5:17
which is over against G .... Lk 8:26
through the midst of Samaria and G ... Lk 17:11
beginning from G to this place............. Lk 23:5
When Pilate heard of G, he asked .... Lk 23:6
manner that followed him from G ...... Lk 23:49
also, which came with him from G ...... Lk 23:55
unto you when he was yet in G .... Lk 24:6
Jesus would go forth into G............. Jn 1:43
there was a marriage in Cana of G....... Jn 2:1
miracles did Jesus in Cana of G .... Jn 2:11
Judaea, and departed again into G ...... Jn 4:3
departed thence, and went into G ...... Jn 4:43
Then when he was come into G......... Jn 4:45
Jesus came again into Cana of G ...... Jn 4:46
was come out of Judaea into G .... Jn 4:47
he was come out of Judaea into G ...... Jn 4:54
Jesus went over the sea of G .... Jn 6:1
these things Jesus walked in G............. Jn 7:1
unto them, he abode still in G .... Jn 7:9
said, Shall Christ come out of G......... Jn 7:41
said unto him, Art thou also of G......... Jn 7:52
for out of G ariseth no prophet............. Jn 7:52
which was of Bethsaida of G .... Jn 12:21
and Nathanael of Cana in G .... Jn 21:2
Which also said, Ye men of G .... Acts 1:11
of G in the days of the taxing............. Acts 5:37
rest throughout all Judaea and G......... Acts 9:31
all Judaea, and began from G .... Acts 10:37
up with him from G to Jerusalem....... Acts 13:31

GALL

among you a root that beareth g .... Deut 29:18
their grapes are grapes of g............. Deut 32:32
poureth out my g upon the ground....... Job 16:13
it is the g of asps within him .... Job 20:14
sword cometh out of his g............. Job 20:25
They gave me also g for my meat......... Ps 69:21
and given us water of g to drink......... Jer 8:14
and give them water of g to drink....... Jer 9:15
and make them drink the water of g ... Jer 23:15
me, and compassed me with g............. Lam 3:5
my misery, the wormwood and the g ... Lam 3:19
ye have turned judgment into g......... Amos 6:12
vinegar to drink mingled with g......... Mt 27:34
thou art in the g of bitterness............. Acts 8:23

GALLANT

neither shall g ship pass thereby .... Is 33:21

GALLERIES

the king is held in the g............. Song 7:5
the g thereof on the one side and .... Eze 41:15
the g round about on their three......... Eze 41:16
for the g were higher than these,......... Eze 42:5

GALLERY

was g against g in three............. Eze 42:3

GALLEY

wherein shall go no g with oars......... Is 33:21

GALLIM (gal´-lim) A city in Benjamin.
the son of Laish, which was of G......... 1Sa 25:44
up thy voice, O daughter of G .... Is 10:30

GALLIO (gal´-le-o) A Roman proconsul of
Achaia.
when G was the deputy of Achaia, ... Acts 18:12
G said unto the Jews, If it were......... Acts 18:14
G cared for none of those things......... Acts 18:17

GALLOWS

Let a g be made of fifty cubits............. Est 5:14
and he caused the g to be made............. Est 6:4
that he had prepared for him............. Est 6:4
the g fifty cubits high, which .... Est 7:9
on the g that he had prepared for ...... Est 7:10
him they have hanged upon the g ...... Est 8:7
ten sons be hanged upon the g .... Est 9:13
sons should be hanged on the g .... Est 9:25

GAMAD See GAMMADIMS.

GAMALIEL (gam-a´-le-el)
1. A chief of Manasseh.
G the son of Pedahzur............. Num 1:10
shall be G the son of Pedahzur............. Num 2:20
day offered G the son of Pedahzur ...... Num 7:54

---

offering of G the son of Pedahzur......... Num 7:59
was G the son of Pedahzur............. Num 10:23
2. A noted Rabbinic teacher.
the council, a Pharisee, named G......... Acts 5:34
up in this city at the feet of G............. Acts 22:3

GAMMAD See GAMMADIMS.

GAMMADIM See GAMMADIMS.

GAMMADIMS (gam´-ma-dims) Defenders of
Tyre.
and the G were in thy towers .... Eze 27:11

GAMUL (ga´-mul) See BETH-GAMUL. A
sanctuary servant in David's time.
Jachin, the two and twentieth to G... 1Chr 24:17

GAP

stand in the g before me for the .... Eze 22:30

GAPED

They have g upon me with their .... Job 16:10
They g upon me with their mouths,....... Ps 22:13

GAPS

Ye have not gone up into the g......... Eze 13:5

GARDEN

God planted a g eastward in Eden ...... Gen 2:8
life also in the midst of the g............. Gen 2:9
went out of Eden to water the g......... Gen 2:10
put him into the g of Eden to............. Gen 2:15
Of every tree of the g thou............. Gen 2:16
not eat of every tree of the g............. Gen 3:1
the fruit of the trees of the g............. Gen 3:2
which is in the midst of the g............. Gen 3:3
in the g in the cool of the day .... Gen 3:8
amongst the trees of the g .... Gen 3:8
said, I heard thy voice in the g............. Gen 3:10
sent him forth from the g of Eden ...... Gen 3:23
east of the g of Eden Cherubim......... Gen 3:24
even as the g of the LORD............. Gen 13:10
it with thy foot, as a g of herbs......... Deut 11:10
I may have it for a g of herbs 1Kin 21:2
he fled by the way of the g house....... 2Kin 9:27
buried in the g of his own house......... 2Kin 21:18
his own house, in the g of Uzza......... 2Kin 21:18
in his sepulchre in the g of Uzza......... 2Kin 21:26
walls, which is by the king's g............. 2Kin 25:4
pool of Siloah by the king's g............. Neh 3:15
in the g in the court of the .... Est 1:5
his wrath went into the palace g......... Est 7:7
g into the place of the banquet............. Est 7:8
branch shooteth forth in his g............. Job 8:16
A g inclosed is my sister, my .... Song 4:12
blow upon my g, that the spices......... Song 4:16
Let my beloved come into his g......... Song 4:16
I am come into my g, my sister .... Song 5:1
beloved is gone down into his g......... Song 6:2
I went down into the g of nuts to......... Song 6:11
as a lodge in a g of cucumbers......... Is 1:8
as a g that hath no water............. Is 1:30
her desert like the g of the LORD......... Is 51:3
and thou shalt be like a watered g ...... Is 58:11
as the g causeth the things that .... Is 61:11
soul shall be as a watered g .... Jer 31:12
night, by the way of the king's g......... Jer 39:4
walls, which was by the king's g .... Jer 52:7
tabernacle, as if it were of a g............. Lam 2:6
hast been in Eden the g of God .... Eze 28:13
The cedars in the g of God could......... Eze 31:8
nor any tree in the g of God was......... Eze 31:8
Eden, that were in the g of God......... Eze 31:9
is become like the g of Eden............. Eze 36:35
the land is as the g of Eden............. Joel 2:3
a man took, and cast into his g .... Lk 13:19
the brook Cedron, where was a g......... Jn 18:1
not I see thee in the g with him......... Jn 18:26
he was crucified there was a g .... Jn 19:41
in the g a new sepulchre, wherein....... Jn 19:41

GARDENER

She, supposing him to be the g............. Jn 20:15

GARDENS

as g by the river's side, as the .... Num 24:6
I made me g and orchards, and I......... Eccl 2:5
A fountain of g, a well of living......... Song 4:15
beds of spices, to feed in the g............. Song 6:2
Thou that dwellest in the g .... Song 8:13
for the g that ye have chosen............. Is 1:29
that sacrificeth in g, and burneth ...... Is 65:3
purify themselves in the g behind......... Is 66:17
and plant g, and eat the fruit of .... Jer 29:5
and plant g, and eat the fruit of......... Jer 29:28
when your g and your vineyards and... Amos 4:9
they shall also make g, and eat......... Amos 9:14

GAREB (ga´-reb)
1. A "mighty man" of David.
Ira an Ithrite, G an Ithrite, ... 2Sa 23:38
Ira the Ithrite, G the Ithrite,............. 1Chr 11:40
2. A hill near Jerusalem.
over against it upon the hill G .... Jer 31:39

GARLANDS

g unto the gates, and would have ...... Acts 14:13

GARLICK

leeks, and the onions, and the g......... Num 11:5

GARMENT

And Shem and Japheth took a g .... Gen 9:23
out red, all over like an hairy g......... Gen 25:25
And she caught him by his g .... Gen 39:12
and he left his g in her hand............. Gen 39:12

he had left his *g* in her hand .... Gen 39:13
cried, that he left his *g* with me ...... Gen 39:15
And she laid up his *g* by her .... Gen 39:16
cried, that he left his *g* with me ...... Gen 39:18
priest shall put on his linen *g* .... Lev 6:10
of the blood thereof upon any *g* .... Lev 6:27
The *g* also that the plague of .... Lev 13:47
a woollen *g*, or a linen *g* .... Lev 13:47
be greenish or reddish in the *g* .... Lev 13:49
if the plague be spread in the *g* .... Lev 13:51
He shall therefore burn that *g* .... Lev 13:52
the plague be not spread in the *g* ..... Lev 13:53
he shall rend it out of the *g* .... Lev 13:56
And if it appear still in the *g* .... Lev 13:57
And the *g*, either warp, or woof, ... Lev 13:58
in a *g* of woollen or linen .... Lev 13:59
And for the leprosy of a *g* .... Lev 14:55
And every *g*, and every skin, ... Lev 15:17
neither shall a *g* mingled of .... Lev 19:19
shall a man put on a woman's *g* ...... Deut 22:5
not wear a *g* of divers sorts .... Deut 22:11
the spoils a goodly Babylonish *g* ..... Josh 7:21
of Zerah, and the silver, and the *g* .... Josh 7:24
And they spread a *g*, and did cast ..... Judg 8:25
she had a *g* of divers colours 2Sa 13:18
rent her *g* of divers colours that 2Sa 13:19
Joab's *g* that he had put on was 2Sa 20:8
he had clad himself with a new *g* 1Kin 11:29
caught the new *g* that was on him 1Kin 11:30
hasted, and took every man his *g* 2Kin 9:13
I heard this thing, I rent my *g* .... Ezr 9:3
and having rent my *g* and my mantle, ... Ezr 9:5
with a *g* of fine linen and purple ...... Esth 8:15
as a *g* that is moth eaten .... Job 13:28
of my disease is my *g* changed .... Job 30:18
I made the cloud the *g* thereof .... Job 38:9
and they stand as a *g* .... Job 38:14
can discover the face of his *g* .... Job 41:13
I made sackcloth also my *g* .... Ps 69:11
violence covereth them as a *g* .... Ps 73:6
of them shall wax old like a *g* .... Ps 102:26
thyself with light as with a *g* .... Ps 104:2
it with the deep as with a *g* .... Ps 104:6
with cursing like as with his *g* .... Ps 109:18
him as the *g* which covereth him ...... Ps 109:19
Take his *g* that is surety for a .... Prov 20:16
taketh away a *g* in cold weather ...... Prov 25:20
Take his *g* that is surety for a .... Prov 27:13
who hath bound the waters in a *g* ..... Prov 30:4
lo, they all shall wax old as a *g* .... Is 50:9
the earth shall wax old like a *g* .... Is 51:6
moth shall eat them up like a *g* .... Is 51:8
the *g* of praise for the spirit of .... Is 61:3
as a shepherd putteth on his *g* .... Jer 43:12
hath covered the naked with a *g* ...... Eze 18:7
hath covered the naked with a *g* ...... Eze 18:16
whose *g* was white as snow, and the .. Dan 7:9
ye pull off the robe with the *g* .... Mic 2:8
holy flesh in the skirt of his *g* .... Hag 2:12
they wear a rough *g* to deceive .... Zec 13:4
one covereth violence with his *g* ...... Mal 2:16
piece of new cloth unto an old *g* ...... Mt 9:16
to fill it up taketh from the *g* .... Mt 9:16
him, and touched the hem of his *g* .... Mt 9:20
herself, If I may but touch his *g* .... Mt 9:21
might only touch the hem of his *g* .... Mt 14:36
man which had not on a wedding *g* ... Mt 22:11
in hither not having a wedding *g* ...... Mt 22:12
a piece of new cloth on an old *g* ...... Mk 2:21
press behind, and touched his *g* .... Mk 5:27
it were but the border of his *g* .... Mk 6:56
And he, casting away his *g* .... Mk 10:50
back again for to take up his *g* .... Mk 13:16
side, clothed in a long white *g* .... Mk 16:5
a piece of a new *g* upon an old .... Lk 5:36
and touched the border of his *g* .... Lk 8:44
hath no sword, let him sell his *g* ...... Lk 22:36
Cast thy *g* about thee, and follow .... Acts 12:8
all shall wax old as doth a *g* .... Heb 1:11
hating even the *g* spotted by the ...... Jude 23
clothed with a *g* down to the foot ..... Rev 1:13

GARMENTS

and be clean, and change your *g* ...... Gen 35:2
put her widow's *g* off from her .... Gen 38:14
put on the *g* of her widowhood .... Gen 38:19
he washed his *g* in wine, and his ...... Gen 49:11
thou shalt make holy *g* for Aaron ..... Ex 28:2
make Aaron's *g* to consecrate him ..... Ex 28:3
these are the *g* which they shall .... Ex 28:4
they shall make holy *g* for Aaron ...... Ex 28:4
And thou shalt take the *g*, and put .... Ex 29:5
it upon Aaron, and upon his *g* .... Ex 29:21
upon the *g* of his sons with him .... Ex 29:21
and he shall be hallowed, and his *g* ... Ex 29:21
his sons, and his sons' *g* with him ..... Ex 29:21
the holy *g* of Aaron shall be his .... Ex 29:29
the holy *g* for Aaron the priest, ... Ex 31:10
the *g* of his sons, to minister in .... Ex 31:10
the holy *g* for Aaron the priest, ... Ex 35:19
the *g* of his sons, to minister in .... Ex 35:19
his service, and for the holy *g* .... Ex 35:21
and made the holy *g* for Aaron .... Ex 39:1
the holy *g* for Aaron the priest, ... Ex 39:41
Aaron the priest, and his sons' *g* ...... Ex 39:41
shalt put upon Aaron the holy *g* .... Ex 40:13
his *g*, and put on other *g* .... Lev 6:11
and his sons with him, and the *g* ...... Lev 8:2
it upon Aaron, and upon his *g* .... Lev 8:30
and upon his sons' *g* with him .... Lev 8:30
and sanctified Aaron, and his *g* .... Lev 8:30

his sons, and his sons' *g* with him ..... Lev 8:30
these are holy *g* .... Lev 16:4
and shall put off the linen *g* .... Lev 16:23
the holy place, and put on his *g* .... Lev 16:24
linen clothes, even the holy *g* .... Lev 16:32
is consecrated to put on the *g* .... Lev 21:10
g throughout their generations .... Num 15:38
And strip Aaron of his *g*, and put ..... Num 20:26
And Moses stripped Aaron of his *g* .... Num 20:28
their feet, and old *g* upon them .... Josh 9:5
and these our *g* and our shoes are ..... Josh 9:13
sheets and thirty change of *g* .... Judg 14:12
sheets and thirty change of *g* .... Judg 14:13
gave change of *g* unto them which ... Judg 14:19
and gave it to David, and his *g* 1Sa 18:4
and cut off their *g* in the middle 2Sa 10:4
the king arose, and tare his *g* 2Sa 13:31
silver, and vessels of gold, and *g* 1Kin 10:25
of silver, and two changes of *g* 2Kin 5:22
two bags, with two changes of *g* 2Kin 5:23
to receive money, and to receive *g* 2Kin 5:26
and, lo, all the way was full of *g* 2Kin 7:15
And changed his prison *g* 2Kin 25:29
cut off their *g* in the midst hard 1Chr 19:4
silver, and one hundred priests' *g* ..... Ezr 2:69
five hundred and thirty priests' *g* ..... Neh 7:70
and threescore and seven priests' *g* ... Neh 7:72
How thy *g* are warm, when he .... Job 37:17
They part my *g* among them, ... Ps 22:18
All thy *g* smell of myrrh, and .... Ps 45:8
went down to the skirts of his *g* ...... Ps 133:2
Let thy *g* be always white. .... Eccl 9:8
the smell of thy *g* is like the .... Song 4:11
noise, and *g* rolled in blood .... Is 9:5
put on thy beautiful *g*, O .... Is 52:1
Their webs shall not become *g* .... Is 59:6
he put on the *g* of vengeance for ..... Is 59:17
me with the *g* of salvation .... Is 61:10
Edom, with dyed *g* from Bozrah ..... Is 63:1
thy *g* like him that treadeth in .... Is 63:2
shall be sprinkled upon my *g* .... Is 63:3
were not afraid, nor rent their *g* ...... Jer 36:24
And changed his prison *g* .... Jer 52:33
that men could not touch their *g* ...... Lam 4:14
of thy *g* thou didst take, and .... Eze 16:16
And tookest thy broidered *g* .... Eze 16:18
and put off their broidered *g* .... Eze 16:18
lay their *g* wherein they minister ..... Eze 42:14
and shall put on other *g*, and shall .... Eze 42:14
shall be clothed with linen *g* .... Eze 44:17
their *g* wherein they ministered .... Eze 44:19
shall not sanctify the people with *g* ... Eze 44:19
and their hats, and their other *g* ...... Dan 3:21
And rend your heart, and not your *g* .. Joel 2:13
Joshua was clothed with filthy *g* ...... Zec 3:3
Take away the filthy *g* from him ...... Zec 3:4
his head, and clothed him with *g* ..... Zec 3:5
spread their *g* in the way .... Mt 21:8
and enlarge the borders of their *g* .... Mt 23:5
crucified him, and parted his *g* .... Mt 27:35
They parted my *g* among them, ... Mt 27:35
to Jesus, and cast their *g* on him ..... Mk 11:7
And many spread their *g* in the way ... Mk 11:8
crucified him, they parted his *g* .... Mk 15:24
they cast their *g* upon the colt .... Lk 19:35
men stood by them in shining *g* ...... Lk 24:4
from supper, and laid aside his *g* ..... Jn 13:4
their feet, and had taken his *g* .... Jn 13:12
had crucified Jesus, took his *g* .... Jn 19:23
g which Dorcas made, while she ...... Acts 9:39
and your *g* are motheaten .... Jas 5:2
which have not defiled their *g* .... Rev 3:4
that watcheth, and keepeth his *g* ..... Rev 16:15

GARMITE

GARMITE (*gar'-mite*) *A descendant of Judah.*
Naham, the father of Keilah the G...... 1Chr 4:19

GARNER

and gather his wheat into the *g* .... Mt 3:12
will gather the wheat into his *g* .... Lk 3:17

GARNERS

That our *g* may be full, affording .... Ps 144:13
the *g* are laid desolate, the .... Joel 1:17

GARNISH

g the sepulchres of the righteous ..... Mt 23:29

GARNISHED

he *g* the house with precious 2Chr 3:6
his spirit he hath *g* the heavens ...... Job 26:13
he findeth it empty, swept, and *g* .... Mt 12:44
cometh, he findeth it swept and *g* .... Lk 11:25
g with all manner of precious .... Rev 21:19

GARRISON

where is the *g* of the Philistines 1Sa 10:5
Jonathan smote the *g* of the 1Sa 13:3
smitten a *g* of the Philistines 1Sa 13:4
the *g* of the Philistines went out 1Sa 13:23
us go over to the Philistines' *g* 1Sa 14:1
go over unto the Philistines' *g* 1Sa 14:6
unto the *g* of these uncircumcised ... 1Sa 14:6
unto the *g* of the Philistines. 1Sa 14:11
the men of the *g* answered 1Sa 14:12
the *g*, and the spoilers, they also 1Sa 14:15
the *g* of the Philistines was then 2Sa 23:14
the Philistines' *g* was then at 1Chr 11:16
city of the Damascenes with a *g* 2Cor 11:32

GARRISONS

Then David put *g* in Syria of.......... 2Sa 8:6
And he put *g* in Edom................. 2Sa 8:14
throughout all Edom put he *g*......... 2Sa 8:14
Then David put *g* in 1Chr 18:6
And he put *g* in Edom................. 1Chr 18:13
set *g* in the land of Judah, and in 2Chr 17:2
thy strong *g* shall go down to the .... Eze 26:11

GASHMU

GASHMU (*gash'-mu*) *See* GESHEM. *A Samaritan in Nehemiah's time.*
G saith it, that thou and the Jews..... Neh 6:6

GAT

Abraham *g* up early in the morning ... Gen 19:27
cloud, and *g* him up into the mount... Ex 24:18
Moses *g* him into the camp, he and ... Num 11:30
g them up into the top of the .... Num 14:40
So they *g* up from the tabernacle .... Num 16:27
Abimelech *g* him up to mount .... Judg 9:48
g them up to the top of the tower .... Judg 9:51
rose up, and *g* him unto his place .... Judg 19:28
g him up from Gilgal unto Gibeah 1Sa 13:15
his men *g* them up unto the hold..... 1Sa 24:22
they *g* them away, and no man saw ... 1Sa 26:12
g them away through the plain all..... 2Sa 4:7
David *g* him a name when he 2Sa 8:13
every man *g* him up upon his mule, ... 2Sa 13:29
g him home to his house, to his 2Sa 17:23
the people *g* them by stealth that 2Sa 19:3
with clothes, but he *g* no heat 1Kin 1:1
the pains of hell *g* hold upon me ..... Ps 116:3
I *g* me men singers and women....... Eccl 2:8
We *g* our bread with the peril of ..... Lam 5:9

GATAM

GATAM (*ga'-tam*) *A son of Eliphaz*
were Teman, Omar, Zepho, and G ..... Gen 36:11
Duke Korah, duke G, and duke .... Gen 36:16
Teman, and Omar, Zephi, and G 1Chr 1:36

GATE

and Lot sat in the *g* of Sodom. .... Gen 19:1
possess the *g* of his enemies .... Gen 22:17
that went in at the *g* of his city ...... Gen 23:10
that went in at the *g* of his city ...... Gen 23:18
the *g* of those which hate them ...... Gen 24:60
God, and this is the *g* of heaven...... Gen 28:17
son came unto the *g* of their .... Gen 34:20
went out of the *g* of his city .... Gen 34:24
went out of the *g* of his city .... Gen 34:24
of the *g* shall be fifteen cubits. .... Ex 27:14
for the *g* of the court shall be .... Ex 27:16
Moses stood in the *g* of the camp .... Ex 32:26
out from *g* to *g* throughout the ..... Ex 32:27
side of the *g* were fifteen cubits ..... Ex 38:14
for the other side of the *g* .... Ex 38:15
the hanging for the *g* of the .... Ex 38:18
and the sockets of the court *g* .... Ex 38:31
and the hanging for the court *g* ...... Ex 39:40
up the hanging at the court *g* .... Ex 40:8
set up the hanging of the court *g* .... Ex 40:33
the door of the *g* of the court .... Num 4:26
city, and unto the *g* of his place...... Deut 21:19
the elders of the city in the *g* .... Deut 22:15
both out unto the *g* of that city ...... Deut 22:24
go up to the *g* unto the elders .... Deut 25:7
the time of shutting of the *g* .... Josh 2:5
were gone out, they shut the *g* ...... Josh 2:7
before the *g* even unto Shebarim, ... Josh 7:5
the entering of the *g* of the city ...... Josh 8:29
the entering of the *g* of the city ...... Josh 20:4
the entering of the *g* of the city ...... Judg 9:35
even unto the entering of the *g* ...... Judg 9:40
the entering of the *g* of the city ...... Judg 9:44
all night in the *g* of the city .... Judg 16:2
the doors of the *g* of the city .... Judg 16:3
stood by the entering of the *g*. .... Judg 18:16
stood in the entering of the *g*. .... Judg 18:17
Then went Boaz up to the *g* .... Ruth 4:1
and from the *g* of his place .... Ruth 4:10
all the people that were in the *g* ...... Ruth 4:11
backward by the side of the *g* 1Sa 4:18
Saul drew near to Samuel in the *g* 1Sa 9:18
scrabbled on the doors of the *g* 1Sa 21:13
the *g* to speak with him quietly 2Sa 3:27
array at the entering in of the *g* 2Sa 10:8
even unto the entering of the *g* 2Sa 11:23
and stood beside the way of the *g* ... 2Sa 15:2
And the king stood by the side. 2Sa 18:4
the roof over the *g* unto the wall 2Sa 18:24
went up to the chamber over the *g* ... 2Sa 18:33
the king arose, and sat in the *g* 2Sa 19:8
the king doth sit in the *g* 2Sa 19:8
of Beth-lehem, which by the *g* 2Sa 23:15
of Beth-lehem, that was by the *g* 2Sa 23:16
when he came to the *g* of the city 1Kin 17:10
the entrance of the *g* of Samaria 1Kin 22:10
for a shekel, in the *g* of Samaria 2Kin 7:1
men at the entering in of the *g* 2Kin 7:3
to have the charge of the *g* 2Kin 7:17
people trode upon him in the *g* 2Kin 7:17
this time in the *g* of Samaria 2Kin 7:18
people trode upon him in the *g* 2Kin 7:20
And as Jehu entered in at the *g* 2Kin 9:31
in of the *g* until the morning 2Kin 10:8
part shall be at the *g* of Sur 2Kin 11:6
part at the *g* behind the guard 2Kin 11:6
came by the way of the *g* of the 2Kin 11:19
of Ephraim unto the corner *g* 2Kin 14:13
He built the higher *g* of the 2Kin 15:35
g of Joshua the governor of the 2Kin 23:8
left hand at the *g* of the city 2Kin 23:8

way of the *g* between two walls......... 2Kin 25:4
waited in the king's *g* eastward.......... 1Chr 9:18
of Beth-lehem, that is at the *g*........... 1Chr 11:17
of Beth-lehem, that was by the *g*......... 1Chr 11:18
in array before the *g* of the city......... 1Chr 19:9
of their fathers, for every *g*............. 2Chr 26:13
with the *g* Shallecheth, by the.......... 1Chr 26:16
also by their courses at every *g*......... 2Chr 8:14
entering in the *g* of Samaria............ 2Chr 18:9
part at the *g* of the foundation.......... 2Chr 23:5
the horse *g* by the king's house......... 2Chr 23:15
the high *g* into the king's house........ 2Chr 23:20
set it without at the *g* of the........... 2Chr 24:8
g of Ephraim to the corner *g*............ 2Chr 25:23
corner *g*, and at the valley *g*........... 2Chr 26:9
He built the high *g* of the house........ 2Chr 27:3
the street of the *g* of the city........... 2Chr 32:6
to the entering in at the fish *g*.......... 2Chr 33:14
and the porters waited at every *g*...... 2Chr 35:15
by night by the *g* of the valley.......... Neh 2:13
went on to the *g* of the fountain........ Neh 2:14
and entered by the *g* of the valley...... Neh 2:15
and they builded the sheep *g*........... Neh 3:1
But the fish *g* did the sons of........... Neh 3:3
Moreover the old *g* repaired............ Neh 3:6
The valley *g* repaired Hanun, and..... Neh 3:13
on the wall unto the dung *g*............. Neh 3:13
But the dung *g* repaired Malchiah..... Neh 3:14
But the *g* of the fountain................ Neh 3:15
the water *g* toward the east............. Neh 3:26
the horse *g* repaired the priests........ Neh 3:28
the keeper of the east *g*................. Neh 3:29
over against the *g* Miphkad............. Neh 3:31
sheep *g* repaired the goldsmiths....... Neh 3:32
that was before the water *g*............. Neh 8:1
that was before the water *g* from....... Neh 8:3
and in the street of the water *g*......... Neh 8:16
in the street of the *g* of Ephraim....... Neh 8:16
upon the wall toward the dung *g*....... Neh 12:31
And at the fountain *g*, which was...... Neh 12:37
even unto the water *g* eastward......... Neh 12:37
And from above the *g* of Ephraim...... Neh 12:39
the old *g*, and above the fish *g*........ Neh 12:39
of Meah, even unto the sheep *g*........ Neh 12:39
they stood still in the prison *g*.......... Neh 12:39
then Mordecai sat in the king's *g*...... Est 2:19
Mordecai sat in the king's *g*............ Est 2:21
that were in the king's *g*................ Est 3:2
which were in the king's *g*.............. Est 3:3
And came even before the king's *g*..... Est 4:2
king's *g* clothed with sackcloth......... Est 4:2
which was before the king's *g*.......... Est 4:6
over against the *g* of the house......... Est 5:1
saw Mordecai in the king's *g*........... Est 5:9
the Jew sitting at the king's *g*.......... Est 5:13
Jew, that sitteth at the king's *g*........ Est 6:10
came again to the king's *g*.............. Est 6:12
and they are crushed in the *g*........... Job 5:4
out to the *g* through the city............ Job 29:7
when I saw my help in the *g*............ Job 31:21
sit in the *g* speak against me........... Ps 69:12
This *g* of the Lord, into which......... Ps 118:20
speak with the enemies in the *g*........ Ps 127:5
his *g* seeketh destruction............... Prov 17:19
oppress the afflicted in the *g*........... Prov 22:22
he openeth not his mouth in the *g*..... Prov 24:7
Heshbon, by the *g* of Bath-rabbim..... Song 7:4
Howl, O *g*; cry, O city................. Is 14:31
set themselves in array at the *g*........ Is 22:7
the *g* is smitten with destruction....... Is 24:12
that turn the battle to the *g*............ Is 28:6
for him that reproveth in the *g*......... Is 29:21
Stand in the *g* of the Lord's............ Jer 7:2
stand in the *g* of the children of....... Jer 17:19
is by the entry of the east *g*............ Jer 19:2
were in the high *g* of Benjamin........ Jer 20:2
of the new *g* of the Lord's house...... Jer 26:10
Hananeel unto the *g* of the corner..... Jer 31:38
of the horse *g* toward the east......... Jer 31:40
of the new *g* of the Lord's house...... Jer 36:10
when he was in the *g* of Benjamin..... Jer 37:13
then sitting in the *g* of Benjamin...... Jer 38:7
came in, and sat in the middle *g*....... Jer 39:3
by the *g* betwixt the two walls......... Jer 39:4
of the *g* between the two walls......... Jer 52:7
The elders have ceased from the *g*..... Lam 5:14
to the door of the inner *g*............. Eze 8:3
behold northward at the *g* of the....... Eze 8:5
g of the Lord's house which was...... Eze 8:14
came from the way of the higher *g*.... Eze 9:2
of the east *g* of the Lord's house...... Eze 10:19
the east *g* of the Lord's house......... Eze 11:1
behold at the door of the *g* five........ Eze 11:1
and he stood in the *g*.................. Eze 11:1
Then came he unto the *g* which........ Eze 40:6
measured the threshold of the *g*........ Eze 40:6
and the other threshold of the *g*........ Eze 40:6
the threshold of the *g* the............. Eze 40:7
of the *g* within was one reed........... Eze 40:7
also the porch of the *g* within.......... Eze 40:8
measured he the porch of the *g*......... Eze 40:9
and the porch of the *g* was inward..... Eze 40:9
the little chambers of the *g*............ Eze 40:10
The breadth of the entry of the *g*....... Eze 40:11
and the length of the *g*, thirteen........ Eze 40:11
He measured then the *g* from the...... Eze 40:13
of the court round about the *g*.......... Eze 40:14
from the face of the *g* of the........... Eze 40:15
of the inner *g* were fifty cubits........ Eze 40:15
posts within the *g* round about.......... Eze 40:16

g unto the forefront of the inner...... Eze 40:19
the *g* of the outward court that......... Eze 40:20
after the measure of the first *g*......... Eze 40:21
that looketh toward the east........... Eze 40:22
the *g* of the inner court was over...... Eze 40:23
against the *g* toward the north......... Eze 40:23
from *g* to *g* an hundred cubits......... Eze 40:23
behold a *g* toward the south............ Eze 40:24
there was a *g* in the inner court........ Eze 40:27
he measured from *g* to *g* toward...... Eze 40:27
to the inner court by the south *g*....... Eze 40:28
he measured the south *g* according.... Eze 40:28
he measured the *g* according to........ Eze 40:32
And he brought me to the north *g*...... Eze 40:35
in the porch of the *g* were two......... Eze 40:39
up to the entry of the north *g*........... Eze 40:40
which was at the porch of the *g*........ Eze 40:40
that side, by the side of the *g*.......... Eze 40:41
without the inner *g* were the............ Eze 40:44
was at the side of the north *g*........... Eze 40:44
the breadth of the *g* was three......... Eze 40:48
g whose prospect is toward the........ Eze 42:15
Afterward he brought me to the *g*...... Eze 43:1
even the *g* that looketh toward......... Eze 43:4
the house by the way of the *g*.......... Eze 43:4
g of the outward sanctuary which..... Eze 44:1
This *g* shall be shut, it shall............ Eze 44:2
by the way of the porch of that *g*...... Eze 44:3
of the north *g* before the house........ Eze 44:4
posts of the *g* of the inner court....... Eze 45:19
The *g* of the inner court that........... Eze 46:1
of the porch of that *g* without......... Eze 46:2
shall stand by the post of the *g*........ Eze 46:2
worship at the threshold of the *g*...... Eze 46:2
but the *g* shall not be shut until....... Eze 46:2
worship at the door of this *g*........... Eze 46:3
by the way of the porch of that *g*...... Eze 46:8
in by the way of the north *g* to......... Eze 46:9
go out by the way of the south *g*....... Eze 46:9
by the way of the south *g* shall........ Eze 46:9
forth by the way of the north *g*......... Eze 46:9
way of the *g* whereby he came in...... Eze 46:9
one shall then open him the *g*.......... Eze 46:12
going forth one shall shut the *g*........ Eze 46:12
which was at the side of the *g*.......... Eze 46:19
out of the way of the *g* northward..... Eze 47:2
utter *g* by the way that looketh........ Eze 47:2
one *g* of Reuben....................... Eze 48:31
one *g* of Judah, one *g* of Levi.......... Eze 48:31
one *g* of Joseph...................... Eze 48:32
one *g* of Benjamin, one *g* of Dan....... Eze 48:32
one *g* of Simeon..................... Eze 48:33
of Issachar, one *g* of Zebulun......... Eze 48:33
one *g* of Gad....................... Eze 48:34
of Asher, one *g* of Naphtali........... Eze 48:34
Daniel sat in the *g* of the king......... Dan 2:49
hate him that rebuketh in the *g*........ Amos 5:10
poor in the *g* from their right.......... Amos 5:12
and establish judgment in the *g*........ Amos 5:15
not have entered into the *g* of my...... Obad 13
is come unto the *g* of my people....... Mic 1:9
the Lord unto the *g* of Jerusalem...... Mic 1:9
up, and have passed through the *g*..... Mic 2:13
noise of a cry from the fish *g*.......... Zeph 1:10
from Benjamin's *g* unto the place..... Zec 14:10
the first *g*, unto the corner *g*.......... Zec 14:10
Enter ye in at the strait *g*.............. Mt 7:13
for wide is the *g*, and broad is......... Mt 7:13
Because strait is the *g*, and............ Mt 7:14
he came nigh to the *g* of the city...... Lk 7:12
to enter in at the strait *g*.............. Lk 13:24
Lazarus, which was laid at his *g*....... Lk 16:20
whom they laid daily at the *g* of...... Acts 3:2
at the Beautiful *g* of the temple....... Acts 3:10
house, and stood before the *g*......... Acts 10:17
they came unto the iron *g* that........ Acts 12:10
knocked at the door of the *g*........... Acts 12:13
she opened not the *g* for gladness..... Acts 12:14
told how Peter stood before the *g*...... Acts 12:14
own blood, suffered without the *g*..... Heb 13:12
every several *g* was of one pearl...... Rev 21:21

GATES

thy stranger that is within thy *g*....... Ex 20:10
were fenced with high walls, *g*......... Deut 3:5
thy stranger that is within thy *g*........ Deut 5:14
posts of thy house, and on thy *g*........ Deut 6:9
of thine house, and upon thy *g*......... Deut 11:20
the Levite that is within your *g*......... Deut 12:12
kill and eat flesh in all thy *g*........... Deut 12:15
thy *g* the tithe of thy corn.............. Deut 12:17
the Levite that is within thy *g*.......... Deut 12:18
thee, and thou shalt eat in thy *g*....... Deut 12:21
the stranger that is in thy *g*............ Deut 14:21
the Levite that is within thy *g*.......... Deut 14:27
and shalt lay it up within thy *g*........ Deut 14:28
the widow, which are within thy *g*..... Deut 14:29
g in thy land which the Lord thy...... Deut 15:7
Thou shalt eat it within thy *g*.......... Deut 15:22
the passover within any of thy *g*....... Deut 16:5
the Levite that is within thy *g*.......... Deut 16:11
the widow, that are within thy *g*....... Deut 16:14
shalt thou make then in all thy *g*....... Deut 16:18
within any of thy *g* which the......... Deut 17:2
that wicked thing, unto thy *g*.......... Deut 17:5
of controversy within thy *g*............ Deut 17:8
any of thy *g* out of all Israel........... Deut 18:6
he shall choose in one of thy *g*........ Deut 23:16
that are in thy land within thy *g*....... Deut 24:14
that they may eat within thy *g*......... Deut 26:12

shall besiege thee in all thy *g*.......... Deut 28:52
all thy *g* throughout all thy land...... Deut 28:52
shall distress thee in all thy *g*......... Deut 28:55
shall distress thee in thy *g*............ Deut 28:57
thy stranger that is within thy *g*....... Deut 31:12
son shall he set up the *g* of it.......... Josh 6:26
then was war in the *g*................. Judg 5:8
of the Lord go down to the *g*.......... Judg 5:11
the valley, and to the *g* of Ekron...... 1Sa 17:52
entering into a town that hath *g*....... 1Sa 23:7
And David sat between the two *g*...... 2Sa 18:24
set up the *g* thereof in his............ 1Kin 16:34
down the high places of the *g*......... 2Kin 23:8
service, keepers of the *g* of the........ 1Chr 9:19
porters in the *g* were two hundred.... 1Chr 9:22
of the *g* of the house of the Lord..... 1Chr 9:23
the nails for the doors of the *g*........ 1Chr 22:3
fenced cities, with walls, *g*........... 2Chr 8:5
about them walls, and towers, *g*...... 2Chr 14:7
at the *g* of the house of the Lord..... 2Chr 23:19
to praise in the *g* of the tents.......... 2Chr 31:2
the *g* thereof are burned with......... Neh 1:3
the *g* thereof are consumed with...... Neh 2:3
g of the palace which appertained.... Neh 2:8
the *g* thereof were consumed with.... Neh 2:13
the *g* thereof are burned with......... Neh 2:17
not set up the doors upon the *g*....... Neh 6:1
Let not the *g* of Jerusalem be......... Neh 7:3
and their brethren that kept the *g*..... Neh 11:19
ward at the thresholds of the *g*....... Neh 12:25
and purified the people, and the *g*.... Neh 12:30
that when the *g* of Jerusalem......... Neh 13:19
that the *g* should be shut............. Neh 13:19
of my servants set I at the *g*.......... Neh 13:19
they should come and keep the *g*..... Neh 13:22
Have the *g* of death been opened..... Job 38:17
liftest me up from the *g* of death...... Ps 9:13
in the *g* of the daughter of Zion....... Ps 9:14
Lift up your heads, O ye *g*............ Ps 24:7
Lift up your heads, O ye *g*............ Ps 24:9
The Lord loveth the *g* of Zion........ Ps 87:2
Enter into his *g* with................ Ps 100:4
For he hath broken the *g* of brass..... Ps 107:16
draw near unto the *g* of death........ Ps 107:18
Open to me the *g* of righteousness.... Ps 118:19
Our feet shall stand within thy *g*...... Ps 122:2
strengthened the bars of thy *g*......... Ps 147:13
in the openings of the *g*............. Prov 1:21
She crieth at the *g*, at the entry...... Prov 8:3
me, watching daily at my *g*........... Prov 8:34
wicked at the *g* of the righteous...... Prov 14:19
Her husband is known in the *g*........ Prov 31:23
her own works praise her in the *g*..... Prov 31:31
at our *g* are all manner of............ Song 7:13
her shall lament and mourn........... Is 3:26
may go into the *g* of the nobles....... Is 13:2
Open ye the *g*, that the righteous..... Is 26:2
I shall go to the *g* of the grave....... Is 38:10
open before him the two leaved *g*..... Is 45:1
and the *g* shall not be shut........... Is 45:1
break in pieces the *g* of brass........ Is 45:2
thy *g* of carbuncles, and all thy...... Is 54:12
Therefore thy *g* shall be open........ Is 60:11
walls Salvation, and thy *g* Praise..... Is 60:18
Go through, go through the *g*......... Is 62:10
entering of the *g* of Jerusalem....... Jer 1:15
in at these *g* to worship the Lord.... Jer 7:2
and the *g* thereof languish........... Jer 14:2
with a fan in the *g* of the land....... Jer 15:7
in all the *g* of Jerusalem............. Jer 17:19
that enter in by these *g*.............. Jer 17:20
bring it in by the *g* of Jerusalem..... Jer 17:21
bring in no burden through the *g*..... Jer 17:24
into the *g* of this city kings.......... Jer 17:25
even entering in at the *g* of.......... Jer 17:27
I kindle a fire in the *g* thereof....... Jer 17:27
people that enter in by these *g*....... Jer 22:4
the *g* of this house kings sitting...... Jer 22:4
forth beyond the *g* of Jerusalem..... Jer 22:19
which have neither *g* nor bars........ Jer 49:31
her high *g* shall be burned with...... Jer 51:58
all her *g* are desolate................ Lam 1:4
Her *g* are sunk into the ground....... Lam 2:9
entered into the *g* of Jerusalem...... Lam 4:12
of the sword against all their *g*....... Eze 21:15
battering rams against the *g*.......... Eze 21:22
that was the *g* of the people......... Eze 26:2
when he shall enter into thy *g*........ Eze 26:10
and having neither bars nor *g*........ Eze 38:11
g over against the length of the...... Eze 40:18
of the *g* was the lower pavement..... Eze 40:18
were by the posts of the *g*........... Eze 40:38
charge at the *g* of the house......... Eze 44:11
in at the *g* of the inner court......... Eze 44:17
in the *g* of the inner court........... Eze 44:17
the *g* of the city shall be after....... Eze 48:31
three *g* northward.................. Eze 48:31
four hundred and three *g*............ Eze 48:32
measures; and three *g*.............. Eze 48:33
five hundred, with their three *g*...... Eze 48:34
and foreigners entered into his *g*..... Obad 11
The *g* of the rivers shall be.......... Nah 2:6
the *g* of thy land shall be set........ Nah 3:13
of truth and peace in your *g*.......... Zec 8:16
the *g* of hell shall not prevail........ Mt 16:18
And they watched the *g* day......... Acts 9:24
oxen and garlands unto the *g*......... Acts 14:13
great and high, and had twelve *g*..... Rev 21:12
at the twelve angels, and names..... Rev 21:12
On the east three *g*................. Rev 21:13

on the north three g................................Rev 21:13
on the south three g................................Rev 21:13
and on the west three g..............................Rev 21:13
the g thereof, and the wall.........................Rev 21:15
the twelve g were twelve pearls.....................Rev 21:21
the g of it shall not be shut at....................Rev 21:25
in through the g into the city......................Rev 22:14

GATH (*gath*) See GATH-HEPHER, GATH-RIMMON,
GITTITE, MORESHETH-GATH. *A royal Philistine
city.*
only in Gaza, in G, and in Ashdod,.................Josh 11:22
of Israel be carried about unto G....................1Sa 5:8
one, for Askelon one, for G one......................1Sa 6:17
to Israel, from Ekron even unto G....................1Sa 7:14
Philistines, named Goliath, of G....................1Sa 17:4
the champion, the Philistine of G..................1Sa 17:23
the way to Shaaraim, even unto G...................1Sa 17:52
and went to Achish the king of G...................1Sa 21:10
afraid of Achish the king of G.....................1Sa 21:12
the son of Maoch, king of G.........................1Sa 27:2
And David dwelt with Achish at G....................1Sa 27:3
Saul that David was fled to G.......................1Sa 27:4
alive, to bring tidings to G.......................1Sa 27:11
Tell it not in G, publish it not....................2Sa 1:20
men which came after him from G....................2Sa 15:18
And there was yet a battle in G.....................2Sa 21:20
four were born to the giant in G...................2Sa 21:22
Achish son of Maachah king of G....................1Kin 2:39
Behold, thy servants be in G.......................1Kin 2:39
went to G to Achish to seek his....................1Kin 2:40
and brought his servants from G....................1Kin 2:40
had gone from Jerusalem to G.......................1Kin 2:41
went up, and fought against G.....................2Kin 12:17
whom the men of G that were born....................1Chr 7:21
drove away the inhabitants of G.....................1Chr 8:13
and subdued them, and took G........................1Chr 18:1
And yet again there was war at G...................1Chr 20:6
were born unto the giant in G......................1Chr 20:8
And G, and Mareshah, and Ziph,......................2Chr 11:8
and brake down the wall of G.......................2Chr 26:6
the Philistines took him in G........................Ps 56:t
then go down to G of the...........................Amos 6:2
Declare ye it not at G, weep ye......................Mic 1:10

GATHER
eaten, and thou shalt g it to thee..................Gen 6:21
said unto his brethren, G stones...................Gen 31:46
they shall g themselves together...................Gen 34:30
let them g all the food of those....................Gen 41:35
G yourselves together, that I may...................Gen 49:1
G yourselves together, and hear,....................Gen 49:2
the elders of Israel together,......................Ex 3:16
them go and g straw for themselves...................Ex 5:7
to g stubble instead of straw.......................Ex 5:12
g thy cattle, and all that thou,....................Ex 9:19
a g certain rate every day, that...................Ex 16:4
be twice as much as they g daily...................Ex 16:5
G of it every man according to....................Ex 16:16
Six days ye shall g it............................Ex 16:26
on the seventh day for to g.......................Ex 16:27
shalt g in the fruits thereof......................Ex 23:10
g thou all the congregation.........................Lev 8:3
field, neither shalt thou g the....................Lev 19:9
neither shalt thou g every grape...................Lev 19:10
neither shalt thou g any gleaning..................Lev 23:22
and g in the fruit thereof.........................Lev 25:3
neither g the grapes of thy vine...................Lev 25:5
nor g the grapes in it of thy.....................Lev 25:11
not sow, nor g in our increase....................Lev 25:20
thou shalt g the whole assembly....................Num 8:9
shall g themselves unto thee......................Num 10:4
G unto me seventy men of the......................Num 11:16
a man that is clean shall g up....................Num 19:9
g thou the assembly together,.....................Num 20:8
G the people together, and I will.................Num 21:16
G me the people together, and I....................Deut 4:10
that thou mayest g in thy corn....................Deut 11:14
thou shalt g all the spoil of it..................Deut 13:16
shalt not g the grapes thereof....................Deut 28:30
field, and shalt g but little in..................Deut 28:38
of the wine, nor g the grapes.....................Deut 28:39
g thee from all the nations,......................Deut 30:3
will the LORD thy God g thee.......................Deut 30:3
G the people together, men, and...................Deut 31:12
G unto me all the elders of your..................Deut 31:28
g after the reapers among the.......................Ruth 2:7
G all Israel to Mizpeh, and I will...................1Sa 7:5
will g all Israel unto my lord.....................2Sa 3:21
Now therefore g the rest of the...................2Sa 12:28
g to me all Israel unto mount....................1Kin 18:19
out into the field to g herbs.....................2Kin 4:39
I will g thee unto thy fathers,...................2Kin 22:20
that they may g themselves unto...................1Chr 13:2
g us together, and deliver us from.................1Chr 16:35
David commanded to g together the...................2Chr 22:2
of all Israel money to repair......................2Chr 24:5
I will g thee to thy fathers, and.................2Chr 34:28
that they should g themselves.......................Ezr 10:7
yet will I g them from thence, and..................Neh 1:9
heart to g together the nobles......................Neh 7:5
to g into them out of the fields..................Neh 12:44
that they may g together all the....................Est 2:3
g together all the Jews that are...................Est 4:16
city to g themselves together........................Est 8:11
or g together, then who can........................Job 11:10
they g the vintage of the wicked....................Job 24:6
if he g unto himself his spirit....................Job 34:14
thy seed, and g it into thy barn...................Job 39:12
G not my soul with sinners, nor.....................Ps 26:9
and knoweth not who shall g them.....................Ps 39:6

G my saints together unto me.........................Ps 50:5
They g themselves together, they....................Ps 56:6
They g themselves together.........................Ps 94:21
they g themselves together, and.....................Ps 104:22
That thou givest them they g......................Ps 104:28
g us from among the heathen, to...................Ps 106:47
he shall g it for him that will....................Prov 28:8
sinner he giveth travail, to........................Eccl 2:26
a time to g stones together.........................Eccl 3:5
in the gardens, and to g lilies....................Song 6:2
of Gebim g themselves to flee......................Is 10:31
g together the dispersed of Judah..................Is 11:12
and hatch, and g under her shadow...................Is 34:15
he shall g the lambs with his arm...................Is 40:11
the east, and g thee from the west..................Is 43:5
all these g themselves together.....................Is 49:18
with great mercies will I g thee....................Is 54:7
they shall surely g together........................Is 54:15
whosoever shall g together..........................Is 54:15
Yet will I g others to him,.........................Is 56:8
all they g themselves together.......................Is 60:4
g out the stones...................................Is 62:10
come, that I will g all nations....................Is 66:18
g together, and say, Assemble........................Jer 4:5
g yourselves to flee out of the.....................Jer 6:1
The children g wood, and the.......................Jer 7:18
harvestman, and none shall g them..................Jer 9:22
G up thy wares out of the land, O..................Jer 10:17
I will g the remnant of my flock...................Jer 23:3
I will g you from all the nations..................Jer 29:14
g them from the coasts of the......................Jer 31:8
that scattered Israel will g him...................Jer 31:10
Behold, I will g them out of all...................Jer 32:37
g ye wine, and summer fruits, and...................Jer 40:10
and none shall g up him that.......................Jer 49:5
G ye together, and come against....................Jer 49:14
bright the arrows; g the shields...................Jer 51:11
I will even g you from the people...................Eze 11:17
therefore I will g all thy lovers..................Eze 16:37
I will even g them round about.....................Eze 16:37
will g you out of the countries....................Eze 20:34
g you out of the countries.........................Eze 20:41
therefore I will g you in mine.....................Eze 22:19
As they g silver, and brass, and...................Eze 22:20
so will I g you in mine anger and..................Eze 22:20
Yea, I will g you, and blow upon...................Eze 22:21
G the pieces thereof into it,......................Eze 24:4
I g the Egyptians from the people..................Eze 29:13
g them from the countries, and....................Eze 34:13
g you out of all countries, and....................Eze 36:24
will g them on every side, and....................Eze 37:21
g yourselves on every side to my...................Eze 39:17
sent to g together the princes......................Dan 3:2
the nations, now will I g them......................Hos 8:10
Egypt shall g them up, Memphis......................Hos 9:6
assembly, g the elders and all the.................Joel 1:14
all faces shall g blackness........................Joel 2:6
G the people, sanctify the.........................Joel 2:16
the children, and those that.......................Joel 2:16
I will also g all nations..........................Joel 3:2
g yourselves together round about..................Mic 1:7
I will surely g the remnant of......................Mic 2:12
I will g her that is driven out,....................Mic 4:6
for he shall g them as the.........................Mic 4:12
Now g thyself in troops, O.........................Mic 5:1
the faces of them all g blackness..................Nah 2:10
they shall g the captivity as the...................Hab 1:9
net, and g them in their drag......................Hab 1:15
O yourselves together, yea,.........................Zeph 2:1
g together, O nation not desired...................Zeph 2:1
determination is to g the nations..................Zeph 3:8
I will g them that are sorrowful...................Zeph 3:18
g her that was driven out..........................Zeph 3:19
even in the time that I g you......................Zeph 3:20
I will hiss for them, and g them...................Zec 10:8
Egypt, and g them out of Assyria...................Zec 10:10
For I will g all nations against....................Zec 14:2
g his wheat into the garner.........................Mt 3:12
do they reap, nor g into barns......................Mt 6:26
Do men g grapes of thorns, or.......................Mt 7:16
thou then that we go and g them up..................Mt 13:28
lest while ye g up the tares........................Mt 13:29
G ye together first the tares, and..................Mt 13:30
but g the wheat into my barn.......................Mt 13:30
they shall g out of his kingdom....................Mt 13:41
they shall g together his elect....................Mt 24:31
g where I have not strawed.........................Mt 25:26
shall g together his elect from....................Mk 13:27
will g the wheat into his garner....................Lk 3:17
For of thorns men do not g figs.....................Lk 6:44
of a bramble bush g they grapes....................Lk 6:44
as a hen doth g her brood under....................Lk 13:34
G up the fragments that remain,.....................Jn 6:12
but that also he should g..........................Jn 11:52
men g them, and cast them into the.................Jn 15:6
g together in one all things in....................Eph 1:10
the clusters of the vine of the...................Rev 14:18
to g them to the battle of that...................Rev 16:14
g yourselves together unto the....................Rev 19:17
to g them together to battle.......................Rev 20:8

GATHERED
be g together unto one place........................Gen 1:9
their substance that they had g....................Gen 13:6
and was g to his people...........................Gen 25:8
and was g unto his people.........................Gen 25:17
And thither were all the flocks g...................Gen 29:3
the cattle should be g together....................Gen 29:7
all the flocks be g together......................Gen 29:8
Laban g together all the men of....................Gen 29:22
was g unto his people, being old...................Gen 35:29

he g up all the food of the seven.................Gen 41:48
Joseph g corn as the sand of the.................Gen 41:49
Joseph g up all the money that.....................Gen 47:14
I am to be g unto my people........................Gen 49:29
he g up his feet into the bed, and................Gen 49:33
ghost, and was g unto his people..................Gen 49:33
g together all the elders of the....................Ex 4:29
they g them together upon heaps......................Ex 8:14
the waters were g together.........................Ex 15:8
children of Israel did so, and g...................Ex 16:17
he that g much had nothing over,...................Ex 16:18
he that g little had no lack.......................Ex 16:18
they g every man according to his..................Ex 16:18
they g it every morning, every.....................Ex 16:21
day they g twice as much bread.....................Ex 16:22
when thou hast g in thy labours....................Ex 23:16
the people g themselves together...................Ex 32:1
all the sons of Levi g themselves..................Ex 32:26
Moses g all the congregation of....................Ex 35:1
the assembly was g together........................Lev 8:4
when ye have g in the fruit of....................Lev 23:39
when ye are g together within.....................Lev 26:25
congregation is to be g together...................Num 10:7
g it, and ground it in mills, or...................Num 11:8
of the sea be g together for them..................Num 11:22
g the seventy men of the elders...................Num 11:24
next day, and they g the quails...................Num 11:32
that g least g ten homers.........................Num 11:32
that are g together against me....................Num 14:35
they found a man that g sticks....................Num 15:32
they g themselves together........................Num 16:3
all thy company are g together.....................Num 16:11
Korah g all the congregation......................Num 16:19
congregation was g against Moses...................Num 16:42
they g themselves together.........................Num 20:2
Aaron g the congregation together..................Num 20:10
Aaron shall be g unto his people...................Num 20:24
Aaron shall be g unto his people...................Num 20:26
but Sihon g all his people........................Num 21:23
g themselves together against the..................Num 27:3
also shalt be g unto thy people...................Num 27:13
as Aaron thy brother was g........................Num 27:13
shalt thou be g unto thy people....................Num 31:2
that thou hast g in thy corn......................Deut 11:14
goest up, and be g unto thy people.................Deut 32:50
Hor, and was g unto his people....................Deut 32:50
tribes of Israel were g together...................Deut 33:5
That they g themselves together....................Josh 9:2
g themselves together, and went up.................Josh 10:5
are g together against us.........................Josh 10:6
of the children of Israel g.......................Josh 22:12
Joshua g all the tribes of Israel..................Josh 24:1
g their meat under my table........................Judg 1:7
were g unto their fathers.........................Judg 2:10
he g unto him the children of.....................Judg 3:13
Sisera g together all his.........................Judg 4:13
of the east were g together.......................Judg 6:33
and Abi-ezer was g after him......................Judg 6:34
who also was g after him..........................Judg 6:35
the men of Israel g themselves.....................Judg 7:23
of Ephraim g themselves together...................Judg 7:24
all the men of Shechem g together..................Judg 9:6
g their vineyards, and trode the...................Judg 9:27
tower of Shechem were g together...................Judg 9:47
children of Ammon were g together..................Judg 10:17
there were g vain men to Jephthah..................Judg 11:3
but Sihon g all his people........................Judg 11:20
the men of Ephraim g themselves...................Judg 12:1
Then Jephthah g together all the...................Judg 12:4
g them together for to offer a.....................Judg 16:23
to Micah's house were g together...................Judg 18:22
was g together as one man.........................Judg 20:1
of Israel were g against the city..................Judg 20:11
But the children of Benjamin g....................Judg 20:14
and g all the lords of the..........................1Sa 5:8
g together all the lords of the.....................1Sa 5:11
they g together to Mizpeh, and......................1Sa 7:6
Israel were g together to Mizpeh....................1Sa 7:7
of Israel g themselves together....................1Sa 8:4
the Philistines g themselves......................1Sa 13:5
that the Philistines g themselves..................1Sa 13:11
he g an host, and smote the.......................1Sa 14:48
Saul g the people together, and...................1Sa 15:4
Now the Philistines g together....................1Sa 17:1
were g together at Shochoh, which..................1Sa 17:1
the men of Israel were g together..................1Sa 17:2
And Jonathan's lad g up the arrows..................1Sa 20:38
g themselves unto him..............................1Sa 22:2
the Israelites were g together.....................1Sa 25:1
that the Philistines g their.......................1Sa 28:1
the Philistines g themselves......................1Sa 28:4
Saul g all Israel together, and....................1Sa 28:4
Now the Philistines g together......................1Sa 29:1
the children of Benjamin g.........................2Sa 2:25
when he had g all the people.......................2Sa 2:30
David g together all the chosen.....................2Sa 6:1
they g themselves together.........................2Sa 10:15
he g all Israel together, and.....................2Sa 10:17
David g all the people together...................2Sa 12:29
that came unto him were g.........................2Sa 17:11
Israel be generally g unto thee....................2Sa 17:11
and they were g together, and went.................2Sa 20:14
they g the bones of them that.....................2Sa 21:13
were there g together to battle....................2Sa 23:9
the Philistines were g together....................2Sa 23:11
Solomon g together chariots and...................1Kin 10:26
he g men unto him, and became.....................1Kin 11:24
the prophets together unto.......................1Kin 18:20
of Syria g all his host together...................1Kin 20:1
of Israel the prophets together...................1Kin 22:6

they g all that were able to put 2Kin 3:21
g thereof wild gourds his lap 2Kin 4:39
king of Syria g all his host 2Kin 6:24
Jehu g all the people together, ... 2Kin 10:18
of the door have g of the people. 2Kin 22:4
Thy servants have g the money. 2Kin 22:9
thou shalt be g into thy grave in. 2Kin 22:20
they g unto him all the elders of 2Kin 23:1
Then all Israel g themselves to. 1Chr 11:1
were g together to battle. 1Chr 11:13
So David g all Israel together, ... 1Chr 13:5
David g all Israel together to 1Chr 15:3
And the children of Ammon g 1Chr 19:7
he g all Israel, and passed over. 1Chr 19:17
he g together all the princes of. 1Chr 23:2
Solomon g chariots and horsemen 2Chr 1:14
he g of the house of Judah and 2Chr 11:1
that were g together to Jerusalem. 2Chr 12:5
there are g unto him vain men, ... 2Chr 13:7
he g all Judah and Benjamin, and 2Chr 15:9
So they g themselves together at 2Chr 15:10
g together of prophets four 2Chr 18:5
Judah g themselves together, to. 2Chr 20:4
g the Levites out of all the 2Chr 23:2
he g together the priests and the 2Chr 24:5
by day, and g money in abundance. 2Chr 24:11
Moreover Amaziah g Judah together. 2Chr 25:5
Ahaz g together the vessels of 2Chr 28:24
g them together into the east 2Chr 29:4
they g their brethren, and 2Chr 29:15
g the rulers of the city, and went. 2Chr 29:20
people g themselves together to. 2Chr 30:3
So there was g much people 2Chr 32:4
g them together to him in the 2Chr 32:6
had g of the hand of Manasseh 2Chr 34:9
they have g together the money 2Chr 34:17
thou shalt be g to thy grave in. 2Chr 34:28
g together all the elders of 2Chr 34:29
the people g themselves together ...... Ezr 3:1
I g together out of Israel chief ...... Ezr 7:28
I g them together to the river ...... Ezr 8:15
Benjamin g themselves together ...... Ezr 10:9
all my servants were g thither ...... Neh 5:16
all the people g themselves ...... Neh 8:1
on the second day were g together ...... Neh 8:13
the singers g themselves together ...... Neh 12:28
I g them together, and set them in. ...... Neh 13:11
when many maidens were g together ...... Est 2:8
when the virgins were g together ...... Est 2:19
The Jews g themselves together in ...... Est 9:2
g themselves together on the ...... Est 9:15
provinces g themselves together ...... Est 9:16
they have g themselves together ...... Job 16:10
lie down, but he shall not be g ...... Job 27:19
the nettles they were g together. ...... Job 30:7
and g themselves together ...... Ps 35:15
the objects g themselves together ...... Ps 35:15
of the people are g together ...... Ps 47:9
the mighty are g against me. ...... Ps 59:3
When the people are g together, ... Ps 102:22
g them out of the lands, from th ...... Ps 107:3
are they g together for war ...... Ps 140:2
and herbs of the mountains are g ...... Prov 27:25
who hath g the wind in his fists ...... Prov 30:4
I g me also silver and gold, and. ...... Eccl 2:8
I have g my myrrh with my spice ...... Song 5:1
g out the stones thereof, and. ...... Is 5:2
are left, have I g all the earth. ...... Is 10:14
kingdoms of nations g together ...... Is 13:4
ye g together the waters of the. ...... Is 22:9
And they shall be g together ...... Is 24:22
as prisoners are g in the pit ...... Is 24:22
and ye shall be g one by one ...... Is 27:12
your spoil shall be g like the. ...... Is 33:4
shall the vultures also be g ...... Is 34:15
and his spirit it hath g them ...... Is 34:16
Let all the nations be g together. ...... Is 43:9
let them all be g together ...... Is 44:11
to him, Though Israel be not g ...... Is 49:5
beside those that are g unto him ...... Is 56:8
shall be g together unto thee ...... Is 60:7
they that have g it shall eat it. ...... Is 62:9
the nations shall be g into it. ...... Jer 3:17
they shall not be g, nor be ...... Jer 8:2
shall not be lamented, neither g ...... Jer 25:33
all the people were g against ...... Jer 26:9
g wine and summer fruits very much. ...... Jer 40:12
that all the Jews which are g ...... Jer 40:15
When I shall have g the house of ...... Eze 28:25
not be brought together, nor g ...... Eze 29:5
is g out of many people, against ...... Eze 38:8
that are g out of the nations ...... Eze 38:12
hast thou g thy company to take a ...... Eze 38:13
g them out of their enemies'. ...... Eze 39:27
but I have g them unto their own ...... Eze 39:28
were g together, saw these. ...... Dan 3:3
being g together, saw these men, ... Dan 3:27
children of Israel be g together. ...... Hos 1:11
people shall be g against them. ...... Hos 10:10
for she g it of the hire of an. ...... Mic 1:7
many nations are g against thee. ...... Mic 4:11
they have g the summer fruits. ...... Mic 7:1
earth be g together against ...... Zec 12:3
round about shall be g together ...... Zec 14:14
when he had g all the chief ...... Mt 2:4
were g together with him, so that. ...... Mt 13:2
As therefore the tares are g ...... Mt 13:40
into the sea, and g of every kind ...... Mt 13:47
the good into vessels, but cast ...... Mt 13:48
three are g together in my name ...... Mt 18:20

g together all as many as they ...... Mt 22:10
to silence, they were g together. ...... Mt 22:41
the Pharisees were g together ...... Mt 22:41
I have g thy children together. ...... Mt 23:37
will the eagles be g together ...... Mt 24:28
before him shall be g all nations. ...... Mt 25:32
when they were g together ...... Mt 27:17
g unto him the whole band of ...... Mt 27:27
all the city was g together at. ...... Mk 1:33
straightway many were g together. ...... Mk 2:2
there was g unto him a great ...... Mk 4:1
side, much people g unto him ...... Mk 5:21
the apostles g themselves ...... Mk 6:30
when much people were g together ...... Lk 8:4
the people were g thick together ...... Lk 11:29
when there were g together an ...... Lk 12:1
I have g thy children together. ...... Lk 13:34
the younger son g all together ...... Lk 15:13
will the eagles be g together ...... Lk 17:37
and found the eleven g together ...... Lk 24:33
Therefore they g them together ...... Jn 6:13
Then g the chief priests and the ...... Jn 11:47
were g together at Jerusalem ...... Acts 4:6
the rulers were g together ...... Acts 4:26
of Israel, were g together ...... Acts 4:27
where many were g together ...... Acts 12:12
had g the church together, they ...... Acts 14:27
when they had g the multitude. ...... Acts 15:30
a company, and set all the city. ...... Acts 17:5
where they were g together ...... Acts 20:8
when Paul had g a bundle of ...... Acts 28:3
Christ, when ye are g together 1Cor 5:4
He that had g much had nothing 2Cor 8:15
he that had g little had no lack 2Cor 8:15
g the vine of the earth, and cast. ...... Rev 14:19
he g them together into a place ...... Rev 16:16
g together to make war against ...... Rev 19:19

GATHERER
herdman, and a g of sycomore fruit... Amos 7:14

GATHEREST
When thou g the grapes of thy ...... Deut 24:21

GATHERETH
he that g the ashes of the heifer ...... Num 19:10
He g the waters of the sea. ...... Ps 33:7
his heart g iniquity to itself. ...... Ps 41:6
he g together the outcasts of ...... Ps 147:2
g her food in the harvest ...... Prov 6:8
The that g in summer is a wise son. ...... Prov 10:5
but he that g by labour shall. ...... Prov 13:11
as one g eggs that are left, have ...... Is 10:14
as when the harvestman g the corn ...... Is 17:5
it shall be as he that g ears in ...... Is 17:5
The Lord God which g the outcasts ...... Is 56:8
the mountains, and no man g them. ...... Nah 3:18
but g unto him all nations, and. ...... Hab 2:5
he that g not with me scattereth ...... Mt 12:30
even as a hen g her chickens. ...... Mt 23:37
he that g not with me scattereth ...... Lk 11:23
g fruit unto life eternal. ...... Jn 4:36

GATHERING
the g together of the waters. ...... Gen 1:10
him shall the g of the people be. ...... Gen 49:10
they that found him g sticks. ...... Num 15:33
widow woman was there g of sticks. 1Kin 17:10
I am g two sticks, that I may go. 1Kin 17:12
were three days in g of the spoil 2Chr 20:25
shall fail, the g shall not come. ...... Is 32:10
like the g of the caterpillar. ...... Is 33:4
g where thou hast not strawed ...... Mt 25:24
assuredly g that the Lord had. ...... Acts 16:10
by our g together unto him, ... 2Th 2:1

GATHERINGS
that there be no g when I come 1Cor 16:2

GATH-HEPHER (gath-he´-fer) See GITTAH-
HEPHER. A town in Zebulun.
the prophet, which was of G 2Kin 14:25

GATH-RIMMON (gath-rim´-mon)
1. A Levitical town in Dan.
And Jehud, and Bene-berak, and G ...... Josh 19:45
2. A Levitical town in Manasseh.
her suburbs, G with her suburbs ...... Josh 21:24
suburbs, G with her suburbs ...... Josh 21:25
suburbs, G with her suburbs 1Chr 6:69

GAVE
Adam g names to all cattle, and to ...... Gen 2:20
g also unto her husband with her ...... Gen 3:6
she g me of the tree, and I did. ...... Gen 3:12
And he g him tithes of all ...... Gen 14:20
g her to her husband Abram to be. ...... Gen 16:3
and good, and g it unto a young man. ...... Gen 18:7
g them unto Abraham, and restored. ...... Gen 20:14
g it unto Hagar, putting it on. ...... Gen 21:14
with water, and g the lad drink. ...... Gen 21:19
g them unto Abimelech. ...... Gen 21:27
upon her hand, and g him drink. ...... Gen 24:18
g straw and provender for the. ...... Gen 24:32
and raiment, and g them to Rebekah. ...... Gen 24:53
he g also to her brother and to. ...... Gen 24:53
Abraham g all that he had unto. ...... Gen 25:5
Abraham had, Abraham g gifts. ...... Gen 25:6
Then Abraham g up the ghost. ...... Gen 25:8
he g up the ghost, and died. ...... Gen 25:17
Then Jacob g Esau bread and. ...... Gen 25:34
she g the savoury meat and the. ...... Gen 27:17
which God g unto Abraham ...... Gen 28:4
he blessed him he g him a charge ...... Gen 28:6

Laban g unto his daughter Leah ...... Gen 29:24
he g him Rachel his daughter to ...... Gen 29:28
Laban g to Rachel his daughter ...... Gen 29:29
she g him Bilhah her handmaid to ...... Gen 30:4
her maid, and g her Jacob to wife. ...... Gen 30:9
g them into the hand of his sons. ...... Gen 30:35
they g unto Jacob all the strange. ...... Gen 35:4
And the land which I g Abraham ...... Gen 35:12
Isaac g up the ghost, and died, and. ...... Gen 35:29
he g it her, and came in unto her, ... Gen 38:18
because that I g her not to ...... Gen 38:26
g him favour in the sight of the. ...... Gen 39:21
I g the cup into Pharaoh's hand ...... Gen 40:11
he g the cup into Pharaoh's hand ...... Gen 40:21
he g him to wife Asenath the ...... Gen 41:45
g them water, and they washed ...... Gen 43:24
he g their asses provender. ...... Gen 43:24
Joseph g them wagons, according ...... Gen 45:21
g them provision for the way ...... Gen 45:21
To all of them he g each man ...... Gen 45:22
but to Benjamin he g three ...... Gen 45:22
whom Laban g to Leah his daughter. ...... Gen 46:18
which Laban g unto Rachel his ...... Gen 46:25
g them a possession in the land ...... Gen 47:11
Joseph g them bread in exchange ...... Gen 47:17
portion which Pharaoh g them ...... Gen 47:22
he g Moses Zipporah his daughter. ...... Ex 2:21
g them a charge unto the children ...... Ex 6:13
the LORD g the people favour in. ...... Ex 11:3
the LORD g the people favour in ...... Ex 12:36
but it g light by night to these. ...... Ex 14:20
he g unto Moses, when he had made. ...... Ex 31:18
So they g it me ...... Ex 32:24
he g them in commandment all that ...... Ex 34:32
Moses g commandment, and they. ...... Ex 36:6
Moses g the money of them that ...... Num 3:51
oxen, and g them unto the Levites. ...... Num 7:6
four oxen he g unto the sons of ...... Num 7:7
eight oxen he g unto the sons of ...... Num 7:8
unto the sons of Kohath he g none. ...... Num 7:9
g it unto the seventy elders ...... Num 11:25
their princes g him a rod apiece ...... Num 17:6
g him a charge, as the LORD ...... Num 27:23
Moses g the tribute, which was. ...... Num 31:41
g them unto the Levites, which. ...... Num 31:47
Moses g unto them, even to the. ...... Num 32:33
of other names unto the cities ...... Num 32:38
Moses g Gilead unto Machir the. ...... Num 32:40
which the LORD g unto them ...... Deut 2:12
g I unto the Reubenites and to the ...... Deut 3:12
g I unto the half tribe of ...... Deut 3:13
And I g Gilead unto Machir. ...... Deut 3:15
unto the Gadites I g from Gilead. ...... Deut 3:16
that the LORD g me the two tables. ...... Deut 9:11
and the LORD g them unto me. ...... Deut 10:4
I g my daughter unto this man to ...... Deut 22:16
g it for an inheritance unto the. ...... Deut 29:8
he g Joshua the son of Nun a ...... Deut 31:23
Moses g you on this side Jordan ...... Josh 1:14
g you on this side Jordan toward ...... Josh 1:15
Joshua g it for an inheritance ...... Josh 4:36
g it for a possession unto the. ...... Josh 12:6
which Joshua g unto the tribes of ...... Josh 12:7
inheritance, which Moses g them ...... Josh 13:8
the servant of the LORD g them ...... Josh 13:8
of Levi he g none inheritance ...... Josh 13:14
Moses g inheritance unto the ...... Josh 13:24
Moses g inheritance unto the half ...... Josh 13:29
Levi Moses g not any inheritance. ...... Josh 13:33
but unto the Levites he g none ...... Josh 14:3
therefore they g no part unto the. ...... Josh 14:4
g unto Caleb the son of Jephunneh ...... Josh 14:13
he g a part among the children of ...... Josh 15:13
he g him Achsah his daughter to. ...... Josh 15:17
he g her the upper springs, and. ...... Josh 15:19
g them an inheritance among the. ...... Josh 17:4
the servant of the LORD g them ...... Josh 18:7
the children of Israel g an ...... Josh 19:49
g him the city which he asked ...... Josh 19:50
the children of Israel g unto the. ...... Josh 21:3
the children of Israel g by lot. ...... Josh 21:8
they g out of the tribe of the. ...... Josh 21:9
they g them the city of Arba the. ...... Josh 21:11
g they to Caleb the son of. ...... Josh 21:12
Thus they g to the children of ...... Josh 21:13
g the tribe of Simeon with her ...... Josh 21:21
they g Golan in Bashan with her. ...... Josh 21:27
the LORD g unto Israel all the. ...... Josh 21:43
the LORD g them rest round about, ... Josh 21:44
g you on the other side Jordan ...... Josh 22:4
g Joshua among their brethren on. ...... Josh 22:7
his seed, and g him Isaac. ...... Josh 24:3
I g unto Isaac Jacob and Esau ...... Josh 24:4
g Esau mount Seir, to. ...... Josh 24:4
I g them into your hand, that ye. ...... Judg 1:4
he g him Achsah his daughter to. ...... Judg 1:13
Caleb g her the upper springs and ...... Judg 1:15
they g Hebron unto Caleb, as. ...... Judg 1:20
g their daughters to their sons. ...... Judg 3:6
g him drink, and covered him. ...... Judg 4:19
He asked water, and she g him milk. ...... Judg 5:25
before you, and g you their land ...... Judg 6:9
they g him threescore and ten ...... Judg 9:4
and g them, and they did eat ...... Judg 14:9
g change of garments unto them ...... Judg 14:19
therefore I g her to thy. ...... Judg 15:2
g them to the founder, who made. ...... Judg 17:4
g a provender unto the asses ...... Judg 19:21
for the men of Israel g place to ...... Judg 20:36

they g them wives which they had.... Judg 21:14
g to her that she had reserved......... Ruth 2:18
six measures of barley g he me.......... Ruth 3:17
shoe, and g it to his neighbour.......... Ruth 4:7
the LORD g her conception, and she..... Ruth 4:13
women her neighbours g it a name..... Ruth 4:17
he g to Peninnah his wife, and to...... 1Sa 1:4
unto Hannah he g a worthy portion..... 1Sa 1:5
g her son suck until she weaned........ 1Sa 1:23
Bring the portion which I g thee........ 1Sa 9:23
Samuel, God g him another heart...... 1Sa 10:9
g it to David, and his garments,........ 1Sa 18:4
they g them in full tale to the.......... 1Sa 18:27
Saul g him Michal his daughter to..... 1Sa 18:27
Jonathan g his artillery unto his....... 1Sa 20:40
So the priest g him hallowed............ 1Sa 21:6
g him victuals, and g him the.......... 1Sa 22:10
Then Achish g him Ziklag that day 1Sa 27:6
g him bread, and he did eat............ 1Sa 30:11
they g him a piece of a cake of........ 1Sa 30:12
I g thee thy master's house, and....... 2Sa 12:8
g thee the house of Israel and of..... 2Sa 12:8
king g all the captains charge......... 2Sa 18:5
Joab g up the sum of the number...... 2Sa 24:9
And God g Solomon wisdom and........ 1Ki 4:29
So Hiram g Solomon cedar trees and ... 1Ki 5:10
Solomon g Hiram twenty thousand.... 1Ki 5:11
thus g Solomon to Hiram year by...... 1Ki 5:11
the LORD g Solomon wisdom, as he 1Ki 5:12
that then king Solomon g Hiram....... 1Ki 9:11
she g the king an hundred and........ 1Ki 10:10
queen of Sheba g to king Solomon 1Ki 10:10
king Solomon g unto the queen of 1Ki 10:13
Solomon g her of his royal bounty.... 1Ki 10:13
which g him an house, and............ 1Ki 11:18
him victuals, and g him land.......... 1Ki 11:18
so that he g him to wife the........... 1Ki 11:19
old men's counsel that they g him..... 1Ki 12:13
he g a sign the same day, saying,..... 1Ki 13:3
the house of David, and g thee........ 1Ki 14:8
which he g to their fathers, and...... 1Ki 14:15
g unto the people, and they did...... 1Ki 19:21
And he g him his hand................. 2Ki 10:15
upon him, and g him the testimony... 2Ki 11:12
they g the money, being told,......... 2Ki 12:11
But they g that to the workmen,...... 2Ki 12:14
the LORD g Israel a saviour, so........ 2Ki 13:5
Menahem g Pul a thousand talents ... 2Ki 15:19
his servant, and g him presents....... 2Ki 17:3
Hezekiah g him all the silver.......... 2Ki 18:15
g it to the king of Assyria............. 2Ki 18:16
the land which I g their fathers....... 2Ki 21:8
Hilkiah g the book to Shaphan, and.. 2Ki 22:8
Jehoiakim g the silver and the........ 2Ki 23:35
and they g judgment upon him........ 1Ch 6:32
Sheshan g his daughter to Jarha....... 1Ch 2:35
they g them Hebron in the land of 1Ch 6:55
they g to Caleb the son of............. 1Ch 6:56
Aaron they g the cities of Judah....... 1Ch 6:57
the children of Israel g to the........ 1Ch 6:64
they g by lot out of the tribe of....... 1Ch 6:65
they g unto them, of the cities........ 1Ch 6:67
they g also Gezer with her............. 1Ch 6:67
David g a commandment, and they.. 1Ch 14:12
Joab g the sum of the number of...... 1Ch 21:5
So David g to Ornan for the place..... 1Ch 21:25
God g to Heman fourteen sons and... 1Ch 25:5
Then David g to Solomon his son...... 1Ch 28:11
He g of gold by weight for things...... 1Ch 28:14
by weight he g gold for the............ 1Ch 28:16
for the golden basons he g gold....... 1Ch 28:17
g for the service of the house of...... 1Ch 29:7
g them to the treasure of the......... 1Ch 29:8
she g the king an hundred and........ 2Chr 9:9
the queen of Sheba g king Solomon.. 2Chr 9:9
king Solomon g to the queen of...... 2Chr 9:12
counsel which the old men g him...... 2Chr 10:8
he g them victual in abundance....... 2Chr 11:23
g the kingdom over Israel to.......... 2Chr 13:5
Then the men of Judah g a shout...... 2Chr 13:15
the LORD g them rest round about.... 2Chr 15:15
for his God g him rest round.......... 2Chr 30:30
their father g them great gifts........ 2Chr 21:3
but the kingdom g he to Jehoram.... 2Chr 21:3
g him the testimony, and made him.. 2Chr 23:11
Jehoiada g it to such as did the....... 2Chr 24:12
the Ammonites g gifts to Uzziah..... 2Chr 26:8
the children of Ammon g him the..... 2Chr 27:5
g them to eat and to drink, and...... 2Chr 28:15
g it unto the king of Assyria.......... 2Chr 28:21
who therefore g them up to........... 2Chr 30:7
the princes g to the congregation.... 2Chr 30:24
unto him, and he g him a sign........ 2Chr 32:24
they g it to the workmen that........ 2Chr 34:10
artificers and builders g they it...... 2Chr 34:11
Josiah g to the people, of the......... 2Chr 35:7
his princes g willingly unto the...... 2Chr 35:8
g unto the priests for the............. 2Chr 35:8
g unto the Levites for passover....... 2Chr 35:9
he g them all into his hand............ 2Chr 36:17
They g after their ability unto........ Ezr 2:69
They g money also unto the masons.. Ezr 3:7
he g them into the hand of........... Ezr 5:12
Artaxerxes g unto Ezra the priest .... Ezr 7:11
they g their hands that they......... Ezr 10:19
the wine, and g it unto the king...... Neh 2:1
g them the king's letters.............. Neh 2:9
That I g my brother Hanani, and...... Neh 7:2
of the fathers g unto the work........ Neh 7:70
The Tirshatha g to the treasure...... Neh 7:70

g to the treasure of the work......... Neh 7:71
g was twenty thousand drams of..... Neh 7:72
g the sense, and caused them to...... Neh 8:8
companies of them that g thanks..... Neh 12:31
g thanks went over against them..... Neh 12:38
that g thanks in the house of God.... Neh 12:40
g the portions of the singers and.... Neh 12:47
they g them drink in vessels of....... Est 1:7
he speedily g her her things for...... Est 2:9
g gifts, according to the state........ Est 2:18
g it unto Haman the son of........... Est 3:10
g him a commandment to Mordecai,. Est 4:5
Also he g him the copy of the......... Est 4:8
g him commandment unto Mordecai. Est 4:10
from Haman, and g it unto Mordecai. Est 8:2
the LORD g, and the LORD hath........ Job 1:21
my servant, and he g me no answer... Job 19:16
eye saw me, it g witness to me........ Job 29:11
Unto me men g ear, and waited, and.. Job 29:21
I g ear to your reasons, whilst........ Job 32:11
also the LORD g Job twice as much... Job 42:10
every man also g him a piece of...... Job 42:11
their father g them inheritance...... Job 42:15
and the Highest g his voice............ Ps 18:13
The Lord g the word..................... Ps 68:11
They g me also gall for my meat...... Ps 69:21
in my thirst they g me vinegar to.... Ps 69:21
and he g ear unto me.................. Ps 77:1
g them drink as out of the great..... Ps 78:15
for he g them their own desire....... Ps 78:29
He g also their increase unto the..... Ps 78:46
He g up their cattle also to the....... Ps 78:48
but g their life over to the........... Ps 78:50
He g his people over also unto....... Ps 78:62
So I g them up unto their own........ Ps 81:12
and the ordinance that he g them.... Ps 99:7
He g them hail for rain, and.......... Ps 105:32
g them the lands of the heathen..... Ps 105:44
And he g them their request.......... Ps 106:15
he g them into the hand of the....... Ps 106:41
g their land for an heritage, an...... Ps 135:12
g their land for an heritage.......... Ps 136:21
When he g to the sea his decree,..... Prov 8:29
I g my heart to seek and search...... Eccl 1:13
I g my heart to know wisdom, and... Eccl 1:17
shalt return unto God who g it........ Eccl 12:7
he g good heed, and sought out, and.. Eccl 12:9
called him, but he g me no answer... Song 5:6
the nations before him, and made... Is 41:2
he g them as the dust to his........... Is 41:2
Who g Jacob for a spoil, and.......... Is 42:24
I g Egypt for thy ransom,.............. Is 43:3
I g my back to the smiters, and my... Is 50:6
the land that I g to your fathers...... Jer 7:7
unto the place which I g to you....... Jer 7:14
land that I g unto their fathers....... Jer 16:15
from thine heritage that I g thee..... Jer 17:4
you, and the city that I g you......... Jer 23:39
off the land that I g unto them....... Jer 24:10
land that I g to their fathers.......... Jer 30:3
g the evidence of the purchase....... Jer 32:12
g it to Baruch the scribe, the........ Jer 36:32
where he g judgment upon him...... Jer 39:5
g them vineyards and fields at the.. Jer 39:10
a charge concerning Jeremiah to..... Jer 39:11
of the guard g him victuals........... Jer 40:5
as I g Zedekiah king of Judah......... Jer 44:30
where he g judgment upon him...... Jer 52:9
mine elders g up the ghost in the... Lam 1:19
My meat also which I g thee.......... Eze 16:19
I g them my statutes, and shewed... Eze 20:11
Moreover also I g them my........... Eze 20:25
Wherefore I g them also statutes.... Eze 20:25
the land that I g to your fathers..... Eze 36:28
g them into the hand of their........ Eze 39:23
g unto the king of Judah, and........ Dan 1:2
God g Jehoiakim king of............... Dan 1:2
the prince of the eunuchs g names... Dan 1:7
for he g unto Daniel the name of..... Dan 1:7
and g them pulse......................... Dan 1:16
God g them knowledge and skill in.. Dan 1:17
g him many great gifts, and made... Dan 2:48
O thou king, the most high God g... Dan 5:18
And for the majesty that he g them.. Dan 5:19
g thanks before his God, as he....... Dan 6:10
did not know that I g her corn....... Hos 2:8
I g thee a king in mine anger, and... Hos 13:11
But ye g the Nazarites wine to....... Amos 2:12
I g them to him for the fear.......... Mal 2:5
he commandment to depart unto.... Mt 8:18
he g them power against unclean.... Mt 10:1
g the loaves to his disciples, and.... Mt 14:19
g thanks, and brake them............. Mt 15:36
g to his disciples, and the............ Mt 15:36
who g thee this authority............. Mt 21:23
unto one he g five talents, to......... Mt 25:15
I was an hungred, and ye g me meat . Mt 25:35
I was thirsty, and ye g me drink...... Mt 25:35
or thirsty, and g thee drink........... Mt 25:37
an hungred, and ye g me no meat.... Mt 25:42
was thirsty, and ye g me no drink.... Mt 25:42
g it to the disciples, and said........ Mt 26:26
g thanks, and g it to them............. Mt 26:27
that betrayed him g them a sign...... Mt 26:48
g them for the potter's field, as...... Mt 27:10
They g him vinegar to drink.......... Mt 27:34
it on a reed, and g him to drink...... Mt 27:48
they g large money unto the......... Mt 28:12
g also to them which were with..... Mk 6:41
And forthwith Jesus g them leave.... Mk 5:13
g them power over unclean spirits... Mk 6:7

a charger, and g it to the damsel..... Mk 6:28
the damsel g it to her mother........ Mk 6:28
g them to his disciples to set.......... Mk 6:41
g thanks, and brake.................... Mk 8:6
g to his disciples to set before....... Mk 8:6
who g thee this authority to do...... Mk 11:28
g authority to his servants, and...... Mk 13:34
g to them, and said, Take, eat........ Mk 14:22
had given thanks, he g it to them.... Mk 14:23
they g him to drink wine mingled.... Mk 15:23
g him to drink, saying, Let alone..... Mk 15:36
a loud voice, and g up the ghost...... Mk 15:37
g up the ghost, he said, Truly........ Mk 15:39
he g the body to Joseph.............. Mk 15:45
she coming in that instant g......... Lk 2:38
he g it again to the minister, and.... Lk 4:20
g also to them that were with him.... Lk 6:4
many that were blind he g sight...... Lk 7:21
g them power and authority over.... Lk 9:1
g to the disciples to set before....... Lk 9:16
g them to the host, and said unto.... Lk 10:35
and no man g unto him............... Lk 15:16
they saw it, g praise unto God........ Lk 18:43
or who is he that g thee this......... Lk 20:2
g thanks, and said, Take this, and.... Lk 22:17
g thanks, and brake it................. Lk 22:19
g unto them, saying, This is my...... Lk 22:19
Pilate g sentence that it should...... Lk 23:24
and the paps which never g suck..... Lk 23:29
said thus, he g up the ghost.......... Lk 23:46
it, and brake, and g to them.......... Lk 24:30
they g him a piece of a broiled...... Lk 24:42
to them g he power to become the .. Jn 1:12
that he g his only begotten Son,..... Jn 3:16
that Jacob g to his son Joseph........ Jn 4:5
which g us the well, and drank....... Jn 4:12
He g them bread from heaven to..... Jn 6:31
Moses g you not that bread from.... Jn 6:32
Moses therefore g unto you.......... Jn 6:32
which g them me, is greater than.... Jn 10:29
he g me a commandment, what I..... Jn 12:49
he g it to Judas Iscariot, the.......... Jn 13:26
as the Father g me commandment,.. Jn 14:31
which g counsel to the Jews, that.... Jn 18:14
But Jesus g him no answer............ Jn 19:9
bowed his head, and g up the ghost.. Jn 19:30
and Pilate g him leave................. Jn 19:38
And they g forth their lots........... Acts 1:26
as the Spirit g them utterance........ Acts 2:4
he g heed unto them, expecting to... Acts 3:5
with great power g the apostles..... Acts 4:33
fell down, and g up the ghost........ Acts 5:5
he g him none inheritance in it...... Acts 7:5
And he g him the covenant of........ Acts 7:8
g him favour and wisdom in the..... Acts 7:10
g them up to worship the host of.... Acts 7:42
the people with one accord g heed... Acts 8:6
To whom they all g heed, from the.. Acts 8:10
he g her his hand, and lifted her..... Acts 9:41
which g much alms to the people,... Acts 10:2
Forasmuch then as God g them the.. Acts 11:17
And the people g a shout, saying,.... Acts 12:22
because he g not God the glory....... Acts 12:23
eaten of worms, and g up the ghost.. Acts 12:23
after that he g unto them judges,.... Acts 13:20
God g unto them Saul the son of..... Acts 13:21
to whom also he g testimony......... Acts 13:22
which g testimony unto the word.... Acts 14:3
g us rain from heaven, and.......... Acts 14:17
a audience to Barnabas and Paul,.... Acts 15:12
we g no such commandment......... Acts 15:24
they g him audience unto this....... Acts 22:22
g commandment to his accusers..... Acts 23:30
I g my voice against them............ Acts 26:10
g him liberty to go unto his.......... Acts 27:3
g thanks to God in presence of...... Acts 27:35
Wherefore God also g them up to.... Rom 1:24
For this cause God g them up unto... Rom 1:26
God g them over to a reprobate..... Rom 1:28
even as the Lord g to every man..... 1Cor 3:5
but God g the increase................ 1Cor 3:6
but first g their own selves to....... 2Cor 8:5
Who g himself for our sins, that..... Gal 1:4
To whom we g place by subjection,.. Gal 2:5
they g to me and Barnabas the...... Gal 2:9
who loved me, and g himself for me.. Gal 2:20
but God g it to Abraham by.......... Gal 3:18
g him to be the head over all........ Eph 1:22
captive, and g gifts unto men....... Eph 4:8
And he g some, apostles.............. Eph 4:11
the church, and g himself for it..... Eph 5:25
we g you by the Lord Jesus........... 1Th 4:2
Who g himself a ransom for all,..... 1Ti 2:6
Who g himself for us, that he....... Titus 2:14
Abraham g a tenth part of all....... Heb 7:4
Abraham g the tenth of the spoils... Heb 7:4
of which no man g attendance at.... Heb 7:13
g commandment concerning his..... Heb 11:22
us, and we g them reverence......... Heb 12:9
again, and the heaven g rain........ Jas 5:18
up from the dead, and g him glory... 1Pet 1:21
another, as he g us commandment... 1Jn 3:23
the record that God g of his Son..... 1Jn 5:10
when I g all diligence to write....... Jude 3
Christ, which God g unto him........ Rev 1:1
g her space to repent of her......... Rev 2:21
g glory to the God of heaven......... Rev 11:13
the dragon g him his power, and.... Rev 13:2
which g power unto the beast........ Rev 13:4
one of the four beasts g unto the ... Rev 15:7

GAVEST

woman whom thou g to be with me	Gen 3:12
which thou g unto their fathers.........	1Kin 8:34
which thou g unto our fathers.........	1Kin 8:48
which thou g unto their fathers.........	1Kin 8:48
the land which thou g to them.........	2Chr 6:25
which thou g unto our fathers.........	2Chr 6:31
which thou g unto their fathers,.........	2Chr 6:38
g it to the seed of Abraham thy.........	2Chr 20:7
g him the name of Abraham.........	Neh 9:7
g them right judgments, and true	Neh 9:13
g them bread from heaven for.........	Neh 9:15
Thou g also thy good spirit to.........	Neh 9:20
g them water for their thirst.........	Neh 9:20
Moreover thou g them kingdoms.........	Neh 9:22
g them into their hands, with.........	Neh 9:24
mercies thou g them saviours.........	Neh 9:27
therefore g thou them into the.........	Neh 9:28
great goodness that thou g them.........	Neh 9:35
fat land which thou g before them......	Neh 9:35
for the land that thou g unto our......	Neh 9:36
G thou the goodly wings unto the	Job 39:13
thou g it him, even length of	Ps 21:4
g him to be meat to the people	Ps 74:14
thou g me no water for my feet	Lk 7:44
Thou g me no kiss	Lk 7:45
and yet thou never g me a kid.........	Lk 15:29
Wherefore then g not thou my	Lk 19:23
the work which thou g me to do	Jn 17:4
which thou g me out of the world......	Jn 17:6
they were, and thou g them me.........	Jn 17:6
them the words which thou g me......	Jn 17:8
those that thou g me I have kept......	Jn 17:12
which thou g me I have given them......	Jn 17:22
Of them which thou g me have I	Jn 18:9

GAY

him that weareth the g clothing...	Jas 2:3

GAZA (ga'-zah) See AZZAH, GAZITES.
1. A royal Philistine city.

as thou comest to Gerar, unto G.........	Gen 10:19
from Kadesh-barnea even unto G.........	Josh 10:41
only in G, in Gath, and in Ashdod,......	Josh 11:22
G with her towns and her villages......	Josh 15:47
Also Judah took G with the coast......	Judg 1:18
Then went Samson to G, and saw......	Judg 16:1
eyes, and brought him down to G......	Judg 16:21
for Ashdod one, for G one.........	Josh 6:17
the Philistines, even unto G.........	2Kin 18:8
before that Pharaoh smote G.........	Jer 47:1
Baldness is come upon G.........	Jer 47:5
For three transgressions of G.........	Amos 1:6
will send a fire on the wall of G.........	Amos 1:7
For G shall be forsaken, and.........	Zeph 2:4
G also shall see it, and be very	Zec 9:5
and the king shall perish from G......	Zec 9:5
goeth down from Jerusalem unto G......	Acts 8:26

2. A city in Ephraim.

the earth, till thou come unto G.........	Judg 6:4
also and the towns thereof, unto G......	1Chr 7:28

GAZATHITES (ga'-zath-ites) See GAZITES.
Inhabitants of Gaza.

the G, and the Ashdothites, and......	Josh 13:3

GAZE

break through unto the LORD to g......	Ex 19:21

GAZER (ga'-zur) See GEZER. A Canaanite city.

from Geba until thou come to G.........	2Sa 5:25
Philistines from Gibeon even to G......	1Chr 14:16

GAZEZ (ga'-zez) A son of Caleb.

bare Haran, and Moza, and G.........	1Chr 2:46
and Haran begat G.........	1Chr 2:46

GAZING

why stand ye g up into heaven......	Acts 1:11

GAZINGSTOCK

vile, and will set thee as a g.........	Nah 3:6
were made a g both by reproaches	Heb 10:33

GAZITES (ga'-zites) See GAZATHITES.
Inhabitants of Gaza.

And it was told the G, saying,.........	Judg 16:2

GAZZAM (gaz'-zam) A family of exiles.

of Nekoda, the children of G.........	Ezr 2:48
The children of G, the children......	Neh 7:51

GEBA (ghe'-bah) See GABA, GIBEAH, GIBEON. A
Levitical city in Benjamin.

her suburbs, G with her suburbs,......	Josh 21:17
of the Philistines that was in G.........	1Sa 13:3
from G until thou come to Gazer......	2Sa 5:25
Asa built with them G of Benjamin...	1Kin 15:22
from G to Beer-sheba, and took.........	2Kin 23:8
G with her suburbs, and Alemeth......	1Chr 6:60
fathers of the inhabitants of G.........	1Chr 8:6
and he built therewith G and Mizpah...	2Chr 16:6
Benjamin from G dwelt at Michmash	Neh 11:31
Gilgal, and out of the fields of G.........	Neh 12:29
have taken up their lodging at G.........	Is 10:29
G to Rimmon south of Jerusalem......	Zec 14:10

GEBAL (ghe'-bal) See GIBLITES.
1. An Edomite territory.

G, and Ammon, and Amalek.........	Ps 83:7

2. A Phoenician trade city.

The ancients of G and the wise men	Eze 27:9

GEBALITES See GIBLITES.

GEBER See EZION-GEBER.
1. Father of an officer of Solomon.

The son of G, in Ramoth-gilead.........	1Kin 4:13

2. The son of Uri.

The son of Uri was in the	1Kin 4:19

GEBIM (ghe'-bim) A city in Benjamin.

the inhabitants of G gather.........	Is 10:31

GEDALIAH (ghed-a-li'-ah)
1. Son of Ahikam.

them he made G the son of Ahikam .	2Kin 25:22
of Babylon had made G governor......	2Kin 25:22
there came to G to Mizpah.........	2Kin 25:23
G ware to them, and to their men,...	2Kin 25:24
and ten men with him, and smote G	2Kin 25:25
committed him unto G the son of......	Jer 39:14
Go back also to G the son of.........	Jer 40:5
Then went Jeremiah unto G the son	Jer 40:6
the king of Babylon had made G......	Jer 40:7
Then they came to G to Mizpah......	Jer 40:8
G the son of Ahikam the son of......	Jer 40:9
that he had set over them G the......	Jer 40:11
came to the land of Judah, to G.........	Jer 40:12
the fields, came to G to Mizpah,......	Jer 40:13
But G the son of Ahikam believed......	Jer 40:14
spake to G in Mizpah secretly.........	Jer 40:15
But G the son of Ahikam said unto...	Jer 40:16
came unto G the son of Ahikam to...	Jer 41:1
smote G the son of Ahikam the son...	Jer 41:2
that were with him, even with G......	Jer 41:3
second day after he had slain G......	Jer 41:4
Come to G the son of Ahikam.........	Jer 41:6
whom he had slain because of G.........	Jer 41:9
committed to G the son of Ahikam...	Jer 41:10
he had slain G the son of Ahikam...	Jer 41:16
had slain G the son of Ahikam.........	Jer 41:18
of the guard had left with G the......	Jer 43:6

2. A son of Jeduthun.

G, and Zeri, and Jeshaiah,.........	1Chr 25:3
to G, to G, who with his	1Chr 25:9

3. Priest who married a foreigner.

and Eliezer, and Jarib, and G.........	Ezr 10:18

4. Grandfather of Zephaniah.

the son of Cushi, the son of G.........	Zeph 1:1

5. A prince who had Jeremiah imprisoned.

G the son of Pashur, and Jucal the......	Jer 38:1

GEDEON (ghed'-e-on) See GIDEON. Greek form
of Gideon.

time would fail me to tell of G.........	Heb 11:32

GEDER (ghe'-dur) See BETH-GADER, GEDERITE,
GEDOR. A Canaanite city.

the king of G, one.........	Josh 12:13

GEDERAH (ghed'-e-rah) See GEDERATHITE. A
city in Judah.

And Sharaim, and Adithaim, and G......	Josh 15:36

GEDERATHITE (ghed'-e-rath-ite) An
inhabitant of Gederah.

and Johanan, and Josabad the G.........	1Chr 12:4

GEDERITE (ghed'-e-rite) An inhabitant of
Geder.

low plains was Baal-hanan the G.........	1Chr 27:28

GEDEROTH (ghed'-e-roth) A town in Judah.

And G, Beth-dagon,.........	Josh 15:41
Beth-shemesh, and Ajalon, and G......	2Chr 28:18

GEDEROTHAIM (ghed-e-ro-tha'-im) A town
in Judah.

And Adithaim, and Gederah, and G...	Josh 15:36

GEDOR (ghe'-dor) See GEDER.
1. A city in Judah.

Halhul, Beth-zur, and G,.........	Josh 15:58

2. Hometown of Jeroham.

the sons of Jeroham of G.........	1Chr 12:7

3. Son of Jehiel.

And G, and Ahio, and Zacher.........	1Chr 8:31
And G, and Ahio, and Zechariah, and...	1Chr 9:37

4. A descendant of Judah.

And Penuel the father of G.........	1Chr 4:4
bare Jered the father of G.........	1Chr 4:18

5. A place in Judah.

And they went to the entrance of G...	1Chr 4:39

GE-HARASHIM See CHARASHIM.

GEHAZI (ghe-ha'-zi) A servant of Elisha.

he said to G his servant, Call.........	2Kin 4:12
G answered, Verily she hath no.........	2Kin 4:14
that he said to G his servant.........	2Kin 4:25
but G came near to thrust her.........	2Kin 4:27
Then he said to G, Gird up thy.........	2Kin 4:29
G passed on before them, and laid......	2Kin 4:31
And he called G, and said, Call.........	2Kin 4:36
But G, the servant of Elisha the......	2Kin 5:20
So G followed after Naaman.........	2Kin 5:21
unto him, Whence comest thou, G...	2Kin 5:25
the king talked with G the	2Kin 8:4
G said, My lord, O king, this is......	2Kin 8:5

GELILOTH (ghel'-il-oth) Place on boundary of
Benjamin and Judah.

and went forth toward G, which is	Josh 18:17

GEMALLI (ghe-mal'-li) One of the twelve
spies.

tribe of Dan, Ammiel the son of G	Num 13:12

GEMARIAH (ghem-a-ri'-ah)
1. Son of Shaphan.

in the chamber of G the son of.........	Jer 36:10
When Michaiah the son of G.........	Jer 36:11
G the son of Shaphan, and Zedekiah ...	Jer 36:12
G had made intercession to the......	Jer 36:25

2. Son of Hilkiah.

G the son of Hilkiah, (whom.........	Jer 29:3

GENDER

thy cattle g with a diverse kind.........	Lev 19:19
knowing that they do g strifes.........	2Ti 2:23

GENDERED

frost of heaven, who hath g it.........	Job 38:29

GENDERETH

Their bull g, and faileth not	Job 21:10
which g to bondage, which is Agar......	Gal 4:24

GENEALOGIES

All these were reckoned by g in......	1Chr 5:17
in all by their g fourscore.........	1Chr 7:5
were reckoned by their g twenty......	1Chr 7:7
So all Israel were reckoned by g.........	1Chr 9:1
and of Iddo the seer concerning g......	2Chr 12:15
reckoned by g among the Levites......	2Chr 31:19
give heed to fables and endless g.........	1Ti 1:4
But avoid foolish questions, and g......	Titus 3:9

GENEALOGY

their habitations, and their g.........	1Chr 4:33
the g is not to be reckoned after......	1Chr 5:1
when the g of their generations.........	1Chr 5:7
of them, after their g by their.........	1Chr 7:9
the number throughout the g of......	1Chr 7:40
by their g in their villages.........	1Chr 9:22
Beside their g of males, from.........	2Chr 31:16
Both to the g of the priests by.........	2Chr 31:17
to the g of all their little ones.........	2Chr 31:18
those that were reckoned by g.........	Ezr 2:62
this is the g of them that went.........	Ezr 8:1
by g of the males an hundred.........	Ezr 8:3
that they might be reckoned by g......	Neh 7:5
I found a register of the g of.........	Neh 7:5
those that were reckoned by g.........	Neh 7:64

GENERAL

the g of the king's army was Joab......	1Chr 27:34
To the g assembly and church of......	Heb 12:23

GENERALLY

Israel be g gathered unto thee	2Sa 17:11
There shall be lamentation g upon......	Jer 48:38

GENERATION

righteous before me in this g.........	Gen 7:1
But in the fourth g they shall.........	Gen 15:16
Ephraim's children of the third g......	Gen 50:23
all his brethren, and all that g.........	Ex 1:6
with Amalek from g to g.........	Ex 17:16
fourth g of them that hate me.........	Ex 20:5
unto the third and to the fourth g......	Ex 34:7
unto the third and fourth g.........	Num 14:18
forty years, until all the g.........	Num 32:13
of this evil g see that good land.........	Deut 1:35
until all the g of the men of war......	Deut 2:14
fourth g of them that hate me,......	Deut 5:9
even to his tenth g shall they not......	Deut 23:2
even to their tenth g shall they.........	Deut 23:3
of the LORD in their third g.........	Deut 23:8
So that the g to come of your.........	Deut 29:22
they are a perverse and crooked g......	Deut 32:5
for they are a very froward g.........	Deut 32:20
also all that g were gathered.........	Judg 2:10
there arose another g after them.........	Judg 2:10
g shall sit on the throne of.........	2Kin 10:30
of Israel unto the fourth g.........	2Kin 15:12
and kept throughout every g.........	Est 9:28
them from this g for ever.........	Ps 12:7
God is in the g of the righteous......	Ps 14:5
be accounted to the Lord for a g......	Ps 22:30
This is the g of them that seek.........	Ps 24:6
ye may tell it to the g following.........	Ps 48:13
shall go to the g of his fathers.........	Ps 49:19
shewed thy strength unto this g.........	Ps 71:18
against the g of thy children.........	Ps 73:15
shewing to the g to come the.........	Ps 78:4
That the g to come might know.........	Ps 78:6
a stubborn and rebellious g.........	Ps 78:8
a g that set not their heart.........	Ps 78:8
long was I grieved with this g.........	Ps 95:10
be written for the g to come.........	Ps 102:18
in the g following let their name.........	Ps 109:13
the g of the upright shall be.........	Ps 112:2
One g shall praise thy works to.........	Ps 145:4
doth the crown endure to every g......	Prov 27:24
There is a g that curseth their.........	Prov 30:11
There is a g that are pure in.........	Prov 30:12
There is a g, O how lofty are.........	Prov 30:13
There is a g, whose teeth are as......	Prov 30:14
passeth away, and another g cometh...	Eccl 1:4
be dwelt in from g to g.........	Is 13:20
from g to g it shall lie.........	Is 34:10
from g to g shall they.........	Is 34:17
my salvation from g to g.........	Is 51:8
and who shall declare his g.........	Is 53:8
O g, see ye the word of the LORD......	Jer 2:31
and forsaken the g of his wrath......	Jer 7:29
be dwelt in from g to g.........	Jer 50:39
thy throne from g to g.........	Lam 5:19
dominion is from g to g.........	Dan 4:3
kingdom is from g to g.........	Dan 4:34
and their children another g.........	Joel 1:3

and Jerusalem from *g* to .... Joel 3:20
The book of the *g* of Jesus Christ.......... Mt 1:1
O *g* of vipers, who hath warned.............. Mt 3:7
whereunto shall I liken this *g*............... Mt 11:16
O *g* of vipers, how can ye, being............ Mt 12:34
adulterous *g* seeketh after a sign........... Mt 12:39
rise in judgment with this *g*................ Mt 12:41
up in the judgment with this *g*.............. Mt 12:42
it be also unto this wicked *g*............... Mt 12:45
adulterous *g* seeketh after a sign........... Mt 16:4
said, O faithless and perverse *g*............ Mt 17:17
ye *g* of vipers, how can ye escape........... Mt 23:33
things shall come upon this *g*............... Mt 23:36
This *g* shall not pass, till all............. Mt 24:34
Why doth this *g* seek after a sign........... Mk 8:12
no sign be given unto this *g*................ Mk 8:12
in this adulterous and sinful *g*............. Mk 8:38
him, and saith, O faithless *g*............... Mk 9:19
that this *g* shall not pass, till............ Mk 13:30
fear him from *g* to *g*...................... Lk 1:50
O *g* of vipers, who hath warned.............. Lk 3:7
shall I liken the men of this *g*............. Lk 7:31
said, O faithless and perverse *g*............ Lk 9:41
began to say, This is an evil *g*............. Lk 11:29
also the Son of man be to this *g*............ Lk 11:30
judgment with the men of this *g*............. Lk 11:31
up in the judgment with this *g*.............. Lk 11:32
world, may be required of this *g*............ Lk 11:50
It shall be required of this *g*.............. Lk 11:51
g wiser than the children of .... Lk 16:8
things, and be rejected of this *g*........... Lk 17:25
This *g* shall not pass away, till............ Lk 21:32
yourselves from this untoward *g*............. Acts 2:40
and who shall declare his *g*................. Acts 8:33
his own *g* by the will of God................ Acts 13:36
I was aggrieved with that *g*................. Heb 3:10
But ye are a chosen *g*, a royal.............. 1Pet 2:9

GENERATIONS

These are the *g* of the heavens and.......... Gen 2:4
This is the book of the *g* of Adam........... Gen 5:1
These are the *g* of Noah..................... Gen 6:9
a just man and perfect in his *g*............. Gen 6:9
that is with you, for perpetual *g*........... Gen 9:12
Now these are the *g* of the sons............. Gen 10:1
the sons of Noah, after their *g*............. Gen 10:32
These are the *g* of Shem..................... Gen 11:10
Now these are the *g* of Terah................ Gen 11:27
g for an everlasting covenant............... Gen 17:7
and thy seed after thee in their *g*.......... Gen 17:9
you, every man child in your *g*.............. Gen 17:12
Now these are the *g* of Ishmael.............. Gen 25:12
their names, according to their *g*........... Gen 25:13
And these are the *g* of Isaac................ Gen 25:19
Now these are the *g* of Esau................. Gen 36:1
these are the *g* of Esau the .... Gen 36:9
These are the *g* of Jacob.................... Gen 37:2
and this is my memorial unto all *g*.......... Ex 3:15
sons of Levi according to their *g*........... Ex 6:16
of Levi according to their *g*................ Ex 6:19
to the LORD throughout your *g*............... Ex 12:14
your *g* by an ordinance for ever............. Ex 12:17
the children of Israel in their *g*........... Ex 12:42
omer of it to be kept for your *g*............ Ex 16:32
the LORD, to be kept for your *g*............. Ex 16:33
g on the behalf of the children............. Ex 27:21
g at the door of the tabernacle............. Ex 29:42
before the LORD throughout your *g*........... Ex 30:8
upon it throughout your *g*................... Ex 30:10
and to his seed throughout their *g*.......... Ex 30:21
oil unto me throughout your *g*............... Ex 30:31
me and you throughout your *g*................ Ex 31:13
the sabbath throughout their *g*.............. Ex 31:16
priesthood throughout their *g*............... Ex 40:15
g throughout all your dwellings............. Lev 3:17
be a statute for ever in your *g*............. Lev 6:18
for ever throughout your *g*.................. Lev 7:36
for ever throughout your *g*.................. Lev 10:9
ever unto them throughout their *g*........... Lev 17:7
in their *g* that hath any blemish............ Lev 21:17
be of all your seed among your *g*............ Lev 22:3
your *g* in all your dwellings................ Lev 23:14
your dwellings throughout your *g*............ Lev 23:21
your *g* in all your dwellings................ Lev 23:31
be a statute for ever in your *g*............. Lev 23:41
That your *g* may know that I made............ Lev 23:43
be a statute for ever in your *g*............. Lev 24:3
that bought it throughout his *g*............. Lev 25:30
Israel's eldest son, by their *g*............. Num 1:20
children of Simeon, by their *g*.............. Num 1:22
the children of Gad, by their *g*............. Num 1:24
the children of Judah, by their *g*........... Num 1:26
children of Issachar, by their *g*............ Num 1:28
children of Zebulun, by their *g*............. Num 1:30
children of Ephraim, by their *g*............. Num 1:32
children of Manasseh, by their *g*............ Num 1:34
children of Benjamin, by their *g*............ Num 1:38
children of Dan, by their *g*................. Num 1:38
the children of Asher, by their *g*........... Num 1:40
of Naphtali, throughout their *g*............. Num 1:42
These also are the *g* of Aaron............... Num 3:1
for ever throughout your *g*.................. Num 10:8
whosoever be among you, in your *g*........... Num 15:14
an ordinance for ever in your *g*............. Num 15:15
LORD an heave offering in your *g*............ Num 15:21
and henceforward among your *g*............... Num 15:23
their garments throughout their *g*........... Num 15:38
for ever throughout your *g*.................. Num 18:23
your *g* in all your dwellings................ Num 35:29
his commandments to a thousand *g*............ Deut 7:9
old, consider the years of many *g*.......... Deut 32:7

our *g* after us, that we might do............ Josh 22:27
to us or to our *g* in time to come........... Josh 22:28
Only that the *g* of the children............. Judg 3:2
Now these are the *g* of Pharez............... Ruth 4:18
These are their *g*........................... 1Chr 1:29
genealogy of their *g* was reckoned........... 1Chr 5:7
valiant men of might in their *g*............. 1Chr 7:2
And with them, by their *g*, after............ 1Chr 7:4
after their genealogy by their *g*............ 1Chr 7:9
heads of the fathers, by their *g*............ 1Chr 8:28
brethren, according to their *g*.............. 1Chr 9:9
were chief throughout their *g*............... 1Chr 9:34
he commanded to a thousand *g*................ 1Chr 16:15
according to the *g* of his fathers........... 1Chr 26:31
and his sons' sons, even four *g*............. Job 42:16
thoughts of his heart to all *g*.............. Ps 33:11
name to be remembered in all *g*.............. Ps 45:17
and their dwelling places to all *g*.......... Ps 49:11
and his years as many *g*..................... Ps 61:6
and moon endure, throughout all *g*........... Ps 72:5
shew forth thy praise to all *g*.............. Ps 79:13
draw out thine anger to all *g*............... Ps 85:5
known thy faithfulness to all *g*............. Ps 89:1
and build up thy throne to all *g*............ Ps 89:4
been our dwelling place in all *g*............ Ps 90:1
and his truth endureth to all *g*............. Ps 100:5
and thy remembrance unto all *g*.............. Ps 102:12
thy years are throughout all *g*.............. Ps 102:24
he commanded to a thousand *g*................ Ps 105:8
unto all *g* for evermore..................... Ps 106:31
Thy faithfulness is unto all *g*.............. Ps 119:90
O LORD, throughout all *g*.................... Ps 135:13
endureth throughout all *g*................... Ps 145:13
even thy God, O Zion, unto all *g*............ Ps 146:10
calling the *g* from the beginning............ Is 41:4
the ancient days, in the *g* of old........... Is 51:9
up the foundations of many *g*................ Is 58:12
excellency, a joy of many *g*................. Is 60:15
cities, the desolations of many *g*........... Is 61:4
it, even to the years of many *g*............. Joel 2:2
So all the *g* from Abraham to................ Mt 1:17
Abraham to David are fourteen *g*............. Mt 1:17
away into Babylon are fourteen *g*............ Mt 1:17
unto Christ are fourteen *g*.................. Mt 1:17
from henceforth all *g* shall call............ Lk 1:48
hath been hid from ages and from *g*.......... Col 1:26

GENNESARET (*ghen-nes'-a-ret*) See
CHINNERETH. *Same as Galilee.*
they came into the land of G.................. Mt 14:34
they came into the land of G.................. Mk 6:53
of God, he stood by the lake of G............. Lk 5:1

GENTILE (*jen'-tile*) See GENTILES. *A non-Jew.*
The Jew first, and also of the G.............. Rom 2:9
The Jew first, and also to the G.............. Rom 2:10

GENTILES
of the G divided in their lands............... Gen 10:5
which dwelt in Harosheth of the G............. Judg 4:2
from Harosheth of the G unto the.............. Judg 4:13
the host, unto Harosheth of the G............. Judg 4:16
to it shall the G seek........................ Is 11:10
bring forth judgment to the G................. Is 42:1
the people, for a light of the G.............. Is 42:6
give thee for a light to the G................ Is 49:6
I will lift up mine hand to the G............. Is 49:22
and thy seed shall inherit the G.............. Is 54:3
the G shall come to thy light, and........... Is 60:3
the forces of the G shall come................ Is 60:5
unto thee the forces of the G................. Is 60:11
shalt also suck the milk of the G............. Is 60:16
ye shall eat the riches of the G.............. Is 61:6
seed shall be known among the G............... Is 61:9
the G shall see thy righteousness............. Is 62:2
the glory of the G like a flowing............. Is 66:12
declare my glory among the G.................. Is 66:19
destroyer of the G is on his way.............. Jer 4:7
of the G that can cause ruin.................. Jer 14:22
the G shall come unto thee from............... Jer 16:19
the prophet against the G..................... Jer 46:1
and her princes are among the G............... Lam 2:9
their defiled bread among the G............... Eze 4:13
the G as a vessel wherein is no............... Hos 8:8
Proclaim ye this among the G.................. Joel 3:9
of Jacob shall be among the G in.............. Mic 5:8
to cast out the horns of the G................ Zec 1:21
name shall be great among the G............... Mal 1:11
because the lordship over them................ Mt 10:42
A light to lighten the G, and the............ Lk 2:32
he shall be delivered unto the G.............. Lk 18:32
shall be trodden down of the G................ Lk 21:24
the times of the G be fulfilled............... Lk 21:24
The kings of the G exercise................... Lk 22:25
go unto the dispersed among the G............. Jn 7:35
the G, and teach the G........................ Jn 7:35
and Pontius Pilate, with the G................ Acts 4:27
into the possession of the G.................. Acts 7:45
me, to bear my name before the G.............. Acts 9:15
because that on the G also was................ Acts 10:45
G had also received the word of............... Acts 11:1
Then hath God also to the G................... Acts 11:18
the G besought that these words............... Acts 13:42

life, lo, we turn to the G.................... Acts 13:46
set thee to be a light of the G............... Acts 13:47
when the G heard this, they were.............. Acts 13:48
unbelieving Jews stirred up the G............. Acts 14:2
was an assault made both of the G............. Acts 14:5
the door of faith unto the G.................. Acts 14:27
declaring the conversion of the G............. Acts 15:3
that the G by my mouth should................. Acts 15:7
had wrought among the G by them............... Acts 15:12
God at the first did visit the G.............. Acts 15:14
seek after the Lord, and all the G............ Acts 15:17
among the G are turned to God................. Acts 15:19
which are of the G in Antioch................. Acts 15:23
henceforth I will go unto the G............... Acts 18:6
him into the hands of the G................... Acts 21:11
among the G by his ministry................... Acts 21:19
are among the G to forsake Moses.............. Acts 21:21
As touching the G which believe............... Acts 21:25
send thee far hence unto the G................ Acts 22:21
from the people, and from the G............... Acts 26:17
of Judaea, and then to the G.................. Acts 26:20
unto the people, and to the G................. Acts 26:23
of God is sent unto the G..................... Acts 28:28
you also, even as among other G............... Rom 1:13
For when the G, which have not................ Rom 2:14
among the G through you, as it is............. Rom 2:24
have before proved both Jews and G............ Rom 3:9
is he not also of the G...................... Rom 3:29
Yes, of the G also............................ Rom 3:29
the Jews only, but also of the G.............. Rom 9:24
That the G, which followed not................ Rom 9:30
fall salvation is come unto the G............. Rom 11:11
of them the riches of the G................... Rom 11:12
For I speak to you G, inasmuch as............. Rom 11:13
as I am the apostle of the G.................. Rom 11:13
the fulness of the G be come in............... Rom 11:25
that the G might glorify God for.............. Rom 15:9
will confess to thee among the G.............. Rom 15:9
And again he saith, Rejoice, ye G............. Rom 15:10
again, Praise the Lord, all ye G.............. Rom 15:11
shall rise to reign over the G................ Rom 15:12
in him shall the G trust...................... Rom 15:12
minister of Jesus Christ to the G............. Rom 15:16
up of the G might be acceptable............... Rom 15:16
by me, to make the G obedient................. Rom 15:18
For if the G have been made................... Rom 15:27
also all the churches of the G................ Rom 16:4
not so much as named among the G.............. 1Cor 5:1
the things which the G sacrifice.............. 1Cor 10:20
neither to the Jews, nor to the G............. 1Cor 10:32
Ye know that ye were G, carried............... 1Cor 12:2
one body, whether we be Jews or G............. 1Cor 12:13
gospel which I preach among the G............. Gal 2:2
was mighty in me toward the G................. Gal 2:8
from James, he did eat with the G............. Gal 2:12
Jew, livest after the manner of G............. Gal 2:14
thou the G to live as do the Jews............. Gal 2:14
nature, and not sinners of the G.............. Gal 2:15
on the G through Jesus Christ................. Gal 3:14
being in time past G in the flesh............. Eph 2:11
of Jesus Christ for you G..................... Eph 3:1
That the G should be fellowheirs.............. Eph 3:6
the G the unsearchable riches of.............. Eph 3:8
walk not as other G walk, in the.............. Eph 4:17
glory of this mystery among the G............. Col 1:27
to the G that they might be saved............. 1Th 2:16
even as the G which know not God.............. 1Th 4:5
a teacher of the G in faith................... 1Ti 2:7
of angels, preached unto the G................ 1Ti 3:16
an apostle, and a teacher of the G............ 2Ti 1:11
and that all the G might hear................. 2Ti 4:17
conversation honest among the G............... 1Pet 2:12
to have wrought the will of the G............. 1Pet 4:3
forth, taking nothing of the G................ 3Jn 7
for it is given unto the G.................... Rev 11:2

GENTLE
But we were *g* among you, even as............ 1Th 2:7
but be *g* unto all men, apt to............... 2Ti 2:24
no man, to be no brawlers, but *g*............ Titus 3:2
is first pure, then peaceable, *g*............ Jas 3:17
not only to the good and *g*.................. 1Pet 2:18

GENTLENESS
and thy *g* hath made me great................ 2Sa 22:36
up, and thy *g* hath made me great............ Ps 18:35
g of Christ, who in presence am............. 2Cor 10:1
joy, peace, longsuffering, *g*................ Gal 5:22

GENTLY
Deal *g* for my sake with the young........... 2Sa 18:5
shall *g* lead those that are with............ Is 40:11

GENUBATH (*ghen'-u-bath*) *Son of Hadad.*
of Tahpenes bare him G his son................ 1Kin 11:20
G was in Pharaoh's household.................. 1Kin 11:20

GERA (*ghe'-rah*) *A son of Bela.*
Belah, and Becher, and Ashbel, G.............. Gen 46:21
up a deliverer, Ehud the son of G............. Judg 3:15
name was Shimei, the son of G................. 2Sa 16:5
And Shimei the son of G, a.................... 2Sa 19:16
Shimei the son of G fell down................. 2Sa 19:18
with thee Shimei the son of G................. 1Kin 2:8
sons of Bela were, Addar, and G............... 1Chr 8:3
And G, and Shephuphan, and Huram.............. 1Chr 8:5
And Naaman, and Ahiah, and G.................. 1Chr 8:7

GERAHS
(a shekel is twenty *g*....................... Ex 30:13
twenty *g* shall be the shekel................ Lev 27:25
(the shekel is twenty *g*..................... Num 3:47
the sanctuary, which is twenty *g*........... Num 18:16

And the shekel shall be twenty g....... Eze 45:12

GERAR (ghe´-rar) A city in Gaza.
from Sidon, as thou comest to G.......... Gen 10:19
Kadesh and Shur, and sojourned in G . Gen 20:1
and Abimelech king of G sent.............. Gen 20:2
king of the Philistines unto G............. Gen 26:1
And Isaac dwelt in G.......................... Gen 26:6
his tent in the valley of G.................... Gen 26:17
the herdmen of G did strive with....... Gen 26:20
Then Abimelech went to him from G. Gen 26:26
went with him pursued them unto G 2Chr 14:13
all the cities round about G................ 2Chr 14:14

GERGESENES (ghur´-ghes-enes´) Inhabitants
   of an area near Sea of Galilee.
side into the country of the G............. Mt 8:28

GERIZIM (gher´-iz-im) A mountain in central
   Palestine.
put the blessing upon mount G.......... Deut 11:29
upon mount G to bless the people...... Deut 27:12
half of them over against mount G ..... Josh 8:33
and stood in the top of mount G........ Judg 9:7

GERSHOM (ghur´-shom) See GERSHON.
  1. Firstborn son of Moses.
a son, and he called his name G.......... Ex 2:22
which the name of the one was G....... Ex 18:3
The sons of Moses were, G................. 1Chr 23:15
Of the sons of G, Shebuel was the..... 1Chr 23:16
And Shebuel the son of G, the son 1Chr 26:24
  2. A son of Levi.
G, Kohath, and Merari......................... 1Chr 6:1
be the names of the sons of G............ 1Chr 6:17
son of G.. 1Chr 6:20
The son of Jahath, the son of G......... 1Chr 6:43
to the sons of G throughout their....... 1Chr 6:62
Unto the sons of G were given out 1Chr 6:71
Of the sons of G 1Chr 15:7
  3. A descendant of Phinehas.
                        Ezr 8:2
  4. Father of Jonathan.
and Jonathan, the son of G .... Judg 18:30

GERSHON (ghur´-shon) See GERSHOM,
  GERSHONITE. A form of Gershom 2.
G, Kohath, and Merari....................... Gen 46:11
G, and Kohath, and Merari................. Ex 6:16
The sons of G.................................... Ex 6:17
G, and Kohath, and Merari................. Num 3:17
the sons of G by their families............ Num 3:18
Of G was the family of the................. Num 3:21
Of G in the tabernacle of the............. Num 3:25
also the son of the sons of G.............. Num 4:22
of G in the tabernacle of the.............. Num 4:28
were numbered of the sons of G .... Num 4:38
of the families of the sons of G........... Num 4:41
oxen he gave unto the sons of G .... Num 7:7
and the sons of G and the sons of ..... Num 10:17
of G, the family of the....................... Num 26:57
the children of G had by lot out.......... Josh 21:6
And unto the children of G................. Josh 21:27
G, Kohath, and Merari....................... 1Chr 6:1
among the sons of Levi, namely, G 1Chr 23:6

GERSHONITE (ghur´-shon-ites) See
  GERSHONITES. Descendant of Gershom 2.
the sons of the G Laadan, chief........... 1Chr 26:21
fathers, even of Laadan the G............. 1Chr 26:21
Lord, by the hand of Jehiel the G....... 2Chr 29:8

GERSHONITES (ghur´-shon-ites)
these are the families of the G............ Num 3:21
The families of the G shall pitch .... Num 3:23
G shall be Eliasaph the son of........... Num 3:24
service of the families of the G........... Num 4:24
the service of the sons of the G.......... Num 4:27
of Gershon, the family of the G........... Num 26:57
All the cities of the G according.......... Josh 21:33
Of the G were, Laadan, and Shimei.... 1Chr 23:7
and of the G.................................... 2Chr 29:12

GERUTH See CHIMHAM.

GERUTH KIMHAM See CHIMHAM.

GESHAM (ghe´-sham) A son of Jahdai.
Regem, and Jotham, and G................ 1Chr 2:47

GESHAN See GESHAM.

GESHEM (ghe´-shem) See GASHMU. An
  opponent of Nehemiah.
G the Arabian, heard it, they.............. Neh 2:19
G the Arabian, and the rest of our ...... Neh 6:1
G sent unto me, saying, Come, let...... Neh 6:2

GESHUR (ghe´-shur) See GESHURITES. A
  kingdom in Bashan.
the daughter of Talmai king of G........ 2Sa 3:3
the son of Amminud, king of G 2Sa 13:37
So Absalom fled, and went to G......... 2Sa 13:38
So Joab arose and went to G.............. 2Sa 14:23
say, Wherefore am I come from G....... 2Sa 14:32
a vow while I abode at G in Syria....... 2Sa 15:8
And he took G, and Aram, with the 1Chr 2:23
the daughter of Talmai king of G........ 1Chr 3:2

GESHURI (ghesh´-u-ri) See GESHURITES.
  1. Inhabitants of Geshur.
of Argob unto the coasts of G .... Deut 3:14
  2. A people dwelling between Arabia and
   Philistia.
of the Philistines, and all G................. Josh 13:2

GESHURITES (ghesh´-u-rites)
  1. Inhabitants of Geshur.
Bashan, unto the border of the G........ Josh 12:5
and Gilead, and the border of the G.... Josh 13:11
of Israel expelled not the G................ Josh 13:13
but the G and the Maachathites .... Josh 13:13
  2. Same as Geshuri 2.
his men went up, and invaded the G.... 1Sa 27:8

GET
G thee out of thy country, and.......... Gen 12:1
said, Up, g you out of this place .... Gen 19:14
g thee into the land of Moriah .... Gen 22:2
g thee out from this land, and.......... Gen 31:13
saying, G me this damsel to wife...... Gen 34:4
g you possessions therein............... Gen 34:10
g you down thither, and buy for us.... Gen 42:2
g up in peace unto your.................. Gen 44:17
g you unto the land of Canaan......... Gen 45:17
so g them up out of the land........... Ex 11:10
g you unto your burdens................. Ex 5:4
g you straw where ye can find it...... Ex 5:11
g thee unto Pharaoh in the............. Ex 7:15
G thee from me, take heed to .... Ex 10:28
G thee out, and all the people......... Ex 11:8
g you forth from among my people,... Ex 12:31
I will g me honour upon Pharaoh,..... Ex 14:17
g thee down, and thou shalt come,... Ex 19:24
said unto Moses, Go, g thee down.... Ex 32:7
he be poor, and cannot g so much ... Lev 14:21
pigeons, such as he is able to g....... Lev 14:22
young pigeons, such as he can g ..... Lev 14:31
Even such as he is able to g............ Lev 14:31
whose hand is not able to g that ...... Lev 14:32
beside that that his hand shall g ...... Num 6:21
G you up this way southward, and.... Num 13:17
g you into the wilderness by the....... Num 14:25
saying, G you up from about the....... Num 16:24
G you up from among this.............. Num 16:45
of Balak, G you into your land .... Num 22:13
thee, I will g me back again............. Num 22:34
G thee up into this mount Abarim,.... Num 27:12
g you over the brook Zered .... Deut 2:13
G thee up into the top of Pisgah,..... Deut 3:27
G you into your tents again.............. Deut 5:30
giveth thee power to g wealth.......... Deut 8:18
g thee down quickly from hence....... Deut 9:12
g thee up into the place which.......... Deut 17:8
shall g up above thee very high........ Deut 28:43
G thee up into this mountain............ Deut 32:49
G you to the mountain, lest the........ Josh 2:16
Lord said unto Joshua, G thee up..... Josh 7:10
then g thee up to the wood.............. Josh 17:15
g you unto your tents, and unto....... Josh 22:4
g thee down unto the host............... Judg 7:9
now therefore g her for me to.......... Judg 14:2
unto his father, G her for me............ Judg 14:3
to morrow g you early on your way.... Judg 19:9
thee, and g thee down to the floor.... Ruth 3:3
Now therefore g you up.................. 1Sa 9:13
g you down from among the............ 1Sa 15:6
in thine eyes, let me g away for........ 1Sa 20:29
g thee into the land of Judah........... 1Sa 22:5
David made haste to g away for....... 1Sa 23:26
G you up to Carmel, and go to 1Sa 25:5
lest he g him fenced cities, and........ 2Sa 20:6
that my lord the king may g heat 1Kin 1:2
g thee in unto king David, and say.... 1Kin 1:13
g thee to Anathoth, unto thine......... 1Kin 2:26
speed to g him up to his chariot....... 1Kin 12:18
and g thee to Shiloh........................ 1Kin 14:2
g thee to thine own house............... 1Kin 14:12
G thee hence, and turn thee............ 1Kin 17:3
to Zarephath, which......................... 1Kin 17:9
Ahab, G thee up, eat and drink........ 1Kin 18:41
g thee down, that the rain stop........ 1Kin 18:44
g thee to the prophets of thy........... 2Kin 3:13
them alive, and g into the city.......... 2Kin 7:12
speed to g him up to his chariot....... 2Chr 10:18
So didst thou g thee a name............. Neh 9:10
thy precepts I g understanding......... Ps 119:104
G wisdom, g understanding.............. Prov 4:5
therefore g wisdom........................ Prov 4:7
all thy getting g understanding......... Prov 4:7
A wound and dishonour shall he g .... Prov 6:33
is it to g wisdom than gold.............. Prov 16:16
to g understanding rather to be........ Prov 16:16
in the hand of a fool to g wisdom ..... Prov 17:16
ways, and g a snare to thy soul........ Prov 22:25
A time to g, and a time to lose .... Eccl 3:6
Let us g up early to the................... Song 7:12
g thee unto this treasurer, even........ Isa 22:15
G you out of the way, turn aside...... Isa 30:11
shalt say unto it, G thee hence......... Isa 30:22
g thee up into the high mountain...... Isa 40:9
g thee into darkness, O daughter ..... Isa 47:5
I will g me unto the great men.......... Jer 5:5
g thee a linen girdle, and put it......... Jer 13:1
a potter's earthen bottle, and.......... Jer 19:1
g ye, horsemen, and stand forth....... Jer 46:4
Moab, that it may flee and g away.... Jer 48:9
g you far off, dwell deep, O ye .... Jer 49:30
g you up unto the wealthy nation,..... Jer 49:31
me about, that I cannot g out.......... Lam 3:7
g thee unto the house of Israel......... Eze 3:4
g you far from the Lord................... Eze 11:15
said, G you far off from the Lord....... Eze 11:15
souls, to g dishonest gain .... Eze 22:27
let the beasts g away from under...... Dan 4:14
come, g you down............................ Joel 3:13

I will g them praise and fame in......... Zeph 3:19
G you hence, walk to and fro............. Zec 6:7
unto him, G thee hence, Satan.......... Mt 4:10
his disciples to g into a ship.............. Mt 14:22
Peter, G thee behind me, Satan........ Mt 16:23
his disciples to g into the ship........... Mk 6:45
saying, G thee behind me, Satan...... Mk 8:33
unto him, G thee behind me, Satan... Lk 4:8
about, and lodge, and g victuals....... Lk 9:12
G thee out, and depart hence............ Lk 13:31
G thee out of thy country, and......... Acts 7:3
g thee down, and go with them,........ Acts 10:20
g thee quickly out of Jerusalem......... Acts 22:18
first into the sea, and g to land......... Acts 27:43
Lest Satan should g an advantage.... 2Cor 2:11
a year, and buy and sell, and g gain.. Jas 4:13

GETHER (ghe´-ther) A son of Aram.
Uz, and Hul, and G, and Mash.......... Gen 10:23
and Uz, and Hul, and G..................... 1Chr 1:17

GETHSEMANE (gheth-sem´-a-ne) A garden
  near Jerusalem.
with them unto a place called G......... Mt 26:36
came to a place which was named G... Mk 14:32

GETTETH
Whosoever g up to the gutter, and 2Sa 5:8
the man that g understanding............ Prov 3:13
a scorner g to himself shame............. Prov 9:7
a wicked man g himself a blot............ Prov 9:7
heareth reproof g understanding........ Prov 15:32
heart of the prudent g knowledge ..... Prov 18:15
He that g wisdom loveth his own....... Prov 19:8
so he that g riches, and not by .... Jer 17:11
he that g up out of the pit shall......... Jer 48:44

GETTING
had gotten, the cattle of his g........... Gen 31:18
with all thy g get understanding........ Prov 4:7
The g of treasures by a lying............. Prov 21:6

GEUEL (ghe-u´-el) A son of Machi.
tribe of Gad, G the son of Machi .... Num 13:15

GEZER (ghe´-zur) See GAZER, GEZRITES. A
  Canaanite city.
Then Horam king of G came up to ..... Josh 10:33
the king of G, one.......................... Josh 12:12
of Beth-horon the nether, and to G.... Josh 16:3
the Canaanites that dwelt in G.......... Josh 16:10
and G with her suburbs..................... Josh 21:21
Canaanites that dwelt in G .... Judg 1:29
Canaanites dwelt in G among them ... Judg 1:29
and Hazor, and Megiddo, and G 1Kin 9:15
of Egypt had gone up, and taken G.... 1Kin 9:16
And Solomon built G, and Beth-horon 1Kin 9:17
they gave also G with her suburbs.... 1Chr 6:67
Naaran, and westward G................... 1Chr 7:28
war at G with the Philistines.............. 1Chr 20:4

GEZRITES (ghez´-rites) Inhabitants of Gezer.
invaded the Geshurites, and the G...... 1Sa 27:8

GHOST
Then Abraham gave up the g............. Gen 25:8
and he gave up the g and died,......... Gen 25:17
And Isaac gave up the g, and died,.... Gen 35:29
into the bed, and yielded up the g ..... Gen 49:33
why did I not give up the g when...... Job 3:11
Oh that I had given up the g............. Job 10:18
be as the giving up of the g.............. Job 11:20
my tongue, I shall give up the g........ Job 13:19
yea, man giveth up the g, and.......... Job 14:10
she hath given up the g................... Jer 15:9
elders gave up the g in the city......... Lam 1:19
found with child of the Holy G........... Mt 1:18
conceived in her is of the Holy G....... Mt 1:20
shall baptize you with the Holy G...... Mt 3:11
G shall not be forgiven unto men....... Mt 12:31
speaketh against the Holy G............. Mt 12:32
a loud voice, yielded up the g........... Mt 27:50
and of the Son, and of the Holy G..... Mt 28:19
shall baptize you with the Holy G...... Mk 1:8
the Holy G hath never forgiveness.... Mk 3:29
David himself said by the Holy G....... Mk 12:36
not yet speak, but the Holy G............ Mk 13:11
a loud voice, and gave up the g .... Mk 15:37
he so cried out, and gave up the g.... Mk 15:39
shall be filled with the Holy G........... Lk 1:15
The Holy G shall come upon thee,..... Lk 1:35
was filled with the Holy G................. Lk 1:41
was filled with the Holy G................. Lk 1:67
and the Holy G was upon him .... Lk 2:25
revealed unto him by the Holy G....... Lk 2:26
shall baptize you with the Holy G...... Lk 3:16
the Holy G descended in a bodily ...... Lk 3:22
the Holy G returned from Jordan....... Lk 4:1
Holy G it shall not be forgiven.......... Lk 12:10
For the Holy G shall teach you in ...... Lk 12:12
said thus, he gave up the g.............. Lk 23:46
which baptizeth with the Holy G........ Jn 1:33
for the Holy G was not yet given .... Jn 7:39
Comforter, which is the Holy G.......... Jn 14:26
bowed his head, and gave up the g.... Jn 19:30
unto them, Receive ye the Holy G ..... Jn 20:22
after that he through the Holy G....... Acts 1:2
by the Holy G not many days hence... Acts 1:5
that the Holy G is come upon you...... Acts 1:8
which the Holy G by the mouth of..... Acts 1:16
were all filled with the Holy G........... Acts 2:4
Father the promise of the Holy G...... Acts 2:33
receive the gift of the Holy G............ Acts 2:38
Peter, filled with the Holy G.............. Acts 4:8

were all filled with the Holy G .... Acts 4:31
thine heart to lie to the Holy G .... Acts 5:3
words fell down, and gave up the g .... Acts 5:5
at his feet, and yielded up the g .... Acts 5:10
and so is also the Holy G, whom .... Acts 5:32
honest report, full of the Holy G .... Acts 6:3
full of faith and of the Holy G .... Acts 6:5
ye do always resist the Holy G .... Acts 7:51
But he, being full of the Holy G .... Acts 7:55
they might receive the Holy G .... Acts 8:15
them, and they received the Holy G.. Acts 8:17
hands the Holy G was given .... Acts 8:18
hands, he may receive the Holy G...... Acts 8:19
and be filled with the Holy G .... Acts 9:17
and in the comfort of the Holy G .... Acts 9:31
Jesus of Nazareth with the Holy G ..... Acts 10:38
the Holy G fell on all them which .... Acts 10:44
poured out the gift of the Holy G....... Acts 10:45
received the Holy G as well as we....... Acts 10:47
the Holy G fell on them, as on us......... Acts 11:15
shall be baptized with the Holy G....... Acts 11:16
a good man, and full of the Holy G..... Acts 11:24
eaten of worms, and gave up the g.... Acts 12:23
Lord, and fasted, the Holy G said .... Acts 13:2
being sent forth by the Holy G .... Acts 13:4
Paul,) filled with the Holy G .... Acts 13:9
with joy, and with the Holy G .... Acts 13:52
witness, giving them the Holy G .... Acts 15:8
For it seemed good to the Holy G .... Acts 15:28
Holy G to preach the word in Asia ...... Acts 16:6
the Holy G since ye believed................ Acts 19:2
heard whether there be any Holy G..... Acts 19:2
them, the Holy G came on them........... Acts 19:6
Save that the Holy G witnesseth .... Acts 20:23
Holy G hath made you overseers......... Acts 20:28
and said, Thus saith the Holy G .... Acts 21:11
Well spake the Holy G by Esaias......... Acts 28:25
the Holy G which is given unto us....... Rom 5:5
bearing me witness in the Holy G .... Rom 9:1
and peace, and joy in the Holy G .... Rom 14:17
through the power of the Holy G......... Rom 15:13
being sanctified by the Holy G............ Rom 15:16
but which the Holy G teacheth 1Cor 2:13
of the Holy G which is in you............... 1Cor 6:19
is the Lord, but by the Holy G 1Cor 12:3
by kindness, by the Holy G 2Cor 6:6
and the communion of the Holy G 2Cor 13:14
also in power, and in the Holy G 1Th 1:5
with joy of the Holy G 1Th 1:6
the Holy G which dwelleth in us 2Ti 1:14
and renewing of the Holy G .... Titus 3:5
miracles, and gifts of the Holy G .... Heb 2:4
Wherefore (as the Holy G saith .... Heb 3:7
were made partakers of the Holy G.... Heb 6:4
The Holy G this signifying, that .... Heb 9:8
Whereof the Holy G also is a................ Heb 10:15
the Holy G sent down from heaven..... 1Pet 1:12
as they were moved by the Holy G 2Pet 1:21
Father, the Word, and the Holy G 1Jn 5:7
holy faith, praying in the Holy G .... Jude 20

GIAH (ghi'-ah) A place near the wilderness of Gibeon.
that lieth before G by the way of 2Sa 2:24

GIANT
which was of the sons of the g 2Sa 21:16
which was of the sons of the g 2Sa 21:18
and he also was born to the g 2Sa 21:20
four were born to the g in Gath 2Sa 21:22
that was of the children of the g 1Chr 20:4
and he also was the son of the g 1Chr 20:6
were born unto the g in Gath 1Chr 20:8
he runneth upon me like a g .... Job 16:14

GIANTS
There were g in the earth in .... Gen 6:4
And there we saw the g .... Num 13:33
sons of Anak, which come of the g .... Num 13:33
Which also were accounted g .... Deut 2:11
also was accounted a land of g........... Deut 2:20
g dwelt therein in old time .... Deut 2:20
remained of the remnant of g .... Deut 3:11
which was called the land of g .... Deut 3:13
which was of the remnant of the g.... Josh 12:4
remained of the remnant of the g..... Josh 13:12
of the valley of the g northward .... Josh 15:8
of the Perizzites and of the g .... Josh 17:15
the valley of the g on the north .... Josh 18:16

GIBALITES See Giblites.

GIBBAR (ghib'-bar) See Gibeon. A family of exiles.
The children of G, ninety and five........ Ezr 2:20

GIBBETHON (ghib'-be-thon) A town in Dan.
And Eltekeh, and G, and Baalath, ... Josh 19:44
her suburbs, G with her suburbs,........ Josh 21:23
and Baasha smote him at G, which 1Kin 15:27
and all Israel laid siege to G 1Kin 15:27
people were encamped against G 1Kin 16:15
And Omri went up from G, and all 1Kin 16:17

GIBEA (ghib'-e-ah) See Gibeah. Son of Sheva,
of Machbenah, and the father of G..... 1Chr 2:49

GIBEAH (ghib'-e-ah) A city in Judah.
Cain, G, and Timnah............................. Josh 15:57
we will pass over to G........................... Judg 19:12
places to lodge all night, in G.............. Judg 19:13
upon them when they were by G......... Judg 19:14
to go in and to lodge in G.................... Judg 19:15
and he sojourned in G........................... Judg 19:16

I came into G that belongeth to........... Judg 20:4
the men of G rose against me, and...... Judg 20:5
the thing which we will do to G............ Judg 20:9
when they come to G of Benjamin...... Judg 20:10
of Belial, which are in G........................ Judg 20:13
together out of the cities unto G......... Judg 20:14
beside the inhabitants of G .... Judg 20:15
morning, and encamped against G...... Judg 20:19
array to fight against them at G.......... Judg 20:20
of Benjamin came forth out of G........ Judg 20:21
them out of G the second day............. Judg 20:25
set liers in wait round about G............ Judg 20:29
put themselves in array against G ...... Judg 20:30
and the other to G in the field............. Judg 20:31
even out of the meadows of G............. Judg 20:33
there came against G ten thousand.... Judg 20:34
wait which they had set beside G........ Judg 20:36
in wait hasted, and rushed upon G..... Judg 20:37
against G toward the sunrising............ Judg 20:43
And Saul also went home to G .... Judg 20:26
came the messengers to G of Saul...... 1Sa 10:26
with Jonathan in G of Benjamin......... 1Sa 13:2
up from Gilgal unto G of Benjamin.... 1Sa 13:15
with them, abode in G of Benjamin.... 1Sa 13:16
in the uttermost part of G under......... 1Sa 14:2
other southward over against G.......... 1Sa 14:5
of Saul in G of Benjamin looked.......... 1Sa 14:16
went up to his house to G of Saul....... 1Sa 15:34
(now Saul abode in G under a tree...... 1Sa 22:6
came up the Ziphites to Saul to G 1Sa 23:19
the Ziphites came unto Saul to G 1Sa 26:1
house of Abinadab that was in G......... 2Sa 6:3
house of Abinadab was at G 2Sa 6:4
up unto the LORD in G of Saul.............. 2Sa 21:6
of G of the children of Benjamin......... 2Sa 23:29
Ithai the son of Ribai of G 1Chr 11:31
the daughter of Uriel of G................... 2Chr 13:2
of G Saul is fled................................... Is 10:29
Blow ye the cornet in G, and the........ Hos 5:8
themselves, as in the days of G............ Hos 9:9
hast sinned from the days of G............ Hos 10:9
the battle in G against the.................... Hos 10:9

GIBEAH (ghib'-e-ath) See Gibeah,
Gibeathite. Same as Gibeah.
and Jebusi, which is Jerusalem, G ...... Josh 18:28

GIBEATH-HAARALOTH See Gibeath.

GIBEATHITE (ghib'-e-ath-ite) An inhabitant
of Gibeah.
Joash, the sons of Shemaah the G....... 1Chr 12:3

GIBEON (ghib'-e-on) See Geba, Gibeah,
Gibeonite.
1. A Hivite city.
when the inhabitants of G heard......... Josh 9:3
Now their cities were G, and............... Josh 9:17
how the inhabitants of G had made.... Josh 10:1
because G was a great city, as .... Josh 10:2
and help me, that we may smite G ..... Josh 10:4
their hosts, and encamped before G.. Josh 10:5
the men of G sent unto Joshua to....... Josh 10:6
them with a great slaughter at G .... Josh 10:10
Sun, stand thou still upon G .... Josh 10:12
country of Goshen, even unto G .... Josh 10:41
the Hivites the inhabitants of G.......... Josh 11:19
2. A city in Benjamin.
G, and Ramah, and Beeroth,................ Josh 18:25
G with her suburbs, Geba with her .... Josh 21:17
Saul, went out from Mahanaim to G.. 2Sa 2:12
and met together by the pool of G 2Sa 2:13
Helkath-hazzurim, which is in G 2Sa 2:16
by the way of the wilderness of G 2Sa 2:24
brother Asahel at G in the battle......... 2Sa 3:30
at the great stone which is in G 2Sa 20:8
the king went to G to sacrifice............ 1Kin 3:4
In G the LORD appeared to Solomon... 1Kin 3:5
as he had appeared unto him at G 1Kin 9:2
at G dwelt the father of Gibeon.......... 1Chr 8:29
in G dwelt the father of Gibeon,......... 1Chr 9:35
Philistines from G even to Gazer......... 1Chr 14:16
in the high place that was at G 1Chr 16:39
season in the high place at G 1Chr 21:29
to the high place that was at G 2Chr 1:3
place that was at G to Jerusalem........ 2Chr 1:13
the Meronothite, the men of G .... Neh 3:7
The children of G, ninety and five....... Neh 7:25
be wroth as in the valley of G .... Is 28:21
Azur the prophet, which was of G....... Jer 28:1
by the great waters that are in G .... Jer 41:12
whom he had brought again from G ... Jer 41:16

GIBEONITE (ghib'-e-on-ite) See Gibeonites.
An inhabitant of Gibeon.
Abdon the son of G 1Chr 12:4
unto them repaired Melatiah the G.... Neh 3:7

GIBEONITES (ghib'-e-on-ites)
house, because he slew the G............... 2Sa 21:1
And the king called the G, and said.... 2Sa 21:2
(now the G were not of the................... 2Sa 21:2
Wherefore David said unto the G 2Sa 21:3
the G said unto him, We will have....... 2Sa 21:4
them into the hands of the G 2Sa 21:9

GIBLITES (ghib'-lites) Inhabitants of Gebal.
And the land of the G, and all............. Josh 13:5

GIDDALTI (ghid-dal'-ti) A son of Heman.
Hananiah, Hanani, Eliathah, G 1Chr 25:4
The two and twentieth to G................. 1Chr 25:29

GIDDEL (ghid'-del)
1. A family of exiles.
The children of G, the children .... Ezr 2:47
of Hanan, the children of G .... Neh 7:49
2. Servants of Solomon
of Darkon, the children of G .... Ezr 2:56
of Darkon, the children of G .... Neh 7:58

GIDEON (ghid'-e-on) See Gedeon, Jerubbaal.
A judge of Israel.
his son G threshed wheat by the........ Judg 6:11
G said unto him, Oh my Lord, if .... Judg 6:13
G went in, and made ready a kid,....... Judg 6:19
when G perceived that he was an....... Judg 6:22
Lord, G said, Alas, O Lord God.......... Judg 6:22
Then G built an altar there unto......... Judg 6:24
Then G took ten men of his .... Judg 6:27
G the son of Joash hath done this...... Judg 6:29
Spirit of the LORD came upon G......... Judg 6:34
G said unto God, If thou wilt.............. Judg 6:36
G said unto God, Let not thine .... Judg 6:39
Then Jerubbaal, who is G, and all...... Judg 7:1
And the LORD said unto G, The........... Judg 7:2
And the LORD said unto G, The........... Judg 7:4
and the LORD said unto G, Every .... Judg 7:5
And the LORD said unto G, By the....... Judg 7:7
when G was come, behold, there....... Judg 7:13
the sword of G the son of Joash......... Judg 7:14
when G heard the telling of the .... Judg 7:15
The sword of the LORD, and of G .... Judg 7:18
So G, and the hundred men that....... Judg 7:19
The sword of the LORD, and of G .... Judg 7:20
G sent messengers throughout all.... Judg 7:24
Zeeb to G on the other side .... Judg 7:25
G came to Jordan, and passed over,. Judg 8:4
G said, Therefore when the LORD...... Judg 8:7
G went up by the way of them that.. Judg 8:11
G the son of Joash returned from..... Judg 8:13
G arose, and slew Zebah and .... Judg 8:21
the men of Israel said unto G .... Judg 8:22
G said unto them, I will not rule....... Judg 8:23
G said unto them, I would desire..... Judg 8:24
G made an ephod thereof, and put.. Judg 8:27
which thing became a snare unto G.. Judg 8:27
forty years in the days of G .... Judg 8:28
G had threescore and ten sons of.... Judg 8:30
G the son of Joash died in a good.... Judg 8:32
to pass, as soon as G was dead......... Judg 8:33
the house of Jerubbaal, namely,....... Judg 8:35

GIDEONI (ghid-e-o'-ni) A Benjamite who
counted the people.
Abidan the son of G .... Num 1:11
shall be Abidan the son of G .... Num 2:22
the ninth day Abidan the son of G.... Num 7:60
offering of Abidan the son of G .... Num 7:65
Benjamin was Abidan the son of G.... Num 10:24

GIDOM (ghi'-dom) A place near Bethel.
and pursued hard after them unto G. Judg 20:45

GIER
and the pelican, and the g, eagle,...... Lev 11:18
the g eagle, and the cormorant,......... Deut 14:17

GIFT
Ask me never so much dowry and g .. Gen 34:12
And thou shalt take no g .... Ex 23:8
for the g blindeth the wise, and........ Ex 23:8
given the Levites as a g to Aaron ...... Num 8:19
are given as a g for the LORD............. Num 18:6
office unto you as a service of g......... Num 18:7
the heave offering of their g.............. Num 18:11
respect persons, neither take a g...... Deut 16:19
for a g doth blind the eyes of............. Deut 16:19
or hath he given us any g 2Sa 19:42
of Tyre shall be there with a g .... Ps 45:12
A g is as a precious stone in the........ Prov 17:8
A wicked man taketh a g out of .... Prov 17:23
A man's g maketh room for .... Prov 18:16
A g in secret pacifieth anger .... Prov 21:14
of a false g is like clouds.................... Prov 25:14
his labour, it is the g of God .... Eccl 3:13
this is the g of God .... Eccl 5:19
and a g destroyeth the heart .... Eccl 7:7
give a g unto any of his sons .... Eze 46:16
But if he give a g of his .... Eze 46:17
if thou bring thy g to the altar........... Mt 5:23
Leave there thy g before the .... Mt 5:24
and then come and offer thy g.......... Mt 5:24
offer the g that Moses commanded,. Mt 8:4
father or his mother, It is a g .... Mt 15:5
swearth by the g that is upon it........ Mt 23:18
for whether is greater, the g............. Mt 23:19
the altar that sanctifieth the g .... Mt 23:19
It is Corban, that is to say, a g........... Mk 7:11
her, If thou knewest the g of God..... Jn 4:10
receive the g of the Holy Ghost........ Acts 2:38
thou hast thought that the g of....... Acts 8:20
out the g of the Holy Ghost .... Acts 10:45
them the like g as he did unto us...... Acts 11:17
impart unto you some spiritual g .... Rom 1:11
offence, so also is the free g............. Rom 5:15
the g by grace, which is by one......... Rom 5:15
by one that sinned, so is the g .... Rom 5:16
but the free g is of many................... Rom 5:16
the g of righteousness shall .... Rom 5:17
the free g came upon all men........... Rom 5:18
but the g of God is eternal life.......... Rom 6:23
So that ye come behind in no g 1Cor 1:7
man hath his proper g of God........... 1Cor 7:7
though I have the g of prophecy....... 1Cor 13:2
that for the g bestowed upon us 2Cor 1:11

that we would receive the g 2Cor 8:4
be unto God for his unspeakable g 2Cor 9:15
it is the g of God .... Eph 2:8
according to the g of the grace ...... Eph 3:7
to the measure of the g of Christ .... Eph 4:7
Not because I desire a g .... Phil 4:17
Neglect not the g that is in thee 1Ti 4:14
that thou stir up the g of God 2Ti 1:6
and have tasted of the heavenly g .... Heb 6:4
good g and every perfect g .... Jas 1:17
As every man hath received the g 1Pet 4:10

GIFTS
which Abraham had, Abraham gave g ... Gen 25:6
shall hallow in all their holy g ..... Ex 28:38
of the LORD, and beside your g .... Lev 23:38
Out of all your g ye shall offer...... Num 18:29
David's servants, and brought g 2Sa 8:2
servants to David, and brought g 2Sa 8:6
David's servants, and brought g 1Chr 18:2
David's servants, and brought g 1Chr 18:6
of persons, nor taking of g 2Chr 19:7
gave them great g of silver.......... 2Chr 21:3
And the Ammonites gave g to Uzziah ... 2Chr 26:8
many brought g unto the LORD to 2Chr 32:23
to the provinces, and gave g .... Est 2:18
one to another, and g to the poor .... Est 9:22
thou hast received g for men .... Ps 68:18
of Sheba and Seba shall offer g ...... Ps 72:10
though thou givest many g .... Prov 6:35
but he that hateth g shall live...... Prov 15:27
is a friend to him that giveth g .... Prov 19:6
that receiveth g overthroweth it ..... Prov 29:4
every one loveth g, and followeth .... Is 1:23
They give g to all whores............ Eze 16:33
givest thy g to all thy lovers....... Eze 16:33
And I polluted them in their own g ... Eze 20:26
For when ye offer your g, when ye .... Eze 20:31
my holy name no more with your g ..... Eze 20:39
have they taken g to shed blood ..... Eze 22:12
thereof, ye shall receive of me g .... Dan 2:6
man, and gave him many great g .... Dan 2:48
Let thy g be to thyself, and give .... Dan 5:17
they presented unto him g .... Mt 2:11
to give good g unto your children .... Mt 7:11
to give good g unto your children .... Lk 11:13
casting their g into the treasury .... Lk 21:1
adorned with goodly stones and g ..... Lk 21:5
For the g and calling of God are ..... Rom 11:29
Having then g differing according..... Rom 12:6
Now concerning spiritual g 1Cor 12:1
Now there are diversities of g 1Cor 12:4
to another the g of healing by 1Cor 12:9
then g of healings, helps,........... 1Cor 12:28
Have all the g of healing............ 1Cor 12:30
But covet earnestly the best g 1Cor 12:31
charity, and desire spiritual g 1Cor 14:1
as ye are zealous of spiritual g 1Cor 14:12
captive, and gave g unto men......... Eph 4:8
g of the Holy Ghost, according to .... Heb 2:4
to God, that he may offer both g ..... Heb 5:1
priest is ordained to offer g .... Heb 8:3
that offer g according to the law .... Heb 9:9
in which were offered both g......... Heb 9:9
God testifying of his g.............. Heb 11:4
shall send g one to another .... Rev 11:10

GIHON (ghi'-hon)
  1. A river in the Garden of Eden.
the name of the second river is G..... Gen 2:13
  2. A place near Jerusalem.
own mule, and bring him down to G 1Kin 1:33
David's mule, and brought him to G ... 1Kin 1:38
have anointed him king in G.......... 1Kin 1:45
the upper watercourse of G 2Chr 32:30
of David, on the west side of G....... 2Chr 33:14

GILALAI (ghil'-a-lahee) *A priest who dedicated
    the wall.*
Shemaiah, and Azareel, Milalai, G .... Neh 12:36

GILBOA (ghil-bo'-ah)
  1. A district in Manasseh.
together, and they pitched in G....... 1Sa 28:4
Philistines had slain Saul in G 2Sa 21:12
  2. A mountain near the valley Jezreel.
and fell down slain in mount G 1Sa 31:1
his three sons fallen in mount G 1Sa 31:8
I happened by chance upon mount G 2Sa 1:6
Ye mountains of G, let there be...... 2Sa 1:21
and fell down slain in mount G 1Chr 10:1
and his sons fallen in mount G 1Chr 10:8

GILEAD (ghil'-e-ad) See GILEADITE, GILEAD'S,
    JABESH-GILEAD, RAMOTH-GILEAD.
  1. District east of the Jordan River.
of Ishmeelites came from G with ...... Gen 37:25
land of Jazer, and the land of G ..... Num 32:1
shall be there in the cities of G .... Num 32:26
the land of G for a possession....... Num 32:29
the son of Manasseh went to G........ Num 32:39
Moses gave G unto Machir the son...... Num 32:40
that is by the river, even unto G .... Deut 2:36
the cities of the plain, and all G ... Deut 3:10
the rest of G, and all Bashan,....... Deut 3:13
And I gave G unto Machir .... Deut 3:15
unto the Gadites I gave from G .... Deut 3:16
and Ramoth in G, of the Gadites ...... Deut 4:43
LORD shewed him all the land of G .... Deut 34:1
of the river, and from half G .... Josh 12:2
and the Maachathites, and half G ..... Josh 12:5
And G, and the border of the......... Josh 13:11
was Jazer, and all the cities of G ... Josh 13:25

And half G, and Ashtaroth .... Josh 13:31
a man of war, therefore he had G ..... Josh 17:1
to Manasseh, beside the land of G .... Josh 17:5
Manasseh's sons had the land of G .... Josh 17:6
Ramoth in G and out of the tribe of .. Josh 20:8
to go unto the country of G .... Josh 22:9
of Manasseh, into the land of G ...... Josh 22:13
of Manasseh, unto the land of G....... Josh 22:15
of Gad, out of the land of G .... Josh 22:32
G abode beyond Jordan .... Judg 5:17
day, which are in the land of G ...... Judg 10:4
of the Amorites, which is in G .... Judg 10:8
together, and encamped in G .... Judg 10:17
princes of G said one to another,.... Judg 10:18
over all the inhabitants of G .... Judg 10:18
the elders of G went to fetch .... Judg 11:5
said unto the elders of G .... Judg 11:7
the elders of G said unto .... Judg 11:8
over all the inhabitants of G .... Judg 11:8
said unto the elders of G .... Judg 11:9
the elders of G said unto .... Judg 11:10
went with the elders of G .... Judg 11:11
Jephthah, and he passed over G .... Judg 11:29
and passed over Mizpeh of G .... Judg 11:29
from Mizpeh of G he passed over ...... Judg 11:29
together all the men of G .... Judg 12:4
the men of G smote Ephraim,.......... Judg 12:4
that the men of G said unto him....... Judg 12:5
buried in one of the cities of G ..... Judg 12:7
to Beer-sheba, with the land of G .... Judg 20:1
Jordan to the land of Gad and G 1Sa 13:7
And made him king over G, and over ... 2Sa 2:9
Absalom pitched in the land of G 2Sa 17:26
Then they came to G, and to the 2Sa 24:6
son of Manasseh, which are in G 1Kin 4:13
of Uri was in the country of G 1Kin 4:19
who was of the inhabitants of G 1Kin 17:1
Know ye that Ramoth in G is ours...... 1Kin 22:3
eastward, all the land of G 2Kin 10:33
is by the river Arnon, even G 2Kin 10:33
Kedesh, and Hazor, and G 2Kin 15:29
and twenty cities in the land of G ... 1Chr 2:22
were multiplied in the land of G 1Chr 5:9
throughout all the east land of G 1Chr 5:10
And they dwelt in G in Bashan 1Chr 5:16
Ramoth in G with her suburbs, and 1Chr 6:80
men of valour at Jazer of G 1Chr 26:31
the half tribe of Manasseh in G 1Chr 27:21
G is mine, and Manasseh is mine....... Ps 60:7
     2. A mountain range in Gilead 1.
flock of goats that appear from G .... Song 4:1
Is there no balm in G .... Jer 8:22
Thou art G unto me, and the head ..... Jer 22:6
Go up into G, and take balm, O .... Jer 46:11
satisfied upon mount Ephraim and G ... Jer 50:19
and from Damascus, and from G .... Eze 47:18
G is a city of them that work .... Hos 6:8
Is there iniquity in G .... Hos 12:11
because they have threshed G with .... Amos 1:3
up the women with child of G .... Amos 1:13
and Benjamin shall possess G .... Obad 19
let them feed in Bashan and G .... Mic 7:14
bring them into the land of G .... Zec 10:10
     2. A mountain range in Gilead 1.
set his face toward the mount G ...... Gen 31:21
they overtook him in the mount G ..... Gen 31:23
pitched in the mount of G .... Gen 31:25
the river Arnon, and half mount G .... Deut 3:12
and depart early from mount G .... Judg 7:3
goats, that appear from mount G ...... Song 4:1
     3. Son of Machir.
and Machir begat G .... Num 26:29
of G come the family of the .... Num 26:29
These are the sons of G .... Num 26:30
the son of Hepher, the son of G ...... Num 27:1
the families of the children of G .... Num 36:1
of Manasseh, the father of G .... Josh 17:1
the son of Hepher, the son of G ...... Josh 17:3
of Machir the father of G 1Chr 2:21
sons of Machir the father of G 1Chr 2:23
bare Machir the father of G 1Chr 7:14
These were the sons of G, the son 1Chr 7:17
     4. Father of Jephthah.
and G begat Jephthah .... Judg 11:1
     5. A chief of Gad.
the son of Jaroah, the son of G 1Chr 5:14

GILEADITE (ghil'-e-ad-ite) See GILEADITES. A
    descendant of Gilead.
After after him arose Jair, a G ...... Judg 10:3
Now Jephthah the G was a mighty ...... Judg 11:1
the G four days in a year .... Judg 11:40
Then died Jephthah the G, and was .... Judg 12:7
and Barzillai the G of Rogelim 2Sa 17:27
Barzillai the G came down from 2Sa 19:31
unto the sons of Barzillai the G 1Kin 2:7
the daughters of Barzillai the G ..... Ezr 2:61
of Barzillai the G to wife .... Neh 7:63

GILEADITES (ghil'-e-ad-ites)
Gilead come the family of the G ...... Num 26:29
Ye G are fugitives of Ephraim .... Judg 12:4
the G took the passages of Jordan.... Judg 12:5
and with him fifty men of G 2Kin 1:13

GILEAD'S (ghil'-e-ads) Refers to Gilead 4.
And G wife bare him sons.............. Judg 11:2

GILGAL (ghil'-gal)
  1. A place near Jericho.
in the champaign over against G....... Deut 11:30

the first month, and encamped in G ... Josh 4:19
of Jordan, did Joshua pitch in G ..... Josh 4:20
place is called G unto this day....... Josh 5:9
children of Israel encamped in G ..... Josh 5:10
sent unto Joshua to the camp to G .... Josh 10:6
So Joshua ascended from G .... Josh 10:7
and went up from G all night .... Josh 10:9
with him, unto the camp to G .... Josh 10:15
with him, unto the camp to G .... Josh 10:43
of Judah came unto Joshua in G .... Josh 14:6
and so northward, looking toward G ... Josh 15:7
the LORD came up from G to Bochim ... Judg 2:1
from the quarries that were by G ..... Judg 3:19
year in circuit to Beth-el, and G 1Sa 7:16
thou shalt go down before me to G 1Sa 10:8
people, Come, and let us go to G 1Sa 11:14
And all the people went to G 1Sa 11:15
Saul king before the LORD in G 1Sa 11:15
called together after Saul to G 1Sa 13:7
As for Saul, he was yet in G 1Sa 13:7
but Samuel came not to G 1Sa 13:8
will come down now upon me to G 1Sa 13:12
gat him up from G unto Gibeah of 1Sa 13:15
and passed on, and gone down to G 1Sa 15:12
unto the LORD thy God in G 1Sa 15:21
in pieces before the LORD in G 1Sa 15:33
And Judah came to G, to go to meet ... 2Sa 19:15
Then the king went on to G 2Sa 19:40
Also from the house of G, and out.... Neh 12:29
and come not ye unto G, neither go ... Hos 4:15
All their wickedness is in G .... Hos 9:15
they sacrifice bullocks in G .... Hos 12:11
at G multiply transgression.......... Amos 4:4
not Beth-el, nor enter into G .... Amos 5:5
for G shall surely go into .... Amos 5:5
answered him from Shittim unto G ..... Mic 6:5
     2. A city between Dor and Tirsa.
the king of the nations of G .... Josh 12:23
     3. A city north of Joppa.
went to Joshua unto the camp at G .... Josh 9:6
     4. A place south of Ebal and Gerizim.
Elijah went with Elisha from G 2Kin 2:1
And Elisha came again to G 2Kin 4:38

GILO See GILOH.

GILOH (ghi'-loh) See GILONITE. A town in
    Judah.
And Goshen, and Holon, and G......... Josh 15:51
from his city, even from G 2Sa 15:12

GILONITE (ghi'-lo-nite) An inhabitant of
    Giloh.
Absalom sent for Ahithophel the G 2Sa 15:12
Eliam the son of Ahithophel the G 2Sa 23:34

GIMZO (ghim'-zo) A city in Judah.
G also and the villages thereof 2Chr 28:18

GIN
The g shall take him by the heel,..... Job 18:9
the houses of Israel, for a g .... Is 8:14
the earth, where no g is for him ..... Amos 3:5

GINATH (ghi'-nath) Father of Tibni.
followed Tibni the son of G 1Kin 16:21
that followed Tibni the son of G 1Kin 16:22

GINNETHO (ghin'-ne-tho) See GINNETHON. A
    priest who renewed the covenant.
Iddo, G, Abijah,..................... Neh 12:4

GINNETHOI See GINNETHO.

GINNETHON (ghin'-ne-thon) See GINNETHO.
    Same as Ginnetho.
Daniel, G, Baruch,................... Neh 10:6
of G, Meshullam,..................... Neh 12:16

GINS
they have set g for me .... Ps 140:5
the g of the workers of iniquity .... Ps 141:9

GIRD
g him with the curious girdle of .... Ex 29:5
thou shalt g them with girdles,...... Ex 29:9
he did g it under his raiment........ Judg 3:16
G ye on every man his sword.......... 1Sa 25:13
g you with sackcloth, and mourn 2Sa 3:31
G up thy loins, and take my staff ... 2Kin 4:29
G up thy loins, and take this box ... 2Kin 9:1
G up now thy loins like a man........ Job 38:3
G up thy loins now like a man........ Job 40:7
G thy sword upon thy thigh, O........ Ps 45:3
g yourselves, and ye shall be .... Is 8:9
g yourselves, and ye shall be .... Is 8:9
shall themselves with sackcloth ..... Is 15:3
g sackcloth upon your loins.......... Is 32:11
Thou therefore g up thy loins .... Jer 1:17
For this g you with sackcloth,....... Jer 4:8
g thee with sackcloth, and wallow ... Jer 6:26
of Rabbah, g you with sackcloth ..... Jer 49:3
They shall also g themselves with ... Eze 7:18
g them with sackcloth, and they ..... Eze 27:31
they shall not g themselves with .... Eze 44:18
G yourselves, and lament, ye .... Joel 1:13
unto you, that he shall g himself ... Lk 12:37
g thyself, and serve me, till I ..... Lk 17:8
hands, and another shall g thee ..... Jn 21:18
G thyself, and bind on thy sandals .. Acts 12:8
Wherefore g up the loins of your 1Pet 1:13

GIRDED
with your loins g, your shoes on .... Ex 12:11
g him with the girdle, and clothed .. Lev 8:7
he g him with the curious girdle .... Lev 8:7

g them with girdles, and put .... Lev 8:13
shall be g with a linen girdle, ... Lev 16:4
when ye had g on every man his .... Deut 1:41
that stumbled are g with strength 1Sa 2:4
a child, g with a linen ephod 1Sa 2:18
David g his sword upon his armour 1Sa 17:39
they g on every man his sword 1Sa 25:13
David also g on his sword 1Sa 25:13
David was g with a linen ephod 2Sa 6:14
that he had put on was g unto him 2Sa 20:8
be being g with a new sword, ... 2Sa 21:16
For thou hast g me with strength 2Sa 22:40
he g up his loins, and ran before 1Kin 18:46
So they g sackcloth on their 1Kin 20:32
one had his sword g by his side .... Neh 4:18
For thou hast g me with strength .... Ps 18:39
sackcloth, and g me with gladness .... Ps 30:11
being g with power .... Ps 65:6
wherewith he hath g himself .... Ps 93:1
wherewith he is g continually .... Ps 109:19
I g thee, though thou hast not .... Is 45:5
they have g themselves with .... Lam 2:10
I g thee about with fine linen, ... Eze 16:10
G with girdles upon their loins, ... Eze 23:15
whose loins were g with fine gold .... Dan 10:5
Lament like a virgin g with .... Joel 1:8
Let your loins be g about .... Lk 12:35
and took a towel, and g himself .... Jn 13:4
with the towel wherewith he was g .... Jn 13:5
breasts g with golden girdles. .... Rev 15:6

GIRDEDST
thou g thyself, and walkedst .... Jn 21:18

GIRDETH
Let not him that g on his harness 1Kin 20:11
g their loins with a girdle .... Job 12:18
It is God that g me with strength. .... Ps 18:32
She g her loins with strength, and .... Prov 31:17

GIRDING
of a stomacher a g of sackcloth .... Is 3:24
baldness, and to g with sackcloth. .... Is 22:12

GIRDLE
A broidered coat, a mitre, and a g .... Ex 28:4
the curious g of the ephod, which .... Ex 28:8
above the curious g of the ephod .... Ex 28:27
above the curious g of the ephod .... Ex 28:28
shalt make the g of needlework .... Ex 28:39
with the curious g of the ephod, ... Ex 29:5
the curious g of his ephod, that .... Ex 39:5
above the curious g of the ephod .... Ex 39:20
above the curious g of the ephod .... Ex 39:21
a g of fine twined linen, and blue .... Ex 39:29
coat, and girded him with the g, ... Lev 8:7
with the curious g of the ephod .... Lev 8:7
and shall be girded with a linen g .... Lev 16:4
sword, and to his bow, and to his g 1Sa 18:4
ten shekels of silver, and a g 2Sa 18:11
upon it a g with a sword fastened 2Sa 20:8
his g that was about his loins 1Kin 2:5
girt with a g of leather about 2Kin 1:8
and girdeth their loins with a g, ... Job 12:18
for a g wherewith he is girded .... Ps 109:19
and instead of a g a rent .... Is 3:24
neither shall the g of their .... Is 5:27
shall be the g of his loins. .... Is 11:5
faithfulness the g of his reins .... Is 11:5
and strengthen him with thy g .... Is 22:21
unto me, Go and get thee a linen g .... Jer 13:1
So I got a g according to the. .... Jer 13:2
Take the g that thou hast got, ... Jer 13:4
take the g from thence, which I .... Jer 13:6
took the g from the place where I .... Jer 13:7
behold, the g was marred, it was .... Jer 13:7
them, shall even be as this g .... Jer 13:10
For as the g cleaveth to the. .... Jer 13:11
a leathern g about his loins .... Mt 3:4
with a g of a skin about his .... Mk 1:6
come unto us, he took Paul's g, ... Acts 21:11
bind the man that oweth this g .... Acts 21:11
about the paps with a golden g .... Rev 1:13

GIRDLES
and thou shalt make for them a g .... Ex 28:40
And thou shalt gird them with g .... Ex 29:9
upon them, and girded them with a g .... Lev 8:13
delivereth g unto the merchant. .... Prov 31:24
Girded with g upon their loins, ... Eze 23:15
breasts girded with golden g .... Rev 15:6

GIRGASHITE (*ghur'-gash-ite*) See
GIRGASHITES, GIRGASITE. *A Canaanite tribe.*
also, and the Amorite, and the G..... .... 1Chr 1:14

GIRGASHITES (*ghur'-gash-ites*)
and the Canaanites, and the G..... .... Gen 15:21
thee, the Hittites, and the G..... .... Deut 7:1
and the Perizzites, and the G..... .... Josh 3:10
and the Hittites, and the G..... .... Josh 24:11
and the Jebusites, and the G..... .... Neh 9:8

GIRGASITE (*ghur'-ga-site*) See GIRGASHITE.
Same as Girgashite.
and the Amorite, and the G..... .... Gen 10:16

GIRL
sold a g for wine, that they .... Joel 3:3

GIRLS
g playing in the streets thereof. .... Zec 8:5

GIRT
g with a girdle of leather about 2Kin 1:8
he g his fisher's coat unto him, (.............. Jn 21:7

your loins g about with truth .... Eph 6:14
g about the paps with a golden .... Rev 1:13

GIRZITES See GEZRITES.

GISHPA See GISPA.

GISPA (*ghis'-pah*) *An overseer of the Nethinim.*
G were over the Nethinims .... Neh 11:21

GISPHA See GISPA.

GITTAH-HEPHER (*ghit''-tah-he'-fer*) See
GATH-HEPHER. *A town in Zebulun.*
passeth on along on the east to G. .... Josh 19:13

GITTAIM (*ghit-ta'-im*)
1. *A city of refuge.*
And the Beerothites fled to G. 2Sa 4:3
2. *A Benjamite city.*
Hazor, Ramah, G, ... Neh 11:33

GITTITE (*ghit'-tite*) See GITTITES, GITTITH. *An inhabitant of Gath.*
into the house of Obed-edom the G..... .... 2Sa 6:10
of Obed-edom the G three months..... .... 2Sa 6:11
Then said the king to Ittai the G..... .... 2Sa 15:19
Ittai the G passed over, and all 2Sa 15:22
under the hand of Ittai the G..... .... 2Sa 18:2
slew the brother of Goliath the G 2Sa 21:19
into the house of Obed-edom the G 1Chr 13:13
the brother of Goliath the G..... .... 1Chr 20:5

GITTITES
the Eshkalonites, the G, and the..... .... Josh 13:3
all the Pelethites, and all the G. 2Sa 15:18

GITTITH (*ghit'-tith*) *A musical instrument.*
To the chief Musician upon G..... .... Ps 8:t
To the chief Musician upon G..... .... Ps 81:t
To the chief Musician upon G..... .... Ps 84:t

GIVE See PREFACE.
of all that thou shalt g me I .... Gen 28:22
Every man shall g as he is able .... Deut 16:17
g thanks unto the LORD 1Chr 16:34
I shall g thee the heathen for .... Ps 2:8
he shall g thee the desires of .... Ps 37:4
O God, do we g .... Ps 75:1
unto thee do we g thanks. .... Ps 75:1
For he shall g his angels charge .... Ps 91:11
g me thine heart, and let thine .... Prov 23:26
lambs as he shall be able to g .... Eze 46:5
to the lambs as he is able to g .... Eze 46:11
He shall g his angels charge .... Mt 4:6
G us this day our daily bread..... .... Mt 6:11
or what shall a man g in exchange..... .... Mt 16:26
Or what shall a man g in exchange..... .... Mk 8:37
g to the poor, and thou shalt have .... Mk 10:21
G, and it shall be given unto you. .... Lk 6:38
G us day by day our daily bread.... .... Lk 11:3
I shall g him shall never thirst..... .... Jn 4:14
but the water that I shall g .... Jn 4:14
the Son of man shall g unto you..... .... Jn 6:27
with you, my peace I g unto you..... .... Jn 14:27
but such as I have g I thee .... Acts 3:6
more blessed to g than to receive..... .... Acts 20:35
him also freely g us all things..... .... Rom 8:32
shall g account of himself to God .... Rom 14:12
in his heart, so let him g 2Cor 9:7
In every thing g thanks: 1Th 5:18
I will g thee a crown of life. .... Rev 2:10
to g every man according as his .... Rev 22:12

GIVEN See PREFACE.

GIVER
so with the g of usury to him..... .... Is 24:2
for God loveth a cheerful g 2Cor 9:7

GIVEST
brother, and thou g him nought..... .... Deut 15:9
thou g unto him from him. .... Deut 15:10
be righteous, what g thou him. .... Job 35:7
Thou g thy mouth to evil, and thy .... Ps 50:19
g them tears to drink in great..... .... Ps 80:5
That thou g them they gather..... .... Ps 104:28
thou g them their meat in due .... Ps 145:15
content, though thou g many gifts..... .... Prov 4:35
thou g him not warning, nor .... Eze 3:18
but thou g thy gifts to all thy .... Eze 16:33
and in that thou g a reward..... .... Eze 16:34
For thou verily g thanks well..... .... 1Cor 14:17

GIVETH
he g goodly words .... Gen 49:21
therefore he g you on the sixth..... .... Ex 16:29
which the LORD thy God g thee..... .... Ex 20:12
of every man that g it willingly .... Ex 25:2
that g any of his seed unto .... Lev 20:2
when he g of his seed unto Molech .... Lev 20:4
all that any man g of such unto .... Lev 27:9
whatsoever any man g the priest .... Num 5:10
land which the LORD our God g us..... .... Deut 2:29
LORD God of your fathers g you..... .... Deut 4:1
which the LORD thy God g thee..... .... Deut 4:21
which the LORD thy God g thee..... .... Deut 4:40
which the LORD thy God g thee..... .... Deut 5:16
for it is he that g thee power to..... .... Deut 8:18
that the LORD thy God g thee not .... Deut 9:6
good land which the LORD g you..... .... Deut 11:17
which the LORD your God g you..... .... Deut 11:31
thy fathers g thee to possess it..... .... Deut 12:1
which the LORD thy God g you..... .... Deut 12:9
LORD your God g you to inherit .... Deut 12:10
when he g you rest from all your .... Deut 12:10
g thee a sign or a wonder, ... Deut 13:1
God g thee for an inheritance to..... .... Deut 15:4

which the LORD thy God g thee .... Deut 15:7
which the LORD thy God g thee..... .... Deut 16:5
which the LORD thy God g thee..... .... Deut 16:18
which the LORD thy God g thee..... .... Deut 16:20
which the LORD thy God g thee..... .... Deut 17:2
which the LORD thy God g thee..... .... Deut 17:14
which the LORD thy God g thee..... .... Deut 18:9
land the LORD thy God g thee..... .... Deut 19:1
LORD thy God g thee to possess it..... .... Deut 19:2
LORD thy God g thee to inherit..... .... Deut 19:3
which the LORD thy God g thee for..... .... Deut 19:10
LORD thy God g thee to possess it..... .... Deut 19:14
LORD thy God g thee to possess it..... .... Deut 21:1
which the LORD thy God g thee for..... .... Deut 21:23
g it in her hand, and sendeth her..... .... Deut 24:3
which the LORD thy God g thee for..... .... Deut 24:4
which the LORD thy God g thee..... .... Deut 25:15
God g thee for an inheritance to..... .... Deut 25:19
thy God g thee for an inheritance .... Deut 26:1
land that the LORD thy God g thee..... .... Deut 26:2
which the LORD thy God g thee..... .... Deut 27:2
which the LORD thy God g thee..... .... Deut 27:3
which the LORD thy God g thee..... .... Deut 28:8
LORD your God g you to possess it..... .... Josh 1:11
which the LORD your God g them..... .... Josh 1:15
Chemosh thy god g thee to possess..... .... Judg 11:24
Cursed be he that g a wife to..... .... Judg 21:18
Who g rain upon the earth, and..... .... Job 5:10
man g up the ghost, and where is..... .... Job 14:10
the Almighty g them understanding..... .... Job 32:8
For g a good account of any of..... .... Job 33:13
When he g quietness, who then can .... Job 34:29
maker, who g songs in the night..... .... Job 35:10
There they cry, but none g answer..... .... Job 35:12
but g right to the poor..... .... Job 36:6
he g meat in abundance..... .... Job 36:31
deliverance g he to his king..... .... Ps 18:50
the righteous sheweth mercy, and g..... .... Ps 37:21
of Israel is he that g strength..... .... Ps 68:35
The entrance of thy words g light..... .... Ps 119:130
it g understanding unto the..... .... Ps 119:130
for so he g his beloved sleep..... .... Ps 127:2
Who g food to all flesh..... .... Ps 136:25
It is he that g salvation unto..... .... Ps 144:10
which g food to the hungry..... .... Ps 146:7
He g to the beast his food, and to..... .... Ps 147:9
for g not know like word..... .... Ps 147:16
For the LORD g wisdom..... .... Prov 2:6
but he g grace unto the lowly..... .... Prov 3:34
Good understanding g favour..... .... Prov 13:15
A wicked doer g heed to false..... .... Prov 17:4
a liar g ear to a naughty tongue..... .... Prov 17:4
is a friend to him that g gifts..... .... Prov 19:6
but the righteous g and spareth..... .... Prov 21:26
for he g of his bread to the poor..... .... Prov 22:9
he that g to the rich, shall..... .... Prov 22:16
when it g his colour in the cup,..... .... Prov 23:31
his lips that g a right answer..... .... Prov 24:26
so is he that g honour to a fool..... .... Prov 26:8
He that g unto the poor shall not..... .... Prov 28:27
g meat to her household, and a..... .... Prov 31:15
For God g to a man that is good..... .... Eccl 2:26
but to the sinner he g travail..... .... Eccl 2:26
days of his life, which God g him,..... .... Eccl 5:18
yet God g him not power to eat .... Eccl 6:2
that wisdom g life to them that..... .... Eccl 7:12
which God g him under the sun..... .... Eccl 8:15
He g power to the faint..... .... Is 40:29
he that g breath unto the people..... .... Is 42:5
the LORD our God, that g rain,..... .... Jer 5:24
wages, and g him not for his work..... .... Jer 22:13
which g the sun for a light by..... .... Jer 31:35
He g his cheek to him that..... .... Lam 3:30
he g wisdom unto the wise, and..... .... Dan 2:21
g it to whomsoever he will, and..... .... Dan 4:17
g it to whomsoever he will,..... .... Dan 4:25
g it to whomsoever he will..... .... Dan 4:32
Woe unto him that g his neighbour .... Hab 2:15
if light unto all that are in..... .... Mt 5:15
for God g not the Spirit by..... .... Jn 3:34
but my Father g you the true..... .... Jn 6:32
heaven, and g life unto the world..... .... Jn 6:33
the Father g me shall come to me..... .... Jn 6:37
the good shepherd g his life for..... .... Jn 10:11
not as the world g, give I unto..... .... Jn 14:27
and g them, and fish likewise..... .... Jn 21:13
seeing he g to all life, and..... .... Acts 17:25
he that g, let him do it with..... .... Rom 12:8
to the Lord, for he g God thanks..... .... Rom 14:6
he eateth not, and g God thanks..... .... Rom 14:6
but God that g the increase..... .... 1Cor 3:7
So then he that g her in marriage..... .... 1Cor 7:38
but he that g her not in marriage..... .... 1Cor 7:38
But God g it a body as it hath..... .... 1Cor 15:38
which g us the victory through..... .... 1Cor 15:57
killeth, but the spirit g life..... .... 2Cor 3:6
who g us richly all things to..... .... 1Ti 6:17
that g to men liberally, and..... .... Jas 1:5
But he g more grace..... .... Jas 4:6
but g grace unto the humble..... .... Jas 4:6
it as of the ability which God g..... .... 1Pet 4:11
proud, and g grace to the humble..... .... 1Pet 5:5
for the Lord God g them light..... .... Rev 22:5

GIVING
And when she had done g him drink..... .... Gen 24:19
in g him food and raiment..... .... Deut 10:18
g him a double portion of all..... .... Deut 21:17
his people in g them bread..... .... Ruth 1:6
in g food for my household..... .... 1Kin 5:9
by g him according to his..... .... 2Chr 6:23

and g thanks unto the LORD .... Ezr 3:11
shall be as the g up of the ghost .... Job 11:20
g in marriage, until the day that .... Mt 24:38
shall be as his feet, g him thanks .... Lk 17:16
g out that himself was some great .... Acts 8:9
g them the Holy Ghost, even as he .... Acts 15:8
strong in faith, g glory to God .... Rom 4:20
the g of the law, and the service .... Rom 9:4
even things without life g sound 1Cor 14:7
say Amen at thy g of thanks 1Cor 14:16
G no offence in any thing, that 2Cor 6:3
but rather g of thanks .... Eph 5:4
G thanks always for all things .... Eph 5:20
with me as concerning g and .... Phil 4:15
G thanks unto the Father, which .... Col 1:12
g thanks to God and the Father by .... Col 3:17
g of thanks, be made for all men 1Ti 2:1
g heed to seducing spirits, and 1Ti 4:1
Not g heed to Jewish fables, and .... Titus 1:14
of our lips g thanks to his name .... Heb 13:15
g honour unto the wife, as unto 1Pet 3:7
g all diligence, add to your 2Pet 1:5
g themselves over to fornication,.... Jude 7

GIZONITE (ghi'-zo-nite) *A bodyguard of David.*
The sons of Hashem the G, ... 1Chr 11:34

GLAD
he will be g in his heart .... Ex 4:14
And the priest's heart was g .... Judg 18:20
and they were g 1Sa 11:9
g of heart for all the goodness 1Kin 8:66
people away into their tents, g 2Chr 7:10
that day joyful and with a g heart .... Est 5:9
city of Shushan rejoiced and was g .... Est 8:15
rejoice exceedingly, and are g .... Job 3:22
The righteous see it, and are g .... Job 22:19
I will be g and rejoice in thee .... Ps 9:2
rejoice, and Israel shall be g .... Ps 14:7
Therefore my heart is g, and my .... Ps 16:9
exceeding g with thy countenance .... Ps 21:6
I will be g and rejoice in thy .... Ps 31:7
Be g in the LORD, and rejoice, ye.... Ps 32:11
shall hear thereof, and be g .... Ps 34:2
Let them shout for joy, and be g .... Ps 35:27
seek thee rejoice and be g in thee .... Ps 40:16
whereby they have made thee g .... Ps 45:8
shall make g the city of God.... .... Ps 46:4
let the daughters of Judah be g .... Ps 48:11
rejoice, and Israel shall be g .... Ps 53:6
righteous shall be g in the LORD .... Ps 64:10
O let the nations be g and sing .... Ps 67:4
But let the righteous be g .... Ps 68:3
humble shall see this, and be g .... Ps 69:32
seek thee rejoice and be g in thee .... Ps 70:4
may rejoice and be g all our days .... Ps 90:14
Make us g according to the days .... Ps 90:15
hast made me g through thy work .... Ps 92:4
rejoice, and let the earth be g .... Ps 96:11
multitude of isles be g thereof .... Ps 97:1
Zion heard, and was g .... Ps 97:8
that maketh g the heart of man.... Ps 104:15
I will be g in the LORD .... Ps 104:34
Egypt was g when they departed .... Ps 105:38
Then are they g because they be .... Ps 107:30
the will rejoice and be g in it .... Ps 118:24
there will be g when they see me .... Ps 119:74
I was g when they said unto me, ... Ps 122:1
whereof we are g .... Ps 126:3
A wise son maketh a g father .... Prov 10:1
but a good word maketh it g .... Prov 12:25
A wise son maketh a g father .... Prov 15:20
he that is g at calamities shall.... Prov 17:5
father and thy mother shall be g .... Prov 23:25
heart be g when he stumbleth .... Prov 24:17
son, be wise, and make my heart g .... Prov 27:11
we will be g and rejoice in the, ... Song 1:4
have waited for him, we will be g .... Is 25:9
place shall be g for them .... Is 35:1
And Hezekiah was g of them .... Is 39:2
But be ye g and rejoice for ever .... Is 65:18
be g with her, all ye that love .... Is 66:10
making him very g .... Jer 20:15
were with him, then they were g .... Jer 41:13
Because ye were g, because ye, ... Jer 50:11
they are g that thou hast done it .... Lam 1:21
Rejoice and be g, O daughter of.... Lam 4:21
was the king exceeding g for him .... Dan 6:23
They make the king g with their.... Hos 7:3
be g and rejoice .... Joel 2:21
Be g then, ye children of Zion, ... Joel 2:23
was exceeding g of the gourd .... Jonah 4:6
therefore they rejoice and are g .... Hab 1:15
be g and rejoice with all the .... Zeph 3:14
children shall see it, and be g .... Zec 10:7
Rejoice, and be exceeding g .... Mt 5:12
when they heard it, they were g .... Mk 14:11
and to shew thee these g tidings .... Lk 1:19
shewing the g tidings of the .... Lk 8:1
we should make merry, and be g .... Lk 15:32
And they were g, and covenanted to .... Lk 23:8
saw Jesus, he was exceeding g .... Jn 8:56
and he saw it, and was g .... Jn 8:56
I am g for your sakes that I was .... Jn 11:15
Then were the disciples g .... Jn 20:20
heart, and my tongue was g .... Acts 2:26
had seen the grace of God, was g .... Acts 11:23
And we declare unto you g tidings.... Acts 13:32
Gentiles heard this, they were g .... Acts 13:48

bring g tidings of good things .... Rom 10:15
I am g therefore on your behalf .... Rom 16:19
I am g of the coming of Stephanas 1Cor 16:17
who is he then that maketh me g 2Cor 2:2
For we are g, when we are weak, ... 2Cor 13:9
ye may be g also with exceeding 1Pet 4:13
Let us be g and rejoice, and give .... Rev 19:7

GLADLY
did many things, and heard him g .... Mk 6:20
And the common people heard him g .... Mk 12:37
the people g received him .... Lk 8:40
Then they that g received his.... .... Acts 2:41
the brethren received us g .... Acts 21:17
For ye suffer fools g, seeing ye 2Cor 11:19
Most g therefore will I rather.... .... 2Cor 12:9
And I will very g spend and be 2Cor 12:15

GLADNESS
Also in the day of your g .... Num 10:10
and with g of heart, for the .... Deut 28:47
into the city of David with g 1Chr 16:27
strength and g are in his place 1Chr 16:27
the Lord on that day with great g 1Chr 29:22
And they sang praises with g 2Chr 29:30
bread seven days with great g 2Chr 30:21
they kept other seven days with g 2Chr 30:23
And there was very great g .... Neh 8:17
to keep the dedication with g .... Neh 12:27
The Jews had light, and g, and joy,.... Est 8:16
came, the Jews had joy and g .... Est 8:17
and made it a day of feasting and g .... Est 9:17
and made it a day of feasting and g .... Est 9:18
made it a day of feasting and g .... Est 9:19
Thou hast put g in my heart .... Ps 4:7
my sackcloth, and girded me with g .... Ps 30:11
the oil of g above thy fellows .... Ps 45:7
With g and rejoicing shall they be .... Ps 45:15
Make me to hear joy and g .... Ps 51:8
g for the upright in heart.... .... Ps 97:11
Serve the LORD with g .... Ps 100:2
with joy, and his chosen with g .... Ps 105:43
rejoice in the g of thy nation.... .... Ps 106:5
hope of the righteous shall be g .... Prov 10:28
in the day of the g of his heart .... Song 3:11
g is taken away, and joy out of.... .... Is 16:10
And behold joy and g, slaying oxen, ... Is 22:13
of heart, as when one goeth .... Is 30:29
they shall obtain joy and g .... Is 35:10
g shall be found therein, ... Is 51:3
they shall obtain g and joy .... Is 51:11
voice of mirth, and the voice of g .... Jer 7:34
voice of mirth, and the voice of g .... Jer 16:9
voice of mirth, and the voice of g .... Jer 25:10
Sing with g for Jacob, and shout.... .... Jer 31:7
voice of joy, and the voice of g .... Jer 33:11
g is taken from the plentiful.... .... Joel 1:16
g from the house of our God .... Joel 1:16
be to the house of Judah joy and g .... Zec 8:19
immediately receive it with g .... Mt 13:20
And thou shalt have joy and g .... Lk 1:14
house, did eat their meat with g .... Acts 2:46
she opened not the gate for g .... Acts 12:14
filling our hearts with food and g .... Acts 14:17
therefore in the Lord with all g .... Phil 2:29
the oil of g above thy fellows .... Heb 1:9

GLASS
strong, and as a molten looking g .... Job 37:18
For now we see through a g 1Cor 13:12
as in a g the glory of the Lord 2Cor 3:18
beholding his natural face in a g .... Jas 1:23
was a sea of glass unto crystal.... .... Rev 4:6
were a sea of a mingled with fire .... Rev 15:2
his name, stand on the sea of g.... .... Rev 15:2
was pure gold, like unto clear g .... Rev 21:18
gold, as it were transparent g .... Rev 21:21

GLASSES
The g, and the fine linen, and the.... .... Is 3:23

GLEAN
And thou shalt not g thy vineyard .... Lev 19:10
thou shalt not g it afterward.... .... Deut 24:21
g ears of corn after him in whose .... Ruth 2:2
And she said, I pray you, let me g .... Ruth 2:7
Go not to g in another field, ... Ruth 2:8
And when she was risen up to g .... Ruth 2:15
Let her g even among the sheaves, ... Ruth 2:15
leave them, that she may g them .... Ruth 2:16
g unto the end of barley harvest.... .... Ruth 2:23
They shall throughly g the .... Jer 6:9

GLEANED
they g of them in the highways,.... .... Judg 20:45
g in the field after the reapers.... .... Ruth 2:3
So she g in the field until even, ... Ruth 2:17
even, and beat out that she had g .... Ruth 2:17
mother in law saw what she had g .... Ruth 2:18
her, Where hast thou g to day .... Ruth 2:19

GLEANING
thou gather any g of thy harvest .... Lev 23:22
Is not the g of the grapes of.... .... Judg 8:2
Yet g grapes shall be left in it, ... Is 17:6
as the g grapes when the vintage.... .... Is 24:13
they not leave some g grapes .... Jer 49:9

GLEANINGS
thou gather the g of thy harvest .... Lev 19:9

GLEDE
And the g, and the kite, and the .... Deut 14:13

GLISTERING
g stones, and of divers colours,.... .... 1Chr 29:2
and his raiment was white and g .... Lk 9:29

GLITTER
it is furbished that it may g .... Eze 21:10

GLITTERING
If I whet my g sword, and mine.... .... Deut 32:41
the g sword cometh out of his .... Job 20:25
the g spear and the shield .... Job 39:23
to consume because of the g .... Eze 21:28
the bright sword and the g spear .... Nah 3:3
and at the shining of thy g spear .... Hab 3:11

GLOOMINESS
A day of darkness and of g .... Joel 2:2
a day of darkness and g, a day of.... .... Zeph 1:15

GLORIEST
Wherefore g thou in the valleys, ... Jer 49:4

GLORIED
But let him that g glory in this.... .... Jer 9:24
as it is written, He that g 1Cor 1:31
But he that g, let him glory in 2Cor 10:17

GLORIFIED
before all the people I will be g .... Lev 10:3
thou art g .... Is 26:15
Jacob, and g himself in Israel.... .... Is 44:23
O Israel, in whom I will be g .... Is 49:3
for he hath g thee .... Is 55:5
of Israel, because he hath g thee .... Is 60:9
work of my hands, that I may be g .... Is 60:21
of the LORD, that he might be g .... Is 61:3
sake, said, Let the LORD be g .... Is 66:5
I will be g in the midst of thee, ... Eze 28:22
renown the day that I shall be g .... Eze 39:13
are all thy ways, haat thou not g .... Dan 5:23
pleasure in it, and I will be g .... Hag 1:8
g God, which had given such power .... Mt 9:8
and they g the God of Israel .... Mt 15:31
g God, saying, We never saw it on .... Mk 2:12
their synagogues, being g of all.... .... Lk 4:15
were all amazed, and they g God.... .... Lk 5:26
and they g God, saying, That a.... .... Lk 7:16
she was made straight, and g God .... Lk 13:13
back, and with a loud voice g God .... Lk 17:15
to God, saying, Certainly this.... .... Lk 23:47
because that Jesus was not yet g .... Jn 7:39
the Son of God might be g thereby .... Jn 11:4
but when Jesus was g, then .... Jn 12:16
that the Son of man should be g .... Jn 12:23
heaven, saying, I have both g it.... .... Jn 12:28
said, Now is the Son of man g .... Jn 13:31
man g, and God is g in him .... Jn 13:31
If God be g in him, God shall.... .... Jn 13:32
the Father may be g in the Son.... .... Jn 14:13
Herein is my Father g, that ye .... Jn 15:8
I have g thee on the earth.... .... Jn 17:4
and I am g in them .... Jn 17:10
our fathers, hath g his Son Jesus .... Acts 3:13
for all men g God for that which .... Acts 4:21
g God, saying, Then hath God also .... Acts 11:18
glad, and g the word of the Lord .... Acts 13:48
they g the Lord, and said unto him .... Acts 21:20
they g him not as God, neither.... .... Rom 1:21
that we may be also g together.... .... Rom 8:17
whom he justified, them he also g .... Rom 8:30
And they g God in me .... Gal 1:24
shall come to be g in his saints.... .... 2Th 1:10
Lord Jesus Christ may be g in you,.... .... 2Th 1:12
may have free course, and be g 2Th 3:1
So also Christ g not himself to.... .... Heb 5:5
may be g through Jesus Christ.... .... 1Pet 4:11
of, but on your part he is g 1Pet 4:14
How much she hath g herself.... .... Rev 18:7

GLORIFIETH
Whoso offereth praise g me .... Ps 50:23

GLORIFY
all ye the seed of Jacob, g him .... Ps 22:23
deliver thee, and thou shalt g me .... Ps 50:15
and shall g thy name .... Ps 86:9
I will g thy name for evermore .... Ps 86:12
Wherefore g ye the LORD in the .... Is 24:15
shall the strong people g thee .... Is 25:3
will the house of thy glory.... .... Is 60:7
I will also g them, and they shall .... Jer 30:19
g your Father which is in heaven .... Mt 5:16
Father, g thy name .... Jn 12:28
glorified it, and will g it again.... .... Jn 12:28
God shall also g him in himself .... Jn 13:32
and shall straightway g him .... Jn 13:32
He shall g me .... Jn 16:14
the hour is come; g thy Son, ... Jn 17:1
that thy Son also may g thee .... Jn 17:1
g thou me with thine own self .... Jn 17:5
by what death he should g God.... .... Jn 21:19
with one mind and one mouth g God .... Rom 15:6
might g God for his mercy .... Rom 15:9
therefore g God in your body, and.... .... 1Cor 6:20
they g God for your profession.... .... 2Cor 9:13
g God in the day of visitation.... .... 1Pet 2:12
but let him g God on this behalf 1Pet 4:16
fear thee, O Lord, and g thy name .... Rev 15:4

GLORIFYING
And the shepherds returned, g .... Lk 2:20
returned to his own house, g God .... Lk 5:25
his sight, and followed him, g God .... Lk 18:43

GLORIOUS
O LORD, is become g in power .... Ex 15:6
g in holiness, fearful in praises.... .... Ex 15:11
thou that mayest fear this g .... Deut 28:58
How g was the king of Israel 2Sa 6:20

thank thee, and praise thy g name..... 1Chr 29:13
and blessed be thy g name, which..... Neh 9:5
the riches of his g kingdom .... Est 1:4
king's daughter is all g within .... Ps 45:13
make his praise g .... Ps 66:2
And blessed be his g name for ever....... Ps 72:19
Thou art more g and excellent than .... Ps 76:4
G things are spoken of thee, O................. Ps 87:3
His work is honourable and g .... Ps 111:3
I will speak of the g honour of .... Ps 145:5
the g majesty of his kingdom .... Ps 145:12
of the LORD be beautiful and g .... Is 4:2
and his rest shall be g .... Is 11:10
he shall be for a g throne to his......... Is 22:23
whose g beauty is a fading flower .... Is 28:1
the g beauty, which is on the .... Is 28:4
cause his g voice to be heard................ Is 30:30
But there the g LORD will be unto .... Is 33:21
yet shall I be g in the eyes of .... Is 49:5
will make the place of my feet g .... Is 60:13
this that is g in his apparel.................... Is 63:1
hand of Moses with his g arm .... Is 63:12
people, to make thyself a g name .... Is 63:14
A g high throne from the .... Jer 17:12
made very g in the midst of the .... Eze 27:25
and he shall stand in the g land .... Dan 11:16
shall enter also into the g land............ Dan 11:41
the seas in the g holy mountain .... Dan 11:45
a things that were done by him .... Lk 13:17
g liberty of the children of God .... Rom 8:21
and engraven in stones, was g 2Cor 3:7
of the spirit be rather g 2Cor 3:8
g had no glory in this respect................. 2Cor 3:10
if that which is done away was g 2Cor 3:11
that which remaineth is g 2Cor 3:11
light of the g gospel of Christ 2Cor 4:4
present it to himself a g church.............. Eph 5:27
be fashioned like unto his g body......... Phil 3:21
might, according to his g power.............. Col 1:11
According to the g gospel of the 1Ti 1:11
the g appearing of the great God........... Titus 2:13

hath g gotten all this g .... Gen 31:1
my father of all my g in Egypt.............. Gen 45:13
said unto Pharaoh, G over me .... Ex 8:9
ye shall see the g of the LORD .... Ex 16:7
the g of the LORD appeared in the .... Ex 16:10
the g of the LORD abode upon................ Ex 24:16
the sight of the g of the LORD .... Ex 24:17
for Aaron thy brother for g .... Ex 28:2
shalt thou make for them, for g .... Ex 28:40
shall be sanctified by my g .... Ex 29:43
I beseech thee, shew me thy g .... Ex 33:18
while my g passeth by, that I................. Ex 33:22
the g of the LORD filled the.................... Ex 40:34
the g of the LORD filled the.................... Ex 40:35
the g of the LORD shall appear .... Lev 9:6
the g of the LORD appeared unto .... Lev 9:23
the g of the LORD appeared in the .... Num 14:10
be filled with the g of the LORD........... Num 14:21
those men which have seen my g .... Num 14:22
the g of the LORD appeared unto .... Num 16:19
LORD our God hath shewed us his g .... Num 16:42
the g of the LORD appeared unto .... Num 20:6
LORD our God hath shewed us his g .... Deut 5:24
His g is like the firstling of .... Deut 33:17
g to the LORD God of Israel, and .... Josh 7:19
make them inherit the throne of g 1Sa 2:8
The g is departed from Israel 1Sa 4:21
The g is departed from Israel 1Sa 4:22
ye shall give g unto the God of 1Sa 6:5
for the g of the LORD had filled 1Kin 8:11
g of this, and tarry at home.................... 2Kin 14:10
G ye in his holy name 1Chr 16:10
Declare his g among the heathen 1Chr 16:24
G and honour are in his presence 1Chr 16:27
the people, give unto the LORD g 1Chr 16:28
the LORD the g due unto his name 1Chr 16:29
the holy name, and g in thy praise....... 1Chr 16:35
of a throughout all countries 1Chr 22:5
greatness, and the power, and the g..... 1Chr 29:11
for the g of the LORD had filled 2Chr 5:14
the g of the LORD filled the.................... 2Chr 7:1
because the g of the LORD had 2Chr 7:2
the g of the LORD upon the house,........ 2Chr 7:3
told them of the g of his riches............... Est 5:11
He hath stripped me of my g .... Job 19:9
My g was fresh in me, and my bow....... Job 29:20
the g of his nostrils is terrible.............. Job 39:20
and array thyself with g and beauty...... Job 40:10
my g, and the lifter up of mine .... Ps 3:3
long will ye turn my g into shame .... Ps 4:2
who hast set thy g above the .... Ps 8:5
and hast crowned him with g .... Ps 8:5
heart is glad, and my g rejoiceth .... Ps 16:9
The heavens declare the g of God.......... Ps 19:1
His g is great in thy salvation.............. Ps 21:5
the King of g shall come in .... Ps 24:7
Who is this King of g .... Ps 24:8
the King of g shall come in .... Ps 24:9
Who is this King of g .... Ps 24:10
of hosts, he is the King of g .... Ps 24:10
O ye mighty, give unto the LORD g ...... Ps 29:1
the LORD the g due unto his name .... Ps 29:2
the God of g thundereth .... Ps 29:3

doth every one speak of his g .... Ps 29:9
To the end that my g may sing .... Ps 30:12
thigh, O most mighty, with thy g .... Ps 45:3
when the g of his house is...................... Ps 49:16
his g shall not descend after him .... Ps 49:17
let thy g be above all the earth .... Ps 57:5
Awake up, my g .... Ps 57:8
let thy g be above all the earth .... Ps 57:11
In God is my salvation and my g .... Ps 62:7
To see thy power and thy g .... Ps 63:2
that one sweareth by him shall g .... Ps 63:11
all the upright in heart shall g .... Ps 64:10
whole earth be filled with his g .... Ps 72:19
and afterward receive me to g .... Ps 73:24
his g into the enemy's hand .... Ps 78:61
salvation, for the g of thy name .... Ps 79:9
the LORD will give grace and g .... Ps 84:11
that g may dwell in our land .... Ps 85:9
For thou art the g of their .... Ps 89:17
Thou hast made his g to cease .... Ps 89:44
the g unto their children .... Ps 90:16
Declare his g among the heathen,.......... Ps 96:3
the people, give unto the LORD g .... Ps 96:7
the LORD the g due unto his name .... Ps 96:8
and all the people see his g .... Ps 97:6
all the kings of the earth thy g........... Ps 102:15
up Zion, he shall appear in his g .... Ps 102:16
The g of the LORD shall endure .... Ps 104:31
G ye in his holy name............................ Ps 105:3
nation, that I may g with thine........... Ps 106:5
Thus they changed their g into .... Ps 106:20
and give praise, even with my g .... Ps 108:1
thy g above all the earth...................... Ps 108:5
and his g above the heavens .... Ps 113:4
unto us, but unto thy name give g ...... Ps 115:1
for great is the g of the LORD .... Ps 138:5
speak of the g of thy kingdom .... Ps 145:11
his g is above the earth and .... Ps 148:13
Let the saints be joyful in g .... Ps 149:5
The wise shall inherit g .... Prov 3:35
a crown of g shall she deliver to........... Prov 4:9
The hoary head is a crown of g........... Prov 16:31
the g of children are their .... Prov 17:6
it is his g to pass over a .... Prov 19:11
The g of young men is their .... Prov 20:29
It is the g of God to conceal a .... Prov 25:2
search their own g is not g .... Prov 25:27
men do rejoice, there is great g .... Prov 28:12
LORD, and for the g of his majesty .... Is 2:10
for the g of his majesty, when he.......... Is 2:19
for the g of his majesty, when he........... Is 2:21
to provoke the eyes of his g .... Is 3:8
for upon all the g shall be a .... Is 4:5
and their g, and their multitude,........... Is 5:14
the whole earth is full of his g .... Is 6:3
the king of Assyria, and all his g .... Is 8:7
and where will ye leave your g .... Is 10:3
and the g of his high looks.................... Is 10:12
under his g he shall kindle a .... Is 10:16
shall consume the g of his forest.......... Is 10:18
the g of kingdoms, the beauty of.......... Is 13:19
even all of them, lie in g .... Is 14:18
the g of Moab shall be contemned,....... Is 16:14
they shall be as the g of the .... Is 17:3
that the g of Jacob shall be made.......... Is 17:4
expectation, and of Egypt their g .... Is 20:5
all the g of Kedar shall............................ Is 21:16
thy g shall be the shame of thy .... Is 22:18
all the g of his father's house................ Is 22:24
it, to stain the pride of all g .... Is 23:9
songs, even g to the righteous................ Is 24:16
LORD of hosts be for a crown of g .... Is 28:5
the g of Lebanon shall be given .... Is 35:2
they shall see the g of the LORD .... Is 35:2
the g of the LORD shall be........................ Is 40:5
shalt g in the Holy One of Israel .... Is 41:16
my g will I not give to another,........... Is 42:8
for I have created him for my g .... Is 43:7
Israel be justified, and shall g .... Is 45:25
salvation in Zion for Israel my g .... Is 46:13
I will not give my g unto another .... Is 48:11
the g of the LORD shall be thy .... Is 58:8
his g from the rising of the sun............. Is 59:19
the g of the LORD is risen upon .... Is 60:1
shall he seen upon thee .... Is 60:2
I will glorify the house of my g .... Is 60:7
The g of Lebanon shall come unto....... Is 60:13
light, and thy God thy g .... Is 60:19
and thy g be thy boast............................. Is 61:6
righteousness, and all kings thy g .... Is 62:2
of g in the hand of thy God .... Is 62:3
of thy holiness and of thy g .... Is 63:15
with the abundance of her g .... Is 66:11
the g of the Gentiles like a .... Is 66:11
and they shall come, and see my g....... Is 66:18
my fame, neither have seen my g .... Is 66:19
declare my g among the Gentiles.......... Is 66:19
my people have changed their g .... Jer 2:11
in him, and in him shall they g .... Jer 4:2
nor the wise man g in his wisdom........ Jer 9:23
let the mighty man g in his might........ Jer 9:23
not the rich man g in his riches........... Jer 9:23
let him that glorieth g in this .... Jer 9:24
and for a praise, and for a g .... Jer 13:11
Give g to the LORD your God,.............. Jer 13:16
down, even the crown of your g .... Jer 13:18
not disgrace the throne of thy g .... Jer 14:21
Ah lord! or, Ah his g! .... Jer 22:18
Dibon, come down from thy g .... Jer 48:18

the likeness of the g of the LORD .... Eze 1:28
Blessed be the g of the LORD from .... Eze 3:12
the g of the LORD stood there, as......... Eze 3:23
as the g which I saw by the river .... Eze 3:23
the g of the God of Israel was .... Eze 8:4
the g of the God of Israel was .... Eze 9:3
Then the g of the God of Israel .... Eze 10:4
of the brightness of the LORD's g .... Eze 10:4
Then the g of the LORD departed .... Eze 10:18
the g of the God of Israel was .... Eze 10:19
the g of the God of Israel was .... Eze 11:22
the g of the LORD went up from .... Eze 11:23
which is the g of all lands .... Eze 20:6
which is the g of all lands .... Eze 20:15
strength, the joy of their g .... Eze 24:25
frontiers, the g of the country............... Eze 25:9
I shall set g in the land of the .... Eze 26:20
To whom art thou thus like in g .... Eze 31:18
I will set my g among the heathen ...... Eze 39:21
the g of the God of Israel came........... Eze 43:2
and the earth shined with his g .... Eze 43:2
the g of the LORD came into the.......... Eze 43:4
the g of the LORD filled the .... Eze 43:5
the g of the LORD filled the .... Eze 44:4
kingdom, power, and strength, and g... Dan 2:37
for the g of my kingdom, mine .... Dan 4:36
father a kingdom and majesty, and g... Dan 5:18
and they took his g from him .... Dan 5:20
was given him dominion, and g .... Dan 7:14
of taxes in the g of the kingdom .... Dan 11:20
acknowledge and increase with g....... Dan 11:39
will I change their g into shame .... Hos 4:7
their g shall fly away like a.................. Hos 9:11
rejoiced on it, for the g thereof .... Hos 10:5
come unto Adullam the g of Israel...... Mic 1:15
have ye taken away my g for ever .... Mic 2:9
g out of all the pleasant .... Nah 2:9
knowledge of the g of the LORD......... Hab 2:14
Thou art filled with shame for g .... Hab 2:16
spewing shall be on thy g .... Hab 2:16
His g covered the heavens, and the ...... Hab 3:3
saw this house in her first g .... Hag 2:3
and I will fill this house with g .... Hag 2:7
The g of this latter house shall .... Hag 2:9
will be the g in the midst of her .... Zec 2:5
for their g is spoiled.............................. Zec 2:8
and he shall bear the g, and shall ...... Zec 6:13
that the g of the house of David .... Zec 12:7
the g of the inhabitants of .... Zec 12:7
to give g unto my name, saith the ...... Mal 2:2
of the world, and the g of them .... Mt 4:8
that they may have a g of men .... Mt 6:2
kingdom, and the power, and the g ...... Mt 6:13
his g was not arrayed like one of .... Mt 6:29
Son of man shall come in the g of....... Mt 16:27
shall sit in the throne of his g............. Mt 19:28
of heaven with power and great g .... Mt 24:30
Son of man shall come in his g .... Mt 25:31
he sit upon the throne of his g .... Mt 25:31
when he cometh in the g of his........... Mk 8:38
other on thy left hand, in thy g .... Mk 10:37
the clouds with great power and g ..... Mk 13:26
the g of the LORD shone round............. Lk 2:9
G to God in the highest, and on .... Lk 2:14
the g of thy people Israel .... Lk 2:32
I give thee, and the g of them................ Lk 4:6
when he shall come in his own g .... Lk 9:26
Who appeared in g, and spake of .... Lk 9:31
they were awake, they saw his g .... Lk 9:32
that Solomon in all his g was not....... Lk 12:27
that returned to give g to God .... Lk 17:18
in heaven, and g in the highest .... Lk 19:38
in a cloud with power and great g ...... Lk 21:27
things, and to enter into his g .... Lk 24:26
among us, (and we beheld his g .... Jn 1:14
the g as of the only begotten of........... Jn 1:14
and manifested forth his g .... Jn 2:11
of himself seeketh his own g .... Jn 7:18
that seeketh his g that sent him........... Jn 7:18
And I seek not mine own g .... Jn 8:50
unto death, but for the g of God .... Jn 11:4
thou shouldest see the g of God .... Jn 11:40
said Esaias, when he saw his g .... Jn 12:41
g which I had with thee before .... Jn 17:5
the g which thou gavest me I have ..... Jn 17:22
that they may behold my g .... Jn 17:24
The God of g appeared unto our......... Acts 7:2
into heaven, and saw the g of God..... Acts 7:55
because he gave not God the g .... Acts 12:23
not see for the g of that light .... Acts 22:11
And changed the g of the .... Rom 1:23
in well doing seek for g and .... Rom 2:7
But g, honour, and peace, to every ...... Rom 2:10
through my lie unto his g .... Rom 3:7
and come short of the g of God .... Rom 3:23
by works, he hath whereof to g .... Rom 4:2
strong in faith, giving g to God .... Rom 4:20
rejoice in hope of the g of God .... Rom 5:2
but we g in tribulations also .... Rom 5:3
the dead by the g of the Father .... Rom 6:4
g which shall be revealed in us........... Rom 8:18
pertaineth the adoption, and the g...... Rom 9:4
of his g on the vessels of mercy......... Rom 9:23
he had afore prepared unto g .... Rom 9:23
to whom be g for ever .... Rom 11:36
also received us to the g of God .... Rom 15:7
g through Jesus Christ in those.......... Rom 15:17
be g through Jesus Christ for .... Rom 16:27
no flesh should g in his presence...... 1Cor 1:29

glorieth, let him g in the Lord 1Cor 1:31
before the world unto our g 1Cor 2:7
not have crucified the Lord of g 1Cor 2:8
Therefore let no man g in men 1Cor 3:21
didst receive it, why dost thou g 1Cor 4:7
gospel, I have nothing to g of 1Cor 9:16
ye do, do all to the g of God 1Cor 10:31
as he is the image and g of God 1Cor 11:7
but the woman is the g of the man 1Cor 11:7
have long hair, it is a g to her 1Cor 11:15
but the g of the celestial is one 1Cor 15:40
the g of the terrestrial is 1Cor 15:40
There is one g of the sun 1Cor 15:41
another g of the moon 1Cor 15:41
and another g of the stars 1Cor 15:41
differeth from another star in g 1Cor 15:41
it is raised in g 1Cor 15:43
him Amen, unto the g of God by us 2Cor 1:20
for the g of his countenance 2Cor 3:7
which g was to be done away 2Cor 3:7
ministration of condemnation be g 2Cor 3:9
of righteousness exceed in g 2Cor 3:9
glorious had no g in this respect 2Cor 3:10
by reason of the g that excelleth 2Cor 3:10
as in a glass the g of the Lord 2Cor 3:18
the same image from g to g 2Cor 3:18
the g of God in the face of Jesus 2Cor 4:6
of many redound to the g of God 2Cor 4:15
exceeding and eternal weight of g 2Cor 4:17
you occasion to g on our behalf 2Cor 5:12
answer them which g in appearance 2Cor 5:12
by us to the g of the same Lord 2Cor 8:19
the churches, and the g of Christ 2Cor 8:23
glorieth, let him g in the Lord 2Cor 10:17
that wherein they g, they may be 2Cor 11:12
g after the flesh, I will g also 2Cor 11:18
If I must needs g, I will g 2Cor 11:30
expedient for me doubtless to g 2Cor 12:1
Of such an one will I g 2Cor 12:5
yet of myself I will not g 2Cor 12:5
For though I would desire to g 2Cor 12:6
will I rather g in my infirmities 2Cor 12:9
to be known of g for ever and ever .... Gal 1:5
Let us not be desirous of vain g .... Gal 5:26
that they may g in your flesh .... Gal 6:13
But God forbid that I should g .... Gal 6:14
the praise of the g of his grace .... Eph 1:6
should be to the praise of his g .... Eph 1:12
unto the praise of his g .... Eph 1:14
Jesus Christ, the Father of g .... Eph 1:17
what the riches of the g of his .... Eph 1:18
for you, which is your g .... Eph 3:13
according to the riches of his g .... Eph 3:16
Unto him be g in the church by .... Eph 3:21
are by Jesus Christ, unto the g .... Phil 1:11
to the g of God the Father .... Phil 2:11
whose g is in their shame, who .... Phil 3:19
his riches in g by Christ Jesus .... Phil 4:19
God and our Father be g for ever .... Phil 4:20
the g of this mystery among the .... Col 1:27
is Christ in you, the hope of g .... Col 1:27
ye also appear with him in g .... Col 3:4
Nor of men sought we g, neither 1Th 2:6
called you unto his kingdom and g 1Th 2:12
For ye are our g and joy 1Th 2:20
So that we ourselves g in you in 2Th 1:4
Lord, and from the g of his power 2Th 1:9
to the obtaining of the g of our 2Th 2:14
be honour and g for ever and ever 1Ti 1:17
in the world, received up into g 1Ti 3:16
is in Christ Jesus with eternal g 2Ti 2:10
to whom be g for ever and ever 2Ti 4:18
Who being the brightness of his g .... Heb 1:3
thou crownedst him with g .... Heb 2:7
of death, crowned with g and .... Heb 2:9
in bringing many sons unto g .... Heb 2:10
worthy of more g than Moses .... Heb 3:3
of g shadowing the mercyseat .... Heb 9:5
to whom be g for ever and ever .... Heb 13:21
Lord Jesus Christ, the Lord of g .... Jas 2:1
g not, and lie not against the .... Jas 3:14
g at the appearing of Jesus 1Pet 1:7
with joy unspeakable and full of g 1Pet 1:8
and the g that should follow 1Pet 1:11
up from the dead, and gave him g 1Pet 1:21
all the g of man as the flower of 1Pet 1:24
For what g is it, if, when ye 1Pet 2:20
when his g shall be revealed, ye 1Pet 4:13
for the spirit of g and of God 1Pet 4:14
of the g that shall be revealed 1Pet 5:1
a crown of g that fadeth not away 1Pet 5:4
his eternal g by Christ Jesus 1Pet 5:10
To him be g and dominion for ever 1Pet 5:11
of him that hath called us to g 2Pet 1:3
from God the Father honour and g 2Pet 1:17
voice to him from the excellent g 2Pet 1:17
To him be g both now and for ever 2Pet 3:18
of his g with exceeding joy .... Jude 24
only wise God our Saviour, be g .... Jude 25
to him be g and dominion for ever .... Rev 1:6
And when those beasts give g .... Rev 4:9
art worthy, O Lord, to receive g .... Rev 4:11
and strength, and honour, and g .... Rev 5:12
saying, Blessing, and honour, and g .... Rev 5:13
Blessing, and g, and wisdom, and .... Rev 7:12
gave g to the God of heaven .... Rev 11:13
voice, Fear God, and give g to him .... Rev 14:7
with smoke from the g of God .... Rev 15:8
they repented not to give him g .... Rev 16:9
earth was lightened with his g .... Rev 18:1

Salvation, and g, and honour, and .... Rev 19:1
Having the g of God .... Rev 21:11
for the g of God did lighten it, ... Rev 21:23
of the earth do bring their g .... Rev 21:24
And they shall bring the g .... Rev 21:26

GLORYING
Your g is not good 1Cor 5:6
any man should make my g void 1Cor 9:15
toward you, great is my g of you 2Cor 7:4
I am become a fool in g 2Cor 12:11

GLUTTON
is g, and a drunkard .... Deut 21:20
the g shall come to poverty .... Prov 23:21

GLUTTONOUS
and say, Behold a man g .... Mt 11:19
and ye say, Behold a g man .... Lk 7:34

GNASH
he shall g with his teeth, and .... Ps 112:10
thy hiss and the g the teeth .... Lam 2:16

GNASHED
they g upon me with their teeth .... Ps 35:16
they g on him with their teeth .... Acts 7:54

GNASHETH
he g upon me with his teeth .... Job 16:9
g upon him with his teeth .... Ps 37:12
g with his teeth, and pineth away .... Mk 9:18

GNASHING
shall be weeping and g of teeth .... Mt 8:12
shall be weeping and g of teeth .... Mt 13:42
shall be wailing and g of teeth .... Mt 13:50
shall be weeping and g of teeth .... Mt 22:13
shall be weeping and g of teeth .... Mt 24:51
shall be weeping and g of teeth .... Mt 25:30
of teeth, when ye shall hear .... Lk 13:28

GNAT
blind guides, which strain at a g .... Mt 23:24

GNAW
they g not the bones till the .... Zeph 3:3

GNAWED
they g their tongues for pain, ... Rev 16:10

GO See PREFACE.

GOAD
six hundred men with an ox g .... Judg 3:31

GOADS
for the axes, and to sharpen the g 1Sa 13:21
The words of the wise are as g .... Eccl 12:11

GOAH See GOATH.

GOAT
a she g of three years old, and a .... Gen 15:9
And if his offering be a g .... Lev 4:24
his hand upon the head of the g .... Lev 4:24
fat, of ox, or of sheep, or of g .... Lev 7:23
people's offering, and took the g .... Lev 9:15
sought the g of the sin offering .... Lev 10:16
Aaron shall bring the g upon .... Lev 16:9
But the g, on which the lot fell .... Lev 16:10
he kill the g of the sin offering .... Lev 16:15
bullock, and the blood of the g .... Lev 16:18
altar, he shall bring the live g .... Lev 16:20
hands upon the head of the live g .... Lev 16:21
them upon the head of the g .... Lev 16:21
the g shall bear upon him all .... Lev 16:22
let go the g in the wilderness .... Lev 16:22
he that let go the g for the .... Lev 16:26
the g for the sin offering, whose .... Lev 17:3
that killeth an ox, or lamb, or g .... Lev 17:3
a bullock, or a sheep, or a g .... Lev 22:27
then he shall bring a she g of .... Num 15:27
a sheep, the firstling of a g .... Num 18:17
one g for a sin offering, to make .... Num 28:22
And one g for a sin offering .... Num 28:30
And one g for a sin offering .... Num 29:28
And one g for a sin offering .... Num 29:31
And one g for a sin offering .... Num 29:34
And one g for a sin offering .... Num 29:38
the ox, the sheep, and the g .... Deut 14:4
and the fallow deer, and the wild g .... Deut 14:5
an he g also .... Prov 30:31
every day a g for a sin offering .... Eze 43:25
an he g came from the west on the .... Dan 8:5
the g had a notable horn between .... Dan 8:5
the he g waxed very great .... Dan 8:8
the rough g is the king of Grecia .... Dan 8:21

GOATH (go'-ath) A place near Jerusalem.
and shall compass about to G .... Jer 31:39

GOATS
thence two kids of the g .... Gen 27:9
the kids of the g upon his hands .... Gen 27:16
spotted and speckled among the g .... Gen 30:32
speckled and spotted among the g .... Gen 30:33
the he g that were ringstraked, ... Gen 30:35
all the she g that were speckled .... Gen 31:38
thy she g have not cast their .... Gen 31:38
Two hundred she g .... Gen 32:14
and twenty he g .... Gen 32:14
coat, and killed a kid of the g .... Gen 37:31
out from the sheep, or from the g .... Ex 12:5
namely, the sheep, or the g of the .... Lev 1:10
his offering, a kid of the g .... Lev 4:23
his offering, a kid of the g .... Lev 4:28
flock, a lamb or a kid of the g .... Lev 5:6

a kid of the g for a sin offering .... Lev 9:3
one kid of the g for a sin offering .... Lev 16:5
And he shall take the two g .... Lev 16:7
shall cast lots upon the two g .... Lev 16:7
beeves, of the sheep, or of the g .... Lev 22:19
kid of the g for a sin offering .... Lev 23:19
Enoch of the g for a sin offering .... Num 7:16
two oxen, five rams, five he g .... Num 7:17
One kid of the g for a sin .... Num 7:22
two oxen, five rams, five he g .... Num 7:23
One kid of the g for a sin .... Num 7:28
two oxen, five rams, five he g .... Num 7:29
One kid of the g for a sin .... Num 7:34
two oxen, five rams, five he g .... Num 7:35
One kid of the g for a sin .... Num 7:40
two oxen, five rams, five he g .... Num 7:41
One kid of the g for a sin .... Num 7:46
two oxen, five rams, five he g .... Num 7:47
One kid of the g for a sin .... Num 7:52
two oxen, five rams, five he g .... Num 7:53
One kid of the g for a sin .... Num 7:58
two oxen, five rams, five he g .... Num 7:59
One kid of the g for a sin .... Num 7:64
two oxen, five rams, five he g .... Num 7:65
One kid of the g for a sin .... Num 7:70
two oxen, five rams, five he g .... Num 7:71
One kid of the g for a sin .... Num 7:76
two oxen, five rams, five he g .... Num 7:77
One kid of the g for a sin .... Num 7:82
two oxen, five rams, five he g .... Num 7:83
One kid of the g for a sin .... Num 7:87
the kids of the g for sin .... Num 7:88
the rams sixty, the he g sixty .... Num 15:24
one kid of the g for a sin .... Num 28:15
And one kid of the g, to make an .... Num 28:30
one kid of the g for a sin .... Num 29:5
One kid of the g for a sin .... Num 29:11
one kid of the g for a sin .... Num 29:16
One kid of the g for a sin .... Num 29:19
one kid of the g for a sin .... Num 29:25
rams of the breed of Bashan, and g .... Deut 32:14
men upon the rocks of the wild g 1Sa 24:2
thousand sheep, and a thousand g 1Sa 25:2
thousand and seven hundred he g 2Chr 17:11
and seven lambs, and seven he g 2Chr 29:21
they brought forth the he g for 2Chr 29:21
for all Israel, twelve he g .... Ezr 6:17
twelve he g for a sin offering .... Ezr 8:35
wild g of the rock bring forth .... Job 39:1
nor he g out of thy folds .... Ps 50:9
of bulls, or drink the blood of g .... Ps 50:13
I will offer bullocks with g .... Ps 66:15
hills are a refuge for the wild g .... Ps 104:18
the g are the price of the field .... Prov 27:26
thy hair is as a flock of g .... Song 4:1
of g that appear from Gilead .... Song 6:5
bullocks, or of lambs, or of he g .... Is 1:11
and with the blood of lambs and g .... Is 34:6
be as the g before the flocks .... Jer 50:8
slaughter, like rams with he g .... Jer 51:40
with thee in lambs, and rams, and g .... Eze 27:21
between the rams and the he g .... Eze 34:17
earth, of rams, of lambs, and of g .... Eze 39:18
the g without blemish for a sin .... Eze 43:22
a kid of the g daily for a sin .... Eze 43:25
shepherds, and I punished the g .... Zec 10:3
divideth his sheep from the g .... Mt 25:32
right hand, but the g on the left .... Mt 25:33
Neither by the blood of g .... Heb 9:12
For if the blood of bulls and of g .... Heb 9:13
took the blood of calves and of g .... Heb 9:19
of g should take away sins .... Heb 10:4

GOATS'
and fine linen, and g hair, ... Ex 25:4
thou shalt make curtains of g .... Ex 26:7
and fine linen, and g hair, ... Ex 35:6
g hair, and red skins of rams, ... Ex 35:23
them up in wisdom spun g hair .... Ex 35:26
he made curtains of g hair for .... Ex 36:14
of skins, and all work of g hair: .... Num 31:20
put a pillow of g hair for his 1Sa 19:13
with a pillow of g hair for his 1Sa 19:16
thou shalt have g milk enough for .... Prov 27:27

GOATSKINS
wandered about in sheepskins and g .... Heb 11:37

GOB (gob) A place where David battled the Philistines.
battle with the Philistines at G 2Sa 21:18
battle in G with the Philistines 2Sa 21:19

GOBLET
Thy navel is like a round g .... Song 7:2

GOD (god) See PREFACE. See also GODDESS, GODHEAD, GOD'S, GODS, GOD-WARD. Creator and Ruler of the world, Israel, and the church.
G called the dry land Earth .... Gen 1:10
and G saw that it was good .... Gen 1:10
Enoch walked with G after he .... Gen 5:22
And Enoch walked with G .... Gen 5:24
for G took him .... Gen 5:24
spake unto her, Thou G seest me .... Gen 16:13
G said unto Moses, I AM THAT I AM .... Ex 3:14
G is not a man, that he should .... Num 23:19
For the LORD thy G is a consuming .... Deut 4:24
Ye shall not G our G is one LORD .... Deut 6:4
The LORD our G is one LORD .... Deut 6:4
the LORD thy G with all thine heart .... Deut 6:5
the LORD your G is G of gods .... Deut 10:17
The eternal G is thy refuge, and .... Deut 33:27

For who is G, save the LORD 2Sa 22:32
and who is a rock, save our G 2Sa 22:32
if the LORD be G, follow him 1Kin 18:21
they said, The LORD is, he is the G..... 1Kin 18:39
O LORD G of Israel, which................ 2Kin 19:15
O LORD G of our fathers 2Chr 20:6
art not thou G in heaven 2Chr 20:6
And thou sayest, How doth G know... Job 22:13
said in his heart, There is no G .... Ps 14:1
For who is G save the LORD.............. Ps 18:31
or who is a rock save our G.............. Ps 18:31
heavens declare the glory of G.......... Ps 19:1
My G, my G, why hast thou .... Ps 22:1
My soul thirsteth for G .... Ps 42:2
for the living G............................ Ps 42:2
G is our refuge and strength, a .... Ps 46:1
Be still, and know that I am G........... Ps 46:10
Create in me a clean heart, O G .... Ps 51:10
said in his heart, There is no G .... Ps 53:1
In G I will praise his word................ Ps 56:4
in G I have put my trust................. Ps 56:4
Blessed be G, which hath not .... Ps 66:20
a doorkeeper in the house of my G .... Ps 84:10
to everlasting, thou art G .... Ps 90:2
For the LORD is a great G .... Ps 95:3
Know ye that the LORD he is G.......... Ps 100:3
the courts of the house of our G........ Ps 135:2
O give thanks unto the G of gods ...... Ps 136:2
Search me, O G, and know my heart... Ps 139:23
that people, whose G is the LORD ...... Ps 144:15
hath the G of Jacob for his help .... Ps 146:5
whose hope is in the LORD his G........ Ps 146:5
and take the name of my G in vain .... Prov 30:9
hasty to utter any thing before G ...... Eccl 5:2
Fear G, and keep his commandments .. Eccl 12:13
Behold, G is my salvation .... Is 12:2
for I am thy G.............................. Is 41:10
and beside me there is no G............ Is 44:6
for I am G, and there is none else ...... Is 45:22
Spirit of the Lord G is upon me.......... Is 61:1
Let us now fear the LORD our G .... Jer 5:24
and will be their G, and they shall ..... Jer 31:33
I am the LORD your G...................... Eze 20:19
know that I am the LORD your G......... Eze 20:20
for I am G, and not man .... Hos 11:9
arise, call upon thy G..................... Jonah 1:6
and to walk humbly with thy G .... Mic 6:8
Will a man rob G........................... Mal 3:8
being interpreted is, G with us .... Mt 1:23
Ye cannot serve G and mammon .... Mt 6:24
is none good but one, that is, G......... Mt 19:17
I am the G of Abraham .... Mt 22:32
the Lord thy G with all thy heart....... Mt 22:37
that is to say, My G, my G .... Mt 27:46
for there is one G.......................... Mk 12:32
being interpreted, My G, my G .... Mk 15:34
For with G nothing shall be .... Lk 1:37
Glory to G in the highest, and on ...... Lk 2:14
the Lord thy G with all thy heart....... Lk 10:27
Ye cannot serve G and mammon .... Lk 16:13
all, Art thou then the Son of G .... Lk 22:70
was with G, and the Word was G........ Jn 1:1
G is a Spirit .... Jn 4:24
we have one Father, even G .... Jn 8:41
ask of G, G will give it thee .... Jn 4:10
ye believe in G, believe also in .... Jn 11:22
might know thee the only true G .... Jn 17:3
and said unto him, My Lord and my G . Jn 20:28
ought to obey G rather than men....... Acts 5:29
heaven, and saw the glory of G......... Acts 7:55
standing on the right hand of G .... Acts 7:55
because he gave not G the glory .... Acts 12:23
inscription, TO THE UNKNOWN G ..... Acts 17:23
because the love of G is shed .... Rom 5:5
But G commendeth his love toward .... Rom 5:8
G forbid. How shall we .... Rom 6:2
but the gift of G is eternal life .... Rom 6:23
as are led by the Spirit of G .... Rom 8:14
they are the sons of G.................... Rom 8:14
If G be for us, who can be .... Rom 8:31
give account of himself to G .... Rom 14:12
But to us there is but one G 1Cor 8:6
him, that G may be all in all 1Cor 15:28
Blessed be G, even the Father of 2Cor 1:3
mercies, and the G of all comfort....... 2Cor 1:3
For we are unto G a sweet savour 2Cor 2:15
we have a building of G, an.............. 2Cor 5:1
that G was in Christ, reconciling........ 2Cor 5:19
for G loveth a cheerful giver 2Cor 9:7
Thanks be unto G for his 2Cor 9:15
G is not mocked............................ Gal 6:7
For it is G which worketh in you .... Phil 2:13
But my G shall supply all your .... Phil 4:19
let the peace of G rule in your .... Col 3:15
not as pleasing men, but G 1Th 2:4
and one mediator between G 1Ti 2:5
G was manifest in the flesh,............. 1Ti 3:16
glorious appearing of the great G...... Titus 2:13
therefore, G, even thy G .... Heb 1:9
but he that built all things is G .... Heb 3:4
not ashamed to be called their G....... Heb 11:16
For our G is a consuming fire............ Heb 12:29
believest that there is one G............ Jas 2:19
that G is light, and in him is no 1Jn 1:5
is born of G doth not commit sin 1Jn 3:9
sin, because he is born of G 1Jn 3:9
the children of G are manifest 1Jn 3:10
not righteousness is not of G 1Jn 3:10
for love is of G............................. 1Jn 4:7
because that G sent his only 1Jn 4:9

No man hath seen G at any time 1Jn 4:12
G is love.................................... 1Jn 4:16
love dwelleth in G, and G in him........ 1Jn 4:16
Jesus is the Christ is born of G 1Jn 5:1
that G hath given to us eternal.......... 1Jn 5:11
not the Son of G hath not life 1Jn 5:12
on the name of the Son of G 1Jn 5:13
G shall wipe away all tears from........ Rev 7:17
Saying with a loud voice, Fear G........ Rev 14:7
G shall wipe away all tears from........ Rev 21:4
and I will be his G, and he shall......... Rev 21:7

GODDESS
Ashtoreth the g of the Zidonians 1Kin 11:5
Ashtoreth the g of the Zidonians 1Kin 11:33
great g Diana should be despised....... Acts 19:27
a worshipper of the great g Diana ..... Acts 19:35
nor blasphemers of your g .... Acts 19:37

GODHEAD *That which is divine.*
that the G is like unto gold .... Acts 17:29
made, even his eternal power and G... Rom 1:20
all the fulness of the G bodily........... Col 2:9

GODLINESS
quiet and peaceable life in all g 1Ti 2:2
professing g) with good works........... 1Ti 2:10
great is the mystery of g 1Ti 3:16
and exercise thyself rather unto g 1Ti 4:7
but g is profitable unto all 1Ti 4:8
doctrine which is according to g 1Ti 6:3
truth, supposing that gain is g 1Ti 6:5
But g with contentment is great 1Ti 6:6
and follow after righteousness, g 1Ti 6:11
Having a form of g, but denying 2Ti 3:5
of the truth which is after g............. Titus 1:1
that pertain unto life and g 2Pet 1:3
and to patience g 2Pet 1:6
And to g brotherly kindness.............. 2Pet 1:7
be in all holy conversation and g 2Pet 3:11

GODLY
apart him that is g for himself........... Ps 4:3
for the g man ceaseth .... Ps 12:1
this shall every one that is g .... Ps 32:6
That he might seek a g seed .... Mal 2:15
g sincerity, not with fleshly.............. 2Cor 1:12
were made sorry after a g manner 2Cor 7:9
For g sorrow worketh repentance....... 2Cor 7:10
that ye sorrowed after a g sort 2Cor 7:11
jealous over you with a g jealousy 2Cor 11:2
rather than g edifying which is 1Ti 1:4
all that will live g in Christ 2Ti 3:12
live soberly, righteously, and g .... Titus 2:12
with reverence and g fear .... Heb 12:28
deliver the g out of temptations........ 2Pet 2:9
on their journey after a g sort........... 3Jn 6

GOD'S *Refers to God I.*
for a pillar, shall be G house............. Gen 28:22
and he said, Am I in G stead............. Gen 30:2
saw them, he said, This is G host....... Gen 32:2
G anger was kindled because he .... Num 22:22
for the judgment is G .... Deut 1:17
the battle is not yours, but G 2Chr 20:15
and into an oath, to walk in G law ..... Neb 10:29
according to thy wish in G stead .... Job 33:6
My righteousness is more than G .... Job 35:2
I have yet to speak on G behalf .... Job 36:2
for it is G throne .... Mt 5:34
and unto God the things that are G..... Mt 22:21
and to God the things that are G........ Mk 12:17
for the kingdom of G sake............... Lk 18:29
and unto God the things which be G ... Lk 20:25
He that is of God heareth G words ..... Jn 8:47
said, Revilest thou G high priest........ Acts 23:4
thing to the charge of G elect .... Rom 8:33
being ignorant of G righteousness ..... Rom 10:3
for they are G ministers .... Rom 13:6
ye are G husbandry, ye are G............ 1Cor 3:9
and Christ is G 1Cor 3:23
and in your spirit, which are G........... 1Cor 6:20
according to the faith of G elect......... Titus 1:1
as being lords over G heritage 1Pet 5:3

GODS
be opened, and ye shall be as g .... Gen 3:5
wherefore hast thou stolen my g .... Gen 31:30
whomsoever thou findest thy g .... Gen 31:32
the strange g that are among you...... Gen 35:2
g which were in their hand .... Gen 35:4
against all the g of Egypt I will.......... Ex 12:12
unto thee, O LORD, among the g .... Ex 15:11
the LORD is greater than all g .... Ex 18:11
shalt have no other g before me........ Ex 20:3
not make with me g of silver .... Ex 20:23
shall ye make unto you g of gold .... Ex 20:23
Thou shalt not revile the g .... Ex 22:28
no mention of the name of other g ..... Ex 23:13
shalt not bow down to their g .... Ex 23:24
with them, nor with their g .... Ex 23:32
for if thou serve their g .... Ex 23:33
and said unto him, Up, make us g ...... Ex 32:1
and they said, These be thy g........... Ex 32:4
and said, These be thy g................. Ex 32:8
For they said unto me, Make us g ...... Ex 32:23
sin, and have made them g of gold .... Ex 32:31
they go a whoring after their g .... Ex 34:15
and do sacrifice unto their g .... Ex 34:15
go a whoring after their g .... Ex 34:16
sons go a whoring after their g .... Ex 34:16
Thou shalt make thee no molten g ..... Ex 34:17
nor make to yourselves molten g .... Lev 19:4

unto the sacrifices of their g .... Num 25:2
did eat, and bowed down to their g .... Num 25:2
upon their g also the LORD .... Num 33:4
And there ye shall serve g .... Deut 4:28
shalt have none other g before me..... Deut 5:7
Ye shall not go after other g .... Deut 6:14
of the g of the people which are .... Deut 6:14
me, that they may serve other g .... Deut 7:4
neither shalt thou serve their g .... Deut 7:16
their g shall ye burn with fire .... Deut 7:25
thy God, and walk after other g .... Deut 8:19
For the LORD your God is God of g ..... Deut 10:17
ye turn aside, and serve other g .... Deut 11:16
you this day, to go after other g .... Deut 11:28
ye shall possess served their g .... Deut 12:2
down the graven images of their g ..... Deut 12:3
thou enquire not after their g .... Deut 12:30
did these nations serve their g .... Deut 12:30
have burnt in the fire to their g .... Deut 12:31
saying, Let us go after other g .... Deut 13:2
Let us go and serve other g .... Deut 13:6
of the g of the people which are .... Deut 13:7
Let us go and serve other g .... Deut 13:13
And hath gone and served other g ..... Deut 17:3
speak in the name of other g............ Deut 18:20
which they have done unto their g ..... Deut 20:18
to go after other g to serve them ...... Deut 28:14
and there shalt thou serve other g..... Deut 28:36
and there thou shalt serve other g..... Deut 28:64
serve the g of these nations............. Deut 29:18
For they went and served other g ...... Deut 29:26
g whom they knew not .... Deut 29:26
be drawn away, and worship other g .. Deut 30:17
go a whoring after the g of the .... Deut 31:16
that they are turned unto other g ...... Deut 31:18
then will they turn unto other g .... Deut 31:20
him to jealousy with strange g .... Deut 32:16
to g whom they knew not .... Deut 32:17
to new g that came newly up, whom .. Deut 32:17
he shall say, Where are their g .... Deut 32:37
God of g, the LORD God of g .... Josh 22:22
mention of the names of their g .... Josh 23:7
and have gone and served other g ..... Josh 23:16
and they served other g .... Josh 24:2
put away the g which your fathers ..... Josh 24:14
whether the g which your fathers ...... Josh 24:15
or the g of the Amorites, in .... Josh 24:15
the LORD, to serve other g............... Josh 24:16
the LORD, and serve strange g .... Josh 24:20
the strange g which are among you ... Josh 24:23
their g shall be a snare unto you .... Judg 2:3
of Egypt, and followed other g .... Judg 2:12
go a whoring after the g of the .... Judg 2:17
that they are turned unto other g ...... Judg 2:19
following other g to serve them .... Judg 2:19
to their sons, and served their g .... Judg 3:6
They chose new g .... Judg 5:8
fear not the g of the Amorites,.......... Judg 6:10
the g of Syria .... Judg 10:6
the g of Zidon .... Judg 10:6
the g of Moab.............................. Judg 10:6
the g of the children of Ammon .... Judg 10:6
the g of the Philistines, and .... Judg 10:6
forsaken me, and served other g .... Judg 10:13
cry unto the g which ye have .... Judg 10:14
the strange g from among them .... Judg 10:16
the man Micah had an house of g....... Judg 17:5
have taken away my g .... Judg 18:24
unto her people, and unto her g .... Ruth 1:15
out of the hand of these mighty G 1Sa 4:8
these are the G that smote the 1Sa 4:8
from off you, and from off your g 1Sa 6:5
then put away the strange g 1Sa 7:3
forsaken me, and served other g 1Sa 8:8
Philistine cursed David by his g......... 1Sa 17:43
LORD, saying, Go, serve other g 1Sa 26:19
I saw g ascending out of the 1Sa 28:13
from the nations and their g 2Sa 7:23
you, but go and serve other g 1Kin 9:6
and have taken hold upon other g...... 1Kin 9:9
away your heart after their g 1Kin 11:4
away his heart after other g 1Kin 11:4
and sacrificed unto their g 1Kin 11:8
he should not go after other g 1Kin 11:10
behold thy g, O Israel, which 1Kin 12:28
hast gone and made thee other g 1Kin 14:9
And call ye on the name of your g 1Kin 18:24
and call on the name of your g.......... 1Kin 18:25
saying, So let the g do to me............ 1Kin 19:2
The g do so unto me, and more also ... 1Kin 20:10
The, g are g of the hills 1Kin 20:23
Their g are g of the hills.................. 1Kin 20:23
nor sacrifice unto other g 2Kin 5:17
of Egypt, and had feared other g 2Kin 17:7
every nation made g of their own 2Kin 17:29
Anammelech, the g of Sepharvaim 2Kin 17:31
the LORD, and served their own g 2Kin 17:33
saying, Ye shall not fear other g 2Kin 17:35
and ye shall not fear other g 2Kin 17:37
neither shall ye fear other g 2Kin 17:38
Hath any of the g of the nations 2Kin 18:33
Where are the g of Hamath 2Kin 18:34
where are the g of Sepharvaim.......... 2Kin 18:34
among all the g of the countries........ 2Kin 18:35
Have the g of the nations................ 2Kin 19:12
have cast their g into the fire 2Kin 19:18
for they were no g, but the works 2Kin 19:18
have burned incense unto other g 2Kin 22:17
went a whoring after the g of the...... 1Chr 5:25

armour in the house of their *g*.............1Chr 10:10
when they had left their *g* there 1Chr 14:12
also is to be feared above all *g* 1Chr 16:25
For all the *g* of the people are 1Chr 16:26
for great is our God above all *g* 2Chr 2:5
you, and shall go and serve other *g* ...2Chr 7:19
of Egypt, and laid hold on other *g* 2Chr 7:22
which Jeroboam made you for a 2Chr 13:8
be a priest of them that are no *g* 2Chr 13:9
away the altars of the strange *g* 2Chr 14:3
that he brought the *g* of the 2Chr 25:14
Seir, and set them up to be his *g* 2Chr 25:14
sought after the *g* of the people 2Chr 25:15
they sought after the *g* of Edom 2Chr 25:20
sacrificed unto the *g* of Damascus 2Chr 28:23
Because the *g* of the kings of 2Chr 28:23
to burn incense unto other *g* 2Chr 28:25
were the *g* of the nations of 2Chr 28:25
the *g* of those nations that my 2Chr 32:14
As the *g* of the nations of other 2Chr 32:17
as against the *g* of the people of 2Chr 32:19
And he took away the strange *g* 2Chr 33:15
have burned incense unto other *g* 2Chr 34:25
put them in the house of his *g* ....Ezr 1:7
he judgeth among the *g* ....Ps 82:1
I have said, Ye are *g* ....Ps 82:6
Among the *g* there is none like ....Ps 86:8
God, and a great King above all *g* ......Ps 95:3
he is to be feared above all *g* ....Ps 96:4
For all the *g* of the nations are ....Ps 96:5
worship him, all ye *g* ....Ps 97:7
thou art exalted far above all *g* ....Ps 97:9
and that our Lord is above all *g* ....Ps 135:5
O give thanks unto the God of *g* ....Ps 136:2
before the *g* will I sing praise ....Ps 138:1
all the graven images of her *g* he ....Is 21:9
Hath any of the *g* of the nations ....Is 36:18
Where are the *g* of Hamath ....Is 36:19
where are the *g* of Sepharvaim ....Is 36:19
among all the *g* of these lands ....Is 36:20
Have the *g* of the nations ....Is 37:12
have cast their *g* into the fire ....Is 37:19
for they were no *g*, but the work ....Is 37:19
that we may know that ye are *g* ....Is 41:23
the molten images, Ye are our *g* ....Is 42:17
have burned incense unto other *g* ....Jer 1:16
their *g*, which are yet no *g* ....Jer 2:11
But where are thy *g* that thou ....Jer 2:28
number of thy cities are thy *g* ....Jer 2:28
and sworn by them that are no *g* ....Jer 5:7
and served strange *g* in your land ....Jer 5:19
walk after other *g* to your hurt ....Jer 7:6
after other *g* whom ye know not ....Jer 7:9
out drink offerings unto other *g* ....Jer 7:18
The *g* that have no made the ....Jer 10:11
went after other *g* to serve them ....Jer 11:10
cry unto the *g* unto whom they ....Jer 11:12
number of thy cities were thy *g* ....Jer 11:13
heart, and walk after other *g* ....Jer 13:10
and have walked after other *g* ....Jer 16:11
there shall ye serve other *g* day ....Jer 16:13
Shall a man make a unto himself ....Jer 16:20
and they are no *g* ....Jer 16:20
burned incense in it unto other *g* ....Jer 19:4
out drink offerings unto other *g* ....Jer 19:13
their God, and worshipped other *g* ......Jer 22:9
not after other *g* to serve them ....Jer 25:6
out drink offerings unto other *g* ....Jer 32:29
not after other *g* to serve them ....Jer 35:15
in the houses of the *g* of the ....Jer 43:12
the houses of the *g* of the ....Jer 43:13
burn incense, and to serve other *g* ......Jer 44:3
to burn no incense unto other *g* ....Jer 44:5
unto other *g* in the land of Egypt ....Jer 44:8
had burned incense unto other *g* ....Jer 44:15
Pharaoh, and Egypt, with their *g* ....Jer 46:25
him that burneth incense to his *g* ....Jer 48:35
it before the king, except the *g* ....Dan 2:11
is, that your God is a God of *g* ....Dan 2:47
they serve not thy *g*, nor worship ....Dan 3:12
Abed-nego, do not ye serve my *g* ....Dan 3:14
that we will not serve thy *g* ....Dan 3:18
whom is the spirit of the holy *g* ....Dan 4:8
spirit of the holy *g* is in thee ....Dan 4:9
spirit of the holy *g* is in thee ....Dan 4:18
wine, and praised the *g* of gold ....Dan 5:4
whom is the spirit of the holy *g* ....Dan 5:11
wisdom, like the wisdom of the *g* ....Dan 5:11
the spirit of the *g* is in thee ....Dan 5:14
thou hast praised the *g* of silver ....Dan 5:23
carry captives into Egypt their *g* ....Dan 11:8
things against the God of *g* ....Dan 11:36
of Israel, who look to other *g* ....Hos 3:1
work of our hands, Ye are our *g* ....Hos 14:3
out of the house of thy *g* will I ....Nah 1:14
famish all the *g* of the earth ....Zeph 2:11
in your law, I said, Ye are *g* ....Jn 10:34
If he called them *g*, unto whom ....Jn 10:35
Make us *g* to go before us ....Acts 7:40
The *g* are come down to us in the ....Acts 14:11
to be a setter forth of strange *g* ....Acts 17:18
people, saying that they be no *g* ....Acts 19:26
though there be that are called *g* 1Cor 8:5
or in earth, (as there be *g* many 1Cor 8:5
them which by nature are no *g* ....Gal 4:8

Be thou for the people to G.....................Ex 18:19
trust have we through Christ to G..........2Cor 3:4
your faith to G is spread abroad 1Th 1:8

as thou *g*, unto Sodom, and.................Gen 10:19
as thou *g* unto Sephar a mount of ......Gen 10:30
Egypt, as thou *g* toward Assyria..........Gen 25:18
thee in all places whither thou *g*..........Gen 28:15
and whither *g* thou ....Gen 32:17
When thou *g* to return into Egypt,......Ex 4:21
is it not in that thou *g* with us ....Ex 34:12
of the land whither thou *g*...................Num 14:14
land whither thou *g* to possess it........Deut 7:1
whither thou *g* in to possess it,............Deut 11:10
land whither thou *g* to possess it........Deut 11:29
whither thou *g* to possess them,.........Deut 12:29
When thou *g* out to battle against......Deut 20:1
When thou *g* forth to war against........Deut 21:10
land whither thou *g* to possess it........Deut 23:20
shalt thou be when thou *g* out.............Deut 28:6
shalt thou be when thou *g* out.............Deut 28:19
whither thou *g* to possess it ....Deut 28:21
land whither thou *g* to possess it........Deut 28:63
land whither thou *g* to possess it........Deut 30:16
in the mount whither thou *g* up..........Deut 32:50
prosper whithersoever thou *g*..............Josh 1:7
is with thee whithersoever thou *g* ....Josh 1:9
that thou *g* to take a wife of thou ....Judg 14:3
the old man said, Whither *g* thou ....Judg 19:17
for whither thou *g*, I will go ....Ruth 1:16
of the land, as thou *g* to Shur ....Is 27:8
strength, when thou *g* on thy way........1Sa 28:22
Wherefore *g* thou also with us.............2Sa 15:19
be, that on the day thou *g* out.............1Kin 2:37
a certain, on the day thou *g* out..........1Kin 2:42
g not forth with our armies....................Ps 44:9
When thou *g*, thy steps shall not ....Prov 4:12
When thou *g*, it shall lead thee.............Prov 6:22
when thou *g* to the house of God.........Eccl 5:1
in the grave, whither thou *g*.................Eccl 9:10
prey in all places whither thou *g*...........Jer 45:5
Then said I, Whither *g* thou ....Zec 2:2
follow thee whithersoever thou *g*..........Mt 8:19
follow thee whithersoever thou *g*..........Lk 9:57
When thou *g* with thine adversary........Lk 12:58
and *g* thou thither again ....Jn 11:8
unto him, Lord, whither *g* thou............Jn 13:36
Lord, we know not whither thou *g*.......Jn 14:5
of you asketh me, Whither *g* thou.........Jn 16:5

that is it which *g* toward the ....Gen 2:14
with the present that *g* before me.........Gen 32:20
as the cattle that *g* before me ....Gen 33:14
Behold thy father in law *g* up to ....Gen 38:13
lo, he *g* out unto the water....................Ex 7:15
unto him thy that the sun *g* down.........Ex 22:26
when he *g* in unto the holy place,.........Ex 28:29
when he *g* in before the LORD..............Ex 28:30
sound shall be heard when he *g* in........Ex 28:35
thing that a upon all four.........................Lev 11:21
whatsoever *g* upon his paws, among.....Lev 11:27
Whatsoever *g* upon the belly, and.........Lev 11:42
whatsoever *g* upon all four, or..............Lev 11:42
Moreover he that *g* into the house.........Lev 14:46
and of him whose seed *g* from him........Lev 15:32
of the congregation when he *g* in..........Lev 16:17
that *g* unto the holy things,...................Lev 22:3
or a man whose seed *g* from him...........Lev 22:4
when it *g* out in the jubile,....................Lev 27:21
when a wife *g* aside to another..............Num 5:29
that *g* down to the dwelling of Ar..........Num 21:15
LORD your God which *g* before you ......Deut 1:30
is he which *g* over before thee...............Deut 9:3
by the way where the sun *g* down ....Deut 11:30
As when a man *g* into the wood............Deut 19:5
your God is he that *g* with you ....Deut 20:4
When the host *g* forth against ....Deut 23:9
pledge again when the sun *g* down........Deut 24:13
the way that a *g* to Beth-horon.............Josh 10:10
that *g* up to Seir, even unto...................Josh 11:17
mount Halak, that *g* up to Seir..............Josh 12:7
to the wilderness that *g* up from............Josh 16:1
g out from Beth-el to Luz, and..............Josh 16:2
a down westward to the coast of.............Josh 16:3
thee *g* out to Daberath, and *g*............Josh 19:12
g out to Remmon-methoar to Neah......Josh 19:13
g out to Cabul on the left hand...........Josh 19:27
g out from thence to Hukkok, and........Josh 19:34
sun when he *g* forth in his might..........Judg 5:31
of which one *g* up to the house of.........Judg 20:31
that *g* up from Beth-el to Shechem .....Judg 21:19
if it *g* up by the way of his own.............1Sa 6:9
law, and *g* at thy bidding, and is...........1Sa 22:14
part is that *g* down to the battle............1Sa 30:24
that when my master *g* into the 2Kin 5:18
be ye with the king as he *g* out.............2Kin 11:8
of Millo, which *g* down to Silla 2Kin 12:20
he cometh in, and when he *g* out..........2Chr 23:7
the walls, and this work *g* fast on..........Ezr 5:8
so be that a down to the grave..................Job 7:9
he *g* by me, and I see him not................Job 9:11
Which *g* in company with the ....Job 34:8
the sound that *g* out of his mouth.........Job 37:2
he *g* on to meet the armed men.............Job 39:21
Out of his nostrils *g* smoke...................Job 41:20
a flame *g* out of his mouth...................Job 41:21
that *g* not out of feigned lips................Ps 17:1
when he *g* abroad, he telleth it..............Ps 41:6
as *g* on still in his trespasses.................Ps 68:21
Thy fierce wrath *g* over me.....................Ps 88:16
A fire *g* before him, and burneth...........Ps 97:3
Man *g* forth unto his work and to.........Ps 104:23

He that *g* forth and weepeth..................Ps 126:6
His breath *g* forth, he returneth............Ps 146:4
So he that *g* in to his.............................Prov 6:29
He *g* after her straightway....................Prov 7:22
as an ox *g* to the slaughter, or..............Prov 7:22
When it *g* well with the righteous..........Prov 11:10
Pride *g* before destruction, and an.......Prov 16:18
He that *g* about as a talebearer ....Prov 20:19
As a thorn *g* up into the hand of..........Prov 26:9
no wood is, there the fire *g* out..............Prov 26:20
her candle *g* not out by night................Prov 31:18
also ariseth, and the sun *g* down...........Eccl 1:5
The wind *g* toward the south, and........Eccl 1:6
the spirit of man that *g* upward ....Eccl 3:21
that *g* downward to the earth................Eccl 3:21
because man *g* to his long home,..........Eccl 12:5
that *g* down sweetly, causing the...........Song 7:9
From the time that it *g* forth it ....Is 28:19
as when one *g* with a pipe to come ....Is 30:29
to go forth out of my mouth....................Is 55:11
whosoever *g* therein shall not ....Is 59:8
As a beast *g* down into the valley ....Is 63:14
every one that *g* out thence shall ....Jer 5:6
for the day *g* away, for the....................Jer 6:4
but he that *g* out, and falleth to ....Jer 21:9
but weep sore for him that *g* away ....Jer 22:10
of the LORD *g* forth with fury ....Jer 23:19
but he that *g* forth to the ....Jer 38:2
g forth out of our own mouth ....Jer 44:17
every one that *g* by it shall be..............Jer 49:17
every one that *g* by Babylon shall.........Jer 50:13
but none *g* to the battle ....Eze 7:14
but their heart *g* after their ....Eze 33:31
as one *g* up to the entry of the ....Eze 40:40
as one *g* into them from the utter........Eze 42:9
day that he *g* into the sanctuary ....Eze 44:27
as one *g* to Hamath, Hazar-enan,.........Eze 48:1
are as the light that *g* forth..................Hos 6:5
This is the curse that *g* forth................Zec 5:3
and see what is this that *g* forth...........Zec 5:5
This as spirit that *g* forth.....................Zec 5:6
and I say to this man, Go, and he *g*......Mt 8:9
Then *g* he, and taketh with himself ......Mt 12:45
he hideth, and for joy thereof *g*............Mt 13:44
Not that which *g* into the mouth..........Mt 15:11
in at the mouth *g* into the belly ....Mt 15:17
Howbeit this kind *g* not out but ....Mt 17:21
into the mountains, and seeketh ....Mt 18:12
it had been good for that man...................Mt 26:24
as unto whom it is written ....Mt 28:7
he *g* before you into Galilee ....Mk 14:28
he *g* up into a mountain, and ....Mk 3:13
g out into the draught, purging.............Mk 7:19
The Son of man indeed *g*, as it is..........Mk 14:21
he *g* straightway to him, and saith........Mk 14:45
Peter that he *g* before you into.............Mk 16:7
and I say unto one, Go, and he *g*...........Lk 7:8
Then *g* he, and taketh to him seven .....Lk 11:26
And truly the Son of man *g*...................Lk 22:22
whence it cometh, and whither it *g* ....Jn 3:8
who *g* about to kill thee ....Jn 7:20
he *g* before them, and the sheep...........Jn 10:4
She *g* unto the grave to weep ....Jn 11:31
darkness knoweth not whither he *g* ......Jn 12:35
the south unto the way that *g* ....Acts 8:26
But brother *g* to law with brother..........1Cor 6:6
Who *g* a warfare any time at his............1Cor 9:7
g his way, and straightway ....Jas 1:24
and knoweth not whither he *g* ....Jn 2:11
the Lamb whithersoever he *g* ....Rev 14:4
of the seven, and *g* into perdition..........Rev 17:11
out of his mouth *g* a sharp sword..........Rev 19:15

See HAMON-GOG, MAGOG.
1. Son of Shemaiah.
G his son, Shimei his son.........................1Chr 5:4
2. A prince of Scythia.
of man, set thy face against G..................Eze 38:2
Behold, I am against thee, O G................Eze 38:3
of man, prophesy and say unto G.............Eze 38:14
shall be sanctified in thee, O G................Eze 38:16
to pass at the same time when G.............Eze 38:18
son of man, prophesy against G...............Eze 39:1
Behold, I am against thee, O G................Eze 39:1
that I will give unto G a place..................Eze 39:11
and there shall they bury G.....................Eze 39:11
the four quarters of the earth, G.............Rev 20:8

See NATIONS.

See NATIONS.

g on still toward the south......................Gen 12:9
And when the sun was *g* down...............Gen 15:12
g to carry it down to Egypt....................Gen 37:25
until the *g* down of the sun ....Ex 17:12
enemy's ox or his ass *g* astray...............Ex 23:4
six branches *g* out of the sides..............Ex 37:18
branches *g* out of the candlestick..........Ex 37:19
to the six branches *g* out of it................Ex 37:21
g upon all four, shall be an ....Lev 11:20
g over into the land which the ....Num 32:7
the *g* forth thereof shall be from............Num 34:8
at the *g* down of the sun, at the............Deut 16:6
Rejoice, Zebulun, in thy *g* out...............Deut 33:18
sea toward the *g* down of the sun..........Josh 1:4
after the ark, the priests a on...................Josh 6:9
the city, a about in ....Josh 6:11
ark of the LORD, the priests *g* on..........Josh 6:13
and smote them in the *g* down..............Josh 7:5
were in the *g* down to Beth-horon,.........Josh 10:11
the time of the *g* down of the sun..........Josh 10:27
is before the *g* up to Adummim..............Josh 15:7

over against the *g* up of Adummim .... Josh 18:17
this day I am *g* the way of all .... Josh 23:14
was from the *g* up to Akrabbim .... Judg 1:36
but I am now *g* to the house of .... Judg 19:18
said unto her, Up, and let us be *g* .... Judg 19:28
young maidens *g* out to draw water 1Sa 9:11
as they were *g* down to the end of 1Sa 9:27
three men *g* up to God to Beth-el 1Sa 10:3
as the host was *g* forth to the 1Sa 17:20
hast been upright, and thy *g* out 1Sa 29:6
in *g* he turned not to the right 2Sa 2:19
thee, and to know thy *g* out 2Sa 3:25
a *g* in the tops of the mulberry 2Sa 5:24
as she was *g* to fetch it, he 1Kin 17:11
host about the *g* down of the sun 1Kin 22:36
as he was *g* up by the way, there 2Kin 2:23
And they did so at the *g* up to Gur 2Kin 9:27
I know thy abode, and thy *g* out 2Kin 19:27
of *g* in the tops of the mulberry 1Chr 14:15
by the causeway of the *g* up 1Chr 26:16
returned from *g* against Jeroboam 2Chr 11:4
time of the sun *g* down he died 2Chr 18:34
the *g* up to the armoury at the .... Neh 3:19
to the *g* up of the corner .... Neh 3:31
between the *g* up of the corner .... Neh 3:32
at the *g* up of the wall, above ...... Neh 12:37
the LORD, and said, From *g* to .... Job 1:7
the LORD, and said, From *g* to .... Job 2:2
him from *g* down to the pit .... Job 33:24
his soul from *g* into the pit .... Job 33:28
His *g* forth is from the end of .... Ps 19:6
the sun unto the *g* down thereof .... Ps 50:1
the sun knoweth his *g* down .... Ps 104:19
the *g* down of the same the LORD's .... Ps 113:3
The LORD shall preserve thy *g* out .... Ps 121:8
be no breaking in, nor *g* out .... Ps 144:14
g down to the chambers of death .... Prov 7:27
prudent man looketh well to his *g* .... Prov 14:15
well, yea, four are comely in *g* ...... Prov 30:29
shall be darkened in his *g* forth ...... Is 13:10
I know thy abode, and thy *g* out .... Is 37:28
For in the *g* up of Luhith .... Is 48:5
for in the *g* down of Horonaim the .... Jer 48:5
the children of Judah together, *g* .... Jer 50:4
Dan also and Javan *g* to and fro .... Eze 27:19
the *g* up to it had eight steps .... Eze 40:31
the *g* up to it had eight steps .... Eze 40:34
the *g* up to it had eight steps .... Eze 40:37
with every *g* forth of the .... Eze 44:5
after his *g* forth one shall shut .... Eze 46:12
he laboured till the *g* down of .... Dan 6:14
that from the *g* forth of the .... Dan 9:25
his *g* forth is prepared as the .... Hos 6:3
and he found a ship *g* to Tarshish .... Jonah 1:3
g down of the same my name shall .... Mal 1:11
g on from thence, he saw other .... Mt 4:21
Jesus *g* up to Jerusalem took the .... Mt 20:17
Rise, let us be *g* .... Mt 26:46
Now when they were *g*, behold, ... Mt 28:11
for there were many coming and *g* .... Mk 6:31
were in the way *g* up to Jerusalem .... Mk 10:32
g to make war against another .... Lk 14:31
And as he was now *g* down, his ...... Jn 4:51
g through the midst of them, and .... Jn 8:59
coming in and *g* out at Jerusalem .... Acts 9:28
These *g* before tarried for us at .... Acts 20:5
about to establish their own .... Rom 10:3
beforehand, *g* before to judgment 1Ti 5:24
g before for the weakness .... Heb 7:18
For *ye* were as sheep *g* astray 1Pet 2:25
g after strange flesh, are set .... Jude 7

GOINGS

Moses wrote their *g* out according .... Num 33:2
journeys according to their *g* out .... Num 33:2
the *g* out of it shall be at the .... Num 34:5
the *g* forth of the border shall .... Num 34:8
the *g* out of it shall be at .... Num 34:9
the *g* out of it shall be at the .... Num 34:12
the *g* out thereof were at .... Josh 15:4
the *g* out of the border were at .... Josh 15:11
the *g* out thereof are at the sea .... Josh 16:3
the *g* out thereof were at the sea .... Josh 16:8
the *g* out thereof were at .... Josh 18:12
the *g* out of it were at .... Josh 18:14
of man, and he seeth all his *g* .... Job 34:21
Hold up my *g* in thy paths, that .... Ps 17:5
upon a rock, and established my *g* .... Ps 40:2
They have seen thy *g*, O God .... Ps 68:24
even the *g* of my God, my King, in .... Ps 68:24
have purposed to overthrow my *g* .... Ps 140:4
LORD, and he pondereth all his *g* .... Prov 5:21
Man's *g* are of the LORD .... Prov 20:24
there is no judgment in their *g* .... Is 59:8
all their *g* out were both .... Eze 42:11
the *g* out thereof, and the comings .... Eze 43:11
these are the *g* out of the city .... Eze 48:30
whose *g* forth have been from of .... Mic 5:2

GOLAN (gō'-lan) *A Levitical city in Manasseh.*
G in Bashan, of the Manassites .... Deut 4:43
G in Bashan out of the tribe of .... Josh 20:8
gave G in Bashan with her suburbs .... Josh 21:27
G in Bashan with her suburbs, and 1Chr 6:71

GOLD

land of Havilah, where there is *g*...... Gen 2:11
the *g* of that land is good .... Gen 2:12
in cattle, in silver, and in *g* .... Gen 13:2
hands of ten shekels weight of *g* .... Gen 24:22
flocks, and herds, and silver, and *g* .... Gen 24:35

jewels of silver, and jewels of *g* ...... Gen 24:53
put a *g* chain about his neck .... Gen 41:42
of thy lord's house silver or *g* ...... Gen 44:8
jewels of silver, and jewels of *g* ...... Ex 3:22
jewels of silver, and of jewels of *g* .... Ex 11:2
jewels of silver, and jewels of *g* ...... Ex 12:35
shall ye make unto you gods of *g* .... Ex 20:23
g, and silver, and brass, ... Ex 25:3
thou shalt overlay it with pure *g* .... Ex 25:11
upon it a crown of *g* round about .... Ex 25:11
shalt cast four rings of *g* for it ...... Ex 25:12
wood, and overlay them with *g* ...... Ex 25:13
shalt make a mercy seat of pure *g* .... Ex 25:17
shalt make two cherubims of *g* ...... Ex 25:18
thou shalt overlay it with pure *g* .... Ex 25:24
thereto a crown of *g* round about .... Ex 25:24
shalt make for it four rings of *g* .... Ex 25:26
wood, and overlay them with *g* ...... Ex 25:28
of pure *g* shalt thou make them .... Ex 25:29
make a candlestick of pure *g* ...... Ex 25:31
be one beaten work of pure *g* .... Ex 25:36
thereof, shall be of pure *g* .... Ex 25:38
talent of pure *g* shall he make it .... Ex 25:39
thou shalt make fifty taches of *g* .... Ex 26:6
shalt overlay the boards with *g* .... Ex 26:29
make their rings of *g* for places .... Ex 26:29
shalt overlay the bars with *g* ...... Ex 26:29
of shittim wood overlaid with *g* .... Ex 26:32
their hooks shall be of *g* .... Ex 26:32
wood, and overlay them with *g* .... Ex 26:37
and their hooks shall be of *g* ...... Ex 26:37
And they shall take *g*, and blue, and .... Ex 28:5
And they shall make the ephod of *g* .... Ex 28:6
even of *g*, of blue, and purple, and .... Ex 28:8
them to be set in ouches of *g* .... Ex 28:11
And thou shalt make ouches of *g* .... Ex 28:13
two chains of pure *g* at the ends .... Ex 28:14
of *g*, of blue, and of purple, and .... Ex 28:15
be set in *g* in their inclosings ...... Ex 28:20
ends of wreathen work of pure *g* .... Ex 28:22
the breastplate two rings of *g* ...... Ex 28:23
g in the two rings which are on .... Ex 28:24
And thou shalt make two rings of *g* .... Ex 28:26
other rings of *g* thou shalt make .... Ex 28:27
bells of *g* between them round ...... Ex 28:33
thou shalt make a plate of pure *g* .... Ex 28:36
thou shalt overlay it with pure *g* .... Ex 30:3
unto it a crown of *g* round about .... Ex 30:3
wood, and overlay them with *g* .... Ex 30:5
cunning works, to work in *g* .... Ex 31:4
unto them, Whosoever hath any *g* .... Ex 32:24
sin, and have made them gods of *g* .... Ex 32:31
g, and silver, and brass, ... Ex 35:5
and tablets, all jewels of *g* .... Ex 35:22
an offering of *g* unto the LORD .... Ex 35:22
curious works, to work in *g* .... Ex 35:32
And he made fifty taches of *g* ...... Ex 36:13
And he overlaid the boards with *g* .... Ex 36:34
made their rings of *g* to be .... Ex 36:34
bars, and overlaid the bars with *g* .... Ex 36:34
wood, and overlaid them with *g* .... Ex 36:36
their hooks were of *g* .... Ex 36:36
chapiters and their fillets with *g* .... Ex 36:38
he overlaid it with pure *g* within .... Ex 37:2
made a crown of *g* to it round .... Ex 37:2
And he cast for it four rings of *g* .... Ex 37:3
wood, and overlaid them with *g* .... Ex 37:4
he made the mercy seat of pure *g* .... Ex 37:6
And he made two cherubims of *g* .... Ex 37:7
And he overlaid it with pure *g* ...... Ex 37:11
a crown of *g* round about .... Ex 37:11
made a crown of *g* for the border .... Ex 37:12
And he cast for it four rings of *g* .... Ex 37:13
wood, and overlaid them with *g* .... Ex 37:15
covers to cover withal, of pure *g* .... Ex 37:16
he made the candlestick of pure *g* .... Ex 37:17
beaten work of *g* made he it ...... Ex 37:22
and his snuffdishes, of pure *g* ...... Ex 37:23
Of a talent of pure *g* made he it .... Ex 37:24
And he overlaid it with pure *g* ...... Ex 37:26
unto it a crown of *g* round about .... Ex 37:26
he made two rings of *g* for it ...... Ex 37:27
wood, and overlaid with *g* .... Ex 37:28
All the *g* that was occupied for .... Ex 38:24
even the *g* of the offering, was ...... Ex 38:24
And he made the ephod of *g* .... Ex 39:2
did beat the *g* into thin plates .... Ex 39:3
of *g*, blue, and purple, and scarlet .... Ex 39:5
stones inclosed in ouches of *g* ...... Ex 39:6
of *g*, blue, and purple, and scarlet .... Ex 39:8
ouches of *g* in their inclosings ...... Ex 39:13
ends, of wreathen work of pure *g* .... Ex 39:15
And they made two ouches of *g* .... Ex 39:16
ouches of *g*, and two *g* rings ...... Ex 39:16
put the two wreathen chains of *g* .... Ex 39:17
And they made two rings of *g* ...... Ex 39:19
And they made bells of pure *g* ...... Ex 39:25
plate of the holy crown of pure *g* .... Ex 39:30
thou shalt set the altar of *g* for .... Ex 40:5
the spoon of ten shekels of *g* ...... Num 7:14
One spoon of *g* of ten shekels, ... Num 7:20
silver bowls, twelve spoons of *g* .... Num 7:84
all the *g* of the spoons was an ...... Num 7:86
the candlestick was of beaten ...... Num 8:4
me his house full of silver and *g* .... Num 22:18
me his house full of silver and *g* .... Num 24:13
Only the *g*, and the silver, the .... Num 31:22
man hath gotten, of jewels of *g* .... Num 31:50
the priest took the *g* of them ...... Num 31:51
all the *g* of the offering that.......... Num 31:52

Eleazar the priest took the *g* of ...... Num 31:54
the silver or *g* that is on them ...... Deut 7:25
thy *g* is multiplied, and all that .... Deut 8:13
multiply to himself silver and *g* .... Deut 17:17
idols, wood and stone, silver and *g* .... Deut 29:17
But all the silver, and *g* .... Josh 6:19
only the silver, and the *g* .... Josh 6:24
a wedge of *g* of fifty shekels ...... Josh 7:21
and the garment, and the wedge of *g*.. Josh 7:24
cattle, with silver, and with *g* ...... Josh 22:8
and seven hundred shekels of *g* .... Judg 8:26
and put the jewels of *g*, which ye 1Sa 6:8
and the coffer with the mice of *g* 1Sa 6:11
it, wherein the jewels of *g* were 1Sa 6:15
ornaments of *g* upon your apparel 2Sa 1:24
David took the shields of *g* that 2Sa 8:7
of silver, and vessels of *g* 2Sa 8:10
g that he had dedicated of all 2Sa 8:11
of *g* with the precious stones 1Kin 12:30
will have no silver nor *g* of Saul 2Sa 21:4
and he overlaid it with pure *g* 1Kin 6:20
the house within with pure *g* were 1Kin 6:21
the chains of *g* before the oracle 1Kin 6:21
and he overlaid it with *g* 1Kin 6:21
whole house he overlaid with *g* 1Kin 6:22
by the oracle he overlaid with *g* 1Kin 6:22
he overlaid the cherubims with *g* 1Kin 6:28
of the house he overlaid with *g* 1Kin 6:32
flowers, and overlaid them with *g* 1Kin 6:32
spread *g* upon the cherubims, and 1Kin 6:32
covered them with *g* fitted upon 1Kin 6:35
altar of *g*, and the table of 1Kin 7:48
And the candlesticks of pure *g* 1Kin 7:49
and the lamps, and the tongs of *g* 1Kin 7:49
spoons, and the censers of pure *g* 1Kin 7:50
and the hinges of *g*, both for the 1Kin 7:50
even the silver, and the *g* 1Kin 7:51
trees and fir trees, and with *g* 1Kin 9:11
to the king sixscore talents of *g* 1Kin 9:14
Ophir, and fetched from thence *g* 1Kin 9:28
that bare spices, and very much *g* 1Kin 10:2
an hundred and twenty talents of *g* 1Kin 10:10
Hiram, that brought *g* from Ophir 1Kin 10:11
Now the weight of *g* that came to 1Kin 10:14
threescore and six talents of *g* 1Kin 10:14
two hundred targets of beaten *g* 1Kin 10:16
shekels of *g* went to one target 1Kin 10:16
three hundred shields of beaten *g* 1Kin 10:17
three pound of *g* went to one 1Kin 10:17
and overlaid it with the best *g* 1Kin 10:18
drinking vessels were of *g* 1Kin 10:21
forest of Lebanon were of pure *g* 1Kin 10:21
the navy of Tharshish, bringing *g* 1Kin 10:22
of silver, and vessels of *g* 1Kin 10:25
counsel, and made two calves of *g* 1Kin 12:28
of *g* which Solomon had made 1Kin 14:26
house of the LORD, silver, and *g* 1Kin 15:15
the *g* that were left in the 1Kin 15:18
thee a present of silver and *g* 1Kin 15:19
Thy silver and thy *g* is mine 1Kin 20:3
deliver me thy silver, and thy *g* 1Kin 20:5
and for my silver, and for my *g* 1Kin 20:7
of Tharshish to go to Ophir for *g* 1Kin 22:48
and six thousand pieces of *g* 2Kin 5:5
and carried thence silver, and *g* 2Kin 7:8
trumpets, any vessels of *g* 2Kin 12:13
all the *g* that was found in the 2Kin 12:18
And he took all the *g* and silver, ... 2Kin 14:14
g that was found in the house of 2Kin 16:8
of silver and thirty talents of *g* 2Kin 18:14
time all Hezekiah cut off the *g* 2Kin 18:16
things, the silver, and the *g* 2Kin 20:13
of silver, and a talent of *g* 2Kin 23:33
the silver and the *g* to Pharaoh 2Kin 23:35
the *g* of the people of the land, ... 2Kin 23:35
of which Solomon king of Israel 2Kin 24:13
such things as were of *g*, in *g* 2Kin 25:15
David took the shields of *g* that 1Chr 18:7
him all manner of vessels of *g* 1Chr 18:10
the *g* that he brought from all 1Chr 18:11
found it to weigh a talent of *g* 1Chr 20:2
hundred shekels of *g* by weight 1Chr 21:25
an hundred thousand talents of *g* 1Chr 22:14
Of the *g*, the silver, and the 1Chr 22:16
of *g* by weight for things of *g* 1Chr 28:14
weight for the candlesticks of *g* 1Chr 28:15
and for their lamps of *g* 1Chr 28:15
by weight he gave *g* for the 1Chr 28:16
Also pure *g* for the fleshhooks, ... 1Chr 28:17
gave *g* by weight for every bason 1Chr 28:17
of incense refined *g* by weight 1Chr 28:18
g fo: the pattern of the chariot 1Chr 28:18
g for things to be made of *g* 1Chr 29:2
of mine own proper good, of *g* 1Chr 29:3
three thousand talents of *g*, of 1Chr 29:4
of the *g* of Ophir, and seven 1Chr 29:4
The for things of *g*, and the 1Chr 29:5
of God of *g* five thousand talents 1Chr 29:7
at Jerusalem as plenteous as 2Chr 1:15
a man cunning to work in *g* 2Chr 2:7
man of Tyre, skilful to work in *g* 2Chr 2:14
he overlaid it within with pure *g* 2Chr 3:4
which he overlaid with fine *g* 2Chr 3:5
and the *g* was of Parvaim 2Chr 3:6
and the doors thereof, with *g* 2Chr 3:7
and he overlaid it with fine *g* 2Chr 3:8
the nails was fifty shekels of *g* 2Chr 3:9
the upper chambers with *g* 2Chr 3:9
work, and overlaid them with *g* 2Chr 3:10
of *g* according to their form 2Chr 4:7

And he made a hundred basons of g .. 2Chr 4:8
before the oracle, of pure g 2Chr 4:20
he of g, and that perfect g 2Chr 4:21
spoons, and the censers, of pure g .. 2Chr 4:22
house of the temple, were of g 2Chr 4:22
and the silver, and the g, and all 2Chr 5:1
hundred and fifty talents of g 2Chr 8:18
g in abundance, and precious 2Chr 9:9
which brought g from Ophir 2Chr 9:10
Now the weight of g that came to 2Chr 9:13
and threescore and six talents of g ... 2Chr 9:13
of the country brought g and 2Chr 9:14
two hundred targets of beaten g 2Chr 9:15
of beaten g went to one target 2Chr 9:15
shields made he of beaten g 2Chr 9:16
shekels of g went to one shield 2Chr 9:16
ivory, and overlaid it with pure g 2Chr 9:17
the throne, with a footstool of g 2Chr 9:18
vessels of king Solomon were of g ... 2Chr 9:20
forest of Lebanon were of pure g 2Chr 9:20
the ships of Tarshish bringing g 2Chr 9:21
of silver, and vessels of g 2Chr 9:24
of g which Solomon had made 2Chr 12:9
the candlesticks of g with the 2Chr 13:11
had dedicated, silver, and g 2Chr 15:18
g out of the treasures of the 2Chr 16:2
I have sent thee silver and g 2Chr 16:3
great gifts of silver, and of g 2Chr 21:3
and spoons, and vessels of g 2Chr 24:14
And he took all the g and the 2Chr 25:24
treasures for silver, and for g 2Chr 32:27
of silver and a talent of g 2Chr 36:3
help him with silver, and with g ..... Ezr 1:4
with vessels of silver, with g .... Ezr 1:6
thirty chargers of g, a thousand ..... Ezr 1:9
Thirty basons of g, silver basons .... Ezr 1:10
All the vessels of g and of silver ..... Ezr 1:11
and one thousand drams of g .... Ezr 2:69
And the vessels also of g and .... Ezr 7:15
And to carry the silver and g .... Ezr 7:15
g that thou canst find in all the ..... Ezr 7:16
the rest of the silver and the g ...... Ezr 7:18
unto them the silver, and the g ..... Ezr 8:25
and of g an hundred talents .... Ezr 8:26
Also twenty basons of g, of a .... Ezr 8:27
of fine copper, precious as g .... Ezr 8:27
the g are a freewill offering .... Ezr 8:28
weight of the silver, and the g ...... Ezr 8:30
day was the silver and the g .... Ezr 8:33
treasure a thousand drams of g ..... Neh 7:71
work twenty thousand drams of g ... Neh 7:71
was twenty thousand drams of g .... Neh 7:72
the beds were of g and silver, ... Est 1:6
gave them drink in vessels of g ..... Est 1:7
white, and with a great crown of g .. Est 8:15
Or with princes that had g .... Job 3:15
Then shalt thou lay up g as dust .... Job 22:24
the g of Ophir as the stones of ..... Job 22:24
tried me, I shall come forth as g ..... Job 23:10
a place for g where they find it ..... Job 28:1
and it hath dust of g .... Job 28:6
It cannot be gotten for g .... Job 28:15
be valued with the g of Ophir .... Job 28:16
The g and the crystal cannot equal .. Job 28:17
shall not be for jewels of fine g ..... Job 28:17
shall it be valued with pure g .... Job 28:19
If I have made g my hope .... Job 31:24
or have said to the fine g .... Job 31:24
no, not g, nor all the forces of ...... Job 36:19
and every one an earring of g .... Job 42:11
to be desired are they than g .... Ps 19:10
yea, than much fine g .... Ps 19:10
a crown of pure g on his head .... Ps 21:3
did stand the queen in g of Ophir ... Ps 45:9
her clothing is of wrought g .... Ps 45:13
and her feathers with yellow g ...... Ps 68:13
hath given of the g of Sheba .... Ps 72:15
them forth also with silver and g ... Ps 105:37
Their idols are silver and g .... Ps 115:4
unto me than thousands of g .... Ps 119:72
I love thy commandments above g .. Ps 119:127
yea, above fine g .... Ps 119:127
of the heathen are silver and g ..... Ps 135:15
and the gain thereof than fine g ..... Prov 3:14
and knowledge rather than choice g . Prov 8:10
My fruit is better than g .... Prov 8:19
yea, than fine g .... Prov 8:19
As a jewel of g in a swine's .... Prov 11:22
better is it to get wisdom than g .... Prov 16:16
for silver, and the furnace for g ..... Prov 17:3
There is g, and a multitude of .... Prov 20:15
favour rather than silver and g ...... Prov 22:1
apples of g in pictures of silver ..... Prov 25:11
As an earring of g, and an .... Prov 25:12
of g, and an ornament of fine g ..... Prov 25:12
for silver, and the furnace for g .... Prov 27:21
I gathered me also silver and g ..... Eccl 2:8
jewels, thy neck with chains of g ... Song 1:10
borders of g with studs of silver ... Song 1:11
silver, the bottom thereof of g ...... Song 3:10
His head is as the most fine g .... Song 5:11
His hands are as rings set with g ... Song 5:14
set upon sockets of fine g .... Song 5:15
land also is full of silver and g ..... Is 2:7
of silver, and his idols of g .... Is 2:20
a man more precious than fine g .... Is 13:12
and as for g, they shall not .... Is 13:17
of thy molten images of g .... Is 30:22
of silver, and idols of g .... Is 31:7

things, the silver, and the g .... Is 39:2
spreadeth it over with g, and .... Is 40:19
They lavish g out of the bag, and ..... Is 46:6
they shall bring g and incense .... Is 60:6
their g with them, unto the name ..... Is 60:9
For brass I will bring g, and for .... Is 60:17
deckest thee with ornaments of g .... Jer 4:30
deck it with silver and with g .... Jer 10:4
g from Uphaz, the work of the .... Jer 10:9
that which was of g it a .... Jer 52:19
How is the g become dim .... Lam 4:1
how is the most fine g changed .... Lam 4:1
of Zion, comparable to fine g .... Lam 4:2
and their g shall be removed .... Eze 7:19
their g shall not be able to .... Eze 7:19
Thus wast thou decked with g .... Eze 16:13
taken thy fair jewels of my g .... Eze 16:17
and with all precious stones, and g .. Eze 27:22
the riches, and hast gotten g .... Eze 28:4
emerald, and the carbuncle, and g ... Eze 28:13
to carry away silver and g .... Eze 28:13
This image's head was of fine g .... Dan 2:32
the brass, the silver, and the g .... Dan 2:35
Thou art this head of g .... Dan 2:38
the clay, the silver, and the g .... Dan 2:45
the king made an image of g .... Dan 3:1
wine, and praised the gods of g .... Dan 5:4
have a chain of g about his neck ...... Dan 5:7
have a chain of g about thy neck ...... Dan 5:16
praised the gods of silver, and g ...... Dan 5:23
put a chain of g about his neck .... Dan 5:29
were girded with fine g of Uphaz .... Dan 10:5
vessels of silver and of g .... Dan 11:8
knew not shall he honour with g ..... Dan 11:38
power over the treasures of g .... Dan 11:43
and multiplied her silver and g .... Hos 2:8
their g have they made them idols .... Hos 8:4
ye have taken my silver and my g .... Joel 3:5
of silver, take the spoil of g .... Nah 2:9
Behold, it is laid over with g .... Hab 2:19
g shall be able to deliver them .... Zeph 1:18
the g is mine, saith the LORD of ...... Hag 2:8
and behold a candlestick all of g ..... Zec 4:2
Then take silver and g, and make ..... Zec 6:11
fine g as the mire of the streets .... Zec 9:3
and will try them as g is tried .... Zec 13:9
shall be gathered together, g .... Zec 14:14
sons of Levi, and purge them as g .... Mal 3:3
g, and frankincense, and myrrh .... Mt 2:11
Provide neither g, nor silver .... Mt 10:9
swear by the g of the temple .... Mt 23:16
for whether is greater, the g .... Mt 23:17
the temple that sanctifieth the g ..... Mt 23:17
said, Silver and g have I none .... Acts 3:6
that the Godhead is like unto g .... Acts 17:29
coveted no man's silver, or g .... Acts 20:33
man build upon this foundation g 1Cor 3:12
not with braided hair, or g 1Ti 2:9
there are not only vessels of g 2Ti 2:20
overlaid round about with g .... Heb 9:4
your assembly a man with a g ring ... Jas 2:2
Your g and silver is cankered .... Jas 5:3
precious than of g that perisheth 1Pet 1:7
things, as silver and g, from your 1Pet 1:18
the hair, and of wearing of g 1Pet 3:3
to buy of me g tried in the fire .... Rev 3:18
had on their heads crowns of g .... Rev 4:4
were as it were crowns like g .... Rev 9:7
not worship devils, and idols of g .... Rev 9:20
scarlet colour, and decked with g .... Rev 17:4
The merchandise of g, and silver ..... Rev 18:12
and scarlet, and decked with g .... Rev 18:16
and the city was pure g, like unto ... Rev 21:18
the street of the city was pure g ...... Rev 21:21

GOLDEN

that the man took a g earring of ...... Gen 24:22
thou shalt make a g crown to the ..... Ex 25:25
A g bell and a pomegranate .... Ex 28:34
a g bell and a pomegranate, upon ..... Ex 28:34
two g rings shalt thou make to it ..... Ex 30:4
them, Break off the g earrings .... Ex 32:2
g earrings which were in their .... Ex 32:3
And they made two rings or rings ..... Ex 39:20
the g altar, and the anointing oil ..... Ex 39:38
he put the g altar in the tent of .... Ex 40:26
forefront, did he put the g plate ...... Lev 8:9
upon the g altar they shall .... Num 4:11
One g spoon of ten shekels, full ...... Num 7:26
One g spoon of ten shekels, full ...... Num 7:32
One g spoon of ten shekels, full ...... Num 7:38
One g spoon of ten shekels, full ...... Num 7:44
One g spoon of ten shekels, full ...... Num 7:50
One g spoon of ten shekels, full ...... Num 7:56
One g spoon of ten shekels, full ...... Num 7:62
One g spoon of ten shekels, full ...... Num 7:68
One g spoon of ten shekels, full ...... Num 7:74
One g spoon of ten shekels, full ...... Num 7:80
The g spoons were twelve, full of ..... Num 7:86
(For they had g earrings, because ..... Judg 8:24
the weight of the g earrings that ..... Judg 8:26
g emerods, and five g mice 1Sa 6:4
these are the g emerods which 1Sa 6:17
the g mice, according to the 1Sa 6:18
the g calves that were in Beth-el 2Kin 10:29
for the g basons he gave gold by 1Chr 28:17
the g altar also, and the tables 2Chr 4:8
and there are with you g calves 2Chr 13:8
And also let the g and silver .... Ezr 6:5
king shall hold out the g sceptre ..... Est 4:11
g sceptre that was in his hand .... Est 5:2

out the g sceptre toward Esther .... Est 8:4
or the g bowl be broken, or the .... Eccl 12:6
a man than the g wedge of Ophir ..... Is 13:12
the g city ceased .... Is 14:4
Babylon hath been a g cup in the .... Jer 51:7
down and worship the g image that .. Dan 3:5
worshipped the g image that .... Dan 3:7
fall down and worship the g image ... Dan 3:10
nor worship the g image which .... Dan 3:12
nor worship the g image which I ..... Dan 3:14
nor worship the g image which .... Dan 3:18
wine, commanded to bring the g ..... Dan 5:2
Then they brought the g vessels ...... Dan 5:3
g pipes empty the oil out of .... Zec 4:12
Which had the g censer, and the ..... Heb 9:4
wherein was the g pot that had .... Heb 9:4
I saw seven g candlesticks .... Rev 1:12
about the paps with a g girdle .... Rev 1:13
hand, and the seven g candlesticks .. Rev 1:20
midst of the seven g candlesticks .... Rev 2:1
a vials full of odours, which are ...... Rev 5:8
at the altar, having a g censer .... Rev 8:3
the g altar which was before the ..... Rev 9:13
the g altar which is before God .... Rev 9:14
man, having on his head a g crown .. Rev 14:14
breasts girded with g girdles .... Rev 15:6
unto the seven angels seven g .... Rev 15:7
having a g cup in her hand full .... Rev 17:4
had a reed to measure the city .... Rev 21:15

GOLDSMITH

the g spreadeth it over with gold ..... Is 40:19
So the carpenter encouraged the g ... Is 41:7
in the balance, and hire a g .... Is 46:6

GOLDSMITH'S

the g son unto the place of .... Neh 3:31

GOLDSMITHS

the son of Harhaiah, of the g .... Neh 3:8
the sheep gate repaired the g .... Neh 3:32

GOLGOTHA (gŏl´-go-thah) See CALVARY. Hill
where Jesus was crucified.

were come unto a place called G ...... Mt 27:33
they bring him unto the place G ...... Mk 15:22
which is called in the Hebrew G ...... Jn 19:17

GOLIATH (go-lī´-ath) Philistine warrior killed
by David.

camp of the Philistines, named G 1Sa 17:4
G by name, out of the armies of 1Sa 17:23
The sword of G the Philistine, ... 1Sa 21:9
him the sword of G the Philistine 1Sa 22:10
slew the brother of G the Gittite 2Sa 21:19
the brother of G the Gittite 1Chr 20:5

GOMER (go´-mer)
1. Son of Japheth.

G, and Magog, and Madai, and Javan,. Gen 10:2
And the sons of G .... Gen 10:3
G, and Magog, and Madai, and Javan,. 1Chr 1:5
And the sons of G 1Chr 1:6
2. Descendants of Gomer 1.
G, and all his bands .... Eze 38:6
3. Wife of Hosea.
took G the daughter of Diblaim .... Hos 1:3

GOMORRAH (go-mor´-rah) See GOMORRHA.
City destroyed by God.

as thou goest, unto Sodom, and G .... Gen 10:19
the LORD destroyed Sodom and G ..... Gen 13:10
Sodom, and with Birsha king of G .... Gen 14:2
Sodom, and the king of G .... Gen 14:8
of Sodom and G fled, and fell there .. Gen 14:10
took all the goods of Sodom and G ... Gen 14:11
G is great, and because their sin ..... Gen 18:20
upon G brimstone and fire from the .. Gen 19:24
And he looked toward Sodom and G .. Gen 19:28
like the overthrow of Sodom, and G . Deut 29:23
of Sodom, and of the fields of G ...... Deut 32:32
we should have been like unto G ..... Is 1:9
law of our God, ye people of G .... Is 1:10
as when God overthrew Sodom and G. Is 13:19
and the inhabitants thereof as G ..... Jer 23:14
As in the overthrow of Sodom and G. Jer 49:18
As God overthrew Sodom and G .... Jer 50:40
you, as God overthrew Sodom and G Amos 4:11
and the children of Ammon as G ...... Zeph 2:9
G into ashes condemned them with .. 2Pet 2:6

GOMORRHA (go-mor´-rah) See GOMORRAH.
Greek form of Gomorrah.

In the day of judgment, than .... Mt 10:15
G in the day of judgment, than .... Mk 6:11
Sodoma, and been made like unto G .. Rom 9:29
Even as Sodom and G, and the cities .. Jude 7

GONE

Jacob was yet scarce g out from ...... Gen 27:30
mother, and was g to Padan-aram .... Gen 28:7
though thou wouldest needs be g ...... Gen 31:30
our daughter, and we will be g .... Gen 34:17
of your households, and be g .... Gen 42:33
when they were g out of the city, ... Gen 44:4
the prey, my son, thou art g up .... Gen 49:9
As soon as I am g out of the city, ... Ex 9:29
herds, as ye have said, and be g ...... Ex 12:31
And when the dew that lay was g up .. Ex 16:14
the children of Israel were g .... Ex 19:1
Moses, until he was g into the .... Ex 33:8
after whom they have g a whoring .... Lev 17:7
if thou hast not g aside to .... Num 5:19
But if thou hast g aside to .... Num 5:20

G

when Moses was g into the.................... Num 7:89
when we have g to search it...................... Num 13:32
is wrath g out from the LORD.................. Num 16:46
there is a fire g out of Heshbon............... Num 21:28
When I was g up into the mount to........... Deut 9:9
are g out from among you, and have......... Deut 13:13
And hath g and served other gods,............ Deut 17:3
That which is g out of thy lips................ Deut 23:23
shall be when ye be g over Jordan........... Deut 27:4
he seeth that their power is g.................. Deut 32:36
pursued after them were g out................... Josh 2:7
before us, until we were g over............... Josh 4:23
commanded you, and have g...................... Josh 23:16
When he was g out, his servants.............. Judg 3:24
Abinoam was g up to mount Tabor............ Judg 4:12
is not the LORD g out before thee............. Judg 4:14
and the priest, and ye are g away............ Judg 18:24
of Israel were g up to Mizpeh................... Judg 20:3
of the LORD is g out against me............... Ruth 1:13
in law is g back unto her people.............. Ruth 1:15
knew not that Jonathan was g................... 1Sa 14:3
now, and see who is g from us.................. 1Sa 14:17
is g about, and passed on........................... 1Sa 15:12
and g down to Gilgal.................................. 1Sa 15:12
have g the way which the LORD............... 1Sa 15:20
And as soon as the land was g.................. 1Sa 20:41
when the wine was g out of Nabal............ 1Sa 25:37
in the morning the people had g................. 2Sa 2:27
Wherefore hast thou g in unto my............ 2Sa 3:7
him away, and he was g in peace.............. 2Sa 3:22
him away, and he is g in peace................. 2Sa 3:23
sent him away, and he is quite g............... 2Sa 3:24
ark of the LORD had g six paces............... 2Sa 6:13
Amnon said unto her, Arise, be g............. 2Sa 13:15
They be g over the brook of water........... 2Sa 17:20
them that was not g over Jordan.............. 2Sa 17:22
and the men of Israel were g away.......... 2Sa 23:9
So when they had g through all.............. 2Sa 24:8
For he is g down this day, and................. 1Kin 1:25
had g from Jerusalem to Gath................... 1Kin 2:41
Pharaoh king of Egypt had g up.............. 1Kin 9:16
host was g up to bury the slain................ 1Kin 11:15
And when he was g, a lion met him......... 1Kin 13:24
for thou hast g and made thee.................. 1Kin 14:9
away dung, till it be all g........................ 1Kin 14:10
pass, as soon as I am g from thee............ 1Kin 18:12
was busy here and there, he was g........... 1Kin 20:40
whither he is g down to possess.............. 1Kin 21:18
the messenger that was g to call.............. 1Kin 22:13
that bed on which thou art g up............... 2Kin 1:4
that bed on which thou art g up............... 2Kin 1:6
that bed on which thou art g up............... 2Kin 1:16
to pass, when they were over.................... 2Kin 2:9
And the Syrians had g out by.................. 2Kin 5:2
and g forth, behold, an host...................... 2Kin 6:15
therefore are they g out of the................. 2Kin 7:12
afore Isaiah was g out into the................ 2Kin 20:4
by which it had g down in the.................. 2Kin 20:11
for God is g forth before thee to.............. 1Chr 14:15
but have g from tent to tent, and............ 1Chr 17:5
of their feasting were g about................... Job 1:5
shall I arise, and the night be g.............. Job 7:4
me on every side, and I am g................... Job 19:10
Neither have I g back from the............... Job 23:12
for a little while, but are g....................... Job 24:24
up, they are g away from men................. Job 28:4
They are all g aside, they are.................. Ps 14:3
Their line is g out through all.................. Ps 19:4
iniquities are g over mine head.............. Ps 38:4
mine eyes, it also is g from me................ Ps 38:10
for I had g with the multitude, I............. Ps 42:4
and thy billows are g over me.................. Ps 42:7
God is g up with a shout, the................... Ps 47:5
after he had g in to Bath-sheba............... Ps 51:1
Every one of them is g back...................... Ps 53:3
as for me, my feet were almost g............ Ps 73:2
is his mercy clean g for ever.................... Ps 77:8
thing that is g out of my lips................... Ps 89:34
wind passeth over it, and it is g............. Ps 103:16
I am g like the shadow when it.............. Ps 109:23
I have g astray like a lost sheep............ Ps 119:176
the stream had g over our soul................ Ps 124:4
proud waters had g over our soul........... Ps 124:5
at home, he is g a long journey............... Prov 7:19
but when he is g his way, then he.......... Prov 20:14
g from the place of the holy, and............ Eccl 8:10
is past, the rain is over and g.................. Song 2:11
had withdrawn himself, and was g......... Song 5:6
Whither is thy beloved g, O thou........... Song 6:1
My beloved is g down into his............... Song 6:2
anger, they are g away backward............ Is 1:4
my people are g into captivity................ Is 5:13
They are g over the passage..................... Is 10:29
He is g up to Bajith, and to Dibon........ Is 15:2
For the cry is g round about Dibon....... Is 15:8
out, they are g over the sea..................... Is 16:8
are wholly g up to the housetops........... Is 22:1
the mirth of the land is g........................ Is 24:11
which is g down in the sun dial............. Is 38:8
by which degrees it was g down............. Is 38:8
that he had not g with his feet............... Is 41:3
the word is g out of my mouth in......... Is 45:23
themselves are g into captivity.............. Is 46:2
my salvation is g forth, and mine......... Is 51:5
All we like sheep have g astray.............. Is 53:6
to another than me, and art g up............ Is 57:8
me, that they are g far from me............. Jer 2:5
I have not g after Baalim......................... Jer 2:23
she is g up upon every high.................... Jer 3:6
he is g forth from his place to................ Jer 4:7

they are revolted and g........................... Jer 5:23
beast are fled; they are g.......................... Jer 9:10
my children are g forth of me................ Jer 10:20
and the cry of Jerusalem is g up............ Jer 14:2
the LORD, thou art g backward.............. Jer 15:6
her sun is g down while it was............... Jer 15:9
g forth into all the land.......................... Jer 23:15
of the LORD is g forth in fury............... Jer 23:19
g forth with you into captivity............... Jer 29:16
army, which are g up from you.............. Jer 34:21
Now while he was not yet g back......... Jer 40:5
Egypt, whither ye be g to dwell............. Jer 44:8
which are g into the land of.................... Jer 44:14
that are g into the land of Egypt............ Jer 44:28
neither hath he g into captivity............. Jer 48:11
g up out of her cities, and his................ Jer 48:15
men are g down to the slaughter........... Jer 48:15
thy plants are g over the sea................... Jer 48:32
they have g from mountain to hill......... Jer 50:6
Judah is g into captivity because.......... Lam 1:3
her children are g into captivity............ Lam 1:5
they are g without strength..................... Lam 1:6
my young men are g into captivity........ Lam 1:18
the morning is g forth.............................. Eze 7:10
Israel was g up from the cherub............ Eze 9:3
Ye have not g up into the gaps............... Eze 13:5
fire is g out of a rod of her.................... Eze 19:14
because thou hast g a whoring............... Eze 23:30
and whose scum is not g out of it......... Eze 24:6
earth are g down from his shadow........ Eze 31:12
they are g down, they lie......................... Eze 32:21
which are g down uncircumcised............ Eze 32:24
which are g down to hell with.............. Eze 32:27
which are g down with the slain............ Eze 32:30
are g forth out of his land...................... Eze 36:20
the heathen, whither they be g.............. Eze 37:21
are g away far from me........................... Eze 44:10
Chaldeans, The thing is g from me........ Dan 2:5
ye see the thing is g from me................ Dan 2:8
which was g forth to slay the................. Dan 2:14
and when I am g forth, lo, the................ Dan 10:20
they have g a whoring from under......... Hos 4:12
For they are g up to Assyria, a............. Hos 8:9
for thou hast g a whoring from............. Hos 9:1
they are g because of destruction.......... Hos 9:6
When will the new moon be g................ Amos 8:5
But Jonah was g down into the.............. Jonah 1:5
for they are g into captivity................... Mic 1:16
the gate, and are g out by it.................. Mic 2:13
are g away from mine ordinances......... Mal 3:7
Ye shall not have g over the.................. Mt 10:23
unclean spirit is g out of a man........... Mt 12:43
And when they were g over, they......... Mt 14:34
sheep, and one of them be g astray....... Mt 18:12
and seeketh that which is g astray....... Mt 18:12
for our lamps are g out........................... Mt 25:8
when he was g out into the porch........ Mt 26:71
when he had g a little farther............... Mk 1:19
that virtue had g out of him................. Mk 5:30
the devil is g out of thy........................ Mk 7:29
house, she found the devil g out.......... Mk 7:30
when he was g forth into the way........ Mk 10:17
as the angels were g away from........... Lk 2:15
the fishermen were g out of them........ Lk 5:2
that virtue is g out of me....................... Lk 8:46
to pass, when the devil was g out........ Lk 11:14
unclean spirit is g out of a man.......... Lk 11:24
That he was g to be guest with a........ Lk 19:7
as though he would have g further...... Lk 24:28
(For his disciples were g away............. Jn 4:8
his disciples were g away into............. Jn 6:22
But when his brethren were g up......... Jn 7:10
behold, the world is g after him.......... Jn 12:19
Therefore, when he was g out.............. Jn 13:31
when they had g through the isle......... Acts 13:6
when the Jews were g out of the......... Acts 13:42
Now when they had g throughout....... Acts 16:6
the hope of their gains was g............... Acts 16:19
g up, and saluted the church, he......... Acts 18:22
when he had g over those parts,.......... Acts 20:2
among whom I have g preaching the.. Acts 20:25
Who also hath g about to profane....... Acts 24:6
And when they were g aside................ Acts 26:31
when they had g a little further,......... Acts 27:28
They are all g out of the way,............. Rom 3:12
Who is g into heaven, and is on........... 1Pet 3:22
are g astray, following the way............ 2Pet 2:15
prophets are g out into the world....... 1Jn 4:1
for they have g in the way of.............. Jude 11

GOOD See PREFACE.

GOODLIER
of Israel a g person than he.................. 1Sa 9:2

GOODLIEST
your g young men, and your asses........ 1Sa 8:16
also and thy children, even the g......... 1Kin 20:3

GOODLINESS
all the g thereof is as the....................... Is 40:6

GOODLY
Rebekah took g raiment of her.............. Gen 27:15
And Joseph was a g person, and well.. Gen 39:6
he giveth g words.................................... Gen 49:21
she saw him that he was a g child...... Ex 2:2
g bonnets of fine linen, and linen........ Ex 39:28
first day the boughs of g trees.............. Lev 23:40
How g are thy tents, O Jacob, and..... Num 24:5
dwelt, and all their g castles................. Num 31:10
that g mountain, and Lebanon.............. Deut 3:25
g cities, which thou buildedst............... Deut 6:10

art full, and hast built g houses.......... Deut 8:12
the spoils a g Babylonish garment...... Josh 7:21
Saul, a choice young man, and a g..... 1Sa 9:2
countenance, and g to look to.............. 1Sa 16:12
And he slew an Egyptian, a g man..... 2Sa 23:21
and he also was a very g man.............. 1Kin 1:6
with the g vessels of the house............ 2Chr 36:10
all the g vessels thereof........................ 2Chr 36:19
Gavest thou the g wings unto the....... Job 39:13
yea, I have a g heritage......................... Ps 16:6
thereof were like the g cedars.............. Ps 80:10
a g heritage of the hosts of.................. Jer 3:19
olive tree, fair, and of g fruit.............. Jer 11:16
fruit, that it might be a g vine............ Eze 17:8
and bear fruit, and be a g cedar.......... Eze 17:23
his land they have made g images...... Hos 10:1
your temples my g pleasant things.... Joel 3:5
them as his g horse in the battle........ Zec 10:3
a price that I was prised at of............. Zec 11:13
a merchant man, seeking g pearls....... Mt 13:45
how it was adorned with g stones...... Lk 21:5
in apparel, and there come in............. Jas 2:2
g are departed from thee, and thou.... Rev 18:14

GOODMAN
For the g is not at home, he is........... Prov 7:19
against the g of the house.................... Mt 20:11
that if the g of the house had............. Mt 24:43
in, say ye to the g of the house.......... Mk 14:14
that if the g of the house had............. Lk 12:39
shall say unto the g of the house....... Lk 22:11

GOODNESS
the g which the LORD had done to..... Ex 18:9
make all my g pass before thee.......... Ex 33:19
longsuffering, and abundant in g....... Ex 34:6
that what g the LORD shall do............ Num 10:32
according to all the g which he......... Judg 8:35
promised this g unto thy servant....... 2Sa 7:28
glad of heart for all the g that........... 1Kin 8:66
promised this g unto thy servant....... 1Chr 17:26
and let thy saints rejoice in g............ 2Chr 6:41
merry in heart for the g that the........ 2Chr 7:10
the acts of Hezekiah, and his g.......... 2Chr 32:32
the acts of Josiah, and his g.............. 2Chr 35:26
themselves in thy great g.................... Neh 9:25
in thy great g that thou gavest.......... Neh 9:35
my g extendeth not to thee................ Ps 16:2
him with the blessings of g............... Ps 21:3
Surely g and mercy shall follow me.. Ps 23:6
I had believed to see the g of............ Ps 27:13
Oh how great is thy g, which thou... Ps 31:19
is full of the g of the LORD............... Ps 33:5
the g of God endureth continually..... Ps 52:1
satisfied with the g of thy house...... Ps 65:4
Thou crownest the year with thy g.. Ps 65:11
prepared of thy g for the poor........... Ps 68:10
would praise the LORD for his g....... Ps 107:8
and filleth the hungry soul with g... Ps 107:9
would praise the LORD for his g....... Ps 107:15
would praise the LORD for his g....... Ps 107:21
would praise the LORD for his g....... Ps 107:31
My g, and my fortress........................ Ps 144:2
utter the memory of thy great g........ Ps 145:7
will proclaim every one his own g... Prov 20:6
the great g toward the house of........ Is 63:7
fruit thereof and the g thereof.......... Jer 2:7
together to the g of the LORD............ Jer 31:12
shall be satisfied with my g.............. Jer 31:14
fear and tremble for all the g........... Jer 33:9
Lord and his g in the latter days...... Hos 3:5
for your g is as a morning cloud....... Hos 6:4
according to the g of his land........... Hos 10:1
For how great is his g, and how........ Zec 9:17
thou the riches of his g and.............. Rom 2:4
not knowing that the g of God........... Rom 2:4
Behold therefore the g and................ Rom 11:22
but toward thee, g..................... .... Rom 11:22
if thou continue in his g.................... Rom 11:22
that ye also are full of g................... Rom 15:14
longsuffering, gentleness, g............... Gal 5:22
fruit of the Spirit is in all g.............. Eph 5:9
all the good pleasure of his g............ 2Th 1:11

GOODNESS'
remember thou me for thy g sake....... Ps 25:7

GOODS
And they took all the g of Sodom....... Gen 14:11
son, who dwelt in Sodom, and his g.. Gen 14:12
And he brought back all the g.............. Gen 14:16
again his brother Lot, and his g.......... Gen 14:16
persons, and take the g to thyself....... Gen 14:21
for a...the g of his master were.......... Gen 24:10
all his g which he had gotten............. Gen 31:18
took their cattle, and their g.............. Gen 46:6
his hand unto his neighbour's g......... Ex 22:8
his hand unto his neighbour's g......... Ex 22:11
unto Korah, and all their g.................. Num 16:32
all their flocks, and all their g.......... Num 31:9
for their cattle, and for their g.......... Num 35:3
shall make thee plenteous in g........... Deut 28:11
and thy wives, and all thy g............... 2Chr 21:14
silver, and with gold, and with g....... Ezr 1:4
of silver, with gold, with g................ Ezr 1:6
that of the king's, g, even of the....... Ezr 6:8
or to confiscation of g, or to............. Ezr 7:26
and possessed houses full of all g..... Neh 9:25
his hands shall restore their g........... Job 20:10
shall no man look for his g................ Job 20:21
his g shall flow away in the day....... Job 20:28
When g increase, they are.................. Eccl 5:11

which have gotten cattle and g .... Eze 38:12
and gold, to take away cattle and g ... Eze 38:13
Therefore their g shall become a ...... Zeph 1:13
man's house, and spoil his g .... Mt 12:29
make him ruler over all his g .... Mt 24:47
and delivered unto them his g .... Mt 25:14
man's house, and spoil his g .... Mk 3:27
away thy g ask them not again .... Lk 6:30
his palace, his g are in peace .... Lk 11:21
I bestow all my fruits and my g .... Lk 12:18
thou hast much g laid up for many ... Lk 12:19
portion of g that falleth to me .... Lk 15:12
unto him that he had wasted his g ... Lk 16:1
the half of my g I give to the .... Lk 19:8
And sold their possessions and g ..... Acts 2:45
bestow all my g to feed the poor 1Cor 13:3
joyfully the spoiling of your g .... Heb 10:34
I am rich, and increased with g .... Rev 3:17

GOPHER
Make thee an ark of g wood .... Gen 6:14

GORE
If an ox g a man or a woman, that ...... Ex 21:28

GORED
Whether he have g a son .... Ex 21:31
or have g a daughter, according .... Ex 21:31

GORGEOUS
him, and arrayed him in a g robe .... Lk 23:11

GORGEOUSLY
captains and rulers clothed most g .... Eze 23:12
they which are g apparelled .... Lk 7:25

GOSHEN (go'-shen)
1. A district of Egypt.
thou shalt dwell in the land of G .... Gen 45:10
Joseph, to direct his face unto G .... Gen 46:28
and they came into the land of G ...... Gen 46:28
to meet Israel his father, to G .... Gen 46:29
ye may dwell in the land of G .... Gen 46:34
behold, they are in the land of G .... Gen 47:1
servants dwell in the land of G .... Gen 47:4
in the land of G let them dwell .... Gen 47:6
of Egypt, in the country of G .... Gen 47:27
herds, they left in the land of G .... Gen 50:8
sever in that day the land of G .... Ex 8:22
Only in the land of G, where the .... Ex 9:26
2. A district in southern Palestine.
Gaza, and all the country of G .... Josh 10:41
country, and all the land of G .... Josh 11:16
3. A town in Judea.
And G, and Holon, and Giloh .... Josh 15:51

GOSPEL
preaching the g of the kingdom, ... Mt 4:23
preaching the g of the kingdom, ... Mt 9:35
poor have the g preached to .... Mt 11:5
this g of the kingdom shall be .... Mt 24:14
Wheresoever this g shall be .... Mt 26:13
of the g of Jesus Christ, the Son .... Mk 1:1
preaching the g of the kingdom of .... Mk 1:14
repent ye, and believe the g .... Mk 1:15
the g must first be published .... Mk 13:10
Wheresoever this g shall be .... Mk 14:9
preach the g to every creature .... Mk 16:15
me to preach the g to the poor .... Lk 4:18
to the poor the g is preached .... Lk 7:22
the towns, preaching the g .... Lk 9:6
in the temple, and preached the g .... Lk 20:1
preached the g in many villages, ... Acts 8:25
And there they preached the g .... Acts 14:7
had preached the g to that city .... Acts 14:21
should near the word of the g .... Acts 15:7
us for to preach the g unto them ...... Acts 16:10
to testify the g of the grace of .... Acts 20:24
separated unto the g of God .... Rom 1:1
my spirit in the g of his Son .... Rom 1:9
I am ready to preach the g to you ..... Rom 1:15
am not ashamed of the g of Christ .... Rom 1:16
by Jesus Christ according to my g ..... Rom 2:16
them that preach the g of peace, ... Rom 10:15
they have not all obeyed the g .... Rom 10:16
As concerning the g, they are .... Rom 11:28
ministering the g of God .... Rom 15:16
fully preached the g of Christ .... Rom 15:19
so have I strived to preach the g .... Rom 15:20
the blessing of the g of Christ .... Rom 15:29
to stablish you according to my g ..... Rom 16:25
to baptize, but to preach the g 1Cor 1:17
I have begotten you through the g 1Cor 4:15
we should hinder the g of Christ 1Cor 9:12
the g should live of the g 1Cor 9:14
For though I preach the g 1Cor 9:16
is unto me, if I preach not the g 1Cor 9:16
of the g is committed unto me 1Cor 9:17
Verily that, when I preach the g 1Cor 9:18
I may make the g of Christ 1Cor 9:18
I abuse not my power in the g 1Cor 9:18
I declare unto you the g which I 1Cor 15:1
to Troas to preach Christ's g 2Cor 2:12
But if our g be hid, it is hid to 2Cor 4:3
light of the glorious g of Christ 2Cor 4:4
brother, whose praise is in the g 2Cor 8:18
subjection unto the g of Christ 2Cor 9:13
also in preaching the g of Christ 2Cor 10:14
To preach the g in the regions 2Cor 10:16
have not received, or another g 2Cor 11:4
to you the g of God freely 2Cor 11:7
grace of Christ unto another g .... Gal 1:6
and would pervert the g of Christ ..... Gal 1:7

preach any other g unto you than ..... Gal 1:8
g unto you than that ye have .... Gal 1:9
that the g which was preached of ...... Gal 1:11
that which I preach among the .... Gal 2:2
that the truth of the g might .... Gal 2:5
when they saw that the g of the .... Gal 2:7
as the g of the circumcision was .... Gal 2:7
according to the truth of the g .... Gal 2:14
before the g unto Abraham .... Gal 3:8
the g unto you at the first .... Gal 4:13
of truth, the g of your salvation .... Eph 1:13
of his promise in Christ by the g .... Eph 3:6
the preparation of the g of peace ..... Eph 6:15
make known the mystery of the g ..... Eph 6:19
For your fellowship in the g from ...... Phil 1:5
defence and confirmation of the g ... Phil 1:7
unto the furtherance of the g .... Phil 1:12
I am set for the defence of the g .... Phil 1:17
be as it becometh the g of Christ ..... Phil 1:27
together for the faith of the g .... Phil 1:27
he hath served with me in the g .... Phil 4:3
that in the beginning of the g .... Phil 4:15
in the word of the truth of the g .... Col 1:5
moved away from the hope of the g .. Col 1:23
For our g came not unto you in 1Th 1:5
the g of God with much contention ... 1Th 2:2
God to be put in trust with the g 1Th 2:4
not the g of God only, but also 1Th 2:8
we preached unto you the g of God ... 1Th 2:9
fellowlabourer in the g of Christ 1Th 3:2
that obey not the g of our Lord 2Th 1:8
Whereunto he called you by our g 2Th 2:14
the glorious g of the blessed God 1Ti 1:11
of the afflictions of the g 2Ti 1:8
to light through the g 2Ti 1:10
from the dead according to my g 2Ti 2:8
unto me in the bonds of the g .... Philem 13
For unto us was the g preached .... Heb 4:2
g unto you with the Holy Ghost 1Pet 1:12
by the g is preached unto you 1Pet 1:25
For for this cause was the g 1Pet 4:6
them that obey not the g of God 1Pet 4:17
having the everlasting to .... Rev 14:6

GOSPEL'S
his life for my sake and the g .... Mk 8:35
or lands, for my sake, and the g .... Mk 10:29
And this I do for the g sake 1Cor 9:23

GOT
which he had in the land of .... Gen 36:6
her hand, and fled, and g him out ..... Gen 39:12
with me, and fled, and g him out ...... Gen 39:15
For they g not the land in .... Ps 44:3
I g me servants and maidens, ... Eccl 2:7
So I g a girdle according to the .... Jer 13:2
Take the girdle that thou hast g .... Jer 13:4

GOTTEN
I have a man from the Lord .... Gen 4:1
souls that they had g in Haran .... Gen 12:5
father's hath he g all this glory, ... Gen 31:1
and all his goods which he had g ...... Gen 31:18
which he had a g in Padan-aram, for . Gen 31:18
which they had a in the land of .... Gen 46:6
when I have a me honour upon .... Ex 14:18
thing which he hath deceitfully g ...... Lev 6:4
the Lord, what every man hath a .... Num 31:50
mine hand hath g me this wealth ...... Deut 8:17
If he be g into a city, then 2Sa 17:13
It cannot be g for gold, neither .... Job 28:15
and because mine hand had much .... Job 31:25
holy arm, hath g him the victory .... Ps 98:1
Wealth by vanity shall be .... Prov 13:11
An inheritance may be g hastily .... Prov 20:21
have gotten wisdom than all they ..... Eccl 1:16
the abundance they have g .... Is 15:7
that he hath a are gotten .... Jer 48:36
thou hast g thee riches, and hast ...... Eze 28:4
thee riches, and hast g gold .... Eze 28:4
the nations, which have g cattle .... Eze 38:12
hast g thee renown, as at this .... Dan 9:15
that after we were g from them, ... Acts 21:1
them that had g the victory over .... Rev 15:2

GOURD
And the Lord God prepared a g .... Jonah 4:6
Jonah was exceeding glad of the g .... Jonah 4:6
it smote the g that it withered. .... Jonah 4:7
thou well to be angry for the g .... Jonah 4:9
Lord, Thou hast had pity on the g ..... Jonah 4:10

GOURDS
thereof wild g his lap full. 2Kin 4:39

GOVERN
Dost thou now g the kingdom of 1Kin 21:7
Shall even he that hateth right g ...... Job 34:17
and g the nations upon earth .... Ps 67:4

GOVERNMENT
the g shall be upon his shoulder .... Is 9:6
Of the increase of his g and peace .... Is 9:7
I will commit thy g into his hand, ... Is 22:21
lust of uncleanness, and despise g 2Pet 2:10

GOVERNMENTS
then gifts of healings, helps, g 1Cor 12:28

GOVERNOR
And Joseph was the g over the land .. Gen 42:6
he is g over all the land of .... Gen 45:26
which was the g of his house 1Kin 18:3

back unto Amon the g of the city 1Kin 22:26
gate of Joshua the g of the city 2Kin 23:8
of Babylon had made Gedaliah g 2Kin 25:23
unto the Lord to be the chief g 1Chr 29:22
to every g in all Israel, the 2Chr 1:2
back to Amon the g of the city 2Chr 18:25
Azrikam the g of the house, and 2Chr 28:7
and Maaseiah the g of the city 2Chr 34:8
g on this side the river, and .... Ezr 5:3
g on this side the river, and .... Ezr 5:6
Sheshbazzar, whom he had made g ... Ezr 5:14
Tatnai, g beyond the river, ... Ezr 6:6
let the g of the Jews and the .... Ezr 6:7
g on this side the river .... Ezr 6:13
of the g on this side the river .... Neh 3:7
be their g in the land of Judah .... Neh 5:14
have not eaten the bread of the g .... Neh 5:14
required not I the bread of the g .... Neh 5:18
and in the days of Nehemiah the g .... Neh 12:26
he is the g among the nations .... Ps 22:28
who was also chief g in the house ..... Jer 20:1
their g shall proceed from the .... Jer 30:21
made g over the cities of Judah .... Jer 40:5
the son of Ahikam g in the land .... Jer 40:7
Babylon had made g over the land .... Jer 41:2
of Babylon made g in the land .... Jer 41:18
g of Judah, and to Joshua the son .... Hag 1:1
g of Judah, and the spirit of .... Hag 1:14
g of Judah, and to Joshua the son .... Hag 2:2
g of Judah, saying, I will shake .... Hag 2:21
and he shall be as a g in Judah. .... Zec 9:7
offer it now unto thy g .... Mal 1:8
for out of thee shall come a G .... Mt 2:6
him to Pontius Pilate the g .... Mt 27:2
And Jesus stood before the g .... Mt 27:11
and the g asked him, saying, Art thou Mt 27:11
that the g marvelled greatly .... Mt 27:14
Now at that feast the g was wont ...... Mt 27:15
The g answered and said unto them, . Mt 27:21
the g said, Why, what evil hath .... Mt 27:23
Then the soldiers of the g took .... Mt 27:27
made when Cyrenius was g of Syria ... Lk 2:2
Pontius Pilate being g of Judaea .... Lk 3:1
the power and authority of the g .... Lk 20:20
and bear unto the g of the feast .... Jn 2:8
the g of the feast called the .... Jn 2:9
and he made him g over Egypt .... Acts 7:10
bring him safe unto Felix the g .... Acts 23:24
g Felix sendeth greeting .... Acts 23:26
and delivered the epistle to the g ..... Acts 23:33
when the g had read the letter, ... Acts 23:34
who informed the g against Paul .... Acts 24:1
after that the g had beckoned .... Acts 24:10
the king rose up, and the g .... Acts 26:30
In Damascus the g under Aretas, ... 2Cor 11:32
helm, whithersoever the g listeth ...... Jas 3:4

GOVERNOR'S
And if this come to the g ears, ... Mt 28:14

GOVERNORS
heart is toward the g of Israel .... Judg 5:9
out of Machir came down g .... Judg 5:14
and of the g of the country. 1Kin 10:15
for the g of the sanctuary, and 1Chr 24:5
g of the house of God, were 1Chr 24:5
of the country brought gold and 2Chr 9:14
g of the people, and all the 2Chr 23:20
to the g on this side the river .... Ezr 8:36
me to the g beyond the river .... Neh 2:7
I came to the g beyond the river .... Neh 2:9
But the former g that had been .... Neh 5:15
to the g that were over every .... Est 3:12
chief of the g over all the wise .... Dan 2:48
together the princes, the g .... Dan 3:2
the princes, the g, and .... Dan 3:3
And the princes, g, and captains, ... Dan 3:27
presidents of the kingdom, the g ...... Dan 6:7
the g of Judah shall say in their .... Zec 12:5
In that day will I make the g of .... Zec 12:6
And ye shall be brought before g ...... Mt 10:18
g until the time appointed of the ...... Gal 4:2
Or unto g, as unto them that are 1Pet 2:14

GOYIM See Nations.

GOZAN (go'-zan) An Assyrian city.
and in Habor by the river of G 2Kin 17:6
and in Habor by the river of G 2Kin 18:11
G, and Haran, and Rezeph 2Kin 19:12
Habor, and Hara, and to the river G ... 1Chr 5:26
my fathers have destroyed, as G .... Is 37:12

GRACE
But Noah found g in the eyes of .... Gen 6:8
servant hath found g in thy sight ...... Gen 19:19
that I may find g in thy sight. .... Gen 32:5
These are to find g in the sight .... Gen 33:8
now I have found g in thy sight .... Gen 33:10
let me find g in the sight of my .... Gen 33:15
let me find g in your eyes, and .... Gen 34:11
And Joseph found g in his master ...... Gen 39:4
let us find g in the sight of my .... Gen 47:25
now I have found g in thy sight .... Gen 47:29
now I have found g in your eyes. .... Gen 50:4
hast also found g in my sight. .... Ex 33:12
if I have found g in thy sight. .... Ex 33:13
that I may find g in thy sight. .... Ex 33:13
people have found g in thy sight .... Ex 33:16
for thou hast found g in my sight ...... Ex 33:17
now I have found g in thy sight .... Ex 34:9
if we have found g in thy sight. .... Num 32:5
now I have found g in thy sight .... Judg 6:17

G

him in whose sight I shall find g........... Ruth 2:2
Why have I found g in thine eyes........ Ruth 2:10
handmaid find g in thy sight.............. 1Sa 1:18
that I have found g in thine eyes........ 1Sa 20:3
I have now found g in thine eyes......... 1Sa 27:5
that I have found a g in thine eyes....... 2Sa 14:22
that I may find g in thy sight............ 2Sa 16:4
now for a little space g hath............. Ezr 9:8
all the women, and she obtained g........ Est 2:17
g is poured into thy lips................. Ps 45:2
the LORD will give g and glory........... Ps 84:11
be an ornament of g unto thine head...... Prov 1:9
unto thy soul, and g to thy neck......... Prov 3:22
but he giveth g unto the lowly........... Prov 3:34
to thine head an ornament of g........... Prov 4:9
for the g of his lips the king........... Prov 22:11
sword found g in the wilderness.......... Jer 31:2
crying, G, g unto it..................... Zec 4:7
of Jerusalem, the spirit of g............ Zec 12:10
the g of God was upon him................ Lk 2:40
of the Father,) full of g................ Jn 1:14
all we received, and g for g............. Jn 1:16
the law was given by Moses, but g........ Jn 1:17
great g was upon them all................ Acts 4:33
he came, and had seen the g of God.. Acts 11:23
them to continue in the g of God.. Acts 13:43
testimony unto the word of his g.... Acts 14:3
had been recommended to the g of.. Acts 14:26
the g of the Lord Jesus Christ we...... Acts 15:11
by the brethren unto the g of God...... Acts 15:40
much which had believed through g .. Acts 18:27
the gospel of the g of God.............. Acts 20:24
to God, and to the word of his g........ Acts 20:32
By whom we have received g.............. Rom 1:5
G to you and peace from God our...... Rom 1:7
Being justified freely by his g......... Rom 3:24
is the reward not reckoned of g......... Rom 4:4
of faith, that it might be by g......... Rom 4:16
into this g wherein we stand............. Rom 5:2
g of God, and the gift by g............. Rom 5:15
they which receive abundance of g....... Rom 5:17
abounded, g did much more abound....... Rom 5:20
even so might g reign through........... Rom 5:21
in sin, that g may abound............... Rom 6:1
not under the law, but under g.......... Rom 6:14
not under the law, but under g.......... Rom 6:15
according to the election of g.......... Rom 11:5
And if by g, then is it no more of...... Rom 11:6
otherwise g is no more g................ Rom 11:6
be of works, then is it no more g....... Rom 11:6
through the g given unto me, to......... Rom 12:3
to the g that is given to us............ Rom 12:6
because of the g that is given to....... Rom 15:15
The g of our Lord Jesus Christ be....... Rom 16:20
The g of our Lord Jesus Christ be....... Rom 16:24
G be unto you, and peace, from God .. 1Cor 1:3
for the g of God which is given......... 1Cor 1:4
According to the g of God which...... 1Cor 3:10
For if I by g be a partaker, why.... 1Cor 10:30
But by the g of God I am what I 1Cor 15:10
his g which was bestowed upon me .. 1Cor 15:10
but the g of God which was with...... 1Cor 15:10
The g of our Lord Jesus Christ be.... 1Cor 16:23
G be to you and peace from God our .. 2Cor 1:2
wisdom, but by the g of God............. 2Cor 1:12
that the abundant g might through .. 2Cor 4:15
receive not the g of God in vain........ 2Cor 6:1
we do you to wit of the g of God........ 2Cor 8:1
finish in you the same g also........... 2Cor 8:6
see that ye abound in this g also....... 2Cor 8:7
For ye know the g of our Lord........... 2Cor 8:9
to travel with us with this g........... 2Cor 8:19
to make all g abound toward you......... 2Cor 9:8
for the exceeding g of God in you....... 2Cor 9:14
My g is sufficient for thee............. 2Cor 12:9
The g of the Lord Jesus Christ,....... 2Cor 13:14
G be to you and peace from God the ..... Gal 1:3
him that called you into the g of....... Gal 1:6
womb, and called me by his g............ Gal 1:15
perceived the g that was given.......... Gal 2:9
I do not frustrate the g of God......... Gal 2:21
ye are fallen from g.................... Gal 5:4
the g of our Lord Jesus Christ be....... Gal 6:18
G be to you, and peace, from............ Eph 1:2
the praise of the glory of his g........ Eph 1:6
according to the riches of his g........ Eph 1:7
with Christ, (by g ye are saved......... Eph 2:5
his g in his kindness toward us......... Eph 2:7
For by g are ye saved through........... Eph 2:8
of the dispensation of the g of......... Eph 3:2
the g of God given unto me the g........ Eph 3:7
of all saints, is this g given.......... Eph 3:8
unto every one of us is given g......... Eph 4:7
may minister g unto the hearers......... Eph 4:29
G be with all them that love our........ Eph 6:24
G be unto you, and peace, from God .. Phil 1:2
ye all are partakers of my g............ Phil 1:7
The g of our Lord Jesus Christ be...... Phil 4:23
G be unto you, and peace, from God .. Col 1:2
knew the g of God in truth.............. Col 1:6
singing with g in your hearts to........ Col 3:16
Let your speech be alway with g......... Col 4:6
G be with you......................... Col 4:18
G be unto you, and peace, from.......... 1Th 1:1
The g of our Lord Jesus Christ be....... 1Th 5:28
G unto you, and peace, from God 2Th 1:2
according to the g of our God........... 2Th 1:12
and good hope through g................. 2Th 2:16
The g of our Lord Jesus Christ be....... 2Th 3:18
G, mercy, and peace, from God our 1Ti 1:2

the g of our Lord was exceeding......... 1Ti 1:14
G be with thee......................... 1Ti 6:21
G, mercy, and peace, from God the .. 2Ti 1:2
according to his own purpose and g...... 2Ti 1:9
be strong in the g that is in........... 2Ti 2:1
G be with you......................... 2Ti 4:22
G, mercy, and peace, from God the .. Titus 1:4
For the g of God that bringeth.......... Titus 2:11
That being justified by his g........... Titus 3:7
G be with you all...................... Titus 3:15
G to you, and peace, from God our .. Philem 3
The g of our Lord Jesus Christ be.... Philem 25
that he by the g of God should.......... Heb 2:9
come boldly unto the throne of g........ Heb 4:16
find g to help in time of need.......... Heb 4:16
done despite unto the Spirit of g....... Heb 10:29
lest any man fail of the g of God....... Heb 12:15
cannot be moved, let us have g.......... Heb 12:28
the heart be established with g......... Heb 13:9
G be with you all...................... Heb 13:25
the g of the fashion of it.............. Jas 1:11
But he giveth more g.................... Jas 4:6
but giveth g unto the humble............ Jas 4:6
G unto you, and peace, be............... 1Pet 1:2
the prophesied of the g that........... 1Pet 1:10
hope to the end for the g that is....... 1Pet 1:13
heirs together of the g of life......... 1Pet 3:7
stewards of the manifold g of God....... 1Pet 4:10
proud, and giveth g to the humble....... 1Pet 5:5
But the God of all g, who hath.......... 1Pet 5:10
that this is the true g of God.......... 1Pet 5:12
G and peace be multiplied unto you .. 2Pet 1:2
But grow in g, and in the............... 2Pet 3:18
G be with you, mercy, and peace,........ 2Jn 3
turning the g of our God into........... Jude 4
G be unto you, and peace, from him .. Rev 1:4
the g of our Lord Jesus Christ be.... Rev 22:21

GRACIOUS

God be g unto thee, my son.............. Gen 43:29
for I am g.............................. Ex 22:27
be g to whom I will be g................ Ex 33:19
LORD, The LORD God, merciful and g..... Ex 34:6
upon thee, and be g unto thee........... Num 6:25
tell whether God will be g to me........ 2Sa 12:22
And the LORD was g unto them............ 2Kin 13:23
for the LORD your God is g.............. 2Chr 30:9
thou art a God ready to pardon, g....... Neh 9:17
for thou art a g and merciful God....... Neh 9:31
Then he is g unto him, and saith,....... Job 33:24
Hath God forgotten to be g.............. Ps 77:9
a God full of compassion, and g......... Ps 86:15
The LORD is merciful and g.............. Ps 103:8
the LORD is g and full of............... Ps 111:4
he is g, and full of compassion,........ Ps 112:4
G is the LORD, and righteous............ Ps 116:5
The LORD is g, and full of.............. Ps 145:8
A woman retaineth honour................ Prov 11:16
words of a wise man's mouth are g...... Eccl 10:12
wait, that he may be g unto you......... Is 30:18
he will be very g unto thee at.......... Is 30:19
O LORD, be g unto us.................... Is 33:2
how g shalt thou be when pangs.......... Jer 22:23
for he is g and merciful, slow to....... Joel 2:13
be g unto the remnant of Joseph......... Amos 5:15
for I knew that thou art a g............ Jonah 4:2
God that he will be g unto us........... Mal 1:9
wondered at the g words which........... Lk 4:22
ye have tasted that the Lord is g .. 1Pet 2:3

GRACIOUSLY

God hath g given thy servant............ Gen 33:5
Because God hath dealt g with me........ Gen 33:11
and grant me thy law g.................. Ps 119:29
all iniquity, and receive us g.......... Hos 14:2

GRAFF

God is able to g them in again.......... Rom 11:23

GRAFFED

wert g in among them, and with.......... Rom 11:17
broken off, that I might be g in........ Rom 11:19
still in unbelief, shall be g in........ Rom 11:23
wert g contrary to nature into a........ Rom 11:24
be g into their own olive tree.......... Rom 11:24

GRAIN

the least g fall upon the earth......... Amos 9:9
is like to a g of mustard seed.......... Mt 13:31
have faith as a g of mustard seed....... Mt 17:20
It is like a g of mustard seed.......... Mk 4:31
It is like a g of mustard seed,......... Lk 13:19
had faith as a g of mustard seed........ Lk 17:6
body that shall be, but bare g.......... 1Cor 15:37
of wheat, or of some other g............ 1Cor 15:37

GRANDMOTHER

which dwelt first in thy g Lois......... 2Ti 1:5

GRANT

shall a redemption for the land......... Lev 25:24
The LORD g you that ye may find......... Ruth 1:9
the God of Israel g thee thy............ Isa 1:17
to Oran, to the place of this........... 1Chr 21:22
thou shalt g it me for the full......... 1Chr 21:22
them, but I will g them some............ 2Chr 12:7
according to the g that they had........ Ezr 3:7
g him mercy in the sight of this........ Neh 1:11
please the king to g my petition....... Est 5:8
that God would g me the thing........... Job 6:8
g thee according to thine own........... Ps 20:4
O LORD, and g us thy salvation.......... Ps 85:7
and g me thy law graciously............. Ps 119:29

G not, O LORD, the desires of the....... Ps 140:8
G that these my two sons may sit,....... Mt 20:21
G unto us that we may sit, one on....... Mk 10:37
g unto thy servants, that with.......... Acts 4:29
and consolation g you to be............. Rom 15:5
That he would g you, according to....... Eph 3:16
The Lord g unto him that he may......... 2Ti 1:18
I g to sit with me in my throne......... Rev 3:21

GRANTED

God g him that which he requested.. 1Chr 4:10
and knowledge is g unto thee.......... 2Chr 1:12
the king g him all his request.......... Ezr 7:6
And the king g me, according to......... Neh 2:8
and it shall be g thee.................. Est 5:2
and it shall be g thee.................. Est 7:2
Wherein the king g the Jews which....... Est 8:11
and it shall be g thee.................. Est 9:12
let it be g to the Jews which are....... Est 9:13
Thou hast g me life and favour, and.. Job 10:12
of the righteous shall be g............. Prov 10:24
a murderer to be g unto you............ Acts 3:14
Gentiles g repentance unto life....... Acts 11:18
g signs and wonders to be done by ...... Acts 14:3
to her was g that she should be......... Rev 19:8

GRAPE

gather every g of thy vineyard.......... Lev 19:10
drink the pure blood of the g........... Deut 32:14
off his unripe g as the vine............ Job 15:33
the tender g give a good smell.......... Song 2:13
whether the tender g appear............. Song 7:12
the sour g is ripening in the........... Is 18:5
The fathers have eaten a sour g........ Jer 31:29
every man that eateth the sour g....... Jer 31:30

GRAPEGATHERER

hand as a g into the baskets............ Jer 6:9

GRAPEGATHERERS

If g come to thee, would they not....... Jer 49:9
if the g came to thee, would they....... Obad 5

GRAPEGLEANINGS

fruits, as the g of the vintage......... Mic 7:1

GRAPES

thereof brought forth ripe g............ Gen 40:10
and I took the g, and pressed them...... Gen 40:11
and his clothes in the blood of g....... Gen 49:11
neither gather the g of thy vine....... Lev 25:5
nor gather the g in it of thy........... Lev 25:11
liquor of g, nor eat moist g............ Num 6:3
was the time of the firstripe g......... Num 13:20
a branch with one cluster of g.......... Num 13:23
because of the cluster of g which...... Num 13:24
then thou mayest eat g thy fill......... Deut 23:24
gatherest the g of thy vineyard......... Deut 24:21
and shalt not gather the g thereof.. Deut 24:21
of the wine, nor gather the g........... Deut 28:39
their g are g of gall................... Deut 32:32
the g of Ephraim better than the........ Judg 8:2
their vineyards, and trode the g........ Judg 9:27
as also wine, g and figs, and all....... Neh 13:15
for our vines have tender g............. Song 2:15
and thy breasts to clusters of g........ Song 7:7
that it should bring forth g............ Is 5:2
and it brought forth wild g............. Is 5:2
that it should bring forth g............ Is 5:4
brought it forth wild g................. Is 5:4
Yet gleaning g shall be left in......... Is 17:6
as the gleaning g when the.............. Is 24:13
there shall be no g on the vine......... Jer 8:13
a shout, as they that tread the g....... Jer 25:30
they not leave some gleaning g.......... Jer 49:9
The fathers have eaten a sour g......... Eze 18:2
Israel like g in the wilderness......... Hos 9:10
the treader of g him that soweth.. Amos 9:13
thee, would they not leave some g....... Obad 5
Do men gather g of thorns............... Mt 7:16
of a bramble bush gather they g......... Lk 6:44
for her g are fully ripe............... Rev 14:18

GRASS

said, Let the earth bring forth g....... Gen 1:11
And the earth brought forth g........... Gen 1:12
ox licketh up the g of the field........ Num 22:4
I will send g in thy fields for......... Deut 11:15
nor any g groweth therein, like......... Deut 29:23
and as the showers upon the g........... Deut 32:2
as the tender g springing out of....... 2Sa 23:4
we may find g to save the horses....... 1Kin 18:5
they were as the g of the field......... 2Kin 19:26
as th... g on the house tops, and as.. 2Kin 19:26
offspring as the g of the earth......... Job 5:25
the wild ass bray when he hath g........ Job 6:5
he eateth g as an ox.................... Job 40:15
shall soon be cut down like the g....... Ps 37:2
down like rain upon the mown g.......... Ps 72:6
flourish like g of the earth............ Ps 72:16
they are like g which groweth up........ Ps 90:5
When the wicked spring as the g......... Ps 92:7
is smitten, and withered like g......... Ps 102:4
and I am withered like g................ Ps 102:11
for man, his days are as g.............. Ps 103:15
He causeth the g to grow for the........ Ps 104:14
similitude of an ox that eateth g....... Ps 106:20
be as the g upon the housetops......... Ps 129:6
who maketh g to grow upon the........... Ps 147:8
his favour is as dew upon the g......... Prov 19:12
the tender g sheweth itself, and....... Prov 27:25
the g faileth, there is no green........ Is 15:6

GRASSHOPPER

shall be *g* with reeds and rushes	Is 35:7
they were as the *g* of the field	Is 37:27
as the *g* on the housetops, and as	Is 37:27
All flesh is *g*, and all the	Is 40:6
The *g* withereth, the flower	Is 40:7
surely the people is *g*	Is 40:7
The *g* withereth, the flower	Is 40:8
shall spring up as among the *g*	Is 44:4
of the *g* he shall make as a *g*	Jer 14:5
it, because there was no *g*	Jer 14:5
did fail, because there was no *g*	Jer 14:6
are grown fat as the heifer at *g*	Jer 50:11
in the tender *g* of the field	Dan 4:15
the beasts in the *g* of the earth	Dan 4:15
in the tender *g* of the field	Dan 4:23
shall make thee to eat *g* as oxen	Dan 4:25
shall make thee to eat *g* as oxen	Dan 4:32
from men, and did eat *g* as oxen	Dan 4:33
they fed him with *g* like oxen	Dan 5:21
end of eating the *g* of the land	Amos 7:2
LORD, as the showers upon the *g*	Mic 5:7
rain, to every one *g* in the field	Zec 10:1
God so clothe the *g* of the field	Mt 6:30
multitude to sit down on the *g*	Mt 14:19
by companies upon the green *g*	Mk 6:39
If then God so clothe the *g*	Lk 12:28
Now there was much *g* in the place	Jn 6:10
of the *g* he shall pass away	Jas 1:10
heat, but it withereth the *g*	Jas 1:11
For all flesh is as *g*, and all the	1Pet 1:24
glory of man as the flower of *g*	1Pet 1:24
The *g* withereth, and the flower	1Pet 1:24
up, and all green *g* was burnt up	Rev 8:7
not hurt the *g* of the earth	Rev 9:4

GRASSHOPPER

his kind, and the *g* after his kind	Lev 11:22
Canst thou make him afraid as a *g*	Job 39:20
the *g* shall be a burden, and	Eccl 12:5

GRASSHOPPERS

and we were in our own sight as *g*	Num 13:33
they came as *g* for multitude	Judg 6:5
the valley like *g* for multitude	Judg 7:12
the inhabitants thereof are as *g*	Is 40:22
because they are more than the *g*	Jer 46:23
he formed *g* in the beginning of	Amos 7:1
and thy captains as the great *g*	Nah 3:17

GRATE

for it a *g* of network of brass	Ex 27:4
burnt offering, with his brasen *g*	Ex 35:16
of network under the compass	Ex 38:4
the four ends of the *g* of brass	Ex 38:5
altar, and the brasen *g* for it	Ex 38:30
his *g* of brass, his staves, and	Ex 39:39

GRAVE

And Jacob set a pillar upon her *g*	Gen 35:20
of Rachel's *g* unto this day	Gen 35:20
into the *g* unto my son mourning	Gen 37:35
gray hairs with sorrow to the *g*	Gen 42:38
gray hairs with sorrow to the *g*	Gen 44:29
our father with sorrow to the *g*	Gen 44:31
in my *g* which I have digged for	Gen 50:5
g on them the names of the	Ex 28:9
g upon it, like the engravings of	Ex 28:36
body, or a bone of a man, or a *g*	Num 19:16
or one slain, or one dead, or a *g*	Num 19:18
he bringeth down to the *g*	1Sa 2:6
voice, and wept at the *g* of Abner	2Sa 3:32
be buried by the *g* of my father	2Sa 19:37
head go down to the *g* in peace	1Kin 2:6
thou down to the *g* with blood	1Kin 2:9
he laid his carcase in his own *g*	1Kin 13:30
of Jeroboam shall come to the *g*	1Kin 14:13
be gathered into thy *g* in peace	2Kin 22:20
that can skill to *g* with the	2Chr 2:7
also to *g* any manner of graving	2Chr 2:14
be gathered to thy *g* in peace	2Chr 34:28
glad, when they can find the *g*	Job 3:22
shalt come to thy *g* in a full age	Job 5:26
to the *g* shall come up no more	Job 7:9
carried from the womb to the *g*	Job 10:19
thou wouldest hide me in the *g*	Job 14:13
If I wait, the *g* is mine house	Job 17:13
and in a moment go down to the *g*	Job 21:13
Yet shall he be brought to the *g*	Job 21:32
so doth the *g* those which have	Job 24:19
not stretch out his hand to the *g*	Job 30:24
his soul draweth near unto the *g*	Job 33:22
in the *g* who shall give thee	Ps 6:5
brought up my soul from the *g*	Ps 30:3
and let them be silent in the *g*	Ps 31:17
Like sheep they are laid in the *g*	Ps 49:14
in the *g* from their dwelling	Ps 49:14
my soul from the power of the *g*	Ps 49:15
my life draweth nigh unto the *g*	Ps 88:3
like the slain that lie in the *g*	Ps 88:5
be declared in the *g*	Ps 88:11
his soul from the hand of the *g*	Ps 89:48
us swallow them up alive as the *g*	Prov 1:12
The *g*; and the barren	Prov 30:16
knowledge, nor wisdom, in the *g*	Eccl 9:10
jealousy is cruel as the *g*	Song 8:6
Thy pomp is brought down to the *g*	Is 14:11
thy *g* like an abominable branch	Is 14:19
I shall go to the gates of the *g*	Is 38:10
For the *g* cannot praise thee	Is 38:18
he made his *g* with the wicked, and	Is 53:9
my mother might have been my *g*	Jer 20:17
down to the *g* I caused a mourning	Eze 31:15

GRAVECLOTHES

forth, bound hand and foot with *g*	Jn 11:44

GRAVED

he *g* cherubims, lions, and palm	1Kin 7:36
and *g* cherubims on the walls	2Chr 3:7

GRAVEL

his mouth shall be filled with *g*	Prov 20:17
of thy bowels like the *g* thereof	Is 48:19
broken my teeth with *g* stones	Lam 3:16

GRAVEN

not make unto thee any *g* image	Ex 20:4
writing of God, *g* upon the tables	Ex 32:16
inclosed in ouches of gold, *g*	Ex 39:6
of gold, *g*, as signets are *g*	Ex 39:6
make you no idols nor *g* image	Lev 26:1
yourselves, and make you a *g* image	Deut 4:16
with you, and make you a *g* image	Deut 4:23
yourselves, and make a *g* image	Deut 4:25
shalt not make thee any *g* image	Deut 5:8
burn their *g* images with fire	Deut 7:5
The *g* images of their gods shall	Deut 7:25
down the *g* images of their gods	Deut 12:3
that maketh any *g* or molten image	Deut 27:15
for my son, to make a *g* image	Judg 17:3
who made thereof a *g* image	Judg 17:4
a *g* image, and a molten image	Judg 18:14
in thither, and took the *g* image	Judg 18:17
the *g* image, and went in the midst	Judg 18:20
up the *g* image by the *g* image	Judg 18:30
they set them up Micah's *g* image	Judg 18:31
LORD, and served their *g* images	2Kin 17:41
he set a *g* image of the grove	2Kin 21:7
g images, before he was humbled	2Chr 33:19
had beaten the *g* images into	2Chr 34:7
That they were *g* with an iron pen	Job 19:24
to jealousy with their *g* images	Ps 78:58
be all they that serve *g* images	Ps 97:7
whose *g* images did excel them of	Is 10:10
all the *g* images of her gods he	Is 21:9
of thy *g* images of silver	Is 30:22
The workman melteth a *g* image	Is 40:19
workman to prepare a *g* image	Is 40:20
neither my praise to *g* images	Is 42:8
ashamed, that trust in *g* images	Is 42:17
They that make a *g* image are all	Is 44:9
or molten a *g* image that is	Is 44:10
he maketh it a *g* image, and	Is 44:15
he maketh a god, even his *g* image	Is 44:17
set up the wood of their *g* image	Is 45:20
my *g* image, and my molten image	Is 48:5
I have *g* thee upon the palms of	Is 49:16
me to anger with their *g* images	Jer 8:19
is confounded by the *g* image	Jer 10:14
it is *g* upon the table of their	Jer 17:1
for it is the land of *g* images	Jer 50:38
is confounded by the *g* image	Jer 51:17
upon the *g* images of Babylon	Jer 51:47
do judgment upon her *g* images	Jer 51:52
and burned incense to *g* images	Hos 11:2
all the *g* images thereof shall be	Mic 1:7
Thy *g* images also will I cut off	Mic 5:13
gods will I cut off the *g* image	Nah 1:14
What profiteth the *g* image that	Hab 2:18
that the maker thereof hath a *g*	Hab 2:18
stone, *g* by art and man's device	Acts 17:29

GRAVE'S

are scattered at the *g* mouth	Ps 141:7

GRAVES

Because there were no *g* in Egypt	Ex 14:11
the powder thereof upon the *g* of	2Kin 23:6
strowed it upon the *g* of them	2Chr 34:4
extinct, the *g* are ready for me	Job 17:1
Which remain among the *g*, and	Is 65:4
of Jerusalem, out of their *g*	Jer 8:1
into the *g* of the common people	Jer 26:23
his *g* are about him	Eze 32:22
Whose *g* are set in the sides of	Eze 32:23
her are round about him	Eze 32:25
her *g* are round about him	Eze 32:26
O my people, I will open your *g*	Eze 37:12
you to come up out of your *g*	Eze 37:12
LORD, when I have opened your *g*	Eze 37:13
and brought you up out of your *g*	Eze 37:13
Gog a place there of *g* in Israel	Eze 39:11
And the *g* were opened	Mt 27:52
came out of the *g* after his	Mt 27:53
for ye are as a which appear not	Lk 11:44
are in the *g* shall hear his voice	Jn 5:28
their dead bodies to be put in *g*	Rev 11:9

GRAVETH

that *g* an habitation for himself	Is 22:16

GRAVING

and fashioned it with a *g* tool	Ex 32:4
also to grave any manner of *g*	2Chr 2:14

I will engrave the *g* thereof	Zec 3:9

GRAVINGS

of it were *g* with their borders	1Kin 7:31

GRAVITY

children in subjection with all *g*	1Ti 3:4
doctrine shewing uncorruptness, *g*	Titus 2:7

GRAY

then shall ye bring down my *g*	Gen 42:38
ye shall bring down my *g* hairs	Gen 44:29
servants shall bring down the *g*	Gen 44:31
also with the man of *g* hairs	Deut 32:25
g hairs are here and there upon	Hos 7:9

GRAYHEADED

and I am old and *g*	1Sa 12:2
With us are both the *g* and very	Job 15:10

GREASE

Their heart is as fat as *g*	Ps 119:70

GREAT See PREFACE.

GREATER

the *g* light to rule the day, and	Gen 1:16
punishment is *g* than I can bear	Gen 4:13
There is none *g* in this house	Gen 39:9
the throne will I be *g* than thou	Gen 41:40
brother shall be *g* than he	Gen 48:19
that the LORD is *g* than all gods	Ex 18:11
and will make of thee a *g* nation	Num 14:12
heart, saying, The people is *g*	Deut 1:28
out nations from before thee *g*	Deut 4:38
and the Jebusites, seven nations *g*	Deut 7:1
to go in to possess nations *g*	Deut 9:1
a nation mightier and *g* than they	Deut 9:14
and ye shall possess *g* nations	Deut 11:23
and because it was *g* than AJ	Josh 10:2
had there not been now a much *g*	1Sa 14:30
wherewith he hated her was *g* than	2Sa 13:15
a *g* than the other that thou didst	2Sa 13:16
make his throne *g* than the throne	1Kin 1:37
make his throne *g* than thy throne	1Kin 1:47
So David waxed *g* and *g*	1Chr 11:9
So David waxed *g* and *g*	1Chr 11:9
the *g* house he cieled with fir	2Chr 3:5
man Mordecai waxed *g* and *g*	Est 9:4
thee, that God is *g* than man	Job 33:12
a *g* than the punishment of the sin	Lam 4:6
and thou shalt see *g* abominations	Eze 8:6
thou shalt see *g* abominations	Eze 8:13
thou shalt see *g* abominations	Eze 8:15
thee *g* settle shall be four cubits	Eze 43:14
a multitude *g* than the former	Dan 11:13
or their border *g* than your	Amos 6:2
shall be *g* than of the former	Hag 2:9
risen a *g* than John the Baptist	Mt 11:11
kingdom of heaven is *g* than he	Mt 11:11
place is one *g* than the temple	Mt 12:6
behold, a *g* than Jonas is here	Mt 12:41
behold, a *g* than Solomon is here	Mt 12:42
ye shall receive the *g* damnation	Mt 23:14
for whether is *g*, the gold, or	Mt 23:17
for whether is *g*, the gift, or	Mt 23:19
becometh a tree, so that the birds	Mt 13:32
other commandment *g* than these	Mk 12:31
these shall receive a damnation	Mk 12:40
born of women there is not a *g*	Lk 7:28
the kingdom of God is *g* than he	Lk 7:28
behold, a *g* than Solomon is here	Lk 11:31
behold, a *g* than Jonas is here	Lk 11:32
pull down my barns, and build *g*	Lk 12:18
same shall receive *g* damnation	Lk 20:47
For whether is *g*, he that sitteth	Lk 22:27
thou shalt see *g* things than	Jn 1:50
Art thou *g* than our father Jacob	Jn 4:12
will shew him *g* works than these	Jn 5:20
But I have *g* witness than that of	Jn 5:36
Art thou *g* than our father	Jn 8:53
which gave them me, is *g* than all	Jn 10:29
servant is not *g* than his lord	Jn 13:16
is sent *g* than he that sent him	Jn 13:16
g works than these shall he do	Jn 14:12
for my Father is *g* than I	Jn 14:28
G love hath no man than this	Jn 15:13
servant is not *g* than his lord	Jn 15:20
we unto thee hath the *g* sin	Jn 19:11
to lay upon you no *g* burden than	Acts 15:28
for *g* is he that prophesieth than	1Cor 14:5
of whom the *g* part remain unto	1Cor 15:6
because he could swear by no *g*	Heb 6:13
For men verily swear by the *g*	Heb 6:16
of good things to come, by a *g*	Heb 9:11
the reproach of Christ *g* riches	Heb 11:26
shall receive the *g* condemnation	Jas 3:1
angels, which are *g* in power	2Pet 2:11
God is *g* than our heart, and	1Jn 3:20
because *g* is he that is in you	1Jn 4:4
of men, the witness of God is *g*	1Jn 5:9
I have no *g* joy than to hear that	3Jn 4

GREATEST

hundred, and the *g* one a thousand	1Chr 12:14
for hitherto the *g* part of them	1Chr 12:29
so that this man was the *g* of all	Job 1:3
g of them every one is given to	Jer 6:13
the *g* is given to covetousness	Jer 8:10
least of them unto the *g* of them	Jer 31:34
from the least even unto the *g*	Jer 42:1
from the least even to the *g*	Jer 42:8
from the least even unto the *g*	Jer 44:12
from the *g* of them even to the	Jonah 3:5
is the *g* among herbs, and	Mt 13:32

Who is the g in the kingdom of............ Mt 18:1
the same is g in the kingdom of............ Mt 18:4
But he that is g among you shall............ Mt 23:11
themselves, who should be the g............ Mk 9:34
them, which of them should be g............ Lk 9:46
of them should be accounted the g............ Lk 22:24
but he that is g among you............ Lk 22:26
heed, from the least to the g............ Acts 8:10
but the g of these is charity............ 1Cor 13:13
know me, from the least to the g............ Heb 8:11

GREATLY

I will g multiply thy sorrow and............ Gen 3:16
were increased g upon the earth............ Gen 7:18
And he pressed upon them g............ Gen 19:3
the LORD hath blessed my master g............ Gen 24:35
Then Jacob was g afraid and............ Gen 32:7
and the whole mount quaked g............ Ex 19:18
anger of the LORD was kindled g............ Num 11:10
and the people mourned g............ Num 14:39
for the LORD shall g bless thee............ Deut 15:4
neither shall he g multiply to............ Deut 17:17
That they feared g, because............ Josh 10:2
and they were g distressed............ Judg 2:15
Israel was g impoverished because............ Judg 6:6
and his anger was kindled g............ 1Sa 11:6
all the men of Israel rejoiced g............ 1Sa 11:15
all the people g feared the LORD............ 1Sa 12:18
and he loved him g............ 1Sa 16:21
they were dismayed, and g afraid............ 1Sa 17:11
afraid, and his heart g trembled............ 1Sa 28:5
And David was g distressed............ 1Sa 30:6
because the men were g ashamed............ 2Sa 10:5
David's anger was g kindled............ 2Sa 12:5
I have sinned g in that I have............ 2Sa 24:10
and his kingdom was established g............ 1Kin 2:12
of Solomon, that he rejoiced g............ 1Kin 5:7
(Now Obadiah feared the LORD g............ 1Kin 18:3
of their fathers increased g............ 1Chr 4:38
is the LORD, and g to be praised............ 1Chr 16:25
for the men were g ashamed............ 1Chr 19:5
said unto God, I have sinned g............ 1Chr 21:8
anger was g kindled against Judah............ 2Chr 25:10
humbled himself g before the God............ 2Chr 33:12
For the thing which I g feared is............ Job 3:25
thy latter end should g increase............ Job 8:7
salvation how g shall he rejoice............ Ps 21:1
therefore my heart g rejoiceth............ Ps 28:7
I am bowed down g............ Ps 38:6
the king g desire thy beauty............ Ps 45:11
he is g exalted............ Ps 47:9
g to be praised in the city of............ Ps 48:1
I shall not be g moved............ Ps 62:2
thou g enrichest it with the............ Ps 65:9
My lips shall g rejoice when I............ Ps 71:23
was wroth, and g abhorred Israel............ Ps 78:59
God is g to be feared in the............ Ps 89:7
the LORD is great, and g to be praised............ Ps 96:4
And he increased his people g............ Ps 105:24
so that they are multiplied g............ Ps 107:38
LORD, that delighteth g in his............ Ps 112:1
I was g afflicted............ Ps 116:10
proud have had me g in derision............ Ps 119:51
is the LORD, and g to be praised............ Ps 145:3
of the righteous shall g rejoice............ Prov 23:24
back, they shall be g ashamed............ Is 42:17
I will g rejoice in the LORD, my............ Is 61:10
shalt not that land be g polluted............ Jer 3:1
surely thou hast g deceived this............ Jer 4:10
we are g confounded, because we............ Jer 9:19
they shall be g ashamed............ Jer 20:11
and my sabbaths they g polluted............ Eze 20:13
hath g offended, and revenged............ Eze 25:12
was king Belshazzar g troubled............ Dan 5:9
for thou art g beloved............ Dan 9:23
a man g beloved, understand the............ Dan 10:11
O man g beloved, fear not............ Dan 10:19
thou art g despised............ Obad 2
is near, it is near, and hasteth g............ Zeph 1:14
Rejoice g, O daughter of Zion............ Zec 9:9
that the governor marvelled g............ Mt 27:14
that were done, they feared g............ Mt 27:54
And besought him g, saying, My............ Mk 5:23
and them that wept and wailed g............ Mk 5:38
were g amazed, and running to him............ Mk 9:15
ye therefore do g err............ Mk 12:27
rejoiceth g because of the............ Jn 3:29
is called Solomon's, g wondering............ Acts 3:11
multiplied in Jerusalem g............ Acts 6:7
I g desired him to come unto you............ 1Cor 16:12
how g I long after you all in the............ Phil 1:8
But I rejoiced in the Lord g............ Phil 4:10
desiring g to see us, as we also............ 1Th 3:6
G desiring to see thee, being............ 2Ti 1:4
for he hath g withstood our words............ 2Ti 4:15
Wherein ye g rejoice, though now............ 1Pet 1:6
I rejoiced g that I found of thy............ 2Jn 4
For I rejoiced g, when the............ 3Jn 3

GREATNESS

in the g of thine excellency thou............ Ex 15:7
by the g of thine arm they shall............ Ex 15:16
according unto the g of thy mercy............ Num 14:19
begun to shew thy servant thy g............ Deut 3:24
hath shewed us his glory and his g............ Deut 5:24
thou hast redeemed through thy g............ Deut 9:26
of the LORD your God, his g............ Deut 11:2
ascribe ye g unto our God............ Deut 32:3
heart, hast thou done all this g............ 1Chr 17:19
people, to make thee a name of g............ 1Chr 17:21

Thine, O LORD, is the g, and the............ 1Chr 29:11
the one half of the g of thy............ 2Chr 9:6
the g of the burdens laid upon............ 2Chr 24:27
according to the g of thy mercy............ Neh 13:22
declaration of the g of Mordecai............ Est 10:2
through the g of thy power shall............ Ps 66:3
Thou shalt increase my g, and............ Ps 71:21
according to the g of thy power............ Ps 79:11
and his g is unsearchable............ Ps 145:3
and I will declare thy g............ Ps 145:6
him according to his excellent g............ Ps 150:2
in the g of his folly he shall go............ Prov 5:23
by names by the g of his might............ Is 40:26
art wearied in the g of thy way............ Is 57:10
in the g of his strength............ Is 63:1
For the g of thine iniquity are............ Jer 13:22
Whom art thou like in g of thy............ Eze 31:2
Thus was he fair in his g............ Eze 31:7
in g among the trees of Eden............ Eze 31:18
for thy g is grown, and reacheth............ Dan 4:22
the g of the kingdom under the............ Dan 7:27
what is the exceeding g of his............ Eph 1:19

GREAVES

he had g of brass upon his legs,............ 1Sa 17:6

GRECIA See GRECIANS, GREECE. Latin form of Greece.

the rough goat is the king of G............ Dan 8:21
lo, the prince of G shall come............ Dan 10:20
up all against the realm of G............ Dan 11:2

GRECIANS See GREEKS.
1. Inhabitants of Greece.

Jerusalem have sold unto the G............ Joel 3:6
2. Hellenistic Jews.
of the G against the Hebrews............ Acts 6:1
Jesus, and disputed against the G............ Acts 9:29
come to Antioch, spake unto the G............ Acts 11:20

GREECE See GRECIA. Peninsula south of the Balkans.

O Zion, against thy sons, O G............ Zec 9:13
much exhortation, he came into G............ Acts 20:2

GREEDILY

He coveteth g all the day long............ Prov 21:26
thou hast g gained of thy............ Eze 22:12
ran g after the error of Balaam............ Jude 11

GREEDINESS

to work all uncleanness with g............ Eph 4:19

GREEDY

as a lion that is g of his prey............ Ps 17:12
of every one that is g of gain............ Prov 1:19
He that is g of gain troubleth............ Prov 15:27
they are g dogs which can never............ Is 56:11
no striker, not g of filthy lucre............ 1Ti 3:3
much wine, not g of filthy lucre............ 1Ti 3:8

GREEK See GREEKS.
1. A native of Greece.

written over him in letters of G............ Lk 23:38
and it was written in Hebrew, and G............ Jn 19:20
but his father was a G............ Acts 16:1
knew all that his father was a G............ Acts 16:3
the Jew first, and also to the G............ Rom 1:16
between the Jew and the G............ Rom 10:12
Titus, who was with me, being a G............ Gal 2:3
There is neither Jew nor G............ Gal 3:28
Where there is neither G nor Jew............ Col 3:11
2. A language.
Who said, Canst thou speak G............ Acts 21:37
but in the G tongue hath his name............ Rev 9:11
3. A female.
The woman was a G, a............ Mk 7:26

GREEKS See GRECIANS. Plural of Greek 1.

there were certain G among them............ Jn 12:20
Jews and also of the G believed............ Acts 14:1
of the devout G a great multitude............ Acts 17:4
of honourable women which were G............ Acts 17:12
and persuaded the Jews and the G............ Acts 18:4
Then all the G took Sosthenes,............ Acts 18:17
of the Lord Jesus, both Jews and G............ Acts 19:10
G also dwelling at Ephesus............ Acts 19:17
to the Jews, and also to the G............ Acts 20:21
further brought G also into the............ Acts 21:28
I am debtor both to the G............ Rom 1:14
sign, and the G seek after wisdom............ 1Cor 1:22
and unto the G foolishness............ 1Cor 1:23
which are called, both Jews and G............ 1Cor 1:24

GREEN

have given every g herb for meat............ Gen 1:30
even as the g herb have I given............ Gen 9:3
Jacob took him rods of g poplar............ Gen 30:37
not any g thing in the trees............ Ex 10:15
offering of thy firstfruits g............ Lev 2:14
nor g ears, until the selfsame............ Lev 23:14
the hills, and under every g tree............ Deut 12:2
If they bind me with seven g............ Judg 16:7
brought up for her seven g withs............ Judg 16:8
high hill, and under every g tree............ 1Kin 14:23
the hills, and under every g tree............ 2Kin 16:4
high hill, and under every g tree............ 2Kin 17:10
of the field, and as the g herb............ 2Kin 19:26
the hills, and under every g tree............ 2Chr 28:4
Where were white, g, and blue,............ Est 1:6
He is g before the sun, and his............ Job 8:16
and his branch shall not be g............ Job 15:32
he searcheth after every g thing............ Job 39:8
me to lie down in g pastures............ Ps 23:2
grass, and wither as the g herb............ Ps 37:2

himself like a g bay tree............ Ps 37:35
But I am like a g olive tree in............ Ps 52:8
also our bed is g............ Song 1:16
fig tree putteth forth her g figs............ Song 2:13
faileth, there is no g thing............ Is 15:6
of the field, and as the g herb............ Is 37:27
with idols under every g tree............ Is 57:5
under every g tree thou wanderest............ Jer 2:20
mountain and under every g tree............ Jer 3:6
the strangers under every g tree............ Jer 3:13
A olive tree, fair, and of............ Jer 11:16
their groves by the g trees upon............ Jer 17:2
cometh, but her leaf shall be g............ Jer 17:8
mountains, and under every g tree............ Eze 6:13
tree, have dried up the g tree............ Eze 17:24
shall devour every g tree in thee............ Eze 20:47
I am like a g fir tree............ Hos 14:8
by companies upon the g grass............ Mk 6:39
they do these things in a g tree............ Lk 23:31
up, and all g grass was burnt up............ Rev 8:7
of the earth, neither any g thing............ Rev 9:4

GREENISH

if the plague be g or reddish in............ Lev 13:49
or g reddish, which in sight are............ Lev 14:37

GREENNESS

Whilst it is yet in his g............ Job 8:12

GREET

to Nabal, and g him in my name............ 1Sa 25:5
G Priscilla and Aquila my helpers............ Rom 16:3
Likewise g the church that is in............ Rom 16:5
G Mary, who bestowed much labour............ Rom 16:6
G Amplias my beloved in the Lord............ Rom 16:8
G them that be of the household............ Rom 16:11
All the brethren g you............ 1Cor 16:20
G ye one another with an holy............ 1Cor 16:20
G one another with an holy kiss............ 2Cor 13:12
brethren which are with me g you............ Phil 4:21
physician, and Demas, g you............ Col 4:14
G all the brethren with an holy............ 1Th 5:26
G them that love us in the faith............ Titus 3:15
G ye one another with a kiss of............ 1Pet 5:14
of thy elect sister g thee............ 2Jn 13
G the friends by name............ 3Jn 14

GREETETH

Eubulus g thee, and Pudens, and............ 2Ti 4:21

GREETING

brethren send g unto the brethren............ Acts 15:23
governor Felix sendeth g............ Acts 23:26
which are scattered abroad, g............ Jas 1:1

GREETINGS

g in the markets, and to be called............ Mt 23:7
synagogues, and g in the markets............ Lk 11:43
love g in the markets, and the............ Lk 20:46

GREW

herb of the field before it g............ Gen 2:5
that which g upon the ground............ Gen 19:25
And the child g, and was weaned............ Gen 21:8
and he g, and dwelt in the............ Gen 21:20
And the boys g............ Gen 25:27
g until he became very great............ Gen 26:13
had possessions therein, and g............ Gen 47:27
the more they multiplied and g............ Ex 1:12
And the child g, and she brought............ Ex 2:10
and his wife's sons g up, and they............ Judg 11:2
and the child g, and the LORD............ Judg 13:24
child Samuel g before the LORD............ 1Sa 2:21
And the child Samuel g on, and was............ 1Sa 2:26
And Samuel g, and the LORD was with............ 1Sa 3:19
g great, and the LORD God of hosts............ 2Sa 5:10
it g up together with him, and............ 2Sa 12:3
And it g, and became a spreading............ Eze 17:6
wither in the furrows where it g............ Eze 17:10
The tree g, and was strong, and the............ Dan 4:11
tree that thou sawest, which g............ Dan 4:20
among thorns, and the thorns g up............ Mk 4:7
bettered, but rather g worse............ Mk 5:26
And the child g, and waxed strong............ Lk 1:80
And the child g, and waxed strong............ Lk 2:40
and it g, and waxed a great tree............ Lk 13:19
sworn to Abraham, the people g............ Acts 7:17
But the word of God g and............ Acts 12:24
So mightily g the word of God and............ Acts 19:20

GREY

beauty of old men is the g head............ Prov 20:29

GREYHEADED

Now also when I am old and g............ Ps 71:18

GREYHOUND

A............ Prov 30:31

GRIEF

Which were a g of mind unto Isaac............ Gen 26:35
and g have I spoken hitherto............ 1Sa 1:16
That this shall be no g unto thee............ 1Sa 25:31
know his own sore and his own g............ 2Chr 6:29
saw that his g was very great............ Job 2:13
O that my g were throughly............ Job 6:2
of my lips should assuage your g............ Job 16:5
I speak, my g is not asswaged............ Job 16:6
Mine eye is consumed because of g............ Ps 6:7
mine eye is consumed with g............ Ps 31:9
For my life is spent with g............ Ps 31:10
they talk to the g of those whom............ Ps 69:26
foolish son is a g to his father............ Prov 17:25
For in much wisdom is much g............ Eccl 1:18
are sorrows, and his travail a g............ Eccl 2:23

GRIEFS
shall be a heap in the day of g .... Is 17:11
of sorrows, and acquainted with g .... Is 53:3
he hath put him to g .... Is 53:10
before me continually is g .... Jer 6:7
but I said, Truly this is a g .... Jer 10:19
LORD hath added g to my sorrow .... Jer 45:3
But though he cause g, yet will .... Lam 3:32
head, to deliver him from his g .... Jonah 4:6
But if any have caused g, he hath 2Cor 2:5
may do it with joy, and not with g .... Heb 13:17
conscience toward God endure g 1Pet 2:19

GRIEFS
Surely he hath borne our g .... Is 53:4

GRIEVANCE
iniquity, and cause me to behold g .... Hab 1:3

GRIEVE
thine eyes, and to g thine heart 1Sa 2:33
from evil, that it may not g me 1Chr 4:10
and g him in the desert .... Ps 78:40
nor g the children of men .... Lam 3:33
g not the holy Spirit of God, ... Eph 4:30

GRIEVED
earth, and it g him at his heart .... Gen 6:6
and the men were g, and they were .... Gen 34:7
Now therefore be not g, nor angry .... Gen 45:5
The archers have sorely g him .... Gen 49:23
they were g because of the .... Ex 1:12
thine heart shall not be g when .... Deut 15:10
his soul was g for the misery of .... Judg 10:16
and why is thy heart g 1Sa 1:8
And it g Samuel 1Sa 15:11
Jonathan know this, lest he be g 1Sa 20:3
for he was g for David, because 1Sa 20:34
the soul of all the people was g 1Sa 30:6
how the king was g for his son 2Sa 19:2
it g them exceedingly that there .... Neh 2:10
neither be ye g .... Neh 8:11
And it g me sore .... Neh 13:8
Then was the queen exceedingly g .... Est 4:4
commune with thee, wilt thou be g .... Job 4:2
was not my soul g for the poor .... Job 30:25
Thus my heart was g, and I was .... Ps 73:21
long was I g with this generation .... Ps 95:10
The wicked shall see it, and be g .... Ps 112:10
the transgressors, and was g .... Ps 119:158
am not I g with those that rise .... Ps 139:21
g in spirit, and a wife of youth, ... Is 54:6
therefore thou wast not g .... Is 57:10
them, but they have not g .... Jer 5:3
I Daniel was g in my spirit in .... Dan 7:15
therefore he shall be g, and .... Dan 11:30
but they are not g for the .... Amos 6:6
being g for the hardness of their .... Mk 3:5
at that saying, and went away a .... Mk 10:22
Peter was g because he said unto .... Jn 21:17
Being g that they taught the .... Acts 4:2
But Paul, being g, turned and said .... Acts 16:18
if thy brother be g with thy meat .... Rom 14:15
not that ye should be g, but that 2Cor 2:4
caused grief, he hath not g me 2Cor 2:5
Wherefore I was g with that .... Heb 3:10
with whom was he g forty years .... Heb 3:17

GRIEVETH
for it g me much for your sakes .... Ruth 1:13
it g him to bring it again to his .... Prov 26:15

GRIEVING
nor any g thorn of all that are .... Eze 28:24

GRIEVOUS
for the famine was g in the land .... Gen 12:10
and because their sin is very g .... Gen 18:20
the thing was very g in Abraham's .... Gen 21:11
Let it not be g in thy sight .... Gen 21:12
for it shall be very g .... Gen 41:31
This is a g mourning to the .... Gen 50:11
there came a g swarm of flies .... Ex 8:24
there shall be a very g murrain .... Ex 9:3
cause it to rain a very g hail .... Ex 9:18
mingled with the hail, very g .... Ex 9:24
very g were they .... Ex 10:14
which cursed me with a g curse in 1Kin 2:8
Thy father made our yoke g 1Kin 12:4
thou the g service of thy father 1Kin 12:4
Thy father made our yoke g 2Chr 10:4
ease thou somewhat the g 2Chr 10:4
His ways are always g .... Ps 10:5
which speak g things proudly and .... Ps 31:18
but g words stir up anger .... Prov 15:1
Correction is g unto him that .... Prov 15:10
under the sun is a g evil .... Eccl 2:17
his life shall be g unto him .... Is 15:4
A g vision is declared unto me .... Is 21:2
They are all g revolters, walking .... Jer 6:28
my wound is g .... Jer 10:19
great breach, with a very g blow .... Jer 14:17
They shall die of g deaths .... Jer 16:4
forth in fury, even a g whirlwind .... Jer 23:19
is incurable, and thy wound is g .... Jer 30:12
thy wound is g .... Nah 3:19
g to be borne, and lay them on .... Mt 23:4
men with burdens g to be borne .... Lk 11:46
shall g wolves enter in among you .... Acts 20:29
g complaints against Paul, which .... Acts 25:7
to you, to me indeed is not g .... Phil 3:1
seemeth to be joyous, but g .... Heb 12:11
and his commandments are not g 1Jn 5:3
g sore upon the men which had the .... Rev 16:2

GRIEVOUSLY
afterward did more g afflict her .... Is 9:1
it shall fall upon the head of .... Jer 23:19
Jerusalem hath g sinned .... Lam 1:8
for I have g rebelled .... Lam 1:20
against me by trespassing g .... Eze 14:13
sick of the palsy, g tormented .... Mt 8:6
my daughter is g vexed with a .... Mt 15:22

GRIEVOUSNESS
that write g which they have .... Is 10:1
bent bow, and from the g of war .... Is 21:15

GRIND
he did g in the prison house .... Judg 16:21
Then let my wife g unto another .... Job 31:10
and g the faces of the poor .... Is 3:15
Take the millstones, and g meal .... Is 47:2
They took the young men to g .... Lam 5:13
fall, it will g him to powder .... Mt 21:44
fall, it will g him to powder .... Lk 20:18

GRINDERS
the g cease because they are few, ... Eccl 12:3

GRINDING
when the sound of the g is low .... Eccl 12:4
Two women shall be g at the mill .... Mt 24:41
Two women shall be g together .... Lk 17:35

GRISLED
were ringstraked, speckled, and g .... Gen 31:10
are ringstraked, speckled, and g .... Gen 31:12
and in the fourth chariot g .... Zec 6:3
the g go forth toward the south .... Zec 6:6

GROAN
Men g from out of the city, and .... Job 24:12
all her land the wounded shall g .... Jer 51:52
he shall g before him with the .... Eze 30:24
How do the beasts g .... Joel 1:18
we ourselves g within ourselves .... Rom 8:23
For in this we g, earnestly 2Cor 5:2
that are in this tabernacle do g 2Cor 5:4

GROANED
he g in the spirit, and was .... Jn 11:33

GROANETH
we know that the whole creation g .... Rom 8:22

GROANING
And God heard their g, and God .... Ex 2:24
I have also heard the g of the .... Ex 6:5
my stroke is heavier than my g .... Job 23:2
I am weary with my g .... Ps 6:6
my g is not hid from thee .... Ps 38:9
my g my bones cleave to my skin .... Ps 102:5
To hear the g of the prisoner .... Ps 102:20
Jesus therefore again g in .... Jn 11:38
in Egypt, and I have heard their g .... Acts 7:34

GROANINGS
of their g by reason of them that .... Judg 2:18
the g of a deadly wounded man .... Eze 30:24
us with g which cannot be uttered .... Rom 8:26

GROPE
And thou shalt g at noonday .... Deut 28:29
in the noonday as in the night, ... Job 5:14
They g in the dark without light, ... Job 12:25
We g for the wall like the blind, ... Is 59:10
we g as if we had no eyes .... Is 59:10

GROPETH
as the blind g in darkness .... Deut 28:29

GROSS
earth, and g darkness the people .... Is 60:2
of death, and make it g darkness .... Jer 13:16
this people's heart is waxed g .... Mt 13:15
heart of this people is waxed g .... Acts 28:27

GROUND
there was not a man to till the g .... Gen 2:5
watered the whole face of the g .... Gen 2:6
formed man of the dust of the g .... Gen 2:7
out of the g made the LORD God to .... Gen 2:9
out of the g the LORD God formed .... Gen 2:19
cursed is the g for thy sake .... Gen 3:17
till thou return unto the g .... Gen 3:19
to till the g from whence he was .... Gen 3:23
but Cain was a tiller of the g .... Gen 4:2
the g an offering unto the LORD .... Gen 4:3
blood crieth unto me from the g .... Gen 4:10
When thou tillest the g, it shall .... Gen 4:12
because of the g which the LORD .... Gen 5:29
which was upon the face of the g .... Gen 7:23
abated from off the face of the g .... Gen 8:8
behold, the face of the g was dry .... Gen 8:13
g and by for man's sake .... Gen 8:21
and bowed himself toward the g .... Gen 18:2
with his face toward the g .... Gen 19:1
and that which grew upon the g .... Gen 19:25
himself to the g seven times .... Gen 33:3
wife, that he spilled it on the g .... Gen 38:9
down every man his sack to the g .... Gen 44:11
and they fell before him on the g .... Gen 44:14
whereon thou standest is holy g .... Ex 3:5
he said, Cast it on the g .... Ex 4:3
he cast it on the g, and it .... Ex 4:3
also the g whereon they are .... Ex 8:21
the fire ran along upon the g .... Ex 9:23
of Israel shall go on dry g .... Ex 14:16
midst of the sea upon the dry g .... Ex 14:22
small as the hoar frost on the g .... Ex 16:14
g it in powder, and strawed it .... Ex 32:20

thing that creepeth on the g .... Lev 20:25
g it in mills, or beat it in a .... Num 11:8
that the g clave asunder that was .... Num 16:31
any thing that creepeth on the g .... Deut 4:18
g it very small, even until it .... Deut 9:21
shalt pour it upon the g as water .... Deut 15:23
the way in any tree, or on the g .... Deut 22:6
the body, and the fruit of thy g .... Deut 28:4
cattle, and in the fruit of thy g .... Deut 28:11
foot upon the g for delicateness .... Deut 28:56
on dry g in the midst of Jordan .... Josh 3:17
Israelites passed over on dry g .... Josh 3:17
in a parcel of g which Jacob .... Josh 24:32
and fastened it into the g .... Judg 4:21
upon all the g let there be dew .... Judg 6:39
and there was dew on all the g .... Judg 6:40
and fell on their faces to the g .... Judg 13:20
destroyed down to the g of the .... Judg 20:21
destroyed down to the g of the .... Judg 20:25
face, and bowed herself to the g .... Ruth 2:10
none of his words fall to the g 1Sa 3:19
the g before the ark of the LORD 1Sa 5:4
and will set them to ear his g 1Sa 8:12
and there was honey upon the g 1Sa 14:25
and calves, and slew them on the g 1Sa 14:32
hair of his head fall to the g 1Sa 14:45
son of Jesse liveth upon the g 1Sa 20:31
and fell on his face to the g 1Sa 20:41
face, and bowed herself to the g 1Sa 25:23
stuck in the g at his bolster 1Sa 26:7
he stooped with his face to the g 1Sa 28:14
should I smite thee to the g 2Sa 2:22
line, casting them down to the g 2Sa 8:2
she fell on her face to the g 2Sa 14:4
and are as water spilt on the g 2Sa 14:14
And Joab fell to the g on his face 2Sa 14:22
his face to the g before the king 2Sa 14:33
him as the dew falleth on the g 2Sa 17:12
mouth, and spread g corn thereon 2Sa 17:19
thou not smite him there to the g 2Sa 18:11
and shed out his bowels to the g 2Sa 20:10
was a piece g of full of lentiles 2Sa 23:11
he stood in the midst of the g 2Sa 23:12
the king on his face upon the g 2Sa 24:20
the king with his face to the g 1Kin 1:23
in the clay g between Succoth and 1Kin 7:46
that they sow went over on dry g 1Kin 2:8
themselves to the g before him 2Kin 2:15
water is naught, and the g barren 2Kin 2:19
feet, and bowed herself to the g 2Kin 4:37
and cast him into the plat of a 2Kin 9:26
king of Israel, Smite upon the g 2Kin 13:18
was a parcel of g full of barley 1Chr 11:13
to David with his face to the g 1Chr 21:21
the g was Ezri the son of Chelub 1Chr 27:26
in the clay g between Succoth and 2Chr 4:17
faces to the g upon the pavement 2Chr 7:3
his head with his face to the g 2Chr 20:18
with their faces to the g .... Neh 8:6
to bring the firstfruits of our g .... Neh 10:35
tithes of our g unto the Levites .... Neh 10:37
his head, and fell down upon the g .... Job 1:20
with him upon the g seven days .... Job 2:13
doth trouble spring out of the g .... Job 5:6
and the stock thereof die in the g .... Job 14:8
he poureth out my gall upon the g .... Job 16:13
snare is laid for him in the g .... Job 18:10
satisfy the desolate and waste g .... Job 38:27
swalloweth the g with fierceness .... Job 39:24
place of thy name to the g .... Ps 74:7
his crown by casting it to the g .... Ps 89:39
and cast his throne down to the g .... Ps 89:44
and devoured the fruit of their g .... Ps 105:35
and the watersprings into dry g .... Ps 107:33
water, and dry g into watersprings .... Ps 107:35
smitten my life down to the g .... Ps 143:3
casteth the wicked down to the g .... Ps 147:6
desolate shall sit upon the g .... Is 3:26
how art thou cut down to the g .... Is 14:12
gods he hath broken unto the g .... Is 21:9
down, lay low, and bring to the g .... Is 25:12
he layeth it low, even to the g .... Is 26:5
open and break the clods of his g .... Is 28:24
down, and shalt speak out of the g .... Is 29:4
a familiar spirit, out of the g .... Is 29:4
that thou shalt sow the g withal .... Is 30:23
the g shall eat clean provender .... Is 30:24
the parched g shall become a pool .... Is 35:7
thirsty, and floods upon the dry g .... Is 44:3
daughter of Babylon, sit on the g .... Is 47:1
thou hast laid thy body as the g .... Is 51:23
and as a root out of a dry g .... Is 53:2
Jerusalem, Break up your fallow g .... Jer 4:3
field, and upon the fruit of the g .... Jer 7:20
they are black unto the g .... Jer 14:2
Because the g is chapt, for there .... Jer 14:4
they shall be dung upon the g .... Jer 25:33
and the beast that are upon the g .... Jer 27:5
hath brought them down to the g .... Lam 2:2
Her gates are sunk into the g .... Lam 2:9
daughter of Zion sit upon the g .... Lam 2:10
hang down their heads to the g .... Lam 2:10
old lie on the g in the streets .... Lam 2:21
thy face, that thou see not the g .... Eze 12:6
he see not the g with his eyes .... Eze 12:12
morter, and bring it down to the g .... Eze 13:14
fury, she was cast down to the g .... Eze 19:12
wilderness, in a dry and thirsty g .... Eze 19:13
she poured it not upon the g .... Eze 24:7
garrisons shall go down to the g .... Eze 26:11

G

they shall sit upon the *g* .... Eze 26:16
I will cast thee to the *g* .... Eze 28:17
and every wall shall fall to the *g* .... Eze 38:20
from the *g* up to the windows, and .... Eze 41:16
From the *g* unto above the door .... Eze 41:20
and the middlemost from the *g* .... Eze 42:6
from the bottom upon the *g* even .... Eze 43:14
whole earth, and touched not the *g* .... Dan 8:5
but he cast him down to the *g* .... Dan 8:7
the host and of the stars to the *g* .... Dan 8:10
it cast down the truth to the *g* .... Dan 8:12
sleep on my face toward the *g* .... Dan 8:18
my face, and my face toward the *g* .... Dan 10:9
me, I set my face toward the *g* .... Dan 10:15
with the creeping things of the *g* .... Hos 2:18
break up your fallow *g* .... Hos 10:12
be cut off, and fall to the *g* .... Amos 3:14
Who shall bring me down to the *g* .... Obad 3
that which the *g* bringeth forth .... Hag 1:11
the *g* shall give her increase, and .... Zec 8:12
not destroy the fruits of your *g* .... Mal 3:11
fall on the *g* without your Father .... Mt 10:29
But other fell into good *g* .... Mt 13:8
g is he that heareth the word .... Mt 13:23
multitude to sit down on the *g* .... Mt 15:35
And some fell on stony *g*, where it .... Mk 4:5
And other fell on good *g*, and did .... Mk 4:8
which are sown on stony *g* .... Mk 4:16
are they which are sown on good *g* .... Mk 4:20
a man should cast seed into the *g* .... Mk 4:26
the people to sit down on the *g* .... Mk 8:6
and he fell on the *g*, and wallowed .... Mk 9:20
a little, and fell on the *g* .... Mk 14:35
And other fell on good *g*, and .... Lk 8:8
But that on the good *g* are they .... Lk 8:15
The *g* of a certain rich man .... Lk 12:16
why cumbereth it the *g* .... Lk 13:7
him, I have bought a piece of *g* .... Lk 14:18
And shall lay thee even with the *g* .... Lk 19:44
of blood falling down to the *g* .... Lk 22:44
near to the parcel of *g* that .... Jn 4:5
and with his finger wrote on the *g* .... Jn 8:6
stooped down, and wrote on the *g* .... Jn 8:8
had thus spoken, he spat on the *g* .... Jn 9:6
a corn of wheat fall into the *g* .... Jn 12:24
went backward, and fell to the *g* .... Jn 18:6
where thou standest is holy *g* .... Acts 7:33
And I fell unto the *g*, and heard a .... Acts 22:7
God, the pillar and *g* of the truth 1Ti 3:15

GROUNDED
where the *g* staff shall pass .... Is 30:32
ye, being rooted and *g* in love, ... Eph 3:17
If ye continue in the faith *g* .... Col 1:23

GROVE
Abraham planted a *g* in Beer-sheba .... Gen 21:33
a *g* of any trees near unto the .... Deut 16:21
cut down the *g* that is by it .... Judg 6:25
the *g* which thou shalt cut down .... Judg 6:26
the *g* was cut down that was by it .... Judg 6:28
cut down the *g* that was by it .... Judg 6:30
she had made an idol in a *g* 1Kin 15:13
And Ahab made a *g* 1Kin 16:33
remained the *g* also in Samaria 2Kin 13:6
even two calves, and made a *g* 2Kin 17:16
up altars for Baal, and made a *g* 2Kin 21:3
he set a graven image of the *g* 2Kin 21:7
were made for Baal, and for the *g* 2Kin 23:4
he brought out the *g* from the 2Kin 23:6
the women wove hangings for the *g* 2Kin 23:7
small to powder, and burned the *g* 2Kin 23:15
she had made an idol in a *g* 2Chr 15:16

GROVES
their images, and cut down their *g* .... Ex 34:13
their images, and cut down their *g* .... Deut 7:5
and burn their *g* with fire .... Deut 12:3
God, and served Baalim and the *g* .... Judg 3:7
because they have made their *g* 1Kin 14:15
them high places, and images, and *g*. ... 1Kin 14:23
prophets of the *g* four hundred 1Kin 18:19
g in every high hill, and under 2Kin 17:10
the images, and cut down the *g* 2Kin 18:4
the images, and cut down the *g* 2Chr 14:3
the high places and *g* out of Judah 2Chr 17:6
taken away the *g* out of the land 2Chr 19:3
God of their fathers, and served *g* 2Chr 24:18
in pieces, and cut down the *g* 2Chr 31:1
up altars for Baalim, and made *g* 2Chr 33:3
he built high places, and set up *g* 2Chr 33:19
from the high places, and the *g* 2Chr 34:3
and the *g*, and the carved images, ... 2Chr 34:4
broken down the altars and the *g* 2Chr 34:7
fingers have made, either the *g* .... Is 17:8
that are beaten in sunder, the *g* .... Is 27:9
their *g* by the green trees upon .... Jer 17:2
I will pluck up thy *g* out of the .... Mic 5:14

GROW
g every tree that is pleasant to .... Gen 2:9
let them *g* into a multitude in .... Gen 48:16
locks of the hair of his head *g* .... Num 6:5
to *g* again after he was shaven .... Judg 16:22
although he make it not to *g* 2Sa 23:5
such things as *g* of themselves. 2Kin 19:29
why should damage *g* to the hurt .... Ezr 4:22
Can the rush *g* up without mire .... Job 8:11
can the flag *g* without water .... Job 8:11
out of the earth shall others *g* .... Job 8:19
g out of the dust of the earth .... Job 14:19

Let thistles *g* instead of wheat, ... Job 31:40
good liking, they *g* up with corn. .... Job 39:4
he shall *g* like a cedar in .... Ps 92:12
the grass to *g* for the cattle .... Ps 104:14
grass to *g* upon the mountains. .... Ps 147:8
nor how the bones do *g* in the .... Eccl 11:5
a Branch shall *g* out of his roots. .... Is 11:1
shalt thou make thy plant to *g* .... Is 17:11
For he shall *g* up before him as a .... Is 53:2
they *g*, yea, they bring forth .... Jer 12:2
righteousness to *g* up unto David .... Jer 33:15
nor suffer their locks to *g* long .... Eze 44:20
shall *g* all trees for meat, whose .... Eze 47:12
he shall *g* as the lily, and cast. .... Hos 14:5
as the corn, and *g* as the vine. .... Hos 14:7
not laboured, neither madest it *g* .... Jonah 4:10
he shall *g* up out of his place, ... Zec 6:12
g up as calves of the stall. .... Mal 4:2
lilies of the field, how they *g* .... Mt 6:28
Let both *g* together until the .... Mt 13:30
unto it, Let no fruit *g* on thee .... Mt 21:19
and *g* up, he knoweth not how .... Mk 4:27
Consider the lilies how they *g* .... Lk 12:27
of them whereunto this would *g* .... Acts 5:24
may *g* up into him in all things, ... Eph 4:15
the word, that ye may *g* thereby. 1Pet 2:2
But *g* in grace, and in the 2Pet 3:18

GROWTH
which *g* for you out of the field. .... Ex 10:5
freckled spot that *g* in the skin. .... Lev 13:39
That which *g* of its own accord of .... Lev 25:5
reap that which *g* of itself in it .... Lev 25:11
beareth, nor any grass *g* therein .... Deut 29:23
the day *g* to an end, lodge here, ... Judg 19:9
When the dust *g* into hardness .... Job 38:38
they are like grass which *g* up .... Ps 90:5
morning it flourisheth, and *g* up .... Ps 90:6
which withereth afore it *g* up. .... Ps 129:6
eat this year such as *g* of itself .... Is 37:30
But when it is sown, it *g* up .... Mk 4:32
building fitly framed together *g* .... Eph 2:21
that your faith *g* exceedingly 2Th 1:3

GROWN
house, till Shelah my son be *g* .... Gen 38:11
for she saw that Shelah was *g* .... Gen 38:14
in those days, when Moses was *g* .... Ex 2:11
for they were not *g* up .... Ex 9:32
there is black hair *g* up therein. .... Lev 13:37
art waxen fat, thou art *g* thick .... Deut 32:15
tarry for them till they were *g* .... Ruth 1:13
at Jericho until your beards be *g* 2Sa 10:5
young men that were *g* up with 1Kin 12:8
the young men that were *g* up with. 1Kin 12:10
And when the child was *g*, it fell 2Kin 4:18
as corn blasted before it be *g* up 2Kin 19:26
at Jericho until your beards be *g* 1Chr 19:5
our trespass is *g* up unto the .... Ezr 9:6
be as plants *g* up in their youth. .... Ps 144:12
it was all *g* over with thorns, and .... Prov 24:31
as corn blasted before it be *g* up .... Is 37:27
because ye are *g* fat as the. .... Jer 50:11
are fashioned, and thine hair is *g* .... Eze 16:7
It is thou, O king, that art *g* .... Dan 4:22
for thy greatness is *g*, and .... Dan 4:22
till his hairs were *g* like .... Dan 4:33
but when it is *g*, it is the .... Mt 13:32

GROWTH
the shooting up of the latter *g* .... Amos 7:1
it was the latter *g* after the. .... Amos 7:1

GRUDGE
nor bear any *g* against the .... Lev 19:18
g if they be not satisfied. .... Ps 59:15
G not one against another, ... Jas 5:9

GRUDGING
one to another without *g* 1Pet 4:9

GRUDGINGLY
not *g*, or of necessity 2Cor 9:7

GUARD
of Pharaoh's, and captain of the *g* ...... Gen 37:36
of Pharaoh, captain of the *g* .... Gen 39:1
the house of the captain of the *g* .... Gen 40:3
the captain of the *g* charged................... Gen 40:4
servant to the captain of the *g* .... Gen 41:12
And David set him over his *g* 2Sa 23:23
the hands of the chief of the *g* 1Kin 14:27
that the *g* bare them, and brought....... 1Kin 14:28
them back into the *g* chamber 1Kin 14:28
offering, that Jehu said to the *g* 2Kin 10:25
and the *g* and the captains cast. 2Kin 10:25
with the captains and the *g* 2Kin 11:4
part at the gate behind the *g* 2Kin 11:6
the *g* stood, every man with his 2Kin 11:11
Athaliah heard the noise of the *g* 2Kin 11:13
and the captains, and the *g* 2Kin 11:19
gate of the *g* to the king's house 2Kin 11:19
Nebuzar-adan, captain of the *g* 2Kin 25:8
were with the captain of the *g* 2Kin 25:10
the captain of the *g* carry away. 2Kin 25:11
But the captain of the *g* left of 2Kin 25:12
the captain of the *g* took away 2Kin 25:15
the captain of the *g* took Seraiah 2Kin 25:18
captain of the *g* took these. 2Kin 25:20
and David set him over his *g* 1Chr 11:25
the hands of the chief of the *g* 2Chr 12:10
the *g* came and fetched them, and. 2Chr 12:11
them again into the *g* chamber 2Chr 12:11

the night they may be a *g* to us .... Neh 4:22
men of the *g* which followed me .... Neh 4:23
of *g* carried away captive into .... Jer 39:9
g left of the poor of the people .... Jer 39:10
Nebuzar-adan the captain of the *g* ...... Jer 39:11
the captain of the *g* sent......................... Jer 39:13
the *g* had let him go from Ramah .... Jer 40:1
captain of the *g* took Jeremiah .... Jer 40:2
of the *g* gave him victuals. .... Jer 40:5
g had committed to Gedaliah the .... Jer 41:10
g had left with Gedaliah the son .... Jer 43:6
Nebuzar-adan, captain of the *g* .... Jer 52:12
were with the captain of the *g* .... Jer 52:14
g carried away captive certain of .... Jer 52:15
the captain of the *g* left certain .... Jer 52:16
took the captain of the *g* away. .... Jer 52:19
the captain of the *g* took Seraiah .... Jer 52:24
the captain of the *g* took them .... Jer 52:25
the *g* carried away captive of the .... Jer 52:30
thee, and be thou a *g* unto them. .... Eze 38:7
the captain of the king's *g* .... Dan 2:14
prisoners to the captain of the *g* .... Acts 28:16

GUARD'S
in the captain of the *g* house. .... Gen 41:10

GUDGODAH (*gud-go'-dah*) See Hor-
HAGIDGAD. *A wilderness encampment of
Israel.*
From thence they journeyed unto G... .. Deut 10:7
from G to Jotbath, a land of................... Deut 10:7

GUEST
That he was gone to be *g* with a .... Lk 19:7

GUESTCHAMBER
The Master saith, Where is the *g* .... Mk 14:14
saith unto thee, Where is the *g* .... Lk 22:11

GUESTS
all the *g* that were with him 1Kin 1:41
all the *g* that were with Adonijah 1Kin 1:49
that her *g* are in the depths of .... Prov 9:18
a sacrifice, he hath bid his *g* .... Zeph 1:7
the wedding was furnished with *g* .... Mt 22:10
the king came in to see the *g* .... Mt 22:11

GUIDE
or canst thou *g* Arcturus with his .... Job 38:32
The meek will he *g* in judgment .... Ps 25:9
thy name's sake lead me, and *g* me .... Ps 31:3
I will *g* thee with mine eye .... Ps 32:8
he will be our *g* even unto death .... Ps 48:14
was thou, a man mine equal, my *g* ...... Ps 55:13
Thou shalt *g* me with thy counsel, ... Ps 73:24
he will *g* his affairs with. .... Ps 112:5
forsaketh the *g* of her youth .... Prov 2:17
Which having no *g*, overseer, or .... Prov 6:7
of the upright shall *g* them .... Prov 11:3
wise, and *g* thine heart in the way ...... Prov 23:19
springs of water shall he *g* them. .... Is 49:10
There is none to *g* her among all. .... Is 51:18
the Lord shall *g* thee continually. .... Is 58:11
thou art the *g* of my youth .... Jer 3:4
put ye not confidence in a *g* .... Mic 7:5
to *g* our feet into the way of .... Lk 1:79
he will *g* you into all truth .... Jn 16:13
which was *g* to them that took. .... Acts 1:16
I, except some man should *g* me .... Acts 8:31
thou thyself art a *g* of the blind. .... Rom 2:19
the house, give none occasion 1Ti 5:14

GUIDED
thou hast *g* them in thy strength. .... Ex 15:13
other, and *g* them on every side. 2Chr 32:22
I have *g* her from my mother's .... Job 31:18
g them in the wilderness like a .... Ps 78:52
g them by the skilfulness of his .... Ps 78:72

GUIDES
Woe unto you, ye blind *g*, which .... Mt 23:16
Ye blind *g*, which strain at a. .... Mt 23:24

GUIDING
head, *g* his hands wittingly .... Gen 48:14

GUILE
his neighbour, to slay him with *g* .... Ex 21:14
and in whose spirit there is no *g* .... Ps 32:2
evil, and thy lips from speaking *g*. ...... Ps 34:13
a depart not from her streets .... Ps 55:11
Israelite indeed, in whom is no *g* .... Jn 1:47
being crafty, I caught you with *g* 2Cor 12:16
nor of uncleanness, nor in *g* 1Th 2:3
laying aside all malice, and all *g* 1Pet 2:1
neither was *g* found in his mouth. 1Pet 2:22
and his lips that they speak no *g* 1Pet 3:10
And in their mouth was found no *g* .... Rev 14:5

GUILT
but thou shalt put away the *g* of .... Deut 19:13
So shalt thou put away the *g* of .... Deut 21:9

GUILTINESS
shouldest have brought *g* upon us .... Gen 26:10

GUILTLESS
g that taketh his name in vain .... Ex 20:7
shall the man be *g* from iniquity .... Num 5:31
be *g* before the LORD, and before ...... Num 32:22
g that taketh his name in vain .... Deut 5:11
be upon his head, and we will be *g* ..... Josh 2:19
the LORD's anointed, and be *g* 1Sa 26:9
my kingdom are *g* before the LORD 2Sa 3:28
and the king and his throne be *g* 2Sa 14:9
Now therefore hold him not *g* 1Kin 2:9

GUILTY

We are verily *g* concerning our .... Gen 42:21
that will by no means clear the *g*........ Ex 34:7
should not be done, and are *g* .... Lev 4:13
which should not be done, and is *g* ...... Lev 4:22
ought not to be done, and be *g* .... Lev 4:27
he also shall be unclean, and *g* .... Lev 5:2
knoweth of it, then he shall be *g* .... Lev 5:3
he shall be *g* in one of these............. Lev 5:4
when he shall be *g* in one of .... Lev 5:5
he wist it not, yet is he *g* .... Lev 5:17
because he hath sinned, and is *g* .... Lev 6:4
the LORD, and that person be *g* .... Num 5:6
and by no means clearing the *g* .... Num 14:18
he shall not be *g* of blood .... Num 35:27
a murderer, which is *g* of death .... Num 35:31
at this time, that ye should be *g* .... Judg 21:22
and being *g*, they offered a ram of ...... Ezr 10:19
he curse thee, and thou be found *g* .... Prov 30:10
Thou art become *g* in thy blood......... Eze 22:4
them, and hold themselves not *g* .... Zec 11:5
the gift that is upon it, he is *g* .... Mt 23:18
and said, He is *g* of death .... Mt 26:66
condemned him to be *g* of death .... Mk 14:64
the world may become *g* before God... Rom 3:19
shall be *g* of the body and blood 1Cor 11:27
in one point, he is *g* of all .... Jas 2:10

GULF

and you there is a great *g* fixed.......... Lk 16:26

GUNI (gu´-ni) See GUNITES.

1. A son of Naphtali.
Jahzeel, and G, and Jezer, and............ Gen 46:24
of G, the family of the Gunites............ Num 26:48
Jahziel, and G, and Jezer, and.............. 1Chr 7:13
2. Father of Abdiel.
the son of Abdiel, the son of G........... 1Chr 5:15

GUNITES (gu´-nites) *Descendants of Guni 1.*
of Guni, the family of the................... Num 26:48

GUR (gur) See GUR-BAAL. *A hill near Ibleam.*
they did so at the going up to G........... 2Kin 9:27

GUR-BAAL (gur-ba´-al) *Place in western Arabia.*
the Arabians that dwelt in G............... 2Chr 26:7

GUSH
our eyelids *g* out with waters............ Jer 9:18

GUSHED
till the blood *g* out upon them 1Kin 18:28
the rock, that the waters *g* out........... Ps 78:20
the rock, and the waters *g* out........... Ps 105:41
rock also, and the waters *g* out.......... Is 48:21
midst, and all his bowels *g* out.......... Acts 1:18

GUTTER
Whosoever getteth up to the *g*........... 2Sa 5:8

GUTTERS
g in the watering troughs when .... Gen 30:38
the eyes of the cattle in the *g*........... Gen 30:41

H

HA
saith among the trumpets, H, h .... Job 39:25

HAAHASHTARI (ha-a-hash´-te-ri) *A son of Naarah.*
and Hepher, and Temeni, and H......... 1Chr 4:6

HABAIAH (hab-ah´-yah) *A family of exiles.*
the children of H, the children .... Ezr 2:61
the children of H, the children .... Neh 7:63

HABAKKUK (hab´-ak-kuk) *A prophet of Judah.*
The burden which H the prophet .... Hab 1:1
A prayer of H the prophet upon .... Hab 3:1

HABAZINIAH (hab-az-in-i´-ah) *Head of a Rechabite family.*
the son of Jeremiah, the son of H .... Jer 35:3

HABAZZINIAH See HABAZINIAH.

HABERGEON
it, as it were the hole of an h............. Ex 28:32
of the robe, as the hole of an h........... Ex 39:23
the spear, the dart, nor the h............. Job 41:26

HABERGEONS
and spears, and helmets, and h.......... 2Chr 26:14
shields, and the bows, and the h......... Neh 4:16

HABITABLE
Rejoicing in the h part of his............. Prov 8:31

HABITATION
God, and I will prepare him an h........ Ex 15:2
in thy strength unto thy holy h.......... Ex 15:13
without the camp shall his h be .... Lev 13:46
even unto his h shall ye seek............ Deut 12:5
Look down from thy holy h.............. Deut 26:15
which I have commanded in my h 1Sa 2:29
thou shalt see an enemy in my h........ 1Sa 2:32
and shew me both it, and his h.......... 2Sa 15:25
have built an house of h for thee........ 2Chr 6:2

faces from the h of the LORD 2Chr 29:6
Israel, whose h is in Jerusalem........... Ezr 7:15
but suddenly I cursed his h................ Job 5:3
and thou shalt visit thy h................. Job 5:24
make the h of thy righteousness .... Job 8:6
shall be scattered upon his h .... Job 18:15
I have loved the h of thy house .... Ps 26:8
From the place of his h .... Ps 33:14
the widows, is God in his holy h......... Ps 68:5
Let their h be desolate...................... Ps 69:25
Be thou my strong h, whereunto I...... Ps 71:3
judgment are the h of thy throne........ Ps 89:14
refuge, even the most High, thy h....... Ps 91:9
judgment are the h of his throne........ Ps 97:2
fowls of the heaven have their h .... Ps 104:12
that they might go to a city of h......... Ps 107:7
they may prepare a city for h .... Ps 107:36
an h for the mighty God of Jacob........ Ps 132:5
he hath desired it for his h................. Ps 132:13
but he blesseth the h of the just......... Prov 3:33
the LORD be in the h of the wicked...... Prov 3:33
that graveth an h for himself in.......... Is 22:16
the h forsaken, and left like a............ Is 27:10
shall dwell in a peaceable h .... Is 32:18
shall see Jerusalem a quiet h .... Is 33:20
and it shall be an h of dragons........... Is 34:13
in the h of dragons, where each .... Is 35:7
behold from the h of thy holiness ...... Is 63:15
Thine h is in the midst of deceit......... Jer 9:6
him, and have made his h desolate...... Jer 10:25
utter his voice from his holy h........... Jer 25:30
he shall mightily roar upon his h .... Jer 25:30
O h of justice, and mountain of .... Jer 31:23
shall be an h of shepherds .... Jer 33:12
and dwelt in the h of Chimham.......... Jer 41:17
against the h of the strong .... Jer 49:19
the h of justice, even the LORD.......... Jer 50:7
will bring Israel again to his h .... Jer 50:19
Jordan unto the h of the strong .... Jer 50:44
make their h desolate with them........ Jer 50:45
Pathros, into the land of their h......... Eze 29:14
fowls of the heaven had their h .... Dan 4:21
of the rock, whose h is high .... Obad 3
and moon stood still in their h.......... Hab 3:11
he is raised up out of his holy h .... Zec 2:13
Let his h be desolate, and let no .... Acts 1:20
and the bounds of their h.................. Acts 17:26
an h of God through the Spirit........... Eph 2:22
estate, but left their own h................ Jude 6
and is become the h of devils .... Rev 18:2

HABITATIONS
according to their h in the land .... Gen 36:43
of cruelty are in their h.................... Gen 49:5
in all your h shall ye eat................... Ex 12:20
your h upon the sabbath day .... Ex 35:3
Ye shall bring out of your h two .... Lev 23:17
be come into the land of your h .... Num 15:2
These were their h, and their 1Chr 4:33
the h that were found there, and 1Chr 4:41
h were, Beth-el and the towns........... 1Chr 7:28
are full of the h of cruelty.................. Ps 74:20
their camp, round about their h.......... Ps 78:28
forth the curtains of thine h............... Is 54:2
for the h of the wilderness a.............. Jer 9:10
or who shall enter into our h............. Jer 21:13
the peaceable h are cut down .... Jer 25:37
make their h desolate with them........ Jer 49:20
swallowed up all the h of Jacob......... Lam 2:2
toward Diblath, in all their h .... Eze 6:14
h of the shepherds shall................... Amos 1:2
receive you into everlasting .... Lk 16:9

---

3. A son of Ishmael.
Mishma, and Dumah, Massa, H......... 1Chr 1:30
4. An early king of Edom.
was dead, H reigned in his stead......... 1Chr 1:50
H died also............................... 1Chr 1:51

HADADEZER (had-ad-e´zer) See HADAREZER. *King of Zobah.*
David smote also H, the son of 2Sa 8:3
came to succour H king of Zobah........ 2Sa 8:5
that were on the servants of H............. 2Sa 8:7
and from Berothai, cities of H............. 2Sa 8:8
had smitten all the host of H.............. 2Sa 8:9
because he had fought against H 2Sa 8:10
for H had wars with Toi 2Sa 8:10
of Amalek, and of the spoil of H......... 2Sa 8:12
from his lord H king of Zobah............ 1Kin 11:23

HADADRIMMON (ha´´-dad-rim´-mom) *A place in the valley of Megiddo.*
as the mourning of H in the .... Zec 12:11

HADAR (ha´-dar) See HADAD.
1. A son of Ishmael.
H, and Tema, Jetur, Naphish, and...... Gen 25:15
2. An early king of Edom.
died, and H reigned in his stead........ Gen 36:39

HADAREZER (had-a-re´-zer) See HADADEZER. *Another name for Hadadezer.*
H sent, and brought out the 2Sa 10:16
of the host of H went before them....... 2Sa 10:16
to H saw that they were smitten......... 2Sa 10:19
David smote H king of Zobah unto...... 1Chr 18:3
came to help H king of Zobah............ 1Chr 18:5
that were on the servants of H............ 1Chr 18:7
and from Chun, cities of H 1Chr 18:8
all the host of H king of Zobah.......... 1Chr 18:9
because he had fought against H 1Chr 18:10
(for H had war with Toi 1Chr 18:10
of the host of H went before them 1Chr 19:16
when the servants of H saw that........ 1Chr 19:19

HADASHAH (had´-a-shah) *A town in Judah.*
Zenan, and H, and Migdal-gad,......... Josh 15:37

HADASSAH (ha-das´-sah) See ESTHER. *Another name for Esther.*
And he brought up H, that is,............ Est 2:7

HADATTAH (ha-dat´-tah) See HAZOR-HADATTAH. *Another name for Hazor.*
And Hazor, H, and Kerioth, and......... Josh 15:25

HADES

HADID (ha´-did) *A city in Benjamin.*
The children of Lod, H, and Ono, ... Ezr 2:33
The children of Lod, H, and Ono, ... Neh 7:37
H, Zeboim, Neballat, ... Neh 11:34

HADLAI (had´-la-i) *Father of Amasa.*
of Shallum, and Amasa the son of H .. 2Chr 28:12

HADORAM (ha-do´-ram) See ADORAM.
1. A son of Joktan.
And H, and Uzal, and Diklah,............ Gen 10:27
H also, and Uzal, and Diklah,............ 1Chr 1:21
2. A son of Tou.
He sent H his son to king David,....... 1Chr 18:10
3. An officer of Rehoboam.
Then king Rehoboam sent H that....... 2Chr 10:18

HADRACH (ha´-drak) *A district in Syria.*
word of the LORD in the land of H...... Zec 9:1

HADST
little which thou h before I came .... Gen 30:30
surely thou h sent me away now .... Gen 31:42
that thou h utterly hated her .... Judg 15:2
thee, except thou h hasted................ 1Sa 25:34
God liveth, unless thou h spoken 2Sa 2:27
then h thou smitten Syria till............ 2Kin 13:19
Syria till thou h consumed it............ 2Kin 13:19
with us till thou h consumed us........ Ezr 9:14
which thou h sworn to give them....... Neh 9:15
concerning which thou h promised..... Neh 9:23
because thou h a favour unto them..... Ps 44:3
thou, O God, which h cast us off .... Ps 60:10
or ever thou h formed the earth .... Ps 90:2
thou h removed it far unto all........... Is 26:15
O that thou h hearkened to my .... Is 48:18
thou h a whore's forehead, thou........ Jer 3:3
For thou h cast me into the deep, ... Jonah 2:3
Saying, If thou h known, even.......... Lk 19:42
if thou h been here, my brother .... Jn 11:21
if thou h been here, my brother .... Jn 11:32
as if thou h not received it 1Cor 4:7
neither h pleasure therein .... Heb 10:8

HA-ELEPH See ELEPH.

HAFT
the h also went in after the .... Judg 3:22

HAGAB (ha´-gab) See HAGABA. *A family of exiles.*
The children of H, the children .... Ezr 2:46

HAGABA (hag-a-bah) *Same as Hagab.*
of Lebana, the children of H............. Neh 7:48

HAGABAH (hag´-a-bah) See HAGABA. *Same as Hagab.*
of Lebanah, the children of H............ Ezr 2:45

HAGAR (ha´-gar) *Sarah's handmaid.*
an Egyptian, whose name was H........ Gen 16:1
wife took H her maid the Egyptian ..... Gen 16:3

And he went in unto *H*, and she ...... Gen 16:4
And he said, *H*, Sarai's maid,.......... Gen 16:8
his son's name, which *H* bare.......... Gen 16:15
when *H* bare Ishmael to Abram ...... Gen 16:16
saw the son of *H* the Egyptian......... Gen 21:9
of water, and gave it unto *H* .... Gen 21:14
of God called to *H* out of heaven ..... Gen 21:17
unto her, What aileth thee, *H* .... Gen 21:17
whom *H* the Egyptian, Sarah's .... Gen 25:12

HAGARENES (*haga-renes'*) See HAGARITES. *A people east of the Jordan.*
of Moab, and the *H* .... Ps 83:6

HAGARITES (*hag'a-rites*) *Same as Hagarenes.*
of Saul they made war with the *H* 1Chr 5:10
And they made war with the *H* 1Chr 5:19
the *H* were delivered into their.......... 1Chr 5:20

HAGERITE (*hag'-e-rite*) See HAGARITES. Haggeri. *Family of David's herdsmen.*
over the flocks was Jaziz the *H*.......... 1Chr 27:31

HAGGAI (*hag'-ga-i*) *A prophet.*
H the prophet, and Zechariah the ..... Ezr 5:1
the prophesying of *H* the prophet ..... Ezr 6:14
came the word of the LORD by *H* ...... Hag 1:1
word of the LORD by *H* the prophet .. Hag 1:3
and the words of *H* the prophet......... Hag 1:12
Then spake *H* the LORD's messenger... Hag 1:13
word of the LORD by the prophet *H*... Hag 2:1
word of the LORD by *H* the prophet .. Hag 2:10
Then said *H*, If one that is .... Hag 2:13
Then answered *H*, and said, So is ...... Hag 2:14
the LORD came unto *H* in the four...... Hag 2:20

HAGGEDOLIM See NEH 12:14

HAGGERI (*hag'-gher-i*) See HAGGERITE. *Father of Mibhar.*
of Nathan, Mibhar the son of *H* 1Chr 11:38

HAGGI (*hag'-ghi*) See HAGGITES. *A son of Gad.*
Ziphion, and *H*, Shuni, and Ezbon,.... Gen 46:16
of *H*, the family of the Haggites......... Num 26:15

HAGGIAH (*hag-ghi'-ah*) *A descendant of Merari.*
H his son, Asaiah his son 1Chr 6:30

HAGGITES (*hag'-ghites*) See HAGGI. *Descendants of Haggi.*
of Haggi, the family of the *H* .... Num 26:15

HAGGITH (*hag'-ghith*) *A wife of David.*
the fourth, Adonijah the son of *H* 2Sa 3:4
the son of *H* exalted himself 1Kin 1:5
Adonijah the son of *H* doth reign 1Kin 1:11
Adonijah the son of *H* came to.......... 1Kin 2:13
the fourth, Adonijah the son of *H* 1Chr 3:2

HAGRI See HAGGERI.

HAGRITE See HAGERITE.

HAGRITES See HAGARITES.

HAI (*ha'-i*) See AI. *A form of Ai.*
on the west, and *H* on the east........... Gen 12:8
beginning, between Beth-el and *H* ..... Gen 13:3

HAIL
it to rain a very grievous *h* .... Ex 9:18
the *h* shall come down upon them, ... Ex 9:19
that there may be *h* in all the............. Ex 9:22
and the LORD sent thunder and *h* ...... Ex 9:23
the LORD rained *h* upon the land .... Ex 9:23
h, and fire mingled with the *h* .... Ex 9:24
the *h* smote throughout all the.......... Ex 9:25
the *h* smote every herb of the........... Ex 9:25
of Israel were, was there no *h* .... Ex 9:26
no more mighty thunderings and *h* ... Ex 9:28
neither shall there be any more *h* ..... Ex 9:29
h ceased, and the rain was not.......... Ex 9:33
saw that the rain and the *h*............... Ex 9:34
remaineth unto you from the *h* .... Ex 10:5
even all that the *h* hath left .... Ex 10:12
of the trees which the *h* had left........ Ex 10:15
thou seen the treasures of the *h* .... Job 38:22
h stones and coals of fire................... Ps 18:12
h stones and coals of fire................... Ps 18:13
He destroyed their vines with *h* .... Ps 78:47
up their cattle also to the *h*............... Ps 78:48
He gave them *h* for rain, and............. Ps 105:32
Fire, and *h*; snow, and vapours .... Ps 148:8
one, which as a tempest of *h*............. Is 28:2
the *h* shall sweep away the refuge .... Is 28:17
When it shall *h*, coming down on....... Is 32:19
with *h* in all the labours of your......... Hag 2:17
he came to Jesus, and said, *H*........... Mt 26:49
him, and mocked him, saying, *H*........ Mt 27:29
Jesus met them, saying, All *h* .... Mt 28:9
And began to salute him, *H* .... Mk 15:18
came in unto her, and said, *H*........... Lk 1:28
And said, *H*, King of the Jews .... Jn 19:3
sounded, and there followed *h*.......... Rev 8:7
and an earthquake, and great *h*......... Rev 11:19
upon men a great *h* out of heaven..... Rev 16:21
because of the plague of the *h* .... Rev 16:21

HAILSTONES
h than they whom the children of ...... Josh 10:11
with scattering, and tempest, and *h* .. Is 30:30
and ye, O great *h*, shall fall............... Eze 13:11
great *h* in my fury to consume it .... Eze 13:13

and overflowing rain, and great *h* ..... Eze 38:22

HAIR
and fine linen, and goats' *h* .... Ex 25:4
h to be a covering upon the .... Ex 26:7
and fine linen, and goats' *h* .... Ex 35:6
and fine linen, and goats' *h* .... Ex 35:23
them up in wisdom spun goats' *h* ..... Ex 35:26
of goats' *h* for the tent over the .... Ex 36:14
when the *h* in the plague is .... Lev 13:3
the *h* thereof be not turned white...... Lev 13:4
and it have turned the *h* white .... Lev 13:10
the *h* thereof be turned white........... Lev 13:20
if the *h* in the bright spot be .... Lev 13:25
there be no white *h* in the bright .... Lev 13:26
and there be in it a yellow thin *h* ...... Lev 13:30
and that there is no black *h* in it........ Lev 13:31
and there be in it no yellow *h*............ Lev 13:32
shall not seek for yellow *h*................. Lev 13:36
there is black *h* grown up therein...... Lev 13:37
the man whose *h* is fallen off his ...... Lev 13:40
he that hath his *h* fallen off .... Lev 13:41
clothes, and shave off all his *h*.......... Lev 14:8
shave all his *h* off his head .... Lev 14:9
even all his *h* he shall shave off .... Lev 14:9
locks of the *h* of his head grow......... Num 6:5
shall take the *h* of the head of .... Num 6:18
after the *h* of his separation is.......... Num 6:19
of skins, and all work of goats' *h*....... Num 31:20
Howbeit the *h* of his head began ...... Judg 16:22
sling stones at an *h* breadth.............. Judg 20:16
there shall not one *h* of his head....... 1Sa 14:45
of goats' *h* for his bolster 1Sa 19:13
of goats' *h* for his bolster 1Sa 19:16
there shall not one *h* of thy son 2Sa 14:11
because the *h* was heavy on him,....... 2Sa 14:26
he weighed the *h* of his head at........ 2Sa 14:26
there shall not an *h* of him fall 1Kin 1:52
and plucked off the *h* of my head...... Ezr 9:3
of them, and plucked off their *h*......... Neh 13:25
the *h* of my flesh stood up .... Job 4:15
thy *h* is as a flock of goats,............... Song 4:1
thy *h* is as a flock of goats that .... Song 6:5
the *h* of thine head like purple .... Song 7:5
and instead of well set *h* baldness .... Is 3:24
the head, and the *h* of the feet .... Is 7:20
to them that plucked off the *h*........... Is 50:6
Cut off thine *h*, O Jerusalem, and ..... Jer 7:29
to weigh, and divide the *h*................. Eze 5:1
thine *h* is grown, whereas thou .... Eze 16:7
nor was an *h* of their head singed..... Dan 3:27
the *h* of his head like the pure........... Dan 7:9
John had his raiment of camel's *h*..... Mt 3:4
not make one *h* white or black.......... Mt 5:36
John was clothed with camel's *h*....... Mk 1:6
not an *h* of your head perish.............. Lk 21:18
and wiped his feet with her *h* .... Jn 11:2
and wiped his feet with her *h* .... Jn 12:3
for there shall not an *h* fall .... Acts 27:34
you, that, if a man have long *h* 1Cor 11:14
But if a woman have long *h* 1Cor 11:15
for her *h* is given her for a 1Cor 11:15
not with broided *h*, or gold, or.......... 1Ti 2:9
adorning of plaiting the *h*.................. 1Pet 3:3
became black as sackcloth of *h*......... Rev 6:12
they had *h* as the *h* of women,.......... Rev 9:8

HAIRS
gray *h* with sorrow to the grave......... Gen 42:38
gray *h* with sorrow to the grave......... Gen 44:29
shall bring down the gray *h* of........... Gen 44:31
there be no white *h* therein .... Lev 13:21
also with the man of gray *h*............... Deut 32:25
are more than the *h* of mine head..... Ps 40:12
are more than the *h* of mine head..... Ps 69:4
even to hoar *h* will I carry you .... Is 46:4
till his *h* were grown like................... Dan 4:33
gray *h* are here and there upon him .. Hos 7:9
But the very *h* of your head are .... Mt 10:30
wipe them with the *h* of her head ..... Lk 7:38
wiped them with the *h* of her head ... Lk 7:44
But even the very *h* of your head ...... Lk 12:7
his *h* were white like wool, as .... Rev 1:14

HAIRY
red, all over like an *h* garment........... Gen 25:25
Esau my brother is a *h* man .... Gen 27:11
him not, because his hands were *h* .... Gen 27:23
answered him, He was an *h* man 2Kin 1:8
the *h* scalp of such an one as .... Ps 68:21

HAKELDAMA See ACELDAMA.

HAKKATAN (*hak'-ka-tan*) *A family of exiles.*
Johanan the son of *H*, and with him ... Ezr 8:12

HAKKOZ (*hak'-koz*) See KOZ. *A sanctuary servant.*
The seventh to *H*, the eighth to 1Chr 24:10

HAKUPHA (*ha-ku'-fah*) *A family of exiles.*
of Bakbuk, the children of *H* .... Ezr 2:51
of Bakbuk, the children of *H* .... Neh 7:53

HALAH (*ha'-lah*) *An Assyrian district.*
into Assyria, and placed them in *H*.... 2Kin 17:6
unto Assyria, and put them in *H*......... 2Kin 18:11
Manasseh, and brought them unto *H* . 1Chr 5:26

HALAK (*ha'-lak*) *A mountain in southern Canaan.*
Even from the mount *H*, that goeth .. Josh 11:17
of Lebanon even unto the mount *H*.... Josh 12:7

HALE
lest he *h* thee to the judge, and........ Lk 12:58

HALF
earring of *h* a shekel weight.............. Gen 24:22
Moses took *h* of the blood, and put ... Ex 24:6
h of the blood he sprinkled on........... Ex 24:6
a *h* shall be the length thereof,.......... Ex 25:10
a *h* the breadth thereof..................... Ex 25:10
a cubit and a *h* the height thereof ..... Ex 25:10
a *h* shall be the length thereof,.......... Ex 25:17
cubit and a *h* the breadth thereof ..... Ex 25:17
a cubit and a *h* the height thereof ..... Ex 25:23
the *h* curtain that remaineth,............. Ex 26:12
a *h* shall be the breadth of one,......... Ex 26:16
h a shekel after the shekel of .... Ex 30:13
an *h* shekel shall be the .... Ex 30:13
not give less than *h* a shekel,............ Ex 30:15
and of sweet cinnamon *h* so much .... Ex 30:23
of a board one cubit and a *h* .... Ex 36:21
a *h* was the length of it, and a .... Ex 37:1
a *h* the breadth of it .... Ex 37:1
a cubit and a *h* the height of it.......... Ex 37:1
a *h* was the length thereof, and......... Ex 37:6
cubit and a *h* the breadth thereof ..... Ex 37:10
a cubit and a *h* the height thereof ..... Ex 37:10
h a shekel, after the shekel of .... Ex 38:26
h of it in the morning, and *h*.............. Lev 6:20
of whom the flesh is *h* consumed...... Num 12:12
mingled with *h* an hin of oil............... Num 15:9
a drink offering *h* an hin of wine .... Num 15:10
half an hin of wine .... Num 15:10
Take it of their *h*, and give it .... Num 31:29
And of the children of Israel's *h* .... Num 31:30
And the *h*, which was the portion ...... Num 31:36
And of the children of Israel's *h* .... Num 31:42
(Now the *h* that pertained unto .... Num 31:43
of the children of Israel's *h* .... Num 31:47
unto *h* the tribe of Manasseh the ..... Num 32:33
nine tribes, and to the *h* tribe .... Num 34:13
h the tribe of Manasseh have .... Num 34:14
the *h* tribe have received their .... Num 34:15
h mount Gilead, and the cities........... Deut 3:12
gave I unto the *h* tribe of .... Deut 3:13
unto the river Arnon in the valley ...... Deut 3:16
to the *h* tribe of Manasseh .... Deut 29:8
to *h* the tribe of Manasseh, spake .... Josh 1:12
h the tribe of Manasseh, passed....... Josh 4:12
h of them over against mount .... Josh 8:33
h of them over against mount Ebal ... Josh 8:33
from *h* Gilead, even unto the............. Josh 12:2
h Gilead, the border of Sihon,........... Josh 12:5
and the *h* tribe of Manasseh............. Josh 12:6
and the *h* tribe of Manasseh............. Josh 13:7
h the land of the children of .... Josh 13:25
unto the *h* tribe of Manasseh .... Josh 13:29
of the *h* tribe of the children of .... Josh 13:29
h Gilead, and Ashtaroth, and Edrei,... Josh 13:31
even to the one *h* of the children ...... Josh 13:31
nine tribes, and for the *h* tribe .... Josh 14:2
an *h* tribe on the other side............... Josh 14:3
to the *h* tribe of Manasseh, have ...... Josh 18:7
out of the *h* tribe of Manasseh,......... Josh 21:5
out of the *h* tribe of Manasseh in ..... Josh 21:6
out of the *h* tribe of Manasseh .... Josh 21:25
out of the other *h* tribe of .... Josh 21:27
and the *h* tribe of Manasseh,............. Josh 22:1
Now to the one *h* of the tribe of........ Josh 22:7
but unto the other *h* thereof gave...... Josh 22:7
h the tribe of Manasseh returned,..... Josh 22:9
the *h* tribe of Manasseh built .... Josh 22:10
the *h* tribe of Manasseh have .... Josh 22:11
to the *h* tribe of Manasseh, into .... Josh 22:13
to the *h* tribe of Manasseh, unto ...... Josh 22:15
the *h* tribe of Manasseh answered,... Josh 22:21
as it were an *h* acre of land 1Sa 14:14
off the one *h* of their beards 2Sa 10:4
neither if *h* of us die, will they 2Sa 18:3
also *h* the people of Israel 2Sa 19:40
give *h* to the one, and *h* to the 1Kin 3:25
work of the base, a cubit and an *h* 1Kin 7:31
a wheel was a cubit and *h* a cubit 1Kin 7:32
a round compass of *h* a cubit high 1Kin 7:35
and, behold, the *h* was not told me ... 1Kin 10:7
thou wilt give me *h* thine house 1Kin 13:8
captain of *h* his chariots,................... 1Kin 16:9
h of the people followed Tibni 1Kin 16:21
and *h* followed Omri.......................... 1Kin 16:21
Haroeh, and *h* of the Manahethites,... 1Chr 2:52
h of the Manahethites, the 1Chr 2:54
h the tribe of Manasseh,................... 1Chr 5:18
the children of the *h* tribe of 1Chr 5:23
the *h* tribe of Manasseh, and............ 1Chr 5:26
cities given out of the *h* tribe of........ 1Chr 6:61
out of the *h* tribe of Manasseh,......... 1Chr 6:61
out of the *h* tribe of Manasseh,......... 1Chr 6:70
family of the *h* tribe of Manasseh 1Chr 6:71
the *h* tribe of Manasseh................... 1Chr 12:31
the *h* tribe of Manasseh, for 1Chr 12:37
the *h* tribe of Manasseh, Joel 1Chr 27:20
Of the *h* tribe of Manasseh in 1Chr 27:21
the ruler of the greatness of thy....... 2Chr 9:6
the ruler of the *h* part of .... Neh 3:9
the ruler of the *h* part of .... Neh 3:12
ruler of the *h* part of Beth-zur .... Neh 3:16
the ruler of the *h* part of Keilah .... Neh 3:17
the ruler of the *h* part of Keilah .... Neh 3:18
together unto the *h* thereof .... Neh 4:6
that the *h* of my servants wrought,.... Neh 4:16
the other *h* of them held both the,.... Neh 4:16

h of them held the spears from............ Neh 4:21
h of the princes of Judah,.................. Neh 12:32
the *h* of the people upon the wall....... Neh 12:38
the *h* of the rulers with me................ Neh 12:40
their children spake *h* in the.............. Neh 13:24
thee to the *h* of the kingdom.............. Est 5:3
even to the *h* of the kingdom............. Est 5:6
even to the *h* of the kingdom............. Est 7:2
shall not live out *h* their days.............. Ps 55:23
Samaria committed *h* of thy sins......... Eze 16:51
an *h* long, and a cubit and an *h*......... Eze 40:42
about it shall be a cubit........................ Eze 43:17
be for a time, times, and an *h*............. Dan 12:7
barley, and an *h* homer of barley........ Hos 3:2
h of the city shall go forth into........... Zec 14:2
h of the mountain shall remove.......... Zec 14:4
and *h* of it toward the south.............. Zec 14:4
h of them toward the former sea,........ Zec 14:8
h of them toward the hinder sea......... Zec 14:8
it thee, unto the *h* of my kingdom....... Mk 6:23
and departed, leaving him *h* dead...... Lk 10:30
the *h* of my goods I give to the........... Lk 19:8
about the space of *h* an hour............. Rev 8:1
dead bodies three days and an *h*........ Rev 11:9
an *h* the Spirit of life from God............ Rev 11:11
h a time, from the face of the............... Rev 12:14

HALHUL (*hal'-hul*) *A city in Judah.*
H, Beth-zur, and Gedor,...................... Josh 15:58

HALI (*ha'-li*) *A town in Asher.*
And their border was Heikath, and *H* Josh 19:25

HALING
h men and women committed them to. Acts 8:3

HALL
took Jesus into the common *h*............ Mt 27:27
soldiers led him away into the *h*.......... Mk 15:16
a fire in the midst of the *h*.................. Lk 22:55
Caiaphas unto the *h* of judgment....... Jn 18:28
went not into the judgment *h*.............. Jn 18:28
entered into the judgment *h* again...... Jn 18:33
And went again into the judgment *h*.... Jn 18:39
to be kept in Herod's judgment *h*........ Acts 23:35

HALLOHESH (*ha-lo'-hesh*) See HALOHESH.
Father of Shallum.
H, Pileha, Shobek,............................... Neh 10:24

HALLOW
shall *h* in all their holy gifts.................. Ex 28:38
thou shalt do unto them to *h* them...... Ex 29:1
that is therein, and shalt *h* it............... Lev 25:10
h it from the uncleanness of the.......... Lev 16:19
those things which they *h* unto me....... Lev 22:2
of Israel *h* unto the LORD.................... Lev 22:3
I am the Lord which *h* you................... Lev 22:32
ye shalt *h* the fiftieth year, and.......... Lev 25:10
shall *h* his head that same day.......... Num 6:11
The same day did the king *h* the....... 1Kin 8:64
but *h* ye the sabbath day, as I........... Jer 17:22
but *h* the sabbath day, to do............. Jer 17:24
unto me to *h* the sabbath day............ Jer 17:27
And *h* my sabbaths........................... Eze 20:20
and they shall *h* my sabbaths............ Eze 44:24

HALLOWED
blessed the sabbath day, and it........... Ex 20:11
and he shall be *h*, and his garments... Ex 29:21
she shall touch no *h* thing................... Lev 12:4
profaned the *h* thing of the LORD,....... Lev 19:8
but I will be *h* among the.................... Lev 22:32
in the land of Egypt I *h* unto me.......... Num 3:13
every man's *h* things shall be his........ Num 5:10
for they are *h*..................................... Num 16:38
the LORD, therefore they are *h*............ Num 16:38
the things of the children of................. Num 18:8
even the *h* part thereof out of it.......... Num 18:29
I have brought away the *h* things....... Deut 26:13
mine hand, but there is *h* bread......... 1Sa 21:4
So the priest gave him *h* bread.......... 1Sa 21:6
I have *h* this house, which thou......... 1Kin 9:3
house, which I have *h* for my name.... 1Kin 9:7
all the *h* things that Jehoshaphat....... 2Kin 12:18
dedicated, and his own *h* things......... 2Kin 12:18
Moreover Solomon *h* the middle of..... 2Chr 7:7
LORD which he had *h* in Jerusalem.... 2Chr 36:14
art in heaven, *H* be thy name............ Mt 6:9
art in heaven, *H* be thy name............ Lk 11:2

HALOHESH (*ha-lo'-hesh*) See HALLOHESH.
Same as Hallohesh.
him repaired Shallum the son of *H*...... Neh 3:12

HALT
How long *h* ye between two................ 1Kin 18:21
For I am ready to *h*, and my sorrow..... Ps 38:17
to enter into life *h* or maimed............. Mt 18:8
for thee to enter *h* into life................. Mk 9:45
the poor, and the maimed, and the *h*... Lk 14:21
of impotent folk, of blind, *h*................. Jn 5:3

HALTED
upon him, and he *h* upon his thigh...... Gen 32:31
I will make her that *h* a remnant......... Mic 4:7

HALTETH
LORD, will I assemble her that *h*.......... Mic 4:6
and I will save her that *h*.................... Zeph 3:19

HALTING
All my familiars watched for my *h*....... Jer 20:10

HAM (*ham*)
   1. *A son of Noah.*
and Noah begat Shem, *H*, and Japheth Gen 5:32

And Noah begat three sons, Shem, H... Gen 6:10
day entered Noah, and Shem, and H.... Gen 7:13
forth of the ark, were Shem, and H....... Gen 9:18
H is the father of Canaan..................... Gen 9:18
And H, the father of Canaan, saw......... Gen 9:22
of the sons of Noah, Shem, H............... Gen 10:1
And the sons of H................................ Gen 10:6
These are the sons of H, after.............. Gen 10:20
Karnaim, and the Zuzims in H............... Gen 14:5
Noah, Shem, and Japheth.................... 1Chr 1:4
The sons of H...................................... 1Chr 1:8
   2. *Descendants and land of Ham.*
for they of H had dwelt there of........... 1Chr 4:40
strength in the tabernacles of H........... Ps 78:51
Jacob sojourned in the land of H.......... Ps 105:23
them, and wonders in the land of H...... Ps 105:27
Wondrous works in the land of H.......... Ps 106:22

HANAN (*ha'-man*) See HAMATHITE.
   Prime minister under King Ahasuerus.
H the son of Hammedatha the............. Est 3:1
gate, bowed, and reverenced H........... Est 3:2
not unto them, that they told H............. Est 3:4
when H saw that Mordecai bowed......... Est 3:5
then was H full of wrath....................... Est 3:5
wherefore H sought to destroy all........ Est 3:6
before H from day to day, and from...... Est 3:7
H said unto king Ahasuerus, There....... Est 3:8
gave it unto H the son of..................... Est 3:10
And the king said unto H, The.............. Est 3:11
H had commanded unto the king's....... Est 3:12
the king and H sat down to drink.......... Est 3:15
that H had promised to pay to the........ Est 4:7
H come this day unto the banquet........ Est 5:4
Cause H to make haste, that he........... Est 5:5
H came to the banquet that Esther....... Est 5:5
H come to the banquet that I............... Est 5:8
Then went H forth that day joyful......... Est 5:9
but when H saw Mordecai in the........... Est 5:9
Nevertheless H refrained himself......... Est 5:10
H told them of the glory of his............. Est 5:11
H said moreover, Yea, Esther the......... Est 5:12
And the thing pleased H...................... Est 5:14
Now H was come into the outward....... Est 6:4
Behold, H standeth in the court............ Est 6:5
So H came in.. Est 6:6
Now H thought in his heart, To............. Est 6:6
H answered the king, For the man........ Est 6:7
Then the king said to H, Make.............. Est 6:10
Then took H the apparel and the.......... Est 6:11
But H hasted to his house.................... Est 6:12
H told Zeresh his wife and all his......... Est 6:13
hasted to bring H unto the................... Est 6:14
H came to banquet with Esther the...... Est 7:1
and enemy is this wicked H................. Est 7:6
Then H was afraid before the king........ Est 7:6
H stood up to make request for............ Est 7:7
H was fallen upon the bed whereon..... Est 7:8
which H had made for Mordecai,.......... Est 7:9
king, standeth in the house of H.......... Est 7:9
So they hanged H on the gallows......... Est 7:10
Ahasuerus give the house of H the...... Est 8:1
ring, which he had taken from H........... Est 8:2
set Mordecai over the house of H........ Est 8:2
the mischief of H the Agagite.............. Est 8:3
by H the son of Hammedatha the......... Est 8:5
have given Esther the house of H........ Est 8:7
The ten sons of H done in..................... Est 9:10
the palace, and the ten sons of H........ Est 9:12
Because H the son of Hammedatha,..... Est 9:24

HAMAN'S (*ha'-mans*)
king's mouth, they covered H face....... Est 7:8
let H ten sons be hanged upon the....... Est 9:13
and they hanged H ten sons................. Est 9:14

HAMATH (*ha'-math*) See HAMATHITE,
   HAMATH-ZOBAH, HEMATH. *A capital of Syria.*
Zin unto Rehob, as men come to H...... Num 13:21
border unto the entrance of H.............. Num 34:8
Hermon unto the entering into H.......... Josh 13:5
unto the entering in of H...................... Judg 3:3
When Toi king of H heard that.............. 2Sa 8:9
in of H unto the river of Egypt.............. 1Kin 8:65
of H unto the sea of the plain.............. 2Kin 14:25
how he recovered Damascus, and H.... 2Kin 14:28
Cuthah, and from Ava, and from H....... 2Kin 17:24
the men of H made Ashima,................. 2Kin 17:30
Where are the gods of H, and.............. 2Kin 18:34
Where is the king of H, and the........... 2Kin 19:13
bands at Riblah in the land of H........... 2Kin 23:33
them at Riblah in the land of H............. 2Kin 25:21
Hadarezer king of Zobah unto H........... 1Chr 18:3
Now when Toi king of H heard how....... 1Chr 18:9
till a man come over against H............ 2Chr 7:8
way of Hethlon, as one goeth to H....... Eze 47:16
store cities, which he built in H............ 2Chr 8:4
is not H as Arpad................................. Is 10:9
Elam, and from Shinar, and from H....... Is 11:11
Where are the gods of H and Arphad.... Is 36:19
Where is the king of H, and the........... Is 37:13
to Riblah in the land of H..................... Jer 39:5
H is confounded, and Arpad................ Jer 49:23
to Riblah in the land of H..................... Jer 52:9
death in Riblah in the land of H........... Jer 52:27
H, Berothah, Sibraim, which is............. Eze 47:16
of Damascus and the border of H......... Eze 47:17
northward, and the border of H............ Eze 47:17
northward, to the coast of H................ Eze 48:1
from thence go ye to H the great......... Amos 6:2
H also shall border thereby.................. Zec 9:2

HAMATHITE
and the Zemarite, and the H................ Gen 10:18
and the Zemarite, and the H................ 1Chr 1:16

HAMATH-ZOBAH (*ha''-math-zo'-bah*) *Full*
   name of Hamath.
And Solomon went to H, and............... 2Chr 8:3

HAMITES See HAM.

HAMMATH (*ham'-math*) *A city in Naphtali.*
cities are Ziddim, Zer, and H................ Josh 19:35

HAMMEDATHA (*ham-med'-a-thah*) *Father of*
   Haman.
Haman the son of H the Agagite.......... Est 3:1
Haman the son of H the Agagite.......... Est 3:10
by Haman the son of H the Agagite...... Est 8:5
ten sons of Haman the son of H........... Est 9:10
Because Haman the son of H................ Est 9:24

HAMMELECH (*ham'-me-lek*) *Father of*
   Jerahmeel
commanded Jerahmeel the son of H.... Jer 36:26
dungeon of Malchiah the son of H........ Jer 38:6

HAMMER
took an *h* in her hand, and went.......... Judg 4:21
her right hand to the workmen's *h*....... Judg 5:26
with the *h* she smote Sisera, she........ Judg 5:26
so that there was neither *h* nor........... 1Kin 6:7
the *h* him that smote the anvil........... Is 41:7
like a *h* that breaketh the rock........... Jer 23:29
How is the *h* of the whole earth......... Jer 50:23

HAMMERS
thereof at once with axes and *h*......... Ps 74:6
coals, and fashioneth it with *h*............ Is 44:12
fasten it with nails and with *h*............ Jer 10:4

HAMMOLEKETH (*ham-mol'-e-keth*)
   Daughter of Machir.
And his sister H bare Ishod................. 1Chr 7:18

HAMMON (*ham'-mon*)
   1. *A city in Asher.*
And Hebron, and Rehob, and H............ Josh 19:28
   2. *A city in Naphtali.*
H with her suburbs, and Kirjathaim...... 1Chr 6:76

HAMMOTH-DOR (*ham''-moth-dor'*) *Same as*
   Hammon 2.
H with her suburbs, and Kartan............ Josh 21:32

HAMMUEL See HAMUEL.

HAMONAH (*ha-mo'-nah*) *Place where Gog is*
   buried.
the name of the city shall be H............. Eze 39:16

HAMON-GOG (*ha''-mon-gog*) *Same as*
   Hamonah.
shall call it The valley of H.................. Eze 39:11
have buried it in the valley of H............ Eze 39:15

HAMOR (*ha'-mor*) See EMMOR, HAMOR'S.
   Father of Shechem.
at the hand of the children of H............ Gen 33:19
Shechem the son of H the Hivite.......... Gen 34:2
Shechem spake unto his father H......... Gen 34:4
H the father of Shechem went out........ Gen 34:6
H communed with them, saying, The.... Gen 34:8
H his father deceitfully, and said.......... Gen 34:13
And their words pleased H, and........... Gen 34:18
H and Shechem his son came............. Gen 34:20
unto H and unto Shechem................... Gen 34:24
And they slew H and Shechem............ Gen 34:26
Jacob bought of the sons of H the....... Josh 24:32
serve the men of H the father of.......... Judg 9:28

HAMOR'S (*ha'-mors*)
pleased Hamor, and Shechem H son .. Gen 34:18

HAMRAN See AMRAN.

HAMUEL (*ha-mu'-el*) *Son of Mishma.*
H his son, Zacchur his son,.................. 1Chr 4:26

HAMUL (*ha'-mul*) See HAMULITES. *A son of*
   Pharez.
sons of Pharez were Hezron and H...... Gen 46:12
of H, the family of the Hamulites........ Num 26:21
Hezron, and H..................................... 1Chr 2:5

HAMULITES (*ha'-mu-lites*) *Descendants of*
   Hamul
of Hamul, the family of the H............... Num 26:21

HAMUTAL (*ha-mu'-tal*) *Mother of King*
   Jehoahaz.
And his mother's name was H.............. 2Kin 23:31
And his mother's name was H.............. 2Kin 24:18
his mother's name was H the.............. Jer 52:1

HANAMEEL See HANAMEEL.

HANAMEEL (*ha-nam-e-el*) *Son of Shallum.*
H the son of Shallum thine uncle........ Jer 32:7
So H mine uncle's son came to me...... Jer 32:8
the field of H my uncle's son................ Jer 32:9
in the sight of H mine uncle's.............. Jer 32:12

HANAMEL See HANAMEEL.

HANAN (*ha'-nan*) See BAAL-HANAN, BEN-
   HANAN, ELON-BETH-HANAN.
   1. *A son of Shashak.*
And Abdon, and Zichri, and H.............. 1Chr 8:23
   2. *A son of Azel.*
and Sheariah, and Obadiah, and H...... 1Chr 8:38
and Sheariah, and Obadiah, and H...... 1Chr 9:44

H

3. A "mighty man" of David.
H the son of Maachah, and 1Chr 11:43
4. Family of exiles.
of Shalmai, the children of H............... Ezr 2:46
The children of H, the children .... Neh 7:49
5. A priest who assisted Ezra.
Kelita, Azariah, Jozabad, H.................... Neh 8:7
6. A Levite who renewed the covenant.
Hodijah, Kelita, Pelaiah, H................. Neh 10:10
next to them was H the son of .... Neh 13:13
7. A chief who renewed the covenant.
Pelatiah, H, Anaiah, ... Neh 10:22
8. Another chief who renewed the covenant.
And Ahijah, H, Anan,......................... Neh 10:26
9. Son of Igdaliah.
into the chamber of the sons of H ...... Jer 35:4

HANANEAL See HANANEEL.

HANANEEL (*ha-nan'-e-el*) *A tower on
Jerusalem's wall.*
it, unto the tower of H........................... Neh 3:1
the fish gate, and the tower of H ...... Neh 12:39
of H unto the gate of the corner .... Jer 31:38
from the tower of H unto the .... Zec 14:10

HANANEL See HANANEEL.

HANANI (*ha-na'-ni*)
1. A son of Heman.
Shebuel, and Jerimoth, Hananiah, H... 1Chr 25:4
the eighteenth to H, he, his sons 1Chr 25:25
2. A prophet.
at that time H the seer came to 2Chr 16:7
3. Father of Jehu.
Jehu the son of H against Baasha 1Kin 16:1
of H came the word of the LORD........ 1Kin 16:7
Jehu the son of H the seer went........ 2Chr 19:2
in the book of Jehu the son of H 2Chr 20:34
4. Married a foreigner in exile.
of Immer; H, and Zebadiah .... Ezr 10:20
5. Brother of Nehemiah.
That H, one of my brethren, came,...... Neh 1:2
That I gave my brother H, and........... Neh 7:2
6. A priest.
Maai, Nethaneel, and Judah, H......... Neh 12:36

HANANIAH (*han-a-ni'-ah*) See SHADRACH.
1. A son of Heman.
Uzziel, Shebuel, and Jerimoth, H 1Chr 25:4
The sixteenth to H, he, his sons,....... 1Chr 25:23
Meraiah; of Jeremiah, H..................... Neh 12:12
Hear now, H, The LORD hath .... Jer 28:15
2. A captain of King Uzziah.
the ruler, under the hand of H.......... 2Chr 26:11
3. Father of Zedekiah.
Shaphan, and Zedekiah the son of H .. Jer 36:12
4. A false prophet.
that H the son of Azur the .... Jer 28:1
H in the presence of the priests .... Jer 28:5
Then H the prophet took the yoke ..... Jer 28:10
H spake in the presence of all .... Jer 28:11
after that H the prophet had............. Jer 28:12
Go and tell H, saying, Thus saith ...... Jer 28:13
Jeremiah unto H the prophet .... Jer 28:15
So H the prophet died the same........ Jer 28:17
5. Grandfather of Irijah.
son of Shelemiah, the son of H .... Jer 37:13
6. Son of Shashak.
And H, and Elam, and Antothijah,..... 1Chr 8:24
7. Hebrew form of Shadrach.
the children of Judah, Daniel, H........ Dan 1:6
and to H, of Shadrach........................ Dan 1:7
eunuchs had set over Daniel, H......... Dan 1:11
all was found none like Daniel, H....... Dan 1:19
and made the thing known to H......... Dan 2:17
8. A son of Zerubbabel.
Meshullam, and H, and Shelomith...... 1Chr 3:19
And the sons of H 1Chr 3:21
9. Married a foreigner in exile.
Jehohanan, H, Zabbai, and Athlai ...... Ezr 10:28
10. A rebuilder of Jerusalem's wall.
repaired H the son of one of the .... Neh 3:8
11. Another rebuilder of Jerusalem's wall.
After him repaired H the son of......... Neh 3:30
12. A governor of Nehemiah.
H the ruler of the palace, charge....... Neh 7:2
13. An Israelite who renewed the covenant.
Hoshea, H, Hashub, ... Neh 10:23
14. A priest.
Elioenai, Zechariah, and H................ Neh 12:41

HAND See PREFACE.

HANDBREADTH
a border of an h round about............. Ex 37:12
And the thickness of it was an h......... 2Chr 4:5
thou hast made my days as an h .... Ps 39:5

HANDED
him while he is weary and weak h 2Sa 17:2

HANDFUL
his h of the flour thereof .... Lev 2:2
the priest shall take his h of it........... Lev 5:12
And he shall take of it his h .... Lev 6:15
offering, and took an h thereof.......... Lev 9:17
shall take an h of the offering,........... Num 5:26
but an h of meal in a barrel, and........ 1Kin 17:12
There shall be an h of corn in............ Ps 72:16
Better is an h with quietness, ... Eccl 4:6
as the h after the harvestman, and.... Jer 9:22

HANDFULS
the earth brought forth by h .... Gen 41:47
Take to you h of ashes of the............ Ex 9:8
some of the h of purpose for her .... Ruth 2:16
of Samaria shall suffice for h 1Kin 20:10
among my people for h of barley .... Eze 13:19

HANDKERCHIEFS
brought unto the sick h or aprons ..... Acts 19:12

HANDLE
father of all such as h the harp.......... Gen 4:21
they that h the pen of the writer .... Judg 5:14
the battle, that could h shield............ 1Chr 12:8
forth to war, that could h spear 2Chr 25:5
They have hands, but they h not........ Ps 115:7
they that h the law knew me not........ Jer 2:8
and the Libyans, that h the shield...... Jer 46:9
and the Lydians, that h and bend....... Jer 46:9
And all that h the oar, the................ Eze 27:29
h me, and see .... Lk 24:39
taste not; h not.............................. Col 2:21

HANDLED
to be furbished, that it may be h .... Eze 21:11
and sent him away shamefully h .... Mk 12:4
looked upon, and our hands have h 1Jn 1:1

HANDLES
myrrh, upon the h of the lock............ Song 5:5

HANDLETH
He that h a matter wisely shall .... Prov 16:20
him that h the sickle in the time........ Jer 50:16
shall he stand that h the bow .... Amos 2:15

HANDLING
and shields, all of them h swords....... Eze 38:4
nor h the word of God deceitfully....... 2Cor 4:2

HANDMAID
and she had an h, an Egyptian,.......... Gen 16:1
Hagar the Egyptian, Sarah's h .... Gen 25:12
Leah Zilpah his maid for an h............. Gen 29:24
Bilhah his h to be her maid................ Gen 29:29
she gave him Bilhah her h to wife...... Gen 30:4
And the sons of Bilhah, Rachel's h ..... Gen 35:25
And the sons of Zilpah, Leah's h........ Gen 35:26
ass may rest, and the son of thy h..... Ex 23:12
and wine also for me, and for thy h ... Judg 19:19
hast spoken friendly unto thine h...... Ruth 2:13
she answered, I am Ruth thine h........ Ruth 3:9
therefore thy skirt over thine h......... Ruth 3:9
look on the affliction of thine h 1Sa 1:11
me, and not forget thine h................. 1Sa 1:11
give unto thine h a man child 1Sa 1:11
Count not thine h for a daughter....... 1Sa 1:16
Let thine h find grace in thy.............. 1Sa 1:18
and let thine h, I pray thee,.............. 1Sa 25:24
and hear the words of thine h 1Sa 25:24
but I thine h saw not the young 1Sa 25:25
thine h hath brought unto my lord..... 1Sa 25:27
forgive the trespass of thine h 1Sa 25:28
my lord, then remember thine h 1Sa 25:31
let thine h be a servant to wash........ 1Sa 25:41
thine h hath obeyed thy voice, and.... 1Sa 28:21
also unto the voice of thine h............ 1Sa 28:22
thy h had two sons, and they two...... 2Sa 14:6
family is risen against thine h 2Sa 14:7
Then the woman said, Let thine h...... 2Sa 14:12
thy h said, I will now speak unto........ 2Sa 14:15
will perform the request of his h 2Sa 14:15
to deliver his h out of the hand 2Sa 14:16
Then thine h said, The word of my..... 2Sa 14:17
words in the mouth of thine h 2Sa 14:19
him, Hear the words of thine h.......... 2Sa 20:17
lord, O king, swear unto thine h........ 1Kin 1:13
by the LORD thy God unto thine h...... 1Kin 1:17
beside me, while thine h slept 1Kin 3:20
Thine h hath not any thing in the...... 2Kin 4:2
of God, do not lie unto thine h.......... 2Kin 4:16
and save the son of thine h............... Ps 86:16
servant, and the son of thine h......... Ps 116:16
an h that is heir to her mistress........ Prov 30:23
his servant, and every man his h....... Jer 34:16
said, Behold the h of the Lord........... Lk 1:38

HANDMAIDEN
regarded the low estate of his h .... Lk 1:48

HANDMAIDENS
Then the h came near, they and........ Gen 33:6
I be not like unto one of thine h .... Ruth 2:13
on my h I will pour out in those......... Acts 2:18

HANDMAIDS
and unto Rachel, and unto the two h.. Gen 33:1
And he put the h and their children ... Gen 33:2
the eyes of the h of his servants....... Ps 123:2
of the LORD for servants and h .... Is 14:2
and caused the servants and the h .... Jer 34:11
subjection for servants and for h ...... Jer 34:11
be unto you for servants and h .... Jer 34:16
upon the h in those days will I .... Joel 2:29

HANDS
our work and toil of our h.................. Gen 5:29
and submit thyself under her h .... Gen 16:9
innocency of my h have I done .... Gen 20:5
two bracelets for her h .... Gen 24:22
and bracelets upon his sister's h .... Gen 24:30
face, and the bracelets upon her h .... Gen 24:47
the kids of the goats upon his h .... Gen 27:16
but the h are the h of Esau............... Gen 27:22
him not, because his h were hairy ...... Gen 27:23

as his brother Esau's h .... Gen 27:23
affliction and the labour of my h........ Gen 31:42
he delivered him out of their h .... Gen 37:21
he might rid him out of their h........... Gen 37:22
bought him of the h of the................ Gen 39:1
brought down in our h to buy food .... Gen 43:22
head, guiding his h wittingly .... Gen 48:14
the arms of his h were made .... Gen 49:24
the h of the mighty God of Jacob ...... Gen 49:24
spread abroad my h unto the LORD .... Ex 9:29
spread abroad his h unto the LORD .... Ex 9:33
which thy h have established .... Ex 15:17
But Moses' h were heavy.................... Ex 17:12
and Aaron and Hur stayed up his h ... Ex 17:12
his h were steady until the going ...... Ex 17:12
his sons shall put their h upon.......... Ex 29:10
their h upon the head of the ram ...... Ex 29:15
their h upon the head of the ram ...... Ex 29:19
shalt put all in the h of Aaron .... Ex 29:24
and in the h of his sons .... Ex 29:24
shalt receive them of their h .... Ex 29:25
and his sons shall wash their h .... Ex 30:19
So they shalt wash their h .... Ex 30:21
he cast the tables out of his h.......... Ex 32:19
hearted did spin with their h .... Ex 35:25
Aaron and his sons washed their h .... Ex 40:31
h upon the head of the bullock .... Lev 4:15
His own h shall bring the.................. Lev 7:30
his sons laid their h upon the .... Lev 8:14
his sons laid their h upon the .... Lev 8:18
his sons laid their h upon the .... Lev 8:22
upon the thumbs of their right h .... Lev 8:24
And he put all upon Aaron's h........... Lev 8:27
and upon his sons' h......................... Lev 8:27
Moses took them from off their h ...... Lev 8:28
and hath not rinsed his h in water..... Lev 15:11
his h full of sweet incense................. Lev 16:12
Aaron shall lay both his h upon......... Lev 16:21
him lay their h upon his head .... Lev 24:14
the offering of memorial in her h ...... Num 5:18
them upon the h of the Nazarite .... Num 6:19
put their h upon the Levites .... Num 8:10
the Levites shall lay their h .... Num 8:12
and he smote his h together............. Num 24:10
And he laid his h upon him............... Num 27:23
the fruit of the land in their h .... Deut 1:25
God delivered into our h Og also....... Deut 3:3
serve gods, the work of men's h .... Deut 4:28
of the covenant were in my two h ..... Deut 9:15
and cast them out of my two h......... Deut 9:17
that thou puttest thine h unto.......... Deut 12:18
and in all the works of thine h.......... Deut 16:15
The h of the witnesses shall be......... Deut 17:7
afterward the h of all the people ...... Deut 17:7
hath delivered it into thine h .... Deut 20:13
shall wash their h over the .... Deut 21:6
Our h have not shed this blood,........ Deut 21:7
hath delivered them into thine h....... Deut 21:10
thee in all the work of thine h .... Deut 24:19
LORD, the work of the h of the.......... Deut 27:15
anger through the work of your h...... Deut 31:29
let his h be sufficient for him .... Deut 33:7
and accept the work of his h............. Deut 33:11
for Moses had laid his h upon him .... Deut 34:9
delivered into our h all the land .... Josh 2:24
he delivered them into the h of .... Judg 2:14
he sold them into the h of thine........ Judg 2:14
us into the h of the Midianites.......... Judg 6:13
give the Midianites into their h .... Judg 7:2
afterward shall thine h be................. Judg 7:11
the pitchers that were in their h .... Judg 7:19
and held the lamps in their left h ..... Judg 7:20
in their right h to blow withal .... Judg 7:20
into your h the princes of Midian ...... Judg 8:3
Are the h of Zebah and Zalmunna .... Judg 8:6
Are the h of Zebah and Zalmunna .... Judg 8:15
h of all their enemies on every .... Judg 8:34
to the deserving of his h................... Judg 9:16
into the h of the Philistines .... Judg 10:7
into the h of the children of .... Judg 10:7
the children of Ammon into mine h.... Judg 11:30
LORD delivered them into his h.......... Judg 11:32
delivered me not out of their h .... Judg 12:3
me not, I put my life in my h .... Judg 12:3
and a meat offering at our h .... Judg 13:23
And he took thereof in his h............. Judg 14:9
his hands loosed from off his h .... Judg 15:14
delivered into our h our enemy .... Judg 16:24
for God hath given it into your h....... Judg 18:10
her h were upon the threshold .... Judg 19:27
both the palms of his h were cut 1Sa 5:4
out of the h of the Philistines 1Sa 7:14
thou shalt receive of their h 1Sa 10:4
of Israel by the h of messengers........ 1Sa 11:7
And Jonathan climbed up upon his h.. 1Sa 14:13
the h of them that spoiled them 1Sa 14:48
and he will give you into our h 1Sa 17:47
and feigned himself mad in their h 1Sa 21:13
me into the h of my master 1Sa 30:15
now let your h be strengthened 2Sa 2:7
Thy h were not bound, nor thy.......... 2Sa 3:34
his h were feeble, and all the............ 2Sa 4:1
slew them, and cut off their h 2Sa 4:12
then shalt the h of all that are 2Sa 16:21
them into the h of the Gibeonites...... 2Sa 21:9
of my h hath he recompensed me 2Sa 22:21
He teacheth my h to war 2Sa 22:35
they cannot be taken with h 2Sa 23:6
spread forth his h toward heaven 1Kin 8:22
spread forth his h toward this 1Kin 8:38

with his h spread up to heaven 1Kin 8:54
committed them unto the h of the .. 1Kin 14:27
to anger with the work of his h 1Kin 16:7
poured water on the h of Elijah 2Kin 3:11
his eyes, and his h upon his h 2Kin 4:34
at his h that which he brought 2Kin 5:20
And Joram turned his h, and fled, ... 2Kin 9:23
the feet, and the palms of her h 2Kin 9:35
I have brought into your h escape .. 2Kin 10:24
and they clapped their h, and said .. 2Kin 11:12
And they laid h on her 2Kin 11:16
into the h of them that did the 2Kin 12:11
put his h upon the king's h 2Kin 13:16
no gods, but the work of men's h 2Kin 19:18
with all the works of their h 2Kin 22:17
there is no wrong in mine h 1Chr 12:17
of Asaph under the h of Asaph 1Chr 25:2
under the h of their father 1Chr 25:3
All these were under the h of 1Chr 25:6
to be made by the h of artificers ... 1Chr 29:5
who hath with his h fulfilled 2Chr 6:4
of Israel, and spread forth his h 2Chr 6:12
spread forth his h toward heaven .. 2Chr 6:13
spread forth his h in this house 2Chr 6:29
by the h of his servants ships 2Chr 8:18
committed them to the h of the 2Chr 12:10
and let not your h be weak 2Chr 15:7
So they laid h on her 2Chr 23:15
and they laid their h upon them 2Chr 29:23
were the work of the h of man 2Chr 32:19
with all the works of their h 2Chr 34:25
sprinkled the blood from their h 2Chr 35:11
their h with vessels of silver .... Ezr 1:6
the h of the people of Judah .... Ezr 4:4
fast on, and prospereth in their h .. Ezr 5:8
to strengthen their h in the work ... Ezr 6:22
spread out my h unto the LORD my Ezr 9:5
they gave their h that they would ... Ezr 10:19
their h for this good work .... Neh 2:18
one of his h wrought in the work .... Neh 4:17
Their h shall be weakened from ..... Neh 6:9
therefore, O God, strengthen my h Neh 6:9
Amen, with lifting up their h .... Neh 8:6
and gavest them into their h .... Neh 9:24
do so again, I will lay h on you ...... Neh 13:21
scorn to lay h on Mordecai alone ... Est 3:6
talents of silver to the h of .... Est 3:9
they laid not their h on the prey .... Est 9:16
hast blessed the work of his h .... Job 1:10
thou hast strengthened the weak h Job 4:3
so that their h cannot perform .... Job 5:12
he woundeth, and his h make whole Job 5:18
and make my h never so clean .... Job 9:30
despise the work of thine h .... Job 10:3
Thine h have made me and fashioned Job 10:8
and stretch out thine h toward him.. Job 11:13
a desire to the work of thine h .... Job 14:15
me over into the h of the wicked .... Job 16:11
Not for any injustice in mine h ...... Job 16:17
is he that will strike h with me ...... Job 17:3
hath clean h shall be stronger ...... Job 17:9
his h shall restore their goods ...... Job 20:10
by the pureness of thine h .... Job 22:30
Men shall clap their h at him .... Job 27:23
the strength of their h profit me .... Job 30:2
any blot hath cleaved to mine h .... Job 31:7
they all are the work of his h .... Job 34:19
sin, he clappeth his h among us .... Job 34:37
if there be iniquity in my h .... Ps 7:3
dominion over the works of thy h ... Ps 8:6
snared in the work of his own h ..... Ps 9:16
of my h hath he recompensed me .. Ps 18:20
cleanness of my h in his eyesight .. Ps 18:24
He teacheth my h to war, so that ... Ps 18:34
they pierced my h and my feet .... Ps 22:16
He that hath clean h, and a pure ... Ps 24:4
I will wash mine h in innocency ..... Ps 26:6
In whose h is mischief, and their ... Ps 26:10
when I lift up my h toward thy .... Ps 28:2
them after the work of their h .... Ps 28:4
LORD, not the operation of his h .... Ps 28:5
out our h to a strange god .... Ps 44:20
O clap your h, all ye people .... Ps 47:1
He hath put forth his h against ...... Ps 55:20
violence of your h in the earth .... Ps 58:2
I will lift up my h in thy name .... Ps 63:4
soon stretch out her h unto God .... Ps 68:31
vain, and washed my h in innocency Ps 73:13
men of might have found their h .... Ps 76:5
them by the skilfulness of his h .... Ps 78:72
his h were delivered from the .... Ps 81:6
have stretched out my h unto thee .. Ps 88:9
thou the work of our h upon us ...... Ps 90:17
the work of our h establish thou .... Ps 90:17
shall bear thee up in their h .... Ps 91:12
triumph in the works of thy h .... Ps 92:4
his h formed the dry land .... Ps 95:5
Let the floods clap their h .... Ps 98:8
the heavens are the work of thy h .. Ps 102:25
The works of his h are verity .... Ps 111:7
and gold, the work of men's h .... Ps 115:4
They have h, but they handle not ... Ps 115:7
My h also will I lift up unto thy ...... Ps 119:48
Thy h have made me and fashioned Ps 119:73
put forth their h unto iniquity .... Ps 125:3
shalt eat the labour of thine h .... Ps 128:2
Lift up your h in the sanctuary, ... Ps 134:2
and gold, the work of men's h .... Ps 135:15
not the works of thine own h .... Ps 138:8
O LORD, from the h of the wicked .. Ps 140:4

the lifting up of my h as the .... Ps 141:2
I muse on the work of thy h .... Ps 143:5
I stretch forth my h unto thee .... Ps 143:6
which teacheth my h to war .... Ps 144:1
little folding of the h to sleep .... Prov 6:10
h that shed innocent blood, ... Prov 6:17
the recompence of a man's h shall.. Prov 12:14
plucketh it down with her h .... Prov 14:1
void of understanding striketh h ... Prov 17:18
for his h refuse to labour .... Prov 21:25
thou one of them that strike h .... Prov 22:26
little folding of the h to sleep .... Prov 24:33
The spider taketh hold with her h .. Prov 30:28
and worketh willingly with her h ... Prov 31:13
with the fruit of her h she .... Prov 31:16
She layeth her h to the spindle ...... Prov 31:19
and her h hold the distaff .... Prov 31:19
reacheth forth her h to the needy ... Prov 31:20
Give her of the fruit of her h .... Prov 31:31
the works that my h had wrought .... Eccl 2:11
The fool foldeth his h together ...... Eccl 4:5
than both the h full with travail .... Eccl 4:6
and destroy the work of thine h ..... Eccl 5:6
snares and nets, and her h as bands Eccl 7:26
through idleness of the h the .... Eccl 10:18
my h dropped with myrrh, and my .. Song 5:5
His h are as gold rings set with ..... Song 5:14
the work of the h of a cunning ...... Song 7:1
And when ye spread forth your h .... Is 1:15
your h are full of blood .... Is 1:15
worship the work of their own h .... Is 2:8
of his h shall be given him .... Is 3:11
consider the operation of his h ..... Is 5:12
Therefore shall all h be faint .... Is 13:7
to the altars, the work of his h ...... Is 17:8
and Assyria the work of my h .... Is 19:25
forth his h in the midst of them .... Is 25:11
spreadeth forth his h to swim .... Is 25:11
with the spoils of their h .... Is 25:11
his children, the work of mine h .... Is 29:23
which your own h have made unto .. Is 31:7
that shaketh his h from holding .... Is 33:15
Strengthen ye the weak h, and ..... Is 35:3
no gods, but the work of men's h ... Is 37:19
or thy work, He hath no h .... Is 45:9
the work of my h command ye me .. Is 45:11
I, even my h, have stretched out .... Is 45:12
thee upon the palms of my h .... Is 49:16
of the field shall clap their h .... Is 55:12
For your h are defiled with blood ... Is 59:3
the act of violence is in their h ..... Is 59:6
of thy planting, the work of my h ... Is 60:21
I have spread out my h all the .... Is 65:2
long enjoy the work of their h .... Is 65:22
the works of their own h .... Jer 1:16
him, and thine h upon thine head ... Jer 2:37
herself, that spreadeth her h .... Jer 4:31
our h wax feeble .... Jer 6:24
the work of the h of the workman ... Jer 10:3
and of the h of the founder .... Jer 10:9
by the h of them that seek their .... Jer 19:7
weapons of war that are in your h .. Jer 21:4
also the h of evildoers, that .... Jer 23:14
to anger with the works of your h .. Jer 25:6
works of your h to your own hurt ... Jer 25:7
to the works of their own h .... Jer 25:14
every man with his h on his loins .. Jer 30:6
and buyest the work of their h .... Jer 32:30
the h of him that telleth them .... Jer 33:13
for thus he weakeneth the h of ...... Jer 38:4
the h of all the people, in .... Jer 38:4
wrath with the works of your h ...... Jer 44:8
children for feebleness of h .... Jer 47:3
upon all the h shall be cuttings, ... Jer 48:37
of them, and his h waxed feeble .... Jer 50:43
hath delivered me into their h .... Lam 1:14
Zion spreadeth forth her h .... Lam 1:17
that pass by clap their h at thee ... Lam 2:15
lift up thy h toward him for the ..... Lam 2:19
our h unto God in the heavens .... Lam 3:41
according to the work of their h ..... Lam 3:64
the work of the h of the potter .... Lam 4:2
a moment, and no h stayed on her.. Lam 4:6
The h of the pitiful women have ..... Lam 4:10
they had the h of a man under ...... Eze 1:8
All h shall be feeble, and .... Eze 7:17
I will give it into the h of the .... Eze 7:21
the h of the people of the land ...... Eze 7:27
put it into the h of him that was ... Eze 10:7
body, and their backs, and their ... Eze 10:12
the likeness of the h of a man ...... Eze 10:21
you into the h of strangers .... Eze 11:9
strengthened the h of the wicked ... Eze 13:22
and I put bracelets upon thy h .... Eze 16:11
through all thy h be feeble, and .... Eze 21:7
and smite thine h together .... Eze 21:14
I will also smite mine h together ... Eze 21:17
endure, or can thine h be strong ... Eze 22:14
adultery, and blood is in their h .... Eze 23:37
which put bracelets upon their h ... Eze 23:42
and blood is in their h .... Eze 23:45
Because thou hast clapped thine h Eze 25:6
a stone was cut out without h .... Dan 2:34
cut out of the mountain without h .. Dan 2:45
shall deliver you out of my h .... Dan 3:15
knees and upon the palms of my h . Dan 10:10
say any more to the work of our h .. Hos 14:3
nor have laid h on their .... Obad 13
the violence that is in their h .... Jonah 3:8
more worship the work of thine h ... Mic 5:13

may do evil with both h earnestly ... Mic 7:3
thee shall clap the h over thee ...... Nah 3:19
voice, and lifted up his h on high ... Hab 3:10
to Zion, Let not thine h be slack ... Zeph 3:16
and upon all the labour of the h .... Hag 1:11
and so is every work of their h ...... Hag 2:14
hail in all the labours of your h .... Hag 2:17
The h of Zerubbabel have laid the .. Zec 4:9
his h shall also finish it .... Zec 4:9
Let your h be strong, ye that .... Zec 8:9
not, but let your h be strong .... Zec 8:13
What are these wounds in thine h .. Zec 13:6
in their h they shall bear thee ...... Mt 4:6
not their h when they eat bread .... Mt 15:2
unwashen h defileth not a man .... Mt 15:20
be betrayed into the h of men ...... Mt 17:22
rather than having two h or two .... Mt 18:8
and he laid h on him, and took him Mt 18:28
that he should put his h on them .. Mt 19:13
And he laid his h on them, and .... Mt 19:15
when they sought to lay h on him .. Mt 21:46
is betrayed into the h of sinners ... Mt 26:45
laid h on Jesus, and took him ...... Mt 26:50
him with the palms of their h .... Mt 26:67
washed his h before the multitude .. Mt 27:24
thee, come and lay thy h on her .... Mk 5:23
mighty works are wrought by his h .. Mk 6:2
laid his h upon a few sick folk ..... Mk 6:5
that is to say, with unwashen, h ... Mk 7:2
except they wash their h oft .... Mk 7:3
but eat bread with unwashen h ..... Mk 7:5
put his h upon him, he asked him .. Mk 8:23
he put his h again upon his eyes .. Mk 8:25
is delivered into the h of men ...... Mk 9:31
than having two h to go into hell .. Mk 9:43
put his h upon them, and blessed .. Mk 10:16
is betrayed into the h of sinners ... Mk 14:41
And they laid their h on him .... Mk 14:46
this temple that is made with h .... Mk 14:58
will build another made without h .. Mk 14:58
him with the palms of their h .... Mk 14:65
they shall lay h on the sick .... Mk 16:18
in their h they shall bear thee ...... Lk 4:11
no h to him on every one of .... Lk 4:40
did eat, rubbing them in their h .... Lk 6:1
be delivered into the h of men ...... Lk 9:44
And he laid his h on her .... Lk 13:13
same hour sought to lay h on him .. Lk 20:19
they shall lay their h on you .... Lk 21:12
stretched forth no h against me .... Lk 22:53
into thy h I commend my spirit ..... Lk 23:46
into the h of sinful men, and be ... Lk 24:7
Behold my h and my feet, that ..... Lk 24:39
thus spoken, he shewed them his h. Lk 24:40
to Bethany, and he lifted up his h .. Lk 24:50
but no man laid h on him, because .. Jn 7:30
but no man laid h on him .... Jn 7:44
and no man laid h on him .... Jn 8:20
had given all things into his h ...... Jn 13:3
no my feet only, but also my h ...... Jn 13:9
and they smote him with their h .... Jn 19:3
said, he shewed unto them his h .. Jn 20:20
in his h the print of the nails .... Jn 20:25
hither thy finger, and behold my h .. Jn 20:27
thou shalt stretch forth thy h .... Jn 21:18
by wicked h have crucified and .... Acts 2:23
And they laid h on them, and put .. Acts 4:3
by the h of the apostles were .... Acts 5:12
laid their h on the apostles, and .. Acts 5:18
prayed, they laid their h on them .. Acts 6:6
in the works of their own h .... Acts 7:41
not in temples made with h .... Acts 7:48
Then laid they their h on them ...... Acts 8:17
h the Holy Ghost was given .... Acts 8:18
power, that on whomsoever I lay h .. Acts 8:19
and putting his h on him said ...... Acts 9:17
the elders by the h of Barnabas ... Acts 11:30
h to vex certain of the church ...... Acts 12:1
And his chains fell off from his h .. Acts 12:7
prayed, and laid their h on them ... Acts 13:3
and wonders to be done by their h.. Acts 14:3
not in temples made with h .... Acts 17:24
is worshipped with men's h .... Acts 17:25
Paul had laid his h upon them, ... Acts 19:6
special miracles by the h of Paul .. Acts 19:11
be no gods, which are made with h . Acts 19:26
that these h have ministered unto.. Acts 20:34
Paul's girdle, and bound his own h . Acts 21:11
him into the h of the Gentiles ...... Acts 21:11
all the people, and laid h on him,.. Acts 24:7
took him away out of our h .... Acts 24:7
own h the tackling of the ship ...... Acts 27:19
and prayed, and laid his h on him .. Acts 28:8
into the h of the Romans .... Acts 28:17
forth my h unto a disobedient ...... Rom 10:21
And labour, working with our own h. 1Cor 4:12
of God, an house not made with h .. 2Cor 5:1
by the wall, and escaped his h 2Cor 11:33
the right h of fellowship .... Gal 2:9
the flesh made by h .... Eph 2:11
working with his h the thing .... Eph 4:28
the circumcision made without h .. Col 2:11
and to work with your own h 1Th 4:11
every where, lifting up holy h 1Ti 2:8
on of the h of the presbytery 1Ti 4:14
Lay h suddenly on no man, neither .. 1Ti 5:22
in thee by the putting on of my h .. 2Ti 1:6
heavens are the works of thy h ..... Heb 1:10
set him over the works of thy h .... Heb 2:7
of baptisms, and of laying on of h . Heb 6:2

tabernacle, not made with *h*................ Heb 9:11
into the holy places made with *h*........ Heb 9:24
fall into the *h* of the living God........ Heb 10:31
lift up the *h* which hang down........... Heb 12:12
Cleanse your *h*, ye sinners.................. Jas 4:8
our *h* have handled, of the Word...... 1Jn 1:1
white robes, and palms in their *h*...... Rev 7:9
not of the works of their *h*................ Rev 9:20
their foreheads, or in their *h*............. Rev 20:4

HANDSTAVES
the bows and the arrows, and the *h*..... Eze 39:9

HANDWRITING
Blotting out the *h* of ordinances........ Col 2:14

HANDYWORK
and the firmament sheweth his *h*........ Ps 19:1

HANES (ha´-nees) See TAHPANES. *A place in Egypt.*
and his ambassadors came to *H*.......... Is 30:4

HANG
thee, and shall *h* thee on a tree........ Gen 40:19
shall *h* over the backside of the........ Ex 26:12
it shall *h* over the sides of the.......... Ex 26:13
thou shalt *h* it upon four pillars........ Ex 26:32
thou shalt *h* up the vail under.......... Ex 26:33
h up the hanging at the court........... Ex 40:8
h them up before the LORD against.... Num 25:4
to death, and thou *h* him on a tree..... Deut 21:22
thy life shall *h* in doubt before........ Deut 28:66
we will *h* them up unto the LORD...... 2Sa 21:6
to speak unto the king to *h*.............. Est 6:4
Then the king said, H him thereon...... Est 7:9
whereon there *h* a thousand............. Song 4:4
they shall *h* upon him all the........... Is 22:24
the virgins of Jerusalem *h* down...... Lam 2:10
pin of it to *h* any vessel thereon....... Eze 15:3
two commandments *h* all the law..... Mt 22:40
the venomous beast *h* on his hand.... Acts 28:4
lift up the hands which *h* down........ Heb 12:12

HANGED
But he *h* the chief baker................... Gen 40:22
unto mine office, and him he *h*......... Gen 41:13
(for he that is *h* is accursed of........ Deut 21:23
the king of Ai he *h* on a tree............ Josh 8:29
them, and *h* them on five trees......... Josh 10:26
h them up over the pool in Hebron... 2Sa 4:12
h himself, and died, and was buried... 2Sa 17:23
Behold, I saw Absalom *h* in an oak.... 2Sa 18:10
they *h* them in the hill before........... 2Sa 21:9
where the Philistines had *h* them..... 2Sa 21:12
the bones of them that were *h*........... 2Sa 21:13
set up, let him be *h* thereon.............. Ezr 6:11
they were both *h* on a tree................ Est 2:23
that Mordecai may be *h* thereon...... Est 5:14
So they *h* Haman on the gallows....... Est 7:10
him they have *h* upon the gallows,.... Est 8:7
ten sons be *h* upon the gallows......... Est 9:13
and they *h* Haman's ten sons............ Est 9:14
sons should be *h* on the gallows........ Est 9:25
We *h* our harps upon the willows...... Ps 137:2
Princes are *h* up by their hand......... Lam 5:12
they *h* the shield and helmet in....... Eze 27:10
they *h* their shields upon thy.......... Eze 27:11
a millstone were *h* about his neck..... Mt 18:6
and departed, and went and *h* himself. Mt 27:5
a millstone were *h* about his neck..... Mk 9:42
a millstone were *h* about his neck..... Lk 17:2
which were *h* railed on him.............. Lk 23:39
whom ye slew and *h* on a tree.......... Acts 5:30
whom they slew and *h* on a tree........ Acts 10:39

HANGETH
and *h* the earth upon nothing........... Job 26:7
is every one that *h* on a tree............. Gal 3:13

HANGING
thou shalt make an *h* for the door..... Ex 26:36
thou shalt make for the *h* five.......... Ex 26:37
shall be an *h* of twenty cubits.......... Ex 27:16
the *h* for the door at the.................. Ex 35:15
the *h* for the door of the court.......... Ex 35:17
he made an *h* for the tabernacle....... Ex 36:37
the *h* for the gate of the court.......... Ex 38:18
the *h* for the tabernacle door........... Ex 39:38
the *h* for the court gate, his............. Ex 39:40
put the *h* of the door to the.............. Ex 40:5
hang up the *h* at the court gate........ Ex 40:8
he set up the *h* at the door of.......... Ex 40:28
set up the *h* of the court gate........... Ex 40:33
the *h* for the door of the.................. Num 3:25
wherewith they minister, and the *h*... Num 3:31
the *h* for the door of the................. Num 4:25
the *h* for the door of the gate of...... Num 4:26
they were *h* upon the trees until....... Josh 10:26

HANGINGS
be *h* for the court of fine twined...... Ex 27:9
be *h* of an hundred cubits long......... Ex 27:11
side shall be *h* of fifty cubits........... Ex 27:12
The *h* of one side of the gate............ Ex 27:14
side shall be *h* fifteen cubits............ Ex 27:15
The *h* of the court, his pillars,.......... Ex 35:17
the *h* of the court were of................ Ex 38:9
side the *h* were an hundred cubits..... Ex 38:11
west side were *h* of fifty cubits......... Ex 38:12
The *h* of the one side of the gate....... Ex 38:14
hand, were *h* of fifteen cubits.......... Ex 38:15
All the *h* of the court round.............. Ex 38:16
answerable to the *h* of the court....... Ex 38:18

The *h* of the court, his pillars,.......... Ex 39:40
the *h* of the court, and the.............. Num 3:26
the *h* of the court, and the.............. Num 4:26
the women wove *h* for the grove....... 2Kin 23:7
were white, green, and blue, *h*.......... Est 1:6

HANIEL (ha´-ne-el) See HANNIEL. *A son of Ulla.*
Arah, and H, and Rezia....................... 1Chr 7:39

HANNAH (han´-nah) *Mother of Samuel.*
the name of the one was H................. 1Sa 1:2
children, but H had no children.......... 1Sa 1:2
But unto H he gave a worthy.............. 1Sa 1:5
for he loved H.................................. 1Sa 1:5
Elkanah her husband to her, H........... 1Sa 1:8
So H rose up after they had eaten....... 1Sa 1:9
Now H, she spake in her heart............ 1Sa 1:13
H answered and said, No, my lord,...... 1Sa 1:15
and Elkanah knew H his wife.............. 1Sa 1:19
come about after H had conceived...... 1Sa 1:20
But H went not up.............................. 1Sa 1:22
H prayed, and said, My heart.............. 1Sa 2:1
And the LORD visited H, so that.......... 1Sa 2:21

HANNATHON (han´-na-thon) *A city in Zebulun.*
it on the north side to H..................... Josh 19:14

HANNIEL (han´-ne-el) See HANIEL. *A prince of Manasseh.*
of Manasseh, for the son of Ephod...... Num 34:23

HANOCH (ha´-nok) See HANOCHITES, HENOCH.
1. A son of Midian.
Ephah, and Epher, and H, and Abidah, Gen 25:4
2. A son of Reuben.
H, and Phallu, and Hezron, and Carmi Gen 46:9
H, and Pallu, Hezron, and Carmi......... Ex 6:14
H, of whom cometh the family of....... Num 26:5
the firstborn of Israel were, H............ 1Chr 5:3

HANOCHITES (ha´-nok-ites) *Descendants of Hanoch 2.*
whom cometh the family of the H....... Num 26:5

HANUN (ha´-nun)
1. A king of Ammon.
H his son reigned in his stead............ 2Sa 10:1
kindness unto H the son of Nahash..... 2Sa 10:2
of Ammon said unto H their............... 2Sa 10:3
Wherefore H took David's servants..... 2Sa 10:4
kindness unto H the son of Nahash..... 1Chr 19:2
of the children of Ammon to H........... 1Chr 19:3
the children of Ammon said to H........ 1Chr 19:3
Wherefore H took David's servants..... 1Chr 19:4
themselves odious to David, H........... 1Chr 19:6
2. A son of Zalaph.
H the sixth son of Zalaph,.................. Neh 3:30
3. A rebuilder of Jerusalem's wall.
The valley gate repaired H................. Neh 3:13

HAP
her *h* was to light on a part of.......... Ruth 2:3

HAPHRAIM (haf-ra´-im) *A city in Issachar.*
And H, and Shihon, and Anaharath,... Josh 19:19

HAPLY
if the people had eaten freely.............. 1Sa 14:30
if *h* he might find any thing.............. Mk 11:13
Lest *h*, after he hath laid the............ Lk 14:29
lest *h* ye be found even to fight........ Acts 5:39
if *h* they might feel after him,.......... Acts 17:27
Lest *h* if they of Macedonia come.... 2Cor 9:4

HAPPEN
h to thee for this thing..................... 1Sa 28:10
There shall no evil *h* to the just........ Prov 12:21
forth, and shew us what shall *h*........ Is 41:22
what things should *h* unto him........ Mk 10:32

HAPPENED
it was a chance that *h* to us.............. 1Sa 6:9
As I *h* by chance upon mount............ 2Sa 1:6
there is to be there a man of.............. 2Sa 20:1
him of all that had *h* unto the.......... Est 4:7
therefore this evil is *h* unto you....... Jer 44:23
of all these things which had *h*......... Lk 24:14
at that which had *h* unto him........... Acts 3:10
blindness in part is *h* to Israel......... Rom 11:25
Now all these things *h* unto them..... 1Cor 10:11
that the things which *h* unto me........ Phil 1:12
some strange thing *h* unto you.......... 1Pet 4:12
But it is *h* unto them according........ 2Pet 2:22

HAPPENETH
also that one event *h* to them all...... Eccl 2:14
As it *h* to the fool.......................... Eccl 2:15
so it *h* even to me.......................... Eccl 2:15
unto whom it *h* according to the...... Eccl 8:14
to whom it *h* according to the.......... Eccl 8:14
but time and chance *h* to them all..... Eccl 9:11

HAPPIER
But she is *h* if she so abide,.............. 1Cor 7:40

HAPPIZZEZ See APHSES.

HAPPY
H am I, for the daughters will.......... Gen 30:13
H art thou, O Israel.......................... Deut 33:29
H are thy men, *h* are these............. 1Kin 10:8
H are thy men, and *h* are these....... 2Chr 9:7
h is the man whom God correcteth.... Job 5:17
H is the man that hath his quiver...... Ps 127:5
h shalt thou be, and it shall be......... Ps 128:2
h shall he be, that rewardeth........... Ps 137:8

H shall he be, that taketh and.......... Ps 137:9
H is that people, that is in such........ Ps 144:15
h is that people, whose God is.......... Ps 144:15
H is he that hath the God of............. Ps 146:5
H is the man that findeth wisdom,..... Prov 3:13
h is every one that retaineth her....... Prov 3:18
*h*ath mercy on the poor, *h* is he...... Prov 14:21
trusteth in the LORD, *h* is he............ Prov 16:20
H is the man that feareth alway......... Prov 28:14
he that keepeth the law, *h* is he........ Prov 29:18
wherefore are all they *h* that........... Jer 12:1
And now we call the proud *h*............ Mal 3:15
things, *h* are ye if ye do them........... Jn 13:17
I think myself *h*, king Agrippa,........ Acts 26:2
H is he that condemneth not............ Rom 14:22
for righteousness' sake, *h* are ye....... 1Pet 3:14
for the name of Christ, *h* are ye........ 1Pet 4:14

HARA (ha´-rah) *An Assyrian province.*
them unto Halah, and Habor, and H... 1Chr 5:26

HARADAH (har´-a-dah) *A Hebrew encampment in the wilderness.*
mount Shapher, and encamped in H. Num 33:24
And they removed from H, and......... Num 33:25

HARAN (ha´-ran) See BETH-HARAN, CHARRAN.
1. A son of Terah.
and begat Abram, Nahor, and H......... Gen 11:26
Terah begat Abram, Nahor, and H...... Gen 11:27
and H begat Lot............................. Gen 11:27
H died before his father Terah in........ Gen 11:28
wife, Milcah, the daughter of H.......... Gen 11:29
and Lot the son of H his son's son...... Gen 11:31
2. A Levite.
Shelomith, and Haziel, and H............ 1Chr 23:9
3. A son of Caleb.
Ephah, Caleb's concubine, bare H....... 1Chr 2:46
and H begat Gazez.......................... 1Chr 2:46
4. A city in northern Mesopotamia.
and they came unto H, and dwelt....... Gen 11:31
and Terah died in H.......................... Gen 11:32
old when he departed out of H........... Gen 12:4
souls that they had gotten in H........... Gen 12:5
thou to Laban my brother to H........... Gen 27:43
from Beer-sheba, and went toward H... Gen 28:10
And they said, Of H are we................ Gen 29:4
Gozan, and H, and Rezeph............... 2Kin 19:12
have destroyed, as Gozan, and H........ Is 37:12
H, and Canneh, and Eden, the........... Eze 27:23

HARARITE (har´-a-rite) *Native of the hill country of Judah.*
was Shammah the son of Agee the H.. 2Sa 23:11
Shammah the H, Ahiam the son of..... 2Sa 23:33
Ahiam the son of Sharar the H........... 2Sa 23:33
Jonathan the son of Shage the H......... 1Chr 11:34
Ahiam the son of Sacar the H............. 1Chr 11:35

HARBONA (har-bo´-nah) See HARBONAH. *A servant of King Ahasuerus.*
he commanded Mehuman, Biztha, H... Est 1:10

HARBONAH (har-bo´-nah) See HARBONA. *Same as Harbona.*
And H, one of the chamberlains,........ Est 7:9

HARD
Is any thing too *h* for the LORD........ Gen 18:14
travailed, and she had *h* labour......... Gen 35:16
to pass, when she was in *h* labour..... Gen 35:17
their lives bitter with *h* bondage...... Ex 1:14
the *h* causes they brought unto........ Ex 18:26
he take off *h* by the backbone.......... Lev 3:9
the cause that is too *h* for you......... Deut 1:17
It shall not seem *h* unto thee........... Deut 15:18
matter too *h* for thee in judgment.... Deut 17:8
us, and laid upon us *h* bondage........ Deut 26:6
went *h* unto the door of the house... Judg 9:52
pursued *h* after them unto Gidom,.... Judg 20:45
even they also followed *h* after......... 1Sa 14:22
Philistines followed *h* upon Saul...... 1Sa 31:2
and horsemen followed *h* after him... 2Sa 1:6
sons of Zeruiah be too *h* for me....... 2Sa 3:39
Amnon thought it *h* for him to do.... 2Sa 13:2
to prove him with *h* questions.......... 1Kin 10:1
h by the palace of Ahab king of....... 1Kin 21:1
said, Thou hast asked a *h* thing........ 2Kin 2:10
Philistines followed *h* after Saul...... 1Chr 10:2
in the midst *h* by their buttocks........ 1Chr 19:4
with *h* questions at Jerusalem........... 2Chr 9:1
as *h* as a piece of the nether............ Job 41:24
hast shewed thy people *h* things....... Ps 60:3
My soul followeth *h* after thee.......... Ps 63:8
Thy wrath lieth *h* upon me.............. Ps 88:7
they utter and speak *h* things.......... Ps 94:4
but the way of transgressors is *h*...... Prov 13:15
from the *h* bondage wherein thou..... Is 14:3
there is nothing too *h* for thee.......... Jer 32:17
is there any thing too *h* for me......... Jer 32:27
of an *h* language, but to the............. Eze 3:5
of an *h* language, whose words........ Eze 3:6
dreams, and shewing of *h* sentences.. Dan 5:12
rowed *h* to bring it to the land......... Jonah 1:13
knew thee that thou art an *h* man..... Mt 25:24
how *h* is it for them that trust.......... Mk 10:24
this, said, This is an *h* saying........... Jn 6:60
it is *h* for thee to kick against.......... Acts 9:5
house joined *h* to the synagogue...... Acts 18:7
it is *h* for thee to kick against.......... Acts 26:14
h to be uttered, seeing ye are.......... Heb 5:11
some things *h* to be understood........ 2Pet 3:16

of all their h speeches which .... Jude 15

HARDEN
but I will h his heart, that he.......... Ex 4:21
I will h Pharaoh's heart, and.......... Ex 7:3
I will h Pharaoh's heart, that he .... Ex 14:4
I will h the hearts of the.......... Ex 14:17
thou shalt not h thine heart.......... Deut 15:7
was of the LORD to h their hearts.......... Josh 11:20
then do ye h your hearts, as the.......... 1Sa 6:6
I would h myself in sorrow.......... Job 6:10
H not your heart, as in the.......... Ps 95:8
H not your hearts, as in the.......... Heb 3:8
h not your hearts, as in the.......... Heb 3:15
hear his voice, h not your hearts.......... Heb 4:7

HARDENED
he h Pharaoh's heart, that he.......... Ex 7:13
unto Moses, Pharaoh's heart is h.......... Ex 7:14
and Pharaoh's heart was h, neither .... Ex 7:22
he h his heart, and hearkened not.......... Ex 8:15
and Pharaoh's heart was h this time.......... Ex 8:19
Pharaoh h his heart at this time.......... Ex 8:32
And the heart of Pharaoh was h.......... Ex 9:7
the LORD h the heart of Pharaoh,.......... Ex 9:12
h his heart, he and his servants.......... Ex 9:34
And the heart of Pharaoh was h.......... Ex 9:35
for I have h his heart, and.......... Ex 10:1
But the LORD h Pharaoh's heart,.......... Ex 10:20
But the LORD h Pharaoh's heart,.......... Ex 10:27
the LORD h Pharaoh's heart, so.......... Ex 11:10
the LORD h the heart of Pharaoh.......... Ex 14:8
for the LORD thy God h his spirit.......... Deut 2:30
and Pharaoh h their hearts.......... 1Sa 6:6
but h their necks, like to the.......... 2Kin 17:14
h his heart from turning unto the.......... 2Chr 36:13
h their necks, and hearkened not.......... Neh 9:16
but h their necks, and in their.......... Neh 9:17
h their neck, and would not hear.......... Neh 9:29
who hath h himself against him,.......... Job 9:4
She is h against her young ones,.......... Job 39:16
h our heart from thy fear.......... Is 63:17
their ear, but h their neck.......... Jer 7:26
because they have h their necks.......... Jer 17:23
lifted up, and his mind in h pride .... Dan 5:20
for their heart was h .... Mk 6:52
have ye your heart yet h .... Mk 8:17
their eyes, and h their heart.......... Jn 12:40
But when divers were h, and.......... Acts 19:9
lest any of you be h through the.......... Heb 3:13

HARDENETH
A wicked man h his face.......... Prov 21:29
but he that h his heart shall .... Prov 28:14
being often reproved h his neck .... Prov 29:1
have mercy, and whom he will he h.......... Rom 9:18

HARDER
A brother offended is h to be won .... Prov 18:19
made their faces h than a rock .... Jer 5:3
As an adamant h than flint have I.......... Eze 3:9

HARDHEARTED
house of Israel are impudent and h.......... Eze 3:7

HARDLY
And when Sarai dealt h with her .... Gen 16:6
when Pharaoh would h let us go.......... Ex 13:15
through it, h bestead and hungry.......... Is 8:21
That a rich man shall h enter.......... Mt 19:23
How h shall they that have riches.......... Mk 10:23
bruising him h departeth from him .... Lk 9:39
How h shall they that have riches.......... Lk 18:24
h passing it, came unto a place.......... Acts 27:8

HARDNESS
When the dust groweth into h.......... Job 38:38
Moses because of the h of your .... Mt 19:8
grieved for the h of their hearts.......... Mk 3:5
For the h of your heart he wrote.......... Mk 10:5
h of heart, because they believed.......... Mk 16:14
But after thy h and impenitent.......... Rom 2:5
Thou therefore endure h, as a.......... 2Ti 2:3

HARE
And the h, because he cheweth the.......... Lev 11:6
as the camel, and the h, and the.......... Deut 14:7

HAREPH (ha'-ref) A son of Caleb.
H the father of Beth-gader.......... 1Chr 2:51

HARETH (ha'-reth) Forest land in Judah.
and came into the forest of H 1Sa 22:5

HARHAIAH (har-ha-i'-ah) Father of Uzziel.
him repaired Uzziel the son of H.......... Neh 3:8

HARHAS (har'-has) See HASRAH. Grandfather of Shallum.
the son of Tikvah, the son of H.......... 2Kin 22:14

HARHUR (har'-hur) A family in exile.
of Hakupha, the children of H .... Ezr 2:51
of Hakupha, the children of H .... Neh 7:53

HARIM (ha'-rim)
1. A priest.
The third to H, the fourth to 1Chr 24:8
The children of H, a thousand and .... Ezr 2:39
And of the sons of H.......... Ezr 10:21
Malchijah the son of H, and Hashub.......... Neh 3:11
The children of H, a thousand and.......... Neh 7:42
Of H, Adna; of Meraioth.......... Neh 12:15
2. A family in exile.
The children of H, three hundred .... Ezr 2:32
The children of H, three hundred .... Neh 7:35
3. Married a foreigner in exile.

And of the sons of H.......... Ezr 10:31
4. An Israelite who renewed the covenant.
H, Meremoth, Obadiah,.......... Neh 10:5
5. A family who renewed the covenant.
Malluch, H, Baanah.......... Neh 10:27

HARIPH (ha'-rif) See JORAH.
1. A family of exiles.
The children of H, an hundred and.......... Neh 7:24
2. An Israelite who renewed the covenant.
H, Anathoth, Nebai,.......... Neh 10:19

HARLOT
deal with our sister as with an h.......... Gen 34:31
her, he thought her to be an h.......... Gen 38:15
place, saying, Where is the h.......... Gen 38:21
There was no h in this place.......... Gen 38:21
that there was no h in this place.......... Gen 38:22
daughter in law hath played the h.......... Gen 38:24
woman, or profane, or an h.......... Lev 21:14
only Rahab the h shall live.......... Josh 6:17
And Joshua saved Rahab the h alive.......... Josh 6:25
valour, and he was the son of an h .... Judg 11:1
Samson to Gaza, and saw there an h.......... Judg 16:1
a woman with the attire of an h .... Prov 7:10
is the faithful city become an h .... Is 1:21
years shall Tyre sing as an h .... Is 23:15
thou h that hast been forgotten.......... Is 23:16
thou wanderest, playing the h.......... Jer 2:20
thou h with thy many lovers.......... Jer 3:1
tree, and there hath played the h .... Jer 3:6
but went and played the h also.......... Jer 3:8
playest the h because of thy.......... Eze 16:15
and playedst the h thereupon.......... Eze 16:16
thou hast played the h with them.......... Eze 16:28
and hast not been as an h, in that.......... Eze 16:31
Wherefore, O h, hear the word of .... Eze 16:35
thee to cease from playing the h.......... Eze 16:41
played the h when she was mine.......... Eze 23:5
played the h in the land of Egypt.......... Eze 23:19
unto a woman that playeth the h.......... Eze 23:44
their mother hath played the h .... Hos 2:5
thou shalt not play the h .... Hos 3:3
Though thou, Israel, play the h .... Hos 4:15
and have given a boy for an h.......... Joel 3:3
wife shall be an h in the city.......... Amos 7:17
gathered it of the hire of an h.......... Mic 1:7
shall return to the hire of an h .... Mic 1:7
whoredoms of the wellfavoured h .... Nah 3:4
and make them the members of an h.......... 1Cor 6:15
is joined to an h is one body.......... 1Cor 6:16
By faith the h Rahab perished not .... Heb 11:31
Rahab the h justified by works.......... Jas 2:25

HARLOT'S
went, and came into an h house.......... Josh 2:1
the country, Go into the h house .... Josh 6:22

HARLOTS
came there two women, that were h.......... 1Kin 3:16
with h spendeth his substance .... Prov 29:3
whores, and they sacrifice with h.......... Hos 4:14
the h go into the kingdom of God.......... Mt 21:31
publicans and the h believed him .... Mt 21:32
hath devoured thy living with h.......... Lk 15:30
THE GREAT, THE MOTHER OF H.......... Rev 17:5

HARLOTS'
by troops in the h houses.......... Jer 5:7

HARM
and this pillar unto me, for h.......... Gen 31:52
he shall make amends for the h.......... Lev 5:16
his enemy, neither sought his h.......... Num 35:23
for I will no more do thee h.......... 1Sa 26:21
do us more h than did Absalom.......... 2Sa 20:6
And there was no h in the pot.......... 2Kin 4:41
anointed, and do my prophets no h.......... 1Chr 16:22
anointed, and do my prophets no h .... Ps 105:15
cause, if he have done thee no h.......... Prov 3:30
look well to him, and do him no h.......... Jer 39:12
voice, saying, Do thyself no h.......... Acts 16:28
Crete, and to have gained this h.......... Acts 27:21
beast into the fire, and felt no h.......... Acts 28:5
saw no h come to him, they.......... Acts 28:6
shewed or spake any h of thee.......... Acts 28:21
And who is he that will h you.......... 1Pet 3:13

HAR-MAGEDON See ARMAGEDDON.

HARMLESS
wise as serpents, and h as doves.......... Mt 10:16
That ye may be blameless and h .... Phil 2:15
priest became us, who is holy, h.......... Heb 7:26

HARNEPHER (har-ne'-fur) A son of Zophah.
H, and Shual, and Beri.......... 1Chr 7:36

HARNESS
on his h boast himself as he that 1Kin 20:11
between the joints of the h.......... 1Kin 22:34
and vessels of gold, and raiment, h.......... 2Chr 9:24
between the joints of the h.......... 2Chr 18:33
H the horses.......... Jer 46:4

HARNESSED
up h out of the land of Egypt.......... Ex 13:18

HAROD (ha'-rod) See HARODITE. A spring of water.
and pitched beside the well of H.......... Judg 7:1

HARODITE (ha-ro'-dite) See HARORITE. Family name of two of David's "mighty men."
Shammah the H, Elika the H 2Sa 23:25

HAROEH (ha-ro'-eh) See REAIAH. A son of Shobal.
H, and half of the Manahethites.......... 1Chr 2:52

HARORITE (ha-ro'-rite) Family name of a "mighty man."
Shammoth the H, Helez the 1Chr 11:27

HAROSHETH (ha'ro-sheth) A city in Galilee.
which dwelt in H of the Gentiles .... Judg 4:2
from H of the Gentiles unto the .... Judg 4:13
the host, unto H of the Gentiles.......... Judg 4:16

HARP
of all such as handle the h .... Gen 4:21
songs, with tabret, and with h .... Gen 31:27
and a tabret, and a pipe, and a h 1Sa 10:5
who is a cunning player on an h 1Sa 16:16
upon Saul, that David took an h 1Sa 16:23
Jeduthun, who prophesied with a h 1Chr 25:3
They take the timbrel and h .... Job 21:12
My h also is turned to mourning,.......... Job 30:31
Praise the LORD with h .... Ps 33:2
upon the h will I praise thee, O .... Ps 43:4
open my dark saying upon the h .... Ps 49:4
awake, psaltery and h .... Ps 57:8
unto thee will I sing with the h .... Ps 71:22
the pleasant h with the psaltery .... Ps 81:2
upon the h with a solemn sound .... Ps 92:3
Sing unto the LORD with the h .... Ps 98:5
with the h, and the voice of a .... Ps 98:5
Awake, psaltery and h .... Ps 108:2
praise upon the h unto our God.......... Ps 147:7
unto him with the timbrel and h .... Ps 149:3
praise him with the psaltery and h .... Ps 150:3
And the h, and the viol, the tabret.......... Is 5:12
shall sound like an h for Moab .... Is 16:11
Take an h, go about the city,.......... Is 23:16
endeth, the joy of the h ceaseth .... Is 24:8
the sound of the cornet, flute, h .... Dan 3:5
the sound of the cornet, flute, h .... Dan 3:7
the sound of the cornet, flute, h .... Dan 3:10
the sound of the cornet, flute, h .... Dan 3:15
giving sound, whether pipe or h.......... 1Cor 14:7

HARPED
it be known what is piped or h.......... 1Cor 14:7

HARPERS
I heard the voice of h harping.......... Rev 14:2
And the voice of h, and musicians,.......... Rev 18:22

HARPING
of harpers h with their harps.......... Rev 14:2

HARPS
made of fir wood, even on h.......... 2Sa 6:5
h also and psalteries for singers.......... 1Kin 10:12
might, and with singing, and with h 1Chr 13:8
of musick, psalteries and h.......... 1Chr 15:16
with h on the Sheminith to excel.......... 1Chr 15:21
a noise with psalteries and h 1Chr 15:28
Jeiel with psalteries and with h 1Chr 16:5
who should prophesy with h.......... 1Chr 25:1
with cymbals, psalteries, and h 1Chr 25:6
having cymbals and psalteries and h.......... 2Chr 5:12
and to the king's palace, and h 2Chr 9:11
to Jerusalem with psalteries and h 2Chr 20:28
with psalteries, and with h 2Chr 29:25
cymbals, psalteries, and with h .... Neh 12:27
We hanged our h upon the willows .... Ps 137:2
Lamb, having every one of them h .... Rev 5:8
of harpers harping with their h .... Rev 14:2
sea of glass, having the h of God.......... Rev 15:2

HARROW
or will he h the valleys after .... Job 39:10

HARROWS
under h of iron, and under axes of 2Sa 12:31
with h of iron, and with axes 1Chr 20:3

HARSHA (har'-shah) A family of exiles.
of Mehida, the children of H .... Ezr 2:52
of Mehida, the children of H .... Neh 7:54

HART
as of the roebuck, and as of the h.......... Deut 12:15
the h is eaten, so thou shalt eat.......... Deut 12:22
The h, and the roebuck, and the.......... Deut 14:5
as the roebuck, and as the h .... Deut 15:22
As the h panteth after the water .... Ps 42:1
is like a roe or a young h .... Song 2:9
h upon the mountains of Bether .... Song 2:17
like to a roe or to a young h .... Song 8:14
shall the lame man leap as an h .... Is 35:6

HARTS
and an hundred sheep, beside h.......... 1Kin 4:23
like h that find no pasture .... Lam 1:6

HARUM (ha'-rum) Father of Aharhel.
families of Aharhel the son of H 1Chr 4:8

HARUMAPH (ha-ru'-maf) Father of Jedaiah.
repaired Jedaiah the son of H .... Neh 3:10

HARUPHITE (ha'-ru-fite) A Korhite soldier.
and Shephatiah the H.......... 1Chr 12:5

HARUZ (ha'ruz) Father of Meshullemeth.
the daughter of H of Jotbah.......... 2Kin 21:19

HARVEST
earth remaineth, seedtime and h.......... Gen 8:22
went in the days of wheat h.......... Gen 30:14

shall neither be earing nor *h* .... Gen 45:6
And the feast of *h*, the .... Ex 23:16
time and in *h* thou shalt rest .... Ex 34:21
of the firstfruits of wheat *h* .... Ex 34:22
when ye reap the *h* of your land .... Lev 19:9
gather the gleanings of thy *h* .... Lev 19:9
you, and shall reap the *h* thereof ...... Lev 23:10
of your *h* unto the priest .... Lev 23:10
when ye reap the *h* of your land .... Lev 23:22
thou gather any gleaning of thy *h* ..... Lev 23:22
of thy *h* thou shalt not reap .... Lev 25:5
cuttest down thine *h* in thy field .... Deut 24:19
all his banks all the time of *h* .... Josh 3:15
after, in the time of wheat *h* .... Judg 15:1
in the beginning of barley *h* .... Ruth 1:22
until they have ended all my *h* .... Ruth 2:21
of barley *h* and of wheat *h* .... Ruth 2:23
their wheat *h* in the valley 1Sa 6:13
ear his ground, and to reap his *h* 1Sa 8:12
Is it not wheat *h* to day 1Sa 12:17
put to death in the days of *h* 2Sa 21:9
in the beginning of barley *h* 2Sa 21:9
from the beginning of *h* until 2Sa 21:10
came to David in the *h* time unto 2Sa 23:13
Whoso *h* the hungry eateth up, and ... Job 5:5
and gathereth her food in the *h* .... Prov 6:8
but he that sleepeth in *h* is a .... Prov 10:5
therefore shall he beg in *h* .... Prov 20:4
the cold of snow in the time of *h* .... Prov 25:13
snow in summer, and as rain in *h* ...... Prov 26:1
thee according to the joy in *h* .... Is 9:3
fruits and for thy *h* is fallen .... Is 16:9
but the *h* shall be a heap in the .... Is 17:11
a cloud of dew in the heat of *h* .... Is 18:4
For afore the *h*, when the bud is .... Is 18:5
for in the *h* of the river, is her .... Is 23:3
And they shall eat up thine *h* .... Jer 5:17
us the appointed weeks of the *h* .... Jer 5:24
The *h* is past, the summer is .... Jer 8:20
the sickle in the time of *h* .... Jer 50:16
and the time of her *h* shall come .... Jer 51:33
Judah, he hath set an *h* for thee .... Hos 6:11
because the *h* of the field is .... Joel 1:11
in the sickle, for the *h* is ripe .... Joel 3:13
were yet three months to the *h* .... Amos 4:7
The *h* truly is plenteous, but the ...... Mt 9:37
ye therefore the Lord of the *h* .... Mt 9:38
send forth labourers into his *h* .... Mt 9:38
both grow together until the *h* .... Mt 13:30
in the time of *h* I will say to .... Mt 13:30
the *h* is the end of the world .... Mt 13:39
the sickle, because the *h* is come ...... Mk 4:29
The *h* truly is great, but the .... Lk 10:2
ye therefore the Lord of the *h* .... Lk 10:2
send forth labourers into his *h* .... Lk 10:2
yet four months, and then cometh *h*.. Jn 4:35
for they are white already to *h* .... Jn 4:35
for the *h* of the earth is ripe .... Rev 14:15

HARVESTMAN

as when the *h* gathereth the corn .... Is 17:5
and as the handful after the *h* .... Jer 9:22

HAS

the words which thou *h* heard 2Kin 22:18

HASADIAH (has-a-di'-ah) A son of
Zerubbabel.
and Ohel, and Berechiah, and 1Chr 3:20

HASENUAH (has-e-nu'-ah) See SENUAH.
Father of Hodaviah.
the son of Hodaviah, the son of *H* 1Chr 9:7

HASHABIAH (hash-a-bi'-ah)
1. Son of Amaziah.
The son of *H*, the son of Amaziah, ... 1Chr 6:45
2. A Merarite Levite.
the son of Azrikam, the son of *H* 1Chr 9:14
3. A son of Jeduthun.
Gedaliah, and Zeri, and Jeshaiah, *H* ... 1Chr 25:3
The twelfth to *H*, he, his sons,........... 1Chr 25:19
4. A descendant of Hebron.
And of the Hebronites, *H* and his 1Chr 26:30
5. Son of Kemuel.
the Levites, *H* the son of Kemuel 1Chr 27:17
6. A Levite chief.
And Nethaneel, his brethren, and *H*... 2Chr 35:9
7. A Levite in exile.
And *H*, and with him Jeshaiah of the .. Ezr 8:19
8. A chief priest.
of the priests, Sherebiah, *H* .... Ezr 8:24
9. A rebuilder of Jerusalem's wall.
Next unto him repaired *H*, the .... Neh 3:17
10. A Levite who renewed the covenant.
Micha, Rehob, *H*, ... Neh 10:11
11. Son of Bunni.
the son of Azrikam, the son of *H* .... Neh 11:15
12. Another Levite.
the son of Bani, the son of *H* .... Neh 11:22
13. A priest in Joiakim's time.
Of Hilkiah, *H* .... Neh 12:21
14. A chief Levite.
H, Sherebiah, and Jeshua the son ..... Neh 12:24

HASHABNAH (hash-ab'-nah) A clan leader
who renewed the covenant.
Rehum, *H*, Maaseiah, ... Neh 10:25

HASHABNIAH See HASHABIAH.

HASHABNIAH (hash-ab-ni'-ah)
1. Father of Hattush.
him repaired Hattush the son of *H* ..... Neh 3:10

2. A Levite.
Jeshua, and Kadmiel, Bani, *H*, ... Neh 9:5

HASHBADANA (hash-bad'-a-nah) A priest.
and Malchiah, and Hashum, and *H*..... Neh 8:4

HASHBADDANAH See HASHBADANA.

HASHEM (ha'-shem) Father of several "mighty
men."
The sons of *H* the Gizonite, ... 1Chr 11:34

HASHMONAH (hash-mo'-nah) A Hebrew
encampment in the wilderness.
from Mithcah, and pitched in *H* .... Num 33:29
And they departed from *H*, and .... Num 33:30

HASHUB (ha'-shub) See HASSHUB.
1. Father of Shemaiah.
Shemaiah the son of *H*, the son of ..... Neh 11:15
2. Son of Pahath-moab.
H the son of Pahath-moab, ... Neh 3:11
3. A rebuilder of Jerusalem's wall.
H over against their house. .... Neh 3:23
4. A clan leader who renewed the covenant.
Hoshea, Hananiah, *H*, ... Neh 10:23

HASHUBAH (hash-u'-bah) A son of
Zerubbabel.
And *H*, and Ohel, and Berechiah, and . 1Chr 3:20

HASHUM (ha'-shum)
1. A family of exiles.
The children of *H*, two hundred........... Ezr 2:19
Of the sons of *H*, ... Ezr 10:33
The children of *H*, three hundred....... Neh 7:22
2. A priest.
and Mishael, and Malchiah, and *H*..... Neh 8:4
3. A clan leader who renewed the covenant.
Hodijah, *H*, Bezai, ... Neh 10:18

HASHUPHA (hash-u'-fah) See HASUPHA. A
family of exiles.
of Ziha, the children of *H* .... Neh 7:46

HASRAH (has'-rah) See HARHAS. Same as
Harhas.
the son of Tikvath, the son of *H* 2Chr 34:22

HASSENAAH (has-se-na'-ah) See SENAAH.
Father of some rebuilders of Jerusalem's wall.
fish gate did the sons of *H* build......... Neh 3:3

HASSENUAH See SENUAH.

HASSHUB (hash'-ub) See HASHUB. Father of
Shemaiah.
Shemaiah the son of *H*, the son of 1Chr 9:14

HASSOPHERETH See SOPHERETH.

HAST See PREFACE.

HASTE

H thee, escape thither .... Gen 19:22
And she made *h*, and let down her ..... Gen 24:46
And Joseph made *h* .... Gen 43:30
H ye, and go up to my father, and ...... Gen 45:9
and ye shall *h* and bring down my ..... Gen 45:13
called for Moses and Aaron in *h* .... Ex 10:16
and ye shall eat it in *h* .... Ex 12:11
send them out of the land in *h* .... Ex 12:33
And Moses made *h*, and bowed his .... Ex 34:8
out of the land of Egypt in *h* .... Deut 16:3
that shall come upon them make *h* .... Deut 32:35
What ye have seen me do, make *h* ..... Judg 9:48
the woman made *h*, and ran. .... Judg 13:10
make *h* now, for he came to day to 1Sa 9:12
after she fed, Make speed, *h* 1Sa 20:38
the king's business required *h* 1Sa 21:8
David made *h* to get away for fear 1Sa 23:26
Saul, saying, *H* thee, and come 1Sa 23:27
Then Abigail made *h*, and took two ... 1Sa 25:18
to pass, as she made *h* to flee 2Sa 4:4
Syrians had cast away in their *h* 2Kin 7:15
for God commanded me to make *h* 2Chr 35:21
they went up in *h* to Jerusalem .... Ezr 4:23
king said, Cause Haman to make *h* .... Est 5:5
the king said to Haman, Make *h* .... Est 6:10
to answer, and for this I make *h* .... Job 20:2
O my strength, *h* thee to help me .... Ps 22:19
For I said in my *h*, I am cut off .... Ps 31:22
Make *h* to help me, O Lord my .... Ps 38:22
O LORD, make *h* to help me .... Ps 40:13
Make *h*, O God, to deliver me .... Ps 70:1
make *h* to help me, O LORD .... Ps 70:1
make *h* unto me, O God .... Ps 70:5
O my God, make *h* for my help .... Ps 71:12
I said in my *h*, All men are liars .... Ps 116:11
I made *h*, and delayed not to keep .... Ps 119:60
make *h* unto me. .... Ps 141:1
to evil, and make *h* to shed blood ...... Prov 1:16
but he that maketh *h* to be rich .... Prov 28:20
Make *h*, my beloved, and be thou ...... Song 8:14
that believeth shall not make *h* .... Is 28:16
Thy children shall make *h* .... Is 49:17
For ye shall not go out with *h* .... Is 52:12
they make *h* to shed innocent .... Is 59:7
And let them make *h*, and take up a .. Jer 9:18
in Daniel before the king in *h* .... Dan 2:25
was astonied, and rose up in *h* .... Dan 3:24
went in *h* unto the den of lions .... Dan 6:19
they shall make *h* to the wall, ... Nah 2:5
straightway with *h* unto the king, ... Mk 6:25
went into the hill country with *h* .... Lk 1:39
And they came with *h*, and found ...... Lk 2:16
said unto him, Zacchaeus, make *h* ..... Lk 19:5

And he made *h*, and came down, and.. Lk 19:6
saying unto me, Make *h* .... Acts 22:18

HASTED

and he *h* to dress it .... Gen 18:7
and she *h*, and let down her pitcher .. Gen 24:18
And she *h*, and emptied her pitcher ... Gen 24:20
And the taskmasters *h* them .... Ex 5:13
and the people *h* and passed over...... Josh 4:10
king of Ai saw it, that they *h* .... Josh 8:14
into the city, and took it, and *h* .... Josh 8:19
h not to go down about a whole.......... Josh 10:13
And the liers in wait *h*, and rushed ... Judg 20:37
nigh to meet David, that David *h*......... 1Sa 17:48
And when Abigail saw David, she *h* 1Sa 25:23
hurting thee, except thou hadst *h* 1Sa 25:34
And he *h*, and took the ashes away ... 1Kin 20:41
Then they *h*, and took every man 2Kin 9:13
himself *h* also to go out, because 2Chr 26:20
But Haman *h* to his house mourning... Est 6:12
h to bring Haman unto the banquet ... Est 6:14
or if my foot hath *h* to deceit............. Job 31:5
they were troubled, and *h* away .... Ps 48:5
voice of thy thunder they *h* away .... Ps 104:7
for he *h*, if it were possible for .... Acts 20:16

HASTEN

H hither Micaiah the son of Imlah 1Kin 22:9
year, and see that ye *h* the matter...... 2Chr 34:5
that *h* after another god .... Ps 16:4
I would *h* my escape from the. .... Ps 55:8
eat, or who else can *h* hereunto .... Eccl 2:25
h his work, that we may see it. .... Is 5:19
I the LORD will *h* it in his time. .... Is 60:22
for I will *h* my word to perform .... Jer 1:12

HASTENED

Abraham *h* into the tent unto. .... Gen 18:6
arose, then the angels *h* Lot .... Gen 19:15
Howbeit the Levites *h* it not 2Chr 24:5
being *h* by the king's commandment... Est 3:15
mules and camels went out, being *h*.. Est 8:14
I have not *h* from being a pastor .... Jer 17:16

HASTENETH

The captive exile *h* that he may .... Is 51:14

HASTETH

as the eagle that *h* to the prey .... Job 9:26
he drinketh up a river, and *h* not .... Job 40:23
as a bird *h* to the snare, and. .... Prov 7:23
the that *h* with his feet sinneth. .... Prov 19:2
He that *h* to be rich hath an evil. .... Prov 28:22
h to his place where he arose............. Eccl 1:5
to come, and his affliction *h* fast .... Jer 48:16
fly as the eagle that *h* to eat. .... Hab 1:8
h greatly, even the voice of the .... Zeph 1:14

HASTILY

they brought him *h* out of the .... Gen 41:14
without driving them out *h* .... Judg 2:23
Then he called *h* unto the young .... Judg 9:54
And the man came in *h*, and told Eli... 1Sa 4:14
come from him, and did *h* catch it...... 1Kin 20:33
may be gotten *h* at the beginning ...... Prov 20:21
Go not forth *h* to strive, lest. .... Prov 25:8
they saw Mary, that she rose up *h*...... Jn 11:31

HASTING

judgment, and *h* righteousness .... Is 16:5
h unto the coming of the day of 2Pet 3:12

HASTY

but he that is *h* of spirit. .... Prov 14:29
every one that is *h* only to want. .... Prov 21:5
thou a man that is *h* in his words .... Prov 29:20
let not thine heart be *h* to utter .... Eccl 5:2
Be not *h* in thy spirit to be .... Eccl 7:9
Be not *h* to go out of his sight .... Eccl 8:3
as the *h* fruit before the summer .... Is 28:4
is the decree so *h* from the king. .... Dan 2:15
h nation, which shall march .... Hab 1:6

HASUPHA (has-u'-fah) A family of exiles.
of Ziha, the children of *H* .... Ezr 2:43

HATACH (ha'-tak) A servant of King
Ahasuerus.
Then called Esther for *H*, one of .... Est 4:5
So *H* went forth to Mordecai unto ...... Est 4:6
H came and told Esther the words ...... Est 4:9
Again Esther spake unto *H* .... Est 4:10

HATCH

owl make her nest, and lay, and *h* ..... Is 34:15
They *h* cockatrice' eggs, and weave ... Is 59:5

HATCHETH

sitteth on eggs, and *h* them not. .... Jer 17:11

HATE

the gate of those which *h* them. .... Gen 24:60
come ye to me, seeing ye *h* me. .... Gen 26:27
Joseph will peradventure *h* us. .... Gen 50:15
generation of them that *h* me. .... Ex 20:5
Thou shalt not *h* thy brother in. .... Lev 19:17
they that *h* you shall reign over .... Lev 26:17
let them that *h* thee flee before. .... Num 10:35
generation of them that *h* me .... Deut 5:9
them that *h* him to their face .... Deut 7:10
them upon all them that *h* thee .... Deut 7:15
But if any man *h* his neighbour .... Deut 19:11
and go in unto her, and *h* her, ... Deut 22:13

And if the latter husband *h* her.......... Deut 24:3
enemies, and on them that *h* thee.......... Deut 30:7
and will reward them that *h* me.......... Deut 32:41
him, and of them that *h* him.......... Deut 33:11
elders of Gilead, Did not ye *h* me.......... Judg 11:7
him, and said, Thou dost but *h* me.......... Judg 14:16
I might destroy them that *h* me ... 2Sa 22:41
but I *h* him.......... 1Kin 22:8
but I *h* him.......... 2Chr 18:7
and love them that *h* the LORD.......... 2Chr 19:2
They that *h* thee shall be clothed.......... Job 8:22
which I suffer of them that *h* me.......... Ps 9:13
I might destroy them that *h* me.......... Ps 18:40
shall find out those that *h* thee.......... Ps 21:8
they *h* me with cruel hatred.......... Ps 25:19
that that *h* the righteous shall.......... Ps 34:21
the eye that *h* me without a cause.......... Ps 35:19
that that *h* me wrongfully are.......... Ps 38:19
All that *h* me whisper together.......... Ps 41:7
they which *h* us spoil for.......... Ps 44:10
upon me, and in wrath they *h* me.......... Ps 55:3
let them also that *h* him flee.......... Ps 68:1
They that *h* me without a cause.......... Ps 69:4
be delivered from them that *h* me.......... Ps 69:14
they that *h* thee have lifted up.......... Ps 83:2
that they which *h* me may see it.......... Ps 86:17
face, and plague them that *h* him.......... Ps 89:23
Ye that love the LORD, *h* evil.......... Ps 97:10
I *h* the work of them that turn.......... Ps 101:3
their heart to *h* his people.......... Ps 105:25
see my desire upon them that *h* me..... Ps 118:7
therefore I *h* every false way.......... Ps 119:104
I *h* vain thoughts.......... Ps 119:113
and I *h* every false way.......... Ps 119:128
I *h* and abhor lying.......... Ps 119:163
and turned back that *h* Zion.......... Ps 129:5
I *h* them, O LORD, that *h* thee.......... Ps 139:21
I *h* them with perfect hatred.......... Ps 139:22
scorning, and fools *h* knowledge.......... Prov 1:22
These six things doth the LORD *h*.......... Prov 6:16
The fear of the LORD is to *h* evil.......... Prov 8:13
way, and the froward mouth, do I *h* .. Prov 8:13
all they that *h* me love death.......... Prov 8:36
a scorner, lest he *h* thee.......... Prov 9:8
the brethren of the poor do *h* him.......... Prov 19:7
he be weary of thee, and so *h* thee..... Prov 25:17
The bloodthirsty *h* the upright.......... Prov 29:10
A time to love, and a time to *h*.......... Eccl 3:8
I *h* robbery for burnt offering.......... Is 61:8
this abominable thing that I *h*.......... Jer 44:4
unto the will of them that *h* thee..... Eze 16:27
the dream be to them that *h* thee..... Dan 4:19
They *h* him that rebuketh in the.......... Amos 5:10
H the evil, and love the good, and ..... Amos 5:15
I *h*, I despise your feast days,.......... Amos 5:21
of Jacob, and *h* his palaces.......... Amos 6:8
Who *h* the good, and love the evil.......... Mic 3:2
for all these are things that I *h*.......... Zec 8:17
thy neighbour, and *h* thine enemy .. Mt 5:43
you, do good to them that *h* you.......... Mt 5:44
for either he will *h* the one.......... Mt 6:24
another, and shall *h* one another.......... Mt 24:10
and from the hand of all that *h* us ..... Lk 1:71
are ye, when men shall *h* you.......... Lk 6:22
do good to them which *h* you.......... Lk 6:27
h not his father, and mother, and.......... Lk 14:26
for either he will *h* the one.......... Lk 16:13
The world cannot *h* you.......... Jn 7:7
If the world *h* you, ye know that.......... Jn 15:18
but what I *h*, that do I.......... Rom 7:15
my brethren, if the world *h* you.......... 1Jn 3:13
the Nicolaitans, which I also *h*.......... Rev 2:6
the Nicolaitans, which thing I *h*.......... Rev 2:15
beast, these shall *h* the whore.......... Rev 17:16

HATED

Esau in Jacob because of the.......... Gen 27:41
when the LORD saw that Leah was *h*.... Gen 29:31
the LORD hath heard that I was *h*.......... Gen 29:33
than all his brethren, they *h*.......... Gen 37:4
and they *h* him yet the more.......... Gen 37:5
they *h* him yet the more for his.......... Gen 37:8
him, and shot at him, and *h* him.......... Gen 49:23
and said, Because the LORD *h* us.......... Deut 1:27
and *h* him not in times past.......... Deut 4:42
them, and because he *h* them.......... Deut 9:28
whom he *h* not in time past.......... Deut 19:4
inasmuch as he *h* him not in time..... Deut 19:6
wives, one beloved, and another *h*..... Deut 21:15
both the beloved and the *h*.......... Deut 21:15
firstborn son be hers that was *h*.......... Deut 21:15
firstborn before the son of the *h*..... Deut 21:16
son of the *h* for the firstborn.......... Deut 21:17
and *h* him not beforetime.......... Josh 20:5
that thou hadst utterly *h* her.......... Judg 15:2
that are *h* of David's soul, he.......... 2Sa 5:8
Then Amnon *h* her exceedingly.......... 2Sa 13:15
h her was greater than the love.......... 2Sa 13:15
for absalom *h* Amnon, because he..... 2Sa 13:22
enemy, and from them that *h* me.......... 2Sa 22:18
had rule over them that *h* them.......... Est 9:1
they would unto those that *h* them..... Est 9:5
the destruction of him that *h* me.......... Job 31:29
enemy, and from them which *h* me..... Ps 18:17
I have *h* the congregation of.......... Ps 26:5
I have *h* them that regard lying.......... Ps 31:6
hast put them to shame that *h* us..... Ps 44:7
neither was it he that *h* me.......... Ps 55:12
from the hand of him that *h* us.......... Ps 106:10
they that *h* them ruled over them..... Ps 106:41
For that they *h* knowledge.......... Prov 1:29

How have I *h* instruction, and my ..... Prov 5:12
and a man of wicked devices is *h*..... Prov 14:17
The poor is *h* even of his own.......... Prov 14:20
Therefore I *h* life.......... Eccl 2:17
I *h* all my labour which I had.......... Eccl 2:18
thou hast been forsaken and *h*.......... Is 60:15
Your brethren that *h* you, that.......... Is 66:5
therefore have I *h* it.......... Jer 12:8
with all them that thou hast *h*.......... Eze 16:37
sith thou hast not *h* blood.......... Eze 35:6
for there I *h* them.......... Hos 9:15
I *h* Esau, and laid his mountains.......... Mal 1:3
ye shall be *h* of all men for my.......... Mt 10:22
ye shall be *h* of all nations for.......... Mt 24:9
ye shall be *h* of all men for my.......... Mk 13:13
But his citizens *h* him, and sent a .. Lk 19:14
ye shall be *h* of all men for my.......... Lk 21:17
ye know that it *h* me before it.......... Jn 15:18
me before it *h* you.......... Jn 15:18
seen and *h* both me and my Father..... Jn 15:24
They *h* me without a cause.......... Jn 15:25
and the world hath *h* them, because ... Jn 17:14
have I loved, but Esau have I *h*.......... Rom 9:13
no man ever yet *h* his own flesh.......... Eph 5:29
righteousness, and *h* iniquity.......... Heb 1:9

HATEFUL

his iniquity be found to be *h*.......... Ps 36:2
living in malice and envy, *h*.......... Titus 3:3
a cage of every unclean and *h* bird... Rev 18:2

HATEFULLY

And they shall deal with thee *h*.......... Eze 23:29

HATERS

The *h* of the LORD should have.......... Ps 81:15
h of God, despiteful, proud,.......... Rom 1:30

HATEST

thine enemies, and *h* thy friends..... 2Sa 19:6
thou *h* all workers of iniquity.......... Ps 5:5
righteousness, and *h* wickedness.......... Ps 45:7
Seeing thou *h* instruction.......... Ps 50:17
into the hand of them whom thou *h*.. Eze 23:28
that thou *h* the deeds of the.......... Rev 2:6

HATETH

h thee lying under his burden.......... Ex 23:5
not be slack to him that *h* him.......... Deut 7:10
to the LORD, which he *h*, have.......... Deut 12:31
which the LORD thy God *h*.......... Deut 16:22
this man to wife, and he *h* her.......... Deut 22:16
teareth me in his wrath, who *h* me..... Job 16:9
Shall even he that *h* right govern... Job 34:17
that loveth violence his soul *h*.......... Ps 11:5
long dwelt with him that *h* peace..... Ps 120:6
he that *h* suretiship is sure.......... Prov 11:15
but he that *h* reproof is brutish.......... Prov 12:1
A righteous man *h* lying.......... Prov 13:5
he that *h* his son.......... Prov 13:24
he that *h* reproof shall die.......... Prov 15:10
but he that *h* gifts shall live.......... Prov 15:27
He that *h* dissembleth with his.......... Prov 26:24
A lying tongue *h* those that are.......... Prov 26:28
but he that *h* covetousness shall..... Prov 28:16
with a thief is his own soul.......... Prov 29:24
your appointed feasts my soul *h*.......... Is 1:14
saith that he *h* putting away.......... Mal 2:16
one that doeth evil *h* the light.......... Jn 3:20
but in it is, because I testify of.......... Jn 7:7
he that *h* his life in this world.......... Jn 12:25
world, therefore the world *h* you..... Jn 15:19
he that *h* me my Father.......... Jn 15:23
his brother, is in darkness.......... Jn 2:9
But he that *h* his brother is in.......... 1Jn 2:11
Whosoever *h* his brother is a.......... 1Jn 3:15
h his brother, he is a liar.......... 1Jn 4:20

HATH See PREFACE.

HATHACH See HATACH.

HATHATH (ha'-thath) Son of Othniel.

sons of Othniel;.......... 1Chr 4:13

HATING

God, men of truth, *h* covetousness..... Ex 18:21
envy, hateful, and *h* one another.......... Titus 3:3
h even the garment spotted by the..... Jude 23

HATIPHA (hat'-if-ah) A family of exiles.

of Neziah, the children of H.......... Ezr 2:54
of Neziah, the children of H.......... Neh 7:56

HATITA (hat'-it-ah) A family of exiles.

of Akkub, the children of H.......... Ezr 2:42
of Akkub, the children of H.......... Neh 7:45

HATRED

But if he thrust him of *h*.......... Num 35:20
so that the *h* wherewith he hated..... 2Sa 13:15
and they hate me with cruel *h*.......... Ps 25:19
me about also with words of *h*.......... Ps 109:3
evil for good, and *h* for my love.......... Ps 109:5
I hate them with perfect *h*.......... Ps 139:22
H stirreth up strifes.......... Prov 10:12
He that hideth *h* with lying lips,..... Prov 10:18
is covered, whose *h* is covered.......... Prov 26:26
Whose *h* is covered by deceit, his..... Prov 26:26
or *h* by all that is before them.......... Eccl 9:1
Also their love, and their *h*.......... Eccl 9:6
to destroy it for the old *h*.......... Eze 25:15
thou hast had a perpetual *h*.......... Eze 35:5
used out of thy *h* against them.......... Eze 35:11
of thine iniquity, and the great *h*.......... Hos 9:7
h in the house of his God.......... Hos 9:8

Idolatry, witchcraft, *h*, variance.......... Gal 5:20

HATS

coats, their hosen, and their *h*.......... Dan 3:21

HATTIL (hat'-til) A family of exiles.

of Shephatiah, the children of H.......... Ezr 2:57
of Shephatiah, the children of H.......... Neh 7:59

HATTUSH (hat'-tush)

1. A son of Shemaiah.

H, and Igeal, and Bariah, and.......... 1Chr 3:22
the sons of David; H.......... Ezr 8:2

3. A priest.

Amariah, Malluch, H.......... Neh 12:2

4. A rebuilder of Jerusalem's wall.

repaired H the son of Hashabniah...... Neh 3:10

5. Renewed the covenant.

H, Shebaniah, Malluch,.......... Neh 10:4

HAUGHTILY

neither shall ye go *h*.......... Mic 2:3

HAUGHTINESS

the *h* of men shall be bowed down,..... Is 2:11
the *h* of men shall be made low.......... Is 2:17
lay low the *h* of the terrible.......... Is 13:11
even of his *h*, and his pride, and..... Is 16:6
his pride, and the *h* of his heart...... Jer 48:29

HAUGHTY

but thine eyes are upon the *h*.......... 2Sa 22:28
Lord, my heart is not *h*, nor mine..... Ps 131:1
an *h* spirit before a fall.......... Prov 16:18
destruction the heart of man is *h*..... Prov 18:12
h scorner is his name, who.......... Prov 21:24
the daughters of Zion are *h*.......... Is 3:16
down, and the *h* shall be humbled..... Is 10:33
the *h* people of the earth do.......... Is 24:4
And they were *h*, and committed.......... Eze 16:50
thou shalt no more be *h* because..... Zeph 3:11

HAUNT

and see his place where his *h*.......... 1Sa 23:22
himself and his men were wont to *h*... 1Sa 30:31
terror to be on all that *h* it.......... Eze 26:17

HAURAN (hau'-ran) A province south of Damascus.

which is by the coast of H.......... Eze 47:16
east side ye shall measure from H...... Eze 47:18

HAVE See PREFACE.

HAVEN

shall dwell at the *h* of the sea.......... Gen 49:13
and he shall be for an *h* of ships..... Gen 49:13
them unto their desired *h*.......... Ps 107:30
because the *h* was not commodious .. Acts 27:12
which is an *h* of Crete, and lieth..... Acts 27:12

HAVENS

place which is called The fair *h*.......... Acts 27:8

HAVILAH (hav'-il-ah)

1. A son of Cush.

Seba, and H, and Sabtah,.......... Gen 10:7
Seba, and H, and Sabta, and Raamah,... 1Chr 1:9

2. A son of Joktan.

And Ophir, and H, and Jobab.......... Gen 10:29
And Ophir, and H, and Jobab.......... 1Chr 1:23

3. A land west of Ural.

compasseth the whole land of H.......... Gen 2:11

4. A district east of Amalek.

And they dwelt from H unto Shur...... Gen 25:18
from H until thou comest to Shur...... 1Sa 15:7

HAVING

h Beth-el on the west, and Hai on..... Gen 12:8
h his uncleanness upon him, even..... Lev 7:20
lie with a woman *h* her sickness.......... Lev 20:18
h his uncleanness upon him, that..... Lev 22:3
or *h* a wen, or scurvy, or scabbed..... Lev 22:22
a trance, but *h* his eyes open.......... Num 24:4
a trance, but *h* his eyes open.......... Num 24:16
h the two tables in mine hand.......... Deut 10:3
their thumbs and their great.......... Judg 1:7
h his servant with him, and a.......... Judg 19:3
ye stay for them from *h* husbands..... Ruth 1:13
h his spear in his hand, and all..... 1Sa 22:6
h three thousand chosen men of.......... 1Sa 26:2
h put on their robes, in a void.......... 1Kin 22:10
h for their captains Pelatiah, and..... 1Chr 4:42
h a drawn sword in his hand.......... 1Chr 21:16
h wards one against another, to..... 2Chr 9:18
h cymbals and psalteries and harps,... 2Chr 5:12
h Judah and Benjamin on his side..... 2Chr 11:12
every man *h* his weapon in his.......... 2Chr 23:10
h rent my garment and my mantle, I ... Ezr 9:5
h knowledge, and *h* understanding... Neh 10:28
h the oversight of the chamber of..... Neh 13:4
mourning, and *h* his head covered..... Est 6:12
h sorrow in my heart daily.......... Ps 13:2
Which *h* no guide, overseer, or.......... Prov 6:7
h separated himself, seeketh and..... Prov 18:1
h a live coal in his hand, which..... Is 6:6
threshing instrument *h* teeth.......... Is 41:15
h their beards shaven, and their..... Jer 41:5
h cut themselves, with offerings..... Jer 41:5
h neither bars nor gates.......... Eze 38:11
at the side of the east gate *h*.......... Eze 40:44
h charge at the gates of the.......... Eze 44:11
The ram which thou sawest *h* two..... Dan 8:20
of Saphir, *h* thy shame naked.......... Mic 1:11
he is just, and *h* salvation.......... Zec 9:9
he taught them as one *h* authority..... Mt 7:29

authority, h soldiers under me............. Mt 8:9
abroad, as sheep h no shepherd........... Mt 9:36
h with them those that were lame,...... Mt 15:30
rather than h two hands or two........... Mt 18:8
rather than h two eyes to be cast........ Mt 18:9
in hither not h a wedding garment...... Mt 22:12
h no children, his brother shall.......... Mt 22:24
h no issue, left his wife unto............. Mt 22:25
woman h an alabaster box of very...... Mt 26:7
were as sheep not h a shepherd.......... Mk 6:34
h nothing to eat, Jesus called........... Mk 8:1
H eyes, see ye not........................ Mk 8:18
and h ears, hear ye not................... Mk 8:18
than h two hands to go into hell,...... Mk 9:43
than h two feet to be cast into.......... Mk 9:45
than h two eyes to be cast into.......... Mk 9:47
a fig tree afar off h leaves.............. Mk 11:13
H yet therefore one son, his............ Mk 12:6
h heard them reasoning together....... Mk 12:28
there came a woman h an alabaster.... Mk 14:3
a linen cloth cast about his............. Mk 14:51
h had perfect understanding of......... Lk 1:3
No man also h drunk old wine........... Lk 5:39
h under me soldiers, and I say.......... Lk 7:8
h heard the word, keep it, and.......... Lk 8:15
a woman h an issue of blood............ Lk 8:43
h put his hand to the plough, and..... Lk 9:62
h no part dark, the whole shall......... Lk 11:36
h an hundred sheep, if he lose......... Lk 15:4
Either what woman h ten pieces of.... Lk 15:8
h a servant plowing or feeding........ Lk 17:7
h received the kingdom, then he....... Lk 19:15
h a wife, and he die without........... Lk 20:28
h examined him before you, have...... Lk 23:14
h said thus, he gave up the ghost..... Lk 23:46
h seen all the things that he did...... Jn 4:45
tongue Bethesda, h five porches....... Jn 5:2
this man letters, h never learned..... Jn 7:15
h loved his own which were in the.... Jn 13:1
the devil h now put into the........... Jn 13:2
He then h received the sop went...... Jn 13:30
h received a band of men and......... Jn 18:3
Simon Peter h a sword drew it........ Jn 18:10
h loosed the pains of death........... Acts 2:24
h received of the Father the.......... Acts 2:33
h favour with all the people.......... Acts 2:47
h raised up his Son Jesus, sent...... Acts 3:26
H land, sold it, and brought the..... Acts 4:37
h made Blastus the king's............ Acts 12:20
h stoned Paul, drew him out of....... Acts 14:19
h received such a charge, thrust.... Acts 16:24
h shorn his head in Cenchrea......... Acts 18:18
Paul h passed through the upper..... Acts 19:1
h caught Gaius and Aristarchus,..... Acts 19:29
h a good report of all the Jews..... Acts 22:12
h understood that he was a Roman... Acts 23:27
h more perfect knowledge of that.... Acts 24:22
h received authority from the....... Acts 26:10
H therefore obtained help of God,... Acts 26:22
fasting, h taken nothing............. Acts 27:33
h not the law, are a law unto....... Rom 2:14
neither h done any good or evil,.... Rom 9:11
H then gifts differing according.... Rom 12:6
But now h no more place in these.... Rom 15:23
h a great desire these many years... Rom 15:23
h a matter against another, go to... 1Cor 6:1
h no necessity, but hath power...... 1Cor 7:37
h his head covered, dishonoureth.... 1Cor 11:4
h given more abundant honour to.... 1Cor 12:24
h confidence in you all, that my.... 2Cor 2:3
We h the same spirit of faith,...... 2Cor 4:13
as h nothing, and yet possessing.... 2Cor 6:10
H therefore these promises dearly... 2Cor 7:1
always h all sufficiency in all..... 2Cor 9:8
h in a readiness to revenge all..... 2Cor 10:6
but h hope, when your faith is...... 2Cor 10:15
h begun in the Spirit, are ye now... Gal 3:3
H predestinated us unto the......... Eph 1:5
H made known unto us the mystery... Eph 1:9
h no hope, and without God in the.. Eph 2:12
H abolished in his flesh the........ Eph 2:15
h slain the enmity thereby.......... Eph 2:16
The understanding darkened,......... Eph 4:18
not h spot, or wrinkle, or any...... Eph 5:27
evil day, and h done all, to stand.. Eph 6:13
h your loins girt about with........ Eph 6:14
truth, and h on the breastplate of.. Eph 6:14
h a desire to depart, and to be..... Phil 1:23
h this confidence, I know that I.... Phil 1:25
H the same conflict which ye saw.... Phil 1:30
the same love, being of one......... Phil 2:2
not h mine own righteousness,....... Phil 3:9
h received of Epaphroditus the...... Phil 4:18
h made peace through the blood of... Col 1:20
h forgiven you all trespasses....... Col 2:13
h spoiled principalities and........ Col 2:15
bands h nourishment ministered,.... Col 2:19
h received the word in much......... 1Th 1:6
From which some h swerved have...... 1Ti 1:6
which some h put away concerning.... 1Ti 1:19
h his children in subjection with... 1Ti 3:4
h their conscience seared with a.... 1Ti 4:2
h promise of the life that now is... 1Ti 4:8
h been the wife of one man,......... 1Ti 5:9
H damnation, because they have...... 1Ti 5:12
h food and raiment let us be........ 1Ti 6:8
h this seal, The Lord knoweth....... 2Ti 2:19
H a form of godliness, but.......... 2Ti 3:5
teachers, h itching ears,........... 2Ti 4:3
h loved this present world, and is.. 2Ti 4:10

h faithful children not accused...... Titus 1:6
h no evil thing to say of you........ Titus 2:8
h confidence in thy obedience I...... Philem 21
h neither beginning of days, nor.... Heb 7:3
h obtained eternal redemption for... Heb 9:12
For the law h a shadow of good...... Heb 10:1
H therefore, brethren, boldness..... Heb 10:19
h an high priest over the house..... Heb 10:21
h our hearts sprinkled from an...... Heb 10:22
not h received the promises......... Heb 11:13
but h seen them afar off, and were.. Heb 11:13
h obtained a good report through.... Heb 11:39
God h provided some better thing.... Heb 11:40
Whom h not seen, ye love............ 1Pet 1:8
H your conversation honest among.... 1Pet 2:12
h compassion one of another, love... 1Pet 3:8
H a good conscience................. 1Pet 3:16
h escaped the corruption that is.... 2Pet 1:4
H eyes full of adultery, and that... 2Pet 2:14
H many things to write unto you,.... 2Jn 12
h saved the people out of the....... Jude 5
h men's persons in admiration....... Jude 16
sensual, h not the Spirit........... Jude 19
h seven horns and seven eyes,....... Rev 5:6
h every one of them harps, and...... Rev 5:8
h the seal of the living God........ Rev 7:2
at the altar, h a golden censer..... Rev 8:3
h breastplates of fire, and of...... Rev 9:9
h seven heads and ten horns, and.... Rev 12:3
h great wrath, because he knoweth... Rev 12:12
h seven heads and ten horns, and.... Rev 13:1
h his Father's name written in...... Rev 14:1
h the everlasting gospel to......... Rev 14:6
h on his head a golden crown, and... Rev 14:14
heaven, he also h a sharp sickle.... Rev 14:17
seven angels h the seven last....... Rev 15:1
sea of glass, h the harps of God.... Rev 15:2
h the seven plagues, clothed in..... Rev 15:6
h their breasts girded with......... Rev 15:6
h seven heads and ten horns......... Rev 17:3
a golden cup in her hand full h..... Rev 17:4
down from heaven, h great power..... Rev 18:1
h the key of the bottomless pit..... Rev 20:1
H the glory of God.................. Rev 21:11

HAVOCK
he made h of the church, entering.... Acts 8:3

HAVOTH-JAIR (ha''-voth-ja'-ir) See BASHAN-
HAVOTH. Villages in Gilead.
towns thereof, and called them H..... Num 32:41
which are called H unto this day..... Judg 10:4

HAWK
And the owl, and the night h......... Lev 11:16
cuckow, and the h after his kind,.... Lev 11:16
And the owl, and the night h......... Deut 14:15
cuckow, and the h after his kind,.... Deut 14:15
Doth the h fly by thy wisdom, and.... Job 39:26

HAY
The h appeareth, and the tender...... Prov 27:25
for the h is withered away, the...... Is 15:6
silver, precious stones, wood, h..... 1Cor 3:12

HAZAEL (ha'-za-el) A king of Syria.
anoint H to be king over Syria....... 1Kin 19:15
the sword of H shall Jehu slay....... 1Kin 19:17
And the king said unto H, Take a..... 2Kin 8:8
So H went to meet him, and took a.... 2Kin 8:9
H said, Why weepeth my lord.......... 2Kin 8:12
H said, But what, is thy servant..... 2Kin 8:13
and H reigned in his stead........... 2Kin 8:15
H king of Syria in Ramoth-gilead..... 2Kin 8:28
he fought against H king of Syria.... 2Kin 8:29
because of H king of Syria........... 2Kin 9:14
he fought with H king of Syria....... 2Kin 9:15
H smote them in all the coasts of.... 2Kin 10:32
Then H king of Syria went up, and.... 2Kin 12:17
H set his face to go up to........... 2Kin 12:17
sent it to H king of Syria........... 2Kin 12:18
into the hand of H king of Syria..... 2Kin 13:3
hand of Ben-hadad the son of H....... 2Kin 13:3
But H king of Syria oppressed........ 2Kin 13:22
So H king of Syria died.............. 2Kin 13:24
Ben-hadad the son of H the cities.... 2Kin 13:25
king of Israel to war against H...... 2Chr 22:5
he fought with H king of Syria....... 2Chr 22:6
send a fire into the house of H...... Amos 1:4

HAZAIAH (ha-za-i'-ah) Son of Adaiah.
the son of Colhozeh, the son of...... Neh 11:5

HAZAR-ADDAR (ha''-zar-ad'-dar) See ADDAR.
A place in southern Palestine.
and shall go on to H, and pass on.... Num 34:4

HAZARDED
Men that have h their lives for...... Acts 15:26

HAZAR-ENAN (ha''-zar-e'-nan) A village in
northeastern Palestine.
goings out of it shall be at H....... Num 34:9
east border from H to Shepham........ Num 34:10
border from the sea shall be H....... Eze 47:17
as one goeth to Hamath, H............ Eze 48:1

HAZAR-GADDAH (ha''-zar-gad'-dah) A town
in Judah.
And H, and Heshmon.................. Josh 15:27

HAZAR-HATTICON (ha''-zar-hat'-ti-con) A
place in Hauran.
H, which is by the coast of......... Eze 47:16

HAZARMAVETH (ha-zar-ma'-veth) A son of
Joktan.
begat Almodad, and Sheleph, and H... Gen 10:26
begat Almodad, and Sheleph, and H... 1Chr 1:20

HAZAR-SHUAL (ha''-zar-shoo'-al) A town in
Judah.
And H, and Beer-sheba, and.......... Josh 15:28
And H, and Balah, and Azem,......... Josh 19:3
at Beer-sheba, and Moladah, and H... 1Chr 4:28
And at H, and at Beer-sheba, and in.. Neh 11:27

HAZAR-SUSAH (ha''-zar-soo'-sah) See
HAZAR-SUSIM. A city in Judah.
Ziklag, and Beth-marcaboth, and H... Josh 19:5

HAZAR-SUSIM (ha''-zar-soo'-sim) See
HAZAR-SUSAH. Same as Hazar-susah.
And at Beth-marcaboth, and H........ 1Chr 4:31

HAZAZON-TAMAR (haz''-a-zon-ta'-mar) See
HAZEZON-TAMAR. A name for En-gedi.
and, behold, they be in H, which.... 2Chr 20:2

HAZEL
rods of green poplar, and of the h... Gen 30:37

HAZELELPONI (haz-el-el-po'-ni) Sister of the
sons of Etam.
and the name of their sister was H.. 1Chr 4:3

HAZER-HATTICON See HAZAR-HATTICON.

HAZERIM (haz'-e-rim) A district near Gaza.
And the Avims which dwelt in H...... Deut 2:23

HAZEROTH (haz'-e-roth) A Hebrew
encampment in the wilderness.
from Kibroth-hattaavah unto H....... Num 11:35
and abode at H...................... Num 11:35
the people removed from H........... Num 12:16
and encamped at H................... Num 33:17
And they departed from H, and....... Num 33:18
Paran, and Tophel, and Laban, and H. Deut 1:1

HAZEZON-TAMAR (haz''-e-zon-ta'-mar) See
EN-GEDI, HAZAZON-TAMAR. Same as Hazazon-
tamar.
the Amorites, that dwelt in H....... Gen 14:7

HAZIEL (ha'-ze-el) A Levite.
Shelomith, and H, and Haran, three.. 1Chr 23:9

HAZO (ha'-zo) A son of Nahor.
And Chesed, and H, and Pildash, and. Gen 22:22

HAZOBEBAH See HAZELELPONI.

HAZOR (ha'-zor) See BAAL-HAZOR, EN-HAZOR,
HEZRON.
1. A fortified city in Naphtali.
when Jabin king of H had heard...... Josh 11:1
that time turned back, and took H.... Josh 11:10
for H beforetime was the head of.... Josh 11:10
and he burnt H with fire............ Josh 11:11
burned none of them, save H only.... Josh 11:13
the king of H, one.................. Josh 12:19
And Adamah, and Ramah, and H........ Josh 19:36
king of Canaan, that reigned in H... Judg 4:2
peace between Jabin the king of H... Judg 4:17
Sisera, captain of the host of H.... 1Sa 12:9
and the wall of Jerusalem, and H.... 1Kin 9:15
H, Ramah, Gittaim,.................. Neh 11:33
2. A city in Judah.
And Kedesh, and H, and Ithnan,...... Josh 15:23
and Janoah, and Kedesh, and H....... 2Kin 15:29
3. Another town in Judah.
And H, Hadattah, and Kerioth, and... Josh 15:25
and Kerioth, and Hezron, which is H. Josh 15:25
4. Where the Benjamites lived after the Exile.
and concerning the kingdoms of H.... Jer 49:28
5. An area in eastern Arabia.
dwell deep, O ye inhabitants of H... Jer 49:30
shall be a dwelling for dragons,.... Jer 49:33

HAZZELELPONI See HAZELELPONI.

HE (hay) See PREFACE. A Hebrew letter.

HEAD
it shall bruise thy h, and thou..... Gen 3:15
And the man bowed down his h........ Gen 24:26
And I bowed down my h, and.......... Gen 24:48
shall Pharaoh lift up thine h....... Gen 40:13
I had three white baskets on my h... Gen 40:16
them out of the basket upon my h.... Gen 40:17
lift up thy h from off thee......... Gen 40:19
he lifted up the h of the chief..... Gen 40:20
bowed himself upon the bed's h...... Gen 47:31
hand, and laid it upon Ephraim's h.. Gen 48:14
his left hand upon Manasseh's h..... Gen 48:14
right hand upon the h of Ephraim.... Gen 48:17
Ephraim's h unto Manasseh's h....... Gen 48:18
put thy right hand upon his h....... Gen 48:18
they shall be on the h of Joseph.... Gen 49:26
on the crown of the h of him that... Gen 49:26
And the people bowed the h.......... Ex 12:27
above the h of it unto one ring..... Ex 26:24
shalt put the mitre upon his h...... Ex 29:6
oil, and pour it upon his h......... Ex 29:7
hands upon the h of the bullock..... Ex 29:10
their hands upon the h of the ram... Ex 29:15
unto his pieces, and unto his h..... Ex 29:17
their hands upon the h of the ram... Ex 29:19
bowed his h toward the earth, and... Ex 34:8
coupled together at the h thereof... Ex 36:29
upon the h of the burnt offering.... Lev 1:4

sons, shall lay the parts, the *h* .... Lev 1:8
it into his pieces, with his *h* .... Lev 1:12
the altar, and wring off his *h* .... Lev 1:15
hand upon the *h* of his offering .... Lev 3:2
hand upon the *h* of his offering .... Lev 3:8
lay his hand upon the *h* of it .... Lev 3:13
lay his hand upon the bullock's *h* .... Lev 4:4
and all his flesh, with his *h* .... Lev 4:11
h of the bullock before the LORD .... Lev 4:15
his hand upon the *h* of the goat .... Lev 4:24
upon the *h* of the sin offering .... Lev 4:29
upon the *h* of the sin offering .... Lev 4:33
and wring off his *h* from his neck .... Lev 5:8
And he put the mitre upon his *h* .... Lev 8:9
the anointing oil upon Aaron's *h* .... Lev 8:12
the *h* of the bullock for the sin .... Lev 8:14
their hands upon the *h* of the ram .... Lev 8:18
and Moses burnt the *h*, and the .... Lev 8:20
their hands upon the *h* of the ram .... Lev 8:22
with the pieces thereof, and the *h* .... Lev 9:13
from his *h* even to his foot .... Lev 13:12
a plague upon the *h* or the beard .... Lev 13:29
a leprosy upon the *h* or beard .... Lev 13:30
whose hair is fallen off his *h* .... Lev 13:40
the part of his *h* toward his face .... Lev 13:41
And if there be in the bald *h* .... Lev 13:42
a leprosy sprung up in his bald *h* .... Lev 13:42
be white reddish in his bald *h* .... Lev 13:43
his plague is in his *h* .... Lev 13:44
his *h* bare, and he shall put a .... Lev 13:45
shave all his hair off his *h* .... Lev 14:9
hand he shall pour upon the *h* of .... Lev 14:18
hand he shall put upon the *h* of .... Lev 14:29
hands upon the *h* of the live goat .... Lev 16:21
them upon the *h* of the goat .... Lev 16:21
shalt rise up before the hoary *h* .... Lev 19:32
not make baldness upon their *h* .... Lev 21:5
upon whose *h* the anointing oil .... Lev 21:10
garments, shall not uncover his *h* .... Lev 21:10
him lay their hands upon his *h* .... Lev 24:14
every one *h* of the house of his .... Num 1:4
LORD, and uncover the woman's *h* .... Num 5:18
shall no razor come upon his *h* .... Num 6:5
locks of the hair of his *h* grow .... Num 6:5
of his God is upon his *h* .... Num 6:7
defiled the *h* of his consecration .... Num 6:9
then he shall shave his *h* in the .... Num 6:9
shall hallow his *h* that same day .... Num 6:11
the Nazarite shall shave the *h* of .... Num 6:18
hair of the *h* of his separation .... Num 6:18
for one rod shall be for the *h* of .... Num 17:3
and he bowed down his *h*, and fell .... Num 22:31
he was *h* over a people, and of a .... Num 25:15
the *h* slippeth from the helve, and .... Deut 19:5
and she shall shave her *h*, and pare ...... Deut 21:12
And the LORD shall make thee the *h* ...... Deut 28:13
that is over thy *h* shall be brass .... Deut 28:23
of thy foot unto the top of thy *h* .... Deut 28:35
he shall be the *h*, and thou shalt .... Deut 28:44
come upon the *h* of Joseph .... Deut 33:16
upon the top of the *h* of him that .... Deut 33:20
the arm with the crown of the *h* .... Deut 33:20
his blood shall be upon his *h* .... Josh 2:19
his blood shall be on our *h* .... Josh 2:19
was the *h* of all those kingdoms .... Josh 11:10
each one was an *h* of the house of .... Josh 22:14
smote Sisera, she smote off his *h* .... Judg 5:26
of a millstone upon Abimelech's *h* .... Judg 9:53
he shall be *h* over all the .... Judg 10:18
be our *h* over all the inhabitants .... Judg 11:8
them before me, shall I be your *h* .... Judg 11:9
Gilead, and the people made him *h* ...... Judg 11:11
and no razor shall come on his *h* .... Judg 13:5
seven locks of my *h* with the web .... Judg 16:13
hath not come a razor upon mine *h* ...... Judg 16:17
off the seven locks of his *h* .... Judg 16:19
Howbeit the hair of his *h* began .... Judg 16:22
shall no razor come upon his *h* 1Sa 1:11
rent, and with earth upon his *h* 1Sa 4:12
the *h* of Dagon and both the palms 1Sa 5:4
and oil, and poured it upon his *h* 1Sa 10:1
hair of his *h* fall to the ground 1Sa 14:45
wast thou not made the *h* of the 1Sa 15:17
had an helmet of brass upon his *h* 1Sa 17:5
his spear's *h* weighed six hundred.......... 1Sa 17:7
put an helmet of brass upon his *h* 1Sa 17:38
thee, and take thine *h* from thee 1Sa 17:46
him, and cut off his *h* therewith 1Sa 17:51
And David took the *h* of the 1Sa 17:54
him before Saul with the *h* of the 1Sa 17:57
of Nabal upon his own *h* 1Sa 25:39
thee keeper of mine *h* for ever 1Sa 28:2
And they cut off his *h*, and 2Sa 4:7
clothes rent, and earth upon his *h* 2Sa 1:2
the crown that was upon his *h* 2Sa 1:10
unto him, Thy blood be upon thy *h* 2Sa 1:16
every one his fellow by the *h* 2Sa 2:16
and said, Am I a dog's *h*, which 2Sa 3:8
Let it rest on the *h* of Joab 2Sa 3:29
and beheaded him, and took his *h* 2Sa 4:7
they brought the *h* of Ish-bosheth 2Sa 4:8
Behold the *h* of Ish-bosheth 2Sa 4:8
they took the *h* of Ish-bosheth 2Sa 4:12
their king's crown from off his *h* 2Sa 12:30
and it was set on David's *h* 2Sa 12:30
And Tamar put ashes on her *h* 2Sa 13:19
on her, and laid her hand on her *h* 2Sa 13:19
his *h* there was no blemish in him 2Sa 14:25
And when he polled his *h*, (for it 2Sa 14:26
he weighed the hair of his *h* 2Sa 14:26

he went up, and had his *h* covered 2Sa 15:30
with him covered every man his *h* 2Sa 15:30
coat rent, and earth upon his *h* 2Sa 15:32
I pray thee, and take off his *h* 2Sa 16:9
his *h* caught hold of the oak, and 2Sa 18:9
his *h* shall be thrown to thee 2Sa 20:21
they cut off the *h* of Sheba the 2Sa 20:22
kept me to be *h* of the heathen 2Sa 22:44
let not his hoar *h* go down to the 1Kin 2:6
but his hoar *h* bring thou down to 1Kin 2:9
return his blood upon his own *h* 1Kin 2:32
return upon the *h* of Joab 1Kin 2:33
upon the *h* of his seed for ever 1Kin 2:33
blood shall be upon thine own *h* 1Kin 2:37
thy wickedness upon thine own *h* 1Kin 2:44
to bring his way upon his *h* 1Kin 8:32
and a cruse of water at his *h* 1Kin 19:6
away thy master from thy *h* to day 2Kin 2:3
away thy master from thy *h* to day 2Kin 2:5
said unto him, Go up, thou bald *h* 2Kin 2:23
go up, thou bald *h* 2Kin 2:23
unto his father, My *h*, my *h* 2Kin 4:19
the ax *h* fell into the water 2Kin 6:5
until an ass's *h* was sold for 2Kin 6:25
if the *h* of Elisha the son of 2Kin 6:31
hath sent to take away mine *h* 2Kin 6:32
box of oil, and pour it on his *h* 2Kin 9:3
and he poured the oil on his *h* 2Kin 9:6
painted her face, and tired her *h* 2Kin 9:30
hath shaken her *h* at thee 2Kin 19:21
began to reign did lift up the *h* 2Kin 25:27
had stripped him, they took his *h* 1Chr 10:9
fastened his *h* in the temple of 1Chr 10:10
of their king from off his *h* 1Chr 20:2
and it was set upon David's *h* 1Chr 20:2
thou art exalted as *h* above all 1Chr 29:11
his way upon his own *h* 2Chr 6:23
Jehoshaphat bowed his *h* with his 2Chr 20:18
and plucked off the hair of my *h* .... Ezr 9:3
are increased over our *h*, and our .... Ezr 9:6
their reproach upon their own *h* .... Neh 4:4
he set the royal crown upon her *h* .... Est 2:17
royal which is set upon his *h* .... Est 6:8
mourning, and having his *h* covered ...... Est 6:12
should return upon his own *h* .... Est 9:25
rent his mantle, and shaved his *h* .... Job 1:20
yet will I not lift up my *h* .... Job 10:15
you, and shake mine *h* at you .... Job 16:4
and taken the crown from my *h* .... Job 19:9
his *h* reach unto the clouds .... Job 20:6
When his candle shined upon my *h* ...... Job 29:3
or his *h* with fish spears .... Job 41:7
glory, and the lifter up of mine *h* .... Ps 3:3
shall return upon his own *h* .... Ps 7:16
hast made me the *h* of the heathen ...... Ps 18:43
a crown of pure gold on his *h* .... Ps 21:3
out the lip, they shake the *h* .... Ps 22:7
thou anointest my *h* with oil .... Ps 23:5
now shall mine *h* be lifted up .... Ps 27:6
iniquities are gone over mine *h* .... Ps 38:4
are more than the hairs of mine *h* .... Ps 40:12
shaking of the *h* among the people ...... Ps 44:14
also is the strength of mine *h* .... Ps 60:7
shall wound the *h* of his enemies .... Ps 68:21
are more than the hairs of mine *h* .... Ps 69:4
hate them have lifted up the *h* .... Ps 83:2
also is the strength of mine *h* .... Ps 108:8
therefore shall he lift up the *h* .... Ps 110:7
become the *h* stone of the corner .... Ps 118:22
the precious ointment upon the *h* .... Ps 133:2
covered my *h* in the day of battle .... Ps 140:7
As for the *h* of those that .... Ps 140:9
oil, which shall not break my *h* .... Ps 141:5
an ornament of grace unto thy *h* .... Prov 1:9
to thine *h* an ornament of grace .... Prov 4:9
are upon the *h* of the just .... Prov 10:6
upon the *h* of him that selleth it .... Prov 11:26
The hoary *h* is a crown of glory .... Prov 16:31
beauty of old men is the grey *h* .... Prov 20:29
heap coals of fire upon his *h* .... Prov 25:22
The wise man's eyes are in his *h* .... Eccl 2:14
let thy *h* lack no ointment .... Eccl 9:8
His left hand is under my *h* .... Song 2:6
for my *h* is filled with dew, and .... Song 5:2
His *h* is as the most fine gold .... Song 5:11
Thine *h* upon thee is like Carmel .... Song 7:5
the hair of thine *h* like purple .... Song 7:5
left hand should be under my *h* .... Song 8:3
the whole *h* is sick, and the whole ...... Is 1:5
the *h* there is no soundness in it .... Is 1:6
of the *h* of the daughters of Zion .... Is 3:17
For the *h* of Syria is Damascus, ... Is 7:8
the *h* of Damascus is Rezin .... Is 7:8
the *h* of Ephraim is Samaria, and .... Is 7:9
the *h* of Samaria is Remaliah's .... Is 7:9
by the king of Assyria, the *h* .... Is 7:20
LORD will cut off from Israel *h* .... Is 9:14
and honourable, he is the *h* .... Is 9:15
for Egypt, which the *h* or tail .... Is 19:15
which are on the *h* of the fat .... Is 28:1
which is on the *h* of the fat .... Is 28:4
hath shaken her *h* at thee .... Is 37:22
joy shall be upon their *h* .... Is 51:11
they lie at the *h* of all the .... Is 51:20
it to bow down his *h* as a bulrush .... Is 58:5
an helmet of salvation upon his *h* .... Is 59:17
have broken the crown of thy *h* .... Jer 2:16
him, and thine hands upon thine *h* ...... Jer 2:37
Oh that my *h* were waters, and mine .... Jer 9:1
shall be astonished, and wag his *h* ...... Jer 18:16

unto me, the *h* of Lebanon .... Jer 22:6
upon the *h* of the wicked .... Jer 23:19
pain upon the *h* of the wicked .... Jer 30:23
For every *h* shall be bald, and .... Jer 48:37
the crown of the *h* of the .... Jer 48:45
the *h* of Jehoiachin king of Judah ...... Jer 52:31
wag their *h* at the daughter of .... Lam 2:15
Waters flowed over mine *h* .... Lam 3:54
The crown is fallen from our *h* .... Lam 5:16
and cause it to pass upon thine *h* .... Eze 5:1
and took me by a lock of mine *h* .... Eze 8:3
recompense their way upon their *h* ...... Eze 9:10
firmament that was above the *h* of ...... Eze 10:1
the *h* looked they followed it .... Eze 10:11
make kerchiefs upon the *h* of .... Eze 13:18
and a beautiful crown upon thine *h* ...... Eze 16:12
high place at every *h* of the way .... Eze 16:25
place in the *h* of every way .... Eze 16:31
recompense thy way upon thine *h* .... Eze 16:43
will I recompense upon his own *h* .... Eze 17:19
choose it at the *h* of the way to .... Eze 21:19
at the *h* of the two ways, to use .... Eze 21:21
the tire of thine *h* upon thee .... Eze 24:17
every *h* was made bald, and every .... Eze 29:18
his blood shall be upon his own *h* .... Eze 33:4
was a door in the *h* of the way .... Eze 42:12
make me endanger my *h* to the king .... Dan 1:10
the visions of thy *h* upon thy bed .... Dan 2:28
This image's *h* was of fine gold, ... Dan 2:32
Thou art this *h* of gold .... Dan 2:38
nor was an hair of their *h* singed .... Dan 3:27
the visions of my *h* troubled me .... Dan 4:5
the visions of mine *h* in my bed .... Dan 4:10
the visions of my *h* upon my bed .... Dan 4:13
and visions of his *h* upon his bed .... Dan 7:1
the hair of his *h* like the pure .... Dan 7:9
the visions of my *h* troubled me .... Dan 7:15
the ten horns that were in his *h* .... Dan 7:20
and appoint themselves one *h* .... Hos 1:11
your recompence upon your own *h* .... Joel 3:4
your recompence upon your own *h* .... Joel 3:7
of the earth on the *h* of the poor .... Amos 2:7
loins, and baldness upon every *h* .... Amos 8:10
and cut them in the *h*, all of them ...... Amos 9:1
shall return upon thine own *h* .... Obad 15
the weeds were wrapped about my *h* .... Jonah 2:5
it might be a shadow over his *h* .... Jonah 4:6
the sun beat upon the *h* of Jonah .... Jonah 4:8
and the LORD on the *h* of them .... Mic 2:13
thou woundedst the *h* out of the .... Hab 3:13
his staves the *h* of his villages .... Hab 3:14
so that no man did lift up his *h* .... Zec 1:21
them set a fair mitre upon his *h* .... Zec 3:5
they set a fair mitre upon his *h* .... Zec 3:5
set them upon the *h* of Joshua the ...... Zec 6:11
Neither shalt thou swear by thy *h* .... Mt 5:36
when thou fastest, anoint thine *h* .... Mt 6:17
man hath not where to lay his *h* .... Mt 8:20
hairs of your *h* are all numbered .... Mt 10:30
John Baptist's *h* in a charger .... Mt 14:8
his *h* was brought in a charger, ... Mt 14:11
is become the *h* of the corner .... Mt 21:42
ointment, and poured it on his *h* .... Mt 26:7
of thorns, they put it upon his *h* .... Mt 27:29
the reed, and smote him on the *h* .... Mt 27:30
set up over his *h* his accusation .... Mt 27:37
The *h* of John the Baptist .... Mk 6:24
charger the *h* of John the Baptist .... Mk 6:25
and commanded his *h* to be brought .... Mk 6:27
brought his *h* in a charger, and .... Mk 6:28
stones, and wounded him in the *h* .... Mk 12:4
is become the *h* of the corner .... Mk 12:10
the box, and poured it on his *h* .... Mk 14:3
of thorns, and put it about his *h* .... Mk 15:17
smote him on the *h* with a reed .... Mk 15:19
wipe them with the hairs of her *h* .... Lk 7:38
them with the hairs of her *h* .... Lk 7:44
My *h* with oil thou didst not .... Lk 7:46
man hath not where to lay his *h* .... Lk 9:58
hairs of your *h* are all numbered .... Lk 12:7
is become the *h* of the corner .... Lk 20:17
not an hair of your *h* perish .... Lk 21:18
only, but also my hands and my *h* .... Jn 13:9
of thorns, and put it on his *h* .... Jn 19:2
and he bowed his *h*, and gave up the .... Jn 19:30
the napkin, that was about his *h* .... Jn 20:7
white sitting, the one at the *h* .... Jn 20:12
is become the *h* of the corner .... Acts 4:11
having shorn his *h* in Cenchrea .... Acts 18:18
fall from the *h* of any of you .... Acts 27:34
shalt heap coals of fire on his *h* .... Rom 12:20
that the *h* of every man is Christ 1Cor 11:3
the *h* of the woman is the man 1Cor 11:3
and the *h* of Christ is God 1Cor 11:3
prophesying, having his *h* covered 1Cor 11:4
uncovered dishonoureth her *h* 1Cor 11:5
indeed ought not to cover his *h* 1Cor 11:7
on her *h* because of the angels 1Cor 11:10
nor again the *h* to the feet. 1Cor 12:21
gave him to be the *h* over all .... Eph 1:22
him in all things, which is the *h* .... Eph 4:15
the husband is the *h* of the wife .... Eph 5:23
as Christ is the *h* of the church .... Eph 5:23
he is the *h* of the body, the .... Col 1:18
in him, which is the *h* of all .... Col 2:10
And not holding the *H*, from which .... Col 2:19
same is made the *h* of the corner 1Pet 2:7
His *h* and his hairs were white .... Rev 1:14
and a rainbow was upon his *h* .... Rev 10:1
upon her *h* a crown of twelve .... Rev 12:1

HEADBANDS

having on his *h* a golden crown, ... Rev 14:14
on his *h* were many crowns .... Rev 19:12

HEADBANDS

ornaments of the legs, and the *h* .... Is 3:20

HEADLONG

of the froward is carried *h* .... Job 5:13
that they might cast him down *h* .... Lk 4:29
and falling *h*, he burst asunder in .... Acts 1:18

HEADS

was parted, and became into four *h* .... Gen 2:10
And they bowed down their *h* .... Gen 43:28
then they bowed their *h* and .... Ex 4:31
These be the *h* of their fathers .... Ex 6:14
these are the *h* of the fathers of .... Ex 6:25
made them *h* over the people, ... Ex 18:25
his sons, Uncover not your *h* .... Lev 10:6
not round the corners of your *h* .... Lev 19:27
fathers, *h* of thousands in Israel .... Num 1:16
h of the house of their fathers, ... Num 7:2
hands upon the *h* of the bullocks .... Num 8:12
which are *h* of the thousands of .... Num 10:4
all those men were *h* of the .... Num 13:3
Take all the *h* of the people, and .... Num 25:4
Moses spake unto the *h* of the .... Num 30:1
and made them *h* over you .... Deut 1:15
even all the *h* of your tribes, and .... Deut 5:23
when the *h* of the people and the .... Deut 33:5
he came with the *h* of the people .... Deut 33:21
Israel, and put dust upon their *h* .... Josh 7:6
the *h* of the fathers of the .... Josh 14:1
the *h* of the fathers of the .... Josh 19:51
Then came near the *h* of the .... Josh 21:1
unto the *h* of the fathers of the .... Josh 21:1
said unto the *h* of the thousands .... Josh 22:21
h of the thousands of Israel .... Josh 22:30
for their elders, and for their *h* .... Josh 23:2
elders of Israel, and for their *h* .... Josh 24:1
Midian, and brought the *h* of Oreb .... Judg 7:25
they lifted up their *h* no more. .... Judg 8:28
did God render upon their *h* .... Judg 9:57
it not be with the *h* of these men 1Sa 29:4
all the *h* of the tribes, the 1Kin 8:1
on our loins, and ropes upon our *h* 1Kin 20:31
loins, and put ropes on their *h* 1Kin 20:32
take ye the *h* of the men your 2Kin 10:6
put their *h* in baskets, and sent 2Kin 10:7
brought the *h* of the king's sons. 2Kin 10:8
these were the *h* of the house of 1Chr 5:24
h of the house of their fathers 1Chr 5:24
h of their father's house, to wit 1Chr 7:2
h of the house of their fathers, ... 1Chr 7:9
h of the house of their fathers, ... 1Chr 7:9
by the *h* of their fathers, mighty 1Chr 7:11
h of their father's house, choice 1Chr 7:40
these are the *h* of the fathers of 1Chr 8:6
were his sons, *h* of the fathers 1Chr 8:10
who were *h* of the fathers of the 1Chr 8:13
These were *h* of the fathers, by 1Chr 8:28
h of the house of their fathers, ... 1Chr 9:13
Saul to the jeopardy of our *h* 1Chr 12:19
the *h* of them were two hundred 1Chr 12:32
fathers, and bowed down their *h* 1Chr 29:20
put them on the *h* of the pillars 2Chr 3:16
all the *h* of the tribes, the 2Chr 5:2
Then certain of the *h* of the 2Chr 28:12
gladness, and they bowed their *h* 2Chr 29:30
and they bowed their *h*, and .... Neh 8:6
dust upon their *h* toward heaven .... Job 2:12
Lift up your *h*, O ye gates .... Ps 24:7
Lift up your *h*, O ye gates .... Ps 24:9
caused men to ride over our *h* .... Ps 66:12
thou brakest the *h* of the dragons .... Ps 74:13
Thou brakest the *h* of leviathan .... Ps 74:14
upon me they shaked their *h*. .... Ps 109:25
he shall wound the *h* over many .... Ps 110:6
on all their *h* shall be baldness. .... Is 15:2
and everlasting joy upon their *h*. .... Is 35:10
and confounded, and covered their *h* ...... Jer 14:3
ashamed, they covered their *h*. .... Jer 14:4
have cast up dust upon their *h* .... Lam 2:10
hang down their *h* to the ground. .... Lam 2:10
of the firmament upon the *h* of .... Eze 1:22
forth over their *h* above .... Eze 1:25
firmament that was over their *h* .... Eze 1:25
h was the likeness of a throne .... Eze 1:26
and baldness upon all their *h* .... Eze 7:18
their way upon their own *h*, ... Eze 11:21
have I recompensed upon their *h* .... Eze 22:31
in dyed attire upon their *h* .... Eze 23:15
and beautiful crowns upon their *h* .... Eze 23:42
your tires shall be upon your *h* .... Eze 24:23
shall cast up dust upon their *h* .... Eze 27:30
laid their swords under their *h* .... Eze 32:27
have linen bonnets upon their *h* .... Eze 44:18
Neither shall they shave their *h* .... Eze 44:20
they shall only poll their *h* .... Eze 44:20
the beast had also four *h* .... Dan 7:6
O *h* of Jacob, and ye princes of .... Mic 3:1
ye *h* of the house of Jacob, and. .... Mic 3:9
The *h* thereof judge for reward, ... Mic 3:11
by reviled him, wagging their *h* .... Mt 27:39
by railed on him, wagging their *h* .... Mk 15:29
then look up, and lift up your *h* .... Lk 21:28
Your blood be upon your own *h*, ... Acts 18:6
them, that they may shave their *h* .... Acts 21:24
had on their *h* crowns of gold .... Rev 4:4
on their *h* were as it were crowns .... Rev 9:7
the *h* of the horses were as the .... Rev 9:17
the horses were as the *h* of lions .... Rev 9:17

HEADSTONE

the *h* thereof with shoutings .... Zec 4:7

HEADY

Traitors, *h*, highminded, lovers 2Ti 3:4

HEAL

H her now, O God, I beseech thee. .... Num 12:13
wound, and I *h* .... Deut 32:39
behold, I will *h* thee. 2Kin 20:5
the sign that the LORD will *h* me 2Kin 20:8
their sin, and will *h* their land. 2Chr 7:14
O LORD, *h* me .... Ps 6:2
h my soul .... Ps 41:4
h the breaches thereof .... Ps 60:2
A time to kill, and a time to *h* .... Eccl 3:3
he shall smite and *h* it. .... Is 19:22
of them, and shall *h* them .... Is 19:22
have seen his ways, and will *h* him .... Is 57:18
and I will *h* him .... Is 57:19
I will *h* your backslidings. .... Jer 3:22
If me, O LORD, and I shall be .... Jer 17:14
I will *h* thee of thy wounds, ... Jer 30:17
who can *h* thee? .... Lam 2:13
yet could he not *h* you, nor cure .... Hos 5:13
for he hath torn, and he will *h* us. ...... Hos 6:1
I will *h* their backsliding, I .... Hos 14:4
nor *h* that that is broken, nor .... Zec 11:16
unto him, I will come and *h* him .... Mt 8:7
to *h* all manner of sickness and .... Mt 10:1
H the sick, cleanse the lepers, ... Mt 10:8
Is it lawful to *h* on the sabbath. .... Mt 12:10
be converted, and I should *h* them. .... Mt 13:15
whether he would *h* him on the .... Mk 3:2
And to have power to *h* sicknesses .... Mk 3:15
sent me to *h* the brokenhearted, ... Lk 4:18
proverb, Physician, *h* thyself .... Lk 4:23
of the Lord was present to *h* them .... Lk 5:17
whether he would *h* on the sabbath. .... Lk 6:7
he would come and *h* his servant .... Lk 7:3
kingdom of God, and to *h* the sick .... Lk 9:2
the sick that are therein, and .... Lk 10:9
Is it lawful to *h* on the sabbath. .... Lk 14:3
he would come down, and *h* his son .... Jn 4:47
be converted, and I should *h* them .... Jn 12:40
stretching forth thine hand to *h* .... Acts 4:30
be converted, and I should *h* them. .... Acts 28:27

HEALED

God Abimelech, and his wife, and .... Gen 20:17
cause him to be thoroughly *h* .... Ex 21:19
skin thereof, was a boil, and is .... Lev 13:18
the scall is *h*, he is clean. .... Lev 13:37
of leprosy be *h* in the leper .... Lev 14:3
clean, because the plague is *h* .... Lev 14:48
itch, whereof thou canst not be *h*. .... Deut 28:27
a sore botch that cannot be *h*. .... Deut 28:35
then ye shall be *h*, and it shall 1Sa 6:3
the Loan, I have *h* these waters 2Kin 2:21
the waters were *h* unto this day 2Kin 2:22
king Joram went back to be *h* in 2Kin 8:29
king Joram was returned to be *h* 2Kin 9:15
he returned to be *h* in Jezreel 2Chr 22:6
to Hezekiah, and *h* the people 2Chr 30:20
unto thee, and thou hast *h* me .... Ps 30:2
h them, and delivered them from .... Ps 107:20
their heart, and convert, and be *h* .... Is 6:10
and with his stripes we are *h* .... Is 53:5
They have *h* also the hurt of the .... Jer 6:14
For they have *h* the hurt of the .... Jer 8:11
incurable, which refuseth to be *h* .... Jer 15:18
Heal me, O LORD, and I shall be *h* .... Jer 17:14
her pain, if so be she may be *h* .... Jer 51:8
h Babylon, but she is not *h* .... Jer 51:9
it shall not be bound up to be *h* .... Eze 30:21
neither have ye *h* that which was. .... Eze 34:4
the sea, the waters shall be *h* .... Eze 47:8
for they shall be *h* .... Eze 47:9
marishes thereof shall not be *h*. .... Eze 47:11
When I would have *h* Israel. .... Hos 7:1
but they knew not that I *h* them. .... Hos 11:3
and he *h* them .... Mt 4:24
only, and my servant shall be *h* .... Mt 8:8
his servant was *h* in the selfsame .... Mt 8:13
his word, and *h* all that were sick .... Mt 8:16
followed him, and he *h* them all. .... Mt 12:15
he *h* him, insomuch that the blind .... Mt 12:22
toward them, and he *h* their sick. .... Mt 14:14
and he *h* them .... Mt 15:30
and he *h* them there .... Mt 19:2
he *h* many that were sick of .... Mk 1:34
For he had *h* many .... Mk 3:10
hands on her, that she may be *h* .... Mk 5:23
that she was *h* of that plague. .... Mk 5:29
upon a few sick folk, and *h* them. .... Mk 6:5
many that were sick, and *h* them .... Mk 6:13
on every one of them, and *h* them .... Lk 4:40
hear, and to be *h* by him of their .... Lk 5:15
to be *h* of their diseases. .... Lk 6:17
and they were *h* .... Lk 6:18

virtue out of him, and *h* them all. .... Lk 6:19
a word, and my servant shall be *h*. .... Lk 7:7
which had been *h* of evil spirits. .... Lk 8:2
was possessed of the devils was *h*. .... Lk 8:36
neither could be *h* of any .... Lk 8:43
him, and how she was *h* immediately .... Lk 8:47
h them that had need of healing .... Lk 9:11
h the child, and delivered him .... Lk 9:42
Jesus had *h* on the sabbath day .... Lk 13:14
in them therefore come and be *h* .... Lk 13:14
took him, and *h* him, and let him go. ..... Lk 14:4
them, when he saw that he was *h*, ... Lk 17:15
And he touched his ear, and *h* him .... Lk 22:51
he that was *h* wist not who it was. .... Jn 5:13
lame man which was *h* held Peter .... Acts 3:11
which was *h* standing with them, ... Acts 4:14
and they were *h* every one. .... Acts 5:16
and that were lame, were *h* .... Acts 8:7
that he had faith to be *h* .... Acts 14:9
laid his hands on him, and *h* him .... Acts 28:8
in the island, came, and were *h* .... Acts 28:9
but let it rather be *h* .... Heb 12:13
one for another, that ye may be *h* .... Jas 5:16
by whose stripes ye were *h* 1Pet 2:24
and his deadly wound was *h* .... Rev 13:3
beast, whose deadly wound was *h* .... Rev 13:12

HEALER

swear, saying, I will not be an *h* .... Is 3:7

HEALETH

for I am the LORD that *h* thee. .... Ex 15:26
who is all thy diseases .... Ps 103:3
He *h* the broken in heart, and .... Ps 147:3
h the stroke of their wound .... Is 30:26

HEALING

us, and there is no *h* for us .... Jer 14:19
and for the time of *h*, and behold. .... Jer 14:19
thou hast no *h* medicines .... Jer 30:13
There is no *h* of thy bruise. .... Nah 3:19
arise with *h* in his wings .... Mal 4:2
h all manner of sickness and all .... Mt 4:23
h every sickness and every disease .... Mt 9:35
the gospel, and *h* every where .... Lk 9:6
and healed them that had need of *h* .... Lk 9:11
whom this miracle of *h* was shewed .... Acts 4:22
h all that were oppressed of the .... Acts 10:38
the gifts of *h* by the same Spirit. 1Cor 12:9
Have all the gifts of *h* 1Cor 12:30
were for the *h* of the nations .... Rev 22:2

HEALINGS

that miracles, then gifts of *h* 1Cor 12:28

HEALTH

servant our master is in good *h* .... Gen 43:28
Joab said to Amasa, Art thou in *h* 2Sa 20:9
who is the *h* of my countenance, ... Ps 42:11
who is the *h* of my countenance, ... Ps 43:5
thy saving *h* among all nations. .... Ps 67:2
It shall be *h* to thy navel, and .... Prov 3:8
them, and *h* to all their flesh .... Prov 4:22
but the tongue of the wise is *h* .... Prov 12:18
but a faithful ambassador is *h*. .... Prov 13:17
to the soul, and *h* to the bones .... Prov 16:24
thine *h* shall spring forth .... Is 58:8
and for a time of *h*, and behold .... Jer 8:15
why then is not the *h* of the .... Jer 8:22
For I will restore *h* unto thee, ... Jer 30:17
Behold, I will bring it *h*, ... Jer 33:6
for this is for your *h* .... Acts 27:34
thou mayest prosper and be in *h* 3Jn 2

HEAP

and they took stones, and made an *h* ...... Gen 31:46
and they did eat there upon the *h*. .... Gen 31:46
This *h* is a witness between me and .... Gen 31:48
said to Jacob, Behold this *h* .... Gen 31:51
This *h* be witness, and this pillar .... Gen 31:52
will not pass over this *h* to thee .... Gen 31:52
thou shalt not pass over this *h* .... Gen 31:52
the floods stood upright as an *h*. .... Ex 15:8
and it shall be an *h* for ever .... Deut 13:16
I will *h* mischiefs upon them .... Deut 32:23
and they shall stand upon an *h*. .... Josh 3:13
rose up upon an *h* very far from. .... Josh 3:16
a great *h* of stones unto this day .... Josh 7:26
Ai, and made it an *h* for ever. .... Josh 8:28
raise thereon a great *h* of stones .... Josh 8:29
down at the end of the *h* of corn. .... Ruth 3:7
laid a very great *h* of stones 2Sa 18:17
His roots are wrapped about the *h* .... Job 8:17
I could *h* up words against you, ... Job 16:4
Though he *h* up silver as the dust. .... Job 27:16
hypocrites in heart *h* up wrath .... Job 36:13
of the sea together as an *h* .... Ps 33:7
made the waters to stand as an *h*. .... Ps 78:13
For thou shalt *h* coals of fire. .... Prov 25:22
travail, to gather and to *h* up. .... Eccl 2:26
thy belly is like an *h* of wheat .... Song 7:2
city, and it shall be a ruinous *h* .... Is 17:1
shall be a *h* in the day of grief .... Is 17:11
For thou hast made of a city an *h* .... Is 25:2
shall be builded upon her own *h* .... Jer 30:18
and it shall be a desolate *h* .... Jer 49:2
H on wood, kindle the fire, ... Eze 24:10
make Samaria an *h* of the field .... Mic 1:6
for they shall *h* dust, and take it .... Hab 1:10
through the *h* of great waters. .... Hab 3:15
came to an *h* of twenty measures .... Hag 2:16
shalt *h* coals of fire on his head. .... Rom 12:20
they *h* to themselves teachers 2Ti 4:3

HEAPED
h up silver as the dust, and fine .... Zec 9:3
Ye have h treasure together for .... Jas 5:3

HEAPETH
he h up riches, and knoweth not .... Ps 39:6
nations, and h unto him all people............ Hab 2:5

HEAPS
gathered them together upon h............ Ex 8:14
h upon h, with the jaw of an .... Judg 15:16
Lay ye them in two h at the 2Kin 10:8
fenced cities into ruinous h............ 2Kin 19:25
Lord their God, and laid them by h............ 2Chr 31:6
to lay the foundation of the h............ 2Chr 31:7
and the princes came and saw the h............ 2Chr 31:8
and the Levites concerning the h............ 2Chr 31:9
revive the stones out of the h of .... Neh 4:2
which are ready to become h............ Job 15:28
they have laid Jerusalem on h............ Ps 79:1
defenced cities into ruinous h............ Is 37:26
And I will make Jerusalem h............ Jer 9:11
and Jerusalem shall become h............ Jer 26:18
up waymarks, make thee high h............ Jer 31:21
cast her up as h, and destroy; her .... Jer 50:26
And Babylon shall become h............ Jer 51:37
their altars are as h in the .... Hos 12:11
and Jerusalem shall become h............ Mic 3:12

HEAR See PREFACE.
and I will make them h my words............ Deut 4:10
have not known any thing, may h............ Deut 31:13
when ye h the sound of the .... Josh 6:5
for I h of your evil dealings by 1Sa 2:23
until noon, saying, O Baal, h us............ 1Kin 18:26
then will I h from heaven............ 2Chr 7:14
H my words, O ye wise men............ Job 34:2
The Lord h thee in the day of .... Ps 20:1
H, O Lord, when I cry with my............ Ps 27:7
for who, say they, doth h............ Ps 59:7
Come and h, all ye that fear God,............ Ps 66:16
I will h what God the Lord will .... Ps 85:8
A wise man will h, and will............ Prov 1:5
H instruction, and be wise, and............ Prov 8:33
Let us h the conclusion of the .... Eccl 12:13
H ye indeed, but understand not .... Is 6:9
H, ye that are far off, what I .... Is 33:13
h, and your soul shall live .... Is 55:3
He that heareth, let him h............ Eze 3:27
h the prayer of thy servant, and............ Dan 9:17
that hath ears to h, let him; h............ Mt 11:15
h ye him............ Mt 17:5
And ye shall h of wars and rumours... Mt 24:6
and hearing they may h, and not............ Mk 4:12
such as h the word, and receive it............ Mk 4:20
he maketh both the deaf to h............ Mk 7:37
But when ye shall h of wars............ Lk 21:9
when the dead shall h the voice .... Jn 5:25
and they that h shall live............ Jn 5:25
and the sheep h his voice .... Jn 10:3
My sheep h my voice, and I know............ Jn 10:27
And if any man h my words, and............ Jn 12:47
how h we every man in our own............ Acts 2:8
we do h them speak in our tongues... Acts 2:11
together to h the word of God............ Acts 13:44
to tell, or to h some new thing............ Acts 17:21
how shall they h without a............ Rom 10:14
let every man be swift to h............ Jas 1:19
if any man h my voice, and open .... Rev 3:20

HEARD See PREFACE.
they h the voice of the Lord God............ Gen 3:8
God h their groaning, and God............ Ex 2:24
have h their cry by reason of .... Ex 3:7
and the Lord h it............ Num 11:1
And the Lord h it............ Num 12:2
that hath h the voice of the .... Deut 5:26
all that we have h with our ears............ 2Sa 7:22
I sought the Lord, and he h me............ Ps 34:4
But I, as a deaf man, h not............ Ps 38:13
Zion h, and was glad............ Ps 97:8
of the turtle is h in our land .... Song 2:12
have ye not h?............ Is 40:21
had not h shall they consider............ Is 52:15
unto the Lord, and he h me............ Jonah 2:2
Ye have h that it was said by............ Mt 5:21
for thy prayer is h............ Lk 1:13
darkness shall be h in the light............ Lk 12:3
And what he hath seen and h............ Jn 3:32
for we have h them ourselves, and............ Jn 4:42
because that every man h them............ Acts 2:6
of them which h the word believed... Acts 4:4
h a voice saying unto him, Saul,............ Acts 9:4
h a voice saying unto me, Saul,............ Acts 22:7
but they h not the voice of him............ Acts 22:9
I h a voice speaking unto me, and............ Acts 26:14
in him of whom they have not h............ Rom 10:14
Eye hath not seen, nor ear h............ 1Cor 2:9
If so be that ye have h him............ Eph 4:21
with faith in them that h it............ Heb 4:2
Ye have h of the patience of Job,............ Jas 5:11
the beginning, which we have h............ 1Jn 1:1
h declare we unto you, that ye............ 1Jn 1:3
how thou hast received it, and h............ Rev 3:3
John saw these things, and h them............ Rev 22:8
And when I had h and seen, I fell............ Rev 22:8

HEARDEST
thou h his words out of the midst............ Deut 4:36
for thou h in that day how the............ Josh 14:12
when thou h what I spake against............ 2Kin 22:19
when thou h his words against............ 2Chr 34:27
h their cry by the Red sea............ Neh 9:9

thee, thou h them from heaven............ Neh 9:27
thee, thou h them from heaven............ Neh 9:28
nevertheless thou h the voice of............ Ps 31:22
declared my ways, and thou h me............ Ps 119:26
the day when thou h them not............ Is 48:7
Yea, thou h not............ Is 48:8
hell cried I, and thou h my voice............ Jonah 2:2

HEARER
if any be a h of the word .... Jas 1:23
he being not a forgetful h............ Jas 1:25

HEARERS
(For not the h of the law are............ Rom 2:13
it may minister grace unto the h............ Eph 4:29
but to the subverting of the h............ 2Ti 2:14
not h only, deceiving your own............ Jas 1:22

HEAREST
Ruth, H thou not, my daughter .... Ruth 2:8
Wherefore h thou men's words,............ 1Sa 24:9
when thou h them............ 1Kin 8:30
and when thou h, forgive............ 1Kin 8:30
and when thou h, forgive............ 2Chr 6:21
in the daytime, but thou h not............ Ps 22:2
O thou that h prayer, unto thee............ Ps 65:2
unto him, H thou what these say............ Mt 21:16
H thou not how many things they............ Mt 27:13
thou h the sound thereof, but............ Jn 3:8
And I knew that thou h me always............ Jn 11:42

HEARETH
for that he h your murmurings............ Ex 16:7
for that the Lord h your............ Ex 16:8
disallow her in the day that he h............ Num 30:5
when he h the words of this curse... Deut 29:19
for thy servant h............ 1Sa 3:9
for thy servant h............ 1Sa 3:10
every one that h it shall tingle............ 1Sa 3:11
that whosoever h it will say............ 2Sa 17:9
and Judah, that whosoever h of it............ 2Kin 21:12
he h the cry of the afflicted............ Job 34:28
The righteous cry, and the Lord h............ Ps 34:17
Thus I was as a man that h not............ Ps 38:14
For the Lord h the poor, and............ Ps 69:33
Blessed is the man that h me............ Prov 8:34
A wise son h his father's............ Prov 13:1
but a scorner h not rebuke............ Prov 13:1
but the poor h not rebuke............ Prov 13:8
but he that h the prayer of the............ Prov 15:29
The ear that h the reproof of............ Prov 15:31
but he that h reproof getteth............ Prov 15:32
answereth a matter before he h it............ Prov 18:13
but he that h me shall dwell............ Prov 1:33
Lest he that h it put thee to............ Prov 25:10
he h cursing, and bewrayeth it not... Prov 29:24
there is none that h your words............ Is 41:26
opening the ears, but he h not............ Is 42:20
this place, the which whosoever h............ Jer 19:3
he that h, let him hear............ Eze 3:27
Then whosoever h the sound of the... Eze 33:4
Therefore whosoever h these............ Mt 7:24
every one that h these sayings of............ Mt 7:26
When any one h the word of the............ Mt 13:19
the same is he that h the word............ Mt 13:20
the thorns is he that h the word............ Mt 13:22
good ground is he that h the word... Mt 13:23
h my sayings, and doeth them, I............ Lk 6:47
But he that h, and doeth not, is............ Lk 6:49
He that h you h me............ Lk 10:16
him, rejoiceth greatly because............ Jn 3:29
I say unto you, He that h my word............ Jn 5:24
He that is of God h God's words............ Jn 8:47
we know that God h not sinners............ Jn 9:31
God, and doeth his will, him he h............ Jn 9:31
that is of the truth h my voice............ Jn 18:37
me to be, or that he h of me............ 2Cor 12:6
of the world, and the world h them... 1Jn 4:5
he that knoweth God h us............ 1Jn 4:6
he that is not of God h not us............ 1Jn 4:6
according to his will, he h us............ 1Jn 5:14
And let him that h say, Come............ Rev 22:17
h the words of the prophecy of............ Rev 22:18

HEARING
law before all Israel in their h............ Deut 31:11
for in our h the king charged............ 2Sa 18:12
there was neither voice, nor h............ 2Kin 4:31
Surely thou hast spoken in mine h............ Job 33:8
heard of thee by the h of the ear............ Job 42:5
The h ear, and the seeing eye, the............ Prov 20:12
away his ear from h the law............ Prov 28:9
seeing, nor the ear filled with h............ Eccl 1:8
reprove after the h of his ears............ Is 11:3
I was bowed down at the h of it............ Is 21:3
stoppeth his ears from h of blood............ Is 33:15
to the others he said in mine h............ Eze 9:5
it was cried unto them in my h............ Eze 10:13
but of h the words of the Lord............ Amos 8:11
h they hear not, neither do they............ Mt 13:13
By h ye shall hear, and shall not............ Mt 13:14
and their ears are dull of h............ Mt 13:15
and h they may hear, and not............ Mk 4:12
many h him were astonished,............ Mk 6:2
midst of the doctors, both h them............ Lk 2:46
h they might not understand............ Lk 8:10
h the multitude pass by, he asked............ Lk 18:36
Ananias h these words fell down,............ Acts 5:5
things which Philip spake, h............ Acts 8:6
h a voice, but seeing no man............ Acts 9:7
of the Corinthians h believed............ Acts 18:8
reserved unto the h of Augustus............ Acts 25:21
was entered into the place of h............ Acts 25:23

H ye shall hear, and shall not............ Acts 28:26
and their ears are dull of h............ Acts 28:27
So then faith cometh by h............ Rom 10:17
and h by the word of God............ Rom 10:17
were an eye, where were the h............ 1Cor 12:17
If the whole were h, where were............ 1Cor 12:17
of the law, or by the h of faith............ Gal 3:2
of the law, or by the h of faith............ Gal 3:5
H of thy love and faith, which............ Philem 5
uttered, seeing ye are dull of h............ Heb 5:11
among them, in seeing and h............ 2Pet 2:8

HEARKEN
wives of Lamech, h unto my speech...... Gen 4:23
said unto thee, h unto her voice............ Gen 21:12
My lord, h unto me............ Gen 23:15
But if ye will not h unto us............ Gen 34:17
h unto Israel your father............ Gen 49:2
they shall h to thy voice............ Ex 3:18
believe me, nor h unto my voice............ Ex 4:1
neither h to the voice of the............ Ex 4:8
neither h unto thy voice, that............ Ex 4:9
and how shall Pharaoh h unto me............ Ex 6:30
But Pharaoh shall not h unto you............ Ex 7:4
neither did he h unto them............ Ex 7:22
Pharaoh shall not h unto you............ Ex 11:9
If thou wilt diligently h to the............ Ex 15:26
H now unto my voice, I will give............ Ex 18:19
But if ye will not h unto me............ Lev 26:14
not yet for all this h unto me............ Lev 26:18
unto me, and will not h unto me............ Lev 26:21
will not for all this h unto me............ Lev 26:27
h unto me, thou son of Zippor............ Num 23:18
Lord would not h to your voice............ Deut 1:45
Now therefore h, O Israel, unto............ Deut 4:1
if ye h to these judgments, and............ Deut 7:12
If ye shall h diligently unto my............ Deut 11:13
Thou shalt not h unto the words............ Deut 13:3
consent unto him, nor h unto him............ Deut 13:8
When thou shalt h to the voice of... Deut 13:18
Only if thou carefully h unto this... Deut 15:5
will not h unto the priest that............ Deut 17:12
unto him ye shall h............ Deut 18:15
that whosoever will not h unto my... Deut 18:19
him, will not h unto them............ Deut 21:18
thy God would not h unto Balaam............ Deut 23:5
judgments, and to h unto his voice... Deut 26:17
Israel, saying, Take heed, and h............ Deut 27:9
if thou shalt h diligently unto............ Deut 28:1
if thou shalt h unto the voice of............ Deut 28:2
if that thou h unto the............ Deut 28:13
if thou wilt not h unto the voice of Deut 28:15
If thou shalt h unto the voice of............ Deut 30:10
things, so will we h unto thee............ Josh 1:17
will not h unto thy words in all............ Josh 1:18
But I would not h unto Balaam............ Josh 24:10
would not h unto their judges............ Judg 2:17
to know whether they would h unto... Judg 3:4
H unto me, ye men of Shechem,............ Judg 9:7
that God may h unto you............ Judg 9:7
king of Edom would not h thereto............ Judg 11:17
But the men would not h to him............ Judg 19:25
h to the voice of their brethren............ Judg 20:13
H unto the voice of the people in............ 1Sa 8:7
Now therefore h unto their voice............ 1Sa 8:9
H unto their voice, and make them... 1Sa 8:22
now therefore h thou unto the............ 1Sa 15:1
to h than the fat of rams............ 1Sa 15:22
h thou also unto the voice of............ 1Sa 28:22
H thou also unto the voice of............ 1Sa 30:24
For who will h unto you in this............ 1Sa 30:24
he would not h unto our voice............ 2Sa 12:18
he would not h unto her voice............ 2Sa 13:14
But he would not h unto her............ 2Sa 13:16
to h unto the cry and to the............ 1Kin 8:28
that thou mayest h unto the............ 1Kin 8:29
h thou to the supplication of thy............ 1Kin 8:30
to h unto them in all that they............ 1Kin 8:52
if thou wilt h unto all that I............ 1Kin 11:38
H not unto him, nor consent............ 1Kin 20:8
And he said, H, O people, every............ 1Kin 22:28
if ye will h unto my voice, take............ 2Kin 10:6
Howbeit they did not h, but they............ 2Kin 17:40
H not to Hezekiah............ 2Kin 18:31
h not unto Hezekiah, for he............ 2Kin 18:32
to h unto the cry and the prayer............ 2Chr 6:19
to h unto the prayer which thy............ 2Chr 6:21
H therefore unto the............ 2Chr 6:21
the king would not h unto them............ 2Chr 10:16
And he said, H, all ye people............ 2Chr 18:33
he said, H ye all Judah, and ye............ 2Chr 20:15
but they would not h............ 2Chr 33:10
Shall we then h unto you to do............ Neh 13:27
h to the pleadings of my lips............ Job 13:6
Therefore I said, H to me............ Job 32:10
my speeches, and h to all my words... Job 33:1
Mark well, O Job, h unto me............ Job 33:31
If not, h unto me............ Job 33:33
Therefore h unto me, ye men of............ Job 34:10
h to the voice of my words............ Job 34:16
me, and let a wise man h unto me............ Job 34:34
H unto this, O Job............ Job 37:14
H unto the voice of my cry, my............ Ps 5:2
Come, ye children, h unto me............ Ps 34:11
O daughter, and consider, and............ Ps 45:10
Which wilt not h to the voice of............ Ps 58:5
O Israel, if thou wilt h unto me............ Ps 81:8
my people would not h to my voice... Ps 81:11
H unto me now therefore, O ye............ Prov 7:24
Now therefore h unto me, O ye............ Prov 8:32
H unto thy father that begat thee,... Prov 23:22
If a ruler h to lies, all his............ Prov 29:12

H

the companions *h* to thy voice............ Song 8:13
h, and hear my speech........................... Is 28:23
ears of them that hear shall *h*............. Is 32:3
and *h*, ye people.................................... Is 34:1
H not to Hezekiah.................................. Is 36:16
who will *h* and hear for the time........ Is 42:23
H unto me, O house of Jacob, and.... Is 46:3
H unto me, ye stouthearted, that...... Is 46:12
H unto me, O Jacob and Israel, my .... Is 48:12
and *h*, ye people, from far .... Is 49:1
H to me, ye that follow after.............. Is 51:1
H unto me, my people.......................... Is 51:4
H unto me, ye that know...................... Is 51:7
h diligently unto me, and eat ye........ Is 55:2
uncircumcised, and they cannot *h*..... Jer 6:10
H to the sound of the trumpet............ Jer 6:17
But they said, We will not *h*.............. Jer 6:17
but they will not *h* to thee................. Jer 7:27
unto me, I will not *h* unto them .... Jer 11:11
that they may not *h* unto me.............. Jer 16:12
pass, if ye diligently *h* unto me......... Jer 17:24
But if ye will not *h* unto me to .... Jer 17:27
h to the voice of them that................. Jer 18:19
H not unto the words of the............... Jer 23:16
If so be they will *h*, and turn.............. Jer 26:3
If ye will not *h* to me, to walk........... Jer 26:4
To *h* to the words of my servants...... Jer 26:5
Therefore *h* not ye to your................... Jer 27:9
Therefore *h* not unto the words of..... Jer 27:14
H not to the words of your.................. Jer 27:16
H not unto them................................... Jer 27:17
neither *h* to your dreams which ye..... Jer 29:8
unto me, and I will *h* unto you........... Jer 29:12
instruction to *h* to my words.............. Jer 35:13
did *h* unto the words of the LORD,...... Jer 37:2
counsel, wilt thou not *h* unto me....... Jer 38:15
the LORD, we will not *h* unto thee ..... Jer 44:16
of Israel will not *h* unto thee............. Eze 3:7
for they will not *h* unto me............... Eze 3:7
me, and would not *h* unto me............. Eze 20:8
also, if ye will not *h* unto me............. Eze 20:39
O LORD, *h* and do............................... Dan 9:19
and *h*, ye house of Israel..................... Hos 5:1
because they did not *h* unto him........ Hos 9:17
h, O earth, and all that therein........... Mic 1:2
nor *h* unto me, saith the LORD............ Zec 1:4
But they refused to *h*, and pulled...... Zec 7:11
H; Behold, there went........................... Mk 4:3
H unto me every one of you, and........ Mk 7:14
known unto you, and *h* to my words .. Acts 2:14
to *h* unto you more than unto God.... Acts 4:19
Men, brethren, and fathers, *h*............. Acts 7:2
of the gate, a damsel came to *h*........ Acts 12:13
Men and brethren, *h* unto me............. Acts 15:13
H, my beloved brethren, Hath not...... Jas 2:5

HEARKENED
Because thou hast *h* unto the............ Gen 3:17
Abram *h* to the voice of Sarai .... Gen 16:2
And Abraham *h* unto Ephron.............. Gen 23:16
God *h* unto Leah, and she conceived.. Gen 30:17
God *h* to her, and opened her womb.. Gen 30:22
unto Shechem his son *h* all that....... Gen 34:24
that he *h* not unto her, to lie by....... Gen 39:10
but they *h* not unto Moses for.......... Ex 6:9
of Israel have not *h* unto me............ Ex 6:12
heart, that he *h* not unto them.......... Ex 7:13
his heart, and *h* not unto them.......... Ex 8:15
hardened, and he *h* not unto them.... Ex 8:19
of Pharaoh, and he *h* not unto them.. Ex 9:12
they *h* not unto Moses....................... Ex 16:20
So Moses *h* to the voice of his.......... Ex 18:24
times, and have not *h* to my voice.... Num 14:22
the LORD *h* to the voice of Israel....... Num 21:3
But the LORD *h* not at that................. Deut 1:43
him not, nor *h* to his voice................. Deut 9:23
the LORD *h* unto me at that time...... Deut 10:10
h unto observers of times, and.......... Deut 18:14
but I have *h* to the voice of the......... Deut 26:14
the children of Israel *h* unto him....... Josh 1:17
According as we *h* unto Moses in....... Josh 1:17
that the LORD *h* unto the voice of..... Josh 10:14
and have not *h* unto my voice............ Judg 2:20
king of the children of Ammon *h*...... Judg 11:28
God *h* to the voice of Manoah............ Judg 13:9
Notwithstanding they *h* not............... 1Sa 2:25
I have *h* unto your voice in all............ 1Sa 12:1
Saul *h* unto the voice of Jonathan...... 1Sa 19:6
I have *h* to thy voice, and have......... 1Sa 25:35
have *h* unto thy words which thou..... 1Sa 28:21
and he *h* unto their voice................... 1Sa 28:23
Wherefore the king *h* not unto the.... 1Kin 12:15
saw that the king *h* not unto them .. 1Kin 12:16
They *h* therefore to the word of........ 1Kin 12:24
So Ben-hadad *h* unto king Asa,......... 1Kin 15:20
he *h* unto their voice, and did so...... 1Kin 20:25
the LORD, and the LORD *h* unto him... 2Kin 13:4
And the king of Assyria *h* unto......... 2Kin 16:9
Hezekiah *h* unto them, and shewed... 2Kin 20:13
But they *h* not.................................... 2Kin 21:9
not *h* unto the words of this book..... 2Kin 22:13
So the king *h* not unto the people..... 2Chr 10:15
Ben-hadad *h* unto king Asa, and....... 2Chr 16:4
Then the king *h* unto them................. 2Chr 24:17
hast not *h* unto my counsel................. 2Chr 25:16
the LORD *h* to Hezekiah, and healed.. 2Chr 30:20
h not unto the words of Necho 2Chr 35:22
h not to thy commandments,............. Neh 9:16
h not unto thy commandments, but.. Neh 9:29
nor *h* unto thy commandments, and.. Neh 9:34
he *h* not unto them, that they .... Est 3:4

that he had *h* unto my voice............. Job 9:16
Oh that my people had *h* unto me..... Ps 81:13
h not unto the voice of the LORD....... Ps 106:25
he *h* diligently with much heed.......... Is 21:7
O that thou hadst *h* to my................. Is 48:18
they have not *h* unto my words......... Jer 6:19
But they *h* not, nor inclined.............. Jer 7:24
Yet they *h* not unto me, nor............. Jer 7:26
I *h* and heard, but they spake not...... Jer 8:6
but ye have not *h*............................... Jer 25:3
but ye have not *h*, nor inclined.......... Jer 25:4
Yet ye have not *h* unto me................ Jer 25:7
sending them, but ye have not *h*....... Jer 26:5
they have not *h* to my words............ Jer 29:19
yet they have not *h* to receive.......... Jer 32:33
but your fathers *h* not unto me.......... Jer 34:14
Ye have not *h* unto me, in................ Jer 34:17
but ye *h* not unto me......................... Jer 35:14
inclined your ear, nor *h* unto me....... Jer 35:15
this people hath not *h* unto me......... Jer 35:16
but they *h* not.................................... Jer 36:31
But he *h* not to him............................ Jer 37:14
But they *h* not, nor inclined.............. Jer 44:5
them, they would have *h* unto thee... Eze 3:6
Neither have we *h* unto thy.............. Dan 9:6
and the LORD *h*, and heard it, and a.. Mal 3:16
Sirs, ye should have *h* unto me......... Acts 27:21

HEARKENEDST
because thou *h* not unto the voice..... Deut 28:45

HEARKENETH
But whoso *h* unto me shall dwell....... Prov 1:33
but he that *h* unto counsel is.............. Prov 12:15

HEARKENING
h unto the voice of his word............... Ps 103:20

HEART See PREFACE.
of the thoughts of his *h* was only ...... Gen 6:5
hath he filled with wisdom of *h*.......... Ex 35:35
and to serve him with all your *h*....... Deut 11:13
and to serve him with all your *h*....... Josh 22:5
My *h* rejoiceth in the LORD, mine....... 1Sa 2:1
Samuel, God gave him another *h*........ 1Sa 10:9
serve the LORD with all your *h*........... 1Sa 12:20
but the LORD looketh on the *h*........... 1Sa 16:7
and who followed me with all his *h*.. 1Kin 14:8
and said to him, Is thine *h* right....... 2Kin 10:15
they were not of double *h*................... 1Chr 12:33
let the *h* of them rejoice that............. 1Chr 16:10
my God, that thou triest the *h*........... 1Chr 29:17
of their fathers with all their *h*.......... 2Chr 15:12
his God, he did it with all his *h*......... 2Chr 31:21
is nothing else but sorrow of *h*.......... Neh 2:2
He is wise in *h*, and mighty in............ Job 9:4
the widow's *h* to sing for joy............. Job 29:13
hath given understanding to the *h*..... Job 38:36
The fool hath said in his *h*.................. Ps 14:1
hath clean hands, and a pure *h*.......... Ps 24:4
against me, my *h* shall not fear.......... Ps 27:3
unto them that are of a broken *h*....... Ps 34:18
he knoweth the secrets of the *h*........ Ps 44:21
Create in me a clean *h*, O God............ Ps 51:10
of every one of them, and the *h*........ Ps 64:6
they have more than *h* could wish..... Ps 73:7
For their *h* was not right with............ Ps 78:37
let the *h* of them rejoice that............. Ps 105:3
Search me, O God, and know my *h*..... Ps 139:23
Keep thy *h* with all diligence............. Prov 4:23
The *h* knoweth his own bitterness...... Prov 14:10
For as he thinketh in his *h*................. Prov 23:7
My son, give me thine *h*, and let....... Prov 23:26
a wise man's *h* discerneth both.......... Eccl 8:5
and drink thy wine with a merry *h*.... Eccl 9:7
and gladness of *h*, as when one......... Is 30:29
and no man layeth it to *h*.................. Is 57:1
to revive the *h* of the contrite........... Is 57:15
my *h* maketh a noise in me................ Jer 4:19
that triest the reins and the *h*........... Jer 11:20
The *h* is deceitful above all................ Jer 17:9
I will give them an *h* to know me...... Jer 24:7
return unto me with their whole *h*.... Jer 24:7
And I will give them one *h*................. Jer 32:39
Give them sorrow of *h*, thy curse...... Lam 3:65
And I will give them one *h*................. Eze 11:19
and make you a new *h* and a new..... Eze 18:31
A new *h* also will I give you, and....... Eze 36:26
strangers, uncircumcised in *h*............ Eze 44:7
And rend your *h*, and not your........... Joel 2:13
he shall turn the *h* of the................... Mal 4:6
Blessed are the pure in *h*.................... Mt 5:8
is, there will your *h* be also............... Mt 6:21
for I am meek and lowly in *h*............ Mt 11:29
of the *h* the mouth speaketh............. Mt 12:34
For out of the *h* proceed evil............. Mt 15:19
the Lord thy God with all thy *h*........ Mt 22:37
from within, out of the *h* of men...... Mk 7:21
For the hardness of your *h* he........... Mk 10:5
the Lord thy God with all thy *h*........ Mk 12:30
h bringeth forth that which is........... Lk 6:45
the Lord thy God with all thy *h*........ Lk 10:27
is, there will your *h* be also............... Lk 12:34
slow of *h* to believe all that the........ Lk 24:25
Let not your *h* be troubled................ Jn 14:1
Let not your *h* be troubled................ Jn 14:27
with gladness and singleness of *h*..... Acts 2:46
stiffnecked and uncircumcised in *h*... Acts 7:51
shalt believe in thine *h* that God........ Rom 10:9
For with the *h* man believeth unto... Rom 10:10
have entered into the *h* of man......... 1Cor 2:9
but in singleness of *h*, fearing............ Col 3:22

is charity out of a pure *h*.................... 1Ti 1:5
the thoughts and intents of the *h*...... Heb 4:12
true *h* in full assurance of faith......... Heb 10:22
For if our *h* condemn.......................... 1Jn 3:20
God is greater than our *h*.................... 1Jn 3:20

HEARTED
speak unto all that are wise *h*............ Ex 28:3
that are wise *h* I have put wisdom.... Ex 31:6
every wise *h* among you shall come.. Ex 35:10
women, as many as were willing *h*.... Ex 35:22
wise *h* did spin with their hands....... Ex 35:25
and Aholiab, and every wise *h* man.. Ex 36:1
and Aholiab, and every wise *h* man.. Ex 36:2
every wise *h* man among them that.. Ex 36:8

HEARTH
it, and make cakes upon the *h*........... Gen 18:6
and my bones are burned as an *h*...... Ps 102:3
a sherd to take fire from the *h*........... Is 30:14
fire on the *h* burning before him....... Jer 36:22
into the fire that was on the *h*........... Jer 36:23
in the fire that was on the *h*.............. Jer 36:23
like an *h* of fire among the wood...... Zec 12:6

HEARTILY
And whatsoever ye do, do it *h*............ Col 3:23

HEART'S
wicked boasts of his *h* desire............. Ps 10:3
Thou hast given him his *h* desire........ Ps 21:2
my *h* desire and prayer to God for..... Rom 10:1

HEARTS
of bread, and comfort ye your *h*........ Gen 18:5
harden the *h* of the Egyptians........... Ex 14:17
in the *h* of all that are wise.............. Ex 31:6
send a faintness into their *h* in......... Lev 26:36
their uncircumcised *h* be humbled..... Lev 26:41
let not your *h* faint, fear not............. Deut 20:3
Set your *h* unto all the words............ Deut 32:46
our *h* did melt, neither did there....... Josh 2:11
wherefore the *h* of the people........... Josh 7:5
was of the LORD to harden their *h*..... Josh 11:20
and ye know in all your *h* and in...... Josh 23:14
their *h* inclined to follow................... Judg 9:3
to pass, when their *h* were merry...... Judg 16:25
as they were making their *h* merry.. Judg 19:22
then do ye harden your *h*, as the....... 1Sa 6:6
and Pharaoh hardened their *h*............ 1Sa 6:6
unto the LORD with all your *h*............ 1Sa 7:3
prepare your *h* unto the LORD, and.... 1Sa 7:3
of men, whose *h* God had touched 1Sa 10:26
stole the *h* of the men of Israel 2Sa 15:6
The *h* of the men of Israel are.......... 2Sa 15:13
knowest the *h* of all the children 1Kin 8:39
he may incline our *h* unto him 1Kin 8:58
for the LORD searcheth all *h*.............. 1Chr 28:9
walk before thee with all their *h*....... 2Chr 6:14
the *h* of the children of men.............. 2Chr 6:30
of Israel such as set their *h* to.......... 2Chr 11:16
h unto the God of their fathers 2Chr 20:33
sinned, and curse God in their *h*........ Job 1:5
the righteous God trieth the *h*........... Ps 7:9
but mischief is in their *h*.................... Ps 28:3
He fashioneth their *h* alike................ Ps 33:15
Let them not say in their *h*................ Ps 35:25
They said in their *h*, Let us............... Ps 74:8
we may apply our *h* unto wisdom..... Ps 90:12
them that are upright in their *h*........ Ps 125:4
then the *h* of the children of men..... Prov 15:11
but the LORD trieth the *h*................... Prov 17:3
but the LORD pondereth the *h*........... Prov 21:2
unto those that be of heavy *h*........... Prov 31:6
and their *h*, that they cannot............. Is 44:18
parts, and write it in their *h*.............. Jer 31:33
but I will put my fear in their *h*......... Jer 32:40
For ye dissembled in your *h*............... Jer 42:20
the mighty men's *h* in Moab at.......... Jer 48:41
that prophesy out of their own *h*....... Eze 13:2
also vex the *h* of many people .... Eze 32:9
both these kings *h* shall be to........... Dan 11:27
their *h* that I remember all their........ Hos 7:2
they made their *h* as an adamant...... Zec 7:12
in your *h* against his neighbour......... Zec 8:17
Wherefore think ye evil in your *h*...... Mt 9:4
if ye from your *h* forgive not............. Mt 18:35
h suffered you to put away your....... Mt 19:8
there, and reasoning in their *h*.......... Mk 2:6
reason ye these things in your *h*........ Mk 2:8
for the hardness of their *h*................. Mk 3:5
the word that was sown in their *h*.... Mk 4:15
to turn the *h* of the fathers to........... Lk 1:17
in the imagination of their *h*............. Lk 1:51
them laid them up in their *h*.............. Lk 1:66
of many *h* may be revealed............... Lk 2:35
all men mused in their *h* of John ...... Lk 3:15
them, What reason ye in your *h*........ Lk 5:22
away the word out of their *h*............. Lk 8:12
but God knoweth your *h*.................... Lk 16:15
Settle it therefore in your *h*............... Lk 21:14
Men's *h* failing them for fear, and .... Lk 21:26
lest at any time your *h* be................. Lk 21:34
why do thoughts arise in your *h*........ Lk 24:38
which knowest the *h* of all men......... Acts 1:24
in their *h* turned back again into....... Acts 7:39
seasons, filling our *h* with food......... Acts 14:17
the word that was sown in their *h*.... Acts 15:8
them, purifying their *h* by faith........ Acts 15:9
through the lusts of their own *h*........ Rom 1:24
of the law written in their *h*............. Rom 2:15
our *h* by the Holy Ghost which is...... Rom 5:5
he that searcheth the *h* knoweth...... Rom 8:27

deceive the *h* of the simple............ Rom 16:18
manifest the counsels of the *h*.......... 1Cor 4:5
earnest of the Spirit in our *h*............ 2Cor 1:22
are our epistle written in our *h*.......... 2Cor 3:2
of darkness, hath shined in our *h*........ 2Cor 4:6
that ye are in our *h* to die................ 2Cor 7:3
the Spirit of his Son into your *h*.......... Gal 4:6
may dwell in your *h* by faith............ Eph 3:17
and that he might comfort your *h*........ Eph 6:22
understanding, shall keep your *h*........ Phil 4:7
That their *h* might be comforted......... Col 2:2
the peace of God rule in your *h*.......... Col 3:15
with grace in your *h* to the Lord........ Col 3:16
your estate, and comfort your *h*.......... Col 4:8
men, but God, which trieth our *h*........ 1Th 2:4
h unblameable in holiness before.......... 1Th 3:13
Comfort your *h*, and stablish you........ 2Th 2:17
your *h* into the love of God............... 2Th 3:5
Harden not your *h*, as in the............ Heb 3:8
hear his voice, harden not your *h*........ Heb 3:15
hear his voice, harden not your *h*........ Heb 4:7
mind, and write them in their *h*.......... Heb 8:10
I will put my laws into their *h*............ Heb 10:16
having our *h* sprinkled from an.......... Heb 10:22
envying and strife in your *h*............. Jas 3:14
and purify your *h*, ye double............ Jas 4:8
ye have nourished your *h*, as in a........ Jas 5:5
ye also patient; stablish your *h*.......... Jas 5:8
sanctify the Lord God in your *h*.......... 1Pet 3:15
and the day star arise in your *h*......... 2Pet 1:19
and shall assure our *h* before him....... 1Jn 3:19
he which searcheth the reins and *h*...... Rev 2:23
put in their *h* to fulfil his will............ Rev 17:17

HEARTS'
them up unto their own *h* lust............ Ps 81:12

HEARTY
of a man's friend by *h* counsel........... Prov 27:9

HEAT
seedtime and harvest, and cold and *h*... Gen 8:22
the tent door in the *h* of the day......... Gen 18:1
what meaneth the *h* of this great........ Deut 29:24
and devoured with burning *h*............ Deut 32:24
Ammonites until the *h* of the day........ 1Sa 11:11
came about the *h* of the day to.......... 2Sa 4:5
him with clothes, but he gat no *h*........ 1Kin 1:1
that my lord the king may get *h*.......... 1Kin 1:2
h consume the snow waters................ Job 24:19
me, and my bones are burned with *h*.... Job 30:30
is nothing hid from the *h* thereof........ Ps 19:6
lie together, then they have *h*............ Eccl 4:11
shadow in the daytime from the *h*....... Is 4:6
place like a clear *h* upon herbs.......... Is 18:4
cloud of dew in the *h* of harvest......... Is 18:4
the storm, a shadow from the *h*.......... Is 25:4
as the *h* in a dry place.................... Is 25:5
even the *h* with the shadow of a......... Is 25:5
neither shall the *h* nor sun smite........ Is 49:10
and shall not see when *h* cometh........ Jer 17:8
he cast out in the day to the *h*........... Jer 36:30
In their *h* I will make their............... Jer 51:39
bitterness, in the *h* of my spirit.......... Eze 3:14
commanded that they should *h* the...... Dan 3:19
borne the burden and *h* of the day....... Mt 20:12
blow, ye say, There will be *h*............. Lk 12:55
there came a viper out of the *h*.......... Acts 28:3
no sooner risen with a burning *h*........ Jas 1:11
shall melt with fervent *h*................. 2Pet 3:10
shall melt with fervent *h*................. 2Pet 3:12
the sun light on them, nor any *h*......... Rev 7:16
And men were scorched with great *h*.... Rev 16:9

HEATED
more than it was wont to be *h*........... Dan 3:19
as an oven *h* by the baker, who......... Hos 7:4

HEATH
shall be like the *h* in the desert......... Jer 17:6
be like the *h* in the wilderness.......... Jer 48:6

HEATHEN
shall be of the *h* that are round......... Lev 25:44
And I will scatter you among the *h*...... Lev 26:33
And ye shall perish among the *h*........ Lev 26:38
of Egypt in the sight of the *h*........... Lev 26:45
be left few in number among the *h*...... Deut 4:27
hast kept me to be head of the *h*........ 2Sa 22:44
unto thee, O LORD, among the *h*......... 2Sa 22:50
to the abominations of the *h*............. 2Kin 16:3
walked in the statutes of the *h*.......... 2Kin 17:8
as did the *h* whom the LORD.............. 2Kin 17:11
went after the *h* that were round........ 2Kin 17:15
after the abominations of the *h*.......... 2Kin 21:2
Declare his glory among the *h*.......... 1Chr 16:24
and deliver us from the *h*................ 1Chr 16:35
over all the kingdoms of the *h*.......... 2Chr 20:6
the *h* whom the LORD had cast out...... 2Chr 28:3
unto the abominations of the *h*.......... 2Chr 33:2
to err, and to do worse than the *h*...... 2Chr 33:9
all the abominations of the *h*............ 2Chr 36:14
filthiness of the *h* of the land........... Ezr 6:21
Jews, which were sold unto the *h*....... Neh 5:8
the reproach of the *h* our enemies...... Neh 5:9
among the *h* that are about us.......... Neh 5:17
It is reported among the *h*............... Neh 6:6
all the *h* that were about us saw........ Neh 6:16
Why do the *h* rage, and the people...... Ps 2:1
thee the *h* for thine inheritance........ Ps 2:8
Thou hast rebuked the *h*, thou.......... Ps 9:5
The *h* are sunk down in the pit.......... Ps 9:15
let the *h* be judged in thy sight.......... Ps 9:19

the *h* are perished out of his............ Ps 10:16
hast made me the head of the *h*......... Ps 18:43
unto thee, O LORD, among the *h*......... Ps 18:49
the counsel of the *h* to nought.......... Ps 33:10
drive out the *h* with thy hand........... Ps 44:2
and hast scattered us among the *h*...... Ps 44:11
makest us a byword among the *h*........ Ps 44:14
The *h* raged, the kingdoms were........ Ps 46:6
I will be exalted among the *h*............ Ps 46:10
God reigneth over the *h*.................. Ps 47:8
Israel, awake to visit all the *h*........... Ps 59:5
shalt have all the *h* in derision.......... Ps 59:8
He cast out the *h* also before............ Ps 78:55
the *h* are come into thine............... Ps 79:1
the *h* that have not known thee......... Ps 79:6
Wherefore should the *h* say.............. Ps 79:10
let him be known among the *h* in........ Ps 79:10
thou hast cast out the *h*, and........... Ps 80:8
He that chastiseth the *h*, shall.......... Ps 94:10
Declare his glory among the *h*.......... Ps 96:3
Say among the *h* that the LORD.......... Ps 96:10
shewed in the sight of the *h*............. Ps 98:2
So the *h* shall fear the name of......... Ps 102:15
And gave them the lands of the *h*....... Ps 105:44
But were mingled among the *h*.......... Ps 106:35
gave them into the hand of the *h*....... Ps 106:41
and gather us from among the *h*........ Ps 106:47
He shall judge among the *h*............. Ps 110:6
give them the heritage of the *h*......... Ps 111:6
Wherefore should the *h* say.............. Ps 115:2
then said they among the *h*.............. Ps 126:2
The idols of the *h* are silver............ Ps 135:15
To execute vengeance upon the *h*....... Ps 149:7
the lords of the *h* have broken.......... Is 16:8
scatter them also among the *h*.......... Jer 9:16
Learn not the way of the *h*.............. Jer 10:2
for the *h* are dismayed at them......... Jer 10:2
upon the *h* that know thee not.......... Jer 10:25
Ask ye now among the *h*, who hath..... Jer 18:13
an ambassador is sent unto the *h*....... Jer 49:14
will make thee small among the *h*....... Jer 49:15
she dwelleth among the *h*, she......... Lam 1:3
the *h* entered into her sanctuary....... Lam 1:10
wandered, they said among the *h*....... Lam 4:15
shadow we shall live among the *h*...... Lam 4:20
I will bring the worst of the *h*........... Eze 7:24
of the *h* that are round about you...... Eze 11:12
cast them far off among the *h*........... Eze 11:16
among the *h* whither they come......... Eze 12:16
forth among the *h* for thy beauty....... Eze 16:14
not be polluted before the *h*............. Eze 20:9
not be polluted before the *h*............. Eze 20:14
be polluted in the sight of the *h*........ Eze 20:22
I would scatter them among the *h*...... Eze 20:23
that ye say, We will be as the *h*......... Eze 20:32
be sanctified in you before the *h*....... Eze 20:41
I made thee a reproach unto the *h*...... Eze 22:4
I will scatter thee among the *h*.......... Eze 22:15
in thyself in the sight of the *h*.......... Eze 22:16
hast gone a whoring after the *h*......... Eze 23:30
deliver thee for a spoil to the *h*......... Eze 25:7
of Judah is like unto all the *h*.......... Eze 25:8
the *h* in the sight of the *h*............. Eze 25:15
it shall be the time of the *h*............. Eze 30:3
hand of the mighty one of the *h*......... Eze 31:11
his shadow in the midst of the *h*........ Eze 31:17
shall no more be a prey to the *h*........ Eze 34:28
bear the shame of the *h* any more....... Eze 34:29
unto the residue of the *h*................ Eze 36:3
of the *h* that are round about........... Eze 36:4
against the residue of the *h*............. Eze 36:5
ye have borne the shame of the *h*....... Eze 36:6
Surely the *h* that are about you,........ Eze 36:7
thee the shame of the *h* any more....... Eze 36:15
And I scattered them among the *h*...... Eze 36:19
And when they entered unto the *h*...... Eze 36:20
Israel had profaned among the *h*....... Eze 36:21
ye have profaned among the *h*.......... Eze 36:22
which was profaned among the *h*....... Eze 36:23
the *h* shall know that I am the........... Eze 36:23
I will take you from among the *h*........ Eze 36:24
reproach of famine among the *h*........ Eze 36:30
Then the *h* that are left round.......... Eze 36:36
of Israel from among the *h*.............. Eze 37:21
the *h* shall know that I the LORD........ Eze 37:28
that the *h* may know me, when I........ Eze 38:16
the *h* shall know that I am the........... Eze 39:7
I will set my glory among the *h*......... Eze 39:21
all the *h* shall see my judgment........ Eze 39:21
the *h* shall know that the house......... Eze 39:23
be led into captivity among the *h*....... Eze 39:28
that the *h* should rule over them........ Joel 2:17
make you a reproach among the *h*...... Joel 2:19
yourselves, and come, all ye *h*......... Joel 3:11
Let the *h* be wakened, and come up.... Joel 3:12
to judge all the *h* round about.......... Joel 3:12
remnant of Edom, and all the *h*......... Amos 9:12
an ambassador is sent among the *h*.... Obad 1
have made thee small among the *h*..... Obad 2
the LORD is near upon all the *h*......... Obad 15
so shall all the *h* drink.................. Obad 16
in anger and fury upon the *h*........... Mic 5:15
Behold ye among the *h*, and regard..... Hab 1:5
thou didst thresh the *h* in anger....... Hab 3:12
even all the isles of the *h*............... Zeph 2:11
strength of the kingdoms of the *h*...... Hag 2:22
with the *h* that are at ease.............. Zec 1:15
as ye were a curse among the *h*........ Zec 8:13
he shall speak peace unto the *h*........ Zec 9:10
the wealth of all the *h* round............ Zec 14:14

the LORD will smite the *h* that.......... Zec 14:18
name shall be great among the *h*....... Mal 1:11
my name is dreadful among the *h*...... Mal 1:14
not vain repetitions, as the *h* do........ Mt 6:7
let him be unto thee as an *h* man....... Mt 18:17
hast said, Why did the *h* rage........... Acts 4:25
countrymen, in perils by the *h*......... 2Cor 11:26
I might preach him among the *h*........ Gal 1:16
that we should go unto the *h*........... Gal 2:9
would justify the *h* through faith....... Gal 3:8

HEAVE
and the shoulder of the *h* offering....... Ex 29:27
for it is an *h* offering.................... Ex 29:28
it shall be an *h* offering from........... Ex 29:28
even their *h* offering unto the........... Ex 29:28
for an *h* offering unto the LORD......... Lev 7:14
h offering of the sacrifices of............ Lev 7:32
the *h* shoulder have I taken of.......... Lev 7:34
h shoulder shall ye eat in a............... Lev 10:14
The *h* shoulder and the wave breast.... Lev 10:15
the wave breast and *h* shoulder........ Num 6:20
ye shall offer up an *h* offering.......... Num 15:19
of your dough for an *h* offering......... Num 15:20
as ye do the *h* offering of the.......... Num 15:20
threshingfloor, so shall ye *h* it......... Num 15:20
an *h* offering in your generations...... Num 15:21
h offerings of all the hallowed.......... Num 18:8
the *h* offering of their gift............. Num 18:11
All the *h* offerings of the holy......... Num 18:19
as an *h* offering unto the LORD......... Num 18:24
then ye shall offer up an *h*............. Num 18:26
this your *h* offering shall be.......... Num 18:27
Thus ye also shall offer an *h*........... Num 18:28
h offering to Aaron the priest........... Num 18:28
every *h* offering of the LORD............ Num 18:29
for an *h* offering of the LORD........... Num 31:29
which was the LORD's *h* offering...... Num 31:41
h offerings of your hand, and your...... Deut 12:6
the *h* offering of thine hand............ Deut 12:11
or *h* offering of thine hand............. Deut 12:17

HEAVED
which is waved, and which is *h* up...... Ex 29:27
When ye have *h* the best thereof....... Num 18:30
When ye have *h* from it the best........ Num 18:32

HEAVEN See PREFACE.
the beginning God created the *h*........ Gen 1:1
And God called the firmament *H*........ Gen 1:8
of God, and this is the gate of *h*........ Gen 28:17
I have talked with you from *h*........... Ex 20:22
Behold, the *h* and the *h* of............. Deut 10:14
for the precious things of *h*............. Deut 33:13
behold, the *h* and of........................ 1Kin 8:27
the LORD would make windows in *h*... 2Kin 7:2
then will I hear from *h*, and will....... 2Chr 7:14
and he waketh in the circuit of *h*...... Job 22:14
Whom have I in *h* but thee............. Ps 73:25
For who in the *h* can be compared..... Ps 89:6
For as the *h* is high above the.......... Ps 103:11
The *h*, even the heavens, are the...... Ps 115:16
time to every purpose under the *h*..... Eccl 3:1
for God is in *h*, and thou upon......... Eccl 5:2
meted out *h* with the span, and........ Is 40:12
The *h* is my throne, and the earth...... Is 66:1
Do not I fill *h* and earth................. Jer 23:24
If *h* above can be measured, and....... Jer 31:37
out the *h* by his understanding........ Jer 51:15
put thee out, I will cover the *h*......... Eze 32:7
to his will in the army of *h*............. Dan 4:35
of man came with the clouds of *h*...... Dan 7:13
Therefore the *h* over you is............ Hag 1:10
not open you the windows of *h*........ Mal 3:10
for the kingdom of *h* is at hand........ Mt 3:2
for great is your reward in *h*........... Mt 5:12
For verily I say unto you, Till *h*........ Mt 5:18
Swear not at all; neither by *h*.......... Mt 5:34
Our Father which art in *h*................ Mt 6:9
thee the keys of the kingdom of *h*..... Mt 16:19
the sign of the Son of man in *h*........ Mt 24:30
H and earth shall pass away, but........ Mt 24:35
and coming in the clouds of *h*.......... Mt 26:64
earth to the uttermost part of *h*....... Mk 13:27
the *h* was opened, and the............. Mk 14:62
and praying, the *h* was opened........ Lk 3:21
Father, I have sinned against *h*........ Lk 15:18
Hereafter ye shall see *h* open.......... Jn 1:51
He gave them bread from *h* to eat..... Jn 6:31
Whom the *h* must receive until the.... Acts 3:21
name under *h* given among men....... Acts 4:12
H is my throne, and earth is my......... Acts 7:49
from *h* against all ungodliness........ Rom 1:18
whether in *h* or in earth, (as.......... 1Cor 8:5
the second man is the Lord from *h*.... 1Cor 15:47
an one caught up to the third *h*........ 2Cor 12:2
Of whom the whole family in *h*........ Eph 3:15
knee should bow, of things in *h*....... Phil 2:10
all things created, that are in *h*....... Col 1:16
firstborn, which are written in *h*...... Heb 12:23
are three that bear record in *h*........ 1Jn 5:7
behold, a door was opened in *h*....... Rev 4:1
there was silence in *h* about the...... Rev 8:1
the temple of God was opened in *h*.... Rev 11:19
appeared a great wonder in *h*......... Rev 12:1
for the first *h* and the first............. Rev 21:1

HEAVENLY
your *h* Father will also forgive......... Mt 6:14
yet your *h* Father feedeth them........ Mt 6:26
for your *h* Father knoweth that........ Mt 6:32
which my *h* Father hath not........... Mt 15:13

So likewise shall my *h* Father do....... Mt 18:35
of the *h* host praising God .... Lk 2:13
how much more shall your *h* Father..... Lk 11:13
if I tell you of *h* things .... Jn 3:12
not disobedient unto the *h* vision .... Acts 26:19
and as is the *h*, such are they 1Cor 15:48
such are they also that are *h*................ 1Cor 15:48
also bear the image of the *h*................. 1Cor 15:49
blessings in *h* places in Christ .... Eph 1:3
own right hand in the *h* places .... Eph 1:20
in *h* places in Christ Jesus .... Eph 2:6
powers in *h* places might be known..... Eph 3:10
preserve me unto his *h* kingdom......... 2Ti 4:18
partakers of the *h* calling .... Heb 3:1
and have tasted of the *h* gift .... Heb 6:4
the example and shadow of *h* things ... Heb 8:5
but the *h* things themselves with .... Heb 9:23
a better country, that is, an *h*.............. Heb 11:16
the *h* Jerusalem, and to an .... Heb 12:22

HEAVEN'S

eunuchs for the kingdom of *h* sake ..... Mt 19:12

HEAVENS

Thus the *h* and the earth were .... Gen 2:1
are the generations of the *h* .... Gen 2:4
LORD God made the earth and the *h* ..... Gen 2:4
the heaven of *h* is the LORD's th'y .... Deut 10:14
Give ear, O ye *h*, and I will speak........ Deut 32:1
also his *h* shall drop down dew .... Deut 33:28
the *h* dropped, the clouds also .... Judg 5:4
He bowed the *h* also, and came down... 2Sa 22:10
heaven of *h* cannot contain thee........... 1Kin 8:27
but the LORD made the *h* 1Chr 16:26
Let the *h* be glad, and let the 1Chr 16:31
Israel like to the stars of the *h*............. 1Chr 27:23
heaven of *h* cannot contain him 2Chr 2:6
the heaven of *h* cannot contain 2Chr 6:18
Then hear thou from the *h*..................... 2Chr 6:25
Then hear thou from the *h*..................... 2Chr 6:33
hear thou from the *h* their prayer 2Chr 6:35
Then hear thou from the *h*..................... 2Chr 6:39
trespass is grown up unto the *h*............ Ezr 9:6
hast made heaven, the heaven of *h*...... Neh 9:6
Which alone spreadeth out the *h* .... Job 9:8
till the *h* be no more, they shall .... Job 14:12
the *h* are not clean in his sight .... Job 15:15
his excellency mount up to the *h* .... Job 20:6
spirit he hath garnished the *h* .... Job 26:13
Look unto the *h*, and see .... Job 35:5
that sitteth in the *h* shall laugh............ Ps 2:4
hast set thy glory above the *h*............... Ps 8:1
When I consider thy *h*, the work .... Ps 8:3
He bowed the *h* also, and came down... Ps 18:9
The LORD also thundered in the *h*......... Ps 18:13
He declare the glory of God .... Ps 19:1
word of the LORD were the *h* made....... Ps 33:6
Thy mercy, O LORD, is in the *h*............. Ps 36:5
He shall call to the *h* from above .... Ps 50:4
And the *h* shall declare his.................... Ps 50:6
thou exalted, O God, above the *h*.......... Ps 57:5
For thy mercy is great unto the *h*......... Ps 57:10
thou exalted, O God, above the *h*.......... Ps 57:11
rideth upon the *h* by his name JAH ...... Ps 68:4
the *h* also dropped at the...................... Ps 68:8
that rideth upon the *h* of *h* .... Ps 68:33
set their mouth against the *h* .... Ps 73:9
thou establish in the very *h* .... Ps 89:2
the *h* shall praise thy wonders, O .... Ps 89:5
The *h* are thine, the earth also.............. Ps 89:11
but the LORD made the *h*........................ Ps 96:5
Let the *h* rejoice, and let the .... Ps 96:11
The *h* declare his righteousness............ Ps 97:6
the *h* are the work of thy hands .... Ps 102:25
hath prepared his throne in the *h*......... Ps 103:19
out the *h* like a curtain .... Ps 104:2
thy mercy is great above the *h*............. Ps 108:4
thou exalted, O God, above the *h* .... Ps 108:5
nations, and his glory above the *h* .... Ps 113:4
But our God is in the *h* .... Ps 115:3
The heaven, even the *h*, are the........... Ps 115:16
O thou that dwellest in the *h*................ Ps 123:1
To him that by wisdom made the *h*...... Ps 136:5
Bow thy *h*, O LORD, and come down .... Ps 144:5
Praise ye the LORD from the *h*.............. Ps 148:1
Praise him, ye *h* of *h*.......................... Ps 148:4
and ye waters that be above the *h*........ Ps 148:4
hath he established the *h* .... Prov 3:19
When he prepared the *h*, I was............. Prov 8:27
Hear, O *h*, and give ear, O earth .... Is 1:2
is darkened in the *h* thereof................... Is 5:30
Therefore I will shake the *h* .... Is 13:13
the *h* shall be rolled together as .... Is 34:4
stretcheth out the *h* as a curtain .... Is 40:22
the LORD, he that created the *h*............ Is 42:5
Sing, O ye *h*... Is 44:23
that stretcheth forth the *h* alone .... Is 44:24
Drop down, ye *h*, from above, and....... Is 45:8
hands, have stretched out the *h* .... Is 45:12
saith the LORD that created the *h*......... Is 48:13
my right hand hath spanned the *h* .... Is 48:13
Sing, O *h*.. Is 49:13
I clothe the *h* with blackness, and........ Is 50:3
Lift up your eyes to the *h*...................... Is 51:6
for the *h* shall vanish away like............ Is 51:6
that hath stretched forth the *h*............. Is 51:13
mine hand, that I may plant the *h* .... Is 51:16
For as the *h* are higher than the .... Is 55:9
Oh that thou wouldest rend the *h*........ Is 64:1
For, behold, I create new *h*................... Is 65:17
For as the new *h* and the new earth .... Is 66:22

Be astonished, O ye *h*, at this............... Jer 2:12
and the *h*, and they had no light .... Jer 4:23
all the birds of the *h* were fled .... Jer 4:25
mourn, and the *h* above be black......... Jer 4:28
both the fowl of the *h* and the............. Jer 9:10
The gods that have not made the *h*..... Jer 10:11
the earth, and from under these *h* .... Jer 10:11
out the *h* by his discretion.................... Jer 10:12
is a multitude of waters in the *h* .... Jer 10:13
or can the *h* give showers.................... Jer 14:22
is a multitude of waters in the *h*......... Jer 51:16
with our hands unto God in the *h* .... Lam 3:41
from under the *h* of the LORD.............. Lam 3:66
that the *h* were opened, and I saw ...... Eze 1:1
have known that the *h* do rule .... Dan 4:26
saith the LORD, I will hear the *h* .... Hos 2:21
the *h* shall tremble .... Joel 2:10
And I will shew wonders in the *h*........ Joel 2:30
and the *h* and the earth shall shake..... Joel 3:16
His glory covered the *h*, and the .... Hab 3:3
while, and I will shake the *h* .... Hag 2:6
Judah, saying, I will shake the *h*......... Hag 2:21
are the four spirits of the *h* .... Zec 6:5
the *h* shall give their dew.................... Zec 8:12
which stretcheth forth the *h* .... Zec 12:1
the *h* were opened unto him, and he ... Mt 3:16
powers of the *h* shall be shaken.......... Mt 24:29
of the water, he saw the *h* opened ...... Mk 1:10
in the *h* that faileth not........................ Lk 12:33
David is not ascended into the *h*......... Acts 2:34
said, Behold, I see the *h* opened......... Acts 7:56
made with hands, eternal in the *h* 2Cor 5:1
that ascended up far above all *h* .... Eph 4:10
the *h* are the works of thine............... Heb 1:10
priest, that is passed into the *h* .... Heb 4:14
and made higher than the *h* .... Heb 7:26
throne of the Majesty in the *h* .... Heb 8:1
h should be purified with these.......... Heb 9:23
the word of God the *h* were of old 2Pet 3:5
But the *h* and the earth, which are 2Pet 3:7
in the which the *h* shall pass 2Pet 3:10
wherein the *h* being on fire shall 2Pet 3:12
to his promise, look for new *h*............ 2Pet 3:13
Therefore rejoice, ye *h*, and ye.......... Rev 12:12

HEAVIER

For now it would be *h* than the .... Job 6:3
my stroke is *h* than my groaning .... Job 23:2
fool's wrath is *h* than them both.......... Prov 27:3

HEAVILY

wheels, that they drave them *h*........... Ex 14:25
I bowed down *h*, as one that .... Ps 35:14
hast thou very *h* laid thy yoke............ Is 47:6

HEAVINESS

sacrifice I arose up from my *h* .... Ezr 9:5
complaint, I will leave off my *h*.......... Job 9:27
and I am full of *h*.................................. Ps 69:20
My soul melteth for *h*.......................... Ps 119:28
son is the *h* of his mother.................... Prov 10:1
H in the heart of man maketh it .... Prov 12:25
and the end of that mirth is *h* .... Prov 14:13
Ariel, and there shall be *h* .... Is 29:2
of praise for the spirit of *h*.................. Is 61:3
That I have great *h* and continual........ Rom 9:2
would not come again to you in *h* 2Cor 2:1
after you all, and was full of *h*............ Phil 2:26
to mourning, and your joy to *h* .... Jas 4:9
ye are in *h* through manifold............... 1Pet 1:6

HEAVY

But Moses' hands were *h* .... Ex 17:12
for this thing is too *h* for thee .... Ex 18:18
alone, because it is too *h* for me .... Num 11:14
for he was an old man, and *h*.............. 1Sa 4:18
LORD was *h* upon them of Ashdod 1Sa 5:6
the hand of God was very *h* there 1Sa 5:11
because the hair was *h* on him 2Sa 14:26
his *h* yoke which he put upon us,....... 1Kin 12:4
Thy father made our yoke *h*................. 1Kin 12:10
father did lade you with a *h* yoke....... 1Kin 12:11
My father made your yoke *h*................ 1Kin 12:14
I am sent to thee with *h* tidings 1Kin 14:6
of Israel went to his house *h*............... 1Kin 20:43
And Ahab came into his house *h* 1Kin 21:4
his *h* yoke that he put upon us,.......... 2Chr 10:4
Thy father made our yoke *h* 2Chr 10:10
my father put a *h* yoke upon you....... 2Chr 10:11
My father made your yoke *h*............... 2Chr 10:14
bondage was *h* upon this people......... Neh 5:18
shall my hand be *h* upon thee............. Job 33:7
and night thy hand was *h* upon me..... Ps 32:4
as an *h* burden they are too *h*.......... Ps 38:4
burden they are too *h* for me .... Ps 38:4
that singeth songs to an *h* heart .... Prov 25:20
A stone is *h*, and the sand weighty..... Prov 27:3
unto those that be of *h* hearts .... Prov 31:6
people fat, and make their ears *h* .... Is 6:10
thereof shall be *h* upon it .... Is 24:20
anger, and the burden thereof is *h*...... Is 30:27
your carriages were *h* loaden............. Is 46:1
wickedness, to undo the *h* burdens..... Is 58:6
neither his ear *h*, that it cannot .... Is 59:1
he hath made my chain *h* .... Lam 3:7
are *h* laden, and I will give you.......... Mt 11:28
For they bind *h* burdens and .... Mt 23:4
began to be sorrowful and very *h*....... Mt 26:37
for their eyes were *h* .... Mt 26:43
were amazed, and to be very *h* .... Mk 14:33
again, (for their eyes were *h*............... Mk 14:40
were with him were *h* with sleep........ Lk 9:32

HEBER (*he'-bur*) See EBER, HEBER'S, HEBERITES.

1. A son of Beriah.

H, and Malchiel... Gen 46:17
of *H*, the family of the Heberites............. Num 26:45
H, and Malchiel, who is the father........... 1Chr 7:31
H begat Japhlet, and Shomer, and........... 1Chr 7:32
of Phalec, which was the son of *H*........... Lk 3:35

2. Husband of Jael.

Now *H* the Kenite, which was of .... Judg 4:11
of Jael the wife of *H* the Kenite .... Judg 4:17
and the house of *H* the Kenite................. Judg 4:17
Jael the wife of *H* the Kenite be .... Judg 5:24

3. A son of Ezra.

H the father of Socho, and....................... 1Chr 4:18

4. A son of Elpaal.

and Meshullam, and Hezeki, and *H*........ 1Chr 8:17

5. A head of a Gadite family.

and Jachan, and Zia, and *H*..................... 1Chr 5:13

6. A son of Shashak.

And Ishpan, and *H*, and Eliel, ... 1Chr 8:22

HEBERITES (*he'-bur-ites*) Descendants of Heber.

of Heber, the family of the *H*................... Num 26:45

HEBER'S (*he'-burs*) Refers to Heber 2.

Then Jael *H* wife took a nail of .... Judg 4:21

HEBREW (*he'-broo*) See HEBREWESS, HEBREWS.

1. Descendants of Jacob.

had escaped, and told Abram the *H*......... Gen 14:13
in an *H* unto us to mock us....................... Gen 39:14
The *H* servant, which thou hast .... Gen 39:17
there with us a young man, an *H*............. Gen 41:12
of Egypt spake to the *H* midwives........... Ex 1:15
of a midwife to the *H* women.................. Ex 1:16
Because the *H* women are not as .... Ex 1:19
to thee a nurse of the *H* women .... Ex 2:7
he spied an Egyptian smiting an *H* .... Ex 2:11
If thou buy an *H* servant, six .... Ex 21:2
an *H* man, or an *H* woman, be .... Deut 15:12
being an *H* or an Hebrewess, go .... Jer 34:9
ye go every man his brother an *H*........... Jer 34:14
And he said unto them, I am an *H*........... Jonah 1:9
of Benjamin, an *H* of the Hebrews .... Phil 3:5

2. A language.

letters of Greek, and Latin, and *H* .... Lk 23:38
called in the *H* tongue Bethesda............. Jn 5:2
called the Pavement, but in the *H* .... Jn 19:13
which is called in the *H* Golgotha........... Jn 19:17
and it was written in *H*, and Greek,........ Jn 19:20
spake unto them in the *H* tongue............ Acts 21:40
he spake in the *H* tongue to them........... Acts 22:2
me, and saying in the *H* tongue .... Acts 26:14
name in the *H* tongue is Abaddon........... Rev 9:11
called in the *H* tongue Armageddon........ Rev 16:16

HEBREWESS (*he'-broo-ess*)

being an Hebrew or an *H*, go free.......... Jer 34:9

HEBREWS (*he'-brooz*) See HEBREWS'.

away out of the land of the *H* .... Gen 40:15
might not eat bread with the *H*................ Gen 43:32
two men of the *H* strove together .... Ex 2:13
God of the *H* hath met with us .... Ex 3:18
The God of the *H* hath met with us.......... Ex 5:3
The LORD God of the *H* hath sent........... Ex 7:16
Thus saith the LORD God of the *H*.......... Ex 9:1
Thus saith the LORD God of the *H*.......... Ex 9:13
Thus saith the LORD God of the *H*.......... Ex 10:3
great shout in the camp of the *H* 1Sa 4:6
be not servants unto the *H* 1Sa 4:9
the land, saying, Let the *H* hear 1Sa 13:3
some of the *H* went over Jordan to 1Sa 13:7
Lest the *H* make them swords or............. 1Sa 13:19
the *H* come forth out of the holes........... 1Sa 14:11
Moreover the *H* that were with the......... 1Sa 14:21
Philistines, What do these *H* here 1Sa 29:3
of the Grecians against the *H*.................. Acts 6:1
Are they *H*.. 2Cor 11:22
of Benjamin, an Hebrew of the *H*........... Phil 3:5
Written to the *H* from Italy by .... Heb s

HEBREWS' (*he'-brooz*)

This is one of the *H* children................... Ex 2:6

HEBRON (*he'-brun*) See HEBRONITES.

1. A city in Asher.

And *H*, and Rehob.................................... Josh 19:28

2. A city in Judah.

the plain of Mamre, which is in *H*.......... Gen 13:18
the same is *H* in the land of.................... Gen 23:2
the same is *H* in the land of.................... Gen 23:19
the city of Arbah, which is *H*.................. Gen 35:27
he sent him out of the vale of *H*.............. Gen 37:14
by the south, and came unto *H*............... Num 13:22
(Now *H* was built seven years................ Num 13:22
sent unto Hoham king of *H*..................... Josh 10:3
king of Jerusalem, the king of *H*............ Josh 10:5
king of Jerusalem, the king of *H*............ Josh 10:23
and all Israel with him, unto *H*.............. Josh 10:36
as he had done to *H*, so he did to.......... Josh 10:39
from the mountains, from *H*.................... Josh 11:21
the king of *H*, one........................... Josh 12:10
of Jephunneh *H* for an inheritance .... Josh 14:13
H therefore became the.......................... Josh 14:14
And the name of *H* before was .... Josh 14:15
father of Anak, which city is *H*.............. Josh 15:13
and Kirjath-arba, which is *H* .... Josh 15:54
and Kirjath-arba, which is *H*.................. Josh 20:7
father of Anak, which city is *H*.............. Josh 21:11
the priest *H* with her suburbs................ Josh 21:13

the Canaanites that dwelt in *H*............ Judg 1:10
(now the name of *H* before was............ Judg 1:10
they gave *H* unto Caleb, as Moses........ Judg 1:20
top of an hill that is before *H*............ Judg 16:3
And to them which were in *H*............. 1Sa 30:31
And he said, Unto *H*................... 2Sa 2:1
and they dwelt in the cities of *H*........ 2Sa 2:3
in *H* over the house of Judah was....... 2Sa 2:11
they came to *H* at break of day........ 2Sa 2:32
And unto David were sons born in *H*.... 2Sa 3:2
These were born to David in *H*.......... 2Sa 3:5
speak in the ears of David in *H*......... 2Sa 3:19
So Abner came to David to *H*........... 2Sa 3:20
but Abner was not with David in *H*...... 2Sa 3:22
and when Abner was returned to *H*...... 2Sa 3:27
And they buried Abner in *H*............. 2Sa 3:32
heard that Abner was dead in *H*......... 2Sa 4:1
of Ish-bosheth unto David in *H*......... 2Sa 4:8
hanged them up over the pool in *H*...... 2Sa 4:12
it in the sepulchre of Abner in *H*........ 2Sa 4:12
tribes of Israel to David unto *H*......... 2Sa 5:1
of Israel came to the king to *H*.......... 2Sa 5:3
with them in *H* before the LORD........ 2Sa 5:3
In *H* he reigned over Judah seven....... 2Sa 5:5
after he was come from *H*.............. 2Sa 5:13
I have vowed unto the LORD, in *H*....... 2Sa 15:7
So he arose, and went to *H*............. 2Sa 15:9
shall say, Absalom reigneth in *H*........ 2Sa 15:10
seven years reigned he in *H*............. 1Kin 2:11
which were born unto him in *H*......... 1Chr 3:1
Amram, Izhar, and *H*, and Uzziel........ 1Chr 6:2
they gave them *H* in the land of........ 1Chr 6:55
the cities of Judah, namely, *H*........... 1Chr 6:57
themselves to David unto *H*............ 1Chr 11:1
elders of Israel to the king to *H*......... 1Chr 11:3
with them in *H* before the LORD......... 1Chr 11:3
to the war, and came to David to *H*..... 1Chr 12:23
came with a perfect heart to *H*......... 1Chr 12:38
seven years reigned he in *H*............. 1Chr 29:27
And Zorah, and Aijalon, and *H*........... 2Chr 11:10
   3. A son of *Kohath*.
Amram, and Izhar, and *H*, and Uzziel.... Ex 6:18
Amram, and Izehar, *H*, and Uzziel....... Num 3:19
These six were born unto him in *H*...... 1Chr 3:4
were, Amram, and Izhar, and *H*.......... 1Chr 6:18
Amram, Izhar, *H*, and Uzziel, four....... 1Chr 23:12
Of the sons of *H*...................... 1Chr 23:19
And the sons of *H*..................... 1Chr 24:23
   4. A son of *Mareshah*.
Son of Mareshah the father of *H*........ 1Chr 2:42
And the sons of *H*..................... 1Chr 2:43
Of the sons of *H*...................... 1Chr 15:9

HEBRONITES (*he'-brun-ites*) *Descendants of
Hebron 3.*
and the family of the *H*, and the........ Num 3:27
the Libnites, the family of the *H*........ Num 26:58
the Izharites, the *H*, and the........... 1Chr 26:23
And of the *H*, Hashabiah and his........ 1Chr 26:30
Among the *H* was Jerijah the chief...... 1Chr 26:31
even among the *H*, according to the... 1Chr 26:31

HEDGE
Hast not thou made an *h* about him .... Job 1:10
slothful man is as an *h* of thorns........ Prov 15:19
and whoso breaketh an *h*, a serpent ... Eccl 10:8
I will take away the *h* thereof.......... Is 5:5
neither made up the *h* for the.......... Eze 13:5
them, that should make up the *h* ...... Eze 22:30
I will *h* up thy way with thorns,........ Hos 2:6
upright is sharper than a thorn *h* ...... Mic 7:4
set an *h* about it, and digged a......... Mk 12:1

HEDGED
way is hid, and whom God hath *h* in .... Job 3:23
He hath *h* me about, that I cannot ...... Lam 3:7
it round about, and digged a............ Mt 21:33

HEDGES
that dwelt among plants and *h*......... 1Chr 4:23
hast thou then broken down her *h* ..... Ps 80:12
Thou hast broken down all his *h*........ Ps 89:40
lament, and run to and fro by the *h*..... Jer 49:3
camp in the *h* in the cold day.......... Nah 3:17
Go out into the highways and *h*........ Lk 14:23

HEED
Take *h* that thou speak not to.......... Gen 31:24
Take thou *h* that thou speak not....... Gen 31:29
take *h* to thyself, see my face no....... Ex 10:28
Take *h* to yourselves, that ye go....... Ex 19:12
Take *h* to thyself, lest thou make...... Ex 34:12
Must I not take *h* to speak that........ Num 23:12
take ye good *h* unto yourselves .... Deut 2:4
Only take *h* to thyself, and keep....... Deut 4:9
therefore good *h* unto yourselves ..... Deut 4:15
Take *h* unto yourselves, lest ye .... Deut 4:23
Take *h* to yourselves, that your .... Deut 11:16
Take *h* to thyself that thou offer...... Deut 12:13
Take *h* to thyself that thou.......... Deut 12:19
Take *h* to thyself that thou be........ Deut 12:30
Take *h* in the plague of leprosy,....... Deut 24:8
unto all Israel, saying, Take *h*......... Deut 27:9
But take diligent *h* to do the.......... Josh 22:5
Take good *h* therefore unto........... Josh 23:11
take *h* to thyself until the............ 1Sa 19:2
But Amasa took no *h* to the sword 2Sa 20:10
thy children take *h* to their way....... 1Kin 2:4
thy children take *h* to their way....... 1Kin 8:25
But Jehu took no *h* to walk in the..... 2Kin 10:31
if thou takest *h* to fulfil the.......... 1Chr 22:13
Take *h* now;........................ 1Chr 28:10
yet so that thy children take *h*........ 2Chr 19:6

to the judges, Take *h* what ye do....... 2Chr 19:6
take *h* and do it...................... 2Chr 19:7
so that they will take *h* to do......... 2Chr 33:8
Take *h* now that ye fail not to do..... 2Chr 33:8
Take *h*, regard not iniquity........... Job 36:21
I said, I will take *h* to my ways........ Ps 39:1
by taking *h* thereto according to ..... Ps 119:9
doer giveth *h* to false lips............ Prov 17:4
Also take no *h* unto all words......... Eccl 7:21
yea, he gave good *h*, and sought ..... Eccl 12:9
And say unto him, Take *h*, and be .... Is 7:4
hearkened diligently with much *h*..... Is 21:7
Take ye *h* every one of his............ Jer 9:4
Take *h* to yourselves, and bear no .... Jer 17:21
let us not give *h* to any of his........ Jer 18:18
Give *h* to me, O LORD, and hearken ... Jer 18:19
left off to take *h* to the LORD......... Hos 4:10
Therefore take *h* to your spirit........ Mal 2:15
therefore take *h* to your spirit........ Mal 2:16
Take *h* that ye do not your alms....... Mt 6:1
Then Jesus said unto them, Take *h* ... Mt 16:6
Take *h* that ye despise not one of .... Mt 18:10
Take *h* that no man deceive you ...... Mt 24:4
unto them, Take *h* what ye hear ...... Mk 4:24
he charged them, saying, Take *h* ..... Mk 8:15
Take *h*, lest any man deceive you..... Mk 13:5
But take *h* to yourselves............. Mk 13:9
But take ye *h*........................ Mk 13:23
Take ye *h*, watch and pray........... Mk 13:33
Take *h* therefore how ye hear........ Lk 8:18
Take *h* therefore that the light....... Lk 11:35
And he said unto them, Take *h* ...... Lk 12:15
Take *h* to yourselves................ Lk 17:3
Take *h* that ye be not deceived....... Lk 21:8
take *h* to yourselves, lest at any ..... Lk 21:34
he gave it unto them, expecting to..... Acts 3:5
take *h* to yourselves what ye........ Acts 5:35
h unto those things which Philip...... Acts 8:6
To whom they all gave *h*, from the ... Acts 8:10
Take *h* therefore unto yourselves,..... Acts 20:28
saying, Take *h* what thou doest...... Acts 23:26
take *h* lest he also spare not......... Rom 11:21
But let every man take *h* how he..... 1Cor 3:10
But take *h* lest by any means this 1Cor 8:9
he standeth take *h* lest he fall....... 1Cor 10:12
take *h* that ye be not consumed...... Gal 5:15
Take *h* to the ministry which thou ... Col 4:17
Neither give *h* to fables and......... 1Ti 1:4
giving *h* to seducing spirits, and..... 1Ti 4:1
Take *h* unto thyself, and unto the ... 1Ti 4:16
Not giving *h* to Jewish fables, and ... Titus 1:14
h to the things which we have....... Heb 2:1
Take *h*, brethren, lest there be....... Heb 3:12
ye do well that ye take *h*............ 2Pet 1:19

the *h* in the breadth was five.......... Ex 38:18
or on the *h* of his stature............ 1Sa 16:7
whose *h* was six cubits and a span 1Sa 17:4
the *h* thereof thirty cubits........... 1Kin 6:2
and twenty cubits in the *h* thereof 1Kin 6:20
The *h* of the one cherub was ten...... 1Kin 6:26
the *h* thereof thirty cubits, upon 1Kin 7:2
the *h* of the one chapter was 1Kin 7:16
the *h* of the other chapter was....... 1Kin 7:16
about, and his *h* was five cubits...... 1Kin 7:23
and three cubits the *h* of............ 1Kin 7:27
the *h* of a wheel was a cubit and 1Kin 7:32
come up to the *h* of the mountains ... 2Kin 19:23
The *h* of the one pillar was.......... 2Kin 25:17
the *h* of the chapiter three......... 2Kin 25:17
the *h* was an hundred and twenty 2Chr 3:4
and ten cubits the *h* thereof......... 2Chr 4:2
and five cubits the *h* thereof........ 2Chr 4:2
and raised it up a very great *h* 2Chr 33:14
the *h* thereof threescore cubits,...... Ezr 6:3
Is not God in the *h* of heaven........ Job 22:12
behold the *h* of the stars, how...... Job 22:12
down from the *h* of his sanctuary ... Ps 102:19
The heaven for *h*, and the earth..... Prov 25:3
in the depth, or in the *h* above...... Is 7:11
come up to the *h* of the mountains .. Is 37:24
enter into the *h* of his border....... Is 37:24
come and sing in the *h* of Zion...... Jer 31:12
that holdest the *h* of the hill....... Jer 49:16
fortify the *h* of her strength........ Jer 51:53
the *h* of one chapter was eighteen ... Jer 52:22
In the mountain of the *h* of......... Jer 17:23
the appeared in her *h* with the....... Eze 19:11
the mountain of the *h* of Israel...... Eze 20:40
Therefore his *h* was exalted above ... Eze 31:5
thou hast lifted up thyself in *h* ...... Eze 31:10
his heart is lifted up in his *h*........ Eze 31:10
exalt themselves for their *h* .... Eze 31:14
their trees stand up in their *h* ...... Eze 31:14
and the valleys with thy *h*.......... Eze 32:5
and the *h*, one reed.................. Eze 40:5
I saw also the *h* of the house........ Eze 41:8
whose *h* was threescore cubits, and .. Dan 3:1
earth, and the *h* thereof was great ... Dan 4:10
the *h* thereof reached unto heaven .. Dan 4:11
whose *h* reached unto the heaven,.... Dan 4:20
whose *h* was like the *h* of......... Amos 2:9
was like the *h* of the cedars......... Amos 2:9
Nor *h*, nor depth, nor any other...... Rom 8:39
and length, and depth, and *h*........ Eph 3:18
breadth and the *h* of it are equal ..... Rev 21:16

HEIGHTS

praise him in the *h*................... Ps 148:1
ascend above the *h* of the clouds ...... Is 14:14

HEINOUS

For this is an *h* crime................. Job 31:11

HEIR

one born in my house is mine *h*........ Gen 15:3
saying, This shall not be thine *h*....... Gen 15:4
thine own bowels shall be thine *h*..... Gen 15:4
shall not be *h* with my son........... Gen 21:10
and we will destroy the *h* also........ 2Sa 14:7
that is *h* to her mistress............. Prov 30:23
hath he no *h*?....................... Jer 49:1
then shall Israel be *h* unto them...... Jer 49:2
Yet will I bring an *h* unto thee........ Mic 1:15
among themselves, This is the *h*..... Mt 21:38
among themselves, This is the *h*..... Mk 12:7
themselves, saying, This is the *h* .... Lk 20:14
he should be the *h* of the world...... Rom 4:13
Now I say, That the *h*, as long as..... Gal 4:1
then an *h* of God through Christ...... Gal 4:7
of the bondwoman shall not be *h*..... Gal 4:30
he hath appointed *h* of all things...... Heb 1:2
became *h* of the righteousness....... Heb 11:7

HEIRS

be heir unto them that were his *h* ..... Jer 49:2
if they which are of the law be *h*...... Rom 4:14
And if children, then *h*.............. Rom 8:17
of God, and joint-heirs with.......... Rom 8:17
h according to the promise......... Gal 3:29
we should be made *h* according to ... Titus 3:7
them who shall be *h* of salvation...... Heb 1:14
abundantly to shew unto the *h* of.... Heb 6:17
the *h* with him of the same......... Heb 11:9
h of the kingdom which he hath...... Jas 2:5
as being *h* together of the grace...... 1Pet 3:7

HELAH (*he'-lah*) A wife of Asher.
father of Tekoa had two wives, *H* 1Chr 4:5
And the sons of *H* were, Zereth, and ... 1Chr 4:7

HELAM (*he'-lam*) A place east of the Jordan.
and they came to *H*................. 2Sa 10:16
passed over Jordan, and came to *H* 2Sa 10:17

HELBAH (*hel'-bah*) A town in Asher.
of Ahlab, nor of Achzib, nor of *H*...... Judg 1:31

HELBON (*hel'-bon*) City near Damascus.
in the wine of *H*, and white wool...... Eze 27:18

HELD

man wondering at her *h* his peace.... Gen 24:21
Jacob *h* his peace until they were .... Gen 34:5
he *h* up his father's hand, to........ Gen 48:17
when Moses *h* up his hand, that..... Ex 17:11
the loops *h* one curtain to.......... Ex 36:12
And Aaron *h* his peace............. Lev 10:3

h his peace at her in the day	Num 30:7
h his peace at her, and disallowed	Num 30:11
because he *h* his peace at her to	Num 30:14
the lamps in their left hands,	Judg 7:20
the lad that *h* him by the hand	Judg 16:26
And when she *h* it, he measured six	Ruth 3:15
But he *h* his peace	1Sa 10:27
he *h* a feast in his house, like	1Sa 25:36
for Joab *h* back the people	2Sa 18:16
And at that time Solomon *h* a feast	1Kin 8:65
But the people *h* their peace	2Kin 18:36
and *h* three thousand baths	2Chr 4:5
half of them *h* both the spears	Neh 4:16
and with the other hand *h* a weapon	Neh 4:17
half of them *h* the spears from	Neh 4:21
Then *h* they their peace, and found	Neh 5:8
the king *h* out to Esther the	Est 5:2
I had *h* my tongue, although the	Est 7:4
Then the king *h* out the golden	Est 8:4
My foot hath *h* his steps, his way	Job 23:11
The nobles *h* their peace, and	Job 29:10
whose mouth must be *h* in with bit	Ps 32:9
I *h* my peace, even from good	Ps 39:2
thy mercy, O LORD, *h* me up	Ps 94:18
I *h* him, and would not let him go,	Song 3:4
the king is *h* in the galleries	Song 7:5
But they *h* their peace, and	Is 57:11
have not I *h* my peace even of old	Is 57:11
took them captives *h* them fast	Jer 50:33
when he *h* up his right hand and	Dan 12:7
h a council against him, how they	Mt 12:14
But Jesus *h* his peace	Mt 26:63
h him by the feet, and worshipped	Mt 28:9
But they *h* their peace	Mk 3:4
But they *h* their peace	Mk 9:34
But he *h* his peace, and answered	Mk 14:61
the morning the chief priests *h* a	Mk 15:1
And they *h* their peace	Lk 14:4
at his answer, and *h* their peace	Lk 20:26
the men that *h* Jesus mocked him,	Lk 22:63
lame man which *h* healed Peter	Acts 3:11
they *h* their peace, and glorified	Acts 11:18
part *h* with the Jews, and part	Acts 14:4
And after they had *h* their peace,	Acts 15:13
that being dead wherein we were *h*,	Rom 7:6
and for the testimony which they *h*,	Rev 6:9

HELDAI (hel'-dahee) See HELED, HELEM.
1. A sanctuary servant.
month was *H* the Netophathite | 1Chr 27:15
2. An honored exile.
them of the captivity, even of *H* | Zec 6:10

HELEB (he'-leb) See HELED. A 'mighty man' of David.
H the son of Baanah, a | 2Sa 23:29

HELECH See HELEK.

HELED (he'-led) See HELEB, HELDAI. Same as Heleb.
H the son of Baanah the | 1Chr 11:30

HELEK (he'-lek) See HELEKITES. A son of Gilead.
of *H*, the family of the Helekites | Num 26:30
Abiezer, and for the children of *H* | Josh 17:2

HELEKITES (he'-lek-ites) Descendants of Helek.
of Helek, the family of the | Num 26:30

HELEM (he'-lem)
1. A descendant of Asher.
And the sons of his brother *H* | 1Chr 7:35
2. Same as Heldai.
And the crowns shall be to *H* | Zec 6:14

HELEPH (he'-lef) A town in Naphtali.
Their coast was from *H* | Josh 19:33

HELEZ (he'-lez)
1. A 'mighty man' of David.
The Paltite, Ira the son of | 2Sa 23:26
the Paltite, *H* the Pelonite, | 1Chr 11:27
seventh month was *H* the Pelonite | 1Chr 27:10
2. A son of Azariah.
And Azariah begat *H*, and Helez | 1Chr 2:39
begat Helez, and *H* begat Eleasah, | 1Chr 2:39

HELI (he'-li) See ELI. Father of Joseph; ancestor of Jesus.
of Joseph, which was the son of *H* | Lk 3:23

HELKAI (hel'-kahee) A priest.
Adna; of Meraioth, *H* | Neh 12:15

HELKATH (hel'-kath) See HELKATH-HAZZURIM, HUKOK. A town in Asher.
And their border was *H*, and Hali, | Josh 19:25
H with her suburbs, and Rehob with | Josh 21:31

HELKATH-HAZZURIM (hel'-kath-haz'zu-rim) A plain near the pool of Gibeon.
wherefore that place was called *H* | 2Sa 2:16

HELL
and shall burn unto the lowest *h* | Deut 32:22
The sorrows of *h* compassed me | 2Sa 22:6
deeper than *h* | Job 11:8
H is naked before him, and | Job 26:6
The wicked shall be turned into *h* | Ps 9:17
thou wilt not leave my soul in *h* | Ps 16:10
The sorrows of *h* compassed me | Ps 18:5
and let them go down quick into *h* | Ps 55:15
my soul from the lowest *h* | Ps 86:13
the pains of *h* gat hold upon me | Ps 116:3

if I make my bed in *h*, behold,	Ps 139:8
her steps take hold on *h*	Prov 5:5
Her house is the way to *h*	Prov 7:27
her guests are in the depths of *h*	Prov 9:18
H and destruction are before thee	Prov 15:11
that he may depart from *h* beneath	Prov 15:24
and shalt deliver his soul from *h*	Prov 23:14
H and destruction are never full	Prov 27:20
Therefore *h* hath enlarged herself	Is 5:14
H from beneath is moved for thee	Is 14:9
thou shalt be brought down to *h*	Is 14:15
with *h* are we at agreement	Is 28:15
agreement with *h* shall not stand	Is 28:18
didst debase thyself even unto *h*	Is 57:9
when I cast him down to *h* with	Eze 31:16
They also went down into *h* with	Eze 31:17
of *h* with them that help him	Eze 32:21
which are gone down to *h* with,	Eze 32:27
Though they dig into *h*, thence	Amos 9:2
out of the belly of *h* I cried	Jonah 2:2
who enlargeth his desire as *h*	Hab 2:5
shall be in danger of *h* fire	Mt 5:22
whole body should be cast into *h*	Mt 5:29
whole body should be cast into *h*	Mt 5:30
to destroy both soul and body in *h*	Mt 10:28
shalt be brought down to *h*	Mt 11:23
the gates of *h* shall not prevail	Mt 16:18
two eyes to be cast into *h* fire	Mt 18:9
the child of *h* than yourselves	Mt 23:15
can ye escape the damnation of *h*	Mt 23:33
having two hands to go into *h*	Mk 9:43
having two feet to be cast into *h*	Mk 9:45
two eyes to be cast into *h* fire	Mk 9:47
killed hath power to cast into *h*	Lk 12:5
in *h* he lift up his eyes, being	Lk 16:23
thou wilt not leave my soul in *h*,	Acts 2:27
that his soul was not left in *h*	Acts 2:31
and it is set on fire of *h*	Jas 3:6
sinned, but cast them down into *h*	2Pet 2:4
and have the keys of *h* and of death	Rev 1:18
was Death, and *H* followed with him	Rev 6:8
h delivered up the dead which	Rev 20:13
h were cast into the lake of fire	Rev 20:14

HELLENISTS See GRECIANS.

HELM
turned about with a very small *h* | Jas 3:4

HELMET
he had an *h* of brass upon his | 1Sa 17:5
he put an *h* of brass upon his | 1Sa 17:38
an *h* of salvation upon his head | Is 59:17
and shield and *h* round about | Eze 23:24
hanged the shield and *h* in thee | Eze 27:10
all of them with shield and *h*, | Eze 38:5
take the *h* of salvation, and the | Eph 6:17
and for an *h*, the hope of | 1Th 5:8

HELMETS
the host shields, and spears, and *h* | 2Chr 26:14
and stand forth with your *h* | Jer 46:4

HELON (he'-lon) Father of Eliab.
Eliab the son of *H* | Num 1:9
Eliab the son of *H* shall be, | Num 2:7
the third day Eliab the son of *H*, | Num 7:24
offering of Eliab the son of *H* | Num 7:29
of Zebulun was Eliab the son of *H*. | Num 10:16

HELP
I will make him an *h* meet for him | Gen 2:18
was not found an *h* meet for him | Gen 2:20
of thy father, who shall *h* thee | Gen 49:25
of my father, said he, was mine *h*. | Ex 18:4
and wouldest forbear to *h* him | Ex 23:5
thou shalt surely *h* with him to | Ex 23:5
thou shalt surely *h* him to lift | Deut 22:4
h you, and be your protection | Deut 32:38
be thou an *h* to him from his, | Deut 33:7
rideth upon the heaven in thy *h*, | Deut 33:26
by the LORD, the shield of thy *h*, | Deut 33:29
mighty men of valour, and *h* them, | Josh 1:14
h me, that we may smite Gibeon | Josh 10:4
us quickly, and save us, and *h* us | Josh 10:6
of Gezer came up to *h* Lachish | Josh 10:33
came not to the *h* of the LORD | Judg 5:23
to the *h* of the LORD against the | Judg 5:23
the sun be hot, ye shall have *h* | 1Sa 11:9
for me, then thou shalt *h* me | 2Sa 10:11
thee, then I will come and *h* thee | 2Sa 10:11
So the Syrians feared to *h* the | 2Sa 10:19
and did obeisance, and said, *H* | 2Sa 14:4
cried a woman unto him, saying, *H* | 2Kin 6:26
h thee, whence shall I *h* thee | 2Kin 6:27
be come peaceably unto me to *h* me, | 1Chr 12:17
day there came to David to *h* him, | 1Chr 12:22
came to *h* Hadarezer king of Zobah. | 1Chr 18:5
for me, then thou shalt *h* me | 1Chr 19:12
for thee, then I will *h* thee. | 1Chr 19:12
neither would the Syrians *h* | 1Chr 19:19
of Israel to *h* Solomon his son. | 1Chr 22:17
it is nothing with thee to *h* | 2Chr 14:11
us, O LORD our God | 2Chr 14:11
Shouldest thou *h* the ungodly, | 2Chr 19:2
together, to ask *h* of the LORD. | 2Chr 20:4
then thou wilt hear and... | 2Chr 20:9
for God hath power to *h*, and to | 2Chr 25:8
to *h* the king against the enemy | 2Chr 26:13
the kings of Assyria to *h* him. | 2Chr 28:16
gods of the kings of Syria *h* them, | 2Chr 28:23
to them, that they may *h* me | 2Chr 28:23

brethren the Levites did *h* them	2Chr 29:34
and they did *h* him	2Chr 32:3
us is the LORD our God to *h* us	2Chr 32:8
of his place *h* him with silver	Ezr 1:4
horsemen to *h* us against the	Ezr 8:22
Is not my *h* in me	Job 6:13
neither will he *h* the evil doers.	Job 8:20
and him that had none to *h* him	Job 29:12
when I saw my *h* in the gate	Job 31:21
There is no *h* for him in God	Ps 3:2
H, LORD; for the godly	Ps 12:1
Send thee *h* from the sanctuary,	Ps 20:2
for there is none to *h*	Ps 22:11
O my strength, haste thee to *h* me.	Ps 22:19
thou hast been my *h*	Ps 27:9
he is our *h* and our shield	Ps 33:20
buckler, and stand up for mine *h*.	Ps 35:2
And the LORD shall *h* them, and	Ps 37:40
Make haste to *h* me, O Lord my	Ps 38:22
O LORD, make haste to *h* me.	Ps 40:13
thou art my *h* and my deliverer	Ps 40:17
him for the *h* of his countenance	Ps 42:5
Arise for our *h*, and redeem us for	Ps 44:26
a very present *h* in trouble	Ps 46:1
God shall *h* her, and that right.	Ps 46:5
awake to *h* me, and behold	Ps 59:4
Give us *h* from trouble	Ps 60:11
for vain is the *h* of man	Ps 60:11
Because thou hast been my *h*	Ps 63:7
make haste to me, O God	Ps 70:1
thou art my *h* and my deliverer	Ps 70:5
O my God, make haste for my *h*	Ps 71:12
H us, O God of our salvation, for	Ps 79:9
I have laid *h* upon one that is	Ps 89:19
Unless the LORD had been my *h*	Ps 94:17
fell down, and there was none to *h*.	Ps 107:12
Give us *h* from trouble	Ps 108:12
for vain is the *h* of man	Ps 108:12
H me, O LORD my God	Ps 109:26
he is their *h* and their shield	Ps 115:9
he is their *h* and their shield	Ps 115:10
he is their *h* and their shield	Ps 115:11
my part with them that *h* me	Ps 118:7
h thou me	Ps 119:86
Let thine hand *h* me	Ps 119:173
and let thy judgments *h* me	Ps 119:175
hills, from whence cometh my *h*.	Ps 121:1
My *h* cometh from the LORD, which	Ps 121:2
Our *h* is in the name of the LORD,	Ps 124:8
son of man, in whom there is no *h*.	Ps 146:3
hath the God of Jacob for his *h*	Ps 146:5
he hath not another to *h* him up	Eccl 4:10
to whom will ye flee for *h*	Is 10:3
whither we flee for *h* to be,	Is 20:6
nor be an *h* nor profit, but a	Is 30:5
For the Egyptians shall *h* in vain	Is 30:7
them that go down to Egypt for *h*,	Is 31:1
against the *h* of them that work,	Is 31:2
yea, I will *h* thee	Is 41:10
I will *h* thee	Is 41:13
I will *h* thee, saith the LORD, and	Is 41:14
from the womb, which will *h* thee	Is 44:2
For the Lord GOD will *h* me.	Is 50:7
Behold, the Lord GOD will *h* me.	Is 50:9
I looked, and there was none to *h*	Is 63:5
which is come forth to *h* you	Jer 37:7
of the enemy, and none did *h* her	Lam 1:7
eyes as yet failed for our vain *h*	Lam 4:17
all that are about him to *h* him	Eze 12:14
of hell with them that *h* him	Eze 32:21
the chief princes, came to *h* me,	Dan 10:13
shall be holpen with a little *h*	Dan 11:34
to his end, and none shall *h* him	Dan 11:45
but in me is thine *h*	Hos 13:9
him, saying, Lord, *h* me.	Mt 15:25
have compassion on us, and *h* us	Mk 9:22
h thou mine unbelief	Mk 9:24
that they should come and *h* them	Lk 5:7
bid her therefore that she *h* me	Lk 10:40
Come over into Macedonia, and *h* us.	Acts 16:9
Crying out, Men of Israel, *h*.	Acts 21:28
therefore obtained *h* of God	Acts 26:22
h those women which laboured with	Phil 4:3
find grace to *h* in time of need.	Heb 4:16

HELPED
h them, and married their flock | Ex 2:17
Hitherto hath the LORD *h* us | 1Sa 7:12
and they following Adonijah *h* him. | 1Kin 1:7
thirty and two kings that *h* him | 1Kin 20:16
they were *h* against them, and the | 1Chr 5:20
but they *h* them not | 1Chr 12:19
they *h* David against the band of... | 1Chr 12:21
when God *h* the Levites that bare | 1Chr 15:26
cried out, and the Lord *h* him. | 2Chr 18:31
every one *h* to destroy another | 2Chr 20:23
God *h* him against the Philistines | 2Chr 26:7
for he was marvellously *h*, | 2Chr 26:15
but he *h* him not | 2Chr 28:21
and Shabbethai the Levite *h* them, | Ezr 10:15
officers of the king, *h* the Jews | Est 9:3
How hast thou *h* him that is... | Job 26:2
heart trusted in him, and I am *h* | Ps 28:7
I was brought low, and he *h* me. | Ps 116:6
for thou hast *h* me | Ps 118:13
They *h* every one his neighbour | Is 41:6
a day of salvation have I *h* thee | Is 49:8
they *h* forward the affliction. | Zec 1:15
h them much which had believed, | Acts 18:27
And the earth *h* the woman, and the | Rev 12:16

HELPER

any left, nor any h for Israel	2Kin 14:26
my calamity, they have no h......	Job 30:13
thou art the h of the fatherless	Ps 10:14
LORD, be thou my h	Ps 30:10
Behold, God is mine h	Ps 54:4
poor also, and him that hath no h	Ps 72:12
Zidon every h that remaineth	Jer 47:4
our h in Christ, and Stachys my	Rom 16:9
may boldly say, The Lord is my h	Heb 13:6

HELPERS

the mighty men, h of the war	1Chr 12:1
unto thee, and peace be to thine h	1Chr 12:18
the proud h do stoop under him......	Job 9:13
when all her h shall be destroyed......	Eze 30:8
Put and Lubim were thy h	Nah 3:9
Aquila my h in Christ Jesus......	Rom 16:3
your faith, but are h of your joy......	2Cor 1:24

HELPETH

for thy God h thee	1Chr 12:18
hand, both he that h shall fall......	Is 31:3
the Spirit also h our infirmities......	Rom 8:26
and to every one that h with us......	1Cor 16:16

HELPING

were the prophets of God h them......	Ezr 5:2
why art thou so far from h me......	Ps 22:1
Ye also h together by prayer for......	2Cor 1:11

HELPS

they had taken up, they used h......	Acts 27:17
then gifts of healings, h......	1Cor 12:28

HELVE

and the head slippeth from the h......	Deut 19:5

HEM

beneath upon the h of it thou......	Ex 28:33
round about the h thereof......	Ex 28:33
upon the h of the robe round......	Ex 28:34
upon the h of the robe, round......	Ex 39:25
round about the h of the robe to......	Ex 39:26
touched the h of his garment......	Mt 9:20
only touch the h of his garment......	Mt 14:36

HEMAM (he´-mam) See HOMAM. A son of Lotan.

children of Lotan were Hori and H......	Gen 36:22

HEMAN (he´-man)
1. A son of Zerah.

than Ethan the Ezrahite, and H......	1Kin 4:31
Zimri, and Ethan, and H, and Calcol,......	1Chr 2:6
Of H: the sons of......	1Chr 25:4

2. A son of Joel.

H a singer, the son of Joel, the......	1Chr 6:33
appointed H the son of Joel......	1Chr 15:17
So the singers, H, Asaph, and......	1Chr 15:19
And with them H and Jeduthun, and......	1Chr 16:41
with them H and Jeduthun......	1Chr 16:42
of the sons of Asaph, and of H......	1Chr 25:1
All these were the sons of H the......	1Chr 25:5
God gave to H fourteen sons and......	1Chr 25:5
order to Asaph, Jeduthun, and H......	1Chr 25:6
all of them of Asaph, of H......	2Chr 5:12
And of the sons of H......	2Chr 29:14
of David, and Asaph, and H, and......	2Chr 35:15
Maschil of H the Ezrahite......	Ps 88:t

HEMATH (he´-math) See HAMATH.
1. Same as Hamath.

Egypt even unto the entering of H......	1Chr 13:5
in of H unto the river of the......	Amos 6:14
2. Father of the Kenites and Rechabites.
are the Kenites that came of H......	1Chr 2:55

HEMDAN (hem´-dan) See AMRAM. Son of Dishon.

H, and Eshban, and Ithran, and......	Gen 36:26

HEMLOCK

as h in the furrows of the field......	Hos 10:4
the fruit of righteousness into h......	Amos 6:12

HEMS

they made upon the h of the robe......	Ex 39:24

HEN (hen) A son of Zephaniah.

to H the son of Zephaniah, for a......	Zec 6:14
even as a h gathereth her......	Mt 23:37
as a h doth gather her brood......	Lk 13:34

HENA (he´-nah) A city on the Euphrates.

are the gods of Sepharvaim, H......	2Kin 18:34
of the city of Sepharvaim, of H......	2Kin 19:13
king of the city of Sepharvaim, H......	Is 37:13

HENADAD (hen´-a-dad) A Levite.

the sons of H, with their sons and......	Ezr 3:9
brethren, Bavai the son of H......	Neh 3:18
Binnui the son of H another piece......	Neh 3:24
Azaniah, Binnui of the sons of H......	Neh 10:9

HENCE

the man said, They are departed h......	Gen 37:17
Pharaoh ye shall not go forth h......	Gen 42:15
ye shall carry up my bones from h......	Gen 50:25
afterwards he will let you go h......	Ex 11:1
thrust you out h altogether......	Ex 11:1
carry up my bones away h with you......	Ex 13:19
unto Moses, Depart, and go up h......	Ex 33:1
go not with me, carry us not up h......	Ex 33:15
get thee down quickly from h......	Deut 9:12
Take you h out of the midst of......	Josh 4:3
Depart not h, I pray thee, until......	Judg 6:18

another field, neither go from h......	Ruth 2:8
Get thee h, and turn thee eastward......	1Kin 17:3
recover strength, before I go h......	Ps 39:13
shalt say unto it, Get thee h......	Is 30:22
Take from h thirty men with thee,......	Jer 38:10
and he said, Get you h, walk to and......	Zec 6:7
saith Jesus unto him, Get thee h......	Mt 4:10
Remove h to yonder place......	Mt 17:20
of God, cast thyself down from h......	Lk 4:9
him, Get thee out, and depart h......	Lk 13:31
would pass from h to you cannot......	Lk 16:26
sold doves, Take these things h......	Jn 2:16
therefore said unto them, Depart h......	Jn 7:3
Arise, let us go h......	Jn 14:31
but now is my kingdom not from h......	Jn 18:36
Sir, if thou have borne him h......	Jn 20:15
the Holy Ghost not many days h......	Acts 1:5
send thee far h unto the Gentiles......	Acts 22:21
come they not h, even of your......	Jas 4:1

HENCEFORTH

it shall not h yield unto thee......	Gen 4:12
must the children of Israel h......	Num 18:22
Ye shall h return no more that......	Deut 17:16
shalt h commit no more any such......	Deut 19:20
I also will not h drive out any......	Judg 2:21
for thy servant will h offer......	2Kin 5:17
therefore from h thou shalt have......	2Chr 16:9
his people from h even for ever......	Ps 125:2
Israel hope in the LORD from h......	Ps 131:3
with justice from h even for ever......	Is 9:7
for h there shall no more come......	Is 52:1
seed, saith the LORD, from h......	Is 59:21
thou shalt no more h bereave them......	Eze 36:12
over them in mount Zion from h......	Mic 4:7
unto you, Ye shall not see me h......	Mt 23:39
I will not drink h of this fruit......	Mt 26:29
from h all generations shall call......	Lk 1:48
from h thou shalt catch men......	Lk 5:10
For from h there shall be five in......	Lk 12:52
from h ye know him, and have seen......	Jn 14:7
H I call you not servants......	Jn 15:15
that they speak h to no man in......	Acts 4:17
from h I will go unto the......	Acts 18:6
that h we should not serve sin......	Rom 6:6
should not h live unto themselves......	2Cor 5:15
Wherefore h know we no man after......	2Cor 5:16
yet now h know we him no more......	2Cor 5:16
From h let no man trouble me......	Gal 6:17
That we h be no more children,......	Eph 4:14
that ye h walk not as other......	Eph 4:17
H there is laid up for me a crown......	2Ti 4:8
From h expecting till his enemies......	Heb 10:13
dead which die in the Lord from h......	Rev 14:13

HENCEFORWARD

and h among your generations......	Num 15:23
no fruit grow on thee h for ever......	Mt 21:19

HENNA See CAMPHIRE.

HENOCH (he´-nok) See ENOCH. Same as Enoch.

Enoch,	
H, Methuselah, Lamech,......	1Chr 1:3
Ephah, and Epher, and H, and......	1Chr 1:33

HEPHER (he´-fer) See GATH-HEPHER, HEPHERITES.
1. A son of Gilead.

and of H, the family of the......	Num 26:32
the son of H had no sons, but......	Num 26:33
of Zelophehad, the son of H......	Num 27:1
Shechem, and for the children of H......	Josh 17:2
But Zelophehad, the son of H......	Josh 17:3
2. A son of Naarah.
And Naarah bare him Ahuzam, and H......	1Chr 4:6
3. A mighty man of David.
the Mecherathite, Ahijah the......	1Chr 11:36
4. A Canaanite city.
the king of H, one......	Josh 12:17
Sochoh, and all the land of H......	1Kin 4:10

HEPHERITES (he´-fer-ites) Descendants of Hepher 1.

and of Hepher, the family of the H......	Num 26:32

HEPHZI-BAH (hef´-zi-bah)
1. Wife of King Hezekiah.

And his mother's name was H......	2Kin 21:1
2. A symbolic name for Jerusalem.
but thou shalt be called H......	Is 62:4

HER See PREFACE.

HERALD

Then an h cried aloud, To you it......	Dan 3:4

HERB

the h yielding seed, and the fruit......	Gen 1:11
h yielding seed after his kind,......	Gen 1:12
given you every h bearing seed......	Gen 1:29
have given every green h for meat......	Gen 1:30
every h of the field before it......	Gen 2:5
thou shalt eat the h of the field......	Gen 3:18
even as the green h have I given......	Gen 9:3
upon every h of the field,......	Ex 9:22
hail smote every h of the field......	Ex 9:25
eat every h of the land, even all......	Ex 10:12
they did eat every h of the land......	Ex 10:15
the small rain upon the tender h......	Deut 32:2
of the field, and as the green h......	2Kin 19:26
it withereth before any other h......	Job 8:12
of the tender h to spring forth......	Job 38:27
grass, and wither as the green h......	Ps 37:2
and h for the service of man......	Ps 104:14

HERBS

or in the h of the field, through......	Ex 10:15
with bitter h they shall eat it......	Ex 12:8
with unleavened bread and bitter h......	Num 9:11
with thy foot, as a garden of h......	1Kin 21:2
I may have it for a garden of h......	1Kin 21:2
out into the field to gather h......	2Kin 4:39
eat up all the h in their land......	Ps 105:35
is a dinner of h where love is......	Prov 15:17
of the mountains are gathered......	Prov 27:25
place like a clear heat upon h......	Is 18:4
for thy dew is as the dew of h,......	Is 26:19
and hills, and dry up all their h......	Is 42:15
the h of every field wither, for......	Jer 12:4
grown, it is the greatest among h......	Mt 13:32
and becometh greater than all h......	Mk 4:32
mint and rue and all manner of h......	Lk 11:42
another, who is weak, eateth h......	Rom 14:2
bringeth forth h meet for them by......	Heb 6:7

HERD

And Abraham ran unto the h......	Gen 18:7
of the cattle, even of the h......	Lev 1:2
be a burnt sacrifice of the h......	Lev 1:3
offering, if he offer it of the h......	Lev 3:1
And concerning the tithe of the h......	Lev 27:32
savour unto the LORD, of the h......	Num 15:3
then thou shalt kill of thy h......	Deut 12:21
males that come of thy h and of......	Deut 15:19
thy God, of the flock and the h......	Deut 16:2
came after the h out of the field......	1Sa 11:5
of his own flock and of his own h......	2Sa 12:4
young of the flock and of the h......	Jer 31:12
h nor flock, taste any thing......	Jonah 3:7
there shall be no h in the stalls......	Hab 3:17
then an h of many swine feeding......	Mt 8:30
us to go away into the h of swine......	Mt 8:31
they went into the h of swine......	Mt 8:32
behold, the whole h of swine ran......	Mt 8:32
a great h of swine feeding......	Mk 5:11
the h ran violently down a steep......	Mk 5:13
there was there an h of many......	Lk 8:32
the h ran violently down a steep......	Lk 8:33

HERDMAN

but I was an h, and a gatherer of......	Amos 7:14

HERDMEN

between the h of Abram's cattle......	Gen 13:7
cattle and the h of Lot's cattle......	Gen 13:7
and between my h and thy h......	Gen 13:8
the h of Gerar did strive with......	Gen 26:20
Gerar did strive with Isaac's h......	Gen 26:20
the chiefest of the h that......	1Sa 21:7
who was among the h of Tekoa......	Amos 1:1

HERDS

went with Abram, had flocks, and......	Gen 13:5
and he hath given him flocks, and h......	Gen 24:35
of flocks, and possession of h......	Gen 26:14
was with him, and the flocks, and h......	Gen 32:7
and h with young are with me......	Gen 33:13
children, and thy flocks, and thy h......	Gen 45:10
brought their flocks, and their h......	Gen 46:32
and their flocks, and their h......	Gen 47:1
and for the cattle of the h......	Gen 47:17
my lord also hath our h of cattle......	Gen 47:18
ones, and their flocks, and their h......	Gen 50:8
flocks and with our h will we go......	Ex 10:9
your flocks and your h be stayed......	Ex 10:24
Also take your flocks and your h......	Ex 12:32
and flocks, and h, even very much......	Ex 34:3
nor h feed before that mount......	Ex 34:3
the h be slain for them, to......	Num 11:22
And when thy h and thy flocks......	Deut 8:13
and the firstlings of your h......	Deut 12:6
of thy h or of thy flock, for any......	Deut 12:17
oil, and the firstlings of thy h......	Deut 14:23
took all the flocks and the h......	1Sa 30:20
had exceeding many flocks and h......	2Sa 12:2
over the h that fed in Sharon was......	1Chr 27:29
over the h that were in the......	1Chr 27:29
of flocks and h in abundance......	2Chr 32:29
law, and the firstlings of our h......	Neh 10:36
thy flocks, and look well to thy h......	Prov 27:23
a place for the h to lie down in......	Is 65:10
their flocks and their h, their......	Jer 3:24
eat up thy flocks and thine h......	Jer 5:17
with their h to seek the LORD......	Hos 5:6
the h of cattle are perplexed,......	Joel 1:18

HERE

Have I also h looked after him......	Gen 16:13
unto Lot, Hast thou h any besides......	Gen 19:12
and thy two daughters, which are h......	Gen 19:15
Now therefore swear unto me by......	Gen 21:23
and he said, Behold, h I am......	Gen 22:1
men, Abide ye h with the ass......	Gen 22:5
and he said, H am I, my son......	Gen 22:7
and he said, H am I......	Gen 22:11
I stand h by the well of water......	Gen 24:13
and said unto him, Behold, h am I......	Gen 27:1
and he said, H am I......	Gen 27:18
And I said, H am I......	Gen 31:11
set it h before my brethren and......	Gen 31:37
And he said to him, H am I......	Gen 37:13
h also have I done nothing that......	Gen 40:15
one of your brethren h with me......	Gen 42:33
And he said, H am I......	Gen 46:2
h is seed for you, and ye shall......	Gen 47:23

And he said, H am I .... Ex 3:4
the elders, Tarry ye h for us............. Ex 24:14
shall it be known h that I .... Ex 33:16
the mountain, saying, Lo, we be h..... Num 14:40
Lodge h this night, and I will.............. Num 22:8
you, tarry ye also h this night............. Num 22:19
Build me h seven altars, and.............. Num 23:1
and prepare me h seven oxen............. Num 23:1
Stand h by thy burnt offering............. Num 23:15
Build me h seven altars, and.............. Num 23:29
prepare me h seven bullocks and........ Num 23:29
go to war, and shall ye sit h............... Num 32:6
build sheepfolds h for our cattle......... Num 32:16
are all of us h alive this day.............. Deut 5:3
as for thee, stand thou h by me.......... Deut 5:31
the things that we do h this day.......... Deut 12:8
But with him that standeth h with....... Deut 29:15
that is not h with us this day............... Deut 29:15
for you h before the LORD our God...... Josh 18:6
that I may h cast lots for you............. Josh 18:8
which are h mentioned by name.......... Josh 21:9
thee, and say, Is there any man h........ Judg 4:20
and what hast thou h.......................... Judg 18:3
day groweth to an end, lodge h.......... Judg 19:9
h is my daughter a maiden, and his.... Judg 19:24
give h your advice and counsel........... Judg 20:7
but abide h fast by my maidens.......... Ruth 2:8
turn aside, sit down h......................... Ruth 4:1
the city, and said, Sit ye down h......... Ruth 4:2
am the woman that stood by thee h..... 1Sa 1:26
and he answered, H am I 1Sa 3:4
he ran unto Eli, and said, H am I........ 1Sa 3:5
and went to Eli, and said, H am I........ 1Sa 3:6
and went to Eli, and said, H am I........ 1Sa 3:8
And he answered, H am I 1Sa 3:16
I have h at hand the fourth part.......... 1Sa 9:8
and said unto them, Is the seer h....... 1Sa 9:11
Behold, h I am.................................... 1Sa 12:3
man his sheep, and slay them h.......... 1Sa 14:34
Jesse, Are h all thy children................ 1Sa 16:11
is there not h under thine hand........... 1Sa 21:8
it is h wrapped in a cloth behind......... 1Sa 21:9
for there is no other save that h.......... 1Sa 21:9
And he answered, H am I 1Sa 22:12
Behold, we be afraid h in Judah.......... 1Sa 23:3
What do these Hebrews h.................... 1Sa 29:3
And I answered, H am I 2Sa 1:7
Tarry h to day also, and to morrow..... 2Sa 11:12
h am I, let him do to me as................. 2Sa 15:26
unto him, Turn aside, and stand h...... 2Sa 18:30
three days, and be thou h present....... 2Sa 20:4
h be oxen for burnt sacrifice, and....... 2Sa 24:22
but I will die h.................................... 1Kin 2:30
thy lord, Behold, Elijah is h................. 1Kin 18:8
thy lord, Behold, Elijah is h................. 1Kin 18:11
thy lord, Behold, Elijah is h................. 1Kin 18:14
said unto him, What doest thou h........ 1Kin 19:9
him, and said, What doest thou h....... 1Kin 19:13
And as thy servant was busy h............ 1Kin 20:40
Is there not h a prophet of the............ 1Kin 22:7
Elijah said unto Elisha, Tarry h........... 2Kin 2:2
said unto him, Elisha, tarry h.............. 2Kin 2:4
unto him, Tarry, I pray thee, h............ 2Kin 2:6
Is there not h a prophet of the............ 2Kin 3:11
H is Elisha the son of Shaphat............ 2Kin 3:11
Why sit we h until we die.................... 2Kin 7:3
and if we sit still h, we die also........... 2Kin 7:4
look that there be h with you.............. 2Kin 10:23
thy people, which are present h.......... 1Chr 29:17
Is there not h a prophet of the............ 2Chr 18:6
h shall thy proud waves be stayed...... Job 38:11
go, and say unto thee, H we are.......... Job 38:35
h will I dwell..................................... Ps 132:14
Then said I, H am I............................ Is 6:8
h cometh a chariot of men, with a...... Is 21:9
What hast thou h................................ Is 22:16
and whom hast thou h, that thou........ Is 22:16
hast hewed thee out a sepulchre h..... Is 22:16
h a little, and there a little.................. Is 28:10
h a little, and there a little.................. Is 28:13
Now therefore, what have I h.............. Is 52:5
cry, and he shall say, H I am.............. Is 58:9
the house of Israel committeth h........ Eze 8:6
abominations which they commit h...... Eze 8:9
yea, gray hairs are h and there........... Hos 7:9
behold, a greater than Jonas is h........ Mt 12:41
a greater than Solomon is h............... Mt 12:42
Give me h John Baptist's head in....... Mt 14:8
We have h but five loaves, and two.... Mt 14:17
you, There be some standing h........... Mt 16:28
Lord, it is good for us to be h............. Mt 17:4
let us make h three tabernacles.......... Mt 17:4
Why stand ye h all the day idle........... Mt 20:6
be left h one stone upon another........ Mt 24:2
you, Lo, h is Christ, or there............... Mt 24:23
unto the disciples, Sit ye h................. Mt 26:36
tarry ye h, and watch with me............ Mt 26:38
He is not h..................................... Mt 28:6
and are not his sisters h with us.......... Mk 6:3
with bread h in the wilderness............. Mk 8:4
be some of them that stand h............. Mk 9:1
Master, it is good for us to be h.......... Mk 9:5
of stones and what buildings are h...... Mk 13:1
shall say to you, Lo, h is Christ.......... Mk 13:21
saith to his disciples, Sit ye h............. Mk 14:32
tarry ye h, and watch............................ Mk 14:34
he is not h...................................... Mk 16:6
do also h in thy country...................... Lk 4:23
for we are h in a desert place.............. Lk 9:12

a truth, there be some standing h....... Lk 9:27
Master, it is good for us to be h.......... Lk 9:33
a greater than Solomon is h............... Lk 11:31
behold, a greater than Jonas is h........ Lk 11:32
Neither shall they say, Lo h................ Lk 17:21
And they shall say to you, See h......... Lk 17:23
h is thy pound, which I have kept........ Lk 19:20
Lord, behold, here are two swords...... Lk 22:38
He is not h, but is risen..................... Lk 24:6
unto them, Have ye h any meat.......... Lk 24:41
There is a lad h, which hath five......... Jn 6:9
Jesus, Lord, if thou hadst been h........ Jn 11:21
him, Lord, if thou hadst been h.......... Jn 11:32
this man stand h before you whole..... Acts 4:10
the eunuch said, See, h is water......... Acts 8:36
And he said, Behold, I am h............... Acts 9:10
h he hath authority from the.............. Acts 9:14
are we all h present before God.......... Acts 10:33
for we are all h.................................. Acts 16:28
ought to have been h before thee....... Acts 24:19
Or else let these same h say............... Acts 24:20
men which are h present with us........ Acts 25:24
me, both at Jerusalem, and also h...... Acts 25:24
you all things which are done h.......... Col 4:9
h men that die receive tithes............. Heb 7:8
For h have we no continuing city........ Heb 13:14
Sit thou h in a good place................... Jas 2:3
or sit h under my footstool................. Jas 2:3
time of your sojourning h h................ 1Pet 1:17
H is the patience and the faith of....... Rev 13:10
H is wisdom...................................... Rev 13:18
H is the patience of the saints............ Rev 14:12
h are they that keep the..................... Rev 14:12
h is the mind which hath wisdom........ Rev 17:9

HEREAFTER
the things that are to come h.............. Is 41:23
h also, if ye will not hearken............... Eze 20:39
bed, what should come to pass h........ Dan 2:29
king what shall come to pass h........... Dan 2:45
H shall ye see the Son of man............ Mt 26:64
man eat fruit of thee h for ever.......... Mk 11:14
H shall the Son of man sit on the....... Lk 22:69
H ye shall see heaven open, and........ Jn 1:51
but thou shalt know h........................ Jn 13:7
H I will not talk much with you........... Jn 14:30
should h believe on him to life............ 1Ti 1:16
the things which shall be h................. Rev 1:19
shew these things which must be h..... Rev 4:1
there come two woes more h.............. Rev 9:12

HEREBY
H ye shall be proved.......................... Gen 42:15
H shall I know that ye are true............ Gen 42:33
H ye shall know that the LORD........... Num 16:28
H ye shall know that the living............ Josh 3:10
yet am I not h justified....................... 1Cor 4:4
h we do know that we know him, if..... 1Jn 2:3
h know we that we are in him............. 1Jn 2:5
H perceive we the love of God,........... 1Jn 3:16
h we know that we are of the.............. 1Jn 3:19
h we know that he abideth in us,........ 1Jn 3:24
H know ye the Spirit of God................ 1Jn 4:2
H know we the spirit of truth, and...... 1Jn 4:6
H know we that we dwell in him,........ 1Jn 4:13

HEREIN
Only h will the men consent unto........ Gen 34:22
H thou hast done foolishly................... 2Chr 16:9
h is that saying true, One soweth........ Jn 4:37
Why h is a marvellous thing, that........ Jn 9:30
H is my Father glorified, that ye......... Jn 15:8
h do I exercise myself, to have............ Acts 24:16
And h I give my advice........................ 2Cor 8:10
H is love, not that we loved God,........ 1Jn 4:10
H is our love made perfect, that......... 1Jn 4:17

HEREOF
the fame h went abroad into all.......... Mt 9:26
And by reason h he ought, as for....... Heb 5:3

HERES (he´-res) See KIR-HERES, TIMMATH-
HERES. A mountain in Judah.
would dwell in mount H in Aijalon ..... Judg 1:35

HERESH (he´-resh) A Levite.
And Bakbakkar, H, and Galal, and..... 1Chr 9:15

HERESIES
there must be also h among you......... 1Cor 11:19
wrath, strife, seditions, h................... Gal 5:20
privily shall bring in damnable h......... 2Pet 2:1

HERESY
after the way which they call h............ Acts 24:14

HERETH See HARETH.

HERETICK
man that is an h after the first............ Titus 3:10

HERETOFORE
I am not eloquent, neither h............... Ex 4:10
people straw to make brick, as h........ Ex 5:7
the bricks, which they did make h....... Ex 5:8
both yesterday and to day, as h.......... Ex 5:14
for ye have not passed this way h....... Josh 3:4
a people which thou knewest not h..... Ruth 2:11
hath not been such a thing h.............. 1Sa 4:7
write to them which h have sinned...... 2Cor 13:2

HEREUNTO
can eat, or who else can hasten h....... Eccl 2:25
For even h were ye called................... 1Pet 2:21

HEREWITH
and yet thou wast not satisfied h........ Eze 16:29
in mine house, and prove me now h.... Mal 3:10

HERITAGE
and I will give it you for an h.............. Ex 6:8
he h appointed unto him by God......... Job 20:29
the h of oppressors, which they.......... Job 27:13
yea, I have a goodly h........................ Ps 16:6
thou hast given me the h of those....... Ps 61:5
O LORD, and afflict thine h................. Ps 94:5
give them the h of the heathen............ Ps 111:6
have I taken as an h for ever.............. Ps 119:111
Lo, children are an h of the LORD....... Ps 127:3
And gave their land for an h............... Ps 135:12
a h unto Israel his people.................... Ps 135:12
And gave their land for an h............... Ps 136:21
Even an h unto Israel his servant....... Ps 136:22
This is the h of the servants of........... Is 54:17
feed thee with the h of Jacob thy....... Is 58:14
made mine h an abomination.............. Jer 2:7
a goodly h of the hosts of.................. Jer 3:19
mine house, I have left mine h............ Jer 12:7
Mine h is unto me as a lion in............ Jer 12:8
Mine h is unto me as a speckled......... Jer 12:9
them again, every man to his h........... Jer 12:15
from thine h that I gave thee.............. Jer 17:4
O ye destroyers of mine h.................. Jer 50:11
and give not thine h to reproach........ Joel 2:17
for my people and for my h Israel....... Joel 3:2
and his house, even a man and his h... Mic 2:2
thy rod, the flock of thine h............... Mic 7:14
of the remnant of his h...................... Mic 7:18
his h waste for the dragons of............ Mal 1:3
as being lords over God's h................ 1Pet 5:3

HERITAGES
cause to inherit the desolate h............ Is 49:8

HERMAS (her´-mas) A Christian acquaintance
of Paul.
Salute Asyncritus, Phlegon, H.......... Rom 16:14

HERMES (her´-mees) A Christian
acquaintance of Paul.
Phlegon, Hermas, Patrobas, H............ Rom 16:14

HERMOGENES (her-mof´-e-nees) A false
Christian teacher.
of whom are Phygellus and H............. 2Ti 1:15

HERMON
the river of Arnon unto mount H......... Deut 3:8
(Which H the Sidonians call................ Deut 3:9
even unto mount Sion which is H........ Deut 4:48
to the Hivite under H in the land........ Josh 11:3
valley of Lebanon under mount H....... Josh 11:17
from the river Arnon unto mount H..... Josh 12:1
And reigned in mount H, and in.......... Josh 12:5
from Baal-gad under mount H unto..... Josh 13:5
and Maachathites, and all mount H.... Josh 13:11
and Senir, and unto mount H............. 1Chr 5:23
H shall rejoice in thy name................. Ps 89:12
As the dew of H, and as the dew......... Ps 133:3
from the top of Shenir and H.............. Song 4:8

HERMONITES (her´-mon-ites) See HERMON.
Inhabitants of Mt. Hermon.
the land of Jordan, and of the H......... Ps 42:6

HEROD (her´-od) See HERODIANS, HEROD'S.
1. Herod the Great.
Judaea in the days of H the king........ Mt 2:1
When H the king had heard these....... Mt 2:3
Then H, when he had privily.............. Mt 2:7
that they should not return to H......... Mt 2:12
for H will seek the young child........... Mt 2:13
And was there until the death of H..... Mt 2:15
Then H, when he saw that he was...... Mt 2:16
But when H was dead, behold, an...... Mt 2:19
in the room of his father H................ Mt 2:22
There was in the days of H................ Lk 1:5
No, nor yet H: for I sent.................... Lk 23:15
2. Herod Antipas.
At that time H the tetrarch heard........ Mt 14:1
For H had laid hold on John, and....... Mt 14:3
danced before them, and pleased H.... Mt 14:6
And king H heard of him.................... Mk 6:14
But when H heard thereof, he said,.... Mk 6:16
For H himself had sent forth and........ Mk 6:17
For John had said unto H, It is........... Mk 6:18
For H feared John, knowing that........ Mk 6:20
that H on his birthday made a............. Mk 6:21
came in, and danced, and pleased H... Mk 6:22
Pharisees, and of the leaven of H....... Mk 8:15
H being tetrarch of Galilee, and......... Lk 3:1
But H the tetrarch, being.................... Lk 3:19
all the evils which H had done............ Lk 3:19
Now H the tetrarch heard of all.......... Lk 9:7
H said, John have I beheaded............. Lk 9:9
for H will kill thee.............................. Lk 13:31
jurisdiction, he sent him to H............. Lk 23:7
And when H saw Jesus, he was.......... Lk 23:8
H with his men of war set him at........ Lk 23:11
H were made friends together............. Lk 23:12
whom H had thought good, Herod...... Acts 4:27
brought up with H the tetrarch........... Acts 13:1
3. Herod Agrippa I.
Now about that time H the king......... Acts 12:1
when H would have brought him.......... Acts 12:6
delivered me out of the hand of H....... Acts 12:11
when H had sought for him, and......... Acts 12:19
H was highly displeased with them..... Acts 12:20
And upon a set day H, arrayed in....... Acts 12:21

HERODIANS (he-ro´-de-uns) Hellenizing Jews.
him their disciples with the H	Mt 22:16
counsel with the H against him	Mk 3:6
of the Pharisees and of the H	Mk 12:13

HERODIAS (he-ro´-de-as) See HERODIAS'.
Granddaughter of Herod 1.
the daughter of H danced before	Mt 14:6
Therefore H had a quarrel against	Mk 6:19
daughter of the said H came in	Mk 6:22
for H his brother Philip's wife	Lk 3:19

HERODIAS' (he-ro´-de-as)
and put him in prison for H sake	Mt 14:3
and bound him in prison for H sake	Mk 6:17

HERODION (he-ro´-de-on) A relative of Paul.
Salute H my kinsman	Rom 16:11

HEROD'S (her´-ods)
1. Refers to Herod 2.
But when H birthday was kept, the	Mt 14:6
the wife of Chuza H steward	Lk 8:3
he belonged unto H jurisdiction	Lk 23:7
2. Refers to Herod 3.
him to be kept in H judgment hall	Acts 23:35

HERON
the h after her kind, and the	Lev 11:19
the h after her kind, and the	Deut 14:18

HERS
firstborn son be h that was hated	Deut 21:15
damsels of h that went after her	1Sa 25:42
saying, Restore all that was h	2Kin 8:6
ones, as though they were not h	Job 39:16

HERSELF
Therefore Sarah laughed within h	Gen 18:12
and she, even she h said, He is my	Gen 20:5
she took a vail, and covered h	Gen 24:65
her with a vail, and wrapped h	Gen 38:14
came down to wash h at the river	Ex 2:5
she shall number to h seven days	Lev 15:28
if she profane h by playing the	Lev 21:9
the thrust h unto the wall, and	Num 22:25
bind h by a bond, being in her	Num 30:3
yea, she returned answer to h	Judg 5:29
bowed h to the ground, and said	Ruth 2:10
husband were dead, she bowed h	1Sa 4:19
face, and bowed h to the ground	1Sa 25:23
bowed h on her face to the earth	1Sa 25:41
the roof he saw a woman washing h	2Sa 11:2
shall feign h to be another woman	1Kin 14:5
bowed h to the ground, and took up	2Kin 4:37
time she lifteth up h on high	Job 39:18
and the swallow a nest for h	Ps 84:3
She maketh h coverings of	Prov 31:22
Therefore hell hath enlarged h	Is 5:14
find for h a place of rest	Is 34:14
bride adorneth h with her jewels	Is 61:10
Israel hath justified h more than	Jer 3:11
of Zion, that bewaileth h	Jer 4:31
feeble, and turneth h to flee	Jer 49:24
idols against h to defile h	Eze 22:3
all their idols she defiled h	Eze 23:7
She hath weaned h with lies	Eze 24:12
she decked h with her earrings and	Hos 2:13
Tyrus did build h a strong hold	Zec 9:3
For she said within h, If I may	Mt 9:21
earth bringeth forth fruit of h	Mk 4:28
hid h five months, saying	Lk 1:24
and could in no wise lift up h	Lk 13:11
had thus said, she turned h back	Jn 20:14
She turned h, and saith unto him	Jn 20:16
Through faith also Sara h	Heb 11:11
which calleth h a prophetess	Rev 2:20
How much she hath glorified h	Rev 18:7
and his wife hath made h ready	Rev 19:7

HESED (he´-sed) See JUSHAB-HESED. Father of
an officer of Solomon.
The son of H, in Aruboth	1Kin 4:10

HESHBON (hesh´-bon) A Levitical city in
Reuben and Gad.
the cities of the Amorites, in H	Num 21:25
For H was the city of Sihon the	Num 21:26
in proverbs say, Come into H	Num 21:27
For there is a fire gone out of H	Num 21:28
H is perished even unto Dibon, and	Num 21:30
of the Amorites, which dwelt at H	Num 21:34
Dibon, and Jazer, and Nimrah, and H	Num 32:3
And the children of Reuben built H	Num 32:37
of the Amorites, which dwelt in H	Deut 1:4
hand Sihon the Amorite, king of H	Deut 2:24
king of H with words of peace	Deut 2:26
But Sihon king of H would not let	Deut 2:30
of the Amorites, which dwelt at H	Deut 3:2
as we did unto Sihon king of H	Deut 3:6
of the Amorites, who dwelt at H	Deut 4:46
this place, Sihon the king of H	Deut 29:7
beyond Jordan, to Sihon king of H	Josh 9:10
of the Amorites, who dwelt in H	Josh 12:2
the border of Sihon king of H	Josh 12:5
the Amorites, which reigned in H	Josh 13:10
H, and all her cities that are in	Josh 13:17
the Amorites, which reigned in H	Josh 13:21
from H unto Ramath-mizpeh, and	Josh 13:26
of the kingdom of Sihon king of H	Josh 13:27
H with her suburbs, Jazer with	Josh 21:39
of the Amorites, king of H	Judg 11:19
While Israel dwelt in H and her	Judg 11:26
H with her suburbs, and Jazer with	1Chr 6:81

and the land of the king of H .... Neh 9:22
eyes like the fishpools in H .... Song 7:4
And H shall cry, and Elealeh .... Is 15:4
For the fields of H languish .... Is 16:8
water thee with my tears, O H .... Is 16:9
in H they have devised evil .... Jer 48:2
From the cry of H even unto .... Jer 48:34
shadow of H because of the force ... Jer 48:45
a fire shall come forth out of H ..... Jer 48:45
Howl, O H, for Ai is spoiled .... Jer 49:3

HESHMON (hesh´-mon) See AZMON. A town in
Judah.
And Hazar-gaddah, and H, and	Josh 15:27

HESLI See ESLI.

HETH (heth) Son of Canaan.
begat Sidon his firstborn, and H	Gen 10:15
dead, and spake unto the sons of H	Gen 23:3
the children of H answered	Gen 23:5
land, even to the children of H	Gen 23:7
dwelt among the children of H	Gen 23:10
the audience of the children of H	Gen 23:10
in the audience of the sons of H	Gen 23:16
the presence of the children of H	Gen 23:18
a buryingplace by the sons of H	Gen 23:20
purchased of the sons of H	Gen 25:10
because of the daughters of H	Gen 27:46
take a wife of the daughters of H	Gen 27:46
was from the children of H	Gen 49:32
begat Zidon his firstborn, and H	1Chr 1:13

HETHLON (heth´-lon) A place in northern
Palestine.
from the great sea, the way of H	Eze 47:15
end to the coast of the way of H	Eze 48:1

HEW
H thee two tables of stone like	Ex 34:1
H thee two tables of stone like	Deut 10:1
ye shall h down the graven images	Deut 12:3
wood with his neighbour to h wood	Deut 19:5
command thou that they h me cedar	1Kin 5:6
h timber like unto the Sidonians	1Kin 5:6
and Hiram's builders did h them	1Kin 5:18
he set masons to h wrought stones	1Chr 22:2
thousand to h in the mountain	2Chr 2:2
H ye down trees, and cast a mount	Jer 6:6
H down the tree, and cut off his	Dan 4:14
H the tree down, and destroy it	Dan 4:23

HEWED
he h two tables of stone like	Ex 34:4
h two tables of stone like unto	Deut 10:3
h them in pieces, and sent them	1Sa 11:7
Samuel h Agag in pieces before	1Sa 15:33
h stones, to lay the foundation	1Kin 5:17
court with three rows of h stone	1Kin 6:36
to the measures of h stones	1Kin 7:9
after the measures of h stones	1Kin 7:11
was with three rows of h stone	1Kin 7:12
h stone to repair the breaches of	2Kin 12:12
that thou hast h thee out a	Is 22:16
h them out cisterns, broken	Jer 2:13
Therefore have I h them by the	Hos 6:5

HEWER
from the h of thy wood unto the	Deut 29:11

HEWERS
but let them be h of wood	Josh 9:21
h of wood and drawers of water for	Josh 9:23
made them that day h of wood	Josh 9:27
thousand h in the mountains	2Chr 2:18
h of stone, and to buy timber and	2Kin 12:12
workmen with thee in abundance, h	1Chr 22:15
the h that cut timber, twenty	2Chr 2:10
thousand to be h in the mountain	2Chr 2:18
her with axes, as h of wood	Jer 46:22

HEWETH
against him that h therewith	Is 10:15
as he that h him out an sepulchre	Is 22:16
He h him down cedars, and taketh	Is 44:14

HEWN
shalt not build it of h stone	Ex 20:25
h stone to repair the house	2Kin 22:6
gave they it, to buy h stone	2Chr 34:11
she hath h out her seven pillars	Prov 9:1
but we will build with h stones	Is 9:10
ones of stature shall be h down	Is 10:33
Lebanon is ashamed and h down	Is 33:9
unto the rock whence ye are h	Is 51:1
inclosed my ways with h stone	Lam 3:9
the four tables were of h stone	Eze 40:42
ye have built houses of h stone	Amos 5:11
not forth good fruit is h down	Mt 3:10
not forth good fruit is h down	Mt 7:19
which he had h out in the rock	Mt 27:60
which was h out of a rock	Mk 15:46
not forth good fruit is h down	Lk 3:9
a sepulchre that was h in stone	Lk 23:53

HEZAI (hez´-e-ki) A Benjamite.
And Zebadiah, and Meshullam, and H	1Chr 8:17

HEZEKIAH (hez-e-ki´-ah) See EZEKIAS.
Hizkiah.
1. Son of King Ahaz.
H his son reigned in his stead	2Kin 16:20
that H the son of Ahaz king of	2Kin 18:1
in the fourth year of king H	2Kin 18:9
even in the sixth year of H	2Kin 18:10
in the fourteenth year of king H	2Kin 18:13

H king of Judah sent to the king 2Kin 18:14
H king of Judah three hundred 2Kin 18:14
H gave him all the silver that 2Kin 18:15
At that time did H cut off the 2Kin 18:16
from the pillars which H king of 2Kin 18:16
king H with a great host against 2Kin 18:17
said unto them, Speak ye now to H ... 2Kin 18:19
whose altars H hath taken away 2Kin 18:22
the king, Let not H deceive you 2Kin 18:29
Neither let H make you trust in 2Kin 18:30
Hearken not to H 2Kin 18:31
and hearken not unto H, when he 2Kin 18:32
to H with their clothes rent, and ... 2Kin 18:37
to pass, when king H heard it 2Kin 19:1
they said unto him, Thus saith H 2Kin 19:3
servants of king H came to Isaiah ... 2Kin 19:5
he sent messengers again unto H 2Kin 19:9
shall ye speak to H king of Judah ... 2Kin 19:10
H received the letter of the hand ... 2Kin 19:14
H went up into the house of the 2Kin 19:14
H prayed before the LORD, and said .. 2Kin 19:15
Isaiah the son of Amoz sent to H 2Kin 19:20
those days was H sick unto death 2Kin 20:1
And H wept sore 2Kin 20:3
tell H the captain of my people 2Kin 20:5
H said unto Isaiah, What shall be 2Kin 20:8
H answered, It is a light thing 2Kin 20:10
sent letters and a present unto H 2Kin 20:12
he had heard that H had been sick ... 2Kin 20:12
H hearkened unto them, and shewed ... 2Kin 20:13
dominion, that H shewed them not 2Kin 20:13
Isaiah the prophet unto king H 2Kin 20:14
H said, They are come from a far 2Kin 20:14
H answered, All the things that 2Kin 20:15
And Isaiah said unto H, Hear the 2Kin 20:16
the rest of the acts of H, and all .. 2Kin 20:20
And H slept with his fathers 2Kin 20:21
which H his father had destroyed 2Kin 21:3
H his son, Manasseh his son 1Chr 3:13
in the days of H king of Judah 1Chr 4:41
H his son reigned in his stead 2Chr 28:27
Then they went in to H the king 2Chr 29:18
H the king rose early, and 2Chr 29:20
H commanded to offer the burnt 2Chr 29:27
Moreover H the king and the 2Chr 29:30
Then H answered and said, Now ye 2Chr 29:31
H rejoiced, and all the people 2Chr 29:36
H sent to all Israel and Judah, and . 2Chr 30:1
But H prayed for them, saying 2Chr 30:18
And the LORD hearkened to H 2Chr 30:20
H spake comfortably unto all the 2Chr 30:22
For H king of Judah did give to 2Chr 30:24
multiplied the courses of the 2Chr 31:2
when H and the princes came 2Chr 31:8
Then H questioned with the 2Chr 31:9
Then H commanded to prepare 2Chr 31:11
at the commandment of H the king 2Chr 31:13
thus did H throughout all Judah 2Chr 31:20
when H saw that Sennacherib was 2Chr 32:2
upon the words of H king of Judah ... 2Chr 32:8
unto H king of Judah, and to all 2Chr 32:9
Doth not H persuade you to give 2Chr 32:11
Hath not the same H taken away 2Chr 32:12
therefore let not H deceive you 2Chr 32:15
God, and against his servant H 2Chr 32:16
so shall not the God of H deliver ... 2Chr 32:17
And for this cause H the king 2Chr 32:20
Thus the LORD saved H and the 2Chr 32:22
presents to H king of Judah 2Chr 32:23
In those days H was sick to the 2Chr 32:24
But H rendered not again 2Chr 32:25
Notwithstanding H humbled himself ... 2Chr 32:26
not upon them in the days of H 2Chr 32:26
H had exceeding much riches and 2Chr 32:27
This same H also stopped the 2Chr 32:30
H prospered in all his works 2Chr 32:30
Now the rest of the acts of H 2Chr 32:32
H slept with his fathers, and they .. 2Chr 32:33
H his father had broken down 2Chr 33:3
which the men of H king of Judah .... Prov 25:1
of Uzziah, Jotham, Ahaz, and H ...... Is 1:1
in the fourteenth year of king H ... Is 36:1
unto king H with a great army .... Is 36:2
said unto them, Say ye now to H ..... Is 36:7
whose altars H hath taken away ...... Is 36:7
the king, Let not H deceive you ..... Is 36:14
Neither let H make you trust in ..... Is 36:15
Hearken not to H .... Is 36:16
Beware lest H persuade you .... Is 36:18
to H with their clothes rent, and ... Is 36:22
to pass, when king H heard it .... Is 37:1
they said unto him, Thus saith H .... Is 37:3
servants of king H came to Isaiah ... Is 37:5
heard it, he sent messengers to H ... Is 37:9
shall ye speak to H king of Judah ... Is 37:10
H received the letter from the ...... Is 37:14
H went up unto the house of the ..... Is 37:14
H prayed unto the LORD, saying ...... Is 37:15
the son of Amoz sent unto H .... Is 37:21
those days was H sick unto death .... Is 38:1
Then H turned his face toward the ... Is 38:2
And H wept sore .... Is 38:3
Go, and say to H, Thus saith the .... Is 38:5
The writing of H king of Judah ...... Is 38:9
H also had said, What is the sign ... Is 38:22
sent letters and a present to H ..... Is 39:1
was glad of them, and shewed .... Is 39:2
dominion, that H shewed them not .... Is 39:2

Isaiah the prophet unto king *H* .... Is 39:3
H said, They are come from a far .... Is 39:3
H answered, All that is in mine ...... Is 39:4
Then said Isaiah to *H*, Hear the ...... Is 39:5
Then said *H* to Isaiah, Good is .... Is 39:8
the son of *H* king of Judah .... Jer 15:4
in the days of *H* king of Judah .... Jer 26:18
Did *H* king of Judah and all Judah .... Jer 26:19
of Uzziah, Jotham, Ahaz, and *H* .... Hos 1:1
in the days of Jotham, Ahaz, and *H* ... Mic 1:1
2. A son of Neariah.
Elioenai, and *H*, and Azrikam, three ... 1Chr 3:23
3. A family of exiles.
The children of Ater of *H* .... Ezr 2:16
The children of Ater of *H* .... Neh 7:21

HEZION (*he´-zi-on*) Grandfather of King
Benhadad of Syria.
the son of Tabrimon, the son of *H* 1Kin 15:18

HEZIR (*he´-zir*)
1. A sanctuary servant.
The seventeenth to *H*, the 1Chr 24:15
2. An Israelite who renewed the covenant.
Magpiash, Meshullam, *H*, ... Neh 10:20

HEZRAI (*hez´-rahee*) See HEZRO. *A mighty
man of David.*
H the Carmelite, Paarai the 2Sa 23:35

HEZRO (*hez´-ro*) See HEZRAI. *Same as Hezrai.*
H the Carmelite, Naarai the son 1Chr 11:37

HEZRON (*hez´-ron*) See HAZOR, HEZRONITES,
HEZRON's.
1. *Son of Pharez.*
And the sons of Pharez were *H* .... Gen 46:12
Of *H*, the family of the .... Num 26:6
of *H*, the family of the .... Num 26:21
Pharez begat *H*, ... Ruth 4:18
H begat Ram, and Ram begat .... Ruth 4:19
of Pharez; *H*, and Hamul 1Chr 2:5
The sons also of *H*, that were 1Chr 2:9
Caleb the son of *H* begat children 1Chr 2:18
afterward *H* went in to the 1Chr 2:21
And after that *H* was dead in 1Chr 2:24
Jerahmeel the firstborn of *H* were 1Chr 2:25
Pharez, and Carmi, and Hur, and 1Chr 4:1
2. *A son of Reuben.*
Hanoch, and Phallu, and *H*, and Carmi . Gen 46:9
Hanoch, and Pallu, *H*, and Carmi...... Ex 6:14
Israel were, Hanoch, and Pallu, *H* 1Chr 5:3
3. *A town in Judah.*
and passed along to *H*, and went up.... Josh 15:3
Hazor, Hadattah, and Kerioth, and *H* .. Josh 15:25

HEZRONITES (*hez´-ron-ites*) *Descendants of
Hezron 2.*
Of Hezron, the family of the *H* .... Num 26:6
of Hezron, the family of the *H* .... Num 26:21

HEZRON'S (*hez´-ronz*) *Refers to Hezron 2.*
then Abiah *H* wife bare him Ashur 1Chr 2:24

HID
his wife *h* themselves from the .... Gen 3:8
and I *h* myself .... Gen 3:10
and from thy face shall I be *h*........ Gen 4:14
Jacob *h* them under the oak which ..... Gen 35:4
child, she *h* him three months .... Ex 2:2
Egyptian, and *h* him in the sand ...... Ex 2:12
And Moses *h* his face .... Ex 3:6
the thing be *h* from the eyes of ...... Lev 4:13
withal, and it be *h* from .... Lev 5:3
with an oath, and it be *h* from him.... Lev 5:4
it be *h* from the eyes of her .... Num 5:13
and of treasures in the sand .... Deut 33:19
h them, and said thus, There came .... Josh 2:4
h them with the stalks of flax .... Josh 2:6
because she *h* the messengers that .... Josh 6:17
because she *h* the messengers .... Josh 6:25
they are *h* in the earth in the .... Josh 7:21
it was *h* in his tent, and the .... Josh 7:22
h themselves in a cave at .... Josh 10:16
are found *h* in a cave at Makkedah .... Josh 10:17
the cave wherein they had been *h* ..... Josh 10:27
for he *h* himself .... Judg 9:5
every whit, and *h* nothing from him.... 1Sa 3:18
he hath *h* himself among the stuff 1Sa 10:22
holes where they had *h* themselves 1Sa 14:11
had *h* themselves in mount Ephraim 1Sa 14:22
So David *h* himself in the field 1Sa 20:24
he is *h* now in some pit, or in 2Sa 17:9
is no matter *h* from the king 2Sa 18:13
was not any thing *h* from the king 1Kin 10:3
h them by fifty in a cave, and fed ... 1Kin 18:4
how I *h* an hundred men of the 1Kin 18:13
and the LORD hath *h* it from me........ 2Kin 4:27
and she hath *h* her son 2Kin 6:29
gold, and raiment, and went and *h* it . 2Kin 7:8
thence also, and went and *h* it 2Kin 7:8
and they *h* him, even him and his 2Kin 11:2
he was with her in the house of 2Kin 11:3
four sons with him *h* themselves 1Chr 21:20
there was nothing *h* from Solomon 2Chr 9:2
him, (for he was *h* in Samaria 2Chr 22:9
h him from Athaliah, so that she 2Chr 22:11
he was with them *h* in the house 2Chr 22:12
nor *h* sorrow from mine eyes .... Job 3:10
for it more than for *h* treasures ..... Job 3:21
given to a man whose way is *h* .... Job 3:23
Thou shalt be *h* from the scourge ..... Job 5:21
the ice, and wherein the snow is *h* ... Job 6:16
things hast thou *h* in thine heart .... Job 10:13

their fathers, and have not *h* it ..... Job 15:18
For thou hast *h* their heart from ..... Job 17:4
shall be *h* in his secret places ...... Job 20:26
the thing that is *h* bringeth he ...... Job 28:11
Seeing it is *h* from the eyes of ...... Job 28:21
young men saw me, and *h* themselves ... Job 29:8
The waters are as *h* with a stone, ... Job 38:30
in the net which they *h* is their ..... Ps 9:15
thou filest with thy *h* treasure ...... Ps 17:14
there is nothing *h* from the heat...... Ps 19:6
neither hath he *h* his face from ...... Ps 22:24
and mine iniquity have I not *h* .... Ps 32:5
they *h* for me their net in a pit ..... Ps 35:7
net that he hath *h* catch himself ..... Ps 35:8
and my groaning is not *h* from thee ... Ps 38:9
I have not *h* thy righteousness .... Ps 40:10
I would have *h* myself from him .... Ps 55:12
and my sins are not *h* from thee ...... Ps 69:5
Thy word have I *h* in mine heart ...... Ps 119:11
My substance was not *h* from thee ..... Ps 139:15
The proud have *h* a snare for me ...... Ps 140:5
for her as for *h* treasures .... Prov 2:4
falsehood have we *h* ourselves .... Is 28:15
of their prudent men shall be *h* ...... Is 29:14
My way is *h* from the LORD, and my .... Is 40:27
they are *h* in prison houses .... Is 42:22
shadow of his hand hath he *h* me ...... Is 49:2
in his quiver hath he *h* me .... Is 49:2
I *h* not my face from shame and .... Is 50:6
we *h* as it were our faces from .... Is 53:3
In a little wrath I *h* my face .... Is 54:8
I *h* me, and was wroth, and he went ... Is 57:17
your sins have *h* his face from .... Is 59:2
for thou hast *h* thy face from us, ... Is 64:7
because they are *h* from mine eyes .... Is 65:16
h it by Euphrates, as the LORD .... Jer 13:5
from the place where I had *h* it ...... Jer 13:7
they are not *h* from my face .... Jer 16:17
their iniquity *h* from mine eyes ...... Jer 16:17
take me, and *h* snares for my feet .... Jer 18:22
I have *h* my face from this city ...... Jer 33:5
but the LORD *h* them .... Jer 36:26
upon these stones that I have *h*....... Jer 43:10
have *h* there from my .... Ps 55:1
therefore *h* I my face from them, ... Eze 39:23
unto them, and *h* my face from them ... Eze 39:24
and Israel is not *h* from me, ... Hos 5:3
his sin is *h* .... Hos 13:12
shall be *h* from mine eyes .... Hos 13:14
though they be *h* from my sight in .... Amos 9:3
thou shalt be *h*, thou also shalt ..... Nah 3:11
it may be ye shall be *h* in the .... Zeph 2:3
is set on an hill cannot be *h*. .... Mt 5:14
and *h*, that shall not be known .... Mt 10:26
because thou hast *h* these things ..... Mt 11:25
h in three measures of meal, till, ... Mt 13:33
like unto treasure *h* in a field ...... Mt 13:44
the earth, and *h* his lord's money .... Mt 25:18
h thy talent in the earth .... Mt 25:25
For there is nothing *h*, which .... Mk 4:22
but he could not be *h* .... Mk 7:24
h herself five months, saying, ... Lk 1:24
neither any thing *h*, that shall ...... Lk 8:17
the woman saw that she was not *h*, ... Lk 8:47
it was *h* from them, that they .... Lk 9:45
that thou hast *h* these things, ... Lk 10:21
neither *h*, that shall not be .... Lk 12:2
h in three measures of meal, till .... Lk 13:21
and this saying was *h* from them, ... Lk 18:34
now they are *h* from thine eyes .... Lk 19:42
but Jesus *h* himself, and went out, ... Jn 8:59
But if our gospel be *h*, it is *h* 2Cor 4:3
of the world hath been *h* in God ...... Eph 3:9
which hath been *h* from ages, ... Col 1:26
In whom are *h* all the treasures ...... Col 2:3
your life is *h* with Christ in God .... Col 3:3
that are otherwise cannot be *h*. 1Ti 5:25
was *h* three months of his parents.... Heb 11:23
h themselves in the dens and in ...... Rev 6:15

HIDDAI (*hid´-dahee*) See HURAI. *A mighty man
of David.*
H of the brooks of Gaash, ... 2Sa 23:30

HIDDEKEL (*hid´-de-kel*) *A name for the Tigris
River.*
the name of the third river is *H* ..... Gen 2:14
of the great river, which is *H* .... Dan 10:4

HIDDEN
things, and if it be *h* from thee, ... Lev 5:2
this day, it is not *h* from thee...... Deut 30:11
Or as an *h* untimely birth I had ...... Job 3:16
of years is to the oppressor .... Job 15:20
times are not *h* from the Almighty .... Job 24:1
in the *h* part thou shalt make me...... Ps 51:6
and consulted against thy *h* ones ..... Ps 83:3
when the wicked rise, a man is *h* ..... Prov 28:12
h riches of secret places, that ...... Is 45:3
even *h* things, and thou didst not..... Is 48:6
how are his *h* things sought up .... Obad 6
of these things are *h* from him, ... Acts 26:26
in a mystery, even the *h* wisdom 1Cor 2:7
to light the *h* things of darkness 1Cor 4:5
the *h* things of dishonesty, ... 2Cor 4:2
let it be the *h* man of the heart 1Pet 3:4
will I give to eat of the *h* manna .... Rev 2:17

HIDE
Shall I *h* from Abraham that thing..... Gen 18:17
We will not *h* it from my lord, ... Gen 47:18
when she could not longer *h* him ...... Ex 2:3

But the bullock, and his *h*, ... Lev 8:17
the *h* he burnt with fire without ..... Lev 9:11
ways *h* their eyes from the man .... Lev 20:4
h themselves from thee, be .... Deut 7:20
go astray, and *h* thyself from them ... Deut 22:1
thou mayest not *h* thyself .... Deut 22:3
the way, and *h* thyself from them ..... Deut 22:4
I will *h* my face from them, and ...... Deut 31:17
I will surely *h* my face in that ...... Deut 31:18
I will *h* my face from them, I .... Deut 32:20
h yourselves there three days, ... Josh 2:16
h it not from me .... Josh 7:19
to *h* it from the Midianites .... Judg 6:11
I pray thee *h* it not from me 1Sa 3:17
if thou *h* any thing from me of 1Sa 3:17
people did *h* themselves in caves 1Sa 13:6
in a secret place, and *h* thyself. 1Sa 19:2
my father *h* this thing from me 1Sa 20:2
that I may *h* myself in the field 1Sa 20:5
h thyself when the business was 1Sa 20:19
Doth not David *h* himself with us 1Sa 23:19
Doth not David *h* himself in the 1Sa 26:1
H not from me, I pray thee, the 2Sa 14:18
h thyself by the brook Cherith, ... 1Kin 17:3
an inner chamber to *h* thyself 1Kin 22:25
camp to *h* themselves in the field. ... 2Kin 7:12
an inner chamber to *h* thyself 2Chr 18:24
then I will not *h* myself from .... Job 13:20
thou wouldest *h* me in the grave, ... Job 14:13
though he *h* it under his tongue....... Job 20:12
the earth *h* themselves together ...... Job 24:4
his purpose, and *h* pride from man..... Job 33:17
of iniquity may *h* themselves .... Job 34:22
H them in the dust together .... Job 40:13
long wilt thou *h* thy face from me..... Ps 13:1
h me under the shadow of thy .... Ps 17:8
he shall *h* me in his pavilion .... Ps 27:5
of his tabernacle shall he *h* me....... Ps 27:5
H not thy face from me .... Ps 27:9
thou didst *h* thy face, and I was ..... Ps 30:7
Thou shalt *h* them in the secret ...... Ps 31:20
H thy face from my sins, and blot, ... Ps 51:9
Dost not David *h* himself with us ..... Ps 54:1
and *h* not thyself from my .... Ps 55:1
they *h* themselves, they mark my ...... Ps 56:6
H me from the secret counsel of ...... Ps 64:2
h not thy face from thy servant ...... Ps 69:17
We will not *h* them from their .... Ps 78:4
wilt thou *h* thyself for ever .... Ps 89:46
H not thy face from me in that day ... Ps 102:2
h not thy commandments from me .... Ps 119:19
h not thy face from me, lest I be .... Ps 143:7
I flee unto thee to *h* me .... Ps 143:9
h my commandments with thee .... Prov 2:1
the wicked rise, men *h* themselves .... Prov 28:28
I will *h* mine eyes from you, ... Is 1:15
h thee in the dust, for fear of ...... Is 2:10
their sin as Sodom, they *h* it .... Is 3:9
h the outcasts .... Is 16:3
h thyself as it were for a little .... Is 26:20
to *h* their counsel from the LORD ..... Is 29:15
that thou *h* not thyself from .... Is 58:7
h it there in a hole of the rock ..... Jer 13:4
which I commanded thee to *h* there .... Jer 13:5
Can any *h* himself in secret .... Jer 23:24
Go, *h* thee, thou and Jeremiah .... Jer 36:19
h nothing from me .... Jer 38:14
is it not from us, and we will not ..... Jer 38:25
h them in the clay in the .... Jer 43:9
he shall not be able to *h* himself. ... Jer 49:10
h not thine ear at my breathing, ... Lam 3:56
secret that they can *h* from thee ..... Eze 28:3
the garden of God could not *h* him .... Eze 31:8
Neither will I *h* my face any more .... Eze 39:29
so that they fled to *h* themselves .... Dan 10:7
though they *h* themselves in the ...... Amos 9:3
he will even *h* his face from them .... Mic 3:4
that they shall *h* themselves from .... Jn 12:36
a multitude of sins. .... Jas 5:20
h us from the face of him that .... Rev 6:16

HIDEST
Wherefore *h* thou thy face, and .... Job 13:24
why *h* thou thyself in times of .... Ps 10:1
Wherefore *h* thou thy face, and .... Ps 44:24
why *h* thou thy face from me .... Ps 88:14
Thou *h* thy face, they are .... Ps 104:29
thou art a God that *h* thyself .... Is 45:15

HIDETH
lurking places where he *h* himself.... 1Sa 23:23
he *h* himself on the right hand, ... Job 23:9
when he *h* his face, who then can ..... Job 34:29
Who is he that *h* counsel without ..... Job 42:3
he *h* his face .... Ps 10:11
because he *h* not from these .... Ps 139:12
A slothful man *h* his hand in his ..... Prov 19:24
foreseeth the evil, and *h* himself..... Prov 22:3
The slothful *h* his hand in his .... Prov 26:15
foreseeth the evil, and *h* himself..... Prov 27:12
Whosoever *h* her *h* the wind, ... Prov 27:16
but he that *h* his eyes shall have .... Prov 28:27
that *h* his face from the house of .... Is 8:17
which when a man hath found, he *h* .... Mt 13:44

HIDING
by *h* mine iniquity in my bosom .... Job 31:33
Thou art my *h* place .... Ps 32:7
Thou art my *h* place and thy shield ... Ps 119:114
waters shall overflow the *h* place .... Is 28:17
be as an *h* place from the wind .... Is 32:2

and there was the h of his power........ Hab 3:4

HIEL (hi'-el) A Bethelite.
In his days did H the Beth-elite........ 1Kin 16:34

HIERAPOLIS (hi-e-rap'-o-lis) A city in Phrygia.
are in Laodicea, and them in H............ Col 4:13

HIGGAION (hig-gah'-yon) A musical notation.
work of his own hands. H. .... Ps 9:16

HIGH See PREFACE.

HIGHER
and his king shall be h than Agag...... Num 24:7
upward he was h than any of the 1Sa 9:2
he was h than any of the people 1Sa 10:23
He built the h gate of the house........ 2Kin 15:35
the wall, and on the h places.............. Neh 4:13
the clouds which are h than thou...... Job 35:5
me to the rock that is h than I.......... Ps 61:2
h than the kings of the earth............ Ps 89:27
for he that is h than the highest ...... Eccl 5:8
and there be h than they.................. Eccl 5:8
the heavens are h than the earth ..... Is 55:9
so are my ways h than your ways ..... Is 55:9
the scribe, in the h court.................. Jer 36:10
came from the way of the h gate...... Eze 9:2
the galleries were h than these........ Eze 42:5
the shall be the h place of the.......... Eze 43:13
but one was h than the other............ Dan 8:3
and the h came up last..................... Dan 8:3
say unto thee, Friend, go up h.......... Lk 14:10
soul be subject unto the h powers.... Rom 13:1
and made h than the heavens........... Heb 7:26

HIGHEST
heavens, and the H gave his voice.... Ps 18:13
the h himself shall establish her....... Ps 87:5
not the h part of the dust of the...... Prov 8:26
upon the h places of the city............ Prov 9:3
is higher than the h regardeth.......... Eccl 5:8
took the h branch of the cedar......... Eze 17:3
I will also take of the h branch........ Eze 17:22
chamber to the h by the midst.......... Eze 41:7
Hosanna in the h............................... Mt 21:9
Hosanna in the h............................... Mk 11:10
shall be called the Son of the H........ Lk 1:32
thee, and the power of the H shall .... Lk 1:35
be called the prophet of the H.......... Lk 1:76
Glory to God in the h, and on.......... Lk 2:14
ye shall be the children of the H....... Lk 6:35
sit not down in the h room............... Lk 14:8
in heaven, and glory in the h........... Lk 19:38
the h seats in the synagogues, and.... Lk 20:46

HIGHLY
Hail, thou that art h favoured.......... Lk 1:28
for that which is h esteemed............ Lk 16:15
Herod was h displeased with them.... Acts 12:20
more h than he ought to think.......... Rom 12:3
God also hath h exalted him............ Phil 2:9
to esteem them very h in love for 1Th 5:13

HIGHMINDED
Be not h, but fear............................ Rom 11:20
in this world, that they be not h...... 1Ti 6:17
Traitors, heady, h, lovers of............ 2Ti 3:4

HIGHNESS
by reason of his h I could not.......... Job 31:23
even them that rejoice in my h......... Is 13:3

HIGHWAY
on the east side of the h that.......... Judg 21:19
Beth-shemesh, and went along the h .. 1Sa 6:12
in blood in the midst of the h.......... 2Sa 20:12
Amasa out of the h into the field..... 2Sa 20:13
When he was removed out of the h ... 2Sa 20:13
which is in the h of the fuller's....... 2Kin 18:17
The h of the upright is to depart..... Prov 16:17
in the h of the fuller's field............ Is 7:3
there shall be an h for the.............. Is 11:16
be a h out of Egypt to Assyria......... Is 19:23
an h shall be there, and a way, and.. Is 35:8
in the h of the fuller's field............ Is 36:2
in the desert a h for our God.......... Is 40:3
set thine heart toward the h........... Jer 31:21
sat by the h side begging............... Mk 10:46

HIGHWAYS
the h were unoccupied, and the...... Judg 5:6
kill, as at other times, in the h....... Judg 20:31
them from the city unto the h.......... Judg 20:32
them in the h five thousand men..... Judg 20:45
The h lie waste, the wayfaring......... Is 33:8
a way, and my h shall be exalted..... Is 49:11
cast up, cast up the h..................... Is 62:10
and they shall say in all the h......... Amos 5:16
Go ye therefore into the h.............. Mt 22:9
servants went out into the h........... Mt 22:10
the servant, Go out into the h......... Lk 14:23

HILEN (hi'-len) See HOLON. A Levitical city in Judah.
H with her suburbs, Debir with........ 1Chr 6:58

HILKIAH (hil-ki'-ah) See HELKAI, HILKIAH'S.
1. Father of Eliakim.
out to them Eliakim the son of H..... 2Kin 18:18
Then said Eliakim the son of H........ 2Kin 18:26
Then came Eliakim the son of H....... 2Kin 18:37
And Shallum begat H....................... 1Chr 6:13
and H begat Azariah....................... 1Chr 6:13
Of H, Hashabiah; of Jedaiah........... Neh 12:21

my servant Eliakim the son of H...... Is 22:20
Then came Eliakim, the son of H...... Is 36:22
2. A High Priest.
Go up to the high priest, that.......... 2Kin 22:4
H the high priest said unto.............. 2Kin 22:8
H gave the book to Shaphan, and he.. 2Kin 22:8
H the priest hath delivered me a...... 2Kin 22:10
the king commanded H the priest..... 2Kin 22:12
So H the priest, and Ahikam, and 2Kin 22:14
king commanded H the high priest.... 2Kin 23:4
The priest found in the house........... 2Chr 23:24
And Azariah the son of H, the son.... 1Chr 9:11
they came to H the high priest......... 2Chr 34:9
The priest found a book of the......... 2Chr 34:14
H answered and said to Shaphan the.. 2Chr 34:15
H delivered the book to Shaphan..... 2Chr 34:15
The priest hath given me a book...... 2Chr 34:18
And the king commanded H, and...... 2Chr 34:20
And H, and they that the king had ... 2Chr 35:8
H and Zechariah and Jehiel, rulers... 2Chr 35:8
the son of Azariah, the son of H...... Ezr 7:1
Shaphan, and Gemariah the son of H. Jer 29:3
3. A descendant of Merari.
the son of Amaziah, the son of H..... 1Chr 6:45
4. A son of Hosah.
H the second, Tebaliah the third,..... 1Chr 26:11
5. A priest who assisted Ezra.
Shema, and Anaiah, and Urijah, and H. Neh 8:4
Seraiah the son of H, the son of...... Neh 11:11
Sallu, Amok, H, Jedaiah.................. Neh 12:7
6. Father of Jeremiah.
words of Jeremiah the son of H........ Jer 1:1

HILKIAH'S (hil-ki'-ahs) Refers to Hilkiah 1.
H son, which was over the house,..... Is 36:3

HILL
the h with the rod of God in mine.... Ex 17:10
Hur went up to the top of the h....... Ex 17:10
and builded an altar under the h...... Ex 24:4
presumed to go up unto the h top .... Num 14:44
Canaanites which dwelt in that h...... Num 14:45
ye were ready to go up into the h..... Deut 1:41
went presumptuously up into the h... Deut 1:43
Israel at the h of the foreskins........ Josh 5:3
the h country from Lebanon unto..... Josh 13:6
was drawn from the top of the h...... Josh 15:9
The h is not enough for us.............. Josh 17:16
near the h that lieth on the............ Josh 18:13
from the h that lieth before............ Josh 18:14
in the h country of Judah, with....... Josh 21:11
the north side of the h of Gaash...... Josh 24:30
they buried him in a h that............ Josh 24:33
on the north side of the h Gaash..... Judg 2:9
by the h of Moreh, in the valley...... Judg 7:1
top of an h that is before Hebron.... Judg 16:3
the house of Abinadab in the h....... 1Sa 7:1
as they went up the h to the city 1Sa 9:11
thou shalt come to the h of God...... 1Sa 10:5
when they came thither to the h...... 1Sa 10:10
h of Hachilah, which is on............. 1Sa 23:19
came down by the covert of the h.... 1Sa 26:3
hide himself in the h of Hachilah 1Sa 26:1
Saul pitched in the h of Hachilah 1Sa 26:3
stood on the top of an h afar off...... 1Sa 26:13
they were come to the h of Ammah... 2Sa 2:24
and stood on the top of an h............ 2Sa 2:25
the way of the h side behind him..... 2Sa 13:34
a little past the top of the h........... 2Sa 16:1
them in the h before the LORD......... 2Sa 21:9
in the h that is before Jerusalem..... 1Kin 11:7
and groves, on every high h............ 1Kin 14:23
he bought the h Samaria of Shemer.. 1Kin 16:24
of silver, and built on the h............ 1Kin 16:24
name of Shemer, owner of the h...... 1Kin 16:24
behold, he sat on the top of an h..... 2Kin 1:9
came to the man of God to the h...... 2Kin 4:27
images and groves in every high h.... 2Kin 17:10
my king upon my holy h of Zion...... Ps 2:6
and he heard me out of his holy h.... Ps 3:4
who shall dwell in thy holy h.......... Ps 15:1
ascend into the h of the LORD.......... Ps 24:3
the Hermonites, from the h Mizar.... Ps 42:6
let them bring me unto thy holy h.... Ps 43:3
h of God is as the h of Bashan........ Ps 68:15
an high h as the h of Bashan........... Ps 68:15
this is the h which God desireth...... Ps 68:16
our God, and worship at his holy h... Ps 99:9
and to the h of frankincense........... Song 4:6
a vineyard in a very fruitful h......... Is 5:1
of Zion, the h of Jerusalem............. Is 10:32
mountain, and as an ensign on an h.. Is 30:17
mountain, and upon every high h..... Is 30:25
mount Zion, and for the h thereof ... Is 31:4
mountain and h shall be made low.... Is 40:4
when upon every high h and under... Jer 2:20
every mountain, and from every h.... Jer 16:16
over against it upon the h Gareb...... Jer 31:39
that holdest the height of the h....... Jer 49:16
they have gone from mountain to h... Jer 50:6
their altars, upon every high h........ Eze 6:13
them, then they saw every high h..... Eze 20:28
mountains, and upon every high h.... Eze 34:6
round about my h a blessing........... Eze 34:26
that is set on an h cannot be hid..... Mt 5:14
went into the h country with.......... Lk 1:39
all the h country of Judaea............. Lk 1:65
and h shall be brought low............. Lk 3:5
h whereon their city was built......... Lk 4:29
they were come down from the h..... Lk 9:37
stood in the midst of Mars' h.......... Acts 17:22

HILLEL (hil'-lel) Father of Abdon.
And after him Abdon the son of H..... Judg 12:13
And Abdon the son of H the............. Judg 12:15

HILL'S
on the h side over against him......... 2Sa 16:13

HILLS
and all the high h, that were........... Gen 7:19
utmost bound of the everlasting h.... Gen 49:26
him, and from the h I behold him .... Num 23:9
thereunto, in the plain, in the h...... Deut 1:7
that spring out of valleys and h....... Deut 8:7
out of whose h thou mayest dig....... Deut 8:9
go to possess it, is a land of h........ Deut 11:11
the high mountains, and upon the h.. Deut 12:2
precious things of the lasting h........ Deut 33:15
on this side Jordan, in the h........... Josh 9:1
smote all the country of the h......... Josh 10:40
Joshua took all that land, the h....... Josh 11:16
him, Their gods are gods of the h..... 1Kin 20:23
said, The LORD is God of the h......... 1Kin 20:28
all Israel scattered upon the h........ 1Kin 22:17
in the high places, and on the h...... 2Kin 16:4
in the high places, and on the h...... 2Chr 28:4
or wast thou made before the h....... Job 15:7
foundations also of the h moved...... Ps 18:7
and the cattle upon a thousand h..... Ps 50:10
the little h rejoice on every............ Ps 65:12
Why leap ye, ye high h................... Ps 68:16
to the people, and the little h......... Ps 72:3
The h were covered with the........... Ps 80:10
the strength of the h is his also...... Ps 95:4
The h melted like wax at the.......... Ps 97:5
let the h be joyful together............ Ps 98:8
valleys, which run among the h....... Ps 104:10
He watereth the h from his............. Ps 104:13
The high h are a refuge for the....... Ps 104:18
he toucheth the h, and they smoke... Ps 104:32
rams, and the little h like lambs...... Ps 114:4
and ye little h, like lambs.............. Ps 114:6
will lift up mine eyes unto the h..... Ps 121:1
mountains, skipping upon the h....... Ps 148:9
before the h was I brought forth...... Prov 8:25
mountains, skipping upon the.......... Song 2:8
and shall be exalted above the h...... Is 2:2
upon all the h that are lifted up...... Is 2:14
the h did tremble, and their........... Is 5:25
on all h that shall be digged........... Is 7:25
in scales, and the h in a balance..... Is 40:12
and shalt make the h as chaff......... Is 41:15
I will make waste mountains and h... Is 42:15
shall depart, and the h be removed... Is 54:10
the h shall break forth before......... Is 55:12
and blasphemed me upon the h....... Jer 16:5
is salvation hoped for from the h..... Jer 3:23
and all the h moved lightly............. Jer 4:24
the green trees upon the high h...... Jer 17:2
Goto the mountains, and to the h..... Eze 6:3
in thy h, and in thy valleys, and..... Eze 35:8
Goto the mountains, and to the h..... Eze 36:4
unto the mountains, and to the h..... Eze 36:6
and burn incense upon the h.......... Hos 4:13
and to the h, Fall on us.................. Hos 10:8
the h shall flow with milk, and....... Joel 3:18
wine, and all the h shall melt.......... Amos 9:13
it shall be exalted above the h........ Mic 4:1
and let the h hear thy voice............ Mic 6:1
and the h, and the earth is............. Nah 1:5
the perpetual h did bow................. Hab 3:6
and a great crashing from the h...... Zeph 1:10
and to the h, Cover us.................... Lk 23:30

HIM See PREFACE.

HIMSELF See PREFACE.

HIN
fourth part of an h of beaten oil..... Ex 29:40
the fourth part of an h of wine........ Ex 29:40
sanctuary, and of oil olive an h....... Ex 30:24
a just ephah, and a just h............... Lev 19:36
of wine, the fourth part of a h........ Lev 23:13
the fourth part of an h of oil.......... Num 15:4
the fourth part of an h of wine....... Num 15:4
the third part of an h of oil............ Num 15:6
the third part of an h of wine......... Num 15:7
mingled with half an h of oil........... Num 15:9
drink offering half an h of wine...... Num 15:10
fourth part of an h of beaten oil..... Num 28:5
part of an h for the one lamb.......... Num 28:7
half an h of wine unto a bullock...... Num 28:14
the third part of an h unto a ram.... Num 28:14
a fourth part of an h unto a lamb.... Num 28:14
measure, the sixth part of an h....... Eze 4:11
ram, and an h of oil for an ephah.... Eze 45:24
give, and an h of oil to an ephah..... Eze 46:5
unto, and an h of oil to an ephah.... Eze 46:7
give, and an h of oil to an ephah..... Eze 46:11
and the third part of an h of oil...... Eze 46:11

HIND
Naphtali is a h let loose................. Gen 49:21
Let her be as the loving h.............. Prov 5:19
the h also calved in the field........... Jer 14:5

HINDER
me not, seeing the LORD hath.......... Gen 24:56
h thee from coming unto me............ Num 22:16
wherefore Abner with the h end of ... 2Sa 2:23
all their h parts were inward.......... 1Kin 7:25
all their h parts were inward.......... 2Chr 4:4

against Jerusalem, and to h it .... Neh 4:8
he taketh away, who can h him .... Job 9:12
together, then who can h him .... Job 11:10
smote his enemies in the h parts .... Ps 78:66
his h part toward the utmost sea, ... Joel 2:20
and half of them toward the h sea .... Zec 14:8
he was in the h part of the ship, ... Mk 4:38
what doth h me to be baptized .... Acts 8:36
but the h part was broken with .... Acts 27:41
lest we should h the gospel of 1Cor 9:12
who did h thou that ye should not .... Gal 5:7

HINDERED
these men, that they be not h .... Ezr 6:8
them that were entering in ye h .... Lk 11:52
been much h from coming to you .... Rom 15:22
but Satan h us 1Th 2:18
that your prayers be not h 1Pet 3:7

HINDERETH
anger, is persecuted, and none h .... Is 14:6

HINDERMOST
after, and Rachel and Joseph h .... Gen 33:2
the h of the nations shall be a .... Jer 50:12

HINDMOST
They shall go h with their .... Num 2:31
the way, and smote the h of thee .... Deut 25:18
enemies, and smite the h .... Josh 10:19

HINDS
thou mark when the h do calve .... Job 39:1
of the LORD maketh the h to calve .... Ps 29:9
by the h of the field, that ye .... Song 2:7
by the h of the field, that ye .... Song 3:5

HINDS'
He maketh my feet like h feet 2Sa 22:34
He maketh my feet like h feet .... Ps 18:33
he will make my feet like h feet .... Hab 3:19

HINGES
the h of gold, both for the doors 1Kin 7:50
As the door turneth upon his h .... Prov 26:14

HINNOM (hin'-nom) A valley near Jerusalem.
of H unto the south side of the .... Josh 15:8
before the valley of H westward .... Josh 15:8
before the valley of the son of H .... Josh 18:16
and descended to the valley of H .... Josh 18:16
the valley of the children of H 2Kin 23:10
in the valley of the son of H 2Chr 28:3
in the valley of the son of H 2Chr 33:6
Beer-sheba unto the valley of H .... Neh 11:30
is in the valley of the son of H .... Jer 7:31
nor the valley of the son of H .... Jer 7:32
unto the valley of the son of H .... Jer 19:2
nor The valley of the son of H .... Jer 19:6
are in the valley of the son of H .... Jer 32:35

HIP
And he smote them h and thigh with . Judg 15:8

HIRAH (hi'-rah) A friend of Judah.
Adullamite, whose name was H. .... Gen 38:1
his friend H the Adullamite. .... Gen 38:12

HIRAM (hi'-ram) See HIRAM'S, HURAM.
1. A king of Tyre.
H king of Tyre sent messengers to 2Sa 5:11
H king of Tyre sent his servants 1Kin 5:1
for H was ever a lover of David. 1Kin 5:1
And Solomon sent to H, saying, ... 1Kin 5:2
when H heard the words of Solomon, . 1Kin 5:7
H sent to Solomon, saying, I have 1Kin 5:8
So H gave Solomon cedar trees and 1Kin 5:10
Solomon gave H twenty thousand 1Kin 5:11
gave Solomon to H year by year 1Kin 5:11
and there was peace between H 1Kin 5:12
(Now the king of Tyre had 1Kin 9:11
H twenty cities in the land of 1Kin 9:11
H came out from Tyre to see the 1Kin 9:12
H sent to the king sixscore 1Kin 9:14
H sent in the navy his servants, ... 1Kin 9:27
And the navy also of H, that 1Kin 10:11
of Tharshish with the navy of H 1Kin 10:22
Now H king of Tyre sent 1Chr 14:1
2. An architect.
sent and fetched H out of Tyre 1Kin 7:13
H made the lavers, and the shovels 1Kin 7:40
So H made an end of doing all the 1Kin 7:40
which H made to king Solomon for 1Kin 7:45

HIRAM'S (hi'-rams) Refers to Hiram 1.
H builders did hew them, and the 1Kin 5:18

HIRE
Leah said, God hath given me my h ... Gen 30:18
and of such shall be my h .... Gen 30:32
come for my h before thy face .... Gen 30:33
The ringstreaked shall be thy h .... Gen 31:8
an hired thing, it came for his h. .... Ex 22:15
shalt not bring the h of a whore .... Deut 23:18
his day thou shalt give him his h. .... Deut 24:15
unto thee will I give h for thy 1Kin 5:6
of silver to h them chariots 1Chr 19:6
Tyre, and she shall turn to her h. .... Is 23:17
her h shall be holiness to the .... Is 23:18
in the balance, and h a goldsmith .... Is 46:6
harlot, in that thou scornest h. .... Eze 16:31
also shalt give no h any more .... Eze 16:41
gathered it of the h of an harlot, ... Mic 1:7
return to the h of an harlot. .... Mic 1:7
the priests thereof teach for h .... Mic 3:11
h for man, nor any h for beast .... Zec 8:10

into h labourers into his vineyard .... Mt 20:1
labourers, and give them their h. .... Mt 20:8
the labourer is worthy of his h .... Lk 10:7
the h of the labourers who have .... Jas 5:4

HIRED
for surely I have h thee with my .... Gen 30:16
an h servant shall not eat .... Ex 12:45
if it be an h thing, it came for .... Ex 22:15
the wages of him that is h shall .... Lev 19:13
or an h servant, shall not eat of .... Lev 22:10
thy maid, and for thy h servant .... Lev 25:6
But as an h servant, and as a .... Lev 25:40
according to the time of an h. .... Lev 25:50
as a yearly h servant shall he be .... Lev 25:53
worth a double h servant to thee. .... Deut 15:18
because they h against thee .... Deut 23:4
oppress an h servant that is poor .... Deut 24:14
wherewith Abimelech h vain .... Judg 9:4
Micah with me, and hath h me, ... Judg 18:4
have h out themselves for bread 1Sa 2:5
h the Syrians of Beth-rehob, and ... 2Sa 10:6
the king of Israel hath h against 2Kin 7:6
So they h thirty and two thousand 1Chr 19:7
h masons and carpenters to repair 2Chr 24:12
He h also an hundred thousand 2Chr 25:6
h counsellors against them, to .... Ezr 4:5
for Tobiah and Sanballat had h him .. Neh 6:12
Therefore was he h, that I should ...... Neh 6:13
but h Balaam against them, that ...... Neh 13:2
Lord shave with a razor that is h ...... Is 7:20
Also her h men are in the midst ...... Jer 46:21
Ephraim hath h lovers .... Hos 8:9
though they have h among the .... Hos 8:10
him, because no man hath h us. .... Mt 20:7
were h about the eleventh hour ...... Mt 20:9
in the ship with the h servants. ...... Mk 1:20
How many h servants of my .... Lk 15:17
make me as one of thy h servants. ... Lk 15:19
whole years in his own h house ...... Acts 28:30

HIRELING
days also like the days of an h .... Job 7:1
as a h looketh for the reward of ...... Job 7:2
till he shall accomplish, as an h ...... Job 14:6
three years, as the years of an h. ...... Is 16:14
according to the years of an h ...... Is 21:16
that oppress the h in his wages ...... Mal 3:5
But he that is an h, and not the ...... Jn 10:12
h fleeth, because he is an h .... Jn 10:13

HIRES
all the h thereof shall be burned ...... Mic 1:7

HIREST
h them, that they may come unto ...... Eze 16:33

HIS See PREFACE.

HISS
shall be astonished, and shall h 1Kin 9:8
shall h him out of his place. .... Job 27:23
will h unto them from the end of ...... Is 5:26
that the LORD shall h for the fly ...... Is 7:18
h because of all the plagues. .... Jer 19:8
shall h at all the plagues .... Jer 49:17
and h at all her plagues .... Jer 50:13
they h and wag their head at the ...... Lam 2:15
they h and gnash the teeth .... Lam 2:16
among the people shall h at these ... Eze 27:36
one that passeth by her shall h ...... Zeph 2:15
I will h them, and gather them, ... Zec 10:8

HISSING
trouble, to astonishment, and to h ... 2Chr 29:8
land desolate, and a perpetual h ...... Jer 18:16
make this city desolate, and an h ...... Jer 19:8
them an astonishment, and an h ...... Jer 25:9
desolation, an astonishment, an h ... Jer 25:18
and an astonishment, and an h ...... Jer 29:18
dragons, an astonishment, and an h ... Jer 51:37
and the inhabitants thereof an h ...... Mic 6:16

HIT
Saul, and the archers h him 1Sa 31:3
Saul, and the archers h him 1Chr 10:3

HITHER
they shall come h again .... Gen 15:16
your youngest brother come h .... Gen 42:15
yourselves, that ye sold me h ...... Gen 45:5
now it was not you that sent me h ... Gen 45:8
haste and bring down my father ...... Gen 45:13
And he said, Draw not nigh h .... Ex 3:5
there came men in h to-night of ...... Josh 2:2
the children of Israel, Come h ...... Josh 3:9
and bring the description h to me ... Josh 18:6
Gazites, saying, Samson is come h ... Judg 16:2
said unto him, Who brought thee h ... Judg 18:3
We will not turn aside h into the ... Judg 19:12
and bring h every man his ox, and ... Ruth 2:14
Bring h a burnt offering to me, ... 1Sa 13:9
Ahiah, Bring h the ark of God 1Sa 14:18
Bring me h every man his ox, and ... 1Sa 14:34
Let us draw near h unto God 1Sa 14:36
And Saul said, Draw ye near h 1Sa 14:38
Bring ye h to me Agag the king of ... 1Sa 15:32
will not sit down till he come h 1Sa 16:11
he said, Why camest thou down h ... 1Sa 17:28
the priest, Bring h the ephod 1Sa 23:9
I pray thee, bring me h the ephod ... 1Sa 30:7
have brought them h unto my lord ... 2Sa 1:10
lame, thou shalt not come in h 2Sa 5:6
I sent unto thee, saying, Come h ... 2Sa 14:32

pray you, unto Joab, Come near h 2Sa 20:16
Hasten h Micaiah the son of Imlah ... 1Kin 22:9
waters, and they were divided h. 2Kin 2:8
smitten the waters, they parted h 2Kin 2:14
saying, The man of God is come h ... 2Kin 8:7
to David, Thou shalt not come h 1Chr 11:5
shall not bring in the captives h 2Chr 28:13
of Assur, which brought us up h ...... Ezr 4:2
Therefore his people return h ...... Ps 73:10
bring h the timbrel, the pleasant ... Ps 81:2
is simple, let him turn in h ...... Prov 9:4
is simple, let him turn in h. ...... Prov 9:16
it be said unto thee, Come up h ...... Prov 25:7
But draw near h, ye sons of the ...... Is 57:3
them unto thee art thou brought h ... Eze 40:4
high God, come forth, and come h ... Dan 3:26
art thou come h to torment us ...... Mt 8:29
He said, Bring them h to me ...... Mt 14:18
bring him h to me .... Mt 17:17
how camest thou in h not having a ... Mt 22:12
and straightway he will send him h ... Mk 11:3
Bring thy son h. .... Lk 9:41
the city, and bring in h the poor ...... Lk 14:21
bring h the fatted calf, and kill ...... Lk 15:23
I should reign over them, bring h ... Lk 19:27
loose him, and bring him h. ...... Lk 19:30
not, neither come h to draw ...... Jn 4:15
Go, call thy husband, and come h ... Jn 4:16
him, Rabbi, when camest thou h ...... Jn 6:25
Reach h thy finger, and behold my ... Jn 20:27
reach h thy hand, and thrust it ...... Jn 20:27
came h for that intent, that he ...... Acts 9:21
Call h Simon, whose surname is ...... Acts 10:32
world upside down are come h also ... Acts 17:6
For ye have brought h these men ...... Acts 19:37
Therefore, when they were come h ... Acts 25:17
which said, Come up h, and I will ...... Rev 4:1
saying unto them, Come up h ...... Rev 11:12
with me, saying unto me, Come h ...... Rev 17:1
and talked with me, saying, Come h ... Rev 21:9

HITHERTO
behold, h thou wouldest not hear ...... Ex 7:16
as the LORD hath blessed me h ...... Josh 17:14
H thou hast mocked me .... Judg 16:13
and grief have I spoken h 1Sa 1:16
H hath the LORD helped us 1Sa 7:12
that thou hast brought me h 1Sa 7:18
have been thy father's servant h 2Sa 15:34
Who h waited in the king's gate 1Chr 9:18
for h the greatest part of them 1Chr 12:29
that thou hast brought me h. 1Chr 17:16
H shalt thou come, but no further .... Job 38:11
h have I declared thy wondrous ...... Ps 71:17
terrible from their beginning h. ...... Is 18:2
terrible from their beginning h. ...... Is 18:7
H is the end of the matter. .... Dan 7:28
them, My Father worketh h .... Jn 5:17
H have ye asked nothing in my ...... Jn 16:24
to come unto you, (but was let h ...... Rom 1:13
for h ye were not able to bear it 1Cor 3:2

HITTITE (hit'-tite) See HITTITES. A descendant
of Heth.
Ephron the H answered Abraham in . Gen 23:10
of Ephron the son of Zohar the H. ...... Gen 25:9
the daughter of Beeri the H. ...... Gen 26:34
the daughter of Elon the H ...... Gen 26:34
Adah the daughter of Elon the H ...... Gen 36:2
is in the field of Ephron the H ...... Gen 49:29
the H for a possession of a ...... Gen 49:30
of a buryingplace of Ephron the H ... Gen 50:13
Hivite, the Canaanite, and the H.. ...... Ex 23:28
Canaanite, the Amorite, and the H ... Ex 33:2
and the Canaanite, and the H. ...... Ex 34:11
sea over against Lebanon, the H ...... Josh 9:1
west, and to the Amorite, and the H . Josh 11:3
David and said to Ahimelech the H ... 1Sa 26:6
of Eliam, the wife of Uriah the H 2Sa 11:3
Joab, saying, Send me Uriah the H ... 2Sa 11:6
and Uriah the H died also 2Sa 11:17
servant Uriah the H is dead also 2Sa 11:21
servant Uriah the H is dead also 2Sa 11:24
killed Uriah the H with the sword 2Sa 12:9
of Uriah the H to be thy wife. 2Sa 12:10
Uriah the H: thirty and seven 2Sa 23:39
only in the matter of Uriah the H 1Kin 15:5
that were left of the Hittites, ... 2Chr 8:7

HITTITES (hit'-tites)
And the H, and the Perizzites, and .... Gen 15:20
place of the Canaanites, and the H..... Ex 3:8
land of the Canaanites, and the H..... Ex 3:17
land of the Canaanites, and the H.... Ex 13:5
in unto the Amorites, and the H ...... Ex 23:23
and the H, and the Jebusites, and ... Num 13:29
many nations before thee, the H ...... Deut 7:1
namely, the H, and the Amorites, ... Deut 20:17
Euphrates, all the land of the H. ...... Josh 1:4
you the Canaanites, and the H ...... Josh 3:10
the H, the Amorites, and the ...... Josh 12:8
and the Canaanites, and the H ...... Josh 24:11
man went into the land of the H ...... Judg 1:26
dwelt among the Canaanites, H ...... Judg 3:5
that were left of the Amorites, H 1Kin 9:20
and so for all the kings of the H. 1Kin 10:29
Edomites, Zidonians, and H 1Kin 11:1
against us the kings of the H 2Kin 7:6
horses for all the kings of the H 2Chr 1:17
people that were left of the H........ 2Chr 8:7

even of the Canaanites, the *H* .... Ezr 9:1
the land of the Canaanites, the *H* ...... Neh 9:8

HIVITE (*hi'-vite*) *A descendant of Canaan.*
And the *H*, and the Arkite, and the ... Gen 10:17
Shechem the son of Hamor the *H* .... Gen 34:2
Anah the daughter of Zibeon the *H* .... Gen 36:2
thee, which shall drive out the *H* ..... Ex 23:28
Hittite, and the Perizzite, the *H* ...... Ex 33:2
and the Perizzite, and the *H* .... Ex 34:11
Canaanite, the Perizzite, the *H* .... Josh 9:1
to the *H* under Hermon in the land .... Josh 11:3
And the *H*, and the Arkite, and the 1Chr 1:15

HIVITES (*hi'-vites*)
and the Perizzites, and the *H* .... Ex 3:8
and the Perizzites, and the *H* .... Ex 3:17
and the Amorites, and the *H* .... Ex 13:5
and the Canaanites, the *H* .... Ex 23:23
and the Perizzites, and the *H* .... Deut 7:1
and the Perizzites, the *H* .... Deut 20:17
and the Hittites, and the *H* .... Josh 3:10
the men of Israel said unto the *H* ..... Josh 9:7
save the *H* the inhabitants of .... Josh 11:19
Canaanites, the Perizzites, the *H* ..... Josh 12:8
and the Girgashites, the *H* .... Josh 24:11
the *H* that dwelt in mount Lebanon ... Judg 3:3
and Amorites, and Perizzites, and *H* .. Judg 3:5
and to all the cities of the *H* 2Sa 24:7
Amorites, Hittites, Perizzites, *H* 1Kin 9:20
and the Perizzites, and the *H* 2Chr 8:7

HIZKI See HEZEKI.

HIZKIAH (*hiz-ki'-ah*) See HEZEKIAH, HIZKIJAH.
An ancestor of Zephaniah.
the son of Amariah, the son of .... Zeph 1:1

HIZKIJAH (*hiz-ki'-jah*) See HIZKIAH. *An
Israelite who renewed the covenant.*
Ater, Azzur, ... Neh 10:17

HO
unto whom he said, *H*, such a one .... Ruth 4:1
H, every one that thirsteth, come. ..... Is 55:1
H, h, come forth, and flee from .... Zec 2:6

HOAR
as small as the *h* frost on the .... Ex 16:14
let not his *h* head go down to the 1Kin 2:6
but his *h* head bring thou down to ... 1Kin 2:9
scattereth the *h* frost like ashes. ..... Ps 147:16
even to *h* hairs will I carry you .... Is 46:4

HOARY
shalt rise up before the *h* head .... Lev 19:32
The *h* frost of heaven, who hath ...... Job 38:29
one would think the deep to be *h* .... Job 41:32
The *h* head is a crown of glory, ... Prov 16:31

HOBAB (*ho'-bab*) See JETHRO. *Another name
for Jethro.*
And Moses said unto *H*, the son of ... Num 10:29
of *H* the father in law of Moses, ... Judg 4:11

HOBAH (*ho'-bah*) *Place where Abraham
pursued the five kings.*
them, and pursued them unto *H* .... Gen 14:15

HOBAIAH See HABAIAH.

HOD (*hod*) *A son of Zophah.*
Bezer, and *H*, and Shamma, and 1Chr 7:37

HODAIAH (*ho-da-i'-ah*) See HODAVIAH. *A royal
descendant of Judah.*
And the sons of Elioenai were, ... 1Chr 3:24

HODAVIAH (*ho-da-vi'-ah*) See HODAIAH,
HODIAH.
    1. A chief of Manasseh.
and Azriel, and Jeremiah, and 1Chr 5:24
    2. Son of Hassenuah.
son of Meshullam, the son of *H*. 1Chr 9:7
    3. A family of exiles.
and Kadmiel, the children of *H* .... Ezr 2:40

HODESH (*ho'-desh*) *Wife of Shaharaim.*
And he begat of *H* his wife 1Chr 8:9

HODEVAH (*ho-de'-vah*) See HODAVIAH. *A
family of exiles.*
Kadmiel, and the children of *H* .... Neh 7:43

HODIAH (*ho-di'-ah*) See HODIJAH. *A wife of
Mered.*
of his wife *H* the sister of Naham 1Chr 4:19

HODIJAH (*ho-di'-jah*) See HODIAH.
    1. A Levite.
Jamin, Akkub, Shabbethai, *H* .... Neh 8:7
Bani, Hashabniah, Sherebiah, *H* ...... Neh 9:5
And their brethren, Shebaniah, *H* ..... Neh 10:10
H, Bani, Beninu .... Neh 10:13
    2. A leader of the people.
H, Hashum, Bezai, ... Neh 10:18

HOGLAH (*hog'-lah*) See BETH-HOGLAH. *A
daughter of Zelophehad.*
were Mahlah, and Noah, *H*, Milcah,. Num 26:33
Noah, and *H*, and Milcah .... Num 27:1
For Mahlah, Tirzah, and *H*, and ..... Num 36:11
his daughters, Mahlah, and Noah, *H*,. Josh 17:3

HOHAM (*ho'-ham*) *An Amorite king.*
sent unto *H* king of Hebron .... Josh 10:3

HOISED
h up the mainsail to the wind, and ... Acts 27:40

HOLD
the men laid *h* upon his hand, and... Gen 19:16
the lad, and *h* him in thine hand .... Gen 21:18
his hand took *h* on Esau's heel ...... Gen 25:26
that they may *h* a feast unto the ..... Ex 5:1
them go, and wilt *h* them still... ..... Ex 9:2
for we must *h* a feast unto the ...... Ex 10:9
for you, and ye shall *h* your peace. .. Ex 14:14
sorrow shall take *h* on the .... Ex 15:14
trembling shall take *h* upon them. ... Ex 15:15
for the LORD will not *h* him .... Ex 20:7
loops may take *h* one of another .... Ex 26:5
father shall *h* his peace at her .... Num 30:4
his peace at her from day to .... Num 30:7
for the LORD will not *h* him .... Deut 5:11
father and his mother lay *h* on ...... Deut 21:19
lay *h* on her, and lie with her, and... Deut 22:28
and mine hand take *h* on judgment. . Deut 32:41
they entered into an *h* of the .... Judg 9:46
Abimelech, and put them to the *h* ... Judg 9:49
set the *h* on fire upon them. .... Judg 9:49
Samson took *h* of the two middle .... Judg 16:29
If thy peace, lay thine hand upon ..... Judg 18:19
laid *h* on his concubine, and .... Judg 19:29
that thou hast upon thee, and *h* it ... Ruth 3:15
he laid *h* upon the skirt of his 1Sa 15:27
the while that David was in the *h*... 1Sa 22:4
unto David, Abide not in the *h* 1Sa 22:5
and his men gat them up unto the *h*... 1Sa 23:29
Then David took *h* on his clothes. ... 2Sa 1:11
lay thee *h* on one of the young...... 2Sa 2:21
how then should I *h* up my face to ... 2Sa 2:22
good tidings, I took *h* of him. 2Sa 4:10
David took the strong *h* of Zion. 2Sa 5:7
of it, and went down to the *h* 2Sa 5:17
the ark of God, and took *h* of it 2Sa 6:6
unto him to eat, he took *h* of her. ... 2Sa 13:11
but *h* now thy peace, my sister... ... 2Sa 13:20
and his head caught *h* of the oak ... 2Sa 18:9
And David was then in an *h* 2Sa 23:14
And came to the strong *h* of Tyre.... 2Sa 24:7
caught *h* on the horns of the 1Kin 1:50
he hath caught *h* on the horns of ... 1Kin 1:51
Now therefore *h* him not guiltless ... 1Kin 2:9
caught *h* on the horns of the 1Kin 2:28
have taken *h* upon other gods, and... 1Kin 9:9
the altar, saying, Lay *h* on him. 1Kin 13:4
h ye your peace 2Kin 2:3
h ye your peace 2Kin 2:5
he took *h* of his own clothes, and.... 2Kin 2:12
door, and *h* him fast at the door.... 2Kin 6:32
good tidings, and we *h* our peace.... 2Kin 7:9
And David was then in the *h*. 1Chr 11:16
to the wilderness men of might 1Chr 12:8
and Judah to the *h* unto David 1Chr 12:16
put forth his hand to *h* the ark 1Chr 13:9
and laid *h* on other gods, and 2Chr 7:22
If your peace, for the day is holy ..... Neh 8:11
shall *h* out the golden sceptre. .... Est 4:11
Teach me, and I will *h* my tongue.... Job 6:24
he shall *h* it fast, but it shall .... Job 8:15
that thou wilt not *h* me innocent ..... Job 9:28
thy lies make men *h* their peace?..... Job 11:3
ye would altogether *h* your peace .... Job 13:5
H your peace, let me alone, that .... Job 13:13
if I *h* my tongue, I shall give up .... Job 13:19
righteous also shall *h* on his way .... Job 17:9
and trembling taketh *h* on my flesh.. Job 21:6
My righteousness I *h* fast .... Job 27:6
Terrors take *h* on him as waters,... Job 27:20
affliction have taken *h* upon me. ..... Job 30:16
h thy peace, and I will speak. .... Job 33:31
h thy peace, and I shall teach .... Job 33:33
and justice take *h* on thee. .... Job 36:17
That it might take *h* of the ends..... Job 38:13
him that layeth at him cannot *h*. .... Job 41:26
If up my goings in thy paths, that .... Ps 17:5
Take *h* of shield and buckler, and ... Ps 35:2
h not thy peace at my tears .... Ps 39:12
iniquities have taken *h* upon me. .... Ps 40:12
Fear took *h* upon them, and .... Ps 48:6
thy wrathful anger take *h* of them.. Ps 69:24
h not thy peace, and be not still,.... Ps 83:1
h not thy peace, O God of my .... Ps 83:1
the pains of hell gat *h* upon me ..... Ps 116:3
Horror hath taken *h* upon me. ...... Ps 119:53
If thou me up, and I shall be safe .... Ps 119:117
and anguish have taken *h* on me .... Ps 119:143
me, and thy right hand shall *h* me... Ps 139:10
neither take they *h* of the paths..... Prov 2:19
life to them that lay *h* upon her ..... Prov 3:18
Take fast *h* of instruction .... Prov 4:13
her steps take *h* on hell .... Prov 5:5
spider taketh *h* with her hands...... Prov 30:28
and her hands *h* the distaff .... Prov 31:19
to lay *h* on folly, till I might........ Eccl 2:3
Thou shalt even take *h* of this .... Eccl 7:18
They all *h* swords, being expert ..... Song 3:8
I will take *h* of the boughs........... Song 7:8
When a man shall take *h* of his ...... Is 4:1
women shall take *h* of one man...... Is 4:1
lay *h* on the prey, and shall carry... Is 5:29
and sorrows shall take *h* of them .... Is 13:8
pangs have taken *h* upon me. .... Is 21:3
Or let him take *h* of my strength .... Is 27:5

over to his strong *h* for fear.......... Is 31:9
thy God will *h* thy right hand .... Is 41:13
will *h* thine hand, and will keep. .... Is 42:6
son of man that layeth *h* on it ...... Is 56:2
me, and take *h* of my covenant ..... Is 56:4
it, and taketh *h* of my covenant ..... Is 56:6
Zion's sake will I not *h* my peace ... Is 62:1
which shall never *h* their peace ..... Is 62:6
up himself to take *h* of thee. .... Is 64:7
wilt thou *h* thy peace, and afflict.... Is 64:12
cisterns, that can *h* no water .... Jer 2:13
I cannot *h* my peace, because thou ... Jer 4:19
They shall lay *h* on bow and spear ... Jer 6:23
anguish hath taken *h* of us .... Jer 6:24
they *h* fast deceit, they refuse ...... Jer 8:5
astonishment hath taken *h* on me ... Jer 8:21
They shall *h* the bow and the lance ... Jer 50:42
anguish took *h* of him, and pangs ... Jer 50:43
When they took *h* of thee by thy .... Eze 29:7
to make it strong to *h* the sword .... Eze 30:21
about, that they might have *h* .... Eze 41:6
but they had not *h* in the wall of.... Eze 41:6
Then shall he say, *H* thy tongue. ..... Amos 6:10
the strong *h* of the daughter of ...... Mic 4:8
and thou shalt take *h*, but shalt ..... Mic 6:14
a strong *h* in the day of trouble...... Nah 1:7
they shall deride every strong *h* ..... Hab 1:10
If thy peace at the presence of .... Zeph 1:7
they not take *h* of your fathers ...... Zec 1:6
that ten men shall take *h* out of .... Zec 8:23
even shall take *h* of the skirt of ..... Zec 8:23
did build herself a strong *h* .... Zec 9:3
Turn you to the strong *h*, ye .... Zec 9:12
them, and *h* themselves not guilty.... Zec 11:5
they shall lay *h* every one on the ... Zec 14:13
or else he will *h* to the one. .... Mt 6:24
day, will he not lay *h* on it .... Mt 12:11
For Herod had laid *h* on John .... Mt 14:3
because they should *h* their peace ... Mt 20:31
for all *h* John as a prophet .... Mt 21:26
same is her: *h* him fast. .... Mt 26:48
the temple, and ye laid no *h* on me.. Mt 26:55
they that had laid *h* on Jesus led.... Mt 26:57
H thy peace, and come out of him.... Mk 1:25
it, they went out to lay *h* on him ... Mk 3:21
laid *h* upon John, and bound him in ... Mk 6:17
be, which they have received of ...... Mk 7:4
ye *h* the tradition of men, as the.... Mk 7:8
him that he should *h* his peace...... Mk 10:48
And they sought to lay *h* on him. ... Mk 12:12
and the young men laid *h* on him ... Mk 14:51
If thy peace, and come out of him .... Lk 4:35
or else he will *h* to the one. .... Lk 16:13
him, that he should *h* his peace...... Lk 18:39
if these should *h* their peace .... Lk 19:40
they might take *h* of his words ...... Lk 20:20
they could not take *h* of his .... Lk 20:26
they laid *h* upon one Simon, a ...... Lk 23:26
put them in *h* unto the next day .... Acts 4:3
with the hand to *h* their peace ...... Acts 12:17
but speak, and *h* not thy peace ...... Acts 18:9
of men, who *h* the truth in .... Rom 1:18
by, let the first *h* his peace. 1Cor 14:30
and *h* such in reputation .... Phil 2:29
h fast that which is good 1Th 5:21
the traditions which ye have.......... 2Th 2:15
lay *h* on eternal life, whereunto 1Ti 6:12
they may lay *h* on eternal life: 1Ti 6:19
H fast the form of sound words,..... 2Ti 1:13
if we *h* fast the confidence and ..... Heb 3:6
if we *h* the beginning of our .... Heb 3:14
let us *h* fast our profession. .... Heb 4:14
lay *h* upon the hope set before us ... Heb 6:18
Let us *h* fast the profession of ...... Heb 10:23
that *h* the doctrine of Balaam .... Rev 2:14
them that *h* the doctrine of the...... Rev 2:15
have already *h* fast till I come....... Rev 2:25
and heard, and *h* fast, and repent ... Rev 3:3
h that fast which thou hast, that.... Rev 3:11
the *h* of every foul spirit, and ...... Rev 18:2
he laid *h* on the dragon, that old ... Rev 20:2

HOLDEN
Surely there was not *h* such a 2Kin 23:22
was *h* to the LORD in Jerusalem 2Kin 23:23
be *h* in cords of affliction .... Job 36:8
and thy right hand hath *h* me up ... Ps 18:35
have I been *h* up from the womb ... Ps 71:6
thou hast *h* me by my right hand ... Ps 73:23
he shall be *h* with the cords of ..... Prov 5:22
I have long time *h* my peace........ Is 42:14
Cyrus, whose right hand I have *h* ... Is 45:1
But their eyes were *h* that they ..... Lk 24:16
that he should be *h* of it .... Acts 2:24
Yea, he shall be *h* up .... Rom 14:4

HOLDEST
h thy peace at this time, then....... Est 4:14
thy face, and *h* me for thine enemy... Job 13:24
Thou makest my eyes waking .... Ps 77:4
that *h* the height of the hill .... Jer 49:16
h thy tongue when the wicked ...... Hab 1:13
thou *h* my name, and hast not ..... Rev 2:13

HOLDETH
still he *h* fast his integrity,.......... Job 2:3
He *h* back the face of his throne, ... Job 26:9
Which *h* our soul in life, and .... Ps 66:9
man of understanding *h* his peace... Prov 11:12
when he *h* his peace, is counted.... Prov 17:28
there is none that *h* with me in ..... Dan 10:21
him that *h* the sceptre from the .... Amos 1:5

him that *h* the sceptre from.................. Amos 1:8
These things saith he that *h* the .... Rev 2:1

HOLDING
his hands from *h* of bribes................... Is 33:15
I am weary with *h* in........................ Jer 6:11
h the tradition of the elders .... Mk 7:3
H forth the word of life................... Phil 2:16
not *h* the Head, from which all .... Col 2:19
H faith, and a good conscience............ 1Ti 1:19
H the mystery of the faith in a 1Ti 3:9
H fast the faithful word as he .... Titus 1:9
h the four winds of the earth,............. Rev 7:1

HOLDS
whether in tents, or in strong *h*......... Num 13:19
mountains, and caves, and strong *h*..... Judg 6:2
in the wilderness in strong *h*............ 1Sa 23:14
with us in strong *h* in the wood 1Sa 23:19
and dwelt in strong *h* at En-gedi........ 1Sa 23:29
their strong *h* wilt thou set on.......... 2Kin 8:12
And he fortified the strong *h* 2Chr 11:11
hast brought his strong *h* to ruin .... Ps 89:40
to destroy the strong *h* thereof.......... Is 23:11
and he shall destroy thy strong *h*....... Jer 48:18
the strong *h* are surprised, and........ Jer 48:41
they have remained in their *h* .... Jer 51:30
strong *h* of the daughter of Judah........ Lam 2:2
he hath destroyed his strong *h*.......... Lam 2:5
they brought him into *h*, that his........ Eze 19:9
his devices against the strong *h*......... Dan 11:24
most strong *h* with a strange god .... Dan 11:39
and throw down all thy strong *h*........ Mic 5:11
All thy strong *h* shall be like.......... Nah 3:12
the siege, fortify thy strong *h*........... Nah 3:14
to the pulling down of strong *h*......... 2Cor 10:4

HOLE
shall be an *h* in the top of it............ Ex 28:32
work round about the *h* of it .... Ex 28:32
as it were the *h* of an habergeon,....... Ex 28:32
there was an *h* in the midst of........... Ex 39:23
as the *h* of an habergeon, with a .... Ex 39:23
with a band round about the *h*.......... Ex 39:23
bored a *h* in the lid of it, and......... 2Kin 12:9
in his hand by the *h* of the door .... Song 5:4
shall play on the *h* of the asp .... Is 11:8
to the *h* of the pit whence ye are....... Is 51:1
hide it there in a *h* of the rock.......... Jer 13:4
I looked, behold a *h* in the wall......... Eze 8:7

HOLE'S
nest in the sides of the *h* mouth......... Jer 48:28

HOLES
h where they had hid themselves.......... 1Sa 14:11
shall go into the *h* of the rocks.......... Is 2:19
in the *h* of the rocks, and upon .... Is 7:19
they are all of them snared in *h*......... Is 42:22
out of the *h* of the rocks .... Jer 16:16
their *h* like worms of the earth......... Mic 7:17
and filled his *h* with prey.............. Nah 2:12
wages to put it into a bag with *h* ...... Hag 1:6
shall consume away in their *h* .... Zec 14:12
saith unto him, The foxes have *h*....... Mt 8:20
Jesus said unto him, Foxes have *h* ...... Lk 9:58

HOLIER
for I am in than thou...................... Is 65:5

HOLIEST
which is called the *H* of all............ Heb 9:3
that the way into the *h* of all .... Heb 9:8
into the *h* by the blood of Jesus......... Heb 10:19

HOLILY
are witnesses, and God also, how *h*...... 1Th 2:10

HOLINESS
Who is like thee, glorious in *h*........ Ex 15:11
of a signet, *H* TO THE LORD .... Ex 28:36
of a signet, *H* TO THE LORD .... Ex 39:30
the LORD in the beauty of *h* 1Chr 16:29
should praise the beauty of *h*.......... 2Chr 20:21
they sanctified themselves in *h*......... 2Chr 31:18
the LORD in the beauty of *h*........... Ps 29:2
at the remembrance of his *h*........... Ps 30:4
sitteth upon the throne of his *h*......... Ps 47:8
our God, in the mountain of his *h*...... Ps 48:1
God hath spoken in his *h* .... Ps 60:6
Once have I sworn by my *h* that I..... Ps 89:35
h becometh thine house, O LORD,..... Ps 93:5
the LORD in the beauty of *h* .... Ps 96:9
at the remembrance of his *h*........... Ps 97:12
God hath spoken in his *h*............. Ps 108:7
in the beauties of *h* from the .... Ps 110:3
her hire shall be to the LORD .... Is 23:18
it shall be called The way of *h* .... Is 35:8
drink it in the courts of my *h* .... Is 62:9
from the habitation of thy *h*............ Is 63:15
The people of thy *h* have.............. Is 63:18
Israel was *h* unto the LORD, and...... Jer 2:3
and because of the words of his *h*...... Jer 23:9
of justice, and mountain of *h* .... Jer 31:23
The LORD God hath sworn by his *h*.... Amos 4:2
deliverance, and there shall be *h*...... Obad 17
of the horses, *H* UNTO THE LORD ...... Zec 14:20
in Judah shall be *h* unto the LORD ..... Zec 14:21
the *h* of the LORD which he loved...... Mal 2:11
In *h* and righteousness before him,...... Lk 1:75
or *h* we had made this man to walk .... Acts 3:12
according to the spirit of *h* .... Rom 1:4
servants to righteousness unto *h*....... Rom 6:19
to God, ye have your fruit unto *h*....... Rom 6:22

perfecting *h* in the fear of God 2Cor 7:1
in righteousness, and true *h*............ Eph 4:24
unblameable in *h* before God 1Th 3:13
us unto uncleanness, but unto *h* 1Th 4:7
and charity and *h* with sobriety 1Ti 2:15
be in behaviour as becometh *h* .... Titus 2:3
we might be partakers of his *h*.......... Heb 12:10
Follow peace with all men, and *h* .... Heb 12:14

HOLLOW
he touched the *h* of his thigh............ Gen 32:25
the *h* of Jacob's thigh was out of .... Gen 32:25
which is upon the *h* of the thigh......... Gen 32:32
because he touched the *h* of.............. Gen 32:32
H with boards shalt thou make it........ Ex 27:8
he made the altar *h* with boards......... Ex 38:7
walls of the house with *h* strakes .... Lev 14:37
But God clave an *h* place that was....... Judg 15:19
the waters in the *h* of his hand.......... Is 40:12
was four fingers: it was *h* .... Jer 52:21

HOLON (*ho'-lon*) See HILEN.
1. A Levitical city in Judah.
And Goshen, and *H*, and Giloh.......... Josh 15:51
H with her suburbs, and Debir with..... Josh 21:15
2. A Moabite city.
upon *H*, and upon Jahazah, and upon... Jer 48:21

HOLPEN
they have *h* the children of Lot .... Ps 83:8
because thou, LORD, hast *h* me........... Ps 86:17
he that is *h* shall fall down, and......... Is 31:3
they shall be *h* with a little............ Dan 11:34
He hath *h* his servant Israel, in......... Lk 1:54

HOLY See PREFACE.
whereon thou standest is *h* ground ...... Ex 3:5
the sabbath day, to keep it *h*........... Ex 20:8
for it is *h* unto you .... Ex 31:14
ye may put difference between *h* .... Lev 10:10
yourselves, and ye shall be .... Lev 11:44
yourselves therefore, and be ye *h* ...... Lev 20:7
place whereon thou standest is *h* .... Josh 5:15
There is none *h* as the LORD 1Sa 2:2
that this is an *h* man of God 2Kin 4:9
he will bear him from his *h*............ Ps 20:6
his ways, and *h* in all his works........ Ps 145:17
another, and said, *H*, *h*............... Is 6:3
Lord in the *h* mount at Jerusalem....... Is 27:13
his *h* arm in the eyes of all the......... Is 52:10
doing thy pleasure on my *h* day .... Is 58:13
put no difference between the *h* .... Eze 22:26
in her is of the *H* Ghost............... Mt 1:20
baptize you with the *H* Ghost........... Mt 3:11
not that which is *h* unto the dogs .... Mt 7:6
baptize you with the *H* Ghost........... Mk 1:8
of his Father with the *h* angels......... Mk 8:38
shall be filled with the *H* Ghost .... Lk 1:15
The *H* Ghost shall come upon thee,...... Lk 1:35
therefore also that *h* thing which .... Lk 1:35
baptize you with the *H* Ghost .... Lk 3:16
Jesus being full of the *H* Ghost.......... Lk 4:1
the *H* One of God....................... Lk 4:34
his Father's, and of the *h* angels........ Lk 9:26
which baptizeth with the *H* Ghost ...... Jn 1:33
for the *H* Ghost was not yet given....... Jn 7:39
unto them, Receive ye the *H* Ghost...... Jn 20:22
the *H* Ghost not many days hence........ Acts 1:5
were all filled with the *H* Ghost........ Acts 2:4
receive the gift of the *H* Ghost......... Acts 2:38
thine heart to lie to the *H* Ghost .... Acts 5:3
where thou standest is *h* ground .... Acts 7:33
ye do always resist the *H* Ghost .... Acts 7:51
of Nazareth with the *H* Ghost.......... Acts 10:38
For it seemed good to the *H* Ghost ...... Acts 15:28
Have ye received the *H* Ghost........... Acts 19:2
be *h*, the lump is also *h*.............. Rom 11:16
your bodies a living sacrifice, *h*......... Rom 12:1
and peace, and joy in the *H* Ghost ...... Rom 14:17
of the world, that we should be *h* .... Eph 1:4
but that it should be *h* and............. Eph 5:27
through death, to present you *h* .... Col 1:22
every where, lifting up *h* hands......... 1Ti 2:8
and called us with an *h* calling.......... 2Ti 1:9
high priest became us, who is *h*......... Heb 7:26
so be ye *h* in all manner of............. 1Pet 1:15
an *h* priesthood, to offer up 1Pet 2:5
ye to be in all *h* conversation.......... 2Pet 3:11
These things saith he that is *h* .... Rev 3:7
that is *h*, let him be *h* still............ Rev 22:11

HOLYDAY
with a multitude that kept *h*............ Ps 42:4
in drink, or in respect of an *h*........... Col 2:16

HOMAM (*ho'-mam*) See HEMAM. A son of
Lotan.
of Lotan; Hori, and *H*................ 1Chr 1:39

HOME
by her, until his lord came *h*........... Gen 39:16
of his house, Bring these men *h* .... Gen 43:16
And when Joseph came *h*, they .... Gen 43:26
field, and shall not be brought *h* .... Ex 9:19
mother, whether she be born at *h*....... Lev 18:9
shalt bring her *h* to thine house......... Deut 21:12
he shall be free at *h* one year .... Deut 24:5
father's household, *h* unto thee......... Josh 2:18
If ye bring me *h* again to fight .... Judg 11:9
your way, that thou mayest go *h*........ Judg 19:9
hath brought me *h* again empty......... Ruth 1:21
And they went unto their own *h*......... 1Sa 2:20
and bring their calves from them 1Sa 6:7

and shut up their calves at *h*........... 1Sa 6:10
And Saul also went *h* to Gibeah........ 1Sa 10:26
no more *h* to his father's house 1Sa 18:2
And Saul went *h*...................... 1Sa 24:22
Then David sent *h* to Tamar 2Sa 13:7
not fetch *h* again his banished 2Sa 14:13
gat him *h* to his house, to his 2Sa 17:23
in Lebanon, and two months at *h*....... 1Kin 5:14
Come *h* with me, and refresh........... 1Kin 13:7
Come *h* with me, and eat bread......... 1Kin 13:15
glory of this, and tarry at *h*........... 2Kin 14:10
I bring the ark of God *h* to me......... 1Chr 13:12
So David brought not the ark *h* to....... 1Chr 13:13
him out of Ephraim, to go *h* again 2Chr 25:10
they returned *h* in great anger 2Chr 25:10
abide now at *h*....................... 2Chr 25:19
and when he came *h*, he sent and .... Est 5:10
that he will bring *h* thy seed........... Job 39:12
tarried at *h* divided the spoil........... Ps 68:12
For the goodman is not at *h*............ Prov 7:19
will come *h* at the day appointed .... Prov 7:20
because man goeth to his long *h*........ Eccl 12:5
that he should carry him *h*............ Jer 39:14
bereaveth, at *h* there is as death........ Lam 1:20
a proud man, neither keepeth at *h* ..... Hab 2:5
and when ye brought it *h*, I did .... Hag 1:9
lieth at *h* sick of the palsy .... Mt 8:6
Go *h* to thy friends, and tell them...... Mk 5:19
which are at *h* at my house............ Lk 9:61
And when he cometh *h*, he calleth...... Lk 15:6
disciple took her unto his own *h* .... Jn 19:27
went away again unto their own *h* ..... Jn 20:10
and they returned *h* again............. Acts 21:6
any man hunger, let him eat at *h* 1Cor 11:34
let them ask their husbands at *h*....... 1Cor 14:35
whilst we are at *h* in the body 2Cor 5:6
learn first to shew piety at *h*........... 1Ti 5:4
be discreet, chaste, keepers at *h* .... Titus 2:5

HOMEBORN
One law shall be to him that is *h*....... Ex 12:49
is he a *h* slave?...................... Jer 2:14

HOMER
a *h* of barley seed shall be............ Lev 27:16
the seed of an *h* shall yield an.......... Is 5:10
contain the tenth part of an *h* .... Eze 45:11
the ephah the tenth part of an *h*........ Eze 45:11
thereof shall be after the *h* .... Eze 45:11
part of an ephah of an *h* of wheat...... Eze 45:13
of an ephah of an *h* of barley........... Eze 45:13
which is an *h* of ten homers .... Eze 45:14
for ten baths are an *h*................. Eze 45:14
an *h* of barley, and an half *h*.......... Hos 3:2

HOMERS
gathered least gathered ten *h* .... Num 11:32

HONEST
ground are they, which in an *h*......... Lk 8:15
among you seven men of *h* report ...... Acts 6:3
Provide things *h* in the sight of .... Rom 12:17
Providing for *h* things, not only 2Cor 8:21
that ye should do that which is *h* 2Cor 13:7
are true, whatsoever things are *h*....... Phil 4:8
conversation *h* among the Gentiles...... 1Pet 2:12

HONESTLY
Let us walk *h*, as in the day .... Rom 13:13
That ye may walk *h* toward them 1Th 4:12
in all things willing to live *h*.......... Heb 13:18

HONESTY
life in all godliness and *h*............. 1Ti 2:2

HONEY
a little balm, and a little *h*........... Gen 43:11
a land flowing with milk and *h*........ Ex 3:8
a land flowing with milk and *h*........ Ex 3:17
a land flowing with milk and *h*........ Ex 13:5
of it was like wafers made with *h*...... Ex 16:31
a land flowing with milk and *h*........ Ex 33:3
shalt burn no leaven, nor any *h*........ Lev 2:11
land that floweth with milk and *h*...... Lev 20:24
surely it floweth with milk and *h*...... Num 13:27
land which floweth with milk and *h*.... Num 14:8
land that floweth with milk and *h*...... Num 16:13
land that floweth with milk and *h*...... Num 16:14
land that floweth with milk and *h*...... Deut 6:3
a land of oil olive, and *h*.............. Deut 8:8
land that floweth with milk and *h*...... Deut 11:9
land that floweth with milk and *h*...... Deut 26:9
land that floweth with milk and *h*...... Deut 26:15
land that floweth with milk and *h*...... Deut 27:3
that floweth with milk and *h*........... Deut 31:20
him to suck *h* out of the rock .... Deut 32:13
land that floweth with milk and *h*...... Josh 5:6
h in the carcase of the lion........... Judg 14:8
h out of the carcase of the lion .... Judg 14:9
went down, What is sweeter than *h* ..... Judg 14:18
there was *h* upon the ground........... 1Sa 14:25
the wood, behold, the *h* dropped........ 1Sa 14:26
I tasted a little of this *h*............. 1Sa 14:29
I did but taste a little *h* with 1Sa 14:43
And *h*, and butter, and sheep, and 2Sa 17:29
and cracknels, and a cruse of *h*........ 1Kin 14:3
a land of oil olive and of *h*........... 2Kin 18:32
of corn, wine, and oil, and *h*........... 2Chr 31:5
the floods, the brooks of *h*............ Job 20:17
sweeter also than *h* and the *h* .... Ps 19:10
with *h* out of the rock should I .... Ps 81:16
yea, sweeter than *h* to my mouth .... Ps 119:103
My son, eat thou *h*, because it is ...... Prov 24:13

HONEYCOMB *(cont.)*

Hast thou found h?........................Prov 25:16
It is not good to eat much h.............Prov 25:27
h and milk are under thy tongue........Song 4:11
have eaten my honeycomb with my h...Song 5:1
h shall he eat, that he may know........Is 7:15
h shall every one eat that is...............Is 7:22
a land flowing with milk and h...........Jer 11:5
a land flowing with milk and h...........Jer 32:22
and of barley, and of oil, and of h.......Jer 41:8
in my mouth as h for sweetness.........Eze 3:3
thou didst eat fine flour, and h..........Eze 16:13
thee, fine flour, and oil, and h...........Eze 16:19
for them, flowing with milk and h......Eze 20:6
them, flowing with milk and h...........Eze 20:15
wheat of Minnith, and Pannag, and h..Eze 27:17
and his meat was locusts and wild h...Mt 3:4
and he did eat locusts and wild h.......Mk 1:6
shall be in thy mouth sweet as h........Rev 10:9
and it was in my mouth sweet as h......Rev 10:10

HONEYCOMB

in his hand, and dipped it in an h.......1Sa 14:27
sweeter also than honey and the h......Ps 19:10
of a strange woman drop as an h........Prov 5:3
Pleasant words are as an h................Prov 16:24
and the h, which is sweet to thy.........Prov 24:13
The full soul loatheth an h...............Prov 27:7
lips, O my spouse, drop as the h.........Song 4:11
I have eaten my h with my honey.......Song 5:1
of a broiled fish, and of an h..............Lk 24:42

HONOUR

unto their assembly, mine h..............Gen 49:6
and I will get me h upon Pharaoh......Ex 14:17
I have gotten me h upon Pharaoh......Ex 14:18
H thy father and thy mother.............Ex 20:12
nor h the person of the mighty..........Lev 19:15
h the face of the old man, and...........Lev 19:32
promote thee unto very great h.........Num 22:17
able indeed to promote thee to h......Num 22:37
to promote thee unto great h...........Num 24:11
Lord hath kept thee back from h.......Num 24:11
put some of thine h upon him...........Num 27:20
H thy father and thy mother, as.........Deut 5:16
in praise, and in name, and in h.........Deut 26:19
takest shall not be for thine h...........Judg 4:9
wherewith by me they h God...........Judg 9:9
come to pass we may do thee h..........Judg 13:17
for them that h me I will h...............1Sa 2:30
yet h me now, I pray thee, before......1Sa 15:30
of, of them shall I be had in h............2Sa 6:22
thou that David doth h thy father......2Sa 10:3
hast not asked, both riches, nor h.......1Kin 3:13
Glory and h are in his presence.........1Chr 16:27
to thee for the h of thy servant.........1Chr 17:18
thou that David doth h thy father......1Chr 19:3
h come of thee, and thou reignest......1Chr 29:12
age, full of days, riches, and h...........1Chr 29:28
not asked riches, wealth, or h............2Chr 1:11
give thee riches, and wealth, and h....2Chr 1:12
he had riches and h in abundance......2Chr 17:5
h in abundance, and joined...............2Chr 18:1
be for thine h from the Lord God......2Chr 26:18
had exceeding much riches and h.......2Chr 32:27
Jerusalem did him h at his death........2Chr 32:33
the h of his excellent majesty............Est 1:4
shall give to their husbands h............Est 1:20
And the king said, What h and..........Est 6:3
man whom the king delighteth to h...Est 6:6
to do h more than to myself..............Est 6:6
man whom the king delighteth to h...Est 6:7
whom the king delighteth to h..........Est 6:9
man whom the king delighteth to h...Est 6:9
man whom the king delighteth to h...Est 6:11
light, and gladness, and joy, and h.....Est 8:16
His sons come to h, and he knoweth...Job 14:21
earth, and lay mine h in the dust........Ps 7:5
hast crowned him with glory and h.....Ps 8:5
h and majesty hast thou laid upon......Ps 21:5
the place where thine h dwelleth........Ps 26:8
man being in h abideth not................Ps 49:12
Man that is in h, and.......................Ps 49:20
Sing forth the h of his name..............Ps 66:2
praise and with thy h all the day........Ps 71:8
I will deliver him, and h him..............Ps 91:15
H and majesty are before him...........Ps 96:6
thou art clothed with h....................Ps 104:1
his horn shall be exalted with h.........Ps 112:9
of the glorious h of thy majesty.........Ps 145:5
this h have all his saints...................Ps 149:9
H the Lord with thy substance, and...Prov 3:9
and in her left hand riches and h........Prov 3:16
she shall bring thee to h...................Prov 4:8
thou give thine h unto others............Prov 5:9
Riches and h are with me.................Prov 8:18
A gracious woman retaineth h...........Prov 11:16
of people is the king's h...................Prov 14:28
and before h is humility...................Prov 15:33
and before h is humility...................Prov 18:12
It is an h for a man to cease..............Prov 20:3
findeth life, righteousness, and h.......Prov 21:21
fear of the Lord are riches, and h......Prov 22:4
but the h of kings is to search...........Prov 25:2
so h is not seemly for a fool...............Prov 26:1
so is he that giveth h to a fool...........Prov 26:8
but h shall uphold the humble in........Prov 29:23
Strength and h are her clothing.........Prov 31:25
hath given riches, wealth, and h.........Eccl 6:2
is in reputation for wisdom and h......Eccl 10:1
mouth, and with their lips do h me.....Is 29:13
The beast of the field shall h me........Is 43:20

and shalt h him, not doing thine........Is 58:13
h before all the nations of.................Jer 33:9
of me gifts and rewards and great h....Dan 2:6
power, and for the h of my majesty....Dan 4:30
the glory of my kingdom, mine h.......Dan 4:36
the King of heaven, all whose............Dan 4:37
and majesty, and glory, and h............Dan 5:18
not give the h of the kingdom...........Dan 11:21
shall he h the God of forces...............Dan 11:38
knew not shall he h with gold...........Dan 11:38
I be a father, where is mine h.............Mal 1:6
them, A prophet is not without h.......Mt 13:57
saying, H thy father and mother........Mt 15:4
h not his father or his mother,...........Mt 15:6
H thy father and thy mother:............Mt 19:19
them, A prophet is not without h.......Mk 6:4
H thy father and thy mother.............Mk 7:10
not, H thy father and mother............Mk 10:19
H thy father and thy mother.............Lk 18:20
hath no h in his own country.............Jn 4:44
That all men should h the Son...........Jn 5:23
even as they h the Father..................Jn 5:23
I receive not h from men..................Jn 5:41
which receive h one of another,.........Jn 5:44
seek not the h that cometh from........Jn 5:44
but I h my Father, and ye do..............Jn 8:49
h myself, my h is nothing.................Jn 8:54
serve me, him will my Father h..........Jn 12:26
in well doing seek for glory and h......Rom 2:7
But glory, h, and peace, to every........Rom 2:10
lump to make one vessel unto h.........Rom 9:21
in h preferring one another...............Rom 12:10
to whom fear; h to whom.................Rom 13:7
these we bestow more abundant h......1Cor 12:23
h to that part which lacked...............1Cor 12:24
By h and dishonour, by evil report....2Cor 6:8
H thy father and mother...................Eph 6:2
not in any h to the satisfying of.........Col 2:23
his vessel in sanctification and..........1Th 4:4
the only wise God, be h and glory......1Ti 1:17
H widows that are widows indeed......1Ti 5:3
be counted worthy of double h..........1Ti 5:17
their own masters worthy of all h......1Ti 6:1
to whom be h and power everlasting...1Ti 6:16
and some to h, and some to...............2Ti 2:20
he shall be a vessel unto h.................2Ti 2:21
crownedst him with glory and h........Heb 2:7
of death, crowned with glory and h....Heb 2:9
house hath more h than the house......Heb 3:3
no man taketh this h unto himself......Heb 5:4
might be found unto praise and h.......1Pet 1:7
H all men....................................1Pet 2:17
If the king.....................................1Pet 2:17
giving h unto the wife, as unto..........1Pet 3:7
he received from God the Father h.....2Pet 1:17
when those beasts give glory and h.....Rev 4:9
O Lord, to receive glory and h...........Rev 4:11
and wisdom, and strength, and h........Rev 5:12
heard I saying, Blessing, and h...........Rev 5:13
and wisdom, and thanksgiving, and h..Rev 7:12
Salvation, and glory, and h...............Rev 19:1
glad and rejoice, and give h to him.....Rev 19:7
do bring their glory and h into it........Rev 21:24
glory and h of the nations into it........Rev 21:26

HONOURABLE

he was more h than all the house........Gen 34:19
more, and more h than they...............Num 22:15
a man of God, and he is an h man.......1Sa 9:6
bidding, and is h in thine house..........1Sa 22:14
Was he not most h of three................2Sa 23:19
He was more h than the thirty,...........2Sa 23:23
a great man with his master, and h.....2Kin 5:1
Jabez was more h than his..................1Chr 4:9
he was more h than the two...............1Chr 11:21
he was h among the thirty, but...........1Chr 11:25
and the h man dwelt in it...................Job 22:8
daughters were among thy h women...Ps 45:9
His work is h and glorious.................Ps 111:3
captain of fifty, and the h man...........Is 3:3
and the base against the h.................Is 3:5
their h men are famished, and...........Is 5:13
The ancient and h, he is the head.......Is 9:15
are the h of the earth.......................Is 23:8
contempt all the h of the earth..........Is 23:9
magnify the law, and make it h..........Is 42:21
in my sight, thou hast been h.............Is 43:4
delight, the holy of the Lord, h..........Is 58:13
and they cast lots for her h men.........Nah 3:10
an h counsellor, which also...............Mk 15:43
lest a more h man than thou be..........Lk 14:8
h women, and the chief men of the....Acts 13:50
also of h women which were Greeks...Acts 17:12
ye are h, but we are despised.............1Cor 4:10
body, which we think to be less h.......1Cor 12:23
Marriage is h in all, and the bed........Heb 13:4

HONOURED

I will be h upon Pharaoh, and upon....Ex 14:4
that regardeth reproof shall be h........Prov 13:18
waiteth on his master shall be h.........Prov 27:18
neither hast thou h me with thy........Is 43:23
all that h her despise her,...................Lam 1:8
the faces of elders were not h............Lam 5:12
h him that liveth for ever, whose.......Dan 4:34
also h us with many honours.............Acts 28:10
or one member be h, all the...............1Cor 12:26

HONOUREST

h thy sons above me, to make.............1Sa 2:29

HONOURETH

but he h them that fear the Lord........Ps 15:4
is better than he that h himself...........Prov 12:9

but he that h him hath mercy on........Prov 14:31
A son h his father, and a servant........Mal 1:6
mouth, and h me with their lips..........Mt 15:8
This people h me with their lips,........Mk 7:6
He that h not the Son h not...............Jn 5:23
it is my Father that h me..................Jn 8:54

HONOURS

Who also honoured us with many h....Acts 28:10

HOODS

and the fine linen, and the h...............Is 3:23

HOOF

shall not an h be left behind...............Ex 10:26
Whatsoever parteth the h, and is........Lev 11:3
cud, or of them that divide the h.........Lev 11:4
the cud, but divideth not the h...........Lev 11:4
the cud, but divideth not the h...........Lev 11:6
the cud, but divideth not the h...........Lev 11:6
the swine, though he divide the h.......Lev 11:7
every beast which divideth the h........Lev 11:26
And every beast that parteth the h.....Deut 14:6
of them that divide the cloven h.........Deut 14:7
the cud, but divide not the h..............Deut 14:8
swine, because it divideth the h..........Deut 14:8

HOOFS

or bullock that hath horns and............Ps 69:31
their horses' h shall be counted..........Is 5:28
of the h of his strong horses...............Jer 47:3
With the h of his horses shall he.........Eze 26:11
nor the h of beasts trouble them.........Eze 32:13
iron, and I will make thy h brass.........Mic 4:13

HOOK

I will put my h in thy nose................2Kin 19:28
thou draw out leviathan with an h......Job 41:1
Canst thou put an h into his nose.......Job 41:2
will I put my h in thy nose................Is 37:29
go thou to the sea, and cast an h........Mt 17:27

HOOKS

their h shall be of gold, upon.............Ex 26:32
gold, and their h shall be of gold.......Ex 26:37
the h of the pillars and their..............Ex 27:10
the h of the pillars and their..............Ex 27:11
their h shall be of silver,....................Ex 27:17
their h were of gold..........................Ex 36:36
five pillars of it with their h...............Ex 36:38
the h of the pillars and their..............Ex 38:11
the h of the pillars and their..............Ex 38:11
the h of the pillars and their..............Ex 38:17
their h of silver, and the...................Ex 38:19
shekels he made h for the pillars........Ex 38:28
But I will put h in thy jaws................Eze 29:4
put it into thy jaws, and I will...........Eze 38:4
And within were h, an hand broad,....Eze 40:43
that he will take you away with h.......Amos 4:2

HOPE

If I should say, I have h.....................Ruth 1:12
yet now there is h in Israel................Ezr 10:2
thy fear, thy confidence, thy h...........Job 4:6
So the poor hath h, and iniquity.........Job 5:16
in my strength, that I should h...........Job 6:11
shuttle, and are spent without h.........Job 7:6
and the hypocrite's h shall perish.......Job 8:13
Whose h shall be cut off, and.............Job 8:14
be secure, because there is h.............Job 11:18
their h shall be as the giving up.........Job 11:20
For there is h of a tree, if it..............Job 14:7
and thou destroyest the h of man......Job 14:19
And where is now my h.....................Job 17:15
as for my h, who shall see it..............Job 17:15
mine h hath he removed like a...........Job 19:10
For what is the h of the....................Job 27:8
If I have made gold my h, or have......Job 31:24
Behold, the h of him is in vain...........Job 41:9
my flesh also shall rest in h...............Ps 16:9
thou didst make me h when I was......Ps 22:9
heart, all ye that h in the Lord...........Ps 31:24
upon them that h in his mercy...........Ps 33:18
us, according as we h in thee..............Ps 33:22
For in thee, O Lord, do I h................Ps 38:15
my h is in thee.................................Ps 39:7
h thou in God..................................Ps 42:5
h thou in God..................................Ps 42:11
h in God...Ps 43:5
For out my h, O Lord God.................Ps 71:5
But I will h continually, and will........Ps 71:14
they might set their h in God.............Ps 78:7
which thou hast caused me to h..........Ps 119:49
but I h in thy word...........................Ps 119:81
I h in thy word.................................Ps 119:114
and let me not be ashamed of my h.....Ps 119:116
doth wait, and in his word do I h........Ps 130:5
Let Israel h in the Lord....................Ps 130:7
Let Israel h in the Lord....................Ps 131:3
whose h is in the Lord his God...........Ps 146:5
him, in those that h in his mercy........Ps 147:11
The h of the righteous shall be..........Prov 10:28
the h of unjust men perisheth............Prov 11:7
H deferred maketh the heart sick,.......Prov 13:12
than of a fool there is more h.............Prov 14:32
Chasten thy son while there is h........Prov 19:18
there is more h of a fool than of.........Prov 26:12
there is more h of a fool than of.........Prov 29:20
to all the living there is h..................Eccl 9:4
the pit cannot h for thy truth............Is 38:18
saidst thou not, There is no h............Is 57:10
but thou saidst, There is no h............Jer 2:25
O the h of Israel, the saviour............Jer 14:8

H

the LORD, and whose *h* the LORD is...... Jer 17:7
the *h* of Israel, all that forsake .... Jer 17:13
thou art my *h* in the day of evil .... Jer 17:17
And they said, There is no *h* .... Jer 18:12
there is *h* in thine end, saith .... Jer 31:17
the LORD, the *h* of their fathers .... Jer 50:7
my *h* is perished from the LORD .... Lam 3:18
to my mind, therefore have I *h* .... Lam 3:21
therefore will I *h* in him .... Lam 3:24
is good that a man should both *h* .... Lam 3:26
if so be there may be *h* .... Lam 3:29
they have made others to *h* that .... Eze 13:6
her *h* was lost, then she took .... Eze 19:5
bones are dried, and our *h* is lost .... Eze 37:11
valley of Achor for a door of *h*............... Hos 2:15
LORD will be the *h* of his people .... Joel 3:16
strong hold, ye prisoners of *h* .... Zec 9:12
to them of whom ye *h* to receive .... Lk 6:34
also my flesh shall rest in *h* .... Acts 2:26
the *h* of their gains was gone .... Acts 16:19
of the *h* and resurrection of the .... Acts 23:6
have *h* toward God, which they .... Acts 24:15
am judged for the *h* of the .... Acts 26:6
God day and night, *h* to come .... Acts 26:7
all *h* that we should be saved was .... Acts 27:20
because that for the *h* of Israel .... Acts 28:20
Who against *h* believed in *h* .... Rom 4:18
Who against *h* believed in *h* .... Rom 4:18
rejoice in *h* of the glory of God .... Rom 5:2
experience; and experience, *h* .... Rom 5:4
And *h* maketh not ashamed .... Rom 5:5
who hath subjected the same in *h* .... Rom 8:20
For we are saved by *h* .... Rom 8:24
but *h* that is seen is not *h* .... Rom 8:24
man seeth, why doth he yet *h* for .... Rom 8:24
But if we *h* for that we see not,............. Rom 8:25
Rejoicing in *h* .... Rom 12:12
of the scriptures might have *h*............... Rom 15:4
Now the God of *h* fill you with .... Rom 15:13
that ye may abound in *h*, through .... Rom 15:13
he that ploweth should plow in *h* 1Cor 9:10
that he that thresheth in *h* 1Cor 9:10
h should be partaker of his *h* 1Cor 9:10
And now abideth faith, *h*, charity,.......... 1Cor 13:13
life only we have *h* in Christ 1Cor 15:19
our *h* of you is stedfast, knowing 2Cor 1:7
Seeing then that we have such *h* 2Cor 3:12
but having *h*, when your faith is 2Cor 10:15
the *h* of righteousness by faith .... Gal 5:5
know what is the *h* of his calling .... Eph 1:18
covenants of promise, having no *h* .... Eph 2:12
called in one *h* of your calling............... Eph 4:4
to my earnest expectation and my *h* ...... Phil 1:20
Him therefore I *h* to send .... Phil 2:23
For the *h* which is laid up for .... Col 1:5
away from the *h* of the gospel .... Col 1:23
is Christ in you, the *h* of glory .... Col 1:27
patience of *h* in our Lord Jesus 1Th 1:3
For what is our *h*, or joy, or 1Th 2:19
even as others which have no *h*............. 1Th 4:13
for an helmet, the *h* of salvation 1Th 5:8
and good *h* through grace, ... 2Th 2:16
Lord Jesus Christ, which is our *h*........... 1Ti 1:1
In *h* of eternal life, which God .... Titus 1:2
Looking for that blessed *h* .... Titus 2:13
to the *h* of eternal life .... Titus 3:7
of the *h* firm unto the end,.................. Heb 3:6
full assurance of *h* unto the end,........... Heb 6:11
lay hold upon the *h* set before us .... Heb 6:18
Which *h* we have as an anchor of .... Heb 6:19
the bringing in of a better *h* did .... Heb 7:19
h by the resurrection of Jesus 1Pet 1:3
h to the end for the grace that 1Pet 1:13
your faith and *h* might be in God 1Pet 1:21
h that is in you with meekness 1Pet 3:15
this *h* in him purifieth himself 1Jn 3:3

HOPED

Jews to have power over them............... Est 9:1
confounded because they had *h*............ Job 6:20
For I have *h* in thy judgments .... Ps 119:43
because I have *h* in thy word .... Ps 119:74
I *h* in thy word .... Ps 119:147
I have *h* for thy salvation, and,............. Ps 119:166
is salvation *h* for from the hills,............ Jer 3:23
he *h* to have seen some miracle .... Lk 23:8
He *h* also that money should have .... Acts 24:26
And this they did, not as we *h* 2Cor 8:5
is the substance of things *h* for .... Heb 11:1

HOPE'S

For which *h* sake, king Agrippa,........... Acts 26:7

HOPETH

h all things, endureth all things............. 1Cor 13:7

HOPHNI

(hof´-ni) *A son of Eli.*
And the two sons of Eli,........................ 1Sa 1:3
come upon thy two sons, on *H*.............. 1Sa 2:34
and the two sons of Eli,........................ 1Sa 4:4
and the two sons of Eli, *H*................... 1Sa 4:11
people, and thy two sons also, *H*.......... 1Sa 4:17

HOR

(hor) *See* HOR-HAGIDGAD.
1. A mountain in Moab.
and came unto mount *H* .... Num 20:22
unto Moses and Aaron in mount *H*......... Num 20:23
and bring them up unto mount *H* .... Num 20:25
mount *H* in the sight of all the.............. Num 20:27

mount *H* by the way of the Red sea .... Num 21:4
Kadesh, and pitched in mount *H* .... Num 33:37
the priest went up into mount *H* .... Num 33:38
years old when he died in mount *H*........ Num 33:39
And they departed from mount *H* .... Num 33:41
Aaron thy brother died in mount *H*........ Deut 32:50
2. A hill in northern Israel.
shall point out for your mount *H*........... Num 34:7
From mount *H* ye shall point out .... Num 34:8

HORAM

(ho´-ram) *A Canaanite king.*
Then *H* king of Gezer came up to .... Josh 10:33

HOREB

(ho´-reb) *See* SINAI. *A mountain range in Sinai.*
to the mountain of God, even to *H* .... Ex 3:1
thee there upon the rock in *H* .... Ex 17:6
of their ornaments by the mount *H* .... Ex 33:6
H by the way of mount Seir unto .... Deut 1:2
LORD our God spake unto us in *H* .... Deut 1:6
And when we departed from *H* .... Deut 1:19
before the LORD thy God in *H* .... Deut 4:10
in *H* out of the midst of the fire............ Deut 4:15
God made a covenant with us in *H* .... Deut 5:2
Also in *H* ye provoked the LORD to .... Deut 9:8
of the LORD thy God in *H* in the .... Deut 18:16
which he made with them in *H* .... Deut 29:1
stone, which Moses put there at *H* 1Kin 8:9
nights unto *H* the mount of God............ 1Kin 19:8
which Moses put therein at *H*............... 2Chr 5:10
They made a calf in *H*, and................. Ps 106:19
unto him in *H* for all Israel .... Mal 4:4

HOREM

(ho´-rem) *A city in Naphtali.*
And Iron, and Migdal-el, *H*, and .... Josh 19:38

HORESH

See ZIPH.

HOR-HAGIDGAD

(hor-hag-id´-gad) *An encampment of Israel in the wilderness.*
Bene-jaakan, and encamped at *H* .... Num 33:32
And they went from *H*, and pitched........ Num 33:33

HORI

(ho´-ri) *See* HORITE.
1. Son of Lotan.
And the children of Lotan were *H* .... Gen 36:22
are the dukes that came of *H* .... Gen 36:30
H, and Homam, ... 1Chr 1:39
2. Father of Shaphat.
of Simeon, Shaphat the son of *H* .... Num 13:5

HORIMS

(ho´-rims) *See* HORITES. *Inhabitants of Mt. Seir.*
The *H* also dwelt in Seir .... Deut 2:12
destroyed the *H* from before them .... Deut 2:22

HORITE

(ho´-rite) *See* HORI, HORITES. *An inhabitant of Mt. Seir.*
These are the sons of Seir the *H* .... Gen 36:20

HORITES

(ho´-rites) *See* HORIMS. *Same as Horims.*
the *H* in their mount Seir, unto .... Gen 14:6
these are the dukes of the *H* .... Gen 36:29
are the dukes that came of the *H* .... Gen 36:29

HORMAH

(hor´-mah) *See* ZEPHATH. *A Canaanite royal town.*
and discomfited them, even unto *H* .... Num 14:45
he called the name of the place *H* .... Num 21:3
you in Seir, even unto *H* .... Deut 1:44
The king of *H*, one .... Josh 12:14
And Eltolad, and Chesil, and *H* .... Josh 15:30
And Eltolad, and Bethul, and *H* .... Josh 19:4
the name of the city was called *H* .... Judg 1:17
And to them which were in *H* 1Sa 30:30
And at Bethuel, and at *H*, and at 1Chr 4:30

HORN

to push with his *h* in time past.............. Ex 21:29
a long blast with the ram's *h*................. Josh 6:5
mine *h* is exalted in the LORD 1Sa 2:1
exalt the *h* of his anointed.................... 1Sa 2:10
fill thine *h* with oil, and go, I 1Sa 16:1
Then Samuel took the *h* of oil 1Sa 16:13
the *h* of my salvation, my high 2Sa 22:3
Zadok the priest took an *h* of oil 1Kin 1:39
words of God, to lift up the *h* 1Chr 25:5
skin, and defiled my *h* in the dust......... Job 16:15
the *h* of my salvation, and my high .... Ps 18:2
to the wicked, Lift not up the *h* .... Ps 75:4
Lift not up your *h* on high .... Ps 75:5
thy favour our *h* shall be exalted .... Ps 89:17
in my name shall his *h* be exalted .... Ps 89:24
But my *h* shalt thou exalt like .... Ps 92:10
exalt like the *h* of an unicorn .... Ps 92:10
h of his people shall be exalted .... Ps 112:9
will I make the *h* of David to bud .... Ps 132:17
also exalteth the *h* of his people .... Ps 148:14
The *h* of Moab is cut off, and his .... Jer 48:25
fierce anger all the *h* of Israel .... Lam 2:3
he hath set up the *h* of thine .... Lam 2:17
In that day will I cause the *h* of .... Eze 29:21
up among them another little *h* .... Dan 7:8
in this *h* were eyes like the man .... Dan 7:8
The great words which the *h* spake........ Dan 7:11
even of that *h* that had eyes, and .... Dan 7:20
the same *h* made war with the .... Dan 7:21
had a notable *h* between his eyes .... Dan 8:5
strong, the great *h* was broken .... Dan 8:8
one of them came forth a little *h* .... Dan 8:9
the great *h* that is between his .... Dan 8:21
for I will make thine *h* iron.................. Mic 4:13
which lifted up their *h* over the .... Zec 1:21
hath raised up an *h* of salvation .... Lk 1:69

HORNET

God will send the *h* among them........... Deut 7:20
And I sent the *h* before you.................. Josh 24:12

HORNETS

And I will send *h* before thee................ Ex 23:28

HORNS

ram caught in a thicket by his *h*............ Gen 22:13
thou shalt make the *h* it upon .... Ex 27:2
his *h* shall be of the same .... Ex 27:2
put it upon the *h* of the altar .... Ex 29:12
the *h* thereof shall be of the .... Ex 30:2
round about, and the *h* thereof............. Ex 30:3
make an atonement upon the *h* of .... Ex 30:10
the *h* thereof were of the same .... Ex 37:25
round about, and the *h* of it................. Ex 37:26
he made the *h* thereof on the four .... Ex 38:2
the *h* thereof were of the same .... Ex 38:2
h of the altar of sweet incense............. Lev 4:7
the *h* of the altar is before.................. Lev 4:18
put it upon the *h* of the altar of .... Lev 4:25
put it upon the *h* of the altar of .... Lev 4:30
put it upon the *h* of the altar of .... Lev 4:34
put it upon the *h* of the altar .... Lev 8:15
and put it upon the *h* of the altar .... Lev 9:9
put it upon the *h* of the altar .... Lev 16:18
h are like the *h* of unicorns .... Deut 33:17
Chenaanah had made him *h* of iron....... 2Chr 18:10
the ark seven trumpets of rams' *h*......... Josh 6:4
before the ark of the LORD .... Josh 6:6
rams' *h* passed on before the LORD....... Josh 6:8
h before the ark of the LORD went........ Josh 6:13
caught hold on the *h* of the altar 1Kin 1:50
caught hold on the *h* of the altar 1Kin 1:51
caught hold on the *h* of the altar 1Kin 2:28
of Chenaanah made him *h* of iron......... 1Kin 22:11
Chenaanah had made him *h* of iron....... 2Chr 18:10
me from the *h* of the unicorns .... Ps 22:21
than an ox or bullock that hath *h* .... Ps 69:31
All the *h* of the wicked also will .... Ps 75:10
but the *h* of the righteous shall............ Ps 75:10
even unto the *h* of the altar .... Ps 118:27
upon the *h* of your altars .... Jer 17:1
there for a present *h* of ivory .... Eze 27:15
all the diseased with your *h* .... Eze 34:21
altar and upward shall be four *h* .... Eze 43:15
and put it on the four *h* of it................ Eze 43:20
and four *h*....................................... Dan 7:7
I considered the *h*, and, behold, ... Dan 7:8
first *h* plucked up by the roots............. Dan 7:8
of the ten *h* that were in his .... Dan 7:20
the ten *h* out of this kingdom are .... Dan 7:24
the river a ram which had two *h* .... Dan 8:3
and the two *h* were high .... Dan 8:3
he came to the ram that had two *h* .... Dan 8:6
smote the ram, and brake his two *h*...... Dan 8:7
two *h* are the kings of Media .... Dan 8:20
the *h* of the altar shall be cut .... Amos 3:14
taken to us *h* by our own strength .... Amos 6:13
he had *h* coming out of his hand .... Hab 3:4
eyes, and saw, and behold four *h* .... Zec 1:18
These are the *h* which have .... Zec 1:19
These are the *h* which have .... Zec 1:21
to cast out the *h* of the Gentiles .... Zec 1:21
it had been slain, having seven *h*.......... Rev 5:6
h of the golden altar which is............... Rev 9:13
having seven heads and ten *h* .... Rev 12:3
sea, having seven heads and ten *h*........ Rev 13:1
upon his *h* ten crowns, and upon.......... Rev 13:1
he had two *h* like a lamb, and he .... Rev 13:11
having seven heads and ten *h* .... Rev 17:3
hath the seven heads and ten *h*............ Rev 17:7
the ten *h* which thou sawest upon .... Rev 17:12
the ten *h* which thou sawest upon .... Rev 17:16

HORONAIM

(hor-o-na´-im) *See* HOLON. *A Moabite city.*
for in the way of *H* they shall .... Is 15:5
A voice of crying shall be from *H*........... Jer 48:3
for in the going down of *H* the.............. Jer 48:5
voice, from Zoar even unto *H* .... Jer 48:34

HORONITE

(ho´-ron-ite) *A native of Horonaim.*
When Sanballat the *H*, and Tobiah........ Neh 2:10
But when Sanballat the *H*, and .... Neh 2:19
was son in law to Sanballat the *H* .... Neh 13:28

HORRIBLE

day, that, biteth *h* my tempest .... Ps 11:6
me up also out of an *h* pit.................... Ps 40:2
h thing is committed in the land .... Jer 5:30
Israel hath done a very *h* thing............. Jer 18:13
prophets of Jerusalem an *h* thing .... Jer 23:14
I have seen an *h* thing in the .... Hos 6:10

HORRIBLY

be afraid, be ye very desolate,............... Jer 2:12
kings shall be *h* afraid for thee .... Eze 32:10

HORROR

an *h* of great darkness fell upon .... Gen 15:12
upon me, and *h* hath overwhelmed me... Ps 55:5
h hath taken hold upon me because ...... Ps 119:53
sackcloth, and *h* shall cover them......... Eze 7:18

HORSE

the *h*, that biteth the *h* heels .... Gen 49:17
the *h* and his rider hath the LORD thrown Ex 15:1
For the *h* of Pharaoh went in with .... Ex 15:19
the *h* and his rider hath the LORD thrown Ex 15:21
an *h* for an hundred and fifty............... 1Kin 10:29
escaped on an *h* with the horsemen...... 1Kin 20:20
h for *h*, and chariot for 1Kin 20:25

HORSEBACK

that thou hast lost, I for h	1Kin 20:25
an h for an hundred and fifty	2Chr 1:17
of the h gate by the king's house	2Chr 23:15
From above the h gate repaired	Neh 3:28
the h that the king rideth upon	Est 6:8
h be delivered to the hand of one	Est 6:9
and take the apparel and the h	Est 6:10
took Haman the apparel and the h	Est 6:11
on high, she scorneth the h	Job 39:18
Hath thou given the h strength	Job 39:19
Be ye not as the h, or as the	Ps 32:9
An h is a vain thing for safety	Ps 33:17
h are cast into a dead sleep	Ps 76:6
not in the strength of the h	Ps 147:10
The h is prepared against the day	Prov 21:31
A whip for the h, a bridle for	Prov 26:3
bringeth forth the chariot and h	Is 43:17
as an h in the wilderness, that	Is 63:13
as the h rusheth into the battle	Jer 8:6
of the h gate toward the east	Jer 31:40
thee will I break in pieces the h	Jer 51:21
that rideth the h deliver himself	Amos 2:15
behold a man riding upon a red h	Zec 1:8
the h from Jerusalem, and the	Zec 9:10
as his goodly h in the battle	Zec 10:3
smite every h with astonishment	Zec 12:4
will smite every h of the people	Zec 12:4
so shall be the plague of the h	Zec 14:15
And I saw, and behold a white h	Rev 6:2
went out another h that was red	Rev 6:4
And I beheld, and lo a black h	Rev 6:5
And I looked, and behold a pale h	Rev 6:8
even unto the h bridles, by the	Rev 14:20
opened, and behold a white h	Rev 19:11
war against him that sat on the h	Rev 19:19
sword of him that sat upon the h	Rev 19:21

HORSEBACK

there went one on h to meet him	2Kin 9:18
Then he sent out a second on h	2Kin 9:19
bring him on h through the street	Est 6:9
brought him on h through the	Est 6:11
and sent letters by posts on h	Est 8:10

HORSEHOOFS

Then were the h broken by the	Judg 5:22

HORSELEACH

The h hath two daughters, crying	Prov 30:15

HORSEMAN

And Joram said, Take an h, and send	2Kin 9:17
The h lifteth up both the bright	Nah 3:3

HORSEMEN

up with him both chariots and h	Gen 50:9
and chariots of Pharaoh, and his h	Ex 14:9
upon his chariots, and upon his h	Ex 14:17
upon his chariots, and upon his h	Ex 14:18
horses, his chariots, and his h	Ex 14:23
their chariots, and upon their h	Ex 14:26
and covered the chariots, and the h	Ex 14:28
with his h into the sea, and the	Ex 15:19
chariots and h unto the Red sea	Josh 24:6
for his chariots, and to be his h	1Sa 8:11
chariots, six thousand h	1Sa 13:5
h followed hard after him	2Sa 1:6
chariots, and seven hundred h	2Sa 8:4
the Syrians, and forty thousand h	2Sa 10:18
and he prepared him chariots and h	1Kin 1:5
chariots, and twelve thousand h	1Kin 4:26
his chariots, and cities for his h	1Kin 9:19
rulers of his chariots, and his h	1Kin 9:22
gathered together chariots and h	1Kin 10:26
chariots, and twelve thousand h	1Kin 10:26
escaped on an horse with the h	1Kin 20:20
of Israel, and the h thereof	2Kin 2:12
people to Jehoahaz but fifty h	2Kin 13:7
of Israel, and the h thereof	2Kin 13:14
on Egypt for chariots and for h	2Kin 18:24
chariots, and seven thousand h	1Chr 18:4
h out of Mesopotamia, and out of	1Chr 19:6
Solomon gathered chariots and h	2Chr 1:14
chariots, and twelve thousand h	2Chr 1:14
cities, and the cities of the h	2Chr 8:6
and captains of his chariots and h	2Chr 8:9
and chariots, and twelve thousand h	2Chr 9:25
and threescore thousand h	2Chr 12:3
with very many chariots and h	2Chr 16:8
h to help us against the enemy in	Ezr 8:22
captains of the army and h with me	Neh 2:9
saw a chariot with a couple of h	Is 21:7
of men, with a couple of h	Is 21:9
quiver with chariots of men and h	Is 22:6
the h shall set themselves in	Is 22:7
cart, nor bruise it with his h	Is 28:28
and in h, because they are very	Is 31:1
on Egypt for chariots and for h	Is 36:9
shall flee for the noise of the h	Jer 4:29
and get up, ye h, and stand forth	Jer 46:4
young men, h riding upon horses	Eze 23:6
h riding upon horses, all of them	Eze 23:12
and with chariots, and with h	Eze 26:7
shall shake at the noise of the h	Eze 26:10
in thy fairs with horses and h	Eze 27:14
and all thine army, horses and h	Eze 38:4
with chariots, and with h	Dan 11:40
by battle, by horses, nor by h	Hos 1:7
and so, so shall they run	Joel 2:4
their h shall spread themselves	Hab 1:8
their h shall come from far	Hab 1:8
h threescore and ten, and spearmen	Acts 23:23
they left the h to go with him	Acts 23:32

the h were two hundred thousand	Rev 9:16

HORSES

gave them bread in exchange for h	Gen 47:17
which is in the field, upon the h	Ex 9:3
pursued after them, all the h	Ex 14:9
of the sea, even all Pharaoh's h	Ex 14:23
the army of Egypt, unto their h	Deut 11:4
shall not multiply h to himself	Deut 17:16
the end that he should multiply h	Deut 17:16
against thine enemies, and seest h	Deut 20:1
sea shore in multitude, with h	Josh 11:4
thou shalt hough their h, and burn	Josh 11:6
he houghed their h, and burnt	Josh 11:9
David houghed all the chariot h	2Sa 8:4
prepared him chariots and h	2Sa 15:1
stalls of h for his chariots	1Kin 4:26
Barley also and straw for the h	1Kin 4:28
garments, and armour, and spices, h	1Kin 10:25
Solomon had h brought out of	1Kin 10:28
we may find grass to save the h	1Kin 18:5
and two kings with him, and h	1Kin 20:1
Israel went out, and smote the h	1Kin 20:21
as thy people, my h as thy h	1Kin 22:4
h of fire, and parted them both	2Kin 2:11
thy people, and my h as thy h	2Kin 3:7
So Naaman came with his h	2Kin 5:9
compassed the city both with h	2Kin 6:15
the mountain was full of h	2Kin 6:17
of chariots, and a noise of h	2Kin 7:6
and left their tents, and their h	2Kin 7:7
but h tied, and asses tied, and the	2Kin 7:10
thee, five of the h that remain	2Kin 7:13
They took therefore two chariot h	2Kin 7:14
on the wall, and on the h	2Kin 9:33
there are with you chariots and h	2Kin 10:2
the h came into the king's house	2Kin 11:16
And they brought him on h	2Kin 14:20
will deliver thee two thousand h	2Kin 18:23
he took away the h that the kings	2Kin 23:11
also houghed all the chariot h	1Chr 18:4
Solomon had h brought out of	2Chr 1:16
so brought they out h for all the	2Chr 1:17
and raiment, harness, and spices, h	2Chr 9:24
had four thousand stalls for h	2Chr 9:25
unto Solomon h out of Egypt	2Chr 9:28
And they brought him upon h	2Chr 25:28
Their h were seven hundred thirty	Ezr 2:66
Their h, seven hundred thirty and	Neh 7:68
trust in chariots, and some in h	Ps 20:7
I have seen servants upon h	Eccl 10:7
to a company of h in Pharaoh's	Song 1:9
their land is also full of h	Is 2:7
for we will flee upon h	Is 30:16
and stay on h, and trust in	Is 31:1
and their h flesh, and not spirit	Is 31:3
I will give thee two thousand h	Is 36:8
LORD out of all nations upon h	Is 66:20
his h are swifter than eagles	Jer 4:13
They were as fed h in the morning	Jer 5:8
and they ride upon h, set in array	Jer 6:23
of his h was heard from Dan	Jer 8:16
how canst thou contend with h	Jer 12:5
David, riding in chariots and on h	Jer 17:25
David, riding in chariots and on h	Jer 22:4
Harness the h, and get up, ye	Jer 46:4
Come up, ye h, and rage, ye	Jer 46:9
of the hoofs of his strong h	Jer 47:3
A sword is upon their h, and upon	Jer 50:37
sea, and they shall ride upon h	Jer 50:42
cause the h to come up as the	Jer 51:27
Egypt, that they might give him h	Eze 17:15
young men, horsemen riding upon h	Eze 23:6
horsemen riding upon h, all of	Eze 23:12
issue is like the issue of h	Eze 23:20
all of them riding upon h	Eze 23:23
of kings from the north, with h	Eze 26:7
his h their dust shall cover thee	Eze 26:10
With the hoofs of his h shall he	Eze 26:11
traded in thy fairs with h	Eze 27:14
thee forth, and all thine army, h	Eze 38:4
thee, all of them riding upon h	Eze 38:15
be filled at my table with h	Eze 39:20
nor by sword, nor by battle, by h	Hos 1:7
we will not ride upon h	Hos 14:3
of them is as the appearance of h	Joel 2:4
sword, and have taken away your h	Amos 4:10
Shall h run upon the rock	Amos 6:12
that I will cut off thy h out of	Mic 5:10
the wheels, and of the prancing h	Nah 3:2
Their h also are swifter than the	Hab 1:8
that thou didst ride upon thine h	Hab 3:8
walk through the sea with thine h	Hab 3:15
and the h and their riders shall	Hag 2:22
and behind him were there red h	Zec 1:8
In the first chariot were red h	Zec 6:2
and in the second chariot black h	Zec 6:2
And in the third chariot white h	Zec 6:3
fourth chariot grisled and bay h	Zec 6:3
The black h which are therein go	Zec 6:6
them, and the riders on h shall be	Zec 10:5
there be upon the bells of the h	Zec 14:20
like unto h prepared unto battle	Rev 9:7
of many h running to battle	Rev 9:9
And thus I saw the h in the vision	Rev 9:17
the heads of the h were as the	Rev 9:17
wheat, and beasts, and sheep, and h	Rev 18:13
heaven followed him upon white h	Rev 19:14
of mighty men, and the flesh of h	Rev 19:18

HORSES'

their h hoofs shall be counted	Is 5:28
we put his in the h mouths	Jas 3:3

HOSAH (ho'-sah)

1. A city in Asher.

and the coast turneth to H	Josh 19:29

2. A Levite.

of Jeduthun and H to be porters	1Chr 16:38
Also H, of the children of Merari	1Chr 26:10
brethren of H were thirteen	1Chr 26:11
H the lot came forth westward	1Chr 26:16

HOSANNA

saying, H to the son of David	Mt 21:9
H in the highest	Mt 21:9
and saying, H to the son of David	Mt 21:15
that followed, cried, saying, H	Mk 11:9
H in the highest	Mk 11:10
forth to meet him, and cried, H	Jn 12:13

HOSEA (ho-se'-ah) See HOSHEA, OSEE, OSHEA.

A prophet.

word of the LORD that came unto H	Hos 1:1
of the word of the LORD by H	Hos 1:2
and the LORD said to H, Go, take	Hos 1:2

HOSEN

bound in their coats, their h	Dan 3:21

HOSHAIAH (ho-sha-i'-ah)

1. Helped dedicate the wall.

And after them went H, and half of	Neh 12:32

2. Father of Jezaniah.

Kareah, and Jezaniah the son of H	Jer 42:1
Then spake Azariah the son of H	Jer 43:2

HOSHAMA (ho-sha'-mah) Father of Jeconiah.

Pedaiah, and Shenazar, Jecamiah, H	1Chr 3:18

HOSHEA (ho-she'-ah) See HOSEA.

1. Original name of Joshua.

people, he, and H the son of Nun	Deut 32:44

2. An Ephraimite ruler.

of Ephraim, H the son of Azaziah	1Chr 27:20

3. Last king of Israel.

And H the son of Elah made a	2Kin 15:30
H the son of Elah to reign in	2Kin 17:1
H became his servant, and gave him	2Kin 17:3
of Assyria found conspiracy in H	2Kin 17:4
In the ninth year of H the king	2Kin 17:6
of H son of Elah king of Israel	2Kin 18:1
of H son of Elah king of Israel	2Kin 18:9
ninth year of H king of Israel	2Kin 18:10

4. An Israelite who renewed the covenant.

H, Hananiah, Hashub	Neh 10:23

HOSPITALITY

given to h	Rom 12:13
of good behaviour, given to h	1Ti 3:2
But a lover of h, a lover of good	Titus 1:8
Use h one to another without	1Pet 4:9

HOST

finished, and all the h of them	Gen 2:1
of his h spake unto Abraham	Gen 21:22
the chief captain of his h	Gen 21:32
them, he said, This is God's h	Gen 32:2
upon Pharaoh, and upon all his h	Ex 14:4
upon Pharaoh, and upon all his h	Ex 14:17
h of the Egyptians through the	Ex 14:24
troubled the h of the Egyptians	Ex 14:24
all the h of Pharaoh that came	Ex 14:28
his h hath he cast into the sea	Ex 15:4
the dew lay round about the h	Ex 16:13
And his h, and those that were	Num 2:4
And his h, and those that were	Num 2:6
And his h, and those that were	Num 2:8
And his h, and those that were	Num 2:11
And his h, and those that were	Num 2:13
And his h, and those that were	Num 2:15
And his h, and those that were	Num 2:19
And his h, and those that were	Num 2:21
And his h, and those that were	Num 2:23
And his h, and those that were	Num 2:26
And his h, and those that were	Num 2:28
And his h, and those that were	Num 2:30
old, all that enter into the h	Num 4:3
over his h was Nahshon the son of	Num 10:14
over the h of the tribe of	Num 10:15
over the h of the tribe of	Num 10:16
over his h was Elizur the son of	Num 10:18
over the h of the tribe of	Num 10:19
over the h of the tribe of	Num 10:20
over his h was Elishama the son	Num 10:22
over the h of the tribe of	Num 10:23
over the h of the tribe of	Num 10:24
over his h was Ahiezer the son of	Num 10:25
over the h of the tribe of	Num 10:26
over the h of the tribe of	Num 10:27
wroth with the officers of the h	Num 31:14
were over thousands of the h	Num 31:48
were waxed out from among the h	Deut 2:14
to destroy them from among the h	Deut 2:15
stars, even all the h of heaven	Deut 4:19
moon, or any of the h of heaven	Deut 17:3
When the h goeth forth against	Deut 23:9
Pass through the h, and command	Josh 1:11
the officers went through the h	Josh 3:2
but as captain of the h of the	Josh 5:14
of the LORD's h said unto Joshua	Josh 5:15
even all the h that was on the	Josh 10:5
to Joshua to the h at Shiloh	Josh 18:9
the captain of whose h was Sisera	Judg 4:2

and all his chariots, and all his *h*...........	Judg 4:15
the chariots, and after the *h*...................	Judg 4:16
all the *h* of Sisera fell upon the...........	Judg 4:16
so that the *h* of the Midianites...........	Judg 7:1
the *h* of Midian was beneath him...........	Judg 7:8
Arise, get thee down unto the *h*...........	Judg 7:9
Phurah thy servant down to the *h*.........	Judg 7:10
to go down unto the *h*...........................	Judg 7:11
the armed men that were in the *h*......	Judg 7:11
tumbled into the *h* of Midian............	Judg 7:13
delivered Midian, and all the *h*.........	Judg 7:14
and returned into the *h* of Israel......	Judg 7:15
into your hand the *h* of Midian...........	Judg 7:15
all the *h* ran, and cried, and.............	Judg 7:21
fellow, even throughout all the *h*......	Judg 7:22
the *h* fled to Beth-shittah in...............	Judg 7:22
Jogbehah, and smote the *h*................	Judg 8:11
for the *h* was secure............................	Judg 8:11
and discomfited all the *h*...................	Judg 8:12
of the *h* in the morning watch............	1Sa 11:11
Sisera, captain of the *h* of Hazor......	1Sa 12:9
And there was trembling in the *h*.......	1Sa 14:15
the *h* of the Philistines went on........	1Sa 14:19
And he gathered an *h*, and smote the..	1Sa 14:48
of the captain of his *h* was Abner......	1Sa 14:50
as the *h* was going forth to the.........	1Sa 17:20
the *h* of the Philistines this day........	1Sa 17:46
unto Abner, the captain of the *h*.......	1Sa 17:55
son of Ner, the captain of his *h*	1Sa 26:5
when Saul saw the *h* of the...............	1Sa 28:5
h of Israel into the hand of the.........	1Sa 28:19
me in the *h* is good in my sight.........	1Sa 29:6
son of Ner, captain of Saul's *h*.........	2Sa 2:8
all the *h* that was with him were.......	2Sa 3:23
to smite the *h* of the Philistines........	2Sa 5:24
smitten all the *h* of Hadadezer..........	2Sa 8:9
the son of Zeruiah was over the *h*.....	2Sa 8:16
all the *h* of the mighty men..............	2Sa 10:7
Shobach the captain of the *h* of........	2Sa 10:16
Shobach the captain of their *h*..........	2Sa 10:18
captain of the *h* instead of Joab.......	2Sa 17:25
h before me continually in the...........	2Sa 19:13
Joab was over all the *h* of Israel......	2Sa 20:23
through the *h* of the Philistines.........	2Sa 23:16
said to Joab the captain of the *h*......	2Sa 24:2
and against the captains of the *h*......	2Sa 24:4
the captains of the *h* went out...........	2Sa 24:4
and Joab the captain of the *h*...........	1Kin 1:19
sons, and the captains of the *h*........	1Kin 1:25
Ner, captain of the *h* of Israel.........	1Kin 2:32
Jether, captain of the *h* of Judah.....	1Kin 2:32
Jehoiada in his room over the *h*........	1Kin 2:35
son of Jehoiada was over the *h*	1Kin 4:4
Joab the captain of the *h* was..........	1Kin 11:15
the captain of the *h* was dead..........	1Kin 11:21
made Omri, the captain of the *h*.......	1Kin 16:16
Syria gathered all his *h* together......	1Kin 20:1
all the *h* of heaven standing by........	1Kin 22:19
hand, and carry me out of the *h*.......	1Kin 22:34
a proclamation throughout the *h*.......	1Kin 22:36
and there was no water for the *h*......	2Kin 3:9
king, or to the captain of the *h*........	2Kin 4:13
captain of the *h* of the king of.........	2Kin 5:1
horses, and chariots, and a great *h*...	2Kin 6:14
an *h* compassed the city both with....	2Kin 6:15
king of Syria gathered all his *h*........	2Kin 6:24
us fall unto the *h* of the Syrians........	2Kin 7:4
For the LORD had made the *h* of........	2Kin 7:6
even the noise of a great *h*...............	2Kin 7:6
sent after the *h* of the Syrians..........	2Kin 7:14
captains of the *h* were sitting...........	2Kin 9:5
hundreds, the officers of the *h*..........	2Kin 11:15
and worshipped all the *h* of heaven..	2Kin 17:16
with a great *h* against Jerusalem......	2Kin 18:17
and worshipped all the *h* of heaven..	2Kin 21:3
he built altars for all the *h* of heaven	2Kin 21:5
grove, and for all the *h* of heaven....	2Kin 23:4
and to all the *h* of heaven.................	2Kin 23:5
of Babylon came, he, and all his *h*....	2Kin 25:1
and the principal scribe of the *h*.......	2Kin 25:19
being over the *h* of the LORD............	1Chr 9:19
the *h* of the Philistines encamped.....	1Chr 11:15
through the *h* of the Philistines.........	1Chr 11:18
sons of Gad, captains of the *h*	1Chr 12:14
valour, and were captains in the *h*....	1Chr 12:21
a great *h*, like the *h* of God...........	1Chr 12:22
to smite the *h* of the Philistines........	1Chr 14:15
and they smote the *h* of the..............	1Chr 14:16
the *h* of Hadarezer king of Zobah.....	1Chr 18:9
the son of Zeruiah was over the *h*.....	1Chr 18:15
all the *h* of the mighty men..............	1Chr 19:8
Shophach the captain of the *h* of......	1Chr 19:16
Shophach the captain of the *h*...........	1Chr 19:18
the captains of the *h* separated........	1Chr 26:26
and the captains of the *h*..................	1Chr 26:26
of the *h* for the first month...............	1Chr 27:3
The third captain of the *h* for...........	1Chr 27:5
with an *h* of a thousand thousand.....	2Chr 14:9
before the LORD, and before his *h*.....	2Chr 14:13
therefore is the *h* of the king of.......	2Chr 16:7
Ethiopians and the Lubims a huge *h*...	2Chr 16:8
all the *h* of heaven standing on.........	2Chr 18:18
thou mayest carry me out of the *h*....	2Chr 18:33
hundreds that were set over the *h*.....	2Chr 23:14
that the *h* of Syria came up.............	2Chr 24:23
a very great *h* into their hand...........	2Chr 24:24
Uzziah had an *h* of fighting men.......	2Chr 26:11
them throughout all the *h* shields......	2Chr 26:14
before the *h* that came to Samaria....	2Chr 28:9
and worshipped all the *h* of heaven ...	2Chr 33:3
he built altars for all the *h* of.........	2Chr 33:5
of the *h* of the king of Assyria..........	2Chr 33:11
of heaven, with all their *h*...............	Neh 9:6
the *h* of heaven worshippeth thee.....	Neh 9:6
Though an *h* should encamp against...	Ps 27:3
all the *h* of them by the breath........	Ps 33:6
saved by the multitude of an *h*.........	Ps 33:16
Pharaoh and his *h* in the Red sea......	Ps 136:15
mustereth the *h* of the battle............	Is 13:4
h of the high ones that are on...........	Is 24:21
all the *h* of heaven shall be..............	Is 34:4
all their *h* shall fall down, as............	Is 34:4
bringeth out their *h* by number.........	Is 40:26
all their *h* have I commanded...........	Is 45:12
all the *h* of heaven, whom they.........	Jer 8:2
incense unto all the *h* of heaven........	Jer 19:13
As the *h* of heaven cannot be............	Jer 33:22
destroy ye utterly all her *h*...............	Jer 51:3
and the principal scribe of the *h*.......	Jer 52:25
of speech, as the noise of an *h*..........	Eze 1:24
great, even to the *h* of heaven..........	Dan 8:10
and it cast down some of the *h*..........	Dan 8:10
even to the prince of the *h*................	Dan 8:11
an *h* was given him against the.........	Dan 8:12
the *h* to be trodden under foot..........	Dan 8:13
the captivity of this *h* of the.............	Obad 20
them that worship the *h* of heaven....	Zeph 1:5
of the heavenly *h* praising God..........	Lk 2:13
two pence, and gave them to the *h*....	Lk 10:35
up to worship the *h* of heaven...........	Acts 7:42
Gaius mine *h*, and of the whole.........	Rom 16:23

HOSTAGES

of the king's house, and *h*..............	2Kin 14:14
the *h* also, and returned to..............	2Chr 25:24

HOSTS

that all the *h* of the LORD went.........	Ex 12:41
own standard, throughout their *h*......	Num 1:52
their *h* were six hundred thousand.....	Num 2:32
all the camps throughout their *h*.......	Num 10:25
and went up, they and all their *h*......	Josh 10:5
they and all their *h* with them..........	Josh 11:4
their *h* with them, about fifteen........	Judg 8:10
the *h* of the children of the east.......	Judg 8:10
unto the LORD of *h* in Shiloh.............	1Sa 1:3
vowed a vow, and said, O LORD of *h* ..	1Sa 1:11
of the covenant of the LORD of *h*.......	1Sa 4:4
Thus saith the LORD of *h*, I...............	1Sa 15:2
thee in the name of the LORD of *h*.....	1Sa 17:45
and the LORD God of *h* was with him..	2Sa 5:10
of *h* that dwelleth between the..........	2Sa 6:2
in the name of the LORD of *h*............	2Sa 6:18
David, Thus saith the LORD of *h*.........	2Sa 7:8
The LORD of *h* is the God over..........	2Sa 7:26
For thou, O LORD of *h*, God of...........	2Sa 7:27
two captains of the *h* of Israel..........	1Kin 2:5
sent the captains of the *h* which.......	1Kin 15:20
said, As the LORD of *h* liveth............	1Kin 18:15
jealous for the LORD God of *h*...........	1Kin 19:10
jealous for the LORD God of *h*...........	1Kin 19:14
said, As the LORD of *h* liveth............	2Kin 3:14
of the LORD of *h* shall do this...........	2Kin 19:31
for the LORD of *h* was with him.........	1Chr 11:9
David, Thus saith the LORD of *h*	1Chr 17:7
The LORD of *h* is the God of..............	1Chr 17:24
The LORD of *h*, he is the King of........	Ps 24:10
The LORD of *h* is with us...................	Ps 46:7
The LORD of *h* is with us...................	Ps 46:11
seen in the city of the LORD of *h*.......	Ps 48:8
Thou therefore, O LORD God of *h*.......	Ps 59:5
wait on thee, O LORD of *h*.................	Ps 69:6
O LORD God of *h*, how long wilt.........	Ps 80:4
Turn us again, O God of *h*.................	Ps 80:7
we beseech thee, O God of *h*.............	Ps 80:14
Turn us again, O LORD God of *h*.........	Ps 80:19
are thy tabernacles, O LORD of *h*......	Ps 84:1
even thine altars, O LORD of *h*..........	Ps 84:3
O LORD God of *h*, hear my prayer......	Ps 84:8
O LORD of *h*, blessed is the man.......	Ps 84:12
O LORD God of *h*, who is a strong......	Ps 89:8
Bless ye the LORD, all ye his *h*..........	Ps 103:21
thou, O God, go forth with our *h*.......	Ps 108:11
praise ye him, all his *h*....................	Ps 148:2
Except the LORD of *h* had left...........	Is 1:9
saith the Lord, the LORD of *h*............	Is 1:24
For the day of the LORD of *h*.............	Is 2:12
behold, the Lord, the LORD of *h*........	Is 3:1
saith the Lord God of *h*.....................	Is 3:15
LORD of *h* is the house of Israel........	Is 5:7
In mine ears said the LORD of *h*........	Is 5:9
But the LORD of *h* shall be................	Is 5:16
away the law of the LORD of *h*..........	Is 5:24
holy, holy, is the LORD of *h*..............	Is 6:3
have seen the King, the LORD of *h*.....	Is 6:5
Sanctify the LORD of *h* himself..........	Is 8:13
in Israel from the LORD of *h*.............	Is 8:18
the LORD of *h* will perform this..........	Is 9:7
do they seek the LORD of *h*...............	Is 9:13
Lord of *h* is the land darkened..........	Is 9:19
shall the Lord, the Lord of *h*.............	Is 10:16
For the Lord GOD of *h* shall make......	Is 10:23
thus saith the Lord God of *h*.............	Is 10:24
the LORD of *h* shall stir up a.............	Is 10:26
Behold, the Lord, the LORD of *h*........	Is 10:33
the LORD of *h* mustereth the host......	Is 13:4
in the wrath of the LORD of *h*...........	Is 13:13
against them, saith the LORD of *h*.....	Is 14:22
destruction, saith the LORD of *h*........	Is 14:23
The LORD of *h* hath sworn, saying,.....	Is 14:24
For the LORD of *h* hath purposed.......	Is 14:27
of Israel, saith the LORD of *h*............	Is 17:3
LORD of *h* of a people scattered........	Is 18:7
of the name of the LORD of *h*............	Is 18:7
saith the Lord, the Lord of *h*.............	Is 19:4
of *h* hath purposed upon Egypt.........	Is 19:12
of the hand of the LORD of *h*............	Is 19:16
of the counsel of the LORD of *h*.........	Is 19:17
Canaan, and swear to the LORD of *h*..	Is 19:18
LORD of *h* in the land of Egypt.........	Is 19:20
Whom the LORD of *h* shall bless........	Is 19:25
I have heard of the LORD of *h*...........	Is 21:10
GOD of *h* in the valley of vision........	Is 22:5
the Lord God of *h* call to weeping.....	Is 22:12
in mine ears by the LORD of *h*...........	Is 22:14
ye die, saith the Lord GOD of *h*.........	Is 22:14
Thus saith the Lord God of *h*.............	Is 22:15
In that day, saith the LORD of *h*........	Is 22:25
The LORD of *h* hath purposed it,........	Is 23:9
when the LORD of *h* shall reign in......	Is 24:23
make unto all people a feast of..........	Is 25:6
LORD of *h* be for a crown of glory......	Is 28:5
the LORD God of *h* a consumption.....	Is 28:22
cometh forth from the LORD of *h*.......	Is 28:29
of the LORD of *h* with thunder..........	Is 29:6
so shall the LORD of *h* come down......	Is 31:4
the LORD of *h* defend Jerusalem........	Is 31:5
O LORD of *h*, God of Israel, that........	Is 37:16
of the LORD of *h* shall do this...........	Is 37:32
Hear the word of the LORD of *h*........	Is 39:5
and his redeemer the LORD of *h*........	Is 44:6
nor reward, saith the LORD of *h*........	Is 45:13
the LORD of *h* is his name.................	Is 47:4
The LORD of *h* is his name................	Is 48:2
The LORD of *h* is his name................	Is 51:15
the LORD of *h* is his name.................	Is 54:5
in thee, saith the Lord God of *h*........	Jer 2:19
heritage of the *h* of nations..............	Jer 3:19
thus saith the LORD God of *h*.............	Jer 5:14
For thus hath the LORD of *h* said......	Jer 6:6
Thus saith the LORD of *h*, They.........	Jer 6:9
Thus saith the LORD of *h*, the God.....	Jer 7:3
Thus saith the LORD of *h*, the God.....	Jer 7:21
driven them, saith the LORD of *h*......	Jer 8:3
thus saith the LORD of *h*, Behold,......	Jer 9:7
thus saith the LORD of *h*, the God.....	Jer 9:15
Thus saith the LORD of *h*,.................	Jer 9:17
The LORD of *h* is his name................	Jer 10:16
For the LORD of *h*, that planted.........	Jer 11:17
But, O LORD of *h*, that judgest.........	Jer 11:20
thus saith the LORD of *h*, Behold,......	Jer 15:16
by thy name, O LORD God of *h*..........	Jer 15:16
For thus saith the LORD of *h*.............	Jer 16:9
Thus saith the LORD of *h*, the God.....	Jer 19:3
them, Thus saith the LORD of *h*.........	Jer 19:11
Thus saith the LORD of *h*, the God.....	Jer 19:15
But, O LORD of *h*, that triest the.......	Jer 20:12
thus saith the LORD of *h*...................	Jer 23:15
Thus saith the LORD of *h*, Hearken.....	Jer 23:16
God, of the LORD of *h* our God...........	Jer 23:36
thus saith the LORD of *h*...................	Jer 25:8
them, Thus saith the LORD of *h*.........	Jer 25:27
them, Thus saith the LORD of *h*.........	Jer 25:28
of the earth, saith the LORD of *h*.......	Jer 25:29
Thus saith the LORD of *h*, Behold,......	Jer 25:32
saying, Thus saith the LORD of *h*.......	Jer 26:18
masters, Thus saith the LORD of *h*.....	Jer 27:4
intercession to the LORD of *h*............	Jer 27:18
LORD of *h* concerning the pillars........	Jer 27:19
Yea, thus saith the LORD of *h*...........	Jer 27:21
Thus speaketh the LORD of *h*.............	Jer 28:2
For thus saith the LORD of *h*.............	Jer 28:14
Thus saith the LORD of *h*, the God.....	Jer 29:4
For thus saith the LORD of *h*.............	Jer 29:8
Thus saith the LORD of *h*, the God.....	Jer 29:21
Thus speaketh the LORD of *h*.............	Jer 29:25
in that day, saith the LORD of *h*........	Jer 30:8
Thus saith the LORD of *h*, the God.....	Jer 31:23
The LORD of *h* is his name................	Jer 31:35
Thus saith the LORD of *h*, the God.....	Jer 32:14
For thus saith the LORD of *h*.............	Jer 32:15
the Mighty God, the LORD of *h*..........	Jer 32:18
shall say, Praise the LORD of *h*.........	Jer 33:11
Thus saith the LORD of *h*...................	Jer 33:12
Thus saith the LORD of *h*, the God.....	Jer 35:13
thus saith the LORD God of *h*............	Jer 35:17
Thus saith the LORD of *h*...................	Jer 35:18
thus saith the LORD of *h*, the God.....	Jer 35:19
Thus saith the LORD, the God of *h*.....	Jer 38:17
saying, Thus saith the LORD of *h*.......	Jer 39:16
Thus saith the LORD of *h*, the God.....	Jer 42:15
For thus saith the LORD of *h*.............	Jer 42:18
them, Thus saith the LORD of *h*.........	Jer 43:10
thus saith the LORD, the God of *h*.....	Jer 44:2
thus saith the LORD, the God of *h*.....	Jer 44:7
thus saith the LORD of *h*, the God.....	Jer 44:11
Thus saith the LORD of *h*, the God.....	Jer 44:25
is the day of the Lord GOD of *h*.........	Jer 46:10
for the Lord GOD of *h* hath a............	Jer 46:10
King, whose name is the LORD of *h*.....	Jer 46:18
The LORD of *h*, the God of Israel,......	Jer 46:25
Moab thus saith the LORD of *h*..........	Jer 48:1
King, whose name is the LORD of *h*.....	Jer 48:15
thee, saith the Lord GOD of *h*...........	Jer 49:5
Edom, thus saith the LORD of *h*.........	Jer 49:7
in that day, saith the LORD of *h*........	Jer 49:26
Thus saith the LORD of *h*...................	Jer 49:35
thus saith the LORD of *h*, Behold,......	Jer 50:18
of *h* in the land of the Chaldeans......	Jer 50:25
proud, saith the Lord GOD of *h*.........	Jer 50:31

Thus saith the LORD of h............ Jer 50:33
the LORD of h is his name............ Jer 50:34
of his God, of the LORD of h............ Jer 51:5
The LORD of h hath sworn by............ Jer 51:14
the LORD of h is his name............ Jer 51:19
For thus saith the LORD of h............ Jer 51:33
King, whose name is the LORD of h............ Jer 51:57
Thus saith the LORD of h............ Jer 51:58
Even the Lord God of h............ Hos 12:5
saith the Lord GOD, The God of h............ Amos 3:13
the earth, The LORD, The God of h............ Amos 4:13
and so the LORD, the God of h............ Amos 5:14
of h will be gracious unto the............ Amos 5:15
Therefore the LORD, the God of h............ Amos 5:16
LORD, whose name is The God of h............ Amos 5:27
saith the LORD the God of h............ Amos 6:8
saith the LORD the God of h............ Amos 6:14
the Lord GOD of h to be that............ Amos 9:5
of the LORD of h hath spoken it............ Mic 4:4
against thee, saith the LORD of h............ Nah 2:13
against thee, saith the LORD of h............ Nah 3:5
is it not of the LORD of h that............ Hab 2:13
as I live, saith the LORD of h............ Zeph 2:9
the people of the LORD of h............ Zeph 2:10
Thus speaketh the LORD of h............ Hag 1:2
thus saith the LORD of h............ Hag 1:5
Thus saith the LORD of h............ Hag 1:7
saith the LORD of h............ Hag 1:9
in the house of the LORD of h............ Hag 1:14
am with you, saith the LORD of h............ Hag 2:4
For thus saith the LORD of h............ Hag 2:6
with glory, saith the LORD of h............ Hag 2:7
gold is mine, saith the LORD of h............ Hag 2:8
the former, saith the LORD of h............ Hag 2:9
I give peace, saith the LORD of h............ Hag 2:9
Thus saith the LORD of h............ Hag 2:11
In that day, saith the LORD of h............ Hag 2:23
chosen thee, saith the LORD of h............ Hag 2:23
them, Thus saith the LORD of h............ Zec 1:3
ye unto me, saith the LORD of h............ Zec 1:3
unto you, saith the LORD of h............ Zec 1:3
saying, Thus saith the LORD of h............ Zec 1:14
Like as the LORD of h thought to............ Zec 1:16
answered and said, O LORD of h............ Zec 1:12
saying, Thus saith the LORD of h............ Zec 1:12
built in it, saith the LORD of h............ Zec 1:16
saying, Thus saith the LORD of h............ Zec 1:17
For thus saith the LORD of h............ Zec 2:8
that the LORD of h hath sent me............ Zec 2:9
LORD of h hath sent me unto thee............ Zec 2:11
Thus saith the LORD of h............ Zec 3:7
thereof, saith the LORD of h............ Zec 3:9
In that day, saith the LORD of h............ Zec 3:10
by my spirit, saith the LORD of h............ Zec 4:6
LORD of h hath sent me unto you............ Zec 4:9
it forth, saith the LORD of h............ Zec 4:6
Thus speaketh the LORD of h............ Zec 6:12
LORD of h hath sent me unto you............ Zec 6:15
in the house of the LORD of h............ Zec 7:3
the word of the LORD of h unto me............ Zec 7:4
Thus speaketh the LORD of h............ Zec 7:9
the words which the LORD of h............ Zec 7:12
a great wrath from the LORD of h............ Zec 7:12
not hear, saith the LORD of h............ Zec 7:13
word of the LORD of h came to me............ Zec 8:1
Thus saith the LORD of h............ Zec 8:2
the LORD of h in the holy mountain............ Zec 8:3
Thus saith the LORD of h............ Zec 8:4
Thus saith the LORD of h............ Zec 8:6
saith the LORD of h............ Zec 8:6
Thus saith the LORD of h............ Zec 8:7
Thus saith the LORD of h............ Zec 8:9
house of the LORD of h was laid............ Zec 8:9
former days, saith the LORD of h............ Zec 8:11
For thus saith the LORD of h............ Zec 8:14
me to wrath, saith the LORD of h............ Zec 8:14
of the LORD of h came unto me............ Zec 8:18
Thus saith the LORD of h............ Zec 8:19
Thus saith the LORD of h............ Zec 8:20
LORD, and to seek the LORD of h............ Zec 8:21
seek the LORD of h in Jerusalem............ Zec 8:22
Thus saith the LORD of h............ Zec 8:23
The LORD of h shall defend them............ Zec 9:15
for the LORD of h hath visited............ Zec 10:3
in the LORD of h their God............ Zec 12:5
in that day, saith the LORD of h............ Zec 13:2
is my fellow, saith the LORD of h............ Zec 13:7
worship the King, the LORD of h............ Zec 14:16
worship the King, the LORD of h............ Zec 14:17
be holiness unto the LORD of h............ Zec 14:21
in the house of the LORD of h............ Zec 14:21
thus saith the LORD of h, They............ Mal 1:4
saith the LORD of h unto you............ Mal 1:6
saith the LORD of h............ Mal 1:8
saith the LORD of h............ Mal 1:9
in you, saith the LORD of h............ Mal 1:10
the heathen, saith the LORD of h............ Mal 1:11
at it, saith the LORD of h............ Mal 1:13
a great King, saith the LORD of h............ Mal 1:14
unto my name, saith the LORD of h............ Mal 2:2
be with Levi, saith the LORD of h............ Mal 2:4
is the messenger of the LORD of h............ Mal 2:7
of Levi, saith the LORD of h............ Mal 2:8
an offering unto the LORD of h............ Mal 2:12
his garment, saith the LORD of h............ Mal 2:16
shall come, saith the LORD of h............ Mal 3:1
fear not me, saith the LORD of h............ Mal 3:5
unto you, saith the LORD of h............ Mal 3:7
now herewith, saith the LORD of h............ Mal 3:10
in the field, saith the LORD of h............ Mal 3:11
land, saith the LORD of h............ Mal 3:12
mournfully before the LORD of h............ Mal 3:14
be mine, saith the LORD of h............ Mal 3:17
burn them up, saith the LORD of h............ Mal 4:1
do this, saith the LORD of h............ Mal 4:3

HOT

And when the sun waxed h, it............ Ex 16:21
And my wrath shall wax h, and I............ Ex 22:24
my wrath may wax h against them............ Ex 32:10
wrath wax h against thy people............ Ex 32:11
and Moses' anger waxed h, and he............ Ex 32:19
not the anger of my lord wax h............ Ex 32:22
skin whereof there is a h burning............ Lev 13:24
h displeasure, wherewith the LORD............ Deut 9:19
the slayer, while his heart is............ Deut 19:6
This our bread we took h for our............ Josh 9:12
of the LORD was h against Israel............ Judg 2:14
of the LORD was h against Israel............ Judg 2:20
of the LORD was h against Israel............ Judg 3:8
not thine anger be h against me............ Judg 6:39
of the LORD was h against Israel............ Judg 10:7
morrow, by that time the sun be h............ 1Sa 11:9
to put h bread in the day when it............ 1Sa 21:6
be opened until the sun be h............ Neh 7:3
when it is h, they are consumed............ Job 6:17
chasten me in thy displeasure............ Ps 6:1
chasten me in thy h displeasure............ Ps 38:1
My heart was h within me............ Ps 39:3
and their flocks to h thunderbolts............ Ps 78:48
Can one go upon h coals, and his............ Prov 6:28
that the brass of it may be h............ Eze 24:11
and the furnace exceeding h............ Dan 3:22
They are all h as an oven............ Hos 7:7
conscience seared with a h iron............ 1Ti 4:2
that thou art neither cold nor h............ Rev 3:15
I would thou wert cold or h............ Rev 3:15
lukewarm, and neither cold nor h............ Rev 3:16

HOTHAM (ho'-tham) See HOTHAN. A son of Heber.
begat Japhlet, and Shomer, and H............ 1Chr 7:32

HOTHAN (ho'-than) See HOTHAM. Father of Shama and Jehiel.
Jehiel the sons of H the Aroerite............ 1Chr 11:44

HOTHIR (ho'-thir) A son of Heman.
Joshbekashah, Mallothi, H............ 1Chr 25:4
The one and twentieth to H............ 1Chr 25:28

HOTLY
thou hast so h pursued after me............ Gen 31:36

HOTTEST
in the forefront of the h battle............ 2Sa 11:15

HOUGH
thou shalt h their horses, and............ Josh 11:6

HOUGHED
he h their horses, and burnt their............ Josh 11:9
David h all the chariot horses............ 2Sa 8:4
David also h all the chariot............ 1Chr 18:4

HOUR
worshippeth shall the same h be............ Dan 3:6
ye shall be cast the same h into............ Dan 3:15
was astonied for one h, and his............ Dan 4:19
The same h was the thing............ Dan 4:33
In the same h came forth fingers............ Dan 5:5
was healed in the selfsame h............ Mt 8:13
woman was made whole from that h............ Mt 9:22
that same h what ye shall speak............ Mt 10:19
was made whole from that very h............ Mt 15:28
child was cured from that very h............ Mt 17:18
And he went out about the third h............ Mt 20:3
out about the sixth and ninth h............ Mt 20:5
about the eleventh h he went out............ Mt 20:6
were hired about the eleventh h............ Mt 20:9
These last have wrought but one h............ Mt 20:12
h knoweth no man, no, not the............ Mt 24:36
not what h your Lord doth come............ Mt 24:42
for in such an h as ye think not............ Mt 24:44
in an h that he is not aware of............ Mt 24:50
h wherein the Son of man cometh............ Mt 25:13
could ye not watch with me one h............ Mt 26:40
the h is at hand, and the Son of............ Mt 26:45
In that same h said Jesus to the............ Mt 26:55
Now from the sixth h there was............ Mt 27:45
all the land unto the ninth h............ Mt 27:45
about the ninth h Jesus cried............ Mt 27:46
shall be given you in that h............ Mk 13:11
that h knoweth no man, no, not............ Mk 13:32
man except from him............ Mk 13:35
couldest not thou watch one h............ Mk 14:37
it is enough, the h is come............ Mk 14:41
And it was the third h, and they............ Mk 15:25
And when the sixth h was come............ Mk 15:33
the whole land until the ninth h............ Mk 15:33
at the ninth h Jesus cried with a............ Mk 15:34
in that same h he cured many of............ Lk 7:21
In that h Jesus rejoiced in............ Lk 10:21
the same h what ye ought to say............ Lk 12:12
known what h the thief would come............ Lk 12:39
cometh at an h when ye think not............ Lk 12:40
at an h when he is not aware............ Lk 12:46
the scribes the same h sought to............ Lk 20:19
And when the h was come, he sat............ Lk 22:14
but this is your h, and the power............ Lk 22:53
about the space of one h after............ Lk 22:59
And it was about the sixth h............ Lk 23:44
all the earth until the ninth h............ Lk 23:44
they rose up the same h............ Lk 24:33

for it was about the tenth h............ Jn 1:39
mine h is not yet come............ Jn 2:4
and it was about the sixth h............ Jn 4:6
the h cometh, when ye shall............ Jn 4:21
But the h cometh, and now is, when............ Jn 4:23
them the h when he began to amend............ Jn 4:52
the seventh h the fever left him............ Jn 4:52
knew that it was at the same h............ Jn 4:53
The h is coming, and now is, when............ Jn 5:25
for the h is coming, in the which............ Jn 5:28
because his h was not yet come............ Jn 7:30
for his h was not yet come............ Jn 8:20
The h is come, that the Son of............ Jn 12:23
Father, save me from this h............ Jn 12:27
for this cause came I unto this h............ Jn 12:27
when Jesus knew that his h was............ Jn 13:1
sorrow, because her h is come............ Jn 16:21
the h cometh, yea, is now come............ Jn 16:32
and said, Father, the h is come............ Jn 17:1
passover, and about the sixth h............ Jn 19:14
from that h that disciple took............ Jn 19:27
it is but the third h of the day............ Acts 2:15
h of prayer, being the ninth h............ Acts 3:1
evidently about the ninth h of............ Acts 10:3
to pray about the sixth h............ Acts 10:9
ago I was fasting until this h............ Acts 10:30
at the ninth h I prayed in my............ Acts 10:30
And he came out the same h............ Acts 16:18
took them the same h of the night............ Acts 16:33
the same h I looked up upon him............ Acts 22:13
at the third h of the night............ Acts 23:23
this present h we both hunger............ 1Cor 4:11
of the idol unto this h eat it as............ 1Cor 8:7
why stand we in jeopardy every h............ 1Cor 15:30
by subjection, no, not for an h............ Gal 2:5
know what h I will come upon thee............ Rev 3:3
thee from the h of temptation............ Rev 3:10
about the space of half an h............ Rev 8:1
which were prepared for an h............ Rev 9:15
the same h was there a great............ Rev 11:13
for the h of his judgment is come............ Rev 14:7
as kings one h with the beast............ Rev 17:12
for in one h is thy judgment come............ Rev 18:10
For in one h so great riches is............ Rev 18:17
for in one h is she made desolate............ Rev 18:19

HOURS
Are there not twelve h in the day............ Jn 11:9
about the space of three h after............ Acts 5:7
the space of two h cried out............ Acts 19:34

HOUSE See PREFACE.
kindred, and from thy father's h............ Gen 12:1
is none other but the h of God............ Gen 28:17
Egypt, out of the h of bondage............ Ex 13:3
shalt not covet thy neighbour's h............ Ex 20:17
thou covet thy neighbour's h............ Deut 5:21
Why is the h of God forsaken............ Neh 13:11
to the h appointed for all living............ Job 30:23
I will dwell in the h of the LORD............ Ps 23:6
walked unto the h of God in............ Ps 55:14
zeal of thine h hath eaten me up............ Ps 69:9
Yea, the sparrow hath found an h............ Ps 84:3
Let us go into the h of the LORD............ Ps 122:1
Wisdom hath builded her h............ Prov 9:1
but the h of the righteous shall............ Prov 12:7
The h of the wicked shall be............ Prov 14:11
better to go to the h of mourning............ Eccl 7:2
keepers of the h shall tremble............ Eccl 12:3
unto them that join h to h............ Is 5:8
for mine h shall be called an............ Is 56:7
Our holy and our beautiful h............ Is 64:11
winter h with the summer h............ Amos 3:15
to the h of the God of Jacob............ Mic 4:2
houses, and this h lie waste............ Hag 1:4
light unto all that are in the h............ Mt 5:15
which built his h upon a rock............ Mt 7:24
winds blew, and beat upon that h............ Mt 7:27
And when ye come into an h............ Mt 10:12
every city or h divided against............ Mt 12:25
one enter into a strong man's h............ Mt 12:29
My h shall be called the h of............ Mt 21:13
your h is left unto you desolate............ Mt 23:38
at thy h with my disciples............ Mt 26:18
if a h be divided against itself............ Mk 3:25
He is like a man which built an h............ Lk 6:48
Go not from h to h............ Lk 10:7
h divided against a h falleth............ Lk 11:17
come in, that my h may be filled............ Lk 14:23
light a candle, and sweep the h............ Lk 15:8
this man went down to his h............ Lk 18:14
of h merchandise............ Jn 2:16
zeal of thine h hath eaten me up............ Jn 2:17
the h was filled with the odour............ Jn 12:3
In my Father's h are many............ Jn 14:2
it filled all the h where they............ Acts 2:2
and breaking bread from h to h............ Acts 2:46
earthly h of this tabernacle were............ 2Cor 5:1
an h not made with hands, eternal............ 2Cor 5:1
wandering about from h to h............ 1Ti 5:13
But in a great h there are not............ 2Ti 2:20
must begin at the h of God............ 1Pet 4:17

HOUSEHOLD
his h after him, and they shall............ Gen 18:19
thou found of all thy h stuff............ Gen 31:37
Then Jacob said unto his h............ Gen 35:2
lest thou, and thy h, and all that............ Gen 45:11
brethren, and all his father's h............ Gen 47:12
man and his h came with Jacob............ Ex 1:1
if the h be too little for the............ Ex 12:4
for himself, and for his h............ Lev 16:17

upon Pharaoh, and upon all his *h*...... Deut 6:22
shalt rejoice, thou, and thine *h*...... Deut 14:26
LORD shall choose, thou and thy *h*...... Deut 15:20
brethren, and all thy father's *h*...... Josh 2:18
harlot alive, and her father's *h*...... Josh 6:25
the *h* which the LORD shall take...... Josh 7:14
And he brought his *h* man by man...... Josh 7:18
because he feared his father's *h*...... Judg 6:27
thy life, with the lives of thy *h*...... Judg 18:25
our master, and against all his *h*...... 1Sa 25:17
and his men, every man with his *h*...... 1Sa 27:3
bring up, every man with his *h*...... 2Sa 2:3
blessed Obed-edom, and all his *h*...... 2Sa 6:11
David returned to bless his *h*...... 2Sa 6:20
forth, and all his *h* after him...... 2Sa 15:16
be for the king's *h* to ride on...... 2Sa 16:2
put his *h* in order, and hanged...... 2Sa 17:23
boat to carry over the king's *h*...... 2Sa 19:18
have brought the king, and his *h*...... 2Sa 19:41
And Ahishar was over the *h*...... 1Kin 4:6
victuals for the king and his *h*...... 1Kin 4:7
desire, in giving food for my *h*...... 1Kin 5:9
of wheat for food to his *h*...... 1Kin 5:11
h among the sons of Pharaoh...... 1Kin 11:20
we may go and tell the king's *h*...... 2Kin 7:9
Arise, and go thou and thine *h*...... 2Kin 8:1
and she went with her *h*, and...... 2Kin 8:2
of Hilkiah, which was over the *h*...... 2Kin 18:18
of Hilkiah, which was over the *h*...... 2Kin 18:37
Eliakim, which was over the *h*...... 2Kin 19:2
one principal *h* being taken for...... 1Chr 24:6
the *h* stuff of Tobiah out of the...... Neh 13:8
the asses, and a very great *h*...... Job 1:3
thy food, for the food of thy *h*...... Prov 27:27
night, and giveth meat to her *h*...... Prov 31:15
not afraid of the snow for her *h*...... Prov 31:21
for all her *h* are clothed with...... Prov 31:21
looketh well to the ways of her *h*...... Prov 31:27
of Hilkiah, which was over the *h*...... Is 36:22
sent Eliakim, who was over the *h*...... Is 37:2
shall they cast them of his *h*...... Mt 10:25
foes shall be they of his own *h*...... Mt 10:36
lord hath made ruler over his *h*...... Mt 24:45
lord shall make ruler over his *h*...... Lk 12:42
he called two of his *h* servants...... Acts 10:7
when she was baptized, and her *h*...... Acts 16:15
them which are of Aristobulus' *h*...... Rom 16:10
that be of the *h* of Narcissus...... Rom 16:11
baptized also the *h* of Stephanas...... 1Cor 1:16
them who are of the *h* of faith...... Gal 6:10
the saints, and of the *h* of God...... Eph 2:19
they that are of Caesar's *h*...... Phil 4:22
Aquila, and the *h* of Onesiphorus...... 2Ti 4:19

HOUSEHOLDER

So the servants of the *h* came...... Mt 13:27
is like unto a man that is an *h*...... Mt 13:52
is like unto a man that is an *h*...... Mt 20:1
There was a certain *h*, which...... Mt 21:33

HOUSEHOLDS

food for the famine of your *h*...... Gen 42:33
And take your father and your *h*...... Gen 45:18
your food, and for them of your *h*...... Gen 47:24
it in every place, ye and your *h*...... Num 18:31
and swallowed them up, and their *h*...... Deut 11:6
put your hand unto, ye and your *h*...... Deut 12:7
LORD shall take shall come by *h*...... Josh 7:14

HOUSES

corn for the famine of your *h*...... Gen 42:19
feared God, that he made them *h*...... Ex 1:21
be the heads of their fathers' *h*...... Ex 6:14
the frogs from thee and thy *h*...... Ex 8:9
depart from thee, and from thy *h*...... Ex 8:11
and the frogs died out of the *h*...... Ex 8:13
and upon thy people, and into thy *h*...... Ex 8:21
the *h* of the Egyptians shall be...... Ex 8:21
Pharaoh, and into his servants' *h*...... Ex 8:24
and his cattle flee into the *h*...... Ex 9:20
And they shall fill thy *h*...... Ex 10:6
the *h* of all thy servants...... Ex 10:6
the *h* of all the Egyptians...... Ex 10:6
on the upper door posts of the *h*...... Ex 12:7
a token upon the *h* where ye are...... Ex 12:13
put away leaven out of your *h*...... Ex 12:15
be no leaven found in your *h*...... Ex 12:19
come in unto your *h* to smite you...... Ex 12:23
who passed over the *h* of the...... Ex 12:27
the Egyptians, and delivered our *h*...... Ex 12:27
But the *h* of the villages which...... Lev 25:31
the *h* of the cities of their...... Lev 25:32
for the *h* of the cities of the...... Lev 25:33
throughout the *h* of their fathers...... Num 4:22
and swallowed them up, and their *h*...... Num 16:32
according to their fathers' *h*...... Num 17:6
We will not return unto our *h*...... Num 32:18
h full of all good things, which...... Deut 6:11
art full, and hast built goodly *h*...... Deut 8:12
in their cities, and in their *h*...... Deut 19:1
for our provision out of our *h* on...... Josh 9:12
that there is in these *h* an ephod...... Judg 18:14
the men that were in the *h* near...... Judg 18:22
when Solomon had built the two *h*...... 1Kin 9:10
against all the *h* of the land...... 1Kin 13:32
house, and the *h* of thy servants...... 1Kin 20:6
put them in the *h* of the high...... 2Kin 17:29
them in the *h* of the high places...... 2Kin 17:32
brake down the *h* of the sodomites...... 2Kin 23:7
all the *h* also of the high places...... 2Kin 23:19
all the *h* of Jerusalem, and every...... 2Kin 25:9
David made him *h* in the city of...... 1Chr 15:1

of the *h* thereof, and of the......1Chr 28:11
overlay the walls of the *h* withal......1Chr 29:4
to the *h* of their fathers......2Chr 25:5
to floor the *h* which the kings of......2Chr 34:11
by the *h* of your fathers, after......2Chr 35:4
daughters, your wives, and your *h*......Neh 4:14
our lands, vineyards, and *h*......Neh 5:3
their oliveyards, and their *h*......Neh 5:11
and the *h* were not builded......Neh 7:4
possessed *h* full of all goods......Neh 9:25
after the *h* of our fathers, at......Neh 10:34
sons went and feasted in their *h*......Job 1:4
who filled their *h* with silver......Job 3:15
in them that dwell in *h* of clay......Job 4:19
in *h* which no man inhabiteth......Job 15:28
Their *h* are safe from fear......Job 21:9
filled their *h* with good things......Job 22:18
In the dark they dig through *h*......Job 24:16
that their *h* shall continue for......Ps 49:11
the *h* of God in possession......Ps 83:12
we shall fill our *h* with spoil......Prov 1:13
make they their *h* in the rocks......Prov 30:26
I builded me *h*......Eccl 2:4
spoil of the poor is in your *h*......Is 3:14
Of a truth many *h* shall be......Is 5:9
the *h* without man, and the land be......Is 6:11
offence to both the *h* of Israel......Is 8:14
their *h* shall be spoiled, and......Is 13:16
their *h* shall be full of doleful......Is 13:21
shall cry in their desolate *h*......Is 13:22
on the tops of their *h*, and in......Is 15:3
have numbered the *h* of Jerusalem......Is 22:10
the *h* have ye broken down to......Is 22:10
upon all the *h* of joy in the......Is 32:13
and they are full in prison *h*......Is 42:22
And they shall build *h*, and inhabit......Is 65:21
by troops in the harlots' *h*......Jer 5:7
so are their *h* full of deceit......Jer 5:27
their *h* shall be turned unto......Jer 6:12
out of your *h* on the sabbath day......Jer 17:22
Let a cry be heard from their *h*......Jer 18:22
the *h* of Jerusalem......Jer 19:13
the *h* of the kings of Judah......Jer 19:13
because of all the *h* upon whose......Jer 19:13
Build ye *h*, and dwell in them......Jer 29:5
build ye *h*, and dwell in them......Jer 29:28
H and fields and vineyards shall be......Jer 32:15
this city, and burn it with the *h*......Jer 32:29
concerning the *h* of this city......Jer 33:4
concerning the *h* of the kings of......Jer 33:4
Nor to build *h* for us to dwell in......Jer 35:9
the *h* of the people, with fire......Jer 39:8
in the *h* of the gods of Egypt......Jer 43:12
and the *h* of the gods of the......Jer 43:13
all the *h* of Jerusalem, and all......Jer 52:13
all the *h* of the great men......Jer 52:13
to strangers, our *h* to aliens......Lam 5:2
and they shall possess their *h*......Eze 7:24
let us build *h*......Eze 11:3
they shall burn thine *h* with fire......Eze 16:41
and burn up their *h* with fire......Eze 23:47
walls, and destroy thy pleasant *h*......Eze 26:12
safely therein, and shall build *h*......Eze 28:26
walls and in the doors of the *h*......Eze 33:30
It shall be a place for their *h*......Eze 45:4
your *h* shall be made a dunghill......Dan 2:5
their *h* shall be made a dunghill......Dan 3:29
and I will place them in their *h*......Hos 11:11
they shall climb up upon the *h*......Joel 2:9
the *h* of ivory shall perish, and......Amos 3:15
the great *h* shall have an end......Amos 3:15
ye have built *h* of hewn stone......Amos 5:11
the *h* of Achzib shall be a lie to......Mic 1:14
and *h*, and take them away......Mic 2:2
ye cast out from their pleasant *h*......Mic 2:9
their masters' *h* with violence......Zeph 1:9
a booty, and their *h* a desolation......Zeph 1:13
they shall also build *h*, but not......Zeph 1:13
in the *h* of Ashkelon shall they......Zeph 2:7
O ye, to dwell in your cieled *h*......Hag 1:4
the *h* rifled, and the women......Zech 14:2
soft clothing are in kings' *h*......Mt 11:8
And every one that hath forsaken *h*......Mt 19:29
for ye devour widows' *h*, and for a......Mk 12:40
them away fasting to their own *h*......Mk 8:3
hundredfold now in this time, *h*......Mk 10:30
Which devour widows' *h*, and for a......Mk 12:40
they may receive me into their *h*......Lk 16:4
Which devour widows' *h*, and for a......Lk 20:47
of lands or *h* sold them, and......Acts 4:34
have ye not *h* to eat and to drink......1Cor 11:22
children and their own *h* well......1Ti 3:12
sort are they which creep into *h*......2Ti 3:6
be stopped, who subvert whole *h*......Titus 1:11

HOUSETOP

to dwell in a corner of the *h*......Prov 21:9
to dwell in the corner of the *h*......Prov 25:24
Let him which is on the *h* not......Mt 24:17
let him that is on the *h* not go......Mk 13:15
multitude, they went upon the *h*......Lk 5:19
day, he which shall be upon the *h*......Lk 17:31
Peter went up upon the *h* to pray......Acts 10:9

HOUSETOPS

them be as the grass upon the *h*......Ps 129:6
thou art wholly gone up to the *h*......Is 22:1
green herb, as the grass on the *h*......Is 37:27
generally upon all the *h* of Moab......Jer 48:38
the host of heaven upon the *h*......Zeph 1:5
ear, that preach ye upon the *h*......Mt 10:27

shall be proclaimed upon the *h*......Lk 12:3

HOW See PREFACE.

HOWBEIT

H Sisera fled away on his feet to......Judg 4:17
H the king of the children of......Judg 11:28
H the hair of his head began to......Judg 16:22
h the name of the city was Laish......Judg 18:29
H we may not give them wives of......Judg 21:18
h there is a kinsman nearer than......Ruth 3:12
h yet protest solemnly unto them......1Sa 8:9
H he refused to turn aside......2Sa 2:23
H, because by this deed thou hast......2Sa 12:14
H he would not hearken unto her......2Sa 13:14
h he would not go, but blessed......2Sa 13:25
h he attained not unto the first......2Sa 23:19
the kingdom is turned about, and......1Kin 2:15
H I believed not the words, until......1Kin 10:7
H I will not rend away all the......1Kin 11:13
h let me go in any wise......1Kin 11:22
H I will not take the whole......1Kin 11:34
h the slingers went about it, and......2Kin 3:25
the LORD hath shewed me that he......2Kin 8:10
H from the sins of Jeroboam the......2Kin 10:29
H there were not made for the......2Kin 12:13
H the high places were not taken......2Kin 14:4
H the high places were not taken......2Kin 15:35
H every nation made gods of their......2Kin 17:29
H they did not hearken, but they......2Kin 17:40
H there was no reckoning made......2Kin 22:7
h he attained not to the first......1Chr 11:21
H the LORD God of Israel chose me......1Chr 28:4
H I believed not their words......2Chr 9:6
the king of Israel stayed......2Chr 18:34
H the high places were not taken......2Chr 20:33
H the LORD would not destroy the......2Chr 21:7
h they buried him in the city of......2Chr 21:20
H the Levites hastened it not......2Chr 24:5
h he entered not into the temple......2Chr 27:2
H in the business of the......2Chr 32:31
H thou art just in all that is......Neh 9:33
h our God turned the curse into a......Neh 13:2
H he will not stretch out his......Job 30:24
H he meaneth not so, neither doth......Is 10:7
H I sent unto you all my servants......Jer 44:4
H this kind goeth not out but by......Mt 17:21
H Jesus suffered him not, but......Mk 5:19
H in vain do they worship me......Mk 7:7
(*H* there came other boats from......Jn 6:23
H no man spake openly of him for......Jn 7:13
H we know this man whence he is......Jn 7:27
H Jesus spake of his death......Jn 11:13
H when he, the Spirit of truth......Jn 16:13
H many of them which heard the......Acts 4:4
H the most High dwelleth not in......Acts 7:48
H, as the disciples stood round......Acts 14:20
H certain men clave unto him, and......Acts 17:34
H we must be cast upon a certain......Acts 27:26
H they looked when he should have......Acts 28:6
H we speak wisdom among them that......1Cor 2:6
H there is not in every man that......1Cor 8:7
h in the spirit he speaketh......1Cor 14:2
h in malice be ye children, but......1Cor 14:20
H that was not first which is......1Cor 15:46
H whereinsoever any is bold, (I......2Cor 11:21
H then, when ye knew not God, ye......Gal 4:8
H for this cause I obtained mercy......1Ti 1:16
h not all that came out of Egypt......Heb 3:16

HOWL

H ye; for the day of the LORD......Is 13:6
H, O gate......Is 14:31
Moab shall *h* over Nebo, and over......Is 15:2
their streets, every one shall *h*......Is 15:3
h for Moab, every one shall *h*......Is 16:7
H, ye ships of Tarshish......Is 23:1
h, ye inhabitants of the isle......Is 23:6
H, ye ships of Tarshish......Is 23:14
rule over them make them to *h*......Is 52:5
shall *h* for vexation of spirit......Is 65:14
you with sackcloth, lament and *h*......Jer 4:8
H, ye shepherds, and cry......Jer 25:34
inhabitants of the land shall *h*......Jer 47:2
h and cry; tell ye it......Jer 48:20
Therefore will I *h* for Moab......Jer 48:31
They shall *h*, saying, How is it......Jer 48:39
H, O Heshbon, for Ai is spoiled......Jer 49:3
h for her; take balm......Jer 51:8
Cry and *h*, son of man......Eze 21:12
H ye, Woe worth the day......Eze 30:2
and *h*, all ye drinkers of wine......Joel 1:5
h, O ye vinedressers, for the......Joel 1:11
h, ye ministers of the altar......Joel 1:13
Therefore I will wail and *h*......Mic 1:8
H, ye inhabitants of Maktesh, for......Zeph 1:11
H, fir tree; for the cedar......Zech 11:2
h, O ye oaks of Bashan......Zech 11:2
h for your miseries that shall......Jas 5:1

HOWLED

when they *h* upon their beds......Hos 7:14

HOWLING

and in the waste *h* wilderness......Deut 32:10
the *h* thereof unto Eglaim, and the......Is 15:8
the *h* thereof unto Beer-elim......Is 15:8
an *h* from the principal of the......Jer 25:36
an *h* from the second, and a great......Zeph 1:10
a voice of the *h* of the shepherds......Zech 11:3

HOWLINGS
the temple shall be *h* in that day.......... Amos 8:3

HOWSOEVER
h let all thy wants lie upon me........... Judg 19:20
of Zadok yet again to Joab, But *h*........ 2Sa 18:22
But *h*, said he, let me run................. 2Sa 18:23
not be cut off, *h* I punished them.......... Zeph 3:7

HOZAI See SEERS.

HUBBAH See JUHUBBAH.

HUGE
Ethiopians and the Lubims a *h* host...... 2Chr 16:8

HUKKOK (*huk´-kok*) See HELKATH, HUKOK. *A place in Naphtali.*
and goeth out from thence to *H*........... Josh 19:34

HUKOK (*hu´-kok*) See HUKKOK. *A city in Asher.*
H with her suburbs, and Rehob with .. 1Chr 6:75

HUL (*hul*) *A son of Aram.*
Uz, and *H*, and Gether, and Mash...... Gen 10:23
and Lud, and Aram, and Uz, and *H*...... 1Chr 1:17

HULDAH (*hul´-dah*) *A prophetess.*
went unto *H* the prophetess, the........ 2Kin 22:14
went to *H* the prophetess, the........... 2Chr 34:22

HUMBLE
refuse to *h* thyself before me............. Ex 10:3
to *h* thee, and to prove thee, to......... Deut 8:2
knew not, that he might *h* thee.......... Deut 8:16
h ye them, and do with them what .... Judg 19:24
shall *h* themselves, and pray, and...... 2Chr 7:14
thou didst *h* thyself before God,....... 2Chr 34:27
and he shall save the *h* person.......... Job 22:29
forgetteth not the cry of the *h*........... Ps 9:12
forget not the *h*........................... Ps 10:12
hast heard the desire of the *h*........... Ps 10:17
the *h* shall hear thereof, and be........ Ps 34:2
The *h* shall see this, and be glad....... Ps 69:32
h thyself, and make sure thy............ Prov 6:3
be of an *h* spirit with the lowly......... Prov 16:19
shall uphold the *h* in spirit............... Prov 29:23
that is of a contrite and *h* spirit........ Is 57:15
to revive the spirit of the *h*.............. Is 57:15
the queen, if yourselves, sit down....... Jer 13:18
Whosoever therefore shall *h*............ Mt 18:4
he that shall *h* himself shall be......... Mt 23:12
my God will *h* me among you, and.... 2Cor 12:21
but giveth grace unto the *h*.............. Jas 4:6
H yourselves in the sight of the......... Jas 4:10
proud, and giveth grace to the *h*....... 1Pet 5:5
H yourselves therefore under the 1Pet 5:6

HUMBLED
their uncircumcised hearts be *h*......... Lev 26:41
he *h* thee, and suffered thee to......... Deut 8:3
of her, because thou hast *h* her........ Deut 21:14
because he hath *h* his neighbour's..... Deut 22:24
because he hath *h* her, he may not.... Deut 22:29
thou hast *h* thyself before the.......... 2Kin 22:19
Israel and the king *h* themselves....... 2Chr 12:6
LORD saw that they *h* themselves...... 2Chr 12:7
saying, They have *h* themselves........ 2Chr 12:7
And when he *h* himself, the wrath 2Chr 12:12
and of Zebulun *h* themselves............ 2Chr 30:11
Notwithstanding Hezekiah *h*............. 2Chr 32:26
h himself greatly before the God....... 2Chr 33:12
and graven images, before he was *h*.. 2Chr 33:19
h not himself before the LORD, as...... 2Chr 33:23
Manasseh his father had *h* himself..... 2Chr 33:23
h not himself before Jeremiah the...... 2Chr 36:12
I *h* my soul with fasting................... Ps 35:13
The lofty looks of man shall be *h*....... Is 2:11
and the mighty man shall be *h*.......... Is 5:15
the eyes of the lofty shall be *h*......... Is 5:15
down, and the haughty shall be *h*...... Is 10:33
not be *h* even unto this day............. Jer 44:10
in remembrance, and is *h* in me......... Lam 3:20
in thee have they *h* her that was...... Eze 22:10
another in thee hath *h* his sister........ Eze 22:11
hast not *h* thine heart, though.......... Dan 5:22
he *h* himself, and became obedient ..... Phil 2:8

HUMBLEDST
h thyself before me, and didst........... 2Chr 34:27

HUMBLENESS
kindness, *h* of mind, meekness.......... Col 3:12

HUMBLETH
thou now Ahab *h* himself before me .. 1Kin 21:29
because he *h* himself before me, I...... 1Kin 21:29
h himself, that the poor may fall...... Ps 10:10
Who *h* himself to behold the............ Ps 113:6
down, and the great man *h* himself .... Is 2:9
he that *h* himself shall be................ Lk 14:11
he that *h* himself shall be................ Lk 18:14

HUMBLY
I *h* beseech thee that I may find........ 2Sa 16:4
mercy, and to walk *h* with thy God .... Mic 6:8

HUMILIATION
In his *h* his judgment was taken........ Acts 8:33

HUMILITY
and before honour is *h*..................... Prov 15:33
and before honour is *h*..................... Prov 18:12
By *h* and the fear of the LORD are...... Prov 22:4
the Lord with all *h* of mind.............. Acts 20:19
of your reward in a voluntary *h*......... Col 2:18

of wisdom in will worship, and *h*....... Col 2:23
to another, and be clothed with *h* 1Pet 5:5

HUMTAH (*hum´-tah*) *A city in Judah.*
And *H*, and Kirjath-arba, which is ..... Josh 15:54

HUNDRED See PREFACE.

HUNDREDFOLD
and received in the same year an *h* .... Gen 26:12
how many soever they be, an *h*........ 2Sa 24:3
and brought forth fruit, some an *h*..... Mt 13:8
and bringeth forth, some an *h*.......... Mt 13:23
name's sake, shall receive an *h*........ Mt 19:29
receive an *h* now in this time........... Mk 10:30
and sprang up, and bare fruit an *h*..... Lk 8:8

HUNDREDS
of thousands, and rulers of *h*............ Ex 18:21
rulers of thousands, rulers of *h*......... Ex 18:25
thousands, and captains over *h*........ Num 31:14
of thousands, and captains of *h*........ Num 31:48
and of the captains of *h*, was........... Num 31:52
the captains of thousands and of *h* ... Num 31:54
thousands, and captains over *h*........ Deut 1:15
of thousands, and captains of *h*........ 1Sa 22:7
of the Philistines passed on by *h* 1Sa 29:2
and captains of *h* over them............. 2Sa 18:1
and all the people came out by *h*...... 2Sa 18:4
sent and fetched the rulers over *h* 2Kin 11:4
the captains over the *h* did............. 2Kin 11:9
to the captains over *h* did............... 2Kin 11:10
commanded the captains of the *h*...... 2Kin 11:15
And he took the rulers over *h*.......... 2Kin 11:19
the captains of thousands and *h*....... 1Chr 13:1
the captains over thousands and *h* ... 1Chr 26:26
and captains of thousands and *h*...... 1Chr 27:1
the captains, and captains over the *h*... 1Chr 28:1
and took the captains of *h*.............. 2Chr 23:1
to the captains of *h* spears............. 2Chr 23:9
of *h* that were set over the host...... 2Chr 23:14
And he took the captains of *h*.......... 2Chr 23:20
thousands, and captains over *h*........ 2Chr 25:5
And they sat down in ranks, by *h* ..... Mk 6:40

HUNDREDTH
In the six *h* year of Noah's life,........ Gen 7:11
And it came to pass in the six *h*....... Gen 8:13
also the *h* part of the money, and..... Neh 5:11

HUNGER
kill this whole assembly with *h*......... Ex 16:3
thee, and suffered thee to *h*............ Deut 8:3
shall send against thee, in *h*............ Deut 28:48
They shall be burnt with *h*.............. Deut 32:24
bread from heaven for their *h*.......... Neh 9:15
young lions do lack, and suffer *h*...... Ps 34:10
and an idle soul shall suffer *h*.......... Prov 19:15
They shall not *h* nor thirst.............. Is 49:10
he is like to die for *h* in the............. Jer 38:9
the trumpet, nor have *h* of bread ..... Jer 42:14
that faint for *h* in the top of........... Lam 2:19
than they that be slain with *h*......... Lam 4:9
more consumed with *h* in the land .... Eze 34:29
Blessed are they which do *h*............ Mt 5:6
Blessed are ye that *h* now............... Lk 6:21
for ye shall *h*.............................. Lk 6:25
and to spare, and I perish with *h*..... Lk 15:17
that cometh to me shall never *h*....... Jn 6:35
Therefore if thine enemy *h*.............. Rom 12:20
unto this present hour we both *h*...... 1Cor 4:11
And if any man *h*, let him eat at...... 1Cor 11:34
in watchings often, in *h*.................. 2Cor 11:27
to kill with sword, and with *h*.......... Rev 6:8
They shall *h* no more, neither.......... Rev 7:16

HUNGERBITTEN
His strength shall be *h*, and............. Job 18:12

HUNGERED
he returned into the city, he *h*......... Mt 21:18
they were ended, he afterward *h*...... Lk 4:2

HUNGRED
nights, he was afterward an *h*.......... Mt 4:2
and his disciples were an *h*............. Mt 12:1
what David did, when he was an *h* .... Mt 12:3
For I was an *h*, and ye gave me....... Mt 25:35
Lord, when saw we thee an *h*.......... Mt 25:37
For I was an *h*, and ye gave me no.... Mt 25:42
Lord, when saw we thee an *h*.......... Mt 25:44
when he had need, and was an *h*...... Mk 2:25
David did, when himself was an *h*..... Lk 6:3

HUNGRY
and they that were *h* ceased............ 1Sa 2:5
for they said, The people is *h*.......... 2Sa 17:29
They know that we be *h*................. 2Kin 7:12
Whose harvest the *h* eateth up........ Job 5:5
hast withholden bread from the *h*..... Job 22:7
take away the sheaf from the *h*....... Job 24:10
If I were *h*, I would not tell............ Ps 50:12
H and thirsty, their soul fainted....... Ps 107:5
filleth the *h* soul with goodness....... Ps 107:9
And there he maketh the *h* to dwell... Ps 107:36
which giveth food to the *h*.............. Ps 146:7
to satisfy his soul when he is *h*........ Prov 6:30
If thine enemy be *h*, give him.......... Prov 25:21
but to the *h* soul every bitter.......... Prov 27:7
through it, hardly bestead and *h*....... Is 8:21
pass, that when they shall be *h*....... Is 8:21
snatch on the right hand, and be *h* ... Is 9:20
even be as when an *h* man dreameth... Is 29:8

to make empty the soul of the *h*....... Is 32:6
yea, he is *h*, and his strength........... Is 44:12
it not to deal thy bread to the *h*....... Is 58:7
thou draw out thy soul to the *h*....... Is 58:10
shall eat, but ye shall be *h*.............. Is 65:13
hath given his bread to the *h*........... Eze 18:7
but hath given his bread to the *h*..... Eze 18:16
were come from Bethany, he was *h*... Mk 11:12
filled the *h* with good things............ Lk 1:53
And he became very *h*, and would .... Acts 10:10
and one is *h*, and another is............ 1Cor 11:21
both to be full and to be *h*.............. Phil 4:12

HUNT
to the field to *h* for venison............ Gen 27:5
as when one doth *h* a partridge in 1Sa 26:20
Wilt thou *h* the prey for the lion....... Job 38:39
evil shall *h* the violent man to.......... Ps 140:11
the adulteress will *h* for the............ Prov 6:26
they shall *h* them from every........... Jer 16:16
They *h* our steps, that we cannot..... Lam 4:18
head of every stature to *h* souls....... Eze 13:18
Will ye *h* the souls of my people,...... Eze 13:18
wherewith ye there *h* the souls to .... Eze 13:20
souls that ye *h* to make them fly ...... Eze 13:20
they *h* every man his brother with .... Mic 7:2

HUNTED
be no more in your hand to *h*........... Eze 13:21

HUNTER
He was a mighty *h* before the LORD .... Gen 10:9
the mighty *h* before the LORD........... Gen 10:9
and Esau was a cunning *h*, a man of . Gen 25:27
as a roe from the hand of the *h*........ Prov 6:5

HUNTERS
and after will I send for many *h*........ Jer 16:16

HUNTEST
yet thou *h* my soul to take it 1Sa 24:11
Thou *h* me as a fierce lion............... Job 10:16

HUNTETH
that sojourn among you, which *h*...... Lev 17:13

HUNTING
his brother came in from his *h*.......... Gen 27:30
not that which he took in *h*............. Prov 12:27

HUPHAM (*hu´-fam*) See HUPPIM, HUPHAMITES. *A son of Benjamin.*
of *H*, the family of the................... Num 26:39

HUPHAMITES (*hu´-fam-ites*) *Descendants of hupham.*
of Hupham, the family of the *H*........ Num 26:39

HUPPAH (*hup´-pah*) *A priest.*
The thirteenth to *H*, the.................. 1Chr 24:13

HUPPIM (*hup´-pim*) See HUPHAM. *Head of a Benjamite family.*
Ehi, and Rosh, Muppim, and *H*......... Gen 46:21
Shuppim also, and *H*, the children 1Chr 7:12
took to wife the sister of *H*............. 1Chr 7:15

HUR (*hur*)
1. Assisted Moses at Rephidim.
H went up to the top of the hill......... Ex 17:10
H stayed up his hands, the one on..... Ex 17:12
behold, Aaron and *H* are with you ..... Ex 24:14
2. A son of Caleb.
the son of Uri, the son of *H*............. Ex 31:2
the son of Uri, the son of *H*............. Ex 35:30
the son of Uri, the son of *H*............. Ex 38:22
him Ephrath, which bare him *H*......... 1Chr 2:19
H begat Uri, and Uri begat.............. 1Chr 4:4
the son of Uri, the son of *H*............. 2Chr 1:5
3. A Midianite king.
Evi, and Rekem, and Zur, and *H*........ Num 31:8
Evi, and Rekem, and Zur, and *H*....... Josh 13:21
4. An officer of Solomon.
The son of *H*, in mount Ephraim...... 1Kin 4:8
5. Father of Caleb.
the sons of Caleb the son of *H*......... 1Chr 2:50
These are the sons of *H*, the........... 1Chr 4:4
6. A descendant of Judah.
Pharez, Hezron, and Carmi, and *H* 1Chr 4:1
7. A rebuilder of Jerusalem's wall.
repaired Rephaiah the son of *H*......... Neh 3:9

HURAI (*hu´-rahee*) See HIDDAI. *A mighty man of David.*
H of the brooks of Gaash, Abiel........ 1Chr 11:32

HURAM (*hu´-ram*) See HIRAM.
1. Son of Bela.
And Gera, and Shephuphan, and *H*..... 1Chr 8:5
2. Same as Hiram 1.
Solomon sent to *H* the king of.......... 2Chr 2:3
Then *H* the king of Tyre answered..... 2Chr 2:11
H said moreover, Blessed be the....... 2Chr 2:12
understanding, of *H* my father's,...... 2Chr 2:13
That the cities which *H* had.............. 2Chr 8:2
H sent him by the hands of his......... 2Chr 8:18
And the servants also of *H*.............. 2Chr 9:10
Tarshish with the servants of *H*........ 2Chr 9:21
3. Same as Hiram 2.
H made the pots, and the shovels,..... 2Chr 4:11
H finished the work that he was........ 2Chr 4:11
did *H* his father make to king........... 2Chr 4:16

H

HURAM-ABI See HURAM.

HURI (hu´-ri) *Father of Abihail.*
children of Abihail the son of H 1Chr 5:14

HURL
or h at him by laying of wait, ... Num 35:20

HURLETH
as a storm h him out of his place .... Job 27:21

HURLING
hand and the left in h stones 1Chr 12:2

HURT
wounding, and a young man to my h .. Gen 4:23
That thou wilt do us no h .... Gen 26:29
but God suffered him not to h me......... Gen 31:7
the power of my hand to do you h....... Gen 31:29
h a woman with child, so that her....... Ex 21:22
And if one man's ox h another's .... Ex 21:35
and it die, or be h, or driven........... Ex 22:10
of his neighbour, and it be h .... Ex 22:14
neither have I h one of them........... Num 16:15
then he will turn and do you h .... Josh 14:20
there is peace to thee, and no h........ 1Sa 20:21
Behold, David seeketh thy h........... 1Sa 24:9
we h them not, neither was there 1Sa 25:7
good unto us, and we were not h....... 1Sa 25:15
rise against thee to do thee h........... 2Sa 18:32
shouldest thou meddle to thy h 2Kin 14:10
shouldest thou meddle to thine h 2Chr 25:19
damage grow to the h of the kings .... Ezr 4:22
and such as sought their h.............. Est 9:2
may h a man as thou art............... Job 35:8
He that sweareth to his own h......... Ps 15:4
to confusion that devise my h......... Ps 35:4
together that rejoice at mine h......... Ps 35:26
they that seek my h speak............. Ps 38:12
against me do they devise my h........ Ps 41:7
to confusion, that desire my h......... Ps 70:2
and dishonour that seek my h......... Ps 71:13
unto shame, that seek my h........... Ps 71:24
Whose feet they h with fetters........ Ps 105:18
for the owners thereof to their h....... Eccl 5:13
ruleth over another to his own h ...... Eccl 8:9
stones shall be h therewith............ Eccl 10:9
They shall not h nor destroy in........ Is 11:9
lest any h it, I will keep it............. Is 27:3
They shall not h nor destroy in........ Is 65:25
They have healed also the h of .... Jer 6:14
walk after other gods to your hurt..... Jer 7:6
For they have healed the h of the ..... Jer 8:11
For the h of the daughter of my....... Jer 8:21
the daughter of my people am I h...... Jer 8:21
Woe is me for my h................... Jer 10:19
kingdoms of the earth for their h...... Jer 24:9
and I will do you no h................ Jer 25:6
works of your hands to your own h.... Jer 25:7
welfare of this people, but the h....... Jer 38:4
of the fire, and they have no h........ Dan 3:25
mouths, that they have not h me....... Dan 6:22
thee, O king, have I done no h......... Dan 6:22
no manner of h was found upon him... Dan 6:23
deadly thing, it shall not h them....... Mk 16:18
he came out of him, and him not...... Lk 4:35
nothing shall by any means h you...... Lk 10:19
man shall set on thee to h thee........ Acts 18:10
that this voyage will be with h......... Acts 27:10
not be h of the second death......... Rev 2:11
see thou h not the oil and the........ Rev 6:6
whom it was given to h the earth...... Rev 7:2
H not the earth, neither the sea,....... Rev 7:3
not h the grass of the earth........... Rev 9:4
power was to h men five months...... Rev 9:10
had heads, and with them they do h... Rev 9:19
And if any man will h them........... Rev 11:5
and if any man will h them........... Rev 11:5

HURTFUL
h unto kings and provinces, and....... Ezr 4:15
his servant from the h sword.......... Ps 144:10
h lusts, which drown men in.......... 1Ti 6:9

HURTING
hath kept me back from h thee........ 1Sa 25:34

HUSBAND
and gave also unto her h with her..... Gen 3:6
and thy desire shall be to thy h........ Gen 3:16
gave her to her h Abram to be his..... Gen 16:3
now therefore my h will love me....... Gen 29:32
time will my h be joined unto me...... Gen 29:34
matter that thou hast taken my h ..... Gen 30:15
I have given my maiden to my h....... Gen 30:18
now will my h dwell with me.......... Gen 30:20
Surely a bloody h art thou to me...... Ex 4:25
she said, A bloody h thou art.......... Ex 4:26
the woman's h will lay upon him...... Ex 21:22
is a bondmaid, betrothed to an h ..... Lev 19:20
unto him, which hath had no h........ Lev 21:3
take a woman put away from her h.... Lev 21:7
it be hid from the eyes of her h....... Num 5:13
with another instead of thy h.......... Num 5:19
aside to another instead of thy h...... Num 5:20
lain with thee beside thine h.......... Num 5:20
have done trespass against her h...... Num 5:27
aside to another instead of her h...... Num 5:29
And if she had at all an h............. Num 30:6
her h heard it, and held his peace..... Num 30:7
But if her h disallowed her on......... Num 30:8
her h heard it, and held his peace..... Num 30:11
But if her h hath utterly made........ Num 30:12
her h hath made them void............ Num 30:12

her h may establish it .... Num 30:13
or her h may make it void............ Num 30:13
But if her h altogether hold his....... Num 30:14
shalt go in unto her, and be her h..... Deut 21:13
with a woman married to an h........ Deut 22:22
a virgin be betrothed unto an h....... Deut 22:23
And if the latter h hate her........... Deut 24:3
or if the latter h die, which.......... Deut 24:3
Her former h, which sent her away.... Deut 24:4
her h out of the hand of him that..... Deut 25:11
the evil toward the h of her bosom.... Deut 28:56
Then the woman came and told her h Judg 13:6
but Manoah her h was not with her ... Judg 13:9
haste, and ran, and shewed her h ..... Judg 13:10
unto Samson's wife, Entice thy h...... Judg 14:15
her h arose, and went after her,....... Judg 19:3
the h of the woman that was slain .... Judg 20:4
And Elimelech Naomi's h died......... Ruth 1:3
was left of her two sons and her h.... Ruth 1:5
each of you in the house of her h..... Ruth 1:9
for I am too old to have an h......... Ruth 1:12
I should have an h also to night...... Ruth 1:12
in law since the death of thine h...... Ruth 2:11
Then said Elkanah her h to her....... 1Sa 1:8
for she said unto her h, I will........ 1Sa 1:22
Elkanah her h said unto her, Do...... 1Sa 1:23
when she came up with her h to...... 1Sa 2:19
her h were dead, she bowed.......... 1Sa 4:19
of her father in law and her h......... 1Sa 4:21
But she told not her h Nabal......... 1Sa 25:19
sent, and took her from her h......... 2Sa 3:15
her h went with her along weeping.... 2Sa 3:16
heard that Uriah her h was dead...... 2Sa 11:26
she mourned for her h................ 2Sa 11:26
a widow woman, and mine h is dead .. 2Sa 14:5
shall not leave to my h neither........ 2Sa 14:7
saying, Thy servant my h is dead...... 2Kin 4:1
And she said unto her h, Behold...... 2Kin 4:9
hath no child, and her h is old........ 2Kin 4:14
And she called unto her h, and said .. 2Kin 4:22
is it well with thy h................. 2Kin 4:26
woman is a crown to her h........... Prov 12:4
The heart of her h doth safely........ Prov 31:11
Her h is known in the gates, when.... Prov 31:23
her h also, and he praiseth her........ Prov 31:28
For thy Maker is thine h.............. Is 54:5
departeth from her h, so have ye...... Jer 3:20
for even the h with the wife.......... Jer 6:11
although I was an h unto them........ Jer 31:32
taketh strangers instead of her h...... Eze 16:32
daughter, that loatheth her h......... Eze 16:45
or for sister that hath had no h....... Eze 44:25
not my wife, neither am I her h....... Hos 2:2
I will go and return to my first h..... Hos 2:7
sackcloth for the h of her youth...... Joel 1:8
Jacob begat Joseph the h of Mary..... Mt 1:16
Then Joseph her h, being a just...... Mt 1:19
if a woman shall put away her h...... Mk 10:12
had lived with an h seven years....... Lk 2:36
from her h committeth adultery....... Lk 16:18
saith unto her, Go, call thy h......... Jn 4:16
answered and said, I have no h........ Jn 4:17
Thou hast well said, I have no h....... Jn 4:17
whom thou now hast is not thy h..... Jn 4:18
have buried thy h are at the door..... Acts 5:9
her forth, buried her by her h......... Acts 5:10
an h is bound by the law to her...... Rom 7:2
law to her h so long as he liveth...... Rom 7:2
but if the h be dead, she is.......... Rom 7:2
is loosed from the law of her h....... Rom 7:2
So then if, while her h liveth......... Rom 7:3
but if her h be dead, she is free...... Rom 7:3
and let every woman have her own h.. 1Cor 7:2
Let the h render unto the wife....... 1Cor 7:3
likewise also the wife unto the h..... 1Cor 7:3
power of her own body, but the h 1Cor 7:4
likewise also the h hath not......... 1Cor 7:4
not the wife depart from her h........ 1Cor 7:10
or be reconciled to her h............ 1Cor 7:11
let not the h put away his wife....... 1Cor 7:11
for the unbelieving h is.............. 1Cor 7:14
wife is sanctified by the h........... 1Cor 7:14
whether thou shalt save thy h........ 1Cor 7:16
world, how she may please her h...... 1Cor 7:34
the law as long as her h liveth....... 1Cor 7:39
but if her h be dead, she is.......... 1Cor 7:39
for I have espoused you to one h..... 2Cor 11:2
children than she which hath a....... Gal 4:27
For the h is the head of the wife..... Eph 5:23
wife see that she reverence her h..... Eph 5:33
the h of one wife, vigilant,.......... 1Ti 3:2
the h of one wife, having............ Titus 1:6
as a bride adorned for her h......... Rev 21:2

HUSBANDMAN
And Noah began to be an h, and he.. Gen 9:20
thee will I break in pieces the h...... Jer 51:23
they shall call the h to mourning..... Amos 5:16
say, I am no prophet, I am an h...... Zec 13:5
true vine, and my Father is the h..... Jn 15:1
The h that laboureth must be........ 2Ti 2:6
the h waiteth for the precious........ Jas 5:7

HUSBANDMEN
the land to be vinedressers and h..... 2Kin 25:12
h also, and vine dressers in the...... 2Chr 26:10
the cities thereof together, h........ Jer 31:24
land for vinedressers and for h....... Jer 52:16
Be ye ashamed, O ye h.............. Joel 1:11
built a tower, and let it out to....... Mt 21:33

he sent his servants to the h......... Mt 21:34
the h took his servants, and beat..... Mt 21:35
But when he saw the son............ Mt 21:38
what will he do unto those h......... Mt 21:40
let out his vineyard unto other h..... Mt 21:41
built a tower, and let it out to h..... Mk 12:1
season he sent to the h a servant..... Mk 12:2
h of the fruit of the vineyard........ Mk 12:2
But those h said among themselves... Mk 12:7
he will come and destroy the h....... Mk 12:9
a vineyard, and let it forth to h...... Lk 20:9
season he sent a servant to the h .... Lk 20:10
but the h beat him, and sent him.... Lk 20:10
But when the h saw him, they....... Lk 20:14
He shall come and destroy these h ... Lk 20:16

HUSBANDRY
for he loved h.................... 2Chr 26:10
ye are God's h, ye are God's........ 1Cor 3:9

HUSBAND'S
And if she vowed in her h house..... Num 30:10
her h brother shall go in unto....... Deut 25:5
the duty of an h brother unto her.... Deut 25:7
My h brother refuseth to raise up.... Deut 25:7
perform the duty of my h brother.... Deut 25:7
And Naomi had a kinsman of her h... Ruth 2:1

HUSBANDS
my womb, that they may be your h ... Ruth 1:11
ye stay for them from having h....... Ruth 1:13
despise their h in their eyes......... Est 1:17
shall give to their h honour......... Est 1:20
sons, and give your daughters to h... Jer 29:6
thy sisters, which loathed their h..... Eze 16:45
For thou hast had five h............ Jn 4:18
let them ask their h at home........ 1Cor 14:35
submit yourselves unto your own h... Eph 5:22
be to their own h in every thing..... Eph 5:24
H, love your wives, even as.......... Eph 5:25
submit yourselves unto your own h... Col 3:18
H, love your wives, and be not....... Col 3:19
the deacons be the h of one wife..... 1Ti 3:12
to be sober, to love their h.......... Titus 2:4
good, obedient to their own h........ Titus 2:5
be in subjection to your own h....... 1Pet 3:1
in subjection unto their own h....... 1Pet 3:5
Likewise, ye h, dwell with them...... 1Pet 3:7

HUSHAH (hu´-shah) See HUSHATHITE, SHUAH.
A son of Ezer.
of Gedor, and Ezer, the father of H... 1Chr 4:4

HUSHAI (hu´-shaee) *Friend and advisor of
David.*
H the Archite came to meet him...... 2Sa 15:32
So H David's friend came into the 2Sa 15:37
when H the Archite, David's......... 2Sa 16:16
that H said unto Absalom, God...... 2Sa 16:16
And Absalom said to H, Is this thy.... 2Sa 16:17
And H said unto Absalom, Nay....... 2Sa 16:18
Call now H the Archite also, and..... 2Sa 17:5
when H was come to Absalom....... 2Sa 17:6
H said unto Absalom, The counsel.... 2Sa 17:7
For, said H, thou knowest thy....... 2Sa 17:8
The counsel of H the Archite is...... 2Sa 17:14
Then said H unto Zadok and to...... 2Sa 17:15
Baanah the son of H was in Asher.... 1Kin 4:16
H the Archite was the king's......... 1Chr 27:33

HUSHAM (hu´-sham) *A king of Edom.*
H of the land of Temani reigned...... Gen 36:34
H died, and Hadad the son of Bedad . Gen 36:35
H of the land of the Temanites....... 1Chr 1:45
when H was dead, Hadad the son of.. 1Chr 1:46

HUSHATHITE (hu´-shath-ite) *A descendant of
Hushah.*
then Sibbechai the H slew Saph...... 2Sa 21:18
the Anethothite, Mebunnai the H..... 2Sa 23:27
Sibbecai the H, Ilai the Ahohite...... 1Chr 11:29
time Sibbechai the H slew Sippai..... 1Chr 20:4
eighth month was Sibbecai the H..... 1Chr 27:11

HUSHIM (hu´-shim) See SHUHAM.
1. A son of Dan.
the sons of Dan: H................ Gen 46:23
2. A Benjamite.
Huppim, the children of Ir, and H.... 1Chr 7:12
3. A wife of Shaharaim.
H and Baara were his wives.......... 1Chr 8:8
of H he begat Abitub, and Elpaal..... 1Chr 8:11

HUSHITES See HUSHIM.

HUSK
from the kernels even to the h....... Num 6:4
ears of corn in the h thereof......... 2Kin 4:42

HUSKS
with the h that the swine did eat..... Lk 15:16

HUZ
H his firstborn, and Buz his......... Gen 22:21

HUZZAB (huz´-zab) *A region in Assyria.*
H shall be led away captive, she...... Nah 2:7

HYMENAEUS (hy-men-e´-us) *A false Christian
teacher.*
Of whom is H and Alexander........ 1Ti 1:20
of whom is H and Philetus.......... 2Ti 2:17

HYMN
And when they had sung an h........ Mt 26:30
And when they had sung an h........ Mk 14:26

HYMNS

to yourselves in psalms and *h*............... Eph 5:19
one another in psalms and *h*............... Col 3:16

HYPOCRISIES

all malice, and all guile, and *h*............... 1Pet 2:1

HYPOCRISY

will work iniquity, to practise *h*............... Is 32:6
men, but within ye are full of *h*............... Mt 23:28
But he, knowing their *h*, said............... Mk 12:15
of the Pharisees, which is *h*............... Lk 12:1
Speaking lies in *h*............... 1Ti 4:2
without partiality, and without *h*............... Jas 3:17

HYPOCRITE

for an *h* shall not come before............... Job 13:16
stir up himself against the *h*............... Job 17:8
the joy of the *h* but for a moment............... Job 20:5
For what is the hope of the *h*............... Job 27:8
That the *h* reign not, lest the............... Job 34:30
An *h* with his mouth destroyeth............... Prov 11:9
for every one is an *h* and an............... Is 9:17
Thou *h*, first cast out the beam............... Mt 7:5
Thou *h*, cast out first the beam............... Lk 6:42
answered him, and said, Thou *h*............... Lk 13:15

HYPOCRITE'S

and the *h* hope shall perish............... Job 8:13

HYPOCRITES

of *h* shall be desolate, and fire............... Job 15:34
But the *h* in heart heap up wrath............... Job 36:13
fearfulness hath surprised the *h*............... Is 33:14
as the *h* do in the synagogues and............... Mt 6:2
thou shalt not be as the *h* are............... Mt 6:5
when ye fast, be not, as the *h*............... Mt 6:16
Ye *h*, well did Esaias prophesy of............... Mt 15:7
O ye *h*, ye can discern the face............... Mt 16:3
and said, Why tempt ye me, ye *h*............... Mt 22:18
unto you, scribes and Pharisees, *h*............... Mt 23:13
unto you, scribes and Pharisees, *h*............... Mt 23:14
unto you, scribes and Pharisees, *h*............... Mt 23:15
unto you, scribes and Pharisees, *h*............... Mt 23:23
unto you, scribes and Pharisees, *h*............... Mt 23:25
unto you, scribes and Pharisees, *h*............... Mt 23:27
unto you, scribes and Pharisees, *h*............... Mt 23:29
him his portion with the *h*............... Mt 24:51
hath Esaias prophesied of you *h*............... Mk 7:6
unto you, scribes and Pharisees, *h*............... Lk 11:44
Ye *h*, ye can discern the face of............... Lk 12:56

HYPOCRITICAL

With *h* mockers in feasts, they............... Ps 35:16
will send him against an *h* nation............... Is 10:6

HYSSOP

And ye shall take a bunch of *h*............... Ex 12:22
and cedar wood, and scarlet, and *h*............... Lev 14:4
wood, and the scarlet, and the *h*............... Lev 14:6
and cedar wood, and scarlet, and *h*............... Lev 14:49
take the cedar wood, and the *h*............... Lev 14:51
the cedar wood, and with the *h*............... Lev 14:52
shall take cedar wood, and *h*............... Num 19:6
And a clean person shall take *h*............... Num 19:18
is in Lebanon even unto the *h*............... 1Kin 4:33
Purge me with *h*, and I shall be............... Ps 51:7
with vinegar, and put it upon *h*............... Jn 19:29
with water, and scarlet wool, and *h*............... Heb 9:19

I

I See PREFACE.

IBHAR (*ib'-har*) *A son of David.*
I also, and Elishua, and Nepheg, and............ 2Sa 5:15
I also, and Elishama, and Eliphelet 1Chr 3:6
And *I*, and Elishua, and Elpalet,............ 1Chr 14:5

IBLEAM (*ib'-le-am*) *A city in Asher.*
Beth-shean and her towns, and *I* ...... Josh 17:11
towns, nor the inhabitants of *I* .... Judg 1:27
going up to Gur, which is by *I* 2Kin 9:27

IBNEIAH (*ib-ne-i'-ah*) *A son of Jeroham.*
I the son of Jeroham, and Elah the 1Chr 9:8

IBNIJAH (*ib-ni'-jah*) *A family of exiles.*
the son of Reuel, the son of *I* 1Chr 9:8

IBRI (*ib'-ri*) *A descendant of Levi.*
Shoham, and Zaccur, and *I* 1Chr 24:27

IBSAM See JIBSAM.

IBZAN (*ib'-zan*) *A judge of Israel.*
after him *I* of Beth-lehem judged ...... Judg 12:8
Then died *I*, and was buried at............ Judg 12:10

ICE

are blackish by reason of the *i*............... Job 6:16
Out of whose womb came the *i*............... Job 38:29
casteth forth his *i* like morsels............... Ps 147:17

I-CHABOD (*ik'-a-bod*) See I-CHABOD's. *Son of Phinehas.*
And she named the child *I*, saying......... 1Sa 4:21

ICHABOD See I-CHABOD.

I-CHABOD'S (*ik'-a-bods*)
I brother, the son of Phinehas,............... 1Sa 14:3

ICONIUM (*i-co'-ne-um*) *A city in Asia Minor.*
feet against them, and came unto *I* ...... Acts 13:51
And it came to pass in *I*, that............... Acts 14:1
certain Jews from Antioch and *I* ...... Acts 14:19
returned again to Lystra, and to *I* ...... Acts 14:21
brethren that were at Lystra and *I*...... Acts 16:2
came unto me at Antioch, at *I* 2Ti 3:11

IDALAH (*id'-a-lah*) *A town in Zebulun.*
and Nahallal, and Shimron, and *I* ...... Josh 19:15

IDBASH (*id'-bash*) *A son of Abi-etam.*
Jezreel, and Ishma, and *I*............... 1Chr 4:3

IDDO (*id'-do*)
1. Father of Ahinadab.
the son of *I* had Mahanaim............... 1Kin 4:14
2. A descendant of Gershom.
I his son, Zerah his son,............... 1Chr 6:21
3. A son of Zechariah.
in Gilead, *I* the son of Zechariah............... 1Chr 27:21
4. A seer.
in the visions of *I* the seer............... 2Chr 9:29
and of *I* the seer concerning............... 2Chr 12:15
in the story of the prophet *I*............... 2Chr 13:22
5. An ancestor of Zechariah.
and Zechariah the son of *I* .... Ezr 5:1
prophet and Zechariah the son of *I*...... Ezr 6:14
the son of *I* the prophet, saying,............... Zec 1:1
the son of *I* the prophet, saying,............... Zec 1:7
6. A Nethinim chief in exile.
The chief at the place Casiphia .... Ezr 8:17
them what they should say unto *I* ...... Ezr 8:17
7. A priest.
Of *I*, Zechariah;............... Neh 12:4
I, Ginnetho, Abijah,............... Neh 12:16

IDLE

for they be *i*............... Ex 5:8
he said, Ye are *i*, ye are *i*............... Ex 5:17
an *i* soul shall suffer hunger ...... Prov 19:15
That every *i* word that men shall............... Mt 12:36
standing *i* in the marketplace............... Mt 20:3
out, and found others standing............... Mt 20:6
Why stand ye here all the day *i*............... Mt 20:6
words seemed to them as *i* tales............... Lk 24:11
And whilst they learn to be *i*............... 1Ti 5:13
and not only *i*, but tattlers also............... 1Ti 5:13

IDLENESS

and eateth not the bread of *i*............... Prov 31:27
through *i* of the hands the house...... Eccl 10:18
and abundance of *i* was in her............... Eze 16:49

IDOL

she had made an *i* in a grove............... 1Kin 15:13
and Asa destroyed her *i*, and burnt...... 1Kin 15:13
she had made an *i* in a grove............... 2Chr 15:16
and Asa cut down her *i*............... 2Chr 15:16
the *i* which he had made, in the............... 2Chr 33:7
the *i* out of the house of the............... 2Chr 33:15
Mine *i* hath done them, and my............... Is 48:5
incense, as if he blessed an *i*............... Is 66:3
man Coniah a despised broken *i*...... Jer 22:28
Woe to the *i* shepherd that............... Zec 11:17
and offered sacrifice unto the *i* ...... Acts 7:41
we know that an *i* is nothing in............... 1Cor 8:4
the *i* unto this hour eat it as a............... 1Cor 8:7
it as a thing offered unto an *i* 1Cor 8:7
that the *i* is any thing, or that 1Cor 10:19

IDOLATER

fornicator, or covetous, or an *i* 1Cor 5:11
nor covetous man, who is an *i*............... Eph 5:5

IDOLATERS

or extortioners, or with *i*............... 1Cor 5:10
neither fornicators, nor *i*............... 1Cor 6:9
Neither be ye *i*, as were some of 1Cor 10:7
whoremongers and idolaters, and *i*...... Rev 21:8
whoremongers, and murderers, and *i*... Rev 22:15

IDOLATRIES

banquetings, and abominable *i*............... 1Pet 4:3

IDOLATROUS

And he put down the *i* priests............... 2Kin 23:5

IDOLATRY

stubbornness is as iniquity and *i*...... 1Sa 15:23
he saw the city wholly given to *i* ...... Acts 17:16
my dearly beloved, flee from *i* 1Cor 10:14
I, witchcraft, hatred, variance,............... Gal 5:20
and covetousness, which is *i*............... Col 3:5

IDOL'S

sit at meat in the *i* temple............... 1Cor 8:10

IDOLS

Turn ye not unto *i*, nor make to ...... Lev 19:4
make you no *i* nor graven image ...... Lev 26:1
upon the carcases of your *i*............... Lev 26:30
their abominations, and their *i* ...... Deut 29:17
it in the house of their *i*............... 1Sa 31:9
removed all the *i* that his............... 1Kin 15:12
very abominably in following *i*............... 1Kin 21:26
For they served *i*, whereof the...... 2Kin 17:12
made Judah also to sin with his *i*...... 2Kin 21:11
served the *i* that his father............... 2Kin 21:21
wizards, and the images, and the *i*...... 2Kin 23:24
to carry tidings unto their *i* 1Chr 10:9
all the gods of the people are *i* 1Chr 16:26
put away the abominable *i* out of 2Chr 15:8
fathers, and served groves and *i*...... 2Chr 24:18
cut down all the *i* throughout all 2Chr 34:7

all the gods of the nations are *i* ...... Ps 96:5
that boast themselves of *i* .... Ps 97:7
And they served their *i*............... Ps 106:36
sacrificed unto the *i* of Canaan...... Ps 106:38
Their *i* are silver and gold, the...... Ps 115:4
The *i* of the heathen are silver...... Ps 135:15
Their land also is full of *i* .... Is 2:8
the *i* he shall utterly abolish .... Is 2:18
a man shall cast his *i* of silver......... Is 2:20
his *i* of gold, which they made......... Is 2:20
hath found the kingdoms of the *i* ...... Is 10:10
I have done unto Samaria and her *i* ...Is 10:11
so do to Jerusalem and her *i* .... Is 10:11
the *i* of Egypt shall be moved at...... Is 19:1
and they shall seek to the *i* .... Is 19:3
shall cast away his *i* of silver............ Is 31:7
his *i* of gold, which your own............ Is 31:7
together that are makers of *i*............ Is 45:16
their *i* were upon the beasts, and...... Is 46:1
with *i* under every green tree............ Is 57:5
her *i* are confounded, her images ...... Jer 50:2
and they are mad upon their *i* ...... Jer 50:38
down your slain men before your *i*...... Eze 6:4
children of Israel before their *i* ...... Eze 6:5
your *i* may be broken and cease, and...Eze 6:6
which go a whoring after their *i* ...... Eze 6:9
their *i* round about their altars ...... Eze 6:13
offer sweet savour to all their *i* ...... Eze 6:13
all the *i* of the house of Israel,............ Eze 8:10
set up their *i* in their heart............ Eze 14:3
setteth up his *i* in his heart............ Eze 14:4
to the multitude of his *i* .... Eze 14:4
estranged from me through their *i*...... Eze 14:5
and turn yourselves from your *i* ...... Eze 14:6
and setteth up his *i* in his heart......... Eze 14:7
lovers, and with all the *i* of thy......... Eze 16:36
to the *i* of the house of Israel............ Eze 18:6
hath lifted up his eyes to the *i* ...... Eze 18:12
to the *i* of the house of Israel............ Eze 18:15
yourselves with the *i* of Egypt ...... Eze 20:7
did they forsake the *i* of Egypt ...... Eze 20:8
their heart went after their *i* ...... Eze 20:16
defile yourselves with their *i* ...... Eze 20:18
eyes were after their fathers' *i* ...... Eze 20:24
yourselves with all your *i* .... Eze 20:31
Go ye, serve ye every one his *i* ...... Eze 20:39
with your gifts, and with your *i* ...... Eze 20:39
maketh *i* against herself to............ Eze 22:3
in thine *i* which thou hast made...... Eze 22:4
with all their *i* she defiled............ Eze 23:7
thou art polluted with their *i* ...... Eze 23:30
with their *i* have they committed...... Eze 23:37
slain their children to their *i* ...... Eze 23:39
ye shall bear the sins of your *i* ...... Eze 23:49
I will also destroy the *i* .... Eze 30:13
lift up your eyes toward your *i*............ Eze 33:25
for their *i* wherewith they had ...... Eze 36:18
filthiness, and from all your *i* ...... Eze 36:25
themselves any more with their *i*...... Eze 37:23
astray away from me after their *i*...... Eze 44:10
unto them before their *i*, and............ Eze 44:12
Ephraim is joined to *i*............... Hos 4:17
their gold have they made them *i*...... Hos 8:4
and *i* according to their own............ Hos 13:2
What have I to do any more with *i*...... Hos 14:8
all the *i* thereof will I lay............ Mic 1:7
trusteth therein, to make dumb *i*...... Hab 2:18
For the *i* have spoken vanity, and...... Zec 10:2
names of the *i* out of the land,............ Zec 13:2
they abstain from pollutions of ...... Acts 15:20
abstain from meats offered to *i* ...... Acts 15:29
from things offered to *i*, and from...... Acts 21:25
thou that abhorrest *i*, dost thou ...... Rom 2:22
as touching things offered unto *i*...... 1Cor 8:1
are offered in sacrifice unto *i* 1Cor 8:4
things which are offered to *i* 1Cor 8:10
in sacrifice to *i* as any thing 1Cor 10:19
is offered in sacrifice unto *i* 1Cor 10:28
carried away unto these dumb *i* 1Cor 12:2
hath the temple of God with *i* 2Cor 6:16
to God from *i* to serve the living...... 1Th 1:9
children, keep yourselves from *i* 1Jn 5:21
to eat things sacrificed unto *i* ...... Rev 2:14
to eat things sacrificed unto *i* ...... Rev 2:20
of *i* of gold, and silver, and brass,...... Rev 9:20

IDUMAEA (*i-doo-me'-ah*) See IDUMEA. *Greek form of Edom.*
And from Jerusalem, and from ...... Mk 3:8

IDUMEA (*i-doo-me'-ah*) See EDOM, IDUMAEA. *Same as Edom.*
behold, it shall come down upon *I* ...... Is 34:5
great slaughter in the land of *I* ...... Is 34:6
desolate, O mount Seir, and all *I* ...... Eze 35:15
of the heathen, and against all *I*...... Eze 36:5

IEZERITES

IF See PREFACE.

IGAL (*i'-gal*) See IGEAL.
1. One of the twelve spies.
of Issachar, *I* the son of Joseph ...... Num 13:7
2. A mighty man of David.
I the son of Nathan of Zobah,............ 2Sa 23:36

IGDALIAH (*ig-da-li'-ah*) *Father of Hanan.*
the sons of Hanan, the son of *I* ...... Jer 35:4

IGEAL (*ig'-e-al*) See IGAL. *A royal descendant of Judah.*
Hattush, and *I*, and Bariah, and 1Chr 3:22

IGNOMINY
also contempt, and with *i* reproach .... Prov 18:3

IGNORANCE
If a soul shall sin through *i*.................... Lev 4:2
of Israel sin through *i*, and the............ Lev 4:13
done somewhat through *i* against........ Lev 4:22
the common people sin through *i* .... Lev 4:27
a trespass, and sin through *i* .... Lev 5:15
concerning his *i* wherein he erred....... Lev 5:18
if ought be committed by *i* .... Num 15:24
for it is *i* .... Num 15:25
before the LORD, for their *i*................ Num 15:25
seeing all the people were in *i* .... Num 15:26
And if any soul sin through *i*................ Num 15:27
he sinneth by *i* before the LORD .... Num 15:28
for him that sinneth through *i*.............. Num 15:29
I wot that through *i* ye did it .... Acts 3:17
the times of this *i* God winked at....... Acts 17:30
God through the *i* that is in them .... Eph 4:18
to the former lusts in your *i* 1Pet 1:14
to silence the *i* of foolish men........... 1Pet 2:15

IGNORANT
So foolish was I, and *i*.......................... Ps 73:22
they are all *i*, they are all dumb.......... Is 56:10
father, though Abraham be *i* of us....... Is 63:16
and *i* men, they marvelled................... Acts 4:13
Now I would not have you *i* .... Rom 1:13
For they being *i* of God's.................... Rom 10:3
ye should be *i* of this mystery .... Rom 11:25
I would not that ye should be *i* 1Cor 10:1
brethren, I would not have you *i* 1Cor 12:1
any man be *i*, let him be *i* 1Cor 14:38
have you *i* of our trouble which 2Cor 1:8
for we are not *i* of his devices............ 2Cor 2:11
But I would not have you to be *i* 1Th 4:13
Who can have compassion on the *i*.... Heb 5:2
For this they willingly are *i* of 2Pet 3:5
be not *i* of this one thing, that............ 2Pet 3:8

IGNORANTLY
for the soul that sinneth *i*................... Num 15:28
Whoso killeth his neighbour *i* .... Deut 19:4
Whom therefore ye *i* worship............. Acts 17:23
because I did it *i* in unbelief............... 1Ti 1:13

IIM (*i'-im*) See IJE-ABARIM.
1. A Hebrew encampment in the wilderness.
And they departed from *I*, and .... Num 33:45
2. A town in Judah.
Baalah, and *I*, and Azem,.................... Josh 15:29

IJE-ABARIM (*i'-je-ab'-a-rim*) See IIM. Same as
Iim I.
from Oboth, and pitched at *I* .... Num 21:11
from Oboth, and pitched in *I*.............. Num 33:44

IJON (*i'-jon*) A town in Naphtali.
the cities of Israel, and smote *I* 1Kin 15:20
king of Assyria, and took *I* 2Kin 15:29
and they smote *I*, and Dan, and 2Chr 16:4

IKKESH (*ik'-kesh*) Father of Ira.
Ira the son of *I* the Tekoite................. 2Sa 23:26
Ira the son of *I* the Tekoite................. 1Chr 11:28
was Ira the son of *I* the Tekoite........... 1Chr 27:9

ILAI (*i'-lahee*) See ZALMON. A "mighty man" of
David.
the Hushathite, *I* the Ahohite,............ 1Chr 11:29

ILL
I favoured and leanfleshed...................... Gen 41:3
the *i* favoured and leanfleshed............. Gen 41:4
very *i* favoured and leanfleshed,.......... Gen 41:19
the *i* favoured kine did eat up.............. Gen 41:20
but they were still *i* favoured .... Gen 41:21
i favoured kine that came up .... Gen 41:27
Wherefore dealt ye so *i* with me......... Gen 43:6
or blind, or have any *i* blemish............ Deut 15:21
it shall go *i* with him that is................. Job 20:26
so that it went *i* with Moses for.......... Ps 106:32
it shall be *i* with him............................ Is 3:11
but if it seem *i* unto thee to................. Jer 40:4
his *i* savour shall come up,.................. Joel 2:20
themselves *i* in their doings................. Mic 3:4
Love worketh no *i* to his...................... Rom 13:10

ILLUMINATED
days, in which, after ye were *i*............ Heb 10:32

ILLYRICUM (*il-lir'-ic-um*) A Roman Adriatic
province.
Jerusalem, and round about unto *I*...... Rom 15:19

IMAGE
said, Let us make man in our *i* .... Gen 1:26
So God created man in his own *i* .... Gen 1:27
in the *i* of God created he him............. Gen 1:27
in his own likeness, after his *i*............ Gen 5:3
for in the *i* of God made he man......... Gen 9:6
not make unto thee any graven *i*......... Ex 20:4
make you no idols nor graven *i*........... Lev 26:1
neither rear you up a standing *i*.......... Lev 26:1
up any *i* of stone in your land............. Lev 26:1
and make you a graven *i*, the.............. Deut 4:16
with you, and make you a graven *i*..... Deut 4:23
yourselves, and make a graven *i*......... Deut 4:25
shalt not make thee any graven *i*........ Deut 5:8
shalt thou set thee up any *i*................. Deut 9:12
maketh any graven or molten *i*............ Deut 27:15
make a graven *i* and a molten *i*........ Judg 17:3
a graven *i* and a molten *i*................. Judg 17:4
a graven *i*, and a molten *i*............... Judg 18:14

in thither, and took the graven *i*........ Judg 18:17
and the teraphim, and the graven *i*.... Judg 18:17
house, and fetched the carved *i*......... Judg 18:18
and the teraphim, and the molten *i*.... Judg 18:18
and the teraphim, and the graven *i*.... Judg 18:20
of Dan set up the graven *i*................. Judg 18:30
they set them up Micah's graven *i*..... Judg 18:31
And Michal took an *i*, and laid it 1Sa 19:13
behold, there was an *i* in the bed 1Sa 19:16
for he put away the *i* of Baal 2Kin 3:2
And they brake down the *i* of Baal..... 2Kin 10:27
he set a graven *i* of the grove 2Kin 21:7
he made two cherubims of a work 2Chr 3:10
And he set a carved *i*, the idol........... 2Chr 33:7
an *i* was before mine eyes, there ...... Job 4:16
thou shalt despise their *i* .... Ps 73:20
Horeb, and worshipped the molten *i*.. Ps 106:19
The workman melteth a graven *i* .... Is 40:19
workman to prepare a graven *i*.......... Is 40:20
a graven *i* are all their vanity .... Is 42:17
or molten a graven *i* that is .... Is 44:10
he maketh it a graven *i*, and............. Is 44:15
maketh a god, even his graven *i* .... Is 44:17
set up the wood of their graven *i*...... Is 45:20
hath done them, and my graven *i*...... Is 48:5
my graven *i*, and my molten *i*........ Is 48:5
is confounded by the graven *i*........... Jer 10:14
for his molten *i* is falsehood.............. Jer 10:14
is confounded by the graven *i*........... Jer 51:17
for his molten *i* is falsehood............. Jer 51:17
was the seat of the *i* of jealousy....... Eze 8:3
this *i* of jealousy in the entry .... Eze 8:5
king, sawest, and behold a great *i*.... Dan 2:31
This great *i*, whose brightness.......... Dan 2:31
which smote the *i* upon his feet .... Dan 2:34
the *i* became a great mountain .... Dan 2:35
the king made an *i* of gold .... Dan 3:1
i which Nebuchadnezzar the king..... Dan 3:2
unto the dedication of the *i* that ...... Dan 3:3
they stood before the *i* that .... Dan 3:3
worship the golden *i* that .... Dan 3:5
worshipped the golden *i* that .... Dan 3:7
fall down and worship the golden *i*... Dan 3:10
golden *i* which thou hast set up .... Dan 3:12
the golden *i* which I have set up ...... Dan 3:14
worship the *i* which I have made...... Dan 3:15
golden *i* which thou hast made up .... Dan 3:18
a sacrifice, and without an *i*.............. Hos 3:4
gods will I cut off the graven *i* .... Nah 1:14
the graven *i* and the molten *i*........ Nah 1:14
What profiteth the graven *i* that ...... Hab 2:18
the molten *i*, and a teacher of .... Hab 2:18
saith unto them, Whose is this *i* .... Mt 22:20
saith unto them, Whose is this *i* .... Mk 12:16
Whose *i* and superscription hath it.... Lk 20:24
of the *i* which fell down from............. Acts 19:35
an *i* made like to corruptible man...... Rom 1:23
be conformed to the *i* of his Son ...... Rom 8:29
bowed the knee to the *i* of Baal......... Rom 11:4
head, forasmuch as he is the *i*........... 1Cor 11:7
we have borne the *i* of the earthy...... 1Cor 15:49
also bear the *i* of the heavenly.......... 1Cor 15:49
the same *i* from glory to glory 2Cor 3:18
of Christ, who is the *i* of God............ 2Cor 4:4
Who is the *i* of the invisible God .... Col 1:15
the *i* of him that created him.............. Col 3:10
the express *i* of his person, and......... Heb 1:3
not the very *i* of the things, can........ Heb 10:1
should make an *i* to the beast............ Rev 13:14
give life unto the *i* of the beast......... Rev 13:15
that the *i* of the beast should............ Rev 13:15
i of the beast should be killed.......... Rev 13:15
man worship the beast and his *i* .... Rev 14:9
who worship the beast and his *i* .... Rev 14:11
over the beast, and over his *i*............. Rev 15:2
upon them which worshipped his *i* ... Rev 16:2
and them that worshipped his *i* .... Rev 19:20
the beast, neither his *i*, neither......... Rev 20:4

IMAGERY
man in the chambers of his *i*............... Eze 8:12

IMAGE'S
This *i* head was of fine gold, his .... Dan 2:32

IMAGES
Rachel had stolen the *i* that were .... Gen 31:19
Now Rachel had taken the *i* .... Gen 31:34
he searched, but found not the *i*........ Gen 31:35
them, and quite break down their *i*.... Ex 23:24
their altars, break their *i*.................... Ex 34:13
high places, and cut down your *i*........ Lev 26:30
and destroy all their molten *i*............ Num 33:52
altars, and break down their *i* .... Deut 7:5
and burn their graven *i* with fire........ Deut 7:5
The graven *i* of their gods shall......... Deut 7:25
down the graven *i* of their gods........ Deut 12:3
ye shall make *i* of your emerods....... 1Sa 6:5
i of your mice that mar the land 1Sa 6:5
of gold and the *i* of their emerods..... 1Sa 6:11
And there they left their *i* 2Sa 5:21
made thee other gods, and molten *i*.. 1Kin 14:9
also built them high places, and *i*..... 1Kin 14:23
they brought forth the *i* out of.......... 2Kin 10:26
his *i* brake they in pieces................... 2Kin 11:18
And they set them up *i* and groves.... 2Kin 17:10
their God, and made them molten *i*... 2Kin 17:16
LORD, and served their graven *i*........ 2Kin 17:41
the high places, and brake the *i*......... 2Kin 18:4
And he brake in pieces the *i* 2Kin 23:14
spirits, and the wizards, and the *i*..... 2Kin 23:24
high places, and brake down the *i*..... 2Chr 14:3

of Judah the high places and the *i*...... 2Chr 14:5
his *i* in pieces, and slew Mattan 2Chr 23:17
and made also molten *i* for Baalim 2Chr 28:2
Judah, and brake the *i* in pieces........ 2Chr 31:1
and set up groves and graven *i*.......... 2Chr 33:19
I which Manasseh his father had.......... 2Chr 33:22
carved *i*, and the molten *i*.............. 2Chr 34:3
and the *i*, that were on high above.... 2Chr 34:4
carved *i*, and the molten *i*.............. 2Chr 34:4
beaten the graven *i* into powder 2Chr 34:7
to jealousy with their graven *i*.......... Ps 78:58
be all they that serve graven *i*........... Ps 97:7
whose graven *i* did excel them of...... Is 10:10
made, either the groves, or the *i*....... Is 17:8
all the graven *i* of her gods he .... Is 21:9
groves and *i* shall not stand up .... Is 27:9
of thy graven *i* silver .... Is 30:22
ornament of thy molten *i* of gold ...... Is 30:22
their molten *i* are wind and............... Is 41:29
neither my praise to graven *i* .... Is 42:8
ashamed, that trust in graven *i* .... Is 42:17
i, that say to the molten *i*............... Is 42:17
me to anger with their graven *i* .... Jer 8:19
break also the *i* of Beth-shemesh ...... Jer 43:13
her *i* are broken in pieces .... Jer 50:2
for it is the land of graven *i* .... Jer 50:38
upon the graven *i* of Babylon............ Jer 51:47
do judgment upon her graven *i*.......... Jer 51:52
and your *i* shall be broken................. Eze 6:4
your *i* may be cut down, and your...... Eze 6:6
be all they that made the *i* of .... Eze 7:20
and madest to thyself *i* of men .... Eze 16:17
bright, he consulted with *i*................. Eze 21:21
the *i* of the Chaldeans pourtrayed...... Eze 23:14
I will cause their *i* to cease out......... Eze 30:13
his land they have made goodly *i*...... Hos 10:1
altars, he shall spoil their *i*............... Hos 10:2
and burned incense to graven *i*.......... Hos 11:2
them molten *i* of their silver .... Hos 13:2
of your Moloch and Chiun your *i*....... Amos 5:26
all the graven *i* thereof shall be .... Mic 1:7
Thy graven *i* also will I cut off,......... Mic 5:13
thy standing *i* out of the midst.......... Mic 5:13

IMAGINATION
that every *i* of the thoughts of........... Gen 6:5
for the *i* of man's heart is evil........... Gen 8:21
I walk in the *i* of mine heart .... Deut 29:19
for I know their *i* which they go........ Deut 31:21
keep this for ever in the *i* of............. 1Chr 29:18
after the *i* of their evil heart .... Jer 3:17
in the *i* of their evil heart, and.......... Jer 7:24
after the *i* of their own heart............ Jer 9:14
one in the *i* of their evil heart .... Jer 11:8
walk in the *i* of their heart .... Jer 13:10
one after the *i* of his evil heart .... Jer 16:12
one do the *i* of his evil heart .... Jer 18:12
after the *i* of his own heart .... Jer 23:17
proud in the *i* of their hearts............ Lk 1:51

IMAGINATIONS
all the *i* of the thoughts...................... 1Chr 28:9
An heart that deviseth wicked *i*......... Prov 6:18
and all their *i* against me .... Lam 3:60
O LORD, and all their *i* against me ..... Lam 3:61
but became vain in their *i*.................. Rom 1:21
Casting down *i*, and every high......... 2Cor 10:5

IMAGINE
Do ye *i* to reprove words, and the ..... Job 6:26
which ye wrongfully *i* against me ...... Job 21:27
the people a vain thing......................... Ps 2:1
i deceits all the day long.................... Ps 38:12
How long will ye *i* mischief............... Ps 62:3
Which *i* mischiefs in their heart........ Ps 140:2
in the heart of them that *i* evil.......... Prov 12:20
yet do they *i* mischief against me ..... Hos 7:15
What do ye *i* against the LORD .... Nah 1:9
let none of you *i* evil against............. Zec 7:10
let none of you *i* evil in your............. Zec 8:17
rage, and the people *i* vain things...... Acts 4:25

IMAGINED
them, which they have *i* to do .... Gen 11:6
in the devices that they have *i* .... Ps 10:2
that a mischievous device,.................... Ps 21:11

IMAGINETH
that *i* evil against the LORD,............... Nah 1:11

IMLA (*im'-lah*) See IMLAH. Father of Michaiah.
the same is Micaiah the son of *I* 2Chr 18:7
quickly Micaiah the son of *I* 2Chr 18:8

IMLAH (*im'-lah*) See IMLA. Same as Imla.
yet one man, Micaiah the son of *I* 1Kin 22:8
hither Micaiah the son of *I*................. 1Kin 22:9

IMMANUEL (*im-man'-u-el*) See EMMANUEL. A
Messianic name.
a son, and shall call his name *I*.......... Is 7:14
fill the breadth of thy land, O *I* .... Is 8:8

IMMEDIATELY
they *i* left the ship and their .... Mt 4:22
i his leprosy was cleansed.................. Mt 8:3
i Jesus stretched forth his hand,........ Mt 14:31
i their eyes received sight, and.......... Mt 20:34
i after the tribulation of those........... Mt 24:29
And *i* the cock crew............................ Mt 26:74
i the spirit driveth him into the .... Mk 1:12
And *i* his fame spread abroad............. Mk 1:28
the fever left her, and she .... Mk 1:31
i the leprosy departed from him,....... Mk 1:42

i when Jesus perceived in his.................. Mk 2:8
i he arose, took up the bed, and.............. Mk 2:12
i it sprang up, because it had no.............. Mk 4:5
they have heard, Satan cometh i.............. Mk 4:15
i receive it with gladness...................... Mk 4:16
word's sake, i they are offended.............. Mk 4:17
i he putteth in the sickle........................ Mk 4:29
i there met him out of the tombs............ Mk 5:2
i knowing in himself that virtue.............. Mk 5:30
i the king sent an executioner,................ Mk 6:27
i he talked with them, and saith.............. Mk 6:50
i he received his sight, and...................... Mk 10:52
And i, while he yet spake, cometh.......... Mk 14:43
And his mouth was opened i.................... Lk 1:64
i he arose and ministered unto................ Lk 4:39
i the leprosy departed from him.............. Lk 5:13
i he rose up before them, and took.......... Lk 5:25
did beat vehemently, and i it fell............ Lk 6:49
i her issue of blood stanched.................. Lk 8:44
him, and how she was healed i................ Lk 8:47
they may open unto him i........................ Lk 12:36
i she was made straight, and.................... Lk 13:13
i he received his sight, and...................... Lk 18:43
kingdom of God should i appear.............. Lk 19:11
peace, the stones would i cry out.......... Lk 19:40
And i, while he yet spake, the................ Lk 22:60
i the man was made whole, and took...... Jn 5:9
i the ship was at the land........................ Jn 6:21
received the sop went i out.................... Jn 13:30
and i the cock crew............................ Jn 18:27
forth, and entered into a ship i.............. Jn 21:3
i his feet and ancle bones...................... Acts 3:7
i there fell from his eyes as i.................. Acts 9:18
And he arose i.................................. Acts 9:34
i therefore I sent to thee........................ Acts 10:33
i there were three men already.............. Acts 11:11
i the angel of the Lord smote him.......... Acts 12:23
i there fell on him a mist and a.............. Acts 13:11
i we endeavoured to go into.................... Acts 16:10
i all the doors were opened, and............ Acts 16:26
the brethren i sent away Paul and.......... Acts 17:10
then i the brethren sent away................ Acts 17:14
Who i took soldiers and centurions........ Acts 21:32
i I conferred not with flesh and.............. Gal 1:16
And i I was in the spirit........................ Rev 4:2

IMMER (im'-mur)
1. Father of Meshillemeth.
son of Meshillemeth, the son of I.......... 1Chr 9:12
2. The children of I, a thousand............ Ezr 2:37
And of the sons of I................................ Ezr 10:20
The children of I, a thousand.................. Neh 7:40
son of Meshillemoth, the son of I.......... Neh 11:13
2. A sanctuary servant.
to Bilgah, the sixteenth to I.................... 1Chr 24:14
3. An exile.
Tel-harsa, Cherub, Addan, and I............ Ezr 2:59
Tel-harsha, Cherub, Addon, and I.......... Neh 7:61
4. Father of Zadok.
son of I over against his house................ Neh 3:29
5. A priest.
Pashur the son of I the priest.................. Jer 20:1

IMMORTAL
Now unto the King eternal, i.................. 1Ti 1:17

IMMORTALITY
seek for glory and honour and i.............. Rom 2:7
and this mortal must put on i.................. 1Cor 15:53
this mortal shall have put on i................ 1Cor 15:54
Who only hath i, dwelling in the............ 1Ti 6:16
i to light through the gospel.................... 2Ti 1:10

IMMUTABILITY
of promise the i of his counsel.............. Heb 6:17

IMMUTABLE
That by two i things, in which it............ Heb 6:18

IMNA (im'-nah)
I, and Shelesh, and Amal........................ 1Chr 7:35

IMNAH (im'-nah) See IMNAH, JIMNA. A son of Helem.
1. Son of Asher.
I, and Ishuai, and Ishuai, and Beriah .. 1Chr 7:30
2. Father of Kore.
I, and Kore the son of I the Levite........ 2Chr 31:14

IMPART
let him i to him that hath none................ Lk 3:11
that I may i unto you some...................... Rom 1:11

IMPARTED
wisdom, neither hath he i to her............ Job 39:17
were willing to have i unto you.............. 1Th 2:8

IMPEDIMENT
deaf, and had an i in his speech.............. Mk 7:32

IMPENITENT
i heart treasurest up unto........................ Rom 2:5

IMPERIOUS
the work of an i whorish woman............ Eze 16:30

IMPLACABLE
without natural affection, i.................... Rom 1:31

IMPLEAD
let them i one another............................ Acts 19:38

IMPORTUNITY
yet because of his i he will rise.............. Lk 11:8

IMPOSE
it shall not be lawful to i toll................ Ezr 7:24

IMPOSED
i on them until the time of...................... Heb 9:10

IMPOSSIBLE
and nothing shall be i unto you.............. Mt 17:20
unto them, With men this is i................ Mk 19:26

upon them saith, With men it is i.......... Mk 10:27
with God nothing shall be i.................... Lk 1:37
It is i but that offences will.................... Lk 17:1
The things which are i with men............ Lk 18:27
For it is i for those who were................ Heb 6:4
in which it was i for God to lie.............. Heb 6:18
faith it is i to please him........................ Heb 11:6

IMPOTENT
lay a great multitude of i folk................ Jn 5:3
The i man answered him, Sir, I.............. Jn 5:7
the good deed done to the i man............ Acts 4:9
i in his feet, being a cripple.................... Acts 14:8

IMPOVERISH
they shall i thy fenced cities,................ Jer 5:17

IMPOVERISHED
Israel was greatly i because of.............. Judg 6:6
He that is so i that he hath no................ Is 40:20
Whereas Edom saith, We are i................ Mal 1:4

IMPRISONED
I said, Lord, they know that I I.............. Acts 22:19

IMPRISONMENT
to confiscation of goods, or to i.............. Ezr 7:26
leprosy, moreover of bonds and i.......... Heb 11:36

IMPRISONMENTS
In stripes, in i, in tumults, in................ 2Cor 6:5

IMPUDENT
with an i face said unto him,................ Prov 7:13
For they are i children and...................... Eze 2:4
for all the house of Israel are i.............. Eze 3:7

IMPUTE
let not the king i any thing unto............ 1Sa 22:15
Let not my lord i iniquity unto................ 2Sa 19:19
to whom the Lord will not i sin.............. Rom 4:8

IMPUTED
neither shall it be i unto him.................. Lev 7:18
blood shall be i unto that man................ Lev 17:4
might be i unto them also........................ Rom 4:11
therefore it was i to him for.................. Rom 4:22
sake alone, that it was i to him.............. Rom 4:23
us also, to whom it shall be i.................. Rom 4:24
but sin is not i when there is no.............. Rom 5:13
God, and it was i unto him for................ Jas 2:23

IMPUTETH
unto whom the Lord i not iniquity........ Ps 32:2
unto whom God i righteousness............ Rom 4:6

IMPUTING
i this his power unto his god.................. Hab 1:11
not i their trespasses unto...................... 2Cor 5:19

IMRAH (im'-rah) A chief of Asher.
and Shual, and Beri, and I,.................... 1Chr 7:36

IMRI (im'-ri)
1. Son of Bani.
the son of Omri, the son of I.................. 1Chr 9:4
2. Father of Zaccur.
them builded Zaccur the son of I............ Neh 3:2

IN See PREFACE.

INASMUCH
i as he hated him not in time.................. Deut 19:6
i as thou followedst not young................ Ruth 3:10
i as ye have done it unto one of............ Mt 25:40
i as ye did it not to one of the................ Mt 25:45
i as I am the apostle of the...................... Rom 11:13
i as both in my bonds, and in the.......... Phil 1:7
i as he who hath builded the.................. Heb 3:3
i as not without an oath he was............ Heb 7:20
i as ye are partakers of Christ's............ 1Pet 4:13

INCENSE
for anointing oil, and for sweet i............ Ex 25:6
make an altar to burn i upon.................. Ex 30:1
thereon sweet i every morning................ Ex 30:7
lamps, he shall burn i upon it................ Ex 30:7
at even, he shall burn i upon it.............. Ex 30:8
a perpetual i before the Lord................ Ex 30:8
shall offer no strange i thereon.............. Ex 30:9
and his vessels, and the altar of i.......... Ex 30:27
his furniture, and the altar of i.............. Ex 31:8
sweet i for the holy place...................... Ex 31:11
anointing oil, and for the sweet i.......... Ex 35:8
the i altar, and his staves, and.............. Ex 35:15
the anointing oil, and the sweet i.......... Ex 35:15
anointing oil, and for the sweet i.......... Ex 35:28
he made the i altar of shittim................ Ex 37:25
the pure i of sweet spices,.................... Ex 37:29
the anointing oil, and the sweet i.......... Ex 39:38
set the altar of gold for the i................ Ex 40:5
And he burnt sweet i thereon................ Ex 40:27
altar of sweet i before the Lord............ Ex 40:5
put i thereon, and offered strange........ Lev 10:1
full of sweet i beaten small.................... Lev 16:12
he shall put the i upon the fire.............. Lev 16:13
that the cloud of the i may cover.......... Lev 16:13
oil for the light, and the sweet i............ Num 4:16
of ten shekels of gold, full of i.............. Num 7:14
of gold of ten shekels, full of i.............. Num 7:20
spoon of ten shekels, full of i................ Num 7:26
spoon of ten shekels, full of i................ Num 7:32
spoon of ten shekels, full of i................ Num 7:38
spoon of ten shekels, full of i................ Num 7:44
spoon of ten shekels, full of i................ Num 7:50
spoon of ten shekels, full of i................ Num 7:56
spoon of ten shekels, full of i................ Num 7:62
spoon of ten shekels, full of i................ Num 7:68

spoon of ten shekels, full of i................ Num 7:74
spoon of ten shekels, full of i................ Num 7:80
spoons were twelve, full of i.................. Num 7:86
put i in them before the Lord so............ Num 16:7
put i in them, and bring ye before........ Num 16:17
laid i thereon, and stood in the.............. Num 16:18
and fifty men that offered i.................... Num 16:35
near to offer i before the Lord.............. Num 16:40
from off the altar, and put on i.............. Num 16:46
and he put on i, and made an................ Num 16:47
they shall put i before thee.................... Deut 33:10
offer upon mine altar, to burn i............ 1Sa 2:28
and burnt i in high places...................... 1Kin 3:3
he burnt i upon the altar that................ 1Kin 9:25
his strange wives, which burnt i............ 1Kin 11:8
upon the altar, and burnt i.................... 1Kin 12:33
stood by the altar to burn i.................... 1Kin 13:1
high places that burn i upon thee.......... 1Kin 13:2
burnt i yet in the high places................ 1Kin 22:43
burnt i in the high places...................... 2Kin 12:3
burnt i on the high places...................... 2Kin 14:4
burnt i still on the high places.............. 2Kin 15:4
burned i still in the high places............ 2Kin 15:35
burnt i in the high places, and on.......... 2Kin 16:4
there they burnt i in all the.................... 2Kin 17:11
of Israel did burn i to it........................ 2Kin 18:4
have burned i unto other gods,............ 2Kin 22:17
burnt i in the high places in the............ 2Kin 23:5
them also that burned i unto Baal........ 2Kin 23:5
where the priests had burned i.............. 2Kin 23:8
offering, and on the altar of i................ 1Chr 6:49
to burn i before the Lord, to.................. 1Chr 23:13
for the altar of i refined gold................ 1Chr 28:18
and to burn before him sweet i.............. 2Chr 2:4
burnt sacrifices and sweet i.................. 2Chr 13:11
them, and burned i unto them................ 2Chr 25:14
burn i upon the altar of i...................... 2Chr 26:16
to burn i unto the Lord, but to.............. 2Chr 26:18
that are consecrated to burn i................ 2Chr 26:18
a censer in his hand to burn i................ 2Chr 26:19
the Lord, from beside the i altar.......... 2Chr 26:19
Moreover he burnt i in the valley.......... 2Chr 28:3
burnt i in the high places, and on.......... 2Chr 28:4
places to burn i unto other gods............ 2Chr 28:25
have not burned i nor offered................ 2Chr 29:7
minister unto him, and burn i................ 2Chr 29:11
the altars for i took they away.............. 2Chr 30:14
one altar, and burn i upon it.................. 2Chr 32:12
have burned i unto other gods,.............. 2Chr 34:25
of fatlings, with the i of rams................ Ps 66:15
be set forth before thee as i.................. Ps 141:2
i is an abomination unto me.................... Is 1:13
offering, nor wearied thee with i............ Is 43:23
they shall bring gold and i...................... Is 60:6
burneth i upon altars of brick................ Is 65:3
which have burned i in the...................... Is 65:7
he that burneth i, as if he...................... Is 66:3
have burned i unto other gods, and........ Jer 1:16
cometh there to me i from Sheba.......... Jer 6:20
burn i unto Baal, and walk after............ Jer 7:9
the gods unto whom they offer i............ Jer 11:12
even altars to burn i unto Baal.............. Jer 11:13
to anger in offering i unto Baal............ Jer 11:17
and meat offerings, and i, and................ Jer 17:26
me, they have burned i to vanity.......... Jer 18:15
have burned i in it unto other................ Jer 19:4
i unto all the host of heaven.................. Jer 19:13
they have offered i unto Baal................ Jer 32:29
in their hand, to bring them to.............. Jer 41:5
in that they went to burn i.................... Jer 44:3
to burn no i unto other gods.................. Jer 44:5
burning i unto other gods in the............ Jer 44:8
had burned i unto other gods.................. Jer 44:15
to burn i unto the queen of.................... Jer 44:17
to burn i to the queen of heaven.......... Jer 44:18
when we burned i to the queen of.......... Jer 44:19
The i that ye burned in the.................... Jer 44:21
Because ye have burned i, and.............. Jer 44:23
to burn i to the queen of heaven.......... Jer 44:25
and him that burneth i to his gods........ Jer 48:35
and a thick cloud of i went up................ Eze 8:11
mine oil and mine i before them............ Eze 16:18
whereupon thou hast set mine i............ Eze 23:41
wherein she burned i to them................ Hos 2:13
burn i upon the hills, under oaks.......... Hos 4:13
burned i to graven images...................... Hos 11:2
net, and burn i unto their drag.............. Hab 1:16
in every place i shall be offered............ Mal 1:11
his iot was to burn i when he................ Lk 1:9
praying without at the time of i............ Lk 1:10
the right side of the altar of i................ Lk 1:11
there was given unto him much i.......... Rev 8:3
And the smoke of the i, which came...... Rev 8:4

INCENSED
all they that were i against thee............ Is 41:11
all that are i against him shall.............. Is 45:24

INCLINE
i your heart unto the Lord God of........ Josh 24:23
That he may i our hearts unto him........ 1Kin 8:58
i thine ear unto me, and hear my.......... Ps 17:6
and consider, and i thine ear to............ Ps 45:10
I will i mine ear to a parable.................. Ps 49:4
i thine ear unto me, and save me.......... Ps 71:2
i your ears to the words of my.............. Ps 78:1
i thine ear unto my cry.......................... Ps 88:2
i thine ear unto my testimonies,............ Ps 119:36
I not my heart to any evil thing,............ Ps 141:4
So that thou i thine ear unto.................. Prov 2:2
i thine ear unto my sayings.................... Prov 4:20

I thine ear, O LORD, and hear .... Is 37:17
I your ear, and come unto me .... Is 55:3
O my God, *I* thine ear, and hear .... Dan 9:18

INCLINED
and their hearts *i* to follow .... Judg 9:3
he *i* unto me, and heard my cry .... Ps 40:1
Because he hath *i* his ear unto me .... Ps 116:2
I have *i* mine heart to perform .... Ps 119:112
nor *i* mine ear to them that .... Prov 5:13
nor *i* their ear, but walked in .... Jer 7:24
nor *i* their ear, but hardened .... Jer 7:26
nor *i* their ear, but walked every .... Jer 11:8
neither *i* their ear, but made .... Jer 17:23
hearkened, nor *i* your ear to hear .... Jer 25:4
not unto me, neither *i* their ear .... Jer 34:14
but ye have not *i* your ear .... Jer 35:15
nor *i* their ear to turn from .... Jer 44:5

INCLINETH
For her house *i* unto death .... Prov 2:18

INCLOSE
we will *i* her with boards of .... Song 8:9

INCLOSED
onyx stones *i* in ouches of gold .... Ex 39:6
they were *i* in ouches of gold in .... Ex 39:13
Thus they *i* the Benjamites round ...... Judg 20:43
They are *i* in their own fat .... Ps 17:10
assembly of the wicked have *i* me .... Ps 22:16
A garden *i* is my sister, my .... Song 4:12
He hath *i* my ways with hewn stone ..... Lam 3:9
they *i* a great multitude of .... Lk 5:6

INCLOSINGS
shall be set in gold in their *i* .... Ex 28:20
in ouches of gold in their *i* .... Ex 39:13

INCONTINENCY
Satan tempt you for your *i* 1Cor 7:5

INCONTINENT
trucebreakers, false accusers, *i* 2Ti 3:3

INCORRUPTIBLE
but we an *i* 1Cor 9:25
and the dead shall be raised *i* 1Cor 15:52
To an inheritance *i*, and undefiled 1Pet 1:4
not of corruptible seed, but of *i* 1Pet 1:23

INCORRUPTION
it is raised in *i* 1Cor 15:42
neither doth corruption inherit *i* 1Cor 15:50
this corruptible must put on *i* 1Cor 15:53
corruptible shall have put on *i* 1Cor 15:54

INCREASE
And it shall come to pass in the *i* .... Gen 47:24
may yield unto you the *i* thereof .... Lev 19:25
shall all the *i* thereof be meat .... Lev 25:7
ye shall eat the *i* thereof out of .... Lev 25:12
thou shalt *i* the price thereof .... Lev 25:16
not sow, nor gather in our *i* .... Lev 25:20
Take thou no usury of him, or *i* .... Lev 25:36
nor lend him thy victuals for *i* .... Lev 25:37
and the land shall yield her *i* .... Lev 26:4
your land shall not yield her *i* .... Lev 26:20
as the *i* of the threshingfloor .... Num 18:30
as the *i* of the winepress .... Num 18:30
an *i* of sinful men, to augment .... Num 32:14
thee, and that ye may *i* mightily .... Deut 6:3
the *i* of thy kine, and the flocks .... Deut 7:13
beasts of the field *i* upon thee .... Deut 7:22
truly tithe all the *i* of thy seed .... Deut 14:22
tithe of thine *i* the same year .... Deut 14:28
shall bless thee in all thine *i* .... Deut 16:15
tithes of thine *i* the third year .... Deut 26:12
the *i* of thy kine, and the flocks .... Deut 28:4
the *i* of thy kine, and the flocks .... Deut 28:18
the *i* of thy kine, or flocks .... Deut 28:51
he might eat the *i* of the fields .... Deut 32:13
consume the earth with her *i* .... Deut 32:22
and destroyed the *i* of the earth .... Judg 6:4
I thine army, and come out .... Judg 9:29
all the *i* of thine house shall 1Sa 2:33
the LORD had said he would *i* 1Chr 27:23
over the *i* of the vineyards for 1Chr 27:27
of all the *i* of the field 2Chr 31:5
also for the *i* of corn, and wine 2Chr 32:28
to *i* the trespass of Israel .... Ezr 10:10
it yieldeth much *i* unto the kings .... Neh 9:37
thy latter end should greatly *i* .... Job 8:7
The *i* of his house shall depart .... Job 20:28
and would root out all mine *i* .... Job 31:12
dost not *i* thy wealth by their .... Ps 44:12
if riches *i*, set not your heart .... Ps 62:10
Then shall the earth yield her *i* .... Ps 67:6
Thou shalt *i* my greatness, and .... Ps 71:21
they *i* in riches .... Ps 73:12
He gave also their *i* unto the .... Ps 78:46
and our land shall yield her *i* .... Ps 85:12
which may yield fruits of *i* .... Ps 107:37
The LORD shall *i* you more .... Ps 115:14
man will hear, and will *i* learning .... Prov 1:5
the firstfruits of all thine *i* .... Prov 3:9
man, and he will *i* in learning .... Prov 9:9
that gathereth by labour shall *i* .... Prov 13:11
but much *i* is by the strength of .... Prov 14:4
with the *i* of his lips shall he .... Prov 18:20
the poor to *i* his riches, and he .... Prov 22:16
when they perish, the righteous *i* .... Prov 28:28
he that loveth abundance with *i* .... Eccl 5:10
When goods *i*, they are increased .... Eccl 5:11
be many things that *i* vanity .... Eccl 6:11

Of the *i* of his government and .... Is 9:7
The meek also shall *i* their joy .... Is 29:19
and bread of the *i* of the earth .... Is 30:23
didst *i* thy perfumes, and didst .... Is 57:9
LORD, and the firstfruits of his *i* .... Jer 2:3
and they shall be fruitful and *i* .... Jer 23:3
I will *i* the famine upon you, and .... Eze 5:16
usury, neither hath taken any *i* .... Eze 18:8
forth upon usury, and hath taken *i* ...... Eze 18:13
hath not received usury nor *i* .... Eze 18:17
thou hast taken usury and *i* .... Eze 22:12
and the earth shall yield her *i* .... Eze 34:27
and they shall *i* and bring fruit .... Eze 36:11
call for the corn, and will *i* .... Eze 36:29
the *i* of the field, that ye shall .... Eze 36:30
I will *i* them with men like a .... Eze 36:37
the *i* thereof shall be for food .... Eze 48:18
shall acknowledge and *i* with glory ..... Dan 11:39
commit whoredom, and shall not *i* .... Hos 4:10
and the ground shall give her *i* .... Zec 8:12
they shall *i* as they have .... Zec 10:8
said unto the Lord, *I* our faith .... Lk 17:5
He must *i*, but I must decrease .... Jn 3:30
that God gave the *i* 1Cor 3:6
but God that giveth the *i* 1Cor 3:7
sown, and *i* the fruits of your 2Cor 9:10
maketh *i* of the body unto the .... Eph 4:16
increaseth with the *i* of God .... Col 2:19
And the Lord make you to *i* 1Th 3:12
you, brethren, that ye *i* more 1Th 4:10
for they will *i* unto more 2Ti 2:16

INCREASED
and the waters *i*, and bare up the .... Gen 7:17
were *i* greatly upon the earth .... Gen 7:18
it is now *i* unto a multitude .... Gen 30:30
the man *i* exceedingly, and had .... Gen 30:43
i abundantly, and multiplied, and .... Ex 1:7
from before thee, until thou be *i* .... Ex 23:30
of the Philistines went on and *i* 1Sa 14:19
for the people *i* continually with 2Sa 15:12
And the battle *i* that day 1Kin 22:35
house of their fathers *i* greatly 1Chr 4:38
they *i* from Bashan unto 1Chr 5:23
And the battle *i* that day 2Chr 18:34
iniquities are *i* over our head .... Ezr 9:6
and his substance is *i* in the land .... Job 1:10
how are they *i* that trouble me .... Ps 3:1
that their corn and their wine *i* .... Ps 4:7
when the glory of his house is *i* .... Ps 49:16
And he *i* his people greatly .... Ps 105:24
the years of thy life shall be *i* .... Prov 9:11
i more than all that were before .... Eccl 2:9
they are *i* that eat them .... Eccl 5:11
the nation, and not *i* the joy .... Is 9:3
Thou hast *i* the nation, O LORD .... Is 26:15
thou hast *i* the nation .... Is 26:15
alone, and blessed him, and *i* him .... Is 51:2
i in the land, in those days, ... Jer 3:16
many, and their backslidings are *i* .... Jer 5:6
Their widows are *i* to me above .... Jer 15:8
that ye may be *i* there, and not .... Jer 29:6
because thy sins were *i* .... Jer 30:14
because thy sins were *i*, I have .... Jer 30:15
hath *i* in the daughter of Judah .... Lam 2:5
bud of the field, and thou hast *i* .... Eze 16:7
hast *i* thy whoredoms, to provoke .... Eze 16:26
And that she *i* her whoredoms .... Eze 23:14
traffick hast thou *i* thy riches .... Eze 28:5
so *i* from the lowest chamber to .... Eze 41:7
and fro, and knowledge shall be *i* .... Dan 12:4
As they were *i*, so they sinned .... Hos 4:7
of his fruit he hath *i* the altars .... Hos 10:1
fig trees and your olive trees *i* .... Amos 4:9
shall increase as they have *i* .... Zec 10:8
yield fruit that sprang up and *i* .... Mk 4:8
Jesus *i* in wisdom and stature, and ...... Lk 2:52
And the word of God *i* .... Acts 6:7
But Saul *i* the more in strength, ... Acts 9:22
the faith, and *i* in number daily .... Acts 16:5
having hope, when your faith is *i* 2Cor 10:15
i with goods, and have need of .... Rev 3:17

INCREASEST
i thine indignation upon me .... Job 10:17

INCREASETH
For it *i*. Thou huntest me .... Job 10:16
He *i* the nations, and destroyeth .... Job 12:23
up against thee *i* continually .... Ps 74:23
is that scattereth, and yet *i* .... Prov 11:24
sweetness of the lips *i* learning .... Prov 16:21
i the transgressors among men .... Prov 23:28
a man of knowledge *i* strength .... Prov 24:5
unjust gain *i* his substance, he .... Prov 28:8
are multiplied, transgression *i* .... Prov 29:16
he that *i* knowledge *i* sorrow .... Eccl 1:18
that have no might he *i* strength .... Is 40:29
he daily *i* lies and desolation .... Hos 12:1
Woe to him that *i* that which is .... Hab 2:6
i with the increase of God .... Col 2:19

INCREASING
i in the knowledge of God .... Col 1:10

INCREDIBLE
it be thought a thing *i* with you .... Acts 26:8

INCURABLE
in his bowels with an *i* disease 2Chr 21:18
my wound is *i* without .... Job 34:6
my pain perpetual, and my wound *i* ..... Jer 15:18
saith the LORD, Thy bruise is *i* .... Jer 30:12

thy sorrow is *i* for the multitude .... Jer 30:15
For her wound is *i* .... Mic 1:9

INDEBTED
forgive every one that is *i* to us .... Lk 11:4

INDEED
thy wife shall bear thee a son *i* .... Gen 17:19
And yet *i* she is my sister .... Gen 20:12
Shalt thou *i* reign over us .... Gen 37:8
or shalt thou *i* have dominion .... Gen 37:8
thy brethren *i* come to bow down .... Gen 37:10
For *i* I was stolen away out of .... Gen 40:15
we came *i* down at the first time .... Gen 43:20
and whereby *i* he divineth .... Gen 44:5
if ye will obey my voice .... Ex 19:5
if thou shalt *i* obey his voice .... Ex 23:22
ye should *i* have eaten it in the .... Lev 10:18
Hath the Lord *i* spoken only by .... Num 12:2
If thou wilt *i* deliver this .... Num 21:2
am I not able *i* to promote thee .... Num 22:37
For *i* the hand of the LORD was .... Deut 2:15
hated, which is *i* the firstborn .... Deut 21:16
I I have sinned against the LORD .... Josh 7:20
If thou wilt *i* look on the 1Sa 1:11
I said *i* that thy house, and the 1Sa 2:30
I am *i* a widow woman, and mine 2Sa 14:5
bring me again *i* to Jerusalem 2Sa 15:8
But will God *i* dwell on the earth 1Kin 8:27
Thou hast *i* smitten Edom, and 2Kin 14:10
Oh that thou wouldest bless me *i* 1Chr 4:10
that have sinned and done evil *i* 1Chr 21:17
be it *i* that I have erred, mine .... Job 19:4
If *i* ye will magnify yourselves .... Job 19:5
Do ye speak righteousness, O .... Ps 58:1
and tell this people, Hear ye *i* .... Is 6:9
and see ye *i*, but perceive not .... Is 6:9
For if ye do this thing *i* .... Jer 22:4
I baptize you with water unto .... Mt 3:11
Which *i* is the least of all seeds .... Mt 13:32
them, Ye shall drink *i* of my cup .... Mt 20:23
which *i* appear beautiful outward, ... Mt 23:27
the spirit *i* is willing, but the .... Mt 26:41
I have baptized you with water .... Mk 1:8
unto you, That Elias is *i* come .... Mk 9:13
Ye shall *i* drink of the cup that .... Mk 10:39
John, that he was a prophet *i* .... Mk 11:32
The Son of man *i* goeth, as it is .... Mk 14:21
I *i* baptize you with water .... Lk 3:16
for they *i* killed them, and ye .... Lk 11:48
And we *i* justly; for we .... Lk 23:41
Saying, The Lord is risen *i* .... Lk 24:34
of him, Behold an Israelite *i* .... Jn 1:47
and know that this is *i* the Christ .... Jn 4:42
For my flesh is meat *i* .... Jn 6:55
and my blood is drink *i* .... Jn 6:55
Do the rulers know *i* that this is .... Jn 7:26
word, then are ye my disciples *i* .... Jn 8:31
make you free, ye shall be free *i* .... Jn 8:36
for that *i* a notable miracle hath .... Acts 4:16
John *i* baptized with water .... Acts 1:11,16
that were with me saw *i* the light .... Acts 22:9
yourselves to be dead *i* unto sin .... Rom 6:11
the law of God, neither *i* can be .... Rom 8:7
All things *i* are pure .... Rom 14:20
For a man *i* ought not to cover 1Cor 11:7
For I be accepted the exhortation 2Cor 8:17
and *i* bear with me 2Cor 11:1
Some *i* preach Christ even of envy ...... Phil 1:15
For I he was sick nigh unto death .... Phil 2:27
to me *i* is not grievous, but for .... Phil 3:1
Which things have *i* a shew of .... Col 2:23
i ye do it toward all the 1Th 4:10
Honour widows that are widows *i* 1Ti 5:3
Now she that is a widow *i* 1Ti 5:5
relieve them that are widows *i* 1Ti 5:16
living stone, disallowed *i* of men 1Pet 2:4

INDIA (*in'-de-ah*) *Eastern boundary of the Persian Empire.*
reigned from *I* even unto Ethiopia .... Est 1:1
which are from *I* unto Ethiopia .... Est 8:9

INDIGNATION
anger, and in wrath, and in great *i* ...... Deut 29:28
there was great *i* against Israel 2Kin 3:27
he was wroth, and took great *i* .... Neh 4:1
he was full of *i* against Mordecai .... Est 5:9
me, and increasest thine *i* upon me ..... Job 10:17
Pour out thine *i* upon them .... Ps 69:24
of his anger, wrath, and *i* .... Ps 78:49
Because of thine *i* and thy wrath .... Ps 102:10
the staff in their hand is mine *i* .... Is 10:5
the *i* shall cease, and mine anger .... Is 10:25
the LORD, and the weapons of his *i* ..... Is 13:5
moment, until the *i* be overpast .... Is 26:20
his lips are full of *i*, and his .... Is 30:27
with the *i* of his anger, and with .... Is 30:30
For the *i* of the LORD is upon all .... Is 34:2
and his *i* toward his enemies .... Is 66:14
shall not be able to abide his *i* .... Jer 10:10
for thou hast filled me with *i* .... Jer 15:17
forth the weapons of his *i* .... Jer 50:25
hath despised in the *i* of his .... Lam 2:6
I will pour out mine *i* upon thee .... Eze 21:31
nor rained upon in the day of *i* .... Eze 22:24
I poured out mine *i* upon them .... Eze 22:31
shall be in the last end of the *i* .... Dan 8:19
have *i* against the holy covenant .... Dan 11:30
till the *i* be accomplished .... Dan 11:36
I will bear the *i* of the LORD .... Mic 7:9
Who can stand before his *i* .... Nah 1:6

didst march through the land in *i*	Hab 3:12
to pour upon them mine *i*	Zeph 3:8
thou hast had *i* these threescore	Zec 1:12
whom the LORD hath *i* for ever	Mal 1:4
they were moved with *i* against	Mt 20:24
his disciples saw it, they had *i*	Mt 26:8
some that had *i* within themselves	Mk 14:4
of the synagogue answered with *i*	Lk 13:14
Sadducees,) and were filled with *i*	Acts 5:17
but obey unrighteousness, *i*	Rom 2:8
of yourselves, yea, what *i*	2Cor 7:11
for of judgment and fiery *i*	Heb 10:27
mixture into the cup of his *i*	Rev 14:10

INDITING

My heart is *i* a good matter	Ps 45:1

INDUSTRIOUS

the young man that he was *i*	1Kin 11:28

INEXCUSABLE

Therefore thou art *i*, O man,	Rom 2:1

INFALLIBLE

his passion by many *i* proofs	Acts 1:3

INFAMOUS

shall mock thee, which art *i*	Eze 22:5

INFAMY

shame, and thine *i* turn not away	Prov 25:10
and are an *i* of the people	Eze 36:3

INFANT

but slay both man and woman, *i*	1Sa 15:3
be no more thence an *i* of days	Is 65:20

INFANTS

as *i* which never saw light	Job 3:16
their *i* shall be dashed in pieces	Hos 13:16
And they brought unto him also *i*	Lk 18:15

INFERIOR

I am not *i* to you	Job 12:3
I am not *i* unto you	Job 13:2
arise another kingdom *i* to thee	Dan 2:39
ye were *i* to other churches	2Cor 12:13

INFIDEL

hath he that believeth with an *i*	2Cor 6:15
the faith, and is worse than an *i*	1Ti 5:8

INFINITE

and thine iniquities are *i*	Job 22:5
his understanding is *i*	Ps 147:5
were her strength, and it was *i*	Nah 3:9

INFIRMITIES

saying, Himself took our *i*	Mt 8:17
and to be healed by him of their *i*	Lk 5:15
hour he cured many of their *i*	Lk 7:21
been healed of evil spirits and *i*	Lk 8:2
the Spirit also helpeth our *i*	Rom 8:26
ought to bear the *i* of the weak	Rom 15:1
the things which concern mine *i*	2Cor 11:30
I will not glory, but in mine *i*	2Cor 12:5
will I rather glory in my *i*	2Cor 12:9
Therefore I take pleasure in *i*	2Cor 12:10
stomach's sake and thine often *i*	1Ti 5:23
touched with the feeling of our *i*	Heb 4:15

INFIRMITY

for her *i* shall she be unclean	Lev 12:2
And I said, This is my *i*	Ps 77:10
of a man will sustain his *i*	Prov 18:14
had a spirit of *i* eighteen years	Lk 13:11
thou art loosed from thine *i*	Lk 13:12
was there, which had an *i* thirty	Jn 5:5
because of the *i* of your flesh	Rom 6:19
Ye know how through *i* of the	Gal 4:13
himself also is compassed with *i*	Heb 5:2
men high priests which have *i*	Heb 7:28

INFLAME

until night, till wine *i* them	Is 5:11

INFLAMMATION

for it is an *i* of the burning	Lev 13:28
and with a fever, and with an *i*	Deut 28:22

INFLICTED

punishment, which was *i* of many	2Cor 2:6

INFLUENCES

thou bind the sweet *i* of Pleiades	Job 38:31

INFOLDING

a great cloud, and a fire *i* itself	Eze 1:4

INFORM

according to all that they *i* thee	Deut 17:10

INFORMED

And he *i* me, and talked with me, and	Dan 9:22
And they are *i* of thee, that thou	Acts 21:21
they were *i* concerning thee	Acts 21:24
who *i* the governor against Paul	Acts 24:1
of the Jews *i* him against Paul	Acts 25:2
and the elders of the Jews *i* me	Acts 25:15

INGATHERING

and the feast of *i*, which is in	Ex 23:16
the feast of *i* at the year's end	Ex 34:22

INHABIT

the land which ye shall *i*	Num 35:34
the wicked shall not *i* the earth	Prov 10:30
the villages that Kedar doth *i*	Is 42:11
shall build houses, and *i* them	Is 65:21
shall not build, and another *i*	Is 65:22
but shall *i* the parched places in	Jer 17:6
Thou daughter that dost *i* Dibon	Jer 48:18
they that *i* those wastes of the	Eze 33:24
build the waste cities, and *i* them	Amos 9:14
also build houses, but not *i* them	Zeph 1:13

INHABITANT

The flood breaketh out from the *i*	Job 28:4
even great and fair, without *i*	Is 5:9
the cities be wasted without *i*	Is 6:11
of Samaria, that say in the	Is 9:9
Cry out and shout, thou *i* of Zion	Is 12:6
the *i* of this isle shall say in	Is 20:6
are upon thee, O *i* of the earth	Is 24:17
the *i* shall not say, I am sick	Is 33:24
his cities are burned without *i*	Jer 2:15
shall be laid waste, without an *i*	Jer 4:7
of Judah desolate, without an *i*	Jer 9:11
of the land, O *i* of the fortress	Jer 10:17
O *i* of the valley, and rock of	Jer 21:13
O *i* of Lebanon, that makest thy	Jer 22:23
shall be desolate without an *i*	Jer 26:9
without man, and without *i*	Jer 33:10
Judah a desolation without an *i*	Jer 34:22
and a curse, without an *i*	Jer 44:22
be waste and desolate without an *i*	Jer 46:19
O *i* of Aroer, stand by the way	Jer 48:19
of Moab, saith the LORD	Jer 48:43
Babylon a desolation without an *i*	Jer 51:29
Babylon, shall the *i* of Zion say	Jer 51:35
and an hissing, without an *i*	Jer 51:37
cut off the *i* from the plain of	Amos 1:5
I will cut off the *i* from Ashdod	Amos 1:8
thou *i* of Saphir, having thy	Mic 1:11
the *i* of Zaanan came not forth in	Mic 1:11
For the *i* of Maroth waited	Mic 1:12
O thou *i* of Lachish, bind the	Mic 1:13
heir unto thee, O *i* of Mareshah	Mic 1:15
thee, that there shall be no *i*	Zeph 2:5
is no man, that there is none *i*	Zeph 3:6

INHABITANTS

all the *i* of the cities, and that	Gen 19:25
to stink among the *i* of the land	Gen 34:30
when the *i* of the land, the	Gen 50:11
take hold on the *i* of Palestina	Ex 15:14
all the *i* of Canaan shall melt	Ex 15:15
for I will deliver the *i* of the	Ex 23:31
thou make a covenant with the *i*	Ex 34:12
a covenant with the *i* of the land	Ex 34:15
land itself vomiteth out her *i*	Lev 18:25
the land unto all the *i* thereof	Lev 25:10
land that eateth up the *i* thereof	Num 13:32
tell it to the *i* of this land	Num 14:14
because of the *i* of the land	Num 32:17
the *i* of the land from before you	Num 33:52
dispossess the *i* of the land	Num 33:53
the *i* of the land from before you	Num 33:55
withdrawn the *i* of their city	Deut 13:13
Thou shalt surely smite the *i* of	Deut 13:15
that all the *i* of the land faint	Josh 2:9
for even all the *i* of the country	Josh 2:24
all the *i* of the land shall hear	Josh 7:9
all the *i* of Ai in the field	Josh 8:24
utterly destroyed all the *i* of Ai	Josh 8:26
when the *i* of Gibeon heard what	Josh 9:3
all the *i* of our country spake to	Josh 9:11
to destroy all the *i* of the land	Josh 9:24
how the *i* of Gibeon had made	Josh 10:1
save the Hivites the *i* of Gibeon	Josh 11:19
All the *i* of the hill country	Josh 13:6
went up thence to the *i* of Debir	Josh 15:15
the Jebusites the *i* of Jerusalem	Josh 15:63
hand unto the *i* of En-tappuah	Josh 17:7
the *i* of Dor and her towns	Josh 17:11
the *i* of En-dor and her towns, and	Josh 17:11
the *i* of Taanach and her towns, and	Josh 17:11
the *i* of Megiddo and her towns	Josh 17:11
drive out the *i* of those cities	Josh 17:12
he went against the *i* of Debir	Judg 1:11
drave out the *i* of the mountain	Judg 1:19
not drive out the *i* of the valley	Judg 1:19
drive out the *i* of Beth-shean	Judg 1:27
and her towns, nor the *i* of Dor	Judg 1:27
nor the *i* of Ibleam and her towns,	Judg 1:27
nor the *i* of Megiddo and her towns	Judg 1:27
Zebulun drive out the *i* of Kitron	Judg 1:30
nor the *i* of Nahalol	Judg 1:30
Asher drive out the *i* of Accho	Judg 1:31
nor the *i* of Zidon, nor of Ahlab,	Judg 1:31
the Canaanites, the *i* of the land	Judg 1:32
drive out the *i* of Beth-shemesh	Judg 1:33
nor the *i* of Beth-anath	Judg 1:33
the Canaanites, the *i* of the land	Judg 1:33
the *i* of Beth-shemesh and of	Judg 1:33
no league with the *i* of this land	Judg 2:2
The *i* of the villages ceased,	Judg 5:7
the *i* of his villages in Israel	Judg 5:11
curse ye bitterly the *i* thereof	Judg 5:23
be head over all the *i* of Gilead	Judg 10:18
our head over all the *i* of Gilead	Judg 11:8
Amorites, the *i* of that country	Judg 11:21
sword, beside the *i* of Gibeah	Judg 20:15
of the *i* of Jabesh-gilead there	Judg 21:9
smite the *i* of Jabesh-gilead with	Judg 21:10
they found among the *i* of	Judg 21:12
thee, saying, Buy it before the *i*	Ruth 4:4
to the *i* of Kirjath-jearim	1Sa 6:21
So David saved the *i* of Keilah	1Sa 23:5
were of old the *i* of the land	1Sa 27:8
when the *i* of Jabesh-gilead heard	1Sa 31:11
the Jebusites, the *i* of the land	2Sa 5:6
who was of the *i* of Gilead	1Kin 17:1
nobles who were the *i* in his city	1Kin 21:11
Therefore their *i* were of small	2Kin 19:26
this place, and upon the *i* thereof	2Kin 22:16
place, and against the *i* thereof	2Kin 22:19
all the *i* of Jerusalem with him	2Kin 23:2
of the fathers of the *i* of Geba	1Chr 8:6
the fathers of the *i* of Aijalon	1Chr 8:13
who drove away the *i* of Gath	1Chr 8:13
Now the first *i* that dwelt in	1Chr 9:2
Jebusites were, the *i* of the land	1Chr 11:4
the *i* of Jebus said to David,	1Chr 11:5
for he hath given the *i* of the	1Chr 22:18
upon all the *i* of the countries	2Chr 15:5
who didst drive out the *i* of this	2Chr 20:7
ye *i* of Jerusalem, and thou king	2Chr 20:15
the *i* of Jerusalem fell before	2Chr 20:18
me, O Judah, and ye *i* of Jerusalem	2Chr 20:20
up against the *i* of mount Seir	2Chr 20:23
had made an end of the *i* of Seir	2Chr 20:23
caused the *i* of Jerusalem to	2Chr 21:11
the *i* of Jerusalem to go a	2Chr 21:13
the *i* of Jerusalem made Ahaziah	2Chr 22:1
the *i* of Jerusalem from the hand	2Chr 22:22
the *i* of Jerusalem, so that the	2Chr 32:26
the *i* of Jerusalem did him honour	2Chr 32:33
the *i* of Jerusalem to err, and to	2Chr 33:9
this place, and upon the *i* thereof	2Chr 34:24
place, and against the *i* thereof	2Chr 34:27
place, and upon the *i* of the same	2Chr 34:28
the *i* of Jerusalem, and the	2Chr 34:30
thou *i* of Jerusalem according	2Chr 34:30
the *i* of Jerusalem did according	2Chr 35:18
present, and the *i* of Jerusalem	2Chr 35:18
accusation against the *i* of Judah	Ezr 4:6
Hanun, and the *i* of Zanoah	Neh 3:13
watches of the *i* of Jerusalem	Neh 7:3
before them the *i* of the land	Neh 9:24
the waters, and the *i* thereof	Job 26:5
let all the *i* of the world stand	Ps 33:8
give ear, all ye *i* of the world	Ps 49:1
all the *i* thereof are dissolved	Ps 75:3
Philistines with the *i* of Tyre	Ps 83:7
O *i* of Jerusalem, and mon of Judah	Is 5:3
for a snare to the *i* of Jerusalem	Is 8:14
put down the *i* like a valiant man	Is 10:13
the *i* of Gebim gather themselves	Is 10:31
All ye *i* of the world, and	Is 18:3
The *i* of the land of Tema brought	Is 21:14
be a father to the *i* of Jerusalem	Is 22:21
Be still, ye *i* of the isle	Is 23:2
howl, ye *i* of the isle	Is 23:6
scattereth abroad the *i* thereof	Is 24:1
is defiled under the *i* thereof	Is 24:5
therefore the *i* of the earth are	Is 24:6
the *i* of the world will learn	Is 26:9
neither have the *i* of the world	Is 26:18
out of his place to punish the *i*	Is 26:21
Therefore their *i* were of small	Is 37:27
no more with the *i* of the world	Is 38:11
the *i* thereof are as grasshoppers	Is 40:22
the isles, and the *i* thereof	Is 42:10
let the *i* of the rock sing, let	Is 42:11
for too narrow by reason of the *i*	Is 49:19
forth upon all the *i* of the land	Jer 1:14
ye men of Judah and *i* of Jerusalem	Jer 4:4
my hand upon the *i* of the land	Jer 6:12
the bones of the *i* of Jerusalem	Jer 8:1
I will sing out the *i* of the	Jer 10:18
Judah, and to the *i* of Jerusalem	Jer 11:2
and among the *i* of Jerusalem	Jer 11:9
i of Jerusalem go, and cry unto	Jer 11:12
will fill all the *i* of this land	Jer 13:13
all the *i* of Jerusalem, with	Jer 13:13
the *i* of Jerusalem, that	Jer 17:20
of Judah, and the *i* of Jerusalem	Jer 17:25
to the *i* of Jerusalem, saying,	Jer 18:11
kings of Judah, and *i* of Jerusalem	Jer 19:3
to the *i* thereof, and even make	Jer 19:12
I will smite the *i* of this city	Jer 21:6
the *i* thereof as Gomorrah	Jer 23:14
to all the *i* of Jerusalem, saying	Jer 25:2
land, and against the *i* thereof	Jer 25:9
sword upon all the *i* of the earth	Jer 25:29
against all the *i* of the earth	Jer 25:30
this city, and upon the *i* thereof	Jer 26:15
of Judah, and the *i* of Jerusalem	Jer 32:32
the *i* of Jerusalem, Will ye not	Jer 35:13
upon all the *i* of Jerusalem all	Jer 35:17
upon the *i* of Jerusalem, and upon	Jer 36:31
forth upon the *i* of Jerusalem	Jer 42:18
destroy the city and the *i* thereof	Jer 46:8
all the *i* of the land shall howl	Jer 47:2
back, dwell deep, O *i* of Dedan	Jer 49:8
purposed against the *i* of Teman	Jer 49:20
O ye *i* of Hazor, saith the LORD	Jer 49:30
it, and against the *i* of Pekod	Jer 50:21
and disquiet the *i* of Babylon	Jer 50:34
upon the *i* of Babylon, and upon	Jer 50:35
he spake against the *i* of Babylon	Jer 51:12
to all the *i* of Chaldea all their	Jer 51:24
and my blood upon the *i* of Chaldea	Jer 51:35
all the *i* of the world, would not	Lam 4:12
whom the *i* of Jerusalem have said	Eze 11:15
Lord God of the *i* of Jerusalem	Eze 12:19
so will I give the *i* of Jerusalem	Eze 15:6
strong in the sea, she and her	Eze 26:17
The *i* of Zidon and Arvad were thy	Eze 27:8
All the *i* of the isles shall be	Eze 27:35

I

all the i of Egypt shall know .... Eze 29:6
all the i of the earth are .... Dan 4:35
and among the i of the earth .... Dan 4:35
to the i of Jerusalem, and unto .... Dan 9:7
with the i of the land, because .... Hos 4:1
The i of Samaria shall fear .... Hos 10:5
and give ear, all ye i of the land .... Joel 1:2
all the i of the land into the .... Joel 1:14
let all the i of the land tremble .... Joel 2:1
the i thereof have spoken lies, ... Mic 6:12
and the i thereof an hissing .... Mic 6:16
and upon all the i of Jerusalem .... Zeph 1:4
ye i of Maktesh, for all the .... Zeph 1:11
Woe unto the i of the sea coast, ... Zeph 2:5
people, and the i of many cities .... Zec 8:20
the i of one city shall go to .... Zec 8:21
no more pity the i of the land .... Zec 11:6
The i of Jerusalem shall be my .... Zec 12:5
the glory of the i of Jerusalem .... Zec 12:7
LORD defend the i of Jerusalem .... Zec 12:8
upon the i of Jerusalem, the .... Zec 12:10
to the i of Jerusalem for sin and .... Zec 13:1
the i of the earth have been made... Rev 17:2

INHABITED
Seir the Horite, who i the land. .... Gen 36:20
until they came to a land i .... Ex 16:35
iniquities unto a land not i .... Lev 16:22
the Canaanites that i Zephath .... Judg 1:17
the Jebusites that i Jerusalem .... Judg 1:21
eastward he i unto the entering 1Chr 5:9
It shall never be i, neither .... Is 13:20
to Jerusalem, Thou shalt be i .... Is 44:26
not in vain, he formed it to be i .... Is 45:18
make the desolate cities to be i .... Is 54:3
make there desolate, a land not i .... Jer 6:8
in a salt land and not i .... Jer 17:6
and cities which are not i .... Jer 22:6
and afterward it shall be i .... Jer 46:26
of The LORD it shall not be i .... Jer 50:13
and it shall be no more i for ever .... Jer 50:39
that are i shall be laid waste. .... Eze 12:20
that wast i of seafaring men, the... Eze 26:17
like the cities that are not i .... Eze 26:19
to the pit, that thou be not i .... Eze 26:20
neither shall it be i forty years .... Eze 29:11
in all the i places of the .... Eze 34:13
and the cities shall be i, and the .... Eze 36:10
are become fenced, and are i .... Eze 36:35
desolate places that are now i .... Eze 38:12
Jerusalem shall be i as towns .... Zec 2:4
prophets, when Jerusalem was i .... Zec 7:7
when men i the south and the plain... Zec 7:7
Gaza, and Ashkelon shall not be i ...... Zec 9:5
Jerusalem shall be i again in her .... Zec 12:6
i in her place, from Benjamin's .... Zec 14:10
but Jerusalem shall be safely i .... Zec 14:11

INHABITERS
to the i of the earth by reason. .... Rev 8:13
Woe to the i of the earth and of .... Rev 12:12

INHABITEST
O thou that i the praises of .... Ps 22:3

INHABITETH
and in houses where no man i .... Job 15:28
high and lofty One that i eternity .... Is 57:15

INHABITING
to the people the wilderness .... Ps 74:14

INHERIT
to give thee this land to i it .... Gen 15:7
shall I know that I shall i it .... Gen 15:8
that thou mayest i the land .... Gen 28:4
thou be increased, and i the land ...... Ex 23:30
seed, and they shall i it for ever .... Ex 32:13
Ye shall i their land, and I will .... Lev 20:24
to i them for a possession .... Lev 25:46
I have given to the Levites to i .... Num 18:24
of their fathers they shall i .... Num 26:55
For we will not i with them on .... Num 32:19
tribes of your fathers ye shall i. .... Num 33:54
the land which ye shall i by lot .... Num 34:13
for he shall cause Israel to i it .... Deut 1:38
that thou mayest i his land .... Deut 2:31
he shall cause them to i the land ...... Deut 3:28
the LORD your God giveth you to i. ... Deut 12:10
i the land which the LORD thy God... Deut 16:20
the LORD thy God giveth thee to i. ... Deut 19:3
which thou shalt i in the land. .... Deut 19:14
his sons to i that which he hath. ...... Deut 21:16
and thou shalt cause them to i it. ..... Deut 31:7
but one lot and one portion to i. ...... Josh 17:14
Thou shalt not i in our father's. .... Judg 11:2
to make them i the throne of 1Sa 2:8
which thou hast given us to i 2Chr 20:11
and his seed shall i the earth. .... Ps 25:13
the LORD, they shall i the earth. ...... Ps 37:9
But the meek shall i the earth. .... Ps 37:11
blessed of him shall i the earth. ...... Ps 37:22
The righteous shall i the land, ... Ps 37:29
he shall exalt thee to i the land .... Ps 37:34
also of his servants shall i it .... Ps 69:36
for thou shalt i all nations. .... Ps 82:8
The wise shall i glory .... Prov 3:35
those that love me to i substance, ... Prov 8:21
his own house shall i the wind. .... Prov 11:29
The simple i folly .... Prov 14:18
to cause to i the desolate .... Is 49:8
and thy seed shall i the Gentiles. ..... Is 54:3
land, and shall i my holy mountain. ... Is 57:13

they shall i the land for ever, ... Is 60:21
and mine elect shall i it, and my... Is 65:9
fields to them that shall i them .... Jer 8:10
have caused my people Israel to i ..... Jer 12:14
why them doth their king i Gad .... Jer 49:1
whereby ye shall i the land .... Eze 47:13
And ye shall i it, one as well as .... Eze 47:14
the LORD shall i Judah his .... Zec 2:12
for they shall i the earth. .... Mt 5:5
and shall i everlasting life .... Mt 19:29
i the kingdom prepared for you .... Mt 25:34
I do that I may i eternal life .... Mk 10:17
what shall I do to i eternal life .... Lk 10:25
what shall I do to i eternal life. .... Lk 18:18
shall not i the kingdom of God. 1Cor 6:9
shall i the kingdom of God 1Cor 6:10
blood cannot i the kingdom of God.. 1Cor 15:50
doth corruption i incorruption 1Cor 15:50
shall not i the kingdom of God .... Gal 5:21
faith and patience i the promises. .... Heb 6:12
that ye should i a blessing 1Pet 3:9
overcometh shall i all things .... Rev 21:7

INHERITANCE
Is there yet any portion or i for .... Gen 31:14
name of their brethren in their i .... Gen 48:6
them in the mountain of thine i .... Ex 15:17
our sin, and take us for thine i .... Ex 34:9
ye shall take them as an i for .... Lev 25:46
and honey, or given us i of fields ..... Num 16:14
shalt have no i in their land .... Num 18:20
thine i among the children of .... Num 18:20
all the tenth in Israel for an i .... Num 18:21
children of Israel they have no i ...... Num 18:23
of Israel they shall have no i .... Num 18:24
given you from them for your i .... Num 18:26
an i according to the number of ..... Num 26:53
many thou shalt give the more i ..... Num 26:54
to few thou shalt give the less i ..... Num 26:54
to every one shall his i be given. .... Num 26:54
because there was no i given them ... Num 26:62
give them a possession of an i ...... Num 27:7
thou shalt cause the i of their .... Num 27:8
then ye shall cause his i to pass. .... Num 27:8
give his i unto his brethren .... Num 27:9
then ye shall give his i unto his .... Num 27:10
then ye shall give his i unto his .... Num 27:11
have inherited every man his i ..... Num 32:18
because our i is fallen to us on .... Num 32:19
that the possession of our i on .... Num 32:32
lot for an i among your families. ... Num 33:54
the more ye shall give the more i .. Num 33:54
fewer ye shall give the less i ...... Num 33:54
every man's i shall be in the ...... Num 33:54
that shall fall unto you for an i .... Num 34:2
fathers, have received their i ...... Num 34:14
of Manasseh have received their i .. Num 34:14
their i on this side Jordan near .... Num 34:15
tribe, to divide the land by i ...... Num 34:18
LORD commanded to divide the i .. Num 34:29
give unto the Levites of the i of ... Num 35:2
to his i which he inheriteth .... Num 35:8
an i by lot to the children of ...... Num 36:2
by the LORD to give the i of ...... Num 36:3
then shall their i be taken from ... Num 36:3
taken from the i of our fathers. ... Num 36:3
shall be put to the i of the .... Num 36:3
it be taken from the lot of our i .. Num 36:3
i be put unto the i of .... Num 36:4
so shall their i be taken away ... Num 36:4
be taken away from the i of the .. Num 36:4
So shall not the i of the .... Num 36:7
shall keep himself to the i of ... Num 36:7
that possesseth an i in any tribe .. Num 36:8
every man the i of his fathers. ... Num 36:8
Neither shall the i remove from .. Num 36:9
shall keep himself to his own i ... Num 36:9
their i remained in the tribe of ... Num 36:12
to be unto him a people of i ..... Deut 4:20
LORD thy God giveth thee for an i .. Deut 4:21
to give thee their land for an i ... Deut 4:38
destroy not thy people and thine i . Deut 9:26
they are thy people and thine i ... Deut 9:29
no part nor i with his brethren ... Deut 10:9
the LORD is his i, according as ... Deut 10:9
yet come to the rest and to the i .. Deut 12:9
as he hath no part nor i with you. . Deut 12:12
he hath no part nor i with thee. .. Deut 14:27
he hath no part nor i with thee. .. Deut 18:1
the for an i to possess it. .... Deut 15:4
have no part nor i with Israel ... Deut 18:1
the LORD made by fire, and his i. . Deut 18:1
have no i among their brethren .. Deut 18:2
the LORD is their i, as he hath .. Deut 18:2
LORD thy God giveth thee for an i . Deut 19:10
of old time have set in thine i ... Deut 19:14
thy God doth give thee for an i ... Deut 20:16
LORD thy God giveth thee for an i . Deut 21:23
LORD thy God giveth thee for an i . Deut 24:4
thee for an i to possess it .... Deut 25:19
LORD thy God giveth thee for an i . Deut 26:1
gave it for an i unto the .... Deut 29:8
divided to the nations their i .... Deut 32:8
Jacob is the lot of his i .... Deut 32:9
even the i of the congregation of . Deut 33:4
thou divide for an i the land ..... Josh 1:6
Joshua gave it for an i unto ...... Josh 11:23
lot unto the Israelites for an i ... Josh 13:6
for an i unto the nine tribes ..... Josh 13:7
the Gadites have received their i . Josh 13:8
the tribe of Levi he gave none i .. Josh 13:14

Israel made by fire are their i ...... Josh 13:14
i according to their families .... Josh 13:15
This was the i of the children of ... Josh 13:23
Moses gave i unto the tribe of ..... Josh 13:24
This is the i of the children of .... Josh 13:28
Moses gave i unto the half tribe ... Josh 13:29
for i in the plains of Moab .... Josh 13:32
of Levi Moses gave non any i ..... Josh 13:33
LORD God of Israel was their i .... Josh 13:33
Israel, distributed for i to them ... Josh 14:1
By lot was their i, as the LORD ... Josh 14:2
had given the i of two tribes ..... Josh 14:3
Levites he gave none i among them . Josh 14:3
have trodden shall be thine i ..... Josh 14:9
son of Jephunneh Hebron for an i .. Josh 14:13
Hebron therefore became the i of . Josh 14:14
This is the i of the tribe of the ... Josh 15:20
Manasseh and Ephraim, took their i. Josh 16:4
of their i on the east side was. ... Josh 16:5
This is the i of the tribe of the ... Josh 16:8
of Ephraim were among the i of .. Josh 16:9
give us an i among our brethren .. Josh 17:4
an i among the brethren of their .. Josh 17:4
Manasseh had an i among his sons... Josh 17:6
had not yet received their i ...... Josh 18:2
it according to the i of their ..... Josh 18:4
priesthood of the LORD is their i . Josh 18:7
have received their i beyond ..... Josh 18:7
This was the i of the children of .. Josh 18:20
This is the i of the children of ... Josh 18:28
and their i was within the .... Josh 19:1
the i of the children of Judah .... Josh 19:1
And they had in their i Beer-sheba . Josh 19:2
This is the i of the tribe of the ... Josh 19:8
the i of the children of Simeon ... Josh 19:9
i within the i of them .... Josh 19:9
border of their i was unto Sarid .. Josh 19:10
This is the i of the children of ... Josh 19:16
This is the i of the tribe of the ... Josh 19:23
This is the i of the tribe of the ... Josh 19:31
This is the i of the tribe of the ... Josh 19:39
And the coast of their i was Zorah . Josh 19:41
This is the i of the tribe of the ... Josh 19:48
the land for i by their coasts. .... Josh 19:49
i to Joshua the son of Nun among . Josh 19:49
divided for an i by lot in Shiloh .. Josh 19:51
unto the Levites out of their i .... Josh 21:3
to be an i for your tribes, from ... Josh 23:4
depart, every man unto his i ..... Josh 24:28
border of his i in Timnath-serah .. Josh 24:30
it became the i of the children ... Josh 24:32
unto his i to possess the land .... Judg 2:6
border of his i in Timnath-heres .. Judg 2:9
sought them an i to dwell in. ..... Judg 18:1
for unto that day all their i had. .. Judg 18:1
the country of the i of Israel ..... Judg 18:30
There must be an i for them that... Judg 21:17
went and returned unto their i ... Judg 21:23
from thence every man to his i ... Judg 21:24
the name of the dead upon his i .. Ruth 4:5
for myself, lest I mar mine own i . Ruth 4:6
the name of the dead upon his i .. Ruth 4:10
thee to be captain over his i 1Sa 10:1
from abiding in the i of the LORD . 1Sa 26:19
son together out of the i of God .. 2Sa 14:16
neither have we i in the son of ... 2Sa 20:1
thou swallow up the i of the LORD. 2Sa 20:19
ye may bless the i of the LORD. .. 2Sa 21:3
hast given to thy people for an i .. 1Kin 8:36
they be thy people, and thine i ... 1Kin 8:51
of the earth, to be thine i 1Kin 8:53
neither have we i in the son of ... 1Kin 12:16
that I should give the i of my 1Kin 21:3
not give thee the i of my fathers .. 1Kin 21:4
forsake the remnant of mine i 2Kin 21:14
land of Canaan, the lot of your i .. 1Chr 16:18
leave it for an i for your 1Chr 28:8
given unto thy people for an i 2Chr 6:27
we have none i in the son of 2Chr 10:16
leave it for an i to your .... Ezra 9:12
of Judah, every one in his i ..... Neh 11:20
what i of the Almighty from on ... Job 31:2
gave them i among their brethren. . Job 42:15
give thee the heathen for thine i .. Ps 2:8
The LORD is the portion of mine i . Ps 16:5
Save thy people, and bless thine i . Ps 28:9
whom he hath chosen for his own i . Ps 33:12
their i shall be for ever .... Ps 37:18
He shall choose our i for us ...... Ps 47:4
thou didst confirm thine i .... Ps 68:9
the rod of thine i, which thou .... Ps 74:2
the plains of them all by line ..... Ps 78:55
and was wroth with his i .... Ps 78:62
Jacob his people, and Israel his i. Ps 78:71
the heathen are come into thine i . Ps 79:1
neither will he forsake his i ..... Ps 94:14
land of Canaan, the lot of your i .. Ps 105:11
that I may glory with thine i ..... Ps 106:5
that he abhorred his own i .... Ps 106:40
A good man leaveth an i to his ... Prov 13:22
part of one i among the brethren . Prov 17:2
and riches are the i of fathers ... Prov 19:14
An i may be gotten hastily at the . Prov 20:21
Wisdom is good with an i .... Eccl 7:11
of my hands, and Israel mine i ... Is 19:25
my people, I have polluted mine i . Is 47:6
sake, the tribes of thine i .... Is 63:17
given for an i unto your fathers .. Jer 3:18
and Israel is the rod of his i .... Jer 10:16
that touch the i which I have .... Jer 12:14

they have filled mine *i* with the .... Jer 16:18
for the right of *i* is thine .... Jer 32:8
and Israel is the rod of his *i* .... Jer 51:19
Our *i* is turned to strangers, our .... Lam 5:2
thou shalt take thine *i* in........................... Eze 22:16
the land is given us for *i*........................... Eze 33:24
at the *i* of the house of Israel.................... Eze 35:15
thee, and thou shalt be their *i*................... Eze 36:12
And it shall be unto them for an *i*............. Eze 44:28
I am their *i*.. Eze 44:28
divide by lot the land for *i*........................ Eze 45:1
the *i* thereof shall be his sons'.................. Eze 46:16
it shall be their possession by *i*................. Eze 46:16
of his *i* to one of his servants.................... Eze 46:17
but his *i* shall be his sons' for................... Eze 46:17
of the people's *i* by oppression................. Eze 46:18
sons *i* out of his own possession.............. Eze 46:18
land shall fall unto you for *i*..................... Eze 47:14
it by lot for an *i* unto you .... Eze 47:22
they shall have *i* with you among............. Eze 47:22
there shall ye give him his *i*...................... Eze 47:23
unto the tribes of Israel for *i* .... Eze 48:29
him, and let us seize on his *i*.................... Mt 21:38
kill him, and the *i* shall be ours................ Mk 12:7
that he divide the *i* with me...................... Lk 12:13
kill him, that the *i* may be ours................. Lk 20:14
And he gave him none *i* in it...................... Acts 7:5
to give you an *i* among all them............... Acts 20:32
i among them which are sanctified.......... Acts 26:18
For if the *i* be of the law, it is................... Gal 3:18
whom also we have obtained an *i*............. Eph 1:11
our *i* until the redemption of the............. Eph 1:14
the glory of his *i* in the saints.................. Eph 1:18
hath any *i* in the kingdom of..................... Eph 5:5
of the *i* of the saints in light .... Col 1:12
shall receive the reward of the *i*............... Col 3:24
as he hath by *i* obtained a more............... Heb 1:4
receive the promise of eternal *i*................ Heb 9:15
he should after receive for an *i*................. Heb 11:8
To an *i* incorruptible, and 1Pet 1:4

INHERITANCES
These are the *i*, which Eleazar .... Josh 19:51

INHERITED
have *i* every man his inheritance .... Num 32:18
of Israel *i* in the land of Canaan .... Josh 14:1
they *i* the labour of the people.................. Ps 105:44
Surely our fathers have *i* lies.................... Jer 16:19
Abraham was one, and he *i* the land .... Eze 33:24
when he would have *i* the blessing.......... Heb 12:17

INHERITETH
to his inheritance which he *i* .... Num 35:8

INHERITOR
out of Judah an *i* of my mountains........... Is 65:9

INIQUITIES
confess your own all the *i* of the .... Lev 16:21
their *i* unto a land not inhabited .... Lev 16:22
also in the *i* of their fathers....................... Lev 26:39
for a year, shall ye bear your *i*.................. Num 14:34
for our *i* are increased over our .... Ezr 9:6
and for our *i* have we, our kings,.............. Ezr 9:7
us less than our *i* deserve .... Ezr 9:13
sins, and the *i* of their fathers................... Neh 9:2
How many are mine *i* and sins.................. Job 13:23
me to possess the *i* of my youth .... Job 13:26
and thine *i* infinite..................................... Job 22:5
For mine *i* are gone over mine .... Ps 38:4
mine *i* have taken hold upon me,............. Ps 40:12
my sins, and blot out all mine *i* .... Ps 51:9
They search out *i* .... Ps 64:6
I prevail against me....................................... Ps 65:3
remember not against us former *i*............ Ps 79:8
Thou hast set our *i* before thee................ Ps 90:8
Who forgiveth all thine *i*........................... Ps 103:3
rewarded us according to our *i* .... Ps 103:10
and because of their *i*, are .... Ps 107:17
If thou, LORD, shouldest mark *i*................ Ps 130:3
redeem Israel from all his *i*....................... Ps 130:8
His own *i* shall take the wicked............... Prov 5:22
thou hast wearied me with thine *i*........... Is 43:24
Behold, for your *i* have ye sold .... Is 50:1
he was bruised for our *i*............................ Is 53:5
for he shall bear their *i*............................. Is 53:11
But your *i* have separated between.......... Is 59:2
and as for our *i*, we know them,............... Is 59:12
and our *i*, like the wind, have.................... Is 64:6
consumed us, because of our *i*.................. Is 64:7
Your *i*, and the *i* of your............................ Is 65:7
Your *i* have turned away these .... Jer 5:25
to the *i* of their forefathers....................... Jer 11:10
though our *i* testify against us,................. Jer 14:7
and I will pardon all their *i*...................... Jer 33:8
the *i* of her priests, that have.................... Lam 4:13
and we have borne their *i*......................... Lam 5:7
but ye shall pine away for your *i*.............. Eze 24:23
by the multitude of thine *i*....................... Eze 28:18
but their *i* shall be upon their................... Eze 32:27
in your own sight for your *i*...................... Eze 36:31
I will also cause you to dwell....................... Eze 36:33
they may be ashamed of their *i*................. Eze 43:10
thine *i* by shewing mercy to the............... Dan 4:27
that we might turn from our *i*.................... Dan 9:13
for the *i* of our fathers,.............................. Dan 9:16
I will punish you for your *i*........................ Amos 3:2
he will subdue our *i*................................... Mic 7:19
away every one of you from his *i*............. Acts 3:26
are they whose *i* are forgiven................... Rom 4:7
their *i* will I remember no more................ Heb 8:12
i will I remember no more......................... Heb 10:17

and God hath remembered her *i*.............. Rev 18:5

INIQUITY
for the *i* of the Amorites is not .... Gen 15:16
be consumed in the *i* of the city .... Gen 19:15
found out the *i* of thy servants................. Gen 44:16
visiting the *i* of the fathers........................ Ex 20:5
may bear the *i* of the holy things.............. Ex 28:38
that they bear not *i*, and die...................... Ex 28:43
mercy for thousands, forgiving *i* .... Ex 34:7
visiting the *i* of the fathers........................ Ex 34:7
and pardon our *i* and our sin, and........... Ex 34:9
it, then he shall bear his *i*......................... Lev 5:1
is he guilty, and shall bear his *i*............... Lev 5:17
eateth of it shall bear his *i*........................ Lev 7:18
to bear the *i* of the congregation............. Lev 10:17
then he shall bear his *i*.............................. Lev 17:16
I do visit the *i* thereof upon it................... Lev 18:25
that eateth it shall bear his *i*.................... Lev 19:8
he shall bear his *i*...................................... Lev 20:17
they shall bear their *i*................................ Lev 20:19
them to bear the *i* of trespass.................. Lev 22:16
in their *i* in your enemies' lands .... Lev 26:39
If they shall confess their *i*....................... Lev 26:40
the *i* of their fathers, with......................... Lev 26:40
of the punishment of their *i*...................... Lev 26:41
of the punishment of their *i*...................... Lev 26:43
bringing *i* to remembrance........................ Num 5:15
shall the man be guiltless from *i*.............. Num 5:31
and this woman shall bear her *i*............... Num 5:31
and of great mercy, forgiving *i*................. Num 14:18
visiting the *i* of the fathers........................ Num 14:18
of this people according............................... Num 14:19
his *i* shall be upon him............................. Num 15:31
shall bear the *i* of the sanctuary.............. Num 18:1
bear the *i* of your priesthood .... Num 18:1
and they shall bear their *i*......................... Num 18:23
He hath not beheld *i* in Jacob................... Num 23:21
then he shall bear her *i*............................. Num 30:15
visiting the *i* of the fathers........................ Deut 5:9
rise up against a man for any *i*.................. Deut 19:15
a God of truth and without *i*...................... Deut 32:4
Is the *i* of Peor too little for...................... Josh 22:17
man perished not alone in his *i*................ Josh 22:20
ever for the *i* which he knoweth 1Sa 3:13
that the *i* of Eli's house shall.................... 1Sa 3:14
and stubbornness is as *i* and.................... 1Sa 15:23
what is mine *i*?.. 1Sa 20:1
if there be in me *i*, slay me....................... 1Sa 20:8
my lord, upon me let this be 1Sa 25:24
If he commit *i*, I will chasten.................... 2Sa 7:14
the *i* be on me, and on my father's.......... 2Sa 14:9
and if there be any *i* in me........................ 2Sa 14:32
Let not my lord impute *i* unto me............ 2Sa 19:19
and have kept myself from mine *i*........... 2Sa 22:24
take away the *i* of thy servant.................. 2Sa 24:10
do away the *i* of thy servant.................... 1Chr 21:8
for there is no *i* with the LORD................ 2Chr 19:7
And cover not their *i*, and let not............. Neh 4:5
as I have seen, that they plow *i*................ Job 4:8
hope, and I stoppeth her mouth .... Job 5:16
I pray you, let it not be............................... Job 6:29
Is there *i* in my tongue.............................. Job 6:30
and take away mine *i*................................. Job 7:21
That thou enquirest after mine *i*............... Job 10:6
wilt not acquit me from mine *i*................. Job 10:14
the less than thine *i* deserveth................. Job 11:6
If *i* be in thine hand, put it far .... Job 11:14
a bag, and thou sewest up mine *i*............ Job 14:17
For thy mouth uttereth thine *i*.................. Job 15:5
man, which drinketh *i* like water.............. Job 15:16
The heaven shall reveal his *i*.................... Job 20:27
layeth up his *i* for his children................. Job 21:19
thou shalt put away *i* far from.................. Job 22:23
punishment to the workers of *i*................. Job 31:3
it is an *i* to be punished by........................ Job 31:11
This also were an *i* to be.......................... Job 31:28
by hiding mine *i* in my bosom.................. Job 31:33
neither is there *i* in me.............................. Job 33:9
in company with the workers of *i*............. Job 34:8
Almighty, that he should commit *i*........... Job 34:10
workers of *i* may hide themselves............ Job 34:22
if I have done *i*, I will do no..................... Job 34:32
that they return from *i*.............................. Job 36:10
Take heed, regard not *i*............................. Job 36:21
who can say, Thou hast wrought *i*........... Job 36:23
thou hatest all workers of *i*....................... Ps 5:5
from me, all ye workers of *i*...................... Ps 6:8
if there be *i* in my hands........................... Ps 7:3
Behold, he travaileth with *i*...................... Ps 7:14
all the workers of *i* no knowledge............ Ps 14:4
him, and I kept myself from mine *i*.......... Ps 18:23
sake, O LORD, pardon mine *i*................... Ps 25:11
wicked, and with the workers of *i*............ Ps 28:3
faileth because of mine *i*.......................... Ps 31:10
unto whom the LORD imputeth not *i*........ Ps 32:2
thee, and mine *i* have I not hid................. Ps 32:5
thou forgavest the *i* of my sin.................. Ps 32:5
until his *i* be found to be........................... Ps 36:2
The words of his mouth are *i*.................... Ps 36:3
There are the workers of *i* fallen.............. Ps 36:12
envious against the workers of *i*............... Ps 37:1
For I will declare mine *i*............................ Ps 38:18
rebukes dost correct man for his *i*........... Ps 39:11
in heart gathereth *i* to itself..................... Ps 41:6
when the *i* of my heels shall .... Ps 49:5
Wash me throughly from mine *i*............... Ps 51:2
Behold, I was shapen in *i*.......................... Ps 51:5
they, and have done abominable *i*........... Ps 53:1
the workers of *i* no knowledge................. Ps 53:4
for they cast *i* upon me, and in................ Ps 55:3

Shall they escape by *i*................................ Ps 56:7
Deliver me from the workers of *i*.............. Ps 59:2
insurrection of the workers of *i*................. Ps 64:2
If I regard *i* in my heart............................ Ps 66:18
Add *i* unto their *i*...................................... Ps 69:27
of compassion, forgave their *i* .... Ps 78:38
hast forgiven the *i* of thy people.............. Ps 85:2
the rod, and their *i* with stripes............... Ps 89:32
all the workers of *i* do flourish................ Ps 92:7
workers of *i* shall be scattered................ Ps 92:9
the workers of *i* boast themselves........... Ps 94:4
for me against the workers of *i*................ Ps 94:16
Shall the throne of *i* have .... Ps 94:20
shall bring upon them their own *i*............ Ps 94:23
our fathers, we have committed *i*............. Ps 106:6
and were brought low for their *i*.............. Ps 106:43
all *i* shall stop her mouth......................... Ps 107:42
Let the *i* of his fathers be.......................... Ps 109:14
They also do no *i*....................................... Ps 119:3
let not any *i* have dominion over.............. Ps 119:133
put forth their hands unto *i*...................... Ps 125:3
them forth with the workers of *i*............... Ps 125:5
wicked works with men that work *i*.......... Ps 141:4
and the gins of the workers of *i*............... Ps 141:9
shall be to the workers of *i*....................... Prov 10:29
By mercy and truth *i* is purged................. Prov 16:6
mouth of the wicked devoureth *i*.............. Prov 19:28
shall be to the workers of *i*....................... Prov 21:15
He that soweth *i* shall reap....................... Prov 22:8
righteousness, that *i* was there .... Eccl 3:16
nation, a people laden with *i*.................... Is 1:4
it is *i*, even the solemn meeting .... Is 1:13
that draw *i* with cords of vanity............... Is 5:18
thine *i* is taken away, and thy sin............ Is 6:7
evil, and the wicked for their *i*................. Is 13:11
for the *i* of their fathers............................ Is 14:21
Surely this *i* shall not be purged.............. Is 22:14
of the earth for their *i*............................... Is 26:21
shall the *i* of Jacob be purged.................. Is 27:9
all that watch for *i* are cut off.................. Is 29:20
Therefore this *i* shall be to you................ Is 30:13
the help of them that work *i*..................... Is 31:2
villany, and his heart will work *i*............. Is 32:6
therein shall be forgiven their *i*............... Is 33:24
that her *i* is pardoned............................... Is 40:2
hath laid on him the *i* of us all................. Is 53:6
For the *i* of his covetousness was............ Is 57:17
blood, and your fingers with *i*.................. Is 59:3
mischief, and bring forth *i*........................ Is 59:4
their works are works of *i*......................... Is 59:6
their thoughts are thoughts of *i*............... Is 59:7
LORD, neither remember *i* for ever.......... Is 64:9
What *i* have your fathers found in .... Jer 2:5
yet thine *i* is marked before me,.............. Jer 2:22
Only acknowledge thine *i*, that................ Jer 3:13
and weary themselves to commit *i*........... Jer 9:5
thine *i* are thy skirts discovered............. Jer 13:22
he will now remember their *i*.................... Jer 14:10
and the *i* of our fathers.............................. Jer 14:20
or what is our *i*.. Jer 16:10
neither is their *i* hid from mine .... Jer 16:17
first I will recompense their *i*................... Jer 16:18
forgive not their *i*, neither blot................. Jer 18:23
saith the LORD, for their *i*......................... Jer 25:12
one, for the multitude of thine *i*............... Jer 30:14
for the multitude of thine *i*....................... Jer 30:15
every one shall die for his own *i*.............. Jer 31:30
for I will forgive their *i*............................. Jer 31:34
recompensest the *i* of the fathers............ Jer 32:18
cleanse them from all their *i*..................... Jer 33:8
that I may forgive their *i*........................... Jer 36:3
seed and his servants for their *i*.............. Jer 36:31
the *i* of Israel shall be sought................... Jer 50:20
be not cut off in her *i*................................ Jer 51:6
they have not discovered thine *i*.............. Lam 2:14
For the punishment of the *i*...................... Lam 4:6
of thine *i* is accomplished......................... Lam 4:22
he will visit thine *i*, O daughter............... Lam 4:22
wicked man shall die in his *i*.................... Eze 3:18
wicked way, he shall die in his *i*.............. Eze 3:19
his righteousness, and commit *i*............... Eze 3:20
lay the *i* of the house of Israel................. Eze 4:4
upon it thou shalt bear their *i*................... Eze 4:5
upon thee the years of their *i*................... Eze 4:5
bear the *i* of the house of Israel.............. Eze 4:6
thou shalt bear the *i* of the....................... Eze 4:6
and consume away for their *i*................... Eze 4:17
himself in the *i* of his life......................... Eze 7:13
mourning, every one for his *i*................... Eze 7:16
is the stumblingblock of their *i*................ Eze 7:19
The *i* of the house of Israel and .... Eze 9:9
of their *i* before their face........................ Eze 14:4
of his *i* before his face, and..................... Eze 14:4
of his *i* before his face, and..................... Eze 14:7
bear the punishment of their *i*.................. Eze 14:10
this was the *i* of thy sister........................ Eze 16:49
hath withdrawn his hand from *i*............... Eze 18:8
not die for the *i* of his father.................... Eze 18:17
lo, even he shall die in his *i*..................... Eze 18:18
the son bear the *i* of the father................ Eze 18:19
not bear the *i* of the father........................ Eze 18:20
the father bear the *i* of the son................ Eze 18:20
righteousness, and committeth *i*.............. Eze 18:24
righteousness, and committeth *i*.............. Eze 18:26
for his *i* that he hath done shall.............. Eze 18:26
so *i* shall not be your ruin......................... Eze 18:30
he will call to remembrance the *i*............. Eze 21:23
have made your *i* to be remembered........ Eze 21:24
when *i* shall have an end,.......................... Eze 21:25
when their *i* shall have an end................. Eze 21:29

created, till i was found in thee .... Eze 28:15
by the i of thy traffick .... Eze 28:18
bringeth their i to remembrance .... Eze 29:16
them, he is taken away in his i .... Eze 33:6
wicked man shall die in his i .... Eze 33:9
his way, he shall die in his i .... Eze 33:9
own righteousness, and commit i .... Eze 33:13
but for his i that he hath .... Eze 33:13
of life, without committing i .... Eze 33:15
righteousness, and committeth i .... Eze 33:18
the time that their i had an end .... Eze 35:5
went into captivity for their i .... Eze 39:23
they shall even bear their i .... Eze 44:10
house of Israel to fall into i .... Eze 44:12
God, and they shall bear their i .... Eze 44:12
have sinned, and have committed i .... Dan 9:5
and to make reconciliation for i .... Dan 9:24
they set their heart on their i .... Hos 4:8
Israel and Ephraim fall in their i .... Hos 5:5
is a city of them that work i .... Hos 6:8
then the i of Ephraim was .... Hos 7:1
now will he remember their i .... Hos 8:13
mad, for the multitude of thine i .... Hos 9:7
he will remember their i, he will .... Hos 9:9
of i did not overtake them .... Hos 10:9
wickedness, ye have reaped i .... Hos 10:13
find none i in me that were sin .... Hos 12:8
is there i in Gilead .... Hos 12:11
The i of Ephraim is bound up .... Hos 13:12
for thou hast fallen by thine i .... Hos 14:1
say unto him, Take away all i .... Hos 14:2
Woe to them that devise i .... Mic 2:1
with blood, and Jerusalem with i .... Mic 3:10
like unto thee, that pardoneth i .... Mic 7:18
Why dost thou shew me i, and cause.. Hab 1:3
evil, and canst not look on i .... Hab 1:13
blood, and stablisheth a city by i .... Hab 2:12
he will not do i .... Zeph 3:5
remnant of Israel shall not do i .... Zeph 3:13
caused thine i to pass from thee .... Zec 3:4
I will remove the i of that land .... Zec 3:9
i was not found in his lips .... Mal 2:6
and did turn many away from i .... Mal 2:6
depart from me, ye that work i .... Mt 7:23
that offend, and them which do i .... Mt 13:41
ye are full of hypocrisy and i .... Mt 23:28
because i shall abound, the love .... Mt 24:12
from me, all ye workers of i .... Lk 13:27
a field with the reward of i .... Acts 1:18
bitterness, and in the bond of i .... Acts 8:23
uncleanness and to i unto i .... Rom 6:19
Rejoiceth not in i, but rejoiceth 1Cor 13:6
mystery of i doth already work 2Th 2:7
the name of Christ depart from i 2Ti 2:19
he might redeem us from all i .... Titus 2:14
loved righteousness, and hated i .... Heb 1:9
tongue is a fire, a world of i .... Jas 3:6
But was rebuked for his i 2Pet 2:16

INJURED
ye have not i me at all .... Gal 4:12

INJURIOUS
blasphemer, and a persecutor, and i 1Ti 1:13

INJUSTICE
Not for any i in mine hands .... Job 16:17

INK
I wrote them with i in the book .... Jer 36:18
by us, written not with i 2Cor 3:3
I would not write with paper and i 2Jn 12
to write, but I will not with i 3Jn 13

INKHORN
with a writer's i by his side .... Eze 9:2
had the writer's i by his side .... Eze 9:3
which had the i by his side .... Eze 9:11

INN
give his ass provender in the i .... Gen 42:27
to pass, when we came to the i .... Gen 43:21
came to pass by the way in the i .... Ex 4:24
was no room for them in the i .... Lk 2:7
own beast, and brought him to an i .... Lk 10:34

INNER
the cherubims within the i house 1Kin 6:27
he built the i court with these 1Kin 6:36
both for the i court of the house 1Kin 7:12
both for the doors of the i house 1Kin 7:50
into the city, into an i chamber 1Kin 20:30
into an i chamber to hide thyself 1Kin 22:25
and carry him to an i chamber 2Kin 9:2
of the i parlours thereof, and of 1Chr 28:11
the i doors thereof for the most 2Chr 4:22
into an i chamber to hide thyself 2Chr 18:24
the priests went into the i part 2Chr 29:18
unto the king into the i court .... Est 4:11
stood in the i court of the .... Est 5:1
to the door of the i gate .... Eze 8:3
he brought me into the i court of .. Eze 8:16
and the cloud filled the i court .... Eze 10:3
of the i gate were fifty cubits .... Eze 40:15
forefront of the i court without .. Eze 40:19
the gate of the i court was over .. Eze 40:23
in the i court toward the south .... Eze 40:27
he brought me to the i court by .. Eze 40:28
into the i court toward the east .. Eze 40:32
without the i gate were the .... Eze 40:44

of the singers in the i court .... Eze 40:44
hundred cubits, with the i temple .... Eze 41:15
the door, even unto the i house .... Eze 41:17
cubits which were for the i court .... Eze 42:15
an end of measuring the i house .... Eze 42:15
and brought me into the i court .... Eze 43:5
in at the gates of the i court .... Eze 44:17
in the gates of the i court .... Eze 44:17
when they enter into the i court .... Eze 44:21
the sanctuary, unto the i court .... Eze 44:27
posts of the gate of the i court .... Eze 45:19
The gate of the i court that .... Eze 46:1
thrust them into the i prison .... Acts 16:24
might by his Spirit in the i man .... Eph 3:16

INNERMOST
into the i parts of the belly .... Prov 18:8
into the i parts of the belly .... Prov 26:22

INNOCENCY
i of my hands have I done this .... Gen 20:5
I will wash mine hands in i .... Ps 26:6
in vain, and washed my hands in i . Ps 73:13
as before him i was found in me .... Dan 6:22
will it be ere they attain to i .... Hos 8:5

INNOCENT
and the i and righteous slay thou .... Ex 23:7
That I blood be not shed in the .... Deut 19:10
the guilt of i blood from Israel .... Deut 19:13
lay not i blood unto thy people .... Deut 21:8
guilt of i blood from among you .... Deut 21:9
taketh reward to slay an i person .. Deut 27:25
wilt thou sin against i blood 1Sa 19:5
thou mayest take away the i blood .. 1Kin 2:31
Manasseh shed i blood very much 2Kin 21:16
also for the i blood that he shed .. 2Kin 24:4
he filled Jerusalem with i blood 2Kin 24:4
thee, who ever perished, being i .... Job 4:7
will laugh at the trial of the i .... Job 9:23
know that thou wilt not hold me i . Job 9:28
the i shall stir up himself .... Job 17:8
the i laugh them to scorn .... Job 22:19
shall deliver the island of the i .... Job 22:30
the i shall divide the silver .... Job 27:17
without transgression, I am i .... Job 33:9
places doth he murder the i .... Ps 10:8
nor taketh reward against the i .... Ps 15:5
I shall be i from the great .... Ps 19:13
righteous, and condemn the i blood . Ps 94:21
shed i blood, even the blood of .... Ps 106:38
privily for the i without cause .... Prov 1:11
and hands that shed i blood .... Prov 6:17
toucheth her shall not be i .... Prov 6:29
haste to be rich shall not be i .... Prov 28:20
they make haste to shed i blood .... Is 59:7
Yet thou sayest, Because I am i .... Jer 2:35
shed not i blood in this place .... Jer 7:6
neither shed i blood in this .... Jer 22:3
and for to shed i blood, and for .... Jer 22:17
bring i blood upon yourselves .... Jer 26:15
have shed i blood in their land .... Joel 3:19
life, and lay not upon us i blood .. Jonah 1:14
that I have betrayed the i blood .... Mt 27:4
I am i of the blood of this just .. Mt 27:24

INNOCENTS
blood of the souls of the poor i .... Jer 2:34
this place with the blood of i .... Jer 19:4

INNUMERABLE
him, as there are i before him .... Job 21:33
For i evils have compassed me .... Ps 40:12
wherein are things creeping i .... Ps 104:25
than the grasshoppers, and are i .... Jer 46:23
together an i multitude of people .... Lk 12:1
sand which is by the sea shore i .... Heb 11:12
to an i company of angels .... Heb 12:22

INORDINATE
corrupt in her i love than she .... Eze 23:11
i affection, evil concupiscence .... Col 3:5

INQUISITION
The judges shall make diligent i .... Deut 19:18
When he maketh i for blood, he .... Ps 9:12

INSCRIPTION
I found an altar with this i .... Acts 17:23

INSIDE
covered within on the i with wood 1Kin 6:15

INSOMUCH
i that he abhorred his own .... Ps 106:40
i that he regardeth not the .... Mal 2:13
i that the ship was covered with .... Mt 8:24
i that the blind and dumb both .... Mt 12:22
i that they were astonished, and .... Mt 13:54
i that the multitude wondered .... Mt 15:31
i that, if it were possible, they .... Mt 24:24
i that the governor marvelled .... Mt 27:14
i that they questioned among .... Mk 1:27
i that Jesus could no more openly .... Mk 1:45
i that there was no room to .... Mk 2:2
i that they were all amazed, and .... Mk 2:12
i that they pressed upon him for .... Mk 3:10
i that many said, He is dead .... Mk 9:26
i that they trode one upon .... Lk 12:1
i as that field is called in .... Acts 1:19
i that they brought forth the .... Acts 5:15
i that we despaired even of 2Cor 1:8
i that we desired Titus, that as 2Cor 8:6
i that Barnabas also was carried .... Gal 2:13

INSPIRATION
the i of the Almighty giveth them .... Job 32:8
scripture is given by i of God 2Ti 3:16

INSTANT
yea, it shall be at an i suddenly .... Is 29:5
breaking cometh suddenly at an i .... Is 30:13
At what i I shall speak .... Jer 18:7
And at what i I shall speak .... Jer 18:9
she coming in that i gave thanks .... Lk 2:38
they were i with loud voices .... Lk 23:23
continuing i in prayer .... Rom 12:12
be i in season, out of season 2Ti 4:2

INSTANTLY
to Jesus, they besought him i .... Lk 7:4
i serving God day and night, hope .... Acts 26:7

INSTEAD
and closed up the flesh i thereof .... Gen 2:21
me another seed i of Abel .... Gen 4:25
let thy servant abide i of the .... Gen 44:33
he shall be to thee i of a mouth .... Ex 4:16
and thou shalt be to him i of God .... Ex 4:16
to gather stubble i of straw .... Ex 5:12
i of all the firstborn .... Num 3:12
i of all the firstborn among the .... Num 3:41
the cattle of the Levites i of .... Num 3:41
Take the Levites i of all the .... Num 3:45
of the Levites i of their cattle .... Num 3:45
with another i of thy husband .... Num 5:19
aside to another i of thy husband .... Num 5:20
aside to another i of her husband .... Num 5:29
if such as open every womb .... Num 8:16
even i of the firstborn of all .... Num 8:16
and thou mayest be to us i of eyes .. Num 10:31
take her, I pray thee, i of her .... Judg 15:2
captain of the host i of Joab 2Sa 17:25
servant king of David my father 1Kin 3:7
made him king i of his father 2Kin 14:21
i of the children of Israel 2Kin 17:24
as king i of David his father 1Chr 29:23
I of which king Rehoboam made 2Chr 12:10
the king be queen i of Vashti .... Est 2:4
and made her queen i of Vashti .... Est 2:17
Let thistles grow i of wheat .... Job 31:40
and cockle i of barley .... Job 31:40
Of thy fathers shall be thy .... Ps 45:16
that i of sweet smell there shall .... Is 3:24
and i of a girdle a rent .... Is 3:24
i of well set hair baldness .... Is 3:24
i of a stomacher a girding of .... Is 3:24
and burning i of beauty .... Is 3:24
I of the thorn shall come up .... Is 55:13
i of the brier shall come up the .... Is 55:13
which reigned i of Josiah his .... Jer 22:11
the son of Josiah reigned i of .... Jer 37:1
taketh strangers i of her husband .... Eze 16:32

INSTRUCT
his voice, that he might i thee .... Deut 4:36
also thy good spirit to i them .... Neh 9:20
with the Almighty i him .... Job 40:2
my reins also i me in the night .... Ps 16:7
I will i thee and teach thee in .... Ps 32:8
my mother's house, who would i me .... Song 8:2
For his God doth i him .... Is 28:26
among the people shall i many .... Dan 11:33
of the Lord, that he may i him 1Cor 2:16

INSTRUCTED
he i him, he kept him as the .... Deut 32:10
wherein Jehoiada the priest i him 2Kin 12:2
he i about the song, because he 1Chr 15:22
were i in the songs of the LORD 1Chr 25:7
i for the building of the house 2Chr 3:3
Behold, thou hast i many, and thou .... Job 4:3
be i, ye judges of the earth .... Ps 2:10
mine ear to them that i me .... Prov 5:13
and when the wise is i, he .... Prov 21:11
i me that I should not walk in .... Is 8:11
took he counsel, and who i him .... Is 40:14
Be thou i, O Jerusalem, lest my .... Jer 6:8
and after that I was i, I smote .... Jer 31:19
i unto the kingdom of heaven is .... Mt 13:52
being before i of her mother .... Mt 14:8
things, wherein thou hast been i .... Lk 1:4
This man was i in the way of the .... Acts 18:25
excellent, being i out of the law .... Rom 2:18
all things I am i both to be full .... Phil 4:12

INSTRUCTER
an i of every artificer in brass .... Gen 4:22

INSTRUCTERS
ye have ten thousand i in Christ 1Cor 4:15

INSTRUCTING
In meekness i those that oppose 2Ti 2:25

INSTRUCTION
ears of men, and sealeth their i .... Job 33:16
Seeing thou hatest i, and castest .... Ps 50:17
To know wisdom and i .... Prov 1:2
To receive the i of wisdom .... Prov 1:3
but fools despise wisdom and i .... Prov 1:7
hear the i of thy father, and .... Prov 1:8
the i of a father, and attend to .... Prov 4:1
Take fast hold of i .... Prov 4:13
And say, How have I hated i .... Prov 5:12
He shall die without i .... Prov 5:23
reproofs of i are the way of life .... Prov 6:23
Receive my i, and not silver .... Prov 8:10
Hear i, and be wise, and refuse it .... Prov 8:33

Give *i* to a wise man, and he will...... Prov 9:9
in the way of life that keepeth *i*..... Prov 10:17
Whoso loveth *i* loveth knowledge..... Prov 12:1
A wise man heareth his father's *i*..... Prov 13:1
shall be to him that refuseth *i*......... Prov 13:18
A fool despiseth his father's *i*......... Prov 15:5
He that refuseth *i* despiseth his..... Prov 15:32
of the LORD is the *i* of wisdom....... Prov 15:33
but the *i* of fools is folly............... Prov 16:22
Hear counsel, and receive *i*........... Prov 19:20
to hear the *i* that causeth to err..... Prov 19:27
Apply thine heart unto *i*, and....... Prov 23:12
also wisdom, and *i*, and................. Prov 23:23
I looked upon it, and received *i*..... Prov 24:32
might not hear, nor receive *i*......... Jer 17:23
have not hearkened to receive *i*..... Jer 32:33
Will ye not receive *i* to hearken..... Jer 35:13
be a reproach and a taunt, an *i*..... Eze 5:15
for that me, thou wilt receive *i*..... Zeph 3:7
for *i* in righteousness..................... 2Ti 3:16

INSTRUCTOR
An *i* of the foolish, a teacher of..... Rom 2:20

INSTRUMENT
If he smite him with an *i* of iron..... Num 35:16
psaltery and an *i* of ten strings....... Ps 33:2
Upon an *i* of ten strings, and upon..... Ps 92:3
an *i* of ten strings will I sing......... Ps 144:9
not threshed with a threshing *i*..... Is 28:27
sharp threshing *i* having teeth..... Is 41:15
bringeth forth an *i* for his work..... Is 54:16
voice, and can play well on an *i*..... Eze 33:32

INSTRUMENTS
i of cruelty are in their................... Gen 49:5
the pattern of all the *i* thereof....... Ex 25:9
they shall keep all the *i* of the....... Num 3:8
shall take all the *i* of ministry....... Num 4:12
all the *i* of their service, and......... Num 4:26
and their cords, with all their *i*..... Num 4:32
by name ye shall reckon the *i* of..... Num 4:32
it, and all the *i* thereof, both......... Num 7:1
to the war, with the holy *i*............. Num 31:6
harvest, and to make his *i* of war..... 1Sa 8:12
and *i* of his chariots....................... 1Sa 8:12
with joy, and with *i* of musick....... 1Sa 18:6
all manner of *i* made of fir wood..... 2Sa 6:5
burnt sacrifice, and the threshing *i*..... 2Sa 24:22
other *i* of the oxen for wood......... 2Sa 24:22
flesh with the *i* of the oxen........... 1Kin 19:21
all the *i* of the sanctuary, and..... 1Chr 9:29
expert in war, with all *i* of......... 1Chr 12:33
with all manner of *i* of war for..... 1Chr 12:37
be the singers with *i* of musick..... 1Chr 15:16
a sound, and with musical *i* of God..... 1Chr 16:42
and the threshing *i* for wood....... 1Chr 21:23
the LORD with the *i* which I made..... 1Chr 23:5
for all *i* of all manner of............... 1Chr 28:14
for all *i* of silver by weight........... 1Chr 28:14
for all *i* of every kind of............... 1Chr 28:14
and the fleshhooks, and all the *i*..... 2Chr 4:16
silver, and the gold, and all the *i*..... 2Chr 5:1
i of musick, and praised the LORD..... 2Chr 5:13
also with *i* of musick of the LORD..... 2Chr 7:6
also the singers with *i* of musick..... 2Chr 23:13
Levites stood with the *i* of David..... 2Chr 29:26
with the *i* ordained by David king..... 2Chr 29:27
singing with loud *i* unto the LORD..... 2Chr 30:21
that could skill of *i* of musick....... 2Chr 34:12
with the musical *i* of David the..... Neh 12:36
prepared for him the *i* of death..... Ps 7:13
the players on *i* followed after..... Ps 68:25
the players on *i* shall be there..... Ps 87:7
praise him with stringed *i*............. Ps 150:4
of the sons of men, as musical *i*..... Eccl 2:8
The *i* also of the churl are evil..... Is 32:7
sing my songs to the stringed *i*..... Is 38:20
whereupon also they laid the *i*..... Eze 40:42
neither were *i* of musick brought..... Dan 6:18
Gilead with threshing *i* of musick..... Amos 1:3
invent to themselves *i* of musick..... Amos 6:5
the chief singer on my stringed *i*..... Hab 3:19
yet the *i* of a foolish shepherd..... Zec 11:15
yield ye your members as *i* of....... Rom 6:13
the dead, and your members as *i* of..... Rom 6:13

INSURRECTION
time hath made *i* against kings..... Ezr 4:19
from the *i* of the workers of....... Ps 64:2
them that had made *i* with him..... Mk 15:7
who had committed murder in the *i*..... Mk 15:7
The Jews made *i* with one accord..... Acts 18:12

INTEGRITY
in the *i* of my heart and innocency..... Gen 20:5
didst thou in the *i* of thy heart..... Gen 20:6
in *i* of heart, and in uprightness..... 1Kin 9:4
and still he holdeth fast his *i*..... Job 2:3
Dost thou still retain thine *i*..... Job 2:9
I will not remove mine *i* from me..... Job 27:5
balance, that God may know mine *i*..... Job 31:6
according to mine *i* that is in me..... Ps 7:8
Let *i* and uprightness preserve me..... Ps 25:21
for I have walked in mine *i*........... Ps 26:1
as for me, I will walk in mine *i*..... Ps 26:11
me, thou upholdest me in mine *i*..... Ps 41:12
according to the *i* of his heart..... Ps 78:72
The *i* of the upright shall guide..... Prov 11:3
is the poor that walketh in his *i*..... Prov 19:1
The just man walketh in his *i*..... Prov 20:7

INTELLIGENCE
have *i* with them that forsake the..... Dan 11:30

INTEND
did not *i* to go up against them..... Josh 22:33
ye *i* to add more to our sins and..... 2Chr 28:13
i to bring this man's blood upon..... Acts 5:28
ye *i* to do as touching these men..... Acts 5:35

INTENDED
For they *i* evil against thee......... Ps 21:11

INTENDEST
i thou to kill me, as thou.............. Ex 2:14

INTENDING
i to build a tower, sitteth not..... Lk 14:28
i after Easter to bring him forth..... Acts 12:4
Assos, there *i* to take in Paul....... Acts 20:13

INTENT
to the *i* that the LORD might..... 2Sa 17:14
to the *i* that he might destroy..... 2Kin 10:19
to the *i* that he might let none..... 2Chr 16:1
for to the *i* that I might shew..... Eze 40:4
to the *i* that the living may know..... Dan 4:17
there, to the *i* ye may believe..... Jn 11:15
for what *i* he spake this unto him..... Jn 13:28
and came hither for that *i*......... Acts 9:21
for what *i* ye have sent for me..... Acts 10:29
to the *i* we should not lust after..... 1Cor 10:6
To the *i* that now unto the........... Eph 3:10

INTENTS
have performed the *i* of his heart..... Jer 30:24
of the thoughts and *i* of the heart..... Heb 4:12

INTERCESSION
made *i* for the transgressors......... Is 53:12
for them, neither make *i* to......... Jer 7:16
let them now make *i* to the LORD..... Jer 27:18
Gemariah had made *i* to the king..... Jer 36:25
i for us with groanings which....... Rom 8:26
because he maketh *i* for the......... Rom 8:27
of God, who also maketh *i* for us..... Rom 8:34
how he maketh *i* to God against..... Rom 11:2
he ever liveth to make *i* for them..... Heb 7:25

INTERCESSIONS
of all, supplications, prayers, *i*..... 1Ti 2:1

INTERCESSOR
and wondered that there was no *i*..... Is 59:16

INTERMEDDLE
stranger doth not *i* with his joy..... Prov 14:10

INTERMEDDLETH
seeketh and *i* with all wisdom..... Prov 18:1

INTERMISSION
and ceaseth not, without any *i*..... Lam 3:49

INTERPRET
that could *i* them unto Pharaoh..... Gen 41:8
according to his dream he did *i*..... Gen 41:12
and there is none that can *i*......... Gen 41:15
canst understand a dream to *i*..... Gen 41:15
do all *i*?..................................... 1Cor 12:30
with tongues, except he *i*............. 1Cor 14:5
unknown tongue pray that he may *i*..... 1Cor 14:13
and let one *i*............................... 1Cor 14:27

INTERPRETATION
according to the *i* of his dream..... Gen 40:5
unto him, This is the *i* of it........ Gen 40:12
baker saw that the *i* was good..... Gen 40:16
and said, This is the *i* thereof..... Gen 40:18
according to the *i* of his dream..... Gen 41:11
the *i* thereof, that he worshipped..... Judg 7:15
To understand a proverb, and the *i*..... Prov 1:6
and who knoweth the *i* of a thing..... Eccl 8:1
the dream, and we will shew the *i*..... Dan 2:4
me the dream, with the *i* thereof..... Dan 2:6
the *i* thereof, ye shall receive..... Dan 2:6
me the dream, and the *i* thereof..... Dan 2:6
and we will shew the *i* of it........ Dan 2:7
that ye can shew me the *i* thereof..... Dan 2:9
that he would shew the king the *i*..... Dan 2:16
I will shew unto the king the *i*..... Dan 2:24
make known unto the king the *i*..... Dan 2:25
I have seen, and the *i* thereof..... Dan 2:26
make known the *i* to the king..... Dan 2:30
we will tell the *i* thereof before..... Dan 2:36
is certain, and the *i* thereof sure..... Dan 2:45
known unto me the *i* of the dream..... Dan 4:6
make known unto me the *i* thereof..... Dan 4:9
I have seen, and the *i* thereof..... Dan 4:9
declare the *i* thereof, forasmuch..... Dan 4:18
able to make known unto me the *i*..... Dan 4:18
or the *i* thereof, trouble thee..... Dan 4:19
the *i* thereof to thine enemies..... Dan 4:19
This is the *i*, O king, and this is..... Dan 4:24
writing, and shew me the *i* thereof..... Dan 5:7
known to the king the *i* thereof..... Dan 5:8
be called, and he will shew the *i*..... Dan 5:12
make known unto me the *i* thereof..... Dan 5:15
could not shew the *i* of the thing..... Dan 5:15
and make known to me the *i* thereof..... Dan 5:16
and make known to him the *i*..... Dan 5:17
This is the *i* of the thing......... Dan 5:26
made me know the *i* of the things..... Dan 7:16
be called Cephas, which is by *i*..... Jn 1:42
pool of Siloam, (which is by *i*)..... Jn 9:7
which by *i* is called Dorcas......... Acts 9:36
is his name by *i*) withstood them..... Acts 13:8
to another the *i* of tongues......... 1Cor 12:10
hath a revelation, hath an *i*......... 1Cor 14:26
first being by *i* King of............... Heb 7:2
the scripture is of any private *i*..... 2Pet 1:20

INTERPRETATIONS
unto them, Do not *i* belong to God..... Gen 40:8
of thee, that thou canst make *i*..... Dan 5:16

INTERPRETED
as Joseph had *i* to them............... Gen 40:22
him, and he *i* to us our dreams..... Gen 41:12
and it came to pass, as he *i* to us..... Gen 41:13
tongue, and *i* in the Syrian tongue..... Ezr 4:7
name Emmanuel, which being *i* is..... Mt 1:23
which is, being *i*, Damsel, I say..... Mk 5:41
place Golgotha, which is, being *i*..... Mk 15:22
which is, being *i*, My God, my God..... Mk 15:34
Rabbi, (which is to say, being *i*..... Jn 1:38
the Messias, which is, being *i*..... Jn 1:41
Barnabas, (which is, being *i*......... Acts 4:36

INTERPRETER
a dream, and there is no *i* of it..... Gen 40:8
for he spake unto them by an *i*..... Gen 42:23
be a messenger with him, an *i*..... Job 33:23
But if there be no *i*, let him..... 1Cor 14:28

INTERPRETING
of dreams, and shewing of hard..... Dan 5:12

INTO See PREFACE.

INTREAT
i for me to Ephron the son of..... Gen 23:8
I the LORD, that he may take away..... Ex 8:8
when shall I *i* for thee, and for..... Ex 8:9
very far away: *i* for me.............. Ex 8:28
I will *i* the LORD that the swarms..... Ex 8:29
i the LORD (for it is enough)..... Ex 9:28
i the LORD your God, that he may..... Ex 10:17
I me not to leave thee, or to..... Ruth 1:16
the LORD, who shall *i* for him..... 1Sa 2:25
I now the face of the LORD thy..... 1Kin 13:6
the people shall *i* thy favour..... Ps 45:12
Many will *i* the favour of the..... Prov 19:6
Being defamed, we *i*................... 1Cor 4:13
I thee also, true yokefellow..... Phil 4:3
an elder, but *i* him as a father..... 1Ti 5:1

INTREATED
Isaac *i* the LORD for his wife........ Gen 25:21
and the LORD was *i* of him, and..... Gen 25:21
out from Pharaoh, and *i* the LORD..... Ex 8:30
out from Pharaoh, and *i* the LORD..... Ex 10:18
Then Manoah *i* the LORD, and said..... Judg 13:8
after that God was *i* for the land..... 2Sa 21:14
So the LORD was *i* for the land..... 2Sa 24:25
the battle, and he was *i* of them..... 1Chr 5:20
and he was *i* of him, and heard his..... 2Chr 33:13
also, and how God was *i* of him..... 2Chr 33:19
and he was *i* of us..................... Ezr 8:23
I *i* him with my mouth............... Job 19:16
though I *i* for the children's..... Job 19:17
I *i* thy favour with my whole..... Ps 119:58
LORD, and he shall be *i* of them..... Is 19:22
came his father and, and *i* him..... Lk 15:28
i that the word should not be..... Heb 12:19
gentle, and easy to be *i*, full of..... Jas 3:17

INTREATIES
The poor useth *i*......................... Prov 18:23

INTREATY
Praying us with much *i* that we..... 2Cor 8:4

INTRUDING
i into those things which he hath..... Col 2:18

INVADE
thou wouldest not let Israel *i*..... 2Chr 20:10
he will *i* them with his troops..... Hab 3:16

INVADED
the Philistines have *i* the land..... 1Sa 23:27
the Geshurites, and the Gezrites..... 1Sa 27:8
the Amalekites had *i* the scuth..... 1Sa 30:1
the bands of the Moabites came..... 2Kin 13:20
The Philistines also had *i* the..... 2Chr 28:18

INVASION
We made an *i* upon the south of..... 1Sa 30:14

INVENT
i to themselves instruments of..... Amos 6:5

INVENTED
i by cunning men, to be on the..... 2Chr 26:15

INVENTIONS
thou tookest vengeance of their *i*..... Ps 99:8
him to anger with their *i*............. Ps 106:29
went a whoring with their own *i*..... Ps 106:39
and find out knowledge of witty *i*..... Prov 8:12
but they have sought out many *i*..... Eccl 7:29

INVENTORS
i of evil things, disobedient to..... Rom 1:30

INVISIBLE
For the *i* things of him from the..... Rom 1:20
Who is the image of the *i* God..... Col 1:15
that are in earth, visible and..... Col 1:16
King eternal, immortal, *i*............ 1Ti 1:17
endured, as seeing him who is *i*..... Heb 11:27

INVITED
since I said, I have *i* the people..... 1Sa 9:24
Absalom *i* all the king's sons..... 2Sa 13:23
to morrow am I *i* unto her also..... Est 5:12

INWARD

is in the side of the ephod *i*	Ex 28:26
was on the side of the ephod *i*	Ex 39:19
it is fret *i*, whether it be bare	Lev 13:55
built round about from Millo and *i*	2Sa 5:9
and all their hinder parts were *i*	1Kin 7:25
their feet, and their faces were *i*	2Chr 3:13
and all their hinder parts were *i*	2Chr 4:4
All my *i* friends abhorred me	Job 19:19
hath put wisdom in the *i* parts	Job 38:36
their *i* part is very wickedness	Ps 5:9
Their *i* thought is, that their	Ps 49:11
desirest truth in the *i* parts	Ps 51:6
both the *i* thought of every one	Ps 64:6
searching all the *i* parts of the	Prov 20:27
so do stripes the *i* parts of the	Prov 20:30
mine *i* parts for Kir-haresh	Is 16:11
will put my law in their *i* parts	Jer 31:33
and the porch of the gate was *i*	Eze 40:9
and windows were round about *i*	Eze 40:16
Then went he *i*, and measured the	Eze 41:3
a walk of ten cubits breadth *i*	Eze 42:4
but your *i* part is full of	Lk 11:39
in the law of God after the *i* man	Rom 7:22
yet the *i* man is renewed day by	2Cor 4:16
his *i* affection is more abundant	2Cor 7:15

INWARDLY

their mouth, but they curse *i*	Ps 62:4
but *i* they are ravening wolves	Mt 7:15
But he is a Jew, which is one *i*	Rom 2:29

INWARDS

all the fat that covereth the *i*	Ex 29:13
in pieces, and wash the *i* of him	Ex 29:17
and the fat that covereth the *i*	Ex 29:22
But his *i* and his legs shall he	Lev 1:9
But he shall wash the *i* and the	Lev 1:13
the fat that covereth the *i*	Lev 3:3
and all the fat that is upon the *i*	Lev 3:3
and the fat that covereth the *i*	Lev 3:9
and all the fat that is upon the *i*	Lev 3:9
the fat that covereth the *i*	Lev 3:14
and all the fat that is upon the *i*	Lev 3:14
the fat that covereth the *i*	Lev 4:8
and all the fat that is upon the *i*	Lev 4:8
head, and with his legs, and his *i*	Lev 4:11
and the fat that covereth the *i*	Lev 7:3
all the fat that was upon the *i*	Lev 8:16
And he washed the *i* and the legs in	Lev 8:21
all the fat that was upon the *i*	Lev 8:25
And he did wash the *i* and the legs,	Lev 9:14
and that which covereth the *i*	Lev 9:19

IOB See JOB.

IPHEDEIAH (*if-e-di'-ah*) *A son of Shashak.*
And *I*, and Penuel, the sons of.......... 1Chr 8:25

IPHTAH See JIPHTAH.

IPHTAH EL See JIPHTHAH-EL.

IR (*ur*) See IR-NAHASH, IR-SHEMESH. *Father of Machir.*
and Huppim, the children of *I*.......... 1Chr 7:12

IRA (*i'-rah*)
1. An officer of David.
I also the Jairite was a chief 2Sa 20:26
2. A mighty man of David.
the son of Ikkesh the Tekoite, ... 2Sa 23:26
I an Ithrite, Gareb an Ithrite, ... 2Sa 23:38
the son of Ikkesh the Tekoite, ... 1Chr 11:28
the Ithrite, Gareb the Ithrite, ... 1Chr 11:40
the son of Ikkesh the Tekoite 1Chr 27:9

IRAD (*i'-rad*) *Son of Enoch.*
And unto Enoch was born *I* .... Gen 4:18
and *I* begat Mehujael.......... Gen 4:18

IRAM (*i'-ram*) *An Edomite leader.*
Duke Magdiel, duke *I* .... Gen 36:43
Duke Magdiel, duke *I* 1Chr 1:54

IRI (*i'-ri*) *A son of Bela.*
and Uzziel, and Jerimoth, and *I*.......... 1Chr 7:7

IRIJAH (*i-ri'-jah*) *A captain of the guard.*
ward was there, whose name was *I* .... Jer 37:13
so *I* took Jeremiah, and brought .... Jer 37:14

IR-NAHASH (*ur-na'-hash*) *A descendant of Chelub.*
and Tehinnah the father of *I* 1Chr 4:12

IRON (*i'-ron*) *A city in Naphtali.*
And *I*, and Migdal-el, Horem, and.......... Josh 19:38
A metal.
of every artificer in brass and *i* .... Gen 4:22
and I will make your heaven as *i* .... Lev 26:19
and the silver, the brass, the *i* .... Num 31:22
smite him with an instrument of *i* .... Num 35:16
his bedstead was a bedstead of *i* .... Deut 3:11
you forth out of the *i* furnace.......... Deut 4:20
a land whose stones are *i* .... Deut 8:9
not lift up any *i* tool upon them.......... Deut 27:5
that is under thee shall be *i* .... Deut 28:23
put a yoke of *i* upon thy neck .... Deut 28:48
Thy shoes shall be *i* and brass .... Deut 33:25
and gold, and vessels of brass and *i* .... Josh 6:19
and the vessels of brass and of *i* .... Josh 6:24
which no man hath lift up any *i* .... Josh 8:31
of the valley have chariots of *i* .... Josh 17:16
though they have *i* chariots .... Josh 17:18
gold, and with brass, and with *i* .... Josh 22:8
because they had chariots of *i* .... Judg 1:19
he had nine hundred chariots of *i* .... Judg 4:3

even nine hundred chariots of *i*	Judg 4:13
weighed six hundred shekels of *i*	1Sa 17:7
of iron, and under axes of *i*	2Sa 12:31
touch them must be fenced with *i*	2Sa 23:7
any tool of *i* heard in the house	1Kin 6:7
the midst of the furnace of *i*	1Kin 8:51
of Chenaanah made him horns of *i*...	1Kin 22:11
and the *i* did swim	2Kin 6:6
with saws, and with harrows of *i*	1Chr 20:3
David prepared *i* in abundance for	1Chr 22:3
and of brass and *i* without weight	1Chr 22:14
silver, and the brass, and the *i*	1Chr 22:16
the *i* for things of iron, and wood,	1Chr 29:2
brass, the iron for things of *i*	1Chr 29:2
one hundred thousand talents of *i*	1Chr 29:7
in silver, and in brass, and in *i*	2Chr 2:7
and in silver, in brass, in *i*	2Chr 2:14
Chenaanah made him horns of *i*	2Chr 18:10
LORD, and also such as wrought *i*	2Chr 24:12
they were graven with an *i* pen	Job 19:24
He shall flee from the *i* weapon	Job 20:24
Is taken out of the earth, and	Job 28:2
his bones are like bars of *i*	Job 40:18
He esteemeth *i* as straw, and brass	Job 41:27
shalt break them with a rod of *i*	Ps 2:9
he was laid in *i*	Ps 105:18
being bound in affliction and *i*	Ps 107:10
and cut the bars of *i* in sunder	Ps 107:16
and their nobles with fetters of *i*	Ps 149:8
i sharpeneth iron	Prov 27:17
Iron sharpeneth *i*	Prov 27:17
If the *i* be blunt, and he do not	Eccl 10:10
the thickets of the forest with *i*	Is 10:34
and cut in sunder the bars of *i*	Is 45:2
and thy neck is an *i* sinew	Is 48:4
for *i* I will bring silver, and for	Is 60:17
for wood brass, and for stones *i*	Is 60:17
an *i* pillar, and brasen walls	Jer 1:18
they are brass and *i*	Jer 6:28
land of Egypt, from the *i* furnace	Jer 11:4
Shall *i* break the northern iron	Jer 15:12
Shall iron break the northern *i*	Jer 15:12
Judah is written with a pen of *i*	Jer 17:1
shalt make for them yokes of *i*	Jer 28:13
I have put a yoke of *i* upon the	Jer 28:14
take thou unto thee an *i* pan	Eze 4:3
it for a wall of *i* between thee	Eze 4:3
all they are brass, and tin, and *i*	Eze 22:18
gather silver, and brass, and *i*	Eze 22:20
with silver, *i*, tin, and lead,	Eze 27:12
bright *i*, cassia, and calamus,	Eze 27:19
legs of iron, his feet part of *i*	Dan 2:33
upon his feet that were of *i*	Dan 2:34
Then was the *i*, the clay, the	Dan 2:35
kingdom shall be strong as *i*	Dan 2:40
forasmuch as *i* breaketh in pieces	Dan 2:40
as *i* that breaketh all these,	Dan 2:40
of potters' clay, and part of *i*	Dan 2:41
be in it of the strength of the *i*	Dan 2:41
sawest the *i* mixed with miry clay	Dan 2:41
toes of the feet were part of *i*	Dan 2:42
whereas thou sawest *i* mixed with...	Dan 2:43
even as *i* is not mixed with clay	Dan 2:43
and that it brake in pieces the *i*	Dan 2:45
the earth, even with a band of *i*	Dan 4:15
the earth, even with a band of *i*	Dan 4:23
and of silver, of brass, of *i*	Dan 5:4
of silver, and gold, of brass, *i*	Dan 5:23
and it had great *i* teeth	Dan 7:7
dreadful, whose teeth were of *i*	Dan 7:19
with threshing instruments of *i*	Amos 1:3
for I will make thine horn *i*	Mic 4:13
they came unto the *i* gate that...	Acts 12:10
conscience seared with a hot *i*	1Ti 4:2
shall rule them with a rod of *i*	Rev 2:27
as it were breastplates of *i*	Rev 9:9
rule all nations with a rod of *i*	Rev 12:5
precious wood, and of brass, and *i*	Rev 18:12
shall rule them with a rod of *i*	Rev 19:15

IRONS
thou fill his skin with barbed *i*.......... Job 41:7

IRPEEL (*ur'-pe-el*) *A city in Benjamin.*
And Rekem, and *I*, and Taralah, ... Josh 18:27

IR-SHEMESH (*ur-she'-mesh*) *A city in Dan.*
was Zorah, and Eshtaol, and *I* .... Josh 19:41

IRU (*i'-ru*) *A son of Caleb.*
I, Elah, and Naam 1Chr 4:15

IS See MIDFACE.

ISAAC (*i'-za-ak*) See ISAAC'S. *Son of Abraham and Sarah.*
and thou shalt call his name *I*.......... Gen 17:19
covenant will I establish with *I*.......... Gen 17:21
him, whom Sarah bare to him, *I*.......... Gen 21:3
his son *I* being eight days old .... Gen 21:4
when his son *I* was born unto him.......... Gen 21:5
the same day that *I* was weaned .... Gen 21:8
be heir with my son, even with *I* .... Gen 21:10
for in *I* shall thy seed be called .... Gen 21:12
now thy son, thine only son *I* .... Gen 22:2
I his son, and clave the wood for .... Gen 22:3
and laid it upon *I* his son .... Gen 22:6
I spake unto Abraham his father, ... Gen 22:7
bound *I* his son, and laid him on .... Gen 22:9
and take a wife unto my son *I* .... Gen 24:4
hast appointed for thy servant *I* .... Gen 24:14
I came from the way of the well .... Gen 24:62
I went out to meditate in the .... Gen 24:63

up her eyes, and when she saw *I*......	Gen 24:64
the servant told *I* all things........	Gen 24:66
I brought her into his mother.........	Gen 24:67
I was comforted after his...........	Gen 24:67
gave all that he had unto *I*.........	Gen 25:5
and sent them away from *I* his son...	Gen 25:6
And his sons *I* and Ishmael buried....	Gen 25:9
that God blessed his son *I*...........	Gen 25:11
I dwelt by the well Lahai-roi.........	Gen 25:11
And these are the generations of *I*...	Gen 25:19
Abraham begat *I*.....................	Gen 25:19
I was forty years old when he........	Gen 25:20
I intreated the LORD for his wife.....	Gen 25:21
I was threescore years old when......	Gen 25:26
I loved Esau, because he did eat.....	Gen 25:28
I went unto Abimelech king of the....	Gen 26:1
And *I* dwelt in Gerar................	Gen 26:6
I was sporting with Rebekah his......	Gen 26:8
And Abimelech called *I*, and said,...	Gen 26:9
I said unto him, Because I said,......	Gen 26:9
Then *I* sowed in that land, and......	Gen 26:12
And Abimelech said unto *I*, Go from..	Gen 26:16
I departed thence, and pitched his...	Gen 26:17
I digged again the wells of water....	Gen 26:18
I said unto them, Wherefore come.....	Gen 26:27
I sent them away, and they..........	Gen 26:31
Which were a grief of mind unto *I*...	Gen 26:35
came to pass, that when *I* was old...	Gen 27:1
Rebekah heard when *I* spake to......	Gen 27:5
I said unto his son, How is it.......	Gen 27:20
I said unto Jacob, Come near, *I*.....	Gen 27:21
Jacob went near unto *I* his father...	Gen 27:22
his father *I* said unto him, Come....	Gen 27:26
as soon as *I* had made an end of....	Gen 27:30
from the presence of *I* his father...	Gen 27:30
I his father said unto him, Who.....	Gen 27:32
I trembled very exceedingly, and.....	Gen 27:33
I answered and said unto Esau,.......	Gen 27:37
I his father answered and said......	Gen 27:39
And Rebekah said to *I*, I am weary...	Gen 27:46
I called Jacob, and blessed him,.....	Gen 28:1
And I sent away Jacob.................	Gen 28:5
Esau saw that *I* had blessed Jacob...	Gen 28:6
Canaan pleased not *I* his father.....	Gen 28:8
thy father, and the God of *I*.......	Gen 28:13
for to go to *I* his father in the....	Gen 31:18
God of Abraham, and the fear of *I*...	Gen 31:42
sware by the fear of his father *I*...	Gen 31:53
Abraham, and God of my father *I*.....	Gen 32:9
land which I gave Abraham and *I*.....	Gen 35:12
Jacob came unto *I* his father unto...	Gen 35:27
where Abraham and *I* sojourned......	Gen 35:27
the days of *I* were an hundred and..	Gen 35:28
I gave up the ghost, and died, and...	Gen 35:29
unto the God of his father *I*.......	Gen 46:1
I did walk, the God which fed me......	Gen 48:15
the name of my fathers Abraham and *I*	Gen 48:16
there they buried *I* and Rebekah.....	Gen 49:31
which he sware to Abraham, to *I*.....	Gen 50:24
his covenant with Abraham, with *I*...	Ex 2:24
the God of Abraham, the God of *I*....	Ex 3:6
The God of Abraham, the God of *I*....	Ex 3:15
fathers, the God of Abraham, of *I*...	Ex 3:16
the God of Abraham, the God of *I*....	Ex 4:5
I appeared unto Abraham, unto *I*.....	Ex 6:3
swear to give it to Abraham, to *I*...	Ex 6:8
Remember Abraham, and Israel,........	Ex 32:13
which I sware unto Abraham, to *I*....	Ex 33:1
Jacob, and also my covenant with *I*..	Lev 26:42
I sware unto Abraham, unto *I*.......	Num 32:11
unto your fathers, Abraham, *I*......	Deut 1:8
thy fathers, to Abraham, to *I*......	Deut 6:10
unto thy fathers, Abraham,...........	Deut 9:5
Remember thy servants, Abraham, *I*...	Deut 9:27
thy fathers, to Abraham, to *I*......	Deut 29:13
thy fathers, to Abraham, to *I*......	Deut 30:20
I sware unto Abraham, unto *I*.......	Deut 34:4
his seed, and gave him...............	Josh 24:3
And I gave unto *I* Jacob and Esau....	Josh 24:4
and said, Loro God of Abraham, *I*....	1Kin 18:36
of his covenant with Abraham, *I*....	2Kin 13:23
I, and Ishmael.....................	1Chr 1:28
And Abraham begat *I*................	1Chr 1:34
The sons of *I*......................	1Chr 1:34
Abraham, and of his oath unto *I*.....	1Chr 16:16
O Loro God of Abraham, *I*, and of....	1Chr 29:18
unto the LORD God of Abraham, and *I*.	2Chr 30:6
with Abraham, and his oath unto *I*...	Ps 105:9
over the seed of Abraham, *I*........	Jer 33:26
places of *I* shall be desolate......	Amos 7:9
thy word against the house of *I*....	Amos 7:16
Abraham begat *I*....................	Mt 1:2
and *I* begat Jacob..................	Mt 1:2
shalt sit down with Abraham, and....	Mt 8:11
God of Abraham, and the God of *I*....	Mt 22:32
God of Abraham, and the God of *I*....	Mk 12:26
of Jacob, which was the son of *I*....	Lk 3:34
when ye shall see Abraham, and *I*....	Lk 13:28
God of Abraham, and the God of *I*....	Lk 20:37
The God of Abraham, and of *I*.......	Acts 3:13
and so Abraham begat *I*............	Acts 7:8
and *I* begat Jacob..................	Acts 7:8
God of Abraham, and the God of *I*....	Acts 7:32
In *I* shall thy seed be called......	Rom 9:7
by one, even by our father *I*.......	Rom 9:10
as I was, are the children of........	Gal 4:28
dwelling in tabernacles with *I*......	Heb 11:9
when he was tried, offered up *I*.....	Heb 11:17
That in *I* shall thy seed be........	Heb 11:18
By faith *I* blessed Jacob and Esau...	Heb 11:20

when he had offered *I* his son .... Jas 2:21

ISAAC'S (i'-za-aks)
I servants digged in the valley, ... Gen 26:19
Gerar did strive with *I* herdmen .... Gen 26:20
there *I* servants digged a well .... Gen 26:25
that *I* servants came, and told him .... Gen 26:32

ISAIAH (i-za'-yah) See ESAIAS. *A prophet.*
to *I* the prophet the son of Amoz 2Kin 19:2
of king Hezekiah came to *I* 2Kin 19:5
I said unto them, Thus shall ye 2Kin 19:6
Then *I* the son of Amoz sent to 2Kin 19:20
the prophet *I* the son of Amoz 2Kin 20:1
Then *I* was gone out into the 2Kin 20:4
I said, Take a lump of figs 2Kin 20:7
And Hezekiah said unto *I*, What 2Kin 20:8
I said, This sign shalt thou have 2Kin 20:9
I the prophet cried unto the LORD 2Kin 20:11
Then came *I* the prophet unto king 2Kin 20:14
I said unto Hezekiah, Hear the 2Kin 20:16
Then said Hezekiah unto *I* 2Kin 20:19
did *I* the prophet, the son of 2Chr 26:22
the prophet *I* the son of Amoz, ... 2Chr 32:20
in the vision of *I* the prophet 2Chr 32:32
The vision of *I* the son of Amoz, ... Is 1:1
The word that *I* the son of Amoz .... Is 2:1
Then said the LORD unto *I* .... Is 7:3
which *I* the son of Amoz did see .... Is 13:1
the LORD by *I* the son of Amoz .... Is 20:2
as my servant *I* hath walked naked .... Is 20:3
unto *I* the prophet the son of .... Is 37:2
of king Hezekiah came to *I* .... Is 37:5
I said unto them, Thus shall ye .... Is 37:6
Then *I* the son of Amoz sent unto .... Is 37:21
I the prophet the son of Amoz .... Is 38:1
came the word of the LORD to *I* .... Is 38:4
For *I* had said, Let them take a .... Is 38:21
Then came *I* the prophet unto king ...... Is 39:3
Then said *I* to Hezekiah, Hear the ...... Is 39:5
Then said Hezekiah to *I*, Good is .... Is 39:8

ISCAH (is'-cah) See SARAH. *A daughter of Haran.*
of Milcah, and the father of *I* .... Gen 11:29

ISCARIOT (is-car'-e-ot) See JUDAS. *Disciple who betrayed Jesus.*
Simon the Canaanite, and Judas *I* .... Mt 10:4
one of the twelve, called Judas *I* .... Mt 26:14
And Judas *I*, which also betrayed .... Mk 3:19
And Judas *I*, one of the twelve, ... Mk 14:10
the brother of James, and Judas *I* .... Lk 6:16
Satan into Judas surnamed *I* .... Lk 22:3
spake of Judas *I* the son of Simon .... Jn 6:71
one of his disciples, Judas *I* .... Jn 12:4
now put into the heart of Judas *I* .... Jn 13:2
the sop, he gave it to Judas *I* .... Jn 13:26
Judas saith unto him, not *I* .... Jn 14:22

ISHBAH (ish'-bah) *Father of Eshtemoa.*
and *I* the father of Eshtemoa ....

ISHBAK (ish'-bak) *A son of Abraham.*
and Medan, and Midian, and *I*, ... Gen 25:2
and Medan, and Midian, and *I* 1Chr 1:32

ISHBI-BENOB (ish'-bi-be'-nob) *A Philistine giant.*
And *I*, which was of the sons of 2Sa 21:16

ISH-BOSHETH (ish-bo'-sheth) See ESH-BAAL. *Son of Saul.*
took *I* the son of Saul, and 2Sa 2:8
I Saul's son was forty years old 2Sa 2:10
the servants of *I* the son of Saul........... 2Sa 2:12
pertained to *I* the son of Saul............. 2Sa 2:15
I said to Abner, Wherefore hast.......... 2Sa 3:7
very wroth for the words of *I* 2Sa 3:8
sent messengers to *I* Saul's son........... 2Sa 3:14
I sent, and took her from her.............. 2Sa 3:15
heat of the day to the house of *I*........... 2Sa 4:5
head of *I* unto David to Hebron 2Sa 4:8
Behold the head of *I* the son of 2Sa 4:8
But they took the head of *I* 2Sa 4:12

ISHI (i'-shi)
1. A descendant of Pharez.
I 1Chr 2:31
And the sons of *I*........................... 1Chr 2:31
2. A descendant of Judah.
And the sons of *I* were, Zoheth, and... 1Chr 4:20
3. A Simeonite.
and Uzziel, the sons of *I* 1Chr 4:42
4. A head of Manasseh.
their fathers, even Epher, and *I*......... 1Chr 5:24
5. A symbolic name for Israel.
LORD, that thou shalt call me *I* .... Hos 2:16

ISHIAH (i-shi'-ah) See ISHIJAH, ISSHIAH. *A son of Izrahiah.*
Michael, and Obadiah, and Joel, *I* 1Chr 7:3

ISHIJAH (i-shi'-jah) See ISHIAH, JESIAH. *Married a foreigner in exile.*
Eliezer, *I*, Malchiah, Shemaiah, ... Ezr 10:31

ISHMA (ish'-mah) *A descendant of Caleb.*
Jezreel, and *I*, and Idbash 1Chr 4:3

ISHMAEL (ish'-ma-el) See ISHMAELITE, ISHMAEL'S.
1. Son of Abraham and Hagar.
a son, and shalt call his name *I* .... Gen 16:11
son's name, which Hagar bare, *I*.......... Gen 16:15
old, when Hagar bare *I* to Abram....... Gen 16:16

O that *I* might live before thee .... Gen 17:18
And as for *I*, I have heard thee............ Gen 17:20
And Abraham took *I* his son .... Gen 17:23
I his son was thirteen years old,......... Gen 17:25
Abraham circumcised, and *I* his son... Gen 17:26
I buried him in the cave of................ Gen 25:9
these are the generations of *I*............ Gen 25:12
are the names of the sons of *I*............ Gen 25:13
the firstborn of *I*, Nebaioth............... Gen 25:13
These are the sons of *I*, and these...... Gen 25:16
are the years of the life of *I*.............. Gen 25:17
Then went Esau unto *I*, and took....... Gen 28:9
the daughter of *I* Abraham's son .... Gen 28:9
Isaac, and *I* 1Chr 1:28
The firstborn of *I*, Nebaioth............. 1Chr 1:29
These are the sons of *I*.................... 1Chr 1:31
2. A ruler of Judah.
and Zebadiah the son of *I*, and 2Chr 19:11
3. Son of Azel.
and these, Azrikam, Bocheru, and *I* ... 1Chr 8:38
and these, Azrikam, Bocheru, and *I* ... 1Chr 9:44
4. A captain who aided Joash.
I the son of Jehohanan, and.............. 2Chr 23:1
5. Married a foreigner in exile.
Elioenai, Maaseiah, *I*, Nethaneel,...... Ezr 10:22
6. The son of Nethaniah.
even *I* the son of Nethaniah, and........ 2Kin 25:23
that *I* the son of Nethaniah, the......... 2Kin 25:25
even *I* the son of Nethaniah, and........ Jer 40:8
I the son of Nethaniah to slay............ Jer 40:14
thee, and I will slay *I* the son of......... Jer 40:15
for thou speakest falsely of *I*............. Jer 40:16
that *I* the son of Nethaniah came to.... Jer 41:1
Then arose *I* the son of Nethaniah ..... Jer 41:2
I also slew all the Jews that............... Jer 41:3
I the son of Nethaniah went forth....... Jer 41:6
that *I* the son of Nethaniah slew .... Jer 41:7
found among them that said unto *I* .... Jer 41:8
Now the pit wherein *I* had cast.......... Jer 41:9
I the son of Nethaniah filled it.......... Jer 41:9
Then *I* carried away captive all......... Jer 41:10
I the son of Nethaniah carried.......... Jer 41:10
heard of all the evil that *I* .... Jer 41:11
went to fight with *I* the son of .... Jer 41:12
I saw Johanan the son of Kareah........ Jer 41:13
So all the people that *I* had............. Jer 41:14
But *I* the son of Nethaniah............. Jer 41:15
from *I* the son of Nethaniah .... Jer 41:16
because *I* the son of Nethaniah .... Jer 41:18

ISHMAELITE (ish'-ma-el-ite) *Descendants of Ishmael 1.*
the camels also was Obil the *I* 1Chr 27:30

ISHMAELITES (ish'-ma-el-ites) See ISHMEELITES.
earrings, because they were *I*............ Judg 8:24
The tabernacles of Edom, and the *I*.... Ps 83:6

ISHMAEL'S (ish'-ma-els) *Refers to Ishmael 1.*
And Bashemath *I* daughter, sister...... Gen 36:3

ISHMAIAH (ish-ma-i'-ah) See ISMAIAH. *A prince of Zebulun.*
Of Zebulun, *I* the son of Obadiah 1Chr 27:19

ISHMEELITE (ish'-me-el-ite) See ISHMAELITE, ISHMEELITES. *Same as Ishmaelite.*
father of Amasa was Jether the *I*....... 2Chr 2:17

ISHMEELITES (ish'-me-el-ites) See ISHMAELITES.
a company of *I* came from Gilead....... Gen 37:25
Come, and let us sell him to the *I*...... Gen 37:27
sold Joseph to the *I* for twenty......... Gen 37:28
bought him of the hands of the *I*...... Gen 39:1

ISHMERAI (ish'-me-rahee) *A chief of Benjamin.*
I also, and Jezliah, and Jobab, the..... 1Chr 8:18

ISHOD (i'-shod) *A son of Hammoleketh.*
And his sister Hammoleketh bare *I*.... 1Chr 7:18

ISHPAH See ISPAH.

ISHPAN (ish'-pan) *A son of Shashak.*
And *I*, and Heber, and Eliel,............. 1Chr 8:22

ISH-TOB (ish'-tob) *A district of Aram.*
men, and of *I* twelve thousand men 2Sa 10:6
of Zoba, and of Rehob, and *I*............ 2Sa 10:8

ISHUAH (ish'-u-ah) See ISUAH. *A son of Asher.*
Jimnah, and *I*, and Isui, and Beriah,... Gen 46:17

ISHUAI
Imnah, and Isuah, and *I*, and Beriah,.. 1Chr 7:30

ISHUI (ish'-u-i) See ISHUAI, JESUI. *A son of Saul.*
sons of Saul were Jonathan, and *I* 1Sa 14:49

ISLAND
deliver the *i* of the innocent.............. Job 22:30
with the wild beasts of the *i* .... Is 34:14
certain *i* which is called Clauda .... Acts 27:16
we must be cast upon a certain *i* .... Acts 27:26
knew that the *i* was called Melita ...... Acts 28:1
of the chief man of the *i* .... Acts 28:7
also, which had diseases in the *i* .... Acts 28:9
every *i* moved out of their places........ Rev 6:14
i *i* were *i* fled away, and the .... Rev 16:20

ISLANDS
Hamath, and from the *i* of the sea..... Is 11:11
the wild beasts of the *i* shall .... Is 13:22

Keep silence before me, O *i* .... Is 41:1
and declare his praise in the *i* .... Is 42:12
and I will make the rivers *i* .... Is 42:15
to the *i* he will repay recompence .... Is 59:18
beasts of the *i* shall dwell there .... Jer 50:39

ISLE
of this *i* shall say in that day .... Is 20:6
Be still, ye inhabitants of the *i* .... Is 23:2
howl, ye inhabitants of the *i* .... Is 23:6
gone through the *i* unto Paphos .... Acts 13:6
had wintered in the *i* .... Acts 28:11
was in the *i* that is called.................. Rev 1:9

ISLES
By these were the *i* of the .... Gen 10:5
land, and upon the *i* of the sea .... Est 10:1
of the *i* shall bring presents.............. Ps 72:10
multitude of *i* be glad thereof .... Ps 97:1
God of Israel in the *i* of the sea .... Is 24:15
he taketh up the *i* as a very .... Is 40:15
The *i* saw it, and feared .... Is 41:5
the *i* shall wait for his law................ Is 42:4
the *i*, and the inhabitants thereof ...... Is 42:10
Listen, O *i*, unto me .... Is 49:1
the *i* shall wait upon me, and on .... Is 51:5
Surely the *i* shall wait for me,........... Is 60:9
to the *i* afar off, that have not .... Is 66:19
For pass over the *i* of Chittim .... Jer 2:10
the kings of the *i* which are .... Jer 25:22
and declare it in the *i* afar off........... Jer 31:10
Shall not the *i* shake at the .... Eze 26:15
Now shall the *i* tremble in the .... Eze 26:18
the *i* that are in the sea shall............ Eze 26:18
merchant of the people for many *i* .... Eze 27:3
brought out of the *i* of Chittim .... Eze 27:6
purple from the *i* of Elishah was .... Eze 27:7
many *i* were the merchandise of .... Eze 27:15
All the inhabitants of the *i* .... Eze 27:35
that dwell carelessly in the *i* .... Eze 39:6
shall he turn his face unto the *i* .... Dan 11:18
even all the *i* of the heathen .... Zeph 2:11

ISMACHIAH (is-ma-ki'-ah) *A temple servant.*
and Jozabad, and Eliel, and *I*........... 2Chr 31:13

ISMAIAH (is-ma-i'-ah) See ISHMAIAH. *A warrior in David's army.*
I the Gibeonite, a mighty man.......... 1Chr 12:4

ISPAH (is'-pah) *A son of Beriah.*
And Michael, and Ispah, and Joha, the.. 1Chr 8:16

ISRAEL (iz'-ra-el) See PREFACE. See also EL-ELOHE-ISRAEL, ISRAELITE, ISRAEL'S, JACOB, JESHURUN.
1. Name given to Jacob.
be called no more Jacob, but *I* .... Gen 32:28
Jacob, but I shall be thy name .... Gen 35:10
and he called his name *I* .... Gen 35:10
2. People descended from Jacob.
these are the twelve tribes of *I* .... Gen 49:28
I is my son, even my firstborn .... Ex 4:22
should obey his voice to let *I* go .... Ex 5:2
the LORD, neither will I let *I* go .... Ex 5:2
not let the children of *I* go................ Ex 10:20
Thus did all the children of *I* .... Ex 12:50
pursued after the children of *I* .... Ex 14:8
the children of *I* went into the........... Ex 14:22
Thus the LORD saved *I* that day .... Ex 14:30
Moses brought *I* from the Red sea ..... Ex 15:22
shalt say unto the children of *I* .... Ex 20:22
a covenant with thee and with *I* .... Ex 34:27
the children of *I* did according.......... Num 1:54
my name upon the children of *I* .... Num 6:27
I vowed a vow unto the LORD, and...... Num 21:2
I joined himself unto Baal-peor .... Num 25:3
of the LORD was kindled against *I* .... Num 25:3
Hear, O *I*: The LORD our God .... Deut 6:4
And his name shall be called in *I* ...... Deut 25:10
Happy art thou, O *I* .... Deut 33:29
the LORD God of *I* in mount Ebal ..... Josh 8:30
the LORD gave unto *I* all that........... Josh 21:43
the children of *I* again did evil .... Judg 4:1
If thou wilt save *I* by mine hand .... Judg 6:36
Behold, ye are all children of *I* .... Judg 20:7
The glory is departed from *I* 1Sa 4:21
So the LORD saved *I* that day 1Sa 14:23
thee, Thou shalt feed my people *I* 2Sa 5:2
and thou shalt be a captain over *I* 2Sa 5:2
dwell among the children of *I* 1Kin 6:13
and will not forsake my people *I* 1Kin 6:13
And he said, Lord God of *I* 1Kin 8:23
O ye seed of *I* his servant................ 1Chr 16:13
Jerusalem over all *I* forty years 2Chr 9:30
to *I* for an everlasting covenant .... Ps 105:10
O *I*, trust thou in the LORD .... Ps 115:9
he that keepeth *I* shall neither .... Ps 121:4
that shall rule my people *I* .... Mt 2:6
the lost sheep of the house of .... Mt 10:6
the lost sheep of the house of *I* .... Mt 15:24
many of the children of *I* shall.......... Lk 1:16
thou art the King of *I* .... Jn 1:49
Blessed is the King of *I* that .... Jn 12:13
promise raised unto *I* a Saviour .... Acts 13:23
of *I* I am bound with this chain......... Acts 28:20
Esaias also crieth concerning *I* .... Rom 9:27
I hath not obtained that *I* seeketh..... Rom 11:7
And so all *I* shall be saved,.............. Rom 11:26
new covenant with the house of *I*...... Heb 8:8
3. The ten northern tribes.
not the army of *I* go with thee.......... 2Chr 25:7
for the LORD is not with *I* 2Chr 25:7

ISRAELITE (iz'-ra-el-ite) See ISRAELITES, ISRAELITISH. *A member of Israel 3.*
the name of the *I* that was slain ...... Num 25:14
son, whose name was Ithra an *I*...... 2Sa 17:25
saith of him, Behold an *I* indeed...... Jn 1:47
For *I* also am an *I*, of the seed ...... Rom 11:1

ISRAELITES (iz'-ra-el-ites)
one of the cattle of the *I* dead ...... Ex 9:7
all that are *I* born shall dwell ...... Lev 23:42
all the *I* passed over on dry...... Josh 3:17
that all the *I* returned unto Ai,...... Josh 8:24
lot unto the *I* for an inheritance ...... Josh 13:6
dwell among the *I* until this day ...... Josh 13:13
ground of the *I* that day twenty...... Judg 20:21
unto all the *I* that came thither 1Sa 2:14
But all the *I* went down to the 1Sa 13:20
be with the *I* that were with Saul 1Sa 14:21
all the *I* were gathered together,...... 1Sa 25:1
the *I* pitched by a fountain which 1Sa 29:1
and all the *I* were troubled...... 2Sa 4:1
the *I* rose up and smote the...... 2Kin 3:24
of the *I* that are consumed...... 2Kin 7:13
in their cities were, the *I*...... 1Chr 9:2
Who are *I*...... Rom 9:4
Are they *I*...... 2Cor 11:22

ISRAELITISH
And the son of an *I* woman, whose...... Lev 24:10
and this son of the *I* woman...... Lev 24:10
the *I* woman's son blasphemed the...... Lev 24:11

ISRAEL'S (iz'-ra-els)
1. Refers to Israel 1.
his right hand toward *I* left hand...... Gen 48:13
his left hand toward *I* right hand...... Gen 48:13
of Reuben, Israel and son, by their...... Num 1:20
2. Refers to Israel 2.
and to the Egyptians for *I* sake ...... Ex 18:8
And of the children of *I* half ...... Num 31:30
And of the children of *I* half ...... Num 31:42
Even of the children of *I* half...... Num 31:47
blood unto thy people of *I* charge...... Deut 21:8
his kingdom for his people *I* sake...... 2Sa 5:12
3. Refers to Israel 3.
the king of *I* servants answered...... 2Kin 3:11

ISSACHAR (is'-sa-kar)
1. A son of Jacob.
and she called his name *I*...... Gen 30:18
Simeon, and Levi, and Judah, and *I*...... Gen 35:23
And the sons of *I*...... Gen 46:13
I is a strong ass couching down...... Gen 49:14
I, Zebulun, and Benjamin,...... Ex 1:3
Reuben, Simeon, Levi, and Judah, *I*...... 1Chr 2:1
Now the sons of *I* were, Tola, and...... 1Chr 7:1
2. Descendants of Issachar 1.
Of *I*...... Num 1:8
Of the children of *I*, by their...... Num 1:28
of them, even of the tribe of *I*...... Num 1:29
unto him shall be the tribe of *I*...... Num 2:5
be captain of the children of *I*...... Num 2:5
the son of Zuar, prince of *I*...... Num 7:18
I was Nethaneel the son of Zuar...... Num 10:15
Of the tribe of *I*, Igal the son...... Num 13:7
Of the sons of *I* after their...... Num 26:23
These are the families of *I*...... Num 26:25
of the tribe of the children of *I*...... Num 26:25
Simeon, and Levi, and Judah, and *I*...... Deut 27:12
and *I*, in thy tents...... Deut 33:18
on the north, and in *I* on the east...... Josh 17:10
And Manasseh had in *I* and in Asher...... Josh 17:11
And the fourth lot came out to *I*...... Josh 19:17
for the children of *I* according...... Josh 19:17
of *I* according to their families ...... Josh 19:23
of the families of the tribe of *I*...... Josh 21:6
And out of the tribe of *I*, Kishon...... Josh 21:28
the princes of *I* were with...... Judg 5:15
even *I*, and also Barak,...... Judg 5:15
Puah, the son of Dodo, a man of *I*...... Judg 10:1
the son of Paruah, in *I*...... 1Kin 4:17
son of Ahijah, of the house of *I*...... 1Kin 15:27
families out of the tribe of *I*...... 1Chr 6:62
And out of the tribe of *I*...... 1Chr 6:72
of *I* were valiant men of might...... 1Chr 7:5
And of the children of *I*, which 1Chr 12:32
that were nigh them, even unto *I*...... 1Chr 12:40
of *I*, Omri the son of Michael...... 1Chr 27:18
many of Ephraim, and Manasseh, *I*...... 2Chr 30:18
unto the west side, *I* a portion...... Eze 48:25
And by the border of *I*, from the...... Eze 48:26
one gate of Simeon, one gate of *I*...... Eze 48:33
Of the tribe of *I* were sealed...... Rev 7:7
3. A porter of the tabernacle.
the seventh, Peulthai the...... 1Chr 26:5

ISSHIAH (is-shi'-ah) See ISAIAH, JESIAH.
1. A descendant of Moses.
sons of Rehabiah, the first was *I*...... 1Chr 24:21
2. A Levite.
The brother of Micah was *I*...... 1Chr 24:25
of the sons of *I*...... 1Chr 24:25

ISSHIJAH See ISHIJAH.

ISSHOD See ISHOD.

ISSUE
And thy *i*, which thou begettest ...... Gen 48:6
cleansed from the *i* of her blood...... Lev 12:7
hath a running *i* out of his flesh...... Lev 15:2
because of his *i* he is unclean...... Lev 15:2
shall be his uncleanness in his *i*...... Lev 15:3
whether his flesh run with his *i*...... Lev 15:3

his flesh be stopped from his *i*...... Lev 15:3
whereon he lieth that hath the *i*...... Lev 15:4
hath the *i* shall wash his clothes ...... Lev 15:6
hath the *i* shall wash his clothes ...... Lev 15:7
if he that hath the *i* spit upon...... Lev 15:8
that hath the *i* shall be unclean...... Lev 15:9
he toucheth that hath the *i*...... Lev 15:11
that he toucheth which hath the *i*...... Lev 15:12
when he that hath an *i*...... Lev 15:13
an *i* is cleansed of his *i*...... Lev 15:13
for him before the LORD for his *i*...... Lev 15:15
And if a woman have an *i*...... Lev 15:19
her *i* in her flesh be blood, she...... Lev 15:19
if a woman have an *i* of her blood...... Lev 15:25
all the days of the *i* of her...... Lev 15:25
she lieth all the days of her *i*...... Lev 15:26
But if she be cleansed of her *i*...... Lev 15:28
Lord for the *i* of her uncleanness ...... Lev 15:30
is the law of him that hath an *i*...... Lev 15:32
flowers, and of him that hath an *i*...... Lev 15:33
is a leper, or hath a running *i*...... Num 5:2
and every one that hath an *i*...... Num 5:2
house of Joab one that hath an *i*...... 2Sa 3:29
thy sons that shall *i* from thee...... 2Kin 20:18
house, the offspring and the *i*...... Is 22:24
thy sons that shall *i* from the...... Is 39:7
i is like the *i* of horses...... Eze 23:20
These waters *i* out toward the...... Eze 47:8
with an *i* of blood twelve years...... Mt 9:20
a wife, deceased, and having no *i*...... Mt 22:25
which had an *i* of blood twelve...... Mk 5:25
a woman having an *i* of blood ...... Lk 8:43
immediately her *i* of blood...... Lk 8:44

ISSUED
the other *i* out of the city,...... Josh 8:22
as if it had *i* out of the womb...... Job 38:8
waters *i* out from under the...... Eze 47:1
they they *i* out of the sanctuary...... Eze 47:12
A fiery stream *i* and came forth...... Dan 7:10
and out of their mouths *i* fire...... Rev 9:17
which *i* out of their mouths...... Rev 9:18

ISSUES
the Lord belong the *i* from death...... Ps 68:20
for out of it are the *i* of life...... Prov 4:23

ISUAH (is'-u-ah) See ISHUAH. *A son of Asher.*
Imnah, and *I*, and Ishuai, and Beriah... 1Chr 7:30

ISUI (is'-u-i) See ISHUI. *A son of Asher.*
Jimnah, and Ishuah, and *I*, and...... Gen 46:17

IT See PREFACE.

ITALIAN (it-al'-yan)
of the band called the *I* band...... Acts 10:1

ITALY (it'-a-lee) *Homeland of most Roman citizens.*
in Pontus, lately come from *I*...... Acts 18:2
that we should sail into *I*...... Acts 27:1
ship of Alexandria sailing into *I*...... Acts 27:6
They of *I* salute you...... Heb 13:24
to the Hebrews from *I* by Timothy ...... Heb s

ITCH
and with the scab, and with the *i*...... Deut 28:27

ITCHING
teachers, having *i* ears...... 2Ti 4:3

ITHAI (ith'-a-i) See ITTAI. *A mighty man of David.*
I the son of Ribai of Gibeah,...... 1Chr 11:31

ITHAMAR (ith'-a-mar) *A son of Aaron.*
Nadab, and Abihu, Eleazar, and *I*...... Ex 6:23
Nadab and Abihu, Eleazar and *I*...... Ex 28:1
of the Levites, by the hand of *I*...... Ex 38:21
Aaron, and unto Eleazar and unto *I*...... Lev 10:6
Aaron, and unto Eleazar and unto *I*...... Lev 10:12
and he was angry with Eleazar and *I*... Lev 10:16
and Abihu, Eleazar, and *I*...... Num 3:2
I ministered in the priest's...... Num 3:4
shall be under the hand of *I* the...... Num 4:28
under the hand of *I* the son of...... Num 4:33
under the hand of *I* the son of...... Num 7:8
Nadab, and Abihu, Eleazar, and *I*...... Num 26:60
Nadab, and Abihu, Eleazar, and *I*...... 1Chr 6:3
Nadab, and Abihu, Eleazar, and *I*...... 1Chr 24:1
I executed the priest's office...... 1Chr 24:2
and Ahimelech of the sons of *I*...... 1Chr 24:3
of Eleazar than of the sons of *I*...... 1Chr 24:4
eight among the sons of *I*...... 1Chr 24:4
of Eleazar, and of the sons of *I*...... 1Chr 24:5
for Eleazar, and one taken for *I*...... 1Chr 24:6
of the sons of *I*...... Ezr 8:2

ITHIEL (ith'-e-el)
1. Son of Jesaiah.
the son of Maaseiah, the son of *I*...... Neh 11:7
2. Person mentioned in Proverbs.
the man spake unto *I*, even unto ...... Prov 30:1
spake unto Ithiel, even unto *I*...... Prov 30:1

ITHLAH See JETHLAH.

ITHMAH (ith'-mah) *A mighty man of David.*
sons of Elnaam, and the Moabite,...... 1Chr 11:46

ITHNAN (ith'-nan) *A town in Judah.*
And Kedesh, and Hazor, and *I*,...... Josh 15:23

ITHRA (ith'-rah) See JETHER. *Father of Amasa.*
whose name was *I* an Israelite...... 2Sa 17:25

ITHRAN (ith'-ran)
1. A son of Dishon.
Hemdan, and Eshban, and *I*, and...... Gen 36:26

Amram, and Eshban, and *I*...... 1Chr 1:41
2. A son of Zophah.
Shamma, and Shilshah, and *I*...... 1Chr 7:37

ITHREAM (ith'-re-am) *A son of David.*
And the sixth, *I*, by Eglah David's...... 2Sa 3:5
the sixth, *I* by Eglah his wife...... 1Chr 3:3

ITHRITE (ith'-rite) See ITHRITES. *A descendant of Jether.*
Ira an *I*, Gareb an *I*...... 2Sa 23:38
Ira an *I*, Gareb an *I*...... 2Sa 23:38
Ira the *I*, Gareb the *I*,...... 1Chr 11:40
Ira the *I*, Gareb the *I*,...... 1Chr 11:40

ITHRITES (ith'-rites)
the *I*, and the Puhites, and the 1Chr 2:53

ITS
That which groweth of *i* own...... Lev 25:5

ITSELF
his kind, whose seed is in *i*...... Gen 1:11
fruit, whose seed was in *i*...... Gen 1:12
fat of the beast that dieth of *i*...... Lev 7:24
that eateth that which died of *i*...... Lev 17:15
the land *i* vomiteth out her...... Lev 18:25
That which dieth of *i*, or is torn ...... Lev 22:8
that which groweth of *i* in it...... Lev 25:11
eat of any thing that dieth of *i*...... Deut 14:21
were of the very base *i*...... 1Kin 7:34
A land of darkness, as darkness *i*...... Job 10:22
his heart gathereth iniquity to *i*...... Ps 41:6
even Sinai *i* was moved at the...... Ps 68:8
but that his heart may discover *i*...... Prov 18:2
the cup, when it moveth *i* aright...... Prov 23:31
his right hand, which bewrayeth *i*...... Prov 27:16
and the tender grass sheweth *i*...... Prov 27:25
Shall the ax boast *i* against him...... Is 10:15
or shall the saw magnify *i*...... Is 10:15
as if the rod should shake *i*...... Is 10:15
as if the staff should lift up *i*...... Is 10:15
this year such as groweth of *i*...... Is 37:30
your soul delight *i* in fatness...... Is 55:2
neither shall thy moon withdraw *i*...... Is 60:20
And there shall dwell in Judah *i*...... Jer 31:24
cloud, and a fire infolding *i*...... Eze 1:4
eaten of that which dieth of *i*...... Eze 4:14
base, that it might not lift *i*...... Eze 17:14
neither shall it exalt *i* any more...... Eze 29:15
of any thing that is dead of *i*...... Eze 44:31
and it raised up *i* on one side...... Dan 7:5
take thought for the things of *i*...... Mt 6:34
i is brought to desolation ...... Mt 12:25
divided against *i* shall not stand...... Mt 12:25
if a kingdom be divided against *i*... Mk 3:24
if a house be divided against *i*...... Mk 3:25
i is brought to desolation...... Lk 11:17
the branch cannot bear fruit of *i*...... Jn 15:4
wrapped together in a place by *i*...... Jn 20:7
i could not contain the books...... Jn 21:25
The Spirit *i* beareth witness with... Rom 8:16
Because the creature *i* also shall... Rom 8:21
but the Spirit *i* maketh...... Rom 8:26
there is nothing unclean of *i*...... Rom 14:14
Doth not even nature *i* teach you...... 1Cor 11:14
charity vaunteth not *i*, is not...... 1Cor 13:4
Doth not behave *i* unseemly...... 1Cor 13:5
i against the knowledge of God 2Cor 10:5
unto the edifying of *i* in love...... Eph 4:16
but this leaven *i* how to appear...... Heb 9:24
of all men, and of the truth *i*...... 3Jn 12

ITTAH-KAZIN (it'-tah-ka'-zin) *A city in Zebulun.*
the east to Gittah-hepher, to *I*...... Josh 19:13

ITTAI (it'-ta-i) See ITHAI.
1. A Philistine in David's army.
said the king to *I* the Gittite...... 2Sa 15:19
I answered the king, and said, As...... 2Sa 15:21
And David said to *I*, Go and pass...... 2Sa 15:22
I the Gittite passed over, and all... 2Sa 15:22
under the hand of *I* the Gittite...... 2Sa 18:2
commanded Joab and Abishai and *I*... 2Sa 18:5
king charged thee and Abishai and *I*... 2Sa 18:12
2. A mighty man of David.
I the son of Ribai out of Gibeah...... 2Sa 23:29

ITURAEA (i-tu-re'-ah) *A province near Mt. Hermon.*
his brother Philip tetrarch of *I*...... Lk 3:1

IVAH (i'-vah) See AHAVA, AVA. *A Mesopotamian district.*
gods of Sepharvaim, Hena, and *I*...... 2Kin 18:34
city of Sepharvaim, of Hena, and *I*... 2Kin 19:13
city of Sepharvaim, Hena, and *I*...... Is 37:13

IVORY
the king made a great throne of *i*... 1Kin 10:18
bringing gold, and silver, *i*...... 1Kin 10:22
the *i* house which he made, and all... 1Kin 22:39
the king made a great throne of *i*... 2Chr 9:17
bringing gold, and silver, *i*...... 2Chr 9:21
out of the *i* palaces...... Ps 45:8
his belly is as bright *i* overlaid...... Song 5:14
Thy neck is as a tower of *i*...... Song 7:4
have made thy benches of *i*...... Eze 27:6
thee for a present forth *i*...... Eze 27:15
and the houses of *i* shall perish...... Amos 3:15
That lie upon beds of *i*, and...... Amos 6:4
wood, and all manner vessels of *i*... Rev 18:12

IZEHAR (iz'-e-har) See IZEHARITES, IZHAR. *A son of Kohath.*
Amram, and *I*, Hebron, and Uzziel...... Num 3:19

IZEHARITES (iz'-e-har-ites) See IZHARITE.
Descendants of Izehar.
Amramites, and the family of the I .... Num 3:27

IZHAR (iz'-har) See IZEHAB, IZHARITES. *Same as Izehar.*
Amram, and I, and Hebron, and Uzziel .. Ex 6:18
And the sons of I .... Ex 6:21
Now Korah, the son of I, the son...... Num 16:1
Amram, I, and Hebron, and Uzziel 1Chr 6:2
sons of Kohath were, Amram, and I ... 1Chr 6:18
The son of I, the son of Kohath, ... 1Chr 6:38
Amram, I, Hebron, and Uzziel, four .. 1Chr 23:12
Of the sons of I 1Chr 23:18

IZHARITES (iz'-har-ites) See IZEHARITES. *Same as Izeharites.*
Of the I; Shelomoth 1Chr 24:22
Of the Amramites, and the I 1Chr 26:23
Of the I, Chenaniah and his sons 1Chr 26:29

IZLIAH See JEZLIAH.

IZRAHIAH (iz-ra-hi'-ah) See JEZRAHIAH. *Grandson of Tola.*
the sons of Uzzi; I 1Chr 7:3
and the sons of I 1Chr 7:3

IZRAHITE (iz'-ra-hite) See EZRAHITE. *Family name of Shamhuth.*
fifth month was Shamhuth the I 1Chr 27:8

IZRI (iz'-ri) See ZERI. *A sanctuary servant.*
The fourth to I, he, his sons, and...... 1Chr 25:11

IZZIAH See JEZIAH.

J

JAAKAN (ja'-a-kan) See AKAN, BENE-JAAKAN. *A son of Ezer.*
of the children of J to Mosera .... Deut 10:6

JAAKOBAH (ja-ak'-o-bah) *A descendant of Simeon.*
And Elioenai, and J, and Jeshohaiah,.. 1Chr 4:36

JAALA (ja'-a-lah) See JAALAH. *A family of exiles.*
The children of J, the children .... Neh 7:58

JAALAH (ja'-a-lah) See JAALA. *Same as Jaala.*
The children of J, the children .... Ezr 2:56

JAALAM (ja'-a-lam) *A son of Esau.*
And Aholibamah bare Jeush, and J ..... Gen 36:5
and she bare to Esau Jeush, and J ..... Gen 36:14
duke Jeush, duke J, duke Korah .... Gen 36:18
Eliphaz, Reuel, and Jeush, and J 1Chr 1:35

JAANAI (ja'-a-nahee) *A Gadite.*
chief, and Shapham the next, and J ... 1Chr 5:12

JAAR See WOOD.

JAARE-OREGIM (ja'-a-re-or'-eg-im) See JAIR. *Father of Elhanan.*
where Elhanan the son of J 2Sa 21:19

JAASAU (ja-a'-saw) *Married a foreigner in exile.*
Mattaniah, Mattenai, and J .... Ezr 10:37

JAASIEL (ja-a'-se-el) *A son of Abner.*
of Benjamin, J the son of Abner 1Chr 27:21

JAASU See JAASAU.

JAAZANIAH (ja-az-a-ni'-ah) See JEZANIAH.
I. *A son of a Maachathite.*
J the son of a Maachathite, they...... 2Kin 25:23
II. *A chief Rechabite.*
Then I took J the son of Jeremiah ..... Jer 35:3
III. *Son of Shaphan.*
them stood J the son of Shaphan ..... Eze 8:11
IV. *Son of Azur.*
whom I saw J the son of Azur............ Eze 11:1

JAAZER (ja-a'-zer) See JAZER. *A city in Gilead.*
And Moses sent to spy out J .... Num 21:32
And Atroth, and Shophan, and J, and .... Num 32:35

JAAZIAH (ja-a-zi'-ah) *A descendant of Merari.*
the sons of J; Beno.............................. 1Chr 24:26
The sons of Merari by J 1Chr 24:27

JA-AZIEL See BEN.

JAAZIEL (ja-a'-ze-el) See AZIEL. *A priest.*
degree, Zechariah, Ben, and J 1Chr 15:18

JABAL (ja'-bal) *A son of Adah.*
And Adah bare J .... Gen 4:20

JABBOK (jab'-bok) *A brook in Bashan.*
sons, and passed over the ford J........ Gen 32:22
his land from Arnon unto J .... Num 21:24
nor unto any place of the river J .... Deut 2:37
the border even unto the river J .... Deut 3:16
Gilead, even unto the river J .... Josh 12:2
of Egypt, from Arnon even unto J ...... Judg 11:13
Amorites, from Arnon even unto J ...... Judg 11:22

JABESH (ja'-besh) See JABESH-GILEAD.
I. *A city in Gad.*
all the men of J said unto Nahash 1Sa 11:1
And the elders of J said unto him 1Sa 11:3
him the tidings of the men of J 1Sa 11:5

came and shewed it to the men of J... 1Sa 11:9
Therefore the men of J said................. 1Sa 11:10
wall of Beth-shan, and came to J 1Sa 31:12
and buried them under a tree at J...... 1Sa 31:13
of his sons, and brought them to J..... 1Chr 10:12
their bones under the oak in J 1Chr 10:12
II. *Father of Shallum.*
Shallum the son of J conspired.......... 2Kin 15:10
Shallum the son of J began to 2Kin 15:13
Shallum the son of J in Samaria......... 2Kin 15:14

JABESH-GILEAD (ja'-besh-ghil'-e-ad) *Same as Jabesh I.*
the camp from J to the assembly .... Judg 21:8
of the inhabitants of J there................ Judg 21:9
smite the inhabitants of J with........... Judg 21:10
of J four hundred young virgins.......... Judg 21:12
had saved alive of the women of J ..... Judg 21:14
came up, and encamped against J 1Sa 11:1
shall ye say unto the men of J 1Sa 11:9
of J heard of that which the................ 1Sa 31:11
That the men of J were they that....... 2Sa 2:4
sent messengers unto the men of J ... 2Sa 2:5
his son from the men of J 2Sa 21:12
when all J heard all that the.............. 1Chr 10:11

JABEZ (ja'-bez)
I. *A city in Judah.*
of the scribes which dwelt at J 1Chr 2:55
II. *Head of a family of Judah.*
J was more honourable than his 1Chr 4:9
and his mother called his name J 1Chr 4:9
J called on the God of Israel,............. 1Chr 4:10

JABIN (ja'-bin) See JABIN'S.
I. *A king of Hazor.*
when J king of Hazor had heard .... Josh 11:1
II. *Another king of Hazor.*
into the hand of J king of Canaan...... Judg 4:2
peace between J the king of Hazor .... Judg 4:17
So God subdued on that day J the ..... Judg 4:23
prevailed against J the king of........... Judg 4:24
had destroyed J king of Canaan......... Judg 4:24
as to Sisera, as to J, at the............... Ps 83:9

JABIN'S
Sisera, the captain of J army.............. Judg 4:7

JABNEEL (jab'-ne-el) See JABNEH.
I. *A city in Judah.*
mount Baalah, and went out unto J .. Josh 15:11
II. *A city in Naphtali.*
and Adami, Nekeb, and J.................... Josh 19:33

JABNEH (jab'-neh) See JABNEEL. *A Philistine city.*
wall of Gath, and the wall of J........... 2Chr 26:6

JACAN See JACHAN.

JACHAN (ja'-kan) See AKAN. *Head of a Gadite family.*
and Sheba, and Jorai, and J 1Chr 5:13

JACHIN (ja'-kin) See JACHINITES, JARIB.
I. *A son of Simeon.*
Jemuel, and Jamin, and Ohad, and J . Gen 46:10
Jemuel, and Jamin, and Ohad, and J.. Ex 6:15
of J, the family of the .... Num 26:12
II. *A pillar of Solomon's Temple.*
and called the name thereof J 1Kin 7:21
name of that on the right hand J........ 2Chr 3:17
III. *A family of exiles.*
Jedaiah, and Jehoiarib, and J 1Chr 9:10
Jedaiah the son of Joiarib, J .... Neh 11:10
IV. *A sanctuary servant.*
The one and twentieth to J 1Chr 24:17

JACHINITES (ja'-kin-ites) *Descendants of Jachin I.*
of Jachin, the family of the J .... Num 26:12

JACINTH
breastplates of fire, and of j.............. Rev 9:17
the eleventh, a j .... Rev 21:20

JACOB (ja'-cub) See ISRAEL, JACOB'S, JAMES.
I. *Son of Isaac and Rebekah.*
and his name was called J .... Gen 25:26
J was a plain man, dwelling in .... Gen 25:27
but Rebekah loved J .... Gen 25:28
And J sod pottage .... Gen 25:29
And Esau said to J, Feed me, I .... Gen 25:30
J said, Sell me this day thy .... Gen 25:31
J said, Swear to me this day.............. Gen 25:33
and he sold his birthright unto J .... Gen 25:33
Then J gave Esau bread and pottage. Gen 25:34
And Rebekah spake unto J her son .... Gen 27:6
J said to Rebekah his mother,............ Gen 27:11
put them upon J her younger son...... Gen 27:15
into the hand of her son J.................. Gen 27:17
J said unto his father, I am Esau .... Gen 27:19
And Isaac said unto J, Come near,..... Gen 27:21
J went near unto Isaac his father....... Gen 27:22
had made an end of blessing J .... Gen 27:30
J was yet scarce gone out from .... Gen 27:30
said, Is not he rightly named J........... Gen 27:36
Esau hated J because of the .... Gen 27:41
then will I slay my brother J .... Gen 27:41
called J her younger son, and said .... Gen 27:42
if J take a wife of the daughters........ Gen 27:46
And Isaac called J, and blessed him .. Gen 28:1
And Isaac sent away J......................... Gen 28:5
Esau saw that Isaac had blessed J..... Gen 28:6
that J obeyed his father and his .... Gen 28:7
J went out from Beer-sheba, and....... Gen 28:10
J awaked out of his sleep, and he ..... Gen 28:16

J rose up early in the morning,.......... Gen 28:18
J vowed a vow, saying, If God............ Gen 28:20
Then J went on his journey, and........ Gen 29:1
said unto them, My brethren,............. Gen 29:4
when J saw Rachel the daughter of ... Gen 29:10
that J went near, and rolled the .... Gen 29:10
J kissed Rachel, and lifted up his ...... Gen 29:11
J told Rachel that he was her .... Gen 29:12
the tidings of J his sister's son .... Gen 29:13
And Laban said unto J, Because......... Gen 29:15
And J loved Rachel .... Gen 29:18
J served seven years for Rachel......... Gen 29:20
J said unto Laban, Give me my .... Gen 29:21
J did so, and fulfilled her week .... Gen 29:28
saw that she bare J no children .... Gen 30:1
and said unto J, Give me children,..... Gen 30:1
and J went in unto her........................ Gen 30:4
Bilhah conceived, and bare J a son.... Gen 30:5
again, and bare J a second son .... Gen 30:7
her maid, and gave her J to wife....... Gen 30:9
Zilpah Leah's maid bare J a son......... Gen 30:10
Leah's maid bare J a second son .... Gen 30:12
J came out of the field in the............ Gen 30:16
and bare J the fifth son .... Gen 30:17
again, and bare J the sixth son .... Gen 30:19
that J said unto Laban, Send me........ Gen 30:25
her maid, and gave her J to .... Gen 30:35
journey betwixt himself and J .... Gen 30:36
J fed the rest of Laban's flocks .... Gen 30:36
J took him rods of green poplar,........ Gen 30:37
J did separate the lambs, and set ..... Gen 30:40
that J laid the rods before the........... Gen 30:41
J hath taken away all that was........... Gen 31:1
J beheld the countenance of Laban ... Gen 31:2
And the LORD said unto J, Return........ Gen 31:3
And Laban called Rachel and Leah .... Gen 31:4
unto me in a dream, saying, J .... Gen 31:11
Then J rose up, and set his sons .... Gen 31:17
J stole away unawares to Laban........ Gen 31:20
on the third day that J was fled......... Gen 31:22
speak not to J either good or bad ..... Gen 31:24
Then Laban overtook J .... Gen 31:25
Now J had pitched his tent in the ...... Gen 31:25
And Laban said to J, What hast.......... Gen 31:26
speak not to J either good or bad ..... Gen 31:29
J answered and said to Laban,........... Gen 31:31
For J knew not that Rachel had .... Gen 31:32
J was wroth, and chode with Laban ... Gen 31:36
J answered and said to Laban, What.. Gen 31:36
And Laban answered and said unto J . Gen 31:43
J took a stone, and set it up for......... Gen 31:46
J said unto his brethren, Gather......... Gen 31:46
but J called it Galeed .... Gen 31:47
And Laban said to J, Behold this........ Gen 31:51
J sware by the fear of his father........ Gen 31:53
Then J offered sacrifice upon the....... Gen 31:54
J went on his way, and the angels .... Gen 32:1
when J saw them, he said, This is...... Gen 32:2
J sent messengers before him to .... Gen 32:3
Thy servant J saith thus, I have .... Gen 32:4
And the messengers returned to J ..... Gen 32:6
Then J was greatly afraid and .... Gen 32:7
J said, O God of my father................. Gen 32:9
thy servant J is behind us .... Gen 32:20
And J was left alone .... Gen 32:24
And he said, J .... Gen 32:28
name shall be called no more J .... Gen 32:28
J asked him, and said, Tell me, I ...... Gen 32:29
J called the name of the place........... Gen 32:30
J lifted up his eyes, and looked,........ Gen 33:1
J said, Nay, I pray thee, if now .... Gen 33:10
J journeyed to Succoth, and built ...... Gen 33:17
J came to Shalem, a city of................ Gen 33:18
of Leah, which she bare unto J .... Gen 34:1
unto Dinah the daughter of J .... Gen 34:3
J heard that he had defiled Dinah ..... Gen 34:5
J held his peace until they were .... Gen 34:5
out unto J to commune with him .... Gen 34:6
the sons of J came out of the .... Gen 34:7
the sons of J answered Shechem and. Gen 34:13
sore, that two of the sons of J .... Gen 34:25
The sons of J came upon the slain .... Gen 34:27
J said to Simeon and Levi, Ye have ... Gen 34:30
And God said unto J, Arise, go up ..... Gen 35:1
Then J said unto his household,......... Gen 35:2
they gave unto J all the strange .... Gen 35:4
J hid them under the oak which .... Gen 35:4
not pursue after the sons of J .... Gen 35:5
So J came to Luz, which is in the ...... Gen 35:6
And God appeared unto J again .... Gen 35:9
God said unto him, Thy name is J ...... Gen 35:10
shall not be called any more J........... Gen 35:10
J set up a pillar in the place,............. Gen 35:14
J called the name of the place........... Gen 35:15
J set a pillar upon her grave.............. Gen 35:20
Now the sons of J were twelve .... Gen 35:22
these are the sons of J, which .... Gen 35:26
J came unto Isaac his father unto ..... Gen 35:27
and his sons Esau and J buried him... Gen 35:29
from the face of his brother J .... Gen 36:6
J dwelt in the land wherein his.......... Gen 37:1
These are the generations of J .... Gen 37:2
J rent his clothes, and put .... Gen 37:34
Now when J saw that there was .... Gen 42:1
J said unto his sons, Why do ye .... Gen 42:1
J sent not with his brethren .... Gen 42:4
they came unto J their father .... Gen 42:29
J their father said unto them, Me....... Gen 42:36
of Canaan unto J their father............. Gen 45:25
the spirit of J their father.................. Gen 45:27

of the night, and said, J.............. Gen 46:2
J rose up from Beer-sheba............. Gen 46:5
of Israel carried J.................... Gen 46:5
of Canaan, and came into Egypt, J.... Gen 46:6
Israel, which came into Egypt, J...... Gen 46:8
she bare unto J in Padan-aram........ Gen 46:15
and these she bare unto J............. Gen 46:18
of Rachel, which were born to J....... Gen 46:25
and she bare these unto J............. Gen 46:25
souls that came with J into Egypt.... Gen 46:26
all the souls of the house of J........ Gen 46:27
And Joseph brought in J his father.... Gen 47:7
and J blessed Pharaoh................. Gen 47:7
And Pharaoh said unto J, How old..... Gen 47:8
J said unto Pharaoh, The days of...... Gen 47:9
J blessed Pharaoh, and went out...... Gen 47:10
J lived in the land of Egypt........... Gen 47:28
so the whole age of J was an......... Gen 47:28
And one told J, and said, Behold,..... Gen 48:2
J said unto Joseph, God Almighty..... Gen 48:3
J called unto his sons, and said,...... Gen 49:1
together, and hear, ye sons of J....... Gen 49:2
I will divide them in J, and........... Gen 49:7
the hands of the mighty God of J..... Gen 49:24
when J had made an end of............ Gen 49:33
to Abraham, to Isaac, and to J........ Gen 50:24
man and his household came with J.... Ex 1:1
the loins of J were seventy souls...... Ex 1:5
Abraham, with Isaac, and with J...... Ex 2:24
the God of Isaac, and the God of J.... Ex 3:6
the God of Isaac, and the God of J.... Ex 3:15
God of Abraham, of Isaac, and of J... Ex 3:16
the God of Isaac, and the God of J.... Ex 4:5
Abraham, unto Isaac, and unto J...... Ex 6:3
it to Abraham, to Isaac, and to J..... Ex 6:8
that thou say to the house of J....... Ex 19:3
unto Abraham, to Isaac, and to J..... Ex 33:1
I remember my covenant with J....... Lev 26:42
Abraham, unto Isaac, and unto J..... Num 32:11
fathers, Abraham, Isaac, and J........ Deut 1:8
to Abraham, to Isaac, and to J........ Deut 6:10
thy fathers, Abraham, Isaac, and J.... Deut 9:5
servants, Abraham, Isaac, and J...... Deut 9:27
to Abraham, to Isaac, and to J........ Deut 29:13
to Abraham, to Isaac, and to J........ Deut 30:20
Abraham, unto Isaac, and unto J..... Deut 34:4
And I gave unto Isaac J and Esau..... Josh 24:4
but J and his children went down..... Josh 24:4
in a parcel of ground which J......... Josh 24:32
When J was come into Egypt, and.... 1Sa 12:8
with Abraham, Isaac, and J........... 2Kin 13:23
yet I loved J,......................... Mal 1:2
and Isaac begat J..................... Mt 1:2
J begat Judas and his brethren........ Mt 1:2
down with Abraham, and Isaac, and J. Mt 8:11
the God of Isaac, and the God of J.... Mt 22:32
the God of Isaac, and the God of J.... Mk 12:26
over the house of J for ever.......... Lk 1:33
Which was the son of J, which was.... Lk 3:34
shall see Abraham, and Isaac, and J.. Lk 13:28
the God of Isaac, and the God of J.... Lk 20:37
that J gave to his son Joseph......... Jn 4:5
thou greater than our father J........ Jn 4:12
of Abraham, and of Isaac, and of J.... Acts 3:13
and Isaac begat J..................... Acts 7:8
J begat the twelve patriarchs......... Acts 7:8
But when J heard that there was..... Acts 7:12
and called his father J to him......... Acts 7:14
So J went down into Egypt, and...... Acts 7:15
the God of Isaac, and the God of J.... Acts 7:32
a tabernacle for the God of J......... Acts 7:46
J have I loved, but Esau have I....... Rom 9:13
turn away ungodliness from J........ Rom 11:26
in tabernacles with Isaac and J....... Heb 11:9
By faith Isaac blessed J and Esau..... Heb 11:20
By faith J, when he was a dying...... Heb 11:21
2. Father of Joseph; ancestor of Jesus.
and Matthan begat J................. Mt 1:15
J begat Joseph the husband of....... Mt 1:16
3. Descendants of Jacob.
east, saying, Come, curse me J....... Num 23:7
Who can count the dust of J.......... Num 23:10
He hath not beheld iniquity in J...... Num 23:21
there is no enchantment against J.... Num 23:23
this time it shall be said of J......... Num 23:23
How goodly are thy tents, O J........ Num 24:5
there shall come a Star out of J...... Num 24:17
Out of J shall come he that shall..... Num 24:19
J is the lot of his inheritance........ Deut 32:9
of the congregation of J............. Deut 33:4
They shall teach J thy judgments..... Deut 33:10
the fountain of J shall be upon a..... Deut 33:28
the anointed of the God of J......... 2Sa 23:1
of the tribes of the sons of J......... 1Kin 18:31
LORD commanded the children of J... 2Kin 17:34
his servant, ye children of J.......... 1Chr 16:13
confirmed the same to J for a law.... 1Chr 16:17
J shall rejoice, and Israel shall....... Ps 14:7
name of the God of J defend thee.... Ps 20:1
all ye the seed of J, glorify him...... Ps 22:23
seek him, that seek thy face, O J..... Ps 24:6
command deliverances for J.......... Ps 44:4
the God of J is our refuge............ Ps 46:7
the God of J is our refuge............ Ps 46:11
the excellency of J whom he loved.... Ps 47:4
J shall rejoice, and Israel shall....... Ps 53:6
in J unto the ends of the earth....... Ps 59:13
will sing praises to the God of J...... Ps 75:9
At thy rebuke, O God of J............ Ps 76:6
thy people, the sons of J............. Ps 77:15

he established a testimony in J........ Ps 78:5
so a fire was kindled against J........ Ps 78:21
brought him to feed J his people...... Ps 78:71
For they have devoured J, and laid... Ps 79:7
a joyful noise unto the God of J....... Ps 81:1
Israel, and a law of the God of J...... Ps 81:4
give ear, O God of J.................. Ps 84:8
brought back the captivity of J....... Ps 85:1
more than all the dwellings of J...... Ps 87:2
shall the God of J regard it........... Ps 94:7
judgment and righteousness in J..... Ps 99:4
ye children of J his chosen............ Ps 105:6
the same unto J for a law............. Ps 105:10
J sojourned in the land of Ham....... Ps 105:23
the house of J from a people of....... Ps 114:1
at the presence of the God of J....... Ps 114:7
and vowed unto the mighty God of J.. Ps 132:2
for the mighty God of J.............. Ps 132:5
LORD hath chosen J unto himself..... Ps 135:4
hath the God of J for his help........ Ps 146:5
He sheweth his word unto J.......... Ps 147:19
to the house of the God of J.......... Is 2:3
O house of J, come ye, and let us..... Is 2:5
thy people the house of J............. Is 2:6
his face from the house of J.......... Is 8:17
The Lord sent a word into J.......... Is 9:8
as are escaped of the house of J...... Is 10:20
return, even the remnant of J........ Is 10:21
For the LORD will have mercy on J... Is 14:1
shall cleave to the house of J........ Is 14:1
that the glory of J shall be made..... Is 17:4
them that come of J to take root..... Is 27:6
shall the iniquity of J be purged..... Is 27:9
concerning the house of J............ Is 29:22
J shall not now be ashamed,.......... Is 29:22
and sanctify the Holy One of J....... Is 29:23
Why savest thou, O J, and speakest.. Is 40:27
I whom I have chosen, the seed of J.. Is 41:8
Fear not, thou worm J, and ye men... Is 41:14
reasons, saith the King of J.......... Is 41:21
Who gave J for a spoil, and Israel.... Is 42:24
the LORD that created thee, O J...... Is 43:1
thou hast not called upon me, O J.... Is 43:22
have given J to the curse, and....... Is 43:28
Yet now hear, O J my servant....... Is 44:1
Fear not, O J, my servant............ Is 44:2
call himself by the name of J......... Is 44:5
Remember these, O J and Israel...... Is 44:21
for the LORD hath redeemed J........ Is 44:23
For J my servant's sake, and......... Is 45:4
I said not unto the seed of J.......... Is 45:19
Hearken unto me, O house of J....... Is 46:3
Hear ye this, O house of J............ Is 48:1
Hearken unto me, O J and Israel,.... Is 48:12
LORD hath redeemed his servant J.... Is 48:20
to bring J again to him, Though...... Is 49:5
to raise up the tribes of J............ Is 49:6
thy Redeemer, the mighty One of J.. Is 49:26
and the house of J their sins......... Is 58:1
with the heritage of J thy father..... Is 58:14
that turn from transgression in J..... Is 59:20
thy Redeemer, the mighty One of J.. Is 60:16
will bring forth a seed out of J....... Is 65:9
word of the LORD, O house of J....... Jer 2:4
Declare this in the house of J......... Jer 5:20
the portion of J is not like them...... Jer 10:16
for they have eaten up J, and........ Jer 10:25
fear thou not, O my servant J........ Jer 30:10
J shall return, and shall be in....... Jer 30:10
Sing with gladness for J, and........ Jer 31:7
For the LORD hath redeemed J........ Jer 31:11
will I cast away the seed of J......... Jer 33:26
the seed of Abraham, Isaac, and J.... Jer 33:26
But fear not thou, O my servant J.... Jer 46:27
J shall return, and be in rest and.... Jer 46:27
O J my servant, saith the LORD....... Jer 46:28
The portion of J is not like them..... Jer 51:19
LORD hath commanded concerning J.. Lam 1:17
up all the habitations of J............ Lam 2:2
he burned against J like a........... Lam 2:3
unto the seed of the house of J...... Eze 20:5
that I have given to my servant J.... Eze 28:25
I have given unto J my servant....... Eze 37:25
I bring again the captivity of J....... Eze 39:25
plow, and J shall break his clods..... Hos 10:11
will punish J according to his........ Hos 12:2
J fled into the country of Syria,...... Hos 12:12
ye, and testify in the house of J...... Amos 3:13
I abhor the excellency of J........... Amos 6:8
by whom shall J arise................ Amos 7:2
by whom shall J arise................ Amos 7:5
hath sworn by the excellency of J.... Amos 8:7
utterly destroy the house of J........ Amos 9:8
brother J shame shall cover thee..... Obad 10
the house of J shall possess.......... Obad 17
the house of J shall be a fire,........ Obad 18
transgression of J is all this......... Mic 1:5
What is the transgression of J........ Mic 1:5
that art named the house of J........ Mic 2:7
I will surely assemble, O J........... Mic 2:12
Hear, I pray you, O heads of J....... Mic 3:1
of might, to declare unto J his....... Mic 3:8
you, ye heads of the house of J...... Mic 3:9
and to the house of the God of J..... Mic 4:2
the remnant of J shall be in the..... Mic 5:7
the remnant of J shall be among,.... Mic 5:8
Thou wilt perform the truth to J..... Mic 7:20
turned away the excellency of J...... Nah 2:2
out of the tabernacles of J........... Mal 2:12
ye sons of J are not consumed....... Mal 3:6

JACOB'S (ja′-cubs)
1. Refers to Jacob 1.
and said, The voice is J voice......... Gen 27:22
Syrian, the brother of Rebekah, J.... Gen 28:5
J anger was kindled against.......... Gen 30:2
were Laban's, and the stronger J..... Gen 30:42
And Laban went into J tent.......... Gen 31:33
shalt say, They be thy servant J...... Gen 32:18
the hollow of J thigh was out of..... Gen 32:25
he touched the hollow of J thigh..... Gen 32:32
Israel in lying with J daughter....... Gen 34:7
he had defiled J daughter............ Gen 34:7
J firstborn, and Simeon, and Levi,... Gen 35:23
J heart fainted, for he believed...... Gen 45:26
Reuben, J firstborn.................. Gen 46:8
The sons of Rachel J wife............ Gen 46:19
besides J sons' wives, all the........ Gen 46:26
Was not Esau J brother.............. Mal 1:2
Now J well was there................. Jn 4:6
2. Refers to Jacob 3.
it is even the time of J trouble....... Jer 30:7
again the captivity of J tents......... Jer 30:18

JADA (ja′-dah) A grandson of Jerahmeel.
sons of Onam were, Shammai, and J.. 1Chr 2:28
the sons of J the brother of.......... 1Chr 2:32

JADAH See JARAH.

JADAI See JADAU.

JADAU (ja′-daw) Married a foreigner in exile.
Mattithiah, Zabad, Zebina, J........ Ezr 10:43

JADDAI See JADAU.

JADDUA (jad′-du-ah)
1. A Levite.
Meshezabeel, Zadok, J,.............. Neh 10:21
2. A priest.
Jonathan, and Jonathan begat J...... Neh 12:11
Joiada, and Johanan, and J........... Neh 12:22

JADON (ja′-don) A repairer of Jerusalem's wall.
J the Meronothite, the men of........ Neh 3:7

JAEL (ja′-el) The wife of Heber.
of J the wife of Heber the Kenite..... Judg 4:17
J went out to meet Sisera, and...... Judg 4:18
Then J Heber's wife took a nail...... Judg 4:21
J came out to meet him, and said.... Judg 4:22
son of Anath, in the days of J........ Judg 5:6
Blessed above women shall J be...... Judg 5:24

JAGUR (ja′-gur) A town in Judah.
were Kabzeel, and Eder, and J....... Josh 15:21

JAH (jah) See JEHOVAH. A shortened form of Jehovah.
upon the heavens by his name J...... Ps 68:4

JAHALALEEL See JEHALEEL.

JAHATH (ja′-hath)
1. A descendant of Judah.
Reaiah the son of Shobal begat J..... 1Chr 4:2
and J begat Ahumai, and Lahad...... 1Chr 4:2
2. A descendant of Gershom.
J his son, Zimmah his son,........... 1Chr 6:20
The son of J, the son of Gershom,.... 1Chr 6:43
3. Another descendant of Gershom.
the sons of Shimei were, J........... 1Chr 23:10
J was the chief, and Zizah the....... 1Chr 23:11
4. A descendant of Kohath.
the sons of Shelomoth; J............. 1Chr 24:22
5. A descendant of Merari.
and the overseers of them were J.... 2Chr 34:12

JAHAZ (ja′-haz) See JAHAZA, JAHAZAH, JAHZAH.
A Levitical city in Reuben.
and he came to J, and fought........ Num 21:23
and all his people, to fight at J...... Deut 2:32
people together, and pitched in J.... Judg 11:20
voice shall be heard even unto J..... Is 15:4
even unto Elealeh, and even unto J.. Jer 48:34

JAHAZA (ja-ha′-zah) See JAHAZ. Same as Jahaz.
And J, and Kedemoth.................. Josh 13:18

JAHAZAH (ja-ha′-zah) See JAHAZ. Same as Jahaz.
suburbs, and J with her suburbs,.... Josh 21:36
upon Holon, and upon J, and upon... Jer 48:21

JAHAZIAH (ja-ha-zi′-ah) Son of Tikvah.
J the son of Tikvah were employed... Ezr 10:15

JAHAZIEL (ja-ha′-ze-el)
1. A captain in David's army.
and J, and Johanan, and............. 1Chr 12:4
2. A priest.
the priests with trumpets............ 1Chr 16:6
3. A son of Hebron.
the third, and Jekameam the........ 1Chr 23:19
the third, and Jekameam the fourth... 1Chr 24:23
4. A Levite.
Then upon J the son of Zechariah,... 2Chr 20:14
5. A family of exiles.
the son of J, and with him three..... Ezr 8:5

JAHDAI (jah′-dahee) A descendant of Caleb.
And the sons of J..................... 1Chr 2:47

JAHDIEL (jah′-de-el) Head of a family of Manasseh.
and Jeremiah, and Hodaviah, and J.. 1Chr 5:24

JAHDO (jah'-do) *Son of Buz.*
son of Jeshishai, the son of J 1Chr 5:14

JAHLEEL (jah'-le-el) See JAHLEELITES. *A son of Zebulun.*
Sered, and Elon, and .... Gen 46:14
of J, the family of the .... Num 26:26

JAHLEELITES (jah'-le-el-ites) *Descendants of Jahleel.*
of Jahleel, the family of the .... Num 26:26

JAHMAI (jah'-mahee) *A son of Tola.*
and Rephaiah, and Jeriel, and J 1Chr 7:2

JAHZAH (jah'-zah) See JAHAZ. *A Levitical city in Reuben.*
suburbs, and J with her suburbs, ... 1Chr 6:78

JAHZEEL (jah-ze-el) See JAHZEELITES, JAHZIEL. *A son of Naphtali.*
J, and Guni, and Jezer, and Shillem... Gen 46:24
of J, the family of the .... Num 26:48

JAHZEELITES (jah'-ze-el-ites) *Descendants of Jahzeel.*
of Jahzeel, the family of the .... Num 26:48

JAHZEIAH See JAHAZIAH.

JAHZERAH (jah'-ze-rah) See AHAZAI. *The son of Meshullam.*
the son of Adiel, the son of J 1Chr 9:12

JAHZIEL (jah'-ze-el) See JAHZEEL. *Same as Jahzeel*
J, and Guni, and Jezer, and Shallum,.. 1Chr 7:13

JAILER
charging the j to keep them............... Acts 16:23

JAIR (ja'-ur) See HAVOTH-JAIR, JAARE-OREGIM, JAIRITE.
1. A descendant of Judah and Manasseh.
J the son of Manasseh went and......... Num 32:41
J the son of Manasseh took all........... Deut 3:14
towns of J the son of Manasseh 1Kin 4:13
And Segub begat J, who had three 1Chr 2:22
2. A judge.
And after him arose J, a Gileadite ...... Judg 10:3
J died, and was buried in Camon .... Judg 10:5
3. A district in Bashan.
of Bashan, and all the towns of J .... Josh 13:30
and Aram, with the towns of J 1Chr 2:23
4. Father of Mordecai.
name was Mordecai, the son of J .... Est 2:5
5. Father of Elhanan.
Elhanan the son of J slew Lahmi 1Chr 20:5

JAIRITE (ja'-ur-ite) *A descendant of Jair 1.*
Ira also the J was a chief ruler 2Sa 20:26

JAIRUS (ja-i'-rus) *A ruler of a synagogue.*
of the synagogue, J by name .... Mk 5:22
behold, there came a man named J ...... Lk 8:41

JAKAN (ja'-kan) See AKAN, JAAKAN. *A son of Ezer.*
Bilhan, and Zavan, and J 1Chr 1:42

JAKEH (ja'-keh) *Father of Agur.*
The words of Agur the son of J.......... Prov 30:1

JAKIM (ja'-kim)
1. Son of Shimhi.
And J, and Zichri, and Zabdi,........... 1Chr 8:19
2. A sanctuary servant.
to Eliashib, the twelfth to J............. 1Chr 24:12

JAKIN See JACHINITES.

JAKINITE See JACHINITES.

JALAM See JAALAM.

JALON (ja'-lon) *A son of Ezra.*
Jether, and Mered, and Epher, and J... 1Chr 4:17

JAMBRES (jam'-brees) *An opponent of Moses.*
J withstood Moses, so do these........... 2Ti 3:8

JAMES (james) See JACOB.
1. Son of Zebedee.
J the son of Zebedee, and John his...... Mt 4:21
J the son of Zebedee, and John his...... Mt 10:2
six days Jesus taketh Peter, J.......... Mt 17:1
he saw J the son of Zebedee, and....... Mk 1:19
house of Simon and Andrew, with J..... Mk 1:29
And J the son of .... Mk 3:17
and John the brother of J .... Mk 3:17
and J, and John the brother of J .... Mk 5:37
Jesus taketh with him Peter, and ...... Mk 9:2
And J and John, the sons of Zebedee .. Mk 10:35
but to be much displeased with J .... Mk 10:41
against the temple, Peter and J .... Mk 13:3
And he taketh with him Peter and J.... Mk 14:33
And so was also J, and John, the....... Lk 5:10
Peter, and Andrew his brother, J .... Lk 6:14
no man to go in, save Peter, and J ...... Lk 8:51
he took Peter and John and J .... Lk 9:28
and his disciples J and John............. Acts 1:13
where abode both Peter, and J........... Acts 1:13
he killed J the brother of John.......... Acts 12:2
2. Son of Alphaeus.
J the son of Alphaeus, and .... Mt 10:3
J the son of Alphaeus, and .... Mk 3:18
J the son of Alphaeus, and .... Lk 6:15
J the son of Alphaeus, and Simon ...... Acts 1:13
3. Brother of Jesus.
and his brethren, J, and Joses, and..... Mt 13:55

and Mary the mother of J and Joses... Mt 27:56
the son of Mary, the brother of J .... Mk 6:3
and Mary the mother of J the less ...... Mk 15:40
and Mary the mother of J, and.......... Mk 16:1
And Judas the brother of J .... Lk 6:16
Joanna, and Mary the mother of J ...... Lk 24:10
and Judas the brother of J .... Acts 1:13
said, Go shew these things unto J .... Acts 12:17
J answered, saying, Men and .... Acts 15:13
Paul went in with us unto J .... Acts 21:18
After that, he was seen of J 1Cor 15:7
save J the Lord's brother .... Gal 1:19
And when J, Cephas, and John, who..... Gal 2:9
before that certain came from J .... Gal 2:12
J, a servant of God and of the .... Jas 1:1
of Jesus Christ, and brother of J .... Jude 1

JAMIN (ja'-min) See JAMINITES.
1. A son of Simeon.
Jemuel, and J, and Ohad, and Jachin, Gen 46:10
Jemuel, and J, and Ohad, and Jachin,.. Ex 6:15
of J, the family of the Jaminites........ Num 26:12
sons of Simeon were, Nemuel, and J... 1Chr 4:24
2. A descendant of Hezron.
of Jerahmeel were, Maaz, and J 1Chr 2:27
3. A priest.
Jeshua, and Bani, and Sherebiah,...... Neh 8:7

JAMINITES (ja'-min-ites) *Descendants of Jamin.*
of Jamin, the family of the J .... Num 26:12

JAMLECH (jam'-lek) *A royal descendant of Simeon.*
and J and Joshah the 1Chr 4:34

JANAI See JAANAI.

JANGLING
have turned aside unto vain j 1Ti 1:6

JANNA (jan'-nah) *Father of Melchi; ancestor of Jesus.*
of Melchi, which was the son of J .... Lk 3:24

JANNAI See JANNA.

JANNES (jan'-nees) *An opponent of Moses.*
Now as J and Jambres withstood........ 2Ti 3:8

JANOAH (ja-no'-ah) See JANOHAH. *A city in Naphtali.*
Ijon, and Abel-beth-maachah, and J ... 2Kin 15:29

JANOHAH (ja-no'-hah) See JANOAH. *A city between Ephraim and Manasseh.*
and passed by it on the east to J .... Josh 16:6
And it went down from J to Ataroth... Josh 16:7

JANUM (ja'-num) *A city in Judah.*
And J, and Beth-tappuah .... Josh 15:53

JAPHETH (ja'-feth) *A son of Noah.*
and Noah begat Shem, Ham, and J ..... Gen 5:32
begat three sons, Shem, Ham, and...... Gen 6:10
Noah, and Shem, and Ham, and J ...... Gen 7:13
the ark, were Shem, and Ham, and J ... Gen 9:18
J took a garment, and laid it upon...... Gen 9:23
God shall enlarge J, and he shall........ Gen 9:27
the sons of Noah, Shem, Ham, and J... Gen 10:1
The sons of J; Gomer .... Gen 10:2
Eber, the brother of J the elder......... Gen 10:21
Noah, Shem, Ham, and J 1Chr 1:4
The sons of J; Gomer 1Chr 1:5

JAPHIA (ja-fi'-ah)
1. An Amorite king.
unto J king of Lachish, and unto........ Josh 10:3
2. A town in Zebulun.
out to Daberath, and goeth up to J ..... Josh 19:12
3. A son of David.
also, and Elishua, and Nepheg, and J ... 2Sa 5:15
And Nogah, and Nepheg, and J 1Chr 3:7
And Nogah, and Nepheg, and J 1Chr 14:6

JAPHLET (jaf'-let) See JAPHLETI. *A grandson of Beriah.*
And Heber begat J, and Shomer, and.. 1Chr 7:32
And the sons of J 1Chr 7:33
These are the children of J 1Chr 7:33

JAPHLETI (jaf-let-i) See JAPHLET. *A landmark in Ephraim.*
down westward to the coast of J .... Josh 16:3

JAPHLETITES See JAPHLETI.

JAPHO (ja'-fo) See JOPPA. *A city in Dan.*
Rakkon, with the border before J .... Josh 19:46

JARAH (ja'-rah) See JEHOADAH. *A son of Ahaz.*
And Ahaz begat J 1Chr 9:42
and J begat Alemeth, and Azmaveth, and. 1Chr 9:42

JAREB (ja'-reb) *An Assyrian king.*
the Assyrian, and sent to king J .... Hos 5:13
Assyria for a present to king J .... Hos 10:6

JARED (ja'-red) See JERED.
1. A descendant of Seth.
sixty and five years, and begat J .... Gen 5:15
after he begat J eight hundred........... Gen 5:16
J lived an hundred sixty and two .... Gen 5:18
J lived after he begat Enoch .... Gen 5:19
all the days of J were nine .... Gen 5:20
2. Father of Enoch; ancestor of Jesus.
of Enoch, which was the son of J .... Lk 3:37

JARESIAH *A descendant of Benjamin.*
And J, and Eliah, and Zichri, the 1Chr 8:27

JARHA (jar'-hah) *An Egyptian servant.*
an Egyptian, whose name was J......... 1Chr 2:34
daughter to J his servant to wife 1Chr 2:35

JARIB (ja'-rib) See JACHIN.
1. A son of Simeon.
Simeon were, Nemuel, and Jamin, J... 1Chr 4:24
2. One of exiles.
and for Elnathan, and for J.............. Ezr 8:16
3. Married a foreigner.
Maaseiah, and Eliezer, and J............ Ezr 10:18

JARMUTH (jar'-muth) See REMETH.
1. A city in Judah.
Hebron, and unto Piram king of J ...... Josh 10:3
the king of Hebron, the king of J .... Josh 10:5
the king of Hebron, the king of J .... Josh 10:23
The king of J, one.......................... Josh 12:11
J, and Adullam, Socoh, and Azekah,.. Josh 15:35
J with her suburbs, En-gannim .... Josh 21:29
En-rimmon, and at Zareah, and at J ... Neh 11:29
2. A Levitical city.
the son of Huri, the son of J 1Chr 5:14

JAROAH (ja-ro'-ah) *A descendant of Gad.*
the son of Huri, the son of J 1Chr 5:14

JASHAR See JASHER.

JASHEN (ja'-shen) See HASHEM. *Father of several "mighty men" of David.*
the Shaalbonite, of the sons of 2Sa 23:32

JASHER (ja'-shur) *A book of songs.*
not this written in the book of J .... Josh 10:13
it is written in the book of J 2Sa 1:18

JASHOBEAM (jash-o'-be-am)
1. A "mighty man" of David.
J, a Hachmonite, the chief of the....... 1Chr 11:11
month was J the son of Zabdiel......... 1Chr 27:2
2. Another "mighty man" of David.
and Azareel, and Joezer, and J 1Chr 12:6

JASHUB (ja'-shub) See JASHUBI-LEHEM, JOB, JASHUBITES, SHEAR-JASHUB.
1. A son of Issachar.
Of J, the family of the.................... Num 26:24
Issachar were, Tola, and Puah, J 1Chr 7:1
2. Married a foreigner in exile.
Meshullam, Malluch, and Adaiah, J ... Ezr 10:29

JASHUBI-LEHEM See JASHUBI-LEHEM.

JASHUBI-LEHEM (jash'-u-bi-le'-hem) *A descendant of Shelah.*
had the dominion in Moab, and J 1Chr 4:22

JASHUBITES (jash'-u-bites) *Descendants of Jashub.*
Of Jashub, the family of the J .... Num 26:24

JASIEL (ja-se-el) *A "mighty man" of David.*
and Obed, and J the Mesobaite......... 1Chr 11:47

JASON (ja'-sun)
1. A Christian in Thessalonica.
and assaulted the house of J .... Acts 17:5
they found them not, they drew J .... Acts 17:6
Whom J hath received: .... Acts 17:7
when they had taken security of J ...... Acts 17:9
2. A relative of Paul.
my worldfellow, and Lucius, and J ..... Rom 16:21

JASPER
row a beryl, and an onyx, and a j....... Ex 28:20
row a beryl, an onyx, and a j .... Ex 39:13
the beryl, the onyx, and the j .... Eze 28:13
precious, even like a j stone .... Rev 4:3
of the wall of it was of j .... Rev 21:18
The first foundation was j .... Rev 21:19

JATHNIEL (jath'-ne-el) *A son of Meshelemiah.*
Zebadiah the third, J the fourth,....... 1Chr 26:2

JATTIR (jat'-tur) *A Levitical city in Judah.*
And in the mountains, Shamir, and J ... Josh 15:48
J with her suburbs, and Eshtemoa..... Josh 21:14
and to them which were in J 1Sa 30:27
and Libnah with her suburbs, and J ... 1Chr 6:57

JAVAN (ja'-van)
1. A son of Japheth.
Gomer, and Magog, and Madai, and... Gen 10:2
And the sons of J........................... Gen 10:4
Gomer, and Magog, and Madai, and J. 1Chr 1:5
And the sons of J........................... 1Chr 1:7
2. Descendants of Javan 1.
that drew the bow, to Tubal, and J..... Is 66:19
3. A city in southern Arabia.
J, Tubal, and Meshech, they were...... Eze 27:13
J going to and fro occupied in thy...... Eze 27:19

JAVELIN
and took a j in his hand.................. Num 25:7
there was a j in Saul's hand 1Sa 18:10
And Saul cast the j 1Sa 18:11
his house with his j in his hand 1Sa 19:9
David even to the wall with the j 1Sa 19:10
he smote the j into the wall 1Sa 19:10
Saul cast a j at him to smite him 1Sa 20:33

JAW
with the j of an ass have I slain .... Judg 15:16
an hollow place that was in the j .... Judg 15:19
or bore his j through with a............. Job 41:2
their j teeth as knives, to .... Prov 30:14

JAWBONE
And he found a new j of an ass.......... Judg 15:15
With the j of an ass, heaps upon....... Judg 15:16
cast away the j out of his hand.......... Judg 15:17

JAWS
I brake the j of the wicked, and........ Job 29:17
and my tongue cleaveth to my j......... Ps 22:15
a bridle in the j of the people........... Is 30:28
But I will put hooks in thy j............. Eze 29:4
back, and put hooks into thy j........... Eze 38:4
that take off the yoke on their j........ Hos 11:4

JAZER (ja'-zur) See JAAZER. A Levitical city in
Gad.
and when they saw the land of J...... Num 32:1
Ataroth, and Dibon, and J, and...... Num 32:3
And their coast was J, and all the..... Josh 13:25
her suburbs, J with her suburbs....... Josh 21:39
of the river of Gad, and toward J..... 2Sa 24:5
suburbs, and J with her suburbs...... 1Chr 6:81
men of valour at J of.................... 1Chr 26:31
they are come even unto J............. Is 16:8
weeping of J the vine of Sibmah...... Is 16:9
for thee with the weeping of J......... Jer 48:32
they reach even to the sea of J....... Jer 48:32

JAZIZ (ja'-ziz) Overseer of David's flocks.
the flocks was J the Hagerite........... 1Chr 27:31

JEALOUS
for I the LORD thy God am a j God... Ex 20:5
whose name is J, is a j God............. Ex 34:14
he be j of his wife, and she be........ Num 5:14
he be j of his wife, and she be......... Num 5:14
he be j over his wife, and shall....... Num 5:30
is a consuming fire, even a j God..... Deut 4:24
for I the LORD thy God am a j God.... Deut 5:9
(For the LORD thy God is a j God...... Deut 6:15
he is a j God............................. Josh 24:19
I have been very j for the LORD...... 1Kin 19:10
I have been very j for the LORD...... 1Kin 19:14
will be j for my holy name............. Eze 39:25
will the LORD be j for his land........ Joel 2:18
God is j, and the LORD revengeth.... Nah 1:2
I am j for Jerusalem and for Zion..... Zec 1:14
I was j for Zion with great............. Zec 8:2
I was j for her with great fury......... Zec 8:2
For I am j over you with godly........ 2Cor 11:2

JEALOUSIES
This is the law of j, when a wife....... Num 5:29

JEALOUSY
And the spirit of j come upon him..... Num 5:14
if the spirit of j come upon him....... Num 5:14
for it is an offering of j................. Num 5:15
hands, which is the j offering.......... Num 5:15
the j offering out of the woman's..... Num 5:25
the spirit of j cometh upon him....... Num 5:30
the children of Israel in my j.......... Num 25:11
they shall smoke against that........ Deut 29:20
him to j with strange gods............ Deut 32:16
They have moved me to j with that.. Deut 32:21
I will move them to j with those...... Deut 32:21
they provoked him to j with their.... 1Kin 14:22
moved him to j with their graven.... Ps 78:58
shall thy j burn like fire................ Ps 79:5
For j is the rage of a man.............. Prov 6:34
is cruel as the grave.................... Song 8:6
he shall stir up j like a man of........ Is 42:13
of j, which provoketh to j............. Eze 8:3
this image of j in the entry........... Eze 8:5
will give thee blood in fury and j..... Eze 16:38
my j shall depart from thee, and I... Eze 16:42
And I will set my j against thee...... Eze 23:25
Surely in the fire of my j have I...... Eze 36:5
Behold, I have spoken in my j........ Eze 36:6
For in my j and in the fire of my..... Eze 38:19
be devoured by the fire of his j...... Zeph 1:18
be devoured with the fire of my..... Zeph 3:8
and for Zion with a great j............. Zec 1:14
was jealous for Zion with great j..... Zec 8:2
I will provoke you to j by them....... Rom 10:19
for to provoke them to j................ Rom 11:11
Do we provoke the Lord to j.......... 1Cor 10:22
am jealous over you with godly...... 2Cor 11:2

JEARIM (je'-a-rim) See KIRJATH-JEARIM. A
mountain in Judah.
along unto the side of mount J........ Josh 15:10

JEATERAI (je-at'-e-rahee) A descendant of
Gershom.
his son, Zerah his son, J his son...... 1Chr 6:21

JEATHERAI See JEATERAI.

JEBERECHIAH (je-ber'-e-ki'-ah) Father of
Zechariah.
priest, and Zechariah the son of J..... Is 8:2

JEBEREKIAH See JEBERECHIAH.

JEBUS (je'-bus) See JEBUSI, JEBUSITE,
JERUSALEM. Original name of Jerusalem.
departed, and came over against J.... Judg 19:10
And when they were by J, the day..... Judg 19:11
went to Jerusalem, which is J.......... 1Chr 11:4
inhabitants of J said to David.......... 1Chr 11:5

JEBUSI (jeb'-u-si) See JEBUSITE. Same as Jebus.
to the side of J on the south............ Josh 18:16
And Zelah, Eleph, and J, which is..... Josh 18:28

JEBUSITE (jeb'-u-site) See JEBUSITES.
Descendant of Canaan.
And the J, and the Amorite, and the.. Gen 10:16
Perizzite, the Hivite, and the J........ Ex 33:2
and the Hivite, and the J............... Ex 34:11
Perizzite, the Hivite, and the J........ Josh 9:1
the J in the mountains, and to the.... Josh 11:3
unto the south side of the J............ Josh 15:8
threshingplace of Araunah the J...... 2Sa 24:16
threshingfloor of Araunah the J....... 2Sa 24:18
The J also, and the Amorite, and..... 1Chr 11:4
the threshingfloor of Ornan the J..... 1Chr 21:15
the threshingfloor of Ornan the J..... 1Chr 21:18
the threshingfloor of Ornan the J..... 1Chr 21:28
in Judah, and Ekron as a J.............. Zec 9:7

JEBUSITES (jeb'-u-sites)
and the Girgashites, and the J........ Gen 15:21
and the Hivites, and the J.............. Ex 3:8
and the Hivites, and the J.............. Ex 3:17
and the Hivites, and the J.............. Ex 13:5
Canaanites, the Hivites, and the J.... Ex 23:23
and the Hittites, and the J............. Num 13:29
and the Hivites, and the J.............. Deut 7:1
Perizzites, the Hivites, and the J..... Deut 20:17
and the Amorites, and the J........... Josh 3:10
Perizzites, the Hivites, and the J.... Josh 12:8
As for the J the inhabitants of........ Josh 15:63
but the J dwell with the children..... Josh 15:63
the Hivites, and the J................... Josh 24:11
the J that inhabited Jerusalem....... Judg 1:21
but the J dwell with the children.... Judg 1:21
and Perizzites, and Hivites, and J... Judg 3:5
turn in into this city of J............... Judg 19:11
men went to Jerusalem unto the J... 2Sa 5:6
to the gutter, and smiteth the J...... 2Sa 5:8
Perizzites, Hivites, and J.............. 1Kin 9:20
where the J were, the inhabitants... 1Chr 11:4
the first shall be chief................. 1Chr 11:6
and the Hivites, and the J............. 2Chr 8:7
Hittites, the Perizzites, the J......... Ezr 9:1
and the Perizzites, and the J......... Neh 9:8

JECAMIAH (jek-a-mi'-ah) See JEKAMIAH. A son
of Jeconiah.
also, and Pedaiah, and Shenazar,... 1Chr 3:18

JECHILIAH See JECHOLIAH.

JECHOLIAH (jek-o-li'-ah) See JECOLIAH.
Mother of Uzziah.
mother's name was J of Jerusalem... 2Kin 15:2

JECHONIAS (jek-o-ni'-as) See JECONIAH. Greek
form of Jeconiah.
And Josias begat J and his brethren... Mt 1:11
to Babylon, J begat Salathiel.......... Mt 1:12

JECOLIAH (jek-o-li'-ah) See JECHOLIAH. Same
as Jecholiah.
name also was J of Jerusalem.......... 2Chr 26:3

JECONIAH (jek-o-ni'-ah) See CONIAH,
JECHONIAS, JEHOIACHIN. A king of Judah.
J his son, Zedekiah his son............ 1Chr 3:16
And the sons of J......................... 1Chr 3:17
carried away with J king of Judah.... Est 2:6
had carried away captive J the...... Jer 24:1
J the son of Jehoiakim king of........ Jer 27:20
J the son of Jehoiakim king of........ Jer 28:4
(After that J the king, and the........ Jer 29:2

JEDAIAH (jed-a-i'-ah)
1. A descendant of Simeon.
the son of Allon, the son of J.......... 1Chr 4:37
2. A rebuilder of Jerusalem's wall.
repaired J the son of Harumaph...... Neh 3:10
3. A priest in Jerusalem.
J, and Jehoiarib, and Jachin......... 1Chr 9:10
to Jehoiarib, the second to J......... 1Chr 24:7
the children of J, of the house....... Ezr 2:36
the children of J, of the house....... Neh 7:39
4. A family of exiles.
J the son of Joiarib, Jachin........... Neh 11:10
Shemaiah, and Joiarib, J.............. Neh 12:6
Mattenai; of J, Uzzi..................... Neh 12:19
of Heldai, of Tobijah, and of J....... Zec 6:10
to Helem, and to Tobijah, and to J... Zec 6:14
5. A priest.
Sallu, Amok, Hilkiah, J................ Neh 12:7
of J, Nethaneel......................... Neh 12:21

JEDIAEL (jed-e-a'-el)
1. A son of Benjamin.
Bela, and Becher, and J, three....... 1Chr 7:6
The sons also of J...................... 1Chr 7:10
All these the sons of J, by the........ 1Chr 7:11
2. A "mighty man" of David.
J the son of Shimri, and Joha his... 1Chr 11:45
3. A warrior in David's army.
Adnah, and Jozabad, and J........... 1Chr 12:20
4. Son of Meshelemiah.
the second, Zebadiah the third...... 1Chr 26:2

JEDIDAH (jed-i'-dah) Mother of King Josiah.
And his mother's name was J.......... 2Kin 22:1

JEDIDIAH (jed-i-di'-ah) Another name for
Solomon.
he called his name J, because........ 2Sa 12:25

JEDUTHUN (jed'-u-thun) A Levite.
the son of Galal, the son of J.......... 1Chr 9:16
Obed-edom also the son of J.......... 1Chr 16:38
with them Heman and J................. 1Chr 16:41
J with trumpets and cymbals for..... 1Chr 16:42
the sons of J were porters............. 1Chr 16:42
of Asaph, and Heman, and of J...... 1Chr 25:1
Of J: the sons of J....................... 1Chr 25:3
under the hands of their father J.... 1Chr 25:3
to the king's order to Asaph, J....... 1Chr 25:6
of them of Asaph, of Heman, of J.... 2Chr 5:12
and of the sons of J..................... 2Chr 29:14
and Heman, and J the king's seer.... 2Chr 35:15
the son of Galal, the son of J......... Neh 11:17
To the chief Musician, even to J...... Ps 39:t
To the chief Musician, to J............. Ps 62:t
To the chief Musician, to J............. Ps 77:t

JEEZER (je-e'-zur) See ABIEZER, JEEZERITES. A
son of Gilead.
of J: the family of the................... Num 26:30

JEEZERITES (je-e'-zur-ites) Descendants of
Jeezer.
of Jeezer, the family of the............ Num 26:30

JEGAR-SAHADUTHA
And Laban called it J.................... Gen 31:47

JEHALELEEL (je-hal-e'-le-el) See JEHALELEL.
A descendant of Judah.
And the sons of J........................ 1Chr 4:16

JEHALELEL (je-hal'-e-lel) See JEHALELEEL. A
descendant of Merari.
of Abdi, and Azariah the son of J.... 2Chr 29:12

JEHALLELEL See JEHALELEL.

JEHDEIAH (jeh-di'-ah)
1. A sanctuary servant.
the sons of Shubael; J.................. 1Chr 24:20
2. A herdsman of David.
the asses was J the Meronothite..... 1Chr 27:30

JEHEZEKEL (je-hez'-e-kel) See EZEKIEL. A
sanctuary servant.
to Pethahiah, the twentieth to J...... 1Chr 24:16

JEHEZKEL See JEHEZEKEL.

JEHIAH (je-hi'-ah) See JEHIEL. A priest.
J were doorkeepers for the ark....... 1Chr 15:24

JEHIEL (je-hi'-el) See JEHIAH, JEIEL, JEHIELI
1. A Levite.
and Jaaziel, and Shemiramoth, and J 1Chr 15:18
and Aziel, and Shemiramoth, and J.. 1Chr 15:20
Jeiel, and Shemiramoth, and J....... 1Chr 16:5
2. A Gershonite.
the chief was J, and Zetham, and.... 1Chr 23:8
by the hand of J the Gershonite..... 1Chr 29:8
3. A friend of David's son.
J the son of Hachmoni was with..... 1Chr 27:32
4. Son of King Jehoshaphat.
of Jehoshaphat, Azariah, and J...... 2Chr 21:2
5. A son of Heman.
sons of Heman; J, and Shimei....... 1Chr 29:14
6. A Levite in Hezekiah's time.
J, and Azaziah, and Nahath.......... 2Chr 31:13
7. A chief priest.
Hilkiah and Zechariah and J.......... 2Chr 35:8
8. A family of exiles.
Obadiah the son of J, and with him... Ezr 8:9
9. The father of Shechaniah.
And Shechaniah the son of J.......... Ezr 10:2
10. A son of Harim.
and Elijah, and Shemaiah, and J..... Ezr 10:21
11. A man of Elam's family who married a
foreigner.
Mattaniah, Zechariah, and J.......... Ezr 10:26
12. Father of Obadiah.
dwelt the father of Gibeon, J......... 1Chr 9:35
13. A "mighty man" of David.
J the sons of Hothan the Aroerite.... 1Chr 11:44

JEHIELI (je-hi'-el-i) See JEHIEL. A sanctuary
servant.
of Laadan the Gershonite, were J.... 1Chr 26:21
The sons of J; Zetham, and........... 1Chr 26:22

JEHIELITES See JEHIELI.

JEHIZKIAH (je-hiz-ki'-ah) See HEZEKIAH. A
son of Shallum.
the son of Shallum, and Amasa...... 2Chr 28:12

JEHOADAH (je-ho'-a-dah) See JARAH. Son of
Ahaz.
And Ahaz begat J........................ 1Chr 8:36
J begat Alemeth, and Azmaveth, and 1Chr 8:36

JEHOADDAH See JEHOADAH.

JEHOADDAN (je-ho-ad'-dan) Mother of King
Amaziah.
mother's name was J of Jerusalem... 2Kin 14:2
mother's name was J of Jerusalem... 2Chr 25:1

JEHOADDIN See JEHOADDAN.

JEHOAHAZ (je-ho'-a-haz) See AHAZIAH,
JOAHAZ, SHALLUM.
1. Son of King Jehu.
his son reigned in his stead........... 2Kin 10:35
son of Ahaziah king of Judah J....... 2Kin 13:1
J besought the LORD, and the LORD.. 2Kin 13:4
people to J but fifty horsemen........ 2Kin 13:7
Now the rest of the acts of J.......... 2Kin 13:8
And J slept with his fathers........... 2Kin 13:9
Judah began Jehoash the son of J... 2Kin 13:10
Israel all the days of J.................. 2Kin 13:22
Jehoash the son of J took again...... 2Kin 13:25

the hand of J his father by war 2Kin 13:25
J king of Israel reigned Amaziah 2Kin 14:1
the son of J son of Jehu, king of 2Kin 14:8
the death of Jehoash son of J 2Kin 14:17
and sent to Joash, the son of J 2Chr 25:17
of J king of Israel fifteen years 2Chr 25:25
   2. Son of King Josiah.
the land took J the son of Josiah 2Kin 23:30
J was twenty and three years old........ 2Kin 23:31
name to Jehoiakim, and took J away .. 2Kin 23:34
J was twenty and three years old 2Chr 36:2
Necho took J his brother, and 2Chr 36:4
   3. A son of King Jehoram.
was never a son left him, save J 2Chr 21:17
the son of Joash, the son of J 2Chr 25:23

JEHOASH (je-ho'-ash) See JOASH.
   1. A king of Judah.
Seven years old was J when he 2Kin 11:21
year of Jehu J began to reign 2Kin 12:1
J did that which was right in the 2Kin 12:2
J said to the priests, All the 2Kin 12:4
twentieth year of king J the 2Kin 12:6
Then king J called for Jehoiada 2Kin 12:7
J king of Judah took all the 2Kin 12:18
the son of J the son of Ahaziah, ... 2Kin 14:13
   2. A king of Israel.
J the son of Jehoahaz to reign............ 2Kin 13:10
J the son of Jehoahaz took again........ 2Kin 13:25
Then Amaziah sent messengers to J .. 2Kin 14:8
J the king of Israel sent to 2Kin 14:9
Therefore J king of Israel went 2Kin 14:11
J king of Israel took Amaziah 2Kin 14:13
of the acts of J which he did 2Kin 14:15
J slept with his fathers, and was 2Kin 14:16
J son of Jehoahaz king of Israel 2Kin 14:17

JEHOHANAN (je-ho'-ha-nan)
   1. A sanctuary servant.
the sixth, Elioenai the seventh 1Chr 26:3
   2. A chief captain.
And next to him was J the captain 2Chr 17:15
   3. Father of Ishmael.
Jeroham, and Ishmael the son of J 2Chr 23:1
   4. Married a foreigner in exile.
J, Hananiah, Zabbai, and Athlai........ Ezr 10:28
   5. A priest in exile.
Meshullam; of Amariah, J .... Neh 12:13
   6. A priest who dedicated the wall.
and Eleazar, and Uzzi, and J .... Neh 12:42

JEHOIACHIN (je-hoy'-a-kin) See CONIAH,
JECONIAH, JECONIAS, JEHOIACHIN'S. A king of
Judah.
J his son reigned in his stead 2Kin 24:6
J was eighteen years old when he........ 2Kin 24:8
the king of Judah went out to.............. 2Kin 24:12
And he carried away J to Babylon 2Kin 24:15
the captivity of J king of Judah 2Kin 25:27
of J king of Judah out of prison 2Kin 25:27
J his son reigned in his stead 2Chr 36:8
J was eight years old when he 2Chr 36:9
the captivity of J king of Judah .... Jer 52:31
up the head of J king of Judah .... Jer 52:31

JEHOIACHIN'S (je-hoy'-a-kins)
fifth year of J captivity.................... Eze 1:2

JEHOIADA (je-hoy'-a-dah) See BERECHIAS,
JOIADA.
   1. Father of Benaiah.
Benaiah the son of J was over 2Sa 8:18
Benaiah the son of J was over the 2Sa 20:23
And Benaiah the son of J, and 2Sa 23:20
things did Benaiah the son of J 2Sa 23:22
priest, and Benaiah the son of J 1Kin 1:8
priest, and Benaiah the son of J 1Kin 1:26
prophet, and Benaiah the son of J 1Kin 1:32
the son of J answered the king 1Kin 1:36
prophet, and Benaiah the son of J 1Kin 1:38
prophet, and Benaiah the son of J 1Kin 1:44
the hand of Benaiah the son of J 1Kin 2:25
Solomon sent Benaiah the son of J .. 1Kin 2:29
So Benaiah the son of J went up........ 1Kin 2:34
of J in his room over the host............ 1Kin 2:35
commanded Benaiah the son of J 1Kin 2:46
the son of J was over the host............ 1Kin 4:4
Benaiah the son of J was over the 1Chr 11:22
things did Benaiah the son of J 1Chr 11:24
Benaiah the son of J was over the 1Chr 18:17
month was Benaiah the son of J 1Chr 27:5
   2. A high priest.
And the seventh year J sent............ 2Kin 11:4
that J the priest commanded 2Kin 11:9
sabbath, and came to J the priest 2Kin 11:9
But J the priest commanded the...... 2Kin 11:15
J made a covenant between the 2Kin 11:17
J the priest instructed him 2Kin 12:2
Jehoash called for J the priest.......... 2Kin 12:7
But J the priest took a chest, and 2Kin 12:9
Jehoram, the wife of J the priest...... 2Chr 22:11
And in the seventh year J 2Chr 23:1
that J the priest had commanded 2Chr 23:8
J the priest dismissed not................ 2Chr 23:8
Moreover J the priest delivered 2Chr 23:9
J and his sons anointed him 2Chr 23:11
Then J the priest brought out the 2Chr 23:14
J made a covenant between................ 2Chr 23:16
Also J appointed the offices of 2Chr 23:18
LORD all the days of J the priest...... 2Chr 24:2
And J took for him two wives............ 2Chr 24:3
the king called for J the chief 2Chr 24:6
J gave it to such as did the work...... 2Chr 24:12

of the money before the king and J.... 2Chr 24:14
continually all the days of J.............. 2Chr 24:14
But J waxed old, and was full of........ 2Chr 24:15
Now after the death of J came.......... 2Chr 24:17
for the kindness which J his............ 2Chr 24:20
not the kindness which J his............ 2Chr 24:22
blood of the sons of J........................ 2Chr 24:25
   3. A captain in David's army.
J was the leader of the Aaronites 1Chr 12:27
   4. Son of Benaiah.
was J the son of Benaiah, and 1Chr 27:34
   5. A rebuilder of Jerusalem's wall.
gate repaired J the son of Paseah...... Neh 3:6
   6. A pre-exilic priest.
in the stead of J the priest .... Jer 29:26

JEHOIAKIM (je-hoy'-a-kim) See ELIAKIM,
JOIAKIM. A king of Judah.
father, and turned his name to J 2Kin 23:34
J gave the silver and the gold to 2Kin 23:35
J was twenty and five years old 2Kin 23:36
J became his servant three years 2Kin 24:1
Now the rest of the acts of J 2Kin 24:5
So J slept with his fathers.................. 2Kin 24:6
according to all that J had done........ 2Kin 24:19
firstborn Johanan, the second J 1Chr 3:15
And the sons of J 1Chr 3:16
and turned his name to J.................... 2Chr 36:4
J was twenty and five years old 2Chr 36:5
Now the rest of the acts of J 2Chr 36:8
it came also in the days of J .... Jer 1:3
thus saith the LORD concerning J...... Jer 22:18
though Coniah the son of J king........ Jer 22:24
the son of J king of Judah .... Jer 24:1
of Judah in the fourth year of J .... Jer 25:1
the beginning of the reign of J .... Jer 26:1
when J the king, with all his .... Jer 26:21
J the king sent men unto Egypt, ... Jer 26:22
and brought him unto J the king .... Jer 26:23
the beginning of the reign of J .... Jer 27:1
captive Jeconiah the son of J .... Jer 27:20
the son of J king of Judah .... Jer 28:4
from the Lord in the days of J .... Jer 35:1
to pass in the fourth year of J .... Jer 36:1
to pass in the fifth year of J .... Jer 36:9
which J the king of Judah hath........ Jer 36:28
thou shalt say to J king of Judah...... Jer 36:29
saith the LORD of J king of Judah .... Jer 36:30
the son of J king of Judah .... Jer 36:32
instead of Coniah the son of J.......... Jer 37:1
in the fourth year of J the son .... Jer 45:1
smote in the fourth year of J .... Jer 46:2
according to all that J had done........ Dan 1:1
the reign of J king of Judah came .... Dan 1:1
the Lord gave J king of Judah .... Dan 1:2

JEHOIARIB (je-hoy'-a-rib) See JOIARIB.
   1. A priest.
Jedaiah, and J, and Jachin,.............. 1Chr 9:10
   2. A sanctuary servant.
Now the first lot came forth to J 1Chr 24:7

JEHONADAB (je-hon'-a-dab) See JONADAB. A
son of Rechab.
he lighted on J the son of Rechab...... 2Kin 10:15
And J answered, It is,........................ 2Kin 10:15
The son of Rechab, into the 2Kin 10:15

JEHONATHAN (je-hon'-a-than) See JONATHAN.
   1. A storehouse servant.
castles, was J the son of Uzziah........ 1Chr 27:25
   2. A Levite teacher.
and Asahel, and Shemiramoth, and J.. 2Chr 17:8
of Shemaiah, J............................... Neh 12:18

JEHORAM (je-ho'-ram) See HADORAM, JORAM.
   1. A king of Judah.
J his son reigned in his stead 1Kin 22:50
J the son of Jehoshaphat king of 2Kin 1:17
J the son of Jehoshaphat king of 2Kin 8:16
of J king of Judah began to reign 2Kin 8:25
Ahaziah the son of J king of 2Kin 8:29
things that Jehoshaphat, and J 2Chr 21:1
J the son of Jehoshaphat.................. 2Chr 21:3
but the kingdom gave he to J 2Chr 21:3
Now when J was risen up to the 2Chr 21:4
J was thirty and two years old.......... 2Chr 21:5
Then J went forth with his 2Chr 21:9
the Lord wrought up against J the 2Chr 21:16
son of J king of Judah reigned 2Chr 22:1
Azariah the son of J king of 2Chr 22:6
the daughter of king J, the wife 2Chr 22:11
   2. A son of Ahab.
J reigned in his stead in the.............. 2Kin 1:17
Now J the son of Ahab began to...... 2Kin 3:1
king J went out of Samaria the........ 2Kin 3:6
smote J between his arms, and the .. 2Kin 9:24
went with J the son of Ahab king.... 2Chr 22:5
see J the son of Ahab at Jezreel........ 2Chr 22:6
he went out with J against Jehu...... 2Chr 22:7
   3. A priest.
and with them Elishama and J 2Chr 17:8

JEHOSHABEATH (je-ho-shab'-e-ath) See
JEHOSHEBA. A daughter of King Jehoram.
But J, the daughter of the king,........ 2Chr 22:11
So J, the daughter of king 2Chr 22:11

JEHOSHAPHAT (je-hosh'-a-fat) See JOSAPHAT,
JOSAPHAT.
   1. David's recorder.
J the son of Ahilud was recorder...... 2Sa 8:16

J the son of Ahilud was recorder........ 2Sa 20:24
J the son of Ahilud, the recorder...... 1Kin 4:3
J the son of Ahilud, recorder............ 1Kin 18:15
   2. An officer of Solomon.
the son of Paruah, in Issachar 1Kin 4:17
   3. A king of Judah.
J his son reigned in his stead 1Kin 15:24
that J the king of Judah came 1Kin 22:2
And he said unto J, Wilt thou go...... 1Kin 22:4
J said to the king of Israel, I............ 1Kin 22:4
J said unto the king of Israel,.......... 1Kin 22:5
J said, Is there not here a.................. 1Kin 22:7
And the king of Israel said unto J 1Kin 22:8
J said, Let not the king say.............. 1Kin 22:8
J the king of Judah sat each on 1Kin 22:10
And the king of Israel said unto J 1Kin 22:18
the king of Judah went up to 1Kin 22:29
And the king of Israel said unto J 1Kin 22:30
captains of the chariots saw J 1Kin 22:32
and J cried out 1Kin 22:32
J the son of Asa began to reign........ 1Kin 22:41
J was thirty and five years old.......... 1Kin 22:42
J made peace with the king of 1Kin 22:44
Now the rest of the acts of J 1Kin 22:45
J made ships of Tharshish to go 1Kin 22:48
Ahaziah the son of Ahab unto J 1Kin 22:49
But J would not.............................. 1Kin 22:49
J slept with his fathers, and was 1Kin 22:50
year of J king of Judah, and 2Kin 1:17
the son of J king of Judah................ 2Kin 3:7
year of J king of Judah, and 2Kin 3:7
sent to J the king of Judah, ... 2Kin 3:7
But J said, Is there not here a............ 2Kin 3:11
I said, The word of the LORD is 2Kin 3:12
So the king of Israel and J................ 2Kin 3:12
presence of J the king of Judah 2Kin 3:14
J being then king of Judah................ 2Kin 8:16
Jehoram the son of J king of............ 2Kin 8:16
all the hallowed things that J 2Kin 12:18
his son, Asa his son, J his son,.......... 1Chr 3:10
son reigned in his stead, ... 2Chr 17:1
And the LORD was with J, because 2Chr 17:3
all Judah brought to J presents 2Chr 17:5
that they made no war against J 2Chr 17:10
Philistines brought J presents 2Chr 17:11
J waxed great exceedingly................ 2Chr 17:12
Now J had riches and honour in 2Chr 18:1
Israel said unto J king of Judah........ 2Chr 18:3
J said unto the king of Israel............ 2Chr 18:3
But J said, Is there not here a 2Chr 18:6
And the king of Israel said unto J 2Chr 18:7
J said, Let not the king say so.......... 2Chr 18:7
J king of Judah sat either of 2Chr 18:9
And the king of Israel said to J 2Chr 18:17
J the king of Judah went up to 2Chr 18:28
And the king of Israel said unto J 2Chr 18:29
captains of the chariots saw J 2Chr 18:31
but J cried out, and the LORD 2Chr 18:31
J the king of Judah returned to........ 2Chr 19:1
to meet him, and said to king J 2Chr 19:2
And J dwelt at Jerusalem.................. 2Chr 19:4
did J set of the Levites, and of.......... 2Chr 19:8
came against J to battle.................... 2Chr 20:1
Then there came some that told J 2Chr 20:2
J feared, and set himself to seek...... 2Chr 20:3
J stood in the congregation of.......... 2Chr 20:5
of Jerusalem, and thou king J 2Chr 20:15
J bowed his head with his face to 2Chr 20:18
J stood and said, Hear me, O Judah.. 2Chr 20:20
And when J and his people came to.. 2Chr 20:27
J in the forefront of them, to go...... 2Chr 20:27
So the realm of J was quiet.............. 2Chr 20:30
And J reigned over Judah 2Chr 20:31
Now the rest of the acts of J 2Chr 20:34
after this did J king of Judah 2Chr 20:35
of Mareshah prophesied against J.... 2Chr 20:37
Now J slept with his fathers, and.... 2Chr 21:1
And he had brethren the sons of J .. 2Chr 21:2
were the sons of J king of Israel...... 2Chr 21:2
in the ways of J thy father 2Chr 21:12
said they, he is the son of J 2Chr 22:9
   4. Father of Jehu.
the son of J the son of Nimshi.......... 2Kin 9:2
So Jehu the son of J the son of 2Kin 9:14
   5. A priest.
Shebaniah, and J, and 1Chr 15:24
   6. A valley near Jerusalem.
them down into the valley of J .... Joel 3:2
and come up to the valley of J .... Joel 3:12

JEHOSHEBA (je-hosh'-e-bah) See
JEHOSHABEATH. Same as Jehoshabeath.
But J, the daughter of king Joram 2Kin 11:2

JEHOSHUA (je-hosh'-u-ah) See JEHOSHUAH,
JOSHUA. Same as Joshua, son of Nun.
called Oshea the son of Nun J .... Num 13:16

JEHOSHUAH (je-hosh'-u-ah) Same as Joshua,
son of Nun.
Non his son, J his son 1Chr 7:27

JEHOVAH (je-ho'-vah) See GOD, JAH, JEHOVAH-
JIREH, JEHOVAH-NISSI, JEHOVAH-SHALOM,
LORD. A name for God.
but by my name J was I not known .... Ex 6:3
that thou, whose name alone is J ...... Ps 83:18
for the Lord J is my strength and...... Is 12:2
for in the Lord J is everlasting .... Is 26:4

JEHOVAH-JIREH (je-ho'-vah-ji'-reh) Mt.
Moriah.
called the name of that place J.......... Gen 22:14

J

JEHOVAH-NISSI (je-ho'-vah-nis'-si) *An altar built by Moses.*
altar, and called the name of it *J* .... Ex 17:15

JEHOVAH-SHALOM (je-ho'-vah-sha'-lom) *An altar built by Gideon.*
unto the Lord, and called it *J* .... Judg 6:24

JEHOZABAD (je-hoz'-a-bad) *See* JOZABAD.
1. Son of Shomer.
J the son of Shomer, his servants 2Kin 12:21
J the son of Shimrith a Moabitess 2Chr 24:26
2. A son of Obed-edom.
J the second, Joah the third, and 1Chr 26:4
3. A general of Jehoshaphat.
And next him was *J* 2Chr 17:18

JEHOZADAK (je-hoz'-a-dak) *Great-grandson of Hilkiah.*
begat Seraiah, and Seraiah begat *J* 1Chr 6:14
J went into captivity, when the 1Chr 6:15

JEHU (je-hu)
1. A son of Hanani.
to *J* the son of Hanani against 1Kin 16:1
the word of Hanani came the word... .... 1Kin 16:7
against Baasha by *J* the prophet 1Kin 16:12
J the son of Hanani the seer went 2Chr 19:2
the book of *J* the son of Hanani 2Chr 20:34
2. A king of Israel.
J the son of Nimshi shalt thou... .... 1Kin 19:16
the sword of Hazael shall *J* slay 1Kin 19:17
the sword of *J* shall Elisha slay 1Kin 19:17
look out there *J* the son of 2Kin 9:2
I said, Unto which of all us 2Kin 9:5
Then *J* came forth to the servants... .... 2Kin 9:11
with trumpets, saying, *J* is king... .... 2Kin 9:13
So *J* the son of Jehoshaphat the... .... 2Kin 9:14
I said, If it be your minds, then... .... 2Kin 9:15
So *J* rode in a chariot, and went... .... 2Kin 9:16
spied the company of *J* as he came... .... 2Kin 9:17
I said, What hast thou to do with... .... 2Kin 9:18
I answered, What hast thou to do... .... 2Kin 9:19
driving of *J* the son of Nimshi... .... 2Kin 9:20
and they went out against *J* 2Kin 9:21
it came to pass, when Joram saw *J* 2Kin 9:22
that he said, Is it peace, *J* 2Kin 9:22
I drew a bow with his full... .... 2Kin 9:24
Then said *J* to Bidkar his captain 2Kin 9:25
I followed after him, and said, ... 2Kin 9:27
when *J* was come to Jezreel, ... 2Kin 9:30
as I entered in at the gate, she... .... 2Kin 9:31
I wrote letters, and sent to 2Kin 10:1
up of the children, sent to *J* 2Kin 10:6
J slew all that remained of 2Kin 10:11
I met with the brethren of 2Kin 10:13
I gathered all the people 2Kin 10:18
but *J* shall serve him much 2Kin 10:18
But *J* did it in subtilty, to the 2Kin 10:19
I said, Proclaim a solemn 2Kin 10:20
I sent through all Israel 2Kin 10:21
I went, and Jehonadab the son of... .... 2Kin 10:23
I appointed fourscore men without... .... 2Kin 10:24
that *J* said to the guard and to 2Kin 10:25
Thus *J* destroyed Baal out of 2Kin 10:28
I departed not from after them, ... 2Kin 10:29
And the Lord said unto *J*, Because... .... 2Kin 10:30
But *J* took no heed to walk in the 2Kin 10:31
Now the rest of the acts of *J* 2Kin 10:34
And *J* slept with his fathers 2Kin 10:35
the time that *J* reigned over... .... 2Kin 10:36
year of *J* Jehoash began to reign... .... 2Kin 12:1
of Judah Jehoahaz the son of *J* 2Kin 13:1
the son of Jehoahaz son of *J* 2Kin 14:8
of the Lord which he spake by *J* 2Kin 15:12
against *J* the son of Nimshi 2Chr 22:7
when *J* was executing judgment, ... 2Chr 22:8
in Samaria,) and brought him to *J* 2Chr 22:9
the son of Jehoahaz, the son of *J* 2Chr 25:17
of Jezreel upon the house of *J* .... Hos 1:4
3. A son of Obed.
begat Jehu, and *J* begat Azariah,... .... 1Chr 2:38
4. Of Judah.
J the son of Joshibiah, the son of 1Chr 4:35
5. A warrior in David's army.
and Berachah, and the Antothite,... .... 1Chr 12:3

JEHUBBAH (je-hub'-bah) *A descendant of Shamer.*
Ahi, and Rohgah, *J*, and Aram... .... 1Chr 7:34

JEHUCAL (je-hu'-kal) *See* JUCAL. *A son of Shelemiah.*
king sent *J* the son of Shelemiah .... Jer 37:3

JEHUD (je'-hud) *A city in Dan.*
And *J*, and Bene-berak, and... .... Josh 19:45

JEHUDI (je-hu'-di) *Son of Nethaniah.*
sent *J* the son of Nethaniah .... Jer 36:14
So the king sent *J* to fetch the... .... Jer 36:21
J read it in the ears of the king .... Jer 36:21
that when *J* had read three or .... Jer 36:23

JEHUDIJAH (je-hu-di'-jah) *See* HODIAH. *A descendant of Judah.*
his wife *J* bare Jered the father... .... 1Chr 4:18

JEHUSH (je'-hush) *See* JEUSH. *A descendant of King Saul.*
J the second, and Eliphelet the... .... 1Chr 8:39

JEIEL (je-i'-el) *See* JEHIEL, JEUEL.
1. A chief Reubenite.
was reckoned, were the chief, *J* 1Chr 5:7

2. *A Levite gatekeeper.*
and Obed-edom, and *J* 1Chr 15:18
and Obed-edom, and *J* 1Chr 15:21
and next to him Zechariah, *J* 1Chr 16:5
with psalteries and with harps... .... 1Chr 16:5
3. A Levite of the Asaph family.
the son of Benaiah, the son of... .... 2Chr 20:14
4. A scribe.
by the hand of *J* the scribe 2Chr 26:11
Shimri, and *J*, and of the sons... .... 2Chr 29:13
6. A chief Levite.
his brethren, and Hashabiah and *J*... .... 2Chr 35:9
7. An exile.
names are these, Eliphelet, *J*... .... Ezr 8:13
8. Married a foreigner in exile.
J, Mattithiah, Zabad, Zebina,... .... Ezr 10:43

JEKABZEEL (je-kab'-ze-el) *See* KABZEEL. *A city in Judah.*
in the villages thereof, and at *J*... .... Neh 11:25

JEKAMEAM (je-kam'-e-am) *Son of Hebron.*
the third, and *J* the fourth 1Chr 23:19
Jahaziel the third, *J* the fourth... .... 1Chr 24:23

JEKAMIAH (je-ka-mi'-ah) *See* JECAMIAH. *A descendant of Shallum.*
And Shallum begat *J* 1Chr 2:41
and *J* begat Elishama 1Chr 2:41

JEKUTHIEL (je-ku'-the-el) *A descendant of Ezra.*
Socho, and *J* the father of Zanoah 1Chr 4:18

JEMIMA (je-mi'-mah) *A daughter of Job.*
called the name of the first, *J*... .... Job 42:14

JEMIMAH See JEMIMA.

JEMUEL (je-mu'-el) *See* NEMUEL. *A son of Simeon.*
J, and Jamin, and Ohad, and Jachin,... Gen 46:10
J, and Jamin, and Ohad, and Jachin,... Ex 6:15

JEOPARDED
Naphtali were a people that *j*... .... Judg 5:18

JEOPARDY
men that were in *j* of their lives 2Sa 23:17
that have put their lives in *j* 1Chr 11:19
for with the *j* of their lives 1Chr 11:19
master Saul to the *j* of our heads 1Chr 12:19
filled with water, and were in *j* ...... Lk 8:23
And why stand we in *j* every hour 1Cor 15:30

JEPHTHAE (jef'-thah-e) *See* JEPHTHAH. *Same as Jephthah.*
of Barak, and of Samson, and of *J*...... Heb 11:32

JEPHTHAH (jef'-thah) *See* JEPHTHAE, JIPHTHAH-EL. *A judge.*
Now *J* the Gileadite was a mighty...... Judg 11:1
and Gilead begat *J* .... Judg 11:1
grew up, and they thrust out *J* ...... Judg 11:2
Then *J* fled from his brethren, and ...... Judg 11:3
there were gathered vain men to *J* ...... Judg 11:3
to fetch *J* out of the land of Tob ...... Judg 11:5
And they said unto *J*, Come, and be ...... Judg 11:6
J said unto the elders of Gilead, ... Judg 11:7
the elders of Gilead said unto *J* ...... Judg 11:8
J said unto the elders of Gilead, ... Judg 11:9
the elders of Gilead said unto *J* ...... Judg 11:10
Then *J* went with the elders of ...... Judg 11:11
J uttered all his words before ...... Judg 11:11
And *J* sent messengers unto the king...... Judg 11:12
answered unto the messengers of *J* ...... Judg 11:13
J sent messengers again unto the ...... Judg 11:14
And said unto him, Thus saith *J* ...... Judg 11:15
the words of *J* which he sent him ...... Judg 11:28
Spirit of the Lord came upon *J* ...... Judg 11:29
J vowed a vow unto the Lord, and, ... Judg 11:30
So *J* passed over unto the .... Judg 11:32
J came to Mizpeh unto his house, ... Judg 11:34
to lament the daughter of *J* the ...... Judg 11:40
and went northward, and said unto *J*...... Judg 12:1
J said unto them, I and my people ...... Judg 12:2
Then *J* gathered together all the ...... Judg 12:4
J judged Israel six years .... Judg 12:7
Then died *J* the Gileadite, and was...... Judg 12:7
sent Jerubbaal, and Bedan, and *J* 1Sa 12:11

JEPHUNNEH (je-fun'-neh)
1. Father of Caleb.
of Judah, Caleb the son of *J* .... Num 13:6
son of Nun, and Caleb the son of *J*...... Num 14:6
therein, save Caleb the son of *J*...... Num 14:30
the son of Nun, and Caleb the son of *J*...... Num 14:38
of them, save Caleb the son of *J*...... Num 26:65
Caleb the son of *J* the Kenezite... ...... Num 32:12
of Judah, Caleb the son of *J* ...... Num 34:19
Save Caleb the son of *J* .... Deut 1:36
Caleb the son of *J* the Kenezite... ...... Josh 14:6
of *J* Hebron for an inheritance ...... Josh 14:13
of *J* the Kenezite unto this day...... Josh 14:14
unto Caleb the son of *J* he gave a... ...... Josh 15:13
the son of *J* for his possession... ...... Josh 21:12
And the sons of Caleb the son of *J*...... 1Chr 4:15
2. Head of an Asherite family.
J, and Pispah, and Ara 1Chr 7:38

JERAH (je'-rah) *A son of Joktan.*
and Hazarmaveth, and *J* .... Gen 10:26
and Sheleph, and Hazarmaveth, and *J*... 1Chr 1:20

JERAHMEEL (je-rah'-me-el) *See* JERAHMEELITES.
1. A son of Hezron.
and Ram, and Chelubai 1Chr 2:9
the sons of *J* the firstborn of 1Chr 2:25
J had also another wife, whose... .... 1Chr 2:26
of Ram the firstborn of *J* were... .... 1Chr 2:27
These were the sons of *J* 1Chr 2:33
of Caleb the brother of *J* were... .... 1Chr 2:42
2. A son of Kish.
the son of Kish was *J* 1Chr 24:29
3. An officer of Jehoiakim.
commanded *J* the son of Hammelech... Jer 36:26

JERAHMEELITES (je-rah'-me-el-ites)
Descendants of Jerahmeel.
and against the south of the *J* 1Sa 27:10
which were in the cities of the *J* 1Sa 30:29

JERED (je'-red) *See* JARED.
1. A descendant of Seth.
Kenan, Mahalaleel, *J* 1Chr 1:2
2. A descendant of Ezra.
bare *J* the father of Gedor 1Chr 4:18

JEREMAI (jer'-e-mahee) *Married a foreigner in exile.*
Mattathah, Zabad, Eliphelet, *J* ...... Ezr 10:33

JEREMIAH (jer-e-mi'-ah) *See* JEREMIAH'S, JEREMIAS, JEREMY.
1. Father of Hamutal.
the daughter of *J* of Libnah 2Kin 23:31
the daughter of *J* of Libnah 2Kin 24:18
the daughter of *J* of Libnah ...... Jer 52:1
2. Head of a Manassite family.
Ishi, and Eliel, and Azriel, and *J* 1Chr 5:24
3. A warrior in David's army.
J, and Jahaziel, and Johanan... .... 1Chr 12:4
4. A Gadite warrior.
the fourth, *J* the fifth, ... 1Chr 12:10
5. Another Gadite warrior.
the tenth, Machbanai the... .... 1Chr 12:13
6. A prophet.
And I lamented for Josiah 2Chr 35:25
humbled not himself before *J* the 2Chr 36:12
mouth of the Lord by the mouth of *J*...... 2Chr 36:21
mouth of *J* might be accomplished... ...... 2Chr 36:22
the mouth of *J* might be fulfilled ...... Ezr 1:1
The words of *J* the son of Hilkiah ...... Jer 1:1
the Lord came unto me, saying, *J* ...... Jer 1:11
word that came to *J* from the Lord ...... Jer 7:1
word that came to *J* from the Lord ...... Jer 11:1
came to *J* concerning the dearth... ...... Jer 14:1
which came to *J* from the Lord ...... Jer 18:1
let us devise devices against *J* ...... Jer 18:18
Then came *J* from Tophet, whither ...... Jer 19:14
heard that *J* prophesied these ...... Jer 20:1
Then Pashur smote *J* the prophet ...... Jer 20:2
brought forth *J* out of the stocks ...... Jer 20:3
Then said *J* unto him, The Lord ...... Jer 20:3
which came unto *J* from the Lord ...... Jer 21:1
Then said *J* unto them, Thus shall ...... Jer 21:3
Lord unto me, What seest thou, *J* ...... Jer 24:3
The word that came to *J* .... Jer 25:1
The which *J* the prophet spake ...... Jer 25:2
which *J* hath prophesied against ...... Jer 25:13
all the people heard *J* speaking ...... Jer 26:7
when *J* had made an end of .... Jer 26:8
J in the house of the Lord .... Jer 26:9
Then spake *J* unto all the princes ...... Jer 26:12
according to all the words of *J* ...... Jer 26:20
the son of Shaphan was with *J* ...... Jer 26:24
this word unto *J* from the Lord ...... Jer 27:1
Then the prophet *J* said unto the ...... Jer 28:5
Even the prophet *J* said, Amen ...... Jer 28:6
the prophet *J* went his way .... Jer 28:11
the Lord came unto *J* the prophet ...... Jer 28:12
off the neck of the prophet *J* ...... Jer 28:12
Then said the prophet *J* unto ...... Jer 28:15
the words of the letter that *J* ...... Jer 29:1
thou not reproved *J* of Anathoth ...... Jer 29:27
in the ears of *J* the prophet ...... Jer 29:29
came the word of the Lord unto *J* ...... Jer 29:30
word that came to *J* from the Lord ...... Jer 30:1
The word that came to *J* from the... ...... Jer 32:1
The prophet was shut up in the ...... Jer 32:2
J said, The word of the Lord came... ...... Jer 32:6
came the word of the Lord unto *J* ...... Jer 32:26
Lord came unto *J* the second time, ... Jer 33:1
the word of the Lord came unto *J* ...... Jer 33:19
the word of the Lord came to *J* ...... Jer 33:23
which came unto *J* from the Lord ...... Jer 34:1
Then *J* the prophet spake all ...... Jer 34:6
that came unto *J* from the Lord ...... Jer 34:8
the Lord came to *J* from the Lord... ...... Jer 34:12
The word which came unto *J* from... ...... Jer 35:1
I took Jaazaniah the son of *J* ...... Jer 35:3
came the word of the Lord unto *J* ...... Jer 35:12
J said unto the house of the... ...... Jer 35:18
word came unto *J* from the Lord ...... Jer 36:1
Then *J* called Baruch the son of ...... Jer 36:4
commanded *J*, saying, I am ...... Jer 36:5
as *J* had commanded him, and ...... Jer 36:8
that *J* the prophet commanded him... ...... Jer 36:8
in the house of the Lord .... Jer 36:10
Baruch, hide thee, thou and *J* ...... Jer 36:19
the scribe and *J* the prophet. ...... Jer 36:26
of the word of the Lord came to *J* ...... Jer 36:27
Baruch wrote at the mouth of *J* ...... Jer 36:27
Then took *J* another roll, and gave... ...... Jer 36:32
all the words of the book which... ...... Jer 36:32

which he spake by the prophet J....... Jer 37:2
the priest to the prophet J................. Jer 37:3
Now J came in and went out among....... Jer 37:4
of the LORD unto the prophet J............. Jer 37:6
Then J went forth out of .... Jer 37:12
he took J the prophet, saying,............. Jer 37:13
Then said J, It is false........................... Jer 37:14
so Irijah took J, and brought him unto ... Jer 37:14
the princes were wroth with J............. Jer 37:15
When J was entered into the................. Jer 37:16
J had remained there many days............ Jer 37:16
And J said, There is .... Jer 37:17
Moreover J said unto king .... Jer 37:18
that they should commit J into............. Jer 37:21
Thus J remained in the court of .... Jer 37:21
heard the words that J had spoken......... Jer 38:1
Then took they J, and cast him.............. Jer 38:6
and they let down J with cords.............. Jer 38:6
so J sunk in the mire............................ Jer 38:6
they had put J in the dungeon............... Jer 38:7
they have done to J the prophet............ Jer 38:9
take up J the prophet out of the .... Jer 38:10
by cords into the dungeon to J.............. Jer 38:11
the Ethiopian said unto J...................... Jer 38:12
And J did so.. Jer 38:12
So they drew up J with cords................. Jer 38:13
J remained in the court of the .... Jer 38:13
took J the prophet unto him into.......... Jer 38:14
and the king said unto J, I will............. Jer 38:14
Then J said unto Zedekiah, If I............. Jer 38:15
the king sware secretly unto J............... Jer 38:16
Then said J unto Zedekiah, Thus .... Jer 38:17
And Zedekiah the king said unto J........ Jer 38:19
But J said, They shall not...................... Jer 38:20
Then said Zedekiah unto J..................... Jer 38:24
Then came all the princes unto J.......... Jer 38:27
So J abode in the court of the .... Jer 38:28
J to Nebuzar-adan the captain of.......... Jer 39:11
took J out of the court of the .... Jer 39:14
the word of the LORD came unto J......... Jer 39:15
word that came to J from the LORD....... Jer 40:1
the captain of the guard took J............. Jer 40:2
Then went J unto Gedaliah the son....... Jer 40:6
said unto J the prophet, Let, we........... Jer 42:2
Then J the prophet said unto them....... Jer 42:5
Then they said to J, The LORD be.......... Jer 42:5
the word of the LORD came unto J .... Jer 42:7
that when J had made an end of .... Jer 43:1
all the proud men, saying unto J .... Jer 43:2
J the prophet, and Baruch the son........ Jer 43:6
of the LORD unto J in Tahpanhes.......... Jer 43:8
The word that came to J........................ Jer 44:1
of Egypt, in Pathros, answered J .... Jer 44:15
Then J said unto all the people,............ Jer 44:20
Moreover J said unto all the.................. Jer 44:24
The word that J the prophet spake....... Jer 45:1
words in a book at the mouth of J........ Jer 45:1
came to J the prophet against the......... Jer 46:1
the LORD spake to J the prophet........... Jer 46:13
came to J the prophet against the......... Jer 47:1
word of the LORD that came to J........... Jer 49:34
of the Chaldeans by J the prophet........ Jer 50:1
The word which J the prophet................ Jer 51:59
So J wrote in a book all the evil............ Jer 51:60
J said to Seraiah, When thou................. Jer 51:61
Thus far are the words of J.................... Jer 51:64
of the LORD came to J the prophet........ Dan 9:2

JEREMIAH'S *(jer-e-mi′-ahz) Refers to
Jeremiah 6.*
yoke from off the prophet J neck.......... Jer 28:10

JEREMIAS *(jer-e-mi′-as) See* JEREMIAH. *Greek
form of Jeremiah.*
and others, J, or one of the.................... Mt 16:14

JEREMOTH *(jer′-e-moth) See* JERIMOTH.
1. A son of Beriah.
And Ahio, Shashak, and J,..................... 1Chr 8:14
2. A son of Elam.
and Jehiel, and Abdi, and J................... Ezr 10:26
3. Another who married a foreigner in exile.
Eliashib, Mattaniah, and J.................... Ezr 10:27
4. A son of Mushi.
Mahli, and Eder, and J, three............... 1Chr 23:23
5. A sanctuary servant.
The fifteenth to J, his sons,.................. 1Chr 25:22

JEREMY *(jer′-e-mee) See* JEREMIAH. *Latin form
of Jeremiah.*
which was spoken by J the prophet........ Mt 2:17
which was spoken by J the prophet........ Mt 27:9

JERIAH *(je-ri′-ah) See* JERIJAH. *A descendant of
Hebron.*
J the first, Amariah the second,............ 1Chr 23:19
J the first, Amariah the second,............ 1Chr 24:23

JERIBAI *(jer′-ib-ahee) A 'mighty man' of
David.*
Eliel the Mahavite, and J, and.............. 1Chr 11:46

JERICHO *(jer′-ik-o) A city in Benjamin.*
of Moab on this side Jordan by J........... Num 22:1
plains of Moab by Jordan near J............ Num 26:3
plains of Moab by Jordan near J............ Num 26:63
Moab, which are by Jordan near J......... Num 31:12
plains of Moab by Jordan near J............ Num 33:48

plains of Moab by Jordan, near J........... Num 33:50
this side Jordan near J eastward........... Num 34:15
plains of Moab by Jordan near J............ Num 35:1
plains of Moab by Jordan near J............ Num 36:13
of Moab, that is over against J............... Deut 32:49
of Pisgah, that is over against J............. Deut 34:1
and the plain of the valley of J............. Deut 34:3
saying, Go view the land, even J........... Josh 2:1
And it was told the king of Rahab........ Josh 2:3
the king of J sent unto Rahab............... Josh 2:3
passed over right against J.................... Josh 3:16
unto battle, to the plains of J............... Josh 4:13
Gilgal, in the east border of J............... Josh 4:19
month at even in the plains of J........... Josh 5:10
to pass, when Joshua was by J.............. Josh 6:1
Now J was straitly shut up.................... Josh 6:1
I have given into thine hand J............... Josh 6:2
which Joshua sent to spy out J............. Josh 6:25
riseth up and buildeth this city J.......... Josh 6:26
And Joshua sent men from J to Ai......... Josh 7:2
and her king as thou didst unto J......... Josh 8:2
heard what Joshua had done unto J...... Josh 9:3
as he had done to J and her king,......... Josh 10:1
as he did unto the king of J.................. Josh 10:28
as he did unto the king of J.................. Josh 10:30
The king of J, one.................................. Josh 12:9
on the other side Jordan, by J.............. Josh 13:32
of Joseph fell from Jordan by J............. Josh 16:1
unto the water of J on the east............. Josh 16:1
from J throughout mount Beth-el......... Josh 16:1
and to Naarath, and came to J.............. Josh 16:7
the side of J on the north side.............. Josh 18:12
to their families were J, and................. Josh 18:21
other side Jordan by J eastward............ Josh 20:8
went over Jordan, and came unto J...... Josh 24:11
the men of J fought against you,........... Josh 24:11
Tarry at J until your beards be.............. 2Sa 10:5
did Hiel the Beth-elite build J............... 1Kin 16:34
for the LORD hath sent me to J............. 2Kin 2:4
So they came to J................................... 2Kin 2:5
that were at J came to Elisha................ 2Kin 2:15
which were to view at J saw him.......... 2Kin 2:15
to him, (for he tarried at J.................... 2Kin 2:18
overtook him in the plains of J............. 2Kin 25:5
And on the other side Jordan by J......... 1Chr 6:78
Tarry at J until your beards be.............. 1Chr 19:5
upon asses, and brought them to J 2Chr 28:15
The children of J, three hundred.......... Ezr 2:34
unto him builded the men of J.............. Neh 3:2
The children of J, three hundred.......... Neh 7:36
Zedekiah in the plains of J..................... Jer 39:5
Zedekiah in the plains of J..................... Jer 52:8
And as they departed from J................. Mt 20:29
And they came to J................................. Mk 10:46
as he went out of J with his,................. Mk 10:46
man went down from Jerusalem to J.... Lk 10:30
that as he was come nigh unto J........... Lk 18:35
Jesus entered and passed through J...... Lk 19:1
By faith the walls of J fell down........... Heb 11:30

JERIEL *(je-ri′-el) A son of Tola.*
Uzzi, and Rephaiah, and J, and............ 1Chr 7:2

JERIJAH *(je-ri′-jah) Same as* JERIAH.
the Hebronites was J the chief.............. 1Chr 26:31

JERIMOTH *(jer′-im-oth) See* JEREMOTH.
1. A son of Bela.
Ezbon, and Uzzi, and Uzziel, and J....... 1Chr 7:7
2. A son of Becher.
and Elioenai, and Omri, and J............... 1Chr 7:8
3. A warrior in David's army.
Eluzai, and J, and Bealiah, and............. 1Chr 12:5
4. A son of Mushi.
Mahli, and Eder, and J......................... 1Chr 24:30
5. A sanctuary servant.
Mattaniah, Uzziel, Shebuel, and J......... 1Chr 25:4
6. A Naphtalite ruler.
of Naphtali, J the son of Azriel............. 1Chr 27:19
7. A son of David.
of J the son of David to wife................. 2Chr 11:18
8. A Temple servant.
and Nahath, and Asahel, and J............. 2Chr 31:13

JERIOTH *(je′-re-oth) A wife of Caleb.*
of Azubah his wife, and of J.................. 1Chr 2:18

JEROBOAM *(jer-o-bo′-am) See* JEROBOAM'S.
1. A king of Israel.
J the son of Nebat, an Ephrathite.......... 1Kin 11:26
the man J was a mighty man of............. 1Kin 11:28
time when J went out of Jerusalem....... 1Kin 11:29
And he said to J, Take thee ten............ 1Kin 11:31
sought therefore to kill J...................... 1Kin 11:40
J arose, and fled into Egypt, unto......... 1Kin 11:40
when J the son of Nebat, who was........ 1Kin 12:2
king Solomon, and J dwelt in Egypt..... 1Kin 12:2
And J and all the congregation of......... 1Kin 12:3
So J and all the people came to............ 1Kin 12:12
Shilonite unto J the son of Nebat......... 1Kin 12:15
heard that J was come again................. 1Kin 12:20
Then J built Shechem in mount............ 1Kin 12:25
J said in his heart, Now shall............... 1Kin 12:26
J ordained a feast in the eighth........... 1Kin 12:32
J stood by the altar to burn................. 1Kin 13:1
when king J heard the saying of........... 1Kin 13:4
After this thing J returned not.............. 1Kin 13:33
became sin unto the house of J............. 1Kin 13:34
Abijah the son of J fell sick.................. 1Kin 14:1
J said to his wife, Arise, I pray............. 1Kin 14:2
be not known to be the wife of J.......... 1Kin 14:4
the wife of J cometh to ask a............... 1Kin 14:5
he said, Come in, thou wife of J........... 1Kin 14:6

Go, tell J, Thus saith the LORD............. 1Kin 14:7
bring evil upon the house of J.............. 1Kin 14:10
will cut off from J him that.................. 1Kin 14:10
the remnant of the house of J.............. 1Kin 14:10
Him that dieth of J in the city.............. 1Kin 14:11
for he only of J shall come to............... 1Kin 14:13
God of Israel in the house of J.............. 1Kin 14:13
cut off the house of J that day.............. 1Kin 14:14
up because of the sins of J.................... 1Kin 14:16
And the rest of the acts of J.................. 1Kin 14:19
the days which J reigned were two....... 1Kin 14:20
Rehoboam and J all their days.............. 1Kin 14:30
in the eighteenth year of king J........... 1Kin 15:1
J all the days of his life........................ 1Kin 15:6
there was war between Abijam and J.... 1Kin 15:7
in the twentieth year of J king............. 1Kin 15:9
Nadab the son of J began to reign........ 1Kin 15:25
that he smote all the house of J........... 1Kin 15:29
he left not to J any that........................ 1Kin 15:29
of the sins of J which he sinned............ 1Kin 15:30
LORD, and walked in the way of J.......... 1Kin 15:34
thou hast walked in the way of J.......... 1Kin 16:2
the house of J the son of Nebat............ 1Kin 16:3
in being like the house of J.................. 1Kin 16:7
LORD, in walking in the way of J........... 1Kin 16:19
all the way of J the son of Nebat.......... 1Kin 16:26
in the sins of J the son of Nebat.......... 1Kin 16:31
the house of J the son of Nebat............ 1Kin 21:22
in the way of J the son of Nebat.......... 1Kin 22:52
the sins of J the son of Nebat.............. 2Kin 3:3
the house of J the son of Nebat............ 2Kin 9:9
the sins of J the son of Nebat.............. 2Kin 10:29
departed not from the sins of J............ 2Kin 10:31
the sins of J the son of Nebat.............. 2Kin 13:2
from the sins of the house of J............. 2Kin 13:6
the sins of J the son of Nebat.............. 2Kin 13:11
the sins of J the son of Nebat.............. 2Kin 14:24
the sins of J the son of Nebat.............. 2Kin 15:9
the sins of J the son of Nebat.............. 2Kin 15:18
the sins of J the son of Nebat.............. 2Kin 15:24
the sins of J the son of Nebat.............. 2Kin 15:28
they made J the son of Nebat king....... 2Kin 17:21
J drave Israel from following the.......... 2Kin 17:21
in all the sins of J which he did............ 2Kin 17:22
place which J the son of Nebat............. 2Kin 23:15
seer against J the son of Nebat............ 2Chr 9:29
when J the son of Nebat, who was....... 2Chr 10:2
that J returned out of Egypt................. 2Chr 10:2
So J and all Israel came and spake....... 2Chr 10:3
So J and all the people came to............ 2Chr 10:12
Shilonite to J the son of Nebat............ 2Chr 10:15
and returned from going against J........ 2Chr 11:4
for J and his sons had cast them.......... 2Chr 11:14
Rehoboam and J continually.................. 2Chr 12:15
king J began Abijah to reign over......... 2Chr 13:1
there was war between Abijah and J..... 2Chr 13:2
J also set the battle in array................. 2Chr 13:3
Ephraim, and said, Hear me, thou J...... 2Chr 13:4
Yet J the son of Nebat, the................... 2Chr 13:6
which J made you for gods.................... 2Chr 13:8
But J caused an ambushment to........... 2Chr 13:13
it came to pass, that God smote J......... 2Chr 13:15
And Abijah pursued after J.................... 2Chr 13:19
Neither did J recover strength.............. 2Chr 13:20
2. Another king of Israel, son of Jehoash.
and J sat upon his throne...................... 2Kin 13:13
J his son reigned in his stead............... 2Kin 14:16
the son of Joash king of Judah J.......... 2Kin 14:23
by the hand of J the son of Joash........ 2Kin 14:27
Now the rest of the acts of J................ 2Kin 14:29
J slept with his fathers, even................ 2Kin 14:29
seventh year of J king of Israel............ 2Kin 15:1
of J reign over Israel in Samaria.......... 2Kin 15:8
in the days of J king of Israel............... Hos 1:1
in the days of J the son of Joash.......... Amos 1:1
the house of J with the sword.............. Amos 7:9
Beth-el sent to J king of Israel............. Amos 7:10
I shall die by the sword, and............... Amos 7:11

JEROBOAM'S *(jer-o-bo′-ams) Refers to
Jeroboam 1.*
J wife did so, and arose, and went........ 1Kin 14:4
J wife arose, and departed, and............ 1Kin 14:17

JEROHAM *(je-ro′-ham)*
1. Grandfather of Samuel.
name was Elkanah, the son of J............ 1Sa 1:1
J his son, Elkanah his son..................... 1Chr 6:27
The son of Elkanah, the son of J........... 1Chr 6:34
2. Head of a Benjamite family.
Eliah, and Zichri, the sons of J............. 1Chr 8:27
3. A descendant of Benjamin.
And Ibneiah the son of J, and Elah....... 1Chr 9:8
4. A family of exiles.
And Adaiah the son of J, the son.......... 1Chr 9:12
and Adaiah the son of J, the son.......... Neh 11:12
5. A warrior in David's army.
Zebadiah, the sons of J of Gedor.......... 1Chr 12:7
6. Father of Azareel.
Of Dan, Azareel the son of J................. 1Chr 27:22
7. Father of Azariah.
of hundreds, Azariah the son of J......... 2Chr 23:1

JERUBBAAL *(je-rub′-ba-al) See* GIDEON,
JERUBBESHETH. *Another name for Gideon.*
on that day he called him J................... Judg 6:32
Then J, who is Gideon, and all the....... Judg 7:1
J the son of Joash went and dwelt....... Judg 8:29
they kindness to the house of J............ Judg 8:35
Abimelech the son of J went to............ Judg 9:1
either that all the sons of J.................. Judg 9:2

slew his brethren the sons of J............... Judg 9:5
the youngest son of J was left............... Judg 9:5
and if ye have dealt well with J............. Judg 9:16
dealt truly and sincerely with J............ Judg 9:19
and ten sons of J might come............... Judg 9:24
is not he the son of J......................... Judg 9:28
the curse of Jotham the son of J........... Judg 9:57
And the Lord sent J, and Bedan, and.... 1Sa 12:11

JERUBBESHETH (je-rub´-be-sheth) See
JERUBBAAL. *Another name for Gideon.*
Who smote Abimelech the son of J...... 2Sa 11:21

JERUEL (je-ru´-el) *A wilderness in Judah.*
brook, before the wilderness of J........ 2Chr 20:16

JERUSALEM (je-ru´-sa-lem) See PREFACE.
SEE ALSO JERUSALEM'S,SALEM. *City where the
Temple was located.*
carried the ark of God again to J.......... 2Sa 15:29
said, In J will I put my name............... 2Kin 21:4
his son, in this house, and in J............. 2Kin 21:7
And he carried away all J, and all......... 2Kin 24:14
built the house of the Lord in J............ 1Chr 6:32
that they may dwell in J for ever......... 1Chr 23:25
But I have chosen J, that my name...... 2Chr 6:6
me to build me an house at J.............. Ezr 1:2
house of the Lord which is at J........... Ezr 2:68
the house of God which is at J............ Ezr 5:2
So I came to J, and was there............ Neh 2:11
out of Zion, which dwelleth at J.......... Ps 135:21
For J is ruined, and Judah is.............. Is 3:8
on thy beautiful garments, O J........... Is 52:1
is a wilderness, J a desolation............ Is 64:10
O J, wash thine heart from................ Jer 4:14
be saved, and J shall dwell safely....... Jer 33:16
and brake down the walls of J........... Jer 39:8
from J eight hundred thirty............... Jer 52:29
J remembered in the days of her......... Lam 1:7
J hath grievously sinned................... Lam 1:8
came wise men from the east to J....... Mt 2:1
was troubled, and all J with him......... Mt 2:3
O J, J, thou that killest..................... Mt 23:37
they brought him to J, to.................. Lk 2:22
they went up to J after the............... Lk 2:42
child Jesus tarried behind in J............ Lk 2:43
O J, J, which killest the................... Lk 13:34
among all nations, beginning at J........ Lk 24:47
but tarry ye in the city of J............... Lk 24:49
be witnesses unto me before in J........ Acts 1:8
And there were dwelling at J Jews....... Acts 2:5
against the church which was at J....... Acts 8:1
and elders which were at J................ Acts 16:4
But now I go unto J to minister.......... Rom 15:25
But J which is above is free............... Gal 4:26
of the living God, the heavenly J......... Heb 12:22
city of my God, which is new J........... Rev 3:12
I John saw the holy city, new J.......... Rev 21:2
me that great city, the holy J............ Rev 21:10

JERUSALEM'S (je-ru´-sa-lems)
for J sake which I have chosen........... 1Kin 11:13
for J sake, the city which I have......... 1Kin 11:32
for J sake I will not rest, until............ Is 62:1

JERUSHA (je-ru´-shah) See JERUSHAH. *Mother
of King Jotham of Judah.*
And his mother's name was J............. 2Kin 15:33

JERUSHAH (je-ru´-shah) See JERUSHA. *Same
as Jerusha.*
His mother's name also was J............. 2Chr 27:1

JESAIAH (jes-a-i´ah) See ISAIAH, JESHAIAH.
1. *Grandson of Zerubbabel.*
Hananiah, Pelatiah, and J................. 1Chr 3:21
2. *A family of exiles.*
the son of Ithiel, the son of J............. Neh 11:7

JESHAIAH (jesh-a-i´-ah) See JESAIAH.
1. *A sanctuary servant.*
Gedaliah, and Zeri, and J.................. 1Chr 25:3
The eighth to J, he, his sons, and....... 1Chr 25:15
2. *A grandson of Eliezer.*
J his son, and Joram his son, and....... 1Chr 26:25
3. *An Elamite exile.*
J the son of Athaliah, and with.......... Ezr 8:7
4. *A Merarite exile.*
with him J of the sons of Merari......... Ezr 8:19

JESHANAH (jesh-a´-nah) *A city near Bethel.*
J with the towns thereof, and............ 2Chr 13:19

JESHARELAH (je-shar´-e-lah) See ASARELAH.
A sanctuary servant.
The seventh to J, he, his sons,.......... 1Chr 25:14

JESHEBEAB (je-sheb´-e-ab) *A sanctuary
servant.*
to Huppah, the fourteenth to J.......... 1Chr 24:13

JESHER (je´-shur) *A son of Caleb.*
J, and Shobab, and Ardon................. 1Chr 2:18

JESHIMON (jesh´-im-on)
1. *A place in the Sinai.*
of Pisgah, which looketh toward J...... Num 21:20
of Peor, that looketh toward J........... Num 23:28
2. *A place in the wilderness of Judah.*
which is on the south of J................. 1Sa 23:19
in the plain on the south of J............ 1Sa 23:24
of Hachilah, which is before J............ 1Sa 26:1
of Hachilah, which is before J............ 1Sa 26:3

JESHISHAI (jesh´-i-shahee) *Ancestor of a
Gadite family.*
the son of Michael, the son of J......... 1Chr 5:14

JESHOHAIAH (je-sho-ha-i´-ah) *A descendant
of Simeon.*
And Elioenai, and Jaakobah, and J...... 1Chr 4:36

JESHUA (jesh´-u-ah) See JESHUAH, JOSHUA.
1. *A sanctuary servant.*
of Jediah, of the house of J............... Ezr 2:36
of Jediah, of the house of J............... Neh 7:39
2. *A Levite in Hezekiah's time.*
The ninth to J, the tenth to.............. 1Chr 24:11
him were Eden, and Miniamin, and J... 2Chr 31:15
the children of J and Kadmiel, and...... Ezr 2:40
the children of J, of Kadmiel, and....... Neh 7:43
3. *A priest in exile.*
J, Nehemiah, Seraiah, Reelaiah.......... Ezr 2:2
Then stood up J the son of................ Ezr 3:2
J the son of Jozadak, and................. Ezr 3:8
Then stood J with his sons and his..... Ezr 3:9
But Zerubbabel, and J, and the rest.... Ezr 4:3
J the son of Jozadak, and began to..... Ezr 5:2
of the sons of J the son of................ Ezr 10:18
Who came with Zerubbabel, J............ Neh 7:7
the son of Sheaitiel, and J................. Neh 12:1
their brethren in the days of J........... Neh 12:7
J begat Joiakim, Joiakim also............. Neh 12:10
the days of Joiakim the son of J......... Neh 12:26
4. *Father of Jozabad.*
them was Jozabad the son of J.......... Ezr 8:33
5. *A family of exiles.*
Pahath-moab, of the children of J...... Ezr 2:6
Pahath-moab, of the children of J...... Neh 7:11
6. *Father of Ezer.*
to him repaired Ezer the son of J....... Neh 3:19
7. *A priest who assisted Ezra.*
Also J, and Bani, and Sherebiah,........ Neh 8:7
the stairs, of the Levites,................. Neh 9:4
Then the Levites, J, and Kadmiel,....... Neh 9:5
J, Binnui, Kadmiel, Sherebiah,........... Neh 12:8
The son of Kadmiel, with their........... Neh 12:24
8. *Same as Joshua, son of Nun.*
for since the days of J the son.......... Neh 8:17
9. *A Levite who renewed the covenant.*
both J the son of Azaniah, Binnui,...... Neh 10:9
10. *A city in Benjamin.*
And at J, and at Moladah, and in....... Neh 11:26

JESHURUN (jesh´-u-run) *Another name for the
people Israel.*
But J waxed fat, and kicked............... Deut 32:15
And he was king in J, when the.......... Deut 33:5
is none like unto the God of J............ Deut 33:26

JESIAH (je-si´-ah) See ISHIAH.
1. *A warrior in David's army.*
Elkanah, and J, and Azareel, and....... 1Chr 12:6
2. *A descendant of Uzziel.*
Micah the first, and J, the second...... 1Chr 23:20

JESIMIEL (je-sim´-e-el) *A descendant of
Simeon.*
and Asaiah, and Adiel, and J............. 1Chr 4:36

JESSE (jes´-se) *Father of David.*
he is the father of J, the father......... Ruth 4:17
begat J, and J begat David................ Ruth 4:22
send thee to J the Beth-lehemite........ 1Sa 16:1
call J to the sacrifice, and I.............. 1Sa 16:3
And he sanctified J and his sons,....... 1Sa 16:5
Then J called Abinadab, and made...... 1Sa 16:8
Then J made Shammah to pass by....... 1Sa 16:9
J made seven of his sons to pass....... 1Sa 16:10
And Samuel said unto J, The Lord...... 1Sa 16:10
And Samuel said unto J, Are here....... 1Sa 16:11
And Samuel said unto J, Send and...... 1Sa 16:11
seen a son of J the Beth-lehemite...... 1Sa 16:18
Saul sent messengers unto J............. 1Sa 16:19
I took an ass laden with bread, and.... 1Sa 16:20
And Saul sent to J, saying, Let........... 1Sa 16:22
whose name was J; and he had.......... 1Sa 17:12
the three eldest sons of J went.......... 1Sa 17:13
J said unto David his son, Take......... 1Sa 17:17
and went, as J had commanded him.... 1Sa 17:20
thy servant J the Beth-lehemite......... 1Sa 17:58
cometh not the son of J to meat........ 1Sa 20:27
son of J to thine own confusion......... 1Sa 20:30
son of J liveth upon the ground......... 1Sa 20:31
will the son of J give every one......... 1Sa 22:7
made a league with the son of J........ 1Sa 22:8
I saw the son of J coming to Nob....... 1Sa 22:9
against me, thou and the son of J...... 1Sa 22:13
and who is the son of J.................... 1Sa 25:10
we inheritance in the son of J........... 2Sa 20:1
David the son of J said, and the........ 2Sa 23:1
we inheritance in the son of J........... 1Kin 12:16
Boaz begat Obed, and Obed begat J... 1Chr 2:12
J begat his firstborn Eliab, and.......... 1Chr 2:13
kingdom unto David the son of J........ 1Chr 10:14
and on thy side, thou son of J........... 1Chr 12:18
Thus David the son of J reigned......... 1Chr 29:26
none inheritance in the son of J......... 2Chr 10:16
daughter of Eliab the son of J........... 2Chr 11:18
of David the son of J are ended......... Ps 72:20
forth a rod out of the stem of J......... Is 11:1
day there shall be a root of J............ Is 11:10
and Obed begat J.......................... Mt 1:5
and J begat David the king............... Mt 1:6
Which was the son of J, which was..... Lk 3:32
I have found David the son of J.......... Acts 13:22
saith, There shall be a root of J......... Rom 15:12

JESSIAH See JESIAH.

JESTING
nor foolish talking, nor j................... Eph 5:4

JESUI (jes´-u-i) See ISHUI, JESUITES. *A
descendant of Asher.*
Of Jesui, the family of the J............... Num 26:44

JESUITES (jes´-u-ites) *Descendants of Jesui.*
Of Jesui, the family of the J............... Num 26:44

JESURUN (jes´-u-run) See JESHURUN. *Same as
Jeshurun.*
and thou, J, whom I have chosen....... Is 44:2

JESUS (je´-zus) See PREFACE. SEE ALSO BAR-
JESUS, CHRIST, JESUS', JUSTUS.
1. *The Christ.*
of the generation of J Christ.............. Mt 1:1
and thou shalt call his name J............ Mt 1:21
and he called his name J.................. Mt 1:25
But J said unto him, Get thee............ Mt 4:10
What have we to do with thee, J........ Mt 8:29
But J said unto them, A prophet........ Mt 13:57
J to shew unto his disciples.............. Mt 16:21
And J rebuked the devil.................... Mt 17:18
J called a little child unto him,.......... Mt 18:2
But J said, Suffer little..................... Mt 19:14
J said unto him, If thou wilt be.......... Mt 19:21
This is J the prophet of Nazareth....... Mt 21:11
J took bread, and blessed it, and....... Mt 26:26
was also with J of Nazareth.............. Mt 26:71
J stood before the governor.............. Mt 27:11
J held his peace, Thou sayest............ Mt 27:11
with J which is called Christ.............. Mt 27:22
THIS IS J THE KING OF THE JEWS...... Mt 27:37
for I know that ye seek J.................. Mt 28:5
met them, saying, All hail................. Mt 28:9
J came and spake unto them, saying... Mt 28:18
What have I to do with thee, J.......... Mk 5:7
But J said unto them, A prophet........ Mk 6:4
And J said, I am........................... Mk 14:62
thou also wast with J of Nazareth..... Mk 14:67
a son, and shalt call his name J........ Lk 1:31
do with thee, thou J of Nazareth...... Lk 4:34
What have I to do with thee, J......... Lk 8:28
And J, perceiving the thought of...... Lk 9:47
Then said J unto him, Go, and do..... Lk 10:37
J said unto him, Receive thy............ Lk 18:42
Then said J, Father, forgive them..... Lk 23:34
And he said unto J, Lord, remember.. Lk 23:42
grace and truth came by J Christ...... Jn 1:17
J saith unto them, My meat is to...... Jn 4:34
Then said J unto him, Except ye....... Jn 4:48
J answered and said unto them,....... Jn 6:29
J said unto them, I am the bread...... Jn 6:35
J answered, Ye neither know me,...... Jn 8:19
said unto her, I am the................... Jn 11:25
J wept.. Jn 11:35
him, saying, Sir, we would see J....... Jn 12:21
J cried and said, He that................. Jn 12:44
I knowing that the Father had.......... Jn 13:3
J said, Now is the Son of man......... Jn 13:31
J saith unto him, I am the way,........ Jn 14:6
J answered, I have told you that....... Jn 18:8
J answered, Thou sayest that I am.... Jn 18:37
But J gave him no answer................ Jn 19:9
saw J standing, and knew not that.... Jn 20:14
and knew not that it was J.............. Jn 20:14
believe that J is the Christ.............. Jn 20:31
this same J, which is taken up........ Acts 1:11
This J hath God raised up,............. Acts 2:32
God, having raised up his Son J....... Acts 3:26
I believe that J Christ is the........... Acts 8:37
the scriptures that J was Christ....... Acts 18:28
I am J of Nazareth, whom thou....... Acts 22:8
confess with thy mouth the Lord J.... Rom 10:9
the body the dying of the Lord J...... 2Cor 4:10
that the life also of J might be......... 2Cor 4:11
by him, as the truth is in J............. Eph 4:21
That at the name of J every knee..... Phil 2:10
confess that J Christ is Lord............ Phil 2:11
do all in the name of the Lord J....... Col 3:17
For if we believe that J died........... 1Th 4:14
that Christ J came into the world...... 1Ti 1:15
confess that J is the Son of God....... 1Jn 4:15
Whosoever believeth that J is the..... 1Jn 5:1
who confess not that J Christ is....... 2Jn 7
Even so, come, Lord J.................... Rev 22:20
2. *Joshua, son of Nun.*
For is J had given them rest,........... Heb 4:8
3. *Justus, a Roman Christian.*
And J, which is called Justus, who.... Col 4:11

JESUS' (je´-zus) *Refers to the Christ.*
and cast them down at J feet.......... Mt 15:30
who also himself was J disciple........ Mt 27:57
saw it, he fell down at J knees........ Lk 5:8
and he fell down at J feet.............. Lk 8:41
Mary, which also sat at J feet......... Lk 10:39
and they came not for J sake only.... Jn 12:9
Now there was leaning on J bosom... Jn 13:23
He then lying on J breast saith........ Jn 13:25
your servants for J sake................. 2Cor 4:5
delivered unto death for J sake....... 2Cor 4:11

JETHER (je´-thur) See HOBAB, ITHRA, ITHRITES,
JETHRO, RAGUEL.
1. *A son of Gideon.*

he said unto J his firstborn, Up, ... Judg 8:20
   2. Father of Amasa.
Ner, and unto Amasa the son of J....... 1Kin 2:5
of Israel, and Amasa the son of J....... 1Kin 2:32
of Amasa was J the Ishmeelite....... 1Chr 2:17
   3. A son of Jerahmeel.
J, and Jonathan 1Chr 2:32
and J died without children 1Chr 2:32
   4. A son of Ezra.
And the sons of Ezra were, J............. 1Chr 4:17
   5. A descendant of Asher.
And the sons of J 1Chr 7:38

JETHETH (je′-theth) *A prince of Edom.*
duke Timnah, duke Alvah, duke J......... Gen 36:40
duke Timnah, duke Aliah, duke J 1Chr 1:51

JETHLAH (jeth′-lah) *A city in Dan.*
And Shaalabbin, and Ajalon, and J...... Josh 19:42

JETHRO (je′-thro) See JETHER. *Father-in-law of Moses.*
the flock of J his father in law .... Ex 3:1
returned to J his father in law, ... Ex 4:18
J said to Moses, Go in peace .... Ex 4:18
When J, the priest of Midian, ... Ex 18:1
Then J, Moses' father in law, ... Ex 18:2
And J, Moses' father in law, came....... Ex 18:5
father in law J am come unto thee....... Ex 18:6
J rejoiced for all the goodness .... Ex 18:9
J said, Blessed be the LORD, who,....... Ex 18:10
And J, Moses' father in law, took .... Ex 18:12

JETUR (je′-tur)
   1. A son of Ishmael.
Hadar, and Tema, J, Naphish, and .... Gen 25:15
J, Naphish, and Kedemah 1Chr 1:31
   2. Descendants of Jetur.
war with the Hagarites, with J............... 1Chr 5:19

JEUEL (je-u′-el) See JEIEL. *A descendant of Zerah.*
J, and their brethren, six hundred......... 1Chr 9:6

JEUSH (je′-ush) See JEHUSH.
   1. A son of Esau.
And Aholibamah bare J, and Jaalam,... Gen 36:5
and she bare to Esau J, and Jaalam,... Gen 36:14
duke J, duke Jaalam, duke Korah .... Gen 36:18
Eliphaz, Reuel, and J, and Jaalam,..... 1Chr 1:35
   2. Grandson of Jediael.
J, and Benjamin, and Ehud, and.......... 1Chr 7:10
   3. A sanctuary servant.
Shimei were, Jahath, Zina, and J 1Chr 23:10
but J and Beriah had not many sons .. 1Chr 23:11
   4. A son of Rehoboam.
J, and Shamariah, and Zaham 2Chr 11:19

JEUZ (je′-uz) *Son of Shaharaim.*
And J, and Shachia, and Mirma 1Chr 8:10

JEW (jew) See JEWESS, JEWISH, JEWS. *Post-exilic term for the Israelites.*
the palace there was a certain J............. Est 2:5
he had told them that he was a J.......... Est 3:4
the J sitting at the king's gate............... Est 5:13
and do even so to Mordecai the J .... Est 6:10
the queen and to Mordecai the J .... Est 8:7
of Abihail, and Mordecai the J .... Est 9:29
according as Mordecai the J .... Est 9:31
For Mordecai the J was next unto ...... Est 10:3
them, to wit, of a J his brother .... Jer 34:9
of the skirt of him that is a J .... Zec 8:23
How is it that thou, being a J .... Jn 4:9
Pilate answered, Am I a J .... Jn 18:35
a man that is a J to keep company .... Acts 10:28
sorcerer, a false prophet, a J .... Acts 13:6
And found a certain J named Aquila.... Acts 18:2
a certain J named Apollos, born .... Acts 18:24
were seven sons of one Sceva, a J ...... Acts 19:14
when they knew that he was a J .... Acts 19:34
I am a man which am a J of Tarsus...... Acts 21:39
I am verily a man which am a J .... Acts 22:3
to the J first, and also to the .... Rom 1:16
that doeth evil, of the J first.................. Rom 2:9
that worketh good, to the J first........... Rom 2:10
Behold, thou art called a J .... Rom 2:17
For he is not a J, which is one .... Rom 2:28
But he is a J, which is one...................... Rom 2:29
What advantage then hath the J .... Rom 3:1
is no difference between the J............... Rom 10:12
And unto the Jews I became as a J 1Cor 9:20
them all, If thou, being a J .... Gal 2:14
There is neither J nor Greek................... Gal 3:28
there is neither Greek nor J .... Col 3:11

JEWEL
As a j of gold in a swine's snout........... Prov 11:22
of knowledge are a precious j .... Prov 20:15
I put a j on thy forehead, and .... Eze 16:12

JEWELS
servant forth j of silver, and .... Gen 24:53
j of gold, and raiment, and gave.......... Gen 24:53
j of silver, and j of gold, ... Ex 3:22
j of silver, and j of gold, ... Ex 12:2
of the Egyptians j of silver .... Ex 12:35
and j of gold, and raiment..................... Ex 12:35
rings, and tablets, all j of gold............. Num 31:50
gotten, of j of gold, chains, and........... Num 31:50
gold of them, even all wrought j .... Num 31:51
and put the j of gold, which ye 1Sa 6:8
wherein the j of gold were, and 1Sa 6:15
the dead bodies, and precious j............ 2Chr 20:25
and for all manner of pleasant j 2Chr 32:27

shall not be for j of fine gold .... Job 28:17
cheeks are comely with rows of j .... Song 1:10
joints of thy thighs are like j .... Song 7:1
The rings, and nose j .... Is 3:21
bride adorneth herself with her j .... Is 61:10
also taken thy fair j of my gold .... Eze 16:17
clothes, and shall take thy fair j .... Eze 16:39
clothes, and take away thy fair j .... Eze 23:26
with her earrings and her j .... Hos 2:13
in that day when I make up my j .... Mal 3:17

JEWESS (jew′-ess) *A female Jew.*
of a certain woman, which was a J...... Acts 16:1
his wife Drusilla, which was a J .... Acts 24:24

JEWISH (jew′-ish) *Of or relating to the Jews.*
Not giving heed to J fables .... Titus 1:14

JEWRY (jew′-ree) See JUDEA. *Of or relating to the Jews.*
king my father brought out of J .... Dan 5:13
people, teaching throughout all J .... Lk 23:5
for he would not walk in J .... Jn 7:1

JEWS (jews) See JEWS′
Syria, and drave the J from Elath 2Kin 16:6
Gedaliah, that he died, and the J 2Kin 25:25
that the J which came up from .... Ezr 4:12
in haste to Jerusalem unto the J .... Ezr 4:23
unto the J that were in Judah .... Ezr 5:1
God was upon the elders of the J .... Ezr 5:5
let the governor of the J .... Ezr 6:7
the elders of the J build this .... Ezr 6:7
J for the building of this house .... Ezr 6:8
And the elders of the J builded .... Ezr 6:14
concerning the J that had escaped....... Neh 1:2
had I as yet told it to the J .... Neh 2:16
indignation, and mocked the J .... Neh 4:1
and said, What do these feeble J .... Neh 4:2
that when the J which dwelt by............. Neh 4:12
have redeemed our brethren the J .... Neh 5:1
and an hundred and fifty of the J .... Neh 5:8
that thou and the J think to rebel........ Neh 6:6
In those days also saw I J that .... Neh 13:23
J that were throughout the whole........ Est 3:6
and to cause to perish, all J .... Est 3:13
was great mourning among the J .... Est 4:3
the king's treasures for the J .... Est 4:7
king's house, more than all the J .... Est 4:13
arise to the J from another place .... Est 4:14
gather together all the J that .... Est 4:16
Mordecai be of the seed of the J .... Est 6:13
that he had devised against the J .... Est 8:3
J that were in all the king's................... Est 8:5
he laid his hand upon the J .... Est 8:7
Write ye also for the J, as it .... Est 8:8
Mordecai commanded unto the J......... Est 8:9
to the J according to their .... Est 8:9
the J which were in every city to .... Est 8:11
that the J should be ready .... Est 8:13
The J had light, and gladness, and...... Est 8:16
the J had joy and gladness, a .... Est 8:17
the people of the land became J .... Est 8:17
the fear of the J fell upon them .... Est 8:17
J hoped to have power over them .... Est 9:1
that the J had rule over them .... Est 9:1
The J gathered themselves .... Est 9:2
of the king, helped the J .... Est 9:3
Thus the J smote all their...................... Est 9:5
in Shushan the palace the J slew......... Est 9:6
of Hammedatha, the enemy of the J.... Est 9:10
The J have slain and destroyed .... Est 9:12
let it be granted to the J .... Est 9:13
For the J that were in Shushan............. Est 9:15
But the other J that were in .... Est 9:16
But the J that were at Shushan .... Est 9:18
Therefore the J of the villages, ... Est 9:19
sent letters unto all the J that .... Est 9:20
As the days wherein the J rested .... Est 9:22
the J undertook to do as they had....... Est 9:23
Agagite, the enemy of all the J .... Est 9:24
against the J to destroy them .... Est 9:24
which he devised against the J .... Est 9:25
The J ordained, and took upon them ... Est 9:27
should not fail from among the J .... Est 9:28
sent the letters unto all the J .... Est 9:30
Ahasuerus, and great among the J ...... Est 10:3
before all the J that sat in the .... Jer 32:12
I am afraid of the J that are .... Jer 38:19
when all the J that were in Moab......... Jer 40:11
Even all the J returned out of .... Jer 40:12
that all the J which are gathered .... Jer 40:15
slew all the J that were with him .... Jer 41:3
the J which dwelt in the land of .... Jer 44:1
the seventh year three thousand J .... Jer 52:28
of the J seven hundred forty .... Jer 52:30
came near, and accused the J .... Dan 3:8
There are certain J whom thou............. Dan 3:12
is he that is born King of the J............. Mt 2:2
Art thou the King of the J .... Mt 27:11
him, saying, Hail, King of the J .... Mt 27:29
THIS IS JESUS THE KING OF THE J... Mt 27:37
among the J until this day .... Mt 28:15
For the Pharisees, and all the J .... Mk 7:3
him, Art thou the King of the J .... Mk 15:2
unto you the King of the J .... Mk 15:9
whom ye call the King of the J .... Mk 15:12
salute him, Hail, King of the J .... Mk 15:18
written over, THE KING OF THE J...... Mk 15:26
sent unto him the elders of the J .... Lk 7:3
Art thou the King of the J .... Lk 23:3

If thou be the king of the J .... Lk 23:37
THE KING OF THE J .... Lk 23:38
of Arimathaea, a city of the J .... Lk 23:51
when the J sent priests and .... Jn 1:19
manner of the purifying of the J .... Jn 2:6
Then answered the J and said unto ..... Jn 2:18
Then said the J, Forty and six .... Jn 2:20
named Nicodemus, a ruler of the J ...... Jn 3:1
and the J about purifying .... Jn 3:25
for the J have no dealings with .... Jn 4:9
for salvation is of the J .... Jn 4:22
this there was a feast of the J .... Jn 5:1
The J therefore said unto him .... Jn 5:10
told the J that it was Jesus, ... Jn 5:15
did the J persecute Jesus....................... Jn 5:16
Therefore the J sought the more .... Jn 5:18
And the passover, a feast of the J ...... Jn 6:4
The J then murmured at him, ... Jn 6:41
The J therefore strove among .... Jn 6:52
because the J sought to kill him........... Jn 7:1
Then the J sought him at the .... Jn 7:11
openly of him for fear of the J .... Jn 7:13
the J marvelled, saying, How .... Jn 7:15
Then said the J among themselves,..... Jn 7:35
Then said the J, Will he kill .... Jn 8:22
to those J which believed on him,....... Jn 8:31
Then answered the J, and said unto .... Jn 8:48
Then said the J unto him, Now we ...... Jn 8:52
Then said the J unto him, Thou............ Jn 8:57
But the J did not believe....................... Jn 9:18
because they feared the J .... Jn 9:22
for the J had agreed already, ... Jn 9:22
among the J for these sayings............... Jn 10:19
Then came the J round about him, ... Jn 10:24
Then the J took up stones again .... Jn 10:31
answered them, saying, For a .... Jn 10:33
the J of late sought to stone .... Jn 11:8
many of the J came to Martha and ..... Jn 11:19
The J then which were with her in....... Jn 11:31
the J also weeping which came .... Jn 11:33
Then said the J, Behold how he .... Jn 11:36
Then many of the J which came to ..... Jn 11:45
walked no more openly among the J ... Jn 11:54
Much people of the J therefore .... Jn 12:9
of him many of the J went away,......... Jn 12:11
and as I said unto the J, Whither .... Jn 13:33
and officers of the J took Jesus, ... Jn 18:12
he, which gave counsel to the J........... Jn 18:14
whither the J always resort .... Jn 18:20
The J therefore said unto him, It .... Jn 18:31
him, Art thou the King of the J .... Jn 18:33
should not be delivered to the J .... Jn 18:36
he went out again unto the J .... Jn 18:38
unto you the King of the J .... Jn 18:39
And said, Hail, King of the J .... Jn 19:3
The J answered him, We have a law.... Jn 19:7
but the J cried out, saying, If .... Jn 19:12
and he saith unto the J, Behold .... Jn 19:14
OF NAZARETH THE KING OF THE J.. Jn 19:19
title then read many of the J .... Jn 19:20
chief priests of the J to Pilate.............. Jn 19:21
Write not, The King of the J .... Jn 19:21
that he said, I am King of the J .... Jn 19:21
The J therefore, because it was........... Jn 19:31
but secretly for fear of the J .... Jn 19:38
as the manner of the J is to bury .... Jn 19:40
were assembled for fear of the J .... Jn 20:19
were dwelling at Jerusalem J .... Acts 2:5
Cyrene, and strangers of Rome, ... Acts 2:10
confounded the J which dwelt at.......... Acts 9:22
the J took counsel to kill him............... Acts 9:23
among all the nation of the J .... Acts 10:22
he did both in the land of the J .... Acts 10:39
word to none but unto the J only .... Acts 11:19
because he saw it pleased the J .... Acts 12:3
of the people of the J .... Acts 12:11
of God in the synagogues of the J .... Acts 13:5
when the J were gone out of the.......... Acts 13:42
was broken up, many of the J .... Acts 13:43
But when the J saw the multitudes ..... Acts 13:45
But the J stirred up the devout .... Acts 13:50
into the synagogue of the J .... Acts 14:1
a great multitude both of the J .... Acts 14:1
But the unbelieving J stirred up .... Acts 14:2
and part held with the J, and part...... Acts 14:4
also of the J with their rulers, ... Acts 14:5
thither certain J from Antioch .... Acts 14:19
J which were in those quarters .... Acts 16:3
saying, These men, being J .... Acts 16:20
where was a synagogue of the J .... Acts 17:1
But the J which believed not,............... Acts 17:5
went into the synagogue of the J .... Acts 17:10
But when the J of Thessalonica .... Acts 17:13
he in the synagogue with the J .... Acts 17:17
all J to depart from Rome..................... Acts 18:2
every sabbath, and persuaded the J ... Acts 18:4
testified to the J that Jesus was.......... Acts 18:5
made insurrection with one .... Acts 18:12
his mouth, Gallio said unto the J........ Acts 18:14
wrong or wicked lewdness, O ye J .... Acts 18:14
synagogue, and reasoned with the J ... Acts 18:19
For he mightily convinced the J .... Acts 18:28
word of the Lord Jesus, both J .... Acts 19:10
Then certain of the vagabond J .... Acts 19:13
And this was known to all the J .... Acts 19:17
the J putting him forward .... Acts 19:33
when the J laid wait for him, as.......... Acts 20:3
me by the lying in wait of the J .... Acts 20:19
Testifying both to the J, and to .... Acts 20:21
So shall the J at Jerusalem bind .... Acts 21:11

how many thousands of J there are.... Acts 21:20
that thou teachest all the J .... Acts 21:21
the J which were of Asia, when........ Acts 21:27
of all the J which dwelt there.......... Acts 22:12
wherefore he was accused of the J ... Acts 22:30
certain of the J banded together....... Acts 23:12
The J have agreed to desire thee...... Acts 23:20
This man was taken of the J .... Acts 23:27
that the J laid wait for the man....... Acts 23:30
all the J throughout the world.......... Acts 24:5
the J also assented, saying that....... Acts 24:9
Whereupon certain J from Asia........ Acts 24:18
willing to shew the J a pleasure....... Acts 24:27
the chief of the J informed him........ Acts 25:2
The J which came down from.......... Acts 25:7
Neither against the law of the J ...... Acts 25:8
willing to do the J a pleasure.......... Acts 25:9
to the J have I done no wrong, as.... Acts 25:10
the elders of the J informed me....... Acts 25:15
of the J have I dealt with me.......... Acts 25:24
whereof I am accused of the J .... Acts 26:2
questions which are among the J ..... Acts 26:3
at Jerusalem, know all the J .... Acts 26:4
Agrippa, I am accused of the J .... Acts 26:7
For these causes the J caught me .... Acts 26:21
the chief of the J together.............. Acts 28:17
But when the J spake against it,...... Acts 28:19
the J departed, and had great......... Acts 28:29
for we have before proved both J .... Rom 3:9
Is he the God of the J only.............. Rom 3:29
he hath called, not of the J only...... Rom 9:24
For the J require a sign, and the...... 1Cor 1:22
unto the J a stumblingblock, and..... 1Cor 1:23
them which are called, both J 1Cor 1:24
unto the J I became as a Jew,......... 1Cor 9:20
as a Jew, that I might gain the J 1Cor 9:20
none offence, neither to the J 1Cor 10:32
body, whether we be J or Gentiles... 1Cor 12:13
Of the J five times received I 2Cor 11:24
the other J dissembled likewise....... Gal 2:13
of Gentiles, and not as do the J ..... Gal 2:14
the Gentiles to live as do the J ...... Gal 2:14
We who are J by nature, and not..... Gal 2:15
even as they have of the J 1Th 2:14
of them which say they are J .... Rev 2:9
of Satan, which say they are J .... Rev 3:9

JEWS' (jews)
talk not with us in the J 2Kin 18:26
a loud voice in the J language......... 2Kin 18:28
the J speech unto the people of....... 2Chr 32:18
could not speak in the J language.... Neh 13:24
the Agagite, the J enemy .... Est 3:10
the J enemy unto Esther the queen... Est 8:1
speak not to us in the J language .... Is 36:11
a loud voice in the J language......... Is 36:13
the J passover was at hand, and...... Jn 2:13
Now the J feast of tabernacles........ Jn 7:2
the J passover was nigh at hand...... Jn 11:55
because of the J preparation day..... Jn 19:42
in time past in the J religion........... Gal 1:13
profited in the J religion above........ Gal 1:14

JEZANIAH (jez-a-ni'-ah) See JAAZANIAH. A
Jewish captain.
J the son of a Maachathite, they...... Jer 40:8
J the son of Hoshaiah, and all the... Jer 42:1

JEZEBEL (jez'-e-bel) See JEZEBEL'S. Wife of
King Ahab.
that he took to wife J the 1Kin 16:31
when J cut off the prophets of......... 1Kin 18:4
told my lord what I did when J 1Kin 18:13
Ahab told J all that Elijah had........ 1Kin 19:1
Then J sent a messenger unto 1Kin 19:2
But J his wife came to him, and...... 1Kin 21:5
J his wife said unto him, Dost......... 1Kin 21:7
did as J had sent unto them, and.... 1Kin 21:11
Then they sent to J, saying,........... 1Kin 21:14
when J heard that Naboth was........ 1Kin 21:15
that J said to Ahab, Arise, take...... 1Kin 21:15
of J also spake the LORD, saying..... 1Kin 21:23
The dogs shall eat J by the wall..... 1Kin 21:23
whom J his wife stirred up............. 1Kin 21:25
of the LORD, at the hand of J 2Kin 9:7
the dogs shall eat J in the............. 2Kin 9:10
as the whoredoms of thy mother J ... 2Kin 9:22
come to Jezreel, J heard of it......... 2Kin 9:30
shall dogs eat the flesh of J 2Kin 9:36
the carcase of J shall be as dung.... 2Kin 9:37
they shall not say, This is J 2Kin 9:37
thou sufferest that woman J .... Rev 2:20

JEZEBEL'S (jez'-e-bels)
hundred, which eat at J table.......... 1Kin 18:19

JEZER (je'-zur) See JEZERITES. A son of
Naphtali.
Jahzeel, and Guni, and J, and........ Gen 46:24
Of J, the family of the Jezerites...... Num 26:49
Jahziel, and Guni, and J.............. 1Chr 7:13

JEZERITES (je'-zur-ites) Descendants of Jezer.
Of Jezer, the family of the J .... Num 26:49

JEZIAH (je-zi'-ah) Married a foreigner in exile.
Ramiah, and J, and Malchiah, and .. Ezr 10:25

JEZIEL (je'-ze-el) A warrior in David's army.
and J, and Pelet, the sons of.......... 1Chr 12:3

JEZLIAH (jez-li'-ah) A son of Elpaal.
Ishmerai also, and J, and Jobab,..... 1Chr 8:18

JEZOAR (je-zo'-ar) See ZOAR. A son of Helah.
sons of Helah were, Zereth, and J.... 1Chr 4:7

JEZRAHIAH (jez-ra-hi'-ah) See IZRAHIAH. A
priest.
sang loud, with J their overseer ...... Neh 12:42

JEZREEL (jez'-re-el) See JEZREELITE.
1. A city in Judah.
And J, and Jokdeam, and Zanoah,... Josh 15:56
and pitched in the valley of J .... Judg 6:33
David also took Ahinoam of J 1Sa 25:43
by a fountain which is in J 1Sa 29:1
And the Philistines went up to J 1Sa 29:11
2. A city in Issachar.
And their border was toward J .... Josh 19:18
and over the Ashurites, and over J... 2Sa 2:9
came of Saul and Jonathan out of J.. 2Sa 4:4
which is by Zartanah beneath J 1Kin 4:12
And Ahab rode, and went to J 1Kin 18:45
before Ahab to the entrance of J 1Kin 18:46
had a vineyard, which was in J 1Kin 21:1
eat Jezebel by the wall of J 1Kin 21:23
J of the wounds which the Syrians.... 2Kin 8:29
to see Joram the son of Ahab in J ... 2Kin 8:29
eat Jezebel in the portion of J 2Kin 9:10
was returned to be healed in J 2Kin 9:15
of the city to go to tell it in J 2Kin 9:15
rode in a chariot, and went to J 2Kin 9:16
a watchman on the tower in J 2Kin 9:17
And when Jehu was come to J 2Kin 9:30
In the portion of J shall dogs......... 2Kin 9:36
of the field in the portion of J 2Kin 9:37
to Samaria, unto J their king.......... 2Kin 10:1
come to me to J by to morrow this... 2Kin 10:6
in baskets, and sent them to J 2Kin 10:7
of the house of Ahab in J 2Kin 10:11
J because of the wounds which........ 2Chr 22:6
see Jehoram the son of Ahab at J.... 2Chr 22:6
3. A plain.
they who are of the valley of J .... Josh 17:16
bow of Israel in the valley of J .... Hos 1:5
and they shall hear J .... Hos 2:22
4. A descendant of Etam.
and J, and Ishma, and Idbash........ 1Chr 4:3
5. Symbolic name for Hosea's eldest son.
unto him, Call his name J .... Hos 1:4
6. Symbolic name for Hosea's eldest son.
blood of J upon the house of Jehu... Hos 1:4
for great shall be the day of J .... Hos 1:11

JEZREELITE (jez'-re-el-ite) See JEZREELITESS.
An inhabitant of Jezreel.
that Naboth the J had a vineyard..... 1Kin 21:1
Naboth the J had spoken to him...... 1Kin 21:4
Because I spake unto Naboth the J... 1Kin 21:6
thee the vineyard of Naboth the J.... 1Kin 21:7
of the vineyard of Naboth the J 1Kin 21:15
to the vineyard of Naboth the J 1Kin 21:16
in the portion of Naboth the 2Kin 9:21
of the field of Naboth the J 2Kin 9:25

JEZREELITESS (jez'-re-el-i-tess) A female
Jezreelite.
with his two wives, Ahinoam the J... 1Sa 27:3
taken captives, Ahinoam the J......... 1Sa 30:5
his two wives also, Ahinoam the J ... 2Sa 2:2
was Amnon, of Ahinoam the J 2Sa 3:2
firstborn Amnon, of Ahinoam the J.. 1Chr 3:1

JIBSAM (jib'-sam) A son of Tola.
and Jeriel, and Jahmai, and.......... 1Chr 7:2

JIDLAPH (jid'-laf) A son of Nahor.
Chesed, and Hazo, and Pildash, and J Gen 22:22

JIMNA (jim'-nah) See JIMNAH, JIMNITES.
A son of Asher.
of J, the family of the Jimnites...... Num 26:44

JIMNAH (jim'-nah) See JIMNA. Same as Jimna.
J, and Ishuah, and Isui, and Beriah,.. Gen 46:17

JIMNITES (jim'-nites) Descendants of Jimna.
of Jimna, the family of the J .... Num 26:44

JIPHTAH (jif'-tah) See JEPHTHAH, JIPHTHAH-EL.
A city in Judah.
And J, and Ashnah, and Nezib,....... Josh 15:43

JIPHTHAH-EL (jif'-thah-el) A valley in
Zebulun.
thereof are in the valley of J .... Josh 19:14
to the valley of J toward the.......... Josh 19:27

JOAB (jo'-ab) See ATAROTH, HOUSE, JOAB'S.
1. Commander of David's army.
the son of Zeruiah, brother to J....... 1Sa 26:6
J the son of Zeruiah, and the.......... 2Sa 2:13
And Abner said to J, Let the young... 2Sa 2:14
And J said, Let them arise............. 2Sa 2:14
three sons of Zeruiah there, J 2Sa 2:18
hold up my face to J thy brother..... 2Sa 2:22
J also and Abishai pursued after...... 2Sa 2:24
Then Abner called to J, and said,..... 2Sa 2:26

J said, As God liveth, unless 2Sa 2:27
So J blew a trumpet, and all the...... 2Sa 2:28
J returned from following Abner 2Sa 2:30
And J and his men went all night,.... 2Sa 3:22
J came from pursuing a troop, and... 2Sa 3:22
When J and all the host that was 2Sa 3:23
with him were come, they told J 2Sa 3:23
When J came to the king, and said,.. 2Sa 3:24
when J was come out from David,.... 2Sa 3:26
J took him aside in the gate to....... 2Sa 3:27
Let it rest on the head of J 2Sa 3:29
house of J one that hath an issue ... 2Sa 3:29
So J and Abishai his brother slew 2Sa 3:30
And David said to J, and to all the... 2Sa 3:31
J the son of Zeruiah was over the.... 2Sa 8:16
when David heard of it, he sent J.... 2Sa 10:7
When J saw that the front of the..... 2Sa 10:9
J drew nigh, and the people that..... 2Sa 10:13
So J returned from the children....... 2Sa 10:14
to battle, that David sent J 2Sa 11:1
And J wrote in a letter, saying, Send 2Sa 11:6
And J sent Uriah to David 2Sa 11:6
David demanded of him how J did.... 2Sa 11:7
and my lord J, and the servants of.. 2Sa 11:11
that David wrote a letter to J 2Sa 11:14
when J observed the city, that he.... 2Sa 11:16
city went out, and fought with J 2Sa 11:17
Then J sent and told David all the... 2Sa 11:18
David all that J had sent him for..... 2Sa 11:22
Thus shalt thou say unto J 2Sa 11:25
J fought against Rabbah of the........ 2Sa 12:26
J sent messengers to David, and...... 2Sa 12:27
Now J the son of Zeruiah.............. 2Sa 14:1
J sent to Tekoah, and fetched......... 2Sa 14:2
So J put the words in her mouth...... 2Sa 14:3
Is not the hand of J with thee in..... 2Sa 14:19
for thy servant J, he bade me, and.. 2Sa 14:19
thy servant J done this thing.......... 2Sa 14:20
And the king said unto J, Behold,.... 2Sa 14:21
I fell to the ground on his face,...... 2Sa 14:22
Today thy servant J knoweth.......... 2Sa 14:22
So J arose and went to Geshur, and. 2Sa 14:23
Therefore Absalom sent for J 2Sa 14:29
Then J arose, and came to Absalom.. 2Sa 14:31
And Absalom answered J, Behold, I.. 2Sa 14:32
So J came to the king, and told....... 2Sa 14:33
captain of the host instead of J 2Sa 17:25
the people under the hand of J 2Sa 18:2
And the king commanded J and....... 2Sa 18:5
a certain man saw it, and told J 2Sa 18:10
J said unto the man that told him.... 2Sa 18:11
And the man said unto J, Though I... 2Sa 18:12
Then said J, I may not tarry thus.... 2Sa 18:14
J blew the trumpet, and the people.. 2Sa 18:16
for J held back the people............. 2Sa 18:16
J said unto him, Thou shalt not...... 2Sa 18:20
Then said J to Cushi, Go tell the..... 2Sa 18:21
And Cushi bowed himself unto J 2Sa 18:21
the son of Zadok yet again to J 2Sa 18:22
J said, Wherefore wilt thou run,...... 2Sa 18:22
When J sent the king's servant,...... 2Sa 18:29
And it was told J, Behold, the........ 2Sa 19:1
J came into the house to the king.... 2Sa 19:5
me continually in the room of J 2Sa 19:13
J said to Amasa, Art thou in.......... 2Sa 20:9
J took Amasa, by the beard with..... 2Sa 20:9
So J and Abishai his brother.......... 2Sa 20:10
him, and said, Be thou for J 2Sa 20:11
is for David, let him go after J 2Sa 20:11
all the people went on after J 2Sa 20:13
were with J battered the wall.......... 2Sa 20:15
say, I pray you, unto J, Come........ 2Sa 20:16
her, the woman said, Art thou J 2Sa 20:17
J answered and said, Far be it,....... 2Sa 20:20
And the woman said unto J, Behold,. 2Sa 20:21
of Bichri, and cast it out to J 2Sa 20:21
J returned to Jerusalem unto the..... 2Sa 20:22
Now J was over all the host of....... 2Sa 20:23
And Abishai, the brother of J 2Sa 23:18
of J was one of the thirty 2Sa 23:24
armourbearer to J the son of.......... 2Sa 23:37
For the king said to J the............. 2Sa 24:2
J said unto the king, Now the........ 2Sa 24:3
king's word prevailed against J 2Sa 24:4
And J and the captains of the host... 2Sa 24:4
J gave up the sum of the number.... 2Sa 24:9
he conferred with J the son of........ 1Kin 1:7
J the captain of the host.............. 1Kin 1:19
when J heard the sound of the........ 1Kin 1:41
J the son of Zeruiah did to me........ 1Kin 2:5
and for J the son of Zeruiah........... 1Kin 2:22
The tidings came to J 1Kin 2:28
for J had turned after Adonijah,...... 1Kin 2:28
J fled unto the tabernacle of the..... 1Kin 2:28
it was told king Solomon that J 1Kin 2:29
word again, saying, Thus said J 1Kin 2:30
the innocent blood, which J shed..... 1Kin 2:31
return upon the head of J 1Kin 2:33
J the captain of the host was......... 1Kin 11:15
(For six months did J remain.......... 1Kin 11:16
that J the captain of the host......... 1Kin 11:21
Abishai, and J, and Asahel, three.... 1Chr 2:16
So J the son of Zeruiah went......... 1Chr 11:6
I repaired the rest of the city,........ 1Chr 11:8
And Abishai the brother of J 1Chr 11:20
were, Asahel the brother of J 1Chr 11:26
of J the son of Zeruiah................. 1Chr 11:39
J the son of Zeruiah was over the ... 1Chr 18:15
when David heard of it, he sent....... 1Chr 19:8
Now when J saw that the battle...... 1Chr 19:10

So J and the people that were with... 1Chr 19:14
Then J came to Jerusalem.................... 1Chr 19:15
J led forth the power of the army,........ 1Chr 20:1
J smote Rabbah, and destroyed it........ 1Chr 20:1
And David said to J and to the............. 1Chr 21:2
I answered, The LORD make his............. 1Chr 21:3
king's word prevailed against J............ 1Chr 21:4
Wherefore J departed, and went........... 1Chr 21:4
I gave the sum of the number of........... 1Chr 21:5
king's word was abominable to J........... 1Chr 21:6
J the son of Zeruiah........................... 1Chr 26:28
month was Asahel the brother of J........ 1Chr 27:7
J the son of Zeruiah began to.............. 1Chr 27:24
general of the king's army was J........... 1Chr 27:34
when J returned, and smote of Edom..... Ps 60:t
    2. A descendant of Caleb.
Ataroth, the house of J, and half........... 1Chr 2:54
    3. A grandson of Kenaz.
and Seraiah begat J, the father of........ 1Chr 4:14
    4. A family of exiles with Zerubbabel.
of the children of Jeshua and J............. 1Chr 3:9 (Ezr 2:6)
of the children of Jeshua and J............. Neh 7:11
    5. A family of exiles with Ezra.
Of the sons of J.................................... Ezr 8:9

JOAB'S (*jo'-abs*) *Refers to Joab 1.*
J field is near mine, and he hath......... 2Sa 14:30
sister to Zeruiah J mother................... 2Sa 17:25
J brother, and a third part under......... 2Sa 18:2
bare J armour compassed about.......... 2Sa 18:15
And there went out after him J men..... 2Sa 20:7
J garment that he had put on was....... 2Sa 20:8
to the sword that was in J hand........... 2Sa 20:10
one of J men stood by him, and.......... 2Sa 20:11

JOAH (*jo'-ah*) *See ETHAN.*
J the son of Asaph the recorder......... 2Kin 18:18
son of Hilkiah, and Shebna, and J...... 2Kin 18:26
J the son of Asaph the recorder,........ 2Kin 18:37
house, and Shebna the scribe, and J... Is 36:3
J unto Rabshakeh, Speak, I pray........ Is 36:11
and Shebna the scribe, and J............. Is 36:22
    2. A descendant of Gershom.
J his son, Iddo his son, Zerah 1Chr 6:21
J the son of Zimmah.......................... 2Chr 29:12
and Eden the son of J........................ 2Chr 29:12
    3. A sanctuary servant.
J the third, and Zacar the fourth,....... 1Chr 26:4
    4. A Levite.
the son of Joahaz the recorder,.......... 2Chr 34:8

JOAHAZ (*jo'-a-haz*) *See JEHOAHAZ. Father of Joah.*
and Joah the son of J the recorder.... 2Chr 34:8

JOANAN See JOANNA.

JOANNA (*jo-an'-nah*)
    1. A female disciple.
J the wife of Chuza Herod's................ Lk 8:3
It was Mary Magdalene, and J............. Lk 24:10
    2. An ancestor of Jesus.
Which was the son of J, which was..... Lk 3:27

JOASH (*jo'-ash*) *See JEHOASH.*
    1. A son of Becher.
Zemira, and J, and Eliezer, and.......... 1Chr 7:8
    2. A sanctuary servant.
and over the cellars of oil was J........ 1Chr 27:28
    3. Father of Gideon.
pertained unto J the Abi-ezrite........... Judg 6:11
Gideon the son of J hath done............ Judg 6:29
the men of the city said unto J........... Judg 6:30
J said unto all that stood.................. Judg 6:31
the sword of Gideon the son of J........ Judg 7:14
Gideon the son of J returned from...... Judg 8:13
And Jerubbaal the son of J went........ Judg 8:29
Gideon the son of J died in a............ Judg 8:32
in the sepulchre of J his father......... Judg 8:32
    4. A son of King Ahab.
the city, and to J the king's son........ 1Kin 22:26
the city, and to J the king's son........ 2Chr 18:25
    5. A son of King Ahaziah.
took J the son of Ahaziah, and........ 2Kin 11:2
And the rest of the acts of J............. 2Kin 12:19
slew J in the house of Millo,.............. 2Kin 12:20
twentieth year of J the son of.......... 2Kin 13:1
seventh year of J king of Judah........ 2Kin 13:10
the son of J king of Judah................ 2Kin 14:1
to all things as J his father did......... 2Kin 14:3
Amaziah the son of J king of J 2Kin 14:17
year of Amaziah the son of J king... 2Kin 14:23
son, Ahaziah his son, J his son,........ 1Chr 3:11
took J the son of Ahaziah, and......... 2Chr 22:11
J was seven years old when he......... 2Chr 24:1
J did that which was right in the...... 2Chr 24:2
that J was minded to repair the....... 2Chr 24:4
Thus J the king remembered not....... 2Chr 24:22
they executed judgment against J..... 2Chr 24:24
king of Judah, the son of J............... 2Chr 25:23
Amaziah the son of J king of........... 2Chr 25:25
    6. A king of Israel.
J his son reigned in his stead.......... 2Kin 13:9
And the rest of the acts of J............. 2Kin 13:12
And J slept with his fathers............. 2Kin 13:13
J was buried in Samaria with the.... 2Kin 13:13
J the king of Israel came down........ 2Kin 13:14
Three times did J beat him............... 2Kin 13:25
In the second year of J son of......... 2Kin 14:1
of Judah Jeroboam the son of J........ 2Kin 14:23
the hand of Jeroboam the son of J... 2Kin 14:27
Judah took advice, and sent to J...... 2Chr 25:17

J king of Israel sent to Amaziah........ 2Chr 25:18
So J the king of Israel went up......... 2Chr 25:21
the king of Israel took Amaziah........ 2Chr 25:23
J son of Jehoahaz king of Israel........ 2Chr 25:25
the days of Jeroboam the son of J..... Hos 1:1
the son of J king of Israel................ Amos 1:1
    7. A descendant of Shelah.
and the men of Chozeba, and J.......... 1Chr 4:22
    8. A captain in David's army.
The chief was Ahiezer, then J............ 1Chr 12:3

JOATHAM (*jo'-a-tham*) *See JOTHAM. Ancestor of Joseph, husband of Mary.*
and Ozias begat J............................ Mt 1:9
and Ozias begat J............................ Mt 1:9

JOAZCAR See JOZACHAR.

JOB (*jobe*) *See JASHUB, JOB'S.*
    1. A descendant of Issachar.
Tola, and Phuvah, and J................... Gen 46:13
    2. A righteous sufferer.
the land of Uz, whose name was J..... Job 1:1
were gone about, that J sent............ Job 1:5
for J said, It may be that my............. Job 1:5
Thus did J continually...................... Job 1:5
Hast thou considered my servant J.... Job 1:8
Doth J fear God for nought............... Job 1:9
And there came a messenger unto J... Job 1:14
Then J arose, and rent his mantle,... Job 1:20
In all this J sinned not, nor.............. Job 1:22
Hast thou considered my servant J.... Job 2:3
smote J with sore boils from the...... Job 2:7
this did not J sin with his lips........ Job 2:10
After this opened J his mouth.......... Job 3:1
And J spake, and said,..................... Job 3:2
But J answered and said,................. Job 6:1
Then J answered and said,............... Job 9:1
And J answered and said,................. Job 12:1
Then J answered and said,............... Job 16:1
Then J answered and said,............... Job 19:1
But J answered and said,................. Job 21:1
Then J answered and said,............... Job 23:1
But J answered and said,................. Job 26:1
Moreover J continued his parable,.... Job 27:1
Moreover J continued his parable,.... Job 29:1
The words of J are ended................. Job 31:40
three men ceased to answer J.......... Job 32:1
against J was his wrath kindled,....... Job 32:2
no answer, and yet had condemned J... Job 32:3
had waited till J had spoken............ Job 32:4
was none of you that convinced J..... Job 32:12
Wherefore, J, I pray thee, hear......... Job 33:1
Mark well, O J, hearken unto me...... Job 33:31
For J hath said, I am righteous......... Job 34:5
What man is like J, who drinketh...... Job 34:7
J hath spoken without knowledge,.... Job 34:35
My desire is that J may be tried...... Job 34:36
Therefore doth J open his mouth...... Job 35:16
Hearken unto this, O J.................... Job 37:14
answered J out of the whirlwind...... Job 38:1
Moreover the LORD answered J......... Job 40:1
Then J answered the LORD, and said.. Job 40:3
LORD unto J out of the whirlwind...... Job 40:6
Then J answered the LORD, and said.. Job 42:1
had spoken these words unto J......... Job 42:7
is right, as my servant J hath.......... Job 42:7
seven rams, and go to my servant J... Job 42:8
my servant J shall pray for you,...... Job 42:8
which is right, like my servant J...... Job 42:8
the LORD also accepted J................. Job 42:9
LORD turned the captivity of J......... Job 42:10
also the LORD gave J twice as........ Job 42:10
end of J more than his beginning..... Job 42:12
so fair as the daughters of J............ Job 42:15
After this lived J an hundred........... Job 42:16
So J died, being old and full of........ Job 42:17
three men, Noah, Daniel, and J........ Eze 14:14
Though Noah, Daniel, and J............ Eze 14:20
have heard of the patience of J....... Jas 5:11

JOBAB (*jo'-bab*)
    1. A son of Joktan.
And Ophir, and Havilah, and J.......... Gen 10:29
And Ophir, and Havilah, and J.......... 1Chr 1:23
    2. A king of Edom.
J the son of Zerah of Bozrah........... Gen 36:33
J died, and Husham of the land of... Gen 36:34
J the son of Zerah of Bozrah........... 1Chr 1:44
when J was dead, Husham of the..... 1Chr 1:45
    3. A Canaanite king.
that he sent to J king of Madon...... Josh 11:1
    4. A son of Shaharaim.
And he begat of Hodesh his wife, J.. 1Chr 8:9
    5. A son of Elpaal.
Ishmerai also, and Jezliah, and J..... 1Chr 8:18

JOB'S (*jobes*) *Refers to Job 2.*
Now when J three friends heard of... Job 2:11

JOCHEBED (*jok'-e-bed*) *Wife of Amram.*
Amram took Jtook J his father's....... Ex 6:20
of Amram's wife was J..................... Num 26:59

JODA See JUDA.

JOED (*jo'-ed*) *A son of Pedaiah.*
son of Meshullam, the son of J........ Neh 11:7

JOEL (*jo'-el*)
    1. A son of Samuel.
the name of his firstborn was J....... 1Sa 8:2
Heman a singer, the son of J........... 1Chr 6:33
appointed Heman the son of J.......... 1Chr 15:17

---

    2. A Simeonite.
And J, and Jehu the son of Josibiah... 1Chr 4:35
    3. Father of Shemaiah.
The sons of J................................. 1Chr 5:4
the son of Shema, the son of J........ 1Chr 5:8
    4. A chief Gadite.
J the chief, and Shapham the next,.. 1Chr 5:12
    5. A Kohathite.
The son of Elkanah, the son of J...... 1Chr 6:36
    6. A descendant of Tola.
Michael, and Obadiah, and J............ 1Chr 7:3
    7. A 'mighty man' of David.
J the brother of Nathan, Mibhar,...... 1Chr 11:38
    8. A Gershomite.
the chief, and his brethren an.......... 1Chr 15:7
Levites, for Uriel, Asaiah, and J........ 1Chr 15:11
chief was Jehiel, and Zetham, and J.. 1Chr 23:8
    9. A treasurer of the Temple.
his brother, which were over........... 1Chr 26:22
    10. A prince of Manasseh.
of Manasseh, J the son of Pedaiah... 1Chr 27:20
    11. A Kohathite who cleansed the Temple.
J the son of Azariah, of the sons...... 2Chr 29:12
    12. Married a foreigner in exile.
Eliezer, Zidelna, Jadau, and J........... Ezr 10:43
    13. An overseer of the Benjamites.
J the son of Zichri was their............ Neh 11:9
    14. A prophet.
that came to J the son of Pethuel.... Joel 1:1
which was spoken by the prophet J.. Acts 2:16

JOELAH (*jo-e'-lah*) *A member of David's band.*
and J, and Zebadiah, the sons of...... 1Chr 12:7

JOEZER (*jo-e'-zer*) *A warrior in David's army.*
and Jesiah, and Azareel, and J......... 1Chr 12:6

JOGBEHAH (*jog'-be-hah*) *A place in Gad.*
Atroth, Shophan, and Jaazer, and J... Num 32:35
tents on the east of Nobah and J..... Judg 8:11

JOGLI (*jog'-li*) *A Danite prince.*
of Dan, Bukki the son of J............... Num 34:22

JOHA (*jo'-hah*)
    1. Son of Beriah.
And Michael, and Ispah, and J......... 1Chr 8:16
    2. A 'mighty man' of David.
J his brother, the Tizite,................. 1Chr 11:45

JOHANAN (*jo-ha'-nan*) *See JEHOHANAN, JOHN.*
    1. A son of Kareah.
J the son of Careah, and Seraiah...... 2Kin 25:23
the son of Nethaniah, and J............ Jer 40:8
Moreover J the son of Kareah, and... Jer 40:13
Then J the son of Kareah spake to.... Jer 40:15
said unto J the son of Kareah.......... Jer 40:16
But when J the son of Kareah, and... Jer 41:11
Ishmael saw J the son of Kareah...... Jer 41:13
went unto J the son of Kareah......... Jer 41:14
escaped from J with eight men........ Jer 41:15
Then took J the son of Kareah, and.. Jer 41:16
J the son of Kareah, and Jezaniah... Jer 42:1
Then called he J the son of............. Jer 42:8
J the son of Kareah, and all the...... Jer 43:2
So J the son of Kareah, and all....... Jer 43:4
But J the son of Kareah, and all...... Jer 43:5
    2. A son of King Josiah.
of Josiah were, the firstborn J......... 1Chr 3:15
    3. A son of Elioenai.
and Pelaiah, and Akkub, and J......... 1Chr 3:24
    4. A grandson of Ahimaaz.
begat Azariah, and Azariah begat J... 1Chr 6:9
J begat Azariah, (he it is that......... 1Chr 6:10
    5. A warrior in David's army.
and Jeremiah, and Jahaziel, and J.... 1Chr 12:4
    6. A Gadite warrior in David's army.
the eighth, Elzabad the ninth,.......... 1Chr 12:12
    7. An Ephraimite.
of Ephraim, Azariah the son of J...... 2Chr 28:12
    8. An exile with Ezra.
The son of Hakkatan, and with........ Ezr 8:12
    9. A priest in exile with Ezra.
chamber of J the son of Eliashib...... Ezr 10:6
    10. A son of Tobiah.
his son J had taken the daughter..... Neh 6:18
    11. A priest in exile with Zerubbabel.
days of Eliashib, Joiada, and J......... Neh 12:22
the days of J the son of Eliashib...... Neh 12:23

JOHN (*jon*) *See BAPTIST, JEHOHANAN, JOHN'S, MARK.*
    1. The Baptizer.
In those days came J the Baptist...... Mt 3:1
the same J had his raiment of......... Mt 3:4
from Galilee to Jordan unto J.......... Mt 3:13
But J forbad him, saying, I have...... Mt 3:14
heard that J was cast into prison..... Mt 4:12
came to him the disciples of J.......... Mt 9:14
Now when J had heard in the.......... Mt 11:2
shew J again those things which...... Mt 11:4
unto the multitudes concerning J..... Mt 11:7
a greater than J the Baptist............ Mt 11:11
from the days of J the Baptist......... Mt 11:12
the law and the prophets until J...... Mt 11:13
For J came neither eating nor.......... Mt 11:18
servants, This is J the Baptist......... Mt 14:2
For Herod had laid hold on J............ Mt 14:3
said unto him, It is not................... Mt 14:4
Give me here J Baptist's head in...... Mt 14:8
sent, and beheaded J in the prison... Mt 14:10
say that thou art J the Baptist......... Mt 16:14
spake unto them of J the Baptist...... Mt 17:13

The baptism of J, whence was it........ Mt 21:25
for all hold J was a prophet.............. Mt 21:26
For I came unto you in the way of....... Mt 21:32
J did baptize in the wilderness,.......... Mk 1:4
J was clothed with camel's hair,......... Mk 1:6
and was baptized of J in Jordan........ Mk 1:9
Now after that J was put in............. Mk 1:14
And the disciples of J and of the....... Mk 2:18
him, Why do the disciples of J........... Mk 2:18
That J the Baptist was risen from...... Mk 6:14
heard thereof, he said, It is J.......... Mk 6:16
sent forth and laid hold upon J........ Mk 6:17
For J had said unto Herod, It is......... Mk 6:18
For Herod feared J, knowing that..... Mk 6:20
said, The head of J the Baptist......... Mk 6:24
charger the head of J the Baptist..... Mk 6:25
And they answered, J the Baptist..... Mk 8:28
The baptism of J, was it from........... Mk 11:30
for all men counted J, that he........... Mk 11:32
and thou shalt call his name J.......... Lk 1:13
but he shall be called J.................. Lk 1:60
and wrote, saying, His name is J...... Lk 1:63
the word of God came unto J the..... Lk 3:2
men mused in their hearts of J......... Lk 3:15
J answered, saying unto them all,..... Lk 3:16
all, that he shut up J in prison.......... Lk 3:20
do the disciples of J fast often.......... Lk 5:33
the disciples of J shewed him of...... Lk 7:18
J calling unto him two of his............ Lk 7:19
J Baptist hath sent us unto thee,..... Lk 7:20
tell J what things ye have seen......... Lk 7:22
the messengers of J were departed.... Lk 7:24
unto the people concerning J............ Lk 7:24
prophet than J the Baptist............... Lk 7:28
baptized with the baptism of J......... Lk 7:29
For J the Baptist came neither........ Lk 7:33
that J was risen from the dead......... Lk 9:7
And Herod said, J have I beheaded... Lk 9:9
answering said, J the Baptist.......... Lk 9:19
as J also taught his disciples........... Lk 11:1
law and the prophets were until J.... Lk 16:16
The baptism of J, was it from.......... Lk 20:4
be persuaded that J was a prophet... Lk 20:6
sent from God, whose name was J..... Jn 1:6
I bare witness of him, and cried,...... Jn 1:15
And this is the record of J.............. Jn 1:19
J answered them, saying, I.............. Jn 1:26
Jordan, where J was baptizing......... Jn 1:28
The next day J seeth Jesus coming.... Jn 1:29
I bare record, saying, I saw the....... Jn 1:32
Again the next day after J stood...... Jn 1:35
of the two which heard J speak....... Jn 1:40
J also was baptizing in Aenon......... Jn 3:23
For J was not yet cast into............. Jn 3:24
And they came unto J, and said unto.. Jn 3:26
J answered and said, A man can...... Jn 3:27
and baptized more disciples than J.... Jn 4:1
Ye sent unto J, and he bare............ Jn 5:33
greater witness than that of J.......... Jn 5:36
place where J at first baptized......... Jn 10:40
him, and said, J did no miracle......... Jn 10:41
but all things that J spake of........... Jn 10:41
For J truly baptized with water....... Acts 1:5
Beginning from the baptism of J..... Acts 1:22
the baptism which J preached.......... Acts 10:37
J indeed baptized with water........... Acts 11:16
When J had first preached before..... Acts 13:24
as J fulfilled his course, he.............. Acts 13:25
knowing only the baptism of J......... Acts 18:25
J verily baptized with the............... Acts 19:4
   2. Son of Zebedee.
J his brother, in a ship with............ Mt 4:21
son of Zebedee, and J his brother..... Mt 10:2
J his brother, and J his brother....... Mk 1:19
J his brother, who also were in........ Mk 1:19
Simon and Andrew, with James and J.. Mk 1:29
and J the brother of James.............. Mk 3:17
James, and J the brother of James.... Mk 5:37
with him Peter, and James, and J..... Mk 9:2
J answered him, saying, Master,....... Mk 9:38
And James and J, the sons of.......... Mk 10:35
much displeased with James and J.... Mk 10:41
the temple, Peter and James and J.... Mk 13:3
with him Peter and James and J...... Mk 14:33
And so was also James, and J......... Lk 5:10
and Andrew his brother, James and J.. Lk 6:14
go in, save Peter, and James, and J.. Lk 8:51
these sayings, he took Peter and J.... Lk 9:28
J answered and said, Master, we..... Lk 9:49
I saw this, they said, Lord,............. Lk 9:54
And he sent Peter and J, saying, Go.. Lk 22:8
abode both Peter, and James, and J.. Acts 1:13
J went up together into the............ Acts 3:1
J about to go into the temple........... Acts 3:3
his eyes upon him with J, said,........ Acts 3:4
which was healed held Peter and J... Acts 3:11
saw the boldness of Peter and J....... Acts 4:13
J answered and said unto them,....... Acts 4:19
they sent unto them Peter and J...... Acts 8:14
the brother of J with the sword....... Acts 12:2
And when James, Cephas, and J....... Gal 2:9
by his angel unto his servant J........ Rev 1:1
J to the seven churches which are.... Rev 1:4
I J, who also your brother, and........ Rev 1:9
J saw the holy city, new................ Rev 21:2
I J saw these things, and heard....... Rev 22:8
   3. A relative of Annas the priest.
high priest, and Caiaphas, and J...... Acts 4:6
   4. Surnamed Mark.
the house of Mary the mother of J.... Acts 12:12

ministry, and took with them J........ Acts 12:25
they had also J to their minister....... Acts 13:5
J departing from them returned to.... Acts 13:13
determined to take with them J........ Acts 15:37

JOHN'S (*jonz*) *Refers to John 1.*
between some of J disciples............. Jn 3:25
And they said, Unto J baptism........ Acts 19:3

JOIADA (*joy'-a-dah*) See **JEHOIADA**. *A priest
with Zerubbabel.*
Eliashib, and Eliashib begat J.......... Neh 12:10
J begat Jonathan, and Jonathan....... Neh 12:11
in the days of Eliashib, J............... Neh 12:22
And one of the sons of J, the son...... Neh 13:28

JOIAKIM (*joy'-a-kim*) See **JEHOIAKIM**. *Another
priest with Zerubbabel.*
and Jeshua begat J....................... Neh 12:10
J also begat Eliashib.................... Neh 12:10
And in the days of J were priests..... Neh 12:12
the days of J the son of Jeshua....... Neh 12:26

JOIARIB (*joy'-a-rib*) See **JEHOIARIB**.
   1. A messenger for Ezra.
also for J, and for Elnathan, men..... Ezr 8:16
   2. A descendant of Perez.
the son of Adaiah, the son of J........ Neh 11:5
   3. Father of Jedaiah.
Jedaiah the son of J, Jachin........... Neh 11:10
Shemaiah, and J, Jedaiah,.............. Neh 12:6
And of J, Mattenai...................... Neh 12:19

JOIN
they J also unto our enemies, and.... Ex 1:10
J himself with Ahaziah king of........ 2Chr 20:35
J in affinity with the people of........ Ezr 9:14
Though hand J in hand, the wicked... Prov 11:21
though hand J in hand, he shall...... Prov 16:5
unto them that J house to house...... Is 5:8
him, and J his enemies together...... Is 9:11
that J themselves to the LORD, to.... Is 56:6
let us J ourselves to the LORD in..... Jer 50:5
J them one to another into one....... Eze 37:17
they shall J themselves together...... Dan 11:6
durst no man J himself to them....... Acts 5:13
J thyself to this chariot................ Acts 8:29
he assayed to J himself to the........ Acts 9:26

JOINED
All these were J together in the,...... Gen 14:3
they J battle with them in the......... Gen 14:8
time will my husband be J unto me... Gen 29:34
J at the two edges thereof.............. Ex 28:7
and so it shall be J together........... Ex 28:7
that they may be J unto thee.......... Num 18:2
And they shall be J unto thee......... Num 18:4
Israel J himself unto Baal-peor........ Num 25:3
men that were J unto Baal-peor....... Num 25:5
and when they J battle, Israel was.... Isa 4:2
of the wheels were J to the base...... 1Kin 7:32
because they about the battle was J.. 1Kin 20:29
and J affinity with Ahab................ 2Chr 18:1
he J himself with him to make........ 2Chr 20:36
Because thou hast J thyself with..... 2Chr 20:37
thereof, and J the foundations......... Ezr 4:12
all the wall was J together unto...... Neh 4:6
upon all such as J themselves......... Est 9:27
let it not be J unto the days of........ Job 3:6
They are one to another, they........ Job 41:17
of his flesh are J together.............. Job 41:23
Assur also is J with them.............. Ps 83:8
They J themselves also unto........... Ps 106:28
For to him that is J to all the......... Eccl 9:4
every one that is J unto them......... Is 13:15
strangers shall be J with them........ Is 14:1
Thou shalt not be J with them in..... Is 14:20
that hath J himself to the LORD,..... Is 56:3
Their wings were J one to another.... Eze 1:9
every one were J one to another...... Eze 1:11
courts J of forty cubits long........... Eze 46:22
Ephraim is J to idols.................... Hos 4:17
many nations shall be J to the........ Zec 2:11
therefore God hath J together......... Mt 19:6
therefore God hath J together......... Mk 10:9
J himself to a citizen of that........... Lk 15:15
about four hundred, J themselves..... Acts 5:36
whose house J hard to the............. Acts 18:7
but that ye be perfectly J.............. 1Cor 1:10
is J to an harlot is one body........... 1Cor 6:16
But he that is J unto the Lord is..... 1Cor 6:17
the whole body fitly J together,....... Eph 4:16
shall be J unto his wife, and they.... Eph 5:31

JOINING
J to the wing of the other cherub..... 2Chr 3:12

JOININGS
doors of the gates, and for the J...... 1Chr 22:3

JOINT
of Jacob's thigh was out of J.......... Gen 32:25
and all my bones are out of J.......... Ps 22:14
broken tooth, and a foot out of J..... Prov 25:19
by that which every J supplieth....... Eph 4:16

JOINT-HEIRS
heirs of God, and J with Christ....... Rom 8:17

JOINTS
between the J of the harness........... 1Kin 22:34
between the J of the harness........... 2Chr 18:33
the J of thy thighs are like............. Song 7:1
so that the J of his loins were........ Dan 5:6
from which all the body by J.......... Col 2:19

of soul and spirit, and of the J....... Heb 4:12

JOKDEAM (*jok'-de-am*) *A city in Judah.*
And Jezreel, and J, and Zanoah,..... Josh 15:56

JOKIM (*jo'-kim*) *A descendant of Shelah.*
And J, and the men of Chozeba, and... 1Chr 4:22

JOKMEAM (*jok'-me-am*) See **JOKNEAM**. *A
Levitical city in Ephraim.*
J with her suburbs, and Beth-horon... 1Chr 6:68

JOKNEAM (*jok'-ne-am*) See **JOKMEAM**,
KIBZAIM.
   1. A Levitical city in Zebulun.
the king of J of Carmel, one........... Josh 12:22
to the river that is before J............ Josh 19:11
J with her suburbs, and Kartah,..... Josh 21:34
   2. A Levitical city in Ephraim.
unto the place that is beyond J....... 1Kin 4:12

JOKSHAN (*jok'-shan*) *A son of Abraham.*
And she bare him Zimran, and J..... Gen 25:2
And J begat Sheba, and Dedan........ Gen 25:3
she bare Zimran, and J, and Medan,... 1Chr 1:32
And the sons of J......................... 1Chr 1:32

JOKTAN (*jok'-tan*) *A son of Eber.*
and his brother's name was J.......... Gen 10:25
J begat Almodad, and Sheleph, and... Gen 10:26
all these were the sons of J............ Gen 10:29
and his brother's name was J.......... 1Chr 1:19
J begat Almodad, and Sheleph, and... 1Chr 1:20
All these were the sons of J............ 1Chr 1:23

JOKTHEEL (*jok'-the-el*) See **SELAH**.
   1. A city in Judah.
And Dilean, and Mizpeh, and J....... Josh 15:38
   2. Another name for Petra in Edom.
the name of it J unto this day......... 2Kin 14:7

JONA (*jo'-nah*) See **BAR-JONA**, **JONAH**, **JONAS**.
Greek form of Jonah.
said, Thou art Simon the son of J..... Jn 1:42

JONADAB (*jon'-a-dab*) See **JEHONADAB**.
   1. Son of Shimeah.
had a friend, whose name was J....... 2Sa 13:3
and J was a very subtil man............ 2Sa 13:3
J said unto him, Lay thee down on... 2Sa 13:5
And J, the son of Shimeah David's... 2Sa 13:32
J said unto the king, Behold, the..... 2Sa 13:35
   2. Son of Rechab.
for J the son of Rechab our............ Jer 35:6
have we obeyed the voice of J the.... Jer 35:8
that J our father commanded us...... Jer 35:10
The words of J the son of Rechab,.... Jer 35:14
Because the sons of J the son of...... Jer 35:16
the commandment of J your father... Jer 35:18
The son of Rechab shall not........... Jer 35:19

JONAH (*jo'-nah*) See **JONA**, **JONAS**. *A prophet.*
by the hand of his servant J........... Jer 14:25
came unto J the son of Amittai........ Jonah 1:1
But J rose up to flee unto.............. Jonah 1:3
But J was gone down into the......... Jonah 1:5
cast lots, and the lot fell upon J...... Jonah 1:7
So they took up J, and cast him...... Jonah 1:15
a great fish to swallow up J........... Jonah 1:17
J was in the belly of the fish.......... Jonah 1:17
Then J prayed unto the LORD his..... Jonah 2:1
it vomited out J upon the dry......... Jonah 2:10
LORD came unto J the second time... Jonah 3:1
So J arose, and went unto Nineveh,.. Jonah 3:3
J began to enter into the city a....... Jonah 3:4
But it displeased J exceedingly....... Jonah 4:1
So J went out of the city, and sat.... Jonah 4:5
and made it to come up over J........ Jonah 4:6
So J was exceeding glad of the........ Jonah 4:6
the sun beat upon the head of J...... Jonah 4:8
And God said to J, Doest thou well... Jonah 4:9

JONAM See **JONAN**.

JONAN (*jo'-nan*) *Ancestor of Joseph, husband
of Mary.*
of Joseph, which was the son of J..... Lk 3:30

JONAS (*jo'-nas*) See **JONA**, **JONAH**.
   1. Same as Jonah.
it, but the sign of the prophet J....... Mt 12:39
For as J was three days and three.... Mt 12:40
repented at the preaching of J........ Mt 12:41
behold, a greater than J is here....... Mt 12:41
it, but the sign of the prophet J....... Mt 16:4
it, but the sign of J the prophet...... Lk 11:29
For as J was a sign unto the.......... Lk 11:30
repented at the preaching of J........ Lk 11:32
behold, a greater than J is here....... Lk 11:32
   2. Father of Peter.
to Simon Peter, son of J................ Jn 21:15
the second time, Simon, son of J...... Jn 21:16
the third time, Simon, son of J........ Jn 21:17

JONATHAN (*jon'-a-than*) See **JEHONATHAN**,
JONATHAN'S.
   1. A Levite.
and J, the son of Gershom, the son... Judg 18:30
   2. Son of Saul.
a thousand were with J in Gibeah.... 1Sa 13:2
J smote the garrison of the........... 1Sa 13:3
J his son, and the people that........ 1Sa 13:16
people that were with Saul and J.... 1Sa 13:22
with J his son was there found....... 1Sa 13:22
that J the son of Saul said unto...... 1Sa 14:1
people knew not that J was gone..... 1Sa 14:3
by which J sought to go over unto.... 1Sa 14:4

J said to the young man that bare...... 1Sa 14:6
Then said J, Behold, we will pass 1Sa 14:8
men of the garrison answered J...... 1Sa 14:12
J said unto his armourbearer...... 1Sa 14:12
J climbed up upon his hands and 1Sa 14:13
and they fell before J...... 1Sa 14:13
And that first slaughter, which J 1Sa 14:14
when they had numbered, behold, J... 1Sa 14:17
that were with Saul and J...... 1Sa 14:21
But J heard not when his father...... 1Sa 14:27
Then said J, My father hath 1Sa 14:29
Israel, though it be in J my son 1Sa 14:39
J my son will be on the other...... 1Sa 14:40
And Saul and J were taken...... 1Sa 14:41
Cast lots between me and J my son... 1Sa 14:42
And J was taken 1Sa 14:42
Then Saul said to J, Tell me what 1Sa 14:43
J told him, and said, I did but 1Sa 14:43
for thou shalt surely die, J...... 1Sa 14:44
said unto Saul, Shall J die 1Sa 14:45
So the people rescued J, that he...... 1Sa 14:49
Now the sons of Saul were J...... 1Sa 14:49
that the soul of J was knit with...... 1Sa 18:1
J loved him as his own soul...... 1Sa 18:1
Then J and David made a covenant, ... 1Sa 18:3
J stripped himself of the robe...... 1Sa 18:4
And Saul spake to J his son...... 1Sa 19:1
But J Saul's son delighted much 1Sa 19:2
J told David, saying, Saul my 1Sa 19:2
J spake good of David unto Saul 1Sa 19:4
hearkened unto the voice of J...... 1Sa 19:6
J called David, and Jonathan...... 1Sa 19:7
J shewed him all those things 1Sa 19:7
J brought David to Saul, and he 1Sa 19:7
Ramah, and came and said before J 1Sa 20:1
Let not J know this, lest he be...... 1Sa 20:3
Then said J unto David...... 1Sa 20:4
And David said unto J, Behold, to..... 1Sa 20:5
J said, Far be it from thee 1Sa 20:9
Then said David to J, Who shall...... 1Sa 20:10
J said unto David, Come, and let...... 1Sa 20:11
J said unto David, O Lord God of..... 1Sa 20:12
The Lord do so and much more to J .. 1Sa 20:13
So J made a covenant with the 1Sa 20:16
J caused David to swear again,...... 1Sa 20:17
Then J said to David, To morrow...... 1Sa 20:18
J arose, and Abner sat by Saul's...... 1Sa 20:25
and Saul said unto J his son...... 1Sa 20:27
J answered Saul, David earnestly 1Sa 20:28
anger was kindled against J...... 1Sa 20:30
J answered Saul his father, and 1Sa 20:32
whereby J knew that it was...... 1Sa 20:33
So J arose from the table in...... 1Sa 20:34
that J went out into the field at 1Sa 20:35
of the arrow which J had shot 1Sa 20:37
J cried after the lad, and said, ... 1Sa 20:37
J cried after the lad, Make speed... 1Sa 20:38
only J and David knew the matter... 1Sa 20:39
J gave his artillery unto his lad 1Sa 20:40
J said to David, Go in peace, ... 1Sa 20:42
and J went into the city...... 1Sa 20:42
J Saul's son arose, and went to...... 1Sa 23:16
the wood, and J went to his house 1Sa 23:18
and the Philistines slew J...... 1Sa 31:2
Saul and J his son are dead also 2Sa 1:4
that Saul and J his son be dead 2Sa 1:5
for J his son, and for the people 2Sa 1:12
over Saul and over J his son...... 2Sa 1:17
the bow of J turned not back, and ... 2Sa 1:22
J were lovely and pleasant in 2Sa 1:23
O J, thou wast slain in thine...... 2Sa 1:25
distressed for thee, my brother J 2Sa 1:26
And J, Saul's son, had a son that 2Sa 4:4
J out of Jezreel, and his name 2Sa 4:4
J hath yet a son, which is lame 2Sa 9:3
when Mephibosheth, the son of J 2Sa 9:6
kindness for J thy father's sake 2Sa 9:7
the son of J the son of Saul...... 2Sa 21:7
David and J the son of Saul...... 2Sa 21:7
the bones of J his son from the 2Sa 21:12
of Saul and the bones of J his son ... 2Sa 21:13
J his son buried they in the...... 2Sa 21:14
Kish begat Saul, and Saul begat J ... 1Chr 8:33
the son of J was Merib-baal 1Chr 8:34
and Saul begat J, and Malchi-shua, ... 1Chr 9:39
the son of J was Merib-baal 1Chr 9:40
and the Philistines slew J...... 1Chr 10:2
  3. A son of Abiathar.
thy son, and J the son of Abiathar ... 2Sa 15:27
Zadok's son, and J Abiathar's son ... 2Sa 15:36
Now J and Ahimaaz stayed by...... 2Sa 17:17
they said, Where is Ahimaaz and J ... 2Sa 17:20
J the son of Abiathar the priest 1Kin 1:42
J answered and said to Adonijah, ... 1Kin 1:43
  4. A son of Shimea.
J the son of Shimeah the brother ... 2Sa 21:21
J the son of Shimea David's...... 1Chr 20:7
  5. A "mighty man" of David.
of the sons of Jashen, J...... 2Sa 23:32
J the son of Shage the Hararite,... 1Chr 11:34
  6. A son of Jada.
Shammai; Jether, and J...... 1Chr 2:32
And the sons of J...... 1Chr 2:33
  7. An uncle of David.
Also J David's uncle was a 1Chr 27:32
  8. A family of exiles.
Ebed the son of J, and with him ... Ezr 8:6
  9. Son of Asahel.
Only J the son of Asahel and ...... Ezr 10:15
  10. A descendant of Jeshua.

And Joiada begat J...... Neh 12:11
and J begat Jaddua ...... Neh 12:11
  11. A priest descended from Melicu.
Of Melicu, J...... Neh 12:14
  *12. A priest descended from Shemaiah,
  namely, Zechariah the son of J...... Neh 12:35
  13. A scribe.*
in the house of J the scribe ...... Jer 37:15
to the house of J the scribe ...... Jer 37:20
  14. A son of Kareah.
J the sons of Kareah, and Seraiah...... Jer 40:8

JONATHAN'S (*jon'-a-thans*) Refers to Jonathan 2.
J lad gathered up the arrows, and...... 1Sa 20:38
may shew him kindness for J sake 2Sa 9:1
not cause me to return to J house ...... Jer 38:26

JONATH-ELEM-RECHOKIM (*jo''-nath-e'-lem-re-ko'-kim*) A musical notation.
To the chief Musician upon J...... Ps 56:t

JOPPA (*jop'-pah*) A seaport in Dan.
it to thee in flotes by sea to J...... 2Chr 2:16
from Lebanon to the sea of J...... Ezr 3:7
of the Lord, and went down to J...... Jonah 1:3
Now there was at J a certain...... Acts 9:36
forasmuch as Lydda was nigh to J...... Acts 9:38
And it was known throughout all J ... Acts 9:42
days in J with one Simon a tanner...... Acts 9:43
And now send men to J, and call for ..Acts 10:5
unto them, he sent them to J...... Acts 10:8
brethren then J accompanied him...... Acts 10:23
Send therefore to J, and call...... Acts 10:32
I was in the city of J praying...... Acts 11:5
and said unto him, Send men to J... Acts 11:13

JORAH (*jo'-rah*) See HARIPH. *A family of exiles.*
The children of J, an hundred and ... Ezr 2:18

JORAI (*jo'-rahee*) *Head of a Gadite family.*
and Meshullam, and Sheba, and J ... 1Chr 5:13

JORAM (*jo'-ram*) See JEHORAM.
  1. A son of Toi.
Then Toi sent J his son unto king...... 2Sa 8:10
J brought with him vessels of 2Sa 8:10
  2. Same as Jehoram.
So J went over to Zair, and all 2Kin 8:21
And the rest of the acts of J...... 2Kin 8:23
J slept with his fathers, and was ... 2Kin 8:24
Jehosheba, the daughter of king J ... 2Kin 11:2
J his son, Ahaziah his son, Joash ... 1Chr 3:11
and Josaphat begat J...... Mt 1:8
and J begat Ozias...... Mt 1:8
  3. A son of Ahab.
in the fifth year of J the son of 2Kin 8:16
In the twelfth year of J the son...... 2Kin 8:25
he went with J the son of Ahab to ... 2Kin 8:28
and the Syrians wounded J...... 2Kin 8:28
king J went back to be healed in 2Kin 8:29
see J the son of Ahab in Jezreel...... 2Kin 8:29
son of Nimshi conspired against J 2Kin 9:14
(Now J had kept Ramoth-gilead, he ... 2Kin 9:14
But king J was returned to be...... 2Kin 9:15
for J lay there...... 2Kin 9:16
of Judah was come down to see J 2Kin 9:16
J said, Take an horseman, and send ... 2Kin 9:17
And J said, Make ready...... 2Kin 9:21
J king of Israel and Ahaziah king 2Kin 9:21
when J saw Jehu, that he said, Is ... 2Kin 9:22
J turned his hands, and fled, and...... 2Kin 9:23
in the eleventh year of J the son 2Kin 9:29
and the Syrians smote J...... 2Chr 22:5
Ahaziah was of God by coming to J ... 2Chr 22:7
  4. A descendant of Eliezer.
J his son, and Zichri his son, and...... 1Chr 26:25

JORDAN (*jor'-dan*) *A river that runs from the Sea of Galilee to the Dead Sea.*
and beheld all the plain of J...... Gen 13:10
Lot chose him all the plain of J...... Gen 13:11
my staff I passed over this J...... Gen 32:10
of Atad, which is beyond J...... Gen 50:10
Abel-mizraim, which is beyond J ...... Gen 50:11
by the sea, and by the coast of J ...... Num 13:29
of Moab on this side J by Jericho ... Num 22:1
plains of Moab by J near Jericho...... Num 26:3
plains of Moab by J near Jericho...... Num 26:63
Moab, which are by J near Jericho ... Num 31:12
and bring us not over J...... Num 32:5
with them on yonder side J...... Num 32:19
to us on this side J eastward...... Num 32:19
you armed over J before the Lord ...... Num 32:21
Reuben will pass with you over J ...... Num 32:29
on this side J may be ours...... Num 32:32
plains of Moab by J near Jericho...... Num 33:48
And they pitched by J...... Num 33:49
Moses in the plains of Moab by J ...... Num 33:50
over J into the land of Canaan...... Num 33:51
And the border shall go down to J... Num 34:12
this side J near Jericho eastward...... Num 34:15
plains of Moab by J near Jericho...... Num 35:1
When ye be come over J into the...... Num 35:10
give three cities on this side J...... Num 35:14
plains of Moab by J near Jericho...... Num 36:13
on this side J in the wilderness...... Deut 1:1
On this side J, in the land of...... Deut 1:5
until I shall pass over J into...... Deut 2:29
the land that was on this side J...... Deut 3:8
The plain also, and J the...... Deut 3:17
your God hath given them beyond J ... Deut 3:20
the good land that is beyond J...... Deut 3:25

for thou shalt not go over this J ...... Deut 3:27
sware that I should not go over J ...... Deut 4:21
this land, I must not go over J...... Deut 4:22
ye go over J to possess it...... Deut 4:26
this side J toward the sunrising...... Deut 4:41
On this side J, in the valley...... Deut 4:46
this side J toward the sunrising...... Deut 4:47
the plain on this side J eastward...... Deut 4:49
Thou art to pass over J this day...... Deut 9:1
Are they not on the other side J ...... Deut 11:30
For ye shall pass over J to go in ...... Deut 11:31
But when ye go over J, and dwell...... Deut 12:10
J unto the land which the Lord...... Deut 27:2
shall ye when ye be gone over J...... Deut 27:4
people, when ye are come over J...... Deut 27:12
over J to go to possess it...... Deut 30:18
me, Thou shalt not go over this J...... Deut 31:2
ye go over J to possess it...... Deut 31:13
ye go over J to possess it...... Deut 32:47
therefore arise, go over this J...... Josh 1:2
days ye shall pass over this J...... Josh 1:11
Moses gave you on this side J...... Josh 1:14
this side J toward the sunrising...... Josh 1:15
then the way to J unto the fords ...... Josh 2:7
that were on the other side J...... Josh 2:10
from Shittim, and came to J...... Josh 3:1
to the brink of the water of J...... Josh 3:8
J, ye shall stand still in J...... Josh 3:8
passeth over before you into J...... Josh 3:11
shall rest in the waters of J...... Josh 3:13
that the waters of J shall be cut ...... Josh 3:13
from their tents, to pass over J...... Josh 3:14
bare the ark were come unto J...... Josh 3:15
(for J overfloweth all his banks...... Josh 3:15
on dry ground in the midst of J...... Josh 3:17
people were passed clean over J...... Josh 3:17
people were clean passed over J...... Josh 4:1
you hence out of the midst of J...... Josh 4:3
Lord your God into the midst of J...... Josh 4:5
That the waters of J were cut off...... Josh 4:7
when it passed over J...... Josh 4:7
the waters of J were cut off...... Josh 4:7
stones out of the midst of J...... Josh 4:8
twelve stones in the midst of J...... Josh 4:9
the ark stood in the midst of J...... Josh 4:10
that they come up out of J...... Josh 4:16
saying, Come up out of J...... Josh 4:17
come up out of the midst of J...... Josh 4:18
that the waters of J returned...... Josh 4:18
the people came up out of J on ...... Josh 4:19
stones, which they took out of J...... Josh 4:20
came over this J on dry land...... Josh 4:22
the waters of J from before you...... Josh 4:23
were on the side of J westward...... Josh 5:1
of J from before the children of...... Josh 5:1
at all brought this people over J ...... Josh 7:7
and dwelt on the other side J...... Josh 7:7
kings which were on this side J...... Josh 9:1
the Amorites, that were beyond J ...... Josh 9:10
J toward the rising of the sun...... Josh 12:1
smote on this side J on the west ...... Josh 12:7
beyond J eastward, even as Moses ...... Josh 12:7
of the children of Reuben was J...... Josh 13:23
of Sihon king of Heshbon, ... Josh 13:27
on the other side J eastward...... Josh 13:27
of Moab, on the other side J...... Josh 13:32
an half tribe on the other side J...... Josh 14:3
salt sea, even unto the end of J...... Josh 15:5
sea at the uttermost part of J...... Josh 15:5
of Joseph fell from J by Jericho...... Josh 16:1
came to Jericho, and went out at J ... Josh 16:7
which were on the other side J...... Josh 17:5
inheritance beyond J on the east...... Josh 18:7
on the north side was from J...... Josh 18:19
salt sea at the south end of J...... Josh 18:19
J was the border of it on the...... Josh 18:20
of their border were at J...... Josh 18:22
the outgoings thereof were at J...... Josh 19:33
to Judah upon J toward the ...... Josh 19:34
on the other side J by Jericho...... Josh 20:8
Lord gave you on the other side J ...... Josh 22:4
brethren on this side J westward...... Josh 22:7
they came unto the borders of J...... Josh 22:10
built there an altar by J...... Josh 22:10
of Canaan, in the borders of J...... Josh 22:11
hath made J a border between us...... Josh 22:25
for your tribes, from J with all...... Josh 23:4
which dwelt on the other side J...... Josh 24:8
And ye went over J, and came unto ... Josh 24:11
took the fords of J toward Moab...... Judg 3:28
Gilead abode beyond J...... Judg 5:17
the waters unto Beth-barah and J ..... Judg 7:24
the waters unto Beth-barah and J ..... Judg 7:24
to Gideon on the other side J...... Judg 8:4
And Gideon came to J, and passed...... Judg 8:4
J in the land of the Amorites...... Judg 10:8
to fight also against Judah...... Judg 10:9
Arnon even unto Jabbok, and unto J ... Judg 11:13
from the wilderness even unto J...... Judg 11:22
of J before the Ephraimites...... Judg 12:5
and slew him at the passages of J ...... Judg 12:6
went over J to the land of Gad...... 1Sa 13:7
that were on the other side J...... 1Sa 31:7
the plain, and passed over J...... 2Sa 2:29
Israel together, and passed over J 2Sa 10:17
with him, and they passed over J 2Sa 17:22
of them that was not gone over J 2Sa 17:22
And Absalom passed over J, he and ... 2Sa 17:24
the king returned, and came to J 2Sa 19:15
king, to conduct the king over J...... 2Sa 19:15

they went over *J* before the king 2Sa 19:17
the king, as he was come over *J* 2Sa 19:31
went over *J* with the king 2Sa 19:31
to conduct him over *J* 2Sa 19:31
a little way over *J* with the king 2Sa 19:36
And all the people went over *J* 2Sa 19:39
all David's men with him, over *J* 2Sa 19:41
king, from *J* even to Jerusalem 2Sa 20:2
And they passed over *J*, and pitched 2Sa 24:5
but he came down to meet me at *J* 1Kin 2:8
In the plain of *J* did the king 1Kin 7:46
brook Cherith, that is before *J* 1Kin 17:3
brook Cherith, that is before *J* 1Kin 17:5
for the LORD hath sent me to *J* 2Kin 2:6
and they two stood by *J* 2Kin 2:7
back, and stood by the bank of *J* 2Kin 2:13
wash in *J* seven times, and thy 2Kin 5:10
dipped himself seven times in *J* 2Kin 5:14
Let us go, we pray thee, unto *J* 2Kin 6:2
And when they came to *J*, they cut 2Kin 6:4
And they went after them unto *J* 2Kin 7:15
From *J* eastward, all the land of 2Kin 10:33
And on the other side *J* by Jericho 1Chr 6:78
on the east side of *J* 1Chr 6:78
went over *J* in the first month 1Chr 12:15
And on the other side of *J* 1Chr 12:37
all Israel, and passed over *J* 1Chr 19:17
them of Israel on this side *J* 1Chr 26:30
In the plain of *J* did the king 2Chr 4:17
he can draw up *J* into his mouth .... Job 40:23
remember thee from the land of *J* .... Ps 42:6
J was driven back .... Ps 114:3
thou *J*, that thou wast driven .... Ps 114:5
by the way of the sea, beyond *J* .... Is 9:1
wilt thou do in the swelling of *J* .... Jer 12:5
a lion from the swelling of *J* .... Jer 49:19
of *J* unto the habitation of the .... Jer 50:44
and from the land of Israel by *J* .... Eze 47:18
for the pride of *J* is spoiled .... Zec 11:3
and all the region round about *J* .... Mt 3:5
And were baptized of him in *J* .... Mt 3:6
Jesus from Galilee to *J* unto John .... Mt 3:13
by the way of the sea, beyond *J* .... Mt 4:15
and from Judaea, and from beyond *J* .... Mt 4:25
the coasts of Judaea beyond *J* .... Mt 19:1
baptized of him in the river of *J* .... Mk 1:5
and was baptized of John in *J* .... Mk 1:9
and from Idumaea, and from beyond *J* .... Mk 3:8
Judaea by the farther side of *J* .... Mk 10:1
came into all the country about *J* .... Lk 3:3
of the Holy Ghost returned from *J* .... Lk 4:1
were done in Bethabara beyond *J* .... Jn 1:28
he that was with thee beyond *J* .... Jn 3:26
went away again beyond *J* into the .... Jn 10:40

JORIM (jo'-rim) *Son of Matthat; ancestor of Jesus.*
Eliezer, which was the son of *J* .... Lk 3:29

JORKEAM See JORKOAM.

JORKOAM (jor'-ko-am) *A descendant of Hebron.*
begat Raham, the father of *J* 1Chr 2:44

JOSABAD (jos'-a-bad) See JOZABAD. *A warrior in David's army.*
and Johanan, and *J* the Gederathite, ... 1Chr 12:4

JOSAPHAT (jos'-a-fat) See JEHOSHAPHAT. *Son of Asa; ancestor of Jesus.*
And Asa begat *J* .... Mt 1:8
and *J* begat Joram .... Mt 1:8

JOSE (jo'-ze) See JOSES. *Son of Eliezer; ancestor of Jesus.*
Which was the son of *J*, which was .... Lk 3:29

JOSEDECH See JOSEPH.

JOSEDECH (jos'-e-dek) See JOZADAK. *Father of Joshua, the priest.*
Judah, and to Joshua the son of *J* .... Hag 1:1
Shealtiel, and Joshua the son of *J* .... Hag 1:12
the spirit of Joshua the son of *J* .... Hag 1:14
Judah, and to Joshua the son of *J* .... Hag 2:2
and be strong, O Joshua, son of *J* .... Hag 2:4
the head of Joshua the son of *J* .... Zec 6:11

JOSEPH (jo'-zef) See BARSABAS, JOSEPH'S.
1. *Son of Jacob and Rachel.*
And she called his name *J* .... Gen 30:24
to pass, when Rachel had born *J* .... Gen 30:25
after, and Rachel and *J* hindermost .... Gen 33:2
and after came *J* near and Rachel, ... Gen 33:7
sons of Rachel; *J*, and Benjamin .... Gen 35:24
J, being seventeen years old, was .... Gen 37:2
J brought unto his father their .... Gen 37:2
Now Israel loved *J* more than all .... Gen 37:3
J dreamed a dream, and he told it .... Gen 37:5
And Israel said unto *J*, Do not thy .... Gen 37:13
J went after his brethren, and .... Gen 37:17
when *J* was come unto his brethren, ... Gen 37:23
they stript *J* out of his coat .... Gen 37:23
lifted up *J* out of the pit, and .... Gen 37:28
sold *J* to the Ishmeelites for .... Gen 37:28
and they brought *J* into Egypt .... Gen 37:28
and, behold, *J* was not in the pit .... Gen 37:29
J is without doubt rent in pieces .... Gen 37:33
J was brought down to Egypt .... Gen 39:1
And the LORD was with *J*, and he was .... Gen 39:2
J found grace in his sight, and he .... Gen 39:4
J was a goodly person, and well .... Gen 39:6
wife cast her eyes upon *J* .... Gen 39:7

as she spake to *J* day by day .... Gen 39:10
that *J* went into the house to do .... Gen 39:11
But the LORD was with *J*, and .... Gen 39:21
the place where *J* was bound .... Gen 39:21
of the guard charged *J* with them. .... Gen 40:4
I came in unto them in the .... Gen 40:6
And *J* said unto them, Do not .... Gen 40:8
chief butler told his dream to *J* .... Gen 40:9
J said unto him, This is the .... Gen 40:12
was good, he said unto *J*, I also .... Gen 40:16
J answered and said, This is the .... Gen 40:18
as *J* had interpreted to them .... Gen 40:22
not the chief butler remember *J* .... Gen 40:23
Then Pharaoh sent and called *J* .... Gen 41:14
And Pharaoh said unto *J*, I have .... Gen 41:15
J answered Pharaoh, saying, It is .... Gen 41:16
And Pharaoh said unto *J*, In my .... Gen 41:17
J said unto Pharaoh, The dream of .... Gen 41:25
And Pharaoh said unto *J*, Forasmuch .... Gen 41:39
And Pharaoh said unto *J*, See, I .... Gen 41:41
J went out over all the land of .... Gen 41:45
J was thirty years old when he .... Gen 41:46
J went out from the presence of .... Gen 41:46
J gathered corn as the sand of .... Gen 41:49
unto *J* were born two sons before .... Gen 41:50
And *J* called the name of the .... Gen 41:51
to come, according as *J* had said .... Gen 41:54
unto all the Egyptians, Go unto *J* .... Gen 41:55
J opened all the storehouses, and .... Gen 41:56
into Egypt to *J* for to buy corn. .... Gen 41:57
J was the governor over the land, ... Gen 42:6
J saw his brethren, and he knew .... Gen 42:7
And *J* knew his brethren, but they .... Gen 42:8
J remembered the dreams which he .... Gen 42:9
And *J* said unto them, That is it .... Gen 42:14
And *J* said unto them the third day, ... Gen 42:18
J knew not that *J* understood them .... Gen 42:23
Then *J* commanded to fill their .... Gen 42:25
J is not, and Simeon is not, and ye .... Gen 42:36
down to Egypt, and stood before *J* .... Gen 43:15
when *J* saw Benjamin with them, he .... Gen 43:16
And the man did as *J* bade .... Gen 43:17
present against *J* came at noon .... Gen 43:25
when *J* came home, they brought .... Gen 43:26
And *J* made haste .... Gen 43:30
to the word that *J* had spoken .... Gen 44:2
J said unto his steward, Up, ... Gen 44:4
J said unto them, What deed is .... Gen 44:15
Then *J* could not refrain himself .... Gen 45:1
And *J* made himself known unto .... Gen 45:1
J said unto his brethren .... Gen 45:3
I am *J*; doth my father .... Gen 45:3
J said unto his brethren, Come .... Gen 45:4
I am *J* your brother, whom ye sold, ... Gen 45:4
unto him, Thus saith thy son *J* .... Gen 45:9
And Pharaoh said unto *J*, Say unto .... Gen 45:17
J gave them wagons, according to .... Gen 45:21
is yet alive, and he is governor .... Gen 45:26
they told him all the words of *J* .... Gen 45:27
which *J* had sent to carry him .... Gen 45:27
J my son is yet alive .... Gen 45:28
I shall put his hand upon thine .... Gen 46:4
Jacob's wife; *J*, and Benjamin .... Gen 46:19
unto *J* in the land of Egypt were .... Gen 46:20
And the sons of *J*, which were born .... Gen 46:27
he sent Judah before him unto *J* .... Gen 46:28
J made ready his chariot, and went .... Gen 46:29
And Israel said unto *J*, Now let me .... Gen 46:30
J said unto his brethren, and unto .... Gen 46:31
Then *J* came and told Pharaoh, and .... Gen 47:1
And Pharaoh spake unto *J*, saying, ... Gen 47:5
J brought in Jacob his father, and .... Gen 47:7
J placed his father and his .... Gen 47:11
J nourished his father, and his .... Gen 47:12
and *J* brought the money into .... Gen 47:14
all the Egyptians came unto *J* .... Gen 47:15
And *J* said, Give your cattle .... Gen 47:16
they brought their cattle unto *J* .... Gen 47:17
J gave them bread in exchange for .... Gen 47:17
J bought all the land of Egypt .... Gen 47:20
Then *J* said unto the people, ... Gen 47:23
J made it a law over the land of .... Gen 47:26
and he called his son *J*, and said .... Gen 47:29
these things, that one told *J* .... Gen 48:1
thy son *J* cometh unto thee .... Gen 48:2
And Jacob said unto *J*, God .... Gen 48:3
J said unto his father, They are .... Gen 48:9
And Israel said unto *J*, I had not .... Gen 48:11
J brought them out from between .... Gen 48:12
I took them both, Ephraim in his .... Gen 48:13
And he blessed *J*, and said, God .... Gen 48:15
when *J* saw that his father laid .... Gen 48:17
J said unto his father, Not so, ... Gen 48:18
And Israel said unto *J*, Behold, I .... Gen 48:21
J is a fruitful bough, even a .... Gen 49:22
they shall be on the head of *J* .... Gen 49:26
J fell upon his father's face, and .... Gen 50:1
J commanded his servants the .... Gen 50:2
spake unto the house of Pharaoh .... Gen 50:4
J went up to bury his father .... Gen 50:7
And all the house of *J*, and his .... Gen 50:8
J returned into Egypt, he and his .... Gen 50:14
J will peradventure hate us, and .... Gen 50:15
And they sent a messenger unto *J* .... Gen 50:16
So shall ye say unto *J*, Forgive, ... Gen 50:17
J wept when they spake unto him. .... Gen 50:17
J said unto them, Fear not .... Gen 50:19
J dwelt in Egypt, he, and his .... Gen 50:22

J lived an hundred and ten years .... Gen 50:22
J saw Ephraim's children of the .... Gen 50:23
J said unto his brethren, I die .... Gen 50:24
J took an oath of the children of .... Gen 50:25
So *J* died, being an hundred and .... Gen 50:26
for *J* was in Egypt already .... Ex 1:5
J died, and all his brethren, and .... Ex 1:6
king over Egypt, which knew not *J* .... Ex 1:8
took the bones of *J* with him .... Ex 13:19
families of Manasseh the son of *J* .... Num 27:1
tribe of Manasseh the son of *J* .... Num 32:33
The prince of the children of *J* .... Num 34:23
the sons of Manasseh the son of *J* .... Num 36:12
Levi, and Judah, and Issachar, and *J* .... Deut 27:12
the children of *J* were two tribes .... Josh 14:4
the lot of the children of *J* fell .... Josh 16:1
So the children of *J*, Manasseh and .... Josh 16:4
for he was the firstborn of *J* .... Josh 17:1
the son of *J* by their families .... Josh 17:2
the children of *J* spake unto .... Josh 17:14
And the children of *J* said .... Josh 17:16
And the bones of *J*, which the .... Josh 24:32
Dan, *J*, and Benjamin, Naphtali, ... 1Chr 2:2
He sent a man before them, even *J* .... Ps 105:17
that Jacob gave to his son *J* .... Jn 4:5
with envy, sold *J* into Egypt .... Acts 7:9
at the second time *J* was made .... Acts 7:13
Then sent *J*, and called his father .... Acts 7:14
king arose, which knew not *J* .... Acts 7:18
dying, blessed both the sons of *J* .... Heb 11:21
By faith *J*, when he died, made .... Heb 11:22

2. *Descendants of Joseph.*
Of the children of *J* .... Num 1:10
Of the children of *J*, namely, of .... Num 1:32
Of the tribe of *J*, namely, of the .... Num 13:11
The sons of *J* after their .... Num 26:28
sons of *J* after their families .... Num 26:37
of the families of the sons of *J* .... Num 36:1
of the sons of *J* hath said .... Num 36:5
of *J* he said, Blessed of the LORD .... Deut 33:13
blessing came upon the head of *J* .... Deut 33:16
Joshua spake unto the house of *J* .... Josh 17:17
the house of *J* shall abide in .... Josh 18:5
of Judah and the children of *J* .... Josh 18:11
inheritance of the children of *J* .... Josh 24:32
And the house of *J*, they also went .... Judg 1:22
the house of *J* sent to descry .... Judg 1:23
hand of the house of *J* prevailed. .... Judg 1:35
this day of all the house of *J* to 2Sa 19:20
all the charge of the house of *J* 1Kin 11:28
the son of *J*, in the land of 1Chr 5:1
children of *J* the son of Israel 1Chr 7:29
people, the sons of Jacob and *J* .... Ps 77:15
he refused the tabernacle of *J* .... Ps 78:67
thou that leadest Joseph like a flock .... Ps 80:1
he ordained in *J* for a testimony .... Ps 81:5
stick, and write upon it, For *J* .... Eze 37:16
I will take the stick of *J* .... Eze 37:19
I shall have two portions .... Eze 47:13
and one gate of *J*, one gate of .... Eze 48:32
out like fire in the house of *J* .... Amos 5:6
be gracious unto the remnant of *J* .... Amos 5:15
grieved for the affliction of *J* .... Amos 6:6
a fire, and the house of *J* a flame .... Obad 18
and I will save the house of *J* .... Zec 10:6
Of the tribe of *J* were sealed .... Rev 7:8

3. *A spy sent to the Promised Land.*
of Issachar, Igal the son of *J* .... Num 13:7

4. *A son of Asaph.*
Zaccur, and *J*, and Nethaniah, and 1Chr 25:2
lot came forth for Asaph to *J* 1Chr 25:9

5. *Married a foreigner in exile.*
Shallum, Amariah, and *J* .... Ezr 10:42

6. *A priest.*
Jonathan; of Shebaniah, *J* .... Neh 12:14

7. *Husband of Mary, the mother of Jesus.*
Jacob begat *J* the husband of Mary .... Mt 1:16
his mother Mary was espoused to *J* .... Mt 1:18
Then *J* her husband, being a just .... Mt 1:19
unto him in a dream, saying, *J* .... Mt 1:20
Then *J* being raised from sleep .... Mt 1:24
Lord appeareth to *J* in a dream .... Mt 2:13
in a dream to *J* in Egypt, ... Mt 2:19
to a man whose name was *J* .... Lk 1:27
J also went up from Galilee, out .... Lk 2:4
with haste, and found Mary, and *J* .... Lk 2:16
And *J* and his mother marvelled at .... Lk 2:33
and *J* and his mother knew not of it. .... Lk 2:43
(as was supposed) the son of *J* .... Lk 3:23
Jesus of Nazareth, the son of *J* .... Jn 1:45
Is not this Jesus, the son of *J* .... Jn 6:42

8. *A disciple of Jesus.*
a rich, man of Arimathaea, named *J* .... Mt 27:57
when *J* had taken the body, he .... Mt 27:59
J of Arimathaea, an honourable .... Mk 15:43
centurion, he gave the body to *J* .... Mk 15:45
behold, there was a man named *J* .... Lk 23:50
after this *J* of Arimathaea, being .... Jn 19:38

9. *Son of Mattathias; ancestor of Jesus.*
of Janna, which was the son of *J* .... Lk 3:24

10. *Son of Juda; ancestor of Jesus.*
of Semei, which was the son of *J* .... Lk 3:26

11. *Son of Jonan; ancestor of Jesus.*
of Juda, which was the son of *J* .... Lk 3:30

12. *A nominee for Judas' apostleship.*
J called Barsabas, who was .... Acts 1:23

JOSEPH'S (jo'-zefs)
1. *Refers to Joseph 1.*
And they took *J* coat, and killed a .... Gen 37:31
the Egyptian's house for *J* sake .... Gen 39:5

he left all that he had in J hand .... Gen 39:6
J master took him, and put him .... Gen 39:20
of the prison committed to J hand .... Gen 39:22
his hand, and put it upon J hand .... Gen 41:42
And Pharaoh called J name .... Gen 41:45
J ten brethren went down to buy .... Gen 42:3
J brother, Jacob sent not with .... Gen 42:4
J brethren came, and bowed down .... Gen 42:6
man brought the men into J house .... Gen 43:17
they were brought into J house .... Gen 43:18
near to the steward of J house .... Gen 43:19
And brought the men into J house .... Gen 43:24
and his brethren came to J house .... Gen 44:14
saying, J brethren are come .... Gen 45:16
And Israel beheld J sons, and said, ... Gen 48:8
when J brethren saw that their .... Gen 50:15
were brought up upon J knees .... Gen 50:23
but the birthright was J 1Chr 5:2
J kindred was made known unto .... Acts 7:13
   2. *Refers to Joseph 7.*
And they said, Is not this J son .... Lk 4:22

JOSES (jo´-zez) See JOSE.
   1. *A brother of Jesus.*
and his brethren, James, and J.......... Mt 13:55
Mary, the brother of James, and J.......... Mk 6:3
   2. *Same as Barnabas.*
and Mary the mother of James and J.......... Mt 27:56
mother of James the less and of J.......... Mk 15:40
Mary the mother of J beheld where.......... Mk 15:47
And J, who by the apostles was.......... Acts 4:36

JOSHAH (jo´-shah) *A descendant of Simeon.*
Jamlech, and J the son of Amaziah,.......... 1Chr 4:34

JOSHAPHAT (josh´-a-fat) See JEHOSHAPHAT.
JOSAPHAT. *A "mighty man" of David.*
of Maachah, and J the Mithnite,.......... 1Chr 11:43

JOSHAVIAH (josh-a-vi´-ah) *A "mighty man" of David.*
the Mahavite, and Jeribai, and J.......... 1Chr 11:46

JOSHBEKASHAH (josh-bek´-a-shah) *A sanctuary servant.*
Giddalti, and Romamti-ezer, J.......... 1Chr 25:4
The seventeenth to J, he, his.......... 1Chr 25:24

JOSHEB-BASSHEBETH See ADINO.

JOSHUA (josh´-u-ah) See HOSEA, HOSHEA, JEHOSHUAH, JESHUA, JESHUAH, JESUS, OSEA, OSHEA.
   1. *Son of Nun.*
And Moses said unto J, Choose us.......... Ex 17:9
So J did as Moses had said to him,.......... Ex 17:10
J discomfited Amalek and his.......... Ex 17:13
and rehearse it in the ears of J.......... Ex 17:14
Moses rose up, and his minister J.......... Ex 24:13
when J heard the noise of the.......... Ex 32:17
but his servant J, the son of Nun.......... Ex 33:11
J the son of Nun, the servant of.......... Num 11:28
J the son of Nun and Caleb the.......... Num 14:6
of Jephunneh, and J the son of Nun.......... Num 14:30
But J the son of Nun, and Caleb.......... Num 14:38
of Jephunneh, and J the son of Nun.......... Num 26:65
Take thee J the son of Nun, a man.......... Num 27:18
and he took J, and set him before.......... Num 27:22
the Kenezite, and J the son of Nun.......... Num 32:12
J the son of Nun, and the son of.......... Num 32:28
the priest, and J the son of Nun.......... Num 34:17
But J the son of Nun, which.......... Deut 1:38
I commanded J at that time,.......... Deut 3:21
But charge J, and encourage him,.......... Deut 3:28
and J, he shall go over before.......... Deut 31:3
And Moses called unto J, and said.......... Deut 31:7
call J, and present yourselves in.......... Deut 31:14
J went, and presented themselves.......... Deut 31:14
he gave J the son of Nun a charge.......... Deut 31:23
J the son of Nun was full of the.......... Deut 34:9
LORD spake unto J the son of Nun.......... Josh 1:1
Then J commanded the officers of.......... Josh 1:10
the tribe of Manasseh, spake J.......... Josh 1:12
And they answered J, saying, All.......... Josh 1:16
J the son of Nun sent out of.......... Josh 2:1
came to J the son of Nun, and told.......... Josh 2:23
And they said unto J, Truly the.......... Josh 2:24
J rose early in the morning;.......... Josh 3:1
J said unto the people, Sanctify.......... Josh 3:5
J spake unto the priests, saying,.......... Josh 3:6
And the LORD said unto J, This day.......... Josh 3:7
J said unto the children of.......... Josh 3:9
J said, Hereby ye shall know that.......... Josh 3:10
that the LORD spake unto J.......... Josh 4:1
Then J called the twelve men,.......... Josh 4:4
J said unto them, Pass over.......... Josh 4:5
of Israel did so as J commanded.......... Josh 4:8
Jordan, as the LORD spake unto J.......... Josh 4:8
J set up twelve stones in the.......... Josh 4:9
that the LORD commanded J to.......... Josh 4:10
to all that Moses commanded J.......... Josh 4:10
J in the sight of all Israel.......... Josh 4:14
And the LORD spake unto J, saying,.......... Josh 4:15
J therefore commanded the priests.......... Josh 4:17
of Jordan, did J pitch in Gilgal.......... Josh 4:20
At that time the LORD said unto J.......... Josh 5:2
J made him sharp knives, and.......... Josh 5:3
this is the cause why J did circumcise.......... Josh 5:4
their stead, them J circumcised.......... Josh 5:7
And the LORD said unto J, This day.......... Josh 5:9
when J was by Jericho, that he.......... Josh 5:13
J went unto him, and said unto him.......... Josh 5:13
J fell on his face to the earth,.......... Josh 5:14

of the LORD's host said unto J.......... Josh 5:15
And J did so.......... Josh 5:15
And the LORD said unto J, See, I.......... Josh 6:2
J the son of Nun called the.......... Josh 6:6
when J had spoken unto the people.......... Josh 6:8
J had commanded the people,.......... Josh 6:10
J rose early in the morning, and.......... Josh 6:12
J said unto the people, Shout.......... Josh 6:16
But J had said unto the two men.......... Josh 6:22
J saved Rahab the harlot alive,.......... Josh 6:25
which J sent to spy out Jericho.......... Josh 6:25
J adjured them at that time,.......... Josh 6:26
So the LORD was with J.......... Josh 6:27
J sent men from Jericho to Ai,.......... Josh 7:2
And they returned to J, and said.......... Josh 7:3
J rent his clothes, and fell to.......... Josh 7:6
J said, Alas, O Lord GOD,.......... Josh 7:7
And the LORD said unto J, Get thee.......... Josh 7:10
So J rose up early in the morning.......... Josh 7:16
J said unto Achan, My son, give.......... Josh 7:19
And Achan answered J, and said,.......... Josh 7:20
So J sent messengers, and they ran.......... Josh 7:22
the tent, and brought them unto J.......... Josh 7:23
And J, and all Israel with him,.......... Josh 7:24
J said, Why hast thou troubled us.......... Josh 7:25
And the LORD said unto J, Fear.......... Josh 8:1
So J arose, and all the people of.......... Josh 8:3
J chose out thirty thousand.......... Josh 8:3
J therefore sent them forth:.......... Josh 8:9
but J lodged that night among the.......... Josh 8:9
J rose up early in the morning,.......... Josh 8:10
J went that night into the midst.......... Josh 8:13
And J and all Israel made as if.......... Josh 8:15
and they pursued after J, and were.......... Josh 8:16
And the LORD said unto J, Stretch.......... Josh 8:18
J stretched out the spear that he.......... Josh 8:18
And when J and all Israel saw that.......... Josh 8:21
took alive, and brought him to J.......... Josh 8:23
For J drew not his hand back,.......... Josh 8:26
of the LORD which he commanded J.......... Josh 8:27
J burnt Ai, and made it an heap.......... Josh 8:28
J commanded that they should take.......... Josh 8:29
Then J built an altar unto the.......... Josh 8:30
which J read not before all the.......... Josh 8:35
together, to fight with J.......... Josh 9:2
of Gibeon heard what J had done.......... Josh 9:3
they went to J unto the camp at.......... Josh 9:6
And they said unto J, We are thy.......... Josh 9:8
J said unto them, Who are ye.......... Josh 9:8
J made peace with them, and made a.......... Josh 9:15
J called for them, and he spake.......... Josh 9:22
And they answered J, and said,.......... Josh 9:24
J made them that day hewers of.......... Josh 9:27
had heard how J had taken Ai.......... Josh 10:1
for it hath made peace with J.......... Josh 10:4
sent unto J to the camp to Gilgal.......... Josh 10:6
So J ascended from Gilgal, he, and.......... Josh 10:7
And the LORD said unto J, Fear.......... Josh 10:8
J therefore came unto them.......... Josh 10:9
Then spake J to the LORD in the.......... Josh 10:12
J returned, and all Israel with.......... Josh 10:15
And it was told J, saying, The.......... Josh 10:17
J said, Roll great stones upon.......... Josh 10:18
And it came to pass, when J.......... Josh 10:20
camp to J at Makkedah in peace.......... Josh 10:21
Then said J, Open the mouth of.......... Josh 10:22
brought out those kings unto J.......... Josh 10:23
that J called for all the men of.......... Josh 10:24
And J said unto them, Fear not, nor.......... Josh 10:25
afterward J smote them, and slew.......... Josh 10:26
that J commanded, and they took.......... Josh 10:27
that day J took Makkedah, and.......... Josh 10:28
Then J passed from Makkedah, and.......... Josh 10:29
J passed from Libnah, and all.......... Josh 10:31
J smote him and his people, until.......... Josh 10:33
J and all Israel with him unto.......... Josh 10:34
J went up from Eglon, and all.......... Josh 10:36
J returned, and all Israel with.......... Josh 10:38
So J smote all the country of the.......... Josh 10:40
J smote them from Kadesh-barnea.......... Josh 10:41
their land did J take at one time,.......... Josh 10:42
And the LORD said unto J, Be not.......... Josh 11:6
So J came, and all the people of.......... Josh 11:7
J did unto them as the LORD bade.......... Josh 11:9
at that time turned back, and.......... Josh 11:10
did J take, and smote them with.......... Josh 11:12
that did J burn.......... Josh 11:13
Moses command J, and so did J.......... Josh 11:15
So J took all that land, the.......... Josh 11:16
J made war a long time with all.......... Josh 11:18
And at that time came J, and cut.......... Josh 11:21
J destroyed them utterly with.......... Josh 11:21
So J took the whole land,.......... Josh 11:23
J gave it for an inheritance unto.......... Josh 11:23
the kings of the country which J.......... Josh 12:7
which J gave unto the tribes of.......... Josh 12:7
Now J was old and stricken in.......... Josh 13:1
J the son of Nun, and the heads of.......... Josh 14:1
J blessed him, and gave unto Caleb.......... Josh 14:13
the commandment of the LORD to J.......... Josh 15:13
before J the son of Nun, and.......... Josh 17:4
children of Joseph spake unto J.......... Josh 17:14
J answered them, If thou be a.......... Josh 17:15
J spake unto the house of Joseph,.......... Josh 17:17
J said unto the children of.......... Josh 18:3
J charged them that went to.......... Josh 18:8
came again to J to the host at.......... Josh 18:9
J cast lots for them in Shiloh.......... Josh 18:10

there J divided the land unto the.......... Josh 18:10
to J the son of Nun among them.......... Josh 19:49
J the son of Nun, and the heads of.......... Josh 19:51
The LORD also spake unto J.......... Josh 20:1
unto J the son of Nun, saying,.......... Josh 21:1
Then J called the Reubenites, and.......... Josh 22:1
So J blessed them, and sent them,.......... Josh 22:6
the other half thereof gave J.......... Josh 22:7
when J sent them away also unto.......... Josh 22:7
that J waxed old and stricken in.......... Josh 23:1
J called for all Israel, and for.......... Josh 23:2
J gathered all the tribes of.......... Josh 24:1
J said unto all the people, Thus.......... Josh 24:2
J said unto the people, Ye cannot.......... Josh 24:19
And the people said unto J.......... Josh 24:21
J said unto the people, Ye are.......... Josh 24:22
And the people said unto J.......... Josh 24:24
So J made a covenant with the.......... Josh 24:25
J wrote these words in the book.......... Josh 24:26
J said unto all the people,.......... Josh 24:27
So J let the people depart, every.......... Josh 24:28
that J the son of Nun, the.......... Josh 24:29
served the LORD all the days of J.......... Josh 24:31
of the elders that overlived J.......... Josh 24:31
the death of J it came to pass.......... Judg 1:1
when J had let the people go, the.......... Judg 2:6
served the LORD all the days of J.......... Judg 2:7
of the elders that outlived J.......... Judg 2:7
J the son of Nun, the servant of.......... Judg 2:8
nations which J left when he died.......... Judg 2:21
be them into the hand of J.......... Judg 2:23
he spake by J the son of Nun.......... 1Kin 16:34
   2. *A Bethshemite.*
the cart came into the field of J.......... 1Sa 6:14
unto this day in the field of J.......... 1Sa 6:18
   3. *A governor of Jerusalem.*
of J the governor of the city.......... 2Kin 23:8
   4. *A High Priest.*
to J the son of Josedech, the.......... Hag 1:1
J the son of Josedech, the high.......... Hag 1:12
the spirit of J the son of.......... Hag 1:14
to J the son of Josedech, the.......... Hag 2:2
and be strong, O J, son of.......... Hag 2:4
he shewed me J the high priest.......... Zec 3:1
Now J was clothed with filthy.......... Zec 3:3
of the LORD protested unto J.......... Zec 3:6
O J the high priest, thou, and thy.......... Zec 3:8
stone that I have laid before J.......... Zec 3:9
the head of J the son of Josedech.......... Zec 6:11

JOSIAH (jo-si´-ah) See JOSIAS.
   1. *A king of Judah.*
the house of David, J for thee.......... 1Kin 13:2
made J his son king in his stead.......... 2Kin 21:24
J his son reigned in his stead.......... 2Kin 21:26
J was eight years old when he.......... 2Kin 22:1
in the eighteenth year of king J.......... 2Kin 22:3
as J turned himself, he spied the.......... 2Kin 23:16
I took away, and did to them.......... 2Kin 23:19
in the eighteenth year of king J.......... 2Kin 23:23
did J put away, that he might.......... 2Kin 23:24
Now the rest of the acts of J.......... 2Kin 23:28
and king J went against him.......... 2Kin 23:29
land took Jehoahaz the son of J.......... 2Kin 23:30
made Eliakim the son of J king in.......... 2Kin 23:34
Jehoahaz the son of J his father.......... 2Kin 23:34
Amon his son, J his son.......... 1Chr 3:14
And the sons of J were, the.......... 1Chr 3:15
made J his son king in his stead.......... 2Chr 33:25
J was eight years old when he.......... 2Chr 34:1
J took away all the abominations.......... 2Chr 34:33
Moreover J kept a passover unto.......... 2Chr 35:1
J gave to the people, of the.......... 2Chr 35:7
to the commandment of king J.......... 2Chr 35:16
keep such a passover as J kept.......... 2Chr 35:18
reign of J was this passover kept.......... 2Chr 35:19
when J had prepared the temple,.......... 2Chr 35:20
and J went out against him.......... 2Chr 35:20
Nevertheless J would not turn his.......... 2Chr 35:22
And the archers shot at king J.......... 2Chr 35:23
Judah and Jerusalem mourned for J.......... 2Chr 35:24
And Jeremiah lamented for J.......... 2Chr 35:25
the singing women spake of J in.......... 2Chr 35:25
Now the rest of the acts of J.......... 2Chr 35:26
land took Jehoahaz the son of J.......... 2Chr 36:1
J the son of Amon king of Judah.......... Jer 1:2
the son of J king of Judah.......... Jer 1:3
the son of J king of Judah.......... Jer 1:3
unto me in the days of J the king.......... Jer 3:6
the son of J king of Judah.......... Jer 22:11
reigned instead of J his father.......... Jer 22:11
the son of J king of Judah.......... Jer 22:18
From the thirteenth year of J the.......... Jer 25:3
of J king of Judah came this word.......... Jer 26:1
of J king of Judah came this word.......... Jer 27:1
the son of J king of Judah.......... Jer 36:1
the son of J king of Judah.......... Jer 36:2
unto thee, from the days of J.......... Jer 36:2
the son of J king of Judah.......... Jer 36:9
king Zedekiah the son of J.......... Jer 37:1
the son of J king of Judah.......... Jer 45:1
the son of J king of Judah.......... Jer 46:2
in the days of J the son of Amon,.......... Zeph 1:1
   2. *A son of Zephaniah.*
house of J the son of Zephaniah.......... Zec 6:10

JOSIAS (jo-si´-as) See JOSIAH. *Son of Amon; ancestor of Jesus.*
and Amon begat J.......... Mt 1:10
J begat Jechonias and his brethren.......... Mt 1:11

JOSIBIAH *(jos-ib-i'-ah)* A Simeonite.
And Joel, and Jehu the son of J 1Chr 4:35

JOSIPHIAH *(jos-if-i'-ah)* A family of exiles.
the son of J, and with him an.................. Ezr 8:10

JOT
one *j* or one tittle shall in no .... Mt 5:18

JOTBAH *(jot'-bah)* A place near Hebron.
the daughter of Haruz of J 2Kin 21:19

JOTBATH *(jot'-bath)* An
encampment during the Exodus.
and from Gudgodah to J, a land of...... Deut 10:7

JOTBATHAH *(jot'-ba-thah)* See JOTBATH.
Same as Jotbath.
Hor-hagidgad, and pitched in J....... Num 33:33
And they removed from J, and......... Num 33:34

JOTHAM *(jo'-tham)* See JOATHAM.
1. A son of Gideon.
notwithstanding yet J the.................. Judg 9:5
And when they told it to J.................. Judg 9:7
J ran away, and fled, and went to...... Judg 9:21
curse of J the son of Jerubbaal........ Judg 9:57
2. Father of King Ahaz.
J the king's son was over the........... 2Kin 15:5
J his son reigned in his stead........... 2Kin 15:7
year of J the son of Uzziah.............. 2Kin 15:30
Remaliah king of Israel began J....... 2Kin 15:32
Now the rest of the acts of J........... 2Kin 15:36
J slept with his fathers, and............ 2Kin 15:38
of J king of Judah began to reign.... 2Kin 16:1
son, Azariah his son, J his son,........ 1Chr 3:12
in the days of J king of Judah.......... 1Chr 5:17
J his son was over the king's............ 2Chr 26:21
J his son reigned in his stead........... 2Chr 26:23
J was twenty and five years old....... 2Chr 27:1
So J became mighty, because he....... 2Chr 27:6
Now the rest of the acts of J........... 2Chr 27:7
J slept with his fathers, and they..... 2Chr 27:9
in the days of Uzziah, J, Ahaz,......... Is 1:1
in the days of Ahaz the son of J....... Is 7:1
Been, in the days of Uzziah, J........... Hos 1:1
the Morasthite in the days of J......... Mic 1:1
3. A descendant of Caleb.
and J, and Gesham, and Pelet........... 1Chr 2:47

JOURNEY
had made his *j* prosperous or not...... Gen 24:21
Then Jacob went on his *j*, and came.... Gen 29:1
set three days' *j* betwixt himself...... Gen 30:36
pursued after him seven days' *j* ..... Gen 31:23
And he said, Let us take our *j*,......... Gen 33:12
Israel took his *j* with all that......... Gen 46:1
three days' *j* into the wilderness..... Ex 3:18
three days' *j* into the desert, and.... Ex 5:3
three days' *j* into the wilderness..... Ex 8:27
And they took their *j* from Succoth... Ex 13:20
And they took their *j* from Elim...... Ex 16:1
dead body, or be in a *j* afar off....... Num 9:10
that is clean, and is not in a *j* .... Num 9:13
the south side shall take their *j* ...... Num 10:6
they first took their *j* according..... Num 10:13
mount of the LORD three days' *j* ..... Num 10:33
before them in the three days' *j* ..... Num 10:33
as it were a day's *j* on this side...... Num 11:31
were a day's *j* on the other side...... Num 11:31
went three days' *j* in the............... Num 33:8
they took their *j* out of the............ Num 33:12
(There are eleven days' *j* from....... Deut 1:2
Turn you, and take your *j*, and go.... Deut 1:7
take your *j* into the wilderness....... Deut 1:40
took our *j* into the wilderness by.... Deut 2:1
Rise ye up, take your *j*, and pass..... Deut 2:24
children of Israel took their *j*......... Deut 10:6
take thy *j* before the people,.......... Deut 10:11
Take victuals with you for the *j* ...... Josh 9:11
old by reason of the very long *j* ..... Josh 9:13
notwithstanding that *j* that thou..... Judg 4:9
And the LORD sent thee on a *j* 1Sa 15:18
Uriah, Cannot thou not from thy *j*.... 2Sa 11:10
he is pursuing, or he is in a *j* 1Kin 18:27
a day's *j* into the wilderness.......... 1Kin 19:4
because the *j* is too great for......... 1Kin 19:7
a compass of seven days' *j* 2Kin 3:9
Then Solomon came from his *j* to.... 2Chr 1:13
him,) For how long shall thy *j* be.... Neh 2:6
not at home, he is gone a long *j* ..... Prov 7:19
great city of three days' *j* .... Jonah 3:3
to enter into the city a day's *j* .... Jonah 3:4
Nor scrip for your *j*, neither two..... Mt 10:10
and straightway took his *j*............. Mt 25:15
should take nothing for their *j* .... Mk 6:8
of man is as a man taking a far *j* .... Mk 13:34
in the company, went a day's *j* ...... Lk 2:44
them, Take Nothing for your *j* .... Lk 9:3
of mine in his *j* is come to me........ Lk 11:6
took his *j* into a far country, and.... Lk 15:13
being wearied with his *j*................ Jn 4:6
from Jerusalem a sabbath day's *j* ... Acts 1:12
morrow, as they went on their *j* .... Acts 10:9
to pass, that, as I made my *j* .... Acts 22:6
I might have a prosperous *j* by....... Rom 1:10
Whensoever I take my *j* into Spain... Rom 15:24
for I trust to see you in my *j* .... Rom 15:24
me on my *j* whithersoever I go....... 1Cor 16:6
and Apollos on their *j* diligently...... Titus 3:13
on their *j* after a godly sort........... 3Jn 6

JOURNEYED
as they *j* from the east, that.......... Gen 11:2
And Abram *j*, going on still toward... Gen 12:9
and Lot *j* east .... Gen 13:11
Abraham *j* from thence toward the.... Gen 20:1
Jacob *j* to Succoth, and built him.... Gen 33:17
And they *j*: and the terror............. Gen 35:5
And they *j* from Beth-el................ Gen 35:16
And Israel *j*, and spread his tent..... Gen 35:21
the children of Israel *j* from.......... Ex 12:37
of the children of Israel *j* from....... Ex 17:1
then they *j* not till the day that...... Ex 40:37
that the children of Israel *j* .... Num 9:17
the LORD the children of Israel *j* ..... Num 9:18
the charge of the LORD, and *j* not,... Num 9:19
commandment of the LORD they *j* .... Num 9:20
up in the morning, then they *j* .... Num 9:21
the cloud was taken up, they *j* .... Num 9:21
abode in their tents, and *j* not........ Num 9:22
but when it was taken up, they *j* ..... Num 9:22
commandment of the LORD by *j* ...... Num 9:23
And the people *j* from................. Num 11:35
the people *j* not till Miriam was..... Num 12:15
j from Kadesh, and came unto........ Num 20:22
they *j* from mount Hor by the way.... Num 21:4
they *j* from Oboth, and pitched at... Num 21:11
they *j* from Rissah, and pitched in... Num 33:22
From thence they *j* unto Gudgodah.... Deut 10:7
And the children of Israel *j* .... Josh 9:17
to the house of Micah, as he *j* .... Judg 17:8
But a certain Samaritan, as he *j* ..... Lk 10:33
And as he *j*, he came near Damascus... Acts 9:3
the men which *j* with him stood...... Acts 9:7
about me and them which *j* with me.... Acts 26:13

JOURNEYING
and for the *j* of the camps............ Num 10:2
We are *j* unto the place of which.... Num 10:29
teaching, and *j* toward Jerusalem.... Lk 13:22

JOURNEYINGS
Thus were the *j* of the children...... Num 10:28
In *j* often, in perils of waters,........ 2Cor 11:26

JOURNEYS
he went on his *j* from the south...... Gen 13:3
wilderness of Sin, after their *j* .... Ex 17:1
Israel went onward in all their *j* ..... Ex 40:36
of Israel, throughout all their *j* ...... Ex 40:38
shall blow an alarm for their *j* .... Num 10:6
children of Israel took their *j* .... Num 10:12
These are the *j* of the children....... Num 33:1
goings out according to their *j* .... Num 33:2
these are their *j* according to........ Num 33:2

JOY
king Saul, with tabrets, with *j* 1Sa 18:6
pipes, and rejoiced with great *j* 1Kin 1:40
for there was *j* in Israel............... 1Chr 12:40
by lifting up the voice with *j* 1Chr 15:16
of the house of Obed-edom with *j* ... 1Chr 15:25
king also rejoiced with great *j* 1Chr 29:9
now have I seen with *j* thy people.... 1Chr 29:17
to go again to Jerusalem with *j* 2Chr 20:27
So there was great *j* in Jerusalem.... 2Chr 30:26
and many shouted aloud for *j* .... Ezr 3:12
the noise of the shout of *j* from...... Ezr 3:13
of this house of God with *j* .... Ezr 6:16
bread seven days with *j* .... Ezr 6:22
for the *j* of the LORD is your.......... Neh 8:10
made them rejoice with great *j* ...... Neh 12:43
so that the *j* of Jerusalem was........ Neh 12:43
Jews had light, and gladness, and *j* ... Est 8:16
his decree came, the Jews had *j* ..... Est 8:17
turned unto them from sorrow to *j* ... Est 9:22
make them days of feasting and *j* ... Est 9:22
Behold, this is the *j* of his way...... Job 8:19
the *j* of the hypocrite but for a...... Job 20:5
the widow's heart to sing for *j* ...... Job 29:13
and he shall see his face with *j* ...... Job 33:26
all the sons of God shouted for *j* .... Job 38:7
is turned into *j* before him............ Job 41:22
let them ever shout for *j* .... Ps 5:11
in thy presence is fulness of *j* .... Ps 16:11
The king shall *j* in thy strength,..... Ps 21:1
in his tabernacle sacrifices of *j* ...... Ps 27:6
but *j* cometh in the morning.......... Ps 30:5
and shout for *j*, all ye that are....... Ps 32:11
Let them shout for *j*, and be glad,.... Ps 35:27
house of God, with the voice of *j* .... Ps 42:4
of God, unto God my exceeding *j* .... Ps 43:4
the *j* of the whole earth, is........... Ps 48:2
Make me to hear *j* and gladness...... Ps 51:8
unto me the *j* of thy salvation....... Ps 51:12
they shout for *j*, they also sing....... Ps 65:13
the nations be glad and sing for *j* ... Ps 67:4
brought forth his people with *j* ...... Ps 105:43
that sow in tears shall reap in *j* ..... Ps 126:5
and let thy saints shout for *j* .... Ps 132:9
saints shall shout aloud for *j* .... Ps 132:16
not Jerusalem above my chief *j* ...... Ps 137:6
to the counsellors of peace is *j* ...... Prov 12:20
doth not intermeddle with his *j* ..... Prov 14:10
Folly is *j* to him that is................ Prov 15:21
A man hath *j* by the answer of his.... Prov 15:23
and the father of a fool hath no *j* .... Prov 17:21
It is *j* to the just to do.............. Prov 21:15
a wise child shall have *j* of him...... Prov 23:24
withheld not my heart from any *j* .... Eccl 2:10
sight wisdom, and knowledge, and *j*.... Eccl 2:26
him in the *j* of his heart.............. Eccl 5:20
Go thy way, eat thy bread with *j* .... Eccl 9:7

nation, and not increased the *j* ...... Is 9:3
they *j* before thee according to...... Is 9:3
according to the *j* in harvest......... Is 9:3
have no *j* in their young men......... Is 9:17
Therefore with *j* shall ye draw....... Is 12:3
j out of the plentiful field............ Is 16:10
And behold *j* and gladness, slaying.... Is 22:13
the *j* of the harp ceaseth............. Is 24:8
all *j* is darkened, the mirth of....... Is 24:11
increase their *j* in the LORD........... Is 29:19
houses of *j* in the joyous city........ Is 32:13
a *j* of wild asses, a pasture of....... Is 32:14
and rejoice even with *j* and.......... Is 35:2
everlasting *j* upon their heads........ Is 35:10
they shall obtain *j* and gladness,..... Is 35:10
j and gladness shall be found........ Is 51:3
everlasting *j* shall be upon their..... Is 51:11
they shall obtain gladness and *j* ..... Is 51:11
Break forth into *j*, sing together..... Is 52:9
For ye shall go out with *j* .... Is 55:12
a *j* of many generations.............. Is 60:15
the oil of *j* for mourning, the....... Is 61:3
everlasting *j* shall be unto them..... Is 61:7
shall sing for *j* of heart............. Is 65:14
a rejoicing, and her people a *j* ...... Is 65:18
in Jerusalem, and *j* in my people.... Is 65:19
but he shall appear to your *j* .... Is 66:5
rejoice for *j* with her, all ye......... Is 66:10
and thy word was unto me the *j* ..... Jer 15:16
I will turn their mourning into *j* ..... Jer 31:13
And it shall be to me a name of *j* .... Jer 33:9
The voice of *j*, and the voice of...... Jer 33:11
of him, thou skippedst for *j* .... Jer 48:27
And *j* and gladness is taken from..... Jer 48:33
praise not left, the city of my *j* ..... Jer 49:25
beauty, The *j* of the whole earth..... Lam 2:15
The *j* of our heart is ceased.......... Lam 5:15
the *j* of their glory, the desire...... Eze 24:25
with the *j* of all their heart......... Eze 36:5
Rejoice not, O Israel, for *j* .... Hos 9:1
because *j* is withered away from..... Joel 1:12
cut off before our eyes, yea, *j* ...... Joel 1:16
I will *j* in the God of my............. Hab 3:18
he will rejoice over thee with *j* ..... Zeph 3:17
he will *j* over thee with singing..... Zeph 3:17
shall be to the house of Judah *j* ..... Zec 8:19
rejoiced with exceeding great *j* ..... Mt 2:10
word, and anon with *j* receiveth it.... Mt 13:20
for *j* thereof goeth and selleth....... Mt 13:44
enter thou into the *j* of thy lord..... Mt 25:21
enter thou into the *j* of thy lord..... Mt 25:23
sepulchre with fear and great *j* ...... Mt 28:8
And thou shalt have *j* and gladness.... Lk 1:14
the babe leaped in my womb for *j* ... Lk 1:44
bring you good tidings of great *j* .... Lk 2:10
ye in that day, and leap for *j* .... Lk 6:23
hear, receive the word with *j* .... Lk 8:13
the seventy returned again with *j* ... Lk 10:17
that likewise *j* shall be in............ Lk 15:7
there is *j* in the presence of the..... Lk 15:10
while they yet believed not for *j* .... Lk 24:41
to Jerusalem with great *j* .... Lk 24:52
this my *j* therefore is fulfilled....... Jn 3:29
that my *j* might remain in you, and.... Jn 15:11
that your *j* might be full............. Jn 15:11
sorrow shall be turned into *j* .... Jn 16:20
for *j* that a man is born into the..... Jn 16:21
your *j* no man taketh from you....... Jn 16:22
receive, that your *j* may be full..... Jn 16:24
have my *j* fulfilled in themselves.... Jn 17:13
me full of *j* with thy countenance.... Acts 2:28
And there was great *j* in that city.... Acts 8:8
the disciples were filled with *j* ...... Acts 13:52
they caused great *j* unto all the..... Acts 15:3
I might finish my course with *j* ...... Acts 20:24
but we also *j* in God through our..... Rom 5:11
and peace, and *j* in the Holy Ghost... Rom 14:17
God of hope fill you with all *j* .... Rom 15:13
you with *j* by the will of God........ Rom 15:32
faith, but are helpers of your *j* 2Cor 1:24
that my *j* is the *j* of you all........ 2Cor 2:3
that my *j* is the *j* of you all........ 2Cor 2:3
more joyed we for the *j* of Titus..... 2Cor 7:13
The abundance of their *j* and their.... 2Cor 8:2
fruit of the Spirit is love, *j* .... Gal 5:22
for you all making request with *j* ... Phil 1:4
your furtherance and *j* of faith...... Phil 1:25
Fulfil ye my *j*, that ye be............ Phil 2:2
and service of your faith, I *j* .... Phil 2:17
For the same cause also do ye *j* ..... Phil 2:18
beloved and longed for, my *j* .... Phil 4:1
with *j* of the Holy Ghost............. 1Th 1:6
For what is our hope, or *j* 1Th 2:19
For ye are our glory and *j* 1Th 2:20
for all the *j* wherewith we *j* 1Th 3:9
for all the *j* wherewith we *j* 1Th 3:9
that I may be filled with *j* 2Ti 1:4
For we have great *j* and.............. Philem 7
let me have *j* of thee in the Lord.... Philem 20
who for the *j* that was set before.... Heb 12:2
that they may do it with *j* .... Heb 13:17
count it all *j* when ye fall into....... Jas 1:2
mourning, and your *j* to heaviness.... Jas 4:9
ye rejoice with *j* unspeakable....... 1Pet 1:8
may be glad also with exceeding *j* ... 1Pet 4:13
unto you, that your *j* may be full.... 1Jn 1:4
to face, that our *j* may be full....... 2Jn 12
I have no greater *j* than to hear..... 3Jn 4
of his glory with exceeding *j* .... Jude 24

JOYED
exceedingly the more *j* we for the 2Cor 7:13

JOYFUL
king, and went unto their tents *j* 1Kin 8:66
for the LORD had made them *j* .... Ezr 6:22
Then went Haman forth that day *j* .... Est 5:9
let no *j* voice come therein............. Job 3:7
that love thy name be *j* in thee......... Ps 5:11
And my soul shall be *j* in the LORD..... Ps 35:9
shall praise thee with *j* lips.............. Ps 63:5
Make a *j* noise unto God, all ye .... Ps 66:1
make a *j* noise unto the God of .... Ps 81:1
the people that know the *j* sound......... Ps 89:15
let us make a *j* noise to the rock .... Ps 95:1
make a *j* noise unto him with............ Ps 95:2
Let the field be *j*, and all that .... Ps 96:12
Make a *j* noise unto the LORD, all...... Ps 98:4
make a *j* noise before the LORD......... Ps 98:6
let the hills be *j* together................. Ps 98:8
Make a *j* noise unto the LORD, all...... Ps 100:1
to be a *j* mother of children .... Ps 113:9
of Zion be *j* in their King............... Ps 149:2
Let the saints be *j* in glory .... Ps 149:5
In the day of prosperity be *j* .... Eccl 7:14
and be *j*, O earth.......................... Is 49:13
make them *j* in my house of prayer..... Is 56:7
my soul shall be *j* in my God............ Is 61:10
I am exceeding *j* in all our 2Cor 7:4

JOYFULLY
Live *j* with the wife whom thou.......... Eccl 9:9
and came down, and received him *j* ..... Lk 19:6
took *j* the spoiling of your goods......... Heb 10:34

JOYFULNESS
not the LORD thy God with *j* .... Deut 28:47
patience and longsuffering with *j* .... Col 1:11

JOYING
am I with you in the spirit, ... Col 2:5

JOYOUS
a tumultuous city, a *j* city............... Is 22:2
Is this your *j* city, whose................. Is 23:7
the houses of joy in the *j* city .... Is 32:13
for the present seemeth to be *j* .... Heb 12:11

JOZABAD/1
2. *Another warrior in David's army.*
to him of Manasseh, Adnah, and *J* 1Chr 12:20
and Jediael, and Michael, and *J* 1Chr 12:20
3. *A Chief Levite in Josiah's time.*
and Asahel, and Jerimoth, and *J* 2Chr 31:13
4. *An exile with Ezra.*
and Hashabiah and Jeiel and *J* 2Chr 35:9
5. *A priest.*
with them was *J* the son of Jeshua..... Ezr 8:33
6. *A Levite.*
Maaseiah, Ishmael, Nethaneel, *J* .... Ezr 10:22
7. *A priest who helped Ezra.*
J, and Shimei, and Kelaiah, (the........ Ezr 10:23
8. *A chief Levite in exile.*
Maaseiah, Kelita, Azariah, *J* .... Neh 8:7
9. *A chief Levite in exile.*
And Shabbethai and *J*, of the chief...... Neh 11:16

JOZACHAR (*joz'-a-kar*) See ZABAD. *Son of Shimeath.*
For *J* the son of Shimeath, and........... 2Kin 12:21

JOZADAK (*joz'-a-dak*) See JEHOZADAK, JOSEDECH. *A priest with Zerubbabel.*
Then stood up Jeshua the son of *J* ...... Ezr 3:2
Sheaitiel, and Jeshua the son of *J* ...... Ezr 3:8
Sheaitiel, and Jeshua the son of *J* ...... Ezr 5:2
the son of Jeshua the son of *J* .... Ezr 10:18
the son of Jeshua, the son of *J* .... Neh 12:26

JUBAL (*ju'-bal*) *Son of Adah.*
And his brother's name was *J* .... Gen 4:21

JUBILE
j to sound on the tenth day of .... Lev 25:9
it shall be a *j* unto you.................. Lev 25:10
A *j* shall that fiftieth year be........... Lev 25:11
For it is the *j*............................ Lev 25:12
in the year of this *j* ye shall .... Lev 25:13
the number of years after the *j*......... Lev 25:15
bought it until the year of *j*............. Lev 25:28
in the *j* it shall go out, and he .... Lev 25:28
it shall not go out in the *j*.............. Lev 25:30
and they shall go out in the *j*........... Lev 25:31
shall go out in the year of *j*............ Lev 25:33
serve thee unto the year of *j*............ Lev 25:40
sold to him unto the year of *j*.......... Lev 25:50
but few years unto the year of *j*........ Lev 25:52
he shall go out in the year of *j*......... Lev 25:54
his field from the year of *j*.............. Lev 27:17
he sanctify his field after the *j*......... Lev 27:18
even unto the year of the *j*.............. Lev 27:18
field, when it goeth out in the *j*........ Lev 27:21
even unto the year of the *j*.............. Lev 27:23
In the year of the *j* the field........... Lev 27:24
when the *j* of the children of........... Num 36:4

JUCAL (*ju'-kal*) See JEHUCAL. *An enemy of Jeremiah.*
J the son of Shelemiah, and Pashur..... Jer 38:1

JUCE
wine of the *j* of my pomegranate .... Song 8:2

JUDA (*ju'-dah*) See JUDAH.
1. *Greek form of Judah, the tribe.*
thou Bethlehem, in the land of *J*........ Mt 2:6

---

the least among the princes of *J* .... Mt 2:6
with haste, into a city of *J* .... Lk 1:39
that our Lord sprang out of *J* .... Heb 7:14
the Lion of the tribe of *J* .... Rev 5:5
Of the tribe of *J* were sealed........... Rev 7:5
2. *A brother of Jesus.*
of James, and Joses, and of *J* .... Mk 6:3
3. *Son of Jacob; an ancestor of Jesus.*
of Phares, which was the son of *J* ..... Lk 3:33

JUDAEA *A Roman province.*
J in the days of Herod the king .... Mt 2:1
said unto him, In Bethlehem of *J* .... Mt 2:5
that Archelaus did reign in *J* .... Mt 2:22
preaching in the wilderness of *J* .... Mt 3:1
out to him Jerusalem, and all *J* .... Mt 3:5
and from Jerusalem, and from *J* .... Mt 4:25
the coasts of *J* beyond Jordan........... Mt 19:1
be in *J* flee into the mountains.......... Mt 24:16
out unto him all the land of *J* .... Mk 1:5
Galilee followed him, and from *J* .... Mk 3:7
cometh to the coasts of *J* by .... Mk 10:1
be in *J* flee to the mountains .... Mk 13:14
the days of Herod, the king of *J* .... Lk 1:5
all the hill country of *J* .... Lk 1:65
of the city of Nazareth, into *J* .... Lk 2:4
Pilate being governor of *J* .... Lk 3:1
of every town of Galilee, and *J* .... Lk 5:17
multitude of people out of all *J* .... Lk 6:17
him went forth throughout all *J* .... Lk 7:17
are in *J* flee to the mountains........... Lk 21:21
his disciples into the land of *J* .... Jn 3:22
He left *J*, and departed again into ...... Jn 4:3
was come out of *J* into Galilee.......... Jn 4:47
he was come out of *J* into Galilee...... Jn 4:54
him, Depart hence, and go into *J* .... Jn 7:3
disciples, Let us go into *J* again......... Jn 11:7
the moth in Jerusalem, and in all *J* .... Acts 1:8
dwellers in Mesopotamia, and in *J* ..... Acts 2:9
and said unto them, Ye men of *J* ...... Acts 2:14
throughout the regions of *J* .... Acts 8:1
churches rest throughout all *J* .... Acts 9:31
was published throughout all *J* .... Acts 10:37
brethren that were in *J* heard........... Acts 11:1
the brethren which dwelt in *J* .... Acts 11:29
he went down from *J* to Caesarea...... Acts 12:19
down from *J* taught the brethren........ Acts 15:1
down from *J* a certain prophet.......... Acts 21:10
and throughout all the coasts of *J* ...... Acts 26:20
letters out of *J* concerning thee......... Acts 28:21
them that do not believe in *J* .... Rom 15:31
to be brought on my way toward *J*...... 2Cor 1:16
of *J* which were in Christ .... Gal 1:22
which in *J* are in Christ Jesus.......... 1Th 2:14

JUDAH (*ju'-dah*) See PREFACE. SEE ALSO BETHLEHEM-JUDAH, JUDA, JUDAH'S, JUDAS, JUDEA, JUDE.
1. *Son of Jacob and Leah.*
therefore she called his name *J* .... Gen 29:35
J said unto Israel his father............. Gen 43:8
J, thou art he whom thy brethren ...... Gen 49:8
2. *The tribe and its land.*
And this is the blessing of *J* .... Deut 33:7
of *J* according to their families.......... Josh 15:20
David king over the house of *J* 2Sa 2:4
In *J* is God known........................ Ps 76:1
of Israel and the house of *J* .... Heb 8:8
3. *The southern kingdom after the revolt of the ten northern tribes.*
of David, but the tribe of *J* only 1Kin 12:20
that dwelt in the cities of *J* 2Chr 10:17
the wrath of the LORD was upon *J* 2Chr 29:8
is ruined, and *J* is fallen .... Is 3:8
the word of the LORD, all ye of *J* ...... Jer 7:2
concerning Israel and concerning *J* ..... Jer 30:4
In those days shall *J* be saved.......... Jer 33:16
Thus *J* was carried away captive........ Jer 52:27
J is gone into captivity because .... Lam 1:3
For three transgressions of *J* .... Amos 2:4

David spake before concerning *J* .... Acts 1:16
from which *J* by transgression .... Acts 1:25
2. *A brother of Jesus.*
James, and Joses, and Simon, and *J*..... Mt 13:55
3. *A disciple of Jesus.*
J, the brother of James, and Judas...... Lk 6:16
J saith unto him, not Iscariot,.......... Jn 14:22
and *J* the brother of James............. Acts 1:13
4. *A seditious Galilean.*
After this man rose up *J* of .... Acts 5:37
5. *Lodged Paul in Damascus.*
house of *J* for one called Saul........... Acts 9:11
6. *Surnamed Barsabas.*
J surnamed Barsabas, and Silas,........ Acts 15:22
We have sent therefore *J* and Silas..... Acts 15:27
And *J* and Silas, being prophets......... Acts 15:32
and Jacob begat *J* and his brethren..... Mt 1:2
J begat Phares and Zara of Thamar..... Mt 1:3

JUDE (*jood*) See JUDAS. *A brother of Jesus.*
J, the servant of Jesus Christ,........... Jude 1

JUDEA (*ju-de'-ah*) See JEWRY, JUDAH. *Southern portion of Israel.*
we went into the province of *J* .... Ezr 5:8

JUDEAN See JUDEA.

JUDGE
whom they shall serve, will I *j*......... Gen 15:14
the LORD *j* between me and thee....... Gen 16:5
Shall not the *J* of all the earth......... Gen 18:25
sojourn, and he will needs be a *j* ...... Gen 19:9
that they may *j* betwixt us both........ Gen 31:37
God of their father, *j* betwixt us .... Gen 31:53
Dan shall *j* his people, as one of ...... Gen 49:16
made thee a prince and a *j* over us .... Ex 2:14
The LORD look upon you, and *j* .... Ex 5:21
that Moses said to *j* the people......... Ex 18:13
I *j* between one and another, and I .... Ex 18:16
let them *j* the people at all .... Ex 18:22
every small matter they shall *j* .... Ex 18:22
shalt thou *j* thy neighbour.............. Lev 19:15
shall *j* between the slayer .... Num 35:24
j righteously between every man .... Deut 1:16
they shall *j* the people with just....... Deut 16:18
unto the *j* that shall be in those .... Deut 17:9
the LORD thy God, or unto the *j* ...... Deut 17:12
that the judges may *j* them .... Deut 25:1
that the *j* shall cause him to lie........ Deut 25:2
For the LORD shall *j* his people........ Deut 32:36
then the LORD was with the *j* .... Judg 2:18
enemies all the days of the *j* .... Judg 2:18
came to pass, when the *j* was dead .... Judg 2:19
the LORD the *J* be *j* this day .... Judg 11:27
the LORD shall *j* the ends of the........ 1Sa 2:10
another, the *j* shall *j* him 1Sa 2:25
will *j* his house for ever for the 1Sa 3:13
now make us a king to *j* us like 1Sa 8:5
they said, Give us a king to *j* us....... 1Sa 8:6
and that our king may *j* us 1Sa 8:20
The LORD *j* between me and thee, and . 1Sa 24:12
The LORD therefore be *j*................. 1Sa 24:15
j between me and thee, and see, and... 1Sa 24:15
Oh that I were made *j* in the land 2Sa 15:4
heart to *j* thy people, that I may 1Kin 3:9
for who is able to *j* this thy so 1Kin 3:9
for the throne where he might *j* 1Kin 7:7
thy servants, condemning the............ 1Kin 8:32
because he cometh to *j* the earth....... 1Chr 16:33
for who can *j* this thy people,.......... 2Chr 1:10
that thou mayest *j* my people 2Chr 1:11
thy servants, by requiting the 2Chr 6:23
for ye *j* not for man, but for the....... 2Chr 19:6
O our God, wilt thou not *j* them....... 2Chr 20:12
which may *j* all the people that........ Ezr 7:25
I would make supplication to my *j*..... Job 9:15
can he *j* through the dark cloud........ Job 22:13
I be delivered for ever from my *j*...... Job 23:7
iniquity to be punished by the *j*........ Job 31:28
The LORD shall *j* the people............ Ps 7:8
j me, O LORD, according to my......... Ps 7:8
And he shall *j* the world in............. Ps 9:8
To *j* the fatherless and the.............. Ps 10:18
j me, O LORD............................ Ps 26:1
j me, O LORD my God, according to.... Ps 35:24
j me, O God, and plead my cause...... Ps 43:1
earth, that he may *j* his people........ Ps 50:4
for God is *j* himself..................... Ps 50:6
thy name, and *j* me by thy strength ... Ps 54:1
do ye *j* uprightly, O ye sons of......... Ps 58:1
for thou shalt *j* the people............. Ps 67:4
a *j* of the widows, is God in his........ Ps 68:5
He shall *j* thy people with............... Ps 72:2
He shall *j* the poor of the people....... Ps 72:4
congregation I will *j* uprightly.......... Ps 75:2
But God is the *j*......................... Ps 75:7
How long will ye *j* unjustly............. Ps 82:2
Arise, O God, *j* the earth............... Ps 82:8
up thyself, thou *J* of the earth.......... Ps 94:2
he shall *j* the people righteously....... Ps 96:10
he he cometh to *j* the earth............ Ps 96:13
he shall *j* the world with............... Ps 96:13
for he cometh to *j* the earth............ Ps 98:9
shall he *j* the world, and the........... Ps 98:9
He shall *j* among the heathen, he...... Ps 110:6
For the LORD will *j* his people.......... Ps 135:14
j righteously, and plead the cause...... Prov 31:9
God shall *j* the righteous and the....... Eccl 3:17
j the fatherless, plead for the.......... Is 1:17
they *j* not the fatherless,............... Is 1:23
he shall *j* among the nations, and ..... Is 2:4

JUDGED

man, and the man of war, the *j* .... Is 3:2
and standeth to *j* the people .... Is 3:13
of Jerusalem, and men of Judah, *j* .... Is 5:3
he shall not *j* after the sight of .... Is 11:3
righteousness shall he *j* the poor .... Is 11:4
For the LORD is our *j*, the LORD .... Is 33:22
and mine arms shall *j* the people .... Is 51:5
they *j* not the cause, the cause .... Jer 5:28
right of the needy do they not *j* .... Jer 5:28
j thou my cause .... Lam 3:59
will *j* thee according to thy ways .... Eze 7:3
I will *j* thee according to thy .... Eze 7:8
to their deserts will I *j* them .... Eze 7:27
I will *j* you in the border of .... Eze 11:10
but I will *j* you in the border of .... Eze 11:11
And I will *j* thee, as women that .... Eze 16:38
Therefore I will *j* you, O house .... Eze 18:30
Wilt thou *j* them, son of man, ... Eze 20:4
son of man, wilt thou *j* them .... Eze 20:4
I will *j* thee in the place where .... Eze 21:30
Now, thou son of man, wilt thou *j* .... Eze 22:2
wilt thou *j* the bloody city .... Eze 22:2
they shall *j* thee according to .... Eze 23:24
Son of man, wilt thou *j* Aholah .... Eze 23:36
they shall *j* them after the .... Eze 23:45
to thy doings, shall they *j* thee .... Eze 24:14
I will *j* you every one after his .... Eze 33:20
I *j* between cattle and cattle, ... Eze 34:17
will *j* between the fat cattle and .... Eze 34:20
I will *j* between cattle and cattle, ... Eze 34:22
they shall *j* it according to my .... Eze 44:24
for there will I sit to *j* all the .... Joel 3:12
I will cut off the *j* from the .... Amos 2:3
mount Zion to *j* the mount of Esau .... Obad 21
The heads thereof *j* for reward .... Mic 3:11
he shall *j* among many people, and .... Mic 4:3
they shall smite the *j* of Israel .... Mic 5:1
the *j* asketh for a reward .... Mic 7:3
then thou shalt also *j* my house .... Zec 3:7
adversary deliver thee to the *j* .... Mt 5:25
the *j* deliver thee to the officer .... Mt 5:25
J not, that ye be not judged .... Mt 7:1
For with what judgment ye *j* .... Mt 7:2
J not, and ye shall not be judged .... Lk 6:37
who made me a *j* or a divider over .... Lk 12:14
yourselves *j* ye not what is right .... Lk 12:57
lest he hale thee to the *j* .... Lk 12:58
the *j* deliver thee to the officer .... Lk 12:58
Saying, There was in a city a *j* .... Lk 18:2
Hear what the unjust *j* saith .... Lk 18:6
of thine own mouth will I *j* thee .... Lk 19:22
as I hear, I *j* .... Jn 5:30
J not according to the appearance .... Jn 7:24
but *j* righteous judgment .... Jn 7:24
Doth our law *j* any man, before it .... Jn 7:51
Ye *j* after the flesh .... Jn 8:15
I *j* no man .... Jn 8:15
And yet if I *j*, my judgment is .... Jn 8:16
many things to say and to *j* of you .... Jn 8:26
and believe not, I *j* him not .... Jn 12:47
for I came not to *j* the world .... Jn 12:47
the same shall *j* him in the last .... Jn 12:48
j him according to your law .... Jn 18:31
unto you more than unto God, *j* ye .... Acts 4:19
they shall be in bondage will I *j* .... Acts 7:7
made thee a ruler and a *j* over us .... Acts 7:27
Who made thee a ruler and a *j* .... Acts 7:35
of God to be the *J* of quick .... Acts 10:42
you, and *j* yourselves unworthy of .... Acts 13:46
in the which he will *j* the world .... Acts 17:31
I will be no *j* of such matters .... Acts 18:15
thou to *j* me after the law .... Acts 23:3
many years a *j* unto this nation .... Acts 24:10
In the day when God shall *j* the .... Rom 2:16
j thee, who by the letter and .... Rom 2:27
then how shall God *j* the world .... Rom 3:6
eateth not *j* him that eateth .... Rom 14:3
But why dost thou *j* thy brother .... Rom 14:10
therefore *j* one another any more .... Rom 14:13
but *j* this rather, that no man .... Rom 14:13
yea, I *j* not mine own self 1Cor 4:3
Therefore *j* nothing before the 1Cor 4:5
For what have I to do to *j* them 1Cor 5:12
do not ye *j* them that are within 1Cor 5:12
that the saints shall *j* the world 1Cor 6:2
are ye unworthy to *j* the smallest 1Cor 6:2
ye not that we shall *j* angels 1Cor 6:3
set them to *j* who are least 1Cor 6:4
be able to *j* between his brethren 1Cor 6:5
j ye what I say 1Cor 10:15
J in yourselves 1Cor 11:13
For if we would *j* ourselves 1Cor 11:31
two or three, and let the other *j* 1Cor 14:29
because we thus *j*, that if one 2Cor 5:14
no man therefore *j* you in meat .... Col 2:16
Christ, who shall *j* the quick 2Ti 4:1
which the Lord, the righteous *j* 2Ti 4:8
The Lord shall *j* his people .... Heb 10:30
in heaven, and to God the *J* of all .... Heb 12:23
and adulterers God will *j* .... Heb 13:4
but if thou *j* the law, thou art .... Jas 4:11
not a doer of the law, but a *j* .... Jas 4:11
the *j* standeth before the door .... Jas 5:9
him that is ready to *j* the quick 1Pet 4:5
holy and true, dost thou not *j* .... Rev 6:10
and in righteousness he doth *j* .... Rev 19:11

JUDGED

And Rachel said, God hath *j* me .... Gen 30:6
they *j* the people at all seasons .... Ex 18:26
small matter they *j* themselves .... Ex 18:26
he *j* Israel, and went out to war .... Judg 3:10
she *j* Israel at that time .... Judg 4:4
he *j* Israel twenty and three years .... Judg 10:2
j Israel twenty and two years .... Judg 10:3
Jephthah *j* Israel six years .... Judg 12:7
him Ibzan of Beth-lehem *j* Israel .... Judg 12:8
And he *j* Israel seven years .... Judg 12:9
him Elon, a Zebulonite, *j* Israel .... Judg 12:11
and he *j* Israel ten years .... Judg 12:11
Hillel, a Pirathonite, *j* Israel .... Judg 12:13
and he *j* Israel eight years .... Judg 12:14
he *j* Israel in the days of the .... Judg 15:20
And he *j* Israel twenty years .... Judg 16:31
he had *j* Israel forty years 1Sa 4:18
Samuel *j* the children of Israel 1Sa 7:6
Samuel *j* Israel all the days of 1Sa 7:15
j Israel in all those places 1Sa 7:16
and there he *j* Israel 1Sa 7:17
the judgment which the king had *j* 1Kin 3:28
days of the judges that *j* Israel 2Kin 23:22
let the heathen be *j* in thy sight .... Ps 9:19
nor condemn him when he is *j* .... Ps 37:33
When he shall be *j*, let him be .... Ps 109:7
He *j* the cause of the poor and .... Jer 22:16
break wedlock and shed blood are *j* .... Eze 16:38
which hast *j* thy sisters, bear .... Eze 16:52
the wounded shall be *j* in the .... Eze 28:23
among them, when I have *j* thee .... Eze 35:11
to their doings I *j* thee .... Eze 36:19
and against our judges that *j* us .... Dan 9:12
Judge not, that ye be not *j* .... Mt 7:1
judgment ye judge, ye shall be *j* .... Mt 7:2
Judge not, and ye shall not be *j* .... Lk 6:37
unto him, Thou hast rightly *j* .... Lk 7:43
the prince of this world is *j* .... Jn 16:11
If ye have *j* me to be faithful to .... Acts 16:15
would have *j* according to our law .... Acts 24:6
there be *j* of these things before .... Acts 25:9
seat, where I ought to be *j* .... Acts 25:10
there be *j* of these matters .... Acts 25:20
am I for the hope of the promise .... Acts 26:6
in the law shall be *j* by the law .... Rom 2:12
mightest overcome when thou art *j* .... Rom 3:4
why yet am I also *j* as a sinner .... Rom 3:7
yet he himself is *j* of no man 1Cor 2:15
thing that I should be *j* of you 1Cor 4:3
have *j* already, as though I were 1Cor 5:3
and if the world shall be *j* by you 1Cor 6:2
for why is my liberty *j* 1Cor 10:29
ourselves, we should not be *j* 1Cor 11:31
But when we are *j*, we are 1Cor 11:32
convinced of all, he is *j* of all 1Cor 14:24
because she *j* him faithful who .... Heb 11:11
shall be *j* by the law of liberty .... Jas 2:12
that they might be *j* according to 1Pet 4:6
the dead, that they should be *j* .... Rev 11:18
be, because thou hast *j* thus .... Rev 16:5
for he hath *j* the great whore, ... Rev 19:2
the dead were *j* out of those .... Rev 20:12
they were *j* every man according .... Rev 20:13

JUDGES

master shall bring him unto the *j* .... Ex 21:6
he shall pay as the *j* determine .... Ex 21:22
house shall be brought unto the *j* .... Ex 22:8
parties shall come before the *j* .... Ex 22:9
whom the *j* shall condemn, he .... Ex 22:9
Moses said unto the *j* of Israel .... Num 25:5
And I charged your *j* at that time .... Deut 1:16
J and officers shalt thou make .... Deut 16:18
LORD, before the priests and the *j* .... Deut 19:17
the *j* shall make diligent .... Deut 19:18
thy *j* shall come forth, and they .... Deut 21:2
that the *j* may judge them .... Deut 25:1
our enemies themselves being *j* .... Deut 32:31
elders, and officers, and their *j* .... Josh 8:33
for their heads, and for their *j* .... Josh 23:2
for their heads, and for their *j* .... Josh 24:1
Nevertheless the LORD raised up *j* .... Judg 2:16
would not hearken unto their *j* .... Judg 2:17
And when the LORD raised them up *j* .... Judg 2:18
pass in the days when the *j* ruled .... Ruth 1:1
he made his sons *j* over Israel 1Sa 8:1
they were *j* in Beer-sheba 1Sa 8:2
j to be over my people Israel 2Sa 7:11
days of the *j* that judged Israel 2Kin 23:22
a word to any of the *j* of Israel 1Chr 17:6
j to be over my people Israel 1Chr 17:10
six thousand were officers and *j* 1Chr 23:4
over Israel, for officers and *j* 1Chr 26:29
and of hundreds, and for the *j* 2Chr 1:2
he set *j* in the land throughout 2Chr 19:5
And said to the *j*, Take heed what 2Chr 19:6
thine hand, set magistrates and *j* .... Ezr 7:25
the *j* thereof, until the fierce .... Ezr 10:14
the faces of the *j* thereof .... Job 9:24
spoiled, and maketh the *j* fools .... Job 12:17
iniquity to be punished by the *j* .... Job 31:11
be instructed, ye *j* of the earth .... Ps 2:10
When their *j* are overthrown in .... Ps 141:6
princes, and all *j* of the earth .... Ps 148:11
even all the *j* of the earth .... Prov 8:16
restore thy *j* as at the first .... Is 1:26
he maketh the *j* of the earth as .... Is 40:23
governors, and the captains, the *j* .... Dan 3:2
the governors, and captains, the *j* .... Dan 3:3
against our *j* that judged us, by .... Dan 9:12
an oven, and have devoured their *j* .... Hos 7:7
thy *j* of whom thou saidst, Give .... Hos 13:10
her *j* are evening wolves .... Zeph 3:3
therefore they shall be your *j* .... Mt 12:27
therefore shall they be your *j* .... Lk 11:19
after that he gave unto them *j* .... Acts 13:20
are become *j* of evil thoughts .... Jas 2:4

JUDGEST

speakest, and be clear when thou *j* .... Ps 51:4
that *j* righteously, that triest .... Jer 11:20
O man, whosoever thou art that *j* .... Rom 2:1
for wherein thou *j* another .... Rom 2:1
for thou that *j* doest the same .... Rom 2:1
that *j* them which do such things, ... Rom 2:3
Who art thou that *j* another man's .... Rom 14:4
who art thou that *j* another .... Jas 4:12

JUDGETH

seeing he *j* those that are high .... Job 21:22
For by them *j* he the people .... Job 36:31
God *j* the righteous, and God is .... Ps 7:11
he is a God that *j* in the earth .... Ps 58:11
he *j* among the gods .... Ps 82:1
king that faithfully *j* the poor .... Prov 29:14
For the Father *j* no man, but hath .... Jn 5:22
there is one that seeketh and *j* .... Jn 8:50
not my words, hath one that *j* him .... Jn 12:48
he that is spiritual *j* all things 1Cor 2:15
but he that *j* me is the Lord 1Cor 4:4
But them that are without God *j* 1Cor 5:13
j his brother, speaketh evil of .... Jas 4:11
evil of the law, and *j* the law .... Jas 4:11
j according to every man's work 1Pet 1:17
himself to him that *j* righteously 1Pet 2:23
strong is the Lord God who *j* her .... Rev 18:8

JUDGING

house, *j* the people of the land 2Kin 15:5
house, *j* the people of the land 2Chr 26:21
thou satest in the throne *j* right .... Ps 9:4
in the tabernacle of David, *j* .... Is 16:5
the twelve tribes of Israel .... Mt 19:28
sit on thrones *j* the twelve .... Lk 22:30

JUDGMENT

of the LORD, to do justice and *j* .... Gen 18:19
gods of Egypt I will execute *j* .... Ex 12:12
according to this *j* shall it be .... Ex 21:31
to decline after many to wrest .... Ex 23:2
the *j* of thy poor in his cause .... Ex 23:6
of *j* with cunning work .... Ex 28:15
breastplate of *j* upon his heart .... Ex 28:29
in the breastplate of the Urim .... Ex 28:30
Aaron shall bear the *j* of the .... Ex 28:30
shall do no unrighteousness in *j* .... Lev 19:15
shall do no unrighteousness in .... Lev 19:35
children of Israel a statute of *j* .... Num 27:11
the *j* of Urim before the LORD .... Num 27:21
before the congregation in *j* .... Num 35:12
of *j* unto you throughout your .... Num 35:29
Ye shall not respect persons in *j* .... Deut 1:17
for the *j* is God's .... Deut 1:17
execute the *j* of the fatherless .... Deut 10:18
judge the people with just *j* .... Deut 16:18
Thou shalt not wrest *j* .... Deut 16:19
a matter too hard for thee in *j* .... Deut 17:8
shall shew thee the sentence of *j* .... Deut 17:9
according to the *j* which they .... Deut 17:11
not pervert the *j* of the stranger .... Deut 24:17
between men, and they come unto *j* .... Deut 25:1
perverteth the *j* of the stranger .... Deut 27:19
for all his ways are *j* .... Deut 32:4
and mine hand take hold on *j* .... Deut 32:41
before the congregation for *j* .... Josh 20:6
of Israel came up to her for *j* .... Judg 4:5
on white asses, ye that sit in *j* .... Judg 5:10
and took tithes, and perverted *j* 1Sa 8:3
and David executed *j* and justice 2Sa 8:15
came to the king for *j*, then 2Sa 15:2
that came to the king for *j* 2Sa 15:6
understanding to discern *j* 1Kin 3:11
all Israel heard of the *j* which 1Kin 3:28
wisdom of God was in him, to do *j* 1Kin 3:28
might judge, even the porch of *j* 1Kin 7:7
made he the king, to do *j* 1Kin 10:9
said unto him, So shall thy *j* be 1Kin 20:40
and they gave *j* upon him 2Kin 25:6
over all Israel, and executed *j* 1Chr 18:14
he thee king over them, to do *j* 2Chr 9:8
LORD, who is with you in the *j* 2Chr 19:6
for the *j* of the LORD, and for 2Chr 19:8
cometh upon us, as the sword, ... 2Chr 20:9
j upon the house of Ahab, and 2Chr 22:8
So they executed *j* against Joash 2Chr 24:24
let *j* be executed speedily upon .... Ezr 7:26
toward all that knew law and *j* .... Est 1:13
Doth God pervert *j* .... Job 8:3
and if of *j*, who shall set me a .... Job 9:19
and we should come together in *j* .... Job 9:32
and bringest me into *j* with thee .... Job 14:3
I cry aloud, but there is no *j* .... Job 19:7
that ye may know there is a *j* .... Job 19:29
will he enter with thee into *j* .... Job 22:4
liveth, who hath taken away my *j* .... Job 27:2
my *j* was as a robe and a diadem .... Job 29:14
neither do the aged understand *j* .... Job 32:9
Let us choose to us *j* .... Job 34:4
and God hath taken away my *j* .... Job 34:5
with the Almighty pervert *j* .... Job 34:12
he should enter into *j* with God .... Job 34:23
not see him, yet *j* is before him .... Job 35:14
fulfilled the *j* of the wicked .... Job 36:17
j and justice take hold on thee .... Job 36:17
he is excellent in power, and in *j* .... Job 37:23
Wilt thou also disannul my *j* .... Job 40:8

ungodly shall not stand in the *j* .... Ps 1:5
awake for me to the *j* that thou .... Ps 7:6
he hath prepared his throne for *j* .... Ps 9:7
he shall minister to the people .... Ps 9:8
known by the *j* which he executeth ...... Ps 9:16
The meek will he guide in *j* .... Ps 25:9
He loveth righteousness and *j* .... Ps 33:5
Stir up thyself, and awake to my *j* ...... Ps 35:23
light, and thy *j* as the noonday .... Ps 37:6
For the LORD loveth *j*, and .... Ps 37:28
and his tongue talketh of *j* .... Ps 37:30
righteousness and thy poor with *j* ...... Ps 72:2
Thou didst cause *j* to be heard .... Ps 76:8
When God arose to *j*, to save all .... Ps 76:9
j are the habitation of thy .... Ps 89:14
But *j* shall return unto .... Ps 94:15
j are the habitation of his .... Ps 97:2
The king's strength also loveth *j* ...... Ps 99:4
equity, thou executest *j* and .... Ps 99:4
I will sing of mercy and *j* .... Ps 101:1
j for all that are oppressed .... Ps 103:6
Blessed are they that keep *j* .... Ps 106:3
stood up Phinehas, and executed *j* ...... Ps 106:30
of his hands are verity and *j* .... Ps 111:7
Teach me good *j* and knowledge .... Ps 119:66
when wilt thou execute *j* on them ...... Ps 119:84
I have done *j* and justice .... Ps 119:121
quicken me according to thy *j* .... Ps 119:149
For there are set thrones of *j* .... Ps 122:5
enter not into *j* with thy servant ...... Ps 143:2
Which executeth *j* for the .... Ps 146:7
execute upon them the *j* written ...... Ps 149:9
of wisdom, justice, and *j*, and .... Prov 1:3
He keepeth the paths of *j* .... Prov 2:8
understand righteousness, and *j* ...... Prov 2:9
in the midst of the paths of *j* .... Prov 8:20
that is destroyed for want of *j* .... Prov 13:23
his mouth transgresseth not in *j* ...... Prov 16:10
bosom to pervert the ways of *j* .... Prov 17:23
to overthrow the righteous in *j* ...... Prov 18:5
An ungodly witness scorneth *j* .... Prov 19:28
j scattereth away all evil with .... Prov 20:8
is more acceptable to the LORD .... Prov 21:3
because they refuse to do *j* .... Prov 21:7
It is joy to the just to do *j* .... Prov 21:15
to have respect of persons in *j* .... Prov 24:23
Evil men understand not *j* .... Prov 28:5
The king by *j* establisheth the .... Prov 29:4
but every man's *j* cometh from the .... Prov 29:26
pervert the *j* of any of the .... Prov 31:5
saw under the sun the place of *j* ...... Eccl 3:16
poor, and violent perverting of *j* ...... Eccl 5:8
heart discerneth both time and *j* ...... Eccl 8:5
every purpose there is time and *j* ...... Eccl 8:6
things God will bring thee into *j* ...... Eccl 11:9
God shall bring every work into *j* ...... Eccl 12:14
seek *j*, relieve the oppressed .... Is 1:17
it was full of *j* .... Is 1:21
Zion shall be redeemed with *j* .... Is 1:27
The LORD will enter into *j* with .... Is 3:14
midst thereof by the spirit of *j* .... Is 4:4
and he looked for *j*, but behold .... Is 5:7
of hosts shall be exalted in *j* .... Is 5:16
it, and to establish it with *j* .... Is 9:7
To turn aside the needy from *j* .... Is 10:2
Take counsel, execute *j* .... Is 16:3
of David, judging, and seeking *j* ...... Is 16:5
j to him that sitteth in *j* .... Is 28:6
er in vision, they stumble in *j* .... Is 28:7
I also will I lay to the line, and .... Is 28:17
for the LORD is a God of *j* .... Is 30:18
and princes shall rule in *j* .... Is 32:1
Then *j* shall dwell in the .... Is 32:16
he hath filled Zion with *j* .... Is 33:5
upon the people of my curse, to *j* ...... Is 34:5
and taught him in the path of *j* ...... Is 40:14
my *j* is passed over from my God ...... Is 40:27
let us come near together to *j* .... Is 41:1
bring forth *j* to the Gentiles .... Is 42:1
he shall bring forth *j* unto truth ...... Is 42:3
till he have set *j* in the earth .... Is 42:4
yet surely my *j* is with the LORD ...... Is 49:4
I will make my *j* to rest for a .... Is 51:4
was taken from prison and from *j* ...... Is 53:8
thee in *j* thou shalt condemn .... Is 54:17
Thus saith the LORD, Keep ye *j* .... Is 56:1
there is no *j* in their goings .... Is 59:8
Therefore is *j* far from us .... Is 59:9
we look for *j*, but there is none .... Is 59:11
j is turned away backward, and ...... Is 59:14
him that there was no *j* .... Is 59:15
For I the LORD love *j*, I hate .... Is 61:8
The LORD liveth, in truth, in *j* .... Jer 4:2
if there be any that executeth *j* ...... Jer 5:1
the LORD, nor the *j* of their God ...... Jer 5:4
the LORD, and the *j* of their God ...... Jer 5:5
throughly execute *j* between a man .... Jer 7:5
people know not the *j* of the LORD ...... Jer 8:7
which exercise lovingkindness, *j* ...... Jer 9:24
O LORD, correct me, but with *j* .... Jer 10:24
Execute *j* in the morning, and .... Jer 21:12
Execute ye *j* and righteousness, and.... Jer 22:3
thy father eat and drink, and do *j* ...... Jer 22:15
and prosper, and shall execute *j* ...... Jer 23:5
and he shall execute *j* and .... Jer 33:15
Hamath, where he gave *j* upon him .... Jer 39:5
is come upon the plain country......... Jer 48:21
Thus far is the *j* of Moab .... Jer 48:47
they whose *j* was not to drink of ...... Jer 49:12
for her *j* reacheth unto heaven, ... Jer 51:9

that I will do *j* upon the graven .... Jer 51:47
that I will do *j* upon her graven ...... Jer 51:52
where he gave *j* upon him............ Jer 52:9
hath executed true *j* between man .... Eze 18:8
for they had executed *j* upon her ...... Eze 23:10
I will set *j* before them, and they ...... Eze 23:24
I will feed them with *j* .... Eze 34:16
see my *j* that I have executed .... Eze 39:21
controversy they shall stand in *j* ...... Eze 44:24
violence and spoil, and execute *j* ...... Eze 45:9
works are truth, and his ways *j* ...... Dan 4:37
the *j* was set, and the books were...... Dan 7:10
I was given to the saints of the .... Dan 7:22
But the *j* shall sit, and they .... Dan 7:26
unto me in righteousness, and in *j* .... Hos 2:19
for *j* is toward you, because ye............ Hos 5:1
is oppressed and broken in *j* .... Hos 5:11
thus *j* springeth up as hemlock in .... Hos 10:4
keep mercy and *j*, and wait on thy .... Hos 12:6
Ye who turn *j* to wormwood............ Amos 5:7
good, and establish *j* in the gate...... Amos 5:15
But let *j* run down as waters, and...... Amos 5:24
for ye have turned *j* into gall............ Amos 6:12
Is it not for you to know *j* .... Mic 3:1
the spirit of the LORD, and of *j* ...... Mic 3:8
the house of Israel, that abhor *j* ...... Mic 3:9
my cause, and execute *j* for me ...... Mic 7:9
slacked, and *j* doth never go forth ...... Hab 1:4
therefore wrong *j* proceedeth .... Hab 1:4
their *j* and their dignity shall .... Hab 1:7
thou hast ordained them for *j* .... Hab 1:12
earth, which have wrought his *j* ...... Zeph 2:3
doth he bring his *j* to light .... Zeph 3:5
of hosts, saying, Execute true *j* ...... Zec 7:9
execute the *j* of truth and peace ...... Zec 8:16
or, Where is the God of *j* .... Mal 2:17
And I will come near to you to *j* ...... Mal 3:5
kill shall be in danger of the *j* .... Mt 5:21
cause shall be in danger of the *j* ...... Mt 5:22
For with what *j* ye judge, ye .... Mt 7:2
Sodom and Gomorrha in the day of *j*.... Mt 10:15
for Tyre and Sidon at the day of *j* ...... Mt 11:22
the land of Sodom in the day of *j* ...... Mt 11:24
he shall shew *j* to the Gentiles............ Mt 12:18
till he send forth *j* unto victory ...... Mt 12:20
account thereof in the day of *j* .... Mt 12:36
rise in *j* with this generation............ Mt 12:41
up in the *j* with this generation............ Mt 12:42
weightier matters of the law, *j* .... Mt 23:23
he was set down on the *j* seat .... Mt 27:19
Sodom and Gomorrha in the day of *j*.... Mk 6:11
for Tyre and Sidon at the *j* .... Lk 10:14
the south shall rise up in the *j* ...... Lk 11:31
up in the *j* with this generation............ Lk 11:32
manner of herbs, and pass over *j* ...... Lk 11:42
hath committed all *j* unto the Son ...... Jn 5:22
him authority to execute *j* also............ Jn 5:27
and my *j* is just .... Jn 5:30
appearance, but judge righteous *j* ...... Jn 7:24
And yet if I judge, my *j* is true .... Jn 8:16
For *j* I am come into this world, ... Jn 9:39
Now is the *j* of this world............ Jn 12:31
sin, and of righteousness, and of *j* ...... Jn 16:8
Of *j*, because the prince of this .... Jn 16:11
from Caiaphas unto the hall of *j* ...... Jn 18:28
went not into the *j* hall, lest .... Jn 18:28
entered into the *j* hall again............ Jn 18:33
And went again into the *j* hall .... Jn 19:9
sat down in the *j* seat in a place ...... Jn 19:13
humiliation his was taken away............ Acts 8:33
and brought him to the *j* seat............ Acts 18:12
And he drave them from the *j* seat ...... Acts 18:16
and beat him before the *j* seat............ Acts 18:17
him to be kept in Herod's *j* hall ...... Acts 23:35
to come, Felix trembled, and............ Acts 24:25
the *j* seat commanded Paul to be ...... Acts 25:6
Paul, I stand at Caesar's *j* seat............ Acts 25:10
desiring to have *j* against him .... Acts 25:15
on the morrow I sat on the *j* seat ...... Acts 25:17
Who knowing the *j* of God, that ...... Rom 1:32
But we are sure that the *j* of God ...... Rom 2:2
thou shalt escape the *j* of God .... Rom 2:3
of the righteous *j* of God............ Rom 2:5
for the *j* was by one to .... Rom 5:16
of one *j* came upon all men to............ Rom 5:18
stand before the *j* seat of Christ ...... Rom 14:10
in the same mind and in the same *j* 1Cor 1:10
be judged of you, or of man's *j* 1Cor 4:3
yet I give my *j*, as one that hath...... 1Cor 7:25
If she so abide, after my *j* 1Cor 7:40
before the *j* seat of Christ 2Cor 5:10
troubleth you shall bear his *j* .... Gal 5:10
and more in knowledge and in all *j* .... Phil 1:9
token of the righteous *j* of God............ 2Th 1:5
beforehand, going before to *j* 1Ti 5:24
of the dead, and of eternal *j* .... Heb 6:2
once to die, but after this the *j* .... Heb 9:27
certain fearful looking for of *j* .... Heb 10:27
and draw you before the *j* seats ...... Jas 2:6
that hath shewed no mercy............ Jas 2:13
and mercy rejoiceth against *j* .... Jas 2:13
For the time is come that *j* must 1Pet 4:17
whose *j* now of a long time............ 2Pet 2:3
darkness, to be reserved unto *j* 2Pet 2:4
unto the day of *j* to be punished...... 2Pet 2:9
unto fire against the day of *j* 2Pet 3:7
may have boldness in the day of *j*...... 1Jn 4:17
unto the *j* of the great day............ Jude 6
To execute *j* upon all, and to............ Jude 15
for the hour of his *j* is come............ Rev 14:7

I will shew unto thee the *j* of .... Rev 17:1
for in one hour is thy *j* come............ Rev 18:10
them, and *j* was given unto them......... Rev 20:4

JUDGMENTS

out arm, and with great *j* .... Ex 6:6
of the land of Egypt by great *j* .... Ex 7:4
Now these are the *j* which thou............ Ex 21:1
words of the LORD, and all the *j* ...... Ex 24:3
Ye shall do my *j*, and keep mine......... Lev 18:4
keep my statutes, and my *j* .... Lev 18:5
keep my statutes and my *j*, and ...... Lev 18:26
all my statutes, and all my *j* .... Lev 19:37
keep all my statutes, and all my *j* ...... Lev 20:22
do my statutes, and keep my *j* .... Lev 25:18
or if your soul abhor my *j* .... Lev 26:15
even because they despised my *j* ...... Lev 26:43
These are the statutes and *j* .... Lev 26:46
gods also the LORD executed *j* .... Num 33:4
of blood according to these *j* .... Num 35:24
are the commandments and the *j* ...... Num 36:13
unto the statutes and unto the *j* ...... Deut 4:1
I have taught you statutes and *j* ...... Deut 4:5
j so righteous as all this law, ... Deut 4:8
time to teach you statutes and *j* ...... Deut 4:14
and the statutes, and the *j* .... Deut 4:45
j which I speak in your ears this ...... Deut 5:1
and the statutes, and the *j* .... Deut 5:31
the statutes, and the *j*, which .... Deut 6:1
and the statutes, and the *j* .... Deut 6:20
and the statutes, and the *j* .... Deut 7:11
to pass, if ye hearken to these *j* ...... Deut 7:12
his commandments, and his *j* .... Deut 8:11
charge, and his statutes, and his *j* ...... Deut 11:1
j which I set before you this day ...... Deut 11:32
These are the statutes and *j* .... Deut 12:1
thee to do these statutes and *j* ...... Deut 26:16
and his commandments, and his *j* ...... Deut 26:17
and his statutes and his *j*, that ...... Deut 30:16
They shall teach Jacob thy *j* .... Deut 33:10
of the LORD, and his *j* with Israel ...... Deut 33:21
For all his *j* were before me 2Sa 22:23
and his commandments, and his *j* 1Kin 2:3
in my statutes, and execute my *j* 1Kin 6:12
and his statutes, and his *j* 1Kin 8:58
and wilt keep my statutes and my *j* 1Kin 9:4
and to keep my statutes and my *j* 1Kin 11:33
wonders, and the *j* of his mouth 1Chr 16:12
his *j* are in all the earth............ 1Chr 16:14
j which the LORD charged Moses......... 1Chr 22:13
to do my commandments and my *j* 1Chr 28:7
shalt observe my statutes and my *j* 2Chr 7:17
commandment, statutes and *j* 2Chr 19:10
to teach in Israel statutes and *j* ...... Ezr 7:10
nor the statutes, nor the *j* .... Neh 1:7
heaven, and gavest them right *j* ...... Neh 9:13
but sinned against thy *j* .... Neh 9:29
of the LORD our Lord, and his *j* ...... Neh 10:29
thy *j* are far above out of his............ Ps 10:5
For all his *j* were before me, and ...... Ps 18:22
the *j* of the LORD are true and............ Ps 19:9
thy *j* are a great deep .... Ps 36:6
Judah be glad, because of thy *j* ...... Ps 48:11
Give the king thy *j*, O God, and............ Ps 72:1
my law, and walk not in my *j* .... Ps 89:30
Judah rejoiced because of thy *j* ...... Ps 97:8
wonders, and the *j* of his mouth ...... Ps 105:5
his *j* are in all the earth............ Ps 105:7
have learned thy righteous *j* .... Ps 119:7
I declared all the *j* of thy mouth......... Ps 119:13
it hath unto thy *j* at all times............ Ps 119:20
thy *j* have I laid before me............ Ps 119:30
for thy *j* are good............ Ps 119:39
for I have hoped in thy *j* .... Ps 119:43
I remembered thy *j* of old............ Ps 119:52
thee because of thy righteous *j* ...... Ps 119:62
that thy *j* are right, and that .... Ps 119:75
I have not departed from thy *j* ...... Ps 119:102
that I will keep thy righteous *j* ...... Ps 119:106
mouth, O God, and teach me thy *j* .... Ps 119:108
and I am afraid of thy *j* .... Ps 119:120
O LORD, and upright are thy *j* .... Ps 119:137
quicken me according to thy *j* ...... Ps 119:156
thy righteous *j* endureth for ever ...... Ps 119:160
thee because of thy righteous *j* ...... Ps 119:164
and let thy *j* help me............ Ps 119:175
his statutes and his *j* unto Israel...... Ps 147:19
and as for his *j*, they have not............ Ps 147:20
J are prepared for scorners, and ...... Prov 19:29
Yea, in the way of thy *j*, O LORD,......... Is 26:8
for when thy *j* are in the earth, ... Is 26:9
I will utter my *j* against them............ Jer 1:16
let me talk with thee of thy *j* .... Jer 12:1
she hath changed my *j* into............ Eze 5:6
for they have refused my *j* .... Eze 5:6
statutes, neither have kept my *j* ...... Eze 5:7
have done according to the *j* of ...... Eze 5:7
will execute *j* in the midst of............ Eze 5:8
and I will execute *j* in thee .... Eze 5:10
shall execute *j* in thee in anger......... Eze 5:15
and will execute *j* among you............ Eze 11:9
statutes, neither executed my *j* ...... Eze 11:12
my four sore *j* upon Jerusalem......... Eze 14:21
execute *j* upon thee in the sight......... Eze 16:41
in my statutes, and hath kept my *j* .... Eze 18:9
nor increase, hath executed my *j* ...... Eze 18:17
my statutes, and shewed them my *j* .... Eze 20:11
statutes, and they despised my *j* ...... Eze 20:13
Because they despised my *j* .... Eze 20:16
fathers, neither observe their *j* ...... Eze 20:18
walk in my statutes, and keep my *j* .... Eze 20:19

J

neither kept my *j* to do them .... Eze 20:21
they had not executed my *j* .... Eze 20:24
j whereby they should not live .... Eze 20:25
judge thee according to their *j* .... Eze 23:24
And I will execute *j* upon Moab .... Eze 25:11
I shall have executed *j* in her .... Eze 28:22
when I have executed *j* upon all .... Eze 28:26
in Zoan, and I will execute *j* in No........... Eze 30:14
Thus will I execute *j* in Egypt................... Eze 30:19
statutes, and ye shall keep my *j* .... Eze 36:27
they shall also walk in my *j* .... Eze 37:24
shall judge it according to thy *j* .... Eze 44:24
from thy precepts and from thy *j* .... Dan 9:5
thy *j* are as the light that goeth .... Hos 6:5
The LORD hath taken away thy *j* .... Zeph 3:15
Israel, with the statutes and *j* .... Mal 4:4
how unsearchable are his *j* .... Rom 11:33
If then ye have *j* of things 1Cor 6:4
for thy *j* are made manifest........................ Rev 15:4
true and righteous are thy *j* .... Rev 16:7
For true and righteous are his *j* .... Rev 19:2

JUDITH (*ju'-dith*) *A wife of Esau.*
wife *J* the daughter of Beeri the .... Gen 26:34

JULIA (*ju'-le-ah*) *A Christian acquaintance of*
Paul.
Salute Philologus, and *J*, Nereus, ... Rom 16:15

JULIUS (*ju'-le-us*) *A Roman centurion.*
other prisoners unto one named *J*............... Acts 27:1
J courteously entreated Paul, and .... Acts 27:3

JUMPING
horses, and of the *j* chariots .... Nah 3:2

JUNIA (*ju'-ne-ah*) *A Christian acquaintance of*
Paul.
Salute Andronicus and *J*, my...................... Rom 16:7

JUNIPER
came and sat down under a *j* tree.............. 1Kin 19:4
as he lay and slept under a *j* tree............... 1Kin 19:5
bushes, and *j* roots for their meat .... Job 30:4
of the mighty, with coals of *j* .... Ps 120:4

JUPITER (*ju'-pit-ur*) *Chief god of the Romans.*
And they called Barnabas, *J* .... Acts 14:12
Then the priest of *J*, which was .... Acts 14:13
the image which fell down from *J* .... Acts 19:35

JURISDICTION
that he belonged unto Herod's *j* .... Lk 23:7

JUSHAB-HESED (*ju''-shab-he'-sed*) *A son of*
Zerubbabel.
and Berechiah, and Hasadiah, *J* 1Chr 3:20

JUST
Noah was a *j* man and perfect in .... Gen 6:9
j balances, *j* weights .... Lev 19:36
a *j* ephah, and a *j* hin, shall .... Lev 19:36
judge the people with *j* judgment.............. Deut 16:18
is altogether *j* shalt thou follow .... Deut 16:20
j weight, a perfect and.................................. Deut 25:15
j measure shalt thou have .... Deut 25:15
of truth and without iniquity, *j* .... Deut 32:4
He that ruleth over men must be *j* 2Sa 23:3
Howbeit thou art *j* in all that is .... Neh 9:33
mortal man be more *j* than God .... Job 4:17
but how should man be *j* with God .... Job 9:2
the *j* upright man is laughed to .... Job 12:4
but the *j* shall put it on, and the .... Job 27:17
Behold, in this thou art not *j* .... Job 33:12
thou condemn him that is most *j* .... Job 34:17
but establish the *j* .... Ps 7:9
The wicked plotteth against the *j* .... Ps 37:12
blesseth the habitation of the *j* .... Prov 3:33
But the path of the *j* is as the .... Prov 4:18
teach a *j* man, and he will............................ Prov 9:9
are upon the head of the *j* .... Prov 10:6
The memory of the *j* is blessed .... Prov 10:7
The tongue of the *j* is as choice................. Prov 10:20
The mouth of the *j* bringeth forth .... Prov 10:31
but a *j* weight is his delight .... Prov 11:1
shall the *j* be delivered................................ Prov 11:9
but the *j* shall come out of .... Prov 12:13
shall no evil happen to the *j* .... Prov 12:21
the sinner is laid up for the *j* .... Prov 13:22
A *j* weight and balance are the .... Prov 16:11
and he that condemneth the *j* .... Prov 17:15
Also to punish the *j* is not good .... Prov 17:26
first in his own cause seemeth *j* .... Prov 18:17
The *j* man walketh in his .... Prov 20:7
It is joy to the *j* to do judgment................ Prov 21:15
For a *j* man falleth seven times, ... Prov 24:16
but the *j* seek his soul .... Prov 29:10
man is an abomination to the *j*................... Prov 29:27
there is a *j* man that perisheth .... Eccl 7:15
there is not a *j* man upon earth.................. Eccl 7:20
that there be *j* men, unto whom it .... Eccl 8:14
The way of the *j* is uprightness................. Is 26:7
dost weigh the path of the *j* .... Is 26:7
turn aside the *j* for a thing of .... Is 29:21
a *j* God and a Saviour .... Is 45:21
of the *j* in the midst of her .... Lam 4:13
But if a man be *j*, and do that .... Eze 18:5
he is *j*, he shall surely live, ... Eze 18:9
Ye shall have *j* balances, and a................. Eze 45:10
a *j* ephah, and a *j* bath .... Eze 45:10
and the *j* shall walk in them .... Hos 14:9
they afflict the *j*, they take a..................... Amos 5:12
but the *j* shall live by his faith .... Hab 2:4
The *j* LORD is in the midst .... Zeph 3:5
he is *j*, and having salvation .... Zec 9:9

Joseph her husband, being a *j* man........... Mt 1:19
good, and sendeth rain on the *j* .... Mt 5:45
sever the wicked from among the *j* .... Mt 13:49
nothing to do with that *j* man.................... Mt 27:19
of the blood of this *j* person....................... Mt 27:24
John, knowing that he was a *j* man........... Mk 6:20
to the wisdom of the *j* .... Lk 1:17
and the same man was *j* and devout,....... Lk 2:25
at the resurrection of the *j* .... Lk 14:14
nine *j* persons, which need no .... Lk 15:7
should feign themselves *j* men .... Lk 20:20
and he was a good man, and a *j* .... Lk 23:50
and my judgment is *j* .... Jn 5:30
ye denied the Holy One and the *J* .... Acts 3:14
before of the coming of the *J* One............ Acts 7:52
a *j* man, and one that feareth God, ... Acts 10:22
know his will, and see that *J* One............. Acts 22:14
of the dead, both of the *j* .... Acts 24:15
The *j* shall live by faith .... Rom 1:17
of the law are *j* before God........................ Rom 2:13
whose damnation is *j* .... Rom 3:8
that he might be *j*, and the .... Rom 3:26
and the commandment holy, and *j*............. Rom 7:12
The *j* shall live by faith .... Gal 3:11
honest, whatsoever things are *j* .... Phil 4:8
your servants that which is *j* .... Col 4:1
a lover of good men, sober, *j* .... Titus 1:8
received a *j* recompence of reward .... Heb 2:2
Now the *j* shall live by faith .... Heb 10:38
the spirits of *j* men made perfect............... Heb 12:23
Ye have condemned and killed the *j* .... Jas 5:6
the *j* for the unjust, that he 1Pet 3:18
And delivered *j* Lot, vexed with 2Pet 2:7
j to forgive us our sins, and to 1Jn 1:9
j and true are thy ways, thou King.......... Rev 15:3

JUSTICE
keep the way of the LORD, to do *j* .... Gen 18:19
he executed the *j* of the LORD .... Deut 33:21
judgment and *j* unto all his people 2Sa 8:15
come unto me, and I would do him *j* 2Sa 15:4
he thee king, to do judgment and *j* 1Kin 10:9
and *j* among all his people 1Chr 18:14
over them, to do judgment and *j* 2Chr 9:8
or doth the Almighty pervert *j* .... Job 8:3
judgment and *j* take hold on thee............. Job 36:17
and in judgment, and in plenty of *j* .... Job 37:23
do *j* to the afflicted and needy .... Ps 82:3
J and judgment are the habitation............ Ps 89:14
I have done judgment and *j* .... Ps 119:121
the instruction of wisdom, *j* .... Prov 1:3
kings reign, and princes decree *j* .... Prov 8:15
To do *j* and judgment is more.................... Prov 21:3
j in a province, marvel not at..................... Eccl 5:8
with *j* from henceforth even for .... Is 9:7
LORD, Keep ye judgment, and do *j* .... Is 56:1
ask of me the ordinances of *j* .... Is 58:2
None calleth for *j*, nor any......................... Is 59:4
us, neither doth *j* overtake us.................... Is 59:9
backward, and *j* standeth afar off.............. Is 59:14
eat and drink, and do judgment and *j* ...... Jer 22:15
judgment and *j* in the earth........................ Jer 23:5
bless thee, O habitation of *j* .... Jer 31:23
the LORD, and execute judgment of *j* .... Jer 50:7
spoil, and execute judgment of *j* .... Eze 45:9

JUSTIFICATION
and was raised again for our *j* .... Rom 4:25
gift is of many offences unto *j* .... Rom 5:16
came upon all men unto *j* of life .... Rom 5:18

JUSTIFIED
and should a man full of talk be *j* .... Job 11:2
I know that I shall be *j* .... Job 13:18
How then can man be *j* with God .... Job 25:4
because he *j* himself rather than .... Job 32:2
mightest be *j* when thou speakest............. Ps 51:4
sight shall no man living be *j* .... Ps 143:2
witnesses, that they may be *j* .... Is 43:9
thou, that thou mayest be *j* .... Is 43:26
shall all the seed of Israel be *j* .... Is 45:25
The backsliding Israel hath *j* .... Jer 3:11
hast *j* thy sisters in all thine .... Eze 16:51
in that thou hast *j* thy sisters..................... Eze 16:52
But wisdom is *j* of her children .... Mt 11:19
For by thy words thou shalt be *j* .... Mt 12:37
j God, being *j* against you .... Lk 7:29
But wisdom is *j* of all her .... Lk 7:35
his house *j* rather than the other............... Lk 18:14
believe are *j* from all things .... Acts 13:39
not be *j* by the law of Moses..................... Acts 13:39
the doers of the law shall be *j* .... Rom 2:13
thou mightest be *j* in thy sayings.............. Rom 3:4
shall no flesh be *j* in his sight..................... Rom 3:20
Being *j* freely by his grace .... Rom 3:24
we conclude that a man is *j* by .... Rom 3:28
For if Abraham were *j* by works .... Rom 4:2
Therefore being *j* by faith.......................... Rom 5:1
being now *j* by his blood, we..................... Rom 5:9
and whom he called, them he also *j* .... Rom 8:30
and whom he *j*, them he also..................... Rom 8:30
yet am I not hereby *j* 1Cor 4:4
but ye are *j* in the name of the 1Cor 6:11
is not *j* by the works of the law .... Gal 2:16
that we might be *j* by the faith .... Gal 2:16
of the law shall no flesh be *j*...................... Gal 2:16
But that no man is *j* by the law .... Gal 3:11
that we might be *j* by faith .... Gal 3:24
whosoever of you are *j* by the law .... Gal 5:4
j in the Spirit, seen of angels,.................... 1Ti 3:16
That being *j* by his grace, ... Titus 3:7

not Abraham our father *j* by works .... Jas 2:21
then how that by works a man is *j*............ Jas 2:24
not Rahab the harlot *j* by works .... Jas 2:25

JUSTIFIER
the *j* of him which believeth in................. Rom 3:26

JUSTIFIETH
He that *j* the wicked, and he that .... Prov 17:15
He is near that *j* me .... Is 50:8
on him that *j* the ungodly........................... Rom 4:5
It is God that *j* .... Rom 8:33

JUSTIFY
for I will not *j* the wicked........................... Ex 23:7
then they shall *j* the righteous................... Deut 25:1
If I myself, mine own mouth .... Job 9:20
God forbid that I should *j* you .... Job 27:5
speak, for I desire to *j* thee .... Job 33:32
Which *j* the wicked for reward, and......... Is 5:23
shall my righteous servant *j* many .... Is 53:11
But he, willing to *j* himself .... Lk 10:29
Ye are they which *j* yourselves .... Lk 16:15
which shall *j* the circumcision by.............. Rom 3:30
would *j* the heathen through faith .... Gal 3:8

JUSTIFYING
j the righteous, to give him 1Kin 8:32
by *j* the righteous, by giving him 2Chr 6:23

JUSTLE
they shall *j* one against another .... Nah 2:4

JUSTLY
LORD require of thee, but to do *j* .... Mic 6:8
And we indeed *j*; for we receive................ Lk 23:41
and God also, how holily and *j* 1Th 2:10

JUSTUS (*jus'-tus*) See BARSABAS, JESUS.
1. Surname for Barsabas.
Barsabas, who was surnamed *J* .... Acts 1:23
2. A Corinthian Christian.
a certain man's house, named *J* .... Acts 18:7
3. A Christian acquaintance of Paul.
And Jesus, which is called *J* .... Col 4:11

JUTTAH (*jut'-tah*) *A city in Judah.*
Maon, Carmel, and Ziph, and *J* .... Josh 15:55
and *J* with her suburbs, ... Josh 21:16

K

KABZEEL (*kab'-ze-el*) See JEKABZEEL. *A city*
in Judah.
coast of Edom southward were *K* .... Josh 15:21
the son of a valiant man, of *K* 2Sa 23:20
the son of a valiant man of *K* 1Chr 11:22

KADESH (*ka'-desh*) See EN-MISHPAT, KADESH-
BARNEA, KEDESH. *A place in the wilderness,*
south of Judah.
and came to En-mishpat, which is *K* .... Gen 14:7
behold, it is between *K* and Bered............. Gen 16:14
country, and dwelled between *K* .... Gen 20:1
the wilderness of Paran, to *K*..................... Num 13:26
and the people abode in *K* .... Num 20:1
from *K* unto the king of Edom................... Num 20:14
and, behold, we are in *K*, a city................. Num 20:16
congregation, journeyed from *K* .... Num 20:22
in *K* in the wilderness of Zin .... Num 27:14
the wilderness of Zin, which is *K* .... Num 33:36
And they removed from *K*, and .... Num 33:37
So ye abode in *K* many days...................... Deut 1:46
unto the Red sea, and came to *K* .... Judg 11:16
and Israel abode in *K* .... Judg 11:17
LORD shaketh the wilderness of *K* .... Ps 29:8
even to the waters of strife in *K* .... Eze 47:19
unto the waters of strife in *K* .... Eze 48:28

KADESH-BARNEA (*ka''-desh-bar'-ne-ah*) See
KADESH. *Same as Kadesh.*
sent them from *K* to see the land.............. Num 32:8
shall be from the south to *K* .... Num 34:4
by the way of mount Seir unto *K*.............. Deut 1:2
and we came to *K*.. Deut 1:19
the space in which we came from *K* .... Deut 2:14
when the LORD sent you from *K*................. Deut 9:23
smote them from *K* even unto Gaza.......... Josh 10:41
of God concerning me and thee in *K*........ Josh 14:6
me from *K* to espy out the land................. Josh 14:7
up on the south side unto *K*........................ Josh 15:3

KADMIEL (*kad'-me-el*)
1. An exile.
the children of Jeshua and *K*...................... Ezr 2:40
the children of Jeshua, of *K*....................... Neh 7:43
2. A helper of the Temple.
with his sons and his brethren, *K* .... Ezr 3:9
3. A Levite with Nehemiah.
the Levites, Jeshua, and *K* .... Neh 9:4
Then the Levites, Jeshua, and *K* .... Neh 9:5
Binnui of the sons of Henadad, *K* .... Neh 10:9
Jeshua, Binnui, *K*, Sherebiah, ... Neh 12:8
Sherebiah, and Jeshua the son of *K* .... Neh 12:24

KADMONITES (*kad'-mo-nites*) *A Phoenician*
tribe.
and the Kenizzites, and the *K*.................... Gen 15:19

KAIN See Cain.

KAIWAN See Chiun.

KALLAI (kal'-la-i) *A priest.*
Of Sallai, of Amok .... Neh 12:20

KAMON See Camon.

KANAH (ka'-nah)
  1. A brook between Ephraim and Manasseh.
Tappuah westward unto the river K.... Josh 16:8
coast descended unto the river K ...... Josh 17:9
  2. A city in Asher.
Rehob, and Hammon, and K............... Josh 19:28

KAREAH (ha'-re-ah) See Careah. *A captain of the Jews.*
Johanan and Jonathan the sons of K.. Jer 40:8
Moreover Johanan the son of K......... Jer 40:13
Then Johanan the son of K spake...... Jer 40:15
said unto Johanan the son of K......... Jer 40:16
But when Johanan the son of K........ Jer 41:11
Ishmael saw Johanan the son of K.... Jer 41:13
and went unto Johanan the son of K.. Jer 41:14
Then took Johanan the son of K....... Jer 41:16
forces, and Johanan the son of K...... Jer 42:1
called he Johanan the son of K......... Jer 42:8
Hoshaiah, and Johanan the son of K.. Jer 43:2
So Johanan the son of K, and all....... Jer 43:4
But Johanan the son of K, and all...... Jer 43:5

KARKA See Karkaa.

KARKAA (kar'-ka-ah) *A city in Judah.*
Adar, and fetched a compass to K..... Josh 15:3

KARKOR (kar'-kor) *A Gadite city.*
Now Zebah and Zalmunna were in K. Judg 8:10

KARNAIM (kar'-na-im) See Ashteroth. *A city in Og.*
smote the Rephaims in Ashteroth K... Gen 14:5

KARTAH (kar'-tah) See Kattath. *A Levitical city in Zebulun.*
suburbs, and K with her suburbs,....... Josh 21:34

KARTAN (kar'-tan) See Kirjathaim. *A Levitical city in Naphtali.*
suburbs, and K with her suburbs,....... Josh 21:32

KATTATH (kat'-tath) See Kartah, Kitron. *A city in Zebulun.*
And K, and Nahallal........................... Josh 19:15

KEBAR See Chebar.

KEDAR (ke'-dar)
  1. A son of Ishmael.
and K, and Adbeel, and Mibsam,........ Gen 25:13
then K, and Adbeel, and Mibsam,....... 1Chr 1:29
  2. The tribe.
that I dwell in the tents of K............... Ps 120:5
of Jerusalem, as the tents of K........... Song 1:5
and all the glory of K shall fail.......... Is 21:16
mighty men of the children of K......... Is 21:17
the villages that K doth inhabit.......... Is 42:11
All the flocks of K shall.................... Is 60:7
and send unto K, and consider........... Jer 2:10
Concerning K, and concerning the .... Jer 49:28
Arise ye, go up to K, and spoil.......... Jer 49:28
Arabia, and all the princes of K......... Eze 27:21

KEDEMAH (ked'-e-mah) *A son of Ishmael.*
and Tema, Jetur, Naphish, and K....... Gen 25:15
Jetur, Naphish, and K........................ 1Chr 1:31

KEDEMOTH (ked'-e-moth)
  1. A wilderness in Reuben.
out of the wilderness of K unto .... Deut 2:26
  2. A Levitical city in Reuben.
And Jahaza, and K, and Mephaath,.... Josh 13:18
K with her suburbs, and Mephaath.... Josh 21:37
K also with her suburbs, and............ 1Chr 6:79

KEDESH (ke'-desh) See Kadesh, Kedesh-Naphtali, Kishion.
  1. A Canaanite city.
The king of K, one............................. Josh 12:22
And K, and Edrei, and En-hazor,....... Josh 19:37
  2. A city of refuge in Naphtali.
they appointed K in Galilee in .... Josh 20:7
K in Galilee with her suburbs, to....... Josh 21:32
arose, and went with Barak to K .... Judg 4:9
called Zebulun and Naphtali to K ..... Judg 4:10
plain of Zaanaim, which is by K........ Judg 4:11
and Janoah, and K, and Hazor, and... 2Kin 15:29
K in Galilee with her suburbs, and.... 1Chr 6:76
  3. A Levitical city in Naphtali.
K with her suburbs, Daberath with ... 1Chr 6:72
  4. A city in Judah.
And K, and Hazor, and Ithnan,........... Josh 15:23

KEDESH-NAPHTALI (ke''-desh-naf''-ta-li)
Same as Kedesh 2.
Barak the son of Abinoam out of K.. Judg 4:6

KEDOLAOMER See Chedorlaomer.

KEEP
of Eden to dress it and to k it .... Gen 2:15
to k the way of the tree of life........... Gen 3:24
to k them alive with............................ Gen 6:19
come unto thee, to k them alive:........ Gen 6:20
to k seed alive upon the face of......... Gen 7:3
Abraham, Thou shalt k my covenant.. Gen 17:9
is my covenant, which ye shall k .... Gen 17:10
they shall k the way of the Lord,....... Gen 18:19

will k thee in all places whither........ Gen 28:15
will k me in this way that I go............ Gen 28:20
I will again feed and k thy flock......... Gen 30:31
k that thou hast unto thyself.............. Gen 33:9
let them k food in the cities............... Gen 41:35
whom the Egyptians in bondage....... Ex 6:5
ye shall k it up until the.................... Ex 12:6
ye shall k it a feast to the Lord.......... Ex 12:14
ye shall k it a feast by an.................. Ex 12:14
that ye shall k this service................ Ex 12:25
congregation of Israel shall k it........ Ex 12:47
will k the passover to the Lord,......... Ex 12:48
and then let him come near and k it... Ex 12:48
that thou shalt k this service in .... Ex 13:5
Thou shalt therefore k this............... Ex 13:10
k all his statutes, I will put............... Ex 15:26
refuse ye to k my commandments..... Ex 16:28
k my covenant, then ye shall be a..... Ex 19:5
love me, and k my commandments.... Ex 20:6
the sabbath day, to k it holy............. Ex 20:8
his neighbour money or stuff to k..... Ex 22:7
or a sheep, or any beast, to k........... Ex 22:10
K thee far from a false matter:.......... Ex 23:7
Three times thou shalt k a feast....... Ex 23:14
Thou shalt k the feast of................... Ex 23:15
to k thee in the way, and to bring...... Ex 23:20
Verily my sabbaths ye shall k.......... Ex 31:13
Ye shall k the sabbath therefore ...... Ex 31:14
of Israel shall k the sabbath............. Ex 31:16
of unleavened bread shalt thou k...... Ex 34:18
that which was delivered him to k .... Lev 6:2
that which was delivered him to k .... Lev 6:4
k the charge of the Lord, that ye....... Lev 8:35
k mine ordinances, to walk............. Lev 18:4
Ye shall therefore k my statutes....... Lev 18:5
Ye shall therefore k my statutes....... Lev 18:26
shall ye k mine ordinance................ Lev 18:30
and his father, and k my sabbaths.... Lev 19:3
Ye shall k my statutes..................... Lev 19:19
Ye shall k my sabbaths, and............ Lev 19:30
ye shall k my statutes, and do.......... Lev 20:8
shall therefore k all my statutes....... Lev 20:22
shall therefore k mine ordinance..... Lev 22:9
shall ye k my commandments.......... Lev 22:31
ye shall k a feast unto the Lord........ Lev 23:39
ye shall k it a feast unto the............. Lev 23:41
then shall the land k a sabbath......... Lev 25:2
k my judgments, and do them.......... Lev 25:18
Ye shall k my sabbaths, and............ Lev 26:2
k my commandments, and do them.. Lev 26:3
the Levites shall k the charge of...... Num 1:53
And they shall k his charge.............. Num 3:7
they shall k all the instruments........ Num 3:8
k the charge of the sanctuary........... Num 3:28
The Lord bless thee, and k thee........ Num 6:24
to k the charge, and shall do no .... Num 8:26
k the passover at his appointed......... Num 9:2
ye shall k it in his appointed............ Num 9:3
ceremonies thereof, shall ye k it...... Num 9:3
that they should k the passover........ Num 9:4
that they could not k the.................. Num 9:6
yet he shall k the passover unto ...... Num 9:10
month at even they shall k it............. Num 9:11
of the passover they shall k it.......... Num 9:12
and forbeareth to k the passover...... Num 9:13
will k the passover unto the Lord...... Num 9:14
And they shall k thy charge............. Num 18:3
k the charge of the tabernacle of ..... Num 18:4
ye shall k the charge of the.............. Num 18:5
thy sons with thee shall k your......... Num 18:7
ye shall k a feast unto the Lord......... Num 29:12
with him, k alive for yourselves....... Num 31:18
which k the charge of the................. Num 31:30
to himself to the inheritance of .... Num 36:7
k himself to his own inheritance....... Num 36:9
that ye may k the commandments of... Deut 4:2
K therefore and do them.................. Deut 4:6
k thy soul diligently, lest thou......... Deut 4:9
Thou shalt k therefore his................ Deut 4:40
day, that ye may keep them, and k ... Deut 5:1
me and k my commandments............ Deut 5:10
K the sabbath day to sanctify it,....... Deut 5:12
thee to k the sabbath day................. Deut 5:15
k all my commandments always,...... Deut 5:29
to k all his statutes and his.............. Deut 6:2
Ye shall diligently k the .... Deut 6:17
because he would k the oath which... Deut 7:8
k his commandments to a thousand.. Deut 7:9
therefore k the commandments......... Deut 7:11
hearken to these judgments, and k... Deut 7:12
shall k unto thee the covenant......... Deut 7:12
thou wouldest k his commandments.. Deut 8:2
Therefore thou shalt k the............... Deut 8:6
To k the commandments.................. Deut 10:13
k his charge, and his statutes, and... Deut 11:1
Therefore shall ye k all the.............. Deut 11:8
For if ye shall diligently k all .... Deut 11:22
k his commandments, and obey his.. Deut 13:4
to k all his commandments which I... Deut 13:18
k the passover unto the Lord thy...... Deut 16:1
thou shalt k the feast of weeks......... Deut 16:10
Seven days shalt thou k a solemn.... Deut 16:15
to k all the words of this law............ Deut 17:19
If thou shalt k all these.................... Deut 19:9
then k thee from every wicked .... Deut 23:9
gone out of thy lips thou shalt k ...... Deut 23:23
thou shalt therefore k and do them... Deut 26:16
to k his statutes, and his.................. Deut 26:17
that thou shouldest k all his............ Deut 26:17
K all the commandments which I..... Deut 27:1

if thou shalt k the commandments.... Deut 28:9
to k his commandments and his....... Deut 28:45
K therefore the words of this............ Deut 29:9
to k his commandments and his....... Deut 30:10
to k his commandments and his....... Deut 30:16
in any wise k yourselves from the.... Deut 6:18
and set men by it for to k them.......... Josh 10:18
to k his commandments, and to........ Josh 22:5
ye therefore very courageous to k.... Josh 23:6
whether they will k the way of.......... Judg 2:22
as their fathers did k it.................... Judg 2:22
who said, K silence......................... Judg 3:19
Thou shalt k fast by my young men... Ruth 2:21
He will k the feet of his saints,......... 1Sa 2:9
his son to k the ark of the Lord 1Sa 7:1
and with one full line to k alive......... 2Sa 8:2
were concubines, to k the house 2Sa 15:16
which he hath left to k the house...... 2Sa 16:21
I have no son to k my name in.......... 2Sa 18:18
whom he had left to k the house....... 2Sa 20:3
k the charge of the Lord thy God,...... 1Kin 2:3
to k his statutes, and his.................. 1Kin 2:3
my ways, to k my statutes and my.... 1Kin 3:14
k all my commandments to walk in ... 1Kin 6:12
k with my servant David my............. 1Kin 8:25
to k his commandments, and his....... 1Kin 8:58
to k his commandments, as at this.... 1Kin 8:61
thee, and with k my statutes and my.. 1Kin 9:4
will not k my commandments and my. 1Kin 9:6
to k my statutes and my judgments,.. 1Kin 11:33
my sight, to k my statutes and my.... 1Kin 11:38
man unto me, and said, K this man... 1Kin 20:39
so shall ye k the watch of the.......... 2Kin 11:6
even they shalt k the watch of.......... 2Kin 11:7
k my commandments.......................... 2Kin 17:13
to k his commandments and his........ 2Kin 23:3
K the passover unto the Lord your.... 2Kin 23:21
that thou wouldest k me from evil.... 1Chr 4:10
thousand, which could k rank.......... 1Chr 12:33
men of war, that could k rank........... 1Chr 12:38
that thou mayest k the law of the 1Chr 22:12
that they should k the charge of 1Chr 23:32
and in the audience of our God, k 1Chr 28:8
fathers, k this for ever in the............ 1Chr 29:18
to k his commandments, thy............. 1Chr 29:19
k with thy servant David my............ 2Chr 6:16
for we k the charge of the Lord......... 2Chr 13:11
no power to k still the kingdom........ 2Chr 22:9
shall k the watch of the Lord............ 2Chr 23:6
now ye purpose to k under the......... 2Chr 28:10
to k the passover unto the Lord......... 2Chr 30:1
to k the passover in the second....... 2Chr 30:2
they could not k it at that time.......... 2Chr 30:3
that they should come to k the......... 2Chr 30:5
at Jerusalem much people to k the ... 2Chr 30:13
counsel to k other seven days........... 2Chr 30:23
to k his commandments, and his....... 2Chr 34:31
to k the passover, and to offer.......... 2Chr 35:16
did all the kings of Israel k.............. 2Chr 35:18
k them, until ye weigh them............. Ezr 8:29
k my commandments, and do them... Neh 1:9
to k the dedication with gladness..... Neh 12:27
k the gates, to sanctify the.............. Neh 13:22
neither k they the king's laws.......... Est 3:8
that they should k the fourteenth..... Est 9:21
that they would k these two days...... Est 9:27
that thou wouldest k me secret........ Job 14:13
but k it still within his mouth.......... Job 20:13
Thou shalt k them, O Lord, thou...... Ps 12:7
K me as the apple of the eye,........... Ps 17:8
K back thy servant also from........... Ps 19:13
none can k alive his own soul.......... Ps 22:29
truth unto such as k his covenant .... Ps 25:10
O k my soul, and deliver me............ Ps 25:20
thou shalt k them secretly in a........ Ps 31:20
to k them alive in famine................. Ps 33:19
K thy tongue from evil, and thy........ Ps 34:13
k not silence.................................. Ps 35:22
he his way, and he shall exalt thee... Ps 37:34
I will k my mouth with a bridle,........ Ps 39:1
will preserve him, and k him alive.... Ps 41:2
come, and shall not k silence.......... Ps 50:3
of God, but k his commandments...... Ps 78:7
K not thou silence, O God................ Ps 83:1
My mercy will I k for him for............. Ps 89:28
and k not my commandments........... Ps 89:31
to k thee in all thy ways.................. Ps 91:11
neither will he k his anger for.......... Ps 103:9
To such as k his covenant, and to,... Ps 103:18
his statutes, and k his laws............. Ps 105:45
Blessed are they that k judgment.... Ps 106:3
the barren woman to k house.......... Ps 113:9
are they that k his testimonies....... Ps 119:2
us to k thy precepts diligently......... Ps 119:4
were directed to k thy statutes........ Ps 119:5
I will k thy statutes........................ Ps 119:8
that I may live, and k thy word......... Ps 119:17
I shall k it unto the end................... Ps 119:33
and I shall k thy law....................... Ps 119:34
So shall I k thy law continually....... Ps 119:44
said that I would k thy words........... Ps 119:57
delayed not to k thy commandments. Ps 119:60
and of them that k thy precepts....... Ps 119:63
but I will k thy precepts with my...... Ps 119:69
so shall I k the testimony of thy...... Ps 119:88
because I k thy precepts................. Ps 119:100
evil way, that I might k thy word...... Ps 119:101
that I will k thy righteous............... Ps 119:106
for I will k the commandments of .... Ps 119:115
therefore doth my soul k them......... Ps 119:129

so will I k thy precepts............... Ps 119:134
eyes, because they k not thy law........ Ps 119:136
I will k thy statutes.................. Ps 119:145
I will k thy testimonies............... Ps 119:146
except the LORD k the city............. Ps 127:1
thy children will k my covenant....... Ps 132:12
K me, O LORD, from the hands of...... Ps 140:4
K the door of my lips.................. Ps 141:3
K me from the snares which they...... Ps 141:9
thee, understanding shall k thee....... Prov 2:11
k the paths of the righteous............ Prov 2:20
let thine heart k my commandments.... Prov 3:1
k sound wisdom and discretion......... Prov 3:21
shall k thy foot from being taken...... Prov 3:26
k my commandments, and live......... Prov 4:4
love her, and she shall k thee.......... Prov 4:6
let her not go: k her................... Prov 4:13
k them in the midst of thine........... Prov 4:21
K thy heart with all diligence.......... Prov 4:23
and that thy lips may k knowledge..... Prov 5:2
k thy father's commandment, and...... Prov 6:20
thou sleepest, it shall k thee........... Prov 6:22
To k thee from the evil woman,........ Prov 6:24
My son, k my words, and lay up my ... Prov 7:1
K my commandments, and live......... Prov 7:2
That they may k thee from the......... Prov 7:5
blessed are they that k my ways....... Prov 8:32
he that doth k his soul shall be......... Prov 22:5
thing if thou k them within thee....... Prov 22:18
but such as k the law contend.......... Prov 28:4
a time to k, and a time to cast......... Eccl 3:6
a time to k silence, and a time to....... Eccl 3:7
K thy foot when thou goest to the...... Eccl 5:1
I counsel thee to k the king's.......... Eccl 8:2
Fear God, and k his commandments ... Eccl 12:13
those that k the fruit thereof.......... Song 8:12
Thou wilt k him in perfect peace,...... Is 26:3
I the LORD do it....................... Is 27:3
hurt it, I will k it night and day....... Is 27:3
K silence before me, O islands......... Is 41:1
hold thine hand, and will k thee....... Is 42:6
and to the south, K not back........... Is 43:6
K ye judgment, and do justice......... Is 56:1
the eunuchs that k my sabbaths........ Is 56:4
of the LORD, k not silence,............. Is 62:6
I will not k silence, but will............ Is 65:6
will he k it to the end................. Jer 3:5
I will not k anger for ever............. Jer 3:12
k him, as a shepherd doth his.......... Jer 31:10
I will k nothing back from you......... Jer 42:4
sit upon the ground, and k silence..... Lam 2:10
k mine ordinances, and do them....... Eze 11:20
k all my statutes, and do that.......... Eze 18:21
k my judgments, and do them.......... Eze 20:19
ye shall k my judgments, and do ...... Eze 36:27
that they may k the whole form........ Eze 43:11
me, and they shall k my charge........ Eze 44:16
and they shall k my laws and my ...... Eze 44:24
to them that k his commandments..... Dan 9:4
k mercy and judgment, and wait on... Hos 12:6
shall k silence in that time............. Amos 5:13
k the doors of thy mouth from her .... Mic 7:5
k thy solemn feasts, perform thy....... Nah 1:15
k the munition, watch the way,........ Nah 2:1
let all the earth k silence.............. Hab 2:20
ways, and if thou wilt k my charge..... Zec 3:7
house, and shalt also k my courts...... Zec 3:7
for to k cattle from my youth.......... Zec 13:5
to k the feast of tabernacles........... Zec 14:16
up to k the feast of tabernacles........ Zec 14:18
up to k the feast of tabernacles........ Zec 14:19
priest's lips should k knowledge....... Mal 2:7
into life, k the commandments......... Mt 19:17
I will k the passover at thy............ Mt 26:18
that ye may k your own tradition...... Mk 7:9
charge over thee, to k thee............. Lk 4:10
k it, and bring forth fruit with......... Lk 8:15
hear the word of God, and k it......... Lk 11:28
and k thee in on every side,........... Lk 19:43
if a man k my saying, he shall......... Jn 8:51
If a man k my saying, he shall......... Jn 8:52
but I know him, and k his saying...... Jn 8:55
shall k it unto life eternal............. Jn 12:25
If ye love me, k my commandments... Jn 14:15
a man love me, he will k my words ... Jn 14:23
If ye k my commandments, ye shall... Jn 15:10
my saying, they will k yours also...... Jn 15:20
k through thine own name those....... Jn 17:11
shouldest k them from the evil......... Jn 17:15
to k back part of the price of.......... Acts 5:3
a man that is a Jew to k company ..... Acts 10:28
quaternions of soldiers to k him....... Acts 12:4
them to k the law of Moses............ Acts 15:5
must be circumcised, and k the law ... Acts 15:24
from which if ye k yourselves,......... Acts 15:29
them the decrees for to k............... Acts 16:4
the jailer to k them safely............. Acts 16:23
I must by all means k this feast........ Acts 18:21
save only that they k themselves....... Acts 21:25
commanded a centurion to k Paul..... Acts 24:23
profiteth, if thou k the law,........... Rom 2:25
k the righteousness of the law......... Rom 2:26
Therefore let us k the feast............ 1Cor 5:8
written unto you not to k company 1Cor 5:11
heart that he will k his virgin.......... 1Cor 7:37
But I k under my body, and bring 1Cor 9:27
k the ordinances, as I delivered....... 1Cor 11:2
let him k silence in the church......... 1Cor 14:28
Let your women k silence in the 1Cor 14:34
if ye k in memory what I preached 1Cor 15:2

unto you, and so will I k myself....... 2Cor 11:9
who are circumcised k the law......... Gal 6:13
Endeavouring to k the unity of......... Eph 4:3
shall k your hearts and minds......... Phil 4:7
stablish you, and k you from evil...... 2Th 3:3
k thyself pure....................... 1Ti 5:22
That thou k this commandment........ 1Ti 6:14
k that which is committed to thy...... 1Ti 6:20
to k that which I have committed...... 2Ti 1:12
thee k by the Holy Ghost which 2Ti 1:14
to k himself unspotted from the....... Jas 1:27
whosoever shall k the whole law...... Jas 2:10
him, if we k his commandments....... 1Jn 2:3
because we k his commandments, and . 1Jn 3:22
love God, and k his commandments... 1Jn 5:2
that we k his commandments.......... 1Jn 5:3
children, k yourselves from idols...... 1Jn 5:21
K yourselves in the love of............ Jude 21
is able to k you from falling........... Jude 24
k those things which are written....... Rev 1:3
I also will k thee from the hour....... Rev 3:10
which k the commandments of God,... Rev 12:17
here are they that k the............... Rev 14:12
of them which k the sayings of........ Rev 22:9

KEEPER
And Abel was a k of sheep, but........ Gen 4:2
Am I my brother's k................... Gen 4:9
the sight of the k of the prison........ Gen 39:21
the k of the prison committed to...... Gen 39:22
The k of the prison looked not to...... Gen 39:23
and left the sheep with a k............ 1Sa 17:20
the hand of the k of the carriage...... 1Sa 17:22
make thee k of mine head for ever.... 1Sa 28:2
son of Harhas, k of the wardrobe..... 2Kin 22:14
son of Hasrah, k of the wardrobe..... 2Chr 34:22
Asaph the k of the king's forest....... Neh 2:8
the k of the east gate................. Neh 3:29
chamberlain, k of the women......... Est 2:3
custody of Hegai, k of the women..... Est 2:8
the k of the women, appointed........ Est 2:15
and as a booth that the k maketh...... Job 27:18
The LORD is thy k.................... Ps 121:5
made me the k of the vineyards....... Song 1:6
son of Shallum, the k of the door..... Jer 35:4
the k of the prison awaking out....... Acts 16:27
the k of the prison told this........... Acts 16:36

KEEPERS
be k of the watch of the king's........ 2Kin 11:5
which the k of the door have taken.... 2Kin 22:4
the k of the door, to bring forth....... 2Kin 23:4
and the three k of the door........... 2Kin 25:18
k of the gates of the tabernacle....... 1Chr 9:19
of the LORD, were k of the entry...... 1Chr 9:19
the k of the door, who sought to...... Est 6:2
In the day when the k of the.......... Eccl 12:3
the k of the walls took away my....... Song 5:7
he let out the vineyard unto k......... Song 8:11
As k of a field, are they against....... Jer 4:17
and the three k of the door........... Jer 52:24
the k of the charge of the house...... Eze 40:45
the k of the charge of the altar....... Eze 40:46
but ye have set k of my charge in..... Eze 44:8
But I will make them k of the......... Eze 44:14
for fear of him the k did shake........ Mt 28:4
the k standing without before the..... Acts 5:23
the k before the door kept the........ Acts 12:6
found him not, he examined the k .... Acts 12:19
k at home, good, obedient to......... Titus 2:5

KEEPEST
who k covenant and mercy with thy .. 1Kin 8:23
which k covenant, and shewest....... 2Chr 6:14
who k covenant and mercy, let not ... Neh 9:32
walkest orderly, and k the law........ Acts 21:24

KEEPETH
and he die not, but k his bed.......... Ex 21:18
which k covenant and mercy with..... Deut 7:9
and, behold, he k the sheep........... 1Sa 16:11
that k covenant and mercy for them .. Neh 1:5
He k back his soul from the pit,....... Job 33:18
He k all his bones................... Ps 34:20
he that k thee will not slumber....... Ps 121:3
he that k Israel shall neither.......... Ps 121:4
which k truth for ever................ Ps 146:6
He k the paths of judgment, and...... Prov 2:8
way of life that k instruction......... Prov 10:17
He that k his mouth k his............ Prov 13:3
that k his mouth k his life............ Prov 13:3
Righteousness k him that is.......... Prov 13:6
he that k his way preserveth his...... Prov 16:17
he that k understanding shall......... Prov 19:8
He that k the commandment k........ Prov 19:16
Whoso k his mouth and his tongue... Prov 21:23
his tongue k his soul from............ Prov 21:23
he that k thy soul, doth not he........ Prov 24:12
Whoso k the fig tree shall eat......... Prov 27:18
Whoso k the law is a wise son........ Prov 28:7
but he that k company with........... Prov 29:3
but a wise man k it in till............. Prov 29:11
but he that k the law, happy is........ Prov 29:18
Whoso k the commandment shall..... Eccl 8:5
which k the truth may enter in........ Is 26:2
that k the sabbath from polluting..... Is 56:2
k his hand from doing any evil........ Is 56:2
every one that k the sabbath from.... Is 56:6
cursed be he that k back his.......... Jer 48:10
k silence, because he hath borne..... Lam 3:28
is a proud man, neither k at home.... Hab 2:5
a strong man armed k his palace...... Lk 11:21

law, and yet none of you k the law ... Jn 7:19
because he k not the sabbath day..... Jn 9:16
k them, he it is that loveth me........ Jn 14:21
loveth me not k not my sayings....... Jn 14:24
k not his commandments, is a liar 1Jn 2:4
But whoso k his word, in him......... 1Jn 2:5
he that k his commandments......... 1Jn 3:24
that is begotten of God k himself..... 1Jn 5:18
k my works unto the end, to him..... Rev 2:26
k his garments, lest he walk.......... Rev 16:15
blessed is he that k the sayings....... Rev 22:7

KEEPING
K mercy for thousands, forgiving...... Ex 34:7
k the charge of the sanctuary......... Num 3:28
k the charge of the sanctuary for..... Num 3:38
in not k his commandments, and his . Deut 8:11
we were with them k the sheep....... 1Sa 25:16
were porters k the ward at the........ Neh 12:25
in k of them there is great............ Ps 19:11
but that by k of his covenant it....... Eze 17:14
k the covenant and mercy to them ... Dan 9:4
k watch over their flock by night..... Lk 2:8
but the k of the commandments of ... 1Cor 7:19
k of their souls to him in well........ 1Pet 4:19

KEHELATHAH *(ke-hel'-a-thah)* An Israelites
encampment in the wilderness.
from Rissah, and pitched in K......... Num 33:22
And they went from K, and pitched... Num 33:23

KEILAH *(ki'-lah)*
   1. A city in Judah.
And K, and Achzib, and Mareshah ... Josh 15:44
the Philistines fight against K......... 1Sa 23:1
smite the Philistines, and save K..... 1Sa 23:2
to K against the armies of the......... 1Sa 23:3
him and said, Arise, go down to K.... 1Sa 23:4
So David and his men went to K...... 1Sa 23:5
David saved the inhabitants of K...... 1Sa 23:5
of Ahimelech fled to David to K...... 1Sa 23:6
Saul that David was come to K........ 1Sa 23:7
together to war, to go down to K...... 1Sa 23:8
that Saul seeketh to come to K....... 1Sa 23:10
Will the men of K deliver me up...... 1Sa 23:11
Will the men of K deliver me........ 1Sa 23:12
arose and departed out of K.......... 1Sa 23:13
that David was escaped from K....... 1Sa 23:13
the ruler of the half part of K........ Neh 3:17
the ruler of the half part of K........ Neh 3:18
   2. A descendant of Caleb.
the father of K the Garmite........... 1Chr 4:19

KELAIAH *(kel'-i-yah)* See **KELITA.** *Married a
foreigner in exile.*
Jozabad, and Shimei, and K, the...... Ezr 10:23

KELAL See **CHELAL.**

KELITA *(kel'-i-tah)* See **KELAIAH.**
   1. Married a foreigner in exile.
and Kelaiah, (the same is K,.......... Ezr 10:23
   2. A priest who assisted Ezra.
Shabbethai, Hodijah, Maaseiah, K .... Neh 8:7
   3. A Levite who renewed the covenant.
brethren, Shebaniah, Hodijah, K ..... Neh 10:10

KELUB See **CHELUB.**

KELUHI See **CHELLUH.**

KEMUEL *(kem-u'-el)*
   1. A son of Nahor.
brother, and K the father of Aram,.... Gen 22:21
   2. An Ephraimite prince.
of Ephraim, K the son of Shiphtan.... Num 34:24
   3. Father of Hashabiah.
Levites, Hashabiah the son of K....... 1Chr 27:17

KENAANAH See **CHENAANAH.**

KENAN *(ke'-nan)* See **CAINAN.** *Son of Enosh.*
K, Mahalaleel, Jered,................ 1Chr 1:2

KENANI See **CHENANI.**

KENANIAH See **CHENANIAH.**

KENATH *(ke'-nath)* See **NOBAH.** *A city in
Bashan.*
And Nobah went and took K.......... Num 32:42
towns of Jair, from them, with K..... 1Chr 2:23

KENAZ *(ke'-naz)* See **KENEZITE.**
   1. A son of Eliphaz.
Omar, Zepho, and Gatam, and K...... Gen 36:11
duke Omar, duke Zepho, duke K ..... Gen 36:15
and Omar, Zephi, and Gatam, K...... 1Chr 1:36
   2. A duke of Edom.
Duke K, duke Teman, duke Mibzar,... Gen 36:42
Duke K, duke Teman, duke Mibzar,... 1Chr 1:53
   3. Brother of Caleb.
And Othniel the son of K, the......... Josh 15:17
And Othniel the son of K, Caleb's.... Judg 1:13
them, even Othniel the son of K ...... Judg 3:9
And Othniel the son of K died........ Judg 3:11
And the sons of K.................... 1Chr 4:13
   4. A grandson of Caleb.
and the sons of Elah, even K.......... 1Chr 4:15

KENEZITE *(ken'-e-zite)* See **KENIZZITES.**
   Descendants of Jephunneh.
Caleb the son of Jephunneh the K .... Num 32:12
of Jephunneh the K said unto him..... Josh 14:6
of Jephunneh the K unto this day..... Josh 14:14

KENITE (ken'-ite) See **KENITES**. *A member of a Canaanite tribe.*
the *K* shall be wasted, until............. Num 24:22
And the children of the *K*, Moses'......... Judg 1:16
Now Heber the *K*, which was of the..... Judg 4:11
of Jael the wife of Heber the *K*........... Judg 4:17
Hazor and the house of Heber the *K*... Judg 4:17
Jael the wife of Heber the *K* he.......... Judg 5:24

KENITES (ken'-ites) See **MIDIANITES**.
The *K*, and the Kenizzites, and the..... Gen 15:19
And he looked on the *K*....................... Num 24:21
had severed himself from the *K*.......... Judg 4:11
And Saul said unto the *K*, Go,............. 1Sa 15:6
So the *K* departed from among the...... 1Sa 15:6
and against the south of the *K*............ 1Sa 27:10
which were in the cities of the *K*......... 1Sa 30:29
These are the *K* that came of............. 1Chr 2:55

KENIZZITE See **KENIZZITES**.

KENIZZITES (ken'-iz-zites) See **KENEZITE**. *A Canaanite tribe in Abraham's time.*
The Kenites, and the *K*, and the......... Gen 15:19

KENNIZZITE See **KENIZZITES**.

KEPHER AMMONI See **CHEPHAR-HAAMMONAI**.

KEPHIRAH See **CHEPHIRAH**.

KEPT
k my charge, my commandments, my.. Gen 26:5
father's sheep: for she *k* them............ Gen 29:9
neither hath he *k* back any thing......... Gen 39:9
and ye shall be *k* in prison................... Gen 42:16
Now Moses *k* the flock of Jethro......... Ex 3:1
for you to be *k* until the morning......... Ex 12:6
it to be *k* for your generations............ Ex 16:32
to be *k* for your generations............... Ex 16:33
up before the Testimony, to be *k*........ Ex 16:34
owner, and he hath not *k* him in.......... Ex 21:29
and he hath not *k* him in.................... Ex 21:36
be *k* close, and she be defiled, and..... Num 5:13
they *k* the passover on the................. Num 9:5
wherefore are we *k* back, that we...... Num 9:7
Israel *k* the charge of the LORD, and... Num 9:19
they *k* the charge of the LORD, and.... Num 9:23
to be *k* for a token against the........... Num 17:10
place, and it shall be *k* for the............ Num 19:9
the LORD hath *k* thee back from......... Num 24:11
which *k* the charge of the................... Num 31:47
he *k* him as the apple of his eye........ Deut 32:10
thy word, and *k* thy covenant............. Deut 33:9
k the passover on the fourteenth....... Josh 5:10
behold, the LORD hath *k* me alive....... Josh 14:10
Ye have *k* all that Moses the.............. Josh 22:2
but have *k* the charge of the.............. Josh 22:3
So she *k* fast by the maidens of......... Ruth 2:23
it been *k* for thee since I said............. 1Sa 9:24
thou hast not *k* the commandment...... 1Sa 13:13
because thou hast not *k* that............. 1Sa 13:14
Thy servant *k* his father's sheep,........ 1Sa 17:34
if the young men have *k*.................... 1Sa 21:4
Of a truth women have been *k* from.... 1Sa 21:5
Surely in vain have I *k* all that............ 1Sa 25:21
which hast *k* me this day from............ 1Sa 25:33
which hath *k* me back from hurting...... 1Sa 25:34
hath *k* his servant from evil............... 1Sa 25:39
hast thou not *k* thy lord this.............. 1Sa 26:15
because ye have not *k* your master..... 1Sa 26:16
the young man that *k* the watch.......... 2Sa 13:34
For I have *k* the ways of the LORD...... 2Sa 22:22
have *k* myself from mine iniquity......... 2Sa 22:24
thou hast *k* me to be head of the........ 2Sa 22:44
thou not *k* the oath of the LORD......... 1Kin 2:43
thou hast *k* for him this great............. 1Kin 3:6
Who hast *k* with thy servant David..... 1Kin 8:24
but he *k* not that which the LORD....... 1Kin 11:10
and thou hast not *k* my covenant....... 1Kin 11:11
he *k* my commandments..................... 1Kin 11:34
hast not *k* the commandment which.... 1Kin 13:21
who *k* my commandments, and who.... 1Kin 14:8
which *k* the door of the king's............. 1Kin 14:27
(Now Joram had *k* Ramoth-gilead....... 2Kin 9:14
the priests that *k* the door put........... 2Kin 12:9
k not the commandments................... 2Kin 17:19
but *k* his commandments, which the.... 2Kin 18:6
word of the LORD, which he *k* not...... 1Chr 10:13
while he yet *k* himself close............... 1Chr 12:1
k the ward of the house of Saul......... 1Chr 12:29
Thou which hast *k* with thy............... 2Chr 6:15
Solomon *k* the feast seven days......... 2Chr 7:8
for they *k* the dedication of the.......... 2Chr 7:9
that *k* the entrance of the king's........ 2Chr 12:10
k the feast of unleavened bread......... 2Chr 30:21
they *k* other seven days with............. 2Chr 30:23
which the Levites that *k*.................... 2Chr 34:9
have not *k* the word of the LORD....... 2Chr 34:21
Moreover Josiah *k* a passover unto..... 2Chr 35:1
k the passover at that time............... 2Chr 35:17
that *k* in Israel from the days of......... 2Chr 35:18
keep such a passover as Josiah *k*....... 2Chr 35:18
of Josiah was this passover *k*............. 2Chr 35:18
as she lay desolate she *k* sabbath..... 2Chr 36:21
They *k* also the feast of................... Ezr 3:4
k the dedication of this house of....... Ezr 6:16
captivity *k* the passover upon the...... Ezr 6:19
k the feast of unleavened bread......... Ezr 6:22
have not *k* the commandments, nor.... Neh 1:7
they *k* the feast seven days, and....... Neh 8:18
k thy law, nor hearkened unto thy...... Neh 9:34
their brethren that *k* the gates.......... Neh 11:19

the porters *k* the ward of their.......... Neh 12:45
which *k* the concubines...................... Est 2:14
Teresh, of those which *k* the door...... Est 2:21
k throughout every generation........... Est 9:28
held his steps, his way have I *k*......... Job 23:11
k close from the fowls of the air........ Job 28:21
and *k* silence at my counsel.............. Job 29:21
that I *k* silence, and went not out...... Job 31:34
I have *k* me from the paths of the...... Ps 17:4
For I have *k* the ways of the LORD..... Ps 18:21
I *k* myself from mine iniquity.............. Ps 18:23
thou hast *k* me alive, that I.............. Ps 30:3
When I *k* silence, my bones waxed..... Ps 32:3
with a multitude that *k* holyday......... Ps 42:4
hast thou done, and I *k* silence.......... Ps 50:21
They *k* not the covenant of God,......... Ps 78:10
God, and *k* not his testimonies.......... Ps 78:56
they *k* his testimonies, and the.......... Ps 99:7
for I have *k* thy testimonies............... Ps 119:22
in the night, and have *k* thy law......... Ps 119:55
I had, because I *k* thy precepts......... Ps 119:56
but now have I *k* thy word................ Ps 119:67
because they *k* not thy word............. Ps 119:158
My soul hath *k* thy testimonies.......... Ps 119:167
I have *k* thy precepts and thy............ Ps 119:168
eyes desired I *k* not from them........... Eccl 2:10
riches *k* for the owners thereof.......... Eccl 5:13
mine own vineyard have I not *k*.......... Song 1:6
night when a holy solemnity is *k*......... Is 30:29
forsaken me, and have not *k* my law... Jer 16:11
k all his precepts, and done.............. Jer 35:18
neither have *k* my judgments............. Eze 5:7
hath *k* my judgments, to deal............ Eze 18:9
hath *k* all my statutes, and hath........ Eze 18:19
neither *k* my judgments to do them..... Eze 20:21
ye have not *k* the charge of mine....... Eze 44:8
that *k* the charge of my sanctuary...... Eze 44:15
which have *k* my charge, which......... Eze 48:11
and whom he would he *k* alive........... Dan 5:19
but I *k* the matter in my heart........... Dan 7:28
a wife, and for a wife he *k* sheep....... Hos 12:12
and he *k* his wrath for ever............... Amos 1:11
have not *k* his commandments, and.... Amos 2:4
For the statutes of Omri are *k*........... Mic 6:16
as ye have not *k* my ways, but.......... Mal 2:9
ordinances, and have not *k* them....... Mal 3:7
it that we have *k* his ordinance.......... Mal 3:14
And they that *k* them fled, and went.. Mt 8:33
utter things which have been *k*.......... Mt 13:35
But when Herod's birthday was *k*...... Mt 14:6
things have I *k* from my youth up....... Mt 19:20
neither was any thing *k* secret.......... Mk 4:22
and *k* that saying with..................... Mk 9:10
But Mary *k* all these things, and......... Lk 2:19
but his mother *k* all these................ Lk 2:51
he was *k* bound with chains and in..... Lk 8:29
they *k* it close, and told no man........ Lk 9:36
these have I *k* from my youth up........ Lk 18:21
which I have *k* laid up in a............... Lk 19:20
but thou hast *k* the good wine........... Jn 2:10
day of my burying hath she *k* this...... Jn 12:7
even as I have *k* my Father's............ Jn 15:10
if they have *k* my saying, they.......... Jn 15:20
and they have *k* thy word................. Jn 17:6
the world, I *k* them in thy name......... Jn 17:12
that thou gavest me I have *k*............ Jn 17:12
and spake unto her that *k* the door.... Jn 18:16
damsel that *k* the door unto Peter...... Jn 18:17
k back part of the price, his............. Acts 5:2
of angels, and have not *k* it............. Acts 7:53
which had *k* his bed eight years,........ Acts 9:33
Peter therefore was *k* in prison......... Acts 12:5
before the door *k* the prison............. Acts 12:6
Then all the multitude *k* silence........ Acts 15:12
how I *k* back nothing that was........... Acts 20:20
to them, they *k* the more silence....... Acts 22:2
k the raiment of them that slew......... Acts 22:20
he commanded him to be *k*............... Acts 24:23
that Paul should be *k* at Caesarea..... Acts 25:4
I commanded him to be *k* till I........... Acts 25:21
k them from their purpose............... Acts 27:43
himself with a soldier that *k* him........ Acts 28:16
which was *k* secret since the............ Rom 16:25
in all things I have *k* myself............... 2Cor 11:9
governor under Aretas the king *k*....... 2Cor 11:32
we were *k* under the law, shut up...... Gal 3:23
my course, I have *k* the faith............ 2Ti 4:7
Through faith he *k* the passover........ Heb 11:28
which is of you *k* back by fraud.......... Jas 5:4
Who are *k* by the power of God......... 1Pet 1:5
by the same word are *k* in store........ 2Pet 3:7
the angels which *k* not their.............. Jude 6
hast *k* my word, and hast not........... Rev 3:8
Because thou hast *k* the word of....... Rev 3:10

KERAN See **CHERAN**.

KERCHIEFS
make *k* upon the head of every......... Eze 13:18
Your *k* also will I tear, and................ Eze 13:21

KEREN-HAPPUCH (ke'-ren-hap'-puk) *A daughter of Job.*
and the name of the third, *K*.............. Job 42:14

KERETHITE See **CHERETHITES**.

KERETHITES See **CHERETHITES**.

KERIOTH (ke'-re-oth) See **ISCARIOT**, **KIRIOTH**.
1. *A city in Judah.*
And Hazor, Hadattah, and *K*, and....... Josh 15:25
2. *A city in Moab.*

And upon *K*, and upon Bozrah, and..... Jer 48:24
K is taken, and the strong holds......... Jer 48:41

KERIOTH HEZRON

KERITH See **CHERITH**.

KERNELS
from the *k* even to the husk.............. Num 6:4

KEROS (ke'-ros) *A family of exiles.*
The children of *K*, the children........... Ezr 2:44
The children of *K*, the children........... Neh 7:47

KERUB See **CHERUB**.

KESALON See **CHESALON**.

KESED See **CHESED**.

KESIL See **CHESIL**.

KESULLOTH See **CHESULLOTH**.

KETTLE
he struck it into the pan, or *k*............ 1Sa 2:14

KETURAH (ket-u'-rah) *A wife of Abraham.*
took a wife, and her name was *K*........ Gen 25:1
All these were the children of *K*.......... Gen 25:4
Now the sons of *K*, Abraham's........... 1Chr 1:32
All these are the sons of *K*................ 1Chr 1:33

KEY
therefore they took a *k*, and.............. Judg 3:25
the *k* of the house of David will.......... Is 22:22
taken away the *k* of knowledge.......... Lk 11:52
true, he that hath the *k* of David....... Rev 3:7
to him was given the *k* of the............ Rev 9:1
having the *k* of the bottomless.......... Rev 20:1

KEYS
the *k* of the kingdom of heaven......... Mt 16:19
and have the *k* of hell and of death... Rev 1:18

KEZIA (ke-zi'-ah) *A daughter of Job.*
and the name of the second, *K*.......... Job 42:14

KEZIAH See **KEZIA**.

KEZIB See **CHEZIB**.

KEZIZ (ke'-ziz) *A valley in Benjamin.*
Beth-hoglah, and the valley of *K*......... Josh 18:21

KIBROTH-HATTAAVAH (kib'-roth-hat-ta'-a-vah) *A Hebrew encampment in the wilderness.*
called the name of that place *K*.......... Num 11:34
journeyed from *K* unto Hazeroth......... Num 11:35
desert of Sinai, and pitched at *K*........ Num 33:16
And they departed from *K*, and.......... Num 33:17
at Taberah, and at Massah, and at *K*.. Deut 9:22

KIBZAIM (kib-za'-im) See **JOKMEAM**. *A Levitical city in Ephraim.*
K with her suburbs, and Beth-horon .. Josh 21:22

KICK
Wherefore *k* ye at my sacrifice and.... 1Sa 2:29
for thee to *k* against the pricks.......... Acts 9:5
for thee to *k* against the pricks.......... Acts 26:14

KICKED
But Jeshurun waxed fat, and *k*.......... Deut 32:15

KID
killed a *k* of the goats, and............... Gen 37:31
will send thee a *k* from the flock........ Gen 38:17
Judah sent the *k* by the hand of........ Gen 38:20
behold, I sent this *k*, and thou.......... Gen 38:23
seethe a *k* in his mother's milk.......... Ex 23:19
seethe a *k* in his mother's milk.......... Ex 34:26
a *k* of the goats, a male without........ Lev 4:23
a *k* of the goats, a female................. Lev 4:28
a lamb or a *k* of the goats, for........... Lev 5:6
Take ye a *k* of the goats for a............ Lev 9:3
Then ye shall sacrifice one *k* of......... Lev 23:19
One *k* of the goats for a sin............... Num 7:16
One *k* of the goats for a sin............... Num 7:22
One *k* of the goats for a sin............... Num 7:28
One *k* of the goats for a sin............... Num 7:34
One *k* of the goats for a sin............... Num 7:40
One *k* of the goats for a sin............... Num 7:46
One *k* of the goats for a sin............... Num 7:52
One *k* of the goats for a sin............... Num 7:58
One *k* of the goats for a sin............... Num 7:64
One *k* of the goats for a sin............... Num 7:70
One *k* of the goats for a sin............... Num 7:76
One *k* of the goats for a sin............... Num 7:82
one ram, or for a lamb, or a *k*............ Num 15:11
one *k* of the goats for a sin............... Num 15:24
one *k* of the goats for a sin............... Num 28:15
one *k* of the goats, to make an.......... Num 28:30
one *k* of the goats for a sin............... Num 29:5
one *k* of the goats for a sin............... Num 29:11
One *k* of the goats for a sin............... Num 29:16
one *k* of the goats for a sin............... Num 29:19
one *k* of the goats for a sin............... Num 29:25
seethe a *k* in his mother's milk.......... Deut 14:21
Gideon went in, and made ready a *k* .. Judg 6:19
have made ready a *k* for thee............ Judg 13:15
So Manoah took a *k* with a meat....... Judg 13:19
him as he would have rent a *k*........... Judg 14:6
Samson visited his wife with a *k*......... Judg 15:1
and a bottle of wine, and a............... 1Sa 16:20
leopard shall lie down with the *k*........ Is 11:6
a *k* of the goats without blemish........ Eze 43:22

a k of the goats daily for a sin............ Eze 45:23
and yet thou never gavest me a k...... Lk 15:29

KIDNEYS
is above the liver, and the two k........ Ex 29:13
above the liver, and the two k........... Ex 29:22
And the two k, and the fat that is ...... Lev 3:4
caul above the liver, with the k......... Lev 3:4
And the two k, and the fat that is ...... Lev 3:10
caul above the liver, with the k......... Lev 3:10
And the two k, and the fat that is ...... Lev 3:15
caul above the liver, with the k......... Lev 3:15
And the two k, and the fat that is ...... Lev 4:9
caul above the liver, with the k......... Lev 4:9
And the two k, and the fat that is ...... Lev 7:4
is above the liver, with the k........... Lev 7:4
above the liver, and the two k........... Lev 8:16
above the liver, and the two k........... Lev 8:25
But the fat, and the k, and the.......... Lev 9:10
covereth the inwards, and the k......... Lev 9:19
goats, with the fat of k of wheat .... Deut 32:14
with the fat of the k of rams .... Is 34:6

KIDON

KIDRON (kid'-ron) A brook near Jerusalem.
himself passed over the brook K........ 2Sa 15:23
out, and passed over the brook K....... 1Kin 2:37
idol, and burnt it by the brook K........ 1Kin 15:13
Jerusalem in the fields of K............. 2Kin 23:4
Jerusalem, unto the brook K............ 2Kin 23:6
and burned it at the brook K........... 2Kin 23:6
the dust of them into the brook K....... 2Kin 23:12
it, and burnt it at the brook K.......... 2Chr 15:16
it out abroad into the brook K.......... 2Chr 29:16
and cast them into the brook K......... 2Chr 30:14
the fields unto the brook K............. Jer 31:40

KIDS
thence two good k of the goats........ Gen 27:9
she put the skins of the k of the .... Gen 27:16
of the children of Israel two k.......... Lev 16:5
the k of the goats for sin.............. Num 7:87
to Beth-el, one carrying three k........ 1Sa 10:3
them like two little flocks of k......... 1Kin 20:27
people, of the flock, lambs and k....... 2Chr 35:7
feed thy k beside the shepherds'...... Song 1:8

KILEAB See CHILEAB.

KILION See CHILION.

KILION'S See CHILION'S.

KILL
lest any finding him should k him....... Gen 4:15
and they will k me, but they will....... Gen 12:12
the place should k me for Rebekah ..... Gen 26:7
himself, purposing to k thee .... Gen 27:42
and said, Let us not k him .... Gen 37:21
it be a son, then ye shall k him .... Ex 1:16
intendest thou to k me, as thou .... Ex 2:14
Lord met him, and sought to k him ..... Ex 4:24
Israel shall k it in the evening......... Ex 12:6
your families, and k the passover...... Ex 12:21
to k this whole assembly with .... Ex 16:3
us up out of Egypt, to k us........... Ex 17:3
Thou shalt not k....................... Ex 20:13
or a sheep, and k it, or sell it .... Ex 22:1
I will k you with the sword........... Ex 22:24
thou shalt k the bullock before........ Ex 29:11
Then shalt thou k the ram............. Ex 29:20
he shall k the bullock before the ...... Lev 1:5
he shall k it on the side of the........ Lev 1:11
and k it at the door of the .... Lev 3:2
k it before the tabernacle of the ...... Lev 3:8
k it before the tabernacle of the ...... Lev 3:13
k the bullock before the Lord......... Lev 4:4
k it in the place where they k .... Lev 4:24
where they k the burnt offering....... Lev 4:33
In the place where they k the......... Lev 7:2
they k the trespass offering.......... Lev 7:2
where he shall k the sin offering...... Lev 14:13
he shall k the burnt offering.......... Lev 14:19
he shall k the lamb of the .... Lev 14:25
he shall k the one of the birds....... Lev 14:50
shall k the bullock of the............ Lev 16:11
Then shall he k the goat of the....... Lev 16:15
seed unto Molech, and k him not..... Lev 20:4
thereto, thou shalt k the woman...... Lev 20:16
be cow or ewe, ye shall not k it ...... Lev 22:28
k me, I pray thee, out of hand........ Num 11:15
Now if thou shalt k all this.......... Num 14:15
to k us in the wilderness, except..... Num 14:16
mine hand, for now would I k thee..... Num 22:29
Now therefore k every male among.... Num 31:17
k every woman that hath known....... Num 31:17
revenger of blood k the slayer....... Num 35:27
which should k his neighbour........ Deut 4:42
Thou shalt not k...................... Deut 5:17
Notwithstanding thou mayest k...... Deut 12:15
then thou shalt k of thy herd........ Deut 12:21
But thou shalt surely k him........... Deut 13:9
and I, I make alive................... Deut 32:39
If the Lord were pleased to k us...... Judg 13:23
but surely we will not k thee......... Judg 15:13
when it is day, we shall k him........ Judg 16:2
to smite of the people, and k........ Judg 20:31
k of the men of Israel................ Judg 20:39
if Saul hear it, he will k me.......... 1Sa 16:2
able to fight with me, and to k me 1Sa 17:9
k him, then shall ye be our........... 1Sa 17:9
that they should k David............. 1Sa 19:1
Saul my father seeketh to k thee..... 1Sa 19:2

why should I k thee.................. 1Sa 19:17
and some bade me k thee............ 1Sa 19:17
God, that thou wilt neither k me 1Sa 30:15
then k him, fear not................. 2Sa 13:28
his brother, that we may k him 2Sa 14:7
any iniquity in me, let him k me 2Sa 14:32
us shall thou k any man in Israel 2Sa 21:4
sought therefore to k Jeroboam 1Kin 11:40
king of Judah, and they shall k me... 1Kin 12:27
clothes, and said, Am I God, to k 2Kin 5:7
and if they k us, we shall but die 2Kin 7:4
followeth her k with the sword 2Kin 11:15
So k the passover, and sanctify 2Chr 35:6
provinces, to destroy, to k .... Est 3:13
they watched the house to k him .... Ps 59:1
A time to k, and a time to heal ...... Eccl 3:3
I will k thy root with famine, and ... Is 14:30
let them k sacrifices................ Is 29:1
the wool, ye k them that are fed..... Eze 34:3
of old time, Thou shalt not k........ Mt 5:21
whosoever shall k shall be in .... Mt 5:21
And fear not them which k the body .. Mt 10:28
but are not able to k the soul....... Mt 10:28
And they shall k him, and the third... Mt 17:23
come, let us k him, and let us....... Mt 21:38
and some of them ye shall k......... Mt 23:34
to be afflicted, and shall k you...... Mt 24:9
take Jesus by subtilty, and k him.... Mt 26:4
to save life, or to k................. Mk 3:4
hands of men, and they shall k him .. Mk 9:31
Do not commit adultery, Do not k ... Mk 10:19
spit upon him, and shall k him....... Mk 10:34
come, let us k him, and the .... Mk 12:7
afraid of them that k the body....... Lk 12:4
for Herod will k thee................ Lk 13:31
hither the fatted calf, and k it....... Lk 15:23
Do not commit adultery, Do not k ... Lk 18:20
come, let us k him, that the .... Lk 20:14
sought how they might k him .... Lk 22:2
the Jews sought the more to k him .. Jn 5:18
because the Jews sought to k him ... Jn 7:1
Why go ye about to k me............ Jn 7:19
who goeth about to k thee.......... Jn 7:20
not this he, whom they seek to k .... Jn 7:25
said the Jews, Will he k himself..... Jn 8:22
but ye seek to k me, because my.... Jn 8:37
But now ye seek to k me, a man .... Jn 8:40
not, but for to steal, and to k .... Jn 10:10
Wilt thou k me, as thou diddest..... Acts 7:28
the Jews took counsel to k him ..... Acts 9:23
the gates day and night to k him .... Acts 9:24
Rise, Peter; k, and eat.............. Acts 10:13
And as they went about to k him .... Acts 21:31
he come near, are ready to k him ... Acts 23:15
laying wait in the way to k him ..... Acts 25:3
the temple, and went about to k me.. Acts 26:21
counsel was to k the prisoners ..... Acts 27:42
commit adultery, Thou shalt not k ... Rom 13:9
adultery, said also, Do not k........ Jas 2:11
commit no adultery, yet if thou k.... Jas 2:11
ye k, and desire to have, and....... Jas 4:2
I will k her children with death ..... Rev 2:23
and that they should k one another.. Rev 6:4
to k with sword, and with hunger.... Rev 6:8
given that they should not k them ... Rev 9:5
shall overcome them, and k them ... Rev 11:7

KILLED
k a kid of the goats, and dipped..... Gen 37:31
that he hath k a man or a woman..... Ex 21:29
shall be k before the Lord.......... Lev 4:15
is k shall the sin offering be........ Lev 6:25
sin offering be k before the Lord.... Lev 6:25
And he is k; and Moses.............. Lev 8:19
that one of the birds be k in........ Lev 14:5
that was k over the running water.... Lev 14:6
Ye have k the people of the Lord .... Num 16:41
whosoever hath k any person....... Num 31:19
k thee not, know thou and see that .. 1Sa 24:11
that I have k for my shearers........ 1Sa 25:11
k it, and took flour, and kneaded.... 1Sa 28:24
thou hast k Uriah the Hittite........ 2Sa 12:9
and smote the Philistine, and k 2Sa 21:17
and because he k him................ 1Kin 16:7
k him, in the twenty and seventh.... 1Kin 16:10
Thus saith the Lord, Hast thou k 1Kin 21:19
he k him, and reigned in his room ... 2Kin 15:25
k Shophach the captain of the 1Chr 19:18
Ahab k sheep and oxen for him in ... 2Chr 18:2
that had k the king his father....... 2Chr 25:3
So they k the bullocks, and the 2Chr 29:22
when they had k the rams........... 2Chr 29:22
they k also the lambs, and they..... 2Chr 29:22
And the priests k them, and they ... 2Chr 29:24
Then they k the passover on the 2Chr 30:15
they k the passover on the 2Chr 35:1
they k the passover, and the........ 2Chr 35:11
k the passover for all the .... Ezr 6:20
sake are we k all the day long...... Ps 44:22
She hath k her beasts.............. Prov 9:2
thou hast k, and not pitied......... Lam 2:21
chief priests and scribes, and be k .. Mt 16:21
k another, and stoned another...... Mt 21:35
my oxen and my fatlings are k ...... Mt 22:4
of them which k the prophets ...... Mt 23:31
against him, and would have k him .. Mk 6:19
priests, and scribes, and be k....... Mk 8:31
and after that he is k, he shall...... Mk 9:31
and him they k, and many others.... Mk 12:5
k him, and cast him out of the ...... Mk 12:8
when they k the passover, his ...... Mk 14:12

prophets, and your fathers k them ... Lk 11:47
for they indeed k them, and ye ...... Lk 11:48
which after he hath k hath power..... Lk 12:5
thy father hath k the fatted calf ..... Lk 15:27
thou hast k for him the fatted .... Lk 15:30
him out of the vineyard, and k him... Lk 20:15
when the passover must be k .... Lk 22:7
k the Prince of life, whom God ...... Acts 3:15
he k James the brother of John ...... Acts 12:2
sword, and would have k himself..... Acts 16:27
nor drink till they had k Paul........ Acts 23:12
nor drink till they have k him........ Acts 23:21
and should have been k of them ..... Acts 23:27
sake we are k all the day long .... Rom 8:36
they have k thy prophets, and .... Rom 11:3
as chastened, and not k............. 2Cor 6:9
Who both k the Lord Jesus, and 1Th 2:15
Ye have condemned and k the just ... Jas 5:6
that should be k as they were .... Rev 6:11
three was the third part of men k .... Rev 9:18
k by these plagues yet repented..... Rev 9:20
them, he must in this manner be k ... Rev 11:5
sword must be k with the sword ..... Rev 13:10
image of the beast should be k....... Rev 13:15

KILLEDST
kill me, as thou k the Egyptian ...... Ex 2:14
me into thine hand, thou k me not ... 1Sa 24:18

KILLEST
thou that k the prophets, and....... Mt 23:37
which k the prophets, and stonest.... Lk 13:34

KILLETH
that k an ox, or lamb, or goat,...... Lev 17:3
or that k it out of the camp......... Lev 17:3
he that k any man shall surely be.... Lev 24:17
he that k a beast shall make it ...... Lev 24:18
And he that k a beast, he shall...... Lev 24:21
and he that k a man, he shall be..... Lev 24:21
which k any person at unawares..... Num 35:11
that every one that k any person..... Num 35:15
Whoso k any person, the murderer... Num 35:30
Whoso k his neighbour ignorantly,... Deut 19:4
slayer that k any person unawares... Josh 20:3
that whosoever k any person at ..... Josh 20:9
The Lord k, and maketh alive........ 1Sa 2:6
shall be, that the man who k him..... 1Sa 17:25
to the man that k this Philistine..... 1Sa 17:26
it be done to the man that k him..... 1Sa 17:27
For wrath k the foolish man, and..... Job 5:2
rising with the light k the poor...... Job 24:14
The desire of the slothful k him ..... Prov 21:25
He that k an ox is as if he slew ..... Is 66:3
that whosoever k you will think...... Jn 16:2
for the letter k, but the spirit....... 2Cor 3:6
he that k with the sword must be ... Rev 13:10

KILLING
him in the k of his brethren......... Judg 9:24
Levites had the charge of the k...... 2Chr 30:17
k sheep, eating flesh, and .... Is 22:13
By swearing, and lying, and k........ Hos 4:2
beating some, and k some........... Mk 12:5

KILMAD See CHILMAD.
KIMHAM See CHIMHAM.

KIN
to any that is near of k to him .... Lev 18:6
for he uncovereth his near k......... Lev 20:19
But for his k, that is near unto...... Lev 21:2
if any of his k come to redeem it .... Lev 25:25
or any that is nigh of k unto him..... Lev 25:49
her, The man is near of k unto us.... Ruth 3:20
the king is near of k to us........... 2Sa 19:42
own country, and among his own k... Mk 6:4

KINAH (ki'-nah) A city in Judah.
And K, and Dimonah, and Adadah,... Josh 15:22

KIND
tree yielding fruit after his k .... Gen 1:11
and herb yielding seed after his k ... Gen 1:11
seed was in itself, after his k ...... Gen 1:12
forth abundantly, after their k ...... Gen 1:21
and every winged fowl after his k ... Gen 1:21
the living creature after his k ...... Gen 1:24
and beast of the earth after his k ... Gen 1:24
his k, and cattle after their k .... Gen 1:25
upon the earth after his k .... Gen 1:25
Of fowls after their k .... Gen 6:20
and of cattle after their k .... Gen 6:20
thing of the earth after his k ...... Gen 6:20
They, and every beast after his k ... Gen 7:14
and all the cattle after their k ..... Gen 7:14
upon the earth after his k .... Gen 7:14
and every fowl after his k .... Gen 7:14
vulture, and the kite after his k .... Lev 11:14
Every raven after his k .... Lev 11:15
cuckow, and the hawk after his k ... Lev 11:16
the stork, the heron after her k .... Lev 11:19
the locust after his k .... Lev 11:22
and the bald locust after his k ..... Lev 11:22
and the beetle after his k .... Lev 11:22
and the grasshopper after his k .... Lev 11:22
and the tortoise after his k .... Lev 11:29
cattle gender with a diverse k ..... Lev 19:19
kite, and the vulture after his k .... Deut 14:13
And every raven after his k .... Deut 14:14
cuckow, and the hawk after his k ... Deut 14:15
stork, and the heron after her k .... Deut 14:18
instruments of every k of service... 1Chr 28:14

If thou be *k* to this people, and...... 2Chr 10:7
sellers of all *k* of ware lodged...... Neh 13:20
trees in them of all *k* of fruits...... Eccl 2:5
the multitude of all *k* of riches...... Eze 27:12
the sea, and gathered of every *k*...... Mt 13:47
Howbeit this *k* goeth not out but...... Mt 17:21
This *k* can come forth by nothing,...... Mk 9:29
for he is *k* unto the unthankful...... Lk 6:35
Charity suffereth long, and is *k*...... 1Cor 13:4
there is one *k* of flesh of men...... 1Cor 15:39
And be ye *k* one to another,...... Eph 4:32
truth, that we should be a *k* of...... Jas 1:18
For every *k* of beasts, and of...... Jas 3:7

KINDLE
Ye shall *k* no fire throughout...... Ex 35:3
is a contentious man to *k* strife...... Prov 26:21
shall *k* in the thickets of the...... Is 9:18
under his glory he shall *k* a...... Is 10:16
a stream of brimstone, doth *k* it...... Is 30:33
shall the flame *k* upon thee......... Is 43:2
Behold, all ye that *k* a fire....... Is 50:11
wood, and the fathers *k* the fire...... Jer 7:18
then will I *k* a fire in the gates...... Jer 17:27
I will *k* a fire in the forest....... Jer 21:14
to *k* meat offerings, and to do...... Jer 33:18
I will *k* a fire in the houses of...... Jer 43:12
I will *k* a fire in the wall of....... Jer 49:27
I will *k* a fire in his cities, and...... Jer 50:32
I will *k* a fire in thee, and it...... Eze 20:47
k the fire, consume the flesh, and...... Eze 24:10
But I will *k* a fire in the wall...... Amos 1:14
stubble, and they shall *k* in them...... Obad 18
neither do ye *k* fire on mine....... Mal 1:10

KINDLED
anger is *k* against Rachel......... Gen 30:2
that his wrath was *k*........... Gen 39:19
of the LORD was *k* against Moses...... Ex 4:14
he that *k* the fire shall surely...... Ex 22:6
the burning which the LORD hath *k*...... Lev 10:6
and his anger was *k*......... Num 11:1
anger of the LORD was *k* greatly...... Num 11:10
the LORD was *k* against the people... Num 11:33
of the LORD was *k* against them...... Num 12:9
God's anger was *k* because he went.. Num 22:22
and Balaam's anger was *k*, and he.... Num 22:27
anger was *k* against Balaam......... Num 24:10
of the LORD was *k* against Israel..... Num 25:3
Lord's anger was *k* the same time.... Num 32:10
LORD's anger was *k* against Israel.... Num 32:13
LORD thy God be *k* against thee..... Deut 6:15
of the LORD be *k* against you...... Deut 7:4
the LORD's wrath be *k* against you.... Deut 11:17
the LORD was *k* against this land.... Deut 29:27
Then my anger shall be *k* against.... Deut 31:17
For a fire is *k* in mine anger....... Deut 32:22
the anger of the LORD was *k*...... Josh 7:1
of the LORD be *k* against you....... Josh 23:16
the son of Ebed, his anger was *k*.... Judg 9:30
And his anger was *k*............ Judg 14:19
and his anger was *k* greatly...... 1Sa 11:6
Eliab's anger was *k* against David.... 1Sa 17:28
anger was *k* against Jonathan...... 1Sa 20:30
of the LORD was *k* against Uzzah..... 2Sa 6:7
was greatly *k* against the man....... 2Sa 12:5
coals were *k* by it........... 2Sa 22:9
before him were coals of fire *k*...... 2Sa 22:13
of the LORD was *k* against Israel..... 2Sa 24:1
of the LORD was *k* against Israel..... 2Kin 13:3
of the LORD that is *k* against us.... 2Kin 22:13
shall be *k* against this place...... 2Kin 22:17
his anger was *k* against Judah....... 2Kin 23:26
of the LORD was *k* against Uzza..... 1Chr 13:10
anger was greatly *k* against Judah.... 2Chr 25:10
of the LORD was *k* against Amaziah.. 2Chr 25:15
He hath also *k* his wrath against... Job 19:11
Then was *k* the wrath of Elihu the.. Job 32:2
against Job was his wrath *k*....... Job 32:2
his three friends was his wrath *k*.... Job 32:3
three men, then his wrath was *k*.... Job 32:5
My wrath is *k* against thee, and.... Job 42:7
when his wrath is *k* but a little.... Ps 2:12
coals were *k* by it........... Ps 18:8
so a fire was *k* against Jacob....... Ps 78:21
a fire was *k* in their company...... Ps 106:18
of the LORD *k* against his people.... Ps 106:40
when their wrath was *k* against us... Ps 124:3
of the LORD is against his people..... Is 5:25
and in the sparks that ye have *k*.... Is 50:11
tumult he hath *k* fire upon it....... Jer 11:16
for a fire is *k* in mine anger....... Jer 15:14
for ye have *k* a fire in mine....... Jer 17:4
was *k* in the cities of Judah and.... Jer 44:6
hath *k* a fire in Zion, and it hath.. Lam 4:11
see that I the LORD have *k* it....... Eze 20:48
mine anger is *k* against them....... Hos 8:5
me, my repentings are *k* together.... Hos 11:8
Mine anger was *k* against the....... Zec 10:3
what will I, if it be already *k*...... Lk 12:49
when they had *k* a fire in the..... Lk 22:55
for they *k* a fire, and received us... Acts 28:2

KINDLETH
His breath *k* coals, and a flame..... Job 41:21
yea, he *k* it, and baketh bread...... Is 44:15
great a matter a little fire *k*....... Jas 3:5

KINDLY
And now if ye will deal *k* and truly... Gen 24:49
and spake *k* unto the damsel....... Gen 34:3
hand under my thigh, and deal *k*.... Gen 47:29

them, and spake *k* unto them...... Gen 50:21
us the land, that we will deal *k*.... Josh 2:14
the LORD deal *k* with you, as ye.... Ruth 1:8
shalt deal *k* with thy servant....... Ruth 1:8
And he spake *k* to him, and set his.. 2Kin 25:28
spake *k* unto him, and set his...... Jer 52:32
Be *k* affectioned one to another..... Rom 12:10

KINDNESS
This is thy *k* which thou shalt...... Gen 20:13
but according to the *k* that I....... Gen 21:23
shew *k* unto my master Abraham..... Gen 24:12
thou hast shewed *k* unto my master.. Gen 24:14
be well with thee, and shew *k*...... Gen 40:14
LORD, since I have shewed you *k*..... Josh 2:12
shew *k* unto my father's house....... Josh 2:12
Neither shewed they *k* to the....... Judg 8:35
not left off his *k* to the living..... Ruth 2:20
for thou hast shewed more *k* in.... Ruth 3:10
for ye shewed *k* to all the....... 1Sa 15:6
I live shew me the *k* of the LORD... 1Sa 20:14
off thy *k* from my house for ever.... 1Sa 20:15
have shewed this *k* unto your lord... 2Sa 2:5
And now the LORD shew *k* and truth.. 2Sa 2:6
and I also will requite you this *k*.... 2Sa 2:6
which against Judah do shew *k*...... 2Sa 3:8
shew him *k* for Jonathan's sake..... 2Sa 9:1
I may shew the *k* of God unto him... 2Sa 9:3
for I will surely shew thee *k* for.... 2Sa 9:7
I will shew *k* unto Hanun the son... 2Sa 10:2
have shewed this *k* unto thee....... 2Sa 10:2
Is this thy *k* to thy friend......... 2Sa 16:17
But shew *k* unto the sons of....... 1Kin 2:7
hast kept for him this great *k*...... 1Kin 3:6
I will shew *k* unto Hanun the son... 1Chr 19:2
because his father shewed *k* to me... 1Chr 19:2
the king remembered not the *k*...... 2Chr 24:22
slow to anger, and of great *k*....... Neh 9:17
him, and she obtained *k* of him..... Est 2:9
his marvellous *k* in a strong city.... Ps 31:21
For his mercuful *k* is great........ Ps 117:2
thy merciful *k* be for my comfort,... Ps 119:76
it shall be a *k*.............. Ps 141:5
The desire of a man is his *k*....... Prov 19:22
and in her tongue is the law of *k*... Prov 31:26
but with everlasting *k* will I...... Is 54:8
but my *k* shall not depart from..... Is 54:10
of the youth, the love of *k*....... Jer 2:2
slow to anger, and of great *k*...... Joel 2:13
slow to anger, and of great *k*...... Jonah 4:2
people shewed us no little *k*....... Acts 28:2
knowledge, by longsuffering, by *k*... 2Cor 6:6
riches of his grace in his *k*....... Eph 2:7
and beloved, bowels of mercies, *k*.. Col 3:12
But after that the *k* and love of.... Titus 3:4
And to godliness brotherly *k*...... 2Pet 1:7
And to brotherly *k* charity....... 2Pet 1:7

KINDRED
out of thy country, and from thy *k*.. Gen 12:1
go unto my country, and to my *k*.... Gen 24:4
house, and from the land of my *k*... Gen 24:7
my father's house, and to my *k*.... Gen 24:38
take a wife for my son of my *k*.... Gen 24:40
my oath, when thou comest to my *k*. Gen 24:41
land of thy fathers, and to thy *k*... Gen 31:3
and return unto the land of thy *k*... Gen 31:13
unto thy country, and to thy *k*..... Gen 32:9
of our state, and of our *k*........ Gen 43:7
to mine own land, and to my *k*.... Num 10:30
and they brought out all her *k*..... Josh 6:23
who was of the *k* of Elimelech..... Ruth 2:3
And now is not Boaz of our *k*...... Ruth 3:2
the *k* of Saul, three thousand....... 1Chr 12:29
not shewed her people nor her *k*.... Est 2:10
yet shewed her *k* nor her people.... Est 2:20
to see the destruction of my *k*...... Est 8:6
the Buzite, of the *k* of Ram....... Job 32:2
thy brethren, the men of thy *k*..... Eze 11:15
There is none of thy *k* that is..... Lk 1:61
were of the *k* of the high priest.... Acts 4:6
out of thy country, and from thy *k*.. Acts 7:3
Joseph's *k* was made known unto.... Acts 7:13
father Jacob to him, and all his *k*.. Acts 7:14
same dealt subtilly with our *k*...... Acts 7:19
God by thy blood out of every *k*.... Rev 5:9
earth, and to every nation, and *k*... Rev 14:6

KINDREDS
ye *k* of the people, give unto the.... 1Chr 16:28
all the *k* of the nations shall...... Ps 22:27
O ye *k* of the people, give unto.... Ps 96:7
all the *k* of the earth be blessed.... Acts 3:25
all *k* of the earth shall wail...... Rev 1:7
number, of all nations, and *k*...... Rev 7:9
And they of the people and *k*...... Rev 11:9
and power was given him over all *k*.. Rev 13:7

KINDS
upon the earth, after their *k*...... Gen 8:19
divers *k* of spices prepared by..... 2Chr 16:14
I will appoint over them four *k*.... Jer 15:3
shall be according to their *k*...... Eze 47:10
all *k* of musick, ye fall down and.. Dan 3:5
all *k* of the earth shall wail....... Dan 3:7
all *k* of musick, ye shall down..... Dan 3:10
all *k* of musick, ye fall down and.. Dan 3:15
to another divers *k* of tongues..... 1Cor 12:10
so many *k* of voices in the world,.. 1Cor 14:10

KINE
camels with their colts, forty *k*.... Gen 32:15
the river seven well favoured *k*.... Gen 41:2

seven other *k* came up after them... Gen 41:3
stood by the other *k* upon the..... Gen 41:3
leanfleshed *k* did eat up the....... Gen 41:4
the seven well favoured and fat *k*... Gen 41:4
came up out of the river seven *k*... Gen 41:18
seven other *k* came up after them,.. Gen 41:19
the ill favoured *k* did eat up the... Gen 41:20
did eat up the first seven fat *k*.... Gen 41:20
The seven good *k* are seven years... Gen 41:26
ill favoured *k* that came up after... Gen 41:27
thine oil, the increase of thy *k*.... Deut 7:13
thy cattle, the increase of thy *k*... Deut 28:4
thy land, the increase of thy *k*.... Deut 28:18
or oil, or the increase of thy *k*.... Deut 28:51
Butter of *k*, and milk of sheep,... Deut 32:14
a new cart, and take two milch *k*... 1Sa 6:7
tie the *k* to the cart, and bring..... 1Sa 6:7
and took two milch *k*, and tied them.. 1Sa 6:10
the *k* took the straight way to...... 1Sa 6:12
offered the *k* a burnt offering...... 1Sa 6:14
butter, and sheep, and cheese of *k*.. 2Sa 17:29
ye *k* of Bashan, that are in the.... Amos 4:1

KING See PREFACE.
and the shout of a *k* is among them.. Num 23:21
now make us a *k* to judge us like.. 1Sa 8:5
the people that asked of him a *k*.... 1Sa 8:10
shouted, and said, God save the *k*... 1Sa 10:24
there they made Saul *k* before the... 1Sa 11:15
David *k* over the house of Judah.... 2Sa 2:4
and they made David *k* over the.... 2Sa 16:16
and say, God save *k* Solomon...... 1Kin 1:34
come to Shechem to make him *k*.... 1Kin 12:1
and they made him *k*, and anointed. 2Kin 11:12
hands, and said, God save the *k*.... 2Kin 11:12
Nebuchadnezzar *k* of Babylon came.. 2Kin 25:1
and with all Israel, to make him *k*.. 1Chr 11:10
Now the acts of David the *k*....... 1Chr 29:29
for thou hast made me a over a..... 2Chr 1:9
so the *k* and all the people....... 2Chr 7:5
all Israel come to make him *k*...... 2Chr 10:1
to the commandment of the *k*...... 2Chr 8:15
bring him to the *k* of terrors...... Job 18:14
Yet have I set my *k* upon my holy ... Ps 2:6
The LORD is *K* for ever and ever.... Ps 10:16
the *K* of glory shall come in....... Ps 24:7
Who is this *K* of glory......... Ps 24:8
of hosts, he is the *K* of glory...... Ps 24:10
For God is my *K* of old, working.... Ps 74:12
of Zion be joyful in their *K*....... Ps 149:2
son, fear thou the LORD and the *k*.. Prov 24:21
man do that cometh after the *k*.... Eccl 2:12
when thy *k* is a child, and thy..... Eccl 10:16
Curse not the *k*, no not in thy..... Eccl 10:20
for mine eyes have seen the *K*..... Is 6:5
living God, and an everlasting *k*.... Jer 10:10
the LORD shall be *k* over all the... Zec 14:9
year to year to worship the *K*..... Zec 14:16
is he that is born *K* of the Jews.... Mt 2:2
for it is the city of the great *K*.... Mt 5:35
thy *K* cometh unto thee, meek, and... Mt 21:5
Art thou the *K* of the Jews....... Mt 27:11
Or what *k*, going to make war...... Lk 14:31
Blessed be the *K* that cometh in.... Lk 19:38
that he himself is Christ a *K*...... Lk 23:2
him by force, to make him a *k*..... Jn 6:15
said unto him, Art thou a *k* then... Jn 18:37
Thou sayest that I am a *k*........ Jn 18:37
unto the Jews, Behold your *K*..... Jn 19:14
saying that there is another *k*..... Acts 17:7
Now unto the *K* eternal, immortal,.. 1Ti 1:17
the *K* of kings, and Lord of lords... 1Ti 6:15
K OF KINGS................ Rev 19:16

KINGDOM
the beginning of his *k* was Babel... Gen 10:10
on me and on my *k* a great sin..... Gen 20:9
shall be unto me a *k* of priests.... Ex 19:6
Agag, and his *k* shall be exalted.... Num 24:7
the *k* of Sihon king of the....... Num 32:33
the *k* of Og king of Bashan, the... Num 32:33
of Argob, the *k* of Og in Bashan... Deut 3:4
cities of the *k* of Og in Bashan.... Deut 3:10
and all Bashan, being the *k* of Og.. Deut 3:13
stitteth upon the throne of his *k*.... Deut 17:18
he may prolong his days in his *k*.. Deut 17:20
All the *k* of Og in Bashan, which... Josh 13:12
all the *k* of Sihon king of the.... Josh 13:21
the rest of the *k* of Sihon king.... Josh 13:27
all the *k* of Og king of Bashan,... Josh 13:30
cities of the *k* of Og in Bashan,... Josh 13:31
But of the matter of the *k*........ 1Sa 10:16
the people the manner of the *k*.... 1Sa 10:25
to Gilgal, and renew the *k* there... 1Sa 11:14
thy *k* upon Israel for ever....... 1Sa 13:13
But now thy *k* shall not continue... 1Sa 13:14
So Saul took the *k* over Israel...... 1Sa 14:47
The LORD hath rent the *k* of...... 1Sa 15:28
what can he have more but the *k*... 1Sa 18:8
not be established, nor thy *k*....... 1Sa 20:31
that the *k* of Israel shall be....... 1Sa 24:20
hath rent the *k* out of thine hand.. 1Sa 28:17
To translate the *k* from the house.. 2Sa 3:10
my *k* are guiltless before the...... 2Sa 3:28
that he had exalted his *k* for his... 2Sa 5:12
bowels, and I will establish his *k*.. 2Sa 7:12
the throne of his *k* for ever...... 2Sa 7:13
thy *k* shall be established for...... 2Sa 7:16
restore me the *k* of my father..... 2Sa 16:3
the LORD hath delivered the *k*..... 2Sa 16:8
sitteth on the throne of the *k*...... 1Kin 1:46

his *k* was established greatly 1Kin 2:12
Thou knewest that the *k* was mine 1Kin 2:15
howbeit the *k* is turned about, and 1Kin 2:15
ask for him the *k* also 1Kin 2:22
the *k* was established in the hand 1Kin 2:46
of thy *k* upon Israel for ever 1Kin 9:5
was not the like made in any *k* 1Kin 10:20
will surely rend the *k* from thee 1Kin 11:11
I will not rend away all the *k*............... 1Kin 11:13
I will rend the *k* out of the hand.......... 1Kin 11:31
take the whole *k* out of his hand 1Kin 11:34
But I will take the *k* out of his 1Kin 11:35
to bring the *k* again to Rehoboam 1Kin 12:21
Now shall the *k* return to the 1Kin 12:26
rent the *k* away from the house of 1Kin 14:8
liveth, there is no nation or *k*............... 1Kin 18:10
he took an oath of the *k* and 1Kin 18:10
thou now govern the *k* of Israel.......... 1Kin 21:7
as soon as the *k* was confirmed in 2Kin 14:5
him to confirm the *k* in his hand.......... 2Kin 15:19
turned the *k* unto David the son........... 1Chr 10:14
themselves with him in his *k* 1Chr 11:10
to turn the *k* of Saul to him, ... 1Chr 12:23
for his *k* was lifted up on high, ... 1Chr 14:2
from one *k* to another people 1Chr 16:20
and I will establish his *k* 1Chr 17:11
in mine house and in my *k* for ever 1Chr 17:14
of his *k* over Israel for ever 1Chr 22:10
of the *k* of the LORD over Israel.......... 1Chr 28:5
I will establish his *k* for ever 1Chr 28:7
thine is the *k*, O LORD, and thou 1Chr 29:11
David was strengthened in his *k* 2Chr 1:1
the LORD, and an house for his *k* 2Chr 2:1
the LORD, and an house for his *k*.......... 2Chr 2:12
I stablish the throne of thy *k*............... 2Chr 7:18
was not the like made in any *k* 2Chr 9:19
bring the *k* again to Rehoboam 2Chr 11:1
they strengthened the *k* of Judah 2Chr 11:17
Rehoboam had established the *k* 2Chr 12:1
k over Israel to David for ever 2Chr 13:5
now ye think to withstand the *k* 2Chr 13:8
the *k* was quiet before him.................. 2Chr 14:5
LORD established the *k* in his hand...... 2Chr 17:5
but the *k* gave he to Jehoram 2Chr 21:3
risen up to the *k* of his father 2Chr 21:4
had no power to keep still the *k* 2Chr 22:9
the king upon the throne of the *k* 2Chr 23:20
when the *k* was established to him 2Chr 25:3
for a sin offering for the *k* 2Chr 29:21
for no god of any nation or *k* was 2Chr 32:15
him again to Jerusalem into his *k* 2Chr 33:13
the reign of the *k* of Persia................ 2Chr 36:20
proclamation throughout all his *k* 2Chr 36:22
proclamation throughout all his *k* ...... Ezr 1:1
have not served thee in their *k* .... Neh 9:35
sat on the throne of his *k* .... Est 1:2
the riches of his glorious *k* .... Est 1:4
and which sat the first in the *k*............ Est 1:14
in all the provinces of his *k* .... Est 2:3
the whole *k* of Ahasuerus, even .... Est 3:6
in all the provinces of thy *k* .... Est 3:8
to the *k* for such a time as this .... Est 4:14
given thee to the half of the *k* .... Est 5:3
of the *k* it shall be performed.............. Est 5:6
even to the half of the *k* .... Est 7:2
provinces of the *k* of Ahasuerus .... Est 9:30
For the *k* is the LORD's........................ Ps 22:28
of thy *k* is a right sceptre................... Ps 45:6
and his *k* ruleth over all....................... Ps 103:19
from one *k* to another people.............. Ps 105:13
shall speak of the glory of thy *k*.......... Ps 145:11
and the glorious majesty of his *k* .... Ps 145:12
Thy *k* is an everlasting *k* .... Ps 145:13
is born in his *k* becometh poor .... Eccl 4:14
throne of David, and upon his *k* .... Is 9:7
the *k* from Damascus, and the .... Is 17:3
city, and *k* against *k* .... Is 19:2
call the nobles thereof to the *k*............ Is 34:12
k that will not serve thee shall.......... Is 60:12
a nation, and concerning a *k*................ Jer 18:7
a nation, and concerning a *k*................ Jer 18:9
k which will not serve the same .... Jer 27:8
he hath polluted the *k* and the .... Lam 2:2
and thou didst prosper into a *k* .... Eze 16:13
That the *k* might be base, that it .... Eze 17:14
and they shall be there a base *k* .... Eze 29:14
God of heaven hath given thee a *k* ...... Dan 2:37
arise another *k* inferior to thee .... Dan 2:39
and another third *k* of brass................ Dan 2:39
the fourth *k* shall be strong as............ Dan 2:40
of iron, the *k* shall be divided.............. Dan 2:41
so the *k* shall be partly strong............ Dan 2:42
the God of heaven set up a *k* .... Dan 2:44
the *k* shall not be left to other .... Dan 2:44
his *k* is an everlasting *k*,.................. Dan 4:3
most High ruleth in the *k* of men .... Dan 4:17
and his *k* shall rule over all .... Dan 4:18
most High ruleth in the *k* of men .... Dan 4:25
thy *k* shall be sure unto thee,.............. Dan 4:26
in the palace of the *k* of Babylon .... Dan 4:29
of the *k* by the might of my power...... Dan 4:30
The *k* is departed from thee................ Dan 4:31
most High ruleth in the *k* of men .... Dan 4:32
his *k* is from generation to.................. Dan 4:34
and for the glory of my *k*, mine .... Dan 4:36
and I was established in my *k*.............. Dan 4:36
shall be the third ruler in the *k* .... Dan 5:7
There is a man in thy *k*, in whom........ Dan 5:11
shalt be the third ruler in the *k* .... Dan 5:16
Nebuchadnezzar thy father a *k* .... Dan 5:18

high God ruled in the *k* of men .... Dan 5:21
God hath numbered thy *k*, and.......... Dan 5:26
Thy *k* is divided, and given to the ...... Dan 5:28
be the third ruler in the *k* .... Dan 5:29
And Darius the Median took the *k*...... Dan 5:31
to set over the *k* an hundred .... Dan 6:1
which should be over the whole *k*........ Dan 6:1
against Daniel concerning the *k*.......... Dan 6:4
All the presidents of the *k*.................. Dan 6:7
dominion of my *k* men tremble............ Dan 6:26
his *k* that which shall not be .... Dan 6:26
him dominion, and glory, and a *k* .... Dan 7:14
his *k* that which shall not be.............. Dan 7:14
of the most High shall take the *k*........ Dan 7:18
and possess the *k* for ever.................. Dan 7:18
that the saints possessed the *k* .... Dan 7:22
shall be the fourth *k* upon earth .... Dan 7:23
the ten horns out of this *k* are............ Dan 7:24
And the *k* and dominion...................... Dan 7:27
the greatness of the *k* under the .... Dan 7:27
whose *k* is an everlasting *k* .... Dan 7:27
And in the latter time of their *k* .... Dan 8:23
But the prince of the *k* of Persia .... Dan 10:13
his *k* shall be broken, and shall .... Dan 11:4
for his *k* shall be plucked up, ... Dan 11:4
the south shall come into his *k* .... Dan 11:9
with the strength of his whole *k* .... Dan 11:17
of taxes in the glory of the *k*.............. Dan 11:20
not give the honour of the *k*................ Dan 11:21
obtain the *k* by flatteries.................... Dan 11:21
the *k* of the house of Israel................ Hos 1:4
Lord GOD are upon the sinful *k*............ Amos 9:8
the *k* shall be the LORD's.................... Obad 21
the *k* shall come to the daughter .... Mic 4:8
for the *k* of heaven is at hand............ Mt 3:2
for the *k* of heaven is at hand............ Mt 4:17
and preaching the gospel of the *k*...... Mt 4:23
for theirs is the *k* of heaven.............. Mt 5:3
for theirs is the *k* of heaven.............. Mt 5:10
the least in the *k* of heaven .... Mt 5:19
called great in the *k* of heaven .... Mt 5:19
case enter into the *k* of heaven.......... Mt 5:20
Thy *k* come.. Mt 6:10
For thine is the *k*, and the power,........ Mt 6:13
But seek ye first the *k* of God .... Mt 6:33
shall enter into the *k* of heaven.......... Mt 7:21
and Jacob, in the *k* of heaven .... Mt 8:11
But the children of the *k* shall............ Mt 8:12
and preaching the gospel of the *k*...... Mt 9:35
The *k* of heaven is at hand .... Mt 10:7
he that is least in the *k* of .... Mt 11:11
k of heaven suffereth violence .... Mt 11:12
Every *k* divided against itself is.......... Mt 12:25
how shall then his *k* stand .... Mt 12:26
then the *k* of God is come unto............ Mt 12:28
the mysteries of the *k* of heaven .... Mt 13:11
any one heareth the word of the *k*...... Mt 13:19
The *k* of heaven is likened unto a ...... Mt 13:24
The *k* of heaven is like to a .... Mt 13:31
The *k* of heaven is like unto................ Mt 13:33
seed are the children of the *k* .... Mt 13:38
of his *k* all things that offend .... Mt 13:41
the sun in the *k* of their Father .... Mt 13:43
the *k* of heaven is like unto .... Mt 13:44
the *k* of heaven is like unto .... Mt 13:45
the *k* of heaven is like unto a .... Mt 13:47
k of heaven is like unto a man.......... Mt 13:52
thee the keys of the *k* of heaven .... Mt 16:19
the Son of man coming in his *k* .... Mt 16:28
the greatest in the *k* of heaven .... Mt 18:1
not enter into the *k* of heaven .... Mt 18:3
is greatest in the *k* of heaven .... Mt 18:4
Therefore is the *k* of heaven.............. Mt 18:23
for of such is the *k* of heaven .... Mt 19:14
hardly enter into the *k* of heaven........ Mt 19:23
man to enter into the *k* of God............ Mt 19:24
For the *k* of heaven is like unto .... Mt 20:1
the other on the left, in thy *k* .... Mt 20:21
go into the *k* of God before you .... Mt 21:31
The *k* of God shall be taken from ...... Mt 21:43
The *k* of heaven is like unto a .... Mt 22:2
for ye shut up the *k* of heaven............ Mt 23:13
nation, and *k* against *k* .... Mt 24:7
this gospel of the *k* shall be .... Mt 24:14
Then shall the *k* of heaven be............ Mt 25:1
For the *k* of heaven is as a man .... Mt 25:14
inherit the *k* prepared for you .... Mt 25:34
it new with you in my Father's .... Mt 26:29
the gospel of the *k* of God .... Mk 1:14
and the *k* of God is at hand .... Mk 1:15
if a *k* be divided against itself, ... Mk 3:24
that *k* cannot stand .... Mk 3:24
know the mystery of the *k* of God........ Mk 4:11
And he said, So is the *k* of God .... Mk 4:26
shall we liken the *k* of God .... Mk 4:30
it thee, unto the half of my *k*.............. Mk 6:23
seen the *k* of God come with power .... Mk 9:1
into the *k* of God with one eye............ Mk 9:47
for of such is the *k* of God .... Mk 10:14
the *k* of God as a little child .... Mk 10:15
riches enter into the *k* of God .... Mk 10:23
riches to enter into the *k* of God .... Mk 10:24
man to enter into the *k* of God .... Mk 10:25
Blessed be the *k* of our father............ Mk 11:10
art not far from the *k* of God .... Mk 12:34
nation, and *k* against *k*.................... Mk 13:8
I drink it new in the *k* of God.............. Mk 14:25
also waited for the *k* of God .... Mk 15:43
of his *k* there shall be no end............ Lk 1:33

I must preach the *k* of God to.............. Lk 4:43
for yours is the *k* of God...................... Lk 6:20
the *k* of God is greater than he .... Lk 7:28
the glad tidings of the *k* of God............ Lk 8:1
the mysteries of the *k* of God .... Lk 8:10
sent them to preach the *k* of God........ Lk 9:2
spake unto them of the *k* of God.......... Lk 9:11
death, till they see the *k* of God .... Lk 9:27
go thou and preach the *k* of God.......... Lk 9:60
back, is fit for the *k* of God.................. Lk 9:62
The *k* of God is come nigh unto .... Lk 10:9
that the *k* of God is come nigh............ Lk 10:11
Thy *k* come.. Lk 11:2
Every *k* divided against itself is.......... Lk 11:17
himself, how shall his *k* stand............ Lk 11:18
no doubt the *k* of God is come .... Lk 11:20
But rather seek ye the *k* of God .... Lk 12:31
good pleasure to give you the *k* .... Lk 12:32
Unto what is the *k* of God like............ Lk 13:18
shall I liken the *k* of God .... Lk 13:20
all the prophets, in the *k* of God .... Lk 13:28
and shall sit down in the *k* of God ...... Lk 13:29
shall eat bread in the *k* of God .... Lk 14:15
time the *k* of God is preached.............. Lk 16:16
when the *k* of God should come, he...... Lk 17:20
The *k* of God cometh not with............ Lk 17:20
the *k* of God is within you.................. Lk 17:21
for of such is the *k* of God .... Lk 18:16
k of God as a little child shall............ Lk 18:17
riches enter into the *k* of God .... Lk 18:24
man to enter into the *k* of God .... Lk 18:25
for the *k* of God's sake,........................ Lk 18:29
the *k* of God should immediately;........ Lk 19:11
to receive for himself a *k* .... Lk 19:12
returned, having received the *k*............ Lk 19:15
nation, and *k* against *k* .... Lk 21:10
know ye that the *k* of God is nigh ...... Lk 21:31
it be fulfilled in the *k* of God.............. Lk 22:16
until the *k* of God shall come .... Lk 22:18
And I appoint unto you a *k* .... Lk 22:29
eat and drink at my table in my *k* ...... Lk 22:30
me when thou comest into thy *k* .... Lk 23:42
himself waited for the *k* of God .... Lk 23:51
again, he cannot see the *k* of God ...... Jn 3:3
he cannot enter into the *k* of God........ Jn 3:5
My *k* is not of this world .... Jn 18:36
if my *k* were of this world, then.......... Jn 18:36
but now is my *k* not from hence .... Jn 18:36
things pertaining to the *k* of God .... Acts 1:3
restore again the *k* to Israel................ Acts 1:6
things concerning the *k* of God............ Acts 8:12
enter into the *k* of God .... Acts 14:22
things concerning the *k* of God............ Acts 19:8
have gone preaching the *k* of God ...... Acts 20:25
and testified the *k* of God.................. Acts 28:23
Preaching the *k* of God, and .... Acts 28:31
For the *k* of God is not meat and........ Rom 14:17
For the *k* of God is not in word,.......... 1Cor 4:20
shall not inherit the *k* of God 1Cor 6:9
shall inherit the *k* of God 1Cor 6:10
have delivered up the *k* to God 1Cor 15:24
blood cannot inherit the *k* of God 1Cor 15:50
shall not inherit the *k* of God .... Gal 5:21
inheritance in the *k* of Christ .... Eph 5:5
us into the *k* of his dear Son .... Col 1:13
fellow workers unto the *k* of God .... Col 4:11
who hath called you unto his *k*............ 1Th 2:12
be counted worthy of the *k* of God 2Th 1:5
dead at his appearing and his *k*.......... 2Ti 4:1
preserve me unto his heavenly *k*.......... 2Ti 4:18
is the sceptre of thy *k* .... Heb 1:8
a *k* which cannot be moved................ Heb 12:28
heirs of the *k* which he hath................ Jas 2:5
the everlasting *k* of our Lord 2Pet 1:11
in tribulation, and in the *k* .... Rev 1:9
the *k* our God, and the power of .... Rev 12:10
his *k* was full of darkness.................... Rev 16:10
which have received no *k* as yet,.......... Rev 17:12
give their *k* unto the beast,................ Rev 17:17

KINGDOMS

all the *k* whither thou passest .... Deut 3:21
into all the *k* of the earth.................... Deut 28:25
was the head of all those *k* .... Josh 11:10
and out of the hand of all *k* 1Sa 10:18
Solomon reigned over all *k* from.......... 1Kin 4:21
of all the *k* of the earth...................... 2Kin 19:15
that all the *k* of the earth may............ 2Kin 19:19
over all the *k* of the countries 1Chr 29:30
service of the *k* of the countries 2Chr 12:8
k of the lands that were round............ 2Chr 17:10
over all the *k* of the heathen.............. 2Chr 20:6
on all the *k* of those countries............ 2Chr 20:29
All the *k* of the earth hath the 2Chr 36:23
given me all the *k* of the earth............ Ezr 1:2
Moreover thou gavest them *k* .... Neh 9:22
heathen raged, the *k* were moved ...... Ps 46:6
Sing unto God, ye *k* of the earth........ Ps 68:32
upon the *k* that have not called.......... Ps 79:6
are gathered together, and the *k* .... Ps 102:22
of Bashan, and all the *k* of Canaan .... Ps 135:11
hath found the *k* of the idols.............. Is 10:10
a tumultuous noise of the *k* of .... Is 13:4
And Babylon, the glory of *k*,.............. Is 13:19
to tremble, that did shake *k*................ Is 14:16
hand over the sea, he shook the *k* ...... Is 23:11
k of the world upon the face of .... Is 23:17
of all the *k* of the earth...................... Is 37:16
that all the *k* of the earth may............ Is 37:20
no more be called, The lady of *k* .... Is 47:5
over the nations and over the *k* .... Jer 1:10

families of the *k* of the north .... Jer 1:15
of the nations, and in all their *k* .... Jer 10:7
removed into all *k* of the earth .... Jer 15:4
the *k* of the earth for their hurt .... Jer 24:9
all the *k* of the world, which are .... Jer 25:26
countries, and against great *k* .... Jer 28:8
removed to all the *k* of the earth .... Jer 29:18
all the *k* of the earth of his .... Jer 34:1
into all the *k* of the earth .... Jer 34:17
and concerning the *k* of Hazor .... Jer 49:28
and with thee will I destroy *k* .... Jer 51:20
against her the *k* of Ararat .... Jer 51:27
It shall be the basest of the *k* .... Eze 29:15
into two *k* any more at all .... Eze 37:22
in pieces and consume all these *k* .... Dan 2:44
which shall be diverse from all *k* .... Dan 7:23
four *k* shall stand up out of the .... Dan 8:22
be they better than these *k* .... Amos 6:2
thy nakedness, and the *k* thy shame ..... Nah 3:5
that I may assemble the *k* .... Zeph 3:8
I will overthrow the throne of *k* .... Hag 2:22
strength of the *k* of the heathen .... Hag 2:22
him all the *k* of the world .... Mt 4:8
shewed unto him all the *k* of the .... Lk 4:5
Who through faith subdued *k* .... Heb 11:33
The *k* of this world are become .... Rev 11:15
are become the *k* of our Lord .... Rev 11:15

KINGLY

he was deposed from his *k* throne .... Dan 5:20

KING'S

of Shaveh, which is the *k* dale .... Gen 14:17
a place where the *k* prisoners .... Gen 39:20
we will go by the *k* high way .... Num 20:17
will go along by the *k* high way .... Num 21:22
now therefore be the *k* son in law 1Sa 18:22
light thing to be a *k* son in law 1Sa 18:23
to be avenged of the *k* enemies 1Sa 18:25
David well to be the *k* son in law 1Sa 18:26
that he might be the *k* son in law 1Sa 18:27
he cometh not unto the *k* table 1Sa 20:29
because the *k* business required 1Sa 21:2
David, which is the *k* son in law 1Sa 22:14
be to deliver him into the *k* hand 1Sa 23:20
And now see where the *k* spear is 1Sa 26:16
and said, Behold the *k* spear 1Sa 26:22
at my table, as one of the *k* sons 2Sa 9:11
eat continually at the *k* table 2Sa 9:13
upon the roof of the *k* house 2Sa 11:2
Uriah departed out of the *k* house 2Sa 11:8
k house with all the servants of 2Sa 11:9
if so be that the *k* wrath arise 2Sa 11:20
some of the *k* servants be dead, ... 2Sa 11:24
he took their *k* crown from off 2Sa 12:30
Why art thou, being the *k* son 2Sa 13:4
the *k* daughters that were virgins 2Sa 13:18
and Absalom invited all the *k* sons 2Sa 13:23
all the *k* sons go with him 2Sa 13:27
Then all the *k* sons arose 2Sa 13:29
Absalom hath slain all the *k* sons 2Sa 13:30
all the young men the *k* sons 2Sa 13:33
that all the *k* sons are dead 2Sa 13:33
the king, Behold, the *k* sons come 2Sa 13:35
the *k* sons came, and lifted up 2Sa 13:36
the *k* heart was toward Absalom 2Sa 14:1
own house, and saw not the *k* face 2Sa 14:24
shekels after the *k* weight 2Sa 14:26
Jerusalem, and saw not the *k* face 2Sa 14:28
therefore let me see the *k* face 2Sa 14:32
the *k* servants said unto the king 2Sa 15:15
shalt hear out of the *k* house 2Sa 15:35
be for the *k* household to ride on 2Sa 16:2
forth mine hand against the *k* son 2Sa 18:12
a pillar, which is in the *k* dale 2Sa 18:18
because the *k* son is dead 2Sa 18:20
When Joab sent the *k* servant 2Sa 18:29
to carry over the *k* household 2Sa 19:18
we eaten at all of the *k* cost 2Sa 19:42
Notwithstanding the *k* servant 2Sa 24:4
all his brethren the *k* sons 1Kin 1:9
the men of Judah the *k* servants 1Kin 1:9
and hath called all the *k* sons 1Kin 1:19
And she came into the *k* presence 1Kin 1:28
him to ride upon the *k* mule 1Kin 1:44
moreover the *k* servants came to 1Kin 1:47
a seat to be set for the *k* mother 1Kin 2:19
officer, and the *k* friend 1Kin 4:5
the *k* house, and all Solomon's 1Kin 9:1
of the LORD, and the *k* house 1Kin 9:10
of the LORD, and for the *k* house 1Kin 10:12
the *k* merchants received the 1Kin 10:28
he was of the *k* seed in Edom 1Kin 11:14
the hand was restored him again 1Kin 13:6
and the treasures of the *k* house 1Kin 14:26
kept the door of the *k* house 1Kin 14:27
and the treasures of the *k* house 1Kin 15:18
into the palace of the *k* house 1Kin 16:18
burnt the *k* house over him with 1Kin 16:18
shall deliver it into the *k* hand 1Kin 22:12
the city, and to Joash the *k* son 1Kin 22:26
we may go and tell the *k* household 2Kin 7:9
told it to the *k* house within 2Kin 7:11
for she is a *k* daughter 2Kin 9:34
Now the *k* sons, being seventy 2Kin 10:6
them, that they took the *k* sons 2Kin 10:7
brought the heads of the *k* sons 2Kin 10:8
among the *k* sons which were slain 2Kin 11:2
LORD, and shewed them the *k* son 2Kin 11:4
of the watch of the *k* house 2Kin 11:5
And he brought forth the *k* son 2Kin 11:12

the horses came into the *k* house 2Kin 11:16
gate of the guard to the *k* house 2Kin 11:19
with the sword beside the *k* house 2Kin 11:20
in the chest, that the *k* scribe 2Kin 12:10
of the LORD, and in the *k* house 2Kin 12:18
Put his hands upon the *k* hands 2Kin 13:16
in the treasures of the *k* house 2Kin 14:14
Jotham the *k* son was over the 2Kin 15:5
in the palace of the *k* house 2Kin 15:25
in the treasures of the *k* house 2Kin 16:8
the *k* burnt sacrifice, and his 2Kin 16:15
entry without, turned he 2Kin 16:18
in the treasures of the *k* house 2Kin 18:15
for the *k* commandment was, saying 2Kin 18:36
and Asahiah a servant of the *k* 2Kin 22:12
and the treasures of the *k* house 2Kin 24:13
the *k* mother, and the *k* wives 2Kin 24:15
walls, which is by the *k* garden 2Kin 25:4
the *k* house, and all the houses of 2Kin 25:9
them that were in the *k* presence 2Kin 25:19
waited in the *k* gate eastward 1Chr 9:18
Nevertheless the *k* word prevailed 1Chr 21:4
for the *k* word was abominable to 1Chr 21:6
the *k* seer in the words of God 1Chr 25:5
according to the *k* order to Asaph 1Chr 25:6
over the *k* treasures was Azmaveth .. 1Chr 27:25
of Hachmoni was with the *k* sons 1Chr 27:32
Ahithophel was the *k* counsellor 1Chr 27:33
the Archite was the *k* companion 1Chr 27:33
general of the *k* army was Joab 1Chr 27:34
with the rulers of the *k* work 2Chr 8:15
the *k* merchants received the 2Chr 1:16
house of the LORD, and the *k* house 2Chr 7:11
of the LORD, and to the palace 2Chr 9:11
For the *k* ships went to Tarshish 2Chr 9:21
and the treasures of the *k* house 2Chr 12:9
kept the entrance of the *k* house 2Chr 12:10
of the LORD and of the *k* house 2Chr 12:11
will deliver it into the *k* hand 2Chr 18:5
the city, and to Joash the *k* son 2Chr 18:25
of Judah, for all the *k* matters 2Chr 19:11
that was found in the *k* house 2Chr 21:3
among the *k* sons that were slain 2Chr 22:1
the *k* son shall reign, as the 2Chr 23:3
part shall be at the *k* house 2Chr 23:5
Then they brought out the *k* son 2Chr 23:11
of the horse gate by the *k* house 2Chr 23:15
the high gate into the *k* house 2Chr 23:20
at the *k* commandment they made a 2Chr 24:8
the *k* office by their hand of 2Chr 24:11
the *k* scribe and the high priest's 2Chr 24:11
Art thou made of the *k* counsel 2Chr 25:16
and the treasures of the *k* house 2Chr 25:24
Hananiah, one of the *k* captains 2Chr 28:7
his son was over the *k* house 2Chr 28:7
Ephraim, slew Maaseiah the *k* son 2Chr 28:7
of David, and of Gad the *k* seer 2Chr 29:25
He appointed also the *k* portion 2Chr 31:3
and Asaiah a servant of the *k* 2Chr 34:20
these were of the *k* substance 2Chr 35:7
according to the *k* commandment 2Chr 35:10
and Jeduthun the *k* seer 2Chr 35:15
maintenance from the *k* palace .... Ezr 4:14
for us to see the *k* dishonour .... Ezr 4:14
made in the *k* treasure house .... Ezr 5:17
be given out of the *k* house .... Ezr 6:4
that of the *k* goods, even of the .... Ezr 6:8
it out of the *k* treasure house .... Ezr 7:20
a thing as this in the *k* heart .... Ezr 7:27
before all the *k* mighty princes .... Ezr 7:28
they delivered the *k* commissions .... Ezr 8:36
unto the *k* lieutenants, and to .... Ezr 8:36
Pul his son was *k* cupbearer .... Neh 1:11
Asaph the keeper of the *k* forest .... Neh 2:8
river, and gave them the *k* letters ...... Neh 2:9
of the fountain, and to the *k* pool ...... Neh 3:15
as also the *k* words that he had .... Neh 3:15
pool of Siloah by the *k* garden .... Neh 3:15
lieth out from the *k* high house .... Neh 3:25
borrowed money for the *k* tribute .... Neh 5:4
For it was the *k* commandment .... Neh 11:23
was at the *k* hand in all matters .... Neh 11:24
of the garden of the *k* palace .... Est 1:5
Vashti refused to come at the *k* .... Est 1:12
(for so was the *k* manner toward .... Est 1:13
and Media, which saw the *k* face .... Est 1:14
this day unto all the *k* princes .... Est 1:18
when the *k* decree which he shall .... Est 1:20
letters into all the *k* provinces .... Est 1:22
Then said the *k* servants that .... Est 2:2
custody of Hege the *k* chamberlain .... Est 2:3
when the *k* commandment and his .... Est 2:8
was brought also unto the *k* house .... Est 2:8
be given her, out of the *k* house .... Est 2:9
of the women unto the *k* house .... Est 2:13
the *k* chamberlain, which kept the .... Est 2:14
but what Hegai the *k* chamberlain .... Est 2:15
then Mordecai sat in the *k* gate .... Est 2:19
while Mordecai sat in the *k* gate .... Est 2:21
two of the *k* chamberlains, which .... Est 2:21
all the *k* servants, that were in .... Est 3:2
servants, that were in the *k* gate .... Est 3:2
Then the *k* servants, which were .... Est 3:3
which were in the *k* gate .... Est 3:3
thou the *k* commandment .... Est 3:3
neither keep they the *k* laws .... Est 3:8
for the *k* profit to suffer them .... Est 3:8
to bring it into the *k* treasuries ...... Est 3:9
Then were the *k* scribes called on ...... Est 3:12
commanded unto the *k* lieutenants .... Est 3:12

and sealed with the *k* ring .... Est 3:12
by posts into all the *k* provinces ...... Est 3:13
hastened by the *k* commandment .... Est 3:15
And came even before the *k* gate .... Est 4:2
the *k* gate clothed with sackcloth .... Est 4:2
whithersoever the *k* commandment .... Est 4:3
one of the *k* chamberlains, whom .... Est 4:5
city, which was before the *k* gate .... Est 4:6
to the *k* treasuries for the Jews .... Est 4:7
All the *k* servants, and the people ...... Est 4:11
and the people of the *k* provinces ...... Est 4:11
thou shalt escape in the *k* house .... Est 4:13
in the inner court of the *k* house .... Est 5:1
over against the *k* house .... Est 5:1
Haman saw Mordecai in the *k* gate .... Est 5:9
the Jew sitting at the *k* gate .... Est 5:13
two of the *k* chamberlains, the .... Est 6:2
Then said the *k* servants that .... Est 6:3
the outward court of the *k* house .... Est 6:4
the *k* servants said unto him, ... Est 6:5
one of the *k* most noble princes .... Est 6:9
Jew, that sitteth at the *k* gate .... Est 6:10
Mordecai came again to the *k* gate .... Est 6:12
came the *k* chamberlains, and .... Est 6:14
not countervail the *k* damage .... Est 7:4
the word went out of the *k* mouth .... Est 7:8
Then was the *k* wrath pacified .... Est 7:10
which are in all the *k* provinces .... Est 8:5
as it liketh you, in the *k* name .... Est 8:8
and seal it with the *k* ring .... Est 8:8
which is written in the *k* name .... Est 8:8
and sealed with the *k* ring .... Est 8:8
Then were the *k* scribes called at ...... Est 8:9
and sealed it with the *k* ring .... Est 8:10
pressed on by the *k* commandment .... Est 8:14
whithersoever the *k* commandment .... Est 8:17
when the *k* commandment and his .... Est 9:1
Mordecai was great in the *k* house .... Est 9:4
in the rest of the *k* provinces .... Est 9:12
k provinces gathered themselves .... Est 9:16
in the heart of the *k* enemies .... Ps 45:5
The *k* daughter is all glorious .... Ps 45:13
shall enter into the *k* palace .... Ps 45:15
Thou wilt prolong the *k* life .... Ps 61:6
thy righteousness unto the *k* son .... Ps 72:1
The *k* strength also loveth .... Ps 99:4
of people is the *k* honour .... Prov 14:28
The *k* favour is toward a wise .... Prov 14:35
of the *k* countenance is life .... Prov 16:15
The *k* wrath is as the roaring of ...... Prov 19:12
The *k* heart is in the hand of the ...... Prov 21:1
thee to keep the *k* commandment .... Eccl 8:2
for the *k* commandment was, saying ...... Is 36:21
LORD unto the *k* house of Judah .... Jer 22:6
then they came up from the *k* .... Jer 26:10
he went down into the *k* house .... Jer 36:12
eunuchs which was in the *k* house .... Jer 38:7
went forth out of the *k* house .... Jer 38:22
night, by the way of the *k* garden ...... Jer 39:4
the Chaldeans burned the *k* house .... Jer 39:8
even the *k* daughters, and all the ...... Jer 41:10
the *k* daughters, and every person ...... Jer 43:6
walls, which was by the *k* garden .... Jer 52:7
house of the LORD, and the *k* house ...... Jer 52:13
them that were near the *k* person ...... Jer 52:25
And hath taken of the *k* seed .... Eze 17:13
of Israel, and of the *k* seed .... Dan 1:3
in them to stand in the *k* palace .... Dan 1:4
a daily provision of the *k* meat .... Dan 1:5
with the portion of the *k* meat .... Dan 1:8
eat of the portion of the *k* meat .... Dan 1:8
did eat the portion of the *k* meat ...... Dan 1:15
earth that can shew the *k* matter .... Dan 2:10
Arioch the captain of the *k* guard ...... Dan 2:14
and said to Arioch the *k* captain .... Dan 2:15
made known unto us the *k* matter .... Dan 2:23
Therefore because the *k* .... Dan 3:22
the *k* counsellors, being gathered ...... Dan 3:27
him, and have changed the *k* word .... Dan 3:28
While the word was in the *k* mouth ...... Dan 4:31
of the wall of the *k* palace .... Dan 5:5
Then the *k* countenance was .... Dan 5:6
Then came in all the *k* wise men .... Dan 5:8
the king concerning the *k* decree .... Dan 6:12
I rose up, and did the *k* business ...... Dan 8:27
for the *k* daughter of the south .... Dan 11:6
latter growth after the *k* mowings ...... Amos 7:1
for it is the *k* chapel .... Amos 7:13
and it is the *k* court .... Amos 7:13
the *k* children, and all such as .... Zeph 1:8
Hananeel unto the *k* winepresses .... Zec 14:10
having made Blastus the *k* .... Acts 12:20
was nourished by the *k* country .... Acts 12:20
not afraid of the *k* commandment .... Heb 11:23

KINGS

the *k* that were with him, and .... Gen 14:5
four *k* with five .... Gen 14:9
the *k* of Sodom and Gomorrah fled, ... Gen 14:10
of the *k* that were with him, at .... Gen 14:17
thee, and *k* shall come out of thee ...... Gen 17:6
k of people shall be of her .... Gen 17:16
k shall come out of thy loins .... Gen 35:11
these are the *k* that reigned in .... Gen 36:31
And they slew the *k* of Midian .... Num 31:8
the *k* of Midian; Evi, and five *k* ...... Num 31:8
and Hur, and Reba, five *k* of Midian ..... Num 31:8
k of the Amorites the land that .... Deut 3:8
God hath done unto these two *k* .... Deut 3:21
two *k* of the Amorites, which were ...... Deut 4:47
deliver their *k* into thine hand .... Deut 7:24
k of the Amorites, and unto the .... Deut 31:4

unto the two *k* of the Amorites .... Josh 2:10
when all the *k* of the Amorites .... Josh 5:1
all the *k* of the Canaanites, ... Josh 5:1
when all the *k* which were on this .... Josh 9:1
did to the two *k* of the Amorites .... Josh 9:10
the five *k* of the Amorites .... Josh 10:5
for all the *k* of the Amorites .... Josh 10:6
But these five *k* fled, and hid .... Josh 10:16
The five *k* are found hid in a .... Josh 10:17
bring out those five *k* unto me. .... Josh 10:22
five *k* unto him out of the cave .... Josh 10:23
brought out those *k* unto Joshua .... Josh 10:24
feet upon the necks of these *k* .... Josh 10:24
and of the springs, and all their *k* .... Josh 10:40
And all these *k* and their land did .... Josh 10:42
to the *k* that were on the north .... Josh 11:2
when all these *k* were met .... Josh 11:5
those *k*, and all the *k* of them .... Josh 11:12
and all their *k* he took, and smote .... Josh 11:17
war a long time with all those *k* .... Josh 11:18
Now these are the *k* of the land .... Josh 12:1
those are the *k* of the country .... Josh 12:7
all the *k* thirty and one .... Josh 12:24
even the two *k* of the Amorites .... Josh 24:12
said, Threescore and ten *k* .... Judg 1:7
Hear, O ye *k* .... Judg 5:3
The *k* came and fought .... Judg 5:19
then fought the *k* of Canaan in .... Judg 5:19
Zebah and Zalmunna, *k* of Midian .... Judg 8:5
them, and took the two *k* of Midian .... Judg 8:12
that was on the *k* of Midian .... Judg 8:26
Edom, and against the *k* of Zobah..... 1Sa 14:47
unto the *k* of Judah unto this day 1Sa 27:6
when all the *k* that were servants 2Sa 10:19
at the time when *k* go forth to 2Sa 11:1
shall not be any among the *k* like 1Kin 3:13
over all the *k* on this side the 1Kin 4:24
from all *k* of the earth, which 1Kin 4:34
and of all the *k* of Arabia 1Kin 10:15
all the *k* of the earth for riches 1Kin 10:23
so for all the *k* of the Hittites, ... 1Kin 10:29
for the *k* of Syria, did they 1Kin 10:29
the chronicles of the *k* of Israel 1Kin 14:19
the chronicles of the *k* of Judah 1Kin 14:29
the chronicles of the *k* of Judah 1Kin 15:7
the chronicles of the *k* of Israel 1Kin 15:23
the chronicles of the *k* of Judah 1Kin 15:31
the chronicles of the *k* of Israel 1Kin 16:5
the chronicles of the *k* of Israel 1Kin 16:14
the chronicles of the *k* of Judah 1Kin 16:20
the chronicles of the *k* of Judah 1Kin 16:27
k of Israel that were before him 1Kin 16:33
two *k* with him, and horses, and 1Kin 20:1
the *k* in the pavilions, that he 1Kin 20:12
in the pavilions, he and the *k* 1Kin 20:16
thirty and two *k* that helped him 1Kin 20:16
And do this thing, Take the *k* away, ... 1Kin 20:24
we have heard that the *k* of the 1Kin 20:31
house of Israel are merciful *k* 1Kin 20:31
the chronicles of the *k* of Judah 1Kin 22:45
the chronicles of the *k* of Israel 2Kin 1:18
called these three *k* together 2Kin 3:10
called these three *k* together 2Kin 3:13
k were come up to fight against 2Kin 3:21
the *k* are surely slain, and they 2Kin 3:23
against us the *k* of the Hittites 2Kin 7:6
the *k* of the Egyptians, to come 2Kin 7:6
in the way of the *k* of Israel 2Kin 8:18
the chronicles of the *k* of Judah 2Kin 8:23
two *k* stood not before him 2Kin 10:4
the chronicles of the *k* of Israel 2Kin 10:34
And he sat on the throne of the *k* 2Kin 11:19
k of Judah, had dedicated, and his 2Kin 12:18
the chronicles of the *k* of Judah 2Kin 12:19
the chronicles of the *k* of Israel 2Kin 13:8
the chronicles of the *k* of Israel 2Kin 13:12
in Samaria with the *k* of Israel 2Kin 13:13
the chronicles of the *k* of Israel 2Kin 14:15
in Samaria with the *k* of Israel 2Kin 14:16
the chronicles of the *k* of Judah 2Kin 14:18
the chronicles of the *k* of Judah 2Kin 14:28
even with the *k* of Israel 2Kin 14:29
the chronicles of the *k* of Judah 2Kin 15:6
the chronicles of the *k* of Israel 2Kin 15:11
the chronicles of the *k* of Israel 2Kin 15:21
the chronicles of the *k* of Judah 2Kin 15:26
the chronicles of the *k* of Israel 2Kin 15:31
the chronicles of the *k* of Israel 2Kin 15:36
in the way of the *k* of Israel 2Kin 16:3
the chronicles of the *k* of Judah 2Kin 16:19
but not as the *k* of Israel that 2Kin 17:2
of the *k* of Israel, which they 2Kin 17:8
like him among all the *k* of Judah 2Kin 18:5
thou hast heard what the *k* of 2Kin 19:11
the *k* of Assyria have destroyed 2Kin 19:17
the chronicles of the *k* of Judah 2Kin 20:20
the chronicles of the *k* of Judah 2Kin 21:17
whom the *k* of Judah had ordained 2Kin 23:5
k of Judah had given to the sun 2Kin 23:11
which the *k* of Judah had made, and 2Kin 23:12
which the *k* of Israel had made to 2Kin 23:19
all the days of the *k* of Judah 2Kin 23:22
nor of the *k* of Judah 2Kin 23:22
the chronicles of the *k* of Judah 2Kin 23:28
the chronicles of the *k* of Judah 2Kin 24:5
k that were with him in Babylon 2Kin 25:28
Now these are the *k* that reigned 1Chr 1:43

in the book of the *k* of Israel 1Chr 9:1
he reproved *k* for their sakes, ... 1Chr 16:21
the *k* that were come were by 1Chr 19:9
the time that *k* go out to battle 1Chr 20:1
such as none of the *k* have had 2Chr 1:12
for all the *k* of the Hittites, ... 2Chr 1:17
for the *k* of Syria, by their 2Chr 1:17
all the *k* of Arabia and governors 2Chr 9:14
all the *k* of the earth in riches 2Chr 9:22
all the *k* of the earth sought the 2Chr 9:23
he reigned over all the *k* from 2Chr 9:26
in the book of the *k* of Judah 2Chr 16:11
in the book of the *k* of Israel 2Chr 20:34
in the way of the *k* of Israel 2Chr 21:6
in the way of the *k* of Israel 2Chr 21:13
not in the sepulchres of the *k* 2Chr 21:20
in the city of David among the *k* 2Chr 24:16
not in the sepulchres of the *k* 2Chr 24:25
in the story of the book of the *k* 2Chr 24:27
in the book of the *k* of Judah 2Chr 25:26
burial which belonged to the *k* 2Chr 26:23
in the book of the *k* of Israel 2Chr 27:7
in the ways of the *k* of Israel 2Chr 28:2
unto the *k* of Assyria to help him 2Chr 28:16
gods of the *k* of Syria help them 2Chr 28:23
in the book of the *k* of Judah 2Chr 28:26
the sepulchres of the *k* of Israel 2Chr 28:27
of the hand of the *k* of Assyria 2Chr 30:6
Why should the *k* of Assyria come 2Chr 32:4
and in the book of the *k* of Judah 2Chr 32:32
in the book of the *k* of Israel 2Chr 33:18
the *k* of Judah had destroyed 2Chr 34:11
neither did all the *k* of Israel 2Chr 35:18
in the book of the *k* of Israel 2Chr 35:27
in the book of the *k* of Israel 2Chr 36:8
endamage the revenue of the *k* .... Ezr 4:13
city, and hurtful unto *k* and .... Ezr 4:15
hath made insurrection against *k* ..... Ezr 4:19
been mighty *k* also over Jerusalem ..... Ezr 4:20
damage grow to the hurt of the *k* ..... Ezr 4:22
name to dwell there destroy all *k* ..... Ezr 6:12
Artaxerxes, king of *k*, unto Ezra ..... Ezr 7:12
for our iniquities have we, our *k* ..... Ezr 9:7
the hand of the *k* of the lands ..... Ezr 9:7
in the sight of the *k* of Persia ..... Ezr 9:9
into their hands, with their *k* ..... Neh 9:24
that hath come upon us, on our *k* ..... Neh 9:32
since the time of the *k* of ..... Neh 9:32
Neither have our *k*, our princes, ... Neh 9:34
the *k* whom thou hast set over us ..... Neh 9:37
the chronicles of the *k* of Media ..... Est 10:2
With *k* and counsellors of the ..... Job 3:14
He looseth the bond of *k*, and ..... Job 12:18
but with *k* are they on the throne. ..... Job 36:7
The *k* of the earth set themselves ..... Ps 2:2
Be wise now therefore, O ye *k* ..... Ps 2:10
the *k* were assembled, they passed ..... Ps 48:4
K of armies did flee apace ..... Ps 68:12
the Almighty scattered *k* in it ..... Ps 68:14
shall *k* bring presents unto thee. ..... Ps 68:29
The *k* of Tarshish and of the isles ..... Ps 72:10
the *k* of Sheba and Seba shall ..... Ps 72:10
all *k* shall fall down before him. ..... Ps 72:11
is terrible to the *k* of the earth. ..... Ps 76:12
higher than the *k* of the earth. ..... Ps 89:27
all the *k* of the earth thy glory. ..... Ps 102:15
he reproved *k* for their sakes. ..... Ps 105:14
in the chambers of their *k* ..... Ps 105:30
through *k* in the day of his wrath ..... Ps 110:5
of thy testimonies also before *k* ..... Ps 119:46
great nations, and slew mighty *k* ..... Ps 135:10
To him which smote great *k* ..... Ps 136:17
And slew famous *k* ..... Ps 136:18
All the *k* of the earth shall ..... Ps 138:4
he that giveth salvation unto *k* ..... Ps 144:10
K of the earth, and all people ..... Ps 148:11
To bind their *k* with chains ..... Ps 149:8
By me *k* reign, and princes decree ..... Prov 8:15
to *k* to commit wickedness ..... Prov 16:12
lips are the delight of *k* ..... Prov 16:13
he shall stand before *k* ..... Prov 22:29
but the honour of *k* is to search ..... Prov 25:2
the heart of *k* is unsearchable ..... Prov 25:3
ways to that which destroyeth *k* ..... Prov 31:3
It is not for *k*, O Lemuel, it is ..... Prov 31:4
it is not for *k* to drink wine ..... Prov 31:4
and the peculiar treasure of *k* ..... Eccl 2:8
Ahaz, and Hezekiah, *k* of Judah ..... Is 1:1
shall be forsaken of both her *k* ..... Is 7:16
Are not my princes altogether *k* ..... Is 10:8
thrones all the *k* of the nations. ..... Is 14:9
All the *k* of the nations, even ..... Is 14:18
of the wise, the son of ancient *k* ..... Is 19:11
the *k* of the earth upon the earth. ..... Is 24:21
thou hast heard what the *k* of ..... Is 37:11
the *k* of Assyria have laid waste. ..... Is 37:18
him, and made him rule over *k* ..... Is 41:2
and I will loose the loins of *k* ..... Is 45:1
K shall see and arise, princes. ..... Is 49:7
k shall be thy nursing fathers, ... Is 49:23
the *k* shall shut their mouths at ..... Is 52:15
k to the brightness of thy rising. ..... Is 60:3
their *k* shall minister unto thee. ..... Is 60:10
that *k* may be brought ..... Is 60:11
and shalt suck the breast of *k* ..... Is 60:16
righteousness, and all *k* thy glory. ..... Is 62:2
land, against the *k* of Judah ..... Jer 1:18
they, their *k*, their princes, and. ..... Jer 2:26
out the bones of the *k* of Judah ..... Jer 8:1
even the *k* that sit upon David's ..... Jer 13:13

whereby the *k* of Judah came in, ... Jer 17:19
ye *k* of Judah, and all Judah, and .... Jer 17:20
into the gates of this city *k* .... Jer 17:25
O *k* of Judah, and inhabitants of .... Jer 19:3
nor the *k* of Judah, and have .... Jer 19:4
and the houses of the *k* of Judah .... Jer 19:13
all the treasures of the *k* of .... Jer 20:5
k sitting upon the throne of .... Jer 22:4
great *k* shall serve themselves of ..... Jer 25:14
the *k* thereof, and the princes .... Jer 25:18
all the *k* of the land of Uz, and ..... Jer 25:20
all the *k* of the land of the .... Jer 25:20
all the *k* of Tyrus .... Jer 25:22
all the *k* of Zidon .... Jer 25:22
the *k* of the isles which are .... Jer 25:22
all the *k* of Arabia .... Jer 25:24
all the *k* of the mingled people ..... Jer 25:24
all the *k* of Zimri .... Jer 25:25
and all the *k* of Elam .... Jer 25:25
and all the *k* of the Medes .... Jer 25:25
all the *k* of the north, far and ..... Jer 25:26
great *k* shall serve themselves of ..... Jer 27:7
me to anger, they, their *k* .... Jer 32:32
the houses of the *k* of Judah .... Jer 33:4
the former *k* which were before .... Jer 34:5
the wickedness of the *k* of Judah ..... Jer 44:9
done, we, and our fathers, our *k* ..... Jer 44:17
ye, and your fathers, your *k* .... Jer 44:21
with their gods, and their *k* .... Jer 46:25
many *k* shall be raised up from ..... Jer 50:41
the spirit of the *k* of the Medes ..... Jer 51:11
nations with the *k* of the Medes ..... Jer 51:28
k that were with him in Babylon ..... Jer 52:32
The *k* of the earth, and all the ..... Lam 4:12
king of Babylon, a king of *k* ..... Eze 26:7
thou didst enrich the *k* of the ..... Eze 27:33
their *k* shall be sore afraid, ... Eze 27:35
ground, I will lay thee before *k* ..... Eze 28:17
their *k* shall be horribly afraid ..... Eze 32:10
There is Edom, her *k*, and all her ..... Eze 32:29
defile, neither they, nor their *k* ..... Eze 43:7
of their *k* in their high places. ..... Eze 43:7
and the carcases of their *k* ..... Eze 43:9
removeth *k*, and setteth up *k* ..... Dan 2:21
Thou, O king, art a king of *k* ..... Dan 2:37
in the days of these *k* shall the ..... Dan 2:44
is a God of gods, and a LORD of *k* ..... Dan 2:47
which are four, are four *k* ..... Dan 7:17
are ten *k* that shall arise ..... Dan 7:24
first, and he shall subdue three *k* ..... Dan 7:24
two horns are the *k* of Media ..... Dan 8:20
which spake in thy name to our *k* ..... Dan 9:6
confusion of face, to our *k* ..... Dan 9:8
there with the *k* of Persia ..... Dan 10:13
stand up yet three *k* in Persia ..... Dan 11:2
k of Judah, and in the days of ..... Hos 1:1
all their *k* are fallen. ..... Hos 7:7
They have set up *k*, but not by me ..... Hos 8:4
k of Judah, which he saw ..... Mic 1:1
shall be a lie to the *k* of Israel ..... Mic 1:14
And they shall scoff at the *k* ..... Hab 1:10
k for my sake, for a testimony ..... Mt 10:18
of whom do the *k* of the earth ..... Mt 17:25
k for my sake, for a testimony ..... Mk 13:9
k have desired to see those. ..... Lk 10:24
prisons, being brought before *k* ..... Lk 21:12
The *k* of the Gentiles exercise ..... Lk 22:25
The *k* of the earth stood up, and ..... Acts 4:26
my name before the Gentiles, and *k* ..... Acts 9:15
ye have reigned as *k* without us 1Cor 4:8
For *k*, and for all that are in 1Ti 2:2
and only Potentate, the King of *k* 1Ti 6:15
from the slaughter of the *k* ..... Heb 7:1
the prince of the *k* of the earth. ..... Rev 1:5
And hath made us *k* and priests unto ..... Rev 1:6
And hast made us unto our God *k* ..... Rev 5:10
the *k* of the earth, and the great ..... Rev 6:15
and nations, and tongues, and *k* ..... Rev 10:11
that the way of the *k* of the east ..... Rev 16:12
go forth unto the *k* of the earth ..... Rev 16:14
With whom the *k* of the earth have ..... Rev 17:2
And there are seven *k* ..... Rev 17:10
horns which thou sawest are ten *k* ..... Rev 17:12
but receive power as *k* one hour ..... Rev 17:12
he is Lord of lords, and King of *k* ..... Rev 17:14
reigneth over the *k* of the earth. ..... Rev 17:18
the *k* of the earth have committed ..... Rev 18:3
the *k* of the earth, who have ..... Rev 18:9
thigh a name written, KING OF *K*... Rev 19:16
That ye may eat the flesh of *k* ..... Rev 19:18
the *k* of the earth, and their ..... Rev 19:19
the *k* of the earth do bring their ..... Rev 21:24

KINGS'

K daughters were among thy .... Ps 45:9
her hands, and is in *k* palaces ..... Prov 30:28
both these *k* hearts shall be to ..... Dan 11:27
soft clothing are in *k* houses. ..... Mt 11:8
live delicately, are in *k* courts. ..... Lk 7:25

KINNERETH See CINNEROTH.

KINSFOLK

My *k* have failed, and my familiar. ..... Job 19:14
and they sought him among their *k*..... Lk 2:44

KINSFOLKS

against a wall, neither of his *k* 1Kin 16:11
and all his great men, and his *k* 2Kin 10:11
by parents, and brethren, and *k* ..... Lk 21:16

KINSMAN

But if the man have no *k* to	Num 5:8
his *k* that is next to him of his	Num 27:11
Naomi had a *k* of her husband's, a......	Ruth 2:1
for thou art a near *k*	Ruth 3:9
it is true that I am thy near *k*	Ruth 3:12
there is a *k* nearer than I	Ruth 3:12
perform unto thee the part of a *k*	Ruth 3:13
not do the part of a *k* to thee	Ruth 3:13
will I do the part of a *k* to thee	Ruth 3:13
the *k* of whom Boaz spake came by ...	Ruth 4:1
And he said unto the *k*, Naomi, ...	Ruth 4:3
the *k* said, I cannot redeem it	Ruth 4:6
Therefore he *k* said unto Boaz, ...	Ruth 4:8
left thee this day without a *k*	Ruth 4:14
his *k* whose ear Peter cut	Jn 18:26
Salute Herodion my *k*	Rom 16:11

KINSMAN'S

let him do the *k* part	Ruth 3:13

KINSMEN

of kin unto us, one of our next *k*	Ruth 2:20
and my *k* stand afar off	Ps 38:11
nor thy brethren, neither thy *k*	Lk 14:12
and had called together his *k*	Acts 10:24
my *k* according to the flesh	Rom 9:3
Salute Andronicus and Junia, my *k* ...	Rom 16:7
and Jason, and Sosipater, my *k*	Rom 16:21

KINSWOMAN

she is thy father's near *k*	Lev 18:12
for she is thy mother's near *k*	Lev 18:13
and call understanding thy *k*	Prov 7:4

KINSWOMEN

for they are her near *k*	Lev 18:17

KIOS See CHIOS.

KIR (kur) See KIR-HARESH.

1. An Assyrian district on the Kur River.

the people of it captive to *K*	2Kin 16:9
shall go into captivity unto *K*	Amos 1:5
Caphtor, and the Syrians from *K*	Amos 9:7

2. A Moabite city.

because in the night *K* of Moab is	Is 15:1

3. Inhabitants of Kir 1.

and *K* uncovered the shield	Is 22:6

KIR-HARASETH (kur-har'-a-seth) See KIR-HARESETH. A Moabite city.

only in *K* left they the stones.	2Kin 3:25

KIR-HARESETH (kur-har'-e-seth) See KIR-HARESH. Same as Kir-haraseth.

foundations of *K* shall ye mourn	Is 16:7

KIR-HARESH (kur-ha'-resh) See KIR-HARASETH, KIR-HARESETH, KIR-HERES. Same as Kir-haraseth.

Moab, and mine inward parts for *K*. ...	Is 16:11

KIR-HERES (kur-he'-res) See KIR-HARESH.

shall mourn for the men of *K*.	Jer 48:31
sound like pipes for the men of *K*.	Jer 48:36

KIRIATH See KIRJATH.

KIRIATHAIM (kir-e-a-thay'-im) See KIRTAN, KIRJATHAIM.

1. A town east of the Jordan.

in Ham, and the Emims in Shaveh *K* ...	Gen 14:5

2. A city in Reuben.

is confounded and taken	Jer 48:1
And upon *K*, and upon	Jer 48:23
Beth-jeshimoth, Baal-meon, and *K*	Eze 25:9

KIRIATH ARBA See KIRJATH-ARBA.

KIRIATH-ARBA See KIRJATH-ARBA.

KIRIATH-ARIM See KIRJATH-ARIM.

KIRIATH-BAAL See KIRJATH-BAAL.

KIRIATH-JEARIM See KIRJATH.

KIRIATH-SANNAH See KIRJATH-SANNAH.

KIRIATH-SEPHER See KIRJATH-SEPHER.

KIRIOTH (kir'-e-oth) See KERIOTH. A Moabite city.

it shall devour the palaces of *K*	Amos 2:2

KIRJATH (kur'-jath) See KIRJATH-ARIM, KIRJATH-BAAL, KIRJATH-JEARIM. Short form of Kirjath-jearim.

which is Jerusalem, Gibeath, and *K*...	Josh 18:28

KIRJATHAIM (jur'-jath-a'-im)

1. A city in Reuben.

built Heshbon, and Elealeh, and *K*	Num 32:37
And *K*, and Sibmah	Josh 13:19

2. A Levitical city in Naphtali.

suburbs, and *K* with her suburbs	1Chr 6:76

KIRJATH-ARBA (kur'-jath-ar'-bah) See HEBRON. A city in Judah.

And Sarah died in *K*	Gen 23:2
the name of Hebron before was *K*	Josh 14:15
And Hamath, and *K*, which	Josh 15:54
in mount Ephraim, and *K*	Josh 20:7
the name of Hebron before was *K*......	Judg 1:10
the children of Judah dwelt at *K*	Neh 11:25

KIRJATH-ARIM (kur'-jath-a'-rim) See KIRJATH-JEARIM. Same as Kiriath-jearim.

The children of *K*, Chephirah, and	Ezr 2:25

KIRJATH-BAAL (kur'-jath-ba'-al) See BAALAH, KIRJATH-JEARIM. Same as Kiriath-jearim.

K, which is Kirjath-jearim, and	Josh 15:60
the goings out thereof were at *K*.	Josh 18:14

KIRJATH-HUZOTH (kur'-jath-hu'-zoth) Residence of Balak, king of Edom.

with Balak, and they came unto *K*.	Num 22:39

KIRJATH-JEARIM (kur'-jath-je'-a-rim) See KIRIATH, KIRJATH-ARIM, KIRJATH-BAAL.

1. A city in Judah.

and Chephirah, and Beeroth, and *K*....	Josh 9:17
was drawn to Baalah, which is *K*	Josh 15:9
Kirjath-baal, which is *K*, and	Josh 15:60
were at Kirjath-baal, which is *K*	Josh 18:14
quarter was from the end of *K*	Josh 18:15
And they went up, and pitched in *K*. ...	Judg 18:12
behold, it is behind *K*	Judg 18:12
to the inhabitants of *K*, saying, ...	1Sa 6:21
And the men of *K* came, and brought...	1Sa 7:1
to pass, while the ark abode in *K*	1Sa 7:2
to bring the ark of God from *K*	1Chr 13:5
Israel, to Baalah, that is, to *K*.	1Chr 13:6
K to the place which David had	2Chr 1:4
The men of *K*, Chephirah, and	Neh 7:29
Urijah the son of Shemaiah of *K*	Jer 26:20

2. A descendant of Caleb.

Shobal the father of *K*, ...	1Chr 2:50
Shobal the father of *K* had sons.	1Chr 2:52
And the families of *K*	1Chr 2:53

KIRJATH-SANNAH (kur'-jath-san'-nah) A city in Judah.

And Dannah, and *K*, which is Debir...	Josh 15:49

KIRJATH-SEPHER (kur'-jath-se'-fer) See DEBIR, KIRJATH-SANNAH. Same as Kiriath-sannah.

and the name of Debir before was *K*....	Josh 15:15
And Caleb said, He that smiteth *K*......	Josh 15:16
and the name of Debir before was *K*....	Judg 1:11
And Caleb said, He that smiteth *K*......	Judg 1:12

KISH (kish)

1. Father of King Saul.

man of Benjamin, whose name was *K* ...	1Sa 9:1
the asses of *K* Saul's father were	1Sa 9:3
K said to Saul his son, Take now	1Sa 9:3
that is come unto the son of *K*.	1Sa 10:11
for the son of *K* was taken	1Sa 10:21
And *K* was the father of Saul	1Sa 14:51
in the sepulchre of *K* his father	2Sa 21:14
And Ner begat *K*	1Chr 8:33
K begat Saul.	1Chr 8:33
And Ner begat *K*	1Chr 9:39
and *K* begat Saul	1Chr 9:39
because of Saul the son of *K*	1Chr 12:1
the seer, and Saul the son of *K*	1Chr 26:28

2. Son of Abi-Gibeon.

firstborn son Abdon, and Zur, and *K*. ...	1Chr 8:30
son Abdon, then Zur, and *K*...............	1Chr 9:36

3. A sanctuary servant.

of Mahli; Eleazar, and *K*.	1Chr 23:21
brethren the sons of *K* took them	1Chr 23:22
Concerning *K*: the son of Kish	1Chr 24:29

4. A Levite.

K the son of Abdi, and Azariah the.....	2Chr 29:12

5. An ancestor of Mordecai.

the son of Shimei, the son of	Est 2:5

KISHI (kish'-i) See KUSHAIAH. Father of Ethan.

Ethan the son of *K*, ...	1Chr 6:44

KISHION (kish'-e-on) See KEDESH, KISHON.

A Levitical city in Issachar.

And Rabbith, and *K*, and Abez, ...	Josh 19:20

KISHON (ki'-shon) See KISHION, KISON.

1. Same as Kishion.

K with her suburbs, Dabareh with	Josh 21:28
the Gentiles unto the river of *K*	Judg 4:13
The river of *K* swept them away, ...	Judg 5:21
that ancient river, the river *K*	Judg 5:21
brought them down to the brook *K*	1Kin 18:40

2. A brook near Mt. Tabor.

draw unto thee to the river *K*	Judg 4:7

KISLEV See CHISLEU.

KISLON See CHISLON.

KISLOTH TABOR See CHISLOTH-TABOR.

KISON (ki'-son) See KISHON. Same as Kishon 2.

as to Jabin, at the brook of *K*.	Ps 83:9

KISS

Come near now, and *k* me, my son ...	Gen 27:26
hast not suffered me to *k* my sons.....	Gen 31:28
with the right hand to *k* him	2Sa 20:9
k my father and my mother	1Kin 19:20
K the Son, lest he be angry, and	Ps 2:12
Every man shall *k* his lips that	Prov 24:26
Let him *k* me with the kisses of	Song 1:2
find thee without, I would *k* thee.	Song 8:1
men that sacrifice *k* the calves	Hos 13:2
saying, Whomsoever I shall *k*, ...	Mt 26:48
saying, Whomsoever I shall *k*	Mk 14:44
Thou gavest me no *k*	Lk 7:45
in hath not ceased to *k* my feet	Lk 7:45
and drew near unto Jesus to *k* him....	Lk 22:47
thou the Son of man with a *k*	Lk 22:48
Salute one another with an holy *k*	Rom 16:16
ye one another with an holy *k*	1Cor 16:20

Greet one another with an holy *k*......	2Cor 13:12
all the brethren with an holy *k*	1Th 5:26
one another with a *k* of charity	1Pet 5:14

KISSED

And he came near, and *k* him	Gen 27:27
Jacob & Rachel, and lifted up his	Gen 29:11
k him, and brought him to his	Gen 29:13
k his sons and his daughters, and	Gen 31:55
and fell on his neck, and *k* him	Gen 33:4
Moreover he *k* all his brethren,.........	Gen 45:15
he *k* them, and embraced them	Gen 48:10
face, and wept upon him, and *k* him ...	Gen 50:1
him in the mount of God, and *k* him ...	Ex 4:27
law, and did obeisance, and *k* him	Ex 18:7
Then she *k* them	Ruth 1:9
Orpah *k* her mother in law	Ruth 1:14
k him, and said, Is it not because......	1Sa 10:1
they *k* one another, and wept one	1Sa 20:41
and the king *k* Absalom	2Sa 14:33
his hand, and took him, and *k* him	2Sa 15:5
the king *k* Barzillai, and blessed	2Sa 19:39
every mouth which hath not *k* him.....	1Kin 19:18
or my mouth hath *k* my hand.	Job 31:27
and peace have *k* each other	Ps 85:10
k him, and with an impudent face	Prov 7:13
master; and *k* him	Mt 26:49
Master, master; and *k* him	Mk 14:45
k his feet, and anointed them with.....	Lk 7:38
and fell on his neck, and *k* him, ...	Lk 15:20
and fell on Paul's neck, and *k* him, ...	Acts 20:37

KISSES

but the *k* of an enemy are	Prov 27:6
kiss me with the *k* of his mouth........	Song 1:2

KITE

vulture, and the *k* after his kind	Lev 11:14
And the glede, and the *k*, and the	Deut 14:13

KITHLISH (kith'-lish) A city in Judah.

And Cabbon, and Lahmam, and *K*	Josh 15:40

KITRON (ki'-tron) See KATTAH. A city in Zebulun.

drive out the inhabitants of *K*	Judg 1:30

KITTIM (kit'-tim) See CHITTIM. A son of Javan.

Elishah, and Tarshish, *K*, and	Gen 10:4
Elishah, and Tarshish, *K*, and	1Chr 1:7

KIYYUN See CHIUN.

KNEAD

k it, and make cakes upon the	Gen 18:6
the women *k* their dough, to make	Jer 7:18

KNEADED

k it, and did bake unleavened	1Sa 28:24
k it, and made cakes in his sight, ...	2Sa 13:8
raising after he hath *k* the dough	Hos 7:4

KNEADINGTROUGHS

into thine ovens, and into thy *k*..........	Ex 8:3
their *k* being bound up in their	Ex 12:34

KNEE

they cried before him, Bow the *k*	Gen 41:43
That unto me every *k* shall bow	Is 45:23
and they bowed the *k* before him, ...	Mt 27:29
bowed the *k* to the image of Baal	Rom 11:4
every *k* shall bow to me, and every....	Rom 14:11
name of Jesus every *k* should bow....	Phil 2:10

KNEEL

he made his camels to *k* down	Gen 24:11
let us *k* before the LORD our	Ps 95:6

KNEELED

k down upon his knees before all	2Chr 6:13
he *k* upon his knees three times a	Dan 6:10
k to him, and asked him, Good	Mk 10:17
cast, and *k* down, and prayed, ...	Lk 22:41
he *k* down, and cried with a loud	Acts 7:60
all forth, and *k* down, and prayed	Acts 9:40
he *k* down, and prayed with them......	Acts 20:36
we *k* down on the shore, and prayed...	Acts 21:5

KNEELING

from *k* on his knees with his	1Kin 8:54
k down to him, and saying, ...	Mt 17:14
k down to him, and saying unto him ...	Mk 1:40

KNEES

and she shall bear upon my *k*	Gen 30:3
them out from between his *k*	Gen 48:12
were brought up upon Joseph's *k*	Gen 50:23
LORD shall smite thee in the *k*	Deut 28:35
boweth down upon his *k* to drink, ...	Judg 7:5
down upon their *k* to drink water	Judg 7:6
And she made him sleep upon her *k* ...	Judg 16:19
from kneeling on his *k* with his	1Kin 8:54
and put his face between his *k*	1Kin 18:42
all the *k* which have not bowed	1Kin 19:18
fell on his *k* before Elijah, and	2Kin 1:13
mother, he sat on her *k* till noon	2Kin 4:20
kneeled down upon his *k* before	2Chr 6:13
and my mantle, I fell upon my *k*	Ezr 9:5
Why did the *k* prevent me	Job 3:12
hast strengthened the feeble *k*	Job 4:4
My *k* are weak through fasting...........	Ps 109:24
hands, and confirm the feeble *k*	Is 35:3
sides, and be dandled upon her *k*	Is 66:12
all *k* shall be weak as water	Eze 7:17
all *k* shall be weak as water	Eze 21:7
the waters were to the *k*	Eze 47:4
his *k* smote one against another.......	Dan 5:6

upon his _k_ three times a day................ Dan 6:10
me, which set me upon my _k_................ Dan 10:10
the _k_ smite together, and much........... Nah 2:10
bowing their _k_ worshipped him........... Mk 15:19
saw it, he fell down at Jesus' _k_............ Lk 5:8
For this cause I bow my _k_ unto............ Eph 3:14
which hang down, and the feeble _k_ .... Heb 12:12

KNEW

they _k_ that they were naked................. Gen 3:7
And Adam _k_ Eve his wife.................... Gen 4:1
And Cain _k_ his wife............................. Gen 4:17
And Adam _k_ his wife again................. Gen 4:25
so Noah _k_ that the waters were........... Gen 8:11
_k_ what his younger son had done.......... Gen 9:24
and I _k_ it not.................................... Gen 28:16
For Jacob _k_ not that Rachel had........... Gen 31:32
And he _k_ it, and said, It is my............. Gen 37:33
Onan _k_ that the seed should not........... Gen 38:9
(for he _k_ not that she was his.............. Gen 38:16
And he _k_ her again no more................ Gen 38:26
he _k_ not ought he had, save the........... Gen 39:6
he _k_ them, but made himself............... Gen 42:7
Joseph _k_ his brethren.......................... Gen 42:8
his brethren, but they _k_ not him.......... Gen 42:8
they _k_ not that Joseph understood...... Gen 42:23
over Egypt, which he _k_ not................. Ex 1:8
for I _k_ not that thou stoodest in......... Num 22:34
_k_ the knowledge of the most High,...... Num 24:16
manna, which thy fathers _k_ not........... Deut 8:16
LORD from the day that I _k_ you........... Deut 9:24
them, gods whom they _k_ not................ Deut 29:26
to gods whom they _k_ not, to new......... Deut 32:17
brethren, nor _k_ his own children.......... Deut 33:9
whom the LORD _k_ face to face............ Deut 34:10
which is not the LORD, nor yet the........ Judg 2:10
such as before _k_ nothing thereof.......... Judg 3:2
and she _k_ no man............................... Judg 11:39
For Manoah _k_ not that he was an........ Judg 13:16
Then Manoah _k_ that he was an........... Judg 13:21
his mother _k_ not that it was of........... Judg 14:4
they _k_ the voice of the young man...... Judg 18:3
and they _k_ her, and abused her all...... Judg 19:25
but they _k_ not that evil was near....... Judg 20:34
Elkanah _k_ Hannah his wife................. 1Sa 1:19
they _k_ not the LORD........................... 1Sa 2:12
from Dan even to Beer-sheba _k_........... 1Sa 3:20
when all that _k_ him beforetime........... 1Sa 10:11
the people _k_ not that Jonathan........... 1Sa 14:3
_k_ that the LORD was with David,......... 1Sa 18:28
for if I certainly that evil................... 1Sa 20:9
whereby Jonathan _k_ that it was......... 1Sa 20:33
But the lad _k_ not any thing................ 1Sa 20:39
Jonathan and David _k_ the matter....... 1Sa 20:39
for thy servant _k_ nothing of all......... 1Sa 22:15
and because they _k_ when he fled........ 1Sa 22:17
I _k_ it that day, when Doeg the........... 1Sa 22:22
David and Saul secretly....................... 1Sa 23:9
away, and no man saw it, nor _k_ it...... 1Sa 26:12
Saul _k_ David's voice, and said, Is...... 1Sa 26:17
but David _k_ it not............................. 2Sa 3:26
where he _k_ that valiant men were....... 2Sa 11:16
_k_ ye not that they would shoot........... 2Sa 11:20
and they _k_ not any thing.................... 2Sa 15:11
tumult, but I _k_ not what it was.......... 2Sa 18:29
a people which I _k_ not shall.............. 2Sa 22:44
but the king _k_ her not....................... 1Kin 1:4
he _k_ him, and fell on his face, and..... 1Kin 18:7
for they _k_ them not........................... 2Kin 4:39
Then Manasseh _k_ that the LORD he ... 2Chr 33:13
the rulers _k_ not whither I went.......... Neh 2:16
which _k_ the times, (for so was........... Est 1:13
manner toward all that _k_ law............ Est 1:13
_k_ him not, they lifted up their............ Job 2:12
Oh that I _k_ where I might find.......... Job 23:3
the cause which I _k_ not..................... Job 29:16
wonderful for me, which I _k_ not......... Job 42:3
to my charge things that I _k_ not........ Ps 35:11
against me, and I _k_ it not.................. Ps 35:15
thou sayest, Behold, we _k_ it not......... Prov 24:12
blind by a way that they _k_ not.......... Is 42:16
on fire round about, yet he _k_ not....... Is 42:25
Because I _k_ that thou art.................. Is 48:4
shouldest say, Behold, I _k_ them......... Is 48:7
for I _k_ that thou wouldest deal.......... Is 48:8
nations that _k_ not thee shall run....... Is 55:5
formed thee in the belly I _k_ thee....... Jer 1:5
they that handle the law _k_ me not..... Jer 2:8
I _k_ not that they had devised............. Jer 11:19
Then I _k_ that this was the word.......... Jer 32:8
slain Gedaliah, and no man _k_ it......... Jer 41:4
serve other gods, whom they _k_ not..... Jer 44:3
Then all the men which _k_ that........... Jer 44:15
I _k_ that they were the cherubims....... Eze 10:20
he _k_ their desolate palaces, and......... Eze 19:7
till he _k_ that the most high God......... Dan 5:21
Now when Daniel _k_ that the.............. Dan 6:10
a god whom his fathers _k_ not............ Dan 11:38
have made princes, and I _k_ it not...... Hos 8:4
but they _k_ not that I healed them....... Hos 11:3
For the men _k_ that he fled from......... Jonah 1:10
for I _k_ that thou art a gracious......... Jonah 4:2
all the nations whom they _k_ not........ Zec 7:14
me _k_ that it was the word of the....... Zec 11:11
_k_ her not till she had brought........... Mt 1:25
profess unto them, I never _k_ you........ Mt 7:23
But when Jesus _k_ it, he withdrew....... Mt 12:15
Jesus _k_ their thoughts, and said........ Mt 12:25
they _k_ him not, but have done........... Mt 17:12
_k_ not until the flood came, and.......... Mt 24:39
I _k_ thee that thou art an hard........... Mt 25:24

For he _k_ that for envy they had......... Mt 27:18
to speak, because they _k_ him.............. Mk 1:34
saw them departing, and many _k_ him.. Mk 6:33
And when they _k_, they say, Five,....... Mk 6:38
the ship, straightway they _k_ him........ Mk 6:54
And when Jesus _k_ it, he saith unto.... Mk 8:17
for they _k_ that he had spoken the...... Mk 12:12
For he _k_ that the chief priests........... Mk 15:10
when he _k_ it of the centurion, he....... Mk 15:45
Joseph and his mother _k_ not of it...... Lk 2:43
for they _k_ that he was Christ............. Lk 4:41
But he _k_ their thoughts, and said....... Lk 6:8
when she _k_ that Jesus sat at meat...... Lk 7:37
And the people, when they _k_ it.......... Lk 9:11
which _k_ his lord's will, and............... Lk 12:47
But he that _k_ not, and did commit..... Lk 12:48
neither _k_ they the things which......... Lk 18:34
as soon as he _k_ that he belonged...... Lk 23:7
eyes were opened, and they _k_ him..... Lk 24:31
by him, and the world _k_ him not....... Jn 1:10
And I _k_ him not................................. Jn 1:31
And I _k_ him not................................. Jn 1:33
made wine, and _k_ not whence it was.. Jn 2:9
servants which drew the water _k_....... Jn 2:9
unto them, because he _k_ all men........ Jn 2:24
for he _k_ what was in man................. Jn 2:25
When therefore the Lord _k_ how the.... Jn 4:1
So the father _k_ that it was at........... Jn 4:53
_k_ that he had been now a long.......... Jn 5:6
for he himself _k_ what he would do..... Jn 6:6
When Jesus _k_ in himself that his....... Jn 6:61
For Jesus _k_ from the beginning......... Jn 6:64
I _k_ that thou hearest me always......... Jn 11:42
if any man _k_ where he were, he......... Jn 11:57
therefore _k_ that he was there............. Jn 11:57
when Jesus _k_ that his hour was......... Jn 13:1
For he _k_ who should betray him........ Jn 13:11
Now no man at the table _k_ for.......... Jn 13:28
Now Jesus _k_ that they were............... Jn 16:19
which betrayed him, _k_ the place........ Jn 18:2
For as yet they _k_ not........................ Jn 20:9
and _k_ not that it was Jesus.............. Jn 20:14
but the disciples _k_ not that it........... Jn 21:4
they _k_ that it was he which sat......... Acts 3:10
king arose, which _k_ not Joseph......... Acts 7:18
Which when the brethren _k_................ Acts 9:30
when she _k_ Peter's voice, she........... Acts 12:14
rulers, because they _k_ him not.......... Acts 13:27
for they _k_ all that his father............. Acts 16:3
the more part _k_ not wherefore......... Acts 19:32
But when they _k_ that he was a Jew ... Acts 19:34
after he _k_ that he was a Roman,....... Acts 22:29
Which _k_ me from the beginning,........ Acts 26:5
it was day, they _k_ not the land......... Acts 27:39
then they _k_ that the island was........ Acts 28:1
Because that, when they _k_ God......... Rom 1:21
God the world by wisdom _k_ not God.. 1Cor 1:21
of the princes of this world _k_........... 1Cor 2:8
to be sin for us, who _k_ no sin........... 2Cor 5:21
I _k_ a man in Christ above................. 2Cor 12:2
I such a man, (whether in the............. 2Cor 12:3
Howbeit then, when ye _k_ not............. Gal 4:8
_k_ the grace of God in truth............... Col 1:6
For I would that ye _k_ what great...... Col 2:1
us not, because it _k_ him not.............. 1Jn 3:1
though ye once _k_ this, how that......... Jude 5
had a name written, that no man _k_ .. Rev 19:12

KNEWEST

thee with manna, which thou _k_ not.... Deut 8:3
which thou _k_ not heretofore............... Ruth 2:11
for thou _k_ that they dealt................ Neh 9:10
within me, then thou _k_ my path........ Ps 142:3
yea, thou _k_ not................................. Is 48:8
heart, though thou _k_ all this............. Dan 5:22
thou _k_ that I reap where I sowed...... Mt 25:26
Thou _k_ that I was an austere man,.... Lk 19:22
because thou _k_ not the time of......... Lk 19:44
If thou _k_ the gift of God, and who.... Jn 4:10

KNIFE

took the fire in his hand, and a _k_..... Gen 22:6
took the _k_ to slay his son................. Gen 22:10
come into his house, he took a _k_....... Judg 19:29
put a _k_ to thy throat, if thou be....... Prov 23:2
part, and smite about it with a _k_...... Eze 5:1
part, and smite about it with a _k_...... Eze 5:2

KNIT

the city, _k_ together as one man......... Judg 20:11
was _k_ with the soul of David............ 1Sa 18:1
mine heart shall be _k_ unto you.......... 1Chr 12:17
great sheet _k_ at the four corners...... Acts 10:11
being _k_ together in love, and unto..... Col 2:2
_k_ together, increaseth with the.......... Col 2:19

KNIVES

unto Joshua, Make thee sharp _k_........ Josh 5:2
And Joshua made him sharp _k_........... Josh 5:3
after their manner with _k_.................. 1Kin 18:28
of silver, nine and twenty _k_.............. Ezr 1:9
swords, and their jaw teeth as _k_....... Prov 30:14

KNOCK

_k_, and it shall be opened unto you...... Mt 7:7
_k_, and it shall be opened unto you...... Lk 11:9
to _k_ at the door, saying, Lord,.......... Lk 13:25
Behold, I stand at the door, and _k_..... Rev 3:20

KNOCKED

as Peter _k_ at the door of the............. Acts 12:13

KNOCKETH

is the voice of my beloved that _k_...... Song 5:2
to him that _k_ it shall be opened........ Mt 7:8

to him that _k_ it shall be opened........ Lk 11:10
that when he cometh and _k_, they...... Lk 12:36

KNOCKING

But Peter continued _k_........................ Acts 12:16

KNOP

made like unto almonds, with a _k_..... Ex 25:33
in the other branch, with a _k_............ Ex 25:33
there shall be a _k_ under two............. Ex 25:35
a _k_ under two branches of the........... Ex 25:35
a _k_ under two branches of the........... Ex 25:35
of almonds in one branch, a _k_.......... Ex 37:19
almonds in another branch, a _k_......... Ex 37:19
a _k_ under two branches of the........... Ex 37:21
a _k_ under two branches of the........... Ex 37:21
a _k_ under two branches of the........... Ex 37:21

KNOPS

and his branches, his bowls, his _k_..... Ex 25:31
like unto almonds, with their _k_......... Ex 25:34
Their _k_ and their branches shall....... Ex 25:36
and his branch, his bowls, his _k_........ Ex 37:17
bowls made like almonds, his _k_......... Ex 37:20
Their _k_ and their branches were of... Ex 37:22
house within was carved with _k_........ 1Kin 6:18
about there were _k_ compassing it...... 1Kin 7:24
the _k_ were cast in two rows, when.... 1Kin 7:24

KNOW See PREFACE.

tree, of _k_ good and evil.................... Gen 3:22
for now I _k_ that thou fearest God...... Gen 22:12
that thou mightest _k_ that the............ Deut 4:35
to _k_ whether ye love the LORD.......... Deut 13:3
Now Samuel did not yet _k_ the LORD .. 1Sa 3:7
I _k_ thy pride, and the naughtiness.... 1Sa 17:28
earth may _k_ that the LORD is God..... 1Kin 8:60
For I _k_ that my redeemer liveth,....... Job 19:25
And thou sayest, How doth God _k_..... Job 22:13
Be still, and _k_ that I am God........... Ps 46:10
And they say, How doth God _k_.......... Ps 73:11
_k_ ye that the LORD he is God........... Ps 100:3
Search me, O God, and _k_ my heart ... Ps 139:23
But I _k_ thy abode, and thy going...... Is 37:28
my people shall _k_ my name............... Is 52:6
therefore they shall _k_ in that........... Is 52:6
ye shall _k_ that I am the LORD........... Eze 6:7
and thou shalt _k_ the LORD................ Hos 2:20
let not thy left hand _k_ what thy....... Mt 6:3
Ye shall _k_ them by their fruits......... Mt 7:16
by their fruits ye shall _k_ them.......... Mt 7:20
for ye _k_ not what hour your LORD..... Mt 24:42
for ye _k_ neither the day nor the....... Mt 25:13
with an oath, I do not _k_ the man...... Mt 26:72
him, saying, Woman, I _k_ him not...... Lk 22:57
for they _k_ not what they do.............. Lk 23:34
_k_ that this is indeed the Christ,........ Jn 4:42
I _k_ them, and they follow me............ Jn 10:27
_k_ ye what I have done to you............ Jn 13:12
If ye _k_ these things, happy are......... Jn 13:17
I go ye _k_, and the way ye _k_........... Jn 14:4
It is not for you to _k_ the times......... Acts 1:7
we _k_ that all things work.................. Rom 8:28
neither can he _k_ them, because......... 1Cor 2:14
For we _k_ in part, and we prophesy.... 1Cor 13:9
but then shall I even as also I............. 1Cor 13:12
for I _k_ whom I have believed, and..... 2Ti 1:12
Whereas ye _k_ not what shall be on.... Jas 4:14
hereby we do _k_ that we _k_ him........ 1Jn 2:3
hereby _k_ we that we are in him......... 1Jn 2:5
that ye may _k_ that ye have.............. 1Jn 5:13
We _k_ that whosoever is born of......... 1Jn 5:18

KNOWEST

for thou _k_ my service which I........... Gen 30:26
Thou _k_ how I have served thee, and.. Gen 30:29
If thou _k_ any men of activity........... Gen 47:6
_k_ thou not yet that Egypt is............ Ex 10:7
thou _k_ the people, that they are...... Ex 32:22
forasmuch as thou _k_ how we are to .. Num 10:31
whom thou _k_ to be the elders of...... Num 11:16
Thou _k_ all the travel that hath........ Num 20:14
diseases of Egypt, which thou _k_....... Deut 7:15
of the Anakims, whom thou _k_.......... Deut 9:2
Only the trees which thou _k_ that...... Deut 20:20
a nation which thou _k_ not eat up...... Deut 28:33
Thou _k_ the thing that the LORD........ Josh 14:6
_k_ thou not that the Philistines......... Judg 15:11
thou _k_ what Saul hath done, how..... 1Sa 28:9
How _k_ thou that Saul and Jonathan.. 2Sa 1:5
_k_ thou not that it will be................. 2Sa 2:26
Thou _k_ Abner the son of Ner, that.... 2Sa 3:25
for thou, Lord God, _k_ thy servant..... 2Sa 7:20
thou _k_ thy father and his men,......... 2Sa 17:8
my lord the king, thou _k_ it not........ 1Kin 1:18
Moreover thou _k_ also what Joab....... 1Kin 2:5
_k_ what thou oughtest to do unto...... 1Kin 2:9
Thou _k_ that the kingdom was mine,.. 1Kin 2:15
Thou _k_ all the wickedness which...... 1Kin 2:44
Thou _k_ how that David my father.... 1Kin 5:3
for thou _k_ that there is not.............. 1Kin 5:6
to his ways, whose heart thou _k_....... 1Kin 8:39
_k_ the hearts of all the children......... 1Kin 8:39
_k_ thou that the LORD will take......... 2Kin 2:3
_k_ thou that the LORD will take......... 2Kin 2:5
for thou, even thou only, _k_ the........ 2Kin 6:30
for thou _k_ thy servant...................... 1Chr 17:18
all his ways, whose heart thou _k_...... 2Chr 6:30
(for thou only _k_ the hearts of.......... 2Chr 6:30
Thou _k_ that I am not wicked........... Job 10:7
What _k_ thou, that we know not......... Job 15:9
_k_ thou not this of old, since man...... Job 20:4
therefore speak what thou _k_............. Job 34:33
the measures thereof, if thou _k_........ Job 38:5

KNOWETH

declare if thou *k* it all .... Job 38:18
K thou it, because thou wast then .... Job 38:21
K thou the ordinances of heaven .... Job 38:33
K thou the time when the wild .... Job 39:1
or *k* thou the time when they .... Job 39:2
refrained my lips, O LORD, thou *k* .... Ps 40:9
O God, thou *k* my foolishness .... Ps 69:5
Thou *k* my downsitting and mine .... Ps 139:2
lo, O LORD, thou *k* it altogether .... Ps 139:4
for thou *k* not what a day may .... Prov 27:1
for thou *k* not what evil shall be .... Eccl 11:2
As thou *k* not what is the way of .... Eccl 11:5
even so thou *k* not the works of .... Eccl 11:5
for thou *k* not whether shall .... Eccl 11:6
call a nation that thou *k* not .... Is 55:5
nation whose language thou *k* not ...... Jer 5:15
But thou, O LORD, *k* me .... Jer 12:3
into a land which thou *k* not .... Jer 15:14
O LORD, thou *k* .... Jer 15:15
in the land which thou *k* not .... Jer 17:4
thou *k*: that which came .... Jer 17:16
thou *k* all their counsel against .... Jer 18:23
mighty things, which thou *k* not .... Jer 33:3
And I answered, O Lord God, thou *k* ..... Eze 37:3
K thou wherefore I come unto thee .... Dan 10:20
unto me, *K* thou not what these be .... Zec 4:5
and said, *K* thou not what these be ...... Zec 4:13
K thou that the Pharisees were .... Mt 15:12
Thou *k* the commandments, Do not .... Mk 10:19
Thou *k* the commandments, Do not .... Lk 18:20
shalt thrice deny that thou *k* .... Lk 22:34
saith unto him, Whence *k* thou me ...... Jn 1:48
of Israel, and *k* not these things ...... Jn 3:10
him, What I do thou *k* not now .... Jn 13:7
we sure that thou *k* all things .... Jn 16:30
k thou not that I have power to .... Jn 19:10
thou *k* that I love thee .... Jn 21:15
thou *k* that I love thee .... Jn 21:16
unto him, Lord, thou *k* all things ...... Jn 21:17
thou *k* that I love thee .... Jn 21:17
which *k* the hearts of all men .... Acts 1:24
no wrong, as thou very well *k* .... Acts 25:10
k his will, and approvest the .... Rom 2:18
For what *k* thou, O wife, whether 1Cor 7:16
or how *k* thou, O man, whether 1Cor 7:16
This thou *k*, that all they which 2Ti 1:15
me at Ephesus, thou *k* very well 2Ti 1:18
k not that thou art wretched, and ...... Rev 3:17
And I said unto him, Sir, thou *k* .... Rev 7:14

KNOWETH

My lord *k* that the children are .... Gen 33:13
when he *k* of it, then he shall be ...... Lev 5:3
when he *k* of it, then he shall be ...... Lev 5:4
he *k* thy walking through this .... Deut 2:7
but no man *k* of his sepulchre .... Deut 34:6
gods, the LORD God of gods, he *k* .... Josh 22:22
ever for the iniquity which he *k* 1Sa 3:13
Thy father certainly *k* that I 1Sa 20:3
and that also Saul my father *k* 1Sa 23:17
Today thy servant *k* that I have 2Sa 14:22
for all Israel *k* that thy father 2Sa 17:10
reign, and David our lord *k* it not 1Kin 1:11
who *k* whether thou art come to .... Est 4:14
For he *k* vain men .... Job 11:11
who *k* not such things as these .... Job 12:3
Who *k* not in all these that the .... Job 12:9
come to honour, and he *k* it not .... Job 14:21
he *k* that the day of darkness is .... Job 15:23
the place of him that *k* not God .... Job 18:21
But he *k* the way that I take .... Job 23:10
There is a path which no fowl *k* .... Job 28:7
Man *k* not the price thereof .... Job 28:13
and he *k* the place thereof .... Job 28:23
Therefore he *k* their works .... Job 34:25
yet he *k* it not in great .... Job 35:15
For the LORD *k* the way of the .... Ps 1:6
The LORD *k* the days of the .... Ps 37:18
k not who shall gather them .... Ps 39:6
for he *k* the secrets of the heart ...... Ps 44:21
among us any that *k* how long .... Ps 74:9
Who *k* the power of thine anger .... Ps 90:11
A brutish man *k* not .... Ps 92:6
The LORD *k* the thoughts of man .... Ps 94:11
For he *k* our frame .... Ps 103:14
the sun *k* his going down .... Ps 104:19
but the proud he *k* afar off .... Ps 138:6
and that my soul *k* right well .... Ps 139:14
k not that it is for his life .... Prov 7:23
she is simple, and *k* nothing .... Prov 9:13
But he *k* not that the dead are .... Prov 9:18
The heart *k* his own bitterness .... Prov 14:10
who *k* the ruin of them both .... Prov 24:22
who *k* whether he shall be a wise .... Eccl 2:19
Who *k* the spirit of man that .... Eccl 3:21
that *k* to walk before the living .... Eccl 6:8
For who *k* what is good for man in ...... Eccl 6:12
k that thou thyself likewise hast ...... Eccl 7:22
who *k* the interpretation of a .... Eccl 8:1
For he *k* not that which shall be .... Eccl 8:7
no man *k* either love or hatred by ...... Eccl 9:1
For man also *k* not his time .... Eccl 9:12
because he *k* not how to go to the ...... Eccl 10:15
The ox *k* his owner, and the ass .... Is 1:3
and who *k* us? .... Is 29:15
the heaven *k* her appointed times ...... Jer 8:7
k me, that I am the LORD which .... Jer 9:24
he *k* what is in the darkness, and ...... Dan 2:22
his strength, and he *k* it not .... Hos 7:9
and there upon him, yet he *k* not .... Hos 7:9
Who *k* if he will return and repent ..... Joel 2:14

he *k* them that trust in him .... Nah 1:7
the unjust *k* no shame .... Zeph 3:5
for your Father *k* what things ye .... Mt 6:8
for your heavenly Father *k* that .... Mt 6:32
no man *k* the Son, but the Father .... Mt 11:27
neither *k* any man the Father, ... Mt 11:27
hour *k* no man, no, not the angels ...... Mt 24:36
spring and grow up, he *k* not how .... Mk 4:27
of that day and that hour *k* no man ..... Mk 13:32
no man *k* who the Son is, but the .... Lk 10:22
your Father *k* that ye have need .... Lk 12:30
but God *k* your hearts .... Lk 16:15
How *k* this man letters, having .... Jn 7:15
cometh, no man *k* whence he is .... Jn 7:27
But this people who *k* not the .... Jn 7:49
As the Father *k* me, even so know .... Jn 10:15
darkness *k* not whither he goeth .... Jn 12:35
it seeth him not, neither *k* him .... Jn 14:17
for the servant *k* not what his .... Jn 15:15
he *k* that he saith true, that ye .... Jn 19:35
which *k* the hearts, bare them .... Acts 15:8
what man is there that *k* not how .... Acts 19:35
For the king *k* of these things, ... Acts 26:26
he that searcheth the hearts *k* .... Rom 8:27
For what man *k* the things of a 1Cor 2:11
so the things of God *k* no man 1Cor 2:11
The Lord *k* the thoughts of the 1Cor 3:20
any man think that he *k* any thing 1Cor 8:2
he *k* nothing yet as he ought to 1Cor 8:2
I love you not? God *k* 2Cor 11:11
for evermore, *k* that I lie not 2Cor 11:31
I cannot tell: God *k* 2Cor 12:2
I cannot tell: God *k* 2Cor 12:3
The Lord *k* them that are his 2Ti 2:19
to him that *k* to do good, and .... Jas 4:17
The Lord *k* how to deliver the 2Pet 2:9
k not whither he goeth, because 1Jn 2:11
therefore the world *k* us not 1Jn 3:1
than our heart, and *k* all things 1Jn 3:20
he that *k* God heareth us 1Jn 4:6
loveth is born of God, and *k* God 1Jn 4:7
He that loveth not *k* not God 1Jn 4:8
which no man *k* saving the that .... Rev 2:17
because he *k* that he hath but a .... Rev 12:12

KNOWING

shall be as gods, *k* good and evil ...... Gen 3:5
my father David not *k* thereof 1Kin 2:32
Jesus *k* their thoughts said, ... Mt 9:4
not *k* the scriptures, nor the .... Mt 22:29
immediately *k* in himself that .... Mk 5:30
k what was done in her, came and .... Mk 5:33
k that he was a just man and an .... Mk 6:20
k their hypocrisy, said unto them ...... Mk 12:15
him to scorn, *k* that she was dead ...... Lk 8:53
not *k* what he said .... Lk 9:33
k their thoughts, said unto them, ... Lk 11:17
Jesus *k* that the Father had given ...... Jn 13:3
k all things that should come .... Jn 18:4
Jesus *k* that all things were now .... Jn 19:28
k that it was the Lord .... Jn 21:12
k that God had sworn with an oath ...... Acts 2:30
not *k* what was done, came in .... Acts 5:7
k only the baptism of John .... Acts 18:25
not *k* the things that shall .... Acts 20:22
Who *k* the judgment of God, that .... Rom 1:32
not *k* that the goodness of God .... Rom 2:4
that tribulation worketh .... Rom 5:3
K this, that our old man is .... Rom 6:6
K that Christ being raised from .... Rom 6:9
k the time, that now it is high .... Rom 13:11
And our hope of you is stedfast, *k* 2Cor 1:7
K that he which raised up the 2Cor 4:14
k that, whilst we are at home in 2Cor 5:6
K therefore the terror of the 2Cor 5:11
K that a man is not justified by .... Gal 2:16
k that whatsoever good thing any ...... Eph 6:8
k that your Master also is in .... Eph 6:9
k that I am set for the defence .... Phil 1:17
K that of the Lord ye shall .... Col 3:24
k that ye also have a Master in .... Col 4:1
K, brethren beloved, your 1Th 1:4
K this, that the law is not made 1Ti 1:9
k nothing, but doting about 1Ti 6:4
k that they do gender strifes 2Ti 2:23
k of whom thou hast learned them 2Ti 3:14
K that he that is such is .... Titus 3:11
k that thou wilt also do more .... Philem 21
k in yourselves that ye have in .... Heb 10:34
went out, not *k* whither he went .... Heb 11:8
K this, that the trying of your .... Jas 1:3
k that ye shall receive the .... Jas 3:1
k that ye are thereunto called, ... 1Pet 3:9
k that the same afflictions are 1Pet 5:9
K that shortly I must put off 2Pet 1:14
K this first, that no prophecy of 2Pet 1:20
K this first, that there shall 2Pet 3:3

KNOWLEDGE

garden, and the tree of *k* of good ...... Gen 2:9
But of the tree of the *k* of good .... Gen 2:17
and in understanding, and in *k* .... Ex 31:3
wisdom, in understanding, and in *k* .... Ex 35:31
he hath sinned, come to his *k* .... Lev 4:23
he hath sinned, come to his *k* .... Lev 4:28
without the *k* of the congregation ...... Num 15:24
knew the *k* of the most High, ... Num 24:16
in that day had no *k* between good ...... Deut 1:39
that thou shouldest take *k* of me .... Ruth 2:10
be he that did take *k* of thee .... Ruth 2:19
the LORD is a God of *k* 1Sa 2:3

take *k* of all the lurking places 1Sa 23:23
shipmen that had *k* of the sea 1Kin 9:27
Give me now wisdom and *k*, that I 2Chr 1:10
k for thyself, that thou mayest 2Chr 1:11
Wisdom and *k* is granted unto thee 2Chr 1:12
and servants that had *k* of the sea 2Chr 8:18
taught the good *k* of the LORD 2Chr 30:22
daughters, every one having *k* .... Neh 10:28
Should a wise man utter vain *k* .... Job 15:2
we desire not the *k* of thy ways .... Job 21:14
Shall any teach God *k* .... Job 21:22
and my lips shall utter *k* clearly ...... Job 33:3
give ear unto me, ye that have *k* .... Job 34:2
Job hath spoken without *k* .... Job 34:35
he multiplieth words without *k* .... Job 35:16
I will fetch my *k* from afar .... Job 36:3
that is perfect in *k* is with thee ...... Job 36:4
and they shall die without *k* .... Job 36:12
of him which is perfect in *k* .... Job 37:16
counsel by words without *k* .... Job 38:2
he that hideth counsel without *k* .... Job 42:3
all the workers of iniquity no *k* .... Ps 14:4
and night unto night sheweth *k* .... Ps 19:2
Have the workers of iniquity no *k* ...... Ps 53:4
is there *k* in the most High .... Ps 73:11
he that teacheth man *k*, shall not ...... Ps 94:10
Teach me good judgment and *k* .... Ps 119:66
Such is too wonderful for me .... Ps 139:6
is man, that thou takest *k* of him ...... Ps 144:3
to the simple, to the young man *k* ...... Prov 1:4
of the LORD is the beginning of *k* ...... Prov 1:7
their scorning, and fools hate *k* ...... Prov 1:22
For that they hated *k*, and did not ..... Prov 1:29
Yea, if thou criest after *k* .... Prov 2:3
of the LORD, and find the *k* of God ..... Prov 2:5
out of his mouth cometh *k* .... Prov 2:6
k is pleasant unto thy soul .... Prov 2:10
By his *k* the depths are broken up ...... Prov 3:20
and that thy lips may keep *k* .... Prov 5:2
and right to them that find *k* .... Prov 8:9
k rather than choice gold .... Prov 8:10
find out *k* of witty inventions .... Prov 8:12
and the *k* of the holy is .... Prov 9:10
Wise men lay up *k* .... Prov 10:14
but through *k* shall the just be .... Prov 11:9
Whoso loveth instruction loveth *k* ...... Prov 12:1
A prudent man concealeth *k* .... Prov 12:23
Every prudent man dealeth with *k* .... Prov 13:16
but *k* is easy unto him that .... Prov 14:6
not in him the lips of *k* .... Prov 14:7
the prudent are crowned with *k* .... Prov 14:18
tongue of the wise useth *k* aright ...... Prov 15:2
The lips of the wise disperse *k* .... Prov 15:7
that hath understanding seeketh *k* ...... Prov 15:14
He that hath *k* spareth his words .... Prov 17:27
heart of the prudent getteth *k* .... Prov 18:15
and the ear of the wise seeketh *k* ...... Prov 18:15
Also, that the soul be without *k* .... Prov 19:2
and he will understand *k* .... Prov 19:25
to err from the words of *k* .... Prov 19:27
but the lips of *k* are a precious .... Prov 20:15
is instructed, he receiveth *k* .... Prov 21:11
The eyes of the LORD preserve *k* .... Prov 22:12
and apply thine heart unto my *k* .... Prov 22:17
excellent things in counsels and *k* .... Prov 22:20
and thine ears to the words of *k* .... Prov 23:12
by *k* shall the chambers be filled ...... Prov 24:4
a man of *k* increaseth strength .... Prov 24:5
So shall the *k* of wisdom be unto .... Prov 24:14
k the state thereof shall be .... Prov 28:2
nor have the *k* of the holy .... Prov 30:3
great experience of wisdom and *k* ...... Eccl 1:16
increaseth *k* increaseth sorrow .... Eccl 1:18
labour is in wisdom, and in *k* .... Eccl 2:21
is good in his sight wisdom, and *k* ..... Eccl 2:26
but the excellency of *k* is .... Eccl 7:12
is no work, nor device, nor *k* .... Eccl 9:10
he still taught the people *k* .... Eccl 12:9
captivity, because they have no *k* ...... Is 5:13
the child shall have *k* to cry .... Is 8:4
counsel and might, the spirit of *k* ..... Is 11:2
be full of the *k* of the LORD .... Is 11:9
Whom shall he teach *k* .... Is 28:9
of the rash shall understand *k* .... Is 32:4
k shall be the stability of thy .... Is 33:6
path of judgment, and taught him *k* ..... Is 40:14
his heart, neither is there *k* nor ...... Is 44:19
and maketh their *k* foolish .... Is 44:25
they have no *k* that set up the .... Is 45:20
Thy wisdom and thy *k*, it hath .... Is 47:10
by his *k* shall my righteous .... Is 53:11
our soul, and thou takest no *k* .... Is 58:3
which shall feed you with *k* .... Jer 3:15
but to do good they have no *k* .... Jer 4:22
Every man is brutish in his *k* .... Jer 10:14
And the LORD hath given me *k* of it ..... Jer 11:18
Every man is brutish by his *k* .... Jer 51:17
in all wisdom, and cunning in *k* .... Dan 1:4
four children, God gave them *k* .... Dan 1:17
k to them that know understanding ...... Dan 2:21
as an excellent spirit, and *k* .... Dan 5:12
and fro, and *k* shall be increased ...... Dan 12:4
mercy, nor *k* of God in the land .... Hos 4:1
are destroyed for lack of *k* .... Hos 4:6
because thou hast rejected *k* .... Hos 4:6
the *k* of God more than burnt .... Hos 6:6
the *k* of the glory of the LORD .... Hab 2:14
the priest's lips should keep *k* .... Mal 2:7
men of that place had *k* of him .... Mt 14:35
To give *k* of salvation unto his .... Lk 1:77

K

KNOWN

ye have taken away the key of *k*...... Lk 11:52
and they took *k* of them, that they ... Acts 4:13
had *k* that the word of God was...... Acts 17:13
mayest take *k* of all these things...... Acts 24:8
having more perfect *k* of that way.... Acts 24:22
not like to retain God in their *k* ..... Rom 1:28
babes, which hast the form of *k* ...... Rom 2:20
for by the law is the *k* of sin .... Rom 3:20
of God, but not according to *k* .... Rom 10:2
both of the wisdom and *k* of God .... Rom 11:33
of goodness, filled with all *k* .... Rom 15:14
in all utterance, and in all *k* 1Cor 1:5
idols, we know that we all have *k* ... 1Cor 8:1
K puffeth up, but charity 1Cor 8:1
there is not in every man that *k* 1Cor 8:7
hast *k* sit at meat in the idol's 1Cor 8:10
through thy *k* shall the weak.......... 1Cor 8:11
the word of *k* by the same Spirit..... 1Cor 12:8
all mysteries, and all *k* 1Cor 13:2
whether there be *k*, it shall.......... 1Cor 13:8
you either by revelation, or by *k* 1Cor 14:6
for some have not the *k* of God 1Cor 15:34
of his *k* by us in every place.......... 2Cor 2:14
to give the light of the *k* of the 2Cor 4:6
By pureness, by *k*, by 2Cor 6:6
in faith, and utterance, and *k* 2Cor 8:7
itself against the *k* of God 2Cor 10:5
I be rude in speech, yet not in *k* 2Cor 11:6
and revelation in the *k* of him....... Eph 1:17
ye may understand my *k* in the ...... Eph 3:4
love of Christ, which passeth *k* ...... Eph 3:19
of the *k* of the Son of God, unto .... Eph 4:13
may abound yet more and more in *k*. Phil 1:9
of the *k* of Christ Jesus my Lord .... Phil 3:8
the *k* of his will in all wisdom....... Col 1:9
and increasing in the *k* of God....... Col 1:10
all the treasures of wisdom and *k*.... Col 2:3
which is renewed in *k* after the ..... Col 3:10
to come unto the *k* of the truth 1Ti 2:4
to come to the *k* of the truth........ 2Ti 3:7
have received the *k* of the truth..... Heb 10:26
man and endued with *k* among you.. Jas 3:13
dwell with them according to *k* 1Pet 3:7
unto you through the *k* of God 2Pet 1:2
through the *k* of him that hath....... 2Pet 1:3
and to virtue *k* 2Pet 1:5
And to *k* temperance 2Pet 1:6
in the *k* of our Lord Jesus Christ 2Pet 1:8
world through the *k* of the Lord..... 2Pet 2:20
in the *k* of our Lord and Saviour..... 2Pet 3:18

KNOWN

daughters which have not *k* man...... Gen 19:8
virgin, neither had any man *k* her ... Gen 24:16
it could not be *k* that they had....... Gen 41:21
the plenty shall not be *k* in the...... Gen 41:31
made himself *k* unto his brethren.... Gen 45:1
and said, Surely this thing is *k* ...... Ex 2:14
name JEHOVAH was I not *k* to them .. Ex 6:3
Or if it be *k* that the ox hath .... Ex 21:36
wherein shall it be *k* that there I ... Ex 33:16
they have sinned against it, is *k* .... Lev 4:14
whether he hath seen or *k* of it ..... Lev 5:1
myself *k* unto him in a vision .... Num 12:6
that hath *k* man by lying with him .. Num 31:17
that have not *k* a man by lying....... Num 31:18
had not *k* man by lying with him .... Num 31:35
k among your tribes, and I will....... Deut 1:13
of your tribes, wise men, and *k* ...... Deut 1:15
your children which have not *k* ...... Deut 1:39
other gods, which ye have not *k* ..... Deut 11:28
other gods, which thou hast not *k* ... Deut 13:2
other gods, which thou hast not *k* ... Deut 13:6
other gods, which ye have not *k* ...... Deut 13:13
it be not *k* who hath slain him....... Deut 21:1
thou nor thy fathers have *k* .... Deut 28:36
thou nor thy fathers have *k* .... Deut 28:64
which have not *k* any thing .... Deut 31:13
which had *k* all the works of the .... Josh 24:31
had not *k* all the wars of Canaan .... Judg 3:1
So his strength was not *k* .... Judg 16:9
that had *k* no man by lying with ..... Judg 21:12
make not thyself *k* unto the man.... Ruth 3:3
Let it not be *k* that a woman came.. Ruth 3:14
it shall be *k* to you why his hand.... 1Sa 6:3
that thou mayest make *k* unto me ... 1Sa 28:15
and the thing was not *k* 2Sa 17:19
that thou be not *k* to be the wife... 1Kin 14:2
let it be *k* this day that thou 1Kin 18:36
make *k* his deeds among the people.. 1Chr 16:8
in making *k* all these great............ 1Chr 17:19
Be it *k* unto the king, that the ...... Ezr 4:12
Be it *k* now unto the king, that,..... Ezr 4:13
Be it *k* unto the king, that we .... Ezr 5:8
heard that it was *k* unto us .... Neh 4:15
madest *k* unto them thy holy .... Neh 9:14
And the thing was *k* to Mordecai..... Est 2:22
The LORD is *k* by the judgment........ Ps 9:16
whom I have not *k* shall serve me ... Ps 18:43
thou hast *k* my soul in .... Ps 31:7
God is *k* in her palaces for a .... Ps 48:3
That thy way may be *k* upon earth .. Ps 67:2
Thou hast *k* my reproach, and my ... Ps 69:19
in Judah is God *k* ....Ps 76:1
and thy footsteps are not *k* .... Ps 77:19
Which we have heard and *k*, and our Ps 78:3
make them *k* to their children....... Ps 78:5
the heathen that have not *k* thee.... Ps 79:6
let him be *k* among the heathen in . Ps 79:10
thy wonders be *k* in the dark .... Ps 88:12
I make *k* thy faithfulness to all...... Ps 89:1
high, because he hath *k* my name..... Ps 91:14
heart, and they have not *k* my ways.. Ps 95:10
LORD hath made *k* his salvation........ Ps 98:2
He made *k* his ways unto Moses,...... Ps 103:7
make *k* his deeds among the people . Ps 105:1
make his mighty power to be *k* .... Ps 106:8
those that have *k* thy testimonies ... Ps 119:79
I have *k* of old that thou hast .... Ps 119:152
thou hast searched me, and *k* me..... Ps 139:1
To make *k* to the sons of men his.... Ps 145:12
judgments, they have not *k* them..... Ps 147:20
I will make *k* my words unto you..... Prov 1:23
perverteth his ways shall be *k* .... Prov 10:9
A fool's wrath is presently *k* .... Prov 12:16
in the midst of fools is made *k* ...... Prov 14:33
Even a child is *k* by his doings........ Prov 20:11
I have made *k* to thee this day,...... Prov 22:19
Her husband is *k* in the gates .... Prov 31:23
a fool's voice is *k* by multitude ...... Eccl 5:3
not seen the sun, nor *k* any thing.... Eccl 6:5
and it is *k* that it is man .... Eccl 6:10
this is *k* in all the earth .... Is 12:5
And the LORD shall be *k* to Egypt...... Is 19:21
children shall make *k* thy truth ...... Is 38:19
Have ye not *k*? .... Is 40:21
Hast thou not *k*? .... Is 40:28
in paths that they have not *k* .... Is 42:16
They have not *k* nor understood...... Is 44:18
thee, though thou hast not *k* me ..... Is 45:4
thee, though thou hast not *k* me ..... Is 45:5
shall be *k* among the Gentiles .... Is 61:9
to make thy name *k* to thine......... Is 64:2
shall be *k* toward his servants .... Is 66:14
is foolish, they have not *k* me .... Jer 4:22
for they have *k* the way of the ...... Jer 5:5
they nor their fathers have *k* .... Jer 9:16
they nor their fathers have *k* .... Jer 19:4
pass, then shall the prophet be *k* .... Jer 28:9
they are not *k* in the streets .... Lam 4:8
made myself *k* unto them in the ..... Eze 20:5
sight I made myself *k* unto them .... Eze 20:9
countries which thou hast not *k* ..... Eze 32:9
I will make myself *k* among them .... Eze 35:11
the Lord GOD, be it *k* unto you....... Eze 36:32
I will be *k* in the eyes of many ...... Eze 38:23
name *k* in the midst of my people ... Eze 39:7
will not make *k* unto me the dream . Dan 2:5
will not make *k* unto me the dream . Dan 2:9
Arioch made the thing *k* to Daniel ... Dan 2:15
and made the thing *k* to Hananiah... Dan 2:17
hast made *k* unto me now what we ... Dan 2:23
for thou hast now made *k* unto us ... Dan 2:23
that will make *k* unto the king .... Dan 2:25
Art thou able to make *k* unto me .... Dan 2:26
secrets, and maketh *k* to the king ... Dan 2:28
that revealeth secrets maketh *k* ..... Dan 2:29
the interpretation to the king........ Dan 2:30
the great God hath made *k* to the ... Dan 2:45
be it *k* unto thee, O king, that ...... Dan 3:18
that they might make *k* unto me..... Dan 4:6
but they did not make *k* unto me .... Dan 4:7
make *k* unto me the interpretation .. Dan 4:18
have *k* that the heavens do rule...... Dan 4:26
nor make *k* to the king the .... Dan 5:8
make *k* unto me the interpretation .. Dan 5:15
make *k* to me the interpretation .... Dan 5:16
make *k* to him the interpretation ... Dan 5:17
them, and they have not *k* the LORD.. Hos 5:4
made *k* that which shall surely be ... Hos 5:9
You only have I *k* of all the .... Amos 3:2
place is not *k* where they are......... Nah 3:17
in the midst of the years make *k* .... Hab 3:2
day which shall be *k* to the God...... Zec 14:7
and told, that shall not be *k* .... Mt 10:26
But if ye had *k* what this meaneth... Mt 12:7
that they should not make him *k* .... Mt 12:16
for the tree is *k* by his fruit.......... Mt 12:33
k in what watch the thief would..... Mt 24:43
that they should not make *k* .... Mk 3:12
the Lord hath made *k* unto us......... Lk 2:15
they made *k* abroad the saying ...... Lk 2:17
every tree is *k* by his own fruit...... Lk 6:44
were a prophet, would have *k* who .. Lk 7:39
thing hid, that shall not be *k* .... Lk 8:17
neither hid, that shall not be *k* ...... Lk 12:2
k what hour the thief would come .. Lk 12:39
Saying, If thou hadst *k*, even......... Lk 19:42
hast not *k* the things which are ...... Lk 24:18
how he was *k* of them in breaking ... Lk 24:35
he himself seeketh to be *k* openly ... Jn 7:4
if ye had *k* me, ye should have ...... Jn 8:19
ye should have *k* my Father also..... Jn 8:19
Yet ye have not *k* him .... Jn 8:55
and know my sheep, and am *k* of mine Jn 10:14
If ye had *k* me, ye should have ...... Jn 14:7
ye should have *k* my Father also..... Jn 14:7
you, and yet hast thou not *k* me ..... Jn 14:9
my Father I have made *k* unto you... Jn 15:15
they have not *k* the Father .... Jn 16:3
Now they have *k* that all things...... Jn 17:7
have *k* surely that I came out of ..... Jn 17:8
Father, the world hath not *k* thee.... Jn 17:25
but I have *k* thee, and these have.... Jn 17:25
these have *k* that thou hast sent .... Jn 17:25
that disciple was *k* unto the high .... Jn 18:15
which was *k* unto the high priest .... Jn 18:16
it was *k* unto all the dwellers at..... Acts 1:19
be this *k* unto you, and hearken to... Acts 2:14
Thou hast made *k* to me the ways.... Acts 2:28
Be it *k* unto you all, and to all ...... Acts 4:10
Joseph was made *k* to his brethren.... Acts 7:13
kindred was made *k* unto Pharaoh .... Acts 7:13
their laying await was *k* of Saul....... Acts 9:24
it was *k* throughout all Joppa.......... Acts 9:42
Be it *k* unto you therefore, men....... Acts 13:38
K unto God are all his works from .... Acts 15:18
this was *k* to all the Jews and........ Acts 19:17
because he would have *k* the .... Acts 22:30
when I would have *k* the cause .... Acts 23:28
Be it *k* therefore unto you, that ..... Acts 28:28
Because that which may be *k* of ...... Rom 1:19
the way of peace have they not *k* .... Rom 3:17
Nay, I had not *k* sin, but by the ..... Rom 7:7
for I had not *k* lust, except the...... Rom 7:7
his wrath, and to make his power *k* .. Rom 9:22
that he might make *k* the riches ..... Rom 9:23
For who hath *k* the mind of the ..... Rom 11:34
made *k* to all nations for the .... Rom 16:26
for had they *k* it, they would not.... 1Cor 2:8
For who hath *k* the mind of the 1Cor 2:16
love God, the same is *k* of him 1Cor 8:3
shall I know even as also I am *k* 1Cor 13:12
how shall it be *k* what is piped 1Cor 14:7
how shall it be *k* what is spoken 1Cor 14:9
epistle written in our hearts, *k* 2Cor 3:2
though we have *k* Christ after the ... 2Cor 5:16
As unknown, and yet well *k*........... 2Cor 6:9
But now, after that ye have *k* God ... Gal 4:9
or rather are *k* of God................. Gal 4:9
Having made *k* unto us the mystery . Eph 1:9
he made *k* unto me the mystery ..... Eph 3:3
not made *k* unto the sons of men.... Eph 3:5
be *k* by the church the manifold ..... Eph 3:10
to make *k* the mystery of the .... Eph 6:19
shall make *k* to you all things........ Eph 6:21
your moderation be *k* unto all men.. Phil 4:5
your requests be made *k* unto God... Phil 4:6
To whom God would make *k* what is . Col 1:27
They shall make *k* unto you all ...... Col 4:9
But thou hast fully *k* my doctrine.... 2Ti 3:10
thou hast *k* the holy scriptures 2Ti 3:15
me the preaching might be fully *k* ... 2Ti 4:17
and they have not *k* my ways......... Heb 3:10
when we made *k* unto you the power. 2Pet 1:16
have *k* the way of righteousness...... 2Pet 2:21
than, after they have *k* it............. 2Pet 2:21
because ye have *k* him that is 1Jn 2:13
because ye have *k* the Father......... 1Jn 2:13
because ye have *k* him that is 1Jn 2:14
hath not seen him, neither *k* him 1Jn 3:6
And we have *k* and believed the love 1Jn 4:16
all they that have *k* the truth 2Jn 1
which have not *k* the depths of...... Rev 2:24

KOA (ko´-ah) An obscure tribe.

Chaldeans, Pekod, and Shoa, and K .... Eze 23:23

KOHATH (ko´-hath) See KOHATHITES. A son of Levi.

Gershon, K, and Merari .... Gen 46:11
Gershon, K, and Merari .... Ex 6:16
and the sons of K .... Ex 6:18
life of K were an hundred thirty ..... Ex 6:18
Gershon, and K, and Merari........... Num 3:17
the sons of K by their families....... Num 3:19
of K was the family of the............ Num 3:27
The families of the sons of K......... Num 3:29
of K from among the sons of Levi.... Num 4:2
of K in the tabernacle of the .... Num 4:4
the sons of K shall come to bear..... Num 4:15
of K in the tabernacle of the .... Num 4:15
unto the sons of K he gave none.... Num 7:9
the son of Izhar, the son of K .... Num 16:1
of K, the family of the .... Num 26:57
And K begat Amram...................... Num 26:58
the rest of the children of K had ... Josh 21:5
the families of the children of K .... Josh 21:20
remained of the children of K .... Josh 21:26
the children of K that remained...... Josh 21:26
Gershon, K, and Merari................. 1Chr 6:1
and the sons of K 1Chr 6:2
Gershom, K, and Merari 1Chr 6:16
the son of K, the son of 1Chr 6:22
and the sons of K were, Amram, and . 1Chr 6:18
The sons of K 1Chr 6:22
The son of Izhar, the son of K 1Chr 6:38
And unto the sons of K, which were . 1Chr 6:61
K had cities of their coasts out...... 1Chr 6:66
of the remnant of the sons of K 1Chr 6:70
Of the sons of K 1Chr 15:5
sons of Levi, namely, Gershon, K 1Chr 23:6
the son of K 1Chr 23:12

KOHATHITES (ko´-hath-ites) Descendants of Kohath.

these are the families of the K....... Num 3:27
K shall be Elizaphan the son of ..... Num 3:30
of the K from among the Levites..... Num 4:18
of the K after their families .... Num 4:34
numbered of the families of the K... Num 4:37
the K set forward, bearing the....... Num 10:21
of Kohath, the family of the K ...... Num 26:57
out for the families of the K......... Josh 21:10
being of the families of the K .... Josh 21:10
Of the sons of K 1Chr 6:33
Aaron, of the families of the K 1Chr 6:54
brethren, of the sons of K 1Chr 9:32
Levites, of the children of the K..... 2Chr 20:19
of Azariah, of the sons of the K 2Chr 29:12
Meshullam, of the sons of the K 2Chr 34:12

KOLAIAH (ko-la-i´-ah)

I. A family of exiles.
the son of Pedaiah, the son of K...... Neh 11:7

2. Father of Ahab.

of Israel, of Ahab the son of K.............. Jer 29:21

KORAH (ko'-rah) See CORE, KORAHITE, KORE.

1. A son of Esau.

bare Jeush, and Jaalam, and K...........	Gen 36:5
to Esau Jeush, and Jaalam, and K......	Gen 36:14
duke Jeush, duke Jaalam, duke K......	Gen 36:18
Reuel, and Jeush, and Jaalam, and K..	1Chr 1:35

2. A son of Eliphaz.

Duke K, duke Gatam, and duke........... Gen 36:16

3. A conspirator against Moses.

K, and Nepheg, and Zichri.................	Ex 6:21
And the sons of K.............................	Ex 6:24
Now K, the son of Izhar, the son......	Num 16:1
And he spake unto K and unto all......	Num 16:5
Take you censers, K, and all his........	Num 16:6
And Moses said unto K, Hear, I.........	Num 16:8
And Moses said unto K......................	Num 16:16
K gathered all the congregation........	Num 16:19
up from about the tabernacle of K.....	Num 16:24
gat up from the tabernacle of K........	Num 16:27
the men that appertained unto K.......	Num 16:32
that he be not as K, and as his.........	Num 16:40
that died about the matter of K........	Num 16:49
against Aaron in the company of K....	Num 26:9
swallowed them up together with K....	Num 26:10
the children of K died not.................	Num 26:11
the LORD in the company of K...........	Num 27:3
the son of Ebiasaph, the son of K.....	1Chr 6:37
the son of Ebiasaph, the son of K.....	1Chr 9:19

4. A son of Hebron.

K, and Tappuah, and Rekem.............. 1Chr 2:43

5. A grandson of Kohath.

K his son, Assir his son,....................	1Chr 6:22
Maschil, for the sons of K..................	Ps 42:t
chief Musician for the sons of K........	Ps 44:t
Shoshannim, for the sons of K..........	Ps 45:t
chief Musician for the sons of K........	Ps 46:t
A Psalm for the sons of K..................	Ps 47:t
A Song and Psalm for the sons of K..	Ps 48:t
A Psalm for the sons of K..................	Ps 49:t
A Psalm for the sons of K..................	Ps 84:t
A Psalm for the sons of K..................	Ps 85:t
A Psalm or Song for the sons of K.....	Ps 87:t
of K to the chief Musician upon.........	Ps 88:t

KORAHITE (ko'-ra-hite) See KORAHITES, KORE.

A descendant of Korah.

the firstborn of Shallum the K........... 1Chr 9:31

KORAHITES (ko'-ra-hites) See KORATHITES, KORITES.

of the house of his father, the K........ 1Chr 9:19

KORATHITES (ko'-ra-thites) See KORAHITES.

Same as Korahites.

the Mushites, the family of the K....... Num 26:58

KORAZIN See CHORAZIN.

KORE (ko'-re)

1. Father of Shallum.

And Shallum the son of K, the son.....	1Chr 9:19
was Meshelemiah the son of K..........	1Chr 26:1
the porters among the sons of K.......	1Chr 26:19

2. A Temple servant.

K the son of Imnah the Levite,........... 2Chr 31:14

KORHITES (kor'-hites) See KORAHITES. Same as Korahites.

these are the families of the K..........	Ex 6:24
and Joezer, and Jashobeam, the K....	1Chr 12:6
Of the K was Meshelemiah the son....	1Chr 26:1
and of the children of K.....................	2Chr 20:19

KOUM See CUMI.

KOZ (coz) See HAKKOZ.

1. A family of priests.

of Habaiah, the children of K.............	Ezr 2:61
of Habaiah, the children of K.............	Neh 7:63

2. Father of two rebuilders of the wall.

the son of Urijah, the son of K...........	Neh 3:4
Urijah the son of K another piece.......	Neh 3:21

KUSHAIAH (cu-shah'-yah) See KISHI. Father of Ethan.

brethren, Ethan the son of K.............. 1Chr 15:17

L

LAADAH (la'-a-dah) Son of Shelah.

L the father of Mareshah, and the..... 1Chr 4:21

LAADAN (la'-a-dan) See LIBNI.

1. A descendant of Ephraim.

L his son, Ammihud his son,.............. 1Chr 7:26

2. A descendant of Gershon.

Of the Gershonites were, L.................	1Chr 23:7
The sons of L....................................	1Chr 23:8
the chief of the fathers of L...............	1Chr 23:9
As concerning the sons of L..............	1Chr 26:21
the sons of the Gershonite L.............	1Chr 26:21
even of L the Gershonite, were..........	1Chr 26:21

LABAN (la'-ban) See LABAN'S, LIBNAH.

1. Father of Rachel.

had a brother, and his name was L....	Gen 24:29
L ran out unto the man, unto the.......	Gen 24:29

Then L and Bethuel answered and......	Gen 24:50
the sister to L the Syrian....................	Gen 25:20
flee thou to L my brother to..............	Gen 27:43
of L thy mother's brother...................	Gen 28:2
and he went to Padan-aram unto L....	Gen 28:5
Know ye L the son of Nahor...............	Gen 29:5
of L his mother's brother....................	Gen 29:10
the sheep of L his mother's...............	Gen 29:10
flock of L his mother's brother...........	Gen 29:10
when L heard the tidings of Jacob.....	Gen 29:13
he told L all these things..................	Gen 29:13
L said to him, Surely thou art my......	Gen 29:14
L said unto Jacob, Because thou.......	Gen 29:15
And L had two daughters...................	Gen 29:16
L said, It is better that I give.............	Gen 29:19
And Jacob said unto L, Give me my....	Gen 29:21
L gathered together all the men........	Gen 29:22
L gave unto his daughter Leah..........	Gen 29:24
and he said to L, What is this...........	Gen 29:25
L said, It must not be so done in.......	Gen 29:26
L gave to Rachel his daughter..........	Gen 29:29
Joseph, that Jacob said unto L.........	Gen 30:25
L said unto him, I pray thee, if.........	Gen 30:27
L said, Behold, I would it might........	Gen 30:34
all the brown in the flock of L...........	Gen 30:40
Jacob beheld the countenance of L....	Gen 31:2
seen all that L doeth unto thee.........	Gen 31:12
L went to shear his sheep.................	Gen 31:19
away unawares to L the Syrian.........	Gen 31:20
it was told L on the third day............	Gen 31:22
God came to L the Syrian in a...........	Gen 31:24
Then L overtook Jacob......................	Gen 31:25
L with his brethren pitched in...........	Gen 31:25
L said to Jacob, What hast thou........	Gen 31:26
And Jacob answered and said to L....	Gen 31:31
L went into Jacob's tent, and into.....	Gen 31:33
L searched all the tent, but..............	Gen 31:34
Jacob was wroth, and chode with L...	Gen 31:36
and Jacob answered and said to L....	Gen 31:36
L answered and said unto Jacob,......	Gen 31:43
L called it Jegar-sahadutha.............	Gen 31:47
L said, This heap is a witness..........	Gen 31:48
L said to Jacob, Behold this heap.....	Gen 31:51
And early in the morning L rose up....	Gen 31:55
L departed, and returned unto his.....	Gen 31:55
thus, I have sojourned with L............	Gen 32:4
whom L gave to Leah his daughter,....	Gen 46:18
L gave unto Rachel his....................	Gen 46:25

2. A Hebrew encampment in the wilderness.

between Paran, and Tophel, and L..... Deut 1:1

LABAN'S (la'-bans) Refers to Laban 1.

and Jacob fed the rest of L flocks.....	Gen 30:36
and put them not unto L cattle..........	Gen 30:40
so the feebler were L, and the..........	Gen 30:42
And he heard the words of L sons......	Gen 31:1

LABOUR

the l of my hands, and rebuked........	Gen 31:42
travailed, and she had hard l...........	Gen 35:16
to pass, when she was in hard l........	Gen 35:17
the men, that they may l therein.......	Ex 5:9
Six days shalt thou l, and do all.......	Ex 20:9
Six days thou shalt l, and do all.......	Deut 5:13
on our affliction, and our..................	Deut 26:7
not all the people to l thither............	Josh 7:3
you a land for which ye did not l.......	Josh 24:13
be a guard to us, and l on the day....	Neh 4:22
man from his house, and from his l...	Neh 5:13
I be wicked, why then l I in vain........	Job 9:29
or wilt thou leave thy l to him..........	Job 39:11
her l is in vain without fear..............	Job 39:16
and their l unto the locust...............	Ps 78:46
years, yet is their strength l............	Ps 90:10
to his l until the evening..................	Ps 104:23
inherited the l of the people.............	Ps 105:44
brought down their heart with l.........	Ps 107:12
and let the strangers spoil his l........	Ps 109:11
they l in vain that build it.................	Ps 127:1
shalt eat the l of the hands..............	Ps 128:2
That our oxen may be strong to l.......	Ps 144:14
The l of the righteous tendeth to......	Prov 10:16
gathereth by l shall increase...........	Prov 13:11
In all l there is profit.......................	Prov 14:23
for his hands refuse to l..................	Prov 21:25
L not to be rich..............................	Prov 23:4
profit hath a man of all his l.............	Eccl 1:3
All things are full of l......................	Eccl 1:8
for my heart rejoiced in all my l.......	Eccl 2:10
this was my portion of all my l.........	Eccl 2:10
on the l that I had l laboured to........	Eccl 2:11
I hated all my l which I had..............	Eccl 2:18
all my l wherein I have laboured.......	Eccl 2:19
the l which I took under the sun.......	Eccl 2:20
is a man whose l is in wisdom..........	Eccl 2:21
For what hath man of all his l...........	Eccl 2:22
make his soul enjoy good in his l......	Eccl 2:24
and enjoy the good of all his l..........	Eccl 3:13
yet is there no end of all his l..........	Eccl 4:8
neither saith he, For whom do I l......	Eccl 4:8
have a good reward for their l...........	Eccl 4:9
and shall take nothing of his l..........	Eccl 5:15
l that he taketh under the sun.........	Eccl 5:18
portion, and to rejoice in his l.........	Eccl 5:19
All the l of man is for his mouth........	Eccl 6:7
him of his l the days of his life........	Eccl 8:15
though a man l to seek it out............	Eccl 8:17
to l in it which thou takest under.....	Eccl 9:9
The l of the foolish wearieth............	Eccl 10:15
l not to comfort me, because of........	Is 22:4
The l of Egypt, and merchandise of...	Is 45:14
your l for that which satisfieth..........	Is 55:2

They shall not l in vain, nor..............	Is 65:23
For shame hath devoured the l of......	Jer 3:24
I forth out of the womb to see l.........	Jer 20:18
and the people shall l in vain............	Jer 51:58
we l, and have no rest.....................	Lam 5:5
and shall take away all thy l.............	Eze 23:29
him the land of Egypt for his l...........	Eze 29:20
l to bring forth, O daughter of..........	Mic 4:10
people shall l in the very fire............	Hab 2:13
the l of the olive shall fail, and.........	Hab 3:17
and upon all the l of the hands.........	Hag 1:11
Come unto me, all ye that l...............	Mt 11:28
that whereon ye bestowed no l.........	Jn 4:38
L not for the meat which..................	Jn 6:27
Mary, who bestowed much l on us.....	Rom 16:6
and Tryphosa, who l in the Lord........	Rom 16:12
own reward according to his own l.....	1Cor 3:8
And l, working with our own hands....	1Cor 4:12
your l is not in vain in the Lord..........	1Cor 15:58
Wherefore we l, that, whether..........	2Cor 5:9
have bestowed upon you l in vain......	Gal 4:11
but rather let him l, working.............	Eph 4:28
flesh, this is the fruit of my l............	Phil 1:22
my brother, and companion in l........	Phil 2:25
Whereunto I also l, striving..............	Col 1:29
l of love, and patience of hope in.....	1Th 1:3
For ye remember, brethren, our l......	1Th 2:9
tempted you, and our l be in vain......	1Th 3:5
to know them which l among you.......	1Th 5:12
but wrought with l and travail...........	2Th 3:8
For therefore we both l and suffer.....	1Ti 4:10
especially they which l in the word....	1Ti 5:17
Let us l therefore to enter into..........	Heb 4:11
l of love, which ye have shewed........	Heb 6:10
I know thy works, and thy l...............	Rev 2:2

LABOURED

So we l in the work.........................	Neh 4:21
That which he l for shall he..............	Job 20:18
on the labour that I had l to do.........	Eccl 2:11
all my labour wherein I have l..........	Eccl 2:19
yet to a man that hath not l..............	Eccl 2:21
wherein he hath l under the sun.......	Eccl 2:22
hath he that hath l for the wind.......	Eccl 5:16
thou hast l from thy youth...............	Is 47:12
unto thee with whom thou hast l.......	Is 47:15
I have l in vain, I have spent my.......	Is 49:4
wine, for the which thou hast l.........	Is 62:8
he l till the going down of the..........	Dan 6:14
for the which thou hast not l............	Jonah 4:10
other men l, and ye are entered.......	Jn 4:38
Persis, which l much in the Lord.......	Rom 16:12
but I l more abundantly than they.....	1Cor 15:10
run in vain, neither l in vain.............	Phil 2:16
which l with me in the gospel...........	Phil 4:3
and for my name's sake hast l..........	Rev 2:3

LABOURER

for the l is worthy of his hire............	Lk 10:7
The l is worthy of his reward............	1Ti 5:18

LABOURERS

is plenteous, but the l are few..........	Mt 9:37
send forth l into his harvest.............	Mt 9:38
to hire l into his vineyard.................	Mt 20:1
with the l for a penny a day..............	Mt 20:2
unto his steward, Call the l..............	Mt 20:8
truly is great, but the l are few.........	Lk 10:2
send forth l into his harvest.............	Lk 10:2
For we are l together with God..........	1Cor 3:9
the hire of the l who have reaped.....	Jas 5:4

LABOURETH

He that l for himself........................	Prov 16:26
He that l for himself........................	Prov 16:26
that worketh in that wherein he l......	Eccl 3:9
one that helpeth with us, and l........	1Cor 16:16
The husbandman that l must be........	2Ti 2:6

LABOURING

The sleep of a l man is sweet..........	Eccl 5:12
how that so l ye ought to support.....	Acts 20:35
always l fervently for you in.............	Col 4:12
for l night and day, because we........	1Th 2:9

LABOURS

harvest, the firstfruits of thy l..........	Ex 23:16
in thy l out of the field....................	Ex 23:16
fruit of thy land, and all thy l............	Deut 28:33
thy l be in the house of a................	Prov 5:10
pleasure, and exact all your l..........	Is 58:3
this city, and all the l thereof..........	Jer 20:5
in all my l they shall find none.........	Hos 12:8
hail in all the l of your hands...........	Hag 2:17
and ye are entered into their l..........	Jn 4:38
imprisonments, in tumults, in l........	2Cor 6:5
that is, of other men's l...................	2Cor 10:15
in l more abundant, in stripes..........	2Cor 11:23
that they may rest from their l..........	Rev 14:13

LACE

of the ephod with a l of blue............	Ex 28:28
And thou shalt put it on a blue l.......	Ex 28:37
of the ephod with a l of blue............	Ex 39:21
And they tied unto it a l of blue........	Ex 39:31

LACHISH (la'-kish) An Amorite city.

Jarmuth, and unto Japhia king of L...	Josh 10:3
king of Jarmuth, the king of L...........	Josh 10:5
king of Jarmuth, the king of L...........	Josh 10:23
and all Israel with him, unto L..........	Josh 10:31
the LORD delivered L into the..........	Josh 10:32
king of Gezer came up to help L.......	Josh 10:33
from L Joshua passed unto Eglon.....	Josh 10:34
to all that he had done to L..............	Josh 10:35

LACK

the king of L, one .... Josh 12:11
L, and Bozkath, and Eglon, ... Josh 15:39
and he fled to L 2Kin 14:19
but they sent after him to L 2Kin 14:19
sent to the king of Assyria to L 2Kin 18:14
Rab-shakeh from L to king 2Kin 18:17
heard that he was departed from L . 2Kin 19:8
And Adoraim, and L, and Azekah, .. 2Chr 11:9
and he fled to L 2Chr 25:27
but they sent to L after him 2Chr 25:27
he himself laid siege against L 2Chr 32:9
and in their villages, at L .... Neh 11:30
of Assyria sent Rabshakeh from L . Is 36:2
heard that he was departed from L . Is 37:8
Judah that were left, against L ...... Jer 34:7
O thou inhabitant of L, bind the .... Mic 1:13

LACK

Peradventure there shall I five ..... Gen 18:28
all the city for I of five .... Gen 18:28
he that gathered little had no I ...... Ex 16:18
thou shalt not I any thing in it ...... Deut 8:9
old lion perisheth for I of prey ...... Job 4:11
God, they wander for I of meat ..... Job 38:41
The young lions do I, and suffer .... Ps 34:10
giveth unto the poor shall not I ..... Prov 28:27
and let thy head I no ointment ...... Eccl 9:8
is destroyed for I of knowledge ..... Hos 4:6
what I I yet .... Mt 19:20
that had gathered little had no I 2Cor 8:15
to supply your I of service .... Phil 2:30
and that ye may have I of nothing .. 1Th 4:12
If any of you I wisdom, let him ...... Jas 1:5

LACKED

thou hast I nothing .... Deut 2:7
there I of David's servants. 2Sa 2:30
by the morning light there I not 2Sa 17:22
they I nothing 1Kin 4:27
him, But what hast thou I with me . 1Kin 11:22
so that they I nothing. .... Neh 9:21
away, because it I moisture .... Lk 8:6
scrip, and shoes, I ye any thing. .... Lk 22:35
was there any among them that I .... Acts 4:34
honour to that part which I 1Cor 12:24
careful, but ye I opportunity .... Phil 4:10

LACKEST

said unto him, One thing thou I ..... Mk 10:21
.unto him, Yet I thou one thing. .... Lk 18:22

LACKETH

there I not one man of us .... Num 31:49
on the sword, or that I bread 2Sa 3:29
with a woman I understanding .... Prov 6:32
honoureth himself, and I bread ...... Prov 12:9
But he that I these things is 2Pet 1:9

LACKING

to be I from thy meat offering .... Lev 2:13
superfluous or I in his parts .... Lev 22:23
be to day one tribe I in Israel .... Judg 21:3
And there was nothing I to them 1Sa 30:19
dismayed, neither shall they be I .... Jer 23:4
for that which was I on your part 1Cor 16:17
for that which was I to me the 2Cor 11:9
that which is I in your faith 1Th 3:10

LAD

in thy sight because of the I .... Gen 21:12
And God heard the voice of the I .... Gen 21:17
the voice of the I where he is .... Gen 21:17
Arise, lift up the I, and hold him, ... Gen 21:18
with water, and gave the I drink ..... Gen 21:19
And God was with the I .... Gen 21:20
the will go yonder and worship, ... Gen 22:5
Lay not thine hand upon the I .... Gen 22:12
the I was with the sons of Bilhah .... Gen 37:2
his father, Send the I with me .... Gen 43:8
The I cannot leave his father .... Gen 44:22
father, and the I be not with us, ... Gen 44:30
seeth that the I is not with us .... Gen 44:31
surety for the I unto my father .... Gen 44:32
of the I a bondman to my lord .... Gen 44:33
let the I go up with his brethren. .... Gen 44:33
father, and the I be not with me, ... Gen 44:34
Samson said unto the I that held .... Judg 16:26
And, behold, I will send a I 1Sa 20:21
If I expressly say unto the I, ... 1Sa 20:21
David, and a little I with him. 1Sa 20:35
And he said unto his I, Run, find. ... 1Sa 20:36
And as the I ran, he shot an arrow .. 1Sa 20:36
when the I was come to the place. ... 1Sa 20:37
shot, Jonathan cried after the I 1Sa 20:37
And Jonathan cried after the I 1Sa 20:38
Jonathan's I gathered up the 1Sa 20:38
But the I knew not any thing 1Sa 20:39
gave his artillery unto his I 1Sa 20:40
And as soon as the I was gone. 1Sa 20:41
Nevertheless as I saw them 2Sa 17:18
And he said to a I, Carry him to 2Kin 4:19
There is a I here, which hath .... Jn 6:9

LADAN See LAADAN.

LADDER

behold a I set up on the earth, ... Gen 28:12

LADE

I your beasts, and go, get you .... Gen 45:17
did I you with a heavy yoke, ... 1Kin 12:11
for ye I men with burdens. .... Lk 11:46

LADED

they I their asses with the corn, ... Gen 42:26
I every man his ass, and returned ... Gen 44:13
bare burdens, with those that I ...... Neh 4:17
they I us with such things as .... Acts 28:10

LADEN

ten asses I with the good things ..... Gen 45:23
and ten she asses I with corn .... Gen 45:23
And Jesse took an ass I with bread .. 1Sa 16:20
a people I with iniquity, a seed ...... Is 1:4
all ye that labour and are heavy I, .. Mt 11:28
captive silly women I with sins....... 2Ti 3:6

LADETH

to him that I himself with thick...... Hab 2:6

LADIES

Her wise I answered her, yea, she.. Judg 5:29
Likewise shall the I of Persia .... Est 1:18

LADING

bringing in sheaves, and I asses ..... Neh 13:15
and much damage, not only of the I.. Acts 27:10

LAD'S

life is bound up in the I life .... Gen 44:30

LADS

me from all evil, bless the I .... Gen 48:16

LADY

more be called, The I of kingdoms .. Is 47:5
saidst, I shall be a I for ever .... Is 47:7
The elder unto the elect I, ... 2Jn 1
And now I beseech thee, I, not as ... 2Jn 5

LAEL (la´-el) A Levite.

shall be Eliasaph the son of L......... Num 3:24

LAHAD (la´-had) Great-grandson of Shobal.

and Jahath begat Ahumai, and L 1Chr 4:2

LAHAI-ROI (la-hah´-ee-roy) See BEER-LAHAIROI. A well in Paran.

came from the way of the well L ..... Gen 24:62
and Isaac dwelt by the well L.......... Gen 25:11

LAHMAM (lah´-mam) A city in Judah.

And Cabbon, and L, and Kithlish, ... Josh 15:40

LAHMAS See LAHMAM.

LAHMI (lah´-mi) See BETHLEHEMITE. A brother of Goliath.

slew L the brother of Goliath the 1Chr 20:5

LAID

I it upon both their shoulders, ... Gen 9:23
I each piece one against another ..... Gen 15:10
the men I hold upon his hand, and .. Gen 19:16
and I it upon Isaac his son .... Gen 22:6
I the wood in order, and bound. ..... Gen 22:9
I him on the altar upon the wood .... Gen 22:9
that Jacob I the rods before the ...... Gen 30:41
I by her wail from her, and put on.... Gen 38:19
she I up his garment by her, ... Gen 39:16
I up the food in the cities .... Gen 41:48
every city, I he up in the same .... Gen 41:48
I it upon Ephraim's head, who was .. Gen 48:14
I his right hand upon the head of ..... Gen 48:17
I in the flags by the .... Ex 2:3
there more work be I upon the men.. Ex 5:9
they I it up till the morning, as ...... Ex 16:24
so Aaron I it up before the .... Ex 16:34
I before their faces all these. .... Ex 19:7
If there be I on him a sum of .... Ex 21:30
his life whatsoever is I upon him. ... Ex 21:30
of Israel he I not his hand. .... Ex 24:11
his sons I their hands upon the ...... Lev 8:14
his sons I their hands upon the ...... Lev 8:18
his sons I their hands upon the ...... Lev 8:22
I incense thereon, and stood in. ..... Num 16:18
Moses I up the rods before the .... Num 17:7
we have I them waste even unto ..... Num 21:30
he I his hands upon him, and gave .. Num 27:23
us, and I upon us hard bondage ...... Deut 26:6
which the LORD hath I upon it .... Deut 29:22
Is not this I up in store with me ..... Deut 32:34
for Moses had I his hands upon. ..... Deut 34:9
which she had I in order upon the ... Josh 2:6
And before they were I down.......... Josh 2:8
they lodged, and I them down there. Josh 4:8
I them out before the LORD .... Josh 7:23
I great stones in the cave's .... Josh 10:27
their blood be I upon Abimelech .... Judg 9:24
they I wait against Shechem in ...... Judg 9:34
I wait in the field, and looked, ... Judg 9:43
I it on his shoulder, and said, ... Judg 9:48
I wait for him all night in the .... Judg 16:2
I hold on his concubine, and .... Judg 19:29
uncovered his feet, and I her down . Ruth 3:7
of barley, and I it on her .... Ruth 3:15
I it in her bosom, and became. ...... Ruth 4:16
when Eli was I down in his place, ... 1Sa 3:2
Samuel was I down to sleep; 1Sa 3:3
they I the ark of the LORD upon. 1Sa 6:11
book, and I it up before the LORD .. 1Sa 10:25
how he I wait for him in the way, ... 1Sa 15:2
Amalek, and I wait in the valley. 1Sa 15:5
he I hold upon the skirt of his 1Sa 15:27
I it in the bed, and put a pillow....... 1Sa 19:13
David I up these words in his 1Sa 21:12
cakes of figs, and I them on asses... 1Sa 25:18
and he was I down 1Sa 28:23
I her hand on her head, and went ... 2Sa 13:19
I a very great heap of stones 2Sa 18:17

I it in her bosom 1Kin 3:20
I her dead child in my bosom......... 1Kin 3:20
of the voice of the LORD I 1Kin 6:37
an oath be I upon him to cause 1Kin 8:31
I it upon the ass, and brought it 1Kin 13:29
he I his carcase in his own grave 1Kin 13:30
all Israel I siege to Gibbethon 1Kin 15:27
he I the foundation thereof in 1Kin 16:34
abode, and I him upon his own bed . 1Kin 17:19
I him on the wood, and said, Fill 1Kin 18:33
eat and drink, and I him down again. 1Kin 19:6
he I him down upon his bed, and 1Kin 21:4
I him on the bed of the man and 2Kin 4:21
I the staff upon the face of the 2Kin 4:31
child was dead, and I upon his bed .. 2Kin 4:32
I them upon two of his servants 2Kin 5:23
the LORD I this burden upon him 2Kin 9:25
And they I hands on her. 2Kin 11:16
I it out to the carpenters 2Kin 12:11
for all that was I out for the 2Kin 12:12
I it on the boil, and he recovered. ... 2Kin 20:7
have I up in store unto this day. 2Kin 20:17
an oath be I upon him to make him . 2Chr 6:22
and I hold on other gods, and 2Chr 7:22
I him in the bed which was filled 2Chr 16:14
So they I hands on her. 2Chr 23:15
I upon Israel in the wilderness. 2Chr 24:9
of the burdens I upon him 2Chr 24:27
they I their hands upon them. 2Chr 29:23
their God, and I them by heaps 2Chr 31:6
(but he himself I siege against 2Chr 32:9
temple of the LORD was not yet I .... Ezr 3:6
And when the builders I the .... Ezr 3:10
of the house of the LORD was I. ...... Ezr 3:11
house was I before their eyes.......... Ezr 3:12
timber is I in the walls, and this ..... Ezr 5:8
I the foundation of the house of ...... Ezr 5:16
treasures were I up in Babylon. ...... Ezr 6:1
foundations thereof be strongly I. ... Ezr 6:3
who also I the beams thereof, and ... Neh 3:3
they I the beams thereof, and set .... Neh 3:6
they I the meat offerings .... Neh 13:5
because he I his hand upon the ...... Est 8:7
but on the spoil I they not their ...... Est 9:10
on the prey they I not their hand. ... Est 9:15
but they I not their hands on the .... Est 9:16
the king Ahasuerus I a tribute. ...... Est 10:1
my calamity I in the balances......... Job 6:2
The snare is I for him in the .... Job 18:10
I their hand on their mouth .... Job 29:9
or if I have I wait at my. .... Job 31:9
Where wast thou when I I the......... Job 38:4
Who hath I the measures thereof, ... Job 38:5
or who I the corner stone thereof... Job 38:6
I I me down and slept................... Ps 3:5
and majesty hast thou I upon him.... Ps 21:5
that they have I privily for me. .... Ps 31:4
which thou hast I up for them......... Ps 31:19
they I to my charge things that I. .... Ps 35:11
sheep they are I in the grave;.......... Ps 49:14
to be I in the balance, they are. ...... Ps 62:9
they have I Jerusalem on heaps. ..... Ps 79:1
I waste his dwelling place. .... Ps 79:7
Thou hast I me in the lowest pit, ... Ps 88:6
I have I help upon one that is .... Ps 89:19
Of old hast thou I the foundation.... Ps 102:25
Who I the foundations of the .... Ps 104:5
he was I in iron. .... Ps 105:18
thy judgments have I I before me. .. Ps 119:30
The wicked have I a snare for me. ... Ps 119:110
before, and I thine hand upon me. .. Ps 139:5
snares which they have I for me. ..... Ps 141:9
they privily I a snare for me. .... Ps 142:3
the sinner is I up for the just.......... Prov 13:22
old, which I have I up for thee. .... Song 7:13
he I it upon my mouth, and said, ... Is 6:7
he hath I up his carriages. .... Is 10:28
saying, Since thou art I down .... Is 14:8
the night Ar of Moab is I waste. ..... Is 15:1
the night Kir of Moab is I waste, ... Is 15:1
and that which they have I up .... Is 15:7
for it is I waste, so that there. .... Is 23:1
for your strength is I waste. .... Is 23:14
shall not be treasured nor I up. ...... Is 23:18
have I waste all the nations .... Is 37:18
have I up in store until this day. ..... Is 39:6
him, yet he I is not to heart. .... Is 42:25
temple, Thy foundation shall be I. .. Is 44:28
hast thou very heavily I thy yoke .... Is 47:6
Mine hand also hath I the .... Is 48:13
I the foundations of the earth......... Is 51:13
thou hast I thy body as the. .... Is 51:23
the LORD hath I on him the. .... Is 53:6
me, nor I it to thy heart. .... Is 57:11
the pleasant things are I waste .... Is 64:11
and thy cities shall be I waste .... Jer 4:7
should this city be I waste. .... Jer 27:17
but they I up the roll in the .... Jer 36:20
I have I a snare for thee, and .... Jer 50:24
they I wait for us in the .... Lam 4:19
For I have I upon thee the years ..... Eze 4:5
the cities shall be I waste .... Eze 6:6
that your altars may be I waste........ Eze 6:6
whom ye have I in the midst of it. ... Eze 11:7
are inhabited shall be I waste .... Eze 12:20
and he I waste their cities .... Eze 19:7
replenished, now she I waste. .... Eze 26:2
among the cities that are I waste ..... Eze 29:12
be thou I with the uncircumcised. ... Eze 32:19
they have I their swords under .... Eze 32:27

LAIDST
which with their might are l by........ Eze 32:29
he shall be l in the midst of the........ Eze 32:32
when I have l the land most........ Eze 33:29
saying, They are l desolate........ Eze 35:12
my hand that I have l upon them........ Eze 39:21
whereupon also they l the........ Eze 40:42
l upon the mouth of the den........ Dan 6:17
their jaws, and I meat unto them........ Hos 11:4
He hath l my vine waste, and........ Joel 1:7
clods, the garners are l desolate........ Joel 1:17
l to pledge by every altar........ Amos 2:8
of Israel shall be l waste........ Amos 7:9
bread have l a wound under thee........ Obad 7
nor have l hands on their........ Obad 13
he l his robe from him, and........ Jonah 3:6
he hath l siege against us........ Mic 5:1
thee, and say, Nineveh is l waste........ Nah 3:7
it is l over with gold and silver........ Hab 2:19
from before a stone was l upon a........ Hag 2:15
of the LORD's temple was l........ Hag 2:18
stone that I have l before Joshua........ Zec 3:9
l the foundation of this house........ Zec 4:9
for they l the pleasant land........ Zec 7:14
house of the LORD of hosts was l........ Zec 8:9
l his mountains and his heritage........ Mal 1:3
now also the ax is l unto the........ Mt 3:10
house, he saw his wife's mother l........ Mt 8:14
For Herod had l hold on John........ Mt 14:3
he l hands on him, and took him by........ Mt 18:28
he l his hands on them, and........ Mt 19:15
l hands on Jesus, and took him........ Mt 26:50
the temple, and ye l no hold on me........ Mt 26:55
they that had l hold on Jesus led........ Mt 26:57
l it in his own new tomb, which........ Mt 27:60
save that he l his hands upon a........ Mk 6:5
l hold upon John, and bound him in........ Mk 6:17
up his corpse, and l it in a tomb........ Mk 6:29
they l the sick in the streets........ Mk 6:56
and her daughter l upon the bed........ Mk 7:30
they l their hands on him, and........ Mk 14:46
and the young men l hold on him........ Mk 14:51
l him in a sepulchre which was........ Mk 15:46
of Joses behold where he was l........ Mk 15:47
behold the place where they l him........ Mk 16:6
them l them up in their heart........ Lk 1:66
clothes, and l him in a manger........ Lk 2:7
now also the axe is l unto the........ Lk 3:9
he l his hands on every one of........ Lk 4:40
l the foundation on a rock........ Lk 6:48
much goods l up for many years........ Lk 12:19
And he l his hands on her........ Lk 13:13
after he hath l the foundation........ Lk 14:29
which was l at his gate, full of........ Lk 16:20
I have kept l up in a napkin........ Lk 19:20
man, taking up that l l not down........ Lk 19:22
they l hold upon one Simon, a........ Lk 23:26
and on him they l the cross........ Lk 23:26
l it in a sepulchre that was hewn........ Lk 23:53
wherein never man before was l........ Lk 23:53
sepulchre, and how his body was l........ Lk 24:12
the linen clothes l by themselves........ Jn 7:30
but no man l hands on him........ Jn 7:30
but no man l hands on him........ Jn 7:44
and no man l hands on him........ Jn 8:20
And said, Where have ye l him........ Jn 11:34
the place where the dead was l........ Jn 11:41
supper, and l aside his garments........ Jn 13:4
wherein was never man yet l........ Jn 19:41
There l they Jesus therefore........ Jn 19:42
we know not where they have l him........ Jn 20:2
I know not where they have l him........ Jn 20:13
tell me where thou hast l him........ Jn 20:15
and fish l thereon, and bread........ Jn 21:9
whom they l daily at the gate of........ Acts 3:2
they l hands on them, and put them........ Acts 4:3
l them down at the apostles' feet........ Acts 4:35
it at the apostles' feet........ Acts 4:37
l it at the apostles' feet........ Acts 5:2
l them on beds and couches, that........ Acts 5:15
l their hands on the apostles, and........ Acts 5:18
they l their hands on them........ Acts 6:6
l in the sepulchre that Abraham........ Acts 7:16
the witnesses l down their........ Acts 7:58
Then l they their hands on them........ Acts 8:17
they l her in an upper chamber........ Acts 9:37
l their hands on them, they sent........ Acts 13:3
the tree, and l him in a sepulchre........ Acts 13:29
was l unto his fathers, and saw........ Acts 13:36
when they had l many stripes upon........ Acts 16:23
when Paul had l his hands upon........ Acts 19:6
And when the Jews l wait for him........ Acts 20:3
the people, and l hands on him........ Acts 21:27
but to have nothing l to his........ Acts 23:29
that the Jews l wait for the man........ Acts 23:30
l many and grievous complaints........ Acts 25:7
the crime l against him........ Acts 25:16
signify the crimes l against him........ Acts 25:27
l them on the fire, there came a........ Acts 28:3
l his hands on him, and healed him........ Acts 28:8
my life l down their own necks........ Rom 16:4
I have l the foundation, and........ 1Cor 3:10
can no man lay than that is l........ 1Cor 3:11
for necessity is l upon me........ 1Cor 9:16
which is l up for you in heaven........ Col 1:5
Henceforth there is l up for me a........ 2Ti 4:8
it may not be l to their charge........ 2Ti 4:16
in the beginning have l the........ Heb 1:10
because he l down his life for us........ 1Jn 3:16
he l his right hand upon me........ Rev 1:17
the l hold on the dragon, that old........ Rev 20:2

LAIDST
thou l affliction upon our loins........ Ps 66:11

LAIN
woman, if no man have l with thee........ Num 5:19
some man have l with thee beside........ Num 5:20
woman that hath l by man........ Judg 21:11
For now should I have l still........ Job 3:13
he found that he had l in the........ Jn 11:17
where the body of Jesus had l........ Jn 20:12

LAISH (la'-ish) See DAN, LESHEM.
1. Same as the city of Dan.
five men departed, and came to L........ Judg 18:7
went to spy out the country of L........ Judg 18:14
which he had, and came unto L........ Judg 18:27
of the city was L at the first........ Judg 18:29
cause it to be heard unto L........ Is 10:30
2. Father of Phaltiel.
wife, to Phalti the son of L........ 1Sa 25:44
even from Phaltiel the son of L........ 2Sa 3:15

LAKE
he stood by the l of Gennesaret........ Lk 5:1
saw two ships standing by the l........ Lk 5:2
over unto the other side of the l........ Lk 8:22
down a storm of wind on the l........ Lk 8:23
down a steep place into the l........ Lk 8:33
both were cast alive into a l of........ Rev 19:20
them was cast into the l of fire........ Rev 20:10
hell were cast into the l of fire........ Rev 20:14
life was cast into the l of fire........ Rev 20:15
in the l which burneth with fire........ Rev 21:8

LAKKUM See LAKUM.

LAKUM (la'-kum) A city in Naphtali.
Adami, Nekeb, and Jabneel, unto L........ Josh 19:33

LAMA
saying, Eli, Eli, l sabachthani........ Mt 27:46
saying, Eloi, Eloi, l sabachthani........ Mk 15:34

LAMB
but where is the l for a burnt........ Gen 22:7
himself a l for a burnt offering........ Gen 22:8
shall take to them every man a l........ Ex 12:3
their fathers, a l for an house........ Ex 12:3
household be too little for the l........ Ex 12:4
shall make your count for the l........ Ex 12:4
Your l shall be without blemish........ Ex 12:5
take you a l according to your........ Ex 12:21
an ass thou shalt redeem with a l........ Ex 13:13
The one l thou shalt offer in the........ Ex 29:39
the other l thou shalt offer at........ Ex 29:39
with the one l a tenth deal of........ Ex 29:40
the other l thou shalt offer at........ Ex 29:41
an ass thou shalt redeem with a l........ Ex 34:20
he l offer a l for his offering........ Lev 3:7
if he bring a l for a sin........ Lev 4:32
as the fat of the l is taken away........ Lev 4:35
a l or a kid of the goats, for a........ Lev 5:6
And if he be not able to bring a l........ Lev 5:7
and a calf and a l, both of the........ Lev 9:3
she shall bring a l of the first........ Lev 12:6
if she be not able to bring a l........ Lev 12:8
one ewe l of the first year........ Lev 14:10
And the priest shall take one he l........ Lev 14:12
he shall slay the l in the place........ Lev 14:13
then he shall take one l for a........ Lev 14:21
the l of the trespass offering........ Lev 14:24
he shall kill the l of the........ Lev 14:25
Israel, that killeth an ox, or l........ Lev 17:3
Either a bullock or a l that hath........ Lev 22:23
he l without blemish of the first........ Lev 23:12
shalt bring a l of the first year........ Num 6:12
one he l of the first year........ Num 6:14
one ewe l of the first year........ Num 6:14
one of the first year, for a........ Num 7:15
one of the first year, for a........ Num 7:21
one of the first year, for a........ Num 7:27
one of the first year, for a........ Num 7:33
one of the first year, for a........ Num 7:39
one of the first year, for a........ Num 7:45
one of the first year, for a........ Num 7:51
one of the first year, for a........ Num 7:57
one of the first year, for a........ Num 7:63
one of the first year, for a........ Num 7:69
one of the first year, for a........ Num 7:75
one of the first year, for a........ Num 7:81
offering or sacrifice, for one l........ Num 15:11
or for one ram, or for a l........ Num 15:11
The one l shalt thou offer in the........ Num 28:4
the other l shalt thou offer at........ Num 28:8
part of an hin for the one l........ Num 28:7
the other l shalt thou offer at........ Num 28:8
for meat offering unto one l........ Num 28:13
a fourth part of an hin unto a l........ Num 28:14
deal shalt thou offer for every l........ Num 28:21
A several tenth deal unto one l........ Num 28:29
And one tenth deal for one l........ Num 29:4
A several tenth deal for one l........ Num 29:10
to each l of the fourteen lambs........ Num 29:15
and Samuel took a sucking l........ 1Sa 7:9
took a ewe l of the flock........ 2Sa 12:4
nothing, save one little ewe l........ 2Sa 12:3
but took the poor man's l........ 2Sa 12:4
he shall restore the l fourfold........ 2Sa 12:6
wolf also shall dwell with the l........ Is 11:6
Send ye the l to the ruler of the........ Is 16:1
brought as a l to the slaughter........ Is 53:7
the l shall feed together, and the........ Is 65:25
he that sacrificeth a l, as if he........ Is 66:3

But I was like a l or an ox that........ Jer 11:19
one l out of the flock, out of........ Eze 45:15
of a l of the first year without........ Eze 46:13
Thus shall they prepare the l........ Eze 46:15
feed them as a l in a large place........ Hos 4:16
and saith, Behold the L of God........ Jn 1:29
he saith, Behold the L of God........ Jn 1:36
like a l dumb before his shearer........ Acts 8:32
as of a l without blemish and........ 1Pet 1:19
stood a L as it had been slain........ Rev 5:6
elders fell down before the L........ Rev 5:8
Worthy is the L that was slain to........ Rev 5:12
throne, and unto the L for ever........ Rev 5:13
I saw when the L opened one of........ Rev 6:1
and from the wrath of the L........ Rev 6:16
the throne, and before the L........ Rev 7:9
upon the throne, and unto the L........ Rev 7:10
them white in the blood of the L........ Rev 7:14
For the L which is in the midst........ Rev 7:17
him by the blood of the L........ Rev 12:11
in the book of life of the L........ Rev 13:8
and he had two horns like a L........ Rev 13:11
a L stood on the mount Sion, and........ Rev 14:1
the L whithersoever he goeth........ Rev 14:4
firstfruits unto God and to the L........ Rev 14:4
and in the presence of the L........ Rev 14:10
of God, and the song of the L........ Rev 15:3
These shall make war with the L........ Rev 17:14
the L shall overcome them........ Rev 17:14
for the marriage of the L is come........ Rev 19:7
unto the marriage supper of the L........ Rev 19:9
of the twelve apostles of the L........ Rev 21:14
the L are the temple of it........ Rev 21:22
the L is the light thereof........ Rev 21:23
of the throne of God and of the L........ Rev 22:1
of God and of the L shall be in it........ Rev 22:3

LAMB'S
shew the bride, the L wife........ Rev 21:9
are written in the L book of life........ Rev 21:27

LAMBS
Abraham set seven ewe l of the........ Gen 21:28
ewe l which thou hast set by........ Gen 21:30
For these seven ewe l shalt thou........ Gen 21:30
And Jacob did separate the l........ Gen 30:40
two l of the first year day by........ Ex 29:38
take two he l without blemish........ Lev 14:10
offer with the bread seven l........ Lev 23:18
two l of the first year l........ Lev 23:19
before the LORD, with the two l........ Lev 23:20
goats, five l of the first year........ Num 7:17
goats, five l of the first year........ Num 7:23
goats, five l of the first year........ Num 7:29
goats, five l of the first year........ Num 7:35
goats, five l of the first year........ Num 7:41
goats, five l of the first year........ Num 7:47
goats, five l of the first year........ Num 7:53
goats, five l of the first year........ Num 7:59
goats, five l of the first year........ Num 7:65
goats, five l of the first year........ Num 7:71
goats, five l of the first year........ Num 7:77
goats, five l of the first year........ Num 7:83
the l of the first year twelve........ Num 7:87
the l of the first year sixty........ Num 7:88
two l of the first year without........ Num 28:3
on the sabbath day two l of the........ Num 28:9
seven l of the first year without........ Num 28:11
seven l of the first year........ Num 28:19
lamb, throughout the seven l........ Num 28:21
seven l of the first year........ Num 28:27
one lamb, throughout the seven l........ Num 28:29
seven l of the first year without........ Num 29:2
one lamb, throughout the seven l........ Num 29:4
one lamb, throughout the seven l........ Num 29:8
fourteen l of the first year........ Num 29:13
to each lamb of the fourteen l........ Num 29:15
fourteen l of the first year........ Num 29:17
for the rams, and for the l........ Num 29:18
fourteen l of the first year........ Num 29:20
for the rams, and for the l........ Num 29:21
fourteen l of the first year........ Num 29:23
for the rams, and for the l........ Num 29:24
fourteen l of the first year........ Num 29:26
for the rams, and for the l........ Num 29:27
fourteen l of the first year........ Num 29:29
for the rams, and for the l........ Num 29:30
fourteen l of the first year........ Num 29:32
for the rams, and for the l........ Num 29:33
seven l of the first year without........ Num 29:36
for the ram, and for the l........ Num 29:37
and milk of sheep, with fat of l........ Deut 32:14
and of the fatlings, and the l........ 1Sa 15:9
of Israel an hundred thousand l........ 2Kin 3:4
a thousand rams, and a thousand l........ 1Chr 29:21
and seven rams, and seven l........ 2Chr 29:21
they killed also the l, and they........ 2Chr 29:22
an hundred rams, and two hundred l........ 2Chr 29:32
to the people, of the flock, l........ 2Chr 35:7
young bullocks, and rams, and l........ Ezr 6:9
two hundred rams, four hundred l........ Ezr 6:17
with this money bullocks, rams, l........ Ezr 7:17
and six rams, seventy and seven l........ Ezr 8:35
the LORD shall be as the fat of l........ Ps 37:20
rams, and the little hills like l........ Ps 114:4
and ye little hills, like l........ Ps 114:6
he shall gather the l with his........ Is 40:11
Then shall the l feed after their........ Is 5:17
fatness, and with the blood of l........ Is 34:6

shall gather the *l* with his arm .... Is 40:11
them down like *l* to the slaughter .... Jer 51:40
they occupied with thee in *l* .... Eze 27:21
of the earth, of rams, of *l* .... Eze 39:18
shall be six *l* without blemish .... Eze 46:4
the meat offering for the *l* as he .... Eze 46:5
bullock without blemish, and six *l* ...... Eze 46:6
for the *l* according as his hand .... Eze 46:7
to the *l* as he is able to give, ... Eze 46:11
eat the *l* out of the flock, and, ... Amos 6:4
send you forth as *l* among wolves ...... Lk 10:3
He saith unto him, Feed my *l* .... Jn 21:15

LAME

a blind man, or a *l*, or he that .... Lev 21:18
blemish therein, as if it be *l* .... Deut 15:21
had a son that was *l* of his feet 2Sa 4:4
flee, that he fell, and became *l* 2Sa 4:4
thou take away the blind and the *l* 2Sa 5:6
smiteth the Jebusites, and the *l* 2Sa 5:8
the *l* shall not come into the 2Sa 5:8
yet a son, which is *l* on his feet 2Sa 9:3
and was *l* on both his feet 2Sa 9:13
because thy servant is *l* 2Sa 19:26
the blind, and feet was *l* to the *l* ...... Job 29:15
The legs of the *l* are not equal .... Prov 26:7
the *l* take the prey .... Is 33:23
Then shall the *l* man leap as an .... Is 35:6
and with them the blind and the *l* ...... Jer 31:8
and if ye offer the *l* and sick, is .... Mal 1:8
that which was torn, and the *l* .... Mal 1:13
the *l* walk, the lepers are .... Mt 11:5
with them those that were the *l* .... Mt 15:30
the *l* to walk, and the blind to .... Mt 15:31
the *l* came to him in the temple .... Mt 21:14
the *l* walk, the lepers are .... Lk 7:22
call the poor, the maimed, the *l*, ... Lk 14:13
a certain man *l* from his mother's ...... Acts 3:2
as the *l* man which was healed .... Acts 3:11
with palsies, and that were *l* .... Acts 8:7
lest that which is *l* be turned .... Heb 12:13

LAMECH *(la´-mek)* A son of Methuselah.

and Methuselah begat *L* .... Gen 4:18
L took unto him two wives, ... Gen 4:19
L said unto his wives, Adah and .... Gen 4:23
ye wives of *L*, hearken unto my .... Gen 4:23
truly L seventy and sevenfold .... Gen 4:24
eighty and seven years, and begat *L* ... Gen 5:25
he begat L seven hundred eighty .... Gen 5:26
L lived an hundred eighty and two ...... Gen 5:28
L lived after he begat Noah five .... Gen 5:30
all the days of L were seven .... Gen 5:31
Henoch, Methuselah, *L* 1Chr 1:3
of Noe, which was the son of *L* .... Lk 3:36

LAMENT

of Israel went yearly to the .... Judg 11:40
And her gates shall *l* and mourn .... Is 3:26
angle into the brooks shall *l* .... Is 19:8
They shall *l* for the teats, for .... Is 32:12
this gird you with sackcloth, *l* .... Jer 4:8
neither go to *l* nor bemoan them, ... Jer 16:5
neither shall men *l* for them .... Jer 16:6
They shall not *l* for him, saying, ... Jer 22:18
they shall not *l* for him, saying, ... Jer 22:18
and they will *l* thee, saying, Ah .... Jer 34:5
L and run to and fro by the hedges ...... Jer 49:3
made the rampart and the wall to *l* .... Lam 2:8
I over thee, saying, What city is .... Eze 27:32
wherewith they shall *l* her .... Eze 32:16
of the nations shall *l* her .... Eze 32:16
they shall *l* for her, even for .... Eze 32:16
L like a virgin girded with .... Joel 1:8
Gird yourselves, and *l*, ye priests, ... Joel 1:13
I with a doleful lamentation, and .... Mic 2:4
unto you, That ye shall weep and *l* .... Jn 16:20
I for her, when they shall see .... Rev 18:9

LAMENTABLE

he cried with a *l* voice unto .... Dan 6:20

LAMENTATION

with a great and very sore *l* .... Gen 50:10
lamented with this *l* over Saul 2Sa 1:17
and their widows made no *l* .... Ps 78:64
as for an only son, most bitter *l* .... Jer 6:26
take up a *l* on high places .... Jer 7:29
habitations of the wilderness a *l* .... Jer 9:10
and every one her neighbour *l* .... Jer 9:20
A voice was heard in Ramah, *l* .... Jer 31:15
There shall be *l* generally upon .... Jer 48:38
daughter of Judah mourning and *l* ..... Lam 2:5
Moreover take thou up a *l* for the ...... Eze 19:1
is a *l*, and shall be for a *l* .... Eze 19:14
they shall take up a *l* for thee .... Eze 26:17
son of man, take up a *l* for Tyrus .... Eze 27:2
they shall take up a *l* for thee, ... Eze 27:32
take up a *l* upon the king of .... Eze 28:12
take up a *l* for Pharaoh king of .... Eze 32:2
This is the *l* wherewith they; .... Eze 32:16
I take up against you, even a *l* .... Amos 5:1
as are skilful of *l* to wailing .... Amos 5:16
and all your songs into *l* .... Amos 8:10
you, and lament with a doleful *l* .... Mic 2:4
Rama was there a voice heard, *l* .... Mt 2:18
burial, and made great *l* over him ..... Acts 8:2

LAMENTATIONS

of Josiah in their *l* this day 2Chr 35:25
behold, they are written in the *l* 2Chr 35:25
and there was written therein *l* .... Eze 2:10

LAMENTED

and the people *l*, because the LORD 1Sa 6:19
house of Israel *l* after the LORD 1Sa 7:2
I him, and buried him in his house. 1Sa 25:1
was dead, and all Israel had *l* him. 1Sa 28:3
David *l* with this lamentation 2Sa 1:17
the king *l* over Abner, and said,........ 2Sa 3:33
And Jeremiah *l* for Josiah 2Chr 35:25
they shall not be *l* .... Jer 16:4
they shall not be *l*, neither .... Jer 25:33
unto you, and ye have not *l*. .... Mt 11:17
which also bewailed and *l* him .... Lk 23:27

LAMP

a burning *l* that passed between .... Gen 15:17
to cause the *l* to burn always. .... Ex 27:20
ere the *l* of God went out in the 1Sa 3:3
For thou art my *l*, O LORD 2Sa 22:29
his God give him a *l* in Jerusalem 1Kin 15:4
to slip with his feet is as a *l* .... Job 12:5
Thy word is a *l* unto my feet .... Ps 119:105
ordained a *l* for mine anointed .... Ps 132:17
For the commandment is a *l* .... Prov 6:23
but the *l* of the wicked shall be .... Prov 13:9
his *l* shall be put out in obscure .... Prov 20:20
thereof as a *l* that burneth. .... Is 62:1
heaven, burning as it were a *l* .... Rev 8:10

LAMPS

shalt make the seven *l* thereof. .... Ex 25:37
and they shall light the *l* thereof .... Ex 25:37
when he dresseth the *l*, he shall .... Ex 30:7
when Aaron lighteth the *l* at even. ..... Ex 30:8
light, and his furniture, and his *l* .... Ex 35:14
And he made his seven *l*, and his ...... Ex 37:23
candlestick, with the *l* thereof .... Ex 39:37
even with the *l* to be set in .... Ex 39:37
and light the *l* thereof .... Ex 40:4
he lighted the *l* before the LORD .... Ex 40:25
the light, to cause the *l* to burn .... Lev 24:2
He shall order the *l* upon the .... Lev 24:4
of the light, and his *l*, and his .... Num 4:9
him, When thou lightest the *l* .... Num 8:2
the seven *l* shall give light over .... Num 8:2
he lighted the *l* thereof over .... Num 8:3
and *l* within the pitchers .... Judg 7:16
held the *l* in their left hands, ... Judg 7:20
the flowers, and the *l*, ... 1Kin 7:49
of gold, and for their *l* of gold, ... 1Chr 28:15
candlestick, and for the *l* thereof 1Chr 28:15
and also for the *l* thereof 1Chr 28:15
the candlesticks with their *l*, ... 2Chr 4:20
And the flowers, and the *l*, and the 2Chr 4:21
of gold with the *l* thereof 2Chr 13:11
of the porch, and put out the *l* 2Chr 29:7
Out of his mouth go burning *l* .... Job 41:19
fire, and like the appearance of *l* .... Eze 1:13
and his eyes as *l* of fire .... Dan 10:6
top of it, and his seven *l* thereon .... Zec 4:2
and seven pipes to the seven *l* .... Zec 4:2
ten virgins, which took their *l* .... Mt 25:1
that were foolish took their *l* .... Mt 25:3
oil in their vessels with their *l* .... Mt 25:4
virgins arose, and trimmed their *l* ..... Mt 25:7
for our *l* are gone out. .... Mt 25:8
there were seven *l* of fire .... Rev 4:5

LANCE

They shall hold the bow and the *l* ..... Jer 50:42

LANCETS

their manner with knives and *l* 1Kin 18:28

LAND See PREFACE.

LANDED

And when he had *l* at Caesarea .... Acts 18:22
sailed into Syria, and *l* at Tyre .... Acts 21:3

LANDING

l at Syracuse, we tarried there .... Acts 28:12

LANDMARK

not remove thy neighbour's *l* .... Deut 19:14
that removeth his neighbour's *l* .... Deut 27:17
Remove not the ancient *l*, which .... Prov 22:28
Remove not the old *l* .... Prov 23:10

LANDMARKS

Some remove the *l* .... Job 24:2

LANDS

the Gentiles divided in their *l* .... Gen 10:5
after their tongues, in their *l* .... Gen 10:31
and the dearth was in all *l* .... Gen 41:54
the famine was so sore in all *l* .... Gen 41:57
my lord, but our bodies, and our *l* ..... Gen 47:18
wherefore they sold not their *l* .... Gen 47:22
hearts in the *l* of their enemies .... Lev 26:36
their iniquity in your enemies' *l* .... Lev 26:39
restore those *l* again peaceably .... Judg 11:13
of Assyria have done to all *l* 2Kin 19:11
destroyed the nations and their *l* 2Kin 19:17
fame of David went out into all *l* 1Chr 14:17
out of Egypt, and out of all *l* 2Chr 9:28
manner of the nations of other *l* 2Chr 13:9
the *l* that were round about Judah 2Chr 17:10
unto all the people of other *l* 2Chr 32:13
gods of the nations of those *l* 2Chr 32:13
deliver their *l* out of mine hand 2Chr 32:13
gods of the nations of other *l* 2Chr 32:17
from the people of the *l*, doing .... Ezr 9:1
with the people of those *l* .... Ezr 9:2
the hand of the kings of the *l* .... Ezr 9:7
filthiness of the people of the *l* .... Ezr 9:11

said, We have mortgaged our *l* .... Neh 5:3
tribute, and that upon our *l* .... Neh 5:4
for other men have our *l* and .... Neh 5:5
to them, even this day, their *l* .... Neh 5:11
the hand of the people of the *l* .... Neh 9:30
of the *l* unto the law of God .... Neh 10:28
they call their *l* after their own. .... Ps 49:11
a joyful noise unto God, all ye *l* .... Ps 66:1
noise unto the LORD, all ye *l* .... Ps 100:1
gave them the *l* of the heathen .... Ps 105:44
and to scatter them in the *l* .... Ps 106:27
And gathered them out of the *l* .... Ps 107:3
among all the gods of these *l* .... Is 36:20
all *l* by destroying them utterly .... Is 37:11
from all the *l* whither he had .... Jer 16:15
now have I given all these *l* into .... Jer 27:6
which is the glory of all *l* .... Eze 20:6
which is the glory of all *l* .... Eze 20:15
them out of their enemies' *l* .... Eze 39:27
or wife, or children, or *l* .... Mt 19:29
or wife, or children, or *l* .... Mk 10:29
and mothers, and children, and *l* ...... Mk 10:30
of *l* or houses sold them, and .... Acts 4:34

LANES

l of the city, and bring in hither .... Lk 14:21

LANGUAGE

And the whole earth was of one *l* ...... Gen 11:1
is one, and they have all one *l* .... Gen 11:6
down, and there confound their *l* ...... Gen 11:7
confound the *l* of all the earth .... Gen 11:9
to thy servants in the Syrian *l* 2Kin 18:26
talk not with us in the Jews' *l* 2Kin 18:26
with a loud voice in the Jews' *l* 2Kin 18:28
and could not speak in the Jews' *l* ..... Neh 13:24
according to the *l* of each people .... Neh 13:24
and to every people after their *l* .... Est 1:22
to the *l* of every people. .... Est 1:22
and to every people after their *l* .... Est 3:12
unto every people after their *l* .... Est 8:9
writing, and according to their *l* .... Est 8:9
There is no speech nor *l*, where .... Ps 19:3
where I heard a *l* that I. .... Ps 81:5
Jacob from a people of strange *l* .... Ps 114:1
of Egypt speak the *l* of Canaan. .... Is 19:18
unto thy servants in the Syrian *l* .... Is 36:11
and speak not to us in the Jews' *l* ...... Is 36:11
with a loud voice in the Jews' *l* .... Is 36:13
a nation whose *l* thou knowest not .... Jer 5:15
a strange speech and of an hard *l* ...... Eze 3:5
a strange speech and of an hard *l* ...... Eze 3:6
That every people, nation, and *l* .... Dan 3:29
I turn to the people a pure *l* .... Zeph 3:9
man heard them speak in his own *l* ... Acts 2:6

LANGUAGES

O people, nations, and *l* .... Dan 3:4
the people, the nations, and the *l* ...... Dan 3:7
unto all people, nations, and *l* .... Dan 4:1
him, all people, nations, and *l* .... Dan 5:19
unto all people, nations, and *l* .... Dan 6:25
that all people, nations, and *l* .... Dan 7:14
hold out of all *l* of the nations .... Zec 8:23

LANGUISH

For the fields of Heshbon *l* .... Is 16:8
nets upon the waters shall *l* .... Is 19:8
haughty people of the earth do *l* .... Is 24:4
mourneth, and the gates thereof *l* ...... Jer 14:2
one that dwelleth therein shall *l* .... Hos 4:3

LANGUISHED

they *l* together. .... Lam 2:8

LANGUISHETH

earth *l* and fadeth away, the world *l* ... Is 24:4
The new wine mourneth, the vine *l* ... Is 24:7
The earth mourneth and *l* .... Is 33:9
She that hath borne seven *l* .... Jer 15:9
new wine is dried up, the oil *l* .... Joel 1:10
is dried up, and the fig tree *l* .... Joel 1:12
Bashan *l*, and Carmel .... Nah 1:4
and the flower of Lebanon *l* .... Nah 1:4

LANGUISHING

strengthen him upon the bed of *l* ...... Ps 41:3

LANTERNS

Pharisees, cometh thither with *l* .... Jn 18:3

LAODICEA *(la-od-i-se´-ah)* Chief city of Phrygia.

I have for you, and for them that at *L* .... Col 2:1
for you, and them that are in *L* .... Col 4:13
the brethren which are in *L* .... Col 4:15
likewise read the epistle from *L* .... Col 4:16
to Timothy was written from *L* .... 1Ti s
and into Philadelphia, and unto *L* ...... Rev 1:11

LAODICEANS *(la-od-i-se´-uns)* Inhabitants of Laodicea.

read also in the church of the *L* .... Col 4:16
of the church of the *L* write. .... Rev 3:14

LAP

thereof wild gourds his *l* full. 2Kin 4:39
Also I shook my *l*, and said, So. .... Neh 5:13
The lot is cast into the *l* .... Prov 16:33

LAPIDOTH *(lap´-i-doth)* Husband of Deborah. a prophetess, the wife of *L* .... Judg 4:4

LAPPED

And the number of them that *l* .... Judg 7:6
men that *l* will I save you .... Judg 7:7

LAPPETH
Every one that l of the water............... Judg 7:5
water with his tongue, as a dog l......... Judg 7:5

LAPPIDOTH See LAPIDOTH.

LAPWING
heron after her kind, and the l............. Lev 11:19
heron after her kind, and the l.......... Deut 14:18

LARGE
behold, it is l enough for them............. Gen 34:21
that land unto a good land and a l......... Ex 3:8
a people secure, and to a l land.......... Judg 18:10
me forth also into a l place.............. 2Sa 22:20
people, The work is great and l........... Neh 4:19
Now the city was l and great.............. Neh 7:4
thou gavest them, and in the l............ Neh 9:35
me forth also into a l place.............. Ps 18:19
thou hast set my feet in a l room......... Ps 31:8
me, and set me in a l place............... Ps 118:5
thee like a ball into a l country......... Is 22:18
thy cattle feed in l pastures............. Is 30:23
he hath made it deep and l................ Is 30:33
l chambers, and cutteth him out........... Jer 22:14
of thy sister's cup deep and l............ Eze 23:32
feed them as a lamb in a l place.......... Hos 4:16
they gave l money unto the................ Mt 28:12
he will shew you a l upper room........... Mk 14:15
he shall shew you a l upper room.......... Lk 22:12
Ye see how l a letter I have.............. Gal 6:11
the length is as l as the breadth......... Rev 21:16

LARGENESS
l of heart, even as the sand that......... 1Kin 4:29

LASCIVIOUSNESS
wickedness, deceit, l, an evil............ Mk 7:22
l which they have committed............... 2Cor 12:21
fornication, uncleanness, l............... Gal 5:19
have given themselves unto l.............. Eph 4:19
the Gentiles, when we walked in l......... 1Pet 4:3
the grace of our God into l............... Jude 4

LASEA (la-se'-ah) A city on Crete,
nigh whereunto was the city of L.......... Acts 27:8

LASHA (la'-shah) A place in southern Canaan.
and Zeboim, even unto L.................. Gen 10:19

LASHARON (lash'-ar-on) A Canaanite town.
the king of L, one...................... Josh 12:18

LAST
shall befall you in the l days........... Gen 49:1
but he shall overcome at the l........... Gen 49:19
and let my l end be like his............ Num 23:10
Why are ye the l to bring the........... 2Sa 19:11
ye the l to bring back the king......... 2Sa 19:12
Now these be the l words of David....... 2Sa 23:1
For by the l words of David the......... 1Chr 23:27
of David the king, first and l......... 1Chr 29:29
the acts of Solomon, first and l........ 2Chr 9:29
the acts of Rehoboam, first and l....... 2Chr 12:15
the acts of Asa, first and l........... 2Chr 16:11
acts of Jehoshaphat, first and l........ 2Chr 20:34
the acts of Amaziah, first and l........ 2Chr 25:26
of the acts of Uzziah, first and l...... 2Chr 26:22
and of all his ways, first and l........ 2Chr 28:26
And his deeds, first and l, behold...... 2Chr 35:27
of the l sons of Adonikam, whose........ Ezr 8:13
from the first day unto the l day....... Neh 8:18
And thou mourn at the l, when thy....... Prov 5:11
At the l it biteth like a serpent....... Prov 23:32
shall come to pass in the l days........ Is 2:2
LORD, the first, and with the l......... Is 41:4
I am the first, and I am the l.......... Is 44:6
I am the first, I also am the l......... Is 48:12
said, He shall not see our l end........ Jer 12:4
I this Nebuchadrezzar king of........... Jer 50:17
the remembereth not her l end........... Lam 1:9
But at the l Daniel came in............. Dan 4:8
other, and the higher came up l......... Dan 8:3
in the l end of the indignation........ Dan 8:19
I will slay the l of them with......... Amos 9:1
But in the l days it shall come......... Mic 4:1
the l state of that man is worse....... Mt 12:45
many that are first shall be l......... Mt 19:30
and the l shall be first............... Mt 19:30
from the l unto the first.............. Mt 20:8
These l have wrought but one hour...... Mt 20:12
I will give unto this l, even as....... Mt 20:14
So the l shall be first............... Mt 20:16
shall be first, and the first l....... Mt 20:16
But l of all he sent unto them........ Mt 21:37
l of the woman died also.............. Mt 22:27
At the l came two false witnesses..... Mt 26:60
so the l error shall be worse......... Mt 27:64
first, the same shall be l of all..... Mk 9:35
many that are first shall be l........ Mk 10:31
and the l first........................ Mk 10:31
he sent also l unto them.............. Mk 12:6
l of all the woman died also.......... Mk 12:22
the l state of that man is worse...... Lk 11:26
thou hast paid the very l mite........ Lk 12:59
there are l which shall be first...... Lk 13:30
there are first which shall be l...... Lk 13:30
l of all the woman died also.......... Lk 20:32
raise it up again at the l day........ Jn 6:39
will raise him up at the l day........ Jn 6:40
I will raise him up at the l day...... Jn 6:44
I will raise him up at the l day...... Jn 6:54
In the l day, that great day of....... Jn 7:37
at the eldest, even unto the l........ Jn 8:9

in the resurrection at the l day...... Jn 11:24
same shall judge him in the l day..... Jn 12:48
shall come to pass in the l days...... Acts 2:17
hath set forth us the apostles l...... 1Cor 4:9
of all he was seen of me also......... 1Cor 15:8
The l enemy that shall be............. 1Cor 15:26
the l Adam was made a quickening...... 1Cor 15:45
of an eye, at the l trump............. 1Cor 15:52
that now at the l your care of me..... Phil 4:10
that in the l days perilous times..... 2Ti 3:1
Hath in these l days spoken unto...... Heb 1:2
treasure together for the l days...... Jas 5:3
to be revealed in the l time.......... 1Pet 1:5
manifest in these l times for you..... 1Pet 1:20
shall come in the l days scoffers..... 2Pet 3:3
Little children, it is the l time..... 1Jn 2:18
we know that it is the l time......... 1Jn 2:18
should be mockers in the l time....... Jude 18
and Omega, the first and the l........ Rev 1:11
I am the first and the l.............. Rev 1:17
things saith the first and the l...... Rev 2:8
the l to be more than the first...... Rev 2:19
angels having the seven l plagues..... Rev 15:1
vials full of the seven l plagues..... Rev 21:9
and the end, the first and the l...... Rev 22:13

LASTED
seven days, while their feast l....... Judg 14:17

LASTING
precious things of the l hills........ Deut 33:15

LATCHET
nor the l of their shoes be........... Is 5:27
the l of whose shoes I am not......... Mk 1:7
the l of whose shoes I am not......... Lk 3:16
whose shoe's I am not worthy to....... Jn 1:27

LATE
thou to rise up early, to sit up l.... Ps 127:2
Even of l my people is risen up....... Mic 2:8
the Jews of l sought to stone......... Jn 11:8

LATELY
I come from Italy, with his wife...... Acts 18:2

LATIN (lat'-in) Language spoken by the
Romans.
in letters of Greek, and L............ Lk 23:38
written in Hebrew, and Greek, and L... Jn 19:20

LATTER
believe the voice of the l sign....... Ex 4:8
do to thy people in the l days........ Num 24:14
but his l end shall be that he........ Num 24:20
upon thee, even in the l days......... Deut 4:30
to do thee good at thy l end.......... Deut 8:16
the l rain, that thou mayest.......... Deut 11:14
if the l husband hate her, and....... Deut 24:3
or if the l husband die, which....... Deut 24:3
will befall you in the l days........ Deut 31:29
they would consider their l end...... Deut 32:29
the l end than at the beginning...... Ruth 3:10
will be bitterness in the l end...... 2Sa 2:26
yet thy l end should arise........... Job 8:7
stand at the l day upon the earth.... Job 19:25
mouth wide as for the l rain......... Job 29:23
So the LORD blessed the l end of..... Job 42:12
is as a cloud of the l rain......... Prov 16:15
thou mayest be wise in thy l end..... Prov 19:20
them, and know the l end of them..... Is 41:22
didst remember the l end of it....... Is 47:7
hath been hurt in l end............. Jer 3:3
rain, both the former and the l...... Jer 5:24
in the l days ye shall consider..... Jer 30:24
in the l days ye shall consider..... Jer 48:47
captivity of Moab in the l days..... Jer 48:47
shall come to pass in the l days.... Jer 49:39
in the l years thou shalt consider.. Eze 38:16
it shall be in the l days.......... Eze 38:16
what shall be in the l days........ Dan 2:28
in the l time of their kingdom..... Dan 8:23
befall thy people in the l days.... Dan 10:14
not be as the former, or as the l.. Dan 11:29
and his goodness in the l days..... Hos 3:5
unto us as the rain, as the l...... Hos 6:3
the l rain in the first month...... Joel 2:23
the shooting up of the l growth.... Amos 7:1
it was the l growth after the...... Amos 7:1
The glory of this l house shall.... Hag 2:9
rain in the time of the l rain..... Zec 10:1
that in the l times some shall..... 1Ti 4:1
he receive the early and l rain.... Jas 5:7
the l end is worse with them than.. 2Pet 2:20

LATTICE
a window, and cried through the l.... Judg 5:28
Ahaziah fell down through a l in..... 2Kin 1:2
shewing himself through the l........ Song 2:9

LAUD
and l him, all ye people............. Rom 15:11

LAUGH
Abraham, Wherefore did Sarah l....... Gen 18:13
but thou didst l..................... Gen 18:15
Sarah said, God hath made me to l.... Gen 21:6
that all that hear will l with me.... Gen 21:6
and famine thou shalt l.............. Job 5:22
he will l at the trial of the....... Job 9:23
the innocent l them to scorn........ Job 22:19
sitteth in the heavens shall l...... Ps 2:4
they that see me l me to scorn...... Ps 22:7
The LORD shall l at him............. Ps 37:13
see, and fear, and shall l at him... Ps 52:6

But thou, O LORD, shalt l at them.... Ps 59:8
our enemies l among themselves...... Ps 80:6
I also will l at your calamity...... Prov 1:26
foolish man, whether he rage or l... Prov 29:9
A time to weep, and a time to l..... Eccl 3:4
for ye shall l...................... Lk 6:21
Woe unto you that now l............. Lk 6:25

LAUGHED
Abraham fell upon his face, and l.... Gen 17:17
Therefore Sarah l within herself.... Gen 18:12
Sarah denied, saying, I l not....... Gen 18:15
despised thee, and l thee to scorn.. 2Kin 19:21
but they l them to scorn, and....... 2Chr 30:10
they l us to scorn, and despised.... Neh 2:19
just upright man is l to scorn...... Job 12:4
If I l on them, they believed it.... Job 29:24
despised thee, and l thee to scorn.. Is 37:22
thou shalt be l to scorn and had.... Eze 23:32
And they l him to scorn............. Mt 9:24
And they l him to scorn............. Mk 5:40
they l him to scorn, knowing that... Lk 8:53

LAUGHETH
he l at the shaking of a spear...... Job 41:29

LAUGHING
Till he fill thy mouth with l....... Job 8:21

LAUGHTER
Then was our mouth filled with l.... Ps 126:2
Even in l the heart is sorrowful.... Prov 14:13
I said of l, It is mad............. Eccl 2:2
Sorrow is better than l............ Eccl 7:3
a pot, so is the l of the fool..... Eccl 7:6
A feast is made for l, and wine.... Eccl 10:19
let your l be turned to mourning... Jas 4:9

LAUNCH
L out into the deep, and let down... Lk 5:4

LAUNCHED
And they l forth................... Lk 8:22
were gotten from thence, and had l.. Acts 21:1
into a ship of Adramyttium, we l... Acts 27:2
had launched from thence.......... Acts 27:4

LAVER
Thou shalt also make a l of brass.. Ex 30:18
with all his vessels, and the l.... Ex 30:28
with all his furniture, and the l.. Ex 31:9
staves, and all his vessels, the l. Ex 35:16
And he made the l of brass......... Ex 38:8
staves, and all his vessels, the l. Ex 39:39
thou shalt set the l between the... Ex 40:7
And thou shalt anoint the l........ Ex 40:11
he set the l between the tent of... Ex 40:30
and all his vessels, both the l.... Lev 8:11
under the l were undersetters...... 1Kin 7:30
one l contained forty baths....... 1Kin 7:38
and every l was four cubits....... 1Kin 7:38
every one of the ten bases one l... 1Kin 7:38
removed the l from off them....... 2Kin 16:17

LAVERS
Then made he ten l of brass....... 1Kin 7:38
And Hiram made the l, and the..... 1Kin 7:40
ten bases, and ten l on the bases. 1Kin 7:43
He made also ten l, and put five... 2Chr 4:6
and l made he upon the bases...... 2Chr 4:14

LAVISH
They l gold out of the bag, and... Is 46:6

LAW
son, and Sarai his daughter in l... Gen 11:31
son, and put on, and spake unto his Gen 19:12
out, and spake unto his sons in l.. Gen 19:14
that mocked unto his sons in l..... Gen 19:14
Judah to Tamar his daughter in l... Gen 38:11
Behold thy father in l goeth up.... Gen 38:13
that she was his daughter in l..... Gen 38:16
Tamar thy daughter in l hath....... Gen 38:24
she sent to her father in l........ Gen 38:25
Joseph made it a l over the land... Gen 47:26
flock of Jethro his father in l.... Ex 3:1
to Jethro his father in l.......... Ex 4:18
One l shall be to him that is...... Ex 12:49
that the LORD's l may be in thy.... Ex 13:9
whether they will walk in my l..... Ex 16:4
of Midian, Moses' father in l...... Ex 18:1
Then Jethro, Moses' father in l.... Ex 18:2
And Jethro, Moses' father in l..... Ex 18:5
I thy father in l Jethro am come... Ex 18:6
went out to meet his father in l... Ex 18:7
Moses told his father in l all..... Ex 18:8
And Jethro, Moses' father in l..... Ex 18:12
with Moses' father in l before God. Ex 18:12
when Moses' father in l saw all.... Ex 18:14
Moses said unto his father in l.... Ex 18:15
Moses' father in l said unto him... Ex 18:17
to the voice of his father in l.... Ex 18:24
Moses let his father in l depart... Ex 18:27
give thee tables of stone, and a l. Ex 24:12
This is the l of the burnt........ Lev 6:9
this is the l of the meat......... Lev 6:14
this is the l of the sin offering. Lev 6:25
Likewise this is the l of the..... Lev 7:1
there is one l for them........... Lev 7:7
this is the l of the sacrifice of. Lev 7:11
This is the l of the.............. Lev 7:37
This is the l of the beasts, and.. Lev 11:46
This is the l for her that hath... Lev 12:7
This is the l of the plague of.... Lev 13:59
This shall be the l of the leper.. Lev 14:2

This is the *l* of him in whom is ...... Lev 14:32
This is the *l* for all manner of ...... Lev 14:54
this is the *l* of leprosy ...... Lev 14:57
This is the *l* of him that hath an ...... Lev 15:32
nakedness of thy daughter in *l* ...... Lev 18:15
a man lie with his daughter in *l* ...... Lev 20:12
Ye shall have one manner of *l* ...... Lev 24:22
This is the *l* of jealousies, when ...... Num 5:29
shall execute upon her all this *l* ...... Num 5:30
this is the *l* of the Nazarite, ... Num 6:13
This is the *l* of the Nazarite who ...... Num 6:21
do after the *l* of his separation ...... Num 6:21
the Midianite, Moses' father in *l* ...... Num 10:29
One *l* and one manner shall be for ...... Num 15:16
Ye shall have one *l* for him that ...... Num 15:29
This is the ordinance of the *l* ...... Num 19:2
This is the *l*, when a man dieth ...... Num 19:14
This is the ordinance of the *l* ...... Num 31:21
began Moses to declare this *l* ...... Deut 1:5
so righteous as all this *l* ...... Deut 4:8
this is the *l* which Moses set ...... Deut 4:44
to the sentence of the *l* which ...... Deut 17:11
I in a book out of that which is ...... Deut 17:18
to keep all the words of this *l* ...... Deut 17:19
upon them all the words of this *l* ...... Deut 27:3
the words of this *l* very plainly ...... Deut 27:8
that lieth with his mother in *l* ...... Deut 27:23
the words of this *l* to do them ...... Deut 27:26
to do all the words of this *l* ...... Deut 28:58
not written in the book of this *l* ...... Deut 28:61
are written in this book of the *l* ...... Deut 29:21
we may do all the words of this *l* ...... Deut 29:29
are written in this book of the *l* ...... Deut 30:10
And Moses wrote this *l*, and ...... Deut 31:9
thou shalt read this *l* before all ...... Deut 31:11
to do all the words of this *l* ...... Deut 31:12
the words of this *l* in a book ...... Deut 31:24
Take this book of the *l*, and put ...... Deut 31:26
to do, all the words of this *l* ...... Deut 32:46
hand went a fiery *l* for them ...... Deut 33:2
Moses commanded us a *l*, even the ...... Deut 33:4
thy judgments, and Israel thy *l* ...... Deut 33:10
to do according to all the *l* ...... Josh 1:7
This book of the *l* shall not ...... Josh 1:8
in the book of the *l* of Moses ...... Josh 8:31
stones a copy of the *l* of Moses ...... Josh 8:32
he read all the words of the *l* ...... Josh 8:34
is written in the book of the *l* ...... Josh 8:34
to do the commandment and the *l* ...... Josh 8:34
in the book of the *l* of Moses ...... Josh 23:6
words in the book of the *l* of God ...... Josh 24:26
of the Kenite, Moses' father in *l* ...... Judg 1:16
of Hobab the father in *l* of Moses ...... Judg 4:11
the son in *l* of the Timnite, ... Judg 15:6
And his father in *l*, the damsel's ...... Judg 19:4
father said unto his son in *l* ...... Judg 19:5
depart, his father in *l* urged him ...... Judg 19:7
and his servant, his father in *l* ...... Judg 19:9
she arose with her daughters in *l* ...... Ruth 1:6
her two daughters in *l* with her ...... Ruth 1:7
said unto her two daughters in *l* ...... Ruth 1:8
and Orpah kissed her mother in *l* ...... Ruth 1:14
thy sister in *l* is gone back unto ...... Ruth 1:15
return thou after thy sister in *l* ...... Ruth 1:15
the Moabitess, her daughter in *l* ...... Ruth 1:22
in *l* since the death of thine ...... Ruth 2:11
her mother in *l* saw what she had ...... Ruth 2:18
And her mother in *l* said unto her ...... Ruth 2:19
she shewed her mother in *l* with ...... Ruth 2:19
Naomi said unto her daughter in *l* ...... Ruth 2:20
said unto Ruth her daughter in *l* ...... Ruth 2:22
and dwelt with her mother in *l* ...... Ruth 2:23
her mother in *l* said unto her ...... Ruth 3:1
all that her mother in *l* bade her ...... Ruth 3:6
when she came to her mother in *l* ...... Ruth 3:16
Go not empty unto thy mother in *l* ...... Ruth 3:17
for thy daughter in *l*, which ...... Ruth 4:15
And his daughter in *l*, Phinehas' 1Sa 4:19
taken, and that her father in *l* 1Sa 4:19
and because of her father in *l* 1Sa 4:21
I should be son in *l* to the king 1Sa 18:18
son in *l* in the one of the twain 1Sa 18:21
therefore be the king's son in *l* 1Sa 18:22
thing to be a king's son in *l* 1Sa 18:23
well to be the king's son in *l* 1Sa 18:26
he might be the king's son in *l* 1Sa 18:27
which is the king's son in *l* 1Sa 22:14
it is written in the *l* of Moses 1Kin 2:3
the son in *l* of the house of Ahab 2Kin 8:27
took no heed to walk in the *l* of 2Kin 10:31
in the book of the *l* of Moses 2Kin 14:6
according to all the *l* which I 2Kin 17:13
their ordinances, or after the *l* 2Kin 17:34
and the ordinances, and the *l* 2Kin 17:37
according to all the *l* that my 2Kin 21:8
of the *l* in the house of the LORD 2Kin 22:8
the words of the book of the *l* 2Kin 22:11
I which were written in the book 2Kin 23:24
according to all the *l* of Moses 2Kin 23:25
his daughter in *l* bare him Pharez 1Chr 2:4
the same to Jacob for a *l* 1Chr 16:17
is written in the *l* of Moses 1Chr 16:40
keep the *l* of the LORD thy God 1Chr 22:12
need to their way to walk in my *l* 2Chr 6:16
he forsook the *l* of the LORD 2Chr 12:1
of their fathers, and to do the *l* 2Chr 14:4
a teaching priest, and without *l* 2Chr 15:3
had the book of the *l* of the LORD 2Chr 17:9
between blood and blood, between 2Chr 19:10
it is written in the *l* of Moses 2Chr 23:18

in the *l* in the book of Moses 2Chr 25:4
according to the *l* of Moses the 2Chr 30:16
is written in the *l* of the LORD 2Chr 31:3
encouraged in the *l* of the LORD 2Chr 31:4
of the house of God, and in the *l* 2Chr 31:21
them, according to the whole *l* 2Chr 33:8
the *l* of the LORD given by Moses 2Chr 34:14
of the *l* in the house of the LORD 2Chr 34:15
king had heard the words of the *l* 2Chr 34:19
was written in the *l* of the LORD 2Chr 35:26
in the *l* of Moses the man of God ...... Ezr 3:2
a ready scribe in the *l* of Moses ...... Ezr 7:6
heart to seek the *l* of the LORD ...... Ezr 7:10
a scribe of the *l* of the God of ...... Ezr 7:12
according to the *l* of thy God ...... Ezr 7:14
the scribe of the *l* of the God of ...... Ezr 7:21
will not do the *l* of thy God ...... Ezr 7:26
the *l* of the king, let judgment ...... Ezr 7:26
let it be done according to the *l* ...... Ezr 10:3
because he was the son in *l* of ...... Neh 6:18
bring the book of the *l* of Moses ...... Neh 8:1
Ezra the priest brought the *l* ...... Neh 8:2
attentive unto the book of the *l* ...... Neh 8:3
the people to understand the *l* ...... Neh 8:7
read in the book of the *l* of God ...... Neh 8:8
read in the book of the *l* distinctly ...... Neh 8:8
they heard the words of the *l* ...... Neh 8:9
to understand the words of the *l* ...... Neh 8:13
they found written in the *l* which ...... Neh 8:14
read in the book of the *l* of God ...... Neh 8:18
read in the book of the *l* of the ...... Neh 9:3
cast thy *l* behind their backs, and ...... Neh 9:26
bring them again unto thy *l* ...... Neh 9:29
nor our fathers, kept thy *l* ...... Neh 9:34
of the lands unto the *l* of God ...... Neh 10:28
into an oath, to walk in God's *l* ...... Neh 10:29
God, as it is written in the *l* ...... Neh 10:34
cattle, as it is written in the *l* ...... Neh 10:36
portions of the *l* for the priests ...... Neh 12:44
pass, when they had heard the *l* ...... Neh 13:3
was son in *l* to Sanballat the ...... Neh 13:28
drinking was according to the *l* ...... Est 1:8
manner toward all that knew *l* ...... Est 1:13
the queen Vashti according to *l* ...... Est 1:15
there is one of his to put him ...... Est 4:11
which is not according to the *l* ...... Est 4:16
the *l* from his mouth, and lay up ...... Job 22:22
delight is in the *l* of the LORD ...... Ps 1:2
in his *l* doth he meditate day and ...... Ps 1:2
The *l* of the LORD is perfect, ... Ps 19:7
The *l* of his God is in his heart ...... Ps 37:31
yea, thy *l* is within my heart ...... Ps 40:8
Give ear, O my people, to my *l* ...... Ps 78:1
Jacob, and appointed a *l* in Israel ...... Ps 78:5
God, and refused to walk in his *l* ...... Ps 78:10
and a *l* of the God of Jacob, ... Ps 81:4
If his children forsake my *l* ...... Ps 89:30
and teachest him out of thy *l* ...... Ps 94:12
which frameth mischief by a *l* ...... Ps 94:20
the same unto Jacob for a *l* ...... Ps 105:10
who walk in the *l* of the LORD ...... Ps 119:1
wondrous things out of thy *l* ...... Ps 119:18
and grant me thy *l* graciously ...... Ps 119:29
and I shall keep thy *l* ...... Ps 119:34
So shall I keep thy *l* continually ...... Ps 119:44
have I not declined from thy *l* ...... Ps 119:51
of the wicked that forsake thy *l* ...... Ps 119:53
in the night, and have kept thy *l* ...... Ps 119:55
but I have not forgotten thy *l* ...... Ps 119:61
but I delight in thy *l* ...... Ps 119:70
The *l* of thy mouth is better unto ...... Ps 119:72
for thy *l* is my delight ...... Ps 119:77
for me, which are not after thy *l* ...... Ps 119:85
Unless thy *l* had been my delights ...... Ps 119:92
O how love I thy *l* ...... Ps 119:97
yet do I not forget thy *l* ...... Ps 119:109
but thy *l* do I love ...... Ps 119:113
for they have made void thy *l* ...... Ps 119:126
eyes, because they keep not thy *l* ...... Ps 119:136
and thy *l* is the truth ...... Ps 119:142
they are far from thy *l* ...... Ps 119:150
for I do not forget thy *l* ...... Ps 119:153
but thy *l* do I love ...... Ps 119:163
peace have they which love thy *l* ...... Ps 119:165
and thy *l* is my delight ...... Ps 119:174
forsake not the *l* of thy mother ...... Prov 1:8
My son, forget not my *l* ...... Prov 3:1
doctrine, forsake ye not my *l* ...... Prov 4:2
forsake not the *l* of thy mother ...... Prov 6:20
my *l* as the apple of thine eye ...... Prov 6:23
The *l* of the wise is a fountain ...... Prov 13:14
forsake the *l* praise the wicked ...... Prov 28:4
as keep the *l* contend with them ...... Prov 28:4
Whoso keepeth the *l* is a wise son ...... Prov 28:7
away his ear from hearing the *l* ...... Prov 28:9
but he that keepeth the *l* ...... Prov 29:18
Lest they drink, and forget the *l* ...... Prov 31:5
her tongue is the *l* of kindness ...... Prov 31:26
give ear unto the *l* of our God ...... Is 1:10
out of Zion shall go forth the *l* ...... Is 2:3
away the *l* of the LORD of hosts ...... Is 5:24
seal the *l* among my disciples ...... Is 8:16
To the *l* and to the testimony ...... Is 8:20
will not hear the *l* of the LORD ...... Is 30:9
and the idles shall not be in *l* ...... Is 42:4
he will magnify the *l*, and make it ...... Is 42:21
were they obedient unto his *l* ...... Is 42:24
for a *l* shall proceed from me, and ...... Is 51:4
the people in whose heart is my *l* ...... Is 51:7
that handle the *l* knew me not ...... Jer 2:8

unto my words, nor to my *l* ...... Jer 6:19
the *l* of the LORD is with us ...... Jer 8:8
my *l* which I set before them ...... Jer 9:13
me, and have not kept my *l* ...... Jer 16:11
for the *l* shall not perish from ...... Jer 18:18
hearken to me, to walk in my *l* ...... Jer 26:4
I will put my *l* in their inward ...... Jer 31:33
was sealed according to the *l* ...... Jer 32:11
voice, neither walked in thy *l* ...... Jer 32:23
they feared, nor walked in his *l* ...... Jer 44:10
of the LORD, nor walked in his *l* ...... Jer 44:23
the *l* is no more ...... Lam 2:9
but the *l* shall perish from the ...... Eze 7:26
lewdly defiled his daughter in *l* ...... Eze 22:11
Her priests have violated my *l* ...... Eze 22:26
This is the *l* of the house ...... Eze 43:12
this is the *l* of the house ...... Eze 43:12
him concerning the *l* of his God ...... Dan 6:5
according to the *l* of the Medes ...... Dan 6:8
according to the *l* of the Medes ...... Dan 6:12
that the *l* of the Medes and ...... Dan 6:15
Israel have transgressed thy *l* ...... Dan 9:11
the *l* of Moses the servant of God ...... Dan 9:11
it is written in the *l* of Moses ...... Dan 9:13
hast forgotten the *l* of thy God ...... Hos 4:6
and trespassed against my *l* ...... Hos 8:1
to him the great things of my *l* ...... Hos 8:12
have despised the *l* of the LORD ...... Amos 2:4
for the *l* shall go forth of Zion, ... Mic 4:2
the daughter in *l* against her ...... Mic 7:6
against her mother in *l* ...... Mic 7:6
Therefore the *l* is slacked ...... Hab 1:4
they have done violence to the *l* ...... Zeph 3:4
now the priests concerning the *l* ...... Hag 2:11
lest they should hear the *l* ...... Zec 7:12
The *l* of truth was in his mouth, ... Mal 2:6
should seek the *l* at his mouth ...... Mal 2:7
caused many to stumble at the *l* ...... Mal 2:8
but have been partial in the *l* ...... Mal 2:9
Remember ye the *l* of Moses my ...... Mal 4:4
that I am come to destroy the *l* ...... Mt 5:17
shall in no wise pass from the *l* ...... Mt 5:18
if any man will sue thee at the *l* ...... Mt 5:40
for this is the *l* and the prophets ...... Mt 7:12
the daughter in *l* against her ...... Mt 10:35
against her mother in *l* ...... Mt 10:35
the *l* prophesied until John ...... Mt 11:13
Or have ye not read in the *l* ...... Mt 12:5
is the great commandment in the *l* ...... Mt 22:36
two commandments hang all the *l* ...... Mt 22:40
the weightier matters of the *l* ...... Mt 23:23
the *l* of Moses were accomplished ...... Lk 2:22
is written in the *l* of the Lord ...... Lk 2:23
is said in the *l* of the Lord, ... Lk 2:24
for him after the custom of the *l* ...... Lk 2:27
according to the *l* of the Lord ...... Lk 2:39
and doctors of the *l* sitting by ...... Lk 5:17
him, What is written in the *l* ...... Lk 10:26
the mother in *l* against her ...... Lk 12:53
against her daughter in *l* ...... Lk 12:53
the daughter in *l* against her ...... Lk 12:53
against her mother in *l* ...... Lk 12:53
The *l* and the prophets were until ...... Lk 16:16
than one tittle of the *l* to fail ...... Lk 16:17
were written in the *l* of Moses ...... Lk 24:44
For the *l* was given by Moses, but ...... Jn 1:17
found him, of whom Moses in the *l* ...... Jn 1:45
Did not Moses give you the *l* ...... Jn 7:19
and yet none of you keepeth the *l* ...... Jn 7:19
that the *l* of Moses should not be ...... Jn 7:23
who knoweth not the *l* are cursed ...... Jn 7:49
Doth our *l* judge any man, before ...... Jn 7:51
Now Moses in the *l* commanded us ...... Jn 8:5
It is also written in your *l* ...... Jn 8:17
them, Is it not written in your *l* ...... Jn 10:34
We have heard out of the *l* that ...... Jn 12:34
that is written in their *l* ...... Jn 15:25
he was father in *l* to Caiaphas ...... Jn 18:13
and judge him according to your *l* ...... Jn 18:31
Jews answered him, We have a *l* ...... Jn 19:7
by our *l* he ought to die, because ...... Jn 19:7
named Gamaliel, a doctor of the *l* ...... Acts 5:34
against this holy place, and the *l* ...... Acts 6:13
Who have received the *l* by the ...... Acts 7:53
And after the reading of the *l* ...... Acts 13:15
be justified by the *l* of Moses ...... Acts 13:39
them to keep the *l* of Moses ...... Acts 15:5
be circumcised, and keep the *l* ...... Acts 15:24
to worship God contrary to the *l* ...... Acts 18:13
of words and names, and of your *l* ...... Acts 18:15
the *l* is open, and there are ...... Acts 19:38
and they are all zealous of the *l* ...... Acts 21:20
walkest orderly, and keepest the *l* ...... Acts 21:24
against the people, and the *l* ...... Acts 21:28
manner of the *l* of the fathers, ... Acts 22:3
a devout man according to the *l* ...... Acts 22:12
thou to judge me after the *l* ...... Acts 23:3
to be smitten contrary to the *l* ...... Acts 23:3
accused of questions of their *l* ...... Acts 23:29
have judged according to our *l* ...... Acts 24:6
things which are written in the *l* ...... Acts 24:14
Neither against the *l* of the Jews ...... Acts 25:8
Jesus, both out of the *l* of Moses ...... Acts 28:23
I shall also perish without *l* ...... Rom 2:12
shall be judged by the *l* ...... Rom 2:12
of the *l* are just before God ...... Rom 2:13
doers of the *l* shall be justified ...... Rom 2:13
Gentiles, which have not the *l* ...... Rom 2:14
the things contained in the *l* ...... Rom 2:14
these, having not the *l* ...... Rom 2:14

the *l*, are a *l* unto themselves .... Rom 2:14
of the *l* written in their hearts .... Rom 2:15
called a *law*, and restest in the *l* .... Rom 2:17
being instructed out of the *l* .... Rom 2:18
and of the truth in the *l* .... Rom 2:20
that makest thy boast of the *l* .... Rom 2:23
through breaking the *l* .... Rom 2:23
profiteth, if thou keep the *l* .... Rom 2:25
but if thou be a breaker of the *l* .... Rom 2:25
keep the righteousness of the *l* .... Rom 2:26
is by nature, if it fulfil the *l* .... Rom 2:27
dost transgress the *l* .... Rom 2:27
what things soever the *l* saith .... Rom 3:19
saith to them who are under the *l* .... Rom 3:19
of the *l* there shall no flesh be .... Rom 3:20
for by the *l* is the knowledge of .... Rom 3:20
God without the *l* is manifested .... Rom 3:21
being witnessed by the *l* .... Rom 3:21
By what *l* .... Rom 3:27
but by the *l* of faith .... Rom 3:27
faith without the deeds of the *l* .... Rom 3:28
make void the *l* through faith .... Rom 3:31
yea, we establish the *l* .... Rom 3:31
or to his seed, through the *l* .... Rom 4:13
they which are of the *l* be heirs .... Rom 4:14
Because the *l* worketh wrath .... Rom 4:15
for where no *l* is, there is no .... Rom 4:15
to that only which is of the *l* .... Rom 4:16
(For until the *l* sin was in the .... Rom 5:13
is not imputed when there is no *l* .... Rom 5:13
Moreover the *l* entered, that the .... Rom 5:20
for ye are not under the *l* .... Rom 6:14
because we are not under the *l* .... Rom 6:15
I speak to them that know the *l* .... Rom 7:1
how that the *l* hath dominion .... Rom 7:1
l to her husband so long as he .... Rom 7:2
loosed from the *l* of her husband .... Rom 7:2
be dead, she is free from that *l* .... Rom 7:3
to the *l* by the body of Christ .... Rom 7:4
of sins, which were by the *l* .... Rom 7:5
now we are delivered from the *l* .... Rom 7:6
Is the *l* sin .... Rom 7:7
I had not known sin, but by the *l* .... Rom 7:7
known lust, except the *l* had said .... Rom 7:7
For without the *l* sin was dead .... Rom 7:8
I was alive without the *l* once .... Rom 7:9
Wherefore the *l* is holy, and the .... Rom 7:12
we know that the *l* is spiritual .... Rom 7:14
unto the *l* that it is good .... Rom 7:16
I find them a *l*, that, when I .... Rom 7:21
For I delight in the *l* of God .... Rom 7:22
But I see another *l* in my members .... Rom 7:23
warring against the *l* of my mind .... Rom 7:23
into me captivity to the *l* of sin .... Rom 7:23
mind I myself serve the *l* of God .... Rom 7:25
but with the flesh the *l* of sin .... Rom 7:25
For the *l* of the Spirit of .... Rom 8:2
made me free from the *l* of sin .... Rom 8:2
For what the *l* could not do .... Rom 8:3
of the *l* might be fulfilled in us .... Rom 8:4
it is not subject to the *l* of God .... Rom 8:7
covenants, and the giving of the *l* .... Rom 9:4
after the *l* of righteousness .... Rom 9:31
to the *l* of righteousness .... Rom 9:31
as it were by the works of the *l* .... Rom 9:32
For Christ is the end of the *l* .... Rom 10:4
righteousness which is of the *l* .... Rom 10:5
another hath fulfilled the *l* .... Rom 13:8
love is the fulfilling of the *l* .... Rom 13:10
to go *l* before the unjust, and not 1Cor 6:1
brother goeth to *l* with brother 1Cor 6:6
ye go to *l* one with another 1Cor 6:7
The wife is bound by the *l* as 1Cor 7:39
or saith not the *l* the same also 1Cor 9:8
it is written in the *l* of Moses 1Cor 9:9
are under the *l*, as under the *l* 1Cor 9:20
gain them that are under the *l* 1Cor 9:20
are without *l*, as without *l* 1Cor 9:21
l, (being not without *l* to God 1Cor 9:21
but under the *l* to Christ 1Cor 9:21
gain them that are without *l* 1Cor 9:21
In the *l* it is written, With men 1Cor 14:21
obedience, as also saith the *l* 1Cor 14:34
and the strength of sin is the *l* 1Cor 15:56
justified by the works of the *l* .... Gal 2:16
and not by the works of the *l* .... Gal 2:16
for by the works of the *l* .... Gal 2:16
For I through the *l* am dead to .... Gal 2:19
through the *l* am dead to the *l* .... Gal 2:19
if righteousness come by the *l* .... Gal 2:21
the Spirit by the works of the *l* .... Gal 3:2
doeth he it by the works of the *l* .... Gal 3:5
of the *l* are under the curse .... Gal 3:10
in the book of the *l* to do them .... Gal 3:10
by the *l* in the sight of God .... Gal 3:11
And the *l* is not of faith .... Gal 3:12
us from the curse of the *l* .... Gal 3:13
before of God in Christ, the *l* .... Gal 3:17
if the inheritance be of the *l* .... Gal 3:18
Wherefore then serveth the *l* .... Gal 3:19
Is the *l* then against the .... Gal 3:21
for if there had been a *l* given .... Gal 3:21
should have been by the *l* .... Gal 3:21
came, we were kept under the *l* .... Gal 3:23
Wherefore the *l* was our .... Gal 3:24
made of a woman, made under the *l* .... Gal 4:4
redeem them that were under the *l* .... Gal 4:5
ye that desire to be under the *l* .... Gal 4:21
do ye not hear the *l* .... Gal 4:21
he is a debtor to do the whole *l* .... Gal 5:3

of you are justified by the *l* .... Gal 5:4
For all the *l* is fulfilled in one .... Gal 5:14
Spirit, ye are not under the *l* .... Gal 5:18
against such there is no *l* .... Gal 5:23
and so fulfil the *l* of Christ .... Gal 6:2
who are circumcised keep the *l* .... Gal 6:13
even the *l* of commandments .... Eph 2:15
as touching the *l*, a Pharisee .... Phil 3:5
righteousness which is in the *l* .... Phil 3:6
righteousness, which is of the *l* .... Phil 3:9
Desiring to be teachers of the *l* 1Ti 1:7
But we know that the *l* is good 1Ti 1:8
that the *l* is not made for a 1Ti 1:9
and strivings about the *l* .... Titus 3:9
of the people received the *l* .... Heb 7:5
it the people received the *l* .... Heb 7:11
necessity a change also of the *l* .... Heb 7:12
not after the *l* of a carnal .... Heb 7:16
For the *l* made nothing perfect .... Heb 7:19
For the *l* maketh men high priests .... Heb 7:28
the oath, which was since the *l* .... Heb 7:28
offer gifts according to the *l* .... Heb 8:4
all the people according to the *l* .... Heb 9:19
are by the *l* purged with blood .... Heb 9:22
For the *l* having a shadow of good .... Heb 10:1
which are offered by the *l* .... Heb 10:8
He that despised Moses' *l* died .... Heb 10:28
into the perfect *l* of liberty .... Jas 1:25
If ye fulfil the royal *l* .... Jas 2:8
the *l* as transgressors .... Jas 2:9
whosoever shall keep the whole *l* .... Jas 2:10
become a transgressor of the *l* .... Jas 2:11
be judged by the *l* of liberty .... Jas 2:12
evil of the *l*, and judgeth the *l* .... Jas 4:11
but if thou judge the *l* .... Jas 4:11
thou art not a doer of the *l* .... Jas 4:11
sin transgresseth also the *l* 1Jn 3:4
sin is the transgression of the *l* 1Jn 3:4

LAWFUL
it shall not be *l* to impose toll .... Ezr 7:24
or the *l* captive delivered .... Is 49:24
be just, and do that which is *l* .... Eze 18:5
the son hath done that which is *l* .... Eze 18:19
statutes, and do that which is *l* .... Eze 18:21
and doeth that which is *l* .... Eze 18:27
his sin, and do that which is *l* .... Eze 33:14
he hath done that which is *l* .... Eze 33:16
wickedness, and do that which is *l* .... Eze 33:19
not *l* to do upon the sabbath day .... Mt 12:2
which was not *l* for him to eat .... Mt 12:4
Is it *l* to heal on the sabbath .... Mt 12:10
Wherefore it is *l* to do well on .... Mt 12:12
It is not *l* for thee to have her .... Mt 14:4
Is it *l* for a man to put away his .... Mt 19:3
Is it not *l* for me to do what .... Mt 20:15
Is it *l* to give tribute unto .... Mt 22:17
It is not *l* for to put them into .... Mt 27:6
sabbath day that which is not *l* .... Mk 2:24
which is not *l* to eat but for the .... Mk 2:26
Is it *l* to do good on the sabbath .... Mk 3:4
It is not *l* for thee to have thy .... Mk 6:18
Is it *l* for a man to put away his .... Mk 10:2
Is it *l* to give tribute to Caesar .... Mk 12:14
not *l* to do on the sabbath days .... Lk 6:2
which it is not *l* to eat but for .... Lk 6:4
Is it *l* on the sabbath days to do .... Lk 6:9
Is it *l* to heal on the sabbath .... Lk 14:3
Is it *l* for us to give tribute .... Lk 20:22
it is not *l* for thee to carry thy .... Jn 5:10
It is not *l* for us to put any man .... Jn 18:31
which are not *l* for us to receive .... Acts 16:21
be determined in a *l* assembly .... Acts 19:39
Is it *l* for you to scourge a man .... Acts 22:25
All things are *l* unto me, but all 1Cor 6:12
all things are *l* for me, but I 1Cor 6:12
All things are *l* for me, but all 1Cor 10:23
all things are *l* for me, but all 1Cor 10:23
which it is not *l* for a man to 2Cor 12:4

LAWFULLY
law is good, if a man use it *l* 1Ti 1:8
not crowned, except he strive *l* 2Ti 2:5

LAWGIVER
nor a *l* from between his feet .... Gen 49:10
it, by the direction of the *l* .... Num 21:18
there, in a portion of the *l* .... Deut 33:21
Judah is my *l* .... Ps 60:7
Judah is my *l* .... Ps 108:8
is our judge, the LORD is our *l* .... Is 33:22
There is one *l*, who is able to .... Jas 4:12

LAWLESS
a righteous man, but for the *l* 1Ti 1:9

LAWS
my statutes, and my *l* .... Gen 26:5
to keep my commandments and my *l* .... Ex 16:28
the statutes of God, and his *l* .... Ex 18:16
shalt teach them ordinances and *l* .... Ex 18:20
the statutes and judgments and *l* .... Lev 26:46
all such as know the *l* of thy God .... Ezr 7:25
them right judgments, and true *l* .... Neh 9:13
them precepts, statutes, and *l* .... Neh 9:14
among the *l* of the Persians .... Est 1:19
their *l* are diverse from all .... Est 3:8
neither keep they the king's *l* .... Est 3:8
his statutes, and keep his *l* .... Ps 105:45
they have transgressed the *l* .... Is 24:5
thereof, and all the *l* thereof .... Eze 43:11
of the LORD, and all the *l* thereof .... Eze 44:5
and they shall keep my *l* and my .... Eze 44:24

and think to change times and *l* .... Dan 7:25
LORD our God, to walk in his *l* .... Dan 9:10
I will put my *l* into their mind .... Heb 8:10
I will put my *l* into their hearts .... Heb 10:16

LAWYER
Then one of them, which was a *l* .... Mt 22:35
And, behold, a certain *l* stood up .... Lk 10:25
Bring Zenas the *l* and Apollos on .... Titus 3:13

LAWYERS
I rejected the counsel of God .... Lk 7:30
Then answered one of the *l* .... Lk 11:45
he said, Woe unto you also, ye *l* .... Lk 11:46
Woe unto you, *l* .... Lk 11:52
Jesus answering spake unto the *l* .... Lk 14:3

LAY
But before they *l* down, the men .... Gen 19:4
went in, and *l* with her father .... Gen 19:33
he perceived not when she *l* down .... Gen 19:33
I yesternight with my father .... Gen 19:34
the younger arose, and *l* with him .... Gen 19:35
he perceived not when she *l* down .... Gen 19:35
L not thine hand upon the lad .... Gen 22:12
l down in that place to sleep .... Gen 28:11
And he *l* with her that night .... Gen 30:16
l with her, and defiled her .... Gen 34:2
l with Bilhah his father's .... Gen 35:22
wilderness, and *l* no hand upon him .... Gen 37:22
l up corn under the hand of .... Gen 41:35
heretofore, ye shall *l* upon them .... Ex 5:8
that I may *l* my hand upon Egypt .... Ex 7:4
the dew *l* round about the host .... Ex 16:13
when the dew that *l* was gone up .... Ex 16:14
there *l* a small round thing .... Ex 16:14
that which remaineth over *l* up .... Ex 16:23
l it up before the LORD, to be .... Ex 16:33
woman's husband will *l* upon him .... Ex 21:22
shalt thou *l* upon him usury .... Ex 22:25
the wood in order upon the fire .... Lev 1:7
shall *l* the parts, the head, and .... Lev 1:8
the priest shall *l* them in order .... Lev 1:12
and *l* frankincense thereon .... Lev 2:15
he shall *l* his hand upon the head .... Lev 3:2
he shall *l* his hand upon the head .... Lev 3:8
he shall *l* his hand upon the head .... Lev 3:13
shall *l* his hand upon .... Lev 4:4
of the congregation shall *l* their .... Lev 4:15
he shall *l* his hand upon the .... Lev 4:24
he shall *l* his hand upon the .... Lev 4:29
he shall *l* his hand upon the .... Lev 4:33
the burnt offering in order .... Lev 6:12
Aaron shall *l* both his hands upon .... Lev 16:21
let all that heard him *l* their .... Lev 24:14
the Levites shall *l* their hands .... Num 8:12
l not the sin upon us, wherein we .... Num 12:11
thou shalt *l* them up in the .... Num 17:4
them up without the camp in a .... Num 19:9
he *l* down as a lion, and as a .... Num 24:9
spirit, and I thine hand upon them .... Num 27:18
but will *l* them upon all their .... Deut 7:15
Therefore shall ye *l* up these my .... Deut 11:18
your God shall *l* the fear of you .... Deut 11:25
shalt *l* it up within thy gates .... Deut 14:28
I not innocent blood unto thy .... Deut 21:8
his mother I hold on him, and .... Deut 21:19
the man that I with the woman .... Deut 22:22
only that I with her shall die .... Deut 22:25
I hold on her, and *l* with her .... Deut 22:28
Then the man that I with her .... Deut 22:29
he shall *l* the foundation thereof .... Josh 6:26
laid an ambush for the city .... Josh 8:2
all that I near Ashdod, with .... Josh 15:46
her tent, behold, Sisera *l* dead .... Judg 4:22
feet he bowed, he fell, he *l* down .... Judg 5:27
I them upon this rock, and pour .... Judg 6:20
east *l* along in the valley like .... Judg 7:12
it, that the tent *l* along .... Judg 7:13
because she *l* sore upon him .... Judg 14:17
Samson *l* till midnight, and arose .... Judg 16:3
I thine hand upon thy mouth, and .... Judg 18:19
uncover his feet, and *l* thee down .... Ruth 3:4
and, behold, a woman *l* at his feet .... Ruth 3:8
she *l* at his feet until the .... Ruth 3:14
how they *l* with the women that 1Sa 2:22
And he went and *l* down 1Sa 3:5
went and *l* down in his place 1Sa 3:9
Samuel *l* until the morning, and 1Sa 3:15
the LORD, and *l* it upon the cart 1Sa 6:8
l it for a reproach upon all 1Sa 11:2
l down naked all that day and all 1Sa 19:24
beheld the place where Saul *l* 1Sa 26:5
Saul *l* in the trench, and his 1Sa 26:5
Saul *l* sleeping within the trench 1Sa 26:7
the people *l* round about him 1Sa 26:7
I thee hold on one of the young 2Sa 2:21
who *l* on a bed at noon 2Sa 4:5
he *l* on his bed in his bedchamber 2Sa 4:7
in unto him, and he *l* with her 2Sa 11:4
I in his bosom, and was unto him 2Sa 12:3
I all night upon the earth 2Sa 12:16
went in unto her, and *l* with her 2Sa 12:24
I thee down on thy bed, and make 2Sa 13:5
So Amnon *l* down, and made himself 2Sa 13:6
she, forced her, and *l* with her 2Sa 13:14
his garments, and *l* on the earth 2Sa 13:31
sustenance while he *l* at Mahanaim 2Sa 19:32
to *l* the foundation of the house 1Kin 5:17
that I on forty five pillars 1Kin 7:3
the altar, saying, L *l* hold on him 1Kin 13:4
I my bones beside his bones 1Kin 13:31

l it on wood, and put no fire...... 1Kin 18:23
l it on wood, and put no fire...... 1Kin 18:23
And as he l and slept under a 1Kin 19:5
l in sackcloth, and went softly 1Kin 21:27
into the chamber, and l there...... 2Kin 4:11
l my staff upon the face of the...... 2Kin 4:29
l upon the child, and put his...... 2Kin 4:34
for Joram l there...... 2Kin 9:16
L ye them in two heaps at the...... 2Kin 10:8
be to l waste fenced cities into...... 2Kin 19:25
to l the foundation of the heaps...... 2Chr 31:7
for as long as she l desolate she...... 2Chr 36:21
of such as l in wait by the way...... Ezr 8:31
so again, I will l hands on you...... Neh 13:21
sought to l hand on the king...... Est 2:21
he thought scorn to l hands on...... Est 3:6
many l in sackcloth and ashes...... Est 4:3
who sought to l hand on the kings...... Est 6:2
to l hand on such as sought their...... Est 9:2
that might l his hand upon us...... Job 9:33
L down now, put me in a surety...... Job 17:3
l your hand upon your mouth...... Job 21:5
l up his words in thine heart...... Job 22:22
Then shalt thou l up gold as dust...... Job 22:24
the dew l all night upon my...... Job 29:19
For he will not l upon man more...... Job 34:23
I will l mine hand upon my mouth...... Job 40:4
L thine hand upon him, remember...... Job 41:8
I will both l me down in peace,...... Ps 4:8
l mine honour in the dust...... Ps 7:5
after my life l snares for me...... Ps 38:12
they that l wait for my soul take...... Ps 71:10
where she may l her young...... Ps 84:3
l them down in their dens...... Ps 104:22
let us l wait for blood, let us...... Prov 1:11
they l wait for their own blood...... Prov 1:18
life to them that l hold upon her...... Prov 3:18
l up my commandments with thee...... Prov 7:1
Wise men l up knowledge...... Prov 10:14
l not wait, O wicked man, against...... Prov 24:15
l thine hand upon thy mouth...... Prov 30:32
to l hold on folly, till I might...... Eccl 2:3
the living will l it to his heart...... Eccl 7:2
And I will l it waste...... Is 5:6
that l field to field, till there...... Is 5:8
l hold of the prey, and shall...... Is 5:29
they shall l their hand upon Edom...... Is 11:14
anger, to l the land desolate...... Is 13:9
will l low the haughtiness of the...... Is 13:11
David will l l upon his shoulder...... Is 22:22
l low, and bring to the ground,...... Is 25:12
l l in Zion for a foundation a...... Is 28:16
also will l l to the...... Is 28:17
will l siege against thee with a...... Is 29:3
l a snare for him that reproveth...... Is 29:21
which the LORD shall l upon him....... Is 30:32
the great owl make her nest, and l...... Is 34:15
of dragons, where each l shall...... Is 35:7
that thou shouldest be to l waste...... Is 37:26
l it for a plaister upon the boil...... Is 38:21
so that thou didst not l these...... Is 47:7
l the foundations of the earth,...... Is 51:16
I will l thy stones with fair...... Is 54:11
l thy foundations with sapphires...... Is 54:11
they l wait, as he that setteth...... Jer 5:26
I will l stumblingblocks before...... Jer 6:21
They shall l hold on bow and spear...... Jer 6:23
l l a stumblingblock before him,...... Eze 3:20
l it before thee, and pourtray...... Eze 4:1
l siege against it, and build a...... Eze 4:2
thou shalt l siege against it...... Eze 4:3
l the iniquity of the house of...... Eze 4:4
I will l bands upon thee, and thou...... Eze 4:8
I will l the dead carcases of the...... Eze 6:5
she l down among lions, she...... Eze 19:2
for in her youth they l with her...... Eze 23:8
I will l my vengeance upon Edom...... Eze 25:14
when I shall l my vengeance upon...... Eze 25:17
and they shall l thy stones...... Eze 26:12
l away their robes, and put off...... Eze 26:16
I will l thee before kings, that...... Eze 28:17
I will l thy flesh upon the...... Eze 32:5
For I will l thee land most...... Eze 33:28
I will l thy cities waste, and...... Eze 35:4
it, and l no famine upon you...... Eze 36:29
whereas it l desolate in the...... Eze 36:34
I will l sinews upon you, and will...... Eze 37:6
there shall they l the most holy...... Eze 42:13
but there they shall l their...... Eze 42:14
l them in the holy chambers, and...... Eze 44:19
they l themselves down upon...... Amos 2:8
and he l, and was fast asleep...... Jonah 1:5
l not upon us innocent blood...... Jonah 1:14
idols l herself will l desolate...... Mic 1:7
they shall l their hand upon...... Mic 7:16
they shall l hold every one on...... Zec 14:13
and if ye will not l it to heart,...... Mal 2:2
because ye do not l it to heart...... Mal 2:2
L not up for yourselves treasures...... Mt 6:19
But l up for yourselves treasures...... Mt 6:20
man hath not where to l his head...... Mt 8:20
l thy hand upon her, and she shall...... Mt 9:18
day, will he not l hold on it...... Mt 12:11
they sought to l hands on him...... Mt 21:46
l them on men's shoulders...... Mt 23:4
see the place where the Lord l...... Mt 28:6
wife's mother l sick of a fever...... Mk 1:30
wherein the sick of the palsy l...... Mk 2:4
they went out to l hold on him...... Mk 3:21
l thy hands on her, that she may...... Mk 5:23

And they sought to l hold on him...... Mk 12:12
which I bound with them that had...... Mk 15:7
they shall l hands on the sick,...... Mk 16:18
him in, and to l him before him...... Lk 5:18
and took up that whereon he l...... Lk 5:25
years of age, and she l a dying...... Lk 8:42
man hath not where to l his head...... Lk 9:58
shall l thee even with the ground...... Lk 19:44
hour sought to l hands on him...... Lk 20:19
they shall l their hands on you,...... Lk 21:12
in these l a great multitude of,...... Jn 5:3
I l down my life for the sheep...... Jn 10:15
because I l down my life, that I...... Jn 10:17
but I l down of myself...... Jn 10:18
I have power to l it down,...... Jn 10:18
was a cave, and a stone l upon it...... Jn 11:38
I will l down my life for thy...... Jn 13:37
Wilt thou l down my life for my...... Jn 13:38
that a man l down his life for...... Jn 15:13
l not this sin to their charge...... Acts 7:60
that on whomsoever l hands...... Acts 8:19
to l upon you no greater burden,...... Acts 15:28
and no small tempest l on us...... Acts 27:20
of Publius l sick of a fever...... Acts 28:8
Who shall l any thing to the...... Rom 8:33
l l in Sion a stumblingstone and...... Rom 9:33
can no man l than that is laid...... 1Cor 3:11
one of you l by him in store...... 1Cor 16:2
ought not to l up for the parents...... 2Cor 12:14
hands suddenly on no man,...... 1Ti 5:22
l hold on eternal life, whereunto...... 1Ti 6:12
that they may l hold on eternal...... 1Ti 6:19
who have fled for refuge to l...... Heb 6:18
let us l aside every weight, and...... Heb 12:1
Wherefore l apart all filthiness,...... Jas 1:21
l l in Sion a chief corner stone,...... 1Pet 2:6
we ought to l down our lives for...... 1Jn 3:16

LAYEDST

takest up that thou l not down...... Lk 19:21

LAYEST

that thou l the burden of all...... Num 11:11
wherefore then l thou a snare for...... 1Sa 28:9

LAYETH

God l up his iniquity for his...... Job 21:19
yet God l not folly to them...... Job 24:12
of him that l at him cannot hold...... Job 41:26
he l up the depth in storehouses,...... Ps 33:7
Who l the beams of his chambers...... Ps 104:3
He l up sound wisdom for the...... Prov 2:7
but a fool l open his folly...... Prov 13:16
lips, and l up deceit within him...... Prov 26:24
She l her hands to the spindle,...... Prov 31:19
the lofty city, he l it low...... Is 26:5
he l it low, even to the ground,...... Is 26:5
the son of man that l hold on it...... Is 56:2
and no man l it to heart,...... Is 57:1
mouth, but in hand he l his wait...... Jer 9:8
because no man l it to heart,...... Jer 12:11
l the foundation of the earth, and...... Zec 12:1
So is he that l up treasure for...... Lk 12:21
he l it on his shoulders,...... Lk 15:5

LAYING

or hurl at him by l of wait...... Num 35:20
him any thing without l of wait...... Num 35:22
they commune of l snares privily...... Ps 64:5
For l aside the commandment of...... Mk 7:8
L wait for him, and seeking to...... Lk 11:54
when Simon saw that through the...... Acts 8:18
But their l await was known of...... Acts 9:24
I wait in the way to kill him...... Acts 25:3
with the l on of the hands of the...... 1Ti 4:14
L up in store for themselves a...... 1Ti 6:19
not l again the foundation of...... Heb 6:1
and of l on of hands, and of...... Heb 6:2
Wherefore l aside all malice, and...... 1Pet 2:1

LAZARUS (laz'-a-rus)

1. Name for a beggar in a parable of Jesus.
Was a certain beggar named L...... Lk 16:20
afar off, and L in his bosom...... Lk 16:23
have mercy on me, and send L...... Lk 16:24
things, and likewise L evil things...... Lk 16:25
2. Man raised from the dead by Jesus.
a certain man was sick, named L...... Jn 11:1
hair, whose brother L was sick...... Jn 11:2
loved Martha, and her sister, and L...... Jn 11:5
unto them, Our friend L sleepeth...... Jn 11:11
unto them plainly, L is dead...... Jn 11:14
he cried with a loud voice, L...... Jn 11:43
where L was which had been dead,...... Jn 12:1
but L was one of them that sat at...... Jn 12:2
but that they might see L also...... Jn 12:9
they might put L also to death...... Jn 12:10
when he called L out of his grave...... Jn 12:17

LEAD

I will l on softly, according as...... Gen 33:14
of a cloud, to l them the way...... Ex 13:21
they sank as l in the mighty...... Ex 15:10
the people unto the place of...... Ex 32:34
them, and which may l them out...... Num 27:17
the iron, the tin, and the l,...... Num 31:22
whither the LORD shall l you...... Deut 4:27
of the armies to l the people...... Deut 20:9
whither the LORD shall l thee...... Deut 28:37
So the LORD alone did l him,...... Deut 32:12
thy captivity captive, thou son...... Judg 5:12
that they may l them away...... Is 30:22
before them that l them captive,...... 2Chr 30:9

them by day, to l them in the way...... Neh 9:19
pen and l in the rock for ever...... Job 19:24
L me, O LORD, in thy...... Ps 5:8
L me in thy truth, and teach me...... Ps 25:5
l me in a plain path, because of...... Ps 27:11
for thy name's sake l me, and...... Ps 31:3
let them l me...... Ps 43:3
who will l me into Edom...... Ps 60:9
l me to the rock that is higher...... Ps 61:2
who will l me into Edom...... Ps 108:10
the LORD shall l them forth with...... Ps 125:5
Even there shall thy hand l me...... Ps 139:10
l me in the way everlasting...... Ps 139:24
l me into the land of uprightness....... Ps 143:10
When thou goest, it shall l thee...... Prov 6:22
l l in the way of righteousness,...... Prov 8:20
I would l thee, and bring thee...... Song 8:2
they which l thee cause thee to...... Is 3:12
and a little child shall l them...... Is 11:6
l away the Egyptians prisoners...... Is 20:4
shall gently l those that are...... Is 40:11
I will l them in paths that they...... Is 42:16
hath mercy on them shall l them...... Is 49:10
I will l him also, and restore...... Is 57:18
so didst thou l thy people...... Is 63:14
the l is consumed of the fire...... Jer 6:29
l l in the way of righteousness,...... Jer 31:9
he shall l Zedekiah to Babylon,...... Jer 32:5
are brass, and tin, and iron, and l...... Eze 22:18
silver, and brass, and iron, and l...... Eze 22:20
with silver, iron, tin, and l...... Eze 27:12
her maids shall l her as with the...... Nah 2:7
there was lifted up a talent of l...... Zec 5:7
he cast the weight of l upon the...... Zec 5:8
l us not into temptation, but...... Mt 6:13
And if the blind l the blind...... Mt 15:14
But when they shall l you,...... Mk 13:11
take him, and l him away safely...... Mk 14:44
them, Can the blind l the blind...... Lk 6:39
And l us not into temptation,...... Lk 11:4
stall, and l him away to watering....... Lk 13:15
seeking some to l him by the hand...... Acts 13:11
we not power to l about a sister...... 1Cor 9:5
that we may l a quiet and...... 1Ti 2:2
l captive silly women laden with...... 2Ti 3:6
l them out of the land of Egypt...... Heb 8:9
them, and shall l them unto living...... Rev 7:17

LEADER

was the l of the Aaronites...... 1Chr 12:27
and hundreds, and with every l...... 1Chr 13:1
for a witness to the people, a l...... Is 55:4

LEADERS

mighty men of valour, and the l...... 2Chr 32:21
For the l of this people cause...... Is 9:16
they be blind l of the blind...... Mt 15:14

LEADEST

thou that l Joseph like a flock...... Ps 80:1

LEADETH

unto the way that l to Ophrah...... 1Sa 13:17
He l counsellors away spoiled, and...... Job 12:17
He l princes away spoiled, and...... Job 12:19
he l me beside the still waters...... Ps 23:2
he l me in the paths of...... Ps 23:3
l him into the way that is not...... Prov 16:29
which l thee by the way that thou...... Is 48:17
that l to destruction, and many...... Mt 7:13
which l unto life, and few there...... Mt 7:14
l them up into an high mountain...... Mk 9:2
own sheep by name, and l them out...... Jn 10:3
iron gate that l unto the city...... Acts 12:10
of God l thee to repentance...... Rom 2:4
He that l into captivity shall go...... Rev 13:10

LEAF

mouth was an olive l pluckt off...... Gen 8:11
of a shaken l shall chase them...... Lev 26:36
Wilt thou break a l driven to...... Job 13:25
his l also shall not wither...... Ps 1:3
shall be as an oak whose l fadeth...... Is 1:30
as the l falleth off from the...... Is 34:4
and we all do fade as a l...... Is 64:6
the fig tree, and the l shall begin...... Jer 8:13
cometh, but her l shall be green...... Jer 17:8
whose l shall not fade, neither...... Eze 47:12
l the thereof for medicine...... Eze 47:12

LEAGUE

now therefore make ye a l with us...... Josh 9:6
and how shall we make a l with you...... Josh 9:7
therefore now make ye a l with us...... Josh 9:11
made a l with them, to let them...... Josh 9:15
after they had made a l with them...... Josh 9:16
ye shall make no l with the...... Judg 2:2
made a l with the son of Jesse...... 1Sa 22:8
saying also, Make thy l with me...... 2Sa 3:12
I will make a l with thee...... 2Sa 3:13
that they may make a l with thee...... 2Sa 3:21
king David made a l with them in...... 2Sa 5:3
and they two made a l together...... 1Kin 5:12
There is a l between me and thee,...... 1Kin 15:19
break thy l with Baasha king of...... 1Kin 15:19
There is a l between me and thee,...... 2Chr 16:3
break thy l with Baasha king of...... 2Chr 16:3
For thou shalt be in l with the...... Job 5:23
the men of the land that is in l...... Eze 30:5
after the l made with him he...... Dan 11:23

LEAH (le'-ah) See LEAH's. *Wife of Jacob.*
the name of the elder was *L*	Gen 29:16
L was tender eyed	Gen 29:17
that he took *L* his daughter	Gen 29:23
Laban gave unto his daughter	Gen 29:24
in the morning, behold, it was *L*	Gen 29:25
he loved also Rachel more than *L*	Gen 29:30
the LORD saw that *L* was hated	Gen 29:31
L conceived, and bare a son, and	Gen 29:32
When *L* saw that she had left	Gen 30:9
And *L* said, A troop cometh	Gen 30:11
L said, Happy am *I*, for the	Gen 30:13
and brought them unto his mother *L.*	Gen 30:14
Then Rachel said to *L*, Give me, I	Gen 30:14
L went out to meet him, and said	Gen 30:16
And God hearkened unto *L*, and she	Gen 30:17
L said, God hath given me my hire	Gen 30:18
L conceived again, and bare Jacob	Gen 30:19
L said, God hath endued me with a	Gen 30:20
L to the field unto his flock	Gen 31:4
L answered and said unto him, Is	Gen 31:14
And he divided the children unto *L*	Gen 33:1
and their children foremost, and *L.*	Gen 33:2
L also with her children came	Gen 33:7
And Dinah the daughter of *L.*	Gen 34:1
The sons of *L*; Reuben	Gen 35:23
These be the sons of *L*, which she	Gen 46:15
whom Laban gave to *L* his daughter	Gen 46:18
and there I buried *L.*	Gen 49:31
thine house like Rachel and like *L.*	Ruth 4:11

LEAH'S (le'-ahs)
Zilpah *L* maid bare Jacob a son	Gen 30:10
Zilpah *L* maid bare Jacob a second	Gen 30:12
into Jacob's tent, and into *L* tent	Gen 31:33
Then went he out of *L* tent	Gen 31:33
And the sons of Zilpah, *L* handmaid	Gen 35:26

LEAN
And the *I* and the ill favoured kine	Gen 41:20
land is, whether it be fat or *I*	Num 13:20
standeth, that I may *I* upon them	Judg 16:26
the king's son, *I* from day to day	2Sa 13:4
upon Egypt, on which if a man *I*	2Kin 18:21
He shall *I* upon his house, but it	Job 8:15
and I not unto thine own	Prov 3:5
fatness of his flesh shall wax *I*	Is 17:4
whereon if a man *I*, it will go	Is 36:6
cattle and between the *I* cattle	Eze 34:20
yet will they *I* upon the LORD	Mic 3:11

LEANED
behold, Saul *I* upon his spear	2Sa 1:6
king *I* answered the man of God	2Kin 7:2
the lord on whose hand he *I* on	2Kin 7:17
and when they *I* upon thee, thou	Eze 29:7
I his hand on the wall, and a	Amos 5:19
which also *I* on his breast at	Jn 21:20

LEANETH
or that *I* on a staff, or that	2Sa 3:29
he *I* on my hand, and I bow myself	2Kin 5:18

LEANFLESHED
of the river, ill favoured and *I*	Gen 41:3
I kine did eat up the seven well	Gen 41:4
poor and very ill favoured and *I*	Gen 41:19

LEANING
wilderness, *I* upon her beloved	Song 8:5
Now there was *I* on Jesus' bosom	Jn 13:23
I upon the top of his staff	Heb 11:21

LEANNESS
my *I* rising up in me beareth	Job 16:8
but sent *I* into their soul	Ps 106:15
hosts, send among his fat ones *I*	Is 10:16
But I said, My *I*, my *I*	Is 24:16

LEANNOTH (le-an'-noth) *A musical choir.*
chief Musician upon Mahalath *L*	Ps 88:t

LEAP
all the rams which *I* upon the	Gen 31:12
to *I* withal upon the earth	Lev 11:21
he shall *I* from Bashan	Deut 33:22
lamps, and sparks of fire *I* out	Job 41:19
Why *I* ye, ye high hills	Ps 68:16
shall the lame man *I* as an hart	Is 35:6
tops of mountains shall they *I*	Joel 2:5
all those that *I* on the threshold	Zeph 1:9
ye in that day, and *I* for joy	Lk 6:23

LEAPED
the rams which *I* upon the cattle	Gen 31:10
by my God have I *I* over a wall	2Sa 22:30
they *I* upon the altar which was	1Kin 18:26
and by my God have I *I* over a wall	Ps 18:29
of Mary, the babe *I* in her womb	Lk 1:41
the babe *I* in my womb for joy	Lk 1:44
And he *I* and walked	Acts 14:10
the evil spirit was *I* them	Acts 19:16

LEAPING
a window, and saw king David *I*	2Sa 6:16
he cometh *I* upon the mountains	Song 2:8
he *I* up stood, and walked, and	Acts 3:8
into the temple, walking, and *I*	Acts 3:8

LEARN
that they may *I* to fear me all	Deut 4:10
ears this day, that ye may *I* them	Deut 5:1
that thou mayest *I* to fear the	Deut 14:23
that he may *I* to fear the LORD	Deut 17:19
thou shalt not *I* to do after the	Deut 18:9
they may hear, and that they may *I*	Deut 31:12

LEATHER
a girdle of *I* about his loins	2Kin 1:8

LEATHERN
I girdle about his loins	Mt 3:4

LEAVE
shall a man *I* his father and his	Gen 2:24
for I will not *I* thee, until I	Gen 28:15

I to fear the LORD your God, as	Deut 31:13
that I might *I* thy statutes	Ps 119:71
that I may *I* thy commandments	Ps 119:73
Lest thou *I* his ways, and get a	Prov 22:25
L to do well	Is 1:17
neither will they *I* war any more	Is 2:4
of the world will *I* righteousness	Is 26:9
yet will he not *I* righteousness	Is 26:10
that murmured shall *I* doctrine	Is 29:24
L not the way of the heathen, and	Jer 10:2
I the ways of my people, to swear	Jer 12:16
neither shall they *I* war any more	Mic 4:3
I what that meaneth, I will have	Mt 9:13
Take my yoke upon you, and *I* of me	Mt 11:29
Now *I* a parable of the fig tree	Mt 24:32
Now *I* a parable of the fig tree	Mk 13:28
that ye might *I* in us not to	1Cor 4:6
one by one, that all may *I*	1Cor 14:31
And if they will *I* any thing	1Cor 14:35
This only would I *I* of you	Gal 3:2
that they may *I* not to blaspheme	1Ti 1:20
Let the woman *I* in silence with	1Ti 2:11
let them *I* first to shew piety at	1Ti 5:4
And withal they *I* to be idle	1Ti 5:13
let ours also *I* to maintain good	Titus 3:14
no man could *I* that song but the	Rev 14:3

LEARNED
for I have *I* by experience that	Gen 30:27
the heathen, and *I* their works	Ps 106:35
when I shall have *I* thy righteous	Ps 119:7
neither *I* wisdom, nor have the	Prov 30:3
men deliver to one that is *I*	Is 29:11
is delivered to him that is not *I*	Is 29:12
and he saith, I am not *I*	Is 29:12
hath given me the tongue of the *I*	Is 50:4
mine ear to hear as the *I*	Is 50:4
lion, and it *I* to catch the prey	Eze 19:3
I to catch the prey, and devoured	Eze 19:6
hath of the Father, cometh unto	Jn 6:45
this man letters, having never *I*	Jn 7:15
Moses was *I* in all the wisdom of	Acts 7:22
to the doctrine which ye have *I*	Rom 16:17
But ye have not so *I* Christ	Eph 4:20
things, which ye have both *I*	Phil 4:9
for I have *I*, in whatsoever state	Phil 4:11
As ye also *I* of Epaphras our dear	Col 1:7
in the things which thou hast *I*	2Ti 3:14
knowing of whom thou hast *I* them	2Ti 3:14
yet *I* he obedience by the things	Heb 5:8

LEARNING
man will hear, and will increase *I*	Prov 1:5
man, and he will increase in *I*	Prov 9:9
of the lips increaseth *I*	Prov 16:21
mouth, and addeth *I* to his lips	Prov 16:23
and the wise man's mouth teach the	Dan 1:4
them knowledge and skill in all *I*	Dan 1:17
much *I* doth make thee mad	Acts 26:24
aforetime were written for our *I*	Rom 15:4
Ever *I*, and never able to come to	2Ti 3:7

LEAST
with us a few days, at the *I* ten	Gen 24:55
of the *I* of all the mercies	Gen 32:10
he that gathered *I* gathered ten	Num 11:32
at the *I* such as before knew	Judg 3:2
I am the *I* in my father's house	Judg 6:15
my family the *I* of all the	Judg 6:15
kept themselves at *I* from women	1Sa 21:4
of the *I* of my master's servants	2Kin 18:24
one of the *I* was over an hundred	1Chr 12:14
of the *I* of my master's servants	Is 36:9
For from the *I* of them even unto	Jer 6:13
for every one from the *I* even	Jer 8:10
from the *I* of them unto	Jer 31:34
from the *I* even unto the greatest	Jer 42:1
from the *I* even to the greatest	Jer 42:8
from the *I* even unto the greatest	Jer 44:12
Surely the *I* of the flock shall	Jer 49:20
Surely the *I* of the flock shall	Jer 50:45
yet shall not the *I* grain fall	Amos 9:9
of them even to the *I* of them	Jonah 3:5
not be *I* among the princes	Mt 2:6
break one of these *I* commandments	Mt 5:19
he shall be called the *I* in the	Mt 5:19
notwithstanding he that is *I* in	Mt 11:11
indeed is the *I* of all seeds	Mt 13:32
one of the *I* of these my brethren	Mt 25:40
it not to one of the *I* of these	Mt 25:45
but he that is *I* in the kingdom	Lk 7:28
for he that is *I* among you all	Lk 9:48
able to do that thing which is *I*	Lk 16:10
is *I* is faithful also in much	Lk 16:10
in the *I* is unjust also in much	Lk 16:10
at *I* in this thy day, the things	Lk 19:42
that at the *I* the shadow of Peter	Acts 5:15
from the *I* to the greatest	Acts 8:10
who are I esteemed in the church	1Cor 6:4
For I am the *I* of the apostles	1Cor 15:9
am less than the *I* of all saints	Eph 3:8
from the *I* to the greatest	Heb 8:11

Let me now *I* with thee some of	Gen 33:15
I one of your brethren here with	Gen 42:33
lord, The lad cannot *I* his father	Gen 44:22
for if he should *I* his father	Gen 44:22
Let no man *I* of it till the	Ex 16:19
what they *I* the beasts of the	Ex 23:11
he shall not *I* any of it until	Lev 7:15
holy place, and shall *I* them there	Lev 16:23
thou shalt *I* them for the poor and	Lev 19:10
ye shall *I* none of it until the	Lev 22:30
thou shalt *I* them unto the poor	Lev 23:22
They shall *I* none of it unto the	Num 9:12
And he said, *L* us not, I pray thee	Num 10:31
to give me *I* to go with you	Num 22:13
he will yet again *I* them in the	Num 32:15
also shall not *I* thee either corn	Deut 28:51
of his children which he shall *I*	Deut 28:54
I them in the lodging place	Josh 4:3
Should I *I* my fatness, wherewith	Judg 9:9
unto them, Should I *I* my wine	Judg 9:13
said, Intreat me not to *I* thee	Ruth 1:16
them, that she may glean them	Ruth 2:16
lest my father *I* caring for the	1Sa 9:5
let us not *I* a man of them	1Sa 14:36
David earnestly asked *I* of me	1Sa 20:6
David earnestly asked *I* of me to	1Sa 20:28
if I *I* all that pertain to him	1Sa 25:22
shall not *I* to my husband neither	2Sa 14:7
let him not *I* us, nor forsake us	1Kin 8:57
soul liveth, I will not *I* thee	2Kin 2:2
soul liveth, I will not *I* thee	2Kin 2:4
soul liveth, I will not *I* thee	2Kin 2:6
soul liveth, I will not *I* thee	2Kin 4:30
shall eat, and shall *I* thereof	2Kin 4:43
Neither did he *I* of the people to	2Kin 13:7
I it for an inheritance for your	1Chr 28:8
to *I* us a remnant to escape, and	Ezr 9:8
I it for an inheritance to your	Ezr 9:12
pray you, let us *I* off this usury	Neh 5:10
the work cease, whilst I *I* it	Neh 6:3
that we would *I* the seventh year	Neh 10:31
days obtained I *I* of the king	Neh 13:6
I will *I* off my heaviness, and	Job 9:27
I will *I* my complaint upon myself	Job 10:1
to thee will *I* thou labour to him	Job 39:11
thou wilt not *I* my soul in hell	Ps 16:10
the rest of their substance to	Ps 17:14
I me not, neither forsake me, O	Ps 27:9
LORD will not *I* him in his hand	Ps 37:33
and *I* their wealth to others	Ps 49:10
I me not to thine oppressors	Ps 119:121
I not my soul destitute	Ps 141:8
Who *I* the paths of uprightness	Prov 2:13
therefore *I* off contention	Prov 17:14
because I should *I* it unto the	Eccl 2:18
shall he *I* it for his portion	Eccl 2:21
up against thee, *I* not thy place	Eccl 10:4
and where will ye *I* your glory	Is 10:3
ye shall *I* your name for a curse	Is 65:15
that I might *I* my people, and go	Jer 9:2
I us not	Jer 14:9
shall *I* them in the midst of his	Jer 17:11
Will a man *I* the snow of Lebanon	Jer 18:14
will not *I* thee altogether	Jer 30:11
of Judah, to *I* you none to remain	Jer 44:7
yet will I not *I* thee wholly	Jer 46:28
the cities, and dwell in the	Jer 48:28
would they not *I* some gleaning	Jer 49:9
L thy fatherless children, I will	Jer 49:11
Yet will I *I* a remnant, that ye	Eze 6:8
But I will *I* a few men of them	Eze 12:16
jewels, and *I* thee naked and bare	Eze 16:39
I will *I* you there, and melt you	Eze 22:20
shall *I* thee naked and bare	Eze 23:29
I will *I* thee thrown into the	Eze 29:5
Then will I *I* thee upon the land	Eze 32:4
I but the sixth part of thee, and	Eze 39:2
Nevertheless *I* the stump of his	Dan 4:15
yet *I* the stump of the roots	Dan 4:23
whereas they commanded to *I* the	Dan 4:26
shall he *I* his blood upon him	Hos 12:14
and *I* a blessing behind him	Joel 2:14
by a thousand shall *I* an hundred	Amos 5:3
forth by an hundred shall *I* ten	Amos 5:3
I off righteousness in the earth	Amos 5:7
would they not *I* some grapes	Obad 5
I will also *I* in the midst of	Zeph 3:12
that it shall *I* them neither root	Mal 4:1
L there thy gift before the altar	Mt 5:24
and *I* the ninety and nine	Mt 18:12
this cause shall a man *I* father	Mt 19:5
not to *I* the other undone	Mt 23:23
And forthwith Jesus gave them *I*	Mk 5:13
cause shall a man *I* his father	Mk 10:7
I his wife behind him	Mk 12:19
I no children, that his brother	Mk 12:19
not to *I* the other undone	Lk 11:42
doth not *I* the ninety and nine in	Lk 15:4
they shall not *I* in thee one	Lk 19:44
I will not *I* you comfortless	Jn 14:18
Peace I *I* with you, my peace I	Jn 14:27
I *I* the world, and go to the	Jn 16:28
to his own, and shall *I* me alone	Jn 16:32
and Pilate gave him *I*	Jn 19:38
thou wilt not *I* my soul in hell	Acts 2:27
that we should *I* the word of God	Acts 6:2
then took his *I* of the brethren	Acts 18:18
we had taken our *I* one of another	Acts 21:6
dwell with her, let her not *I* him	1Cor 7:13
but taking my *I* of them, I went	2Cor 2:13

L

cause shall a man *l* his father .... Eph 5:31
he hath said, I will never *l* thee .... Heb 13:5
which is without the temple *l* out .... Rev 11:2

LEAVED
open before him the two *l* gates .... Is 45:1

LEAVEN
put away *l* out of your houses .... Ex 12:15
be no *l* found in your houses .... Ex 12:19
neither shall there be *l* seen .... Ex 13:7
the blood of my sacrifice with *l* .... Ex 34:25
the LORD, shall be made with *l* .... Lev 2:11
for ye shall burn no *l*, nor any .... Lev 2:11
It shall not be baken with *l* .... Lev 6:17
eat it without *l* beside the altar .... Lev 10:12
they shall be baken with *l* .... Lev 23:17
sacrifice of thanksgiving with *l* .... Amos 4:5
kingdom of heaven is like unto *l* .... Mt 13:33
beware of the *l* of the Pharisees .... Mt 16:6
beware of the *l* of the Pharisees .... Mt 16:11
them not beware of the *l* of bread .... Mt 16:12
beware of the *l* of the Pharisees, ... Mk 8:15
and of the *l* of Herod .... Mk 8:15
ye of the *l* of the Pharisees .... Lk 12:1
It is like *l*, which a woman took .... Lk 13:21
little *l* leaveneth the whole lump 1Cor 5:6
Purge out therefore the old *l* 1Cor 5:7
us keep the feast, not with old *l* 1Cor 5:8
neither with the *l* of malice 1Cor 5:8
A little *l* leaveneth the whole .... Gal 5:9

LEAVENED
for whosoever eateth *l* bread from .... Ex 12:15
whosoever eateth that which is *l* .... Ex 12:19
Ye shall eat nothing *l* .... Ex 12:20
took their dough before it was *l* .... Ex 12:34
out of Egypt, for it was not *l* .... Ex 12:39
there shall no *l* bread be eaten .... Ex 13:3
there shall no *l* bread be seen .... Ex 13:7
of my sacrifice with *l* bread .... Ex 23:18
l bread with the sacrifice of .... Lev 7:13
Thou shalt eat no *l* bread with it .... Deut 16:3
there shall be no *l* bread seen .... Deut 16:4
kneaded the dough, until it be *l* .... Hos 7:4
of meal, till the whole was *l* .... Mt 13:33
of meal, till the whole was *l* .... Lk 13:21

LEAVENETH
a little leaven *l* the whole lump 1Cor 5:6
A little leaven *l* the whole lump .... Gal 5:9

LEAVES
and they sewed fig *l* together .... Gen 3:7
the two *l* of the one door were 1Kin 6:34
the two *l* of the other door were 1Kin 6:34
in them, when they cast their *l* .... Is 6:13
Jehudi had read three or four *l* .... Jer 36:23
wither in all the *l* of her spring .... Eze 17:9
two *l* apiece, two turning *l* .... Eze 41:24
two *l* for the one door .... Eze 41:24
and two *l* for the other door .... Eze 41:24
The *l* thereof were fair, and the .... Dan 4:12
off his branches, shake off his *l* .... Dan 4:14
Whose *l* were fair, and the fruit .... Dan 4:21
but *l* only, and said unto it, Let .... Mt 21:19
is yet tender, and putteth forth *l* .... Mt 24:32
a fig tree afar off having *l* .... Mk 11:13
to it, he found nothing but *l* .... Mk 11:13
is yet tender, and putteth forth *l* .... Mk 13:28
the *l* of the tree were for the .... Rev 22:2

LEAVETH
Which *l* her eggs in the earth, and .... Job 39:14
A good man *l* an inheritance to .... Prov 13:22
a sweeping rain which *l* no food .... Prov 28:3
idol shepherd that *l* the flock .... Zec 11:17
Then the devil *l* him, and, behold, ... Mt 4:11
coming, and *l* the sheep, and fleeth ...... Jn 10:12

LEAVING
l Nazareth, he came and dwelt in .... Mt 4:13
him, and departed, *l* him half dead ...... Lk 10:30
l the natural use of the woman, ... Rom 1:27
Therefore *l* the principles of the .... Heb 6:1
l us an example, that ye should 1Pet 2:21

LEBANA (*leb´-a-nah*) See LEBANAH. A family of exiles.
The children of L, the children .... Neh 7:48

LEBANAH (*leb´-a-nah*) Same as Lebana.
The children of L, the children .... Ezr 2:45

LEBANON (*leb´-a-non*) Chief mountain range in Syria.
land of the Canaanites, and unto L .... Deut 1:7
that goodly mountain, and L .... Deut 3:25
from the wilderness and L, from .... Deut 11:24
this L even unto the great river, ... Josh 1:4
of the great sea over against L .... Josh 9:1
valley of L, under mount Hermon .... Josh 11:17
of L even unto the mount Halak .... Josh 12:7
land of the Giblites, and all L .... Josh 13:5
from L unto Misrephoth-maim. .... Josh 13:6
the Hivites that dwelt in mount L .... Judg 3:3
and devour the cedars of L .... Judg 9:15
in L even unto the hyssop that 1Kin 4:33
they hew me cedar trees out of L 1Kin 5:6
them down from L unto the sea 1Kin 5:9
And he sent them to L in 1Kin 5:14
a month they were in L, and two 1Kin 5:14
also the house of the forest of L 1Kin 7:2
to build in Jerusalem, and in L 1Kin 9:19
in the house of the forest of L 1Kin 10:17

the forest of L were of pure gold 1Kin 10:21
The thistle that was in L sent to 2Kin 14:9
sent to the cedar that was in L 2Kin 14:9
by a wild beast that was in L 2Kin 14:9
the mountains, to the sides of L 2Kin 19:23
trees, and algum trees, out of L 2Chr 2:8
can skill to cut timber in L 2Chr 2:8
And we will cut wood out of L 2Chr 2:16
to build in Jerusalem, and in L 2Chr 8:6
in the house of the forest of L 2Chr 9:16
the forest of L were of pure gold 2Chr 9:20
The thistle that was in L sent to 2Chr 25:18
sent to the cedar that was in L 2Chr 25:18
by a wild beast that was in L 2Chr 25:18
trees from L to the sea of Joppa .... Ezr 3:7
the LORD breaketh the cedars of L .... Ps 29:5
L and Sirion like a young unicorn. .... Ps 29:6
fruit thereof shall shake like L .... Ps 72:16
he shall grow like a cedar in L .... Ps 92:12
the cedars of L, which he hath .... Ps 104:16
a chariot of the wood of L. .... Song 3:9
Come with me from L, my spouse, ... Song 4:8
with me from L .... Song 4:8
garments is like the smell of L .... Song 4:11
living waters, and streams from L .... Song 4:15
his countenance is as L, ... Song 5:15
thy nose is as the tower of L .... Song 7:4
And upon all the cedars of L .... Is 2:13
L shall fall by a mighty one .... Is 10:34
at thee, and the cedars of L .... Is 14:8
L shall be turned into a fruitful .... Is 29:17
L is ashamed and hewn down .... Is 33:9
the glory of L shall be given .... Is 35:2
the mountains, to the sides of L .... Is 37:24
L is not sufficient to burn, nor .... Is 40:16
The glory of L shall come unto .... Is 60:13
Will a man leave the snow of L .... Jer 18:14
Gilead unto me, and the head of L .... Jer 22:6
Go up to L, and cry .... Jer 22:20
O inhabitant of L, that makest .... Jer 22:23
had divers colours, came unto L .... Eze 17:3
from L to make mast for thee .... Eze 27:5
a cedar in L with fair branches .... Eze 31:3
I caused L to mourn for him, and .... Eze 31:15
of Eden, the choice and best of L .... Eze 31:16
and cast forth his roots as L .... Hos 14:5
the olive tree, and his smell as L .... Hos 14:6
thereof shall be as the wine of L .... Hos 14:7
and the flower of L languisheth. .... Nah 1:4
violence of L shall cover thee .... Hab 2:17
them into the land of Gilead and L .... Zec 10:10
Open thy doors, O L, that the .... Zec 11:1

LEBAOTH (*leb´-a-oth*) See BETH-LEBAOTH. A city in Judah.
And L, and Shilhim, and Ain, and .... Josh 15:32

LEBBAEUS (*leb-be´-us*) See JUDAS,
THADDAEUS. Same as Thaddaeus.
James the son of Alphaeus, and L .... Mt 10:3

LEB-KAMAI See MIDST.

LEBONAH (*le-bo´-nah*) A city in Ephraim.
to Shechem, and on the south of L .. Judg 21:19

LECAH (*le´-cah*) Son of Er.
of Judah were, Er the father of L 1Chr 4:21

LED
the LORD *l* me to the house of my .... Gen 24:27
which had *l* me in the right way .... Gen 24:48
he *l* the flock to the backside of .... Ex 3:1
that God *l* them not through the .... Ex 13:17
But God *l* the people about, ... Ex 13:18
Thou in thy mercy hast *l* forth .... Ex 15:13
l thee these forty years in the .... Deut 8:2
Who *l* thee through that great and .... Deut 8:15
I have *l* you forty years in the .... Deut 29:5
he *l* him about, he instructed him .... Deut 32:10
l him throughout all the land of .... Josh 24:3
which *l* them away captive, and 1Kin 8:48
But he *l* them to Samaria 2Kin 6:19
Joab *l* forth the power of the 1Chr 20:1
l forth his people, and went to 2Chr 25:11
thou hast *l* captivity captive .... Ps 68:18
also he *l* them with a cloud, ... Ps 78:14
he *l* them on safely, so that they .... Ps 78:53
so he *l* them through the depths, ... Ps 106:9
he *l* them forth by the right way, ... Ps 107:7
To him which *l* his people through ...... Ps 136:16
I have *l* thee in right paths .... Prov 4:11
they that are *l* of them are .... Is 9:16
he *l* them through the deserts .... Is 48:21
joy, and be *l* forth with peace .... Is 55:12
That they by the right hand of .... Is 63:12
That *l* them through the deep, as .... Is 63:13
that *l* us through the wilderness, ... Jer 2:6
when he *l* thee by the way .... Jer 2:17
whither they have *l* him captive .... Jer 22:12
which *l* the seed of the house of .... Jer 23:8
He hath *l* me, and brought me into .... Lam 3:2
l them with him to Babylon .... Eze 17:12
which caused them to be *l* into .... Eze 39:28
I me about the way without unto .... Eze 47:2
I you forty years through the .... Amos 2:10
Israel shall surely be *l* away .... Amos 7:11
And Huzzab shall be *l* away captive, ... Nah 2:7
Then was Jesus *l* up of the spirit .... Mt 4:1
that had laid hold on Jesus *l* him .... Mt 26:57
had *l* him away, and delivered him .... Mt 27:2
l him away to crucify him .... Mt 27:31
hand, and *l* him out of the town .... Mk 8:23

they *l* Jesus away to the high .... Mk 14:53
the soldiers *l* him away into the .... Mk 15:16
him, and *l* him out to crucify him. .... Mk 15:20
was *l* by the Spirit into the .... Lk 4:1
l him unto the brow of the hill .... Lk 4:29
shall be *l* away captive into all .... Lk 21:24
l him, and brought him into the .... Lk 22:54
l him into their council, saying, ... Lk 22:66
them arose, and *l* him unto Pilate .... Lk 23:1
as they *l* him away, they laid .... Lk 23:26
I with him to be put to death .... Lk 23:32
he *l* them out as far as to .... Lk 24:50
l him away to Annas first .... Jn 18:13
they *l* Jesus from Caiaphas .... Jn 18:28
And they took Jesus, and *l* him away ...... Jn 19:16
He was *l* as a sheep to the .... Acts 8:32
but they *l* him by the hand, and .... Acts 9:8
Paul was to be *l* into the castle .... Acts 21:37
being *l* by the hand of them that .... Acts 22:11
For as many as are *l* by the .... Rom 8:14
dumb idols, even as ye were *l* 1Cor 12:2
But if ye be *l* of the Spirit, ye .... Gal 5:18
he *l* captivity captive, and gave .... Eph 4:8
l away with divers lusts, ... 2Ti 3:6
being *l* away with the error of 2Pet 3:17

LEDDEST
over us, thou wast he that *l* out 2Sa 5:2
was king, thou wast he that *l* out 1Chr 11:2
Moreover thou *l* them in the day .... Neh 9:12
Thou *l* thy people like a flock by .... Ps 77:20
l out into the wilderness four .... Acts 21:38

LEDGES
and the borders were between the *l* 1Kin 7:28
were between the *l* were lions 1Kin 7:29
upon the *l* there was a base above 1Kin 7:29
the top of the base the *l* thereof 1Kin 7:35
on the plates of the *l* thereof 1Kin 7:36

LEEKS
and the melons, and the *l*, and the ...... Num 11:5

LEES
things, a feast of wines on the *l* .... Is 25:6
of wines on the *l* well refined .... Is 25:6
and he hath settled on his *l* .... Jer 48:11
men that are settled on their *l* .... Zeph 1:12

LEFT
they *l* off to build the city .... Gen 11:8
if thou wilt take the *l* hand, ... Gen 13:9
hand, then I will go to the *l* .... Gen 13:9
which is on the *l* hand of .... Gen 14:15
he *l* off talking with him, and God .. Gen 17:22
as soon as he had *l* communing. .... Gen 18:33
who hath not *l* destitute my .... Gen 24:27
to the right hand, or to the *l* .... Gen 24:49
and *l* bearing. .... Gen 29:35
Leah saw that she had *l* bearing .... Gen 30:9
company which is *l* shall escape. .... Gen 32:8
And Jacob was *l* alone .... Gen 32:24
he *l* all that he had in Joseph's .... Gen 39:6
he *l* his garment in her hand, and ...... Gen 39:12
he had *l* his garment in her hand ...... Gen 39:13
that he *l* his garment with me, and ...... Gen 39:15
that he *l* his garment with me, and ...... Gen 39:18
very much, until he *l* numbering .... Gen 41:49
brother is dead, and he is *l* alone ...... Gen 42:38
the eldest, and *l* at the youngest .... Gen 44:12
he alone is *l* of his mother, and .... Gen 44:20
there is not ought *l* in the sight. .... Gen 47:18
right hand toward Israel's *l* hand ...... Gen 48:13
Manasseh in his *l* hand toward .... Gen 48:13
his *l* hand upon Manasseh's head, ... Gen 48:14
they *l* in the land of Goshen. .... Gen 50:8
why is it that ye have *l* the man .... Ex 2:20
word of the LORD *l* his servants. .... Ex 9:21
even all that the hail hath *l* .... Ex 10:12
of the trees which the hail had *l* ...... Ex 10:15
shall not an hoof be *l* behind. .... Ex 10:26
their right hand, and on their *l* .... Ex 14:22
their right hand, and on their *l* .... Ex 14:29
but some of them *l* of it until .... Ex 16:20
passover be *l* unto the morning. .... Ex 34:25
that which is *l* of the meat .... Lev 2:10
Ithamar, his sons that were *l* .... Lev 10:12
sons of Aaron which were *l* alive ...... Lev 10:16
into the palm of his own *l* hand .... Lev 14:15
in the oil that is in his *l* hand .... Lev 14:16
into the palm of his own *l* hand .... Lev 14:26
his *l* hand seven times before the .... Lev 14:27
upon them that are *l* alive of you ...... Lev 26:36
they that are *l* of you shall pine ...... Lev 26:39
The land also shall be *l* of them, ... Lev 26:43
to the right hand nor to the *l* .... Num 20:17
they that are *l* of you shall .... Num 21:35
to the right hand or to the *l* .... Num 22:26
unto the right hand nor to the *l* .... Deut 2:27
every city, we *l* none to remain. .... Deut 2:34
until none was *l* to him remaining. ...... Deut 3:3
ye shall be *l* few in number among ...... Deut 4:27
to the right hand, nor to the *l* .... Deut 5:32
among them, until they that are *l* ...... Deut 7:20
to the right hand, nor to the *l* .... Deut 17:11
to the right hand, or to the *l* .... Deut 17:20
to the right hand, or to the *l* .... Deut 28:14
hath nothing *l* him in the siege .... Deut 28:55
ye shall be *l* few in number, ... Deut 28:62
and there is none shut up, or *l* .... Deut 32:36
it to the right hand or to the *l* .... Josh 1:7
l them without the camp of Israel ...... Josh 6:23

was not a man in Ai or Beth-el......	Josh 8:17
they l the city open, and pursued......	Josh 8:17
until he had l him none remaining......	Josh 10:33
he l none remaining, according to......	Josh 10:37
he l none remaining......	Josh 10:39
he l none remaining, but utterly......	Josh 10:40
until they l them none remaining......	Josh 11:8
there was not any l to breathe......	Josh 11:11
neither l they any to breathe......	Josh 11:14
he l nothing undone of all that......	Josh 11:15
There was none of the Anakims l......	Josh 11:22
goeth out to Cabul on the l hand......	Josh 19:27
Ye have not l your brethren these......	Josh 22:3
to the right hand or to the l......	Josh 23:6
which Joshua l when he died......	Judg 2:21
the Lord l those nations, without......	Judg 2:23
are the nations which the Lord l......	Judg 3:1
And Ehud put forth his l hand......	Judg 3:21
and there was not a man l......	Judg 4:16
l no sustenance for Israel......	Judg 6:4
held the lamps in their l hands......	Judg 7:20
all that were l of all the hosts......	Judg 8:10
youngest son of Jerubbaal was l......	Judg 9:5
hand, and of the other with his l......	Judg 16:29
and she was l, and her two sons......	Ruth 1:3
the woman was l of her two sons......	Ruth 1:5
then she l gleaning unto her......	Ruth 2:18
and how thou hast l thy father......	Ruth 2:11
did eat, and was sufficed, and l......	Ruth 2:14
who hath not l off his kindness......	Ruth 2:20
which hath not l thee this day......	Ruth 4:14
that every one that is l in thine......	1Sa 2:36
the stump of Dagon was l to him......	1Sa 5:4
to the right hand or to the l......	1Sa 6:12
said, Behold that which is l......	1Sa 9:24
thy father hath l the care of the......	1Sa 10:2
two of them were not l together......	1Sa 11:11
l the sheep with a keeper, and......	1Sa 17:20
David l his carriage in the hand......	1Sa 17:22
with whom hast thou l those few......	1Sa 17:28
surely there had not been l unto......	1Sa 25:34
l neither man nor woman alive, and......	1Sa 27:9
those that were l behind stayed......	1Sa 30:9
and my master l me, because three......	1Sa 30:13
nor to the l from following Abner......	2Sa 2:19
to thy right hand or to the l......	2Sa 2:21
there they l their images, and......	2Sa 5:21
that is l of the house of Saul......	2Sa 9:1
and there is not one of them l......	2Sa 13:30
shall quench thy coal which is l......	2Sa 14:7
the l from ought that my lord the......	2Sa 14:19
the king l ten women, which were......	2Sa 15:16
on his right hand and on his l......	2Sa 16:6
which he hath l to keep the house......	2Sa 16:21
shall not be l so much as one......	2Sa 17:12
whom he had l to keep the house......	2Sa 20:3
and he set up the l pillar......	1Kin 7:21
five on the l side of the house......	1Kin 7:39
Solomon l all the vessels......	1Kin 7:47
the right side, and five on the l......	1Kin 7:49
that were l of the Amorites......	1Kin 9:20
were l after them in the land......	1Kin 9:21
I in Israel, and will take away......	1Kin 14:10
the gold that were l in the......	1Kin 15:18
that he l off building of Ramah......	1Kin 15:21
he l not to Jeroboam any that......	1Kin 15:29
he l him not one that breath......	1Kin 16:11
that there was no breath l in him......	1Kin 17:17
to Judah, and l his servant there......	1Kin 19:3
and I, even I only, am l......	1Kin 19:10
and I, even I only, am l......	1Kin 19:14
Yet I have l me seven thousand in......	1Kin 19:18
he l the oxen, and ran after......	1Kin 19:20
thousand of the men that were l......	1Kin 20:30
that is shut up and l in Israel......	1Kin 21:21
him on his right hand and on his l......	1Kin 22:19
only in Kir-haraseth l they the......	2Kin 3:25
I thereof, according to the word......	2Kin 4:44
l their tents, and their horses......	2Kin 7:7
which are l in the city, (behold,......	2Kin 7:13
of Israel that are l in it......	2Kin 7:13
since the day that she l the land......	2Kin 8:6
that is shut up and l in Israel......	2Kin 9:8
until he l him none remaining......	2Kin 10:11
neither l he any of them......	2Kin 10:14
was not a man l that came not......	2Kin 10:21
to the l corner of the temple......	2Kin 11:11
was not any shut up, nor any l......	2Kin 14:26
they l all the commandments of......	2Kin 17:16
there was none l but the tribe of......	2Kin 17:18
prayer for the remnant that are l......	2Kin 19:4
nothing shall be l, saith the......	2Kin 20:17
to the right hand or to the l......	2Kin 22:2
which were on a man's l hand at......	2Kin 23:8
people that were l in the city......	2Kin 25:11
But the captain of the guard l of......	2Kin 25:12
king of Babylon had l, even over......	2Kin 25:22
of Merari stood on the l hand......	1Chr 6:44
which were l of the family of......	1Chr 6:61
the l in hurling stones and......	1Chr 12:2
that are l in all the land of......	1Chr 13:2
when they had l their gods there,......	1Chr 14:12
So he l there before the ark of......	1Chr 16:37
right hand, and the other on the l......	2Chr 3:17
and the name of that on the l Boaz......	2Chr 3:17
the right hand, and five on the l......	2Chr 4:6
the right hand, and five on the l......	2Chr 4:7
the right side, and five on the l......	2Chr 4:8
that were l of the Hittites......	2Chr 8:7
who were l after them in the land......	2Chr 8:8

For the Levites l their suburbs......	2Chr 11:14
therefore have l also i you in......	2Chr 12:5
that he l off building of Ramah......	2Chr 16:5
on his right hand and on his l......	2Chr 18:18
that there was never a son l him......	2Chr 21:17
to the l side of the temple......	2Chr 23:10
they l the house of the Lord God......	2Chr 24:18
(for they l him in great diseases......	2Chr 24:25
other ten thousand l alive did......	2Chr 25:12
So the armed men l the captives......	2Chr 28:14
enough to eat, and have l plenty......	2Chr 31:10
that which is l is this great......	2Chr 31:10
was done in the land, God l him......	2Chr 32:31
to the right hand, nor to the l......	2Chr 34:2
and for them that are l in Israel......	2Chr 34:21
which were l of the captivity, and......	Neh 1:2
The remnant that are l of the......	Neh 1:3
there was no breach l therein......	Neh 6:1
and on his l hand, Pedaiah, and......	Neh 8:4
Shall have made of his meat be l......	Job 20:21
him that is l in his tabernacle......	Job 20:26
On the l hand, where he doth work......	Job 23:9
they l off speaking......	Job 32:15
he hath l off to be wise, and to......	Ps 36:3
there was not one of them l......	Ps 106:11
in her l hand riches and honour......	Prov 3:16
to the right hand nor to the l......	Prov 4:27
but a child l to himself bringeth......	Prov 29:15
but a fool's heart at his l......	Eccl 10:2
His l hand is under my head, and......	Song 2:6
His l hand should be under my......	Song 8:3
the daughter of Zion is l as a......	Is 1:8
l unto us a very small remnant......	Is 1:9
pass, that he that is l in Zion......	Is 4:3
one eat that is l in the land......	Is 7:22
and he shall eat on the l hand......	Is 9:20
as one gathereth eggs that are l......	Is 10:14
of his people, which shall be l......	Is 11:11
of his people, which shall be l......	Is 11:16
gleaning grapes shall be l in it......	Is 17:6
they shall be l together unto the......	Is 18:6
earth are burned, and few men l......	Is 24:6
In the city is l desolation......	Is 24:12
forsaken, and l like a wilderness......	Is 27:10
till ye be l as a beacon upon the......	Is 30:17
hand, and when ye turn to the l......	Is 30:21
multitude of the city shall be l......	Is 32:14
prayer for the remnant that is l......	Is 37:4
nothing shall be l, saith the......	Is 39:6
Behold, I was l alone......	Is 49:21
on the right hand and on the l......	Is 54:3
house, I have l mine heritage......	Jer 12:7
such as are l in this city from......	Jer 21:7
are l in the house of the Lord......	Jer 27:18
The people which were l of the......	Jer 31:2
the cities of Judah that were l......	Jer 38:22
all the women that are l in the......	Jer 38:22
So they l off speaking with him......	Jer 38:27
the captain of the guard l of the......	Jer 39:10
people that were l in the land......	Jer 40:6
Babylon had l a remnant of Judah......	Jer 40:11
(for we are l but a few of many,......	Jer 42:2
the captain of the guard had......	Jer 43:6
But since we l off to burn......	Jer 44:18
How is the city of praise not l......	Jer 49:25
let nothing of her be l......	Jer 50:26
the captain of the guard l......	Jer 52:16
the face of an ox on the l side......	Eze 1:10
Lie thou also upon thy l side......	Eze 4:4
were slaying them, and I was l......	Eze 9:8
therein shall be l a remnant that......	Eze 14:22
that dwell at thy l hand......	Eze 16:46
on the right hand, or on the l......	Eze 21:16
Neither l she her whoredoms......	Eze 23:8
ye have l shall fall by the sword......	Eze 24:21
near thee turn off, and have l him......	Eze 31:12
from his shadow, and have l him......	Eze 31:12
Then the heathen that are l round......	Eze 36:36
smite thy bow out of thy l hand......	Eze 39:3
have l none of them any more......	Eze 39:28
that which was l was the place of......	Eze 41:9
were toward the place that was l......	Eze 41:11
was l was five cubits round about......	Eze 45:15
that are l in the breadth over......	Dan 2:44
shall not be l to other people......	Dan 2:44
Therefore I was l alone, and saw......	Dan 10:8
neither is there breath l in me......	Dan 10:17
his l hand unto heaven, and sware......	Dan 12:7
because they have l off to take......	Hos 4:10
that there shall not be a man l......	Hos 9:12
hath l the locust eaten......	Joel 1:4
hath l the cankerworm eaten......	Joel 1:4
hath l the caterpiller eaten......	Joel 1:4
their right hand and their l hand......	Jonah 4:11
Who is l among you that saw this......	Hag 2:3
the other upon the l side thereof......	Zec 4:11
and upon the l side thereof......	Zec 4:11
on the right hand and on the l......	Zec 12:6
but the third shall be l therein......	Zec 13:8
that every one that is l of all......	Zec 14:16
And they straightway l their nets......	Mt 4:20
And they immediately l the ship......	Mt 4:22
let not thy l hand know what thy......	Mt 6:3
her hand, and the fever l her......	Mt 8:15
that was l seven baskets full......	Mt 15:37
And he l them, and departed......	Mt 16:4
right hand, and the other on the l......	Mt 20:23
sit on my right hand, and on my l......	Mt 21:17
he l them, and went out of the......	Mt 21:17

and l them, and went their way......	Mt 22:22
l his wife unto his brother......	Mt 22:25
your house is l unto you desolate......	Mt 23:38
There shall not be l here one......	Mt 24:2
shall be taken, and the other l......	Mt 24:40
shall be taken, and the other l......	Mt 24:41
hand, but the goats on the l......	Mt 25:33
say also unto them on the l hand......	Mt 25:41
he l them, and went away again, and......	Mt 26:44
right hand, and another on the l......	Mt 27:38
they l their father Zebedee in......	Mk 1:20
and immediately the fever l her......	Mk 1:31
meat that was l seven baskets......	Mk 8:8
he l them, and entering into the......	Mk 8:13
say unto him, Lo, we have l all......	Mk 10:28
hand, and the other on thy l hand......	Mk 10:37
on my l hand is not mine to give......	Mk 10:40
and they l him, and went their way......	Mk 12:12
took a wife, and dying l no seed......	Mk 12:20
and died, neither l he any seed......	Mk 12:21
the seven had her, and l no seed......	Mk 12:22
there shall not be l one stone......	Mk 13:2
journey, who l his house, and gave......	Mk 13:34
he l the linen cloth, and fled......	Mk 14:52
right hand, and the other on his l......	Mk 15:27
l all, and followed him......	Lk 4:39
Now when he had l speaking......	Lk 5:4
he l all, rose up, and followed......	Lk 5:28
sister hath l me to serve alone......	Lk 10:40
your house is l unto you desolate......	Lk 13:35
be taken, and the other shall be l......	Lk 17:34
shall be taken, and the other l......	Lk 17:35
shall be taken, and the other l......	Lk 17:36
Peter said, Lo, we have l all,......	Lk 18:28
There is no man that hath l house......	Lk 18:29
they l no children, and died......	Lk 20:31
not be l one stone upon another......	Lk 21:6
right hand, and the other on the l......	Lk 23:33
He l Judaea, and departed again......	Jn 4:3
The woman then l her waterpot......	Jn 4:28
the seventh hour the fever l him......	Jn 4:52
and Jesus was l alone, and the......	Jn 8:9
the Father hath not l me alone......	Jn 8:29
that his soul was not l in hell......	Acts 2:31
Nevertheless he l not himself......	Acts 14:17
came to Ephesus, and l them there......	Acts 18:19
we l it on the l hand, and......	Acts 21:3
Cyprus, we l it on the l hand......	Acts 21:3
soldiers, they l beating of Paul......	Acts 21:32
On the morrow they l the horsemen......	Acts 23:32
the Jews a pleasure, l Paul bound......	Acts 24:27
a certain man l in bonds by Felix......	Acts 25:14
Lord of Sabaoth had l us a seed......	Rom 9:29
I am l alone, and they seek my......	Rom 11:3
on the right hand and on the l......	2Cor 6:7
it good to be l at Athens alone......	1Th 3:1
The cloke that I l at Troas with......	2Ti 4:13
have l l at Miletum sick......	2Ti 4:20
For this cause l I thee in Crete,......	Titus 1:5
he l nothing that is not put......	Heb 2:8
a promise being l us of entering......	Heb 4:1
but l their own habitation, he......	Jude 6
thou hast l thy first love......	Rev 2:4
sea, and his l foot on the earth,......	Rev 10:2

LEFTEST

therefore l thou them in the hand......	Neh 9:28

LEFTHANDED

son of Gera, a Benjamite, a man l......	Judg 3:15
were seven hundred chosen men l......	Judg 20:16

LEG

thy locks, make bare the l......	Is 47:2

LEGION

he answering, said, My name is L......	Mk 5:9
with the devil, and had the L......	Mk 5:15
and said, L......	Lk 8:30

LEGIONS

me more than twelve l of angels......	Mt 26:53

LEGS

his head with his l, and with the......	Ex 12:9
wash the inwards of him, and his l......	Ex 29:17
his l shall he wash in water......	Lev 1:9
the inwards and the l with water......	Lev 1:13
with his head, and with his l......	Lev 4:11
the inwards and the l in water......	Lev 8:21
he did wash the inwards and the l......	Lev 9:14
which have l above their feet, to......	Lev 11:21
thee in the knees, and in the l......	Deut 28:35
had greaves of brass upon his l......	1Sa 17:6
not pleasure in the l of a man......	Ps 147:10
The l of the lame are not equal......	Prov 26:7
His l are as pillars of marble,......	Song 5:15
and the ornaments of the l......	Is 3:20
His l of iron, his feet part of......	Dan 2:33
that their l might be broken......	Jn 19:31
brake the l of the first, and of......	Jn 19:32
already, they brake not his l......	Jn 19:33

LEHAB

begat Ludim, and Anamim, and L......	Gen 10:13
begat Ludim, and Anamim, and L......	1Chr 1:11

LEHABIM See LEHAB.

LEHABITES See LEHAB.

LEHI (le'-hi) See RAMATH-LEHI. A district near
Jerusalem.

Judah, and spread themselves in L......	Judg 15:9

L

And when he came unto *L*, the .... Judg 15:14
which is in *L* unto this day .... Judg 15:19

LEISURE
they had no *l* so much as to eat .... Mk 6:31

LEMUEL (lem´-u-el) *A king mentioned in Proverbs.*
The words of king *L*, the prophecy .... Prov 31:1
It is not for kings, O *L*, it is .... Prov 31:4

LEND
If thou *l* money to any of my .... Ex 22:25
nor *l* him thy victuals for .... Lev 25:37
thou shalt *l* unto many nations, ... Deut 15:6
shalt surely *l* him sufficient for .... Deut 15:8
Thou shalt not *l* upon usury to .... Deut 23:19
stranger thou mayest *l* upon usury .... Deut 23:20
thou shalt not *l* upon usury .... Deut 23:20
When thou dost *l* thy brother any .... Deut 24:10
the man to whom thou dost *l* shall .... Deut 24:11
thou shalt *l* unto many nations, ... Deut 28:12
He shall *l* to thee, and thou shalt .... Deut 28:44
and thou shalt not *l* to him .... Deut 28:44
if ye *l* to them of whom ye hope .... Lk 6:34
for sinners also *l* to sinners .... Lk 6:34
ye your enemies, and do good, and *l* .... Lk 6:35
him, Friend, *l* me three loaves .... Lk 11:5

LENDER
The borrower is servant to the *l*, ... Prov 22:7
as with the *l*, so with .... Is 24:2

LENDETH
Every creditor that *l* ought unto .... Deut 15:2
He is ever merciful, and *l* .... Ps 37:26
A good man sheweth favour, and *l* .... Ps 112:5
upon the poor *l* unto the LORD .... Prov 19:17

LENGTH
The *l* of the ark shall be three .... Gen 6:15
through the land in the *l* of it .... Gen 13:17
and a half shall be the *l* thereof .... Ex 25:10
and a half made be the *l* thereof .... Ex 25:17
two cubits shall be the *l* thereof .... Ex 25:23
The *l* of one curtain shall be .... Ex 26:2
The *l* of one curtain shall be .... Ex 26:8
the *l* of the curtains of the tent .... Ex 26:13
cubits shall be the *l* of a board .... Ex 26:16
I there shall be hangings of an .... Ex 27:11
The *l* of the court shall be an .... Ex 27:18
a span shall be the *l* thereof .... Ex 28:16
A cubit shall be the *l* thereof .... Ex 30:2
The *l* of one curtain was twenty .... Ex 36:9
The *l* of one curtain was thirty .... Ex 36:15
The *l* of a board was ten cubits, ... Ex 36:21
cubits and a half was the *l* of it .... Ex 37:1
and a half was the *l* thereof .... Ex 37:6
two cubits was the *l* thereof .... Ex 37:10
the *l* of it was a cubit, and .... Ex 37:25
five cubits was the *l* thereof .... Ex 38:1
and twenty cubits was the *l* .... Ex 38:18
a span was the *l* thereof, and a .... Ex 39:9
nine cubits was the *l* thereof .... Deut 3:11
is thy life, and the *l* of thy days .... Deut 30:20
which had two edges, of a cubit *l* .... Judg 3:16
the *l* thereof was threescore 1Kin 6:2
twenty cubits was the *l* 1Kin 6:3
forepart was twenty cubits in *l* 1Kin 6:20
the *l* thereof was an hundred 1Kin 7:2
the *l* thereof was fifty cubits, ... 1Kin 7:6
four cubits was the *l* of one base. 1Kin 7:27
The *l* by cubits after The 2Chr 3:3
the *l* of it was according to the 2Chr 3:4
the *l* whereof was according to 2Chr 3:8
twenty cubits the *l* thereof 2Chr 4:1
in *l* of days understanding .... Job 12:12
even *l* of days for ever and ever .... Ps 21:4
For *l* of days, and long life, and .... Prov 3:2
For *l* of days is her right hand .... Prov 3:16
have him become his son as the *l* .... Prov 29:21
in the *l* of his branches .... Eze 31:7
the *l* of the gate, thirteen .... Eze 40:11
the *l* of the gates was the lower .... Eze 40:18
north, he measured the *l* thereof .... Eze 40:20
the *l* thereof was fifty cubits, ... Eze 40:21
the *l* was fifty cubits, and the .... Eze 40:25
the *l* was fifty cubits, and the .... Eze 40:36
The *l* of the porch was twenty .... Eze 40:49
and he measured the *l* thereof .... Eze 41:2
So he measured the *l* thereof .... Eze 41:4
the *l* thereof ninety cubits, ... Eze 41:12
he measured the *l* of the building. .... Eze 41:15
high, and the *l* thereof two cubits, ... Eze 41:22
the *l* thereof was forty cubits, ... Eze 41:22
Before the *l* of an hundred cubits .... Eze 42:2
the *l* thereof was fifty cubits .... Eze 42:7
For the *l* of the chambers that .... Eze 42:8
the *l* shall be the *l* of five, ... Eze 45:1
the sanctuary five hundred in *l*, ... Eze 45:2
shalt thou measure the *l* of five .... Eze 45:3
the five and twenty thousand in *l*, ... Eze 45:5
the *l* shall be over against one .... Eze 45:7
in *l* as one of the other parts, ... Eze 48:8
of five and twenty thousand in *l* .... Eze 48:9
five and twenty thousand in *l* .... Eze 48:10
five and twenty thousand in *l* .... Eze 48:13
have five and twenty thousand in *l* .... Eze 48:13
all the *l* shall be five and twenty .... Eze 48:13
the residue in *l* over against the .... Eze 48:18
thereof, and what is the *l* thereof. .... Eze 48:20
the *l* thereof is twenty cubits, ... Zec 5:2
The *l* thereof is twenty cubits, ... Zec 5:2
if by any means now at *l* I might .... Rom 1:10

saints what is the breadth, and *l* .... Eph 3:18
the *l* is as large as the breadth .... Rev 21:16
The *l* and the breadth and the .... Rev 21:16

LENGTHEN
did walk, then I will *l* thy days 1Kin 3:14
I thy cords, and strengthen thy .... Is 54:2

LENGTHENED
that thy days may be *l* in the .... Deut 25:15

LENGTHENING
if it may be a *l* of thy .... Dan 4:27

LENT
so that they *l* unto them such .... Ex 12:36
of any thing that is *l* upon usury .... Deut 23:19
also I have *l* him to the LORD 1Sa 1:28
liveth he shall be *l* to the LORD 1Sa 1:28
the loan which is *l* to the LORD 1Sa 2:20
I have neither *l* on usury .... Jer 15:10
nor men have *l* to me on usury .... Jer 15:10

LENTILES
gave Esau bread and pottage of *l* .... Gen 25:34
and parched corn, and beans, and *l* 2Sa 17:28
was a piece of ground full of *l* 2Sa 23:11
wheat, and barley, and beans, and *l* .... Eze 4:9

LEOPARD
the *l* shall lie down with the kid .... Is 11:6
a *l* shall watch over their cities .... Jer 5:6
his skin, or the *l* his spots. .... Jer 13:23
I beheld, and lo another, like a *l* .... Dan 7:6
as a *l* by the way will I observe .... Hos 13:7
which I saw was like unto a *l* .... Rev 13:2

LEOPARDS
dens, from the mountains of the *l* .... Song 4:8
also are swifter than the *l* .... Hab 1:8

LEPER
the *l* in whom the plague is, his .... Lev 13:45
the *l* in the day of his cleansing .... Lev 14:2
of leprosy be healed in the *l* .... Lev 14:3
of the seed of Aaron is a *l* .... Lev 22:4
they put out of the camp every *l* .... Num 5:2
hath an issue, or that is a *l*, ... 2Sa 3:29
man in valour, but he was a *l* 2Kin 5:1
over the place, and recover the *l*, ... 2Kin 5:11
his presence a *l* as white as snow. 2Kin 5:27
so that he was a *l* unto the day 2Kin 15:5
Uzziah the king was a *l* unto the 2Chr 26:21
in a several house, being a *l*. 2Chr 26:21
for they said, He is a *l*. 2Chr 26:23
And, behold, there came a *l* .... Mt 8:2
in the house of Simon the *l*, ... Mt 26:6
And there came a *l* to him, ... Mk 1:40
in the house of Simon the *l* .... Mk 14:3

LEPERS
And when these *l* came to the 2Kin 7:4
Heal the sick, cleanse the *l*, ... Mt 10:8
the *l* are cleansed, and the deaf .... Mt 11:5
many *l* were in Israel in the time .... Lk 4:27
the *l* are cleansed, the deaf hear .... Lk 7:22
there met him ten men that were *l* .... Lk 17:12

LEPROSY
of his flesh like the plague of *l* .... Lev 13:2
in his flesh, it is a plague of *l* .... Lev 13:3
it is a *l* .... Lev 13:8
When the plague of *l* is in a man .... Lev 13:9
It is an old *l* in the skin of his .... Lev 13:11
if a break out abroad in the .... Lev 13:12
the *l* cover all the skin of him .... Lev 13:12
the *l* have covered all his .... Lev 13:13
it is a *l* .... Lev 13:15
it is a plague of *l* broken out of .... Lev 13:20
it is a *l* broken out of the .... Lev 13:25
it is the plague of *l* .... Lev 13:25
it is the plague of *l* .... Lev 13:27
even a *l* upon the head or beard. .... Lev 13:30
it is a *l* sprung up in his skin. .... Lev 13:42
as the *l* appeareth in the skin of .... Lev 13:43
also that the plague of *l* is in .... Lev 13:47
it is a plague of *l*, and shall be .... Lev 13:49
the plague is a fretting *l* .... Lev 13:51
for it is a fretting *l* .... Lev 13:52
of *l* in a garment of woollen or .... Lev 13:59
of the plague of *l* be healed in. .... Lev 14:3
cleansed from the *l* seven times. .... Lev 14:7
of him in whom is the plague of *l* .... Lev 14:32
I put the plague of *l* in a house .... Lev 14:34
it is a fretting *l* in the house. .... Lev 14:44
law for all manner of plague of *l* .... Lev 14:54
for the *l* of a garment, and of a .... Lev 14:55
this is the law of *l* .... Lev 14:57
him have the plague of *l* .... Deut 24:8
for he would recover him of his *l* 2Kin 5:3
thou mayest recover him of his *l* 2Kin 5:6
unto me to recover a man of his *l* 2Kin 5:7
The therefore of Naaman shall 2Kin 5:27
the *l* even rose up in his 2Chr 26:19
And immediately his *l* was cleansed. .... Mk 8:3
immediately the *l* departed from .... Mk 1:42
city, behold a man full of *l* .... Lk 5:12
immediately the *l* departed from .... Lk 5:13

LEPROUS
behold, his hand was *l* as snow .... Ex 4:6
He is a *l* man, he is unclean. .... Lev 13:44
and, behold, Miriam became *l* .... Num 12:10
Miriam, and, behold, she was *l* .... Num 12:10
there were four *l* men at the 2Kin 7:3

he was *l* in his forehead, and they 2Chr 26:20

LESHEM (le´-shem) *See* LAISH. *Same as Laish. of Dan went up to fight against L .... Josh 19:47
it, and dwelt therein, and called L .... Josh 19:47

LESS
and gathered, some more, some *l* .... Ex 16:17
not give *l* than half a shekel .... Ex 30:15
thou shalt give the *l* inheritance .... Num 26:54
ye shall give the *l* inheritance .... Num 33:54
nothing of all this, *l* or more. 1Sa 22:15
l or more, until the morning 1Sa 25:36
how much *l* this house that I have 1Kin 8:27
how much *l* this house which I 2Chr 6:18
how much *l* shall your God deliver. 2Chr 32:15
us I than our iniquities deserve .... Ezr 9:13
How much *l* in them than dwell in .... Job 4:19
How much *l* shall I answer him, and .... Job 9:14
that God exacteth of thee *l* than .... Job 11:6
How much *l* man, that is a worm .... Job 25:6
How much *l* to him that accepteth .... Job 34:19
much *l* do lying lips a prince .... Prov 17:7
much *l* for a servant to have rule .... Prov 19:10
are counted to him I than nothing. .... Is 40:17
how much *l* shall it be meet yet .... Eze 15:5
is I than all the seeds that be .... Mk 4:31
and Mary the mother of James the *L*. .... Mk 15:40
which we think to be *l* honourable. 1Cor 12:23
I love you, the *l* I be loved. 2Cor 12:15
who am I than the least of all. .... Eph 3:8
and that I may be the *l* sorrowful .... Phil 2:28
it is blessed of the better .... Heb 7:7

LESSER
the *l* light to rule the night .... Gen 1:16
and for the treading of *l* cattle .... Is 7:25
from the *l* I settle even to the .... Eze 43:14

LEST
shall ye touch it, *l* ye die .... Gen 3:3
he put forth his hand, and take .... Gen 3:22
any finding him should kill him. .... Gen 4:15
I we be scattered abroad upon the .... Gen 11:4
thou shouldest say, I have made. .... Gen 14:23
I thou be consumed in the .... Gen 19:15
the mountain, I thou be consumed. .... Gen 19:17
I some evil take me, and I die .... Gen 19:19
I said he, the men of the place .... Gen 26:7
Because I said, L I die for her .... Gen 26:9
he will come and smite me, and .... Gen 32:11
I that he should give seed to his .... Gen 38:9
L peradventure he die also, as .... Gen 38:11
take it to her, I we be shamed .... Gen 38:23
L peradventure mischief befall. .... Gen 42:4
I peradventure I see the evil .... Gen 44:34
I thou, and thy household, and all .... Gen 45:11
I they multiply, and it come to .... Ex 1:10
I he fall upon us with pestilence. .... Ex 5:3
L peradventure the people repent. .... Ex 13:17
I they break through unto the .... Ex 19:21
the LORD break forth upon them. .... Ex 19:22
I he break forth upon them .... Ex 19:24
I not God speak with us, I we die .... Ex 20:19
I the land become desolate, and .... Ex 23:29
I they make thee sin against me. .... Ex 23:33
I consume thee in the way. .... Ex 33:3
I thou make a covenant with the .... Ex 34:12
I it be for a snare in the midst .... Ex 34:12
L thou make a covenant with the .... Ex 34:15
I ye die, and I wrath come upon .... Lev 10:6
I wrath come upon all the people. .... Lev 10:6
of the congregation, I ye die .... Lev 10:7
of the congregation, I ye die .... Lev 10:9
the land fall to whoredom, and .... Lev 19:29
I they bear sin for it, and die .... Num 18:22
touch any holy thing, I they die. .... Num 4:15
things are covered, I they die. .... Num 4:20
I ye be consumed in all their .... Num 16:26
I the earth swallow us up also. .... Num 16:34
I they bear sin, and die .... Num 18:32
the children of Israel, I ye die. .... Num 18:32
I come out against thee with .... Num 20:18
I ye be smitten before your .... Deut 1:42
I thou forget the things which .... Deut 4:9
I they depart from thy heart all .... Deut 4:9
I ye corrupt yourselves, and make .... Deut 4:16
I thou lift up thine eyes unto .... Deut 4:19
I ye forget the covenant of the .... Deut 4:23
Then beware I thou forget the .... Deut 6:12
The anger of the LORD thy God .... Deut 6:15
of the beasts of the field .... Deut 7:22
thee, I thou be snared therein .... Deut 7:25
I thou be a cursed thing like it .... Deut 7:26
I when thou hast eaten and art .... Deut 8:12
The land whence thou broughtest .... Deut 9:28
person quickly from off the .... Deut 11:17
L the avenger of the blood pursue .... Deut 19:6
I he die in the battle, and .... Deut 20:5
I he die in the battle, and .... Deut 20:6
I he die in the battle, and .... Deut 20:7
I his brethren's heart faint as .... Deut 20:8
the fruit of thy seed which. .... Deut 22:9
I he cry against thee unto the .... Deut 24:15
I thou exceed, and beat .... Deut 25:3
L there should be among you man, ... Deut 29:18
I there should be among you a .... Deut 29:18
I their adversaries should behave .... Deut 32:27
I they should say, Our hand is .... Deut 32:27
mountain, I the pursuers meet you .... Josh 2:16
I ye make yourselves accursed, ... Josh 6:18

l wrath be upon us, because of........Josh 9:20
unto you, l ye deny your God........Josh 24:27
l Israel taunt themselves against........Judg 7:2
l we burn thee and thy father's........Judg 14:15
l angry fellows run upon thee, and........Judg 18:25
l I mar mine own inheritance........Ruth 4:6
l my father leave caring for the........1Sa 9:5
L the Hebrews make them swords or........1Sa 13:19
l I destroy you with them........1Sa 15:6
know this, l be grieved........1Sa 20:3
L they should tell on us, saying,........1Sa 27:11
battle, l in the battle he be an........1Sa 29:4
l these uncircumcised come and........1Sa 31:4
l the daughters of the........2Sa 1:20
rejoice, l the daughters of the........2Sa 1:20
l I take the city, and it be........2Sa 13:25
l we be chargeable unto thee........2Sa 13:25
any more, l they destroy my son........2Sa 14:11
l he overtake us suddenly, and........2Sa 15:14
the king be swallowed up, and........2Sa 17:16
l he get him fenced cities, and........2Sa 20:6
l peradventure the Spirit of the........2Kin 2:16
l these uncircumcised come and........1Chr 10:4
L ye should say, We have found........Job 32:13
not, l the people be ensnared........Job 34:30
beware l he take thee away with........Job 36:18
l I deal with you after your........Job 42:8
l he be angry, and ye perish from........Ps 2:12
l he tear you like a lion,........Ps 7:2
l I sleep the sleep of death........Ps 13:3
l mine enemy say, I have........Ps 13:4
l, if thou be silent to me, l........Ps 28:1
l they come near unto thee........Ps 32:9
l otherwise they should rejoice........Ps 38:16
l I tear you in pieces, and there........Ps 50:22
Slay them not, l my people forget........Ps 59:11
l thou dash thy foot against a........Ps 91:12
wrath, l he should destroy them........Ps 106:23
l the righteous put forth their........Ps 125:3
l they exalt themselves........Ps 140:8
l I be like unto them that go........Ps 143:7
L thou shouldest ponder the path........Prov 5:6
L thou give thine honour unto........Prov 5:9
l strangers be filled with thy........Prov 5:10
not a scorner, l he hate thee........Prov 9:8
not sleep, l thou come to poverty........Prov 20:13
L thou learn his ways, and get a........Prov 22:25
L the LORD see it, and it........Prov 24:18
l thou know not what to do in the........Prov 25:8
L that heareth it put thee to........Prov 25:10
l thou be filled therewith, and........Prov 25:16
l he be weary of thee, and so hate........Prov 25:17
l thou also be like unto him........Prov 26:4
l he be wise in his own conceit........Prov 26:5
l he reprove thee, and thou be........Prov 30:6
L l be full, and deny thee, and say........Prov 30:9
or l I be poor, and steal, and take........Prov 30:9
l he curse thee, and thou be found........Prov 30:10
L they drink, and forget the law,........Prov 31:5
l thou hear thy servant curse........Eccl 7:21
l they see with their eyes, and........Is 6:10
l hurt it, I will keep it........Is 27:3
l your bands be made strong........Is 28:22
Beware l Hezekiah persuade you,........Is 36:18
l thou shouldest say, Mine idol........Is 48:5
l thou shouldest say, Behold, I........Is 48:7
l I confound thee before them........Jer 1:17
l my fury come forth like fire,........Jer 4:4
l my soul depart from thee........Jer 6:8
l I make thee desolate, a land........Jer 6:8
l thou bring me to nothing........Jer 10:24
l my fury go out like fire, and........Jer 21:12
the scribe, l I die there........Jer 37:20
l they deliver me into their hand........Jer 38:19
l your heart faint, and ye fear........Jer 51:46
L I strip her naked, and set her........Hos 2:3
l he break out like fire in the........Amos 5:6
l they should hear the law, and........Zec 7:12
l I come and smite the earth with........Mal 4:6
l at any time thou dash thy foot........Mt 4:6
l at any time the adversary........Mt 5:25
l they trample them under their........Mt 7:6
l at any time they should see........Mt 13:15
while ye gather up the tares,........Mt 13:29
fasting, l they faint in the way........Mt 15:32
l we should offend them, go thou........Mt 17:27
l there be not enough for us and........Mt 25:9
l there be an uproar among the........Mt 26:5
his disciples come by night, and........Mt 27:64
l they should throng him........Mk 3:9
l at any time they should be........Mk 4:12
Take heed l any man deceive you........Mk 13:5
l coming suddenly he find you........Mk 13:36
l there be an uproar of the........Mk 14:2
l ye enter into temptation........Mk 14:38
l at any time thou dash thy foot........Lk 4:11
l they should believe and be saved........Lk 8:12
l he hale thee to the judge, and........Lk 12:58
a more honourable man than thou........Lk 14:8
l they also bid thee again, and a........Lk 14:12
l, haply, after he hath laid the........Lk 14:29
l they also come into this place........Lk 16:28
l by her continual coming she........Lk 18:5
l at any time your hearts be........Lk 21:34
l ye enter into temptation........Lk 22:46
l his deeds should be reproved........Jn 3:20
l a worse thing come unto thee........Jn 5:14
light, l darkness come upon you........Jn 12:35
l they should be put out of the........Jn 12:42
hall, l they should be defiled........Jn 18:28

l they should have been stoned........Acts 5:26
l haply ye be found even to fight........Acts 5:39
l that come upon you, which is........Acts 13:40
fearing l they should have been........Acts 23:10
fearing l they should fall into........Acts 27:17
Then fearing l we should have........Acts 27:29
l any of them should swim out, and........Acts 27:42
l they should see with their eyes........Acts 28:27
take heed l he also spare not........Rom 11:21
l ye should be wise in your own........Rom 11:25
l I should build upon another........Rom 15:20
L any should say that I had........1Cor 1:15
l the cross of Christ should be........1Cor 1:17
But take heed l by any means this........1Cor 8:9
l I make my brother to offend........1Cor 8:13
l we should hinder the gospel of........1Cor 9:12
l that by any means, when I have........1Cor 9:27
l he standeth take heed l he fall........1Cor 10:12
And I wrote this same unto you, l........2Cor 2:3
l perhaps such a one should be........2Cor 2:7
L Satan should get an advantage........2Cor 2:11
l through the light of the glorious........2Cor 4:4
l your boasting of you should be........2Cor 9:3
L haply if they of Macedonia come........2Cor 9:4
l by any means, as the serpent........2Cor 11:3
l any man should think of me........2Cor 12:6
l I should be exalted above........2Cor 12:7
l I should be exalted above........2Cor 12:7
For I fear, l, when I come, I........2Cor 12:20
l there be debates, envyings,........2Cor 12:20
And l, when I come again, my God........2Cor 12:21
l being present I should use........2Cor 13:10
l by any means I should run, or........Gal 2:2
l I have bestowed upon you labour........Gal 4:11
only l they should suffer........Gal 6:12
of works, l any man should boast........Eph 2:9
l I should have sorrow upon........Phil 2:27
l any man should beguile you with........Col 2:4
Beware l any man spoil you........Col 2:8
to anger, l they be discouraged........Col 3:21
l by some means the tempter have........1Th 3:5
l being lifted up with pride he........1Ti 3:6
l he fall into reproach and the........1Ti 3:7
l at any time we should let them........Heb 2:1
l there be in any of you an evil........Heb 3:12
l any of you be hardened through........Heb 3:13
Let us therefore fear, l, a........Heb 4:1
l any man fall after the same........Heb 4:11
l he that destroyed the firstborn........Heb 11:28
l ye be wearied and faint in your........Heb 12:3
l that which is lame be turned........Heb 12:13
Looking diligently l any man fail........Heb 12:15
l any root of bitterness........Heb 12:15
L there be any fornicator, or........Heb 12:16
brethren, l ye be condemned........Jas 5:9
l ye fall into condemnation........Jas 5:12
beware l ye also, being led away........2Pet 3:17
l he walk naked, and they see his........Rev 16:15

LET See PREFACE.

LETHEK See HOMER.

that David wrote a l to Judah,........2Sa 11:14
And he wrote in the l, saying, Set........2Sa 11:15
l will send a l unto the king of........2Kin 5:5
he brought the l to the king of........2Kin 5:6
Now when this l is come unto thee........2Kin 5:6
the king of Israel had read the l........2Kin 5:7
as soon as this l cometh to you........2Kin 10:2
Then he wrote a l the second time........2Kin 10:6
l came to them, that........2Kin 10:7
Hezekiah received the l of the........2Kin 19:14
the writing of the l was written........Ezr 4:7
of the l that they sent unto him........Ezr 4:8
The l which ye sent us hath........Ezr 4:18
l was read before Rehum, and........Ezr 4:23
by l concerning this matter........Ezr 5:5
The copy of the l that Tatnai........Ezr 5:6
They sent a l unto him, wherein........Ezr 5:7
Now this is the copy of the l........Ezr 7:11
l unto Asaph the keeper of the........Neh 2:8
time with an open l in his hand........Neh 6:5
for all the words of this l........Est 9:26
to confirm this second l of Purim........Est 9:29
Hezekiah received the l from the........Is 37:14
l that Jeremiah the prophet sent........Jer 29:1
in the ears of Jeremiah the........Jer 29:29
he wrote a l after this manner........Acts 23:25
when the governor had read the l........Acts 23:34
the law, judge thee, who by the l........Rom 2:27
in the spirit, and not in the l........Rom 2:29
and not in the oldness of the l........Rom 7:6
not of the l, but of the spirit........2Cor 3:6
for the l killeth, but the spirit........2Cor 3:6
though I made you sorry with a l........2Cor 7:8
Ye see how large a l I have........Gal 6:11
nor by l as from us, as that the........2Th 2:2
for I have written a l unto you........Heb 13:22

LETTERS
So she wrote l in Ahab's name, and........1Kin 21:8
sent the l unto the elders and to........1Kin 21:8
And she wrote in the l, saying,........1Kin 21:9
Baladan, king of Babylon, sent l........2Kin 20:12
wrote l also to Ephraim and........2Chr 30:1
wrote l to the l from the king........2Chr 30:6

He wrote also l to rail on the........2Chr 32:17
king, let l be given me to the........Neh 2:7
river, and gave them the king's........Neh 2:9
of Judah sent many l unto Tobiah........Neh 6:17
the l of Tobiah came unto them........Neh 6:17
Tobiah sent l to put me in fear........Neh 6:19
For he sent l into all the king's........Est 1:22
the l were sent by posts into all........Est 3:13
the l devised by Haman the son of........Est 8:5
sent l by posts on horseback, and........Est 8:10
sent l unto all the Jews that........Est 9:20
he commanded by l that his wicked........Est 9:25
he sent the l unto all the Jews,........Est 9:30
Baladan, king of Babylon, sent l........Is 39:1
Because thou hast sent l in thy........Jer 29:25
written over him in l of Greek........Lk 23:38
saying, How knoweth this man l........Jn 7:15
desired of him l to Damascus to........Acts 9:2
they wrote l by them after this........Acts 15:23
I received l unto the brethren........Acts 22:5
We neither received l out of........Acts 28:21
ye shall approve by your l........1Cor 16:3
or l of commendation from you........2Cor 3:1
as if I would terrify you by l........2Cor 10:9
For his l, say they, are weighty........2Cor 10:10
in word by l when we are absent........2Cor 10:11

LETTEST
l such words go out of thy mouth........Job 15:13
with a cord which thou l down........Job 41:1
now l thou thy servant depart in........Lk 2:29

LETTETH
hands escape, he that l him go........2Kin 10:24
strife is as when one l out water........Prov 17:14
only he who now l will let........2Th 2:7

LETTING
deceitfully any more in not l the........Ex 8:29

LETUSHIM (le-tu'-shim) A son of Dedan.
sons of Dedan were Asshurim, and L........Gen 25:3

LETUSHITES See LETUSHIM.

LEUMMIM (le-um'-mim) A son of Dedan.
were Asshurim, and Letushim, and L........Gen 25:3

LEVI (le'-vi) See LEVITE, LEVITICAL, MATTHEW.
  1. A son of Jacob.
therefore was his name called L........Gen 29:34
of the sons of Jacob, Simeon and L........Gen 34:25
And Jacob said to Simeon and L........Gen 34:30
firstborn, and Simeon, and L........Gen 35:23
Simeon and L are brethren........Gen 49:5
Reuben, Simeon, L, and Judah,........Ex 1:2
are the names of the sons of L........Ex 6:16
life of L were an hundred thirty........Ex 6:16
were the sons of L by their names........Num 3:17
Hear, I pray you, ye sons of L........Num 16:8
was Jochebed, the daughter of L........Num 26:59
her mother bare to L in Egypt........Num 26:59
the son of Kohath, the son of L........1Chr 6:38
the son of Gershom, the son of L........1Chr 6:43
the son of Merari, the son of L........1Chr 6:47
son of Mahli, the son of L........Ezr 8:18
  2. The tribe.
And the sons of L........Gen 46:11
went a man of the house of L........Ex 2:1
and took to wife a daughter of L........Ex 2:1
these are the families of L........Ex 6:19
all the sons of L gathered........Ex 32:26
the children of L did according........Ex 32:28
shalt not number the tribe of L........Num 1:49
Bring the tribe of L near........Num 1:49
Number the children of L after........Num 3:15
Kohath from among the sons of L........Num 4:2
too much upon you, ye sons of L........Num 16:8
Hear, I pray you, ye sons of L........Num 16:8
brethren the sons of L with thee........Num 16:10
Aaron's name upon the rod of L........Num 17:3
for the house of L was budded........Num 17:8
brethren also of the tribe of L........Num 18:2
I have given the children of L........Num 18:21
the LORD separated the tribe of L........Deut 10:8
Wherefore L hath no part nor........Deut 10:9
Levites, and all the tribe of L........Deut 18:1
the sons of L shall come near........Deut 21:5
Simeon, and L, and Judah, and........Deut 27:12
l unto the priests the sons of L........Deut 31:9
of L he said, Let thy Thummim and........Deut 33:8
Only unto the tribe of L he gave........Josh 13:14
But unto the tribe of L Moses........Josh 13:33
who were of the children of L........Josh 21:10
which were not of the sons of L........1Chr 12:31
Reuben, Simeon, L, and Judah,........1Chr 2:1
The sons of L; Gershon........1Chr 6:1
The sons of L; Gershom........1Chr 6:16
companies of the children of L........1Chr 9:18
the children of L four thousand........1Chr 12:26
But L and Benjamin counted he not........1Chr 21:6
into courses among the sons of L........1Chr 23:6
sons were named of the tribe of L........1Chr 23:14
These were the sons of L after........1Chr 23:24
rest of the sons of L were these........1Chr 24:20
found there none of the sons of L........Ezr 8:15
the children of L shall bring the........Neh 10:39
The sons of L, the chief of the........Neh 12:23
Bless the LORD, O house of L........Ps 135:20
sons of Zadok among the sons of L........Eze 40:46
one gate of Judah, one gate of L........Eze 48:31
family of the house of L apart........Zec 12:13
that my covenant might be with L........Mal 2:4

LEVIATHAN

have corrupted the covenant of L	Mal 2:8
he shall purify the sons of L	Mal 3:3
they that are of the sons of L	Heb 7:5
L also, who receiveth tithes,	Heb 7:9
Of the tribe of L were sealed	Rev 7:7
3. Some as Matthew the apostle.	
he saw L the son of Alphaeus,	Mk 2:14
forth, and saw a publican, named L	Lk 5:27
I made him a great feast in his	Lk 5:29
4. Father of Matthat; ancestor of Jesus.	
Matthat, which was the son of L	Lk 3:24
5. Father of another Matthat; ancestor of Jesus.	
Matthat, which was the son of L	Lk 3:29

LEVIATHAN

thou draw out l with an hook	Job 41:1
brakest the heads of l in pieces	Ps 74:14
there is that l, whom thou hast	Ps 104:26
punish l the piercing serpent	Is 27:1
even l that crooked serpent	Is 27:1

LEVITE (le'-vite) See LEVITES, LEVITICAL. *A descendant of Levi.*

Is not Aaron the L thy brother	Ex 4:14
the L that is within your gates	Deut 12:12
the L that is within thy gates	Deut 12:18
that thou forsake not the L as	Deut 12:19
the L that is within thy gates	Deut 14:27
And the L, (because he hath no	Deut 14:29
the L that is within thy gates,	Deut 16:11
and thy maidservant, and the L	Deut 16:14
if a L come from any of thy gates	Deut 18:6
unto thine house, thou, and the L	Deut 26:11
and hast given it unto the L	Deut 26:12
also have given them unto the L	Deut 26:13
the family of Judah, who was a L	Judg 17:7
I am a L of Beth-lehem-judah, and	Judg 17:9
So the L went in	Judg 17:10
the L was content to dwell with,	Judg 17:11
And Micah consecrated the L	Judg 17:12
seeing I have a L to my priest	Judg 17:13
the voice of the young man the L	Judg 18:3
the house of the young man the L	Judg 18:15
that there was a certain L	Judg 19:1
And the L, the husband of the	Judg 20:4
a L of the sons of Asaph, came	2Chr 20:14
which Cononiah the L was ruler	2Chr 31:12
And Kore the son of Imnah the L	2Chr 31:14
and Shabbethai the L helped them.	Ezr 10:15
And likewise a L, when he was at	Lk 10:32
The son of consolation,) a L	Acts 4:36

LEVITES

the L according to their families	Ex 6:25
Moses, for the service of the L	Ex 38:21
the cities of the L, and the	Lev 25:32
may the L redeem at any time.	Lev 25:32
And if a man purchase of the L	Lev 25:33
L are their possession among the	Lev 25:33
But the L after the tribe of	Num 1:47
the L over the tabernacle of	Num 1:50
forward, the L shall take it down	Num 1:51
be pitched, the L shall set it up	Num 1:51
But the L shall pitch round about,	Num 1:53
the L shall keep the charge of	Num 1:53
of the L in the midst of the camp	Num 2:17
But the L were not numbered among.	Num 2:33
thou shalt give the L unto Aaron	Num 3:9
I have taken the L from among the	Num 3:12
therefore the L shall be mine	Num 3:12
These are the families of the L	Num 3:20
be chief over the chief of the L	Num 3:32
All that were numbered of the L	Num 3:39
thou shalt take the L for me (I	Num 3:41
the cattle of the L instead of	Num 3:41
Take the L instead of all the	Num 3:45
the cattle of the L instead of	Num 3:45
and the L shall be mine	Num 3:45
Israel, which are more than the L	Num 3:46
them that were redeemed by the L	Num 3:49
the Kohathites from among the L	Num 4:18
those that were numbered of the L	Num 4:46
thou shalt give them unto the L	Num 7:5
the oxen, and gave them unto the L	Num 7:6
Take the L from among the	Num 8:6
thou shalt bring the L before the	Num 8:9
shalt bring the L before the Lord.	Num 8:10
shall put their hands upon the L	Num 8:10
Aaron shall offer the L before	Num 8:11
the L shall lay their hands upon	Num 8:12
to make an atonement for the L	Num 8:12
thou shalt set the L before Aaron,	Num 8:13
the L from among the children of	Num 8:14
and the L shall be mine	Num 8:14
after that shall the L go in to	Num 8:15
I have taken the L for all the	Num 8:18
I have given the L as a gift to	Num 8:19
did to the L according unto all	Num 8:20
commanded Moses concerning the L.	Num 8:20
the L were purified, and they	Num 8:21
after that went the L in to do	Num 8:22
commanded Moses concerning the L.	Num 8:22
is it that belongeth unto the L.	Num 8:24
unto the L touching their charge.	Num 8:26
the L from among the children of	Num 18:6
But the L shall do the service of	Num 18:23
I have given to the L to inherit.	Num 18:24
Thus speak unto the L, and say	Num 18:26
unto the L as the increase of the.	Num 18:30
of the L after their families	Num 26:57
These are the families of the L	Num 26:58

beasts, and give them unto the L	Num 31:30
of beast, and gave them unto the L.	Num 31:47
that they give unto the L of the	Num 35:2
ye shall give also unto the L	Num 35:4
which ye shall give unto the L	Num 35:6
which ye shall give unto the L	Num 35:6
give to the L shall be forty	Num 35:7
give of his cities unto the L	Num 35:8
shalt come unto the priests the L	Deut 17:9
which is before the priests the L	Deut 17:18
The priests the L, and all the	Deut 18:1
God, as all his brethren the L do.	Deut 18:7
the priests the L shall teach you.	Deut 24:8
the priests the L spake unto all	Deut 27:9
the L shall speak, and say unto	Deut 27:14
That Moses commanded the L	Deut 31:25
and the priests the L bearing it	Josh 3:3
side before the priests the L	Josh 8:33
but unto the L he gave none	Josh 14:3
no part unto the L in the land.	Josh 14:4
But the L have no part among you.	Josh 18:7
of the L unto Eleazar the priest	Josh 21:1
of Israel gave unto the L out of	Josh 21:3
the priest, which were of the L	Josh 21:4
of Israel gave by lot unto the L	Josh 21:8
the L which remained of the	Josh 21:20
Gershon, of the families of the L	Josh 21:27
of Merari, the rest of the L	Josh 21:34
of the families of the L, were by	Josh 21:40
All the cities of the L within	Josh 21:41
the L look down the ark of the	1Sa 6:15
all the L were with him, bearing	2Sa 15:24
did the priests and the L bring up	1Kin 8:4
the L according to their fathers	1Chr 6:19
Their brethren also the L were	1Chr 6:48
children of Israel gave to the L	1Chr 6:64
the Israelites, the priests, L	1Chr 9:2
And of the L	1Chr 9:14
For these L, the four chief	1Chr 9:26
And Mattithiah, one of the L	1Chr 9:31
chief of the fathers of the L	1Chr 9:33
These chief fathers of the L were	1Chr 9:34
L which are in their cities and	1Chr 13:2
to carry the ark of God but the L	1Chr 15:2
the children of Aaron, and the L	1Chr 15:4
the priests, and for the L	1Chr 15:11
the chief of the fathers of the L	1Chr 15:12
the L sanctified themselves to	1Chr 15:14
the children of the L bare the	1Chr 15:15
to appoint their brethren to be	1Chr 15:16
So the L appointed Heman the son	1Chr 15:17
And Chenaniah, chief of the L	1Chr 15:22
when God helped the L that bare	1Chr 15:26
all the L that bare the ark, and	1Chr 15:27
he appointed certain of the L	1Chr 16:4
Israel, with the priests and the L	1Chr 23:2
Now the L were numbered from the	1Chr 23:3
And also unto the L	1Chr 23:26
by the last words of David the L	1Chr 23:27
the scribe, one of the L, wrote	1Chr 24:6
the fathers of the priests and L	1Chr 24:6
of the L after the house of their	1Chr 24:30
the fathers of the priests and L	1Chr 24:31
Eastward were six L, northward	1Chr 26:17
And of the L, Ahijah was over the	1Chr 26:20
Of the L, Hashabiah the son of	1Chr 27:17
courses of the priests and the L	1Chr 28:13
courses of the priests and the L	1Chr 28:21
and the L took up the ark	2Chr 5:4
did the priests and the L bring up	2Chr 5:5
Also the L which were the singers	2Chr 5:12
the L also with instruments of	2Chr 7:6
the L to their charges, to praise	2Chr 8:14
L concerning any matter, or	2Chr 8:15
the L that were in all Israel	2Chr 11:13
For the L left their suburbs and	2Chr 11:14
Lord, the sons of Aaron, and the L	2Chr 13:10
the L wait upon their business	2Chr 13:10
And with them he sent L, even	2Chr 17:8
and Tobijah, and Tob-adonijah, L	2Chr 17:8
did Jehoshaphat set of the L	2Chr 19:8
also the L shall be officers	2Chr 19:11
And the L, of the children of the	2Chr 20:19
gathered the L out of all the	2Chr 23:2
of the priests and of the L	2Chr 23:4
and they that minister of the L	2Chr 23:6
the L shall compass the king	2Chr 23:7
So the L and all Judah did	2Chr 23:8
by the hand of the priests the L	2Chr 23:18
together the priests and the L	2Chr 24:5
Howbeit the L hastened it not	2Chr 24:5
of the L to bring in out of Judah	2Chr 24:6
office by the hand of the L	2Chr 24:11
brought in the priests and the L	2Chr 29:4
And said unto them, Hear me, ye L	2Chr 29:5
Then the L arose, Mahath the son	2Chr 29:12
the L took it, to carry it out	2Chr 29:16
he set the L in the house of the	2Chr 29:25
the L stood with the instruments	2Chr 29:26
the princes commanded the L to	2Chr 29:30
brethren the L did help them	2Chr 29:34
for the L were more upright in	2Chr 29:34
the L were ashamed, and sanctified	2Chr 30:3
received of the hand of the L	2Chr 30:16
therefore the L had the charge of	2Chr 30:17
that taught the good knowledge	2Chr 30:22
Judah, with the priests and the L	2Chr 30:25
Then the priests the L arose	2Chr 30:27
the L after their courses, every	2Chr 31:2

L for burnt offerings and for	2Chr 31:2
portion of the priests and the L	2Chr 31:4
the L concerning the heaps	2Chr 31:9
the L from twenty years old and	2Chr 31:17
by genealogies among the L	2Chr 31:19
which the L that kept the doors	2Chr 34:9
were Jahath and Obadiah, the L	2Chr 34:12
and other of the L, all that could	2Chr 34:12
of the L there were scribes, and	2Chr 34:13
and the priests, and the L	2Chr 34:30
said unto the L that taught all	2Chr 35:3
division of the families of the L	2Chr 35:5
to the priests, and to the L	2Chr 35:5
Jeiel and Jozabad, chief of the L	2Chr 35:9
gave unto the L for passover	2Chr 35:9
the L in their courses, according	2Chr 35:10
their hands, and the L flayed them.	2Chr 35:11
therefore the L prepared for	2Chr 35:14
brethren the L prepared for them	2Chr 35:14
kept, and the priests, and the L	2Chr 35:18
and the priests, and the L	2Chr 35:18
The L: the children.	Ezr 2:40
So the priests, and the L, and some	Ezr 2:70
brethren the priests and the L	Ezr 3:8
and appointed the L, from twenty	Ezr 3:8
sons and their brethren the L	Ezr 3:9
the L the sons of Asaph with	Ezr 3:10
But many of the priests and L	Ezr 3:12
of Israel, the priests, and the L	Ezr 6:16
the L in their courses, for the	Ezr 6:18
the L were purified together, all	Ezr 6:20
and of the priests, and the L	Ezr 7:7
of Israel, and of his priests and L	Ezr 7:13
touching any of the priests and L	Ezr 7:24
for the service of the L, two	Ezr 8:20
the chief of the priests and the L	Ezr 8:29
the L the weight of the silver,	Ezr 8:30
and Noadiah the son of Binnui, L	Ezr 8:33
Israel, and the priests, and the L	Ezr 8:1
and made the chief priests, the L	Ezr 10:5
Also of the L	Ezr 10:23
After him repaired the L, Rehum	Neh 3:17
singers and the L were appointed,	Neh 7:1
The L: the children.	Neh 7:43
So the priests, and the L, and the	Neh 7:73
Jozabad, Hanan, Pelaiah, and the L	Neh 8:7
the L that taught the people.	Neh 8:9
So the L stilled all the people,	Neh 8:11
the people, the priests, and the L	Neh 8:13
up upon the stairs, of the L	Neh 9:4
Then the L, Jeshua, and Kadmiel,	Neh 9:5
and our princes, L, and priests,	Neh 9:38
And L: both Jeshua	Neh 10:9
of the people, the priests, the L	Neh 10:28
the lots among the priests, the L	Neh 10:34
tithes of our ground unto the L	Neh 10:37
that the same L might have the	Neh 10:38
son of Aaron shall be with the L	Neh 10:38
when the L take tithes.	Neh 10:38
the L shall bring up the tithe of	Neh 10:38
Israel, the priests, and the L	Neh 11:3
Also of the L	Neh 11:15
and Jozabad, of the chief of the L	Neh 11:16
All the L in the holy city were	Neh 11:18
Israel, of the priests, and the L	Neh 11:20
The overseer also of the L	Neh 11:22
of the L were divisions in Judah,	Neh 11:36
and the L that went up with	Neh 12:1
Moreover the L: Jeshua.	Neh 12:8
The L in the days of Eliashib,	Neh 12:22
And the chief of the L	Neh 12:24
the L out of all their places	Neh 12:27
the L purified themselves, and	Neh 12:30
of the law for the priests and L	Neh 12:44
priests and for the L that waited	Neh 12:44
sanctified holy things unto the L	Neh 12:47
the L sanctified them unto the	Neh 12:47
commanded to be given to the L	Neh 13:5
of the L had not been given them.	Neh 13:10
for the L and the singers, that	Neh 13:10
and Zadok the scribe, and of the L	Neh 13:13
I commanded the L that they	Neh 13:22
of the priesthood, and of the L	Neh 13:29
the wards of the priests and the L	Neh 13:30
take of them for priests and for L	Is 66:21
I want a man before me to offer	Jer 33:18
with the L the priests, my	Jer 33:21
the L that minister unto me	Jer 33:22
L that be of the seed of Zadok	Eze 43:19
the L that are gone away far from	Eze 44:10
But the priests the L, the sons	Eze 44:15
of breadth, shall also the L	Eze 45:5
went astray, as the L went astray	Eze 48:11
most holy by the border of the L	Eze 48:12
the priests the L shall have five	Eze 48:13
from the possession of the L	Eze 48:22
L from Jerusalem to ask him, Who	Jn 1:19

LEVITICAL (le-vit'-i-cal) *Belonging to the Levites.*

were by the L priesthood, (for	Heb 7:11

LEVY

l a tribute unto the Lord of the	Num 31:28
raised a l out of all Israel	1Kin 5:13
the l was thirty thousand men	1Kin 5:13
and Adoniram was over the l	1Kin 5:14
which Solomon king Solomon raised	1Kin 9:15
upon those did Solomon l a	1Kin 9:21

LEWD

which are ashamed of thy l way	Eze 16:27
and unto Aholibah, the l women	Eze 23:44

took unto them certain *l* fellows............ Acts 17:5

LEWDLY
another hath *l* defiled his................... Eze 22:11

LEWDNESS
for they have committed *l*................... Judg 20:6
she hath wrought *l* with many.............. Jer 11:15
the *l* of thy whoredom, and thine......... Jer 13:27
thou shalt not commit this *l*................ Jer 16:43
Thou hast borne thy *l* and thine.......... Eze 16:58
the midst of thee they commit *l*........... Eze 22:9
to remembrance the *l* of thy youth....... Eze 23:21
I make thy *l* to cease from thee........... Eze 23:27
shall be discovered, both thy *l*............ Eze 23:29
therefore bear thou also thy *l*............. Eze 23:35
Thus will I cause *l* to cease out......... Eze 23:48
be taught not to do after your *l*........... Eze 23:48
shall recompense your *l* upon you....... Eze 23:49
In thy filthiness is *l*........................ Eze 24:13
now will I discover her *l* in the............ Hos 2:10
for they commit *l*............................ Hos 6:9
a matter of wrong or wicked *l*.............. Acts 18:14

LIAR
not so now, who will make me a *l*.......... Job 24:25
a *l* giveth ear to a naughty................. Prov 17:4
and a poor man is better than a *l*........ Prov 19:22
thee, and thou be found a *l*................ Prov 30:6
thou be altogether unto me as a *l*....... Jer 15:18
for he is a *l*, and the father of............ Jn 8:44
I shall be a *l* like unto you................. Jn 8:55
God be true, but every man a *l*............ Rom 3:4
have not sinned, we make him a *l*........ 1Jn 1:10
not his commandments, is a *l*............. 1Jn 2:4
Who is a *l* but he that denieth............ 1Jn 2:22
and hateth his brother, he is a *l*......... 1Jn 4:20
not God hath made him a *l*................ 1Jn 5:10

LIARS
shall be found *l* unto thee................. Deut 33:29
I said in my haste, All men are *l*......... Ps 116:11
frustrateth the tokens of the *l*............ Is 44:25
A sword is upon the *l*...................... Jer 50:36
mankind, for menstealers, for *l*........... 1Ti 1:10
said, The Cretians are alway *l*............ Titus 1:12
and are not, and hast found them *l*...... Rev 2:2
sorcerers, and idolaters, and all *l*........ Rev 21:8

LIBERAL
The *l* soul shall be made fat............... Prov 11:25
person shall be no more called *l*......... Is 32:5
But the *l* deviseth *l* things............... Is 32:8
by *l* things shall he stand................. Is 32:8
for your *l* distribution unto them......... 2Cor 9:13

LIBERALITY
to bring your *l* unto Jerusalem........... 1Cor 16:3
unto the riches of their *l*................... 2Cor 8:2

LIBERALLY
furnish him out of thy flock................ Deut 15:14
of God, that giveth to all men *l*........... Jas 1:5

LIBERTINES (*lib´-ur-tins*) *Former Jewish slaves.*
is called the synagogue of the *L*.......... Acts 6:9

LIBERTY
proclaim *l* throughout all the............ Lev 25:10
And I will walk at *l*.......................... Ps 119:45
to proclaim *l* to the captives, and....... Is 61:1
to proclaim *l* unto them................... Jer 34:8
in proclaiming *l* every man to his....... Jer 34:16
he had set at *l* at their pleasure......... Jer 34:16
unto me, in proclaiming *l*.................. Jer 34:17
behold, I proclaim a *l* for you............ Jer 34:17
it shall be his to the year of *l*............ Eze 46:17
to set at *l* them that are bruised......... Lk 4:18
keep Paul, and to let him have *l*........ Acts 24:23
This man might have been set at.......... Acts 26:32
gave him *l* to go unto his friends........ Acts 27:3
glorious *l* of the children of God........ Rom 8:21
she is at *l* to be married to whom....... 1Cor 7:39
means this *l* of yours become a......... 1Cor 8:9
for why is my *l* judged of another....... 1Cor 10:29
Spirit of the Lord is, there is *l*............ 2Cor 3:17
I which we have in Christ Jesus........... Gal 2:4
Stand fast therefore in the *l*.............. Gal 5:1
ye have been called unto *l*................ Gal 5:13
only use not *l* for an occasion to....... Gal 5:13
our brother Timothy is set at *l*........... Heb 13:23
looketh into the perfect law of *l*......... Jas 1:25
shall be judged by the law of *l*........... Jas 2:12
not using your *l* for a cloke of........... 1Pet 2:16
While they promise them *l*................ 2Pet 2:19

LIBNAH (*lib´-nah*) See LABAN.
1. A Hebrew encampment in the wilderness.
Rimmon-parez, and pitched in *L*........ Num 33:20
And they removed from *L*, and......... Num 33:21
2. A Levitical city in Judah.
and all Israel with him, unto *L*.......... Josh 10:29
unto Libnah, and fought against *L*...... Josh 10:29
And Joshua passed from *L*, and all.... Josh 10:31
to all that he had done to *L*.............. Josh 10:32
as he had done also to *L*, and to....... Josh 10:39
The king of *L*, one......................... Josh 12:15
L, and Ether, and Ashan.................. Josh 15:42
and *L* with her suburbs................... Josh 21:13
Then *L* revolted at the same time....... 2Kin 8:22
king of Assyria warring against *L*....... 2Kin 19:8
the daughter of Jeremiah of *L*........... 2Kin 23:31
the daughter of Jeremiah of *L*........... 2Kin 24:18
L with her suburbs and Jattir, and..... 1Chr 6:57
The same time also did *L* revolt......... 2Chr 21:10

king of Assyria warring against *L*....... Is 37:8
the daughter of Jeremiah of *L*........... Jer 52:1

LIBNI (*lib´-ni*) See LAADAN, LIBNITES.
1. Son of Gershom.
L, and Shimi, according to their......... Ex 6:17
their families; *L*, and Shimei............. Num 3:18
of Gershom; *L*, and Shimei............... 1Chr 6:17
L his son, Jahath his son, Zimmah.... 1Chr 6:20
2. Grandson of Merari.
L his son, Shimei his son, Uzza........ 1Chr 6:29

LIBNITES (*lib´-nites*) *Descendants of Libni.*
Gershon was the family of the *L*........ Num 3:21
the family of the *L*, the family.......... Num 26:58

LIBYA (*lib´-e-ah*) See LIBYANS. *A land in north Africa.*
Ethiopia, and *L*, and Lydia, and all.... Eze 30:5
Persia, Ethiopia, and *L* with them...... Eze 38:5
and in the parts of *L* about Cyrene...... Acts 2:10

LIBYANS (*lib´-e-uns*) See LEHABIM. *Inhabitants of Libya.*
the Ethiopians and the *L*, that.......... Jer 46:9
and the *L*, and the Ethiopians shall... Dan 11:43

LICE
that it may become *l* throughout........ Ex 8:16
the earth, and it became *l* in man...... Ex 8:17
l throughout all the land of............... Ex 8:17
enchantments to bring forth *l*........... Ex 8:18
so there were *l* upon man, and upon.. Ex 8:18
flies, and *l* in all their coasts........... Ps 105:31

LICENCE
And when he had given him *l*............ Acts 21:40
have I to answer for himself.............. Acts 25:16

LICK
Now shall this company *l* up all........ Num 22:4
of Naboth shall dogs *l* thy blood....... 1Kin 21:19
and his enemies shall *l* the dust....... Ps 72:9
l up the dust of thy feet................... Is 49:23
They shall *l* the dust like a.............. Mic 7:17

LICKED
l up the water that was in the........... 1Kin 18:38
In the place where dogs *l* the........... 1Kin 21:19
and the dogs *l* up his blood............. Num 22:38
the dogs came and *l* his sores.......... Lk 16:21

LICKETH
as the ox *l* up the grass of the.......... Num 22:4

LID
and bored a hole in the *l* of.............. 2Kin 12:9

LIE
we will *l* with him, that we may......... Gen 19:32
I with him, that we may preserve......... Gen 19:34
Therefore he shall *l* with thee to....... Gen 30:15
and she said, *L* with me.................. Gen 39:7
to *l* by her, or to be with her............ Gen 39:10
by his garment, saying, *L* with me.... Gen 39:12
he came in unto me to *l* with me....... Gen 39:14
But I will *l* with my fathers, and........ Gen 47:30
if a man *l* not in wait, but God......... Ex 21:13
I with her, he shall surely endow........ Ex 22:16
thou shalt let it rest and *l* still........ Ex 23:11
l unto his neighbour in............... Lev 6:2
shall *l* with seed of copulation......... Lev 15:24
if any man *l* with her at all, and....... Lev 15:24
Moreover thou shalt not *l*................ Lev 18:20
Thou shalt not *l* with mankind......... Lev 18:22
Neither shalt thou *l* with any........... Lev 18:23
before a beast to *l* down thereto....... Lev 18:23
falsely, neither *l* one to another........ Lev 19:11
if a man *l* with his daughter in......... Lev 20:12
If a man also *l* with mankind............ Lev 20:13
if a man *l* with a beast, he shall....... Lev 20:15
l down thereto, thou shalt kill.......... Lev 20:16
if a man shall *l* with a woman.......... Lev 20:18
if a man shall *l* with his sister.......... Lev 20:20
in the land, and ye shall *l* down........ Lev 26:6
a man *l* with her carnally, and.......... Num 5:13
then the camps that *l* on the east..... Num 10:5
then the camps that *l* on the............ Num 10:6
is not a man, that he should *l*........... Num 23:19
he shall not *l* down until he eat........ Num 23:24
l in wait for him, and rise up............ Deut 19:11
her in the city, and *l* with her........... Deut 22:23
the man force her, and *l* with her...... Deut 22:25
l with her, and they be found........... Deut 22:28
Judge shall cause him to *l* down....... Deut 25:2
and another man shall *l* with her....... Deut 28:30
in this book shall *l* upon him........... Deut 29:20
ye shall *l* in wait against the............ Josh 8:4
and they were to *l* in ambush.......... Josh 8:9
set them to *l* in ambush between...... Josh 8:12
thee, and *l* in wait in the field......... Judg 9:32
let all thy wants *l* upon me............. Judg 19:20
l in wait in the vineyards................ Judg 21:20
mark the place where he shall *l*........ Ruth 3:4
he went to *l* down at the end of........ Ruth 3:7
l down until the morning................ Ruth 3:13
l down again..................................... 1Sa 3:5
l down again..................................... 1Sa 3:6
Eli said unto Samuel, Go, *l* down...... 1Sa 3:9
of Israel will not *l* nor repent.......... 1Sa 15:29
to *l* in wait, as at this day.............. Isa 22:8
to *l* in wait, as at this day.............. 1Sa 22:13
and to drink, and to *l* with my wife.... 2Sa 11:11
at even he went out to *l* on his......... 2Sa 11:13
he shall *l* with thy wives in the........ 2Sa 12:11
Come *l* with me, my sister.............. 2Sa 13:11

let her *l* in thy bosom, that my........ 1Kin 1:2
do not *l* unto thine handmaid.......... 2Kin 4:16
for it is evident unto you if I *l*.......... Job 6:28
When I *l* down, I say, When shall..... Job 7:4
Also thou shalt *l* down, and none..... Job 11:19
which shall *l* down with him in........ Job 20:11
They shall *l* down alike in the......... Job 21:26
The rich man shall *l* down.............. Job 27:19
Should I *l* against my right............. Job 34:6
abide in the covert to *l* in wait........ Job 38:40
He maketh me to *l* down in green..... Ps 23:2
I even among them that are set......... Ps 57:4
they *l* in wait for my soul............... Ps 59:3
and men of high degree are a *l*........ Ps 62:9
the slain that *l* in the grave............ Ps 88:5
that I will not *l* unto David.............. Ps 89:35
proud have forged a *l* against me..... Ps 119:69
yea, thou shalt *l* down, and thy....... Prov 3:24
wicked are to *l* in wait for blood...... Prov 12:6
A faithful witness will not *l*............. Prov 14:5
if two *l* together, then they have....... Eccl 4:11
he shall *l* all night betwixt my......... Song 1:13
leopard shall *l* down with the kid...... Is 11:6
young ones shall *l* down together..... Is 11:7
of the desert shall *l* there............... Is 13:21
l in glory, every one in his own........ Is 14:18
the needy shall *l* down in safety....... Is 14:30
be for flocks, which shall *l* down...... Is 17:2
feed, and there shall he *l* down........ Is 27:10
The highways I waste, the................ Is 33:8
to generation it shall *l* waste.......... Is 34:10
they shall *l* down together, they...... Is 43:17
is there not a *l* in my right hand...... Is 44:20
ye shall *l* down in sorrow............... Is 50:11
they *l* at the head of all the............ Is 51:20
people, children that will not *l*........ Is 63:8
place for the herds to *l* down in....... Is 65:10
We *l* down in our shame, and our..... Jer 3:25
For they prophesy a *l* unto you........ Jer 27:10
for they prophesy a *l* unto you........ Jer 27:14
yet they prophesy a *l* in my name..... Jer 27:15
for they prophesy a *l* unto you........ Jer 27:16
this people to trust in a *l*................ Jer 28:15
which prophesy a *l* unto you in my.... Jer 29:21
and he caused you to trust in a *l*...... Jer 29:31
causing their flocks to *l* down.......... Jer 33:12
the old *l* on the ground in the......... Lam 2:21
L thou also upon thy left side.......... Eze 4:4
of the days that thou shalt *l*............ Eze 4:4
I again on thy right side, and............ Eze 4:6
that thou shalt *l* upon thy side........ Eze 4:6
whiles they divine a *l* unto thee....... Eze 21:29
thou shalt *l* in the midst of the........ Eze 28:8
they *l* uncircumcised, slain by........ Eze 32:21
they shall not *l* with the mighty....... Eze 32:27
shalt *l* with them that are slain........ Eze 32:28
they shall *l* with the................... Eze 32:29
they *l* uncircumcised with them....... Eze 32:30
there shall they *l* in a good fold....... Eze 34:14
and I will cause them to *l* down....... Eze 34:15
will make them to *l* down safely....... Hos 2:18
an oven, whiles they *l* in wait......... Hos 7:6
l all night in sackcloth, ye............. Joel 1:13
That *l* upon beds of ivory, and......... Amos 6:4
be a *l* to the kings of Israel............ Mic 1:14
in the spirit and falsehood do *l*........ Mic 2:11
they all *l* in wait for blood.............. Mic 7:2
the end it shall speak, and not *l*...... Hab 2:3
shall they *l* down in the evening...... Zeph 2:7
flocks shall *l* down in the midst...... Zeph 2:14
a place for beasts to *l* down in......... Zeph 2:15
l down, and none shall make them.... Zeph 3:13
houses, and this house I waste......... Hag 1:4
and the diviners have seen a *l*......... Zec 10:2
When Jesus saw him *l*, and knew..... Jn 5:6
When he speaketh a *l*, he speaketh.. Jn 8:44
and seeth the linen clothes *l*........... Jn 20:6
heart to *l* to the Holy Ghost............ Acts 5:3
for there *l* in wait for him.............. Acts 23:21
changed the truth of God into a *l*..... Rom 1:25
through my *l* unto his glory............ Rom 3:7
I *l* not, my conscience also............ Rom 9:1
evermore, knoweth that I *l* not........ 2Cor 11:31
you, behold, before God, I *l* not....... Gal 1:20
whereby they *l* in wait to deceive..... Eph 4:14
L not one to another, seeing that..... Col 3:9
that they should believe a *l*............ 2Th 2:11
the truth in Christ, and I *l* not......... 1Ti 2:7
life, which God, that cannot *l*.......... Titus 1:2
it was impossible for God to *l*......... Heb 6:18
not, and *l* not against the truth....... Jas 3:14
him, and walk in darkness, we *l*...... 1Jn 1:6
that no *l* is of the truth.................. 1Jn 2:21
things, and is truth, and is no *l*....... 1Jn 2:27
are Jews, and are not, but do *l*........ Rev 3:9
their dead bodies shall *l* in the....... Rev 11:8
abomination, or maketh a *l*............ Rev 21:27
and whosoever loveth and maketh a *l* Rev 22:15

LIED
But he *l* unto him......................... 1Kin 13:18
they *l* unto him with their.............. Ps 78:36
or feared, that thou hast *l*............. Is 57:11
thou hast not *l* unto men, but......... Acts 5:4

LIEN
lightly have *l* with thy wife............. Gen 26:10
Though ye have *l* among the pots...... Ps 68:13
where thou hast not been *l* with....... Jer 3:2

LIERS
their *l* in wait on the west of........... Josh 8:13
l in ambush against him behind....... Josh 8:14

the men of Shechem set *l* in wait ...... Judg 9:25
there were *l* in wait abiding in .... Judg 16:12
Israel set *l* in wait round about .... Judg 20:29
the *l* in wait of Israel came .... Judg 20:33
the *l* in wait which they had set .... Judg 20:36
the *l* in wait hasted, and rushed .... Judg 20:37
the *l* in wait drew themselves .... Judg 20:37
the *l* in wait, that they should .... Judg 20:38

LIES

thou hast mocked me, and told me *l* .... Judg 16:10
thou hast mocked me, and told me *l*. ... Judg 16:13
Should thy *l* make men hold their .... Job 11:3
But ye are forgers of *l*, ye are .... Job 13:4
nor such as turn aside to *l* .... Ps 40:4
soon as they be born, speaking *l* .... Ps 58:3
they delight in *l* .... Ps 62:4
that speak *l* shall be stopped .... Ps 63:11
he that telleth *l* shall not tarry .... Ps 101:7
A false witness that prophesied *l* .... Prov 6:19
but a false witness will utter *l* .... Prov 14:5
a deceitful witness speaketh *l* .... Prov 14:25
that speaketh *l* shall not escape .... Prov 19:5
he that speaketh *l* shall perish .... Prov 19:9
If a ruler hearken to *l*, all his .... Prov 29:12
Remove far from me vanity and *l* .... Prov 30:8
and the prophet that teacheth *l* .... Is 9:15
but his *l* shall not be so .... Is 16:6
for we have made *l* our refuge .... Is 28:15
shall sweep away the refuge of *l* .... Is 28:17
your lips have spoken *l*, your .... Is 59:3
they trust in vanity, and speak *l* .... Is 59:4
tongues like their bow for *l* .... Jer 9:3
taught their tongue to speak *l* .... Jer 9:5
prophets prophesy *l* in my name .... Jer 14:14
our fathers have inherited *l* .... Jer 16:19
to whom thou hast prophesied *l* .... Jer 20:6
commit adultery, and walk in *l* .... Jer 23:14
said, that prophesy *l* in my name .... Jer 23:25
of the prophets that prophesy *l* .... Jer 23:26
cause my people to err by their *l* .... Jer 23:32
his *l* shall not so effect it .... Jer 48:30
ye have spoken vanity, and seen *l* .... Eze 13:8
that see vanity, and that divine *l* .... Eze 13:9
to my people that hear your *l* .... Eze 13:19
Because with *l* ye have made the .... Eze 13:22
divining *l* unto them, saying, ... Eze 22:28
She hath wearied herself with *l* .... Eze 24:12
they shall speak *l* at one table .... Dan 11:27
and the princes with their *l* .... Hos 7:3
yet they have spoken *l* against me .... Hos 7:13
ye have eaten the fruit of *l* .... Hos 10:13
compasseth me about with *l* .... Hos 11:12
he daily increaseth *l* and .... Hos 12:1
their *l* caused them to err, after .... Amos 2:4
inhabitants thereof have spoken *l* .... Mic 6:12
it is all full of *l* and robbery .... Nah 3:1
molten image, and a teacher of *l* .... Hab 2:18
not do iniquity, nor speak *l* .... Zeph 3:13
for thou speakest *l* in the name .... Zec 13:3
Speaking *l* in hypocrisy 1Ti 4:2

LIEST

the land whereon thou *l*, to thee .... Gen 28:13
by the way, and when thou *l* down........ Deut 6:7
by the way, when thou *l* down............... Deut 11:19
wherefore *l* thou thus upon thy .... Josh 7:10
When thou *l* down, thou shalt not........ Prov 3:24

LIETH

doest not well, sin *l* at the door .... Gen 4:7
of the deep that *l* under......................... Gen 49:25
Whosoever *l* with a beast shall............. Ex 22:19
I concerning it, and sweareth................... Lev 6:3
he that *l* in the house shall wash .... Lev 14:47
whereon he *l* that hath the issue, ... Lev 15:4
every thing that she *l* upon in............... Lev 15:20
bed whereon he *l* shall be unclean....... Lev 15:24
Every bed whereon she *l* all the .... Lev 15:26
of him that *l* with her that is................. Lev 15:33
whosoever *l* carnally with a woman...... Lev 19:20
the man that *l* with his father's............ Lev 20:11
as he *l* with a woman, both of.............. Lev 20:13
as long as it *l* desolate......................... Lev 26:34
As long as it *l* desolate it shall .... Lev 26:35
while she *l* desolate without them .... Lev 26:43
l upon the border of Moab..................... Num 21:15
Cursed be he that *l* with his.................. Deut 27:20
Cursed be he that *l* with his sister........ Deut 27:22
be that *l* with his sister........................ Deut 27:22
Cursed be he that *l* with his................. Deut 27:23
l before the valley of Hinnom................ Josh 15:8
Michmethah, that *l* before Shechem..... Josh 17:7
near the hill that *l* on the south............ Josh 18:13
from the hill that *l* before..................... Josh 18:14
l before the valley of the son of............ Josh 18:16
which *l* in the south of Arad.................. Judg 1:16
see wherein his great strength *l* .... Judg 16:5
wherein thy great strength *l* .... Judg 16:6
me wherein thy great strength *l* .... Judg 16:15
the valley that *l* by Beth-rehob............. Judg 18:28
And it shall be, when he *l* down........... Ruth 3:4
that *l* before Giah by the way of 2Sa 2:24
l in the midst of the river of 2Sa 24:5
l waste, and the gates thereof are .... Neh 2:3
we are in, how Jerusalem *l* waste......... Neh 2:17
the tower which *l* out from the.............. Neh 3:25
the east, and the tower that *l* out......... Neh 3:26
the great tower that *l* out...................... Neh 3:27
So man *l* down, and riseth not.............. Job 14:12
He *l* under the shady trees, in.............. Job 40:21
He *l* in wait secretly as a lion............... Ps 10:9

he *l* in wait to catch the poor............... Ps 10:9
now that he *l* he shall rise up in........... Ps 41:8
Thy wrath *l* hard upon me, and thou .... Ps 88:7
l in wait at every corner....................... Prov 7:12
She also *l* in wait as for a prey,............ Prov 23:28
thou shalt be as he that *l* down............ Prov 23:34
or as he that *l* upon the top of a .... Prov 23:34
which *l* toward the north, and............... Eze 9:2
the great dragon that *l* in the............... Eze 29:3
from her that *l* in thy bosom................. Mic 7:5
my servant *l* at home sick of the .... Mt 8:6
My little daughter *l* at the point............ Mk 5:23
the region that *l* round about............... Acts 14:6
l toward the south west and north........ Acts 27:12
be possible, as much as *l* in you.......... Rom 12:18
the whole world *l* in wickedness............ 1Jn 5:19
the city foursquare, and the .... Rev 21:16

LIEUTENANTS

commissions unto the king's *l* .... Ezr 8:36
had commanded unto the king's *l* .... Est 3:12
unto the Jews, and to the *l* .... Est 8:9
rulers of the provinces, and the *l* .... Est 9:3

LIFE

the moving creature that hath *l* .... Gen 1:20
the earth, wherein there is *l* .... Gen 1:30
into his nostrils the breath of *l* .... Gen 2:7
the tree of *l* also in the midst............... Gen 2:9
thou eat all the days of thy *l*................. Gen 3:14
eat of it all the days of thy *l* .... Gen 3:17
and take also of the tree of *l* .... Gen 3:22
to keep the way of the tree of *l* .... Gen 3:24
flesh, wherein is the breath of *l* .... Gen 6:17
six hundredth year of Noah's *l* .... Gen 7:11
flesh, wherein is the breath of *l* .... Gen 7:15
nostrils was the breath of *l* .... Gen 7:22
But flesh with the *l* thereof.................... Gen 9:4
will I require the *l* of man .... Gen 9:5
thee according to the time of *l* .... Gen 18:10
thee, according to the time of *l* .... Gen 18:14
that he said, Escape for thy *l*................ Gen 19:17
shewed unto me in saving my *l* .... Gen 19:19
were the years of the *l* of Sarah .... Gen 23:1
of Abraham's *l* which he lived............... Gen 25:7
are the years of the *l* of Ishmael.......... Gen 25:17
I am weary of my *l* because of the .... Gen 27:46
land, what good shall my *l* do me .... Gen 27:46
to face, and my *l* is preserved.............. Gen 32:30
By the *l* of Pharaoh ye shall not .... Gen 42:15
or else by the *l* of Pharaoh................... Gen 42:16
seeing that his *l* is bound up in............ Gen 44:30
is bound up in the lad's *l* .... Gen 44:30
send me before you to preserve *l* .... Gen 45:5
days of the years of my *l* been............. Gen 47:9
l of my fathers in the days of .... Gen 47:9
me all my *l* long unto this day.............. Gen 48:15
men are dead which sought thy *l* .... Ex 4:19
the years of the *l* of Levi were.............. Ex 6:16
the years of the *l* of Kohath were......... Ex 6:18
the years of the *l* of Amram were......... Ex 6:20
then thou shalt give *l* for .... Ex 21:23
give for the ransom of his *l* .... Ex 21:30
For the *l* of the flesh is in the .... Lev 17:11
For it is the *l* of all flesh .... Lev 17:14
blood of it is for the *l* thereof............... Lev 17:14
for the *l* of all flesh is the .... Lev 17:14
beside the other in her *l* time............... Lev 18:18
for the *l* of a murderer, which is........... Num 35:31
thy heart all the days of thy *l* .... Deut 4:9
son's son, all the days of thy *l* .... Deut 6:2
for the blood is the *l* .... Deut 12:23
not eat the *l* with the flesh.................... Deut 12:23
of Egypt all the days of thy *l* .... Deut 16:3
therein all the days of his *l* .... Deut 17:19
but *l* shall go for *l*, eye for................. Deut 19:21
l) to employ them in the siege.............. Deut 20:19
for he taketh a man's *l* to pledge......... Deut 24:6
thy *l* shall hang in doubt before........... Deut 28:66
have none assurance of thy *l* .... Deut 28:66
I have set before thee this day *l* .... Deut 30:15
you, that I have set before you *l* .... Deut 30:19
therefore choose *l*, that both................ Deut 30:19
for he is thy *l*, and the length of.......... Deut 30:20
because it is your *l* .... Deut 32:47
before thee all the days of thy *l* .... Josh 1:5
Our *l* for yours, if ye utter not.............. Josh 2:14
Moses, all the days of his *l* .... Josh 4:14
for you, and adventured his *l* far......... Judg 9:17
I put my *l* in my hands, and passed..... Judg 12:3
than they which he slew in his *l* .... Judg 16:30
run upon thee, and thou lose thy *l*........ Judg 18:25
he came to restore of thy *l* .... Ruth 4:15
the LORD all the days of his *l* 1Sa 1:11
Israel all the days of his *l* 1Sa 7:15
and what is my *l*, or my father's........... 1Sa 18:18
For he did put his *l* in his hand............ 1Sa 19:5
thy father, that he seeketh my *l* 1Sa 20:1
seeketh my *l* seeketh thy *l* 1Sa 22:23
Saul was come out to seek his *l* 1Sa 23:15
bundle of *l* with the LORD thy God 1Sa 25:29
as thy *l* was much set by this day........ 1Sa 26:24
so let my *l* be much set by in the 1Sa 26:24
then layest thou a snare for my *l* 1Sa 28:9
and I have put my *l* in my hand........... 1Sa 28:21
because my *l* is yet whole in me 2Sa 1:9
thine enemy, which sought thy *l* 2Sa 4:8
for the *l* of his brother whom he 2Sa 14:7
shall be, whether in death or *l* 2Sa 15:21
forth of my bowels, seeketh my *l* 2Sa 16:11
falsehood against mine own *l* 2Sa 18:13

which this day have saved thy *l* 2Sa 19:5
that thou mayest save thine own *l* 1Kin 1:12
and the *l* of thy son Solomon................ 1Kin 1:12
this word against his own *l* 1Kin 2:23
hast not asked for thyself long *l* 1Kin 3:11
hast asked the *l* of thine enemies......... 1Kin 3:11
Solomon all the days of his *l* 1Kin 4:21
his *l* for David my servant's sake 1Kin 11:34
him all the days of his *l* 1Kin 15:5
and Jeroboam all the days of his *l* 1Kin 15:6
if I make not thy *l* as the *l* 1Kin 19:2
that, he arose, and went for his *l* 1Kin 19:3
now, O LORD, take away my *l* 1Kin 19:4
and they seek my *l*, to take it 1Kin 19:10
and they seek my *l*, to take it 1Kin 19:14
peradventure he will save thy *l* 1Kin 20:31
then shall thy *l* be for his *l*,............... 1Kin 20:39
thy *l* shall go for his *l* 1Kin 20:42
man of God, I pray thee, let my *l* 2Kin 1:13
the *l* of these fifty thy servants 2Kin 1:13
therefore let my *l* now be...................... 2Kin 1:14
according to the time of *l* 2Kin 4:16
her, according to the time of *l* 2Kin 4:17
as it was, and fled for their *l* 2Kin 7:7
whose son he had restored to *l* 2Kin 8:1
he had restored a dead body to *l* 2Kin 8:5
whose son he had restored to *l* 2Kin 8:5
son, whom Elisha restored to *l* 2Kin 8:5
his *l* shall be for the *l* 2Kin 10:24
I shall be for the *l* of him 2Kin 10:24
before him all the days of his *l* 2Kin 25:29
every day, all the days of his *l* 2Kin 25:30
nor the *l* of thine enemies,................... 2Chr 1:11
hast thou asked long *l* 2Chr 1:11
and pray for the *l* of the king............... Ezr 6:10
go into the temple to save his *l* .... Neh 6:11
let my *l* be given me at my.................... Est 7:3
for his *l* to Esther the queen................ Est 7:7
together, and to stand for their *l* .... Est 8:11
a man hath will he give for his *l* .... Job 2:4
but save his *l* .... Job 2:6
I unto the bitter in soul........................... Job 3:20
end, that I should prolong my *l* .... Job 6:11
O remember that my *l* is wind.............. Job 7:7
and death rather than my *l* .... Job 7:15
I would despise my *l* .... Job 9:21
My soul is weary of my *l* .... Job 10:1
Thou hast granted me *l* and favour,..... Job 10:12
teeth, and put my *l* in mine hand .... Job 13:14
riseth up, and no man is sure of *l* .... Job 24:22
owners thereof to lose their *l*................ Job 31:39
of the Almighty hath given me *l* .... Job 33:4
his *l* from perishing by the sword .... Job 33:18
So that his *l* abhorreth bread, and....... Job 33:20
grave, and his *l* to the destroyers......... Job 33:22
his *l* shall see the light......................... Job 33:28
not the *l* of the wicked.......................... Job 36:6
their *l* is among the unclean.................. Job 36:14
tread down my *l* upon the earth............ Ps 7:5
Thou wilt shew me the path of *l* .... Ps 16:11
have their portion in this *l* .... Ps 17:14
He asked *l* of thee, and thou................ Ps 21:4
follow me all the days of my *l* .... Ps 23:6
sinners, nor my *l* with bloody men .... Ps 26:9
the LORD is the strength of my *l* .... Ps 27:1
of the LORD all the days of my *l* .... Ps 27:4
in his favour is *l* .... Ps 30:5
For my *l* is spent with grief, and,.......... Ps 31:10
they devised to take away my *l* .... Ps 31:13
What man is he that desireth *l* .... Ps 34:12
with thee is the fountain of *l* .... Ps 36:9
seek after my *l* lay snares for me......... Ps 38:12
and my prayer unto the God of my *l*..... Ps 42:8
Thou wilt prolong the king's *l*................ Ps 61:6
lovingkindness is better than *l* .... Ps 63:3
preserve my *l* from fear of the.............. Ps 64:1
Which holdeth our soul in *l* .... Ps 66:9
but gave their *l* over to the .... Ps 78:50
my *l* draweth nigh unto the grave .... Ps 88:3
With long *l* will I satisfy him,................ Ps 91:16
redeemeth thy *l* from destruction .... Ps 103:4
Jerusalem all the days of thy *l* .... Ps 128:5
the blessing, even *l* for evermore......... Ps 133:3
smitten my *l* down to the ground.......... Ps 143:3
away the *l* of the owners thereof .... Prov 1:19
take they hold of the paths of *l* .... Prov 2:19
For length of days, and long *l*............... Prov 3:2
She is a tree of *l* to them that .... Prov 3:18
So shall they be *l* unto thy soul........... Prov 3:22
the years of thy *l* shall be many .... Prov 4:10
for she is thy *l* .... Prov 4:13
For they are *l* unto those that .... Prov 4:22
for out of it are the issues of *l* .... Prov 4:23
shouldest ponder the path of *l* .... Prov 5:6
of instruction are the way of *l* .... Prov 6:23
will hunt for the precious *l* .... Prov 6:26
knoweth not that it is for his *l* .... Prov 7:23
For whoso findeth me findeth *l* .... Prov 8:35
the years of thy *l* shall be .... Prov 9:11
of a righteous man is a well of *l* .... Prov 10:11
of the righteous tendeth to *l* .... Prov 10:16
He is in the way of *l* that .... Prov 10:17
As righteousness tendeth to *l* .... Prov 11:19
of the righteous is a tree of *l* .... Prov 11:30
man regardeth the *l* of his beast.......... Prov 12:10
In the way of righteousness is *l* .... Prov 12:28
keepeth his mouth keepeth his *l* .... Prov 13:3
of a man's *l* are his riches.................... Prov 13:8
desire cometh, it is a tree of *l* .... Prov 13:12
of the wise is a fountain of *l* .... Prov 13:14

of the LORD is a fountain of l .... Prov 14:27
sound heart is the l of the flesh .... Prov 14:30
A wholesome tongue is a tree of l ...... Prov 15:4
The way of l is above to the wise .... Prov 15:24
of l abideth among the wise .... Prov 15:31
of the king's countenance is l .... Prov 16:15
is a wellspring of l unto him .... Prov 16:22
l are in the power of the tongue .... Prov 18:21
The fear of the LORD tendeth to l .... Prov 19:23
righteousness and mercy findeth l ...... Prov 21:21
LORD are riches, and honour, and l ..... Prov 22:4
and not evil all the days of her l .... Prov 31:12
heaven all the days of their l .... Eccl 2:3
Therefore I hated l .... Eccl 2:17
rejoice, and to do good in his l .... Eccl 3:12
the sun all the days of his l .... Eccl 5:18
much remember the days of his l .... Eccl 5:20
what is good for man in this l .... Eccl 6:12
all the days of his vain l which .... Eccl 6:12
that wisdom giveth l to them that ...... Eccl 7:12
his l in his wickedness .... Eccl 7:15
of his labour the days of his l .... Eccl 8:15
the days of the l of thy vanity .... Eccl 9:9
for that is thy portion in this l .... Eccl 9:9
his l shall be grievous unto him .... Is 15:4
I have cut off like a weaver my l .... Is 38:12
things is the l of my spirit .... Is 38:16
of our l in the house of the LORD .... Is 38:20
men for thee, and people for thy l ...... Is 43:4
hast found the l of thine hand .... Is 57:10
thee, they will seek thy l .... Jer 4:30
shall be chosen rather than l by .... Jer 8:3
men of Anathoth, that seek thy l .... Jer 11:21
hand of those that seek their l .... Jer 21:7
I set before you the way of l .... Jer 21:8
his l shall be unto him for a .... Jer 21:9
the hand of them that seek thy l .... Jer 22:25
hand of them that seek their l .... Jer 34:20
hand of them that seek their l .... Jer 34:21
he shall have his l for a prey .... Jer 38:2
hand of these men that seek thy l ...... Jer 38:16
but thy l shall be for a prey .... Jer 38:18
the hand of them that seek his l .... Jer 44:30
his enemy, and that sought his l .... Jer 44:30
but thy l will I give unto thee .... Jer 45:5
and before them that seek their l .... Jer 49:37
before him all the days of his l .... Jer 52:33
his death, all the days of his l .... Jer 52:34
for the l of thy young children .... Lam 2:19
have cut off my l in the dungeon .... Lam 3:53
thou hast redeemed my l .... Lam 3:58
his wicked way, to save his l .... Eze 3:18
himself in the iniquity of his l .... Eze 7:13
wicked way, by promising him l .... Eze 13:22
moment, every man for his own l .... Eze 32:10
robbed, walk in the statutes of l .... Eze 33:15
awake, some to everlasting l .... Dan 12:2
us not perish for this man's l .... Jonah 1:14
brought up my l from corruption .... Jonah 2:6
I beseech thee, my l from me .... Jonah 4:3
My covenant was with him of l .... Mal 2:5
which sought the young child's l .... Mt 2:20
you, Take no thought for your l .... Mt 6:25
Is not the l more than meat, and .... Mt 6:25
is the way, which leadeth unto l .... Mt 7:14
that findeth his l shall lose it .... Mt 10:39
he that loseth his l for my sake .... Mt 10:39
will save his l shall lose it .... Mt 16:25
whosoever will lose his l for my .... Mt 16:25
to enter into l halt or maimed .... Mt 18:8
thee to enter into l with one eye .... Mt 18:9
I do, that I may have eternal l .... Mt 19:16
but if thou wilt enter into l .... Mt 19:17
and shall inherit everlasting l .... Mt 19:29
to give his l a ransom for many .... Mt 20:28
but the righteous into l eternal .... Mt 25:46
to save l, or to kill .... Mk 3:4
will save his l shall lose it .... Mk 8:35
shall lose his l for my sake .... Mk 8:35
for thee to enter into l maimed .... Mk 9:43
for thee to enter halt into l .... Mk 9:45
I do that I may inherit eternal l .... Mk 10:17
and in the world to come eternal l ..... Mk 10:30
to give his l a ransom for many .... Mk 10:45
before him, all the days of our l .... Lk 1:75
to save l, or to destroy it .... Lk 6:9
and riches and pleasures of this l ...... Lk 8:14
will save his l shall lose it .... Lk 9:24
will lose his l for my sake .... Lk 9:24
shall I do to inherit eternal l .... Lk 10:25
for a man's l consisteth not in .... Lk 12:15
you, Take no thought for your l .... Lk 12:22
The l is more than meat, and the .... Lk 12:23
sisters, yea, and his own l also .... Lk 14:26
seek to save his l shall lose it .... Lk 17:33
lose his l shall preserve it .... Lk 17:33
shall I do to inherit eternal l .... Lk 18:18
the world to come l everlasting .... Lk 18:30
drunkenness, and cares of this l .... Lk 21:34
In him was l .... Jn 1:4
the l was the light of men .... Jn 1:4
not perish, but have eternal l .... Jn 3:15
perish, but have everlasting l .... Jn 3:16
on the Son hath everlasting l .... Jn 3:36
not the Son shall not see l .... Jn 3:36
springing up into everlasting l .... Jn 4:14
and gathereth fruit unto l eternal ..... Jn 4:36
that sent me, hath everlasting l .... Jn 5:24
but is passed from death unto l .... Jn 5:24
as the Father hath l in himself .... Jn 5:26

to the Son to have l in himself .... Jn 5:26
good, unto the resurrection of l .... Jn 5:29
them ye think ye have eternal l .... Jn 5:39
come to me, that ye might have l .... Jn 5:40
which endureth unto everlasting l ..... Jn 6:27
and giveth l unto the world .... Jn 6:33
unto them, I am the bread of l .... Jn 6:35
on him, may have everlasting l .... Jn 6:40
on me hath everlasting l .... Jn 6:47
I am that bread of l .... Jn 6:48
will give for the l of the world .... Jn 6:51
his blood, ye have no l in you .... Jn 6:53
drinketh my blood, hath eternal l ...... Jn 6:54
they are spirit, and they are l .... Jn 6:63
thou hast the words of eternal l .... Jn 6:68
but shall have the light of l .... Jn 8:12
I am come that they might have l .... Jn 10:10
giveth his l for the sheep .... Jn 10:11
and I lay down my l for the sheep ...... Jn 10:15
love me, because I lay down my l .... Jn 10:17
And I give unto them eternal l .... Jn 10:28
I am the resurrection, and the l .... Jn 11:25
that loveth his l shall lose it .... Jn 12:25
he that hateth his l in this .... Jn 12:25
shall keep it unto l eternal .... Jn 12:25
his commandment is l everlasting ..... Jn 12:50
I will lay down my l for thy sake .... Jn 13:37
thou lay down thy l for my sake .... Jn 13:38
I am the way, the truth, and the l ...... Jn 14:6
lay down his l for his friends .... Jn 15:13
that he should give eternal l to .... Jn 17:2
And this is l eternal, that they .... Jn 17:3
ye might have l through his name ..... Jn 20:31
made known to me the ways of l .... Acts 2:28
And killed the Prince of l .... Acts 3:15
people all the words of this l .... Acts 5:20
for his l is taken from the earth .... Acts 8:33
granted repentance unto l .... Acts 11:18
unworthy of everlasting l .... Acts 13:46
ordained to eternal l believed .... Acts 13:48
thing, seeing he giveth to all l .... Acts 17:25
for his l is in him .... Acts 20:10
count l my dear unto myself .... Acts 20:24
My manner of l from my youth .... Acts 26:4
no loss of any man's l among you ..... Acts 27:22
honour and immortality, eternal l ..... Rom 2:7
we shall be saved by his l .... Rom 5:10
shall reign in l by one, Jesus .... Rom 5:17
all men unto justification of l .... Rom 5:18
l by Jesus Christ our Lord .... Rom 5:21
also should walk in newness of l ...... Rom 6:4
and the end everlasting l .... Rom 6:22
l through Jesus Christ our Lord .... Rom 6:23
which was ordained to l, I found ...... Rom 7:10
of l in Christ Jesus hath made me ... Rom 8:2
but to be spiritually minded is l .... Rom 8:6
but the Spirit is l because of .... Rom 8:10
that neither death, nor l .... Rom 8:38
am left alone, and they seek my l ..... Rom 11:3
of them be, but l from the dead .... Rom 11:15
Who have for my l laid down their .... Rom 16:4
or Cephas, or the world, or l 1Cor 3:22
things that pertain to this l 1Cor 6:3
of things pertaining to this l 1Cor 6:4
things without l giving sound 1Cor 14:7
If in this l only we have hope in 1Cor 15:19
that we despaired even of l 2Cor 1:8
other the savour of l unto l 2Cor 2:16
killeth, but the spirit giveth l 2Cor 3:6
that the l also of Jesus might be 2Cor 4:10
that the l also of Jesus might be 2Cor 4:11
death worketh in us, but l in you 2Cor 4:12
might be swallowed up of l 2Cor 5:4
the l which I now live in the .... Gal 2:20
given which could have given l .... Gal 3:21
the Spirit reap l everlasting .... Gal 6:8
being alienated from the l of God ..... Eph 4:18
in my body, whether it be by l .... Phil 1:20
Holding forth the word of l .... Phil 2:16
unto death, not regarding his l .... Phil 2:30
whose names are in the book of l ...... Phil 4:3
your l is hid with Christ in God .... Col 3:3
When Christ, who is our l .... Col 3:4
believe on him to l everlasting 1Ti 1:16
peaceable l in all godliness and 1Ti 2:2
promise of the l that now is 1Ti 4:8
of faith, lay hold on eternal l 1Ti 6:12
they may lay hold on eternal l 1Ti 6:19
of l which is in Christ Jesus 2Ti 1:1
death, and hath brought l and 2Ti 1:10
with the affairs of this l 2Ti 2:4
known my doctrine, manner of l 2Ti 3:10
In hope of eternal l, which God, ... Titus 1:2
to the hope of eternal l .... Titus 3:7
beginning of days, nor end of l .... Heb 7:3
after the power of an endless l .... Heb 7:16
their dead raised to l again .... Heb 11:35
he shall receive the crown of l .... Jas 1:12
For what is your l .... Jas 4:14
heirs together of the grace of l 1Pet 3:7
For he that will love l, and see 1Pet 3:10
For the time past of our l may 1Pet 4:3
us all things that pertain unto l 2Pet 1:3
have handled, of the Word of l 1Jn 1:1
(For the l was manifested, and we ... 1Jn 1:2
and shew unto you that eternal l 1Jn 1:2
of the eyes, and the pride of l 1Jn 2:16
hath promised us, even eternal l 1Jn 2:25
we have passed from death unto l 1Jn 3:14
hath eternal l abiding in him 1Jn 3:15

because he laid down his l for us 1Jn 3:16
God hath given to us eternal l 1Jn 5:11
and this l is in his Son 1Jn 5:11
He that hath the Son hath l 1Jn 5:12
not the Son of God hath not l 1Jn 5:12
may know that ye have eternal l 1Jn 5:13
he shall give him l for them that 1Jn 5:16
is the true God, and eternal l 1Jn 5:20
Lord Jesus Christ unto eternal l .... Jude 21
I give to eat of the tree of l .... Rev 2:7
and I will give thee a crown of l .... Rev 2:10
out his name out of the book of l ...... Rev 3:5
which were in the sea, and had l ...... Rev 8:9
an half the Spirit of l from God .... Rev 11:11
of l of the Lamb slain from the .... Rev 13:8
he had power to give l unto the .... Rev 13:15
of l from the foundation of the .... Rev 17:8
opened, which is the book of l .... Rev 20:12
found written in the book of l .... Rev 20:15
fountain of the water of l freely .... Rev 21:6
written in the Lamb's book of l .... Rev 21:27
me a pure river of water of l .... Rev 22:1
river, was there the tree of l .... Rev 22:2
may have right to the tree of l .... Rev 22:14
him take the water of l freely .... Rev 22:17
his part out of the book of l .... Rev 22:19

LIFETIME
Now Absalom in his l had taken 2Sa 18:18
remember that thou in thy l .... Lk 16:25
all their l subject to bondage .... Heb 2:15

LIFT
it was l up above the earth .... Gen 7:17
L up now thine eyes, and look from .. Gen 13:14
I have l up mine hand unto the .... Gen 14:22
he l up his eyes and looked, and, ... Gen 18:2
him, and l up her voice, and wept .... Gen 21:16
up the lad, and hold him in .... Gen 21:18
L up now thine eyes, and see, all .... Gen 31:12
shall Pharaoh l up thine head .... Gen 40:13
l up thy head from off thee .... Gen 40:19
without thee shall no man l up .... Gen 41:44
But I thou up thy rod, and stretch ... Ex 14:16
for if thou l up thy tool upon it .... Ex 20:25
The LORD l up his countenance .... Num 6:26
wherefore then I eye up yourselves .. Num 16:3
l up himself as a young lion .... Num 23:24
l up thine eyes westward, and .... Deut 3:27
lest thou l up thine eyes unto .... Deut 4:19
help him to l them up again .... Deut 22:4
thou shalt not l up any iron tool..... Deut 27:5
For I l up my hand to heaven, and... Deut 32:40
which no man hath l up any iron..... Josh 8:31
he l up his spear against eight 2Sa 23:8
wherefore l up thy prayer for the 2Kin 19:4
l up the head of Jehoiachin king 2Kin 25:27
words of God, to l up the horn 1Chr 25:5
blush to l up my face to thee, my .... Ezr 9:6
yet will I not l up my head .... Job 10:15
For then shalt thou l up thy face ..... Job 11:15
shalt l up thy face unto God .... Job 22:26
Canst thou l up thy voice to the ...... Job 38:34
I thou up the light of thy .... Ps 4:6
up thyself because of the rage .... Ps 7:6
O God, l up thine hand .... Ps 10:12
L up your heads, O ye gates .... Ps 24:7
L up your heads, O ye gates .... Ps 24:9
even l them up, ye everlasting .... Ps 24:9
thee, O LORD, do I l up my soul .... Ps 25:1
when I l up my hands toward thy .... Ps 28:2
them also, and l them up for ever .... Ps 28:9
I will l up my hands in thy name ..... Ps 63:4
L up thy feet unto the perpetual ..... Ps 74:3
to the wicked, L not up the horn ...... Ps 75:5
L not up your horn on high .... Ps 75:5
thee, O Lord, do I l up my soul .... Ps 86:4
the floods l up their waves .... Ps 93:3
L up thyself, thou judge of the .... Ps 94:2
therefore shall he l up the head ...... Ps 110:7
My hands also will I l up unto .... Ps 119:48
I will l up mine eyes unto the .... Ps 121:1
Unto thee I l up mine eyes, O .... Ps 123:1
L up your hands in the sanctuary, .. Ps 134:2
for I l up my soul unto thee .... Ps 143:8
the one will l up his fellow .... Eccl 4:10
nation shall not l up sword .... Is 2:4
he will l up an ensign to the .... Is 5:26
itself against them that l it up .... Is 10:15
if the staff should l up itself .... Is 10:15
shall l up his staff against thee ...... Is 10:24
so shall he l it up after the .... Is 10:26
L up thy voice, O daughter of .... Is 10:30
L ye up a banner upon the high ...... Is 13:2
They shall l up their voice, they ..... Is 24:14
now will I l up myself .... Is 33:10
wherefore l up thy prayer for the .... Is 37:4
l up thy voice with strength .... Is 40:9
l it up, be not afraid .... Is 40:9
L up your eyes on high, and behold. Is 40:26
He shall not cry, nor l up .... Is 42:2
cities thereof l up their voice .... Is 42:11
L up thine eyes round about, and.... Is 49:18
I will l up mine hand to the .... Is 49:22
L up your eyes to the heavens, and. Is 51:6
Thy watchmen shall l up the voice .. Is 52:8
l up thy voice like a trumpet, and ... Is 58:1
shall l up a standard against him... Is 59:19
L up thine eyes round about, and.... Is 60:4
l up a standard for the people .... Is 62:10
L up thine eyes unto the high .... Jer 3:2

neither l up cry nor prayer for.............. Jer 7:16
neither l up a cry or prayer for............. Jer 11:14
L up your eyes, and behold them.............. Jer 13:20
l up thy voice in Bashan, and cry............ Jer 22:20
they shall l up a shout against.............. Jer 51:14
l up thy hands toward him for the............ Lam 2:19
Let us l up our heart with our............... Lam 3:41
l up thine eyes now the way.................. Eze 8:5
the cherubims l up their wings............... Eze 11:22
that it might not l itself up................ Eze 17:14
l up to the voice with shouting.............. Eze 21:22
so that thou shalt not l up thine............ Eze 23:27
l up the buckler against thee................ Eze 26:8
l up your eyes toward your idols,............ Eze 33:25
nation shall not l up a sword................ Mic 4:3
so that no man did l up his head............. Zec 1:21
L up now thine eyes, and see what............ Zec 5:5
not lay hold on it, and l it out............. Mt 12:11
and could in no wise l up herself............ Lk 13:11
in hell he l up his eyes, being.............. Lk 16:23
would not l up so much as his................ Lk 18:13
then look up, and l up your heads............ Lk 21:28
L up your eyes, and look on the.............. Jn 4:35
Wherefore l up the hands which.............. Heb 12:12
of the Lord, and he shall l you up........... Jas 4:10

LIFTED

Lot l up his eyes, and beheld all........... Gen 13:10
third day Abraham l up his eyes............. Gen 22:4
Abraham l up his eyes, and looked,.......... Gen 22:13
he l up his eyes, and saw, and,............. Gen 24:63
Rebekah l up her eyes, and when............. Gen 24:64
Esau l up his voice, and wept............... Gen 27:38
and l up his voice, and wept................ Gen 29:11
that I l up mine eyes, and saw in........... Gen 31:10
Jacob l up his eyes, and looked,............ Gen 33:1
he l up his eyes, and saw the............... Gen 33:5
they l up their eyes and looked,............ Gen 37:25
l up Joseph out of the pit, and............. Gen 37:28
he heard that I l up my voice............... Gen 39:15
as I l up my voice and cried, that......... Gen 39:18
he l up the head of the chief............... Gen 40:20
he l up his eyes, and saw.................. Gen 43:29
he l up the rod, and smote the............. Ex 7:20
of Israel l up their eyes.................. Ex 14:10
Aaron l up his hand toward the............. Lev 9:22
the congregation l up their voice......... Num 14:1
Moses l up his hand, and with his......... Num 20:11
Balaam l up his eyes, and he saw.......... Num 24:2
Then thine heart be l up, and thou........ Deut 8:14
be not l up above his brethren............ Deut 17:20
feet were l up unto the day............... Josh 4:18
that he l up his eyes and looked,......... Josh 5:13
that the people l up their voice.......... Judg 2:4
so that they l up their heads no.......... Judg 8:28
l up his voice, and cried, and said....... Judg 9:7
And when he had l up his eyes,........... Judg 19:17
l up their voices, and wept sore......... Judg 21:2
they l up their voice, and wept.......... Ruth 1:9
he l up himself, and said unto........... Ruth 1:14
they l up their eyes, and saw the........ 1Sa 6:13
all the people l up their voices,....... 1Sa 11:4
Saul l up his voice, and wept,........... 1Sa 24:16
were with him l up their voice........... 1Sa 30:4
the king l up his voice, and said........ 2Sa 3:32
that kept the watch l up his eyes........ 2Sa 13:34
came, and l up their voice and wept...... 2Sa 13:36
l up his eyes, and looked, and........... 2Sa 18:24
l up their hand against my lord.......... 2Sa 18:28
hath l up his hand against the.......... 2Sa 20:21
thou also hast l me up on high.......... 2Sa 22:49
he l up his spear against three......... 2Sa 23:18
even he l up his hand against the....... 1Kin 11:26
this was the cause that he l up......... 1Kin 11:27
he l up his face to the window,........ 2Kin 9:32
and thine heart hath l thee up......... 2Kin 14:10
voice, and l up thine eyes on high..... 2Kin 19:22
he l up his spear against three....... 1Chr 11:11
for his kingdom was l up on........... 1Chr 14:2
David l up his eyes, and saw the...... 1Chr 21:16
when they l up their voice with...... 2Chr 5:13
his heart was l up in the ways of.... 2Chr 17:6
his heart was l up to his............ 2Chr 26:16
for his heart was l up............... 2Chr 32:25
when they l up their eyes afar....... Job 2:12
they l up their voice, and wept...... Job 2:12
If I have l up my hand against....... Job 31:21
or l up myself when evil found....... Job 31:29
who hath not l up his soul unto...... Ps 24:4
and be ye l up, ye everlasting....... Ps 24:7
now shall mine head be l up above.... Ps 27:6
for thou hast l me up, and hast...... Ps 30:1
hath l up his heel against me........ Ps 41:9
l up axes upon the thick trees....... Ps 74:5
that hate thee have l up the head.... Ps 83:2
The floods have l, O Lord, the....... Ps 93:3
the floods have l up their voice..... Ps 93:3
for thou hast l me up, and cast me... Ps 102:10
Therefore he l up his hand........... Ps 106:26
and their eyelids are l up........... Prov 30:13
and upon every one that is l up...... Is 2:12
l up, and upon all the oaks of....... Is 2:13
upon all the hills that are l up..... Is 2:14
l up, and his train filled the....... Is 6:1
Lord, when thy hand is l up.......... Is 26:11
voice, and l up thine eyes on high... Is 37:23
is l up even to the skies............ Jer 51:9
l up the head of Jehoiachin king..... Jer 52:31
were l up from the earth, the........ Eze 1:19
the earth, the wheels were l up...... Eze 1:19
the wheels were l up................. Eze 1:20

when those were l up from the........ Eze 1:21
the wheels were l up over against.... Eze 1:21
So the spirit l me up, and took me... Eze 3:14
the spirit l me up between the....... Eze 8:3
So I l up mine eyes the way.......... Eze 8:5
And the cherubims were l up.......... Eze 10:15
when the cherubims l up their........ Eze 10:16
and when they were l up.............. Eze 10:17
these l up themselves also........... Eze 10:17
the cherubims l up their wings,...... Eze 10:19
Moreover the spirit l me up.......... Eze 11:1
neither hath l up his eyes to the.... Eze 18:6
hath l up his eyes to the idols,..... Eze 18:12
neither hath l up his eyes to the.... Eze 18:15
l up mine hand unto the seed of...... Eze 20:5
when I l up mine hand unto them,..... Eze 20:5
In the day that I l up mine hand..... Eze 20:6
Yet also I l up my hand unto them.... Eze 20:15
I l up mine hand unto them also...... Eze 20:23
for the which I l up mine hand to.... Eze 20:28
the country for the which I l up..... Eze 20:42
Because thine heart is l up.......... Eze 28:2
thine heart is l up because of....... Eze 28:5
Thine heart was l up because of...... Eze 28:17
Because thou hast l up thyself in.... Eze 31:10
his heart is l up in his height...... Eze 31:10
I have l up mine hand, Surely the.... Eze 36:7
therefore have I l up mine hand,..... Eze 44:12
concerning the which I l up mine..... Eze 47:14
l up mine eyes unto heaven........... Dan 4:34
But when his heart was l up.......... Dan 5:20
But hast l up thyself against the.... Dan 5:23
it was l up from the earth, and..... Dan 7:4
Then I l up mine eyes, and saw, and.. Dan 8:3
Then I l up mine eyes, and looked,... Dan 10:5
his heart shall be l up............. Dan 11:12
Thine hand shall be l up upon....... Mic 5:9
his soul which is l up is not....... Hab 2:4
voice, and l up his hands on high... Hab 3:10
Then I l up mine eyes, and saw, and. Zec 1:18
which l up their horn over the...... Zec 1:21
I l up mine eyes again, and looked.. Zec 2:1
l up mine eyes, and looked, and..... Zec 5:1
there was l up a talent of lead..... Zec 5:7
Then I l up mine eyes, and looked,.. Zec 5:9
they l up the ephah between the..... Zec 5:9
I l up mine eyes, and looked, and... Zec 6:1
l up as an ensign upon his land..... Zec 9:16
and it shall be l up, and inhabited. Zec 14:10
And when they had l up their eyes,.. Mt 17:8
took her by the hand, and l her up.. Mk 1:31
took him by the hand, and l him up.. Mk 9:27
he l up his eyes on his disciples... Lk 6:20
of the company l up her voice...... Lk 11:27
they l up their voices, and said,.. Lk 17:13
he l up his hands, and blessed..... Lk 24:50
as Moses l up the serpent in the... Jn 3:14
so must the Son of man be l up..... Jn 3:14
When Jesus then l up his eyes...... Jn 6:5
he l up himself, and said unto..... Jn 8:7
When Jesus had l up himself........ Jn 8:10
When ye have l up the Son of man,.. Jn 8:28
Jesus l up his eyes, and said,..... Jn 11:41
if I be l up from the earth, will.. Jn 12:32
thou, The Son of man must be l up.. Jn 12:34
me hath l up his heel against me... Jn 13:18
l up his eyes to heaven, and said.. Jn 17:1
l up his voice, and said unto them, Acts 2:14
by the right hand, and l him up.... Acts 3:7
they l up their voice to God with.. Acts 4:24
l her up, and when he had called... Acts 9:41
they l up their voices, saying in.. Acts 14:11
then l up their voices, and said,.. Acts 22:22
lest being l up with pride he...... 1Ti 3:6
upon the earth l up his hand to.... Rev 10:5

LIFTER

glory, and the l up of mine head.... Ps 3:3

LIFTEST

Thou l me up to the wind............ Job 30:22
thou that l me up from the gates.... Ps 9:13
thou l me up above those that....... Ps 18:48
l up thy voice for understanding.... Prov 2:3

LIFTETH

he bringeth low, and l up........... 1Sa 2:7
l up the beggar from the dunghill... 1Sa 2:8
thine heart l thee up to boast..... 2Chr 25:19
What time she l up herself on...... Job 39:18
which l up the waves thereof....... Ps 107:25
the needy out of the dunghill...... Ps 113:7
The Lord l up the meek............. Ps 147:6
when he l up an ensign on the...... Is 18:3
against him that l himself up in... Jer 51:3
The horseman l up both the bright.. Nah 3:3

LIFTING

for l up his spear against three... 1Chr 11:20
by l up the voice with joy......... 1Chr 15:16
Amen, Amen, with l up their hands,. Neh 8:6
thou shalt say, There is l up...... Job 22:29
the l up of my hands as the........ Ps 141:2
done foolishly in l up thyself..... Prov 30:32
mount up like the l up of smoke.... Is 9:18
at the l up of thyself the......... Is 33:3
l up holy hands, without wrath and. 1Ti 2:8

LIGHT

And God said, Let there be l....... Gen 1:3
and there was l................... Gen 1:3
And God saw the l, that it was.... Gen 1:4
God divided the l from the........ Gen 1:4

And God called the l Day, and the.... Gen 1:5
heaven to give l upon the earth...... Gen 1:15
the greater l to rule the day, and... Gen 1:16
the lesser l to rule the night...... Gen 1:16
heaven to give l upon the earth..... Gen 1:17
to divide the l from the darkness... Gen 1:18
As soon as the morning was l........ Gen 44:3
Israel had l in their dwellings..... Ex 10:23
a pillar of fire, to give them l.... Ex 13:21
but it gave l by night to these..... Ex 14:20
Oil for the l, spices for.......... Ex 25:6
they shall l the lamps thereof,..... Ex 25:37
they may give l over against it..... Ex 25:37
pure oil olive beaten for the l..... Ex 27:20
And oil for the l, and spices for... Ex 35:8
The candlestick also for the l...... Ex 35:14
his lamps, with the oil for the l... Ex 35:14
And spice, and oil for the l....... Ex 35:28
vessels thereof, and the oil for l.. Ex 39:37
and l the lamps thereof............ Ex 40:4
pure oil olive beaten for the l.... Lev 24:2
and cover the candlestick of the l. Num 4:9
pertaineth the oil for the l....... Num 4:16
the seven lamps shall give l over.. Num 8:2
and our soul loatheth this l bread. Num 21:5
Cursed be that setteth l by........ Deut 27:16
l persons, which followed him...... Judg 9:4
where her lord was, till it was l.. Judg 19:26
her nap was to l on a part of the.. Ruth 2:3
and spoil them until the morning l. 1Sa 14:36
Seemeth it to you a l thing to be.. 1Sa 18:23
l any that pisseth against the..... 1Sa 25:22
l any that pisseth against the..... 1Sa 25:34
less or more, until the morning l.. 1Sa 25:36
early in the morning, and have l... 1Sa 29:10
Asahel was as l of foot as a wild.. 2Sa 2:18
we will l upon him as the dew...... 2Sa 17:12
by the morning l there lacked not.. 2Sa 17:22
thou quench not the l of Israel.... 2Sa 21:17
shall be as the l of the morning... 2Sa 23:4
I was against l in three........... 1Kin 7:4
I was against l in three........... 1Kin 7:5
was against l in three ranks....... 1Kin 7:5
David my servant may have a l...... 1Kin 11:36
as if it had been a l thing for.... 1Kin 16:31
this is but a l thing in the....... 2Kin 3:18
if we tarry till the morning l..... 2Kin 7:9
him to give him alway a l.......... 2Kin 8:19
It is a l thing for the shadow to.. 2Kin 20:10
as promised to give a l to him..... 2Chr 21:7
to give them l in the way wherein.. Neh 9:12
of fire by night, to shew them l... Neh 9:19
The Jews had l, and gladness, and.. Est 8:16
neither let the l shine upon it.... Job 3:4
let it look for l, but have none... Job 3:9
as infants which never saw l....... Job 3:16
Wherefore is l given to him that... Job 3:20
Why is l given to a man whose way.. Job 3:23
where the l is as darkness......... Job 10:22
bringeth out to the shadow of...... Job 12:22
They grope in the dark without l... Job 12:25
the l is short because of.......... Job 17:12
the l of the wicked shall be put... Job 18:5
The l shall be dark in his......... Job 18:6
be driven from l into darkness..... Job 18:18
the l shall shine upon thy ways.... Job 22:28
of those that rebel against the l.. Job 24:13
with the l taketh the poor........ Job 24:14
they know not the l.............. Job 24:16
and upon whom doth not his l arise Job 25:3
is hid bringeth he forth to...... Job 28:11
when by his l I walked through... Job 29:3
the l of my countenance they cast Job 29:24
and when I waited for l, there... Job 30:26
pit, and his life shall see the l Job 33:28
with the l of the living........ Job 33:30
he spreadeth his l upon the..... Job 36:30
With clouds he covereth the l... Job 36:32
caused the l of his cloud to.... Job 37:15
bright l which is in the clouds. Job 37:21
the wicked their l is withholden Job 38:15
Where is the way where l dwelleth Job 38:19
By what way is the l parted..... Job 38:24
By his meetings a l doth shine.. Job 41:18
lift thou up the l of thy....... Ps 4:6
For thou wilt l my candle....... Ps 18:28
The Lord is my l and my salvation Ps 27:1
in thy l shall we see l......... Ps 36:9
in thy l shall we see l......... Ps 36:9
forth thy righteousness as the l Ps 37:6
as for the l of mine eyes, it... Ps 38:10
O send out thy l and thy truth.. Ps 43:3
the l of thy countenance, because Ps 44:3
they shall never see l.......... Ps 49:19
before God in the l of the living Ps 56:13
thou hast prepared the l and the Ps 74:16
and all the night with a l of fire Ps 78:14
in the l of thy countenance..... Ps 89:15
sins in the l of thy countenance Ps 90:8
L is sown for the righteous, and Ps 97:11
thyself with l as with a garment Ps 104:2
and fire to give l in the night. Ps 105:39
there ariseth l in the darkness. Ps 112:4
the LORD, which hath shewed us l. Ps 118:27
unto my feet, and a l unto my path Ps 119:105
entrance of thy words giveth l.. Ps 119:130
the night shall be l about me... Ps 139:11
the l are both alike to thee.... Ps 139:12
praise him, all ye stars of l... Ps 148:3
of the just as the shining l.... Prov 4:18

and the law is l...................................... Prov 6:23
The l of the righteous rejoiceth........... Prov 13:9
The l of the eyes rejoiceth the............. Prov 15:30
In the l of the king's.............................. Prov 16:15
as far as I excelleth darkness............... Eccl 2:13
Truly the l is sweet, and a.................... Eccl 11:7
While the sun, or the l, or the.............. Eccl 12:2
let us walk in the l of the LORD............ Is 2:5
for l, and l for darkness........................ Is 5:20
the l is darkened in the heavens.......... Is 5:30
is because there is no l in them............ Is 8:20
in darkness have seen a great l............ Is 9:2
upon them hath the l shined................. Is 9:2
the l of Israel shall be for a................. Is 10:17
thereof shall not give their l................ Is 13:10
shall not cause her l to shine................ Is 13:10
Moreover the l of the moon shall.......... Is 30:26
moon shall be as the l of the sun......... Is 30:26
the l of the sun shall be........................ Is 30:26
as the l of seven days, in the............... Is 30:26
people, for a l of the Gentiles............... Is 42:6
will make darkness l before them......... Is 42:16
I form the l, and create darkness......... Is 45:7
It is a l thing that thou........................ Is 49:6
give thee for a l to the Gentiles............ Is 49:6
walketh in darkness, and hath no l...... Is 50:10
walk in the l of your fire, and in.......... Is 50:11
to rest for a l of the people................. Is 51:4
Then shall thy l break forth as............ Is 58:8
then shall thy l rise in........................... Is 58:10
we wait for l, but behold...................... Is 59:9
for thy l is come, and the glory............ Is 60:1
the Gentiles shall come to thy l........... Is 60:3
sun shall be no more thy l by day........ Is 60:19
shall the moon give l unto thee........... Is 60:19
be unto thee an everlasting l............... Is 60:19
LORD shall be thine everlasting l......... Is 60:20
and the heavens, and they had no l...... Jer 4:23
and, while ye look for l, he turn........... Jer 13:16
and the l of the candle.......................... Jer 25:10
giveth the sun for a l by day................ Jer 31:35
and of the stars for a l by night........... Jer 31:35
me into darkness, but not into l........... Lam 3:2
Is it a l thing to the house of.............. Eze 8:17
In thee have they set l by father......... Eze 22:7
and the moon shall not give her l......... Eze 32:7
and the l dwelleth with him................. Dan 2:22
and in the days of thy father l............. Dan 5:11
of the gods is in thee, and that l......... Dan 5:14
are as the l that goeth forth................. Hos 6:5
of the LORD is darkness, and l.............. Amos 5:18
of the LORD be darkness, and not l...... Amos 5:20
when the morning is l, they.................. Mic 2:1
the LORD shall be a l unto me............... Mic 7:8
he will bring me forth to the l............. Mic 7:9
And his brightness was as the l........... Hab 3:4
at the l of thine arrows they............... Hab 3:11
Her prophets are l and treacherous..... Zeph 3:4
doth he bring his judgment to l........... Zeph 3:5
that the l shall not be clear,............... Zec 14:6
at evening time it shall be l................ Zec 14:7
which sat in darkness saw great l........ Mt 4:16
and shadow of death l is sprung up..... Mt 4:16
Ye are the l of the world..................... Mt 5:14
Neither do men l a candle.................... Mt 5:15
it giveth l unto all that are in............. Mt 5:15
Let your l so shine before men,........... Mt 5:16
The l of the body is the eye................ Mt 6:22
thy whole body shall be full of l......... Mt 6:22
If therefore the l that is in................. Mt 6:23
in darkness, that speak ye in l............ Mt 10:27
yoke is easy, and my burden is l......... Mt 11:30
and his raiment was white as the l...... Mt 17:2
But they made l of it, and went.......... Mt 22:5
and the moon shall not give her l........ Mt 24:29
and the moon shall not give her l........ Mk 13:24
To give l to them that sit in............... Lk 1:79
A l to lighten the Gentiles, and........... Lk 2:32
they which enter in may see the l....... Lk 8:16
they which come in may see the l........ Lk 11:33
The l of the body is the eye............... Lk 11:34
thy whole body also is full of l........... Lk 11:34
the l which is in thee be not............... Lk 11:35
whole body therefore be full of l......... Lk 11:36
the whole shall be full of l.................. Lk 11:36
of a candle doth give thee l................ Lk 11:36
darkness shall be heard in the l.......... Lk 12:3
one piece, doth not l a candle............ Lk 15:8
wiser than the children of l................. Lk 16:8
and the life was the l of men.............. Jn 1:4
the l shineth in darkness.................... Jn 1:5
witness, to bear witness of the L........ Jn 1:7
He was not that L, but was sent......... Jn 1:8
sent to bear witness of that l............. Jn 1:8
That was the true L, which................. Jn 1:9
that is come into the world, and......... Jn 3:19
men loved darkness rather than l........ Jn 3:19
one that doeth evil hateth the l.......... Jn 3:20
neither cometh to the l....................... Jn 3:20
that doeth truth cometh to the l......... Jn 3:21
He was a burning and a shining l........ Jn 5:35
for a season to rejoice in his l............ Jn 5:35
saying, I am the l of the world........... Jn 8:12
but shall have the l of life.................. Jn 8:12
world, I am the l of the world............. Jn 9:5
he seeth the l of this world................. Jn 11:9
because there is no l in him................ Jn 11:10
a little while is the l with you............. Jn 12:35
Walk while ye have the l, lest............. Jn 12:35
ye have l, believe in the l.................. Jn 12:36

that ye may be the children of l.......... Jn 12:36
I am come a l into the world,............... Jn 12:46
round about him a l from heaven........ Acts 9:3
him, and a l shined in the prison......... Acts 12:7
the to be a l of the Gentiles................ Acts 13:47
Then he called for a l, and sprang...... Acts 16:29
heaven a great l round about me........ Acts 22:6
were with me saw indeed the l........... Acts 22:9
not see for the glory of that l............. Acts 22:11
I saw in the way a l from heaven........ Acts 26:13
to turn them from darkness to l.......... Acts 26:18
should shew l unto the people, and..... Acts 26:23
a l of them which are in darkness....... Rom 2:19
and let us put on the armour of l........ Rom 13:12
who both will bring to l the................. 1Cor 4:5
lest the l of the glorious gospel........... 2Cor 4:4
who commanded the l to shine out...... 2Cor 4:6
to give the l of the knowledge of....... 2Cor 4:6
For our l affliction, which is................ 2Cor 4:17
communion hath l with darkness......... 2Cor 6:14
is transformed into an angel of l......... 2Cor 11:14
but now are ye l in the Lord................ Eph 5:8
walk as children of l........................... Eph 5:8
are made manifest by the l................. Eph 5:13
doth make manifest is l....................... Eph 5:13
dead, and Christ shall give thee l....... Eph 5:14
inheritance of the saints in l............... Col 1:12
Ye are all the children of l.................. 1Th 5:5
dwelling in the l which no man........... 1Ti 6:16
immortality to l through the............... 2Ti 1:10
of darkness into his marvellous l......... 1Pet 2:9
as unto a l that shineth in a.............. 2Pet 1:19
declare unto you, that God is l........... 1Jn 1:5
in the l, as he is in the l.................... 1Jn 1:7
past, and the true l now shineth........ 1Jn 2:8
He that saith he is in the l................ 1Jn 2:9
his brother abideth in the l................ 1Jn 2:10
neither shall the sun l on them.......... Rev 7:16
the l of a candle shall shine no.......... Rev 18:23
her l was like unto a stone most........ Rev 21:11
it, and the Lamb is the l thereof........ Rev 21:23
saved shall walk in the l of it............ Rev 21:24
no candle, neither l of the sun.......... Rev 22:5
for the Lord God giveth them l.......... Rev 22:5

LIGHTED

saw Isaac, she l off the camel........... Gen 24:64
he l upon a certain place, and........... Gen 28:11
he l the lamps before the LORD......... Ex 40:25
he l the lamps thereof over.............. Num 8:3
and she l off her ass........................ Judg 1:14
and she l from off her ass................ Judg 4:15
so that Sisera l down off his............. Judg 4:15
l off the ass, and fell before............. 1Sa 25:23
he l down from the chariot to........... 2Kin 5:21
he l on Jehonadab the son of........... 2Kin 10:15
Jacob, and it hath l upon Israel........ Is 9:8
No man, when he hath l a candle...... Lk 8:16
No man, when he hath l a candle...... Lk 11:33

LIGHTEN

peradventure he will l his hand......... 1Sa 6:5
and the LORD will l my darkness......... 2Sa 22:29
that our God may l our eyes.............. Ezr 9:8
I mine eyes, lest I sleep the.............. Ps 13:3
into the sea, to l it off them............. Jonah 1:5
A light to l the Gentiles, and............. Lk 2:32
for the glory of God did l it............... Rev 21:23

LIGHTENED

They looked unto him, and were l...... Ps 34:5
the lightnings l the world................... Ps 77:18
the next day they l the ship.............. Acts 27:18
they l the ship, and cast out............. Acts 27:38
the earth was l with his glory........... Rev 18:1

LIGHTENETH

the l from l both their eyes............... Prov 29:13
that l out of the one part under........ Lk 17:24

LIGHTER

yoke which he put upon us,............... 1Kin 12:4
thy father did put upon us................ 1Kin 12:9
heavy, but make thou it l unto us...... 1Kin 12:10
make thou it somewhat l than us....... 2Chr 10:10
they are altogether l than vanity....... Ps 62:9

LIGHTEST

unto him, When thou l the lamps...... Num 8:2

LIGHTETH

when Aaron l the lamps at even,....... Ex 30:8
l upon his neighbour, that he die....... Deut 19:5
which l every man that cometh.......... Jn 1:9

LIGHTING

shall shew the l down of his arm,....... Is 30:30
like a dove, and l upon him.............. Mt 3:16

LIGHTLY

might l have lien with thy wife.......... Gen 26:10
l esteemed the Rock of his................ Deut 32:15
despise me shall be l esteemed......... 1Sa 2:30
I am a poor man, and l esteemed...... 1Sa 18:23
when at the first he l afflicted........... Is 9:1
and all the hills moved l................... Jer 4:24
that can l speak evil of me............... Mk 9:39

LIGHTNESS

through the l of her whoredom.......... Jer 3:9
err by their lies, and by their l......... Jer 23:32
was thus minded, did l use l............. 2Cor 1:17

LIGHTNING

l, and discomfited them..................... 2Sa 22:15
a way for the l of the thunder........... Job 28:26
his l unto the ends of the earth......... Job 37:3
or a way for the l of thunder............. Job 38:25
Cast forth l, and scatter them............ Ps 144:6
and out of the fire went forth l.......... Eze 1:13
the appearance of a flash of l............ Eze 1:14
his face as the appearance of l.......... Dan 10:6
his arrow shall go forth as the l......... Zec 9:14
For as the l cometh out of the........... Mt 24:27
His countenance was like l................. Mt 28:3
Satan as l fall from heaven................. Lk 10:18
For as the l, that lighteneth out......... Lk 17:24

LIGHTNINGS

that there were thunders and l........... Ex 19:16
saw the thunderings, and the l........... Ex 20:18
Canst thou send l, that they may....... Job 38:35
and he shot out l, and discomfited..... Ps 18:14
the l lightened the world................... Ps 77:18
His l enlightened the world................ Ps 97:4
he maketh l for the rain.................... Ps 135:7
he maketh l with rain, and................ Jer 10:13
he maketh l with rain, and................ Jer 51:16
they shall run like the...................... Nah 2:4
And out of the throne proceeded l...... Rev 4:5
were voices, and thunderings, and l.... Rev 8:5
and there were l, and voices, and....... Rev 11:19
were voices, and thunders, and l........ Rev 16:18

LIGHTS

Let there be l in the firmament.......... Gen 1:14
And let them be for l in the............... Gen 1:15
And God made two great l.................. Gen 1:16
house he made windows of narrow l.... 1Kin 6:4
To him that made great l................... Ps 136:7
All the bright l of heaven will l.......... Eze 32:8
girded about, and your l burning......... Lk 12:35
there were many l in the upper.......... Acts 20:8
whom ye shine as l in the world......... Phil 2:15
cometh down from the Father of l...... Jas 1:17

LIGN

as the trees of l aloes which.............. Num 24:6

LIGURE

And the third row a l, an agate,......... Ex 28:19
And the third row, a l, an agate,........ Ex 39:12

LIKE See PREFACE.

LIKED

he l me to make king over all............ 1Chr 28:4

LIKEMINDED

consolation grant you to be l one....... Rom 15:5
Fulfil ye my joy, that ye be l.............. Phil 2:2
For I have no man l, who will............. Phil 2:20

LIKEN

To whom then will ye l God................ Is 40:18
To whom then will ye l me................. Is 40:25
To whom will ye l me, and make me.... Is 46:5
what thing shall I l to thee................. Lam 2:13
I will l him unto a wise man,.............. Mt 7:24
shall I l this generation..................... Mt 11:16
shall we l the kingdom of God............ Mk 4:30
Whereunto then shall I l the men........ Lk 7:31
Whereunto then shall I l the kingdom.. Lk 13:20

LIKENED

the mighty can be l unto the LORD...... Ps 89:6
I have l the daughter of Zion to......... Jer 6:2
shall be l unto a foolish man,............. Mt 7:26
The kingdom of heaven is l unto a...... Mt 13:24
of heaven l unto a certain king.......... Mt 18:23
of heaven be l unto ten virgins.......... Mt 25:1

LIKENESS

man in our image, after our l............. Gen 1:26
in the l of God made he him.............. Gen 5:1
and begat a son in his own l.............. Gen 5:3
or any l of any thing that is in.......... Ex 20:4
figure, the l of male or female,.......... Deut 4:16
The l of any beast that is on the........ Deut 4:17
the l of any winged fowl that............ Deut 4:17
The l of any thing that creepeth........ Deut 4:18
the l of any fish that is in the........... Deut 4:18
or the l of any thing, which the......... Deut 4:23
or the l of any thing, and shall......... Deut 4:25
or any l of any thing that is in.......... Deut 5:8
when I awake, with thy l.................... Ps 17:15
or what l will ye compare unto.......... Is 40:18
the l of four living creatures,............. Eze 1:5
they had the l of a man.................... Eze 1:5
As for the l of their faces, they......... Eze 1:10
As for the l of the living.................... Eze 1:13
and they four had one l..................... Eze 1:16
the l of the firmament upon the........ Eze 1:22
their heads was the l of a throne....... Eze 1:26
upon the l of the throne was the....... Eze 1:26
the l as the appearance of a man...... Eze 1:26
of the l of the glory of the LORD........ Eze 1:28
lo a l as the appearance of fire.......... Eze 8:2
appearance of the l of a throne.......... Eze 10:1
appearances, they four had one l....... Eze 10:10
the l of the hands of a man was......... Eze 10:21
the l of their faces was the same....... Eze 10:22
come down to us in the l of men........ Acts 14:11
together in the l of his death............. Rom 6:5
also in the l of his resurrection.......... Rom 6:5
own Son in the l of sinful flesh.......... Rom 8:3
and was made in the l of men............ Phil 2:7

L

LIKETH
of thy gates, where it l him best .... Deut 23:16
ye also for the Jews, as it l you .... Est 8:8
for this l you, O ye children of .... Amos 4:5

LIKEWISE
L. shalt thou do with thine oxen, ... Ex 22:30
and l shalt thou make in the .... Ex 26:24
l he made in the uttermost side .... Ex 36:11
L this is the law of the trespass .... Lev 7:1
L when the LORD sent you from .... Deut 9:23
even so will l do .... Deut 12:30
thy maidservant thou shalt do l .... Deut 15:17
thou hast found, shalt thou do l .... Deut 22:3
l I will go with thee into thy .... Judg 1:3
l every one that boweth down upon ...... Judg 7:5
unto them, Look on me, and do l .... Judg 7:17
to Penuel, and spake unto them l .... Judg 8:8
all the people l cut down every .... Judg 9:49
L all the men of Israel which had 1Sa 14:22
messengers, and they prophesied l 1Sa 19:21
he fell l upon his sword, and died 1Sa 31:5
l all the men that were with him 2Sa 1:11
let us hear l what he saith 2Sa 17:5
l did he for all his strange 1Kin 11:8
he fell l on the sword, and died 1Chr 10:5
l from Tibnath, and from Chun, ... 1Chr 18:8
they l fled before Abishai his 1Chr 19:15
and praise the LORD, and l at even 1Chr 23:30
These l cast lots over against 1Chr 24:31
in his course l were twenty 1Chr 27:4
l silver for the tables of silver 1Chr 28:16
l silver by weight for every 1Chr 28:17
all the sons l of king David, ... 1Chr 29:24
the other wing was l five cubits 2Chr 3:11
l, when they had killed the rams, ... 2Chr 29:22
L at the same time said l unto .... Neh 4:22
L l, and my brethren, and my .... Neh 5:10
l, shall the ladies of Persia and .... Est 1:18
l also and my maidens will fast l .... Est 4:16
the furrows l thereof complain .... Job 31:38
l to the small rain, and to the .... Job 37:6
the fool and the brutish person .... Ps 49:10
God shall l destroy thee for ever .... Ps 52:5
thou thyself l hast cursed others .... Eccl 7:22
l cast the young asses .... Is 30:24
L when all the Jews that were in .... Jer 40:11
L, thou son of man, set thy face .... Eze 13:17
round about, and l to the arches .... Eze 40:16
L the people of the land shall .... Eze 46:3
l many, yet thus shall they be .... Nah 1:12
L shall also the Son of man. .... Mt 17:12
So l shall my heavenly Father do .... Mt 18:35
the sixth and ninth hour, and did l .... Mt 20:5
they l received every man a penny .... Mt 20:10
he came to the second, and said l .... Mt 21:30
and they did unto them l .... Mt 21:36
L the second also, and the third, ... Mt 22:26
So l ye, when ye shall see all............... Mt 24:33
l he that had received two, he .... Mt 25:17
L also said all the disciples. .... Mt 26:35
L also the chief priests mocking .... Mt 27:41
these are they l which are sown .... Mk 4:16
and the third l .... Mk 12:21
L also said they all. .... Mk 14:31
L also the chief priests mocking .... Mk 15:31
gave thanks l unto the Lord. .... Lk 2:38
he that hath meat, let him do l .... Lk 3:11
the soldiers l demanded of him, ... Lk 3:14
the disciples of the Pharisees. .... Lk 5:33
do to you, do ye also to them l .... Lk 6:31
l a Levite, when he was at the .... Lk 10:32
Jesus unto him, Go, and do thou l .... Lk 10:37
ye repent, ye shall all l perish .... Lk 13:3
ye repent, ye shall all l perish .... Lk 13:5
So l, whosoever he be of you that .... Lk 14:33
that l joy shall be in heaven................... Lk 15:7
L, I say unto you, there is joy .... Lk 15:10
things, and l Lazarus evil things .... Lk 16:25
So l ye, when ye shall have done .... Lk 17:10
L also as it was in the days of .... Lk 17:28
let him l not return back. .... Lk 17:31
And he said l to him, Be thou also. ...... Lk 19:19
So l ye, when ye see these things .... Lk 21:31
L also the cup after supper, ... Lk 22:20
let him take it, and l his scrip............... Lk 22:36
doeth, these also doeth the Son l .... Jn 5:19
l of the fishes as much as they .... Jn 6:11
bread, and giveth them, and fish l .... Jn 21:13
have l foretold of these days. .... Acts 3:24
l also the men, leaving the .... Rom 1:27
l reckon ye also yourselves to be .... Rom 6:11
L the Spirit also helpeth our .... Rom 8:26
l greet the church that is in .... Rom 16:5
l also the wife unto the husband. 1Cor 7:3
l also the husband hath not power 1Cor 7:4
l also he that is called, being 1Cor 7:22
So l ye, except ye utter by the. 1Cor 14:9
other Jews dissembled l with him. .... Gal 2:13
that ye l read the epistle from .... Col 4:16
L must the deacons be grave, not. 1Ti 3:8
L also the good works of some are 1Ti 5:25
The aged women l, that they be in .... Titus 2:3
Young men l exhort to be sober. .... Titus 2:6
L also himself l took part of. .... Heb 2:14
L also was not Rahab the harlot .... Jas 2:25
L, ye wives, be in subjection to. 1Pet 3:1
L, ye husbands, dwell with them. 1Pet 3:7
arm yourselves l with the same. 1Pet 4:1
L, ye younger, submit yourselves. 1Pet 5:5

l also these filthy dreamers .... Jude 8
third part of it, and the night l .... Rev 8:12

LIKHI (lik´-hi) Son of Shemidah
were, Ahian, and Shechem, and L. 1Chr 7:19

LIKING
Their young ones are in good l .... Job 39:4
l than the children which are of .... Dan 1:10

LILIES
brim of a cup, with flowers of l 1Kin 7:26
brim of a cup, with flowers of l 2Chr 4:5
he feedeth among the l .... Song 2:16
are twins, which feed among the l .... Song 4:5
his lips like l, dropping sweet .... Song 5:13
in the gardens, and to gather l .... Song 6:2
he feedeth among the l .... Song 6:3
an heap of wheat set about with l. .... Song 7:2
Consider the l of the field .... Mt 6:28
Consider the l how they grow .... Lk 12:27

LILY
were of l work in the porch. 1Kin 7:19
the top of the pillars was l work 1Kin 7:22
Sharon, and the l of the valleys .... Song 2:1
As the l among thorns, so is my .... Song 2:2
he shall grow as the l, and cast .... Hos 14:5

LIME
shall be as the burnings of l .... Is 33:12
bones of the king of Edom into l .... Amos 2:1

LIMIT
l thereof round about shall be .... Eze 43:12

LIMITED
God, and l the Holy One of Israel. ...... Ps 78:41

LIMITETH
he l a certain day, saying in................. Heb 4:7

LINE
thou shalt bind this l of scarlet .... Josh 2:18
bound the scarlet l in the window .... Josh 2:21
Moab, and measured them with a l 2Sa 8:2
and with one full l to keep alive. 2Sa 8:2
a l of twelve cubits did compass 1Kin 7:15
a l of thirty cubits did compass. 1Kin 7:23
over Jerusalem the l of Samaria 2Kin 21:13
a l of thirty cubits did compass 2Chr 4:2
who hath stretched the l upon it .... Job 38:5
Their l is gone out through all .... Ps 19:4
divided them an inheritance by l .... Ps 78:55
l upon l, l upon l .... Is 28:10
l upon l, l upon l .... Is 28:13
Judgment also will l lay to the .... Is 28:17
out upon it the l of confusion. .... Is 34:11
hath divided it unto them by l .... Is 34:17
he marketh it out with a l .... Is 44:13
the measuring l shall yet go. .... Jer 31:39
he hath stretched out a l .... Lam 2:8
with a l of flax in his hand, and .... Eze 40:3
when the man that had the l in .... Eze 47:3
and thy land shall be divided by l .... Amos 7:17
l shall be stretched forth upon .... Zec 1:16
with a measuring l in his hand .... Zec 2:1
l of things made ready to our. 2Cor 10:16

LINEAGE
he was of the house and l of David ...... Lk 2:4

LINEN
arrayed him in vestures of fine l .... Gen 41:42
and purple, and scarlet, and fine l .... Ex 25:4
ten curtains of fine twined l .... Ex 26:1
fine twined l of cunning work, ... Ex 26:31
and scarlet, and fine twined l .... Ex 26:36
for the court of fine twined l of. .... Ex 27:9
and scarlet, and fine twined l .... Ex 27:16
five cubits of fine twined l .... Ex 27:18
and purple, and scarlet, and fine l .... Ex 28:5
of scarlet, and of fine twined l .... Ex 28:6
and scarlet, and fine twined l .... Ex 28:8
of scarlet, and of fine twined l .... Ex 28:15
embroider the coat of fine l .... Ex 28:39
shalt make the mitre of fine l .... Ex 28:39
thou shalt make them l breeches. .... Ex 28:42
and purple, and scarlet, and fine l .... Ex 35:6
and purple, and scarlet, and fine l .... Ex 35:23
and scarlet, and of fine l .... Ex 35:25
purple, in scarlet, and in fine l .... Ex 35:35
ten curtains of fine twined l .... Ex 36:8
and scarlet, and fine twined l .... Ex 36:35
and scarlet, and fine twined l .... Ex 36:37
the court were of fine twined l .... Ex 38:9
round about were of fine twined l .... Ex 38:16
and scarlet, and fine twined l .... Ex 38:18
purple, and in scarlet, and fine l .... Ex 38:23
and scarlet, and fine twined l .... Ex 39:2
in the scarlet, and in the fine l .... Ex 39:3
and scarlet, and fine twined l .... Ex 39:5
and scarlet, and fine twined l .... Ex 39:8
purple, and scarlet, and l twined l. ...... Ex 39:24
And a mitre of fine l .... Ex 39:28
and goodly bonnets of fine l .... Ex 39:28
l breeches of fine twined l .... Ex 39:28
l breeches of fine twined l .... Ex 39:28
And a girdle of fine twined l .... Ex 39:29
priest shall put on his l garment. .... Lev 6:10
his l breeches shall he put upon. .... Lev 6:10
a woollen garment, or a l garment. ...... Lev 13:47
of l, or of woollen. .... Lev 13:48
warp or woof, in woollen or in l .... Lev 13:52

in a garment of woollen or l. .... Lev 13:59
He shall put on the holy l coat .... Lev 16:4
he shall have the l breeches upon. ...... Lev 16:4
shall be girded with a l girdle. .... Lev 16:4
with the l mitre shall he be. .... Lev 16:4
and shall put off the l garments .... Lev 16:23
and shall put on the l clothes. .... Lev 16:32
shall a garment mingled of l .... Lev 19:19
as of woollen and l together. .... Deut 22:11
a child, girded with a l 1Sa 2:18
persons that did wear a l ephod 1Sa 22:18
David was girded with a l ephod. 2Sa 6:14
brought out of Egypt, and l yarn. 1Kin 10:28
received the l yarn at a price. 1Kin 10:28
house of them that wrought fine l 1Chr 4:21
was clothed with a robe of fine l 1Chr 15:27
also had upon him an ephod of l. 1Chr 15:27
brought out of Egypt, and l yarn 2Chr 1:16
received the l yarn at a price 2Chr 1:16
in purple, in blue, and in fine l 2Chr 2:14
and purple, and crimson, and fine l 2Chr 3:14
being arrayed in white l 2Chr 5:12
fastened with cords of fine l .... Est 1:6
gold, and with a garment of fine l .... Est 8:15
works, with fine l of Egypt .... Prov 7:16
She maketh fine l, and selleth it. .... Prov 31:24
The glasses, and the fine l .... Is 3:23
me, Go and get thee a l girdle. .... Jer 13:1
man among them was clothed with l .... Eze 9:2
called to the man clothed with l .... Eze 9:3
behold, the man clothed with l .... Eze 9:11
spake unto the man clothed with l .... Eze 10:2
commanded the man clothed with l ...... Eze 10:6
of him that was clothed with l. .... Eze 10:7
l girded thee about with fine l .... Eze 16:10
and thy raiment was of fine l .... Eze 16:13
Fine l with broidered work from .... Eze 27:7
and broidered work, and fine l .... Eze 27:16
shall be clothed with l garments. .... Eze 44:17
They shall have l bonnets upon. .... Eze 44:18
shall have l breeches upon their .... Eze 44:18
behold a certain man clothed in l .... Dan 10:5
one said to the man clothed in l .... Dan 12:6
And I heard the man clothed in l .... Dan 12:7
he wrapped it in a clean l cloth. .... Mt 27:59
having a l cloth cast about his. .... Mk 14:51
And he left the l cloth, and fled .... Mk 14:52
And he bought fine l, and took him .... Mk 15:46
him down, and wrapped him in the l ... Mk 15:46
was clothed in purple and fine l .... Lk 16:19
took it down, and wrapped it in l .... Lk 23:53
he beheld the l clothes laid by .... Lk 24:12
wound it in l clothes with the .... Jn 19:40
in, saw the l clothes lying. .... Jn 20:5
and seeth the l clothes lie, ... Jn 20:6
not lying with the l clothes. .... Jn 20:7
clothed in pure and white l .... Rev 15:6
stones, and of pearls, and fine l .... Rev 18:12
city, that was clothed in fine l .... Rev 18:16
she should be arrayed in fine l .... Rev 19:8
for the fine l is the .... Rev 19:8
white horses, clothed in fine l .... Rev 19:14

LINES
even with two l measured he to 2Sa 8:2
The l are fallen unto me in. .... Ps 16:6

LINGERED
And while he l, the men laid hold .... Gen 19:16
For except we had l, surely now. .... Gen 43:10

LINGERETH
judgment now of a long time l not. 2Pet 2:3

LINTEL
in in the bason, and strike the l .... Ex 12:22
he seeth the blood upon the l .... Ex 12:23
the l and side posts were a fifth. 1Kin 6:31
Smite the l of the door, that the. .... Amos 9:1

LINTELS
shall lodge in the upper l of it .... Zeph 2:14

LINUS (li´-nus) A Christian at Rome.
greeteth thee, and Pudens, and L. 2Ti 4:21

LION
stooped down, he couched as a l .... Gen 49:9
and as an old l .... Gen 49:9
people shall rise up as a great l .... Num 23:24
and lift up himself as a young l .... Num 23:24
He couched, he lay down as a l .... Num 24:9
and as a great l .... Num 24:9
he dwelleth as a l, and teareth. .... Deut 33:20
a young l roared against him .... Judg 14:5
aside to see the carcase of the l. .... Judg 14:8
and honey in the carcase of the l .... Judg 14:8
honey out of the carcase of the l .... Judg 14:9
And what is stronger than a l .... Judg 14:18
father's sheep, and there came a l 1Sa 17:34
Thy servant slew both the l 1Sa 17:36
me out of the paw of the l 1Sa 17:37
heart is as the heart of a l 2Sa 17:10
slew a l in the midst of a pit in 2Sa 23:20
a l met him by the way, and slew 1Kin 13:24
the l also stood by the carcase. 1Kin 13:25
the l standing by the carcase. 1Kin 13:25
hath delivered him unto the l 1Kin 13:26
the l standing by the carcase, ... 1Kin 13:28
the l had not eaten the carcase, ... 1Kin 13:28
from me, a l shall slay thee 1Kin 20:36
a l found him, and slew him. 1Kin 20:36
slew a l in a pit in snowy day 1Chr 11:22

The roaring of the l........................ Job 4:10
and the voice of the fierce l.............. Job 4:10
Thou l perisheth for lack of.............. Job 4:11
Thou huntest me as a fierce l............ Job 10:16
it, nor the fierce l passed by it........... Job 28:8
Wilt thou hunt the prey for the l......... Job 38:39
Lest he tear my soul like a l............... Ps 7:2
wait secretly as a l in his den............ Ps 10:9
Like as a l that is greedy of his.......... Ps 17:12
as it were a young l lurking in............ Ps 17:12
as a ravening and a roaring l.............. Ps 22:13
Thou shalt tread upon the l................ Ps 91:13
the young l and the dragon shalt........ Ps 91:13
wrath is as the roaring of a l............. Prov 19:12
a king is as the roaring of a l............ Prov 20:2
man saith, There is a l without........... Prov 22:13
saith, There is a l in the way............. Prov 26:13
a l is in the streets........................ Prov 26:13
but the righteous are bold as a l......... Prov 28:1
As a roaring l, and a ranging bear...... Prov 28:15
A l which is strongest among............. Prov 30:30
dog is better than a dead l................ Eccl 9:4
Their roaring shall be like a l............. Is 5:29
and the calf and the young l.............. Is 11:6
the l shall eat straw like the ox.......... Is 11:7
And he cried, A l........................... Is 21:8
whence come the young and old l........ Is 30:6
spoken unto me, Like as the l............ Is 31:4
the young l roaring on his prey........... Is 31:4
No l shall be there, nor any............... Is 35:9
till morning, that, as a l................... Is 38:13
the l shall eat straw like the.............. Is 65:25
prophets, like a destroying l.............. Jer 2:30
The l is come up from his thicket........ Jer 4:7
Wherefore a l out of the forest........... Jer 5:6
is unto me as a l in the forest............ Jer 12:8
forsaken his covert, as the l.............. Jer 25:38
he shall come up like a l from........... Jer 49:19
he shall come up like a l from........... Jer 50:44
wait, and as a l in secret places......... Lam 3:10
face of a man, and the face of a l....... Eze 1:10
man, and the third the face of a l....... Eze 10:14
it became a young l, and it............... Eze 19:3
her whelps, and made him a young l... Eze 19:5
the lions, he became a young l........... Eze 19:6
like a roaring l ravening the............. Eze 22:25
art like a young l of the nations......... Eze 32:2
the face of a young l toward the......... Eze 41:19
The first was like a l, and had........... Dan 7:4
For I will be unto Ephraim as a l........ Hos 5:14
as a young l to the house of............. Hos 5:14
he shall roar like a l...................... Hos 11:10
I will be unto them as a l................. Hos 13:7
there will I devour them like a l......... Hos 13:8
whose teeth are the teeth of a l......... Joel 1:6
hath the cheek teeth of a great l........ Joel 1:6
Will a l roar in the forest, when........ Amos 3:4
will a young l cry out of his den........ Amos 3:4
The l hath roared, who will not.......... Amos 3:8
of the mouth of the l two legs.......... Amos 3:12
As if a man did flee from a l............. Amos 5:19
the midst of many people as a l........ Mic 5:8
as a young l among the flocks of....... Mic 5:8
of the young lions, where the l.......... Nah 2:11
even the old l............................. Nah 2:11
The l did tear in pieces enough......... Nah 2:12
out of the mouth of the l............... Nah 2:11
the devil, as a roaring l................. 1Pet 5:8
And the first beast was like a l......... Rev 4:7
the L of the tribe of Juda, the......... Rev 5:5
a loud voice, as when a l roareth...... Rev 10:3
and his mouth as the mouth of a l..... Rev 13:2

LIONESS

A l.. Eze 19:2

LIONESSES

whelps, and strangled for his l......... Nah 2:12

LIONLIKE

acts, he slew two l men of Moab....... 2Sa 23:20
he slew two l men of Moab............. 1Chr 11:22

LION'S

Judah is a l whelp........................ Gen 49:9
of Dan he said, Dan is a l whelp........ Deut 33:22
the stout l whelps are scattered........ Job 4:11
The l whelps have not trodden it....... Job 28:8
Save me from the l mouth............... Ps 22:21
the l whelp, and none made them...... Nah 2:11

LIONS

eagles, they were stronger than l....... 2Sa 1:23
were between the ledges were l......... 1Kin 7:29
and beneath the l and oxen were....... 1Kin 7:29
thereof, he graved cherubims, l........ 1Kin 7:36
two l stood beside the stays............ 1Kin 10:19
twelve l stood there on the one......... 1Kin 10:20
the LORD sent l among them............ 2Kin 17:25
he hath sent l among them.............. 2Kin 17:26
faces were like the faces of l........... 1Chr 12:8
two l standing by the stays............. 2Chr 9:18
twelve l stood there on the one......... 2Chr 9:19
lion, and the teeth of the young l...... Job 4:10
fill the appetite of the young l......... Job 38:39
The young l do lack, and suffer......... Ps 34:10
my darling from the l..................... Ps 35:17
My soul is among l....................... Ps 57:4
the great teeth of the young l.......... Ps 58:6
The young l roar after their prey....... Ps 104:21
they shall roar like young l............. Is 5:29
l upon him that escapeth of Moab...... Is 15:9
The young l roared upon him, and..... Jer 2:15

the l have driven him away............. Jer 50:17
They shall roar together like l.......... Jer 51:38
she lay down among l, she.............. Eze 19:2
her whelps among young l.............. Eze 19:2
up and down among l.................... Eze 19:3
with all the young l thereof............ Eze 38:13
shall be cast into the den of l.......... Dan 6:7
shall be cast into the den of l.......... Dan 6:12
and cast him into the den of l......... Dan 6:16
went in haste unto the den of l........ Dan 6:19
able to deliver thee from the l......... Dan 6:20
they cast them into the den of l....... Dan 6:24
the l had the mastery of them, and... Dan 6:24
Daniel from the power of the l......... Dan 6:27
Where is the dwelling of the l......... Nah 2:11
the feeding place of the young l....... Nah 2:11
sword shall devour thy young l........ Nah 2:13
princes within her are roaring l....... Zeph 3:3
a voice of the roaring of young l...... Zec 11:3
promises, stopped the mouths of l.... Heb 11:33
teeth were as the teeth of l............ Rev 9:8
the horses were as the heads of l..... Rev 9:17

LIONS'

Shenir and Hermon, from the l dens... Song 4:8
they shall yell as l whelps.............. Jer 51:38
angel, and hath shut the l mouths..... Dan 6:22

LIP

put a covering upon his upper l........ Lev 13:45
they shoot out the l, they shake....... Ps 22:7
The l of truth shall be................... Prov 12:19

LIPS

me, who am of uncircumcised l......... Ex 6:12
Behold, I am of uncircumcised l....... Ex 6:30
pronouncing with his l to do evil...... Lev 5:4
or uttered ought out of her l........... Num 30:6
that which she uttered with her l...... Num 30:8
out of her l concerning her vows...... Num 30:12
gone out of thy l thou shalt keep..... Deut 23:23
only her l moved, but her voice....... 1Sa 1:13
thy nose, and my bridle in thy l....... 2Kin 19:28
this did not Job sin with his l.......... Job 2:10
laughing, and thy l with rejoicing..... Job 8:21
speak, and open his l against thee.... Job 11:5
hearken to the pleadings of my l...... Job 13:6
thine own l testify against thee....... Job 15:6
the moving of my l should assuage... Job 16:5
from the commandment of his l........ Job 23:12
My l shall not speak wickedness,...... Job 27:4
I will open my l and answer........... Job 32:20
my l shall utter knowledge............ Job 33:3
With flattering l and with a............ Ps 12:2
shall cut off all flattering l............. Ps 12:3
our l are our own........................ Ps 12:4
nor take up their names into my l..... Ps 16:4
that goeth not out of feigned l........ Ps 17:1
by the word of thy l I have kept...... Ps 17:4
withholden the request of his l........ Ps 21:2
Let the lying l be put to silence...... Ps 31:18
thy l from speaking guile............... Ps 34:13
lo, I have not refrained my l........... Ps 40:9
grace is poured into thy l.............. Ps 45:2
O Lord, open thou my l................. Ps 51:15
swords are in their l..................... Ps 59:7
the words of their l let them.......... Ps 59:12
than life, my l shall praise thee...... Ps 63:3
shall praise thee with joyful l......... Ps 63:5
Which my l have uttered, and my..... Ps 66:14
My l shall greatly rejoice when I..... Ps 71:23
thing that is gone out of my l......... Ps 89:34
he spake unadvisedly with his l....... Ps 106:33
With my l have I declared all the..... Ps 119:13
My l shall utter praise, when......... Ps 119:171
my soul, O LORD, from lying l......... Ps 120:2
adders' poison is under their l......... Ps 140:3
of their own l cover them.............. Ps 140:9
Keep the door of my l................... Ps 141:3
perverse l put far from thee........... Prov 4:24
that thy l may keep knowledge....... Prov 5:2
For the l of a strange woman drop... Prov 5:3
of her l she forced him................. Prov 7:21
the opening of my l shall be.......... Prov 8:6
is an abomination to my l.............. Prov 8:7
In the l of him that hath............... Prov 10:13
that hideth hatred with lying l....... Prov 10:18
he that refraineth his l is wise....... Prov 10:19
The l of the righteous feed many..... Prov 10:21
The l of the righteous know what.... Prov 10:32
by the transgression of his l.......... Prov 12:13
Lying l are abomination to the....... Prov 12:22
wide his l shall have destruction..... Prov 13:3
but the l of the wise shall............. Prov 14:3
not in him the l of knowledge........ Prov 14:7
but the talk of the l tendeth.......... Prov 14:23
The l of the wise disperse............. Prov 15:7
sentence is in the l of the king...... Prov 16:10
Righteous l are the delight of........ Prov 16:13
the l of the increaseth learning...... Prov 16:21
and addeth learning to his l.......... Prov 16:23
in his l there is as a burning......... Prov 16:27
moving his l he bringeth evil to..... Prov 16:30
doer giveth heed to false l........... Prov 17:4
much less do lying l a prince........ Prov 17:7
his l is esteemed a man of........... Prov 17:28
A fool's l enter into contention...... Prov 18:6
his l are the snare of his soul....... Prov 18:7
of his l shall he be filled............. Prov 18:20
than he that is perverse in his l..... Prov 19:1
but the l of knowledge are a......... Prov 20:15
him that flattereth with his l......... Prov 20:19

for the grace of his l the king......... Prov 22:11
shall withal be fitted in thy l.......... Prov 22:18
when thy l speak right things......... Prov 23:16
and their l talk of mischief........... Prov 24:2
Every man shall kiss his l that....... Prov 24:26
and deceive not with thy l............ Prov 24:28
Burning l and a wicked heart are.... Prov 26:23
hateth dissembleth with his l......... Prov 26:24
a stranger, and not thine own l...... Prov 27:2
but the l of a fool will swallow....... Eccl 10:12
Thy l are like a thread of............. Song 4:3
Thy l, O my spouse, drop as the..... Song 4:11
his l like lilies, dropping sweet...... Song 5:13
causing the l of those that are....... Song 7:9
because I am a man of unclean l..... Is 6:5
midst of a people of unclean l........ Is 6:5
said, Lo, this hath touched thy l...... Is 6:7
with the breath of his l shall he..... Is 11:4
For with stammering l and another.. Is 28:11
with their l do honour me, but....... Is 29:13
his l are full of indignation, and.... Is 30:27
thy nose, and my bridle in thy l..... Is 37:29
I create the fruit of the l............. Is 57:19
your l have spoken lies, your........ Is 59:3
out of my l was right before thee... Jer 17:16
The l of those that rose up........... Lam 3:62
upon thy feet, and cover not thy l... Eze 24:17
ye shall not cover your l.............. Eze 24:22
are taken up in the l of talkers...... Eze 36:3
of the sons of men touched my l..... Dan 10:16
we render the calves of our l........ Hos 14:2
yea, they shall all cover their l...... Mic 3:7
my l quivered at the voice........... Hab 3:16
iniquity was not found in his l....... Mal 2:6
For the priest's l should keep........ Mal 2:7
and honoureth me with their l....... Mt 15:8
people honoureth me with their l.... Mk 7:6
poison of asps is under their l....... Rom 3:13
other l will I speak unto this........ 1Cor 14:21
the fruit of our l giving thanks...... Heb 13:15
his l that they speak no guile....... 1Pet 3:10

LIQUOR

shall he drink any l of grapes....... Num 6:3
round goblet, which wanteth not l... Song 7:2

LIQUORS

of thy ripe fruits, and thy l.......... Ex 22:29

LISTED

done unto him whatsoever they l..... Mt 17:12
done unto him whatsoever they l..... Mk 9:13

LISTEN

L, O isles, unto me.................... Is 49:1

LISTETH

The wind bloweth where it l......... Jn 3:8
whithersoever the governor l........ Jas 3:4

LITTERS

horses, and in chariots, and in l.... Is 66:20

LITTLE

Let a l water, I pray you, be........ Gen 18:4
to flee unto, and it is a l one....... Gen 19:20
thither, (is it not a l one............. Gen 19:20
drink a l water of thy pitcher....... Gen 24:17
a l water of thy pitcher to drink.... Gen 24:43
For it was I which thou hadst........ Gen 30:30
their wealth, and all their l ones.... Gen 34:29
there was but a l way to come to... Gen 35:16
them, Go again, buy us a l food.... Gen 43:2
we, and thou, and also our l ones... Gen 43:8
a l balm, and a l honey,.............. Gen 43:11
a child of his old age, a l one....... Gen 44:20
Go again, and buy us a l food....... Gen 44:25
the land of Egypt for your l food... Gen 45:19
their father, and their l ones........ Gen 46:5
and for food for your l ones......... Gen 47:24
but a l way to come unto Ephrath.. Gen 48:7
only their l ones, and their........... Gen 50:8
will nourish you, and your l ones... Gen 50:21
I will let you go, and your l ones... Ex 10:10
let your l ones also go with you..... Ex 10:24
household be too l for the lamb..... Ex 12:4
and he that gathered l had no lack. Ex 16:18
By l and l I will drive them.......... Ex 23:30
And the l owl, and the cormorant,.. Lev 11:17
But your l ones, which ye said...... Num 14:31
their sons, and their l children..... Num 16:27
Midian captives, and their l ones... Num 31:9
kill every male among the l ones... Num 31:17
cattle, and cities for our l ones..... Num 32:16
our l ones shall dwell in the........ Num 32:17
Build you cities for your l ones..... Num 32:24
Our l ones, our wives, our flocks.. Num 32:26
Moreover your l ones, which ye.... Deut 1:39
the l ones, of every city, we........ Deut 2:34
But your wives, and your l ones.... Deut 3:19
before thee by l and l................ Deut 7:22
The l owl, and the great owl, and.. Deut 14:16
the l ones, and the cattle, and all.. Deut 20:14
field, and shall gather but l in...... Deut 28:38
Your l ones, your wives, and thy... Deut 29:11
Your wives, your l ones, and your.. Josh 1:14
the l ones, and the strangers that.. Josh 8:35
of Dan went out too l for them..... Josh 19:47
the iniquity of Peor too l for us.... Josh 22:17
I pray thee, a l water to drink...... Judg 4:19
and departed, and put her l ones... Judg 18:21
that she tarried a l in the house.... Ruth 2:7
his mother made him a l coat....... 1Sa 2:19

I tasted a *l* of this honey 1Sa 14:29
I did but taste a *l* honey with 1Sa 14:43
When thou wast *l* in thine own 1Sa 15:17
with David, and a *l* lad with him 1Sa 20:35
had nothing, save one *l* ewe lamb 2Sa 12:3
and if that had been too *l* 2Sa 12:8
all the *l* ones that were with him 2Sa 15:22
when David was a *l* past the top 2Sa 16:1
Thy servant will go a *l* way over 2Sa 19:36
and I am but a *l* child 1Kin 3:7
was before the LORD was too *l* to........ 1Kin 8:64
Hadad being yet a *l* child 1Kin 11:17
My *l* finger shall be thicker than 1Kin 12:10
a *l* water in a vessel, that I may 1Kin 17:10
a barrel, and a *l* oil in a cruse............ 1Kin 17:12
make me thereof a *l* cake first 1Kin 17:13
there ariseth a *l* cloud out of.............. 1Kin 18:44
them like two *l* flocks of kids 1Kin 20:27
there came forth *l* children out 2Kin 2:23
Let us make a *l* chamber, I pray 2Kin 4:10
of the land of Israel a *l* maid 2Kin 5:2
like unto the flesh of a *l* child 2Kin 5:14
So he departed from him a *l* way........ 2Kin 5:19
unto them, Ahab served Baal a *l* 2Kin 10:18
My *l* finger shall be thicker than........ 2Chr 10:10
the LORD, with their *l* ones 2Chr 20:13
the genealogy of all their *l* ones........ 2Chr 31:18
way for us, and for our *l* ones .... Ezr 8:21
now for a *l* space grace hath been ...... Ezr 9:8
give us a *l* reviving in our .... Ezr 9:8
the trouble seem *l* before thee............ Neh 9:32
l children and women, in one day ...... Est 3:13
would assault them, both *l* ones .... Est 8:11
and mine ear received a *l* thereof ...... Job 4:12
that I may take comfort a *l* .... Job 10:20
forth their *l* ones like a flock.............. Job 21:11
They are exalted for a *l* while.............. Job 24:24
but how *l* a portion is heard of .... Job 26:14
Suffer me a *l*, and I will shew .... Job 36:2
when his wrath is kindled but a *l* ...... Ps 2:12
him a *l* lower than the angels.............. Ps 8:5
For yet a *l* while, and the wicked........ Ps 37:10
A *l* that a righteous man hath is........ Ps 37:16
the *l* hills rejoice on every side............ Ps 65:12
There is *l* Benjamin with their .... Ps 68:27
the *l* hills, by righteousness................ Ps 72:3
rams, and the *l* hills like lambs............ Ps 114:4
and ye *l* hills, like lambs...................... Ps 114:6
dasheth thy *l* ones against the .... Ps 137:9
Yet a *l* sleep, a *l* slumber.................. Prov 6:10
a *l* folding of the hands to sleep .... Prov 6:10
heart of the wicked is *l* worth............ Prov 10:20
Better is *l* with the fear of the .... Prov 15:16
Better is a *l* with righteousness.......... Prov 16:8
Yet a *l* sleep, a *l* slumber.................. Prov 24:33
a *l* folding of the hands to sleep .... Prov 24:33
things which are *l* upon the earth ...... Prov 30:24
sweet, whether he eat *l* or much .... Eccl 5:12
There was a *l* city, and few men .... Eccl 9:14
so doth a *l* folly him that is in............ Eccl 10:1
the *l* foxes, that spoil the vines .... Song 2:15
It was but a *l* that I passed from........ Song 3:4
We have a *l* sister, and she hath .... Song 8:8
For yet a very *l* while, and the............ Is 10:25
a *l* child shall lead them...................... Is 11:6
thyself as it were for a *l* moment ...... Is 26:20
here a *l*, and there a *l*...................... Is 28:10
here a *l*, and there a *l*...................... Is 28:13
Is it not yet a very *l* while.................. Is 29:17
up the isles as a very *l* thing.............. Is 40:15
In a *l* wrath I hid my face from .... Is 54:8
A *l* one shall become a thousand........ Is 60:22
have possessed it but a *l* while .... Is 63:18
sent their *l* ones to the waters .... Jer 14:3
her *l* ones have caused a cry to .... Jer 48:4
yet a *l* while, and the time of her...... Jer 51:33
maids, and *l* children, and women...... Eze 9:6
as a *l* sanctuary in the countries .... Eze 11:16
as if that were a very *l* thing.............. Eze 16:47
sent out her *l* rivers unto all.............. Eze 31:4
every *l* chamber was one reed long .... Eze 40:7
between the *l* chambers were five........ Eze 40:7
the *l* chambers of the gate .... Eze 40:10
The space also before the *l* .... Eze 40:12
the *l* chambers were six cubits on...... Eze 40:12
the gate from the roof of one *l* .... Eze 40:13
narrow windows to the *l* chambers .... Eze 40:16
the *l* chambers thereof were three...... Eze 40:21
the *l* chambers thereof, and the .... Eze 40:29
the *l* chambers thereof, and the .... Eze 40:33
The *l* chambers thereof, the posts...... Eze 40:36
came up among them another *l* horn.. Dan 7:8
one of them came forth a *l* horn........ Dan 8:9
shall be holpen with a *l* help.............. Dan 11:34
for yet a *l* while, and I will .... Hos 1:4
they shall sorrow a *l* for the................ Hos 8:10
and the *l* house with clefts .... Amos 6:11
though thou be *l* among the................ Mic 5:2
Ye have sown much, and bring in *l* .... Hag 1:6
for much, and, lo, it came to *l* .... Hag 1:9
Yet once, it is a *l* while .... Hag 2:6
for I was but a *l* displeased................ Zec 1:15
turn mine hand upon the *l* ones .... Zec 13:7
more clothe you, O ye of *l* faith.......... Mt 6:30
are ye fearful, O ye of *l* faith .... Mt 8:26
I ones a cup of cold water only .... Mt 10:42
said unto him, O thou of *l* faith .... Mt 14:31
said, Seven, and a few *l* fishes .... Mt 15:34
said unto them, O ye of *l* faith .... Mt 16:8
Jesus called a *l* child unto him .... Mt 18:2

and become as *l* children, ye.............. Mt 18:3
humble himself as this *l* child .... Mt 18:4
whoso shall receive one such *l* .... Mt 18:5
these *l* ones which believe in me........ Mt 18:6
despise not one of these *l* ones.......... Mt 18:10
that one of these *l* ones should .... Mt 18:14
there brought unto him *l* children...... Mt 19:13
Suffer *l* children, and forbid them...... Mt 19:14
And he went a *l* farther, and fell........ Mt 26:39
he had gone a *l* farther thence .... Mk 1:19
were also with him other *l* ships........ Mk 4:36
My *l* daughter lieth at the point.......... Mk 5:23
these *l* ones that believe in me .... Mk 9:42
Suffer the *l* children to come .... Mk 10:14
the kingdom of God as a *l* child.......... Mk 10:15
And he went forward a *l*, and fell...... Mk 14:35
a *l* after, they that stood by .... Mk 14:70
thrust out a *l* from the land .... Lk 5:3
but to whom *l* is forgiven.................... Lk 7:47
to forgiven, the same loveth *l*............ Lk 7:47
he clothe you, O ye of *l* faith............ Lk 12:28
Fear not, *l* flock.................................. Lk 12:32
should offend one of these *l* ones...... Lk 17:2
Suffer *l* children to come unto me...... Lk 18:16
a *l* child shall in no wise enter .... Lk 18:17
because he was *l* of stature .... Lk 19:3
hast been faithful in a very *l*.............. Lk 19:17
after a *l* while another saw him.......... Lk 22:58
every one of them may take a *l* .... Jn 6:7
Yet a *l* while am I with you, and........ Jn 7:33
Yet a *l* while is the light with .... Jn 13:33
L children, yet a *l* while I .... Jn 13:33
Yet a *l* while, and the world seeth...... Jn 14:19
A *l* while, and ye shall not see me ...... Jn 16:16
a *l* while, and ye shall see me............ Jn 16:16
A *l* while, and ye shall not see me ...... Jn 16:17
a *l* while, and ye shall see me............ Jn 16:17
in this that he saith, A *l* while............ Jn 16:18
A *l* while, and ye shall not see me ...... Jn 16:19
a *l* while, and ye shall see me............ Jn 16:19
other disciples came in a *l* ship .... Jn 21:8
put the apostles forth a *l* space.......... Acts 5:34
alive, and were not a *l* comforted ...... Acts 20:12
and when they had gone a *l* further .. Acts 27:28
people shewed us no *l* kindness.......... Acts 28:2
Know ye not that a *l* leaven................ 1Cor 5:6
that had gathered *l* had no lack 2Cor 8:15
bear with me a *l* in my folly 2Cor 11:1
me, that I may boast myself a *l* 2Cor 11:16
My *l* children, of whom I travail........ Gal 4:19
A *l* leaven leaveneth the whole .... Gal 5:9
For bodily exercise profiteth *l* 1Ti 4:8
water, but use a *l* wine for thy............ 1Ti 5:23
Thou madest him a *l* lower than........ Heb 2:7
who was made a *l* lower than the........ Heb 2:9
For yet a *l* while, and he that .... Heb 10:37
Even so the tongue is a *l* member...... Jas 3:5
great a matter a *l* fire kindleth .... Jas 3:5
that appeareth for a *l* time.................. Jas 4:14
My *l* children, these things write 1Jn 2:1
children, because your sins are 1Jn 2:12
l children, because ye have known...... 1Jn 2:13
L children, it is the last time................ 1Jn 2:18
And now, *l* children, abide in him...... 1Jn 2:28
L children, let no man deceive 1Jn 3:7
My *l* children, let us not love in.......... 1Jn 3:18
l children, and have overcome them.. 1Jn 4:4
L children, keep yourselves from 1Jn 5:21
for thou hast a *l* strength.................... Rev 3:8
should rest yet for a *l* season.............. Rev 6:11
he had in his hand a *l* book open........ Rev 10:2
take the *l* book which is open in.......... Rev 10:8
said unto him, Give me the *l* book ...... Rev 10:9
I took the *l* book out of the................ Rev 10:10
that he must be loosed a *l* season...... Rev 20:3

LIVE

of life, and eat, and *l* for ever............ Gen 3:22
my soul shall *l* because of thee............ Gen 12:13
that Ishmael might *l* before thee.......... Gen 17:18
and my soul shall *l* .... Gen 19:20
pray for thee, and thou shalt *l* .... Gen 20:7
And by thy sword shalt thou *l*............ Gen 27:40
findest thy gods, let him not *l* .... Gen 31:32
that we may *l*, and not die .... Gen 42:2
them the third day, This do, and *l* ...... Gen 42:18
that we may *l*, and not die, both .... Gen 43:8
doth my father yet *l* .... Gen 45:3
and give us seed, that we may *l* .... Gen 47:19
be a daughter, then she shall *l*............ Ex 1:16
be beast or man, it shall not *l* .... Ex 19:13
then they shall sell the *l* ox................ Ex 21:35
shalt not suffer a witch to *l* .... Ex 22:18
there shall no man see me, and *l*........ Ex 33:20
altar, he shall bring the *l* goat .... Lev 16:20
hands upon the head of the *l* goat...... Lev 16:21
of a man do, he shall *l* in them .... Lev 18:5
that he may *l* with thee...................... Lev 25:35
that thy brother may *l* with thee .... Lev 25:36
do unto them, that they may *l* .... Num 4:19
But as truly as I *l*, all the.................. Num 14:21
Say unto them, As truly as I *l* .... Num 14:28
when he looketh upon it, shall *l*.......... Num 21:8
who shall *l* when God doeth this .... Num 24:23
for to do them, that ye may *l* .... Deut 4:1
that they shall *l* upon the earth .... Deut 4:10
fire, as thou hast heard, and *l*............ Deut 4:33
one of these cities he might *l* .... Deut 4:42
hath commanded you, that ye may *l*.. Deut 5:33
ye observe to do, that ye may *l*.......... Deut 8:1
that man doth not *l* by bread only...... Deut 8:3

the mouth of the LORD doth man *l*...... Deut 8:3
the days that ye *l* upon the earth........ Deut 12:1
thou follow, that thou mayest *l* .... Deut 16:20
shall flee thither, that he may *l* .... Deut 19:4
unto one of those cities, and *l* .... Deut 19:5
all thy soul, that thou mayest *l* .... Deut 30:6
his judgments, that thou mayest *l*...... Deut 30:16
that both thou and thy seed may *l* ...... Deut 30:19
as long as ye *l* in the land.................. Deut 31:13
to heaven, and say, I *l* for ever............ Deut 32:40
Let Reuben *l*, and not die.................... Deut 33:6
only Rahab the harlot shall *l* .... Josh 6:17
a league with them, to let them *l* ...... Josh 9:15
we will even let them *l*, lest .... Josh 9:20
said unto them, Let them *l* .... Josh 9:21
I *l* shew me the kindness of the 1Sa 20:14
not *l* after that he was fallen.............. 2Sa 1:10
to me, that the child may *l*................ 2Sa 12:22
the king, How long have I to *l* 2Sa 19:34
Let my lord king David *l* for ever........ 1Kin 1:31
thee all the days that they *l* in............ 1Kin 8:40
saith, I pray thee, let me *l* 1Kin 20:32
I thou and thy children of the................ 2Kin 4:7
if they save us alive, we shall *l* 2Kin 7:4
shall be wanting, he shall not *l* 2Kin 10:19
olive and of honey, that ye may *l* 2Kin 18:32
for thou shalt die, and not *l*................ 2Kin 20:1
so long as they *l* in the land 2Chr 6:31
the king, Let the king *l* for ever.......... Neh 2:3
for them, that we may eat, and *l*........ Neh 5:2
if a man do, he shall *l* in them .... Neh 9:29
the golden sceptre, that he may *l*........ Est 4:11
I would not *l* alway .... Job 7:16
If a man die, shall he *l* again .... Job 14:14
Wherefore do the wicked *l* .... Job 21:7
not reproach me so long as I *l* .... Job 27:6
your heart shall *l* for ever.................... Ps 22:26
That he should still *l* for ever.............. Ps 49:9
shall not *l* out half their days .... Ps 55:23
Thus will I bless thee while I *l*............ Ps 63:4
your heart shall *l* that seek God.......... Ps 69:32
And he shall *l*, and to him shall be...... Ps 72:15
sing unto the LORD as long as I *l*........ Ps 104:33
I call upon him as long as I *l* .... Ps 116:2
I shall not die, but *l*, and...................... Ps 118:17
with thy servant, that I may *l* .... Ps 119:17
come unto me, that I may *l* .... Ps 119:77
unto thy word, that I may *l*................ Ps 119:116
me understanding, and I shall *l* .... Ps 119:144
Let my soul *l*, and it shall praise .... Ps 119:175
While I *l* will I praise the LORD............ Ps 146:2
keep my commandments, and *l* .... Prov 4:4
Keep my commandments, and *l*.......... Prov 7:2
Forsake the foolish, and *l*.................... Prov 9:6
but he that hateth gifts shall *l*............ Prov 15:27
I many years, so that the days of .... Eccl 6:3
though he *l* a thousand years .... Eccl 6:6
is in their heart while they *l* .... Eccl 9:3
L joyfully with the wife whom .... Eccl 9:9
But if a man *l* many years.................. Eccl 11:8
having a *l* coal in his hand.................. Is 6:6
They are dead, they shall not *l* .... Is 26:14
Thy dead men shall *l*, together............ Is 26:19
for thou shalt die, and not *l* .... Is 38:1
O Lord, by these things men *l* .... Is 38:16
thou recover me, and make me to *l* .... Is 38:16
As I *l*, saith the LORD, thou................ Is 49:18
hear, and your soul shall *l* .... Is 55:3
that besiege you, he shall *l* .... Jer 21:9
As I *l*, saith the LORD, though .... Jer 22:24
and serve him and his people, and *l*.... Jer 27:12
serve the king of Babylon, and *l*.......... Jer 27:17
that ye may *l* many days in the .... Jer 35:7
forth to the Chaldeans shall *l* .... Jer 38:2
his life for a prey, and shall *l*.............. Jer 38:2
princes, then thy soul shall *l* .... Jer 38:17
and thou shalt *l*, and thine house........ Jer 38:17
unto thee, and thy soul shall *l* .... Jer 38:20
As I *l*, saith the King, whose .... Jer 46:18
we shall *l* among the heathen .... Lam 4:20
doth not sin, he shall surely *l* .... Eze 3:21
Wherefore, as I *l*, saith the Lord........ Eze 5:11
the souls alive that should not *l*.......... Eze 13:19
these were in it, as I *l* .... Eze 14:16
three men were in it, as I *l* .... Eze 14:18
and Job, were in it, as I *l* .... Eze 14:20
when thou wast in thy blood, L .... Eze 16:6
when thou wast in thy blood, *l* .... Eze 16:6
As I *l*, saith the Lord GOD, Sodom...... Eze 16:48
As I *l*, saith the Lord GOD, ... Eze 17:16
As I *l*, surely mine oath that he.......... Eze 17:19
As I *l*, saith the Lord GOD, ye............ Eze 18:3
he is just, he shall surely *l* .... Eze 18:9
shall he then *l* .... Eze 18:13
he shall not *l* .... Eze 18:13
of his father, he shall surely *l*............ Eze 18:17
hath done them, he shall surely *l* ...... Eze 18:19
and right, he shall surely *l* .... Eze 18:21
that he hath done he shall *l* .... Eze 18:22
should return from his ways, and *l*...... Eze 18:23
the wicked man doeth, shall he *l* .... Eze 18:24
hath committed, he shall surely *l* ...... Eze 18:28
turn yourselves, and *l* ye .... Eze 18:32
As I *l*, saith the Lord GOD, ... Eze 20:3
a man do, he shall even *l* in them ...... Eze 20:11
a man do, he shall even *l* in them ...... Eze 20:13
a man do, he shall even *l* in them ...... Eze 20:21
whereby they should not *l* .... Eze 20:25
As I *l*, saith the Lord GOD, ... Eze 20:31
As I *l*, saith the Lord GOD, ... Eze 20:33

in them, how should we then *l* .... Eze 33:10
Say unto them, As I *l*, saith the........... Eze 33:11
the wicked turn from his way and *l*..... Eze 33:11
to *l* for his righteousness in the .... Eze 33:12
righteous, that he shall surely *l* .... Eze 33:13
he shall surely *l*, he shall not............. Eze 33:15
he shall surely *l* .... Eze 33:16
and right, he shall *l* thereby.............. Eze 33:19
As I *l*, surely they that are in .... Eze 34:8
As I *l* saith the Lord GOD, surely..... Eze 34:8
Therefore, as I *l*, saith the............... Eze 35:6
Therefore, as I *l*, saith the Lord....... Eze 35:11
me, Son of man, can these bones *l*..... Eze 37:3
to enter into you, and ye shall *l*........ Eze 37:5
put breath in you, and ye shall *l* .... Eze 37:6
upon these slain, that they may *l* ...... Eze 37:9
my spirit in you, and ye shall *l* .... Eze 37:14
the rivers shall come, shall *l* .... Eze 47:9
every thing shall *l* whither the .... Eze 47:9
in Syriack, O king, *l* for ever .... Dan 2:4
O king, *l* for ever .... Dan 3:9
spake and said, O king, *l* for ever..... Dan 5:10
unto him, King Darius, *l* for ever ..... Dan 6:6
unto the king, O king, *l* for ever....... Dan 6:21
us up, and we shall *l* in his sight....... Hos 6:2
Israel, Seek ye me, and ye shall *l* ..... Amos 5:4
Seek the LORD, and ye shall *l* .... Amos 5:6
good, and not evil, that ye may *l* ...... Amos 5:14
is better for me to die than to *l*......... Jonah 4:3
is better for me to die than to *l*......... Jonah 4:8
but the just shall *l* by his faith.......... Hab 2:4
Therefore as I *l*, saith the Lord .... Zeph 2:9
the prophets, do they *l* for ever .... Zec 1:5
they shall *l* with their children.......... Zec 10:9
say unto him, Thou shalt not *l* .... Zec 13:3
Man shall not *l* by bread alone........... Mt 4:4
thy hand upon her, and she shall *l*..... Mt 9:18
and she shall *l* .... Mk 5:23
man shall not *l* by bread alone .... Lk 4:4
I delicately, are in kings'.................. Lk 7:25
this do, and thou shalt........................ Lk 10:28
for all *l* unto him .... Lk 20:38
and they that hear shall *l* .... Jn 5:25
this bread, he shall *l* for ever .... Jn 6:51
sent me, and I *l* by the Father............ Jn 6:57
eateth me, even he shall *l* by me .... Jn 6:57
of this bread shall *l* for ever .... Jn 6:58
he were dead, yet shall he *l* .... Jn 11:25
because I *l*, ye shall *l* also .... Jn 14:19
to the end they might not *l* .... Acts 7:19
For in him we *l*, and move, and have Acts 17:28
it is not fit that he should *l* .... Acts 22:22
that he ought not to *l* any longer...... Acts 25:24
yet vengeance suffereth not to *l* .... Acts 28:4
The just shall *l* by faith.................. Rom 1:17
dead to sin, *l* any longer therein...... Rom 6:2
that we shall also *l* with him .... Rom 6:8
the flesh, to *l* after the flesh............. Rom 8:12
For if ye *l* after the flesh, ye............ Rom 8:13
the deeds of the body, ye shall *l* .... Rom 8:13
those things shall *l* by them .... Rom 10:5
in you, I peaceably with all men........ Rom 12:18
we *l*, we *l* unto the Lord................ Rom 14:8
whether we *l* therefore, or die,......... Rom 14:8
For it is written, As I *l*.................... Rom 14:11
minister about holy things *l* of........ 1Cor 9:13
the gospel should *l* of the gospel...... 1Cor 9:14
For we which *l* are alway................ 2Cor 4:11
that they which *l* should not............ 2Cor 5:15
not henceforth *l* unto themselves..... 2Cor 5:15
as dying, and, behold, we *l* 2Cor 6:9
our hearts to die and *l* with you....... 2Cor 7:3
but we shall *l* with him by the......... 2Cor 13:4
be of one mind, *l* in peace................ 2Cor 13:11
the Gentiles to *l* as do the Jews........ Gal 2:14
the law, that I might *l* unto God....... Gal 2:19
nevertheless I *l* .... Gal 2:20
the life which I now *l* in the .... Gal 2:20
I by the faith of the Son of God........... Gal 2:20
for, The just shall *l* by faith .... Gal 3:11
that doeth them shall *l* in them .... Gal 3:12
If we *l* in the Spirit, let us .... Gal 5:25
thou mayest *l* long on the earth .... Eph 6:3
For to me to *l* is Christ, and to......... Phil 1:21
But if I *l* in the flesh, this is .... Phil 1:22
For now we *l*, if ye stand fast in 1Th 3:8
we should *l* together with him.......... 1Th 5:10
him, we shall also *l* with him 2Ti 2:11
all that will *l* godly in Christ............ 2Ti 3:12
lusts, we should *l* soberly................. Titus 2:12
Now the just shall *l* by faith............ Heb 10:38
unto the Father of spirits, and *l*........ Heb 12:9
all things willing to *l* honestly......... Heb 13:18
say, If the Lord will, we shall *l*........ Jas 4:15
should *l* unto righteousness.............. 1Pet 2:24
That he no longer should *l* the 1Pet 4:2
but *l* according to God in the........... 1Pet 4:6
those that after should *l* ungodly...... 2Pet 2:6
escaped from them when I *l* in error 2Pet 2:18
that we might *l* through him............ 1Jn 4:9
the wound by a sword, and did *l*....... Rev 13:14

LIVED
Adam *l* an hundred and thirty years ... Gen 5:3
that Adam *l* were nine hundred......... Gen 5:5
Seth *l* an hundred and five years,...... Gen 5:6
Seth *l* after he begat Enos eight .... Gen 5:7
Enos *l* ninety years, and begat .... Gen 5:9
Enos *l* after he begat Cainan .... Gen 5:10
Cainan *l* seventy years, and begat..... Gen 5:12
And Cainan *l* after he begat.............. Gen 5:13

And Mahalaleel *l* sixty and five......... Gen 5:15
Mahalaleel *l* after he begat Jared .... Gen 5:16
Jared *l* an hundred sixty and two....... Gen 5:18
Jared *l* after he begat Enoch.............. Gen 5:19
And Enoch *l* sixty and five years,....... Gen 5:21
Methuselah *l* an hundred eighty and... Gen 5:25
Methuselah *l* after he begat .... Gen 5:26
Lamech *l* an hundred eighty and two .. Gen 5:28
Lamech *l* after he begat Noah five...... Gen 5:30
Noah *l* after the flood three.............. Gen 9:28
Shem *l* after he begat Arphaxad......... Gen 11:11
And Arphaxad *l* five and thirty.......... Gen 11:12
Arphaxad *l* after he begat Salah......... Gen 11:13
Salah *l* thirty years, and begat .... Gen 11:14
Salah *l* after he begat Eber four......... Gen 11:15
And Eber *l* four and thirty years,....... Gen 11:16
Eber *l* after he begat Peleg four......... Gen 11:17
Peleg *l* thirty years, and begat .... Gen 11:18
Peleg *l* after he begat Reu two.......... Gen 11:19
And Reu *l* two and thirty years, and .. Gen 11:20
Reu *l* after he begat Serug two.......... Gen 11:21
Serug *l* thirty years, and begat.......... Gen 11:22
Serug *l* after he begat Nahor two....... Gen 11:23
And Nahor *l* nine and twenty years,... Gen 11:24
Nahor *l* after he begat Terah an......... Gen 11:25
Terah *l* seventy years, and begat .... Gen 11:26
Isaac his son, while he yet *l*.............. Gen 25:6
of Abraham's life which he *l* .... Gen 25:7
Jacob *l* in the land of Egypt,............. Gen 47:28
Joseph *l* an hundred and ten years .... Gen 50:22
went to search the land, I still .... Num 14:38
beheld the serpent of brass, he *l*....... Num 21:9
of the fire, as we have, and *l* .... Deut 5:26
I perceive, that if Absalom had *l*....... 2Sa 19:6
Solomon his father while he yet *l* 1Kin 12:6
l after the death of Jehoash son 2Kin 14:17
Solomon his father while he yet *l* 2Chr 10:6
the son of Joash king of Judah *l* 2Chr 25:25
After this I Job an hundred and......... Job 42:16
Though while he *l* he blessed his....... Ps 49:18
breath came into them, and they *l* ..... Eze 37:10
had *l* with an husband seven years.... Lk 2:36
I have *l* in all good conscience .... Acts 23:1
of our religion I *l* a Pharisee............ Acts 26:5
some time, when ye *l* in them .... Col 3:7
Ye have *l* in pleasure on the............. Jas 5:5
I deliciously, so much torment and..... Rev 18:7
I deliciously with her, shall............... Rev 18:9
and they *l* and reigned with Christ.... Rev 20:4
But the rest of the dead *l* not .... Rev 20:5

LIVELY
for they are *l*, and are delivered.......... Ex 1:19
But mine enemies are *l*, and they...... Ps 38:19
who received the *l* oracles to............ Acts 7:38
a *l* hope by the resurrection of.......... 1Pet 1:3
as *l* stones, are built up a................. 1Pet 2:5

LIVER
and the caul that is above the *l*......... Ex 29:13
inwards, and the caul above the *l* ..... Ex 29:22
flanks, and the caul above the *l* .... Lev 3:4
flanks, and the caul above the *l* .... Lev 3:10
flanks, and the caul above the *l* .... Lev 3:15
flanks, and the caul above the *l* .... Lev 4:9
and the caul that is above the *l*......... Lev 7:4
inwards, and the caul above the *l* ..... Lev 8:16
inwards, and the caul above the *l* ..... Lev 8:25
the caul above the *l* of the sin........... Lev 9:10
kidneys, and the caul above the *l*...... Lev 9:19
Till a dart strike through his *l*.......... Prov 7:23
my *l* is poured upon the earth,.......... Lam 2:11
with images, he looked in the *l*......... Eze 21:21

LIVES
blood of your *l* will I require............. Gen 9:5
to save your *l* by a great.................. Gen 45:7
they said, Thou hast saved our *l*....... Gen 47:25
they made their *l* bitter with............ Ex 1:14
have, and deliver our *l* from death .... Josh 2:13
afraid of our *l* because of you,.......... Josh 9:24
I unto the death in the high .... Judg 5:18
with the *l* of thy household.............. Judg 18:25
lovely and pleasant in their *l*............ 2Sa 1:23
the *l* of thy sons and of thy............... 2Sa 19:5
the *l* of thy wives............................ 2Sa 19:5
and the *l* of thy concubines.............. 2Sa 19:5
that went in jeopardy of their *l* 2Sa 23:17
that have put their *l* in jeopardy....... 1Chr 11:19
that brought it 1Chr 11:19
together, and stood for their *l* .... Est 9:16
they lurk privily for their own *l*....... Prov 1:18
hands of them that seek their *l* .... Jer 19:7
and they that seek their *l*................. Jer 19:9
hand of those that seek their *l* .... Jer 46:26
Flee, save your *l*, and be like the ...... Jer 48:6
our *l* because of the sword of the...... Lam 5:9
yet their *l* were prolonged for a .... Dan 7:12
is not come to destroy men's *l* .... Lk 9:56
Men that have hazarded their *l*........ Acts 15:26
lading and ship, but also of our *l*...... Acts 27:10
lay down our *l* for the brethren......... 1Jn 3:16
loved not their *l* unto the death......... Rev 12:11

LIVEST
as long as thou *l* upon the earth......... Deut 12:19
as thou *l*, and as thy soul liveth,....... 2Sa 11:11
I after the manner of Gentiles,............ Gal 2:14
that thou hast a name that thou *l*....... Rev 3:1

LIVETH
that I shall be meat for you................ Gen 9:3
God with talk with man, and he *l*...... Deut 5:24

as the LORD *l*, if ye had saved .... Judg 8:19
a kinsman to thee, as the LORD *l* ...... Ruth 3:13
said, Oh my lord, as thy soul *l*.......... 1Sa 1:26
as long as he *l* he shall be lent 1Sa 1:28
For, as the LORD *l*, which saveth....... 1Sa 14:39
as the LORD *l*, there shall not........... 1Sa 14:45
And Abner said, As thy soul *l*........... 1Sa 17:55
and Saul sware, As the LORD *l*......... 1Sa 19:6
the LORD *l*, and as thy soul *l* 1Sa 20:3
as the LORD *l* 1Sa 20:21
son of Jesse *l* upon the ground......... 1Sa 20:31
say to him that *l* in prosperity.......... 1Sa 25:6
the LORD *l*, and as thy soul *l*......... 1Sa 25:26
deed, as the LORD God of Israel *l*...... 1Sa 25:34
said furthermore, As the LORD *l*....... 1Sa 26:10
As the LORD *l*, ye are worthy to......... 1Sa 26:16
the LORD, saying, As the LORD *l*....... 1Sa 28:10
unto him, Surely, as the LORD *l*....... 1Sa 29:6
And Joab said, As God *l*, unless....... 2Sa 2:27
and said unto them, As the LORD *l*... 2Sa 4:9
as thou livest, and as thy soul *l* 2Sa 11:11
he said to Nathan, As the LORD *l*...... 2Sa 12:5
And he said, As the LORD *l*.............. 2Sa 14:11
answered and said, As thy soul *l*...... 2Sa 14:19
the king, and said, As the LORD *l*..... 2Sa 15:21
and as my lord the king *l* 2Sa 15:21
The LORD *l* 2Sa 22:47
sware, and said, As the LORD *l*......... 1Kin 1:29
Now therefore, as the LORD *l*........... 1Kin 2:24
one saith, This is my son that *l*......... 1Kin 3:23
Ahab, As the LORD God of Israel *l*.... 1Kin 17:1
she said, As the LORD thy God *l*....... 1Kin 17:12
and Elijah said, See, thy son *l*.......... 1Kin 17:23
As the LORD thy God *l*, there is........ 1Kin 18:10
said, As the LORD of hosts *l*............. 1Kin 18:15
And Micaiah said, As the LORD *l*...... 1Kin 22:14
the LORD *l*, and as thy soul *l*......... 2Kin 2:2
the LORD *l*, and as thy soul *l*......... 2Kin 2:4
the LORD *l*, and as thy soul *l*......... 2Kin 2:6
said, As the LORD of hosts *l*............. 2Kin 3:14
the LORD *l*, and as thy soul *l*......... 2Kin 4:30
But he said, As the LORD *l* 2Kin 5:16
but, as the LORD *l*, I will run........... 2Kin 5:20
And Micaiah said, As the LORD *l*...... 2Chr 18:13
For I know that my redeemer *l*.......... Job 19:25
As God *l*, who hath taken away my ... Job 27:2
The LORD *l* .... Ps 18:46
What man is he that *l*, and shall....... Ps 89:48
And thou shalt swear, The LORD *l*..... Jer 4:2
And though they say, The LORD *l*...... Jer 5:2
to swear by my name, The LORD *l*..... Jer 12:16
shall no more be said, The LORD *l*.... Jer 16:14
But, The LORD *l*, that brought up...... Jer 16:15
shall no more say, The LORD *l* .... Jer 23:7
But, The LORD *l*, which brought up ... Jer 23:8
Jeremiah, saying, As the LORD *l*....... Jer 38:16
of Egypt, saying, The Lord GOD *l*..... Jer 44:26
to pass, that every thing that *l*......... Eze 47:9
and honoured him that *l* for ever....... Dan 4:34
sware by him that *l* for ever that....... Dan 12:7
Beth-aven, nor swear, The LORD *l*.... Hos 4:15
and say, Thy god, O Dan, *l*.............. Amos 8:14
and, The manner of Beer-sheba *l*...... Amos 8:14
thy son *l*....................................... Jn 4:50
and told him, saying, Thy son .... Jn 4:53
Jesus said unto him, Thy son .... Jn 4:53
And whosoever *l* and believeth in me . Jn 11:26
in that he *l*, he *l* unto God.............. Rom 6:10
over a man as long as he *l* .... Rom 7:1
to her husband so long as he *l*.......... Rom 7:2
So then if, while her husband *l*......... Rom 7:3
For none of us *l* to himself............... Rom 14:7
the law as long as her husband *l*....... 1Cor 7:39
yet he *l* by the power of God 2Cor 13:4
yet not I, but Christ *l* in me............. Gal 2:20
But she that *l* in pleasure is 1Ti 5:6
in pleasure is dead while she *l*......... 1Ti 5:6
of whom it is witnessed that he *l*...... Heb 7:8
by him, seeing he ever *l* to make...... Heb 7:25
at all while the testator *l*................. Heb 9:17
by the word of God, which *l*............. 1Pet 1:23
I am he that *l*, and was dead............. Rev 1:18
throne, who *l* for ever and ever,....... Rev 4:9
and worship him that *l* for ever .... Rev 4:10
and worshipped him that *l* for ever ... Rev 5:14
And sware by him that *l* for ever....... Rev 10:6
of God, who *l* for ever and ever .... Rev 15:7

LIVING
every *l* creature that moveth,............. Gen 1:21
the *l* creature after his kind.............. Gen 1:24
over every *l* thing that moveth.......... Gen 1:28
and man became a *l* soul.................. Gen 2:7
Adam called every *l* creature............ Gen 2:19
she was the mother of all *l* .... Gen 3:20
of every *l* thing of all flesh,.............. Gen 6:19
every *l* substance that I have............ Gen 7:4
every *l* substance was destroyed....... Gen 7:23
remembered Noah, and every *l* thing . Gen 8:1
every *l* thing that is with thee........... Gen 8:17
smite any more every thing *l*............ Gen 8:21
with every *l* creature that is .... Gen 9:10
every *l* creature that is with you .... Gen 9:12
every *l* creature of all flesh .... Gen 9:15
every *l* creature of all flesh .... Gen 9:16
of any *l* thing which is in the............ Lev 11:10
of every *l* creature that moveth........ Lev 11:46
As for the *l* bird, he shall take .... Lev 14:4
the *l* bird in the blood of the .... Lev 14:6
shall let the *l* bird loose into............ Lev 14:7
the *l* bird, and dip them in the .... Lev 14:51

running water, and with the *l* bird........... Lev 14:52
But he shall let go the *l* bird............... Lev 14:53
or by any manner of *l* thing that .... Lev 20:25
stood between the dead and the *l*...... Num 16:48
hath heard the voice of this *l* God......... Deut 5:26
know that the *l* God is among you ...... Josh 3:10
left off his kindness to the *l* .... Ruth 2:20
defy the armies of the *l* God.............. 1Sa 17:26
defied the armies of the *l* God............ 1Sa 17:36
of their death, *l* in widowhood........... 2Sa 20:3
but the *l* is my son, and the dead 1Kin 3:22
is thy son, and the *l* is my son 1Kin 3:22
is the dead, and my son is the *l* 1Kin 3:23
Divide the *l* child in two, and.......... 1Kin 3:25
the *l* child was unto the king........... 1Kin 3:26
O my lord, give her the *l* child 1Kin 3:26
and said, Give her the *l* child 1Kin 3:27
hath sent to reproach the *l* God 2Kin 19:4
sent him to reproach the *l* God 2Kin 19:16
hand is the soul of every *l* thing .... Job 12:10
is it found in the land of the *l* .... Job 28:13
it is hid from the eyes of all *l* .... Job 28:21
to the house appointed for all *l* .... Job 30:23
with the light of the *l* .... Job 33:30
of the LORD in the land of the *l* .... Ps 27:13
thirsteth for God, for the *l* God .... Ps 42:2
thee out of the land of the *l*........... Ps 52:5
before God in the light of the *l*.......... Ps 56:13
away as with a whirlwind, both *l* .... Ps 58:9
blotted out of the book of the *l* .... Ps 69:28
my flesh crieth out for the *l* God .... Ps 84:2
the LORD in the land of the *l*........... Ps 116:9
my portion in the land of the *l* .... Ps 142:5
sight shall no man *l* be justified .... Ps 143:2
the desire of every *l* thing.............. Ps 145:16
than the *l* which are yet alive .... Eccl 4:2
I considered all the *l* which walk......... Eccl 4:15
that knoweth to walk before the *l* .... Eccl 6:8
the *l* will lay it to his heart .... Eccl 7:2
joined to all the *l* there is hope.......... Eccl 9:4
for a *l* dog is better than a dead......... Eccl 9:4
For the *l* know that they shall .... Eccl 9:5
of gardens, a well of *l* waters........ Song 4:15
written among the *l* in Jerusalem........ Is 4:3
for the *l* to the dead .... Is 8:19
hath sent to reproach the *l* God......... Is 37:4
hath sent to reproach the *l* God......... Is 37:17
the LORD, in the land of the *l* .... Is 38:11
The *l*, the *l*, he shall .... Is 38:19
cut off out of the land of the *l*......... Is 53:8
me the foundation of *l* waters .... Jer 2:13
is the true God, he is the *l* God........ Jer 10:10
him off from the land of the *l*......... Jer 11:19
LORD, the fountain of *l* waters......... Jer 17:13
perverted the words of the *l* God....... Jer 23:36
Wherefore doth a *l* man complain ...... Lam 3:39
the likeness of four *l* creatures......... Eze 1:5
the likeness of the *l* creatures .... Eze 1:13
up and down among the *l* creatures ..... Eze 1:13
the *l* creatures ran and returned........ Eze 1:14
Now as I beheld the *l* creatures........ Eze 1:15
upon the earth by the *l* creatures....... Eze 1:15
when the *l* creatures went, the .... Eze 1:19
when the *l* creatures were lifted........ Eze 1:19
for the spirit of the *l* creature........ Eze 1:20
for the spirit of the *l* creature........ Eze 1:21
l creature was as the colour of .... Eze 1:22
the *l* creatures that touched one....... Eze 3:13
This is the *l* creature that I saw .... Eze 10:15
of the *l* creature was in them.......... Eze 10:17
This is the *l* creature that I saw .... Eze 10:20
set glory in the land of the *l*.......... Eze 26:20
terror in the land of the *l* .... Eze 32:23
their terror in the land of the *l* .... Eze 32:24
was caused in the land of the *l*........ Eze 32:25
their terror in the land of the *l* .... Eze 32:26
the mighty in the land of the *l*........ Eze 32:27
my terror in the land of the *l* .... Eze 32:32
that I have more than any *l* .... Dan 2:30
to the intent that the *l* may know ..... Dan 4:17
O Daniel, servant of the *l* God......... Dan 6:20
for he is the *l* God, and stedfast...... Dan 6:26
Ye are the sons of the *l* God.......... Hos 1:10
that *l* waters shall go out from .... Zec 14:8
the Christ, the Son of the *l* God....... Mt 16:16
the God of the dead, but of the *l*...... Mt 22:32
him, I adjure thee by the *l* God ...... Mt 26:63
of the dead, but the God of the *l*...... Mk 12:27
all that she had, even all her *l* .... Mk 12:44
spent all her *l* upon physicians .... Lk 8:43
And he divided unto them his *l*........ Lk 15:12
his substance with riotous *l* .... Lk 15:13
hath devoured thy *l* with harlots ...... Lk 15:30
a God of the dead, but of the *l*....... Lk 20:38
cast in all the *l* that she had.......... Lk 21:4
Why seek ye the *l* among the dead .... Lk 24:5
he would have given thee *l* water ...... Jn 4:10
then hast thou that *l* water............ Jn 4:11
I am the *l* bread which came down...... Jn 6:51
As the *l* Father hath sent me, and..... Jn 6:57
that Christ, the Son of the *l* God....... Jn 6:69
shall flow rivers of *l* water............. Jn 7:38
these vanities unto the *l* God.......... Acts 14:15
called the children of the *l* God......... Rom 9:26
present your bodies a *l* sacrifice....... Rom 12:1
be Lord both of the dead and *l* .... Rom 14:9
first man Adam was made a *l* soul..... 1Cor 15:45
but with the Spirit of the *l* God........ 2Cor 3:3
ye are the temple of the *l* God........ 2Cor 6:16
as though *l* in the world, are ye...... Col 2:20

to God from idols to serve the *l*......... 1Th 1:9
which is the church of the *l* God......... 1Ti 3:15
because we trust in the *l* God.......... 1Ti 4:10
riches, but in the *l* God, who........... 1Ti 6:17
I in malice and envy, hateful, and........ Titus 3:3
in departing from the *l* God............ Heb 3:12
dead works to serve the *l* God .... Heb 9:14
I way, which he hath consecrated......... Heb 10:20
fall into the hands of the *l* God........ Heb 10:31
and unto the city of the *l* God.......... Heb 12:22
To whom coming, as unto a *l* stone..... 1Pet 2:4
having the seal of the *l* God............ Rev 7:2
them unto *l* fountains of waters........ Rev 7:17
every *l* soul died in the sea............ Rev 16:3

LIZARD
and the chameleon, and the *l*.......... Lev 11:30

LO
and, *l*, in her mouth was an olive....... Gen 8:11
and, *l*, one born in my house is......... Gen 15:3
and, *l*, an horror of great.............. Gen 15:12
lift up his eyes and looked, and, *l*...... Gen 18:2
and, *l*, Sarah thy wife shall have....... Gen 18:10
of the plain, and beheld, and, *l*........ Gen 19:28
behold a well in the field, and, *l*....... Gen 29:2
And he said, *l*, it is yet high day....... Gen 29:7
sheaves in the field, and, *l*............ Gen 37:7
and, *l*, it is even in my sack .... Gen 42:28
l, here is seed for you, and ye......... Gen 47:23
and, *l*, God hath shewed me also....... Gen 48:11
father made me swear, saying, *l*....... Gen 50:5
l, he goeth out unto the water .... Ex 7:15
l, he cometh forth to the water .... Ex 8:20
l, shall we sacrifice the.............. Ex 8:26
And the LORD said unto Moses, *L*....... Ex 19:9
top of the mountain, saying, *L*........ Num 14:40
And Balaam said unto Balak, *L*......... Num 22:38
And he returned unto him and, *l*....... Num 23:6
l, the people shall dwell alone........ Num 23:9
but, *l*, the LORD hath kept thee........ Num 24:11
And, *l*, he hath given occasions of..... Deut 22:17
and now, *l*, I am this day............. Josh 14:10
Behold, I dreamed a dream, and, *l*..... Judg 7:13
For, *l*, thou shalt conceive, and....... Judg 13:5
And when he came, *l*, Eli sat upon 1Sa 4:13
and, *l*, thy father hath left the........ 1Sa 10:2
rod that was in mine hand, and, *l*..... 1Sa 14:43
said Achish unto his servants, *L*....... 1Sa 21:14
and, *l*, the chariots and horsemen..... 2Sa 1:6
l Zadok also, and all the Levites...... 2Sa 15:24
that smote the people, and said, *L*..... 2Sa 24:17
And, *l*, while she yet talked with...... 1Kin 1:22
for, *l*, he hath caught hold on........ 1Kin 1:51
l, I have given thee a wise and an.... 1Kin 3:12
and they said one to another, *L*....... 2Kin 7:6
and, *l*, all the way was full of 2Kin 7:15
said to Nathan the prophet, *L*........ 1Chr 17:1
l, I give thee the oxen also for....... 1Chr 21:23
the acts of Asa, first and last, *l*...... 2Chr 16:11
Thou sayest, *L*, thou hast smitten 2Chr 25:19
and all his wars, and his ways, *l*..... 2Chr 27:7
For, *l*, our fathers have fallen......... 2Chr 29:9
and, *l* we bring into bondage our...... Neh 5:5
And, *l*, I perceived that God had...... Neh 6:12
l, let that night be solitary .... Job 3:7
L this, we have searched it, so....... Job 5:27
L, he goeth by me, and I see him..... Job 9:11
If I speak of strength, *l*............. Job 9:19
l, mine eye hath seen all this........ Job 13:1
l, their good is not in their......... Job 21:16
l, these are parts of his ways........ Job 26:14
l, all these things worketh God...... Job 33:29
l now, his strength is in his......... Job 40:16
For, *l*, the wicked bend their bow..... Ps 11:2
Yet he passed away, and, *l*.......... Ps 37:36
Then said I, *L*, I come .... Ps 40:7
l, I have not refrained my lips....... Ps 40:9
For, *l*, the kings were assembled..... Ps 48:4
l, this is the man that made not..... Ps 52:7
l, then would I wander far off........ Ps 55:7
For, *l*, they lie in wait for my....... Ps 59:3
l, he doth send out his voice, and.... Ps 68:33
For, *l*, they that are far from........ Ps 73:27
For, *l*, thine enemies make a .... Ps 83:2
l, thine enemies, O LORD, for........ Ps 92:9
l, children are an heritage of .... Ps 127:3
l, we heard of it at Ephratah .... Ps 132:6
not a word in my tongue, but, *l*...... Ps 139:4
And, *l*, it was all grown over with.... Prov 24:31
with mine own heart, saying, *L*...... Eccl 1:16
L, this only have I found, that....... Eccl 7:29
For, *l*, the winter is past, the........ Song 2:11
laid it upon my mouth, and said, *L*... Is 6:7
it shall be said in that day, *L*....... Is 25:9
l, thou trustest in the staff of ...... Is 36:6
and, *l*, these from the north and..... Is 49:12
l, they all shall wax old as a........ Is 50:9
For, *l*, I will call all the........... Jer 1:15
I beheld the earth, and, *l*........... Jer 4:23
I beheld the mountains, and, *l*....... Jer 4:24
I beheld, and, *l*, there was no man.... Jer 4:25
I beheld, and, *l*, the fruitful........ Jer 4:26
L, I will bring a nation upon you .... Jer 5:15
L, certainly in vain made he it....... Jer 8:8
l, they have rejected the word of.... Jer 8:9
For, *l*, I begin to bring evil on...... Jer 25:29
For, *l*, the days come, saith the...... Jer 30:3
for, *l*, I will save thee from......... Jer 30:10
and, *l*, all the princes sat there,..... Jer 36:12
For, *l*, I will make thee small........ Jer 49:15

For, *l*, I will raise and cause to......... Jer 50:9
and, *l*, a roll of a book was........... Eze 2:9
Then he said unto me, *L*, I have .... Eze 4:15
a likeness as the appearance of......... Eze 8:2
and, *l*, they put the branch to........ Eze 8:17
and one built up a wall, and, *l*....... Eze 13:10
L, when the wall is fallen, shall...... Eze 13:12
by breaking the covenant, when, *l*..... Eze 17:18
Now, *l*, if he beget a son, that....... Eze 18:14
is not good among his people, *l*....... Eze 18:18
and, *l*, thus have they done in the.... Eze 23:39
and, *l*, they came .... Eze 23:40
for, *l*, it cometh .... Eze 30:9
and, *l*, it shall not be bound up...... Eze 30:21
And, *l*, thou art unto them as a....... Eze 33:32
And when this cometh to pass, (*l*...... Eze 33:33
and, *l*, they were very dry............ Eze 37:2
And when I beheld, *l*, the sinews...... Eze 37:8
me into the outward court, and, *l*..... Eze 40:17
and, *l*, before the temple were an..... Eze 42:8
He answered and said, *L*, I see....... Dan 3:25
I another, like a leopard, which .... Dan 7:6
but, *l*, Michael, one of the chief ..... Dan 10:13
and when I am gone forth, *l*......... Dan 10:20
For, *l*, they are gone because of..... Hos 9:6
sworn by his holiness, that, *l*....... Amos 4:2
For, *l*, he that formeth the.......... Amos 4:13
and, *l*, it was the latter growth..... Amos 7:1
For, *l*, I will command, and I will ... Amos 9:9
For, *l*, I raise up the Chaldeans,..... Hab 1:6
Ye looked for much, and, *l*.......... Hag 1:9
for, *l*, I come, and I will dwell...... Zec 2:10
but, *l*, I will deliver thee unto...... Zec 11:16
For, *l*, I will raise up a............ Zec 11:16
l the star, which they saw.......... Mt 2:9
and, *l*, the heavens were opened..... Mt 3:16
I a voice from heaven, saying,........ Mt 3:17
if any man shall say unto you, *L*.... Mt 24:23
l, there thou hast that is thine..... Mt 25:25
And while he yet spake, *l*, Judas.... Mt 26:47
L, I have told you .... Mt 28:7
and, *l*, I am with you alway, even ... Mt 28:20
Peter began to say unto him, *L*..... Mk 10:28
if any man shall say to you, *L*...... Mk 13:21
or, *l*, he is there .... Mk 13:21
l, he that betrayeth me is at....... Mk 14:42
For, *l*, as soon as the voice of...... Lk 1:44
And, *l*, the angel of the Lord came.... Lk 2:9
And, *l*, a spirit taketh him, and he.... Lk 9:39
Abraham, whom Satan hath bound, *l*... Lk 13:16
answering said to his father, *L*....... Lk 15:29
Neither shall they say, *L* here .... Lk 17:21
or, *l* there .... Lk 17:21
Then Peter said, *L*, we have left..... Lk 18:28
and, *l*, nothing worthy of death is ... Lk 23:15
But, *l*, he speaketh boldly, and ..... Jn 7:26
His disciples said unto him, *L*....... Jn 16:29
unworthy of everlasting life, *l*...... Acts 13:46
and, *l*, God hath given thee all ..... Acts 27:24
Then said I, *L*, I come (in the....... Heb 10:7
Then said he, *L*, I come to do thy ... Heb 10:9
And I beheld, and, *l*, in the midst ... Rev 5:6
And I beheld, and *l* a black horse .... Rev 6:5
had opened the sixth seal, and, *l*.... Rev 6:12
After this I beheld, and, *l*.......... Rev 7:9
And I looked, and, *l*, a Lamb stood ... Rev 14:1

LOADEN
your carriages were heavy *l*............ Is 46:1

LOADETH
who daily *l* us with benefits,.......... Ps 68:19

LOAF
one *l* of bread, and one cake of .... Ex 29:23
to women, to every one a *l* of bread ... 1Chr 16:3
ship with them more than one *l*........ Mk 8:14

LO-AMMI (*lo-am'-mi*) Symbolic name meaning
'Not My People.'
Then said God, Call his name *L*....... Hos 1:9

LOAN
the *l* which is lent to the LORD 1Sa 2:20

LOATHE
I *l* it .... Job 7:16

LOATHETH
our soul *l* this light bread............ Num 21:5
The full soul *l* an honeycomb......... Prov 27:7

LOATHSOME
nostrils, and it be *l* unto you.......... Num 11:20
my skin is broken, and become *l*....... Job 7:5
loins are filled with a *l* disease........ Ps 38:7
but a wicked man is *l*, and cometh..... Prov 13:5

LOAVES
two waves *l* of two tenth deals........ Lev 23:17
l of bread unto the people that........ Judg 8:5
another carrying three *l* of bread 1Sa 10:3
thee, and give thee two *l* of bread 1Sa 10:4
this parched corn, and these ten *l*..... 1Sa 17:17
give me five *l* of bread in mine 1Sa 21:3
made haste, and took two hundred *l*... 1Sa 25:18
upon them two hundred *l* of bread 2Sa 16:1
And take with thee ten *l*, and........ 1Kin 14:3
twenty *l* of barley, and full ears...... 2Kin 4:42
unto him, We have here but five *l*..... Mt 14:17
on the grass, and took the five *l*...... Mt 14:19
gave the *l* to his disciples, and...... Mt 14:19
unto them, How many *l* have ye ...... Mt 15:34
And he took the seven *l* and the...... Mt 15:36

LOCK

the five *l* of the five thousand .... Mt 16:9
Neither the seven *l* of the four .... Mt 16:10
unto them, How many *l* have ye............. Mk 6:38
And when he had taken the five *l* .... Mk 6:41
and blessed, and brake the *l* .... Mk 6:41
they that did eat of the *l* were................. Mk 6:44
not the miracle of the *l* .... Mk 6:52
he asked them, How many *l* have ye...... Mk 8:5
and he took the seven *l*, and gave .... Mk 8:6
the five *l* among five thousand............... Mk 8:19
said, We have no more but five *l* .... Lk 9:13
Then he took the five *l* and the .... Lk 9:16
unto him, Friend, lend me three *l* .... Lk 11:5
here, which hath five barley *l* .... Jn 6:9
And Jesus took the *l* .... Jn 6:11
fragments of the five barley *l* .... Jn 6:13
but because ye did eat of the *l* .... Jn 6:26

LOCK

myrrh, upon the handles of the *l*............. Song 5:5
and took me by a *l* of mine head........... Eze 8:3

LOCKED

the parlour upon him, and *l* them........... Judg 3:23
the doors of the parlour were *l* .... Judg 3:24

LOCKS

shall let the *l* of the hair of.................... Num 6:5
seven *l* of my head with the web .... Judg 16:13
shave off the seven *l* of his head .... Judg 16:19
the *l* thereof, and the bars..................... Neh 3:3
the *l* thereof, and the bars..................... Neh 3:6
the *l* thereof, and the bars..................... Neh 3:13
the *l* thereof, and the bars..................... Neh 3:14
the *l* thereof, and the bars..................... Neh 3:15
hast doves' eyes within thy *l* .... Song 4:1
of a pomegranate within thy *l* .... Song 4:3
my *l* with the drops of the night............ Song 5:2
his *l* are bushy, and black as a .... Song 5:11
are thy temples within thy *l* .... Song 6:7
uncover thy *l*, make bare the leg, ... Is 47:2
nor suffer their *l* to grow long............... Eze 44:20

LOCUST

there remained not one *l* in all .... Ex 10:19
the *l* after his kind, and the bald .... Lev 11:22
the bald *l* after his kind, and the.......... Lev 11:22
for the *l* shall consume *h* .... Deut 28:38
of thy land shall the *l* consume .... Deut 28:42
pestilence, blasting, mildew, *l* 1Kin 8:37
and their labour unto the *l* .... Ps 78:46
I am tossed up and down as the *l*.......... Ps 109:23
hath left hath the *l* eaten........................ Joel 1:4
that which the *l* hath left hath............... Joel 1:4
the years that the *l* hath eaten.............. Joel 2:25

LOCUSTS

will I bring the *l* into thy coast............... Ex 10:4
over the land of Egypt for the *l*.............. Ex 10:12
the east wind brought the *l* .... Ex 10:13
the *l* went up over all the land .... Ex 10:14
them there were no such *l* as they .... Ex 10:14
west wind, which took away the *l* .... Ex 10:19
there be blasting, or mildew, *l* 2Chr 6:28
command the *l* to devour the land 2Chr 7:13
the *l* came, and caterpillars, and .... Ps 105:34
The *l* have no king, yet go they............. Prov 30:27
the *l* shall he run upon them.................. Is 33:4
make thyself many as the *l* .... Nah 3:15
Thy crowned are as the *l*, and thy .... Nah 3:17
and his meat was *l* and wild honey........ Mt 3:4
and he did eat *l* and wild honey............ Mk 1:6
out of the smoke *l* upon the earth.......... Rev 9:3
the shapes of the *l* were like.................. Rev 9:7

LOD A city in Benjamin.

and Shamed, who built Ono, and *L* 1Chr 8:12
The children of *L*, Hadid, and Ono, ... Ezr 2:33
The children of *L*, Hadid, and Ono, ... Neh 7:37
L, and Ono, the valley of .... Neh 11:35

LO-DEBAR (lo-de'-bar) A city in Manasseh.

Machir, the son of Ammiel, in *L*............. 2Sa 9:4
Machir, the son of Ammiel, from *L*......... 2Sa 9:5
and Machir the son of Ammiel of *L*....... 2Sa 17:27

LODGE

thy father's house for us to *l* in............. Gen 24:23
provender enough, and room to *l* in...... Gen 24:25
L here this night, and I will.................... Num 22:8
where ye shall *l* this night .... Josh 4:3
l here, that thine heart may be .... Judg 19:9
city of the Jebusites, and *l* in .... Judg 19:11
of these places to *l* all night.................. Judg 19:13
to go in and to *l* in Gibeah.................... Judg 19:15
only *l* not in the street .... Judg 19:20
Benjamin, I and my concubine, to *l* .... Judg 20:4
and where thou lodgest, I will *l* .... Ruth 1:16
will not *l* with the people........................ 2Sa 17:8
L not this night in the plains of 2Sa 17:16
his servant I within Jerusalem.................. Neh 4:22
them, Why *l* ye about the wall............... Neh 13:21
the naked to *l* without clothing .... Job 24:7
stranger did not *l* in the street............... Job 31:32
let us *l* in the villages............................ Song 7:11
as a *l* in a garden of cucumbers,.......... Is 1:8
the forest in Arabia shall ye *l* .... Is 21:13
l in the monuments, which eat .... Is 65:4
thy vain thoughts *l* within thee .... Jer 4:14
the bittern shall *l* in the upper .... Zeph 2:14
l in the branches thereof....................... Mt 13:32
air may *l* under the shadow of it........... Mk 4:32
and country round about, and *l*.............. Lk 9:12
disciple, with whom we should *l*............ Acts 21:16

LODGED (column 2)

he *l* there that same night...................... Gen 32:13
himself *l* that night in the...................... Gen 32:21
house, named Rahab, and *l* there .... Josh 2:1
I there before they passed over .... Josh 3:1
them unto the place where they *l* .... Josh 4:8
into the camp, and *l* in the camp .... Josh 6:11
but Joshua *l* that night among the......... Josh 8:9
the house of Micah, they *l* there .... Judg 18:2
they did eat and drink, and *l* there .... Judg 19:4
therefore he *l* there again....................... Judg 19:7
thither unto a cave, and *l* there 1Kin 19:9
they *l* round about the house of 1Chr 9:27
sellers of all kind of ware *l* .... Neh 13:20
righteousness *l* in it .... Is 1:21
and he *l* there .... Mt 21:17
the fowls of the air *l* in the................... Lk 13:19
was surnamed Peter, were *l* there .... Acts 10:18
Then called he them in, and *l* them ...... Acts 10:23
he is *l* in the house of one Simon .... Acts 10:32
l us three days courteously .... Acts 28:7
children, if she have *l* strangers............. 1Ti 5:10

LODGEST

and where thou *l*, I will lodge .... Ruth 1:16

LODGETH

He *l* with one Simon a tanner,................ Acts 10:6

LODGING

you, and leave them in the *l* place .... Josh 4:3
took them into his house to *l* .... Judg 19:15
have taken up their *l* at Geba................ Is 10:29
a *l* place of wayfaring men...................... Jer 9:2
there came many to him into his *l* .... Acts 28:23
But withal prepare me also a *l* .... Philem 22

LODGINGS

enter into the *l* of his borders................. 2Kin 19:23

LOFT

l bosom, and carried him up into a *l*.... 1Kin 17:19
and fell down from the third *l* .... Acts 20:9

LOFTILY

they speak *l*... Ps 73:8

LOFTINESS

the *l* of man shall be bowed down, ... Is 2:17
(he is exceeding proud) his *l* .... Jer 48:29

LOFTY

is not haughty, nor mine eyes *l*.............. Ps 131:1
O how I are their eyes .... Prov 30:13
The *l* looks of man shall be .... Is 2:11
upon every one that is proud and *l*......... Is 2:12
the eyes of the *l* shall be....................... Is 5:15
the *l* city, he layeth it low....................... Is 26:5
Upon a *l* and high mountain hast.......... Is 57:7
l One that inhabiteth eternity,................. Is 57:15

LOG

mingled with oil, and one *l* of oil........... Lev 14:10
the *l* of oil, and wave them for a............ Lev 14:12
shall take some of the *l* of oil................. Lev 14:15
a meat offering, and a *l* of oil................ Lev 14:21
of the oil, and the priest shall .... Lev 14:24

LOINS

kings shall come out of thy *l*.................. Gen 35:11
and put sackcloth upon his *l*................... Gen 37:34
Egypt, which came out of his *l*............... Gen 46:26
the *l* of Jacob were seventy souls .... Ex 1:5
with your *l* girded, your shoes on........... Ex 12:11
from the *l* even unto the thighs.............. Ex 28:42
smite through the *l* of them that .... Deut 33:11
upon his *l* in the sheath thereof............ 2Sa 20:8
his girdle that was about his *l* 1Kin 2:5
shall come forth out of thy *l* 1Kin 8:19
be thicker than my father's *l* 1Kin 12:10
and he girded up his *l*, and ran............. 1Kin 18:46
pray thee, put sackcloth on our *l* 1Kin 20:31
they girded sackcloth on their *l* 1Kin 20:32
a girdle of leather about his *l* 2Kin 1:8
he said to Gehazi, Gird up thy *l* 2Kin 4:29
and saith unto him, Gird up thy *l* 2Kin 9:1
shall come forth out of thy *l* 2Chr 6:9
be thicker than my father's *l* 2Chr 10:10
and girdeth their *l* with a girdle............. Job 12:18
If his *l* have not blessed me, and .... Job 31:20
Gird up now thy *l* like a man .... Job 38:3
Gird up thy *l* now like a man................. Job 40:7
Lo now, his strength is in his *l* .... Job 40:16
For my *l* are filled with a .... Ps 38:7
thou laidst affliction upon our *l*.............. Ps 66:11
make their *l* continually to shake........... Ps 69:23
She girdeth her *l* with strength............... Prov 31:17
the girdle of their *l* be loosed................ Is 5:27
shall be the girdle of his *l* .... Is 11:5
the sackcloth from off thy *l* .... Is 20:2
are my *l* filled with pain......................... Is 21:3
and gird sackcloth upon your *l* .... Is 32:11
and will *l* loose the *l* of kings............... Is 45:1
Thou therefore gird up thy *l* .... Jer 1:17
girdle, and put it upon thy *l* .... Jer 13:1
of the Lord, and put it on thy *l*.............. Jer 13:2
hast got, which is upon thy *l* .... Jer 13:4
girdle cleaveth to the *l* of a man........... Jer 13:11
every man with his hands on his *l* .... Jer 30:6
cuttings, and upon the *l* sackcloth .... Jer 48:37
appearance of his *l* even upward .... Eze 1:27
appearance of his *l* even downward....... Eze 1:27
appearance of his *l* even downward....... Eze 8:2
from his *l* even upward, as the.............. Eze 8:2
man, with the breaking of thy *l* .... Eze 21:6

LONG

Girded with girdles upon their *l*.............. Eze 23:15
all their *l* to be at a stand...................... Eze 29:7
have linen breeches upon their *l* .... Eze 44:18
the waters were to the *l* .... Eze 47:4
the joints of his *l* were loosed................ Dan 5:6
whose *l* were girded with fine .... Dan 10:5
bring up sackcloth upon all *l* .... Amos 8:10
watch the way, make thy *l* strong .... Nah 2:1
and much pain is in all *l* .... Nah 2:10
and a leathern girdle about his *l*............ Mt 3:4
a girdle of a skin about his *l*.................. Mk 1:6
Let your *l* be girded about, and .... Lk 12:35
him, that of the fruit of his *l*.................. Acts 2:30
having your *l* girt about with .... Eph 6:14
they come out of the *l* of Abraham........ Heb 7:5
he was yet in the *l* of his father .... Heb 7:10
gird up the *l* of your mind 1Pet 1:13

LOIS (lo'-is) Grandmother of Timothy.

dwelt first in thy grandmother *L* 2Ti 1:5

LONG

when he had been there a *l* time .... Gen 26:8
me all my life *l* unto this day .... Gen 48:15
How *l* wilt thou refuse to humble .... Ex 10:3
How *l* shall this man be a snare .... Ex 10:7
How *l* refuse ye to keep my................... Ex 16:28
when the trumpet soundeth *l* .... Ex 19:13
How *l* refuse ye to keep my................... Ex 16:28
that thy days may be *l* upon the .... Ex 20:12
of shittim wood, five cubits *l* .... Ex 27:1
an hundred cubits *l* for one side .... Ex 27:9
hangings of an hundred cubits *l* .... Ex 27:11
as *l* as she is put apart for her .... Lev 18:19
as *l* as it lieth desolate, and ye .... Lev 26:34
As *l* as it lieth desolate *l* .... Lev 26:35
Let us the cloud abode upon the.............. Num 9:18
when the cloud tarried *l* upon the......... Num 9:19
How *l* will this people provoke me .... Num 14:11
now *l* will it be ere they believe .... Num 14:11
How *l* shall I bear with this evil............. Num 14:27
we have dwelt in Egypt a *l* time .... Num 20:15
Ye have dwelt *l* enough in this............... Deut 1:6
compassed this mountain *l* enough .... Deut 2:3
shall have remained *l* in the land.......... Deut 4:25
l as thou livest upon the earth............... Deut 12:19
And if the way be too *l* for thee .... Deut 14:24
him, because the way is *l* .... Deut 19:6
shalt besiege a city a *l* time................... Deut 20:19
longing for them all the day *l* .... Deut 28:32
of *l* continuance, and sore..................... Deut 28:59
sicknesses, and of *l* continuance .... Deut 28:59
as *l* as ye live in the land .... Deut 31:13
shall cover him all the day *l* .... Deut 33:12
that when they make a *l* blast .... Josh 6:5
by reason of the very *l* journey.............. Josh 9:13
Joshua made war a *l* time with all .... Josh 11:18
How *l* are ye slack to go to.................... Josh 18:3
it came to pass a *l* time after .... Josh 23:1
in the wilderness a *l* season.................. Josh 24:7
Why is his chariot so *l* in coming.......... Judg 5:28
How *l* wilt thou be drunken.................... 1Sa 1:14
as *l* as he liveth he shall be................... 1Sa 1:28
that the time was *l* 1Sa 7:2
How *l* wilt thou mourn for Saul............. 1Sa 16:1
For as *l* as the son of Jesse................... 1Sa 20:31
as *l* as we were conversant with............ 1Sa 25:15
thou found in thy servant so *l* as 1Sa 29:6
how *l* shall it be then, ere thou............. 2Sa 2:26
Now there was *l* war between the 2Sa 3:1
had a *l* time mourned for the dead........ 2Sa 14:2
How *l* have I to live, that I.................... 2Sa 19:34
hast not asked for thyself *l* life 1Kin 3:11
before it, was forty cubits *l* 1Kin 6:17
How *l* halt ye between two.................... 1Kin 18:21
so *l* as the whoredoms of thy 2Kin 9:22
Hast thou not heard *l* ago how *l* 2Kin 19:25
neither yet hast asked *l* life 2Chr 1:11
cherubims were twenty cubits *l* 2Chr 3:11
brasen scaffold, of five cubits *l*.............. 2Chr 6:13
so *l* as they live in the land 2Chr 6:31
Now for a *l* season Israel hath 2Chr 15:3
as *l* as he sought the Lord, God............. 2Chr 26:5
a *l* time in such sort as it was 2Chr 30:5
for as *l* as she lay desolate she 2Chr 36:21
For how shall thy journey be.................... Neh 2:6
so *l* as I see Mordecai the Jew .... Est 5:13
Which *l* for death, but it cometh .... Job 3:21
grant me the thing that I *l* for .... Job 6:8
How *l* wilt thou not depart from .... Job 7:19
How *l* wilt thou speak these .... Job 8:2
how *l* shall the words of thy .... Job 8:2
How *l* will it be ere ye make an .... Job 18:2
How *l* will ye vex my soul, and .... Job 19:2
not reproach me so *l* as I live................ Job 27:6
how *l* will ye turn my glory into............ Ps 4:2
how *l* will ye love vanity, and............... Ps 4:2
but thou, O Lord, how *l*......................... Ps 6:3
How *l* wilt thou forget me, O Lord........ Ps 13:1
how *l* wilt thou hide thy face .... Ps 13:1
How *l* shall I take counsel in my........... Ps 13:2
how *l* shall mine enemy be exalted ...... Ps 13:2
through my roaring all the day *l* .... Ps 32:3
Lord, how *l* wilt thou look on............... Ps 35:17
and of thy praise all the day *l* .... Ps 35:28
I go mourning all the day *l* .... Ps 38:6
and imagine deceits all the day *l*........... Ps 38:12
In God we boast all the day *l* .... Ps 44:8
sake are we killed all the day *l* .... Ps 44:22
How *l* will ye imagine mischief .... Ps 62:3
thy righteousness all the day *l* .... Ps 71:24

shall fear thee as *l* as the sun .... Ps 72:5
peace so *l* as the moon endureth .... Ps 72:7
be continued as *l* as the sun .... Ps 72:17
For all the day I have I been........................ Ps 73:14
among us any that knoweth how *l* .... Ps 74:9
how *l* shall the adversary .... Ps 74:10
How *l*, LORD .... Ps 79:5
how *l* wilt thou be angry against .... Ps 80:4
How *l* will ye judge unjustly, and............... Ps 82:2
How *l*, LORD₂.. Ps 89:46
Return, O LORD, how *l* .... Ps 90:13
With I life will I satisfy him......................... Ps 91:16
how *l* shall the wicked................................. Ps 94:3
how *l* shall the wicked triumph.................. Ps 94:3
How *l* shall they utter and speak............... Ps 94:4
Forty years I was I grieved with .... Ps 95:10
sing unto the LORD as I as I live .... Ps 104:33
I call upon him as I as I live .... Ps 116:2
My soul hath *l* dwelt with him................... Ps 120:6
they made I their furrows............................. Ps 129:3
as those that have been I dead.................... Ps 143:3
How *l*, ye simple ones, will ye .... Prov 1:22
l life, and peace, shall they add .... Prov 3:2
How *l* wilt thou sleep, O sluggard............ Prov 6:9
at home, he is gone a I journey.................... Prov 7:19
coveteth greedily all the day I...................... Prov 21:26
fear of the LORD all the day I .... Prov 23:17
They that tarry *l* at the wine .... Prov 23:30
By *l* forbearing is a prince .... Prov 25:15
because man goeth to his *l* home............... Eccl 12:5
Then said I, Lord, how *l*............................. Is 6:11
unto him that fashioned it I ago .... Is 22:11
Hast thou not heard I ago .... Is 37:26
I have I time holden my peace .... Is 42:14
mine elect shall I enjoy the work .... Is 65:22
How *l* shall I vain thoughts .... Jer 4:14
How *l* shall I see the standard .... Jer 4:21
how *l* shall the land mourn, and .... Jer 12:4
How *l* shall this be in the heart .... Jer 23:26
saying, This captivity is *l* .... Jer 29:28
How *l* wilt thou go about, O thou .... Jer 31:22
how *l* wilt thou cut thyself........................ Jer 47:5
how *l* will it be ere thou be....................... Jer 47:6

fruit, and children of a span *l* .... Lam 2:20
for ever, and forsake us so *l* time............. Lam 5:20
his branches became I because of .... Eze 31:5
reed of six cubits I by the cubit .... Eze 40:5
little chamber was one reed *l*..................... Eze 40:7
it was fifty cubits *l*, and five and............... Eze 40:29
were five and twenty cubits *l*..................... Eze 40:30
it was fifty cubits *l*, and five and............... Eze 40:33
offering, of a cubit and an half *l*.............. Eze 40:42
the court, an hundred cubits *l*................... Eze 40:47
the house, an hundred cubits *l*.................. Eze 41:13
thereof, an hundred cubits *l*...................... Eze 41:13
as I as they, and as broad as they .... Eze 42:11
round about, five hundred reeds *l* .... Eze 42:20
altar shall be twelve cubits *l*..................... Eze 43:16
settle shall be fourteen cubits *l*................ Eze 43:17
nor suffer their locks to grow *l* .... Eze 44:20
and five and twenty thousand *l* .... Eze 45:6
courts joined of forty cubits *l*................... Eze 46:22
How *l* shall be the vision........................... Dan 8:13
but the time appointed was *l* .... Dan 10:1
How *l* shall it be to the end of.................. Dan 12:6
how *l* will it be ere they attain................. Hos 8:5
for he should not stay *l* in.......................... Hos 13:13
how *l* shall I cry, and thou wilt .... Hab 1:2
which is not *l* but how *l*........................... Hab 2:6
how *l* wilt thou not have mercy on .... Zec 1:12
as I as the bridegroom is with .... Mt 9:15
have repented I ago in sackcloth................. Mt 11:21
how *l* shall I be with you............................ Mt 17:17
how *l* shall I suffer you .... Mt 17:17
and for a pretence make I prayer .... Mt 23:14
After a I time the lord of those .... Mt 25:19
as I as they have the bridegroom................ Mk 2:19
how *l* shall I be with you............................ Mk 9:19
how *l* shall I suffer you .... Mk 9:19
How *l* is it ago since this came.................. Mk 9:21
which love to go in *l* clothing .... Mk 12:38
and for a pretence make I prayers.............. Mk 12:40
clothed in a I white garment .... Mk 16:5
he tarried so *l* in the temple .... Lk 1:21
man, which had devils I time .... Lk 8:27
how *l* shall I be with you............................ Lk 9:41
him, though he had I time with .... Lk 18:7
into a far country for a I time....................... Lk 20:9
which desire to walk in I robes .... Lk 20:46
and for a shew make I prayers...................... Lk 20:47
desirous to see him of a I season .... Lk 23:8
been now a I time in that case .... Jn 5:6
As I as I am in the world, I am .... Jn 9:5
How *l* dost thou make us to doubt .... Jn 10:24
Have I been so I time with you.................... Jn 14:9
because that of I time he had .... Acts 8:11
I, time therefore abode they .... Acts 14:3
there they abode I time with the .... Acts 14:28
and as Paul was I preaching......................... Acts 20:9
and talked a I while .... Acts 20:11
But not I after there arose............................ Acts 27:14
But after I abstinence Paul stood................ Acts 27:21
For I I to see you, that I may........................ Rom 1:11
over a man as I as he liveth.......................... Rom 7:1
to her husband so I as he liveth.................. Rom 7:2
sake we are killed all the day I .... Rom 8:36
All day I I have stretched forth .... Rom 10:21
law as I as her husband liveth..................... 1Cor 7:39
you, that, if a man have I hair 1Cor 11:14
But if a woman have I hair 1Cor 11:15

Charity suffereth *l*, and is kind................. 1Cor 13:4
which I after you for the 2Cor 9:14
as I as he is a child, differeth .... Gal 4:1
thou mayest live I on the earth................... Eph 6:3
how greatly I I after you all in..................... Phil 1:8
But if I tarry *l*, that thou............................ 1Ti 3:15
David, To day, after so I a time................... Heb 4:7
hath I patience for it, until he .... Jas 5:7
as I as ye do well, and are not 1Pet 3:6
as I as I am in this tabernacle,.................... 2Pet 1:13
now of a I time lingereth not 2Pet 2:3
with a loud voice, saying, How *l*.............. Rev 6:10

LONGED

the soul of king David I to go 2Sa 13:39
And David I, and said, Oh that one............ 2Sa 23:15
And David I, and said, Oh that one............ 1Chr 11:17
I have I after thy precepts........................... Ps 119:40
for I I for thy commandments .... Ps 119:131
I have I for thy salvation, O......................... Ps 119:174
For he I after you all, and was.................... Phil 2:26
I for, my joy and crown, so stand .... Phil 4:1

LONGEDST

because thou sore I after thy .... Gen 31:30

LONGER

And when she could not I hide him............. Ex 2:3
let you go, and ye shall stay no *l*............... Ex 9:28
any I stand before their enemies................ Judg 2:14
but he tarried I than the set......................... 2Sa 20:5
should I wait for the LORD any *l* 2Kin 6:33
thereof is I than the earth .... Job 11:9
So that the LORD could no I bear .... Jer 44:22
for thou mayest be no I steward .... Lk 16:2
him to tarry I time with them...................... Acts 18:20
that he ought not to live any *l* .... Acts 25:24
dead to sin, live any I therein..................... Rom 6:2
we are no I under a schoolmaster .... Gal 3:25
when we could no I forbear.......................... 1Th 3:1
cause, when I could no I forbear 1Th 3:5
Drink no I water, but use a.......................... 1Ti 5:23
That he no I should live the rest................. 1Pet 4:2
that there should be time no I .... Rev 10:6

LONGETH

son Shechem I for your daughter................ Gen 34:8
because thy soul I for eat flesh .... Deut 12:20
my flesh I for thee in a dry and .... Ps 63:1
My soul I, yea, even fainteth for .... Ps 84:2

LONGING

fail with I for them all the day .... Deut 28:32
For he satisfieth the I soul........................... Ps 107:9
My soul breaketh for the I that................... Ps 119:20

LONGSUFFERING

LORD God, merciful and gracious, *l*.......... Ex 34:6
The LORD is I, and of great mercy,.............. Num 14:18
of compassion, and gracious, *l*.................. Ps 86:15
take me not away in thy *l*.......................... Jer 15:15
his goodness and forbearance and *l*......... Rom 2:4
endured with much I the vessels .... Rom 9:22
By pureness, by knowledge, by *l* 2Cor 6:6
the Spirit is love, joy, peace, *l*................... Gal 5:22
all lowliness and meekness, with *l*........... Eph 4:2
all patience and I with joyfulness .... Col 1:11
humbleness of mind, meekness, *l* .... Col 3:12
Christ might shew forth all *l*..................... 1Ti 1:16
manner of life, purpose, faith, *l* 2Ti 3:10
rebuke, exhort with all *l* 2Ti 4:2
when once the I of God waited in................ 1Pet 3:20
but is I to us-ward, not willing.................... 2Pet 3:9
account that the I of our Lord is................. 2Pet 3:15

LONGWINGED

A great eagle with great wings, *l*.............. Eze 17:3

LOOK

I will I upon it, that I may........................... Gen 9:16
thou art a fair woman to I upon.................. Gen 12:11
I from the place where thou art .... Gen 13:14
I, now toward heaven, and tell the .... Gen 15:5
I not behind thee, neither stay .... Gen 19:17
damsel was very fair to I upon.................... Gen 24:16
because she was fair to I upon.................... Gen 26:7
Wherefore I ye so sadly to day.................... Gen 40:7
let Pharaoh I out a man discreet................ Gen 41:33
Why do ye I one upon another..................... Gen 42:1
for he was afraid to I upon God.................. Ex 3:6
unto them, The LORD I upon .... Ex 5:21
I to it... Ex 10:10
faces shall I one to another......................... Ex 25:20
I that thou make them after their .... Ex 25:40
Moses did I upon all the work, and........... Ex 39:43
the priest shall I on the plague .... Lev 13:3
and the priest shall I on him....................... Lev 13:5
the priest shall I on him.............................. Lev 13:5
the priest shall I on him again.................... Lev 13:6
But if the priest I on it .... Lev 13:21
Then the priest shall I upon it..................... Lev 13:25
But if the priest I on it .... Lev 13:26
the priest shall I upon him the................... Lev 13:27
if the priest I on the plague of .... Lev 13:31
the priest shall I on the plague.................. Lev 13:32
the priest shall I on the scall .... Lev 13:34
Then the priest shall I on him.................... Lev 13:36
Then the priest shall I................................. Lev 13:39
Then the priest shall I upon it..................... Lev 13:43
priest shall I upon the plague..................... Lev 13:50
he shall I on the plague on the................... Lev 13:51
And if the priest shall I, and....................... Lev 13:53
the priest shall I on the plague.................. Lev 13:55
And if the priest I, and, behold,................. Lev 13:56

and the priest shall I, and, behold .... Lev 14:3
he shall I on the plague, and....................... Lev 14:37
again the seventh day, and shall I .... Lev 14:39
Then the priest shall come and I .... Lev 14:44
I upon it, and, behold, the plague............. Lev 14:48
a fringe, that ye may I upon it.................... Num 15:39
I not unto the stubbornness of.................... Deut 9:27
I, down from thy holy habitation,.............. Deut 26:15
people, and thine eyes shall I .... Deut 28:32
them, I, on me, and do likewise.................. Judg 7:17
if thou wilt indeed I on the......................... 1Sa 1:11
I, not on his countenance, or on 1Sa 16:7
countenance, and goodly to I to.................. 1Sa 16:12
I how thy brethren fare, and take 1Sa 17:18
that thou shouldest I upon such a.............. 2Sa 9:8
was very beautiful to I upon....................... 2Sa 11:2
LORD will I on mine affliction..................... 2Sa 16:12
Go up now, I toward the sea 1Kin 18:43
Judah, I would not I toward thee 2Kin 3:14
I, when the messenger cometh,.................. 2Kin 6:32
I out there Jehu the son of......................... 2Kin 9:2
I, even out the best and meetest of............ 2Kin 10:3
I that there be here with you...................... 2Kin 10:23
let us I one another in the face 2Kin 14:8
the God of our fathers I thereon 1Chr 12:17
died, he said, The LORD I upon it............... 2Chr 24:22
for she was fair to I on .... Est 1:11
let it I for light, but have none................... Job 3:9
therefore be content, I upon me................. Job 6:28
shall no man I for his goods .... Job 20:21
I, unto the heavens, and see....................... Job 35:5
I, on every one that is proud, and.............. Job 40:12
my prayer unto thee, and will *l* .... Ps 5:3
they I and stare upon me .... Ps 22:17
I, upon mine affliction and my pain .... Ps 25:18
LORD, how long wilt thou I on..................... Ps 35:17
me, so that I am not able to I up................ Ps 40:12
I down from heaven, and behold, and........ Ps 80:14
I upon the face of thine anointed .... Ps 84:9
shall I down from heaven .... Ps 85:11
him that hath an high I and a .... Ps 101:5
I, thou upon me, and be merciful............... Ps 119:132
as the eyes of servants I unto.................... Ps 123:2
Let thine eyes I right on .... Prov 4:25
let thine eyelids I straight .... Prov 4:25
A proud I, a lying tongue, and..................... Prov 6:17
An high I, and a proud heart, and .... Prov 21:4
I, not thou upon the wine when it .... Prov 23:31
flocks, and I well to thy herds.................... Prov 27:23
those that I out of the windows.................. Eccl 12:3
I, not upon me, because I am black............ Song 1:6
I from the top of Amana, from the .... Song 4:8
return, that we may I upon thee................. Song 6:13
if one I unto the land, behold..................... Is 5:30
of Jacob, and I will I for him....................... Is 8:17
king and their God, and I upward.............. Is 8:21
they shall I unto the earth........................... Is 8:22
thee shall narrowly I upon thee .... Is 14:16
day shall a man I to his Maker................... Is 17:7
he shall not I to the altars, the.................. Is 17:8
Therefore said I, I away from me................ Is 22:4
thou didst I in that day to the .... Is 22:8
but they I not unto the Holy One .... Is 31:1
I, upon Zion, the city of our........................ Is 33:20
and I, ye blind, that ye may see................. Is 42:18
I, unto me, and be ye saved, all .... Is 45:22
I unto the rock whence ye are..................... Is 51:1
I, unto Abraham your father, and.............. Is 51:2
and I upon the earth beneath .... Is 51:6
they all I to their own way.......................... Is 56:11
we I for judgment, but there is.................. Is 59:11
I, down from heaven, and behold .... Is 63:15
but to this man will I I, even to .... Is 66:2
I upon the carcases of the men .... Is 66:24
while ye I for light, he turn it .... Jer 13:16
I well to him, and do him no harm .... Jer 39:12
and I will I well unto thee............................ Jer 40:4
and are fled apace, and I not back .... Jer 46:5
the fathers shall not I back to .... Jer 47:3
Till the LORD I down, and behold.............. Lam 3:50
all of them princes to I on .... Eze 23:15
when they shall I after them .... Eze 29:16
stairs shall I toward the east .... Eze 43:17
whose I was more stout than his................ Dan 7:20
who I to other gods, and love .... Hos 3:1
yet I will I again toward thy .... Jonah 3:4
and let our eye I upon Zion......................... Mic 4:11
Therefore I will I unto the LORD .... Mic 7:7
but none shall I back .... Nah 2:8
that all they that I upon thee...................... Nah 3:7
evil, and canst not I on iniquity .... Hab 1:13
that thou mayest I on their .... Hab 2:15
they shall I upon me whom they................ Zec 12:10
come, or do we I for another....................... Mt 11:3
upon his eyes, and made him I up.............. Mk 8:25
or I we for another .... Lk 7:19
or I we for another .... Lk 7:20
I beseech thee, I upon my son.................... Lk 9:38
begin to come to pass, then I up................ Lk 21:28
up your eyes, and I on the fields .... Jn 4:35
Search, and I .... Jn 7:52
They shall I on him whom they................... Jn 19:37
upon him with John, said, I, on us............ Acts 3:4
or why I ye so earnestly on us,................... Acts 3:12
I ye out among you seven men of .... Acts 6:3
names, and of your law, I ye to it .... Acts 18:15
for I I for him with the brethren 1Cor 16:11
I to the end of that which is........................ 2Cor 3:13
While we I not at the things......................... 2Cor 4:18
Do ye I on things after the.......................... 2Cor 10:7

l not every man on his own things ...... Phil 2:4
whence also we *l* for the Saviour...... Phil 3:20
unto them that *l* for him shall be ...... Heb 9:28
the angels desire to *l* into....................... 1Pet 1:12
I for new heavens and a new earth,...... 2Pet 3:13
seeing that ye *l* for such things,........... 2Pet 3:14
L to yourselves, that we lose not.............. 2Jn 8
sat was to *l* upon like a jasper........... Rev 4:3
the book, neither to *l* thereon........... Rev 5:3
the book, neither to *l* thereon........... Rev 5:4

LOOKED
God *l* upon the earth, and, behold,...... Gen 6:12
the covering of the ark, and *l*............ Gen 8:13
Have I also here *l* after him that ...... Gen 16:13
And he lift up his eyes and *l*............. Gen 18:2
up from thence, and *l* toward Sodom. Gen 18:16
But his wife *l* back from behind...... Gen 19:26
l toward Sodom and Gomorrah .... Gen 19:28
Abraham lifted up his eyes, and *l* ...... Gen 22:13
the Philistines *l* out at a window ...... Gen 26:8
And he *l*, and behold a well in the ...... Gen 29:2
LORD hath *l* upon my affliction........ Gen 29:32
And Jacob lifted up his eyes, and *l* ...... Gen 33:1
and they lifted up their eyes and *l* ...... Gen 37:25
The Keeper of the prison *l* not to...... Gen 39:23
l upon them, and, behold, they...... Gen 40:6
brethren, and *l* on their burdens......... Ex 2:11
he *l* this way and that way, and........... Ex 2:12
God *l* upon the children of Israel ...... Ex 2:25
and he *l*, and, behold, the bush......... Ex 3:2
and that he had *l* upon them .... Ex 4:31
in the morning watch the LORD *l*...... Ex 14:24
that they *l* toward the wilderness ...... Ex 16:10
l after Moses, until he was gone......... Ex 33:8
Aaron *l* upon Miriam, and, behold,...... Num 12:10
that they *l* toward the tabernacle...... Num 16:42
and they *l*, and took every man his...... Num 17:9
when he *l* on Amalek, he took up...... Num 24:20
he *l* on the Kenites, and took up......... Num 24:21
And I *l*, and, behold, ye had sinned...... Deut 9:16
l on our affliction, and our............... Deut 26:7
that he lifted up his eyes and *l*........... Josh 5:13
when the men of Ai *l* behind them ...... Josh 8:20
of Sisera *l* out at a window .... Judg 5:28
And the LORD *l* upon him, and said, ... Judg 6:14
and laid wait in the field, and *l*......... Judg 9:43
and Manoah and his wife *l* on........... Judg 13:19
And Manoah and his wife *l* on it......... Judg 13:20
the Benjamites *l* behind them .... Judg 20:40
because they had *l* into the ark......... 1Sa 6:19
for I have *l* upon my people,.............. 1Sa 9:16
of Saul in Gibeah of Benjamin *l*......... 1Sa 14:16
that he *l* on Eliab, and said,............... 1Sa 16:6
And when the Philistine *l* about,...... 1Sa 17:42
when Saul *l* behind him, David 1Sa 24:8
when he *l* behind him, he saw me,...... 2Sa 1:7
Then Abner *l* behind him, and said,...... 2Sa 2:20
daughter *l* through a window............. 2Sa 6:16
watch lifted up his eyes, and *l*......... 2Sa 13:34
wall, and lifted up his eyes, and *l* 2Sa 18:24
They *l*, but there was none to............. 2Sa 22:42
And Araunah *l*, and saw the king and 2Sa 24:20
And he went up, and *l*, and said, ... 1Kin 18:43
And he *l*, and, behold, there was a 1Kin 19:6
them, and cursed them in the........... 2Kin 2:24
by upon the wall, and the people *l*...... 2Kin 6:30
her head, and *l* out at a window......... 2Kin 9:30
there *l* out to him two or three............. 2Kin 9:32
And when she *l*, behold, the king...... 2Kin 11:14
Amaziah king of Judah *l* one............. 2Kin 14:11
as David came to Ornan, Ornan *l*......... 1Chr 21:21
And when Judah *l* back, behold, the 2Chr 13:14
they *l* unto the multitude, and,......... 2Chr 20:24
And she *l*, and, behold, the king 2Chr 23:13
l upon him, and, behold, he was......... 2Chr 26:20
And I *l*, and rose up, and said unto....... Neh 4:14
sight of all them that *l* upon her......... Est 2:15
The troops of Tema *l*, the............... Job 6:19
When I *l* for good, then evil came....... Job 30:26
The LORD *l* down from heaven upon...... Ps 14:2
They *l* unto him, and were............... Ps 34:5
God *l* down from heaven upon the ...... Ps 53:2
I *l* for some to take pity, but........... Ps 69:20
For he hath *l* down from the........... Ps 102:19
when they *l* upon me they shaked ...... Ps 109:25
I *l* on my right hand, and beheld,...... Ps 142:4
my house I *l* through my casement...... Prov 7:6
I *l* upon it, and received................... Prov 24:32
Then I *l* on all the works that my ...... Eccl 2:11
because the sun hath *l* upon me......... Song 1:6
he *l* that it should bring forth............. Is 5:2
when I *l* that it should bring............. Is 5:4
he *l* for judgment, but behold............. Is 5:7
but ye have not *l* unto the maker ...... Is 22:11
And I *l*, and there was none to help ...... Is 63:5
things which we *l* not for............... Is 64:3
We *l* for peace, but no good came...... Jer 8:15
we *l* for peace, and there is no.......... Jer 14:19
this is the day that we *l* for............. Lam 2:16
And I *l*, and, behold, a whirlwind...... Eze 1:4
And when I *l*, behold, an hand was ...... Eze 2:9
and when I *l*, behold a hole in the ...... Eze 8:7
Then I *l*, and, behold, in the............. Eze 10:9
And when I *l*, behold the four......... Eze 10:11
the head I they followed it............... Eze 10:11
I upon thee, behold, thy time was ...... Eze 16:8
with images, he *l* in the liver......... Eze 21:21
court that I toward the north........... Eze 40:20
and I *l*, and, behold, the glory of ...... Eze 44:4
priests, which *l* toward the north ...... Eze 46:19

be *l* upon before thee, and the............. Dan 1:13
Then I lifted up mine eyes, and............. Dan 10:5
Then I Daniel *l*, and, behold,............. Dan 12:5
But thou shouldest not have *l* on......... Obad 12
thou shouldest not have *l* on............. Obad 13
Ye *l* for much, and, lo, it came to......... Hag 1:9
I lifted up mine eyes again, and *l*......... Zec 2:1
And I said, I have *l*, and behold a...... Zec 4:2
and lifted up mine eyes, and *l*............. Zec 5:1
Then lifted I up mine eyes, and *l*......... Zec 5:9
and lifted up mine eyes, and *l*............. Zec 6:1
when he had *l* round about on them ...... Mk 3:5
he *l* round about on them which...... Mk 3:34
he *l* round about to see her that......... Mk 5:32
he *l* up to heaven, and blessed, and...... Mk 6:41
And he *l* up, and said, I see men as......... Mk 8:24
l on his disciples, he rebuked............. Mk 8:33
when they had *l* round about............. Mk 9:8
Jesus *l* round about, and saith............. Mk 10:23
when he had *l* round about upon......... Mk 11:11
she *l* upon him, and said, And thou...... Mk 14:67
And when they *l*, they saw that the ...... Mk 16:4
me in the days wherein he *l* on me ...... Lk 1:25
I for redemption in Jerusalem............. Lk 2:38
on him, and passed by on the......... Lk 10:32
Jesus came to the place, he *l*............. Lk 19:5
And he *l* up, and saw the rich men...... Lk 21:1
the fire, and earnestly *l* upon him......... Lk 22:56
the Lord turned, and *l* upon Peter ...... Lk 22:61
the disciples *l* one on another............. Jn 13:22
down, and *l* into the sepulchre,......... Jn 20:11
while they *l* stedfastly toward......... Acts 1:10
I up stedfastly into heaven, and......... Acts 7:55
And when he *l* on him, he was............. Acts 10:4
And the same hour I *l* upon him ...... Acts 22:13
Howbeit they *l* when he should......... Acts 28:6
after they had *l* a great while............. Acts 28:6
For he *l* for a city which hath............. Heb 11:10
our eyes, which we have *l* upon......... 1Jn 1:1
After this I *l*, and, behold, a............. Rev 4:1
And I *l*, and behold a pale horse......... Rev 6:8
And I *l*, and, lo, a Lamb stood on......... Rev 14:1
And I *l*, and behold a white cloud, ... Rev 14:14
And after that I *l*, and, behold,......... Rev 15:5

LOOKEST
I narrowly unto all my paths.............. Job 13:27
wherefore I thou upon them that ...... Hab 1:13

LOOKETH
foot, wheresoever the priest *l*............. Lev 13:12
that is bitten, when he I upon it.............. Num 21:8
Pisgah, which *l* toward Jeshimon......... Num 21:20
of Peor, that *l* toward Jeshimon......... Num 23:28
from the bay that *l* southward......... Josh 15:2
a view of the border that *l*............. Josh 18:14
for man I on the outward............... 1Sa 16:7
but the LORD *l* on the heart............. 1Sa 16:7
as a hireling I for the reward of......... Job 7:2
For he *l* to the ends of the earth......... Job 28:24
He I upon men, and if any say, I......... Job 33:27
The LORD *l* from heaven............... Ps 33:13
the place of his habitation he *l*......... Ps 33:14
He I on the earth, and it............... Ps 104:32
prudent man I well to his going......... Prov 14:15
She I well to the ways of her............. Prov 31:27
he I forth at the windows,............... Song 2:9
Who is she that I forth as the......... Song 6:10
Lebanon which *l* toward Damascus ...... Song 7:4
when he that I upon it seeth............. Is 28:4
gate, that I toward the north............. Eze 8:3
Lord's house, which I eastward......... Eze 11:1
the gate which I toward the east......... Eze 40:6
the gate that I toward the east......... Eze 40:22
the gate that I toward the east......... Eze 43:1
sanctuary which I toward the east......... Eze 44:1
gate of the inner court that *l*............. Eze 46:1
the gate that I toward the east......... Eze 46:12
gate by the way that I eastward......... Eze 47:2
That whosoever I on a woman to...... Mt 5:28
in a day when he I not for him............. Mt 24:50
in a day when he I not for him............. Lk 12:46
But whoso I into the perfect law......... Jas 1:25

LOOKING
I toward Gilgal, that is before............. Josh 15:7
three I toward the north, and............. 1Kin 7:25
three I toward the west,............... 1Kin 7:25
three I toward the south............... 1Kin 7:25
and three I toward the east............. 1Kin 7:25
Michal the daughter of Saul I out......... 1Chr 15:29
three I toward the north,............... 2Chr 4:4
three I toward the west.................. 2Chr 4:4
three I toward the south............... 2Chr 4:4
and three I toward the east............. 2Chr 4:4
is strong, and as a molten I glass......... Job 37:18
mine eyes fail with I upward............. Is 38:14
I up to heaven, he blessed, and......... Mk 6:41
I up to heaven, he sighed, and............. Mk 7:34
Jesus I upon them saith, With men......... Mk 10:27
were also women I on afar off............. Mk 15:40
I round about upon them all, he......... Lk 6:10
I up to heaven, he blessed them,......... Lk 9:16
I back, is fit for the kingdom of......... Lk 9:62
I after those things which............... Lk 21:26
I upon Jesus as he walked, he............. Jn 1:36
I in, saw the linen clothes lying............. Jn 20:5
I stedfastly on him, saw his face......... Acts 6:15
I for a promise from thence............... Acts 23:21
I for that blessed hope, and the......... Titus 2:13
certain fearful I for of judgment......... Heb 10:27
L unto Jesus the author and............. Heb 12:2

L diligently lest any man fail of......... Heb 12:15
L for and hasting unto the coming...... 2Pet 3:12
L for the mercy of our Lord Jesus...... Jude 21

LOOKINGGLASSES
of the I of the women assembling,......... Ex 38:8

LOOKS
but will bring down high *l*............... Ps 18:27
The lofty *l* of man shall be............. Is 2:11
and the glory of his high *l*............. Is 10:12
words, nor be dismayed at their *l*....... Eze 2:6
neither be dismayed at their *l*......... Eze 3:9

LOOPS
thou shalt make *l* of blue upon......... Ex 26:4
Fifty I shalt thou make in the......... Ex 26:5
fifty I shalt thou make in the............. Ex 26:5
that the I may take hold of one of......... Ex 26:5
thou shalt make fifty I on the......... Ex 26:10
fifty I in the edge of the............... Ex 26:10
and put the taches into the I............. Ex 26:11
he made I of blue on the edge of......... Ex 36:11
Fifty I made he in one curtain,......... Ex 36:12
fifty I made he in the edge of............. Ex 36:12
the I held one curtain to another......... Ex 36:12
And he made fifty I upon the............. Ex 36:17
fifty I made he upon the edge of......... Ex 36:17

LOOSE
Naphtali is a hind let I................... Gen 49:21
living bird I into the open field.......... Lev 14:7
I his shoe from off his foot, and......... Deut 25:9
L thy shoe from off thy foot............. Josh 5:15
that he would let I his hand............. Job 6:9
they have also let I the bridle............. Job 30:11
Pleiades, or I the bands of Orion......... Job 38:31
to I those that are appointed to......... Ps 102:20
I clothed with a sack of the............. Is 8:2
I will I the loins of kings, to............. Is 45:1
I thyself from the bands of thy......... Is 52:2
to I the bands of wickedness, to......... Is 58:6
I thee this day from the chains......... Jer 40:4
and said, Lo, I see four men I......... Dan 3:25
whatsoever thou shalt I on earth......... Mt 16:19
whatsoever ye shall I on earth............. Mt 18:18
I them, and bring them unto me......... Mt 21:2
I him, and bring him,................... Mk 11:2
and they I him....................... Mk 11:4
I his ox or his ass from the............. Lk 13:15
I him, and bring him hither............. Lk 19:30
any man ask you, Why do ye I him...... Lk 19:31
saith unto them, Why I ye the colt...... Lk 19:33
unto them, L him, and let him go......... Jn 11:44
of his feet I am not worthy to I......... Acts 13:25
him of Paul, that he might I him......... Acts 24:26
book, and to I the seals thereof......... Rev 5:2
to I the seven seals thereof............. Rev 5:5
L the four angels which are bound ...... Rev 9:14

LOOSED
be not I from the ephod............... Ex 28:28
might not be I from the ephod......... Ex 39:21
house of him that hath his shoe I......... Deut 25:10
his bands I from off his hands............. Judg 15:14
Because he hath I my cord............... Job 30:11
or who hath I the bands of the......... Job 39:5
The king sent and I him............... Ps 105:20
I thou hast I my bonds................... Ps 116:16
O ever the silver cord be I............. Eccl 12:6
the girdle of their loins be I............. Is 5:27
Thy tacklings are I.................. Is 33:23
exile hasteneth that he may be I......... Is 51:14
The joints of his loins were I......... Dan 5:6
on earth shall be I in heaven............. Mt 16:19
on earth shall be I in heaven............. Mt 18:18
I him, and forgave him the debt......... Mt 18:27
and the string of his tongue was I......... Mk 7:35
immediately, and his tongue I............. Lk 1:64
thou art I from thine infirmity............. Lk 13:12
be I from this bond on the............. Lk 13:16
having I the pains of death............. Acts 2:24
Paul and his company I from Paphos ...... Acts 13:13
and every one's bands were I............. Acts 16:26
he I him from his bands, and............. Acts 22:30
not have I from Crete, and to have ...... Acts 27:21
the rudder bands, and hoised up......... Acts 27:40
she is I from the law of her............... Rom 7:2
seek not to be I...................... 1Cor 7:27
Art thou I from a wife?................. 1Cor 7:27
And the four angels were I............. Rev 9:15
that he must be I a little season......... Rev 20:3
Satan shall be I out of his............. Rev 20:7

LOOSETH
He I the bond of kings, and............. Job 12:18
The LORD I the prisoners............... Ps 146:7

LOOSING
unto them, What do ye, I the colt......... Mk 11:5
And as they were I the colt............. Lk 19:33
Therefore I from Troas, we came......... Acts 16:11
I thence, they sailed close by......... Acts 27:13

LOP
shall I the bough with terror............. Is 10:33

LORD See PREFACE.
　I. God.
Now the L had said unto Abram,......... Gen 12:1
Is any thing too hard for the L............. Gen 18:14
then shall the L be my God............... Gen 28:21
the name of the L thy God in vain......... Ex 20:7
for the L will not hold him............... Ex 20:7

proclaimed, The L, the L God .... Ex 34:6
know that the L is one L .... Deut 4:35
The L our God is one L .... Deut 6:4
thou forget not the L thy God .... Deut 8:11
to know whether ye love the L .... Deut 13:3
seem evil unto you to serve the L .... Josh 24:15
and my house, we will serve the L .... Josh 24:15
is none holy as the L 1Sa 2:2
And he said, It is the L 1Sa 3:18
For the L will not forsake his 1Sa 12:22
But the L said unto Samuel, Look 1Sa 16:7
for the L seeth not as man seeth 1Sa 16:7
but the L looketh on the heart 1Sa 16:7
the L, he is the God 1Kin 18:39
For the eyes of the L run to 2Chr 16:9
Thou, even thou, art I alone .... Neh 9:6
For who is God save the L .... Ps 18:31
The L is my light and my salvation .... Ps 27:1
The L is the strength of my life ...... Ps 27:1
Wait on the L .... Ps 27:14
wait, I say, on the L .... Ps 27:14
is the nation whose God is the L ...... Ps 33:12
Know ye that the L is God .... Ps 100:3
Bless the L, O my soul .... Ps 103:1
God is the L, which hath shewed .... Ps 118:27
The fear of the L is the .... Prov 1:7
For when the L loveth he .... Prov 3:12
These six things doth the L hate ...... Prov 6:16
The fear of the L is the .... Prov 9:10
may know that thou art the L .... Is 37:20
I, even I, am the L .... Is 43:11
I am the L, your Holy One, the .... Is 43:15
I am the L, and there is none else .... Is 45:5
The L hath made bare his holy arm ..... Is 52:10
whom is the arm of the L revealed ..... Is 53:1
the L hath laid on him the .... Is 53:6
Seek ye the L while he may be .... Is 55:6
Spirit of the L God is upon me .... Is 61:1
the L shall be king over all the ...... Zec 14:9
in that day shall there be one L ...... Zec 14:9
Prepare ye the way of the L .... Mt 3:3
one that saith unto me, L .... Mt 7:21
Prepare ye the way of the L .... Mk 1:3
of man is L also of the sabbath .... Mk 2:28
cried out, and said with tears, L ..... Mk 9:24
The L our God is one L .... Mk 12:29
thou shalt love the L thy God .... Mk 12:30
the angel of the L came upon them ..... Lk 2:9
the glory of the L shone round .... Lk 2:9
a Saviour, which is Christ the L ...... Lk 2:11
The Spirit of the L is upon me .... Lk 4:18
of man is L also of the sabbath .... Lk 6:5
And he said unto him, L, I am .... Lk 22:33
Make straight the way of the L .... Jn 1:23
then Simon Peter answered him, L ...... Jn 6:68
Ye call me Master and L .... Jn 13:13
said unto him, We have seen the L ..... Jn 20:25
answered and said unto him, My L ...... Jn 20:28
saith unto Peter, It is the L .... Jn 21:7
Peter heard that it was the L .... Jn 21:7
seeing him saith to Jesus, L .... Jn 21:21
whom ye have crucified, both .... Acts 2:36
And he said, Who art thou, L .... Acts 9:5
the L said, I am Jesus whom thou ...... Acts 9:5
saying, The will of the L be done ..... Acts 21:14
And I said, Who art thou, L .... Acts 26:15
life through Jesus Christ our L .... Rom 6:23
with thy mouth the L Jesus .... Rom 10:9
for the same L over all is rich .... Rom 10:12
I will repay, saith the L .... Rom 12:19
he might be L both of the dead .... Rom 14:9
written, As I live, saith the L .... Rom 14:11
not have crucified the L of glory 1Cor 2:8
man can say that Jesus is the L 1Cor 12:3
second man is the L from heaven 1Cor 15:47
One L, one faith, one baptism .... Eph 4:5
confess that Jesus Christ is L .... Phil 2:11
worthy of the L unto all pleasing ..... Col 1:10
do, do it heartily, as to the L .... Col 3:23
For the L himself shall descend 1Th 4:16
clouds, to meet the L in the air 1Th 4:17
and so shall we ever be with the L 1Th 4:17
the L so cometh as a thief in the 1Th 5:2
the coming of our L Jesus Christ 2Th 2:1
the King of kings, and L of lords 1Ti 6:15
The L shall judge his people .... Heb 10:30
ye ought to say, If the L will .... Jas 4:15
that the L is very pitiful, and of .... Jas 5:11
him with oil in the name of the L ..... Jas 5:14
sick, and the L shall raise him up .... Jas 5:15
word of the L endureth for ever 1Pet 1:25
is with the L as a thousand years 2Pet 3:8
The L is not slack concerning his 2Pet 3:9
But the day of the L will come as 2Pet 3:10
the L cometh with ten thousands .... Jude 14
L God Almighty, which was, and is ..... Rev 4:8
for the L God omnipotent reigneth ..... Rev 19:6
AND L OF LORDS .... Rev 19:16
Even so, come, L Jesus .... Rev 22:20
2. A human title of honor.
said unto him, Well done, ... Mt 25:21
enter thou into the joy of thy L .... Mt 25:21

LORDLY
brought forth butter in a l dish ...... Judg 5:25

LORD'S
1. Refers to Lord 1.
know how that the earth is the L ...... Ex 9:29
it is the L passover .... Ex 12:11
the sacrifice of the L passover .... Ex 12:27

that the L law may be in thy .... Ex 13:9
the males shall be the L .... Ex 13:12
and said, Who is on the L side .... Ex 32:26
they brought the L offering to .... Ex 35:21
and brass brought the L offering ...... Ex 35:24
all the fat is the L .... Lev 3:16
goat upon which the L lot fell .... Lev 16:9
month at even is the L passover .... Lev 23:5
which should be the L firstling .... Lev 27:26
it is the L .... Lev 27:26
the fruit of the tree, is the L .... Lev 27:30
Is the L hand waxed short .... Num 11:23
all the L people were prophets .... Num 11:29
ye shall give thereof the L heave ..... Num 18:28
the L tribute of the sheep was .... Num 31:37
of which the L tribute was .... Num 31:38
of which the L tribute was .... Num 31:39
of which the L tribute was thirty ..... Num 31:40
which was the L heave offering .... Num 31:41
the L anger was kindled the same ...... Num 32:10
the L anger was kindled against .... Num 32:13
of heavens is the L thy God .... Deut 10:14
then the L wrath be kindled .... Deut 11:17
it is called the L release .... Deut 15:2
For the L portion is his people .... Deut 32:9
which Moses the L servant gave .... Josh 1:15
the captain of the L host said .... Josh 5:15
wherein the L tabernacle dwelleth ..... Josh 22:19
of Ammon, shall surely be the L .... Judg 11:24
pillars of the earth are the L 1Sa 2:8
ye make the L people to 1Sa 2:24
the L priest in Shiloh, wearing 1Sa 14:3
Surely the L anointed is before 1Sa 16:6
for the battle is the L, and he 1Sa 17:47
for me, and fight the L battles 1Sa 18:17
that Saul had slain the L priests 1Sa 22:21
the L anointed, to stretch forth 1Sa 24:10
for he is the L anointed 1Sa 24:10
hath against the L anointed 1Sa 26:9
mine hand against the L anointed 1Sa 26:11
kept your master, the L anointed 1Sa 26:16
mine hand against the L anointed 1Sa 26:23
hand to destroy the L anointed 2Sa 1:14
I have slain the L anointed 2Sa 1:16
because he cursed the L anointed 2Sa 19:21
because of the L oath that was 2Sa 21:7
The L prophets by fifty in a cave 1Kin 18:13
that they should be the L people 2Kin 11:17
The arrow of the L deliverance 2Kin 13:17
the LORD had filled the L house 2Chr 7:2
that they should be the L people 2Chr 23:16
the L throne is in heaven .... Ps 11:4
For the kingdom is the L .... Ps 22:28
The earth is the L, and the .... Ps 24:1
same the L name is to be praised ...... Ps 113:3
are the heavens, are the L .... Ps 115:16
In the courts of the L house .... Ps 116:19
This is the L doing .... Ps 118:23
How shall we sing the L song in a ..... Ps 137:4
just weight and balance are the L ..... Prov 16:11
that the mountain of the L house ...... Is 2:2
it is the day of the L vengeance ...... Is 34:8
L hand double for all her sins .... Is 40:2
and blind as the L servant .... Is 42:19
One shall say, I am the L .... Is 44:5
the L hand is not shortened, that ..... Is 59:1
for they are not the L .... Jer 5:10
Stand in the gate of the L house ...... Jer 7:2
because the L flock is carried .... Jer 13:17
stood in the court of the L house ..... Jer 19:14
Then took I the cup at the L hand ..... Jer 25:17
Stand in the court of the L house ..... Jer 26:2
come to worship in the L house .... Jer 26:2
of the new gate of the L house .... Jer 26:10
the vessels of the L house shall ...... Jer 27:16
all the vessels of the L house .... Jer 28:3
again the vessels of the L house ...... Jer 28:3
the L house upon the fasting day ...... Jer 36:6
words of the LORD in the L house ...... Jer 36:8
of the new gate of the L house .... Jer 36:10
is the time of the L vengeance .... Jer 51:6
been a golden cup in the L hand .... Jer 51:7
the sanctuaries of the L house .... Jer 51:51
so that in the day of the L anger ..... Lam 2:22
It is of the L mercies that we .... Lam 3:22
the L house which was toward the ...... Eze 8:14
the inner court of the L house .... Eze 8:16
of the brightness of the L glory ...... Eze 10:4
of the east gate of the L house .... Eze 10:19
unto the east gate of the L house ..... Eze 11:1
that is desolate, for the L sake ...... Dan 9:17
shall not dwell in the L land .... Hos 9:3
priests, the L ministers, mourn .... Joel 1:9
and the kingdom shall be the L .... Obad 21
The L controversy, and ye strong ...... Mic 6:2
The L voice crieth unto the city ...... Mic 6:9
the cup of the L right hand shall ..... Hab 2:16
in the day of the L sacrifice .... Zeph 1:8
them in the day of the L wrath .... Zeph 1:18
day of the L anger come upon you ...... Zeph 2:2
be hid in the day of the L anger ...... Zeph 2:3
the time that the L house should ...... Hag 1:2
Then spake Haggai the L messenger ..... Hag 1:13
in the L message unto the people ...... Hag 1:13
the pots in the L house shall be ...... Zec 14:20
This was the L doing, and it is .... Mt 21:42
before he had seen the L Christ .... Lk 2:26
therefore, or die, we are the L .... Rom 14:8

being a servant, is the L freeman 1Cor 7:22
be partakers of the L table 1Cor 10:21
For the earth is the L, and the 1Cor 10:26
for the earth is the L, and the 1Cor 10:28
this is not to eat the L supper 1Cor 11:20
ye do shew the L death till he 1Cor 11:26
not discerning the L body 1Cor 11:29
I none, save James the L brother ...... Gal 1:19
ordinance of man for the L sake 1Pet 2:13
I was in the Spirit on the L day ...... Rev 1:10

LORDS
And he said, Behold now, my l .... Gen 19:2
the l of the high places of Arnon ..... Num 21:28
God is God of gods, and Lord of l ..... Deut 10:17
five l of the Philistines .... Josh 13:3
five l of the Philistines, and ah ..... Judg 3:3
the l of the Philistines came up ...... Judg 16:5
Then the l of the Philistines .... Judg 16:8
sent and called for the l of the ...... Judg 16:18
Then the l of the Philistines .... Judg 16:18
Then the l of the Philistines .... Judg 16:23
all the l of the Philistines were ..... Judg 16:27
and the house fell upon the l .... Judg 16:30
gathered all the l of the 1Sa 5:8
all the l of the Philistines 1Sa 5:11
of the l of the Philistines 1Sa 6:4
was on you all, and on your l 1Sa 6:4
the l of the Philistines went 1Sa 6:12
And when the five l of the 1Sa 6:16
belonging to the five l, both of 1Sa 6:18
the l of the Philistines passed 1Sa 7:7
the l of the Philistines passed 1Sa 29:2
the l favour thee not 1Sa 29:7
for the l of the Philistines upon 1Chr 12:19
and his counsellors, and his l .... Ezr 8:25
O give thanks to the Lord of l .... Ps 136:3
the l of the heathen have broken ...... Is 16:8
other l besides thee have had .... Is 26:13
wherefore say my people, We are l ..... Jer 2:31
men, captains and rulers, great l ..... Eze 23:23
and my l sought unto me .... Dan 4:36
feast to a thousand of his l .... Dan 5:1
in him, and his l were astonied .... Dan 5:9
of the words of the king and his l .... Dan 5:10
before thee, and thou, and thy l ...... Dan 5:23
and with the signet of his l .... Dan 6:17
birthday made a supper to his l .... Mk 6:21
there be gods many, and l many) 1Cor 8:5
the King of kings, and Lord of l 1Ti 6:15
Neither as being l over God's 1Pet 5:3
for he is Lord of l, and King of ...... Rev 17:14
KING OF KINGS, AND LORD OF L .... Rev 19:16

LORD'S/1
2. Refers to Lord 2.
him in the ward of his l house .... Gen 40:7
out of thy l house silver or gold ..... Gen 44:8
and we also will be my l bondmen ...... Gen 44:9
behold, we are my l servants .... Gen 44:16
thee, speak a word in my l ears .... Gen 44:18
take thou thy l servants, and 2Sa 20:6
are they not all my l servants 1Chr 21:3
shall be the shame of thy l house ..... Is 22:18
in the earth, and hid his l money ..... Mt 25:18
servant, which knew his l will .... Lk 12:47
one of his l debtors unto him .... Lk 16:5

LORDSHIP
the Gentiles exercise l over them ..... Mk 10:42
the Gentiles exercise l over them ..... Lk 22:25

LO-RUHAMAH (lo-ru-ha'-mah) Symbolic
name meaning 'Not pitied.'
said unto him, Call her name L .... Hos 1:6
Now when she had weaned L .... Hos 1:8

LOSE
thou l thy life, with the lives .... Judg 18:25
that we l not all the beasts 1Kin 18:5
owners thereof to l their life .... Job 31:39
vomit up, and l thy sweet words .... Prov 23:8
A time to get, and a time to l .... Eccl 3:6
that findeth his life shall l it ...... Mt 10:39
he shall in no wise l his reward ...... Mt 10:42
will save his life shall l it .... Mt 16:25
whosoever will l his life for my ...... Mt 16:25
whole world, and l his own soul .... Mt 16:26
will save his life shall l it .... Mk 8:35
but whosoever shall l his life .... Mk 8:35
whole world, and l his own soul .... Mk 8:36
you, he shall not l his reward .... Mk 9:41
will save his life shall l it .... Lk 9:24
but whosoever will l his life for ..... Lk 9:24
l himself, or be cast away .... Lk 9:25
if he l one of them, doth not .... Lk 15:4
if she l one piece, doth not .... Lk 15:8
seek to save his life shall l it ...... Lk 17:33
whosoever shall l his life shall ...... Lk 17:33
hath given me l should l nothing ...... Jn 6:39
that loveth his life shall l it .... Jn 12:25
that we l not those things which 2Jn 8

LOSETH
he that l his life for my sake .... Mt 10:39

LOSS
I bare the l of it .... Gen 31:39
shall pay for the l of his time .... Ex 21:19
shall I know the l of children .... Is 47:8
the l of children, and widowhood ...... Is 47:9
and to have gained this harm and l .... Acts 27:21

LOST

for there shall be no *l* of any	Acts 27:22
be burned, he shall suffer *l*......	1Cor 3:15
me, those I counted *l* for Christ.....	Phil 3:7
I count all things but *l* for the......	Phil 3:8
have suffered the *l* of all things.....	Phil 3:8

LOST

or for any manner of *l* thing.......	Ex 22:9
Or have found that which was *l*......	Lev 6:3
or the *l* thing which he found.......	Lev 6:4
days that were before shall be *l*....	Num 6:12
and with all *l* things of thy........	Deut 22:3
of thy brother's, which he hath *l*....	Deut 22:3
of Kish Saul's father were *l*........	1Sa 9:3
asses that were *l* three days ago....	1Sa 9:20
like the army that thou hast *l*.......	1Kin 20:25
I have gone astray like a *l* sheep....	Ps 119:176
have, after thou hast *l* the other....	Is 49:20
seeing I have *l* my children.........	Is 49:21
My people hath been *l* sheep.......	Jer 50:6
she had waited, and her hope was *l*..	Eze 19:5
have we sought that which was *l*....	Eze 34:4
I will seek that which was *l*.........	Eze 34:16
bones are dried, and our hope is *l*...	Eze 37:11
but if the salt have *l* his savour......	Mt 5:13
But go rather to the *l* sheep of......	Mt 10:6
I am not sent but unto the *l*........	Mt 15:24
is come to save that which was *l*....	Mt 18:11
if the salt have *l* his saltness.......	Mk 9:50
but if the salt have *l* his savour....	Lk 14:34
and go after that which is *l*.........	Lk 15:4
I have found my sheep which was *l*..	Lk 15:6
found the piece which I had *l*.......	Lk 15:9
he was *l*, and is found............	Lk 15:24
and was *l*, and is found...........	Lk 15:32
seek and to save that which was *l*...	Lk 19:10
that remain, that nothing be *l*......	Jn 6:12
I have kept, and none of them is *l*...	Jn 17:12
thou gavest me have I *l* none.......	Jn 18:9
hid, it is hid to them that are *l*......	2Cor 4:3

LOT (lot) See Lot's. Abraham's nephew.

and Haran begat *L*...............	Gen 11:27
L the son of Haran his son's son.....	Gen 11:31
and *L* went with him..............	Gen 12:4
L his brother's son, and their........	Gen 12:5
L with him, into the south.........	Gen 13:1
L also, which went with Abram......	Gen 13:5
And Abram said unto *L*, Let there....	Gen 13:8
L lifted up his eyes, and beheld......	Gen 13:10
Then *L* chose him all the plain of.....	Gen 13:11
and *L* journeyed east.............	Gen 13:11
L dwelled in the cities of the.......	Gen 13:12
after that *L* was separated from.....	Gen 13:14
And they took *L*, Abram's brother's...	Gen 14:12
also brought again his brother *L*.....	Gen 14:16
L sat in the gate of Sodom.........	Gen 19:1
L seeing them rose up to meet......	Gen 19:1
And they called unto *L*, and said.....	Gen 19:5
L went out at the door unto them....	Gen 19:6
pressed sore upon the man, even *L*...	Gen 19:9
pulled *L* into the house to them......	Gen 19:10
And the men said unto *L*, Hast thou..	Gen 19:12
L went out, and spake unto his......	Gen 19:14
arose, then the angels hastened *L*....	Gen 19:15
L said unto them, Oh, not so, my....	Gen 19:18
earth when *L* entered into Zoar......	Gen 19:23
sent *L* out of the midst of the.......	Gen 19:29
the cities in the which *L* dwelt......	Gen 19:29
L went up out of Zoar, and dwelt....	Gen 19:30
of *L* with child by their father......	Gen 19:36
one *l* for the Lord, and the other....	Lev 16:8
the other *l* for the scapegoat.......	Lev 16:8
goat upon which the Lord's *l* fell.....	Lev 16:9
on which the *l* fell to be the.......	Lev 16:10
the land shall be divided by *l*.......	Num 26:55
According to the *l* shall the........	Num 26:56
ye shall divide the land by *l* for.....	Num 33:54
in the place where his *l* falleth......	Num 33:54
land which ye shall inherit by *l*......	Num 34:13
by *l* to the children of Israel.......	Num 36:2
from the *l* of our inheritance.......	Num 36:3
children of *L* for a possession.......	Deut 2:9
children of *L* for a possession.......	Deut 2:19
Jacob is the *l* of his inheritance.....	Deut 32:9
only divide thou it by *l* unto the.....	Josh 13:6
By *l* was their inheritance, as.......	Josh 14:2
This then was the *l* of the tribe.....	Josh 15:1
the *l* of the children of Joseph......	Josh 16:1
There was also a *l* for the tribe.....	Josh 17:1
There was also a *l* for the rest......	Josh 17:2
Why hast thou given me but one *l*....	Josh 17:14
thou shalt not have one *l* only......	Josh 17:17
the *l* of the tribe of the..........	Josh 18:11
the coast of their *l* came forth.....	Josh 18:11
the second *l* came forth to Simeon...	Josh 19:1
the third *l* came up for the........	Josh 19:10
the fourth *l* came out to Issachar....	Josh 19:17
the fifth *l* came out for the........	Josh 19:24
The sixth *l* came out to the........	Josh 19:32
the seventh *l* came out for the......	Josh 19:40
by *l* in Shiloh before the Lord......	Josh 19:51
the *l* came out for the families.....	Josh 21:4
had by *l* out of the tribe of........	Josh 21:4
by *l* out of the families of the......	Josh 21:6
by *l* out of the families of the......	Josh 21:6
unto the Levites these cities........	Josh 21:8
for theirs was the first *l*..........	Josh 21:10
l out of the tribe of Ephraim.......	Josh 21:20
were by their *l* twelve cities.......	Josh 21:40
by *l* these nations that remain.....	Josh 23:4

Come up with me into my *l*.........	Judg 1:3
will go with thee into thy *l*........	Judg 1:3
we will go up by *l* against it........	Judg 20:9
God of Israel, Give a perfect *l*......	1Sa 14:41
for theirs was the *l*..............	1Chr 6:54
the half tribe of Manasseh, by *l*....	1Chr 6:61
sons of Merari were given by *l*......	1Chr 6:63
they gave by *l* out of the tribe.....	1Chr 6:65
the *l* of your inheritance..........	1Chr 16:18
Thus were they divided by *l*.......	1Chr 24:5
Now the first *l* came forth to.......	1Chr 24:7
Now the first *l* came forth for......	1Chr 25:9
the eastward fell to Shelemiah......	1Chr 26:14
and his *l* came out northward.......	1Chr 26:14
Hosah the *l* came forth westward....	1Chr 26:16
they cast Pur, that is, the *l*........	Est 3:7
and had cast Pur, that is, the *L*.....	Est 9:24
thou maintainest my *l*............	Ps 16:5
have holpen the children of *L*.......	Ps 83:8
the *l* of your inheritance..........	Ps 105:11
rest upon the *l* of the righteous....	Ps 125:3
Cast in thy *l* among us............	Prov 1:14
The *l* is cast into the lap..........	Prov 16:33
The *l* causeth contentions to......	Prov 18:18
the *l* of them that rob us..........	Is 17:14
And he hath cast the *l* for them.....	Is 34:17
they, they are thy *l*..............	Is 57:6
This is thy *l*, the portion of thy.....	Jer 13:25
let no *l* fall upon it...............	Eze 24:6
when ye shall divide by *l* the.......	Eze 45:1
that ye shall divide it by *l* for......	Eze 47:22
l unto the tribes of Israel for......	Eze 48:29
stand in thy *l* at the end of the.....	Dan 12:13
lots, and the *l* fell upon Jonah.....	Jonah 1:7
none that shall cast a cord by *l*.....	Mic 2:5
his *l* was to burn incense when he...	Lk 1:9
also as it was in the days of *L*......	Lk 17:28
But the same day that *L* went out....	Lk 17:29
and the *l* fell upon Matthias.......	Acts 1:26
neither part nor *l* in this matter....	Acts 8:21
divided their land to them by *l*.....	Acts 13:19
And delivered just *L*, vexed with....	2Pet 2:7

LOTAN (*lo'-tan*) See LOTAN'S. *Son of Seir.*

L, and Shobal, and Zibeon........	Gen 36:20
And the children of *L* were Hori.....	Gen 36:22
duke *L*, duke Shobal, duke Zibeon...	Gen 36:29
L, and Shobal, and Zibeon, and Anah..	1Chr 1:38
And the sons of *L*................	1Chr 1:39

LOTAN'S (*lo'-tans*)

and *L* sister was Timna............	Gen 36:22
and Timna was *L* sister............	1Chr 1:39

LOTHE

the Egyptians shall *l* to drink of.....	Ex 7:18
they shall *l* themselves for the......	Eze 6:9
ye shall *l* yourselves in your own....	Eze 20:43
shall *l* yourselves in your own......	Eze 36:31

LOTHED

hath thy soul *l* Zion..............	Jer 14:19
which *l* their husbands and their....	Eze 16:45
and my soul *l* them, and their soul...	Zec 11:8

LOTHETH

that *l* her husband and her.........	Eze 16:45

LOTHING

to the *l* of thy person, in the......	Eze 16:5

LOT'S (*lots*)

cattle and the herdmen of *L* cattle..	Gen 13:7
Remember *L* wife................	Lk 17:32

LOTS

Aaron shall cast *l* upon the two.....	Lev 16:8
that I may cast *l* for you here......	Josh 18:6
that I may here cast *l* for you......	Josh 18:8
Joshua cast *l* for them in Shiloh....	Josh 18:10
Cast *l* between me and Jonathan my...	1Sa 14:42
These likewise cast *l* over.........	1Chr 24:31
And they cast *l*, ward against ward...	1Chr 25:8
And they cast *l*, as well the small...	1Chr 26:13
a wise counsellor, they cast *l*......	1Chr 26:14
we cast the *l* among the priests.....	Neh 10:34
rest of the people also cast *l*.......	Neh 11:1
them, and cast *l* upon my vesture...	Ps 22:18
And they have cast *l* for my people..	Joel 3:3
cast *l* upon Jerusalem, even thou....	Obad 11
fellow, Come, and let us cast *l*.....	Jonah 1:7
So they cast *l*, and the lot fell.....	Jonah 1:7
they cast *l* for her honourable.....	Nah 3:10
and parted his garments, casting *l*...	Mt 27:35
upon my vesture did they cast *l*....	Mt 27:35
casting *l* upon them, what every....	Mk 15:24
parted his raiment, and cast *l*......	Lk 23:34
us not rend it, but cast *l* for it.....	Jn 19:24
and for my vesture they did cast *l*...	Jn 19:24
And they gave forth their *l*........	Acts 1:26

LOUD

me, and I cried with a *l* voice.......	Gen 39:14
voice of the trumpet exceeding *l*....	Ex 19:16
the men of Israel with a *l* voice.....	Deut 27:14
Samuel, she cried with a *l*.........	1Sa 1:13
the country wept with a *l* voice.....	2Sa 15:23
and the king cried with a *l* voice....	2Sa 19:4
of Israel with a *l* voice, saying......	1Kin 8:55
cried with a *l* voice in the Jews'....	2Kin 18:28
unto the Lord with a *l* voice........	2Chr 15:14
of Israel with a *l* voice on high.....	2Chr 20:19
singing with *l* instruments unto....	2Chr 30:21
Then they cried with a *l* voice in....	2Chr 32:18

their eyes, wept with a *l* voice......	Ezr 3:12
the people shouted with a *l* shout...	Ezr 3:13
answered and said with a *l* voice....	Ezr 10:12
cried with a *l* voice unto the.......	Neh 9:4
And the singers sang *l*, with.......	Neh 12:42
of the city, and cried with a *l*......	Est 4:1
play skilfully with a *l* noise........	Ps 33:3
make a *l* noise, and rejoice, and....	Ps 98:4
Praise him upon the *l* cymbals.....	Ps 150:5
(She is *l* and stubborn...........	Prov 7:11
his friend with a *l* voice..........	Prov 27:14
cried with a *l* voice in the Jews'....	Is 36:13
cry in mine ears with a *l* voice......	Eze 8:18
also in mine ears with a *l* voice.....	Eze 9:1
my face, and cried with a *l* voice....	Eze 11:13
hour Jesus cried with a *l* voice.....	Mt 27:46
he had cried again with a *l* voice....	Mt 27:50
torn him, and cried with a *l* voice...	Mk 1:26
And cried with a *l* voice, and said...	Mk 5:7
hour Jesus cried with a *l* voice.....	Mk 15:34
And Jesus cried with a *l* voice......	Mk 15:37
And spake out with a *l* voice.......	Lk 1:42
and cried out with a *l* voice........	Lk 4:33
with a *l* voice said, What have I.....	Lk 8:28
with a *l* voice glorified God........	Lk 17:15
praise God with a *l* voice for all....	Lk 19:37
they were instant with *l* voices.....	Lk 23:23
Jesus had cried with a *l* voice......	Lk 23:46
spoken, he cried with a *l* voice.....	Jn 11:43
they cried out with a *l* voice.......	Acts 7:57
down, and cried with a *l* voice......	Acts 7:60
spirits, crying with *l* voice........	Acts 8:7
Said with a *l* voice, Stand.........	Acts 14:10
But Paul cried with a *l* voice.......	Acts 16:28
Festus said with a *l* voice.........	Acts 26:24
angel proclaiming with a *l* voice....	Rev 5:2
Saying with a *l* voice, Worthy is....	Rev 5:12
And they cried with a *l* voice.......	Rev 6:10
he cried with a *l* voice to the.......	Rev 7:2
And cried with a *l* voice, saying.....	Rev 7:10
of heaven, saying with a *l* voice.....	Rev 8:13
And cried with a *l* voice, as when...	Rev 10:3
I heard a *l* voice saying in.........	Rev 12:10
Saying with a *l* voice, Fear God.....	Rev 14:7
them, saying with a *l* voice........	Rev 14:9
crying with a *l* voice to him that....	Rev 14:15
cried with a *l* cry to him that......	Rev 14:18
and he cried with a *l* voice........	Rev 19:17

LOUDER

long, and waxed *l* and I...........	Ex 19:19

LOVE

make me savoury meat, such as I *l*...	Gen 27:4
few days, for the *l* he had to her....	Gen 29:20
therefore my husband will *l* me.....	Gen 29:32
unto thousands of them that *l* me....	Ex 20:6
I *l* my master, my wife, and my......	Ex 21:5
but thou shalt *l* thy neighbour as....	Lev 19:18
thou shalt *l* him as thyself........	Lev 19:34
unto thousands of them that *l* him...	Deut 5:10
thou shalt *l* the Lord thy God.......	Deut 6:5
Lord did not set his *l* upon you......	Deut 7:7
and mercy with them that *l* him.....	Deut 7:9
And he will *l* thee, and bless thee...	Deut 7:13
to *l* him, and to serve the Lord.....	Deut 10:12
delight in thy fathers to *l* them.....	Deut 10:15
L ye therefore the stranger........	Deut 10:19
thou shalt *l* the Lord thy God.......	Deut 11:1
to *l* the Lord your God, and to......	Deut 11:13
to *l* the Lord your God, to walk.....	Deut 11:22
to know whether ye *l* the Lord......	Deut 13:3
to *l* the Lord thy God, and to walk...	Deut 19:9
to *l* the Lord thy God with all......	Deut 30:6
this day to *l* the Lord thy God.......	Deut 30:16
thou mayest *l* the Lord thy God.....	Deut 30:20
to *l* the Lord your God, and to......	Josh 22:5
that ye *l* the Lord your God........	Josh 23:11
but let them that I him be as the.....	Judg 5:31
I thee, when thine heart is not......	Judg 16:15
thee, and all his servants *l* thee....	1Sa 18:22
thy *l* to me was wonderful........	2Sa 1:26
passing the *l* of women...........	2Sa 1:26
I Tamar, my brother Absalom's......	2Sa 13:4
the *l* wherewith he had loved her...	2Sa 13:15
Solomon clave unto these in *l*......	1Kin 11:2
them that hate the Lord...........	2Chr 19:2
and mercy for them that *l* him......	Neh 1:5
how long will ye *l* vanity..........	Ps 4:2
let them also that *l* thy name be....	Ps 5:11
I will *l* thee, O Lord, my.........	Ps 18:1
O I the Lord, all ye his saints.......	Ps 31:23
let such as *l* thy salvation say.....	Ps 40:16
they that *l* his name shall dwell....	Ps 69:36
let such as *l* thy salvation say.....	Ps 70:4
Because he hath set his *l* upon me...	Ps 91:14
Ye that *l* the Lord, hate evil......	Ps 97:10
For my *l* they are my adversaries....	Ps 109:4
evil for good, and hatred for my *l*...	Ps 109:5
I *l* the Lord, because he hath......	Ps 116:1
O how I *l* thy law...............	Ps 119:97
but thy law do I *l*...............	Ps 119:113
therefore I *l* thy testimonies......	Ps 119:119
Therefore I *l* thy commandments....	Ps 119:127
to do unto those that *l* thy name....	Ps 119:132
Consider how I *l* thy precepts.....	Ps 119:159
I will *l* thee, O Lord, my........	Ps 119:163
peace have they which *l* thy law....	Ps 119:165
and I *l* them exceedingly.........	Ps 119:167
they shall prosper that *l* thee......	Ps 122:6
preserveth all them that *l* him.....	Ps 145:20

simple ones, will ye l simplicity............ Prov 1:22
l her, and she shall keep thee............... Prov 4:6
thou ravished always with her l........... Prov 5:19
our fill of l until the morning............ Prov 7:18
I l them that l me.......................... Prov 8:17
that l me to inherit substance............ Prov 8:21
all they that hate me l death.............. Prov 8:36
a wise man, and he will l thee............ Prov 9:8
but l covereth all sins.................... Prov 10:12
is a dinner of herbs where l is........... Prov 15:17
they l him that speaketh right............ Prov 16:13
a transgression seeketh l................. Prov 17:9
they that l it shall eat the............... Prov 18:21
L not sleep, lest thou come to........... Prov 20:13
rebuke is better than secret l............ Prov 27:5
A time to l, and a time to hate............ Eccl 3:8
no man knoweth either l or hatred....... Eccl 9:1
Also their l, and their hatred, and...... Eccl 9:6
for thy l is better than wine.............. Song 1:2
therefore do the virgins l thee........... Song 1:3
remember thy l more than wine......... Song 1:4
the upright l thee......................... Song 1:4
I have compared thee, O my l............ Song 1:9
Behold, thou art fair, my l................ Song 1:15
so is my l among the daughters......... Song 2:2
and his banner over me was l............ Song 2:4
for I am sick of l.......................... Song 2:5
ye stir not up, nor awake my l........... Song 2:7
and said unto me, Rise up, my l.......... Song 2:10
Arise, my l, my fair one, and come...... Song 2:13
ye stir not up, nor awake my l........... Song 3:5
midst thereof being paved with l........ Song 3:10
Behold, thou art fair, my l................ Song 4:1
Thou art all fair, my l..................... Song 4:7
How fair is thy l, my sister, my......... Song 4:10
much better is thy l than wine.......... Song 4:10
Open to me, my sister, my l.............. Song 5:2
ye tell him, that I am sick of l............ Song 5:8
Thou art beautiful, O my l................ Song 6:4
and how pleasant art thou, O l.......... Song 7:6
ye stir not up, nor awake my l........... Song 8:4
for l is strong as death................... Song 8:6
Many waters cannot quench l............ Song 8:7
the substance of his house for l......... Song 8:7
but thou hast in l to my soul............. Is 38:17
to l the name of the LORD, to be........ Is 56:6
For l the LORD l judgment................ Is 61:8
in his l and in his pity he................. Is 63:9
glad with her, all ye that l her........... Is 66:10
the l of thine espousals, when........... Jer 2:2
trimmest thou thy way to seek l........ Jer 2:33
my people l to have it so.................. Jer 5:31
loved thee with an everlasting l......... Jer 31:3
thy time was the time of l................ Eze 16:8
in her inordinate l than she............. Eze 23:11
came to her into the bed of l............ Eze 23:17
with their mouth they shew much l..... Eze 33:31
tender l with the prince of the.......... Dan 1:9
and mercy to them that l him........... Dan 9:4
a woman beloved of her friend......... Hos 3:1
according to the l of the LORD.......... Hos 3:1
other gods, and l flagons of wine....... Hos 3:1
her rulers with shame do l............... Hos 4:18
mine house, I will l them no more...... Hos 9:15
cords of a man, with bands of l......... Hos 11:4
backsliding, I will l them freely.......... Hos 14:4
I the good, and establish judgment..... Amos 5:15
Who hate the good, and l the evil...... Mic 3:2
to l mercy, and to walk humbly......... Mic 6:8
he will rest in his l, he will.............. Zeph 3:17
and l no false oath....................... Zec 8:17
therefore l the truth and peace........ Zec 8:19
Thou shalt l thy neighbour, and........ Mt 5:43
L your enemies, bless them that....... Mt 5:44
For if ye l them which l you,............. Mt 5:46
for they l to pray standing in........... Mt 6:5
will hate the one, and l the other...... Mt 6:24
Thou shalt l thy neighbour as.......... Mt 19:19
shalt l the Lord thy God................. Mt 22:37
Thou shalt l thy neighbour as.......... Mt 22:39
l the uppermost rooms at feasts....... Mt 23:6
the l of many shall wax cold............ Mt 24:12
thou shalt l the Lord thy God........... Mk 12:30
Thou shalt l thy neighbour as.......... Mk 12:31
to l him with all the heart, and......... Mk 12:33
to l his neighbour as himself, is....... Mk 12:33
which l to go in long clothing,.......... Mk 12:38
l salutations in the marketplaces...... Mk 12:38
L your enemies, do good to them...... Lk 6:27
For if ye l them which l you.............. Lk 6:32
also l those that l them.................. Lk 6:32
But l ye your enemies, and do good.... Lk 6:35
which of them will l him most........... Lk 7:42
Thou shalt l the Lord thy God........... Lk 10:27
over judgment and the l of God......... Lk 11:42
for ye l the uppermost seats in......... Lk 11:43
will hate the one, and l the other...... Lk 16:13
l greetings in the markets, and......... Lk 20:46
ye have not the l of God in you......... Jn 5:42
were your Father, ye would l me....... Jn 8:42
Therefore doth my Father l me.......... Jn 10:17
unto you, That ye l one another......... Jn 13:34
you, that ye also l one another.......... Jn 13:34
if ye have l one to another.............. Jn 13:35
If ye l me, keep my commandments..... Jn 14:15
of my Father, and I will l him............ Jn 14:21
and said unto him, If a man l me........ Jn 14:23
and my Father will l him, and we....... Jn 14:23
may know that I l the Father............. Jn 14:31
continue ye in my l....................... Jn 15:9

ye shall abide in my l..................... Jn 15:10
commandments, and abide in his l...... Jn 15:10
That ye l one another, as I have......... Jn 15:12
Greater l hath no man than this,........ Jn 15:13
you, that ye l one another............... Jn 15:17
world, the world would l his own....... Jn 15:19
that the l wherewith thou hast......... Jn 17:26
thou knowest that I l thee............... Jn 21:15
thou knowest that I l thee............... Jn 21:16
thou knowest that I l thee............... Jn 21:17
because the l of God is shed............ Rom 5:5
God commendeth his l toward us....... Rom 5:8
for good to them that l God.............. Rom 8:28
separate us from the l of Christ......... Rom 8:35
to separate us from the l of God........ Rom 8:39
Let l be without dissimulation......... Rom 12:9
one to another with brotherly l........ Rom 12:10
any thing, but to l one another......... Rom 13:8
Thou shalt l thy neighbour as.......... Rom 13:9
l worketh no ill to his neighbour...... Rom 13:10
therefore l is the fulfilling of......... Rom 13:10
for the l of the Spirit, that ye......... Rom 15:30
hath prepared for them that l him..... 1Cor 2:9
come unto you with a rod, or in l....... 1Cor 4:21
But if any man l God, the same is....... 1Cor 8:3
If any man l not the Lord Jesus......... 1Cor 16:22
My l be with you all in Christ........... 1Cor 16:24
but that ye might know the l............ 2Cor 2:4
would confirm your l toward him...... 2Cor 2:8
For the l of Christ constraineth........ 2Cor 5:14
the Holy Ghost, by l unfeigned,........ 2Cor 6:6
all diligence, and in your l to us....... 2Cor 8:7
to prove the sincerity of your l......... 2Cor 8:8
the churches, the proof of your l....... 2Cor 8:24
because I l you not....................... 2Cor 11:11
the more abundantly I l you............. 2Cor 12:15
and the God of l and peace shall be.... 2Cor 13:11
the l of God, and the communion of.... 2Cor 13:14
but faith which worketh by l............ Gal 5:6
but by l serve one another.............. Gal 5:13
Thou shalt l thy neighbour as.......... Gal 5:14
But the fruit of the Spirit is l.......... Gal 5:22
and without blame before him in l...... Eph 1:4
Jesus, and l unto all the saints,......... Eph 1:15
for his great l wherewith he............ Eph 2:4
ye, being rooted and grounded in l..... Eph 3:17
And to know the l of Christ............. Eph 3:19
forbearing one another in l............. Eph 4:2
But speaking the truth in l.............. Eph 4:15
unto the edifying of itself in l.......... Eph 4:16
And walk in l, as Christ also hath...... Eph 5:2
l your wives, even as Christ also....... Eph 5:25
So ought men to l their wives as....... Eph 5:28
so l his wife even as himself............ Eph 5:33
l with faith, from God the Father....... Eph 6:23
that l our Lord Jesus Christ in.......... Eph 6:24
that your l may abound yet more....... Phil 1:9
But the other of l, knowing that....... Phil 1:17
in Christ, if any comfort of l............ Phil 2:1
be likeminded, having the same l....... Phil 2:2
of the l which ye have to all the....... Col 1:4
unto us your l in the Spirit.............. Col 1:8
being knit together in l................. Col 2:2
l your wives, and be not bitter......... Col 3:19
work of faith, and labour of l........... 1Th 1:3
abound in l one toward another,....... 1Th 3:12
But as touching brotherly l ye......... 1Th 4:9
taught of God to l one another......... 1Th 4:9
on the breastplate of faith and l........ 1Th 5:8
highly in l for their work's sake........ 1Th 5:13
received not the l of the truth......... 2Th 2:10
your hearts into the l of God........... 2Th 3:5
l which is in Christ Jesus................ 1Ti 1:14
For the l of money is the root of........ 1Ti 6:10
godliness, faith, l, patience,............ 1Ti 6:11
but of power, and of l, and of a........ 2Ti 1:7
l which is in Christ Jesus................ 2Ti 1:13
them also that l his appearing.......... 2Ti 4:8
be sober, to l their husbands........... Titus 2:4
to l their children.......................... Titus 2:4
of God our Saviour toward man........ Titus 3:4
Greet them that l us in the faith....... Titus 3:15
Hearing of thy l and faith, which....... Philem 5
great joy and consolation in thy l...... Philem 7
forget your work and labour of l........ Heb 6:10
one another to provoke unto l.......... Heb 10:24
Let brotherly l continue................. Heb 13:1
hath promised to them that l him...... Jas 1:12
hath promised to them that l him...... Jas 2:5
Thou shalt l thy neighbour as.......... Jas 2:8
Whom having not seen, ye l............. 1Pet 1:8
unto unfeigned l of the brethren...... 1Pet 1:22
see that ye l one another with a....... 1Pet 1:22
L the brotherhood........................ 1Pet 2:17
l as brethren, be pitiful, be............. 1Pet 3:8
For he that will l life, and see.......... 1Pet 3:10
verily is the l of God perfected........ 1Jn 2:5
L not the world, neither the............ 1Jn 2:15
If any man l the world................... 1Jn 2:15
the l of the Father is not in him....... 1Jn 2:15
what manner of l the Father hath...... 1Jn 3:1
that we should l one another.......... 1Jn 3:11
because we l the brethren.............. 1Jn 3:14
Hereby perceive we the l of God...... 1Jn 3:16
how dwelleth the l of God in him...... 1Jn 3:17
children, let us not l in word........... 1Jn 3:18
l one another, as he gave us............ 1Jn 3:23
Beloved, let us l one another.......... 1Jn 4:7
for l is of God............................. 1Jn 4:7
for God is l................................ 1Jn 4:8

manifested the l of God toward us...... 1Jn 4:9
Herein is l, not that we loved........... 1Jn 4:10
we ought also to l one another........ 1Jn 4:11
If we l one another, God dwelleth...... 1Jn 4:12
us, and his l is perfected in us.......... 1Jn 4:12
believed the l that God hath to......... 1Jn 4:16
God is l..................................... 1Jn 4:16
dwelleth in l dwelleth in God........... 1Jn 4:16
Herein is our l made perfect............ 1Jn 4:17
There is no fear in l...................... 1Jn 4:18
but perfect l casteth out fear.......... 1Jn 4:18
feareth is not made perfect in l........ 1Jn 4:18
We l him, because he first loved...... 1Jn 4:19
I l God, and hateth his brother,........ 1Jn 4:20
how can he l God whom he hath not... 1Jn 4:20
who loveth God l his brother also..... 1Jn 4:21
that we l the children of God........... 1Jn 5:2
children of God, when we l God........ 1Jn 5:2
For this is the l of God, that we....... 1Jn 5:3
children, whom I l in the truth......... 2Jn 1
Son of the Father, in truth and l....... 2Jn 3
beginning, that we l one another...... 2Jn 5
And this is l, that we walk after....... 2Jn 6
Gaius, whom I l in the truth............. 3Jn 1
Mercy unto you, and peace, and l...... Jude 2
Keep yourselves in the l of God....... Jude 21
thou hast left thy first l.................. Rev 2:4
As many as I l, I rebuke and............ Rev 3:19

LOVED

his wife, and he l her.................... Gen 24:67
And Isaac l Esau, because he did...... Gen 25:28
but Rebekah l Jacob..................... Gen 25:28
meat, such as his father l............... Gen 27:14
And Jacob l Rachel...................... Gen 29:18
he l also Rachel more than Leah,...... Gen 29:30
he l the damsel, and spake kindly..... Gen 34:3
Now Israel l Joseph more than all..... Gen 37:3
I him more than all his brethren....... Gen 37:4
because he l thy fathers,................ Deut 4:37
But because the LORD l you............ Deut 7:8
because the LORD thy God l thee..... Deut 23:5
Yea, he l the people...................... Deut 33:3
that he l a woman in the valley........ Judg 16:4
for he l Hannah............................ 1Sa 1:5
and he l him greatly...................... 1Sa 16:21
Jonathan l him as his own soul........ 1Sa 18:1
because he l him as his own soul...... 1Sa 18:3
But all Israel and Judah l David........ 1Sa 18:16
And Michal Saul's daughter l David.... 1Sa 18:20
that Michal Saul's daughter l him...... 1Sa 18:28
to swear again, because he l him....... 1Sa 20:17
for he l him as he........................ 1Sa 20:17
him as he l his own soul................ 1Sa 20:17
and the Lord l him........................ 2Sa 12:24
and Amnon the son of David l her..... 2Sa 13:1
the love wherewith he had l her....... 2Sa 13:15
Solomon l the LORD, walking in........ 1Kin 3:3
the LORD l Israel for ever.............. 1Kin 10:9
But king Solomon l many strange..... 1Kin 11:1
the LORD hath l his people............. 2Chr 2:11
because thy God l Israel, to........... 2Chr 9:8
Rehoboam l Maachah the daughter... 2Chr 11:21
for he l husbandry....................... 2Chr 26:10
the king l Esther above all the......... Est 2:17
they whom I l are turned against...... Job 19:19
I have l the habitation of thy........... Ps 26:8
the excellency of Jacob whom he l..... Ps 47:4
Judah, the mount Zion which he l...... Ps 78:68
As he l cursing, so let it come.......... Ps 109:17
thy commandments, which I have l.... Ps 119:47
thy commandments, which I have l.... Ps 119:48
been honourable, and I have l thee.... Is 43:4
The Lord hath l him...................... Is 48:14
for I have l strangers, and after....... Jer 2:25
host of heaven, whom they have l..... Jer 8:2
Thus have they l to wander............ Jer 14:10
I have l thee with an everlasting..... Jer 31:3
and all them that thou hast l........... Eze 16:37
thou hast l a reward upon every...... Hos 9:1
were according as they l................ Hos 9:10
Israel was a child, then I l him......... Hos 11:1
I have l you, saith the LORD........... Mal 1:2
ye say, Wherein hast thou l us......... Mal 1:2
yet I l Jacob............................... Mal 1:2
holiness of the LORD which he l....... Mal 2:11
Then Jesus beholding him l him....... Mk 10:21
for she l much............................ Lk 7:47
For God so l the world, that he........ Jn 3:16
men l darkness rather than light...... Jn 3:19
Now Jesus l Martha, and her sister... Jn 11:5
the Jews, Behold how he l him......... Jn 11:36
For they l the praise of men more.... Jn 12:43
having l his own which were in........ Jn 13:1
the world, he l them unto the end.... Jn 13:1
of his disciples, whom Jesus l......... Jn 13:23
as I have l you, that ye also........... Jn 13:34
loveth me shall be l of my Father..... Jn 14:21
If ye l me, ye would rejoice,........... Jn 14:28
hath l me, so have I l you............... Jn 15:9
love one another, as I have l you...... Jn 15:12
loveth you, because ye have l me..... Jn 16:27
thou hast sent me, and hast l them... Jn 17:23
as thou hast l me........................ Jn 17:23
thou hast l me may be in them........ Jn 17:26
disciple standing by, whom he l....... Jn 19:26
the other disciple, whom Jesus l...... Jn 20:2
whom Jesus l saith unto Peter........ Jn 21:7
disciple whom Jesus l following....... Jn 21:20
conquerors through him that l us...... Rom 8:37
As it is written, Jacob have I l......... Rom 9:13

LOVEDST

I love you, the less I be I	2Cor 12:15
faith of the Son of God, who I me	Gal 2:20
his great love wherewith he I us	Eph 2:4
in love, as Christ also hath I us	Eph 5:2
even as Christ also I the church	Eph 5:25
even our Father, which hath I us	2Th 2:16
having I this present world, and	2Ti 4:10
Thou hast I righteousness, and	Heb 1:9
son of Bosor, who I the wages of	2Pet 2:15
Herein is love, not that we I God	1Jn 4:10
but that he I us	1Jn 4:11
Beloved, if God so I us, we ought	1Jn 4:11
love him, because he first I us	1Jn 4:19
Unto him that I us, and washed us	Rev 1:5
and to know that I have I thee	Rev 3:9
they I not their lives unto the	Rev 12:11

LOVEDST

thou I their bed where thou	Is 57:8
for thou I me before the	Jn 17:24

LOVELY

Saul and Jonathan were I and	2Sa 1:23
yea, he is altogether I	Song 5:16
a very I young of one that hath a	Eze 33:32
are pure, whatsoever things are I	Phil 4:8

LOVER

for Hiram was ever a I of David	1Kin 5:1
I, and friend hast thou put far	Ps 88:18
But a I of hospitality	Titus 1:8
a I of good men, sober, just,	Titus 1:8

LOVERS

My I and my friends stand aloof	Ps 38:11
played the harlot with many I	Jer 3:1
thy I will despise thee, they	Jer 4:30
for all thy I are destroyed	Jer 22:20
thy I shall go into captivity	Jer 22:22
All thy I have forgotten thee	Jer 30:14
among all her I she hath none to	Lam 1:2
I called for my I, but they	Lam 1:19
givest thy gifts to all thy I	Eze 16:33
through thy whoredoms with thy I	Eze 16:36
therefore I will gather all thy I	Eze 16:37
and she doted on her I, on the	Eze 23:5
her into the hand of her I	Eze 23:9
will raise up thy I against thee	Eze 23:22
she said, I will go after my I	Hos 2:5
And she shall follow after her I	Hos 2:7
lewdness in the sight of her I	Hos 2:10
rewards that my I have given me	Hos 2:12
jewels, and she went after her I	Hos 2:13
Ephraim hath hired I	Hos 8:9
For men shall be I of their own	2Ti 3:2
I of pleasures more than	2Ti 3:4
I of pleasures more than I of God	2Ti 3:4

LOVE'S

Yet for I sake I rather beseech	Philem 9

LOVES

of Korah, A Maschil, A Song of I	Ps 45:t
let us solace ourselves with I	Prov 7:18
there will I give thee my I	Song 7:12

LOVEST

thine only son Isaac, whom thou I	Gen 22:2
dost but hate me, and I me not	Judg 14:16
In that thou I thine enemies, and	2Sa 19:6
Thou I righteousness, and hatest	Ps 45:7
Thou I evil more than good	Ps 52:3
Thou I all devouring words, O	Ps 52:4
with the wife whom thou I all the	Eccl 9:9
behold, he whom thou I is sick	Jn 11:3
I thou me more than these	Jn 21:15
Simon, son of Jonas, I thou me	Jn 21:16
Simon, son of Jonas, I thou me	Jn 21:17
him the third time, I thou me	Jn 21:17

LOVETH

meat for thy father, such as he I	Gen 27:9
his mother, and his father I him	Gen 44:20
I the stranger, in giving him	Deut 10:18
because he I thee and thine house	Deut 15:16
thy daughter in law, which I thee	Ruth 4:15
him that I violence his soul	Ps 11:5
righteous LORD I righteousness	Ps 11:7
He I righteousness and judgment	Ps 33:5
I many days, that he may see good	Ps 34:12
for the LORD I judgment, and	Ps 37:28
The LORD I the gates of Zion more	Ps 87:2
king's strength also I judgment	Ps 99:4
therefore thy servant I thee	Ps 119:140
the LORD I the righteous	Ps 146:8
For whom the LORD I he correcteth	Prov 3:12
I instruction I knowledge	Prov 12:1
but he that I him chasteneth him	Prov 13:24
but he I him that followeth after	Prov 15:9
A scorner I not one that	Prov 15:12
A friend I at all times, and a	Prov 17:17
He I transgression that I strife	Prov 17:19
transgression that I strife	Prov 17:19
getteth wisdom I his own soul	Prov 19:8
He that I pleasure shall be a	Prov 21:17
he that I wine and oil shall not	Prov 21:17
He that I pureness of heart, for	Prov 22:11
Whoso I wisdom rejoiceth his	Prov 29:3
He that I silver shall not be	Eccl 5:10
nor he that I abundance with	Eccl 5:10
Tell me, O thou whom my soul I	Song 1:7
bed I sought him whom my soul I	Song 3:1
I will seek him whom my soul I	Song 3:2
I said, Saw ye him whom my soul I	Song 3:3

but I found him whom my soul I	Song 3:4
every one I gifts, and followeth	Is 1:23
and I to tread out the corn	Hos 10:11
He I to oppress	Hos 12:7
He that I father or mother more	Mt 10:37
he that I son or daughter more	Mt 10:37
For he I our nation, and he hath	Lk 7:5
is forgiven, the same I little	Lk 7:47
The Father I the Son, and hath	Jn 3:35
For the Father I the Son, and	Jn 5:20
He that I his life shall lose it	Jn 12:25
keepeth them, he it is that I me	Jn 14:21
he that I me shall be loved of my	Jn 14:21
the that I me not keepeth not my	Jn 14:24
For the Father himself I you	Jn 16:27
for he that I another hath	Rom 13:8
for God I a cheerful giver	2Cor 9:7
He that I his wife I himself	Eph 5:28
For whom the Lord I he chasteneth	Heb 12:6
He that I his brother abideth in	1Jn 2:10
neither he that I not his brother	1Jn 3:10
He that I not his brother abideth	1Jn 3:14
every one that I is born of God	1Jn 4:7
He that I not knoweth not God	1Jn 4:8
for he that I not his brother	1Jn 4:20
That he who I God love his	1Jn 4:21
every one that I him that begat	1Jn 5:1
I him also that is begotten of	1Jn 5:1
who I to have the preeminence	3Jn 9
and idolaters, and whosoever I	Rev 22:15

LOVING

Let her be as the I hind and	Prov 5:19
I favour rather than silver and	Prov 22:1
lying down, I to slumber	Is 56:10

LOVINGKINDNESS

Shew thy marvellous I, O thou	Ps 17:7
for they I are before mine eyes	Ps 26:3
How excellent is thy I, O God	Ps 36:7
I concerning thy I unto them that	Ps 36:10
I have not concealed thy I	Ps 40:10
let thy I and thy truth	Ps 40:11
will command his I in the daytime	Ps 42:8
We have thought of thy I, O God,	Ps 48:9
me, O God, according to thy I	Ps 51:1
Because thy I is better than life	Ps 63:3
for thy I is good	Ps 69:16
Shall thy I be declared in	Ps 88:11
Nevertheless my I will I not	Ps 89:33
shew forth thy I in the morning	Ps 92:2
who crowneth thee with I	Ps 103:4
understand the I of the LORD	Ps 107:43
Quicken me after thy I	Ps 119:88
my voice according unto thy I	Ps 119:149
me, O LORD, according to thy I	Ps 119:159
and praise thy name for thy I	Ps 138:2
me to hear thy I in the morning	Ps 143:8
I am the LORD which exercise I	Jer 9:24
people, saith the LORD, even I	Jer 16:5
therefore with I have I drawn	Jer 31:3
Thou shewest I unto thousands, and	Jer 32:18
and in judgment, and in I, and in	Hos 2:19

LOVINGKINDNESSES

LORD, thy tender mercies and thy I	Ps 25:6
Lord, where are thy former I	Ps 89:49
I will mention the I of the LORD	Is 63:7
to the multitude of his I	Is 63:7

LOW

and thou shalt come down very I	Deut 28:43
hast brought me very I	Judg 11:35
he bringeth I, and lifteth up	1Sa 2:7
the I plains was Baal-hanan the	1Chr 27:28
are in the I plains in abundance	2Chr 9:27
cattle, both in the I country	2Chr 26:10
the cities of the I country	2Chr 28:18
For the Lord brought Judah I	2Chr 28:19
To set up on high those that be I	Job 5:11
and they are brought I, but	Job 14:21
while, but are gone and brought I	Job 24:24
one that is proud, and bring him I	Job 40:12
Both I and high, rich and poor,	Ps 49:2
Surely men of I degree are vanity	Ps 62:9
for we are brought very I	Ps 79:8
were brought I for their iniquity	Ps 106:43
brought I through oppression,	Ps 107:39
I was brought I, and he helped me	Ps 116:6
Who remembered us in our I estate	Ps 136:23
I am brought very I	Ps 142:6
A man's pride shall bring him I	Prov 29:23
and the rich sit in I place	Eccl 10:6
the sound of the grinding is I	Eccl 12:4
of musick shall be brought I	Eccl 12:4
and he shall be brought I	Is 2:12
of men shall be made I	Is 2:17
will lay I the haughtiness of the	Is 13:11
terrible ones shall be brought I	Is 25:5
walls shall he bring down, lay I	Is 25:12
the lofty city, he layeth it I	Is 26:5
he layeth it I, even to the	Is 26:5
speech shall be I out of the dust	Is 29:4
city shall be I in a place	Is 32:19
city shall be I in a I place	Is 32:19
mountain and hill shall be made I	Is 40:4
O Lucep, out of the I dungeon	Lam 3:55
a spreading vine of I stature	Eze 17:6
tree, have exalted the I tree	Eze 17:24
exalt him that is I, and abase him	Eze 21:26
thee in the I parts of the earth	Eze 26:20
the I estate of his handmaiden	Lk 1:48

and exalted them of I degree	Lk 1:52
mighty shall be brought I	Lk 3:5
but condescend to men of I estate	Rom 12:16
Let the brother of I degree	Jas 1:9
the rich, in that he is made I	Jas 1:10

LOWER

with I, second, and third stories	Gen 6:16
it be in sight I than the skin	Lev 13:20
if it be not I than the skin, but	Lev 13:21
it be no I than the other skin,	Lev 13:26
in sight are I than the wall	Lev 14:37
I in the I places behind the wall	Neh 4:13
him a little I than the angels	Ps 8:5
shall go into the I parts of the	Ps 63:9
I in the presence of the prince	Prov 25:7
together the waters of the I pool	Is 22:9
shout, ye I parts of the earth	Is 44:23
of the gates was the I pavement	Eze 40:18
from the forefront of the I gate	Eze 40:19
higher than these, than the I	Eze 42:5
the I settle shall be two cubits	Eze 43:14
into the I parts of the earth	Eph 4:9
him a little I than the angels	Heb 2:7
who was made a little I than the	Heb 2:9

LOWEST

and shall burn unto the I hell	Deut 32:22
priests of the I of the people	1Kin 12:31
but made again of the I of the	1Kin 13:33
the I of them priests of the high	2Kin 17:32
delivered my soul from the I hell	Ps 86:13
Thou hast laid me in the I pit	Ps 88:6
for the I parts of the earth	Ps 139:15
so increased from the I chamber	Eze 41:7
was restrained more than the I	Eze 42:6
with shame to take the I room	Lk 14:9
go and sit down in the I room	Lk 14:10

LOWETH

or I the ox over his fodder	Job 6:5

LOWINESS

but in I of mind let each esteem	Phil 2:3

LOWING

I as they went, and turned not	1Sa 6:12
the I of the oxen which I hear	1Sa 15:14

LOWLINESS

With all I and meekness, with	Eph 4:2

LOWLY

yet hath he respect unto the I	Ps 138:6
but he giveth grace unto the I	Prov 3:34
but with the I is wisdom	Prov 11:2
be of an humble spirit with the I	Prov 16:19
I, and riding upon an ass, and upon	Zec 9:9
for I am meek and I in heart	Mt 11:29

LOWRING

for the sky is red and I	Mt 16:3

LUBIM (lu'-bim) See LUBIMS. *An African race.*

the L, the Sukkiims, and the	2Chr 12:3
Put and L were thy helpers	Nah 3:9

LUBIMS (lu'-bims) See LEHABIM, LUBIM. *Same as Lubim.*

The L a huge host, with very many 2Chr 16:8

LUCAS (lu'-cas) See LUKE. *Same as Luke.*

city of Macedonia, by Titus and L	2Cor 8
Marcus, Aristarchus, Demas, L	Philem 24

LUCIFER (lu'-sif-ur) *Title applied to king of Babylon.*

art thou fallen from heaven, O L ...... Is 14:12

LUCIUS (lu'-she-us)
  1. A Christian from Cyrene.
  L of Cyrene, and Manaen, which had.. Acts 13:1
  2. A relative of Paul.
  Timotheus my workfellow, and L...... Rom 16:21

LUCRE

ways, but turned aside after I	1Sa 8:3
striker, not greedy of filthy I	1Ti 3:3
much wine, not greedy of filthy I	1Ti 3:8
no striker, not given to filthy I	Titus 1:7
not for filthy I, but of a ready	1Pet 5:2

LUCRE'S

they ought not, for filthy I sake ...... Titus 1:11

LUD (lud) See LUDIM, LYDIA.
  1. Son of Shem.

and Asshur, and Arphaxad, and L	Gen 10:22
and Asshur, and Arphaxad, and L	1Chr 1:17
2. Descendants of Lud I.	
nations, to Tarshish, Pul, and L	Is 66:19
They of Persia and of L and of Phut .. Eze 27:10	

LUDIM (lu'-dim) See LUD. *Son of Mizraim.*

And Mizraim begat L	Gen 10:13
And Mizraim begat L	1Chr 1:11

LUHITH (lu'-hith) *A Moabite city.*

for by the mounting up of L with	Is 15:5
For in the going up of L	Jer 48:5

LUKE (luke) See LUCAS. *A companion of Paul.*

L, the beloved physician, and	Col 4:14
Only L is with me	2Ti 4:11

L

LUKEWARM
So then because thou art *l* .... Rev 3:16

LUMP
And Isaiah said, Take a *l* of figs 2Kin 20:7
said, Let them take a *l* of figs .... Is 38:21
of the same *l* to make one vessel .... Rom 9:21
be holy, the *l* is also holy .... Rom 11:16
leaven leaveneth the whole *l* 1Cor 5:6
leaven, that ye may be a new *l* 1Cor 5:7
leaven leaveneth the whole *l* .... Gal 5:9

LUNATICK
devils, and those which were *l* .... Mt 4:24
for he is *l*, and sore vexed .... Mt 17:15

LURK
let us *l* privily for the innocent .... Prov 1:11
they *l* privily for their own .... Prov 1:18

LURKING
take knowledge of all the *l* 1Sa 23:23
He sitteth in the *l* places of the .... Ps 10:8
a young lion *l* in secret places .... Ps 17:12

LUST
my *l* shall be satisfied upon them .... Ex 15:9
heart his asking meat for their *l* .... Ps 78:18
were not estranged from their *l* .... Ps 78:30
them up unto their own hearts' *l* .... Ps 81:12
L not after her beauty in thine .... Prov 6:25
to *l* after her hath committed .... Mt 5:28
burned in their *l* one toward .... Rom 1:27
for I had not known *l*, except the .... Rom 7:7
we should not *l* after evil things 1Cor 10:6
not fulfil the *l* of the flesh .... Gal 5:16
Not in the *l* of concupiscence 1Th 4:5
he is drawn away of his own *l* .... Jas 1:14
Then when *l* hath conceived, it .... Jas 1:15
Ye *l*, and have not .... Jas 4:2
that is in the world through *l* 2Pet 1:4
the flesh in the *l* of uncleanness 2Pet 2:10
the *l* of the flesh 1Jn 2:16
the *l* of the eyes, and the pride 1Jn 2:16
passeth away, and the *l* thereof 1Jn 2:17

LUSTED
they buried the people that *l* .... Num 11:34
But I exceedingly in the .... Ps 106:14
after evil things, as they also *l* 1Cor 10:6
the fruits that thy soul *l* after .... Rev 18:14

LUSTETH
whatsoever thy soul *l* after .... Deut 12:15
whatsoever thy soul *l* after .... Deut 12:20
gates whatsoever thy soul *l* after .... Deut 12:21
for whatsoever thy soul *l* after .... Deut 14:26
For the flesh *l* against the .... Gal 5:17
that dwelleth in us *l* to envy .... Jas 4:5

LUSTING
that was among them fell a *l* .... Num 11:4

LUSTS
the *l* of other things entering in .... Mk 4:19
the *l* of your father ye will do .... Jn 8:44
through the *l* of their own hearts .... Rom 1:24
should obey it in the *l* thereof .... Rom 6:12
flesh, to fulfil the *l* thereof .... Rom 13:14
flesh with the affections and *l* .... Gal 5:24
times past in the *l* of our flesh .... Eph 2:3
according to the deceitful *l* .... Eph 4:22
and into many foolish and hurtful *l* 1Ti 6:9
Flee also youthful *l* 2Ti 2:22
with sins, led away with divers *l* 2Ti 3:6
but after their own *l* shall they 2Ti 4:3
denying ungodliness and worldly *l* ...... Titus 2:12
deceived, serving divers *l* .... Titus 3:3
even of your *l* that war in your .... Jas 4:1
ye may consume it upon your *l* .... Jas 4:3
the former *l* in your ignorance 1Pet 1:14
pilgrims, abstain from fleshly *l* 1Pet 2:11
time in the flesh to the *l* of men 1Pet 4:2
we walked in lasciviousness, *l* 1Pet 4:3
allure through the *l* of the flesh 2Pet 2:18
walking after their own *l* 2Pet 3:3
walking after their own *l* .... Jude 16
walk after their own ungodly *l* .... Jude 18

LUSTY
about ten thousand men, all *l* .... Judg 3:29

LUZ (luz) See BETH-EL.
1. A Canaanite city.
city was called *L* at the first .... Gen 28:19
So Jacob came to *L*, which is in .... Gen 35:6
me at *L* in the land of Canaan .... Gen 48:3
And goeth out from Beth-el to *L* .... Josh 16:2
toward *L*, to the side of *L* .... Josh 18:13
the name of the city before was *L* ...... Judg 1:23
2. A Hittite city.
and called the name thereof *L* .... Judg 1:26

LYCAONIA (li-ca-o'-ne-ah) *A Roman province
in Asia Minor.*
unto Lystra and Derbe, cities of *L* ...... Acts 14:6
voices, saying in the speech of *L* .... Acts 14:11

LYCAONIAN

LYCIA (lish'-e-ah) *A Roman province in Asia
Minor.*
we came to Myra, a city of *L* .... Acts 27:5

LYDDA (lid'-dah) See LOD. *A city in Judea.*
to the saints which dwelt at *L* .... Acts 9:32
And all that dwelt at *L* and Saron ...... Acts 9:35

forasmuch as *L* was nigh to Joppa, ... Acts 9:38

LYDIA (lid'-e-ah) See LUDIM, LYDIANS.
1. A people in North Africa.
Ethiopia, and Libya, and *L*, and all ..... Eze 30:5
2. A Christian woman.
And a certain woman named *L* .... Acts 16:14
and entered into the house of *L* .... Acts 16:40

LYDIANS (lid'-e-ans) *Same as Lydia 1.*
and the *L*, that handle and bend the ... Jer 46:9

LYING
three flocks of sheep *l* by it .... Gen 29:2
Israel in *l* with Jacob's daughter .... Gen 34:7
hateth thee *l* under his burden .... Ex 23:5
that hath known man by *l* with him, .. Num 31:17
not known a man by *l* with him .... Num 31:18
had not known man by *l* with him ..... Num 31:35
in the field, and it be not .... Deut 21:1
If a man be found *l* with a woman ..... Deut 22:22
were with him, from *l* in wait .... Judg 9:35
Now there were men *l* in wait .... Judg 16:9
known no man by *l* with any male .... Judg 21:12
I will be a *l* spirit in the mouth 1Kin 22:22
the LORD hath put a *l* spirit in 1Kin 22:23
be a *l* spirit in the mouth of all 2Chr 18:21
the LORD hath put a *l* spirit in 2Chr 18:22
hated them that regard *l* vanities ...... Ps 31:6
Let the *l* lips be put to silence .... Ps 31:18
and I rather than to speak .... Ps 52:3
for cursing and *l* which they speak .... Ps 59:12
spoken against me with a *l* tongue ..... Ps 109:2
Remove from me the way of *l* .... Ps 119:29
I hate and abhor *l* .... Ps 119:163
my soul, O LORD, from *l* lips .... Ps 120:2
my *l* down, and art acquainted with ... Ps 139:3
a *l* tongue, and hands that shed .... Prov 6:17
He that hideth hatred with *l* lips ...... Prov 10:18
but a *l* tongue is but for a .... Prov 12:19
L lips are abomination to the .... Prov 12:22
A righteous man hateth *l* .... Prov 13:5
much less do *l* lips a prince .... Prov 17:7
a *l* tongue is a vanity tossed to ...... Prov 21:6
A *l* tongue hateth those that are ...... Prov 26:28
l children, children that will .... Is 30:9
to destroy the poor with *l* words ...... Is 32:7
l down, slow to slumber .... Is 56:10
l against the LORD, and departing ..... Is 59:13
Trust ye not in *l* words, saying, ... Jer 7:4
Behold, ye trust in *l* words .... Jer 7:8
have spoken *l* words in my name, ... Jer 29:23
was unto me as a bear *l* in wait ...... Lam 3:10
l divination, saying, The LORD .... Eze 13:6
have ye not spoken a *l* divination ..... Eze 13:7
by your *l* to my people that hear ...... Eze 13:19
for ye have prepared *l* and corrupt ... Dan 2:9
By swearing, and *l*, and killing, and ... Hos 4:2
They that observe *l* vanities .... Jonah 2:8
man sick of the palsy, *l* on a bed ..... Mt 9:2
in where the damsel was *l* .... Mk 5:40
swaddling clothes, *l* in a manger ...... Lk 2:12
Joseph, and the babe *l* in a manger ... Lk 2:16
He then *l* on Jesus' breast saith .... Jn 13:25
in, saw the linen clothes *l* .... Jn 20:5
not *l* with the linen clothes, but ...... Jn 20:7
me by the *l* in wait of the Jews .... Acts 20:19
son heard of their *l* in wait .... Acts 23:16
Wherefore putting away *l*, speak ...... Eph 4:25
all power and signs and *l* wonders, ... 2Th 2:9

LYSANIAS (li-sa'-ne-as) *Governor of Abilene.*
L the tetrarch of Abilene, ... Lk 3:1

LYSIAS (lis'-e-as) *A Roman commander.*
Claudius *L* unto the most .... Acts 23:26
the chief captain *L* came upon us ...... Acts 24:7
When *L* the chief captain shall .... Acts 24:22

LYSTRA (lis'-trah) *A city in Lycaonia.*
were ware of it, and fled unto *L* .... Acts 14:6
And there sat a certain man at *L* ...... Acts 14:8
many, they returned again to *L* .... Acts 14:21
Then came he to Derbe and *L* .... Acts 16:1
of by the brethren that were at *L* ..... Acts 16:2
me at Antioch, at Iconium, at *L* 2Ti 3:11

M

MAACAH (ma'-a-kah) See MAACHAH.
1. A wife of David.
Absalom the son of *M* the daughter ... 2Sa 3:3
2. A king of Maacah 3.
of king *M* a thousand men, and of 2Sa 10:6
3. A district of Syria.
and Rehob, and Ish-tob, and *M* 2Sa 10:8

MAACATHITE See MAACHATHITE.

MAACHAH (ma'-a-kah) See BETH-MAACHAH,
MAACHA, MAACHATHITE, SYRIA-MAACHAH.
1. A son of Nahor.
and Gaham, and Thahash, and *M* ...... Gen 22:24
2. Father of Achish.
unto Achish son of *M* king of Gath ... 1Kin 2:39
3. Wife of King Rehoboam.
And his mother's name was *M* 1Kin 15:2
And his mother's name was *M* 1Kin 15:10

after her he took *M* the daughter 2Chr 11:21
Rehoboam loved *M* the daughter of 2Chr 11:21
Abijah the son of *M* the chief 2Chr 13:2
4. Mother of King Asa.
also *M* his mother, even her he 1Kin 15:13
also concerning *M* the mother of 2Chr 15:16
5. Concubine of Caleb.
M, Caleb's concubine, bare Sheber 1Chr 2:48
6. A wife of Machir.
Absalom the son of *M* the daughter 1Chr 3:2
7. A wife of Machir.
whose sister's name was *M* 1Chr 7:15
M the wife of Machir bare a son, ... 1Chr 7:16
8. Wife of Jehiel.
whose wife's name was *M* 1Chr 8:29
Jehiel, whose wife's name was *M* 1Chr 9:35
9. Father of Hanan.
Hanan the son of *M*, and Joshaphat.. 1Chr 11:43
10.A district of Syria.
chariots, and the king of *M* 1Chr 19:7
11. Father of Shephatiah.
Shephatiah the son of *M* 1Chr 27:16

MAACHATHI (ma-ak'-a-thi) See
MAACHATHITE. *Inhabitants of Maachah 10.*
unto the coasts of Geshuri and *M* ...... Deut 3:14

MAACHATHITE (ma-ak'-a-thite) See
MAACHATHI, MAACHATHITES. *Same as
Maachathi.*
son of Maachah, the son of the *M* 2Sa 23:34
and Jaazaniah the son of a *M* 2Kin 25:23
the Garmite, and Eshtemoa the *M* 1Chr 4:19
and Jezaniah the son of a *M* .... Jer 40:8

MAACHATHITES
border of the Geshurites and the *M* .... Josh 12:5
the border of the Geshurites and *M* .... Josh 13:11
not the Geshurites, nor the *M* .... Josh 13:13
the *M* dwell among the Israelites ...... Josh 13:13

MAADAI (ma'-a-dahee) *Married a foreigner in
exile.*
M, Amram, and Uel, ... Ezr 10:34

MAADIAH (ma-a-di'-ah) See MOADIAH. *A
priest with Zerubbabel.*
Miamin, *M*, Bilgah, ... Neh 12:5

MAAI (ma'-ahee) *A priest.*
and Azareel, Milalai, Gilalai, *M* .... Neh 12:36

MAALEH-ACRABBIM (ma'-a-leh-ac-rab'-
bim) See AKRABBIM . *A pass on Judah's
southern border.*
went out to the south side to *M* .... Josh 15:3

MAARATH (ma'-a-rath) *A city in Judah.*
And *M*, and Beth-anoth, and Eltekon .. Josh 15:59

MAAREH-GEBA

MAASAI See MAASIAI.

MAASEIAH (ma-a-si'-ah)
1. A priest who relocated the Ark.
and Unni, Eliab, and Benaiah, and *M* .. 1Chr 15:18
Jehiel, and Unni, and Eliab, and *M* 1Chr 15:20
2. Son of Adaiah.
Obed, and *M* the son of Adaiah, and... 2Chr 23:1
3. An officer of King Uzziah.
M the ruler, under the hand of 2Chr 26:11
4. A son of King Ahaz.
slew *M* the king's son, and Azrikam ... 2Chr 28:7
5. A governor of Jerusalem.
M the governor of the city, and 2Chr 34:8
6. A priest who married a foreigner.
M, and Eliezer, and Jarib, and .... Ezr 10:18
M, and Elijah, and Shemaiah, and ..... Ezr 10:21
8. A priest of the Pashur family.
Elioenai, *M*, Ishmael, Nethaneel, ... Ezr 10:22
9. A priest of the Pahath-moab family.
Adna, and Chelal, Benaiah, *M* .... Ezr 10:30
10. Father of Azariah.
the son of Ananiah by his house .... Neh 3:23
11. A priest with Ezra.
and Urijah, and Hilkiah, and *M* .... Neh 8:4
12. Another priest with Ezra.
Akkub, Shabbethai, Hodijah, *M* .... Neh 8:7
13. An Israelite who renewed the covenant.
Rehum, Hashabnah, *M*, ... Neh 10:25
14. A family of exiles.
M the son of Baruch, the son of ...... Neh 11:5
15. A descendant of Benjamin.
the son of Kolaiah, the son of *M* ...... Neh 11:7
16. A priest who dedicated the wall.
Eliakim, *M*, Miniamin, Michaiah, ... Neh 12:41
17. Another priest who dedicated the wall.
M, and Shemaiah .... Neh 12:42
18. Father of Zephaniah.
Zephaniah the son of *M* the priest ..... Jer 21:1
Zephaniah the son of *M* the priest ..... Jer 29:25
Zephaniah the son of *M* the priest ..... Jer 37:3
19. Father of Zedekiah.
and of Zedekiah the son of *M* .... Jer 29:21
20. A Temple officer.
keeper of *M* the son of Shallum .... Jer 35:4
21. Grandfather of Baruch.
the son of Neriah, the son of *M* .... Jer 32:12
the son of Neriah, the son of *M* .... Jer 51:59

MAASIAI (ma-a'-see-ahee) *A family of exiles.*
M the son of Adiel, the son of 1Chr 9:12

MAATH (ma'-ath) *Father of Nagge; ancestor of Jesus.*
Which was the son of M, which was .... Lk 3:26

MAAZ (ma'-az) *A son of Ram.*
firstborn of Jerahmeel were, M............... 1Chr 2:27

MAAZIAH (ma-a-zi'-ah)
  1. A sanctuary servant.
the four and twentieth to M................. 1Chr 24:18
  2. A priest who renewed the covenant.
M, Bilgai, Shemaiah .... Neh 10:8

MACBENAH See **MACHBENAH.**

MACEDONIA (mas-e-do'-nee-ah) See **MACEDONIAN.** *A Roman province north of Greece.*
There stood a man of M, and prayed..... Acts 16:9
him, saying, Come over into M .... Acts 16:9
we endeavoured to go into M................. Acts 16:10
the chief city of that part of M .... Acts 16:12
and Timotheus were come from M ...... Acts 18:5
when he had passed through M .... Acts 19:21
So he sent into M two of them .... Acts 19:22
Gaius and Aristarchus, men of M .... Acts 19:29
and departed for to go into M .... Acts 20:1
he purposed to return through M .... Acts 20:3
For it hath pleased them of M .... Rom 15:26
you, when I shall pass through M 1Cor 16:5
for I do pass through M 1Cor 16:5
And to pass by you into M 2Cor 1:16
to come again out of M unto you 2Cor 1:16
them, I went from thence into M 2Cor 2:13
For, when we were come into M 2Cor 7:5
God bestowed on the churches of M... 2Cor 8:1
which I boast of you to them of M....... 2Cor 9:2
haply if they of M come with me.......... 2Cor 9:4
which came from M supplied 2Cor 11:9
from Philippi, a city of M .... 2Cor s
gospel, when I departed from M .... Phil 4:15
to all that believe in M and 1Th 1:7
word of the Lord not only in M 1Th 1:8
the brethren which are in all M 1Th 4:10
at Ephesus, when I went into M 1Ti 1:3
the Cretians, from Nicopolis of M ...... Titus s

MACEDONIAN (mas-e-do'-nee-an) *An inhabitant of Macedonia.*
a M of Thessalonica, being with .... Acts 27:2

MACHBANAI See **MACBENAI.**

MACHBANNAI (mak'-ba-nahee) *A warrior in David's army.*
the tenth, the eleventh 1Chr 12:13

MACHBENAH See **MACEBENAI.**

MACHBENA See **MACHBENAH.**

MACHBENAH (mak'-be-nah) *A descendant of Caleb.*
Madmannah, Sheva the father of M 1Chr 2:49

MACHI (ma'-ki) *Father of Geuel.*
tribe of Gad, Geuel the son of M .... Num 13:15

MACHIR (ma'-kur) See **MACHIRITE.**
  1. Son of Manasseh.
the children also of M the son of .... Gen 50:23
of M, the family of the......................... Num 26:29
and M begat Gilead .... Num 26:29
the son of Gilead, the son of M .... Num 27:1
the children of M the son of .... Num 32:39
Gilead unto M the son of Manasseh.... Num 32:40
children of Gilead, the son of M .... Num 36:1
And I gave Gilead unto M...................... Deut 3:15
children of M the son of Manasseh .... Josh 13:31
children of M by their families .... Josh 13:31
for M the firstborn of Manasseh, ... Josh 17:1
the son of Gilead, the son of M .... Josh 17:3
out of M came down governors, and ... Judg 5:14
of M the father of Gilead 1Chr 2:21
sons of M the father of Gilead 1Chr 2:23
bare M the father of Gilead 1Chr 7:14
M took to wife the sister of 1Chr 7:15
Maachah the wife of M bare a son 1Chr 7:16
the sons of Gilead, the son of M 1Chr 7:17
  2. Son of Ammiel.
Behold, he is in the house of M........... 2Sa 9:4
fetched him out of the house of M 2Sa 9:5
M the son of Ammiel of Lo-debar, ... 2Sa 17:27

MACHIRITES (ma'-kur-ites) *Descendants of Machir I.*
of Machir, the family of the M .... Num 26:29

MACHNADEBAI (mak-nad'-e-bahee) *Married a foreigner in exile.*
M, Shashai, Sharai, ... Ezr 10:40

MACHPELAH (mak-pe'-lah) *Burial place of Abraham.*
That he may give me the cave of M..... Gen 23:9
field of Ephron, which was in M......... Gen 23:17
of the field of M before Mamre .... Gen 23:19
buried him in the cave of M .... Gen 25:9
cave that is in the field of M................ Gen 49:30
him in the cave of the field of M .... Gen 50:13

MAD
So that thou shalt be m for the............ Deut 28:34
feigned himself m in their hands 1Sa 21:13
servants, Lo, ye see the man is m 1Sa 21:14
Have I need of m men, that ye 1Sa 21:15

to play the m man in my presence...... 1Sa 21:15
came this m fellow to thee................... 2Kin 9:11
they that are m against me are .... Ps 102:8
As a m man who casteth firebrands.... Prov 26:18
I said of laughter, It is m .... Eccl 2:2
oppression maketh a wise man m ...... Eccl 7:7
the liars, and maketh diviners m .... Is 44:25
shall drink, and be moved, and be m... Jer 25:16
the LORD, for every man that is m....... Jer 29:26
they are m upon their idols.................. Jer 50:38
therefore the nations are m .... Jer 51:7
is a fool, the spiritual man is m .... Hos 9:7
said, He hath a devil, and is m .... Jn 10:20
And they said unto her, Thou art m.... Acts 12:15
being exceedingly m against them .... Acts 26:11
much learning doth make thee m........ Acts 26:24
But he said, I am not m, most .... Acts 26:25
will they not say that ye are m 1Cor 14:23

MADAI (ma'-dahee) See **MEDE, MEDIA.** *Son of Japheth.*
Gomer, and Magog, and M................... Gen 10:2
Gomer, and Magog, and M, and Javan, 1Chr 1:5

MADE See PREFACE.

MADEST
m a covenant with him to give the..... Neh 9:8
m known unto them thy holy............... Neh 9:14
Thou m him to have dominion over ... Ps 8:6
that thou m strong for thyself .... Ps 80:15
whom thou m strong for thyself .... Ps 80:17
m to thyself images of men, and .... Eze 16:17
m all their loins to be at a .... Eze 29:7
not laboured, neither m it grow .... Jonah 4:10
before these days m an uproar .... Acts 21:38
Thou m him a little lower than............ Heb 2:7

MADIAN (ma'-de-an) See **MIDIAN.** *Same as Midian 2.*
was a stranger in the land of M .... Acts 7:29

MADMANNAH (mad-man'-nah)
  1. A city in Judah.
And Ziklag, and M, and Sansannah,... Josh 15:31
  2. Grandson of Caleb.
bare also Shaaph the father of M 1Chr 2:49

MADMEN (mad'-men) See **MADMENAH.** *A Moabite city.*
Also thou shalt be cut down, O M .... Jer 48:2

MADMENAH (mad-me'-nah) See **MADMEN.** *A city in Benjamin.*
M is removed .... Is 10:31

MADNESS
The LORD shall smite thee with m ...... Deut 28:28
to know wisdom, and to know m......... Eccl 1:17
myself to behold wisdom, and m .... Eccl 2:12
folly, even of foolishness and m .... Eccl 7:25
m is in their heart while they .... Eccl 9:3
end of his talk is mischievous m .... Eccl 10:13
astonishment, and his rider with m .... Zec 12:4
And they were filled with m .... Lk 6:11
voice forbad the m of the prophet....... 2Pet 2:16

MADON (ma'-don) *A Canaanite city.*
that he sent to Jobab king of M........... Josh 11:1
The king of M, one................................ Josh 12:19

MAGADAN See **MAGDALA.**

MAGBISH (mag'-bish) *A family of exiles.*
The children of M, an hundred............ Ezr 2:30

MAGDALA (mag'-da-lah) See **MAGDALENE.** *A city in Galilee.*
and came into the coasts of M .... Mt 15:39

MAGDALENE (mag'-da-leen) *A woman acquaintance of Jesus.*
Among which was Mary M, and Mary. Mt 27:56
And there was Mary M, and the other. Mt 27:61
day of the week, came Mary M............. Mt 28:1
among whom was Mary M, and Mary.. Mk 15:40
And Mary M and Mary the mother of.. Mk 15:47
when the sabbath was past, Mary M ... Mk 16:1
week, he appeared first to Mary M...... Mk 16:9
and infirmities, Mary called M .... Lk 8:2
It was Mary M, and Joanna, and Mary Lk 24:10
the wife of Cleophas, and Mary M ..... Jn 19:25
of the week cometh Mary M early...... Jn 20:1
Mary M came and told the disciples.... Jn 20:18

MAGDIEL (mag'-de-el) *A duke of Edom.*
Duke M, duke Iram .... Gen 36:43
Duke M, duke Iram 1Chr 1:54

MAGICIAN
that asked such things at any m .... Dan 2:10

MAGICIANS
and called for all the m of Egypt .... Gen 41:8
and I told this unto the m..................... Gen 41:24
now the m of Egypt, they also did...... Ex 7:11
the m of Egypt did so with their .... Ex 7:22
And the m did so with their .... Ex 8:7
And the m did so with their .... Ex 8:18
the m the m said unto Pharaoh, ... Ex 8:19
the m could not stand before .... Ex 9:11
for the boil was upon the m................. Ex 9:11
ten times better than all the m .... Dan 1:20
the king commanded to call the m ..... Dan 2:2
wise men, the astrologers, the m .... Dan 2:27
Then came in the m, the .... Dan 4:7
O Belteshazzar, master of the m .... Dan 4:9

thy father, made master of the m .... Dan 5:11

MAGISTRATE
and there was no m in the land........... Judg 18:7
with thine adversary to the m .... Lk 12:58

MAGISTRATES
God, that is in thine hand, set m .... Ezr 7:25
unto the synagogues, and unto m .... Lk 12:11
And brought them to the m, saying,.... Acts 16:20
the m rent off their clothes, and.......... Acts 16:22
the m sent the serjeants, saying,......... Acts 16:35
The m have sent to let you go .... Acts 16:36
told these words unto the m .... Acts 16:38
and powers, to obey m, to be ready ... Titus 3:1

MAGNIFICAL
for the LORD must be exceeding m 1Chr 22:5

MAGNIFICENCE
her m should be destroyed, whom...... Acts 19:27

MAGNIFIED
sight, and thou hast m thy mercy........ Gen 19:19
On that day the LORD m Joshua in ...... Josh 4:14
And let thy name be m for ever 2Sa 7:26
that thy name may be m for ever 1Chr 17:24
the LORD m Solomon exceedingly in.. 1Chr 29:25
with him, and m him exceedingly....... 2Chr 1:1
so that he was m in the sight of 2Chr 32:23
continually, Let the LORD be m........... Ps 35:27
say continually, The LORD be m.......... Ps 40:16
say continually, Let God be m .... Ps 70:4
for thou hast m thy word above .... Ps 138:2
for he m himself against the LORD ..... Jer 48:26
because he hath m himself against ..... Jer 48:42
for the enemy hath m himself .... Lam 1:9
m himself even to the prince .... Dan 8:11
m themselves against their border ...... Zeph 2:8
m themselves against the people .... Zeph 2:10
The LORD will be m from the .... Mal 1:5
but the people m them .... Acts 5:13
the name of the Lord Jesus was m...... Acts 19:17
also Christ shall be m in my body....... Phil 1:20

MAGNIFY
This day will I begin to m thee .... Josh 3:7
is man, that thou shouldest m him ..... Job 7:17
If indeed ye will m yourselves............ Job 19:5
Remember that thou m his work .... Job 36:24
O m the LORD with me, and let us ...... Ps 34:3
dishonour that m themselves............... Ps 35:26
they m themselves against me .... Ps 38:16
me that did m himself against me ...... Ps 55:12
will m him with thanksgiving .... Ps 69:30
or shall the saw m itself against .... Is 10:15
he will m the law, and make it .... Is 42:21
Thus will I m myself, and sanctify ..... Eze 38:23
he shall m himself in his heart,.......... Dan 8:25
m himself above every god, and .... Dan 11:36
for he shall m himself above all......... Dan 11:37
do not m themselves against Judah.... Zec 12:7
said, My soul doth m the Lord............. Lk 1:46
with tongues, and m God .... Acts 10:46
of the Gentiles, I m mine office .... Rom 11:13

MAGOG (ma'-gog)
  1. A son of Japheth.
Gomer, and M, and Madai, and Javan,. Gen 10:2
Gomer, and M, and Madai, and Javan,. 1Chr 1:5
  2. Descendants of Magog.
face against Gog, the land of M........... Eze 38:2
And I will send a fire on M .... Eze 39:6
quarters of the earth, Gog and M .... Rev 20:8

MAGOR-MISSABIB (ma'''-gor-mis'-sa-bib) *A symbolic name of Pashur.*
not called thy name Pashur, but M...... Jer 20:3

MAGPIASH (mag'-pe-ash) *A chief Israelite who renewed the covenant.*
M, Meshullam, Hezir, ... Neh 10:20

MAHALAH (ma'-ha-lah) See **MAHLAH.** *Great-grandson of Manasseh.*
bare Ishod, and Abiezer, and M........... 1Chr 7:18

MAHALALEEL (ma-hal'-a-le-el) See **MALELEEL.**
  1. Son of Cainan.
lived seventy years, and begat M .... Gen 5:12
after he begat M eight hundred .... Gen 5:13
M lived sixty and five years, and .... Gen 5:15
M lived after he begat Jared .... Gen 5:16
all the days of M were .... Gen 5:17
Kenan, M, Jered, ... 1Chr 1:2
  2. A family of exiles.
son of Shephatiah, the son of M.......... Neh 11:4

MAHALATH (ma'-ha-lath) See **BASHEMATH.**
  1. A daughter of Ishmael.
he had M the daughter of Ishmael....... Gen 28:9
  2. A granddaughter of David.
Rehoboam took him M the daughter .. 2Chr 11:18
  3. A musical choir.
To the chief Musician upon M .... Ps 53:t
chief Musician upon M Leannoth....... Ps 88:t

MAHALI (ma'-ha-li) See **MAHLI.** *Same as Lahli I.*
sons of Merari, M and Mushi................ Ex 6:19

MAHANAIM (ma-ha-na'-im) *A town east of the Jordan.*
called the name of that place M .... Gen 32:2

from *M* unto the border of Debir .... Josh 13:26
And their coast was from *M* .... Josh 13:30
and *M* with her suburbs, ... Josh 21:38
of Saul, and brought him over to *M* 2Sa 2:8
Saul, went out from *M* to Gibeon 2Sa 2:12
all Bithron, and they came to *M* 2Sa 2:29
Then David came to *M* 2Sa 17:24
to pass, when David was come to *M* 2Sa 17:27
of sustenance while he lay at *M* 2Sa 19:32
curse in the day when I went to *M* 1Kin 2:8
Ahinadab the son of Iddo had *M* 1Kin 4:14
suburbs, and *M* with her suburbs,......... 1Chr 6:80

MAHANEH-DAN (*ma'-ha-neh-dan*) *A place in Judah.*
called that place *M* unto this day....... Judg 18:12

MAHARAI (*ma'-ha-rahee*) *A warrior of David.*
the Ahohite, *M* the Netophathite,......... 2Sa 23:28
M the Netophathite, Heled the son..... 1Chr 11:30
month was *M* the Netophathite........ 1Chr 27:13

MAHATH (*ma'-hath*)
1. A descendant of Kohath.
the son of Elkanah, the son of *M*........ 1Chr 6:35
M the son of Amasai, and Joel the ... 2Chr 29:12
2. A Temple servant.
and Eliel, and Ismachiah, and *M*........ 2Chr 31:13

MAHAVITE (*ma'-ha-vite*) *Family name of Eliel.*
Eliel the *M*, and Jeribai, and............. 1Chr 11:46

MAHAZIOTH (*ma-ha'-ze-oth*) *A sanctuary servant.*
Mallothi, Hothir, and *M*.................. 1Chr 25:4
The three and twentieth to *M*.......... 1Chr 25:30

MAHER-SHALAL-HASH-BAZ (*ma''-her-sha''-lal-hash'-baz*) *A son of Isaiah.*
it with a man's pen concerning *M*........... Is 8:1
the LORD to me, Call his name *M*.......... Is 8:3

MAHLAH (*mah'-lah*) *A daughter of Zelophehad.*
daughters of Zelophehad were *M*........ Num 26:33
M, Noah, and Hoglah .... Num 27:1
For *M*, Tirzah, and Hoglah, and .... Num 36:11
are the names of his daughters, *M*...... Josh 17:3

MAHLI (*mah'-li*) See MAHALI, MAHLITES.
1. Son of Merari.
their families; *M*, and Mushi............. Num 3:20
of Merari; *M*, and Mushi................. 1Chr 6:19
M, Libni his son, Shimei his son,....... 1Chr 6:29
M, and Mushi. The sons of *M*.......... 1Chr 23:21
The sons of Merari were *M*............... 1Chr 24:26
Of *M* came Eleazar, who had no......... 1Chr 24:28
understanding, of the sons of *M*......... Ezr 8:18
2. Son of Mushi.
The son of *M*, the son of Mushi,......... 1Chr 6:47
M, and Eder, and Jeremoth, three.... 1Chr 23:23
M, and Eder, and Jerimoth 1Chr 24:30

MAHLITES (*mah'-lites*) *Descendants of Mahli 1.*
Of Merari was the family of the *M*....... Num 3:33
Hebronites, the family of the *M*........ Num 26:58

MAHLON (*mah'-lon*) See MAHLON'S. *A son of Naomi.*
and the name of his two sons *M*.......... Ruth 1:2
And *M* and Chilion died also both of .... Ruth 1:5
Ruth the Moabitess, the wife of *M*...... Ruth 4:10

MAHLON'S (*mah'-lons*)
and all that was Chilion's and *M*........ Ruth 4:9

MAHOL (*ma'-hol*) *Father of some wise men.*
Chalcol, and Darda, the sons of *M*..... 1Kin 4:31

MAHSEIAH See MAASEIAH.

MAID
I pray thee, go in unto my *m* .... Gen 16:2
took Hagar her the *M* the Egyptian ...... Gen 16:3
I have given my *m* into thy bosom........ Gen 16:5
Behold, thy *m* is in thy hand .... Gen 16:6
And he said, Hagar, Sarai's *m* .... Gen 16:8
Leah Zilpah his *m* for an handmaid...... Gen 29:24
Bilhah his handmaid to be her *m*........ Gen 29:29
And she said, Behold my *m* Bilhah ...... Gen 30:3
Bilhah Rachel's *m* conceived again...... Gen 30:7
bearing, she took Zilpah her *m*.......... Gen 30:9
Zilpah Leah's *m* bare Jacob a son .... Gen 30:10
Zilpah Leah's *m* bare Jacob a .... Gen 30:12
flags, she sent her *m* to fetch it .... Ex 2:5
the *m* went and called the child's .... Ex 2:8
a man smite his servant, or his *m* ..... Ex 21:20
his servant, or the eye of his *m* .... Ex 21:26
if a man entice a that is not .... Ex 22:16
But if she bear a *m* child .... Lev 12:5
and for thy servant, and for thy *m* ..... Lev 25:6
came to her, I found her not a *m* .... Deut 22:17
I found not thy daughter a *m* .... Deut 22:17
of the land of Israel a little *m*.......... 2Kin 5:2
thus said the *m* that is of the 2Kin 5:4
the *m* was fair and beautiful .... Est 2:7
why then should I think upon a *m* ...... Job 31:1
and the way of a man with a *m* .... Prov 30:19
as with the *m*, so with her .... Is 24:2
Can a *m* forget her ornaments, or ..... Jer 2:32
in pieces the young man and the *m* .... Jer 51:22
father will go in unto the same *m* ...... Amos 2:7
for the *m* is not dead, but............... Mt 9:24
her by the hand, and the *m* arose...... Mt 9:25
into the porch, another *m* saw him..... Mt 26:71

a m saw him again, and began to........ Mk 14:69
by the hand, and called, saying, *M* ..... Lk 8:54
But a certain *m* beheld him as he .... Lk 22:56

MAIDEN
I have given my *m* to my husband .... Gen 30:18
Behold, here is my daughter a *m*........ Judg 19:24
upon young man or *m* 2Chr 36:17
let the *m* which pleaseth the king ...... Est 2:4
the *m* pleased him, and she .... Est 2:9
thus came every *m* unto the king....... Est 2:13
as the eyes of a *m* unto the hand ...... Ps 123:2
the father and the mother of the *m*..... Lk 8:51

MAIDENS
her *m* walked along by the river's ...... Ex 2:5
but abode here fast by my *m* .... Ruth 2:8
that thou go out with his *m* .... Ruth 2:22
So she kept fast by the *m* of Boaz...... Ruth 2:23
kindred, with whom thou wast........... Ruth 3:2
they found young *m* going out to....... Is 26:10
when many *m* were gathered........... Est 2:8
as belonged to her, and seven *m*....... Est 2:9
I also and my *m* will fast likewise ...... Est 4:16
or wilt thou bind him for thy *m*......... Job 41:5
their *m* were not given to .... Ps 78:63
Both young men, and *m* .... Ps 148:12
She hath sent forth her *m* .... Prov 9:3
and for the maintenance for thy *m*..... Prov 27:27
household, and a portion to her *m* ..... Prov 31:15
I got me servants and *m*, and had ...... Eccl 2:7
but they shall take *m* of the seed....... Eze 44:22
to beat the menservants and *m*........ Lk 12:45

MAID'S
Now when every *m* turn was come to.... Est 2:12

MAIDS
Beside their servants and their *m*...... Ezr 2:65
her *m* unto the best place of the .... Est 2:9
So Esther's *m* and her chamberlains ... Est 4:4
that dwell in mine house, and my *m* ... Job 19:15
the *m* in the cities of Judah .... Lam 5:11
Slay utterly old and young, both *m* ..... Eze 9:6
her *m* shall lead her as with the........ Nah 2:7
men cheerful, and new wine the *m* ..... Zec 9:17
one of the *m* of the high priest......... Mk 14:66

MAIDSERVANT
of the *m* that is behind the mill .... Ex 11:5
thy manservant, nor thy *m* .... Ex 20:10
nor his manservant, nor his *m*.......... Ex 20:17
a man sell his daughter to be a *m* ...... Ex 21:7
ox shall push a manservant or a *m* ..... Ex 21:32
nor thy manservant, nor thy *m*......... Deut 5:14
thy *m* may rest as well as thou .... Deut 5:14
or his manservant, or his *m* .... Deut 5:21
and thy manservant, and thy *m*........ Deut 12:18
also unto thy *m* thou shalt do .... Deut 15:17
and thy manservant, and thy *m* .... Deut 16:11
and thy manservant, and thy *m*........ Deut 16:14
made Abimelech, the son of his *m* ..... Judg 9:18
cause of my manservant or of my *m* ... Job 31:13
manservant, and every man his *m* ..... Jer 34:9
manservant, and every one his *m*...... Jer 34:10

MAIDSERVANT'S
tooth, or his *m* tooth .... Ex 21:27

MAIDSERVANTS
and menservants, and *m*............... Gen 12:16
Abimelech, and his wife, and his *m*..... Gen 20:17
and gold, and menservants, and *m*..... Gen 24:35
and had much cattle, and *m*............ Gen 30:43
and your menservants, and your *m* .... Deut 12:12
take your menservants, and your *m* 1Sa 8:16
of the *m* which thou hast spoken....... 2Sa 6:22
and oxen, and menservants, and *m* 2Kin 5:26
their manservants and their *m* .... Neh 7:67

MAIDSERVANTS'
tent, and into the two *m* tents.......... Gen 31:33

MAIL
and he was armed with a coat of *m*..... 1Sa 17:5
he armed him with a coat of *m* 1Sa 17:38

MAIMED
Blind, or broken, or *m*, or having....... Lev 22:22
that were lame, blind, dumb, *m*......... Mt 15:30
for the to be whole, the lame to .... Mt 15:31
thee to enter into life halt or *m*........ Mt 18:8
for thee to enter into life *m*............ Mk 9:43
a feast, call the poor, the *m*............ Lk 14:13
in hither the poor, and the *m*........... Lk 14:21

MAINSAIL
and hoisted up the *m* to the wind....... Acts 27:40

MAINTAIN
supplication, and *m* their cause......... 1Kin 8:45
dwelling place, and *m* their cause,...... 1Kin 8:49
that he *m* the cause of his 1Kin 8:59
to *m* the house of the LORD............ 1Chr 26:27
supplication, and *m* their cause........ 2Chr 6:35
m their cause, and forgive thy 2Chr 6:39
but I will *m* mine own ways before ..... Job 13:15
I know that the LORD will *m* the....... Ps 140:12
might be careful to *m* good works ..... Titus 3:8
let ours also learn to *m* good .... Titus 3:14

MAINTAINED
For thou hast *m* my right and my ...... Ps 9:4

MAINTAINEST
thou *m* my lot......................... Ps 16:5

MAINTENANCE
Now because we have *m* from the...... Ezr 4:14
for the *m* for thy maidens .... Prov 27:27

MAJESTY
glory, and the victory, and the *m*........ 1Chr 29:11
m as had not been on any king 1Chr 29:25
of his excellent *m* many days........... Est 1:4
with God is terrible *m* .... Job 37:22
Deck thyself now with *m* and .... Job 40:10
m hast thou laid upon him .... Ps 21:5
voice of the LORD is full of *m* .... Ps 29:4
mighty, with thy glory and thy *m*....... Ps 45:3
in thy *m* ride prosperously .... Ps 45:4
reigneth, he is clothed with *m* .... Ps 93:1
Honour and *m* are before him .... Ps 96:6
thou art clothed with honour and *m* ... Ps 104:1
of the glorious honour of thy *m* .... Ps 145:5
the glorious *m* of his kingdom .... Ps 145:12
LORD, and for the glory of his *m* .... Is 2:10
LORD, and for the glory of his *m* .... Is 2:19
LORD, and for the glory of his *m*....... Is 2:21
shall sing for the *m* of the LORD........ Is 24:14
will not behold the *m* of the LORD ..... Is 26:10
of his ornament, he set it in *m* .... Eze 7:20
power, and for the honour of my *m* .... Dan 4:30
excellent *m* was added unto me .... Dan 4:36
thy father a kingdom and *m*............ Dan 5:18
for the *m* that he gave him, all........ Dan 5:19
in the *m* of the name of the LORD...... Mic 5:4
the right hand of the *M* on high .... Heb 1:3
throne of the *M* in the heavens......... Heb 8:1
but were eyewitnesses of his *m*....... 2Pet 1:16
God our Saviour, be glory and *m* ...... Jude 25

MAKAZ (*ma'-kaz*) *A town in Judah.*
The son of Dekar, in *M*, and in 1Kin 4:9

MAKE See PREFACE.

MAKER
a man be more pure than his *m*........ Job 4:17
in so doing *m* would soon take .... Job 32:22
But none saith, Where is God my *m*.... Job 35:10
ascribe righteousness to my *M* .... Job 36:3
us kneel before the LORD our *m*....... Ps 95:6
the poor reproacheth his *M* .... Prov 14:31
the poor reproacheth his *M* .... Prov 17:5
the LORD is the *m* of them all.......... Prov 22:2
the *m* of it as a spark, and they .... Is 1:31
day shall a man look to his *M* .... Is 17:7
not looked unto the thereof .... Is 22:11
unto him that striveth with his *M* ...... Is 45:9
the Holy One of Israel, and his *M* ...... Is 45:11
And forgettest the LORD thy *m* .... Is 51:13
For thy *M* is thine husband............ Is 54:5
Thus saith the LORD the *m* thereof .... Jer 33:2
For Israel hath forgotten his *M*........ Hos 8:14
that the *m* thereof hath graven it ...... Hab 2:18
that the *m* of his work trusteth .... Hab 2:18
whose builder and *m* is God .... Heb 11:10

MAKERS
together that are *m* of idols .... Is 45:16

MAKEST
what *m* thou in this place............... Judg 18:3
m me to possess the iniquities of...... Job 13:26
that thou *m* thy ways perfect........... Job 22:3
only *m* me dwell in safety .... Ps 4:8
thou *m* his beauty to consume away... Ps 39:11
thou *m* us to back from the........... Ps 44:10
Thou *m* us a reproach to our .... Ps 44:13
Thou *m* us a byword among the....... Ps 44:14
thou *m* the outgoings of the .... Ps 65:8
thou *m* it soft with showers .... Ps 65:10
Thou *m* us a strife unto our .... Ps 80:6
Thou *m* darkness, and it is night ..... Ps 104:20
that thou *m* account of him .... Ps 144:3
where thou *m* thy flock to rest at ..... Song 1:7
that fashioneth it, What *m* thou...... Is 45:9
that *m* thy nest in the cedars,........ Jer 22:23
but thou *m* this people to trust ...... Jer 28:15
in thine high place in every .... Eze 16:31
m men as the fishes of the sea,........ Hab 1:14
the *m* him drunken also, that thou .... Hab 2:15
When thou *m* a dinner or a supper,.... Lk 14:12
But when thou *m* a feast, call the..... Lk 14:13
whom *m* thou thyself .... Jn 8:53
thou, being a man, *m* thyself God ..... Jn 10:33
the law, and *m* thy boast of God,...... Rom 2:17
Thou that *m* thy boast of the law,..... Rom 2:23

MAKETH
or who *m* the dumb, or deaf, or ...... Ex 4:11
the priest that *m* atonement .... Lev 7:7
the priest that *m* him clean shall..... Lev 14:11
for it is the blood that *m* an .... Lev 17:11
m his son or his daughter to pass .... Deut 18:10
the city that *m* war with these ...... Deut 20:20
when he *m* his sons to inherit ...... Deut 21:16
m merchandise of him, or selleth..... Deut 24:7
Cursed be the man that *m* any...... Deut 27:15
Cursed be he that *m* the blind to .... Deut 27:18
unto thy God with thine this day ..... Deut 29:12
The LORD killeth, and *m* alive 1Sa 2:6
The LORD *m* poor, and *m* rich 1Sa 2:7
and he *m* my path straight 2Sa 22:33
He *m* my feet like hinds' feet 2Sa 22:34
For he *m* sore, and bindeth up ...... Job 5:18
Which *m* Arcturus, Orion, and...... Job 9:9
spoiled, and *m* the judges fools ..... Job 12:17
he *m* them to stagger like a .... Job 12:25
m collops of fat on his flanks .... Job 15:27
For God *m* my heart soft, and the... Job 23:16
he *m* peace in his high places ...... Job 25:2
and as a booth that the keeper *m* ... Job 27:18
m us wiser than the fowls of .... Job 35:11

For he *m* small the drops of water .... Job 36:27
He *m* the deep to boil like a pot .... Job 41:31
he *m* the sea like a pot of .... Job 41:31
He *m* a path to shine after him .... Job 41:32
When he *m* inquisition for blood, ... Ps 9:12
strength, and my way perfect .... Ps 18:32
He *m* my feet like hinds' feet, and .... Ps 18:33
He *m* me to lie down in green .... Ps 23:2
He *m* them also to skip like a .... Ps 29:6
of the LORD in the hinds to calve .... Ps 29:9
he *m* the devices of the people of .... Ps 33:10
man that *m* the LORD his trust .... Ps 40:4
He *m* wars to cease unto the end .... Ps 46:9
who *m* the clouds his chariot .... Ps 104:3
Who *m* his angels spirits .... Ps 104:4
wine that *m* glad the heart of man .... Ps 104:15
He *m* the storm a calm, so that .... Ps 107:29
there he *m* the hungry to dwell, ... Ps 107:36
m him families like a flock .... Ps 107:41
He *m* the barren woman to keep .... Ps 113:9
he *m* lightnings for the rain .... Ps 135:7
who *m* grass to grow upon the .... Ps 147:8
He *m* peace in thy borders, and .... Ps 147:14
A wise son *m* a glad father .... Prov 10:1
the hand of the diligent *m* rich .... Prov 10:4
it *m* rich, and he addeth no sorrow ...... Prov 10:22
but she that *m* ashamed is as .... Prov 12:4
in the heart of man *m* it stoop .... Prov 12:25
but a good word *m* it glad .... Prov 12:25
There is that *m* himself rich .... Prov 13:7
there is that *m* himself poor .... Prov 13:7
Hope deferred *m* the heart sick, ... Prov 13:12
A merry heart *m* a cheerful .... Prov 15:13
A wise son *m* a glad father .... Prov 15:20
and a good report *m* the bones fat .... Prov 15:30
he *m* even his enemies to be at .... Prov 16:7
A man's gift *m* room for him .... Prov 18:16
Wealth *m* many friends .... Prov 19:4
but he that *m* haste to be rich .... Prov 28:20
She *m* herself coverings of .... Prov 31:22
She *m* fine linen, and selleth it .... Prov 31:24
m from the beginning to the end .... Eccl 3:11
oppression *m* a wise man mad .... Eccl 7:7
a man's wisdom *m* his face to .... Eccl 8:1
for laughter, and wine *m* merry .... Eccl 10:19
not the works of God who *m* all .... Eccl 11:5
every one that *m* mention thereof .... Is 19:17
the LORD *m* the earth empty, and .... Is 24:1
m it waste, and turneth it upside .... Is 24:1
when he *m* all the downs of the .... Is 27:9
he *m* the judges of the earth as .... Is 40:23
which *m* a way in the sea, and a .... Is 43:16
m it after the figure of a man, ... Is 44:13
m a god, and worshipeth it .... Is 44:15
he *m* it a graven image, and .... Is 44:15
And the residue thereof he *m* a god .... Is 44:17
I am the LORD that *m* all things .... Is 44:24
of the liars, and *m* diviners mad .... Is 44:25
and their knowledge foolish .... Is 44:25
and he *m* it a god .... Is 44:17
m it bring forth and bud, that it .... Is 55:10
from evil *m* himself a prey .... Is 59:15
my heart *m* a noise in me .... Jer 4:19
he *m* lightnings with rain, and .... Jer 10:13
m flesh his arm, and whose heart .... Jer 17:5
king of Babylon *m* war against us .... Jer 21:2
m himself a prophet, that thou .... Jer 29:26
which *m* himself a prophet to you .... Jer 29:27
be like the dove that *m* her nest .... Jer 48:28
he *m* lightnings with rain, and .... Jer 51:16
m idols against herself to defile .... Eze 22:3
secrets, and *m* known to the king .... Dan 2:28
he that revealeth secrets *m* known .... Dan 2:29
but *m* his petition three times a .... Dan 6:13
the abomination that *m* desolate .... Dan 11:31
m desolate set up, there .... Dan 12:11
that *m* the morning darkness, and .... Amos 4:13
Seek him that *m* the seven stars .... Amos 5:8
m the day dark with night .... Amos 5:8
m it dry, and drieth up all the .... Nah 1:4
for he *m* his sun to rise on the .... Mt 5:45
he *m* both the deaf to hear, and .... Mk 7:37
then both the new *m* a rent .... Lk 5:36
whosoever *m* himself a king .... Jn 19:12
Aeneas, Jesus Christ *m* thee whole ... Acts 9:34
And hope *m* not ashamed .... Rom 5:5
but the Spirit itself *m* .... Rom 8:26
because he *m* intercession for the .... Rom 8:27
who also *m* intercession for us .... Rom 8:34
how he *m* intercession to God .... Rom 11:2
For who *m* thee to differ from 1Cor 4:7
who is he then that *m* me glad 2Cor 2:2
m manifest the savour of his 2Cor 2:14
they were, it *m* no matter to .... Gal 2:6
m increase of the body unto the .... Eph 4:16
Who *m* his angels spirits, and his .... Heb 1:7
For the law *m* men high priests .... Heb 7:28
the Son, who is consecrated for .... Heb 7:28
so that he *m* fire come down from .... Rev 13:13
worketh abomination, or *m* a lie, ... Rev 21:27
and whosoever loveth and *m* a .... Rev 22:15

MAKHELOTH (mak´-he-loth) An Israelite
encampment in the wilderness.
from Mardakah, and pitched in M, and .... Num 33:25
And they removed from M, and .... Num 33:26

MAKI See MACHI.

MAKING
task in *m* brick both yesterday .... Ex 5:14
in *m* war against it to take it, ... Deut 20:19
Now as they were in their hearts .... Judg 19:22

eating and drinking, and *m* merry 1Kin 4:20
m a noise with psalteries and 1Chr 15:28
in known all these great things 1Chr 17:19
m confession to the LORD God of 2Chr 30:22
Lord is sure, *m* wise the simple .... Ps 19:7
of *m* many books there is no end......... Eccl 12:12
m thinking with their .... Is 3:16
m him very glad .... Jer 20:15
multitude of the wares of thy *m*. .... Eze 27:16
multitude of the wares of thy *m*. .... Eze 27:18
m supplication before his God .... Dan 6:11
swearing falsely in *m* a covenant .... Hos 10:4
in the ephah small, and the shekel .... Amos 8:5
m the desolate because of thy .... Mic 6:13
minstrels and the people *m* a noise ..... Mt 9:23
M the word of God of none effect .... Mk 7:13
Father, himself equal with God .... Jn 5:18
M request, if by any means now ar. .... Rom 1:10
as poor, yet *m* many rich 2Cor 6:10
m mention of you in my prayers .... Eph 1:16
of twain one new man, so *m* peace ..... Eph 2:15
m melody in your heart to the .... Eph 5:19
for you all *m* request with joy .... Phil 1:4
m mention of thee always in my .... Phm 4
m mention of thee always in my .... Philem 4
than an ensample unto those 2Pet 2:6
have compassion, *m* a difference .... Jude 22

MAKIR See MACHIR.

MAKIRITE See MACHIRITES.

MAKKEDAH (mak´-ke-dah) A city in Judah.
smote them to Azekah, and unto M .... Josh 10:10
and hid themselves in a cave at M .... Josh 10:16
are found hid in a cave at M .... Josh 10:17
the camp to Joshua at M in peace............ Josh 10:21
And that day Joshua took M .... Josh 10:28
he did to the king of M as he did .... Josh 10:28
Then Joshua passed from M .... Josh 10:29
The king of M, one, ... Josh 12:16
Beth-dagon, and Naamah, and M .... Josh 15:41

MAKTESH (mak´-tesh) A district near
Jerusalem.
Howl, ye inhabitants of M .... Zeph 1:11

MALACHI (mal´-a-ki) A prophet.
word of the LORD to Israel by M .... Mal 1:1

MALCAM See MALCHAM.

MALCHAM (mal´-kam) See MILCOM.
1. Son of Shaharaim.
Jobab, and Zibia, and Mesha, and M 1Chr 8:9
2. An Ammonite idol.
by the LORD, and that swear by M .... Zeph 1:5

MALCHIAH (mal-ki´-ah) See MALCHIJAH,
MELCHIAH.
1. Father of Baaseiah.
the son of Baaseiah, the son of M 1Chr 9:12
2. A descendant of Parosh.
Eliezer, and Jeziah, and M, and .... Ezr 10:25
the son of Pashur, the son of M .... Neh 11:12
3. Another descendant of Parosh.
Eliezer, Ishijah, M, Shemaiah, ... Ezr 10:31
4. A repairer of Jerusalem's wall.
gate repaired M the son of Rechab .... Neh 3:14
5. Another repairer of Jerusalem's wall.
After him repaired M the .... Neh 3:31
6. A priest who aided Ezra.
hand, Pedaiah, and Mishael, and M .... Neh 8:4
7. A priest who dedicated the wall.
Shelemiah, and Pashur the son of M .... Neh 10:3
Malchijah .... Neh 12:42

MALCHIEL (mal´-ke-el) See MALCHIELITES. A
son of Beriah.
Heber, and M .... Gen 46:17
of M, the family of the .... Num 26:45
Heber, and M, who is the father of 1Chr 7:31

MALCHIELITES (mal´-ke-el-ites) Descendants
of Malchiel.
of Malchiel, the family of the M .... Num 26:45

MALCHIJAH (mal-ki´-jah) See MALCHIAH.
1. A family of exiles.
the son of Pashur, the son of 1Chr 9:12
2. A sanctuary servant.
The fifth to M, the sixth to 1Chr 24:9
3. Married a foreigner in exile.
and Miamin, and Eleazar, and M .... Ezr 10:25
4. A rebuilder of Jerusalem's wall.
M the son of Harim, and Hashub the .... Neh 3:11
5. A priest who dedicated the wall.
Pashur, Amariah, M, ... Neh 10:3
and Uzzi, and Jehohanan, and M .... Neh 12:42

MALCHIRAM (mal´-ki-ram) A descendant of
King Jehoiakim.
M also, and Pedaiah, and Shenazar, ... 1Chr 3:18

MALCHI-SHUA (mal´-ki-shu´-ah) See
MELCHISHUA. A son of King Saul.
and Saul begat Jonathan, and M 1Chr 8:33
and Saul begat Jonathan, and M 1Chr 9:39
slew Jonathan, and Abinadab, and M 1Chr 10:2

MALCHUS (mal´-kus) A servant wounded by
Simon Peter.
The servant's name was M .... Jn 18:10

MALE
m and female created he them .... Gen 1:27
M and female created he them .... Gen 5:2
they shall be *m* and female .... Gen 6:19

take to thee by sevens, the *m* .... Gen 7:2
that are not clean by two, the *m* .... Gen 7:2
also of the air by sevens, the *m* .... Gen 7:3
two unto Noah into the ark, the *m* .... Gen 7:9
And they that went in, went in *m* .... Gen 7:16
money, every *m* among the men of ..... Gen 17:23
as we be, that every *m* of you be .... Gen 34:15
people, if every *m* among us be .... Gen 34:22
every *m* was circumcised, all that ...... Gen 34:24
blemish, a *m* of the first year .... Ex 12:5
whether ox or sheep, that is *m* .... Ex 34:19
let him offer a *m* without blemish .... Lev 1:3
bring it a *m* without blemish .... Lev 1:10
whether it be a *m* or female .... Lev 3:1
m or female, he shall offer if .... Lev 3:6
of the goats, a *m* without blemish ...... Lev 4:23
Every *m* among the priests shall .... Lev 7:6
that hath born a *m* or a female .... Lev 12:7
your own will a *m* without blemish...... Lev 22:19
thy estimation shall be of the *m* .... Lev 27:3
shall be of the *m* twenty shekels .... Lev 27:5
of the *m* five shekels of silver .... Lev 27:6
if it be a *m*, then thy estimation .... Lev 27:7
names, every *m* by their polls .... Num 1:2
every *m* from twenty years old and ... Num 1:20
every *m* from twenty years old and ... Num 1:22
every *m* from a month old and .... Num 3:15
Both *m* and female shall ye put out ... Num 5:3
every *m* shall eat it .... Num 18:10
every *m* among the little ones .... Num 31:17
the likeness of *m* or female .... Deut 4:16
there shall not be *m* or female .... Deut 4:16
thou shalt smite every *m* thereof .... Deut 20:13
these were the *m* children of .... Judg 17:2
Ye shall utterly destroy every *m* .... Judg 21:11
known no man by lying with any *m* ..... Judg 21:12
he had smitten every *m* in Edom 1Kin 11:15
he had cut off every *m* in Edom 1Kin 11:16
which hath in his flock a *m* .... Mal 1:14
them at the beginning made them *m* .. Mt 19:4
of the creation God made them *m* .... Mk 10:6
Every *m* that openeth the womb .... Lk 2:23
there is neither *m* nor female .... Gal 3:28

MALEFACTOR
said unto him, If he were not a *m* .... Jn 18:30

MALEFACTORS
And there were also two others, *m* ...... Lk 23:32
they crucified him, and the *m* .... Lk 23:33
one of the *m* which were hanged .... Lk 23:39

MALELEEL (mal-e-le-el) See MAHALALEEL.
Son of Cainan; ancestor of Jesus.
of Jared, which was the son of M .... Lk 3:37

MALES
city boldly, and slew all the *m* .... Gen 34:25
let all his *m* be circumcised, and .... Ex 12:48
the *m* shall be the LORD'S .... Ex 13:12
that openeth the matrix, being *m* .... Ex 13:15
m shall appear before the LORD .... Ex 23:17
All the *m* among the children of .... Lev 6:18
All the *m* among the priests shall .... Lev 6:29
to the number of all the *m* .... Num 3:22
in the number of all the *m* .... Num 3:28
to the number of all the *m* .... Num 3:34
all the *m* from a month old and .... Num 3:39
m of the children of Israel from .... Num 3:40
all the firstborn *m* by the number .... Num 3:43
all *m* from a month old and upward ... Num 26:62
and they slew all the *m* .... Deut 3:6
All the thrusting *m* that come of .... Deut 15:19
times in a year shall all thy *m* .... Deut 16:16
came out of Egypt, that were *m* .... Josh 5:4
Beside their genealogy of 2Chr 31:16
to all the *m* among the priests 2Chr 31:19
by genealogy of the *m* an hundred ..... Ezr 8:3
and with him two hundred *m* .... Ezr 8:4
and with him three hundred *m* .... Ezr 8:5
of Jonathan, and with him fifty *m* .... Ezr 8:6
Athaliah, and with him seventy *m* ...... Ezr 8:7
Michael, and with him fourscore *m* .... Ezr 8:8
him two hundred and eighteen *m* .... Ezr 8:9
him an hundred and threescore *m* ..... Ezr 8:10
and with him twenty and eight *m* .... Ezr 8:11
and with him an hundred and ten *m* ... Ezr 8:12
and with them threescore *m* .... Ezr 8:13
and Zabbud, and with them seventy *m* .. Ezr 8:14

MALICE
neither with the leaven of *m* 1Cor 5:8
howbeit in *m* be ye children, but... ...... 1Cor 14:20
be put away from you, with all *m* .... Eph 4:31
anger, wrath, *m*, blasphemy, ... Col 3:8
lusts and pleasures, living in *m* .... Titus 3:3
Wherefore laying aside all *m* 1Pet 2:1

MALICIOUS
prating against us with *m* words 3Jn 10

MALICIOUSNESS
wickedness, covetousness, *m* .... Rom 1:29
your liberty for a cloke of *m* 1Pet 2:16

MALIGNITY
envy, murder, debate, deceit, *m* .... Rom 1:29

MALLOTHI (mal´-lo-thi) A son of Heman.
and Romamti-ezer, Joshbekashah, M. .. 1Chr 25:4
The nineteenth to M, he, his sons... ...... 1Chr 25:26

MALLOWS
Who cut up *m* by the bushes, and .... Job 30:4

MALLUCH (mal´-luk) See MELICU.
1. Ancestor of Ethan.
the son of Abdi, the son of M 1Chr 6:44

2. A son of Bani.
Meshullam, M, and Adaiah, Jashub,..... Ezr 10:29
3. A descendant of Harim.
Benjamin, M, and Shemariah.............. Ezr 10:32
4. A priest who renewed the covenant.
Hattush, Shebaniah, M,...................... Neh 10:4
Amariah, M, Hattush,......................... Neh 12:2
5. A clan leader who renewed the covenant.
M, Harim, Baanah.............................. Neh 10:27

MALLUCHI See MELICU.

MALTA See MELITA.

MAMMON
Ye cannot serve God and m................... Mt 6:24
of the m of unrighteousness.................. Lk 16:9
Ye cannot serve God and m................... Lk 16:11
Ye cannot serve God and m................... Lk 16:13

MAMRE *(mam'-re)*
1. A place near Hebron.
came and dwelt in the plain of M.......... Gen 13:18
unto him in the plains of M.................. Gen 18:1
in Machpelah, which was before M....... Gen 23:17
the field of Machpelah before M........... Gen 23:19
the Hittite, which is before M............... Gen 25:9
came unto Isaac his father unto M....... Gen 35:27
of Machpelah, which is before M.......... Gen 49:30
of Ephron the Hittite, before M............ Gen 50:13
2. An Amorite ally of Abraham.
in the plain of M the Amorite.............. Gen 14:13
went with me, Aner, Eshcol, and M...... Gen 14:24

MAN See PREFACE.

MANAEN *(man'-a-en)* A Christian teacher at
Antioch.
Niger, and Lucius of Cyrene, and M .... Acts 13:1

MANAHATH *(man'-a-hath)*
1. A son of Shobal.
Alvan, and M, and Ebal, Shepho, and.. Gen 36:23
Alian, and M, and Ebal, Shephi, and.... 1Chr 1:40
2. A city in Benjamin.
Geba, and they removed them to M...... 1Chr 8:6

MANAHETHITES *(man'-a-heth-ites)*
Descendants of Shobal.
Haroeh, and half of the M.................... 1Chr 2:52
house of Joab, and half of the M.......... 1Chr 2:54

MANASSEH *(ma-nas'-seh)* See MANASSEH'S,
MANASSES, MANASSITES.
1. A son of Joseph.
the name of the firstborn M.................. Gen 41:51
in the land of Egypt were born M......... Gen 46:20
he took with him his two sons, M.......... Gen 48:1
two sons, Ephraim and M..................... Gen 48:5
M in his left hand toward..................... Gen 48:13
for M was the firstborn........................ Gen 48:14
God make thee as Ephraim and as M.... Gen 48:20
and he set Ephraim before M............... Gen 48:20
also of Machir the son of M were......... Gen 50:23
after their families were M................... Num 26:29
Of the sons of M.................................. Num 26:29
the son of Machir, the son of M............ Num 27:1
families of M the son of Joseph............. Num 27:1
the son of M went to Gilead................. Num 32:39
Gilead unto Machir the son of M.......... Num 32:40
And Jair the son of M went.................. Num 32:41
the son of Machir, the son of M............ Num 32:41
Jair the son of M took all the.............. Deut 3:14
descendant of Machir the son of M....... Josh 13:31
for Machir the firstborn of M............... Josh 17:1
of M the son of Joseph by their........... Josh 17:2
the son of Machir, the son of M........... Josh 17:3
the towns of Jair the son of M............. 1Kin 4:13
The.. 1Chr 7:14
the son of Machir, the son of M........... 1Chr 7:17
2. Descendants and land of Manasseh 1.
of M; Gamaliel the son........................ Num 1:10
Of the children of M, by their.............. Num 1:34
of them, even of the tribe of M............ Num 1:35
And by him shall be the tribe of M...... Num 2:20
Of M shall be Gamaliel the son of....... Num 2:20
prince of the children of M................... Num 7:54
of M was Gamaliel the tribe of M........ Num 10:23
Joseph, namely, of the tribe of M........ Num 13:11
These are the families of M.................. Num 26:34
the tribe of M the son of Joseph.......... Num 32:33
half the tribe of M have received......... Num 34:14
the tribe of the children of M.............. Num 34:23
the sons of M the son of Joseph.......... Num 36:12
gave I unto the half tribe of M............ Deut 3:13
and to the half tribe of M.................... Deut 29:8
and they are the thousands of M......... Deut 33:17
and the land of Ephraim, and M.......... Deut 34:2
and to half the tribe of M.................... Josh 1:12
of M, and the half tribe of M............... Josh 4:12
Gadites, and the half tribe of M.......... Josh 12:6
tribes, and the half tribe of M............. Josh 13:7
unto the half tribe of M their families.. Josh 13:29
children of M by their families............. Josh 13:29
of Joseph were two tribes, M............... Josh 14:4
So the children of Joseph, M............... Josh 16:4
inheritance of the children of M.......... Josh 16:9
was also a lot for the tribe of M.......... Josh 17:1
children of M by their families............. Josh 17:2
And there fell ten portions to M.......... Josh 17:5
Because the daughters of M had an..... Josh 17:6
the coast of M was from Asher to........ Josh 17:7
Now M had the land of Tappuah......... Josh 17:8
of M belonged to the children of........ Josh 17:8

Ephraim are among the cities of M...... Josh 17:9
the coast of M also was on the........... Josh 17:9
M had in Issachar and in Asher.......... Josh 17:11
Yet the children of M could not........... Josh 17:12
Joseph, even to Ephraim and to M...... Josh 17:17
and Reuben, and half the tribe of M.... Josh 18:7
in Bashan out of the tribe of M.......... Josh 20:8
and out of the half tribe of M............. Josh 21:5
of the half tribe of M in Bashan......... Josh 21:6
And out of the half tribe of M............. Josh 21:25
M they gave Golan in Bashan with...... Josh 21:27
Gadites, and the half tribe of M......... Josh 22:1
M Moses had given possession in....... Josh 22:7
and the half tribe of M returned......... Josh 22:9
the half tribe of M built there............ Josh 22:10
the half tribe of M have built an......... Josh 22:11
of Gad, and to the half tribe of M...... Josh 22:13
of Gad, and to the half tribe of M...... Josh 22:15
and the half tribe of M answered........ Josh 22:21
of Gad and the children of M spake.... Josh 22:30
of Gad, and to the children of M......... Josh 22:31
Neither did M drive out the................. Judg 1:27
behold, my family is poor in M............ Judg 6:15
sent messengers throughout all M....... Judg 6:35
and out of Asher, and out of all M...... Judg 7:23
and he passed over Gilead, and M...... Judg 11:29
Gadites, and half the tribe of M......... 1Chr 5:18
half tribe of M dwelt in the land........ 1Chr 5:23
Gadites, and the half tribe of M......... 1Chr 5:26
out of the half tribe of M................... 1Chr 6:61
out of the tribe of M in Bashan.......... 1Chr 6:62
And out of the half tribe of M............. 1Chr 6:70
the family of the half tribe of M......... 1Chr 6:71
the borders of the children of M......... 1Chr 7:29
of the children of Ephraim, and M...... 1Chr 9:3
And there fell some of M to David 1Chr 12:19
to Ziklag, there fell to him of M......... 1Chr 12:20
of the thousands that were of M......... 1Chr 12:20
half tribe of M eighteen thousand....... 1Chr 12:31
and of the half tribe of M.................. 1Chr 12:37
Gadites, and the tribe of M................ 1Chr 26:32
Of the half tribe of M, Joel the.......... 1Chr 27:20
Of the half tribe of M in Gilead......... 1Chr 27:21
with them out of Ephraim and M....... 2Chr 15:9
letters also to Ephraim and M............ 2Chr 30:1
Ephraim and M even unto.................. 2Chr 30:10
Nevertheless divers of Asher and M... 2Chr 30:11
even many of Ephraim, and M........... 2Chr 30:18
and Benjamin, in Ephraim also and M 2Chr 31:1
And so did he in the cities of M......... 2Chr 34:6
had gathered of the hand of M.......... 2Chr 34:9
Gilead is mine, and M is mine........... Ps 60:7
M stir up thy strength, and come...... Ps 80:2
M is mine.. Ps 108:8
M, Ephraim; and Ephraim................. Is 9:21
and Ephraim, M................................ Is 9:21
the west side, a portion for M........... Eze 48:4
And by the border of M, from the...... Eze 48:5
3. Grandfather of Jonathan.
the son of Gershom, the son of......... Judg 18:30
4. Son of King Hezekiah.
M his son reigned in his stead.......... 2Kin 20:21
M was twelve years old when he....... 2Kin 21:1
M seduced them to do more evil....... 2Kin 21:9
Because M king of Judah hath done.. 2Kin 21:11
Moreover M shed innocent blood...... 2Kin 21:16
Now the rest of the acts of M........... 2Kin 21:17
M slept with his fathers, and was..... 2Kin 21:18
of the LORD, as his father M did....... 2Kin 21:20
the altars which M had made in the.. 2Kin 23:12
that M had provoked him withal....... 2Kin 23:26
of his sight, for the sins of M........... 2Kin 24:3
son, Hezekiah his son, M his son,.... 1Chr 3:13
M his son reigned in his stead......... 2Chr 32:33
M was twelve years old when he...... 2Chr 33:1
So M made Judah and the............... 2Chr 33:9
Then M knew that the LORD he was. 2Chr 33:13
Now the rest of the acts of M.......... 2Chr 33:18
So M slept with his fathers, and...... 2Chr 33:20
of the LORD, as did M his father...... 2Chr 33:22
which M his father had made........... 2Chr 33:22
as M his father had made before..... 2Chr 33:23
because of M the son of Hezekiah.... Jer 15:4
5. Married a foreigner in exile.
Bezaleel, and Binnui, and M............ Ezr 10:30
6. A descendant of Hashum.
Zabad, Eliphelet, Jeremai, M........... Ezr 10:33

MANASSEH'S *(ma-nas'-sez)*
1. Refers to Manasseh 1.
and his left hand upon M head........ Gen 48:14
from Ephraim's head unto M head.... Gen 48:17
the rest of M sons had the land....... Josh 17:6
2. Refers to Manasseh 2.
Ephraim's, and northward it was M.. Josh 17:10

MANASSES *(ma-nas'-seez)* See MANASSEH.
*1. Greek form of Manasseh; ancestor of
Jesus.*
And Ezekias begat M....................... Mt 1:10
And M begat Amon.......................... Mt 1:10
2. Greek form of Manasseh 2.
Of the tribe of M were sealed.......... Rev 7:6

MANASSITES *(ma-nas'-sites)* Same as
Manasseh 2.
and Golan in Bashan, out the M...... Deut 4:43
the Ephraimites, and among the M... Judg 12:4
and the Reubenites, and the M....... 2Kin 10:33

MANDRAKES
found in the field, and brought........ Gen 30:14
me, I pray thee, of thy son's m....... Gen 30:14
thou take away my son's m also...... Gen 30:15
thee to night for thy son's m........... Gen 30:15
I have hired thee with my son's m.... Gen 30:16
The m give a smell, and at our........ Song 7:13

MANEH
fifteen shekels, shall be your m....... Eze 45:12

MANGER
clothes, and laid him in a m............ Lk 2:7
swaddling clothes, lying in a m........ Lk 2:12
Joseph, and the babe lying in a m... Lk 2:16

MANIFEST
of men, that God might m them........ Eccl 3:18
secret, that shall not be made m...... Lk 8:17
he should be made m to Israel........ Jn 1:31
that his deeds may be made m........ Jn 3:21
of God should be made m in him..... Jn 9:3
love him, and will m myself to him.. Jn 14:21
that thou wilt m thyself unto us...... Jn 14:22
is m to all them that dwell in.......... Acts 4:16
may be known of God is m in them.. Rom 1:19
I was made m unto them that asked. Rom 10:20
But now is made m, and by the....... Rom 16:26
Every man's work shall be made m... 1Cor 3:13
will make m the counsels of the...... 1Cor 4:5
may be made m among you............. 1Cor 11:19
the secrets of his heart made m...... 1Cor 14:25
it is m that he is excepted,............. 1Cor 15:27
maketh m the savour of his............ 2Cor 2:14
Jesus might be made m in our body. 2Cor 4:10
be made m in our mortal flesh........ 2Cor 4:11
but we are made m unto God.......... 2Cor 5:11
are made m in your consciences..... 2Cor 5:11
made m among you in all things...... 2Cor 11:6
Now the works of the flesh are m... Gal 5:19
reproved are made m by the light... Eph 5:13
whatsoever doth make m is light..... Eph 5:13
in Christ are m in all the palace..... Phil 1:13
but now is made m to his saints..... Col 1:26
That I may make it m, as I ought... Col 4:4
Which is a m token of the.............. 2Th 1:5
God was m in the flesh, justified.... 1Ti 3:16
works of some are m beforehand.... 1Ti 5:25
But is now made m by the.............. 2Ti 1:10
folly shall be m unto all men......... 2Ti 3:9
that is not m in his sight............... Heb 4:13
holiest of all was not yet made m... Heb 9:8
but was m in these last times for... 1Pet 1:20
that they might be made m that..... 1Jn 2:19
In this the children of God are m.... 1Jn 3:10
for thy judgments are made m........ Rev 15:4

MANIFESTATION
for the m of the sons of God.......... Rom 8:19
But the m of the Spirit is given..... 1Cor 12:7
but by m of the truth commending. 2Cor 4:2

MANIFESTED
nothing hid, which shall not be m... Mk 4:22
of Galilee, and m forth his glory.... Jn 2:11
I have m thy name unto the men.... Jn 17:6
of God without the law is m........... Rom 3:21
But hath in due times m his word.. Titus 1:3
(For the life was m, and we have... 1Jn 1:2
with the Father, and was m unto us. 1Jn 1:2
ye know that he was m to take...... 1Jn 3:5
this purpose the Son of God was m. 1Jn 3:8
In this was m the love of God........ 1Jn 4:9

MANIFESTLY
Forasmuch as ye are m declared to.. 2Cor 3:3

MANIFOLD
Yet thou in thy m mercies.............. Neh 9:19
according to thy m mercies thou..... Neh 9:27
O LORD, how m are thy works........ Ps 104:24
For I know your m transgressions... Amos 5:12
Who shall not receive m more in..... Lk 18:30
by the church the m wisdom of God. Eph 3:10
heaviness through m temptations.... 1Pet 1:6
stewards of the m grace of God...... 1Pet 4:10

MANKIND
Thou shalt not lie with m............... Lev 18:22
If a man also lie with m, as he....... Lev 20:13
thing, and the breath of all m........ Job 12:10
abusers of themselves with m........ 1Cor 6:9
nor abusers of themselves with m.. 1Ti 1:10
is tamed, and hath been tamed of m. Jas 3:7

MANNA
they said one to another, It is m.... Ex 16:15
Israel called the name thereof M.... Ex 16:31
and put an omer full of m therein... Ex 16:33
of Israel did eat m forty years....... Ex 16:35
they did eat m, until they came..... Ex 16:35
is nothing at all, beside this m....... Num 11:6
the m was as coriander seed, and... Num 11:7
in the night, the m fell upon it...... Num 11:9
to hunger, and fed thee with m...... Deut 8:3
fed thee in the wilderness with m... Deut 8:16
the m ceased on the morrow after.. Josh 5:12
the children of Israel m any more... Josh 5:12
not thy m from their mouth........... Neh 9:20
had rained down m upon them....... Ps 78:24
fathers did eat m in the desert...... Jn 6:31
did eat m in the wilderness........... Jn 6:49
not as your fathers did eat m......... Jn 6:58
was the golden pot that had m....... Heb 9:4

I give to eat of the hidden m .... Rev 2:17

MANNER

with Sarah after the m of women ...... Gen 18:11
far from thee to do after this m .... Gen 18:25
us after the m of all the earth.......... Gen 19:31
womb, and two m of people shall be .. Gen 25:23
On this m shall ye speak unto........... Gen 32:19
After this m did thy servant to .... Gen 39:19
after the former m when thou wast .... Gen 40:13
basket there was of all m of .... Gen 40:17
his father he sent after this m........... Gen 45:23
in all m of service in the field.......... Ex 1:14
they also did in like m with............. Ex 7:11
no m of work shall be done in........... Ex 12:16
with her after the m of daughters....... Ex 21:9
For all m of trespass, whether it .... Ex 22:9
or for any m of lost thing, which....... Ex 22:9
In like m thou shalt deal with.......... Ex 23:11
and in all m of workmanship,........... Ex 31:3
to work in all m of workmanship....... Ex 31:5
to bring for all m of work.............. Ex 35:29
and in all m of workmanship........... Ex 35:31
to make any m of cunning work........ Ex 35:33
of heart, to work all m of work........ Ex 35:35
to know how to work all m of work.... Ex 36:1
offering, according to the m .... Lev 5:10
saying, Ye shall eat no m of fat....... Lev 7:23
ye shall eat no m of blood............. Lev 7:26
it be that eateth any m of blood....... Lev 7:27
and offered it according to the m ..... Lev 9:16
among all m of beasts that go on...... Lev 11:27
ye defile yourselves with any m .... Lev 11:44
for all m of plague of leprosy......... Lev 14:54
you, that eateth any m of blood....... Lev 17:10
eat the blood of no m of flesh........ Lev 17:14
planted all m of trees for food....... Lev 19:23
or by any m of living thing that ..... Lev 20:25
Ye shall do no m of work............. Lev 23:31
Ye shall have one m of law........... Lev 24:22
neither she be taken with the m ...... Num 5:13
and according to the m thereof....... Num 9:14
do these things after this m .... Num 15:13
one m shall be for you, and for ..... Num 15:16
offering, according to the m .... Num 15:24
ye shall do no m of servile work.... Num 28:18
After this m ye shall offer daily.... Num 28:24
offerings, according unto their m ... Num 29:6
to their number, after the m .... Num 29:18
to their number, after the m .... Num 29:21
to their number, after the m .... Num 29:24
to their number, after the m .... Num 29:27
to their number, after the m .... Num 29:30
to their number, after the m .... Num 29:33
to their number, after the m .... Num 29:37
of all m of beasts, and give them... Num 31:30
for ye saw no m of similitude on.... Deut 4:15
this is the m of the release......... Deut 15:2
In like m shalt thou do with his.... Deut 22:3
he that lieth with any m of beast... Deut 27:21
city after the same m seven times... Josh 6:15
What m of men were they whom ye..... Judg 8:18
in like m they sent unto the king .. Judg 11:17
after the m of the Zidonians,....... Judg 18:7
Now this was the m in former time .. Ruth 4:7
shew them the m of the king that ... 1Sa 8:9
This will be the m of the king...... 1Sa 8:11
the people the m of the kingdom..... 1Sa 10:25
people answered him after this m ... 1Sa 17:27
and spake after the same m 1Sa 17:30
him again after the former m 1Sa 17:30
saying, On this m spake David....... 1Sa 18:24
before Samuel in like m, and lay ... 1Sa 19:24
and the bread is in a m common...... 1Sa 21:5
so will be his m all the while he... 1Sa 27:11
played before the LORD on all m 2Sa 6:5
And is this the m of man, O Lord 2Sa 7:19
king, and speak on this m unto him.. 2Sa 14:3
on this m did Absalom to all........ 2Sa 15:6
hath spoken after this m 2Sa 17:6
work of the bases was on this m..... 1Kin 7:28
After this m he made the ten........ 1Kin 7:37
after their m with knives........... 1Kin 18:28
And one said on this m.............. 1Kin 22:20
and another said on that m.......... 1Kin 22:20
What m of man was he which came 2Kin 1:7
stood by a pillar, as the m was..... 2Kin 11:14
know not the m of the God of the ... 2Kin 17:26
not the m of the God of the land ... 2Kin 17:26
them the m of the God of the land .. 2Kin 17:27
after the m of the nations whom 2Kin 17:33
but they did after their former m .. 2Kin 17:40
m of service of the tabernacle of .. 1Chr 6:48
with all m of instruments of war ... 1Chr 12:37
with him all m of vessels of gold... 1Chr 18:10
all m of cunning men for every 1Chr 22:15
cunning men for every m of work..... 1Chr 22:15
for all m of measure and the 1Chr 23:29
of the LORD, according to their m... 1Chr 24:19
instruments of all m of service.... 1Chr 28:14
shall be with thee for all m of 1Chr 28:21
skilful man, for any m of work...... 1Chr 28:21
all m of precious stones, and....... 1Chr 29:2
for all m of work to be made by 1Chr 29:5
also to grave any m of graving...... 2Chr 2:14
after the m before the oracle....... 2Chr 4:20
of the nations of other lands....... 2Chr 13:9
And one spake saying after that m... 2Chr 18:19
and another spake after that m 2Chr 18:19
in their place after their m 2Chr 30:16
you, nor persuade you on this m 2Chr 32:15

for all m of pleasant jewels,....... 2Chr 32:27
and stalls for all m of beasts...... 2Chr 32:28
the work in any m of service........ 2Chr 34:13
said we unto them after this m ..... Ezr 5:4
I answered them after the same m ... Neh 6:4
m the fifth time with an open....... Neh 6:5
assembly, according unto the m ..... Neh 8:18
and the fruit of all m of trees..... Neh 10:37
all m of burdens, which they........ Neh 13:15
all m of ware, and sold on the...... Neh 13:16
(for so was the king's m toward.... Est 1:13
according to the m of the women..... Est 2:12
but abhorreth all m of meat........ Ps 107:18
be full, affording all m of store... Ps 144:13
are all m of pleasant fruits........ Song 7:13
the lambs feed after their m .... Is 5:17
thee, after the m of Egypt.......... Is 10:24
lift it up after the m of Egypt..... Is 10:26
dwell therein shall die in like m .. Is 51:6
After this m will I mar the pride... Jer 13:9
hath been thy m from thy youth...... Jer 22:21
shall remain after the m thereof.... Jer 30:18
after the m of your fathers......... Eze 20:30
after the m of the Babylonians in .. Eze 23:15
them after the m of adulteresses ... Eze 23:45
after the m of women that shed...... Eze 23:45
no m of hurt was found upon him,.... Dan 6:23
pestilence after the m of Egypt..... Amos 4:10
the m of Beer-sheba liveth.......... Amos 8:14
and healing all m of sickness....... Mt 4:23
all m of disease among the people... Mt 4:23
shall say all m of evil against..... Mt 5:11
After this m therefore pray ye...... Mt 6:9
What m of man is this, that even.... Mt 8:27
out, and to heal all m of sickness.. Mt 10:1
of sickness and all m of disease.... Mt 10:1
All m of sin and blasphemy shall.... Mt 12:31
What m of man is this, that even.... Mk 4:41
see what m of stones and what....... Mk 13:1
So ye in like m, when ye shall...... Mk 13:29
cast in her mind what m of .... Lk 1:29
What m of child shall this be....... Lk 1:66
for in the like m did their......... Lk 6:23
What m of woman this is that........ Lk 7:39
to another, What m of man is this .. Lk 8:25
Ye know not what m of spirit ye..... Lk 9:55
all m of herbs, and pass over....... Lk 11:42
and in like m the seven also........ Lk 20:31
What m of communications are........ Lk 24:17
after the m of the purifying of .... Jn 2:6
What m of saying is this that he ... Jn 7:36
as the m of the Jews is to bury..... Jn 19:40
shall so come in like m as ye ...... Acts 1:11
Wherein were all m of fourfooted.... Acts 10:12
circumcised after the m of Moses.... Acts 15:1
letters by them after this m .... Acts 15:23
And Paul, as his m was, went in..... Acts 17:2
after what m I have been with you... Acts 20:18
the m of the law of the fathers..... Acts 22:3
And he wrote a letter after this m.. Acts 23:25
It is not the m of the Romans to ... Acts 25:16
I doubted of such m of questions.... Acts 25:20
My m of life from my youth, which... Acts 26:4
I speak after the m of men .... Rom 6:19
in me all m of concupiscence........ Rom 7:8
gift of God, one after this m 1Cor 7:7
After the same m also he took the .. 1Cor 11:25
If after the m of men I have 1Cor 15:32
were made sorry after a godly m 2Cor 7:9
livest after the m of Gentiles..... Gal 2:14
I speak after the m of men .... Gal 3:15
as ye know what m of men we were.... 1Th 1:5
m of entering in we had unto you.... 1Th 1:9
In like m also, that women adorn... 1Ti 2:9
of life, purpose, faith,............ 2Ti 3:10
together, as the m of some is ...... Heb 10:25
forgetteth what m of man he was..... Jas 1:24
or what m of time the Spirit of 1Pet 1:11
ye holy in all m of conversation... 1Pet 1:15
For after this m in the old time.... 1Pet 3:5
what m of persons ought ye to be ... 2Pet 3:11
what m of love the Father hath...... 1Jn 3:1
the cities about them in like m .... Jude 7
them, be meat in this m be killed .. Rev 11:5
all m vessels of ivory.............. Rev 18:12
with all m of precious stones,...... Rev 21:19
which bare twelve m of fruits....... Rev 22:2

MANNERS

not walk in the m of the nation .... Lev 20:23
day they do after the former m 2Kin 17:34
but have done after the m of the ... Eze 11:12
he their m in the wilderness........ Acts 13:18
communications corrupt good m 1Cor 15:33
in divers m spake in time past...... Heb 1:1

MANOAH (ma-no'-ah) Father of Samson.

of the Danites, whose name was M.... Judg 13:2
Then M intreated the LORD, and...... Judg 13:8
God hearkened to the voice of M..... Judg 13:9
but M her husband was not with...... Judg 13:9
M arose, and went after his wife,... Judg 13:11
M said, Now let thy words come to... Judg 13:12
the angel of the LORD said unto M .. Judg 13:13
M said unto the angel of the LORD .. Judg 13:15
the angel of the LORD said unto M .. Judg 13:16
For M knew not that he was an ...... Judg 13:16
M said unto the angel of the LORD .. Judg 13:17
So M took a kid with a meat......... Judg 13:19
and M and his wife looked on........ Judg 13:19

M and his wife looked on it......... Judg 13:20
the LORD did no more appear to M ... Judg 13:21
Then M knew that he was an angel.... Judg 13:21
M said unto his wife, We shall...... Judg 13:22
the buryingplace of M his father ... Judg 16:31

MAN'S

the ground any more for m sake...... Gen 8:21
for the imagination of m heart is... Gen 8:21
at the hand of every m brother...... Gen 9:5
Whoso sheddeth m blood, by man ..... Gen 9:6
man, and every m hand against him .. Gen 16:12
for she is a m wife................. Gen 20:3
We are all one m sons.............. Gen 42:11
to restore every m money into his.. Gen 42:25
every m bundle of money was in ..... Gen 42:35
every m money was in the mouth of.. Gen 43:21
put every m money in his sack's.... Gen 44:1
for we may not see the m face....... Gen 44:26
unto him, Who hath made m mouth..... Ex 4:11
But every m servant that is........ Ex 12:44
if one m ox hurt another's, that ... Ex 21:35
and shall feed in another m field .. Ex 22:5
it be stolen out of the m house..... Ex 22:7
Upon m flesh shall it not be .... Ex 30:32
offereth any m burnt offering ...... Lev 7:8
if any m seed of copulation go...... Lev 15:16
adultery with another m wife .... Lev 20:10
every m hallowed things shall be ... Num 5:10
If any m wife go aside, and commit.. Num 5:12
write thou every m name upon his ... Num 17:2
come to pass, that the m rod .... Num 17:5
every m inheritance shall be in .... Num 33:54
(is m life) to employ them in the .. Deut 20:19
she may go and be another m wife ... Deut 24:2
for he taketh a m life to pledge.... Deut 24:6
he put a trumpet in every m hand.... Judg 7:16
the LORD set every m sword.......... Judg 7:22
of the m house where her lord was.. Judg 19:26
The m name with whom I.............. Ruth 2:19
thou taken ought of any m hand 1Sa 12:4
every m sword was against his 1Sa 14:20
Let no m heart fail because of 1Sa 17:32
but took the poor m lamb, and 2Sa 12:4
came to a m house in Bahurim,....... 2Sa 17:18
which Amasa was a m son, whose...... 2Sa 17:25
out of the sea, like a m hand....... 1Kin 18:44
m heart to bring into the house 2Kin 12:4
which were on m left hand at........ 2Kin 23:8
which went on m left hand........... 2Kin 23:8
do according to every m pleasure ... Est 1:8
Are thy years as m days,............ Job 10:5
I pray you, accept any m person .... Job 32:21
bread which strengtheneth m heart... Ps 104:15
The rich m wealth is his strong .... Prov 10:15
the recompence of a m hands shall .. Prov 12:14
The ransom of a m life are his ..... Prov 13:8
When a m ways please the LORD, he... Prov 16:7
A m heart deviseth his way.......... Prov 16:9
The words of a m mouth are as....... Prov 18:4
The rich m wealth is his strong .... Prov 18:11
A m gift maketh room for him, and .. Prov 18:16
A m belly shall be satisfied with .. Prov 18:20
are many devices in a m heart ...... Prov 19:21
M goings are of the LORD;........... Prov 20:24
of a m friend by hearty counsel..... Prov 27:9
a m pride bring him low............. Prov 29:23
but every m judgment cometh from ... Prov 29:26
The wise m eyes are in his head..... Eccl 2:14
a m wisdom maketh his face to....... Eccl 8:1
a wise m heart discerneth both...... Eccl 8:5
the poor m wisdom is despised....... Eccl 9:16
A wise m heart is at his right...... Eccl 10:2
of a wise m mouth are gracious...... Eccl 10:12
in it with a m pen concerning....... Is 8:1
and every m heart shall melt........ Is 13:7
go from him, and become another m .. Jer 3:1
for every m word shall be his....... Jer 23:36
given thee cow's dung for m dung.... Eze 4:15
of a m hand under their wings....... Eze 10:8
every m sword shall be against ..... Eze 38:21
the land, when any seeth a m bone .. Eze 39:15
in the m hand a measuring reed of .. Eze 40:5
Let his heart be changed from m .... Dan 4:16
came forth fingers of a m hand ..... Dan 5:5
a m heart was given to it........... Dan 7:4
I heard a m voice between the ...... Dan 8:16
a m uncle shall take him up, and ... Amos 6:10
let us not perish for this m life... Jonah 1:14
a m enemies are the men of his...... Mic 7:6
a m foes shall be they of his own... Mt 10:36
receive a righteous m reward........ Mt 10:41
one enter into a strong m house..... Mt 12:29
can enter into a strong m house..... Mk 3:27
If a m brother die, and leave his... Mk 12:19
as evil, for the Son of m sake ..... Lk 6:22
for a m life consisteth not in ..... Lk 12:15
in that which is another m......... Lk 16:12
which fell from the rich m table.... Lk 16:21
If a m brother die, having.......... Lk 20:28
thou also one of this m disciples .. Jn 18:17
to bring this m blood upon us ...... Acts 5:28
their clothes at a young m feet..... Acts 7:58
and we entered into the m house .... Acts 11:12
Of this m seed hath God according .. Acts 13:23
stone, graven by art and m device .. Acts 17:29
and entered into a certain m house . Acts 18:7
I have coveted no m silver......... Acts 20:33
no loss of any m life among you,.... Acts 27:22
For if by one m offence death ...... Rom 5:17
For as by one m disobedience many .. Rom 5:19

MANSERVANT (cont.)

that judgest another m servant .... Rom 14:4
build upon another m foundation ...... Rom 15:20
with enticing words of m wisdom........ 1Cor 2:4
the words which m wisdom teacheth... 1Cor 2:13
Every m work shall be made............... 1Cor 3:13
every m work of what sort it is 1Cor 3:13
If any m work abide which he hath 1Cor 3:14
If any m work shall be burned, he...... 1Cor 3:15
judged of you, or of m judgment........ 1Cor 4:3
judged of another m conscience.......... 1Cor 10:29
commending ourselves to every m 2Cor 4:2
not to boast in another m line of 2Cor 10:16
God accepteth no m person................. Gal 2:6
Though it be but a m covenant .... Gal 3:15
did we eat any m bread for nought 2Th 3:8
heart, this m religion is vain.............. Jas 1:26
judgeth according to every m work's .. 1Pet 1:17
the dumb ass speaking with m............ 2Pet 2:16

MANSERVANT

thy son, nor thy daughter, thy m........ Ex 20:10
thy neighbour's wife, nor his m.......... Ex 20:17
shall push a m or a maidservant .... Ex 21:32
son, nor thy daughter, nor thy m .... Deut 5:14
that thy m and thy maidservant may . Deut 5:14
house, his field, or his m .... Deut 5:21
son, and thy daughter, and thy m ...... Deut 12:18
son, and thy daughter, and thy m ...... Deut 16:11
son, and thy daughter, and thy m ...... Deut 16:14
of my m or of my maidservant............ Job 31:13
That every man should let his m........ Jer 34:9
that every one should let his m .... Jer 34:10

MANSERVANT'S

And if he smite out his m tooth .... Ex 21:27

MANSERVANTS

Beside their and their m.................... Neh 7:67

MANSIONS

In my Father's house are many .... Jn 14:2

MANSLAYER

which ye shall appoint for the m .... Num 35:6
that the m die not, until he .... Num 35:12

MANSLAYERS

and murderers of mothers, for m 1Ti 1:9

MANTLE

tent, she covered him with a m .... Judg 4:18
laid hold upon the skirt of his m 1Sa 15:27
and he is covered with a m.................. 1Sa 28:14
that he wrapped his face in his m....... 1Kin 19:13
by him, and cast his m upon him....... 1Kin 19:19
And Elijah took his m, and wrapped .. 2Kin 2:8
He took up also the m of Elijah 2Kin 2:13
he took the m of Elijah that fell......... 2Kin 2:14
thing, I rent my garment and my m ... Ezr 9:3
and having rent my garment and my m. Ezr 9:5
Then Job arose, and rent his m........... Job 1:20
and they rent every one his m .... Job 2:12
their own confusion, as with a m .... Ps 109:29

MANTLES

suits of apparel, and the m.................. Is 3:22

MANY See PREFACE.

MAOCH (ma'-ok) Father of Achish.

him unto Achish, the son of M 1Sa 27:2

MAON (ma'-on) See MAONITES.

1. A city in Judah.
M, Carmel, and Ziph, and Juttah,...... Josh 15:55
And there was a man in M, whose 1Sa 25:2
2. A descendant of Caleb.
And the son of Shammai was M 1Chr 2:45
M was the father of Beth-zur............... 1Chr 2:45
3. A wilderness in Judah.
men were in the wilderness of M 1Sa 23:24
and abode in the wilderness of M 1Sa 23:25
David in the wilderness of M.............. 1Sa 23:25

MAONITES (ma'-on-ites) See MEHUNIM. An enemy tribe of Israel.

also, and the Amalekites, and the M . Judg 10:12

MAR

neither shalt thou m the corners........ Lev 19:27
lest I m mine own inheritance............ Ruth 4:6
of your mice that m the land 1Sa 6:5
m every good piece of land with....... 2Kin 3:19
They m my path, they set forward...... Job 30:13
will I m the pride of Judah .... Jer 13:9

MARA (ma'-rah) Another name for Naomi.

Call me not Naomi, call me M .... Ruth 1:20

MARAH (ma'-rah) An Israelite encampment in the wilderness.

And when they came to M, they .... Ex 15:23
not drink of the waters of M .... Ex 15:23
the name of it was called M .... Ex 15:23
of Etham, and pitched in M................ Num 33:8
And they removed from M, and came. Num 33:9

MARALAH (mar'-a-lah) A city in Zebulun.

went up toward the sea, and M .... Josh 19:11

MARANATHA

Christ, let him be Anathema M 1Cor 16:22

MARBLE

stones, and m stones in abundance 1Chr 29:2
to silver rings and pillars of m........... Est 1:6
and blue, and white, and black, m...... Est 1:6
His legs are as pillars of m................. Song 5:15

wood, and of brass, and iron, and m .. Rev 18:12

MARCHED

when thou didst m through the .... Ps 68:7
for they shall m with an army .... Jer 46:22
they shall m every one on his............. Joel 2:7
which shall m through the breadth..... Hab 1:6
Thou didst m through the land in ...... Hab 3:12

MARCHEDST

the Egyptians m after them................ Ex 14:10

MARCHEDST

when thou m out of the field of .... Judg 5:4

MARCUS (mar'-cus) See MARK. Latin form of Mark.

fellowprisoner saluteth you, and M ... Col 4:10
M, Aristarchus, Demas, Lucas, my .... Philem 24
and so doth M my son 1Pet 5:13

MARDUK See MERODACH.

MAREAL See MARALAH.

MARESHAH

1. A city in Judah.
And Keilah, and Achzib, and M .... Josh 15:44
And Gath, and M and Ziph,................. 2Chr 11:8
and came unto M 2Chr 14:9
in the valley of Zephathah at M 2Chr 14:10
Eliezer the son of Dodavah of M 2Chr 20:37
heir unto thee, O inhabitant of M ...... Mic 1:15
2. Father of Hebron.
the sons of the father of....................... 1Chr 2:42
3. A descendant of Shelah.
Lecah, and Laadah the father of M 1Chr 4:21

MARINERS

of Zidon and Arvad were thy m.......... Eze 27:8
m were in thee to occupy thy............. Eze 27:9
thy fairs, thy merchandise, thy m ...... Eze 27:27
And all that handle the oar, the m...... Eze 27:29
Then the m were afraid, and cried..... Jonah 1:5

MARISHES

the m thereof shall not be healed........ Eze 47:11

MARK See MARCUS. Missionary companion of Paul.

And the LORD set a m upon Cain........ Gen 4:15
that thou shalt m the place where ..... Ruth 3:4
thereof, as though I shot at a m.......... Job 16:12
M ye now when Amnon's heart is...... 2Sa 13:28
elders of the land, and said, M 1Kin 20:7
him, Go, strengthen thyself, and m ... 1Kin 20:22
thou set me as a m against thee.......... Job 7:20
to pieces, and set me up for his m ...... Job 16:12
m, and afterwards we will speak .... Job 18:2
M me, and be astonished, and lay ..... Job 21:5
M well, O Job, hearken unto me......... Job 33:31
or canst thou m when the hinds do ... Job 39:1
M the perfect man, and behold the ... Ps 37:37
M ye well her bulwarks, consider...... Ps 48:13
they m my steps, when they wait....... Ps 56:6
shouldest m iniquities, O Lord,.......... Ps 130:3
set me as a m for the arrow .... Lam 3:12
set a m upon the foreheads of the ..... Eze 9:4
near any man upon whom is the m .... Eze 9:6
m well, and behold with thine eyes ... Eze 44:5
m well the entering in of the .... Eze 44:5
of John, whose surname was M .... Acts 12:12
then John, whose surname was M ...... Acts 12:25
then John, whose surname was M ...... Acts 15:37
and so Barnabas took M, and sailed.. Acts 15:39
m them which cause divisions and.... Rom 16:17
I press toward the m for the............... Phil 3:14
m them which walk so as ye have ..... Phil 3:17
Take M, and bring him with thee 2Ti 4:11
to receive a m in their right .... Rev 13:16
or sell, save he that had the m............ Rev 13:17
receive his m in his forehead, or .... Rev 14:9
receiveth the m of his name............... Rev 14:11
and over his image, and over his m ... Rev 15:2
men which had the m of the beast...... Rev 16:2
had received the m of the beast .... Rev 19:20
his m upon their foreheads................. Rev 20:4

MARKED

the LORD, that Eli m her mouth.......... 1Sa 1:12
Hast thou m the old way which .... Job 22:15
which they had m for themselves....... Job 24:16
yet thine iniquity is m before me ...... Jer 2:22
who hath m his word, and heard it .... Jer 23:18
when he m how they chose out the .... Lk 14:7

MARKEST

If I sin, then thou m me, and thou ..... Job 10:14

MARKET

men and vessels of brass in thy m ..... Eze 27:13
traded in thy m wheat of Minnith..... Eze 27:17
cassia, and calamus, were in thy m.... Eze 27:19
did sing of thee in the m .... Eze 27:25
And when they come from the m........ Mk 7:4
Jerusalem by the sheep m a pool........ Jn 5:2
in the m daily with them that met..... Acts 17:17

MARKETH

in the stocks, he m all my paths......... Job 33:11
He m it out with a line....................... Is 44:13
he m it out with the compass, and.... Is 44:13

MARKETPLACE

saw others standing idle in the m ...... Mt 20:3
unto children sitting in the m............ Lk 7:32
them into the m unto the rulers......... Acts 16:19

MARKETPLACES

and love salutations in the m............. Mk 12:38

MARKETS

unto children sitting in the m............ Mt 11:16
And greetings in the m, and to be...... Mt 23:7
synagogues, and greetings in the m .. Lk 11:43
robes, and love greetings in the m..... Lk 20:46

MARKS

dead, nor print any m upon you......... Lev 19:28
my body the m of the Lord Jesus....... Gal 6:17

MAROTH (ma'-roth) A city in Judah.

For the inhabitant of M waited .... Mic 1:12

MARRED

visage was so m more than any man .. Is 52:14
and, behold, the girdle was m............. Jer 13:7
was m in their vine branches............. Jer 18:4
out, and m their vine branches.......... Nah 2:2
spilled, and the bottles will be m....... Mk 2:22

MARRIAGE

her raiment, and her duty of .... Ex 21:10
their maidens were not given to m .... Ps 78:63
king, which made a m for his son ...... Mt 22:2
are ready: come unto the m .... Mt 22:4
as ye shall find, bid to the m.............. Mt 22:9
neither marry, nor are given in m ...... Mt 22:30
drinking, marrying and giving in m .. Mt 24:38
ready went in with him to the m .... Mt 25:10
neither marry, nor are given in m ...... Mk 12:25
wives, they were given in m .... Lk 17:27
world marry, and are given in m .... Lk 20:34
neither marry, nor are given in m ...... Lk 20:35
there was a m in Cana of Galilee .... Jn 2:1
and his disciples, to the m.................. Jn 2:2
that giveth her in m doeth well.......... 1Cor 7:38
giveth her not in m doeth better 1Cor 7:38
M is honourable in all, and the .... Heb 13:4
for the m of the Lamb is come, and ... Rev 19:7
unto the m supper of the Lamb .... Rev 19:9

MARRIAGES

And make ye m with us, and give....... Gen 34:9
shalt thou make m with them .... Deut 7:3
you, and shall make m with their...... Josh 23:12

MARRIED

which m his daughters, and said,....... Gen 19:14
if he were m, then his wife shall .... Ex 21:3
also be m unto a stranger.................... Lev 22:12
woman whom he had m .... Num 12:1
for he had m an Ethiopian woman..... Num 12:1
if they be m to any of the sons .... Num 36:3
were m unto their father's.................. Num 36:11
they were m into the families of........ Num 36:12
with a woman m to an husband .... Deut 22:22
m her, and it come to pass that .... Deut 24:1
whom he m when he was threescore.. 1Chr 2:21
m fourteen wives, and begat twenty . 2Chr 13:21
J lews that had m wives of Ashdod..... Neh 13:23
For an odious woman when she is m . Prov 30:23
than the children of the m wife.......... Is 54:1
in thee, and thy land shall be m......... Is 62:4
for I am m unto you............................ Is 62:5
hath m the daughter of a strange....... Mal 2:11
the first, when he had m a wife .... Mt 22:25
for he had m her................................. Mk 6:17
be m to another, she committeth........ Mk 10:12
And another said, I have m a wife ..... Lk 14:20
they m wives, they were given in ...... Lk 17:27
she be m to another man, she............ Rom 7:3
though she be m to another man........ Rom 7:3
that ye should be m to another .... Rom 7:4
unto the m I command, yet not I 1Cor 7:10
But he that is m careth for the 1Cor 7:33
but she that is m careth for the 1Cor 7:34
liberty to be m to whom she will 1Cor 7:39

MARRIETH

For as a young man m a virgin........... Is 62:5
whoso m her which is put away .... Mt 19:9
m another, committeth adultery .... Lk 16:18
whosoever m that is put away .... Lk 16:18

MARROW

and his bones are moistened with m .. Job 21:24
soul shall be satisfied as with m .... Ps 63:5
to thy navel, and m to thy bones .... Prov 3:8
the lees, of fat things full of m .... Is 25:6
and spirit, and of the joints and m .... Heb 4:12

MARRY

m her, and raise up seed to thy .... Gen 38:8
Let them m to whom they think........ Num 36:6
of their father shall they m................. Num 36:6
not m without unto a stranger........... Deut 25:5
virgin, so shall thy sons m thee .... Is 62:5
whosoever shall m her that is............ Mt 5:32
shall m another, committeth.............. Mt 19:9
his wife, it is not good to m .... Mt 19:10
his brother shall m his wife............... Mk 12:19
the resurrection they neither m .... Mt 22:30
m another, committeth adultery .... Mk 10:11
from the dead, they neither m............ Mk 12:25
The children of this world m .... Lk 20:34
from the dead, neither m, nor are...... Lk 20:35
they cannot contain, let them m......... 1Cor 7:9
it is better to m than to burn 1Cor 7:9
But and if thou m, thou hast not........ 1Cor 7:28
and if a virgin m, she hath not........... 1Cor 7:28
he sinneth not: let them m 1Cor 7:36
Forbidding to m, and commanding to. 1Ti 4:3

against Christ, they will m.................. 1Ti 5:11
that the younger women m, bear 1Ti 5:14

MARRYING
our God in m strange wives .... Neh 13:27
they were eating and drinking, m .... Mt 24:38

MARS' (*marz*) *Refers to a landmark in Athens.*
Paul stood in the midst of Mars' .... Acts 17:22

MARSENA (*mar'-se-nah*) *A prince of Media
and Persia.*
Admatha, Tarshish, Meres, M .... Est 1:14

MART
and she is a m of nations .... Is 23:3

MARTHA (*mar'-thah*) *Sister of Lazarus.*
a certain woman named M received ..... Lk 10:38
But M was cumbered about much .... Lk 10:40
and said unto her, M, M .... Lk 10:41
the town of Mary and her sister M .... Jn 11:1
Now Jesus loved M, and her sister .... Jn 11:5
And many of the Jews came to M .... Jn 11:19
Then M, as soon as she heard that ..... Jn 11:20
Then said M unto Jesus, Lord, if ...... Jn 11:21
M saith unto him, I know that he ...... Jn 11:24
was in that place where M met him .... Jn 11:30
M, the sister of him that was .... Jn 11:39
a supper; and M served .... Jn 12:2

MARTYR
blood of thy m Stephen was shed ... Acts 22:20
wherein Antipas was my faithful m .... Rev 2:13

MARTYRS
with the blood of the m of Jesus .... Rev 17:6

MARVEL
a province, m not at the matter .... Eccl 5:8
and all men did m .... Mk 5:20
M not that I said unto thee, Ye .... Jn 3:7
works than these, that ye may m ...... Jn 5:20
M not at this .... Jn 5:28
I have done one work, and ye all m .... Jn 7:21
men of Israel, why m ye at this .... Acts 3:12
And no m; for Satan himself 2Cor 11:14
I m that ye are so soon removed .... Gal 1:6
M not, my brethren, if the world 1Jn 3:13
unto me, Wherefore didst thou m .... Rev 17:7

MARVELLED
and the men M one at another .... Gen 43:33
They saw it, and so they m .... Ps 48:5
When Jesus heard it, he m .... Mt 8:10
But the men m, saying, What .... Mt 8:27
the multitudes saw it, they m .... Mt 9:8
and the multitudes m, saying, It ...... Mt 9:33
when the disciples saw it, they m ..... Mt 21:20
had heard these words, they m .... Mt 22:22
that the governor m greatly .... Mt 27:14
he m because of their unbelief .... Mk 6:6
And they m at him .... Mk 12:17
so that Pilate m .... Mk 15:5
Pilate m if he were already dead ...... Mk 15:44
m that he tarried so long in the .... Lk 1:21
And they m all .... Lk 1:63
his mother m at those things .... Lk 2:33
he m at him, and turned him about, .. Lk 7:9
he m that he had not first washed ... Lk 11:38
they m at his answer, and held .... Lk 20:26
m that he talked with the woman ..... Jn 4:27
And the Jews m, saying, How .... Jn 7:15
And they were all amazed and m .... Acts 2:7
unlearned and ignorant men, they m ... Acts 4:13

MARVELLOUS
Remember his m works that he hath . 1Chr 16:12
his m works among all nations 1Chr 16:24
m things without number .... Job 10:16
thou shewest thyself m upon me. ..... Job 10:16
I will shew forth all thy m works .... Ps 9:1
Shew thy m lovingkindness, O thou ... Ps 17:7
his m kindness in a strong city .... Ps 31:21
M things did he in the sight of .... Ps 78:12
for he hath done m things .... Ps 98:1
Remember his m works that he hath ... Ps 105:5
it is m in our eyes .... Ps 118:23
m are his works .... Ps 139:14
to do a m work among this people ..... Is 29:14
among this people, even a m work ..... Is 29:14
shall speak m things against the ..... Dan 11:36
will I shew unto him m things .... Mic 7:15
If it be m in the eyes of this .... Zec 8:6
should it also be m in mine eyes ...... Zec 8:6
doing, and it is m in our eyes .... Mt 21:42
doing, and it is m in our eyes .... Mk 12:11
Why herein is a m thing .... Jn 9:30
out of darkness into his m light 1Pet 2:9
sign in heaven, great and m .... Rev 15:1
m are thy works, Lord God .... Rev 15:3

MARVELLOUSLY
for he was m, helped, till he was ... 2Chr 26:15
God thundereth m with his voice .... Job 37:5
heathen, and regard, and wonder m .. Hab 1:5

MARVELS
before all thy people I will do m .... Ex 34:10

MARY (*ma'-ry*)
1. Mother of Jesus.
begat Joseph the husband of M .... Mt 1:16
When as his mother M was espoused .. Mt 1:18
not to take unto thee M thy wife .... Mt 1:20
the young child with M his mother .... Mt 2:11

is not his mother called M .... Mt 13:55
this the carpenter, the son of M .... Mk 6:3
and the virgin's name was M .... Lk 1:27
angel said unto her, Fear not, M .... Lk 1:30
Then said M unto the angel, How ..... Lk 1:34
M said, Behold the handmaid of .... Lk 1:38
M arose in those days, and went ...... Lk 1:39
heard the salutation of M .... Lk 1:41
M said, My soul doth magnify the ..... Lk 1:46
M abode with her about three .... Lk 1:56
To be taxed with M his espoused ...... Lk 2:5
they came with haste, and found M ... Lk 2:16
But M kept all these things, and ...... Lk 2:19
said unto M his mother, Behold, ... Lk 2:34
M the mother of Jesus, and with ..... Acts 1:14

2. A woman of Magdala.
Among which was M Magdalene .... Mt 27:56
And there was M Magdalene, and the.. Mt 28:1
came M Magdalene and the other .... Mt 28:1
among whom was M Magdalene .... Mk 15:40
M Magdalene and Mary the mother of. Mk 15:47
he appeared first to M Magdalene ..... Mk 16:9
M called Magdalene, out of whom .... Lk 8:2
it was M Magdalene, and Joanna, and. Lk 24:10
wife of Cleophas, and M Magdalene .. Jn 19:25
the week cometh M Magdalene early... Jn 20:1
But M stood without at the .... Jn 20:11
Jesus saith unto her, M .... Jn 20:16
M Magdalene came and told the .... Jn 20:18

3. Mother of James and Joses.
M the mother of James and Joses, ... Mt 27:56
Mary Magdalene, and the other M ..... Mt 27:61
the other M to see the sepulchre...... Mt 28:1
M the mother of James the less and .. Mk 15:40
M the mother of Joses beheld........... Mk 15:47
M Magdalene, and Mary the mother .. Mk 16:1
M the mother of James, and Salome, .. Mk 16:1
M the mother of James, and other .... Lk 24:10

4. Wife of Cleophas.
The wife of Cleophas, and Mary .... Jn 19:25

5. Sister of Lazarus.
And she had a sister called M .... Lk 10:39
M hath chosen that good part, ... Lk 10:42
of Bethany, the town of M .... Jn 11:1
(It was that M which anointed the ... Jn 11:2
of the Jews came to Martha and M ... Jn 11:19
but M sat still in the house .... Jn 11:20
called M her sister secretly,.............. Jn 11:28
and comforted her, when they saw M. Jn 11:31
Then when M was come where Jesus . Jn 11:32
many of the Jews which came to M ... Jn 11:45
Then took M a pound of ointment...... Jn 12:3

6. Mother of John Mark.
the house of M the mother of John .. Acts 12:12

7. A Christian in Rome.
Greet M, who bestowed much labour. Rom 16:6

MASCHIL (*mas'-kil*) *A didactic poem.*
A Psalm of David, m M .... Ps 32:t
To the chief Musician, M, for the ..... Ps 42:t
Musician for the sons of Korah, M .... Ps 44:t
for the sons of Korah, A .... Ps 45:t
To the chief Musician, M, A Psalm ... Ps 52:t
chief Musician upon Mahalath, M, ... Ps 53:t
To the chief Musician, on Neginoth, M Ps 54:t
the chief Musician on Neginoth, M .... Ps 55:t
of Asaph .... Ps 74:t
of Asaph .... Ps 78:t
Leannoth, M of Heman the Ezrahite .. Ps 88:t
M of Ethan the Ezrahite .... Ps 89:t
of David .... Ps 142:t

MASH (*mash*) *A son of Aram.*
Uz, and Hul, and Gether, and M .... Gen 10:23

MASHAL (*ma'-shal*) *A Levitical city in Asher.*
M with her suburbs, and Abdon with . 1Chr 6:74

MASONS
cedar trees, and carpenters, and m .. 2Sa 5:11
And to m, and hewers of stone, and.. 2Kin 12:12
carpenters, and builders, and m 2Kin 22:6
and timber of cedars, with m 1Chr 22:2
he set m to hew wrought stones to ... 1Chr 22:2
the house of the Lord, and hired m... 2Chr 24:12
They gave money also unto the m .... Ezr 3:7

MASREKAH (*mas'-re-kah*) *A place in Edom.*
Samlah of M reigned in his stead ..... Gen 36:36
Samlah of M reigned in his stead 1Chr 1:47

MASSA (*mas'-sah*) *A son of Ishmael.*
And Mishma, and Dumah, and M ..... Gen 25:14
Mishma, and Dumah, and Hadad, and. 1Chr 1:30

MASSAH (*mas'-sah*) *See* MERIBAH. *A place in
the wilderness where the Israelites
murmured.*
he called the name of the place M ..... Ex 17:7
your God, as ye tempted him in M ..... Deut 6:16
at Taberah, and at M, and at .... Deut 9:22
one, whom thou didst prove at M ...... Deut 33:8

MAST
he that lieth upon the top of a m ...... Prov 23:34
could not well strengthen their m ...... Is 33:23

MASTER
under the thigh of Abraham his m ..... Gen 24:9
ten camels of the camels of his m ..... Gen 24:10
goods of his m were in his hand .... Gen 24:10
said, O LORD God of my m Abraham.. Gen 24:12
shew kindness unto my m Abraham .. Gen 24:12
hast shewed kindness unto my m ..... Gen 24:14

be the LORD God of my m Abraham... Gen 24:27
left destitute my m of his mercy........ Gen 24:27
LORD hath blessed my m greatly .... Gen 24:35
a son to my m when she was old ...... Gen 24:36
my m made me swear, saying, Thou .. Gen 24:37
And I said unto my m, Peradventure .. Gen 24:39
said, O LORD God of my m Abraham... Gen 24:42
the LORD God of my m Abraham .... Gen 24:48
deal kindly and truly with my m .... Gen 24:49
he said, Send me away unto my m .... Gen 24:54
me away that I may go to my m .... Gen 24:56
the servant had said, It is my m ...... Gen 24:65
the house of his m the Egyptian....... Gen 39:2
his m saw that the LORD was with ..... Gen 39:3
my m wotteth not what is with me .... Gen 39:8
when his m heard the words of his ... Gen 39:19
And Joseph's m took him, and put .... Gen 39:20
If his m have given him a wife, ... Ex 21:4
shall plainly say, I love my m .... Ex 21:5
Then his m shall bring him unto .... Ex 21:6
his m shall bore his ear through ...... Ex 21:6
If she please not her m, who hath ... Ex 21:8
their m thirty shekels of silver .... Ex 21:32
then the m of the house shall be ..... Ex 22:8
m the servant which is escaped........ Deut 23:15
is escaped from his m unto thee ...... Deut 23:15
and the servant said unto his m ..... Judg 19:11
his m said unto him, We will not ..... Judg 19:12
and spake to the m of the house ..... Judg 19:22
the m of the house, went out unto ... 1Sa 24:9
up the arrows, and came to his m 1Sa 20:38
I should do this thing unto my m 1Sa 24:6
break away every man from his m 1Sa 25:10
of the wilderness to salute our m...... 1Sa 25:14
evil is determined against our m 1Sa 25:17
because ye have not kept your m 1Sa 26:16
he reconcile himself unto his m 1Sa 29:4
my left me, because three days 1Sa 30:13
deliver me into the hands of my m.... 1Sa 30:15
for your m Saul is dead, and also 2Sa 2:7
and the LORD said, These have no m.. 1Kin 22:17
away thy m from thy head to day 2Kin 2:3
away thy m from thy head to day 2Kin 2:5
go, we pray thee, and seek thy m 2Kin 2:16
Syria, was a great man with his m 2Kin 5:1
that when my m goeth into the 2Kin 5:18
my m hath spared Naaman this 2Kin 5:20
M my m hath sent me, saying, Behold. 2Kin 5:22
he went in, and stood before his m... 2Kin 5:25
and he cried, and said, Alas, m 2Kin 6:5
servant said unto him, Alas, my m 2Kin 6:15
eat and drink, and go to their m 2Kin 6:22
away, and they went to their m 2Kin 6:23
from Elisha, and came to his m 2Kin 8:14
smite the house of Ahab thy m 2Kin 9:7
but Zimri peace, who slew his m 2Kin 9:31
behold, I conspired against my m 2Kin 10:9
Hath my m sent me to thy m,........... 2Kin 18:27
his m hath sent to reproach the 2Kin 19:4
them, Thus shall ye say to your m 2Kin 19:6
He will fall to his m on Saul to the ... 1Chr 12:19
Chenaniah the m of the song with 1Chr 15:27
and the LORD said, These have no m.. 2Chr 18:16
and the servant is free from his m..... Job 3:19
on his m shall be honoured.............. Prov 27:18
Accuse not a servant unto his m....... Prov 30:10
with the servant, so with his m .... Is 24:2
to my m the king of Assyria, and I.... Is 36:8
Hath my m sent me to thy m .... Is 36:12
his m hath sent to reproach the .... Is 37:4
Thus shall ye say unto your m......... Is 37:6
Ashpenaz the m of his eunuchs........ Dan 1:3
m of the magicians, because I .... Dan 4:9
father, made m of the magicians, ... Dan 5:11
his father, and a servant his m .... Mal 1:6
and if I be a m, where is my fear ...... Mal 1:6
the man that doeth this, the m .... Mal 2:12
scribe came, and said unto him, M ... Mt 8:19
Why eateth your M with publicans... Mt 9:11
The disciple is not above his m......... Mt 10:24
the disciple that he be as his m .... Mt 10:25
the m of the house Beelzebub .... Mt 10:25
The Pharisees answered, saying, M ... Mt 12:38
said, Doth not your m pay tribute...... Mt 17:24
one came and said unto him, Good M. Mt 19:16
with the Herodians, saying, M .... Mt 22:16
Saying, M, Moses said, If a man ...... Mt 22:24
M, which is the great commandment .. Mt 22:36
for one is your M, even Christ .... Mt 23:10
for one is your M, even Christ .... Mt 23:10
The M saith, My time is at hand ...... Mt 26:18
betrayed him, answered and said, M .. Mt 26:25
came to Jesus, and said, Hail, m ..... Mt 26:49
awake him, and say unto him, M ..... Mk 4:38
troublest thou the M any further ...... Mk 5:35
answered and said to Jesus, M .... Mk 9:5
the multitude answered and said, M.. Mk 9:17
And John answered him, saying, M.... Mk 9:38
to him, and asked him, Good M .... Mk 10:17
he answered and said unto him, M ... Mk 10:35
Zebedee, come unto him, saying, M .. Mk 10:35
to remembrance, saith unto him, M.. Mk 11:21
were come, they say unto him, M ..... Mk 12:14
M, Moses wrote unto us, If a .... Mk 12:19
the scribe said unto him, Well, M ..... Mk 12:32
his disciples saith unto him, M .... Mk 13:1
when the m of the house cometh ..... Mk 13:35
The M saith, Where is the .... Mk 14:14
to him, and saith, M .... Mk 14:45
be baptized, and said unto him, M ... Lk 3:12

Simon answering said unto him, *M* .... Lk 5:5
The disciple is not above his *m* .... Lk 6:40
that is perfect shall be as his *m* .... Lk 6:40
And he saith, *M*, say on .... Lk 7:40
and awoke him, saying, *M, m* .... Lk 8:24
they that were with him said, *M* .... Lk 8:45
trouble not the *M* .... Lk 8:49
him, Peter said unto Jesus, *M* .... Lk 9:33
the company cried out, saying, *M* .... Lk 9:38
And John answered and said, *M* .... Lk 9:49
up, and tempted him, saying, *M* .... Lk 10:25
the lawyers, and said unto him, *M* .... Lk 11:45
of the company said unto him, *M* .... Lk 12:13
When once the *m* of the house is .... Lk 13:25
Then the *m* of the house being .... Lk 14:21
their voices, and said, Jesus, *M* .... Lk 17:13
ruler asked him, saying, Good *M* .... Lk 18:18
the multitude said unto him, *M* .... Lk 19:39
And they asked him, saying, *M* .... Lk 20:21
Saying, *M*, Moses wrote unto us............. Lk 20:28
of the scribes answering said, *M* .... Lk 20:39
And they asked him, saying, *M* .... Lk 21:7
The *M* saith unto thee, Where is .... Lk 22:11
is to say, being interpreted, *M* .... Jn 1:38
unto him, Art thou a *m* of Israel .... Jn 3:10
disciples prayed him, saying, *M* .... Jn 4:31
They say unto him, *M*, this woman .... Jn 8:4
disciples asked him, saying, *M* .... Jn 9:2
His disciples say unto him, *M* .... Jn 11:8
The *M* is come, and calleth for .... Jn 11:28
Ye call me *M* and Lord .... Jn 13:13
If I then, your Lord and *M* .... Jn 13:14
which is to say, *M* .... Jn 20:16
the centurion believed the *m* .... Acts 27:11
to his own *m* he standeth or .... Rom 14:4
that your *M* also is in heaven .... Eph 6:9
that ye also have a *M* in heaven .... Col 4:1

MASTERBUILDER
is given unto me, as a wise *m* 1Cor 3:10

MASTERIES
And if a man also strive for *m* 2Ti 2:5

MASTER'S
me to the house of my *m* brethren .... Gen 24:27
Sarah my *m* wife bare a son to my .... Gen 24:36
hath appointed out for my *m* son............. Gen 24:44
me in the right way to take my *m* .... Gen 24:48
and let her be thy *m* son's wife............... Gen 24:51
that his *m* wife cast her eyes.................. Gen 39:7
refused, and said unto his *m* wife .... Gen 39:8
and her children shall be her *m* .... Ex 21:4
my *m* servants that are come with 1Sa 29:10
I have given unto thy *m* son all 2Sa 9:9
that thy *m* son may have food to 2Sa 9:10
but Mephibosheth thy *m* son shall........... 2Sa 9:10
And I gave thee thy *m* house 2Sa 12:8
thy *m* wives into thy bosom, and 2Sa 12:8
king said, And where is thy *m* son........... 2Sa 16:3
sound of his *m* feet behind him 2Kin 6:32
seeing your *m* sons are with you 2Kin 10:2
best and meetest of your *m* sons............ 2Kin 10:3
throne, and fight for your *m* house 2Kin 10:3
the heads of the your *m* sons.................. 2Kin 10:6
of the least of my *m* servants 2Kin 18:24
his owner, and the ass his *m* crib .... Is 1:3
of the least of my *m* servants .... Is 36:9
sanctified, and meet for the *m* use.......... 2Ti 2:21

MASTERS
look unto the hand of their *m* .... Ps 123:2
he refresheth the soul of his *m*................ Prov 25:13
fastened by the *m* of assemblies............. Eccl 12:11
command them to say unto their *m* .... Jer 27:4
Thus shall ye say unto your *m* .... Jer 27:4
the needy, which say to their *m* .... Amos 4:1
No man can serve two *m* .... Mt 6:24
Neither be ye called *m* .... Mt 23:10
No servant can serve two *m* .... Lk 16:13
which brought her *m* much gain by .... Acts 16:16
when her *m* saw that the hope of .... Acts 16:19
are your *m* according to the flesh .... Eph 6:5
And, ye *m*, do the same things unto .... Eph 6:9
your *m* according to the flesh .... Col 3:22
M, give unto your servants that............... Col 4:1
their own *m* worthy of all honour 1Ti 6:1
And they that have believing *m*............... 1Ti 6:2
to be obedient unto their own *m*.............. Titus 2:9
My brethren, be not many *m* .... Jas 3:1
subject to your *m* with all fear................. 1Pet 2:18

MASTERS'
which fill their *m* houses with .... Zeph 1:9
which fall from their *m* table .... Mt 15:27

MASTERY
voice of them that shout for *m* .... Ex 32:18
and the lions had the *m* of them .... Dan 6:24
the *m* is temperate in all things 1Cor 9:25

MASTS
from Lebanon to make *m* for thee............ Eze 27:5

MATE
be gathered, every one with her *m* .... Is 34:15
shall fail, none shall want her *m* .... Is 34:16

MATHUSALA (*ma-thu'-sa-lah*) See
METHUSELAH. *Son of Enoch; ancestor of
Jesus.*
Which was the son of *M*, which was .... Lk 3:37

MATRED (*ma'-tred*) *Mother of Mehetabel.*
was Mehetabel, the daughter of *M* .... Gen 36:39
was Mehetabel, the daughter of *M* 1Chr 1:50

MATRI (*ma'-tri*) *An ancestral family of King
Saul.*
the family of *M* was taken 1Sa 10:21

MATRITE See MATRI.

MATRIX
the LORD all that openeth the *m* .... Ex 13:12
the LORD all that openeth the *m* .... Ex 13:15
that openeth the *m* is mine...................... Ex 34:19
in among the children of Israel .... Num 3:12
that openeth the *m* of all flesh .... Num 18:15

MATTAN (*mat'-tan*)
1. *A priest of Baal.*
slew *M* the priest of Baal before............... 2Kin 11:18
slew *M* the priest of Baal before............... 2Chr 23:17
2. *Father of Shephatiah.*
Then Shephatiah the son of *M* .... Jer 38:1

MATTANAH (*mat'-ta-nah*) *An encampment of
Israel in the wilderness.*
the wilderness they went to *M* .... Num 21:18
And from *M* to Nahaliel .... Num 21:19

MATTANIAH (*mat-ta-ni'-ah*) See ZEDEKIAH.
1. *Same as Zedekiah, king of Judah.*
the king of Babylon made *M* his.............. 2Kin 24:17
2. *A family of exiles.*
M the son of Micah, the son of 1Chr 9:15
the son of Jeiel, the son of *M* 2Chr 20:14
M the son of Micha, the son of .... Neh 11:17
son of Hashabiah, the son of *M* .... Neh 11:22
Kadmiel, Sherebiah, Judah, and *M*.......... Neh 12:8
M, and Bakbukiah, Obadiah,................... Neh 12:25
the son of Shemaiah, the son of *M*.......... Neh 12:35
3. *A sanctuary servant.*
Bukkiah, *M*, Uzziel, Shebuel, and............ 1Chr 25:4
The ninth to *M*, he, his sons, and 1Chr 25:16
4. *A descendant of Asaph.*
Zechariah, and *M* 2Chr 29:13
5. *A descendant of Elam.*
M, Zechariah, and Jehiel, and Abdi,........ Ezr 10:26
6. *A descendant of Zattu.*
Elioenai, Eliashib, *M*, and .... Ezr 10:27
7. *A descendant of Pahath-Moab.*
And *M*, Bezaleel, Binnui, and .... Ezr 10:30
8. *A descendant of Bani.*
M, Mattenai, and Jaasau,........................ Ezr 10:37
9. *Father of Zaccur.*
the son of Zaccur, the son of *M* .... Neh 13:13

MATTATHA (*mat'-ta-thah*) See MATTATHAH.
A son of Nathan; ancestor of Jesus.
of Menan, which was the son of *M* .... Lk 3:31

MATTATHAH (*mat'-ta-thah*) See MATTATHA.
Married a foreigner in exile.
Mattenai, M, Zabad, Eliphelet, ... Ezr 10:33

MATTATHIAH See MATTATHIAS.

MATTATHIAS (*mat-ta-thi'-as*) See
MATTITHIAH.
1. *A son of Amos; ancestor of Jesus.*
Which was the son of *M*, which was .... Lk 3:25
2. *A son of Semei; ancestor of Jesus.*
of Maath, which was the son of *M* .... Lk 3:26

MATTENAI (*mat'-te-nahee*)
1. *A descendant of Hashum.*
M, Mattathah, Zabad, Eliphelet,............... Ezr 10:33
2. *A descendant of Bani.*
Mattaniah, M, and Jaasau, ... Ezr 10:37
3. *A priest.*
And of Joiarib, *M*..................................... Neh 12:19

MATTER
and sware to him concerning that *m* .... Gen 24:9
Is it a small *m* that thou hast.................... Gen 30:15
When they have a *m*, they come............... Ex 18:16
that every great *m* they shall .... Ex 18:22
but every small *m* they shall .... Ex 18:22
but every small *m* they judged................. Ex 18:26
Keep thee far from a false *m*.................... Ex 23:7
that died about the *m* of Korah .... Num 16:49
beguiled you in the *m* of Peor .... Num 25:18
in the *m* of Cozbi, the daughter .... Num 25:18
against the LORD in the *m* of Peor .... Num 31:16
because no more unto the *m* of this *m* ... Deut 3:26
If there arise a *m* too hard for.................. Deut 17:8
shall the *m* be established .... Deut 19:15
and slayeth him, even so is this *m* .... Deut 22:26
thou know how the *m* will fall .... Ruth 3:18
But of the *m* of the kingdom.................... 1Sa 10:16
And as touching the *m* which thou 1Sa 20:23
only Jonathan and David knew the *m* 1Sa 20:39
will hearken unto you in this *m* 1Sa 30:24
said unto him, How went the *m* 2Sa 1:4
for there is no *m* hid from the................... 2Sa 18:13
then be ye angry for this *m* 2Sa 19:42
and so they ended the *m*......................... 2Sa 20:18
The *m* is not so 2Sa 20:21
all times, as the *m* shall require............... 1Kin 8:59
save only in the *m* of Uriah the................ 1Kin 15:5
for every *m* pertaining to God, and.......... 1Chr 26:32
the king in any *m* of the courses 1Chr 27:1
and Levites concerning any *m*................. 2Chr 8:15
year, and see that ye hasten the *m*.......... 2Chr 24:5
till the *m* came to Darius......................... Ezr 5:5

by letter concerning this *m* .... Ezr 5:5
pleasure to us concerning this *m*............. Ezr 5:17
for this *m* belongeth unto thee................. Ezr 10:4
God, trembling because of this *m* .... Ezr 10:9
God for this *m* be turned from us .... Ezr 10:14
Tikvah were employed about this *m*......... Ezr 10:15
the tenth month to examine the *m*............ Ezr 10:16
might have *m* for an evil report................ Neh 6:13
inquisition was made of the *m*................. Est 2:23
they had seen concerning this *m*............. Est 9:26
the root of the *m* is found in me............... Job 19:28
For I am full of *m* .... Job 32:18
My heart is inditing a good *m* .... Ps 45:1
encourage themselves in an evil *m* .... Ps 64:5
faithful spirit concealeth the *m* .... Prov 11:13
He that handleth a *m* wisely shall............ Prov 16:20
an separateth very friends .... Prov 17:9
He that answereth a *m* before he............ Prov 18:13
of kings is to search out a *m* .... Prov 25:2
a province, marvel not at the *m* .... Eccl 5:8
which hath wings shall tell the *m*............. Eccl 10:20
the conclusion of the whole *m*................. Eccl 12:13
for the *m* was not perceived .... Jer 38:27
by his side, reported the *m*...................... Eze 9:11
this of thy whoredoms a small *m*............. Eze 16:20
So he consented to them in this *m* .... Dan 1:14
earth that can shew the king's *m*............. Dan 2:10
made known unto us the king's *m*........... Dan 2:23
careful to answer thee in this *m* .... Dan 3:16
This *m* is by the decree of the................. Dan 4:17
Hitherto is the end of the *m* .... Dan 7:28
but I kept the *m* in my heart .... Dan 7:28
therefore understand the *m* .... Dan 9:23
it much, and to blaze abroad the *m*......... Mk 1:45
asked him again of the same *m*............... Mk 10:10
neither part nor lot in this *m*.................... Acts 8:21
the *m* from the beginning, and .... Acts 11:4
for to consider of this *m*.......................... Acts 15:6
We will hear thee again of this *m* .... Acts 17:32
If it were a *m* of wrong or wicked .... Acts 18:14
have a *m* against any man, the law .... Acts 19:38
will know the uttermost of your *m*............ Acts 24:22
having a *m* against another, go to 1Cor 6:1
yourselves to be clear in this *m* 2Cor 7:11
as a *m* of bounty, and not as of 2Cor 9:5
they were, it maketh no *m* to me.............. Gal 2:6
and defraud his brother in any *m* 1Th 4:6
how great a *m* a little fire........................ Jas 3:5

MATTERS
if any man have any *m* to do .... Ex 24:14
being *m* of controversy within thy .... Deut 17:8
and a man of war, and prudent in *m*........ 1Sa 16:18
the *m* of the war unto the king 2Sa 11:19
him, See, thy *m* are good and right 2Sa 15:3
speakest thou any more of thy *m* 2Sa 19:29
is over you in all *m* of the LORD.............. 2Chr 19:11
of Judah, for all the king's 2Chr 19:11
in all *m* concerning the people................ Neh 11:24
whether Mordecai's *m* would stand......... Est 3:4
the *m* of the fastings and their .... Est 9:31
Esther confirmed these *m* of Purim......... Est 9:32
not account of any of his *m* .... Job 33:13
but they devise deceitful *m*..................... Ps 35:20
do I exercise myself in great *m*............... Ps 131:1
And in all *m* of wisdom and..................... Dan 1:20
dream, and told the sum of the *m*............ Dan 7:1
the weightier *m* of the law .... Mt 23:23
for I will be no judge of such *m* .... Acts 18:15
any thing concerning other *m* .... Acts 19:39
and there be judged of these *m* .... Acts 25:20
unworthy to judge the smallest *m*........... 1Cor 6:2
or as a busybody in other men's *m* 1Pet 4:15

MATTHAN (*mat'-than*) *Son of Eleazar;
ancestor of Jesus.*
and Eleazar begat *M* .... Mt 1:15
and M begat Jacob................................... Mt 1:15

MATTHAT (*mat'-that*)
1. *Son of Levi; an ancestor of Jesus.*
Which was the son of *M*, which was .... Lk 3:24
2. *Father of Jorim; an ancestor of Jesus.*
of Jorim, which was the son of *M* .... Lk 3:29

MATTHEW (*math'-ew*) See LEVI. *A disciple of
Jesus.*
thence, he saw a man, named *M* .... Mt 9:9
Thomas, and *M* the publican .... Mt 10:3
and Philip, and Bartholomew, and *M*....... Mk 3:18
M and Thomas, James the son of............. Lk 6:15
and Thomas, Bartholomew, and *M* .... Acts 1:13

MATTHIAS (*mat'-thias*) *Successor to Judas
Iscariot as apostle.*
who was surnamed Justus, and *M*........... Acts 1:23
and the lot fell upon *M* .... Acts 1:26

MATTITHIAH (*mat-tith-i'-ah*) See
MATTATHIAS.
1. *A son of Shallum.*
And *M*, one of the Levites, who was......... 1Chr 9:31
2. *A Levite gatekeeper.*
and Benaiah, and Maaseiah, and *M*........ 1Chr 15:18
And *M*, and Elipheleh,............................. 1Chr 15:21
and Shemiramoth, and Jehiel, and *M*...... 1Chr 16:5
3. *Son of Jeduthun.*
and Jeshaiah, Hashabiah, and *M*............ 1Chr 25:3
The fourteenth to *M*, he, his sons............ 1Chr 25:21
4. *Married a foreigner in exile.*
Jeiel, M, Zabad, Zebina, Jadau,............... Ezr 10:43
5. *A priest who aided Ezra.*
and beside him stood *M*, and Shema, ... Neh 8:4

MATTOCK
his coulter, and his ax, and his *m* 1Sa 13:20
that shall be digged with the *m* ....Is 7:25

MATTOCKS
Yet they had a file for the *m* 1Sa 13:21
with their *m* round about. 2Chr 34:6

MAUL
against his neighbour is a *m* ....Prov 25:18

MAW
and the two cheeks, and the *m* ....Deut 18:3

MAY See PREFACE.

MAYEST
of the garden thou *m* freely eat. ....Gen 2:16
but that thou *m* bury thy dead ....Gen 23:6
that thou *m* be a multitude of ....Gen 28:3
that thou *m* inherit the land ....Gen 28:4
that thou *m* come in unto me ....Gen 38:16
that thou *m* bring forth my people ....Ex 3:10
that thou *m* know that there is ....Ex 8:10
to the end thou *m* know that I am ....Ex 8:22
that thou *m* know that there is ....Ex 9:14
that thou *m* know how that the ....Ex 9:29
that thou *m* tell in the ears of ....Ex 10:2
that thou *m* bring the causes unto .....Ex 18:19
that thou *m* teach them ....Ex 24:12
that thou *m* bring in thither ....Ex 26:33
that thou *m* offer for a freewill. ....Lev 22:23
that thou *m* use them for ....Num 10:2
that thou *m* be to us instead of eyes ...Num 10:31
from whence thou *m* see them ....Num 23:13
thou *m* curse them from thence. ....Num 23:27
that thou *m* inherit his land ....Deut 2:31
that thou *m* prolong thy days upon ......Deut 4:40
with thee, and that thou *m* go in ....Deut 6:18
thou *m* not consume them at once, ...Deut 7:22
of whose hills thou *m* dig brass. ....Deut 8:9
that thou *m* gather in thy corn, ...Deut 11:14
for thy cattle, that thou *m* eat ....Deut 11:15
Notwithstanding thou *m* kill. ....Deut 12:15
Thou *m* not eat within thy gates ....Deut 12:17
thou *m* eat flesh, whatsoever thy ....Deut 12:20
that thou *m* not eat the life with the ....Deut 12:23
or thou *m* sell it unto an alien ....Deut 14:21
that thou *m* learn to fear the ....Deut 14:23
a foreigner thou *m* exact it again ....Deut 15:3
that thou *m* remember the day when. ..Deut 16:3
Thou *m* not sacrifice the passover. ......Deut 16:5
thou follow, that thou *m* live. ....Deut 16:20
thou *m* not set a stranger over. ....Deut 17:15
for thou *m* eat of them, and thou. ....Deut 20:19
thou *m* not hide thyself. ....Deut 22:3
that thou *m* prolong thy days ....Deut 22:7
a stranger thou *m* lend upon usury. .....Deut 23:20
then thou *m* eat grapes thy fill. ....Deut 23:24
then thou *m* pluck the ears with ....Deut 23:25
that thou *m* be an holy people ....Deut 26:19
that thou *m* go in unto the land ....Deut 27:3
that thou *m* fear this glorious and. ......Deut 28:58
all thy soul, that thou *m* live. ....Deut 30:6
in thy heart, that thou *m* do it. ....Deut 30:14
his judgments, that thou *m* live. ....Deut 30:16
That thou *m* love the Lord thy God. .....Deut 30:20
that thou *m* obey his voice, and. ....Deut 30:20
that thou *m* cleave unto him ....Deut 30:20
that thou *m* dwell in the land ....Deut 30:20
that thou *m* observe to do. ....Josh 1:7
that thou *m* prosper whithersoever. ....Josh 1:7
that thou *m* observe to do. ....Josh 1:8
then *m* thou do to them as thou ....Judg 9:33
that thou *m* go with us, and fight ....Judg 11:6
on your way, that thou *m* go home. .....Judg 19:9
away, that thou *m* go in peace 1Sa 1:17
that thou *m* do to him as it shall. 1Sa 24:4
that thou *m* make known unto me. 1Sa 28:15
that thou *m* have strength, when. 1Sa 28:22
that thou *m* reign over all that 2Sa 3:21
then *m* thou for defeat the. 2Sa 15:34
that thou *m* bring them down. 2Sa 22:28
that thou *m* save thine own life, ...1Kin 1:12
that thou *m* prosper in all that 1Kin 2:3
that thou *m* take away the. 1Kin 2:31
that thou *m* hearken unto the 1Kin 8:29
that thou *m* recover him of his. 2Kin 5:6
him, Thou *m* certainly recover. 2Kin 8:10
that thou *m* keep the law of the 1Chr 22:12
and thou *m* add thereto. 1Chr 22:14
that thou *m* judge my people, over 2Chr 1:11
that thou *m* carry me out of the 2Chr 18:33
That thou *m* buy speedily with ....Ezr 7:17
that thou *m* hear the prayer of ....Neh 1:6
that thou *m* be their king, ...Neh 6:6
me, that thou *m* be righteous. ....Job 40:8
in a time when thou *m* be found ....Ps 32:6
whom thou *m* make princes in all ....Ps 45:16
That thou *m* give him rest from ....Ps 94:13
that thou *m* give them their meat. ....Ps 104:27
with thee, that thou *m* be feared. ....Ps 130:4
That thou *m* walk in the way of ....Prov 2:20
That thou *m* regard discretion, and ....Prov 5:2
that thou *m* be wise in thy latter. ....Prov 19:20
that thou *m* be remembered. ....Is 23:16
thou, that thou *m* be justified. ....Is 43:26
that thou *m* know that I, the LORD ....Is 45:3
profit, if so be, that thou *m* ....Is 47:12
that thou *m* be my salvation unto. ......Is 49:6
That thou *m* say to the prisoners, ...Is 49:9
wickedness, that thou *m* be saved. .....Jer 4:14
among my people, that thou *m* know ...Jer 6:27

cause, that thou *m* be bound up ....Jer 30:13
That thou *m* bear thine own shame, ...Eze 16:54
m be confounded in all that thou. ....Eze 16:54
That thou *m* remember, and be. ....Eze 16:63
that thou *m* look on their. ....Hab 2:15
that thou *m* eat the passover. ....Mk 14:12
that thou *m* be delivered from him.......Lk 12:58
for thou *m* be no longer steward ....Lk 16:2
with all thine heart, thou *m* ....Acts 8:37
m take knowledge of all these. ....Acts 24:8
Because that thou *m* understand. ......Acts 24:11
but if thou *m* be made free, use. 1Cor 7:21
thou *m* live long on the earth. ....Eph 6:3
that thou *m* know how thou. 1Ti 3:15
all things that thou *m* prosper. 3Jn 2
in the fire, that thou *m* be rich. ....Rev 3:18
that thou *m* be clothed, and that. ......Rev 3:18
with eyesalve, that thou *m* see. ....Rev 3:18

MAZZAROTH (*maz'-za-roth*) The twelve signs of the Zodiac.
thou bring forth M in his season ....Job 38:32

ME See PREFACE.

MEADOW
and they fed in a *m* ....Gen 41:2
and they fed in a *m* ....Gen 41:18

MEADOWS
even out of the *m* of Gibeah ....Judg 20:33

MEAH (*me'-ah*) A tower on Jerusalem's wall.
the tower of M they sanctified it. ....Neh 3:1
of Hananeel, and the tower of M. ....Neh 12:39

MEAL
quickly three measures of fine *m* ....Gen 18:6
part of an ephah of barley *m* ....Num 5:15
and threescore measures of *m* 1Kin 4:22
but an handful of *m* in a barrel 1Kin 17:12
The barrel of *m* shall not waste, ...1Kin 17:14
And the barrel of *m* wasted not. 1Kin 17:16
But he said, Then bring *m* 2Kin 4:41
on mules, and on oxen, and meat, *m* ..1Chr 12:40
Take the millstones, and grind *m* ....Is 47:2
the bud shall yield no *m*. ....Hos 8:7
and hid in three measures of *m*. ....Mt 13:33
and hid in three measures of *m*. ....Lk 13:21

MEALTIME
At *m* come thou hither, and eat of ......Ruth 2:14

MEAN
What *m* these seven ewe lambs.........Gen 21:29
What *m* ye by this service. ....Ex 12:26
What *m* the testimonies, and the. ......Deut 6:20
What *m* ye by these stones ....Josh 4:6
come, saying, What *m* these stones ...Josh 4:21
And it came to pass in the *m* while.....1Kin 18:45
he shall not stand before *m* men. ....Prov 22:29
the *m* man moveth down, and the. .....Is 2:9
What *m* ye that ye beat my people. ....Is 3:15
the *m* man shall be brought down, ...Is 5:15
and the sword, not of a *m* man. ....Is 31:8
Know ye not what these things *m*. .....Eze 17:12
What *m* ye, that ye use this. ....Eze 18:2
the rising from the dead should *m*. .....Mk 9:10
In the *m* time, when there. ....Lk 12:1
In the *m* while his disciples. ....Jn 4:31
vision which he had seen should *m*. ...Acts 10:17
therefore what these things *m*. ....Acts 17:20
What *m* ye to weep and to break. ......Acts 21:13
Cilicia, a citizen of no *m* city. ....Acts 21:39
their thoughts the *m* while. ....Rom 2:15
For I *m* not that other men be. 2Cor 8:13

MEANEST
that thou by all this drove. ....Gen 33:8
unto Ziba, What *m* thou by these. 2Sa 16:2
not shew us what thou *m* by these. ....Eze 37:18
and said unto him, What *m* thou. ....Jonah 1:6

MEANETH
What *m* the heat of this great. ....Deut 29:24
What *m* the noise of this great 1Sa 4:6
What *m* the noise of this tumult. 1Sa 4:14
What *m* then this bleating of the. 1Sa 15:14
Howbeit he *m* not so, neither doth. ....Is 10:7
But go ye and learn what that *m*. ....Mt 9:13
But if ye had known what this *m*. ....Mt 12:7
one to another, What *m* this. ....Acts 2:12

MEANING
the vision, and sought for the *m* ....Dan 8:15
m to sail by the coasts of Asia ....Acts 27:2
if I know not the *m* of the voice. 1Cor 14:11

MEANS
that will by no *m* clear the. ....Ex 34:7
by no *m* clearing the guilty, ...Num 14:18
broken by the *m* of the pransings ......Judg 5:22
by what *m* we may prevail against......Judg 16:5
yet doth he devise *m*, that his. 2Sa 14:14
they bring them out by their *m*. 1Kin 10:29
if by any *m* he be missing, then. 1Kin 20:39
the kings of Syria, by their *m*. 2Chr 1:17
by this *m* thou shalt have no. ....Ezr 4:16
can by any *m* redeem his brother ....Ps 49:7
For by *m* of a whorish woman a man. ..Prov 6:26
the priests bear rule by their *m* ....Jer 5:31
this hath been by your *m*. ....Mal 1:9
shalt by no *m* come out thence. ....Mt 5:26
they sought no to bring him in, and. ....Lk 5:18
m he that was possessed of the. ....Lk 8:36
nothing shall by any *m* hurt you. ....Lk 10:19

But by what *m* he now seeth, we........Jn 9:21
by what *m* he is made whole. ....Acts 4:9
I must by all *m* keep this feast. ....Acts 18:21
if by any *m* they might attain to ....Acts 27:12
if by any *m* now at length I might ....Rom 1:10
If by any *m* I may provoke to. ....Rom 11:14
But take heed lest by any *m* this. 1Cor 8:9
that I might by all *m* save some. 1Cor 9:22
lest that by any *m*, when I have 1Cor 9:27
gift bestowed upon us by the *m* of 2Cor 1:11
But I fear, lest by any *m* 2Cor 11:3
lest by any *m* I should run, or. ....Gal 2:2
If by any *m* I might attain unto. ....Phil 3:11
lest by some *m* the tempter have........1Th 3:5
Let no man deceive you by any *m* 2Th 2:3
give you peace always by all *m* 2Th 3:16
that by *m* of death, for the. ....Heb 9:15
m of those miracles which he had. ......Rev 13:14

MEANT
but God *m* it unto good, to bring ....Gen 50:20
and asked what these things *m*. ....Lk 15:26
pass by, he asked what it *m*. ....Lk 18:36

MEARAH (*me'-a-rah*) A place near Sidon.
M that is beside the Sidonians, ...Josh 13:4

MEASURE
of the curtains shall have one *m* ....Ex 26:2
curtains shall be all of one *m*. ....Ex 26:8
in meteyard, in weight, or in *m* ....Lev 19:35
ye shall *m* from without the city ....Num 35:5
they shall *m* unto the cities. ....Deut 21:2
perfect and just *m* shalt thou have .....Deut 25:15
about two thousand cubits by *m* ....Josh 3:4
both the cherubims were of one *m*......1Kin 6:25
of them had one casting, one *m*. 1Kin 7:37
a *m* of fine flour be sold for a. 2Kin 7:1
So a *m* of fine flour was sold for 2Kin 7:16
a *m* of fine flour for a shekel, ...2Kin 7:18
is fried, and for all manner of *m*. 1Chr 23:29
the first *m* was threescore cubits 2Chr 3:3
The *m* thereof is longer than ....Job 11:9
and he weigheth the waters by *m*. ......Job 28:25
the *m* of my days, what it is ....Ps 39:4
them tears to drink in great *m*. ....Ps 80:5
and opened her mouth without *m*. .....Is 5:14
In *m*, when it shooteth forth, ...Is 27:8
the dust of the earth in a *m*. ....Is 40:12
therefore will I *m* their former. ....Is 65:7
but I will correct thee in *m*. ....Jer 30:11
of thee, but correct thee in *m*. ....Jer 46:28
the *m* of thy covetousness. ....Jer 51:13
Thou shalt drink also water by *m*. ......Eze 4:11
and they shall drink water by *m*. ....Eze 4:16
they three were of one *m*. ....Eze 40:10
the posts had one *m* on this side ....Eze 40:10
after the *m* of the first gate ....Eze 40:21
were after the *m* of the gate that. ......Eze 40:22
about within and without, by *m*, ...Eze 41:17
and let them *m* the pattern. ....Eze 43:10
of this *m* shalt thou. ....Eze 45:3
shalt thou the length of five ....Eze 45:3
and the bath shall be of one *m*. ....Eze 45:11
the *m* thereof shall be after the. ....Eze 45:11
these four corners were of one *m*. ......Eze 46:22
east side ye shall *m* from Hauran. ......Eze 47:18
the scant *m* that is abominable. ....Mic 6:10
In Jerusalem, to see what is ....Zec 2:2
and with what *m* ye mete, it shall. ......Mt 7:2
ye up then the *m* of your fathers. ......Mt 23:32
with what *m* ye mete, it shall be. ....Mk 4:24
amazed in themselves beyond *m*. ....Mk 6:51
And were beyond *m* astonished ....Mk 7:37
And they were astonished out of *m*.....Mk 10:26
good *m*, pressed down, and shaken .....Lk 6:38
For with the same *m* that ye mete ....Lk 6:38
not the Spirit by *m* unto him. ....Jn 3:34
dealt to every man the *m* of faith ....Rom 12:3
that we were pressed out of *m* 2Cor 1:8
not boast of things without our *m*. 2Cor 10:13
but according to the *m* of the. 2Cor 10:13
a *m* to reach even unto you 2Cor 10:13
not ourselves beyond our *m*, ...2Cor 10:14
boasting of things without our *m*. 2Cor 10:15
more abundant, in stripes above *m*, ...2Cor 11:23
in through the abundance of the. 2Cor 12:7
lest I should be exalted above *m*. 2Cor 12:7
that beyond *m* I persecuted. ....Gal 1:13
to the *m* of the gift of Christ. ....Eph 4:7
unto the *m* of the stature of the ....Eph 4:13
working in the *m* of every part ....Eph 4:16
A *m* of wheat for a penny, and ....Rev 6:6
m the temple of God, and the altar ......Rev 11:1
the temple leave out, and *m* it not ....Rev 11:2
had a golden reed to *m* the city ....Rev 21:15
according to the *m* of a man. ....Rev 21:17

MEASURED
he *m* six measures of barley, ...Ruth 3:15
m them with a line, casting them. 2Sa 8:2
two lines *m* he to put to death............2Sa 8:2
Who hath *m* the waters in the. ....Is 40:12
If heaven above can be *m*, and the. .....Jer 31:37
neither the sand of the sea *m*. ....Jer 33:22
so he *m* the breadth of the ....Eze 40:5
the threshold of the gate, ...Eze 40:6
the threshold of the gate, ...Eze 40:8
Then he *m* the porch of the gate. ....Eze 40:9
he *m* the breadth of the entry of ....Eze 40:11
he *m* the gate from the roof ....Eze 40:13
Then he *m* the breadth from the ....Eze 40:19

M

as Jesus sat at *m* in his house .... Mk 2:15
they took up of the broken *m* that.......... Mk 8:8
Simon the leper, as he sat at *m*................ Mk 14:3
unto the eleven as they sat at *m*.............. Mk 16:14
and he that hath *m*, let him do.................. Lk 3:11
house, and sat down to *m*............................ Lk 7:36
sat at *m* in the Pharisee's house .... Lk 7:37
they that sat at *m* with him began.......... Lk 7:49
and he commanded to give her *m*............ Lk 8:55
buy *m* for all this people............................ Lk 9:13
and he went in, and sat down to *m*........ Lk 11:37
The life is more than *m*, and the.............. Lk 12:23
and make them to sit down to *m*.............. Lk 12:37
their portion of *m* in due season............ Lk 12:42
of them that sit at *m* with thee................ Lk 14:10
at *m* with him heard these things.......... Lk 14:15
the field, Go and sit down to *m*................ Lk 17:7
is greater, he that sitteth at *m*.............. Lk 22:27
is not he that sitteth at *m*...................... Lk 22:27
to pass, as he sat at *m* with them.......... Lk 24:30
unto them, Have ye here any *m*.............. Lk 24:41
gone away unto the city to buy *m*.......... Jn 4:8
I have *m* to eat that ye know not .... Jn 4:32
My *m* is to do the will of him.................. Jn 4:34
not for the *m* which perisheth................ Jn 6:27
but for that *m* which endureth................ Jn 6:27
For my flesh is *m* indeed, and my.......... Jn 6:55
them, Children, have ye any *m*................ Jn 21:5
did eat their *m* with gladness .... Acts 2:46
And when he had received *m*.................... Acts 9:19
he set *m* before them, and rejoiced...... Acts 16:34
Paul besought them all to take *m*.......... Acts 27:33
I pray you to take some *m*........................ Acts 27:34
cheer, and they also took some *m*.......... Acts 27:36
thy brother be grieved with thy *m*........ Rom 14:15
Destroy not him with thy *m*.................... Rom 14:15
For the kingdom of God is not *m*............ Rom 14:17
For *m* destroy not the work of God ...... Rom 14:20
fed you with milk, and not with *m*........ 1Cor 3:2
But *m* commendeth us not to God 1Cor 8:8
sit at *m* in the idol's temple 1Cor 8:10
if *m* make my brother to offend, I........ 1Cor 8:13
did all eat the same spiritual *m*............ 1Cor 10:3
no man therefore judge you in *m*.......... Col 2:16
need of milk, and not of strong *m*........ Heb 5:12
But strong *m* belongeth to them.......... Heb 5:14
morsel of *m* sold his birthright .... Heb 12:16

MEATS

neither desire thy dainty *m*...................... Prov 23:6
into the draught, purging all *m*.............. Mk 7:19
abstain from *m* offered to idols .... Acts 15:29
M for the belly, and the belly for 1Cor 6:13
for the belly, and the belly for................ 1Cor 6:13
and commanding to abstain from *m*...... 1Ti 4:3
Which stood only in *m* and drinks,........ Heb 9:10
not with *m*, which have not...................... Heb 13:9

MEBUNNAI (*me-bun´-nahee*) See SIBBECHAI. A
'mighty man' of David.
Anethothite, *M* the Hushathite, ... 2Sa 23:27

MECHERATHITE (*me-ker´-ath-ite*) A family
name of a 'mighty man' of David.
Hepher the *M*, Ahijah the Pelonite.... 1Chr 11:36

MECONAH See MEKONAH.

MEDAD (*me´-dad*) *An elder of Israel.*
Eldad, and the name of the other *M*..... Num 11:26
M do prophesy in the camp...................... Num 11:27

MEDAN (*me´-dan*) *A son of Abraham.*
bare him Zimran, and Jokshan, and *M* Gen 25:2
she bare Zimran, and Jokshan, and *M* 1Chr 1:32

MEDDLE

M not with them.. Deut 2:5
them not, nor *m* with them...................... Deut 2:19
why shouldest thou *m* to thy hurt........ 2Kin 14:10
shouldest thou *m* to thine hurt.............. 2Chr 25:19
therefore *m* not with him that .... Prov 20:19
m not with them that are given to ...... Prov 24:21

MEDDLED

contention, before it be *m* with .... Prov 17:14

MEDDLETH

m with strife belonging not to .... Prov 26:17

MEDDLING

forbear thee from *m* with God................ 2Chr 35:21
but every fool will be *m*............................ Prov 20:3

MEDE (*meed*) See MEDES, MEDIAN. *An
inhabitant of Media.*
in the first year of Darius the *M*.......... Dan 11:1

MEDEBA (*med´-e-bah*) *A city in Reuben.*
Nophah, which reacheth unto *M*............ Num 21:30
and all the plain of *M* unto Dibon .... Josh 13:9
the river, and all the plain by *M*............ Josh 13:16
who came and pitched before *M*............ 1Chr 19:7
shall howl over Nebo, and over *M*.......... Is 15:2

MEDES (*meeds*)
Gozan, and in the cities of the *M*.......... 2Kin 17:6
Gozan, and in the cities of the *M*.......... 2Kin 18:11
that is in the province of the *M*............ Ezr 6:2
the laws of the Persians and the *M*...... Est 1:19
I will stir up the *M* against them.......... Is 13:17
Elam, and all the kings of the *M*.......... Jer 25:25
the spirit of the kings of the *M*............ Jer 51:11
nations with the kings of the *M*............ Jer 51:28
is divided, and given to the *M*................ Dan 5:28
according to the law of the *M*................ Dan 6:8

according to the law of the *M*................ Dan 6:12
O king, that the law of the *M*................ Dan 6:15
Ahasuerus, of the seed of the *M*............ Dan 9:1
Parthians, and Medes, and Elamites, and.... Acts 2:9

MEDIA (*me´-de-ah*) See MADAI, MEDE, MEDIAN.
A country north of Persia.
the power of Persia and *M*, the.............. Est 1:3
the seven princes of Persia and *M*........ Est 1:14
M say this day unto all the...................... Est 1:18
the chronicles of the kings of *M*............ Est 10:2
besiege, O *M*.. Is 21:2
two horns are the kings of *M*.................. Dan 8:20

MEDIAN (*me´-de-an*) See MEDE. *A native of
Media.*
Darius the *M* took the kingdom,............ Dan 5:31

MEDIATOR

by angels in the hand of a *m*.................. Gal 3:19
Now a *m* is not a .... Gal 3:20
is not a *m* of one.. Gal 3:20
one *m* between God and men, the man.. 1Ti 2:5
he is the *m* of a better covenant............ Heb 8:6
he is the *m* of the new testament .... Heb 9:15
to Jesus the *m* of the new .... Heb 12:24

MEDICINE

A merry heart doeth good like a *m* ...... Prov 17:22
meat, and the leaf thereof for *m*............ Eze 47:12

MEDICINES

thou hast no healing *m*.............................. Jer 30:13
in vain shalt thou use many *m*................ Jer 46:11

MEDITATE

Isaac went out to *m* in the field .... Gen 24:63
but thou shalt *m* therein day.................. Josh 1:8
and in his law doth he *m* day.................. Ps 1:2
m on thee in the night watches............ Ps 63:6
I will *m* also of all thy work, and.......... Ps 77:12
I will *m* in thy precepts, and have........ Ps 119:15
thy servant did *m* in thy statutes .... Ps 119:23
and I will *m* in thy statutes.................... Ps 119:48
but I will *m* in thy precepts .... Ps 119:78
that I might *m* in thy word...................... Ps 119:148
I *m* on all thy works .... Ps 143:5
Think heart shall *m* terror...................... Is 33:18
not to *m* before what ye shall................ Lk 21:14
M upon these things.................................. 1Ti 4:15

MEDITATION

consider my *m*.. Ps 5:1
the *m* of my heart, be acceptable.......... Ps 19:14
the *m* of my heart shall be of................ Ps 49:3
My *m* of him shall be sweet .... Ps 104:34
it is my *m* all the day................................ Ps 119:97
for thy testimonies are my *m*................ Ps 119:99

MEEK

(Now the man Moses was very *m*............ Num 12:3
The *m* shall eat and be satisfied............ Ps 22:26
The *m* will he guide in judgment.......... Ps 25:9
the *m* will he teach his way.................... Ps 25:9
But the *m* shall inherit the earth.......... Ps 37:11
to save all the *m* of the earth................ Ps 76:9
The LORD lifteth up the *m*........................ Ps 147:6
beautify the *m* with salvation................ Ps 149:4
equity for the *m* of the earth.................. Is 11:4
The *m* also shall increase their.............. Is 29:19
to preach good tidings unto the *m*........ Is 61:1
and turn aside the way of the *m*............ Amos 2:7
all ye *m* of the earth, which have.......... Zeph 2:3
Blessed are the *m*.. Mt 5:5
for I am *m* and lowly in heart................ Mt 11:29
thy King cometh unto thee, *m*................ Mt 21:5
even the ornament of a *m*........................ 1Pet 3:4

MEEKNESS

because of truth and *m* and...................... Ps 45:4
seek righteousness, seek *m*...................... Zeph 2:3
or in love, and in the spirit of *m*.......... 1Cor 4:21
Paul myself beseech you by the *m*........ 2Cor 10:1
M, temperance.. Gal 5:23
such an one in the spirit of *m*................ Gal 6:1
With all lowliness and *m*, with.............. Eph 4:2
kindness, humbleness of mind, *m*........ Col 3:12
faith, love, patience,.................................... 1Ti 6:11
In *m* instructing those that...................... Ti 2:25
shewing all *m* unto all men.................... Titus 3:2
receive with *m* the engrafted word...... Jas 1:21
his works with *m* of wisdom .... Jas 3:13
of the hope that is in you with *m*.......... 1Pet 3:15

MEET

I will make him an help *m* for him........ Gen 2:18
was not found an help *m* for him.......... Gen 2:20
m him after his return from the............ Gen 14:17
he ran to *m* them from the tent............ Gen 18:2
Lot seeing them rose up to *m* them...... Gen 19:1
And the servant ran to *m* her.................. Gen 24:17
that watcheth in the field to *m* us........ Gen 24:65
son, that he ran to *m* him........................ Gen 29:13
and Leah went out to *m* him.................. Gen 30:16
Esau, and also he cometh to *m* thee.... Gen 32:6
Esau ran to *m* him .... Gen 33:4
went up to *m* Israel his father,.............. Gen 46:29
behold, he cometh forth to *m* thee........ Ex 4:14
Go into the wilderness to *m* Moses...... Ex 4:27
Moses said, It is not *m* so to do............ Ex 8:26
went out to *m* his father in law.............. Ex 18:7
out of the camp to *m* with God.............. Ex 19:17
If thou *m* thine enemy's ox or his........ Ex 23:4
And there I will *m* with thee.................. Ex 25:22
where I will *m* with you, to speak........ Ex 29:42

there I will *m* with the children .... Ex 29:43
where I will *m* with thee.......................... Ex 30:6
where I will *m* with thee.......................... Ex 30:36
where I will *m* with you............................ Num 17:4
he went out to *m* unto a city.................. Num 22:36
the LORD will come to *m* me...................... Num 23:3
while I *m* the LORD yonder........................ Num 23:15
went forth to *m* them without the........ Num 31:13
all that are *m* for the war........................ Deut 3:18
mountain, lest the pursuers *m* you...... Josh 2:16
for the journey, and go to *m* them........ Josh 9:11
And Jael went out to *m* Sisera................ Judg 4:18
Sisera, Jael came out to *m* him.............. Judg 4:22
m for the necks of them that take........ Judg 5:30
and they came up to *m* them.................. Judg 6:35
of the doors of my house to *m* me........ Judg 11:31
came out to *m* him with timbrels........ Judg 11:34
saw him, he rejoiced to *m* him.............. Judg 19:3
that they *m* thee not in any other........ Ruth 2:22
there shall *m* thee three men 1Sa 10:3
that thou shalt *m* a company of............ 1Sa 10:5
and Saul went out to *m* him.................... 1Sa 13:10
early to *m* Saul in the morning............ 1Sa 15:12
and came and drew nigh to *m* David .. 1Sa 17:48
the army to *m* the Philistine.................. 1Sa 17:48
was going, Saul with tabrets,.................... 1Sa 18:6
which sent thee this day to *m* me........ 1Sa 25:34
thou hadst hasted and come to *m* me.. 1Sa 25:34
and they went forth to *m* David 1Sa 30:21
to *m* the people that were with............ 1Sa 30:21
of Saul came out to *m* David.................. 2Sa 6:20
it unto David, he sent to *m* them.......... 2Sa 10:5
came to *m* him with his coat rent........ 2Sa 15:32
to Gilgal, to go to *m* the king................ 2Sa 19:15
the men of Judah to *m* king David...... 2Sa 19:17
to go down to *m* my lord the king........ 2Sa 19:20
of Saul came down to *m* the king.......... 2Sa 19:24
come to Jerusalem to *m* the king.......... 2Sa 19:25
he came down to *m* me at Jordan.......... 2Sa 19:20
And the king rose up to *m* her................ 1Kin 2:19
So Obadiah went to *m* Ahab.................... 1Kin 18:16
and Ahab went to *m* Elijah...................... 1Kin 18:16
go down to *m* Ahab king of Israel,........ 1Kin 21:18
go up to *m* the messengers of the........ 2Kin 1:3
him, There came a man up to *m* us...... 2Kin 1:6
man was he which came up to *m* you.. 2Kin 1:7
And they came to *m* him, and bowed .. 2Kin 2:15
to *m* her, and say unto her, Is it 2Kin 4:26
if thou *m* any man, salute him not 2Kin 4:29
Wherefore he went again to *m* him...... 2Kin 4:31
down from the chariot to *m* him............ 2Kin 5:21
again from his chariot to *m* thee.......... 2Kin 5:26
the man of God, and enquire of................ 2Kin 8:8
So Hazael went to *m* him, and took...... 2Kin 8:9
an horseman, and send to *m* them........ 2Kin 9:17
went one on horseback to *m* him.......... 2Kin 9:18
the son of Rechab coming to *m* him 2Kin 10:15
king Ahaz went to Damascus to *m*........ 2Kin 16:10
And David went out to *m* them 1Chr 12:17
And he sent to *m* them................................ 1Chr 19:5
And he went out to Asa, and said............ 2Chr 15:2
Hanani the seer went out to *m* him...... 2Chr 19:2
it was not *m* for us to see the................ Ezr 4:14
Let us *m* together in some one of.......... Neh 6:2
which were *m* to be given her, out........ Neh 6:10
they *m* with darkness in the.................... Est 2:9
Surely it is *m* to be said unto .... Job 34:31
he goeth on to the armed men.................. Job 39:21
Therefore came I forth to *m* thee.......... Prov 7:15
that withholdeth more than is *m*.......... Prov 11:24
bear robbed of her whelps in a man...... Prov 17:12
The rich and poor *m* together .... Prov 22:2
and the deceitful man *m* together........ Prov 29:13
Isaiah, Go forth now to *m* Ahaz............ Is 7:3
for thee to *m* thee at thy coming.......... Is 14:9
m with the wild beasts of the................ Is 34:14
I will not *m* thee as a man...................... Is 47:3
me as seemeth good and *m* unto you.. Jer 26:14
it unto whom it seemed *m* unto me...... Jer 27:5
went forth from Mizpah to *m* them...... Jer 41:6
One post shall run to *m* another............ Jer 51:31
and one messenger to *m* another.......... Jer 51:31
Is it *m* for any work .... Eze 15:4
was whole, it was *m* for no work .... Eze 15:5
shall it be *m* for any work...................... Eze 15:5
I will *m* them as a bear that is .... Hos 13:8
unto thee, prepare to *m* thy God .... Amos 4:12
another angel went out to *m* him.......... Zec 2:3
therefore fruits *m* for repentance........ Mt 3:8
whole city came out to *m* Jesus............ Mt 8:34
and said, It is not *m* to take the............ Mt 15:26
went forth to *m* the bridegroom .... Mt 25:6
go ye out to *m* him.................................... Mt 25:6
for it is not *m* to take the........................ Mk 7:27
there shall *m* you a man bearing a........ Mk 14:13
to *m* him that cometh against him........ Lk 14:31
It was *m* that we should make.............. Lk 15:32
the city, there shall a man *m* you........ Lk 22:10
trees, and went forth to *m* him.............. Jn 12:13
do works *m* for repentance...................... Acts 26:20
they came to *m* us as far as Appii........ Acts 28:15
of their error which was *m*...................... Rom 1:27
that am not *m* to be called an................ 1Cor 15:9
if it be *m* that I go also, they.................. 1Cor 16:4
Even as it is *m* for me to think .... Phil 1:7
which hath made us *m* to be.................... Col 1:12
clouds, to *m* the Lord in the air 1Th 4:17
for you, brethren, as it is *m*.................... 2Th 1:3
m for the master's use, and.................... 2Ti 2:21

bringeth forth herbs *m* for them............ Heb 6:7
Yea, I think it m, as long as I........... 2Pet 1:13

MEETEST
m of your master's sons, and set......... 2Kin 10:3
Thou m him that rejoiceth and............... Is 64:5

MEETETH
When Esau my brother m thee............ Gen 32:17
when he m him, he shall slay him....... Num 35:19
slay the murderer, when he m him ..... Num 35:21

MEETING
was afraid at the m of David............... 1Sa 21:1
it is iniquity, even the solemn m......... Is 1:13

MEGIDDO (*me-ghid'-do*) See MEGIDDON. *A city
on the plain of Jezreel.*
the king of M, one............................... Josh 12:21
towns, and the inhabitants of M......... Josh 17:11
towns, nor the inhabitants of M......... Judg 1:27
in Taanach by the waters of M............. Judg 5:19
to him pertained Taanach and M......... 1Kin 4:12
wall of Jerusalem, and Hazor, and M... 1Kin 9:15
And he fled to M, and died there......... 2Kin 9:27
and he slew him at M, when he had... 2Kin 23:29
him in a chariot dead from M............. 2Kin 23:30
towns, Taanach and her towns, M....... 1Chr 7:29
came to fight in the valley of M......... 2Chr 35:22

MEGIDDON (*me-ghid'-don*) See ARMAGEDDON,
MEGIDDO. *Same as Megiddo.*
of Hadadrimmon in the valley of M..... Zec 12:11

MEHETABEEL (*me-het'-a-be-el*) See
MEHETABEL. *Father of Delaiah.*
the son of Delaiah the son of M........... Neh 6:10

MEHETABEL (*me-het'-a-bel*) See
MEHETABEEL. *Wife of Hadar.*
and his wife's name was M, the........... Gen 36:39
and his wife's name was M............... 1Chr 1:50

MEHIDA (*me-hi'-dah*) *A family of exiles.*
of Bazluth, the children of M............. Ezr 2:52
of Bazlith, the children of M............. Neh 7:54

MEHIR (*me'-hur*) *A son of Chelub.*
the brother of Shuah begat M............ 1Chr 4:11

MEHOLATHITE (*me-ho'-lath-ite*) *An
inhabitant of a city in Issachar.*
given unto Adriel the M to wife........... 1Sa 18:19
Adriel the son of Barzillai the M......... 2Sa 21:8

MEHUJAEL (*me-hu'-ja-el*) *Son of Irad.*
and Irad begat M.............................. Gen 4:18
and M begat Methusael....................... Gen 4:18

MEHUMAN (*me-hu'-man*) *A servant of King
Ahasuerus.*
merry with wine, he commanded M..... Est 1:10

MEHUNIM (*me-hu'-nim*) See MAONITE,
MEHUNIMS, MEUNIM. *A family of exiles.*
of Asnah, the children of M................. Ezr 2:50

MEHUNIMS (*me-hu'-nims*) See MEHUNIM. *A
people who lived in Arabia.*
that dwelt in Gur-baal, and the M....... 2Chr 26:7

ME-JARKON (*me-jar'-kon*) *A city in Dan.*
And M, and Rakkon, with the border ... Josh 19:46

MEKERATHITE See NETOPHATHITE.

MEKONAH (*me-ko'-nah*) *A city in Judah.*
And at Ziklag, and at M, and in the ... Neh 11:28

MELATIAH (*mel-a-ti'-ah*) *A repairer of
Jerusalem's wall.*
them repaired M the Gibeonite............ Neh 3:7

MELCHI (*mel'-ki*) See MELCHI-SHUA,
MELCHIZEDEK.
1. *Son of Janna; ancestor of Jesus.*
of Levi, which was the son of M......... Lk 3:24
2. *Son of Addi; ancestor of Jesus.*
Which was the son of M, which was ... Lk 3:28

MELCHIAH (*mel-ki'-ah*) See MALCHIAH.
Father of Pashur.
sent unto him Pashur the son of M ..... Jer 21:1

MELCHISEDEC (*mel'-ki-shu'-ah*) See
MELCHIZEDEK. *Greek form of Melchizedek.*
for ever after the order of M............... Heb 5:6
high priest after the order of M........... Heb 5:10
for ever after the order of M............... Heb 6:20
For this M, king of Salem, priest......... Heb 7:1
of his father, when M met him............. Heb 7:10
should rise after the order of M........... Heb 7:11
of M there ariseth another priest......... Heb 7:15
for ever after the order of M............... Heb 7:17
for ever after the order of M............... Heb 7:21

MELCHI-SHUA (*mel'-ki-shu'-ah*) See
MALCHISHUA. *A son of King Saul.*
were Jonathan, and Ishui, and M....... 1Sa 14:49
slew Jonathan, and Abinadab, and M... 1Sa 31:2

MELCHIZEDEK (*mel-kiz'-e-dek*) See
MELCHISEDEC. *King and priest of Salem.*
M king of Salem brought forth............ Gen 14:18
for ever after the order of M............... Ps 110:4

MELEA (*mel'-e-ah*) *Son of Menan; an ancestor
of Jesus.*
Which was the son of M, which was ... Lk 3:31

MELECH (*me'-lek*) See EBED-MELECH, HAM-
MELECH, NATHAN-MELECH, REGEM-MELECH. *A
son of Micah.*
sons of Micah were, Pithon, and M 1Chr 8:35
sons of Micah were, Pithon, and M 1Chr 9:41

MELICHU See MELICU.

MELICU (*mel'-i-cu*) See MALLUCH. *A priest.*
Of M, Jonathan................................ Neh 12:14

MELITA (*mel'-i-tah*) *A Mediterranean island.*
knew that the island was called M........ Acts 28:1

MELODY
make sweet m, sing many songs........... Is 23:16
thanksgiving, and the voice of m......... Is 51:3
will not hear the m of thy viols........... Amos 5:23
making m in your heart to................. Eph 5:19

MELONS
the cucumbers, and the m, and the ..... Num 11:5

MELT
of Canaan shall m away....................... Ex 15:15
these things, our hearts did m............. Josh 2:11
me made the heart of the people m....... Josh 14:8
heart of a lion, shall utterly m............ 2Sa 17:10
Let them m away as waters which......... Ps 58:7
gnash with his teeth, and m away......... Ps 112:10
and every man's heart shall m............. Is 13:7
Egypt shall m in the midst of it........... Is 19:1
of hosts, Behold, I will m them........... Jer 9:7
and every heart shall m, and all........... Eze 21:7
to blow the fire upon it, to m it........... Eze 22:20
I will leave you there, and m you......... Eze 22:20
toucheth the land, and it shall m......... Amos 9:5
wine, and all the hills shall m............. Amos 9:13
quake at him, and the hills m............. Nah 1:5
shall m with fervent heat.................... 2Pet 3:10
shall m with fervent heat.................... 2Pet 3:12

MELTED
and when the sun waxed hot, it m....... Ex 16:21
passed over, that their heart m........... Josh 5:1
the hearts of the people m................... Josh 7:5
The mountains m from before the....... Judg 5:5
and, behold, the multitude m away..... Is 14:16
it is m in the midst of my bowels......... Ps 22:14
he uttered his voice, the earth m......... Ps 46:6
The hills m like wax at the................. Ps 97:5
their soul is m because of................... Ps 107:26
shall be m with their blood................. Is 34:3
ye shall be m in the midst.................. Eze 22:21
As silver is m in the midst of.............. Eze 22:22
so shall ye be m in the midst.............. Eze 22:22

MELTETH
As a snail which m, let every one......... Ps 58:8
as wax m before the fire, so let........... Ps 68:2
My soul m for heaviness.................... Ps 119:28
sendeth out his word, and m them....... Ps 147:18
The workman m a graven image, and... Is 40:19
the founder m in vain....................... Jer 6:29
and the heart m, and the knees........... Nah 2:10

MELTING
As when the m fire burneth, the .... Is 64:2

MELZAR (*mel'-zar*) *Babylonian officer charged
with Daniel and his companions.*
These said Daniel to M, whom the....... Dan 1:11
Then M took away the portion of........ Dan 1:16

MEMBER
or hath his privy m cut off.................. Deut 23:1
For the body is not one m................... 1Cor 12:14
And if they were all one m................. 1Cor 12:19
And whether one m suffer, all the....... 1Cor 12:26
or one m be honoured, all the............. 1Cor 12:26
Even so the tongue is a little m........... Jas 3:5

MEMBERS
and all my m are as a shadow............. Job 17:7
in thy book all my m were written ..... Ps 139:16
that one of thy m should perish.......... Mt 5:29
that one of thy m should perish.......... Mt 5:30
yield ye your m as instruments of....... Rom 6:13
dead, and your m as instruments of ... Rom 6:13
your m servants to uncleanness.......... Rom 6:19
even so now yield your m servants ..... Rom 6:19
did work in our m to bring forth......... Rom 7:5
But I see another law in my m............ Rom 7:23
the law of sin which is in my m........... Rom 7:23
For as we have many m in one body ... Rom 12:4
all m have not the same office............ Rom 12:4
every one m one of another............... Rom 12:5
your bodies are the m of Christ.......... 1Cor 6:15
shall I then take the m of Christ.......... 1Cor 6:15
and make them the m of an harlot 1Cor 6:15
the body is one, and hath many m....... 1Cor 12:12
all the m of that one body, being......... 1Cor 12:12
hath made God set the m every........... 1Cor 12:18
But now are they many m, yet but 1Cor 12:20
much more those m of the body........... 1Cor 12:22
those m of the body, which................. 1Cor 12:23
but that the m should have the........... 1Cor 12:25
suffer, all the m suffer with it............ 1Cor 12:26
all the m rejoice with it..................... 1Cor 12:26
of Christ, and m in particular............. 1Cor 12:27
for we are m one of another............... Eph 4:25
For we are m of his body, of his......... Eph 5:30
Mortify therefore your m which......... Col 3:5
so is the tongue among our m............. Jas 3:6
of your lusts that war in your m......... Jas 4:1

MEMORIAL
this is my m unto all generations......... Ex 3:15
day shall be unto you for a m............. Ex 12:14
for a m between thine eyes, that......... Ex 13:9
Write this for a m in a book............... Ex 17:14
of the ephod for stones of m unto....... Ex 28:12
upon his two shoulders for a m........... Ex 28:12
place, for a m before the LORD............ Ex 28:29
that it may be a m unto the............... Ex 30:16
for a m to the children of Israel......... Ex 39:7
burn the m of it upon the altar........... Lev 2:2
the meat offering a m thereof............. Lev 2:9
the priest shall burn the m of it......... Lev 2:16
even a m thereof, and burn it on......... Lev 5:12
a sweet savour, even the m of it......... Lev 6:15
a m of blowing of trumpets, an.......... Lev 23:24
it may be on the bread for a m........... Lev 24:7
of jealousy, an offering of m.............. Num 5:15
the offering of m in her hands............ Num 5:18
the offering, even the m thereof......... Num 5:26
be to you for a m before your God....... Num 10:10
To be a m unto the children of........... Num 16:40
for a m for the children of................. Num 31:54
these stones shall be for a m.............. Josh 4:7
have no portion, nor right, nor m....... Neh 2:20
nor the m of them perish from........... Est 9:28
their m is perished with them............ Ps 9:6
and thy m, O LORD, throughout all ..... Ps 135:13
the LORD is his m............................ Hos 12:5
for a m in the temple of the LORD....... Zec 6:14
hath done, be told for a m of her........ Mt 26:13
shall be spoken of for a m of her........ Mk 14:9
are come up for a m before God......... Acts 10:4

MEMORY
off the m of them from the earth......... Ps 109:15
utter the m of thy great goodness....... Ps 145:7
The m of the just is blessed................ Prov 10:7
for the m of them is forgotten............. Eccl 9:5
and made all their m to perish............ Is 26:14
if ye keep in m what I preached........... 1Cor 15:2

MEMPHIS (*mem'-fis*) See NOPH. *A city in
Egypt.*
gather them up, M shall bury them..... Hos 9:6

MEMUCAN (*mem-u'-can*) *A prince of Media
and Persia.*
Tarshish, Meres, Marsena, and M........ Est 1:14
M answered before the king and the... Est 1:16
did according to the word of M........... Est 1:21

MEN See PREFACE.

MENAHEM (*men'-a-hem*) *Son of Gadi.*
For M the son of Gadi went up........... 2Kin 15:14
Then M smote Tiphsah, and all that... 2Kin 15:16
M the son of Gadi to reign over......... 2Kin 15:17
M gave Pul a thousand talents of....... 2Kin 15:19
M exacted the money of Israel........... 2Kin 15:20
And the rest of the acts of M............. 2Kin 15:21
And M slept with his fathers.............. 2Kin 15:22
of Judah Pekahiah the son of M......... 2Kin 15:23

MENAN (*me'-nan*) *Father of Melea; ancestor of
Jesus.*
of Melea, which was the son of M....... Lk 3:31

MEND
brass to m the house of the LORD........ 2Chr 24:12

MENDING
their father, m their nets.................... Mt 4:21
were in the ship m their nets.............. Mk 1:19

MENE (*me'-ne*) *Part of "the handwriting on the
wall".*
writing that was written, M, M........... Dan 5:25
M, God hath numbered...................... Dan 5:26

MENI See MENAN.

MENNA See MENAN.

MENPLEASERS
Not with eyeservice, as m.................. Eph 6:6
not with eyeservice, as m.................. Col 3:22

MEN'S
the m feet that were with him........... Gen 24:32
Fill the m sacks with food, as............ Gen 44:1
serve gods, the work of m hands......... Deut 4:28
Wherefore hearest thou m words........ 1Sa 24:9
forsook the old m counsel that........... 1Kin 12:13
m bones shall be burnt upon thee...... 1Kin 13:2
no gods, but the work of m hands....... 2Kin 19:18
burned m bones upon them, and......... 2Kin 23:20
and ', 'ld, the work of m hands........... Ps 115:4
and gold, the work of m hands........... Ps 135:15
no gods, but the work of m hands....... Is 37:19
the mighty m hearts in Moab at......... Jer 48:41
because of m blood, and for the......... Hab 2:8
them afraid, because of m blood........ Hab 2:17
borne, and lay them on m shoulders... Mt 23:4
are within full of dead m bones......... Mt 23:27
is not come to destroy m lives........... Lk 9:56
M hearts failing them for fear............ Lk 21:26
is worshipped with m hands.............. Acts 17:25
that is, of other m labours................. 2Cor 10:15
be partaker of other m sins............... 1Ti 5:22
Some m sins are open beforehand....... 1Ti 5:24
as a busybody in other m matters....... 1Pet 4:15
having m persons in admiration......... Jude 16

MENSERVANTS
sheep, and oxen, and the asses, and m Gen 12:16
took sheep, and oxen, and m.............. Gen 20:14

herds, and silver, and gold, and *m* .... Gen 24:35
cattle, and maidservants, and *m* .... Gen 30:43
have oxen, and asses, flocks, and *m* ..... Gen 32:5
she shall not go out as the *m* do .... Ex 21:7
and your daughters, and your *m* .... Deut 12:12
And he will take your *m*, and your 1Sa 8:16
and sheep, and oxen, and *m*, and 2Kin 5:26
and shall begin to beat the *m* .... Lk 12:45

MENSTEALERS
themselves with mankind, for *m* 1Ti 1:10

MENSTRUOUS
shalt cast them away as a *m* cloth .... Is 30:22
is as a *m* woman among them .... Lam 1:17
hath come near to a *m* woman .... Eze 18:6

MENTION
make *m* of me unto Pharaoh, and .... Gen 40:14
make no *m* of the name of other .... Ex 23:13
neither make *m* of the names of .... Josh 23:7
when he made *m* of the ark of God, ... 1Sa 4:18
No *m* shall be made of coral, or .... Job 28:18
I will make *m* of thy .... Ps 71:16
I will make *m* of Rahab and Babylon .... Ps 87:4
make *m* that his name is exalted .... Is 12:4
every one that maketh *m* thereof .... Is 19:17
only will we make *m* of thy name .... Is 26:13
make *m* of the God of Israel, but .... Is 48:1
mother hath he made *m* of my name .... Is 49:1
ye that make *m* of the LORD, ... Is 62:6
I will in the lovingkindness of .... Is 63:7
Make ye *m* to the nations .... Jer 4:16
I said, I will not make *m* of him .... Jer 20:9
of the LORD shall ye *m* no more .... Jer 23:36
for we may not make *m* of the name .... Amos 6:10
m of you always in my prayers. .... Rom 1:9
making *m* of you in my prayers .... Eph 1:16
making *m* of you in our prayers 1Th 1:2
making *m* of thee always in my .... Philem 4
made *m* of the departing of the .... Heb 11:22

MENTIONED
cities which are here *m* by name .... Josh 21:9
These *m* by their names were 1Chr 4:38
who is *m* in the book of the kings 2Chr 20:34
For thy sister Sodom was not *m* by ...... Eze 16:56
they shall not be *m* unto him .... Eze 18:22
that he hath done shall not be *m* .... Eze 18:24
committed shall be *m* unto him. .... Eze 33:16

MENUHOTH See MANAHETHITES.

MEONENIM (me-on'-e-nim) *A place near*
Shechem.
come along by the plain of M .... Judg 9:37

MEONOTHAI (me-on'-o-thahee) *Descendant*
of Judah.
And M begat Ophrah 1Chr 4:14

MEPHAATH (mef'-a-ath) *A Levitical city in*
Reuben.
And Jahaza, and Kedemoth, and M ...... Josh 13:18
suburbs, and M with her suburbs .... Josh 21:37
suburbs, and M with her suburbs 1Chr 6:79
upon Jahazah, and upon M .... Jer 48:21

MEPHIBOSHETH (me-fib'-o-sheth) *See*
MERIBBAAL.
1. *Son of Jonathan.*
And his name was M 2Sa 4:4
Now when M, the son of Jonathan, ... 2Sa 9:6
And David said, M 2Sa 9:6
but M thy master's son shall eat 2Sa 9:10
As for M, said the king, he shall 2Sa 9:11
M had a young son, whose name was... 2Sa 9:12
of Ziba were servants unto M 2Sa 9:12
So M dwelt in Jerusalem 2Sa 9:13
Ziba the servant of M met him 2Sa 16:1
are all that pertained unto M 2Sa 16:4
M the son of Saul came down to 2Sa 19:24
wentest not thou with me, M 2Sa 19:25
M said unto the king, Yea, let 2Sa 19:30
But the king spared M, the son of 2Sa 21:7
2. *Son of Rizpah.*
she bare unto Saul, Armoni and M 2Sa 21:8

MERAB (me'-rab) *Daughter of King Saul.*
the name of the firstborn M 1Sa 14:49
David, Behold my elder daughter M 1Sa 18:17
M Saul's daughter should have 1Sa 18:19

MERAIAH (me-a-i'-ah) *A priest.*
fathers: of Seraiah, M .... Neh 12:12

MERAIOTH (me-rah'-yoth) *See* MEREMOTH.
1. *An ancestor of Azariah.*
Zerahiah, and Zerahiah begat M 1Chr 6:6
M begat Amariah, and Amariah begat... 1Chr 6:7
M his son, Amariah his son, ... 1Chr 6:52
the son of Azariah, the son of M .... Ezr 7:3
2. *Another ancestor of Azariah.*
the son of Zadok, the son of M 1Chr 9:11
the son of Zadok, the son M .... Neh 11:11
3. *A priest in exile.*
of M, Helkai .... Neh 12:15

MERARI (me-rah'-ri) *See* MERARITES. *A son of*
Levi.
Gershon, Kohath, and M .... Gen 46:11
Gershon, and Kohath, and M, ... Ex 6:16
and the sons of M .... Ex 6:19
Gershon, and Kohath, and M, ... Num 3:17
the sons of M by their families .... Num 3:20
Of M was the family of the .... Num 3:33

---

these are the families of M .... Num 3:33
M was Zuriel the son of Abihail .... Num 3:35
charge of the sons of M shall be .... Num 3:36
As for the sons of M, thou shalt .... Num 4:29
of the families of the sons of M .... Num 4:33
of the families of the sons of M .... Num 4:42
of the families of the sons of M .... Num 4:45
oxen he gave unto the sons of M .... Num 7:8
and the sons of M set forward............ Num 10:17
of M, the family of the Merarites .... Num 26:57
The children of M by their .... Josh 21:7
the families of the children of M .... Josh 21:34
children of M by their families .... Josh 21:40
Gershon, Kohath, and M 1Chr 6:1
Gershon, Kohath, and M 1Chr 6:16
The sons of M; Mahli, ... 1Chr 6:19
The sons of M; Mahli, Libni................ 1Chr 6:29
sons of M stood on the left hand 1Chr 6:44
the son of Mushi, the son of M 1Chr 6:47
Unto the sons of M were given by 1Chr 6:63
the rest of the children of M 1Chr 6:77
of Hashabiah, of the sons of M 1Chr 9:14
Of the sons of M 1Chr 15:6
of the sons of M their brethren 1Chr 15:17
namely, Gershon, Kohath, and M 1Chr 23:6
The sons of M; Mahli, ... 1Chr 23:21
sons of M were Mahli 1Chr 24:26
The sons of M by Jaaziah................... 1Chr 24:27
Also Hosah, of the children of M 1Chr 26:10
of Kore, and among the sons of M....... 1Chr 26:19
and of the sons of M, Kish the son...... 2Chr 29:12
the Levites, of the sons of M 2Chr 34:12
men Jeshaiah of the sons of M .... Ezr 8:19

MERARITES (me-ra'-rites) *Descendants of*
Merari.
of Merari, the family of the M .... Num 26:57

MERATHAIM (mer-a-tha'-im) *A symbolic*
name for Babylon.
Go up against the land of M .... Jer 50:21

MERCHANDISE
thou shalt not make *m* of her .... Deut 21:14
of Israel, and maketh *m* of him........... Deut 24:7
For the *m* of it is better than .... Prov 3:14
it is better than the *m* of silver .... Prov 3:14
She perceiveth that her *m* is good ...... Prov 31:18
And her *m* and her hire shall be .... Is 23:18
for her *m* shall be for their own.......... Is 23:18
m of Ethiopia and of the Sabeans, ... Is 45:14
riches, and make a prey of thy *m* .... Eze 26:12
were in thee to occupy thy *m* .... Eze 27:9
isles were the *m* of thine hand .... Eze 27:15
and made of cedar, among thy *m* ...... Eze 27:24
Thy riches, and thy fairs, thy *m* .... Eze 27:27
and the occupiers of thy *m* .... Eze 27:27
of thy riches and of thy *m* .... Eze 27:33
in the depths of the waters thy *m* ...... Eze 27:34
By the multitude of thy *m* they .... Eze 28:16
one to his farm, another to his *m* ...... Mt 22:5
my Father's house an house of *m* ...... Jn 2:16
with feigned words make of you *m* 2Pet 2:3
no man buyeth their *m* any more....... Rev 18:11
The *m* of gold, and silver, and .... Rev 18:12

MERCHANT
silver, current money with the *m* .... Gen 23:16
and deliverdth girdles unto the *m* .... Prov 31:24
with all powders of the *m* .... Song 3:6
a commandment against the city .... Is 23:11
which art a *m* of the people for .... Eze 27:3
Tarshish was thy *m* by reason of .... Eze 27:12
Syria was thy *m* by reason of the .... Eze 27:16
Damascus was thy *m* in the .... Eze 27:18
Dedan was thy *m* in precious............ Eze 27:20
He is a *m*, the balances of deceit .... Hos 12:7
for all the *m* people are cut down ...... Zeph 1:11
of heaven is like unto a *m* man.......... Mt 13:45

MERCHANTMEN
Then there passed by Midianites *m* .... Gen 37:28
Beside that he had of the *m* 1Kin 10:15

MERCHANTS
and of the traffick of the spice *m* 1Kin 10:15
the king's *m* received the linen 1Kin 10:28
the king's *m* received the linen 2Chr 1:16
that which chapmen and *m* brought.... 2Chr 9:14
of the Nethinims, and of the *m*.......... Neh 3:31
repaired the goldsmiths and the *m*..... Neh 3:32
So the *m* and sellers of all kind .... Neh 13:20
shall they part him among the *m* .... Job 41:6
thou whom the *m* of Zidon, that, ... Is 23:2
whose *m* are princes, whose .... Is 23:8
thou hast laboured, even thy *m* .... Is 47:15
he set it in a city of *m* .... Eze 17:4
and Meshech, they were thy *m* .... Eze 27:13
The men of Dedan were thy *m* .... Eze 27:15
land of Israel, they were thy *m* .... Eze 27:17
in these were they thy *m* .... Eze 27:21
The *m* of Sheba and Raamah .... Eze 27:22
Sheba and Raamah, they were thy *m*.. Eze 27:22
the *m* of Sheba, Asshur, and .... Eze 27:23
and Chilmad, were thy *m* .... Eze 27:23
These were thy *m* in all sorts of .... Eze 27:24
The *m* among the people shall hiss.... Eze 27:36
the *m* of Tarshish, with all the .... Eze 38:13
Thou hast multiplied thy *m* above ..... Nah 3:16
the *m* of the earth are waxed rich...... Rev 18:3
the *m* of the earth shall weep and ..... Rev 18:11
The *m* of these things, which were .... Rev 18:15
for thy *m* were the great men of .... Rev 18:23

MERCHANTS'
She is like the *m* ships .... Prov 31:14

MERCIES
worthy of the least of all the *m* .... Gen 32:10
for his *m* are great 2Sa 24:14
for very great are his *m* 1Chr 21:13
remember the *m* of David thy 2Chr 6:42
Yet thou in thy manifold *m* .... Neh 9:19
m thou gavest them saviours .... Neh 9:27
deliver them according to thy *m* .... Neh 9:28
Remember, O LORD, thy tender *m* ...... Ps 25:6
not thou thy tender *m* from me .... Ps 40:11
m blot out my transgressions.............. Ps 51:1
to the multitude of thy tender *m* .... Ps 69:16
he in anger shut up his tender *m*........ Ps 77:9
let thy tender *m* speedily prevent ...... Ps 79:8
I will sing of the *m* of the LORD.......... Ps 89:1
with lovingkindness and tender *m* ..... Ps 103:4
not the multitude of thy *m* .... Ps 106:7
to the multitude of his *m* .... Ps 106:45
Let thy *m* come also unto me, O .... Ps 119:41
Let thy tender *m* come unto me .... Ps 119:77
Great are thy tender *m*, O LORD .... Ps 119:156
his tender *m* are over all his .... Ps 145:9
but the tender *m* of the wicked .... Prov 12:10
but with great *m* will I gather .... Is 54:7
you, even the sure *m* of David .... Is 55:3
on them according to his *m* .... Is 63:7
thy bowels and of thy *m* toward me... Is 63:15
LORD, even lovingkindness and *m*..... Jer 16:5
And I will shew *m* unto you .... Jer 42:12
It is of the LORD's *m* that we are....... Lam 3:22
to the multitude of his *m* .... Lam 3:32
That they would desire *m* of the .... Dan 2:18
To the Lord our God belong *m*.......... Dan 9:9
but for thy great *m* .... Dan 9:18
and in lovingkindness, and in *m* ...... Hos 2:19
I am returned to Jerusalem with *m* .... Zec 1:16
will give you the sure *m* of David ...... Acts 13:34
brethren, by the *m* of God .... Rom 12:1
Jesus Christ, the Father of *m* 2Cor 1:3
of the Spirit, if any bowels and *m*...... Phil 2:1
God, holy and beloved, bowels of *m*.. Col 3:12

MERCIES'
Nevertheless for thy great *m* sake ..... Neh 9:31
oh save me for thy *m* sake .... Ps 6:4
save me for thy *m* sake .... Ps 31:16
help, and redeem us for thy *m* sake ... Ps 44:26

MERCIFUL
the LORD being *m* unto him .... Gen 19:16
The LORD, The LORD God, *m*, ... Ex 34:6
(For the LORD thy God is a *m* God..... Deut 4:31
Be *m*, O LORD, unto thy people .... Deut 21:8
will be *m* unto his land, and to .... Deut 32:43
With the *m* thou wilt shew thyself 2Sa 22:26
thou wilt shew thyself *m* 2Sa 22:26
the house of Israel are *m* kings 1Kin 20:31
LORD your God is gracious and *m*..... 2Chr 30:9
ready to pardon, gracious and *m* ..... Neh 9:17
for thou art a gracious and *m* God .... Neh 9:31
With the *m* thou wilt shew thyself ..... Ps 18:25
thou wilt shew thyself *m* .... Ps 18:25
redeem me, and be *m* unto me. .... Ps 26:11
He is ever *m*, and lendeth .... Ps 37:26
I said, LORD, be *m* unto me .... Ps 41:4
be *m* unto me, and raise me up, ... Ps 41:10
Be *m* unto me, O God .... Ps 56:1
Be *m* unto me, O God, be .... Ps 57:1
be not *m* to any wicked .... Ps 59:5
God be *m* unto us, and bless us ...... Ps 67:1
Be *m* unto me, O Lord .... Ps 86:3
The LORD is *m* and gracious, slow ... Ps 103:8
yea, our God is *m* .... Ps 116:5
For his *m* kindness is great .... Ps 117:2
be *m* unto me according to thy .... Ps 119:58
thy *m* kindness be for my comfort, ... Ps 119:76
be *m* unto me, as thou usest to do ... Ps 119:132
The *m* man doeth good to his own .... Prov 11:17
m men are taken away, none .... Is 57:1
for I am *m*, saith the LORD, and I ..... Jer 3:12
for he is gracious and *m*, slow to ..... Joel 2:13
thou art a gracious God, and .... Jonah 4:2
Blessed are the *m* .... Mt 5:7
Be ye therefore *m*, as your Father ..... Lk 6:36
as your Father also is *m* .... Lk 6:36
saying, God be *m* to me a sinner. ..... Lk 18:13
brethren, that he might be a *m* .... Heb 2:17
For I will be *m* to their .... Heb 8:12

MERCURIUS (mer-cu'-re-us) *A Roman god.*
and Paul, M, because he was the .... Acts 14:12

MERCY
and thou hast magnified thy *m* .... Gen 19:19
left destitute my master of his *m* ...... Gen 24:27
was with Joseph, and shewed him *m*.. Gen 39:21
give you *m* before the man .... Gen 43:14
m thou hast led forth the .... Ex 15:13
shewing unto thousands of them .... Ex 20:6
shalt make a *m* seat of pure gold...... Ex 25:17
in the two ends of the *m* seat .... Ex 25:18
even of the *m* seat shall ye make ..... Ex 25:19
covering the *m* seat with their .... Ex 25:20
toward the *m* seat shall the faces ..... Ex 25:20
thou shalt put the *m* seat above........ Ex 25:21
with thee from above the *m* seat ...... Ex 25:22
thou shalt put the *m* seat upon .... Ex 26:34
before the *m* seat that is over .... Ex 30:6
the *m* seat that is thereupon, and..... Ex 31:7
shew *m* on whom I will shew *m* ..... Ex 33:19

Keeping *m* for thousands,................ Ex 34:7
staves thereof, with the *m* seat,........ Ex 35:12
he made the *m* seat of pure gold,........ Ex 37:6
on the two ends of the *m* seat.......... Ex 37:7
out of the *m* seat made he the.......... Ex 37:8
with their wings over the *m* seat........ Ex 37:9
even to the *m* seatward were the........ Ex 37:9
staves thereof, and the *m* seat,........ Ex 39:35
put the *m* seat above upon the ark...... Ex 40:20
within the vail before the *m* seat...... Lev 16:2
in the cloud upon the *m* seat........... Lev 16:2
of the incense may cover the *m*......... Lev 16:13
finger upon the *m* seat eastward........ Lev 16:14
before the *m* seat shall he............ Lev 16:14
and sprinkle it upon the *m* seat........ Lev 16:14
and before the *m* seat.................. Lev 16:15
m seat that was upon the ark of........ Num 7:89
is longsuffering, and of great *m*....... Num 14:18
unto the greatness of thy *m*............ Num 14:19
shewing *m* unto thousands of them,...... Deut 5:10
with them, nor shew *m* unto them........ Deut 7:2
m with them that love him and keep..... Deut 7:9
the *m* which he sware unto thy.......... Deut 7:12
of his anger, and shew thee *m*.......... Deut 13:17
the city, and we will shew thee *m*...... Judg 1:24
But my *m* shall not depart away......... 2Sa 7:15
m and truth be with thee............... 2Sa 15:20
sheweth *m* to his anointed, unto........ 2Sa 22:51
servant David my father great *m*........ 1Kin 3:6
m with thy servants that walk.......... 1Kin 8:23
for his *m* endureth for ever............ 1Chr 16:34
because his *m* endureth for ever........ 1Chr 16:41
will not take my *m* away from him....... 1Chr 17:13
and of the place of the *m* seat......... 1Chr 28:11
great *m* unto David my father........... 2Chr 1:8
for his *m* endureth for ever............ 2Chr 5:13
shewest *m* unto thy servants, that...... 2Chr 6:14
for his *m* endureth for ever............ 2Chr 7:3
because his *m* endureth for ever........ 2Chr 7:6
for his *m* endureth for ever............ 2Chr 20:21
for his *m* endureth for ever............ Ezr 3:11
hath extended *m* unto me before......... Ezr 7:28
but hath extended *m* unto us in......... Ezr 9:9
m for them that love him............... Neh 1:5
grant him *m* in the sight of this....... Neh 1:11
God, who keepest covenant and *m*........ Neh 9:32
to the greatness of thy *m*.............. Neh 13:22
or for his land, or for *m*.............. Job 37:13
have upon me, and hear my prayer......... Ps 4:1
house in the multitude of thy *m*........ Ps 5:7
Have *m* upon me, O LORD................. Ps 6:2
Have *m* upon me, O LORD................. Ps 9:13
But I have trusted in thy *m*............ Ps 13:5
sheweth *m* to his anointed, to.......... Ps 18:50
through the *m* of the most High he...... Ps 21:7
m shall follow me all the days of...... Ps 23:6
according to thy *m* remember thou....... Ps 25:7
All the paths of the LORD are *m*........ Ps 25:10
thee unto me, and have *m* upon me....... Ps 25:16
have *m* also upon me, and answer me..... Ps 27:7
Hear, O LORD, and have *m* upon me....... Ps 30:10
will be glad and rejoice in thy *m*...... Ps 31:7
Have *m* upon me, O LORD, for I am....... Ps 31:9
m shall compass him about.............. Ps 32:10
him, upon them that hope in his *m*...... Ps 33:18
Let thy *m*, O LORD, be upon us,......... Ps 33:22
Thy *m*, O LORD, is in the heavens....... Ps 36:5
but the righteous shewth *m*............. Ps 37:21
Have *m* upon me, O God, according....... Ps 51:1
I trust in the *m* of God for ever....... Ps 52:8
God shall send forth his *m*............. Ps 57:3
For thy *m* is great unto the............ Ps 57:10
The God of my *m* shall prevent me....... Ps 59:10
aloud of thy *m* in the morning.......... Ps 59:16
is my defence, and the God of my *m*..... Ps 59:17
O prepare *m* and truth, which may....... Ps 61:7
unto thee, O Lord, belongeth *m*......... Ps 62:12
away my prayer, nor his *m* from me...... Ps 66:20
in the multitude of thy *m* hear me...... Ps 69:13
is his *m* clean gone for ever........... Ps 77:8
Shew us thy *m*, O Lord, and grant....... Ps 85:7
M and truth are met together.......... Ps 85:10
plenteous in *m* unto all them that...... Ps 86:5
For great is thy *m* toward me........... Ps 86:13
longsuffering, and plenteous in *m*...... Ps 86:15
O turn unto me, and have *m* upon me..... Ps 86:16
M shall be built up for ever........... Ps 89:2
m and truth shall go before thy........ Ps 89:14
and my *m* shall be with him............. Ps 89:24
My *m* will I keep for him for........... Ps 89:28
O satisfy us early with thy *m*.......... Ps 90:14
thy *m*, O Lord, held me up.............. Ps 94:18
He hath remembered his *m* and his....... Ps 98:3
his *m* is everlasting................... Ps 100:5
I will sing of *m* and judgment.......... Ps 101:1
shalt arise, and have *m* upon Zion...... Ps 102:13
slow to anger, and plenteous in *m*...... Ps 103:8
so great is his *m* toward them.......... Ps 103:11
But the *m* of the LORD is from.......... Ps 103:17
for his *m* endureth for ever............ Ps 106:1
for his *m* endureth for ever............ Ps 107:1
For thy *m* is great above the........... Ps 108:4
be none to extend *m* unto him........... Ps 109:12
that he remembered not to shew *m*....... Ps 109:16
for his *m* is good, deliver............. Ps 109:21
O save me according to thy *m*........... Ps 109:26
thy name give glory, for thy *m*......... Ps 115:1
because his *m* endureth for ever........ Ps 118:1
that his *m* endureth for ever........... Ps 118:2
that thy *m* endureth for ever........... Ps 118:3

that his *m* endureth for ever........... Ps 118:4
for his *m* endureth for ever............ Ps 118:29
earth, O LORD, is full of thy *m*........ Ps 119:64
thy servant according unto thy *m*....... Ps 119:124
God, until that he have *m* upon us...... Ps 123:2
Have *m* upon us, O LORD, have........... Ps 123:3
upon us, O LORD, have *m* upon us........ Ps 123:3
for with the LORD there is *m*........... Ps 130:7
for his *m* endureth for ever............ Ps 136:1
for his *m* endureth for ever............ Ps 136:2
for his *m* endureth for ever............ Ps 136:3
for his *m* endureth for ever............ Ps 136:4
for his *m* endureth for ever............ Ps 136:5
for his *m* endureth for ever............ Ps 136:6
for his *m* endureth for ever............ Ps 136:7
for his *m* endureth for ever............ Ps 136:8
for his *m* endureth for ever............ Ps 136:9
for his *m* endureth for ever............ Ps 136:10
for his *m* endureth for ever............ Ps 136:11
for his *m* endureth for ever............ Ps 136:12
for his *m* endureth for ever............ Ps 136:13
for his *m* endureth for ever............ Ps 136:14
for his *m* endureth for ever............ Ps 136:15
for his *m* endureth for ever............ Ps 136:16
for his *m* endureth for ever............ Ps 136:17
for his *m* endureth for ever............ Ps 136:18
for his *m* endureth for ever............ Ps 136:19
for his *m* endureth for ever............ Ps 136:20
for his *m* endureth for ever............ Ps 136:21
for his *m* endureth for ever............ Ps 136:22
for his *m* endureth for ever............ Ps 136:23
for his *m* endureth for ever............ Ps 136:24
for his *m* endureth for ever............ Ps 136:25
for his *m* endureth for ever............ Ps 136:26
thy *m*, O LORD, endureth for ever....... Ps 138:8
of thy *m* cut off mine enemies, and..... Ps 143:12
slow to anger, and great *m*............. Ps 145:8
him, in those that hope in his *m*....... Ps 147:11
Let not *m* and truth forsake thee....... Prov 3:3
but he that hath *m* on the poor......... Prov 14:21
but *m* and truth shall be to them....... Prov 14:22
honoureth him hath *m* on the poor....... Prov 14:31
By *m* and truth iniquity is purged...... Prov 16:6
M and truth preserve the king.......... Prov 20:28
and his throne is upholden by *m*........ Prov 20:28
in findeth life, righteousness, and...... Prov 21:21
and forsaketh them shall have *m*........ Prov 28:13
neither shall have *m* on their.......... Is 9:17
For the LORD will have *m* on Jacob...... Is 14:1
And in *m* shall the throne be........... Is 16:5
made them will not have *m* on them...... Is 27:11
that he may have *m* upon you............ Is 30:18
thou didst shew them no *m*.............. Is 47:6
for he that hath *m* on them shall....... Is 49:10
will have *m* upon his afflicted......... Is 49:13
kindness will I have *m* on thee......... Is 54:8
the LORD that hath *m* on thee........... Is 54:10
LORD, and he will have *m* upon him...... Is 55:7
in my favour have I had *m* on thee...... Is 60:10
they are cruel, and have no *m*.......... Jer 6:23
not pity, nor spare, nor have *m*........ Jer 13:14
neither have pity, nor have *m*.......... Jer 21:7
have *m* on his dwellingplaces........... Jer 30:18
I will surely have *m* upon him.......... Jer 31:20
for his *m* endureth for ever............ Jer 33:11
to return, and have *m* on them.......... Jer 33:26
you, that he may have *m* upon you....... Jer 42:12
are cruel, and will not shew *m*......... Jer 50:42
have *m* upon the whole house of......... Eze 39:25
by shewing *m* to the poor............... Dan 4:27
m to them that love him, and to........ Dan 9:4
for I will no more have *m* upon......... Hos 1:6
But I will have *m* upon the house....... Hos 1:7
I will not have *m* upon her............. Hos 2:4
I will have *m* upon her that had........ Hos 2:23
upon her that had not obtained *m*....... Hos 2:23
because there is no truth, nor *m*....... Hos 4:1
For I desired *m*, and not sacrifice..... Hos 6:6
in righteousness, reap in *m*............ Hos 10:12
keep *m* and judgment, and wait on....... Hos 12:6
in thee the fatherless findeth *m*....... Hos 14:3
vanities forsake their own *m*........... Jonah 2:8
but to do justly, and to love *m*........ Mic 6:8
ever, because he delighteth in *m*....... Mic 7:18
the *m* to Abraham, which thou hast...... Mic 7:20
in wrath remember *m*.................... Hab 3:2
wilt thou not have *m* on Jerusalem...... Zec 1:12
Execute true judgment, and shew *m*...... Zec 7:9
for I have *m* upon them................. Zec 10:6
for they shall obtain *m*................ Mt 5:7
what that meaneth, I will have *m*....... Mt 9:13
Thou son of David, have *m* on us........ Mt 9:27
what this meaneth, I will have *m*....... Mt 12:7
Have *m* on me, O Lord, thou son of...... Mt 15:22
Lord, have *m* on my son................. Mt 17:15
Have *m* on us, O Lord, thou son of...... Mt 20:30
Have *m* on us, O Lord, thou son of...... Mt 20:31
matters of the law, judgment, *m*........ Mt 23:23
thou son of David, have *m* on me........ Mk 10:47
Thou son of David, have *m* on me........ Mk 10:48
his *m* is on them that fear him......... Lk 1:50
Israel, in remembrance of his *m*........ Lk 1:54
Lord had shewed great *m* upon her....... Lk 1:58
To perform the *m* promised to our....... Lk 1:72
Through the tender *m* of our God........ Lk 1:78
he said, He that shewed *m* on him....... Lk 10:37
have *m* on me, and send Lazarus......... Lk 16:24
said, Jesus, Master, have *m* on us...... Lk 17:13
thou son of David, have *m* on me........ Lk 18:38
Thou son of David, have *m* on me........ Lk 18:39

I will have *m* on whom I will have...... Rom 9:15
have *m* on whom I will have *m*......... Rom 9:15
but of God that sheweth *m*.............. Rom 9:16
Therefore hath he *m* on whom he......... Rom 9:18
on whom he will have *m*................. Rom 9:18
of his glory on the vessels of *m*....... Rom 9:23
yet have now obtained *m* through........ Rom 11:30
that through your *m* they also may...... Rom 11:31
they also may obtain *m*................. Rom 11:31
that he might have *m* upon all.......... Rom 11:32
he that sheweth *m*, with................ Rom 12:8
might glorify God for his *m*............ Rom 15:9
as one that hath obtained *m* of......... 1Cor 7:25
ministry, as we have received *m*........ 2Cor 4:1
this rule, peace be on them, and *m*..... Gal 6:16
But God, who is rich in *m*.............. Eph 2:4
but God had *m* on him................... Phil 2:27
Grace, *m*, and peace, from God our...... 1Ti 1:2
but I obtained *m*, because I did........ 1Ti 1:13
for this cause I obtained *m*............ 1Ti 1:16
Grace, *m*, and peace, from God the...... 2Ti 1:2
The Lord give *m* unto the house of...... 2Ti 1:16
find *m* of the Lord in that day......... 2Ti 1:18
Grace, *m*, and peace, from God the...... Titus 1:4
according to his *m* he saved us......... Titus 3:5
of grace, that we may obtain *m*......... Heb 4:16
Moses' law died without *m* under........ Heb 10:28
he shall have judgment without *m*....... Jas 2:13
that hath shewed no *m*.................. Jas 2:13
m rejoiceth against judgment........... Jas 2:13
easy to be intreated, full of *m*........ Jas 3:17
is very pitiful, and of tender *m*....... Jas 5:11
m hath begotten us again unto a........ 1Pet 1:3
which had not obtained *m*............... 1Pet 2:10
but now have obtained *m*................ 1Pet 2:10
Grace be with you, *m*, and peace........ 2Jn 3
M unto you, and peace, and love, be.... Jude 2
looking for the *m* of our Lord.......... Jude 21

MERCYSEAT
of glory shadowing the *m*............... Heb 9:5

MERED (*me'-red*) A descendant of Judah.
sons of Ezra were, Jether, and *M*....... 1Chr 4:17
daughter of Pharaoh, which *M* took...... 1Chr 4:18

MEREMOTH (*mer'-e-moth*) See MERAIOTH.
1. Son of Uriah the priest.
of *M* the son of Uriah the priest....... Ezr 8:33
them repaired *M* the son of Urijah...... Neh 3:4
After him repaired *M* the son of........ Neh 3:21
2. Married a foreigner in exile.
Vaniah, *M*, Eliashib,................... Ezr 10:36
3. A priest who renewed the covenant.
Harim, *M*, Obadiah,..................... Neh 10:5
Shechaniah, Rehum, *M*,.................. Neh 12:3

MERES (*me'-res*) A prince of Media and Persia.
Shethar, Admatha, Tarshish, *M*.......... Est 1:14

MERIBAH (*mer'-i-bah*) See MASSAH, MERIBAH-KADESH. Same as Meribah-Kadesh.
name of the place Massah, and *M*........ Ex 17:7
This is the water of *M*................. Num 20:13
against my word at the water of *M*...... Num 20:24
that is the water of *M* in Kadesh....... Num 27:14
didst strive at the waters of *M*........ Deut 33:8
I proved thee at the waters of *M*....... Ps 81:7

MERIBAH-KADESH (*mer'-i-bah-ka'-desh*) A place between Zin and Sinai.
of Israel at the waters of *M*........... Deut 32:51

MERIBATH-KADESH See MERIBAH-KADESH.

MERIB-BAAL (*me-rib'-ba-al*) See MEPHIBOSHETH. Son of Jonathan.
And the son of Jonathan was *M*.......... 1Chr 8:34
and *M* begat Micah...................... 1Chr 8:34
And the son of Jonathan was *M*.......... 1Chr 9:40
and *M* begat Micah...................... 1Chr 9:40

MERODACH (*mer'-o-dak*) See BERODACH, EVIL-MERODACH, MERODACH-BALADAN. A Babylonian god of war.
confounded, *M* is broken in pieces...... Jer 50:2

MERODACH-BALADAN (*mer'-o-dak-bal'-a-dan*) See BERODACH-BALADAN. A king of Babylon.
At that time *M*, the son of............. Is 39:1

MEROM (*me'-rom*) A small lake north of the Sea of Chinnereth.
together at the waters of *M*............ Josh 11:5
them by the waters of *M* suddenly....... Josh 11:7

MERONOTHITE (*me-ron'-o-thite*) An inhabitant of a district of Zebulun.
over the asses was Jehdeiah the *M*...... 1Chr 27:30
the Gibeonite, and Jadon the *M*......... Neh 3:7

MEROZ (*me'-roz*) A place near Lake Merom.
Curse ye *M*, said the angel of the...... Judg 5:23

MERRILY
then go thou in *m* with the king........ Est 5:14

MERRY
and were *m* with him.................... Gen 43:34
and trode the grapes, and made *m*....... Judg 9:27
to pass, when their hearts were *m*...... Judg 16:25
night, and let thine heart be *m*........ Judg 19:6
here, that thine heart may be *m*........ Judg 19:9
they were making their hearts *m*........ Judg 19:22
and drunk, and his heart was *m*......... Ruth 3:7
Nabal's heart was *m* within him......... 1Sa 25:36

when Amnon's heart is *m* with wine.......2Sa 13:28
eating and drinking, and making *m*.....1Kin 4:20
bread, and let thine heart be *m*...........1Kin 21:7
m in heart for the goodness that.........2Chr 7:10
heart of the king was *m* with wine........Est 1:10
A *m* heart maketh a cheerful...............Prov 15:13
but he that is of a *m* heart hath.........Prov 15:15
A *m* heart doeth good like a...............Prov 17:22
to eat, and to drink, and to be *m*........Eccl 8:15
and drink thy wine with a *m* heart........Eccl 9:7
for laughter, and make maketh *m*..........Eccl 10:19
and the voice of them that make *m*........Jer 30:19
in the dances of them that make *m*........Jer 31:4
thine ease, eat, drink, and be *m*.........Lk 12:19
and let us eat, and be *m*..................Lk 15:23
And they began to be *m*....................Lk 15:24
I might make *m* with my friends............Lk 15:29
It was meet that we should make *m*........Lk 15:32
Is any *m*?.................................Jas 5:13
rejoice over them, and make *m*.............Rev 11:10

MERRYHEARTED

languisheth, all the *m* do sigh............Is 24:7

MESECH (*me´-sek*) See MESHECH. *A tribe joined to Kedar.*

Woe is me, that I sojourn in *M*............Ps 120:5

MESHA (*me´-shah*)
1. A place in southeastern Arabia.
And their dwelling was from *M*.............Gen 10:30
2. A king of Moab.
M king of Moab was a sheepmaster, *M*......2Kin 3:4
3. A son of Caleb.
M his firstborn, which was the.............1Chr 2:42
4. A son of Shaharaim.
his wife, Jobab, and Zibia, and............1Chr 8:9

MESHACH (*me´-shak*) *A companion of Daniel.*
and to Mishael, of M........................Dan 1:7
the king, and he set Shadrach, M...........Dan 2:49
province of Babylon, Shadrach, M...........Dan 3:13
commanded to bring Shadrach, M.............Dan 3:13
them, Is it true, O Shadrach, M.............Dan 3:14
Shadrach, M, and Abed-nego,................Dan 3:16
was changed against Shadrach, M............Dan 3:19
in his army to bind Shadrach, M............Dan 3:20
men that took up Shadrach, M...............Dan 3:22
And these three men, Shadrach, M...........Dan 3:23
and spake, and said, Shadrach, M...........Dan 3:26
Then Shadrach, M, and Abed-nego,...........Dan 3:26
Blessed be the God of Shadrach, M..........Dan 3:28
against the God of Shadrach, M.............Dan 3:29
the king promoted Shadrach, M..............Dan 3:30

MESHECH (*me´-shek*) See MESECH.
1. A son of Japheth.
Madai, and Javan, and Tubal, and M.........Gen 10:2
Madai, and Javan, and Tubal, and M.........1Chr 1:5
2. A son of Shem.
and Uz, and Hul, and Gether, and M.........1Chr 1:17
3. Descendants of Meschech I.
Javan, Tubal, and M, they were thy.........Eze 27:13
There is M, Tubal, and all her.............Eze 32:26
of Magog, the chief prince of M............Eze 38:2
O Gog, the chief prince of M...............Eze 38:3
O Gog, the chief prince of M...............Eze 39:1

MESHELEMIAH (*me-shel-e-mi´-ah*) See MESHULLAM, SHELEMIAH, SHALLUM. *Father of Zechariah.*
Zachariah the son of M was porter.........1Chr 9:21
Korhites was M the son of Kore.............1Chr 26:1
And the sons of M were, Zechariah..........1Chr 26:2
M had sons and brethren, strong............1Chr 26:9

MESHEZABEEL (*me-shez´-a-be-el*)
1. Father of Berechiah.
son of Berechiah, the son of M.............Neh 3:4
2. An Israelite who renewed the covenant.
M, Zadok, Jaddua,..........................Neh 10:21
And Pethahiah the son of M.................Neh 11:24

MESHEZABEL See MESHEZABEEL.

MESHILLEMITH (*me-shil´-le-mith*) See MESHILLEMOTH. *A family of exiles.*
son of Meshullam, the son of M.............1Chr 9:12

MESHILLEMOTH (*me-shil´-le-moth*) See MESHILLEMITH.
1. Father of Berechiah.
Johanan, Berechiah the son of M............2Chr 28:12
2. A family of exiles.
the son of Ahasai, the son of M............Neh 11:13

MESHOBAB (*me-sho´-bab*) *A chief of Simeon.*
And M, and Jamlech, and Joshah the.........1Chr 4:34

MESHULLAM (*me-shul´-lam*) See MESHILLEMITH.
1. A scribe in Josiah's time.
the son of Azaliah, the son of M...........2Kin 22:3
2. A descendant of Jeconiah.
M, and Hananiah, and Shelomith.............1Chr 3:19
3. Head of a Gadite family.
their fathers were, Michael, and M.........1Chr 5:13
4. A Beniamite of the Elpaal family.
Zebadiah, and M, and Hezekki,..............1Chr 8:17
5. Father of Sallu.
Sallu the son of M, the son of.............1Chr 9:7
6. Son of Shephathiah.
M the son of Shephatiah, the son...........1Chr 9:8
7. Father of Hilkiah.
the son of Hilkiah, the son of M...........1Chr 9:11
the son of Hilkiah, the son of M...........Neh 11:11

8. Son of Meshillemeth.
the son of Jahzerah, the son of M..........1Chr 9:12
9 A Kohathite repairer of the wall.
and Zechariah and M, of the sons of.......2Chr 34:12
10. A clan leader with Ezra.
and for Zechariah, and for M................Ezr 8:16
11. A priest who accounted for the foreign wives.
12. A son of Bani.
M, Malluch, and Adaiah, Jashub, and........Ezr 10:29
13. A son of Berechiah.
repaired M the son of Berechiah............Neh 3:4
After him repaired M the son of............Neh 3:30
of M the son of Berechiah..................Neh 6:18
14. A son of Besodeiah.
Paseah, and M the son of Besodeiah.........Neh 3:6
15. A Levite who aided Ezra.
and Hashhadana, Zechariah, and M...........Neh 8:4
16. A priest who renewed the covenant.
M, Abijah, Mijamin,........................Neh 10:7
17. A clan leader who renewed the covenant.
Magpiash, M, Hezir,........................Neh 10:20
18. A family of exiles.
Sallu the son of M, the son of.............Neh 11:7
19. A priest who dedicated the wall.
Of Ezra, M.................................Neh 12:13
And Azariah, Ezra, and M...................Neh 12:33
20. A descendant of Ginnethon.
of Ginnethon, M............................Neh 12:16
21. A Levite gatekeeper.
and Bakbukiah, Obadiah, M..................Neh 12:25

MESHULLEMETH (*me-shul´-le-meth*) *Mother of King Amon.*
And his mother's name was M................2Kin 21:19

MESOBAITE (*me-so´-ba-ite*) *Family name of Jasiel.*
Eliel, and Obed, and Jasiel the M..........1Chr 11:47

MESOPOTAMIA (*mes-o-po-ta´-me-ah*) See ARAM, NAHARAIM. *Land between the Tigris and Euphrates Rivers.*
and he arose, and went to M................Gen 24:10
the son of Beor of Pethor of M.............Deut 23:4
of Chushan-rishathaim king of M............Judg 3:8
king of M into his hand....................Judg 3:10
chariots and horsemen out of M.............1Chr 19:6
and Elamites, and the dwellers in M........Acts 2:9
father Abraham, when he was in.............Acts 7:2

MESS
but Benjamin's *m* was five times..........Gen 43:34
there followed him a *m* of meat...........2Sa 11:8

MESSAGE
I have a *m* from God unto thee.............Judg 3:20
pass, when Ben-hadad heard this in.........1Kin 20:12
He that sendeth a *m* by the hand..........Prov 26:6
in the LORD's m unto the people............Hag 1:13
sent a *m* after him, saying, We...........Lk 19:14
This then is the *m* which we have.........1Jn 1:5
For this is the *m* that ye heard..........1Jn 3:11

MESSENGER
And they sent a *m* unto Joseph............Gen 50:16
the *m* answered and said, Israel is.......1Sa 4:17
But there came a *m* unto Saul.............2Sa 11:19
And charged the *m*, saying, When..........2Sa 11:19
So the *m* went, and came and shewed.......2Sa 11:22
the *m* said unto David, Surely the........2Sa 11:23
Then David said unto the *m*...............2Sa 11:25
And there came a *m* to David..............2Sa 15:13
Then Jezebel sent a *m* unto Elijah........1Kin 19:2
the *m* that was gone to call..............1Kin 22:13
And Elisha sent a *m* unto him.............2Kin 5:10
but ere the *m* came to him................2Kin 6:32
look, when the *m* cometh, shut the........2Kin 6:32
behold, the *m* came down unto him.........2Kin 6:33
The *m* came to them, but he cometh........2Kin 9:18
And there came a *m*, and told him,........2Kin 9:18
the *m* that went to call Micaiah..........2Chr 18:12
And there came a *m* unto Job..............Job 1:14
If there be a *m* with him, an.............Job 33:23
A wicked *m* falleth into mischief.........Prov 13:17
therefore a cruel *m* shall be sent........Prov 17:11
so is a faithful *m* to them that..........Prov 25:13
or deaf, as my *m* that I sent.............Is 42:19
one *m* to meet another, to shew...........Jer 51:31
from far, unto whom a *m* was sent.........Eze 23:40
Then spake Haggai the LORD's *m* in........Hag 1:13
for he is the *m* of the LORD of...........Mal 2:7
Behold, I will send my *m*, and he.........Mal 3:1
even the *m* of the covenant, whom.........Mal 3:1
I send my *m* before thy face,.............Mt 11:10
I send my *m* before thy face,.............Mk 1:2
I send my *m* before thy face,.............Lk 7:27
the *m* of Satan to buffet me, lest........2Cor 12:7
and fellow soldier, but your *m*...........Phil 2:25

MESSENGERS
Jacob sent *m* before him to Esau..........Gen 32:3
the *m* returned to Jacob, saying,.........Gen 32:6
Moses sent *m* from Kadesh unto the........Num 20:14
Israel sent *m* unto Sihon king of.........Num 21:21
He sent *m* therefore unto Balaam..........Num 22:5
Spake I not also to thy *m* which..........Num 24:12
I sent *m* out of the wilderness of........Deut 2:26
she hid the *m* that we sent...............Josh 6:17
because she hid the *m*, which.............Josh 6:25
So Joshua sent *m*, and they ran...........Josh 7:22
he sent *m* throughout all Manasseh........Judg 6:35

he sent *m* unto Asher, and unto...........Judg 6:35
Gideon sent *m* throughout all.............Judg 7:24
he sent *m* unto Abimelech privily,........Judg 9:31
Jephthah sent *m* unto the king of.........Judg 11:12
answered unto the *m* of Jephthah..........Judg 11:13
Jephthah sent *m* again unto the...........Judg 11:14
Then Israel sent *m* unto the king.........Judg 11:17
Israel sent *m* unto Sihon king of.........Judg 11:19
they sent *m* to the inhabitants of........1Sa 6:21
that we may send *m* unto all the..........1Sa 11:3
Then came the *m* to Gibeah of Saul........1Sa 11:4
of Israel by the hands of..................1Sa 11:7
And they said unto the *m* that came.......1Sa 11:9
the *m* came and shewed it to the..........1Sa 11:9
Wherefore Saul sent *m* unto Jesse.........1Sa 16:19
Saul also sent *m* unto David's............1Sa 19:11
And when Saul sent *m* to take David.......1Sa 19:14
Saul sent the *m* again to see.............1Sa 19:15
when the *m* were come in, behold,.........1Sa 19:16
Saul sent *m* to take David................1Sa 19:20
of God was upon the *m* of Saul,...........1Sa 19:20
it was told Saul, he sent other *m*........1Sa 19:21
Saul sent *m* again the third time,........1Sa 19:21
Behold, David sent *m* out of the..........1Sa 25:42
and she went after the *m* of David........1Sa 25:42
David sent *m* unto the men of.............2Sa 2:5
Abner sent *m* to David on his.............2Sa 3:12
David sent *m* to Ish-bosheth..............2Sa 3:14
he sent *m* after Abner, which.............2Sa 3:26
king of Tyre sent *m* to David.............2Sa 5:11
And David sent *m*, and took her...........2Sa 11:4
And Joab sent *m* to David, and said,......2Sa 12:27
he sent *m* to Ahab king of Israel.........1Kin 20:2
The *m* came again, and said, Thus.........1Kin 20:5
he said unto the *m* of Ben-hadad..........1Kin 20:9
the *m* departed, and brought him..........1Kin 20:9
and he sent *m*, and said unto them,.......2Kin 1:2
go up to meet the *m* of the king..........2Kin 1:3
when the *m* turned back unto him,.........2Kin 1:5
Forasmuch as thou hast sent *m* to.........2Kin 1:16
the *m* returned, and told the king........2Kin 7:15
Then Amaziah sent *m* to Jehoash...........2Kin 14:8
So Ahaz sent *m* to Tiglath-pileser........2Kin 16:7
for he had sent *m* to So king of..........2Kin 17:4
he sent *m* again unto Hezekiah,...........2Kin 19:9
the letter of the hand of the *m*.........2Kin 19:14
By thy *m* thou hast reproached the........2Kin 19:23
king of Tyre sent *m* to David.............1Chr 14:1
David sent *m* to comfort him..............1Chr 19:2
worse before Israel, they sent *m*.........1Chr 19:16
fathers sent to them by his *m*............2Chr 36:15
But they mocked the *m* of God.............2Chr 36:16
I sent *m* unto them, saying, I am.........Neh 6:3
wrath of a king is as *m* of death.........Prov 16:14
then answer the *m* of the nation..........Is 14:32
waters, saying, Go, ye swift *m*...........Is 18:2
he sent *m* to Hezekiah, saying,...........Is 37:9
the letter from the hand of the *m*.......Is 37:14
performeth the counsel of his *m*..........Is 44:26
and didst send thy *m* far off.............Is 57:9
by the hand of the *m* which come..........Jer 27:3
sent *m* unto them into Chaldea............Eze 23:16
In that day shall *m* go forth from........Eze 30:9
the voice of thy *m* shall no more.........Nah 2:13
when the *m* of John were departed,........Lk 7:24
And sent *m* before his face...............Lk 9:52
they are the *m* of the churches,..........2Cor 8:23
when she had received the *m*..............Jas 2:25

MESSES
sent *m* unto them from before him.........Gen 43:34

MESSIAH (*mes-si´-ah*) See MESSIAS. *The great Deliverer of Israel.*
to build Jerusalem unto the M the.........Dan 9:25
and two weeks shall be M be cut off........Dan 9:26

MESSIAS (*mes-si´-as*) See MESSIAH. *Greek form of Messiah.*
unto him, We have found the M..............Jn 1:41
unto him, I know that M cometh.............Jn 4:25

MET
way, and the angels of God *m* him.........Gen 32:1
thou by all this drove which I *m*.........Gen 33:8
God of the Hebrews hath *m* with us........Ex 3:18
in the rain, that the LORD *m* him.........Ex 4:24
m him in the mount of God, and...........Ex 4:27
God of the Hebrews hath *m* with us........Ex 5:3
they *m* Moses and Aaron, who stood........Ex 5:20
And God *m* Balaam.........................Num 23:4
And the LORD *m* Balaam, and put a.........Num 23:16
Because they *m* you not with bread........Deut 23:4
How he *m* thee by the way, and............Deut 25:18
all these kings were *m* together..........Josh 11:5
they *m* together in Asher on the..........Josh 17:10
a company of prophets *m* him..............1Sa 10:10
and she *m* them.............................1Sa 25:20
m together by the pool of Gibeon.........2Sa 2:13
the servant of Mephibosheth *m* him........2Sa 16:1
Absalom *m* the servants of David..........2Sa 18:9
a lion *m* him by the way, and slew........1Kin 13:24
in the way, behold, Elijah *m* him.........1Kin 18:7
m him in the portion of Naboth...........2Kin 9:21
Jehu *m* with the brethren of..............2Kin 10:13
Because they *m* not the children..........Neh 13:2
Mercy and truth are *m* together...........Ps 85:10
there *m* him a woman with the.............Prov 7:10
and it came to pass, as he *m* them,.......Prov 17:12
flee from a lion, and a bear *m* him,......Amos 5:19
there *m* him two possessed with............Mt 8:28
disciples, behold, Jesus *m* them..........Mt 28:9

immediately there m him out of .... Mk 5:2
in a place where two ways m .... Mk 11:4
there m him out of the city a................ Lk 8:27
from the hill, much people m him........ Lk 9:37
there m him ten men that were .... Lk 17:12
going down, his servants m him .... Jn 4:51
Jesus was coming, went and m him.... Jn 11:20
in that place where Martha m him ...... Jn 11:30
this cause the people also m him .... Jn 12:18
was coming in, Cornelius m him........ Acts 10:25
with a spirit of divination m us......... Acts 16:16
daily with them that m with him........ Acts 17:17
when he m with us at Assos, we .... Acts 20:14
into a place where two seas m .... Acts 27:41
who m Abraham returning from the .... Heb 7:1
father, when Melchisedec m him .... Heb 7:10

METE
when they did m it with an omer, ... Ex 16:18
m out the valley of Succoth .... Ps 60:6
m out the valley of Succoth .... Ps 108:7
and with what measure ye m .... Mt 7:2
with what measure ye m, it shall........ Mk 4:24
with the same measure that ye .... Lk 6:38

METED
a nation m out and trodden down,...... Is 18:2
a nation m out and trodden under ...... Is 18:7
m out heaven with the span, and ...... Is 40:12

METEYARD
unrighteousness in judgment, in m .... Lev 19:35

METHEG-AMMAH (me'-theg-am'-mah) A
place in Philistia.
David took M out of the hand of 2Sa 8:1

METHUSAEL (me-thu'-sa-el) A descendant of
Cain.
and Mehujael begat M .... Gen 4:18
and M begat Lamech .... Gen 4:18

METHUSELAH (me-thu'-se-lah) See
MATHUSALA. Of Enoch.
sixty and five years, and begat M ...... Gen 5:21
he begat M three hundred years........ Gen 5:22
M lived an hundred eighty and .... Gen 5:25
M lived after he begat Lamech.......... Gen 5:26
all the days of M were nine .... Gen 5:27
Henoch, M, Lamech,......................... 1Chr 1:3

METHUSHAEL See METHUSAEL.

MEUNIM (me-u'-nim) See MEHUNIM. A family
of exiles.
of Besai, the children of M .... Neh 7:52

MEUNITES See MEHUNIMS.

MEZAHAB (mez'-a-hab) Grandfather of
Mehetabel.
of Matred, the daughter of M .... Gen 36:39
of Matred, the daughter of M 1Chr 1:50

MEZOBAITE See MESOBAITE.

MIAMIN (mi'-a-min) See MIJAMIN, MINIAMIN.
1. Married a foreigner in exile.
and Jeziah, and Malchiah, and M ...... Ezr 10:25
2. A priest with Zerubbabel.
M, Maadiah, Bilgah,......................... Neh 12:5

MIBHAR (mib'-har) A 'mighty man' of David.
of Nathan, the son of Haggeri,......... 1Chr 11:38

MIBSAM (mib'-sam)
1. A son of Ishmael.
and Kedar, and Adbeel, and M.......... Gen 25:13
then Kedar, and Adbeel, and M 1Chr 1:29
2. A son of Simeon.
M his son, Mishma his son................ 1Chr 4:25

MIBZAR (mib'-zar) A descendant of Esau.
Duke Kenaz, duke Teman, duke M .... Gen 36:42
Duke Kenaz, duke Teman, duke M 1Chr 1:53

MICA See MICHA.

MICAH (mi'-cah) See MICAIAH, MICAH'S,
MICHAH.
1. An Ephraimite who set up idols.
mount Ephraim, whose name was M.. Judg 17:1
and they were in the house of M .... Judg 17:4
the man M had an house of gods,...... Judg 17:5
mount Ephraim to the house of M ..... Judg 17:8
M said unto him, Whence comest...... Judg 17:9
M said unto him, Dwell with me,....... Judg 17:10
And M consecrated the Levite .... Judg 17:12
priest, and was in the house of M ..... Judg 17:12
Then said M, Now know I that the .... Judg 17:13
mount Ephraim, to the house of M.... Judg 18:2
When they were by the house of M ... Judg 18:3
Thus and thus dealeth M with me ..... Judg 18:4
and came unto the house of M.......... Judg 18:13
Levite, even unto the house of M ..... Judg 18:15
a good way from the house of M .... Judg 18:22
their faces, and said unto M .... Judg 18:23
when M saw that they were too........ Judg 18:26
took the things which M had made.... Judg 18:27
2. Head of a Reubenite family.
M his son, Reaia his son, Baal........... 1Chr 5:5
3. Son of Merib-baal.
and Merib-baal begat M 1Chr 8:34
And the sons of M were, Pithon, and.. 1Chr 8:35
and Merib-baal begat M 1Chr 9:40
And the sons of M were, Pithon, and.. 1Chr 9:41
4. A family of exiles.
Galal, and Mattaniah the son of M.... 1Chr 9:15

5. A sanctuary servant.
M the first, and Jesiah the second 1Chr 23:20
6. Father of Abdon.
and Abdon the son of M.................... 2Chr 34:20
7. A prophet.
M the Morasthite prophesied in .... Jer 26:18
the M the Morasthite in the days of.... Mic 1:1

MICAH'S (mi'-cahs) Refers to Micah 1.
And these went into M house .... Judg 18:18
to M house were gathered together.... Judg 18:22
they set them up M graven image ..... Judg 18:31

MICAIAH (mi-ka-i'-ah) See MICHA, MICHAIAH.
A prophet who foretold Ahab's fall.
M the son of Imlah, by whom we 1Kin 22:8
Hasten hither M the son of Imlah...... 1Kin 22:9
was gone to call M spake unto him.... 1Kin 22:13
M said, As the LORD liveth, what 1Kin 22:14
And the king said unto him, M 1Kin 22:15
smote M on the cheek, and said, ... 1Kin 22:24
M said, Behold, thou shalt see in 1Kin 22:25
the king of Israel said, Take M 1Kin 22:26
M said, If thou return at all in 1Kin 22:28
the same is M the son of Imla 2Chr 18:7
Fetch quickly M the son of Imla........ 2Chr 18:8
that went to call M spake to him 2Chr 18:12
M said, As the LORD liveth, even....... 2Chr 18:13
king, the king said unto him, M 2Chr 18:14
smote M upon the cheek, and said, ... 2Chr 18:23
M said, Behold, thou shalt see on 2Chr 18:24
king of Israel said, Take ye M 2Chr 18:25
M said, If thou certainly return 2Chr 18:27

MICE
golden emerods, and five golden m.... 1Sa 6:4
images of your m that mar the 1Sa 6:5
and the coffer with the m of gold 1Sa 6:11
And the golden m, according to the.... 1Sa 6:18

MICHA (mi'-cah) See MICAH, MICAIAH.
1. Son of Mephibosheth.
had a young son, whose name was M.. 2Sa 9:12
2. A Levite who renewed the covenant.
M, Rehob, Hashabiah, ... Neh 10:11
3. A family of exiles.
And Mattaniah the son of M .... Neh 11:17
son of Mattaniah, the son of M .... Neh 11:22

MICHAEL (mi'-ka-el)
1. Father of Sethur.
of Asher, Sethur the son of M .... Num 13:13
2. A Gadite who settled in Bashan.
house of their fathers were, ... 1Chr 5:13
3. Son of Jeshishai.
the son of Gilead, the son of M 1Chr 5:14
4. Son of Baaseiah.
The son of M, the son of Baaseiah..... 1Chr 6:40
5. A chief man of Issachar.
and Obadiah, and Joel, Ishiah,......... 1Chr 7:3
6. A Benjamite in Jerusalem.
And M, and Ispah, and Joha, the sons.. 1Chr 8:16
7. A warrior in David's army.
and Jozabad, and Jediael, and M 1Chr 12:20
8. Father of Omri.
of Issachar, Omri the son of M 1Chr 27:18
9. A son of Jehoshaphat.
and Zechariah, and Azariah, and M... 2Chr 21:2
10. A family of exiles.
Zebadiah the son of M, and with ...... Ezr 8:8
11. Angelic messenger who came to Daniel.
but, lo, M, one of the chief .... Dan 10:13
these things, but M your prince........ Dan 10:21
And at that time shall M stand up...... Dan 12:1
Yet M the archangel, when .... Jude 9
M and his angels fought against .... Rev 12:7

MICHAH (mi'-cah) See MICAH, MICHAIAH. A
sanctuary servant.
sons of Uzziel; M................................ 1Chr 24:24
of the sons of M 1Chr 24:24
The brother of M was Isshiah............ 1Chr 24:25

MICHAIAH (mi-ka-i'-ah) See MICHA, MICAIAH.
1. Father of Achbor.
Shaphan, and Achbor the son of M ... 2Kin 22:12
2. Wife of King Rehoboam.
His mother's name also was M the..... 2Chr 13:2
3. A prince of Judah.
and to Nethaneel, and to M 2Chr 17:7
4. A priest with Zerubbabel.
son of Mattaniah, the son of M .... Neh 12:35
Eliakim, Maaseiah, Miniamin, M ...... Neh 12:41
5. Son of Gemariah.
When M the son of Gemariah, the..... Jer 36:11
Then M declared unto them all the ... Jer 36:13

MICHAL (mi'-kal) See EGLAH. A wife of David.
and the name of the younger M......... 1Sa 14:49
M Saul's daughter loved David 1Sa 18:20
Saul gave him M his daughter to 1Sa 18:27
that M Saul's daughter loved him...... 1Sa 18:28
M David's wife told him, saying,....... 1Sa 19:11
So M let David down through a 1Sa 19:12
M took an image, and laid it in 1Sa 19:13
and Saul said unto M, Why hast,....... 1Sa 19:17
M answered Saul, He said unto me, .. 1Sa 19:17
But Saul had given M his daughter ... 1Sa 25:44
first bring M Saul's daughter............ 2Sa 3:13
son, saying, Deliver me my wife M ... 2Sa 3:14
M Saul's daughter looked through..... 2Sa 6:16
M the daughter of Saul came out....... 2Sa 6:20
And David said unto M, It was.......... 2Sa 6:21
Therefore M the daughter of Saul 2Sa 6:23

the five sons of M the daughter......... 2Sa 21:8
that M the daughter of Saul 1Chr 15:29

MICHMAS (mik'-mas) See MICHMASH. Home
of some exiles.
The men of M, an hundred twenty .... Ezr 2:27
The men of M, an hundred and .... Neh 7:31

MICHMASH (mik'-mash) See MICHMAS. A city
near Jerusalem.
two thousand were with Saul in M 1Sa 13:2
and they came up, and pitched in M .. 1Sa 13:5
gathered themselves together at M 1Sa 13:11
but the Philistines encamped in M 1Sa 13:16
went out to the passage of M 1Sa 13:23
situate northward over against M 1Sa 14:5
that day from M to Aijalon................ 1Sa 14:31
of Benjamin from Geba dwelt at M .... Neh 11:31
at M he hath laid up his................... Is 10:28

MICHMETHAH (mik'-me-thah) A city
between Ephraim and Manasseh.
the sea to M on the north side .... Josh 16:6
of Manasseh was from Asher to M..... Josh 17:7

MICHMETHATH See MICHMETHAH.

MICHRI (mik'-ri) Father of Uzzi.
the son of Uzzi, the son of M............ 1Chr 9:8

MICHTAM (mik'-tam) A type of psalm.
M of David .... Ps 16:t
A m of David, when the .... Ps 56:t
M of David, when he fled from .... Ps 57:t
Michtam, Altaschith, M of David ...... Ps 58:t
Musican, Altaschith, M of David ...... Ps 59:t
M of David, to teach .... Ps 60:t

MICMASH See MICHMASH.

MICMETHAH See MICHMETHAH.

MICRI See MICHRI.

MIDDAY
to pass, when m was past, and they .. 1Kin 18:29
gate from the morning until m .... Neh 8:3
At m, O king, I saw in the way a ...... Acts 26:13

MIDDIN (mid'-din) A city in the wilderness
south of Judah.
in the wilderness, Beth-arabah, M..... Josh 15:61

MIDDLE
the m bar in the midst of the .... Ex 26:28
he made the m bar to shoot .... Ex 36:33
from the m of the river, and from...... Josh 12:2
in the beginning of the m watch....... Judg 7:19
people down by the m of the land ..... Judg 9:37
Samson took hold of the two m .... Judg 16:29
out, as out of the m of a sling........... 1Sa 25:29
cut off their garments in the m.......... 2Sa 10:4
the m was six cubits broad, and........ 1Kin 6:6
The door for the m chamber was in ... 1Kin 6:8
winding stairs into the m chamber 1Kin 6:8
out of the m into the third................ 1Kin 6:8
day did the king hallow the m of 1Kin 8:64
was gone out into the m court 2Kin 20:4
m of the court that was before 2Chr 7:7
came in, and sat in the m gate.......... Jer 39:3
were a wheel in the m of a wheel...... Eze 1:16
hath broken down the m wall of .... Eph 2:14

MIDDLEMOST
than the m of the building................. Eze 42:5
lowest and the m from the ground .... Eze 42:6

MIDIAN (mid'-e-an) See MADIAN, MIDIANITE.
1. A son of Abraham.
and Jokshan, and Medan, and .... Gen 25:2
And the sons of M............................ Gen 25:4
and Jokshan, and Medan, and 1Chr 1:32
And the sons of M............................ 1Chr 1:33
2. A nation on the southern border of Israel.
who smote M in the field of Moab..... Gen 36:35
and dwelt in the land of M .... Ex 2:15
Now the priest of M had seven......... Ex 2:16
father in law, the priest of M .... Ex 3:1
And the LORD said unto Moses in M.. Ex 4:19
When Jethro, the priest of M .... Ex 18:1
And Moab said unto the elders of M.. Num 22:4
the elders of M departed with the ..... Num 22:7
people, and of a chief house in M ..... Num 25:15
the daughter of a prince of M .... Num 25:18
and avenge the LORD of M .... Num 31:3
And they slew the kings of M .... Num 31:8
and Hur, and Reba, five kings of M... Num 31:8
took all the women of M captives ..... Num 31:9
Moses smote with the princes of M ... Josh 13:21
into the hand of M seven years .... Judg 6:1
the hand of M prevailed against .... Judg 6:2
the host of M was beneath him in..... Judg 7:8
bread tumbled into the host of M ..... Judg 7:13
his hand hath God delivered M .... Judg 7:14
into your hand the host of M............ Judg 7:15
wine press of Zeeb, and pursued M... Judg 7:25
into your hands the princes of M...... Judg 8:3
Zebah and Zalmunna, kings of M ..... Judg 8:5
them, and took the two kings of M ... Judg 8:12
delivered us from the hand of M ...... Judg 8:22
that was on the kings of M .... Judg 8:26
Thus was M subdued before the .... Judg 8:28
you out of the hand of M .... Judg 9:17
And they arose out of M, and came .. 1Kin 11:18
which smote M in the field of 1Chr 1:46
his oppressor, as in the day of M ..... Is 9:4
of M at the rock of Oreb................... Is 10:26

cover thee, the dromedaries of M............ Is 60:6
of the land of M did tremble.................. Hab 3:7

MIDIANITE (*mid'-e-an-ite*) See MIDIANITES,
MIDIANITISH. A descendant of Midian.
Hobab, the son of Raguel the M........... Num 10:29

MIDIANITES (*mid'-e-an-ites*) See KENITES.
there passed by M merchantmen........... Gen 37:28
the M sold him into Egypt unto............. Gen 37:36
Vex the M, and smite them................... Num 25:17
the children of Israel of the M.............. Num 31:2
war, and let them go against the M...... Num 31:3
And they warred against the M............. Num 31:7
because of the M the children of.......... Judg 6:2
had sown, that the M came up............. Judg 6:3
impoverished because of the M........... Judg 6:6
unto the LORD because of the M.......... Judg 6:7
winepress, to hide it from the M.......... Judg 6:11
us into the hands of the M................... Judg 6:13
Israel from the hand of the M............. Judg 6:14
thou shalt smite the M as one man...... Judg 6:16
Then all the M and the Amalekites...... Judg 6:33
so that the host of the M were on......... Judg 7:1
me to give the M into their hands........ Judg 7:2
deliver the M into thine hand.............. Judg 7:7
the M and the Amalekites..................... Judg 7:12
Manasseh, and pursued after the M.... Judg 7:23
saying, Come down against the M....... Judg 7:24
And they took two princes of the M..... Judg 7:25
thou wentest to fight with the M.......... Judg 8:1
Do unto them as unto the M................. Ps 83:9

MIDIANITISH (*mid'-e-an-i'-tish*) Belonging to
the land of Midian.
a M woman in the sight of Moses........ Num 25:6
that was slain with the M woman......... Num 25:14
the name of the M woman that was...... Num 25:15

MIDNIGHT
About m will I go out into the.............. Ex 11:4
that at m the LORD smote all the.......... Ex 12:29
lay till m, and arose at m.................... Judg 16:3
And it came to pass at m, that the...... Ruth 3:8
And she arose at m, and took my son 1Kin 3:20
the people shall be troubled at m........ Job 34:20
At m I will rise to give thanks............. Ps 119:62
at m there was a cry made, Behold...... Mt 25:6
house cometh, at even, or at m........... Mk 13:35
friend, and shall go unto him at m....... Lk 11:5
at m Paul and Silas prayed, and......... Acts 16:25
and continued his speech until m......... Acts 20:7
about m the shipmen deemed that....... Acts 27:27

MIDST See PREFACE.
firmament in the m of the waters......... Gen 1:6
life also in the m of the garden........... Gen 2:9
upon dry land in the m of the sea........ Ex 14:29
on dry land in the m of the sea............ Ex 15:19
God is in the m of her.......................... Ps 46:5
me not away in the m of my days........ Ps 102:24
lieth down in the m of the sea............. Prov 23:34
One of Israel in the m of thee............. Is 12:6
walking in the m of the fire................. Dan 3:25
the Holy One in the m of thee.............. Hos 11:9
forth as sheep in the m of wolves........ Mt 10:16
him, and set him in the m of them....... Mt 18:2
and set him in the m of them............... Mk 9:36
himself stood in the m of them............ Lk 24:36
came Jesus and stood in the m............ Jn 20:19
being shut, and stood in the m............ Jn 20:26

MIDWIFE
that the m said unto her, Fear............. Gen 35:17
the m took and bound upon his hand Gen 38:28
office of a m to the Hebrew women..... Ex 1:16

MIDWIVES
of Egypt spake to the Hebrew m......... Ex 1:15
But the m feared God, and did not...... Ex 1:17
king of Egypt called for the m............. Ex 1:18
the m said unto Pharaoh, Because...... Ex 1:19
ere the m come in unto them............... Ex 1:19
God dealt well with the m................... Ex 1:20
to pass, because the m feared God..... Ex 1:21

MIGDAL EDER

MIGDAL-EL (*mig'-dal-el*) A city in Naphtali.
And Iron, and M, Horem, and............. Josh 19:38

MIGDAL-GAD (*mig'-dal-gad*) A city in Judah.
Zenan, and Hadashah, and M,............ Josh 15:37

MIGDOL (*mig'-dol*)
1. A place west of the Red Sea.
before Pi-hahiroth, between M............. Ex 14:2
and they pitched before M................... Num 33:7
2. A place in northern Egypt.
land of Egypt, which dwell at M.......... Jer 44:1
ye in Egypt, and publish in M.............. Jer 46:14

MIGHT See PREFACE.
thy works, and according to thy m...... Deut 3:24
all thy soul, and with all thy m............ Deut 6:5
and in thine hand is power and m........ 1Chr 29:12
that I m not sin against thee................ Ps 119:11
of them to do the terrible acts............. Ps 145:6
findeth to do, do it with thy m............. Eccl 9:10
let the mighty man glory in his m......... Jer 9:23
unto Zerubbabel, saying, Not by m..... Zec 4:6
all men through him m be.................... Jn 1:7
the world through him m be saved...... Jn 3:17
I am come that they m have life.......... Jn 10:10
life, and that they m have it more........ Jn 10:10
to be strengthened with m by his........ Eph 3:16

Strengthened with all m,..................... Col 1:11
and honour, and power, and m........... Rev 7:12

MIGHTEST
that thou m know that the LORD he..... Deut 4:35
That thou m fear the LORD thy God..... Deut 6:2
wherewith thou m be bound to........... Judg 16:6
thee, wherewith thou m be bound........ Judg 16:10
tell me wherewith thou m be bound..... Judg 16:13
down that thou m see the battle.......... 1Sa 17:28
that thou m bring them again unto...... Neh 9:29
that thou m still the enemy and........... Ps 8:2
that thou m be justified when.............. Ps 51:4
that thou m answer the words of......... Prov 22:21
that thou m know the thoughts of........ Dan 2:30
thou m be profited by me.................... Mt 15:5
thou m be profited by me.................... Mk 7:11
That thou m know the certainty of....... Lk 1:4
that thou m receive thy sight, and....... Acts 9:17
That thou m be justified in thy............ Rom 3:4
m overcome when thou art judged....... Rom 3:4
that thou m charge some that they...... 1Ti 1:3
that thou by them m war a good.......... 1Ti 1:18

MIGHTIER
for thou art much m than we............... Gen 26:16
of Israel are more and m than we........ Ex 1:9
a greater nation and m than they......... Num 14:12
m than thou art, to bring thee in......... Deut 4:38
nations greater and m than thou.......... Deut 7:1
m than thyself, cities great and........... Deut 9:1
and I will make of thee a nation m...... Deut 9:14
nations and m than yourselves............ Deut 11:23
The LORD on high is m than the.......... Ps 93:4
with him that is m than he.................. Eccl 6:10
but cometh after me is m than I.......... Mt 3:11
cometh one m than I after me............. Mk 1:7
but one m than I cometh, the.............. Lk 3:16

MIGHTIES
who was one of the three m................ 1Chr 11:12
the name among the three m............... 1Chr 11:24

MIGHTIEST
These things did these three m............ 1Chr 11:19

MIGHTILY
thee, and that ye may increase m........ Deut 6:3
twenty years in the m oppressed........ Judg 4:3
of the LORD came m upon him............. Judg 14:6
of the LORD came m upon him............. Judg 15:14
he shall m roar upon his..................... Jer 25:30
with sackcloth, and cry m unto God.... Jonah 3:8
loins strong, fortify thy power m.......... Nah 2:1
For he m convinced the Jews, and....... Acts 18:28
So m grew the word of God and.......... Acts 19:20
working, which worketh in me m......... Col 1:29
he cried m with a strong voice,........... Rev 18:2

MIGHTY
the same became m men which were... Gen 6:4
began to be a m one in the earth......... Gen 10:8
He was a m hunter before the LORD.... Gen 10:9
Even as Nimrod the m hunter.............. Gen 10:9
m nation, and all the nations of........... Gen 18:18
thou art a m prince among us.............. Gen 23:6
the hands of the m God of Jacob........ Gen 49:24
multiplied, and waxed exceeding m..... Ex 1:7
multiplied, and waxed very m.............. Ex 1:20
let you go, no, not by a m hand........... Ex 3:19
there be no more m thunderings.......... Ex 9:28
LORD turned a m strong west wind...... Ex 10:19
they sank as lead in the m waters........ Ex 15:10
the m men of Moab, trembling............ Ex 15:15
great power, and with a m hand.......... Ex 32:11
nor honour the person of the m........... Lev 19:15
for they are too m for me.................... Num 22:6
thy greatness, and thy m hand............ Deut 3:24
and by war, and by a m hand.............. Deut 4:34
with his m power out of Egypt............. Deut 4:37
thee out thence through a m hand....... Deut 5:15
us out of Egypt with a m hand............ Deut 6:21
brought you out with a m hand........... Deut 7:8
the m hand, and the stretched out....... Deut 7:19
is among you, a m God and terrible..... Deut 7:21
destroy them with a m destruction...... Deut 7:23
forth out of Egypt with a m hand........ Deut 9:26
broughtest out by thy m power........... Deut 9:29
Lord of lords, a great God, a m........... Deut 10:17
his m hand, and his stretched out....... Deut 11:2
became there a nation, great, m.......... Deut 26:5
forth out of Egypt with a m hand........ Deut 26:8
And in all that m hand, and in all........ Deut 34:12
all the m men of valour, and help........ Josh 1:14
hand of the Loan, that it is m.............. Josh 4:24
thereof, and the m men of valour........ Josh 6:2
thirty thousand m men of valour......... Josh 8:3
Ai, and all the men thereof were m...... Josh 10:2
him, and all the m men of valour......... Josh 10:7
made me have dominion over the m..... Judg 5:13
the pransings of their m ones............. Judg 5:22
help of the LORD against the m........... Judg 5:23
with thee, thou m man of valour......... Judg 6:12
Gileadite was a m man of valour......... Judg 11:1
a m man of wealth, of the family......... Ruth 2:1
The bows of the m men are broken..... 1Sa 2:4
out of the hand of these m Gods......... 1Sa 4:8
to a Benjamin, a m man of power........ 1Sa 9:1
a m valiant man, and a man of war,.... 1Sa 16:18
how are the m fallen........................... 2Sa 1:19
of the m is vilely cast away................. 2Sa 1:21
the stain, from the fat of the m............ 2Sa 1:22
How are the m fallen in the midst....... 2Sa 1:25

How are the m fallen, and the............. 2Sa 1:27
and all the host of the m men............. 2Sa 10:7
all the m men were on his right........... 2Sa 16:6
and his men, that they be m men........ 2Sa 17:8
that thy father is a m man.................. 2Sa 17:10
the Pelethites, and all the m men........ 2Sa 20:7
names of the m men whom David had. 2Sa 23:8
one of the three m men with David...... 2Sa 23:9
the three m men brake through the..... 2Sa 23:16
things did these three m..................... 2Sa 23:17
the name among three m men............. 2Sa 23:22
the m men which belonged to David.... 1Kin 1:8
prophet, and Benaiah, and the m men 1Kin 1:10
Jeroboam was a m man of valour........ 1Kin 11:28
he was also a m man of valour........... 2Kin 5:1
even of all the m men of wealth.......... 2Kin 15:20
all the m men of valour, even ten........ 2Kin 24:14
the m of the land, those carried.......... 2Kin 24:15
he began to be m upon the earth........ 1Chr 1:10
m men of valour, famous men, and..... 1Chr 5:24
of their fathers, m men of valour........ 1Chr 7:7
m men of valour, was twenty.............. 1Chr 7:9
m men of valour, were seventeen....... 1Chr 7:11
m men of valour, chief of the............. 1Chr 7:40
sons of Ulam were m men of valour.... 1Chr 8:40
chief of the m men whom David had.... 1Chr 11:10
of the m men whom David had........... 1Chr 11:11
and they were among the m men......... 1Chr 12:1
a m man among the thirty, and over.... 1Chr 12:4
for they were all m men of valour....... 1Chr 12:21
m men of valour for the war,.............. 1Chr 12:25
a young man m of valour..................... 1Chr 12:28
hundred, m men of valour, famous...... 1Chr 12:30
and all the host of the m men............. 1Chr 19:8
for they were m men of valour............ 1Chr 26:6
them m men of valour at Jazer of....... 1Chr 26:31
who was m among the thirty, and....... 1Chr 27:6
the officers, and with the m men......... 1Chr 28:1
And all the princes, and the m men..... 1Chr 29:24
thy m hand, and thy stretched out...... 2Chr 6:32
chosen men, being m men of valour.... 2Chr 13:3
But Abijah waxed m, and married....... 2Chr 13:21
all these were m men of valour........... 2Chr 17:13
of war, m men of valour, were in........ 2Chr 17:14
with him m men of valour three.......... 2Chr 17:14
hundred thousand m men of valour.... 2Chr 17:16
Eliada a m man of valour, and with.... 2Chr 17:17
hired also an hundred thousand m...... 2Chr 25:6
m men of valour were two thousand... 2Chr 26:12
that made war with m power.............. 2Chr 26:13
So Jotham became m, because he....... 2Chr 27:6
a m man of Ephraim, slew Maaseiah... 2Chr 28:7
his m men to stop the waters of.......... 2Chr 32:3
cut off all the m men of valour............ 2Chr 32:21
There have been m kings also over...... Ezr 4:20
before all the king's m princes........... Ezr 7:28
made, and unto the house of the m..... Neh 3:16
as a stone into the m waters............... Neh 9:11
our God, the great, the m................... Neh 9:32
m men of valour, an hundred.............. Neh 11:14
mouth, and from the hand of the m..... Job 5:15
Redeem me from the hand of the m..... Job 6:23
wise in heart, and m in strength.......... Job 9:4
spoiled, and overthroweth the m......... Job 12:19
weakeneth the strength of the m......... Job 12:21
become old, yea, are m in power......... Job 21:7
But as for the m man, he had the........ Job 22:8
draweth also the m with his power...... Job 24:22
the m shall be taken away without...... Job 34:20
in pieces m men without number.......... Job 34:24
out by reason of the arm of the m....... Job 35:9
Behold, God is m, and despiseth......... Job 36:5
he is m in strength and wisdom.......... Job 36:5
up himself, the m are afraid................ Job 41:25
and m, the LORD m in battle............... Ps 24:8
Give unto the LORD, O ye m............... Ps 29:1
a m man is not delivered by much....... Ps 33:16
sword upon thy thigh, O most m......... Ps 45:3
The m God, even the LORD, hath........ Ps 50:1
thou thyself in mischief, O m man....... Ps 52:1
the m are gathered against me........... Ps 59:3
out his voice, and that a m voice......... Ps 68:33
mine enemies wrongfully, are m......... Ps 69:4
thou driedst up m rivers...................... Ps 74:15
like a m man that shouteth by............ Ps 78:65
in the congregation of the m............... Ps 82:1
who among the sons of the m can....... Ps 89:6
Thou hast a m arm............................ Ps 89:13
have laid help upon one that is m....... Ps 89:19
the reproach of all the m people......... Ps 89:50
than the m waves of the sea.............. Ps 93:4
can utter the m acts of the LORD........ Ps 106:2
make his m power to be known.......... Ps 106:8
His seed shall be m upon earth.......... Ps 112:2
Sharp arrows of the m, with coals....... Ps 120:4
arrows are in the hand of a m man...... Ps 127:4
and vowed unto the m God of Jacob... Ps 132:2
habitation for the m God of Jacob....... Ps 132:5
great nations, and slew m kings.......... Ps 135:10
and shall declare thy m acts............... Ps 145:4
to the sons of men his m acts............. Ps 145:12
Praise him for his m acts.................... Ps 150:2
to anger is better than the m.............. Prov 16:32
cease, and parteth between the m....... Prov 18:18
man scaleth the city of the m............. Prov 21:22
For their redeemer is m...................... Prov 23:11
the wise more than ten m men........... Eccl 7:19
bucklers, all shields of m men........... Song 4:4
the m One of Israel, Ah, I will........... Is 1:24
The m man, and the man of war, the.. Is 3:2

by the sword, and thy *m* in the war .... Is 3:25
the *m* man shall be humbled, and .... Is 5:15
them that are *m* to drink wine............. Is 5:22
Wonderful, Counsellor, The *m* God .... Is 9:6
remnant of Jacob, unto the *m* God .... Is 10:21
and Lebanon shall fall by a *m* one .... Is 10:34
with his *m* wind shall he shake............ Is 11:15
called my *m* ones for mine anger .... Is 13:3
like the rushing of *m* waters.............. Is 17:12
the *m* men of the children of .... Is 21:17
thee away with a *m* captivity.............. Is 22:17
Behold, the Lord hath a *m* .... Is 28:2
storm, as a flood of *m* waters............. Is 28:2
the LORD, to the *m* One of Israel......... Is 30:29
with the sword, not of a man .... Is 31:8
LORD shall go forth as a *m* man........... Is 42:13
sea, and a path in the *m* waters.......... Is 43:16
the prey be taken from the *m*.............. Is 49:24
of the *m* shall be taken away .... Is 49:25
thy Redeemer, the *m* One of Jacob...... Is 49:26
thy Redeemer, the *m* One of Jacob...... Is 60:16
speak in righteousness, *m* to save .... Is 63:1
it is a *m* nation, it is an .... Jer 5:15
sepulchre, they are all *m* men .... Jer 5:16
neither let the *m* man glory in .... Jer 9:23
as a *m* man that cannot save.............. Jer 14:9
is with me as a *m* terrible one........... Jer 20:11
the king, with all his *m* men............. Jer 26:21
the Great, the *M* God, the LORD of ...... Jer 32:18
Great in counsel, and *m* in .... Jer 32:19
m things, which thou knowest not ...... Jer 33:3
even *m* men of war, and the women,.... Jer 41:16
their *m* ones are beaten down, and ...... Jer 46:5
flee away, nor the *m* man escape .... Jer 46:6
and let the *m* men come forth .... Jer 46:9
for the *m* man hath stumbled.............. Jer 46:12
man hath stumbled against the *m* .... Jer 46:12
How say ye, We are *m* and strong........ Jer 48:14
the *m* men's hearts in Moab at .... Jer 48:41
m men of Edom be as the heart of ...... Jer 49:22
shall be as of a *m* expert man .... Jer 50:9
a sword is upon her *m* men .... Jer 50:36
The *m* men of Babylon have forborn..... Jer 51:30
her *m* men are taken, every one of ..... Jer 51:56
and her rulers, and her *m* men........... Jer 51:57
all my *m* men in the midst of me........ Lam 1:15
hath also taken the *m* of the land....... Eze 17:13
shall Pharaoh with his *m* army........... Eze 17:17
Lord God, surely with a *m* hand .... Eze 20:33
ye are scattered, with a *m* hand .... Eze 20:34
hand of the *m* one of the heathen ...... Eze 31:11
By the swords of the *m* will .... Eze 32:12
The strong among the *m* shall .... Eze 32:21
with the *m* that are fallen of the ...... Eze 32:27
the *m* in the land of the living .... Eze 32:27
a great company, and a *m* army.......... Eze 38:15
Ye shall eat the flesh of the *m*......... Eze 39:18
horses and chariots, with *m* men .... Eze 39:20
he commanded the most *m* men that ..... Dan 3:20
and how *m* are his wonders................ Dan 4:3
And his power shall be, but not....... Dan 8:24
practise, and shall destroy the *m* .... Dan 8:24
the land of Egypt with a *m* hand .... Dan 9:15
a *m* king shall stand up, that........... Dan 11:3
with a very great and *m* army .... Dan 11:25
in the multitude of thy *m* men.......... Hos 10:13
They shall run like *m* men .... Joel 2:7
Prepare war, wake up the *m* men........ Joel 3:9
cause thy *m* ones to come down.......... Joel 3:11
shall the *m* deliver himself .... Amos 2:14
m shall flee away naked in that .... Amos 2:16
transgressions and your *m* sins.......... Amos 5:12
and righteousness as a *m* stream......... Amos 5:24
And thy *m* men, O Teman, shall be...... Obad 9
there was a *m* tempest in the sea....... Jonah 1:4
shield of his *m* men is made red......... Nah 2:3
O *m* God, thou hast established........... Hab 1:12
the *m* man shall cry there .... Zeph 1:14
thy God in the midst of thee is *m*...... Zeph 3:17
made thee as the sword of a *m* man ..... Zec 9:13
And they shall be as *m* men .... Zec 10:5
of Ephraim shall be like a *m* man .... Zec 10:7
because the *m* are spoiled................ Zec 11:2
most of his *m* works were done .... Mt 11:20
for if the *m* works, which were.......... Mt 11:21
for if the *m* works, which have.......... Mt 11:21
man this wisdom, and these *m* works ... Mt 13:54
he did not many *m* works there .... Mt 13:58
therefore *m* works do shew forth .... Mt 14:2
that even such *m* works are............... Mk 6:2
And he could there do no *m* work .... Mk 6:5
therefore *m* works do shew forth .... Mk 6:14
For he that is *m* hath done to me....... Lk 1:49
put down the *m* from their seats......... Lk 1:52
all amazed at the *m* power of God .... Lk 9:43
for if the *m* works had been done...... Lk 10:13
there arose a *m* famine in that .... Lk 15:14
the *m* works that they had seen .... Lk 19:37
which was a prophet *m* in deed .... Lk 24:19
heaven as of a rushing *m* wind.......... Acts 2:2
was *m* in words and in deeds............. Acts 7:22
m in the scriptures, came to .... Acts 18:24
Through *m* signs and wonders, by...... Rom 15:19
men after the flesh, not many *m* 1Cor 1:26
confound the things which are *m* 1Cor 1:27
but *m* through God to the pulling....... 2Cor 10:4
in signs, and wonders, and *m* deeds 2Cor 12:12
is not weak, but is *m* in you............ 2Cor 13:3
the same was *m* in me toward the .... Gal 2:8
to the working of his *m* power.......... Eph 1:19

from heaven with his *m* angels 2Th 1:7
therefore under the *m* hand of God 1Pet 5:6
when she is shaken of a *m* wind.......... Rev 6:13
the chief captains, and the *m* men ...... Rev 6:15
I saw another *m* angel come down .... Rev 10:1
so *m* an earthquake, and so great .... Rev 16:18
great city Babylon, that *m* city......... Rev 18:10
a *m* angel took up a stone like a ...... Rev 18:21
and as the voice of *m* thunderings...... Rev 19:6
captains, and the flesh of *m* men .... Rev 19:18

MIGRON (mi'-gron) A city in Benjamin.
a pomegranate tree which is in M........ 1Sa 14:2
come to Michmash, he is passed to M..... Is 10:28

MIJAMIN (mij'-a-min) See MIAMIN.
    1. A priest in David's time.
to Malchijah, the sixth to M 1Chr 24:9
    2. A priest who renewed the covenant.
Meshullam, Abijah, M, ... Neh 10:7

MIKLOTH (mik'-loth)
    1. A Benjamite in Jerusalem.
And M begat Shimeam 1Chr 8:32
And Ahio, and Zechariah, and M 1Chr 9:37
And M begat Shimeam 1Chr 9:38
    2. A ruler of David's guard.
his course was M also the ruler 1Chr 27:4

MIKNEIAH (mik-ne-i'-ah) A Levite musician.
and Elipheleh, and M 1Chr 15:18
and Elipheleh, and M 1Chr 15:21

MILALAI (mil'-a-lahee) A priest who purified
    the wall.
brethren, Shemaiah, and Azarael, M..... Neh 12:36

MILCAH (mil'-cah)
    1. Daughter of Haran.
and the name of Nahor's wife, M......... Gen 11:29
of Haran, the father of M .... Gen 11:29
told Abraham, saying, Behold, M......... Gen 22:20
these eight M did bear to Nahor........ Gen 22:23
who was born to Bethuel, son of M ..... Gen 24:15
daughter of Bethuel the son of M .... Gen 24:24
Nahor's son, whom M bare unto him...... Gen 24:47
    2. A daughter of Zelophehad.
were Mahlah, and Noah, Hoglah, M...... Num 26:33
Mahlah, Noah, and Hoglah, and M........ Num 27:1
Mahlah, Tirzah, and Hoglah, and M...... Num 36:11
Mahlah, and Noah, Hoglah, M............ Josh 17:3

MILCH
Thirty *m* camels with their colts, ... Gen 32:15
a new cart, and take two *m* kine....... 1Sa 6:7
and took two *m* kine, and tied them 1Sa 6:10

MILCOM (mil'-com) See MALCHAM, MOLECH.
    Chief god of the Ammonites.
after M the abomination of 1Kin 11:5
M the god of the children of............ 1Kin 11:33
for M the abomination of 2Kin 23:13

MILDEW
with and blasting, and with *m* .... Deut 28:22
there be pestilence, blasting,........... 1Kin 8:37
if there be blasting, or *m*............. 2Chr 6:28
smitten you with blasting and *m*........ Amos 4:9
smote you with blasting and with *m*.... Hag 2:17

MILE
shall compel thee to go a *m*............ Mt 5:41

MILETUM (mi-le'-tum) See MILETUS. A city in
    the Roman province of Caria.
Trophimus have I left at M sick......... 2Ti 4:20

MILETUS (mi-le-tus) See MILETUM. Same as
    Miletum.
and the next day we came to M........... Acts 20:15
from M he sent to Ephesus, and .... Acts 20:17

MILK
And he took butter, and *m*, and the .... Gen 18:8
wine, and his teeth white with *m*...... Gen 49:12
large, unto a land flowing with *m*..... Ex 3:8
unto a land flowing with *m* .... Ex 3:17
give thee, a land flowing with *m* ...... Ex 13:5
seethe a kid in his mother's *m*........ Ex 23:19
Unto a land flowing with *m* .... Ex 33:3
seethe a kid in his mother's *m*........ Ex 34:26
it, a land that floweth with *m*........ Lev 20:24
us, and surely it floweth with *m*...... Num 13:27
a land which floweth with *m* .... Num 14:8
out of a land that floweth with *m*..... Num 16:13
into a land that floweth with *m* .... Num 16:14
in the land that floweth with *m*....... Deut 6:3
seed, a land that floweth with *m*...... Deut 11:9
seethe a kid in his mother's *m*........ Deut 14:21
even a land that floweth with *m*....... Deut 26:9
a land that floweth with *m* .... Deut 26:15
thee, a land that floweth with *m*...... Deut 27:3
fathers, that floweth with *m*.......... Deut 31:20
m of sheep, with fat of lambs, and ... Deut 32:14
us, a land that floweth with *m*........ Josh 5:6
And she opened a bottle of *m*.......... Judg 4:19
He asked water, and she gave him *m*.... Judg 5:25
Hast thou not poured me out as *m*...... Job 10:10
His breasts are full of *m*............. Job 21:24
have goats' *m* enough for thy food..... Prov 27:27
of *m* bringeth forth butter............ Prov 30:33
and *m* are under thy tongue............ Song 4:11
I have drunk my wine with my *m*........ Song 5:1
rivers of waters, washed with *m*....... Song 5:12
of *m* that they shall give............. Is 7:22

them that are weaned from the *m* .... Is 28:9
m without money and without price...... Is 55:1
also suck the *m* of the Gentiles .... Is 60:16
that ye may *m* out, and be.............. Is 66:11
give them a land flowing with *m*........ Jer 11:5
give them, a land flowing with *m*....... Jer 32:22
snow, they were whiter than *m*.......... Lam 4:7
espied for them, flowing with *m*........ Eze 20:6
I had given them, flowing with *m*....... Eze 20:15
fruit, and they shall drink thy *m*...... Eze 25:4
and the hills shall flow with *m*........ Joel 3:18
I have fed you with *m*, and not......... 1Cor 3:2
eateth not of the *m* of the flock 1Cor 9:7
are become such as have need of *m*...... Heb 5:12
For every one that useth *m* is.......... Heb 5:13
desire the sincere *m* of the word....... 1Pet 2:2

MILL
maidservant that is behind the *m*........ Ex 11:5
women shall be grinding at the *m*....... Mt 24:41

MILLET
and beans, and lentiles, and *m* .... Eze 4:9

MILLIONS
thou the mother of thousands of *m*..... Gen 24:60

MILLO (mil'-lo)
    1. A fort near Shechem.
together, and all the house of M........ Judg 9:6
men of Shechem, and the house of M...... Judg 9:20
Shechem, and from the house of M........ Judg 9:20
    2. A fort near Jerusalem.
And David built round about from M...... 2Sa 5:9
the LORD, and his own house, and M 1Kin 9:15
then did he build M 1Kin 9:24
Solomon built M, and repaired the...... 1Kin 11:27
and slew Joash in the house of M........ 2Kin 12:20
about, even from M round about 1Chr 11:8
repaired M in the city of David,....... 2Chr 32:5

MILLS
and gathered it, and ground it in *m* .... Num 11:8

MILLSTONE
nether or the upper *m* to pledge .... Deut 24:6
of a *m* upon Abimelech's head........... Judg 9:53
of a *m* upon him from the wall.......... 2Sa 11:21
hard as a piece of the nether *m*........ Job 41:24
a *m* were hanged about his neck .... Mt 18:6
a *m* were hanged about his neck .... Mk 9:42
a *m* were hanged about his neck .... Lk 17:2
took up a stone like a great *m*......... Rev 18:21
the sound of a *m* shall be heard........ Rev 18:22

MILLSTONES
Take the *m*, and grind meal .... Is 47:2
of the bride, the sound of the *m*....... Jer 25:10

MINCING
m as they go, and making a............. Is 3:16

MIND
If it be your *m* that I should .... Gen 23:8
were a grief of *m* unto Isaac .... Gen 26:35
that the *m* of the LORD might be .... Lev 24:12
have not done them of mine own *m*...... Num 16:28
either good or bad of mine own *m* ...... Num 24:13
m unto the place which the LORD....... Deut 18:6
failing of eyes, and sorrow of *m*...... Deut 28:65
them to *m* among all the nations....... Deut 30:1
which is in mine heart and in my *m*.... 1Sa 2:35
days ago, set not thy *m* on them....... 1Sa 9:20
it was in my *m* to build an house...... 1Chr 22:7
perfect heart and with a willing *m*.... 1Chr 28:9
for the people had a *m* to work .... Neh 4:6
But he is in one *m*, and who can....... Job 23:13
Should it be according to thy *m*....... Job 34:33
forgotten as a dead man out of *m*...... Ps 31:12
he bringeth it with a wicked *m*........ Prov 21:27
A fool uttereth all his *m* .... Prov 29:11
whose *m* is stayed on thee............. Is 26:3
bring it again to *m*, O ye .... Is 46:8
be remembered, nor come into *m*........ Is 65:17
neither shall it come to *m* .... Jer 3:16
yet my *m* could not be toward this..... Jer 15:1
it, neither came it into my *m*......... Jer 19:5
not, neither came it into my *m*........ Jer 32:35
them, and came it not into his *m*...... Jer 44:21
and let Jerusalem come unto your *m* .... Jer 51:50
This I recall to my *m*, therefore...... Lam 3:21
the things that come into your *m*...... Eze 11:5
into your *m* shall not be at all,...... Eze 20:32
her *m* was alienated from them......... Eze 23:17
then my *m* was alienated from her,..... Eze 23:18
like as my *m* was alienated from....... Eze 23:18
from whom thy *m* is alienated.......... Eze 23:22
them from whom thy *m* is alienated ..... Eze 23:28
time shall things come into thy *m* ..... Eze 38:10
came into thy *m* upon thy bed.......... Dan 2:29
his *m* hardened in pride, he was .... Dan 5:20
Then shall his *m* change, and he .... Hab 1:11
all thy soul, and with all thy *m*...... Mt 22:37
and clothed, and in his right *m*....... Mk 5:15
all thy soul, and with all thy *m*...... Mk 12:30
Peter called to *m* the word that....... Mk 14:72
cast in her *m* what manner of .... Lk 1:29
Jesus, clothed, and in his right *m*.... Lk 8:35
thy strength, and with all thy *m*...... Lk 10:27
neither be ye of doubtful *m* .... Lk 12:29
the word with all readiness of *m*...... Acts 17:11
the Lord with all humility of *m*....... Acts 20:19
gave them over to a reprobate *m*....... Rom 1:28
warring against the law of my *m*....... Rom 7:23

So then with the *m* I myself serve...... Rom 7:25
do *m* the things of the flesh................ Rom 8:5
Because the carnal *m* is enmity........... Rom 8:7
what is the *m* of the Spirit................... Rom 8:27
who hath known the *m* of the Lord... Rom 11:34
by the renewing of your *m*................. Rom 12:2
Be of the same *m* one toward............ Rom 12:16
M not high things, but condescend..... Rom 12:16
be fully persuaded in his own *m*........ Rom 14:5
That ye may with one *m* and one....... Rom 15:6
in some sort, as putting you in *m*...... Rom 15:15
joined together in the same *m*........... 1Cor 1:10
who hath known the *m* of the Lord.... 1Cor 2:16
But we have the *m* of Christ.............. 1Cor 2:16
your fervent *m* toward me................. 2Cor 7:7
For if there be first a willing *m*........ 2Cor 8:12
and declaration of your ready *m*....... 2Cor 8:19
I know the forwardness of your *m*.... 2Cor 9:2
be of good comfort, be of one *m*........ 2Cor 13:11
desires of the flesh and of the *m*...... Eph 2:3
walk, in the vanity of their *m*............ Eph 4:17
renewed in the spirit of your *m*........ Eph 4:23
with one *m* striving together for...... Phil 1:27
being of one accord, of one *m*........... Phil 2:2
but in lowliness of *m* let each........... Phil 2:3
Let this *m* be in you, which was....... Phil 2:5
rule, let us *m* the same thing........... Phil 3:16
their shame, who *m* earthly things... Phil 3:19
they be of the same *m* in the Lord.... Phil 4:2
enemies in your *m* by wicked works.. Col 1:21
vainly puffed up by his fleshly *m*...... Col 2:18
kindness, humbleness of *m*................ Col 3:12
That ye be not soon shaken in *m*....... 2Th 2:2
and of love, and of a sound *m*........... 2Ti 1:7
but even their *m* and conscience is.. Titus 1:15
Put them in *m* to be subject to......... Titus 3:1
But without thy *m* would I do............ Philem 14
I will put my laws into their *m*.......... Heb 8:10
gird up the loins of your *m*............... 1Pet 1:13
Finally, be ye all of one *m*................ 1Pet 3:8
likewise with the same *m*................. 1Pet 4:1
filthy lucre, but of a ready *m*........... 1Pet 5:2
here is the *m* which hath wisdom..... Rev 17:9
These have one *m*, and shall give..... Rev 17:13

MINDED
was stedfastly *m* to go with her......... Ruth 1:18
that Joash was *m* to repair the......... 2Chr 24:4
which are *m* of their own freewill...... Ezr 7:13
was *m* to put her away privily........... Mt 1:19
shore, into the which they were *m*.... Acts 27:39
For to be carnally *m* is death............ Rom 8:6
but to be spiritually in *m* life............ Rom 8:6
I was *m* to come unto you before...... 2Cor 1:15
When I therefore was thus *m*............ 2Cor 1:17
that ye will be none otherwise *m*...... Gal 5:10
as many as be perfect, be thus *m*..... Phil 3:15
if in any thing ye be otherwise *m*...... Phil 3:15
men likewise exhort to be sober *m*... Titus 2:6
A double *m* man is unstable in all...... Jas 1:8
purify your hearts, ye double *m*....... Jas 4:8

MINDFUL
Be ye *m* always of his covenant....... 1Chr 16:15
neither were *m* of thy wonders......... Neh 9:17
is man, that thou art *m* of him........... Ps 8:4
he will ever be *m* of his covenant..... Ps 111:5
The Lord hath been *m* of us.............. Ps 115:12
hast not been *m* of the rock of......... Is 17:10
being *m* of thy tears, that I may........ 2Ti 1:4
is man, that thou art *m* of him........... Heb 2:6
if they had been *m* of that................ Heb 11:15
That ye may be *m* of the words......... 2Pet 3:2

MINDING
appointed, *m* himself to go afoot....... Acts 20:13

MINDS
it, take advice, and speak your *m*..... Judg 19:30
men, and they be chafed in their *m*... 2Sa 17:8
And Jehu said, If it be your *m*........... 2Kin 9:15
that whereupon they set their *m*...... Eze 24:25
their heart, with despiteful *m*........... Eze 36:5
made their *m* evil affected............... Acts 14:2
come to him, they changed their *m*... Acts 28:6
But their *m* were blinded................. 2Cor 3:14
the *m* of them which believe not...... 2Cor 4:4
so your *m* should be corrupted........ 2Cor 11:3
hearts and *m* through Christ Jesus.... Phil 4:7
disputings of men of corrupt *m*........ 1Ti 6:5
men of corrupt *m*, reprobate............ 2Ti 3:8
in their *m* will I write them.............. Heb 10:16
ye be wearied and faint in your *m*.... Heb 12:3
your pure *m* by way of remembrance.. 2Pet 3:1

MINE See PREFACE.

MINGLE
men of strength to *m* strong drink.... Is 5:22
they shall *m* themselves with the...... Dan 2:43

MINGLED
fire *m* with the hail, very.................. Ex 9:24
m with the fourth part of an hin....... Ex 29:40
cakes of fine flour *m* with oil............ Lev 2:4
fine flour unleavened, *m* with oil...... Lev 2:5
m with oil, and dry, shall all the...... Lev 7:10
unleavened cakes *m* with................ Lev 7:12
cakes *m* with oil, of fine flour......... Lev 7:12
and a meat offering *m* with oil......... Lev 9:4
m with oil, and one log of oil........... Lev 14:10
m with oil for a meat offering.......... Lev 14:21
not sow thy field with *m* seed........... Lev 19:19

shall a garment *m* of linen................ Lev 19:19
deals of fine flour *m* with oil............ Lev 23:13
cakes of fine flour *m* with oil........... Num 6:15
m with oil for a meat offering......... Num 7:13
m with oil for a meat offering......... Num 7:19
m with oil for a meat offering......... Num 7:25
m with oil for a meat offering......... Num 7:31
m with oil for a meat offering......... Num 7:37
m with oil for a meat offering......... Num 7:43
m with oil for a meat offering......... Num 7:49
m with oil for a meat offering......... Num 7:55
m with oil for a meat offering......... Num 7:61
m with oil for a meat offering......... Num 7:67
m with oil for a meat offering......... Num 7:73
m with oil for a meat offering......... Num 7:79
even fine flour *m* with oil................ Num 8:8
of a tenth deal of flour *m* with........ Num 15:4
two tenth deals of flour *m* with....... Num 15:6
flour *m* with half an hin of oil.......... Num 15:9
m with the fourth part of an hin...... Num 28:5
m with oil, and the drink offering.... Num 28:9
m with oil, for one bullock.............. Num 28:12
offering, *m* with oil, for one ram..... Num 28:12
m with oil for a meat offering......... Num 28:13
shall be of flour *m* with oil.............. Num 28:20
meat offering of flour *m* with oil..... Num 28:28
shall be of flour *m* with oil.............. Num 29:3
shall be of flour *m* with oil.............. Num 29:9
shall be of flour *m* with oil.............. Num 29:14
so that the holy seed have *m*............ Ezr 9:2
and *m* my drink with weeping........... Ps 102:9
But were *m* among the heathen, and.. Ps 106:35
she hath *m* her wine....................... Prov 9:2
drink of the wine which I have *m*...... Prov 9:5
The Lord hath *m* a perverse spirit.... Is 19:14
And all the *m* people, and all the...... Jer 25:20
all the kings of the *m* people........... Jer 25:24
upon all the *m* people that are in..... Jer 50:37
and Lydia, and all the *m* people........ Eze 30:5
him vinegar to drink *m* with gall...... Mt 27:34
him to drink wine *m* with myrrh...... Mk 15:23
had *m* with their sacrifices.............. Lk 13:1
fire *m* with blood, and they were..... Rev 8:7
were a sea of glass *m* with fire......... Rev 15:2

MINIAMIN (min´-e-a-min) See Miamin.
I. A Levite.
And next him were Eden, and M 2Chr 31:15
2. A priest with Zerubbabel.
Of M, of Moadiah, Piltai.................... Neh 12:17
Eliakim, Maaseiah, M, Michaiah,...... Neh 12:41

MINISH
Ye shall not *m* ought from your........ Ex 5:19

MINISHED
Again, they are *m* and brought low ... Ps 107:39

MINISTER
And Moses rose up, and his *m* Joshua... Ex 24:13
that he may *m* unto me in the.......... Ex 28:1
that he may *m* unto me in the.......... Ex 28:3
that he may *m* unto me in the.......... Ex 28:4
And it shall be upon Aaron to *m*....... Ex 28:35
that they may *m* unto me in the...... Ex 28:41
the altar to *m* in the holy place....... Ex 28:43
to *m* unto me in the priest's............ Ex 29:1
to *m* in the holy place..................... Ex 29:30
to *m* to me in the priest's office...... Ex 29:44
they come near to the altar to *m*..... Ex 30:20
that they may *m* unto me in the...... Ex 30:30
to *m* in the priest's........................ Ex 31:10
to *m* in the priest's office............... Ex 35:19
about the hem of the robe to *m* in.. Ex 39:26
to *m* in the priest's........................ Ex 39:41
that he may *m* unto me in the........ Ex 40:13
that they may *m* unto me in the...... Ex 40:15
to *m* unto the Lord in the priest's... Lev 7:35
whom he shall consecrate to *m* in.. Lev 16:32
and they shall *m* unto it, and shall.. Num 1:50
to *m* in the priest's office............... Num 3:3
priest, that they may *m* unto him.... Num 3:6
of the sanctuary whereto they *m*.... Num 3:31
thereof, wherewith they *m* unto it... Num 4:9
wherewith they *m* in the sanctuary.. Num 4:12
wherewith they *m* about it............. Num 4:14
But shalt *m* with their brethren....... Num 8:26
the congregation to *m* unto them.... Num 16:9
joined unto thee, and *m* unto thee... Num 18:2
shall *m* before the tabernacle of..... Num 18:2
before the Lord to *m* unto him......... Deut 10:8
the priest that standeth to *m*........... Deut 17:12
to stand to *m* in the name of.......... Deut 18:5
Then he shall *m* in the name of........ Deut 18:7
thy God hath chosen to *m* unto him.. Deut 21:5
Joshua the son of Nun, Moses' *m*..... Josh 1:1
the child did *m* unto the Lord.......... 1Sa 2:11
stand to *m* because of the cloud...... 1Kin 8:11
of God, and to *m* unto him for ever.. 1Chr 15:2
certain of the Levites to *m*.............. 1Chr 16:4
to *m* before the ark continually....... 1Chr 16:37
to *m* unto him, and to bless in his.... 1Chr 23:13
to *m* in the house of the................. 1Chr 26:12
stand to *m* by reason of the cloud... 2Chr 5:14
m before the priests, as the duty..... 2Chr 8:14
which *m* unto the Lord, are the....... 2Chr 13:10
they that *m* of the Levites.............. 2Chr 23:6
of the Lord, even vessels to *m*........ 2Chr 24:14
him, and that ye should *m* unto him. 2Chr 29:11
and for peace offerings, to *m*.......... 2Chr 31:2
unto the priests that *m* in the........ Neh 10:36
sanctuary, and the priests that *m*.... Neh 10:39

he shall *m* judgment to the people... Ps 9:8
of Nebaioth shall *m* unto thee........ Is 60:7
and their kings shall *m* unto thee.... Is 60:10
and the Levites that *m* unto me....... Jer 33:22
near to the Lord to *m* unto him....... Eze 40:46
lay their garments wherein they *m*.. Eze 42:14
to *m* unto me, saith the Lord God,... Eze 43:19
stand before them to *m* unto them... Eze 44:11
come near to me to *m* unto me........ Eze 44:15
to *m* unto me, and they shall keep... Eze 44:16
whiles they *m* in the gates of the.... Eze 44:17
to *m* in the sanctuary, he shall....... Eze 44:27
come near to *m* unto the Lord......... Eze 45:4
among you, let him be your *m*.......... Mt 20:26
to be ministered unto, but to *m*....... Mt 20:28
in prison, and did not *m* unto thee... Mt 25:44
great among you, shall be your *m*..... Mk 10:43
to be ministered unto, but to *m*....... Mk 10:45
and he gave it again to the *m*.......... Lk 4:20
and they had also John to their *m*... Acts 13:5
to *m* or come unto him.................... Acts 24:23
this purpose, to make thee a *m*....... Acts 26:16
For he is the *m* of God to thee......... Rom 13:4
for he is the *m* of God, a................. Rom 13:4
a *m* of the circumcision for the....... Rom 15:8
That I should be the *m* of Jesus....... Rom 15:16
Jerusalem to *m* unto the saints....... Rom 15:25
their duty is also to *m* unto them.... Rom 15:27
m about holy things live of the....... 1Cor 9:13
sower both *m* bread for your food... 2Cor 9:10
is therefore Christ the *m* of sin....... Gal 2:17
Whereof I was made a *m*, according.. Eph 3:7
that it may *m* grace unto the.......... Eph 4:29
faithful *m* in the Lord, shall............ Eph 6:21
is for you a faithful *m* of Christ........ Col 1:7
whereof I Paul am made a *m*........... Col 1:23
Whereof I am made a *m*, according.. Col 1:25
beloved brother, and a faithful *m*.... Col 4:7
m of God, and our fellowlabourer.... 1Th 3:2
which *m* questions, rather than....... 1Ti 1:4
shalt be a good *m* of Jesus Christ..... 1Ti 4:6
sent forth to *m* for them who.......... Heb 1:14
ministered to the saints, and do *m*... Heb 6:10
A *m* of the sanctuary, and of the..... Heb 8:2
but unto us they did *m* the things.... 1Pet 1:12
even so *m* the same one to another... 1Pet 4:10
if any man *m*, let him do it as of....... 1Pet 4:11

MINISTERED
Ithamar *m* in the priest's office....... Num 3:4
Eleazar his son *m* in the priest's..... Deut 10:6
But Samuel *m* before the Lord,........ 1Sa 2:18
the child Samuel *m* unto the Lord... 1Sa 3:1
his servant that *m* unto him........... 2Sa 13:17
cherished the king, and *m* to him..... 1Kin 1:4
the Shunammite *m* unto the king..... 1Kin 1:15
went after Elijah, and *m* unto him... 1Kin 19:21
vessels of brass wherewith they *m*.. 2Kin 25:14
they *m* before the dwelling place.... 1Chr 6:32
that *m* to the king by course........... 1Chr 28:1
that *m* to Ahaziah, he slew them..... 2Chr 22:8
king's servants that *m* unto him...... Est 2:2
king's servants that *m* unto him...... Est 6:3
vessels of brass wherewith they *m*.. Jer 52:18
Because they *m* unto them before.... Eze 44:12
off their garments wherein they *m*.. Eze 44:19
thousand thousands *m* unto him....... Dan 7:10
behold, angels came and *m* unto him.. Mt 4:11
and she arose, and *m* unto them..... Mt 8:15
Son of man came not to be *m* unto... Mt 20:28
and the angels *m* unto him............. Mk 1:13
left her, and she *m* unto them......... Mk 1:31
Son of man came not to be *m* unto... Mk 10:45
followed him, and *m* unto him......... Mk 15:41
she arose and *m* unto them............ Lk 4:39
which *m* unto him of their.............. Lk 8:3
As they *m* to the Lord, and fasted,... Acts 13:2
two of them that *m* unto him.......... Acts 19:22
hands have *m* unto my necessities... Acts 20:34
be the epistle of Christ *m* by us....... 2Cor 3:3
and he that *m* to my wants............. Phil 2:25
and bands having nourishment *m*.... Col 2:19
things he *m* unto me at Ephesus..... 2Ti 1:18
m unto me in the bonds of the........ Philem 13
in that ye have *m* to the saints........ Heb 6:10
For so an entrance shall be *m*......... 2Pet 1:11

MINISTERETH
Now he that *m* seed to the sower...... 2Cor 9:10
that *m* to you the Spirit, and........... Gal 3:5

MINISTERING
had the charge of the *m* vessels....... 1Chr 9:28
of the house, and *m* to the house..... Eze 44:11
Jesus from Galilee, *m* unto him........ Mt 27:55
Or ministry, let us wait on our *m*..... Rom 12:7
m the gospel of God, that the.......... Rom 15:16
fellowship of the *m* to the saints..... 2Cor 8:4
as touching the *m* to the saints....... 2Cor 9:1
Are they not all *m* spirits............... Heb 1:14
And every priest standeth daily *m*... Heb 10:11

MINISTERS
and the attendance of his *m*............ 1Kin 10:5
and the attendance of his *m*............ 2Chr 9:4
or *m* of this house of God, it........... Ezr 7:24
us *m* for the house of our God......... Ezr 8:17
ye *m* of his, that do his pleasure..... Ps 103:21
his *m* a flaming fire........................ Ps 104:4
shall call you the M of our God.......... Is 61:6
the Levites the priests, my *m*.......... Jer 33:21
they shall be *m* in my sanctuary..... Eze 44:11

priests the *m* of the sanctuary .... Eze 45:4
the *m* of the house, have for .... Eze 45:5
where the *m* of the house shall .... Eze 46:24
the priests, the LORD's *m* .... Joel 1:9
howl, ye *m* of the altar .... Joel 1:13
in sackcloth, ye *m* of my God................... Joel 1:13
the *m* of the LORD, weep between .... Joel 2:17
eyewitnesses, and *m* of the word .... Lk 1:2
for they are God's *m*, attending............... Rom 13:6
but *m* by whom ye believed, even........... 1Cor 3:5
of us, as of the *m* of Christ....................... 1Cor 4:1
us able *m* of the new testament 2Cor 3:6
ourselves as the *m* of God........................ 2Cor 6:4
his *m* also be transformed as the 2Cor 11:15
as the *m* of righteousness 2Cor 11:15
Are they *m* of Christ?............................. 2Cor 11:23
spirits, and his *m* a flame of fire............ Heb 1:7

MINISTRATION
days of his *m* were accomplished .... Lk 1:23
were neglected in the daily *m* .... Acts 6:1
But if the *m* of death, written and 2Cor 3:7
How shall not the *m* of the spirit 2Cor 3:8
For if the *m* of condemnation be............ 2Cor 3:9
be glory, much more doth the *m* of 2Cor 3:9
this *m* they glorify God for your 2Cor 9:13

MINISTRY
take all the instruments of *m*................... Num 4:12
came to do the service of the *m*............... Num 4:47
when David praised by their *m* 2Chr 7:6
by the *m* of the prophets .... Hos 12:10
and had obtained part of this *m* .... Acts 1:17
That he may take part of this *m*.............. Acts 1:25
prayer, and to the *m* of the word .... Acts 6:4
when they had fulfilled their *m* .... Acts 12:25
my course with joy, and the *m*............... Acts 20:24
among the Gentiles by his *m*................... Acts 21:19
Or *m*, let us wait on our .... Rom 12:7
themselves to the *m* of the saints 1Cor 16:15
Therefore, seeing we have this *m*........... 2Cor 4:1
to us the *m* of reconciliation 2Cor 5:18
thing, that the *m* be not blamed............. 2Cor 6:3
the saints, for the work of the *m*............. Eph 4:12
Take heed to the *m* which thou.............. Col 4:17
faithful, putting me into the *m*.............. 1Ti 1:12
make full proof of thy *m* 2Ti 4:5
he is profitable to me for the *m* 2Ti 4:11
he obtained a more excellent *m*.............. Heb 8:6
and all the vessels of the *m*..................... Heb 9:21

MINJAMIN See MINIAMIN.

MINNI (min'-ni) *A district in Armenia.*
her the kingdoms of Ararat, M .... Jer 51:27

MINNITH (min'-nith) *An Ammonite city.*
Aroer, even till thou come to M............... Judg 11:33
traded in thy market wheat of M............... Eze 27:17

MINSTREL
But now bring me a 2Kin 3:15
came to pass, when the *m* played 2Kin 3:15

MINSTRELS
the ruler's house, and saw the *m*.............. Mt 9:23

MINT
for ye pay tithe of *m* and anise and .... Mt 23:23
for ye tithe *m* and rue and all................... Lk 11:42

MIPHKAD (mif'-kad) *A gate of Jerusalem.*
over against the gate M, and so .... Neh 3:31

MIRACLE
you, saying, Shew a *m* for you .... Ex 7:9
not the *m* of the loaves .... Mk 6:52
man which shall do a *m* in my name........ Mk 9:39
to have seen some *m* done by him .... Lk 23:8
again the second *m* that Jesus did .... Jn 4:54
had seen the *m* that Jesus did .... Jn 6:14
unto him, and said, John did no *m* .... Jn 10:41
heard that he had done this *m* .... Jn 12:18
m hath been done by them is .... Acts 4:16
on whom this *m* of healing was.............. Acts 4:22

MIRACLES
my glory, and my *m* .... Num 14:22
And his *m*, and his acts, which he........... Deut 11:3
seen, the signs, and those great *m* .... Deut 29:3
where be all his *m* which .... Judg 6:13
This beginning of *m* did Jesus in .... Jn 2:11
when they saw the *m* which he did .... Jn 2:23
can do these *m* that thou doest .... Jn 3:2
because they saw his *m* which he........... Jn 6:2
seek me, not because ye saw the *m*........ Jn 6:26
will he do more *m* than these................... Jn 7:31
a man that is a sinner do such *m* .... Jn 9:16
for this man doeth many *m* .... Jn 11:47
he had done so many *m* before them ..... Jn 12:37
approved of God among you by *m* .... Acts 2:22
wonders and *m* among the people........... Acts 6:8
seeing the *m* which he did....................... Acts 8:6
and wondered, beholding the *m* .... Acts 8:13
and Paul, declaring what *m* .... Acts 15:12
God wrought special *m* by the .... Acts 19:11
To another the working of *m* 1Cor 12:10
thirdly teachers, after that *m* 1Cor 12:28
are all workers of *m*? 1Cor 12:29
worketh *m* among you, doeth he it .... Gal 3:5
and wonders, and with divers *m* .... Heb 2:4
m which he had power to do in the........ Rev 13:14
the spirits of devils, working *m* .... Rev 16:14
prophet that wrought *m* before him ...... Rev 19:20

MIRE
stamp them as the *m* of the street 2Sa 22:43
Can the rush grow up without *m* .... Job 8:11
He hath cast me into the *m* .... Job 30:19
sharp pointed things upon the *m*............. Job 41:30
place in deep *m*, where there is............... Ps 69:2
Deliver me out of the *m*, and let............. Ps 69:14
down like the *m* of the streets................. Is 10:6
rest, whose waters cast up *m*................... Is 57:20
dungeon there was no water, but *m*........ Jer 38:6
so Jeremiah sunk in the *m* .... Jer 38:6
thy feet are sunk in the *m* .... Jer 38:22
down as the *m* of the streets................... Mic 7:10
fine gold as the *m* of the streets............. Zec 9:3
m of the streets in the battle................... Zec 10:5
washed to her wallowing in the *m* 2Pet 2:22

MIRIAM (mir'-e-am) See MARY.
  1. *Sister of Aaron.*
M the prophetess, the sister of .... Ex 15:20
M answered them, Sing ye to the .... Ex 15:21
M and Aaron spake against........................ Num 12:1
Moses, and unto Aaron, and unto M....... Num 12:4
tabernacle, and called Aaron and M....... Num 12:5
M became leprous, white as snow .... Num 12:10
and Aaron looked upon M, and,............... Num 12:10
M was shut out from the camp .... Num 12:15
not till M was brought in again .... Num 12:15
M died there, and was buried there.......... Num 20:1
Aaron and Moses, and M their sister ...... Num 26:59
thy God did unto M by the way .... Deut 24:9
Aaron, and Moses, and M .... Mic 6:4
before thee Moses, Aaron, and M............ Mic 6:4
  2. *A daughter of Ezra.*
and she bare M, and Shammai, and...... 1Chr 4:17

MIRMA (mir'-mah) *Son of Shaharaim.*
And Jeuz, and Shachia, and M................. 1Chr 8:10

MIRMAH See MIRMA.

MIRTH
might have sent thee away with *m*........... Gen 31:27
send portions, and to make great *m*........ Neh 8:12
that wasted us required of us *m*.............. Ps 137:3
and the end of that *m* is heaviness .... Prov 14:13
to now, I will prove thee with *m*............. Eccl 2:1
and of *m*, What doeth it.......................... Eccl 2:2
of fools is in the house of *m*................... Eccl 7:4
Then I commended *m*, because a man .. Eccl 8:15
The *m* of tabrets ceaseth, the .... Is 24:8
the *m* of the land is gone......................... Is 24:11
of Jerusalem, the voice of *m*................... Jer 7:34
and in your days, the voice of *m*............ Jer 16:9
take from them the voice of *m* .... Jer 25:10
should we then make *m*?......................... Eze 21:10
also cause all her *m* to cease.................. Hos 2:11

MIRY
horrible pit, out of the *m* clay .... Ps 40:2
But the *m* places thereof and the .... Eze 47:11
sawest the iron mixed with *m* clay .... Dan 2:41
sawest iron mixed with *m* clay .... Dan 2:43

MISCARRYING
give them a *m* womb and dry breasts...... Hos 9:14

MISCHIEF
Lest peradventure *m* befall him .... Gen 42:4
if *m* befall him by the way in the .... Gen 42:38
m befall him, ye shall bring down .... Gen 44:29
from her, and yet no *m* follow .... Ex 21:22
And if any *m* follow, then thou .... Ex 21:23
For *m* did he bring them out, to .... Ex 32:12
people, that they are set on *m* .... Ex 32:22
secretly practised *m* against him 1Sa 23:9
behold, thou art taken in thy *m* 2Sa 16:8
beside the *m* that Hadad did 1Kin 11:25
and see how this man seeketh *m* 1Kin 20:7
light, some *m* will come upon us........... 2Kin 7:9
But they thought to do me *m* .... Neh 6:2
away the *m* of Haman the Agagite......... Est 8:3
They conceive *m*, and bring forth .... Job 15:35
iniquity, and hath conceived *m* .... Ps 7:14
His *m* shall return upon his own .... Ps 7:16
under his tongue is *m* and vanity........... Ps 10:7
for thou beholdest *m* and spite, to, ... Ps 10:14
In whose hands is *m*, and their .... Ps 26:10
but *m* is in their hearts........................... Ps 28:3
He deviseth *m* upon his .... Ps 36:4
Why boastest thou thyself in *m*............. Ps 52:1
m also and sorrow are in the midst....... Ps 55:10
will ye imagine *m* against a man........... Ps 62:3
thee, which frameth *m* by a law .... Ps 94:20
draw nigh that follow after *m* .... Ps 119:150
let the *m* of their own lips cover........... Ps 140:9
not, except they have done *m* .... Prov 4:16
heart, he deviseth *m* continually........... Prov 6:14
that be swift in running to *m*................. Prov 6:18
It is as sport to a fool to do *m* .... Prov 10:23
but he that seeketh *m*, it shall............... Prov 11:27
the wicked shall be filled with *m*.......... Prov 12:21
A wicked messenger falleth into *m* ...... Prov 13:17
a perverse tongue falleth into *m*........... Prov 17:20
and their lips talk of *m*........................... Prov 24:2
but the wicked shall fall into *m*............. Prov 24:16
his heart shall fall into *m* .... Prov 28:14
and *m* shall fall upon these.................... Is 47:11
they conceive *m*, and bring forth .... Is 59:4
M shall come upon .... Eze 7:26
these are the men that devise *m*............ Eze 11:2
kings' hearts shall be to do *m*................ Dan 11:27
yet do they imagine *m* against me .... Hos 7:15

O full of all subtilty and all *m*................. Acts 13:10

MISCHIEFS
I will heap *m* upon them......................... Deut 32:23
Thy tongue deviseth *m*........................... Ps 52:2
Which imagine *m* in their heart............. Ps 140:2

MISCHIEVOUS
they imagined a *m* device, which .... Ps 21:11
that seek my hurt speak *m* things.......... Ps 38:12
evil shall be called a *m* person .... Prov 24:8
end of his talk is *m* madness................. Eccl 10:13
man, he uttereth his *m* desire................ Mic 7:3

MISERABLE
m comforters are ye all .... Job 16:2
Christ, we are of all men most *m*........... 1Cor 15:19
not that thou art wretched, and *m* .... Rev 3:17

MISERABLY
He will *m* destroy those wicked............. Mt 21:41

MISERIES
of her *m* all her pleasant things............. Lam 1:7
howl for your *m* that shall come............ Jas 5:1

MISERY
was grieved for the *m* of Israel.............. Judg 10:16
light given to him that is in *m* .... Job 3:20
Because thou shalt forget thy *m*............ Job 11:16
and remember his *m* no more .... Prov 31:7
therefore the *m* of man is great............. Eccl 8:6
mine affliction and my *m*, the .... Lam 3:19
and *m* are in their ways.......................... Rom 3:16

MISGAB (mis'-gab) *The mountainous area in Moab.*
M is confounded and dismayed................ Jer 48:1

MISHAEL (mish'-a-el) See MISHAL.
  1. *A son of Uzziel.*
and Elzaphan, and Zithri.......................... Ex 6:22
Moses called M and .... Lev 10:4
of Judah, Daniel, Hananiah, M................ Dan 1:6
and to M, of Meshach .... Dan 1:7
had set over Daniel, Hananiah, M........... Dan 1:11
none like Daniel, Hananiah, M................ Dan 1:19
the thing known to Hananiah, M............. Dan 2:17
  2. *A priest who aided Ezra.*
on his left hand, Pedaiah, and M............. Neh 8:4

MISHAL (mi'-shal) See MISHAEL. *A Levitical city in Asher.*
M with her suburbs, Abdon with .... Josh 21:30

MISHAM (mi'-sham) *Son of Elpaal.*
Eber, and M, and Shamed, who built 1Chr 8:12

MISHEAL (mish'-e-al) *Same as Mishal.*
And Alammelech, and Amad, and M ...... Josh 19:26

MISHMA (mish'-mah) *A son of Ishmeal.*
And M, and Dumah, and Massa,.............. Gen 25:14
M, and Dumah, Massa, Hadad, and........ 1Chr 1:30
son, Mibsam his son, M his son 1Chr 4:25
And the sons of M 1Chr 4:26

MISHMANNAH (mish-man'-nah) *A warrior in David's army.*
M the fourth, Jeremiah the fifth,............. 1Chr 12:10

MISHRAITES (mish'-ra-ites) *A family of Kirjath-jearim.*
and the Shumathites, and the M............... 1Chr 2:53

MISPAR See MIZPAR.

MISPERETH (mis-pe'-reth) See MIZPAR. *An exile with Ezra.*
Nahamani, Mordecai, Bilshan, M .... Neh 7:7

MISREPHOTH-MAIM *Same as Zarephath.*
them unto great Zidon, and unto M .... Josh 11:8
full country from Lebanon unto M.......... Josh 13:6

MISS
at an hair breadth, and not *m* .... Judg 20:16
If thy father at all *m* me......................... 1Sa 20:6

MISSED
and thou shalt be *m*, because thy........... 1Sa 20:18
neither *m* we any thing, as long............ 1Sa 25:15
so that nothing was *m* of all that 1Sa 25:21

MISSING
was there ought *m* unto them................. 1Sa 25:7
if by any means he be *m*, then............... 1Kin 20:39

MIST
there went up a *m* from the earth........... Gen 2:6
immediately there fell on him a *m* .... Acts 13:11
to whom the *m* of darkness is 2Pet 2:17

MISTRESS
her *m* was despised in her eyes............. Gen 16:4
flee from the face of my *m* Sarai.......... Gen 16:8
said unto her, Return to thy *m* .... Gen 16:9
the *m* of the house, fell sick 1Kin 17:17
And she said unto her *m*, Would God.... 2Kin 5:3
a maiden unto the hand of her *m*.......... Ps 123:2
an handmaid that is heir to her *m* .... Prov 30:23
as with the maid, so with her *m*............ Is 24:2
the *m* of witchcrafts, that .... Nah 3:4

MISUSED

m his prophets, until the wrath 2Chr 36:16

MITE

thou hast paid the very last *m* .... Lk 12:59

MITES

poor widow, and she threw in two *m*. . Mk 12:42
widow casting in thither two *m* .... Lk 21:2

MITHCAH *(mith'-cah) An Israelite*
encampment in the wilderness.
from Tarah, and pitched in M .... Num 33:28
And they went from M, and pitched. Num 33:29

MITHCAK See MITHCAH.

MITHNAH See MITHCAH.

MITHNITE *(mith'-nite) Family name of*
Joshaphat.
of Maachah, and Joshaphat the M..... 1Chr 11:43

MITHREDATH *(mith'-re-dath) Treasurer for*
King Cyrus of Persia.
by the hand of M the treasurer .... Ezr 1:8
of Artaxerxes wrote Bishlam, M .... Ezr 4:7

MITRE
a robe, and a broidered coat, a m......... Ex 28:4
lace, that it may be upon the m .... Ex 28:37
forefront of the m it shall be .... Ex 28:37
shalt make the m of fine linen............. Ex 28:39
shalt put the m upon his head............. Ex 29:6
and put the holy crown upon the m .. Ex 29:6
a m of fine linen, and goodly .... Ex 39:28
to fasten it on high upon the m .... Ex 39:31
he put the m upon his head............. Lev 8:9
also upon the m, even upon his......... Lev 8:9
upon the linen m shall he be............. Lev 16:4
them set a fair m upon his head......... Zec 3:5
they set a fair m upon his head......... Zec 3:5

MITYLENE *(mit-i-le'-ne) Major city of the*
island of Lesbos.
we took him in, and came to M .... Acts 20:14

MIXED
a m multitude went up also with .... Ex 12:38
from Israel all the m multitude......... Neh 13:3
that they go to seek m wine............. Prov 23:30
dross, thy wine m with water............. Is 1:22
sawest the iron m with miry clay..... Dan 2:41
thou sawest iron m with miry clay... Dan 2:43
even as iron is not m with clay......... Dan 2:43
he hath m himself among the............. Hos 7:8
not being m with faith in them......... Heb 4:2

MIXT
the m multitude that was among....... Num 11:4

MIXTURE
it is full of m .... Ps 75:8
by night, and brought a m of myrrh ... Jn 19:39
which is poured out without m .... Rev 14:10

MIZAR *(mi'-zar) A hill near Hermon.*
the Hermonites, from the hill M .... Ps 42:6

MIZPAH *(miz'-pah) See* MIZPEH.
1. A city in Gilead.
And M; for he said .... Gen 31:49
2. A city in Benjamin.
with them Geba of Benjamin, and M 1Kin 15:22
the men of Gibeon, and of M............. Neh 3:7
3. A city in Judah.
there came to Gedaliah to M............. 2Kin 25:23
Chaldees that were with him at M..... 2Kin 25:25
and he built therewith Geba and M... 2Chr 16:6
Gedaliah the son of Ahikam to M..... Jer 40:6
Then they came to Gedaliah to M..... Jer 40:6
I will dwell at M to serve the............. Jer 40:10
of Judah, to Gedaliah, unto M............. Jer 40:12
the fields, came to Gedaliah to M..... Jer 40:13
spake to Gedaliah in M secretly......... Jer 40:15
Gedaliah the son of Ahikam to M..... Jer 41:1
they did eat bread together in M..... Jer 41:1
him, even with Gedaliah, at M............. Jer 41:3
went forth from M to meet them....... Jer 41:6
of the people that were in M............. Jer 41:10
all the people that remained in M..... Jer 41:10
away captive from M cast about .... Jer 41:14
the son of Nethaniah, from M............. Jer 41:16
because ye have been a snare on M... Hos 5:1
4. A district ruled by Shallum.
Colhozeh, the ruler of part of M..... Neh 3:15
5. A place ruled by Ezer.
the son of Jeshua, the ruler of M..... Neh 3:19

MIZPAR *(miz'-par) See* MISPERETH. *A clan*
leader with Zerubbabel.
Reelaiah, Mordecai, Bilshan, M............. Ezr 2:2

MIZPEH *(miz'-peh) See* MIZPAH, RAMATH-
MIZPEH.
1. A valley near Mt. Hermon.
under Hermon in the land of M............. Josh 11:3
and unto the valley of M eastward..... Josh 11:8
2. A city in Judah.
And Dilean, and M, and Joktheel,..... Josh 15:38
of Gilead, unto the LORD in M............. Judg 20:1
of Israel were gone up to M............. Judg 20:3
the men of Israel had sworn in M..... Judg 21:1
that came not up to the LORD to M... Judg 21:5
that came not up to M to the LORD... Judg 21:5
said, Gather all Israel to M............. 1Sa 7:5
And they gathered together to M..... 1Sa 7:6

the children of Israel in M............. 1Sa 7:6
were gathered together to M............. 1Sa 7:7
the men of Israel went out of M..... 1Sa 7:11
took a stone, and set it between M... 1Sa 7:12
to Beth-el, and Gilgal, and M............. 1Sa 7:16
together unto the LORD to M............. 1Sa 10:17
3. A city in Benjamin.
And M, and Chephirah, and Mozah,.. Josh 18:26
4. A city in Gad.
together, and encamped in M............. Judg 10:17
his words before the LORD in M......... Judg 11:11
and passed over M of Gilead............. Judg 11:29
from M of Gilead he passed over......... Judg 11:29
Jephthah came unto M to his house. Judg 11:34
5. A city in Moab.
And David sent thence to M of Moab. 1Sa 22:3

MIZRAIM *(miz'-ra-im) See* ABEL-MIZRAIM. *Son*
of Ham.
Cush, and M, and Phut, and Canaan... Gen 10:6
M begat Ludim, and Anamim, and..... Gen 10:13
Cush, and M, Put, and Canaan............. 1Chr 1:8
M begat Ludim, and Anamim, and..... 1Chr 1:11

MIZZAH *(miz'-zah) Son of Reuel.*
Zerah, Shammah, and M .... Gen 36:13
duke Zerah, duke Shammah, duke M Gen 36:17
Nahath, Zerah, Shammah, and M..... 1Chr 1:37

MNASON *(na'-son) A Christian in Jerusalem.*
brought with them one M of Cyprus. Acts 21:16

MOAB *(mo'-ab)*
1. A nation east of Israel.
smote Midian in the field of M......... Gen 36:35
the mighty men of M, trembling......... Ex 15:15
the wilderness which is before M..... Num 21:11
is the border of M, between M............. Num 21:13
Ar, and lieth upon the border of M... Num 21:15
that is in the country of M............. Num 21:20
against the former king of M............. Num 21:26
it hath consumed Ar of M, and the..... Num 21:28
Woe to thee, M .... Num 21:29
pitched in the plains of M on......... Num 22:1
M was sore afraid of the people,..... Num 22:3
M was distressed because of the..... Num 22:3
M said unto the elders of Midian,..... Num 22:4
And the elders of M and the elders... Num 22:7
the princes of M abode with,............. Num 22:8
the son of Zippor, king of M............. Num 22:10
And the princes of M rose up............. Num 22:14
and went with the princes of M..... Num 22:21
out to meet him unto a city of M..... Num 22:36
he, and all the princes of M............. Num 23:6
Balak the king of M hath brought..... Num 23:7
and the princes of M with him......... Num 23:17
and shall smite the corners of M..... Num 24:17
whoredom with the daughters of M.. Num 25:1
of M by Jordan near Jericho............. Num 26:3
O M by Jordan near Jericho............. Num 26:63
unto the camp at the plains of M..... Num 31:12
in Ije-abarim, in the border of M..... Num 33:44
of M by Jordan near Jericho............. Num 33:48
Abel-shittim in the plains of M......... Num 33:49
in the plains of M by Jordan............. Num 33:50
of M by Jordan near Jericho............. Num 35:1
of M by Jordan near Jericho............. Num 36:13
side Jordan, in the land of M............. Deut 1:5
by the way of the wilderness of M... Deut 2:8
over through Ar, the coast of M......... Deut 2:18
of Israel in the land of M............. Deut 29:1
Nebo, which is in the land of M......... Deut 32:49
of M unto the mountain of Nebo..... Deut 34:1
LORD died there in the land of M..... Deut 34:5
him in a valley in the land of M..... Deut 34:6
in the plains of M thirty days............. Deut 34:8
inheritance in the plains of M............. Josh 13:32
the son of Zippor, king of M............. Josh 24:9
the king of M against Israel............. Judg 3:12
the king of M eighteen years............. Judg 3:14
present unto Eglon the king of M..... Judg 3:15
the present unto Eglon king of M..... Judg 3:17
took the fords of Jordan toward M... Judg 3:28
they slew of M at that time about..... Judg 3:29
So M was subdued that day under..... Judg 3:30
gods of Zidon, and the gods of M..... Judg 10:6
took not away the land of M............. Judg 11:15
they sent unto the king of M............. Judg 11:17
land of Edom, and the land of M..... Judg 11:18
by the east side of the land of M..... Judg 11:18
came not within the border of M..... Judg 11:18
for Arnon was the border of M......... Judg 11:18
the son of Zippor, king of M............. Judg 11:25
to sojourn in the country of M......... Ruth 1:1
they came into the country of M..... Ruth 1:2
took them wives of the women of M.. Ruth 1:4
return from the country of M............. Ruth 1:6
M how that the LORD had visited..... Ruth 1:6
returned out of the country of M..... Ruth 1:22
Naomi out of the country of M......... Ruth 2:6
again out of the country of M............. Ruth 4:3
and into the hand of the king of M... 1Sa 12:9
enemies on every side, against M..... 1Sa 14:47
David went thence to Mizpeh of M... 1Sa 22:3
and he said unto the king of M......... 1Sa 22:3
brought them before the king of M... 1Sa 22:4
And he smote M, and measured them... 2Sa 8:2
Of Syria, and of M, and of the......... 2Sa 8:12
he slew two lionlike men of M............. 2Sa 23:20
for Chemosh, the abomination of M.. 1Kin 11:7
Then M rebelled against Israel............. 2Kin 1:1
Mesha king of M was a sheepmaster... 2Kin 3:4

that the king of M rebelled............. 2Kin 3:5
The king of M hath rebelled............. 2Kin 3:7
go with me against M to battle......... 2Kin 3:7
deliver them into the hand of M..... 2Kin 3:10
deliver them into the hand of M..... 2Kin 3:13
now therefore, M, to the spoil............. 2Kin 3:23
when the king of M saw that the..... 2Kin 3:26
smote Midian in the field of M......... 1Chr 1:46
Saraph, who had the dominion in M.. 1Chr 4:22
children in the country of M............. 1Chr 8:8
he slew two lionlike men of M............. 1Chr 11:22
And he smote M 1Chr 18:2
and from M, and from the............. 1Chr 18:11
this also, that the children of M..... 2Chr 20:1
the children of Ammon and of M..... 2Chr 20:10
against the children of Ammon, M... 2Chr 20:22
Ammon and M stood up against the. 2Chr 20:23
of Ashdod, of Ammon, and of M..... Neh 13:23
M is my washpot............................. Ps 60:8
of M, and the Hagarenes................. Ps 83:6
M is my washpot............................. Ps 108:9
lay their hand upon Edom and M..... Is 11:14
The burden of M .... Is 15:1
the night Ar of M is laid waste......... Is 15:1
the night Kir of M is laid waste......... Is 15:1
M shall howl over Nebo, and over..... Is 15:2
armed soldiers of M shall cry out..... Is 15:4
My heart shall cry out for M............. Is 15:5
gone round about the borders of M.. Is 15:8
lions upon him that escapeth of M... Is 15:9
so the daughters of M shall be......... Is 16:2
mine outcasts dwell with thee, M... Is 16:4
We have heard of the pride of M..... Is 16:6
Therefore shall M howl for............. Is 16:7
Therefore shall M howl for M............. Is 16:7
shall sound like an harp for M............. Is 16:11
when it is seen that M is weary......... Is 16:12
concerning M since that time............. Is 16:13
the glory of M shall be contemned... Is 16:14
M shall be trodden down under him.. Is 25:10
and the children of Ammon, and M... Jer 9:26
Edom, and M, and the children of..... Jer 25:21
Against M thus saith the LORD of..... Jer 48:1
shall be no more praise of M............. Jer 48:2
M is destroyed............................. Jer 48:4
Give wings unto M, that it may......... Jer 48:9
M hath been at ease from his......... Jer 48:11
M shall be ashamed of Chemosh, as. Jer 48:13
M is spoiled, and gone up out of..... Jer 48:15
The calamity of M is near to come... Jer 48:16
for the spoiler of M shall come......... Jer 48:18
M is confounded............................. Jer 48:20
it in Arnon, that M is spoiled............. Jer 48:20
all the cities of the land of M............. Jer 48:24
The horn of M is cut off, and his..... Jer 48:25
M also shall wallow in his vomit,..... Jer 48:26
O ye that dwell in M, leave the......... Jer 48:28
We have heard the pride of M............. Jer 48:29
Therefore will I howl for M............. Jer 48:31
and I will cry out for all M............. Jer 48:31
field, and from the land of M............. Jer 48:33
I will cause to cease in M............. Jer 48:35
shall sound for M like pipes............. Jer 48:36
upon all the housetops of M............. Jer 48:38
for I have broken M like a vessel,..... Jer 48:38
how hath M turned the back with..... Jer 48:39
so shall M be a derision and a............. Jer 48:39
and shall spread his wings over M... Jer 48:40
the mighty men's hearts in M at..... Jer 48:41
M shall be destroyed from being a... Jer 48:42
be upon thee, O inhabitant of M..... Jer 48:43
I will bring upon it, even upon M..... Jer 48:44
and shall devour the corner of M..... Jer 48:45
Woe be unto thee, O M .... Jer 48:46
captivity of M in the latter days..... Jer 48:47
Thus far is the judgment of M......... Jer 48:47
Because that M and Seir do say,..... Eze 25:8
the side of M from the cities............. Eze 25:9
I will execute judgments upon M..... Eze 25:11
out of his hand, even Edom, and M.. Dan 11:41
For three transgressions of M............. Amos 2:1
But I will send a fire upon M............. Amos 2:2
M shall die with tumult, with............. Amos 2:2
what Balak king of M consulted......... Mic 6:5
I have heard the reproach of M......... Zeph 2:8
Surely M shall be as Sodom, and..... Zeph 2:9
2. Son of Lot.
bare a son, and called his name M... Gen 19:37

MOABITE *(mo'-ab-ite) See* MOABITES,
MOABITESS, MOABITISH. *An inhabitant of*
Moab.
An Ammonite or M shall not enter .. Deut 23:3
sons of Elnaam, and Ithmah the M.. 1Chr 11:46
M he should not come into the......... Neh 13:1

MOABITES *(mo'-ab-ites)*
the father of the M unto this day..... Gen 19:37
was king of the M at that time......... Num 22:4
said unto me, Distress not the M..... Deut 2:9
but the M call them Emims............. Deut 2:11
The M which dwelt in Ar, did unto... Deut 2:29
your enemies the M into your hand.. Judg 3:28
so the M became David's servants,.. 2Sa 8:2
of Pharaoh, women of the M............. 1Kin 11:1
Chemosh the god of the M............. 1Kin 11:33
deliver the M also into your hand..... 2Kin 3:18
when all the M heard that the............. 2Kin 3:21
the M saw the water on the other..... 2Kin 3:22

Israelites rose up and smote the M...... 2Kin 3:24
they went forward smiting the M 2Kin 3:24
the bands of the M invaded the....... 2Kin 13:20
Chemosh the abomination of the M .. 2Kin 23:13
of the Syrians, and bands of the M.... 2Kin 24:2
the M became David's servants, and... 1Chr 18:2
Jebusites, the Ammonites, the M .... Ezr 9:1

MOABITESS (mo'-ab-i-tess) A female
    Moabite.
So Naomi returned, and Ruth the M .. Ruth 1:22
Ruth the M said unto Naomi, Let........ Ruth 2:2
And Ruth the M said, He said unto...... Ruth 2:21
must buy it also of Ruth the M .... Ruth 4:5
Moreover Ruth the M, the wife of....... Ruth 4:10
Jehozabad the son of Shimrith a M... 2Chr 24:26

MOABITISH (mo'-ab-i-tish) Belonging to the
    Moabites.
It is the M damsel that came back...... Ruth 2:6

MOADIAH (mo-ad-i'-ah) See MAADIAH. A
    priest.
of Miniamin, of M, Piltai............ Neh 12:17

MOCK
in an Hebrew unto us to m us .... Gen 39:14
unto us, came in unto me to m me...... Gen 39:17
mocketh another, do ye so m him......... Job 13:9
and after that I have spoken, m on...... Job 21:3
I will m when your fear cometh.......... Prov 1:26
Fools make a m at sin.................... Prov 14:9
me into their hand, and they m me...... Jer 38:19
saw her, and did m at her sabbaths .... Lam 1:7
be far from thee, shall m thee.......... Eze 22:5
deliver him to the Gentiles to m .... Mt 20:19
And they shall m him, and shall........ Mk 10:34
all that behold it begin to m him....... Lk 14:29

MOCKED
one that m unto his sons in law .... Gen 19:14
the ass, Because thou hast m me......... Num 22:29
Samson, Behold, thou hast m me........ Judg 16:10
Samson, Hitherto thou hast m me....... Judg 16:13
thou hast m me these three times,...... Judg 16:15
pass at noon, that Elijah m them........ 1Kin 18:27
m him, and said unto him, Go up,...... 2Kin 2:23
laughed them to scorn, and m them .. 2Chr 30:10
But they m the messengers of God,.. 2Chr 36:16
great indignation, and m the Jews........ Neh 4:1
I am as one m of his neighbour,........ Job 12:4
saw that he was m of the wise men... Mt 2:16
m him, saying, Hail, King of........... Mt 27:29
And after that they had m him......... Mt 27:31
And when they had m him, they took. Mk 15:20
unto the Gentiles, and shall be........ Lk 18:32
And the men that held Jesus m him .. Lk 22:63
m him, and arrayed him in a........... Lk 23:11
And the soldiers also m him............ Lk 23:36
resurrection of the dead, some m .... Acts 17:32
God is not m .... Gal 6:7

MOCKER
Wine is a m, strong drink is.......... Prov 20:1

MOCKERS
Are there not m with me................ Job 17:2
With hypocritical m in feasts......... Ps 35:16
Now therefore be ye not m............ Is 28:22
sat not in the assembly of the m....... Jer 15:17
should be m in the last time............ Jude 18

MOCKEST
and when thou m, shall no man make.. Job 11:3

MOCKETH
or as one man m another, do ye so.... Job 13:9
He m at fear, and is not................. Job 39:22
Whoso m the poor reproacheth his..... Prov 17:5
The eye that m at his father, and....... Prov 30:17
in derision daily, every one m me...... Jer 20:7

MOCKING
she had born unto Abraham, m........ Gen 21:9
heathen, and a m to all countries...... Eze 22:4
also the chief priests m him............ Mt 27:41
m said among themselves with he.... Mk 15:31
Others m said, These men are full..... Acts 2:13

MOCKINGS
And others had trial of cruel m....... Heb 11:36

MODERATELY
hath given you the former rain in...... Joel 2:23

MODERATION
Let your m be known unto all men .... Phil 4:5

MODEST
adorn themselves in m apparel.......... 1Ti 2:9

MOIST
of grapes, nor eat m grapes............. Num 6:3

MOISTENED
and his bones are m with marrow....... Job 21:24

MOISTURE
my m is turned into the drought........ Ps 32:4
away, because it lacked m............... Lk 8:6

MOLE
lizard, and the snail, and the m......... Lev 11:30

MOLECH (mo'-lek) See MALCHAM, MOLOCH.
    An Ammonite god.
seed pass through the fire to M........ Lev 18:21
giveth any of his seed unto M.......... Lev 20:2
he hath given of his seed unto M...... Lev 20:3
when he giveth of his seed unto M.... Lev 20:4
him, to commit whoredom with M..... Lev 20:5
is before Jerusalem, on the M......... 1Kin 11:7
to pass through the fire to M.......... 2Kin 23:10
to pass through the fire unto M....... Jer 32:35

MOLES
for himself to worship, to the m....... Is 2:20

MOLID (mo'-lid) A descendant of Jerahmeel,
    and she bare him Ahban, and M...... 1Chr 2:29

MOLLIFIED
bound up, neither m with ointment...... Is 1:6

MOLOCH (mo'-loch) See MILCHOM, MOLECH.
    Same as Molech.
borne the tabernacle of your M........ Amos 5:26
ye took up the tabernacle of M......... Acts 7:43

MOLTEN
after he had made it a m calf........... Ex 32:4
they have made them a m calf.......... Ex 32:8
Thou shalt make thee no m gods....... Ex 34:17
nor make to yourselves m gods........ Lev 19:4
and destroy all their m images......... Num 33:52
they have made them a m image....... Deut 9:12
God, and had made you a m calf....... Deut 9:16
that maketh any graven or m image 2Deut 27:15
make a graven image and a m image . Judg 17:3
a graven image and a m image......... Judg 17:4
and a graven image, and a m image .. Judg 18:14
and the teraphim, and the m image... Judg 18:17
and the teraphim, and the m image... Judg 18:18
he made two chapiters of m brass ... 1Kin 7:16
And he made a m sea, ten cubits...... 1Kin 7:23
the laver were undersetters m........ 1Kin 7:30
and their spokes, were all m........... 1Kin 7:33
m images, to provoke me to anger.. 1Kin 14:9
their God, and made them a m calf... 2Kin 17:16
Also he made a m sea of ten........... 2Chr 4:2
made also m images for Baalim........ 2Chr 28:2
carved images, and the m images..... 2Chr 34:3
the m images, he brake in pieces...... 2Chr 34:4
when they had made them a m calf... Neh 9:18
brass is m out of the stone............. Job 28:2
strong, and as a m looking glass...... Job 37:18
Horeb, and worshipped the m image . Ps 106:19
ornament of thy m images of gold.... Is 30:22
their m images are wind and.......... Is 41:29
images, that say to the m images..... Is 42:17
or m a graven image that is............ Is 44:10
my m image, hath commanded them .. Is 48:5
for his m image is falsehood, and..... Jer 10:14
for his m image is falsehood, and..... Jer 51:17
filthiness of it may be m in it........ Eze 24:11
have made them m images of their... Hos 13:2
mountains shall be m under him....... Mic 1:4
the graven image and the m image.... Nah 1:14
the m image, and a teacher of lies.... Hab 2:18

MOMENT
up into the midst of thee in a m........ Ex 33:5
that I may consume them in a m...... Num 16:21
that I may consume them as in a..... Num 16:45
every morning, and try him every m... Job 7:18
joy of the hypocrite but for a m....... Job 20:5
in a m go down to the grave............ Job 21:13
In a m shall they die, and the......... Job 34:20
For his anger endureth but a m......... Ps 30:5
into desolation, as in a m.............. Ps 73:19
but a lying tongue is but for a m..... Prov 12:19
thyself as it were for a little m....... Is 26:20
I will water it every m................. Is 27:3
come to thee in a m in one day...... Is 47:9
For a small m have I forsaken........ Is 54:7
I hid my face from thee for a m....... Is 54:8
spoiled, and my curtains in a........ Jer 4:20
that was overthrown as in a m........ Lam 4:6
and shall tremble at every m......... Eze 26:16
and they shall tremble at every m... Eze 32:10
of the world in a m of time........... Lk 4:5
In a m, in the twinkling of an....... 1Cor 15:52
affliction, which is but for a m....... 2Cor 4:17

---

other m have we brought down in..... Gen 43:22
tell who put our m in our sacks....... Gen 43:22
I had your m......................... Gen 43:23
put every man's m in his sack's....... Gen 44:1
of the youngest, and his corn m....... Gen 44:2
Behold, the m, which we found in .... Gen 44:8
Joseph gathered up all the m that .... Gen 47:14
Joseph brought the m into........... Gen 47:14
when m failed in the land of......... Gen 47:15
for the m faileth.................... Gen 47:15
you for your cattle, if m fail......... Gen 47:16
my lord, how that our m is spent..... Gen 47:18
servant that is bought for m......... Ex 12:44
shall she go out free without m...... Ex 21:11
for he is his m..................... Ex 21:21
there be laid on him a sum of m...... Ex 21:30
give m unto the owner of them....... Ex 21:34
live ox, and divide the m of it....... Ex 21:35
his neighbour m or stuff to keep..... Ex 22:7
he shall pay m according to the...... Ex 22:17
If thou lend m to any of my......... Ex 22:25
m of the children of Israel......... Ex 30:16
priest buy any soul with his........ Lev 22:11
not give him m upon usury.......... Lev 25:37
of the m that he was bought for..... Lev 25:51
the m of thy estimation unto it..... Lev 27:15
shall reckon unto him the m......... Lev 27:18
the m of thy estimation unto it..... Lev 27:19
And thou shalt give the m........... Num 3:48
m of them that were over above..... Num 3:49
children of Israel took he the m..... Num 3:50
Moses gave the m of them that...... Num 3:51
for the m of five shekels, after..... Num 18:16
Ye shall buy meat of them for m.... Deut 2:6
also buy water of them for m........ Deut 2:6
Thou shalt sell me meat for m....... Deut 2:28
and give me water for m, that I..... Deut 2:28
Then shalt thou turn it into m....... Deut 14:25
bind up the m in thine hand, and... Deut 14:25
thou shalt bestow that m for....... Deut 14:26
shalt not sell her at all for m....... Deut 21:14
usury of m, usury of victuals,....... Deut 23:19
they took no gain of m............. Judg 5:19
her, and brought m in their hand.... Judg 16:18
he restored the m unto his mother... Judg 17:4
give thee the worth of it in m....... 1Kin 21:2
him, Give me thy vineyard for m.... 1Kin 21:6
he refused to give thee for m....... 1Kin 21:15
Is it a time to receive m............ 2Kin 5:26
All the m of the dedicated things ... 2Kin 12:4
even the m of every one that........ 2Kin 12:4
the m that every man is set at...... 2Kin 12:4
all the m that cometh into any...... 2Kin 12:4
no more m of your acquaintance..... 2Kin 12:7
receive no more m of the people.... 2Kin 12:8
the door put therein all the m...... 2Kin 12:9
there was much m in the chest...... 2Kin 12:10
told the m that was found in the.... 2Kin 12:10
And they gave the m, being told,.... 2Kin 12:11
of the m that was brought into..... 2Kin 12:13
the m to be bestowed on workmen .. 2Kin 12:14
The trespass m and sin m was...... 2Kin 12:16
Menahem exacted the m of Israel.... 2Kin 15:20
m that was delivered into their..... 2Kin 22:7
the m that was found in the house... 2Kin 22:9
he taxed the land to give the m..... 2Kin 23:35
gather of all Israel m to repair..... 2Chr 24:5
they saw that there was much m 2Chr 24:11
day, and gathered m in abundance... 2Chr 24:11
the rest of the m before the king... 2Chr 24:14
they delivered the m that was...... 2Chr 34:9
when they brought out the m that... 2Chr 34:14
m that was found in the house of... 2Chr 34:17
They gave m also unto the masons,.. Ezr 3:7
buy speedily with this m bullocks.. Ezr 7:17
We have borrowed m for the king's.. Neh 5:4
servants, might exact of them m.... Neh 5:10
also the hundredth part of the m.... Neh 5:11
of the sum of the m that Haman..... Est 4:7
the fruits thereof without m......... Job 31:39
man also gave him a piece of m..... Job 42:11
putteth not out his m to usury...... Ps 15:5
He hath taken a bag of m with him .. Prov 7:20
is a defence, and m is a defence.... Eccl 7:12
but m answereth all things.......... Eccl 10:19
bought me no sweet cane with m.... Is 43:24
and ye shall be redeemed without m. Is 52:3
the waters, and he that hath no m... Is 55:1
come, buy wine and milk without m.. Is 55:1
Wherefore do ye spend m for that... Is 55:2
in Anathoth, and weighed him the m. Jer 32:9
weighed him the m in the balances... Jer 32:10
Gob, Buy thee the field for m....... Jer 32:25
Men shall buy fields for m.......... Jer 32:44
We have drunken our water for m.... Lam 5:4
the prophets thereof divine for m... Mic 3:11
received tribute m to Peter......... Mt 17:24
thou shalt find a piece of m........ Mt 17:27
Shew me the tribute m............. Mt 22:19
in the earth, and hid his lord's m.... Mt 25:18
have put my m to the exchangers... Mt 25:27
they gave large m unto the......... Mt 28:12
So they took the m, and did as..... Mt 28:15
no bread, no m in their purse....... Mk 6:8
people cast m into the treasury..... Mk 12:41
and promised to give him m........ Mk 14:11
scrip, neither bread, neither m...... Lk 9:3
him, to whom he had given the m... Lk 19:15
not thou my m into the bank....... Lk 19:23
glad, and covenanted to give him m. Lk 22:5

MOLADAH (mo-la'-dah) A city in Judah.
Amam, and Shema, and M........... Josh 15:26
Beer-sheba, or Sheba, and M........ Josh 19:2
And they dwelt at Beer-sheba, and M. 1Chr 4:28
And at Jeshua, and at M, and at..... Neh 11:26

MONEYCHANGERS

and the changers of *m* sitting........... Jn 2:14
and poured out the changers' *m*........ Jn 2:15
land, sold it, and brought the *m*.......... Acts 4:37
Abraham bought for a sum of *m* of.... Acts 7:16
was given, he offered them *m*........... Acts 8:18
Thy *m* perish with thee, because...... Acts 8:20
of God may be purchased with........... Acts 8:20
He hoped also that *m* should have.... Acts 24:26
For the love of *m* is the root of........... 1Ti 6:10

MONEYCHANGERS

and overthrew the tables of the *m*.... Mt 21:12
and overthrew the tables of the *m*.... Mk 11:15

MONSTERS

Even the sea *m* draw out the............ Lam 4:3

MONTH

of Noah's life, in the second *m*........ Gen 7:11
the seventeenth day of the *m*........... Gen 7:11
the ark rested in the seventh *m*......... Gen 8:4
on the seventeenth day of the *m*...... Gen 8:4
continually until the tenth *m*............. Gen 8:5
in the tenth *m*, on the first day........ Gen 8:5
on the first day of the *m*................. Gen 8:5
and first year, in the first *m*............ Gen 8:13
the first day of the *m*.................... Gen 8:13
And in the second *m*, on the seven... Gen 8:14
seven and twentieth day of the *m*.... Gen 8:14
abode with him the space of a *m*...... Gen 29:14
This *m* shall be unto you a............. Ex 12:2
be the first *m* of the year to you...... Ex 12:2
In the tenth day of this *m* they....... Ex 12:3
the fourteenth day of the same *m*.... Ex 12:6
In the first *m*, on the fourteenth..... Ex 12:18
fourteenth day of the *m* at even...... Ex 12:18
and twentieth day of the *m* at even.. Ex 12:18
day came ye out in the *m* Abib....... Ex 13:4
shalt keep this service in this *m*...... Ex 13:5
in *m* after their departing out of..... Ex 16:1
In the third *m*, when the children.... Ex 19:1
the time appointed of the *m* Abib.... Ex 23:15
thee, in the time of the *m* Abib....... Ex 34:18
for in the *m* Abib thou camest out... Ex 34:18
the first *m* shalt thou set up the..... Ex 40:2
in the first *m* in the second year..... Ex 40:17
on the first day of the *m*............... Ex 40:17
that in the seventh *m*................... Lev 16:29
m, on the tenth day of the............. Lev 16:29
at even is the LORD's passover....... Lev 23:5
same *m* is the feast of unleavened.. Lev 23:6
Israel, saying, In the seventh *m*..... Lev 23:24
in the first day of the *m*............... Lev 23:24
seventh *m* there shall be a day of... Lev 23:27
in the tenth day of the *m* at even.... Lev 23:32
seventh *m* shall be the feast of...... Lev 23:34
fifteenth day of the seventh *m*....... Lev 23:39
celebrate it in the seventh *m*......... Lev 23:41
on the tenth day of the seventh *m*... Lev 25:9
if it be from a *m* old even unto...... Lev 27:6
on the first day of the second *m*..... Num 1:1
on the first day of the second *m*..... Num 1:18
every male from a *m* old and upward.. Num 3:15
of all the males, from a *m* old........ Num 3:22
of all the males, from a *m* old........ Num 3:28
of all the males, from a *m* old........ Num 3:34
all the males from a *m* old............ Num 3:39
children of Israel from a *m* old....... Num 3:40
the number of names, from a *m* old.. Num 3:43
in the first *m* of the second year..... Num 9:1
In the fourteenth day of this *m*...... Num 9:3
m at even in the wilderness of...... Num 9:5
m at even they shall keep it......... Num 9:11
whether it were two days, or a *m*.... Num 9:22
the twentieth day of the second *m*.. Num 10:11
But even a whole *m*, until it come... Num 11:20
that they may eat a whole *m*......... Num 11:21
from a *m* old shalt thou redeem..... Num 18:16
the desert of Zin in the first *m*....... Num 20:1
thousand, all males from a *m* old.... Num 26:62
m throughout the months of the..... Num 28:14
m is the passover of the LORD....... Num 28:16
day of this *m* is the feast............. Num 28:17
And in the seventh *m*, on the first... Num 29:1
m, on the first day of the *m*........ Num 29:1
the burnt offering of the *m*........... Num 29:6
seventh *m* an holy convocation...... Num 29:7
seventh *m* ye shall have an holy.... Num 29:12
from Rameses in the first *m*.......... Num 33:3
the fifteenth day of the first *m*....... Num 33:3
in the first day of the fifth *m*......... Num 33:38
fortieth year, in the eleventh *m*...... Deut 1:3
m, on the first day of the *m*........ Deut 1:3
Observe the *m* of Abib, and keep.... Deut 16:1
for in the *m* of Abib the LORD thy... Deut 16:1
her father and her mother a full *m*... Deut 21:13
on the tenth day of the first *m*....... Josh 4:19
of the *m* at even in the plains of.... Josh 5:10
which was the second day of the *m*.. 1Sa 20:27
no meat the second day of the *m*.... 1Sa 20:34
each man his in a year made........... 1Kin 4:7
table, every man in his *m*............. 1Kin 4:7
ten thousand a *m* by courses........ 1Kin 5:14
a *m* they were in Lebanon, and two.. 1Kin 5:14
reign over Israel, in the *m* Zif....... 1Kin 6:1
m Zif, which is the second *m*...... 1Kin 6:1
of the LORD laid, in the *m* Zif....... 1Kin 6:37
the eleventh year, in the *m* Bul...... 1Kin 6:38
which is the eighth *m*.................. 1Kin 6:38
at the feast in the *m* Ethanim....... 1Kin 8:2
which is the seventh *m*................ 1Kin 8:2
ordained a feast in the eighth *m*..... 1Kin 12:32

on the fifteenth day of the *m*......... 1Kin 12:32
the fifteenth day of the eighth *m*.... 1Kin 12:33
even in the *m* which he had........... 1Kin 12:33
and he reigned a full *m* in Samaria.. 2Kin 15:13
year of his reign, in the tenth *m*..... 2Kin 25:1
in the tenth day of the *m*.............. 2Kin 25:1
m the famine prevailed in the........ 2Kin 25:3
And in the fifth *m*, on the seventh... 2Kin 25:8
on the seventh day of the *m*.......... 2Kin 25:8
it came to pass in the seventh *m*.... 2Kin 25:25
king of Judah, in the twelfth *m*...... 2Kin 25:27
seven and twentieth day of the *m*... 2Kin 25:27
went over Jordan in the first *m*...... 1Chr 12:15
went out *m* by *m* throughout....... 1Chr 27:1
first *m* was Jashobeam the son of... 1Chr 27:2
of the host for the first *m*............. 1Chr 27:2
the second *m* was Dodai an Ahohite.. 1Chr 27:4
of the host for the third *m* was....... 1Chr 27:4
fourth captain for the fourth *m*....... 1Chr 27:7
fifth *m* was Shamhuth the Izrahite... 1Chr 27:8
m was Ira the son of Ikkesh the..... 1Chr 27:9
seventh *m* was Helez the Pelonite... 1Chr 27:10
m was Sibbecai the Hushathite...... 1Chr 27:11
m was Abiezer the Anetothite....... 1Chr 27:12
m was Maharai the Netophathite..... 1Chr 27:13
captain for the eleventh *m* was...... 1Chr 27:14
m was Heldai the Netophathite...... 1Chr 27:15
In the second day of the second *m*.. 2Chr 3:2
feast which was in the seventh *m*... 2Chr 5:3
m he sent the people away into..... 2Chr 7:10
at Jerusalem in the third *m*.......... 2Chr 15:10
year of his reign, in the first *m*..... 2Chr 29:3
day of the first *m* to sanctify........ 2Chr 29:17
on the eighth day of the *m* came.... 2Chr 29:17
of the first *m* they made an end..... 2Chr 29:17
keep the passover in the second *m*.. 2Chr 30:2
unleavened bread in the second *m*.. 2Chr 30:13
fourteenth day of the second *m*..... 2Chr 30:15
In the third *m* they began to lay..... 2Chr 31:7
and finished them in the seventh *m*.. 2Chr 31:7
the fourteenth day of the first *m*.... 2Chr 35:1
And when the seventh *m* was come.. Ezr 3:1
m began they to offer burnt.......... Ezr 3:6
God at Jerusalem, in the second *m*.. Ezr 3:8
on the third day of the *m* Adar...... Ezr 6:15
the fourteenth day of the first *m*.... Ezr 6:19
came to Jerusalem in the fifth *m*.... Ezr 7:8
m began he to go up from Babylon.. Ezr 7:9
the fifth *m* came he to Jerusalem.... Ezr 7:9
on the twelfth day of the first *m*..... Ezr 8:31
It was the ninth *m*, on the........... Ezr 10:9
on the twentieth day of the *m*....... Ezr 10:9
the tenth *m* to examine the matter.. Ezr 10:16
by the first day of the first *m*........ Ezr 10:17
it came to pass in the *m* Chisleu.... Neh 1:1
And it came to pass in the *m* Nisan.. Neh 2:1
twenty and fifth day of the *m* Elul.. Neh 6:15
and when the seventh *m* came........ Neh 7:73
the first day of the seventh *m*........ Neh 8:2
the feast of the seventh *m*........... Neh 8:14
fourth day of this *m* the children.... Neh 9:1
his house royal in the tenth *m*....... Est 2:16
which is the *m* Tebeth................ Est 2:16
In the first *m*, that is................. Est 3:7
the *m* Nisan, in the twelfth year..... Est 3:7
m to *m*, to the twelfth *m*......... Est 3:7
that is, the *m* Adar.................... Est 3:7
the thirteenth day of the first *m*..... Est 3:12
thirteenth day of the twelfth *m*...... Est 3:13
which is the *m* Adar................... Est 3:13
at that time in the *m* Adar............ Est 8:9
the *m* Sivan, on the three and...... Est 8:9
thirteenth day of the twelfth *m*...... Est 8:12
which is the *m* Adar................... Est 8:12
Now in the twelfth *m*, that is,....... Est 9:1
the *m* Adar, on the thirteenth day... Est 9:1
fourteenth day also of the *m* Adar.. Est 9:15
the thirteenth day of the *m* Adar.... Est 9:17
of the *m* Adar a day of gladness.... Est 9:19
the fourteenth day of the *m* Adar... Est 9:19
the *m* which was turned unto them.. Est 9:22
Jerusalem captive in the fifth *m*..... Jer 1:3
in her *m* they shall find her......... Jer 2:24
fourth year, and in the fifth *m*....... Jer 28:1
the same year in the seventh *m*..... Jer 28:17
king of Judah, in the ninth *m*........ Jer 36:9
in the winterhouse in the ninth *m*... Jer 36:22
king of Judah, in the tenth *m*........ Jer 39:1
year of Zedekiah, in the fourth *m*... Jer 39:2
the ninth day of the *m*................ Jer 39:2
it came to pass in the seventh *m*.... Jer 41:1
year of his reign, in the tenth *m*..... Jer 52:4
m, in the tenth day of the *m*....... Jer 52:4
And in the fourth *m*, in the ninth.... Jer 52:6
m, in the ninth day of the *m*....... Jer 52:6
Now in the fifth *m*, in the tenth..... Jer 52:12
m, in the tenth day of the *m*....... Jer 52:12
king of Judah, in the fifth *m*......... Jer 52:12
five and twentieth day of the *m*..... Jer 52:31
thirtieth year, in the fourth *m*....... Eze 1:1
in the fifth day of the *m*.............. Eze 1:1
In the fifth day of the *m*.............. Eze 1:2
In the sixth year, in the sixth *m*..... Eze 8:1
in the fifth day of the *m*.............. Eze 8:1
the seventh year, in the fifth *m*..... Eze 20:1
the tenth day of the *m*................ Eze 20:1
in the tenth year, in the tenth *m*.... Eze 24:1
in the tenth day of the *m*............. Eze 24:1
year, in the first day of the *m*....... Eze 26:1
In the tenth year, in the tenth *m*.... Eze 29:1

in the twelfth day of the *m*.......... Eze 29:1
and twentieth year, in the first *m*... Eze 29:17
in the first day of the *m*............. Eze 29:17
in the seventh day of the *m*......... Eze 30:20
in the eleventh year, in the third *m*.. Eze 31:1
in the first day of the *m*............. Eze 31:1
twelfth year, in the twelfth *m*....... Eze 32:1
in the first day of the *m*............. Eze 32:1
in the fifteenth day of the *m*........ Eze 32:17
of our captivity, in the tenth *m*..... Eze 33:21
in the fifth day of the *m*............. Eze 33:21
year, in the tenth day of the *m*..... Eze 40:1
In the first *m*, in the first day....... Eze 45:18
in the first day of the *m*............. Eze 45:18
the *m* for every one that erreth...... Eze 45:20
In the first *m*, in the fourteenth.... Eze 45:21
in the fourteenth day of the *m*...... Eze 45:21
In the seventh *m*, in the............ Eze 45:25
in the fifteenth day of the *m*........ Eze 45:25
and twentieth day of the first *m*.... Dan 10:4
now shall a *m* devour them with.... Hos 5:7
and the latter rain in the first *m*.... Joel 2:23
Darius the king, in the sixth *m*...... Hag 1:1
m, in the first day of the *m*........ Hag 1:1
and twentieth day of the sixth *m*.... Hag 1:15
In the seventh *m*, in the one and... Hag 2:1
the one and twentieth day of the *m*.. Hag 2:1
and twentieth day of the ninth *m*.... Hag 2:10
and twentieth day of the ninth *m*.... Hag 2:18
four and twentieth day of the *m*..... Hag 2:20
In the eighth *m*, in the second...... Zec 1:1
twentieth day of the eleventh *m*..... Zec 1:7
which is the *m* Sebat................. Zec 1:7
in the fourth day of the ninth *m*..... Zec 7:1
Should I weep in the fifth *m*......... Zec 7:3
mourned in the fifth and seventh *m*.. Zec 7:5
The fast of the fourth *m*, and the... Zec 8:19
shepherds also I cut off in one *m*.... Zec 11:8
in the sixth *m* the angel Gabriel..... Lk 1:26
and this is the sixth *m* with her..... Lk 1:36
for an hour, and a day, and a *m*...... Rev 9:15
and yielded her fruit every *m*........ Rev 22:2

MONTHLY

the *m* prognosticators, stand up,..... Is 47:13

MONTHS

came to pass about three *m* after.... Gen 38:24
goodly child, she hid him three *m*.... Ex 2:2
be unto you the beginning of *m*...... Ex 12:2
and in the beginnings of your *m*..... Num 10:10
in the beginnings of your *m* ye...... Num 28:11
throughout the *m* of the year........ Num 28:14
let me alone two *m*, that I may go... Judg 11:37
And he sent her away for two *m*...... Judg 11:38
came to pass at the end of two *m*... Judg 11:39
and was there four whole *m*.......... Judg 19:2
abode in the rock Rimmon four *m*.... Judg 20:47
of the Philistines seven *m*............ 1Sa 6:1
was a full year and four *m*........... 1Sa 27:7
of Judah was seven years and six *m*.. 2Sa 2:11
over Judah seven years and six *m*... 2Sa 5:5
of Obed-edom the Gittite three *m*.... 2Sa 6:11
to Jerusalem at the end of nine *m*... 2Sa 24:8
flee three *m* before thine enemies... 2Sa 24:13
were in Lebanon, and two *m* at home.. 1Kin 5:14
(For six *m* did Joab remain there..... 1Kin 11:16
year Israel in Samaria six *m*......... 2Kin 15:8
he reigned three *m* in Jerusalem.... 2Kin 23:31
he reigned in Jerusalem three *m*.... 2Kin 24:8
he reigned seven years and six *m*... 1Chr 3:4
of Obed-edom in his house three *m*.. 1Chr 13:14
or three *m* to be destroyed before.. 1Chr 21:12
throughout all the *m* of the year..... 1Chr 27:1
he reigned three *m* in Jerusalem.... 2Chr 36:2
to reign, and he reigned three *m*.... 2Chr 36:9
after that she had been twelve *m*.... Est 2:12
six *m* with oil of myrrh, and six..... Est 2:12
six *m* with sweet odours, and with.. Est 2:12
not come into the number of the *m*.. Job 3:6
am I made to possess *m* of vanity... Job 7:3
the number of his *m* are with thee... Job 14:5
when the number of his *m* is cut.... Job 21:21
Oh that I were as in *m* past......... Job 29:2
number the *m* that they fulfil........ Job 39:2
seven *m* shall the house of Israel.... Eze 39:12
end of seven *m* shall they search.... Eze 39:14
new fruit according to his *m*......... Eze 47:12
At the end of twelve *m* he walked... Dan 4:29
were yet three *m* to the harvest..... Amos 4:7
conceived, and hid herself five *m*.... Lk 1:24
Mary abode with her about three *m*.. Lk 1:56
was shut up three years and six *m*... Lk 4:25
Say not ye, There are yet four *m*..... Jn 4:35
up in his father's house three *m*..... Acts 7:20
continued there a year and six *m*.... Acts 18:11
boldly for the space of three *m*...... Acts 19:8
And there abode three *m*............. Acts 20:3
after three *m* we departed in a...... Acts 28:11
Ye observe days, and *m*, and times,.. Gal 4:10
was hid three *m* of his parents,..... Heb 11:23
the space of three years and six *m*... Jas 5:17
they should be tormented five *m*..... Rev 9:5
power was to hurt men five *m*........ Rev 9:10
tread under foot forty and two *m*.... Rev 11:2
him to continue forty and two *m*..... Rev 13:5

MONUMENTS

the graves, and lodge in the *m*....... Is 65:4

MOON

and, behold, the sun and the *m*...... Gen 37:9
when thou seest the sun, and the *m*.. Deut 4:19

them, either the sun, or *m* .... Deut 17:3
things put forth by the *m* .... Deut 33:14
and thou, *M*, in the valley of .... Josh 10:12
the *m* stayed, until the people .... Josh 10:13
Behold, to morrow is the new *m* 1Sa 20:5
to David, To morrow is the new *m* 1Sa 20:18
and when the new *m* was come 1Sa 20:24
it is neither new *m*, nor sabbath 2Kin 4:23
Baal, to the sun, and to the *m* 2Kin 23:5
Behold even to the *m*, and it .... Job 25:5
or the *m* walking in brightness .... Job 31:26
the work of thy fingers, the *m* .... Ps 8:3
sun and *m* endure, throughout all ..... Ps 72:5
peace so long as the *m* endureth ...... Ps 72:7
Blow up the trumpet in the new *m* .... Ps 81:3
be established for ever as the *m* ...... Ps 89:37
He appointed the *m* for seasons .... Ps 104:19
thee by day, nor the *m* by night .... Ps 121:6
The *m* and stars to rule by night ...... Ps 136:9
Praise ye him, sun and *m* .... Ps 148:3
the sun, or the light, or the *m* .... Eccl 12:2
as the morning, fair as the *m* .... Song 6:10
and their round tires like the *m* .... Is 3:18
the *m* shall not cause her light .... Is 13:10
Then the *m* shall be confounded ...... Is 24:23
Moreover the light of the *m* shall ..... Is 30:26
shall the *m* give light unto thee .... Is 60:19
shall thy *m* withdraw itself .... Is 60:20
that from one new *m* to another .... Is 66:23
them before the sun, and the *m* .... Jer 8:2
day, and the ordinances of the *m* ..... Jer 31:35
the *m* shall not give her light .... Eze 32:7
of the new *m* it shall be opened .... Eze 46:1
in the day of the new *m* .... Eze 46:6
the *m* shall be dark, and the stars .... Joel 2:10
the *m* into blood, before the .... Joel 2:31
the *m* shall be darkened, and the ..... Joel 3:15
When will the new *m* be gone .... Amos 8:5
m stood still in their habitation .... Hab 3:11
the *m* shall not give her light .... Mt 24:29
the *m* shall not give her light .... Mk 13:24
he signs in the sun, and in the *m* ...... Lk 21:25
the *m* into blood, before that .... Acts 2:20
sun, and another glory of the *m* 1Cor 15:41
of an holyday, or of the new *m* .... Col 2:16
of hair, and the *m* became as blood ... Rev 6:12
and the third part of the *m* .... Rev 8:12
the *m* under her feet, and upon her ... Rev 12:1
need of the sun, neither of the *m* ...... Rev 21:23

MOONS
in the sabbaths, on the new *m* 1Chr 23:31
on the sabbaths, and on the new *m* ... 2Chr 2:4
on the sabbaths, and on the new *m* ... 2Chr 8:13
the sabbaths, and for the new *m* 2Chr 31:3
burnt offering, both of the new *m* ..... Ezr 3:5
of the sabbaths, of the new .... Neh 10:33
the new *m* and sabbaths, the .... Is 1:13
Your new *m* and your appointed ...... Is 1:14
in the feasts, and in the new *m* .... Eze 45:17
in the sabbaths and in the new *m* ..... Eze 46:3
cease, her feast days, her new *m* ..... Hos 2:11

MORASHTITE (*mo'-ras-thite*) Family name of
Micah the prophet.
Micah *M* prophesied in the .... Jer 26:18
Micah the *M* in the days of Jotham .... Mic 1:1

MORDECAI (*mor'-de-cahee*) See **MORDECAI'S.**
1. A clan leader with Zerubbabel.
Nehemiah, Seraiah, Reelaiah, *M* .... Ezr 2:2
Azariah, Raamiah, Nahamani, *M* ...... Neh 7:7
2. Cousin of Esther.
a certain Jew, whose name was *M* ..... Est 2:5
whom *M*, when her father and mother.. Est 2:7
for *M* had charged her that she .... Est 2:10
M walked every day before the .... Est 2:11
of Abihail the uncle of *M* .... Est 2:15
then *M* sat in the king's gate .... Est 2:19
as *M* had charged her .... Est 2:20
Esther at the commandment of *M* ..... Est 2:20
while *M* sat in the king's gate .... Est 2:21
And the thing was known to *M* .... Est 2:22
But *M* bowed not, nor did him .... Est 3:2
in the king's gate, said unto *M* .... Est 3:3
when Haman saw that *M* bowed not ... Est 3:5
scorn to lay hands on *M* alone .... Est 3:6
had shewed him the people of *M* .... Est 3:6
Ahasuerus, even the people of *M* ...... Est 3:6
When *M* perceived all that was .... Est 4:1
M rent his clothes, and put on .... Est 4:1
and sent raiment to clothe *M* .... Est 4:4
and gave him a commandment to *M* ... Est 4:5
So Hatach went forth to *M* unto .... Est 4:6
M told him of all that had .... Est 4:7
and told Esther the words of *M* .... Est 4:9
and gave him commandment unto *M* .. Est 4:10
they told to *M* Esther's words .... Est 4:12
Then *M* commanded to answer Esther.. Est 4:13
bade them return *M* this answer .... Est 4:15
So *M* went his way, and did .... Est 4:17
Haman saw *M* in the king's gate ...... Est 5:9
was full of indignation against *M* ...... Est 5:9
so long as I see *M* the Jew .... Est 5:13
king that *M* may be hanged thereon ... Est 5:14
that *M* had told of Bigthana and ...... Est 6:2
hath been done to *M* for this .... Est 6:3
honour on the gallows that he had ...... Est 6:4
said, and do even so to *M* the Jew .... Est 6:10
and the horse, and arrayed *M* .... Est 6:11
M came again to the king's gate .... Est 6:12
If *M* be of the seed of the Jews, ... Est 6:13

high, which Haman had made for *M* .... Est 7:9
that he had prepared for *M* .... Est 7:10
And *M* came before the king .... Est 8:1
from Haman, and gave it unto *M* ...... Est 8:2
Esther set *M* over the house of .... Est 8:2
to *M* the Jew, Behold, I have .... Est 8:7
that *M* commanded unto the Jews ..... Est 8:9
M went out from the presence of ...... Est 8:15
the fear of *M* fell upon them .... Est 9:3
for *M* was great in the king's .... Est 9:4
for this man *M* waxed greater and ..... Est 9:4
M wrote these things, and sent .... Est 9:20
as *M* had written unto them .... Est 9:23
the *M* the Jew, wrote with all .... Est 9:29
appointed, according as *M* the Jew .... Est 9:31
declaration of the greatness of *M* ..... Est 10:2
For *M* the Jew was next unto king ..... Est 10:3

MORDECAI'S (*mor'-de-cahees*) *Refers to
Mordecai 2.*
the king thereof in *M* name .... Est 2:22
to see whether *M* matters would .... Est 3:4

MORE See PREFACE.

MOREH (*mo'-reh*)
1. A place in Ephraim.
of Sichem, unto the plain of *M* .... Gen 12:6
Gilgal, beside the plains of *M* .... Deut 11:30
2. A place in Issachar.
side of them, by the hill of *M* .... Judg 7:1

MOREOVER
She said *m* unto him, We have both ... Gen 24:25
And say ye *m*, Behold, thy servant .... Gen 32:20
M he kissed all his brethren, and ...... Gen 45:15
They said *m* unto Pharaoh, For to ..... Gen 47:4
M I have given to thee one .... Gen 48:22
M he said, I am the God of thy .... Ex 3:6
God said *m* unto Moses, Thus shalt .... Ex 3:15
the man Moses was very great in .... Ex 11:3
M thou shalt provide out of all .... Ex 18:21
M thou shalt make the tabernacle ..... Ex 26:1
the LORD spake unto Moses, ... Ex 30:22
M the soul that shall touch any .... Lev 7:21
Ye ye shall eat no manner of blood ..... Lev 7:26
the *M* that goeth into the house .... Lev 14:46
M thou shalt not lie carnally .... Lev 18:20
M of the children of the .... Lev 25:45
m we saw the children of Anak .... Num 13:28
M thou hast not brought us into ...... Num 16:14
M it shall come to pass, that I .... Num 33:56
M ye shall take no satisfaction .... Num 35:31
m we have seen the sons of the ...... Deut 1:28
M your little ones, which ye said ...... Deut 1:39
the LORD thy God will send the .... Deut 7:20
M all these curses shall come .... Deut 28:45
M he will bring upon thee all the ...... Deut 28:60
the children of Ammon passed .... Judg 10:9
M Ruth the Moabitess, the wife of .... Ruth 4:10
M his mother made him a little 1Sa 2:19
M as for me, God forbid that I 1Sa 12:23
the Hebrews that were with the 1Sa 14:21
David said *m*, The LORD 1Sa 17:37
And David sware *m*, and said, Thy 1Sa 20:3
M, my father, see, yea, see the 1Sa 24:11
the LORD will also deliver 1Sa 28:19
I would *m* have given thee 2Sa 12:8
Absalom said *m*, Oh that I were 2Sa 15:4
M Ahithophel said unto Absalom, ... 2Sa 17:1
M, if he be gotten into a city 2Sa 17:13
the Philistines had yet war 2Sa 21:15
m the king's servants came to 1Kin 1:47
M thou knowest also what Joab the ... 1Kin 2:5
He said *m*, I have somewhat to say ... 1Kin 2:14
The king said *m* to Shimei 1Kin 2:44
M concerning a stranger, that is 1Kin 8:41
the king made a great throne of 1Kin 10:18
the LORD shall raise him up a 1Kin 14:14
M they reckoned not with the men, ... 2Kin 12:15
M Manasseh shed innocent blood 2Kin 21:16
the altar that was at Beth-el, ... 2Kin 23:15
the workers with familiar 2Kin 23:24
m in time past, even when Saul 1Chr 11:2
M they that were nigh them, even ... 1Chr 12:40
M I will subdue all thine enemies 1Chr 17:10
M, Abishai the son Zeruiah slew 1Chr 18:12
M there are workmen with thee in 1Chr 22:15
M four thousand were porters 1Chr 23:5
M David and the captains of the 1Chr 25:1
the sons of Obed-edom were, ... 1Chr 26:4
M I will establish his kingdom 1Chr 28:7
M, because I have set my 1Chr 29:3
the brasen altar, that Bezaleel 2Chr 1:5
Huram said *m*, Blessed be the LORD ... 2Chr 2:12
M he made an altar of brass, ... 2Chr 4:1
M the candlesticks with their 2Chr 4:20
M concerning the stranger, which 2Chr 6:32
M Solomon hallowed the middle of ... 2Chr 7:7
M the king made a great throne of ... 2Chr 9:17
M he took away the high places and .. 2Chr 17:6
M in Jerusalem did Jehoshaphat 2Chr 19:8
M he made high places in the 2Chr 21:11
M the LORD stirred up against 2Chr 21:16
M Jehoiada the priest delivered 2Chr 23:9
M Amaziah gathered Judah together... 2Chr 25:5
M Uzziah built towers in 2Chr 26:9
M Uzziah had an host of fighting 2Chr 26:11
M he built cities in the 2Chr 27:4
M he burnt incense in the valley 2Chr 28:3
M all the vessels, which king 2Chr 29:19

M Hezekiah the king and the 2Chr 29:30
M he commanded the people that 2Chr 31:4
M he provided him cities, and 2Chr 32:29
M Josiah kept a passover unto the 2Chr 35:1
M all the chief of the priests, ... 2Chr 36:14
M I make a decree what ye shall ...... Ezr 6:8
of Israel: of the sons .... Ezr 10:25
M I said unto the king, If it .... Neh 2:7
the old gate repaired Jehoiada .... Neh 3:6
the Nethinims dwelt in Ophel, ... Neh 3:26
M from the time that I was .... Neh 5:14
M there were at my table an .... Neh 5:17
M in those days the nobles of .... Neh 6:17
M thou leddest them in the day by .... Neh 9:12
M thou gavest them kingdoms and .... Neh 9:22
M the porters, Akkub, Talmon, and .. Neh 11:19
the Levites: Jeshua .... Neh 12:8
Haman said *m*, Yea, Esther the .... Est 5:12
M Job continued his parable, and ..... Job 27:1
M Job continued his parable, and ..... Job 29:1
M the LORD answered Job, and said, .. Job 40:1
M by them is thy servant warned ..... Ps 19:11
Elihu spake *m*, and said. .... Job 35:1
Elihu spake *m*, and said. .... Job 36:1
he refused the tabernacle of .... Ps 78:67
he called for a famine upon the .... Ps 105:16
m I saw under the sun the place ...... Eccl 3:16
The profit of the earth is for .... Eccl 5:9
M he hath not seen the sun, nor ...... Eccl 6:5
And *m*, because the preacher was ..... Eccl 12:9
M the LORD saith, Because the .... Is 3:16
M the LORD spake again unto Ahaz, .. Is 7:10
the LORD said unto me, Take .... Is 8:1
M they that work in fine flax, and .... Is 19:9
M the multitude of thy strangers ..... Is 29:5
M the light of the moon shall be ...... Is 30:26
He said *m*, For there shall be .... Is 39:8
the word of the LORD came unto .... Jer 11:1
the word of the LORD came to me ...... Jer 2:1
M thou shalt say unto them, Thus ..... Jer 8:4
M I will deliver all the strength .... Jer 20:5
M I will take from them the voice ..... Jer 25:10
the word of the LORD came unto .... Jer 33:1
the word of the LORD came to .... Jer 33:23
M Jeremiah said unto king, ... Jer 37:18
M he put out Zedekiah's eyes, and ... Jer 39:7
M Johanan the son of Kareah, and ... Jer 40:13
M Jeremiah said unto all the .... Jer 44:24
M I will cause to cease in Moab, ... Jer 48:35
M he said unto me, Son of man, ... Eze 3:10
M he said unto me, Son of man, ... Eze 3:10
take thou unto thee an iron pan .... Eze 4:3
M he said unto me, Son of man, ... Eze 4:16
M I will make thee waste, and a ...... Eze 5:14
the word of the LORD came unto .... Eze 7:1
the spirit lifted me up, and .... Eze 11:1
the word of the LORD came to me . ... Eze 12:17
M thou hast taken thy sons and thy .. Eze 16:20
Thou hast *m* multiplied thy .... Eze 16:29
the word of the LORD came unto .... Eze 17:11
M take thou up a lamentation for ..... Eze 19:1
M also I gave them my sabbaths, ... Eze 20:12
the word of the LORD came unto .... Eze 20:45
the word of the LORD came unto .... Eze 22:1
The LORD said *m* unto me .... Eze 23:36
M this they have done unto me .... Eze 23:38
the word of the LORD came unto .... Eze 28:11
the word of the LORD came unto .... Eze 35:1
M the word of the LORD came unto ... Eze 36:16
M, thou son of man, take thee one ... Eze 37:16
M I will make a covenant of peace .... Eze 37:26
M, when ye shall divide by lot .... Eze 45:1
M the prince shall not take of .... Eze 48:18
from the possession of the .... Eze 48:22
the word of the LORD came unto .... Zec 4:8
He said *m*, This is the .... Zec 5:6
M when ye fast, be not, as the .... Mt 6:16
M if thy brother shall trespass. .... Mt 18:15
the dogs came and licked his .... Lk 16:21
m also my flesh shall rest in .... Acts 2:26
M these six brethren accompanied .... Acts 11:12
M ye see and hear, that not alone .... Acts 19:26
the law entered, that the .... Rom 5:20
whom he did predestinate, them ...... Rom 8:30
M it is required in stewards, ... 1Cor 4:2
M, brethren, I would not that ye..... 1Cor 10:1
M, brethren, I declare unto you. 1Cor 15:1
M I call God for a record upon my 2Cor 1:23
M, brethren, we do you to wit of 2Cor 8:1
He must have a good report of 1Ti 3:7
M he sprinkled with blood both ...... Heb 9:21
of bonds and imprisonment. .... Heb 11:36
M I will endeavour that ye may be 2Pet 1:15

MORESHETH See MORASHTITE.

MORESHETH-GATH (*mor'-e-sheth-gath*) See
MORASHTITE. *A city in Judah.*
shalt thou give presents to *M* .... Mic 1:14

MORIAH (*mo-ri'-ah*) *The Temple Mount.*
and get thee into the land of *M* .... Gen 22:2
of LORD in Jerusalem in mount *M* 2Chr 3:1

MORNING
and the *m* were the first day. .... Gen 1:5
the *m* were the second day. .... Gen 1:8
and the *m* were the third day. .... Gen 1:13
the *m* were the fourth day. .... Gen 1:19
and the *m* were the fifth day. .... Gen 1:23
and the *m* were the sixth day. .... Gen 1:31
And when the *m* arose, then the ...... Gen 19:15
the *m* to the place where he stood. ... Gen 19:27

Abimelech rose early in the m .... Gen 20:8
And Abraham rose up early in the m.. Gen 21:14
And Abraham rose up early in the m.. Gen 22:3
and they rose up in the m, and he .... Gen 24:54
And they rose up betimes in the m.... Gen 26:31
And Jacob rose up early in the m...... Gen 28:18
And it came to pass, that in the m ... Gen 29:25
early in the m Laban rose up, and .... Gen 31:55
Joseph came in unto them in the m .. Gen 40:6
it came to pass in the m that his ...... Gen 41:8
As soon as the m was light .... Gen 44:3
in the m he shall devour the prey .... Gen 49:27
Get thee unto Pharaoh in the m....... Ex 7:15
Moses, Rise up early in the .... Ex 8:20
Moses, Rise up early in the m.......... Ex 9:13
and when it was m, the east wind .... Ex 10:13
nothing of it remain until the m ...... Ex 12:10
the m ye shall burn with fire............ Ex 12:10
the door of his house until the m..... Ex 12:22
that in the m watch the LORD........... Ex 14:24
his strength when the m appeared ... Ex 14:27
And in the m, then ye shall see .... Ex 16:7
in the m bread to the full .... Ex 16:8
in the m ye shall be filled with .... Ex 16:12
in the m the dew lay round about .... Ex 16:13
Let no man leave of it till the m ...... Ex 16:19
of them left of it until the m............ Ex 16:20
And they gathered it every m .... Ex 16:21
up for you to be kept until the m .... Ex 16:23
And they laid it up till the m .... Ex 16:24
Moses from the m unto the evening .. Ex 18:13
stand by thee from m unto even ...... Ex 18:14
to pass on the third day in the m .... Ex 19:16
my sacrifice remain until the m....... Ex 23:18
LORD, and rose up early in the m..... Ex 24:4
from evening to m before the LORD .. Ex 27:21
of the bread, remain unto the m...... Ex 29:34
lamb thou shalt offer in the m......... Ex 29:39
to the meat offering of the m........... Ex 29:41
thereon sweet incense every m .... Ex 30:7
And be ready in the m, and come up.. Ex 34:2
come up in the m unto mount Sinai .. Ex 34:2
and Moses rose up in the m unto .... Ex 34:4
the passover be left unto the m .... Ex 34:25
unto him free offerings every m ...... Ex 36:3
the altar all night unto the m.......... Lev 6:9
shall burn wood on it every m .... Lev 6:12
perpetual, half of it in the m........... Lev 6:20
not leave any of it until the m .... Lev 7:15
the burnt sacrifice of the m .... Lev 9:17
with thee all night until the m .... Lev 19:13
the m before the LORD continually .. Lev 24:3
shall leave none of it unto the m .... Num 9:12
appearance of fire, until the m......... Num 9:15
cloud abode from even unto the m... Num 9:21
the cloud was taken up in the m ..... Num 9:21
And they rose up early in the m....... Num 14:40
And Balaam rose up in the m .... Num 22:13
And Balaam rose up in the m .... Num 22:21
lamb shalt thou offer in the m......... Num 28:4
as the meat offering of the m .... Num 28:8
the burnt offering in the m.............. Num 28:23
remain all night until the m............. Deut 16:4
and thou shalt turn in the m............ Deut 16:7
In the m thou shalt say, Would .... Deut 28:67
shalt say, Would God it were m........ Deut 28:67
And Joshua rose early in the m........ Josh 3:1
And Joshua rose early in the m........ Josh 6:12
In the m therefore ye shall be .... Josh 7:14
So Joshua rose up early in the m ..... Josh 7:16
And Joshua rose up early in the m ... Josh 8:10
of the city arose early in the m .... Judg 6:28
put to death whilst it is yet m.......... Judg 6:31
And it shall be, that in the m........... Judg 9:33
all the night, saying, In the m.......... Judg 16:2
when they arose early in the m .... Judg 19:5
he arose early in the m on the.......... Judg 19:8
her all the night until the m............. Judg 19:25
And her lord rose up in the m.......... Judg 19:27
of Israel rose up in the m................. Judg 20:19
even from the m until now .... Ruth 2:7
night, and it shall be in the m.......... Ruth 3:13
lie down until the m......................... Ruth 3:13
she lay at his feet until the m .... Ruth 3:14
And they rose up in the m early 1Sa 1:19
And Samuel lay until the m.............. 1Sa 3:15
they arose early on the morrow m.... 1Sa 5:4
midst of the host in the m watch 1Sa 11:11
and spoil them until the m light 1Sa 14:36
rose early to meet Saul in the m...... 1Sa 15:12
And the Philistine drew near m........ 1Sa 17:16
And David rose up early in the m.... 1Sa 17:20
take heed to thyself until the m 1Sa 19:2
him, and to slay him in the m 1Sa 19:11
And it came to pass in the m........... 1Sa 20:35
m light any that pisseth against 1Sa 25:22
m light any that pisseth against 1Sa 25:34
less or more, until the m light......... 1Sa 25:36
But it came to pass in the m............ 1Sa 25:37
now rise up early in the m with 1Sa 29:10
soon as ye be up early in the m....... 1Sa 29:10
rose up early to depart in the m...... 1Sa 29:11
surely then in the m the people 2Sa 2:27
And it came to pass in the m........... 2Sa 11:14
by the m light there lacked not 2Sa 17:22
he shall be as the light of the m...... 2Sa 23:4
riseth, even a m without clouds 2Sa 23:4
For when David was up in the m...... 2Sa 24:11
the m even to the time appointed ... 2Sa 24:15

when I rose in the m to give my 1Kin 3:21
when I had considered it in the m ... 1Kin 3:21
him bread and flesh in the m 1Kin 17:6
bread from even until noon............. 1Kin 18:26
And it came to pass in the m 2Kin 3:20
And they rose up early in the m....... 2Kin 3:22
if we tarry till the m light 2Kin 7:9
in of the gate until the m................ 2Kin 10:9
And it came to pass in the m 2Kin 10:9
altar burn the m burnt offering 2Kin 16:15
and when they arose early in the m .. 2Kin 19:35
thereof every m pertained to them .. 1Chr 9:27
the burnt offering continually m 1Chr 16:40
And to stand every m to thank 1Chr 23:30
and for the burnt offerings m 2Chr 2:4
they burn unto the LORD every m 2Chr 13:11
And they rose early in the m............ 2Chr 20:20
offerings, to wit, for the m 2Chr 31:3
the LORD, even burnt offerings m .... Ezr 3:3
of the m till the stars appeared....... Neh 4:21
gate from the m until midday.......... Neh 8:3
them, and rose up early in the m .... Job 1:5
are destroyed from m to evening .... Job 4:20
thou shouldest visit him every m .... Job 7:18
and thou shalt seek me in the m ..... Job 7:21
forth, thou shalt be as the m........... Job 11:17
For the m is to them even as the m .. Job 24:17
When the m stars sang together,...... Job 38:7
commanded the m since thy days .... Job 38:12
are like the eyelids of the m............ Job 41:18
My voice shalt thou hear in the m ... Ps 5:3
in the m will I direct my prayer ...... Ps 5:3
a night, but joy cometh in the m ..... Ps 30:5
have dominion over them in the m .. Ps 49:14
Evening, and m, and at noon, will I .. Ps 55:17
sing aloud of thy mercy in the m .... Ps 59:16
makest the outgoings of the m .... Ps 65:8
plagued, and chastened every m ...... Ps 73:14
in the m shall my prayer prevent..... Ps 88:13
in the m they are like grass .... Ps 90:5
In the m it flourisheth, and............. Ps 90:6
forth thy lovingkindness, in the m .. Ps 92:2
holiness from the womb of the m .... Ps 110:3
I will early destroy all the.............. Ps 119:147
than they that watch for the m........ Ps 130:6
than they that watch for the m........ Ps 130:6
If I take the wings of the m............. Ps 139:9
hear thy lovingkindness in the m .... Ps 143:8
take our fill of love until the m....... Prov 7:18
loud voice, rising early in the m...... Prov 27:14
and thy princes eat in the m .... Eccl 10:16
In the m sow thy seed, and in the ... Eccl 11:6
she that looketh forth as the m........ Song 6:10
them that rise up early in the m...... Is 5:11
heaven, O Lucifer, son of the m...... Is 14:12
in the m shalt thou make thy seed .. Is 17:11
and before the m he is not.............. Is 17:14
The m cometh, and also the night ... Is 21:12
for m by m shall it pass.................. Is 28:19
be thou their arm every m .... Is 33:2
and when they arose early in the m .. Is 37:36
I reckoned till m, that, as a............ Is 38:13
he wakeneth m by m, he................. Is 50:4
thy light break forth as the m.......... Is 58:8
They were as fed horses in the m..... Jer 5:8
and let him hear the cry in the m.... Jer 20:16
Execute judgment in the m.............. Jer 21:12
They are new every .... Lam 3:23
The m is come unto thee, O thou .... Eze 7:7
the m is gone forth .... Eze 7:10
in the m came the word of the .... Eze 12:8
I spake unto the people in the m .... Eze 24:18
I did in the m as I was commanded .. Eze 24:18
until he came to me in the m .... Eze 33:22
thou shalt prepare it every m.......... Eze 46:13
a meat offering for it every m .... Eze 46:14
every m for a continual burnt......... Eze 46:15
king arose very early in the m .... Dan 6:19
the m which was told is true............ Dan 8:26
going forth is prepared as the m ..... Hos 6:3
for your goodness is as a m cloud ... Hos 6:4
in the m it burneth as a flaming .... Hos 7:6
in a m shall the king of Israel......... Hos 10:15
they shall be as the m cloud............ Hos 13:3
as the m spread upon the .... Joel 2:2
and bring your sacrifices every m.... Amos 4:4
that maketh the m darkness............. Amos 4:13
the shadow of death into the m ...... Amos 5:8
worm when the m rose the next day .. Jonah 4:7
when the m is light, they................ Mic 2:1
every m doth he bring his .... Zeph 3:5
And in the m, It will be foul........... Mt 16:3
the m to hire labourers into his ...... Mt 20:1
Now in the m as he returned into ... Mt 21:18
When the m was come, all the......... Mt 27:1
And in the m, rising up a great ...... Mk 1:35
And in the m, as they passed by,..... Mk 11:20
at the cockcrowing, or in the m....... Mk 13:35
straightway in the m the chief .... Mk 15:1
very early in the m the first day ...... Mk 16:2
in the m to him in the temple......... Lk 21:38
of the week, very early in the .... Lk 24:1
And And early in the m he came..... Jn 8:2
early in the m he came again into.... Jn 8:2
But when the m was now come .... Jn 21:4
into the temple early in the .... Acts 5:21
the prophets, from m till evening ... Acts 28:23
And I will give him the m star .... Rev 2:28
of David, the bright and m star...... Rev 22:16

MORROW
And it came to pass on the m .... Gen 19:34
And he said, To m............................ Ex 8:10
and from his people, to m .... Ex 8:23
and from his people, to m .... Ex 8:29
To m the LORD shall do this thing ... Ex 9:5
the LORD did that thing on the m.... Ex 9:6
to m about this time I will cause .... Ex 9:18
to m will I bring the locusts............ Ex 10:4
To m is the rest of the holy............. Ex 16:23
to m I will stand on the top of .... Ex 17:9
And it came to pass on the m .... Ex 18:13
and sanctify them to day and to the .. Ex 19:10
To m is a feast to the LORD .... Ex 32:5
And they rose up early on the m ..... Ex 32:6
And it came to pass on the m .... Ex 32:30
on the m also the remainder of it ... Lev 7:16
same day ye offer it, and on the m .. Lev 19:6
leave none of it until the m............. Lev 22:30
on the m after the sabbath the .... Lev 23:11
you from the m after the sabbath ... Lev 23:15
Even unto the m after the seventh .. Lev 23:16
Sanctify yourselves against to m .... Num 11:18
To m turn you, and get you into ..... Num 14:25
Even to m the LORD will shew who .. Num 16:5
in them before the LORD to m .... Num 16:7
thou, and they, and Aaron, to m..... Num 16:16
But on the m all the congregation ... Num 16:41
that on the m Moses went into the .. Num 17:8
And it came to pass on the m .... Num 22:41
on the m after the passover the ...... Num 33:3
for to m the LORD will do wonders .. Josh 3:5
land on the m after the passover..... Josh 5:11
the manna ceased on the m after .... Josh 5:12
Sanctify yourselves against to m .... Josh 7:13
for to m about this time will I .... Josh 11:6
that to m he will be wroth with....... Josh 22:18
for he rose up early on the m .... Judg 6:38
And it came to pass on the m .... Judg 9:42
to m get you early on your way....... Judg 19:9
for to m I will deliver them into ..... Judg 20:28
And it came to pass on the m .... Judg 21:4
of Ashdod arose early on the m....... 1Sa 5:3
they arose early on the m morning .. 1Sa 5:4
To m about this time I will send 1Sa 9:16
to m I will let thee go, and will 1Sa 9:19
the men of Jabesh-gilead, To m 1Sa 11:9
To m we will come out unto you,.... 1Sa 11:10
And it was so on the m, that Saul ... 1Sa 11:11
And it came to pass on the m 1Sa 18:10
night, to m thou shalt be slain........ 1Sa 19:11
to m is the new moon, and I should .. 1Sa 20:5
my father about to m any time........ 1Sa 20:12
to David, To m is the new moon..... 1Sa 20:18
And it came to pass on the m 1Sa 20:27
to m shalt thou and thy sons be 1Sa 20:31
And it came to pass on the m 1Sa 31:8
to m I will let thee depart............... 2Sa 11:12
in Jerusalem that day, and the m..... 2Sa 11:12
of them by to m about this time 1Kin 19:2
unto thee to m about this time,....... 1Kin 20:6
day, and we will eat my son to m.... 2Kin 6:28
To m about this time shall a........... 2Kin 7:1
shall be to m about this time in...... 2Kin 7:18
And it came to pass on the m 2Kin 8:15
me to Jezreel to m in the second 2Kin 10:6
And it came to pass on the m 1Chr 10:8
on the m after that day, even a....... 1Chr 29:21
To m go ye down against them........ 2Chr 20:16
to m go out against them 2Chr 20:17
on the m she returned into the .... Est 2:14
I will do to m as the king hath .... Est 5:8
to m am I invited unto her also ...... Est 5:12
to m speak thou unto the king .... Est 5:14
which are in Shushan to do to m .... Est 9:13
come again, and to m I will give ..... Prov 3:28
Boast not thyself of to m................. Prov 27:1
for to m we shall die .... Is 22:13
to m shall be as this day, and......... Is 56:12
And it came to pass on the m .... Jer 20:3
gnaw not the bones till the m .... Zeph 3:3
to m is cast into the oven, shall ...... Mt 6:30
therefore no thought for the m........ Mt 6:34
for the m shall take thought for ..... Mt 6:34
And on the m, when they were come.. Mk 11:12
on the m when he departed, he ...... Lk 10:35
to m is cast into the oven .... Lk 12:28
and I do cures to day and to m ...... Lk 13:32
I must walk to day, and to m .... Lk 13:33
And it came to pass on the m .... Acts 4:5
On the m, as they went on their ..... Acts 10:9
on the m Peter went away with ...... Acts 10:23
the m after they entered into .... Acts 10:24
them, ready to depart on the m ...... Acts 20:7
On the m, because he would have ... Acts 22:30
he bring him down unto you to m ... Acts 23:15
down Paul to m into the council ..... Acts 23:20
On the m they left the horsemen..... Acts 23:32
without any delay on the m I sat .... Acts 25:17
To m, said he, thou shalt hear .... Acts 25:22
And on the m, when Agrippa was .... Acts 25:23
for to m we die 1Cor 15:32
To day or to m we will go into .... Jas 4:13
know not what shall be on the m .... Jas 4:14

MORSEL
And I will fetch a m of bread.......... Gen 18:5
thine heart with a m of bread......... Judg 19:5
and dip my m in the vinegar .... Ruth 2:14
a m of bread, and shall say, To 1Sa 2:36
let me set a m of bread before 1Sa 28:22

a *m* of bread in thine hand............ 1Kin 17:11
Or have eaten my *m* myself alone..... Job 31:17
Better is a dry *m*, and quietness ...... Prov 17:1
The *m* which thou hast eaten shalt ..... Prov 23:8
who for one *m* of meat sold his .... Heb 12:16

MORSELS
He casteth forth his ice like a *m* .... Ps 147:17

MORTAL
Shall *m* man be more just than God...... Job 4:17
therefore reign in your *m* body......... Rom 6:12
your *m* bodies by his Spirit that .... Rom 8:11
this *m* must put on immortality 1Cor 15:53
and this *m* shall have put on 1Cor 15:54
be made manifest in our *m* flesh 2Cor 4:11

MORTALITY
that we might be swallowed up of........ 2Cor 5:4

MORTALLY
smite him *m* that he die, and............ Deut 19:11

MORTAR
it in mills, or beat it in a *m*................ Num 11:8
in a *m* among wheat with a pestle..... Prov 27:22

MORTER
stone, and slime had they for *m*......... Gen 11:3
bitter with hard bondage, in *m*.......... Ex 1:14
and he shall take other *m*, and .... Lev 14:42
and all the *m* of the house............. Lev 14:45
shall come upon princes as upon *m*.... Is 41:25
daubed it with untempered *m* .... Eze 13:10
which daub it with untempered *m* .... Eze 13:11
ye have daubed with untempered *m* .. Eze 13:14
have daubed it with untempered *m* ... Eze 13:15
daubed them with untempered *m* ..... Eze 22:28
go into clay, and tread the *m*............ Nah 3:14

MORTGAGED
We have *m* our lands, vineyards, ... Neh 5:3

MORTIFY
Spirit do ye the deeds of the body...... Rom 8:13
M therefore your members which .... Col 3:5

MOSERA (mo-se'-rah) See **MOSEROTH**. *Where Aaron was buried.*
of the children of Jaakan to *M*.......... Deut 10:6

MOSERAH See **MOSERA**.

MOSEROTH (mo-se'-roth) See **MOSERA**. *An Israelite encampment in the wilderness.*
and encamped at *M*...................... Num 33:30
And they departed from *M*, and......... Num 33:31

MOSES (mo'-zez) See PREFACE. SEE ALSO Moses'. *Led Israel out of Egypt.*
And she called his name *M*............... Ex 2:10
of the bush, and said, *M*, *M* .... Ex 3:4
And God said unto *M*, I AM THAT I ..... Ex 3:14
M took his wife and his sons, and...... Ex 4:20
And *M* and Aaron went in unto......... Ex 7:10
M took the bones of Joseph with....... Ex 13:19
M stretched out his hand over the...... Ex 14:21
And the LORD said unto *M*, Stretch..... Ex 14:26
And the people murmured against *M*... Ex 15:24
M went up unto God, and the LORD..... Ex 19:3
So *M* went down unto the people,...... Ex 19:25
And the LORD said unto *M*, Thus .... Ex 20:22
M wrote all the words of the LORD...... Ex 24:4
M went up into the mount of God....... Ex 24:13
M was in the mount forty days and..... Ex 24:18
when the people saw that *M*............. Ex 32:1
M said unto Aaron, What did this....... Ex 32:21
And the LORD said unto *M*, Hew thee... Ex 34:1
And the LORD said unto *M*, Write....... Ex 34:27
when *M* came down from mount Sinai .. Ex 34:29
M brought Aaron and his sons, and .... Lev 8:6
as the LORD commanded *M* .... Lev 8:9
LORD spake unto *M* in mount Sinai..... Lev 25:1
And the LORD said unto *M*, Number .... Num 3:40
which *M* sent to spy out the land....... Num 13:16
M lifted up his hand, and with his...... Num 20:11
LORD spake unto *M* .... Num 20:12
And the LORD said unto *M*, Take........ Num 27:18
M called unto Joshua, and said .... Deut 31:7
So *M* the servant of the LORD died...... Deut 34:5
Now after the death of *M* the........... Josh 1:1
we hearkened unto *M* in all things..... Josh 1:17
be with thee, as he was with *M*......... Josh 1:17
the stones a copy of the law of *M*...... Josh 8:32
there appeared unto them *M* .... Matt 17:3
appeared unto them Elias with *M*....... Mk 9:4
with him two men, which were *M*....... Lk 9:30
In which time *M* was born, and was.... Acts 7:20
face of *M* for the glory of his........... 2Cor 3:7
as also *M* was faithful in all his......... Heb 3:2
By faith *M*, when he was born, was..... Heb 11:23
By faith *M*, when he was come to...... Heb 11:24
was the sight, that *M* said.............. Heb 12:21
he disputed about the body of *M*....... Jude 9
the song of *M* the servant of God...... Rev 15:3

MOSES'
But *M* hands were heavy .... Ex 17:12
M father in law, heard of all........... Ex 18:1
M father in law, took Zipporah,......... Ex 18:2
M wife, after he had sent.............. Ex 18:2
M father in law, came with his......... Ex 18:5
M father in law, took a burnt........... Ex 18:12
to eat bread with *M* father in law ..... Ex 18:12
when *M* father in law saw all that ..... Ex 18:14
M father in law said unto him,......... Ex 18:17

M anger waxed hot, and he cast the.... Ex 32:19
two tables of testimony in *M* hand..... Ex 34:29
that the skin of *M* face shone.......... Ex 34:35
ram of consecration it was *M* part..... Lev 8:29
M father in law, We are............... Num 10:29
son of Nun, *M* minister, saying,........ Josh 1:1
M father in law, went up out of .... Judg 1:16
and the Pharisees sit in *M* seat........ Mt 23:2
but we are *M* disciples................ Jn 9:28
He that despised *M* law died........... Heb 10:28

MOST
was the priest of the *m* high God...... Gen 14:18
be Abram of the *m* high God........... Gen 14:19
And blessed be the *m* high God........ Gen 14:20
the *m* high God, the possessor of...... Gen 14:22
the holy place and the *m* holy .... Ex 26:33
the testimony in the holy place .... Ex 26:34
and it shall be an altar *m* holy.......... Ex 29:37
it is *m* holy unto the LORD............. Ex 30:10
them, that they may be *m* holy .... Ex 30:29
it shall be unto you *m* holy .... Ex 30:36
and it shall be an altar *m* holy.......... Ex 40:10
it is a thing *m* holy of the............. Lev 2:3
it is a thing *m* holy of the............. Lev 2:10
it is *m* holy, as is the sin.............. Lev 6:17
it is *m* holy.......................... Lev 6:25
it is *m* holy.......................... Lev 6:29
it is *m* holy.......................... Lev 7:1
it is *m* holy.......................... Lev 7:6
for it is *m* holy...................... Lev 10:12
holy place, seeing it is *m* holy......... Lev 10:17
it is *m* holy......................... Lev 14:13
of his God, both of the *m* holy .... Lev 21:22
for it is *m* holy unto him of the....... Lev 24:9
thing is *m* holy unto the LORD......... Lev 27:28
about the *m* holy things .... Num 4:4
approach unto the *m* holy things....... Num 4:19
the thine of the *m* holy things......... Num 18:9
shall be *m* holy for thee and for...... Num 18:9
In the *m* holy place shalt thou......... Num 18:10
knew the knowledge of the *m* High.... Num 24:16
When the *M* High divided to the....... Deut 32:8
the *m* High uttered his voice.......... 2Sa 22:14
Was he not *m* honourable of thine 2Sa 23:19
oracle, even for the *m* holy place...... 1Kin 6:16
the *m* holy place, and for the......... 1Kin 7:50
to the *m* holy place, even under 1Kin 8:6
all the work of the place *m* holy 1Chr 6:49
should sanctify the *m* holy things 1Chr 23:13
And he made the *m* holy house........ 2Chr 3:8
in the *m* holy house he made two 2Chr 3:10
thereof for the *m* holy place.......... 2Chr 4:22
into the *m* holy place, even under 2Chr 5:7
of the LORD, and the *m* holy things ... 2Chr 31:14
not eat of the *m* holy things.......... Ezr 2:63
not eat of the *m* holy things.......... Neh 7:65
one of the king's *m* noble princes...... Est 6:9
thou condemn him that is *m* just...... Job 34:17
to the name of the LORD *m* high....... Ps 7:17
praise to thy name, O thou *m* High .... Ps 9:2
hast made him *m* blessed for ever..... Ps 21:6
through the mercy of the *m* High ...... Ps 21:7
O *m* mighty, with thy glory and thy.... Ps 45:3
of the tabernacles of the *m* High ...... Ps 46:4
For the LORD *m* high is terrible........ Ps 47:2
and pay thy vows unto the *m* High .... Ps 50:14
fight against me, O thou *m* High ...... Ps 56:2
I will cry unto God *m* high............ Ps 57:2
is there knowledge in the *m* High ..... Ps 73:11
of the right hand of the *m* High ...... Ps 77:10
the *m* High in the wilderness.......... Ps 78:17
and provoked the *m* high God......... Ps 78:56
of you are children of the *m* High ..... Ps 82:6
art the *m* high over all the earth...... Ps 83:18
the *m* High shall abide under the...... Ps 91:1
is my refuge, even the *m* High .... Ps 91:9
praises unto thy name, O *m* High ...... Ps 92:1
LORD, art *m* high for evermore........ Ps 92:8
the counsel of the *m* High............ Ps 107:11
M men will proclaim every one....... Prov 20:6
His head is as the *m* fine gold......... Song 5:11
His mouth is *m* sweet................ Song 5:16
which hath a *m* vehement flame....... Song 8:6
I will be like the *m* high.............. Is 14:14
in upright, dost weigh the path of ...... Is 26:7
an only son, *m* bitter lamentation..... Jer 6:26
I am against thee, O thou *m* proud..... Jer 50:31
the *m* proud shall stumble and fall .... Jer 50:32
man before the face of the *m* High .... Lam 3:35
Out of the mouth of the *m* High....... Lam 3:38
how is the *m* fine gold changed....... Lam 4:1
for they are *m* rebellious............. Eze 2:7
and rulers clothed *m* gorgeously ...... Eze 23:12
I will lay the land *m* desolate .... Eze 33:28
and I will make the *m* desolate........ Eze 33:29
and I will make them *m* desolate ...... Eze 33:5
will I make mount Seir *m* desolate ..... Eze 35:7
unto me, This is the *m* holy place...... Eze 41:4
LORD shall eat the *m* holy things....... Eze 42:13
shall they lay the *m* holy things .... Eze 42:13
round about shall be *m* holy.......... Eze 43:12
holy things, in the *m* holy place....... Eze 44:13
the sanctuary and the *m* holy place.... Eze 45:3
thing *m* holy by the border of the..... Eze 48:12
he commanded the *m* mighty men .... Dan 3:20
ye servants of the *m* high God......... Dan 3:26
the living may know that the *m*........ Dan 4:17
this is the decree of the *m* High ...... Dan 4:24
till thou know that the *m* High .... Dan 4:25
until thou know that the *m* High ...... Dan 4:32

unto me, and I blessed the *m* High..... Dan 4:34
O thou king, the *m* high God gave ..... Dan 5:18
till he knew that the *m* high God...... Dan 5:21
the saints of the *m* High.............. Dan 7:18
given to the saints of the *m* High...... Dan 7:22
great words against the *m* High .... Dan 7:25
wear out the saints of the *m* High ..... Dan 7:25
of the saints of the *m* High........... Dan 7:27
prophecy, and to anoint the *m* Holy.... Dan 9:24
and take the *m* fenced cities........... Dan 11:15
Thus shall he do in the *m* strong ...... Dan 11:39
return, but not to the *m* High .... Hos 7:16
they called them to the *m* High........ Hos 11:7
provoked him to anger bitterly.......... Hos 12:14
the *m* upright is sharper than a........ Mic 7:4
m of his mighty works were done...... Mt 11:20
Jesus, thou Son of the *m* high God..... Mk 5:7
are *m* surely believed among us........ Lk 1:1
in order, *m* excellent Theophilus, ... Lk 1:3
which of them will love him *m*......... Lk 7:42
that he, to whom he forgave *m*........ Lk 7:43
Jesus, thou Son of God *m* high......... Lk 8:28
Howbeit the *m* High dwelleth not...... Acts 7:48
the servants of the *m* high God........ Acts 16:17
Sorrowing *m* of all for the words,...... Acts 20:38
the *m* excellent governor Felix......... Acts 23:26
places, *m* noble Felix, with all......... Acts 24:3
that after the *m* straitest sect......... Acts 26:5
I am not mad, *m* noble Festus......... Acts 26:25
be by two, or at the *m* by three....... 1Cor 14:27
we are of all men *m* miserable........ 1Cor 15:19
M gladly therefore will I rather....... 2Cor 12:9
Salem, priest of the *m* high God....... Heb 7:1
yourselves on your *m* holy faith....... Jude 20
manner vessels of *m* precious wood.... Rev 18:12
was like unto a stone *m* precious ...... Rev 21:11

MOTE
why beholdest thou the *m* that is...... Mt 7:3
pull out the *m* out of thine eye........ Mt 7:4
the *m* out of thy brother's eye .... Mt 7:5
why beholdest thou the *m* that is...... Lk 6:41
let me pull out the *m* that is in....... Lk 6:42
see clearly to pull out the *m*.......... Lk 6:42

MOTH
which are crushed before the *m*....... Job 4:19
as a garment that is *m* eaten.......... Job 13:28
He buildeth his house as a *m*.......... Job 27:18
beauty to consume away like a *m* ..... Ps 39:11
the *m* shall eat them up .... Is 50:9
For the *m* shall eat them up like...... Is 51:8
will I be unto Ephraim as a *m*......... Hos 5:12
treasures upon earth, where *m*........ Mt 6:19
where neither *m* nor rust doth .... Mt 6:20
approacheth, neither *m* corrupteth..... Lk 12:33

MOTHEATEN
corrupted, and your garments are *m*... Jas 5:2

MOTHER
a man leave his father and his *m* ...... Gen 2:24
she was the *m* of all living............ Gen 3:20
and she shall be a *m* of nations .... Gen 17:16
but not the daughter of my *m* .... Gen 20:12
his *m* took him a wife out of the...... Gen 21:21
and to her *m* precious things......... Gen 24:53
her *m*, and of her father, Let the...... Gen 24:55
be thou the *m* of thousands of .... Gen 24:60
her into his *m* Sarah's tent............ Gen 24:67
And Jacob said to Rebekah his *m*...... Gen 27:11
his *m* said unto him, Upon me be ..... Gen 27:13
fetched, and brought them to his *m*.... Gen 27:14
his *m* made savoury meat, such as ... Gen 27:14
of Rebekah, Jacob's and Esau's *m* ..... Gen 28:5
Jacob obeyed his father and his *m* .... Gen 28:7
and brought them unto his *m* Leah.... Gen 30:14
me, and the *m* with the children ...... Gen 32:11
Shall I and thy *m* and thy brethren .... Gen 37:10
and he alone is left of his *m*.......... Gen 44:20
maid went and called the child's *m*.... Ex 2:8
Honour thy father and thy *m* .... Ex 20:12
that smiteth his father, or his *m* ...... Ex 21:15
that curseth his father, or his *m* ...... Ex 21:17
father, or the nakedness of thy *m*..... Lev 18:7
she is thy *m*......................... Lev 18:7
thy father, or the daughter of thy *m*... Lev 18:9
Ye shall fear every man his *m* .... Lev 19:3
m shall be surely put to death........ Lev 20:9
hath cursed his father or his *m*........ Lev 20:9
And if a man take a wife and her *m*.... Lev 20:14
near unto him, that is, for his *m*...... Lev 21:2
for his father, or for his *m*........... Lev 21:11
for his father, or for his *m*........... Num 6:7
whom her *m* bare to Levi in Egypt..... Num 26:59
Honour thy father and thy *m*......... Deut 5:16
If thy brother, the son of thy *m*....... Deut 13:6
her father and her *m* a full month..... Deut 21:13
his father, or the voice of his *m*....... Deut 21:18
his *m* lay hold on him, and bring ..... Deut 21:19
father of the damsel, and her *m*...... Deut 22:15
light by his father or his *m*........... Deut 27:16
father, or the daughter of his *m*...... Deut 27:22
he that lieth with his *m* in law ...... Deut 27:23
said unto his father and to his *m* ..... Deut 33:9
save alive my father, and my *m*....... Josh 2:13
shalt bring thy father, and thy *m*...... Josh 2:18
Rahab, and her father, and her *m* ..... Josh 6:23
arose, that I arose a *m* in Israel ...... Judg 5:7
The *m* of Sisera looked out at a .... Judg 5:28
brethren, even the sons of my *m*...... Judg 8:19
up, and told his father and his *m* ..... Judg 14:2

his m said unto him, Is there .... Judg 14:3
his m knew not that it was of the ...... Judg 14:4
down, and his father and his m ...... Judg 14:5
father or his m what he had done... Judg 14:6
and came to his father and m ...... Judg 14:9
not told it my father nor my m ...... Judg 14:16
And he said unto his m, The eleven ... Judg 17:2
his m said, Blessed be thou of ...... Judg 17:2
shekels of silver to his m .... Judg 17:3
his m said, I had wholly .... Judg 17:3
he restored the money unto his m ... Judg 17:4
his m took two hundred shekels of ... Judg 17:4
and Orpah kissed her m in law ...... Ruth 1:14
that thou hast done unto thy m in ... Ruth 2:11
hast left thy father and thy m ...... Ruth 2:11
her m in law saw what she had ...... Ruth 2:18
her m in law said unto her, Where... Ruth 2:19
she shewed her m in law with whom ... Ruth 2:19
and dwelt with her m in law...... Ruth 2:23
Then Naomi her m in law said unto ... Ruth 3:1
to all that her m in law bade her ... Ruth 3:6
And when she came to her m in law... Ruth 3:16
Go not empty unto thy m in law ...... Ruth 3:17
Moreover his m made him a little ... 1Sa 2:19
so shall thy m be childless among ... 1Sa 15:33
of Moab, Let my father and my m ... 1Sa 22:3
sister to Zeruiah Joab's m 2Sa 17:25
the grave of my father and of my m... 2Sa 19:37
destroy a city and a m in Israel ... 2Sa 20:19
his m bare him after Absalom 1Kin 1:6
unto Bath-sheba the m of Solomon ... 1Kin 2:13
to Bath-sheba the m of Solomon ... 1Kin 2:13
a seat to be set for the king's m ... 1Kin 2:19
king said unto her, Ask on, my m ... 1Kin 2:20
answered and said unto his m 1Kin 2:22
she is the m thereof 1Kin 3:27
And also Maachah his m, even her... 1Kin 15:13
and delivered him unto his m 1Kin 17:23
pray thee, kiss my father and my m... 1Kin 19:20
father, and in the way of his m ... 1Kin 22:52
like his father, and like his m 2Kin 3:2
and to the prophets of thy m 2Kin 3:13
said to a lad, Carry him to his m... 2Kin 4:19
him, and brought him to his m 2Kin 4:20
the m of the child said, As the ... 2Kin 4:30
as the whoredoms of thy m Jezebel ... 2Kin 9:22
when Athaliah the m of Ahaziah ... 2Kin 11:1
the king of Babylon, he, and his m ... 2Kin 24:12
to Babylon, and the king's m 2Kin 24:15
she was the m of Onam 1Chr 2:26
his m called his name Jabez 1Chr 4:9
Maachah the m of Asa the king ... 2Chr 15:16
for his m was his counsellor to ... 2Chr 22:3
But when Athaliah the m of 2Chr 22:10
for she had neither father nor m ... Est 2:7
m were dead, took for his own ...... Est 2:7
to the worm, Thou art my m ...... Job 17:14
my m forsake me, then the LORD ... Ps 27:10
as one that mourneth for his m ... Ps 35:14
and in sin did my m conceive me ... Ps 51:5
the sin of his m be blotted out ... Ps 109:14
and to be a joyful m of children... Ps 113:9
a child that is weaned of his m ... Ps 131:2
and forsake not the law of thy m ... Prov 1:8
only beloved in the sight of my m ... Prov 4:3
and forsake not the law of thy m... Prov 6:20
son is the heaviness of his m ...... Prov 10:1
but a foolish man despiseth his m... Prov 15:20
his father, and chaseth away his m ... Prov 19:26
Whoso curseth his father or his m ... Prov 20:20
despise not thy m when she is old ... Prov 23:22
thy m shall be glad, and she that ... Prov 23:25
Whoso robbeth his father or his m ... Prov 28:24
himself bringeth to shame his m ... Prov 29:15
father, and doth not bless their m ... Prov 30:11
and despiseth to obey his m ...... Prov 30:17
prophecy that his m taught him ... Prov 31:1
with the crown wherewith his m ... Song 3:11
she is the only one of her m ...... Song 6:9
that sucked the breasts of my m ... Song 8:1
there thy m brought thee forth ... Song 8:5
to cry, My father, and my m ...... Is 8:4
from the bowels of my m hath he ... Is 49:1
transgressions is your m put away ... Is 50:1
As one whom his m comforteth ... Is 66:13
m of the young men a spoiler at ... Jer 15:8
Woe is me, my m, that thou hast ... Jer 15:10
for their father or for their m ... Jer 16:7
wherein my m bare me be blessed ... Jer 20:14
or that my m might have been my ... Jer 20:17
thy m that bare thee, into ...... Jer 22:26
Your m shall be sore confounded ... Jer 50:12
an Amorite, and thy m an Hittite ... Eze 16:3
against thee, saying, As is the m ... Eze 16:44
your m was an Hittite, and your... Eze 16:45
And say, What is thy m .... Eze 19:2
Thy m is like a vine in thy blood ... Eze 19:10
they set light by father and m ... Eze 22:7
two women, the daughters of one m... Eze 23:2
but for father, or for m, or for ... Eze 44:25
Plead with your m, plead ...... Hos 2:2
For their m hath played the ...... Hos 2:5
night, and I will destroy thy m ... Hos 4:5
the m was dashed in pieces upon ... Hos 10:14
daughter riseth up against her m ... Mic 7:6
in law against her m in law ...... Mic 7:6
his m that begat him shall say ... Zec 13:3
his m that begat him shall thrust ... Zec 13:3
When as his m Mary was espoused ... Mt 1:18
the young child with Mary his m ... Mt 2:11

and take the young child and his m ... Mt 2:13
his m by night, and departed into... Mt 2:14
and take the young child and his m ... Mt 2:20
and took the young child and his m ... Mt 2:21
house, he saw his wife's m laid ... Mt 8:14
and the daughter against her m ... Mt 10:35
in law against her m in law ...... Mt 10:35
He that loveth father or m more ... Mt 10:37
to the people, behold, his m ...... Mt 12:46
one said unto him, Behold, thy m ... Mt 12:47
him that told him, Who is my m ... Mt 12:48
disciples, and said, Behold my m ... Mt 12:49
is my brother, and sister, and m ... Mt 12:50
is not his m called Mary .... Mt 13:55
being before instructed of her m ... Mt 14:8
and she brought it to her m ...... Mt 14:11
saying, Honour thy father and m ... Mt 15:4
and, He that curseth father or m ... Mt 15:4
shall say to his father or his m ... Mt 15:5
And honour not his father or his m ... Mt 15:6
shall a man leave father and m ... Mt 19:5
Honour thy father and thy m ...... Mt 19:19
or sisters, or father, or m ...... Mt 19:29
Then came to him the m of ...... Mt 20:20
Magdalene, and Mary the m of James... Mt 27:56
the m of Zebedee's children ...... Mt 27:56
But Simon's wife's m lay sick of ... Mk 1:30
came then his brethren and his m ... Mk 3:31
they said unto him, Behold, thy m ... Mk 3:32
them, saying, Who is my m ...... Mk 3:33
about him, and said, Behold my m ... Mk 3:34
is my brother, and my sister, and m ... Mk 3:35
the m of the damsel, and them that ... Mk 5:40
went forth, and said unto her m ... Mk 6:24
and the damsel gave it to her m ... Mk 6:28
said, Honour thy father and thy m ... Mk 7:10
and, Whoso curseth father or m ... Mk 7:10
man shall say to his father or m ... Mk 7:11
do ought for his father or his m ... Mk 7:12
shall a man leave his father and m ... Mk 10:7
not, Honour thy father and thy m ... Mk 10:19
or sisters, or father, or m ...... Mk 10:29
Mary the m of James the less and... Mk 15:40
Mary the m of Joses beheld where... Mk 15:47
Magdalene, and Mary the m of James... Mk 16:1
that the m of my Lord should come... Lk 1:43
m answered and said, Not so ...... Lk 1:60
his m marvelled at those things ... Lk 2:33
them, and said unto Mary his m ... Lk 2:34
and Joseph and his m knew not of it ... Lk 2:43
his m said unto him, Son, why ...... Lk 2:48
but his m kept all these sayings ... Lk 2:51
Simon's wife's m was taken with a ... Lk 4:38
out, the only son of his m ...... Lk 7:12
And he delivered him to his m ... Lk 7:15
Then came to him his m and his ... Lk 8:19
him by certain which said, Thy m ... Lk 8:20
answered and said unto them, My m ... Lk 8:21
the father and the m of the maiden ... Lk 8:51
the m against the daughter ...... Lk 12:53
and the daughter against the m ... Lk 12:53
the m in law against her daughter... Lk 12:53
in law against her m in law ...... Lk 12:53
me, and hate not his father, and m ... Lk 14:26
Honour thy father and thy m ...... Lk 18:20
and Joanna, and Mary the m of James... Lk 24:10
and the m of Jesus was there ...... Jn 2:1
the m of Jesus saith unto him ...... Jn 2:3
His m saith unto the servants ...... Jn 2:5
down to Capernaum, he, and his m ... Jn 2:12
Joseph, whose father and m we know ... Jn 6:42
stood by the cross of Jesus his m ... Jn 19:25
When Jesus therefore saw his m ... Jn 19:26
he loved, he saith unto his m ...... Jn 19:26
he to the disciple, Behold thy m ... Jn 19:27
the women, and Mary the m of Jesus ... Acts 1:14
the house of Mary the m of John ... Acts 12:12
chosen in the Lord, and his m ...... Rom 16:13
is free, which is the m of us all ... Gal 4:26
shall a man leave his father and m ... Eph 5:31
Honour thy father and m .... Eph 6:2
grandmother Lois, and thy m Eunice ... 2Ti 1:5
Without father, without m .... Heb 7:3
M OF HARLOTS and .... Rev 17:5

MOTHER'S
told them of her m house these ...... Gen 24:28
was comforted after his m death... Gen 24:67
let thy m sons bow down to thee ... Gen 27:29
the house of Bethuel thy m father ... Gen 28:2
daughters of Laban thy m brother ... Gen 28:2
daughter of Laban thy m brother ... Gen 29:10
the sheep of Laban his m brother ... Gen 29:10
the flock of Laban his m brother ... Gen 29:10
his brother Benjamin, his m son ... Gen 43:29
not seethe a kid in his m milk ...... Ex 23:19
not seethe a kid in his m milk ...... Ex 34:26
the nakedness of thy m sister ...... Lev 18:13
for she is thy m near kinswoman... Lev 18:13
or his m daughter, and see her ... Lev 20:17
the nakedness of thy m sister ...... Lev 20:19
his m name was Shelomith, the ... Lev 24:11
when he cometh out of his m womb ... Num 12:12
to Shechem unto his m brethren ... Judg 9:1
of the house of his m father ...... Judg 9:1
his m brethren spake of him in ... Judg 9:3
unto God from my m womb .... Judg 16:17
Go, return each to her m house ... Ruth 1:8
the confusion of thy m nakedness ... 1Sa 20:30
m name was Zeruah 1Kin 11:26

And his m name was Naamah an... 1Kin 14:21
And his m name was Naamah an... 1Kin 14:31
his m name was Maachah, the... 1Kin 15:2
his m name was Maachah, the... 1Kin 15:10
his m name was Azubah the 1Kin 22:42
his m name was Athaliah, the... 2Kin 8:26
And his m name was Zibiah of ... 2Kin 12:1
his m name was Jehoaddan of ... 2Kin 14:2
his m name was Jecholiah of 2Kin 15:2
his m name was Jerusha, the 2Kin 15:33
His m name also was Abi, the 2Kin 18:2
his m name was Hephzi-bah... 2Kin 21:1
his m name was Meshullemeth, the ... 2Kin 21:19
his m name was Jedidah, the 2Kin 22:1
his m name was Hamutal, the 2Kin 23:31
his m name was Zebudah, the 2Kin 23:36
his m name was Nehushta, the ... 2Kin 24:8
his m name was Hamutal, the 2Kin 24:18
And his m name was Naamah an ... 2Chr 12:13
His m name also was Michaiah the ... 2Chr 13:2
his m name was Azubah the 2Chr 20:31
His m name also was Athaliah the ... 2Chr 22:2
His m name also was Zibiah of ... 2Chr 24:1
his m name was Jehoaddan of ... 2Chr 25:1
His m name also was Jecoliah of ... 2Chr 26:3
His m name also was Jerusham, the ... 2Chr 27:1
his m name was Abijah, the 2Chr 29:1
Naked came I out of my m womb ... Job 1:21
not up the doors of my m womb ... Job 3:10
I have guided her from my m womb ... Job 31:18
hope when I was upon my m breasts... Ps 22:9
thou art my God from my m belly ... Ps 22:10
thou slanderest thine own m son... Ps 50:20
and an alien unto my m children ... Ps 69:8
that took me out of my m bowels ... Ps 71:6
thou hast covered me in my m womb ... Ps 139:13
As he came forth of his m womb ... Eccl 5:15
my m children were angry with me ... Song 1:6
I had brought him into my m house... Song 3:4
and bring thee into my m house ... Song 8:2
is the bill of your m divorcement ... Is 50:1
his m name was Hamutal the ...... Jer 52:1
Thou art thy m daughter, that ... Eze 16:45
were so born from their m womb ... Mt 19:12
Holy Ghost, even from his m womb ... Lk 1:15
the second time into his m womb ... Jn 3:4
his sister, Mary the wife of ...... Jn 19:25
lame from his m womb was carried ... Acts 3:2
being a cripple from his m womb ... Acts 14:8
who separated me from my m womb ... Gal 1:15

MOTHERS
and their queens thy nursing m... Is 49:23
concerning their m that bare them ... Jer 16:3
They say to their m, Where is ... Lam 2:12
fatherless, our m are as widows ... Lam 5:3
and brethren, and sisters, and m ... Mk 10:30
of fathers and murderers of m ... 1Ti 1:9
The elder women as m 1Ti 5:2

MOTHERS'
was poured out into their m bosom ... Lam 2:12

MOTIONS
the m of sins, which were by the ... Rom 7:5

MOULDY
of their provision was dry and m... Josh 9:5
behold, it is dry, and it is m ...... Josh 9:12

MOUNT
goest unto Sephar a m of the east ... Gen 10:30
And the Horites in their m Seir ... Gen 14:6
in the m of the LORD it shall be ... Gen 22:14
set his face toward the m Gilead ... Gen 31:21
they overtook him in the m Gilead... Gen 31:23
had pitched his tent in the m ...... Gen 31:25
pitched in the m of Gilead ...... Gen 31:25
offered sacrifice upon the m ...... Gen 31:54
and tarried all night in the m ... Gen 31:54
Thus dwelt Esau in m Seir ...... Gen 36:8
father of the Edomites in m Seir ... Gen 36:9
went, and met him in the m of God ... Ex 4:27
where he encamped at the m of God ... Ex 18:5
there Israel camped before the m ... Ex 19:2
of all the people upon m Sinai ... Ex 19:11
that ye go not up into the m ...... Ex 19:12
whosoever toucheth the m shall be... Ex 19:12
long, they shall come up to the m ... Ex 19:13
down from the m unto the people ... Ex 19:14
and a thick cloud upon the m ...... Ex 19:16
stood at the nether part of the m ... Ex 19:17
m Sinai was altogether on a smoke... Ex 19:18
the whole m quaked greatly ...... Ex 19:18
m Sinai, on the top of the m ...... Ex 19:20
Moses up to the top of the m ... Ex 19:20
people cannot come up to m Sinai ... Ex 19:23
set bounds about the m .... Ex 19:23
Moses, Come up to me into the m ... Ex 24:12
Moses went up into the m of God ... Ex 24:13
And Moses went up into the m ... Ex 24:15
and a cloud covered the m ...... Ex 24:15
of the LORD abode upon m Sinai ... Ex 24:16
fire on the top of the m in the ... Ex 24:17
cloud, and gat him up into the m ... Ex 24:18
and Moses was in the m forty days... Ex 24:18
which was shewed thee in the m ... Ex 25:40
which was shewed thee in the m ... Ex 26:30
as it was shewed thee in the m ... Ex 27:8
communing with him upon m Sinai ... Ex 31:18
delayed to come down out of the m ... Ex 32:1
turned, and went down from the m ... Ex 32:15
and brake them beneath the m ... Ex 32:19

M

of their ornaments by the *m* Horeb......... Ex 33:6
up in the morning unto *m* Sinai............ Ex 34:2
there to me in the top of the *m*.......... Ex 34:2
man be seen throughout all the *m*......... Ex 34:3
nor herds feed before that *m*.............. Ex 34:3
morning, and went up unto *m* Sinai........ Ex 34:4
when Moses came down from *m* Sinai....... Ex 34:29
when he came down from the *m*............. Ex 34:29
had spoken with him in *m* Sinai........... Ex 34:32
LORD commanded Moses in *m* Sinai......... Lev 7:38
LORD spake unto Moses in *m* Sinai........ Lev 25:1
the children of Israel in *m* Sinai........ Lev 26:46
the children of Israel in *m* Sinai........ Lev 27:34
LORD spake with Moses in *m* Sinai......... Num 3:1
they departed from the *m* of the......... Num 10:33
from Kadesh, and came unto *m* Hor......... Num 20:22
unto Moses and Aaron in *m* Hor........... Num 20:23
son, and bring them up unto *m* Hor....... Num 20:25
they went up into *m* Hor in the.......... Num 20:27
died there in the top of the *m*.......... Num 20:28
they journeyed from *m* Hor by the........ Num 21:4
Get thee up into this Abarim............... Num 27:12
which was ordained in *m* Sinai for....... Num 28:6
and pitched in *m* Shapher................. Num 33:23
And they removed from *m* Shapher......... Num 33:24
from Kadesh, and pitched in *m* Hor....... Num 33:37
m Hor at the commandment of the......... Num 33:38
years old when he died in *m* Hor......... Num 33:39
And they departed from *m* Hor............ Num 33:41
ye shall point out for you *m* Hor........ Num 34:7
From *m* Hor ye shall point out........... Num 34:8
way of the *m* unto Kadesh-barnea......... Deut 1:2
have dwelt long enough in this *m*........ Deut 1:6
go to the *m* of the Amorites, and........ Deut 1:7
we compassed *m* Seir many days........... Deut 2:1
because I have given *m* Seir unto........ Deut 2:5
the river of Arnon unto *m* Hermon........ Deut 3:8
half *m* Gilead, and the cities........... Deut 3:12
even unto *m* Sion which is Hermon........ Deut 3:48
m out of the midst of the fire.......... Deut 5:4
fire, and went out into the *m*........... Deut 5:5
m out of the midst of the fire.......... Deut 5:22
When I was gone up into the *m* to........ Deut 9:9
then I abode in the *m* forty days........ Deut 9:9
the LORD spake with you in the *m*......... Deut 9:10
I turned and came down from the *m*....... Deut 9:15
and the *m* burned with fire.............. Deut 9:15
brook that descended out of the *m*....... Deut 9:21
and come up into me into the *m*.......... Deut 10:1
the first, and went up into the *m*....... Deut 10:3
the LORD spake unto you in the *m*......... Deut 10:4
myself and came down from the *m*......... Deut 10:5
And I stayed in the, according........... Deut 10:10
put the blessing upon *m* Gerizim......... Deut 11:29
and the curse upon *m* Ebal............... Deut 11:29
in *m* Ebal, and thou shalt plaister...... Deut 27:4
These shall stand upon *m* Gerizim........ Deut 27:12
shall stand upon *m* Ebal to curse....... Deut 27:13
this mountain Abarim, unto *m* Nebo....... Deut 32:49
die in the *m* whither thou goest........ Deut 32:50
Aaron thy brother died in *m* Hor......... Deut 32:50
he shined forth from *m* Paran........... Deut 33:2
the LORD God of Israel in *m* Ebal........ Josh 8:30
of them over against *m* Gerizim......... Josh 8:33
half of them over against *m* Ebal........ Josh 8:33
Even from the *m* Halak, that goeth....... Josh 11:17
valley of Lebanon under *m* Hermon........ Josh 11:17
the river Arnon unto *m* Hermon.......... Josh 12:1
And reigned in *m* Hermon, and in........ Josh 12:5
of Lebanon even unto the *m* Halak........ Josh 12:7
from Baal-gad under *m* Hermon unto....... Josh 13:5
all *m* Hermon, and all Bashan unto....... Josh 13:11
in the *m* of the valley................. Josh 13:19
out to the cities of *m* Ephron.......... Josh 15:9
from Baalah westward unto *m* Seir........ Josh 15:10
along unto the side of *m* Jearim........ Josh 15:10
and passed along to *m* Baalah........... Josh 15:11
from Jericho throughout in Beth-el........ Josh 16:1
if *m* Ephraim be too narrow for......... Josh 17:15
even Timnath-serah in *m* Ephraim........ Josh 19:50
Kedesh in Galilee in *m* Naphtali........ Josh 20:7
and Shechem in *m* Ephraim............... Josh 20:7
with her suburbs in *m* Ephraim.......... Josh 21:21
and I gave unto Esau *m* Seir............ Josh 24:4
which is in *m* Ephraim, on the.......... Josh 24:30
which was given him in *m* Ephraim....... Josh 24:33
would dwell in *m* Heres in Aijalon....... Judg 1:35
in the *m* of Ephraim, on the north...... Judg 2:9
Hivites that dwelt in *m* Lebanon........ Judg 3:3
from *m* Baal-hermon unto the............ Judg 3:3
went down with him from the *m*.......... Judg 3:27
Ramah and Beth-el in *m* Ephraim......... Judg 4:5
saying, Go and draw toward *m* Tabor...... Judg 4:6
of Abinoam was gone up to *m* Tabor....... Judg 4:12
So Barak went down from *m* Tabor........ Judg 4:14
and depart early from *m* Gilead......... Judg 7:3
throughout all *m* Ephraim, saying....... Judg 7:24
and stood in the top of *m* Gerizim...... Judg 9:7
Abimelech gat him up to *m* Zalmon....... Judg 9:48
he dwelt in Shamir in *m* Ephraim........ Judg 10:1
in the *m* of the Amalekites............. Judg 12:15
And there was a man of *m* Ephraim........ Judg 17:1
he came to *m* Ephraim to the house...... Judg 17:8
who when they came to *m* Ephraim........ Judg 18:2
they passe., thence unto *m* Ephraim..... Judg 18:13
on the side of *m* Ephraim, who.......... Judg 19:1
even, which was also of *m* Ephraim...... Judg 19:16
toward the side of *m* Ephraim........... Judg 19:18
of *m* Ephraim, and his name was......... 1Sa 1:1

And he passed through *m* Ephraim........ 1Sa 9:4
in *m* Beth-el, and a thousand were...... 1Sa 13:2
had hid themselves in *m* Ephraim........ 1Sa 14:22
and fell down slain in *m* Gilboa....... 1Sa 31:1
his three sons fallen in *m* Gilboa...... 1Sa 31:8
happened by chance upon *m* Gilboa....... 2Sa 1:6
went up by the ascent of *m* Olivet...... 2Sa 15:30
was come to the top of the *m*.......... 2Sa 15:32
but a man of *m* Ephraim, Sheba the...... 2Sa 20:21
The son of Hur, in *m* Ephraim.......... 1Kin 4:8
built Shechem in *m* Ephraim............ 1Kin 12:25
to me all Israel unto *m* Carmel........ 1Kin 18:19
prophets together unto *m* Carmel....... 1Kin 18:20
nights unto Horeb the *m* of God........ 1Kin 19:8
stand upon the *m* before the LORD...... 1Kin 19:11
he went from thence to *m* Carmel....... 2Kin 2:25
unto the man of God in *m* Carmel....... 2Kin 4:25
m Ephraim two young men of the........ 2Kin 5:22
and they that escape out of *m* Zion..... 2Kin 19:31
right hand of the *m* of corruption...... 2Kin 23:13
that were there in the *m*, and sent..... 2Kin 23:16
five hundred men, went to *m* Seir....... 1Chr 4:42
and Senir, and unto *m* Hermon.......... 1Chr 5:23
Shechem in *m* Ephraim with her......... 1Chr 6:67
and fell down slain in *m* Gilboa....... 1Chr 10:1
and his sons fallen in *m* Gilboa....... 1Chr 10:8
the LORD at Jerusalem in *m* Moriah...... 2Chr 3:1
Abijah stood up upon *m* Zemaraim....... 2Chr 13:4
Zemaraim, which is in *m* Ephraim....... 2Chr 13:4
which he had taken from *m* Ephraim...... 2Chr 15:8
from Beer-sheba to *m* Ephraim.......... 2Chr 19:4
m Seir, whom thou wouldest not........ 2Chr 20:10
m Seir, which were come against....... 2Chr 20:22
against the inhabitants of *m* Seir...... 2Chr 20:23
in the *m* of the house of the LORD...... 2Chr 33:15
saying, Go forth unto the *m*........... Neh 8:15
camest down also upon *m* Sinai......... Neh 9:13
excellency *m* up to the heavens......... Job 20:6
Doth the eagle *m* up at thy............ Job 39:27
is *m* Zion, on the sides of the........ Ps 48:2
Let *m* Zion rejoice, let the........... Ps 48:11
this *m* Zion, wherein thou hast........ Ps 74:2
the *m* Zion which he loved............. Ps 78:68
They *m* up to the heaven, they go....... Ps 107:26
in the LORD shall be as *m* Zion........ Ps 125:1
goats, that appear from *m* Gilead...... Song 4:1
every dwelling place of *m* Zion........ Is 4:5
hosts, which dwelleth in *m* Zion....... Is 8:18
they shall *m* up like the lifting...... Is 9:18
his whole work upon *m* Zion........... Is 10:12
the *m* of the daughter of Zion......... Is 10:32
upon the *m* of the congregation....... Is 14:13
unto the *m* of the daughter of........ Is 16:1
of the Lord of hosts, the *m* Zion...... Is 18:7
of hosts shall reign in *m* Zion........ Is 24:23
LORD in the holy *m* at Jerusalem....... Is 27:13
shall rise up as in Perazim............. Is 28:21
lay siege against thee with a *m*....... Is 29:3
be, that fight against *m* Zion......... Is 29:8
come down to fight for *m* Zion......... Is 31:4
and they that escape out of *m* Zion..... Is 37:32
they shall *m* up with wings as......... Is 40:31
affliction from *m* Ephraim............. Jer 4:15
cast a *m* against Jerusalem............ Jer 6:6
upon the *m* Ephraim shall cry.......... Jer 31:6
shall be satisfied upon *m* Ephraim..... Jer 50:19
Babylon should *m* up to heaven......... Jer 51:53
it, and cast a *m* against it........... Eze 4:2
wings *m* up from the earth............. Eze 10:16
against the gates, to cast a *m*........ Eze 21:22
cast a *m* against thee, and lift up..... Eze 26:8
man, set thy face against *m* Seir...... Eze 35:2
O *m* Seir, I am against thee, and I..... Eze 35:3
Thus will I make *m* Seir most.......... Eze 35:7
O *m* Seir, and all Idumea, even all..... Eze 35:15
north shall come, and cast up a *m*..... Dan 11:15
for in *m* Zion and in Jerusalem........ Joel 2:32
out of the *m* of Esau................. Obad 8
the *m* of Esau may be cut off by....... Obad 9
But upon *m* Zion shall be............. Obad 17
south shall possess the *m* of Esau..... Obad 19
m Zion to judge the *m* of Esau....... Obad 21
them in *m* Zion from henceforth........ Mic 4:7
and the Holy One from *m* Paran......... Hab 3:3
in that day upon the *m* of Olives...... Zec 14:4
the *m* of Olives shall cleave in....... Zec 14:4
unto the *m* of Olives, then sent....... Mt 21:1
And as he sat upon the *m* of Olives..... Mt 24:3
went out into the *m* of Olives........ Mt 26:30
at the *m* of Olives, he sendeth....... Mk 11:1
as he sat upon the *m* of Olives....... Mk 13:3
went out into the *m* of Olives........ Mk 14:26
at the *m* called the *m* of.......... Lk 19:29
called the *m* of Olives.............. Lk 19:29
at the descent of the *m* of Olives..... Lk 19:37
abode in the *m* that is called the..... Lk 21:37
that is called the *m* of Olives....... Lk 21:37
he was went, to the *m* of Olives...... Lk 22:39
Jesus went unto the *m* of Olives...... Jn 8:1
from the *m* called Olivet, which...... Acts 1:12
to him in the wilderness of *m*........ Acts 7:30
which spake to him in the *m* Sina...... Acts 7:38
the one from the *m* Sinai, which...... Gal 4:24
this Agar is *m* Sinai in Arabia....... Gal 4:25
pattern shewed to thee in the *m*...... Heb 8:5
unto the *m* that might be touched...... Heb 12:18
But ye are come unto *m* Sion.......... Heb 12:22
we were with him in the holy *m*........ 2Pet 1:18
lo, a Lamb stood on the *m* Sion....... Rev 14:1

MOUNTAIN

unto a *m* on the east of Beth-el....... Gen 12:8
they that remained fled to the *m*..... Gen 14:10
escape to the *m*, lest thou be........ Gen 19:17
and I cannot escape to the *m*......... Gen 19:19
out of Zoar, and dwelt in the *m*...... Gen 19:30
desert, and came to the *m* of God...... Ex 3:1
ye shall serve God upon this *m*....... Ex 3:12
plant them in the *m* of thine........ Ex 15:17
LORD called unto him out of the *m*..... Ex 19:3
of the trumpet, and the *m* smoking..... Ex 20:18
southward, and go up into the *m*...... Num 13:17
gat them up into the top of the *m*..... Num 14:40
the way of the *m* of the Amorites..... Deut 1:19
come unto the *m* of the Amorites...... Deut 1:20
they turned and went up into the *m*.... Deut 1:24
Amorites, which dwelt in that *m*...... Deut 1:44
have compassed this *m* long enough..... Deut 2:3
is beyond Jordan, that goodly *m*...... Deut 3:25
ye came near and stood under the *m*.... Deut 4:11
the *m* burned with fire unto the...... Deut 4:11
(for the *m* did burn with fire,)...... Deut 5:23
Get thee up into this *m* Abarim....... Deut 32:49
shall call the people unto the *m*..... Deut 33:19
plains of Moab unto the *m* of Nebo..... Deut 34:1
said unto them, Get you to the *m*..... Josh 2:16
And they went, and came unto the *m*.... Josh 2:22
returned, and descended from the *m*.... Josh 2:23
the *m* of Israel, and the valley...... Josh 11:16
Now therefore give me this *m*......... Josh 14:12
went up to the top of the *m* that..... Josh 15:8
But the *m* shall be thine............ Josh 17:18
came down to the end of the *m*....... Josh 18:16
is Hebron, in the *m* of Judah........ Josh 20:7
Canaanites, that dwelt in the *m*..... Judg 1:9
out the inhabitants of the *m*........ Judg 1:19
the children of Dan into the *m*...... Judg 1:34
a trumpet in the *m* of Ephraim....... Judg 3:27
stood on a *m* on the one side........ 1Sa 17:3
stood on a *m* on the other side...... 1Sa 17:3
remained in a *m* in the wilderness.... 1Sa 23:14
Saul went on this side of the *m*..... 1Sa 23:26
and his men on that side of the *m*.... 1Sa 23:26
him up, and cast him upon some *m*..... 2Kin 2:16
the *m* was full of horses and........ 2Kin 6:17
thousand to hew in the *m*, and....... 2Chr 2:2
thousand to be hewers in the *m*...... 2Chr 2:18
surely the *m* falling cometh to...... Job 14:18
my soul, Flee as a bird to your *m*.... Ps 11:1
hast made my *m* to stand strong...... Ps 30:7
our God, in the *m* of his holiness.... Ps 48:1
of his sanctuary, even to this *m*..... Ps 78:54
I will get me to the *m* of myrrh...... Song 4:6
the *m* of the Lord's house........... Is 2:2
let us go up to the *m* of the LORD..... Is 2:3
hurt nor destroy in all my holy *m*.... Is 11:9
ye up a banner upon the high *m*....... Is 13:2
in this *m* shall the LORD of hosts..... Is 25:6
he will destroy in this *m* the....... Is 25:7
For in this *m* shall the hand of..... Is 25:10
as a beacon upon the top of a *m*..... Is 30:17
there shall be upon every high *m*..... Is 30:25
to come into the *m* of the LORD...... Is 30:29
shall be exalted, and every *m*....... Is 40:4
get thee up into the high *m*......... Is 40:9
them will I bring to my holy *m*...... Is 56:7
high *m* hast thou set thy bed........ Is 57:7
land, and shall inherit my holy *m*.... Is 57:13
the LORD, that forget my holy *m*...... Is 65:11
hurt nor destroy in all my holy *m*.... Is 65:25
beasts, to my holy *m* Jerusalem...... Is 66:20
she is gone up every high *m*......... Jer 3:6
they shall hunt them from every *m*.... Jer 16:16
O my *m* in the field, I will give..... Jer 17:3
the *m* of the house as the high...... Jer 26:18
of justice, and of holiness.......... Jer 31:23
they have gone from *m* to hill....... Jer 50:6
I am against thee, O destroying *m*..... Jer 51:25
and will make thee a burnt *m*........ Jer 51:25
Because of the *m* of Zion, which..... Lam 5:18
stood upon the *m* which is on the..... Eze 11:23
and will plant it upon an high *m*..... Eze 17:22
In the *m* of the height of Israel..... Eze 17:23
For in mine holy *m*................. Eze 20:40
in the *m* of the height of Israel..... Eze 20:40
thou wast upon the holy *m* of God..... Eze 28:14
as profane out of the *m* of God...... Eze 28:16
and set me upon a very high *m*....... Eze 40:2
Upon the top of the *m* the whole..... Eze 43:12
smote the image became a great *m*..... Dan 2:35
cut out of the *m* without hands...... Dan 2:45
thy city Jerusalem, thy holy *m*...... Dan 9:16
my God for the holy *m* of my God..... Dan 9:20
the seas in the glorious holy *m*..... Dan 11:45
and sound an alarm in my holy *m*..... Joel 2:1
God dwelling in Zion, my holy *m*..... Joel 3:17
that are in the *m* of Samaria....... Amos 4:1
and trust in the *m* of Samaria...... Amos 6:1
as ye have drunk upon my holy *m*..... Obad 16
the *m* of the house as the high..... Mic 3:12
that the *m* of the house of the..... Mic 4:1
let us go up to the *m* of the LORD.... Mic 4:2
sea to sea, and from *m* to *m*....... Mic 7:12
be haughty because of my holy *m*..... Zeph 3:11
Go up to the *m*, and bring wood, and.. Hag 1:8
Who art thou, O great *m*............. Zec 4:7
the *m* of the LORD of hosts......... Zec 8:3
the *m* of the LORD the holy of...... Zec 8:3
half of the *m* shall remove toward.... Zec 14:4
him up into an exceeding high *m*..... Mt 4:8

multitudes, he went up into a *m*............ Mt 5:1
When he was come down from the *m*... Mt 8:1
he went up into a *m* apart to pray.... Mt 14:23
and went up into a *m*, and sat down.... Mt 15:29
them up into an high *m* apart .... Mt 17:1
And as they came down from the *m*.... Mt 17:9
seed, ye shall say unto this *m* .... Mt 17:20
also if ye shall say unto this *m*.......... Mt 21:21
Galilee, into a *m* where Jesus had .... Mt 28:16
And he goeth up into a *m*, and .... Mk 3:13
he departed into a *m* to pray .... Mk 6:46
an high *m* apart by themselves .... Mk 9:2
And as they came down from the *m*.. Mk 9:9
whosoever shall say unto this *m*..... Mk 11:23
shall be filled, and every *m* .... Lk 3:5
taking him up into an high *m*............. Lk 4:5
that he went out into a *m* to pray ..... Lk 6:12
of many swine feeding on the *m* .... Lk 8:32
and went up into a *m* to pray .... Lk 9:28
Our fathers worshipped in this *m*...... Jn 4:20
when ye shall neither in this *m*.......... Jn 4:21
And Jesus went up into a *m*.............. Jn 6:3
again into a *m* himself alone............. Jn 6:15
if so much as a beast touch the *m*..... Heb 12:20
and every *m* and island were moved.... Rev 6:14
as it were a great *m* burning with....... Rev 8:8
the spirit to a great and high *m* .... Rev 21:10

MOUNTAINS
and the *m* were covered .... Gen 7:20
the month, upon the *m* of Ararat....... Gen 8:4
were the tops of the *m* seen............... Gen 8:5
the *m* which I will tell thee of .... Gen 22:2
them out, to slay them in the *m*......... Ex 32:12
and the Amorites, dwell in the *m*...... Num 13:29
out of the *m* of the east, saying......... Num 23:7
and pitched in the *m* of Abarim .... Num 33:47
departed from the *m* of Abarim......... Num 33:48
nor unto the cities in the *m*............... Deut 2:37
their gods, upon the high *m* .... Deut 12:2
on fire the foundations of the *m*........ Deut 32:22
the chief things of the ancient *m*...... Deut 33:15
m are gathered together against........ Josh 10:6
that were on the north of the *m*........ Josh 11:2
and the Jebusite in the *m*.................. Josh 11:3
and cut off the Anakims from the *m*.. Josh 11:21
Anab, and from all the *m* of Judah .... Josh 11:21
and from all the *m* of Israel............... Josh 11:21
In the *m*, and in the valleys, and .... Josh 12:8
And in the *m*, Shamir, and Jattir, ... Josh 15:48
up through the *m* westward .... Josh 18:12
The melted from before the LORD .... Judg 5:5
them the dens which are in the *m*...... Judg 6:2
wait for him in the top of the *m*........ Judg 9:25
people down from the top of the *m*... Judg 9:36
of the *m* as if they were men............. Judg 9:36
I may go up and down upon the *m*.... Judg 11:37
bewailed her virginity upon the *m*..... Judg 11:38
doth hunt a partridge in the *m*.......... 1Sa 1:21
Ye *m* of Gilboa, let there be no.......... 2Sa 1:21
thousand hewers in the *m*................. 1Kin 5:15
a great and strong wind rent the *m*... 1Kin 19:11
am come up to the height of the *m*.... 2Kin 19:23
as swift as the roes upon the *m*......... 1Chr 12:8
all Israel scattered upon the *m*.......... 2Chr 18:16
high places in the *m* of Judah 2Chr 21:11
also, and vine dressers in the *m*......... 2Chr 26:10
he built cities in the *m* of Judah 2Chr 27:4
Which removeth the *m*, and they....... Job 9:5
are wet with the showers of the *m*.... Job 24:8
he overturneth the *m* by the roots..... Job 28:9
The range of the *m* is his pasture...... Job 39:8
Surely the *m* bring him forth food ..... Job 40:20
righteousness is like the great *m*....... Ps 36:6
though the *m* be carried into the....... Ps 46:2
though the *m* shake with the .... Ps 46:3
I know all the fowls of the *m*............. Ps 50:11
his strength setteth fast the *m*........... Ps 65:6
The *m* shall bring peace to the.......... Ps 72:3
the earth upon the top of the *m*........ Ps 72:16
and excellent than the *m* of prey....... Ps 76:4
the flame setteth the *m* on fire.......... Ps 83:14
His foundation is in the holy *m*......... Ps 87:1
Before the *m* were brought forth,...... Ps 90:2
the waters stood above the *m*............ Ps 104:6
They go up by the *m*........................ Ps 104:8
The *m* skipped like rams, and the...... Ps 114:4
Ye *m*, that ye skipped like rams .... Ps 114:6
As the *m* are round about.................. Ps 125:2
that descended upon the *m* of Zion ... Ps 133:3
touch the *m*, and they shall smoke.... Ps 144:5
maketh grass to grow upon the *m* ..... Ps 147:8
M, and all hills .... Ps 148:9
Before the *m* were settled, before...... Prov 8:25
and herbs of the *m* are gathered .... Prov 27:25
he cometh leaping upon the *m*.......... Song 2:8
a young hart upon the *m* of Bether ... Song 2:17
from the *m* of the leopards............... Song 4:8
a young hart upon the *m* of spices..... Song 8:14
established in the top of the *m*.......... Is 2:2
And upon all the high *m*, and upon ... Is 2:14
The noise of a multitude in the *m*..... Is 13:4
upon my *m* tread him under foot ...... Is 14:25
chaff of the *m* before the wind.......... Is 17:13
he lifteth up an ensign on the *m*....... Is 18:3
together unto the fowls of the *m*....... Is 18:6
the walls, and of crying to the *m*...... Is 22:5
the *m* shall be melted with their........ Is 34:3
I come up to the height of the *m*....... Is 37:24
and weighed the *m* in scales.............. Is 40:12
thou shalt thresh the *m*, and beat ..... Is 41:15

them shout from the top of the *m*..... Is 42:11
I will make waste in hills and .... Is 42:15
break forth into singing, ye *m*........... Is 44:23
And I will make all my *m* a way .... Is 49:11
and break forth into singing, O *m*..... Is 49:13
How beautiful upon the *m* are the..... Is 52:7
For the *m* shall depart, and the......... Is 54:10
the *m* and the hills shall break.......... Is 55:12
that the *m* might flow down at thy.... Is 64:1
the *m* flowed down at thy presence... Is 64:3
have burned incense upon the *m*....... Is 65:7
out of Judah an inheritor of my *m*.... Is 65:9
hills, and from the multitude of *m*.... Jer 3:23
I beheld the *m*, and, lo, they............. Jer 4:24
For the *m* will I take up a.................. Jer 9:10
your feet stumble upon the dark *m*.... Jer 13:16
and from the plain, and from the *m*... Jer 17:26
plant vines upon the *m* of Samaria .... Jer 31:5
Judah, and in the cities of the *m*....... Jer 32:44
In the cities of the *m*, in the............. Jer 33:13
Surely as Tabor is among the *m*........ Jer 46:18
have turned them away on the *m*....... Jer 50:6
they pursued us upon the *m*.............. Lam 4:19
thy face toward the *m* of Israel......... Eze 6:2
Ye *m* of Israel, hear the word of .... Eze 6:3
Thus saith the Lord GOD to the *m*..... Eze 6:3
hill, in all the tops of the *m*.............. Eze 6:13
not the sounding again of the *m*....... Eze 7:7
hath not eaten upon the *m*, ... Eze 7:16
And hath not eaten upon the *m*........ Eze 18:6
but even hath eaten upon the *m*........ Eze 18:11
That hath not eaten upon the *m*........ Eze 18:15
he heard upon the *m* of Israel........... Eze 19:9
and in thee they eat upon the *m*........ Eze 22:9
upon the *m* and in all the valleys....... Eze 31:12
I will lay thy flesh upon the *m*.......... Eze 32:5
thou swimmest, even to the *m*........... Eze 32:6
the *m* of Israel shall be desolate........ Eze 33:28
sheep wandered through all the *m*..... Eze 34:6
feed them upon the *m* of Israel by..... Eze 34:13
upon the high *m* of Israel shall .... Eze 34:14
they feed upon the *m* of Israel........... Eze 34:14
I will fill his *m* with his slain............ Eze 35:8
spoken against the *m* of Israel........... Eze 36:1
prophesy unto the *m* of Israel,.......... Eze 36:1
Ye *m* of Israel, hear the word of .... Eze 36:4
ye *m* of Israel, hear the word of .... Eze 36:6
Thus saith the Lord GOD to the *m*..... Eze 36:6
land of Israel, and say unto the *m*.... Eze 36:8
O *m* of Israel, ye shall shoot .... Eze 36:8
in the land upon the *m* of Israel........ Eze 37:22
people, against the *m* of Israel .... Eze 38:8
the *m* shall be thrown down, and...... Eze 38:20
against him throughout all my *m*....... Eze 38:21
bring thee upon the *m* of Israel......... Eze 39:2
shalt fall upon the *m* of Israel........... Eze 39:4
sacrifice upon the *m* of Israel............ Eze 39:17
sacrifice upon the tops of the *m*........ Hos 4:13
and they shall say to the *m*............... Hos 10:8
as the morning spread upon the *m*..... Joel 2:2
on the tops of *m* shall they leap......... Joel 2:5
that the *m* shall drop down new........ Joel 3:18
yourselves upon the *m* of Samaria..... Amos 3:9
For, lo, he that formeth the *m*........... Amos 4:13
the *m* shall drop sweet wine, and...... Amos 9:13
went down to the bottoms of the *m*... Jonah 2:6
the *m* shall be molten under him,...... Mic 1:4
established in the top of the *m*.......... Mic 4:1
Arise, contend thou before the *m*...... Mic 6:1
Hear ye, O *m*, the LORD's.................. Mic 6:2
The quake at him, and the hills .... Nah 1:5
Behold upon the *m* the feet of him.... Nah 1:15
people is scattered upon the *m*.......... Nah 3:18
the everlasting *m* were scattered........ Hab 3:6
The *m* saw thee, and they trembled ... Hab 3:10
upon the land, and upon the *m*......... Hag 1:11
chariots out from between two *m*...... Zec 6:1
and the *m* were of brass.................... Zec 6:1
shall flee to the valley of the *m*......... Zec 14:5
of the *m* shall reach unto Azal.......... Zec 14:5
And I hated Esau, and laid his *m*....... Mal 1:3
and mine, and goeth into the *m*......... Mt 18:12
be in Judaea flee into the *m*.............. Mt 24:16
night and day, he was in the *m*.......... Mk 5:5
a great herd of swine feeding.............. Mk 5:11
that be in Judaea flee to the *m*.......... Mk 13:14
which are in Judaea flee to the *m*...... Lk 21:21
shall they begin to say to the *m*........ Lk 23:30
faith, so that I could remove *m*......... 1Cor 13:2
they wandered in deserts, and in *m*.... Heb 11:38
the dens and in the rocks of the *m*.... Rev 6:15
And said to the *m* and rocks, Fall...... Rev 6:16
away, and the *m* were not found........ Rev 16:20
The seven heads are seven *m*............. Rev 17:9

MOUNTED
m up from the earth in my sight........ Eze 10:19

MOUNTING
for by the *m* up of Luhith with.......... Is 15:5

MOUNTS
Behold the *m*, they are come unto..... Jer 32:24
which are thrown down by the *m*...... Jer 33:4
him in the war, by casting up *m*........ Jer 17:17

MOURN
and Abraham came to *m* for Sarah..... Gen 23:2
How long wilt thou *m* for Saul.......... 1Sa 16:1
with sackcloth, and *m* before Abner... 2Sa 3:31
prophet came to the city, to *m*.......... 1Kin 13:29
And all Israel shall *m* for him 1Kin 14:13

m not, nor weep.............................. Neh 8:9
together to come to *m* with him......... Job 2:11
that those which *m* may be exalted.... Job 5:11
and his soul within him shall *m*......... Job 14:22
I *m* in my complaint, and make a...... Ps 55:2
thou *m* at the last, when thy............. Prov 5:11
wicked beareth rule, the people *m*..... Prov 29:2
a time to *m*, and a time to dance .... Eccl 3:4
And her gates shall lament and *m*..... Is 3:26
of Kir-hareseth shall ye *m*................. Is 16:7
The fishers also shall *m*, and all........ Is 19:8
I did *m* as a dove............................. Is 38:14
like bears, and *m* sore like doves ...... Is 59:11
to comfort all that *m*....................... Is 61:2
appoint unto them that *m* in Zion ..... Is 61:3
with her, all ye that *m* for her........... Is 66:10
For this shall the earth *m*................. Jer 4:28
How long shall the land *m*............... Jer 12:4
mine heart shall *m* for the men of..... Jer 48:31
The ways of Zion do *m*, because........ Lam 1:4
buyer rejoice, nor the seller *m*........... Eze 7:12
The king shall *m*, and the prince....... Eze 7:27
yet neither shalt thou *m* nor weep..... Eze 24:16
ye shall not *m* nor weep.................... Eze 24:23
and *m* one toward another .... Eze 24:23
and I caused Lebanon to *m* for him ... Eze 31:15
Therefore shall the land *m*................ Hos 4:3
people thereof shall *m* over it............ Hos 10:5
priests, the LORD's ministers, *m*........ Joel 1:9
of the shepherds shall *m*, and the...... Amos 1:2
every one *m* that dwelleth therein...... Amos 8:8
and all that dwell therein shall *m*...... Amos 9:5
pierced, and they shall *m* for him ..... Zec 12:10
And the land shall *m*, every family.... Zec 12:12
Blessed are they that *m*.................... Mt 5:4
children of the bridechamber *m*........ Mt 9:15
all the tribes of the earth *m*.............. Mt 24:30
for ye shall *m* and weep................... Lk 6:25
Be afflicted, and *m*, and weep........... Jas 4:9
earth shall weep and *m* over her .... Rev 18:11

MOURNED
Ioins, and *m* for his son many days ... Gen 37:34
and the Egyptians *m* for him............ Gen 50:3
there they *m* with a great and very ... Gen 50:10
heard these evil tidings, they *m*......... Ex 33:4
and the people *m* greatly.................. Num 14:39
they *m* for Aaron thirty days............. Num 20:29
nevertheless Samuel *m* for Saul......... 1Sa 15:35
And they *m*, and wept, and fasted 2Sa 1:12
was dead, she *m* for her husband....... 2Sa 11:26
David *m* for his son every day........... 2Sa 13:37
had a long time *m* for the dead......... 2Sa 14:2
they *m* over him, saying, Alas, my ... 1Kin 13:30
and all Israel *m* for him, ... 1Kin 14:18
Ephraim their father *m* many days..... 1Chr 7:22
Judah and Jerusalem *m* for Josiah..... 2Chr 35:24
for he *m* because of the .... Ezr 10:6
m certain days, and fasted, and......... Neh 1:4
m in the fifth and seventh month,..... Zec 7:5
we have *m* unto you, and ye have...... Mt 11:17
that had been with him, as they *m*.... Mk 16:10
we have *m* to you, and ye have not ... Lk 7:32
puffed up, and have not rather *m*...... 1Cor 5:2

MOURNER
thee, feign thyself to be a *m*.............. 2Sa 14:2

MOURNERS
as one that comforteth the *m*............ Job 29:25
the *m* go about the streets................ Eccl 12:5
comforts unto him and to his *m*........ Is 57:18
be unto them as the bread of *m*......... Hos 9:4

MOURNETH
the king weepeth and *m* for Absalom.. 2Sa 19:1
as one that *m* for his mother............ Ps 35:14
Mine eye *m* by reason of.................. Ps 88:9
The earth and fadeth away, the .... Is 24:4
The new wine *m*, the vine .... Is 24:7
The earth *m* and languisheth .... Is 33:9
and being desolate it *m* unto me........ Jer 12:11
Judah *m*, and the gates thereof .... Jer 14:2
because of swearing the land *m*......... Jer 23:10
The field is wasted, the land *m*......... Joel 1:10
as one *m* for his only son, and .... Zec 12:10

MOURNFULLY
that we have walked *m* before the .... Mal 3:14

MOURNING
The days of *m* for my father are .... Gen 27:41
down into the grave unto my son *m*... Gen 37:35
when the days of his *m* were past...... Gen 50:4
he made a *m* for his father seven ...... Gen 50:10
saw the *m* in the floor of Atad,......... Gen 50:11
is a grievous *m* to the Egyptians .... Gen 50:11
I have not eaten thereof in my *m*...... Deut 26:14
weeping and *m* for Moses were ended. Deut 34:8
And when the *m* was past, David....... 2Sa 11:27
mourner, and put on now *m* apparel... 2Sa 14:2
turned into *m* unto all the people...... 2Sa 19:2
there was great *m* among the Jews..... Est 4:3
But Haman hasted to his house *m*...... Est 6:12
to joy, and from *m* into a good day.... Est 9:22
who are ready to raise up their *m*...... Job 3:8
I went in without the sun .... Job 30:28
My harp also is turned to *m*............. Job 30:31
turned for me my *m* into dancing ...... Ps 30:11
I go in all the day long....................... Ps 38:6
why go I *m* because of the................ Ps 42:9
Why go I *m* because of the............... Ps 43:2
is better to go to the house of *m*....... Eccl 7:2

of the wise is in the house of *m* .... Eccl 7:4
of hosts call to weeping, and to *m* .... Is 22:12
and sorrow and *m* shall flee away .... Is 51:11
the days of thy *m* shall be ended .... Is 60:20
for ashes, the oil of joy for *m* .... Is 61:3
make thee *m*, as for an only son, ... Jer 6:26
ye, and call for the *m* women............... Jer 9:17
Enter not into the house of *m*.................. Jer 16:5
men tear themselves for them in *m*........ Jer 16:7
for I will turn their *m* into joy .... Jer 31:13
in the daughter of Judah *m*.................... Lam 2:5
our dance is turned into *m*...................... Lam 5:15
therein lamentations, and *m*................. Eze 2:10
of the valleys, all of them *m*................... Eze 7:16
make no *m* for the dead, bind the .... Eze 24:17
down to the grave I caused a *m*............. Eze 31:15
I Daniel was in three full weeks............. Dan 10:2
and with weeping, and with *m*.............. Joel 2:12
shall call the husbandman to *m*............. Amos 5:16
And I will turn your feasts into *m*......... Amos 8:10
make it as the *m* of an only son .... Amos 8:10
the dragons, and *m* as the owls............. Mic 1:8
not forth in the *m* of Beth-ezel............. Mic 1:11
there be a great *m* in Jerusalem .... Zec 12:11
as the *m* of Hadadrimmon in the .... Zec 12:11
and weeping, and great *m*, Rachel .... Mt 2:18
us your earnest desire, your *m* 2Cor 7:7
let your laughter be turned to *m*........... Jas 4:9
come in one day, death, and *m* .... Rev 18:8

MOUSE

the weasel, and the *m*, and the............... Lev 11:29
and the abomination, and the *m*............. Is 66:17

MOUTH

which hath opened her *m* to .... Gen 4:11
in her *m* was an olive leaf pluckt .... Gen 8:11
the damsel, and enquire at her *m*.......... Gen 24:57
great stone was upon the well's *m*......... Gen 29:2
the stone from the well's *m*.................... Gen 29:3
upon the well's *m* in his place .... Gen 29:3
roll the stone from the well's *m*............ Gen 29:8
the stone from the well's *m*.................... Gen 29:10
behold, it was in his sack's *m*................ Gen 42:27
again in the *m* of your sacks.................. Gen 43:12
money was in the *m* of his sack .... Gen 43:21
every man's money in his sack's *m*........ Gen 44:1
in the sack's *m* of the youngest,............ Gen 44:2
that it is my *m* that speaketh................. Gen 45:12
unto him, Who hath made man's *m* ...... Ex 4:11
go, and I will be with thy *m*................... Ex 4:12
unto him, and put words in his *m*.......... Ex 4:15
be with thy *m*, and with his *m*............ Ex 4:15
shall be to thee instead of a *m*.............. Ex 4:16
the LORD's law may be in thy *m*............ Ex 13:9
let it be heard out of thy *m*.................... Ex 23:13
With him will I speak *m* to *m*,............. Num 12:8
With him will I speak *m* to *m*............. Num 12:8
thing, and the earth open her *m*........... Num 16:30
And the earth opened her *m*................... Num 16:32
the LORD opened the *m* of the ass .... Num 22:28
the word that God putteth in my *m*....... Num 22:38
the LORD put a word in Balaam's *m*...... Num 23:5
which the LORD hath put in my *m*......... Num 23:12
Balaam, and put a word in his *m*........... Num 23:16
And the earth opened her *m*................... Num 26:10
all that proceedeth out of your *m*......... Num 30:2
hath proceeded out of your *m*............... Num 32:24
to death by the *m* of witnesses.............. Num 35:30
the *m* of the LORD doth man love......... Deut 8:3
how the earth opened her *m*.................. Deut 11:6
At the *m* of two witnesses, or .... Deut 17:6
but at the *m* of one witness he.............. Deut 17:6
and will put my words in his *m*............. Deut 18:18
at the *m* of two witnesses,..................... Deut 19:15
or at the *m* of three witnesses,............. Deut 19:15
thou hast promised with thy *m*............. Deut 23:23
is very nigh unto thee, in thy *m*........... Deut 30:14
hear, O earth, the words of my *m*......... Deut 32:1
law shall not depart out of thy *m*......... Josh 1:8
any word proceed out of your *m*........... Josh 6:10
not counsel at the *m* of the LORD......... Josh 9:14
stones upon the *m* of the cave.............. Josh 10:18
Open the *m* of the cave, and bring...... Josh 10:22
laid great stones in the cave's *m*.......... Josh 10:27
putting their hand to their *m*................. Judg 7:6
unto him, Where is now thy *m*.............. Judg 9:38
I have opened my *m* unto the LORD...... Judg 11:35
hast opened thy *m* unto the LORD......... Judg 11:36
which hath proceeded out of thy *m*...... Judg 11:36
peace, lay thine hand upon thy *m*........ Judg 18:19
the LORD, that Eli marked her *m*........... 1Sa 1:12
my *m* is enlarged over mine 1Sa 2:1
not arrogancy come out of your *m*....... 1Sa 2:3
but no man put his hand to his *m*........ 1Sa 14:26
and put his hand to his *m*...................... 1Sa 14:27
him, and delivered it out of his *m*........ 1Sa 17:35
for thy *m* hath testified against............ 2Sa 1:16
So Joab put the words in her *m*............ 2Sa 14:3
words in the *m* of thine handmaid....... 2Sa 14:19
a covering over the well's *m*.................. 2Sa 17:19
alone, there is tidings in his *m*............. 2Sa 18:25
and fire out of his *m* devoured............. 2Sa 22:9
the *m* of it within the harness............... 1Kin 7:31
but the *m* thereof was round after........ 1Kin 7:31
also upon the *m* of it were 1Kin 7:31
with his *m* unto David my father.......... 1Kin 8:15
thou speakest also with thy *m*.............. 1Kin 8:24
hast disobeyed the *m* of the LORD........ 1Kin 13:21
of the LORD in thy *m* is truth 1Kin 17:24
every *m* which hath not kissed him 1Kin 19:18

good unto the king with one *m*............ 1Kin 22:13
in the *m* of all his prophets.................. 1Kin 22:22
the *m* of all these thy prophets............ 1Kin 22:23
and put his *m* upon his 2Kin 4:34
and the judgments of his *m*.................. 1Chr 16:12
with his *m* to my father David 2Chr 6:4
and spakest with thy *m*, and hast........ 2Chr 6:15
in the *m* of all his prophets.................. 2Chr 18:21
in the *m* of these thy prophets............ 2Chr 18:22
words of Necho from the *m* of God...... 2Chr 35:22
speaking from the *m* of the LORD......... 2Chr 36:12
of the LORD by the *m* of Jeremiah....... 2Chr 36:21
by the *m* of Jeremiah might be 2Chr 36:22
the word of the LORD by the *m* of .... Ezr 1:1
not thy manna from their *m*.................. Neh 9:20
the word went out of the king's *m*....... Est 7:8
After this opened Job his *m*.................. Job 3:1
poor from the sword, from their *m*....... Job 5:15
hope, and iniquity stoppeth her *m*....... Job 5:16
Therefore I will not refrain my *m*......... Job 7:11
of thy *m* be like a strong wind .... Job 8:2
Till he fill thy *m* with laughing .... Job 8:21
mine own *m* shall condemn me .... Job 9:20
and the *m* taste his meat .... Job 12:11
For thy *m* uttereth thine iniquity .... Job 15:5
Thine own *m* condemneth thee, and... Job 15:6
such words go out of thy *m*.................. Job 15:13
breath of his *m* shall he go away......... Job 15:30
I would strengthen you with my *m*...... Job 16:5
have gaped upon me with their *m* .... Job 16:10
I intreated him with my *m*.................... Job 19:16
wickedness be sweet in his *m*.............. Job 20:12
but keep it still within his *m*................ Job 20:13
and lay your hand upon your *m*........... Job 21:5
I pray thee, the law from his *m* .... Job 22:22
him, and fill my *m* with arguments...... Job 23:4
his *m* more than my necessary food.... Job 23:12
and laid their hand on their *m* .... Job 29:9
cleaved to the roof of their *m*.............. Job 29:10
they opened their *m* wide as for.......... Job 29:23
or my *m* hath kissed my hand............. Job 31:27
(Neither have I suffered my *m* to .... Job 31:30
in the *m* of these three men................. Job 32:5
Behold, now I have opened my *m*........ Job 33:2
my tongue hath spoken in my *m*......... Job 33:2
words, as the *m* tasteth meat .... Job 34:3
doth Job open his *m* in vain................. Job 35:16
the sound that goeth out of his *m*....... Job 37:2
I will lay mine hand upon my *m*.......... Job 40:4
he can draw up Jordan into his *m*....... Job 40:23
Out of his *m* go burning lamps, and.... Job 41:19
and a flame goeth out of his *m*............ Job 41:21
is no faithfulness in their *m*................. Ps 5:9
Out of the *m* of babes and................... Ps 8:2
His *m* is full of cursing and.................. Ps 10:7
that my *m* shall not transgress............. Ps 17:3
with their *m* they speak proudly.......... Ps 17:10
and fire out of his *m* devoured............ Ps 18:8
Let the words of my *m*, and the .... Ps 19:14
Save me from the lion's *m*.................... Ps 22:21
whose *m* must be held with bit........... Ps 32:9
of them by the breath of his *m*............ Ps 33:6
shall continually be in my *m*................ Ps 34:1
opened their *m* wide against me.......... Ps 35:21
The words of his *m* are iniquity .... Ps 36:3
The *m* of the righteous speaketh......... Ps 37:30
a dumb man that openeth not his *m*.... Ps 38:13
in whose *m* are no reproofs.................. Ps 38:14
I will keep my *m* with a bridle .... Ps 39:1
I was dumb, I opened not my *m*.......... Ps 39:9
And he hath put a new song in my *m*.. Ps 40:3
My *m* shall speak of wisdom................ Ps 49:3
take thy covenant in thy *m*.................. Ps 50:16
Thou givest thy *m* to evil .... Ps 50:19
my *m* shall shew forth thy praise........ Ps 51:15
give ear to the words of my *m*............. Ps 54:2
The words of his *m* were smoother...... Ps 55:21
their teeth, O God, in their *m*.............. Ps 58:6
they belch out with their *m*................. Ps 59:7
For the sin of their *m* and the .... Ps 59:12
they bless with their *m*, but they .... Ps 62:4
my *m* shall praise thee with................. Ps 63:5
but the *m* of them that speak lies........ Ps 63:11
my *m* hath spoken, when I was in .... Ps 66:14
I cried unto him with my *m*................. Ps 66:17
not the pit shut her *m* upon me .... Ps 69:15
Let my *m* be filled with thy.................. Ps 71:8
My *m* shall shew forth thy.................... Ps 71:15
They set their *m* against the .... Ps 73:9
your ears to the words of my *m*........... Ps 78:1
I will open my *m* in a parable.............. Ps 78:2
they did flatter him with their *m*......... Ps 78:36
open thy *m* wide, and I will fill .... Ps 81:10
with my *m* will I make known thy .... Ps 89:1
satisfieth thy *m* with good things......... Ps 103:5
and the judgments of his *m*.................. Ps 105:5
and all iniquity shall stop her *m*.......... Ps 107:42
For the *m* of the wicked and the .... Ps 109:2
the *m* of the deceitful are opened........ Ps 109:2
greatly praise the LORD with my *m*...... Ps 109:30
all the judgments of thy *m*................... Ps 119:13
word of truth utterly out of my *m*........ Ps 119:43
The law of thy *m* is better unto .... Ps 119:72
I keep the testimony of thy *m*.............. Ps 119:88
yea, sweeter than honey to my *m*........ Ps 119:103
the freewill offerings of my *m*.............. Ps 119:108
I opened my *m*, and panted................. Ps 119:131
Then was our *m* filled with .... Ps 126:2
tongue cleave to the roof of my *m*....... Ps 137:6
when they hear the words of thy *m*..... Ps 138:4

Set a watch, O LORD, before my *m*....... Ps 141:3
are scattered at the grave's *m*.............. Ps 141:7
Whose *m* speaketh vanity, and their ... Ps 144:8
whose *m* speaketh vanity, and their ... Ps 144:11
My *m* shall speak the praise of .... Ps 145:21
high praises of God be in their *m*......... Ps 149:6
out of his *m* cometh knowledge and ... Prov 2:6
decline from the words of my *m*.......... Prov 4:5
Put away from thee a froward *m*.......... Prov 4:24
her *m* is smoother than oil................... Prov 5:3
depart not from the words of my *m* ..... Prov 5:7
snared with the words of thy *m*............ Prov 6:2
art taken with the words of thy *m*........ Prov 6:2
man, walketh with a froward *m*............ Prov 6:12
and attend to the words of my *m*......... Prov 7:24
For my *m* shall speak truth .... Prov 8:7
All the words of my *m* are in .... Prov 8:8
and the evil way, and the froward *m*.... Prov 8:13
covereth the *m* of the wicked .... Prov 10:6
The *m* of a righteous man is a.............. Prov 10:11
covereth the *m* of the wicked .... Prov 10:11
but the *m* of the foolish is near........... Prov 10:14
The *m* of the just bringeth forth.......... Prov 10:31
but the *m* of the wicked speaketh........ Prov 10:32
An hypocrite with his *m*....................... Prov 11:9
overthrown by the *m* of the wicked..... Prov 11:11
but the *m* of the upright shall.............. Prov 12:6
with good by the fruit of his *m*............ Prov 12:14
eat good by the fruit of his *m*.............. Prov 13:2
keepeth his *m* keepeth his life............. Prov 13:3
In the *m* of the foolish is a rod .... Prov 14:3
but the *m* of fools poureth out .... Prov 15:2
but the *m* of fools feedeth on.............. Prov 15:14
hath joy by the answer of his *m*........... Prov 15:23
but the *m* of the wicked poureth........ Prov 15:28
his *m* transgresseth not in .... Prov 16:10
heart of the wise teacheth his *m*......... Prov 16:23
for his *m* craveth it of him.................. Prov 16:26
of a man's *m* are as deep waters .... Prov 18:4
his *m* calleth for strokes .... Prov 18:6
A fool's *m* is his destruction, and ...... Prov 18:7
satisfied with the fruit of his *m*.......... Prov 18:20
much as bring it to his *m* again........... Prov 19:24
the *m* of the wicked devoureth........... Prov 19:28
but afterwards his *m* shall be .... Prov 20:17
keepeth his *m* and his tongue............. Prov 21:23
The *m* of strange women is a deep..... Prov 22:14
he openeth not his *m* in the gate .... Prov 24:7
so is a parable in the *m* of fools......... Prov 26:7
so is a parable in the *m* of fools......... Prov 26:9
him to bring it again to his *m*............. Prov 26:15
and a flattering *m* worketh ruin.......... Prov 26:28
praise thee, and not thine own *m*....... Prov 27:2
she eateth, and wipeth her *m*............. Prov 30:20
evil, lay thine hand upon thy *m*......... Prov 30:32
Open thy *m* for the dumb in the........ Prov 31:8
Open thy *m*, judge righteously, and... Prov 31:9
She openeth her *m* with wisdom......... Prov 31:26
Be not rash with thy *m*, and let.......... Eccl 5:2
Suffer not thy *m* to cause thy............. Eccl 5:6
the labour of man is for his *m*............ Eccl 6:7
of a wise man's *m* are gracious........... Eccl 10:12
the words of his *m* is foolishness........ Eccl 10:13
kiss me with the kisses of his *m*.......... Song 1:2
His *m* is most sweet .... Song 5:16
the roof of thy *m* like the best........... Song 7:9
for the *m* of the LORD hath spoken..... Is 1:20
opened her *m* without measure.......... Is 5:14
And he laid it upon my *m*, and said.... Is 6:7
shall devour Israel with open *m*......... Is 9:12
and every *m* speaketh folly.................. Is 9:17
moved the wing, or opened the *m*...... Is 10:14
rod with the rod of his *m*.................... Is 11:4
by the *m* of the brooks, and every ...... Is 19:7
people draw near me with their *m*...... Is 29:13
Egypt, and have not asked at my *m*.... Is 30:2
for my *m* it hath commanded, and ..... Is 34:16
for the *m* of the LORD hath spoken..... Is 40:5
gone out of my *m* in righteousness.... Is 45:23
and they went forth out of my *m*........ Is 48:3
he hath made my *m* like a sharp .... Is 49:2
And I have put my words in thy *m*...... Is 51:16
yet he opened not his *m*...................... Is 53:7
is dumb, so he openeth not his *m*....... Is 53:7
neither was any deceit in his *m*.......... Is 53:9
be that goeth forth out of my *m*......... Is 55:11
against whom make ye a wide *m*......... Is 57:4
for the *m* of the LORD hath spoken..... Is 58:14
words which I have put in thy *m*......... Is 59:21
shall not depart out of thy *m*............... Is 59:21
nor out of the *m* of thy seed............... Is 59:21
nor out of the *m* of thy seed's .... Is 59:21
which the *m* of the LORD shall............ Is 62:2
forth his hand, and touched my *m*...... Jer 1:9
I have put my words in thy *m*............. Jer 1:9
will make my words in thy *m* fire .... Jer 5:14
and is cut off from their *m*.................. Jer 7:28
to his neighbour with his *m*................ Jer 9:8
who is he to whom the *m* of the......... Jer 9:12
ear receive the word of his *m*.............. Jer 9:20
thou art near in their *m*, and far......... Jer 12:2
the vile, thou shalt be as my *m*........... Jer 15:19
and not out of the *m* of the LORD....... Jer 23:16
shall speak with him *m* to *m*............ Jer 32:4
shall speak with thee *m* to *m*........... Jer 34:3
Baruch wrote from the *m* of............... Jer 36:4
which thou hast written from my *m* ... Jer 36:6
write all these words at his *m*............. Jer 36:17
these words unto me with his *m*......... Jer 36:18
Baruch wrote at the *m* of Jeremiah..... Jer 36:27

who wrote therein from the *m* of...... Jer 36:32
goeth forth out of our own *m*......... Jer 44:17
shall no more be named in the *m*..... Jer 44:26
in a book at the *m* of Jeremiah....... Jer 45:1
nest in the sides of the hole's *m*..... Jer 48:28
I will bring forth out of his *m*........ Jer 51:44
have opened their *m* against thee..... Lam 2:16
He putteth his *m* in the dust.......... Lam 3:29
Out of the *m* of the most High........ Lam 3:38
to the roof of his *m* for thirst......... Lam 4:4
open thy *m*, and eat that I give....... Eze 2:8
So I opened my *m*, and he caused me ... Eze 3:2
it was in my *m* as honey for......... Eze 3:3
therefore hear the word at my *m*...... Eze 3:17
cleave to the roof of thy *m*........... Eze 3:26
with thee, I will open thy *m*.......... Eze 3:27
there abominable flesh into my *m*..... Eze 4:14
by thy *m* in the day of thy pride...... Eze 16:56
never open thy *m* any more because... Eze 16:63
to open the *m* in the slaughter....... Eze 21:22
In that day shall thy *m* be opened.... Eze 24:27
of the *m* in the midst of them........ Eze 29:21
thou shalt hear the word at my *m*..... Eze 33:7
and had opened my *m*, until he came. Eze 33:22
my *m* was opened, and I was........ Eze 33:22
for with their *m* they shew much..... Eze 33:31
deliver my flock from their *m*......... Eze 34:10
Thus with your *m* ye have boasted.... Eze 35:13
m of the burning fiery furnace........ Dan 3:26
the word was in the king's *m*......... Dan 4:31
and laid upon the *m* of the den....... Dan 6:17
it had three ribs in the *m* of it....... Dan 7:5
a *m* speaking great things............ Dan 7:8
a *m* that spake very great things,..... Dan 7:20
came flesh nor wine in my *m*......... Dan 10:3
then I opened my *m*, and spake, and. Dan 10:16
the names of Baalim out of her *m*..... Hos 2:17
slain them by the words of my *m*..... Hos 6:5
Set the trumpet to thy *m*............. Hos 8:1
for it is cut off from your *m*.......... Joel 1:5
out of the *m* of the lion two legs..... Amos 3:12
for the *m* of the Lord of hosts........ Mic 4:4
tongue is deceitful in their *m*......... Mic 6:12
keep the doors of thy *m* from her..... Mic 7:5
shall lay their hand upon their *m*..... Mic 7:16
even fall into the *m* of the eater..... Nah 3:12
tongue be found in their *m*........... Zeph 3:13
weight of lead upon the *m* thereof.... Zec 5:8
words by the *m* of the prophets....... Zec 8:9
take away his blood out of his *m*..... Zec 9:7
shall consume away in their *m*....... Zec 14:12
The law of truth was in his *m*........ Mal 2:6
they should seek the law at his *m*.... Mal 2:7
proceedeth out of the *m* of God....... Mt 4:4
And he opened his *m*, and taught..... Mt 5:2
of the heart the *m* speaketh.......... Mt 12:34
I will open my *m* in parables......... Mt 13:35
draweth nigh unto me with their *m*... Mt 15:8
goeth into the *m* defileth a man...... Mt 15:11
that which cometh out of the *m*...... Mt 15:11
in at the *m* goeth into the belly...... Mt 15:17
the *m* come forth from the heart...... Mt 15:18
and when thou hast opened his *m*.... Mt 17:27
that in the *m* of two or three......... Mt 18:16
never read, Out of the *m* of babes.... Mt 21:16
his *m* was opened immediately, and... Lk 1:64
As he spake by the *m* of his holy..... Lk 1:70
which proceeded out of his *m*........ Lk 4:22
of the heart his *m* speaketh.......... Lk 6:45
to catch something out of his *m*..... Lk 11:54
Out of thine own *m* will I judge...... Lk 19:22
For I will give you a *m* and wisdom... Lk 21:15
ourselves have heard of his own *m*... Lk 22:71
upon hyssop, and put it to his *m*..... Jn 19:29
by the *m* of David spake before....... Acts 1:16
by the *m* of all his prophets.......... Acts 3:18
which God hath spoken by the *m* of .. Acts 3:21
Who by the *m* of thy servant David... Acts 4:25
shearer, so opened he not his *m*...... Acts 8:32
Then Philip opened his *m*, and....... Acts 8:35
Then Peter opened his *m*, and said,... Acts 10:34
at any time entered into my *m*....... Acts 11:8
that the Gentiles by my *m* should.... Acts 15:7
tell you the same things by *m*........ Acts 15:27
Paul was now about to open his *m*.... Acts 18:14
shouldest hear the voice of his *m*..... Acts 22:14
by him to smite him on the *m*........ Acts 23:2
Whose *m* is full of cursing and........ Rom 3:14
that every *m* may be stopped, and..... Rom 3:19
word is nigh thee, even in thy *m*...... Rom 10:8
confess with thy *m* the Lord Jesus..... Rom 10:9
with the *m* confession is made........ Rom 10:10
one *m* glorify God, even the.......... Rom 15:6
Thou shalt not muzzle the *m* of....... 1Cor 9:9
our *m* is open unto you, our heart,.... 2Cor 6:11
In the *m* of two or three............. 2Cor 13:1
proceed out of your *m*, but that...... Eph 4:29
me, that I may open my *m* boldly..... Eph 6:19
communication out of your *m*........ Col 3:8
consume with the spirit of his *m*..... 2Th 2:8
out of the *m* of the lion............... 2Ti 4:17
Out of the same *m* proceedeth........ Jas 3:10
neither was guile found in his *m*...... 1Pet 2:22
their *m* speaketh great swelling....... Jude 16
out of his *m* went a sharp............ Rev 1:16
them with the sword of my *m*........ Rev 2:16
hot, I will spue thee out of my *m*..... Rev 3:16
For their power is in their *m*.......... Rev 9:19
shall be in thy *m* sweet as honey...... Rev 10:9
it was in my *m* sweet as honey....... Rev 10:10

fire proceedeth out of their *m*......... Rev 11:5
his *m* water as a flood after the....... Rev 12:15
woman, and the earth opened her *m*.. Rev 12:16
the dragon cast out of his *m*......... Rev 12:16
his *m* as the *m* of a lion........... Rev 13:2
and his *m* as the *m* of a lion....... Rev 13:2
him a speaking great things............ Rev 13:5
he opened his *m* in blasphemy....... Rev 13:6
in their *m* was found no guile........ Rev 14:5
come out of the *m* of the dragon..... Rev 16:13
out of the *m* of the beast............ Rev 16:13
out of the *m* of the false prophet..... Rev 16:13
out of his *m* goeth a sharp sword,..... Rev 19:15
sword proceeded out of his *m*........ Rev 19:21

MOUTHS
which we found in our sacks' *m*....... Gen 44:8
put it in their *m*, that this song...... Deut 31:19
put it in their *m* seed............... Deut 31:21
They gaped upon me with their *m*.... Ps 22:13
their meat was yet in their *m*........ Ps 78:30
They have *m*, but they speak not..... Ps 115:5
They have *m*, but they speak not..... Ps 135:16
is there any breath in their *m*........ Ps 135:17
kings shall shut their *m* at him....... Is 52:15
have both spoken with your *m*....... Jer 44:25
have opened their *m* against us....... Lam 3:46
angel, and hath shut the lions' *m*..... Dan 6:22
he that putteth not into their *m*...... Mic 3:5
Whose *m* must be stopped, who....... Titus 1:11
promises, stopped the *m* of lions...... Heb 11:33
we put bits in the horses' *m*......... Jas 3:3
and out of their *m* issued fire........ Rev 9:17
which issued out of their *m*......... Rev 9:18

MOVE
shall not a dog *m* his tongue......... Ex 11:7
of all that *m* in the waters, and...... Lev 11:10
but thou shalt not *m* a sickle........ Deut 23:25
I will *m* them to jealousy with....... Deut 32:21
m him at times in the camp of Dan... Judg 13:25
place of their own, and *m* no more.... 2Sa 7:10
in any more out of the land which..... 2Kin 21:8
let no man *m* his bones.............. 2Kin 23:18
and with hammers, that it not........ Jer 10:4
they shall *m* out of their holes....... Mic 7:17
but they themselves will not *m*...... Mt 23:4
For in him we live, and *m*, and have.. Acts 17:28
But none of these things *m* me...... Acts 20:24

MOVEABLE
the path of life, her ways are *m*....... Prov 5:6

MOVED
the Spirit of God *m* upon the face..... Gen 1:2
flesh died that *m* upon the earth..... Gen 7:21
They have *m* to jealousy with........ Deut 32:21
none *m* his tongue against any of..... Josh 10:21
that she *m* him to ask of her......... Josh 15:18
that she *m* him to ask of her......... Judg 1:14
all the city was *m* about them....... Ruth 1:19
only her lips *m*, but her voice....... 1Sa 1:13
And the king was much *m*, and went. 2Sa 18:33
the foundations of heaven *m*......... 2Sa 22:8
he *m* David against them to say,..... 2Sa 24:1
shall be stable, that it be not *m*..... 1Chr 16:30
place, and shall be *m* no more....... 1Chr 17:9
God *m* them to depart from him..... 2Chr 18:31
that they have *m* sedition within..... Ezr 4:15
nor *m* for him, he was full of........ Est 5:9
and is *m* out of his place............ Job 37:1
they cannot be *m*................... Job 41:23
in his heart, I shall not be *m*........ Ps 10:6
trouble me rejoice when I am *m*...... Ps 13:4
these things shall never be *m*....... Ps 15:5
my right hand, I shall not be *m*...... Ps 16:8
foundations also of the hills *m*...... Ps 18:7
the most High he shall not be *m*..... Ps 21:7
I said, I shall never be *m*............ Ps 30:6
she shall not be *m*.................. Ps 46:5
raged, the kingdoms were *m*......... Ps 46:6
suffer the righteous to be *m*......... Ps 55:22
I shall not be greatly *m*............. Ps 62:2
I shall not be *m*.................... Ps 62:6
and suffereth not our feet to be *m*... Ps 66:9
even Sinai itself was *m* at the....... Ps 68:8
m him to jealousy with their........ Ps 78:58
stablished, that it cannot be *m*...... Ps 93:1
that it shall not be *m*............... Ps 96:10
let the earth be *m*.................. Ps 99:1
Surely he shall not be *m* for ever..... Ps 112:6
will not suffer thy foot to be *m*...... Ps 121:3
of the righteous shall not be *m*...... Prov 12:3
door, and my bowels were *m* for him.. Song 5:4
the posts of the door *m* at the....... Is 6:4
And his heart was *m*, and the heart... Is 7:2
of the wood are *m* with the wind..... Is 7:2
and there was none that *m* the wing.. Is 10:14
Hell from beneath is *m* for thee...... Is 14:9
Egypt shall be *m* at his presence..... Is 19:1
the earth is exceedingly.............. Is 24:19
graven image, that shall not be *m*... Is 40:20
nails, that it should not be *m*....... Is 41:7
and all the hills lightly.............. Jer 4:24
they shall drink, and be *m*.......... Jer 25:16
whose waters are *m* as the rivers..... Jer 46:7
his waters are *m* like the rivers..... Jer 46:8
the earth is *m* at the noise of....... Jer 49:21
taking of Babylon the earth is *m*..... Jer 50:46
he was *m* with choler against him.... Dan 8:7
the south shall be *m* with choler..... Dan 11:11
he was *m* with compassion on them,.. Mt 9:36

was *m* with compassion toward them .. Mt 14:14
servant was *m* with compassion...... Mt 18:27
they were *m* with indignation....... Mt 20:24
Jerusalem, all the city was *m*........ Mt 21:10
m with compassion, put forth his.... Mk 1:41
was *m* with compassion toward them .. Mk 6:34
the chief priests the people........... Mk 15:11
hand, that I should not be *m*........ Acts 2:25
m with envy, sold Joseph into....... Acts 7:9
m with envy, took unto them........ Acts 17:5
And all the city was *m*, and the...... Acts 21:30
be not *m* away from the hope of..... Col 1:23
should be *m* by these afflictions..... 1Th 3:3
m with fear, prepared an ark to...... Heb 11:7
a kingdom which cannot be *m*...... Heb 12:28
as they were *m* by the Holy Ghost.... 2Pet 1:21
island were *m* out of their places..... Rev 6:14

MOVEDST
although thou *m* me against him,..... Job 2:3

MOVER
a *m* of sedition among all the........ Acts 24:5

MOVETH
and every living creature that *m*..... Gen 1:21
thing that *m* upon the earth......... Gen 1:28
upon all that *m* upon the earth,...... Gen 9:2
creature that *m* in the waters........ Lev 11:46
He *m* his tail like a cedar........... Job 40:17
and every thing that *m* therein...... Ps 69:34
the cup, when it *m* itself aright..... Prov 23:31
every thing that liveth, which *m*..... Eze 47:9

MOVING
the *m* creature that hath life......... Gen 1:20
Every *m* thing that liveth shall...... Gen 9:3
the *m* of my lips should assuage...... Job 16:5
m his lips he bringeth evil to....... Prov 16:30
waiting for the *m* of the water....... Jn 5:3

MOWER
Wherewith the *m* filleth not his...... Ps 129:7

MOWINGS
latter growth after the king's *m*...... Amos 7:1

MOWN
down like rain upon the *m* grass..... Ps 72:6

MOZA (mo'-zah)
    1. A son of Caleb.
concubine, bare Haran, and M.......... 1Chr 2:46
    2. Descendant of King Saul.
and Zimri begat M..................... 1Chr 8:36
And M begat Binea.................... 1Chr 8:37
and Zimri begat M..................... 1Chr 9:42
And M begat Binea.................... 1Chr 9:43

MOZAH (mo'-zah) A city in Benjamin.
And Mizpeh, and Chephirah, and M... Josh 18:26

MUCH
for as *m* money as it is worth he...... Gen 23:9
for thou art *m* mightier than we..... Gen 26:16
had *m* cattle, and maidservants, and.. Gen 30:43
Ask me never so *m* dowry and gift,... Gen 34:12
as the sand of the sea, very *m*....... Gen 41:49
five times so *m* as any of their's..... Gen 43:34
as *m* as they can carry, and put...... Gen 44:1
this day, to save *m* people alive...... Gen 50:20
and herds, even very *m* cattle........ Ex 12:38
It is a night to be *m* observed........ Ex 12:42
remained not so *m* as one of them ... Ex 14:28
twice as *m* as they gather daily...... Ex 16:5
that gathered *m* had nothing over.... Ex 16:18
they gathered twice as *m* bread...... Ex 16:22
and of sweet cinnamon half so *m*.... Ex 30:23
The people bring *m* more than....... Ex 36:5
all the work to make it, and too *m*.... Ex 36:7
Aaron have, one as *m* as another..... Lev 7:10
scab spread *m* abroad in the skin..... Lev 13:7
if it spread *m* abroad in the skin..... Lev 13:22
if it be spread *m* abroad in the....... Lev 13:27
But if the scall spread *m* in the...... Lev 13:35
if he be poor, and cannot get so *m*.... Lev 14:21
unto them, Ye take too *m* upon you... Num 16:3
ye take too *m* upon you, ye sons...... Num 16:7
out against him with *m* people....... Num 20:20
the soul of the people was *m*......... Num 21:4
and *m* people of Israel died......... Num 21:6
not so *m* as a footbreadth........... Deut 2:5
(for I know that ye have *m* cattle..... Deut 3:19
Thou shalt carry *m* seed out into..... Deut 28:38
how *m* more after my death......... Deut 31:27
m people, even as the sand that..... Josh 11:4
yet very *m* land to be possessed..... Josh 13:1
of Judah was too *m* for them........ Josh 19:9
Return with *m* riches unto your...... Josh 22:8
your tents, and with very *m* cattle... Josh 22:8
with iron, and with very *m* raiment.. Josh 22:8
for it grieveth me *m* for your......... Ruth 1:13
then take as *m* as thy soul.......... 1Sa 2:16
How *m* more, if haply the people..... 1Sa 14:30
a *m* greater slaughter among the..... 1Sa 14:30
so that his name was *m* set by....... 1Sa 18:30
Saul's son delighted *m* in David..... 1Sa 19:2
LORD do so and *m* more to Jonathan ... 1Sa 20:13
how *m* more then if we come to...... 1Sa 23:3
as thy life was *m* set by this day..... 1Sa 26:24
so let my life be set by in the........ 1Sa 26:24
How *m* more, when wicked men have.. 2Sa 4:11
king David took exceeding *m* brass.... 2Sa 8:8
there came *m* people by the way of... 2Sa 13:34
so *m* praised as Absalom for his...... 2Sa 14:25

how *m* more now may this Benjamite 2Sa 16:11
shall not be left so *m* as one 2Sa 17:12
And the king was *m* moved 2Sa 18:33
and understanding exceeding *m* 1Kin 4:29
how *m* less this house that I have 1Kin 8:27
that bare spices, and very *m* gold 1Kin 10:2
It is too *m* for you to go up to 1Kin 12:28
how *m* rather then, when he saith 2Kin 5:13
but Jehu shall serve him *m* 2Kin 10:18
there was *m* money in the chest 2Kin 12:10
he wrought *m* wickedness in the 2Kin 21:6
shed innocent blood very *m* 2Kin 21:16
brought David very *m* brass 1Chr 18:8
exceeding *m* spoil out of the city 1Chr 20:2
brought *m* cedar wood to David 1Chr 22:4
because thou hast shed *m* blood 1Chr 22:8
Lebanon, as *m* as thou shalt need 2Chr 2:16
how *m* less this house which I 2Chr 6:18
and they carried away very *m* spoil 2Chr 14:13
was exceeding *m* spoil in them 2Chr 14:14
he had *m* business in the cities 2Chr 17:13
of the spoil, it was so *m* 2Chr 20:25
they saw that there was *m* money 2Chr 24:11
to give thee *m* more than this 2Chr 25:9
thousand of them, and took *m* spoil 2Chr 25:13
for he had *m* cattle, both in the 2Chr 26:10
on the wall of Ophel he built *m* 2Chr 27:3
So *m* did the children of Ammon 2Chr 27:5
took also away *m* spoil from them, ... 2Chr 28:8
m people to keep the head of 2Chr 30:13
was gathered *m* people together 2Chr 32:4
of Assyria come, and find *m* water 2Chr 32:4
how *m* less shall your God deliver 2Chr 32:15
Hezekiah had exceeding *m* riches 2Chr 32:27
had given him substance very *m* 2Chr 32:29
he wrought *m* evil in the sight of 2Chr 33:6
transgressed very *m* after all the 2Chr 36:14
and salt without prescribing how *m* .... Ezr 7:22
many, and it is a time of *m* rain .... Ezr 10:13
is decayed, and there is *m* rubbish .... Neh 4:10
they were *m* cast down in their .... Neh 6:16
it yieldeth *m* increase unto the .... Neh 9:37
shall there arise too *m* contempt .... Est 1:18
How *m* less in them that dwell in .... Job 4:19
How *m* less shall I answer him, and ...... Job 9:14
aged men, *m* elder than thy father .... Job 15:10
How *m* more abominable and filthy ...... Job 15:16
How *m* less man, that is a worm .... Job 25:6
and because mine hand had gotten *m* .. Job 31:25
How *m* less to him that accepteth .... Job 34:19
Job twice as *m* as he had before .... Job 42:10
than gold, yea, than *m* fine gold .... Ps 19:10
is not delivered by *m* strength .... Ps 33:16
I will praise thee among *m* people .... Ps 35:18
as *m* as in all riches .... Ps 119:14
I am afflicted very *m* .... Ps 119:107
With her *m* fair speech she caused ...... Prov 7:21
m more the wicked and the sinner ...... Prov 11:31
M food is in the tillage of the .... Prov 13:23
but *m* increase is by the strength .... Prov 14:4
of the righteous is *m* treasure .... Prov 15:6
how *m* more then the hearts of the .... Prov 15:11
How *m* better is it to get wisdom ...... Prov 16:16
m less do lying lips a prince .... Prov 17:7
how *m* more do his friends go far ...... Prov 19:7
m less for a servant to have rule .... Prov 19:10
will not so *m* as bring it to his .... Prov 19:24
how *m* more, when he bringeth it .... Prov 21:27
eat so *m* as is sufficient for .... Prov 25:16
It is not good to eat *m* honey .... Prov 25:27
For in *m* wisdom is *m* grief .... Eccl 1:18
sweet, whether he eat little or *m* .... Eccl 5:12
in darkness, and he hath *m* sorrow .... Eccl 5:17
For he shall not *m* remember the ...... Eccl 5:20
Be not righteous over *m* .... Eccl 7:16
Be not over *m* wicked, neither be .... Eccl 7:17
but one sinner destroyeth *m* good .... Eccl 9:18
By *m* slothfulness the building .... Eccl 10:18
m study is a weariness of the .... Eccl 12:12
how *m* better is thy love than .... Song 4:10
hearkened diligently with *m* heed ...... Is 21:7
pile thereof is fire and *m* wood .... Is 30:33
as this day, and *m* more abundant .... Is 56:12
with nitre, and take thee *m* sope ...... Jer 2:22
thou about so *m* to change thy way .... Jer 2:36
wine and summer fruits very *m* .... Jer 40:12
How *m* more when I send thy four .... Eze 14:21
how *m* less shall it be meet yet .... Eze 15:5
might give him horses and *m* people .. Eze 17:15
which art infamous and *m* vexed ...... Eze 22:5
it containeth *m* .... Eze 23:32
and companies, and *m* people .... Eze 26:7
with their mouth they shew *m* love .. Eze 33:31
wear fair, and the fruit thereof *m* .... Dan 4:12
were fair, and the fruit thereof *m* .... Dan 4:21
unto it, Arise, devour *m* flesh .... Dan 7:5
my cogitations *m* troubled me .... Dan 7:28
a great army and with *m* riches .... Dan 11:13
face the people shall be *m* pained .... Joel 2:6
and also *m* cattle .... Jonah 4:11
m pain is in all loins, and the .... Nah 2:10
Ye have sown *m*, and bring in .... Hag 1:6
Ye looked for *m*, and, lo, it came .... Hag 1:9
have we spoken so *m* against thee .... Mal 3:13
be heard for their *m* speaking .... Mt 6:7
Are ye not *m* better than they .... Mt 6:26
shall he not *m* more clothe you, O .... Mt 6:30
how *m* more shall your Father .... Mt 7:11
how *m* more shall they call them .... Mt 10:25
How *m* then is a man better than a .. Mt 12:12

where they had not *m* earth .... Mt 13:5
have so *m* bread in the wilderness .... Mt 15:33
might have been sold for *m* .... Mt 26:9
out, and began to publish it *m* .... Mk 1:45
not so *m* as about the door .... Mk 2:2
they could not so *m* as eat bread ...... Mk 3:20
ground, where it had not *m* earth .... Mk 4:5
he besought him that he would .... Mk 5:10
m people gathered unto him .... Mk 5:21
in people followed him, and .... Mk 5:24
had no leisure so *m* as to eat .... Mk 6:31
saw *m* people, and was moved with .. Mk 6:34
so *m* the more a great deal they .... Mk 7:36
he was *m* displeased, and said unto .. Mk 10:14
they began to be *m* displeased .... Mk 10:41
and many that were rich cast in *m* .. Mk 12:41
But so *m* the more went there a ...... Lk 5:15
Have ye not read so *m* as this .... Lk 6:3
to sinners, to receive as *m* again ...... Lk 6:34
went with him, and *m* people .... Lk 7:11
m people of the city was with her .... Lk 7:12
you, and *m* more than a prophet ...... Lk 7:26
for she loved *m* .... Lk 7:47
when *m* people were gathered .... Lk 8:4
from the hill, *m* people met him .... Lk 9:37
was cumbered about *m* serving .... Lk 10:40
how *m* more shall your heavenly .... Lk 11:13
thou hast *m* goods laid up for .... Lk 12:19
how *m* more are ye better than the .. Lk 12:24
how *m* more will he clothe you, O .. Lk 12:28
For unto whomsoever *m* is given .... Lk 12:48
of him shall be *m* required .... Lk 12:48
and to whom men have committed *m*.. Lk 12:48
How *m* owest thou unto my lord ...... Lk 16:5
to another, And how *m* owest thou .. Lk 16:7
is least is faithful also in *m* .... Lk 16:10
in the least is unjust also in *m* .... Lk 16:10
would not lift up so *m* as his .... Lk 18:13
but he cried so *m* the more .... Lk 18:39
that he might know how *m* every .... Lk 19:15
to pass, as they were *m* perplexed .. Lk 24:4
because there was *m* water there ...... Jn 3:23
Now there was *m* grass in the .... Jn 6:10
of the fishes as *m* as they would ...... Jn 6:11
there was *m* murmuring among the .. Jn 7:12
M people of the Jews therefore .... Jn 12:9
On the next day *m* people that .... Jn 12:12
it die, it bringeth forth *m* fruit .... Jn 12:24
I will not talk *m* with you .... Jn 14:30
the same bringeth forth *m* fruit ...... Jn 15:5
glorified, that ye bear *m* fruit .... Jn 15:8
whether ye sold the land for so *m* .. Acts 5:8
And she said, Yea, for so *m* .... Acts 5:8
drew away *m* people after him .... Acts 5:37
not so *m* as to set his foot on .... Acts 7:5
how *m* evil he hath done to thy ...... Acts 9:13
which gave *m* alms to the people, .. Acts 10:2
m people was added unto the Lord .. Acts 11:24
the church, and taught *m* people .... Acts 11:26
faith, and that we must through *m* .. Acts 14:22
when there had been *m* disputing .. Acts 15:7
her masters in gain by soothsaying .. Acts 16:16
for I have *m* people in this city ...... Acts 18:10
helped them *m* which had believed.. Acts 18:27
We have not so *m* as heard whether.. Acts 19:2
turned away *m* people .... Acts 19:26
and had given them *m* exhortation .. Acts 20:2
m learning doth make thee mad ...... Acts 26:24
Now when *m* time was spent, and .. Acts 27:9
m damage, not only of the lading .. Acts 27:10
we had *m* work to come by the boat.. Acts 27:16
as *m* as in me is, I am ready to ...... Rom 1:15
M every way: chiefly .... Rom 3:2
M more then, being now justified .... Rom 5:9
m more, being reconciled, we .... Rom 5:10
m more the grace of God, and the .. Rom 5:15
m more they which receive .... Rom 5:17
abounded, grace did *m* more abound .. Rom 5:20
endured with *m* longsuffering the .. Rom 9:22
how *m* more their fulness .... Rom 11:12
how *m* more shall these, which be .. Rom 11:24
as *m* as lieth in you, live .... Rom 12:18
in hindered from coming to you ...... Rom 15:22
Mary, who bestowed *m* labour on us .. Rom 16:6
which laboured in the Lord .... Rom 16:12
and in fear, and in *m* trembling 1Cor 2:3
so *m* as named among the Gentiles .. 1Cor 5:1
how *m* more things that pertain to .. 1Cor 6:3
m more these members of the body,.. 1Cor 12:22
salute you *m* in the Lord, within 1Cor 16:19
For out of *m* affliction and 2Cor 2:4
m more the ministration of 2Cor 3:9
m more that which remaineth is 2Cor 3:11
in *m* patience, in afflictions, in 2Cor 6:4
Praying us with *m* intreaty that 2Cor 8:4
had gathered *m* had nothing over .. 2Cor 8:15
but now *m* more diligent, upon the.. 2Cor 8:22
are *m* more bold to speak the word.. Phil 1:14
but now *m* more in my absence) .... Phil 2:12
the Holy Ghost, and in *m* assurance.. 1Th 1:5
received the word in *m* affliction 1Th 1:6
gospel of God with *m* contention .. 1Th 2:2
not given to *m* wine, not greedy 1Ti 3:8
the coppersmith did me *m* evil 2Ti 4:14
accusers, not given to *m* wine .... Titus 2:3
though I might be *m* bold in .... Philem 8
but now *m* more unto thee, both in.. Philem 16
Being made so *m* better than the .. Heb 1:4
By so *m* was Jesus made a surety .. Heb 7:22
by how *m* also he is the mediator .. Heb 8:6

How *m* more shall the blood of........ Heb 9:14
so *m* the more, as ye see the day .... Heb 10:25
Of how *m* sorer punishment, ... Heb 10:29
shall we not *m* rather be .... Heb 12:9
if so *m* as a beast touch the .... Heb 12:20
m more shall not we escape, if we .. Heb 12:25
of a righteous man availeth *m* ...... Jas 5:16
being *m* more precious than of 1Pet 1:7
through *m* wantonness, those that .. 2Pet 2:18
And I wept *m*, because no man was .. Rev 5:4
was given unto him *m* incense .... Rev 8:3
How *m* she hath glorified herself, .. Rev 18:7
so *m* torment and sorrow give her .. Rev 18:7
great voice of *m* people in heaven.. Rev 19:1

MUFFLERS
and the bracelets, and the *m* .... Is 3:19

MULBERRY
them over against the *m* trees 2Sa 5:23
going in the tops of the *m* trees 2Sa 5:24
them over against the *m* trees 1Chr 14:14
going in the tops of the *m* trees 1Chr 14:15

MULE
every man gat him up upon his *m* .. 2Sa 13:29
And Absalom rode upon a *m*, and the.. 2Sa 18:9
the *m* went under the thick boughs .. 2Sa 18:9
the *m* that was under him went 2Sa 18:9
my son to ride upon mine own *m* .. 1Kin 1:33
to ride upon king David's *m* 1Kin 1:38
him to ride upon the king's *m* 1Kin 1:44
ye not as the horse, or as the *m* .... Ps 32:9
the plague of the horse, of the *m* .. Zec 14:15

MULES
found the *m* in the wilderness .... Gen 36:24
armour, and spices, horses, and *m*.. 1Kin 10:25
m alive, that we lose not all the 1Kin 18:5
on asses, and on camels, and on *m*.. 1Chr 12:40
harness, and spices, horses, and *m* .. 2Chr 9:24
their *m*, two hundred forty and ...... Ezr 2:66
their *m*, two hundred forty and ...... Neh 7:68
on horseback, and riders on *m* ...... Est 8:10
So the posts that rode upon *m* ...... Est 8:14
and in litters, and upon *m* .... Is 66:20
with horses and horsemen and on *m*.. Eze 27:14

MULES'
thy servant two *m* burden of earth.. 2Kin 5:17

MULTIPLIED
and grew, and *m* exceedingly .... Gen 47:27
and increased abundantly, and *m* .. Ex 1:7
afflicted them, the more they *m* .... Ex 1:12
and the people *m*, and waxed very.. Ex 1:20
may be *m* in the land of Egypt ...... Ex 11:9
The LORD your God hath *m* you .... Deut 1:10
and thy silver and thy gold is *m* .... Deut 8:13
and all that thou hast is *m* .... Deut 8:13
That your days may be *m*, and the.. Deut 11:21
m his seed, and gave him Isaac ...... Josh 24:3
were *m* in the land of Gilead 1Chr 5:9
If his children be *m*, it is for .... Job 27:14
or if thy transgressions be *m* .... Job 35:6
Their sorrows shall be *m* that .... Ps 16:4
that hate me wrongfully are *m* ...... Ps 38:19
also, so that they are *m* greatly ...... Ps 107:38
For by me thy days shall be *m*, ... Prov 9:11
When the wicked are *m*, ... Prov 29:16
Thou hast *m* the nation, and not .... Is 9:3
transgressions are *m* before thee .. Is 59:12
shall come to pass, when ye be *m* .. Jer 3:16
Because ye *m* more than the .... Eze 5:7
Ye have *m* your slain in this city .. Eze 11:6
passed by, and in thy whoredoms .. Eze 16:25
Thou hast moreover *m* thy .... Eze 16:29
but thou hast *m* thine .... Eze 16:51
may faint, and their ruins be *m* .... Eze 21:15
Yet she *m* her whoredoms, in ...... Eze 23:19
the field, and his boughs were *m* .. Eze 31:5
have *m* your words against me ...... Eze 35:13
Peace be *m* unto you .... Dan 4:1
Peace be *m* unto you .... Dan 6:25
m her silver and gold, which they .. Hos 2:8
Judah hath *m* fenced cities .... Hos 8:14
I have *m* visions, and used .... Hos 12:10
Thou hast *m* thy merchants above.. Nah 3:16
the number of the disciples was *m*.. Acts 6:1
disciples *m* in Jerusalem greatly .. Acts 6:7
the people grew and *m* in Egypt, .. Acts 7:17
comfort of the Holy Ghost, were *m*.. Acts 9:31
the word of God grew and *m* .... Acts 12:24
Grace unto you, and peace, be *m* .. 1Pet 1:2
peace be *m* unto you through the .. 2Pet 1:2
unto you, and peace, and love, be *m*.. Jude 2

MULTIPLIEDST
Their children also *m* thou as the .. Neh 9:23

MULTIPLIETH
m my wounds without cause .... Job 9:17
us, and *m* his words against God .. Job 34:37
he *m* words without knowledge .... Job 35:16

MULTIPLY
them, saying, Be fruitful, and *m* .... Gen 1:22
and seas, and let fowl *m* in the earth.. Gen 1:22
said unto them, Be fruitful, and *m* .. Gen 1:28
said, I will greatly *m* thy sorrow .... Gen 3:16
when men began to *m* on the face .. Gen 6:1
be fruitful, and *m* upon the earth .. Gen 8:17
said unto them, Be fruitful, and *m*.. Gen 9:1
And you, be ye fruitful, and *m* ...... Gen 9:7

in the earth, and m therein............... Gen 9:7
I will m thy seed exceedingly,......... Gen 16:10
thee, and will m thee exceedingly.... Gen 17:2
and will m him exceedingly............. Gen 17:20
in multiplying I will m thy seed........ Gen 22:17
seed to m as the stars of heaven....... Gen 26:4
m thy seed for my servant................ Gen 26:24
m thee, that thou mayest be a........... Gen 28:3
be fruitful and m,.............................. Gen 35:11
m thee, and I will make of thee a...... Gen 48:4
lest they m, and it come to pass,....... Ex 1:10
m my signs and my wonders in the.... Ex 7:3
beast of the field m against thee........ Ex 23:29
I will m your seed as the stars.......... Ex 32:13
m you, and establish my covenant..... Lev 26:9
thee, and bless thee, and m thee....... Deut 7:13
to do, that ye may live, and m........... Deut 8:1
thy herds and thy flocks m................ Deut 8:13
m thee, as he hath sworn unto thy.... Deut 13:17
But he shall not m horses to............. Deut 17:16
the end that he should m horses........ Deut 17:16
shall he m wives to himself.............. Deut 17:17
he greatly m to himself silver........... Deut 17:17
you to do you good, and to m you..... Deut 28:63
good, and m thee above thy fathers... Deut 30:5
that thou mayest live and m.............. Deut 30:16
neither did all their family m............. 1Chr 4:27
I shall m my days as the sand........... Job 29:18
and I will m them, and they shall...... Jer 30:19
so will I m the seed of David my....... Jer 33:22
I have caused thee to m as the......... Eze 16:7
I will m men upon you, all the.......... Eze 36:10
I will m upon you man and beast...... Eze 36:11
I will m the fruit of the tree,............. Eze 36:30
m them, and will set my sanctuary.... Eze 37:26
at Gilgal m transgression.................. Amos 4:4
m your seed sown, and increase the.. 2Cor 9:10
and multiplying I will m thee............ Heb 6:14

MULTIPLYING
in m I will multiply my seed............ Gen 22:17
thee, and m I will multiply thee........ Heb 6:14

MULTITUDE
it shall not be numbered for m.......... Gen 16:10
that thou mayest be a m of people.... Gen 28:3
and it is now increased unto a m....... Gen 30:30
which cannot be numbered for m....... Gen 32:12
I will make of thee a m of people...... Gen 48:4
let them grow into a m in the........... Gen 48:16
seed shall become a m of nations..... Gen 48:19
a mixed m went up also with them... Ex 12:38
shalt not follow a m to do evil......... Ex 23:2
According to the m of years thou....... Lev 25:16
the mixt m that was among them...... Num 11:4
Gad had a very great m of cattle....... Num 32:1
day as the stars of heaven for m....... Deut 1:10
thee as the stars of heaven for m...... Deut 10:22
were as the stars of heaven for m..... Deut 28:62
that is upon the sea shore in m......... Josh 11:4
army, with his chariots and his m..... Judg 4:7
they came as grasshoppers for m....... Judg 6:5
valley like grasshoppers for m.......... Judg 7:12
as the sand by the sea side for m....... Judg 7:12
which is on the sea shore in m.......... 1Sa 13:5
the melted away, and they went....... 1Sa 14:16
even among the whole m of Israel..... 2Sa 6:19
the sand that is by the sea for m....... 2Sa 17:11
he numbered nor counted for m........ 1Kin 3:8
the sand which is by the sea in m..... 1Kin 4:20
not be told nor numbered for m........ 1Kin 8:5
Hast thou seen all this great m.......... 1Kin 20:13
all this great m into thine hand........ 1Kin 20:28
they are as all the m of Israel........... 2Kin 7:13
they are even as all the m of the....... 2Kin 7:13
With the m of my chariots I am......... 2Kin 19:23
with the remnant of the m................ 2Kin 25:11
like the dust of the earth in m........... 2Chr 1:9
not be told nor numbered for m........ 2Chr 5:6
and ye be a great m, and there are.... 2Chr 13:8
in thy name we go against this m...... 2Chr 14:11
There cometh a great m against........ 2Chr 20:2
by reason of this great m.................. 2Chr 20:15
they looked unto the m, and,............ 2Chr 20:24
away a great m of them captives....... 2Chr 28:5
For a m of the people, even many..... 2Chr 30:18
nor for all the m that is with............ 2Chr 32:7
from Israel all the mixed m.............. Neh 13:3
the m of his children, and all the...... Est 5:11
accepted of the m of his brethren..... Est 10:3
Should not the m of words be.......... Job 11:2
Did I fear a great m, or did the......... Job 31:34
m of years should teach wisdom....... Job 32:7
the m of his bones with strong......... Job 33:19
By reason of the m of oppressions... Job 35:9
He corneth the m of the city............. Job 39:7
thy house in the m of thy mercy....... Ps 5:7
cast them out in the m of their......... Ps 5:10
no king saved by the m of an host.... Ps 33:16
for I had gone with the m................. Ps 42:4
with a m that kept holyday.............. Ps 42:4
in the m of their riches.................... Ps 49:6
according unto the m of thy............. Ps 51:1
the m of the bulls, with the.............. Ps 68:30
in the m of thy mercy hear me, in.... Ps 69:13
to the m of thy tender mercies......... Ps 69:16
unto the m of the wicked................ Ps 74:19
In the m of my thoughts within me.. Ps 94:19
let the m of isles be glad................. Ps 97:1
not the m of thy mercies................. Ps 106:7
according to the m of his mercies.... Ps 106:45

I will praise him among the m........... Ps 109:30
In the m of words there wanteth....... Prov 10:19
but in the m of counsellors there...... Prov 11:14
In the m of people is the king's........ Prov 14:28
but in the m of counsellors they....... Prov 15:22
There is gold, and a m of rubies....... Prov 20:15
in m of counsellors there is.............. Prov 24:6
cometh through the m of business.... Eccl 5:3
voice is known by m of words.......... Eccl 5:3
For in the m of dreams and many..... Eccl 5:7
To what purpose is the m of your..... Is 1:11
their m dried up with thirst.............. Is 5:13
and their glory, and their m.............. Is 5:14
The noise of a m in the mountains... Is 13:4
contemned, with all that great m...... Is 16:14
Woe to the m of many people,......... Is 17:12
Moreover the m of thy strangers...... Is 29:5
the m of the terrible ones shall........ Is 29:5
the m of all the nations shall............ Is 29:7
so shall the m of all the nations....... Is 29:8
when a m of shepherds is called....... Is 31:4
the m of the city shall be left........... Is 32:14
By the m of my chariots am I come.. Is 37:24
for the m of thy sorceries................ Is 47:9
with the m of thy sorceries,............. Is 47:12
wearied in the m of thy counsels..... Is 47:13
The m of camels shall cover thee,... Is 60:6
according to the m of his................. Is 63:7
hills, and from the m of mountains.. Jer 3:23
there is a m of waters in the............ Jer 10:13
they have called a m after thee........ Jer 12:6
for the m of thine iniquity............... Jer 30:14
for the m of thine iniquity............... Jer 30:15
women that stoop by, a great m....... Jer 44:15
Behold, I will punish the m of No.... Jer 46:25
the m of their cattle a spoil............. Jer 49:32
there is a m of waters in the........... Jer 51:16
with the m of thy waves thereof...... Jer 51:42
of Babylon, and the rest of the m.... Jer 52:15
for the m of her transgressions........ Lam 1:5
according to the m of his mercies.... Lam 3:32
them shall remain, nor of their m..... Eze 7:11
wrath is upon all the m thereof........ Eze 7:12
it is touching the whole m thereof... Eze 7:13
wrath is upon all the m thereof........ Eze 7:14
according to the m of his idols........ Eze 14:4
height with the m of her branches... Eze 19:11
a voice of a m being at ease was..... Eze 23:42
of the m of all kind of riches........... Eze 27:12
the m of the wares of thy making.... Eze 27:16
was thy merchant in the m of the..... Eze 27:18
making, for the m of all riches......... Eze 27:18
earth with the m of thy riches......... Eze 27:33
By the m of thy merchandise they... Eze 28:16
by the m of thine iniquities............. Eze 28:18
and he shall take her m, and take.... Eze 29:19
and they shall take away her m........ Eze 30:4
I will also make the m of Egypt....... Eze 30:10
and I will cut off the m of No......... Eze 30:15
king of Egypt, and to his m............ Eze 31:2
long because of the m of waters...... Eze 31:5
him fair by the m of his branches.... Eze 31:9
This is Pharaoh and all his m.......... Eze 31:18
mighty will I cause thy m to fall..... Eze 32:12
all the m thereof shall be................ Eze 32:12
even for Egypt, and for all her m.... Eze 32:16
of man, wait for the m of Egypt...... Eze 32:18
all her m round about her grave,..... Eze 32:22
midst of the slain with all her m..... Eze 32:25
is Meshech, Tubal, and all her m.... Eze 32:26
shall be comforted over all his m.... Eze 32:31
sword, even Pharaoh and all his m... Eze 32:32
shall they bury Gog and all his m.... Eze 39:11
shall be a very great m of fish........ Eze 47:9
his words like the voice of a m....... Dan 10:6
assemble a m of great forces.......... Dan 11:10
and he shall set forth a great m....... Dan 11:11
but the m shall be given into his..... Dan 11:11
And when he hath taken away the m. Dan 11:12
shall set forth a m greater than....... Dan 11:13
for the m of thine iniquity,.............. Hos 9:7
according to the m of his fruit......... Hos 10:1
in the m of thy mighty men............ Hos 10:13
noise by reason of the m of............ Mic 2:12
and there is a m of slain, and a....... Nah 3:3
Because of the m of the whoredoms. Nah 3:4
without walls for the m of men....... Zec 2:4
the whole m stood on the shore...... Mt 13:2
Jesus unto the m in parables.......... Mt 13:34
Then Jesus sent the m away........... Mt 13:36
put him to death, he feared the...... Mt 14:5
went forth, and saw a great m........ Mt 14:14
send the m away, that they may go. Mt 14:15
he commanded the m to sit down on. Mt 14:19
and the disciples to the m............. Mt 14:19
And he called the m, and said unto. Mt 15:10
Insomuch that the m wondered...... Mt 15:31
said, I have compassion on the m... Mt 15:32
as to fill so great a m.................... Mt 15:33
he commanded the m to sit down on. Mt 15:35
and the disciples to the m............. Mt 15:36
And he sent away the m, and took.. Mt 15:39
And when they were come to the m. Mt 17:14
Jericho, a great m followed him...... Mt 20:29
the m rebuked them, because they.. Mt 20:31
a very great m spread their........... Mt 21:8
the m said, This is Jesus the.......... Mt 21:11
hands on him, they feared the m.... Mt 21:46
when the m heard this, they were.. Mt 22:33
Then spake Jesus to the m............ Mt 23:1

and with him a great m with swords. Mt 26:47
elders persuaded the m that they..... Mt 27:20
and washed his hands before the m.. Mt 27:24
all the m resorted unto him, and..... Mk 2:13
a great m from Galilee followed..... Mk 3:7
about Tyre and Sidon, a great m..... Mk 3:8
wait on him because of the m.......... Mk 3:9
the m cometh together again, so..... Mk 3:20
the m sat about him, and they said.. Mk 3:32
was gathered unto him a great m..... Mk 4:1
the whole m was by the sea on the.. Mk 4:1
And when they had sent away the m. Mk 4:36
Thou seest the m thronging thee..... Mk 5:31
And he took him aside from the m... Mk 7:33
those days the m being very great... Mk 8:1
I have compassion on the m........... Mk 8:2
he saw a great m about them:........ Mk 9:14
And one of the m answered said..... Mk 9:17
and with him a great m with swords. Mk 14:43
the crying aloud began to.............. Mk 15:8
the whole m of the people were..... Lk 1:10
there was with the angel a m of..... Lk 2:13
Then said he to the m that came.... Lk 3:7
they inclosed a great m of fishes.... Lk 5:6
bring him in because of the m........ Lk 5:19
a great m of people out of all........ Lk 6:17
the whole m sought to touch him... Lk 6:19
Then the whole m of the country... Lk 8:37
the m throng thee and press thee,.. Lk 8:45
and said unto him, Send the m away. Lk 9:12
the disciples to set before the m.... Lk 9:16
an innumerable m of people.......... Lk 12:1
And hearing the m pass by, he...... Lk 18:36
the whole m of the disciples......... Lk 19:37
from among the m said unto him... Lk 19:39
unto them in the absence of the m. Lk 22:6
And while he yet spake, behold a m. Lk 22:47
the whole m of them arose, and led. Lk 23:1
lay a great m of impotent folk...... Jn 5:3
away, a m being in that place....... Jn 5:13
a great m followed him, because... Jn 6:2
to draw it for the m of fishes........ Jn 21:6
the m came together, and were.... Acts 2:6
the m of them that believed were.. Acts 4:32
There came also a m of the.......... Acts 5:16
the m of the disciples unto them... Acts 6:2
And the saying pleased the whole m. Acts 6:5
that a great m both of the Jews.... Acts 14:1
But the m of the city was divided.. Acts 14:4
Then all the m kept silence.......... Acts 15:12
they had gathered the m together... Acts 15:30
the m rose up together against..... Acts 16:22
because of the devout Greeks a great m. Acts 17:4
evil of that way before the m....... Acts 19:9
they drew Alexander out of the m.. Acts 19:33
the m must needs come together... Acts 21:22
thing, some another, among the m.. Acts 21:34
For the m of the people followed... Acts 21:36
and the m was divided................. Acts 23:7
in the temple, neither with m....... Acts 24:18
about whom all the m of the Jews.. Acts 25:24
many as the stars of the sky in m... Heb 11:12
death, and shall hide a m of sins... Jas 5:20
charity shall cover the m of sins... 1Pet 4:8
this I beheld, and, lo, a great m.... Rev 7:9
as it were the voice of a great m... Rev 19:6

MULTITUDES
draw her and all her m.................. Eze 32:20
M, m in the valley of.................... Joel 3:14
great m of people from Galilee...... Mt 4:25
And seeing the m, he went up into. Mt 5:1
mountain, great m followed him.... Mt 8:1
when Jesus saw great m about him. Mt 8:18
But when the m saw it, they......... Mt 9:8
I'm marvelled, saying, It was....... Mt 9:33
But when he saw the m, he was.... Mt 9:36
to say unto the m concerning John. Mt 11:7
great m followed him, and he....... Mt 12:15
great m were gathered together..... Mt 13:2
side, while he sent the m away...... Mt 14:22
And when he had sent the m away. Mt 14:23
great m came unto him, having..... Mt 15:30
And great m followed him........... Mt 19:2
the m that went before, and that... Mt 21:9
same hour said Jesus to the m...... Mt 26:55
great m came together to hear, and. Lk 5:15
And there went great m with him.. Lk 14:25
the Lord, m both of men and women. Acts 5:14
But when the Jews saw the m....... Acts 13:45
whore sitteth, are peoples, and m.. Rev 17:15

MUNITION
that fight against her and her m..... Is 29:7
keep the m, watch the way, make.. Nah 2:1

MUNITIONS
defence shall be the m of rocks..... Is 33:16

MUPPIM (mup'-pim) See **SHUPPIM**. A son of Benjamin.
Gera, and Naaman, Ehi, and Rosh, M. Gen 46:21

MURDER
places doth he m the innocent........ Ps 10:8
the stranger, and the fatherless...... Ps 94:6
Will ye steal, m, and commit......... Jer 7:9
priests m in the way by consent..... Hos 6:9
Jesus said, Thou shalt do no m...... Mt 19:18
who had committed m in the......... Mk 15:7
made in the city, and for m........... Lk 23:19
m was cast into prison, whom they. Lk 23:25
full of envy, m, debate, deceit,..... Rom 1:29

M

MURDERER

iron, so that he die, he is a m ...... Num 35:16
the m shall surely be put to ...... Num 35:16
he may die, and he is a m ...... Num 35:17
the m shall surely be put to ...... Num 35:17
he may die, and he is a m ...... Num 35:18
the m shall surely be put to ...... Num 35:18
of blood himself shall slay the m..... Num 35:19
for he is a m ...... Num 35:21
of blood shall slay the m ...... Num 35:21
the m shall be put to death by ...... Num 35:30
satisfaction for the life of a m..... Num 35:31
See ye how this son of a m hath 2Kin 6:32
The m rising with the light ...... Job 24:14
bring forth his children to the m ...... Hos 9:13
He was a m from the beginning, and ...... Jn 8:44
desired a m to be granted unto ...... Acts 3:14
No doubt this man is a m ...... Acts 28:4
But let none of you suffer as a m..... 1Pet 4:15
hateth his brother is a m 1Jn 3:15
ye know that no m hath eternal 1Jn 3:15

MURDERERS

the children of the m he slew not..... 2Kin 14:6
lodged in it; but now m ...... Is 1:21
my soul is wearied because of m..... Jer 4:31
his armies, and destroyed those m ...... Mt 22:7
have been now the betrayers and m..... Acts 7:52
four thousand men that were m ...... Acts 21:38
for m of fathers and m of 1Ti 1:9
m of mothers, for manslayers, ... 1Ti 1:9
and the abominable, and m, and ...... Rev 21:8
sorcerers, and whoremongers, and m.. Rev 22:15

MURDERS

heart proceed evil thoughts, m..... Mt 15:19
adulteries, fornications, m ...... Mk 7:21
Envyings, m, drunkenness, ... Gal 5:21
Neither repented they of their m ...... Rev 9:21

MURMUR

what are we, that ye m against us..... Ex 16:7
murmurings which ye m against him ...... Ex 16:8
congregation, which m against me..... Num 14:27
Israel, which they m against me ...... Num 14:27
the congregation to m against him ...... Num 14:36
is Aaron, that ye m against him ...... Num 16:11
whereby they m against you ...... Num 17:5
unto them, M not among yourselves ...... Jn 6:43
Neither m ye, as some of them 1Cor 10:10

MURMURED

the people m against Moses, ... Ex 15:24
of Israel m against Moses ...... Ex 16:2
the people m against Moses, and ...... Ex 17:3
of Israel m against Moses ...... Num 14:2
upward, which have m against me ...... Num 14:29
of Israel m against Moses ...... Num 16:41
ye m in your tents, and said, ... Deut 1:27
against the princes ...... Josh 9:18
But m in their tents, and, ... Ps 106:25
they that m shall learn doctrine ...... Is 29:24
they m against the goodman of the ...... Mt 20:11
And they m against her ...... Mk 14:5
Pharisees m against his disciples ...... Lk 5:30
And the Pharisees and scribes m ...... Lk 15:2
And when they saw it, they all m ...... Lk 19:7
The Jews then m at him, because ...... Jn 6:41
that his disciples m at it ...... Jn 6:61
m such things concerning him ...... Jn 7:32
murmur ye, as some of them also m 1Cor 10:10

MURMURERS

These are m, complainers, walking ...... Jude 16

MURMURING

there was much m among the people..... Jn 7:12
there arose a m of the Grecians ...... Acts 6:1

MURMURINGS

heareth your m against the LORD ...... Ex 16:7
m which ye murmur against him ...... Ex 16:8
your m are not against us, but ...... Ex 16:8
for he hath heard your m ...... Ex 16:9
I have heard the m of the ...... Ex 16:12
I have heard the m of the ...... Num 14:27
the m of the children of Israel ...... Num 17:5
quite take away their m from me..... Num 17:10
Do all things without m and ...... Phil 2:14

MURRAIN

there shall be a very grievous m ...... Ex 9:3

MUSE

I m on the work of thy hands...... Ps 143:5

MUSED

all men m in their hearts of John ...... Lk 3:15

MUSHI

(mu'-shi) See MUSHITES. A son of Merari.
of Merari; Mahali and M ...... Ex 6:19
families; Mahli, and M ...... Num 3:20
Merari; Mahli, and M 1Chr 6:19
The son of Mahli, the son of M 1Chr 6:47
Merari; Mahli, and M 1Chr 23:21
The sons of M; Mahli 1Chr 23:23
sons of Merari were Mahli and M 1Chr 24:26
The sons also of M 1Chr 24:30

MUSHITES

(mu'-shites) The family of Mushi.
Mahlites, and the family of the M..... Num 3:33
the Mahlites, the family of the M...... Num 26:58

MUSICAL

with m instruments of God 1Chr 16:42
with the m instruments of David ...... Neh 12:36
as m instruments, and that of all ...... Eccl 2:8

MUSICIAN

To the chief M on Neginoth ...... Ps 4:t
To the chief M upon Nehiloth, A ...... Ps 5:t
To the chief M upon Sheminith ...... Ps 6:t
To the chief M upon Gittith ...... Ps 8:t
To the chief M upon Muth-labben, ... Ps 9:t
To the chief M, A Psalm of David..... Ps 11:t
To the chief M, A Psalm of David..... Ps 12:t
To the chief M, A Psalm of David..... Ps 13:t
To the chief M, A Psalm of David..... Ps 14:t
To the chief M, A Psalm of David..... Ps 18:t
To the chief M, A Psalm of David..... Ps 19:t
To the chief M, A Psalm of David..... Ps 20:t
To the chief M, A Psalm of David..... Ps 21:t
To the chief M upon Aijeleth ...... Ps 22:t
To the chief M, A Psalm of David..... Ps 31:t
To the chief M, A Psalm of David..... Ps 36:t
To the chief M, even to Jeduthun, ... Ps 39:t
To the chief M, A Psalm of David..... Ps 40:t
To the chief M, A Psalm of David..... Ps 41:t
To the chief M, Maschil, for the ...... Ps 42:t
To the chief M for the sons of ...... Ps 44:t
To the chief M upon Shoshannim, ... Ps 45:t
To the chief M for the sons of ...... Ps 46:t
To the chief M for the sons of ...... Ps 47:t
To the chief M, A Psalm of David..... Ps 49:t
To the chief M, Maschil, A Psalm ...... Ps 51:t
To the chief M, Maschil, A Psalm ...... Ps 52:t
To the chief M upon Mahalath, ... Ps 53:t
To the chief M on Neginoth ...... Ps 54:t
To the chief M on Neginoth ...... Ps 55:t
To the chief M upon ...... Ps 56:t
To the chief M, Al-taschith, ... Ps 57:t
To the chief M, Al-taschith, ... Ps 58:t
To the chief M, Al-taschith, ... Ps 59:t
To the chief M upon Shushan-eduth..... Ps 60:t
To the chief M upon Neginah ...... Ps 61:t
To the chief M, to Jeduthun, A ...... Ps 62:t
To the chief M, A Psalm and Song ...... Ps 65:t
To the chief M, A Song or Psalm ...... Ps 66:t
To the chief M on Neginoth ...... Ps 67:t
To the chief M, A Psalm of David..... Ps 68:t
To the chief M upon Shoshannim, A..... Ps 69:t
To the chief M, A Psalm of David..... Ps 70:t
To the chief M, Al-taschith, A ...... Ps 75:t
To the chief M on Neginoth ...... Ps 76:t
To the chief M, to Jeduthun, A ...... Ps 77:t
To the chief M, A Psalm of David..... Ps 80:t
To the chief M upon Gittith ...... Ps 81:t
To the chief M, A Psalm for the ...... Ps 84:t
To the chief M, A Psalm for the ...... Ps 85:t
To the chief M upon Mahalath Leannoth..... Ps 88:t
To the chief M, A Psalm of David..... Ps 109:t
To the chief M, A Psalm of David..... Ps 139:t
To the chief M, A Psalm of David..... Ps 140:t

MUSICIANS

And the voice of harpers, and m..... Rev 18:22

MUSICK

joy, and with instruments of m 1Sa 18:6
the singers with instruments of m 1Chr 15:16
and cymbals and instruments of m..... 2Chr 5:13
with instruments of m of the LORD 2Chr 7:6
The singers with instruments of m..... 2Chr 23:13
could skill of instruments of m 2Chr 34:12
of m shall be brought low ...... Eccl 12:4
I am their m ...... Lam 3:63
gate, the young men from their m ...... Lam 5:14
dulcimer, and all kinds of m, ... Dan 3:5
psaltery, and all kinds of m, ... Dan 3:7
and dulcimer, and all kinds of m ...... Dan 3:10
and dulcimer, and all kinds of m ...... Dan 3:15
of m brought before him ...... Dan 6:18
to themselves instruments of m ...... Amos 6:5
nigh to the house, he heard m ...... Lk 15:25

MUSING

while I was m the fire burned ...... Ps 39:3

MUST

thy money, m needs be circumcised..... Gen 17:13
m I needs bring thy son again ...... Gen 24:5
It m not be so done in our ...... Gen 29:26
and said, Thou m come in unto me ...... Gen 30:16
If it m be so now, do this ...... Gen 43:11
time drew nigh that Israel m die..... Gen 47:29
for we m hold a feast unto the ...... Ex 10:9
Thou m give us also sacrifices and..... Ex 10:25
for thereof we take to serve ...... Ex 10:26
not with what we m serve the LORD ...... Ex 10:26
save that which every man m eat ...... Ex 12:16
them the way wherein they m walk..... Ex 18:20
walk, and the work that they m do ...... Ex 18:20
it m be put into water, and it ...... Lev 11:32
seven days ye m eat unleavened ...... Lev 23:6
so he m do after the law of his ...... Num 6:21
Neither m the children of Israel..... Num 18:22
m we fetch you water out of this ...... Num 20:10
M I not take heed to speak that ...... Num 23:12
the LORD speaketh, that I m do...... Num 23:26
word again by what way we m go up ...... Num 24:13
But I m die in this land, I m ...... Deut 4:22
But thou m eat them before the ...... Deut 12:18
for thou m go with this people ...... Deut 31:7
thy days approach that thou m die ...... Deut 31:14
may know the way by which ye m go ...... Josh 3:4

But that ye m turn away this day ...... Josh 22:18
thou m offer it unto the LORD ...... Judg 13:16
There m be an inheritance for ...... Judg 21:17
thou m buy it also of Ruth the ...... Ruth 4:5
was in mine hand, and, lo, I m die 1Sa 14:43
For we m needs die, and are 2Sa 14:14
He that ruleth over men m be just 2Sa 23:3
touch them m be fenced with iron 2Sa 23:7
he sleepeth, and m be awaked 1Kin 18:27
thou m go to be with thy fathers..... 1Chr 17:11
LORD m be exceeding magnifical 1Chr 22:5
As thou hast said, so m we do...... Ezr 10:12
whose mouth m be held in with bit ...... Ps 32:9
friends m shew himself friendly ...... Prov 18:24
him, yet thou m do it again ...... Prov 19:19
then m he put to more strength ...... Eccl 10:10
m have a thousand, and those that..... Song 8:12
For precept m be upon precept ...... Is 28:10
they m needs be borne, because ...... Jer 10:5
this is a grief, and I m bear it ...... Jer 10:19
but ye m tread down with your ...... Eze 34:18
but ye m foul the residue with..... Eze 34:18
how that he m go unto Jerusalem ...... Mt 16:21
scribes that Elias m first come ...... Mt 17:10
for it m needs be that offences..... Mt 18:7
all these things m come to pass ...... Mt 24:6
be fulfilled, that thus it m be ...... Mt 26:54
but new wine m be put into new ...... Mk 2:22
Son of man m suffer many things ...... Mk 8:31
scribes that Elias m first come ...... Mk 9:11
that he m suffer many things, and ...... Mk 9:12
for such things m needs be ...... Mk 13:7
the gospel m first be published ...... Mk 13:10
but the scriptures m be fulfilled ...... Mk 14:49
wist ye not that I m be about my..... Lk 2:49
I m preach the kingdom of God to..... Lk 4:43
But new wine m be put into new..... Lk 5:38
The Son of man m suffer many ...... Lk 9:22
Nevertheless I m walk to day ...... Lk 13:33
ground, and I m needs go and see it ...... Lk 14:18
But first m he suffer many things..... Lk 17:25
for to day I m abide at thy house ...... Lk 19:5
when the passover m be killed ...... Lk 22:7
m yet be accomplished in me..... Lk 22:37
(For of necessity he m release ...... Lk 23:17
The Son of man m be delivered ...... Lk 24:7
that all things m be fulfilled ...... Lk 24:44
unto thee, Ye m be born again ...... Jn 3:7
even so m the Son of man be ...... Jn 3:14
He m increase, but I ...... Jn 3:30
increase, but I m decrease ...... Jn 3:30
he m needs go through Samaria ...... Jn 4:4
him m worship him in spirit ...... Jn 4:24
I m work the works of him that ...... Jn 9:4
them also I m bring, and they ...... Jn 10:16
The Son of man m be lifted up ...... Jn 12:34
that he m rise again from the ...... Jn 20:9
this scripture m needs have been ...... Acts 1:16
m one be ordained to be a witness..... Acts 1:22
Whom the heaven m receive until..... Acts 3:21
among men, whereby we m be saved..... Acts 4:12
shalt be told thee what thou m do..... Acts 9:6
he m suffer for my name's sake ...... Acts 9:16
faith, and that we m through much..... Acts 14:22
Ye m be circumcised, and keep the ...... Acts 15:24
Sirs, what m I do to be saved...... Acts 16:30
that Christ m needs have suffered..... Acts 17:3
I m by all means keep this feast ...... Acts 18:21
been there, I m also see Rome ...... Acts 19:21
the multitude m needs come ...... Acts 21:22
so m thou bear witness also at..... Acts 23:11
thou m be brought before Caesar..... Acts 27:24
Howbeit we m be cast upon a ...... Acts 27:26
Wherefore ye m needs be subject, ... Rom 13:5
for then m ye needs go out of the 1Cor 5:10
For there m be also heresies...... 1Cor 11:19
For he m reign, till he hath put..... 1Cor 15:25
corruptible m put on incorruption..... 1Cor 15:53
this mortal m put on immortality..... 1Cor 15:53
For we m all appear before the 2Cor 5:10
If I m needs glory, I will glory..... 2Cor 11:30
A bishop then m be blameless...... 1Ti 3:2
Moreover he m have a good report 1Ti 3:7
Likewise m the deacons be grave, ... 1Ti 3:8
Even so m their wives be grave, ... 1Ti 3:11
The husbandman that laboureth m..... 2Ti 2:6
servant of the Lord m not strive..... 2Ti 2:24
For a bishop m be blameless ...... Titus 1:7
Whose mouths m be stopped...... Titus 1:11
that some m enter therein...... Heb 4:6
there m also of necessity be the ...... Heb 9:16
For then m he often have suffered..... Heb 9:26
to God m believe that he is...... Heb 11:6
as they that m give account ...... Heb 13:17
m begin at the house of God 1Pet 4:17
Knowing that shortly I m put off 2Pet 1:14
which m shortly come to pass...... Rev 1:1
thee things which m be hereafter..... Rev 4:1
Thou m prophesy again before many ...... Rev 10:11
he m in this manner be killed...... Rev 11:5
sword m be killed with the sword ...... Rev 13:10
he m continue a short space ...... Rev 17:10
after that he m be loosed a ...... Rev 20:3
things which m shortly be done ...... Rev 22:6

MUSTARD

is like to a grain of m seed...... Mt 13:31
have faith as a grain of m seed...... Mt 17:20
It is like a grain of m seed...... Mk 4:31
It is like a grain of m seed...... Lk 13:19

ye had faith as a grain of m seed .... Lk 17:6

MUSTERED
which m the people of the land, ... 2Kin 25:19
who m the people of the land. .... Jer 52:25

MUSTERETH
the LORD of hosts m the host of .... Is 13:4

MUTH-LABBEN (muth-lab´-ben) A musical
notation.
To the chief Musician upon M .... Ps 9:t

MUTTER
unto wizards that peep, and that m .... Is 8:19

MUTTERED
your tongue hath m perverseness .... Is 59:3

MUTUAL
you by the m faith both of you .... Rom 1:12

MUZZLE
Thou shalt not m the ox when he ...... Deut 25:4
Thou shalt not m the mouth of the 1Cor 9:9
Thou shalt not m the ox that. 1Ti 5:18

MY See PREFACE.

MYRA (mi´-rah) A city in Lycia.
and Pamphylia, we came to M .... Acts 27:5

MYRRH
bearing spicery and balm and m. .... Gen 37:25
and a little honey, spices, and m .... Gen 43:11
of pure m five hundred shekels .... Ex 30:23
to wit, six months with oil of m .... Est 2:12
All thy garments smell of m. .... Ps 45:8
I have perfumed my bed with m. .... Prov 7:17
A bundle of m is my wellbeloved. ...... Song 1:13
pillars of smoke, perfumed with m. ...... Song 3:6
will get me to the mountain of m. .... Song 4:6
m and aloes, with all the chief .... Song 4:14
have gathered my m with my spice ...... Song 5:1
and my hands dropped with m, ... Song 5:5
my fingers with sweet smelling m .... Song 5:5
lilies, dropping sweet smelling m .... Song 5:13
gold, and frankincense, and m. .... Mt 2:11
him to drink wine mingled with m: ...... Mk 15:23
night, and brought a mixture of m ...... Jn 19:39

MYRTLE
m branches, and palm branches, an .... Neh 8:15
cedar, the shittah tree, and the m .... Is 41:19
brier shall come up the m tree .... Is 55:13
he stood among the m trees that .... Zec 1:8
stood among the m trees answered ...... Zec 1:10
LORD that stood among the m trees ...... Zec 1:11

MYSELF
and I hid m .... Gen 3:10
By m have I sworn, saith the LORD ...... Gen 22:16
wings, and brought you unto m .... Ex 19:4
of Egypt I sanctified them for m. .... Num 8:17
I the LORD will make m known unto. ...... Num 12:6
I am not able to bear you m alone. ...... Deut 1:9
How can I m alone bear your. .... Deut 1:12
And I turned m and came down from .... Deut 10:5
at other times before, and shake m .... Judg 16:20
said, I cannot redeem it for m .... Ruth 4:6
I forced m therefore, and offered 1Sa 13:12
that I may hide m in the field. 1Sa 20:5
from avenging m with mine own 1Sa 25:33
surely go forth with you m also. 2Sa 18:2
have kept m from mine iniquity 2Sa 22:24
surely shew m unto him to day 1Kin 18:15
Jehoshaphat, I will disguise m 1Kin 22:30
I bow m in the house of Rimmon 2Kin 5:18
when I bow down m in the house of 2Kin 5:18
to m for an house of sacrifice 2Chr 7:12
Jehoshaphat, I will disguise m 2Chr 18:29
Then I consulted with me, and I .... Neh 5:7
that ate had prepared but m. .... Est 5:12
to do honour more than to m .... Est 6:6
yea, I would harden m in sorrow .... Job 6:10
then, so that I am a burden to m. .... Job 7:20
If I justify m, mine own mouth .... Job 9:20
off my heaviness, and comfort m .... Job 9:27
If I wash m with snow water, and .... Job 9:30
I will leave my complaint upon m. .... Job 10:1
then I will not hide m from thee .... Job 13:20
mine error remaineth with m .... Job 19:4
Whom I shall see for m, and mine ...... Job 19:27
Or have eaten my morsel m alone ...... Job 31:17
or lifted up m when evil I found. .... Job 31:29
Wherefore I abhor m, and repent in .... Job 42:6
I kept m from mine iniquity. .... Ps 18:23
I behaved m as though he had been .... Ps 35:14
then I would have hid m from him ...... Ps 55:12
I will awake early .... Ps 57:8
I will behave m wisely in a .... Ps 101:2
I m will awake early .... Ps 108:2
but I give m unto prayer .... Ps 109:4
I will delight in thy statutes. .... Ps 119:16
I will delight m in thy .... Ps 119:47
and have comforted m. .... Ps 119:52
I do exercise m in great matters. .... Ps 131:1
I have behaved and quieted m .... Ps 131:2
in mine heart to give m unto wine ...... Eccl 2:3
I turned m to behold wisdom, and ...... Eccl 2:12
I m perceived also that one event. ...... Eccl 2:14
have shewed m wise under the sun .... Eccl 2:20
now will I lift up m .... Is 33:10
I have been still, and refrained m. ...... Is 42:14
This people have I formed for m .... Is 43:21
spreadeth abroad the earth by m. .... Is 44:24

I have sworn by m, the word is .... Is 45:23
I would comfort m against sorrow. ...... Jer 8:18
I m will fight against you with .... Jer 21:5
hear these words, I swear by m. .... Jer 22:5
For I have sworn by m, saith the .... Jer 49:13
I the LORD will answer him by m. .... Eze 14:7
made m known unto them in the .... Eze 20:5
sight I made m known unto them .... Eze 20:9
mine own, and I have made it for m. .... Eze 29:3
I will make m known among them, ... Eze 35:11
I magnify m, and sanctify m. .... Eze 38:23
neither did I anoint m at all .... Dan 10:3
bow m before the high God. .... Mic 6:6
into my bones, and I trembled in m. .... Hab 3:16
in the fifth month, separating m .... Zec 7:3
I m worthy to come unto thee .... Lk 7:7
hands and my feet, that it is I m. .... Lk 24:39
If I bear witness of m, ... Jn 5:31
of God, or whether I speak of m .... Jn 7:17
and I am not come of m, but he. .... Jn 7:28
them, Though I bear record of m .... Jn 8:14
I am one that bear witness of m. .... Jn 8:18
am he, and that I do nothing of .... Jn 8:28
neither came I of m, but he sent .... Jn 8:42
Jesus answered, If I honour m .... Jn 8:54
from me, but I lay it down of m .... Jn 10:18
For I have not spoken of m .... Jn 12:49
come again, and receive you unto m .... Jn 14:3
I speak unto you I speak not of m ...... Jn 14:10
him, and will manifest m to him. .... Jn 14:21
And for their sakes I sanctify m .... Jn 17:19
I m also am a man .... Acts 10:26
count I my life dear unto m, ... Acts 20:24
the more cheerfully answer for m. ...... Acts 24:10
And herein do I exercise m. .... Acts 24:16
I would also hear the man m. .... Acts 25:22
I think m happy, king Agrippa, ... Acts 26:2
because I shall answer for this .... Acts 26:2
I verily thought with me, that I .... Acts 26:9
the mind I m serve the law of God. ...... Rom 7:25
For I could wish that m were. .... Rom 9:3
reserved to m seven thousand men .... Rom 11:4
I m also am persuaded of you, my ...... Rom 15:14
a succourer of many, and of m also .... Rom 16:2
For I know nothing by m. 1Cor 4:4
have in a figure transferred to m. 1Cor 4:6
that all men were even as I m. 1Cor 7:7
yet have I made m servant unto 1Cor 9:19
others, I m should be a castaway 1Cor 9:27
But I determined this with m 2Cor 2:1
Now I Paul m beseech you by the 2Cor 10:1
m that ye might be exalted 2Cor 11:7
in all things I have kept m from 2Cor 11:9
unto you, and so will I keep m. 2Cor 11:9
me, that I may boast me a little 2Cor 11:16
yet of m I will not glory, but in 2Cor 12:5
except it be that I m was not. 2Cor 12:13
I make m a transgressor. .... Gal 2:18
that I also m shall come shortly .... Phil 2:24
I count not m to have apprehended. .... Phil 3:13
a partner, receive him as m .... Philem 17

MYSIA (miz´-ye-ah) A Roman province in Asia
Minor.
After they were come to M .... Acts 16:7
they passing by M came down to .... Acts 16:8

MYSTERIES
the m of the kingdom of heaven .... Mt 13:11
know the m of the kingdom of God. .... Lk 8:10
and stewards of the m of God. 1Cor 4:1
of prophecy, and understand all m 1Cor 13:2
in the spirit he speaketh 1Cor 14:2

MYSTERY
know the m of the kingdom of God. .... Mk 4:11
ye should be ignorant of this m. .... Rom 11:25
to the revelation of the man m. .... Rom 16:25
we speak the wisdom of God in a m 1Cor 2:7
Behold, I shew you a m. 1Cor 15:51
known unto us the m of his will .... Eph 1:9
he made known unto me the m .... Eph 3:3
my knowledge in the m of Christ) .... Eph 3:4
what is the fellowship of the m. .... Eph 3:9
This is a great m. .... Eph 5:32
to make known the m of the gospel .... Eph 6:19
even the m which hath been hid .... Col 1:26
of this m among the Gentiles .... Col 1:27
acknowledgement of the m of God, ... Col 2:2
to speak the m of Christ .... Col 4:3
For the m of iniquity doth 2Th 2:7
Holding the m of the faith in a 1Ti 3:9
great is the m of godliness. 1Ti 3:16
The m of the seven stars which .... Rev 1:20
the m of God should be finished, ... Rev 10:7
forehead was a name written, M .... Rev 17:5
will tell thee the m of the woman .... Rev 17:7

N

NAAM (na´-am) A son of Caleb.
Iru, Elah, and N. 1Chr 4:15

NAAMAH (na´-a-mah) See NAAMATHITE.
1. Sister of Tubal-cain.
and the sister of Tubal-cain was N ...... Gen 4:22
2. Mother of King Rehoboam.

was N an Ammonitess 1Kin 14:21
was N an Ammonitess 1Kin 14:31
was N an Ammonitess 2Chr 12:13
3. A city in Judah.
And Gederoth, Beth-dagon, and N ...... Josh 15:41

NAAMAN (na´-a-man) See NAAMAN'S,
NAAMITES.
1. A son of Benjamin.
and Becher, and Ashbel, Gera, and N. Gen 46:21
2. A son of Bela.
of Bela were Ard and N. .... Num 26:40
and of N, the family of the .... Num 26:40
And Abishua, and N, and Ahoah, ... 1Chr 8:4
3. A son of Bela.
And N, and Ahiah, and Gera, he. 1Chr 8:7
4. A Syrian captain.
Now N, captain of the host of the 2Kin 5:1
sent N my servant to thee 2Kin 5:6
So N came with his horses and with 2Kin 5:9
N was wroth, and went away 2Kin 5:11
N said, Shall there not then, I............... 2Kin 5:17
master hath spared N this Syrian 2Kin 5:20
So Gehazi followed after N 2Kin 5:21
when N saw him running after him, ... 2Kin 5:21
N said, Be content, take two 2Kin 5:23
of N shall cleave unto thee 2Kin 5:27
was cleansed, saving N the Syrian....... Lk 4:27

NAAMAN'S (na´-a-mans) Refers to Naaman 4.
and she waited on N wife...................... 2Kin 5:2

NAAMATHITE (na´-a-math-ite) Family name
of Zophar.
the Shuhite, and Zophar the N .... Job 2:11
Then answered Zophar the N .... Job 11:1
Then answered Zophar the N .... Job 20:1
The Shuhite and Zophar the N went .... Job 42:9

NAAMITES (na´-a-mites) Descendants of
Naaman 3.
and of Naaman, the family of the N. .... Num 26:40

NAARAH (na´-a-rah) See NAARAN, NAARATH. A
wife of Ashur.
Tekoa had two wives, Helah and N...... 1Chr 4:5
N bare him Ahuzam, and Hepher, and . 1Chr 4:6
These were the sons of N...................... 1Chr 4:6

NAARAI (na´-a-rahee) See PAARAI. A 'mighty
man' of David.
Carmelite, N the son of Ezbai,............. 1Chr 11:37

NAARAN (na´-a-ran) A city in Ephraim.
the towns thereof, and eastward N...... 1Chr 7:28

NAARATH (na´-a-rath) See NAARAH, NAARAN.
Same as Naaran.
from Janohah to Ataroth, and to N. .... Josh 16:7

NAASHON (na´-a-shon) See NAHSHON. Brother
of Elisheba.
of Amminadab, sister of N..................... Ex 6:23

NAASSON (na´-as-son) See NAASHON. Father
of Salmon.
and Aminadab begat N......................... Mt 1:4
and N begat Salmon............................. Mt 1:4
of Salmon, which was the son of N...... Lk 3:32

NABAJOTH See NEBAIOTH.

NABAL (na´-bal) See NABAL'S. A wife of David.
Now the name of the man was N 1Sa 25:3
that N did shear his sheep.................... 1Sa 25:4
Get you up to Carmel, and go to N 1Sa 25:5
they spake to N according to all........... 1Sa 25:9
N answered David's servants, and....... 1Sa 25:10
But she told not her husband N........... 1Sa 25:19
regard this man of Belial, even N 1Sa 25:25
N is his name, and folly is with............. 1Sa 25:25
seek evil to my lord, be as N 1Sa 25:26
there had not been left unto N by......... 1Sa 25:34
And Abigail came to N........................... 1Sa 25:36
when the wine was gone out of N 1Sa 25:37
days after, that the LORD smote N....... 1Sa 25:38
when David heard that N was dead...... 1Sa 25:39
of my reproach from the hand of N...... 1Sa 25:39
wickedness of N upon his own head 1Sa 25:39
the wife of N the Carmelite 1Sa 30:5
the wife of N the Carmelite 2Sa 3:3

NABAL'S (na´-balz)
N wife, saying, Behold, David............... 1Sa 25:14
N heart was merry within him for 1Sa 25:36
Abigail the Carmelitess, N wife 1Sa 27:3
Abigail N wife the Carmelite 2Sa 2:2

NABOTH (na´-both) A Jezreelite of Issachar.
the N the Jezreelite had a 1Kin 21:1
And Ahab spake unto N, saying, ... 1Kin 21:2
N said to Ahab, The LORD forbid 1Kin 21:3
because of the word which N the 1Kin 21:4
I spake unto N the Jezreelite 1Kin 21:6
the vineyard of N the Jezreelite 1Kin 21:7
were in his city, dwelling with N, ... 1Kin 21:8
set N on high among the people 1Kin 21:9
set N on high among the people 1Kin 21:12
against him, even against N 1Kin 21:13
N did blaspheme God and the king...... 1Kin 21:13
saying, N is stoned, and is dead. 1Kin 21:14
Jezebel heard that N was stoned......... 1Kin 21:15
the vineyard of N the Jezreelite 1Kin 21:15
for N is not alive, but dead 1Kin 21:15
when Ahab heard that N was dead 1Kin 21:16
the vineyard of N the Jezreelite 1Kin 21:16
he is in the vineyard of N..................... 1Kin 21:18

of N shall dogs lick thy blood 1Kin 21:19
the portion of N the Jezreelite 2Kin 9:21
of the field of N the Jezreelite 2Kin 9:25
seen yesterday the blood of N 2Kin 9:26

NACHON See NACHON'S.

NACHON'S (na'-kons)
they came to N threshingfloor 2Sa 6:6

NACHOR (na'-kor) See NAHOR.
1. Brother of Abraham.
of Abraham, and the father of N .... Josh 24:2
2. Father of Thara; ancestor of Jesus.
of Thara, which was the son of N .... Lk 3:34

NACON See NACHON'S.

NADAB (na'-dab)
1. Son of Aaron.
and she bare him N, and Abihu, ... Ex 6:23
unto the LORD, thou, and Aaron, N, ... Ex 24:1
Then went up Moses, and Aaron, N, ... Ex 24:9
priest's office, even Aaron, N, ... Ex 28:1
And N and Abihu, the sons of Aaron, ... Lev 10:1
N the firstborn, and Abihu, ... Num 3:2
And N and Abihu died before the .... Num 3:4
And unto Aaron was born N, and .... Num 26:60
And N and Abihu died, when they .... Num 26:61
And Abihu, Eleazar, and Ithamar 1Chr 6:3
N, and Abihu, Eleazar, and Ithamar 1Chr 24:1
But N and Abihu died before their 1Chr 24:2
2. Son of King Jeroboam I.
N his son reigned in his stead 1Kin 14:20
N the son of Jeroboam began to 1Kin 15:25
for N and all Israel laid siege to 1Kin 15:27
Now the rest of the acts of N 1Kin 15:31
3. Great-grandson of Jerahmeel.
Shammai; N, and 1Chr 2:28
And the sons of N 1Chr 2:30
4. A descendant of King Saul.
and Zur, and Kish, and Baal, and N 1Chr 8:30
and Kish, and Baal, and Ner, and N 1Chr 9:36

NAGGAI See NAGGE.

NAGGE (nag'-e) See NEARIAH. *Father of Esli; ancestor of Jesus.*
of Esli, which was the son of N .... Lk 3:25

NAHALAL (na'-ha-lal) *A Levitical city in Zebulun.*
her suburbs, N with her suburbs .... Josh 21:35

NAHALIEL (na-ha'-le-el) *An Israelite encampment in the wilderness.*
And from Mattanah to N .... Num 21:19
and from N to Bamoth .... Num 21:19

NAHALLAL (na'-hal-el) See NAHALAL. *Same as Nahalal.*
and N, and Shimron .... Josh 19:15

NAHALOL (na-ha-lol) *Same as Nahalal.*
Kitron, nor the inhabitants of N .... Judg 1:30

NAHAM (na'-ham) See ISHBAH. *A descendant of Caleb.*
his wife Hodiah the sister of N 1Chr 4:19

NAHAMANI (na-ham'-a-ni) *A clan chief with Zerubbabel.*
Nehemiah, Azariah, Raamiah, N .... Neh 7:7

NAHARAI (na'-ha-rahee) See NAHARI. *A 'mighty man' of David.*
N the Berothite, the armourbearer 1Chr 11:39

NAHARI (na'-ha-ri) See NAHARAI. *Same as Naharai.*
N the Beerothite, armourbearer to 2Sa 23:37

NAHASH (na'-hash) See IR-NAHASH.
1. An Ammonite king.
Then N the Ammonite came up, and 1Sa 11:1
all the men of Jabesh said unto N 1Sa 11:1
N the Ammonite answered them, On 1Sa 11:2
when ye saw that N the king of 1Sa 12:12
2. Father of Shobi and Hanun.
kindness unto Hanun the son of N 2Sa 10:2
that Shobi the son of N of Rabbah 2Sa 17:27
that N the king of the children 1Chr 19:1
kindness unto Hanun the son of N 1Chr 19:2
3. Mother of Abigail.
in to Abigail the daughter of N 2Sa 17:25

NAHATH (na'-hath) See TOHU.
1. A son of Reuel.
N, and Zerah, Shammah, and Mizzah .... Gen 36:13
duke N, duke Zerah, duke Shammah, ... Gen 36:17
N, Zerah, Shammah, and Mizzah 1Chr 1:37
2. Son of Zophi.
Zophai his son, and N his son, ... 1Chr 6:26
3. A Temple servant.
And Jehiel, and Azaziah, and N 2Chr 31:13

NAHBI (nah'-bi) *A spy sent to the Promised Land.*
of Naphtali, N the son of Vophsi .... Num 13:14

NAHOR (na'-hor) See NACHOR, NAHOR'S.
1. Grandfather of Abraham.
lived thirty years, and begat N .... Gen 11:22
he begat N two hundred years .... Gen 11:23
N lived nine and twenty years, and .... Gen 11:24
N lived after he begat Terah an .... Gen 11:25
Serug, N, Terah, ... 1Chr 1:26
2. Son of Terah.
seventy years, and begat Abram, N .... Gen 11:26

Terah begat Abram, N, and Haran .... Gen 11:27
And Abram and N took them wives .... Gen 11:29
born children unto thy brother N .... Gen 22:20
these eight Milcah did bear to N .... Gen 22:23
Mesopotamia, unto the city of N .... Gen 24:10
son of Milcah, the wife of N .... Gen 24:15
of Milcah, which she bare unto N .... Gen 24:24
them, Know ye Laban the son of N .... Gen 29:5
God of Abraham, and the God of N .... Gen 31:53

NAHOR'S (na'-hors) *Refers to Nahor 2.*
and the name of N wife, Milcah, ... Gen 11:29
N son, whom Milcah bare unto him .... Gen 24:47

NAHSHON (nah'-shon) See NAASHON, NAASSON. *Son of Amminadab.*
N the son of Amminadab .... Num 1:7
N the son of Amminadab, he .... Num 2:3
day was N the son of Amminadab .... Num 7:12
of N the son of Amminadab .... Num 7:17
over his host was N the son of .... Num 10:14
And Amminadab begat N, and N .... Ruth 4:20
begat N, and N begat Salmon, ... Ruth 4:20
and Amminadab begat N, prince of 1Chr 2:10
N begat Salma, and Salma begat 1Chr 2:11

NAHUM (na'-hum) See NAUM. *A prophet who spoke against Nineveh.*
of the vision of N the Elkoshite .... Nah 1:1

NAIL
Heber's wife took a n of the tent .... Judg 4:21
smote the n into his temples, and .... Judg 4:21
dead, and the n was in his temples, ... Judg 4:22
She put her hand to the .... Judg 5:26
to give us a n in his holy place, ... Ezr 9:8
fasten him as a n in a sure place .... Is 22:23
shall the n that is fastened in .... Is 22:25
the corner, out of him the .... Zec 10:4

NAILING
out of the way, n it to his cross .... Col 2:14

NAILS
shave his head, and pare his n .... Deut 21:12
iron in abundance for the n for 1Chr 22:3
the weight of the n was fifty 2Chr 3:9
as fastened by the masters of .... Eccl 12:11
and be fastened it with n, that it .... Is 41:7
they fasten it with n and with .... Jer 10:4
and his n like birds' claws .... Dan 4:33
were of iron, and his n of brass .... Dan 7:19
in his hands the print of the n .... Jn 20:25
my finger into the print of the n .... Jn 20:25

NAIN (nane) *A city in Galilee.*
that he went into a city called N .... Lk 7:11

NAIOTH (nay'-yoth) *A place in Ramah.*
he and Samuel went and dwelt in N 1Sa 19:18
Behold, David is at N in Ramah 1Sa 19:19
Behold, they be at N in Ramah 1Sa 19:20
And he went thither to N in Ramah 1Sa 19:23
until he came to N in Ramah 1Sa 19:23
And David fled from N 1Sa 20:1

NAKED
And they were both n, the man and .... Gen 2:25
and they knew that they were n .... Gen 3:7
and I was afraid, because I was n .... Gen 3:10
Who told thee that thou wast n .... Gen 3:11
Moses saw that the people were n .... Ex 32:25
(for Aaron had made them n unto .... Ex 32:25
lay down n all that day and all 1Sa 19:24
all that were n among them 2Chr 28:15
for he made Judah n, and 2Chr 28:19
N came I out of my mother's womb, ... Job 1:21
and n shall I return thither .... Job 1:21
stripped the n of their clothing .... Job 22:6
They cause the n to lodge without .... Job 24:7
him to go n without clothing .... Job 24:10
Hell is n before him, and .... Job 26:6
n shall he return to go as he .... Eccl 5:15
And he did so, walking n and .... Is 20:2
my servant Isaiah hath walked n .... Is 20:3
captives, young and old, n .... Is 20:4
when thou seest the n, that thou .... Is 58:7
drunken, and shalt make thyself n .... Lam 4:21
is grown, whereas thou wast n .... Eze 16:7
of thy youth, when thou wast n .... Eze 16:22
thy fair jewels, and leave thee n .... Eze 16:39
hath covered the n with a garment .... Eze 18:7
hath covered the n with a garment .... Eze 18:16
thy labour, and shall leave thee n .... Eze 23:29
Lest I strip her n, and set her as .... Hos 2:3
shall flee away n in that day .... Amos 2:16
and howl, I will go stripped and n .... Mic 1:8
of Saphir, having thy shame n .... Mic 1:11
Thy bow was made quite n, ... Hab 3:9
N, and ye clothed me .... Mt 25:36
or n, and clothed thee not .... Mt 25:38
n, and ye clothed me not .... Mt 25:43
or athirst, or a stranger, or n .... Mt 25:44
linen cloth cast about his n body .... Mk 14:51
linen cloth, and fled from them .... Mk 14:52
coat unto him, (for he was n .... Jn 21:7
they fled out of that house n .... Acts 19:16
both hunger, and thirst, and are n 1Cor 4:11
clothed we shall not be found n 2Cor 5:3
but all things are n and opened .... Heb 4:13
If a brother or sister be .... Jas 2:15
and poor, and blind, and n .... Rev 3:17
his garments, lest he walk n .... Rev 16:15
and shall make her desolate and n .... Rev 17:16

NAKEDNESS
saw the n of his father, and told .... Gen 9:22
covered the n of their father .... Gen 9:23
and they saw not their father's n .... Gen 9:23
to see the n of the land ye are .... Gen 42:9
but to see the n of the land ye .... Gen 42:12
that thy n be not discovered .... Ex 20:26
linen breeches to cover their n .... Ex 28:42
of kin to him, to uncover their n .... Lev 18:6
The n of thy father .... Lev 18:7
or the n of thy mother, shalt .... Lev 18:7
thou shalt not uncover her n .... Lev 18:7
The n of thy father's wife shalt .... Lev 18:8
it is thy father's n .... Lev 18:8
The n of thy sister, the daughter .... Lev 18:9
even their n thou shalt not .... Lev 18:9
The n of thy son's daughter, or .... Lev 18:10
even their n thou shalt not .... Lev 18:10
for theirs is thine own n .... Lev 18:10
The n of thy father's wife's .... Lev 18:11
thou shalt not uncover her n .... Lev 18:11
the n of thy father's sister .... Lev 18:12
the n of thy mother's sister .... Lev 18:13
the n of thy father's brother .... Lev 18:14
the n of thy daughter in law .... Lev 18:15
thou shalt not uncover her n .... Lev 18:15
the n of thy brother's wife .... Lev 18:16
it is thy brother's n .... Lev 18:16
not uncover the n of a woman .... Lev 18:17
daughter, to uncover her n .... Lev 18:17
to vex her, to uncover her n .... Lev 18:19
unto a woman to uncover her n .... Lev 18:19
hath uncovered his father's n .... Lev 20:11
her n, and she see his n .... Lev 20:17
he hath uncovered his sister's n .... Lev 20:17
sickness, and shall uncover her n .... Lev 20:18
the n of thy mother's sister .... Lev 20:19
he hath uncovered his uncle's n .... Lev 20:20
he hath uncovered his brother's n .... Lev 20:21
in hunger, and in thirst, and in n .... Deut 28:48
the confusion of thy mother's n 1Sa 20:30
Thy n shall be uncovered, yea, ... Is 47:3
her, because they have seen her n .... Lam 1:8
skirt over thee, and covered thy n .... Eze 16:8
thy n discovered through thy .... Eze 16:36
and will discover thy n unto them .... Eze 16:37
that they may see all thy n .... Eze 16:37
they discovered their fathers' n .... Eze 22:10
These discovered her n .... Eze 23:10
whoredoms, and discovered her n .... Eze 23:18
the n of thy whoredoms shall be .... Eze 23:29
and may thus given to cover her n .... Hos 2:9
and I will shew the nations thy n .... Nah 3:5
that thou mayest look on their n .... Hab 2:15
or persecution, or famine, or n .... Rom 8:35
in fastings often, in cold and n 2Cor 11:27
the shame of thy n do not appear .... Rev 3:18

NAME See PREFACE.
bless thee, and make thy n great .... Gen 12:2
he said unto him, What is thy n .... Gen 32:27
God said unto him, Thy n is Jacob .... Gen 35:10
Jacob, but Israel shall be thy n .... Gen 35:10
and he called his n Israel .... Gen 35:10
shall say to me, What is his n .... Ex 3:13
this is my n for ever, and this is .... Ex 3:15
Thou shalt not take the n of the .... Ex 20:7
in my sight, and I know thee by n .... Ex 33:17
shall not swear by n falsely .... Lev 19:12
thou profane the n of thy God .... Lev 19:12
they shall put my n upon the .... Num 6:27
Thou shalt not take the n of the .... Deut 5:11
his n shall be called in Israel .... Deut 25:10
whose n is called the n of the n 2Sa 6:2
and have made thee a great n 2Sa 7:9
He shall build an house for my n 2Sa 7:13
called the pillar after his own n 2Sa 18:18
he shall build an house unto my n 1Kin 5:5
the n of the LORD God of Israel 1Kin 8:17
And call ye on the n of your gods 1Kin 18:24
I will call on the n of the LORD 1Kin 18:24
Glory ye in his holy n 1Chr 16:10
people, which are called by my n 2Chr 7:14
blessed be the n of the LORD .... Job 1:21
to the n of the LORD most high .... Ps 7:17
Save me, O God, by thy n, and .... Ps 54:1
I will praise the n of God with a .... Ps 69:30
His n shall endure for ever .... Ps 72:17
is within me, bless his holy n .... Ps 103:1
that cometh in the n of the LORD .... Ps 118:26
Our help is in the n of the LORD .... Ps 124:8
take the n of my God in vain .... Prov 30:9
A good n is better than precious .... Eccl 7:1
my people shall know my n .... Is 52:6
thou shalt be called by a new n .... Is 62:2
they were not called by thy n .... Is 63:19
and thy people are called by thy n .... Dan 9:19
and thou shalt call his n JESUS .... Mt 1:21
and they shall call his n Emmanuel .... Mt 1:23
art in heaven, Hallowed be thy n .... Mt 6:9
are gathered together in my n .... Mt 18:20
For many shall come in my n .... Mt 24:5
that cometh in the n of the Lord .... Mk 11:9
For many shall come in my n .... Mk 13:6
and holy is his n .... Lk 1:49
whatsoever ye shall ask in my n .... Jn 14:13
If ye shall ask any thing in my n .... Jn 14:14
have ye asked nothing in my n .... Jn 16:24
that ye shall ask in my n .... Jn 16:26
keep through thine own n those .... Jn 17:11
in the n of Jesus Christ for the .... Acts 2:38

his *n* through faith in his *n* .... Acts 3:16
for there is none other *n* under .... Acts 4:12
calling on the *n* of the Lord .... Acts 22:16
him a *n* which is above every *n* .... Phil 2:9
That at the *n* of Jesus every knee ...... Phil 2:10
do all in the *n* of the Lord Jesus........ Col 3:17
Let every one that nameth the *n* 2Ti 2:19
on the *n* of his Son Jesus Christ........ 1Jn 3:23
on the *n* of the Son of God 1Jn 5:13
and in the stone a new *n* written........ Rev 2:17
his *n* is called The Word of God........ Rev 19:13

NAMED

which he had in the audience of .... Gen 23:16
said, Is not he rightly *n* Jacob.............. Gen 27:36
and let my name be *n* on them.......... Gen 48:16
house, *n* Rahab, and lodged there ...... Josh 2:1
she *n* the child I-chabod, saying,...... 1Sa 4:21
n Goliath, of Gath, whose height 1Sa 17:4
n Abiathar, escaped, and fled 1Sa 22:20
of Jacob, whom he *n* Israel.............. 2Kin 17:34
his sons were *n* of the tribe of 1Chr 23:14
That which hath been is already .... Eccl 6:10
But ye shall be *n* the Priests of .... Is 61:6
be *n* in the mouth of any man of ...... Jer 44:26
whom the king *n* Belteshazzar........ Dan 5:12
which are *n* chief of the nations,........ Amos 6:1
O thou that art *n* the house of .... Mic 2:7
n Matthew, sitting at the receipt .... Mt 9:9
n Joseph, who also himself was........ Mt 27:57
to a place which was *n* Gethsemane.. Mk 14:32
And there was one *n* Barabbas.......... Mk 15:7
a certain priest *n* Zacharias.............. Lk 1:5
a city of Galilee, *n* Nazareth,............ Lk 1:26
which was so *n* of the angel .... Lk 2:21
n Levi, sitting at the receipt of .... Lk 5:27
twelve, whom also he *n* apostles........ Lk 6:13
Simon, (whom he also *n* Peter............ Lk 6:14
behold, there came a man *n* Jairus,.. Lk 8:41
a certain woman *n* Martha received.... Lk 10:38
was a certain beggar *n* Lazarus........ Lk 16:20
there was a man *n* Zacchaeus .... Lk 19:2
behold, there was a man *n* Joseph.... Lk 23:50
n Nicodemus, a ruler of the Jews ...... Jn 3:1
n Lazarus, of Bethany, the town........ Jn 11:1
n Caiaphas, being the high priest ...... Jn 11:49
But a certain man *n* Ananias.............. Acts 5:1
n Gamaliel, a doctor of the law,........ Acts 5:34
disciple at Damascus, *n* Ananias ...... Acts 9:10
vision a man *n* Ananias coming in .... Acts 9:12
he found a certain man *n* Aeneas ...... Acts 9:33
a certain disciple *n* Tabitha.............. Acts 9:36
stood up one of them *n* Agabus .... Acts 11:28
a damsel came to hearken, *n* Rhoda.. Acts 12:13
a Timotheus, the son of a certain........ Acts 16:1
And a certain woman *n* Lydia............ Acts 16:14
other prisoners unto one *n* Julius ...... Acts 27:1
Areopagite, and a woman *n* Damaris.. Acts 17:34
And found a certain Jew *n* Aquila...... Acts 18:2
a Justus, one that worshipped God.... Acts 18:7
And a certain Jew *n* Apollos............ Acts 18:24
For a certain man *n* Demetrius.......... Acts 19:24
a certain young man *n* Eutychus........ Acts 20:9
a certain prophet, *n* Agabus .... Acts 21:10
with a certain orator *n* Tertullus........ Acts 24:1

NAMELY

his offering be of the flocks, *n* .... Lev 1:10
Of the children of Joseph, *n* .... Num 1:32
cloud covered the tabernacle, *n* .... Num 9:15
Of the tribe of Joseph, *n* .... Num 13:11
n, Evi, and Rekem, and Zur, and Hur, Num 31:8
N, Bezer in the wilderness, in .... Deut 4:43
N, of the gods of the people .... Deut 13:7
n, the Hittites, and the Amorites,...... Deut 20:17
N, five lords of the Philistines,.......... Judg 3:3
to the house of Jerubbaal, *n* .... Judg 8:35
they gave the cities of Judah, *n* 1Chr 6:57
given out of the half tribe, *n* 1Chr 6:61
gates of the house of the LORD, *n* .. 1Chr 9:23
courses among the sons of Levi, *n*.... 1Chr 23:6
n, of the sons of Jeshua the son........ Ezr 10:18
n, Zechariah the son of Jonathan,.... Neh 12:35
provinces of king Ahasuerus, *n* .... Est 8:12
I have seen under the sun, *n*............ Eccl 5:13
with a razor that is hired, *n*.............. Is 7:20
the king sent men into Egypt, *n* .... Jer 26:22
n this, Thou shalt love thy .... Mk 12:31
n, Judas surnamed Barsabas, and .. Acts 15:22
comprehended in this saying, *n* .... Rom 13:9

NAME'S

his people for his great *n* sake 1Sa 12:22
of a far country for thy *n* sake 1Kin 8:41
far country for thy great *n* sake........ 2Chr 6:32
of righteousness for his *n* sake........ Ps 23:3
For thy *n* sake, O LORD, pardon........ Ps 25:11
therefore for thy *n* sake lead me........ Ps 31:3
away our sins, for thy *n* sake............ Ps 79:9
he saved them for his *n* sake............ Ps 106:8
O God the Lord, for thy *n* sake........ Ps 109:21
me, O Lord, for thy *n* sake.............. Ps 143:11
For my *n* sake will I defer mine........ Is 48:9
that cast you out for my *n* sake........ Is 66:5
us, do thou it for my *n* sake............ Jer 14:7
Do not abhor us, for thy *n* sake........ Jer 14:21
But I wrought for my *n* sake.............. Eze 20:9

But I wrought for my *n* sake.............. Eze 20:14
hand, and wrought for my *n* sake...... Eze 20:22
wrought with you for my *n* sake........ Eze 20:44
Israel, but for mine holy *n* sake........ Eze 36:22
be hated of all men for my *n* sake .... Mt 10:22
children, or lands, for my *n* sake...... Mt 19:29
of all nations for my *n* sake .... Mt 24:9
be hated of all men for my *n* sake .... Mk 13:13
kings and rulers for my *n* sake.......... Lk 21:12
be hated of all men for my *n* sake .... Lk 21:17
they do unto you for my *n* sake........ Jn 15:21
he must suffer for my *n* sake............ Acts 9:16
are forgiven you for his *n* sake........ 1Jn 2:12
for his *n* sake they went forth 3Jn 7
for my *n* sake hath laboured, and .... Rev 2:3

NAMES

Adam gave *n* to all cattle, and to ...... Gen 2:20
these are the *n* of the sons of .... Gen 25:13
the sons of Ishmael, by their *n* .... Gen 25:16
of Ishmael, and these are their *n* ...... Gen 25:16
he called their *n* after the *n* .... Gen 26:18
These are the *n* of Esau's sons .... Gen 36:10
these are the *n* of the dukes that...... Gen 36:40
after their places, by their *n* .... Gen 36:40
these are the *n* of the children.......... Gen 46:8
Now these are the *n* of the .... Ex 1:1
these are the *n* of the sons of .... Ex 6:16
grave on them the *n* of the................ Ex 28:9
Six of their *n* on one stone .... Ex 28:10
the other six *n* of the rest on .... Ex 28:10
the *n* of the children of Israel .... Ex 28:11
Aaron shall bear their *n* before........ Ex 28:12
the *n* of the children of Israel .... Ex 28:21
twelve, according to their *n* .... Ex 28:21
Aaron shall bear the *n* of the .... Ex 28:29
with the *n* of the children of .... Ex 39:6
these are the *n* of the children of .... Ex 39:14
twelve, according to their *n* .... Ex 39:14
with the number of their *n* .... Num 1:2
these are the *n* of the men that........ Num 1:5
which are expressed by their *n* .... Num 1:17
according to the number of the .... Num 1:18
according to the number of the .... Num 1:20
according to the number of the .... Num 1:22
according to the number of the .... Num 1:24
according to the number of the .... Num 1:26
according to the number of the .... Num 1:28
according to the number of the .... Num 1:30
according to the number of the .... Num 1:32
according to the number of the .... Num 1:34
according to the number of the .... Num 1:36
according to the number of the .... Num 1:38
according to the number of the .... Num 1:40
these are the *n* of the sons of .... Num 3:2
These are the *n* of the sons of .... Num 3:3
were the sons of Levi by their *n* ...... Num 3:17
these are the *n* of the sons of .... Num 3:18
and take the number of their *n* .... Num 3:40
males by the number of, from a .... Num 3:43
And these were their *n* .... Num 13:4
These are the *n* of the men which .... Num 13:16
the *n* of the daughters of .... Num 26:33
according to the number of *n*,.......... Num 26:53
according to the *n* of the tribes .... Num 26:55
these are the *n* of his daughters........ Num 27:1
(their *n* being changed), and .... Num 32:38
gave other *n* unto the cities .... Num 32:38
These are the *n* of the men which .... Num 34:17
the *n* of the men are these .... Num 34:19
destroy the *n* of them out of that...... Deut 12:3
these are the *n* of his daughters,...... Deut 16:33
mention of the *n* of their gods.......... Josh 23:7
the *n* of his two daughters were........ 1Sa 14:49
the *n* of his three sons that went...... 1Sa 17:13
these be the *n* of those that were...... 2Sa 5:14
These be the *n* of the mighty men 2Sa 23:8
And these are their *n* 1Kin 4:8
These mentioned by their *n* were...... 1Chr 4:38
the *n* of the sons of 1Chr 6:17
which are called by their *n* 1Chr 6:65
whose *n* are these, Azrikam,............ 1Chr 8:38
whose *n* are these, Azrikam,............ 1Chr 9:44
Now these are the *n* of his 1Chr 14:4
by number of *n* by their polls 1Chr 23:24
What are the *n* of the men that........ Ezr 5:4
We asked their *n* also, to certify........ Ezr 5:10
that we might write the *n* of the ...... Ezr 5:10
whose *n* are these, Eliphelet,............ Ezr 8:13
and all of them by their *n*.................. Ezr 10:16
nor take up their *n* into my lips .... Ps 16:4
their lands after their own *n* .... Ps 49:11
he calleth them all by *n* .... Ps 147:4
he calleth them all by *n* by the .... Is 40:26
the *n* of them were Aholah,.............. Eze 23:4
Thus were their *n* .... Eze 23:4
Now these are the *n* of the tribes .... Eze 48:1
the *n* of the tribes of Israel .... Eze 48:31
the prince of the eunuchs gave .... Dan 1:7
For I will take away the *n* of .... Hos 2:17
that I will cut off the *n* of the .... Zec 13:2
These are the *n* of the twelve apostles Mt 10:2
because your *n* are written in .... Lk 10:20
(the number of *n* together were........ Acts 1:15
If it be a question of words and *n*...... Acts 18:15
whose *n* are in the book of life.......... Phil 4:3
Thou hast a few *n* even in Sardis ...... Rev 3:4
have not *n* written in the .... Rev 13:8
full of *n* of blasphemy, having .... Rev 17:3
whose *n* were not written in the........ Rev 17:8

n written thereon, which are the........ Rev 21:12
which are the *n* of the twelve............ Rev 21:12
in them the *n* of the twelve.............. Rev 21:14

NAMETH

Let every one that *n* the name of 2Ti 2:19

NAOMI (na´-o-mee) See NAOMI's. Mother-in-law
of Ruth.
and the name of his wife N .... Ruth 1:2
N said unto her two daughters in........ Ruth 1:8
N said, Turn again, my daughters........ Ruth 1:11
them, and they said, Is this N.............. Ruth 1:19
she said unto them, Call me not N...... Ruth 1:20
why then call ye me N, seeing the...... Ruth 1:21
So N returned, and Ruth the .... Ruth 1:22
N had a kinsman of her husband's,...... Ruth 2:1
And Ruth the Moabitess said unto N.. Ruth 2:2
with N out of the country of Moab...... Ruth 2:6
N said unto her daughter in law,.......... Ruth 2:20
N said unto her, The man is near .... Ruth 2:20
N said unto Ruth her daughter in........ Ruth 2:22
Then N her mother in law said .... Ruth 3:1
And he said unto the kinsman, N........ Ruth 4:3
buyest the field of the hand of N........ Ruth 4:5
and Mahlon's, of the hand of N .... Ruth 4:9
And the women said unto N, Blessed.. Ruth 4:14
N took the child, and laid it in.............. Ruth 4:16
saying, There is a son born to N.......... Ruth 4:17

NAOMI'S (na´-o-meze)
And Elimelech N husband died .... Ruth 1:3

NAPHATH See DOR.

NAPHATH DOR See DOR.

NAPHETH See DOR.

NAPHISH (na´-fish) See NEPHISH. A son of
Ishmael.
Hadar, and Tema, Jetur, N, and.......... Gen 25:15
Jetur, N, and Kedemah...................... 1Chr 1:31

NAPHTALI (naf´-ta-li) See NEPHTHALIM.
1. A son of Jacob.
and she called his name N .... Gen 30:8
handmaid, Dan, and N...................... Gen 35:25
And the sons of N .... Gen 46:24
N is a hind; he loose .... Gen 49:21
Dan, and N, Gad, and Asher.............. Ex 1:4
Dan, Joseph, and Benjamin, N............ 1Chr 2:2
The sons of N 1Chr 7:13
one gate of Dan, one gate of N .... Eze 48:34
2. The tribe and land.
Of N; Ahira the son .... Num 1:15
Of the children of N, throughout .... Num 1:42
of them, even of the tribe of N............ Num 1:43
Then the tribe of N .... Num 2:29
N shall be Ahira the son of Enan........ Num 2:29
Enan, prince of the children of N .... Num 7:78
of N was Ahira the son of Enan.......... Num 10:27
Of the tribe of N, Nahbi the son........ Num 13:14
Of the sons of N after their .... Num 26:48
These are the families of N .... Num 26:50
of the tribe of the children of N .... Num 34:28
and Asher, and Zebulun, Dan, and N.. Deut 27:13
And of Naphtali he said, O N.............. Deut 33:23
And all N, and the land of Ephraim,.... Deut 34:2
lot came out to the children of N .... Josh 19:32
even for the children of N.................. Josh 19:39
of N according to their families .... Josh 19:39
Kedesh in Galilee in mount N .... Josh 20:7
Asher, and out of the tribe of N.......... Josh 21:6
And out of the tribe of N, Kedesh ...... Josh 21:32
Neither did N drive out the .... Judg 1:33
thousand men of the children of N...... Judg 4:6
called Zebulun and N to Kedesh .... Judg 4:10
N were a people that jeoparded.......... Judg 5:18
Asher, and unto Zebulun, and unto N.. Judg 6:35
themselves together out of N.............. Judg 7:23
Ahimaaz was in N 1Kin 4:15
a widow's son of the tribe of N............ 1Kin 7:14
Cinneroth, with all the land of N 1Kin 15:20
and Galilee, all the land of N.............. 2Kin 15:29
Asher, and out of the tribe of N.......... 1Chr 6:62
And out of the tribe of N.................... 1Chr 6:76
of N a thousand captains, and with...... 1Chr 12:34
unto Issachar and Zebulun and N 1Chr 12:40
of N, Jerimoth the son of Azriel.......... 1Chr 27:19
and all the store cities of N................ 2Chr 16:4
Ephraim, and Simeon, even unto N.... 2Chr 34:6
of Zebulun, and the princes of N........ Ps 68:27
land of Zebulun and the land of N...... Is 9:1
the west side, a portion for N.............. Eze 48:3
And by the border of N, from the .... Eze 48:4

NAPHTUHIM (naf´-too-him) Inhabitants of
central Egypt.
and Pathrusim, and Lehabim, and N .. Gen 10:13

NAPKIN
which I have kept laid up in a *n* .... Lk 19:20
his face was bound about with a *n* .... Jn 11:44
And the *n*, that was about his head .. Jn 20:7

NAPTHUHIM
and Anamim, and Lehabim, and N...... 1Chr 1:11

NARCISSUS (nar-sis´-sus) A Christian in
Rome.
that be of the household of N.............. Rom 16:11

NARROW
further, and stood in a *n* place .... Num 22:26
mount Ephraim be too *n* for thee ...... Josh 17:15

house he made windows of n lights...... 1Kin 6:4
and a strange woman is a n pit .... Prov 23:27
shall even now be too n by reason...... Is 49:19
there were n windows to the................ Eze 40:16
the n windows, and the galleries........ Eze 41:16
And there were n windows and palm.. Eze 41:26
n is the way, which leadeth unto........ Mt 7:14

NARROWED
house he made n rests round about...... 1Kin 6:6

NARROWER
the covering n than that he can .... Is 28:20

NARROWLY
lookest n unto all my paths .... Job 13:27
see thee shall n look upon thee .... Is 14:16

NATHAN (na′-than) See NATHAN-MELECH.
1. A son of David.
Shammuah, and Shobab, and N.......... 2Sa 5:14
Shimea, and Shobab, and N, and 1Chr 3:5
and Shobab, N, and Solomon 1Chr 14:4
Mattatha, which was the son of N ..... Lk 3:31
2. A prophet in David's court.
the king said unto N the prophet........ 2Sa 7:2
N said to the king, Go, do all 2Sa 7:3
the word of the Lord came unto N 2Sa 7:4
so did N speak unto David.................. 2Sa 7:17
And the Lord sent N unto David......... 2Sa 12:1
and he said to N, As the Lord 2Sa 12:5
N said to David, Thou art the man 2Sa 12:7
And David said unto N, I have 2Sa 12:13
N said unto David, The Lord also 2Sa 12:13
N departed unto his house................... 2Sa 12:15
sent by the hand of N the prophet....... 2Sa 12:25
N the prophet, and Shimei, and Rei,.... 1Kin 1:8
But N the prophet, and Benaiah, and.. 1Kin 1:10
Wherefore N spake unto Bath-sheba... 1Kin 1:11
N the prophet also came in.................. 1Kin 1:22
saying, Behold N the prophet 1Kin 1:23
N said, My lord, O king, hast.............. 1Kin 1:24
N the prophet, and Benaiah the son 1Kin 1:32
N the prophet anoint him there 1Kin 1:34
N the prophet, and Benaiah the son 1Kin 1:38
N the prophet, and Benaiah the son 1Kin 1:44
The prophet have anointed him 1Kin 1:45
that David said to N the prophet......... 1Chr 17:1
Then N said unto David, Do all.......... 1Chr 17:2
that the word of God came to N......... 1Chr 17:3
so did N speak unto David 1Chr 17:15
and in the book of N the prophet 1Chr 29:29
in the book of N the prophet.............. 2Chr 9:29
the king's seer, and N the prophet 2Chr 29:25
when N the prophet came unto him,.... Ps 51:t
3. Father of Igal.
Igal the son of N of Zobah.................. 2Sa 23:36
4. Father of Azariah.
Azariah the son of N was over the 1Kin 4:5
5. Father of Zabud.
Zabud the son of N was principal 1Kin 4:5
6. Son of Attai.
And Attai begat N 1Chr 2:36
and N begat Zabad 1Chr 2:36
7. Brother of Joel.
Joel-the brother of N, Mibhar the 1Chr 11:38
8. A clan leader with Ezra.
Jarib, and for Elnathan, and for N........ Ezr 8:16
9. Married a foreigner in exile.
And Shelemiah, and N, and Adaiah, ... Ezr 10:39
10. A family leader.
family of the house of N apart............ Zec 12:12

NATHANAEL (na′-than-a-el) See
BARTHOLOMEW. A disciple of Jesus.
Philip findeth N, and saith unto.......... Jn 1:45
N said unto him, Can there any .... Jn 1:46
Jesus saw N coming to him, and .... Jn 1:47
N saith unto him, Whence knowest .... Jn 1:48
N answered and saith unto him,......... Jn 1:49
of Cana in Galilee, and the sons........ Jn 21:2

NATHAN-MELECH (na′-than-me′-lek) A
servant of King Josiah.
the chamber of N the chamberlain 2Kin 23:11

NATION
And I will make of thee a great n ...... Gen 12:2
And also that n, whom they shall ...... Gen 15:14
and I will make him a great n............. Gen 17:20
surely become a great and mighty n ... Gen 18:18
wilt thou slay also a righteous n........ Gen 20:4
of the bondwoman will I make a ...... Gen 21:13
for I will make him a great n.............. Gen 21:18
a n and a company of nations shall.... Gen 35:11
will there make of thee a great n........ Gen 46:3
land of Egypt since it became a .... Ex 9:24
kingdom of priests, and an holy n...... Ex 19:6
strange n he shall have no power .... Ex 21:8
and I will make of thee a great n........ Ex 32:10
that this n is thy people..................... Ex 33:13
in all the earth, nor in any n .... Ex 34:10
neither any of your own n................. Lev 18:26
not walk in the manners of the n ...... Lev 20:23
and will make of thee a greater n...... Num 14:12
Surely this great n is a wise .... Deut 4:6
For what n is there so great, who...... Deut 4:7
what n is there so great, that............. Deut 4:8
take him a n from the midst of .... Deut 4:34
from the midst of another n............... Deut 4:34
I will make of thee a n a mightier ..... Deut 9:14
with a few, and became there a......... Deut 26:5
shall a n which thou knowest not ...... Deut 28:33

unto a n which neither thou nor........ Deut 28:36
bring a n against thee from far .... Deut 28:49
a n whose tongue thou shalt not .... Deut 28:49
A n of fierce countenance, which...... Deut 28:50
them to anger with a foolish n.......... Deut 32:21
For they are a n void of counsel,....... Deut 32:28
what one n in the earth is like 2Sa 7:23
liveth, there is no n or kingdom 1Kin 18:10
took an oath of the kingdom and n.... 1Kin 18:10
Howbeit every n made gods of 2Kin 17:29
every n in their cities wherein 2Kin 17:29
when they went from n to n 1Chr 16:20
what one n in the earth is like 1Chr 17:21
And n was destroyed of n.................. 2Chr 15:6
for no god of any n or kingdom 2Chr 32:15
whether it be done against a n .... Job 34:29
Blessed is the n whose God is the ...... Ps 33:12
my cause against an ungodly n........... Ps 43:1
us cut them off from being a n .... Ps 83:4
they went from one n to another .... Ps 105:13
rejoice in the gladness of thy n.......... Ps 106:5
He hath not dealt so with any n......... Ps 147:20
Righteousness exalteth a n .... Prov 14:34
Ah sinful n, a people laden with .... Is 1:4
n shall not lift up sword against .... Is 2:4
shall not lift up sword against n .... Is 2:4
Thou hast multiplied the n .... Is 9:3
him against an hypocritical n .... Is 10:6
answer the messengers of the n .... Is 14:32
to a n scattered and peeled, to a .... Is 18:2
a n meted out and trodden down,...... Is 18:2
a n meted out and trodden under ...... Is 18:7
that the righteous n may .... Is 26:2
Thou hast increased the n.................. Is 26:15
O Lord, thou hast increased the n ..... Is 26:15
to him whom the n abhorreth............ Is 49:7
and give ear unto me, O my n .... Is 51:4
thou shalt call a n that thou .... Is 55:5
as a n that did righteousness, and ..... Is 58:2
For the n and kingdom that will .... Is 60:12
and a small one a strong n................ Is 60:22
unto a n that was not called by .... Is 65:1
or shall a n be born at once.............. Is 66:8
Hath a n changed their gods.............. Jer 2:11
be avenged on such a n as this.......... Jer 5:9
I will bring a n upon you from.......... Jer 5:15
mighty n, it is an ancient n.............. Jer 5:15
a n whose language thou knowest ..... Jer 5:15
be avenged on such a n as this.......... Jer 5:29
a great n shall be raised from .... Jer 6:22
This is a n that obeyeth not the .... Jer 7:28
be avenged on such a n as this.......... Jer 9:9
pluck up and destroy that n .... Jer 12:17
I shall speak concerning a n .... Jer 18:7
If that n, against whom I have .... Jer 18:8
I shall speak concerning a n .... Jer 18:9
the king of Babylon, and that n......... Jer 25:12
shall go forth from n to n .... Jer 25:32
it shall come to pass, that the n .... Jer 27:8
that n will I punish, saith the .... Jer 27:8
Lord hath spoken against the n .... Jer 27:13
from being a n before me for ever ..... Jer 31:36
should be no more a n before them.... Jer 33:24
let us cut it off from being a n .... Jer 48:2
get you up unto the wealthy n........... Jer 49:31
there shall be no n whither the .... Jer 49:36
there cometh up a n against her......... Jer 50:3
come from the north, and a great ...... Jer 50:41
for a n that could not save us .... Lam 4:17
to a rebellious n that hath................. Eze 2:3
I will make them one n in the .... Eze 37:22
land. That every people, n .... Dan 3:29
shall stand up out of the n .... Dan 8:22
was a n even to that same time......... Dan 12:1
For a n is come up against my land,.. Joel 1:6
I will raise up against you a n.......... Amos 6:14
n shall not lift up a sword................ Mic 4:3
nor lift up a sword against n .... Mic 4:3
that was cast far off a strong n .... Mic 4:7
Chaldeans, that bitter and hasty n..... Hab 1:6
gather together, O n not desired .... Zeph 2:1
coast, the n of the Cherethites........... Zeph 2:5
people, and so is this n before me .... Hag 2:14
have robbed me, even this whole n.... Mal 3:9
given to a n bringing forth the .... Mt 21:43
For n shall rise against n,.................. Mt 24:7
was a Greek, a Syrophenician by n ... Mk 7:26
For n shall rise against n,.................. Mk 13:8
For he loveth our n, and he hath ...... Lk 7:5
N shall rise against n, and .... Lk 21:10
this fellow perverting the n .... Lk 23:2
and take away both our place and n ... Jn 11:48
and that the whole n perish not......... Jn 11:50
that Jesus should die for that n .... Jn 11:51
And not for that n only, but that....... Jn 11:52
Thine own n and the chief priests ..... Jn 18:35
men, out of every n under heaven ..... Acts 2:5
the n to whom they shall be .... Acts 7:7
among all the n of the earth, were ..... Acts 10:22
or come unto one of another n.......... Acts 10:28
But in every n that feareth .... Acts 10:35
unto this n by thy providence........... Acts 24:2
of many years a judge unto this n..... Acts 24:10
I came to bring alms to my n .... Acts 24:17
among mine own n at Jerusalem .... Acts 26:4
I had ought to accuse my n of .... Acts 28:19
by a foolish n I will anger you......... Rom 10:19
many my equals in mine own n........ Gal 1:14
midst of a crooked and perverse n..... Phil 2:15
a royal priesthood, an holy n 1Pet 2:9

and tongue, and people, and n............ Rev 5:9
dwell on the earth, and to every n ..... Rev 7:14

NATIONS
after their families, in their n .... Gen 10:5
in their countries, and in their n......... Gen 10:20
in their lands, after their n................. Gen 10:31
their generations, in their n .... Gen 10:32
by these were the n divided in........... Gen 10:32
king of Elam, and Tidal king of n ..... Gen 14:1
of Elam, and with Tidal king of n ..... Gen 14:5
thou shalt be a father of many n........ Gen 17:4
father of many n have I made thee .... Gen 17:5
and I will make n of thee.................. Gen 17:6
and she shall be a mother of n .... Gen 17:16
all the n of the earth shall be .... Gen 18:18
all the n of the earth be blessed......... Gen 22:18
princes according to their n .... Gen 25:16
Two n are in thy womb, and two...... Gen 25:23
all the n of the earth be blessed......... Gen 26:4
serve thee, and n bow down to thee... Gen 27:29
a company of n shall be of thee,........ Gen 35:11
shall become a multitude of n .... Gen 48:19
I will cast out the n before thee .... Ex 34:24
for in all these the n are .... Lev 18:24
as it spued out the n that were.......... Lev 18:28
then the n which have heard the........ Num 14:15
shall not be reckoned among the n .... Num 23:9
he shall eat up the n his enemies...... Num 24:8
Amalek was the first of the n............ Num 24:20
the fear of thee upon the n that .... Deut 2:25
in the sight of the n, which .... Deut 4:6
unto all n under the whole heaven,.... Deut 4:19
shalt scatter you among the n .... Deut 4:27
To drive out n from before thee .... Deut 4:38
hath cast out many n before thee....... Deut 7:1
seven n greater and mightier than ..... Deut 7:1
heart, These n are more than I........... Deut 7:17
out those n before thee by little........ Deut 7:22
As the n which the Lord.................... Deut 8:20
to go in to possess n greater .... Deut 9:1
n the Lord doth drive them out......... Deut 9:4
the Lord thy God doth drive .... Deut 9:5
out all these n from before you......... Deut 11:23
and ye shall possess greater n........... Deut 11:23
wherein the n which ye shall .... Deut 12:2
cut off the n from before thee .... Deut 12:29
How did these n serve their gods...... Deut 12:30
above all the n that are upon the ...... Deut 14:2
and thou shalt lend unto many n ...... Deut 15:6
and thou shalt reign over many n ..... Deut 15:6
like as all the n that are about.......... Deut 17:14
after the abominations of those n...... Deut 18:9
For these n, which thou shalt .... Deut 18:14
Lord thy God hath cut off the n .... Deut 19:1
are not of the cities of these n.......... Deut 20:15
above all n which he hath made .... Deut 26:19
on high above all n of the earth .... Deut 28:1
and thou shalt lend unto many n ...... Deut 28:12
among all n whither the Lord .... Deut 28:37
among these n shalt thou find no...... Deut 28:65
unto the n which ye passed by.......... Deut 29:16
go and serve the gods of these n ...... Deut 29:18
Even all n shall say, Wherefore .... Deut 29:24
call them to mind among all the n .... Deut 30:1
and gather thee from all the n .... Deut 30:3
destroy these n from before thee ...... Deut 31:3
to the n their inheritance.................. Deut 32:8
Rejoice, O ye n, with his people....... Deut 32:43
the king of the n of Gilgal .... Josh 12:23
unto all these n because of you......... Josh 23:3
you by lot these n that remain.......... Josh 23:4
with all the n that I have cut .... Josh 23:4
That ye come not among these n ...... Josh 23:7
out from before you great n.............. Josh 23:9
unto the remnant of these n .... Josh 23:12
any of these n from before you......... Josh 23:13
n which Joshua left when he died ..... Judg 2:21
Therefore the Lord left those n .... Judg 2:23
Now these are the n which the .... Judg 3:1
a king to judge us like all the n 1Sa 8:5
we also may be like all the n 1Sa 8:20
for those n were of old the 1Sa 8:20
to thee from Egypt, from the n 2Sa 7:23
of all n which he subdued 2Sa 8:11
his fame was in all n round about..... 1Kin 4:31
Of the n concerning which the 1Kin 11:2
in which the Lord cast out before 1Kin 14:24
The n which thus had removed, and.. 2Kin 17:26
after the manner of the n whom 2Kin 17:33
So these n feared the Lord, and........ 2Kin 17:41
Hath any of the gods of the n 2Kin 18:33
Have the gods of the n delivered,...... 2Kin 19:12
of Assyria have destroyed the n 2Kin 19:17
to do more evil than did the n 2Kin 21:9
the fear of him upon all n................ 1Chr 14:17
his marvellous works among all n 1Chr 16:24
and let men say among the n............ 1Chr 16:31
by driving out n from before thy 1Chr 17:21
that he brought from all these n 1Chr 18:11
a proverb and a byword among all n.. 2Chr 7:20
manner of the n of other lands......... 2Chr 13:9
were the gods of the n of those 2Chr 32:13
those n that my fathers utterly 2Chr 32:14
As the gods of the n of other 2Chr 32:17
sight of all n from thenceforth 2Chr 32:23
the rest of the n whom the great ...... Ezr 4:10
scatter you abroad among the n .... Neh 1:8
thou gavest them kingdoms and n..... Neh 9:22
yet among many n was there no .... Neh 13:26
He increaseth the n, and.................. Job 12:23

he enlargeth the *n*, and .... Job 12:23
all the *n* that forget God .... Ps 9:17
that the *n* may know themselves to ...... Ps 9:20
all the kindreds of the *n* shall .... Ps 22:27
and he is the governor among the *n* ..... Ps 22:28
under us, and the *n* under our feet .... Ps 47:3
I will sing unto thee among the *n* .... Ps 57:9
his eyes behold the *n* .... Ps 66:7
thy saving health among all *n* .... Ps 67:2
O let them be glad and sing for .... Ps 67:4
and govern the *n* upon earth .... Ps 67:4
all *n* shall serve him .... Ps 72:11
all *n* shall call him blessed .... Ps 72:17
for thou shalt inherit all *n* .... Ps 82:8
All *n* whom thou hast made shall .... Ps 86:9
all the gods of the *n* are idols .... Ps 96:5
their seed also among the *n* .... Ps 106:27
They did not destroy the *n* .... Ps 106:34
praises unto thee among the *n* .... Ps 108:3
The LORD is high above all *n* .... Ps 113:4
O praise the LORD, all ye *n* .... Ps 117:1
All *n* compassed me about .... Ps 118:10
Who smote great *n*, and slew mighty ..... Ps 135:10
people curse, *n* shall abhor him .... Prov 24:24
and all *n* shall flow unto it .... Is 2:2
And he shall judge among the *n* .... Is 2:4
up an ensign to the *n* from far .... Is 5:26
Jordan, in Galilee of the *n* .... Is 9:1
to destroy and cut off *n* not a few .... Is 10:7
shall set up an ensign for the *n* .... Is 11:12
kingdoms of *n* gathered together .... Is 13:4
he that ruled the *n* in anger .... Is 14:6
thrones all the kings of the *n* .... Is 14:9
ground, which didst weaken the *n* .... Is 14:12
All the kings of the *n*, even all .... Is 14:18
is stretched out upon all the *n* .... Is 14:26
and to the rushing of *n*, that make .... Is 17:12
The *n* shall rush like the rushing .... Is 17:13
and she is a mart of *n* .... Is 23:3
of the terrible *n* shall fear thee .... Is 25:3
vail that is spread over all *n* .... Is 25:7
the *n* that fight against Ariel .... Is 29:7
the multitude of all the *n* be .... Is 29:8
to sift the *n* with the sieve of .... Is 30:28
of thyself the *n* were scattered .... Is 33:3
Come near, ye *n*, to hear .... Is 34:1
of the LORD is upon all *n* .... Is 34:2
Hath any of the gods of the *n* .... Is 36:18
Have the gods of the *n* delivered .... Is 37:12
Assyria have laid waste all the *n* .... Is 37:18
the *n* are as a drop of a bucket .... Is 40:15
All *n* before him are as nothing .... Is 40:17
gave the *n* before him, and made .... Is 41:2
Let all the *n* be gathered .... Is 43:9
holden, to subdue *n* before him .... Is 45:1
ye that are escaped of the *n* .... Is 45:20
holy arm in the eyes of all the *n* .... Is 52:10
So shall he sprinkle many *n* .... Is 52:15
n that knew not thee shall run .... Is 55:5
those *n* shall be utterly wasted .... Is 60:12
to spring forth before all the *n* .... Is 61:11
that the *n* may tremble at thy .... Is 64:2
come, that I will gather all *n* .... Is 66:18
that escape of them unto the *n* .... Is 66:19
the LORD out of all *n* upon horses .... Is 66:20
thee a prophet unto the *n* .... Jer 1:5
have this day set thee over the *n* .... Jer 1:10
all the *n* shall be gathered unto .... Jer 3:17
goodly heritage of the hosts of *n* .... Jer 3:19
I will shake all *n* themselves in .... Jer 4:2
Make ye mention to the *n* .... Jer 4:16
Therefore hear, ye *n*, and know, O .... Jer 6:18
for all these *n* are uncircumcised .... Jer 9:26
would not fear thee, O King of *n* .... Jer 10:7
among all the wise men of the *n* .... Jer 10:7
the *n* shall not be able to abide .... Jer 10:10
many *n* shall pass by this city .... Jer 22:8
against all these *n* round about .... Jer 25:9
these *n* shall serve the king of .... Jer 25:11
hath prophesied against all the *n* .... Jer 25:13
For many *n* and great kings shall .... Jer 25:14
at my hand, and cause all the *n* .... Jer 25:15
hand, and made all the *n* to drink .... Jer 25:17
hath a controversy with the *n* .... Jer 25:31
a curse to all the *n* of the earth .... Jer 26:6
all *n* shall serve him, and his son .... Jer 27:7
and then many *n* and great kings .... Jer 27:7
But the *n* that bring their neck .... Jer 27:11
n within the space of two full .... Jer 28:11
iron upon the neck of all these *n* .... Jer 28:14
I will gather you from all the *n* .... Jer 29:14
among all the *n* whither I have .... Jer 29:18
n whither I have scattered thee .... Jer 30:11
and shout among the chief of the *n* .... Jer 31:7
Hear the word of the LORD, O ye *n* .... Jer 31:10
before all the *n* of the earth .... Jer 33:9
Judah, and against all the *n* .... Jer 36:2
that were returned from all *n* .... Jer 44:8
among all the *n* of the earth .... Jer 44:8
The *n* have heard of thy shame, and... .... Jer 46:12
the *n* whither I have driven them .... Jer 46:28
Declare ye among the *n* .... Jer 50:2
of great *n* from the north country .... Jer 50:9
of the *n* shall be a wilderness .... Jer 50:12
become a desolation among the *n* .... Jer 50:23
and the cry is heard among the *n* .... Jer 51:51
the *n* have drunken of her wine .... Jer 51:7
therefore the *n* are mad .... Jer 51:7
thee will I break in pieces the *n* .... Jer 51:20
blow the trumpet among the *n* .... Jer 51:27

prepare the *n* against her .... Jer 51:27
Prepare against her the *n* with .... Jer 51:28
an astonishment among the *n* .... Jer 51:41
the *n* shall not flow together any .... Jer 51:44
she that was great among the *n* .... Lam 1:1
have set it in the midst of the *n* .... Eze 5:5
into wickedness more than the *n* .... Eze 5:6
the *n* that are round about you .... Eze 5:7
to the judgments of the *n* that .... Eze 5:7
of thee in the sight of the *n* .... Eze 5:8
a reproach among the *n* that are .... Eze 5:14
an astonishment unto the *n* that .... Eze 5:15
escape the sword among the *n* .... Eze 6:8
a whither they shall be carried .... Eze 6:9
I shall scatter them among the *n* .... Eze 12:15
The *n* also heard of him .... Eze 19:4
Then the *n* set against him on .... Eze 19:8
may not be remembered among the *n* ..... Eze 25:10
will cause many *n* to come up .... Eze 26:3
it shall become a spoil to the *n* .... Eze 26:5
upon thee, the terrible of the *n* .... Eze 28:7
scatter the Egyptians among the *n* .... Eze 29:12
exalt itself any more above the *n* .... Eze 29:15
shall no more rule over the *n* .... Eze 29:15
with him, the terrible of the *n* .... Eze 30:11
scatter the Egyptians among the *n* .... Eze 30:23
scatter the Egyptians among the *n* .... Eze 30:26
his shadow dwelt all great *n* .... Eze 31:6
strangers, the terrible of the *n* .... Eze 31:12
I made the *n* to shake at the .... Eze 31:16
art like a young lion of the *n* .... Eze 32:2
bring thy destruction among the *n* .... Eze 32:9
to fall, the terrible of the *n* .... Eze 32:12
of the *n* shall lament her .... Eze 32:16
and the daughters of the famous *n* .... Eze 32:18
thou hast said, These two *n* .... Eze 35:10
up men, and hast bereaved thy *n* .... Eze 36:13
neither bereave thy *n* any more .... Eze 36:14
thou cause thy *n* to fall any more .... Eze 36:15
and they shall be no more two *n* .... Eze 37:22
it is brought forth out of the *n* .... Eze 38:8
that are gathered out of the *n* .... Eze 38:12
be known in the eyes of many *n* .... Eze 38:23
in them in the sight of many *n* .... Eze 39:27
you it is commanded, O people, *n* .... Dan 3:4
of musick, all the people, the *n* .... Dan 3:7
the king, unto all people, *n* .... Dan 4:1
that he gave him, all people, *n* .... Dan 5:19
Darius wrote unto all people, *n* .... Dan 6:25
and a kingdom, that all people, *n* .... Dan 7:14
they have hired among the *n* .... Hos 8:10
shall be wanderers among the *n* .... Hos 9:17
I will also gather all *n*, and will .... Joel 3:2
they have scattered among the *n* .... Joel 3:2
which are named chief of the *n* .... Amos 6:1
the house of Israel among all *n* .... Amos 9:9
many *n* shall come, and say, Come, ... Mic 4:2
and rebuke strong *n* afar off .... Mic 4:3
Now also many *n* are gathered .... Mic 4:11
The *n* shall see and be confounded .... Mic 7:16
that setleth *n* through her .... Nah 3:4
I will shew the *n* thy nakedness .... Nah 3:5
spare continually to slay the *n* .... Hab 1:17
but gathereth unto him all *n* .... Hab 2:5
Because thou hast spoiled many *n* .... Hab 2:8
he beheld, and drove asunder the *n* ...... Hab 3:6
of her, all the beasts of the *n* .... Zeph 2:14
I have cut off the *n* .... Zeph 3:6
determination is to gather the *n* .... Zeph 3:8
I will shake all *n* .... Hag 2:7
and the desire of all *n* shall come .... Hag 2:7
me unto the *n* which spoiled you .... Zec 2:8
many *n* shall be joined to the .... Zec 2:11
all the *n* whom they knew not .... Zec 7:14
strong *n* shall come to seek the .... Zec 8:22
out of all languages of the *n* .... Zec 8:23
the *n* that come against Jerusalem .... Zec 12:9
For I will gather all *n* against .... Zec 14:2
forth, and fight against those *n* .... Zec 14:3
one that is left of all the *n* .... Zec 14:16
the punishment of all *n* that come .... Zec 14:19
all *n* shall call you blessed .... Mal 3:12
hated of all *n* for my name's sake .... Mt 24:9
world for a witness unto all *n* .... Mt 24:14
him shall be gathered all *n* .... Mt 25:32
Go ye therefore, and teach all *n* .... Mt 28:19
of all *n* the house of prayer .... Mk 11:17
first be published among all *n* .... Mk 13:10
do the *n* of the world seek after .... Lk 12:30
be led away captive into all *n* .... Lk 21:24
and upon the earth distress of *n* .... Lk 21:25
preached in his name among all *n* .... Lk 24:47
seven *n* in the land of Chanaan .... Acts 13:19
all *n* to walk in their own ways .... Acts 14:16
hath made of one blood all *n* .... Acts 17:26
to the faith among all *n*, for his .... Rom 1:5
have made thee a father of many *n* .... Rom 4:17
might become the father of many *n* .... Rom 4:18
made known to all *n* for the .... Rom 16:26
In thee shall all *n* be blessed .... Gal 3:8
him will I give power over the *n* .... Rev 2:26
no man could number, of all *n* .... Rev 7:9
again before many peoples, and *n* .... Rev 10:11
n shall see their dead bodies .... Rev 11:9
the *n* were angry, and thy wrath is .... Rev 11:18
to rule all *n* with a rod of iron .... Rev 12:5
all kindreds, and tongues, and *n* .... Rev 13:7
because she made all *n* drink of .... Rev 14:8
for all *n* shall come and worship .... Rev 15:4
and the cities of the *n* fell .... Rev 16:19

are peoples, and multitudes, and *n* .... Rev 17:15
For all *n* have drunk of the wine .... Rev 18:3
thy sorceries were all *n* deceived .... Rev 18:23
with it he should smite the *n* .... Rev 19:15
he should deceive the *n* no more .... Rev 20:3
shall go out to deceive the *n* .... Rev 20:8
the *n* of them which are saved .... Rev 21:24
glory and honour of the *n* into it .... Rev 21:26
were for the healing of the *n* .... Rev 22:2

NATIVE
no more, nor see his *n* country .... Jer 22:10

NATIVITY
father Terah in the land of his *n* .... Gen 11:28
thy mother, and the land of thy *n* .... Ruth 2:11
people, and to the land of our *n* .... Jer 46:16
thy *n* is of the land of Canaan .... Eze 16:3
And as for thy *n*, in the day thou .... Eze 16:4
created, in the land of thy *n* .... Eze 21:30
of Chaldea, the land of their *n* .... Eze 23:15

NATURAL
not dim, nor his *n* force abated .... Deut 34:7
n use into that which is against .... Rom 1:26
leaving *n* use of the woman, ... Rom 1:27
without *n* affection, implacable, ... Rom 1:31
if God spared not the *n* branches .... Rom 11:21
these, which be the *n* branches .... Rom 11:24
But the *n* man receiveth not the 1Cor 2:14
It is sown a *n* body 1Cor 15:44
There is a *n* body, and there is a 1Cor 15:44
is spiritual, but that which is *n* 1Cor 15:46
Without *n* affection, ... 2Ti 3:3
beholding his *n* face in a glass .... Jas 1:23
as *n* brute beasts, made to be 2Pet 2:12

NATURALLY
who will *n* care for your state .... Phil 2:20
but what they know *n*, as brute .... Jude 10

NATURE
use into that which is against *n* .... Rom 1:26
do by *n* the things contained in .... Rom 2:14
not uncircumcision which is by *n* .... Rom 2:27
the olive tree which is wild by *n* .... Rom 11:24
to *n* into a good olive tree .... Rom 11:24
Doth not even *n* itself teach you, ... 1Cor 11:14
We who are Jews by *n*, and not .... Gal 2:15
unto them which by *n* are no gods .... Gal 4:8
were by *n* the children of wrath, ... Eph 2:3
took not on him the *n* of angels .... Heb 2:16
setteth on fire the course of *n*, ... Jas 3:6
be partakers of the divine *n* 2Pet 1:4

NAUGHT
but the water is *n*, and the ground 2Kin 2:19
It is *n*, it is *n*, saith the .... Prov 20:14

NAUGHTINESS
pride, and the *n* of thine heart 1Sa 17:28
shall be taken in their own *n* .... Prov 11:6
filthiness and superfluity of *n* .... Jas 1:21

NAUGHTY
A person, a wicked man, walketh .... Prov 6:12
a liar giveth ear to a *n* tongue .... Prov 17:4
the other basket had very *n* figs .... Jer 24:2

NAUM (*na'-um*) See NAHUM. Father of Amos;
ancestor of Jesus.
of Amos, which was the son of N .... Lk 3:25

NAVEL
force is in the *n* of his belly .... Job 40:16
It shall be health to thy *n* .... Prov 3:8
Thy *n* is like a round goblet, ... Song 7:2
thou wast born thy *n* was not cut .... Eze 16:4

NAVES
their axletrees, and their *n* 1Kin 7:33

NAVY
king Solomon made a *n* of ships in 1Kin 9:26
Hiram sent in the *n* his servants 1Kin 9:27
the *n* also of Hiram, that brought 1Kin 10:11
For the king had at sea a *n* of 1Kin 10:22
of Tharshish with the *n* of Hiram 1Kin 10:22
years came the *n* of Tharshish 1Kin 10:22

NAY
And he said, N; but thou didst .... Gen 18:15
And they said, N; but we will .... Gen 19:2
N, my lord, hear me .... Gen 23:11
And Jacob said, N, I pray thee, if .... Gen 33:10
And they said unto him, N, my lord .... Gen 42:10
And he said unto them, N, but to .... Gen 42:12
And he said, N, ... Num 22:30
And he said, N; but as captain .... Josh 5:14
And the people said unto Joshua, N ...... Josh 24:21
If he said, N, ... Judg 12:5
unto them, and said unto them, N, ... Judg 19:23
my brethren, n, I pray you .... Judg 19:23
n, my daughters; for it .... Ruth 1:13
then he would answer him, N 1Sa 2:16
N, my sons; for it is 1Sa 2:24
and they said, N; but we will 1Sa 8:19
and ye have said unto him, N 1Sa 10:19
against you, ye said unto me, N 1Sa 12:12
And she answered him, N, my 2Sa 13:12
And the king said to Absalom, N 2Sa 16:18
And Hushai said unto Absalom, N 2Sa 16:18
And the king said unto Araunah, N 2Sa 24:24
king, (for he will not say thee n 1Kin 2:17
I pray thee, say me not n 1Kin 2:20
for I will not say thee n 1Kin 2:20

And he said, N; but I 1Kin 2:30
And the other woman said, N 1Kin 3:22
And the other saith, N 1Kin 3:23
king of Israel said unto him, N 2Kin 3:13
And she said, N, my lord, thou man .. 2Kin 4:16
n, but let the shadow return 2Kin 20:10
And king David said to Ornan, N 1Chr 21:24
n, they were not at all ashamed, ... Jer 6:15
n, they were not at all ashamed, ... Jer 8:12
be, Yea, yea; N, n .... Mt 5:37
But he said, N; lest while .... Mt 13:29
I tell you, N; but rather. .... Lk 12:51
I tell you, N; but, except .... Lk 13:3
I tell you, N; but, except .... Lk 13:5
And he said, N, father Abraham. ..... Lk 16:30
others said, N; but he .... Jn 7:12
n verily; but let them .... Acts 16:37
N: but by the law .... Rom 3:27
N, I had not known sin, but by ...... Rom 7:7
N, in all these things we are .... Rom 8:37
N but, O man, who art thou that ..... Rom 9:20
N, ye do wrong, and defraud, and 1Cor 6:8
N, much more those members of the ... 1Cor 12:22
there should be yea yea, and n n 2Cor 1:17
and toward you was not yea and n. ... 2Cor 1:18
and Timotheus, was not yea and n.. ... 2Cor 1:19
be yea; and your n, n .... Jas 5:12

NAZARENE (naz-a-reen') See NAZARENES.
Native to Nazareth.
prophets, He shall be called a N .... Mt 2:23

NAZARENES (naz-a-reens')
a ringleader of the sect of the N. .. Acts 24:5

NAZARETH (naz'-a-reth) See NAZARENE. A
city in Galilee.
came and dwelt in a city called N ... Mt 2:23
And leaving N, he came and dwelt in. Mt 4:13
Jesus the prophet of N of Galilee ... Mt 21:11
fellow was also with Jesus of N ..... Mt 26:71
that Jesus came from N of Galilee ... Mk 1:9
to do with thee, thou Jesus of N .... Mk 1:24
he heard that it was Jesus of N ..... Mk 10:47
And thou also wast with Jesus of N .. Mk 14:67
Ye seek Jesus of N, which was. ...... Mk 16:6
unto a city of Galilee, named N.. .... Lk 1:26
Galilee, out of the city of N.... .... Lk 2:4
into Galilee, to their own city N. ... Lk 2:39
went down with them, and came to N. .. Lk 2:51
And he came to N, where he had ...... Lk 4:16
to do with thee, thou Jesus of N .... Lk 4:34
him, that Jesus of N passeth by ..... Lk 18:37
unto him, Concerning Jesus of N .... Lk 24:19
prophets, did write, Jesus of N .... Jn 1:45
any good thing come out of N .... Jn 1:46
They answered him, Jesus of N ...... Jn 18:5
And they said, Jesus of N .... Jn 18:7
JESUS OF THE .... Jn 19:19
Jesus of N, a man approved of God .. Acts 2:22
name of Jesus Christ of N rise up .. Acts 3:6
by the name of Jesus Christ of N . .. Acts 4:10
that this Jesus of N hath .... Acts 6:14
Jesus of N with the Holy Ghost .... Acts 10:38
he said unto me, I am Jesus of N. .. Acts 22:8
to the name of Jesus of N .... Acts 26:9

NAZARITE (naz'-a-rite) See NAZARITES. Title
applied to one making a special vow of
abstention.
themselves to vow a vow of a N .... Num 6:2
And this is the law of the N..... ... Num 6:13
the N shall shave the head of his. .. Num 6:18
put them upon the hands of the N . .. Num 6:19
after that the N may drink wine .. .. Num 6:20
the law of the N who hath vowed.. .. Num 6:21
be a N unto God from the womb ..... Judg 13:5
for the child shall be a N to God... Judg 13:7
for I have been a N unto God from.. Judg 16:17

NAZARITES (naz'-a-rites)
Her N were purer than snow, they. .. Lam 4:7
and of your young men for N .... Amos 2:11
But ye gave the N wine to drink . .. Amos 2:12

NEAH (ne'-ah) A city in Zebulun.
goeth out to Remmon-methoar to N. .. Josh 19:13

NEAPOLIS (ne-ap'-o-lis) A Macedonian
seaport.
Samothracia, and the next day to N.. Acts 16:11

NEAR
when he was come n to enter into.. Gen 12:11
And Abraham drew n, and said, Wilt. Gen 18:23
Lot, and came n to break the door. Gen 19:9
now, this city is n to flee unto.. Gen 19:20
But Abimelech had not come n her.. Gen 20:4
And Isaac said unto Jacob, Come n. Gen 27:21
Jacob went n unto Isaac his...... Gen 27:22
And he said, Bring it n to me ... Gen 27:25
And he brought it n to him ...... Gen 27:25
Isaac said unto him, Come n now.. Gen 27:26
And he came n, and kissed him.... Gen 27:27
brother, that Jacob went n....... Gen 29:10
until he came n to his brother... Gen 33:3
Then the handmaidens came n...... Gen 33:6
also with her children came n.... Gen 33:7
and after came Joseph n and Rachel, Gen 33:7
even before he came n unto them.. Gen 37:18
they came n to the steward of.... Gen 43:19
Then Judah came n unto him ...... Gen 44:18
Come n to me, I pray you. .... Gen 45:4
And they came n.................. Gen 45:4

and thou shalt be n unto me ...... Gen 45:10
And he brought them n unto him ... Gen 48:10
hand, and brought them n unto him. Gen 48:13
and then let him come n and keep . Ex 12:48
Philistines, although that was n .. Ex 13:17
not n the other all the night. ... Ex 14:20
of Israel, Come n before the LORD. Ex 16:9
which come n to the LORD,......... Ex 19:22
Moses drew n unto the thick ...... Ex 20:21
Moses alone shall come n the LORD. Ex 24:2
or when they come n unto the. .... Ex 28:43
or when they come n to the altar . Ex 30:20
when they came n unto the altar .. Ex 40:32
and all the congregation drew n... Lev 9:5
Aaron, and said unto them, Come n. Lev 10:4
So they went n, and carried them.. Lev 10:5
to any that is n of kin to him.... Lev 18:6
she is thy father's n kinswoman .. Lev 18:12
she is thy mother's n kinswoman .. Lev 18:13
for they are her n kinswomen. .... Lev 18:17
for he uncovereth his n kin ...... Lev 20:19
that is n unto him, that is, for.. Lev 21:2
Bring the tribe of Levi n .... Num 3:6
And the priest shall bring her n.. Num 5:16
will cause him to come n unto him. Num 5:16
will he cause to come n unto him.. Num 16:5
to bring you n to himself to do.. Num 16:9
And he hath brought thee n to him. Num 16:10
come n to offer incense before ... Num 16:40
Whosoever cometh any thing n ..... Num 17:13
of Moab by Jericho .... Num 26:3
of Moab by Jericho .... Num 26:63
which are by Jordan n Jericho .... Num 31:12
of hundreds, came n unto Moses ... Num 31:48
they came n unto him .... Num 32:16
of Moab by Jordan n Jericho...... Num 33:50
by Jordan, n Jericho, saying,..... Num 33:50
side Jordan n Jericho eastward ... Num 34:15
of Moab by Jordan n Jericho ...... Num 35:1
of the sons of Joseph, came n .... Num 36:1
of Moab by Jordan n Jericho. ..... Num 36:13
ye came n unto me every one of ... Deut 1:22
And ye came n and stood under the. Deut 4:11
fire,) that ye came n unto me .... Deut 5:23
Go thou n, and hear all that the.. Deut 5:27
n unto the altar of the LORD thy . Deut 16:21
the sons of Levi shall come n..... Deut 21:5
the wife of the one draweth n for. Deut 25:11
come not n unto it, that ye may... Josh 3:4
war which went with him, Come n.. Josh 10:24
And they came n, and put their feet. Josh 10:24
the sea, all that lay n Ashdod ... Josh 15:46
they came n before Eleazar the ... Josh 17:4
the n hill that lieth on the ..... Josh 18:13
Then came n the heads of the ..... Josh 21:1
to Micah's house were gathered.... Judg 18:22
let us draw n to one of these .... Judg 19:13
came n against the children of ... Judg 20:24
knew not that evil was n them. ... Judg 20:34
The man is n of kin unto us, one.. Ruth 2:20
for thou art a n kinsman......... Ruth 3:9
is true that I am thy n kinsman... Ruth 3:12
was with child, n to be delivered. 1Sa 4:19
the Philistines drew n to battle.. 1Sa 7:10
Then Saul drew n to Samuel in the. 1Sa 9:18
the tribes of Israel to come n... 1Sa 10:20
to come n by their families 1Sa 10:21
Let us draw n hither unto God ... 1Sa 14:36
And Saul said, Draw ye n hither .. 1Sa 14:38
And the Philistine drew n morning. 1Sa 17:16
he drew n to the Philistine...... 1Sa 17:48
came on and drew n unto David 1Sa 17:40
when David came n to the people .. 1Sa 30:21
of the young men, and said, Go n.. 2Sa 1:15
See, Joab's field is n mine 2Sa 14:30
And he came apart, and drew n 2Sa 18:25
the king is n of kin to us 2Sa 19:42
Come n hither, that I may speak .. 2Sa 20:16
And when he was come n unto him .. 2Sa 20:17
the land of the enemy, far or n... 1Kin 8:46
all the people, Come n unto me.... 1Kin 18:30
And all the people came n unto him. 1Kin 18:30
that Elijah the prophet came n ... 1Kin 18:36
because it is n unto my house. ... 1Kin 21:2
the son of Chenaanah went n...... 1Kin 22:24
but Gehazi came n to thrust her... 2Kin 4:27
And his servants came n, and spake. 2Kin 5:13
captives unto a land far off or n. 2Chr 6:36
the son of Chenaanah came n 2Chr 18:23
that were n the Ethiopians 2Chr 21:16
So Esther drew n, and touched the. Est 5:2
his decree drew n to be put in ... Est 9:1
as a prince would I go n unto him. Job 31:37
his soul draweth n unto the grave. Job 33:22
One is so n to another, that no .. Job 41:16
for trouble is n .... Ps 22:11
lest they come n unto thee. ...... Ps 32:9
is good for me to draw n to God .. Ps 73:28
for that thy name is n .... Ps 75:1
they draw n unto the gates of.... Ps 107:18
Thou art n, O LORD .... Ps 119:151
Let my cry come n before thee.... Ps 119:169
of Israel, a people n unto him.... Ps 148:14
through the street n her corner .. Prov 7:8
of the foolish is n destruction.. Prov 10:14
that is n than a brother far off.. Prov 27:10
and her time is n to come, and her. Is 13:22
that draweth n the time of her ... Is 26:17
people draw n me with their mouth. Is 29:13

and, ye that are n, acknowledge my. Is 33:13
Come n, ye nations, to hear...... Is 34:1
let them come n................. Is 41:1
let us come n together to .... Is 41:1
of the earth were afraid, drew n. Is 41:5
drawn n together, ye that are .... Is 45:20
Tell ye, and bring them n........ Is 45:21
I bring n my righteousness .... Is 46:13
Come ye n unto me, hear ye this .. Is 48:16
He is n that justifieth me .... Is 50:8
let him come n to me .... Is 50:8
My righteousness is n .... Is 51:5
for it shall not come n thee. .... Is 54:14
call ye upon him while he is n ... Is 55:6
for my salvation is n to come. ... Is 56:1
But draw n hither, ye sons of the. Is 57:3
is far off, and to him that is n.. Is 57:19
by thyself, come not n to me. .... Is 65:5
thou art n in their mouth, and far. Jer 12:2
the kings of the north, far and n. Jer 25:26
and I will cause him to draw n ... Jer 30:21
even unto the greatest, came n.... Jer 42:1
asked, and draw n to battle ...... Jer 46:3
The calamity of Moab is n to come. Jer 48:16
of the land of Moab, far n .... Jer 48:24
that were n the king's person.... Jer 52:25
Thou drewest n in the day that I.. Lam 3:57
our end is n, our days are .... Eze 6:12
he that is n shall fall by the ... Eze 6:12
is come, the day of trouble is n.. Eze 7:7
time is come, the day draweth n .. Eze 7:12
charge over the city to draw n ... Eze 9:1
but come not n any man upon whom.. Eze 9:6
Which say, It is not n .... Eze 11:3
wife, neither hath come n to a.... Eze 18:6
haat caused thy days to draw n ... Eze 22:4
Those that be n, and those that be. Eze 22:5
For the day is n, even the day of. Eze 30:3
even the day of the LORD is n..... Eze 30:3
which come n to the LORD to ...... Eze 40:46
And they shall not come n unto me. Eze 44:13
nor to come n to any of my holy .. Eze 44:13
they shall come n to me to .... Eze 44:15
and they shall come n to my table. Eze 44:16
which shall come n to minister ... Eze 45:4
time certain Chaldeans came n .... Dan 3:8
Then Nebuchadnezzar came n .... Dan 3:26
Then they came n, and spake before. Dan 6:12
and they brought him n before him. Dan 6:16
I came n unto one of them that ... Dan 7:16
So he came n where I stood....... Dan 8:17
and unto all Israel, that are n .. Dan 9:7
let all the men of war draw n .... Joel 3:9
is n in the valley of decision ... Joel 3:14
the seat of violence to come ..... Amos 6:3
LORD is n upon all the heathen ... Obad 15
The great day of the LORD is n ... Zeph 1:14
it is n, and hasteth greatly ..... Zeph 1:14
she drew not n to her God .... Zeph 3:2
I will come n to you to judgment.. Mal 3:5
when the time of the fruit drew n. Mt 21:34
these things, know that it is n... Mt 24:33
leaves, ye know that summer is n.. Mk 13:28
Then drew n unto him all the ..... Lk 15:1
and when he was come n, he asked .. Lk 18:40
And when he was come n, he beheld. Lk 19:41
and the time draweth n........... Lk 21:8
drew n unto Jesus to kiss him .... Lk 22:47
and reasoned, Jesus himself drew n. Lk 24:15
was baptizing in Aenon n to Salim. Jn 3:23
n to the parcel of ground that ... Jn 4:5
a country n to the wilderness .... Jn 11:54
as he drew n to behold it, the.... Acts 7:31
the Spirit said unto Philip, Go n. Acts 8:29
he journeyed, he came n Damascus.. Acts 9:3
together his kinsmen and n friends. Acts 10:24
Then the chief captain came n..... Acts 21:33
and we, or ever he come n, are ... Acts 23:15
that they drew n to some country.. Acts 27:27
Let us draw n with a true heart... Heb 10:22

NEARER
there is a kinsman n than I....... Ruth 3:12
salvation n than when we believed.. Rom 13:11

NEARAH (ne-a-ri'-ah) See NAGGE.
1. A son of Shemaiah.
and Igeal, and Bariah, and N 1Chr 3:23
And the sons of N 1Chr 3:23
2. A son of Ishi.
for their captains Pelatiah, and N. 1Chr 4:42

NEBAI (ne'-bahee) A renewer of the covenant.
Hariph, Anathoth, N,............. Neh 10:19

NEBAIOTH (ne-bah'-yoth) See NEBAJOTH.
1. A son of Ishmael.
The firstborn of Ishmael, ... 1Chr 1:29
2. Descendants of Ishmael.
the rams of N shall minister unto.. Is 60:7

NEBAJOTH (ne-ba'-joth) See NEBAIOTH. Same
as Nebaioth 1.
the firstborn of Ishmael,........ Gen 25:13
Abraham's son, the sister of N.... Gen 28:9
Ishmael's daughter, sister of N .. Gen 36:3

NEBALLAT (ne-bal'-lat) A Beniamite city.
Hadid, Zeboim,.................. Neh 11:34

NEBAT (ne'-bat) Father of King Jeroboam.
And Jeroboam the son of N, an 1Kin 11:26
pass, when Jeroboam the son of N . 1Kin 12:2

NEBO

unto Jeroboam the son of N........ 1Kin 12:15
of N reigned Abijam over Judah 1Kin 15:1
house of Jeroboam the son of N....... 1Kin 16:3
the way of Jeroboam the son of N.... 1Kin 16:26
the sins of Jeroboam the son of N.... 1Kin 16:31
house of Jeroboam the son of N....... 1Kin 21:22
the way of Jeroboam the son of N.... 1Kin 22:52
the sins of Jeroboam the son of N.... 2Kin 3:3
house of Jeroboam the son of N....... 2Kin 9:9
the sins of Jeroboam the son of N.... 2Kin 10:29
the sins of Jeroboam the son of N.... 2Kin 13:2
the sins of Jeroboam the son of N.... 2Kin 13:11
the sins of Jeroboam the son of N.... 2Kin 14:24
the sins of Jeroboam the son of N.... 2Kin 15:9
the sins of Jeroboam the son of N.... 2Kin 15:18
the sins of Jeroboam the son of N.... 2Kin 15:24
the sins of Jeroboam the son of N.... 2Kin 15:28
made Jeroboam the son of N king..... 2Kin 17:21
place which Jeroboam the son of N .. 2Kin 23:15
against Jeroboam the son of N........ 2Chr 9:29
pass, when Jeroboam the son of N.... 2Chr 10:2
to Jeroboam the son of N 2Chr 10:15
Yet Jeroboam the son of N 2Chr 13:6

NEBO (ne'-bo) See PISGAH, SAMGAR-NEBO.
1. A city in Reuben.
and Elealeh, and Shebam, and N ...... Num 32:3
And N, and Baal-meon, (their names Num 32:38
the mountains of Abarim, before N... Num 33:47
who dwelt in Aroer, even unto N 1Chr 5:8
Moab shall howl over N, and over .... Is 15:2
Woe unto N .... Jer 48:1
upon Dibon, and upon N .... Jer 48:22
2. A mountain east of the Jordan.
mountain Abarim, unto mount N...... Deut 32:49
of Moab unto the mountain of N...... Deut 34:1
3. A city in Judah.
The children of N, fifty and two .... Ezr 2:29
The men of the other N, fifty and..... Neh 7:33
4. A Chaldean idol.
N stoopeth, their idols were upon ..... Is 46:1
5. Father of several who married foreigners.
Of the sons of N............................ Ezr 10:43

NEBO-SARSEKIM See SARSECHIM.

NEBUCHADNEZZAR

NEBUCHADNEZZAR (neb-u-kad-nez'-zar)
See NEBUCHADREZZAR. King of Babylon.
In his days N king of Babylon 2Kin 24:1
At that time the servants of N.......... 2Kin 24:10
N king of Babylon came against....... 2Kin 24:11
that N king of Babylon came, he...... 2Kin 25:1
year of king N king of Babylon 2Kin 25:8
whom N king of Babylon had left,..... 2Kin 25:22
and Jerusalem by the hand of N 1Chr 6:15
him came up N king of Babylon........ 2Chr 36:6
N also carried of the vessels of 2Chr 36:7
the year was expired, king N sent..... 2Chr 36:10
he also rebelled against king N......... 2Chr 36:13
which N had brought forth out of ..... Ezr 1:7
whom N the king of Babylon had ...... Ezr 2:1
the hand of N the king of Babylon.... Ezr 5:12
which N took forth out of the.......... Ezr 5:14
which N took forth out of the.......... Ezr 6:5
whom N the king of Babylon had ...... Neh 7:6
whom N the king of Babylon had ...... Est 2:6
the hand of N the king of Babylon.... Jer 27:6
the same N the king of Babylon .... Jer 27:8
Which N king of Babylon took not,.... Jer 27:20
that N king of Babylon took away ..... Jer 28:3
so will I break the yoke of N............ Jer 28:11
they may serve N king of Babylon..... Jer 28:14
to all the people whom N had.......... Jer 29:1
to N king of Babylon) saying........... Jer 29:3
when N king of Babylon, and .... Jer 34:1
they brought him up to N king of ..... Jer 39:5
N king of Babylon unto Jerusalem.... Dan 1:1
eunuchs brought them in before N.... Dan 1:18
the second year of the reign of N ..... Dan 2:1
N dreamed dreams, wherewith his .... Dan 2:1
maketh known to the king N what .... Dan 2:28
Then the king N fell upon his .... Dan 2:46
N the king made an image of gold,.... Dan 3:1
Then N the king sent to gather .... Dan 3:2
image which N the king had set up... Dan 3:2
image that N the king had set up...... Dan 3:3
the image that N had set up .... Dan 3:3
image that N the king had set up...... Dan 3:5
image that N the king had set up...... Dan 3:7
They spake and said to the king N .... Dan 3:9
Then N in his rage and fury .... Dan 3:13
N spake and said unto them, Is it ..... Dan 3:14
answered and said to the king, O N .. Dan 3:16
Then was N full of fury, and the....... Dan 3:19
Then N the king was astonied, and ... Dan 3:24
Then N came near to the mouth of ... Dan 3:26
Then N spake, and said, Blessed be ... Dan 3:28
N the king, unto all people,............. Dan 4:1
I N was at rest in mine house, and.... Dan 4:4
This dream I king N have seen.......... Dan 4:18
All this came upon the king N.......... Dan 4:28
from heaven, saying, O king N.......... Dan 4:31
was the thing fulfilled upon N.......... Dan 4:33
at the end of the days I N lifted .... Dan 4:34
Now I N praise and extol and honour.. Dan 4:37
N had taken out of the temple......... Dan 5:2
whom the king N thy father............ Dan 5:11
God gave N thy father a kingdom ..... Dan 5:18

NEBUCHADREZZAR

NEBUCHADREZZAR (neb-u-kad-rez'-zar)
See NEBUCHADNEZZAR. Same as
Nebuchadnezzar.
for N king of Babylon maketh war..... Jer 21:2
the hand of N king of Babylon.......... Jer 21:7
the hand of N king of Babylon.......... Jer 22:25
after that N king of Babylon had....... Jer 24:1
first year of N king of Babylon......... Jer 25:1
N the king of Babylon, my servant.... Jer 25:9
the hand of N king of Babylon.......... Jer 29:21
was the eighteenth year of N........... Jer 32:1
the hand of N king of Babylon.......... Jer 32:28
when N king of Babylon came up ...... Jer 35:11
whom N king of Babylon made king... Jer 37:1
came N king of Babylon and all his ... Jer 39:1
Now N king of Babylon gave charge... Jer 39:11
take N the king of Babylon, my......... Jer 43:10
the hand of N king of Babylon.......... Jer 44:30
which N king of Babylon smote in .... Jer 46:2
how N king of Babylon should come.. Jer 46:13
which N king of Babylon shall .... Jer 46:26
the hand of N king of Babylon.......... Jer 49:28
for N king of Babylon hath taken...... Jer 49:30
last this N king of Babylon hath........ Jer 50:17
N the king of Babylon hath .... Jer 51:34
that N king of Babylon came, he....... Jer 52:4
year of N king of Babylon................ Jer 52:12
whom N carried away captive........... Jer 52:28
In the eighteenth year of N he......... Jer 52:29
twentieth year of N Nebuzar-adan.... Jer 52:30
upon Tyrus N king of Babylon.......... Eze 26:7
N king of Babylon caused his army ... Eze 29:18
of Egypt unto N king of Babylon...... Eze 29:19
by the hand of N king of Babylon..... Eze 30:10

NEBUSHASBAN

NEBUSHASBAN (neb-u-shas'-ban) A
Babylonian prince.
captain of the guard sent, and N ...... Jer 39:13

NEBUSHAZBAN See NEBUSHASBAN.

NEBUZAR-ADAN

NEBUZAR-ADAN (neb-u-zar'-a-dan)
Commander of Nebuchadnezzar's army.
king of Babylon, came N, captain 2Kin 25:8
did N the captain of the guard.......... 2Kin 25:11
N captain of the guard took these..... 2Kin 25:20
Then N the captain of the guard....... Jer 39:9
But N the captain of the guard......... Jer 39:10
to N the captain of the guard........... Jer 39:11
So N the captain of the guard.......... Jer 39:13
after that N the captain of the......... Jer 40:1
king of Babylon came N the captain.. Jer 41:10
king of Babylon, came N, captain ..... Jer 43:6
Then N the captain of the guard....... Jer 52:15
But N the captain of the guard......... Jer 52:16
So N the captain of the guard.......... Jer 52:26
year of Nebuchadrezzar N the .... Jer 52:30

NEBUZARADAN See NEBUZAR-ADAN.

NECESSARY

NECESSARY
of his mouth more than my n food.... Job 23:12
It was n that the word of God .... Acts 13:46
burden than these n things .... Acts 15:28
us with such things as were n .... Acts 28:10
seem to be more feeble, are n 1Cor 12:22
it n to exhort the brethren.............. 2Cor 9:5
Yet I supposed it n to send to .... Phil 2:25
to maintain good works for n uses.... Titus 3:14
It was therefore n that the .... Heb 9:23

NECESSITIES

NECESSITIES
hands have ministered unto my n ..... Acts 20:34
patience, in afflictions, in n............ 2Cor 6:4
infirmities, in reproaches, in n 2Cor 12:10

NECESSITY

NECESSITY
(For of n he must release you .... Lk 23:17
Distributing to the n of saints.......... Rom 12:13
in his heart, having no n 1Cor 7:37
for n is laid upon me...................... 1Cor 9:16
not grudgingly, or of n 2Cor 9:7
ye sent once and again unto my n .... Phil 4:16
should not be as it were of n........... Philem 14
there is made of n a change also ...... Heb 7:12
wherefore is it of n that this .... Heb 8:3
there must also of n be the death..... Heb 9:16

NECHO

NECHO (ne'-ko) See PHARAOH-NECHOH. A king
of Egypt.
N king of Egypt came up to fight 2Chr 35:20
words of N from the mouth of God.... 2Chr 35:22
N took Jehoahaz his brother, and..... 2Chr 36:4

NECK

NECK
and upon the smooth of his n .... Gen 27:16
break his yoke from off thy n........... Gen 27:40
and embraced him, and fell on his n.. Gen 33:4
and put a gold chain about his n....... Gen 41:42
upon his brother Benjamin's n .... Gen 45:14
and Benjamin wept upon his n .... Gen 45:14
and he fell on his n, and wept on ..... Gen 46:29
wept on his n a good while.............. Gen 46:29
be in the n of thine enemies .... Gen 49:8
it, then thou shalt break his n .... Ex 13:13
not, then shalt thou break his n .... Lev 5:8
and wring off his head from his n ..... Lev 5:8
heifer's n there in the valley .... Deut 21:4
put a yoke of iron upon thy n .... Deut 28:48
thy rebellion, and thy stiff n .... Deut 31:27
gate, and his n brake, and he died ... Is 4:18
like to the n of their fathers,........... 2Kin 17:14
but he stiffened his n, and.............. 2Chr 36:13
the shoulder, and hardened their n... Neh 9:29
runneth upon him, even on his n ...... Job 15:26
he hath also taken me by my n .... Job 16:12

NEED

thou clothed his n with thunder....... Job 39:19
In his n remaineth strength, and ...... Job 41:22
speak not with a stiff n .... Ps 75:5
thy head, and chains about thy n...... Prov 1:9
bind them about thy n .... Prov 3:3
unto thy soul, and grace to thy n ..... Prov 3:22
heart, and tie them about thy n........ Prov 6:21
often reproved hardeneth his n .... Prov 29:1
thy n with chains of gold................. Song 1:10
Thy n is like the tower of David .... Song 4:4
eyes, with one chain of thy n........... Song 4:9
Thy n is as a tower of ivory.............. Song 7:4
he shall reach even to the n .... Is 8:8
and his yoke from off thy n .... Is 10:27
shall reach to the midst of the n...... Is 30:28
thy n is an iron sinew, and thy .... Is 48:4
thyself from the bands of thy n........ Is 52:2
lamb, as if he cut off a dog's n .... Is 66:3
their ear, but hardened their n .... Jer 7:26
their ear, but made their n stiff........ Jer 17:23
and yokes, and put them upon thy n .. Jer 27:2
that will not put their n under .... Jer 27:8
the nations that bring their n........... Jer 27:11
from off the prophet Jeremiah's n .... Jer 28:10
king of Babylon from the n of all...... Jer 28:11
off the n of the prophet Jeremiah .... Jer 28:12
upon the n of all these nations .... Jer 28:14
break his yoke from off thy n .... Jer 30:8
wreathed, and come up upon my n ... Lam 1:14
thy hands, and a chain on thy n........ Eze 16:11
have a chain of gold about his n ...... Dan 5:7
have a chain of gold about his n ...... Dan 5:16
put a chain of gold about his n .... Dan 5:29
but I passed over upon her fair n ...... Hos 10:11
the foundation unto the n .... Hab 3:13
millstone were hanged about his n.... Mt 18:6
millstone were hanged about his n.... Mk 9:42
and ran, and fell on his n................. Lk 15:20
millstone were hanged about his n.... Lk 17:2
yoke upon the n of the disciples ...... Acts 15:10
wept sore, and fell on Paul's n .... Acts 20:37

NECKS

NECKS
feet upon the n of these kings .... Josh 10:24
put their feet upon the n of them .... Josh 10:24
meet for the n of them that take ..... Judg 5:30
that were on their camels'............... Judg 8:21
that were about their camels' n .... Judg 8:26
given me the n of mine enemies 2Sa 22:41
not hear, but hardened their n .... Neh 3:5
their n to the work of their Lord...... Neh 3:5
proudly, and hardened their n .... Neh 9:16
but hardened their n, and in their .... Neh 9:17
given me the n of mine enemies ...... Ps 18:40
and walk with stretched forth n .... Is 3:16
they have hardened their n.............. Jer 17:23
Bring your n under the yoke of......... Jer 27:12
Our n are under persecution............ Lam 5:5
upon the n of them that are slain ..... Eze 21:29
which ye shall not remove your n .... Mic 2:3
for my life laid down their own n ..... Rom 16:4

NECO See NECHOH.

NECROMANCER

NECROMANCER
spirits, or a wizard, or a n............... Deut 18:11

NEDABIAH

NEDABIAH (ned-a-bi'-ah) Son of Jeconiah.
Shenazar, Jecamiah, Hoshama, and N. 1Chr 3:18

NEED

NEED
lend him sufficient for his n............ Deut 15:8
Have I n of mad men, that ye have... Sa 21:15
Lebanon, as much as thou shalt n 2Chr 2:16
Ye shall not n to fight in this........... 2Chr 20:17
And that which they have n of .... Ezr 6:9
that shall have no n of spoil .... Prov 31:11
I have n to be baptized of thee,........ Mt 3:14
knoweth what things ye have n of..... Mt 6:8
ye have n of all these things .... Mt 6:32
that be whole n not a physician........ Mt 9:12
said unto them, They n not depart.... Mt 14:16
say, The Lord hath n of them........... Mt 21:3
what further n have we of .... Mt 26:65
whole have no n of the physician ..... Mk 2:17
what David did, when he had n .... Mk 2:25
ye that the Lord hath n of him .... Mk 11:3
What n we any further witnesses ..... Mk 14:63
that are whole n not a physician ...... Lk 5:31
healed them that had n of healing .... Lk 9:11
that ye have n of these things.......... Lk 12:30
persons, which n no repentance .... Lk 15:7
Because the Lord hath n of him........ Lk 19:31
they said, The Lord hath n of him .... Lk 19:34
What n we any further witness .... Lk 22:71
we have n of against the feast .... Jn 13:29
to all men, as every man had n .... Acts 2:45
every man according as he had n...... Acts 4:35
because hath n of you..................... Rom 16:2
no n require, let him do what he 1Cor 7:36
the hand, I have no n of thee 1Cor 12:21
to the feet, I have no n of you 1Cor 12:21
For our comely parts have no n 1Cor 12:24
or n we, as some others, epistles 2Cor 3:1
both to abound and to suffer n........ Phil 4:12
your n according to his riches in ...... Phil 4:19
so that we n not to speak any 1Th 1:8
ye n not that I write unto you 1Th 4:9
ye have no n that I write unto.......... 1Th 5:1
find grace to help in time of n .... Heb 4:16
ye have n that one teach you........... Heb 5:12
are become such as have n of milk ... Heb 5:12
what further n was there that .... Heb 7:11

N

NEEDED

For ye have *n* of patience........................ Heb 10:36
though now for a season, if it be 1Pet 1:6
ye *n* not that any man teach you.............. 1Jn 2:27
good, and seeth his brother have *n*........... 1Jn 3:17
with goods, and have *n* of nothing........... Rev 3:17
And the city had no *n* of the sun............. Rev 21:23
they *n* no candle, neither light................ Rev 22:5

NEEDED

n not that any should testify of .... Jn 2:25
hands, as though he *n* any thing............ Acts 17:25

NEEDEST

n not that any man should ask................. Jn 16:30

NEEDETH

And he said, What *n* it .... Gen 33:15
rise and give him as many as he *n* .... Lk 11:8
He that is washed *n* not save to............. Jn 13:10
he may have to give to him that *n*.......... Eph 4:28
a workman that *n* not to be 2Ti 2:15
Who *n* not daily, as those high .... Heb 7:27

NEEDFUL

be *n* for the house of thy God .... Ezr 7:20
But one thing is *n* .... Lk 10:42
That it was *n* to circumcise them, ... Acts 15:5
in the flesh is more *n* for you .... Phil 1:24
things which are *n* to the body............... Jas 2:16
it was *n* for me to write unto you............ Jude 3

NEEDLE

to go through the eye of a *n*.................... Mt 19:24
to go through the eye of a *n*.................... Mk 10:25

NEEDLE'S

for a camel to go through a *n* eye .... Lk 18:25

NEEDLEWORK

fine twined linen, wrought with a *n* .... Ex 26:36
fine twined linen, wrought with *n*............ Ex 27:16
thou shalt make the girdle of *n*............... Ex 28:39
and fine twined linen, of *n*..................... Ex 36:37
for the gate of the court was *n*............... Ex 38:18
blue, and purple, and scarlet, of *n*.......... Ex 39:29
a prey of divers colours of *n*.................. Judg 5:30
divers colours of *n* on both sides .... Judg 5:30
unto the king in raiment of *n*.................. Ps 45:14

NEEDS

thy money, must *n* be circumcised .... Gen 17:13
sojourn, and he will *n* be a judge........... Gen 19:9
must I *n* bring thy son again unto........... Gen 24:5
though thou wouldest *n* be gone .... Gen 31:30
For we must *n* die, and are as................ 2Sa 14:14
they must *n* be borne, because .... Jer 10:5
for it must *n* be that offences................. Mt 18:7
for such things must *n* be....................... Mk 13:7
a piece of ground, and I must *n* go .... Lk 14:18
he must *n* go through Samaria .... Jn 4:4
must *n* have been fulfilled .... Acts 1:16
that Christ must *n* have suffered .... Acts 17:3
multitude must *n* come together .... Acts 21:22
Wherefore ye must *n* be subject............. Rom 13:5
for then must ye *n* go out of the 1Cor 5:10
If I must *n* glory, I will glory 2Cor 11:30

NEEDY

brother, to thy poor, and to thy *n* .... Deut 15:11
hired servant that is poor and *n* .... Deut 24:14
They turn the *n* out of the way............... Job 24:4
the light killeth the poor and *n* .... Job 24:14
For the *n* shall not alway be .... Ps 9:18
poor, for the sighing of the *n* .... Ps 12:5
the *n* from him that spoileth him............ Ps 35:10
bow, to cast down the poor and *n* .... Ps 37:14
But I am poor and *n* .... Ps 40:17
But I am poor and *n* .... Ps 70:5
shall save the children Of the *n*............. Ps 72:4
deliver the *n* when he crieth .... Ps 72:12
He shall spare the poor and *n* .... Ps 72:13
and shall save the souls of the *n*............ Ps 72:13
let the poor and *n* praise thy name .... Ps 74:21
do justice to the afflicted and *n*............. Ps 82:3
Deliver the poor and *n* .... Ps 82:4
for I am poor and *n* .... Ps 86:1
n man, that he might even slay.............. Ps 109:16
For I am poor and *n*, and my heart .... Ps 109:22
lifteth the *n* out of the dunghill.............. Ps 113:7
earth, and the *n* from among men .... Prov 30:14
plead the cause of the poor and *n*.......... Prov 31:9
reacheth forth her hands to the *n*........... Prov 31:20
To turn aside the *n* from judgment .... Is 10:2
the *n* shall lie down in safety .... Is 14:30
strength to the *n* in his distress............. Is 25:4
the poor, and the steps of the *n*............. Is 26:6
even when the *n* speaketh right .... Is 32:7
n seek water, and there is none.............. Is 41:17
the right of the *n* do they not................ Jer 5:28
judged the cause of the poor and *n* .... Jer 22:16
the hand of the poor and *n*.................... Eze 16:49
Hath oppressed the poor and *n*.............. Eze 18:12
and have vexed the poor and *n*.............. Eze 22:29
the poor, which crush the *n*.................... Amos 4:1
this, O ye that swallow up the *n*............. Amos 8:4
the *n* for a pair of shoes .... Amos 8:6

NEESINGS

By his *n* a light doth shine, and .... Job 41:18

NEGEV See SOUTH.

NEGINAH (neg'-i-nah) See NEGINOTH. A *stringed instrument.*
To the chief Musician upon *N* .... Ps 61:t

NEGINOTH (neg'-i-noth) See NEGINAH. *Same as Neginah.*
To the chief Musician on *N* .... Ps 4:t
Musician on *N* upon Sheminith .... Ps 6:t
To the chief Musician on *N* .... Ps 54:t
To the chief Musician on *N* .... Ps 55:t
To the chief Musician on *N* .... Ps 67:t
To the chief Musician on *N* .... Ps 76:t

NEGLECT

if he shall *n* to hear them, tell .... Mt 18:17
but if he *n* to hear the church, ... Mt 18:17
N not the gift that is in thee, ... 1Ti 4:14
if we *n* so great salvation .... Heb 2:3

NEGLECTED

were *n* in the daily ministration .... Acts 6:1

NEGLECTING

and humility, and *n* of the body .... Col 2:23

NEGLIGENT

My sons, be not now *n* 2Chr 29:11
not be *n* to put you always in 2Pet 1:12

NEHELAM See NEHELAMITE.

NEHELAMITE (ne-hel'-am-ite) *Family name of Shemaiah.*
thou also speak to Shemaiah the *N* .... Jer 29:24
LORD concerning Shemaiah the *N* .... Jer 29:31
I will punish Shemaiah the *N* .... Jer 29:32

NEHEMIAH (ne-he-mi'-ah)
1. A clan leader with Zerubbabel.
Jeshua, Nehemiah, Seraiah, ... Ezr 2:2
came with Zerubbabel, Jeshua, *N* .... Neh 7:7
2. Governor of Jerusalem.
The words of *N* the son of....................... Neh 1:1
And *N*, which is the Tirshatha, and.......... Neh 8:9
Now those that sealed were, *N* .... Neh 10:1
and in the days of *N* the governor .... Neh 12:26
Zerubbabel, and in the days of *N*............ Neh 12:47
3. A rebuilder of Jerusalem's wall.
he repaired *N* the son of Azbuk.............. Neh 3:16

NEHILOTH (ne'-hi-loth) *A musical choir or instrument.*
To the chief Musician upon *N* .... Ps 5:t

NEHUM (ne'-hum) See REHUM. *A clan leader with Zerubbabel.*
Bilshan, Mispereth, Bigvai, *N*, ... Neh 7:7

NEHUSHTA (ne-hush'-tah) *Mother of King Jehoiachin.*
And his mother's name was *N* 2Kin 24:8

NEHUSHTAN (ne-hush'-tan) *Name given to the brazen serpents.*
and he called it *N* 2Kin 18:4

NEIEL (ne-i'-el) *A city in Asher.*
the north side of Beth-emek, and *N* .... Josh 19:27

NEIGHBOUR

every woman shall borrow of her *n* .... Ex 3:22
and let every man borrow of his *n* .... Ex 11:2
and every woman of her *n*, jewels .... Ex 11:2
his *n* next unto his house take it .... Ex 12:4
bear false witness against thy *n*............. Ex 20:16
come presumptuously upon his *n*........... Ex 21:14
unto his *n* money or stuff to keep .... Ex 22:7
he shall pay double unto his *n*............... Ex 22:9
a man deliver unto his *n* an ass............. Ex 22:10
And if a man borrow ought of his *n*........ Ex 22:14
his companion, and every man his *n* ...... Ex 22:27
lie unto his *n* in that which was .... Lev 6:2
violence, or hath deceived his *n*............. Lev 6:2
Thou shalt not defraud thy *n* .... Lev 19:13
shalt thou judge thy *n* .... Lev 19:15
stand against the blood of thy *n* .... Lev 19:16
shalt in any wise rebuke thy *n* .... Lev 19:17
thou shalt love thy *n* as thyself .... Lev 19:18
if a man cause a blemish in his *n*........... Lev 24:19
And if thou sell ought unto thy *n* .... Lev 25:14
jubile thou shalt buy of thy *n* .... Lev 25:15
which should kill his *n* unawares........... Deut 4:42
bear false witness against thy *n*............. Deut 5:20
ought unto his *n* shall release it .... Deut 15:2
he shall not exact it of his *n* .... Deut 15:2
Whoso killeth his *n* ignorantly .... Deut 19:4
the wood with his *n* to hew wood .... Deut 19:5
the twelve, and lighteth upon his *n*........ Deut 19:5
But if any man hate his *n*....................... Deut 19:11
when a man resteth against his *n* .... Deut 22:26
into the standing corn of thy *n* .... Deut 23:25
be he that smiteth his *n* secretly .... Deut 27:24
the smote his *n* unwittingly .... Josh 20:5
off his shoe, and gave it to his *n* .... Ruth 4:7
and hath given it to a *n* of thine............ 1Sa 15:28
thine hand, and given it to thy *n* 1Sa 28:17
eyes, and give them unto thy *n* 2Sa 12:11
If any man trespass against his *n*........... 1Kin 8:31
his *n* in the word of the LORD 2Kin 9:30
I am as one mocked of his *n* .... Job 12:4
God, as a man pleadeth for his *n*........... Job 16:21
speak vanity every one with his *n*.......... Ps 12:2
tongue, nor doeth evil to his *n* .... Ps 15:3
up a reproach against his *n* .... Ps 15:3
Whoso privily slandereth his *n*............... Ps 101:5
Say not unto thy *n*, Go, and come.......... Prov 3:28
Devise not evil against thy *n*.................. Prov 3:29
with his mouth destroyeth his *n*............. Prov 11:9
is void of wisdom despiseth his *n*........... Prov 11:12

---

is more excellent than his *n*.................... Prov 12:26
poor is hated even of his own *n* .... Prov 14:20
He tliat despiseth his *n* sinneth............. Prov 14:21
A violent man enticeth his *n*................... Prov 16:29
but is *n* cometh and searcheth him .... Prov 18:17
the poor is separated from his *n* .... Prov 19:4
his *n* findeth no favour in his .... Prov 21:10
against thy *n* without cause .... Prov 24:28
when thy *n* hath put thee to shame .... Prov 25:8
thy cause with thy *n* himself .... Prov 25:9
witness against his *n* is a maul .... Prov 25:18
is the man that deceiveth his *n* .... Prov 26:19
for better is a *n* that is near.................. Prov 27:10
A man that flattereth his *n*..................... Prov 29:5
for this a man is envied of his *n*............. Eccl 4:4
by another, and every one by his *n*........ Is 3:5
and every one against his *n*................... Is 3:5
They helped every one his *n* .... Is 41:6
the *n* and his friend shall perish .... Jer 6:21
judgment between a man and his *n* .... Jer 7:5
Take ye heed every one of his *n*............. Jer 9:4
every *n* will walk with slanders .... Jer 9:4
they will deceive every one his *n*........... Jer 9:5
peaceably to his *n* with his mouth .... Jer 9:8
and every one her *n* lamentation .... Jer 9:20
they shall say every man to his *n*........... Jer 22:8
they tell every man to his *n* .... Jer 23:27
my words every one from his *n* .... Jer 23:30
shall ye say every one to his *n* .... Jer 23:35
teach no more every man his *n*.............. Jer 31:34
liberty every man to his *n*...................... Jer 34:15
brother, and every man to his *n*............. Jer 34:17
the *n* cities thereof, saith the .... Jer 49:18
the *n* cities thereof, saith the .... Jer 50:40
unto him that giveth his *n* drink............. Hab 2:15
every man his *n* under the vine.............. Zech 3:10
all men every one against his *n* .... Zech 8:10
ye every man the truth to his *n*.............. Zech 8:16
evil in your hearts against his *n*............. Zech 8:17
every one on the hand of his *n*.............. Zech 14:13
rise up against the hand of his *n*........... Zech 14:13
been said, Thou shalt love thy *n*............ Mt 5:43
Thou shalt love thy *n* as thyself .... Mt 19:19
Thou shalt love thy *n* as thyself .... Mt 22:39
Thou shalt love thy *n* as thyself .... Mk 12:31
and to love his *n* as himself .... Mk 12:33
and thy *n* as thyself .... Lk 10:27
said unto Jesus, And who is my *n* .... Lk 10:29
was *n* unto him that fell among .... Lk 10:36
But he that did his *n* wrong.................... Acts 7:27
Thou shalt love thy *n* as thyself .... Rom 13:9
Love worketh no ill to his *n* .... Rom 13:10
his *n* for his good to edification .... Rom 15:2
Thou shalt love thy *n* as thyself .... Gal 5:14
speak every man truth with his *n*........... Eph 4:25
shalt not teach every man his *n* .... Heb 8:11
Thou shalt love thy *n* as thyself .... Jas 2:8

NEIGHBOUR'S

Thou shalt not covet thy *n* house........... Ex 20:17
thou shalt not covet thy *n* wife............... Ex 20:17
ass, nor any thing that is thy *n* .... Ex 20:17
put his hand unto his *n* goods .... Ex 22:8
not put his hand unto his *n* goods......... Ex 22:11
all take thy *n* raiment to pledge .... Ex 22:26
not lie carnally with thy *n* wife .... Lev 18:20
adultery with his *n* wife, the .... Lev 20:10
or buyest ought of thy *n* hand .... Lev 25:14
shalt thou desire thy *n* wife .... Deut 5:21
shalt thou covet thy *n* house.................. Deut 5:21
ass, or any thing that is thy *n*................ Deut 5:21
shalt not remove thy *n* landmark .... Deut 19:14
he hath humbled his *n* wife.................... Deut 22:24
thou comest into thy *n* vineyard............ Deut 23:24
a sickle unto thy *n* standing corn .... Deut 23:25
he that removeth his *n* landmark .... Deut 27:17
if I have laid wait at my *n* door .... Job 31:9
So he that goeth in to his *n* wife .... Prov 6:29
thy foot from thy *n* house...................... Prov 25:17
one neighed after his *n* wife................... Jer 5:8
that useth his *n* service without .... Jer 22:13
neither hath defiled his *n* wife .... Eze 18:6
mountains, and defiled his *n* wife .... Eze 18:11
hath not defiled his *n* wife..................... Eze 18:15
abomination with his *n* wife .... Eze 22:11
and ye defile every one his *n* wife .... Eze 33:26
the men every one with his *n* hand........ Zech 11:6

NEIGHBOURS

they heard that they were their *n* .... Josh 9:16
the women her *n* gave it a name, ... Ruth 4:17
the vessels abroad of all thy *n*............... 2Kin 4:3
which speak peace to their *n* .... Ps 28:3
but especially among my *n* .... Ps 31:11
makest us a reproach to our *n*................ Ps 44:13
We are become a reproach to our *n* .... Ps 79:4
render unto our *n* sevenfold into .... Ps 79:12
makest us a strife unto our *n* .... Ps 80:6
he is a reproach to his *n* .... Ps 89:41
the LORD against all mine evil *n* .... Jer 12:14
and his brethren, and his *n* .... Jer 49:10
with the Egyptians thy *n*, great .... Eze 16:26
gained of thy *n* by extortion .... Eze 22:12
unto the Assyrians her *n* .... Eze 23:5
doted upon the Assyrians her *n*............. Eze 23:12
And her *n* and her cousins heard how..... Lk 1:58
thy kinsmen, nor thy rich *n* .... Lk 14:12
calleth together her friends and *n*.......... Lk 15:6
her *n* together, saying, Rejoice .... Lk 15:9
The *n* therefore, and they which .... Jn 9:8

NEIGHBOURS'
adultery with their *n* wives.................. Jer 29:23

NEIGHED
every one *n* after his neighbour's.......... Jer 5:8

NEIGHING
sound of the *n* of his strong ones.......... Jer 8:16

NEIGHINGS
seen thine adulteries, and thy *n*.......... Jer 13:27

NEITHER See PREFACE.

NEKEB (ne'-keb) *A city in Naphtali.*
Allon to Zaanannim, and Adami, N ... Josh 19:33

NEKODA (ne-ko'-dah)
  1. A family of exiles.
of Rezin, the children of N.................. Ezr 2:48
of Rezin, the children of N.................. Neh 7:50
  2. A family of uncertain origin.
of Tobiah, the children of N................. Ezr 2:60
of Tobiah, the children of N................. Neh 7:62

NEMUEL (ne-mu'-el) See JEMUEL, NEMUELITES.
  1. Son of Eliab.
N, and Dathan, and Abiram.............. Num 26:9
  2. A son of Simeon.
of N, the family of the...................... Num 26:12
The sons of Simeon were, N............... 1Chr 4:24

NEMUELITES (ne-mu'-el-ites) *Descendants of Nemuel 2.*
of Nemuel, the family of the N......... Num 26:12

NEPHEG (ne'-feg)
  1. A son of Izhar.
Korah, and N, and Zichri.................. Ex 6:21
  2. A son of David.
Ibhar also, and Elishua, and N........ 2Sa 5:15
And Nogah, and N, and Japhia,........ 1Chr 3:7
And Nogah, and N, and Japhia,........ 1Chr 14:6

NEPHEW
have son nor *n* among his people....... Job 18:19
name, and remnant, and son, and *n*..... Is 14:22

NEPHEWS
And he had forty sons and thirty *n*.... Judg 12:14
if any widow have children or *n*......... 1Ti 5:4

NEPHILIM (ne'-fish) See NAPHISH. *Descendants of Naphish.*
the Hagarites, with Jetur, and N...... 1Chr 5:19

NEPHISHESIM (ne-fish'-e-sim) See NEPHUSIM.
A family of exiles.
of Meunim, the children of N............ Neh 7:52

NEPHISIM See NEPHUSIM.

NEPHTHALIM (nef'-tha-lim) See NAPHTALI.
Country and tribe of Naphtali.
in the borders of Zabulon and N....... Mt 4:13
land of Zabulon, and the land of N.... Mt 4:15

NEPHTOAH (nef-to'-ah) *A stream near Jerusalem.*
the fountain of the water of N........... Josh 15:9
out to the well of waters of N............ Josh 18:15

NEPHUSHESIM See NEPHISHESIM.

NEPHUSIM (ne-fu'-sim) See NEPHISHESIM. *A family of exiles.*
of Meunim, the children of N............ Ezr 2:50

NEPTHALIM
Of the tribe of N were sealed............. Rev 7:6

NER (nur) *Grandfather of King Saul.*
his host was Abner, the son of N....... 1Sa 14:50
N the father of Abner was the son....... 1Sa 14:51
Saul lay, and Abner the son of N........ 1Sa 26:5
people, and to Abner the son of N...... 1Sa 26:14
But Abner the son of N, captain......... 2Sa 2:8
And Abner the son of N, and the........ 2Sa 2:12
the son of N came to the king............ 2Sa 3:23
Thou knowest Abner the son of N...... 2Sa 3:25
the blood of Abner the son of N......... 2Sa 3:28
king to slay Abner the son of N.......... 2Sa 3:37
Israel, unto Abner the son of N.......... 1Kin 2:5
to wit, Abner the son of N.................. 1Kin 2:32
N begat Kish, and Kish begat Saul,.... 1Chr 8:33
then Zur, and Kish, and Baal, and N.. 1Chr 9:36
And N begat Kish............................. 1Chr 9:39
of Kish, and Abner the son of N........ 1Chr 26:28

NERAIAH See NERIAH.

NEREUS (ne'-re-us) *A Christian acquaintance of Paul.*
Salute Philologus, and Julia, N......... Rom 16:15

NERGAL (nur'-gal) See NERGAL-SHAREZER. *War god of Cuth.*
and the men of Cuth made N............. 2Kin 17:30

NERGAL-SHAREZER (nur'-gal-sha-re'-zur)
  1. A Babylonian prince.
and sat in the middle gate, even N..... Jer 39:3
  2. Another Babylonian prince.
Sarsechim, Rab-saris, N, Rab-mag.... Jer 39:3
and Nebushasban, Rab-saris, and N... Jer 39:13

NERI (ne'-ri) *Father of Salathiel; ancestor of Jesus.*
Salathiel, which was the son of N...... Lk 3:27

NERIAH (ne-ri'-ah) *Father of Baruch.*
purchase unto Baruch the son of N.... Jer 32:12
purchase unto Baruch the son of N.... Jer 32:16
called Baruch the son of N................ Jer 36:4
Baruch the son of N did according.... Jer 36:8
So Baruch the son of N took the........ Jer 36:14
Baruch the scribe, the son of N......... Jer 36:32
But Baruch the son of N setteth......... Jer 43:3
prophet, and Baruch the son of N..... Jer 43:6
spake unto Baruch the son of N......... Jer 45:1
commanded Seraiah the son of N...... Jer 51:59

NERO (ne'-ro) *Emperor of Rome.*
brought before N the second time...... 2Ti s

NEST
and thou puttest thy *n* in a rock......... Num 24:21
If a bird's *n* chance to be before........ Deut 22:6
As an eagle stirreth up her *n*............. Deut 32:11
Then I said, I shall die in my *n*.......... Job 29:18
command, and make her *n* on high.... Job 39:27
and the swallow a *n* for herself......... Ps 84:3
a bird that wandereth from her *n*...... Prov 27:8
my hand hath found as a *n* the.......... Is 10:14
wandering bird cast out of the *n*....... Is 16:2
shall the great owl make her *n*......... Is 34:15
that makest thy *n* in the cedars........ Jer 22:23
her *n* in the sides of the hole's......... Jer 48:28
make thy *n* as high as the eagle....... Jer 49:16
thou set thy *n* among the stars......... Obad 4
that he may set his *n* on high........... Hab 2:9

NESTS
Where the birds make their *n*........... Ps 104:17
heaven made their *n* in his boughs... Eze 31:6
and the birds of the air have *n*........ Mt 8:20
holes, and birds of the air have *n*.... Lk 9:58

NET
upon the *n* shalt thou make four....... Ex 27:4
that the *n* may be even to the........... Ex 27:5
is cast into a *n* by his own feet......... Job 18:8
hath compassed me with his *n*........ Job 19:6
in the *n* which they hid is their........ Ps 9:15
when he draweth him into his *n*...... Ps 10:9
shall pluck my feet out of the *n*....... Ps 25:15
Pull me out of the *n* that they......... Ps 31:4
they hid for me their *n* in a pit....... Ps 35:7
let his *n* that he hath hid catch...... Ps 35:8
have prepared a *n* for my steps....... Ps 57:6
Thou broughtest us into the *n*........ Ps 66:11
have spread a *n* by the wayside....... Ps 140:5
Surely in vain the *n* is spread in..... Prov 1:17
wicked desireth the *n* of evil men.... Prov 12:12
spreadeth a *n* for his feet............... Prov 29:5
that are taken in an evil *n*.............. Eccl 9:12
streets, as a wild bull in a *n*........... Is 51:20
he hath spread a *n* for my feet........ Lam 1:13
My *n* also will I spread upon him.... Eze 12:13
And I will spread my *n* upon him.... Eze 17:20
and spread their *n* over him............ Eze 19:8
my *n* over thee with a company of... Eze 32:3
they shall bring thee up in my *n*..... Eze 32:3
Mizpah, and a *n* spread upon Tabor... Hos 5:1
go, I will spread my *n* upon them.... Hos 7:12
every man his brother with a *n*........ Mic 7:2
angle, they catch them in their *n*.... Hab 1:15
they sacrifice unto their *n*.............. Hab 1:16
they therefore empty their *n*........... Hab 1:17
brother, casting a *n* into the sea...... Mt 4:18
of heaven is like unto a *n*............... Mt 13:47
brother casting a *n* into the sea....... Mk 1:16
at thy word I will let down the *n*..... Lk 5:5
and their *n* brake.......................... Lk 5:6
Cast the *n* on the right side of....... Jn 21:6
dragging the *n* with fishes............. Jn 21:8
drew the *n* to land full of great...... Jn 21:11
so many, yet was not the *n* broken... Jn 21:11

NETAIM See PLANTS.

NETHANEEL See NETHANEEL.

NETHANEEL (ne-than'-e-el)
  1. A son of Zuar.
N the son of Zuar............................ Num 1:8
N the son of Zuar shall be................ Num 2:5
the second day N the son of Zuar...... Num 7:18
the offering of N the son of Zuar....... Num 7:23
of Issachar was N the son of Zuar..... Num 10:15
  2. A brother of David.
N the fourth, Raddai the fifth,.......... 1Chr 2:14
  3. A priest who relocated the Ark.
Shebaniah, and Jehoshaphat, and N.. 1Chr 15:24
  4. A sanctuary servant.
Shemaiah the son of N the scribe...... 1Chr 24:6
  5. A son of Obed-edom.
Ammiel the sixth, N the fifth,.......... 1Chr 26:4
  6. A prince of Judah.
Obadiah, and to Zechariah, and to N... 2Chr 17:7
  7. A Levite chief.
Conaniah also, and Shemaiah and N... 2Chr 35:9
  8. Married a foreigner in exile.
Elioenai, Maaseiah, Ishmael, and N... Ezr 10:22
  9. A priest with Zerubbabel.
of Jedaiah, N................................. Neh 12:21
  10. A priest who dedicated the wall.
Milalai, Gilalai, Maai, N.................. Neh 12:36

NETHANIAH

NETHANIAH (neth-a-ni'-ah)
  1. Father of Ishmael.
Mizpah, even Ishmael the son of N... 2Kin 25:23

NETHANIAH (continued)
month, that Ishmael the son of N...... 2Kin 25:25
Mizpah, even Ishmael the son of N.... Jer 40:8
Ishmael the son of N to slay thee....... Jer 40:14
I will slay Ishmael the son of N......... Jer 40:15
the son of N the son of Elishama........ Jer 41:1
Then arose Ishmael the son of N....... Jer 41:2
Ishmael the son of N went forth........ Jer 41:6
Ishmael the son of N slew them......... Jer 41:7
Ishmael the son of N filled it............ Jer 41:9
Ishmael the son of N carried them..... Jer 41:10
Ishmael the son of N had done........... Jer 41:11
fight with Ishmael the son of N.......... Jer 41:12
But Ishmael the son of N escaped....... Jer 41:15
from Ishmael the son of N................ Jer 41:16
because Ishmael the son of N had....... Jer 41:18
  2. A sanctuary servant.
Zaccur, and Joseph, and N, and......... 1Chr 25:2
The fifth to N, he, his sons, and......... 1Chr 25:12
  3. A Levite.
sent Levites, even Shemaiah, and N... 2Chr 17:8
  4. Father of Jehudi.
princes sent Jehudi the son of N........ Jer 36:14

NETHER
stood at the *n* part of the mount...... Ex 19:17
No man shall take the *n* or the........ Deut 24:6
upper springs, and the *n* springs...... Josh 15:19
the coast of Beth-horon the *n*.......... Josh 16:3
south side of the *n* Beth-horon........ Josh 18:13
upper springs and the *n* springs...... Judg 1:15
built Gezer, and Beth-horon the *n*.... 1Kin 9:17
who built Beth-horon the *n*............. 1Chr 7:24
the upper, and Beth-horon the *n*...... 2Chr 8:5
as a piece of the *n* millstone........... Job 41:24
to the *n* parts of the earth, in......... Eze 31:14
in the *n* parts of the earth............. Eze 31:16
unto the *n* parts of the earth........... Eze 31:18
unto the *n* parts of the earth........... Eze 32:18
unto the *n* parts of the earth........... Eze 32:24

NETHERMOST
The *n* chamber was five cubits......... 1Kin 6:6

NETHINIM See NETHINIMS.

NETHINIMS (neth'-in-ims) *Assistants to the Levites.*
the priests, Levites, and the N.......... 1Chr 9:2
The N: the children of Ziha.............. Ezr 2:43
All the N, and the children of........... Ezr 2:58
singers, and the porters, and the N.... Ezr 2:70
singers, and the porters, and the N.... Ezr 7:7
and Levites, singers, porters, N......... Ezr 7:24
Iddo, and to his brethren the N......... Ezr 8:17
Also of the N, whom David and the.... Ezr 8:20
Levites, two hundred and twenty N... Ezr 8:20
Moreover the N dwelt in Ophel,........ Neh 3:26
son unto the place of the N............... Neh 3:31
The N: the children of Ziha.............. Neh 7:46
All the N, and the children of........... Neh 7:60
and some of the people, and the N..... Neh 7:73
the porters, the singers, the N........... Neh 10:28
priests, and the Levites, and the N..... Neh 11:3
But the N dwelt in Ophel................. Neh 11:21
and Ziha and Gispa were over the N.. Neh 11:21

NETOPHAH (ne-to'-fah) See NETOPHATHITE. *A city in Judah.*
The men of N, fifty and six.............. Ezr 2:22
The men of Beth-lehem and N.......... Neh 7:26

NETOPHATHI (ne-to'-fa-thi) See NETOPHATHITE. *An inhabitant of Netophah.*
and from the villages of N............... Neh 12:28

NETOPHATHITE (ne-to'-fa-thite) See NETOPHATI, NETOPHATHITES. *Same as Netophathi.*
Zalmon the Ahohite, Maharai the N ... 2Sa 23:28
Heleb the son of Baanah, a N........... 2Sa 23:29
the son of Tanhumeth the N............. 2Kin 25:23
Maharai the N, Heled the son of....... 1Chr 11:30
Heled the son of Baanah the N......... 1Chr 11:30
the tenth month was Maharai the N.. 1Chr 27:13
twelfth month was Heldai the N....... 1Chr 27:15
and the sons of Ephai the N............. Jer 40:8

NETOPHATHITES (ne-to'-fa-thites)
Beth-lehem, and the N, Ataroth,....... 1Chr 2:54
dwelt in the villages of the N........... 1Chr 9:16

NETS
of checker work, and wreaths of....... 1Kin 7:17
the wicked fall into their own *n*...... Ps 141:10
woman, whose heart is snares and *n*.. Eccl 7:26
they that spread *n* upon the........... Is 19:8
of *n* in the midst of the sea............ Eze 26:5
shalt be a place to spread *n* upon.... Eze 26:14
be a place to spread forth *n*........... Eze 47:10
And they straightway left their *n*.... Mt 4:20
their father, mending their *n*......... Mt 4:21
straightway they forsook their *n*..... Mk 1:18
were in the ship mending their *n*.... Mk 1:19
of them, and were washing their *n*.. Lk 5:2
and let down your *n* for a draught... Lk 5:4

NETTLES
under the *n* they were gathered....... Job 30:7
n had covered the face thereof,........ Prov 24:31
shall come up in her palaces, *n*....... Is 34:13
silver, *n* shall possess them............ Hos 9:6
Gomorrah, and the breeding of *n*.... Zeph 2:9

N

NETWORK
make for it a grate of *n* of brass ..... Ex 27:4
of *n* under the compass thereof ..... Ex 38:4
rows round about upon the one *n* 1Kin 7:18
the belly which was by the *n* 1Kin 7:20
rows of pomegranates for one *n* 1Kin 7:42
chapiter was five cubits, with *n* ..... Jer 52:22
the *n* were an hundred round about ..... Jer 52:23

NETWORKS
and the two *n*, to cover the two 1Kin 7:41
pomegranates for the two *n* 1Kin 7:42
fine flax, and they that weave *n* ..... Is 19:9

NEVER
Ask me *n* so much dowry and gift,.... Gen 34:12
such as I *n* saw in all the land ..... Gen 41:19
it shall *n* go out ..... Lev 6:13
and upon which *n* came yoke ..... Num 19:2
For the poor shall *n* cease out of ..... Deut 15:11
I will *n* break my covenant with ..... Judg 2:1
Is there *n* a woman among the ..... Judg 14:3
green withs that were *n* dried ..... Judg 16:7
new ropes that *n* were occupied ..... Judg 16:11
shall *n* depart from thine house 2Sa 12:10
for he *n* prophesied good unto me, ... 2Chr 18:7
that there was a *n* son left him 2Chr 21:17
as infants which *n* saw light ..... Job 3:16
and make my hands *n* so clean ..... Job 9:30
soul, and *n* eateth with pleasure ..... Job 21:25
for I shall *n* be in adversity ..... Ps 10:6
he will *n* see it ..... Ps 10:11
these things shall *n* be moved ..... Ps 15:5
I said, I shall *n* be moved ..... Ps 30:6
let me *n* be ashamed ..... Ps 31:1
they shall *n* see light ..... Ps 49:19
he shall *n* suffer the righteous ..... Ps 55:22
of charmers, charming *n* so wisely ..... Ps 58:5
let me *n* be put to confusion ..... Ps 71:1
I will *n* forget thy precepts ..... Ps 119:93
The righteous shall *n* be removed ..... Prov 10:30
Hell and destruction are *n* full ..... Prov 27:20
the eyes of man are *n* satisfied ..... Prov 27:20
three things that are *n* satisfied ..... Prov 30:15
It shall *n* be inhabited, neither ..... Is 13:20
of evildoers shall *n* be renowned ..... Is 14:20
it shall *n* be built ..... Is 25:2
dogs which can *n* have enough,.... Is 56:11
which shall *n* hold their peace ..... Is 62:6
thou *n* barest rule over them ..... Is 63:19
confusion shall *n* be forgotten ..... Jer 20:11
David shall *n* want a man to sit ..... Jer 33:17
n open thy mouth any more because ..... Eze 16:63
yet shalt thou *n* be found again ..... Eze 26:21
a terror, and *n* shalt be any more ..... Eze 26:21
and *n* shalt thou be any more ..... Eze 28:19
which shall *n* be destroyed ..... Dan 2:44
such as *n* was since there was a ..... Dan 12:1
and my people shall *n* be ashamed ..... Joel 2:26
and my people shall *n* be ashamed ..... Joel 2:27
Surely I will *n* forget any of ..... Amos 8:7
shall fall, and *n* rise up again ..... Amos 8:14
and judgment doth *n* go forth ..... Hab 1:4
I profess unto them, I *n* knew you ..... Mt 7:23
It was *n* so seen in Israel ..... Mt 9:33
have ye *n* read, Out of the mouth ..... Mt 21:16
Did ye *n* read in the scriptures,.... Mt 21:42
of thee, yet will I *n* be offended ..... Mt 26:33
And he answered him *n* a word ..... Mt 27:14
We *n* saw it on this fashion ..... Mk 2:12
Have ye *n* read what David did, ... Mk 2:25
the Holy Ghost hath *n* forgiveness ..... Mk 3:29
the fire that *n* shall be quenched ..... Mk 9:43
the fire that *n* shall be quenched ..... Mk 9:45
a colt tied, whereon *n* man sat ..... Mk 11:2
that man if he had *n* been born ..... Mk 14:21
thou *n* gavest me a kid, that ..... Lk 15:29
colt tied, whereon yet *n* man sat ..... Lk 19:30
barren, and the wombs that *n* bare ..... Lk 23:29
and the paps which *n* gave suck ..... Lk 23:29
wherein *n* man before was laid ..... Lk 23:53
I shall give him shall *n* thirst ..... Jn 4:14
that cometh to me shall *n* hunger ..... Jn 6:35
believeth on me shall *n* thirst ..... Jn 6:35
man letters, having *n* learned ..... Jn 7:15
N man spake like this man ..... Jn 7:46
were *n* in bondage to any man ..... Jn 8:33
my saying, he shall *n* see death ..... Jn 8:51
he shall *n* taste of death ..... Jn 8:52
and they shall *n* perish, neither ..... Jn 10:28
and believeth in me shall *n* die ..... Jn 11:26
Thou shalt *n* wash my feet,.... Jn 13:8
wherein was *n* man yet laid ..... Jn 19:41
for I have *n* eaten any thing that ..... Acts 10:14
mother's womb, who *n* had walked ..... Acts 14:8
Charity *n* faileth 1Cor 13:8
n able to come to the knowledge 2Ti 3:7
can *n* with those sacrifices which ..... Heb 10:1
which can *n* take away sins ..... Heb 10:11
I will *n* leave thee, nor forsake ..... Heb 13:5
do these things, ye shall *n* fall 2Pet 1:10

NEVERTHELESS
n in the day when I visit I will ..... Ex 32:34
N these shall ye not eat of them ..... Lev 11:4
N a fountain or pit, wherein ..... Lev 11:36
n the people be strong that dwell ..... Num 13:28
n the ark of the covenant of the ..... Num 14:44
n the firstborn of man shalt thou ..... Num 18:15
N the Kenite shall be wasted,.... Num 24:22
n it shall be purified with them,.... Num 31:23
N these ye shall not eat of them ..... Deut 14:7

N the LORD thy God would not ..... Deut 23:5
N the children of Israel expelled ..... Josh 13:13
N my brethren that went up with ..... Josh 14:8
the inhabitants of Beth-shemesh ..... Judg 1:33
N the LORD raised up judges,.... Judg 2:16
N the people refused to obey the ..... Josh 8:19
n Samuel mourned for Saul 1Sa 15:35
N Saul sought not any thing that 1Sa 20:26
the lords favour thee not 1Sa 29:6
N David took the strong hold of 2Sa 5:7
N a lad saw them, and told Absalom... 2Sa 17:18
he would not drink thereof, but 2Sa 23:16
N thou shalt not build the house 1Kin 8:19
N for David's sake did the LORD.... 1Kin 15:4
N Asa's heart was perfect with 1Kin 15:14
N in the time of his old age he 1Kin 15:23
n the high places were not taken 1Kin 22:43
n, if thou see me when I am taken 2Kin 2:10
N he cleaved unto the sins of 2Kin 3:3
N they departed not from the sins 2Kin 13:6
N the priests of the high places 2Kin 23:9
N David took the castle of Zion,.... 1Chr 11:5
N the king's word prevailed 1Chr 21:4
N they shall be his servants 2Chr 12:8
n the heart of Asa was perfect 2Chr 15:17
N there are good things found in 2Chr 19:3
n divers of Asher and Manasseh and.. 2Chr 30:11
N the people did sacrifice still 2Chr 33:17
N Josiah would not turn his face 2Chr 35:22
N we made our prayer unto our God... Neh 4:9
N they were disobedient, and ..... Neh 9:26
N for thy great mercies' sake ..... Neh 9:31
n even him did confederate women ..... Neh 13:26
N Haman refrained himself,.... Est 5:10
n thou heardest the voice of my ..... Ps 31:22
N man being in honour abideth not,.. Ps 49:12
N I am continually with thee ..... Ps 73:23
N they did flatter him with their ..... Ps 78:36
n thy lovingkindness will I not ..... Ps 89:33
N he saved them for his name's ..... Ps 106:8
N he regarded their affliction,.... Ps 106:44
n the counsel of the LORD, that ..... Prov 19:21
n the poor man's wisdom is ..... Eccl 9:16
N the dimness shall not be such ..... Is 9:1
N in those days, saith the LORD,.... Jer 5:18
N the hand of Ahikam the son of ..... Jer 26:24
N hear thou now this word that I ..... Jer 28:7
N Elnathan and Delaiah ..... Jer 36:25
N if thou warn the righteous man,.... Eze 3:21
N I will remember my covenant ..... Eze 16:60
N mine eye spared them from ..... Eze 20:17
N I withdrew mine hand, and ..... Eze 20:22
N leave the stump of his roots in ..... Dan 4:15
N the men rowed hard to bring it ..... Jonah 1:13
n for the oath's sake, and them ..... Mt 14:9
n not as I will, but as thou wilt ..... Mt 26:39
N I say unto you, Hereafter shall ..... Mt 26:64
n not what I will, but what thou ..... Mk 14:36
n at thy word I will let down the ..... Lk 5:5
N I must walk to day, and ..... Lk 13:33
N when the Son of man cometh,.... Lk 18:8
n not my will, but thine, be done ..... Lk 22:42
n let us go unto him ..... Jn 11:15
N among the chief rulers also ..... Jn 12:42
N I tell you the truth ..... Jn 16:7
N he left not himself without ..... Acts 14:17
N the centurion believed the ..... Acts 27:11
N death reigned from Adam to ..... Rom 5:14
N, brethren, I have written the ..... Rom 15:15
N, to avoid fornication, let 1Cor 7:2
N such shall have trouble in the 1Cor 7:28
N he that standeth stedfast in 1Cor 7:37
N we have not used this power 1Cor 9:12
N neither is the man without the 1Cor 11:11
N when it shall turn to the Lord,.... 2Cor 3:16
N God, that comforteth those that 2Cor 7:6
n, being crafty, I caught you 2Cor 12:16
n I live; yet not I ..... Gal 2:20
N what saith the scripture ..... Gal 4:30
N let every one of you in ..... Eph 5:33
n to abide in the flesh is more ..... Phil 1:24
N, whereto we have already ..... Phil 3:16
N I am not ashamed 2Ti 1:12
N the foundation of God standeth 2Ti 2:19
n afterward it yieldeth the ..... Heb 12:11
N we, according to his promise,.... 2Pet 3:13
N I have somewhat against thee, ... Rev 2:4

NEW
arose up a king over Egypt ..... Ex 1:8
ye shall offer a *n* meat offering ..... Lev 23:16
forth the old because of the ..... Lev 26:10
But if the LORD make a *n* thing ..... Num 16:30
when ye bring a *n* meat offering ..... Num 28:26
there that hath built a *n* house ..... Deut 20:5
When thou buildest a *n* house ..... Deut 22:8
When a man hath taken a *n* wife ..... Deut 24:5
to *n* gods that came newly up ..... Deut 32:17
of wine, which we filled, were *n* ..... Josh 9:13
n bottles ready to burst ..... Judg 5:8
they bound him with two *n* cords,.... Judg 15:13
he found a *n* jawbone of an ass,.... Judg 15:15
Delilah bind me fast with *n* ropes,.. Judg 16:11
Delilah therefore took *n* ropes ..... Judg 16:12
Now therefore make a *n* cart 1Sa 6:7
Behold, to morrow is the *n* moon 1Sa 20:5
to David, To morrow is the *n* moon 1Sa 20:18
when the *n* moon was come, the 1Sa 20:27
set the ark of God upon a *n* cart 2Sa 6:3
of Abinadab, drave the *n* cart 2Sa 6:3

he being girded with a *n* sword 2Sa 21:16
had clad himself with a *n* garment 1Kin 11:29
Ahijah caught the *n* garment that 1Kin 11:30
And he said, Bring me a *n* cruse 2Kin 2:20
it is neither *n* moon, nor sabbath 2Kin 4:23
in a *n* cart out of the house of 1Chr 13:7
in the sabbaths, in the *n* moons 1Chr 23:31
the sabbaths, and on the *n* moons 2Chr 2:4
the sabbaths, and on the *n* moons 2Chr 8:13
of the LORD, before the *n* court 2Chr 20:5
the sabbaths, and for the *n* moons 2Chr 31:3
offering, both of the *n* moons ..... Ezr 3:5
stones, and a row of *n* timber ..... Ezr 6:4
of the sabbaths, of the *n* moons ..... Neh 10:33
of the corn, of the *n* wine,.... Neh 10:39
the *n* wine, and the oil, which was .. Neh 13:5
the *n* wine and the oil unto the ..... Neh 13:12
is ready to burst like *n* bottles ..... Job 32:19
Sing unto him a *n* song ..... Ps 33:3
he hath put a *n* song in my mouth,.. Ps 40:3
Blow up the trumpet in the *n* moon .. Ps 81:3
O sing unto the LORD a *n* song ..... Ps 96:1
O sing unto the LORD a *n* song,.... Ps 98:1
I will sing a *n* song unto thee, O ..... Ps 144:9
Sing unto the LORD a *n* song,.... Ps 149:1
shall burst out with *n* wine ..... Prov 3:10
there is no *n* thing under the sun ..... Eccl 1:9
it may be said, See, this is *n* ..... Eccl 1:10
all manner of pleasant fruits, *n* ..... Song 7:13
the *n* moons and sabbaths, the ..... Is 1:13
Your *n* moons and your appointed ..... Is 1:14
The *n* wine mourneth, the vine ..... Is 24:7
I will make thee a *n* sharp ..... Is 41:15
to pass, and *n* things do I declare .. Is 42:9
Sing unto the LORD a *n* song,.... Is 42:10
Behold, I will do a *n* thing ..... Is 43:19
I have shewed thee *n* things from ..... Is 48:6
thou shalt be called by a *n* name ..... Is 62:2
As the *n* wine is found in the ..... Is 65:8
I create *n* heavens and a *n* earth ..... Is 65:17
For as the *n* heavens ..... Is 66:22
the *n* earth, which I will make,.... Is 66:22
that from one *n* moon to another,.... Is 66:23
of the *n* gate of the LORD's house .. Jer 26:10
created a *n* thing in the earth ..... Jer 31:22
that I will make a *n* covenant ..... Jer 31:31
at the entry of the *n* gate of the .. Jer 36:10
They are in every morning ..... Lam 3:23
I will put a *n* spirit within you ..... Eze 11:19
you a *n* heart and a *n* spirit ..... Eze 18:31
A *n* heart also will I give you,.... Eze 36:26
a *n* spirit will I put within you ..... Eze 36:26
in the feasts, and in the *n* moons .. Eze 45:17
in the day of the *n* moon it shall ..... Eze 46:1
in the sabbaths and in the *n* moons .. Eze 46:3
in the day of the *n* moon it shall ..... Eze 46:6
it shall bring forth *n* fruit ..... Eze 47:12
her *n* moons, and her sabbaths, and .. Hos 2:11
n wine take away the heart ..... Hos 4:11
of wine, because of the *n* wine,.... Joel 1:5
the *n* wine is dried up, the oil ..... Joel 1:10
mountains shall drop down *n* wine ..... Joel 3:18
When will the *n* moon be gone ..... Amos 8:5
upon the corn, and upon the *n* wine .. Hag 1:11
men cheerful, and *n* wine the maids .. Zec 9:17
of *n* cloth unto an old garment ..... Mt 9:16
But they put *n* wine into ..... Mt 9:17
wine into *n* bottles,.... Mt 9:17
out of his treasure things *n* ..... Mt 13:52
is my blood of the *n* testament,.... Mt 26:28
until that day when I drink it *n* ..... Mt 26:29
And laid it in his own *n* tomb,.... Mt 27:60
what a doctrine is this ..... Mk 1:27
of *n* cloth on an old garment ..... Mk 2:21
else the *n* piece that filled it ..... Mk 2:21
no man putteth *n* wine into old ..... Mk 2:22
else the *n* wine doth burst the ..... Mk 2:22
but *n* wine must be put into ..... Mk 2:22
wine must be put into *n* bottles ..... Mk 2:22
is my blood of the *n* testament,.... Mk 14:24
drink it *n* in the kingdom of God ..... Mk 14:25
they shall speak with *n* tongues ..... Mk 16:17
piece of a *n* garment upon an old ..... Lk 5:36
then both the *n* maketh a rent ..... Lk 5:36
of the *n* agreeth not with the old ..... Lk 5:36
no man putteth *n* wine into old ..... Lk 5:37
else the *n* wine will burst the ..... Lk 5:37
But *n* wine must be put into ..... Lk 5:38
wine must be put into *n* bottles ..... Lk 5:38
old wine straightway desireth *n* ..... Lk 5:39
This cup is the *n* testament in my .. Lk 22:20
A commandment I give unto you,.... Jn 13:34
and in the garden a *n* sepulchre ..... Jn 19:41
These men are full of *n* wine ..... Acts 2:13
May we know what this *n* doctrine .. Acts 17:19
to tell, or to hear some *n* thing ..... Acts 17:21
leaven, that ye may be a *n* lump 1Cor 5:7
This cup is the *n* testament in my .. 1Cor 11:25
able ministers of the *n* testament .. 2Cor 3:6
be in Christ, he is a *n* creature 2Cor 5:17
behold, all things are become *n* 2Cor 5:17
uncircumcision, but a *n* creature ..... Gal 6:15
in himself of twain one *n* man ..... Eph 2:15
And that ye put on the *n* man,.... Eph 4:24
of an holyday, or of the *n* moon ..... Col 2:16
And have put on the *n* man, which .. Col 3:10
when I will make a *n* covenant ..... Heb 8:8
A *n* covenant, he hath made the ..... Heb 8:13

the mediator of the *n* testament........ Heb 9:15
By a *n* and living way, which he........ Heb 10:20
the mediator of the *n* covenant........ Heb 12:24
his promise, look for *n* heavens........ 2Pet 3:13
a *n* earth, wherein dwelleth........ 2Pet 3:13
I write *n* o commandment unto you........ 1Jn 2:7
a *n* commandment I write unto you,........ 1Jn 2:8
I wrote a *n* commandment unto thee........ 2Jn 5
and in the stone a *n* name written........ Rev 2:17
which is in Jerusalem, which........ Rev 3:12
I will write upon him my *n* name........ Rev 3:12
And they sung a *n* song, saying,........ Rev 5:9
were a *n* song before the throne........ Rev 14:3
I saw a *n* heaven and a *n* earth........ Rev 21:1
n Jerusalem, coming down from God........ Rev 21:2
said, Behold, I make all things *n*........ Rev 21:5

NEWBORN
As *n* babes, desire the sincere........ 1Pet 2:2

NEWLY
not, to new gods that came *n* up........ Deut 32:17
they had but *n* set the watch........ Judg 7:19

NEWNESS
we also should walk in *n* of life........ Rom 6:4
we should serve in *n* of spirit........ Rom 7:6

NEWS
so is good *n* from a far country........ Prov 25:25

NEXT
at this set time in the *n* year........ Gen 17:21
his neighbour *n* unto his house........ Ex 12:4
those that do pitch *n* unto him........ Num 2:5
all that night, and all the *n* day........ Num 11:32
that is *n* to him of his family........ Num 27:11
which is *n* unto the slain man........ Deut 21:3
that are *n* unto the slain man,........ Deut 21:6
kin unto us, one of our *n* kinsmen........ Ruth 2:20
n unto him Abinadab, and the third.... 1Sa 17:13
Israel, and I shall be *n* unto thee........ 1Sa 23:17
unto the evening of the *n* day........ 1Chr 29:21
and I said unto her on the *n* day........ 2Kin 6:29
Joel the chief, and Shapham the *n*..... 1Chr 5:12
n to him Zechariah, Jeiel, and........ 1Chr 16:5
n to him was Jehohanan the........ 2Chr 17:15
n him was Amasiah the son of........ 2Chr 17:16
n him was Jehozabad, and with him.... 2Chr 17:18
and Elkanah that was *n* to the king.... 2Chr 28:7
and Shimei his brother was the *n*..... 2Chr 31:12
n him were Eden........ 2Chr 31:15
n unto him builded the men of........ Neh 3:2
n to them builded Zaccur the son........ Neh 3:2
n unto him repaired Meremoth the.... Neh 3:4
n unto them repaired Meshullam........ Neh 3:4
n unto them repaired Zadok the........ Neh 3:4
n unto them the Tekoites repaired...... Neh 3:5
n unto them repaired Melatiah the..... Neh 3:7
N unto him repaired Uzziel the........ Neh 3:8
N unto him also repaired Hananiah.... Neh 3:8
n unto them repaired Rephaiah the.... Neh 3:9
n unto them repaired Jediah the........ Neh 3:10
n unto them repaired Hattush the...... Neh 3:10
n unto him repaired Shallum the........ Neh 3:12
N unto him repaired Hashabiah........ Neh 3:17
n to him repaired Ezer the son of...... Neh 3:19
n to them was Hanan the son of........ Neh 13:13
the *n* unto him was Carshena,........ Est 1:14
the Jew was *n* unto king Ahasuerus.... Est 10:3
when the morning rose the *n* day....... Jonah 4:7
Now the *n* day, that followed the....... Mt 27:62
them, Let us go into the *n* towns........ Mk 1:38
came to pass, that on the *n* day........ Lk 9:37
The *n* day John seeth Jesus coming.... Jn 1:29
Again the *n* day after John stood,...... Jn 1:35
On the *n* day much people that........ Jn 12:12
put them in hold unto the *n* day........ Acts 4:3
the *n* day he shewed himself unto...... Acts 7:26
be preached to them the *n* sabbath.... Acts 13:42
the *n* sabbath day came almost the.... Acts 13:44
the *n* day he departed with........ Acts 14:20
and the *n* day to Neapolis........ Acts 16:11
came the *n* day over against Chios.... Acts 20:15
the *n* day we arrived at Samos, and.... Acts 20:15
the *n* day we came to Miletus........ Acts 20:15
the *n* day we that were of Paul's........ Acts 21:8
the *n* day purifying himself with........ Acts 21:26
the *n* day sitting on the judgment..... Acts 25:6
the *n* day we touched at Sidon........ Acts 27:3
the *n* day they lightened the ship...... Acts 27:18
we came the *n* day to Puteoli........ Acts 28:13

NEZIAH (ne-zi´-ah) A family of exiles.
The children of N, the children........ Ezr 2:54
The children of N, the children........ Neh 7:56

NEZIB (ne´-zib) A city in Judah.
And Jiphtah, and Ashnah, and N........ Josh 15:43

NIBHAZ (nib´-haz) A god of the Avites.
And the Avites made N and Tartak,... 2Kin 17:31

NIBSHAN (nib´-shan) A city in Judah.
And N, and the city of Salt, and........ Josh 15:62

NICANOR (ni-ca´-nor) A leader in the
  Jerusalem church.
and Philip, and Prochorus, and N........ Acts 6:5

NICODEMUS (ni-co-de´-mus) A Pharisee
  sympathetic to Jesus.
a man of the Pharisees, named N........ Jn 3:1
N saith unto him, How can a man........ Jn 3:4
N answered and said unto him, How.... Jn 3:9

N saith unto them, (he that came........ Jn 7:50
And there came also N, which at........ Jn 19:39

NICOLAITANES (nic-o-la´-i-tans) A group
  condemned in Revelation.
thou hatest the deeds of the N........ Rev 2:6
that hold the doctrine of the N........ Rev 2:15

NICOLAITANS See Nicolaitanes.

NICOLAS (nic´-o-las) A leader in the Jerusalem
  church.
and N a proselyte of Antioch........ Acts 6:5

NICOLAUS See Nicolas.

NICOPOLIS (ni-cop´-o-lis) A city in Thrace.
be diligent to come unto me to N........ Titus 3:12
the Cretians, from N of Macedonia..... Titus s

NIGER (ni´-jur) See Simeon. A Christian
  teacher and prophet at Antioch.
and Simeon that was called N........ Acts 13:1

NIGH
the time drew *n* that Israel must........ Gen 47:29
And he said, Draw not *n* hither........ Ex 3:5
And when Pharaoh drew *n*, the........ Ex 14:10
but they shall not come *n*........ Ex 24:2
soon as he came *n* unto the camp.... Ex 32:19
and they were afraid to come *n* him.... Ex 34:30
all the children of Israel came *n*........ Ex 34:32
sanctified in them that come *n* me..... Lev 10:3
that is *n* unto him, which hath........ Lev 21:3
n to offer the offerings of the........ Lev 21:21
he shall not come *n* to offer the........ Lev 21:21
nor come *n* unto the altar........ Lev 21:23
or any that is *n* of kin unto him........ Lev 25:49
cometh *n* shall be put to death........ Num 1:51
cometh *n* shall be put to death........ Num 3:10
cometh *n* shall be put to death........ Num 3:38
Israel come *n* unto the sanctuary...... Num 8:19
only they shall not come *n* the........ Num 18:3
shall not come *n* unto you........ Num 18:4
cometh *n* shall be put to death........ Num 18:7
come the tabernacle of the........ Num 18:22
I shall behold him, but not *n*........ Num 24:17
unto all the places *n* thereunto........ Deut 1:7
when thou comest *n* over against...... Deut 2:19
who hath God so *n* unto them........ Deut 4:7
n unto thee, or far off from thee........ Deut 13:7
n unto thee, or far off from thee........ Deut 20:2
ye are come *n* unto the battle........ Deut 20:3
When thou comest *n* unto a city to.... Deut 20:10
if thy brother be not *n* unto thee........ Deut 22:2
But the word is very *n* unto thee........ Deut 30:14
were with him, went up, and drew *n*.... Josh 8:11
drew *n* to meet David, David........ 1Sa 17:48
And Joab drew *n*, and the people....... 2Sa 20:10
Wherefore approached ye so *n*........ 2Sa 11:20
why went ye *n* the wall........ 2Sa 11:21
that when any man came *n* to him.... 2Sa 15:5
David drew *n* that he should die........ 1Kin 2:1
be *n* unto the LORD our God day and.. 1Kin 8:59
Moreover they that were *n* them....... 1Chr 12:40
n before the Syrians unto the........ 1Chr 19:14
of the king Ahasuerus, both *n*........ Est 9:20
they shall not come *n* unto him........ Ps 32:6
The LORD is *n* unto them that are...... Ps 34:18
Draw *n* unto my soul, and redeem it.. Ps 69:18
my steps had well *n* slipped........ Ps 73:2
salvation is them that fear him........ Ps 85:9
my life draweth *n* unto the grave........ Ps 88:3
but it shall not come *n* thee........ Ps 91:7
any plague come *n* thy dwelling........ Ps 91:10
They draw *n* that follow after........ Ps 119:150
The LORD is *n* unto all them that...... Ps 145:18
come not *n* the door of her house...... Prov 5:8
come not, nor the years draw *n*........ Eccl 12:1
of the Holy One of Israel draw *n*........ Is 5:19
LORD cometh, for it is *n* at hand........ Joel 2:1
people draweth *n* unto me........ Mt 15:8
came *n* unto the sea of Galilee........ Mt 15:29
when they drew *n* unto Jerusalem..... Mt 21:1
leaves, ye know that summer is *n*...... Mt 24:32
not come *n* unto him for the press.... Mk 2:4
Now there was there *n* unto the........ Mk 5:11
and he was *n* unto the sea........ Mk 5:21
And when they came *n* to Jerusalem.. Mk 11:1
come to pass, know that it is *n*........ Mk 13:29
Now when he came *n* to the gate of.. Lk 7:12
kingdom of God is come *n* unto you.. Lk 10:9
kingdom of God is come *n* unto you.. Lk 10:11
drew *n* to the house, he heard........ Lk 15:25
as he was come *n* unto Jericho........ Lk 18:35
because he was *n* to Jerusalem........ Lk 19:11
when he was come *n* to Bethphage.... Lk 19:29
And when he was come *n*, even now.. Lk 19:37
that the desolation thereof is *n*........ Lk 21:20
for your redemption draweth *n*........ Lk 21:28
that summer is now *n* at hand........ Lk 21:30
the kingdom of God is *n* at hand........ Lk 21:31
feast of unleavened bread drew *n*...... Lk 22:1
they drew *n* unto the village,........ Lk 24:28
a feast of the Jews, was *n*........ Jn 6:4
sea, and drawing *n* unto the ship...... Jn 6:19
n unto the place where they did........ Jn 6:23
Now Bethany was *n* unto Jerusalem.. Jn 11:18
the Jews' passover was *n* at hand........ Jn 11:55
for the sepulchre was *n* at hand........ Jn 19:42
the time of the promise drew *n*........ Acts 7:17
forasmuch as Lydda was *n* to Joppa.. Acts 9:38
drew *n* unto the city, Peter went........ Acts 10:9

was come *n* unto Damascus about.... Acts 22:6
n whereunto was the city of Lasea..... Acts 27:8
The word is *n* thee, even in thy........ Rom 10:8
are made *n* by the blood of Christ...... Eph 2:13
afar off, and to them that were *n*........ Eph 2:17
indeed he was *n* unto death........ Phil 2:27
of Christ he was *n* unto death........ Phil 2:30
is rejected, and is *n* unto cursing........ Heb 6:8
by the which we draw *n* unto God...... Heb 7:19
Draw *n* to God, and he will draw........ Jas 4:8
to God, and he will draw *n* to you...... Jas 4:8
the coming of the Lord draweth *n*...... Jas 5:8

NIGHT
Day, and the darkness he called N....... Gen 1:5
to divide the day from the *n*........ Gen 1:14
and the lesser light to rule the *n*........ Gen 1:16
rule over the day and over the *n*........ Gen 1:18
and day and *n* shall not cease........ Gen 8:22
them, he and his servants, by *n*........ Gen 14:15
servant's house, and tarry all *n*........ Gen 19:2
we will abide in the street all *n*........ Gen 19:2
men which came in to thee this *n*...... Gen 19:5
their father drink wine that *n*........ Gen 19:33
make him drink wine this *n* also........ Gen 19:34
father drink wine that *n* also........ Gen 19:35
came to Abimelech in a dream by *n*.. Gen 20:3
were with him, and tarried all *n*........ Gen 24:54
LORD appeared unto him the same *n*.. Gen 26:24
place, and tarried there all *n*........ Gen 28:11
the to *n* for thy son's mandrakes...... Gen 30:15
And he lay with her that *n*........ Gen 30:16
Laban the Syrian in a dream by *n*..... Gen 31:24
stolen by day, or stolen by *n*........ Gen 31:39
consumed me, and the frost by *n*...... Gen 31:40
tarried all *n* in the mount........ Gen 31:54
And he lodged there that same *n*...... Gen 32:13
lodged that *n* in the company........ Gen 32:21
And he rose up that *n*, and took his.... Gen 32:22
them, each man his dream in one *n*.... Gen 40:5
And we dreamed a dream in one *n*..... Gen 41:11
Israel in the visions of the *n*........ Gen 46:2
at *n* he shall divide the spoil........ Gen 49:27
land all that day, and all that *n*........ Ex 10:13
and eat the flesh in that *n*........ Ex 12:8
through the land of Egypt this *n*........ Ex 12:12
And Pharaoh rose up in the *n*........ Ex 12:30
he called for Moses and Aaron by *n*.. Ex 12:31
It is a *n* to be much observed........ Ex 12:42
this is that *n* of the LORD to be........ Ex 12:42
by *n* in a pillar of fire, to give........ Ex 13:21
to go by day and by *n*........ Ex 13:21
day, nor the pillar of fire by *n*........ Ex 13:22
but it gave light by *n* to these........ Ex 14:20
came not near the other all the *n*...... Ex 14:20
by a strong east wind all that *n*........ Ex 14:21
by day, and fire was on it by *n*........ Ex 40:38
the altar all *n* unto the morning........ Lev 6:9
the morning, and half thereof at *n*..... Lev 6:20
n seven days, and keep the charge..... Lev 8:35
the *n* hawk, and the cuckow, and the.. Lev 11:16
with thee all *n* until the morning........ Lev 19:13
and the appearance of fire by *n*........ Num 9:16
by *n* that the cloud was taken up....... Num 9:21
dew fell upon the camp in the *n*........ Num 11:9
up all that day, and all that *n*........ Num 11:32
and the people wept that *n*........ Num 14:1
and in a pillar of fire by *n*........ Num 14:14
said unto them, Lodge here this *n*..... Num 22:8
you, tarry ye also here this *n*........ Num 22:19
And God came unto Balaam at *n*...... Num 22:20
pitch your tents in, in fire by *n*........ Deut 1:33
n hawk, and the cuckow........ Deut 14:15
thee forth out of Egypt by *n*........ Deut 16:1
remain all *n* until the morning........ Deut 16:4
not remain all *n* upon the tree........ Deut 21:23
that chanceth him by *n*, then........ Deut 23:10
and thou shalt fear day and *n*........ Deut 28:66
shalt meditate therein day and *n*...... Josh 1:8
there came men in hither to *n* of...... Josh 2:2
where ye shall lodge this *n*........ Josh 4:3
of valour, and sent them away by *n*.. Josh 8:3
lodged that *n* among the people........ Josh 8:9
Joshua went that *n* into the midst..... Josh 8:13
and went up from Gilgal all *n*........ Josh 10:9
And it came to pass the same *n*........ Judg 6:25
do it by day, that he did it by *n*........ Judg 6:27
And God did so that *n*........ Judg 6:40
And it came to pass the same *n*........ Judg 7:9
Now therefore go by *n*, thou and...... Judg 9:32
people that were with him, by *n*........ Judg 9:34
laid wait for him all *n* in the........ Judg 16:2
the city, and were quiet all the *n*...... Judg 16:2
I pray thee, and tarry all *n*........ Judg 19:6
evening, I pray you tarry all *n*........ Judg 19:9
the man would not tarry that *n*........ Judg 19:10
of these places to lodge all *n*........ Judg 19:13
her all the *n* until the morning........ Judg 19:25
house round about upon me by *n*..... Judg 20:5
should have an husband also to *n*..... Ruth 1:12
barley to in the threshingfloor........ Ruth 3:2
Tarry this *n*, and it shall be in........ Ruth 3:13
every man his ox with him that *n*...... 1Sa 14:34
down after the Philistines by *n*........ 1Sa 14:36
and he cried unto the LORD all *n*...... 1Sa 15:11
the LORD hath said to me this *n*........ 1Sa 15:16
and David fled, and escaped that *n*... 1Sa 19:10
saying, If thou save not thy *n*........ 1Sa 19:11
naked all that day and all that *n*........ 1Sa 19:24
were a wall unto us both by *n*........ 1Sa 25:16
Abishai came to the people by *n*...... 1Sa 26:7

and they came to the woman by n 1Sa 28:8
bread all the day, nor all the n 1Sa 28:20
they rose up, and went away that n 1Sa 28:25
valiant men arose, and went all n 1Sa 31:12
all that n through the plain 2Sa 2:29
And Joab and his men went all n 2Sa 2:32
them away through the plain all n 2Sa 4:7
And it came to pass that n 2Sa 7:4
in, and lay all n upon the earth 2Sa 12:16
and pursue after David this n 2Sa 17:1
Lodge not this n in the plains of 2Sa 17:16
not tarry one with thee this n 2Sa 19:7
nor the beasts of the field by n 2Sa 21:10
to Solomon in a dream by n 1Kin 3:5
this woman's child died in the n 1Kin 3:19
may be open toward this house n 1Kin 8:29
unto the LORD our God day and n 1Kin 8:59
and they came by n, and compassed.... 2Kin 6:14
And the king arose in the n 2Kin 7:12
and he rose by n, and smote the 2Kin 8:21
And it came to pass that n 2Kin 19:35
all the men of war fled by n by.......... 2Kin 25:4
employed in that work day and n 1Chr 9:33
And it came to pass the same n 1Chr 17:3
In that n did God appear unto............ 2Chr 1:7
be open upon this house day and n 2Chr 6:20
the LORD appeared to Solomon by n.... 2Chr 7:12
and he rose up by n, and smote the.... 2Chr 21:9
offerings and the fat until n 2Chr 35:14
I pray before thee now, day and n...... Neh 1:6
And I arose in the n, I and some...... Neh 2:12
I went out by n by the gate of........... Neh 2:13
went I up in the n by the brook.......... Neh 2:15
set a watch against them day and n.... Neh 4:9
that in the n they may be a guard...... Neh 4:22
in the n will they come to slay........... Neh 6:10
in the n by a pillar of fire, to............ Neh 9:12
neither the pillar of fire by n............. Neh 9:19
nor drink three days, n or day............ Est 4:16
On that n could not the king .... Est 6:1
the n in which it was said, There........ Job 3:3
As for that n, let darkness seize......... Job 3:6
Lo, let that n be solitary .... Job 3:7
from the visions of the n.................... Job 4:13
grope in the noonday as in the n......... Job 5:14
shall I arise, and the n be gone........... Job 7:4
They change the n into day .... Job 17:12
chased away as a vision of the n......... Job 20:8
needy, and in the n is as a thief......... Job 24:14
until the day and n come to an end..... Job 26:10
stealeth him away in the n................. Job 27:20
the dew lay all n upon my branch....... Job 29:19
are pierced in me in the n season....... Job 30:17
In a dream, in a vision of the n.......... Job 33:15
and he overturneth them in the n....... Job 34:25
maker, who giveth songs in the n........ Job 35:10
Desire not the n, when people are...... Job 36:20
his law doth he meditate day and n..... Ps 1:2
all the n make I my bed to swim.......... Ps 6:6
also instruct me in the n seasons........ Ps 16:7
thou hast visited me in the n .... Ps 17:3
n unto n sheweth knowledge.............. Ps 19:2
and in the n season, and am not......... Ps 22:2
weeping may endure for a n............... Ps 30:5
n thy hand was heavy upon me........... Ps 32:4
tears have been my meat day and n..... Ps 42:3
in the n his song shall be with .... Ps 42:8
n they go about it upon the walls........ Ps 55:10
meditate on thee in the n watches....... Ps 63:6
day is thine, the n also is thine .... Ps 74:16
my sore ran in the n, and ceased........ Ps 77:2
to remembrance my song in the n .... Ps 77:6
all the n with a light of fire............... Ps 78:14
I have cried day and n before thee...... Ps 88:1
is past, and as a watch in the n.......... Ps 90:4
not be afraid for the terror by n.......... Ps 91:5
and thy faithfulness every n .... Ps 92:2
Thou makest darkness, and it is n........ Ps 104:20
and fire to give light in the n.............. Ps 105:39
thy name, O LORD, in the n................ Ps 119:55
Mine eyes prevent the n watches........ Ps 119:148
thee by day, nor the moon by n.......... Ps 121:6
which by n stand in the house of........ Ps 134:1
The moon and stars to rule by n......... Ps 136:9
even the n shall be light about .... Ps 139:11
but the n shineth as the day .... Ps 139:12
evening, in the black and dark n......... Prov 7:9
She riseth also while it is yet n........... Prov 31:15
her candle goeth not out by n............ Prov 31:18
heart taketh not rest in the n............. Eccl 2:23
nor n seeth sleep with his eyes.......... Eccl 8:16
he shall lie all n betwixt my .... Song 1:13
By n on my bed I sought him whom.... Song 3:1
thigh because of fear in the n............. Song 3:8
my locks with the drops of the n .... Song 5:2
shining of a flaming fire by n .... Is 4:5
that continue until n, till wine .... Is 5:11
Because in the n Ar of Moab is........... Is 15:1
because in the n Kir of Moab is.......... Is 15:1
make thy shadow as the n in the .... Is 16:3
the n of my pleasure hath he .... Is 21:4
of Seir, Watchman, what of the n....... Is 21:11
Watchman, what of the n .... Is 21:11
The morning cometh, and also the n.... Is 21:12
soul have I desired thee in the n .... Is 26:9
any hurt it, I will keep it n............... Is 27:3
it pass over, by day and by n .... Is 28:19
shall be as a dream of a n vision .... Is 29:7
as in the n when a holy solemnity ..... Is 30:29
shall not be quenched n nor day .... Is 34:10

from day even to n wilt thou make ...... Is 38:12
from day even to n wilt thou make ...... Is 38:13
we stumble at noonday as in the n...... Is 59:10
they shall not be shut day nor n......... Is 60:11
never hold their peace day nor n .... Is 62:6
Arise, and let us go by n, and let....... Jer 6:5
n for the slain of the daughter .... Jer 9:1
turneth aside to tarry for a n............. Jer 14:8
mine eyes run down with tears n........ Jer 14:17
ye serve other gods day and n............ Jer 16:13
and of the stars for a light by n.......... Jer 31:35
the day, and my covenant of the n...... Jer 33:20
not be day and n in their season........ Jer 33:20
my covenant be not with day and n..... Jer 33:25
heat, and in the n to the frost .... Jer 36:30
went forth out of the city by n........... Jer 39:4
if thieves by n, they will .... Jer 49:9
went forth out of the city by n........... Jer 52:7
She weepeth sore in the n................. Lam 1:2
run down like a river day and n........... Lam 2:18
Arise, cry out in the n....................... Lam 2:19
unto Daniel in a n vision .... Dan 2:19
In that n was Belshazzar the king....... Dan 5:30
palace, and passed the n fasting......... Dan 6:18
and said, I saw in my vision by n........ Dan 7:2
After this I saw in the n visions......... Dan 7:7
I saw in the n visions, and, ... Dan 7:13
shall fall with thee in the n .... Hos 4:5
their baker sleepeth all the n............. Hos 7:6
lie all n in sackcloth, ye .... Joel 1:13
and maketh the day dark with n........ Amos 5:8
came to thee, if robbers by n .... Obad 5
up in a n, and perished in a n .... Jonah 4:10
Therefore n shall be unto you........... Mic 3:6
I saw by n, and behold a man.......... Zec 1:8
known to the LORD, not day, nor n..... Zec 14:7
young child and his mother by n........ Mt 2:14
of the n Jesus went unto them......... Mt 14:25
be offended because of me this n...... Mt 26:31
I say unto thee, That this n .... Mt 26:34
day, lest his disciples come by n ...... Mt 27:64
Say ye, His disciples came by n .... Mt 28:13
And should sleep, and rise n .... Mk 4:27
And always, n and day, he was in.... Mk 5:5
of the n he cometh unto them......... Mk 6:48
be offended because of me this n...... Mk 14:27
That this day, even in this n............ Mk 14:30
watch over their flock by n.............. Lk 2:8
God with fastings and prayers n....... Lk 2:37
Master, we have toiled all the n....... Lk 5:5
continued all n in prayer to God....... Lk 6:12
this n thy soul shall be required...... Lk 12:20
in that n there shall be two men...... Lk 17:34
n unto him, though he bear long...... Lk 18:7
at n he went out, and abode in the.. Lk 21:37
The same came to Jesus by n........... Jn 3:2
them, the that came to Jesus by n.... Jn 7:50
the n cometh, when no man can....... Jn 9:4
But if a man walk in the n............... Jn 11:10
and it was n................................... Jn 13:30
at the first came to Jesus by n........ Jn 19:39
that n they caught nothing.............. Jn 21:3
Lord by n opened the prison doors.... Acts 5:19
the gates day and n to kill him........ Acts 9:24
Then the disciples took him by n...... Acts 9:25
the same n Peter was sleeping .... Acts 12:6
vision appeared to Paul in the n ...... Acts 16:9
took them the same hour of the n.... Acts 16:33
Paul and Silas by n unto Berea .... Acts 17:10
Lord to Paul in the n by a vision..... Acts 18:9
I ceased not to warn every one n..... Acts 20:31
the n following the Lord stood by..... Acts 23:11
at the third hour of the n .... Acts 23:23
and brought him by n to Antipatris.. Acts 23:31
instantly serving God day and n....... Acts 26:7
by me this n the angel of God........ Acts 27:23
when the fourteenth n was come..... Acts 27:27
The n is far spent, the day is at..... Rom 13:12
That the Lord Jesus the same n in... 1Cor 11:23
thrice I suffered shipwreck, a n....... 2Cor 11:25
for labouring n and day, because..... 1Th 2:9
N and day praying exceedingly that.. 1Th 3:10
so cometh as a thief in the n.......... 1Th 5:2
we are not of the n, nor of............. 1Th 5:5
they that sleep sleep in the n.......... 1Th 5:7
be drunken are drunken in the n..... 1Th 5:7
wrought with labour and travail n.... 2Th 3:8
in supplications and prayers n......... 1Ti 5:5
of thee in my prayers n and day...... 2Ti 1:3
will come as a thief in the n........... 2Pet 3:10
and they rest not day and n........... Rev 4:8
serve him day and n in his temple... Rev 7:15
part of it, and the n likewise.......... Rev 8:12
them before our God day and n....... Rev 12:10
and they have no rest day nor n...... Rev 14:11
day and n for ever and ever........... Rev 20:10
for there shall be no n there.......... Rev 21:25
And there shall be no n there......... Rev 22:5

NIGHTS

the earth forty days and forty n ...... Gen 7:4
the earth forty days and forty n ...... Gen 7:12
the mount forty days and forty n..... Ex 24:18
the LORD forty days and forty n....... Ex 34:28
the mount forty days and forty n..... Deut 9:9
the end of forty days and forty n..... Deut 9:11
the first, forty days and forty n....... Deut 9:18
the LORD forty days and forty n....... Deut 9:25
first time, forty days and forty n..... Deut 10:10
any water, three days and three n... 1Sa 30:12
forty n unto Horeb the mount of 1Kin 19:8

the ground seven days and seven n...... Job 2:13
wearisome n are appointed to me........ Job 7:3
and I am set in my ward whole n .... Is 21:8
of the fish three days and three n...... Jonah 1:17
had fasted forty days and forty n........ Mt 4:2
three n in the whale's belly................ Mt 12:40
three n in the heart of the earth........ Mt 12:40

NILE See BROOKS, FLOOD, RIVER.

NIMRAH (nim'-rah) See BETH-NIMRAH. *A city
in Gad.*
Ataroth, and Dibon, and Jazer, and N . Num 32:3

NIMRIM (nim'-rim) *A body of water on the
border of God.*
the waters of N shall be desolate............ Is 15:6
also of N shall be desolate.................. Jer 48:34

NIMROD (nim'-rod) *Son of Cush.*
And Cush began N............................... Gen 10:8
Even as N the mighty hunter................ Gen 10:9
And Cush begat N.............................. 1Chr 1:10
the land of N in the entrances............. Mic 5:6

NIMSHI (nim'-shi) *Grandfather of Jehu.*
Jehu the son of N shalt thou.............. 1Kin 19:16
son of Jehoshaphat the son of N.......... 2Kin 9:2
son of N conspired against Joram........ 2Kin 9:14
the driving of Jehu the son of N.......... 2Kin 9:20
Jehoram against Jehu the son of N...... 2Chr 22:7

NINE

that Adam lived were n hundred........... Gen 5:5
the days of Seth were n hundred......... Gen 5:8
the days of Enos were n hundred......... Gen 5:11
the days of Cainan were n hundred...... Gen 5:14
of Jared were n hundred sixty.............. Gen 5:20
n hundred sixty and n years................ Gen 5:27
the days of Noah were n hundred........ Gen 9:29
n years, and begat sons and................ Gen 11:19
And Nahor lived an twenty years,........ Gen 11:24
Abram was ninety years old and n ...... Gen 17:1
Abraham was ninety years old and n.... Gen 17:24
n talents, and seven hundred and........ Ex 38:24
be unto thee forty and n years........... Lev 25:8
n thousand and three hundred............ Num 1:23
n thousand and three hundred............ Num 2:13
And on the fifth day n bullocks........... Num 29:26
to give unto the n tribes.................... Num 34:13
n cubits was the length thereof........... Deut 3:11
an inheritance unto the n tribes.......... Josh 13:7
hand of Moses, for the n tribes........... Josh 14:2
all the cities are twenty and n............ Josh 15:32
n cities with their villages.................. Josh 15:44
n cities with their villages.................. Josh 15:54
n cities out of those two tribes........... Josh 21:16
for he had n hundred chariots of........ Judg 4:3
even n hundred chariots of iron,......... Judg 4:13
Jerusalem at the end of n months....... 2Sa 24:8
twenty and n years in Jerusalem......... 2Kin 14:2
of Jabesh began to reign in the n....... 2Kin 15:13
In the n and thirtieth year of 2Kin 15:17
in Samaria over Israel n years............ 2Kin 17:1
twenty and n years in Jerusalem......... 2Kin 18:2
and Eliada, and Eliphelet, n.............. 1Chr 3:8
n hundred and fifty and six.............. 1Chr 9:9
twenty and n years in Jerusalem........ 2Chr 25:1
twenty years old, and he reigned n.... 2Chr 29:1
a thousand chargers of silver, n......... Ezr 1:9
of Zattu, n hundred forty and five..... Ezr 2:8
n hundred seventy and three............. Ezr 2:36
in all an hundred thirty and n .... Ezr 2:42
Senaah, three thousand n hundred..... Neh 7:38
n hundred seventy and three............. Neh 7:39
n parts to dwell in other cities.......... Neh 11:1
n hundred twenty and eight.............. Neh 11:8
doth he not leave the ninety and n.... Mt 18:12
ninety and n which went not astray.... Mt 18:13
n in the wilderness, and go after....... Lk 15:4
n just persons, which need no .... Lk 15:7
but where are the n .... Lk 17:17

NINETEEN

n years, and begat sons and.............. Gen 11:25
n cities with their villages................. Josh 19:38
lacked of David's servants n men....... 2Sa 2:30

NINETEENTH

which is the n year of king............... 2Kin 25:8
the n to Pethahiah, the twentieth...... 1Chr 24:16
The n to Mallothi, he, his sons,....... 1Chr 25:26
month, which was the n year of .... Jer 52:12

NINETY

And Enos lived n years, and begat..... Gen 5:9
Mahalaleel were eight hundred n........ Gen 5:17
he begat Noah five hundred n............ Gen 5:30
And when Abram was n years old....... Gen 17:1
n is years old, and bear...................... Gen 17:17
And Abraham was n years old........... Gen 17:24
Now Eli was n and eight years old..... 1Sa 4:15
their brethren, six hundred and n....... 1Chr 9:6
children of Ater of Hezekiah, n.......... Ezr 2:16
The children of Gibbar, n.................. Ezr 2:20
servants, were three hundred n......... Ezr 2:58
twelve bullocks for all Israel, n......... Ezr 8:35
children of Ater of Hezekiah, n.......... Neh 7:21
The children of Gibeon, n................. Neh 7:25
servants, were three hundred n......... Neh 7:60
And there were n and six................. Jer 52:23
the days, three hundred and n days... Eze 4:5
n days shalt thou eat thereof........... Eze 4:9
and the length thereof n cubits .... Eze 41:12

a thousand two hundred and n days .. Dan 12:11
astray, doth he not leave the n .... Mt 18:12
more of that sheep, than of the n .... Mt 18:13
one of them, doth not leave the n ...... Lk 15:4
that repenteth, more than over n....... Lk 15:7

NINEVE (nen'-e-ve) See NINEVEH, NINEVITES.
Same as Nineveh.
The men of N shall rise up in the .... Lk 11:32

NINEVEH (nin'-e-veh) See NINEVE. *Capital of Assyria.*
went forth Asshur, and builded N ...... Gen 10:11
And Resen between N and Calah ...... Gen 10:12
went and returned, and dwelt at N.. 2Kin 19:36
went and returned, and dwelt at N... Is 37:37
Arise, go to N, that great city, ... Jonah 1:2
Arise, go unto N, that great city ...... Jonah 3:2
So Jonah arose, and went unto N..... Jonah 3:3
Now N was an exceeding great city .. Jonah 3:3
days, and N shall be overthrown...... Jonah 3:4
So the people of N believed God...... Jonah 3:5
For word came unto the king of N..... Jonah 3:6
published through N by the decree .... Jonah 3:7
And should not I spare N, that .... Jonah 4:11
The burden of N .... Nah 1:1
But N is of old like a pool of .... Nah 2:8
thee, and say, N is laid waste .... Nah 3:7
will make N a desolation, and dry ... Zeph 2:13
The men of N shall rise in .... Mt 12:41

NINEVITES (nin'-e-vites) *Inhabitants of Nineveh.*
as Jonas was a sign unto the N ...... Lk 11:30

NINTH
in the n day of the month at even .... Lev 23:32
yet of old fruit until the n year........ Lev 25:22
On the n day Abidan the son of....... Num 7:60
In the n year of Hoshea the king.... 2Kin 17:6
that is the n year of Hoshea king.... 2Kin 18:10
pass in the n year of his reign........ 2Kin 25:1
on the n day of the fourth month 2Kin 25:3
Johanan the eighth, Elzabad the n .. 1Chr 12:12
The n to Jeshua, the tenth to 1Chr 24:11
The n to Mattaniah, he, his sons.... 1Chr 25:16
The n captain for the n month........ 1Chr 27:12
for the n month was Abiezer the 1Chr 27:12
n year of his reign was diseased..... 2Chr 16:12
It was the n month, on the .... Ezr 10:9
king of Judah, in the n month .... Jer 36:9
in the winterhouse in the n month... Jer 36:22
In the n year of Zedekiah king of .... Jer 39:1
the n day of the month, the city ...... Jer 39:2
pass in the n year of his reign........ Jer 52:4
in the n day of the month, ... Jer 52:6
Again in the n year, in the tenth...... Eze 24:1
and twentieth day of the n month .... Hag 2:10
and twentieth day of the n month .... Hag 2:18
in the fourth day of the n month...... Zec 7:1
sixth and n hour, and did likewise... Mt 20:5
over all the land unto the n hour..... Mt 27:45
about the n hour Jesus cried with ... Mt 27:46
the whole land until the n hour ...... Mk 15:33
at the n hour Jesus cried with a ..... Mk 15:34
all the earth until the n hour .... Lk 23:44
hour of prayer, being the n hour ..... Acts 3:1
n hour of the day an angel of God.... Acts 10:3
at the n hour I prayed in my .... Acts 10:30
the n, a topaz................................. Rev 21:20

NISAN (ni'-san) See ABIB. *First month of the Hebrew year.*
And it came to pass in the month N ..... Neh 2:1
first month, that is, the month N...... Est 3:7

NISROCH (nis'-rok) *An Assyrian god.*
in the house of N his god................ 2Kin 19:37
in the house of N his god................ Is 37:38

NITRE
weather, and as vinegar upon n ...... Prov 25:20
For though thou wash thee with n .... Jer 2:22

NO See PREFACE.

NOADIAH (no-a-di'-ah)
1. Son of Binnui.
N the son of Binnui, Levites .... Ezr 8:33
2. An opponent of Nehemiah.
works, and on the prophetess N..... Neh 6:14

NOAH (no'-ah) See NOAH'S, NOE.
1. Son of Lamech; built the ark.
And he called his name N, saying,.. Gen 5:29
he begat N five hundred ninety ...... Gen 5:30
N was five hundred years old.......... Gen 5:32
N begat Shem, Ham, and Japheth... Gen 5:32
But N found grace in the eyes of .... Gen 6:8
These are the generations of N....... Gen 6:9
N was a just man and perfect in ..... Gen 6:9
generations, and N walked with God .. Gen 6:9
N begat three sons, Shem, Ham, and .. Gen 6:10
And God said unto N, The end of .... Gen 6:13
made an end of......................... Gen 6:22
And the LORD said unto N, Come .... Gen 7:1
N did according unto all that the .... Gen 7:5
N was six hundred years old when .. Gen 7:6
N went in, and his sons, and his..... Gen 7:7
two unto N into the ark, the male ... Gen 7:9
female, as God had commanded N... Gen 7:9
In the selfsame day entered N .... Gen 7:13
and Ham, and Japheth, the sons of N.. Gen 7:13
they went in unto N into the ark .... Gen 7:15
N only remained alive, and they ..... Gen 7:23

And God remembered N, and every .... Gen 8:1
that N opened the window of .... Gen 8:6
so N knew that the waters were ...... Gen 8:11
N removed the covering of the ark.... Gen 8:13
And God spake unto N, saying, ... Gen 8:15
N went forth, and his sons, and his .... Gen 8:18
N builded an altar unto the LORD.... Gen 8:20
And God blessed N and his sons, and.. Gen 9:1
And God spake unto N, and to his... Gen 9:8
And God said unto N, This is the .... Gen 9:17
And the sons of N, that went forth... Gen 9:18
These are the three sons of N'........ Gen 9:19
N began to be an husbandman, and ... Gen 9:20
N awoke from his wine, and knew ... Gen 9:24
N lived after the flood three .... Gen 9:28
all the days of N were nine........... Gen 9:29
the generations of the sons of N .... Gen 10:1
are the families of the sons of N..... Gen 10:32
N, Shem, Ham, and Japheth............ 1Chr 1:4
is as the waters of N unto me........ Is 54:9
of N should no more go over the...... Is 54:9
Though these three men, N .... Eze 14:14
Though N, Daniel, and Job, were in .. Eze 14:20
By faith N, being warned of God ..... Heb 11:7
of God waited in the days of N 1Pet 3:20
but saved N the eighth person, a 2Pet 2:5
2. A daughter of Zelophehad.
of Zelophehad were Mahlah, and N.. Num 26:33
Mahlah, N, and Hoglah, and Milcah,.. Num 27:1
and Hoglah, and Milcah, and N....... Num 36:11
of his daughters, Mahlah, and N..... Josh 17:3

NOAH'S (no'-ahz) *Refers to Noah 1.*
the six hundredth year of N life....... Gen 7:11
N wife, and the three wives of his .... Gen 7:13

NO-AMON See No.

NOB (nob) *A Levitical city in Benjamin.*
Then came David to N to Ahimelech.... 1Sa 21:1
saw the son of Jesse coming to N.... 1Sa 22:9
house, the priests that were in N..... 1Sa 22:11
And N, the city of the priests,........ 1Sa 22:19
And at Anathoth, N, Ananiah,......... Neh 11:32
yet shall he remain at N that day.... Is 10:32

NOBAH (no'-bah) See KENAH, NOPHAH.
1. A Manassite who captured an Amorite city.
N went and took Kenath, and the .... Num 32:42
villages thereof, and called it N ..... Num 32:42
2. A city in the Trachonitis.
dwelt in tents on the east of N ...... Judg 8:11

NOBLE
n Asnapper brought over, and set ... Ezr 4:10
one of the king's most n princes...... Est 6:9
Yet I had planted thee a n vine ...... Jer 2:21
These were more n than those in.... Acts 17:11
places, most n Felix, with all .... Acts 24:3
said, I am not mad, most n Festus ... Acts 26:25
not many mighty, not many n 1Cor 1:26

NOBLEMAN
A certain n went into a far .... Lk 19:12
And there was a certain n, whose.... Jn 4:46
The n saith unto him, Sir, come...... Jn 4:49

NOBLES
upon the n of the children of.......... Ex 24:11
the n of the people digged it, by .... Num 21:18
over the n among the people........... Judg 5:13
to the n that were in his city,......... 1Kin 21:8
the n who were the inhabitants in ... 1Kin 21:11
captains of hundreds, and the n 2Chr 23:20
nor to the priests, nor to the n ...... Neh 2:16
but their n put not their necks....... Neh 3:5
and rose up, and said unto the n.... Neh 4:14
And I said unto the n, and to the.... Neh 4:19
with myself, and I rebuked the n .... Neh 5:7
Moreover in those days the n of ..... Neh 6:17
heart to gather together the n .... Neh 7:5
clave to their brethren, their n .... Neh 10:29
I contended with the n of Judah ..... Neh 13:17
power of Persia and Media, the n.... Est 1:3
The n held their peace, and their.... Job 29:10
Make their n like Oreb, and like .... Ps 83:11
their n with fetters of iron............. Ps 149:8
By me princes rule, and n, even...... Prov 8:16
when thy king is the son of n .... Eccl 10:17
may go into the gates of the n........ Is 13:2
They shall call the n thereof to ...... Is 34:12
and have brought down all their n .. Is 43:14
their n have sent their little .... Jer 14:3
all the n of Judah and Jerusalem.... Jer 27:20
their n shall be of themselves,....... Jer 30:21
Babylon slew all the n of Judah...... Jer 39:6
the decree of the king and his n .... Jonah 3:7
thy n shall dwell in the dust.......... Nah 3:18

NOD (nod) *A land east of Eden.*
LORD, and dwelt in the land of N..... Gen 4:16

NODAB (no'-dab) *Name of tribe east of the Jordan.*
with Jetur, and Nephish, and N...... 1Chr 5:19

NOE (no'-e) See NOAH. *Greek form of Noah.*
But as the days of N were .... Mt 24:37
until the day that N entered into .... Mt 24:38
of Sem, which was the son of N...... Lk 3:36
And as it was in the days of N........ Lk 17:26
until the day that N entered into .... Lk 17:27

NOGAH (no'-gah) *A son of David.*
And N, and Nepheg, and Japhia,...... 1Chr 3:7
And N, and Nepheg, and Japhia,...... 1Chr 14:6

NOHAH (no'-hah) *A son of Benjamin.*
N the fourth, and Rapha the fifth 1Chr 8:2

NOISE
the n of the trumpet, and the .... Ex 20:18
when Joshua heard the n of the ..... Ex 32:17
There is a n of war in the camp....... Ex 32:17
but the n of them that sing do I ..... Ex 32:18
nor make any n with your voice,...... Josh 6:10
the n of archers in the places of .... Judg 5:11
heard the n of the shout, they 1Sa 4:6
What meaneth the n of this great ... 1Sa 4:6
Eli heard the n of the crying 1Sa 4:14
What meaneth the n of this tumult ... 1Sa 4:14
that the n that was in the host 1Sa 14:19
Wherefore is this n of the city 1Kin 1:41
This is the n that ye have heard..... 1Kin 1:45
Syrians to hear a n of chariots....... 2Kin 7:6
a n of horses, even the n of 2Kin 7:6
Athaliah heard the n of the guard ... 2Kin 11:13
making a n with psalteries and...... 1Chr 15:28
heard the n of the people running .. 2Chr 23:12
n of the shout of joy from the .... Ezr 3:13
n of the weeping of the people........ Ezr 3:13
and the n was heard afar off.......... Ezr 3:13
or the n of his tabernacle .... Job 36:29
The n thereof sheweth concerning .. Job 36:33
attentively the n of his voice......... Job 37:2
play skilfully with a loud n .... Ps 33:3
deep at the n of thy waterspouts .... Ps 42:7
in my complaint, and make a n ...... Ps 55:2
they make a n like a dog, and go.... Ps 59:6
and let them make a n like a dog.... Ps 59:14
Which stilleth the n of the seas...... Ps 65:7
the n of their waves, and the .... Ps 65:7
Make a joyful n unto God, all ye ..... Ps 66:1
make a joyful n unto the God of ..... Ps 81:1
than the n of many waters............ Ps 93:4
let us make a joyful n to the .... Ps 95:1
make a joyful n unto him with .... Ps 95:2
Make a joyful n unto the LORD....... Ps 98:4
make a loud n, and rejoice, and .... Ps 98:4
make a joyful n before the LORD .... Ps 98:6
Make a joyful n unto the LORD....... Ps 100:1
of the warrior is with confused n .... Is 9:5
The n of a multitude in the .... Is 13:4
a tumultuous n of the kingdoms of .. Is 13:4
the grave, and the n of thy viols ..... Is 14:11
a n like the n of the seas.............. Is 17:12
the n of them that rejoice endeth ... Is 24:8
that he who fleeth from the n of .... Is 24:18
bring down the n of strangers........ Is 25:5
and with earthquake, and great n ... Is 29:6
abase himself for the n of them ..... Is 31:4
At the n of the tumult the people ... Is 33:3
A voice of n from the city, a.......... Is 66:6
my heart maketh a n in me .... Jer 4:19
flee for the n of the horsemen .... Jer 4:29
the n of the bruit is come, and a .... Jer 10:22
with the n of a great tumult he...... Jer 11:16
A n shall come even to the ends ..... Jer 25:31
Pharaoh king of Egypt is but a n .... Jer 46:17
At the n of the stamping of the ...... Jer 47:3
is moved at the n of their fall........ Jer 49:21
at the cry the n thereof was........... Jer 49:21
At the n of the taking of Babylon .... Jer 50:46
a n of their voice is uttered........... Jer 51:55
they have made a n in the house.... Lam 2:7
I heard the n of their wings,.......... Eze 1:24
like the n of great waters, as......... Eze 1:24
of speech, as the n of an host........ Eze 1:24
I heard also the n of the wings....... Eze 3:13
the n of the wheels over against .... Eze 3:13
them, and a n of a great rushing .... Eze 3:13
thereof, by the n of his roaring ...... Eze 19:7
shake at the n of the horsemen ..... Eze 26:10
I will cause the n of thy songs........ Eze 26:13
and as I prophesied, there was a n .. Eze 37:7
voice was like a n of many waters ... Eze 43:2
Like the n of chariots on the .... Joel 2:5
like the n of a flame of fire........... Joel 2:5
away from me the n of thy songs .... Amos 5:23
they shall make great n by reason .. Mic 2:12
The n of a whip, and the n of......... Nah 3:2
that there shall be the n of a......... Zeph 1:10
and make a n as through wine....... Zec 9:15
and the people making a n,........... Mt 9:23
shall pass away with a great n 2Pet 3:10
as it were the n of thunder........... Rev 6:1

NOISED
his fame was n throughout all the .. Josh 6:27
it was n that he was in the house... Mk 2:1
all these sayings were n abroad...... Lk 1:65
Now when this was n abroad.......... Acts 2:6

NOISOME
fowler, and from the n pestilence .... Ps 91:3
If I cause n beasts to pass............ Eze 14:15
the n beast, and the pestilence,..... Eze 14:21
and there fell a n and grievous....... Rev 16:2

NON (non) See NUN. *Son of Elishama.*
N his son, Jehoshuah his son 1Chr 7:27

NONE
n of us shall withhold from me .... Gen 23:6
this is n other but the house of ...... Gen 28:17
There is n greater in this house ..... Gen 39:9

there was n of the men of the............ Gen 39:11
but there was n that could................. Gen 41:8
there is n that can interpret it........... Gen 41:15
but there was n that could................. Gen 41:24
there is n so discreet and wise as...... Gen 41:39
is n like unto the LORD our God.......... Ex 8:10
is n like me in all the earth................ Ex 9:14
such as there was n like it in............. Ex 9:24
such as there was n like it................. Ex 11:6
n of you shall go out at the door........ Ex 12:22
I will put n of these diseases............. Ex 15:26
sabbath, in it there shall be n............ Ex 16:26
for to gather, and they found n........... Ex 16:27
n shall appear before me empty........... Ex 23:15
n shall appear before me empty........... Ex 34:20
N of you shall approach to any........... Lev 18:6
There shall n be defiled for the.......... Lev 21:1
ye shall leave n of it until the........... Lev 22:30
And if the man have n to redeem it.... Lev 25:26
down, and n shall make you afraid..... Lev 26:6
ye shall flee when n pursueth you...... Lev 26:17
they shall fall when n pursueth.......... Lev 26:36
before a sword, when n pursueth........ Lev 26:37
N devoted, which shall be devoted...... Lev 27:29
unto the sons of Kohath he gave n..... Num 7:9
They shall leave n of it unto the........ Num 9:12
until there was n left him alive.......... Num 21:35
she bound her soul, n of effect.......... Num 30:8
Surely n of the men that came up...... Num 32:11
every city, we left n to remain........... Deut 2:34
we smote him until n was left to........ Deut 3:3
there is n else beside him................. Deut 4:35
there is n else................................... Deut 4:39
Thou shalt have n of the evil gods...... Deut 5:7
will put n of the evil diseases............ Deut 7:15
cried, and there was n to save her..... Deut 22:27
thou shalt have n to rescue them....... Deut 28:31
shalt have n assurance of thy............ Deut 28:66
is gone, and there is n shut up........... Deut 32:36
There is n like unto the God of.......... Deut 33:26
n went out, and n came in................. Josh 6:1
so that they let n of them remain....... Josh 8:22
there shall n of you be freed............. Josh 9:23
n moved his tongue against any of..... Josh 10:21
he let n remain.................................. Josh 10:28
he let n remain in it.......................... Josh 10:30
until he had left him n remaining....... Josh 10:33
he left n remaining, according to....... Josh 10:37
he left n remaining........................... Josh 10:39
he left n remaining, but utterly.......... Josh 10:40
until they left them n remaining........ Josh 11:8
strength, Israel burned n of them....... Josh 11:13
There was n of the Anakims left........ Josh 11:22
of Levi he gave n inheritance............ Josh 13:14
he gave n inheritance among them..... Josh 14:3
But n answered................................. Judg 19:28
there came n to the camp from.......... Judg 21:8
there were n of the inhabitants.......... Judg 21:9
for there is n to redeem it.................. Ruth 4:4
There is n holy as the LORD................ 1Sa 2:2
for there is n beside thee................... 1Sa 2:2
did let n of his words fall to.............. 1Sa 3:19
that there is n like him among........... 1Sa 10:24
So n of the people tasted any............ 1Sa 14:24
David said, There is n like that......... 1Sa 21:9
there is n that sheweth me that.......... 1Sa 22:8
there is n of you that is sorry............ 1Sa 22:8
for there is n like thee, neither.......... 2Sa 7:22
there was n to part them, but the....... 2Sa 14:6
n can turn to the right hand or.......... 2Sa 14:19
was n to be so much praised as.......... 2Sa 14:25
Beware that n touch the young man.... 2Sa 18:12
looked, but there was n to save.......... 2Sa 22:42
so that there was n like thee.............. 1Kin 3:12
is God, and that there is n else.......... 1Kin 8:60
n were of silver................................ 1Kin 10:21
there was n that followed the............ 1Kin 12:20
n was exempted................................ 1Kin 15:22
But there was n like unto Ahab.......... 1Kin 21:25
whom I stand, I will receive n........... 2Kin 5:16
And one of his servants said, N......... 2Kin 6:12
and there shall be n to bury her......... 2Kin 9:10
then let n go forth nor escape............ 2Kin 9:15
until he left him n remaining............. 2Kin 10:11
let n be wanting................................ 2Kin 10:19
you n of the servants of the LORD....... 2Kin 10:23
let n come forth................................ 2Kin 10:25
there was n left but the tribe of........ 2Kin 17:18
so that after him was n like him........ 2Kin 18:5
n remained, save the poorest sort...... 2Kin 24:14
N ought to carry the ark of God......... 1Chr 15:2
there is n like thee, neither is........... 1Chr 17:20
And Eliezer had n other sons............. 1Chr 23:17
a shadow, and there is n abiding........ 1Chr 29:15
such as n of the kings have had......... 2Chr 1:12
there were n such seen before in....... 2Chr 9:11
n were of silver................................ 2Chr 9:20
we have n inheritance in the son....... 2Chr 10:16
n go out or come in to Asa king........ 2Chr 16:1
so that n is able to withstand............ 2Chr 20:6
fallen to the earth, and n escaped...... 2Chr 20:24
But let n come into the house of........ 2Chr 23:6
that n which was unclean in any........ 2Chr 23:19
found there n of the sons of Levi....... Ezr 8:15
n of us put off our clothes................. Neh 4:23
to the law; n did compel.................... Est 1:8
for n might enter into the king's........ Est 4:2
that there is n like him in.................. Job 1:8
that there is n like him in.................. Job 2:3
and n spake a word unto him............. Job 2:13

let it look for light, but have n.......... Job 3:9
there is n that can deliver out........... Job 10:7
down, and n shall make thee afraid.... Job 11:19
because it is n of his......................... Job 18:15
There shall n of his meat be left........ Job 20:21
and him that had n to help him.......... Job 29:12
there was n of you that convinced..... Job 32:12
But n saith, Where is God my........... Job 35:10
but n giveth answer, because of........ Job 35:12
N is so fierce that dare stir him........ Job 41:10
while there is n to deliver................. Ps 7:2
his wickedness till thou find n.......... Ps 10:15
there is n that doeth good.................. Ps 14:1
there is n that doeth good, no,........... Ps 14:3
but there was n to save them............. Ps 18:41
for there is n to help......................... Ps 22:11
n can keep alive his own soul............ Ps 22:29
let n that wait on thee be................... Ps 25:3
devices of the people of n effect....... Ps 33:10
n of them that trust in him shall....... Ps 34:22
n of his steps shall slide.................... Ps 37:31
N of them can by any means redeem.. Ps 49:7
pieces, and there be n to deliver........ Ps 50:22
there is n that doeth good.................. Ps 53:1
there is n that doeth good, no,........... Ps 53:3
to take pity, but there was n............. Ps 69:20
and for comforters, but I found n...... Ps 69:20
let n dwell in their tents.................... Ps 69:25
for there is n to deliver him.............. Ps 71:11
there is n upon earth that I................ Ps 73:25
n of the men of might have found...... Ps 76:5
and there was n to bury them............ Ps 79:3
and Israel would n of me................... Ps 81:11
gods there is n like unto thee............ Ps 86:8
fell down, and there was n to help..... Ps 107:12
Let there be n to extend mercy.......... Ps 109:12
when as yet there was n of them........ Ps 139:16
counsel, and would n of my reproof... Prov 1:25
They would n of my counsel.............. Prov 1:30
N that go unto her return again,........ Prov 2:19
and choose n of his ways.................. Prov 3:31
twins, and n is barren among them.... Song 4:2
together, and n shall quench them...... Is 1:31
N shall be weary nor stumble............ Is 5:27
n shall slumber nor sleep.................. Is 5:27
away safe, and n shall deliver it........ Is 5:29
there was n that moved the wing,...... Is 10:14
is persecuted, and n hindereth.......... Is 14:6
n shall be alone in his appointed....... Is 14:31
down, and n shall make them afraid... Is 17:2
so he shall open, and n shall shut...... Is 22:22
and he shall shut, and n shall open.... Is 22:22
n shall pass through it for ever.......... Is 34:10
but n shall be there, and all her......... Is 34:12
shall fail, n shall want her mate........ Is 34:16
needy seek water, and there is n........ Is 41:17
there is n that sheweth, yea,.............. Is 41:26
there is n that declareth, yea,............ Is 41:26
there is n that heareth your............... Is 41:26
are for a prey, and n delivereth......... Is 42:22
for a spoil, and n saith, Restore........ Is 42:22
there is n that can deliver out........... Is 43:13
n considereth in his heart.................. Is 44:19
I am the LORD, and there is n else...... Is 45:5
west, that there is n beside me.......... Is 45:6
I am the LORD, and there is n else...... Is 45:6
and there is n else, there is no.......... Is 45:14
and there is n else............................ Is 45:18
there is n beside me.......................... Is 45:21
for I am God, and there is n else........ Is 45:22
for I am God, and there is n else........ Is 46:9
I am God, and there is n like me........ Is 46:9
heart, I am, and n else beside me....... Is 47:8
thou hast said, N seeth me................ Is 47:10
heart, I am, and n else beside me....... Is 47:10
n shall save thee............................... Is 47:15
I called, was there n to answer.......... Is 50:2
There is n to guide her among all...... Is 51:18
n considering that the righteous........ Is 57:1
N calleth for justice, nor any............ Is 59:4
look for judgment, but there is n....... Is 59:11
of the people there was n with me..... Is 63:3
I looked, and there was n to help....... Is 63:5
that there was n to uphold................. Is 63:5
there is n that calleth upon thy......... Is 64:7
when I called, n did answer.............. Is 66:4
quench that n can quench it because.. Jer 4:4
they have n understanding................ Jer 4:22
and n shall fray them away................ Jer 7:33
so that n can pass through them........ Jer 9:10
that n passeth through...................... Jer 9:12
and n shall gather them..................... Jer 9:22
as there is n like unto thee................ Jer 10:6
there is n like unto thee.................... Jer 10:7
there is n to stretch forth my............ Jer 10:20
be shut up, and n shall open them..... Jer 13:19
and they shall have n to bury them.... Jer 14:16
burn that n can quench it,................. Jer 21:12
that n doth return from his................ Jer 23:14
is great, so that n is like it............... Jer 30:7
quiet, and n shall make him afraid.... Jer 30:10
There is n to plead thy cause,........... Jer 30:13
that n should serve himself of.......... Jer 34:9
that n should serve themselves of..... Jer 34:10
for unto this day they drink n........... Jer 35:14
He shall have n to sit upon the.......... Jer 36:30
n of them shall remain or escape...... Jer 42:17
Judah, to leave you n to remain........ Jer 44:7
So that n of the remnant of Judah..... Jer 44:14
for n shall return but such as............ Jer 44:14

ease, and n shall make him afraid..... Jer 46:27
n shall tread with shouting................ Jer 48:33
n shall gather up him that................. Jer 49:5
and n shall dwell therein.................. Jer 50:3
n shall return in vain........................ Jer 50:9
sought for, and there shall be n......... Jer 50:20
let n thereof escape.......................... Jer 50:29
and fall, and n shall raise him up...... Jer 50:32
that n shall remain in it,................... Jer 51:62
lovers she hath n to comfort her....... Lam 1:2
because n come to the solemn........... Lam 1:4
of the enemy, and n did help her....... Lam 1:7
there is n to comfort her.................... Lam 1:17
there is n to comfort me.................... Lam 1:21
anger n escaped nor remained........... Lam 2:22
there is n that doth deliver us............ Lam 5:8
n of them shall remain, nor of........... Eze 7:11
but n goeth to the battle.................... Eze 7:14
seek peace, and there be n................ Eze 7:25
There shall n of my words be............ Eze 12:28
N eye pitied thee, to do any of.......... Eze 16:5
whereas n followeth thee to.............. Eze 16:34
hath spoiled n by violence................ Eze 18:7
but I found n..................................... Eze 22:30
To the end that n of all the............... Eze 31:14
N of his sins that he hath.................. Eze 33:16
that n shall pass through................... Eze 33:28
n did search or seek after them......... Eze 34:6
and n shall make them afraid............ Eze 34:28
their land, and n made them afraid.... Eze 39:26
have left n of them any more............ Eze 39:28
them all was found n like Daniel...... Dan 1:19
there is n other that can shew it........ Dan 2:11
n can stay his hand, or say unto....... Dan 4:35
could find n occasion nor fault......... Dan 6:4
there was n that could deliver........... Dan 8:7
the vision, but n understood it.......... Dan 8:27
there is n that holdeth with me......... Dan 10:21
will, and n shall stand before him..... Dan 11:16
to his end, and n shall help him........ Dan 11:45
n of the wicked shall understand...... Dan 12:10
n shall deliver her out of mine......... Hos 2:10
take away, and n shall rescue him..... Hos 5:14
there is n among them that............... Hos 7:7
High, n at all would exalt him.......... Hos 11:7
n iniquity in me that were sin.......... Hos 12:8
I am the LORD your God, and n else... Joel 2:27
there is n to raise her up................... Amos 5:2
there be n to quench it..................... Amos 5:6
there is n understanding in him........ Obad 7
Therefore thou shalt have n that....... Mic 2:5
n evil can come upon us................... Mic 3:11
and n shall make them afraid............ Mic 4:4
in pieces, and n can deliver.............. Mic 5:8
there is n upright among men........... Mic 7:2
but n shall look back....................... Nah 2:8
for there is n end of the store........... Nah 2:9
whelp, and n made them afraid......... Nah 2:11
there is n end of their corpses.......... Nah 3:3
I am, and there is n beside me.......... Zeph 2:15
streets waste, that n passeth by........ Zeph 3:6
man, that there is n inhabitant.......... Zeph 3:6
down, and n shall make them afraid.. Zeph 3:13
clothe you, but there is n warm......... Hag 1:6
let n of you imagine evil against....... Zec 7:10
let n of you imagine evil in your....... Zec 8:17
let n deal treacherously against......... Mal 2:15
seeking rest, and findeth n............... Mt 12:43
God of n effect by your tradition...... Mt 15:6
there is n good but one, that is,........ Mt 19:17
But found n; yea, though................. Mt 26:60
witnesses came, yet found they n...... Mt 26:60
Making the word of God of n............ Mk 7:13
there is n good but one, that is,........ Mk 10:18
There is n other commandment......... Mk 12:31
and there is n other but he,.............. Mk 12:32
and found n...................................... Mk 14:55
There is n of thy kindred that is....... Lk 1:61
let him impart to him that hath n...... Lk 3:11
But unto n of them was Elias sent..... Lk 4:26
n of them was cleansed, saving........ Lk 4:27
and finding n, he saith, I will........... Lk 11:24
sought fruit thereon, and found n...... Lk 13:6
fruit on this fig tree, and find n........ Lk 13:7
That n of those men which were....... Lk 14:24
n is good, save one, that is, God....... Lk 18:19
they understood n of these things..... Lk 18:34
that there was n other boat there....... Jn 6:22
yet n of you keepeth the law............. Jn 7:19
saw n but the woman, he said unto.... Jn 8:10
the works which n other man did...... Jn 15:24
n of you asketh me, Whither goest.... Jn 16:5
n of them is lost, but the son of........ Jn 17:12
thou gavest me have I lost n.............. Jn 18:9
n of the disciples durst ask him,....... Jn 21:12
said, Silver and gold have I n............ Acts 3:6
for there is n other name under......... Acts 4:12
he gave him n inheritance in it,........ Acts 7:5
yet he was fallen upon n of them...... Acts 8:16
that n of these things which ye......... Acts 8:24
preaching the word to n but unto...... Acts 11:19
cared for n of those things................ Acts 18:17
But n of these things move me,......... Acts 20:24
that he should forbid n of his............ Acts 24:23
but if there be n of these things........ Acts 25:11
they brought n accusation of such..... Acts 25:18
saying n other things than those....... Acts 26:22
for I am persuaded that n of.............. Acts 26:26
There is n righteous, no, not one....... Rom 3:10
There is n that understandeth,........... Rom 3:11

there is n that seeketh after God .... Rom 3:11
there is n that doeth good, no,......... Rom 3:12
and the promise made of n effect....... Rom 4:14
Spirit of Christ, he is n of his......... Rom 8:9
word of God hath taken n effect........ Rom 9:6
For n of us liveth to himself, and...... Rom 14:7
God that I baptized in of you........... 1Cor 1:14
Christ should be made of n effect...... 1Cor 1:17
Which n of the princes of this 1Cor 2:8
wives be as though they had n.......... 1Cor 7:29
that there is n other God but one 1Cor 8:4
But I have used n of these things 1Cor 9:15
Give n offence, neither to the 1Cor 10:32
world, and n of them is without........ 1Cor 14:10
For we write n other things unto 2Cor 1:13
But other of the apostles saw I n ..... Gal 1:19
make the promise of n effect........... Gal 3:17
that ye will be n otherwise............ Gal 5:10
See that n render evil for evil 1Th 5:15
give n occasion to the adversary 1Ti 5:14
But let n of you suffer as a 1Pet 4:15
there is n occasion of stumbling 1Jn 2:10
Fear n of those things which thou ..... Rev 2:10
will put upon you n other burden....... Rev 2:24

NOON
these men shall dine with me at n...... Gen 43:16
present against Joseph came at n....... Gen 43:25
who lay on a bed at n.................. 2Sa 4:5
of Baal from morning even until n..... 1Kin 18:26
And it came to pass at n, that......... 1Kin 18:27
And they went out at n................. 1Kin 20:16
he sat on her knees till n............. 2Kin 4:20
Evening, and morning, and at n......... Ps 55:17
makest thy flock to rest at n.......... Song 1:7
arise, and let us go up at n........... Jer 6:4
cause the sun to go down at n.......... Amos 8:9
come nigh unto Damascus about n....... Acts 22:6

NOONDAY
And thou shalt grope at n, as the ..... Deut 28:29
grope in the n as in the night........ Job 5:14
age shall be clearer than the n....... Job 11:17
light, and thy judgment as the n...... Ps 37:6
the destruction that wasteth at n..... Ps 91:6
the night in the midst of the n....... Is 16:3
and thy darkness be as the n.......... Is 58:10
we stumble at n as in the night....... Is 59:10
of the young men a spoiler at n....... Jer 15:8
shall drive out Ashdod at the n....... Zeph 2:4

NOPH (nof) See MEMPHIS. Same as Memphis.
The princes of N are deceived......... Is 19:13
Also the children of N and............ Jer 2:16
Migdol, and at Tahpanhes, and at N.... Jer 44:1
In Migdol, and publish in N........... Jer 46:14
for N shall be waste and desolate..... Jer 46:19
their images to cease out of N........ Eze 30:13
N shall have distresses daily .... Eze 30:16

NOPHAH (no'-fah) See NOBAH. A city in Sihon.
have laid them waste even unto N...... Num 21:30

NOR See PREFACE.

NORTH
west, and to the east, and to the n... Gen 28:14
the n side there shall be twenty ..... Ex 26:20
shalt put the table on the n side .... Ex 26:35
likewise for the n side on the........ Ex 27:11
which is toward the n corner.......... Ex 36:25
for the n side the hangings were...... Ex 38:11
be on the n side by their armies...... Num 2:25
And this shall be your n border....... Num 34:7
this shall be your n border........... Num 34:9
on the n side two thousand cubits .... Num 35:5
and pitched on the n side of Ai....... Josh 8:11
that was on the n of the city......... Josh 8:13
were on the n of the mountains........ Josh 11:2
their border in the n quarter was .... Josh 15:5
along by the n of Beth-arabah......... Josh 15:6
which is Chesalon, on the n side...... Josh 15:10
was to Michmethah on the n side....... Josh 16:6
was on the n side of the river........ Josh 17:9
met together in Asher on the n .... Josh 17:10
abide in their coasts on the n........ Josh 18:5
their border on the n side was........ Josh 18:12
the side of Jericho on the n side..... Josh 18:12
the valley of the giants on the n .... Josh 18:16
was drawn from the n.................. Josh 18:17
of the border were at the n bay....... Josh 18:19
it on the n side to Hannathon......... Josh 19:14
toward the n side of Beth-emek........ Josh 19:27
on the n side of the hill of.......... Josh 24:30
on the n side of the hill Gaash....... Judg 2:9
were on the n side of them............ Judg 7:1
which is on the n side of Beth-el..... 1Kin 7:25
oxen, three looking toward the n...... 1Kin 7:25
put it on the n side of the altar..... 2Kin 16:14
porters, toward the east, west, ... 1Chr 9:24
oxen, three looking toward the n...... 2Chr 4:4
out the n over the empty place........ Job 26:7
and cold out of the n................. Job 37:9
Fair weather cometh out of the n...... Job 37:22
mount Zion, on the sides of the n .... Ps 48:2
The n and the south thou hast......... Ps 89:12
and from the west, from the n......... Ps 107:3
The n wind driveth away rain.......... Prov 25:23
and turneth about unto the n.......... Eccl 1:6
toward the south, or toward the n..... Eccl 11:3

Awake, O n wind....................... Song 4:16
in the sides of the n................. Is 14:31
shall come from the n a smoke......... Is 14:31
I have raised up one from the n....... Is 41:25
I will say to the n, Give up.......... Is 43:6
and, lo, these from the n and from.... Is 49:12
the face thereof is toward the n...... Jer 1:13
Out of the n an evil shall break ..... Jer 1:14
families of the kingdoms of the n..... Jer 1:15
proclaim these words toward the n..... Jer 3:12
n to the land that I have given....... Jer 3:18
for I will bring evil from the n...... Jer 4:6
for evil appeareth out of the n....... Jer 6:1
people cometh from the n country ..... Jer 6:22
commotion out of the n country .... Jer 10:22
behold them that come from the n...... Jer 13:20
of Israel from the land of the n ..... Jer 16:15
of Israel out of the n country........ Jer 23:8
and take all the families of the n.... Jer 25:9
And all the kings of the n............ Jer 25:26
bring them from the n country......... Jer 31:8
fall toward the n by the river........ Jer 46:6
hosts hath a sacrifice in the n....... Jer 46:10
it cometh out of the n................ Jer 46:20
the hand of the people of the n....... Jer 46:24
waters rise up out of the n........... Jer 47:2
For out of the n there cometh up...... Jer 47:2
great nations from the n country ..... Jer 50:9
a people shall come from the n........ Jer 50:41
shall come unto her from the n........ Jer 51:48
a whirlwind came out of the n......... Eze 1:4
gate, that looketh toward the n....... Eze 8:3
eyes now the way toward the n......... Eze 8:5
up mine eyes the way toward the n .... Eze 8:14
house which was toward the n.......... Eze 8:14
gate, which lieth toward the n........ Eze 9:2
to the n shall be burned therein ..... Eze 20:47
all flesh from the south to the n..... Eze 21:4
a king of Babylon, from the n......... Eze 26:7
There be the princes of the n......... Eze 32:30
of Togarmah of the n quarters......... Eze 38:6
from thy place out of the n parts .... Eze 38:15
thee to come up from the n parts ..... Eze 39:2
court that looked toward the n........ Eze 40:20
against the gate toward the n......... Eze 40:23
And he brought me to the n gate....... Eze 40:35
up to the entry of the n gate......... Eze 40:40
was at the side of the n gate......... Eze 40:44
having the prospect toward the n...... Eze 40:44
toward the n for the priests.......... Eze 40:46
the n side, one door toward the n .... Eze 41:11
utter court, the way toward the n .... Eze 42:1
before the building toward the n ..... Eze 42:1
an hundred cubits was the n door...... Eze 42:2
and their doors toward the n.......... Eze 42:4
chambers which were toward the n...... Eze 42:11
The n chambers and the south......... Eze 42:13
He measured the n side, five......... Eze 42:17
of the n gate before the house....... Eze 44:4
entereth in by the way of the n...... Eze 46:9
go forth by the way of the n gate.... Eze 46:9
which looked toward the n............ Eze 46:19
of the land toward the n side........ Eze 47:15
the n northward, and the border of... Eze 47:17
And this is the n side............... Eze 47:17
From the n end to the coast of....... Eze 48:1
toward the n five and twenty......... Eze 48:10
the n side four thousand and five.... Eze 48:16
shall be toward the two hundred...... Eze 48:17
out of the city on the n side........ Eze 48:30
of the n to make an agreement .... Dan 11:6
the fortress of the king of the n.... Dan 11:7
more years than the king of the n.... Dan 11:8
him, even with the king of the n..... Dan 11:11
the king of the n shall return ...... Dan 11:13
So the king of the n shall come...... Dan 11:15
the king of the n shall come......... Dan 11:40
out of the n shall trouble him....... Dan 11:44
from the n even to the east, they.... Amos 8:12
out his hand against the n........... Zeph 2:13
and flee from the land of the n...... Zec 2:6
go forth into the n country.......... Zec 6:8
these that go toward the n........... Zec 6:8
my spirit in the n country.......... Zec 6:8
shall remove toward the n............ Zec 14:4
and from the west, and from the n.... Lk 13:29
toward the south west and n west .... Acts 27:12
on the n three gates................. Rev 21:13

NORTHERN
Shall iron break the n iron.......... Jer 15:12
far off from you the n army.......... Joel 2:20

NORTHWARD
from the place where thou art n ..... Gen 13:14
upon the side of the tabernacle n .... Ex 40:22
of the altar n before the LORD....... Lev 1:11
on the side of the tabernacle n...... Num 3:35
turn you n........................... Deut 2:3
lift up thine eyes westward, and .... Deut 3:27
even unto the borders of Ekron n .... Josh 13:3
from the valley of Achor, and so n... Josh 15:7
and the valley of the giants n ...... Josh 15:8
went out unto the side of Ekron n.... Josh 15:11
n it was Manasseh's, and the sea .... Josh 17:10
the side over against Arabah n....... Josh 18:18
to the side of Beth-hoglah n......... Josh 18:19
themselves together, and went n ..... Judg 12:1
situate n over against Michmash..... 1Sa 14:5
and his lot came out n............... 1Chr 26:14
n four a day, southward four a....... 1Chr 26:17

behold n at the gate of the altar.... Eze 8:5
an hundred cubits eastward and n ..... Eze 40:19
me out of the way of the gate n...... Eze 47:2
toward the east, and the north n..... Eze 47:17
the border of Damascus n............. Eze 48:1
three gates n; one gate.............. Eze 48:31
the ram pushing westward, and n...... Dan 8:4

NOSE
a lame, or he that hath a flat n..... Lev 21:18
I will put my hook in thy n.......... 2Kin 19:28
his n pierceth through snares........ Job 40:24
Canst thou put an hook into his n.... Job 41:2
the wringing of the n bringeth....... Prov 30:33
thy n is as the tower of Lebanon..... Song 7:4
and the smell of thy n like apples... Song 7:8
The rings, and n jewels.............. Is 3:21
will I put my hook in thy n.......... Is 37:29
These are a smoke in my n............ Is 65:5
they put the branch to their n....... Eze 8:17
they shall take away thy n........... Eze 23:25

NOSES
n have they, but they smell not...... Ps 115:6
stop the n of the passengers......... Eze 39:11

NOSTRILS
breathed into his n the breath of.... Gen 2:7
All in whose n was the breath of..... Gen 7:22
with the blast of thy n the .... Ex 15:8
until it come out at your n.......... Num 11:20
went up a smoke out of his n......... 2Sa 22:9
the blast of the breath of his n 2Sa 22:16
breath of his n are they consumed.... Job 4:9
and the spirit of God is in my n .... Job 27:3
the glory of his n is terrible....... Job 39:20
Out of his n goeth smoke, as out..... Job 41:20
went up a smoke out of his n......... Ps 18:8
the blast of the breath of thy n .... Ps 18:15
man, whose breath is in his n........ Is 2:22
The breath of our n, the anointed ... Lam 4:20
your camps to come up unto your n ... Amos 4:10

NOT See PREFACE.

NOTABLE
the goat had a horn between his...... Dan 8:5
for it came up four n ones toward ... Dan 8:8
And they had then a n prisoner....... Mt 27:16
great and n day of the Lord come .... Acts 2:20
for that indeed a n miracle hath .... Acts 4:16

NOTE
n it in a book, that it may be....... Is 30:8
who are of n among the apostles,..... Rom 16:7
n that man, and have no company...... 2Th 3:14

NOTED
is n in the scripture of truth....... Dan 10:21

NOTHING
now n will be restrained from........ Gen 11:6
only unto these men do n............. Gen 19:8
we have done unto thee n but good... Gen 26:29
here also have I done n that they ... Gen 40:15
there shall n die of all that is .... Ex 9:4
ye shall let n of it remain until ... Ex 12:10
Ye shall eat n leavened.............. Ex 12:20
he that gathered much had n over .... Ex 16:18
he shall go out free for n........... Ex 21:2
if he have n, then he shall be ...... Ex 22:3
There shall n cast their young,...... Ex 23:26
n that is made of the vine tree..... Num 6:4
there is n at all, beside this ...... Num 11:6
touch n of theirs, lest ye be....... Num 16:26
Balak the son of Zippor, Let n...... Num 22:16
thou hast lacked n................... Deut 2:7
shalt save alive n that breatheth... Deut 20:16
unto the damsel thou shalt do n..... Deut 22:26
because he hath n left him in the... Deut 28:55
he left n undone of all that the.... Josh 11:15
such as before knew n thereof....... Judg 3:2
This is n else save the sword of.... Judg 7:14
a kid, and he had n in his hand..... Judg 14:6
him every whit, and hid n from him.. 1Sa 3:18
my father will do n either great.... 1Sa 20:2
thy servant knew n of all this...... 1Sa 22:15
so that n was missed of all that ... 1Sa 25:21
wherefore she told him n, less or... 1Sa 25:36
there is n better for me than....... 1Sa 27:1
there was n lacking to them,........ 1Sa 30:19
But the poor man had n, save one ... 2Sa 12:3
God of that which doth cost me n ... 2Sa 24:24
they lacked n....................... 1Kin 4:27
There was n in the ark save the 1Kin 8:9
it was n accounted of in the days .. 1Kin 10:21
And he answered, N.................. 1Kin 11:22
and looked, and said, There is n ... 1Kin 18:43
n but that which is true in the..... 1Kin 22:16
earth n of the word of the LORD..... 2Kin 10:10
there was n in his house, nor in ... 2Kin 20:13
there is n among my treasures....... 2Kin 20:15
n shall be left, saith the LORD..... 2Kin 20:17
There was n in the ark save the 2Chr 5:10
there was n hid from Solomon 2Chr 9:2
it is n with thee to help,.......... 2Chr 14:11
I adjure thee that thou say n but .. 2Chr 18:15
Ye have n to do with us to build ... Neh 2:20
this is n else but sorrow of .... Neh 2:2
their peace, and found n to answer.. Neh 5:8
them, and will require n of them ... Neh 5:12
unto them for whom it is prepared .. Neh 8:10
wilderness, so that they lacked n .. Neh 9:21
she required n but what Hegai the .. Est 2:15

N

Yet all this availeth me *n* .... Est 5:13
unto him, There is in done for him .... Est 6:3
let *n* fail of all that thou hast .... Est 6:10
they go to *n*, and perish .... Job 6:18
are but of yesterday, and know *n* .... Job 8:9
a liar, and make my speech *n* worth .... Job 24:25
and hangeth the earth upon *n* .... Job 26:7
It proffiteth a man *n* that he .... Job 34:9
hast tried me, and shalt find *n* .... Ps 17:3
there is *n* hid from the heat .... Ps 19:6
and mine age is as *n* before thee .... Ps 39:5
he dieth he shall carry *n* away .... Ps 49:17
and *n* shall offend them .... Ps 119:165
there is *n* froward or perverse in .... Prov 8:8
she is simple, and knoweth *n* .... Prov 9:13
Treasures of wickedness profit *n* .... Prov 10:2
the sluggard desireth, and hath *n* .... Prov 13:4
maketh himself rich, yet hath *n* .... Prov 13:7
he beg in harvest, and have *n* .... Prov 20:4
If thou hast to pay, why should .... Prov 22:27
There is *n* better for a man, than .... Eccl 2:24
n can be put to it, nor any thing .... Eccl 3:14
I perceive that there is *n* better .... Eccl 3:22
a son, and there is *n* in his hand .... Eccl 5:14
shall take *n* of his labour, which .... Eccl 5:15
so that he wanteth *n* for his soul .... Eccl 6:2
that man should find *n* after him .... Eccl 7:14
and all her princes shall be *n* .... Is 34:12
there was *n* in his house, nor in .... Is 39:2
there is *n* among my treasures .... Is 39:4
n shall be left, saith the LORD .... Is 39:6
All nations before him are as *n* .... Is 40:17
are counted to him less than *n* .... Is 40:17
That bringeth the princes to *n* .... Is 40:23
they shall be as *n* .... Is 41:11
war against thee shall be as *n* .... Is 41:12
Behold, ye are of *n*, and your work .... Is 41:24
their works are *n* .... Is 41:29
image that is profitable for *n* .... Is 44:10
anger, lest thou bring me to *n* .... Jer 10:24
marred, it was profitable for *n* .... Jer 13:7
this girdle, which is good for *n* .... Jer 13:10
there is *n* too hard for thee .... Jer 32:17
they have done *n* of all that thou .... Jer 32:23
hide *n* from me .... Jer 38:14
poor of the people, which had *n* .... Jer 39:10
I will keep *n* back from you .... Jer 42:4
let *n* of her be left .... Jer 50:26
Is it *n* to you, all ye that pass .... Lam 1:12
their own spirit, and have seen *n* .... Eze 13:3
of the earth are reputed as *n* .... Dan 4:35
yea, and *n* shall escape them .... Joel 2:3
of his den, if he have taken *n* .... Amos 3:4
the earth, and have taken *n* at all .... Amos 3:5
Surely the Lord GOD will do *n* .... Amos 3:7
eyes in comparison of it as *n* .... Hag 2:3
it is theneforth good for *n* .... Mt 5:13
for there is *n* covered, that .... Mt 10:26
now three days, and have *n* to eat .... Mt 15:32
n shall be impossible unto you .... Mt 17:20
found *n* thereon, but leaves only, ... Mt 21:19
swear by the temple, it is *n* .... Mt 23:16
shall swear by the altar, it is *n* .... Mt 23:18
said unto him, Answerest thou *n* .... Mt 26:62
priests and elders, he answered *n* .... Mt 27:12
Have thou *n* to do with that just .... Mt 27:19
saw that he could prevail *n* .... Mt 27:24
him, See thou say *n* to any man .... Mk 1:44
For there is *n* hid, which shall .... Mk 4:22
was *n* bettered, but rather grew .... Mk 5:26
should take *n* for their journey .... Mk 6:8
for they have *n* to eat .... Mk 8:1
There is *n* from without a man, ... Mk 7:15
very great, and having *n* to eat .... Mk 8:1
me three days, and have *n* to eat .... Mk 8:2
This kind can come forth by *n* .... Mk 9:29
came to it, he found *n* but leaves .... Mk 11:13
Jesus, saying, Answerest thou *n* .... Mk 14:60
he held his peace, and answered *n* .... Mk 14:61
but he answered *n* .... Mk 15:3
again, saying, Answerest thou *n* .... Mk 15:4
But Jesus yet answered *n* .... Mk 15:5
For with God *n* shall be .... Lk 1:37
And in those days he did eat *n* .... Lk 4:2
all the night, and have taken *n* .... Lk 5:5
good, and lend, hoping for *n* again .... Lk 6:35
And when they had to pay .... Lk 7:42
For *n* is secret, that shall not .... Lk 8:17
Take *n* for your journey, neither .... Lk 9:3
n shall by any means hurt you .... Lk 10:19
I have *n* to set before him .... Lk 11:6
For there is *n* covered, that .... Lk 12:2
And they said, *N* .... Lk 22:35
but he answered *n* .... Lk 23:9
n worthy of death is done unto .... Lk 23:15
but this man hath done *n* amiss .... Lk 23:41
and said, A man can receive *n* .... Jn 3:27
thou hast *n* to draw with, and the .... Jn 4:11
you, The Son can do *n* of himself .... Jn 5:19
I can of mine own self do *n* .... Jn 5:30
that remain, that *n* be lost .... Jn 6:12
he hath given me I should lose *n* .... Jn 6:39
the flesh profiteth *n* .... Jn 6:63
boldly, and they say *n* unto him .... Jn 7:26
I am he, and that I do *n* of myself .... Jn 8:28
I honour myself, my honour is *n* .... Jn 8:54
were not of God, he could do *n* .... Jn 9:33
said unto them, Ye know *n* at all .... Jn 11:49
Perceive ye how ye prevail *n* .... Jn 12:19
world cometh, and hath *n* in me .... Jn 14:30

for without me ye can do *n* .... Jn 15:5
And in that day ye shall ask me *n* .... Jn 16:23
have ye asked *n* in my name .... Jn 16:24
and in secret have I said *n* .... Jn 18:20
and that night they caught *n* .... Jn 21:3
them, they could say *n* against it .... Acts 4:14
finding *n* how they might punish .... Acts 4:21
down, and go with them, doubting *n* ... Acts 10:20
for *n* common or unclean hath at .... Acts 11:8
bade me go with them, *n* doubting ...... Acts 11:12
there spent their time in *n* else .... Acts 17:21
to be quiet, and to do *n* rashly .... Acts 19:36
how I kept back *n* that was .... Acts 20:20
informed concerning thee, are *n* .... Acts 21:24
that we will eat *n* until we have .... Acts 23:14
but to have *n* laid to his charge .... Acts 23:29
had committed *n* worthy of death .... Acts 25:25
This man doeth *n* worthy of death .... Acts 26:31
continued fasting, having taken *n* .... Acts 27:33
committed *n* against the people .... Acts 28:17
that there is *n* unclean of itself .... Rom 14:14
will bring to *n* the understanding 1Cor 1:19
For I know *n* by myself 1Cor 4:4
Therefore judge *n* before the time 1Cor 4:5
Circumcision is *n*, and 1Cor 7:19
and uncircumcision is *n* 1Cor 7:19
he knoweth *n* yet as he ought to 1Cor 8:2
that an idol is *n* in the world 1Cor 8:4
the gospel, I have *n* to glory of 1Cor 9:16
and have not charity, I am *n* 1Cor 13:2
not charity, it proffiteth me *n* 1Cor 13:3
as having *n*, and yet possessing 2Cor 6:10
might receive damage by us in *n* 2Cor 7:9
that had gathered much had *n* over 2Cor 8:15
for in *n* am I behind the very 2Cor 12:11
chiefest apostles, though I be *n* 2Cor 12:11
For we can do *n* against the truth 2Cor 13:8
in conference added *n* to me .... Gal 2:6
differeth *n* from a servant, ... Gal 4:1
Christ shall profit you *n* .... Gal 5:2
to be something, when he is *n* .... Gal 6:3
that in *n* I shall be ashamed, but .... Phil 1:20
And in *n* terrified by your .... Phil 1:28
Let *n* be done through strife or .... Phil 2:3
Be careful for *n* .... Phil 4:6
and that ye may have lack of *n* 1Th 4:12
n to be refused, if it be 1Ti 4:4
another, doing *n* by partiality 1Ti 5:21
He is proud, knowing *n*, but 1Ti 6:4
For we brought *n* into this world, ... 1Ti 6:7
it is certain we can carry *n* out 1Ti 6:7
defiled and unbelieving is *n* pure .... Titus 1:15
that *n* be wanting unto them .... Titus 3:13
But without thy mind would I do *n* ... Philem 14
he left *n* that is not put under .... Heb 2:8
spake *n* concerning priesthood .... Heb 7:14
For the law made *n* perfect .... Heb 7:19
be perfect, and entire, wanting *n* .... Jas 1:4
let him ask in faith, *n* wavering .... Jas 1:6
forth, taking *n* of the Gentiles 3Jn 7
with goods, and have need of *n* .... Rev 3:17

NOTICE

And all the people took *n* of it 2Sa 3:36
bounty, whereof ye had *n* before 2Cor 9:5

NOTWITHSTANDING

N they hearkened not unto Moses. .... Ex 16:20
N, if he continue a day or two, ... Ex 21:21
N the cities of the Levites, and .... Lev 25:32
N no devoted thing, that a man .... Lev 27:28
N the children of Korah died not .... Num 26:11
N the land shall be divided by .... Num 26:55
N ye would not go up, but .... Deut 1:26
N thou mayest kill and eat flesh .... Deut 12:15
N, if the land of your possession .... Josh 22:19
n the journey that thou takest .... Judg 4:9
n yet Jotham the youngest son of .... Judg 9:5
N they hearkened not unto the 1Sa 2:25
n, if there be in the iniquity, ... 1Sa 20:8
n the princes of the Philistines 1Sa 29:9
the king's word prevailed 2Sa 24:4
N in thy days I will not do it 1Kin 11:12
N they would not hear, but 2Kin 17:14
N the LORD turned not from the 2Kin 23:26
N thou shalt not build the house 2Chr 6:9
N Hezekiah humbled himself for 2Chr 32:26
n I have spoken unto you, rising .... Jer 35:14
N the children rebelled against .... Eze 20:21
N the land shall be desolate .... Mic 7:13
n, being warned of God in a dream .... Mt 2:22
n he that is least in the kingdom. .... Mt 11:11
N, lest we should offend them, go .... Mt 17:27
N be ye sure of this, that the .... Lk 10:11
N in this rejoice not, that the .... Lk 10:20
N it pleased Silas to abide there. .... Acts 15:34
N, that I be not further tedious .... Acts 24:4
n, every way, whether in pretence .... Phil 1:18
N ye have well done, that ye did .... Phil 4:14
N she shall be saved in 1Ti 2:15
N the Lord stood with me, and 2Ti 4:17
n ye give them not those things. .... Jas 2:16
N I have a few things against .... Rev 2:20

NOUGHT

thou therefore serve me for *n* .... Gen 29:15
there shall cleave to *n* of the .... Deut 13:17
brother, and thou givest him *n* .... Deut 15:9
destroy you, and to bring you to *n* ...... Deut 28:63
had brought their counsel to *n* .... Neh 4:15
and said, Doth Job fear God for *n* .... Job 1:9
of the wicked shall come to *n* .... Job 8:22

the mountain falling cometh to *n* .... Job 14:18
a pledge from thy brother for *n* .... Job 22:6
the counsel of the heathen to *n* .... Ps 33:10
Thou sellest thy people for *n* .... Ps 44:12
ye have set at *n* all my counsel .... Prov 1:25
together, and it shall come to *n* .... Is 8:10
the terrible one is brought to *n* .... Is 29:20
aside the just for a thing of *n* .... Is 29:21
be as nothing, and as a thing of *n* .... Is 41:12
are of nothing, and your work of *n* ...... Is 41:24
I have spent my strength for *n* .... Is 49:4
Ye have sold yourselves for *n* .... Is 52:3
my people is taken away for *n* .... Is 52:5
and divination, and a thing of *n* .... Jer 14:14
and Beth-el shall come to *n* .... Amos 5:5
Ye which rejoice in a thing of *n* .... Amos 6:13
that would shut the doors for *n* .... Mal 1:10
kindle fire on mine altar for *n* .... Mal 1:10
many things, and be set at *n* .... Mk 9:12
with his men of war set him at *n* .... Lk 23:11
was set at *n* of you builders .... Acts 4:11
were scattered, and brought to *n* .... Acts 5:36
work be of men, it will come to *n* .... Acts 5:38
craft is in danger to be set at *n* .... Acts 19:27
dost thou set at *n* thy brother .... Rom 14:10
to bring to *n* things that are 1Cor 1:28
of this world, that come to *n* 1Cor 2:6
did we eat any man's bread for *n* 2Th 3:8
hour so great riches is come to *n* .... Rev 18:17

NOURISH

And there will I *n* thee .... Gen 45:11
I will *n* you, and your little ones .... Gen 50:21
that a man shall *n* a young cow .... Is 7:21
neither do I *n* up young men, ... Is 23:4
an ash, and the rain doth *n* it .... Is 44:14

NOURISHED

Joseph *n* his father, and his .... Gen 47:12
lamb, which he had bought and *n* up 2Sa 12:3
the LORD hath spoken, I have *n* .... Is 1:2
she *n* her whelps among young .... Eze 19:2
n up in his father's house three .... Acts 7:20
him up, and *n* him for her own son ..... Acts 7:21
was *n* by the king's country. .... Acts 12:20
n up in the words of faith and of 1Ti 4:6
ye have *n* your hearts, as in a .... Jas 5:5
place, where she is *n* for a time .... Rev 12:14

NOURISHER

thy life, and a *n* of thine old age .... Ruth 4:15

NOURISHETH

but *n* and cherisheth it, even as .... Eph 5:29

NOURISHING

so *n* them three years, that at .... Dan 1:5

NOURISHMENT

and bands having *n* ministered .... Col 2:19

NOVICE

Not a *n*, lest being lifted up 1Ti 3:6

NOW See PREFACE.

NUMBER

so that if a man can *n* the dust .... Gen 13:16
stars, if thou be able to *n* them .... Gen 15:5
and being few in *n*, they shall .... Gen 34:30
for it was without *n* .... Gen 41:49
according to the *n* of the souls .... Ex 12:4
to the *n* of your persons .... Ex 16:16
the *n* of thy days I will fulfil .... Ex 23:26
children of Israel after their *n* .... Ex 30:12
then he shall *n* to himself seven .... Lev 15:13
then she shall *n* to herself seven .... Lev 15:28
sabbath shall ye *n* fifty days. .... Lev 23:16
thou shalt *n* seven sabbaths of .... Lev 25:8
According to the *n* of years after .... Lev 25:15
according unto the *n* of years of .... Lev 25:15
for according to the *n* of the .... Lev 25:16
be according unto the *n* of years .... Lev 25:50
your cattle, and make you few in *n*, ... Lev 26:22
with the *n* of their names, every .... Num 1:2
Aaron shall *n* them by their .... Num 1:3
according to the *n* of the names .... Num 1:18
according to the *n* of the names .... Num 1:20
according to the *n* of the names .... Num 1:22
according to the *n* of the names .... Num 1:24
according to the *n* of the names .... Num 1:26
according to the *n* of the names .... Num 1:28
according to the *n* of the names .... Num 1:30
according to the *n* of the names .... Num 1:32
according to the *n* of the names .... Num 1:34
according to the *n* of the names .... Num 1:36
according to the *n* of the names .... Num 1:38
according to the *n* of the names .... Num 1:40
according to the *n* of the names .... Num 1:42
shalt not *n* the tribe of Levi .... Num 1:49
N the children of Levi after the .... Num 3:15
old and upward shalt thou *n* them .... Num 3:15
to the *n* of all the males .... Num 3:22
In the *n* of all the males, from .... Num 3:28
to the *n* of all the males .... Num 3:34
N all the firstborn of the males .... Num 3:40
take the *n* of their names .... Num 3:40
firstborn males by the *n* of names .... Num 3:43
wherewith the odd *n* of them is to ...... Num 3:48
fifty years old shalt thou *n* them. .... Num 4:23
thou shalt *n* them after their .... Num 4:29
fifty years old shalt thou *n* them. .... Num 4:30
Aaron did *n* according to the .... Num 4:37
Aaron did *n* according to the .... Num 4:41

of you, according to your whole n.	Num 14:29
After the n of the days in which	Num 14:34
According to the n that ye shall	Num 15:12
to every one according to their n	Num 15:12
the n of the fourth part of	Num 23:10
according to the n of names	Num 26:53
shall be according to their n	Num 29:18
shall be according to their n	Num 29:21
shall be according to their n	Num 29:24
shall be according to their n	Num 29:27
shall be according to their n	Num 29:30
shall be according to their n	Num 29:33
shall be according to their n	Num 29:37
was in n three hundred thousand	Num 31:36
left few in n among the heathen	Deut 4:27
ye were more in n than any people	Deut 7:7
weeks shalt thou n unto thee	Deut 16:9
begin to n the seven weeks from	Deut 16:9
to his fault, by a certain n	Deut 25:2
And ye shall be left few in n	Deut 28:62
the n of the children of Israel	Deut 32:8
according unto the n of the	Josh 4:5
according to the n of the lords	Josh 4:8
and their camels were without n	Judg 6:5
the n of them that lapped,	Judg 7:6
and their camels were without n	Judg 7:12
them wives, according to their n	Judg 21:23
according to the n of the lords	1Sa 6:4
according to the n of all the	1Sa 6:18
N now, and see who is gone from us	1Sa 14:17
went over by n twelve of Benjamin	2Sa 2:15
six foes, four and twenty in n	2Sa 21:20
to say, Go, n Israel and Judah	2Sa 24:1
n ye the people, that I may know	2Sa 24:2
I may know the n of the people	2Sa 24:2
to n the people of Israel	2Sa 24:4
the n of the people unto the king	2Sa 24:9
according to the n of the tribes	1Kin 18:31
n thee an army, like the army	1Kin 20:25
whose n was in the days of David	1Chr 7:2
the n of them, after their	1Chr 7:9
the n throughout the genealogy of	1Chr 7:40
this is the n of the mighty men	1Chr 11:11
and provoked David to n Israel	1Chr 21:1
n Israel from Beer-sheba even to	1Chr 21:2
bring the n of them to me, that I	1Chr 21:2
of the n of the people unto David	1Chr 21:5
brass, and the iron, there is no n	1Chr 22:16
their n by their polls, man by	1Chr 23:3
by n of names by their polls	1Chr 23:24
moons, and on the set feasts, by n	1Chr 23:31
the n of the workmen according to	1Chr 25:1
So the n of them, with	1Chr 25:7
children of Israel after their n	1Chr 27:1
But David took not the n of them	1Chr 27:23
the son of Zeruiah began to n	1Chr 27:24
neither was the n put in the	1Chr 27:24
the people were without n that	2Chr 12:3
according to the n of their	2Chr 26:11
The whole n of the chief of the	2Chr 26:12
the n of the burnt offerings	2Chr 29:32
a great n of priests sanctified	2Chr 30:24
to the n of thirty thousand, and	2Chr 35:7
And this is the n of them	Ezr 1:9
The n of the men of the people of	Ezr 2:2
the daily burnt offerings by n	Ezr 3:4
according to the n of the tribes	Ezr 6:17
By n and by weight of every one	Ezr 8:34
The n, I say, of the men of the	Neh 7:7
On that day the n of those that	Est 9:11
according to the n of them all	Job 1:5
not come into the n of the months	Job 3:6
marvellous things without n	Job 5:9
yea, and wonders without n	Job 9:10
the n of his months are with thee	Job 14:5
the n of years is hidden to the	Job 15:20
when the n of his months is cut	Job 21:21
Is there any n of his armies	Job 25:3
unto him the n of my steps	Job 31:37
in pieces mighty men without n	Job 34:24
neither can the n of his years be	Job 36:26
or because the n of thy days is	Job 38:21
Who can n the clouds in wisdom	Job 38:37
Canst thou n the months that they	Job 39:2
So teach us to n our days	Ps 90:12
When they were but a few men in n	Ps 105:12
caterpillers, and that without n	Ps 105:34
they are more in n than the sand	Ps 139:18
He telleth the n of the stars	Ps 147:4
concubines, and virgins without n	Song 6:8
the residue of the n of archers	Is 21:17
that bringeth out their host by n	Is 40:26
the drink offering unto that n	Is 65:11
will I n you to the sword	Is 65:12
for according to the n of thy	Jer 2:28
have forgotten me days without n	Jer 2:32
For according to the n of thy	Jer 11:13
according to the n of the streets	Jer 11:13
Yet a small n that escape the	Jer 44:28
according to the n of the days	Eze 4:4
according to the n of the days	Eze 4:5
according to the n of the days	Eze 4:9
also take thereof a few in n	Eze 5:3
by books the n of the years	Dan 9:2
Yet the n of the children of	Hos 1:10
my land, strong, and without n	Joel 1:6
slain, and a great n of carcases	Nah 3:3
a great n of people, blind	Mk 10:46
being of the n of the twelve	Lk 22:3
down, in n about five thousand	Jn 6:10

(the n of names together were	Acts 1:15
the n of the men was about five	Acts 4:4
to whom a n of men, about four	Acts 5:36
when the n of the disciples was	Acts 6:1
the n of the disciples multiplied	Acts 6:7
a great n believed, and turned	Acts 11:21
faith, and increased in n daily	Acts 16:5
Though the n of the children of	Rom 9:27
dare not make ourselves of the n	2Cor 10:12
the n under threescore years old	1Ti 5:9
the n of them was ten thousand	Rev 5:11
I heard the n of them which were	Rev 7:4
multitude, which no man could n	Rev 7:9
the n of the army of the horsemen	Rev 9:16
and I heard the n of them	Rev 9:16
the beast, or the n of his name	Rev 13:17
count the n of the beast	Rev 13:18
for it is the n of a man	Rev 13:18
his n is six hundred threescore	Rev 13:18
over the n of his name, stand on	Rev 15:2
the n of whom is as the sand of	Rev 20:8

NUMBERED

then shall thy seed also be n	Gen 13:16
it shall not be n for multitude	Gen 16:10
which cannot be n for multitude	Gen 32:12
passeth among them that are n	Ex 30:13
passeth among them that are n	Ex 30:14
were n of the congregation was an	Ex 38:26
for every one that went to be n	Ex 38:26
so he n them in the wilderness of	Num 1:19
Those that were n of them	Num 1:21
those that were n of them	Num 1:22
Those that were n of them	Num 1:23
Those that were n of them	Num 1:24
Those that were n of them	Num 1:25
Those that were n of them	Num 1:27
Those that were n of them	Num 1:29
Those that were n of them	Num 1:31
Those that were n of them	Num 1:33
Those that were n of them	Num 1:35
Those that were n of them	Num 1:37
Those that were n of them	Num 1:39
Those that were n of them	Num 1:41
Those that were n of them	Num 1:43
n, which Moses and Aaron	Num 1:44
were n of the children of Israel	Num 1:45
Even all they that were n were	Num 1:46
fathers were not n among them	Num 1:47
and those that were n of them	Num 2:4
and those that were n thereof	Num 2:6
and those that were n thereof	Num 2:8
All that were n in the camp of	Num 2:9
and those that were n thereof	Num 2:11
and those that were n of them	Num 2:13
and those that were n of them	Num 2:15
All that were n in the camp of	Num 2:16
and those that were n of them	Num 2:19
and those that were n of them	Num 2:21
and those that were n of them	Num 2:23
All that were n of the camp of	Num 2:24
and those that were n thereof	Num 2:26
and those that were n of them	Num 2:28
and those that were n of them	Num 2:30
All they that were n in the camp	Num 2:31
These are those which were n of	Num 2:32
all those that were n of the	Num 2:32
But the Levites were not n among	Num 2:33
Moses n them according to the	Num 3:16
Those that were n of them	Num 3:22
even those that were n of them	Num 3:22
And those that were n of them	Num 3:34
All that were n of the Levites,	Num 3:39
Aaron n at the commandment of the	Num 3:39
Moses n, as the LORD	Num 3:42
those that were n of them	Num 3:43
n the sons of the Kohathites	Num 4:34
those that were n of them by	Num 4:36
were n of the families of the	Num 4:37
those that were n of the sons of	Num 4:38
Even those that were n of them	Num 4:40
These are they that were n of the	Num 4:41
those that were n of the families	Num 4:42
Even those that were n of them	Num 4:44
These be those that were n of the	Num 4:45
According to the word of	Num 4:45
those that were n of the Levites	Num 4:46
and Aaron and the chief of Israel n	Num 4:46
Even those that were n of them	Num 4:48
they were n by the hand of Moses	Num 4:49
thus were they n of him, as the	Num 4:49
and were over them that were n	Num 7:2
and all that were n of you	Num 14:29
they that were n of them were	Num 26:7
to those that were n of them	Num 26:18
to those that were n of them	Num 26:22
to those that were n of them	Num 26:25
to those that were n of them	Num 26:27
and those that were n of them	Num 26:34
those that were n of them	Num 26:37
they that were n of them were	Num 26:41
to those that were n of them	Num 26:43
to those that were n of them	Num 26:47
they that were n of them were	Num 26:50
These were the n of the children	Num 26:51
to those that were n of him	Num 26:54
these are they that were n of the	Num 26:57
those that were n of them were	Num 26:62
for they were not n among the	Num 26:62
are they that were n by Moses	Num 26:63
who n the children of Israel in	Num 26:63
whom Moses and Aaron the priest n	Num 26:64

when they n the children of	Num 26:64
n the people, and went up, he and	Josh 8:10
the children of Benjamin were	Judg 20:15
which were n seven hundred chosen	Judg 20:15
were n four hundred thousand men	Judg 20:17
For the people were n, and, behold	Judg 21:9
when he n them in Bezek, the	1Sa 11:8
Saul n the people that were	1Sa 13:15
And when they had n, behold,	1Sa 14:17
n them in Telaim, two hundred	1Sa 15:4
David n the people that were with	2Sa 18:1
after that he had n the people	2Sa 24:10
that cannot be n nor counted for	1Kin 3:8
not be told nor n for multitude	1Kin 8:5
Then he n the young men of the	1Kin 20:15
after them he n all the people,	1Kin 20:15
that Ben-hadad n the Syrians	1Kin 20:26
And the children of Israel were n	1Kin 20:27
the same time, and n all Israel	2Kin 3:6
that commanded the people to be n	1Chr 21:17
Now the Levites were n from the	1Chr 23:3
were n from twenty years old	1Chr 23:27
Solomon n all the strangers that	2Chr 2:17
David his father had n them	2Chr 2:17
not be told nor n for multitude	2Chr 5:6
he n them from twenty years old	2Chr 25:5
n them unto Sheshbazzar, the	Ezr 1:8
them, they are more than can be n	Ps 40:5
that which is wanting cannot be n	Eccl 1:15
ye have n the houses of Jerusalem	Is 22:10
he was n with the transgressors	Is 53:12
As the host of heaven cannot be n	Jer 33:22
God hath n thy kingdom, and	Dan 5:26
which cannot be measured nor n	Hos 1:10
very hairs of your head are all n	Mt 10:30
he was n with the transgressors	Mk 15:28
very hairs of your head are all n	Lk 12:7
For he was n with us, and had	Acts 1:17
he was n with the eleven apostles	Acts 1:26

NUMBEREST

unto the LORD, when thou n them	Ex 30:12
among them, when thou n them	Ex 30:12
For now thou n my steps	Job 14:16

NUMBERING

sea, very much, until he left n	Gen 41:49
after the n wherewith David his	2Chr 2:17

NUMBERS

these are the n of the bands that	1Chr 12:23
these are the n of them according	2Chr 17:14
for I know not the n thereof	Ps 71:15

NUN (nun) See NON. Father of Joshua.

his servant Joshua, the son of N	Ex 33:11
And Joshua the son of N, the	Num 11:28
of Ephraim, Oshea the son of N	Num 13:8
Oshea the son of N Jehoshua	Num 13:16
And Joshua the son of N, and Caleb,	Num 14:6
Jephunneh, and Joshua the son of N	Num 14:30
But Joshua the son of N, and Caleb,	Num 14:38
Jephunneh, and Joshua the son of N	Num 26:65
Take thee Joshua the son of N,	Num 27:18
Kenezite, and Joshua the son of N	Num 32:12
priest, and Joshua the son of N	Num 32:28
priest, and Joshua the son of N	Num 34:17
But Joshua the son of N, which	Deut 1:38
gave Joshua the son of N a charge	Deut 31:23
he, and Hoshea the son of N	Deut 32:44
Joshua the son of N was full of	Deut 34:9
spake unto Joshua the son of N	Josh 1:1
Joshua the son of N sent out of	Josh 2:1
and came to Joshua the son of N	Josh 2:23
Joshua the son of N called the	Josh 6:6
priest, and Joshua the son of N	Josh 14:1
and before Joshua the son of N	Josh 17:4
to Joshua the son of N among them	Josh 19:49
priest, and Joshua the son of N	Josh 19:51
and unto Joshua the son of N	Josh 21:1
things, that Joshua the son of N	Josh 24:29
And Joshua the son of N, the	Judg 2:8
he spake by Joshua the son of N	1Kin 16:34
of N unto that day had not the	Neh 8:17

NURSE

Rebekah their sister, and her n	Gen 24:59
But Deborah Rebekah's n died	Gen 35:8
call to thee a n of the Hebrew	Ex 2:7
that she may n the child for thee	Ex 2:7
n it for me, and I will give thee	Ex 2:9
in her bosom, and became n unto it	Ruth 4:16
his n took him up, and fled	2Sa 4:4
they hid him, even him and his n	2Kin 11:2
put him and his n in a bedchamber	2Chr 22:11
even as a n cherisheth her	1Th 2:7

NURSED

the woman took the child, and n it	Ex 2:9
daughters shall be n at thy side	Is 60:4

NURSING

as a n father beareth the sucking	Num 11:12
And kings shall be thy n fathers	Is 49:23
and their queens thy n mothers	Is 49:23

NURTURE

but bring them up in the n	Eph 6:4

NUTS

little honey, spices, and myrrh, n	Gen 43:11
I went down into the garden of n	Song 6:11

NYMPHA See NYMPHAS.

NYMPHAS (nim'-fas) A Christian at Colosse.
which are in Laodicea, and N............ Col 4:15

O

O See PREFACE.

OAK

under the o which was by Shechem..... Gen 35:4
buried beneath Beth-el under an o....... Gen 35:8
and set it up there under an o............. Josh 24:26
sat under an o which was............... Judg 6:11
it out unto him under the o............ Judg 6:19
the thick boughs of a great o........... 2Sa 18:9
and his head caught hold of the o...... 2Sa 18:9
I saw Absalom hanged in an o............ 2Sa 18:10
yet alive in the midst of the o......... 2Sa 18:14
and found him sitting under an o....... 1Kin 13:14
their bones under the o in Jabesh...... 1Chr 10:12
be as an o whose leaf fadeth............ Is 1:30
as a teil tree, and as an o............. Is 6:13
and taketh the cypress and the o....... Is 44:14
tree, and under every thick o.......... Eze 6:13

OAKS

of the o which ye have desired......... Is 1:29
up, and upon all the o of Bashan....... Is 2:13
Of the o of Bashan have they made..... Eze 27:6
incense upon the hills, under.......... Hos 4:13
cedars, and he was strong as the o..... Amos 2:9
howl, O ye o of Bashan................. Zec 11:2

OAR

And all that handle the o, the......... Eze 27:29

OARS

wherein shall go no galley with o..... Is 33:21
of Bashan have they made thine o...... Eze 27:6

OATH

shalt be clear from this my o......... Gen 24:8
thou be clear from this my o.......... Gen 24:41
thou shalt be clear from my o......... Gen 24:41
I will perform the o which I......... Gen 26:3
Let there be now an o betwixt us...... Gen 26:28
Joseph took an o of the children...... Gen 50:25
Then shall an o of the LORD be........ Ex 22:11
a man shall pronounce with an o....... Lev 5:4
priest shall charge her by an o....... Num 5:19
the woman with an o of cursing........ Num 5:21
an o among thy people, when........... Num 5:21
or swear an o to bind his soul........ Num 30:2
her soul by a bond with an o.......... Num 30:10
every binding o to afflict the....... Num 30:13
because he would keep the o which..... Deut 7:8
the LORD thy God, and into his o...... Deut 29:12
do I make this covenant and this o.... Deut 29:14
o which thou hast made us swear....... Josh 2:17
o which thou hast made us to.......... Josh 2:20
because of the o which we sware....... Josh 9:20
For they had made a great o........... Judg 21:5
for the people feared the o.......... 1Sa 14:26
charged the people with the o......... 1Sa 14:27
charged the people with an o.......... 1Sa 14:28
LORD's o that was between them........ 2Sa 21:7
thou not kept the o of the LORD....... 1Kin 2:43
be laid upon him to cause............ 1Kin 8:31
the o come before thine altar in..... 1Kin 8:31
he took an o of the kingdom and....... 1Kin 18:10
took an o of them in the house of.... 2Kin 11:4
Abraham, and of his o unto Isaac...... 1Chr 16:16
an o be laid upon him to make him..... 2Chr 6:22
the o come before thine altar in..... 2Chr 6:22
And all Judah rejoiced at the o....... 2Chr 15:15
the priests, and took an o of them.... Neh 5:12
into a curse, and into an o........... Neh 10:29
with Abraham, and his o unto Isaac.... Ps 105:9
and that in regard of the o of God.... Eccl 8:2
sweareth, as he that feareth an o..... Eccl 9:2
That I may perform the o which I...... Jer 11:5
which hast despised the o in.......... Eze 16:59
him, and hath taken an o of him....... Eze 17:13
whose o he despised, and whose........ Eze 17:16
Seeing he despised the o by........... Eze 17:18
surely mine o that he hath............ Eze 17:19
the o that is written in the law..... Dan 9:11
and love no false o................... Zec 8:17
an o to give her whatsoever she....... Mt 14:7
And again he denied with an o......... Mt 26:72
The o which he sware to our.......... Lk 1:73
God hath sworn with an o to him....... Acts 2:30
have bound themselves with an o....... Acts 23:21
an o for confirmation is to them..... Heb 6:16
his counsel, confirmed it by an o..... Heb 6:17
without an o he was made priest....... Heb 7:20
priests were made without an o....... Heb 7:21
but this with an o by him that....... Heb 7:21
but the word of the o, which was..... Heb 7:28
the earth, neither by any other...... Jas 5:12

OATH'S

nevertheless for the o sake........... Mt 14:9
yet for his o sake, and for their..... Mk 6:26

OATHS

sight, to them that have sworn o...... Eze 21:23
according to the o of the tribes...... Hab 3:9
perform unto the Lord thine o......... Mt 5:33

OBADIAH (o-ba-di'-ah)
1. An officer in Ahab's court.
And Ahab called O, which was the...... 1Kin 18:3
(Now O feared the LORD greatly........ 1Kin 18:3
that O took an hundred prophets....... 1Kin 18:4
And Ahab said unto O, Go into the..... 1Kin 18:5
O went another way by himself......... 1Kin 18:6
as O was in the way, behold,.......... 1Kin 18:7
So O went to meet Ahab, and told..... 1Kin 18:16
2. A descendant of David.
the sons of Arnan, the sons of........ 1Chr 3:21
3. A descendant of Tola.
Michael, and O, and Joel, Ishiah,..... 1Chr 7:3
4. Son of Azel.
and Ishmael, and Sheariah, and O...... 1Chr 8:38
and Ishmael, and Sheariah, and O...... 1Chr 9:44
5. Son of Shemaiah.
O the son of Shemaiah, the son of..... 1Chr 9:16
6. A warrior in David's army.
O the second, Eliab the third,........ 1Chr 12:9
7. A prince of Zebulun.
Of Zebulun, Ishmaiah the son of....... 1Chr 27:19
8. A prince of Judah.
even to Ben-hail, and to O........... 2Chr 17:7
9. A Levite in Josiah's time.
of them were Jahath and O, the........ 2Chr 34:12
10. A clan leader with Ezra.
O the son of Jehiel, and with him..... Ezr 8:9
11. A priest who renewed the covenant.
Harim, Meremoth, O,.................. Neh 10:5
12. A Temple gatekeeper.
Mattaniah, and Bakbukiah, O.......... Neh 12:25
13. A prophet.
The vision of O...................... Obad 1

OBAL (o'-bal) *A son of Joktan.*
And O, and Abimael, and Sheba,........ Gen 10:28

OBED (o'-bed) See OBED-EDOM.
1. Father of Jesse.
and they called his name O............ Ruth 4:17
begat Boaz, and Boaz begat O.......... Ruth 4:21
O begat Jesse, and Jesse begat........ Ruth 4:22
And Boaz begat O, and O begat......... 1Chr 2:12
and Booz begat O of Ruth............. Mt 1:5
and O begat Jesse..................... Mt 1:5
of Jesse, which was the son of O...... Lk 3:32
2. A descendant of Judah.
begat Ephlal, and Ephlal begat O..... 1Chr 2:37
O begat Jehu, and Jehu begat......... 1Chr 2:38
3. A "mighty man" of David.
Eliel, and O, and Jasiel the......... 1Chr 11:47
4. A servant's servant.
Othni, and Rephael, and O, Elzabad,... 1Chr 26:7
5. Father of Azariah.
and Azariah the son of O............. 2Chr 23:1

OBED-EDOM (o'-bed-e'-dom)
1. A Levite.
into the house of O the Gittite...... 2Sa 6:10
of O the Gittite three months........ 2Sa 6:11
and the LORD blessed O, and all his... 2Sa 6:11
LORD hath blessed the house of O..... 2Sa 6:12
of O into the city of David with..... 2Sa 6:12
into the house of O the Gittite...... 1Chr 13:13
of O in his house three months....... 1Chr 13:14
the LORD blessed the house of O...... 1Chr 13:14
and O and Jehiah were doorkeepers.... 1Chr 15:24
out of the house of O with joy....... 1Chr 15:25
2. A priest who ministered before the Ark.
and Elipheleh, and Mikneiah, and O.... 1Chr 15:18
and Elipheleh, and Mikneiah, and O.... 1Chr 15:21
Moreover the sons of O were.......... 1Chr 26:4
All these of the sons of O........... 1Chr 26:8
were threescore and two of O......... 1Chr 26:8
To O southward....................... 1Chr 26:15
3. Another priest who relocated the Ark.
and Eliab, and Benaiah, and O........ 1Chr 16:5
O with their brethren, threescore.... 1Chr 16:38
4. Son of Jeduthun.
O also the son of Jeduthun and....... 1Chr 16:38
5. A Temple servant.
found in the house of God with O..... 2Chr 25:24

OBEDIENCE

for o to the faith among all......... Rom 1:5
so by the o of one shall many be..... Rom 5:19
or of o unto righteousness........... Rom 6:16
For your o is come abroad unto....... Rom 16:19
to all nations for the o of faith.... Rom 16:26
they are commanded to be under o..... 1Cor 14:34
he remembereth the o of you all...... 2Cor 7:15
every thought to the o of Christ..... 2Cor 10:5
when your o is fulfilled............. 2Cor 10:6
in thy o I wrote unto thee........... Philem 21
of the Spirit, unto o and........... Heb 5:8
.... 1Pet 1:2

OBEDIENT

hath said will we do, and be o....... Ex 24:7
the children of Israel may be o...... Num 27:20
shalt be o unto his voice........... Deut 4:30
because ye would not be o unto....... Deut 8:20
hear, they shall be o unto me....... 2Sa 22:45
is a wise reprover upon an o ear..... Prov 25:12
If ye be willing and o, ye shall..... Is 1:19
neither were they o unto his law..... Is 42:24
the priests were o to the faith..... Acts 6:7
by me, to make the Gentiles o....... Rom 15:18
whether ye be o in all things....... 2Cor 2:9
be o to them that are your.......... Eph 6:5
became o unto death, even the....... Phil 2:8

o to their own husbands, that the.... Titus 2:5
Exhort servants to be o unto......... Titus 2:9
As o children, not fashioning....... 1Pet 1:14

OBEISANCE

about, and made o to my sheaf........ Gen 37:7
and the eleven stars made o to me.... Gen 37:9
bowed down their heads, and made o... Gen 43:28
meet his father in law, and did o.... Ex 18:7
he fell to the earth, and did o...... 2Sa 1:2
her face to the ground, and did o.... 2Sa 14:4
man came nigh to him to do him o..... 2Sa 15:5
bowed, and did o unto the king....... 1Kin 1:16
of Judah, and made o to the king..... 2Chr 24:17

OBEY

o my voice according to that......... Gen 27:8
only o my voice, and go fetch me..... Gen 27:13
Now therefore, my son, o my voice.... Gen 27:43
that I should o his voice to let..... Ex 5:2
if ye will o my voice indeed, and.... Ex 19:5
o his voice, provoke him not........ Ex 23:21
if thou shalt indeed o his voice.... Ex 23:22
if ye o the commandments of the..... Deut 11:27
if ye will not o the commandments... Deut 11:28
o his voice, and ye shall serve..... Deut 13:4
which will not o the voice of his... Deut 21:18
he will not o our voice............. Deut 21:20
Thou shalt therefore o the voice.... Deut 27:10
because thou wouldest not o the..... Deut 28:62
shalt o his voice according to..... Deut 30:2
o the voice of the LORD, and do..... Deut 30:8
and that thou mayest o his voice.... Deut 30:20
we serve, and his voice will we o... Josh 24:24
refused to o the voice of Samuel.... 1Sa 8:19
o his voice, and not rebel against.. 1Sa 12:14
But if ye will not o the voice of... 1Sa 12:15
thou not o the voice of the LORD.... 1Sa 15:19
to o is better than sacrifice, and.. 1Sa 15:22
And refused to o, neither were...... Neh 9:17
If they o and serve him, they....... Job 36:11
But if they o not, they shall...... Job 36:12
they hear of me, they shall o me.... Ps 18:44
and despiseth to o his mother....... Prov 30:17
children of Ammon shall o them...... Is 11:14
O my voice, and I will be your God... Jer 7:23
O my voice, and do them, according.. Jer 11:4
and protesting, saying, O my voice.. Jer 11:7
But if they will not o, I will...... Jer 12:17
that it o not my voice, then I...... Jer 18:10
o the voice of the LORD your God.... Jer 26:13
but o their father's commandment.... Jer 35:14
O, I beseech thee, the voice of..... Jer 38:20
we will o the voice of the LORD..... Jer 42:6
when we o the voice of the LORD..... Jer 42:6
neither o the voice of the LORD..... Jer 42:13
dominions shall serve and o him..... Dan 7:27
that they might not o thy voice..... Dan 9:11
If ye will diligently o thy voice... Zec 6:15
even the winds and the sea o him.... Mk 8:27
unclean spirits, and they do o him.. Mk 1:27
even the wind and the sea o him..... Mk 4:41
the winds and water, and they o him. Lk 8:25
and it should o you................. Lk 17:6
We ought to o God rather than men... Acts 5:29
God hath given to them that o him... Acts 5:32
To whom our fathers would not o..... Acts 7:39
do not o the truth................. Rom 2:8
but o unrighteousness.............. Rom 2:8
that ye should o it in the lusts.... Rom 6:12
ye yield yourselves servants to o... Rom 6:16
his servants ye are to whom ye o.... Rom 6:16
that ye should not o the truth..... Gal 3:1
that ye should not o the truth..... Gal 5:7
o your parents in the Lord......... Eph 6:1
o your parents in all things....... Col 3:20
o in all things your masters....... Col 3:22
that o not the gospel of our Lord... 2Th 1:8
if any man o not our word by this... 2Th 3:14
to o magistrates, to be ready to... Titus 3:1
unto all them that o him........... Heb 5:9
O them that have the rule over..... Heb 13:17
mouths, that they may o us.......... Jas 3:3
if any o not the word, they also... 1Pet 3:1
them that o not the gospel of God... 1Pet 4:17

OBEYED

because thou hast o my voice........ Gen 22:18
Because that Abraham o my voice..... Gen 26:5
And that Jacob o his father........ Gen 28:7
because they o not the voice of..... Josh 5:6
have o my voice in all that I....... Josh 22:2
but ye have not o my voice......... Judg 2:2
but ye have not o my voice......... Judg 6:10
I have o the voice of the LORD..... 1Sa 15:20
the people, and o their voice...... 1Sa 15:24
thine handmaid hath o thy voice.... 1Sa 28:21
hast not o the voice of the LORD... 1Kin 20:36
Because they o not the voice of.... 2Kin 18:12
and all Israel o him............... 1Chr 29:23
they o the words of the LORD, and.. 2Chr 11:4
have not o the voice of my......... Prov 5:13
tree, and ye have not o my voice... Jer 34:10
have not o the voice of the LORD... Jer 34:25
them, and have not o my voice...... Jer 9:13
Yet they o not, nor inclined....... Jer 11:8
But they o not, neither inclined... Jer 17:23
but they o not thy voice, neither.. Jer 22:23
of them any more, then they o..... Jer 34:10
Thus have we o the voice of....... Jer 35:8
we have dwelt in tents, and have o. Jer 35:10

Because ye have o the commandment. Jer 35:18
have not o his voice, therefore............... Jer 40:3
but ye have not o the voice of .... Jer 42:21
o not the voice of the LORD, to............... Jer 43:4
for they o not the voice of the .... Jer 43:7
have not o the voice of the LORD, ... Jer 44:23
Neither have we o the voice of .... Dan 9:10
for we o not his voice............................ Dan 9:14
She o not the voice .... Zeph 3:2
o the voice of the LORD their God .... Hag 1:12
and all, as many as o him, were .... Acts 5:36
and all, even as many as o him .... Acts 5:37
but ye have o from the heart that.......... Rom 6:17
they have not all o the gospel .... Rom 10:16
my beloved, as ye have always o .... Phil 2:12
receive for an inheritance, o .... Heb 11:8
Even as Sarah o Abraham, calling.......... 1Pet 3:6

OBEYEDST
Because thou o not the voice of 1Sa 28:18
youth, that thou o not my voice.............. Jer 22:21

OBEYETH
that o the voice of his servant,............... Is 50:10
This is a nation that o not the .... Jer 7:28
Cursed be the man that o not the........... Jer 11:3

OBEYING
o the commandments of the LORD .... Judg 2:17
as in o the voice of the LORD................... 1Sa 15:22
in o the truth through the Spirit 1Pet 1:22

OBIL (o'-bil) *An Ishmaelite camel driver.*
camels also was O the Ishmaelite 1Chr 27:30

OBJECT
have been here before thee, and o .... Acts 24:19

OBLATION
if thou bring an o of a meat .... Lev 2:4
if thy o be a meat offering baken .... Lev 2:5
if thy o be a meat offering baken .... Lev 2:7
As for the o of the firstfruits,............... Lev 2:12
every o of thy meat offering .... Lev 2:13
if his o be a sacrifice of peace .... Lev 3:1
offer one out of the whole o for .... Lev 7:14
unto the LORD shall bring his o .... Lev 7:29
will offer his o for all his vows............. Lev 22:18
every o of theirs, every meat .... Num 18:9
brought an o for the LORD...................... Num 31:50
day, and shall do sacrifice and o .... Is 19:21
o chooseth a tree that will not............... Is 40:20
he that offereth an o, as if he .... Is 66:3
they offer burnt offering and an o .... Jer 14:12
every o of all, of every sort of .... Eze 44:30
ye shall offer an o unto the LORD .... Eze 45:1
over against the o of the holy............... Eze 45:6
side of the o of the holy portion........... Eze 45:7
before the o of the holy portion,.......... Eze 45:7
This is the o that ye shall offer .... Eze 45:13
this o for the prince in Israel................ Eze 45:16
The o that ye shall offer unto............... Eze 48:9
the priests, shall be this holy o............ Eze 48:10
this o of the land that is .... Eze 48:12
in length over against the o of .... Eze 48:18
against the o of the holy portion .... Eze 48:18
All the o shall be five and twenty .... Eze 48:20
shall offer the holy o foursquare .... Eze 48:20
and on the other of the holy o.............. Eze 48:21
of the o toward the east border .... Eze 48:21
and it shall be the holy o...................... Eze 48:21
that they should offer an o .... Dan 2:46
about the time of the evening o .... Dan 9:21
the o to cease, and for the .... Dan 9:27

OBLATIONS
to offer their o unto the LORD............... Lev 7:38
to distribute the o of the LORD............. 2Chr 31:14
Bring no more vain o .... Is 1:13
and the firstfruits of your o .... Eze 20:40
of all, of every sort of your o .... Eze 44:30

OBOTH (o'-both) *An Israelite encampment in the wilderness.*
set forward, and pitched in O................ Num 21:10
And they journeyed from O, and............ Num 21:11
from Punon, and pitched in O .... Num 33:43
And they departed from O, and............. Num 33:44

OBSCURE
shall be put out in o darkness............... Prov 20:20

OBSCURITY
of the blind shall see out of o .... Is 29:18
then shall thy light rise in o.................. Is 58:10
we wait for light, but behold o.............. Is 59:9

OBSERVATION
kingdom of God cometh not with o....... Lk 17:20

OBSERVE
And ye shall o the feast of...................... Ex 12:17
therefore shall ye o this day in .... Ex 12:17
ye shall o this thing for an.................... Ex 12:24
to o the sabbath throughout their .... Ex 31:16
O thou that which I command thee .... Ex 34:11
thou shalt o the feast of weeks,............ Ex 34:22
ye use enchantment, nor o times .... Lev 19:26
shall ye o all my statutes....................... Lev 19:37
shall ye o to offer unto me in .... Num 28:2
Ye shall o to do therefore as the .... Deut 5:32
O Israel, and o to do it.......................... Deut 6:3
if we o to do all these .... Deut 6:25
thee this day shall ye o to do .... Deut 8:1
ye shall o to do all the statutes............ Deut 11:32
which ye shall o to do in the................. Deut 12:1

O and hear all these words which I ....Deut 12:28
soever I command you, to o do it......... Deut 12:32
to o to do all these commandments ......Deut 15:5
O the month of Abib, and keep the...... Deut 16:1
and thou shalt o and do these.............. Deut 16:12
Thou shalt o the feast of...................... Deut 16:13
thou shalt o to do according to .... Deut 17:10
that thou o diligently, and do .... Deut 24:8
them, so ye shall o to do...................... Deut 24:8
voice of the LORD thy God, to o........... Deut 28:1
I command thee this day, to o .... Deut 28:13
to o to do all his commandments......... Deut 28:15
If thou wilt not o to do all the............. Deut 28:58
o to do all the words of this law .... Deut 31:12
command your children to o to do .... Deut 32:46
that thou mayest o to do...................... Josh 1:7
night, that thou mayest o to do .... Josh 1:8
that I commanded her let her o............. Judg 13:14
Now the men did diligently o 1Kin 20:33
ye shall o to do for evermore 2Kin 17:37
only if they will o to do........................ 2Kin 21:8
shalt o thy statutes and my 2Chr 7:17
love him and o his commandments...... Neh 1:5
Moses the servant of God, and to o..... Neh 10:29
That they might o his statutes.............. Ps 105:45
will o these things, even they .... Ps 107:43
I shall o it with my whole heart .... Ps 119:34
and let thine eyes o my ways................ Prov 23:26
the swallow o the time of their .... Jer 8:7
neither o their judgments, nor .... Eze 20:18
o my statutes, and do them .... Eze 37:24
leopard by the way will I o them.......... Hos 13:7
They that o lying vanities .... Jonah 2:8
they bid you o, that o .... Mt 23:3
Teaching them to o all things............... Mt 28:20
for us to receive, neither to o............... Acts 16:21
that they o no such thing .... Acts 21:25
Ye o days, and months, and times,....... Gal 4:10
that thou o these things without.......... 1Ti 5:21

OBSERVED
but his father o the saying .... Gen 37:11
It is a night to be much o unto .... Ex 12:42
o of all the children of Israel .... Ex 12:42
not o all these commandments,........... Num 15:22
for they have o thy word, and kept...... Deut 33:9
to pass, when Joab o the city 2Sa 11:16
o times, and used enchantments, and.. 2Kin 21:6
also he o times, and used 2Chr 33:6
I have heard him, and o him................. Hos 14:8
a just man and an holy, and o him .... Mk 6:20
all these have I o from my youth.......... Mk 10:20

OBSERVER
or an o of times, or an enchanter .... Deut 18:10

OBSERVERS
hearkened unto o of times.................... Deut 18:14

OBSERVEST
many things, but thou o not .... Is 42:20

OBSERVETH
He that o the wind shall not sow .... Eccl 11:4

OBSTINATE
his spirit, and made his heart o .... Deut 2:30
Because I knew that thou art o.............. Is 48:4

OBTAIN
be that I may o children by her............ Gen 16:2
shall o favour of the LORD.................... Prov 8:35
they shall o joy and gladness, and....... Is 35:10
they shall o gladness and joy .... Is 51:11
o the kingdom by flatteries.................. Dan 11:21
for they shall o mercy......................... Mt 5:7
accounted worthy to o that world....... Lk 20:35
your mercy they also o mercy .. Rom 11:31
So run, that ye may o 1Cor 9:24
Now they do it to o a corruptible....... 1Cor 9:25
but to o salvation by our Lord 1Th 5:9
sakes, that they may also o the 2Ti 2:10
of grace, that we may o mercy .... Heb 4:16
that they might o a better................... Heb 11:35
and desire to have, and cannot o .... Jas 4:2

OBTAINED
after certain days o I leave of .... Neh 13:6
him, and she o kindness of him .... Est 2:9
Esther o favour in the sight of............. Est 2:15
she o grace and favour in his............... Est 2:17
that she o favour in his sight .... Est 5:2
upon her that had not o mercy............ Hos 2:23
had o part of this ministry.................. Acts 1:17
With a great sum o I this freedom...... Acts 22:28
Having therefore o help of God........... Acts 26:22
that they had o their purpose .... Acts 27:13
Israel hath not o that which he........... Rom 11:7
but the election hath o it.................... Rom 11:7
yet have now o mercy through........... Rom 11:30
as one that hath o mercy of the 1Cor 7:25
also we have o an inheritance .... Eph 1:11
but I o mercy, because I did it 1Ti 1:13
Howbeit for this cause I o mercy 1Ti 1:16
as he hath by inheritance o a............. Heb 1:4
endured, he o the promise .... Heb 6:15
But now hath he o a more.................. Heb 8:6
having o eternal redemption for......... Heb 9:12
by it the elders o a good report.......... Heb 11:2
by which he o witness that he was ..... Heb 11:4
o promises, stopped the mouths of..... Heb 11:33
having o a good report through.......... Heb 11:39
which had not o mercy........................ 1Pet 2:10
but now have o mercy......................... 1Pet 2:10

to them that have o like precious......... 2Pet 1:1

OBTAINETH
A good man o favour of the LORD........ Prov 12:2
thing, and o favour of the LORD .... Prov 18:22

OBTAINING
to the o of the glory of our Lord.......... 2Th 2:14

OCCASION
that he may seek o against us.............. Gen 43:18
do to them as thou shalt find o .... Judg 9:33
that he sought an o against the........... Judg 14:4
that thou do as o serve thee................ 1Sa 10:7
o to the enemies of the LORD to 2Sa 12:14
which thou shalt have to o bestow ...... Ezr 7:20
in her o who can turn her away........... Jer 2:24
ye shall not have o any more to........... Ezr 18:3
princes sought to find o against.......... Dan 6:4
they could find none o nor fault.......... Dan 6:4
find any o against this Daniel.............. Dan 6:5
taking by the commandment,.............. Rom 7:8
taking o by the commandment,........... Rom 7:11
an o to fall in his brother's way .... Rom 14:13
but give you o to glory on our 2Cor 5:12
but by o of the forwardness of........... 2Cor 8:8
o from them which desire o 2Cor 11:12
not liberty for an o to the flesh.......... Gal 5:13
give none o to the adversary to.......... 1Ti 5:14
there is none o of stumbling in........... 1Jn 2:10

OCCASIONED
I have o the death of all the................ 1Sa 22:22

OCCASIONS
give o of speech against her, and........ Deut 22:14
he hath given o of speech against ...... Deut 22:17
Behold, he findeth o against me.......... Job 33:10

OCCUPATION
you, and shall say, What is your o...... Gen 46:33
unto his brethren, What is your o ...... Gen 47:3
What is thine o .... Jonah 1:8
for by their o they were .... Acts 18:3
with the workmen of like o .... Acts 19:25

OCCUPIED
All the gold that was o for the .... Ex 38:24
with new ropes that never were o ...... Judg 16:11
they o in thy fairs with emeralds .... Eze 27:16
going to and fro o in thy fairs........... Eze 27:19
they o with thee in lambs, and.......... Eze 27:21
they o in thy fairs with chief of........ Eze 27:22
them that have been o therein........... Heb 13:9

OCCUPIERS
the o of thy merchandise, and all...... Eze 27:27

OCCUPIETH
how shall he that o the room of......... 1Cor 14:16

OCCUPY
were in thee to o thy merchandise..... Eze 27:9
and said unto them, O till I come....... Lk 19:13

OCCURRENT
is neither adversary nor evil o........... 1Kin 5:4

OCHRAN See OCRAN.

OCRAN (o'-cran) *An Asherite who counted the people.*
Pagiel the son of O............................. Num 1:13
shall be Pagiel the son of O................ Num 2:27
eleventh day Pagiel the son of O........ Num 7:72
offering of Pagiel the son of O........... Num 7:77
of Asher was Pagiel the son of O....... Num 10:26

ODD
wherewith the o number of them is ... Num 3:48

ODED (o'-ded)
1. Father of Azariah.
came upon Azariah the son of O 2Chr 15:1
and the prophecy of the prophet 2Chr 15:8
2. A prophet of Samaria.
LORD was there, whose name was O... 2Chr 28:9

ODIOUS
had made themselves o to David........ 1Chr 19:6
For an o woman when she is .... Prov 30:23

ODOUR
filled with the o of the ointment........ Jn 12:3
you, an o of a sweet smell, a............... Phil 4:18

ODOURS
smell the savour of your sweet o .... Lev 26:31
bed which was filled with sweet o ..... Jer 34:5
myrrh, and six months with sweet o .. Est 2:12
so shall they burn o for thee.............. Jer 34:5
an oblation and sweet o unto him...... Dan 2:46
harps, and golden vials full of o .... Rev 5:8
And cinnamon, and o, and ointments, Rev 18:13

OF See PREFACE.

OFF See PREFACE.

OFFENCE
o of heart unto my lord,..................... 1Sa 25:31
for a rock of o to both the .... Is 8:14
till they acknowledge their o .... Hos 5:15
thou art an o unto me........................ Mt 16:23
to that man by whom the o cometh.... Mt 18:7
a conscience void of o toward God..... Acts 24:16
But not as the o, so also is the .... Rom 5:15
For if through the o of one many ...... Rom 5:15
For if by one man's o death............... Rom 5:17
Therefore as by the o of one .... Rom 5:18

entered, that the o might abound........ Rom 5:20
a stumblingstone and rock of o .... Rom 9:33
for that man who eateth with o .... Rom 14:20
Give none o, neither to the Jews,....... 1Cor 10:32
Giving no o in any thing, that 2Cor 6:3
Have I committed an o in abasing....... 2Cor 11:7
then is the o of the cross ceased........ Gal 5:11
without o till the day of Christ............ Phil 1:10
of stumbling, and a rock of o 1Pet 2:8

OFFENCES
for yielding pacifieth great o .... Eccl 10:4
Woe unto the world because of o .... Mt 18:7
for it must needs be that o come......... Mt 18:7
impossible but that o will come........... Lk 17:1
Who was delivered for our o .... Rom 4:25
is of many o unto justification............ Rom 5:16
o contrary to the doctrine which......... Rom 16:17

OFFEND
I will not o any more......................... Job 34:31
I should o against the generation....... Ps 73:15
and nothing shall o them.................... Ps 119:165
all that devour him shall o .... Jer 2:3
We o not, because they have.............. Jer 50:7
the harlot, yet let not Judah o............ Hos 4:15
and he shall pass over, and o............. Hab 1:11
And if thy right eye o thee .... Mt 5:29
And if thy right hand o thee................ Mt 5:30
of his kingdom all things that o.......... Mt 13:41
lest we should o them, go thou .... Mt 17:27
But whoso shall o one of these........... Mt 18:6
if thy hand or thy foot o thee.............. Mt 18:8
And if thine eye o thee, pluck it .... Mt 18:9
whosoever shall o one of these.......... Mk 9:42
And if thy hand o thee, cut it off......... Mk 9:43
And if thy foot o thee, cut it off.......... Mk 9:45
And if thine eye o thee, pluck it .... Mk 9:47
than that he should o one of .... Lk 17:2
said unto them, Doth this o you.......... Jn 6:61
if meat make my brother to o 1Cor 8:13
lest I make my brother to o................ 1Cor 8:13
yet o in one point, he is guilty .... Jas 2:10
For in many things we o all................. Jas 3:2
If any man o not in word, the .... Jas 3:2

OFFENDED
and what have I o thee, that thou ...... Gen 20:9
his baker had o their lord the .... Gen 40:1
to Lachish, saying, I have o 2Kin 18:14
for whereas we have o 2Chr 28:13
A brother is harder to be won .... Prov 18:19
What have I o against thee, or .... Jer 37:18
vengeance, and hath greatly o........... Eze 25:12
but when he o in Baal, he died........... Hos 13:1
whosoever shall not be o in me.......... Mt 11:6
of the world, by and by he is o........... Mt 13:21
And they were o in him .... Mt 13:57
thou that the Pharisees were o.......... Mt 15:12
And them shall many be o, and shall.. Mt 24:10
All ye shall be o because of me.......... Mt 26:31
men shall be o because of thee.......... Mt 26:33
yet will I never be o........................... Mt 26:33
sake, immediately they are o .... Mk 4:17
And they were o at him .... Mk 6:3
All ye shall be o because of me.......... Mk 14:27
unto him, Although all shall be o........ Mk 14:29
whosoever shall not be o in me.......... Lk 7:23
unto you, that ye should not be o........ Jn 16:1
have I o any thing at all .... Acts 25:8
thy brother stumbleth, or is o............. Rom 14:21
who is o, and I burn not.................... 2Cor 11:29

OFFENDER
That make a man an o for a word ...... Is 29:21
For if I be an o, or have.................... Acts 25:11

OFFENDERS
my son Solomon shall be counted o ... 1Kin 1:21

OFFER
o him there for a burnt offering........... Gen 22:2
Thou shalt not delay to o the.............. Ex 22:29
Thou shalt not o the blood of my .... Ex 23:18
Thou shalt not o the blood of my .... Ex 34:25
thou shalt o every day a bullock........ Ex 29:36
which thou shalt o upon the altar .... Ex 29:38
lamb thou shalt o in the morning........ Ex 29:39
other lamb thou shalt o at even .... Ex 29:39
other lamb thou shalt o at even .... Ex 29:41
Ye shall o no strange incense .... Ex 30:9
Thou shalt not o the blood of my .... Ex 34:25
Every one that did o an offering .... Ex 35:24
let him o a male without blemish......... Lev 1:3
he shall o it of his own .... Lev 1:3
he shall o it at the mouth................... Lev 2:1
ye shall o them unto the LORD............ Lev 2:12
thine offerings thou shalt o salt.......... Lev 2:13
if thou o a meat offering of thy .... Lev 2:14
thou shalt o for the meat................... Lev 2:14
offering, if he o it of the herd............. Lev 3:1
he shall o it without blemish.............. Lev 3:1
he shall o of the sacrifice of .... Lev 3:3
he shall o it without blemish.............. Lev 3:6
If he o a lamb for his offering,........... Lev 3:7
then shall he o it before the.............. Lev 3:7
he shall o of the sacrifice .... Lev 3:9
then he shall o it before the.............. Lev 3:12
he shall o thereof his offering,........... Lev 3:14
o a young bullock for the sin............. Lev 4:14
who shall o that which is for the .... Lev 5:8
he shall o the second for a burnt....... Lev 5:10
Aaron shall o it before the LORD .... Lev 6:14
which they shall o unto the LORD........ Lev 6:20

o for a sweet savour unto the............. Lev 6:21
anointed in his stead shall o it............ Lev 6:22
he shall o of it all the fat.................... Lev 7:3
which he shall o unto the LORD........... Lev 7:11
If he o it for a thanksgiving,............... Lev 7:12
then he shall o with the..................... Lev 7:12
he shall o for his offering.................. Lev 7:13
of it he shall o one out of the............. Lev 7:14
of which men o an offering made....... Lev 7:25
the children of Israel to o their.......... Lev 7:38
and o them before the LORD............... Lev 9:2
o thy sin offering, and thy burnt......... Lev 9:7
o the offering of the people, and .... Lev 9:7
Who shall o it before the LORD,.......... Lev 12:7
o him for a trespass offering, and...... Lev 14:12
priest shall o the sin offering............. Lev 14:19
the priest shall o the burnt .... Lev 14:20
he shall o the one of the................... Lev 14:30
And the priest shall o them............... Lev 15:15
the priest shall o the one for a .... Lev 15:30
Aaron shall o his bullock of the......... Lev 16:6
fell, and o him for a sin offering .... Lev 16:9
o his burnt offering, and the.............. Lev 16:24
to o an offering unto the LORD .... Lev 17:4
which they o in the open field,........... Lev 17:5
o them for peace offerings unto......... Lev 17:5
they shall no more o their.................. Lev 17:7
to o it unto the LORD......................... Lev 17:9
if ye o a sacrifice of peace .... Lev 19:5
ye shall o it at your own will.............. Lev 19:5
be eaten the same day ye o it .... Lev 19:6
the bread of their God, they do o .... Lev 21:6
to o the bread of his God .... Lev 21:17
the priest shall come nigh to o .... Lev 21:21
nigh to o the bread of his God........... Lev 21:21
which they o unto the LORD .... Lev 22:15
that will o his oblation for all .... Lev 22:18
which they will o unto the LORD.......... Lev 22:18
Ye shall o at your own will a .... Lev 22:19
a blemish, that shall ye not o .... Lev 22:20
ye shall not o these unto the .... Lev 22:22
that mayest thou o for a freewill........ Lev 22:23
Ye shall not o unto the LORD that .... Lev 22:24
o the bread of your God of any of ...... Lev 22:25
when ye will o a sacrifice of .... Lev 22:29
the LORD, o it at your own will........... Lev 22:29
But ye shall o an offering made......... Lev 23:8
ye shall o that day when ye wave...... Lev 23:12
ye shall o a new meal offering........... Lev 23:16
ye shall o with the bread seven .... Lev 23:18
but ye shall o an offering made......... Lev 23:25
o an offering made by fire unto.......... Lev 23:27
Seven days ye shall o an offering...... Lev 23:36
ye shall o an offering made by.......... Lev 23:36
to o an offering made by fire,............ Lev 23:37
beast, of which they do not o a .... Lev 27:11
the LORD, and o it upon the altar........ Num 5:25
the priest shall o the one for a .... Num 6:11
he shall o his offering unto the.......... Num 6:14
shall o his sin offering, and his .... Num 6:16
And he shall o the ram for a.............. Num 6:17
the priest shall o also his meat .... Num 6:17
They shall o their offering, each......... Num 7:11
Zuar, prince of Issachar, did o........... Num 7:18
of the children of Zebulun, did o........ Num 7:24
of the children of Reuben, did o......... Num 7:30
of the children of Simeon, did o......... Num 7:36
Aaron shall o the Levites before .... Num 8:11
thou shalt o the one for a sin............. Num 8:12
o them for an offering unto the.......... Num 8:13
them, and o them for an offering........ Num 8:15
that we may not o an offering of........ Num 9:7
o the third part of an hin of .... Num 15:7
will o an offering made by fire,.......... Num 15:14
ye shall o up an heave offering .... Num 15:19
Ye shall o up a cake of the first........ Num 15:20
o one young bullock for a burnt......... Num 15:24
come near to o incense before the..... Num 16:40
which they shall o unto the LORD........ Num 18:12
of Israel o unto the LORD................... Num 18:19
which they o as an heave offering...... Num 18:24
then ye shall o up an heave .... Num 18:26
Thus ye also shall o an heave .... Num 18:28
o every heave offering of the .... Num 18:29
shall ye observe to o unto me in........ Num 28:2
which ye shall o unto the LORD........... Num 28:3
lamb shalt thou o in the morning .... Num 28:4
other lamb shalt thou o at even .... Num 28:4
other lamb shalt thou o at even .... Num 28:8
offering thereof, thou shalt o it .... Num 28:8
of your months ye shall o a burnt ...... Num 28:11
But ye shall o a sacrifice made......... Num 28:19
deals shall ye o for a bullock............ Num 28:20
deal shalt thou o for every lamb........ Num 28:21
Ye shall o these beside the burnt ...... Num 28:23
this manner ye shall o daily .... Num 28:24
But ye shall o the burnt offering .... Num 28:27
Ye shall o them beside the............... Num 28:31
he shall o a burnt offering for a .... Num 29:2
But ye shall o a burnt offering........... Num 29:8
ye shall o a burnt offering,................ Num 29:13
ye shall o twelve young bullocks....... Num 29:17
But ye shall o a burnt offering,.......... Num 29:36
thou o not thy burnt offerings in .... Deut 12:13
there thou shalt o thy burnt............... Deut 12:14
thou shalt o thy burnt offerings,........ Deut 12:27
from them that o a sacrifice.............. Deut 18:3
thou shalt o burnt offerings,.............. Deut 27:6
thou shalt o peace offerings, and ...... Deut 27:7
there they shall o sacrifices of .... Deut 33:19

or if to o thereon burnt offering.......... Josh 22:23
or if to o peace offerings................... Josh 22:23
had made an end to o the present ..... Judg 3:18
o a burnt sacrifice with the wood ...... Judg 6:26
I will o it up for a burnt..................... Judg 11:31
if thou wilt o a burnt offering,............ Judg 13:16
thou must o it unto the LORD.............. Judg 13:16
to o a great sacrifice unto Dagon...... Judg 16:23
went up to o unto the LORD the.......... 1Sa 1:21
husband to o the yearly sacrifice....... 1Sa 2:19
to o upon mine altar, to burn 1Sa 2:28
to o burnt offerings, and to................ 1Sa 10:8
the LORD, I o thee three things........... 2Sa 24:12
o up what seemeth good unto him...... 2Sa 24:22
neither will I o burnt offerings............ 2Sa 24:24
did Solomon o upon that altar 1Kin 9:25
did Solomon o burnt offerings........... 1Kin 9:25
upon thee shall he o the priests........ 1Kin 13:2
o neither burnt offering nor 2Kin 5:17
when they went in to o sacrifices....... 2Kin 10:24
To o burnt offerings unto the 1Chr 16:40
the LORD, I o thee three things........... 1Chr 21:10
nor o burnt offerings without 1Chr 21:24
to o all burnt sacrifices unto 1Chr 23:31
that we should be able to o so........... 1Chr 29:14
here, to o willingly unto thee 1Chr 29:17
to o the burnt offerings of the 2Chr 23:18
to o withal, and spoons, and............ 2Chr 24:14
priests the sons of Aaron to o 2Chr 29:21
Hezekiah commanded to o the burnt.. 2Chr 29:27
to o unto the LORD, as it is 2Chr 35:12
to o burnt offerings upon the............. 2Chr 35:16
to o burnt offerings thereon, as......... Ezr 3:2
to o burnt offerings unto the LORD ..... Ezr 3:6
That they may o sacrifices of............ Ezr 6:10
o them upon the altar of the.............. Ezr 7:17
o up for yourselves a burnt .... Job 42:8
O the sacrifices of righteousness....... Ps 4:5
offerings of blood will I not o .... Ps 16:4
therefore will I o in his...................... Ps 27:6
O unto God thanksgiving.................... Ps 50:14
then shall they o bullocks upon .... Ps 51:19
I will o unto thee burnt...................... Ps 66:15
I will o bullocks with goats................ Ps 66:15
of Sheba and Seba shall o gifts........ Ps 72:10
I will o to thee the sacrifice of .... Ps 116:17
westest thou up to o sacrifice .... Is 57:7
the gods unto whom they o incense ... Jer 11:12
when they o burnt offering and .... Jer 14:12
before me to o burnt offerings............ Jer 33:18
the place where they did o sweet....... Eze 6:13
For when ye o your gifts, when ye ..... Eze 20:31
to o burnt offerings thereon, and .... Eze 43:18
o a kid of the goats without............... Eze 43:22
thou shalt o a young bullock.............. Eze 43:23
thou shalt o them before the God....... Eze 43:24
they shall o them up for a burnt......... Eze 43:24
when ye o my bread, the fat and .... Eze 44:7
before me to o unto me the fat.......... Eze 44:15
he shall o his sin offering,................. Eze 44:27
ye shall o an oblation unto the .... Eze 45:1
is the oblation that ye shall o .... Eze 45:13
ye shall o the tenth part of a .... Eze 45:14
o unto the LORD in the sabbath.......... Eze 46:4
offering which ye shall o of five......... Eze 48:9
The oblation that ye shall o unto....... Eze 48:9
ye shall o the holy oblation................ Eze 48:20
that they should o an oblation............ Dan 2:46
They shall not o wine offerings.......... Hos 9:4
o a sacrifice of thanksgiving.............. Amos 4:5
Though ye o me burnt offerings and... Amos 5:22
that which they o there is.................. Hag 2:14
Ye o polluted bread upon mine .... Mal 1:7
if ye o the blind for sacrifice,............. Mal 1:8
if ye o the lame and sick, is it .... Mal 1:8
it now unto thy governor.................... Mal 1:8
that they may o unto the God of........ Mal 3:3
and then come and o thy gift............. Mt 5:24
the gift that Moses commanded,........ Mt 8:4
o for thy cleansing those things......... Mk 1:44
to o a sacrifice according to .... Lk 2:24
o for thy cleansing, according as....... Lk 5:14
on the one cheek o also the other ..... Lk 6:29
an egg, will he o him a scorpion........ Lk 11:12
to God, that he may o both gifts......... Heb 5:1
also for himself, to o for sins............. Heb 5:3
to o up sacrifice, first for his .... Heb 7:27
priest is ordained to o gifts................ Heb 8:3
this man have somewhat also to o ..... Heb 8:3
that o gifts according to the law......... Heb 9:4
that he should o himself often........... Heb 9:25
By him therefore let us o the .... Heb 13:15
to o up spiritual sacrifices,............... 1Pet 2:5
that he should o it with the............... Rev 8:3

OFFERED
o burnt offerings on the altar .... Gen 8:20
o him up for a burnt offering in .... Gen 22:13
Then Jacob o sacrifice upon the .... Gen 31:54
o sacrifices unto the God of his......... Gen 46:1
which o burnt offerings, and .... Ex 24:5
o burnt offerings, and brought............ Ex 32:6
every man that o .... Ex 35:22
o an offering of gold......................... Ex 35:22
o upon it the burnt offering and.......... Ex 40:29
burnt offering which he hath o............ Lev 7:8
eaten the same day that it is o .... Lev 7:15
o it for sin, as the first...................... Lev 9:15
it according to the manner................ Lev 9:16
o strange fire before the LORD,.......... Lev 10:1
have they o their sin offering............. Lev 10:19

And their meat o and their drink ...... Num 29:33
And one goat for a sin o ...... Num 29:34
beside the continual burnt o ...... Num 29:34
his meat o, and his drink ...... Num 29:34
and his drink o ...... Num 29:34
But ye shall offer a burnt o ...... Num 29:36
Their meat o and their drink ...... Num 29:37
And one goat for a sin o ...... Num 29:38
beside the continual burnt o ...... Num 29:38
and his meat o ...... Num 29:38
and his drink o ...... Num 29:38
for an heave o of the LORD ...... Num 31:29
which was the LORD's heave o ...... Num 31:41
all the gold of the o that they ...... Num 31:52
the heave o of your hand, and all ...... Deut 12:11
or heave o of thine hand ...... Deut 12:17
of a freewill o of thine hand ...... Deut 16:10
even a freewill o, according as ...... Deut 23:23
thereon burnt o or meat ...... Josh 22:23
or meat o, or if ...... Josh 22:23
us an altar, not for burnt o ...... Josh 22:26
I will offer it up for a burnt o ...... Judg 11:31
and if thou wilt offer a burnt o ...... Judg 13:16
Manoah took a kid with a meat o ...... Judg 13:19
would not have received a burnt o ...... Judg 13:23
a meat o at our hands, neither ...... Judg 13:23
men abhorred the o of the LORD 1Sa 2:17
ye at my sacrifice and at mine o 1Sa 2:29
with sacrifice nor o for ever 1Sa 3:14
any wise return him a trespass o 1Sa 6:3
What shall be the trespass o 1Sa 6:4
ye return him for a trespass o 1Sa 6:8
the kine a burnt o unto the LORD 1Sa 6:14
for a trespass o unto the LORD 1Sa 6:17
a burnt o wholly unto the LORD 1Sa 7:9
as Samuel was o up the burnt 1Sa 7:10
up the burnt o 1Sa 7:10
Bring hither a burnt o to me 1Sa 13:9
And he offered the burnt o 1Sa 13:9
an end o of the burnt 1Sa 13:10
the burnt o, behold 1Sa 13:10
therefore, and offered a burnt o 1Sa 13:12
against me, let him accept an o 1Sa 26:19
made an end o of burnt offerings 2Sa 6:18
until the time of the o of the 1Kin 18:29
of the o of the evening sacrifice 1Kin 18:36
when the meat o was offered 2Kin 3:20
him for a burnt o upon the wall 2Kin 3:27
o nor sacrifice unto other gods 2Kin 5:17
an end o of the burnt 2Kin 10:25
the burnt o, that Jehu 2Kin 10:25
And he burnt his burnt o and his 2Kin 16:13
and his meat o 2Kin 16:13
and poured his drink o 2Kin 16:13
altar burn the morning burnt o 2Kin 16:15
and the evening meat o 2Kin 16:15
burnt sacrifice, and his meat o 2Kin 16:15
with the burnt o of all the 2Kin 16:15
of the land, and their meat o 2Kin 16:15
it all the blood of the burnt o 2Kin 16:15
upon the altar of the burnt o 1Chr 6:49
an end o of the burnt offerings 1Chr 16:2
bring an o, and come before him 1Chr 16:29
the burnt o continually morning 1Chr 16:40
wood, and the wheat for the meat o 1Chr 21:23
by fire upon the altar of burnt o 1Chr 21:26
and the altar of the burnt o 1Chr 21:29
altar of the burnt o for Israel 1Chr 22:1
and for the fine flour for meat o 1Chr 23:29
the burnt o they washed in them 2Chr 4:6
heaven, and consumed the burnt o 2Chr 7:1
o according to the commandment of 2Chr 8:13
the LORD, and the altar of burnt o 2Chr 8:12
for a sin o for the kingdom, and 2Chr 29:21
for the sin o before the king 2Chr 29:23
king commanded that the burnt o 2Chr 29:24
the sin o should be made for all 2Chr 29:24
offer the burnt o upon the altar 2Chr 29:27
And when the burnt o began 2Chr 29:27
until the burnt o was finished 2Chr 29:28
they had made an end of o 2Chr 29:29
were for a burnt o the sin o 2Chr 29:32
drink offerings for every burnt o 2Chr 29:35
o peace offerings, and making 2Chr 30:22
busied in o of burnt offerings 2Chr 35:14
beside the freewill o for the ...... Ezr 1:4
offered the continual burnt o ...... Ezr 3:5
a freewill o unto the LORD ...... Ezr 3:5
for a sin o for all Israel ...... Ezr 6:17
with the freewill o of the people ...... Ezr 7:16
o willingly for the house of ...... Ezr 7:16
even the o of the house of our ...... Ezr 8:25
the gold are a freewill o unto ...... Ezr 8:28
twelve he goats for a sin o ...... Ezr 8:35
this was a burnt o unto the LORD ...... Ezr 8:35
and for the continual meat o ...... Neh 10:33
and for the continual burnt o ...... Neh 10:33
and the people, for the wood o ...... Neh 10:34
shall bring the o of the corn ...... Neh 10:39
the house of God, with the meat o ...... Neh 13:9
And for the wood o, at times ...... Neh 13:31
offer up for yourselves a burnt o ...... Job 42:8
and o thou didst not desire ...... Ps 40:6
burnt o and sin o hast ...... Ps 40:6
thou delightest not in burnt o ...... Ps 51:16
burnt o and whole burnt o ...... Ps 51:19
bring an o, and come into his ...... Ps 96:8
thereof sufficient for a burnt o ...... Is 40:16
caused thee to serve with an o ...... Is 43:23
shalt make his soul an o for sin ...... Is 53:10

them hast thou poured a drink o ...... Is 57:6
thou hast offered a meat o ...... Is 57:6
I hate robbery for burnt o ...... Is 61:8
the drink o unto that number ...... Is 65:11
for an o unto the LORD out of all ...... Is 66:20
an o in a clean vessel into the ...... Is 66:20
to anger in o incense unto Baal ...... Jer 11:17
and when they offer burnt o ...... Jer 14:12
the provocation of their o ...... Eze 20:28
where they washed the burnt o ...... Eze 40:38
side, to slay thereon the burnt o ...... Eze 40:39
sin o and the trespass o ...... Eze 40:39
of hewn stone for the burnt o ...... Eze 40:42
wherewith they slew the burnt o ...... Eze 40:42
the tables was the flesh of the o ...... Eze 40:43
most holy things, and the meat o ...... Eze 42:13
sin o, and the trespass o ...... Eze 42:13
God, a young bullock for a sin o ...... Eze 43:19
the bullock also of the sin o ...... Eze 43:21
goats without blemish for a sin o ...... Eze 43:22
up for a burnt o unto the LORD ...... Eze 43:24
every day a goat for a sin o ...... Eze 43:25
they shall slay the burnt o ...... Eze 44:11
he shall offer his sin o ...... Eze 44:27
They shall eat the meat o ...... Eze 44:29
sin o, and the trespass o ...... Eze 44:29
for a meat o, and for a burnt ...... Eze 45:15
and for a burnt o ...... Eze 45:17
he shall prepare the sin o ...... Eze 45:17
and the meat o ...... Eze 45:17
and the burnt o ...... Eze 45:17
take of the blood of the sin o ...... Eze 45:19
of the land a bullock for a sin o ...... Eze 45:22
prepare a burnt o to the LORD ...... Eze 45:23
of the goats daily for a sin o ...... Eze 45:23
he shall prepare a meat o of an ...... Eze 45:24
days, according to the sin o ...... Eze 45:25
according to the burnt o ...... Eze 45:25
and according to the meat o ...... Eze 45:25
priests shall prepare his burnt o ...... Eze 46:2
the burnt o that the prince shall ...... Eze 46:4
the meat o shall be an ephah for ...... Eze 46:5
the meat o for the lambs as he ...... Eze 46:5
he shall prepare a meat o ...... Eze 46:7
in the solemnities the meat o ...... Eze 46:11
o or peace offerings voluntarily ...... Eze 46:12
and he shall prepare his burnt o ...... Eze 46:12
shall daily prepare a burnt o ...... Eze 46:13
a meat o for it every morning ...... Eze 46:14
a meat o continually by a ...... Eze 46:14
prepare the lamb, and the meat o ...... Eze 46:15
morning for a continual burnt o ...... Eze 46:15
trespass o and the sin o ...... Eze 46:20
where they shall bake the meat o ...... Eze 46:20
shall be the o which ye shall ...... Eze 48:8
The meat o and the drink o ...... Joel 1:9
the drink o is cut off from the ...... Joel 1:9
for the meat o and the drink o ...... Joel 1:13
the drink o is withholden from ...... Joel 1:13
even a meat o and a drink o ...... Joel 2:14
a drink o unto the LORD your God ...... Joel 2:14
my dispersed, shall bring mine o ...... Zeph 3:10
will I accept an o at your hand ...... Mal 1:10
offered unto my name, and a pure o ...... Mal 1:11
thus ye brought an o ...... Mal 1:13
him that offereth an o unto the ...... Mal 1:13
he regardeth not the o any more ...... Mal 2:13
the LORD an o in righteousness ...... Mal 3:3
Then shall the o of Judah ...... Mal 3:4
coming to him, and o him vinegar ...... Lk 23:36
until that an o should be offered ...... Acts 21:26
that the o up of the Gentiles ...... Rom 15:16
and hath given himself for us an o ...... Eph 5:2
o thou wouldest not, but a body ...... Heb 10:5
when he said, Sacrifice and o ...... Heb 10:8
o for sin thou wouldest not ...... Heb 10:8
the o of the body of Jesus Christ ...... Heb 10:10
o oftentimes the same sacrifices ...... Heb 10:11
For by one o he hath perfected ...... Heb 10:14
is, there is no more o for sin ...... Heb 10:18

OFFERINGS

and offered burnt o on the altar ...... Gen 8:20
as also sacrifices and burnt o ...... Ex 10:25
sacrifice thereon thy burnt o ...... Ex 20:24
burnt o, and thy peace o ...... Ex 20:24
of Israel, which offered burnt o ...... Ex 24:5
sacrificed peace o of oxen unto ...... Ex 24:5
of the sacrifice of their peace o ...... Ex 29:28
on the morrow, and offered burnt o ...... Ex 32:6
o, and brought peace o ...... Ex 32:6
yet unto him free o every morning ...... Ex 36:3
of the meat o shall be Aaron's ...... Lev 2:3
of the o of the LORD made by fire ...... Lev 2:3
of the o of the LORD made by fire ...... Lev 2:10
with all thine o thou shalt offer ...... Lev 2:13
of the sacrifice of peace o ...... Lev 4:10
fat of the sacrifice of peace o ...... Lev 4:26
from off the sacrifice of peace o ...... Lev 4:31
from the sacrifice of the peace o ...... Lev 4:35
according to the o made by fire o ...... Lev 4:35
according to the o made by fire ...... Lev 4:35
thereon the fat of the peace o ...... Lev 6:12
portion of my o made by fire ...... Lev 6:17
the o of the LORD made by fire ...... Lev 6:18
law of the sacrifice of peace o ...... Lev 7:11
of thanksgiving of his peace o ...... Lev 7:13
the blood of the peace o ...... Lev 7:14
of the sacrifice of his peace o ...... Lev 7:15
o be eaten at all on the third ...... Lev 7:18
flesh of the sacrifice of peace o ...... Lev 7:20

flesh of the sacrifice of peace o ...... Lev 7:21
the sacrifice of his peace o unto ...... Lev 7:29
of the sacrifice of his peace o ...... Lev 7:29
the o of the LORD made by fire ...... Lev 7:30
of the sacrifices of your peace o ...... Lev 7:32
offereth the blood of the peace o ...... Lev 7:33
the sacrifices of their peace o ...... Lev 7:34
out of the o of the LORD made by ...... Lev 7:35
of the sacrifice of the peace o ...... Lev 7:37
a bullock and a ram for peace o ...... Lev 9:4
ram for a sacrifice of peace o ...... Lev 9:18
and the burnt offering, and peace o ...... Lev 9:22
of the o of the LORD made by fire ...... Lev 10:12
peace o of the children of Israel ...... Lev 10:14
the o made by fire of the fat ...... Lev 10:14
them for peace o unto the LORD ...... Lev 17:5
of peace o unto the LORD, ye ...... Lev 19:5
for the o of the LORD made by ...... Lev 21:6
the o of the LORD made by fire ...... Lev 21:21
vows, and for all his freewill o ...... Lev 22:18
offereth a sacrifice of peace o ...... Lev 22:21
meat offering, and their drink o ...... Lev 23:18
year for a sacrifice of peace o ...... Lev 23:19
offering, a sacrifice, and drink o ...... Lev 23:37
and beside all your freewill o ...... Lev 23:38
o of the LORD made by fire by a ...... Lev 24:9
ram without blemish for peace o ...... Num 6:14
meat offering, and their drink o ...... Num 6:15
of peace o unto the LORD, with ...... Num 6:17
the sacrifice of the peace o ...... Num 6:18
And for a sacrifice of peace o ...... Num 7:17
And for a sacrifice of peace o ...... Num 7:23
And for a sacrifice of peace o ...... Num 7:29
And for a sacrifice of peace o ...... Num 7:35
And for a sacrifice of peace o ...... Num 7:41
And for a sacrifice of peace o ...... Num 7:47
And for a sacrifice of peace o ...... Num 7:53
And for a sacrifice of peace o ...... Num 7:59
And for a sacrifice of peace o ...... Num 7:65
And for a sacrifice of peace o ...... Num 7:71
And for a sacrifice of peace o ...... Num 7:77
And for a sacrifice of peace o ...... Num 7:83
of the peace o were twenty ...... Num 7:88
the trumpets over your burnt o ...... Num 10:10
the sacrifices of your peace o ...... Num 10:10
a vow, or peace o unto the LORD ...... Num 15:8
o of all the hallowed things of ...... Num 18:11
with all the wave o of the ...... Num 18:11
All the heave o of the holy ...... Num 18:19
their drink o shall be half an ...... Num 28:14
without blemish) and their drink o ...... Num 28:31
meat offering, and their drink o ...... Num 29:11
offering of it, and their drink o ...... Num 29:11
their drink o for the bullocks ...... Num 29:18
thereof, and their drink o ...... Num 29:19
their drink o for the bullocks ...... Num 29:21
their drink o for the bullocks ...... Num 29:24
their drink o for the bullocks ...... Num 29:27
their drink o for the bullocks ...... Num 29:30
their drink o for the bullocks ...... Num 29:33
their drink o for the bullocks ...... Num 29:33
your vows, and your freewill o ...... Num 29:39
for your burnt o ...... Num 29:39
and for your meat o ...... Num 29:39
and for your drink o ...... Num 29:39
and for your peace o ...... Num 29:39
ye shall bring your burnt o ...... Deut 12:6
heave o of your hand, and your ...... Deut 12:6
and your vows, and your freewill o ...... Deut 12:6
your burnt o, and your sacrifices ...... Deut 12:11
that thou offer not thy burnt o ...... Deut 12:13
thou shalt offer thy burnt o ...... Deut 12:14
thou vowest, nor thy freewill o ...... Deut 12:17
And thou shalt offer thy burnt o ...... Deut 12:27
they shall eat the o of the LORD ...... Deut 18:1
thou shalt offer burnt o thereon ...... Deut 27:6
And thou shalt offer burnt o ...... Deut 27:7
drank the wine of their drink o ...... Deut 32:38
thereon burnt o unto the LORD ...... Josh 8:31
the LORD, and sacrificed peace o ...... Josh 8:31
or if to offer peace o thereon ...... Josh 22:23
Lord before him with our burnt o ...... Josh 22:27
sacrifices, and with our peace o ...... Josh 22:27
our fathers made, not for burnt o ...... Josh 22:28
to build an altar for burnt o ...... Josh 22:29
for burnt o, for meat o ...... Josh 22:29
until even, and offered burnt o ...... Judg 20:26
and peace o before the LORD ...... Judg 20:26
burnt o and peace o ...... Judg 21:4
o made by fire of the children of 1Sa 2:28
of all the o of Israel my people 1Sa 2:29
of Beth-shemesh offered burnt o 1Sa 6:15
down unto thee, to offer burnt o 1Sa 10:8
sacrifice sacrifices of peace o 1Sa 10:8
of peace o before the LORD 1Sa 11:15
burnt offering to me, and peace o 1Sa 13:9
LORD as great delight in burnt o 1Sa 15:22
rain, upon you, nor fields of o 2Sa 1:21
and David offered burnt o and peace 2Sa 6:17
and peace o before the LORD 2Sa 6:17
burnt o and peace o 2Sa 6:18
neither will I offer burnt o unto 2Sa 24:24
burnt o and peace o 2Sa 24:25
a thousand burnt o did Solomon 1Kin 3:4
offer up burnt offering and burnt o 1Kin 3:15
and offered peace o 1Kin 3:15
offered a sacrifice of peace o 1Kin 8:63
for there he offered burnt o 1Kin 8:64
and meat o 1Kin 8:64
and the fat of the peace o 1Kin 8:64

too little to receive the burnt o............. 1Kin 8:64
and meat o.................................... 1Kin 8:64
and the fat of the peace o.................. 1Kin 8:64
a year did Solomon offer burnt o......... 1Kin 9:25
peace o upon the altar which he 1Kin 9:25
in to offer sacrifices and burnt o 2Kin 10:24
the blood of his peace o, upon 2Kin 16:13
meat offering, and their drink o 2Kin 16:15
sacrifices and peace o before God...... 1Chr 16:1
burnt o and the peace o..................... 1Chr 16:2
To offer burnt o unto the LORD............. 1Chr 16:40
thee the oxen also for burnt o............. 1Chr 21:23
nor offer burnt o without cost............. 1Chr 21:24
burnt o and peace o........................... 1Chr 21:26
and offered burnt o unto the LORD....... 1Chr 29:21
lambs, with their drink o.................... 1Chr 29:21
a thousand burnt o upon it................. 2Chr 1:6
and for the burnt o morning............... 2Chr 2:4
for there he offered burnt o................ 2Chr 7:7
and the fat of the peace o.................. 2Chr 7:7
not able to receive the burnt o........... 2Chr 7:7
and the meat o.................................. 2Chr 7:7
Then Solomon offered burnt o unto ... 2Chr 8:12
to offer the burnt o of the LORD........... 2Chr 23:18
they offered burnt o in the house 2Chr 24:14
incense nor offered burnt o in 2Chr 29:7
thank o into the house of the 2Chr 29:31
brought in sacrifices and thank o 2Chr 29:31
as were of a free heart burnt o........... 2Chr 29:31
And the number of the burnt o 2Chr 29:32
could not flay all the burnt o 2Chr 29:34
And also the burnt o were in 2Chr 29:35
with the fat of the peace o................. 2Chr 29:35
the drink o for every burnt................. 2Chr 29:35
brought in the burnt o into the 2Chr 30:15
seven days, offering peace o.............. 2Chr 30:22
priests and Levites for burnt o........... 2Chr 31:2
and for peace o................................. 2Chr 31:2
of his substance for the burnt o 2Chr 31:3
the morning and evening burnt o 2Chr 31:3
the burnt o for the sabbaths, and....... 2Chr 31:3
the o into the house of the LORD.......... 2Chr 31:10
And brought in the o and the tithes.... 2Chr 31:12
was over the freewill o of God............ 2Chr 31:14
and sacrificed thereon peace o 2Chr 33:16
and thank o, and commanded............ 2Chr 33:16
and kids, all for the passover o.......... 2Chr 35:7
for the passover o two thousand 2Chr 35:8
o five thousand small cattle 2Chr 35:8
And they removed the burnt o 2Chr 35:12
the other holy o sod they in pots 2Chr 35:13
busied in offering of burnt o............... 2Chr 35:14
to offer burnt o upon the altar............ 2Chr 35:16
Israel, to offer burnt o thereon.......... Ezr 3:2
they offered burnt o thereon unto...... Ezr 3:3
the LORD, even burnt o morning.......... Ezr 3:3
the daily burnt o by number .... Ezr 3:4
to offer burnt o unto the LORD............. Ezr 3:6
for the burnt o of the God of .... Ezr 6:9
rams, lambs, with their meat o............ Ezr 7:17
and their drink o............................... Ezr 7:17
offered burnt o unto the God of.......... Ezr 8:35
and for the sin o to make an .... Neh 10:33
of our dough, and our o, and the........ Neh 10:37
for the treasures, for the o................. Neh 12:44
aforetime they laid the meat o........... Neh 13:5
and the o of the priests..................... Neh 13:5
offered burnt o according to the .... Job 1:5
their drink o of blood will I not .... Ps 16:4
Remember all thy o, and accept thy ... Ps 20:3
for thy sacrifices or thy burnt o.......... Ps 50:8
go into thy house with burnt o .... Ps 66:13
thee, the freewill o of my mouth........ Ps 119:108
I have peace o with me...................... Prov 7:14
I am full of the burnt o of rams........... Is 1:11
the small cattle of thy burnt o .... Is 43:23
their burnt o and their sacrifices........ Is 56:7
your burnt o are not acceptable......... Jer 6:20
pour out drink o unto other gods........ Jer 7:18
Put your burnt o unto your................. Jer 7:21
concerning burnt o or sacrifices......... Jer 7:22
from the south, bringing burnt o........ Jer 17:26
and sacrifices, and meat o................. Jer 17:26
with fire for burnt o unto Baal............ Jer 19:5
out drink o unto other gods............... Jer 19:13
out drink o unto other gods............... Jer 32:29
a man before me to offer burnt o....... Jer 33:18
and to kindle meat o......................... Jer 33:18
and having cut themselves, with o..... Jer 41:5
and to pour out drink o unto her......... Jer 44:17
and to pour out drink o unto her......... Jer 44:18
and poured out drink o unto her......... Jer 44:19
and pour out drink o unto her............ Jer 44:19
and to pour out drink o unto her .... Jer 44:25
and poured out their drink o.............. Eze 20:28
and there will I require your o............. Eze 20:40
make it, to offer burnt o thereon........ Eze 43:18
make your burnt o upon the altar....... Eze 43:27
upon the altar, and your peace o....... Eze 43:27
a burnt offering, and for peace o........ Eze 45:15
the prince's part to give burnt o........ Eze 45:17
and meat o, and drink .... Eze 45:17
and drink o, in the........................... Eze 45:17
burnt offering, and the peace o......... Eze 45:17
his burnt offering and his peace o...... Eze 46:2
burnt offering or peace o................... Eze 46:12
his burnt offering and his peace o..... Eze 46:12
of God more than burnt o.................. Hos 6:6
for the sacrifices of mine o............... Hos 8:13
not offer wine o to the LORD.............. Hos 9:4

and proclaim and publish the free o.... Amos 4:5
Though ye offer me burnt o................ Amos 5:22
and your meat o................................ Amos 5:22
the peace o of your fat beasts........... Amos 5:22
o in the wilderness forty years,......... Amos 5:25
I come before him with burnt o........... Mic 6:6
In tithes and o.................................. Mal 3:8
is more than all whole burnt o .... Mk 12:33
cast in unto the o of God................... Lk 21:4
to bring alms to my nation, and o...... Acts 24:17
In burnt o and sacrifices for sin.......... Heb 10:6
Sacrifice and offering and burnt o...... Heb 10:8

OFFICE

me he restored unto mine o............... Gen 41:13
When ye do the o of a midwife to ...... Ex 1:16
unto me in the priest's o.................... Ex 28:1
unto me in the priest's o.................... Ex 28:3
unto me in the priest's o.................... Ex 28:4
unto me in the priest's o.................... Ex 28:41
unto me in the priest's o.................... Ex 29:1
the priest's o shall be theirs.............. Ex 29:9
minister to me in the priest's o........... Ex 29:44
unto me in the priest's o.................... Ex 30:30
to minister in the priest's o .... Ex 31:10
to minister in the priest's o .... Ex 35:19
to minister in the priest's o .... Ex 39:41
unto me in the priest's o.................... Ex 40:13
unto me in the priest's o.................... Ex 40:15
unto the LORD in the priest's o............ Lev 7:35
priest's o in his father's stead............ Lev 16:32
to minister in the priest's o .... Num 3:3
ministered in the priest's o in........... Num 3:4
shall wait on their o........................... Num 3:10
to the o of Eleazar the son of............. Num 4:16
o for every thing of the altar .... Num 18:7
I have given your priest's o unto .... Num 18:7
in the priest's o in their stead............ Deut 10:6
o in the temple that Solomon 1Chr 6:10
their o according to their order 1Chr 6:32
seer did ordain in their set o 1Chr 9:22
porters, were in their set o................. 1Chr 9:26
had the set o over the things............. 1Chr 9:31
Because their o was to wait on........... 1Chr 23:28
Ithamar executed the priest's o......... 1Chr 24:2
the priest's o unto the LORD............... 2Chr 11:14
o by the hand of the Levites.............. 2Chr 11:14
of the priests, in their set o............... 2Chr 31:15
for in their set o they........................ 2Chr 31:18
their o was to distribute unto............. Neh 13:13
and let another take his o.................. Ps 109:8
to do the o of a priest unto me,......... Eze 44:13
o before God in the order of his .... Lk 1:8
to the custom of the priest's o........... Lk 1:9
of the Gentiles, I magnify mine o....... Rom 11:13
all members have not the same o....... Rom 12:4
If a man desire the o of a bishop........ 1Ti 3:1
let them use the o of a deacon........... 1Ti 3:10
For they that have used the o of........ 1Ti 3:13
of Levi, who receive the o of the........ Heb 7:5

OFFICER

an o of Pharaoh's, and captain of....... Gen 37:36
an o of Pharaoh, captain of the .... Gen 39:1
and Zebul his o.................................. Judg 9:28
the son of Nathan was principal o 1Kin 4:5
he was the only o which was in.......... 1Kin 4:19
the king of Israel called an o.............. 1Kin 22:9
appointed unto her a certain o.......... 2Kin 8:6
out of the city he took an o that 2Kin 25:19
and the high priest's o came.............. 2Chr 24:11
the judge deliver thee to the o........... Mt 5:25
the judge deliver thee to the o........... Lk 12:58
the o cast thee into prison................. Lk 12:58

OFFICERS

was wroth against two of his o .... Gen 40:2
he asked Pharaoh's o that were......... Gen 40:7
let him appoint o over the land.......... Gen 41:34
of the people, and their o.................. Ex 5:6
the people went out, and their o........ Ex 5:10
the o of the children of Israel,........... Ex 5:14
Then the o of the children of .... Ex 5:15
the o of the children of Israel .... Ex 5:19
of the people, and o over them.......... Num 11:16
was wroth with o of the host .... Num 31:14
the o which were over thousands....... Num 31:48
over tens, and o among your tribes.... Deut 1:15
o shalt thou make them in all thy ...... Deut 16:18
the o shall speak unto the people...... Deut 20:5
the o shall speak further unto .... Deut 20:8
when the o have made an end of........ Deut 20:9
tribes, your elders, and your o .... Deut 29:10
elders of your tribes, and your o .... Deut 31:28
commanded the o of the people......... Josh 1:10
that the o went through the host........ Josh 3:2
all Israel, and their elders, and o....... Josh 8:33
for their judges, and for their o......... Josh 23:2
for their judges, and for their o......... Josh 24:1
your vineyards, and give to his o 1Sa 8:15
the son of Nathan was over his o 1Kin 4:5
had twelve o over all Israel................ 1Kin 4:7
those o provided victual for king....... 1Kin 4:27
unto the place where the o were........ 1Kin 4:28
o which were over the work................ 1Kin 9:23
These were the chief of the o............. 1Kin 9:23
the o of the host, and said unto......... 2Kin 11:15
the priest appointed o over the......... 2Kin 11:18
and his princes, and his o.................. 2Kin 24:12
and the king's wives, and his o.......... 2Kin 24:15
and six thousand were o and judges... 1Chr 23:4
business over Israel, for o................. 1Chr 26:29

were o among them of Israel on........ 1Chr 26:30
their o that served the king in........... 1Chr 27:1
king, and of his sons, with the o........ 1Chr 28:1
the chief of king Solomon's o............. 2Chr 8:10
of Israel called for one of his o 2Chr 18:8
the Levites shall be before you.......... 2Chr 19:11
Levites there were scribes, and o...... 2Chr 34:13
to all the o of his house..................... Est 1:8
let the king appoint o in all the......... Est 2:3
o of the king, helped the Jews........... Est 9:3
I will also make thy o peace............... Is 60:17
that ye should be o in the house .... Jer 29:26
chief priests sent o to take him.......... Jn 7:32
Then came the o to the chief.............. Jn 7:45
The o answered, Never man spake..... Jn 7:46
o from the chief priests and .... Jn 18:3
o of the Jews took Jesus, and............ Jn 18:12
o stood there, who had made a .... Jn 18:18
one of the o which stood by .... Jn 18:22
o saw him, they cried out, saying ..... Jn 19:6
But when the o came, and found........ Acts 5:22
Then went the captain with the o ...... Acts 5:26

OFFICES

thee, into one of the priests' o.......... 1Sa 2:36
to their o in their service................... 1Chr 24:3
And the priests waited on their o....... 2Chr 7:6
Also Jehoiada appointed the o of....... 2Chr 23:18
of my God, and for the o thereof........ Neh 13:14

OFFSCOURING

Thou hast made us as the o............... Lam 3:45
are the o of all things unto this.......... 1Cor 4:13

OFFSPRING

thine o as the grass of the earth .... Job 5:25
their o before their eyes.................... Job 21:8
his o shall not be satisfied with......... Job 27:14
yea, let my o be rooted out................ Job 31:8
of his father's house, the o................ Is 22:24
seed, and my blessing upon thine o ... Is 44:3
the o of thy bowels like the .... Is 48:19
and their o among the people............ Is 61:9
of the LORD, and their o with them..... Is 65:23
have said, For we are also his o .... Acts 17:28
then as we are the o of God............... Acts 17:29
the o of David, and the bright and ..... Rev 22:16

OFT

that as o as he passed by, he............ 2Kin 4:8
How o is the candle of the wicked...... Job 21:17
how o cometh their destruction......... Job 21:17
How o did they provoke him in the .... Ps 78:40
Why do we and the Pharisees fast o... Mt 9:14
the fire, and o into the water .... Mt 17:15
how o shall my brother sin................. Mt 18:21
except they wash their hands o......... Mk 7:3
I punished them o in every .... Acts 26:11
do ye, as o as ye drink it, in.............. 1Cor 11:25
more frequent, in deaths o................ 2Cor 11:23
for he o refreshed me, and was not ... 2Ti 1:16
in the rain that cometh o upon it....... Heb 6:7

OFTEN

that being o reproved hardeneth....... Prov 29:1
the LORD spake o one to another........ Mal 3:16
how o would I have gathered thy ...... Mt 23:37
he had been o bound with fetters...... Mk 5:4
the o disciples of John fast o............. Lk 5:33
how o would I have gathered thy ...... Lk 13:34
For as o as ye eat this bread, and 1Cor 11:26
In journeyings o, in perils of 2Cor 11:26
and painfulness, in watchings o......... 2Cor 11:27
hunger and thirst, in fastings o 2Cor 11:27
walk, of whom I have told you o......... Phil 3:18
sake and thine o infirmities............... 1Ti 5:23
that he should offer himself .... Heb 9:25
For then must he o have suffered....... Heb 9:26
all plagues, as o as they will............. Rev 11:6

OFTENER

wherefore he sent for him the o .... Acts 24:26

OFTENTIMES

things worketh God o with man......... Job 33:29
For o also thine own heart................. Eccl 7:22
For o it had caught him .... Lk 8:29
that o I purposed to come unto.......... Rom 1:13
whom we have o proved diligent in.... 2Cor 8:22
offering o the same sacrifices,........... Heb 10:11

OFTTIMES

for o he falleth into the fire,.............. Mt 17:15
o it hath cast him into the fire,.......... Mk 9:22
for Jesus o resorted thither with....... Jn 18:2

OG (og) *An Amorite king.*
O the king of Bashan went out .... Num 21:33
the kingdom of O king of Bashan....... Num 32:33
O the king of Bashan, which dwelt .... Deut 1:4
O the king of Bashan came out.......... Deut 3:1
delivered into our hands O also......... Deut 3:3
Argob, the kingdom of O in Bashan... Deut 3:4
of the kingdom of O in Bashan .... Deut 3:10
For only O king of Bashan.................. Deut 3:11
Bashan, being the kingdom of O .... Deut 3:13
the land of O king of Bashan, two...... Deut 4:47
O the king of Bashan, came out......... Deut 29:7
them as he did to Sihon and to O ...... Deut 31:4
the other side Jordan, Sihon and O.... Josh 2:10
to O king of Bashan, which was at ..... Josh 9:10
the coast of O king of Bashan............ Josh 12:4
All the kingdom of O in Bashan......... Josh 13:12
the kingdom of O king of Bashan...... Josh 13:30

OH (continued)

of the kingdom of O in Bashan......... Josh 13:31
Amorites, and of O king of Bashan.... 1Kin 4:19
the land of O king of Bashan.......... Neh 9:22
O king of Bashan, and all the......... Ps 135:11
And O the king of Bashan.............. Ps 136:20

OH

O let not the LORD be angry, and I... Gen 18:30
O let not the Lord be angry, and I.... Gen 18:32
And Lot said unto them, O, not so,... Gen 19:18
O, let me escape thither, (is it...... Gen 19:20
O my lord, let thy servant, I......... Gen 44:18
unto the LORD, and said, O............ Ex 32:31
O my Lord, if the LORD be with us.... Judg 6:13
O my Lord, wherewith shall I save.... Judg 6:15
O my lord, as thy soul liveth, my.... 1Sa 1:26
O that I were made judge in the...... 2Sa 15:4
O that one would give me drink of.... 2Sa 23:15
O that thou wouldest bless me........ 1Chr 4:10
O that one would give me drink of.... 1Chr 11:17
O that I might have my request....... Job 6:8
But o that God would speak, and..... Job 11:5
O that ye would altogether hold..... Job 13:5
O that thou wouldest hide me in..... Job 14:13
O that one might plead for a man.... Job 16:21
O that my words were now written... Job 19:23
o that they were printed in a........ Job 19:23
O that I knew where I might find..... Job 23:3
O that I were as in months past,..... Job 29:2
O that we had of his flesh............ Job 31:31
O that one would hear me............. Job 31:35
o save me for thy mercies' sake...... Ps 6:4
O let the wickedness of the.......... Ps 7:9
O that the salvation of Israel........ Ps 14:7
O how great is thy goodness,......... Ps 31:19
O that the salvation of Israel........ Ps 53:6
O that I had wings like a dove........ Ps 55:6
O that my people had hearkened..... Ps 81:13
O that men would praise the LORD ... Ps 107:8
O that men would praise the LORD ... Ps 107:15
O that men would praise the LORD ... Ps 107:21
O that men would praise the LORD ... Ps 107:31
O that thou wouldest rend the........ Is 64:1
O that my head were waters, and..... Jer 9:1
O that I had in the wilderness a...... Jer 9:2
early and sending them, saying, O... Jer 44:4

OHAD (o'-had) A son of Simeon.
Jamin, and O, and Jachin............. Gen 46:10
Jemuel, and Jamin, and O, and Jachin... Ex 6:15

OHEL (o'-hel) A son of Zerubbabel.
and O, and Berechiah,................ 1Chr 3:20

OHOLAH See AHOLAH.

OHOLIAB See AHOLIAB.

OHOLIBAH See AHOLIBAH.

OHOLIBAMAH See AHOLIBAMAH.

OIL

poured o upon the top of it........... Gen 28:18
thereon, and he poured o thereon.... Gen 35:14
O for the light, spices for............ Ex 25:6
the light, spices for anointing o..... Ex 25:6
that they bring the pure o olive...... Ex 27:20
cakes unleavened tempered with o... Ex 29:2
wafers unleavened anointed with o... Ex 29:2
shalt thou take the anointing o...... Ex 29:7
the altar, and of the anointing o.... Ex 29:21
fourth part of an hin of beaten o.... Ex 29:40
sanctuary, and part of o olive an hin... Ex 30:24
make it an o of holy ointment........ Ex 30:25
it shall be an holy anointing o....... Ex 30:25
o unto me throughout your........... Ex 30:31
And the anointing o, and sweet...... Ex 31:11
o for the light, and spices for........ Ex 35:8
light, and spices for anointing o..... Ex 35:8
with the o for the light,.............. Ex 35:14
and his staves, and the anointing o.. Ex 35:15
o for the light, and for the........... Ex 35:28
the light, and for the anointing o.... Ex 35:28
And he made the holy anointing o... Ex 37:29
thereof, and the o for light,......... Ex 37:29
golden altar, and the anointing o... Ex 39:38
thou shalt take the anointing o...... Ex 40:9
and he shall pour o upon it........... Lev 2:1
of the thereof, with all the.......... Lev 2:2
of fine flour mingled with o.......... Lev 2:4
unleavened wafers anointed with o.. Lev 2:4
flour unleavened, mingled with o.... Lev 2:5
it in pieces, and pour o thereon..... Lev 2:6
be made of fine flour with o.......... Lev 2:7
And thou shalt pour o upon it........ Lev 2:15
thereof, and part of the o thereof... Lev 2:16
he shall put no o upon it.............. Lev 5:11
of the o thereof, and all the......... Lev 6:15
In a pan it shall be made with o..... Lev 6:21
meat offering, mingled with o....... Lev 7:10
unleavened cakes mingled with o.... Lev 7:12
with o, and cakes mingled with o.... Lev 7:12
the garments, and the anointing o.. Lev 8:2
And Moses took the anointing o...... Lev 8:10
the anointing o upon Aaron's head.. Lev 8:12
And Moses took of the anointing o.. Lev 8:30
and a meat offering mingled with o.. Lev 9:4
for the anointing o of the LORD...... Lev 10:7
mingled with o, and one log of o..... Lev 14:10
offering, and the log of o............. Lev 14:12
shall take some of the log of o....... Lev 14:15
in the o that is in his left hand..... Lev 14:16

shall sprinkle of the o with his...... Lev 14:16
of the rest of the o that is in........ Lev 14:17
the remnant of the o that is in...... Lev 14:18
with o for a meat offering............ Lev 14:21
a meat offering, and a log of o....... Lev 14:21
offering, and the log of o............. Lev 14:24
the priest shall pour of the o........ Lev 14:26
his right finger some of the o........ Lev 14:27
the priest shall put of the o......... Lev 14:28
the rest of the o that is in the....... Lev 14:29
head the anointing o was poured.... Lev 21:10
o of his God is upon him.............. Lev 21:12
of fine flour mingled with o.......... Lev 23:13
pure o olive beaten for the light..... Lev 24:2
the o vessels thereof,................. Num 4:9
pertaineth the o for the light........ Num 4:16
meat offering, and the anointing o.. Num 4:16
he shall pour no o upon it............ Num 5:15
of fine flour mingled with o.......... Num 6:15
unleavened bread anointed with o... Num 6:15
with o for a meat offering............ Num 7:13
with o for a meat offering............ Num 7:19
with o for a meat offering............ Num 7:25
with o for a meat offering............ Num 7:31
with o for a meat offering............ Num 7:37
with o for a meat offering............ Num 7:43
with o for a meat offering............ Num 7:49
with o for a meat offering............ Num 7:55
with o for a meat offering............ Num 7:61
with o for a meat offering............ Num 7:67
with o for a meat offering............ Num 7:73
with o for a meat offering............ Num 7:79
even fine flour mingled with o....... Num 8:8
of it was as the taste of fresh o..... Num 11:8
the fourth part of an hin of o........ Num 15:4
the third part of an hin of o.......... Num 15:6
mingled with half an hin of o........ Num 15:9
All the best of the o, and all the.... Num 18:12
fourth part of an hin of beaten o.... Num 28:5
a meat offering, mingled with o...... Num 28:9
a meat offering, mingled with o...... Num 28:12
a meat offering, mingled with o...... Num 28:12
deal of flour mingled with o......... Num 28:13
shall be of flour mingled with o..... Num 28:20
offering that of flour mingled with o.. Num 28:28
shall be of flour mingled with o..... Num 29:3
shall be of flour mingled with o..... Num 29:9
shall be of flour mingled with o..... Num 29:14
was anointed with the holy o........ Num 35:25
thy corn, and thy wine, and thine o.. Deut 7:13
a land of o olive, and honey.......... Deut 8:8
thy corn, and thy wine, and thine o.. Deut 11:14
corn, or of the wine, or of thy o..... Deut 12:17
corn, of thy wine, and of thine o.... Deut 14:23
corn, of thy wine, and of thine o.... Deut 18:4
not anoint thyself with the o........ Deut 28:40
thee either corn, wine, or o.......... Deut 28:51
rock, and o out of the flinty rock.... Deut 32:13
and let him dip his foot in o......... Deut 33:24
Then Samuel took a vial of o......... 1Sa 10:1
fill thine horn with o, and go, I..... 1Sa 16:1
Then Samuel took the horn of o..... 1Sa 16:13
he had not been anointed with o..... 2Sa 1:21
and anoint not thyself with o........ 2Sa 14:2
horn of o out of the tabernacle...... 1Kin 1:39
and twenty measures of pure o...... 1Kin 5:11
barrel, and a little o in a cruse...... 1Kin 17:12
neither shall the cruse of o fail...... 1Kin 17:14
neither did the cruse of o fail........ 1Kin 17:16
in the house, save a pot of o.......... 2Kin 4:2
And the o stayed........................ 2Kin 4:6
And he said, Go, sell the............. 2Kin 4:7
take this box of o in thine hand..... 2Kin 9:1
Then take the box of o, and pour.... 2Kin 9:3
and he poured the o on his head..... 2Kin 9:6
and vineyards, a land of o olive...... 2Kin 18:32
flour, and the wine, and the o....... 1Chr 9:29
bunches of raisins, and wine, and... 1Chr 12:40
over the cellars of o was Joash....... 1Chr 27:28
and twenty thousand bath of o....... 2Chr 2:10
the wheat, and the barley, the o..... 2Chr 2:10
and store of victual, and of o........ 2Chr 11:11
firstfruits of corn, wine, and o...... 2Chr 31:5
increase of corn, and wine, and o... 2Chr 32:28
and meat, and drink, and o, unto.... Ezr 3:7
heaven, wheat, salt, wine, and o.... Ezr 6:9
wine, and to an hundred baths of o.. Ezr 7:22
of the corn, the wine, and the o..... Neh 5:11
manner of trees, of wine and of o.... Neh 10:37
corn, of the new wine, and the o.... Neh 10:39
the corn, the new wine, and the o... Neh 13:5
the o unto the treasures.............. Neh 13:12
wit, six months with o of myrrh..... Est 2:12
Which make o within their walls,.... Job 24:11
rock poured me out rivers of o....... Job 29:6
thou anointest my head with o....... Ps 23:5
hath anointed thee with the o........ Ps 45:7
his words were softer than o......... Ps 55:21
with my holy o have I anointed...... Ps 89:20
I shall be anointed with fresh o...... Ps 92:10
o to make his face to shine, and..... Ps 104:15
water, and like o into his bones..... Ps 109:18
it shall be an excellent o............. Ps 141:5
and her mouth is smoother than o... Prov 5:3
wine and o shall not be rich......... Prov 21:17
o in the dwelling of the wise......... Prov 21:20
and the myrtle, and the o tree....... Is 41:19
the o of joy for mourning, the....... Is 61:3
for wheat, and for wine, and for o... Jer 31:12
ye wine, and summer fruits, and o.. Jer 40:10

of wheat, and of barley, and of o.... Jer 41:8
thee, and I anointed thee with o..... Eze 16:9
eat fine flour, and honey, and o...... Eze 16:13
and thou hast set mine o and mine... Eze 16:18
I gave thee, fine flour, and o......... Eze 16:19
hast set mine incense and mine o.... Eze 23:41
and Pannag, and honey, and o........ Eze 27:17
cause their rivers to run like o...... Eze 32:14
ordinance of o, the bath of o......... Eze 45:14
ram, and an hin of o for an ephah... Eze 45:24
offering, and according to the o..... Eze 45:25
give, and an hin of o to an ephah.... Eze 46:5
unto, and an hin of o to an ephah... Eze 46:7
give, and an hin of o to an ephah.... Eze 46:11
and the third part of an hin of o..... Eze 46:14
and the meat offering, and the o..... Eze 46:15
water, my wool and my flax, mine o.. Hos 2:5
I gave her corn, and wine, and o..... Hos 2:8
the corn, and the wine, and the o.... Hos 2:22
and o is carried into Egypt............ Hos 12:1
is dried up, the o languisheth....... Joel 1:10
will send you corn, and wine, and o.. Joel 2:19
shall overflow with wine and o....... Joel 2:24
with ten thousands of rivers of o.... Mic 6:7
thou shalt not anoint thee with o.... Mic 6:15
upon the new wine, and upon the o.. Hag 1:11
bread, or pottage, or wine, or o...... Hag 2:12
the golden o out of themselves...... Zec 4:12
lamps, and took no o with them..... Mt 25:3
But the wise took o in their.......... Mt 25:4
unto the wise, Give us of your o..... Mt 25:8
anointed with o many that were..... Mk 6:13
My head with o thou didst not....... Lk 7:46
bound up his wounds, pouring in o.. Lk 10:34
he said, An hundred measures of o.. Lk 16:6
hath anointed thee with the o of.... Heb 1:9
anointing him with o in the name... Jas 5:14
and see thou hurt not the o........... Rev 6:6
and frankincense, and wine, and o.. Rev 18:13

OILED

of bread, and one cake of o bread... Ex 29:23
cake, and a cake of o bread........... Lev 8:26

OINTMENT

shalt make it an oil of holy o........ Ex 30:25
an o compound after the art of...... Ex 30:25
and the spices, and the precious o... 2Kin 20:13
priests made the o of the spices..... 1Chr 9:30
he maketh the sea like a pot of o.... Job 41:31
like the precious o upon the head... Ps 133:2
O and perfume rejoice the heart..... Prov 27:9
the o of his right hand, which....... Prov 27:16
name is better than precious o....... Eccl 7:1
and let thy head lack no o............. Eccl 9:8
Dead flies cause the o of the......... Eccl 10:1
thy name is as o poured forth........ Song 1:3
up, neither mollified with o.......... Is 1:6
and the spices, and the precious o... Is 39:2
thou wentest to the king with o..... Is 57:9
alabaster box of very precious o..... Mt 26:7
For this o might have been sold...... Mt 26:9
she hath poured this o on my body... Mt 26:12
of o of spikenard very precious...... Mk 14:3
Why was this waste of the o made... Mk 14:4
brought an alabaster box of o........ Lk 7:37
feet, and anointed them with the o.. Lk 7:38
hath anointed my feet with o......... Lk 7:46
which anointed the Lord with o...... Jn 11:2
Mary a pound of o of spikenard...... Jn 12:3
filled with the odour of the o........ Jn 12:3
Why was not this o sold for three.... Jn 12:5

OINTMENTS

of the savour of thy good o thy...... Song 1:3
smell of thine o than all spices...... Song 4:10
themselves with the chief o.......... Amos 6:6
returned, and prepared spices and o.. Lk 23:56
And cinnamon, and odours, and o.... Rev 18:13

OLD

And Noah was five hundred years o.. Gen 5:32
became mighty men which were of o.. Gen 6:4
Noah was six hundred years o when.. Gen 7:6
Shem was an hundred years o......... Gen 11:10
five years o when he departed out... Gen 12:4
me an hiefer of three years o......... Gen 15:9
and a she goat of three years o...... Gen 15:9
and a ram of three years o............ Gen 15:9
shalt be buried in a good o age....... Gen 15:15
was fourscore and six years o........ Gen 16:16
And when Abram was ninety years o.. Gen 17:1
he that is eight days o shall be...... Gen 17:12
him that is an hundred years o....... Gen 17:17
Sarah, that is ninety years o.......... Gen 17:17
And Abraham was ninety years o..... Gen 17:24
his son was thirteen years o.......... Gen 17:25
Now Abraham and Sarah were o...... Gen 18:11
After I am waxed o shall I have...... Gen 18:12
pleasure, my lord being o also....... Gen 18:12
a surely bear a child, which am o.... Gen 18:13
compassed the house round, both o.. Gen 19:4
unto the younger, Our father is o.... Gen 19:31
bare Abraham a son in his o age...... Gen 21:2
his son Isaac being eight days o...... Gen 21:4
And Abraham was an hundred years o.. Gen 21:5
have born him a son in his o age..... Gen 21:7
and seven and twenty years........... Gen 23:1
And Abraham was o, and well........ Gen 24:1
a son to my master when she was o.. Gen 24:36
ghost, and died in a good o age...... Gen 25:8
an o man, and full of years........... Gen 25:8

Isaac was forty years o when he .... Gen 25:20
years o when she bare them .... Gen 25:26
Esau was forty years o when he .... Gen 26:34
to pass, that when Isaac was o .... Gen 27:1
And he said, Behold now, I am o .... Gen 27:2
gathered unto his people, being o .... Gen 35:29
Joseph, being seventeen years o .... Gen 37:2
he was the son of his o age .... Gen 37:3
Joseph was thirty years o when he .... Gen 41:46
the o man of whom we spake .... Gen 43:27
o man, and a child of his o age .... Gen 44:20
said unto Jacob, How o art thou .... Gen 47:8
as a lion, and as an o lion .... Gen 49:9
being an hundred and ten years o .... Gen 50:26
And Moses was fourscore years o .... Ex 7:7
Aaron fourscore and three years o .... Ex 7:7
go with our young and with our o .... Ex 10:9
are numbered, from twenty years o .... Ex 30:14
be numbered, from twenty years o .... Ex 38:26
It is an o leprosy in the skin of .... Lev 13:11
and honour the face of the o man .... Lev 19:32
eat yet of o fruit until the .... Lev 25:22
in ye shall eat of the o store .... Lev 25:22
And ye shall eat o store .... Lev 26:10
bring forth the o because of the .... Lev 26:10
years o even unto sixty years o .... Lev 27:3
o even unto twenty years o .... Lev 27:5
month o even unto five years o .... Lev 27:6
And if it be from sixty years o .... Lev 27:7
From twenty years o and upward, ... Num 1:3
of the names, from twenty years o .... Num 1:18
every male from twenty years o .... Num 1:20
every male from twenty years o .... Num 1:22
of the names, from twenty years o .... Num 1:24
of the names, from twenty years o .... Num 1:26
of the names, from twenty years o .... Num 1:28
of the names, from twenty years o .... Num 1:30
of the names, from twenty years o .... Num 1:32
of the names, from twenty years o .... Num 1:34
of the names, from twenty years o .... Num 1:36
of the names, from twenty years o .... Num 1:38
of the names, from twenty years o .... Num 1:40
of the names, from twenty years o .... Num 1:42
fathers, from twenty years o .... Num 1:45
every male from a month o .... Num 3:15
of all the males, from a month o .... Num 3:22
of all the males, from a month o .... Num 3:28
of all the males, from a month o .... Num 3:34
all the males from a month o .... Num 3:39
children of Israel from a month o .... Num 3:40
number of names, from a month o .... Num 3:43
From thirty years o and upward .... Num 4:3
upward even until fifty years o .... Num 4:3
From thirty years o and upward .... Num 4:23
years o shalt thou number them .... Num 4:23
From thirty years o and upward .... Num 4:30
years o shalt thou number them .... Num 4:30
From thirty years o and upward .... Num 4:35
and upward even unto fifty years o .... Num 4:35
From thirty years o and upward .... Num 4:39
and upward even unto fifty years o .... Num 4:39
From thirty years o and upward .... Num 4:43
and upward even unto fifty years o .... Num 4:43
From thirty years o and upward .... Num 4:47
and upward even unto fifty years o .... Num 4:47
from twenty and five years o .... Num 8:24
whole number, from twenty years o .... Num 14:29
from a month o shalt thou redeem .... Num 18:16
of Israel, from twenty years o .... Num 26:2
the people, from twenty years o .... Num 26:4
all males from a month o .... Num 26:62
out of Egypt, from twenty years o .... Num 32:11
three years o when he died in .... Num 33:39
giants dwelt therein in time .... Deut 2:20
Thy raiment waxed not o upon thee .... Deut 8:4
which they of o time have set in .... Deut 19:14
not regard the person of the o .... Deut 28:50
clothes are not waxen o upon you .... Deut 29:5
shoe is not waxen o upon thy foot .... Deut 29:5
and twenty years o this day .... Deut 31:2
Remember the days of o, consider .... Deut 32:7
and twenty years o when he died .... Deut 34:7
they did eat of the o corn of the .... Josh 5:11
eaten of the o corn of the land .... Josh 5:12
both man and woman, young and o .... Josh 6:21
took o sacks upon their asses, and .... Josh 9:4
their asses, and wine bottles, o .... Josh 9:4
o shoes and clouted upon their .... Josh 9:5
feet, and o garments upon them .... Josh 9:5
our shoes are become o by reason .... Josh 9:13
Now Joshua was o and stricken in .... Josh 13:1
LORD said unto him, Thou art o .... Josh 13:1
Forty years o was I when Moses .... Josh 14:7
day fourscore and five years o .... Josh 14:10
round about, that Joshua waxed o .... Josh 23:1
and said unto them, I am o .... Josh 23:2
other side of the flood in o time .... Josh 24:2
being an hundred and ten years o .... Josh 24:29
being an hundred and ten years o .... Judg 2:8
second bullock of seven years o .... Judg 6:25
son of Joash died in a good o age .... Judg 8:32
there came an o man from his work .... Judg 19:16
the o man said, Whither goest .... Judg 19:17
the o man said, Peace be with .... Judg 19:20
master of the house, the o man .... Judg 19:22
for I am too o to have an husband .... Ruth 1:12
and a nourisher of thine o age .... Ruth 4:15
Now Eli was very o, and heard all 1Sa 2:22
not be an o man in thine house 1Sa 2:31
there shall not be an o man 1Sa 2:32

Eli was ninety and eight years o 1Sa 4:15
for he was an o man, and heavy 1Sa 4:18
came to pass, when Samuel was o 1Sa 8:1
said unto him, Behold, thou art o 1Sa 8:5
and I am o and grayheaded 1Sa 12:2
for an o man in the days of Saul 1Sa 17:12
for those nations were of o the 1Sa 27:8
And she said, An o man cometh up 1Sa 28:14
Saul's son was forty years o when 2Sa 2:10
He was five years o when the 2Sa 4:4
years o when he began to reign 2Sa 5:4
aged man, even fourscore years o 2Sa 19:32
I am this day fourscore years o 2Sa 19:35
They were wont to speak in o time 2Sa 20:18
Now king David was o and stricken 1Kin 1:1
and the king was very o 1Kin 1:15
came to pass, when Solomon was o 1Kin 11:4
Rehoboam consulted with the o men 1Kin 12:6
forsook the counsel of the o men 1Kin 12:8
forsook the o men's counsel that 1Kin 12:13
dwelt an o prophet in Beth-el 1Kin 13:11
city where the o prophet dwelt 1Kin 13:25
the o prophet came to the city 1Kin 13:29
one years o when he began to 1Kin 14:21
o age he was diseased in his feet 1Kin 15:23
five years o when he began to 1Kin 22:42
no child, and her husband is o 2Kin 4:14
two years o was he when he began 2Kin 8:17
twenty years o was Ahaziah when 2Kin 8:26
Seven years o was Jehoash when he 2Kin 11:21
five years o when he began to 2Kin 14:2
which was sixteen years o 2Kin 14:21
Sixteen years o was he when he 2Kin 15:2
twenty years o was he when he 2Kin 15:33
Twenty years o was Ahaz when he 2Kin 16:2
five years o was he when he began 2Kin 18:2
years o when he began to reign 2Kin 21:1
two years o when he began to 2Kin 21:19
years o when he began to reign 2Kin 22:1
three years o when he began to 2Kin 23:31
five years o when he began to 2Kin 23:36
years o when he began to reign 2Kin 24:8
one years o when he began to 2Kin 24:18
when he was threescore years o 1Chr 2:21
they of Ham dwelt there of o 1Chr 4:40
So when David was o and full of 1Chr 23:1
were numbered from twenty years o 1Chr 23:27
of them from twenty years o 1Chr 27:23
And he died in a good o age 1Chr 29:28
the o men that had stood before 2Chr 10:6
counsel which the o men gave him 2Chr 10:8
forsook the counsel of the o men 2Chr 10:13
forty years o when he began to 2Chr 12:13
five years o when he began to 2Chr 20:31
two years o was he when he began 2Chr 21:5
two years o was he when he began 2Chr 21:20
two years o was Ahaziah when he 2Chr 22:2
Joash was seven years o when he 2Chr 24:1
But Jehoiada waxed o, and was full 2Chr 24:15
thirty years o was he when he 2Chr 24:15
five years o when he began to 2Chr 25:1
numbered them from twenty years o 2Chr 25:5
Uzziah, who was sixteen years o 2Chr 26:1
Sixteen years o was Uzziah when 2Chr 26:3
five years o when he began to 2Chr 27:1
twenty years o when he began to 2Chr 27:8
Ahaz was twenty years o when he 2Chr 28:1
he was five and twenty years o 2Chr 29:1
of males, from three years o 2Chr 31:16
The Levites from twenty years o 2Chr 31:17
years o when he began to reign 2Chr 33:1
twenty years o when he began to 2Chr 33:21
years o when he began to reign 2Chr 34:1
three years o when he began to 2Chr 36:2
five years o when he began to 2Chr 36:5
years o when he began to reign 2Chr 36:9
twenty years o when he began to 2Chr 36:11
o man, or him that stooped for 2Chr 36:17
the Levites, from twenty years o .... Ezr 3:8
within the same of o time .... Ezr 4:15
of o time hath made insurrection .... Ezr 4:19
Moreover the o gate repaired .... Neh 3:6
their clothes waxed not o .... Neh 9:21
of Ephraim, and above the o gate .... Neh 12:39
Asaph of o there were chief of .... Neh 12:46
there was an o man, and had no .... Est 3:13
The o lion perisheth for lack of .... Job 4:11
root thereof wax o in the earth .... Job 14:8
Knowest thou not this of o .... Job 20:4
do the wicked live, become o .... Job 21:7
Hast thou marked the o way which .... Job 22:15
in whom o age was perished .... Job 30:2
I am young, and ye are very o .... Job 32:6
So Job died, being o and full of .... Job 42:17
it waxeth o because of all mine .... Ps 6:7
for they have been ever of o .... Ps 25:6
my bones waxed o through my .... Ps 32:3
I have been young, and now am o .... Ps 37:25
in their days, in the times of o .... Ps 44:1
them, even he that abideth of o .... Ps 55:19
of heavens, which were of o .... Ps 68:33
me not off in the time of o age .... Ps 71:9
Now also when I am o and .... Ps 71:18
which thou hast purchased of o .... Ps 74:2
For God is my King of o, working .... Ps 74:12
I have considered the days of o .... Ps 77:5
I will remember thy wonders of o .... Ps 77:11
I will utter dark sayings of o .... Ps 78:2
still bring forth fruit in o age .... Ps 92:14
Thy throne is established of o .... Ps 93:2

Of o hast thou laid the .... Ps 102:25
them shall wax o like a garment .... Ps 102:26
I remembered thy judgments of o .... Ps 119:52
I have known of o that thou hast .... Ps 119:152
I remember the days of o .... Ps 143:5
o men, and children .... Ps 148:12
of his way, before his works of o .... Prov 8:22
children are the crown of o men .... Prov 17:6
the beauty of o men is the grey .... Prov 20:29
and when he is o, he will not .... Prov 22:6
Remove not the o landmark .... Prov 23:10
not thy mother when she is o .... Prov 23:22
it hath been already of o time .... Eccl 1:10
a poor and a wise child than an o .... Eccl 4:13
of pleasant fruits, new and o .... Song 7:13
Zoar, an heifer of three years o .... Is 15:5
Ethiopians captives, young and o .... Is 20:4
walls for the water of the o pool .... Is 22:11
thy counsels of o are .... Is 25:1
o lion, the viper and fiery flying .... Is 30:6
For Tophet is ordained of o .... Is 30:33
neither consider the things of o .... Is 43:18
And even to your o age I am he .... Is 46:4
Remember the former things of o .... Is 46:9
they all shall wax o as a garment .... Is 50:9
earth shall wax o like a garment .... Is 51:6
days, in the generations of o .... Is 51:9
not I held my peace even of o .... Is 57:11
shall build the o waste places .... Is 58:12
And they shall build the o wastes .... Is 61:4
and carried them all the days of o .... Is 63:9
Then he remembered the days of o .... Is 63:11
nor an o man that hath not filled .... Is 65:20
shall die an hundred years o .... Is 65:20
hundred years o shall be accursed .... Is 65:20
For of o time I have broken thy .... Jer 2:20
and see, and ask for the o paths .... Jer 6:16
before thee of o prophesied both .... Jer 28:8
Loeb hath appeared of o unto me .... Jer 31:3
both young men and o together .... Jer 31:13
and took thence o cast clouts .... Jer 38:11
o rotten rags, and let them down .... Jer 38:11
Put now these o cast clouts .... Jer 38:12
be inhabited, as in the days of o .... Jer 46:26
as an heifer of three years o .... Jer 48:34
thee will I break in pieces o .... Jer 51:22
twenty years o when he began to .... Jer 52:1
that she had in the days of o .... Lam 1:7
he had commanded in the days of o .... Lam 2:17
the o lie on the ground in the .... Lam 2:21
flesh and my skin hath he made o .... Lam 3:4
places, as they that be dead of o .... Lam 3:6
renew our days as of o .... Lam 5:21
Slay utterly o and young, both .... Eze 9:6
unto her that was o in adulteries .... Eze 23:43
to destroy it for the o hatred .... Eze 25:15
pit, with the people of o time .... Eze 26:20
earth, in places desolate of o .... Eze 26:20
settle you after your o estates .... Eze 36:11
in o time by my servants the .... Eze 38:17
about threescore and two years o .... Dan 5:31
ye o men, and give ear, all ye .... Joel 1:2
your o men shall dream dreams, ... Joel 2:28
will build it as in the days of o .... Amos 9:11
goings forth have been from of o .... Mic 5:2
with calves of a year o .... Mic 6:6
and Gilead, as in the days of o .... Mic 7:14
our fathers from the days of o .... Mic 7:20
But Nineveh is of o like a pool .... Nah 2:8
where the lion, even the o lion .... Nah 2:11
There shall yet o men .... Zec 8:4
o women dwell in the streets of .... Zec 8:4
the LORD, as in the days of o .... Mal 3:4
coasts thereof, from two years o .... Mt 2:16
it was said by them of o time .... Mt 5:21
it was said by them of o time .... Mt 5:27
hath been said by them of o time .... Mt 5:33
of new cloth unto an o garment .... Mt 9:16
men put new wine into o bottles .... Mt 9:17
of his treasure things new and o .... Mt 13:52
of new cloth on an o garment .... Mk 2:21
it up taketh away from the o .... Mk 2:21
putteth new wine into o bottles .... Mk 2:22
for I am an o man, and my wife .... Lk 1:18
also conceived a son in her o age .... Lk 1:36
And when he was twelve years o .... Lk 2:42
piece of a new garment upon an o .... Lk 5:36
of the new agreeth not with the o .... Lk 5:36
putteth new wine into o bottles .... Lk 5:37
No man also having drunk o wine .... Lk 5:39
for he saith, The o is better .... Lk 5:39
that one of the o prophets was .... Lk 9:8
that one of the o prophets is .... Lk 9:19
yourselves bags which wax not o .... Lk 12:33
can a man be born when he is o .... Jn 3:4
Thou art not yet fifty years o .... Jn 8:57
but when thou shalt be o, thou .... Jn 21:18
your o men shall dream dreams .... Acts 2:17
the man was above forty years o .... Acts 4:22
And when he was full forty years o .... Acts 7:23
For Moses of o time hath in every .... Acts 15:21
an o disciple, with whom we .... Acts 21:16
he was about an hundred years o .... Rom 4:19
that our o man is crucified with .... Rom 6:6
Purge out therefore the o leaven 1Cor 5:7
keep the feast, not with o leaven 1Cor 5:8
in the reading of the o testament 2Cor 3:14
o things are passed away 2Cor 5:17
the former conversation the o man .... Eph 4:22
put off the o man with his deeds .... Col 3:9

o wives' fables, and exercise 1Ti 4:7
number under threescore years o 1Ti 5:9
all shall wax as doth a garment .... Heb 1:11
he hath made the first o .... Heb 8:13
waxeth o is ready to vanish away .... Heb 8:13
in the o time the holy women also 1Pet 3:5
he was purged from his o sins 2Pet 1:9
not in o time by the will of man 2Pet 1:21
And spared not the o world 2Pet 2:5
word of God the heavens were of o 2Pet 3:5
but an o commandment which ye had 1Jn 2:7
The o commandment is the word 1Jn 2:7
who were before of o ordained to .... Jude 4
that o serpent, called the Devil .... Rev 12:9
that o serpent, which is the .... Rev 20:2

OLDNESS
not in the o of the letter .... Rom 7:6

OLIVE
mouth was as an o leaf pluckt off .... Gen 8:11
pure oil o beaten for the light .... Ex 27:20
the sanctuary, and of oil o an hin .... Ex 30:24
pure oil o beaten for the light .... Lev 24:2
o trees, which thou plantedst not .... Deut 6:11
a land of oil o, and honey .... Deut 8:8
When thou beatest thine o tree .... Deut 24:20
Thou shalt have o trees .... Deut 28:40
for thine o shall cast his fruit .... Deut 28:40
and they said unto the o tree .... Judg 9:8
But the o tree said unto them, ... Judg 9:9
he made two cherubims of o tree 1Kin 6:23
oracle he made doors of o tree 1Kin 6:31
The two doors also were of o tree 1Kin 6:32
of the temple posts of o tree 1Kin 6:33
and vineyards, a land of oil o 2Kin 18:32
And over the o trees and the 1Chr 27:28
fetch o branches, and pine .... Neh 8:15
cast off his flower as the o .... Job 15:33
But I am like a green o tree in .... Ps 52:8
thy children like o plants round .... Ps 128:3
it, as the shaking of an o tree .... Is 17:6
be as the shaking of an o tree .... Is 24:13
called thy name, A green o tree .... Jer 11:16
his beauty shall be as the o tree .... Hos 14:6
your o trees increased, the .... Amos 4:9
the labour of the o shall fail .... Hab 3:17
the o tree, hath not brought .... Hag 2:19
two o trees by it, one upon the .... Zec 4:3
What are these two o trees upon .... Zec 4:11
What be these two o branches .... Zec 4:12
off, and thou, being a wild o tree .... Rom 11:17
the root and fatness of the o tree .... Rom 11:17
o tree which is wild by nature .... Rom 11:24
to nature into a good o tree .... Rom 11:24
be graffed into their own o tree .... Rom 11:24
tree, my brethren, bear o berries .... Jas 3:12
These are the two o trees .... Rev 11:4

OLIVES
corn, with the vineyards and o .... Judg 15:5
thou shalt tread the o, but thou .... Mic 6:15
in that day upon the mount of O .... Zec 14:4
the mount of O shall cleave in .... Zec 14:4
to Bethphage, unto the mount of O .... Mt 21:1
And as he sat upon the mount of O .... Mt 24:3
they went out into the mount of O .... Mt 26:30
and Bethany, at the mount of O .... Mk 11:1
of O over against the temple .... Mk 13:3
they went out into the mount of O .... Mk 14:26
the mount called the mount of O .... Lk 19:29
at the descent of the mount of O .... Lk 19:37
that is called the mount of O .... Lk 21:37
as he was wont, to the mount of O .... Lk 22:39
Jesus went unto the mount of .... Jn 8:1

OLIVET See MOUNT, OLIVES. *Hills east of Jerusalem.*
went up by the ascent of mount O 2Sa 15:30
Jerusalem from the mount called O .... Acts 1:12

OLIVEYARD
with thy vineyard, and with thy o .... Ex 23:11

OLIVEYARDS
o which ye planted not do ye eat .... Josh 24:13
and your vineyards, and your o 1Sa 8:14
and to receive garments, and o 2Kin 5:26
lands, their vineyards, their o .... Neh 5:11
wells digged, vineyards, and o .... Neh 9:25

OLYMPAS (o-lim'-pas) *A Christian acquaintance of Paul.*
Nereus, and his sister, and O .... Rom 16:15

OMAR (o'-mar) *A son of Eliphaz.*
the sons of Eliphaz were Teman, O .... Gen 36:11
duke Teman, duke O, duke Zepho, ... Gen 36:15
Teman, and O, Zephi, and Gatam, ... 1Chr 1:36

OMEGA (o'-me-gah) *Last letter of Greek alphabet; a title applied to Jesus.*
I am Alpha and O, the beginning and .... Rev 1:8
Saying, I am Alpha and O, the .... Rev 1:11
I am Alpha and O, the beginning and .... Rev 21:6
I am Alpha and O, the beginning and .... Rev 22:13

OMER
an o for every man, according to .... Ex 16:16
when they did mete it with an o .... Ex 16:18
Fill an o of it to be kept .... Ex 16:32
put an o full of manna therein, ... Ex 16:33
Now an o is the tenth part of an .... Ex 16:36

OMERS
as much bread, two o for one man .... Ex 16:22

OMITTED
have o the weightier matters of .... Mt 23:23

OMNIPOTENT
for the Lord God o reigneth .... Rev 19:6

OMRI (om'-ri)
1. *A king of Israel.*
wherefore all Israel made O 1Kin 16:16
O went up from Gibbethon, and all 1Kin 16:17
and half followed O 1Kin 16:21
O prevailed against the people 1Kin 16:22
so Tibni died, and O reigned 1Kin 16:22
began O to reign over Israel 1Kin 16:23
But O wrought evil in the eyes of 1Kin 16:25
of the acts of O which he did 1Kin 16:27
So O slept with his fathers, and 1Kin 16:28
the son of O to reign over Israel 1Kin 16:29
Ahab the son of O reigned over 1Kin 16:29
Ahab the son of O reigned in 1Kin 16:30
the daughter of O king of Israel 2Kin 8:26
was Athaliah the daughter of O 2Chr 22:2
For the statutes of O are kept .... Mic 6:16
2. *Son of Becher.*
and Eliezer, and Elioenai, and O 1Chr 7:8
3. *A descendant of Pharez.*
the son of Ammihud, the son of O 1Chr 9:4
4. *A ruler of Issachar.*
of Issachar, O the son of Michael 1Chr 27:18

ON See PREFACE.

ONAM (o'-nam)
1. *The sons of Shobal.*
Manahath, and Ebal, Shepho, and O .... Gen 36:23
Manahath, and Ebal, Shephi, and O 1Chr 1:40
2. *Son of Jerahmeel.*
she was the mother of O 1Chr 2:26
And the sons of O were, Shammai, ... 1Chr 2:28

ONAN (o'-nan) *A son of Judah.*
and she called his name O .... Gen 38:4
And Judah said unto O, Go in unto .... Gen 38:8
O knew that the seed should not .... Gen 38:9
Er, and O, and Shelah, and Pharez, ... Gen 46:12
O died in the land of Canaan .... Gen 46:12
The sons of Judah were Er and .... Num 26:19
O died in the land of Canaan .... Num 26:19
Er, and O, and Shelah 1Chr 2:3

ONCE
and I will speak yet but this o .... Gen 18:32
I pray thee, my sin only this o .... Ex 10:17
atonement upon the horns of it o .... Ex 30:10
o in the year shall he make .... Ex 30:10
for all their sins o a year .... Lev 16:34
Moses, and said, Let us go up at o .... Num 13:30
thou mayest not consume them at o .... Deut 7:22
war, and go round about the city o .... Josh 6:3
the city, going about it o .... Josh 6:11
day they compassed the city o .... Josh 6:14
but this o I will, that thou .... Judg 6:39
but this o with the fleece .... Judg 6:39
saying, Come up this o, for he .... Judg 16:18
me, I pray thee, only this o .... Judg 16:28
that I may be at o avenged of the .... Judg 16:28
the spear even to the earth at o .... Isa 36:8
o in three years came the navy of 1Kin 10:22
himself there, not o nor twice 2Kin 6:10
every three years o came the 2Chr 9:21
o in ten days store of all sorts .... Neh 5:18
without Jerusalem o or twice .... Neh 13:20
For God speaketh o, yea twice, ... Job 33:14
O have I spoken .... Job 40:5
God hath spoken o .... Ps 62:11
work thereof at o with axes .... Ps 74:6
thy sight when o thine art angry .... Ps 76:7
O have I sworn by my holiness .... Ps 89:35
in his ways shall fall at o .... Prov 28:18
I will destroy and devour at o .... Is 42:14
or shall a nation be born at o .... Is 66:8
inhabitants of the land at this o .... Jer 10:18
when shall it o be .... Jer 13:27
I will this o cause them to know, ... Jer 16:21
Yet o, it is a little while, and I .... Hag 2:6
When o the master of the house is .... Lk 13:25
And they cried out all at o .... Lk 23:18
that he died, he died unto sin o .... Rom 6:10
For I was alive without the law o .... Rom 7:9
above five hundred brethren at o 1Cor 15:6
o was I stoned, thrice I suffered 2Cor 11:25
the faith which o he destroyed .... Gal 1:23
let it not be o named among you, ... Eph 5:3
even in Thessalonica ye sent o .... Phil 4:16
come unto you, even I Paul, o 1Th 2:18
for those who were o enlightened .... Heb 6:4
for this he did o, when he .... Heb 7:27
high priest alone o every year .... Heb 9:7
entered in o into the holy place .... Heb 9:12
but now o in the end of the world .... Heb 9:26
it is appointed unto men o to die .... Heb 9:27
So Christ was o offered to bear .... Heb 9:28
because that the worshippers o .... Heb 10:2
body of Jesus Christ o for all .... Heb 10:10
Yet o more I shake not the earth .... Heb 12:26
Yet o more, signifieth the .... Heb 12:27
also hath o suffered for sins 1Pet 3:18
when the longsuffering of God 1Pet 3:20
was o delivered unto the saints .... Jude 3
though ye o knew this, how that .... Jude 5

ONE See PREFACE.

ONE'S
of death than the day of o birth .... Eccl 7:1
every o bands were loosed .... Acts 16:26

ONES See PREFACE.

ONESIMUS (o-nes'-i-mus) *A Christian of Colosse.*
With O, a faithful and beloved .... Col 4:9
the Colossians by Tychicus and O .... Col s
I beseech thee for my son O .... Philem 10
from Rome to Philemon, by O .... Philem s

ONESIPHORUS (o-ne-sif'-o-rus) *A Christian of Ephesus.*
give mercy unto the house of O 2Ti 1:16
and Aquila, and the household of O 2Ti 4:19

ONIONS
melons, and the leeks, and the o .... Num 11:5

ONLY
his heart was o evil continually .... Gen 6:5
Noah o remained alive, and they .... Gen 7:23
Save o that which the young men .... Gen 14:24
o unto these men do nothing .... Gen 19:8
thine o son Isaac, whom thou .... Gen 22:2
thy son, thine o son from me .... Gen 22:12
not withheld thy son, thine o son, ... Gen 22:16
o bring not my son thither again .... Gen 24:8
o obey my voice, and go fetch me .... Gen 27:13
O herein will the men consent .... Gen 34:22
o let us consent unto them, and .... Gen 34:23
o in the throne will I be greater .... Gen 41:40
the land of the priests bought .... Gen 47:22
except the land of the priests o .... Gen 47:26
o their little ones, and their .... Gen 50:8
they may remain in the river o .... Ex 8:9
they shall remain in the river o .... Ex 8:11
o ye shall not go very far away .... Ex 8:28
O in the land of Goshen, where .... Ex 9:26
my sin o this once, and intreat .... Ex 10:17
take away from me this death o .... Ex 10:17
o let your flocks and your herds, ... Ex 10:24
that o may be done of you .... Ex 12:16
o he shall pay for the loss of .... Ex 21:19
any god, save unto the LORD o .... Ex 22:20
For that is his covering o .... Ex 22:27
O he shall not go in unto the .... Lev 21:23
O the firstling of the beasts, ... Lev 27:26
O thou shalt not number the tribe .... Num 1:49
the LORD indeed spoken o by Moses ..... Num 12:2
O rebel not ye against the LORD, ... Num 14:9
o they shall not come nigh the .... Num 18:3
I will o, without doing any thing .... Num 20:19
but o the word that I shall speak .... Num 22:35
O the gold, and the silver, the .... Num 31:22
o to the family of the tribe of .... Num 36:6
o I will pass through on my feet .... Deut 2:28
O the cattle we took for a prey .... Deut 2:35
O unto the land of the children .... Deut 3:11
For o Og king of Bashan remained .... Deut 3:11
O take heed to thyself, and keep .... Deut 4:9
o ye heard a voice .... Deut 4:12
that man doth not live by bread o .... Deut 8:3
O the LORD had a delight in thy .... Deut 10:15
O ye shall not eat the blood .... Deut 12:16
O be sure that thou eat not the .... Deut 12:23
O thy holy things which thou hast .... Deut 12:26
O if thou carefully hearken unto .... Deut 15:5
O thou shalt not eat the blood .... Deut 15:23
O the trees which thou knowest .... Deut 20:20
then the man o that lay with her .... Deut 22:25
and thou shalt be above o, and thou .... Deut 28:13
and thou shalt be o oppressed .... Deut 28:29
and thou shalt be o oppressed .... Deut 28:33
Neither with you O God be with thee, ... Deut 29:14
O be thou strong and very .... Josh 1:7
o the LORD thy God be with thee, ... Josh 1:17
o be strong and of a good courage ...... Josh 1:18
o on that day they compassed the .... Josh 6:15
o Rahab the harlot shall live, ... Josh 6:17
o the silver, and the gold, and the .... Josh 6:24
o the spoil thereof, and the .... Josh 8:2
O the cattle and the spoil of that .... Josh 8:27
burned none of them, save Hazor o ...... Josh 11:13
in Gaza, in Gath, and in Ashdod, ... Josh 11:22
o divide thou it by lot unto the .... Josh 13:6
O unto the tribe of Levi he gave .... Josh 13:14
thou shalt not have one lot o .... Josh 17:17
O that the generations of the .... Judg 3:2
and if the dew be on the fleece o .... Judg 6:37
it now be dry o upon the fleece .... Judg 6:39
for it was dry upon the fleece o .... Judg 6:40
deliver us o, we pray thee, this .... Judg 10:15
and she was his o child .... Judg 11:34
o this once, O God, that I may be .... Judg 16:28
o lodge not in the street .... Judg 19:20
o her lips moved, but her voice 1Sa 1:13
o the LORD establish his word 1Sa 1:23
o the stump of Dagon was left to 1Sa 5:4
unto the LORD, and serve him o 1Sa 7:3
Ashtaroth, and served the LORD o 1Sa 7:4
O fear the LORD, and serve him in 1Sa 12:24
o be thou valiant for me, and 1Sa 18:17
thou shalt not o while yet I live 1Sa 20:14
o Jonathan and David knew the 1Sa 20:39
for Ammon o is dead 2Sa 13:32
for Ammon o is dead 2Sa 13:33
and I will smite the king o 2Sa 17:2
deliver him o, and I will depart 2Sa 20:21

returned after him o to spoil. 2Sa 23:10
O the people sacrificed in burnt. 1Kin 3:3
o he sacrificed and burnt incense. 1Kin 3:3
he was the o officer which was in. 1Kin 4:19
(for thou, even thou o, knowest. 1Kin 8:39
David, but the tribe of Judah o. 1Kin 12:20
to do that o which was right in. 1Kin 14:8
for he o of Jeroboam shall come. 1Kin 14:13
save o in the matter of Uriah the. 1Kin 15:5
unto the people, I, even I o. 1Kin 18:22
and I, even I o, am left. 1Kin 19:10
and I, even I o, am left. 1Kin 19:14
save o with the king of Israel. 1Kin 22:31
o in Kir-haraseth left they the. 2Kin 3:25
but the worshippers of Baal o. 2Kin 10:23
left but the tribe of Judah o. 2Kin 17:18
art the LORD God, even thou o. 2Kin 19:19
o if they will observe to do. 2Kin 21:8
O the LORD give thee wisdom and. .. 1Chr 22:12
save o to burn sacrifice before. 2Chr 2:6
(for thou o knowest the hearts of. 2Chr 6:30
save o with the king of Israel. 2Chr 18:30
yet unto the LORD their God o. 2Chr 33:17
O Jonathan the son of Asahel and. .... Ezr 10:15
hath not done wrong to the king o. ... Est 1:16
o upon himself put not forth. .... Job 1:11
I o am escaped alone to tell thee. ...... Job 1:15
I o am escaped alone to tell thee. ...... Job 1:16
I o am escaped alone to tell thee. ...... Job 1:17
I o am escaped alone to tell thee. ...... Job 1:19
O do not two things unto me. .... Job 13:20
a nation, or against a man o. .... Job 34:29
o makest me dwell in safety. .... Ps 4:8
Against thee, thee o, have I. .... Ps 51:4
He o is my rock and my salvation. .... Ps 62:2
They o consult to cast him down. ..... Ps 62:4
My soul, wait thou o upon God. .... Ps 62:5
He o is my rock and my salvation. .... Ps 62:6
righteousness, even of thine o. .... Ps 71:16
who o doeth wondrous things. .... Ps 72:18
O with thine eyes shalt thou. .... Ps 91:8
o beloved in the sight of my. .... Prov 4:3
Let them be o thine own, and not. .... Prov 5:17
desire of the righteous is o good. ...... Prov 11:23
O by pride cometh contention. .... Prov 13:10
of the lips tendeth o to penury. .... Prov 14:23
An evil man seeketh o rebellion. .... Prov 17:11
diligent tend o to plenteousness. ...... Prov 21:5
every one that is hasty o to want. ..... Prov 21:5
this o have I found, that God. .... Eccl 7:29
she is the o one of her mother. .... Song 6:9
o let us be called by thy name. .... Is 4:1
but by thee o will we make. .... Is 26:13
it shall be a vexation o to. .... Is 28:19
thou art the LORD, even thou o. ..... Is 37:20
O acknowledge thine iniquity. .... Jer 3:13
thee mourning, as for an o son. .... Jer 6:26
the children of Judah have o done. ... Jer 32:30
o provoked me to anger with the. .... Jer 32:30
an o evil, behold, is come. .... Eze 7:5
they o shall be delivered, but. .... Eze 14:16
but they o shall be delivered. .... Eze 14:18
they shall o poll their heads. .... Eze 44:20
You o have I known of all the. .... Amos 3:2
it as the mourning of an o son. .... Amos 8:10
as one mourneth for his o son. .... Zec 12:10
God, and him o shalt thou serve. ..... Mt 4:10
And if ye salute your brethren o. ..... Mt 5:47
but speak the word o, and my. .... Mt 8:8
water o in the name of a disciple. .... Mt 10:42
with him, but o for the priests. .... Mt 12:4
o touch the hem of his garment. ..... Mt 14:36
they saw no man, save Jesus o. ...... Mt 17:8
nothing thereon, but leaves o. .... Mt 21:19
ye shall not o do this which is. .... Mt 21:21
angels of heaven, but my Father o. .. Mt 24:36
who can forgive sins but God o. ..... Mk 2:7
Be not afraid, o believe. .... Mk 5:36
for their journey, save a staff o. ...... Mk 6:8
save Jesus o with themselves. .... Mk 9:8
God, and him o shalt thou serve. ... Lk 4:8
the o son of his mother, and she. .... Lk 7:12
For he had one o daughter. .... Lk 8:42
believe o, and she shall be made. ... Lk 8:50
for he is mine o child. .... Lk 9:38
him. Art thou o a stranger in. .... Lk 24:18
the glory as of the o begotten of. ... Jn 1:14
the o begotten Son, which is in. .... Jn 1:18
that he gave his o begotten Son. ... Jn 3:16
name of the o begotten Son of God. Jn 3:18
because he not o had broken the. .. Jn 5:18
the honour that cometh from God o Jn 5:44
And not for that nation o, but. ..... Jn 11:52
they came not for Jesus' sake o. ... Jn 12:9
unto him, Lord, not my feet o. .... Jn 13:9
might know thee the o true God. .. Jn 17:3
o they were baptized in the name. . Acts 8:16
word to none but unto the Jews o. Acts 11:19
knowing o the baptism of John. .. Acts 18:25
So that not o this our craft is. ...... Acts 19:27
for I am ready not to be bound o. . Acts 21:13
save o that they keep themselves. . Acts 21:25
I would to God, that not o thou. .. Acts 26:29
not o of the lading and ship, but. . Acts 27:10
not o do the same, but have. .... Rom 1:32
Is he the God of the Jews o. .... Rom 3:29
then upon the circumcision o. .... Rom 4:9
who are not of the circumcision o. Rom 4:12
not to that o which is of the law. . Rom 4:16
And not o so, but we glory in. .... Rom 5:3

And not o so, but we also joy in. ..... Rom 5:11
not o they, but ourselves also,. .... Rom 8:23
And not o this. .... Rom 9:10
he hath called, not of the Jews o. .... Rom 9:24
not o for wrath, but also for. .... Rom 13:5
unto whom not o I give thanks. ..... Rom 16:4
To God o wise, be glory through. ... Rom 16:27
o in the Lord. 1Cor 7:39
Or I o and Barnabas, have not we. .. 1Cor 9:6
or came it unto you o. 1Cor 14:36
If in this life o we have hope in. 1Cor 15:19
And not by his coming o, but by. ... 2Cor 7:7
not o to do, but also to be. 2Cor 8:10
And not that o, but who was also. .. 2Cor 8:19
not o in the sight of the Lord. 2Cor 8:21
of this service not o supplieth. 2Cor 9:12
But they had heard o, That he. ..... Gal 1:23
O they would that were should. .... Gal 2:10
This o would I learn of you,. .... Gal 3:2
not o when I am present with you. . Gal 4:18
o use not liberty for an occasion. ... Gal 5:13
o lest they should suffer. .... Gal 6:12
not o in this world, but also in. ..... Eph 1:21
O let your conversation be as it. .... Phil 1:27
not o to believe on him, but also. .. Phil 1:29
obeyed, not as in my presence o. .. Phil 2:12
and not on him o, but on me also,. . Phil 2:27
giving and receiving, but ye o. ..... Phil 4:15
These o are my fellow workers. .... Col 4:11
came not unto you in word o. 1Th 1:5
of the Lord not o in word. 1Th 1:8
unto you, not the gospel of God o. 1Th 2:8
o he who now letteth will let,. 2Th 2:7
the o wise God, be honour and. ... 1Ti 1:17
not o idle, but tattlers also and. ... 1Ti 5:13
o Potentate, the King of kings,. ... 1Ti 6:15
Who o hath immortality, dwelling. 1Ti 6:16
there are not o vessels of gold. 2Ti 2:20
and not to me o, but unto all them. 2Ti 4:8
O Luke is with me. 2Ti 4:11
Which stood o in meats and drinks,. Heb 9:10
offered up his o begotten son. ..... Heb 11:17
once more I shake not the earth o. . Heb 12:26
of the word, and not hearers o. ... Jas 1:22
is justified, and not by faith o. .... Jas 2:24
not o to the good and gentle, but. . 1Pet 2:18
and not for ours o, but also for. ... 1Jn 2:2
because that God sent his o. 1Jn 4:9
not by water o, but by water and. . 1Jn 5:6
and not I o, but also ye which. 2Jn 1
and denying the o Lord God. ..... Jude 4
To the o wise God our Saviour, be. Jude 25
but o those men which have not. .. Rev 9:4
for thou o art holy. .... Rev 15:4

ONO (o'-no)
1. A city in Benjamin.
and Shamed, who built O. 1Chr 8:12
The children of Lod, Hadid, and O. Ezr 2:33
The children of Lod, Hadid, and O. Neh 7:37
Lod, and O, the valley of. .... Neh 11:35
2. A valley near Jerusalem.
of the villages in the plain of O. ... Neh 6:2

ONWARD
went o in all their journeys. .... Ex 40:36

ONYCHA
the sweet spices, stacte, and o. ..... Ex 30:34

ONYX
there is bdellium and the o stone. .. Gen 2:12
O stones, and stones to be set in. .. Ex 25:7
And thou shalt take two o stones. . Ex 28:9
the fourth row a beryl, and an o. . Ex 28:20
o stones, and stones to be set for. . Ex 35:9
And the rulers brought o stones. . Ex 35:27
they wrought o stones inclosed in. Ex 39:6
And the fourth row, a beryl, an o. Ex 39:13
o stones, and stones to be set,. ... 1Chr 29:2
of Ophir, with the precious o. .... Job 28:16
and the diamond, the beryl, the o. Eze 28:13

OPEN
in the firmament of heaven. .... Gen 1:20
herself, and sat in an o place. ...... Gen 38:14
And if a man shall o a pit. .... Ex 21:33
bird louse into the o field. .... Lev 14:7
out of the city into the o fields. ... Lev 14:53
which they offer in the o field. .... Lev 17:5
instead of such as o every womb. . Num 8:16
thing, and the earth o her mouth. Num 16:30
every o vessel, which hath no. ... Num 19:15
with a sword in the o fields. ...... Num 19:16
man whose eyes are o hath said. . Num 24:3
a trance, but having his eyes o. .. Num 24:4
man whose eyes are o hath said. . Num 24:15
a trance, but having his eyes o. .. Num 24:16
But thou shalt o thine hand wide. Deut 15:8
Thou shalt o thine hand wide unto. Deut 15:11
o unto thee, then it shall be,. ..... Deut 20:11
The LORD shall o unto thee. .... Deut 28:12
and they left the city o, and. ..... Josh 8:17
O the mouth of the cave, and bring. Josh 10:22
there was no vision. 1Sa 3:1
are encamped in the o fields. 2Sa 11:11
carved with knops and o flowers. 1Kin 6:18
o flowers, within and without. .. 1Kin 6:29
o flowers, and overlaid them with. 1Kin 6:32
and palm trees and o flowers. ... 1Kin 6:35
That thine eyes may be o toward. 1Kin 8:29
That thine eyes may be o unto the. 1Kin 8:52
o his eyes, *hat he may see. 2Kin 6:17

o the eyes of these men, that. 2Kin 6:20
Then o the door, and flee, and. 2Kin 9:3
And he said, O the window eastward. 2Kin 13:17
o, LORD, thine eyes, and see. 2Kin 19:16
eyes may be o upon this house day. . 2Chr 6:20
I beseech thee, thine eyes be o. 2Chr 6:40
Now mine eyes shall be o, and mine. 2Chr 7:15
now be attentive, and thine eyes o. . Neh 1:6
time with an o letter in his hand. ... Neh 6:5
speak, and o his lips against thee. .. Job 11:5
dost thou o thine eyes upon such. .. Job 14:3
I will o my lips and answer. .... Job 32:20
men in the o sight of others. .... Job 34:26
doth Job o his mouth in vain. ...... Job 35:16
Who can o the doors of his face. .. Job 41:14
their throat is an o sepulchre. ...... Ps 5:9
his ears are o unto their cry. .... Ps 34:15
I will o my dark saying upon the. .. Ps 49:4
O Lord, o thou my lips. .... Ps 51:15
I will o my mouth in a parable. .... Ps 78:2
o thy mouth wide, and I will fill. .. Ps 81:10
O to me the gates of. .... Ps 118:19
O thou mine eyes, that I may. .... Ps 119:18
that a fool layeth o his folly. ...... Prov 13:16
o thine eyes, and thou shalt be. .. Prov 20:13
o rebuke is better than secret. .... Prov 27:5
O thy mouth for the dumb in the. Prov 31:8
O thy mouth, judge righteously,. Prov 31:9
O to me, my sister, my love, my. Song 5:2
I rose up to o to my beloved. .... Song 5:5
shall devour Israel with o mouth. Is 9:12
he shall o, and none shall shut. .. Is 22:22
and he shall shut, and none shall o. Is 22:22
the windows from on high are o. . Is 24:18
O ye the gates, that the. .... Is 26:2
doth he o and break the clods of. Is 28:24
o thine eyes, O LORD, and see. . Is 37:17
I will o rivers in high places,. .... Is 41:18
To o the blind eyes, to bring out. Is 42:7
let the earth o, and let them. .... Is 45:1
be o continually. .... Is 45:8
thy gates shall be o continually. . Is 60:11
Their quiver is as an o sepulchre. Jer 5:16
fall as dung upon the o field. .... Jer 9:22
be shut up, and none shall o them. Jer 13:19
and custom, and that which was o. Jer 32:11
and this evidence which is o. .... Jer 32:14
for thine eyes are o upon all the. Jer 32:19
utmost border, o her storehouses. Jer 50:26
o thy mouth, and eat that I give. Eze 2:8
I will o thy mouth, and thou shalt. Eze 3:27
thou wast cast out in the o field. Eze 16:5
never o thy mouth any more. ... Eze 16:63
to o the mouth in the slaughter,. Eze 21:22
I will o the side of Moab from. . Eze 25:9
thou shalt fall upon the o fields. Eze 29:5
cast thee forth upon the o field. Eze 32:4
him that is in the o field will I. . Eze 33:27
were very many in the o valley. Eze 37:2
I will o your graves, and cause. Eze 37:12
Thou shalt fall upon the o fields. Eze 39:5
one shall then o him the gate. .. Eze 46:12
his windows being o in his. .... Dan 6:10
o thine eyes, and behold our. .. Dan 9:18
be set wide o unto thine enemies. Nah 3:13
O thy doors, O Lebanon, that the. Zec 11:1
I will o mine eyes upon the house. Zec 12:4
if I will not o you the windows. . Mal 3:10
I will o my mouth in parables. .. Mt 13:35
saying, Lord, Lord, o to us. ..... Mt 25:11
they may o unto him immediately. Lk 12:36
saying, Lord, Lord, o unto us. .. Lk 13:25
Hereafter ye shall see heaven o. . Jn 1:51
Can a devil o the eyes of the. ... Jn 10:21
and seeing the prison doors o. .. Acts 16:27
Paul was now about to o his mouth. Acts 18:14
against any man, the law is o. ... Acts 19:38
To o their eyes, and to turn them. Acts 26:18
Their throat is an o sepulchre. .. Rom 3:13
with o face beholding as in a. ... 2Cor 3:18
our mouth is o unto you, our. .. 2Cor 6:11
that I may o my mouth boldly, to. Eph 6:19
that God would o unto us a door. Col 4:3
Some men's sins are o beforehand. 1Ti 5:24
afresh, and put him to an o shame. Heb 6:6
his ears are o unto their prayers. 1Pet 3:12
I have set before thee an o door. Rev 3:8
o the door, I will come in to him. Rev 3:20
Who is worthy to o the book. .. Rev 5:2
the earth, was able to o the book. Rev 5:3
no man was found worthy to o. Rev 5:4
hath prevailed to o the book. .. Rev 5:5
book, and to o the seals thereof. Rev 5:9
had in his hand a little book o. Rev 10:2
take the little book which is o. Rev 10:8

OPENED
then your eyes shall be o. .... Gen 3:5
And the eyes of them both were o. Gen 3:7
which hath o her mouth to receive. Gen 4:11
and the windows of heaven were o. Gen 7:11
that Noah o the window of the ark. Gen 8:6
God o her eyes, and she saw a well. Gen 21:19
Leah was hated, he o her womb. Gen 29:31
hearkened to her, and o her womb. Gen 30:22
Joseph o all the storehouses, and. Gen 41:56
as one of them o his sack to give. Gen 42:27
that we o our sacks, and, behold,. Gen 43:21
ground, and o every man his sack. Gen 44:11
And when she had o it, she saw the. Ex 2:6
And the earth o her mouth, and. Num 16:32

the LORD o the mouth of the ass,....... Num 22:28
Then the LORD o the eyes of....... Num 22:31
And the earth o her mouth, and....... Num 26:10
how the earth o her mouth....... Deut 11:6
he o not the doors of the parlour....... Judg 3:25
they took a key, and o them....... Judg 3:25
she o a bottle of milk, and gave....... Judg 4:19
for I have o my mouth unto the....... Judg 11:35
if thou hast o thy mouth unto the....... Judg 11:36
o the doors of the house, and went...... Judg 19:27
the doors of the house of the....... 1Sa 3:15
times, and the child o his eyes....... 2Kin 4:35
The LORD o the eyes of the young....... 2Kin 6:17
the LORD o their eyes, and they....... 2Kin 6:20
And he o the door, and fled....... 2Kin 9:10
And he o it....... 2Kin 13:17
because they o not his....... 2Kin 15:16
o the doors of the house of the....... 2Chr 29:3
be o until the sun be hot....... Neh 7:3
Ezra o the book in the sight of....... Neh 8:5
and when he o it, all the people....... Neh 8:5
not be o till after the sabbath....... Neh 13:19
After this o Job his mouth, and....... Job 3:1
they o their mouth wide as for....... Job 29:23
but I o my doors to the traveller....... Job 31:32
Behold, now I have o my mouth....... Job 33:2
gates of death been o unto thee....... Job 38:17
they o their mouth wide against....... Ps 35:21
I was dumb, I o not my mouth....... Ps 39:9
mine ears hast thou o....... Ps 40:6
above, and the doors of heaven,....... Ps 78:23
He o the rock, and the waters....... Ps 105:41
The earth o and swallowed up....... Ps 106:17
of the deceitful are o against me....... Ps 109:2
I o my mouth, and panted....... Ps 119:131
I o to my beloved....... Song 5:6
o her mouth without measure....... Is 5:14
or o the mouth, or peeped....... Is 10:14
that o not the house of his....... Is 14:17
the eyes of the blind shall be o....... Is 35:5
time that thine ear was not o....... Is 48:8
The Lord GOD hath o mine ear....... Is 50:5
afflicted, yet he o not his mouth....... Is 53:7
for unto thee have I o my cause....... Jer 20:12
The LORD hath o his armoury....... Jer 50:25
All thine enemies have o their....... Lam 2:16
All our enemies have o their....... Lam 3:46
Chebar, that the heavens were o....... Eze 1:1
So I o my mouth, and he caused me....... Eze 3:2
hast o thy feet to every one that....... Eze 16:25
be o to him which is escaped....... Eze 24:27
had o my mouth, until he came to....... Eze 33:22
and my mouth was o, and I was no....... Eze 33:22
LORD, when I have o your graves....... Eze 37:13
shall be shut, it shall not be o....... Eze 44:2
but on the sabbath it shall be o....... Eze 46:1
day of the new moon it shall be o....... Eze 46:1
was set, and the books were o....... Dan 7:10
then I o my mouth, and spake, and....... Dan 10:16
gates of the rivers shall be o....... Nah 2:6
fountain o to the house of David....... Zec 13:1
when they had o their treasures,....... Mt 2:11
lo, the heavens were o unto him....... Mt 3:16
he o his mouth, and taught them,....... Mt 5:2
knock, and it shall be o unto you....... Mt 7:7
him that knocketh it shall be o....... Mt 7:8
And their eyes were o....... Mt 9:30
and when thou hast o his mouth,....... Mt 17:27
him, Lord, that our eyes may be o....... Mt 20:33
And the graves were o....... Mt 27:52
the water, he saw the heavens o....... Mk 1:10
him, Ephphatha, that is, Be o....... Mk 7:34
And straightway his ears were o....... Mk 7:35
And his mouth was o immediately....... Lk 1:64
and praying, the heaven was o....... Lk 3:21
And when he had o the book....... Lk 4:17
knock, and it shall be o unto you....... Lk 11:9
him that knocketh it shall be o....... Lk 11:10
And their eyes were o, and they....... Lk 24:31
while he o to us the scriptures....... Lk 24:32
Then o he their understanding,....... Lk 24:45
unto him, How were thine eyes o....... Jn 9:10
made the clay, and o mine eyes....... Jn 9:14
of him, that he hath o thine eyes....... Jn 9:17
or who hath o his eyes, we know....... Jn 9:21
how o he thine eyes....... Jn 9:26
he is, and yet he hath o mine eyes....... Jn 9:30
o the eyes of one that was born....... Jn 9:32
which o the eyes of the blind,....... Jn 11:37
Lord by night o the prison doors....... Acts 5:19
but when we had o, we found no....... Acts 5:23
said, Behold, I see the heavens o....... Acts 7:56
shearer, so o he not his mouth....... Acts 8:32
Then Philip o his mouth, and began...... Acts 8:35
and when his eyes were o, he saw....... Acts 9:8
And she o her eyes....... Acts 9:40
And saw heaven o, and a certain....... Acts 10:11
Then Peter o his mouth, and said,....... Acts 10:34
which o to them of his own accord....... Acts 12:10
she o not the gate for gladness,....... Acts 12:14
and when they had o the door....... Acts 12:16
how he had o the door of faith....... Acts 14:27
whose heart the Lord o, that she....... Acts 16:14
immediately all the doors were o....... Acts 16:26
door and effectual is o unto me....... 1Cor 16:9
a door was o unto me of the Lord,....... 2Cor 2:12
o unto the eyes of him with whom....... Heb 4:13
behold, a door was o in heaven:....... Rev 4:1
when the Lamb o one of the seals,....... Rev 6:1
when he had o the second seal, I....... Rev 6:3

when he had o the third seal, I....... Rev 6:5
when he had o the fourth seal,....... Rev 6:7
when he had o the fifth seal, I....... Rev 6:9
when he had o the sixth seal,....... Rev 6:12
when he had o the seventh seal,....... Rev 8:1
And he o the bottomless pit....... Rev 9:2
the temple of God was o in heaven...... Rev 11:19
woman, and the earth o her mouth ...... Rev 12:16
he o his mouth in blasphemy....... Rev 13:6
of the testimony in heaven was o....... Rev 15:5
And I saw heaven o, and behold a....... Rev 19:11
and the books were o....... Rev 20:12
and another book was o, which is ...... Rev 20:12

OPENEST

thou o thine hand, they are....... Ps 104:28
Thou o thine hand, and satisfiest....... Ps 145:16

OPENETH

whatsoever o the womb among the .... Ex 13:2
The LORD all that o the matrix....... Ex 13:12
to the LORD all that o the matrix....... Ex 13:15
All that o the matrix is mine....... Ex 34:19
of all the firstborn that o the....... Num 3:12
Every thing that o the matrix in ...... Num 18:15
he o his eyes, and he is not....... Job 27:19
Then he o the ears of men, and....... Job 33:16
He o also their ear to discipline....... Job 36:10
o their ears in oppression....... Job 36:15
a dumb man that o not his mouth....... Ps 38:13
The LORD o the eyes of the blind:....... Ps 146:8
but he that o wide his lips shall ...... Prov 13:3
he o not his mouth in the gate....... Prov 24:7
She o her mouth with wisdom....... Prov 31:26
is dumb, so he o not his mouth....... Is 53:7
the fire all that o the womb....... Eze 20:26
Every male that o the womb shall ...... Lk 2:23
To him the porter o....... Jn 10:3
hath the key of David, he that o....... Rev 3:7
and shutteth, and no man o....... Rev 3:7

OPENING

the o thereof every morning....... 1Chr 9:27
up a man, and there can be no o....... Job 12:14
the o of my lips shall be right....... Prov 8:6
the ears, but he heareth not....... Is 42:20
the o of the prison to them that ...... Is 61:1
And o alleging, that Christ must....... Acts 17:3

OPENINGS

concourse, in the o of the gates....... Prov 1:21

OPENLY

that was o by the way side....... Gen 38:21
his righteousness hath he o....... Ps 98:2
himself shall reward thee o....... Mt 6:4
in secret shall reward thee o....... Mt 6:6
in secret, shall reward thee o....... Mt 6:18
no more o enter into the city....... Mk 1:45
And he spake that saying o....... Mk 8:32
he himself seeketh to be known o....... Jn 7:4
he also up unto the feast, not o....... Jn 7:10
Howbeit no man spake o of him for ...... Jn 7:13
walked no more o among the Jews....... Jn 11:54
him, I spake o to the world....... Jn 18:20
up the third day, and shewed him o....... Acts 10:40
beaten us o uncondemned....... Acts 16:37
powers, he made a shew of them o....... Col 2:15

OPERATION

nor the o of his hands, he shall....... Ps 28:5
consider the o of his hands....... Is 5:12
through the faith of the o of God ...... Col 2:12

OPERATIONS

there are diversities of o....... 1Cor 12:6

OPHEL (o'-fel) A fortified place near Jerusalem.

and on the wall of O he built much 2Chr 27:3
fish gate, and compassed about O 2Chr 33:14
Moreover the Nethinims dwelt in O ...... Neh 3:26
out, even unto the wall of O....... Neh 3:27
But the Nethinims dwelt in O....... Neh 11:21

OPHIR (o'-fur)
1. A son of Joktan.

And O, and Havilah, and Jobab....... Gen 10:29
And O, and Havilah, and Jobab....... 1Chr 1:23
2. A place in southern Arabia.

And they came to O, and fetched....... 1Kin 9:28
Hiram, that brought gold from O....... 1Kin 10:11
brought in from O great plenty of 1Kin 10:11
of Tharshish to go to O for gold....... 1Kin 22:48
talents of gold, of the gold of O....... 1Chr 29:4
with the servants of Solomon to O 2Chr 8:18
which brought gold from O....... 2Chr 9:10
the gold of O as the stones of....... Job 22:24
be valued with the gold of O....... Job 28:16
did stand the queen in gold of O....... Ps 45:9
a man than the golden wedge of O....... Is 13:12

OPHNI (of'-ni) A place in Benjamin.

And Chephar-haammonai, and O....... Josh 18:24

OPHRAH (of'-rah) See APHRAH.
1. A city in Benjamin.

And Avim, and Parah, and O....... Josh 18:23
unto the way that leadeth to O....... 1Sa 13:17
2. A city in Manasseh.

sat under an oak which was in O....... Judg 6:11
it is yet in ''of the Abi-ezrites ...... Judg 6:24
and put it in his city, even in O....... Judg 8:27
father, in O of the Abi-ezrites....... Judg 8:32

went unto his father's house at O....... Judg 9:5
3. Head of a family in Judah.

And Meonothai begat O....... 1Chr 4:14

OPINION

and durst not shew you mine o....... Job 32:6
I also will shew mine o....... Job 32:10
my part, I also will shew mine o....... Job 32:17

OPINIONS

How long halt ye between two o....... 1Kin 18:21

OPPORTUNITY

time he sought o to betray him....... Mt 26:16
sought o to betray him unto them....... Lk 22:6
As we have therefore o, let us do....... Gal 6:10
also careful, but ye lacked o....... Phil 4:10
might have had o to have returned...... Heb 11:15

OPPOSE

those that o themselves....... 2Ti 2:25

OPPOSED

when they o themselves, and....... Acts 18:6

OPPOSEST

hand thou o thyself against me....... Job 30:21

OPPOSETH

Who o and exalteth himself above 2Th 2:4

OPPOSITIONS

o of science falsely so called....... 1Ti 6:20

OPPRESS

wherewith the Egyptians o them....... Ex 3:9
neither vex a stranger, nor o him....... Ex 22:21
Also thou shalt not o a stranger....... Ex 23:9
hand, ye shall not o one another....... Lev 25:14
shall not therefore o one another....... Lev 25:17
thou shalt not o him....... Deut 23:16
Thou shalt not o an hired servant ...... Deut 24:14
and the Maonites, did o you....... Judg 10:12
unto thee that thou shouldest o....... Job 10:3
man of the earth may no more o....... Ps 10:18
From the wicked that o me....... Ps 17:9
let not the proud o me....... Ps 119:122
neither o the afflicted in the....... Prov 22:22
I will feed them that o thee with.... Is 49:26
If ye o not the stranger, the....... Jer 7:6
and I will punish all that o them....... Jer 30:20
princes shall no more o my people.... Eze 45:8
he loveth to o....... Hos 12:7
which o the poor, which crush the ...... Amos 4:1
so they o a man and his house,....... Mic 2:2
And o not the widow, nor the....... Zec 7:10
against those that o the hireling.... Mal 3:5
Do not rich men o you, and draw....... Jas 2:6

OPPRESSED

and thou shalt be only o and....... Deut 28:29
and thou shalt be only o and....... Deut 28:33
by reason of them that o them....... Judg 2:18
mightily o the children of Israel.... Judg 4:3
out of the hand of all that o you....... Judg 6:9
vexed and o the children of Israel.... Judg 10:8
kingdoms, and of them that o you.... Judg 10:12
whom have I o....... 1Sa 12:3
hast not defrauded us, nor o us....... 1Sa 12:4
because the king of Syria o them....... 2Kin 13:4
But Hazael king of Syria o Israel....... 2Kin 13:22
Asa o some of the people the same... 2Chr 16:10
Because he hath o and hath....... Job 20:19
they make the o to cry....... Job 35:9
also will be a refuge for the o....... Ps 9:9
To judge the fatherless and the o... Ps 10:18
O let not the o return ashamed....... Ps 74:21
and judgment for all that are o....... Ps 103:6
Their enemies also o them....... Ps 106:42
executeth judgment for the o....... Ps 146:7
the tears of such as were o....... Eccl 4:1
seek judgment, relieve the o....... Is 1:17
And the people shall be o, every....... Is 3:5
no more rejoice, O thou o virgin....... Is 23:12
O LORD, I am o....... Is 38:14
the Assyrian o them without cause... Is 52:4
He was o, and he was afflicted,....... Is 53:7
burdens, and to let the o go free....... Is 58:6
children of Judah were o together ...... Jer 50:33
And hath not o any, but hath....... Eze 18:7
Hath o the poor and needy, hath....... Eze 18:12
Neither hath o any, hath not....... Eze 18:16
his father, because he cruelly o....... Eze 18:18
yea, they have o the stranger....... Eze 22:29
Ephraim is o and broken in....... Hos 5:11
the o in the midst thereof....... Amos 3:9
him, and avenged him that was....... Acts 7:24
all that were o of the devil....... Acts 10:38

OPPRESSETH

land against the enemy that o you...... Num 10:9
he fighting daily o me....... Ps 56:1
He that o the poor reproacheth....... Prov 14:31
He that o the poor to increase....... Prov 22:16
A poor man that o the poor is....... Prov 28:3

OPPRESSING

of our nativity, from the o sword.... Jer 46:16
for fear of the o sword they....... Jer 50:16
filthy and polluted, to the o city....... Zeph 3:1

OPPRESSION

I have also seen the o wherewith....... Ex 3:9
and our labour, and our o....... Deut 26:7
for he saw the o of Israel....... 2Kin 13:4
and openeth their ears in o....... Job 36:15

OPPRESSIONS

For the o of the poor, for the.................. Ps 12:5
because of the o of the enemy............... Ps 42:9
because of the o of the enemy............... Ps 43:2
our affliction and our o.......................... Ps 44:24
because of the o of the wicked............... Ps 55:3
Trust not in o, and become not.............. Ps 62:10
and speak wickedly concerning o........... Ps 73:8
minished and brought low through o....... Ps 107:39
Deliver me from the o of man................ Ps 119:134
If thou seest the o of the poor............... Eccl 5:8
Surely o maketh a wise man mad........... Eccl 7:7
looked for judgment, but behold o.......... Is 5:7
despise this word, and trust in o............ Is 30:12
thou shalt be far from o.......................... Is 54:14
away from our God, speaking o............... Is 59:13
she is wholly o in the midst of................ Jer 6:6
to shed innocent blood, and for o........... Jer 22:17
they dealt by o with the stranger........... Eze 22:7
people of the land have used o............... Eze 22:29
of the people's inheritance by o............ Eze 46:18

OPPRESSIONS

By reason of the multitude of o............... Job 35:9
considered all the o that are................... Eccl 4:1
he that despiseth the gain of o............... Is 33:15

OPPRESSOR

they hear not the voice of the o............. Job 3:18
of years is hidden to the o...................... Job 15:20
and shall break in pieces the o.............. Ps 72:4
Envy thou not the o, and choose........... Prov 3:31
understanding is also a great o.............. Prov 28:16
of his shoulder, the rod of his o............ Is 9:4
and say, How hath the o ceased............ Is 14:4
day because of the fury of the o............ Is 51:13
and where is the fury of the o............... Is 51:13
spoiled out of the hand of the o............ Jer 21:12
spoiled out of the hand of the o............ Jer 22:3
of the fierceness of the o....................... Jer 25:38
no o shall pass through them any........... Zec 9:8
bow, out of him every o together........... Zec 10:4

OPPRESSORS

' with God, and the heritage of o........... Job 27:13
me, and o seek after my soul................. Ps 54:3
leave me not to mine o........................... Ps 119:121
side of their o there was power............. Eccl 4:1
my people, children are their o.............. Is 3:12
and they shall rule over their o.............. Is 14:2
the o are consumed out of the............... Is 16:4
unto the LORD because of the o............. Is 19:20

OR See PREFACE.

ORACLE

man had enquired at the o of God......... 2Sa 16:23
both of the temple and of the o.............. 1Kin 6:5
for it within, even for the o..................... 1Kin 6:16
the o he prepared in the house.............. 1Kin 6:19
the o in the forepart was twenty............ 1Kin 6:20
the chains of gold before the o.............. 1Kin 6:21
by the o he overlaid with gold............... 1Kin 6:22
And within the o he made two............... 1Kin 6:23
for the entering of the o he made.......... 1Kin 6:31
and five on the left, before the o........... 1Kin 7:49
into the o of the house, to the............... 1Kin 8:6
in the holy place before the o............... 1Kin 8:8
And he made chains, as in the o........... 2Chr 3:16
after the manner before the o................ 2Chr 4:20
to the o of the house, into the............... 2Chr 5:7
seen from the ark before the o.............. 2Chr 5:9
up my hands toward thy holy o.............. Ps 28:2

ORACLES

the lively o to give unto us.................... Acts 7:38
them were committed the o of God....... Rom 3:2
first principles of the o of God............... Heb 5:12
let him speak as the o of God................ 1Pet 4:11

ORATION

throne, and made an o unto them......... Acts 12:21

ORATOR

artificer, and the eloquent o.................. Is 3:3
with a certain o named Tertullus........... Acts 24:1

ORCHARD

plants are an o of pomegranates.......... Song 4:13

ORCHARDS

I made me gardens and o, and I........... Eccl 2:5

ORDAIN

seer did o in their set office.................. 1Chr 9:22
Also I will o a place for my.................... 1Chr 17:9
Lord, thou wilt o peace for us............... Is 26:12
And so o I in all churches..................... 1Cor 7:17
o elders in every city, as I had.............. Titus 1:5

ORDAINED

which was o in mount Sinai for a........... Num 28:6
Jeroboam o a feast in the eighth........... 1Kin 12:32
o a feast unto the children of................ 1Kin 12:33
had o to burn incense in the high.......... 2Kin 23:5
he o him priests for the high................. 2Chr 11:15
singing, as it was o by David................. 2Chr 23:18
with the instruments o by David............ 2Chr 29:27
The Jews o, and took upon them, and... Est 9:27
sucklings hast thou o strength.............. Ps 8:2
and the stars, which thou hast o........... Ps 8:3
This he o in Joseph for a....................... Ps 81:5
I have o a lamp for mine anointed........ Ps 132:17
For Tophet is o of old............................ Is 30:33
I o thee a prophet unto the.................... Jer 1:5
whom the king had o to destroy............ Dan 2:24
thou hast o them for judgment.............. Hab 1:12

he o twelve, that they should be........... Mk 3:14
o you, that ye should go and bring........ Jn 15:16
must one be o to be a witness.............. Acts 1:22
o of God to be the Judge of quick......... Acts 10:42
as many as were o to eternal life.......... Acts 13:48
when they had o them elders in............ Acts 14:23
that were o of the apostles and............. Acts 16:4
by that man whom he hath o................. Acts 17:31
commandment, which was o to life....... Rom 7:10
the powers that be are o of God........... Rom 13:1
which God o before the world unto....... 1Cor 2:7
Even so hath the Lord o that they......... 1Cor 9:14
it was o by angels in the hand of.......... Gal 3:19
which God hath before o that we.......... Eph 2:10
Whereunto I am o a preacher................ 1Ti 2:7
o the first bishop of the church............. 2Ti s
o the first bishop of the church............. Titus s
priest taken from among men is o......... Heb 5:1
high priest is o to offer gifts.................. Heb 8:3
Now when these things were thus o..... Heb 9:6
of old o to this condemnation................ Jude 4

ORDAINETH

he o his arrows against the.................... Ps 7:13

ORDER

there, and laid the wood in o................. Gen 22:9
set in o one against another.................. Ex 26:17
his sons shall o it from evening............. Ex 27:21
with the lamps to be set in o................. Ex 39:37
set in o the things that are to............... Ex 40:4
that are to be set in o upon I................. Ex 40:4
he set the bread in o upon it................. Ex 40:23
lay the wood in o upon the fire............. Lev 1:7
in o upon the wood that is on the......... Lev 1:8
the priest shall lay them in o on........... Lev 1:12
the burnt offering in o upon it............... Lev 6:12
shall Aaron o it from the evening.......... Lev 24:3
He shall o the lamps upon the.............. Lev 24:4
sabbath he shall set it in o.................... Lev 24:8
she had laid in o upon the roof............. Josh 2:6
How shall we o the child, and how....... Judg 13:12
city, and put his household in o............ 2Sa 17:23
And he put the wood in o, and cut....... 1Kin 18:33
he said, Who shall o the battle............. 1Kin 20:14
the LORD, Set thine house in o............ 2Kin 20:1
and the priests of the second o........... 2Kin 23:4
their office according to their o............ 1Chr 6:32
we sought him not after the due o....... 1Chr 15:13
according to the o commanded unto.... 1Chr 23:31
according to the o of the king.............. 1Chr 25:2
to the king's o to Asaph...................... 1Chr 25:6
according to the o of David his............ 2Chr 8:14
set them in o upon the pure table........ 2Chr 13:11
house of the LORD was set in o........... 2Chr 29:35
shadow of death, without any o........... Job 10:22
I would o my cause before him, and.... Job 23:4
me, set thy words in o before me......... Job 33:5
for we cannot o our speech by............ Job 37:19
be reckoned up in o unto thee............. Ps 40:5
set them in o before thine eyes........... Ps 50:21
ever after the o of Melchizedek........... Ps 110:4
O my steps in thy word........................ Ps 119:133
out, and set in o many proverbs.......... Eccl 12:9
and upon his kingdom, to o it.............. Is 9:7
the LORD, Set thine house in o........... Is 38:1
declare it, and set it in o for me........... Is 44:7
O ye the buckler and shield, and......... Jer 46:3
one over another, and thirty in o.......... Eze 41:6
o a declaration of those things........... Lk 1:1
first, to write unto thee in o................. Lk 1:3
before God in the o of his course........ Lk 1:8
and expounded it by o unto them........ Acts 11:4
of Galatia and Phrygia in o................. Acts 18:23
rest will I set in o when I come........... 1Cor 11:34
things be done decently and in o....... 1Cor 14:40
But every man in his own o................ 1Cor 15:23
as I have given o to the churches...... 1Cor 16:1
joying and beholding your o............... Col 2:5
that thou shouldest set in o the......... Titus 1:5
ever after the o of Melchisedec......... Heb 5:6
priest after the o of Melchisedec....... Heb 5:10
ever after the o of Melchisedec......... Heb 6:20
rise after the o of Melchisedec.......... Heb 7:11
be called after the o of Aaron............ Heb 7:11
ever after the o of Melchisedec......... Heb 7:17
ever after the o of Melchisedec......... Heb 7:21

ORDERED

top of this rock, in the o place............ Judg 6:26
o in all things, and sure...................... 2Sa 23:5
Behold now, I have o my cause.......... Job 13:18
of a good man are o by the LORD....... Ps 37:23

ORDERETH

to him that o his conversation............ Ps 50:23

ORDERINGS

These were the o of them in their...... 1Chr 24:19

ORDERLY

that thou thyself also walkest o......... Acts 21:24

ORDINANCE

keep it a feast by an o for ever........... Ex 12:14
your generations by an o for ever....... Ex 12:17
this thing for an o to thee.................... Ex 12:24
the children of Israel for an o.............. Ex 12:43
Thou shalt therefore keep this o......... Ex 13:10
made for them a statute and an o....... Ex 15:25
Therefore shall ye keep mine o.......... Lev 18:30
They shall therefore keep mine o....... Lev 22:9
to the o of the passover, and.............. Num 9:14

ye shall have one o, both for the....... Num 9:14
for an o for ever throughout your....... Num 10:8
One o shall be both for you of........... Num 15:15
an o for ever in your generations...... Num 15:15
and to thy sons, by an o for ever....... Num 18:8
This is the o of the law which............ Num 19:2
This is the o of the law which............ Num 31:21
them a statute and an o in Shechem.. Josh 24:25
an o for Israel unto this day.............. 1Sa 30:25
This is an o for ever to Israel............ 2Chr 2:4
with fire according to the o................ 2Chr 35:13
day, and made them an o in Israel..... 2Chr 35:25
after the o of David king of............... Ezr 3:10
and the o that he gave them............. Ps 99:7
the laws, changed the o, broken....... Is 24:5
and forsook not the o of their God..... Is 58:2
Concerning the o of oil, the bath....... Eze 45:14
by a perpetual o unto the LORD........ Eze 46:14
is it that we have kept his o.............. Mal 3:14
the power, resisteth the o of God...... Rom 13:2
o of man for the Lord's sake............. 1Pet 2:13

ORDINANCES

And thou shalt teach them o............. Ex 18:20
neither shalt ye walk in their o.......... Lev 18:3
do my judgments, and keep mine o.... Lev 18:4
according to all the o of the.............. Num 9:12
their statutes, or after their o........... 2Kin 17:34
And the statutes, and the o............... 2Kin 17:37
the o by the hand of Moses.............. 2Chr 33:8
Also we made o for us, to charge...... Neh 10:32
Knowest thou the o of heaven.......... Job 38:33
this day according to thine o............. Ps 119:91
they ask of me the o of justice......... Is 58:2
the o of the moon and of the stars.... Jer 31:35
If those o depart from before me...... Jer 31:36
not appointed the o of heaven.......... Jer 33:25
in my statutes, and keep mine o....... Eze 11:20
thereof, and all the o thereof........... Eze 43:11
thereof, and all the o thereof........... Eze 43:11
These are the o of the altar in......... Eze 43:18
the o of the house of the LORD....... Eze 44:5
ye are gone away from mine o.......... Mal 3:7
and o of the Lord blameless............ Lk 1:6
me in all things, and keep the o....... 1Cor 11:2
of commandments contained in o.... Eph 2:15
of that was against us, which.......... Col 2:14
in the world, are ye subject to o...... Col 2:20
had also o of divine service............ Heb 9:1
and divers washings, and carnal o.. Heb 9:10

ORDINARY

and have diminished thine o food...... Eze 16:27

OREB (o '-reb)

1. A prince of Midian.
two princes of the Midianites, O....... Judg 7:25
they slew O upon the rock O............ Judg 7:25
Midian, and brought the heads of O... Judg 7:25
hands the princes of Midian, O......... Judg 8:3
Make their nobles like O, and like.... Ps 83:11
2. A rock east of the Jordan.
of Midian at the rock of O................ Is 10:26

OREN (o '-ren) A son of Jerahmeel.
Ram the firstborn, and Bunah, and O.. 1Chr 2:25

ORGAN

all such as handle the harp and o..... Gen 4:21
and rejoice at the sound of the o....... Job 21:12
my o into the voice of them that........ Job 30:31

ORGANS

with stringed instruments and o......... Ps 150:4

ORION (o '-ri'-on) A constellation of stars.
Which maketh Arcturus, O, and........ Job 9:9
Pleiades, or loose the bands of O..... Job 38:31
that maketh the seven stars and O.... Amos 5:8

ORNAMENT

For they shall be an o of grace......... Prov 1:9
give to thine head an o of grace........ Prov 4:9
an o of fine gold, so is a wise........... Prov 25:12
the o of thy molten images of.......... Is 30:22
thee with them all, as with an o....... Is 49:18
As for the beauty of his o............... Eze 7:20
even the o of a meek and quiet........ 1Pet 3:4

ORNAMENTS

and no man did put on him his o....... Ex 33:4
now put off thy o from thee.............. Ex 33:5
of their o by the mount Horeb.......... Ex 33:6
took away the o that were on........... Judg 8:21
beside o, and collars, and purple..... Judg 8:26
who put on o of gold upon your....... 2Sa 1:24
their tinkling o about their feet......... Is 3:18
the o of the legs, and the................ Is 3:20
bridegroom decketh himself with o... Is 61:10
Can a maid forget her o, or a........... Jer 2:32
thou deckest thee with o of gold...... Jer 4:30
and thou art come to excellent o...... Eze 16:7
I decked thee also with o................ Eze 16:11
eyes, and deckest thyself with o..... Eze 23:40

ORNAN (or '-nan) See ARAUNAH. *A Jebusite prince.*
threshingfloor of O the Jebusite....... 1Chr 21:15
threshingfloor of O the Jebusite....... 1Chr 21:18
O turned back, and saw the angel..... 1Chr 21:20
Now O was threshing wheat............. 1Chr 21:20
And as David came to O, O.............. 1Chr 21:21
Then David said to O, Grant me....... 1Chr 21:22
O said unto David, Take it to........... 1Chr 21:23
And king David said to O, Nay.......... 1Chr 21:24

ORPAH

So David gave to O for the place...... 1Chr 21:25
threshingfloor of O the Jebusite...... 1Chr 21:28
threshingfloor of O the Jebusite...... 2Chr 3:1

ORPAH (or'-pah) *Daughter-in-law of Naomi.*
the name of the one was O...... Ruth 1:4
O kissed her mother in law...... Ruth 1:14

ORPHANS
We are orphans and fatherless, our...... Lam 5:3

OSEE (o'-see) *See* HOSEA, JOSHUA, OSHEA.
Greek form of Hoshea.
As he saith also in O, I will...... Rom 9:25

OSHEA (o-she'-ah) *See* HOSHEA, OSEE. *Same as Joshua, son of Nun.*
of Ephraim, O the son of Nun...... Num 13:8
Moses called O the son of Nun...... Num 13:16

OSNAPPAR *See* ASNAPPER.

OSPRAY
eagle, and the ossifrage, and the o...... Lev 11:13
eagle, and the ossifrage, and the o...... Deut 14:12

OSSIFRAGE
the eagle, and the o, and the...... Lev 11:13
The eagle, and the o, and the...... Deut 14:12

OSTRICH
or wings and feathers unto the o...... Job 39:13

OSTRICHES
like the o in the wilderness...... Lam 4:3

OTHER
Adah, and the name of the o Zillah...... Gen 4:19
And he stayed yet o seven days...... Gen 8:10
And he stayed yet o seven days...... Gen 8:12
themselves the one from the o...... Gen 13:11
that are with thee, and with all o...... Gen 20:16
be stronger than the o people...... Gen 25:23
this is none of but the house of...... Gen 28:17
serve with me yet seven o years...... Gen 29:27
served with him yet seven o years...... Gen 29:30
or if thou shalt take o wives...... Gen 31:50
then the o company which is left...... Gen 32:8
seven o kine came up after them...... Gen 41:3
stood by the o kine upon the...... Gen 41:3
seven o kine came up after them,...... Gen 41:19
he may send away your o brethren...... Gen 43:14
o money have we brought down in...... Gen 43:22
Egypt even to the o end thereof...... Gen 47:21
and the name of the o Puah...... Ex 1:15
was turned again as his o flesh...... Ex 4:7
came not near the o all the night...... Ex 14:20
side, and the o on the...... Ex 17:12
on the o side...... Ex 17:12
And the name of the o was Eliezer...... Ex 18:4
they asked each o of their...... Ex 18:7
shalt have no o gods before me...... Ex 20:3
no mention of the name of o gods...... Ex 23:13
and two rings in the o side of it...... Ex 25:12
the o cherub on the...... Ex 25:12
cherub on the o end...... Ex 25:19
the candlestick out of the o side...... Ex 25:32
made like almonds in the o branch...... Ex 25:33
o five curtains shall be coupled...... Ex 26:3
a cubit on the o side of that...... Ex 26:13
of the o side of the tabernacle...... Ex 26:13
on the o side shall be hangings...... Ex 27:15
the o six names of the rest on...... Ex 28:10
names of the rest on the o stone...... Ex 28:10
the o two ends of the two...... Ex 28:25
two o rings of gold thou shalt...... Ex 28:27
against the o coupling thereof...... Ex 28:27
And thou shalt take the o ram...... Ex 29:19
the o lamb thou shalt offer at...... Ex 29:39
the o lamb thou shalt offer at...... Ex 29:41
shall ye make any o like it...... Ex 30:32
on the o were they written...... Ex 32:15
For thou shalt worship no o god...... Ex 34:14
the o five curtains he coupled...... Ex 36:10
for the o side of the tabernacle...... Ex 36:25
of the o side of the tabernacle...... Ex 36:32
boards from the one end to the o...... Ex 36:33
two rings upon the o side of it...... Ex 37:3
cherub on the o end on that side...... Ex 37:8
out of the o side thereof...... Ex 37:18
for the o side of the court gate,...... Ex 38:15
And they made two o golden rings...... Ex 39:20
against the o coupling thereof...... Ex 39:20
the o for a burnt offering...... Lev 5:7
put on o garments, and carry forth...... Lev 6:11
beasts, may be used in any o use...... Lev 7:24
And he brought the o ram, the ram...... Lev 8:22
But all o flying creeping things,...... Lev 11:23
and the o for a sin offering...... Lev 12:8
and it be no lower than the o skin...... Lev 13:26
and the o a burnt offering...... Lev 14:31
the o for a burnt offering, which...... Lev 14:31
And they shall take o stones...... Lev 14:42
and he shall take o morter...... Lev 14:42
the o for a burnt offering...... Lev 15:15
the o for a burnt offering...... Lev 15:30
the o lot for the scapegoat...... Lev 16:8
beside the o in her life time...... Lev 18:18
have separated you from o people...... Lev 20:24
and have severed you from o people...... Lev 20:26
the o shall not rule with rigour...... Lev 25:46
the o for a burnt offering, unto...... Num 6:11
the o for a burnt offering, unto...... Num 8:12
the o did set up the tabernacle...... Num 10:21
Eldad, and the name of the o Medad...... Num 11:26

a day's journey on the o side...... Num 11:31
and pitched on the o side of Arnon...... Num 21:13
he went not, as at o times...... Num 24:1
the o lamb shalt thou offer at...... Num 28:4
the o lamb shalt thou offer at...... Num 28:8
gave o names unto the cities...... Num 32:38
the o tribes of the children of...... Num 36:3
the one side of heaven unto the o...... Deut 4:32
shalt have none o gods before me...... Deut 5:7
Ye shall not go after o gods...... Deut 6:14
me, that they may serve o gods...... Deut 7:4
thy God, and walk after o gods...... Deut 8:19
and ye turn aside, and serve o gods...... Deut 11:16
you this day, to go after o gods...... Deut 11:28
Are they not on the o side Jordan...... Deut 11:30
saying, Let us go after o gods...... Deut 13:2
saying, Let us go and serve o gods...... Deut 13:6
even unto the o end of the earth...... Deut 13:7
saying, Let us go and serve o gods...... Deut 13:13
And hath gone and served o gods...... Deut 17:3
shall speak in the name of o gods...... Deut 18:20
to go after o gods to serve them...... Deut 28:14
and there shalt thou serve o gods...... Deut 28:36
end of the earth even unto the o...... Deut 28:64
and there thou shalt serve o gods...... Deut 28:64
For they went and served o gods...... Deut 29:26
be drawn away, and worship o gods...... Deut 30:17
that they are turned unto o gods...... Deut 31:18
then will they turn unto o gods...... Deut 31:20
that were on the o side Jordan...... Josh 2:10
and dwelt on the o side of Jordan...... Josh 7:7
the o issued out of the city...... Josh 8:22
all o they took in battle...... Josh 11:19
possessed their land on the o...... Josh 12:1
on the o side Jordan eastward...... Josh 13:27
on the o side by Jericho,...... Josh 13:32
half tribe on the o side Jordan...... Josh 14:3
which were on the o side Jordan...... Josh 17:5
on the o side Jordan by Jericho,...... Josh 20:8
out of the o half tribe of...... Josh 21:27
gave you on the o side Jordan...... Josh 22:4
but unto the o half thereof gave...... Josh 22:7
and have gone and served o gods...... Josh 23:16
Your fathers dwelt on the o side...... Josh 24:2
and they served o gods...... Josh 24:2
from the o side of the flood...... Josh 24:3
which dwelt on the o side the flood...... Josh 24:14
served on the o side of the flood,...... Josh 24:15
were on the o side of the flood,...... Josh 24:15
forsake the LORD, and serve o gods...... Josh 24:16
land of Egypt, and followed o gods...... Judg 2:12
they went a whoring after o gods...... Judg 2:17
in following o gods to serve them...... Judg 2:19
let all the o people go every man...... Judg 7:7
to Gideon on the o side Jordan...... Judg 7:25
the two o companies ran upon all...... Judg 9:44
of Israel that were on the o side...... Judg 10:8
forsaken me, and served o gods,...... Judg 10:13
and pitched on the o side of Arnon...... Judg 11:18
me, that came unto me the o day...... Judg 13:10
and be like any o man...... Judg 16:7
will go out as at o times before...... Judg 16:20
hand, and of the o with his left...... Judg 16:29
against Gibeah, as at o times...... Judg 20:30
people, and kill, as at o times...... Judg 20:31
the o to Gibeah in the field,...... Judg 20:31
Orpah, and the name of the o Ruth...... Ruth 1:4
they met thee not in any o field...... Ruth 2:22
and the name of the o Peninnah...... 1Sa 1:2
and stood, and called as at o times...... 1Sa 3:10
forsaken me, and served o gods...... 1Sa 8:8
garrison, that is on the o side...... 1Sa 14:1
and a sharp rock on the o side...... 1Sa 14:4
Bozez, and the name of the o Seneh...... 1Sa 14:4
the o southward over against...... 1Sa 14:5
my son will be on the o side...... 1Sa 14:40
stood on a mountain on the o side...... 1Sa 17:3
with his hand, as at o times...... 1Sa 18:10
he sent o messengers, and they...... 1Sa 19:21
sat upon his seat, as at o times...... 1Sa 20:25
for there is no o save that here...... 1Sa 21:9
David went over to the o side...... 1Sa 26:13
LORD, saying, Go, serve o gods...... 1Sa 26:19
put on o raiment, and he went,...... 1Sa 28:8
they drave before those o cattle...... 1Sa 30:20
were on the o side of the valley...... 1Sa 31:7
that were on the o side Jordan...... 1Sa 31:7
with o delights, who put on...... 2Sa 1:24
the o on the...... 2Sa 2:13
on the o side of the pool...... 2Sa 2:13
and the name of the o Rechab...... 2Sa 4:2
the one rich, and the o poor...... 2Sa 12:1
the o that thou didst unto my...... 2Sa 13:16
them, but the one smote the o...... 2Sa 14:6
in some pit, or in some o place...... 2Sa 17:9
o instruments of the oxen for...... 2Sa 24:22
And the o woman said, Nay...... 1Kin 3:22
And he saith, Nay...... 1Kin 3:23
half to the one, and half to the o...... 1Kin 3:25
But the o said, Let it be neither...... 1Kin 3:26
five cubits the o wing of the...... 1Kin 6:24
part of the o were ten cubits...... 1Kin 6:24
the o cherub was ten cubits,...... 1Kin 6:26
and so was it of the o cherub...... 1Kin 6:26
o cherub touched the o wall...... 1Kin 6:27
leaves of the o door were folding...... 1Kin 6:34
the o pillars and the thick beam...... 1Kin 7:6
one side of the floor to the o...... 1Kin 7:7
the height of the o chapiter was...... 1Kin 7:16
and seven for the o chapiter...... 1Kin 7:17

and so did he for the o chapter...... 1Kin 7:18
round about upon the o chapiter...... 1Kin 7:20
cubits from the one brim to the o...... 1Kin 7:23
you, but go and serve o gods...... 1Kin 9:6
and have taken hold upon o gods...... 1Kin 9:9
on the o upon the six steps...... 1Kin 10:20
away his heart after o gods...... 1Kin 11:4
he should not go after o gods...... 1Kin 11:10
Beth-el, and the o put he in Dan...... 1Kin 12:29
hast gone and made thee o gods...... 1Kin 14:9
and I will dress the o bullock...... 1Kin 18:23
one over against the o seven days...... 1Kin 20:29
on the o side as red as blood...... 2Kin 3:22
nor sacrifice unto o gods...... 2Kin 5:17
the o priests, and said unto them,...... 2Kin 12:7
of Egypt, and had feared o gods...... 2Kin 17:7
saying, Ye shall not fear o gods...... 2Kin 17:35
and ye shall not fear o gods...... 2Kin 17:37
neither shall ye fear o gods...... 2Kin 17:38
have burned incense unto o gods...... 2Kin 22:17
on the o side Jordan by Jericho,...... 1Chr 6:78
o of their brethren, of the sons...... 1Chr 9:32
on the o side of Jordan, of the...... 1Chr 12:37
And Eliezer had none o sons...... 1Chr 23:17
the o wing was likewise five...... 2Chr 3:11
to the wing of the o cherub...... 2Chr 3:11
one wing of the o cherub was five...... 2Chr 3:12
the o wing was five cubits also,...... 2Chr 3:12
to the wing of the o cherub...... 2Chr 3:12
right hand, and the o on the left...... 2Chr 3:17
you, and shall go and serve o gods...... 2Chr 7:19
of Egypt, and laid hold on o gods...... 2Chr 7:22
on the o upon the six steps...... 2Chr 9:19
manner of the nations of o lands...... 2Chr 13:9
with them o beside the Ammonites,...... 2Chr 20:1
ten thousand left alive did the...... 2Chr 25:12
to burn incense unto o gods...... 2Chr 28:25
ended, and until the o priests had...... 2Chr 29:34
took counsel to keep o seven days...... 2Chr 30:23
they kept o seven days with...... 2Chr 30:23
unto all the people of o lands...... 2Chr 32:13
As the gods of the nations of o...... 2Chr 32:17
and from the hand of all o...... 2Chr 32:22
o of the Levites, all that could...... 2Chr 34:12
have burned incense unto o gods,...... 2Chr 34:25
but the o holy offerings and they...... 2Chr 35:13
and ten, and o vessels a thousand...... Ezr 1:10
The children of the o Elam...... Ezr 2:31
Pahath-moab, repaired the o piece...... Neh 3:11
earnestly repaired the o piece...... Neh 3:20
the o half of them held both the...... Neh 4:16
with the o hand held a weapon...... Neh 4:17
for o men have our lands and...... Neh 5:5
The men of the o Nebo, fifty and...... Neh 7:33
The children of the o Elam...... Neh 7:34
nine parts to dwell in o cities...... Neh 11:1
the o company of them that gave...... Neh 12:38
with o things for the purifying...... Est 2:12
But the o Jews that were in the...... Est 9:16
it withereth before any o herb...... Job 8:12
are taken out of the way as all o...... Job 24:24
They are not in trouble as o men...... Ps 73:5
are they plagued like o men...... Ps 73:5
and peace have kissed each o...... Ps 85:10
as the one dieth, so dieth the o...... Eccl 3:19
this hath more rest than the o...... Eccl 6:5
set the one over against the o...... Eccl 7:14
o lords besides thee have had...... Is 26:13
have, after thou hast lost the o...... Is 49:20
have burned incense unto o gods...... Jer 1:16
walk after o gods to your hurt...... Jer 7:6
walk after o gods whom ye know...... Jer 7:9
out drink offerings unto o gods...... Jer 7:18
they went after o gods to serve...... Jer 11:10
even to the o end of the land...... Jer 12:12
their heart, and walk after o gods...... Jer 13:10
LORD, and have walked after o gods...... Jer 16:11
there shall ye serve o gods day...... Jer 16:13
burned incense in unto o gods...... Jer 19:4
out drink offerings unto o gods...... Jer 19:13
their God, and worshipped o gods...... Jer 22:9
the o basket had very naughty...... Jer 24:2
go not after o gods to serve them...... Jer 25:6
even unto the o end of the earth...... Jer 25:33
day, and in Israel, and among o men...... Jer 32:20
out drink offerings unto o gods...... Jer 32:29
go not after o gods to serve them...... Jer 35:15
they were afraid both one and o...... Jer 36:16
burn incense, and to serve o gods...... Jer 44:3
to burn no incense unto o gods...... Jer 44:5
burning incense unto o gods in...... Jer 44:8
had burned incense unto o gods...... Jer 44:15
straight, the one toward the o...... Eze 1:23
from o women in thy whoredoms...... Eze 16:34
The one way or o, either on...... Eze 21:16
the o threshold of the gates...... Eze 40:40
and on the o side, which was at...... Eze 40:40
and six cubits broad on the o side...... Eze 41:1
and five cubits on the o side...... Eze 41:2
on the one side and on the o side...... Eze 41:15
the palm tree on the o side...... Eze 41:19
one as the appearance of the o...... Eze 41:21
and two leaves for the o door...... Eze 41:24
on the one side and on the o side...... Eze 41:24
and shall put on o garments...... Eze 42:14
and they shall put on o garments,...... Eze 44:19
on the o side of the oblation of...... Eze 45:7
trees on the one side and on the o...... Eze 47:7
in length as one of the o parts...... Eze 48:8
on the o side of the holy oblation,...... Eze 48:21

0

there is none o that can shew it ...... Dan 2:11
shall not be left to o people .... Dan 2:44
their o garments, and were cast ...... Dan 3:21
because there is no o God that .... Dan 3:29
of the o which came up, and before .. Dan 7:20
but one was higher than the o. .... Dan 8:3
and, behold, there stood o two. .... Dan 12:5
the o on that side of the bank of ...... Dan 12:5
of Israel, who look to o gods .... Hos 3:1
O Israel, for joy, as o people .... Hos 9:1
where is any o that may save thee .. Hos 13:10
that thou stoodest on the o side ...... Obad 11
the o upon the left side thereof .... Zec 4:3
Beauty, and the o I called Bands ...... Zec 11:7
Then I cut asunder mine o staff ...... Zec 11:14
he saw o two brethren, James the .... Mt 4:21
cheek, turn to him the o also .... Mt 5:39
will hate the one, and love the o ...... Mt 6:24
hold to the one, and despise the o .... Mt 6:24
to depart unto the o side. .... Mt 8:18
when he was come to the o side .... Mt 8:28
was restored whole, like as the o. .... Mt 12:13
seven o spirits more wicked than .... Mt 12:45
But o fell into good ground, and ...... Mt 13:8
to go before him unto the o side. ...... Mt 14:22
disciples were come to the o side. .... Mt 16:5
the o on the left, in thy kingdom. .... Mt 20:21
not o servants more than the o. .... Mt 21:36
his vineyard unto o husbandmen. .... Mt 21:41
Again, he sent forth o servants .... Mt 22:4
and not to leave the o undone. .... Mt 23:23
from one end of heaven to the o ...... Mt 24:31
one shall be taken, and the o left ...... Mt 24:40
one shall be taken, and the o left ...... Mt 24:41
Afterward came the o virgins .... Mt 25:11
same, and made them o five talents. Mt 25:16
two, he also gained o two. .... Mt 25:17
brought o five talents, saying, ... Mt 25:20
I have gained two o talents. .... Mt 25:22
the o Mary, sitting over against ...... Mt 27:61
the o Mary to see the sepulchre. ...... Mt 28:1
hand was restored whole as the o. .... Mk 3:5
o fell on good ground, and did. .... Mk 4:8
the lusts of o things entering in ...... Mk 4:19
Let us pass over unto the o side. ...... Mk 4:35
were also with him o little ships ...... Mk 4:36
over unto the o side of the sea. .... Mk 5:1
again by ship unto the o side. .... Mk 5:21
to go to the o side before unto .... Mk 6:45
many o things there be, which .... Mk 7:4
many o such like things ye do. .... Mk 7:8
ship again departed to the o side ...... Mk 8:13
the o on thy left hand, in thy .... Mk 10:37
There is none o commandment .... Mk 12:31
and there is none o but he. .... Mk 12:32
right hand, and the o on his left. ...... Mk 15:27
many o women which came up with .. Mk 15:41
many o things in his exhortation ...... Lk 3:18
kingdom of God to o cities also. .... Lk 4:43
which were in the o ship. .... Lk 5:7
hand was restored whole as the o. .... Lk 6:10
on the one cheek offer also the o. ...... Lk 6:29
hundred pence, and the o fifty. .... Lk 7:41
o fell on good ground, and sprang .... Lk 8:8
over unto the o side of the lake .... Lk 8:22
the Lord appointed o seventy also .... Lk 10:1
him, he passed by on the o side. ...... Lk 10:31
him, and passed by on the o side. .... Lk 10:32
taketh to him seven o spirits............ Lk 11:26
and not to leave the o undone. .... Lk 11:42
while the o is yet a great way .... Lk 14:32
will hate the one, and love the o ...... Lk 16:13
hold to the one, and despise the o .... Lk 16:13
shineth unto the o part under .... Lk 17:24
be taken, and the o shall be left ...... Lk 17:34
one shall be taken, and the o left .... Lk 17:35
one shall be taken, and the o left .... Lk 17:36
a Pharisee, and the o a publican. .... Lk 18:10
thee, that I am not as o men are, ... Lk 18:11
house justified rather than the o. .... Lk 18:14
many o things blasphemously spake .. Lk 22:65
right hand, and the o on the left. .... Lk 23:33
But the o answering rebuked him, .. Lk 23:40
o women that were with them, ... Lk 24:10
o men laboured, and ye are entered. Jn 4:38
the people which stood on the o. ...... Jn 6:22
that there was none o boat there, ... Jn 6:22
(Howbeit there came o boats from .. Jn 6:23
him on the o side of the sea. .... Jn 6:25
but climbeth up some o way .... Jn 10:1
o sheep I have, which are not of ...... Jn 10:16
the works which none o man did ...... Jn 15:24
Then went out that o disciple .... Jn 18:16
of the o which was crucified with .... Jn 19:32
to the o disciple, whom Jesus .... Jn 20:2
that o disciple, and came to the ...... Jn 20:4
o disciple that did outrun Peter. ...... Jn 20:4
Then went in also that o disciple. .... Jn 20:8
the o at the feet, where the body ...... Jn 20:12
The o disciples therefore said, ... Jn 20:25
many o signs truly did Jesus in ...... Jn 20:30
and two o of his disciples. .... Jn 21:2
the o disciples came in a little .... Jn 21:8
there are also many o things .... Jn 21:25
and began to speak with o tongues. .. Acts 2:4
with many o words did he testify. .... Acts 2:40
is there salvation in any o: .... Acts 4:12
for there is none o name under ...... Acts 4:12
the o apostles answered and said, ... Acts 5:29
of himself, or of some o man .... Acts 8:34

and Barnabas, and certain o of them.. Acts 15:2
in asunder one from the o. .... Acts 15:39
security of Jason, and the o .... Acts 17:9
o some, He seemeth to be a setter .... Acts 17:18
any thing concerning o matters .... Acts 19:39
the o Pharisees, he cried out in .... Acts 23:6
saying none o things than those........ Acts 26:22
certain o prisoners unto one .... Acts 27:1
also, even as among o Gentiles. .... Rom 1:13
nor any o creature, shall be able ...... Rom 8:39
and if there be any o commandment. Rom 13:9
know not whether I baptized any o .. 1Cor 1:16
For o foundation can no man lay....... 1Cor 3:11
Defraud ye not one the o, except...... 1Cor 7:5
that there is none o God but one. 1Cor 8:4
a wife, as well as o apostles........... 1Cor 9:5
say, not thine own, but of the o 1Cor 10:29
taketh before o him supper 1Cor 11:21
well, but the o is not edified 1Cor 14:17
is written, With men of o tongues 1Cor 14:21
o lips will I speak unto this 1Cor 14:21
two o there, and let the o judge 1Cor 14:29
of wheat, or of some o grain 1Cor 15:37
we write none o things unto you 2Cor 1:13
to the o the savour of life unto 2Cor 2:16
I mean not that o men be eased........ 2Cor 8:13
that is, of o men's labours 2Cor 10:15
I robbed o churches, taking 2Cor 11:8
ye were inferior to o churches.......... 2Cor 12:13
have sinned, and to all o, that, ... 2Cor 13:2
preach any o gospel unto you than.... Gal 1:8
If any man preach any o than .... Gal 1:9
But of the o apostles saw I none, ... Gal 1:19
the o Jews dissembled likewise .... Gal 2:13
a bondmaid, the o by a freewoman.... Gal 4:22
are contrary the one to the o. .... Gal 5:17
Which in o ages was not made .... Eph 3:5
walk not as o Gentiles walk. .... Eph 4:17
the palace, and in all o places. .... Phil 1:13
But the o of love, knowing that I ...... Phil 1:17
esteem o better than themselves. ...... Phil 2:3
If any o man thinketh that he .... Phil 3:4
with o my fellowlabourers, whose .... Phil 4:3
you all toward each o aboundeth...... 2Th 1:3
that they teach no o doctrine, ... 1Ti 1:3
if there be any o thing that is 1Ti 1:10
be partaker of o men's sins. 1Ti 5:22
the earth, neither by any o oath. ...... Jas 5:12
as a busybody in o men's matters. 1Pet 4:15
as they do also the o scriptures. 2Pet 3:16
I will put upon you none o burden. .. Rev 2:24
o voices of the trumpet of the .... Rev 8:13
one is, and the o is not yet come ...... Rev 17:10

OTHERS

and out of the earth shall o grow ...... Job 8:19
and let o bow down upon her .... Job 31:10
number, and set o in their stead ...... Job 34:24
wicked men in the open sight of o .... Job 34:26
and leave their wealth to o .... Ps 49:10
thou give thine honour unto o .... Prov 5:9
thyself likewise hast cursed o. .... Eccl 7:22
saith, Yet will I gather o to him .... Is 56:8
houses shall be turned unto o .... Jer 6:12
will I give their wives unto o. .... Jer 8:10
to the o he said in mine hearing, ... Eze 9:5
they have made o to hope that.......... Eze 13:6
o daubed with untempered .... Eze 13:10
which was diverse from all the o. ...... Dan 7:19
up, even four o beside those .... Dan 11:4
only, what do ye more than o .... Mt 5:47
blind, maimed, and many o. .... Mt 15:30
and o, Jeremias, or one of the .... Mt 16:14
saw a standing idle in the.............. Mt 20:3
found o standing idle, and saith ...... Mt 20:6
o cut down branches from the .... Mt 21:8
o smote him with the palms of .... Mt 26:67
He saved o; .... Mk 15:31
O said, That it is Elias. .... Mk 6:15
O said, That it is a prophet, or .... Mk 6:15
and o, One of the prophets............... Mk 8:28
o cut down branches of the trees ...... Mk 11:8
and him they killed, and many o ...... Mk 12:5
and will give the vineyard unto o .... Mk 12:9
with the scribes, He saved o. .... Mk 15:31
of o that sat down with them .... Lk 5:29
steward, and Susanna, and many o .. Lk 8:3
but to o in parables. .... Lk 8:10
and of o, that one of the old.............. Lk 9:8
o say, that one of the old .... Lk 9:19
And o, tempting him, sought of him .. Lk 11:16
were righteous, and despised o .... Lk 18:9
and shall give the vineyard to o ...... Lk 20:16
And there were also two o, ... Lk 23:32
derided him, saying, He saved o ...... Lk 23:35
prepared, and certain o with them. .. Lk 24:1
o said, Nay .... Jn 7:12
O said, This is the Christ .... Jn 7:41
o said, He is like him .... Jn 9:9
O said, How can a man that is a ...... Jn 9:16
O said, These are not the words ...... Jn 10:21
o said, An angel spake to him .... Jn 12:29
or did o tell it thee of me. .... Jn 18:34
o were with him, on either side. ...... Jn 19:18
O mocking said, These men are .... Acts 2:13
of the Lord, with many o also .... Acts 15:35
o said, We will hear these again ...... Acts 17:32
named Damaris, and o with them. .... Acts 17:34
o also, which had diseases in the...... Acts 28:9
If I be not an apostle unto o 1Cor 9:2
If o be partakers of this power 1Cor 9:12

means, when I have preached to o 1Cor 9:27
by my voice I might teach o also. 1Cor 14:19
or need we, as some o, epistles 2Cor 3:1
occasion of the forwardness of o 2Cor 8:8
the children of wrath, even as o ...... Eph 2:3
every man also on the things of o ...... Phil 2:4
neither of you, nor yet of o 1Th 2:6
even as o which have no hope. 1Th 4:13
let us not sleep, as do o 1Th 5:6
before all, that o also may fear 1Ti 5:20
who shall be able to teach o also........ 2Ti 2:2
place every year with blood of o. ...... Heb 9:25
o were tortured, not accepting.......... Heb 11:35
o had trial of cruel mockings and .... Heb 11:36
o save with fear, pulling them. .... Jude 23

OTHERWISE

O I should have wrought falsehood.... 2Sa 18:13
O it shall come to pass, when my 1Kin 1:21
passover o than it was written 2Chr 30:18
lest o they should rejoice over .... Ps 38:16
o ye have no reward of your. .... Mt 6:1
if o, then both the new maketh a ...... Lk 5:36
o grace is no more grace .... Rom 11:6
o work is no more work .... Rom 11:6
o thou also shalt be cut off .... Rom 11:22
if o, yet as a fool receive me, ... 2Cor 11:16
that ye will be none o minded .... Gal 5:10
and if in any thing ye be o minded.... Phil 3:15
and they that are o cannot be hid. 1Ti 5:25
If any man teach o, and consent, ... 1Ti 6:3
o it is of no strength at all. .... Heb 9:17

OTHNI (oth'-ni) A son of Shemiah.
O, and Rephael, and Obed, Elzabad, .. 1Chr 26:7

OTHNIEL (oth'-ne-el)
1. A brother of Caleb.
O the son of Kenaz, the brother ...... Josh 15:17
O the son of Kenaz, Caleb's .... Judg 1:13
even O the son of Kenaz, Caleb's .... Judg 3:9
And O the son of Kenaz died............. Judg 3:11
O, and Seraiah 1Chr 4:13
and the sons of O 1Chr 4:13
2. Tribe or family of Othniel 1.
was Heldai the Netophathite, of O. .. 1Chr 27:15

OUCHES

make them to be set in o of gold ...... Ex 28:11
And thou shalt make o of gold .... Ex 28:13
the wreathen chains to the o .... Ex 28:14
thou shalt fasten in the two o .... Ex 28:25
onyx stones inclosed in o of gold...... Ex 39:6
they were inclosed in o of gold .... Ex 39:13
and they made two o of gold. .... Ex 39:16
chains they fastened in the two o .... Ex 39:18

OUGHT

unto me that o not to be done .... Gen 20:9
which thing o not to be done .... Gen 34:7
and he knew not o he had, save the .. Gen 39:6
there is not o left in the sight.......... Gen 47:18
ye shall not diminish o thereof .... Ex 5:8
yet not o of your work shall be .... Ex 5:11
Ye shall not minish o from your ...... Ex 5:19
thou shalt not carry forth o of .... Ex 12:46
And if a man borrow o of his............ Ex 22:14
And if o of the flesh of the .... Ex 29:34
things which o not to be done .... Lev 4:2
things which o not to be done .... Lev 4:27
whosoever beareth o of the .... Lev 11:25
if o remain until the third day, ... Lev 19:6
if thou sell o unto thy neighbour .... Lev 25:14
or buyest o of thy neighbour's. .... Lev 25:14
if o be committed by ignorance ...... Num 15:24
soul that doeth o presumptuously .... Num 15:30
or uttered o out of her lips, ... Num 30:6
shall ye diminish o from it .... Deut 4:2
o unto his neighbour shall .... Deut 15:2
neither have I taken away o .... Deut 26:14
nor given o thereof for the dead ...... Deut 26:14
There failed not o of any good .... Josh 21:45
if o but death part thee and me ...... Ruth 1:17
thou taken o of any man's hand...... 1Sa 12:4
ye have not found o in my hand 1Sa 12:5
was there o missing unto them 1Sa 25:7
we will not give them o of the 1Sa 30:22
or else, till the sun be down 2Sa 3:35
for no such thing o to be done in 2Sa 13:12
said, Whosoever saith o unto thee .. 2Sa 14:10
from o that my lord the king hath 2Sa 14:19
to know what Israel o to do. 1Chr 15:2
None o to carry the ark of God. 1Chr 15:2
O ye not to know that the LORD...... 2Chr 13:5
o ye not to walk in the fear of .... Neh 5:9
unto him that o to be feared. .... Ps 76:11
thy brother hath o against thee ...... Mt 5:23
And if any man say o unto you .... Mt 21:3
these o ye to have done, and not. .... Mt 23:23
ye suffer him no more to do o for.... Mk 7:12
him, he asked him if he saw o .... Mk 8:23
forgive, if ye have o against any ...... Mk 11:25
prophet, standing where it o not. .... Mk 13:14
these o ye to have done, and not...... Lk 11:42
in the same hour what ye o to say .. Lk 12:12
six days in which men o to work ...... Lk 13:14
o not thus woman, being a .... Lk 13:16
that men o always to pray, and not .. Lk 18:1
O not Christ to have suffered .... Lk 24:26
the place where men o to worship .... Jn 4:20
Hath any man brought him o to eat .. Jn 4:33
ye also o to wash one another's........ Jn 13:14
a law, and by our law he o to die .... Jn 19:7

that o of the things which he ...... Acts 4:32
We o to obey God rather than men ...... Acts 5:29
we o not to think that the ...... Acts 17:29
ye o to be quiet, and to do ...... Acts 19:36
ye o to support the weak, and to ...... Acts 20:35
saying that they o not to ...... Acts 24:19
Who o to have been here before ...... Acts 24:19
object, if they had o against me. ...... Acts 24:19
seat, where I o to be judged ...... Acts 25:10
crying that he o not to live any ...... Acts 25:24
that I o to do many things ...... Acts 26:9
not that I had o to accuse my ...... Acts 28:19
what we should pray for as we o ...... Rom 8:26
more highly than he o to think ...... Rom 12:3
We then that are strong o to bear ...... Rom 15:1
nothing yet as he o to know 1Cor 8:2
For a man indeed o not to cover 1Cor 11:7
For this cause o the woman to 1Cor 11:10
from them of whom I o to rejoice 2Cor 2:3
ye o rather to forgive him 2Cor 2:7
for I o to have been commended 2Cor 12:11
for the children o not to lay up 2Cor 12:14
So o men to love their wives as ...... Eph 5:28
may speak boldly, as I o to speak ...... Eph 6:20
make it manifest, as I o to speak. ...... Col 4:4
know how ye o to answer every man. ...... Col 4:6
received of us how ye o to walk 1Th 4:1
know how ye o to follow us 2Th 3:7
speaking things which they o not 1Ti 5:13
teaching things which they o not. ...... Titus 1:11
wronged thee, or oweth thee o ...... Philem 18
Therefore we o to give thee credit ...... Heb 2:1
And by reason hereof he o, as for ...... Heb 5:3
for the time ye o to be teachers. ...... Heb 5:12
these things o not so to be. ...... Jas 3:10
For that ye o to say, If the Lord ...... Jas 4:15
of persons o ye to be in all holy 2Pet 3:11
in him o himself also so to walk 1Jn 2:6
we o to lay down our lives for 1Jn 3:16
we o also to love one another 1Jn 4:11
We therefore o to receive such, ... 3Jn 8

OUGHTEST
what thou o to do unto him 1Kin 2:9
Thou o therefore to have put my ...... Mt 25:27
shall tell thee what thou o to do. ...... Acts 10:6
o to behave thyself in the house 1Ti 3:15

OUR See PREFACE.

OURS
herdmen, saying, The water is o ...... Gen 26:20
taken from our father, that is o ...... Gen 31:16
and every beast of theirs be o ...... Gen 34:23
on this side Jordan may be o ...... Num 32:32
ye that Ramoth in Gilead is o 1Kin 22:3
high places are o in possession ...... Eze 36:2
and the inheritance shall be o. ...... Mk 12:7
that the inheritance may be o ...... Lk 20:14
Christ our Lord, both theirs and o 1Cor 1:2
even as ye also are o in the day 2Cor 1:14
let us also learn to maintain good ...... Titus 3:14
and not for o only, but also for 1Jn 2:2

OURSELVES
bow down o to thee to the earth ...... Gen 37:10
or how shall we clear o ...... Gen 44:16
But we o will go ready and armed ...... Num 32:17
cattle we took for a prey unto o ...... Deut 2:35
cities, we took for a prey to o ...... Deut 3:7
and we will discover o unto them 1Sa 14:8
let us behave o valiantly for our 1Chr 19:13
but we o together will build unto ...... Ezr 4:3
we might afflict o before our God ...... Ezr 8:21
to charge o yearly with the third ...... Neh 10:32
let us know among o what a good ...... Job 34:4
Let us take to o the houses of ...... Ps 83:12
he that hath made us, and not we o ...... Ps 100:3
let us solace o with loves. ...... Prov 7:18
and under falsehood have we hid o ...... Is 28:15
we will fill o with strong drink. ...... Is 56:12
let us join o to the LORD in a ...... Jer 50:5
for we o have heard of his own. ...... Lk 22:71
for we have heard him, and know ...... Jn 4:42
But we will give o continually to ...... Acts 6:4
We have bound o under a great. ...... Acts 23:14
but o also, which have the ...... Rom 8:23
even we o groan within ...... Rom 8:23
groan within o, waiting for ...... Rom 8:23
of the weak, and not to please o ...... Rom 15:1
For if we would judge o, ... 1Cor 11:31
we o are comforted of God 2Cor 1:4
we had the sentence of death in o 2Cor 1:9
that we should not trust in o 2Cor 1:9
Do we begin again to commend o 2Cor 3:1
of o to think any thing as of 2Cor 3:5
to think any thing as of o 2Cor 3:5
of the truth commending o to 2Cor 4:2
For we preach not o, but Christ 2Cor 4:5
o your servants for Jesus' sake 2Cor 4:5
we commend not o again unto you 2Cor 5:12
For whether we be beside o 2Cor 5:13
o as the ministers of God 2Cor 6:4
let us cleanse o from all 2Cor 7:1
we dare not make o of the number 2Cor 10:12
or compare o with some that 2Cor 10:12
stretch not o beyond our measure 2Cor 10:14
ye that we excuse o unto you 2Cor 12:19
we o also are found sinners, as ...... Gal 2:17
behaved o among you that believe. 2Th 3:7
So that we o glory in you in the 2Th 1:4
for we behaved not o disorderly 2Th 3:7
but to make o an ensample unto 2Th 3:9
For we o also were sometimes ...... Titus 3:3
the assembling of o together ...... Heb 10:25
that we have no sin, we deceive o. 1Jn 1:8

OUT See PREFACE.

OUTCAST
because they called thee an O ...... Jer 30:17

OUTCASTS
together the o of Israel ...... Ps 147:2
and shall assemble the o of Israel. ...... Is 11:12
hide the o ...... Is 16:3
Let mine o dwell with thee, Moab ...... Is 16:4
the o in the land of Egypt, and ...... Is 27:13
gathereth the o of Israel ...... Is 56:8
the o of Elam shall not come. ...... Jer 49:36

OUTER
was heard even to the o court ...... Eze 10:5
shall be cast out into o darkness ...... Mt 8:12
away, and cast him into o darkness ...... Mt 22:13
servant into o darkness ...... Mt 25:30

OUTGOINGS
the o of it were at the sea ...... Josh 17:9
the o of it shall be thine ...... Josh 17:18
the o of the border were at the ...... Josh 18:19
the o thereof are in the valley ...... Josh 18:16
the o of their border were at ...... Josh 19:22
the o thereof are at the sea from ...... Josh 19:29
the o thereof were at Jordan ...... Josh 19:33
thou makest the o of the morning ...... Ps 65:8

OUTLANDISH
even him did o women cause to sin ...... Neh 13:26

OUTLIVED
the days of the elders that o Joshua. ...... Judg 2:7

OUTMOST
curtain that is o in the coupling ...... Ex 26:10
o coast of the salt sea eastward ...... Num 34:3
out unto the o parts of heaven ...... Deut 30:4
four or five in the o fruitful ...... Is 17:6

OUTRAGEOUS
Wrath is cruel, and anger is o ...... Prov 27:4

OUTRUN
and the other disciple did o Peter ...... Jn 20:4

OUTSIDE
Phurah his servant unto the o of ...... Judg 7:11
when I come to the o of the camp ...... Judg 7:17
came unto the o of the camp in ...... Judg 7:19
so on the o toward the great 1Kin 7:9
behold a wall on the o of the ...... Eze 40:5
ye make clean the o of the cup ...... Mt 23:25
that clean the o that the outside ...... Mt 23:26
make clean the o of the cup ...... Lk 11:39

OUTSTRETCHED
a mighty hand, and with an o arm ...... Deut 26:8
fight against you with an o hand ...... Jer 21:5
by my great power and by my o arm ...... Jer 27:5

OUTWARD
a thousand cubits round about ...... Num 35:4
man looketh on the o appearance. 1Sa 16:7
for the o business over Israel 1Chr 26:29
had the oversight of the o ...... Neh 11:16
the o court of the king's house. ...... Est 6:4
brought he me into the o court ...... Eze 40:17
the gate of the o court that ...... Eze 40:20
thereof were toward the o court ...... Eze 40:34
o sanctuary which looketh toward ...... Eze 44:1
which indeed appear beautiful o ...... Mt 23:27
which is o in the flesh ...... Rom 2:28
but though our o man perish 2Cor 4:16
on things after the o appearance 2Cor 10:7
adorning let it not be that o 1Pet 3:3

OUTWARDLY
Even so ye also o appear ...... Mt 23:28
he is not a Jew, which is one o ...... Rom 2:28

OUTWENT
o them, and came together unto him ...... Mk 6:33

OVEN
of a meat offering baken in the o ...... Lev 2:4
offering that is baken in the o ...... Lev 7:9
whether it be o, or ranges for ...... Lev 11:35
shall bake your bread in one o ...... Lev 26:26
o in the time of thine anger ...... Ps 21:9
Our skin was black like an o ...... Lam 5:10
as an o heated by the baker, who ...... Hos 7:4
made ready their heart like an o ...... Hos 7:6
They are all hot as an o, and have ...... Hos 7:7
cometh, that shall burn as an o ...... Mal 4:1
and to morrow is cast into the o ...... Mt 6:30
and to morrow is cast into the o ...... Lk 12:28

OVENS
upon thy people, and into thine o ...... Ex 8:3

OVER See PREFACE.

OVERCAME
o them, and prevailed against them ...... Acts 19:16
me in my throne, even as I also o ...... Rev 3:21
they o him by the blood of the ...... Rev 12:11

OVERCHARGE
that I may not o you all 2Cor 2:5

OVERCHARGED
your hearts be o with surfeiting ...... Lk 21:34

OVERCOME
Gad, a troop shall o him ...... Gen 49:19
but he shall o at the last ...... Gen 49:19
of them that cry for being o ...... Num 13:30
for we are well able to o them ...... Num 13:30
I shall be able to o them ...... Num 22:11
Ahaz, but could not o him 2Kin 16:5
eyes from me, for they have o me ...... Song 6:5
of them that are o with wine ...... Is 28:1
and like a man whom wine hath o ...... Jer 23:9
o him, he taketh from him all his ...... Lk 11:22
I have o the world ...... Jn 16:33
mightest o when thou art judged ...... Rom 3:4
Be not o of evil, but o ...... Rom 12:21
for of whom a man is o, of the 2Pet 2:19
are again entangled therein, and o 2Pet 2:20
because ye have o the wicked one 1Jn 2:13
you, and ye have o the wicked one 1Jn 2:14
little children, and have o them 1Jn 4:4
war against them, and shall o them ...... Rev 11:7
war with the saints, and to o them ...... Rev 13:7
Lamb, and the Lamb shall o them ...... Rev 17:14

OVERCOMETH
is born of God o the world 1Jn 5:4
the victory that o the world 1Jn 5:4
Who is he that o the world 1Jn 5:5
To him that o will I give to eat ...... Rev 2:7
He that o shall not be hurt of ...... Rev 2:11
To him that o will I give to eat ...... Rev 2:17
And he that o, and keepeth my works ...... Rev 2:26
He that o, the same shall be ...... Rev 3:5
Him that o will I make a pillar ...... Rev 3:12
To him that o will I grant to sit ...... Rev 3:21
He that o shall inherit all ...... Rev 21:7

OVERDRIVE
and if men should o them one day ...... Gen 33:13

OVERFLOW
the water of the Red sea to o ...... Deut 11:4
waters, where the floods o me ...... Ps 69:2
Let not the waterflood o me ...... Ps 69:15
he shall o and go over, he shall ...... Is 8:8
shall o with righteousness ...... Is 10:22
waters shall o the hiding places ...... Is 28:17
the rivers, they shall o thee ...... Is 43:2
shall o the land, and all that is ...... Jer 47:2
and one shall certainly come, and o ...... Dan 11:10
destroy him, and his army shall o ...... Dan 11:26
into the countries, and shall o ...... Dan 11:40
and the fats shall o with wine ...... Joel 2:24
for the press is full, the fats o ...... Joel 3:13

OVERFLOWED
gushed out, and the streams o ...... Ps 78:20
being o with water, perished 2Pet 3:6

OVERFLOWETH
(for Jordan o all his banks all ...... Josh 3:15

OVERFLOWING
He bindeth the floods from o ...... Job 28:11
a watercourse for the o of waters ...... Job 38:25
as a flood of mighty waters o ...... Is 28:2
when the o scourge shall pass ...... Is 28:15
when the o scourge shall pass ...... Is 28:18
as an o stream, shall reach to ...... Is 30:28
the north, and shall be an o flood ...... Jer 47:2
there shall be an o shower ...... Eze 13:11
there shall be an o shower ...... Eze 13:13
o rain, and great hailstones, fire ...... Eze 38:22
the o of the water passed by ...... Hab 3:10

OVERFLOWN
when it had o all his banks 1Chr 12:15
foundation was o with a flood ...... Job 22:16
shall they be o from before him ...... Dan 11:22

OVERLAID
of shittim wood o with gold ...... Ex 26:32
he o the boards with gold, and ...... Ex 36:34
the bars, and o the bars with gold ...... Ex 36:34
shittim wood, and o them with gold ...... Ex 36:36
he o their chapiters and their ...... Ex 36:38
he o it with pure gold within and ...... Ex 37:2
o them with gold, to bear the ...... Ex 37:15
he o it with pure gold, both the ...... Ex 37:26
shittim wood, and o them with gold ...... Ex 37:28
and he o it with brass ...... Ex 38:2
wood, and o them with brass ...... Ex 38:6
o their chapiters, and filleted ...... Ex 38:28
because she o it 1Kin 3:19
and he o it with pure gold 1Kin 6:21
So Solomon o the house within 1Kin 6:21
and he o it with gold 1Kin 6:22
And the whole house he o with gold 1Kin 6:22
was by the oracle he o with gold 1Kin 6:22
he o the cherubims with gold 1Kin 6:28
floor of the house he o with gold 1Kin 6:30
he o the doors with gold, and spread gold 1Kin 6:32
ivory, and o it with the best gold 1Kin 10:18
Hezekiah king of Judah had o 2Kin 18:16
he o it within with pure gold 2Chr 3:4
which he o with fine gold and set 2Chr 3:5
He o also the house, the beams 2Chr 3:7
he o it with fine gold, amounting 2Chr 3:8

OVERLAY

he o the upper chambers with gold 2Chr 3:9
image work, and o them with brass 2Chr 3:10
o the doors of them with brass 2Chr 4:9
of ivory, and o it with pure gold 2Chr 9:17
as bright ivory o with sapphires ...... Song 5:14
covenant o round about with gold ...... Heb 9:4

OVERLAY

thou shalt o it with pure gold, ... Ex 25:11
within and without shalt thou o it ...... Ex 25:11
shittim wood, and o them with gold ...... Ex 25:13
thou shalt o it with pure gold ...... Ex 25:24
o them with gold, that the table ...... Ex 25:28
thou shalt o the boards with gold ...... Ex 26:29
thou shalt o the bars with gold ...... Ex 26:29
o them with gold, and their hooks ...... Ex 26:37
thou shalt o it with brass ...... Ex 27:2
wood, and o them with brass ...... Ex 27:6
thou shalt o it with pure gold, ... Ex 30:3
shittim wood, and o them with gold ...... Ex 30:5
to o the walls of the houses 1Chr 29:4

OVERLAYING

the o of their chapiters of ...... Ex 38:17
the o of their chapiters and their ...... Ex 38:19

OVERLIVED

days of the elders that o Joshua ...... Josh 24:31

OVERMUCH

be swallowed up with o sorrow 2Cor 2:7

OVERPASS

they o the deeds of the wicked ...... Jer 5:28

OVERPAST

until these calamities be o ...... Ps 57:1
until the indignation be o ...... Is 26:20

OVERPLUS

restore the o unto the man to ...... Lev 25:27

OVERRAN

the way of the plain, and o Cushi 2Sa 18:23

OVERRUNNING

But with an o flood he will make ...... Nah 1:8

OVERSEE

were appointed to o the vessels 1Chr 9:29
thousand and six hundred to o them 2Chr 2:2

OVERSEER

he made him o over his house, and ...... Gen 39:4
he had made him o in his house ...... Gen 39:5
the son of Zichri was their o ...... Neh 11:9
their o was Zabdiel, the son of ...... Neh 11:14
The o also of the Levites at ...... Neh 11:22
sang loud, with Jezrahiah their o ...... Neh 12:42
Which having no guide, o, or ...... Prov 6:7

OVERSEERS

six hundred o to set the people a 2Chr 2:18
were o under the hand of Cononiah 2Chr 31:13
the o of them were Jahath and 2Chr 34:12
were o of all that wrought the 2Chr 34:13
it into the hand of the o 2Chr 34:17
the Holy Ghost hath made you o ...... Acts 20:28

OVERSHADOW

power of the Highest shall o thee ...... Lk 1:35
passing by might o some of them ...... Acts 5:15

OVERSHADOWED

behold, a bright cloud o them ...... Mt 17:5
And there was a cloud that o them ...... Mk 9:7
there came a cloud, and o them ...... Lk 9:34

OVERSIGHT

peradventure it was an o ...... Gen 43:12
have the o of them that keep the ...... Num 3:32
the o of all the tabernacle, and ...... Num 4:16
that had the o of the house of 2Kin 12:11
that have the o of the house of 2Kin 22:5
that have the o of the house of 2Kin 22:9
their children had the o of the 1Chr 9:23
the o of the house of the Lord 2Chr 34:10
had the o of the outward business ...... Neh 11:16
having the o of the chamber of ...... Neh 13:4
among you, taking the o thereof 1Pet 5:2

OVERSPREAD

and of them was the whole earth o ...... Gen 9:19

OVERSPREADING

for the o of abominations he ...... Dan 9:27

OVERTAKE

when thou dost o them, say ...... Gen 44:4
said, I will pursue, I will o ...... Ex 15:9
o him, because the way is long ...... Deut 19:6
o thee, if thou shalt hearken ...... Deut 28:2
shall come upon thee, and o thee ...... Deut 28:15
o thee, till thou be destroyed ...... Deut 28:45
for ye shall o them ...... Josh 2:5
shall I o them 1Sa 30:8
for thou shalt surely o them 1Sa 30:8
lest he o us suddenly, and bring 2Sa 15:14
us, neither doth justice o us ...... Is 59:9
shall o you there in the land of ...... Jer 42:16
lovers, but she shall not o them ...... Hos 2:7
of iniquity did not o them ...... Hos 10:9
evil shall not o nor prevent us ...... Amos 9:10
the plowman shall o the reaper ...... Amos 9:13
that day should o you as a thief 1Th 5:4

OVERTAKEN

pursued mine enemies, and o them ...... Ps 18:37
if a man be o in a fault ...... Gal 6:1

OVERTAKETH

the sword of thine enemies o thee 1Chr 21:12

OVERTHREW

he o those cities, and all the ...... Gen 19:25
when he o the cities in the which ...... Gen 19:29
the LORD o the Egyptians in the ...... Ex 14:27
which the LORD o in his anger ...... Deut 29:23
But o Pharaoh and his host in the ...... Ps 136:15
shall be as when God o Sodom ...... Is 13:19
be as the cities which the LORD o ...... Jer 20:16
God o Sodom and Gomorrah ...... Jer 50:40
some of you, as God o Sodom ...... Amos 4:11
o the tables of the moneychangers ...... Mt 21:12
o the tables of the moneychangers ...... Mk 11:15
changers' money, and o the tables ...... Jn 2:15

OVERTHROW

also, that I will not o this city ...... Gen 19:21
Lot out of the midst of the o ...... Gen 19:29
but thou shalt utterly o them ...... Ex 23:24
ye shall o their altars, and break ...... Deut 12:3
therein, like the o of Sodom ...... Deut 29:23
and to spy it out, and to o it 2Sa 10:3
strong against the city, and o it 2Sa 11:25
unto thee for to search, and to o 1Chr 19:3
to o them in the wilderness ...... Ps 106:26
To o their seed also among the ...... Ps 106:27
when have purposed to o my goings ...... Ps 140:4
hunt the violent man to o him ...... Ps 140:11
to o the righteous in judgment ...... Prov 18:5
As in the o of Sodom and Gomorrah ...... Jer 49:18
I will o the throne of kingdoms, ... Hag 2:22
I will o the chariots, and those ...... Hag 2:22
if it be of God, ye cannot o it ...... Acts 5:39
and o the faith of some 2Ti 2:18
ashes condemned them with an o 2Pet 2:6

OVERTHROWETH

away spoiled, and the mighty ...... Job 12:19
but wickedness o the sinner ...... Prov 13:6
but God o the wicked for their ...... Prov 21:12
and he o the words of the ...... Prov 22:12
but he that receiveth gifts o it ...... Prov 29:4

OVERTHROWN

of thine excellency thou hast o ...... Ex 15:7
fled before him, and many were o ...... Judg 9:40
some of them be o at the first 2Sa 17:9
and the Ethiopians were o, that 2Chr 14:13
Know now that God hath o me ...... Job 19:6
judges are o in stony places ...... Ps 141:6
but it is o by the mouth of the ...... Prov 11:11
The wicked are o, and are not ...... Prov 12:7
house of the wicked shall be o ...... Prov 14:11
it is desolate, as o by strangers ...... Is 1:7
but let them be o before thee ...... Jer 18:23
that was o as in a moment, and no ...... Lam 4:6
and many countries shall be o ...... Dan 11:41
I have o some of you, as God ...... Amos 4:11
forty days, and Nineveh shall be o ...... Jonah 3:4
for they were o in the wilderness 1Cor 10:5

OVERTOOK

they o him in the mount Gilead ...... Gen 31:23
Then Laban o Jacob ...... Gen 31:25
he o them, and he spake unto them ...... Gen 44:6
o them encamping by the sea, ... Ex 14:9
and o the children of Dan ...... Judg 18:22
but the battle o them ...... Judg 20:42
o him in the plains of Jericho ...... Jer 39:5
o Zedekiah in the plains of ...... Jer 39:5
o Zedekiah in the plains of ...... Jer 52:8
all her persecutors o her between ...... Lam 1:3

OVERTURN

them out, and they o the earth ...... Job 12:15
I will o, o, o ...... Eze 21:27

OVERTURNED

o it, that the tent lay along ...... Judg 7:13

OVERTURNETH

which o them in his anger ...... Job 9:5
he o the mountains by the roots ...... Job 28:9
he o them in the night, so that ...... Job 34:25

OVERWHELM

ye o the fatherless, and ye dig a ...... Job 6:27

OVERWHELMED

come upon me, and horror hath o me ...... Ps 55:5
cry unto thee, when my heart is o ...... Ps 61:2
I complained, and my spirit was o ...... Ps 77:3
but the sea o their enemies ...... Ps 78:53
of the afflicted, when he is o ...... Ps 102:1
Then the waters had o us, the ...... Ps 124:4
When my spirit was o within me ...... Ps 142:3
is my spirit o within me ...... Ps 143:4

OWE

O no man any thing, but to love ...... Rom 13:8

OWED

which o him ten thousand talents ...... Mt 18:24
which o him an hundred pence ...... Mt 18:28
the one o five hundred pence, and ...... Lk 7:41

OWEST

saying, Pay me that thou o ...... Mt 18:28
How much o thou unto my lord ...... Lk 16:5
he to another, And how much o thou ...... Lk 16:7
o unto me even thine own self ...... Philem 19

OWETH

or o thee ought, put that on mine ...... Philem 18

OWL

And the o, and the night hawk, and ...... Lev 11:16
And the little o, and the cormorant ...... Lev 11:17
and the cormorant, and the great o ...... Lev 11:17
And the o, and the night hawk, and ...... Deut 14:15
The little o, and the great ...... Deut 14:16
and the great o ...... Deut 14:16
I am like an o of the desert ...... Ps 102:6
the also and the raven shall ...... Is 34:11
the screech o also shall rest ...... Is 34:14
shall the great o make her nest ...... Is 34:15

OWLS

to dragons, and a companion to o ...... Job 30:29
o shall dwell there, and satyrs ...... Is 13:21
of dragons, and a court for o ...... Is 34:13
honour me, the dragons and the o ...... Is 43:20
the o shall dwell therein ...... Jer 50:39
the dragons, and mourning as the o ...... Mic 1:8

OWN See PREFACE.

OWNER

but the o of the ox shall be quit ...... Ex 21:28
it hath been testified to his o ...... Ex 21:29
his o also shall be put to death ...... Ex 21:29
The o of the pit shall make it ...... Ex 21:34
and give money unto the o of them ...... Ex 21:34
his o hath not kept him in ...... Ex 21:36
the o shall accept thereof, ... Ex 22:11
restitution unto the o thereof ...... Ex 22:12
the o thereof being not with it, ... Ex 22:14
But if the o thereof be with it, ... Ex 22:15
of Shemer, o of the hill, Samaria 1Kin 16:24
The ox knoweth his o, and the ass ...... Is 1:3
the o of the ship, more than ...... Acts 27:11

OWNERS

or have caused the o thereof to ...... Job 31:39
away the life of the o thereof ...... Prov 1:19
good is there to the o thereof ...... Eccl 5:11
riches kept for the o thereof to ...... Eccl 5:13
the o thereof said unto them, Why ...... Lk 19:33

OWNETH

he that o the house shall come and ...... Lev 14:35
bind the man that o this girdle ...... Acts 21:11

OX

nor his maidservant, nor his o ...... Ex 20:17
If an o gore a man or a woman, ... Ex 21:28
then the o shall be surely stoned ...... Ex 21:28
the owner of the o shall be quit ...... Ex 21:28
But if the o were wont to push, ... Ex 21:29
he shall be stoned, and his ...... Ex 21:29
If the o shall push a manservant ...... Ex 21:32
silver, and the o shall be stoned ...... Ex 21:32
an o or an ass fall therein ...... Ex 21:33
if one man's o hurt another's, ... Ex 21:35
then they shall sell the live o ...... Ex 21:35
the dead o also they shall divide ...... Ex 21:35
Or if it be known that the o hath ...... Ex 21:36
he shall surely pay o for o ...... Ex 21:36
If a man shall steal an o, ... Ex 22:1
shall restore five oxen for an o ...... Ex 22:1
his hand alive, whether it be o, ... Ex 22:4
his neighbour an ass, or an o ...... Ex 22:9
enemy's o or his ass going astray ...... Ex 23:4
that thine o and thine ass may ...... Ex 23:12
whether o or sheep, that is male ...... Ex 34:19
shall eat no manner of fat, of o ...... Lev 7:23
of Israel, that killeth an o ...... Lev 17:3
whether it be o, or sheep ...... Lev 27:26
the princes, and for each one an o ...... Num 7:3
as the o licketh up the grass of ...... Num 22:4
nor thy maidservant, nor thine o ...... Deut 5:14
or his maidservant, his o ...... Deut 5:21
the o, the sheep, and the goat, ... Deut 14:4
and the pygarg, and the wild o ...... Deut 14:5
whether it be o or sheep ...... Deut 18:3
o or his sheep go astray, and hide ...... Deut 22:1
ass or his o fall down by the way ...... Deut 22:4
Thou shalt not plow with an o ...... Deut 22:10
Thou shalt not muzzle the o when ...... Deut 25:4
Thine o shall be slain before ...... Deut 28:31
young and old, and o ...... Josh 6:21
six hundred men with an o goad ...... Judg 3:31
for Israel, neither sheep, nor o ...... Judg 6:4
whose o have I taken 1Sa 12:3
Bring me hither every man his o 1Sa 14:34
man his o with him that night 1Sa 14:34
and woman, infant and suckling, o 1Sa 15:3
prepared for me daily was one o ...... Neh 5:18
or loweth the o over his fodder ...... Job 6:5
take the widow's o for a pledge ...... Job 24:3
he eateth grass as an o ...... Job 40:15
an o or bullock that hath horns ...... Ps 69:31
of an o that eateth grass ...... Ps 106:20
as an o goeth to the slaughter, ... Prov 7:22
is by the strength of the o ...... Prov 14:4
where love is, than a stalled o ...... Prov 15:17
lion shall eat straw like the o ...... Is 11:7
forth thither the feet of the o ...... Is 32:20
He that killeth an o as if he ...... Is 66:3
or an o that is brought to the ...... Jer 11:19
the face of an o on the left side ...... Eze 1:10
his o or his ass from the stall ...... Lk 13:15
an ass or an o fallen into a pit ...... Lk 14:5

OXEN

the o that treadeth out the corn.............1Cor 9:9
Thou shalt not muzzle the o that..............1Ti 5:18

OXEN

and he had sheep, and o, and he ....Gen 12:16
And Abimelech took sheep, and o..............Gen 20:14
And Abraham took sheep and o ....Gen 21:27
And I have o, and asses, flocks, and..............Gen 32:5
They took their sheep, and their o..............Gen 34:28
upon the camels, upon the o..............Ex 9:3
offerings, thy sheep, and thine o..............Ex 20:24
he shall restore five o for an ox..............Ex 22:1
shalt thou do with thine o..............Ex 22:30
offerings of o unto the LORD..............Ex 24:5
six covered wagons, and twelve o..............Num 7:3
And Moses took the wagons and the o ....Num 7:6
four o he gave unto the sons of..............Num 7:7
eight o he gave unto the sons of..............Num 7:8
of peace offerings, two o..............Num 7:17
of peace offerings, two o..............Num 7:23
of peace offerings, two o..............Num 7:29
of peace offerings, two o..............Num 7:35
of peace offerings, two o..............Num 7:41
of peace offerings, two o..............Num 7:47
of peace offerings, two o..............Num 7:53
of peace offerings, two o..............Num 7:59
of peace offerings, two o..............Num 7:65
of peace offerings, two o..............Num 7:71
of peace offerings, two o..............Num 7:77
of peace offerings, two o..............Num 7:83
All the o for the burnt offering..............Num 7:87
all the o for the sacrifice of..............Num 7:88
And Balak offered o and sheep, and..............Num 22:40
and prepare me here seven o..............Num 23:1
thy soul lusteth after, for o..............Deut 14:26
sons, and his daughters, and his o..............Josh 7:24
And he took a yoke of o, and hewed.....1Sa 11:7
so shall it be done unto his o..............1Sa 11:7
which a yoke of o might plow..............1Sa 14:14
the spoil, and took sheep, and o..............1Sa 14:32
best of the sheep, and of the o..............1Sa 15:9
the lowing of the o which I hear..............1Sa 15:14
the best of the sheep and of the o..............1Sa 15:15
took of the spoil, sheep and o..............1Sa 15:21
children and sucklings, and o..............1Sa 22:19
and took away the sheep, and the o.....1Sa 27:9
for the o shook it..............2Sa 6:6
gone six paces, he sacrificed o..............2Sa 6:13
here be o for burnt sacrifice, and..............2Sa 24:22
instruments of the o for wood..............2Sa 24:22
the o for fifty shekels of silver.............2Sa 24:24
And Adonijah slew sheep and o..............1Kin 1:9
And he hath slain o and fat cattle.............1Kin 1:19
down this day, and hath slain o..............1Kin 1:25
Ten fat o, and twenty o out of..............1Kin 4:23
It stood upon twelve o, three..............1Kin 7:25
between the ledges were lions, o..............1Kin 7:29
o were certain additions made of..............1Kin 7:29
sea, and twelve o under the sea..............1Kin 7:44
the ark, sacrificing sheep and o..............1Kin 8:5
LORD, two and twenty thousand o..............1Kin 8:63
with twelve yoke of o before him..............1Kin 19:19
And he left the o, and ran after..............1Kin 19:20
from him, and took a yoke of o..............1Kin 19:21
with the instruments of the o..............1Kin 19:21
and vineyards, and sheep, and o..............2Kin 5:26
the brasen o that were under it..............2Kin 16:17
on camels, and on mules, and on o....1Chr 12:40
of raisins, and wine, and oil, and o......1Chr 12:40
for o to be stumbled..............1Chr 13:9
I give thee the o also for burnt..............1Chr 21:23
under it was the similitude of o..............2Chr 4:3
Two rows of o were cast, when it..............2Chr 4:3
It stood upon twelve o, three..............2Chr 4:4
One sea, and twelve o under it..............2Chr 4:15
the ark, sacrificing sheep and o..............2Chr 5:6
of twenty and two thousand o..............2Chr 7:5
they had brought, seven hundred o...2Chr 15:11
o for him in abundance, and for.......2Chr 18:2
things were six hundred o..............2Chr 29:33
also brought in the tithe of o..............2Chr 31:6
small cattle, and three hundred o........2Chr 35:8
small cattle, and five hundred o..............2Chr 35:9
And so did they with the o..............2Chr 35:12
camels, and five hundred yoke of o .....Job 1:3
The o were plowing, and the asses..............Job 1:14
camels, and a thousand yoke of o..............Job 42:12
All sheep and o, yea, and the..............Ps 8:7
That our o may be strong..............Ps 144:14
Where no o are, the crib is clean..............Prov 14:4
be for the sending forth of o..............Is 7:25
behold joy and gladness, slaying o..............Is 22:13
The o likewise and the young asses........Is 30:24
the husbandman and his yoke of o..............Jer 51:23
shall make thee to eat grass as o..............Dan 4:25
shall make thee to eat grass as o..............Dan 4:32
from men, and did eat grass as o..............Dan 4:33
they fed him with grass like o..............Dan 5:21
will one plow there with o..............Amos 6:12
my o and my fatlings are killed,..............Mt 22:4
I have bought five yoke of o..............Lk 14:19
in the temple those that sold o..............Jn 2:14
temple, and the sheep, and the o..............Jn 2:15
was before that city, brought o..............Acts 14:13
Doth God take care for o..............1Cor 9:9

OZEM (o'-zem)

1. Son of Jesse.
O the sixth, David the seventh 1Chr 2:15
2. Son of Jerahmeel.
and Bunah, and Oren, and O, and.......1Chr 2:25

OZIAS (o-zi'-as) See UZZIAH. *Son of Joram; ancestor of Jesus.*
and Joram begat O..............................Mt 1:8
And O begat Joatham..........................Mt 1:9

OZNI (oz'-ni) See OZNITES. *A son of God.*
Of O, the family of the Oznites............Num 26:16

OZNITES (oz'-nites) *Descendants of Ozni.*
Of Ozni, the family of the O...............Num 26:16

P

PAARAI (pa'-ar-ahee) See NAARAI. *A 'mighty man' of David.*
the Carmelite, P the Arbite,...............2Sa 23:35

PACATIANA (pa-ca-she-a'-nah) *A region of Phrygia in Asia Minor.*
is the chiefest city of Phrygia P..............1Ti s

PACES
ark of the LORD had gone six p...........2Sa 6:13

PACIFIED
Then was the king's wrath p..............Est 7:10
when I am p toward thee for all..............Eze 16:63

PACIFIETH
A gift in secret p anger...............Prov 21:14
for yielding p great offences..............Eccl 10:4

PACIFY
but a wise man will p it..............Prov 16:14

PADAN (pa'-dan) See PADAN-ARAM. *Same as Padan-aram.*
And as for ine, when I came from P......Gen 48:7

PADAN-ARAM (pa''-dan-a'-ram) *The plains of Mesopotamia.*
of Bethuel the Syrian of P..............Gen 25:20
Arise, go to P, to the house of..............Gen 28:2
and he went to P unto Laban..............Gen 28:5
Jacob, and sent thee away to P..............Gen 28:6
and his mother, and was gone to P..............Gen 28:7
getting, which he had gotten in P..............Gen 31:18
of Canaan, when he came from P..............Gen 33:18
again, when he came out of P..............Gen 35:9
which were born to him in P..............Gen 35:26
which she bare unto Jacob in P..............Gen 46:15

PADDLE
shalt have a p upon thy weapon.....Deut 23:13

PADON (pa'-don) *A family of exiles.*
of Siaha, the children of P..............Ezr 2:44
of Sia, the children of P..............Neh 7:47

PAGIEL (pa-ghe-el) *An Asherite who counted the people.*
P the son of Ocran..............Num 1:13
Asher shall be P the son of Ocran......Num 2:27
eleventh day, P the son of Ocran......Num 7:72
offering of P the son of Ocran..............Num 7:77
of Asher was P the son of Ocran......Num 10:26

PAHATH-MOAB (pa''-hath-mo'-ab)
1. A family of exiles.
The children of P, of the..............Ezr 2:6
And of the sons of P..............Ezr 10:30
of Harim, and Hashub the son of P ....Neh 3:11
The children of P, of the..............Neh 7:11
2. Another family of exiles.
Of the sons of P..............Ezr 8:4
3. A family who renewed the covenant.
Parosh, P, Elam, Zatthu, Bani,..............Neh 10:14

PAI (pa-i) See PAU. *A city in Edom.*
and the name of his city was P..............1Chr 1:50

PAID
and custom, was p unto them..............Ezra 4:20
so he p the fare thereof, and went......Jonah 1:3
till thou hast p the uttermost..............Mt 5:26
till thou hast p the very last..............Lk 12:59

PAIN
his flesh upon him shall have p..............Job 14:22
travaileth with p all his days..............Job 15:20
also with p upon his bed, and the......Job 33:19
of his bones with strong p..............Job 33:19
Look upon mine affliction and my p...Ps 25:18
took hold upon them there, and p......Ps 48:6
they shall be in p as a woman..............Is 13:8
are my loins filled with p..............Is 21:3
the time of her delivery, is in p..............Is 26:17
with child, we have been in p..............Is 26:18
before her p came, she was..............Is 66:7
hath taken hold of us, and p..............Jer 6:24
they have put themselves to p..............Jer 12:13
Why is my p perpetual, and my..............Jer 15:18
the p as of a woman in travail..............Jer 22:23
it shall fall with p upon the..............Jer 30:23
take balm for her p, if so be she..............Jer 51:8
great p shall be in Ethiopia,..............Eze 30:4
great p shall come upon them, as..............Eze 30:9
Sin shall have great p, and No..............Eze 30:16
Be in p, and labour to bring forth......Mic 4:10
much p is in all loins, and the..............Nah 2:10
travaileth in p together until..............Rom 8:22
they gnawed their tongues for p..............Rev 16:10
neither shall there be any more p..............Rev 21:4

PAINED
My heart is sore p within me..............Ps 55:4
be sorely p at the report of Tyre..............Is 23:5
I am p at my very heart..............Jer 4:19
face the people shall be much p..............Joel 2:6
in birth, and p to be delivered..............Rev 12:2

PAINFUL
to know this, it was too p for me ....Ps 73:16

PAINFULNESS
In weariness and p, in watchings..............2Cor 11:27

PAINS
for her p came upon her..............1Sa 4:19
the p of hell gat hold upon me..............Ps 116:3
up, having loosed the p of death..............Acts 2:24
God of heaven because of their p......Rev 16:11

PAINTED
she p her face, and tired her head........2Kin 9:30
with cedar, and p with vermilion......Jer 22:14

PAINTEDST
p thy eyes, and deckedst thyself......Eze 23:40

PAINTING
thou rentest thy face with p..............Jer 4:30

PAIR
and the poor for a p of shoes..............Amos 2:6
and the needy for a p of shoes..............Amos 8:6
A p of turtledoves, or two young..............Lk 2:24
had a p of balances in his hand..............Rev 6:5

PALACE
into the p of the king's house..............1Kin 16:18
hard by the p of Ahab king of..............1Kin 21:1
in the p of the king's house,..............2Kin 15:25
in the p of the king of Babylon..............2Kin 20:18
for the p is not for man, but for..............1Chr 29:1
these things, and to build the p..............1Chr 29:19
of the LORD, and to the king's p..............2Chr 9:11
maintenance from the king's p..............Ezr 4:14
in the p that is in the province......Ezr 6:2
year, as I was in Shushan the p..............Neh 1:1
p which appertained to the house......Neh 2:8
and Hananiah the ruler of the p..............Neh 7:2
which was in Shushan the p..............Est 1:2
were present in Shushan the p..............Est 1:5
of the garden of the king's p..............Est 1:5
young virgins unto Shushan the p......Est 2:3
Now in Shushan the p there was a......Est 2:5
together unto Shushan the p..............Est 2:8
decree was given in Shushan the p...Est 3:15
his wrath went into the p garden......Est 7:7
p garden into the place of the..............Est 7:8
decree was given at Shushan the p......Est 8:14
And in Shushan the p the Jews slew......Est 9:6
the p was brought before the king......Est 9:11
five hundred men in Shushan the p.....Est 9:12
shall enter into the king's p..............Ps 45:15
after the similitude of a p..............Ps 144:12
will build upon her a p of silver........Song 8:9
a p of strangers to be no city..............Is 25:2
in the p of the king of Babylon..............Is 39:7
the p shall remain after the..............Jer 30:18
in them to stand in the king's p..............Dan 1:4
house, and flourishing in my p..............Dan 4:4
the p of the kingdom of Babylon..............Dan 4:29
of the wall of the king's p..............Dan 5:5
Then the king went to his p..............Dan 6:18
that I was at Shushan in the p..............Dan 8:2
of his p between the seas in the..............Dan 11:45
and ye shall cast them into the p..............Amos 4:3
and the p shall be dissolved..............Nah 2:6
unto the p of the high priest,..............Mt 26:3
afar off unto the high priest's p..............Mt 26:58
Now Peter sat without in the p..............Mt 26:69
even into the p of the high..............Mk 14:54
And as Peter was beneath in the p......Mk 14:66
a strong man armed keepeth his p......Lk 11:21
into the p of the high priest..............Jn 18:15
Christ are manifest in all the p..............Phil 1:13

PALACES
burnt all the p thereof with fire........2Chr 36:19
and cassia, out of the ivory p..............Ps 45:8
is known in her p for a refuge..............Ps 48:3
well her bulwarks, consider her p......Ps 48:13
built his sanctuary like high p..............Ps 78:69
walls, and prosperity within thy p......Ps 122:7
with her hands, and is in kings' p......Prov 30:28
and dragons in their pleasant p..............Is 13:22
they raised up the p thereof..............Is 23:13
Because the p shall be forsaken........Is 32:14
And thorns shall come up in her p......Is 34:13
by night, and let us destroy her p......Jer 6:5
windows, and is entered into our p......Jer 9:21
shall devour the p of Jerusalem......Jer 17:27
shall consume the p of Ben-hadad......Jer 49:27
he hath swallowed up all her p..............Lam 2:5
of the enemy the walls of her p..............Lam 2:7
And he knew their desolate p,..............Eze 19:7
and they shall set their p in thee........Eze 25:4
shall devour the p thereof..............Hos 8:14
shall devour the p of Ben-hadad......Amos 1:4
which shall devour the p thereof......Amos 1:7
which shall devour the p thereof......Amos 1:10
shall devour the p of Bozrah..............Amos 1:12
and it shall devour the p thereof......Amos 1:14
it shall devour the p of Kirioth......Amos 2:2
shall devour the p of Jerusalem......Amos 2:5
Publish in the p at Ashdod..............Amos 3:9

PALAL

in the *p* in the land of Egypt, and...... Amos 3:9
up violence and robbery in their *p*...... Amos 3:10
thee, and thy *p* shall be spoiled...... Amos 3:11
of Jacob, and hate his *p*...... Amos 6:8
and when he shall tread on our *p*...... Mic 5:5

PALAL (pa'-lal) *A rebuilder of Jerusalem's wall.*
P the son of Uzai, over against...... Neh 3:25

PALE
neither shall his face now wax *p*...... Is 29:22
And I looked, and behold a *p* horse...... Rev 6:8

PALENESS
and all faces are turned into *p*...... Jer 30:6

PALESTINA (pal-es-ti'-nah) See PALESTINE,
PHILISTIA. *The west coast of Canaan.*
take hold on the inhabitants of *P*...... Ex 15:14
Rejoice not thou, whole *P*...... Is 14:29
thou, whole P, art dissolved...... Is 14:31

PALESTINE (pal'-es-tine) See PALESTINA.
Same as Palestina.
and Zidon, and all the coasts of *P*...... Joel 3:4

PALLU (pal'-lu) See PALLUITES, PHALLU. *A son
of Reuben.*
Hanoch, and P, Hezron, and Carmi...... Ex 6:14
P, the family of the Palluites...... Num 26:5
And the sons of P...... Num 26:8
of Israel were, Hanoch, and P...... 1Chr 5:3

PALLUITES (pal'-lu-ites) *Descendants of
Pallu.*
of Pallu, the family of the P...... Num 26:5

PALM
and threescore and ten *p* trees...... Ex 15:27
pour it into the *p* of his own...... Lev 14:15
into the *p* of his own left hand...... Lev 14:26
goodly trees, branches of *p* trees...... Lev 23:40
and threescore and ten *p* trees...... Num 33:9
of Jericho, the city of *p* trees...... Deut 34:3
of *p* trees with the children of...... Judg 1:16
and possessed the city of *p* trees...... Judg 3:13
the dwelt under the *p* tree of...... Judg 4:5
p trees and open flowers, within...... 1Kin 6:29
p trees and open flowers, and...... 1Kin 6:32
p trees and open flowers, and...... 1Kin 6:35
cherubims, and upon the *p* trees...... 1Kin 6:35
and *p* trees and open flowers...... 1Kin 6:35
p trees, according to the...... 1Kin 7:36
fine gold, and set thereon *p* trees...... 2Chr 3:5
to Jericho, the city of *p* trees...... 2Chr 28:15
p branches, and branches of thick...... Neh 8:15
shall flourish like the *p* tree...... Ps 92:12
thy stature is like to a *p* tree...... Song 7:7
said, I will go up to the *p* tree...... Song 7:8
They are upright as the *p* tree...... Jer 10:5
and upon each *p* post were *p* trees...... Eze 40:16
and their arches, and their *p* trees...... Eze 40:22
and it had *p* trees, one on this...... Eze 40:26
p trees were upon the posts...... Eze 40:26
p trees were upon the posts...... Eze 40:31
p trees were upon the posts...... Eze 40:34
p trees were upon the posts...... Eze 40:37
toward the *p* tree on the one side...... Eze 41:19
the *p* tree on the other side...... Eze 41:19
p trees made, and on the wall of...... Eze 41:20
p trees, like as were made upon...... Eze 41:25
p trees on the one side and on the...... Eze 41:26
the *p* tree also, and the apple...... Joel 1:12
Took branches of *p* trees, and went...... Jn 12:13
Jesus with his *p* in his hand...... Jn 18:22

PALMERWORM
That which the *p* hath left hath...... Joel 1:4
and the caterpiller, and the *p*...... Joel 2:25
increased, the *p* devoured them...... Amos 4:9

PALMS
both the *p* of his hands were cut...... 1Sa 5:4
the feet, and the *p* of her hands...... 2Kin 9:35
the upon the *p* of my hands...... Is 49:16
knees and upon the *p* of my hands...... Dan 10:10
him with the *p* of their hands...... Mt 26:67
him with the *p* of their hands...... Mk 14:65
white robes, and *p* in their hands...... Rev 7:9

PALSIES
and many taken with *p*, and that...... Acts 8:7

PALSY
lunatick, and those that had the *p*...... Mt 4:24
lieth at home sick of the *p*...... Mt 8:6
to him a man sick of the *p*...... Mt 9:2
faith said unto the sick of the *p*...... Mt 9:2
saith to the sick of the *p*...... Mt 9:6
him, bringing one sick of the *p*...... Mk 2:3
bed wherein the sick of the *p* lay...... Mk 2:4
he said unto the sick of the *p*...... Mk 2:5
to say to the sick of the *p*...... Mk 2:9
(he saith to the sick of the *p*...... Mk 2:10
a man which was taken with a *p*...... Lk 5:18
(he said unto the sick of the *p*...... Lk 5:24
eight years, and was sick of the *p*...... Acts 9:33

PALTI (pal'-ti) *A spy sent to the Promised
Land.*
of Benjamin, the son of Raphu...... Num 13:9

PALTIEL (pal'-te-el) See PHALTIEL. *A chief of
Issachar.*
of Issachar, P the son of Azzan...... Num 34:26

PALTITE (pal'-tite) See PELONITE. *A resident
of Beth-palet.*
Helez the P, Ira the son of...... 2Sa 23:26

PAMPHYLIA (pam-fil'-e-ah) *A province of
Asia Minor.*
Phrygia, and P, in Egypt, and in...... Acts 2:10
Paphos, they came to Perga in P...... Acts 13:13
Pisidia, they came to P...... Acts 14:24
who departed from them from P...... Acts 15:38
over the sea of Cilicia and P...... Acts 27:5

PAN
be a meat offering baken in a *p*...... Lev 2:5
offering baken in the frying *p*...... Lev 2:7
In a *p* it shall be made with oil...... Lev 6:21
in the fryingpan, and in the *p*...... Lev 7:9
And he struck it into the *p*...... 1Sa 2:14
And she took a *p*, and poured them...... 2Sa 13:9
for that which is baked in the *p*...... 1Chr 23:29
take thou unto thee an iron *p*...... Eze 4:3

PANGS
and sorrows shall take hold of...... Is 13:8
p have taken hold upon me, as the...... Is 21:3
upon me, as the *p* of a woman that...... Is 21:3
in pain, and crieth out in her *p*...... Is 26:17
thou be when *p* come upon thee...... Jer 22:23
as the heart of a woman in her *p*...... Jer 48:41
as the heart of a woman in her *p*...... Jer 49:22
p as of a woman in travail...... Jer 50:43
for *p* have taken thee as a woman...... Mic 4:9

PANNAG (pan'-nag) *A place on the Damascus-
Baalbeck road.*
thy market wheat of Minnith, and P...... Eze 27:17

PANS
thou shalt make his *p* to receive...... Ex 27:3
it in a mortar, and baked it in *p*...... Num 11:8
things that were made in the *p*...... 1Chr 9:31
in pots, and in caldrons, and in *p*...... 2Chr 35:13

PANT
That *p* after the dust of the...... Amos 2:7

PANTED
I opened my mouth, and *p*...... Ps 119:131
My heart *p*, fearfulness...... Is 21:4

PANTETH
My heart *p*, my strength faileth...... Ps 38:10
As the hart *p* after the water...... Ps 42:1
so *p* my soul after thee, O God...... Ps 42:1

PAPER
The reeds by the brooks, by the...... Is 19:7
you, I would not write with *p*...... 2Jn 12

PAPHOS (pa'-fos) *Capital of Cyprus.*
had gone through the isle unto P...... Acts 13:6
Paul and his company loosed from P...... Acts 13:13

PAPS
Egyptians for the *p* of thy youth...... Eze 23:21
the *p* which thou hast sucked...... Lk 11:27
the *p* which never gave suck...... Lk 23:29
girt about the *p* with a golden...... Rev 1:13

PARABLE
And he took up his *p*, and said...... Num 23:7
And he took up his *p*, and said...... Num 23:18
And he took up his *p*, and said...... Num 24:3
And he took up his *p*, and said...... Num 24:15
on Amalek, he took up his *p*...... Num 24:20
on the Kenites, and took up his *p*...... Num 24:21
And he took up his *p*, and said...... Num 24:23
Moreover Job continued his *p*...... Job 27:1
Moreover Job continued his *p*...... Job 29:1
I will incline mine ear to a *p*...... Ps 49:4
I will open my mouth in a *p*...... Ps 78:2
so is a *p* in the mouth of fools...... Prov 26:7
so is a *p* in the mouth of fools...... Prov 26:9
speak a *p* unto the house of...... Eze 17:2
utter a *p* unto the rebellious...... Eze 24:3
shall one take up a *p* against you...... Mic 2:4
all these take up a *p* against him...... Hab 2:6
ye therefore the *p* of the sower...... Mt 13:18
Another *p* put he forth unto them...... Mt 13:24
Another *p* put he forth unto them...... Mt 13:31
Another *p* spake he unto them...... Mt 13:33
without a *p* spake he not unto...... Mt 13:34
Declare unto us the *p* of the...... Mt 13:36
unto him, Declare unto us this *p*...... Mt 15:15
Hear another *p*...... Mt 21:33
Now learn a *p* of the fig tree...... Mt 24:32
the twelve asked of him the *p*...... Mk 4:10
unto them, Know ye not this *p*...... Mk 4:13
But without a *p* spake he not unto...... Mk 4:34
asked him concerning the *p*...... Mk 7:17
he had spoken the *p* against them...... Mk 12:12
Now learn a *p* of the fig tree...... Mk 13:28
And he spake also a *p* unto them...... Lk 5:36
And he spake a *p* unto them...... Lk 6:39
of every city, he spake by a *p*...... Lk 8:4
him, saying, What might this *p* be...... Lk 8:9
Now the *p* is this...... Lk 8:11
unto them a *p* to this end...... Lk 12:16
speakest thou this *p* unto us...... Lk 12:41
He spake also this *p*...... Lk 13:6
he put forth a *p* to those which...... Lk 14:7
And he spake this *p* unto them...... Lk 15:3
he spake a *p* unto them to this...... Lk 18:1
he spake this *p* unto certain...... Lk 18:9
things, he added and spake a *p*...... Lk 19:11
he to speak to the people this...... Lk 20:9
he had spoken this *p* against them...... Lk 20:19
And he spake to them a *p*...... Lk 21:29
This *p* spake Jesus unto them...... Jn 10:6

PARABLES
say of me, Doth he not speak *p*...... Eze 20:49
spake many things unto them in *p*...... Mt 13:3
Why speakest thou unto them in *p*...... Mt 13:10
Therefore speak I to them in *p*...... Mt 13:13
Jesus unto the multitude in *p*...... Mt 13:34
saying, I will open my mouth in *p*...... Mt 13:35
when Jesus had finished these *p*...... Mt 13:53
and Pharisees had heard his *p*...... Mt 21:45
and spake unto them again by *p*...... Mt 22:1
unto him, and said unto them in *p*...... Mk 3:23
he taught them many things by *p*...... Mk 4:2
all these things are done in *p*...... Mk 4:11
and how then will ye know all *p*...... Mk 4:13
with many such *p* spake he the...... Mk 4:33
he began to speak unto them by *p*...... Mk 12:1
but to others in *p*...... Lk 8:10

PARADISE
To day shalt thou be with me in *p*...... Lk 23:43
How that he was caught up into *p*...... 2Cor 12:4
is in the midst of the *p* of God...... Rev 2:7

PARAH (pa'-rah) *A city in Benjamin.*
And Avim, and P, and Ophrah...... Josh 18:23

PARAMOURS
For she doted upon their *p*...... Eze 23:20

PARAN (pa'-ran) *A wilderness south of
Canaan.*
he dwelt in the wilderness of P...... Gen 21:21
rested in the wilderness of P...... Num 10:12
and pitched in the wilderness of P...... Num 12:16
them from the wilderness of P...... Num 13:3
Israel, unto the wilderness of P...... Num 13:26
against the Red sea, between P...... Deut 1:1
he shined forth from mount P...... Deut 33:2
went down to the wilderness of P...... 1Sa 25:1
arose out of Midian, and came to P...... 1Kin 11:18
they took men with them out of P...... 1Kin 11:18
and the Holy One from mount P...... Hab 3:3

PARBAR (par'-bar) *A place near the Temple in
Jerusalem.*
At P westward, four at the...... 1Chr 26:18
four at the causeway, and two at P...... 1Chr 26:18

PARCEL
And he bought a *p* of a field...... Gen 33:19
in a *p* of ground which Jacob...... Josh 24:32
of Moab, selleth a *p* of land...... Ruth 4:3
where was a *p* of ground full of...... 1Chr 11:13
themselves in the midst of that *p*...... 1Chr 11:14
near to the *p* of ground that...... Jn 4:5

PARCHED
nor *p* corn, nor green ears, until...... Lev 23:14
a corn in the selfsame day...... Josh 5:11
and he reached her *p* corn, and she...... Ruth 2:14
brethren an ephah of this *p* corn...... 1Sa 17:17
and five measures of *p* corn...... 1Sa 25:18
p corn, and beans, and lentiles, and...... 2Sa 17:28
beans, and lentiles, and *p* pulse...... 2Sa 17:28
the *p* ground shall become a pool...... Is 35:7
but shall inhabit the *p* places in...... Jer 17:6

PARCHMENTS
the books, but especially the *p*...... 2Ti 4:13

PARDON
for he will not *p* your...... Ex 23:21
P our iniquity and our sin, and...... Ex 34:9
P, I beseech thee, the iniquity...... Num 14:19
p my sin, and turn again with me...... 1Sa 15:25
This thing the LORD *p* thy servant...... 2Kin 5:18
the LORD *p* thy servant in this...... 2Kin 5:18
which the LORD would not *p*...... 2Kin 24:4
saying, The God *p* every one...... 2Chr 30:18
but thou art a God ready to *p*...... Neh 9:17
dost thou not *p* my transgression...... Job 7:21
sake, O LORD, *p* mine iniquity...... Ps 25:11
Our God, for he will abundantly *p*...... Is 55:7
and I will *p* it...... Jer 5:1
How shall I *p* thee for this...... Jer 5:7
I will *p* all their iniquities...... Jer 33:8
for I will *p* them whom I reserve...... Jer 50:20

PARDONED
I have *p* according to thy word...... Num 14:20
that her iniquity is *p*...... Is 40:2
thou hast not *p*...... Lam 3:42

PARDONETH
that iniquity, and passeth by...... Mic 7:18

PARE
shave her head, and *p* her nails...... Deut 21:12

PARENTS
shall rise up against their *p*...... Mt 10:21
when the *p* brought in the child...... Mk 13:12
the child in the temple, the *p*...... Lk 2:27
Now his *p* went to Jerusalem every...... Lk 2:41
And her *p* were astonished...... Lk 8:56
no man that hath left house, or *p*...... Lk 18:29
And ye shall be betrayed both by *p*...... Lk 21:16
who did sin, this man, or his *p*...... Jn 9:2
hath this man sinned, nor his *p*...... Jn 9:3
until they called the *p* of him...... Jn 9:18
His *p* answered them and said, We...... Jn 9:20
These words spake his *p*, because...... Jn 9:22
Therefore said his *p*, He is of...... Jn 9:23
of evil things, disobedient to *p*...... Rom 1:30
ought not to lay up for the *p*...... 2Cor 12:14
but the *p* for the children...... 2Cor 12:14

PARLOUR

Children, obey your p in the Lord	Eph 6:1
obey your p in all things	Col 3:20
no, to make our p to provoke their p	1Ti 5:4
blasphemers, disobedient to p	2Ti 3:2
was hid three months of his p	Heb 11:23

PARLOUR

and he was sitting in a summer p	Judg 3:20
shut the doors of the p upon him	Judg 3:23
the doors of the p were locked	Judg 3:24
he opened not the doors of the p	Judg 3:25
and brought them into the p	1Sa 9:22

PARLOURS

and of the inner p thereof	1Chr 28:11

PARMASHTA (par-mash´-tah) A son of Haman.

And P, and Arisai, and Aridai, and	Est 9:9

PARMENAS (par´-me-nas) A leader in the Jerusalem church.

and Nicanor, and Timon, and P	Acts 6:5

PARNACH (par´-nak) A Zebulunite who apportioned the Promised Land.

Zebulun, Elizaphan the son of P	Num 34:25

PAROSH (pa´-rosh) See PHAROSH.
1. A family of exiles.

The children of P, two thousand	Ezr 2:3
The children of P, two thousand	Neh 7:8

2. Married a foreigner in exile.

of the sons of P	Ezr 10:25

3. Father of Pedaiah.

After him Pedaiah the son of P	Neh 3:25

4. A family who renewed the covenant.

P, Pahath-moab, Elam, Zatthu,	Neh 10:14

PARSHANDATHA (par-shan´-da-thah) A son of Haman.

And P, and Dalphon, and Aspatha,	Est 9:7

PART See PREFACE.

PARTAKER

hast been p with adulterers	Ps 50:18
in hope should be p of his hope	1Cor 9:10
that I might be p thereof with	1Cor 9:23
For if I by grace be a p, why am	1Cor 10:30
neither be p of other men's sins	1Ti 5:22
but be thou p of the afflictions	2Ti 1:8
must be first p of the fruits	2Ti 2:6
also a p of the glory that shall	1Pet 5:1
God speed is p of his evil deeds	2Jn 11

PARTAKERS

we would not have been p with	Mt 23:30
made p of their spiritual things	Rom 15:27
If others be p of this power over	1Cor 9:12
at the altar are p with the altar	1Cor 9:13
for we are all p of that one	1Cor 10:17
of the sacrifices p of the altar	1Cor 10:18
ye cannot be p of the Lord's	1Cor 10:21
knowing, that as ye are p of the	2Cor 1:7
p of his promise in Christ by the	Eph 3:6
Be not ye therefore p with them	Eph 5:7
gospel, ye all are p of my grace	Phil 1:7
to be p of the inheritance of the	Col 1:12
and beloved, p of the benefit	1Ti 6:2
as the children are p of flesh	Heb 2:14
p of the heavenly calling	Heb 3:1
For we are made p of Christ	Heb 3:14
were made p of the Holy Ghost,	Heb 6:4
chastisement, whereof all are p	Heb 12:8
we might be p of his holiness	Heb 12:10
inasmuch as ye are p of Christ's	1Pet 4:13
might be p of the divine nature,	2Pet 1:4
that ye be not p of her sins	Rev 18:4

PARTAKEST

with them p of the root and	Rom 11:17

PARTED

and from thence it was p, and	Gen 2:10
of fire, and p them both asunder	2Kin 2:11
waters, they p hither and thither	2Kin 2:14
my that way is the light p	Job 38:24
among the nations, and p my land	Joel 3:2
p his garments, casting lots	Mt 27:35
They p my garments among	Mt 27:35
they p his garments, casting lots	Mk 15:24
they p his raiment, and cast lots	Lk 23:34
he was p from them, and carried up	Lk 24:51
They p my raiment among them, and	Jn 19:24
p them to all men, as every man	Acts 2:45

PARTETH

Whatsoever p the hoof, and is	Lev 11:3
And every beast that p the hoof	Deut 14:6
to cease, and p between the mighty	Prov 18:18

PARTHIANS (par-the´-uns) Inhabitants of Parthia, now Iran.

P, and Medes, and Elamites, and the	Acts 2:9

PARTIAL

ways, but have been p in the law	Mal 2:9
Are ye not then p in yourselves	Jas 2:4

PARTIALITY

another, doing nothing by p	1Ti 5:21
mercy and good fruits, without p	Jas 3:17

PARTICULAR

body of Christ, and members in p	1Cor 12:27
let every one of you in p so love	Eph 5:33

PARTICULARLY

he declared p what things God had	Acts 21:19
of which we cannot now speak p	Heb 9:5

PARTIES

the cause of both p shall come	Ex 22:9

PARTING

Babylon stood at the p of the way	Eze 21:21

PARTITION

He made a p by the chains of gold	1Kin 6:21
the middle wall of p between us	Eph 2:14

PARTLY

be p strong, and p broken	Dan 2:42
and I p believe it	1Cor 11:18
P, whilst ye were made a	Heb 10:33
and p, whilst ye became companions	Heb 10:33

PARTNER

Whoso is p with a thief hateth	Prov 29:24
do enquire of Titus, he is my p	2Cor 8:23
If thou count me therefore a p	Philem 17

PARTNERS

And they beckoned unto their p	Lk 5:7
Zebedee, which were p with Simon	Lk 5:10

PARTRIDGE

doth hunt a p in the mountains	1Sa 26:20
As the p sitteth on eggs, and	Jer 17:11

PARTS See PREFACE.

PARUAH (par´-u-ah) Father of Jehoshaphat.

Jehoshaphat the son of P, in	1Kin 4:17

PARVAIM (par-va´-im) A place rich in gold.

and the gold was gold of P	2Chr 3:6

PARZITES See PHARZITES.

PASACH (pa´-sak) A son of Japhet.

P, and Bimhal, and Ashvath	1Chr 7:33

PAS-DAMMIM (pas-dam´-mim) A place in Judah.

He was with David at P, and there	1Chr 11:13

PASEAH (pa-se´-ah) See PHASEAH.
1. A son of Eshton.

And Eshton begat Beth-rapha, and P	1Chr 4:12

2. A family of exiles.

of Uzza, the children of P	Ezr 2:49

3. Father of Jehoiada.

repaired Jehoiada the son of P	Neh 3:6

PASHUR (pash´-ur)
1. Head of a priestly family.

the son of Jeroham, the son of P	1Chr 9:12
The children of P, a thousand two	Ezr 2:38
And of the sons of P	Ezr 10:22
The children of P, a thousand two	Neh 7:41
son of Zechariah, the son of P	Neh 11:12

2. Father who renewed the covenant.

P, Amariah, Malchijah,	Neh 10:3

3. A son of Immer.

Now P the son of Immer the priest	Jer 20:1
Then P smote Jeremiah the prophet	Jer 20:2
that P brought forth Jeremiah out	Jer 20:3
LORD hath not called thy name P	Jer 20:3
And thou, P, and all that dwell in	Jer 20:6
Mattan, and Gedaliah the son of P	Jer 38:1

4. A son of Melchiah/Malchiah.

unto him P the son of Melchiah	Jer 21:1
the son of Malchiah, heard the	Jer 38:1

PASS See PREFACE.

PASSAGE

give Israel p through his border	Num 20:21
at the p of the children	Josh 22:11
went out to the p of Michmash	1Sa 13:23
They are gone over the p	Is 10:29

PASSAGES

took the p of Jordan before the	Judg 12:5
and slew him at the p of Jordan	Judg 12:6
And between the p, by which	1Sa 14:4
in Bashan, and cry from the	Jer 22:20
that the p are stopped, and the	Jer 51:32

PASSED

Abram p through the land unto the	Gen 12:6
a burning lamp that p between	Gen 15:17
p over the river, and set his face	Gen 31:21
my staff I p over this Jordan	Gen 32:10
sons, and p over the ford Jabbok	Gen 32:22
as he p over Penuel the sun rose	Gen 32:31
he p over before them, and bowed	Gen 33:3
Then there p by Midianites	Gen 37:28
who p over the houses of the	Ex 12:27
the Lord p by before him, and	Ex 34:6
which we p through to search it,	Num 14:7
left, until we have p thy borders	Num 20:17
p through the midst of the sea,	Num 33:8
When ye are p over Jordan into	Deut 2:8
p by the way of the wilderness of	Deut 2:8
of this law, when thou art p over	Deut 27:3
through the nations which ye p by	Deut 29:16
p over, and came to Joshua the son	Josh 2:23
lodged there before they p over	Josh 3:1
for ye have not p this way	Josh 3:4
the people p over right against	Josh 3:16
Israelites p over on dry ground	Josh 3:17
people were p clean over Jordan	Josh 3:17
people were clean p over Jordan	Josh 4:1

when it p over Jordan, the waters	Josh 4:7
and the people hasted and p over	Josh 4:10
all the people were clean p over	Josh 4:11
that the ark of the LORD p over	Josh 4:11
p over armed before the children	Josh 4:12
war p over before the LORD unto	Josh 4:13
before you, until ye were p over	Josh 5:1
of Israel, until we were p over	Josh 5:1
rams' horns p on before the LORD	Josh 6:8
Then Joshua p from Makkedah, and	Josh 10:29
Joshua p from Libnah, and all	Josh 10:31
from Lachish Joshua p unto Eglon	Josh 10:34
p along to Zin, and ascended up on	Josh 15:3
p along to Hezron, and went up to	Josh 15:3
From thence it p toward Azmoth	Josh 15:4
and p along by the north of	Josh 15:6
the border p toward the waters of	Josh 15:7
p along unto the side of mount	Josh 15:7
Beth-shemesh, and p on to Timnah	Josh 15:10
p along to mount Baalah, and went	Josh 15:11
p by it on the east to Janohah	Josh 16:6
p through the land, and described	Josh 18:9
p along toward the side over	Josh 18:18
the border p along to the side of	Josh 18:19
all the people through whom we p	Judg 2:20
p beyond the quarries, and escaped	Judg 3:26
p over, he, and the three hundred	Judg 8:4
Ammon p over Jordan to fight also	Judg 10:9
he p over Gilead, and Manasseh, and	Judg 11:29
p over Mizpeh of Gilead, and from	Judg 11:29
from Mizpeh of Gilead he p over	Judg 11:29
So Jephthah p over unto the	Judg 11:32
p over against the children of	Judg 12:3
they p thence unto mount Ephraim,	Judg 18:13
And they p on and went their way	Judg 19:14
he p through mount Ephraim, and	1Sa 9:4
p through the land of Shalisha,	1Sa 9:4
then they p through the land of	1Sa 9:4
he p through the land of the	1Sa 9:4
pass on before us, (and he p on	1Sa 9:27
the battle p over unto Beth-aven	1Sa 14:23
p on, and gone down to Gilgal	1Sa 15:12
he p over with the six hundred	1Sa 27:2
the Philistines p on by hundreds	1Sa 29:2
his men p on in the rereward with	1Sa 29:2
p over Jordan, and went through	2Sa 2:29
p over Jordan, and came to Helam	2Sa 10:17
all his servants p on beside him,	2Sa 15:18
from Gath, p on before the king,	2Sa 15:18
And Ittai the Gittite p over,	2Sa 15:22
voice, and all the people p over	2Sa 15:23
himself p over the brook Kidron	2Sa 15:23
and all the people p over	2Sa 15:23
with him, and they p over Jordan	2Sa 17:22
Absalom p over Jordan, he and all	2Sa 17:24
they p over Jordan, and pitched in	2Sa 24:5
And, behold, men p by, and saw the	1Kin 13:25
And, behold, the LORD p by,	1Kin 19:11
and Elijah p by him, and cast his	1Kin 19:19
And as the king p by, he cried	1Kin 20:39
on a day, that Elisha p to Shunem	2Kin 4:8
so it was, that as oft as he p by	2Kin 4:8
Gehazi p on before them, and laid	2Kin 4:31
he p by upon the wall, and the	2Kin 6:30
there p by a wild beast that was	2Kin 14:9
p over Jordan, and came upon them,	1Chr 19:17
king Solomon p all the kings of	2Chr 9:22
there p by a wild beast that was	2Chr 25:18
So the posts p from city to city	2Chr 30:10
Then a spirit p before my face	Job 4:15
They are p away as the swift	Job 9:26
and no stranger p among them.	Job 15:19
not the fierce lion p by it	Job 28:8
was before him his thick clouds p	Ps 18:12
Yet he p away, and, lo, he was not	Ps 37:36
assembled, they p by together	Ps 48:4
our days are p away in thy wrath	Ps 90:9
but a little that I p from thence,	Song 3:4
come to Aiath, he is p to Migron,	Is 10:28
my judgment is p over from my God	Is 40:27
He pursued them, and p safely	Is 41:3
a land that no man p through	Jer 2:6
and the holy flesh is p from thee	Jer 11:15
p between the parts thereof,	Jer 34:18
which p between the parts of the	Jer 34:19
he hath p the time appointed	Jer 46:17
When I p by thee, and saw thee	Eze 16:6
Now when I p by thee, and looked,	Eze 16:8
on every one that p by	Eze 16:25
thy feet to every one that p by	Eze 16:25
in the sight of all that p by	Eze 36:34
a river that could not be p over	Eze 47:5
the smell of fire had p on them	Dan 3:27
palace, and p the night fasting	Dan 6:18
but I p over upon her fair neck	Hos 10:11
billows and thy waves p over me	Jonah 2:3
have p through the gate, and are	Mic 2:13
not thy wickedness p continually	Nah 3:19
the overflowing of the water p by	Hab 3:10
that no man p through nor	Zec 7:14
p over, and came into his own city	Mt 9:1
as Jesus p forth from thence, he	Mt 9:9
when they heard that Jesus p by	Mt 20:30
they that p by reviled him,	Mt 27:39
And as he p by, he saw Levi the	Mk 2:14
when Jesus was p over again by	Mk 5:21
place, and now the time is far p	Mk 6:35
the sea, and would have p by them	Mk 6:48
And when they had p over, they	Mk 6:53
thence, and p through Galilee	Mk 9:30

And in the morning, as they p by .... Mk 11:20
one Simon a Cyrenian, who p by .... Mk 15:21
they that p by ruled on the .... Mk 15:29
he p by on the other side .... Lk 10:31
on him, and p by on the other side .... Lk 10:32
that he p through the midst of .... Lk 17:11
entered and p through Jericho .... Lk 19:1
but is p from death unto life .... Jn 5:24
the midst of them, and so p by .... Jn 8:59
And as Jesus p by, he saw a man .... Jn 9:1
as Peter p throughout all .... Acts 9:32
out, and p on through one street .... Acts 12:10
after they had p throughout .... Acts 14:24
they p through Phenice and Samaria .... Acts 15:3
Now when they had p through .... Acts 17:1
For as I p by, and beheld your .... Acts 17:23
Paul having p through the upper .... Acts 19:1
when he had p through Macedonia .... Acts 19:21
so death p upon all men, for that .... Rom 5:12
cloud, and all p through the sea 1Cor 10:1
old things are p away 2Cor 5:17
that is p into the heavens, Jesus .... Heb 4:14
By faith they p through the Red .... Heb 11:29
we have p from death unto life 1Jn 3:14
and the first earth were p away .... Rev 21:1
for the former things are p away .... Rev 21:4

PASSEDST
Wherefore p thou over to fight .... Judg 12:1

PASSENGERS
To call p who go right on their .... Prov 9:15
the valley of the p on the east .... Eze 39:11
it shall stop the noses of the p .... Eze 39:11
and to bury with the p those .... Eze 39:14
the p that pass through the land .... Eze 39:15

PASSEST
all the kingdoms whither thou p .... Deut 3:21
whither thou p over Jordan to go .... Deut 30:18
If thou p on with me, then thou 2Sa 15:33
p over the brook Kidron, thou 1Kin 2:37
When thou p through the waters, I .... Is 43:2

PASSETH
every one that p among them that .... Ex 30:13
Every one that p among them that .... Ex 30:14
come to pass, while my glory p by .... Ex 33:22
of whatsoever p under the rod .... Lev 27:32
p over before you into Jordan .... Josh 3:11
p along unto the borders of Archi .... Josh 16:2
from thence p on along on the .... Josh 19:13
every one that p by it shall be 1Kin 9:8
which p by us continually 2Kin 4:9
of every one that p the account 2Kin 12:4
to every one that p by it 2Chr 7:21
he p on also, but I perceive him .... Job 9:11
for ever against him, and he p .... Job 14:20
my welfare p away as a cloud .... Job 30:15
but the wind p, and cleanseth them ...... Job 37:21
whatsoever p through the paths of .... Ps 8:8
a wind that p away, and cometh not ...... Ps 78:39
For the wind p over it, and it is .... Ps 103:16
days are as a shadow that p away .... Ps 144:4
As the whirlwind p, so is the .... Prov 10:25
He that p by, and meddleth with .... Prov 26:17
One generation p away, and another .... Eccl 1:4
shall be as chaff that p away .... Is 29:5
a wilderness, that none p through .... Jer 9:12
that p away by the wind of the .... Jer 13:24
every one that p thereby shall be .... Jer 18:16
every one that p thereby shall be .... Jer 19:8
and cut off from it him that p out .... Eze 35:7
and as the early dew that p away .... Hos 13:3
p by the transgression of the .... Mic 7:18
every one that p by her shall hiss .... Zeph 2:15
streets waste, that none p by .... Zeph 3:6
army, because of him that p by .... Zec 9:8
him, that Jesus of Nazareth p by .... Lk 18:37
the fashion of this world p away 1Cor 7:31
which p knowledge, that ye might .... Eph 3:19
which p all understanding, shall .... Phil 4:7
And the world p away, and the lust 1Jn 2:17

PASSING
We are p from Beth-lehem-judah .... Judg 19:18
wonderful, p the love of women 2Sa 1:26
people had done p out of the city 2Sa 15:24
of Israel was p by upon the wall 2Kin 6:26
Who p through the valley of Baca .... Ps 84:6
P through the street near her .... Prov 7:8
p over he will preserve it .... Is 31:5
p through the land to bury with .... Eze 39:14
But he p through the midst of .... Lk 4:30
p by might overshadow some of .... Acts 5:15
p through he preached in all the .... Acts 8:40
And, hardly p it, came unto a .... Acts 27:8

PASSION
his p by many infallible proofs .... Acts 1:3

PASSIONS
also are men of like p with you .... Acts 14:15
a man subject to like p as we .... Jas 5:17

PASSOVER
it is the LORD's p .... Ex 12:11
to your families, and kill the p .... Ex 12:21
is the sacrifice of the LORD's p .... Ex 12:27
This is the ordinance of the p .... Ex 12:43
and will keep the p to the LORD .... Ex 12:48
of the p be left unto the morning .... Ex 34:25
month at even is the LORD's p .... Lev 23:5

the p at his appointed season .... Num 9:2
that they should keep the p .... Num 9:4
they kept the p on the fourteenth .... Num 9:5
could not keep the p on that day .... Num 9:6
he shall keep the p unto the LORD .... Num 9:10
of the p they shall keep it .... Num 9:12
and forbeareth to keep the p .... Num 9:13
and will keep the p unto the LORD .... Num 9:14
to the ordinance of the p .... Num 9:14
first month is the p of the LORD .... Num 28:16
on the morrow after the p the .... Num 33:3
keep the p unto the LORD thy God .... Deut 16:1
the p unto the LORD thy God .... Deut 16:2
the p within any of thy gates .... Deut 16:5
shall sacrifice the p at even .... Deut 16:6
kept the p on the fourteenth day .... Josh 5:10
land on the morrow after the p .... Josh 5:11
Keep the p unto the LORD your God 2Kin 23:21
a p from the days of the judges 2Kin 23:22
wherein this p was holden to the 2Kin 23:23
to keep the p unto the LORD God 2Chr 30:1
to keep the p in the second month 2Chr 30:2
they should come to keep the p 2Chr 30:5
Then they killed the p on the 2Chr 30:15
yet did they eat the p otherwise............ 2Chr 30:18
Moreover Josiah kept a p unto the 2Chr 35:1
and they killed the p on the 2Chr 35:1
So kill the p, and sanctify 2Chr 35:6
and kids, all for the p offerings 2Chr 35:7
for the p offerings two thousand 2Chr 35:8
gave unto the Levites for p 2Chr 35:9
And they killed the p, and the 2Chr 35:11
they roasted the p with fire 2Chr 35:13
the same day, to keep the p 2Chr 35:16
present kept the p at that time 2Chr 35:17
there was no p like to that kept 2Chr 35:18
keep such a p as Josiah kept 2Chr 35:18
reign of Josiah was this p kept 2Chr 35:19
of the captivity kept the p upon .... Ezr 6:19
killed the p for all the children .... Ezr 6:20
of the month, ye shall have the p .... Eze 45:21
two days is the feast of the p .... Mt 26:2
we prepare for thee to eat the p .... Mt 26:17
I will keep the p at thy house .... Mt 26:18
and they made ready the p .... Mt 26:19
two days was the feast of the p .... Mk 14:1
bread, when they killed the p .... Mk 14:12
that thou mayest eat the p .... Mk 14:12
shall eat the p with my disciples .... Mk 14:14
and they made ready the p .... Mk 14:16
every year at the feast of the p .... Lk 2:41
drew nigh, which is called the P .... Lk 22:1
when the p must be killed .... Lk 22:7
saying, Go and prepare us the p .... Lk 22:8
shall eat the p with my disciples .... Lk 22:11
and they made ready the p .... Lk 22:13
this p with you before I suffer .... Lk 22:15
the Jews' p was at hand, and Jesus ...... Jn 2:13
when he was in Jerusalem at the p .... Jn 2:23
And the p, a feast of the Jews .... Jn 6:4
the Jews' p was nigh at hand .... Jn 11:55
up to Jerusalem before the p .... Jn 11:55
days before the p came to Bethany .... Jn 12:1
Now before the feast of the p .... Jn 13:1
but that they might eat the p .... Jn 18:28
release unto you one at the p .... Jn 18:39
it was the preparation of the p .... Jn 19:14
For even Christ our p is 1Cor 5:7
Through faith he kept the p .... Heb 11:28

PASSOVERS
the p for every one that was not 2Chr 30:17

PAST
the days of his mourning were p .... Gen 50:4
to push with his horn in time p .... Ex 21:29
on hath used to push in time p .... Ex 21:36
way, until we be p thy borders .... Num 21:22
Emims dwelt therein in times p .... Deut 2:10
ask now of the days that are p .... Deut 4:32
and hated him not in times p .... Deut 4:42
whom he hated not in time p .... Deut 19:4
as he hated him not in time p .... Deut 19:6
the bitterness of death is p 1Sa 15:32
in his presence, as in times p 1Sa 19:7
in times p to be king over you 2Sa 3:17
Also in time p, when Saul was 2Sa 5:2
And when the morning was p 2Sa 11:27
a little p the top of the hill 2Sa 16:1
came to pass, when midday was p 1Kin 18:29
was the ruler over them in time p 1Chr 9:20
And moreover in time p, even when 1Chr 11:2
doeth great things p finding out .... Job 9:10
me secret, until thy wrath be p .... Job 14:13
My days are p, my purposes are .... Job 17:11
On that I were as in months p .... Job 29:2
are but as yesterday when it is p .... Ps 90:4
and God require th that which is p .... Eccl 3:15
For, lo, the winter is p, the .... Song 2:11
The harvest is p, the summer is .... Jer 8:20
place, and the time is now p .... Mt 14:15
And when the sabbath was p .... Mk 16:1
And when the voice was p, Jesus .... Lk 9:36
When they were p the first .... Acts 12:10
Who in times p suffered all .... Acts 14:16
the fast was now already p .... Acts 27:9
the remission of sins that are p .... Rom 3:25
For as ye in times p have not .... Rom 11:30
and his ways p finding out .... Rom 11:33
in time p in the Jews' religion .... Gal 1:13
p now preacheth the faith which .... Gal 1:23

as I have also told you in time p .... Gal 5:21
Wherein in time p ye walked .... Eph 2:2
times p in the lusts of our flesh .... Eph 2:3
in time p Gentiles in the flesh .... Eph 2:11
Who being p feeling have given .... Eph 4:19
the resurrection is p already 2Ti 2:18
Which in time p was to thee .... Philem 11
in time p unto the fathers by the .... Heb 1:1
of a child when she was p age .... Heb 11:11
Which in time p were not a people 1Pet 2:10
For the time p of our life may 1Pet 4:3
because the darkness is p 1Jn 2:8
One woe is p .... Rev 9:12
The second woe is p .... Rev 11:14

PASTOR
from being a p to follow thee .... Jer 17:16

PASTORS
the p also transgressed against .... Jer 2:8
I will give you p according to .... Jer 3:15
For the p are become brutish, and .... Jer 10:21
Many p have destroyed my vineyard .... Jer 12:10
The wind shall eat up all thy p .... Jer 22:22
Woe be unto the p that destroy .... Jer 23:1
against the p that feed my people .... Jer 23:2
and some, p and teachers .... Eph 4:11

PASTURE
have no p for their flocks .... Gen 47:4
to seek p for their flocks 1Chr 4:39
And they found fat p and good, and 1Chr 4:40
because there was p there for 1Chr 4:41
range of the mountains is his p .... Job 39:8
smoke against the sheep of thy p .... Ps 74:1
sheep of thy p will give thee .... Ps 79:13
and we are the people of his p .... Ps 95:7
his people, and the sheep of his p .... Ps 100:3
joy of wild asses, a p of flocks .... Is 32:14
and scatter the sheep of my p .... Jer 23:1
for the LORD hath spoiled their p .... Jer 25:36
become like harts that find no p .... Lam 1:6
I will feed them in a good p .... Eze 34:14
in a fat p shall they feed upon .... Eze 34:14
you to have eaten up the good p .... Eze 34:18
And ye my flock, the flock of my p .... Eze 34:31
According to their p, so were .... Hos 13:6
perplexed, because they have no p ...... Joel 1:18
and shall go in and out, and find p ...... Jn 10:9

PASTURES
oxen, and twenty oxen out of the p 1Kin 4:23
maketh me to lie down in green p .... Ps 23:2
drop upon the p of the wilderness .... Ps 65:12
The p are clothed with flocks .... Ps 65:13
shall thy cattle feed in large p .... Is 30:23
their p shall be in all high .... Is 49:9
your feet the residue of your p .... Eze 34:18
out of the fat p of Israel .... Eze 45:15
devoured the p of the wilderness .... Joel 1:19
devoured the p of the wilderness .... Joel 1:20
for the p of the wilderness do .... Joel 2:22

PATARA (pat'-a-rah) A city in Lycia in Asia
 Minor.
Rhodes, and from thence unto P .... Acts 21:1

PATE
shall come down upon his own p .... Ps 7:16

PATH
by the way, an adder in the p .... Gen 49:17
stood in a p of the vineyards .... Num 22:24
There is a p which no fowl...................... Job 28:7
They mar my p, they set forward .... Job 30:13
He maketh a p to shine after him .... Job 41:32
Thou wilt shew me the p of life .... Ps 16:11
O LORD, and lead me in a plain p .... Ps 27:11
thy p in the great waters, and thy .... Ps 77:19
go in the p of thy commandments .... Ps 119:35
my feet, and a light unto my p .... Ps 119:105
Thou compassest my p and my lying .... Ps 139:3
within me, then thou knewest my p ...... Ps 142:3
refrain thy foot from their p .... Prov 1:15
yea, every good p .... Prov 2:9
not into the p of the wicked .... Prov 4:14
But the p of the just is as the .... Prov 4:18
Ponder the p of thy feet, and let .... Prov 4:26
shouldest ponder the p of life .... Prov 5:6
dost weigh the p of the just .... Is 26:7
the way, turn aside out of the p .... Is 30:11
taught him in the p of judgment .... Is 40:14
sea, and a p in the mighty waters .... Is 43:16
shall walk every one in his p .... Joel 2:8

PAT_ROS (path'-ros) See PATHRUSIM. A name
 for Upper Egypt.
Assyria, and from Egypt, and from P .... Is 11:11
at Noph, and in the country of P .... Jer 44:1
in the land of Egypt, in P .... Jer 44:15
them to return into the land of P .... Eze 29:14
And I will make P desolate .... Eze 30:14

PATHRUS See PATHROS.

PATHRUSIM (path-ru'-sim) A descendant of
 Mizraim.
And P, and Casluhim, (out of whom .... Gen 10:14
P, and Casluhim, (of whom 1Chr 1:12

PATHS
The p of their way are turned .... Job 6:18
So are the p of all that forget .... Job 8:13
and looketh narrowly unto all my p .... Job 13:27
and he hath set darkness in my p .... Job 19:8

nor abide in the p thereof...................... Job 24:13
the stocks, he marketh all my p .... Job 33:11
know the p to the house thereof .... Job 38:20
passeth through the p of the seas........... Ps 8:8
me from the p of the destroyer.............. Ps 17:4
Hold up my goings in thy p .... Ps 17:5
he leadeth me in the p of .... Ps 23:3
teach me thy p .... Ps 27:11
All the p of the LORD are mercy .... Ps 25:10
and thy p drop fatness.......................... Ps 65:11
He keepeth the p of judgment .... Prov 2:8
Who leave the p of uprightness,............ Prov 2:13
and they froward in their p .... Prov 2:15
death, and her p unto the dead.............. Prov 2:18
take they hold of the p of life .... Prov 2:19
keep the p of the righteous................... Prov 2:20
him, and he shall direct thy p .... Prov 3:6
and all her p are peace......................... Prov 3:17
I have led thee in right p .... Prov 4:11
her ways, go not astray in her p............ Prov 7:25
by the way in the places of the p .... Prov 8:2
in the midst of the p of judgment.......... Prov 8:20
ways, and we will walk in his p .... Is 2:3
err, and destroy the way of thy p .... Is 3:12
I will lead them in a that they .... Is 42:16
The Restorer of p to dwell in................. Is 58:12
and destruction are in their p .... Is 59:7
they have made them crooked p .... Is 59:8
and see, and ask for the old p .... Jer 6:16
in their ways from the ancient p .... Jer 18:15
the ancient p, to walk in p .... Jer 18:15
stone, he hath made my p crooked .... Lam 3:9
that she shall not find her p .... Hos 2:6
ways, and we will walk in his p .... Mic 4:2
of the Lord, make his p straight .... Mt 3:3
of the Lord, make his p straight .... Mk 1:3
of the Lord, make his p straight .... Lk 3:4
And make straight p for your feet .... Heb 12:13

PATHWAY
in the p thereof there is no .... Prov 12:28

PATIENCE
have p with me, and I will pay............... Mt 18:26
Have p with me, and I will pay............... Mt 18:29
it, and bring forth fruit with p................ Lk 8:15
In your p possess ye your souls.............. Lk 21:19
that tribulation worketh p .... Rom 5:3
And p, experience................................. Rom 5:4
then do we with p wait for it .... Rom 8:25
our learning, that we through p .... Rom 15:4
Now the God of p and consolation .... Rom 15:5
the ministers of God, in much p 2Cor 6:4
were wrought among you in all p 2Cor 12:12
to his glorious power, unto all p .... Col 1:11
p of hope in our Lord Jesus.................... 1Th 1:3
in the churches of God for your p 2Th 1:4
godliness, faith, love, p 1Ti 6:11
faith, longsuffering, charity, p 2Ti 3:10
sound in faith, in charity, in p .... Titus 2:2
faith and p inherit the promises............ Heb 6:12
For ye have need of p, that................... Heb 10:36
let us run with p the race that .... Heb 12:1
trying of your faith worketh p .... Jas 1:3
But let p have her perfect work,............ Jas 1:4
the earth, and hath long p for it............ Jas 5:7
of suffering affliction, and of p .... Jas 5:10
Ye have heard of the p of Job................ Jas 5:11
and to temperance p............................ 2Pet 1:6
and to p godliness................................ 2Pet 1:6
p of Jesus Christ, was in the.................. Rev 1:9
works, and thy labour, and thy p .... Rev 2:2
And hast borne, and hast p, and for ...... Rev 2:3
and service, and faith, and thy p........... Rev 2:19
thou hast kept the word of my p .... Rev 3:10
Here is the p and the faith of the .... Rev 13:10
Here is the p of the saints .... Rev 14:12

PATIENT
the p in spirit is better than................... Eccl 7:8
To them who by p continuance in .... Rom 2:7
p in tribulation..................................... Rom 12:12
the weak, be p toward all men 1Th 5:14
into the p waiting for Christ 2Th 3:5
but p, not a brawler, not 1Ti 3:3
unto all men, apt to teach, p................. 2Ti 2:24
Be p therefore, brethren, unto .... Jas 5:7
Be ye also p .... Jas 5:8

PATIENTLY
in the LORD, and wait p for him............. Ps 37:7
I waited p for the LORD .... Ps 40:1
I beseech thee to hear me p .... Acts 26:3
And so, after he had p endured............. Heb 6:15
your faults, ye shall take it p 1Pet 2:20
and suffer for it, ye take it p 1Pet 2:20

PATMOS (pat´-mos) An island off the west
coast of Asia Minor.
was in the isle that is called P............... Rev 1:9

PATRIARCH
speak unto you of the P David............... Acts 2:29
unto whom even the p Abraham gave .... Heb 7:4

PATRIARCHS
and Jacob begat the twelve p .... Acts 7:8
And the p, moved with envy, sold........... Acts 7:9

PATRIMONY
which cometh of the sale of his p.......... Deut 18:8

PATROBAS (pat´-ro-bas) A Christian in Rome.
Asyncritus, Phlegon, Hermas, P............ Rom 16:14

PATTERN
after the p of the tabernacle, and .... Ex 25:9
the p of all the instruments .... Ex 25:9

that thou make them after their p.......... Ex 25:40
according unto the p which the .... Num 8:4
Behold the p of the altar of the............. Josh 22:28
the p of it, according to all the.............. 2Kin 16:10
his son the p of the porch...................... 1Chr 28:11
the p of all that he had by the............... 1Chr 28:12
gold for the p of the chariot of 1Chr 28:18
me, even all the works of this p 1Chr 28:19
and let them measure the p .... Eze 43:10
for a p to them which should................. 1Ti 1:16
shewing thyself a p of good works......... Titus 2:7
the p shewed to thee in the mount........ Heb 8:5

PATTERNS
therefore necessary that the p of .... Heb 9:23

PAU (pa´-u) See PAI. City of King Hadar of
Edom.
and the name of his city was P............... Gen 36:39

PAUL (pawl) See PAUL'S, PAULUS, SAUL. The
apostle to the Gentiles.
Then Saul, (who also is called P............. Acts 13:9
when P and his company........................ Acts 13:13
Then P stood up, and beckoning .... Acts 13:16
religious proselytes followed P .... Acts 13:43
things which were spoken by P .... Acts 13:45
P and Barnabas waxed bold .... Acts 13:46
and raised persecution against P .... Acts 13:50
The same heard P speak........................ Acts 14:9
the people saw what P had done .... Acts 14:11
and P, Mercurius, because he was......... Acts 14:12
when the apostles, Barnabas and P .... Acts 14:14
the people, and, having stoned P .... Acts 14:19
When therefore P and Barnabas had ...... Acts 15:2
with them, they determined that P .... Acts 15:2
audience to Barnabas and P .... Acts 15:12
own company to Antioch with P............. Acts 15:22
with our beloved Barnabas and P .... Acts 15:25
P also and Barnabas continued in .... Acts 15:35
some days after P said unto................... Acts 15:36
But P thought not good to take.............. Acts 15:38
P chose Silas, and departed, being........ Acts 15:40
Him would P have to go forth with .... Acts 16:3
vision appeared to P in the night........... Acts 16:9
the things which were spoken of P .... Acts 16:14
The same followed P and us, and .... Acts 16:17
But P, being grieved, turned and .... Acts 16:18
gains was gone, they caught P .... Acts 16:19
And at midnight P and Silas prayed........ Acts 16:25
But P cried with a loud voice,................ Acts 16:28
trembling, and fell down before P .... Acts 16:29
the prison told this saying to.................. Acts 16:36
But P said unto them, They have........... Acts 16:37
And P, as his manner was, went in .... Acts 17:2
believed, and consorted with P .... Acts 17:4
brethren immediately sent away P......... Acts 17:10
of God was preached of P at Berea .... Acts 17:13
the brethren sent away P to go as......... Acts 17:14
they that conducted P brought him........ Acts 17:15
Now while P waited for them at .... Acts 17:16
when P stood in the midst of .... Acts 17:22
So P departed from among them .... Acts 17:33
After these things P departed................ Acts 18:1
P was pressed in the spirit, and............. Acts 18:5
Then spake the Lord to P in the............. Acts 18:9
with one accord against P .... Acts 18:12
when P was now about to open his........ Acts 18:14
P after this tarried there yet a............... Acts 18:18
P having passed through the upper .... Acts 19:1
Then said P, John verily baptized.......... Acts 19:4
when P had laid his hands upon .... Acts 19:6
miracles by the hands of P .... Acts 19:11
you by Jesus whom P preacheth............ Acts 19:13
said, Jesus I know, and P I know........... Acts 19:15
P purposed in the spirit, when he .... Acts 19:21
this P hath persuaded and turned......... Acts 19:26
when P would have entered in unto .... Acts 19:30
P called unto him the disciples,............. Acts 20:1
P preached unto them, ready to............. Acts 20:7
as P was long preaching, he sunk .... Acts 20:9
P went down, and fell on him, and .... Acts 20:10
there intending to take in P .... Acts 20:13
For P had determined to sail by .... Acts 20:16
who said to P through the Spirit, ... Acts 21:4
Then P answered, What mean ye to....... Acts 21:13
the day following P went in with .... Acts 21:18
Then P took the men, and the next .... Acts 21:26
whom they supposed that P had .... Acts 21:29
and they took P, and drew him out........ Acts 21:30
soldiers, they left beating of P .... Acts 21:32
as P was to be led into the .... Acts 21:37
But P said, I am a man which am a........ Acts 21:39
P stood on the stairs, and .... Acts 21:40
P said unto the centurion that .... Acts 22:25
P said, But I was free born..................... Acts 22:28
to appear, and brought P down.............. Acts 22:30
And P, earnestly beholding the.............. Acts 23:1
Then said P unto him, God shall............ Acts 23:3
Then said P, I wist not, brethren........... Acts 23:5
But when P perceived that the one .... Acts 23:6
fearing lest P should have been .... Acts 23:10
him, and said, Be of good cheer, P .... Acts 23:11
nor drink till they had killed P............... Acts 23:12
eat nothing until we have slain P .... Acts 23:14
into the castle, and told P..................... Acts 23:16
Then P called one of the .... Acts 23:17
The prisoner called me unto him........... Acts 23:18
down P to morrow into the council........ Acts 23:20
beasts, that they may set P on.............. Acts 23:24
as it was commanded them, took P .... Acts 23:31
presented P also before him................. Acts 23:33
informed the governor against P............ Acts 24:1

Then P, after that the governor .... Acts 24:10
commanded a centurion to keep P .... Acts 24:23
which was a Jewess, he sent for P .... Acts 24:24
should have been given him of P........... Acts 24:26
the Jews a pleasure, left P bound .... Acts 24:27
The Jews informed him against P........... Acts 25:2
that P should be kept at Caesarea......... Acts 25:4
seat commanded P to be brought.......... Acts 25:6
and grievous complaints against P .... Acts 25:7
the Jews a pleasure, answered P .... Acts 25:9
Then said P, I stand at Caesar's............ Acts 25:10
whom P affirmed to be alive .... Acts 25:19
But when P had appealed to be............. Acts 25:21
commandment P was brought forth .... Acts 25:23
Then Agrippa said unto P, Thou............. Acts 26:1
Then P stretched forth the hand............ Acts 26:1
Festus said with a loud voice, P .... Acts 26:24
Then Agrippa said unto P, Almost.......... Acts 26:28
P said, I would to God, that not............. Acts 26:29
said into Italy, they delivered P .... Acts 27:1
And Julius courteously entreated P .... Acts 27:3
already past, P admonished them,......... Acts 27:9
things which were spoken by P .... Acts 27:11
But after long abstinence P stood.......... Acts 27:21
Saying, Fear not, P .... Acts 27:24
P said to the centurion and to the .... Acts 27:31
P besought them all to take meat,......... Acts 27:33
the centurion, willing to save P .... Acts 27:43
when P had gathered a bundle of.......... Acts 28:3
to whom P entered in, and prayed,........ Acts 28:8
whom when P saw, he thanked God,...... Acts 28:15
but P was suffered to dwell by .... Acts 28:16
that after three days P called................ Acts 28:17
after that P had spoken one word,......... Acts 28:25
P dwelt two whole years in his .... Acts 28:30
A servant of Jesus Christ, ... Rom 1:1
P, called to be an apostle of 1Cor 1:1
every one of you saith, I am of P........... 1Cor 1:12
was P crucified for you.......................... 1Cor 1:13
were ye baptized in the name of P 1Cor 1:13
For while one saith, I am of P 1Cor 3:4
Who then is P, and who is Apollos,........ 1Cor 3:5
Whether P, or Apollos, or Cephas,......... 1Cor 3:22
of me P with mine own hand................. 1Cor 16:21
P, an apostle of Jesus Christ by 2Cor 1:1
Now I P myself beseech you by the 2Cor 10:1
P, an apostle, (not of men, ... Gal 1:1
I P say unto you, that if ye be .... Gal 5:2
P, an apostle of Jesus Christ by .... Eph 1:1
For this cause I P, the prisoner............. Eph 3:1
P and Timotheus, the servants of .... Phil 1:1
P, an apostle of Jesus Christ, ... Col 1:1
whereof I P am made a minister............ Col 1:23
salutation by the hand of me P .... Col 4:18
P, and Silvanus, and Timotheus,........... 1Th 1:1
have come unto you, even I P................ 1Th 2:18
P, and Silvanus, and Timotheus............ 2Th 1:1
The salutation of P with mine own......... 2Th 3:17
P, an apostle of Jesus Christ 1Ti 1:1
P, an apostle of Jesus Christ 2Ti 1:1
when P was brought before Nero .... 2Ti s
P, a servant of God, and an .... Titus 1:1
P, a prisoner of Jesus Christ, and.......... Philem 1
being such an one as P the aged........... Philem 9
I P have written it with mine own .... Philem 19
even as our beloved brother P 2Pet 3:15

PAUL'S (pawls)
P companions in travel, they .... Acts 19:29
all wept sore, and fell on P neck........... Acts 20:37
that were of P company departed.......... Acts 21:8
come unto us, he took P girdle,............. Acts 21:11
when P sister's son heard of .... Acts 23:16
Festus declared P cause unto the.......... Acts 25:14

PAULUS See PAUL. A Roman proconsul
deputy of the country, Sergius P............ Acts 13:7

PAVED
were a p work of a sapphire stone......... Ex 24:10
midst thereof being p with love .... Song 3:10

PAVEMENT
it, and put it upon a p of stones............ 2Kin 16:17
faces to the ground upon the p 2Chr 7:3
gold and silver, upon a p of red............ Est 1:6
a p made for the court round................. Eze 40:17
thirty chambers were upon the p .... Eze 40:18
the p by the side of the gates................ Eze 40:18
of the gates was the lower p.................. Eze 40:18
over against the p which was for .... Eze 42:3
in a place that is called the P .... Jn 19:13

PAVILION
his p round about him were dark........... Ps 18:11
trouble he shall hide me in his p .... Ps 27:5
in a p from the strife of tongues............ Ps 31:20
spread his royal p over them .... Jer 43:10

PAVILIONS
made darkness p round about him........ 2Sa 22:12
he and the kings in the p 1Kin 20:12
drinking himself drunk in the p 1Kin 20:16

PAW
me out of the p of the lion.................... 1Sa 17:37
out of the p of the bear, he will 1Sa 17:37

PAWETH
He p in the valley, and rejoiceth........... Job 39:21

PAWS
And whatsoever goeth upon his p.......... Lev 11:27

PAY
only he shall p for the loss of .... Ex 21:19
and he shall p as the judges .... Ex 21:22

he shall surely p ox for ox .... Ex 21:36
thief be found, let him p double .... Ex 22:7
he shall p double unto his .... Ex 22:9
he shall p money according to the .... Ex 22:17
thy water, then I will p for it .... Num 20:19
God, thou shalt not slack to p it .... Deut 23:21
p my vow, which I have vowed unto ... 2Sa 15:7
thou shalt p a talent of silver 1Kin 20:39
p thy debt, and live thou and thy 2Kin 4:7
make to p tribute until this day 2Chr 8:8
the children of Ammon p unto him 2Chr 27:5
again, then will they not p toll .... Ezr 4:13
I will p ten thousand talents of .... Est 3:9
that Haman had promised to p to .... Est 4:7
thee, and thou shalt p thy vows .... Job 22:27
I will p my vows before them that ...... Ps 22:25
p thy vows unto the most High .... Ps 50:14
I will p thee my vows, ... Ps 66:13
Vow, and p unto the LORD your God ... Ps 76:11
I will p my vows unto the LORD .... Ps 116:14
I will p my vows unto the LORD .... Ps 116:18
he hath given will he p him again........ Prov 19:17
If thou hast nothing to p .... Prov 22:27
a vow unto God, defer not to p it ...... Eccl 5:4
p that which thou hast vowed .... Eccl 5:4
that thou shouldest vow and not p ..... Eccl 5:5
I will p that that I have vowed .... Jonah 2:9
Doth not your master p tribute........... Mt 17:24
But forasmuch as he had not to p ...... Mt 18:25
with me, and I will p thee all............. Mt 18:26
saying, P me that thou owest............. Mt 18:28
with me, and I will p thee all............. Mt 18:29
prison, till he should p the debt .... Mt 18:30
till he should p all that was due .... Mt 18:34
for ye p tithe of mint and anise .... Mt 23:23
And when they had nothing to p .... Lk 7:42
for this cause ye p tribute also .... Rom 13:6

PAYED

this day have I p my vows................. Prov 7:14
tithes, p tithes in Abraham................ Heb 7:9

PAYETH

wicked borroweth, and p not again ..... Ps 37:21

PAYMENT

all that he had, and p to be made....... Mt 18:25

PEACE

thou shalt go to thy fathers in p .... Gen 15:15
man wondering at her held his p........ Gen 24:21
good, and have sent thee away in p .... Gen 26:29
and they departed from him in p......... Gen 26:31
again to my father's house in p.......... Gen 28:21
Jacob held his p until they were......... Gen 34:5
shall give Pharaoh an answer of p....... Gen 41:16
And he said, P be to you, fear not...... Gen 43:23
get you up in p unto your father........ Gen 44:17
And Jethro said to Moses, Go in p...... Ex 4:18
for you, and ye shall hold your p .... Ex 14:14
shall also go to their place in p......... Ex 18:23
thy p offerings, thy sheep, and .... Ex 20:24
sacrificed p offerings of oxen .... Ex 24:5
sacrifice of their p offerings............. Ex 29:28
offerings, and brought p offerings....... Ex 32:6
be a sacrifice of p offering .... Lev 3:1
p offering an offering made by .... Lev 3:3
of p offering unto the LORD be of....... Lev 3:6
p offering an offering made by .... Lev 3:9
of the sacrifice of p offerings........... Lev 4:10
of the sacrifice of p offerings........... Lev 4:26
off the sacrifice of p offerings.......... Lev 4:31
the sacrifice of the p offerings.......... Lev 4:35
the fat of the p offerings................. Lev 6:12
of the sacrifice of p offerings........... Lev 7:11
thanksgiving of his p offerings........... Lev 7:13
the blood of the p offerings.............. Lev 7:14
his p offerings for thanksgiving.......... Lev 7:15
p offerings be eaten all at on .... Lev 7:16
of the sacrifice of p offerings........... Lev 7:20
of the sacrifice of p offerings........... Lev 7:21
p offerings unto the LORD shall .... Lev 7:29
the sacrifice of his p offerings.......... Lev 7:29
sacrifices of your p offerings............ Lev 7:32
the blood of the p offerings.............. Lev 7:33
sacrifices of their p offerings............ Lev 7:34
the sacrifice of the p offerings.......... Lev 7:37
bullock and a ram for p offerings....... Lev 9:4
for a sacrifice of p offerings............. Lev 9:18
burnt offering, and p offerings........... Lev 9:22
And Aaron held his p .... Lev 10:3
of p offerings of the children of .... Lev 10:14
offer them for p offerings unto .... Lev 17:5
of p offerings unto the LORD .... Lev 19:5
offereth a sacrifice of p .... Lev 22:21
for a sacrifice of p offerings............. Lev 23:19
And I will give p in the land .... Lev 26:6
without blemish for p offerings.......... Num 6:14
of p offerings unto the LORD .... Num 6:17
the sacrifice of the p offerings.......... Num 6:18
upon thee, and give thee p .... Num 6:26
And for a sacrifice of p offerings....... Num 7:17
And for a sacrifice of p offerings....... Num 7:23
And for a sacrifice of p offerings....... Num 7:29
And for a sacrifice of p offerings....... Num 7:35
And for a sacrifice of p offerings....... Num 7:41
And for a sacrifice of p offerings....... Num 7:47
And for a sacrifice of p offerings....... Num 7:53
And for a sacrifice of p offerings....... Num 7:59
And for a sacrifice of p offerings....... Num 7:65
And for a sacrifice of p offerings....... Num 7:71
And for a sacrifice of p offerings....... Num 7:77

And for a sacrifice of p offerings........ Num 7:83
of the p offerings were twenty .... Num 7:88
sacrifices of your p offerings............ Num 10:10
or p offerings unto the LORD............. Num 15:8
I give unto him my covenant of p...... Num 25:12
and for your p offerings.................... Num 29:39
father shall hold his p at her .... Num 30:4
held his p at her in the day that....... Num 30:7
heard it, and held his p at her......... Num 30:11
hold his p at her from day to day ..... Num 30:14
because he held his p at her in........ Num 30:14
king of Heshbon with words of p ...... Deut 2:26
it, then proclaim p unto it .... Deut 20:10
be, if it make thee answer of p .... Deut 20:11
And if it will make no p with thee .... Deut 20:12
Thou shalt not seek their p nor........ Deut 23:6
And thou shalt offer p offerings........ Deut 27:7
his heart, saying, I shall have p .... Deut 29:19
LORD, and sacrificed p offerings....... Josh 8:31
And Joshua made p with them.......... Josh 9:15
of Gibeon had made p with Israel...... Josh 10:1
for it hath made p with Joshua........ Josh 10:4
camp to Joshua at Makkedah in p..... Josh 10:21
p with the children of Israel .... Josh 11:19
or if to offer p offerings................. Josh 22:23
and with our p offerings.................. Josh 22:27
for there was p between Jabin the..... Judg 4:17
said unto him, P be unto thee........... Judg 6:23
saying, When I come again in p......... Judg 8:9
when I return in p from the............. Judg 11:31
priest said unto them, Go in p .... Judg 18:6
And they said unto him, Hold thy p.... Judg 18:19
the old man said, P be with thee ..... Judg 19:20
p offerings before the LORD .... Judg 20:26
burnt offerings and p offerings .... Judg 21:4
Eli answered and said, Go in p 1Sa 1:17
there was p between Israel and the... 1Sa 7:14
sacrifices of p offerings.................. 1Sa 11:15
But he held his p 1Sa 10:27
of p offerings before the LORD......... 1Sa 11:15
offering to me, and p offerings......... 1Sa 13:9
thy servant shall have p 1Sa 20:7
away, that thou mayest go in p........ 1Sa 20:13
for there is p to thee, and no......... 1Sa 20:21
Jonathan said to David, Go in p 1Sa 20:42
P be both to thee 1Sa 25:6
p be to thine house 1Sa 25:6
p be unto all that thou hast............ 1Sa 25:6
Go up in p to thine house 1Sa 25:35
Wherefore now return, and go in p.... 1Sa 29:7
and he went in p 2Sa 3:21
him away, and he was gone in p....... 2Sa 3:22
sent him away, and he is gone in p... 2Sa 3:23
p offerings before the LORD 2Sa 6:17
p offerings, he blessed the.............. 2Sa 6:18
they made p with Israel, and 2Sa 10:19
but hold now thy p, my sister......... 2Sa 13:20
the king said unto him, Go in p....... 2Sa 15:9
return into the city in p 2Sa 15:27
so all the people shall be in p 2Sa 17:3
until the day he came again in p 2Sa 19:24
again in p unto his own house........ 2Sa 19:30
burnt offerings and p offerings 2Sa 24:25
and shed the blood of war in p 1Kin 2:5
head p down to the grave in p 1Kin 2:6
shall there be p for ever from......... 1Kin 2:33
offered p offerings, and made a....... 1Kin 3:15
he had p on all sides round about.... 1Kin 4:24
there was p between Hiram and........ 1Kin 5:12
a sacrifice of p offerings................ 1Kin 8:63
and the fat of the p offerings.......... 1Kin 8:64
and the fat of the p offerings.......... 1Kin 8:64
p offerings upon the altar which 1Kin 9:25
Whether they be come out for p 1Kin 20:18
every man to his house in p 1Kin 22:17
of affliction, until I come in p 1Kin 22:27
said, If thou return at all in p 1Kin 22:28
Jehoshaphat made p with the king.... 1Kin 22:44
hold ye your p............................... 2Kin 2:3
hold ye your p............................... 2Kin 2:5
And he said unto him, Go in p 2Kin 5:19
of good tidings, and we hold our p.... 2Kin 7:9
them, and let him say, Is it p 2Kin 9:17
Thus saith the king, Is it p 2Kin 9:18
said, What hast thou to do with p 2Kin 9:18
Thus saith the king, Is it p 2Kin 9:19
What hast thou to do with p 2Kin 9:19
saw Jehu, that he said, Is it p 2Kin 9:22
And he answered, What p, so long ... 2Kin 9:22
the gate, she said, Had Zimri p 2Kin 9:31
the blood of his p offerings............ 2Kin 16:13
But the people held their p 2Kin 18:36
And he said, Is it not good, if p 2Kin 20:19
be gathered into thy grave in p 2Kin 22:20
p, p be unto thee, and p................ 1Chr 12:18
thee, and p be to thine helpers 1Chr 12:18
and p offerings before God.............. 1Chr 16:1
the p offerings, he blessed the 1Chr 16:2
they made p with David.................. 1Chr 19:19
p offerings, and called upon the 1Chr 21:26
be Solomon, and I will give p 1Chr 22:9
and the fat of the p offerings.......... 2Chr 7:7
was no p to him that went out........ 2Chr 15:5
every man to his house in p 2Chr 18:16
affliction, until I return in p 2Chr 18:26
If thou certainly return in p 2Chr 18:27
to his house in p to Jerusalem......... 2Chr 19:1
with the fat of the p offerings......... 2Chr 29:35
offering p offerings, and making 2Chr 30:22
for p offerings, to minister, and 2Chr 31:2

and sacrificed thereon p offerings..... 2Chr 33:16
be gathered to thy grave in p 2Chr 34:28
unto the rest beyond the river, P..... Ezr 4:17
Unto Darius the king, all p .... Ezr 5:7
of the God of heaven, perfect p ...... Ezr 7:12
or seek their p or their wealth .... Ezr 9:12
Then held they their p, and found .... Neh 5:8
the people, saying, Hold your p .... Neh 8:11
holdest thy p at this time............... Est 4:14
of Ahasuerus, with words of .... Est 9:30
speaking p to all his seed .... Est 10:3
the field shall be at p with thee ..... Job 5:23
that thy tabernacle shall be in p ...... Job 5:24
thy lies make men hold their p .... Job 11:3
ye would altogether hold your p ...... Job 13:5
Hold your p, let me alone, that I .... Job 13:13
now thyself with him, and be at p ... Job 22:21
he maketh p in his high places .... Job 25:2
The nobles held their p, and their ... Job 29:10
hold thy p, and I will speak .... Job 33:31
hold thy p, and I shall teach thee ... Job 33:33
I will both lay me down in p .... Ps 4:8
unto him that was at p with me ...... Ps 7:4
which speak p to their neighbours .... Ps 28:3
LORD will bless his people with p...... Ps 29:11
seek p, and pursue it .... Ps 34:14
For they speak not p .... Ps 35:20
themselves in the abundance of p..... Ps 37:11
for the end of that man is p .... Ps 37:37
dumb with silence, I held my p .... Ps 39:2
hold not thy p at my tears............. Ps 39:12
in p from the battle that was .... Ps 55:18
against such as be at p with him .... Ps 55:20
shall bring p to the people .... Ps 72:3
abundance of p so long as the......... Ps 72:7
hold not thy p, and be not still...... Ps 83:1
he will speak p unto his people....... Ps 85:8
and p have kissed each other .... Ps 85:10
Hold not thy p, O God of my .... Ps 109:1
Great p have they which love thy .... Ps 119:165
long dwelt with him that hateth p ... Ps 120:6
I am for p .... Ps 120:7
Pray for the p of Jerusalem............ Ps 122:6
P be within thy walls, and............. Ps 122:7
I will now say, P be within thee ..... Ps 122:8
but p shall be upon Israel .... Ps 125:5
children, and p upon Israel .... Ps 128:6
He maketh p in thy borders, and ..... Ps 147:14
of days, and long life, and p .... Prov 3:2
and all her paths are p .... Prov 3:17
I have p offerings with me .... Prov 7:14
of understanding holdeth his p .... Prov 11:12
to the counsellors of p is joy .... Prov 12:20
his enemies to be at p with him ..... Prov 16:7
a fool, when he holdeth his p .... Prov 17:28
a time of war, and a time of p .... Eccl 3:8
Father, The Prince of P .... Is 9:6
p there shall be no end, upon the .... Is 9:7
Thou wilt keep him in perfect p ...... Is 26:3
LORD, thou wilt ordain p for us........ Is 26:12
that he may make p with me .... Is 27:5
and he shall make p with the .... Is 27:5
work of righteousness shall be p ..... Is 32:17
the ambassadors of p shall weep ..... Is 33:7
But they held their p, and .... Is 36:21
for p I had great bitterness .... Is 38:17
moreover, For there shall be p .... Is 39:8
I have long time holden my p .... Is 42:14
I make p, and create evil............... Is 45:7
then had thy p been as a river, ... Is 48:18
There is no p, saith the LORD, ... Is 48:22
good tidings, that publisheth p .... Is 52:7
of our p was upon him .... Is 53:5
the covenant of my p be removed..... Is 54:10
shall be the p of thy children......... Is 54:13
with joy, and be led forth with p .... Is 55:12
He shall enter into p .... Is 57:2
have not I held my p even of old .... Is 57:11
P, p to him that is far off,............. Is 57:19
There is no p, saith my God to ...... Is 57:21
The way of p they know not .... Is 59:8
goeth therein shall not know p .... Is 59:8
I will also make thy officers p .... Is 60:17
Zion's sake will I not hold my p ...... Is 62:1
never hold their p day nor night ...... Is 62:6
with thou hold thy p, and afflict ..... Is 64:12
I will extend p to her like a .... Is 66:12
saying, Ye shall have p .... Jer 4:10
I cannot hold my p, because thou.... Jer 4:19
people slightly, saying, P, p .... Jer 6:14
when there is no p ....Jer 6:14
peo, p slightly, saying, P, p .... Jer 8:11
when there is no p .... Jer 8:11
We looked for p, but no good came.. Jer 8:15
and if in the land of p, wherein ...... Jer 12:5
no flesh shall have p .... Jer 12:12
give you assured p in this place...... Jer 14:13
we looked for p, and there is no ..... Jer 14:19
taken away my p from this people.... Jer 16:5
LORD hath said, Ye shall have p ...... Jer 23:17
prophet which prophesieth of p .... Jer 28:9
seek the p of the city whither I ..... Jer 29:7
the p thereof shall ye have p .... Jer 29:7
saith the LORD, thoughts of p .... Jer 29:11
trembling, of fear, and not of p ...... Jer 30:5
unto them the abundance of p .... Jer 33:6
But thou shalt die p .... Jer 34:5
shall go forth from thence in p .... Jer 43:12
removed my soul far off from p ...... Lam 3:17
and they shall seek p, and there...... Eze 7:25

have seduced my people, saying, P......... Eze 13:10
and there was no p................................... Eze 13:10
p for her, and there is no p......................... Eze 13:16
make with them a covenant of p with them ... Eze 34:25
make a covenant of p with them................... Eze 37:26
the altar, and your p offerings.................... Eze 43:27
and for p offerings, to make....................... Eze 45:15
and the p offerings, to make....................... Eze 45:17
his p offerings, and he shall........................ Eze 46:2
a voluntary burnt offering or p.................... Eze 46:12
his p offerings, as he did on the................. Eze 46:12
P be multiplied unto you............................. Dan 4:1
P be multiplied unto you............................. Dan 6:25
heart, and by p shall destroy many............. Dan 8:25
p be unto thee, be strong, yea,.................. Dan 10:19
neither will I regard the p........................... Amos 5:22
the men that were at p with thee............... Obad 7
bite with their teeth, and cry, P................. Mic 3:5
And this man shall be the p........................ Mic 5:5
good tidings, that publisheth p.................. Nah 1:15
Hold thy p at the presence of the............... Zeph 1:7
and in this place will I give p..................... Hag 2:9
the counsel of p shall be between............... Zec 6:13
neither was there any p to him.................... Zec 8:10
of truth and in your gates.......................... Zec 8:16
therefore love the truth and p.................... Zec 8:19
he shall speak p unto the heathen............. Zec 9:10
was with him of life and p.......................... Mal 2:5
he walked with me in p and equity,............. Mal 2:6
worthy, let your p come upon it................... Mt 10:13
worthy, let your p return to you.................. Mt 10:13
that I am come to send p on earth.............. Mt 10:34
I came not to send p, but a sword.............. Mt 10:34
because they should hold their p................. Mt 20:31
But Jesus held his p................................... Mt 26:63
rebuked him, saying, Hold thy p................. Mk 1:25
But they held their p................................. Mk 3:4
the wind, and said unto the sea, P............. Mk 4:39
go in p, and be whole of thy....................... Mk 5:34
But they held their p................................. Mk 9:34
and have p one with another...................... Mk 9:50
him that he should hold his p...................... Mk 10:48
But he held his p, and answered................ Mk 14:61
guide our feet into the way of p................... Lk 1:79
God in the highest, and on earth p.............. Lk 2:14
thou thy servant depart in p....................... Lk 2:29
rebuked him, saying, Hold thy p................. Lk 4:35
go in p.. Lk 7:50
go in p.. Lk 8:48
first say, P be to this house........................ Lk 10:5
And if the son of p be there........................ Lk 10:6
your p shall rest upon it............................. Lk 10:6
his palace, his goods are in p..................... Lk 11:21
that I am come to give p on earth............... Lk 12:51
And they held their p.................................. Lk 14:4
and desireth conditions of p....................... Lk 14:32
him, that he should hold his p.................... Lk 18:39
p in heaven, and glory in the...................... Lk 19:38
if these should hold their p......................... Lk 19:40
things which belong unto thy p................... Lk 19:42
at his answer, and held their p.................... Lk 20:26
and saith unto them, P be unto you........... Lk 24:36
P I leave with you, my p I........................... Jn 14:27
you, that in me ye might have p.................. Jn 16:33
and saith unto them, P be unto you............ Jn 20:19
to them again, P be unto you...................... Jn 20:21
the midst, and said, P be unto you............. Jn 20:26
preaching by Jesus Christ.......................... Acts 10:36
these things, they held their p.................... Acts 11:18
with the hand to hold their p...................... Acts 12:17
their friend, desired p................................. Acts 12:20
And after they had held their p................... Acts 15:13
they were let go in p from the.................... Acts 15:33
now therefore depart, and go in p.............. Acts 16:36
but speak, and hold not thy p..................... Acts 18:9
p from God our Father, and from................ Rom 1:7
But glory, honour, and p, to every.............. Rom 2:10
the way of p have they not known.............. Rom 3:17
we have p with God through our................. Rom 5:1
spiritually minded is life and p.................... Rom 8:6
them that preach the gospel of p................ Rom 10:15
but righteousness, and p, and joy.............. Rom 14:17
after the things which make for p............... Rom 14:19
p in believing, that ye may....................... Rom 15:13
Now the God of p be with you.................... Rom 15:33
the God of peace shall bruise Satan.......... Rom 16:20
be of one mind, live in p............................ 1Cor 1:3
but God hath called us to p........................ 1Cor 7:15
by, let the first hold his p.......................... 1Cor 14:30
the author of confusion, but of p................ 1Cor 14:33
but conduct him forth in p......................... 1Cor 16:11
p from God our Father, and from................ 2Cor 1:2
be of one mind, live in p............................ 2Cor 13:11
of love and p shall be with you.................. 2Cor 13:11
p from God the Father, and from................ Gal 1:3
of these fruits is love, joy,......................... Gal 5:22
p be on them, and mercy, and upon.......... Gal 6:16
Grace be to you, and p, from God.............. Eph 1:2
For he is our p, who hath made.................. Eph 2:14
of twain one new man, so making p............ Eph 2:15
preached p to you which were afar............. Eph 2:17
of the Spirit in the bond of p...................... Eph 4:3
preparation of the gospel of p.................... Eph 6:15
P be to the brethren, and love.................... Eph 6:23
Grace be unto you, and p, from God........... Phil 1:2
the p of God, which passeth all................... Phil 4:7
the God of p shall be with you................... Phil 4:9
Grace be unto you, and p, from God........... Col 1:2
having made p through the blood................ Col 1:20
let the p of God rule in your....................... Col 3:15

Grace be unto you, and p, from God........... 1Th 1:1
For when they shall say, P......................... 1Th 5:3
And be at p among yourselves.................... 1Th 5:13
the very God of p sanctify you.................... 1Th 5:23
Grace unto you, and p, from God............... 2Th 1:2
Now the Lord of P himself give................... 2Th 3:16
give you p always by all means.................. 2Th 3:16
Grace, mercy, and p, from God our............ 1Ti 1:2
Grace, mercy, and p, from God the............ 2Ti 1:2
righteousness, faith, charity, p.................. 2Ti 2:22
Grace, mercy, and p, from God our............ Titus 1:4
Grace to you, and p, from our.................... Philem 3
of Salem, which is, King of p...................... Heb 7:2
she had received the spies with p............... Heb 11:31
Follow p with all men, and......................... Heb 12:14
Now the God of p, that brought................. Heb 13:20
of you say unto them, Depart in p............. Jas 2:16
sown in p of them that make p................... Jas 3:18
Grace unto you, and p, be.......................... 1Pet 1:2
let him seek p, and ensue it....................... 1Pet 3:11
P be with you all that are in....................... 1Pet 5:14
p be multiplied unto you through................ 2Pet 1:2
that ye may be found of him in p................ 2Pet 3:14
Grace be with you, mercy, and p................ 2Jn 3
P be to thee.. Jude 2
Mercy unto you, and p, and love, be.......... Jude 2
Grace to you, and p, from him who............ Rev 1:4
thereon to take p from the earth................ Rev 6:4

PEACEABLE
These men are p with us............................ Gen 34:21
I am one of them that are p in.................... 2Sa 20:19
the land was wide, and quiet, and p........... 1Chr 4:40
shall dwell in a p habitation....................... Is 32:18
the p habitations are cut down................... Jer 25:37
p life in all godliness and.......................... 1Ti 2:2
afterward it yieldeth the p fruit of.............. Heb 12:11
from above is first pure, then p.................. Jas 3:17

PEACEABLY
and could not speak p unto him................. Gen 37:4
restore those lands again p....................... Judg 11:13
Rimmon, and to call p unto them................ Judg 21:13
coming, and said, Comest thou p................ 1Sa 16:4
And he said, P.. 1Sa 16:5
And she said, Comest thou p...................... 1Kin 2:13
And he said, P.. 1Kin 2:13
If ye be come p unto me to help................. 1Chr 12:17
one speaketh p to his neighbour................. Jer 9:8
but he shall come in p, and obtain............. Dan 11:21
He shall enter p even upon the.................... Dan 11:24
lieth in you, live p with all men................. Rom 12:18

PEACEMAKERS
Blessed are the p...................................... Mt 5:9

PEACOCKS
and silver, ivory, and apes, and p.............. 1Kin 10:22
and silver, ivory, and apes, and p.............. 2Chr 9:21
thou the goodly wings unto the p............... Job 39:13

PEARL
he had found one p of great price............... Mt 13:46
every several gate was of one p.................. Rev 21:21

PEARLS
shall be made of coral, or of p.................... Job 28:18
cast ye your p before swine....................... Mt 7:6
a merchant man, seeking goodly p.............. Mt 13:45
with broided hair, or gold, or p................... 1Ti 2:9
with gold and precious stones and p........... Rev 17:4
and precious stones, and of p.................... Rev 18:12
gold, and precious stones, and p................ Rev 18:16
And the twelve gates were twelve p............ Rev 21:21

PECULIAR
then ye shall be a p treasure...................... Ex 19:5
to be a p people unto himself..................... Deut 14:2
thee this day to be his p people................. Deut 26:18
and Israel for his p treasure....................... Ps 135:4
the p treasure of kings and of the.............. Eccl 2:8
and purify unto himself a p people............. Titus 2:14
an holy nation, a p people.......................... 1Pet 2:9

PEDAHEL (ped'-a-hel) A Naphtalite who
apportioned the Promised Land.
of Naphtali, P the son of Ammihud........... Num 34:28

PEDAHZUR (pe-dah'-zur) Father of Gamaliel.
Gamaliel the son of P................................. Num 1:10
shall be Gamaliel the son of P.................... Num 2:20
day offered Gamaliel the son of P.............. Num 7:54
offering of Gamaliel the son of P............... Num 7:59
was Gamaliel the son of P.......................... Num 10:23

PEDAIAH (pe-dah'-yah)
1. Grandfather of King Josiah.
the daughter of P of Rumah....................... 2Kin 23:36
2. Descendant of Jeconiah.
Malchiram also, and P, and Shenazar....... 1Chr 3:18
and the sons of P were, Zerubbabel........... 1Chr 3:19
3. Father of Joel.
of Manasseh, Joel the son of P................... 1Chr 27:20
4. Son of Parosh.
After him P the son of Parosh..................... Neh 3:25
5. A priest who aided Ezra.
and on his left hand, P.............................. Neh 8:4
the scribe, and of the Levites, P................. Neh 13:13
6. A family of exiles.
of the son of Joed, the son of P.................. Neh 11:7

PEDIGREES
they declared their p after their.................. Num 1:18

PEELED
to a nation scattered and p......................... Is 18:7
hosts of a people scattered and p............... Is 18:7

bald, and every shoulder was p................... Eze 29:18

PEEP
spirits, and unto wizards that p.................. Is 8:19

PEEPED
wing, or opened the mouth, or p................. Is 10:14

PEKAH (pe'-kah) A king of Israel.
But P the son of Remaliah, a...................... 2Kin 15:25
P the son of Remaliah began to.................. 2Kin 15:27
In the days of P king of Israel.................... 2Kin 15:29
against P the son of Remaliah..................... 2Kin 15:30
And the rest of the acts of P...................... 2Kin 15:31
In the second year of P the son.................. 2Kin 15:32
Syria, and P the son of Remaliah................ 2Kin 15:37
In the seventeenth year of P the................ 2Kin 16:1
P son of Remaliah king of Israel................. 2Kin 16:5
For P the son of Remaliah slew in.............. 2Chr 28:6
P the son of Remaliah, king...................... Is 7:1

PEKAHIAH (pe-ka-hi'-ah) Son of King
Menahem.
P his son reigned in his stead.................... 2Kin 15:22
P the son of Menahem began to................. 2Kin 15:23
And the rest of the acts of P...................... 2Kin 15:26

PEKOD (pe'-kod) Symbolic name for Chaldea.
and against the inhabitants of P................. Jer 50:21
and all the Chaldeans, P, and Shoa............ Eze 23:23

PELAIAH (pel-a-i'-ah)
1. A son of Elioenai.
were, Hodaiah, and Eliashib, and P............ 1Chr 3:24
2. A priest who aided Ezra.
Azariah, Jozabad, Hanan, P....................... Neh 8:7
3. A Levite who renewed the covenant.
Shebaniah, Hodijah, Kelita, P.................... Neh 10:10

PELALIAH (pel-a-li'-ah) A family of exiles.
the son of Jeroham, the son of P................ Neh 11:12

PELATIAH (pel-a-ti'-ah)
1. Son of Hananiah.
of Hananiah, P, and Jesaiah...................... 1Chr 3:21
2. A Simeonite captain.
Seir, having for their captains P................. 1Chr 4:42
3. A family who renewed the covenant.
P, Hanan, Anaiah,..................................... Neh 10:22
4. Son of Benaiah.
P the son of Benaiah, princes of................. Eze 11:1
that P the son of Benaiah died.................... Eze 11:13

PELEG (pe'-leg) See PHALEC. A son of Eber.
the name of one was P................................ Gen 10:25
four and thirty years, and begat P.............. Gen 11:16
after he begat P four hundred..................... Gen 11:17
P lived thirty years, and begat................... Gen 11:18
P lived after he begat Reu two.................... Gen 11:19
the name of the one was P.......................... 1Chr 1:19
Eber, P, Reu,... 1Chr 1:25

PELET (pe'-let) See BETH-PALET.
1. A son of Jahdai.
Jotham, and Gesham, and P........................ 1Chr 2:47
2. A captain in David's army.
and Jeziel, and P, the sons of..................... 1Chr 12:3

PELETH (pe'-leth)
1. Father of On.
of Eliab, and On, the son of P..................... Num 16:1
of Jonathan; P, and Zaza........................... 1Chr 2:33

PELETHITES (pel'-e-thites) A company of
David's bodyguards.
both the Cherethites and the P................... 2Sa 8:18
all the Cherethites, and all the P............... 2Sa 15:18
men, and the Cherethites, and the P......... 2Sa 20:7
the Cherethites and over the P................... 2Sa 20:23
and the Cherethites, and the P................... 1Kin 1:38
and the Cherethites, and the P................... 1Kin 1:44
was over the Cherethites and the P........... 1Chr 18:17

PELICAN
And the swan, and the p, and the.............. Lev 11:18
And the p, and the gier eagle, and............. Deut 14:17
I am like a p of the wilderness.................... Ps 102:6

PELONITE (pel'-o-nite) See PALTITE.
1. Family name of Helez.
the Harorite, Helez the P........................... 1Chr 11:27
the seventh month was Helez the P............ 1Chr 27:10
2. Family name of Ahijah.
the Mecherathite, Ahijah the P.................. 1Chr 11:36

PELUSIUM See SIN.

PEN
that handle the p of the writer.................... Judg 5:14
they were graven with an iron p................. Job 19:24
my tongue is the p of a ready..................... Ps 45:1
in it with a man's p concerning.................. Is 8:1
the p of the scribes is in vain.................... Jer 8:8
Judah is written with a p of iron............... Jer 17:1
not with ink and p write unto thee............ 3Jn 13

PENCE
which owed him an hundred p..................... Mt 18:28
for more than three hundred p................... Mk 14:5
the one owed five hundred p....................... Lk 7:41
he departed, he took out two p................... Lk 10:35
ointment sold for three hundred p.............. Jn 12:5

PENIEL (pe-ni'-el) See PENUEL. Same as
Penuel.
called the name of the place P.................... Gen 32:30

PENINNAH (pe-nin'-nah) A wife of Elkanah.
and the name of the other P........................ 1Sa 1:2
P had children, but Hannah had no............. 1Sa 1:2

P

offered, he gave to P his wife 1Sa 1:4

PENKNIFE

four leaves, he cut it with the p .... Jer 36:23

PENNY

with the labourers for a p a day .... Mt 20:2
hour, they received every man a p .... Mt 20:9
likewise received every man a p .... Mt 20:10
not thou agree with me for a p .... Mt 20:13
And they brought unto him a p .... Mt 22:19
bring me a p, that I may see it .... Mk 12:15
Shew me a p .... Lk 20:24
say, A measure of wheat for a p .... Rev 6:6
three measures of barley for a p .... Rev 6:6

PENNYWORTH

go and buy two hundred p of bread .... Mk 6:37
Two hundred p of bread is not .... Jn 6:7

PENTECOST (pen´-te-cost) Greek name for Feast of Weeks.

when the day of P was fully come .... Acts 2:1
to be at Jerusalem the day of P .... Acts 20:16
I will tarry at Ephesus until P 1Cor 16:8

PENUEL (pe-nu´-el) See PENIEL.

1. Where Jacob wrestled God.
as he passed over P the sun rose .... Gen 32:31
And he went up thence to P .... Judg 8:8
the men of P answered him as the .... Judg 8:8
he spake also unto the men of P .... Judg 8:9
And he beat down the tower of P.......... Judg 8:17
2. Father of Gedor.
P the father of Gedor, and Ezer 1Chr 4:4
3. A son of Shashak.
And Iphedeiah, and P, the sons of 1Chr 8:25

PENURY

of the lips tendeth only to p .... Prov 14:23
but she of her p hath cast in all .... Lk 21:4

PEOPLE See PREFACE.

PEOPLE'S

And he brought the p offering .... Lev 9:15
the p inheritance by oppression .... Eze 46:18
For this p heart is waxed gross, ... Mt 13:15
his own sins, and then for the p .... Heb 7:27

PEOPLES

must prophesy again before many p ...... Rev 10:11
where the whore sitteth, are p .... Rev 17:15

PEOR (pe´-or) See BAAL-PEOR, BETH-PEOR, PEOR'S.

1. A Moabite god.
beguiled you in the matter of P.......... Num 25:18
the LORD in the matter of P............... Num 31:16
iniquity of P too little for us .... Josh 22:17
2. A mountain.
brought Balaam unto the top of P .... Num 23:28

PEOR'S

the day of the plague for P sake .... Num 25:18

PERADVENTURE

P there be fifty righteous within........... Gen 18:24
P there shall lack five of the................ Gen 18:28
P there shall be forty found................. Gen 18:29
P there shall thirty be found................ Gen 18:30
P there shall be twenty found.............. Gen 18:31
P ten shall be found there.................. Gen 18:32
The woman will not be willing............... Gen 24:5
The woman will not follow me.............. Gen 24:39
My father p will feel me, and I .... Gen 27:12
P thou wouldest take by force thy........ Gen 31:31
P he will accept of me...................... Gen 32:20
Lest p he die also, as his.................... Gen 38:11
Lest p mischief befall him.................. Gen 42:4
it was an oversight......................... Gen 43:12
lest p I see the evil that shall .... Gen 44:34
they said, Joseph will p hate us .... Gen 50:15
Lest p the people repent when .... Ex 13:17
p I shall make an atonement for .... Ex 32:30
p I shall prevail, that we may .... Num 22:6
p I shall be able to overcome .... Num 22:11
p it will please God that thou.............. Num 23:27
the Hivites, P ye dwell among us .... Josh 9:7
p he will lighten his hand from 1Sa 6:5
p he can shew us our way that we 1Sa 9:6
p we may find grace to save the 1Kin 18:5
or p he sleepeth, and must be 1Kin 18:27
p he will save thy life.................... 1Kin 20:31
lest p the Spirit of the LORD 2Kin 2:16
P he will be enticed, and we shall .... Jer 20:10
yet p for a good man some would......... Rom 5:7
if God p will give them.................... 2Ti 2:25

PERAZIM (per´-a-zim) Where David defeated the Philistines.

LORD shall rise up as in mount P .... Is 28:21

PERCEIVE

hath not given you an heart to p .... Deut 29:4
This day we p that the LORD is .... Josh 22:31
that ye may p and see that your 1Sa 12:17
for this day I p, that if Absalom 2Sa 19:6
I p that this is an holy man of 2Kin 4:9
passeth on also, but I p him not .... Job 9:11
and backward, but I cannot p him........ Job 23:8
to p the words of understanding .... Prov 1:2
Wherefore I p that there is .... Eccl 3:22
and see ye indeed, but p not................ Is 6:9
a deeper speech than thou canst p........ Is 33:19
ye shall see, and shall not .... Mt 13:14

seeing they may see, and not p .... Mk 4:12
Do ye not p, that whatsoever .... Mk 7:18
p ye not yet, neither understand .... Mk 8:17
for I p that virtue is gone out .... Lk 8:46
I p that thou art a prophet .... Jn 4:19
P ye how ye prevail nothing .... Jn 12:19
For I p that thou art in the gall .... Acts 8:23
Of a truth I p that God is no .... Acts 10:34
I p that in all things are too .... Acts 17:22
I p that this voyage will be with .... Acts 27:10
and seeing ye shall see, and not p ...... Acts 28:26
for I p that the same epistle 2Cor 7:8
Hereby p we the love of God, ... 1Jn 3:16

PERCEIVED

he p not when she lay down, nor .... Gen 19:33
he p not when she lay down, nor .... Gen 19:35
when Gideon p that he was an .... Judg 6:22
Eli p that the LORD had called 1Sa 3:8
Saul p that it was Samuel, and he 1Sa 28:14
David p that the LORD had 2Sa 5:12
David p that the child was dead 2Sa 12:19
p that the king's heart was 2Sa 14:1
p that it was not the king of 1Kin 22:33
David p that the LORD had 1Chr 14:2
p that it was not the king of 2Chr 18:32
I p that God had not sent him .... Neh 6:12
for they p that this work was .... Neh 6:16
p that the portions of the .... Neh 13:10
When Mordecai p all that was done, ... Est 4:1
Hast thou p the breadth of the .... Job 38:18
I p that this also is vexation of .... Eccl 1:17
I myself p also that one event .... Eccl 2:14
nor p by the ear, neither hath .... Is 64:4
counsel of the LORD, and hath p .... Jer 23:18
for the matter was not p .... Jer 38:27
Which when Jesus p, he said unto .... Mt 16:8
they p that he spake of them .... Mt 21:45
But Jesus p their wickedness, and .... Mt 22:18
immediately when Jesus p in his .... Mk 2:8
they p that he had seen a vision .... Lk 1:22
But when Jesus p their thoughts .... Lk 5:22
hid from them, that they p it not .... Lk 9:45
for they p that he had spoken .... Lk 20:19
But he p their craftiness, and .... Lk 20:23
therefore p that they would come .... Jn 6:15
p that they were unlearned and .... Acts 4:13
But when Paul p that the one .... Acts 23:6
Whom I p to be accused of .... Acts 23:29
p the grace that was given unto .... Gal 2:9

PERCEIVEST

when thou p not in him the lips .... Prov 14:7
but p not the beam that is in .... Lk 6:41

PERCEIVETH

low, but he p it not of them, ... Job 14:21
once, yea twice, yet man p it not .... Job 33:14
She p that her merchandise is .... Prov 31:18

PERCEIVING

p that he had answered them well, ... Mk 12:28
the thought of their heart, ... Lk 9:47
p that he had faith to be healed, ... Acts 14:9

PERDITION

of them is lost, but the son of p .... Jn 17:12
is to them an evident token of p .... Phil 1:28
of sin be revealed, the son of p 2Th 2:3
drown men in destruction and p 1Ti 6:9
not of them who draw back unto p .... Heb 10:39
of judgment and p of ungodly men, ... 2Pet 3:7
the bottomless pit, and goeth into p .... Rev 17:8
is of the seven, and goeth into p .... Rev 17:11

PERES (pe´-res) Portion of ´the handwriting on the wall.´

P, Thy kingdom is, ... Dan 5:28

PERESH (pe´-resh) A son of Machir.

a son, and she called his name P........... 1Chr 7:16

PEREZ (pe´-rez) See PEREZ-UZZAH, PHARES.

1. An ancestor of Jashobeam.
Of the children of P was the 1Chr 27:3
2. A son of Judah, same as Pharez.
Mahalaleel, of the children of P .... Neh 11:4
All the sons of P that dwelt at .... Neh 11:6

PEREZITES See PHARZITES.

PEREZ-UZZA (pe´´-rez-uz´-zah) See PEREZ-UZZAH. Where Uzza died.

place is called P to this day 1Chr 13:11

PEREZ-UZZAH (pe´´-rez-uz´-zah) See PEREZ-UZZA. Same as Perez-uzza.

name of the place P to this day 2Sa 6:8

PERFECT

p in his generations, and Noah .... Gen 6:9
walk before me, and be thou p .... Gen 17:1
it shall be p to b................. accepted .... Lev 22:21
Thou shalt be p with the LORD thy .... Deut 18:13
a p and just weight, a p .... Deut 25:15
he is the Rock, his work is p .... Deut 32:4
LORD God of Israel, Give a p lot 1Sa 14:41
As for God, his way is p 2Sa 22:31
And he maketh my way p 2Sa 22:33
be p with the LORD our God 1Kin 8:61
his heart was not p with the LORD........ 1Kin 11:4
his heart was not p with the LORD........ 1Kin 15:3
was p with the LORD all his days........ 1Kin 15:14
thee in truth and with a p heart 2Kin 20:3
came with a p heart to Hebron, to 1Chr 12:38
and serve him with a p heart 1Chr 28:9

because with p heart they offered 1Chr 29:9
unto Solomon my son a p heart 1Chr 29:19
made he of gold, and that p gold 2Chr 4:21
heart of Asa was p all his days 2Chr 15:17
them whose heart is p toward him, ... 2Chr 16:9
faithfully, and with a p heart 2Chr 19:9
the LORD, but not with a p heart 2Chr 25:2
p peace, and but such a time .... Ezr 7:12
and that man was p and upright, and .... Job 1:1
none like him in the earth, a p .... Job 1:8
none like him in the earth, a p .... Job 2:3
God will not cast away a p man .... Job 8:20
if I say, I am p, it shall also .... Job 9:20
Though I were p, yet would I not .... Job 9:21
I said it, He destroyeth the p .... Job 9:22
him, that thou makest thy way p .... Job 22:3
he that is p in knowledge is with .... Job 36:4
of him which is p in knowledge .... Job 37:16
As for God, his way is p .... Ps 18:30
with strength, and maketh my way p .... Ps 18:32
The law of the LORD is p, ... Ps 19:7
Mark the p man, and behold the .... Ps 37:37
they may shoot in secret at the p .... Ps 64:4
behave myself wisely in a p way .... Ps 101:2
within my house with a p heart .... Ps 101:2
he that walketh in a p way .... Ps 101:6
The LORD will p that which............... Ps 138:8
I hate them with a p hatred .... Ps 139:22
land, and the p shall remain in it .... Prov 2:21
more and more unto the p day .... Prov 4:18
of the p shall direct his way .... Prov 11:5
the harvest, when the bud is p .... Is 18:5
Thou wilt keep him in p peace. .... Is 26:3
thee in truth and with a p heart .... Is 38:3
who is blind as he that is p .... Is 42:19
for it was p through my .... Eze 16:14
thou hast said, I am of p beauty .... Eze 27:3
they have made thy beauty p .... Eze 27:4
full of wisdom, and p in beauty .... Eze 28:12
Thou wast p in thy ways from the .... Eze 28:15
Be ye therefore p, even as your .... Mt 5:48
Father which is in heaven is p .... Mt 5:48
said unto him, If thou wilt be p .... Mt 19:21
having had p understanding of all .... Lk 1:3
but every one that is p shall be .... Lk 6:40
that they may be made p in one .... Jn 17:23
p soundness in the presence of .... Acts 3:16
taught according to the p manner .... Acts 22:3
having more p knowledge of that, ... Acts 24:22
is that good, and acceptable, and p .... Rom 12:2
wisdom among them that are p 1Cor 2:6
But when that which is p is come. 1Cor 13:10
my strength is made p in weakness 2Cor 12:9
Be p, be of good comfort, be of 2Cor 13:11
are ye now made p by the flesh........... Gal 3:3
Not that I had already attained, ... Eph 4:13
attained, either were already p .... Phil 3:12
Let us therefore, as many as be p .... Phil 3:15
every man p in Christ Jesus .... Col 1:28
in prayers, that ye may stand p .... Col 4:12
might p that which is lacking in 1Th 3:10
That the man of God may be p 2Ti 3:17
salvation p through sufferings. .... Heb 2:10
And being made p, he became the ...... Heb 5:9
For the law made nothing p .... Heb 7:19
make him that did the service p .... Heb 9:9
more p tabernacle, not made with .... Heb 9:11
make the comers thereunto p .... Heb 10:1
without us should not be made p .... Heb 11:40
to the spirits of just men made p .... Heb 12:23
Make you p in every good work to. ...... Heb 13:21
But let patience have her p work .... Jas 1:4
that ye may be p .... Jas 1:4
every p gift is from above, and .... Jas 1:17
looketh into the p law of liberty .... Jas 1:25
and by works was faith made p .... Jas 2:22
not in word, the same is a p man .... Jas 3:2
have suffered a while, make you p 1Pet 5:10
Herein is our love made p 1Jn 4:17
but p love casteth out fear 1Jn 4:18
feareth is not made p in love 1Jn 4:18
not found thy works p before God .... Rev 3:2

PERFECTED

So the house of the LORD was p........... 2Chr 8:16
and the work was p by them 2Chr 24:13
thy builders have p thy beauty .... Eze 27:4
and sucklings thou hast p praise .... Mt 21:16
and the third day I shall be p .... Lk 13:32
he hath p for ever them that are .... Heb 10:14
him verily is the love of God p 1Jn 2:5
in us, and his love is p in us 1Jn 4:12

PERFECTING

p holiness in the fear of God. 2Cor 7:1
For the p of the saints, for the .... Eph 4:12

PERFECTION

thou find out the Almighty unto p .... Job 11:7
the p thereof upon the earth .... Job 28:3
darkness, and searcheth out all p .... Job 28:3
the p of beauty, God hath shined .... Ps 50:2
I have seen an end of all p .... Ps 119:96
their p for the multitude of thy .... Is 47:9
that men call The p of beauty .... Lam 2:15
this life, and bring no fruit to .... Lk 8:14
of sins, we also wish, even your p 2Cor 13:9
of Christ, let us go on unto p .... Heb 6:1
If therefore p were by the .... Heb 7:11

PERFECTLY

days ye shall consider it p .... Jer 23:20
many as touched were made p whole .... Mt 14:36

unto him the way of God more p .... Acts 18:26
something more p concerning him ...... Acts 23:15
enquire somewhat of him more p ...... Acts 23:20
but that ye be p joined together 1Cor 1:10
For yourselves know p that he 1Th 5:2

PERFECTNESS
charity, which is the bond of p .... Col 3:14

PERFORM
I will p the oath which I sware .... Gen 26:3
not able to p it thyself alone .... Ex 18:18
that enter in to p the service .... Num 4:23
which he commanded you to p .... Deut 4:13
that he may p the word which the..... Deut 9:5
of thy lips thou shalt keep and p ...... Deut 23:23
p the duty of an husband's............... Deut 25:5
he will not p the duty of my .... Deut 25:7
that if he will p unto thee the .... Ruth 3:13
In that day I will p against Eli 1Sa 3:12
p the request of his handmaid........... 2Sa 14:15
then will I p my word with thee,........ 1Kin 6:12
Lord, that he might p his saying 1Kin 12:15
to p the words of this covenant 2Kin 23:3
that he might p the words of the 2Kin 23:24
that the Lord might p his word 2Chr 10:15
to p the words of the covenant 2Chr 34:31
to p my request, let the king and..... Est 5:8
hands cannot p their enterprise .... Job 5:12
which they are not able to p .... Ps 21:11
ever, that I may daily p my vows....... Ps 61:8
I have sworn, and I will p it.............. Ps 119:106
heart to p thy statutes alway .... Ps 119:112
of the Lord of hosts will p this .... Is 9:7
vow a vow unto the Lord, and p it .... Is 19:21
and shall p all my pleasure .... Is 44:28
for I will hasten my word to p it .... Jer 1:12
That I may p the oath which I .... Jer 11:5
the Lord p thy words which thou ...... Jer 28:6
p my good word toward you, in .... Jer 29:10
that I will p that good thing .... Jer 33:14
We will surely p our vows that we .... Jer 44:25
your vows, and surely p your vows ... Jer 44:25
will I say the word, and will p it .... Eze 12:25
Thou wilt p the truth to Jacob,......... Mic 7:20
thy solemn feasts, p thy vows........... Nah 1:15
but shalt p unto the Lord thine .... Mt 5:33
To p the mercy promised to our .... Lk 1:72
promised, he was able also to p ...... Rom 4:21
but how to p that which is good I ..... Rom 7:18
Now therefore p the doing of it 2Cor 8:11
will p it until the day of Jesus .... Phil 1:6

PERFORMANCE
for there shall be a p of those .... Lk 1:45
so there may be a p also out of 2Cor 8:11

PERFORMED
hath not p my commandments........... 1Sa 15:11
I have p the commandment of the 1Sa 15:13
and they p all that the king 2Sa 21:14
the Lord hath p his word that he 1Kin 8:20
The Lord therefore hath p his........... 2Chr 6:10
to his seed, and hast p thy words..... Neh 9:8
because she hath not p the .... Est 1:15
half of the kingdom it shall be p ...... Est 5:6
and it shall be p, even to the .... Est 7:2
and unto thee shall the vow be p ..... Ps 65:1
that when the Lord hath p his .... Is 10:12
till he have p the thoughts of .... Jer 23:20
until he have p the intents of .... Jer 30:24
which have not p the words of the ... Jer 34:18
his sons not to drink wine, are p ...... Jer 35:14
Jonadab the son of Rechab have p ... Jer 35:16
Lord shall be p against Babylon........ Jer 51:29
it, and p it, saith the Lord .... Eze 37:14
day that these things shall be p .... Lk 1:20
when they had p all things .... Lk 2:39
When therefore I have p this .... Rom 15:28

PERFORMETH
that p not this promise, even........... Neh 5:13
For he p the thing that is .... Job 23:14
unto God that p all things for me .... Ps 57:2
p the counsel of his messengers ..... Is 44:26

PERFORMING
or a sacrifice in p a vow .... Num 15:3
or for a sacrifice in p a vow .... Num 15:8

PERFUME
And thou shalt make it a p .... Ex 30:35
as for the p which thou shalt .... Ex 30:37
Ointment and p rejoice the heart ...... Prov 27:9

PERFUMED
I have p my bed with myrrh, aloes..... Prov 7:17
p with myrrh and frankincense,.......... Song 3:6

PERFUMES
ointment, and didst increase thy p .... Is 57:9

PERGA (pur'-gah) Capital of Pamphylia.
they came to P in Pamphylia .... Acts 13:13
But when they departed from P....... Acts 13:14
they had preached the word in P ..... Acts 14:25

PERGAMOS (pur'-ga-mos) A city in Mysia in Asia Minor.
and unto Smyrna, and unto P.......... Rev 1:11
angel of the church in P write.......... Rev 2:12

PERGAMUM See Pergamos.

PERHAPS
if p the thought of thine heart .... Acts 8:22
lest p such a one should be.............. 2Cor 2:7

For p he therefore departed for a ...... Philem 15

PERIDA (per-i'-dah) A family of exiles.
of Sophereth, the children of P .... Neh 7:57

PERIL
We gat our bread with the p of .... Lam 5:9
or famine, or nakedness, or p .... Rom 8:35

PERILOUS
the last days p times shall come....... 2Ti 3:1

PERILS
in p of waters................................... 2Cor 11:26
in p of robbers................................. 2Cor 11:26
in p by mine own countrymen............ 2Cor 11:26
in p by the heathen.......................... 2Cor 11:26
in p in the city................................. 2Cor 11:26
in p in the wilderness...................... 2Cor 11:26
in p in the sea................................. 2Cor 11:26
in p among false brethren 2Cor 11:26

PERISH
that the land p not through the........ Gen 41:36
Lord to gaze, and many of them p .... Ex 19:21
or the eye of his maid, that it p .... Ex 21:26
ye shall p among the heathen, and... Lev 26:38
we die, we p, we all p .... Num 17:12
end shall be that he p for ever........ Num 24:20
Eber, and he also shall p for ever.... Num 24:24
that ye shall soon utterly p from ..... Deut 4:26
this day that ye shall surely p .... Deut 8:19
before your face, so shall ye p .... Deut 8:20
lest ye p quickly from off the .... Deut 11:17
A Syrian ready to p was my father .. Deut 26:5
and until thou p quickly.................... Deut 28:20
shall pursue thee until thou p .... Deut 28:22
this day, that ye shall surely p .... Deut 30:18
until ye p from off this good .... Josh 23:13
ye shall p quickly from off the .... Josh 23:16
So let all thine enemies p .... Judg 5:31
shall descend into battle, and p 1Sa 26:10
I shall now p one day by the hand... 1Sa 27:1
the whole house of Ahab shall p 2Kin 9:8
to kill, and to cause to p .... Est 3:13
and if I p, I p .... Est 4:16
destroyed, to be slain, and to p ...... Est 7:4
to slay, and to cause to p .... Est 8:11
of them p from their seed .... Est 9:28
Let the day p wherein I was born,.... Job 3:3
By the blast of God they p .... Job 4:9
they p for ever without any .... Job 4:20
they go to nothing, and p .... Job 6:18
and the hypocrite's hope shall p ...... Job 8:13
shall p from the earth, and he .... Job 18:17
Yet he shall p for ever like his .... Job 20:7
that was ready to p came upon me .. Job 29:13
If I have seen any p for want of...... Job 31:19
All flesh shall p together .... Job 34:15
they shall p by the sword, and........ Job 36:12
the way of the ungodly shall p .... Ps 1:6
ye p from the way, when his wrath... Ps 2:12
shall fall and p at thy presence ...... Ps 9:3
of the poor shall not p for ever....... Ps 9:18
But the wicked shall p, and the ...... Ps 37:20
When shall he die, and his name .... Ps 41:5
the fool and the brutish person p .... Ps 49:10
he is like the beasts that p .... Ps 49:12
not, is like the beasts that p .... Ps 49:20
so let the wicked p at the .... Ps 68:2
that are far from thee shall p .... Ps 73:27
they p at the rebuke of thy .... Ps 80:16
let them be put to shame, and p ..... Ps 83:17
for, lo, thine enemies shall p .... Ps 92:9
They shall p, but thou shalt............. Ps 102:26
the desire of the wicked shall p ...... Ps 112:10
in that very day his thoughts p .... Ps 146:4
expectation of the wicked shall p .... Prov 10:28
dieth, his expectation shall p .... Prov 11:7
and when the wicked p, there is...... Prov 11:10
and he that speaketh lies shall p .... Prov 19:9
A false witness shall p .... Prov 21:28
but when they p, the righteous........ Prov 28:28
there is no vision, the people p .... Prov 29:18
drink unto him that is ready to p ..... Prov 31:6
those riches p by evil travail .... Eccl 5:14
and made all their memory to p .... Is 26:14
ready to p in the land of Assyria .... Is 27:13
wisdom of their wise men shall p .... Is 29:14
that arrive with these shall p .... Is 41:11
that will not serve thee shall p .... Is 60:12
the heart of the king shall p .... Jer 4:9
neighbour and his friend shall p ...... Jer 6:21
even they shall p from the earth ..... Jer 10:11
of their visitation they shall p .... Jer 10:15
law shall not p from the priest .... Jer 18:18
drive you out, and ye should p .... Jer 27:15
and the remnant in Judah p .... Jer 40:15
the valley also shall p, and the ...... Jer 48:8
of their visitation they shall p .... Jer 51:18
the law shall p from the priest .... Eze 7:26
thee to p out of the countries .... Eze 25:7
his fellows should not p with the .... Dan 2:18
of the Philistines shall p .... Amos 1:8
the flight shall p from the swift .... Amos 2:14
and the houses of ivory shall p .... Amos 3:15
will think upon us, that we p not ..... Jonah 1:6
let us not p for this man's life,........ Jonah 1:14
his fierce anger, that we p not .... Jonah 3:9
and the king shall p from Gaza .... Zec 9:5
that one of thy members should p.... Mt 5:29
that one of thy members should p.... Mt 5:30
Lord, save us: we p .... Mt 8:25

runneth out, and the bottles p.......... Mt 9:17
one of these little ones should p ...... Mt 18:14
the sword shall p with the sword ..... Mt 26:52
Master, carest thou not that we p .... Mk 4:38
spilled, and the bottles shall p .... Lk 5:37
him, saying, Master, master, we p .... Lk 8:24
repent, ye shall all likewise p .... Lk 13:3
repent, ye shall all likewise p .... Lk 13:5
that a prophet p out of Jerusalem .... Lk 13:33
and to spare, and I p with hunger .... Lk 15:17
shall not an hair of your head p .... Lk 21:18
believeth in him should not p .... Jn 3:15
believeth in him should not p .... Jn 3:16
and they shall never p, neither......... Jn 10:28
and that the whole nation p not .... Jn 11:50
unto him, Thy money p with thee...... Acts 8:20
ye despisers, and wonder, and p ...... Acts 13:41
law shall also p without law .... Rom 2:12
is to them that p foolishness 1Cor 1:18
shall the weak brother p, for 1Cor 8:11
that are saved, and in them that p ... 2Cor 2:15
but though our outward man p 2Cor 4:16
Which all are to p with the using...... Col 2:22
of unrighteousness in them that p 2Th 2:10
They shall p; but thou .... Heb 1:11
shall utterly p in their own............... 2Pet 2:12
not willing that any should p 2Pet 3:9

PERISHED
and they p from among the.............. Num 16:33
Heshbon is even unto Dibon, and .... Num 21:30
that man p not alone in his.............. Josh 22:20
fallen, and the weapons of war p 2Sa 1:27
Remember, I pray thee, who ever p ... Job 4:7
profit me, in whom old age was p .... Job 30:2
their memorial is p with them.......... Ps 9:6
the heathen are p out of his land .... Ps 10:16
Which p at En-dor............................ Ps 83:10
then have p in mine affliction......... Ps 119:92
hatred, and their envy, is now p ...... Eccl 9:6
truth is p, and is cut off from......... Jer 7:28
riches that he hath gotten are p ...... Jer 48:36
is counsel p from the prudent .... Jer 49:7
my hope is p from the Lord .... Lam 3:18
the harvest of the field is p .... Joel 1:11
up in a night, and p in a night,....... Jonah 4:10
is thy counsellor p .... Mic 4:9
The good man is p out of the.......... Mic 7:2
into the sea, and p in the waters .... Mt 8:32
which p between the altar and the ... Lk 11:51
after him: he also p .... Acts 5:37
are fallen asleep in Christ are p 1Cor 15:18
By faith the harlot Rahab p not .... Heb 11:31
being overflowed with water, p 2Pet 3:6
p in the gainsaying of Core............. Jude 11

PERISHETH
The old lion p for lack of prey,........ Job 4:11
and the hope of unjust men p .... Prov 11:7
man that p in his righteousness ...... Eccl 7:15
The righteous p, and no man layeth.. Is 57:1
declare it, for what the land p .... Jer 9:12
the people of Chemosh .... Jer 48:46
Labour not for the meat which p ..... Jn 6:27
the grace of the fashion of it p .... Jas 1:11
more precious than of gold that p 1Pet 1:7

PERISHING
and his life from p by the sword...... Job 33:18

PERIZZITE (per'-iz-zite) See Perizzites. A tribe in Judah.
the P dwelled then in the land......... Gen 13:7
Amorite, and the Hittite, and the P.. Ex 33:2
and the Hittite, and the P................ Ex 34:11
the Amorite, the Canaanite, the P ... Josh 9:1
Amorite, and the Hittite, and the P .. Josh 11:3

PERIZZITES (per'-iz-zites)
And the Hittites, and the P.............. Gen 15:20
among the Canaanites and the P ...... Gen 34:30
and the Amorites, and the .... Ex 3:8
and the Amorites, and the P .... Ex 3:17
and the Hittites, and the P............... Ex 23:23
the Canaanites, and the P .... Deut 7:1
the Canaanites, and the Hivites ...... Deut 20:17
and the Hivites, and the P............... Josh 3:10
and the Canaanites, the P .... Josh 12:8
there in the land of the P .... Josh 17:15
you, the Amorites, and the P........... Josh 24:11
and the P into their hand .... Judg 1:4
they slew the Canaanites and the P . Judg 1:5
Hittites, and Amorites, and P........... Judg 3:5
left of the Amorites, Hittites, P........ 1Kin 9:20
and the Amorites, and the P 2Chr 8:7
Canaanites, the Hittites, the P......... Ezr 9:1
Hittites, the Amorites, and the P ..... Neh 9:8

PERJURED
for p persons, and if there be any 1Ti 1:10

PERMISSION
But I speak this by p, and not of 1Cor 7:6

PERMIT
a while with you, if the Lord p 1Cor 16:7
And this will we do, if God p............ Heb 6:3

PERMITTED
Thou art p to speak for thyself .... Acts 26:1
for it is not p unto them to.............. 1Cor 14:34

PERNICIOUS
And many shall follow their p ways... 2Pet 2:2

PERPETUAL
is with you, for p generations,......... Gen 9:12
shall be theirs for a p statute .... Ex 29:9

P

a p incense before the LORD .... Ex 30:8
generations, for a p covenant .... Ex 31:16
It shall be a p statute for your .... Lev 3:17
fine flour for a meat offering p .... Lev 6:20
LORD made by fire by a p statute .... Lev 24:9
for it is their p possession .... Lev 25:34
it shall be a p statute unto them .... Num 19:21
destructions are come to a p end .... Ps 9:6
thy feet unto the p desolations .... Ps 74:3
he put them to a p reproach .... Ps 78:66
bound of the sea by a p decree .... Jer 5:22
slidden back by a p backsliding .... Jer 8:5
Why is my pain p, and my wound .... Jer 15:18
land desolate, and a p hissing .... Jer 18:16
a p shame, which shall not be .... Jer 23:40
and an hissing, and p desolations .... Jer 25:9
and will make it p desolations .... Jer 25:12
cities thereof shall be p desolations .... Jer 49:13
in a p covenant that shall not be .... Jer 50:5
may rejoice, and sleep a p sleep .... Jer 51:39
and they shall sleep a p sleep .... Jer 51:57
Because thou hast had a p hatred .... Eze 35:5
I will make thee p desolations .... Eze 35:9
by a p ordinance unto the LORD .... Eze 46:14
scattered, the p hills did bow .... Hab 3:6
and saltpits, and a p desolation .... Zeph 2:9

PERPETUALLY
and mine heart shall be there p 1Kin 9:3
and mine heart shall be there p 2Chr 7:16
all pity, and his anger did tear p .... Amos 1:11

PERPLEXED
but the city Shushan was p .... Est 3:15
the herds of cattle are p .... Joel 1:18
and he was p, because that it was .... Lk 9:7
as they were much p thereabout .... Lk 24:4
we are p, but not in despair 2Cor 4:8

PERPLEXITY
of p by the Lord GOD of hosts in .... Is 22:5
now shall be there p .... Mic 7:4
earth distress of nations, with p .... Lk 21:25

PERSECUTE
Why do ye p me as God, and are not... Job 19:22
Why p we him, seeing the root of ...... Job 19:28
save me from all them that p me .... Ps 7:1
Let the enemy p my soul, and take .... Ps 7:5
in his pride doth p the poor .... Ps 10:2
enemies, and from them that p me .... Ps 31:15
the way against them that p me .... Ps 35:3
let the angel of the LORD p them .... Ps 35:6
For they p him whom thou hast .... Ps 69:26
p and take him .... Ps 71:11
So p them with thy tempest, and .... Ps 83:15
judgment on them that p me .... Ps 119:84
they p me wrongfully .... Ps 119:86
Let them be confounded that p me ..... Jer 17:18
I will p them with the sword .... Jer 29:18
P and destroy them in anger from .... Lam 3:66
p you, and shall say all manner of .... Mt 5:11
despitefully use you, and p you .... Mt 5:44
But when they p you in this city .... Mt 10:23
and p them from city to city .... Mt 23:34
some of them they shall slay and p ...... Lk 11:49
p you, delivering you up to the .... Lk 21:12
And therefore did the Jews p Jesus ..... Jn 5:16
me, they will also p you .... Jn 15:20
Bless them which p you .... Rom 12:14

PERSECUTED
them that hate thee, which p thee ..... Deut 30:7
but p the poor and needy man, that .... Ps 109:16
Princes have p me without a cause... Ps 119:161
For the enemy hath p my soul .... Ps 143:3
ruled the nations in anger, is p .... Is 14:6
hast covered with anger, and p us ..... Lam 3:43
are p for righteousness' sake .... Mt 5:10
for so p they the prophets which .... Mt 5:12
If they have p me, they will also .... Jn 15:20
prophets have not your fathers p .... Acts 7:52
I p this way unto the death .... Acts 22:4
I p them even unto strange cities...... Acts 26:11
being p, we suffer it 1Cor 4:12
because I p the church of God 1Cor 15:9
P, but not forsaken 2Cor 4:9
measure I p the church of God .... Gal 1:13
That he which p us in times past .... Gal 1:23
p him that was born after the .... Gal 4:29
their own prophets, and have p us 1Th 2:15
he p the woman which brought .... Rev 12:13

PERSECUTEST
him, Saul, Saul, why p thou me .... Acts 9:4
Lord said, I am Jesus whom thou p ...... Acts 9:5
me, Saul, Saul, why p thou me .... Acts 22:7
I am Jesus of Nazareth, whom thou p... Acts 22:8
tongue, Saul, Saul, why p thou me ... Acts 26:14
he said, I am Jesus whom thou p .... Acts 26:15

PERSECUTING
Concerning zeal, p the church .... Phil 3:6

PERSECUTION
Our necks are under p .... Lam 5:5
for when tribulation or p ariseth .... Mt 13:21
when affliction or p ariseth for .... Mk 4:17
at that time there was a great p .... Acts 8:1
the p that arose about Stephen .... Acts 11:19
raised p against Paul and Barnabas..... Acts 13:50
tribulation, or distress, or p .... Rom 8:35
why do I yet suffer p .... Gal 5:11
suffer p for the cross of Christ .... Gal 6:12

in Christ Jesus shall suffer p 2Ti 3:12

PERSECUTIONS
and children, and lands, with p .... Mk 10:30
reproaches, in necessities, in p......... 2Cor 12:10
patience and faith in all your p 2Th 1:4
P, afflictions, which came unto 2Ti 3:11
what p I endured 2Ti 3:11

PERSECUTOR
was before a blasphemer, and a p....... 1Ti 1:13

PERSECUTORS
their p thou threwest into the .... Neh 9:11
his arrows against the p .... Ps 7:13
Many are my p and mine enemies... Ps 119:157
deliver me from my p .... Ps 142:6
visit me, and revenge me of my p .... Jer 15:15
therefore my p shall stumble, and ..... Jer 20:11
all her p overtook her between .... Lam 1:3
Our p are swifter than the eagles ...... Lam 4:19

PERSEVERANCE
and watching thereunto with all p....... Eph 6:18

PERSIA (per'-she-ah) See ELAM, PERSIAN. An
ancient world power located in present-day
Iran.
the reign of the kingdom of P.......... 2Chr 36:20
the first year of Cyrus king of P....... 2Chr 36:22
up the spirit of Cyrus king of P....... 2Chr 36:22
sixth Cyrus king of P 2Chr 36:23
the first year of Cyrus king of P .... Ezr 1:1
up the spirit of Cyrus king of P .... Ezr 1:1
Thus saith Cyrus king of P .... Ezr 1:2
of P bring forth by the hand of .... Ezr 1:8
that they had of Cyrus king of P .... Ezr 3:7
the king of P hath commanded us ...... Ezr 4:3
all the days of Cyrus king of P .... Ezr 4:5
the reign of Darius king of P .... Ezr 4:5
unto Artaxerxes king of P .... Ezr 4:7
of the reign of Darius king of P .... Ezr 4:24
Darius, and Artaxerxes king of P ...... Ezr 6:14
the reign of Artaxerxes king of P .... Ezr 7:1
us in the sight of the kings of P .... Ezr 9:9
the power of P and Media, the .... Est 1:3
Memucan, the seven princes of P .... Est 1:14
Likewise shall the ladies of P .... Est 1:18
of the kings of Media and P .... Est 1:19
They of Persia and of Lud and of Phut. Eze 27:10
P, Ethiopia, and Libya with them .... Eze 38:5
horns are the kings of Media and P.... Dan 8:20
of P a thing was revealed unto .... Dan 10:1
the kingdom of P withstood me one .. Dan 10:13
there with the kings of P .... Dan 10:13
to fight with the prince of P .... Dan 10:20
stand up yet three kings in P .... Dan 11:2

PERSIAN (per'-she-un) A native of Persia.
to the reign of Darius the P .... Neh 12:22
and in the reign of Cyrus the P.......... Dan 6:28

PERSIANS (per'-she-uns) See ELAMITES.
written among the laws of the P .... Est 1:19
and given to the Medes and P .... Dan 5:28
to the law of the Medes and P .... Dan 6:8
to the law of the Medes and P .... Dan 6:12
P is, That no decree may continue ..... Dan 6:15

PERSIS (pur'-sis) A Christian in Rome.
Salute the beloved P, which .... Rom 16:12

PERSON
And Joseph was a goodly p, and well... Gen 39:6
uncircumcised p shall eat thereof .... Ex 12:48
not respect the p of the poor .... Lev 19:15
nor honour the p of the mighty .... Lev 19:15
the LORD, and the p be guilty............. Num 5:6
for an unclean p they shall take .... Num 19:17
a clean p shall take hyssop, and ...... Num 19:18
the clean p shall sprinkle upon........ Num 19:19
whatsoever the unclean p toucheth.... Num 19:22
whosoever hath killed any p .... Num 31:19
which killeth any p at unawares ...... Num 35:11
any p unawares may flee thither ...... Num 35:15
Whoso killeth any p, the murderer... Num 35:30
against any p to cause him to die .... Num 35:30
the clean p shall eat it alike .... Deut 15:22
reward to slay an innocent p .... Deut 27:25
shall not regard the p of the old ..... Deut 28:50
that killeth any p unawares .... Josh 20:3
that whosoever killeth any p .... Josh 20:9
of any p shall flee on the .... Josh 9:2
prudent in matters, and a comely p ... 1Sa 16:18
thy voice, and have accepted thy p 1Sa 25:35
men have slain a righteous p in 2Sa 4:11
neither doth God respect any p 2Sa 14:14
thou go to battle in thine own p 2Sa 17:11
Will ye accept his p .... Job 13:8
and he shall save the humble p .... Job 22:29
I pray you, accept any man's p .... Job 32:21
whose eyes a vile p is condemned ...... Ps 15:4
the fool and the brutish p perish .... Ps 49:10
I will not know a wicked p .... Ps 101:4
one feeble p among their tribes .... Ps 105:37
A naughty p, a wicked man .... Prov 6:12
to accept the p of the wicked .... Prov 18:5
be called a mischievous p .... Prov 24:8
of any p shall flee on the .... Prov 28:17
The vile p shall be no more .... Is 32:5
For the vile p will speak villany .... Is 32:6
every p that Nebuzar-adan the .... Jer 52:25
them that were near the king's p ...... Jer 52:25
field, to the lothing of thy p .... Eze 16:5

take any p from among them, he is... Eze 33:6
at no dead is to defile themselves .... Eze 44:25
estate shall stand up a vile p .... Dan 11:21
with thee, or accept thy p................. Mal 1:8
thou regardest not the p of men .... Mt 22:16
of the blood of this just p .... Mt 27:24
thou regardest not the p of men .... Mk 12:14
acceptest thou the p of any .... Lk 20:21
among yourselves that wicked p 1Cor 5:13
forgave I it in the p of Christ 2Cor 2:10
God accepteth no man's p .... Gal 2:6
no whoremonger, nor unclean p....... Eph 5:5
and the express image of his p .... Heb 1:3
be any fornicator, or profane p .... Heb 12:16
but saved Noah the eighth p 2Pet 2:5

PERSONS
said unto Abram, Give me the p .... Gen 14:21
all the p of his house, and his .... Gen 36:6
according to the number of your p ..... Ex 16:16
the p shall be for the LORD by .... Lev 27:2
upon the p that were there, and .... Num 19:18
of five hundred, both of the p .... Num 31:28
one portion of fifty, of the p .... Num 31:30
thirty and two thousand p in all ...... Num 31:35
the p were sixteen thousand .... Num 31:40
tribute was thirty and two p............ Num 31:40
And sixteen thousand p .... Num 31:46
shall not respect p in judgment .... Deut 1:17
a terrible, which regardeth not p ...... Deut 10:17
Egypt with threescore and ten p .... Deut 10:22
thou shalt not respect p, neither .... Deut 16:19
which are threescore and ten p .... Judg 9:2
Abimelech hired vain and light p ...... Judg 9:4
being threescore and ten p .... Judg 9:5
his sons, threescore and ten p .... Judg 9:18
the men of Israel about thirty p ...... Judg 20:39
bidden, which were about thirty p 1Sa 9:22
five p that did wear a linen 1Sa 22:18
all the p of thy father's house 1Sa 22:22
the king's sons, being seventy p 2Kin 10:6
king's sons, and slew seventy p 2Kin 10:7
LORD our God, nor respect of p 2Chr 19:7
you, if ye do secretly accept p .... Job 13:10
accepteth not the p of princes .... Job 34:19
I have not sat with vain p .... Ps 26:4
accept the p of the wicked .... Ps 82:2
vain p is void of understanding .... Prov 12:11
to have respect of p in judgment ...... Prov 24:23
have a great hurry enough .... Prov 28:21
To have respect of p is not good ...... Prov 28:21
eight hundred thirty and two p .... Jer 52:29
seven hundred forty and five p .... Jer 52:30
all the p were four thousand and ...... Jer 52:30
not the p of the priests, they .... Lam 4:16
building forts, to cut off many p .... Eze 17:17
they traded the p of men and .... Eze 27:13
p that cannot discern between .... Jonah 4:11
are light and treacherous p .... Zeph 3:4
will he regard your p .... Mal 1:9
than over ninety and nine just p .... Lk 15:7
that God is no respecter of p .... Acts 10:34
the Jews, and with the devout p....... Acts 17:17
there is no respect of p with God ..... Rom 2:11
upon us by the means of many p 2Cor 1:11
is there respect of p with him .... Eph 6:9
and there is no respect of p .... Col 3:25
for liars, for perjured p 1Ti 1:10
Lord of glory, with respect of p .... Jas 2:1
But if ye have respect to p .... Jas 2:9
who without respect of p judgeth 1Pet 1:17
what manner of p ought ye to be 2Pet 3:11
having men's p in admiration .... Jude 16

PERSUADE
the LORD said, Who shall p Ahab 1Kin 22:20
the LORD, and said, I will p him 1Kin 22:21
And he said, Thou shalt p him 1Kin 22:22
Doth not Hezekiah p you to give....... 2Chr 32:11
nor p you on this manner, neither 2Chr 32:15
Beware lest Hezekiah p you .... Is 36:18
governor's ears, we will p him .... Mt 28:14
the terror of the Lord, we p men 2Cor 5:11
For do I now p men, or God .... Gal 1:10

PERSUADED
p him to go up with him to 2Chr 18:2
By long forbearing is a prince p .... Prov 25:15
elders p the multitude that they .... Mt 27:20
prophets, neither will they be p .... Lk 16:31
for they be p that John was a .... Lk 20:6
p them to continue in the grace .... Acts 13:43
who p the people, and having........... Acts 14:19
and ·the Jews and the Greeks .... Acts 18:4
all Asia, this Paul hath p................. Acts 19:26
And when he would not be p .... Acts 21:14
for I am p that none of these .... Acts 26:26
And being fully p that, what he......... Rom 4:21
For I am p, that neither death .... Rom 8:38
man be fully p in his own mind........ Rom 14:5
am p by the Lord Jesus, that .... Rom 14:14
And I myself also am p of you .... Rom 15:14
and I am p that in thee also 2Ti 1:5
am p that he is able to keep that 2Ti 1:12
we are p better things of you, and ..... Heb 6:9
were p of them, and embraced them, . Heb 11:13

PERSUADEST
Paul, Almost thou p me to be a ...... Acts 26:28

PERSUADETH
not unto Hezekiah, when he p you...... 2Kin 18:32
This fellow p men to worship God .... Acts 18:13

PERSUADING
p the things concerning the .... Acts 19:8
p them concerning Jesus, both out ..... Acts 28:23

PERSUASION
This p cometh not of him that .... Gal 5:8

PERTAIN
that p unto the LORD, having his .... Lev 7:20
which p unto the LORD, even that .... Lev 7:21
if I leave of all that p to him 1Sa 25:22
in those things which p to God .... Rom 15:17
more things that p to this life 1Cor 6:3
us all things that p unto life 2Pet 1:3

PERTAINED
(Now the half that p unto the .... Num 31:43
a hill that p to Phinehas his son .... Josh 24:33
that p unto Joash the Abi-ezrite .... Judg 6:11
was missed of all that p unto him 1Sa 25:21
which p to Ish-bosheth the son of 2Sa 2:15
master's son all that p to Saul 2Sa 9:9
all that p unto Mephibosheth 2Sa 16:4
to him p Socoh, and all the land 1Kin 4:10
to him p Taanach and Megiddo, and .. 1Kin 4:12
to him p the towns of Jair the 1Kin 4:13
to him also p the region of Argob 1Kin 4:13
made all the vessels that p unto 1Kin 7:48
all that p to the king of Egypt 2Kin 24:7
thereof every morning p to them 1Chr 9:27
that p to the children of 1Chr 11:31
fenced cities which p to Judah 2Chr 12:4
that p to the children of Israel 2Chr 34:33

PERTAINETH
get that which p to his cleansing .... Lev 14:32
priest p the oil for the light .... Num 4:16
not wear that which p unto a man ...... Deut 22:5
wherefore Ziklag p unto the kings 1Sa 27:6
Obed-edom, and all that p unto him ... 2Sa 6:12
to whom p the adoption, and the .... Rom 9:4
are spoken p to another tribe .... Heb 7:13

PERTAINING
were p unto the children of .... Josh 13:31
for every matter p to God 1Chr 26:32
things p to the kingdom of God .... Acts 1:3
as p to the flesh, hath found .... Rom 4:1
of things p to this life, set 1Cor 6:4
high priest in things p to God .... Heb 2:17
for men in things p to God .... Heb 5:1
perfect, as p to the conscience .... Heb 9:9

PERUDA (per'-u-dah) See PERIDA. A family of exiles.
of Sophereth, the children of P .... Ezr 2:55

PERVERSE
because thy way is p before me .... Num 22:32
they are a p and crooked .... Deut 32:5
Thou son of the p rebellious 1Sa 20:30
cannot my taste discern p things .... Job 6:30
perfect, it shall also prove me p .... Job 9:20
and p lips put far from thee .... Prov 4:24
is nothing froward or p in them .... Prov 8:8
but he that is of a p heart shall .... Prov 12:8
but he that is p in his ways .... Prov 14:2
he that hath a p tongue falleth .... Prov 17:20
than he that is p in his lips .... Prov 19:1
thine heart shall utter p things .... Prov 23:33
than he that is p in his ways .... Prov 28:6
but he that is p in his ways .... Prov 28:18
The LORD hath mingled a p spirit .... Is 19:14
p generation, how long shall I be .... Mt 17:17
p generation, how long shall I .... Lk 9:41
men arise, speaking p things .... Acts 20:30
p nation, among whom ye shine as ..... Phil 2:15
P disputings of men of corrupt 1Ti 6:5

PERVERSELY
that which thy servant did p the 2Sa 19:19
We have sinned, and have done p 1Kin 8:47
for they dealt p with me without .... Ps 119:78

PERVERSENESS
neither hath he seen p in Israel .... Num 23:21
but the p of transgressors shall .... Prov 11:3
but p therein is a breach in the .... Prov 15:4
word, and trust in oppression and p ... Is 30:12
lies, your tongue hath muttered p .... Is 59:3
of blood, and the city full of p .... Eze 9:9

PERVERT
p the words of the righteous .... Deut 16:19
Thou shalt not p the judgment of ...... Deut 24:17
Doth God p judgment .... Job 8:3
or doth the Almighty p justice .... Job 8:3
will the Almighty p judgment .... Job 34:12
bosom to p the ways of judgment .... Prov 17:23
p the judgment of any of the .... Prov 31:5
abhor judgment, and p all equity .... Mic 3:9
wilt thou not cease to p the .... Acts 13:10
would p the gospel of Christ .... Gal 1:7

PERVERTED
and took bribes, and p judgment 1Sa 8:3
p that which was right, and it .... Job 33:27
and thy knowledge, it hath p thee ...... Is 47:10
for they have p their way .... Jer 3:21
for ye have p the words of the .... Jer 23:36

PERVERTETH
p the words of the righteous .... Ex 23:8
Cursed be he that p the judgment .... Deut 27:19
but he that p his ways shall be .... Prov 10:9
The foolishness of man p his way .... Prov 19:3

unto me, as one that p the people .... Lk 23:14

PERVERTING
violent p of judgment and justice .... Eccl 5:8
We found this fellow p the nation .... Lk 23:2

PESTILENCE
lest he fall upon us with p .... Ex 5:3
smite thee and thy people with p .... Ex 9:15
I will send the p among you .... Lev 26:25
I will smite them with the p .... Num 14:12
shall make the p cleave unto thee ...... Deut 28:21
be three days p in thy land 2Sa 24:13
So the LORD sent a p upon Israel 2Sa 24:15
in the land famine, if there be p 1Kin 8:37
the sword of the LORD, even the p 1Chr 21:12
So the LORD sent p upon Israel 1Chr 21:14
death in the land, if there be p 2Chr 6:28
or if I send p among my people 2Chr 7:13
us, as the sword, judgment, or p 2Chr 20:9
but gave their life over to the p .... Ps 78:50
the fowler, and from the noisome p ..... Ps 91:3
Nor for the p that walketh in .... Ps 91:6
and by the famine, and by the p .... Jer 14:12
they shall die of a great p .... Jer 21:6
are left in this city from the p .... Jer 21:7
and by the famine, and by the p .... Jer 21:9
the sword, the famine, and the p .... Jer 24:10
and with the famine, and with the p ... Jer 27:8
sword, by the famine, and by the p ..... Jer 27:13
of war, and of evil, and of p .... Jer 28:8
the sword, the famine, and the p .... Jer 29:17
with the famine, and with the p .... Jer 29:18
and of the famine, and of the p .... Jer 32:24
and by the famine, and by the p .... Jer 32:36
the LORD, to the sword, to the p .... Jer 34:17
sword, by the famine, and by the p ..... Jer 38:2
sword, by the famine, and by the p ..... Jer 42:17
sword, by the famine, and by the p ..... Jer 42:22
sword, by the famine, and by the p ..... Jer 44:13
part of thee shall die with the p .... Eze 5:12
and p and blood shall pass through ..... Eze 5:17
sword, by the famine, and by the p ..... Eze 6:11
is far off shall die of the p .... Eze 6:12
The sword is without, and the p .... Eze 7:15
famine and p shall devour him .... Eze 7:15
from the famine, and from the p .... Eze 12:16
Or if I send a p into that land .... Eze 14:19
and the noisome beast, and the p .... Eze 14:21
For I will send into her p .... Eze 28:23
in the caves shall die of the p .... Eze 33:27
I will plead against him with p .... Eze 38:22
the p after the manner of Egypt .... Amos 4:10
Before him went the p, and burning .... Hab 3:5

PESTILENCES
and there shall be famines, and p .... Mt 24:7
divers places, and famines, and p .... Lk 21:11

PESTILENT
we have found this man a p fellow ...... Acts 24:5

PESTLE
in a mortar among wheat with a p ...... Prov 27:22

PETER (pe'-tur) See CEPHAS, PETER'S, SIMON. A disciple of Jesus.
saw two brethren, Simon called P .... Mt 4:18
The first, Simon, who is called P .... Mt 10:2
P answered him and said, Lord, if ...... Mt 14:28
when P was come down out of the ...... Mt 14:29
Then answered P and said unto him, .. Mt 15:15
Simon P answered and said, Thou ...... Mt 16:16
also unto thee, That thou art P .... Mt 16:18
Then P took him, and began to .... Mt 16:22
But he turned, and said unto P .... Mt 16:23
And after six days taketh P .... Mt 17:1
Then answered P, and said unto .... Mt 17:4
received tribute money came to P .... Mt 17:24
P saith unto him, Of strangers .... Mt 17:26
Then came P to him, and said, Lord ... Mt 18:21
Then answered P and said unto him,.. Mt 19:27
P answered and said unto him, ... Mt 26:33
P said unto him, Though I should .... Mt 26:35
And he took with him P and the two... Mt 26:37
them asleep, and saith unto P .... Mt 26:40
But P followed him afar off unto .... Mt 26:58
Now P sat without in the palace .... Mt 26:69
they that stood by, and said to P .... Mt 26:73
P remembered the word of Jesus, ... Mt 26:75
And Simon he surnamed P .... Mk 3:16
no man to follow him, save P .... Mk 5:37
P answereth and saith unto him, ... Mk 8:29
P took him, and began to rebuke .... Mk 8:32
on his disciples, he rebuked P .... Mk 8:33
six days Jesus taketh with him P .... Mk 9:2
P answered and said to Jesus, ... Mk 9:5
Then P began to say unto him, Lo, ... Mk 10:28
P calling to remembrance saith .... Mk 11:21
Olives over against the temple, P .... Mk 13:3
But P said unto him, Although all ...... Mk 14:29
And he taketh with him P and James.. Mk 14:33
them sleeping, and saith unto P .... Mk 14:37
P followed him afar off, even .... Mk 14:54
as P was beneath in the palace, ... Mk 14:66
when she saw P warming himself, ... Mk 14:67
that stood by said again to P .... Mk 14:70
P called to mind the word that .... Mk 14:72
P that he goeth before you into .... Mk 16:7
When Simon P saw it, he fell down .... Lk 5:8
Simon, (whom he also named P .... Lk 6:14
When all denied, and they that .... Lk 8:45
suffered no man to go in, save P .... Lk 8:51

P answering said, The Christ of........... Lk 9:20
after these sayings, he took P.............. Lk 9:28
But P and they that were with him...... Lk 9:32
P said unto Jesus, Master, it is .... Lk 9:33
Then P said unto him, Lord, ... Lk 12:41
Then P said, Lo, we have left all .... Lk 18:28
And he sent P and John, saying, Go ... Lk 22:8
And he said, I tell thee, P .... Lk 22:34
And P followed afar off .... Lk 22:54
together, P sat down among them........ Lk 22:55
And P said, Man, I am not .... Lk 22:60
P said, Man, I know not what thou..... Lk 22:60
the Lord turned, and looked upon P .. Lk 22:61
P remembered the word of the Lord ... Lk 22:61
P went out, and wept bitterly.............. Lk 22:62
Then arose P, and ran unto the .... Lk 24:12
the city of Andrew and P..................... Jn 1:44
Then Simon P answered him, Lord,.... Jn 6:68
P then turned to Simon P .... Jn 13:6
P saith unto him, Lord, dost thou....... Jn 13:6
P saith unto him, Thou shalt .... Jn 13:8
Simon P saith unto him, Lord, not ..... Jn 13:9
Simon P therefore beckoned to him ... Jn 13:24
Simon P said unto him, Lord, ... Jn 13:36
P said unto him, Lord, why cannot ..... Jn 13:37
Then Simon P having a sword drew .... Jn 18:10
Then said Jesus unto P, Put up .... Jn 18:11
Simon P followed Jesus, and so did.... Jn 18:15
But P stood at the door without .... Jn 18:16
kept the door, and brought in P .... Jn 18:16
damsel that kept the door unto P .... Jn 18:17
P stood with them, and warmed......... Jn 18:18
And Simon P stood and warmed........ Jn 18:25
his kinsman whose ear P cut off......... Jn 18:26
P then denied again .... Jn 18:27
she runneth, and cometh to Simon P . Jn 20:2
P therefore went forth, and that .... Jn 20:3
the other disciple did outrun P .... Jn 20:4
Then cometh Simon P following him .. Jn 20:6
There were together Simon P .... Jn 21:2
Simon P saith unto them, I go a........ Jn 21:3
whom Jesus loved saith unto P .... Jn 21:7
Now when Simon P heard that it........ Jn 21:7
Simon P went up, and drew the net ... Jn 21:11
had dined, Jesus saith to Simon P ..... Jn 21:15
P was grieved because he said .... Jn 21:17
Then P, turning about, seeth the .... Jn 21:20
P seeing him saith to Jesus, Lord .... Jn 21:21
an upper room, where abode both P... Acts 1:13
in those days P stood up in the .... Acts 1:15
But P, standing up with the .... Acts 2:14
in their heart, and said unto P .... Acts 2:37
Then P said unto them, Repent, and .. Acts 2:38
Now P and John went up together...... Acts 3:1
Who seeing P and John about to go.... Acts 3:3
And P, fastening his eyes upon him.... Acts 3:4
Then P said, Silver and gold have ...... Acts 3:6
lame man which was healed held P .... Acts 3:11
when P saw it, he answered unto........ Acts 3:12
Then P, filled with the Holy .... Acts 4:8
when they saw the boldness of P........ Acts 4:13
But P and John answered and said .... Acts 4:19
But P said, Ananias, why hath........... Acts 5:3
P answered unto her, Tell me .... Acts 5:8
Then P said unto her, How is it .... Acts 5:9
of P passing by might overshadow ..... Acts 5:15
Then P and the other apostles............. Acts 5:29
of God, they sent unto them P .... Acts 8:14
But P said unto him, Thy money........ Acts 8:20
as P passed throughout all .... Acts 9:32
P said unto him, Aeneas, Jesus .... Acts 9:34
had heard that P was there .... Acts 9:38
Then P arose and went with them ...... Acts 9:39
But P put them all forth, and .... Acts 9:40
and when she saw P, she sat up .... Acts 9:40
for one Simon, whose surname is P .... Acts 10:5
P went up upon the housetop to......... Acts 10:9
came a voice to him, Rise, P .... Acts 10:13
But P said, Not so, Lord .... Acts 10:14
Now while P doubted in himself .... Acts 10:17
Simon, which was surnamed P .... Acts 10:18
While P thought on the vision, ... Acts 10:19
Then P went down to the .... Acts 10:21
on the morrow P went away with .... Acts 10:23
as P was coming in, Cornelius met .... Acts 10:25
But P took him up, saying, Stand ...... Acts 10:26
hither Simon, whose surname is P ..... Acts 10:32
Then P opened his mouth, and said,.. Acts 10:34
While P yet spake these words, ... Acts 10:44
as many as came with P, because ...... Acts 10:45
Then answered P .... Acts 10:46
when P was come up to Jerusalem, ... Acts 11:2
But P rehearsed the matter from .... Acts 11:4
a voice saying unto me, Arise, P .... Acts 11:7
for Simon, whose surname is P .... Acts 11:13
proceeded further to take P also .... Acts 12:3
P therefore was kept in prison .... Acts 12:5
the same night P was sleeping .... Acts 12:6
he smote P on the side, and raised .... Acts 12:7
when P was come to himself, he .... Acts 12:11
as P knocked at the door of the .... Acts 12:13
told how P stood before the gate .... Acts 12:14
But P continued knocking .... Acts 12:16
soldiers, what was become of P .... Acts 12:18
P rose up, and said unto them, Men... Acts 15:7
I went up to Jerusalem to see P .... Gal 1:18
of the circumcision was unto P .... Gal 2:7
in P to the apostleship of the .... Gal 2:8
But when P was come to Antioch, I..... Gal 2:11
I said unto P before them all, If.......... Gal 2:14

P

P, an apostle of Jesus Christ, to 1Pet 1:1
Simon P, a servant and an apostle 2Pet 1:1

PETER'S (pe'-turz)
when Jesus was come into P house ...... Mt 8:14
him, was Andrew, Simon P brother ...... Jn 1:40
Simon P brother, saith unto him, ... Jn 6:8
And when she knew P voice, she .... Acts 12:14

PETHAHIAH (peth-a-hi'-ah)
1. A temporary servant.
The nineteenth to P, the 1Chr 24:16
2. Married a foreigner.
Kelaiah, (the same is Kelita,) P .... Ezr 10:23
3. A Levite who helped Ezra.
Hodijah, Shebaniah, and P .... Neh 9:5
4. An aide to Nehemiah.
P the son of Meshezabeel, of the ...... Neh 11:24

PETHOR (pe'-thor) A city in Mesopotamia.
unto Balaam the son of Beor to P .... Num 22:5
son of Beor of P of Mesopotamia ...... Deut 23:4

PETHUEL Father of Joel the prophet.
that came to Joel the son of P .... Joel 1:1

PETITION
thy p that thou hast asked of him 1Sa 1:17
me my p which I asked of him 1Sa 1:27
And now I ask one p of thee 1Kin 2:16
I desire one small p of thee 1Kin 2:20
banquet of wine, What is thy p .... Est 5:6
answered Esther, and said, My p .... Est 5:7
it please the king to grant my p .... Est 5:8
banquet of wine, What is thy p .... Est 7:2
let my life be given me at my p .... Est 7:3
now what is thy p .... Est 9:12
that whosoever shall ask a p of .... Dan 6:7
p of any God or man within thirty ...... Dan 6:12
but maketh his p three times a .... Dan 6:13

PETITIONS
the Lord fulfil all thy p .... Ps 20:5
have the p that we desired of him 1Jn 5:15

PEULLETHAI See PEULTHAI.

PEULTHAI (pe-ul'-thahee) A sanctuary
servant.
the seventh, P the eighth 1Chr 26:5

PHALEC (fa'-lek) See PELEG. Father of Ragau;
ancestor of Jesus.
of Ragau, which was the son of P .... Lk 3:35

PHALLU (fal'-lu) Son of Reuben.
Hanoch, and P, and Hezron .... Gen 46:9

PHALTI (fal'-ti) See PHALTIEL. Son of Laish.
to P the son of Laish, which was 1Sa 25:44

PHALTIEL (fal'-te-el) See PHALTI. Same as
Phalti.
even from P the son of Laish to 2Sa 3:15

PHANUEL (fan-u'-el) Mother of Anna.
a prophetess, the daughter of P......... Lk 2:36

PHARAOH (fa'-ra-o) See PHARAOH'S, PHARAOH-
HOPHRA, PHARAOH-NECHO.
1. Ruler of Egypt in Abraham's time.
The princes also of P saw her .... Gen 12:15
and commended her before P .... Gen 12:15
And the LORD plagued P and his ...... Gen 12:17
P called Abram, and said, What is ...... Gen 12:18
P commanded his men concerning ..... Gen 12:20
2. Ruler of Egypt in Joseph's time.
and Potiphar, an officer of P .... Gen 39:1
P was wroth against two of his .... Gen 40:2
days shall P lift up thine head .... Gen 40:13
me, and make mention me unto P ..... Gen 40:14
of all manner of bakemeats for P ...... Gen 40:17
Yet within three days shall P .... Gen 40:19
of two full years, that P dreamed ...... Gen 41:1
So P awoke .... Gen 41:4
P awoke, and, behold, it was a .... Gen 41:7
and P told them his dream .... Gen 41:8
that could interpret them unto P ...... Gen 41:8
spake the chief butler unto P .... Gen 41:9
P was wroth with his servants, and ... Gen 41:10
Then P sent and called Joseph, and ... Gen 41:14
his raiment, and came in unto P .... Gen 41:14
P said unto Joseph, I have .... Gen 41:15
And Joseph answered P, saying, It .... Gen 41:16
God shall give P an answer of .... Gen 41:16
P said unto Joseph, In my dream, ... Gen 41:17
And Joseph said unto P .... Gen 41:25
The dream of P is one .... Gen 41:25
God hath shewed P what he is .... Gen 41:25
thing which I have spoken unto P ..... Gen 41:28
is about to do he sheweth unto P ..... Gen 41:28
dream was doubled unto P twice ...... Gen 41:32
Now therefore let P look out a .... Gen 41:33
Let P do this, and let him appoint ..... Gen 41:34
lay up corn under the hand of P .... Gen 41:35
thing was good in the eyes of P .... Gen 41:37
P said unto his servants, Can we ...... Gen 41:38
P said unto Joseph, Forasmuch as .... Gen 41:39
P said unto Joseph, See, I have .... Gen 41:41
P took off his ring from his hand ...... Gen 41:42
P said unto Joseph, I am Pharaoh, ... Gen 41:44
And P called Joseph's name .... Gen 41:45
he stood before P king of Egypt .... Gen 41:46
went out from the presence of P ...... Gen 41:46
the people cried to P for bread .... Gen 41:55
P said unto all the Egyptians, Go ...... Gen 41:55
By the life of P shall not go .... Gen 42:15

the life of P surely ye are spies, ... Gen 42:16
for thou art even as P .... Gen 44:18
Egyptians and the house of P heard ... Gen 45:2
and hath made me a father to P .... Gen 45:8
and it pleased P well, and his .... Gen 45:16
P said unto Joseph, Say unto thy ...... Gen 45:17
according to the commandment of P .. Gen 45:21
in the wagons which P had sent to .... Gen 45:65
house, I will go up, and shew P .... Gen 46:31
when P shall call you, and shall .... Gen 46:33
Then Joseph came and told P .... Gen 47:1
men, and presented them unto P ...... Gen 47:2
P said unto his brethren, What is ...... Gen 47:3
And they said unto P, Thy servants ... Gen 47:3
They said moreover unto P .... Gen 47:4
P spake unto Joseph, saying, Thy ..... Gen 47:5
his father, and set him before P .... Gen 47:7
and Jacob blessed P .... Gen 47:7
P said unto Jacob, How old art .... Gen 47:8
And Jacob said unto P, The days of ... Gen 47:9
And Jacob blessed P .... Gen 47:10
and went out from before P .... Gen 47:10
of Rameses, as P had commanded .... Gen 47:11
our land will be servants unto P .... Gen 47:19
all the land of Egypt for P .... Gen 47:20
had a portion assigned them of P ..... Gen 47:22
their portion which P gave them ...... Gen 47:22
you this day and your land for P .... Gen 47:23
shall give the fifth part unto P .... Gen 47:24
that P should have the fifth part ...... Gen 47:26
Joseph spake unto the house of P .... Gen 50:4
I pray you, in the ears of P .... Gen 50:4
P said, Go up, and bury thy father, ... Gen 50:6
him went up all the servants of P ..... Gen 50:7
in the sight of P king of Egypt. .... Acts 7:10
kindred was made known unto P ...... Acts 7:13
3. Ruler of Egypt during Moses' infancy.
they built for P treasure cities, ... Ex 1:11
And the midwives said unto P .... Ex 1:19
P charged all his people, saying, ... Ex 1:22
the daughter of P came down to ...... Ex 2:5
4. Ruler of Egypt during Moses' adulthood.
Now when P heard this thing, he ..... Ex 2:15
But Moses fled from the face of P .... Ex 2:15
5. Ruler of Egypt when Moses returned to
Egypt.
and I will send thee unto P .... Ex 3:10
Who am I, that I should go unto P .... Ex 3:11
do all those wonders before P .... Ex 4:21
And thou shalt say unto P, Thus ...... Ex 4:22
Moses and Aaron went in, and told P . Ex 5:1
P said, Who is the LORD, that I .... Ex 5:2
P said, Behold, the people of the ...... Ex 5:5
P commanded the same day the ...... Ex 5:6
the people, saying, Thus saith P ...... Ex 5:10
of Israel came and cried unto P .... Ex 5:15
way, as they came forth from P .... Ex 5:20
to be abhorred in the eyes of P .... Ex 5:21
For since I came to P to speak in ...... Ex 5:23
thou see what I will do to P .... Ex 6:1
speak unto P king of Egypt, that ...... Ex 6:11
how then shall P hear me, who am ... Ex 6:12
unto P king of Egypt, to bring .... Ex 6:13
which spake to P king of Egypt .... Ex 6:27
speak thou unto P king of Egypt ...... Ex 6:29
how shall P hearken unto me .... Ex 6:30
See, I have made thee a god to P ...... Ex 7:1
thy brother shall speak unto P .... Ex 7:2
But P shall not hearken unto you, ... Ex 7:4
When P shall speak unto you, ... Ex 7:9
Take thy rod, and cast it before P ..... Ex 7:9
And Moses and Aaron went in unto P . Ex 7:10
Aaron cast down his rod before P ..... Ex 7:10
Then P also called the wise men ...... Ex 7:11
Get thee unto P in the morning .... Ex 7:15
in the river, in the sight of P .... Ex 7:23
P turned and went into his house, ... Ex 7:23
LORD spake unto Moses, Go unto P .. Ex 8:1
Then P called for Moses and Aaron, .. Ex 8:8
And Moses said unto P, Glory over ... Ex 8:9
And Moses and Aaron went out from P . Ex 8:12
which he had brought against P .... Ex 8:12
But when P saw that there was .... Ex 8:15
Then the magicians said unto P .... Ex 8:19
in the morning, and stand before P ... Ex 8:20
of flies into the house of P .... Ex 8:24
P called for Moses and for Aaron, ... Ex 8:25
P said, I will let you go, that .... Ex 8:28
swarms of flies may depart from P ... Ex 8:29
but let not P deal deceitfully .... Ex 8:29
And Moses went out from P, and ...... Ex 8:30
the swarms of flies from P .... Ex 8:31
P hardened his heart at this time ..... Ex 8:32
said unto Moses, Go in unto P .... Ex 9:1
P sent, and, behold, there was not ... Ex 9:7
And the heart of P was hardened ..... Ex 9:7
the heaven in the sight of P .... Ex 9:8
of the furnace, and stood before P ... Ex 9:10
the LORD hardened the heart of P .... Ex 9:12
in the morning, and stand before P ... Ex 9:13
servants of P made his servants ...... Ex 9:20
P sent, and called for Moses and ..... Ex 9:27
Moses went out of the city from P ... Ex 9:33
when P saw that the rain and the ..... Ex 9:34
And the heart of P was hardened ..... Ex 9:35
said unto Moses, Go in unto P .... Ex 10:1
And Moses and Aaron came in unto P . Ex 10:3
himself, and went out from P .... Ex 10:6
Aaron were brought again unto P ..... Ex 10:8

Then P called for Moses and Aaron ... Ex 10:16
And he went out from P, and .... Ex 10:18
P called unto Moses, and said, Go .... Ex 10:24
P said unto him, Get thee from me ... Ex 10:28
I bring one plague more upon P .... Ex 11:1
from the firstborn of P that .... Ex 11:5
went out from P in a great anger ..... Ex 11:8
P shall not hearken unto you, ... Ex 11:9
did all these wonders before P .... Ex 11:10
from the firstborn of P that sat .... Ex 12:29
P rose up in the night, he, and .... Ex 12:30
when P would hardly let us go, ... Ex 13:15
when P had let the people go, ... Ex 13:17
For P will say of the children of .... Ex 14:3
and I will be honoured upon P .... Ex 14:4
and the heart of P and of his .... Ex 14:5
the heart of P king of Egypt .... Ex 14:8
all the horses and chariots of P .... Ex 14:9
when P drew nigh, the children of .... Ex 14:10
and I will get me honour upon P ...... Ex 14:17
I have gotten me honour upon P ...... Ex 14:18
all the host of P that came into ...... Ex 14:28
For the horse of P went in with ...... Ex 15:19
delivered me from the sword of P .... Ex 18:4
all that the LORD had done unto P ... Ex 18:8
and out of the hand of P, who .... Ex 18:10
great and sore, upon Egypt, upon P .. Deut 6:22
from the hand of P king of Egypt... ... Deut 7:8
what the LORD thy God did unto P ... Deut 7:18
of Egypt unto P the king of Egypt ... Deut 11:3
eyes in the land of Egypt unto P ...... Deut 29:2
to do in the land of Egypt to P .... Deut 34:11
and P hardened their hearts 1Sa 6:6
under the hand of P king of Egypt ... 2Kin 17:7
shewedst signs and wonders upon P . Neh 9:10
midst of thee, O Egypt, upon P .... Ps 135:9
But overthrew P and his host in ...... Ps 136:15
For the scripture saith unto P .... Rom 9:17
6. Ruler of Egypt in Solomon's time.
affinity with P king of Egypt 1Kin 3:1
For P king of Egypt had gone up, ... 1Kin 9:16
together with the daughter of P 1Kin 11:1
to Egypt, unto P king of Egypt 1Kin 11:18
great favour in the sight of P 1Kin 11:19
household among the sons of P 1Kin 11:20
host was dead, Hadad said to P 1Kin 11:21
Then P said unto him, But what 1Kin 11:22
brought up the daughter of P out 2Chr 8:11
7. Ruler of Egypt in Isaiah's time.
of P is become brutish: .... Is 19:11
how say ye unto P, I am the son ...... Is 19:11
themselves in the strength of P ...... Is 30:2
the strength of P be your shame ..... Is 30:3
so is P king of Egypt to all that ...... Is 36:6
8. Ruler of Egypt in Jeremiah's time.
so is P king of Egypt unto all. 2Kin 18:21
gave the silver and the gold to P 2Kin 23:35
according to the commandment of P . 2Kin 23:35
sons of Bithiah the daughter of P 1Chr 4:18
P king of Egypt, and his servants, ... Jer 25:19
P king of Egypt is but a noise; .... Jer 46:17
punish the multitude of No, and P .... Jer 46:25
even P, and all them that trust in ..... Jer 46:25
before that P smote Gaza .... Jer 47:1
Neither shall P with his mighty .... Eze 17:17
thy face against P king of Egypt ...... Eze 29:2
P king of Egypt, the great dragon ... Eze 29:3
broken the arm of P king of Egypt ... Eze 30:21
I am against P king of Egypt, and .... Eze 30:22
the arms of P shall fall down. .... Eze 30:25
speak unto P king of Egypt, and to ... Eze 31:2
This is P and all his multitude, ... Eze 31:18
a lamentation for P king of Egypt .... Eze 32:2
P shall see them, and shall be .... Eze 32:31
over all his multitude, even P .... Eze 32:31
are slain with the sword, even P ...... Eze 32:32

PHARAOH-HOPHRA (fa''-ra-o-hof'-rah)
Same as Pharaoh 8.
I will give P king of Egypt into .... Jer 44:30

PHARAOH-NECHO (fa''-ra-o-ne'-ko) See
PHARAOH-NECHOH. Egyptian ruler during
Josiah's time.
the army of P king of Egypt............ Jer 46:2

PHARAOH-NECHOH (fa''-ra-o-ne'-ko) See
PHARAOH-NECHO. Same as Pharaoh-necho.
In his days P king of Egypt went..... 2Kin 23:29
P put him in bands at Riblah in....... 2Kin 23:33
P made Eliakim the son of Josiah 2Kin 23:34
his taxation, to give it unto P 2Kin 23:35

PHARAOH'S (fa'-ra-oze)
the woman was taken into P house... Gen 12:15
unto Potiphar, an officer of P .... Gen 37:36
he asked P officers that were .... Gen 40:7
And P cup was in my hand.............. Gen 40:11
and pressed them into P cup .... Gen 40:11
and I gave the cup into P hand .... Gen 40:11
shalt deliver P cup into his hand ..... Gen 40:13
third day, which was P birthday ...... Gen 40:20
and he gave the cup into P hand ..... Gen 40:21
fame thereof was heard in P house... Gen 45:16
brought the money into P house ..... Gen 47:14
so the land became P .... Gen 47:20
my lord, and we will be P servants ... Gen 47:25
priests only, which became not P ..... Gen 47:26
said his sister to P daughter .... Ex 2:7
P daughter said to her, Go .... Ex 2:8
P daughter said unto her, Take .... Ex 2:9
she brought him unto P daughter..... Ex 2:10

PHARES

which P taskmasters had set over	Ex 5:14
And I will harden P heart, and	Ex 7:3
And he hardened P heart, that he	Ex 7:13
P heart is hardened, he refuseth	Ex 7:14
P heart was hardened, neither did	Ex 7:22
P heart was hardened, and he	Ex 8:19
P servants said unto him, How	Ex 10:7
were driven out from P presence	Ex 10:11
But the LORD hardened P heart	Ex 10:20
But the LORD hardened P heart	Ex 10:27
Egypt, in the sight of P servants	Ex 11:3
and the LORD hardened P heart	Ex 11:10
And I will harden P heart, that he	Ex 14:4
of the sea, even all P horses	Ex 14:23
P chariots and his host hath he	Ex 15:4
We were P bondmen in Egypt	Deut 6:21
they were in Egypt in P house	1Sa 2:27
took P daughter, and brought her	1Kin 3:1
made also an house for P daughter	1Kin 7:8
But P daughter came up out of the	1Kin 9:24
whom Tahpenes weaned in P house..	1Kin 11:20
was in P household among	1Kin 11:20
a company of horses in P chariots	Song 1:9
Then P army was come forth out of	Jer 37:5
P army, which is come forth to	Jer 37:7
from Jerusalem for fear of P army	Jer 37:11
the entry of P house in Tahpanhes	Jer 43:9
but I will break P arms, and he	Eze 30:24
P daughter took him up, and	Acts 7:21
be called the son of P daughter	Heb 11:24

PHARES (fa´-rez) See PHAREZ. Same as Pharez.

And Judas begat P and Zara of	Mt 1:3
and P begat Esrom	Mt 1:3
of Esrom, which was the son of P	Lk 3:33

PHAREZ (fa´-rez) See PEREZ, PHARES, PHARZITES. A son of Judah.

twofold his name was called P	Gen 38:29
Er, and Onan, and Shelah, and P	Gen 46:12
And the sons of P were Hezron	Gen 46:12
of P, the family of the Pharzites	Num 26:20
And the sons of P were	Num 26:21
thy house be like the house of P	Ruth 4:12
these are the generations of P	Ruth 4:18
P begat Hezron,	Ruth 4:18
his daughter in law bare him P	1Chr 2:4
The sons of P	1Chr 2:5
P, Hezron, and Carmi, and Hur, and	1Chr 4:1
children of P the son of Judah	1Chr 9:4

PHARISAIC See PHARISEES.

PHARISEE (far´-i-see) See PHARISEE'S, PHARISAICS. A member of a Jewish sect.

Thou blind P, cleanse first that	Mt 23:26
Now when the P which had bidden	Lk 7:39
a certain P besought him to dine	Lk 11:37
And when the P saw it, he	Lk 11:38
the one a P, and the other a	Lk 18:10
The P stood and prayed thus with	Lk 18:11
there up one in the council, a P	Acts 5:34
I am a P, the son of a P	Acts 23:6
sect of our religion I lived a P	Acts 26:5
as touching the law, a P	Phil 3:5

PHARISEE'S (far´-i-seez)

And he went into the P house	Lk 7:36
Jesus sat at meat in the P house	Lk 7:37

PHARISEES (far´-i-seze) See PHARISEES'. A Jewish sect.

But when he saw many of the P	Mt 3:7
righteousness of the scribes and P	Mt 5:20
And when the P saw it, they said	Mt 9:11
the P fast oft, but thy disciples	Mt 9:14
But the P said, He casteth out	Mt 9:34
But when the P saw it, they said	Mt 12:2
Then the P went out, and held a	Mt 12:14
But when the P heard it, they	Mt 12:24
of the P answered, saying, Master	Mt 12:38
Then came to Jesus scribes and P	Mt 15:1
thou that the P were offended	Mt 15:12
The P also with the Sadducees	Mt 16:1
and beware of the leaven of the P	Mt 16:6
beware of the leaven of the P	Mt 16:11
but of the doctrine of the P	Mt 16:12
The P also came unto him,	Mt 19:3
P had heard his parables, they	Mt 21:45
Then went the P, and took counsel	Mt 22:15
But when the P had heard that he	Mt 22:34
While the P were gathered,	Mt 22:41
and the P sit in Moses' seat	Mt 23:2
But woe unto you, scribes and P	Mt 23:13
Woe unto you, scribes and P	Mt 23:14
Woe unto you, scribes and P	Mt 23:15
Woe unto you, scribes and P	Mt 23:23
Woe unto you, scribes and P	Mt 23:25
Woe unto you, scribes and P	Mt 23:27
Woe unto you, scribes and P	Mt 23:29
P came together unto Pilate,	Mt 27:62
P saw him eat with publicans and	Mk 2:16
of John and of the P used to fast	Mk 2:18
of John and of the P fast, but thy	Mk 2:18
the P said unto him, Behold, why	Mk 2:24
the P went forth, and straightway	Mk 3:6
Then came together unto him the P	Mk 7:1
For the P, and all the Jews,	Mk 7:3
Then the P and scribes asked him,	Mk 7:5
the P came forth, and began to	Mk 8:11
beware of the leaven of the P	Mk 8:15
the P came to him, and asked him,	Mk 10:2

send unto him certain of the P	Mk 12:13
was teaching, that there were P	Lk 5:17
The P began to reason, saying,	Lk 5:21
P murmured against his disciples,	Lk 5:30
likewise the disciples of the P	Lk 5:33
certain of the P said unto them	Lk 6:2
P watched him, whether he would	Lk 6:7
But the P and lawyers rejected the	Lk 7:30
one of the P desired him that he	Lk 7:36
Now do ye P make clean the	Lk 11:39
But woe unto you, P	Lk 11:42
Woe unto you, P	Lk 11:43
Woe unto you, scribes and P	Lk 11:44
and the P began to urge him	Lk 11:53
Beware ye of the leaven of the P	Lk 12:1
day there came certain of the P	Lk 13:31
the house of one of the chief P	Lk 14:1
spake unto the lawyers and P	Lk 14:3
And the P and scribes murmured,	Lk 15:2
the P also, who were covetous,	Lk 16:14
And when he was demanded of the P..	Lk 17:20
some of the P from among the	Lk 19:39
which were sent were of the P	Jn 1:24
There was a man of the P, named	Jn 3:1
the P had heard that Jesus made	Jn 4:1
The P heard that the people	Jn 7:32
and the P and the chief priests	Jn 7:32
to the chief priests and P	Jn 7:45
Then answered them the P, Are ye	Jn 7:47
or of the P believed on him	Jn 7:48
P brought unto him a woman taken	Jn 8:3
The P therefore said unto him,	Jn 8:13
The P therefore said unto him,	Jn 9:13
Then again the P also asked him	Jn 9:15
Therefore said some of the P	Jn 9:16
some of the P which were with him	Jn 9:40
of them went their ways to the P	Jn 11:46
the P a council, and said, What do	Jn 11:47
the P had given a commandment,	Jn 11:57
The P therefore said among	Jn 12:19
but because of the P they did not	Jn 12:42
from the chief priests and P	Jn 18:3
the sect of the P which believed	Acts 15:5
were Sadducees, and the other P	Acts 23:6
arose a dissension between the P	Acts 23:7
but the P confess both	Acts 23:8

PHARISEES' (far´-i-seez)

that were of the P part arose	Acts 23:9

PHAROSH (fa´-rosh) A family of exiles.

of Shechaniah, of the sons of P	Ezr 8:3

PHARPAR (far´-par) A river near Damascus.

Are not Abana and P, rivers of	2Kin 5:12

PHARZITES (far´-zites) Descendants of Pharez.

of Pharez, the family of the P	Num 26:20

PHASEAH (fa-se´-ah) See PASEAH. A family of exiles.

of Uzza, the children of P	Neh 7:51

PHEBE (fe´-be) A Christian acquaintance of Paul.

I commend unto you P our sister	Rom 16:1
sent by P servant of the church	Rom s

PHENICE (fe-ni´-se) See PHENICIA.

1. Same as Phenicia.

Stephen travelled as far as P	Acts 11:19
the church, they passed through P	Acts 15:3

2. A harbor on Crete.

any means they might attain to P	Acts 27:12

PHENICIA (fe-nish´-e-ah) See PHENICE. Coastal region of northern Palestine.

a ship sailing over unto P	Acts 21:2

PHICHOL The commander of Abimelech's army.

P the chief captain of his host	Gen 21:22
P the chief captain of his host,	Gen 21:32
P the chief captain of his army	Gen 26:26

PHICOL (fi´-col) See PHICHOL. A Philistine commander.

PHILADELPHIA (fil-a-del´-fe-ah) A city in Lydia in Asia Minor.

unto Sardis, and unto P	Rev 1:11
angel of the church in P write	Rev 3:7

PHILEMON (fi-le´-mon) A recipient of a New Testament epistle.

unto P our dearly beloved, and	Philem 1
Written from Rome to P, by	Philem s

PHILETUS (fi-le´tus) A false Christian teacher.

of whom is Hymenaeus and P	2Ti 2:17

PHILIP (fil´-ip) See PHILIP'S.

1. An apostle.

P, and Bartholomew,	Mt 10:3
And Andrew, and P, and Bartholomew,	Mk 3:18
his brother, James and John, P	Lk 6:14
forth into Galilee, and findeth P	Jn 1:43
Now P was of Bethsaida, the city	Jn 1:44
P findeth Nathanael, and saith	Jn 1:45
P saith unto him, Come and see	Jn 1:46
him, Before that P called thee	Jn 1:48
come unto him, he saith unto P	Jn 6:5
P answered him, Two hundred	Jn 6:7
The same came therefore to P	Jn 12:21
P cometh and telleth Andrew	Jn 12:22
and again Andrew and P tell Jesus	Jn 12:22

P saith unto him, Lord, shew us	Jn 14:8
and yet hast thou not known me by	Jn 14:9
and James, and John, and Andrew, P	Acts 1:13

2. A son of Herod the Great.

his brother P tetrarch of Ituraea	Lk 3:1

3. The evangelist.

faith and of the Holy Ghost, and P	Acts 6:5
Then P went down to the city of	Acts 8:5
unto those things which P spake	Acts 8:6
But when they believed P	Acts 8:12
was baptized, he continued with P	Acts 8:13
angel of the Lord spake unto P	Acts 8:26
Then the Spirit said unto P	Acts 8:29
P ran thither to him, and heard	Acts 8:30
he desired P that he would come	Acts 8:31
And the eunuch answered P, and said	Acts 8:34
Then P opened his mouth, and began	Acts 8:35
P said, If thou believest with	Acts 8:37
down both into the water, both P	Acts 8:38
Spirit of the Lord caught away P	Acts 8:39
But P was found at Azotus	Acts 8:40
the house of P the evangelist	Acts 21:8

PHILIPPI (fil-ip´-pi) See PHILIPPIANS.

1. A town in northern Palestine.

into the coasts of Caesarea P	Mt 16:13
into the towns of Caesarea P	Mk 8:27

2. A Macedonian city.

And from thence to P, which is the ..	Acts 16:12
we sailed away from P after the	Acts 20:6
was written from P by Stephanus	1Cor s
Corinthians was written from P	2Cor s
in Christ Jesus which are at P	Phil 1:1
entreated, as ye know, at P	1Th 2:2

PHILIPPIANS (fil-ip´-pe-uns) Residents of Philippi 2.

Now ye P know also, that in the	Phil 4:15
It was written to the P from Rome	Phil s

PHILIP'S (fil´-ips) Refers to Philip 2.

sake, his brother P wife	Mt 14:3
sake, his brother P wife	Mk 6:17
for Herodias his brother P wife	Lk 3:19

PHILISTIA (fi-lis´-te-ah) See PALESTINE, PHILISTINE. Land of the Philistines.

P, triumph thou because of me	Ps 60:8
behold P, and Tyre, with Ethiopia	Ps 87:4
over P will I triumph	Ps 108:9

PHILISTIM (fi-lis´-tim) See PHILISTINES. Descendents of Casluhim.

and Casluhim, (out of whom came P.	Gen 10:14

PHILISTINE (fi-lis´-tin) See PHILISTINES. An inhabitant of Philistia.

am not I a P, and ye servants to	1Sa 17:8
the P said, I defy the armies of	1Sa 17:10
Israel heard those words of the P	1Sa 17:11
the P drew near morning and	1Sa 17:16
the P of Gath, Goliath by name,	1Sa 17:23
to the man that killeth this P	1Sa 17:26
for who is this uncircumcised P	1Sa 17:26
in Christ Jesus which are at P	1Sa 17:32
against this P to fight with him	1Sa 17:33
this uncircumcised P shall be as	1Sa 17:36
me out of the hand of this P	1Sa 17:37
and he drew near to the P	1Sa 17:40
the P came on and drew near unto	1Sa 17:41
when the P looked about, and saw	1Sa 17:42
the P said unto David, Am I a dog	1Sa 17:43
the P cursed David by his gods	1Sa 17:43
the P said to David, Come to me,	1Sa 17:44
Then said David to the P, Thou	1Sa 17:45
it came to pass, when the P arose	1Sa 17:48
ran toward the army to meet the P	1Sa 17:48
smote the P in his forehead, that	1Sa 17:49
prevailed over the P with a sling	1Sa 17:50
and with a stone, and smote the P	1Sa 17:50
David ran, and stood upon the P	1Sa 17:51
And David took the head of the P	1Sa 17:54
saw David go forth against the P	1Sa 17:55
from the slaughter of the P	1Sa 17:57
the head of the P in his hand	1Sa 17:57
from the slaughter of the P	1Sa 18:6
life in his hand, and slew the P	1Sa 19:5
said, The sword of Goliath the P	1Sa 21:9
him the sword of Goliath the P	1Sa 22:10
succoured him, and smote the P	2Sa 21:17

PHILISTINES (fil-is´-tinz) See PHILISTIM, PHILISTINES'.

returned into the land of the P	Gen 21:32
king of the P unto Gerar	Gen 26:1
the P of looked out at a window	Gen 26:8
and the P envied him	Gen 26:14
the P had stopped them, and filled	Gen 26:15
for the P had stopped them after	Gen 26:18
the way of the land of the P	Ex 13:17
sea even unto the sea of the P	Ex 23:31
all the borders of the P, and all	Josh 13:2
five lords of the P	Josh 13:3
Namely, five lords of the P	Judg 3:3
which slew of the P six hundred	Judg 3:31
of Ammon, and the gods of the P	Judg 10:6
sold them into the hands of the P	Judg 10:7
children of Ammon, and from the P..	Judg 10:11
the hand of the P forty years	Judg 13:1
Israel out of the hand of the P	Judg 13:5
Timnath the daughters of the P	Judg 14:1
Timnath of the daughters of the P	Judg 14:2
a wife of the uncircumcised P	Judg 14:3

P

sought an occasion against the *P*........ Judg 14:4
for at that time the *P* had .... Judg 14:4
I be more blameless than the *P*........... Judg 15:3
into the standing corn of the *P*............ Judg 15:5
Then the *P* said, Who hath done........... Judg 15:6
the *P* came up, and burnt her and........ Judg 15:6
Then the *P* went up, and pitched in...... Judg 15:9
not that the *P* are rulers over us.......... Judg 15:11
thee into the hand of the *P*................ Judg 15:12
the *P* shouted against him .... Judg 15:14
in the days of the *P* twenty years .... Judg 15:20
lords of the *P* came up unto her .... Judg 16:5
Then the lords of the *P* brought .... Judg 16:8
The *P* be upon thee, Samson............. Judg 16:9
The *P* be upon thee, Samson............. Judg 16:12
The *P* be upon thee, Samson............. Judg 16:14
and called for the lords of the *P*.......... Judg 16:18
lords of the *P* came up unto her .... Judg 16:18
The *P* be upon thee, Samson............. Judg 16:20
But the *P* took him, and put out .... Judg 16:21
Then the lords of the *P* gathered .... Judg 16:23
all the lords of the *P* were there .... Judg 16:27
avenged of the *P* for my two eyes .... Judg 16:28
said, Let me die with the *P*................ Judg 16:30
went out against the *P* to battle........... 1Sa 4:1
and the *P* pitched in Aphek 1Sa 4:1
the *P* put themselves in array 1Sa 4:2
Israel was smitten before the *P* 1Sa 4:2
smitten us to day before the *P*............ 1Sa 4:3
when the *P* heard the noise of the........ 1Sa 4:6
the *P* were afraid, for they said,.......... 1Sa 4:7
quit yourselves like men, O ye *P*.......... 1Sa 4:9
the *P* fought, and Israel was.............. 1Sa 4:10
said, Israel is fled before the *P*............ 1Sa 4:17
the *P* took the ark of God, and........... 1Sa 5:1
When the *P* took the ark of God.......... 1Sa 5:2
all the lords of the *P* unto them 1Sa 5:8
together all the lords of the *P*............. 1Sa 5:11
the country of the *P* seven months........ 1Sa 6:1
the *P* called for the priests and........... 1Sa 6:2
the number of the lords of the *P* 1Sa 6:4
for the *P* had seen it........................ 1Sa 6:16
five lords of the *P* had seen it............. 1Sa 6:16
the *P* returned for a trespass 1Sa 6:17
the *P* belonging to the five lords 1Sa 6:18
The *P* have brought again the ark........ 1Sa 6:21
you out of the hand of the *P* 1Sa 7:3
when the *P* heard that the................. 1Sa 7:7
the lords of the *P* went up 1Sa 7:7
it, they were afraid of the *P* 1Sa 7:7
save us out of the hand of the *P*.......... 1Sa 7:8
the *P* drew near to battle against 1Sa 7:10
thunder on that day upon the *P*.......... 1Sa 7:10
out of Mizpeh, and pursued the *P* 1Sa 7:11
So the *P* were subdued, and they......... 1Sa 7:13
the *P* all the days of Samuel.............. 1Sa 7:13
the cities which the *P* had taken.......... 1Sa 7:14
deliver out of the hands of the *P*.......... 1Sa 7:14
people out of the hand of the *P*........... 1Sa 9:16
where is the garrison of the *P*............. 1Sa 10:5
Hazor, and into the hand of the *P*........ 1Sa 12:9
of the *P* that was in Geba 1Sa 13:3
and the *P* heard of it 1Sa 13:3
had smitten a garrison of the *P*........... 1Sa 13:4
was had in abomination with the *P*....... 1Sa 13:4
the *P* gathered themselves 1Sa 13:5
that the *P* gathered themselves 1Sa 13:11
The *P* will come down now upon me..... 1Sa 13:12
but the *P* encamped in Michmash........ 1Sa 13:16
camp of the *P* in three companies........ 1Sa 13:17
for the *P* said, Lest the Hebrews.......... 1Sa 13:19
the Israelites went down to the *P* 1Sa 13:20
the garrison of the *P* went out to.......... 1Sa 14:11
unto the garrison of the *P*................. 1Sa 14:11
the *P* said, Behold, the Hebrews.......... 1Sa 14:11
was in the host of the *P* went on.......... 1Sa 14:19
were with the *P* before that time 1Sa 14:21
when they heard that the *P* fled........... 1Sa 14:22
greater slaughter among the *P*............ 1Sa 14:30
they smote the *P* that day from............ 1Sa 14:31
us go down after the *P* by night........... 1Sa 14:36
God, Shall I go down after the *P*.......... 1Sa 14:37
Saul went up from following the *P* 1Sa 14:46
the *P* went to their own place............. 1Sa 14:46
kings of Zobah, and against the *P* 1Sa 14:47
the *P* all the days of Saul.................. 1Sa 14:52
Now the *P* gathered together their 1Sa 17:1
the battle in array against the *P* 1Sa 17:2
the *P* stood on a mountain on the........ 1Sa 17:3
champion out of the camp of the *P*....... 1Sa 17:4
of Elah, fighting with the *P* 1Sa 17:19
the *P* had put the battle in array......... 1Sa 17:21
name, out of the armies of the *P* 1Sa 17:23
P this day unto the fowls of the........... 1Sa 17:46
when the *P* saw their champion was...... 1Sa 17:51
and shouted, and pursued the *P* 1Sa 17:52
the wounded of the *P* fell down by 1Sa 17:52
returned from chasing after the *P* 1Sa 17:53
let the hand of the *P* be upon him 1Sa 18:17
hand of the *P* may be against him 1Sa 18:21
but an hundred foreskins of the *P*........ 1Sa 18:25
David fall by the hand of the *P*........... 1Sa 18:25
slew of the *P* two hundred men........... 1Sa 18:27
the princes of the *P* went forth........... 1Sa 18:30
went out, and fought with the *P* 1Sa 19:8
the *P* fought against Keilah, and.......... 1Sa 23:1
Shall I go and smite these *P*.............. 1Sa 23:2
unto David, Go, and smite the *P* 1Sa 23:2
against the armies of the *P*................ 1Sa 23:3
deliver the *P* into thine hand.............. 1Sa 23:4

to Keilah, and fought with the *P*.......... 1Sa 23:5
for the *P* have invaded the land........... 1Sa 23:27
David, and went against the *P* 1Sa 23:28
was returned from following the *P*......... 1Sa 24:1
escape into the land of the *P* 1Sa 27:1
country of the *P* was a full year........... 1Sa 27:7
dwelleth in the country of the *P* 1Sa 27:11
that the *P* gathered their armies........... 1Sa 28:1
the *P* gathered themselves 1Sa 28:4
when Saul saw the host of the *P* 1Sa 28:5
for the *P* make war against me, and...... 1Sa 28:15
with thee into the hand of the *P* 1Sa 28:19
of Israel into the hand of the *P* 1Sa 28:19
Now the *P* gathered together all 1Sa 29:1
the lords of the *P* passed on by........... 1Sa 29:2
Then said the princes of the *P*............ 1Sa 29:3
said unto the princes of the *P* 1Sa 29:3
the princes of the *P* were wroth........... 1Sa 29:4
princes of the *P* said unto him 1Sa 29:4
displease not the lords of the *P* 1Sa 29:7
the princes of the *P* have said 1Sa 29:9
to return into the land of the *P*............ 1Sa 29:11
And the *P* went up to Jezreel.............. 1Sa 29:11
taken out of the land of the *P* 1Sa 30:16
Now the *P* fought against Israel 1Sa 31:1
of Israel fled from before the *P*............ 1Sa 31:1
the *P* followed hard upon Saul and....... 1Sa 31:2
the *P* slew Jonathan, and Abinadab,..... 1Sa 31:2
the *P* came and dwelt in them 1Sa 31:7
when the *P* came to strip the 1Sa 31:8
the land of the *P* round about 1Sa 31:9
that which the *P* had done to Saul........ 1Sa 31:11
the daughters of the *P* rejoice 2Sa 1:20
for an hundred foreskins of the *P*......... 2Sa 3:14
Israel out of the hand of the *P*............ 2Sa 3:18
But when the *P* heard that they 2Sa 5:17
all the *P* came up to seek David.......... 2Sa 5:17
The *P* also came and spread 2Sa 5:18
saying, Shall I go up to the *P* 2Sa 5:19
deliver the *P* into thine hand.............. 2Sa 5:19
the *P* came up yet again, and 2Sa 5:22
thee, to smite the host of the *P* 2Sa 5:24
smote the *P* from Geba until thou 2Sa 5:25
to pass, that David smote the *P*........... 2Sa 8:1
out of the hand of the *P*................... 2Sa 8:1
children of Ammon, and the *P* 2Sa 8:12
us out of the hand of the *P* 2Sa 19:9
where the *P* had hanged them............ 2Sa 21:12
when the *P* had slain Saul in.............. 2Sa 21:12
Moreover the *P* had yet war again........ 2Sa 21:15
with him, and fought against the *P* 2Sa 21:15
again a battle with the *P* at Gob.......... 2Sa 21:18
again a battle in Gob with the *P* 2Sa 21:19
when they defied the *P* that were 2Sa 23:9
smote the *P* until his hand was........... 2Sa 23:10
the *P* were gathered together into 2Sa 23:11
and the people fled from the *P* 2Sa 23:11
and defended it, and slew the *P*.......... 2Sa 23:12
the troop of the *P* pitched in the.......... 2Sa 23:13
the garrison of the *P* was then in 2Sa 23:14
brake through the host of the *P*........... 2Sa 23:16
the river unto the land of the *P* 1Kin 4:21
which belonged to the *P*.................. 1Kin 15:27
which belonged to the *P*.................. 1Kin 16:15
in the land of the *P* seven years........... 2Kin 8:2
returned out of the land of the *P* 2Kin 8:3
He smote the *P*, even unto Gaza.......... 2Kin 18:8
and Cashuhim, (of whom came the *P*.... 1Chr 1:12
Now the *P* fought against Israel 1Chr 10:1
of Israel fled from before the *P* 1Chr 10:1
the *P* followed hard after Saul............ 1Chr 10:2
the *P* slew Jonathan, and Abinadab,..... 1Chr 10:2
the *P* came and dwelt in them 1Chr 10:7
when the *P* came to strip the.............. 1Chr 10:8
the land of the *P* round about 1Chr 10:9
all that the *P* had done to Saul 1Chr 10:11
there the *P* were gathered................. 1Chr 11:13
the people fled from before the *P*......... 1Chr 11:13
and delivered it, and slew the *P* 1Chr 11:14
the host of the *P* encamped in the........ 1Chr 11:15
brake through the host of the *P* 1Chr 11:18
when he came with the *P* against......... 1Chr 12:19
for the lords of the *P* upon............... 1Chr 12:19
when the *P* heard that David was 1Chr 14:8
all the *P* went up to seek David........... 1Chr 14:8
the *P* came and spread themselves 1Chr 14:9
Shall I go up against the *P*................ 1Chr 14:10
the *P* yet again spread themselves 1Chr 14:13
thee to smite the host of the *P* 1Chr 14:15
the *P* from Gibeon even to Gazer 1Chr 14:16
to pass, that David smote the *P*........... 1Chr 18:1
towns out of the hand of the *P* 1Chr 18:1
children of Ammon, and from the *P*...... 1Chr 18:11
arose war at Gezer with the *P* 1Chr 20:4
And there was war again with the *P* 1Chr 20:5
river even unto the land of the *P*.......... 2Chr 9:26
Also some of the *P* brought 2Chr 17:11
Jehoram the spirit of the *P* 2Chr 21:16
forth and warred against the *P*........... 2Chr 26:6
about Ashdod, and among the *P* 2Chr 26:6
And God helped him against the *P*........ 2Chr 26:7
The *P* also had invaded the cities........ 2Chr 28:18
when the *P* took him in Gath............. Ps 56:t
the *P* with the inhabitants of.............. Ps 83:7
and are soothsayers like the *P* .... Is 2:6
Syrians before, and the *P* behind......... Is 9:12
of the *P* toward the west................... Is 11:14
the kings of the land of the *P* .... Jer 25:20
the prophet against the *P*................. Jer 47:1
that cometh to spoil all the *P*............. Jer 47:4

for the LORD will spoil the *P*.............. Jer 47:4
hate thee, the daughters of the *P*......... Eze 16:27
about her, the daughters of the *P*........ Eze 16:57
Because the *P* have dealt by............... Eze 25:15
stretch out mine hand upon the *P*........ Eze 25:16
the remnant of the *P* shall perish......... Amos 1:8
then go down to Gath of the *P* .... Amos 6:2
the *P* from Caphtor, and the .... Amos 9:7
and they of the plain the *P* .... Obad 19
O Canaan, the land of the *P*.............. Zeph 2:5
I will cut off the pride of the *P*............ Zec 9:6

PHILISTINES' *(fĭl-ĭs´-tĭnz)*
sojourned in the *P* land many days .... Gen 21:34
let us go over to the *P* garrison 1Sa 14:1
to go over unto the *P* garrison 1Sa 14:4
the *P* garrison was then at 1Chr 11:16

PHILOLOGUS *(fĭl-ŏl´-o-gŭs)* A Christian in
Rome.
Salute *P*, and Julia, Nereus, and .... Rom 16:15

PHILOSOPHERS
Then certain *p* of the Epicureans, ... Acts 17:18

PHILOSOPHY
lest any man spoil you through *p*.......... Col 2:8

PHINEHAS *(fĭn´-e-has)* See PHINEHAS.
1. A son of Eleazar.
and she bare him *P*.......................... Ex 6:25
And when *P*, the son of Eleazar,.......... Num 25:7
P, the son of Eleazar, the son of .... Num 25:11
The son of Eleazar, the son of.............. Num 31:6
the son of Eleazar the priest, ... Josh 22:13
when *P* the priest, and the princes .... Josh 22:30
The son of Eleazar the priest............... Josh 22:31
The son of Eleazar the priest, ... Josh 22:32
hill that pertained to *P* his son .... Josh 24:33
And *P*, the son of Eleazar, the son .... Judg 20:28
Eleazar begat *P*............................. 1Chr 6:4
P begat Abishua 1Chr 6:4
P his son, Abishua his son,................ 1Chr 6:50
P the son of Eleazar was the.............. 1Chr 9:20
The son of Abishua, the son of .... Ezr 7:5
Of the sons of *P*............................ Ezr 8:2
Then stood up *P*, and executed........... Ps 106:30
2. A son of Eli.
the two sons of Eli, Hophni and *P*........ 1Sa 1:3
upon thy two sons, on Hophni and *P*..... 1Sa 2:34
the two sons of Eli, Hophni and *P*........ 1Sa 4:4
the two sons of Eli, Hophni and *P*........ 1Sa 4:11
and thy two sons also, Hophni and *P*..... 1Sa 4:17
I-chabod's brother, the son of *P* 1Sa 14:3
3. Father of Eleazar.
with him was Eleazar the son of *P*........ Ezr 8:33

PHINEHAS' *(fĭn´-e-has)* Refers to Phinehas 2.
P wife, was with child, near to............. 1Sa 4:19

PHLEGON *(fle´-gon)* A Christian in Rome.
Salute Asyncritus, *P*, Hermas,............ Rom 16:14

PHOENIX See PHENICE.

PHRYGIA *(frĭj´-e-ah)* A Roman province in
Asia Minor.
P, and Pamphylia, in Egypt, and in....... Acts 2:10
when they had gone throughout *P*........ Acts 16:6
P in order, strengthening all the .... Acts 18:23
the chiefest city of *P* Pacatiana .... 1Ti s

PHURAH *(fu´-rah)* A servant of Gideon.
go thou with *P* thy servant down.......... Judg 7:10
Then went he down with *P* his............. Judg 7:11

PHUT *(fut)* See PUT.
1. A son of Ham.
Cush, and Mizraim, and *P*................. Gen 10:6
2. Land of Phut's descendants.
of *P* were in thine army, they were........ Eze 27:10

PHUVAH *(fu´-vah)* See PUAH. A son of
Issachar.
Tola, and *P*, and Job, and Shimron ...... Gen 46:13

PHYGELLUS *(fĭ-jĕl´-lŭs)* An unfaithful
Christian.
of whom are *P* and Hermogenes 2Ti 1:15

PHYGELUS See PHYGELLUS.

PHYLACTERIES
they make broad their *p*, and............. Mt 23:5

PHYSICIAN
is there no *p* there.......................... Jer 8:22
They that be whole need not a *p*.......... Mt 9:12
are whole have no need of the *p*.......... Mk 2:17
say unto me this proverb, *P* .... Lk 4:23
They that are whole need not a *p* .... Lk 5:31
Luke, the beloved *p*, and Demas,......... Col 4:14

PHYSICIANS
the *p* to embalm his father................. Gen 50:2
and the *p* embalmed Israel................ Gen 50:2
not to the LORD, but to the *p*............. 2Chr 16:12
of lies, ye are all *p* of no value............ Job 13:4
suffered many things of many *p* .... Mk 5:26
had spent all her living upon *p*............ Lk 8:43

PI-BESETH *A city in Egypt.*
of P shall fall by the sword .... Eze 30:17

PICK
of the valley shall p it out .... Prov 30:17

PICTURES
you, and destroy all their p .... Num 33:52
apples of gold in p of silver .... Prov 25:11
Tarshish, and upon all pleasant p .... Is 2:16

PIECE
laid each p one against another .... Gen 15:10
beaten out of one p made he them .... Ex 37:7
of a whole p shalt thou make them .... Num 10:2
a certain woman cast a p of a .... Judg 9:53
crouch to him for a p of silver 1Sa 2:36
that I may eat a p of bread 1Sa 2:36
they gave him a p of a cake of 1Sa 30:12
a good p of flesh, and a flagon of 2Sa 6:19
did not a woman cast a p of a 2Sa 11:21
where was a p of ground full of 2Sa 23:11
mar every good p of land with 2Kin 3:19
on every good p of land cast 2Kin 3:25
a good p of flesh, and a flagon of 1Chr 16:3
Pahath-moab, repaired the other p .... Neh 3:11
another p over against the going .... Neh 3:19
earnestly repaired the other p .... Neh 3:20
Urijah the son of Koz another p .... Neh 3:21
the son of Henadad another p .... Neh 3:24
the Tekoites repaired another p .... Neh 3:27
sixth son of Zalaph, another p .... Neh 3:30
as hard as a p of the nether .... Job 41:24
man also gave him a p of money .... Job 42:11
a man is brought to a p of bread .... Prov 6:26
for for a p of bread that man .... Prov 28:21
thy temples are like a p of a .... Song 4:3
As a p of a pomegranate are thy .... Song 6:7
a p of bread out of the bakers' .... Jer 37:21
into it, even every good p .... Eze 24:4
bring it out p by p .... Eze 24:6
lion two legs, or a p of an ear .... Amos 3:12
one p was rained upon .... Amos 4:7
the p whereupon it rained not .... Amos 4:7
No man putteth a p of new cloth .... Mt 9:16
thou shalt find a p of money .... Mt 17:27
No man also seweth a p of new .... Mk 2:21
else the new p that filled it up .... Mk 2:21
No man putteth a p of a new .... Lk 5:36
the p that was taken out of the .... Lk 5:36
him, I have bought a p of a ground .... Lk 14:18
of silver, if she lose one .... Lk 15:8
have found the p which I had lost .... Lk 15:9
they gave him a p of a broiled .... Lk 24:42

PIECES
lamp that passed between those p .... Gen 15:17
brother a thousand p of silver .... Gen 20:16
father, for an hundred p of money .... Gen 33:19
for twenty p of silver .... Gen 37:28
Joseph is without doubt rent in p .... Gen 37:33
and I said, Surely he is torn in p .... Gen 44:28
he gave three hundred p of silver .... Gen 45:22
LORD, hath dashed in p the enemy .... Ex 15:6
If it be torn in p, then let him .... Ex 22:13
And thou shalt cut the ram in p .... Ex 29:17
his legs, and put them unto his p .... Ex 29:17
offering, and cut it into his p .... Lev 1:6
And he shall cut it into his p .... Lev 1:12
Thou shalt part it in p, and pour .... Lev 2:6
the baken p of the meat offering .... Lev 2:6
And he cut the ram into p .... Lev 8:20
and Moses burnt the head, and the p .... Lev 8:20
unto him, with the p thereof .... Lev 9:13
for an hundred p of silver .... Josh 24:32
ten p of silver out of the house .... Judg 9:4
of us eleven hundred p of silver .... Judg 16:5
with her bones, into twelve p .... Judg 19:29
my concubine, and cut her in p .... Judg 20:6
of the LORD shall be broken to p 1Sa 2:10
yoke of oxen, and hewed them in p 1Sa 11:7
Samuel hewed Agag in p before the 1Sa 15:33
on him, and rent it in twelve p 1Kin 11:30
said to Jeroboam, Take thee ten p 1Kin 11:31
for themselves, and cut it in p 1Kin 18:23
in order, and cut the bullock in p 1Kin 18:33
brake in p the rocks before the 1Kin 19:11
clothes, and rent them in two p 2Kin 2:12
silver, and six thousand p of gold 2Kin 5:5
sold for fourscore p of silver 2Kin 6:25
dove's dung for five p of silver 2Kin 6:25
images brake they in p thoroughly 2Kin 11:18
brake in p the brasen serpent 2Kin 18:4
And he brake in p the images 2Kin 23:14
cut in p all the vessels of gold 2Kin 24:13
LORD, that the Chaldees break in p 2Kin 25:13
his altars and his images in p 2Chr 23:17
that they all were broken in p 2Chr 25:12
cut in p the vessels of the 2Chr 28:24
Judah, and brake the images in p 2Chr 31:1
the molten images, he brake in p 2Chr 34:4
me by my neck, and shaken me to p ..... Job 16:12
soul, and break me in p with words ...... Job 19:2
He shall break in p mighty men .... Job 34:24
bones are as strong p of brass .... Job 40:18
them in p like a potter's vessel .... Ps 2:9
soul like a lion, rending it in p .... Ps 7:2
forget God, lest I tear you in p .... Ps 50:22
arrows, let them be as cut in p .... Ps 58:7
submit himself with p of silver .... Ps 68:30
and shall break in p the oppressor .... Ps 72:4
the heads of leviathan in p .... Ps 74:14

Thou hast broken Rahab in p .... Ps 89:10
They break in p thy people .... Ps 94:5
to bring a thousand p of silver .... Song 8:11
ye that ye beat my people to p .... Is 3:15
and ye shall be broken in p .... Is 8:9
and ye shall be broken in p .... Is 8:9
and ye shall be broken in p .... Is 8:9
be dashed to p before their eyes .... Is 13:16
shall dash the young men to p .... Is 13:18
vessel that is broken in p .... Is 30:14
I will break in p the gates of .... Is 45:2
out thence shall be torn in p .... Jer 5:6
that breaketh the rock in p .... Jer 23:29
Merodach is broken in p .... Jer 50:2
her images are broken in p .... Jer 50:2
will I break in p the nations .... Jer 51:20
thee will I break in p the horse .... Jer 51:21
will I break in p the chariot .... Jer 51:21
the also will I break in p man .... Jer 51:21
with thee will I break in p old .... Jer 51:22
will I break in p the young man .... Jer 51:22
I will also break in p with thee .... Jer 51:23
will I break in p the husbandman .... Jer 51:23
thee will I break in p captains .... Jer 51:23
aside my ways, and pulled me in p ...... Lam 3:11
dieth of itself, or is torn in p .... Eze 44:31
for p of bread, to slay the souls .... Eze 13:19
Gather the p thereof into it .... Eze 24:4
thereof, ye shall he cut in p .... Dan 2:5
iron and clay, and brake them to p ...... Dan 2:34
and the gold, broken to p together .... Dan 2:35
forasmuch as iron breaketh in p .... Dan 2:40
all these, shall it break in p .... Dan 2:40
people, but it shall break in p .... Dan 2:44
and that it brake in p the iron .... Dan 2:45
and Abed-nego, shall be cut in p .... Dan 3:29
brake all their bones in p or .... Dan 6:24
it devoured and brake in p .... Dan 7:7
which devoured, brake in p .... Dan 7:19
tread it down, and break it in p .... Dan 7:23
her to me for fifteen p of silver .... Hos 3:2
of Samaria shall be broken in p .... Hos 8:6
was dashed in p upon her children ...... Hos 10:14
infants shall be dashed in p .... Hos 13:16
thereof shall be beaten to p .... Mic 1:7
their bones, and chop them in p .... Mic 3:3
thou shalt beat in p many people .... Mic 4:13
treadeth down, and teareth in p .... Mic 5:8
He that dasheth in p is come up .... Nah 2:1
The lion did tear in p enough for .... Nah 2:12
children also were dashed in p at .... Nah 3:10
for my price thirty p of silver .... Zec 11:12
And I took the thirty p of silver .... Zec 11:13
the fat, and tear their claws in p .... Zec 11:16
with it shall be cut in p .... Zec 12:3
with him for thirty p of silver .... Mt 26:15
brought again the thirty p of .... Mt 27:3
he cast down the p of silver .... Mt 27:5
chief priests took the p of .... Mt 27:6
they took the thirty p of silver .... Mt 27:9
him, and the fetters broken in p .... Mk 5:4
what woman having ten p of silver .... Lk 15:8
it fifty thousand p of silver .... Acts 19:19
have been pulled in p of them .... Acts 23:10
and some on broken p of the ship ...... Acts 27:44

PIERCE
p them through with his arrows .... Num 24:8
it will go into his hand, and p it 2Kin 18:21
it will go into his hand, and p it .... Is 36:6
a sword shall p through thy own .... Lk 2:35

PIERCED
off his head, when she had p .... Judg 5:26
My bones are p in me in the night .... Job 30:17
they p my hands and my feet .... Ps 22:16
look upon me whom they have p .... Zec 12:10
soldiers with a spear p his side .... Jn 19:34
shall look on him whom they p .... Jn 19:37
p themselves through with many 1Ti 6:10
see him, and they also which p him .... Rev 1:7

PIERCETH
his nose p through snares .... Job 40:24

PIERCING
punish leviathan the p serpent .... Is 27:1
p even to the dividing asunder of .... Heb 4:12

PIERCINGS
speaketh like the p of a sword .... Prov 12:18

PIETY
learn first to shew p at home 1Ti 5:4

PIGEON
and a turtledove, and a young p .... Gen 15:9
a burnt offering, and a young p .... Lev 12:6

PIGEONS
of turtledoves, or of young p .... Lev 1:14
two turtledoves, or two young p .... Lev 5:7
two turtledoves, or two young p .... Lev 5:11
bring two turtles, or two young p .... Lev 12:8
two turtledoves, or two young p .... Lev 14:22
turtledoves, or of the young p .... Lev 14:30
two turtledoves, or two young p .... Lev 15:14
her two turtles, or two young p .... Lev 15:29
bring two turtles, or two young p .... Num 6:10
of turtledoves, or two young p .... Lk 2:24

PI-HAHIROTH
that they turn and encamp before P .... Ex 14:2
encamping by the sea, beside P .... Ex 14:9

Etham, and turned again unto P .... Num 33:7
And they departed from before P .... Num 33:8

PILATE *(pi´lat) A Roman procurator of Judea.*
him to Pontius P the governor .... Mt 27:2
Then said P unto him, Hearest .... Mt 27:13
P saith unto them, Whom will ye .... Mt 27:17
P saith unto them, What shall I .... Mt 27:22
When P saw that he could prevail .... Mt 27:24
He went to P, and begged the body .... Mt 27:58
Then P commanded the body to be .... Mt 27:58
and Pharisees came together unto P .... Mt 27:62
P said unto them, Ye have a watch ..... Mt 27:65
him away, and delivered him to P ...... Mk 15:1
P asked him, Art thou the King of ..... Mk 15:2
P asked him again, saying .... Mk 15:4
so that P marvelled .... Mk 15:5
But P answered them, saying, Will ..... Mk 15:9
P answered and said again unto .... Mk 15:12
Then P said unto them, Why, what .... Mk 15:14
And so P, willing to content the .... Mk 15:15
came, and went in boldly unto P .... Mk 15:43
P marvelled if he were already .... Mk 15:44
Pontius P being governor of .... Lk 3:1
whose blood P had mingled with .... Lk 13:1
of them arose, and led him unto P ..... Lk 23:1
P asked him, saying, Art thou the ...... Lk 23:3
Then said P to the chief priests .... Lk 23:4
When P heard of Galilee, he asked .... Lk 23:6
robe, and sent him again to P .... Lk 23:11
And the same day P and Herod were .. Lk 23:12
And P, when he had called together ... Lk 23:13
P therefore, willing to release .... Lk 23:20
P gave sentence that it should be ...... Lk 23:24
This man went unto P, and begged .... Lk 23:52
P then went out unto them, and .... Jn 18:29
Then said P unto them, Take ye .... Jn 18:31
Then P entered into the judgment ...... Jn 18:33
P answered, Am I a Jew .... Jn 18:35
P therefore said unto him, Art .... Jn 18:37
P saith unto him, What is truth .... Jn 18:38
Then P therefore took Jesus, and ...... Jn 19:1
P therefore went forth again, and ...... Jn 19:4
P saith unto them, Behold the man ... Jn 19:5
P saith unto them, Take ye him .... Jn 19:6
When P therefore heard that .... Jn 19:8
Then saith P unto him, Speakest .... Jn 19:10
from thenceforth P sought to .... Jn 19:12
P therefore heard that .... Jn 19:13
P saith unto them, Shall I .... Jn 19:15
P wrote a title, and put it on the .... Jn 19:19
chief priests of the Jews to P .... Jn 19:21
P answered, What I have written I .... Jn 19:22
besought P that their legs might .... Jn 19:31
besought P that he might take .... Jn 19:38
and P gave him leave .... Jn 19:38
denied him in the presence of P .... Acts 3:13
both Herod, and Pontius P .... Acts 4:27
yet desired they P that he should ...... Acts 13:28
who before Pontius P witnessed a 1Ti 6:13

PILDASH *(pil´dash) A son of Nahor.*
And Chesed, and Hazo, and P, and ..... Gen 22:22

PILE
the p thereof is fire and much .... Is 30:33
even make the p for fire great .... Eze 24:9

PILEHA *(pi´le-ah) A renewer of the covenant.*
Hallohesh, P, Shobek .... Neh 10:24

PILGRIMAGE
the years of my p are an hundred ..... Gen 47:9
my fathers in the days of their p ...... Gen 47:9
of Canaan, the land of their p .... Ex 6:4
my songs in the house of my p .... Ps 119:54

PILGRIMS
were strangers and p on the earth .... Heb 11:13
I beseech you, as strangers and p 1Pet 2:11

PILHA See PILEHA.

PILLAR
him, and she became a p of salt .... Gen 19:26
his pillows, and set it up for a p ...... Gen 28:18
stone, which I have set for a p .... Gen 28:22
where thou anointedst the p .... Gen 31:13
a stone, and set it up for a p .... Gen 31:45
this hcap, and behold this p .... Gen 31:51
this p be witness, that I will .... Gen 31:52
heap and this p unto me, for harm .. Gen 31:52
Jacob set up a p in the place .... Gen 35:14
with him, even a p of stone .... Gen 35:14
Jacob set a p upon her grave .... Gen 35:20
that is the p of Rachel's grave ...... Gen 35:20
them by day in a p of a cloud .... Ex 13:21
and by night in a p of fire .... Ex 13:21
away the p of the cloud by day ..... Ex 13:22
nor the p of fire by night, from ..... Ex 13:22
the p of the cloud went from .... Ex 14:19
Egyptians through the p of fire ..... Ex 14:24
the cloudy p descended, and stood .. Ex 33:9
p stand at the tabernacle door ...... Ex 33:10
came down in the p of the cloud ... Num 12:5
by daytime in a p of a cloud .... Num 14:14
and in a p of fire by night .... Num 14:14
the tabernacle in a p of a cloud ... Deut 31:15
the p of the cloud stood over the .. Deut 31:15
of the p that was in Shechem ..... Judg 9:6
out of the city with a p of smoke .. Judg 20:40
and reared up for himself a p 2Sa 18:18
he called the p after his own 2Sa 18:18

and he set up the right p, and.......... 1Kin 7:21
and he set up the left p, and............ 1Kin 7:21
behold, the king stood by a p............ 2Kin 11:14
And the king stood by a p, and made . 2Kin 23:3
of the one p was eighteen cubits........ 2Kin 25:17
the second p with wreathen work 2Kin 25:17
stood at his p at the entering in........ 2Chr 23:13
them in the day by a cloudy p............ Neh 9:12
and in the night by a p of fire............ Neh 9:12
the p of the cloud departed not.......... Neh 9:19
neither the p of fire by night............. Neh 9:19
spake unto them in the cloudy p......... Ps 99:7
a p at the border thereof to the......... Is 19:19
day a defenced city, and an iron p...... Jer 1:18
the height of one p was eighteen .... Jer 52:21
The second p also and the................. Jer 52:22
church of the living God, the p 1Ti 3:15
make a p in the temple of my God...... Rev 3:12

PILLARS

altar under the hill, and twelve p........ Ex 24:4
thou shalt hang it upon four p of ...... Ex 26:32
hanging five p of shittim wood.......... Ex 26:37
And the twenty p thereof and their .... Ex 27:10
the hooks of the p and their............. Ex 27:10
cubits long, and his twenty p .... Ex 27:11
the hooks of the p and their............. Ex 27:11
their p ten, and their sockets ten....... Ex 27:12
their p three, and their sockets .... Ex 27:14
their p three, and their sockets .... Ex 27:15
their p shall be four, and their.......... Ex 27:16
All the p round about the court .... Ex 27:17
and his boards, his bars, his p .... Ex 35:11
The hangings of the court, his p .... Ex 35:17
thereunto four p of shittim wood........ Ex 36:36
the five p of it with their hooks .... Ex 36:38
Their p were twenty, and their.......... Ex 38:10
the hooks of the p and their............. Ex 38:10
their p were twenty, and their.......... Ex 38:11
the hooks of the p and their............. Ex 38:11
of fifty cubits, their p ten .... Ex 38:12
the hooks of the p and their............. Ex 38:12
their p three, and their sockets .... Ex 38:14
their p three, and their sockets .... Ex 38:15
sockets for the p were of brass.......... Ex 38:17
the hooks of the p and their............. Ex 38:17
all the p of the court were................ Ex 38:17
their p were four, and their.............. Ex 38:19
shekels he made hooks for the p........ Ex 38:28
his boards, his bars, and his p .... Ex 39:33
The hangings of the court, his p .... Ex 39:40
bars thereof, and reared up his p ...... Ex 40:18
the p thereof, and the sockets .... Num 3:36
the p of the court round about,.......... Num 3:37
the p thereof, and sockets thereof...... Num 4:31
the p of the court round about,.......... Num 4:32
their altars, and break their p .... Deut 12:3
and they set him between the p .... Judg 16:25
p whereupon the house standeth........ Judg 16:26
p upon which the house stood............ Judg 16:29
for the p of the earth are the............ 1Sa 2:8
cubits, upon four rows of cedar p 1Kin 7:2
with cedar beams upon the p............. 1Kin 7:2
beams, that lay on forty five p 1Kin 7:3
And he made a porch of p 1Kin 7:6
and the other p and the thick beam ... 1Kin 7:6
For he cast two p of brass................ 1Kin 7:15
to set upon the tops of the p 1Kin 7:16
which were upon the top of the p 1Kin 7:17
And he made the p, and two rows 1Kin 7:18
that were upon the top of the p 1Kin 7:19
the chapiters upon the two p had 1Kin 7:20
he set up the p in the porch of.......... 1Kin 7:21
the top of the p was lily work............ 1Kin 7:22
so was the work of the p finished...... 1Kin 7:22
The two p, and the two bowls of........ 1Kin 7:41
that were on the top of the two p 1Kin 7:41
which were upon the top of the p 1Kin 7:42
chapiters that were upon the p 1Kin 7:42
trees p for the house of the LORD 1Kin 10:12
from the p which Hezekiah king of..... 2Kin 18:16
the p of brass that were in the.......... 2Kin 25:13
The two p, one sea, and the bases 2Kin 25:16
made the brasen sea, and the p 2Chr 4:12
before the house two p of finish........ 2Chr 3:15
and put them on the heads of the p ... 2Chr 3:16
he reared up the p before the........... 2Chr 3:17
To wit, the two p, and the pommels ... 2Chr 4:12
were on the top of the two p 2Chr 4:12
which were on the top of the p 2Chr 4:13
chapiters which were upon the p 2Chr 4:13
to oliver rings and p of marble.......... Est 1:6
place, and the p thereof tremble......... Job 9:6
The p of heaven tremble, and are...... Job 26:11
I bear up the p of it .... Ps 75:3
she hath hewn out her seven p .... Prov 9:1
of the wilderness like p of smoke....... Song 3:6
He made the p thereof of silver,........ Song 3:10
His legs are as p of marble............... Song 5:15
Loab of hosts concerning the p .... Jer 27:19
Also the p of brass that were in......... Jer 52:17
The two p, one sea, and twelve .... Jer 52:20
And concerning the p, the height........ Jer 52:21
there were p by the posts, one on...... Eze 40:49
p as the p of the courts.................... Joel 2:30
blood, and fire, and p of smoke.......... Joel 2:30
and John, who seemed to be p .... Gal 2:9
the sun, and his feet as p of fire........ Rev 10:1

PILLED

p white strakes in them, and made..... Gen 30:37
he had p before the flocks in the....... Gen 30:38

PILLOW

put a p of goats' hair for his............. 1Sa 19:13
with a p of goats' hair for his............ 1Sa 19:16
part of the ship, asleep on a p .... Mk 4:38

PILLOWS

that place, and put them for his........ Gen 28:11
stone that he had put for his p .... Gen 28:18
women that sew p to all armholes...... Eze 13:18
Behold, I am against your p .... Eze 13:20

PILOTS

that were in thee, were thy p............ Eze 27:8
thy mariners, and thy p, thy.............. Eze 27:27
at the sound of the cry of thy p .... Eze 27:28
all the p of the sea, shall come .... Eze 27:29

PILTAI
(pil'-tahee) A priest.
of Miniamin, of Moadiah, P................ Neh 12:17

PIN

And she fastened it with the p........... Judg 16:14
went away with the p of the beam ..... Judg 16:14
or will men take a p of it to .... Eze 15:3

PINE

p away in their iniquity in your.......... Lev 26:39
shall they p away with them.............. Lev 26:39
p branches, and myrtle branches........ Neh 8:15
the desert the fir tree, and the p ...... Is 41:19
the tree, and the box together,......... Is 60:13
for these p away, stricken................. Lam 4:9
but ye shall p away for your.............. Eze 24:23
we p away in them, how should we .... Eze 33:10

PINETH

with his teeth, and p away................ Mk 9:18

PINING

will cut me off with p sickness.......... Is 38:12

PINNACLE

setteth him on a p of the temple........ Mt 4:5
set him on a p of the temple, and...... Lk 4:9

PINON

Aholibamah, duke Elah, duke P........... Gen 36:41
Aholibamah, duke Elah, duke P........... 1Chr 1:52

PINS

thereof, and all the p thereof............ Ex 27:19
all the p of the court, shall be .... Ex 27:19
The p of the tabernacle, and the....... Ex 35:18
the p of the court, and their............. Ex 35:18
all the p of the tabernacle, and......... Ex 38:20
The p of the tabernacle, and the....... Ex 38:31
all the p of the court round.............. Ex 38:31
court gate, his cords, and his p .... Ex 39:40
and their sockets, and their p .... Num 3:37
and their sockets, and their p .... Num 4:32
and the wimples, and the crisping p ... Is 3:22

PIPE

a psaltery, and a tabret, and a p 1Sa 10:5
and the viol, the tabret, and p........... Is 5:12
as when one goeth with a p to........... Is 30:29
giving sound, whether p or harp......... 1Cor 14:7

PIPED

him, and the people p with pipes....... 1Kin 1:40
We have p unto you, and ye have...... Mt 11:17
We have p unto you, and ye have...... Lk 7:32
it be known what is p or harped........ 1Cor 14:7

PIPERS

of harpers, and musicians, and of p ... Rev 18:22

PIPES

him, and the people piped with p 1Kin 1:40
heart shall sound for Moab like p ...... Jer 48:36
like p for the men of Kir-heres......... Jer 48:36
of thy p was prepared in thee in....... Eze 28:13
seven p to the seven lamps, which..... Zec 4:2
p empty the golden oil out of............ Zec 4:12

PIRAM
(pi'-ram) An Amorite king.
unto P king of Jarmuth, and unto...... Josh 10:3

PIRATHON
(pir'-a-thon) See PIRATHONITE. A
place in Ephraim.
was buried in P in the land of .... Judg 12:15

PIRATHONITE
(pir'-a-thon-ite) An inhabitant
of Pirathon.
him Abdon the son of Hillel, a P .... Judg 12:13
the son of Hillel the P died .... Judg 12:15
Benaiah the P, Hiddai of the............. 2Sa 23:30
of Benjamin, Benaiah the P 1Chr 11:31
eleventh month was Benaiah the P 1Chr 27:14

PISGAH
(piz'-gah) A mountain peak in Moab.
country of Moab, to the top of P .... Num 21:20
field of Zophim, to the top of P......... Num 23:14
Get thee up into the top of P .... Deut 3:27
the plain, under the springs of P....... Deut 4:49
mountain of Nebo, to the top of........ Deut 34:1

PISHON See PISON.

PISIDIA
(pi-sid'-e-ah) A Roman province in
Asia Minor.
Perga, they came to Antioch in P....... Acts 13:14
they had passed throughout P .... Acts 14:24

PISIDIAN ANTIOCH

PISON
(pi'-son) A river of Eden.
The name of the first is P................. Gen 2:11

PISPA See PISPAH.

PISPAH
(pis'-pah) A son of Jether.
Jephunneh, and P, and Ara 1Chr 7:38

PISS

and drink their own p with you.......... 2Kin 18:27
and drink their own p with you.......... Is 36:12

PISSETH

light any that p against the wall........ 1Sa 25:22
light any that p against the wall........ 1Sa 25:34
him that p against the wall............... 1Kin 14:10
him not one that p against a wall...... 1Kin 16:11
Ahab him that p against the wall....... 1Kin 21:21
Ahab him that p against the wall....... 2Kin 9:8

PIT

slay him, and cast him into some p .... Gen 37:20
but cast him into this p that is.......... Gen 37:22
took him, and cast him into a p .... Gen 37:24
the p was empty, there was no.......... Gen 37:24
and lifted up Joseph out of the p ...... Gen 37:28
And Reuben returned unto the p .... Gen 37:29
behold, Joseph was not in the p .... Gen 37:29
And if a man shall open a p .... Ex 21:33
or if a man shall dig a p .... Ex 21:33
The owner of the p shall make it ...... Ex 21:34
Nevertheless a fountain or p .... Lev 11:36
and they go down quick into the p ..... Num 16:30
them, went down alive into the p ...... Num 16:33
Behold, he is hid now in some p 2Sa 17:9
him into a great p in the wood.......... 2Sa 18:17
the midst of a p in time of snow 2Sa 23:20
slew them at the p of the................. 2Kin 10:14
slew a lion in a p in a snowy day....... 1Chr 11:22
ye dig a p for your friend .... Job 6:27
go down to the bars of the p .... Job 17:16
keepeth back his soul from the p .... Job 33:18
him from going down to the p .... Job 33:24
his soul from going into the p .... Job 33:28
To bring back his soul from the p ...... Job 33:30
He made a p, and digged it, and is .... Ps 7:15
sunk down in the p that they made.... Ps 9:15
like them that go down into the p ...... Ps 28:1
I should not go down to the p............ Ps 30:3
my blood, when I go down to the p .... Ps 30:9
they hid for me their net in a p .... Ps 35:7
me up also out of an horrible p .... Ps 40:2
down into the p of destruction........... Ps 55:23
they have digged a p before me......... Ps 57:6
let not the p shut her mouth upon..... Ps 69:15
with them that go down into the p ..... Ps 88:4
Thou hast laid me in the lowest p ...... Ps 88:6
until the p be digged for the .... Ps 94:13
unto them that go down into the p ..... Ps 143:7
as those that go down into the p .... Prov 1:12
of strange women is a deep p .... Prov 22:14
and a strange woman is a narrow p ... Prov 23:27
Whoso diggeth a p shall fall .... Prov 26:27
shall fall himself into his own p .... Prov 28:10
of any person shall flee to the p .... Prov 28:17
He that diggeth a p shall fall............. Eccl 10:8
to hell, to the sides of the p .... Is 14:15
go down to the stones of the p .... Is 14:19
Fear, and the p, and the snare, are ... Is 24:17
of the fear shall fall into the p .... Is 24:18
up out of the midst of the p .... Is 24:18
prisoners are gathered in the p .... Is 24:22
to take water withal out of the p ...... Is 30:14
it from the p of corruption .... Is 38:17
the p cannot hope for thy truth......... Is 38:18
to the hole of the p whence ye .... Is 51:1
that he should not die in the p .... Is 51:14
they have digged a p for my soul...... Jer 18:20
they have digged a p to take me .... Jer 18:22
cast them into the midst of the p ...... Jer 41:7
Now the p wherein Ishmael had........ Jer 41:9
Fear, and the p, and the snare,......... Jer 48:43
the fear shall fall into the p .... Jer 48:44
the p shall be taken in the snare....... Jer 48:44
he was taken in their p, and they ..... Eze 19:4
he was taken in their p .... Eze 19:8
with them that descend into the p ..... Eze 26:20
with them that go down to the p .... Eze 26:20
shalt bring thee down to the p .... Eze 28:8
with them that go down to the p .... Eze 31:14
with them that descend into the p ..... Eze 31:16
with them that go down into the p ..... Eze 32:18
are set in the sides of the p .... Eze 32:23
with them that go down to the p .... Eze 32:24
with them that go down to the p .... Eze 32:25
with them that go down to the p .... Eze 32:29
with them that descend to the p .... Eze 32:30
out of the p wherein is no water .... Zec 9:11
if it fall into a p on the .... Mt 12:11
an ass or an ox fallen into a p .... Lk 14:5
given the key of the bottomless p ..... Rev 9:1
And he opened the bottomless p......... Rev 9:2
there arose a smoke out of the p ...... Rev 9:2
by reason of the smoke of the p .... Rev 9:2
is the angel of the bottomless p .... Rev 9:11
p shall make war against them .... Rev 11:7
ascend out of the bottomless p .... Rev 17:8
the key of the bottomless p .... Rev 20:1
And cast him into the bottomless p ... Rev 20:3

PITCH

p it within and without with p........... Gen 6:14
and daubed it with slime and with p .. Ex 2:3
of Israel shall p their tents............... Num 1:52
But the Levites shall p round............. Num 1:53
shall p by his own standard.............. Num 2:2
of the congregation shall they p .... Num 2:2
Judah p throughout their armies .... Num 2:3
those that do p next unto him.......... Num 2:5
those which p by him shall be the..... Num 2:12
of the Gershonites shall p behind...... Num 3:23
of the sons of Kohath shall p on....... Num 3:29
these shall p on the side of the........ Num 3:35
out a place to p your tents in .... Deut 1:33

of Jordan, did Joshua p in Gilgal .... Josh 4:20
shall the Arabian p tent there .... Is 13:20
thereof shall be turned into p..................... Is 34:9
thereof shall become burning p.................. Is 34:9
they shall p their tents against .... Jer 6:3

PITCHED

p his tent, having Beth-el on the .... Gen 12:8
plain, and p his tent toward Sodom.... Gen 13:12
p his tent in the valley of Gerar .... Gen 26:17
of the LORD, and p his tent there .... Gen 26:25
Now Jacob had p his tent in the.............. Gen 31:25
brethren p in the mount of Gilead .... Gen 31:25
p his tent before the city .... Gen 33:18
of the LORD, and p in Rephidim.................. Ex 17:1
Sinai, and had p in the wilderness .... Ex 19:2
p it without the camp, afar off.................. Ex 33:7
and when the tabernacle is to be p .... Num 1:51
so they p by their standards, and.......... Num 2:34
children of Israel p their tents .... Num 9:17
commandment of the LORD they p....... Num 9:18
p in the wilderness of Paran .... Num 12:16
Israel set forward, and p in Oboth........ Num 21:10
Oboth, and p at Ije-abarim, in the .... Num 21:11
and p in the valley of Zared .... Num 21:12
p on the other side of Arnon .... Num 21:13
p in the plains of Moab on this .... Num 22:1
from Rameses, and p in Succoth.......... Num 33:5
p in Etham, which is in the edge .... Num 33:6
and they p before Migdol .... Num 33:7
of Etham, and p in Marah....................... Num 33:8
and they p there .... Num 33:9
in the wilderness of Sinai .... Num 33:15
Sinai, and p at Kibroth-hattaavah ...... Num 33:16
from Hazeroth, and p in Rithmah........ Num 33:18
Rithmah, and p at Rimmon-parez........ Num 33:19
and p in Libnah .... Num 33:20
from Libnah, and p at Rissah................ Num 33:21
from Rissah, and p in Kehelathah .... Num 33:22
and p in mount Shapher .... Num 33:23
from Haradah, and p in Makheloth..... Num 33:25
from Tahath, and p at Tarah .... Num 33:27
from Tarah, and p in Mithcah .... Num 33:28
from Mithcah, and p in Hashmonah ... Num 33:29
Moseroth, and p in Bene-jaakan .... Num 33:31
Hor-hagidgad, and p in Jotbathah ..... Num 33:33
p in the wilderness of Zin, which........ Num 33:36
p in mount Hor, in the edge of............ Num 33:37
from mount Hor, and p in Zalmonah .. Num 33:41
from Zalmonah, and p in Punon.......... Num 33:42
from Punon, and p in Oboth .... Num 33:43
p in Ije-abarim, in the border of......... Num 33:44
from Iim, and p in Dibon-gad .... Num 33:45
p in the mountains of Abarim............. Num 33:47
p in the plains of Moab by Jordan...... Num 33:48
And they p by Jordan, from .... Num 33:49
p on the north side of Ai .... Josh 8:11
p together at the waters of Merom ...... Josh 11:5
p his tent unto the plain of .... Judg 4:11
p in the valley of Jezreel .... Judg 6:33
p beside the well of Harod .... Judg 7:1
p on the other side of Arnon, but ...... Judg 11:18
p in Jahaz, and fought against .... Judg 11:20
p in Judah, and spread themselves .... Judg 15:9
p in Kirjath-jearim, in Judah............... Judg 18:12
to battle, and p beside Eben-ezer........... 1Sa 4:1
and the Philistines p in Aphek 1Sa 4:1
p in Michmash, eastward from.............. 1Sa 13:5
p between Shochoh and Azekah, in 1Sa 17:1
p by the valley of Elah, and set 1Sa 17:2
Saul p in the hill of Hachilah,............. 1Sa 26:3
to the place where Saul had p 1Sa 26:5
the people p round about him 1Sa 26:5
together, and came and p in Shunem.. 1Sa 28:4
together, and they p in Gilboa 1Sa 28:4
the Israelites p by a fountain.............. 1Sa 29:1
that David had p for it 2Sa 6:17
Absalom p in the land of Gilead 2Sa 17:26
p in the valley of Rephaim.................. 2Sa 23:13
p in Aroer, on the right side of 2Sa 24:5
the children of Israel p before.......... 1Kin 20:27
they p one over against the other 1Kin 20:29
Jerusalem, and p against it 2Kin 25:1
ark of God, and p for it a tent............ 1Chr 15:1
the tent that David had p for it......... 1Chr 16:1
who came and p before Medeba 1Chr 19:7
for he had p a tent for it at................... 2Chr 1:4
p against it, and built forts................... Jer 52:4
true tabernacle, which the Lord p .... Heb 8:2

PITCHER

whom I shall say, Let down thy p..... Gen 24:14
with her p upon her shoulder............ Gen 24:15
down to the well, and filled her p .... Gen 24:16
drink a little water of thy p .... Gen 24:17
let down her p upon her hand, and .. Gen 24:18
emptied her p into the trough, and... Gen 24:20
a little water of thy p to drink .... Gen 24:43
forth with her p on her shoulder ..... Gen 24:45
let down her p from her shoulder..... Gen 24:46
or the p be broken at the .... Eccl 12:6
you a man bearing a p of water .... Mk 14:13
meet you, bearing a p of water........... Lk 22:10

PITCHERS

in every man's hand, with empty p .... Judg 7:16
and lamps within the p .... Judg 7:16
brake the p that were in their.............. Judg 7:19
blew the trumpets, and brake the p... Judg 7:20
are they esteemed as earthen............. Lam 4:2

PITHOM (pi'-thom) A city in Lower Egypt.
for Pharaoh treasure cities, P..................... Ex 1:11

PITHON (pi'-thon) A son of Micah.
And the sons of Micah were, P............... 1Chr 8:35
And the sons of Micah were, P............... 1Chr 9:41

PITIED
He made them also to be p of all............ Ps 106:46
of Jacob, and hath not p .... Lam 2:2
hath thrown down, and hath not p .... Lam 2:17
thou hast killed, and not p .... Lam 2:21
thou hast slain, thou hast not p .... Lam 3:43
None eye p thee, to do any of.................. Eze 16:5

PITIETH
Like as a father p his children............... Ps 103:13
so the LORD p them that fear him......... Ps 103:13
eyes, and that which your soul p .... Eze 24:21

PITIFUL
The hands of the p women have............. Lam 4:10
that the Lord is very p, and of.................. Jas 5:11
another, love as brethren, be p 1Pet 3:8

PITS
rocks, and in high places, and in p....... 1Sa 13:6
The proud have digged p for me........... Ps 119:85
into deep p, that they rise not.............. Ps 140:10
through a land of deserts and of p .... Jer 2:6
they came to the p, and found no......... Jer 14:3
of the LORD, was taken in their p......... Lam 4:20

PITY
eye shall have no p upon them .... Deut 7:16
neither shall thine eye p him .... Deut 13:8
Thine eye shall not p him.................... Deut 19:13
And thine eye shall not p .... Deut 19:21
hand, thine eye shall not p .... Deut 25:12
thing, and because he had no p 2Sa 12:6
To him that is afflicted p should .... Job 6:14
Have p upon me, have p upon me ...... Job 19:21
and I looked for some to take p .... Ps 69:20
He that hath p upon the poor .... Prov 19:17
it for him that will p the poor .... Prov 28:8
they shall have no p on the fruit .... Is 13:18
in his p he redeemed them.................... Is 63:9
I will not p, nor spare, nor have .... Jer 13:14
For who shall have p upon thee .... Jer 15:5
not spare them, neither have p .... Jer 21:7
spare, neither will I have any p .... Eze 5:11
spare thee, neither will I have p .... Eze 7:4
not spare, neither will I have p .... Eze 7:9
not spare, neither will I have p .... Eze 8:18
your eye spare, neither have ye p ...... Eze 9:5
not spare, neither will I have p .... Eze 9:10
But I had p for mine holy name,........ Eze 36:21
for his land, and p his people............. Joel 2:18
the sword, and did cast off all p .... Amos 1:11
Thou hast had p on the gourd............ Jonah 4:10
and their own shepherds p them not ... Zec 11:5
For I will no more p the .... Zec 11:6
even as I had p on thee......................... Mt 18:33

PLACE See PREFACE.

PLACED
he p at the east of the garden of......... Gen 3:24
Joseph p his father and his .... Gen 47:11
he p in Beth-el the priests of 1Kin 12:32
p them in Halah and in Habor by 2Kin 17:6
p them in the cities of Samaria......... 2Kin 17:24
p in the cities of Samaria, from 2Kin 17:26
which he p in the chariot cities,....... 2Chr 1:14
p them in the temple, five on the..... 2Chr 4:8
he p forces in all the fenced 2Chr 17:2
old, since man was p upon earth...... Job 20:4
the tent which he p among men........ Ps 78:60
that they may be p alone in the .... Is 5:8
which have p the sand for the .... Jer 5:22
he p it by great waters, and set .... Eze 17:5

PLACES See PREFACE.

PLAGUE
I bring one p more upon Pharaoh......... Ex 11:1
the p shall not be upon you to .... Ex 12:13
that there be no p among them........... Ex 30:12
his flesh like the p of leprosy .... Lev 13:3
on the p in the skin of the flesh .... Lev 13:3
the hair in the p is turned white .... Lev 13:3
the p in sight be deeper than the....... Lev 13:3
his flesh, it is a p of leprosy .... Lev 13:3
up him that hath the p seven days .... Lev 13:4
if the p in his sight be at a .... Lev 13:5
the p spread not in the skin .... Lev 13:5
be somewhat dark .... Lev 13:6
the p spread not in the skin .... Lev 13:6
When the p of leprosy is in a man.... Lev 13:9
the skin of him that hath the p .... Lev 13:12
him clean that hath the p .... Lev 13:13
if the p be turned into white .... Lev 13:17
him clean that hath the p .... Lev 13:17
it is a p of leprosy broken out .... Lev 13:20
it is a p .... Lev 13:22
it is the p of leprosy............................ Lev 13:25
it is the p of leprosy............................ Lev 13:27
If a man or woman have a p upon .... Lev 13:29
Then the priest shall see the p .... Lev 13:30
priest look on the p of the scall .... Lev 13:31
the p of the scall seven days .... Lev 13:32
the priest shall look on the p .... Lev 13:34
his p is in his head .... Lev 13:44
And the leper in whom the p is .... Lev 13:45
All the days wherein the p shall ...... Lev 13:46

also that the p of leprosy is in .... Lev 13:47
if the p be greenish or reddish .... Lev 13:49
it is a p of leprosy, and shall be....... Lev 13:50
the priest shall look upon the p........ Lev 13:50
up it that hath the p seven days ...... Lev 13:50
look on the p on the seventh day ..... Lev 13:51
if the p be spread in the garment .... Lev 13:51
the p is a fretting leprosy .... Lev 13:51
thing of skin, wherein the p is .... Lev 13:52
the p be not spread in the .... Lev 13:53
wash the thing wherein the p is ...... Lev 13:54
And the priest shall look on the p ... Lev 13:55
if the p have not changed his .... Lev 13:55
colour, and the p be not spread ...... Lev 13:55
the p be somewhat dark after the.... Lev 13:56
it is a spreading p .... Lev 13:57
that wherein the p is with fire .... Lev 13:57
if the p be departed from them,...... Lev 13:58
This is the law of the p of .... Lev 13:59
if the p of leprosy be healed in .... Lev 14:3
him in whom is the p of leprosy...... Lev 14:32
I put the p of leprosy in a house ..... Lev 14:34
is as it were a p in the house .... Lev 14:35
priest go unto it to see the p .... Lev 14:36
And he shall look on the p .... Lev 14:37
if the p be in the walls of the .... Lev 14:37
if the p be spread in the walls .... Lev 14:39
away the stones in which the p is.... Lev 14:40
if the p come again, and break out .. Lev 14:43
if the p be spread in the house,....... Lev 14:44
the p hath not spread in the .... Lev 14:48
clean, because the p is healed .... Lev 14:48
for all manner of leprosy .... Lev 14:54
that there be no p among the .... Num 8:19
the people with a very great p........ Num 11:33
died by the p before the LORD........ Num 14:37
the p is begun .... Num 16:46
the p was begun among the people... Num 16:47
and the p was stayed .... Num 16:48
in the p were fourteen thousand.... Num 16:49
and the p was stayed .... Num 16:50
So the p was stayed from the .... Num 25:8
that died in the p were twenty....... Num 25:9
the day of the p for Peor's sake .... Num 25:18
And it came to pass after the p ..... Num 26:1
Peor, and there was a p among the.. Num 31:16
Take heed in the p of leprosy .... Deut 24:8
Also every sickness, and every p.... Deut 28:61
although there was a p in the .... Josh 22:17
for one p was on you all, and on 1Sa 6:4
that the p may be stayed from the.. 2Sa 24:21
the p was stayed from Israel 2Sa 24:25
whatsoever p, whatsoever sickness... 1Kin 8:37
every man the p of his own heart ... 1Kin 8:38
that the p may be stayed from 1Chr 21:22
with a great p will the LORD 2Chr 21:14
his face, and p them that hate him... Ps 89:23
neither shall any p come nigh thy .... Ps 91:10
and the p brake in upon them ...... Ps 106:29
and so the p was stayed .... Ps 106:30
this shall be the p wherewith the .. Zec 14:12
And so shall be the p of the horse... Zec 14:15
be in these tents, as this p .... Zec 14:18
there shall be the p, wherewith .... Zec 14:18
that who was healed of that p .... Mk 5:29
go in peace, and be whole of thy p.. Mk 5:34
God because of the p of the hail .... Rev 16:21
for the p thereof was exceeding..... Rev 16:21

PLAGUED
And the LORD p Pharaoh and his... Gen 12:17
the LORD p the people, because ...... Ex 32:35
I p Egypt, according to that........... Josh 24:5
thy people, that they should be p ... 1Chr 21:17
neither are they p like other men... Ps 73:5
all the day long have I been p .... Ps 73:14

PLAGUES
his house with great p because of ... Gen 12:17
send all my p upon thine heart........ Ex 9:14
I will bring seven times more p....... Lev 26:21
LORD will make thy p wonderful.... Deut 28:59
p of thy seed, even great p.............. Deut 28:59
when they see the p of that land .... Deut 29:22
with all the p in the wilderness........ 1Sa 4:8
his because of all the p thereof ...... Jer 19:8
shall hiss at all the p thereof .... Jer 49:17
astonished, and hiss at all her p..... Jer 50:13
O death, I will be thy p .... Hos 13:14
to touch him, as many as had p .... Mk 3:10
many of their infirmities and p .... Lk 7:21
p yet repented not of the works....... Rev 9:20
and to smite the earth with all p ..... Rev 11:6
angels having the seven last p .... Rev 15:1
of the temple, having the seven p ... Rev 15:6
till the seven p of the seven .... Rev 15:8
which hath power over these p .... Rev 16:9
and that ye receive not of her p ..... Rev 18:4
shall her p come in one day .... Rev 18:8
vials full of the seven last p .... Rev 21:9
God shall add unto him the p that ... Rev 22:18

PLAIN
that they found a p in the land........... Gen 11:2
of Sichem, unto the p of Moreh......... Gen 12:6
and beheld all the p of Jordan .... Gen 13:10
Lot chose him all the p of Jordan .... Gen 13:11
dwelled in the cities of the p............ Gen 13:12
came and dwelt in the p of Mamre .. Gen 13:18
for he dwelt in the p of Mamre........ Gen 14:13
neither stay thou in all the p .... Gen 19:17
those cities, and all the p .... Gen 19:25

and toward all the land of the p.......	Gen 19:28
God destroyed the cities of the p	Gen 19:29
and Jacob was a p man, dwelling in	Gen 25:27
in the p over against the Red sea	Deut 1:1
places nigh thereunto, in the p	Deut 1:7
the way of the p from Elath............	Deut 2:8
All the cities of the p, and all........	Deut 3:10
The p also, and Jordan, and the	Deut 3:17
even unto the sea of the p	Deut 3:17
in the p country, of the	Deut 4:43
all the p on this side Jordan	Deut 4:49
even unto the sea of the p............	Deut 4:49
the p of the valley of Jericho,.......	Deut 34:3
came down toward the sea of the p....	Josh 3:16
at a time appointed, before the p......	Josh 8:14
Goshen, and the valley, and the p......	Josh 11:16
Hermon, and all the p on the east	Josh 12:1
And from the p to the sea of	Josh 12:3
east, and unto the sea of the p........	Josh 12:3
all the p of Medeba unto Dibon	Josh 13:9
the river, and all the p by Medeba	Josh 13:16
all her cities that are in the p	Josh 13:17
And all the cities of the p	Josh 13:21
the p out of the tribe of Reuben	Josh 20:8
his tent unto the p of Zaanaim.......	Judg 4:11
by the p of the pillar that was	Judg 9:6
come along by the p of Meonenim ...	Judg 9:37
unto the p of the vineyards, with.....	Judg 11:33
thou shalt come to the p of Tabor	1Sa 10:3
in the p on the south of Jeshimon ...	1Sa 23:24
all that night through the p	2Sa 2:29
them away through the p all night	2Sa 4:7
tarry in the p of the wilderness......	2Sa 15:28
Ahimaaz ran by the way of the p	2Sa 18:23
In the p of Jordan did the king.......	1Kin 7:46
us fight against them in the p	1Kin 20:23
will fight against them in the p	1Kin 20:25
of Hamath unto the sea of the p	2Kin 14:25
king went the way toward the p	2Kin 25:4
In the p of Jordan did the king.......	2Chr 4:17
the priests, the men of the p........	Neh 3:22
of the villages in the p of Ono.......	Neh 6:2
both out of the p country round	Neh 8:14
O LORD, and lead me in a p path	Ps 27:11
They are all p to him that..........	Prov 8:9
way of the righteous made is........	Prov 15:19
he hath made p the face thereof.....	Is 28:25
straight, and the rough places p	Is 40:4
land of Benjamin, and from the p	Jer 17:26
of the valley, and rock of the p......	Jer 21:13
and he went out the way of the p	Jer 39:4
the p shall be destroyed, as the	Jer 48:8
is come upon the p country	Jer 48:21
and they went by the way of the p	Jer 52:7
me, Arise, go forth into the p	Eze 3:22
I arose, and went forth into the p	Eze 3:23
to the vision that I saw in the p	Eze 8:4
he set it up in the p of Dura........	Dan 3:1
the inhabitant from the p of Aven	Amos 1:5
they of the p the Philistines........	Obad 19
make it p upon tables, that he.......	Hab 2:2
Zerubbabel thou shalt become a p....	Zec 4:7
men inhabited the south and the p....	Zec 7:7
a p from Geba to Rimmon south of	Zec 14:10
tongue was loosed, and he spake p	Mk 7:35
down with them, and stood in the p ...	Lk 6:17

PLAINLY

And if the servant shall p say	Ex 21:5
all the words of this law very p	Deut 27:8
Did I p appear unto the house of	1Sa 2:27
He told us p that the asses were	1Sa 10:16
us hath been p read before me.......	Ezr 4:18
shall be ready to speak p	Is 32:4
If thou be the Christ, tell us p......	Jn 10:24
Then said Jesus unto them p........	Jn 11:14
I shall shew you p of the Father.....	Jn 16:25
unto him, Lo, now speakest thou p ...	Jn 16:29
p that they seek a country	Heb 11:14

PLAINNESS

hope, we use great p of speech......	2Cor 3:12

PLAINS

unto him in the p of Mamre	Gen 18:1
pitched in the p of Moab on this.....	Num 22:1
priest spake with them in the p	Num 26:3
the children of Israel in the p	Num 26:63
unto the camp at the p of Moab	Num 31:12
pitched in the p of Moab by	Num 33:48
Abel-shittim in the p of Moab.......	Num 33:49
Moses in the p of Moab by Jordan ...	Num 33:50
LORD spake unto Moses in the p of....	Num 35:1
the children of Israel in the p	Num 36:13
Gilgal, beside the p of Moreh.......	Deut 11:30
Moses went up from the p of Moab ...	Deut 34:1
in the p of Moab thirty days.......	Deut 34:8
unto battle, to the p of Jericho	Josh 4:13
month at even in the p of Jericho ...	Josh 5:10
of the p south of Chinneroth, and ...	Josh 11:2
and in the valleys, and in the p	Josh 12:8
for inheritance in the p of Moab.....	Josh 13:32
night in the p of the wilderness	2Sa 17:16
overtook him in the p of Jericho	2Kin 25:5
trees that were in the low p was	1Chr 27:28
are in the low p in abundance	2Chr 9:27
in the low country, and in the p	2Chr 26:10
Zedekiah in the p of Jericho.......	Jer 39:5
Zedekiah in the p of Jericho.......	Jer 52:8

PLAISTER

morter, and shall p the house	Lev 14:42
stones, and p them with p	Deut 27:2
thou shalt p them with p	Deut 27:4
lay it for a p upon the boil, and	Is 38:21
the candlestick upon the p of the ...	Dan 5:5

PLAISTERED

the house, and after it is p	Lev 14:43
the house, after the house was p	Lev 14:48

PLAITING

outward adorning of p the hair	1Pet 3:3

PLANES

he fitteth it with p, and he	Is 44:13

PLANETS

sun, and to the moon, and to the p ..	2Kin 23:5

PLANKS

floor of the house with p of fir......	1Kin 6:15
there were thick p upon the face	Eze 41:25
chambers of the house, and thick p ..	Eze 41:26

PLANT

every p of the field before it	Gen 2:5
p them in the mountain of thine.....	Ex 15:17
Thou shalt not p thee a grove of	Deut 16:21
thou shalt p a vineyard, and shalt ...	Deut 28:30
Thou shalt p vineyards, and dress ...	Deut 28:39
my people Israel, and will p them ...	2Sa 7:10
p vineyards, and eat the fruits	2Kin 19:29
my people Israel, and will p them ...	1Chr 17:9
and bring forth boughs like a p	Job 14:9
a vineyards, which may yield	Ps 107:37
a time to p, and a time to pluck	Eccl 3:2
the men of Judah his pleasant p	Is 5:7
shalt thou p pleasant plants	Is 17:10
day shalt thou make thy p to grow ...	Is 17:11
p vineyards, and eat the fruit	Is 37:30
I will p in the wilderness the	Is 41:19
that I may p the heavens, and lay ...	Is 51:16
grow up before him as a tender p	Is 53:2
and they shall p vineyards	Is 65:21
they shall not p, and another eat ...	Is 65:22
to throw down, to build, and to p ...	Jer 1:10
of a strange vine unto the	Jer 2:21
a kingdom, to build and to p it	Jer 18:9
and I will p them, and not pluck	Jer 24:6
p gardens, and eat the fruit of	Jer 29:5
p gardens, and eat the fruit of	Jer 29:28
Thou shalt yet p vines upon the	Jer 31:5
the planters shall p, and shall	Jer 31:5
over them, to build, and to p	Jer 31:28
I will p them in this land..........	Jer 32:41
nor p vineyard, nor have any	Jer 35:7
pull you down, and I will p you	Jer 42:10
will p it upon an high mountain.....	Eze 17:22
the height of Israel will I p it	Eze 17:23
build houses, and p vineyards	Eze 28:26
raise up for them a p of renown	Eze 34:29
and p that that was desolate.......	Eze 36:36
he shall p the tabernacles of his ...	Dan 11:45
and they shall p vineyards	Amos 9:14
I will p them upon their land, and ..	Amos 9:15
and they shall p vineyards	Zeph 1:13
But he answered and said, Every p ..	Mt 15:13

PLANTATION

water it by the furrows of her p	Eze 17:7

PLANTED

the LORD God p a garden eastward ...	Gen 2:8
an husbandman, and he p a vineyard ..	Gen 9:20
Abraham p a grove in Beer-sheba,....	Gen 21:33
shall have p all manner of trees	Lev 19:23
light aloes which the LORD hath p ...	Num 24:6
man is he that hath p a vineyard	Deut 20:6
which ye p not do ye eat	Josh 24:13
a tree p by the rivers of water	Ps 1:3
cast out the heathen, and p it	Ps 80:8
which thy right hand hath p	Ps 80:15
Those that be p in the house of	Ps 92:13
He that p the ear, shall he not	Ps 94:9
of Lebanon, which he hath p	Ps 104:16
I p me vineyards.................	Eccl 2:4
I p trees in them of all kind of	Eccl 2:5
time to pluck up that which is p ...	Eccl 3:2
p it with the choicest vine, and	Is 5:2
Yea, they shall not be p	Is 40:24
Yet I had p thee a noble vine,......	Jer 2:21
the LORD of hosts, that p thee......	Jer 11:17
Thou hast p them, yea, they have ...	Jer 12:2
be as a tree p by the waters	Jer 17:8
which I have p I will pluck up	Jer 45:4
land, and p it in a fruitful field ..	Eze 17:5
It was p in a good soil by great	Eze 17:8
Yea, behold, being p, shall it	Eze 17:10
in thy blood, p by the waters	Eze 19:10
now she is p in the wilderness,.....	Eze 19:13
Tyrus, is p in a pleasant place	Hos 9:13
ye have p pleasant vineyards, but ...	Amos 5:11
my heavenly Father hath not p	Mt 15:13
which p a vineyard, and hedged it ...	Mt 21:33
A certain man p a vineyard	Mk 12:1
had a fig tree p in his vineyard	Lk 13:6
the root, and be thou p in the sea ..	Lk 17:6
they bought, they sold, they p	Lk 17:28
A certain man p a vineyard	Lk 20:9
For if we have been p together in ...	Rom 6:5
I have p, Apollos watered	1Cor 3:6

PLANTEDST

and olive trees, which thou p not ...	Deut 6:11
heathen with thy hand, and p them ..	Ps 44:2

PLANTERS

the p shall plant, and shall eat	Jer 31:5

PLANTETH

of her hands she p a vineyard	Prov 31:16
he p an ash, and the rain doth......	Is 44:14
neither is he that p any thing	1Cor 3:7
Now he that p and he that watereth..	1Cor 3:8
who p a vineyard, and eateth not ...	1Cor 9:7

PLANTING

land for ever, the branch of my p ...	Is 60:21
the p of the LORD, that he might	Is 61:3

PLANTINGS

the field, and as p of a vineyard ...	Mic 1:6

PLANTS

and those that dwelt among p	1Chr 4:23
olive p round about thy table	Ps 128:3
be as p grown up in their youth	Ps 144:12
Thy p are an orchard of...........	Song 4:13
down the principal p thereof	Is 17:10
shalt thou plant pleasant p	Is 17:10
thy p are gone over the sea, they ...	Jer 48:32
rivers running round about his p	Eze 31:4

PLAT

and I will requite thee in this p	2Kin 9:26
and cast him into the p of ground ...	2Kin 9:26

PLATE

thou shalt make a p of pure gold....	Ex 28:36
they made the p of the holy crown ...	Ex 39:30
did he put the golden p, the.......	Lev 8:9

PLATES

did beat the gold into thin p.......	Ex 39:3
let them make them broad p for a ...	Num 16:38
they were made broad p for a	Num 16:39
four brasen wheels, and p of brass ..	1Kin 7:30
For on the p of the ledges.........	1Kin 7:36
Silver spread into p is brought	Jer 10:9

PLATTED

when they had p a crown of thorns ..	Mt 27:29
p a crown of thorns, and put it	Mk 15:17
the soldiers p a crown of thorns,....	Jn 19:2

PLATTER

outside of the cup and of the	Mt 23:25
that which is within the cup and p ..	Mt 23:26
the outside of the cup and the p	Lk 11:39

PLAY

eat and to drink, and rose up to p ..	Ex 32:6
to p the whore in her father's......	Deut 22:21
that he shall p with his hand.......	1Sa 16:16
me now a man that can p well.......	1Sa 16:17
to p the mad man in my presence ...	1Sa 21:15
men now arise, and p before us	2Sa 2:14
will I p before the LORD...........	2Sa 6:21
let us p the men for our people,....	2Sa 10:12
all the beasts of the field p	Job 40:20
Wilt thou p with him as with a	Job 41:5
p skilfully with a loud noise.......	Ps 33:3
whom thou hast made to p therein ...	Ps 104:26
shall p on the hole of the asp	Is 11:8
can p well on an instrument........	Eze 33:32
thou shalt not p the harlot	Hos 3:3
p the harlot, yet let not Judah.....	Hos 4:15
to eat and drink, and rose up to p ..	1Cor 10:7

PLAYED

daughter in law hath p the harlot ...	Gen 38:24
his concubine p the whore against ...	Judg 19:2
took an harp, and p with his hand ...	1Sa 16:23
answered one another as they p	1Sa 18:7
David p with his hand, as at	1Sa 18:10
and David p with his hand.........	1Sa 19:9
I have p the fool, and have erred ...	1Sa 26:21
all the house of Israel p before	2Sa 6:5
came to pass, when the minstrel p ..	2Kin 3:15
all Israel p before God with all	1Chr 13:8
but thou hast p the harlot with	Jer 3:1
tree, and there hath p the harlot ...	Jer 3:6
but went and p the harlot also......	Jer 3:8
Thou hast p the whore also with	Eze 16:28
thou hast p the harlot with them,...	Eze 16:28
Aholah p the harlot when she was ...	Eze 23:5
wherein she had p the harlot in	Eze 23:19
their mother hath p the harlot	Hos 2:5

PLAYEDST

p the harlot because of thy	Eze 16:15
and p the harlot thereupon.........	Eze 16:16

PLAYER

who is a cunning p on an harp	1Sa 16:16

PLAYERS

the p on instruments followed	Ps 68:25
As well the singers as the p on	Ps 87:7

PLAYETH

in unto a woman that p the harlot ..	Eze 23:44

PLAYING

profane herself by p the whore......	Lev 21:9
that is cunning in p, and a	1Sa 16:18
saw king David dancing and p	1Chr 15:29
were the damsels p with timbrels ...	Ps 68:25
tree thou wanderest, p the harlot ...	Jer 2:20
thee to cease from p the harlot	Eze 16:41
girls p in the streets thereof	Zec 8:5

PLEA
blood and blood, between *p* and *p* .... Deut 17:8

PLEAD
against him, Will ye *p* for Baal .... Judg 6:31
he that will *p* for him, let him............... Judg 6:31
let him *p* for himself, because .... Judg 6:31
Let Baal *p* against him, because .... Judg 6:32
p my cause, and deliver me out of 1Sa 24:15
who shall set me a time to *p* .... Job 9:19
Who is he that will *p* with me............... Job 13:19
Oh that one might *p* for a man............... Job 16:21
me, and *p* against me my reproach.......... Job 19:5
Will he *p* against me with his............... Job 23:6
p my cause, O LORD, with them .... Ps 35:1
p my cause against an ungodly............... Ps 43:1
Arise, O God, *p* thine own cause .... Ps 74:22
P my cause, and deliver me............... Ps 119:154
For the LORD will *p* their cause .... Prov 22:23
he shall *p* their cause with thee............. Prov 23:11
p the cause of the poor and needy......... Prov 31:9
the fatherless, *p* for the widow .... Is 1:17
The LORD standeth up to *p*................... Is 3:13
let us *p* together....................................... Is 43:26
will the LORD *p* with all flesh................... Is 66:16
Wherefore I will yet *p* with you............... Jer 2:9
your children's children will I *p* .... Jer 2:9
Wherefore will ye *p* with me............... Jer 2:29
I will *p* with thee, because thou........... Jer 2:35
thou, O LORD, when I *p* with thee .... Jer 12:1
nations, he will *p* with all flesh............... Jer 25:31
There is none to *p* thy cause................ Jer 30:13
he shall throughly *p* their cause............. Jer 50:34
I will *p* thy cause, and take............... Jer 51:36
will *p* with him there for his............... Eze 17:20
there will I *p* with you face to............... Eze 20:35
of Egypt, so will I *p* with you................ Eze 20:36
I will *p* against him with................... Eze 38:22
P with your mother,................................. Hos 2:2
will *p* with them there for my............... Joel 3:2
people, and he will *p* with Israel............... Mic 6:2
against him, until he *p* my cause............. Mic 7:9

PLEADED
that hath *p* the cause of my 1Sa 25:39
thou hast *p* the causes of my soul........ Lam 3:58
Like as I *p* with your fathers in.......... Eze 20:36

PLEADETH
as a man *p* for his neighbour................ Job 16:21
thy God that *p* the cause of his .... Is 51:22
for justice, nor any *p* for truth............... Is 59:4

PLEADINGS
and hearken to the *p* of my lips........... Job 13:6

PLEASANT
every tree that is *p* to the sight .... Gen 2:9
and that it was *p* to the eyes.................... Gen 3:6
good, and the land that it was *p*........... Gen 49:15
p in their lives, and in their 2Sa 1:23
very *p* hast thou been unto me............. 2Sa 1:26
whatsoever is *p* in thine eyes 1Kin 20:6
the situation of this city is *p*................. 2Kin 2:19
and for all manner of *p* jewels........... 2Chr 32:27
are fallen unto me in *p* places............... Ps 16:6
the *p* harp with the psaltery................... Ps 81:2
Yea, they despised the *p* land............... Ps 106:24
how *p* it is for brethren to dwell............. Ps 133:1
for it is *p*.. Ps 135:3
knowledge is *p* unto thy soul .... Prov 2:10
be as the loving hind and *p* roe .... Prov 5:19
and bread eaten in secret is *p* .... Prov 9:17
the words of the pure are *p* words......... Prov 15:26
P words are as an honeycomb,............... Prov 16:24
For it is a *p* thing if thou keep............... Prov 22:18
with all precious and *p* riches............... Prov 24:4
a thing it is for the eyes to............... Eccl 11:7
thou art fair, my beloved, yea, *p* .... Song 1:16
of pomegranates, with *p* fruits............... Song 4:13
his garden, and eat his *p* fruits............... Song 4:16
how *p* art thou, O love, for............... Song 7:6
gates are all manner of *p* fruits............... Song 7:13
Tarnish, and upon all *p* pictures............... Is 2:16
and the men of Judah his *p* plant........... Is 5:7
and dragons in their *p* palaces............... Is 13:22
shalt thou plant *p* plants....................... Is 17:10
for the teats, for the *p* fields................... Is 32:12
and all thy borders of *p* stones............... Is 54:12
all our *p* things are laid waste............... Is 64:11
children, and give thee a *p* .... Jer 3:19
they have made my *p* portion a............... Jer 12:10
the *p* places of the wilderness .... Jer 23:10
and ye shall fall like a *p* vessel............... Jer 25:34
is he a *p* child... Jer 31:20
of her miseries all her *p* things............... Lam 1:7
his hand upon all her *p* things............... Lam 1:10
they have given their *p* things............... Lam 1:11
slew all that were *p* to the eye............... Lam 2:4
walls, and destroy thy *p* houses............. Eze 26:12
song of one that hath a *p* voice............... Eze 33:32
the east, and toward the *p* land............... Dan 8:9
I ate no *p* bread, neither came............... Dan 10:3
with precious stones, and *p* things......... Dan 11:38
the *p* places for their silver,................... Hos 9:6
Tyrus, is planted in a *p* place .... Hos 9:13
the treasure of all *p* vessels............... Hos 13:15
your temples my goodly *p* things........... Joel 3:5
ye have planted *p* vineyards............... Amos 5:11
ye cast out from their *p* houses............... Mic 2:9
glory out of all the *p* furniture............... Nah 2:9
for they laid the *p* land desolate............ Zec 7:14
Jerusalem be *p* unto the LORD, as.......... Mal 3:4

PLEASANTNESS
Her ways are ways of *p*, and all............. Prov 3:17

PLEASE
If she *p* not her master, who hath............. Ex 21:8
peradventure it will *p* God that............... Num 23:27
but if it *p* my father to do thee............... 1Sa 20:13
Therefore now let it *p* thee to 2Sa 7:29
or else, if it *p* thee, I will 1Kin 21:6
Now therefore let it *p* the............... 1Chr 17:27
p them, and speak good words to........... 2Chr 10:7
If it *p* the king, and if thy .... Neh 2:5
If it *p* the king, let letters be................... Neh 2:7
If it *p* the king, let there go a................... Est 1:19
If it *p* the king, let it .... Est 3:9
if it *p* the king to grant my................... Est 5:8
if it *p* the king, let my life be................... Est 7:3
if it *p* the king, and if I have................... Est 8:5
If it *p* the king, let it be............................ Est 9:13
that it would *p* God to destroy me........... Job 6:9
children shall seek to *p* the poor .... Job 20:10
This also shall *p* the LORD better .... Ps 69:31
When a man's ways *p* the LORD............... Prov 16:7
up, nor awake my love, till he *p*............... Song 2:7
up, nor awake my love, till he *p*............... Song 3:5
up, nor awake my love, until he *p*......... Song 8:4
they *p* themselves in the children......... Is 2:6
shall accomplish that which I *p*............... Is 55:11
and choose the things that *p* me .... Is 56:4
do always those things that *p* him......... Is 8:29
are in the flesh cannot *p* God................... Rom 8:8
the weak, and not to *p* ourselves............. Rom 15:1
Let every one of us *p* his......................... Rom 15:2
the Lord, how he may *p* the Lord............ 1Cor 7:32
the world, how he may *p* his wife........... 1Cor 7:33
world, how she may *p* her husband......... 1Cor 7:34
Even as I *p* all men in all things............... 1Cor 10:33
or do I seek to *p* men............................. Gal 1:10
they *p* not God, and are contrary............. 1Th 2:15
to *p* God, so ye would abound more......... 1Th 4:1
that he may *p* him who hath chosen......... 2Ti 2:4
to *p* them well in all things..................... Titus 2:9
faith it is impossible to *p* him.................. Heb 11:6

PLEASED
of Canaan *p* not Isaac his father............. Gen 28:8
of God, and thou saw'st it *p* him........... Gen 33:10
And their words *p* Hamor, and............... Gen 34:18
it *p* Pharaoh well, and his....................... Gen 45:16
when Balaam saw that it *p* the............... Num 24:1
And the saying *p* me well......................... Deut 1:23
of Manasseh spake, it *p* them................ Josh 22:30
the thing *p* the children of................... Josh 22:33
If the LORD were to *p* to kill us............... Judg 13:23
and she *p* Samson well............................ Judg 14:7
because it hath *p* the Lord...................... 1Sa 12:22
told Saul, and the thing *p* him............... 1Sa 18:20
it *p* David well to be the king's............... 1Sa 18:26
took notice of it, and it *p* them............... 2Sa 3:36
the king did *p* all the people................... 2Sa 3:36
the saying *p* Absalom well, and all......... 2Sa 17:4
this day, then I had *p* thee well 2Sa 19:6
And the speech of the Lord, that............... 1Kin 3:10
desire which he was *p* to do................... 1Kin 9:1
and they *p* him not.................................. 1Kin 9:12
And the thing the king and all............... 2Chr 30:4
So it *p* the king to send me..................... Neh 2:6
And the saying *p* the king and the........... Est 1:21
And the thing *p* the king......................... Est 2:4
And the maiden *p* him, and she............... Est 2:9
Be *p*, O LORD, to deliver me................... Ps 40:13
Then shalt thou be *p* with the................ Ps 51:19
he hath done whatsoever he hath *p* .... Ps 115:3
Whatsoever the LORD, that did .... Ps 135:6
The LORD is well *p* for his....................... Is 42:21
Yet it *p* the LORD to bruise him............... Is 53:10
It *p* Darius to set over the....................... Dan 6:1
O LORD, hast done as it *p* thee............... Jonah 1:14
Will the LORD be *p* with thousands......... Mic 6:7
will he be *p* with thee, or accept............. Mal 1:8
beloved Son, in whom I am well *p* .... Mt 3:17
in whom my soul is well *p* .... Mt 12:18
danced before them, and *p* Herod........... Mt 14:6
beloved Son, in whom I am well *p* .... Mt 17:5
I am well *p*, in whom I am well............... Mk 1:11
p Herod and them that sat with him...... Mk 6:22
in thee I am well *p*.................................... Lk 3:22
the saying *p* the whole multitude........... Acts 6:5
And because he saw it *p* the Jews........... Acts 12:3
Then it *p* the apostles and elders,......... Acts 15:22
Notwithstanding it *p* Silas to................. Acts 15:34
For even Christ *p* not himself................. Rom 15:3
For it hath *p* them of Macedonia............. Rom 15:26
It hath *p* them verily................................ 1Cor 1:21
it *p* God by the foolishness of................ 1Cor 1:21
she be *p* to dwell with him, let............... 1Cor 7:12
if he be *p* to dwell with her, let............... 1Cor 7:13
many of them God was not well *p*........... 1Cor 10:5
in the body, as it hath *p* him................... 1Cor 12:18
giveth it a body as it hath *p* him............. 1Cor 15:38
for if I yet *p* men, I should not............... Gal 1:10
But when it *p* God, who separated......... Gal 1:15
For it *p* the Father that in him............... Col 1:19
had this testimony, that he *p* God........... Heb 11:5
such sacrifices God is well *p*................... Heb 13:16
beloved Son, in whom I am well *p* 2Pet 1:17

PLEASETH
do to her as it *p* thee............................. Gen 16:6
dwell where it *p* thee............................. Gen 20:15
for she *p* me well................................... Judg 14:3

PLEASING
I be *p* in his eyes, let it be....................... Est 8:5
neither shall they be *p* unto him............. Hos 9:4
worthy of the Lord unto all *p*................... Col 1:10
for this is well *p* unto the Lord .... Col 3:20
not as *p* men, but God, which 1Th 2:4
things that are *p* in his sight................... 1Jn 3:22

PLEASURE
I am waxed old shall I have *p* .... Gen 18:12
grapes thy fill at thine own *p* .... Deut 23:24
heart, and hast *p* in uprightness............. 1Chr 29:17
let the king send his *p* to us................... Ezr 5:17
God of your fathers, and do his *p* .... Ezr 10:11
and over our cattle, at their *p* .... Neh 9:37
do according to every man's *p* .... Est 1:8
For what *p* hath he in his house............. Job 21:21
his soul, and never eateth with *p*........... Job 21:25
Is it any *p* to the Almighty, that............. Job 22:3
a God that hath *p* in wickedness............. Ps 5:4
which hath *p* in the prosperity of............ Ps 35:27
Do good in thy good *p* unto Zion............. Ps 51:18
thy servants take *p* in her stones........... Ps 102:14
ministers of his, that do his *p*................. Ps 103:21
To bind his princes at his *p*..................... Ps 105:22
of all them that have *p* therein............... Ps 111:2
he taketh not *p* in the legs of a............... Ps 147:10
The LORD taketh *p* in them that............. Ps 147:11
the LORD taketh *p* in his people............. Ps 149:4
He that loveth *p* shall be a poor............ Prov 21:17
with mirth, therefore enjoy *p*............... Eccl 2:1
for he hath no *p* in fools......................... Eccl 5:4
shalt say, I have no *p* in them .... Eccl 12:1
the night of my *p* hath he turned............. Is 21:4
and shall perform all my *p* .... Is 44:28
stand, and I will do all my *p* .... Is 46:10
he will do his *p* on Babylon..................... Is 48:14
the *p* of the LORD shall prosper............. Is 53:10
in the day of your fast ye find *p* .... Is 58:3
from doing thy *p* on my holy day............. Is 58:13
own ways, nor finding thine own *p* .... Is 58:13
snuffeth up the wind at her *p* .... Jer 2:24
is he a vessel wherein is no *p* .... Jer 22:28
he had set at liberty at their *p* .... Jer 34:16
like a vessel wherein is no *p* .... Jer 48:38
with whom thou hast taken *p* .... Eze 16:37
Have I any *p* at all that the..................... Eze 18:23
For I have no *p* in the death of............... Eze 18:32
I have no *p* in the death of the............... Eze 33:11
as a vessel wherein is no *p* .... Mal 1:10
and I will take *p* in it, and I will............... Hag 1:8
I have no *p* in you, saith the................... Mal 1:10
good *p* to give you the kingdom............. Lk 12:32
willing to shew the Jews a *p* .... Acts 24:27
willing to do the Jews a *p*....................... Acts 25:9
but have *p* in them that do them............. Rom 1:32
Therefore I take *p* in infirmities 2Cor 12:10
to the good *p* of his will .... Eph 1:5
according to his good *p* which he............. Eph 1:9
to will and to do of his good *p* .... Phil 2:13
all the good *p* of his goodness............... 2Th 1:11
but had *p* in unrighteousness............... 2Th 2:12
But she that liveth in *p* is dead............... 1Ti 5:6
for sin thou hast had no *p* .... Heb 10:6
not, neither hadst *p* therein................... Heb 10:8
my soul shall have no *p* in him .... Heb 10:38
chastened us after their own *p*............... Heb 12:10
Ye have lived in *p* on the earth............... Jas 5:5
as they that count it *p* to riot................... 2Pet 2:13
for thy *p* they are and were..................... Rev 4:11

PLEASURES
prosperity, and their years in *p* .... Job 36:11
hand there are *p* for evermore .... Ps 16:11
them drink of the river of thy *p* .... Ps 36:8
this, thou that art given to *p* .... Is 47:8
p of this life, and bring no fruit .... Lk 8:14
lovers of *p* more than lovers of............... 2Ti 3:4
serving divers lusts and *p* .... Titus 3:3
than to enjoy the *p* of sin for a............... Heb 11:25

PLEDGE
she said, Wilt thou give me a *p* .... Gen 38:17
he said, What *p* shall I give thee............. Gen 38:18
to receive his *p* from the woman's.......... Gen 38:20
take thy neighbour's raiment to *p* .... Ex 22:26
or the upper millstone to *p* .... Deut 24:6
for he taketh a man's life to *p* .... Deut 24:6
go into his house to fetch his *p* .... Deut 24:10
bring out the *p* abroad unto thee........... Deut 24:11
thou shalt not sleep with his *p* .... Deut 24:12
p again when the sun goeth down........... Deut 24:13
nor take a widow's raiment to *p*............. Deut 24:17
brethren fare, and take their *p* 1Sa 17:18
For thou hast taken a *p* from thy............ Job 22:6
they take the widow's ox for a *p*............. Job 24:3
breast, and take a *p* of the poor .... Job 24:9
take a *p* of him for a stranger................ Prov 20:16
take a *p* of him for a strange................. Prov 27:13
hath restored to the debtor his *p* .... Eze 18:7
violence, hath not restored the *p* .... Eze 18:12
any, hath not withholden the *p* .... Eze 18:16
If the wicked restore the *p* .... Eze 33:15
clothes laid to *p* by every altar............... Amos 2:8

PLEDGES
give *p* to my lord the king of 2Kin 18:23
Now therefore give *p*, I pray thee............ Is 36:8

PLEIADES (ple´-ya-dez) *A constellation of stars.*
maketh Arcturus, Orion, and P............... Job 9:9
bind the sweet influences of P................ Job 38:31

PLENTEOUS
of Egypt in the seven p years................. Gen 41:34
in the seven p years the earth............... Gen 41:47
LORD shall make thee p in goods....... Deut 28:11
p in every work of thine hand.............. Deut 30:9
gold at Jerusalem as p as stones.......... 2Chr 1:15
p in mercy unto all them that................ Ps 86:5
and p in mercy, and truth..................... Ps 86:15
slow to anger, and p in mercy................ Ps 103:8
and with him is p redemption................ Ps 130:7
earth, and it shall be fat and p............... Is 30:23
portion is fat, and their meat p............... Hab 1:16
disciples, The harvest truly is p.............. Mt 9:37

PLENTEOUSNESS
And the seven years of p, that was...... Gen 41:53
of the diligent tend only to p................ Prov 21:5

PLENTIFUL
Thou, O God, didst send a p rain........... Ps 68:9
away, and joy out of the p field............. Is 16:10
And I brought you into a p country........ Jer 2:7
is taken from the p field..................... Jer 48:33

PLENTIFULLY
how hast thou p declared the............... Job 26:3
p rewardeth the proud doer................. Ps 31:23
certain rich man brought forth p............ Lk 12:16

PLENTY
the earth, and p of corn and wine......... Gen 27:28
p throughout all the land of................. Gen 41:29
all the p shall be forgotten in............... Gen 41:30
the p shall not be known in the............ Gen 41:31
pit, wherein there is p of water........... Lev 11:36
from Ophir great p of almug trees........ 1Kin 10:11
had enough to eat, and have left p........ 2Chr 31:10
and thou shalt have p of silver............. Job 22:25
in judgment, and in p of justice............ Job 37:23
shall thy barns be filled with p............ Prov 3:10
his land shall have p of bread............... Prov 28:19
for then had we p of victuals................ Jer 44:17
And ye shall eat in p, and be................ Joel 2:26

PLOTTETH
The wicked p against the just, and....... Ps 37:12

PLOUGH
man, having put his hand to the p....... Lk 9:62

PLOW
Thou shalt not p with an ox................ Deut 22:10
which a yoke of oxen might p............... 1Sa 14:14
I have seen, they that p iniquity........... Job 4:8
will not p by reason of the cold.......... Prov 20:4
Doth the plowman p all day to sow...... Is 28:24
Judah shall p, and Jacob shall............. Hos 10:11
will one p there with oxen.................. Amos 6:12
he that ploweth should p in hope........ 1Cor 9:10

PLOWED
If ye had not p with my heifer,........... Judg 14:18
The plowers p upon my back............... Ps 129:3
Zion shall be p like a field.................. Jer 26:18
Ye have p wickedness, ye have........... Hos 10:13
for your sake be p as a field................ Mic 3:12

PLOWERS
The p plowed upon my back................. Ps 129:3

PLOWETH
that he that p should plow in............... 1Cor 9:10

PLOWING
who was p with twelve yoke of............ 1Kin 19:19
Job, and said, The oxen were p............. Job 1:14
the p of the wicked, is sin................ Prov 21:4
having a servant p or feeding.............. Lk 17:7

PLOWMAN
Doth the p plow all day to sow............. Is 28:24
that the p shall overtake the............... Amos 9:13

PLOWMEN
sons of the alien shall be your p........... Is 61:5
the p were ashamed, they covered....... Jer 14:4

PLOWSHARES
shall beat their swords into p................ Is 2:4
Beat your p into swords, and your...... Joel 3:10
shall beat their swords into p............... Mic 4:3

PLUCK
he shall p away his crop with his......... Lev 1:16
quite p down all their high................. Num 33:52
then thou mayest p the ears with........ Deut 23:25
Then will I p them up by the............... 2Chr 7:20
They p the fatherless from the............ Job 24:9
for he shall p my feet out of the.......... Ps 25:15
p thee out of thy dwelling place,......... Ps 52:5
p it out of thy bosom........................ Ps 74:11
which pass by the way do p her.......... Ps 80:12
a time to p up that which is............... Eccl 3:2
I will p them out of their land,............ Jer 12:14
p out the house of Judah from........... Jer 12:14
not obey, I will uproot it................... Jer 12:17
and concerning a kingdom, to p up..... Jer 18:7
hand, yet would I p thee thence.......... Jer 22:24
will plant them, and not p them up...... Jer 24:6
I have watched over them, to p up...... Jer 31:28
I will plant you, and not p you up....... Jer 42:10
which I have planted I will p up........... Jer 45:4

to p it up by the roots thereof............. Eze 17:9
and p off thine own breasts................ Eze 23:34
who p off their skin from off.............. Mic 3:2
I will p up thy groves out of the.......... Mic 5:14
p it out, and cast it from thee............. Mt 5:29
began to p the ears of corn, and......... Mt 12:1
p it out, and cast it from thee............ Mt 18:9
they went, to p the ears of corn......... Mk 2:23
thine eye offend thee, p it out........... Mk 9:47
any man p them out of my hand.......... Jn 10:28
no man is able to p them out of......... Jn 10:29

PLUCKED
p it out of his bosom, and, behold...... Ex 4:7
ye shall be p from off the land.......... Deut 28:63
a man p off his shoe, and gave it........ Ruth 4:7
p the spear out of the Egyptian's....... 2Sa 23:21
p the spear out of the Egyptian's...... 1Chr 11:23
p off the hair of my head and of....... Ezr 9:3
p off their hair, and made them......... Neh 13:25
p the spoil out of his teeth................ Job 29:17
to them that p off the hair................ Is 50:6
for the wicked are not p away........... Jer 6:29
after that I have p them out I........... Jer 12:15
it shall not be p up, nor thrown......... Jer 31:40
But she was p up in fury, she was...... Eze 19:12
till the wings thereof were p.............. Dan 7:4
the first horns p up by the roots........ Dan 7:8
for his kingdom shall be p up.............. Dan 11:4
a firebrand p out of the burning......... Amos 4:11
this a brand p out of the fire.............. Zec 3:2
chains had been p asunder by him...... Mk 5:4
his disciples p the ears of corn.......... Lk 6:1
Be thou p up by the root, and be....... Lk 17:6
ye would have p out your own eyes..... Gal 4:15
twice dead, p up by the roots............. Jude 12

PLUCKETH
but the foolish p it down with........... Prov 14:1

PLUCKT
her mouth was an olive leaf p off....... Gen 8:11

PLUMBLINE
stood upon a wall made by a p.......... Amos 7:7
with a p in his hand......................... Amos 7:7
And I said, A.................................. Amos 7:8
I will set a p in the midst of my......... Amos 7:8

PLUMMET
the p of the house of Ahab............... 2Kin 21:13
line, and righteousness to the p........... Is 28:17
shall see the p in the hand of........... Zec 4:10

PLUNGE
Yet shalt thou p me in the ditch,....... Job 9:31

POCHERETH (po-ke´-reth) *A family of exiles.*
the children of P of Zebaim............... Ezr 2:57
the children of P of Zebaim............... Neh 7:59

POETS
also of your own p have said.............. Acts 17:28

POINT
Behold, I am at the p to die.............. Gen 25:32
ye shall p out for you mount Hor....... Num 34:7
From mount Hor ye shall p out.......... Num 34:8
ye shall p out your east border......... Num 34:10
iron, and with the p of a diamond...... Jer 17:1
I have set the p of the sword............ Eze 21:15
daughter lieth at the p of death........ Mk 5:23
for he was at the p of death............. Jn 4:47
whole law, and yet offend in one p..... Jas 2:10

POINTED
he spreadeth sharp p things upon...... Job 41:30

POINTS
evil, that in all p as he came............. Eccl 5:16
but was in all p tempted like as........ Heb 4:15

POISON
with the p of serpents of the............ Deut 32:24
Their wine is the p of dragons.......... Deut 32:33
the p whereof drinketh up my........... Job 6:4
He shall suck the p of asps............... Job 20:16
p is like the p of a serpent............... Ps 58:4
adders' p is under their lips............... Ps 140:3
the p of asps is under their lips......... Rom 3:13
an unruly evil, full of deadly p........... Jas 3:8

POLE
fiery serpent, and set it upon a p...... Num 21:8
of brass, and put it upon a p............ Num 21:9

POLICY
through his p also he shall cause...... Dan 8:25

POLISHED
p after the similitude of a................ Ps 144:12
he hid me, and made me a p shaft...... Is 49:2
feet like in colour to p brass............ Dan 10:6

POLISHING
rubies, their p was of sapphire......... Lam 4:7

POLL
take five shekels apiece by the p....... Num 3:47
they shall only p their heads............ Eze 44:20
up for the p by their delicate children.... Mic 1:16

POLLED
when he p his head, (for it was........ 2Sa 14:26
at every year's end that he p it........ 2Sa 14:26
heavy on him, therefore he p it....... 2Sa 14:26

POLLS
names, every male by their p.............. Num 1:2
years old and upward, by their p....... Num 1:18
number of the names, by their p....... Num 1:20
number of the names, by their p....... Num 1:22
and their number by their p............ 1Chr 23:3
by number of names by their p........ 1Chr 23:24

POLLUTE
neither shall ye p the holy................ Num 18:32
So ye shall not p the land................ Num 35:33
is called by my name, to p it............. Jer 7:30
and they shall if p.......................... Eze 7:21
they shall p my secret place............. Eze 7:22
will ye p me among my people for...... Eze 13:19
ye p yourselves with all your........... Eze 20:31
but p ye my holy name no more......... Eze 20:39
I will not let them p my holy............ Eze 39:7
to be in my sanctuary, to p it........... Eze 44:7
they shall p the sanctuary of........... Dan 11:31

POLLUTED
thy tool upon it, thou hast p it......... Ex 20:25
p it, according to the word of........... 2Kin 23:16
p the house of the LORD which he..... 2Chr 36:14
therefore were they, as p.................. Ezr 2:62
therefore were they, as p.................. Neh 7:64
and the land was p with blood......... Ps 106:38
I have p mine inheritance, and.......... Is 47:6
for how should my name be p........... Is 48:11
How canst thou say, I am not p......... Jer 2:23
shalt not that land be greatly p......... Jer 3:1
thou hast p the land with thy........... Jer 3:2
p my name, and caused every man.... Jer 34:16
he hath p the kingdom and the......... Lam 2:2
they have p themselves with blood.... Lam 4:14
behold, my soul hath not been p....... Eze 4:14
neither be p any more with all......... Eze 14:11
saw thee p in thine own blood, I....... Eze 16:6
and bare, and wast p in thy blood..... Eze 16:22
not be p before the heathen............ Eze 20:9
and my sabbaths they greatly p........ Eze 20:13
not be p before the heathen............ Eze 20:14
in my statutes, but p my sabbaths.... Eze 20:16
they p my sabbaths......................... Eze 20:21
that it should not be p in the.......... Eze 20:22
had p my sabbaths, and their eyes.... Eze 20:24
I p them in their own gifts, in.......... Eze 20:26
Are ye p after the manner of your.... Eze 20:30
she was p with them, and her mind... Eze 23:17
thou art p with their idols.............. Eze 23:30
idols wherewith they had p it........... Eze 36:18
work iniquity, and is p with blood..... Hos 6:8
all that eat thereof shall be p........... Hos 9:4
and thou shalt die in a p land......... Amos 7:17
because it is p, it shall destroy......... Mic 2:10
Woe to her that is filthy and p......... Zeph 3:1
her priests have p the sanctuary...... Zeph 3:4
Ye offer p bread upon mine altar...... Mal 1:7
and ye say, Wherein have we p thee... Mal 1:7
say, The table of the LORD is p........ Mal 1:12
temple, and hath p his holy place..... Acts 21:28

POLLUTING
keepeth the sabbath from p it............ Is 56:2
keepeth the sabbath from p it............ Is 56:6

POLLUTION
her that was set apart for p............ Eze 22:10

POLLUTIONS
that they abstain from p of idols...... Acts 15:20
the p of the world through the.......... 2Pet 2:20

POLLUX *A Roman god.*
isle, whose sign was Castor and P..... Acts 28:11

POMEGRANATE
A golden bell and a p, a golden......... Ex 28:34
p, a golden bell and a p................... Ex 28:34
A bell and a p, a bell and a............. Ex 39:26
and a p, a bell and a p................... Ex 39:26
part of Gibeah under a p tree........... 1Sa 14:2
a piece of a p within thy locks........ Song 4:3
As a piece of a p are thy temples..... Song 6:7
spiced wine of the juice of my p...... Song 8:2
the p tree, the palm tree also,......... Joel 1:12
vine, and the fig tree, and the p...... Hag 2:19

POMEGRANATES
of it thou shalt make p of blue......... Ex 28:33
the hems of the robe p of blue......... Ex 39:24
the p upon the hem of the robe...... Ex 39:25
robe, round about between the p...... Ex 39:25
and they brought of the p, and of..... Num 13:23
or of figs, or of vines, or of p.......... Num 20:5
and vines, and fig trees, and p......... Deut 8:8
that were upon the top, with p........ 1Kin 7:18
the two pillars had p also about...... 1Kin 7:20
the p were two hundred in rows...... 1Kin 7:20
four hundred p for the two............. 1Kin 7:42
two rows of p for one network........ 1Kin 7:42
upon the chapiter round about,....... 2Kin 25:17
and made an hundred p.................. 2Chr 3:16
four hundred p on the two wreaths... 2Chr 4:13
two rows of p on each wreath, to..... 2Chr 4:13
Thy plants are an orchard of p......... Song 4:13
vine flourished, and the p budded..... Song 6:11
grape appear, and the p bud forth..... Song 7:12
p upon the chapiters round about,.... Jer 52:22
the p were like unto these............. Jer 52:22
were ninety and six p on a side...... Jer 52:23
all the p upon the network were..... Jer 52:23

POMMELS

To wit, the two pillars, and the *p*.............. 2Chr 4:12
two wreaths to cover the two *p* of 2Chr 4:12
to cover the two *p* of the 2Chr 4:13

POMP

and their multitude, and their *p*................... Is 5:14
Thy *p* is brought down to the .... Is 14:11
I will also make the *p* of the .... Eze 7:24
the *p* of her strength shall cease .... Eze 30:18
they shall spoil the *p* of Egypt .... Eze 32:12
the *p* of her strength shall cease .... Eze 33:28
come, and Bernice, with great *p* .... Acts 25:23

PONDER

P the path of thy feet, and let .... Prov 4:26
thou shouldest *p* the path of life .... Prov 5:6

PONDERED

things, and *p* them in her heart................... Lk 2:19

PONDERETH

the LORD, and he *p* all his goings .... Prov 5:21
but the LORD *p* the hearts .... Prov 21:2
doth not he that *p* the heart.................... Prov 24:12

PONDS

their rivers, and upon their *p*...................... Ex 7:19
over the rivers, and over the *p* .... Ex 8:5
that make sluices and *p* for fish............... Is 19:10

PONTIUS (pon´-she-us) The family name of
Pilate.
delivered him to *P* Pilate the..................... Mt 27:2
P Pilate being governor of Judaea .... Lk 3:1
P Pilate, with the Gentiles, and.............. Acts 4:27
who before *P* Pilate witnessed a.............. 1Ti 6:13

PONTUS (pon´-tus) A Roman province in Asia
Minor.
and in Judaea, and Cappadocia, in *P*..... Acts 2:9
Jew named Aquila, born in *P* .... Acts 18:2
strangers scattered throughout *P*.............. 1Pet 1:1

POOL

met together by the *p* of Gibeon 2Sa 2:13
the one on the one side of the *p* 2Sa 2:13
other on the other side of the *p* 2Sa 2:13
them up over the *p* in Hebron.................... 2Sa 4:12
the chariot in the *p* of Samaria 1Kin 22:38
by the conduit of the upper *p* 2Kin 18:17
all his might, and how he made a *p*...... 2Kin 20:20
the fountain, and to the king's *p*............ Neh 2:14
the wall of the *p* of Siloah by .... Neh 3:15
to the *p* that was made, and unto .... Neh 3:16
p in the highway of the fuller's............... Is 7:3
the waters of the lower *p* .... Is 22:9
walls for the water of the old *p* .... Is 22:11
parched ground shall become a *p* .... Is 35:7
by the conduit of the upper *p* in................ Is 36:2
make the wilderness a *p* of water............ Is 41:18
is of old like a *p* of water .... Nah 2:8
Jerusalem by the sheep market a *p*........... Jn 5:2
at a certain season into the *p* .... Jn 5:4
is troubled, to put me into the *p* .... Jn 5:7
going, to wash in the *p* of Siloam .... Jn 9:7
unto me, Go to the *p* of Siloam .... Jn 9:11

POOLS

and upon all their *p* of water .... Ex 7:19
the rain also filleth the *p*........................... Ps 84:6
I made me *p* of water, to water .... Eccl 2:6
for the bittern, and *p* of water .... Is 14:23
islands, and I will dry up the *p* .... Is 42:15

POOR

other kine came up after them, *p*........... Gen 41:19
of my people that is *p* by thee.................. Ex 22:25
countenance a *p* man in his cause........... Ex 23:3
judgment of thy *p* in his cause............... Ex 23:6
that the *p* of thy people may eat............ Ex 23:11
the *p* shall not give less than .... Ex 30:15
And if he be *p*, and cannot get so.......... Lev 14:21
thou shalt leave them for the *p* .... Lev 19:10
not respect the person of the *p* .... Lev 19:15
thou shalt leave them unto the *p* .... Lev 23:22
If thy brother be waxen *p* .... Lev 25:25
And if thy brother be waxen *p* .... Lev 25:35
that dwelleth by thee be waxen *p*......... Lev 25:39
that dwelleth by him wax *p* .... Lev 25:47
there shall be no *p* among you............ Deut 15:4
If there be among you a *p* man of....... Deut 15:7
thine hand from thy *p* brother............. Deut 15:7
eye be evil against thy *p* brother .... Deut 15:9
For the *p* shall never cease out........... Deut 15:11
wide unto thy brother, to thy *p* .... Deut 15:11
And if the man be *p*, thou shalt .... Deut 24:12
an hired servant that is *p* .... Deut 24:14
for he is *p*, and setteth his heart......... Deut 24:15
my family is *p* in Manasseh .... Judg 6:15
not young men, whether *p* or rich .... Ruth 3:10
The LORD maketh *p*, and maketh rich ... 1Sa 2:7
raiseth up the *p* out of the dust 1Sa 2:8
in law, seeing that I am a *p* man......... 1Sa 18:23
the one rich, and the other 2Sa 12:1
But the *p* man had nothing, save.......... 2Sa 12:3
but took the *p* man's lamb..................... 2Sa 12:4
of the guard left of the *p* of the........... 2Kin 25:12
one to another, and gifts to the *p* .... Est 9:22
he saveth the *p* from the sword............ Job 5:15
So the *p* hath hope, and iniquity .... Job 5:16
shall seek to please the *p* .... Job 20:10
oppressed and hath forsaken the *p* .... Job 20:19
the *p* of the earth hide .... Job 24:4
breast, and take a pledge of the *p*........ Job 24:9

with the light killeth the *p*..................... Job 24:14
I delivered the *p* that cried..................... Job 29:12
I was a father to the *p* .... Job 29:16
was not my soul grieved for the *p*......... Job 30:25
withheld the *p* from their desire........... Job 31:16
or any *p* without covering .... Job 31:19
the rich more than the *p* .... Job 34:19
the cry of the *p* to come unto him......... Job 34:28
but giveth right to the *p* .... Job 36:6
the *p* in his affliction, and..................... Job 36:15
the expectation of the *p* shall .... Ps 9:18
in his pride doth persecute the *p* .... Ps 10:2
are privily set against the *p* .... Ps 10:8
he lieth in wait to catch the *p* .... Ps 10:9
he doth catch the *p*, when he .... Ps 10:9
that the *p* may fall by his strong .... Ps 10:10
the *p* committeth himself unto.............. Ps 10:14
For the oppression of the *p* .... Ps 12:5
have shamed the counsel of the *p* .... Ps 14:6
This *p* man cried, and the LORD.............. Ps 34:6
which delivereth the *p* from him............ Ps 35:10
is too strong for him, yea, the *p*............. Ps 35:10
their bow, to cast down the *p* .... Ps 37:14
But I am *p* and needy.............................. Ps 40:17
is he that considereth the *p* .... Ps 41:1
Both low and high, rich and *p* .... Ps 49:2
of thy goodness for the *p* .... Ps 68:10
But I am *p* and sorrowful........................ Ps 69:29
For the LORD heareth the *p* .... Ps 69:33
But I am *p* and needy.............................. Ps 70:5
and thy *p* with judgment......................... Ps 72:2
shall judge the *p* of the people .... Ps 72:4
the *p* also, and him that hath no .... Ps 72:12
He shall spare the *p* and needy, and ...... Ps 72:13
congregation of thy *p* for ever .... Ps 74:19
let the *p* and needy praise .... Ps 74:21
Defend the *p* and fatherless .... Ps 82:3
Deliver the *p* and needy.......................... Ps 82:4
for I am *p* and needy.............................. Ps 86:1
Yet setteth he the *p* on high from......... Ps 107:41
shew mercy, but persecuted the *p* .... Ps 109:16
For I am *p* and needy, and my heart...... Ps 109:22
stand at the right hand of the *p*............ Ps 109:31
dispersed, he hath given to the *p* .... Ps 112:9
raiseth up the *p* out of the dust .... Ps 113:7
I will satisfy her *p* with bread .... Ps 132:15
afflicted, and the right of the *p* .... Ps 140:12
He becometh *p* that dealeth with a .... Prov 10:4
of the *p* is their poverty .... Prov 10:15
there is that maketh himself *p* .... Prov 13:7
but the *p* heareth not rebuke .... Prov 13:8
food is in the tillage of the *p* .... Prov 13:23
The *p* is hated even of his own............. Prov 14:20
but he that hath mercy on the *p* .... Prov 14:21
the *p* reproacheth his Maker .... Prov 14:31
honoureth him hath mercy on the *p*...... Prov 14:31
Whoso mocketh the *p* reproacheth....... Prov 17:5
The *p* useth intreaties .... Prov 18:23
Better is the *p* that walketh in............... Prov 19:1
but the *p* is separated from his .... Prov 19:4
the brethren of the *p* do hate him.......... Prov 19:7
upon the *p* lendeth unto the LORD.......... Prov 19:17
a *p* man is better than a liar .... Prov 19:22
his ears at the cry of the *p*..................... Prov 21:13
loveth pleasure shall be a *p* man .... Prov 21:17
The rich and *p* meet together .... Prov 22:2
The rich ruleth over the *p* .... Prov 22:7
he giveth of his bread to the *p* .... Prov 22:9
the *p* to increase his riches.................... Prov 22:16
Rob not the *p*, because he is *p*............. Prov 22:22
A *p* man that oppresseth the .... Prov 28:3
p is like a sweeping rain which .... Prov 28:3
Better is the *p* that walketh in............... Prov 28:6
it for him that will pity the *p* .... Prov 28:8
but the *p* hath understanding................ Prov 28:11
a wicked ruler over the *p* people .... Prov 28:15
giveth unto the *p* shall not lack............ Prov 28:27
considereth the cause of the *p* .... Prov 29:7
The *p* and the deceitful man meet .... Prov 29:13
that faithfully judgeth the *p* .... Prov 29:14
or lest I be *p*, and steal, and take......... Prov 30:9
to devour the *p* from off the .... Prov 30:14
and plead the cause of the *p* .... Prov 31:9
stretcheth out her hand to the *p* .... Prov 31:20
Better is a *p* and a wise child................ Eccl 4:13
is born in his kingdom becometh *p*....... Eccl 4:14
seest the oppression of the *p* .... Eccl 5:8
what hath the *p*, that knoweth to.......... Eccl 6:8
was found in it a *p* wise man .... Eccl 9:15
no man remembered that same *p* man ... Eccl 9:15
nevertheless the *p* man's wisdom .... Eccl 9:16
the spoil of the *p* is in your .... Is 3:14
and grind the faces of the *p* .... Is 3:15
the right from the *p* of my people .... Is 10:2
be heard unto Laish, O *p* Anathoth ...... Is 10:30
shall he judge the *p*, and reprove .... Is 11:4
the firstborn of the *p* shall feed............ Is 14:30
the *p* of his people shall trust .... Is 14:32
hast been a strength to the *p* .... Is 25:4
it down, even the feet of the *p* .... Is 26:6
the *p* among men shall rejoice in .... Is 29:19
to destroy the *p* with lying words .... Is 32:7
When the *p* and needy seek water,......... Is 41:17
that thou bring the *p* that are................. Is 58:7
ye brought to him that is *p* .... Is 66:2
of the souls of the *p* innocents.............. Jer 2:34
but, Surely these are *p* .... Jer 5:4
from the hand of evildoers....................... Jer 20:13
He judged the cause of the *p* .... Jer 22:16
guard left of the *p* of the people .... Jer 39:10

of the *p* of the land, of them .... Jer 40:7
certain of the *p* of the people................. Jer 52:15
of the land for vinedressers .... Jer 52:16
she strengthen the hand of the *p* .... Eze 16:49
Hath oppressed the *p* and needy, ... Eze 18:12
taken off his hand from the *p* .... Eze 18:17
robbery, and have vexed the *p* .... Eze 22:29
by shewing mercy to the *p* .... Dan 4:27
the *p* for a pair of shoes......................... Amos 2:6
of the earth on the head of the *p* .... Amos 2:7
of Samaria, which oppress the *p*............ Amos 4:1
as your treading is upon the *p* .... Amos 5:11
they turn aside the *p* in the gate .... Amos 5:12
even to make the *p* of the land to .... Amos 8:4
That we may buy the *p* for silver........... Amos 8:6
was as to devour the *p* secretly .... Hab 3:14
a people, and they shall trust in .... Zeph 3:12
the stranger, nor the *p* .... Zec 7:10
even you, O *p* of the flock .... Zec 11:7
so the *p* of the flock that waited .... Zec 11:11
Blessed are the *p* in spirit .... Mt 5:3
the *p* have the gospel preached to.......... Mt 11:5
that thou hast, and give to the *p* .... Mt 19:21
sold for much, and given to the *p* .... Mt 26:9
For ye have the *p* always with you......... Mt 26:11
thou hast, and give to the *p* .... Mk 10:21
And there came a certain *p* widow .... Mk 12:42
That this *p* widow hath cast more......... Mk 12:43
and have been given to the *p* .... Mk 14:5
For ye have the *p* with you always......... Mk 14:7
me to preach the gospel to the *p* .... Lk 4:18
and said, Blessed be ye *p* .... Lk 6:20
to the *p* the gospel is preached .... Lk 7:22
thou makest a feast, call the *p* .... Lk 14:13
city, and bring in hither the *p* .... Lk 14:21
hast, and distribute unto the *p* .... Lk 18:22
half of my goods I give to the *p* .... Lk 19:8
he saw also a certain *p* widow .... Lk 21:2
that this *p* widow hath cast in .... Lk 21:3
hundred pence, and given to the *p* .... Jn 12:5
said, not that he cared for the *p* .... Jn 12:6
For the *p* always ye have with you......... Jn 12:8
he should give something to the *p* .... Jn 13:29
p saints which are at Jerusalem .... Rom 15:26
bestow all my goods to feed the *p* 1Cor 13:3
as *p*, yet making many rich 2Cor 6:10
yet for your sakes he became *p*............. 2Cor 8:9
he hath given to the *p* 2Cor 9:9
that we should remember the *p* .... Gal 2:10
in also a *p* man in vile raiment .... Jas 2:2
and say to the *p*, Stand thou there......... Jas 2:3
Hath not God chosen the *p* of this .... Jas 2:5
But ye have despised the *p* .... Jas 2:6
art wretched, and miserable, and *p* .... Rev 3:17
both small and great, rich and *p* .... Rev 13:16

POORER

But if he be *p* than thy .... Lev 27:8

POOREST

save the *p* sort of the people of 2Kin 24:14

POPLAR

And Jacob took him rods of green *p*... Gen 30:37

POPLARS

upon the hills, under oaks and *p* .... Hos 4:13

POPULOUS

a nation, great, mighty, and *p* .... Deut 26:5
Art thou better than *p* No...................... Nah 3:8

PORATHA (por´-a-thah) A son of Haman.
And *P*, and Adalia, and Aridatha,.......... Est 9:8

PORCH

Ehud went forth through the *p* .... Judg 3:23
the *p* before the temple of the 1Kin 6:3
And he made a *p* of pillars 1Kin 7:6
and the *p* was before them 1Kin 7:6
Then he made a *p* for the throne 1Kin 7:7
judge, even the *p* of judgment 1Kin 7:7
had another court within the *p* 1Kin 7:8
taken to wife, like unto this *p* 1Kin 7:8
LORD, and for the *p* of the house........... 1Kin 7:12
were of lily work in the *p* 1Kin 7:19
pillars in the *p* of the temple 1Kin 7:21
his son the pattern of the *p* 1Chr 28:11
of the *p*, was in the front of 2Chr 3:4
which he had built before the *p* 2Chr 8:12
that was before the *p* of the LORD 2Chr 15:8
they stood by the doors of the *p* 2Chr 29:7
came they to the *p* of the LORD............ 2Chr 29:17
temple of the LORD, between the *p* ...... Eze 8:16
threshold of the gate by the *p* of .... Eze 40:7
and the *p* of the gate within............... Eze 40:8
measured he the *p* of the gate............ Eze 40:8
the *p* of the gate was inward.............. Eze 40:9
p of the inner gate were fifty .... Eze 40:15
in the *p* of the gate were two............. Eze 40:39
which was at the *p* of the gate .... Eze 40:40
brought me to the *p* of the house........ Eze 40:48
and measured each post of the *p* .... Eze 40:48
length of the *p* was twenty cubits ...... Eze 40:49
upon the face of the *p* without........... Eze 41:25
other side, on the sides of the *p*......... Eze 41:26
by the way of their *p* that gate .... Eze 44:3
that this *p* widow hath cast without... Eze 46:2
by the way of the *p* of that gate .... Eze 46:8
of the LORD, weep between the *p* .... Joel 2:17
when he was gone out into the *p* .... Mt 26:71
And he went out into the *p* .... Mk 14:68
in the temple in Solomon's *p* .... Jn 10:23

in the *p* that is called Solomon's......... Acts 3:11
with one accord in Solomon's *p*............ Acts 5:12

PORCHES
temple, and the *p* of the court .... Eze 41:15
tongue Bethesda, having five *p* .... Jn 5:2

PORCIUS (*por'-she-us*) *Family name of Festus.*
But after two years P Festus came ..... Acts 24:27

PORT
the dragon well, and to the dung *p*..... Neh 2:13

PORTER
and the watchman called unto the *p*..... 2Sa 18:26
and called unto the *p* of the city 2Kin 7:10
the son of Meshelemiah was *p* of....... 1Chr 9:21
the *p* toward the east, was over 1Chr 26:14
work, and commanded the *p* to watch Mk 13:34
To him the *p* openeth......................... Jn 10:3

PORTERS
And he called the *p*........................... 2Kin 7:11
the *p* were, Shallum, and Akkub, and. 1Chr 9:17
they were *p* in the companies of........ 1Chr 9:18
p in the gates were two hundred 1Chr 9:22
In four quarters were the *p* 1Chr 9:24
these Levites, the four chief *p* 1Chr 9:26
and Obed-edom, and Jeiel, the *p* 1Chr 15:18
son of Jeduthun and Hosah to be *p*... 1Chr 16:38
And the sons of Jeduthun were *p* 1Chr 16:42
Moreover four thousand were *p*......... 1Chr 23:5
Concerning the divisions of the *p*...... 1Chr 26:1
thee were the divisions of the *p* 1Chr 26:12
of the *p* among the sons of Kore 1Chr 26:19
the *p* also by their courses at........... 2Chr 8:14
Levites, shall be *p* of the doors......... 2Chr 23:4
he set the *p* at the gates of the......... 2Chr 23:19
were scribes, and officers, and *p*...... 2Chr 34:13
the *p* waited at every gate 2Chr 35:15
The children of the *p* .... Ezr 2:42
people, and the singers, and the *p* .... Ezr 2:70
Levites, and the singers, and the *p*.... Ezr 7:7
priests and Levites, singers, *p* .... Ezr 7:24
the *p*; Shallum, and Telem................. Ezr 10:24
I had set up the doors, and the *p* ..... Neh 7:1
The *p*: the children of Shallum .... Neh 7:45
priests, and the Levites, and the *p* ... Neh 7:73
the priests, the Levites, the *p* .... Neh 10:28
priests that minister, and the *p*......... Neh 10:39
Moreover the *p*, Akkub, Talmon, and Neh 11:19
were *p* keeping the ward at the......... Neh 12:25
the *p* kept the ward of their God, ... Neh 12:45
portions of the singers and the *p*...... Neh 12:47
Levites, and the singers, and the *p*.... Neh 13:5

PORTION
the *p* of the men which went with...... Gen 14:24
let them take their *p*.......................... Gen 14:24
Is there yet any *p* or inheritance....... Gen 31:14
for the priests had a a assigned .... Gen 47:22
did eat their *p* which Pharaoh........... Gen 47:22
to thee one *p* above thy brethren...... Gen 48:22
of my offerings made by fire.............. Lev 6:17
This is the *p* of the anointing of .... Lev 7:35
thou shalt take one *p* of fifty............ Num 31:30
which was the *p* of them that went.... Num 31:36
half, Moses took one *p* of fifty......... Num 31:47
a double *p* of all that he hath........... Deut 21:17
For the LORD's *p* is his people........... Deut 32:9
in a *p* of the lawgiver, was he........... Deut 33:21
one *p* to inherit, seeing I am a .... Josh 17:14
Out of the *p* of the children of .... Josh 19:9
unto Hannah he gave a worthy *p*...... 1Sa 1:5
Bring the *p* which I gave in David..... 1Sa 9:23
saying, What *p* have we in David 1Kin 12:16
let a double *p* of thy spirit be........... 2Kin 2:9
eat Jezebel in the *p* of Jezreel 2Kin 9:10
met him in the *p* of Naboth the......... 2Kin 9:21
cast him in the *p* of the field of........ 2Kin 9:25
In the *p* of Jezreel shall dogs 2Kin 9:36
of the field in the *p* of Jezreel 2Kin 9:37
saying, What *p* have we in David 2Chr 10:16
For Ahaz took away a *p* out of the ... 2Chr 28:21
He appointed also the king's *p* 2Chr 31:3
to give the *p* of the priests.............. 2Chr 31:4
his daily *p* for their service in.......... 2Chr 31:16
have no *p* on this side the river .... Ezr 4:16
but ye have no *p*, nor right, nor .... Neh 2:20
that a certain *p* should be for.......... Neh 11:23
and the porters, every day his *p* ...... Neh 12:47
This is the *p* of a wicked man .... Job 20:29
their *p* is cursed in the earth........... Job 24:18
how little a *p* is heard of him .... Job 26:14
This is the *p* of a wicked man .... Job 27:13
For what *p* of God is there from....... Job 31:2
this shall be the *p* of their cup .... Ps 11:6
The LORD is the *p* of mine............... Ps 16:5
which have their *p* in this life......... Ps 17:14
they shall be a *p* for foxes............. Ps 63:10
of my heart, and my *p* for ever....... Ps 73:26
Thou art my *p*, O LORD................... Ps 119:57
my *p* in the land of the living .... Ps 142:5
household, and a *p* to her maidens .. Prov 31:15
this was my *p* of all my labour ...... Eccl 2:10
shall he leave it for his *p*.............. Eccl 3:21
for that is his *p*.............................. Eccl 3:22
for it is his *p*................................. Eccl 5:18
to eat thereof, and to take his *p*..... Eccl 5:19
neither have they any more a *p*...... Eccl 9:6
for that is thy *p* in this life............. Eccl 9:9
Give a *p* to seven, and also to....... Eccl 11:2
This is the *p* of them that spoil....... Is 17:14

I divide him a *p* with the great .... Is 53:12
stones of the stream is thy *p*.......... Is 57:6
they shall rejoice in their *p*............. Is 61:7
The *p* of Jacob is not like them ...... Jer 10:16
they have trodden my *p* under foot ... Jer 12:10
pleasant *p* a desolate wilderness..... Jer 12:10
the *p* of thy measures from me........ Jer 13:25
The *p* of Jacob is not like them ...... Jer 51:19
every day a *p* until the day of........ Jer 52:34
The LORD is my *p*, saith my soul..... Lam 3:24
The LORD, an holy *p* of the land ..... Eze 45:1
The holy *p* of the land shall be....... Eze 45:4
the oblation of the holy *p*............... Eze 45:6
a *p* shall be for the prince on......... Eze 45:7
of the oblation of the holy *p*........... Eze 45:7
before the oblation of the holy *p*..... Eze 45:7
a *p* for Dan.................................... Eze 48:1
unto the west side, a *p* for Asher .... Eze 48:2
the west side, a *p* for Naphtali........ Eze 48:3
the west side, a *p* for Manasseh ..... Eze 48:4
the west side, a *p* for Ephraim........ Eze 48:5
the west side, a *p* for Reuben......... Eze 48:6
unto the west side, a *p* for Judah..... Eze 48:7
the oblation of the holy *p* shall .... Eze 48:18
the oblation of the holy *p*............... Eze 48:18
side, Benjamin shall have a *p*.......... Eze 48:23
west side, Simeon shall have a *p*..... Eze 48:24
unto the west side, Issachar a *p* ..... Eze 48:25
unto the west side, Zebulun a *p* ...... Eze 48:26
side unto the west side, Gad a *p*...... Eze 48:27
with the *p* of the king's meat.......... Dan 1:8
eat of the *p* of the king's meat....... Dan 1:13
did eat the *p* of the king's meat...... Dan 1:15
took away the *p* of their meat......... Dan 1:16
let his *p* be with the beasts in........ Dan 4:15
let his *p* be with the beasts of........ Dan 4:23
they that feed of the *p* of his.......... Dan 11:26
hath changed the *p* of my people... Mic 2:4
because by them their *p* is fat........ Hab 1:16
Judah his *p* in the holy land............ Zec 2:12
appoint him his *p* with the............. Mt 24:51
to give them their *p* of meat in....... Lk 12:42
him his *p* with the unbelievers........ Lk 12:46
give me the *p* of goods that............ Lk 15:12

PORTIONS
They shall have like *p* to eat........... Deut 18:8
And there fell ten *p* to Manasseh .... Josh 17:5
all her sons and her daughters, *p*.... 1Sa 1:4
to give *p* to all the males among..... 2Chr 31:19
send *p* unto them for whom nothing.. Neh 8:10
to eat, and to drink, and to send *p*... Neh 8:12
the *p* of the law for the priests....... Neh 12:44
gave the *p* of the singers and the ... Neh 12:47
I perceived that the *p* of the......... Neh 13:10
of sending *p* one to another........... Est 9:19
of sending *p* one to another, and .. Est 9:22
be over against one of the *p*.......... Eze 45:7
Joseph shall have two *p*................. Eze 47:13
over against the *p* for the prince .... Eze 48:21
inheritance, and these are their *p*.... Eze 48:29
a month devour them with their *p*.... Hos 5:7

POSSESS
thy seed shall *p* the gate of his...... Gen 22:17
let thy seed *p* the gate of those ..... Gen 24:60
I will give it unto you to *p*............... Lev 20:24
Let us go up at once, and *p* it......... Num 13:30
and his seed shall *p* it.................... Num 14:24
of his family, and he shall *p* it........ Num 27:11
I have given you the land to *p* it...... Num 33:53
p the land which the LORD sware..... Deut 1:8
it, as the LORD God of thy................ Deut 1:21
I give it, and they shall *p* it............ Deut 1:39
begin to *p* it, and contend with...... Deut 2:24
begin to *p*, that thou mayest.......... Deut 2:31
hath given you this land to *p* it....... Deut 3:18
until they also *p* the land which ..... Deut 3:20
the land which the LORD God of........ Deut 4:1
in the land whither ye go in to *p* it .. Deut 4:5
land whither ye go over to *p* it....... Deut 4:14
go over, and *p* that good land......... Deut 4:22
ye go over Jordan to *p* it............... Deut 4:26
land which I give them to *p* it......... Deut 5:31
days in the land which ye shall *p*.... Deut 5:33
in the land whither ye go to *p* it...... Deut 6:1
the good land which the LORD.......... Deut 6:18
land whither thou goest to *p* it....... Deut 7:1
the land which the LORD sware.......... Deut 8:1
to go in to *p* nations greater and..... Deut 9:1
hath brought me in to *p* this land.... Deut 9:4
dost thou go to *p* their land............ Deut 9:5
to *p* it for thy righteousness........... Deut 9:6
the land which I have given you........ Deut 9:23
land which I sware unto................... Deut 10:11
in the land, whither ye go to............ Deut 11:8
the land, whither ye go to *p*........... Deut 11:8
whither thou goest in to *p* it.......... Deut 11:10
the land, whither ye go to *p* it....... Deut 11:11
ye shall *p* greater nations and........ Deut 11:23
land whither thou goest to *p*.......... Deut 11:31
to *p* the land which the LORD your .. Deut 11:31
God giveth you, and ye shall *p* it.... Deut 12:1
thy fathers giveth thee to *p*........... Deut 12:1
ye shall *p* served their gods.......... Deut 12:2
whither thou goest to *p* them........ Deut 12:29
thee for an inheritance to *p* it........ Deut 15:4
God giveth thee, and shalt *p* it...... Deut 17:14
these nations, which thou shalt *p*... Deut 18:14
LORD thy God giveth thee to *p* it.... Deut 19:2
LORD thy God giveth thee to *p* it.... Deut 19:14

LORD thy God giveth thee to *p* it..... Deut 21:1
land whither thou goest to *p* it........ Deut 23:20
thee for an inheritance to *p* .... Deut 25:19
land, whither thou goest to *p* it....... Deut 28:21
land whither thou goest to *p* it....... Deut 28:63
possessed, and thou shalt *p* it .... Deut 30:5
land whither thou goest to *p* it....... Deut 30:16
passest over Jordan to go to *p* it.... Deut 30:18
before thee, and thou shalt *p* them .. Deut 31:3
whither ye go over Jordan to *p* it..... Deut 31:13
whither ye go over Jordan to *p* it..... Deut 32:47
p thou the west and the south .... Deut 33:23
Jordan, to go in to *p* the land.......... Josh 1:11
LORD your God giveth you to *p* it..... Josh 1:11
are ye slack to go to *p* the land....... Josh 18:3
ye shall *p* their land, as the............ Josh 23:5
unto Esau mount Seir, to *p* it.......... Josh 24:4
hand, that ye might *p* their land...... Josh 24:8
his inheritance to *p* the land........... Judg 2:6
Israel, and shouldest thou *p* it........ Judg 11:23
Wilt not thou *p* that which.............. Judg 11:24
Chemosh thy god giveth thee to *p*... Judg 11:24
from before us, them will we *p*....... Judg 11:24
to go, and to enter to *p* the land...... Judg 18:9
whither he is gone down to *p* it....... 1Kin 21:18
that ye may *p* this good land, and.... 1Chr 28:8
land, unto which ye go to *p* it.......... Ezr 9:11
them that they should go in to *p*..... Neh 9:15
that they should go in to *p* it .... Neh 9:23
So am I made to *p* months of.......... Job 7:3
makest me to *p* the iniquities of...... Job 13:26
the house of Israel shall *p* them ..... Is 14:2
nor *p* the land, nor fill the face ...... Is 34:11
and the bittern shall *p* it................ Is 34:11
they shall *p* it for ever, from.......... Is 34:17
his trust in me shall *p* the land...... Is 57:13
land they shall *p* the double .... Is 61:7
their fathers, and they shall *p* it..... Jer 30:3
they shall *p* their houses............... Eze 7:24
and shall *p* the land...................... Eze 33:25
and shall *p* the land...................... Eze 33:26
shalt be mine, and we will *p* it........ Eze 35:10
and they shall *p* thee, and thou...... Eze 36:12
the kingdom for ever, even for......... Dan 7:18
silver, nettles shall *p* them............ Hos 9:6
to *p* the land of the Amorite........... Amos 2:10
That they may *p* the remnant of..... Amos 9:12
Jacob shall *p* their possessions...... Obad 17
south shall *p* the mount of Esau ..... Obad 19
they shall *p* the fields of................ Obad 19
and Benjamin shall *p* Gilead........... Obad 19
shall *p* that of the Canaanites......... Obad 20
shall *p* the cities of the south......... Obad 20
to *p* the dwellingplaces that.......... Hab 1:6
remnant of my people shall *p* them.. Zeph 2:9
this people to *p* all these things...... Zec 8:12
I give tithes of all that I *p*............... Lk 18:12
In your patience *p* ye your souls...... Lk 21:19
to *p* his vessel in sanctification....... 1Th 4:4

POSSESSED
p his land from Arnon unto Jabbok... Num 21:24
and they *p* his land........................ Num 21:35
which we *p* at that time, from......... Deut 3:12
they *p* his land, and the land of...... Deut 4:47
into the land which thy fathers *p*..... Deut 30:5
they also have *p* the land which...... Josh 1:15
p their land on the other side .... Josh 12:1
yet very much land to be *p* .... Josh 13:1
p it, and dwelt therein, and called .. Josh 19:47
and they *p* it, and dwelt therein..... Josh 21:43
possession, whereof they were *p*.... Josh 22:9
and *p* the city of palm trees........... Judg 3:13
so Israel *p* all the land of.............. Judg 11:21
they *p* all the coasts of the........... Judg 11:22
they *p* Samaria, and dwelt in the ... 2Kin 17:24
so they *p* the land of Sihon, and.... Neh 9:22
p the land, and thou subduedst...... Neh 9:24
p houses full of all goods, wells..... Neh 9:25
For thou hast *p* my reins.............. Ps 139:13
The LORD *p* me in the beginning of.. Prov 8:22
have *p* it but a little while.............. Is 63:18
shall be *p* again in this land.......... Jer 32:15
And they came in, and *p* it............. Jer 32:23
that the saints *p* the kingdom......... Dan 7:22
and those which were *p* with devils.. Mt 4:24
him many that were *p* with devils.... Mt 8:16
there met him two *p* with devils...... Mt 8:28
befallen to the *p* of the devils......... Mt 8:33
to him a dumb man *p* with a devil.... Mt 9:32
unto him one *p* with a devil............ Mt 12:22
and them that were *p* with devils..... Mk 1:32
see him that was *p* with the devil..... Mk 5:15
to him that was *p* with the devil...... Mk 5:18
he that had been *p* with the devil..... Mk 5:18
was *p* of the devils was healed .... Lk 8:36
the things which he *p* was his own... Acts 4:32
out of many that were *p* with them... Acts 8:7
a certain damsel *p* with a spirit....... Acts 16:16
that buy, as though they *p* not......... 1Cor 7:30

POSSESSEST
p it, and dwellest therein................ Deut 26:1

POSSESSETH
that *p* an inheritance in any............ Num 36:8
of the things which he *p*................. Lk 12:15

POSSESSING
nothing, and yet *p* all things........... 2Cor 6:10

POSSESSION
of Canaan, for an everlasting *p*....... Gen 17:8
give me a *p* of a buryingplace........ Gen 23:4

a *p* of a buryingplace amongst you.... Gen 23:9
Unto Abraham for a *p* in the............. Gen 23:18
made sure unto Abraham for a *p* of ... Gen 23:20
For he had *p* of flocks, and............... Gen 26:14
p of herds, and great store of .... Gen 26:14
in the land of their *p* .... Gen 36:43
gave them a *p* in the land of .... Gen 47:11
after thee for an everlasting *p*........ Gen 48:4
Hittite for a *p* of a buryingplace...... Gen 49:30
bought with the field for a *p* of ...... Gen 50:13
which I give to you for a *p* .... Lev 14:34
in a house of the land of your *p* ..... Lev 14:34
shall return every man unto his *p* .... Lev 25:10
shall return every man unto his *p* .... Lev 25:13
in all the land of your *p* .... Lev 25:24
and hath sold away some of his *p* .... Lev 25:25
that he may return unto his *p* .... Lev 25:27
and he shall return unto his *p* .... Lev 25:28
houses of the cities of their *p* .... Lev 25:32
was sold, and the city of his *p* .... Lev 25:33
p among the children of Israel.......... Lev 25:33
for it is their perpetual *p* .... Lev 25:34
unto the *p* of his fathers shall.......... Lev 25:41
and they shall be your *p* .... Lev 25:45
you, to inherit them for a *p* .... Lev 25:46
some part of a field of his *p* .... Lev 27:16
the *p* thereof shall be the............... Lev 27:21
is not of the fields of his *p* .... Lev 27:22
whom the *p* of the land did belong.... Lev 27:24
beast, and of the field of his *p* .... Lev 27:28
And Edom shall be a *p* .... Num 24:18
also shall be a *p* for his enemies..... Num 24:18
According to the lot shall the *p* .... Num 26:56
Give unto us therefore a *p* among.... Num 27:4
a *p* of an inheritance among their.... Num 27:7
given unto thy servants for a *p* .... Num 32:5
shall be your *p* before the LORD........ Num 32:22
them the land of Gilead for a *p* .... Num 32:29
that the *p* of our inheritance on....... Num 32:32
of their *p* cities to dwell in............. Num 35:2
the *p* of the children of Israel.......... Num 35:8
return into the land of his *p* .... Num 35:28
mount Seir unto Esau for a *p* .... Deut 2:5
give thee of their land for a *p* .... Deut 2:9
unto the children of Lot for a *p* .... Deut 2:19
Israel did unto the land of his *p* ...... Deut 2:12
of the children of Ammon any *p*....... Deut 2:19
unto the children of Lot for a *p* .... Deut 2:19
ye return every man unto his *p* .... Deut 3:20
the substance that was in their *p* .... Deut 11:6
the children of Israel for a *p* .... Deut 32:49
return unto the land of your *p* .... Josh 1:15
it for a *p* unto the Reubenites .... Josh 12:6
a *p* according to their divisions .... Josh 12:7
this was the *p* of the half tribe........ Josh 13:29
the son of Jephunneh for his *p*........ Josh 21:12
of the Levites within the *p* of .... Josh 21:41
tents, and unto the land of your *p* ... Josh 22:4
Moses had given *p* in Bashan .... Josh 22:7
of Gilead, to the land of their *p*....... Josh 22:9
if the land of your *p* be unclean...... Josh 22:19
the land of the *p* of the LORD .... Josh 22:19
dwelleth, and take *p* among us .... Josh 22:19
take *p* of the vineyard of Naboth 1Kin 21:15
the Jezreelite, to take *p* of it 1Kin 21:16
Hast thou killed, and also taken *p* ... 1Kin 21:19
p of the king, and of his sons,........ 1Chr 28:1
left their suburbs and their *p* 2Chr 11:14
to come to cast us out of thy *p* 2Chr 20:11
returned, every man to his *p* .... Neh 11:3
one in his *p* in their cities............... Neh 11:3
parts of the earth for thy *p* .... Ps 2:8
the land in *p* by their own sword ..... Ps 44:3
may dwell there, and have it in *p* .... Ps 69:35
ourselves the houses of God in *p* ..... Ps 83:12
shall have good things in *p* .... Prov 28:10
also make it a *p* for the bittern ...... Is 14:23
unto us in this land given in *p* .... Eze 11:15
to the men of the east for a *p* .... Eze 25:4
Ammonites, and will give them in *p*.. Eze 25:10
ancient high places are ours in *p* .... Eze 36:2
that ye might be a *p* unto the......... Eze 36:3
appointed my land into their *p* .... Eze 36:5
ye shall give them no *p* in Israel...... Eze 44:28
I am their *p* .... Eze 44:28
for a *p* for twenty chambers........... Eze 45:5
ye shall appoint the *p* of the........... Eze 45:6
of the *p* of the city, before the........ Eze 45:7
before the *p* of the city, from......... Eze 45:7
the land shall be his *p* in Israel....... Eze 45:8
shall be their *p* in Israel................. Eze 46:16
to thrust them out of their *p* .... Eze 46:18
sons inheritance out of his own *p* .... Eze 46:18
scattered every man from his *p* ...... Eze 46:18
with the *p* of the city .... Eze 48:20
of the *p* of the city, over................ Eze 48:21
from the *p* of the Levites................ Eze 48:22
from the *p* of the city, being in....... Eze 48:22
with Sapphira his wife, sold a *p* ...... Acts 5:1
he would give it to him for a *p* .... Acts 7:5
Jesus into the *p* of the Gentiles....... Acts 7:45
the redemption of the purchased *p* .. Eph 1:14

POSSESSIONS

ye therein, and get you *p* therein..... Gen 34:10
and they had *p* therein, and grew,... Gen 47:27
they shall have *p* among you in....... Num 32:30
in Maon, whose *p* were in Carmel..... 1Sa 25:2
And their *p* and habitations were,..... 1Chr 7:28
in their *p* in their cities were........... 1Chr 9:2
of flocks and herds in abundance....... 2Chr 32:29

also I had great *p* of great .... Eccl 2:7
of Jacob shall possess their *p*.......... Obad 17
for he had great *p* .... Mt 19:22
for he had great *p* .... Mk 10:22
And sold their *p* and goods, and ...... Acts 2:45
In the same quarters were *p* of....... Acts 28:7

POSSESSOR

high God, *p* of heaven and earth...... Gen 14:19
the *p* of heaven and earth,.............. Gen 14:22

POSSESSORS

Whose *p* slay them, and hold........... Zec 11:5
for as many as were *p* of lands or ... Acts 4:34

POSSIBLE

but with God all things are *p*........... Mt 19:26
insomuch that, if it were *p*.............. Mt 24:24
saying, O my Father, if it be *p*........ Mt 26:39
all things are *p* to him that............ Mk 9:23
for with God all things are *p*........... Mk 10:27
wonders, to seduce, if it were *p*...... Mk 13:22
and prayed that, if it were *p*........... Mk 14:35
all things are *p* unto thee............... Mk 14:36
with men are *p* with God................ Lk 18:27
because it was not *p* that he.......... Acts 2:24
he hasted, if it were *p* for him........ Acts 20:16
they were minded, if it were *p*........ Acts 27:39
If it be *p*, as much as lieth in .... Rom 12:18
record, that, if it had been *p* .... Gal 4:15
For it is not *p* that the blood of ...... Heb 10:4

POST

on the upper door of the houses....... Ex 12:7
to the door, or unto the door *p*........ Ex 21:6
by a *p* of the temple of the LORD...... 1Sa 1:9
Now my days are swifter than a *p* ... Job 9:25
One *p* shall run to meet another,..... Jer 51:31
even unto the *p* of the court .... Eze 40:14
upon each *p* were palm trees .... Eze 40:16
and measured each *p* of the porch... Eze 40:48
and measured the *p* of the door ...... Eze 41:3
their *p* by my posts, and the wall..... Eze 43:8
shalt stand by the *p* of the gate ...... Eze 46:2

POSTERITY

to preserve you a *p* in the earth ...... Gen 45:7
If any man of your *p* or your *p* ...... Num 9:10
I will take away the *p* of Baasha...... 1Kin 16:3
of Baasha, and the *p* of his house.... 1Kin 16:3
thee, and will take away thy............. 1Kin 21:21
yet their *p* approve their sayings...... Ps 49:13
Let his *p* be cut off .... Ps 109:13
and not to his *p*, not according to.... Dan 11:4
hooks, and your *p* with fishhooks..... Amos 4:2

POSTS

and strike it on the two side *p*......... Ex 12:7
the two side *p* with the blood.......... Ex 12:22
the lintel, and on the two side *p*...... Ex 12:23
them upon thy *p* of thine house....... Deut 6:9
upon the door of thine house............ Deut 11:20
gate of the city, and the two *p*........ Judg 16:3
side *p* were a fifth part of the......... 1Kin 6:31
of the temple *p* of olive tree 1Kin 6:33
p were square, with the windows..... 1Kin 7:5
also the house, the beams, the *p* 2Chr 3:7
So the *p* went with the letters.......... 2Chr 30:6
So the *p* passed from city to city 2Chr 30:10
the letters were sent by *p* into........ Est 3:13
The *p* went out, being hastened by .. Est 3:15
and sent letters by *p* on horseback... Est 8:10
So the *p* that rode upon mules and.. Est 8:14
waiting at the *p* of my doors........... Prov 8:34
the *p* of the door moved at the .... Is 6:4
the *p* hast thou set up thy.............. Is 57:8
the *p* thereof, two cubits .... Eze 40:9
the *p* had one measure on this........ Eze 40:10
He made also *p* of threescore......... Eze 40:14
to their *p* within the gate round...... Eze 40:16
the *p* thereof and the arches.......... Eze 40:21
and he measured the *p* thereof ...... Eze 40:22
on that side, upon the *p* thereof ..... Eze 40:26
the *p* thereof, and the arches.......... Eze 40:29
trees were upon the *p* thereof .... Eze 40:31
the *p* thereof, and the arches.......... Eze 40:33
trees were upon the *p* thereof .... Eze 40:34
the *p* thereof, and the arches.......... Eze 40:36
the *p* thereof were toward the .... Eze 40:37
trees were upon the *p* thereof .... Eze 40:37
were by the *p* of the gates............. Eze 40:38
and there were pillars by the *p* .... Eze 40:49
to the temple, and measured the *p* . Eze 41:1
The door *p*, and the narrow windows. Eze 41:16
The *p* of the temple were squared,.. Eze 41:21
thresholds, and their post by my *p* .. Eze 43:8
and put it upon the *p* of the house.. Eze 45:19
upon the *p* of the gate of the .... Eze 45:19
of the door, that the *p* may shake... Amos 9:1

POT

Moses said unto Aaron, Take a *p*...... Ex 16:33
let it be sodden in a brasen *p* .... Lev 6:28
and he put the broth in a *p*............. Judg 6:19
pan, or kettle, or caldron, or *p*........ 1Sa 2:14
in the house, save a *p* of oil............ 2Kin 4:2
his servant, Set on the great *p*........ 2Kin 4:38
shred them into the *p* of pottage..... 2Kin 4:39
of God, there is death in the *p*........ 2Kin 4:40
And he cast it into the *p*................. 2Kin 4:41
And there was no harm in the *p*...... 2Kin 4:41
as out of a seething *p* or caldron..... Job 41:20
maketh the deep to boil like a *p*...... Job 41:31

the sea like a *p* of ointment............ Job 41:31
The fining *p* is for silver, and.......... Prov 17:3
As the fining *p* for silver, and......... Prov 27:21
the crackling of thorns under a *p* ..... Eccl 7:6
and I said, I see a seething *p* .... Jer 1:13
Set on a *p*, set it on, and also......... Eze 24:3
to the *p* whose scum is therein,....... Eze 24:6
chop them in pieces, as for the *p* .... Mic 3:3
every *p* in Jerusalem and in Judah ... Zec 14:21
was the golden *p* that had manna.... Heb 9:4

POTENTATE

who is the blessed and only *P*.......... 1Ti 6:15

POTIPHAR (pot'i-far) A captain of Pharaoh's guard.

sold him into Egypt unto *P*.............. Gen 37:36
and *P*, an officer of Pharaoh,........... Gen 39:1

POTI-PHERAH Priest of On.

the daughter of *P* priest of On......... Gen 41:45
of *P* priest of On bare unto him........ Gen 41:50
of *P* priest of On bare unto him........ Gen 46:20

POTS

Egypt, when we sat by the flesh *p*.... Ex 16:3
the vessels of the altar, the *p*......... Ex 38:3
it be oven, or ranges for *p*.............. Lev 11:35
And the *p*, and the shovels, and the . 1Kin 7:45
And the *p*, and the shovels, and the . 2Kin 25:14
And Huram made the *p*, and the...... 2Chr 4:11
The *p* also, and the shovels, and..... 2Chr 4:16
holy offerings sod they in *p* 2Chr 35:13
Before your *p* can feel the thorns.... Ps 58:9
Though ye have lien among the *p* .... Ps 68:13
hands were delivered from the *p* ...... Ps 81:6
of the Rechabites *p* full of wine....... Jer 35:5
the *p* in the LORD's house shall........ Zec 14:20
as the washing of cups, and *p*........ Mk 7:4
of men, as the washing of *p*............ Mk 7:8

POTSHERD

he took him a *p* to scrape himself.... Job 2:8
My strength is dried up like a *p* ...... Ps 22:15
a *p* covered with silver dross........... Prov 26:23
Let the *p* strive with the................. Is 45:9

POTSHERDS

strive with the *p* of the earth .... Is 45:9

POTTAGE

And Jacob sod *p* .... Gen 25:29
I pray thee, with that same red *p*..... Gen 25:30
gave Esau bread and *p* of lentiles.... Gen 25:34
seethe *p* for the sons of the 2Kin 4:38
and shred them into the pot of *p* 2Kin 4:39
as they were eating of the *p*........... 2Kin 4:40
his skirt do touch bread, or *p* .... Hag 2:12

POTTER

morter, and as the *p* treadeth clay... Is 41:25
we are the clay, and thou our *p*....... Is 64:8
was marred in the hand of the *p* ..... Jer 18:4
seemed good to the *p* to make it ..... Jer 18:4
cannot I do with you as this *p*.......... Jer 18:6
the work of the hands of the *p* .... Lam 4:2
said unto me, Cast it unto the *p*...... Zec 11:13
cast them to the *p* in the house....... Zec 11:13
Hath not the *p* power over the......... Rom 9:21
as the vessels of a *p* shall they .... Rev 2:27

POTTER'S

them in pieces like a *p* vessel .... Ps 2:9
shall be esteemed as the *p* clay ...... Is 29:16
Arise, and go down to the *p* house ... Jer 18:2
Then I went down to the *p* house..... Jer 18:3
as the clay is in the *p* hand............. Jer 18:6
get a *p* earthen bottle, and take...... Jer 19:1
city, as one breaketh a *p* vessel ...... Jer 19:11
and bought with them the *p* field..... Mt 27:7
And gave them for the *p* field.......... Mt 27:10

POTTERS

These were the *p*, and those that..... 1Chr 4:23

POTTERS'

p vessel that is broken in pieces ..... Is 30:14
the feet and toes, part of *p* clay...... Dan 2:41

POUND

three *p* of gold went to one.............. 1Kin 10:17
and five thousand *p* of silver.......... Ezr 2:69
thy *p* hath gained ten pounds .... Lk 19:16
thy *p* hath gained five pounds .... Lk 19:18
Lord, behold, here is thy *p* .... Lk 19:20
stood by, Take from him the *p* .... Lk 19:24
Then took Mary a *p* of ointment of ... Jn 12:3
aloes, about an hundred *p* weight .... Jn 19:39

POUNDS

and two hundred *p* of silver............. Neh 7:71
gold, and two thousand *p* of silver ... Neh 7:72
servants, and delivered them ten *p*.. Lk 19:13
Lord, thy pound hath gained ten *p* ... Lk 19:16
thy pound hath gained five *p* .... Lk 19:18
and give it to him that hath ten *p*.... Lk 19:24
unto him, Lord, he hath ten *p* .... Lk 19:25

POUR

river, and *p* it upon the dry land...... Ex 4:9
p it upon his head, and anoint him... Ex 29:7
p all the blood beside the bottom..... Ex 29:12
neither shall ye *p* drink offering ...... Ex 30:9
he shall *p* oil upon it, and put .... Lev 2:1
it in pieces, and *p* oil thereon .... Lev 2:6
shall *p* all the blood of the .... Lev 4:7
shall *p* out all the blood at the........ Lev 4:18

shall p out his blood at the .... Lev 4:25
shall p out all the blood thereof .... Lev 4:30
shall p out all the blood thereof .... Lev 4:34
p it into the palm of his own .... Lev 14:15
in the priest's hand he shall p .... Lev 14:18
the priest shall p of the oil .... Lev 14:26
they shall p out the dust that .... Lev 14:41
he shall even p out the blood .... Lev 17:13
he shall p no oil upon it, nor .... Num 5:15
He shall p the water out of his .... Num 24:7
ye shall p it upon the earth as .... Deut 12:16
thou shalt p it upon the earth as .... Deut 12:24
thou shalt p it upon the ground .... Deut 15:23
this rock, and p out the broth .... Judg 6:20
p it on the burnt sacrifice, and 1Kin 18:33
shalt p out into all those 2Kin 4:4
P out for the people, that they 2Kin 4:41
p it on his head, and say, Thus 2Kin 9:3
they p down rain according to the .... Job 36:27
things, I p out my soul in me .... Ps 42:4
p out your heart before him .... Ps 62:8
P out thine indignation upon them .... Ps 69:24
P out thy wrath upon the heathen .... Ps 79:6
I will p out my spirit unto you .... Prov 1:23
For I will p water upon him that .... Is 44:3
I will p my spirit upon thy seed .... Is 44:3
above, and let the skies p down .... Is 45:8
I will p it out upon the children .... Jer 6:11
to p out drink offerings unto .... Jer 7:18
P out thy fury upon the heathen .... Jer 10:25
for I will p their wickedness .... Jer 14:16
p out their blood by the force of .... Jer 18:21
p out drink offerings unto her .... Jer 44:17
to p out drink offerings unto her .... Jer 44:18
to p out drink offerings unto her .... Jer 44:19
p out drink offerings unto her .... Jer 44:25
p out thine heart like water .... Lam 2:19
Now will I shortly p out my fury .... Eze 7:8
p out my fury upon it in blood .... Eze 14:19
I will p out my fury upon them .... Eze 20:8
I would p out my fury upon them .... Eze 20:13
I would p out my fury upon them .... Eze 20:21
I will p out mine indignation .... Eze 21:31
it on, and also p water into it .... Eze 24:3
I will p my fury upon Sin, the .... Eze 30:15
therefore I will p out my wrath .... Hos 5:10
that I will p out my spirit upon .... Joel 2:28
those days will I p out my spirit .... Joel 2:29
I will p down the stones thereof .... Mic 1:6
to p upon them mine indignation, ... Zeph 3:8
I will p upon the house of David, ... Zec 12:10
p you out a blessing, that there .... Mal 3:10
I will p out of my Spirit upon .... Acts 2:17
on my handmaidens I will p out in .... Acts 2:18
p out the vials of the wrath of .... Rev 16:1

POURED
and p oil upon the top of it .... Gen 28:18
he p a drink offering thereon .... Gen 35:14
and he p oil thereon. .... Gen 35:14
the rain was not p upon the earth .... Ex 9:33
man's flesh shall it not be p .... Ex 30:32
place, where the ashes are p out .... Lev 4:12
where the ashes are p out shall .... Lev 4:12
he p of the anointing oil upon .... Lev 8:12
p the blood at the bottom of the .... Lev 8:15
p out the blood at the bottom of .... Lev 9:9
head the anointing oil was p .... Lev 21:10
to be p unto the LORD for a drink .... Num 28:7
of thy sacrifices shall be p out .... Deut 12:27
but have p out my soul before the 1Sa 1:15
p it out before the LORD, and 1Sa 7:6
p it upon his head, and kissed him 1Sa 10:1
a pan, and p them out before him 2Sa 13:9
but p it out unto the LORD 2Sa 23:16
that are upon it shall be p out 1Kin 13:3
the ashes p out from the altar 1Kin 13:5
which p water on the hands of 2Kin 3:11
and she p out 2Kin 4:5
So they p out for the men to eat 2Kin 4:40
he p the oil on his head, and said 2Kin 9:6
and p his drink offering, and 2Kin 16:13
but p it out to the LORD 1Chr 11:18
my wrath shall not be p out upon 2Chr 12:7
of the LORD that is p out upon us 2Chr 34:21
shall be p out upon this place. 2Chr 34:25
my roarings are p out like the .... Job 3:24
Hast thou not p me out as milk, ... Job 10:10
the rock p me out rivers of oil .... Job 29:6
And now my soul is p out upon me. .... Job 30:16
I am p out like water, and all my .... Ps 22:14
grace is p into thy lips. .... Ps 45:2
The clouds p out water .... Ps 77:17
I p out my complaint before him .... Ps 142:2
thy name is as ointment p forth .... Song 1:3
they p out a prayer when thy .... Is 26:16
For the LORD hath p out upon you .... Is 29:10
Until the spirit be p upon us .... Is 32:15
Therefore he hath p upon him the .... Is 42:25
because he hath p out his soul .... Is 53:12
them hast thou p a drink offering .... Is 57:6
my fury shall be p out upon this .... Jer 7:20
have p out drink offerings unto .... Jer 19:13
p out drink offerings unto other .... Jer 32:29
my fury hath been p forth upon .... Jer 42:18
shall my fury be p forth upon .... Jer 42:18
my fury and mine anger was p forth .... Jer 44:6
p out drink offerings unto her, ... Jer 44:19
he p out his fury like fire .... Lam 2:4
my liver is p upon the earth, for .... Lam 2:11
when their soul was p out into .... Lam 2:12

p out in the top of every street .... Lam 4:1
he hath p out his fierce anger, ... Lam 4:11
Because thy filthiness was p out .... Eze 16:36
p out there their drink offerings .... Eze 20:28
out arm, and with fury p out .... Eze 20:33
out arm, and with fury p out .... Eze 20:34
LORD have p out my fury upon you .... Eze 22:22
Therefore have I p out mine .... Eze 22:31
p their whoredom upon her .... Eze 23:8
she p it not upon the ground, to .... Eze 24:7
Wherefore I p my fury upon them, ... Eze 36:18
for I have p out my spirit upon .... Eze 39:29
therefore the curse is p upon us. .... Dan 9:11
shall be p upon the desolate .... Dan 9:27
that are p down a steep place... .... Mic 1:4
his fury is p out like fire, and .... Nah 1:6
blood shall be p out as dust .... Zeph 1:17
p it on his head, as he sat at .... Mt 26:7
For in that she hath p this .... Mt 26:12
the box, and p it on his head .... Mk 14:3
p out the changers' money, and .... Jn 2:15
that on the Gentiles also was p .... Acts 10:45
which is p out without mixture .... Rev 14:10
p out his vial upon the earth .... Rev 16:2
the second angel p out his vial .... Rev 16:3
the third angel p out his vial .... Rev 16:4
the fourth angel p out his vial .... Rev 16:8
the fifth angel p out his vial .... Rev 16:10
the sixth angel p out his vial .... Rev 16:12
the seventh angel p out his vial .... Rev 16:17

POUREDST
p out thy fornications on every .... Eze 16:15

POURETH
He p contempt upon princes, and .... Job 12:21
he p out my gall upon the ground .... Job 16:13
but mine eye p out tears unto God .... Job 16:20
and he p out of the same .... Ps 75:8
p out his complaint before the .... Ps 102:t
He p contempt upon princes, and .... Ps 107:40
mouth of fools p out foolishness .... Prov 15:2
of the wicked p out evil things .... Prov 15:28
p them out upon the face of the .... Amos 5:8
p them out upon the face of the .... Amos 9:6
After that he p water into a .... Jn 13:5

POURING
the residue of Israel in thy p .... Eze 9:8
p in oil and wine, and set him on .... Lk 10:34

POURTRAY
thee, and p upon it the city, even .... Eze 4:1

POURTRAYED
p upon the wall round about .... Eze 8:10
when she saw men p upon the wall .... Eze 23:14
of the Chaldeans p with vermilion .... Eze 23:14

POVERTY
and all that thou hast, come to p .... Gen 45:11
So shall thy p come as one that .... Prov 6:11
of the poor is their p .... Prov 10:15
than is meet, but it tendeth to p .... Prov 11:24
P and shame shall be to him that .... Prov 13:18
not sleep, lest thou come to p .... Prov 20:13
and the glutton shall come to p .... Prov 23:21
So shall thy p come as one that .... Prov 24:34
vain persons shall have p enough .... Prov 28:19
not that p shall come upon him. .... Prov 28:22
give me neither p nor riches. .... Prov 30:8
Let him drink, and forget his p .... Prov 31:7
their deep p abounded unto the 2Cor 8:2
ye through his p might be rich 2Cor 8:9
thy works, and tribulation, and p .... Rev 2:9

POWDER
it in the fire, and ground it to p .... Ex 32:20
shall make the rain of thy land p .... Deut 28:24
Kidron, and stamped it small to p 2Kin 23:6
cast the p thereof upon the 2Kin 23:6
place, and stamped it small to p 2Kin 23:15
beaten the graven images into p 2Chr 34:7
fall, it will grind him to p .... Mt 21:44
fall, it will grind him to p .... Lk 20:18

POWDERS
with all p of the merchant. .... Song 3:6

POWER
ye know that with all my p I have .... Gen 31:6
It is in the p of my hand to do .... Gen 31:29
as a prince hast thou p with God .... Gen 32:28
dignity, and the excellency of p .... Gen 49:3
thee up, for to shew in thee my p .... Ex 9:16
O LORD, is become glorious in p .... Ex 15:6
strange nation he shall have no p .... Ex 21:8
of the land of Egypt with great p .... Ex 32:11
I will break the pride of your p .... Lev 26:19
ye shall have no p to stand .... Lev 26:37
let the p of my LORD be great, ... Num 14:17
have I now any p at all to say .... Num 22:38
with his mighty p out of Egypt .... Deut 4:37
And thou say in thine heart, My p .... Deut 8:17
that giveth thee p to get wealth .... Deut 8:18
broughtest out by thy mighty p .... Deut 9:29
he seeth that their p is gone .... Deut 32:36
they had no p to flee this way or .... Josh 8:20
a great people, and hast great p .... Josh 17:17
a Benjamite, a mighty man of p 1Sa 9:1
until they had no more p to weep 1Sa 30:4
God is my strength and p 2Sa 22:33
of the land of Egypt with great p 1Kin 17:36
their inhabitants were of small p 2Kin 19:26

Joab led forth the p of the army 1Chr 20:1
LORD, is the greatness, and the p 1Chr 29:11
and in thine hand is p and might 1Chr 29:12
many, or with them that have no p 2Chr 14:11
and in thine hand is there not p 2Chr 20:6
no p to keep still the kingdom 2Chr 22:9
for God hath p to help, and to 2Chr 25:8
that made war with mighty p 2Chr 26:13
all his p with him), unto 2Chr 32:9
made them to cease by force and p .... Ezr 4:23
but his p and his wrath is against .... Ezr 8:22
thou hast redeemed by thy great p .... Neh 1:10
is it in our p to redeem them. .... Neh 5:5
the p of Persia and Media, the .... Est 1:3
all the p of the people and .... Est 8:11
Jews hoped to have p over them .... Est 9:1
And all the acts of his p and of .... Est 10:2
all that he hath is in thy p .... Job 1:12
and in war from the p of the sword .... Job 5:20
become old, yea, are mighty in p .... Job 21:7
plead against me with his great p .... Job 23:6
also the mighty with his p .... Job 24:22
thou helpest him that is without p .... Job 26:2
He divideth the sea with his p .... Job 26:12
of his p who can understand .... Job 26:14
Behold, God exalteth by his p .... Job 36:22
he is excellent in p, and in .... Job 37:23
not conceal his parts, nor his p .... Job 41:12
so will we sing and praise thy p .... Ps 21:13
my darling from the p of the dog .... Ps 22:20
I have seen the wicked in great p .... Ps 37:35
my soul from the p of the grave .... Ps 49:15
scatter them by thy p .... Ps 59:11
But I will sing of thy p .... Ps 59:16
that p belongeth unto God .... Ps 62:11
To see thy p and thy glory, so as .... Ps 63:2
being girded with p .... Ps 65:6
thy p shall thine enemies submit .... Ps 66:3
He ruleth by his p for ever .... Ps 66:7
strength and p unto his people .... Ps 68:35
thy p to every one that is to .... Ps 71:18
by his p he brought in the south .... Ps 78:26
to the greatness of thy p .... Ps 79:11
Who knoweth the p of thine anger .... Ps 90:11
make his mighty p to be known .... Ps 106:8
be willing in the day of thy p .... Ps 110:3
his people the p of his works .... Ps 111:6
of thy kingdom, and talk of thy p .... Ps 145:11
Great is our Lord, and of great p .... Ps 147:5
him in the firmament of his p .... Ps 150:1
when it is in the p of thine hand .... Prov 3:27
life are in the p of the tongue .... Prov 18:21
of their oppressors there was p .... Eccl 4:1
hath given him p to eat thereof .... Eccl 5:19
giveth him not p to eat thereof .... Eccl 6:2
the word of a king is, there is p .... Eccl 8:4
There is no man that hath p over .... Eccl 8:8
neither hath he p in the day of .... Eccl 8:8
their inhabitants were of small p .... Is 37:27
might, for that he is strong in p .... Is 40:26
He giveth p to the faint .... Is 40:29
and horse, the army and the p .... Is 43:17
from the p of the flame. .... Is 47:14
or have I no p to deliver .... Is 50:2
He hath made the earth by his p .... Jer 10:12
upon the ground, by my great p .... Jer 27:5
and the earth by thy great p .... Jer 32:17
He hath made the earth by his p .... Jer 51:15
even without great p or many .... Eze 17:9
in thee to their p to shed blood .... Eze 22:6
pride of her p shall come down .... Eze 30:6
hath given thee a kingdom, p .... Dan 2:37
whose bodies the fire had no p .... Dan 3:27
the kingdom by the might of my p .... Dan 4:30
Daniel from the p of the lions .... Dan 6:27
ran unto him in the fury of his p .... Dan 8:6
there was no p in the ram to .... Dan 8:7
of the nation, but not in his p .... Dan 8:22
his p shall be mighty .... Dan 8:24
but not by his own p .... Dan 8:24
shall not retain the p of the arm .... Dan 11:6
And he shall stir up his p .... Dan 11:25
But he shall have p over the .... Dan 11:43
scatter the p of the holy people .... Dan 12:7
by his strength he had p with God .... Hos 12:3
he had p over the angel, and .... Hos 12:4
them from the p of the grave .... Hos 13:14
it is in the p of their hand .... Mic 2:1
But truly I am full of p by the .... Mic 3:8
is slow to anger, and great in p .... Nah 1:3
strong, fortify thy p mightily .... Nah 2:1
imputing this his p unto his god .... Hab 1:11
be delivered from the p of evil .... Hab 2:9
and there was the hiding of his p .... Hab 3:4
saying, Not by might, nor by p .... Zec 4:6
and he will smite her in the sea .... Zec 9:4
thine is the kingdom, and the p .... Mt 6:13
hath p on earth to forgive sins .... Mt 9:6
which had given such p unto men .... Mt 9:8
he gave them p against unclean .... Mt 10:1
the scriptures, nor the p of God .... Mt 22:29
in the clouds of heaven with p .... Mt 24:30
sitting on the right hand of p .... Mt 26:64
All p is given unto me in heaven .... Mt 28:18
hath p on earth to forgive sins .... Mk 2:10
to have p to heal sicknesses, and .... Mk 3:15
gave them p over unclean spirits. .... Mk 6:7
the kingdom of God come with p .... Mk 9:1
scriptures, neither the p of God .... Mk 12:24
coming in the clouds with great p .... Mk 13:26

POWERFUL (cont.)

sitting on the right hand of p .... Mk 14:62
p of Elias, to turn the hearts of ...... Lk 1:17
the p of the Highest shall .... Lk 1:35
All this p will I give thee, and .... Lk 4:6
Jesus returned in the p of the .... Lk 4:14
for his word was with p .... Lk 4:32
p he commandeth the unclean .... Lk 4:36
the p of the Lord was present to .... Lk 5:17
hath p upon earth to forgive sins, ... Lk 5:24
together, and gave them p and .... Lk 9:1
all amazed at the mighty p of God .... Lk 9:43
I give unto you p to tread on .... Lk 10:19
and over all the p of the enemy .... Lk 10:19
killed hath p to cast into hell .... Lk 12:5
they might deliver him unto the p .... Lk 20:20
of man coming in a cloud with p .... Lk 21:27
your hour, and the p of darkness .... Lk 22:53
on the right hand of the p of God .... Lk 22:69
ye be endued with p from on high .... Lk 24:49
to them gave he p to become the .... Jn 1:12
I have p to lay it down, and I .... Jn 10:18
I have p to take it again .... Jn 10:18
hast given him p over all flesh .... Jn 17:2
not that I have p to crucify thee .... Jn 19:10
and have p to release thee .... Jn 19:10
have no p at all against me .... Jn 19:11
the Father hath put in his own p .... Acts 1:7
But ye shall receive p, after .... Acts 1:8
as though by our own p or .... Acts 3:12
the midst, they asked, By what .... Acts 4:7
with great p gave the apostles .... Acts 4:33
sold, was it not in thine own p .... Acts 5:4
And Stephen, full of faith and p .... Acts 6:8
This man is the great p of God .... Acts 8:10
Saying, Give me also this p .... Acts 8:19
with the Holy Ghost and with p .... Acts 10:38
from the p of Satan unto God, ... Acts 26:18
to be the Son of God with p .... Rom 1:4
for it is the p of God unto .... Rom 1:16
that are made, even his eternal p .... Rom 1:20
that I might shew my p in thee, ... Rom 9:17
not the potter p over the clay .... Rom 9:21
his wrath, and to make his p known ...... Rom 9:22
For there is no p but of God, ... Rom 13:1
therefore resisteth the p .... Rom 13:2
thou then not be afraid of the p .... Rom 13:3
through the p of the Holy Ghost. .... Rom 15:13
by the p of the Spirit of God .... Rom 15:19
Now to him that is of p .... Rom 16:25
are saved it is the p of God 1Cor 1:18
and Greeks, Christ the p of God 1Cor 1:24
of the Spirit and of p 1Cor 2:4
of men, but in the p of God 1Cor 2:5
which are puffed up, but the p 1Cor 4:19
of God is not in word, but in p 1Cor 4:20
with the p of our Lord Jesus 1Cor 5:4
not be brought under the p of any 1Cor 6:12
also raise up us by his own p 1Cor 6:14
wife hath not p of her own body 1Cor 7:4
hath not p of his own body 1Cor 7:4
but hath p over his own will, and 1Cor 7:37
Have we not p to eat and to drink 1Cor 9:4
Have we not p to lead about a 1Cor 9:5
have not we p to forbear working 1Cor 9:6
be partakers of this p over you, ... 1Cor 9:12
we have not used this p.................. 1Cor 9:12
I abuse not my p in the gospel 1Cor 9:18
have p on her head because of the 1Cor 11:10
all rule and all authority and 1Cor 15:24
it is raised in p 1Cor 15:43
excellency of the p may be of God 2Cor 4:7
word of truth, by the p of God 2Cor 6:7
for their p, I bear record, ... 2Cor 8:3
beyond their p they were willing........ 2Cor 8:3
that the p of Christ may rest 2Cor 12:9
yet he liveth by the p of God 2Cor 13:4
him by the p of God toward you. 2Cor 13:4
according to the p which the Lord 2Cor 13:10
of his p to us-ward who believe .... Eph 1:19
to the working of his mighty p .... Eph 1:19
Far above all principality, and p .... Eph 1:21
to the prince of the p of the air .... Eph 2:2
by the effectual working of his p .... Eph 3:7
according to the p that worketh .... Eph 3:20
Lord, and in the p of his might .... Eph 6:10
the p of his resurrection, and the ...... Phil 3:10
according to his glorious p .... Col 1:11
us from the p of darkness, ... Col 1:13
the head of all principality and .... Col 2:10
you in word only, but also in p 1Th 1:5
Lord, and from the glory of his p 2Th 1:9
and the work of faith with p 2Th 1:11
the working of Satan with all p 2Th 2:9
Not because we have not p 2Th 3:9
whom be honour and p everlasting 1Ti 6:16
but of p, and of love, and of a 2Ti 1:7
gospel according to the p of God 2Ti 1:8
but denying the p thereof 2Ti 3:5
all things by the word of his p .... Heb 1:3
him that had the p of death............. Heb 2:14
but after the p of an endless .... Heb 7:16
Who are kept by the p of God 1Pet 1:5
According as his divine p hath 2Pet 1:3
when we made known unto you the p 2Pet 1:16
angels, which are greater in p 2Pet 2:11
glory and majesty, dominion and p .... Jude 25
will I give p over the nations .... Rev 2:26
to receive glory and honour and p .... Rev 4:11
Lamb that was slain to receive p .... Rev 5:12
and honour, and glory, and p,........... Rev 5:13

p was given to him that sat .... Rev 6:4
p was given unto them over the .... Rev 6:8
and thanksgiving, and honour, and p ..... Rev 7:12
and unto them was given p, as the .... Rev 9:3
the scorpions of the earth have p .... Rev 9:3
their p was to hurt men five .... Rev 9:10
For their p is in their mouth, and ...... Rev 9:19
I will give p unto my men .... Rev 11:3
These have p to shut heaven, that .... Rev 11:6
have p over waters to turn them .... Rev 11:6
hast taken to thee thy great p .... Rev 11:17
our God, and the p of his Christ .... Rev 12:10
and the dragon gave him his .... Rev 13:2
which gave p unto the beast............. Rev 13:4
was given unto him to continue.......... Rev 13:5
p was given him over all kindreds .... Rev 13:7
he exerciseth all the p of the .... Rev 13:12
of those miracles which he had p .... Rev 13:14
he had p to give life unto the .... Rev 13:15
the altar, which had p over fire........ Rev 14:18
the glory of God, and from his p .... Rev 15:8
p was given unto him to scorch .... Rev 16:8
which hath p over these plagues .... Rev 16:9
but receive p as kings one hour .... Rev 17:12
one mind, and shall give their p .... Rev 17:13
down from heaven, having great p .... Rev 18:1
and glory, and honour, and p .... Rev 19:1
such the second death hath no p .... Rev 20:6

POWERFUL

The voice of the LORD is p .... Ps 29:4
say they, are weighty and p 2Cor 10:10
the word of God is quick, and p .... Heb 4:12

POWERS

the p of the heavens shall be .... Mt 24:29
the p that are in heaven shall be .... Mk 13:25
and unto magistrates, and p .... Lk 12:11
for the p of heaven shall be .... Lk 21:26
angels, nor principalities, nor p .... Rom 8:38
soul be subject unto the higher p .... Rom 13:1
the p that be are ordained of God .... Rom 13:1
p in heavenly places might be .... Eph 3:10
against principalities, against p .... Eph 6:12
or principalities, or p .... Col 1:16
spoiled principalities and p .... Col 2:15
be subject to principalities and p ...... Titus 3:1
the p of the world to come, ... Heb 6:5
being made subject unto him 1Pet 3:22

PRACTICES

have exercised with covetous p.......... 2Pet 2:14

PRACTISE

to p wicked works with men that .... Ps 141:4
to p hypocrisy, and to utter error ...... Is 32:6
and shall prosper, and p, and shall..... Dan 8:24
the morning is light, they p it......... Mic 2:1

PRACTISED

secretly p mischief against him 1Sa 23:9
and it p, and prospered .... Dan 8:12

PRAETORIUM (pre-to'-re-um) Palace of the
Roman procurator in Jerusalem.

him away into the hall, called P .... Mk 15:16

PRAISE

she said, Now will I p the LORD .... Gen 29:35
art he whom thy brethren shall p .... Gen 49:8
be holy to p the LORD withal........... Lev 19:24
He is thy p, and he is thy God,......... Deut 10:21
nations which he hath made, in p .... Deut 26:19
P ye the LORD for the avenging of ...... Judg 5:2
I will sing p to the LORD God of........ Judg 5:3
thank and p the LORD God of Israel... 1Chr 16:4
the holy name, and glory in thy p 1Chr 16:35
made, said David, to p therewith 1Chr 23:5
p the LORD, and likewise at even 1Chr 23:30
to give thanks and to p the LORD 1Chr 25:3
thee, and p thy glorious name 1Chr 29:13
the king had made to p the LORD 2Chr 7:6
Levites to their charges, to p 2Chr 8:14
stood up to p the LORD God of.......... 2Chr 20:19
that should p the beauty of 2Chr 20:21
the army, and to say, P the LORD 2Chr 20:21
when they began to sing and to p 2Chr 20:22
and such as taught to sing p 2Chr 23:13
commanded the Levites to sing p 2Chr 29:30
to p in the gates of the tents of 2Chr 31:2
p the LORD, after the .... Ezr 3:10
exalted above all blessing and p .... Neh 9:5
brethren over against them, to p .... Neh 12:24
of the singers, and songs of p .... Neh 12:46
I will p the LORD according to......... Ps 7:17
will sing p to the name of the......... Ps 7:17
I will p thee, O LORD, with my .... Ps 9:1
I will sing p to thy name .... Ps 9:2
That I may shew forth all thy p .... Ps 9:14
so will we sing and p thy power .... Ps 21:13
of the congregation will I p thee ...... Ps 22:22
Ye that fear the LORD, p him .... Ps 22:23
My p shall be of thee in the........... Ps 22:25
they shall p the LORD that seek .... Ps 22:26
and with my song will I p him .... Ps 28:7
shall the dust p thee.................. Ps 30:9
that my glory may sing p to thee....... Ps 30:12
for p is comely for the upright .... Ps 33:1
the LORD with harp..................... Ps 33:2
his p shall continually be in my .... Ps 34:1
I will p thee among much people .... Ps 35:18
of thy p all the day long .... Ps 35:28
in my mouth, even p unto our God....... Ps 40:3

God, with the voice of joy and p....... Ps 42:4
for I shall yet p him for the.......... Ps 42:5
for I shall yet p him, who is the...... Ps 42:11
yea, upon the harp will I p thee....... Ps 43:4
for I shall yet p him, who is the...... Ps 43:5
day long, and p thy name for ever ..... Ps 44:8
shall the people p thee for ever....... Ps 45:17
so is thy p unto the ends of the ...... Ps 48:10
his soul, and men will p thee......... Ps 49:18
Whoso offereth p glorifieth me .... Ps 50:23
my mouth shall shew forth thy p .... Ps 51:15
I will p thee for ever, because........ Ps 52:9
I will p thy name, O LORD.............. Ps 54:6
In God I will p his word, in God,...... Ps 56:4
In God will I p his word............... Ps 56:10
in the LORD will I p his word.......... Ps 56:10
I will sing and give p................. Ps 57:7
I will p thee, O LORD, among the ...... Ps 57:9
So will I sing p unto thy name .... Ps 61:8
than life, my lips shall p thee....... Ps 63:3
my mouth shall p thee with joyful..... Ps 63:5
P waiteth for thee, O God in Sion ..... Ps 65:1
make his p glorious................... Ps 66:2
the voice of his p to be heard........ Ps 66:8
Let the people p thee, O God.......... Ps 67:3
let all the people p thee............. Ps 67:3
Let the people p thee, O God.......... Ps 67:5
let all the people p thee............. Ps 67:5
I will p the name of God with a ...... Ps 69:30
Let the heaven and earth p him........ Ps 69:34
my p shall be continually of thee .... Ps 71:6
Let my mouth be filled with thy p .... Ps 71:8
will yet p thee more and more......... Ps 71:14
I will also p thee with the........... Ps 71:22
let the poor and needy p thy name .... Ps 74:21
the wrath of man shall p thee......... Ps 76:10
forth thy p to all generations........ Ps 79:13
I will p thee, O Lord my God,......... Ps 86:12
shall the dead arise and p thee....... Ps 88:10
the heavens shall p thy wonders....... Ps 89:5
loud noise, and rejoice, and sing p ... Ps 98:4
Let them p thy great and terrible ..... Ps 99:3
A Psalm of p.......................... Ps 100:t
and into his courts with p............ Ps 100:4
shall be created shall p the LORD ..... Ps 102:18
in Zion, and his p in Jerusalem ...... Ps 102:21
I will sing p to my God while I ...... Ps 104:33
P ye the LORD......................... Ps 104:35
P ye the LORD......................... Ps 105:45
P ye the LORD......................... Ps 106:1
who can shew forth all his p.......... Ps 106:2
they sang his p....................... Ps 106:12
holy name, and to triumph in thy p ... Ps 106:47
P ye the LORD......................... Ps 106:48
Oh that men would p the LORD for ...... Ps 107:8
Oh that men would p the LORD for ...... Ps 107:15
Oh that men would p the LORD for ...... Ps 107:21
Oh that men would p the LORD for ...... Ps 107:31
p him in the assembly of the.......... Ps 107:32
I will sing and give p, even with .... Ps 108:1
I will p thee, O LORD, among the...... Ps 108:3
Hold not thy peace, O God of my p ..... Ps 109:1
I will greatly p the LORD with my .... Ps 109:30
I will p him among the multitude ..... Ps 109:30
P ye the LORD......................... Ps 111:1
I will p the LORD with my whole...... Ps 111:1
his p endureth for ever............... Ps 111:10
P ye the LORD......................... Ps 112:1
P ye the LORD......................... Ps 113:1
P, O ye servants of the LORD,......... Ps 113:1
in the name of the LORD............... Ps 113:2
P ye the LORD......................... Ps 113:9
The dead p not the LORD, neither..... Ps 115:17
P the LORD............................ Ps 115:18
P ye the LORD......................... Ps 116:19
O p the LORD, all ye nations.......... Ps 117:1
p him, all ye people.................. Ps 117:1
and thee, and I will p thee........... Ps 117:2
into them, and I will p the LORD ..... Ps 118:19
I will p thee......................... Ps 118:21
Thou art my God, and I will p thee ... Ps 118:28
I will p thee with uprightness of .... Ps 119:7
Seven times a day do I p thee......... Ps 119:164
My lips shall utter p, when thou..... Ps 119:171
my soul live, and it shall p thee.... Ps 119:175
P ye the LORD......................... Ps 135:1
P ye the name of the LORD............. Ps 135:1
p him, O ye servants of the LORD ..... Ps 135:1
P ye the LORD......................... Ps 135:3
P ye the LORD......................... Ps 135:21
I will p thee with my whole heart..... Ps 138:1
the gods will I sing p unto thee ..... Ps 138:1
p thy name for thy lovingkindness .... Ps 138:2
kings of the earth shall p thee....... Ps 138:4
P ye the LORD......................... Ps 139:14
of prison, that I may p thy name...... Ps 142:7
David's Psalm of p.................... Ps 145:t
I will p thy name for ever and........ Ps 145:2
shall p thy works to another.......... Ps 145:4
All thy works shall p thee............ Ps 145:10
shall speak the p of the LORD .... Ps 145:21
P the LORD, O my soul................. Ps 146:1
While I live will I p the LORD........ Ps 146:2
P ye the LORD......................... Ps 146:10
P ye the LORD......................... Ps 147:1
and p is comely....................... Ps 147:1
sing p upon the harp unto our God ... Ps 147:7
P the LORD, O Jerusalem............... Ps 147:12
thy God, O Zion....................... Ps 147:12

P

P ye the LORD .... Ps 147:20
P ye the LORD .... Ps 148:1
P ye the LORD from the heavens .... Ps 148:1
p him in the heights .... Ps 148:1
P ye him, all his angels .... Ps 148:2
p ye him, all his hosts .... Ps 148:2
P ye him, sun and moon .... Ps 148:3
p him, all ye stars of light .... Ps 148:3
P him, ye heavens of heavens, and ...... Ps 148:4
Let them p the name of the LORD .... Ps 148:5
P the LORD from the earth, ye .... Ps 148:7
Let them p the name of the LORD .... Ps 148:13
people, the p of all his saints .... Ps 148:14
P ye the LORD .... Ps 148:14
P ye the LORD .... Ps 149:1
his p in the congregation of .... Ps 149:1
Let them p his name in the dance .... Ps 149:3
P ye the LORD .... Ps 149:9
P ye the LORD .... Ps 150:1
P God in his sanctuary .... Ps 150:1
p him in the firmament of his .... Ps 150:1
P him for his mighty acts .... Ps 150:2
p him according to his excellent .... Ps 150:2
P him with the sound of the .... Ps 150:3
p him with the psaltery and harp .... Ps 150:3
P him with the timbrel and dance .... Ps 150:4
P him with stringed instruments .... Ps 150:4
P him upon the loud cymbals .... Ps 150:5
p him upon the high sounding .... Ps 150:5
thing that hath breath p the LORD .... Ps 150:6
P ye the LORD .... Ps 150:6
Let another man p thee, and not .... Prov 27:2
so is a man to his p .... Prov 27:21
that forsake the law p the wicked .... Prov 28:4
her own works p her in the gates .... Prov 31:31
shalt say, O LORD, I will p thee .... Is 12:1
P the LORD, call upon his name .... Is 12:4
exalt thee, I will p thy name .... Is 25:1
For the grave cannot p thee .... Is 38:18
the living, he shall p thee .... Is 38:19
neither my p to graven images .... Is 42:8
his p from the end of the earth, ... Is 42:10
declare his p in the islands .... Is 42:12
they shall shew forth my p .... Is 43:21
for my p will I refrain for thee, ... Is 48:9
walls Salvation, and thy gates P .... Is 60:18
the garment of p for the spirit .... Is 61:3
p to spring forth before all the .... Is 61:11
make Jerusalem a p in the earth .... Is 62:7
it shall eat it, and p the LORD .... Is 62:9
people, and for a name, and for a p ...... Jer 13:11
for thou art my p .... Jer 17:14
and bringing sacrifices of p .... Jer 17:26
Sing unto the LORD, p ye the LORD ..... Jer 20:13
p ye, and say, O LORD, save thy .... Jer 31:7
shall be to me a name of joy, a p .... Jer 33:9
shall say, P the LORD of hosts .... Jer 33:11
of p into the house of the LORD .... Jer 33:11
There shall be no more p of Moab .... Jer 48:2
How is the city of p not left .... Jer 49:25
how is the p of the whole earth .... Jer 51:41
p thee, O thou God of my fathers, ... Dan 2:23
Now I Nebuchadnezzar p and extol ...... Dan 4:37
p the name of the LORD your God, ... Joel 2:26
and the earth was full of his p .... Hab 3:3
and I will get them p and fame in .... Zeph 3:19
a p among all people of the earth, ... Zeph 3:20
sucklings thou hast perfected p .... Mt 21:16
when they saw it, gave p unto God .... Lk 18:43
p God with a loud voice for all .... Lk 19:37
and said unto him, Give God the p .... Jn 9:24
For they loved the p of men more. .... Jn 12:43
of men more than the p of God .... Jn 12:43
whose p is not of men, but of God. ...... Rom 2:29
and thou shalt have p of the same. ...... Rom 13:3
P the LORD, all ye Gentiles .... Rom 15:11
shall every man have p of God 1Cor 4:5
Now I p you, brethren, that ye. 1Cor 11:2
I declare unto you I p you not 1Cor 11:17
shall I p you in this. 1Cor 11:22
I p you not. 1Cor 11:22
brother, whose p is in the gospel 2Cor 8:18
To the p of the glory of his .... Eph 1:6
should be to the p of his glory .... Eph 1:12
unto the p of his glory .... Eph 1:14
unto the glory and p of God .... Phil 1:11
any virtue, and if there be any p .... Phil 4:8
church will I sing p unto thee. .... Heb 2:12
sacrifice of p to God continually .... Heb 13:15
with fire, might be found unto p 1Pet 1:7
for the p of them that do well 1Pet 2:14
Jesus Christ, to whom be p 1Pet 4:11
P our God, all ye his servants, ... Rev 19:5

PRAISED

people saw him, they p their god .... Judg 16:24
much p as Absalom for his beauty. 2Sa 14:25
the LORD, who is worthy to be p 2Sa 22:4
is the LORD, and greatly to be p 1Chr 16:25
people said, Amen, and p the LORD 1Chr 16:36
four thousand p the LORD with the 1Chr 23:5
p the LORD, saying, For he is 2Chr 5:13
p the LORD, saying, For he is 2Chr 7:3
when David p by their ministry. 2Chr 7:6
the priests p the LORD day by day 2Chr 30:21
great shout, when they p the LORD .... Ezr 3:11
said, Amen, and p the LORD .... Neh 5:13
the LORD, who is worthy to be p .... Ps 18:3
greatly to be p in the city of .... Ps 48:1
and daily shall he be p .... Ps 72:15
LORD is great, and greatly to be p ..... Ps 96:4

same the LORD'S name is to be p .... Ps 113:3
is the LORD, and greatly to be p .... Ps 145:3
feareth the LORD, she shall be p .... Prov 31:30
Wherefore I p the dead which are .... Eccl 4:2
and the concubines, and they p her ...... Song 6:9
house, where our fathers p thee .... Is 64:11
I blessed the most High, and I p .... Dan 4:34
p the gods of gold, and of silver, ... Dan 5:4
thou hast p the gods of silver, ... Dan 5:23
loosed, and he spake, and p God. .... Lk 1:64

PRAISES

in holiness, fearful in p .... Ex 15:11
they sang p with gladness, and 2Chr 29:30
Sing to the LORD, which .... Ps 9:11
heathen, and sing p unto thy name ...... Ps 18:49
that inhabitest the p of Israel .... Ps 22:3
I will sing p unto the LORD .... Ps 27:6
Sing p to God, sing p .... Ps 47:6
p unto our King, sing p .... Ps 47:6
sing ye p with understanding .... Ps 47:7
I will render p unto thee .... Ps 56:12
Sing unto God, sing p to his name .... Ps 68:4
O sing p unto the LORD .... Ps 68:32
I will sing p to the God of Jacob .... Ps 75:9
to come the p of the LORD .... Ps 78:4
to sing p unto thy name, O most .... Ps 92:1
I will sing p unto thee among the .... Ps 108:3
sing p unto his name .... Ps 135:3
strings will I sing p unto thee .... Ps 144:9
I will sing p unto my God while I .... Ps 146:2
it is good to sing p unto our God .... Ps 147:1
let them sing p unto him with the .... Ps 149:3
Let the high p of God be in their. .... Ps 149:6
shew forth the p of the LORD .... Is 60:6
the p of the LORD, according to .... Is 63:7
Silas prayed, and sang p unto God ...... Acts 16:25
that ye should shew forth the p 1Pet 2:9

PRAISETH

her husband also, and he p her .... Prov 31:28

PRAISING

make one sound to be heard in p 2Chr 5:13
p the king, she came to the 2Chr 23:12
they sang together by course in p ...... Ezr 3:11
they will be still p thee .... Ps 84:4
of the heavenly host p God .... Lk 2:13
p God for all the things that .... Lk 2:20
were continually in the temple, p .... Lk 24:53
P God, and having favour with all .... Acts 2:47
walking, and leaping, and p God .... Acts 3:8
people saw him walking and p God ..... Acts 3:9

PRANSING

of the wheels, and of the p horses ...... Nah 3:2

PRANSINGS

broken by the means of the p .... Judg 5:22
the p of their mighty ones .... Judg 5:22

PRATING

but a p fool shall fall. .... Prov 10:8
but a p fool shall fall. .... Prov 10:10
p against us with malicious words 3Jn 10

PRAY

I p thee, that art my sister .... Gen 12:13
I p thee, between me and thee, and ..... Gen 13:8
thyself, I p thee, from me .... Gen 13:9
I p thee, go in unto my maid .... Gen 16:2
I p thee, from thy servant .... Gen 18:3
p you, be fetched, and wash your .... Gen 18:4
I p you, into your servant's .... Gen 19:2
p you, brethren, do not so .... Gen 19:7
I p you, bring them out unto you, ... Gen 19:8
a prophet, and he shall p for thee .... Gen 20:7
wilt give it, I p thee, hear me. .... Gen 23:13
I p thee, thy hand under my thigh .... Gen 24:2
I p thee, send me good speed this .... Gen 24:12
I p thee, that I may drink .... Gen 24:14
I p thee, drink a little water of .... Gen 24:17
tell me, I p thee .... Gen 24:23
I p thee, a little water of thy .... Gen 24:43
unto her, Let me drink, I p thee .... Gen 24:45
I p thee, with that same red .... Gen 25:30
I p thee, that I may feel thee, ... Gen 27:21
I p thee, of thy son's mandrakes .... Gen 30:14
I p thee, if I have found favour .... Gen 30:27
I p thee, from the hand of my .... Gen 32:11
said, Tell me, I p thee, thy name .... Gen 32:29
I p thee, if now I have found .... Gen 33:10
I p thee, my blessing that is .... Gen 33:11
I p thee, pass over before his. .... Gen 33:14
p you give her him to wife. .... Gen 34:8
p you, this dream which I have .... Gen 37:6
I p thee, see whether it be well .... Gen 37:14
I p thee, where they feed their .... Gen 37:16
I p thee, let me come in unto .... Gen 38:16
I p thee, whose are these, the .... Gen 38:25
tell me them, I p you .... Gen 40:8
I p thee, unto me, and make .... Gen 44:14
I p thee, speak a word in my .... Gen 44:18
I p thee, let thy servant abide .... Gen 44:33
Come near to me, I p you. .... Gen 45:4
we p thee, let thy servants dwell. .... Gen 47:4
I p thee, thy hand under my thigh .... Gen 47:29
bury me not, I p thee, in Egypt .... Gen 47:29
I p thee, unto me, and I will. .... Gen 48:9
I p you, in the ears of Pharaoh, ... Gen 50:4
I p thee, and bury my father, and I ..... Gen 50:5

I p thee now, the trespass of thy .... Gen 50:17
we p thee, forgive the trespass .... Gen 50:17
I p thee, by the hand of him whom..... Ex 4:13
I p thee, let me go .... Ex 4:18
we p thee, three days' journey .... Ex 5:3
I p thee, my sin only this once, ... Ex 10:17
I p thee, out of thy book which .... Ex 32:32
I p thee, if I have found grace .... Ex 33:13
my Lord, I p thee, go among us .... Ex 34:9
he said, Leave us not, I p thee. .... Num 10:31
I p thee, let me go over, and see. .... Num 11:15
Hear, I p you, ye sons of Levi............. Num 16:8
I p you, from the tents of these .... Num 16:26
I p thee, through thy country. .... Num 20:17
p unto the LORD, that he take .... Num 21:7
I p thee, curse me this people. .... Num 22:6
I p thee, hinder thee from coming. ..... Num 22:16
I p thee, curse me this people .... Num 22:17
p you, tarry ye also here this. .... Num 22:19
I p thee, with me unto another .... Num 23:13
I p thee, I will bring thee unto .... Num 23:27
I p thee, let me go over, and see. .... Deut 3:25
I p you, swear unto me by the .... Josh 2:12
I p thee, glory to the LORD God .... Josh 7:19
we p thee, the entrance into the .... Judg 1:24
I p thee, a little water to drink .... Judg 4:19
I p thee, until I come unto thee, ... Judg 6:18
I p thee, but this once with the .... Judg 6:39
I p you, loaves of bread unto the ...... Judg 8:5
I p you, in the ears of all the .... Judg 9:2
I p now, and fight with them .... Judg 9:38
us only, we p thee, this day .... Judg 10:15
I p thee, pass through thy land .... Judg 11:17
we p thee, through thy land into .... Judg 11:19
I p thee, and drink not wine nor .... Judg 13:4
I p thee, let us detain thee, ... Judg 13:15
her, I p thee, instead of her .... Judg 15:2
I p thee, wherein thy great .... Judg 16:6
I p thee, wherewith thou mightest .... Judg 16:10
I p thee, and strengthen me .... Judg 16:28
I p thee, only this once, O God, ... Judg 16:28
we p thee, of God, that we may .... Judg 18:5
I p thee, and tarry all night, and ...... Judg 19:6
Comfort thine heart, I p thee. .... Judg 19:8
evening, I p you tarry all night. .... Judg 19:9
I p you, do not so wickedly. .... Judg 19:23
I p you, let me glean and gather. ...... Ruth 2:7
I p thee, into one of the. 1Sa 2:36
I p thee hide it not from me. 1Sa 3:17
will p for you unto the LORD. 1Sa 7:5
I p thee, where the seer's house 1Sa 9:18
I p thee, what Samuel said to 1Sa 10:15
P for thy servants unto the LORD 1Sa 12:19
the LORD in ceasing to p for you. 1Sa 12:23
I p you, how mine eyes have been 1Sa 14:29
I p thee, pardon my sin, and turn 1Sa 15:25
I p thee, before the elders of my 1Sa 15:30
I p thee, stand before me 1Sa 16:22
I p thee, take heed to thyself 1Sa 19:2
And he said, Let me go, I p thee 1Sa 20:29
I p thee, and see my brethren 1Sa 20:29
I p thee, come forth, and be with 1Sa 23:3
I p you, prepare yet, and know and... 1Sa 23:22
I p thee, and see thy servant's 1Sa 25:8
I p thee, speak in thine audience 1Sa 25:24
I p thee, regard this man of 1Sa 25:25
I p thee, forgive the trespass of 1Sa 25:28
I p thee, with the spear even to 1Sa 26:8
I p thee, take thou now the spear 1Sa 26:11
I p thee, let me by the king 1Sa 36:19
I p thee, divine unto me by the 1Sa 28:8
I p thee, hearken thou also unto 1Sa 28:22
I p thee, bring me hither the 1Sa 30:7
I p thee, tell me 2Sa 1:4
I p thee, upon me, and slay me 2Sa 1:9
heart to p this prayer unto thee 2Sa 7:27
I p thee, let my sister Tamar 2Sa 13:5
I p thee, let Tamar my sister 2Sa 13:6
I p thee, speak unto the king 2Sa 13:13
I p thee, let my brother Amnon go.... 2Sa 13:26
I p thee, feign thyself to be a 2Sa 14:2
I p thee, let the king remember 2Sa 14:11
I p thee, speak one word unto my ... 2Sa 14:12
I p thee, the thing that I shall. 2Sa 14:18
I p thee, let me go and pay my vow...2Sa 15:7
I p thee, turn the counsel of 2Sa 15:31
I p thee, and take off his head 2Sa 16:9
I p thee, also run after Cushi 2Sa 18:22
I p thee, turn back again, that I 2Sa 19:37
I p you, unto Joab, Come near 2Sa 20:16
I p thee, be against me, and 2Sa 24:17
I p thee, give thee counsel, that 1Kin 1:12
I p thee, unto Solomon the king, (... 1Kin 2:17
I p thee, say me not nay. 1Kin 2:20
I p thee, be verified, which thou 1Kin 8:26
when they shall p toward this. 1Kin 8:30
thee, and confess thy name, and p. 1Kin 8:33
if they p toward this place, and 1Kin 8:35
shall come and p toward this house 1Kin 8:42
shall p unto the LORD toward the ... 1Kin 8:44
p unto thee toward their land, ... 1Kin 8:48
p for me, that my hand may be 1Kin 13:6
I p thee, and disguise thyself, ... 1Kin 14:2
I p thee, a morsel of bread in 1Kin 17:10
I p thee, a morsel of bread in 1Kin 17:11
I p thee, let this child's soul. 1Kin 17:21
I p thee, kiss my father and my 1Kin 19:20
I p you, and see how this man....... 1Kin 20:7
I p thee, put sackcloth on our. 1Kin 20:31

saith, I p thee, let me live............... 1Kin 20:32
of the LORD, Smite me, I p thee....... 1Kin 20:35
man, and said, Smite me, I p thee.... 1Kin 20:37
I p thee, at the word of the LORD 1Kin 22:5
I p thee, be like the word of one 1Kin 22:13
I p thee, let my life, and the 2Kin 1:13
unto Elisha, Tarry here, I p thee....... 2Kin 2:2
him, Elisha, tarry here, I p thee....... 2Kin 2:4
unto him, Tarry, I p thee, here 2Kin 2:6
I p thee, let a double portion of....... 2Kin 2:9
we p thee, and seek thy master....... 2Kin 2:16
I p thee, the situation of this........... 2Kin 2:19
chamber, I p thee, on the wall 2Kin 4:10
I p thee, one of the young men,....... 2Kin 4:22
I p thee, to meet her, and say......... 2Kin 4:26
I p you, and see how he seeketh a.... 2Kin 5:7
I p thee, take a blessing of thy 2Kin 5:15
I p thee, be given to thy servant...... 2Kin 5:17
I p thee, a talent of silver, and....... 2Kin 5:22
we p thee, unto Jordan, and take..... 2Kin 6:2
I p thee, and go with thy servants.... 2Kin 6:3
I p thee, open his eyes, that he....... 2Kin 6:17
people, I p thee, with blindness 2Kin 6:18
I p thee, five of the horses that....... 2Kin 7:13
I p thee, all the great things.......... 2Kin 8:4
I p thee, give pledges to my lord..... 2Kin 18:23
I p thee, to thy servants in the....... 2Kin 18:26
in his heart to p before God........... Neh 1:6
I p thee, O LORD my God, be on me.. 1Chr 21:17
return and confess thy name, and p.. 2Chr 6:24
yet if they p toward this place,....... 2Chr 6:26
if they come and p in this house...... 2Chr 6:32
they p unto thee toward this city 2Chr 6:34
p unto thee in the land of their....... 2Chr 6:37
p toward their land, which thou....... 2Chr 6:38
shall humble themselves, and p....... 2Chr 7:14
I p thee, at the word of the LORD 2Chr 18:4
I p thee, be like one of theirs........ 2Chr 18:12
p for the life of the king, and of..... Ezr 6:10
which I p before thee now, day and... Neh 1:6
I p thee, thy servant this day......... Neh 1:11
I p you, let us leave off this........... Neh 5:10
I p you, to them, even this day,....... Neh 5:11
I p thee, who ever perished,........... Job 4:7
I p you, let it not be iniquity......... Job 6:29
I p thee, of the former age, and...... Job 8:8
should we have, if we p unto him .... Job 21:15
I p thee, the law from his mouth..... Job 22:22
I p you, accept any man's person,.... Job 32:21
I p thee, hear my speeches, and..... Job 33:1
He shall p unto God, and he will...... Job 33:26
and my servant Job shall p for you... Job 42:8
for unto thee will I p..................... Ps 5:2
p unto thee in a time when thou ...... Ps 32:6
and morning, and at noon, will I p.... Ps 55:17
I p thee, thy merciful kindness .... Ps 119:76
P for the peace of Jerusalem.......... Ps 122:6
I p you, betwixt me and my............ Is 5:3
shall come to his sanctuary to p...... Is 16:12
I p thee, Read this, I p thee........... Is 29:11
saying, Read this, I p thee............. Is 29:12
I p thee, to my master the king....... Is 36:8
I p thee, unto thy servants in......... Is 36:11
p unto a god that cannot save........ Is 45:20
Therefore p not thou for this.......... Jer 7:16
Therefore p not thou for this,......... Jer 11:14
P not for this people for their......... Jer 14:11
I p thee, of the LORD for us............ Jer 21:2
and p unto the LORD for it............. Jer 29:7
p unto me, and I will hearken unto... Jer 29:12
I p thee, that is in Anathoth,......... Jer 32:8
P now unto the LORD our God for..... Jer 37:3
I p thee, O my lord the king,.......... Jer 37:20
I p thee, be accepted before thee ... Jer 37:20
I p thee, and I will slay Ishmael...... Jer 40:15
p for us unto the LORD thy God,...... Jer 42:2
I will p unto the LORD your God....... Jer 42:4
P for us unto the LORD our God....... Jer 42:20
he p unto all people, and behold my. Lam 1:18
I p you, and hear what is the word... Eze 33:30
we p thee, for whose cause this....... Jonah 1:8
I p thee, O LORD, was not this my.... Jonah 4:2
I p you, O heads of Jacob, and ye.... Mic 3:1
I p you, ye heads of the house of.... Mic 3:9
I p you, consider from this day........ Hag 2:15
their men, to p before the LORD...... Zec 7:2
go speedily to p before the LORD..... Zec 8:21
and to p before the LORD............... Zec 8:22
I p you, beseech God that he will..... Mal 1:9
p for them which despitefully use..... Mt 5:44
for they love to p standing in......... Mt 6:5
p to thy Father which is in............ Mt 6:6
But when ye p, use not vain.......... Mt 6:7
After this manner therefore p ye..... Mt 6:9
P ye therefore the Lord of the........ Mt 9:38
up into a mountain apart to p........ Mt 14:23
put his hands on them, and p......... Mt 19:13
But p ye that your flight be not...... Mt 24:20
ye here, while I go and p yonder..... Mt 26:36
Watch and p, that ye enter not...... Mt 26:41
that I cannot now p to my Father .... Mt 26:53
they began to p him to depart out .. Mk 5:17
I p thee, come and lay thy hands..... Mk 5:23
he departed into a mountain to p..... Mk 6:46
soever ye desire, when ye p........... Mk 11:24
p ye that your flight be not in........ Mk 13:18
Take ye heed, watch and p............ Mk 13:33
Sit ye here, while I shall p............ Mk 14:32
Watch ye and p, lest ye enter into .. Mk 14:38
he went out into a mountain to p.... Lk 6:12

p for them which despitefully use..... Lk 6:28
and went up into a mountain to p..... Lk 9:28
ye therefore the Lord of the .... Lk 10:2
unto him, Lord, teach us to p......... Lk 11:1
And he said unto them, When ye p... Lk 11:2
I p thee have me excused.............. Lk 14:18
I p thee have me excused.............. Lk 14:19
I p thee therefore, father, that....... Lk 16:27
end, that men ought always to p..... Lk 18:1
men went up into the temple to p.... Lk 18:10
and p always, that ye may be........ Lk 21:36
them, P that ye enter not into........ Lk 22:40
rise and p, lest ye enter into......... Lk 22:46
I will p the Father, and he shall...... Jn 14:16
that I will p the Father for you....... Jn 16:26
I p for them.............................. Jn 17:9
I p not for the world, but for......... Jn 17:9
I p not that thou shouldest take...... Jn 17:15
Neither p I for these alone, but...... Jn 17:20
p God, if perhaps the thought of.... Acts 8:22
P ye to the Lord for me, that........ Acts 8:24
I p thee, of whom speaketh the...... Acts 8:34
p to about the sixth hour.............. Acts 10:9
I p thee that thou wouldest hear..... Acts 24:4
Wherefore I p you to take some...... Acts 27:34
what we should p for as we ought.... Rom 8:26
p unto God uncovered.................. 1Cor 11:13
tongue p that he may interpret 1Cor 14:13
For if I p in an unknown tongue,...... 1Cor 14:14
I will p with the spirit, and I........ 1Cor 14:15
I will p with the understanding....... 1Cor 14:15
we p you in Christ's stead, be ye.... 2Cor 5:20
Now I p to God that ye do no evil.... 2Cor 13:7
And this I p, that your love may..... Phil 1:9
it, do not cease to p for you......... Col 1:9
P without ceasing...................... 1Th 5:17
I p God your whole spirit and soul... 1Th 5:23
Brethren, p for us..................... 1Th 5:25
also we p always for you, that....... 2Th 1:11
p for us, that the word of the........ 2Th 3:1
therefore that men p every where ... 1Ti 2:8
I p God that it may not be laid...... 2Ti 4:16
P for us................................ Heb 13:18
let him p................................ Jas 5:13
and let them p over him, anointing... Jas 5:14
one for another, that ye may be ..... Jas 5:16
do not say that he shall p for it 1Jn 5:16

PRAYED

So Abraham p unto God................ Gen 20:17
when Moses p unto the LORD,......... Num 11:2
And Moses p for the people............ Num 21:7
I p for Aaron also the same time..... Deut 9:20
I p therefore unto the LORD, and..... Deut 9:26
p unto the LORD, and wept sore...... 1Sa 1:10
For this child I p....................... 1Sa 1:27
And Hannah p, and said, My heart ... 1Sa 2:1
And Samuel p unto the LORD........... 1Sa 8:6
then unto, and p unto the LORD...... 2Kin 4:33
And Elisha p, and said, LORD, I...... 2Kin 6:17
Elisha p unto the LORD, and said..... 2Kin 6:18
Hezekiah p before the LORD, and..... 2Kin 19:15
That which thou hast p to me......... 2Kin 19:20
wall, and p unto the LORD, saying.... 2Kin 20:2
But Hezekiah p for them, saying....... 2Chr 30:18
prophet Isaiah the son of Amoz, p ... 2Chr 32:20
to the death, and p unto the LORD ... 2Chr 32:24
And p unto him......................... 2Chr 33:13
Now when Ezra had p, and when he.. Ezr 10:1
p before the God of heaven,........... Neh 1:4
So I p to the God of heaven .... Neh 2:4
when he p for his friends.............. Job 42:10
Hezekiah p unto the LORD, saying.... Is 37:15
Whereas thou hast p to me against .. Is 37:21
the wall, and p unto the LORD,....... Is 38:2
I p unto the LORD, saying............. Jer 32:16
his knees three times a day, and p... Dan 6:10
I p unto the LORD my God, and made. Dan 9:4
Then Jonah p unto the LORD his...... Jonah 2:1
he p unto God, and said, I........... Jonah 4:2
and fell on his face, and p........... Mt 26:39
away again the second time, and p... Mt 26:42
p the third time, saying the same.... Mt 26:44
into a solitary place, and there p.... Mk 1:35
p him that he might be with him...... Mk 5:18
p that, if it were possible, the....... Mk 14:35
And again he went away, and p....... Mk 14:39
p him that he would thrust out a..... Lk 5:3
himself into the wilderness, and p.... Lk 5:16
And as he p, the fashion of his...... Lk 9:29
p thus with himself, God, I thank.... Lk 18:11
But I have p for thee, that thy....... Lk 22:32
cast, and kneeled down, and p........ Lk 22:41
in an agony he p more earnestly..... Lk 22:44
mean while his disciples p him........ Jn 4:31
And they p, and said, Thou, Lord,.... Acts 1:24
And when they had p, the place was.. Acts 4:31
and when they had p, they laid....... Acts 6:6
for them, that they might............. Acts 8:15
all forth, and kneeled down, and p... Acts 9:40
to the people, and p to God alway... Acts 10:2
at the ninth hour I p in my house... Acts 10:30
Then p they him to tarry certain..... Acts 10:48
when they had fasted and p........... Acts 13:3
and had p with fasting, they......... Acts 14:23
p him, saying, Come over into........ Acts 16:9
And at midnight Paul and Silas p..... Acts 16:25
kneeled down, and p with them all .. Acts 20:36
kneeled down on the shore, and p.... Acts 21:5
even while I p in the temple, I....... Acts 22:17
p me to bring this young man unto... Acts 23:18

to whom Paul entered in, and p...... Acts 28:8
he p earnestly that it might not ..... Jas 5:17
he p again, and the heaven gave..... Jas 5:18

PRAYER

heart to pray this p unto thee........ 2Sa 7:27
respect unto the p of thy servant.... 1Kin 8:28
hearken unto the cry and to the p... 1Kin 8:28
p which thy servant shall make....... 1Kin 8:29
What p and supplication soever be ... 1Kin 8:38
Then hear thou in heaven their p 1Kin 8:45
Then hear thou their p and their..... 1Kin 8:49
made an end of praying all this p.... 1Kin 8:54
said unto him, I have heard thy p ... 1Kin 9:3
wherefore lift up thy p for the....... 2Kin 19:4
thy father, I have heard thy p....... 2Kin 20:5
therefore to the p of thy servant.... 2Chr 6:19
the p which thy servant prayeth...... 2Chr 6:19
to hearken unto the p which thy 2Chr 6:20
Then what p or what supplication,.... 2Chr 6:29
thou from the heavens their p........ 2Chr 6:35
from thy dwelling place, their p 2Chr 6:39
the p that is made in this place 2Chr 6:40
said unto him, I have heard thy p ... 2Chr 7:12
mine ears attent unto the p that 2Chr 7:15
their p came up to his holy.......... 2Chr 30:27
his p unto his God, and the words.... 2Chr 33:18
His p also, and how God was......... 2Chr 33:19
mayest hear the p of thy servant.... Neh 1:6
attentive to the p of thy servant..... Neh 1:11
to the p of thy servants, who........ Neh 1:11
we made our p unto our God......... Neh 4:9
to begin the thanksgiving in p........ Neh 11:17
fear, and restrainest p before God... Job 15:4
also my p is pure..................... Job 16:17
Thou shalt make thy p unto him...... Job 22:27
have mercy upon me, and hear my p.. Ps 4:1
will I direct my p unto thee.......... Ps 5:3
the LORD will receive my p............ Ps 6:9
A P of David.......................... Ps 17:t
unto my cry, give ear unto my p ..... Ps 17:1
my p returned into mine own bosom.. Ps 35:13
Hear my p, O LORD, and give ear..... Ps 39:12
my p unto the God of my life........ Ps 42:8
Hear my p, O God..................... Ps 54:2
Give ear to my p, O God............. Ps 55:1
attend unto my p...................... Ps 61:1
Hear my voice, O God, in my p ...... Ps 64:1
O thou that hearest p, unto thee..... Ps 65:2
attended to the voice of my p........ Ps 66:19
which hath not turned away my p..... Ps 66:20
my p is unto thee, O LORD, in an..... Ps 69:13
p also shall be made for him......... Ps 72:15
angry against the p of thy people.... Ps 80:4
O LORD God of hosts, hear my p ...... Ps 84:8
A P of David.......................... Ps 86:t
Give ear, O LORD, unto my p.......... Ps 86:6
Let my p come before thee........... Ps 88:2
morning shall my p prevent thee..... Ps 88:13
A P of Moses, the man of God........ Ps 90:t
A P of the afflicted, when he is...... Ps 102:t
Hear my p, O LORD, and let my cry ... Ps 102:1
regard the p of the destitute......... Ps 102:17
and not despise their p............... Ps 102:17
but I give myself unto p.............. Ps 109:4
and let his p become sin............. Ps 109:7
Let my p be set forth before thee ... Ps 141:2
for yet my p also shall be in......... Ps 142:t
A P when he was in the cave......... Ps 142:t
Hear my p, O LORD, give ear to my... Ps 143:1
but the p of the upright is his....... Prov 15:8
he heareth the p of the righteous... Prov 15:29
even his p shall be abomination...... Prov 28:9
they poured out a p when thy......... Is 26:16
wherefore lift up thy p for the....... Is 37:4
thy father, I have heard thy p....... Is 38:5
make them joyful in my house of p... Is 56:7
an house of p for all people.......... Is 56:7
lift up cry nor p for them............ Jer 7:16
lift up a cry or p for them,.......... Jer 11:14
and shout, he shutteth out my p ..... Lam 3:8
that our p should not pass........... Lam 3:44
unto the Lord God, to seek by p...... Dan 9:3
yet made we not our p before the ... Dan 9:13
hear the p of thy servant, and his... Dan 9:17
Yea, whiles I was speaking in p...... Dan 9:21
my p came in unto thee, into........ Jonah 2:7
A p of Habakkuk the prophet upon... Hab 3:1
this kind goeth not out but by p..... Mt 17:21
shall be called the house of p........ Mt 21:13
whatsoever ye shall ask in p......... Mt 21:22
and for a pretence make long p...... Mt 23:14
come forth by nothing, but by p...... Mk 9:29
of all nations the house of p......... Mk 11:17
for thy p is heard.................... Lk 1:13
continued all night in p to God...... Lk 6:12
My house is the house of p........... Lk 19:46
And when he rose up from p.......... Lk 22:45
continued with one accord in p....... Acts 1:14
into the temple at the hour of p..... Acts 3:1
give ourselves continually to p....... Acts 6:4
thy p is heard, and thine alms are... Acts 10:31
but p was made without ceasing of... Acts 12:5
where p was wont to be made........ Acts 16:13
it came to pass, as we went to p.... Acts 16:16
p to God for Israel is, that they..... Rom 10:1
continuing instant in p................ Rom 12:12
give yourselves to fasting and p...... 1Cor 7:5
also helping together by p for us..... 2Cor 1:11
And by their p for you, which long ... 2Cor 9:14
Praying always with all p............. Eph 6:18

PRAYERS (continued)

Always in every p of mine for you ...... Phil 1:4
to my salvation through your p .... Phil 1:19
but in every thing by p and.................... Phil 4:6
Continue in p, and watch in the .... Col 4:2
by the word of God and p 1Ti 4:5
the p of faith shall save the .... Jas 5:15
The effectual fervent p of a .... Jas 5:16
therefore sober, and watch unto p 1Pet 4:7

PRAYERS

The p of David the son of Jesse............... Ps 72:20
yea, when ye make many p, I will .... Is 1:15
and for a pretence make long p .... Mk 12:40
with fastings and p night and day .... Lk 2:37
of John fast often, and make p................. Lk 5:33
houses, and for a shew make long p .... Lk 20:47
and in breaking of bread, and in p .... Acts 2:42
And he said unto him, Thy p.................... Acts 10:4
mention of you always in my p .... Rom 1:9
with me in your p to God for me .... Rom 15:30
making mention of you in my p .... Eph 1:16
labouring fervently for you in p .... Col 4:12
making mention of you in our p 1Th 1:2
first of all, supplications, p..................... 1Ti 2:1
supplications and p night and day 1Ti 5:5
remembrance of thee in my p night 2Ti 1:3
mention of thee always in my p .... Philem 4
your p I shall be given unto you .... Philem 22
flesh, when he had offered up p.............. Heb 5:7
that your p be not hindered 1Pet 3:7
and his ears are open unto their p 1Pet 3:12
odours, which are the p of saints............ Rev 5:8
he should offer it with the p of the .... Rev 8:3
came with the p of the saints.................. Rev 8:4

PRAYEST

And when thou, p, thou shalt not be....... Mt 6:5
But thou, when thou p, enter into........... Mt 6:6

PRAYETH

which thy servant p before thee.............. 1Kin 8:28
which thy servant p before thee.............. 2Chr 6:19
thy servant p toward this place............... 2Chr 6:20
p unto it, and saith, Deliver me .... Is 44:17
for, behold, he p...................................... Acts 9:11
But every woman that p or 1Cor 11:5
in an unknown tongue, my spirit p 1Cor 14:14

PRAYING

she continued p before the LORD............ 1Sa 1:12
by thee here, p unto the LORD................. 1Sa 1:26
made an end of p all this prayer.............. 1Kin 8:54
when Solomon had made an end of p 2Chr 7:1
men assembled, and found Daniel p .... Dan 6:11
And whiles I was speaking, and p .... Dan 9:20
And when ye stand p, forgive, if .... Mk 11:25
multitude of the people were p .... Lk 11:10
Jesus also being baptized, and p .... Lk 3:21
came to pass, as he was alone p .... Lk 9:18
as he was p in a certain place.................. Lk 11:1
I was in the city of Joppa p...................... Acts 11:5
many were gathered together p............... Acts 12:12
Every man or p prophesying..................... 1Cor 11:4
P us with much intreaty that we 2Cor 8:4
P always with all prayer and .... Eph 6:18
Jesus Christ, p always for you,................. Col 1:3
Withal p also for us, that God .... Col 4:3
day p exceedingly that we might 1Th 3:10
holy faith, p in the Holy Ghost,................ Jude 20

PREACH

to p of thee at Jerusalem........................ Neh 6:7
to p good tidings unto the meek.............. Is 61:1
p unto it the preaching that I .... Jonah 3:2
From that time Jesus began to p .... Mt 4:17
And as ye go, p, saying, The.................... Mt 10:7
that p ye upon the housetops.................. Mt 10:27
to teach and to p in their cities............... Mt 11:1
p the baptism of repentance for.............. Mk 1:4
towns, that I may p there also .... Mk 1:38
he might send them forth to p .... Mk 3:14
p the gospel to every creature................. Mk 16:15
me to p the gospel to the poor .... Lk 4:18
to p deliverance to the captives,............. Lk 4:18
To p the acceptable year of the .... Lk 4:19
I must p the kingdom of God to............... Lk 4:43
he sent them to p the kingdom of .... Lk 9:2
go thou and p the kingdom of God.......... Lk 9:60
not to teach and p Jesus Christ .... Acts 5:42
commanded us to p unto the people....... Acts 10:42
p unto you that ye should turn................ Acts 14:15
in every city them that p him.................. Acts 15:21
Holy Ghost to p the word in Asia............ Acts 16:6
us for to p the gospel unto them............. Acts 16:10
whom I p unto you, is Christ .... Acts 17:3
I am ready to p the gospel to you............ Rom 1:15
is, the word of faith, which we p .... Rom 10:8
And how shall they p, except they .... Rom 10:15
them that p the gospel of peace............. Rom 10:15
so have I strived to p the gospel .... Rom 15:20
to baptize, but to p the gospel 1Cor 1:17
But we p Christ crucified, unto................ 1Cor 1:23
the gospel should live of the 1Cor 9:14
For though I p the gospel 1Cor 9:16
is unto me, if I p not the gospel 1Cor 9:16
when I p the gospel, I may make 1Cor 9:18
it were I or they, so we p......................... 1Cor 15:11
to Troas to p Christ's gospel.................... 2Cor 2:12
For we p not ourselves, but..................... 2Cor 4:5
To p the gospel in the regions 2Cor 10:16
p any other gospel unto you than .... Gal 1:8
If any man p any other gospel................. Gal 1:9
that I might p him among the.................. Gal 1:16

which I p among the Gentiles................. Gal 2:2
if I yet p circumcision, why do I .... Gal 5:11
that I should p among the....................... Eph 3:8
Some indeed p Christ even of envy........ Phil 1:15
The one p Christ of contention,.............. Phil 1:16
Whom we p, warning every man, and... Col 1:28
P the word 2Ti 4:2
the everlasting gospel to p unto............. Rev 14:6

PREACHED

I have p righteousness in the.................. Ps 40:9
poor have the gospel p to them.............. Mt 11:5
p in all the world for a witness............... Mt 24:14
shall be p in the whole world.................. Mt 26:13
And p, saying, There cometh one........... Mk 1:7
And he p in their synagogues.................. Mk 1:39
and he p the word unto them.................. Mk 2:2
out, and p that men should repent......... Mk 6:12
this gospel shall be p throughout........... Mk 14:9
p every where, the Lord working............ Mk 16:20
exhortation p he unto the people.......... Lk 3:18
he p in the synagogues of Galilee.......... Lk 4:44
to the poor the gospel is p .... Lk 7:22
that time the kingdom of God is p .... Lk 16:16
p the gospel, the chief priests................ Lk 20:1
remission of sins should be p in .... Lk 24:47
which before was p unto you .... Acts 3:20
p through Jesus the resurrection............ Acts 4:2
of Samaria, and p Christ unto them....... Acts 8:5
p the word of the Lord, returned............ Acts 8:25
the gospel in many villages of................ Acts 8:25
scripture, and p unto him Jesus.............. Acts 8:35
through he p in all the cities.................... Acts 8:40
straightway he p Christ in the .... Acts 9:20
how he had p boldly at Damascus.......... Acts 9:27
after the baptism which John p.............. Acts 10:37
they p the word of God in the................ Acts 13:5
When John had first p before his .... Acts 13:24
that through this man is p unto.............. Acts 13:38
be p to them the next sabbath............... Acts 13:42
And there they p the gospel................... Acts 14:7
when they had p the gospel to............... Acts 14:21
when they had p the word in Perga....... Acts 14:25
we have p the word of the Lord............. Acts 15:36
of God was p of Paul at Berea................ Acts 17:13
because he p unto them Jesus, and....... Acts 17:18
Paul p unto them, ready to depart......... Acts 20:7
I have fully p the gospel of .... Rom 15:19
means, when I have p to others.............. 1Cor 9:27
you the gospel which I p unto you.......... 1Cor 15:1
keep in memory what I p unto you.......... 1Cor 15:2
Now if Christ be p that he rose 1Cor 15:12
who was p among you by us, even......... 2Cor 1:19
another Jesus, whom we have not p...... 2Cor 11:4
because I have p to you the..................... 2Cor 11:7
that which we have p unto you................ Gal 1:8
was p of me is not after man................... Gal 1:11
p before the gospel unto Abraham,........ Gal 3:8
infirmity of the flesh I p the .... Gal 4:13
p peace to you which were afar.............. Eph 2:17
or in truth, Christ is p............................. Phil 1:18
which was p to every creature................ Col 1:23
we p unto you the gospel of God............ 1Th 2:9
p unto the Gentiles, believed on............ 1Ti 3:16
For unto us was the gospel p .... Heb 4:2
but the word p did not profit................... Heb 4:2
first p entered not in because of............. Heb 4:6
unto you by them that have p the........... 1Pet 1:12
which by the gospel is p unto you........... 1Pet 1:25
p unto the spirits in prison...................... 1Pet 3:19
p also to them that are dead.................. 1Pet 4:6

PREACHER

The words of the P, the son of................ Eccl 1:1
Vanity of vanities, saith the P................. Eccl 1:2
I the P was king over Israel in................. Eccl 1:12
this have I found, saith the p.................. Eccl 7:27
Vanity of vanities, saith the p................. Eccl 12:8
moreover, because the p was wise......... Eccl 12:9
The sought to find out............................ Eccl 12:10
how shall they hear without a p............. Rom 10:14
Whereunto I am ordained a p.................. 1Ti 2:7
Whereunto I am appointed a p............... 2Ti 1:11
a p of righteousness, bringing in............. 2Pet 2:5

PREACHEST

thou that p a man should not.................. Rom 2:21

PREACHETH

adjure you by Jesus whom Paul p........... Acts 19:13
if he that cometh p another Jesus.......... 2Cor 11:4
now p the faith which once he................ Gal 1:23

PREACHING

unto it the p that I bid thee..................... Jonah 3:2
p in the wilderness of Judaea,................ Mt 3:1
p the gospel of the kingdom, and........... Mt 4:23
p the gospel of the kingdom, and........... Mt 9:35
they repented at the p of Jonas............. Mt 12:41
p the gospel of the kingdom of.............. Mk 1:14
p the baptism of repentance for............ Lk 3:3
every city and village, p and................... Lk 8:1
p the gospel, and healing every............. Lk 9:6
they repented at the p of Jonas............. Lk 11:32
went every where p the word.................. Acts 8:4
p the things concerning the.................... Acts 8:12
Israel, p peace by Jesus Christ .... Acts 10:36
the word to none but unto the............... Acts 11:19
the Grecians, p the Lord Jesus................ Acts 11:20
p the word of the Lord, with many......... Acts 15:35
and as Paul was long p, he sunk............. Acts 20:9
I have gone p the kingdom of God .... Acts 20:25
P the kingdom of God, and teaching...... Acts 28:31

the p of Jesus Christ, according............. Rom 16:25
For the p of the cross is to them............ 1Cor 1:18
of p to save them that believe 1Cor 1:21
my p was not with enticing words.......... 1Cor 2:4
be not risen, then is our p vain............... 1Cor 15:14
also in p the gospel of Christ................... 2Cor 10:14
that by me the p might be fully............... 2Ti 4:17
manifested his word through p .... Titus 1:3

PRECEPT

For p must be upon p,............................. Is 28:10
p upon p; line upon line.......................... Is 28:10
Lord was unto them p upon p.................. Is 28:13
p upon p; line upon line.......................... Is 28:13
me is taught by the p of men.................. Is 29:13
of your heart he wrote you this p .... Mk 10:5
p to all the people according to.............. Heb 9:19

PRECEPTS

sabbath, and commanded them p .... Neh 9:14
us to keep thy p diligently...................... Ps 119:4
I will meditate in thy p, and have.......... Ps 119:15
me to understand the way of thy p........ Ps 119:27
Behold, I have longed after thy p........... Ps 119:40
for I seek thy p .... Ps 119:45
This I had, because I kept thy p.............. Ps 119:56
thee, and of them that keep thy p.......... Ps 119:63
keep thy p with my whole heart............ Ps 119:69
but I will meditate in thy p .... Ps 119:78
but I forsook not thy p............................ Ps 119:87
I will never forget thy p.......................... Ps 119:93
for I have sought thy p............................ Ps 119:94
ancients, because I keep thy p .... Ps 119:100
Through thy p I get understanding......... Ps 119:104
yet I erred not from thy p .... Ps 119:110
Therefore I esteem all thy p .... Ps 119:128
so will I keep thy p .... Ps 119:134
yet do not I forget thy p.......................... Ps 119:141
Consider how I love thy p .... Ps 119:159
I have kept thy p and thy........................ Ps 119:168
for I have chosen thy p............................ Ps 119:173
your father, and kept all his p .... Jer 35:18
even by departing from thy p .... Dan 9:5

PRECIOUS

brother and for his mother p things....... Gen 24:53
for the p things of heaven, for............... Deut 33:13
for the p fruits brought forth by............. Deut 33:14
for the p things put forth by the............ Deut 33:14
for the p things of the lasting................. Deut 33:15
for the p things of the earth and........... Deut 33:16
of the LORD was p in those days............. 1Sa 3:1
because my soul was p in thine.............. 1Sa 26:21
talent of gold with the p stones............ 2Sa 12:30
and very much gold, and p stones 1Kin 10:2
very great store, and p stones 1Kin 10:10
of almug trees, and p stones.................. 1Kin 10:11
thy servants, be p in thy sight................ 2Kin 1:13
let my life now be p in thy sight 2Kin 1:14
all the house of his p things.................... 2Kin 20:13
the p ointment, and all the house 2Kin 20:13
there were p stones in it......................... 1Chr 20:2
and all manner of p stones..................... 1Chr 29:2
they with whom p stones were.............. 1Chr 29:8
house with p stones for beauty.............. 2Chr 3:6
and gold in abundance, and p stones.... 2Chr 9:1
great abundance, and p stones 2Chr 9:9
brought algum trees and p stones......... 2Chr 9:10
p jewels, which they stripped off 2Chr 20:25
of p things, with fenced cities................ 2Chr 21:3
for p stones, and for spices, and............ 2Chr 32:27
with p things, beside all that .... Ezr 1:6
vessels of fine copper, p as gold............ Ezr 8:27
and his eye seeth every p thing............. Job 28:10
gold of Ophir, with the p onyx................ Job 28:16
the redemption of their soul is p .... Ps 49:8
p shall their blood be in his..................... Ps 72:14
P in the sight of the LORD is the............. Ps 116:15
forth and weepeth, bearing p seed .... Ps 126:6
It is like the p ointment upon................. Ps 133:2
How p also are thy thoughts unto .... Ps 139:17
We shall find all p substance .... Prov 1:13
She is more p than rubies....................... Prov 3:15
will hunt for the p life............................ Prov 6:26
substance of a diligent man is p .... Prov 12:27
A gift is as a p stone in the..................... Prov 17:8
lips of knowledge are a p jewel .... Prov 20:15
the chambers be filled with all p .... Prov 24:4
name is better than p ointment............. Eccl 7:1
make a man more p than fine gold........ Is 13:12
stone, a p corner stone, a sure.............. Is 28:16
them the house of his p things............... Is 39:2
the p ointment, and all the house......... Is 39:2
Since thou wast p in my sight................ Is 43:4
take forth the p from the vile................. Jer 15:19
all the p things thereof, and all .... Jer 20:5
The p sons of Zion, comparable to......... Lam 4:2
taken the treasure and p things............. Eze 22:25
in p clothes for chariots......................... Eze 27:20
all spices, and with all p stones .... Eze 27:22
every p stone was thy covering,............. Eze 28:13
with their p vessels of silver and .... Dan 11:8
with p stones, and pleasant things........ Dan 11:38
over all the p things of Egypt................. Dan 11:43
alabaster box of very p ointment........... Mt 26:7
of ointment of spikenard very p............ Mk 14:3
p stones, wood, hay, stubble................. 1Cor 3:12
for the p fruit of the earth...................... Jas 5:7
being much more p than of gold............ 1Pet 1:7
But with the p blood of Christ,............... 1Pet 1:19
of men, but chosen of God, and p......... 1Pet 2:4
a chief corner stone, elect, p.................. 1Pet 2:6

therefore which believe he is p........ 1Pet 2:7
like p faith with us through the........ 2Pet 1:1
us exceeding great and p promises........ 2Pet 1:4
p stones and pearls, having a........ Rev 17:4
p stones, and of pearls, and fine........ Rev 18:12
all manner vessels of most p wood........ Rev 18:12
with gold, and p stones, and pearls........ Rev 18:16
was like unto a stone most p........ Rev 21:11
with all manner of p stones........ Rev 21:19

PREDESTINATE
he also did p to be conformed to........ Rom 8:29
Moreover whom he did p, them he........ Rom 8:30

PREDESTINATED
Having p us unto the adoption of........ Eph 1:5
being p according to the purpose........ Eph 1:11

PREEMINENCE
a man hath no p above a beast........ Eccl 3:19
in all things he might have the p........ Col 1:18
loveth to have the p among them........ 3Jn 9

PREFER
if I p not Jerusalem above my........ Ps 137:6

PREFERRED
he p her and her maids unto the........ Est 2:9
Daniel was p above the presidents........ Dan 6:3
cometh after me is p before me........ Jn 1:15
coming after me is p before me........ Jn 1:27
cometh a man which is p before me........ Jn 1:30

PREFERRING
in honour p one another........ Rom 12:10
without p one before another........ 1Ti 5:21

PREMEDITATE
ye shall speak, neither do ye p........ Mk 13:11

PREPARATION
will therefore now make p for it........ 1Chr 22:5
torches in the day of his p........ Nah 2:3
that followed the day of the p........ Mt 27:62
was come, because it was the p........ Mk 15:42
And that day was the p, and the........ Lk 23:54
it was the p of the passover, and........ Jn 19:14
therefore, because it was the p........ Jn 19:31
because of the Jews' p day........ Jn 19:42
with the p of the gospel of peace........ Eph 6:15

PREPARATIONS
The p of the heart in man, and the........ Prov 16:1

PREPARE
I will p him an habitation........ Ex 15:2
shall p that which they bring in........ Ex 16:5
thou p with the burnt offering a........ Num 15:6
thou shalt p for a meat offering........ Num 15:6
to the number that ye shall p........ Num 15:12
p me here seven oxen and seven........ Num 23:1
p me here seven bullocks and seven........ Num 23:29
Thou shalt p thee a way, and........ Deut 19:3
people, saying, P you victuals........ Josh 1:11
Let us now p to build us an altar........ Josh 22:26
p your hearts unto the LORD, and........ 1Sa 7:3
p yet, and know and see his place........ 1Sa 23:22
P thy chariot, and get thee down........ 1Kin 18:44
shewbread, to p it every sabbath........ 1Chr 9:32
and p their heart unto thee........ 1Chr 29:18
Even to p me timber in abundance........ 2Chr 2:9
Then Hezekiah commanded to p........ 2Chr 31:11
p yourselves by the houses of........ 2Chr 35:4
p your brethren, that they may do........ 2Chr 35:6
banquet that I shall p for them........ Est 5:8
p thyself to the search of their........ Job 8:8
If thou p thine heart, and stretch........ Job 11:13
dust, and p raiment as the clay........ Job 27:16
He may p it, but the just shall........ Job 27:17
thou wilt p their heart, thou........ Ps 10:17
p themselves without my fault........ Ps 59:4
O p mercy and truth, which may........ Ps 61:7
that they may p a city for........ Ps 107:36
P thy work without, and make it........ Prov 24:27
yet they p their meat in the........ Prov 30:25
P slaughter for his children for........ Is 14:21
P the table, watch in the........ Is 21:5
P ye the way of the LORD, make........ Is 40:3
workman to p a graven image........ Is 40:20
ye up, p the way, take up the........ Is 57:14
p ye the way of the people........ Is 62:10
that p a table for that troop, and........ Is 65:11
P ye war against her........ Jer 6:4
p them for the day of slaughter........ Jer 12:3
I will p destroyers against thee........ Jer 22:7
say ye, Stand fast, and p thee........ Jer 46:14
up the watchmen, p the ambushes........ Jer 51:12
p the nations against her, call........ Jer 51:27
P against her the nations with........ Ezk 4:15
thou shalt p thee bread therewith........ Eze 4:15
p thee stuff for removing, and........ Eze 12:3
I will p thee unto blood, and........ Eze 35:6
p thou for thyself, thou, and all........ Eze 38:7
Seven days shalt thou p every day........ Eze 43:25
they shall also p a young bullock........ Eze 43:25
he shall p the sin offering, and........ Eze 45:17
shalt the prince p for himself........ Eze 45:22
days of the feast he shall p a........ Eze 45:23
he shall p a meat offering of an........ Eze 45:24
the priests shall p his burnt........ Eze 46:2
he shall p a meat offering........ Eze 46:12
Now when the prince shall p a........ Eze 46:12
he shall p his burnt offering and........ Eze 46:12
Thou shalt daily p a burnt........ Eze 46:13
thou shalt p it every morning........ Eze 46:13

thou shalt p a meat offering for........ Eze 46:14
Thus shall they p the lamb........ Eze 46:15
P war, wake up the mighty men........ Joel 3:9
p to meet thy God, O Israel........ Amos 4:12
they even p war against him........ Mic 3:5
he shall p the way before me........ Mal 3:1
P ye the way of the Lord, make........ Mt 3:3
which shall p thy way before thee........ Mt 11:10
Where wilt thou that we p to........ Mt 26:17
which shall p thy way before thee........ Mk 1:2
P ye the way of the Lord, make........ Mk 1:3
p that thou mayest eat the........ Mk 14:12
face of the Lord to p his ways........ Lk 1:76
P ye the way of the Lord, make........ Lk 3:4
which shall p thy way before thee........ Lk 7:27
p us the passover, that we may........ Lk 22:8
him, Where wilt thou that we p........ Lk 22:9
I go to p a place for you........ Jn 14:2
a place for you, I will come........ Jn 14:3
who shall p himself to the battle........ 1Cor 14:8
But withal p me also a lodging........ Philem 22

PREPARED
for I have p the house, and room........ Gen 24:31
and the bread, which she had p........ Gen 27:17
neither had they p for themselves........ Ex 12:39
into the place which I have p........ Ex 23:20
the city of Sihon be built and p........ Num 21:27
I have p seven altars, and I have........ Num 23:4
whom he had p of the children of........ Josh 4:4
About forty thousand p for war........ Josh 4:13
this, that Absalom p him chariots........ 2Sa 15:1
he p him chariots and horsemen, and........ 1Kin 1:5
so they p timber and stones to........ 1Kin 5:18
the oracle he p in the house........ 1Kin 6:19
he p great provision for them........ 2Kin 6:23
for their brethren had p for them........ 1Chr 12:39
p a place for the ark of God, and........ 1Chr 15:1
his place, which he had p for it........ 1Chr 15:3
the place that I have p for it........ 1Chr 15:12
David p iron in abundance for........ 1Chr 22:3
So David p abundantly before his........ 1Chr 22:5
in my trouble I have p for the........ 1Chr 22:14
timber also and stone have I p........ 1Chr 22:14
Now I have p with all my might........ 1Chr 29:2
that I have p for the holy house........ 1Chr 29:3
have p to build thee an house for........ 1Chr 29:16
place which David had p for it........ 2Chr 1:4
in the place that David had p in........ 2Chr 3:1
p unto the day of the foundation........ 2Chr 8:16
because he p not his heart to seek........ 2Chr 12:14
divers kinds of spices p by the........ 2Chr 16:14
thousand ready p for the war........ 2Chr 17:18
hast p thine heart to seek God........ 2Chr 19:3
p their hearts unto the God of........ 2Chr 20:33
Uzziah p for them throughout all........ 2Chr 26:14
because he p his ways before the........ 2Chr 27:6
in his transgression, have we p........ 2Chr 29:19
for great God had p the people........ 2Chr 29:36
and they p them........ 2Chr 31:11
So the service was p, and the........ 2Chr 35:10
the Levites p for themselves........ 2Chr 35:15
brethren the Levites p for them........ 2Chr 35:15
of the LORD was p the same day........ 2Chr 35:16
when Josiah had p the temple........ 2Chr 35:16
For Ezra had p his heart to seek........ Ezr 7:10
Now that which was p for me for daily........ Neh 5:18
also fowls were p for me, and once........ Neh 5:18
unto them for whom nothing is p........ Neh 8:10
he had p for him a great chamber........ Neh 13:5
the banquet that I have p for him........ Est 5:4
to the banquet that Esther had p........ Est 5:5
banquet that she had p but myself........ Est 5:12
the gallows that he had p for him........ Est 6:4
the banquet that Esther had p........ Est 6:14
He p it, yea, and searched it out........ Job 28:27
when I p my seat in the street........ Job 29:7
He hath also p for him the........ Ps 7:13
he hath p his throne for judgment........ Ps 9:7
They have p a net for my steps........ Ps 57:6
hast p of thy goodness for the........ Ps 68:10
thou hast p the light and the sun........ Ps 74:16
The LORD hath p his throne in the........ Ps 103:19
When he p the heavens, I was........ Prov 8:27
Judgments are p for scorners........ Prov 19:29
The horse is p against the day of........ Prov 21:31
yea, for the king it is p........ Is 30:33
what he hath p for him that........ Is 64:4
a table p before it, whereupon........ Eze 23:41
of thy pipes was p in thee in the........ Eze 28:13
Be thou p, and prepare for thyself........ Eze 38:7
for ye have p lying and corrupt........ Dan 2:9
and gold, which they p for Baal........ Hos 2:8
going forth is p as the morning........ Hos 6:3
Now the Lord had p a great fish........ Jonah 1:17
And the LORD God p a gourd........ Jonah 4:6
But God p a worm when the morning........ Jonah 4:7
that God p a vehement east wind........ Jonah 4:8
and the defence shall be p........ Nah 2:5
for the LORD hath p a sacrifice........ Zeph 1:7
is it p of my Father........ Mt 20:23
Behold, I have p my dinner........ Mt 22:4
inherit the kingdom p for you........ Mt 25:34
p for the devil and his angels........ Mt 25:41
be given to them for whom it is p........ Mk 10:40
a large upper room furnished and p........ Mk 14:15
ready a people p for the Lord........ Lk 1:17
Which thou hast p before the face........ Lk 2:31
p not himself, neither did........ Lk 12:47
and p spices and ointments........ Lk 23:56

the spices which they had p........ Lk 24:1
which he had afore p unto glory........ Rom 9:23
God hath p for them that love him........ 1Cor 2:9
use, and p unto every good work........ 2Ti 2:21
not, but a body hast thou p me........ Heb 10:5
p an ark to the saving of his........ Heb 11:7
for he hath p for them a city........ Heb 11:16
trumpets p themselves to sound........ Rev 8:6
like unto horses p unto battle........ Rev 9:7
which were p for an hour, and a........ Rev 9:15
where she hath a place p of God........ Rev 12:6
the kings of the east might be p........ Rev 16:12
p as a bride adorned for her........ Rev 21:2

PREPAREDST
Thou p room before it, and didst........ Ps 80:9

PREPAREST
when thou p a bullock for a burnt........ Num 15:8
Thou p a table before me in the........ Ps 23:5
thou p them corn, when thou hast........ Ps 65:9

PREPARETH
That p his heart to seek God, the........ 2Chr 30:19
vanity, and their belly p deceit........ Job 15:35
who p rain for the earth, who........ Ps 147:8

PREPARING
in p him a chamber in the courts........ Neh 13:7
of Noah, while the ark was a p........ 1Pet 3:20

PRESBYTERY
laying on of the hands of the p........ 1Ti 4:14

PRESCRIBED
grievousness which they have p........ Is 10:1

PRESCRIBING
oil, and salt without p how much........ Ezr 7:22

PRESENCE
the p of the LORD God amongst the........ Gen 3:8
went out from the p of the LORD........ Gen 4:16
in the p of all his brethren........ Gen 16:12
in the p of the sons of my people........ Gen 23:11
in the p of the children of Heth........ Gen 23:18
he died in the p of all his........ Gen 25:18
from the p of Isaac his father........ Gen 27:30
went out from the p of Pharaoh........ Gen 41:46
for they were troubled at his p........ Gen 45:3
for why should we die in thy p........ Gen 47:15
were driven out from Pharaoh's p........ Ex 10:11
My p shall go with thee, and I........ Ex 33:14
If thy p go not with me, carry us........ Ex 33:15
departed from the p of Moses........ Ex 35:20
soul shall be cut off from my p........ Lev 22:3
Aaron went from the p of the........ Num 20:6
unto him in the p of the elders........ Deut 25:9
priests, in the p of the people........ Josh 4:11
which he wrote in the p of the........ Josh 8:32
David avoided out of his p twice........ 1Sa 18:11
David to Saul, and he was in his p........ 1Sa 19:7
he slipped away out of Saul's p........ 1Sa 19:10
to play the mad man in my p........ 1Sa 21:15
I not serve in the p of his son........ 2Sa 16:19
I have served in thy father's p........ 2Sa 16:19
so will I be in thy p........ 2Sa 16:19
went out from the p of the king........ 2Sa 24:4
And she came into the king's p........ 1Kin 1:28
the p of all the congregation of........ 1Kin 8:22
fled from the p of king Solomon........ 1Kin 12:2
in the p of the people, saying........ 1Kin 21:13
the p of Jehoshaphat the king of........ 2Kin 3:14
he went out from his p a leper as........ 2Kin 5:27
cast he them from his p at last........ 2Kin 17:20
he had cast them out from his p........ 2Kin 24:20
of them that were in the king's p........ 2Kin 25:19
Glory and honour are in his p........ 1Chr 16:27
sing out at the p of the LORD........ 1Chr 16:33
Aaron in the p of David the king........ 1Chr 24:31
the p of all the congregation of........ 2Chr 6:12
the earth sought the p of Solomon........ 2Chr 9:23
from the p of Solomon the king........ 2Chr 10:2
before this house, and in thy p........ 2Chr 20:9
the altars of Baalim in his p........ 2Chr 34:4
not been beforetime sad in his p........ Neh 2:1
in the p of Ahasuerus the king........ Est 1:10
Mordecai went out from the p of........ Est 8:15
went forth from the p of the LORD........ Job 1:12
forth from the p of the LORD........ Job 2:7
Therefore am I troubled at his p........ Job 23:15
shall fall and perish at thy p........ Ps 9:3
in thy p is fulness of joy........ Ps 16:11
my sentence come forth from thy p........ Ps 17:2
me in the p of mine enemies........ Ps 23:5
of thy p from the pride of man........ Ps 31:20
Cast me not away from thy p........ Ps 51:11
the wicked perish at the p of God........ Ps 68:2
also dropped at the p of God........ Ps 68:8
itself was moved at the p of God........ Ps 68:8
before his p with thanksgiving........ Ps 95:2
like wax at the p of the LORD........ Ps 97:5
at the p of the LORD of the whole........ Ps 97:5
come before his p with singing........ Ps 100:2
at the p of the Lord........ Ps 114:7
at the p of the God of Jacob........ Ps 114:7
now in the p of all his people........ Ps 116:14
now in the p of all his people........ Ps 116:18
whither shall I flee from thy p........ Ps 139:7
the upright shall dwell in thy p........ Ps 140:13
Go from the p of a foolish man........ Prov 14:7
surety in the p of his friend........ Prov 17:18
thyself in the p of the king........ Prov 25:6
of the prince whom thine eyes........ Prov 25:7

strangers devour it in your p.............. Is 1:7
of Egypt shall be moved at his p............ Is 19:1
and the angel of his p saved them.......... Is 63:9
might flow down at thy p................... Is 64:1
the nations may tremble at thy p........... Is 64:2
mountains flowed down at thy p............. Is 64:3
broken down at the p of the LORD.......... Jer 4:26
will ye not tremble at my p................ Jer 5:22
fathers, and cast out of my p............. Jer 23:39
in the p of the priests and of all......... Jer 28:1
Hananiah in the p of the priests.......... Jer 28:5
in the p of all the people that........... Jer 28:5
spake in the p of all the people........... Jer 28:11
in the p of the witnesses that............ Jer 32:12
he had cast them out from his p........... Jer 52:3
of the earth, shall shake at my p.......... Eze 38:20
answered in the p of the king............. Dan 2:27
Tarshish from the p of the LORD.......... Jonah 1:3
Tarshish from the p of the LORD.......... Jonah 1:3
he fled from the p of the LORD........... Jonah 1:10
and the earth is burned at his p........... Nah 1:5
peace at the p of the LORD God........... Zeph 1:7
that stand in the p of God............... Lk 1:19
We have eaten and drunk in thy p........... Lk 13:26
p of them that sit at meat with............ Lk 14:10
there is joy in the p of the............... Lk 15:10
Jesus in the p of his disciples............ Jn 20:30
and denied him in the p of Pilate......... Acts 3:13
soundness in the p of you all.............. Acts 3:16
shall come from the p of the Lord......... Acts 3:19
from the p of the council................. Acts 5:41
thanks to God in p of them all............ Acts 27:35
no flesh should glory in his p............. 1Cor 1:29
who in p am base among you, but.......... 2Cor 10:1
but his bodily p is weak, and his.......... 2Cor 10:10
obeyed, not as in my p only............... Phil 2:12
from you for a short time in p............. 1Th 2:17
Are not even ye in the p of our............ 1Th 2:19
from the p of the Lord, and from.......... 2Th 1:9
to appear in the p of God for us.......... Heb 9:24
you faultless before the p of his.......... Jude 24
brimstone in the p of the holy............. Rev 14:10
angels, and in the p of the Lamb.......... Rev 14:10

PRESENT

his hand a p for Esau his brother......... Gen 32:13
it is a p sent unto my lord Esau.......... Gen 32:18
with the p that goeth before him.......... Gen 32:20
So went the p over before him............. Gen 32:21
then receive my p at my hand.............. Gen 33:10
and carry down the man a p................ Gen 43:11
And the men took that p, and they........ Gen 43:15
they made ready the p against............. Gen 43:25
they brought him the p which was........... Gen 43:26
p thyself there to me in the top........... Ex 34:2
the p may continue to the............... Lev 14:11
p them before the LORD as the............ Lev 16:7
then he shall p himself before............ Lev 27:8
then he shall p the beast before.......... Lev 27:11
p them before Aaron the priest............ Num 3:6
p yourselves in the tabernacle of......... Deut 31:14
a p unto Eglon the king of Moab.......... Judg 3:15
he brought the p unto Eglon king......... Judg 3:17
he had made an end to offer the p........ Judg 3:18
away the people that bare the p.......... Judg 3:18
unto thee, and bring forth my p........... Judg 6:18
there is not a p to bring to the........... 1Sa 9:7
Now therefore p yourselves before......... 1Sa 10:19
the people that were p with him........... 1Sa 13:15
the people that were p with them.......... 1Sa 13:15
in mine hand, or what there is p.......... 1Sa 21:3
Behold a p for you of the spoil........... 1Sa 30:26
three days, and be thou here p............ 2Sa 20:4
given it for a p unto his............... 1Kin 9:16
And they brought every man his p......... 1Kin 10:25
have sent unto thee a p of silver........ 1Kin 15:19
were numbered, and were all p............ 1Kin 20:27
Take a p in thine hand, and go........... 2Kin 8:8
took a p with him, even of every......... 2Kin 8:9
sent it for a p to the king of........... 2Kin 16:8
brought no p to the king of.............. 2Kin 17:4
Make an agreement with me by a p......... 2Kin 18:31
sent letters and a p unto Hezekiah....... 2Kin 20:12
joy thy people, which are p here......... 1Chr 29:17
that were p were sanctified............... 2Chr 5:11
And they brought every man his p......... 2Chr 9:24
all that were p with him bowed........... 2Chr 29:29
children of Israel that were p at......... 2Chr 30:21
all Israel that were p went out......... 2Chr 31:1
all that were p in Jerusalem............. 2Chr 34:32
that were p in Israel to serve........... 2Chr 34:33
offerings, for all that were p........... 2Chr 35:7
children of Israel that were p........... 2Chr 35:17
all Judah and Israel that were p......... 2Chr 35:18
his lords, and all Israel there p........ Ezr 8:25
that were p in Shushan the palace........ Est 1:5
the Jews that are p in Shushan........... Est 4:16
to p themselves before the LORD.......... Job 1:6
to p themselves before the LORD.......... Job 2:1
them to p himself before the LORD........ Job 2:1
a very p help in trouble................. Ps 46:1
In that time shall the p be.............. Is 18:7
Make an agreement with me by a p......... Is 36:16
sent letters and a p to Hezekiah......... Is 39:1
It may be they will p their.............. Jer 36:7
unto whom ye sent me to p your........... Jer 42:9
thee for a p horns of ivory.............. Eze 27:15
for we do not p our supplications........ Dan 9:18
Assyria for a p to the king Jareb........ Hos 10:6
Jerusalem, to p him to the Lord.......... Lk 2:22
of the Lord was p to heal them........... Lk 5:17

There were p at that season some.......... Lk 13:1
manifold more in this p time.............. Lk 18:30
unto you, being yet p with you........... Jn 14:25
are we all here p before God............. Acts 10:33
and all the elders were p................. Acts 21:18
all men which are here p with us......... Acts 25:24
every one, because of the p main......... Acts 28:2
for to will is p with me................. Rom 7:18
would do good, evil is p with me......... Rom 7:21
this p time are not worthy to be......... Rom 8:18
nor powers, nor things p................. Rom 8:38
Even so then at this p time also......... Rom 11:5
that ye p your bodies a living........... Rom 12:1
or life, or death, or things p........... 1Cor 3:22
Even unto this p hour we both............ 1Cor 4:11
but p in spirit, have judged............. 1Cor 5:3
already, as though I were p.............. 1Cor 5:3
this is good for the p distress.......... 1Cor 7:26
greater part remain unto this p.......... 1Cor 15:6
by Jesus, and shall p us with you........ 2Cor 4:14
body, and to be p with the Lord.......... 2Cor 5:8
whether p or absent, we may be........... 2Cor 5:9
when I am p with that confidence......... 2Cor 10:2
we be also in deed when we are p......... 2Cor 10:11
that I may p you as a chaste............. 2Cor 11:2
And when I was p with you, and........... 2Cor 11:9
and foretell you, as if I were p......... 2Cor 13:2
lest being p I should use................ 2Cor 13:10
deliver us from this p evil world........ Gal 1:4
and not only when I am p with you........ Gal 4:18
I desire to be p with you now............ Gal 4:20
That he might p it to himself a.......... Eph 5:27
to p you holy and unblameable and........ Col 1:22
that we may p every man perfect......... Col 1:28
me, having loved this p world............ 2Ti 4:10
and godly, in this p world............... Titus 2:12
was a figure for the time then p......... Heb 9:9
for the p seemeth to be joyous........... Heb 12:11
and be established in the p truth........ 2Pet 1:12
to p you faultless before................ Jude 24

PRESENTED

to Goshen, and p himself unto him........ Gen 46:29
five men, and p them unto Pharaoh........ Gen 47:2
when it is p unto the priest, he......... Lev 2:8
in the day when he p them to............. Lev 7:35
Aaron's sons p unto him the blood........ Lev 9:12
they p the burnt offering unto........... Lev 9:13
Aaron's sons p unto him the blood........ Lev 9:18
shall be p alive before the LORD......... Lev 16:10
p themselves in the tabernacle of........ Deut 31:14
they p themselves before God............. Josh 24:1
unto him under the oak, and p it......... Judg 6:19
p themselves in the assembly of......... Judg 20:2
evening, and p himself forty days........ 1Sa 17:16
p my supplication before the............. Jer 38:26
there they p the provocation of......... Eze 20:28
treasures, they p unto him gifts......... Mt 2:11
the saints and widows, p her alive....... Acts 9:41
governor, and Paul also before him....... Acts 23:33

PRESENTING

p my supplication before the LORD........ Dan 9:20

PRESENTLY

them not fail to burn the fat p.......... 1Sa 2:16
A fool's wrath p is known................ Prov 12:16
p the fig tree withered away............. Mt 21:19
he shall p give me more than............. Mt 26:53
Him therefore I hope to send p........... Phil 2:23

PRESENTS

despised him, and brought him no p....... 1Sa 10:27
they brought p, and served Solomon....... 1Kin 4:21
became his servant, and gave him p....... 2Kin 17:3
Judah brought to Jehoshaphat p........... 2Chr 17:5
Philistines brought Jehoshaphat p........ 2Chr 17:11
p to Hezekiah king of Judah.............. 2Chr 32:23
shall kings bring p unto thee............ Ps 68:29
and of the isles shall bring p........... Ps 72:10
bring p unto him that ought to be........ Ps 76:11
thou give p to Moresheth-gath............ Mic 1:14

PRESERVE

that we may p seed of our father......... Gen 19:32
that we may p seed of our father......... Gen 19:34
did send me before you to p life......... Gen 45:5
God sent me before you to p a............ Gen 45:7
always, that he might p us alive......... Deut 6:24
thou shalt p them from this.............. Ps 12:7
P me, O God.............................. Ps 16:1
Let integrity and uprightness p me....... Ps 25:21
thou shalt p me from trouble............. Ps 32:7
and thy truth continually p me........... Ps 40:11
The LORD will p him, and keep him........ Ps 41:2
mercy and truth, which may p him......... Ps 61:7
p my life from fear of the enemy......... Ps 64:1
p thou those that are appointed.......... Ps 79:11
P my soul................................ Ps 86:2
The LORD shall p thee from all........... Ps 121:7
he shall p thy soul...................... Ps 121:7
The LORD shall p thy going out........... Ps 121:8
p me from the violent man................ Ps 140:1
p me from the violent man................ Ps 140:4
Discretion shall p thee.................. Prov 2:11
her not, and she shall p thee............ Prov 4:6
the lips of the wise shall p them........ Prov 14:3
Mercy and truth by the king.............. Prov 20:28
The eyes of the LORD p knowledge......... Prov 22:12
and passing over he will p it............ Is 31:5
and I will p thee, and give thee......... Is 49:8
children, I will p them alive............ Jer 49:11
shall lose his life shall p it........... Lk 17:33

will p me unto his heavenly.............. 2Ti 4:18

PRESERVED

God face to face, and my life is p....... Gen 32:30
p us in all the way wherein we........... Josh 24:17
LORD hath given us, who hath p us........ 1Sa 30:23
the LORD p David whithersoever he........ 2Sa 8:6
the LORD p David whithersoever he........ 2Sa 8:14
Thus the LORD p David.................... 1Chr 18:6
Thus the LORD p David.................... 1Chr 18:13
thy visitation hath p my spirit.......... Job 10:12
as in the days when God p me............. Job 29:2
they are p for ever...................... Ps 37:28
and to restore the p of Israel........... Is 49:6
Egypt, and by a prophet was he p......... Hos 12:13
into new bottles, and both are p......... Mt 9:17
and both are p........................... Lk 5:38
body be p blameless unto the............. 1Th 5:23
in Jesus Christ, and called.............. Jude 1

PRESERVER

I do unto thee, O thou p of men.......... Job 7:20

PRESERVEST

is therein, and thou p them all.......... Neh 9:6
O LORD, thou p man and beast............. Ps 36:6

PRESERVETH

He p not the life of the wicked.......... Job 36:6
for the LORD p the faithful.............. Ps 31:23
he p the souls of his saints............. Ps 97:10
The LORD p the simple.................... Ps 116:6
The LORD p all them that love him........ Ps 145:20
The LORD p the strangers................. Ps 146:9
and p the way of his saints.............. Prov 2:8
that keepeth his way p his soul.......... Prov 16:17

PRESIDENTS

And over these three p................... Dan 6:2
Daniel was preferred above the p......... Dan 6:3
Then the p and princes sought to......... Dan 6:4
Then these p and princes assembled....... Dan 6:6
All the p of the kingdom, the............ Dan 6:7

PRESS

for the p is full, the fats.............. Joel 3:13
out fifty vessels out of the p........... Hag 2:16
not come nigh unto him for the p......... Mk 2:4
of Jesus, came in the p behind........... Mk 5:27
of him, turned him about in the p........ Mk 5:30
could not come at him for the p.......... Lk 8:19
p thee, and sayest thou, Who............. Lk 8:45
and could not for the p, because......... Lk 19:3
I p toward the mark for the.............. Phil 3:14

PRESSED

And he p upon them greatly............... Gen 19:3
they p sore upon the man, even........... Gen 19:9
p them into Pharaoh's cup, and I......... Gen 40:11
when she p him daily with her............ Judg 16:16
And he p him............................. 2Sa 13:25
But Absalom p him, that he let........... 2Sa 13:27
on by the king's commandment............ Est 8:14
there were their breasts p............... Eze 23:3
I am p under you, as a cart is........... Amos 2:13
as a cart is p that is full of........... Amos 2:13
insomuch that they p upon him for........ Mk 3:10
as the people p upon him to hear......... Lk 5:1
p down, and shaken together, and......... Lk 6:38
Paul was p in the spirit, and............ Acts 18:5
that we were p out of measure............ 2Cor 1:8

PRESSES

thy p shall burst out with new........... Prov 3:10
tread out no wine in their p............. Is 16:10

PRESSETH

fast in me, and thy hand p me sore....... Ps 38:2
preached, and every man p into it........ Lk 16:16

PRESSFAT

when one came to the p for to............ Hag 2:16

PRESUME

which shall p to speak a word in......... Deut 18:20
that durst p in his heart to do.......... Est 7:5

PRESUMED

But they p to go up unto the hill........ Num 14:44

PRESUMPTUOUS

back thy servant also from p sins........ Ps 19:13
P are they, selfwilled, they are......... 2Pet 2:10

PRESUMPTUOUSLY

But if a man come p upon his............. Ex 21:14
But the soul that doeth ought p.......... Num 15:30
LORD, and went p up into the hill........ Deut 1:43
And the man that will do p................ Deut 17:12
hear, and fear, and do no more p......... Deut 17:13
but the prophet hath spoken it p......... Deut 18:22

PRETENCE

and for a p make long prayer............. Mt 23:14
for a p make long prayers................ Mk 12:40
every way, whether in p, or in........... Phil 1:18

PREVAIL

cubits upward did the waters p........... Gen 7:20
peradventure I shall p, that we.......... Num 22:6
what means we may p against him.......... Judg 16:5
for by strength shall no man p........... 1Sa 2:9
but if I p against him, and kill......... 1Sa 17:9
things, and also shalt still p........... 1Sa 26:25
shalt persuade him, and p also........... 1Kin 22:22
let not man p against thee............... 2Chr 14:11
entice him, and thou shalt also p........ 2Chr 18:21

PREVAILED

thou shalt not p against him	Est 6:13
they shall p against him, as a	Job 15:24
and the robber shall p against him.	Job 18:9
let not man p	Ps 9:19
said, With our tongue will we p	Ps 12:4
Iniquities p against me	Ps 65:3
if one p against him, two shall	Eccl 4:12
it, but could not p against it	Is 7:1
but he shall not p	Is 16:12
he shall p against his enemies	Is 42:13
to profit, if ye be thou mayest p	Is 47:12
but they shall not p against thee	Jer 1:19
themselves, yet can they not p	Jer 5:22
but they shall not p against thee	Jer 15:20
we shall p against him, and we	Jer 20:10
stumble, and they shall not p	Jer 20:11
deal against them, and shall p	Dan 11:7
of hell shall not p against it	Mt 16:18
saw that he could p nothing	Mt 27:24
Perceive ye how ye p nothing	Jn 12:19

PREVAILED

And the waters p, and were	Gen 7:18
the waters p exceedingly upon the	Gen 7:19
the waters p upon the earth an	Gen 7:24
with my sister, and I have p	Gen 30:8
he saw that he p not against him.	Gen 32:25
with God and with men, and hast p	Gen 32:28
because the famine p over them	Gen 47:20
have p above the blessings of my	Gen 49:26
held up his hand, that Israel p	Ex 17:11
he let down his hand, Amalek p	Ex 17:11
the hand of the house of Joseph p	Judg 1:35
and his hand p against	Judg 3:10
p against Jabin the king of	Judg 4:24
hand of Midian p against Israel	Judg 6:2
So David p over the Philistine	1Sa 17:50
Surely the men p against us	2Sa 11:23
the king's word p against Joab	2Sa 24:4
Omri p against the people that	1Kin 16:22
month the famine p in the city	2Kin 25:3
For Judah p above his brethren,	1Chr 5:2
the king's word p against Joab.	1Chr 21:4
to Hamath-zobah, and p against it	2Chr 8:3
time, and the children of Judah p	2Chr 13:18
the Ammonites, and p against them	2Chr 27:5
enemy say, I have p against him	Ps 13:4
yet they have not p against me	Ps 129:2
art stronger than I, and hast p	Jer 20:7
thee on, and have p against thee	Jer 38:22
are desolate, because the enemy p	Lam 1:16
the saints, and p against them	Dan 7:21
he had power over the angel, and p	Hos 12:4
deceived thee, and p against thee	Obad 7
of them and of the chief priests p	Lk 23:23
p against them, so that they fled	Acts 19:16
grew the word of God and p	Acts 19:20
hath p to open the book, and to	Rev 5:5
And p not	Rev 12:8

PREVAILEST

Thou p for ever against him, and	Job 14:20

PREVAILETH

my bones, and it p against them	Lam 1:13

PREVENT

Why did the knees p me	Job 3:12
The God of my mercy shall p me	Ps 59:10
thy tender mercies speedily p us	Ps 79:8
morning shall my prayer p thee	Ps 88:13
Mine eyes p the night watches	Ps 119:148
evil shall not overtake nor p us	Amos 9:10
shall not p them which are asleep	1Th 4:15

PREVENTED

The snares of death p me	2Sa 22:6
They p me in the day of my	2Sa 22:19
the days of affliction p me	Job 30:27
Who hath p me, that I should	Job 41:11
the snares of death p me	Ps 18:5
They p me in the day of my	Ps 18:18
I p the dawning of the morning,	Ps 119:147
they p with their broad that I	Is 21:14
come into the house, Jesus p him	Mt 17:25

PREVENTEST

For thou p him with the blessings	Ps 21:3

PREY

from the p, my son, thou art gone	Gen 49:9
the morning he shall devour the p	Gen 49:27
and our children should be a p	Num 14:3
ones, which ye said should be a p	Num 14:31
lie down until he eat of the p	Num 23:24
took all the spoil, and all the p	Num 31:11
brought the captives, and the p	Num 31:12
the sum of the p that was taken	Num 31:26
divide the p into two parts	Num 31:27
being the rest of the p which the.	Num 31:32
ones, which ye said should be a p	Deut 1:39
we took for a p unto ourselves	Deut 2:35
we took for a p to ourselves	Deut 3:7
ye take for a p unto yourselves	Josh 8:2
took for a p unto themselves	Josh 8:27
took for a p unto themselves	Josh 11:14
have they not divided the p	Judg 5:30
to Sisera a p of divers colours,	Judg 5:30
a p of divers colours of	Judg 5:30
every man the earrings of his p	Judg 8:24
every man the earrings of his p	Judg 8:25
and they shall become a p and a	2Kin 21:14
give them for a p in the land of	Neh 4:4

to take the spoil of them for a p	Est 3:13
to take the spoil of them for a p	Est 8:11
but on the p they laid not their	Est 9:15
laid not their hands on the p	Est 9:16
old lion perisheth for lack of p	Job 4:11
the eagle that hasteth to the p	Job 9:26
rising betimes for a p	Job 24:5
Wilt thou hunt the p for the lion	Job 38:39
From thence she seeketh the p	Job 39:29
as a lion that is greedy of his p	Ps 17:12
excellent than the mountains of p	Ps 76:4
young lions roar after their p	Ps 104:21
given us as a p to their teeth	Ps 124:6
She also lieth in wait as for a p	Prov 23:28
shall roar, and lay hold of the p	Is 5:29
that widows may be their p	Is 10:2
take the spoil, and to take the p	Is 10:6
the young lion roaring on his p	Is 31:4
then is the p of a great spoil	Is 33:23
the lame take the p	Is 33:23
they are for a p, and none	Is 42:22
Shall the p be taken from the	Is 49:24
the p of the terrible shall be	Is 49:25
from evil maketh himself a p	Is 59:15
life shall be unto him for a p	Jer 21:9
all that p upon thee will I give	Jer 30:16
upon thee will I give for a p	Jer 30:16
he shall have his life for a p	Jer 38:2
life shall be for a p unto thee	Jer 39:18
a p in all places whither thou	Jer 45:5
hands of the strangers for a p	Eze 7:21
and it learned to catch the p	Eze 19:3
lion, and learned to catch the p	Eze 19:6
a roaring lion ravening the p	Eze 22:25
are like wolves ravening the p	Eze 22:27
make a p of thy merchandise	Eze 26:12
and take her spoil, and take her p	Eze 29:19
because my flock became a p	Eze 34:8
and they shall no more be a p	Eze 34:22
are forsaken, which became a p	Eze 36:4
minds, to cast it out for a p	Eze 36:5
To take a spoil, and to take a p	Eze 38:12
gathered thy company to take a p	Eze 38:13
he shall scatter among them the p	Dan 11:24
in the forest, when he hath no p	Amos 3:4
and filled his holes with p	Nah 2:12
will cut off thy p from the earth.	Nah 2:13
the p departeth not	Nah 3:1
the day that I rise up to the p	Zeph 3:8

PRICE

shall that increase the p thereof	Lev 25:16
thou shalt diminish the p of it	Lev 25:16
the p of his sale shall be	Lev 25:50
p of his redemption out of the	Lev 25:52
him again the p of his redemption	Lev 25:52
or the p of a dog, into the house	Deut 23:18
will surely buy it of thee at a p	2Sa 24:24
received the linen yarn at a p	1Kin 10:28
shalt grant it me for the full p	1Chr 21:22
will verily buy it for the full p	1Chr 21:24
received the linen yarn at a p	1Chr 1:16
Man knoweth not the p thereof	Job 28:13
be weighed for the p thereof	Job 28:15
for the p of wisdom is above	Job 28:18
increase thy wealth by their p	Ps 44:12
Wherefore is there a p in the	Prov 17:16
the goats are the p of the field	Prov 27:26
for her p is far above rubies.	Prov 31:10
not for p nor reward, saith the	Is 45:13
milk without money and without p	Is 55:1
I give to the spoil without a	Jer 15:13
If ye think good, give me my p	Zec 11:12
So they weighed for my p thirty	Zec 11:12
a goodly p that I was prised at	Zec 11:13
he had found one pearl of great p	Mt 13:46
because it is the p of blood	Mt 27:6
the p of him that was valued,	Mt 27:9
And kept back part of the p	Acts 5:2
back part of the p of the land	Acts 5:3
and they counted the p of them	Acts 19:19
For ye are bought with a	1Cor 6:20
Ye are bought with a p	1Cor 7:23
is in the sight of God of great p	1Pet 3:4

PRICES

brought the p of the things that	Acts 4:34

PRICKED

grieved, and I was p in my reins	Ps 73:21
they were p in their heart, and	Acts 2:37

PRICKING

there shall be no more a p brier	Eze 28:24

PRICKS

of them shall be p in your eyes	Num 33:55
for thee to kick against the p	Acts 9:5
for thee to kick against the p	Acts 26:14

PRIDE

I will break the p of your power	Lev 26:19
I know thy p, and the naughtiness	1Sa 17:28
himself for the p of his heart	2Chr 32:26
his purpose, and hide p from man	Job 33:17
because of the p of evil men	Job 35:12
His scales are his p, shut up	Job 41:15
a king over all the children of p	Job 41:34
The wicked in his p doth	Ps 10:2
through the p of his countenance,	Ps 10:4
of thy presence from the p of man	Ps 31:20
not the foot of p come against me	Ps 36:11

let them even be taken in their p	Ps 59:12
Therefore p compasseth them about	Ps 73:6
p, and arrogancy, and the evil way,	Prov 8:13
When p cometh, then cometh shame.	Prov 11:2
Only by p cometh contention	Prov 13:10
of the foolish is a rod of p	Prov 14:3
P goeth before destruction, and an	Prov 16:18
A man's p shall bring him low	Prov 29:23
of Samaria, that say in the p	Is 9:9
We have heard of the p of Moab,	Is 16:6
even of his haughtiness, and his p	Is 16:6
it, to stain the p of all glory	Is 23:9
he shall bring down their p	Is 25:11
Woe to the crown of p, to the	Is 28:1
crown of p, the drunkards of	Is 28:3
manner will I mar the p of Judah	Jer 13:9
and the great p of Jerusalem	Jer 13:9
keep in secret places for your p	Jer 13:17
We have heard the p of Moab	Jer 48:29
and his arrogancy, and his p	Jer 48:29
the p of thine heart, O thou that	Jer 49:16
rod hath blossomed, p hath budded	Eze 7:10
iniquity of thy sister Sodom, p	Eze 16:49
by thy mouth in the day of thy p	Eze 16:56
the p of her power shall come	Eze 30:6
those that walk in p he is able	Dan 4:37
up, and his mind hardened in p	Dan 5:20
the p of Israel doth testify to	Hos 5:5
the p of Israel testifieth to his	Hos 7:10
The p of thine heart hath	Obad 3
This shall they have for their p	Zeph 2:10
thee them that rejoice in thy p	Zeph 3:11
cut off the p of the Philistines.	Zec 9:6
the p of Assyria shall be brought	Zec 10:11
for the p of Jordan is spoiled	Zec 11:3
an evil eye, blasphemy, p	Mk 7:22
lest being lifted up with p he	1Ti 3:6
the p of life, is not of the	1Jn 2:16

PRIEST

he was the p of the most high God	Gen 14:18
daughter of Poti-pherah of On	Gen 41:45
Poti-pherah p of On bare unto him	Gen 41:50
Poti-pherah p of On bare unto him.	Gen 46:20
Now the p of Midian had seven	Ex 2:16
father in law, the p of Midian	Ex 3:1
that son that is p in his stead	Ex 18:1
the holy garments for Aaron the p	Ex 29:30
the holy garments for Aaron the p	Ex 31:10
of Ithamar, son to Aaron the p	Ex 35:19
the holy garments for Aaron the p	Ex 38:21
sons of Aaron the p shall put	Ex 39:41
the p shall burn all on the altar	Lev 1:7
the p shall lay them in order on	Lev 1:9
the p shall bring it all, and burn	Lev 1:12
the p shall bring it unto the	Lev 1:13
the p shall burn it upon the	Lev 1:15
the p shall burn the memorial of	Lev 1:17
when it is presented unto the p	Lev 2:2
the p shall take from the meat	Lev 2:2
the p shall burn the memorial of	Lev 2:9
the p shall burn it upon the	Lev 2:16
the p shall burn them upon the	Lev 3:11
If the p that is anointed do sin	Lev 4:3
the p that is anointed shall take	Lev 4:5
the p shall dip his finger in the	Lev 4:6
the p shall put some of the blood	Lev 4:7
the p shall burn them upon the	Lev 4:10
the p that is anointed shall	Lev 4:16
the p shall dip his finger in	Lev 4:17
the p shall make an atonement for	Lev 4:20
the p shall take of the blood of	Lev 4:25
the p shall make an atonement for	Lev 4:26
the p shall take of the blood	Lev 4:30
the p shall burn it upon the	Lev 4:31
the p shall make an atonement for	Lev 4:31
the p shall take of the blood	Lev 4:34
the p shall burn them upon the	Lev 4:35
the p shall make an atonement for	Lev 4:35
And he shall bring them unto the p	Lev 5:8
the p shall make an atonement	Lev 5:10
Then shall he bring it to the p	Lev 5:12
the p shall take his handful of	Lev 5:12
the p shall make an atonement	Lev 5:13
thereto, and give it unto the p	Lev 5:16
the p shall make an atonement	Lev 5:16
a trespass offering, unto the p	Lev 5:18
a trespass offering, unto the p	Lev 6:6
the p shall put on his linen	Lev 6:10
the p shall burn wood on it every	Lev 6:12
the p of his sons that is	Lev 6:22
the p shall be wholly burnt	Lev 6:23
The p that offereth it for sin	Lev 7:5
the p shall burn them upon the	Lev 7:5
the p that maketh atonement	Lev 7:7
the p that offereth any man's	Lev 7:8
even the p shall have to himself	Lev 7:8
the p shall burn the fat upon the	Lev 7:31
p for an heave offering of the	Lev 7:34
have given them unto Aaron the p,	Lev 7:34
of the congregation, unto the p	Lev 12:6
the p shall make an atonement for	Lev 12:7
shall be brought unto Aaron the p	Lev 13:2
the p shall look on the plague in	Lev 13:3
the p shall look on him, and	Lev 13:3
then the p shall shut up him that	Lev 13:4
the p shall look on him the	Lev 13:5

then the *p* shall shut him up .... Lev 13:5
the *p* shall look on him again the .... Lev 13:6
the *p* shall pronounce him clean .... Lev 13:6
seen of the *p* for his cleansing .... Lev 13:7
he shall be seen of the *p* again .... Lev 13:7
if the *p* see that, behold, the .... Lev 13:8
then the *p* shall pronounce him .... Lev 13:8
he shall be brought unto the *p* .... Lev 13:9
And the *p* shall see him .... Lev 13:10
the *p* shall pronounce him unclean .... Lev 13:11
foot, wheresoever the *p* looketh .... Lev 13:12
Then the *p* shall consider .... Lev 13:13
the *p* shall see the raw flesh, and .... Lev 13:15
white, he shall come unto the *p* .... Lev 13:16
And the *p* shall see him .... Lev 13:17
then the *p* shall pronounce him .... Lev 13:17
reddish, and it be shewed to the *p* .... Lev 13:19
And if, when the *p* seeth it .... Lev 13:21
the *p* shall pronounce him unclean .... Lev 13:20
But if the *p* look on it, and, ... Lev 13:21
then the *p* shall shut him up .... Lev 13:21
then the *p* shall pronounce him .... Lev 13:22
the *p* shall pronounce him clean .... Lev 13:23
Then the *p* shall look upon it .... Lev 13:25
wherefore the *p* shall pronounce .... Lev 13:25
But if the *p* look on it, and, ... Lev 13:26
then the *p* shall shut him up .... Lev 13:26
the *p* shall look upon him the .... Lev 13:27
then the *p* shall pronounce him .... Lev 13:27
the *p* shall pronounce him clean .... Lev 13:28
the *p* shall see the plague .... Lev 13:30
then the *p* shall pronounce him .... Lev 13:30
if the *p* look on the plague of .... Lev 13:31
then the *p* shall shut up him that .... Lev 13:31
in the seventh day the *p* shall .... Lev 13:32
the *p* shall shut up him that hath .... Lev 13:33
in the seventh day the *p* shall .... Lev 13:34
then the *p* shall pronounce him .... Lev 13:34
Then the *p* shall look on him .... Lev 13:36
the *p* shall not seek for yellow .... Lev 13:36
the *p* shall look upon him .... Lev 13:37
Then the *p* shall look .... Lev 13:39
the *p* shall look upon it .... Lev 13:43
the *p* shall pronounce him utterly .... Lev 13:44
and shall be shewed unto the *p* .... Lev 13:49
the *p* shall look upon the plague, ... Lev 13:50
if the *p* shall look, and, behold, ... Lev 13:53
Then the *p* shall command that .... Lev 13:54
the *p* shall look on the plague, ... Lev 13:55
And if the *p* look, and, behold, the .... Lev 13:56
He shall be brought unto the *p* .... Lev 14:2
the *p* shall go forth out of the .... Lev 14:3
the *p* shall look, and, behold, if .... Lev 14:3
Then shall the *p* command to take .... Lev 14:4
the *p* shall command that one of .... Lev 14:5
the *p* that maketh him clean shall .... Lev 14:11
the *p* shall take one he lamb, and, ... Lev 14:12
the *p* shall take some of the .... Lev 14:14
the *p* shall put it upon the top .... Lev 14:14
the *p* shall take some of the log .... Lev 14:15
the *p* shall dip his right finger .... Lev 14:16
p put upon the tip of the right. .... Lev 14:17
the *p* shall make an atonement for .... Lev 14:18
the *p* shall offer the sin .... Lev 14:19
the *p* shall offer the burnt .... Lev 14:20
the *p* shall make an atonement for .... Lev 14:20
day for his cleansing unto the *p* .... Lev 14:23
the *p* shall take the lamb of the .... Lev 14:24
the *p* shall wave them for a wave .... Lev 14:24
the *p* shall take some of the .... Lev 14:25
the *p* shall pour of the oil into .... Lev 14:26
the *p* shall sprinkle with his .... Lev 14:27
the *p* shall put of the oil that .... Lev 14:28
the *p* shall make an atonement for .... Lev 14:31
house shall come and tell the *p* .... Lev 14:35
Then the *p* shall command that .... Lev 14:36
before the *p* go into it to see .... Lev 14:36
afterward the *p* shall go in to .... Lev 14:36
Then the *p* shall go out of the .... Lev 14:38
the *p* shall come again the .... Lev 14:39
Then the *p* shall command that .... Lev 14:40
Then the *p* shall come and look, and.... Lev 14:44
if the *p* shall come in, and look .... Lev 14:48
then the *p* shall pronounce the .... Lev 14:48
and give them unto the *p* .... Lev 15:14
the *p* shall offer them, the one .... Lev 15:15
the *p* shall make an atonement for .... Lev 15:15
pigeons, and bring them unto the *p* ...... Lev 15:29
the *p* shall offer the one for a .... Lev 15:30
the *p* shall make an atonement for .... Lev 15:30
the *p* make an atonement for you .... Lev 16:32
And the *p*, whom he shall anoint, ... Lev 16:32
of the congregation, unto the *p* .... Lev 17:5
the *p* shall sprinkle the blood .... Lev 17:6
the *p* shall make an atonement for .... Lev 19:22
And the daughter of any *p*, if she .... Lev 21:9
is the high *p* among his brethren .... Lev 21:10
of the seed of Aaron the *p* shall .... Lev 21:21
a sojourner of the *p*, or an hired .... Lev 22:10
But if the *p* buy any soul with .... Lev 22:11
it unto the *p* with the holy thing, ... Lev 22:14
of your harvest unto the *p* .... Lev 23:10
the sabbath the *p* shall wave it. .... Lev 23:11
the *p* shall wave them with the .... Lev 23:20
be holy to the LORD for the *p* .... Lev 23:20
present himself before the *p* .... Lev 27:8
and the *p* shall value him .... Lev 27:8
that vowed shall the *p* value him. .... Lev 27:12
present the beast before the *p* .... Lev 27:11
the *p* shall value it, whether it .... Lev 27:12

as thou valuest it, who art the *p* .... Lev 27:12
as the *p* shall estimate it, ... Lev 27:14
as the *p* shall estimate it, so .... Lev 27:14
then the *p* shall reckon unto him. .... Lev 27:18
Then the *p* shall reckon unto him. .... Lev 27:23
present them before Aaron the *p* .... Num 3:6
Eleazar the son of Aaron the *p* .... Num 3:32
the *p* pertaineth the oil for the. .... Num 4:16
of Ithamar the son of Aaron the *p* .... Num 4:28
of Ithamar the son of Aaron the *p* .... Num 4:33
unto the LORD, even to the *p* .... Num 5:8
which they bring unto the *p* .... Num 5:9
whatsoever any man giveth the *p* .... Num 5:10
the man bring his wife unto the *p* .... Num 5:15
the *p* shall bring her near, and .... Num 5:16
the *p* shall take holy water in an .... Num 5:17
the tabernacle the *p* shall take. .... Num 5:17
the *p* shall set the woman before. .... Num 5:18
the *p* shall have in his hand the. .... Num 5:18
the *p* shall charge her by an oath. .... Num 5:19
Then the *p* shall charge the woman ...... Num 5:21
the *p* shall say unto the woman, ... Num 5:21
the *p* shall write these curses in .... Num 5:23
Then the *p* shall take the .... Num 5:25
the *p* shall take an handful of, ... Num 5:26
the *p* shall execute upon her all .... Num 5:30
or two young pigeons, to the *p* .... Num 6:10
the *p* shall offer the one for a .... Num 6:11
the *p* shall bring them before the .... Num 6:16
the *p* shall offer also his meat .... Num 6:17
the *p* shall take the sodden .... Num 6:19
the *p* shall wave them for a wave .... Num 6:20
this is holy for the *p*, with the .... Num 6:20
of Ithamar the son of Aaron the *p* .... Num 7:8
the *p* shall make an atonement for .... Num 15:25
the *p* shall make an atonement for .... Num 15:28
Eleazar the son of Aaron the *p* .... Num 16:37
Eleazar the *p* took the brasen .... Num 16:39
heave offering to Aaron the *p* .... Num 18:28
shall give her unto Eleazar the *p* .... Num 19:3
Eleazar the *p* shall take of her .... Num 19:4
the *p* shall take cedar wood, and .... Num 19:6
Then the *p* shall wash his clothes. .... Num 19:7
the *p* shall be unclean until the. .... Num 19:7
Eleazar, the son of Aaron the *p* .... Num 20:26
Eleazar, the son of Aaron the *p* .... Num 25:11
Eleazar the son of Aaron the *p* .... Num 26:1
Eleazar the *p* spake with them in .... Num 26:3
by Moses and Eleazar the *p* .... Num 26:63
Moses and Aaron the *p* numbered .... Num 26:64
Moses, and before Eleazar the *p* .... Num 27:2
And set him before Eleazar the *p* .... Num 27:19
shall stand before Eleazar the *p* .... Num 27:21
and set him before Eleazar the *p* .... Num 27:22
Phinehas the son of Eleazar the *p* .... Num 31:6
unto Moses, and Eleazar the *p* .... Num 31:12
And Moses, and Eleazar the *p* .... Num 31:13
Eleazar the *p* said unto the men .... Num 31:21
of beast, thou, and Eleazar the *p* .... Num 31:26
and give it unto Eleazar the *p* .... Num 31:29
Eleazar the *p* did as the LORD .... Num 31:31
offering, unto Eleazar the *p* .... Num 31:41
Eleazar the *p* took the gold of .... Num 31:51
Eleazar the *p* took the gold of .... Num 31:54
unto Moses, and to Eleazar the *p* .... Num 32:2
Moses commanded Eleazar the *p* .... Num 32:28
Aaron the *p* went up into mount. .... Num 33:38
Eleazar the *p*, and Joshua the son .... Num 34:17
it unto the death of the high *p* .... Num 35:25
until the death of the high *p* .... Num 35:28
p the slayer shall return into. .... Num 35:28
land, until the death of the *p* .... Num 35:32
will not hearken unto the *p* that. .... Deut 17:12
give unto the *p* the shoulder. .... Deut 18:3
that the *p* shall approach and .... Deut 20:2
thou shalt go unto the *p* that .... Deut 26:3
the *p* shall take the basket out .... Deut 26:4
of Canaan, which Eleazar the *p* .... Josh 14:1
came near before Eleazar the *p* .... Josh 17:4
inheritances, which Eleazar the *p* .... Josh 19:51
p that shall be in those days. .... Josh 20:6
the Levites unto Eleazar the *p* .... Josh 21:1
and the children of Aaron the *p* .... Josh 21:4
the *p* Hebron with her suburbs .... Josh 21:13
Phinehas the son of Eleazar the *p* .... Josh 22:13
And when Phinehas the *p*, and .... Josh 22:30
the *p* said unto the children of .... Josh 22:31
Phinehas the son of Eleazar the *p* .... Josh 22:32
one of his sons, who became his *p* ...... Judg 17:5
me, and be unto me a father and a *p* . Judg 17:10
and the young man became his *p* .... Judg 17:12
seeing I have a Levite to my *p* .... Judg 17:13
and hath hired me, and I am his *p* ...... Judg 18:4
the *p* said unto them, Go in peace ...... Judg 18:6
the stood in the entering of .... Judg 18:17
Then said the *p* unto them .... Judg 18:18
us, and be to us a father and a *p* .... Judg 18:19
be a *p* unto the house of one man ...... Judg 18:19
or that thou be a *p* unto a tribe .... Judg 18:19
my gods which I made, and the *p* .... Judg 18:24
the *p* which he had, and came unto ...... Judg 18:27
Now Eli the *p* sat upon a seat by 1Sa 1:9
unto the LORD before Eli the *p* 1Sa 2:11
brought up the *p* took for himself 1Sa 2:14
Give flesh to roast for the *p* 1Sa 2:15
the tribes of Israel to be my *p* 1Sa 2:28
I will raise me up a faithful *p* 1Sa 2:35
of Eli, the LORD's *p* in Shiloh. 1Sa 14:3
while Saul talked unto the *p* 1Sa 14:19
and Saul said unto the *p*, Withdraw 1Sa 14:19

Then said the *p*, Let us draw near 1Sa 14:36
David to Nob to Ahimelech the *p* 1Sa 21:1
David said unto Ahimelech the *p* 1Sa 21:2
the *p* answered David, and said, ... 1Sa 21:4
And David answered the *p*, and said 1Sa 21:5
So the *p* gave him hallowed bread 1Sa 21:6
the *p* said, The sword of Goliath 1Sa 21:9
king sent to call Ahimelech the *p* 1Sa 22:11
and he said to Abiathar the *p* 1Sa 23:9
And David said to Abiathar the *p* 1Sa 30:7
king said also unto Zadok the *p* 2Sa 15:27
Zeruiah, and with Abiathar the *p* 1Kin 1:7
But Zadok the *p*, and Benaiah the 1Kin 1:8
of the king, and Abiathar the *p* 1Kin 1:19
of the host, and Abiathar the *p* 1Kin 1:25
me thy servant, and Zadok the *p* 1Kin 1:26
David said, Call me Zadok the *p* 1Kin 1:32
And let Zadok the *p* and Nathan the ... 1Kin 1:34
So Zadok the *p*, and Nathan the 1Kin 1:38
Zadok the *p* took an horn of oil 1Kin 1:39
the son of Abiathar the *p* came 1Kin 1:42
hath sent with him Zadok the *p* 1Kin 1:44
And Zadok the *p* and Nathan the 1Kin 1:45
for him, and for Abiathar the *p* 1Kin 2:22
unto Abiathar the *p* said the king 1Kin 2:26
from being *p* unto the LORD 1Kin 2:27
Zadok the *p* did the king put in 1Kin 2:35
Azariah the son of Zadok the *p* 1Kin 4:2
that Jehoiada the *p* commanded. 2Kin 11:9
and came to Jehoiada the *p* 2Kin 11:9
the *p* give king David's spears 2Kin 11:10
But Jehoiada the *p* commanded the 2Kin 11:15
For the *p* had said, Let her not 2Kin 11:15
slew Mattan the *p* of Baal before 2Kin 11:18
the *p* appointed officers over the 2Kin 11:18
Jehoiada the *p* instructed him. 2Kin 12:2
Jehoash called for Jehoiada the *p* 2Kin 12:7
But Jehoiada the *p* took a chest 2Kin 12:9
scribe and the high *p* came up 2Kin 12:10
the *p* the fashion of the altar 2Kin 16:10
Urijah the *p* built an altar 2Kin 16:11
so Urijah the *p* made it against 2Kin 16:11
king Ahaz commanded Urijah the *p* 2Kin 16:15
Thus did Urijah the *p*, according. 2Kin 16:16
Go up to Hilkiah the high *p* 2Kin 22:4
Hilkiah the high *p* said unto 2Kin 22:8
Hilkiah the *p* hath delivered me a 2Kin 22:10
the king commanded Hilkiah the *p* 2Kin 22:12
So Hilkiah the *p*, and Ahikam, and 2Kin 22:14
king commanded Hilkiah the high *p* 2Kin 23:4
in the book that Hilkiah the *p* 2Kin 23:24
guard took Seraiah the chief *p* 2Kin 25:18
and Zephaniah the second *p* 2Kin 25:18
And Zadok the *p*, and his brethren 1Chr 16:39
and the princes, and Zadok the *p* 1Chr 24:6
chief governor, and Zadok to be *p* 1Chr 29:22
the same may be a *p* of them that 2Chr 13:9
true God, and without a teaching *p* 2Chr 15:3
Amariah the chief *p* is over you 2Chr 19:11
the wife of Jehoiada the *p* 2Chr 22:11
that Jehoiada the *p* had commanded.... 2Chr 23:4
for Jehoiada the *p* dismissed not.......... 2Chr 23:8
Moreover Jehoiada the *p* delivered. 2Chr 23:9
Then Jehoiada the *p* brought out. 2Chr 23:14
For the *p* said, Slay her not in 2Chr 23:14
slew Mattan the *p* of Baal before 2Chr 23:17
all the days of Jehoiada the *p* 2Chr 24:2
the son of Jehoiada the *p* 2Chr 24:20
of the sons of Jehoiada the *p* 2Chr 24:25
Azariah the *p* went in after him, ... 2Chr 26:17
And Azariah the chief *p*, and all 2Chr 26:20
Azariah the chief *p* of the house. 2Chr 31:10
they came to Hilkiah the high *p* 2Chr 34:9
Hilkiah the *p* found a book of the 2Chr 34:14
Hilkiah the *p* hath given me a 2Chr 34:18
till there stood up a *p* with Urim .... Ezr 2:63
the son of Aaron the chief *p* .... Ezr 7:5
Artaxerxes gave unto Ezra the *p* .... Ezr 7:11
king of kings, unto Ezra the *p* .... Ezr 7:12
that, whatsoever Ezra the *p* .... Ezr 7:21
Meremoth the son of Uriah the *p* .... Ezr 8:33
And Ezra the *p* stood up, and said ..... Ezr 10:10
And Ezra the *p*, with certain chief ...... Ezr 10:16
Then Eliashib the high *p* rose up. .... Neh 3:1
the house of Eliashib the high *p* .... Neh 3:20
till there stood up a *p* with Urim. .... Neh 7:65
Ezra the *p* brought the law before ...... Neh 8:2
Ezra the *p* the scribe, and the .... Neh 8:9
the *p* the son of Aaron shall be .... Neh 10:38
the governor, and of Ezra the *p* .... Neh 12:26
And before this, Eliashib the *p* .... Neh 13:4
the treasuries, Shelemiah the *p* .... Neh 13:13
the son of Eliashib the high *p* .... Neh 13:28
Thou art a *p* for ever after the .... Ps 110:4
witnesses to record, Uriah the *p* .... Is 8:2
as with the people, so with the *p* .... Is 24:2
the *p* and the prophet have erred .... Is 28:7
the *p* every one dealeth falsely .... Jer 6:13
the *p* every one dealeth falsely .... Jer 8:10
the *p* go about into a land that. .... Jer 14:18
law shall not perish from the *p* .... Jer 18:18
Now Pashur the son of Immer the *p* ... Jer 20:1
the son of Maaseiah the *p* .... Jer 21:1
For both prophet and *p* are profane ..... Jer 23:11
people, or the prophet, or a *p* .... Jer 23:33
And as for the prophet, and the *p* .... Jer 23:34
the son of Maaseiah the *p* .... Jer 29:25
The LORD hath made thee *p* in the .... Jer 29:26
in the stead of Jehoiada the *p* .... Jer 29:26

Zephaniah the *p* read this letter .... Jer 29:29
the *p* to the prophet Jeremiah............... Jer 37:3
guard took Seraiah the chief *p* .... Jer 52:24
and Zephaniah the second *p* .... Jer 52:24
of his anger the king and the *p* .... Lam 2:6
shall the *p* and the prophet be............. Lam 2:20
came expressly unto Ezekiel the *p* .... Eze 1:3
the law shall perish from the *p* .... Eze 7:26
to do the office of a *p* unto me .... Eze 44:13
Neither shall any *p* drink wine .... Eze 44:21
or a widow that had a *p* before .... Eze 44:22
the *p* the first of your dough.............. Eze 44:30
the *p* shall take of the blood of........... Eze 45:19
as they that strive with the *p* .... Hos 4:4
that thou shalt be no *p* to me.............. Hos 4:6
shall be, like people, like *p* .... Hos 4:9
Then Amaziah the *p* of Beth-el.............. Amos 7:10
the son of Josedech, the high *p* .... Hag 1:1
the son of Josedech, the high *p* .... Hag 1:12
the son of Josedech, the high *p* .... Hag 1:14
the son of Josedech, the high *p* .... Hag 2:2
son of Josedech, the high *p*................ Hag 2:4
p standing before the angel of .... Zec 3:1
Hear now, O Joshua the high *p* .... Zec 3:8
the son of Josedech, the high *p*............ Zec 6:11
he shall be a *p* upon his throne .... Zec 6:13
go thy way, shew thyself to the *p* .... Mt 8:4
unto the palace of the high *p* .... Mt 26:3
him away to Caiaphas the high *p* .... Mt 26:57
And the high *p* arose, and said unto........ Mt 26:62
And the high *p* answered and said .... Mt 26:63
Then the high *p* rent his clothes,.......... Mt 26:65
go thy way, shew thyself to the *p* .... Mk 1:44
the days of Abiathar the high *p* .... Mk 2:26
and staves, from the chief *p* .... Mk 14:43
and smote a servant of the high *p* .... Mk 14:47
they led Jesus away to the high *p* .... Mk 14:53
into the palace of the high *p* .... Mk 14:54
the high *p* stood up in the midst,.......... Mk 14:60
Again the high *p* asked him................. Mk 14:61
Then the high *p* rent his clothes,.......... Mk 14:63
one of the maids of the high *p* .... Mk 14:66
a certain *p* named Zacharias, of............ Lk 1:5
but go, and shew thyself to the *p* .... Lk 5:14
came down a certain *p* that way............. Lk 10:31
smote the servant of the high *p* .... Lk 22:50
being the high *p* that same year* .... Jn 11:49
but being high *p* that year .... Jn 11:51
was the high *p* that same year .... Jn 18:13
was known unto the high *p* .... Jn 18:15
into the palace of the high *p* .... Jn 18:15
which was known unto the high *p* .... Jn 18:16
The high *p* then asked Jesus of............. Jn 18:19
Answerest thou the high *p* so............... Jn 18:22
bound unto Caiaphas the high *p* .... Jn 18:24
One of the servants of the high *p* .... Jn 18:26
And Annas the high *p*, and Caiaphas,........ Acts 4:6
were of the kindred of the high *p*.......... Acts 4:6
Then the high *p* rose up, and all .... Acts 5:17
But the high *p* came, and they that .... Acts 5:21
Now when the high *p* came .... Acts 5:27
and the high *p* asked them,................. Acts 5:27
Then said the high *p*, Are these .... Acts 7:1
of the Lord, went unto the high *p* .... Acts 9:1
Then the *p* of Jupiter, which was .... Acts 14:13
As also the high *p* doth bear me .... Acts 22:5
the high *p* Ananias commanded them.......... Acts 23:2
said, Revilest thou God's high *p* .... Acts 23:4
brethren, that he was the high *p* .... Acts 23:5
high *p* descended with the elders........... Acts 24:1
Then the high *p* and the chief *p* .... Acts 25:2
faithful high *p* in things .... Heb 2:17
High *P* of our profession, Christ .... Heb 3:1
then that we have a great high *p* .... Heb 4:14
For we have not an high *p* which............ Heb 4:15
For every high *p* taken from among.......... Heb 5:1
not himself to be made an high *p* .... Heb 5:5
Thou art a *p* for ever after the .... Heb 5:6
Called of God an high *p* after the .... Heb 5:10
made an high *p* for ever after the .... Heb 6:20
and the high *p* asked them,................. Heb 7:1
abideth a *p* continually.................... Heb 7:3
need was there that another *p* .... Heb 7:11
there ariseth another *p*,................... Heb 7:11
Thou art a *p* for ever after the .... Heb 7:17
not without an oath he was made *p* .... Heb 7:20
Thou art a *p* for ever after the .... Heb 7:21
For such an high *p* became us .... Heb 7:26
We have such an high *p*, who is............. Heb 8:1
For every high *p* is ordained to............ Heb 8:3
of the Lord passed over, and the *p* .... Heb 8:4
the high *p* alone once every year .... Heb 9:7
an high *p* of good things to come........... Heb 9:11
as the high *p* entereth into the .... Heb 9:25
And every *p* standeth daily .... Heb 10:11
having an high *p* over the house .... Heb 10:21
sanctuary by the high *p* for sin............ Heb 13:11

PRIESTHOOD

p throughout their generations............. Ex 40:15
and seek ye the *p* also .... Num 16:10
shall bear the iniquity of your *p* .... Num 18:1
the covenant of an everlasting *p* .... Num 25:13
for the *p* of the Lord is their............. Josh 18:7
they, as polluted, put from the *p* .... Ezr 2:62
they, as polluted, but from the *p* .... Neh 7:64
because they have defiled the *p* .... Neh 13:29
and the covenant of the *p* .... Neh 13:29
who receive the office of the *p* .... Heb 7:5
were by the Levitical *p*, (for............. Heb 7:11
For the *p* being changed, there is.......... Heb 7:12

Moses spake nothing concerning *p* .... Heb 7:14
ever, hath an unchangeable *p* .... Heb 7:24
up a spiritual house, an holy *p* 1Pet 2:5
a chosen generation, a royal *p* 1Pet 2:9

PRIEST'S

minister unto me in the *p* office .... Ex 28:1
minister unto me in the *p* office .... Ex 28:3
minister unto me in the *p* office .... Ex 28:4
minister unto me in the *p* office .... Ex 28:41
minister unto me in the *p* office .... Ex 29:1
the office shall be theirs for .... Ex 29:9
to minister to me in the *p* office .... Ex 30:30
sons, to minister in the *p* office .... Ex 31:10
sons, to minister in the *p* office .... Ex 35:19
to minister in the *p* office................ Ex 39:41
minister unto me in the *p* office .... Ex 40:13
minister unto me in the *p* office .... Ex 40:15
and the remnant shall be the *p* .... Lev 2:3
shall be the *p* that offereth it .... Lev 7:9
it shall be the *p* that sprinkleth......... Lev 7:14
unto the Lord in the *p* office .... Lev 7:35
for as the sin offering is the *p* .... Lev 14:13
of the oil that is in the *p* hand.......... Lev 14:18
rest of the oil that is in the *p* .... Lev 14:29
p office in his father's stead .... Lev 16:32
If the *p* daughter also be married .... Lev 22:12
But if the *p* daughter be a widow,.......... Lev 22:13
possession thereof shall be the *p* .... Lev 27:21
to minister in the *p* office .... Num 3:3
Ithamar ministered in the *p* office .... Num 3:4
they shall wait on their *p* office.......... Num 3:10
p office for every thing of the .... Num 18:7
I have given your *p* office unto............ Num 18:7
in the *p* office in his stead .... Deut 10:6
this shall be the *p* due from the .... Deut 18:3
the *p* heart was glad, and he took .... Judg 18:20
the *p* custom with the people was,.......... 1Sa 2:13
the *p* servant came, while the 1Sa 2:13
the *p* servant came, and said to 1Sa 2:15
the office in the temple that 1Chr 6:10
and Ithamar executed the *p* office 1Chr 24:2
the *p* office unto the Lord 2Chr 11:14
the high *p* office came and................. 2Chr 34:11
of your oblations, shall be the *p* .... Eze 44:30
For the *p* lips should keep................. Mal 2:7
and struck a servant of the high *p* .... Mt 26:51
afar off unto the high *p* palace........... Mt 26:58
that while he executed the *p* .... Lk 1:8
to the custom of the *p* office .... Lk 1:9
brought him into the high *p* house.......... Lk 22:54
it, and smote the high *p* servant........... Jn 18:10

PRIESTS

out of the *p* bought he not................. Gen 47:22
for the *p* had a portion assigned .... Gen 47:22
except the land of the *p* only .... Gen 47:26
shall be unto me a kingdom of *p* .... Ex 19:6
And let the *p* also, which come .... Ex 19:22
but let not the *p* and the people .... Ex 19:24
and the *p*, Aaron's sons, shall............. Lev 1:5
And the *p*, Aaron's sons, shall lay .... Lev 1:11
and the *p*, Aaron's sons, shall .... Lev 1:11
bring it to Aaron's sons the *p* .... Lev 2:2
Aaron's sons the *p* shall sprinkle .... Lev 3:2
among the *p* shall eat thereof .... Lev 6:29
among the *p* shall eat thereof .... Lev 7:6
or unto one of his sons the *p* .... Lev 13:2
shall make an atonement for the *p* .... Lev 16:33
Speak unto the *p* the sons of .... Lev 21:1
the *p* which were anointed, whom .... Num 3:3
And the sons of Aaron, the *p*,.............. Num 10:8
shalt come unto the *p* the Levites .... Deut 17:9
which is before the *p* the Levites .... Deut 17:18
The *p* the Levites, and all the .... Deut 18:1
before the Lord, before the *p* .... Deut 19:17
the *p* the sons of Levi shall come .... Deut 21:5
the *p* the Levites shall teach you......... Deut 24:8
the *p* the Levites spake unto all........... Deut 27:9
it unto the *p* the sons of Levi............. Deut 31:9
the *p* the Levites bearing it,.............. Josh 3:3
And Joshua spake unto the .... Josh 3:8
thou shalt command the *p* that .... Josh 3:8
p that bear the ark of the Lord .... Josh 3:13
the *p* bearing the ark of the .... Josh 3:14
the feet of the *p* that bare the .... Josh 3:15
the *p* that bare the ark of the .... Josh 3:17
the *p* which bare the ark of the .... Josh 4:9
For the *p* which bare the ark.............. Josh 4:10
of the Lord passed over, and the *p* .... Josh 4:11
Command the *p* that bear the ark............ Josh 4:16
Joshua therefore commanded the *p* .... Josh 4:18
when the *p* that bare the ark of .... Josh 4:18
seven *p* shall bear before the ark .... Josh 6:4
the *p* shall blow with .... Josh 6:4
the son of Nun called the *p* .... Josh 6:6
let seven *p* bear seven trumpets............ Josh 6:6
that the seven *p* bearing the .... Josh 6:8
the *p* that blew with the trumpets .... Josh 6:9
the *p* going on, and blowing with........... Josh 6:9
the *p* took up the ark of the Lord .... Josh 6:12
seven *p* bearing seven trumpets............. Josh 6:13
the *p* going on, and blowing with........... Josh 6:13
when the *p* blew with the trumpets.......... Josh 6:16
when the *p* blew with the trumpets.......... Josh 6:20
side before the *p* the Levites .... Josh 8:33
of the children of Aaron, the *p*,.......... Josh 21:19
his sons were *p* to the tribe of .... Judg 18:30
the *p* of the Lord, were there 1Sa 1:3
Therefore neither the *p* of Dagon.......... 1Sa 5:5

the Philistines called for the *p*.......... 1Sa 6:2
house, that the *p* were in his 1Sa 22:11
Turn, and slay the *p* of the Lord 1Sa 22:17
to fall upon the *p* of the Lord............. 1Sa 22:17
Turn thou, and fall upon the *p*............. 1Sa 22:18
turned, and he fell upon the *p* 1Sa 22:18
And Nob, the city of the *p* 1Sa 22:19
that Saul had slain the Lord's *p*........... 1Sa 22:21
the son of Abiathar, were the *p* 2Sa 8:17
with thee Zadok and Abiathar the *p* 2Sa 15:35
it to Zadok and Abiathar the *p* 2Sa 15:35
unto Zadok and to Abiathar the *p* 2Sa 17:15
to Zadok and to Abiathar the *p* 2Sa 19:11
and Zadok and Abiathar were the *p*.......... 2Sa 20:25
and Zadok and Abiathar were the *p*.......... 1Kin 4:4
came, and the *p* took up the ark 1Kin 8:3
tabernacle, even those did the *p* 1Kin 8:4
the *p* brought in the ark of the 1Kin 8:6
when the *p* were come out of the 1Kin 8:10
So that the *p* could not stand to 1Kin 8:11
made *p* of the lowest of the 1Kin 12:31
he placed in Beth-el the *p* of the 1Kin 12:32
p of the high places that burn............ 1Kin 13:2
the people *p* of the high places 1Kin 13:33
one of the *p* of the high places 1Kin 13:33
men, and his kinsfolks, and his *p* 2Kin 10:11
all his servants, and all his *p* 2Kin 10:19
And Jehoash said to the *p*, All the 2Kin 12:4
Let the *p* take it to them, every 2Kin 12:5
year of king Jehoash the *p* had 2Kin 12:6
the priest, and the other *p* 2Kin 12:7
the *p* consented to receive no 2Kin 12:8
the *p* that kept the door put 2Kin 12:9
Carry thither one of the *p* whom 2Kin 17:27
Then one of the *p* whom they had 2Kin 17:28
of them *p* of the high places 2Kin 17:32
scribe, and the elders of the *p* 2Kin 19:2
of Jerusalem with him, and the *p* 2Kin 23:2
the *p* of the second order, and the 2Kin 23:4
And he put down the idolatrous *p* 2Kin 23:5
he brought all the *p* out of the 2Kin 23:8
where the *p* had burned incense 2Kin 23:8
Nevertheless the *p* of the high............. 2Kin 23:9
he slew all the *p* of the high 2Kin 23:20
were, the Israelites, the *p*................ 1Chr 9:2
And of the *p*; Jedaiah..................... 1Chr 9:10
some of the sons of the *p* made 1Chr 9:30
and with them also to the *p* 1Chr 13:2
for Zadok and Abiathar the *p* 1Chr 15:11
So the *p* and the Levites 1Chr 15:14
and Benaiah, and Eliezer, the *p* 1Chr 15:24
Jahaziel the *p* with trumpets............... 1Chr 16:6
the priest, and his brethren the *p* 1Chr 16:39
the princes of Israel, with the *p* 1Chr 23:2
the chief of the fathers of the *p* 1Chr 24:6
the chief of the fathers of the *p* 1Chr 24:31
Also for the courses of the *p* 1Chr 28:13
And, behold, the courses of the *p* 2Chr 8:14
the sea was for the *p* to wash in 2Chr 4:6
he made the court of the *p* 2Chr 4:9
the tabernacle, those did the *p* 2Chr 5:5
the *p* brought in the ark of the 2Chr 5:7
when the *p* were come out of the 2Chr 5:11
(for all the *p* that were present 2Chr 5:11
twenty *p* sounding with trumpets............ 2Chr 5:12
So that the *p* could not stand to 2Chr 5:14
let thy *p*, O Lord God, be clothed 2Chr 6:41
the *p* could not enter into the 2Chr 7:2
the *p* waited on their offices............. 2Chr 7:6
the *p* sounded trumpets before 2Chr 7:6
courses of the *p* to their service.......... 2Chr 8:14
praise and minister before the *p* 2Chr 8:14
of the king unto the *p* and Levites........ 2Chr 8:15
And the *p* and the Levites that were 2Chr 11:13
he ordained him *p* for the high 2Chr 11:15
ye not cast out the *p* of the Lord 2Chr 13:9
have made you a *p* after the manner 2Chr 13:9
and the *p*, which minister unto the 2Chr 13:10
his *p* with sounding trumpets to 2Chr 13:12
the *p* sounded with the trumpets,.......... 2Chr 13:14
with them Elishama and Jehoram, *p* 2Chr 17:8
set of the Levites, and of the *p* 2Chr 19:8
entering on the sabbath, of the *p* 2Chr 23:4
the house of the Lord, save the *p* 2Chr 23:6
by the hand of the *p* the Levites 2Chr 23:18
And he gathered together the *p* 2Chr 24:5
with him fourscore *p* of the Lord.......... 2Chr 26:17
but to the *p* the sons of Aaron,........... 2Chr 26:18
and while he was wroth with the *p* 2Chr 26:19
the *p* in the house of their 2Chr 26:19
the chief priest, and all the *p* 2Chr 26:20
And he brought in the *p* and the 2Chr 29:4
the *p* went into the inner part of 2Chr 29:16
he commanded the *p* the sons of 2Chr 29:21
the *p* received the blood, and.............. 2Chr 29:22
the *p* killed them, and they made 2Chr 29:24
David, and the *p* with the trumpets......... 2Chr 29:26
But the *p* were too few, so that,........... 2Chr 29:34
until the other *p* had sanctified 2Chr 29:34
to sanctify themselves than the *p* 2Chr 29:34
the *p* and the Levites were 2Chr 30:15
the *p* sprinkled the blood, which 2Chr 30:16
the *p* praised the Lord day by day 2Chr 30:21
a great number of *p* sanctified............. 2Chr 30:24
congregation of Judah, with the *p* 2Chr 30:25
Then the *p* the Levites arose and........... 2Chr 30:27
appointed the courses of the *p* 2Chr 31:2
according to his service, the *p* 2Chr 31:2

P

to give the portion of the p 2Chr 31:4
Hezekiah questioned with the p 2Chr 31:9
Shecaniah, in the cities of the p 2Chr 31:15
Both to the genealogy of the p by 2Chr 31:17
Also of the sons of Aaron the p 2Chr 31:19
to all the males among the p 2Chr 31:19
bones of the p upon their altars 2Chr 34:5
of Jerusalem, and the p, and the 2Chr 34:30
he set the p in their charges, and 2Chr 35:2
unto the people, to the p 2Chr 35:8
gave unto the p for the passover 2Chr 35:8
the p stood in their place, and 2Chr 35:10
the p sprinkled the blood from 2Chr 35:11
for themselves, and for the p 2Chr 35:14
because the p the sons of Aaron 2Chr 35:14
for the p the sons of Aaron 2Chr 35:14
passover as Josiah kept, and the p 2Chr 35:18
Moreover all the chief of the p 2Chr 36:14
of Judah and Benjamin, and the p ...... Ezr 1:5
The p: the children of .... Ezr 2:36
And of the children of the p .... Ezr 2:61
So the p, and the Levites, and some ... Ezr 2:70
of Jozadak, and his brethren the p .... Ezr 3:2
remnant of their brethren the p .... Ezr 3:8
they set the p in their apparel .... Ezr 3:10
But many of the p and Levites and ..... Ezr 3:12
of the p which are at Jerusalem .... Ezr 6:9
And the children of Israel, the p ..... Ezr 6:16
they set the p in their divisions ..... Ezr 6:18
For the p and the Levites were .... Ezr 6:20
and for their brethren the p .... Ezr 6:20
children of Israel, and of the p ...... Ezr 7:7
the people of Israel, and of his p .... Ezr 7:13
of the people, and of the p .... Ezr 7:16
you, that touching any of the p .... Ezr 7:24
and I viewed the people, and the p .... Ezr 8:15
twelve of the chief of the p .... Ezr 8:24
them before the chief of the p .... Ezr 8:29
So took the p and the Levites the ..... Ezr 8:30
The people of Israel, and the p .... Ezr 9:1
have we, our kings, and our p .... Ezr 9:7
arose Ezra, and made the chief p ...... Ezr 10:5
among the sons of the p there .... Ezr 10:18
told it to the Jews, nor to the p ..... Neh 2:16
rose up with his brethren the p .... Neh 3:1
And after him repaired the p .... Neh 3:22
the horse gate repaired the p .... Neh 3:28
Then I called the p, and took an ...... Neh 5:12
The p: the children of .... Neh 7:39
And of the p: the children .... Neh 7:63
So the p, and the Levites, and the .... Neh 7:73
fathers of all the people, the p ...... Neh 8:13
on our princes, and on our p .... Neh 9:32
our kings, our princes, our p .... Neh 9:34
and our princes, Levites, and p .... Neh 9:38
these were the p .... Neh 10:8
And the rest of the people, the p ..... Neh 10:28
And we cast the lots among the p ...... Neh 10:34
unto the p that minister in the .... Neh 10:36
of wine and of oil, unto the .... Neh 10:37
the p that minister, and the .... Neh 10:39
cities, to wit, Israel, the p .... Neh 11:3
Of the p: Jedaiah .... Neh 11:10
the residue of Israel, of the p .... Neh 11:20
Now these are the p and the .... Neh 12:1
These were the chief of the .... Neh 12:7
And in the days of Joiakim were p ..... Neh 12:12
also the p, to the reign of .... Neh 12:22
And the p and the Levites purified .... Neh 12:30
And the p; Eliakim .... Neh 12:41
the portions of the law for the p ..... Neh 12:44
for Judah rejoiced for the p .... Neh 12:44
and the offerings of the p .... Neh 13:5
and appointed the wards of the p ...... Neh 13:30
Their p fell by the sword .... Ps 78:64
Moses and Aaron among his p .... Ps 99:6
Let thy p be clothed with .... Ps 132:9
also clothe her p with salvation ...... Ps 132:16
the elders of the p covered with ...... Is 37:2
shall he named the P of the LORD ...... Is 61:6
And I will also take of them for p .... Is 66:21
of the p that were in Anathoth in ..... Jer 1:1
thereof, against the p thereof .... Jer 1:18
The p said not, Where is the LORD ..... Jer 2:8
kings, their princes, and their p ..... Jer 2:26
the p shall be astonished, and the ... Jer 4:9
the p bear rule by their means .... Jer 5:31
princes, and the bones of the p .... Jer 8:1
sit upon David's throne, and the p .... Jer 13:13
and of the ancients of the p .... Jer 19:1
So the p and the prophets and all ..... Jer 26:7
unto all the people, that the p .... Jer 26:8
Then spake the p and the prophets ..... Jer 26:11
and all the people unto the p .... Jer 26:16
Also I spake to the p and to all ...... Jer 27:16
LORD, in the presence of the p .... Jer 28:1
Hananiah in the presence of the p ..... Jer 28:5
away captives, and to the p .... Jer 29:1
the priest, and to all the .... Jer 29:25
the soul of the p with fatness .... Jer 31:14
kings, their princes, their p .... Jer 32:32
Neither shall the p the Levites .... Jer 33:18
and with the Levites the p .... Jer 33:21
Jerusalem, the eunuchs, and the p ..... Jer 34:19
forth into captivity with the p .... Jer 48:7
shall go into captivity, and his p .... Jer 49:3
her p sigh, her virgins are .... Lam 1:4
my p and mine elders gave up the ...... Lam 1:19
and the iniquities of her p .... Lam 4:13
not the persons of the p, they .... Lam 4:16

Her p have violated my law, and .... Eze 22:26
is toward the south, is for the p ..... Eze 40:45
is toward the north is for the p ...... Eze 40:46
where the p that approach unto .... Eze 42:13
When the p enter therein, then .... Eze 42:14
thou shalt give to the p .... Eze 43:19
the p shall cast salt upon them, ... Eze 43:24
the p shall make your burnt .... Eze 43:27
But the p the Levites, the sons .... Eze 44:15
The p shall not eat of any thing ...... Eze 44:31
of the land shall be for the p .... Eze 45:4
the p shall prepare his burnt .... Eze 46:2
into the holy chambers of the p .... Eze 46:19
the p shall boil the trespass .... Eze 46:20
And for them, even for the p .... Eze 48:10
It shall be for the p that are .... Eze 48:11
the p the Levites shall have five ..... Eze 48:11
Hear ye this, O p .... Hos 5:1
so the company of p murder in the ..... Hos 6:9
the p thereof that rejoiced on it ..... Hos 10:5
the p, the LORD's ministers .... Joel 1:9
Gird yourselves, and lament, ye p ..... Joel 1:13
Let the p, the ministers of the .... Joel 2:17
the p thereof teach for hire, and .... Mic 3:11
name of the Chemarims with the p ...... Zeph 1:4
her p have polluted the sanctuary ..... Zeph 3:4
Ask now the p concerning the law, ... Hag 2:11
the p answered and said, No, ... Hag 2:12
the p answered and said, It shall ..... Hag 2:13
to speak unto the p which were in ..... Zec 7:3
people of the land, and to the p ...... Zec 7:5
the LORD of hosts unto you, O p .... Mal 1:6
And now, O ye p, this commandment ..... Mal 2:1
he had gathered all the chief p .... Mt 2:4
were with him, but only for the p ..... Mt 12:4
the p in the temple profane the ...... Mt 12:5
things of the elders and chief p ...... Mt 16:21
be betrayed unto the chief p .... Mt 20:18
And when the chief p and scribes ...... Mt 21:15
come into the temple, the chief p ..... Mt 21:23
And when the chief p and Pharisees .... Mt 21:45
assembled together the chief p .... Mt 26:3
Iscariot, went unto the chief p .... Mt 26:14
and staves, from the chief p .... Mt 26:47
Now the chief p, and elders, and ...... Mt 26:59
morning was come, all the chief p ..... Mt 27:1
pieces of silver to the chief p .... Mt 27:3
the chief p took the silver .... Mt 27:6
he was accused of the chief p .... Mt 27:12
But the chief p and elders .... Mt 27:20
also the chief p mocking him .... Mt 27:41
of the preparation, the chief p .... Mt 27:62
shewed unto the chief p all the .... Mt 28:11
not lawful to eat but for the p .... Mk 2:26
of the elders, and of the chief p ..... Mk 8:31
be delivered unto the chief p .... Mk 10:33
chief p heard it, and sought how ...... Mk 11:18
there come to him the chief p .... Mk 11:27
and the chief p and the scribes .... Mk 14:1
the twelve, went unto the chief p ..... Mk 14:10
were assembled all the chief p .... Mk 14:53
And the chief p and all the council ... Mk 14:55
in the morning the chief p held a ..... Mk 15:1
the chief p accused him of many .... Mk 15:3
p had delivered him for envy .... Mk 15:10
But the chief p moved the people, ... Mk 15:11
Likewise also the chief p mocking ..... Mk 15:31
and Caiaphas being the high p .... Lk 3:2
lawful to eat but for the p alone ..... Lk 6:4
rejected of the elders and chief p .... Lk 9:22
Go shew yourselves unto the p .... Lk 17:14
But the chief p and the scribes and ... Lk 19:47
preached the gospel, the chief p ...... Lk 20:1
And the chief p and the scribes the ... Lk 20:19
And the chief p and scribes sought .... Lk 22:2
way, and communed with the chief p .... Lk 22:4
Then Jesus said unto the chief p ...... Lk 22:52
of the people and the chief p .... Lk 22:66
Then said Pilate to the chief p .... Lk 23:4
And the chief p and scribes stood ..... Lk 23:10
had called together the chief p .... Lk 23:13
them and of the chief p prevailed ..... Lk 23:23
And now the chief p and our rulers .... Lk 24:20
of John, when the Jews sent p .... Jn 1:19
the chief p sent officers to take ..... Jn 7:32
came the officers to the chief p ...... Jn 7:45
Then gathered the chief p .... Jn 11:47
Now both the chief p and the .... Jn 11:57
But the chief p consulted that .... Jn 12:10
men and officers from the chief p ..... Jn 18:3
the chief p have delivered thee .... Jn 18:35
When the chief p therefore .... Jn 19:6
The chief p answered, We have no ...... Jn 19:15
Then said the chief p of the Jews ..... Jn 19:21
they spake unto the people, the p ..... Acts 4:1
and reported all that the chief p ..... Acts 4:23
the chief p heard these things, ... Acts 5:24
a great company of the p were .... Acts 6:7
to bind all that call on thy .... Acts 9:14
bring them bound unto the chief p ..... Acts 9:21
Sceva, a Jew, and chief of the p ...... Acts 19:14
bands, and commanded the chief p ...... Acts 22:30
And they came to the chief p .... Acts 23:14
I was at Jerusalem, the chief p .... Acts 25:15
authority from the chief p .... Acts 26:10
and commission from the chief p .... Acts 26:12
[For those p were made without an .... Heb 7:21
And they truly were many p .... Heb 7:23
not daily, as those high p .... Heb 7:27
men high p which have infirmity .... Heb 7:28

seeing that there are p that .... Heb 8:4
the p went always into the first ..... Heb 9:6
kings and p unto God and his Father ... Rev 1:6
made us unto our God kings and p ...... Rev 5:10
power, but they shall be p of God ..... Rev 20:6

PRIESTS

place where the p feet stood firm .... Josh 4:3
the soles of the p feet were .... Josh 4:18
thee, into one of the p offices 1Sa 2:36
it was the p 2Kin 12:16
silver, and one hundred p garments ... Ezr 2:69
five hundred and thirty p garments ... Neh 7:70
and threescore and seven p garments .. Neh 7:72
certain of the p sons with .... Neh 12:35

PRINCE

thou art a mighty p among us .... Gen 23:6
p of the country, saw her, he .... Gen 34:2
And he said, Who made thee a p .... Ex 2:14
each p on his day, for the .... Num 7:11
of Zuar, p of Issachar, did offer ..... Num 7:18
p of the children of Zebulun, did ..... Num 7:24
p of the children of Reuben, did ...... Num 7:30
p of the children of Simeon, did ...... Num 7:36
p of the children of Gad, offered ..... Num 7:42
p of the children of Ephraim .... Num 7:48
p of the children of Manasseh .... Num 7:54
p of the children of Benjamin, ... Num 7:60
p of the children of Dan, offered, ... Num 7:66
p of the children of Asher, ... Num 7:72
p of the children of Naphtali, ... Num 7:78
thyself altogether a p over us .... Num 16:13
him a rod apiece, for each p one ...... Num 17:6
a p of a chief house among the .... Num 25:14
the daughter of a p of Midian .... Num 25:18
shall take one p of every tribe, ... Num 34:18
the p of the tribe of .... Num 34:22
The p of the children of Joseph, ... Num 34:23
the p of the tribe of the, ... Num 34:24
the p of the tribe of the .... Num 34:25
the p of the tribe of the .... Num 34:26
the p of the tribe of the .... Num 34:27
the p of the tribe of the .... Num 34:28
princes, of each chief house a p ...... Josh 22:14
Know ye not that I was a p 2Sa 3:38
but I will make him p all the 1Kin 11:34
made thee p over my people Israel 1Kin 14:7
made thee p over my people Israel 1Kin 16:2
p of the children of Judah 1Chr 2:10
he was p of the Reubenites 1Chr 5:6
unto Sheshbazzar, the p of Judah ...... Ezr 1:8
say, Where is the house of the p ...... Job 21:28
as a p would I go near unto him .... Job 31:37
is the destruction of the p .... Prov 14:28
much less do bring lips a p .... Prov 17:7
will intreat the favour of the p ...... Prov 19:6
the p whom thine eyes have seen .... Prov 25:7
long forbearing is a p persuaded ...... Prov 25:15
The p that wanteth understanding, ... Prov 28:16
Father, The P of Peace .... Is 9:6
And this Seraiah was a quiet p .... Jer 51:59
the p shall be clothed with .... Eze 7:27
concerneth the p in Jerusalem .... Eze 12:10
the p that is among them shall .... Eze 12:12
thou, profane wicked p of Israel, ... Eze 21:25
of man, say unto the p of Tyrus .... Eze 28:2
no more a p of the land of Egypt ...... Eze 30:13
my servant David a p among them .... Eze 34:24
David shall be their p for ever .... Eze 37:25
the chief p of Meshech and Tubal, ... Eze 38:2
the chief p of Meshech and Tubal ...... Eze 38:3
the chief p of Meshech and Tubal ...... Eze 39:1
It is for the p .... Eze 44:3
the p, he shall sit in it to eat ...... Eze 44:3
be for the p on the one side .... Eze 45:7
this oblation for the p in Israel ..... Eze 45:16
shall the p prepare for himself .... Eze 45:22
the p shall enter by the way of .... Eze 46:2
prince that offering that the p .... Eze 46:4
when the p shall enter, he shall ...... Eze 46:8
the p in the midst thereof, when, ... Eze 46:10
now am a p shall the p prepare a ...... Eze 46:12
If the p give a gift unto any of ...... Eze 46:16
after, it shall return to the p .... Eze 46:17
Moreover the p shall not take of ...... Eze 46:18
And the residue shall be for the p .... Eze 48:21
against the portions for the p .... Eze 48:21
of Benjamin, shall be for the p .... Eze 48:22
Unto whom the p of the eunuchs .... Dan 1:7
p of the eunuchs that he might .... Dan 1:8
love with the p of the eunuchs .... Dan 1:9
the p of the eunuchs said unto .... Dan 1:10
whom the p of the eunuchs had set ..... Dan 1:11
then the p of the eunuchs brought ..... Dan 1:18
himself even to the p of the host ..... Dan 8:11
stand up against the P of princes ..... Dan 8:25
the P shall be seven weeks .... Dan 9:25
the people of the p that shall .... Dan 9:26
But the p of the kingdom of .... Dan 10:13
to fight with the p of Persia .... Dan 10:20
the p of Grecia shall come .... Dan 10:20
these things, but Michael your p ...... Dan 10:21
is for p but his own behalf shall ..... Dan 11:18
also the p of the covenant .... Dan 11:22
the great p which standeth for .... Dan 12:1
without a king, and without a p .... Hos 3:4
the p asketh, and the judge asketh .... Mic 7:3
through the p of the devils .... Mt 9:34
by Beelzebub the p of the devils ...... Mt 12:24

by the p of the devils casteth he........ Mk 3:22
now shall the p of this world be .... Jn 12:31
for the p of this world cometh, ... Jn 14:30
because the p of this world is............ Jn 16:11
And killed the P of life, whom God... Acts 3:15
with his right hand to be a P............ Acts 5:31
according to the p of the power......... Eph 2:2
the p of the kings of the earth .... Rev 1:5

PRINCE'S

thy feet with shoes, O p daughter ..... Song 7:1
it shall be the p part to give .... Eze 45:17
the midst of that which is the p .... Eze 48:22

PRINCES

The p also of Pharaoh saw her, and ... Gen 12:15
twelve p shall he beget, and I .... Gen 17:20
twelve p according to their .... Gen 25:16
p of the tribes of their fathers, ... Num 1:16
the p of Israel, being twelve men ...... Num 1:44
That the p of Israel, heads of .... Num 7:2
who were the p of the tribes, and ...... Num 7:2
a wagon for two of the p, and for...... Num 7:3
the p offered for dedicating of .... Num 7:10
even the p offered their offering .... Num 7:10
was anointed, by the p of Israel .... Num 7:84
but with one trumpet, then the p ...... Num 10:4
fifty p of the assembly, famous .... Num 16:2
of all their p according to the .... Num 17:2
every one of their p gave him a .... Num 17:6
The p digged the well, the nobles ..... Num 21:18
the p of Moab abode with Balaam ... Num 22:8
and said unto the p of Balak .... Num 22:13
the p of Moab rose up, and they ...... Num 22:14
And Balak sent yet again p .... Num 22:15
ass, and went with the p of Moab .... Num 22:21
Balaam went with the p of Balak ..... Num 22:35
to the p that were with him .... Num 22:40
he, and all the p of Moab. .... Num 23:6
and the p of Moab with him .... Num 23:17
the priest, and before the p .... Num 27:2
all the p of the congregation, ... Num 31:13
unto the p of the congregation, ... Num 32:2
before Moses, and before the p........ Num 36:1
the p of the congregation sware .... Josh 9:15
because the p of the congregation .... Josh 9:18
murmured against the p .... Josh 9:18
But all the p said unto all the.......... Josh 9:21
the p said unto them, Let them, ... Josh 9:21
as the p had promised them. .... Josh 9:21
Moses smote with the p of Midian ... Josh 13:21
the son of Nun, and before the p...... Josh 17:4
And with him ten p, of each chief .... Josh 22:14
the p of the congregation and .... Josh 22:30
of Eleazar the priest, and the p .... Josh 22:32
give ear, O ye p............................. Judg 5:3
the p of Issachar were with............. Judg 5:15
they took two p of the Midianites .... Judg 7:25
into your hands the p of Midian ...... Judg 8:3
the p of Succoth said, Are the .... Judg 8:6
unto him the p of Succoth .... Judg 8:14
of Gilead said one to another, ... Judg 10:18
the dunghill, to set them among p 1Sa 2:8
Then the p of the Philistines 1Sa 18:30
Then said the p of the 1Sa 29:3
unto the p of the Philistines 1Sa 29:3
the p of the Philistines were 1Sa 29:4
the p of the Philistines said. 1Sa 29:4
notwithstanding the p of the 1Sa 29:9
the p of the children of Ammon 2Sa 10:3
regardest neither p nor honour. 2Sa 13:4
And these were the p which he had .. 1Kin 4:2
of war, and his servants, and his p ... 1Kin 9:22
men of the p of the provinces............ 1Kin 20:14
men of the p of the provinces............ 1Kin 20:15
the young men of the p of the 1Kin 20:17
So these young men of the p of 1Kin 20:19
as the manner was, and the p........... 2Kin 11:14
mother, and his servants, and his p ... 2Kin 24:12
away all Jerusalem, and all the p...... 2Kin 24:14
names were p in their families........... 1Chr 4:38
men of valour, chief of the p 1Chr 7:40
But the p of the children of 1Chr 19:3
David also commanded all the p of .. 1Chr 22:17
together all the p of Israel 1Chr 23:2
them before the king, and the p 1Chr 24:6
These were the p of the tribes of 1Chr 27:22
assembled all the p of Israel 1Chr 28:1
the p of the tribes, and the 1Chr 28:1
also the p and all the people will...... 1Chr 28:21
p of the tribes of Israel, and the....... 1Chr 29:24
And all the p, and the mighty men,.. 1Chr 29:24
to the p of Judah, that went............. 2Chr 12:5
Whereupon the p of Israel 2Chr 12:6
of his reign he sent to his p 2Chr 17:7
and drivers also of the p of Israel 2Chr 21:9
Jehoram went forth with his p 2Chr 21:9
of Ahab, and found the p of Judah.. 2Chr 22:8
at the entering in, and the p............. 2Chr 23:13
And all the p and all the people 2Chr 24:10
of Jehoiada came the p of Judah 2Chr 24:17
destroyed all the p of the people...... 2Chr 24:23
and the spoil before the p 2Chr 28:14
house of the king, and of the p 2Chr 28:21
he commanded the Levites to 2Chr 29:30
king had taken counsel, and his p 2Chr 30:2
his p throughout all Israel and.......... 2Chr 30:6
the p of Israel and the p, by the 2Chr 30:24
the p gave to the congregation a 2Chr 30:24
the p came and saw the heaps, they .. 2Chr 31:8
He took counsel with his p 2Chr 32:3

ambassadors of the p of Babylon 2Chr 32:31
his p gave willingly unto the 2Chr 35:8
of the king, and of his p 2Chr 36:18
and before all the king's mighty p..... Ezr 7:28
the p had appointed for the .... Ezr 8:20
the p came to me, saying, The .... Ezr 9:1
yea, the hand of the p and rulers...... Ezr 9:2
according to the counsel of the p....... Ezr 10:8
upon us, on our kings, on our p .... Neh 9:32
Neither have our kings, our p .... Neh 9:34
and our p, Levites, and priests,......... Neh 9:38
Then I brought up the p of Judah..... Neh 12:31
and half of the p of Judah .... Neh 12:32
made a feast unto all his p .... Est 1:3
p of the provinces, being before ...... Est 1:3
the people and the p her beauty....... Est 1:11
and Memucan, the seven p of Persia.. Est 1:14
answered before the king and the p... Est 1:16
king only, but also to all the p .... Est 1:16
this day unto all the king's p .... Est 1:18
saying pleased the king and the p..... Est 1:21
made a great feast unto all his p ...... Est 2:18
all the p that were with him .... Est 3:1
he had advanced him above the p...... Est 5:11
of one of the king's most noble p...... Job 3:15
Or with p that had gold, who .... Job 3:15
He leadeth p away spoiled, and........ Job 12:19
He poureth contempt upon p .... Job 12:21
He refrained talking, and laid........... Job 29:9
and to p, Ye are ungodly.................. Job 34:18
accepteth not the persons of p .... Job 34:19
mayest make p in all the earth .... Ps 45:16
The p of the people are gathered...... Ps 47:9
the p of Judah and their council, ... Ps 68:27
the p of Zebulun .... Ps 68:27
and the p of Naphtali...................... Ps 68:27
P shall come out of Egypt .... Ps 68:31
He shall cut off the spirit of p .... Ps 76:12
men, and fall like one of the p .... Ps 82:7
yea, all their p as Zebah .... Ps 83:11
To bind his p at his pleasure............ Ps 105:22
He poureth contempt upon p .... Ps 107:40
That he may set him with p .... Ps 113:8
even with the p of his people........... Ps 113:8
than to put confidence in p .... Ps 118:9
P also did sit and speak against .... Ps 119:23
P have persecuted me without a....... Ps 119:161
Put not your trust in p, nor in.......... Ps 146:3
p, and all judges of the earth........... Ps 148:11
kings reign, and p decree justice....... Prov 8:15
By me p rule, and nobles, even all ... Prov 8:16
good, nor to strike p for equity .... Prov 17:26
for a servant to have rule over p ...... Prov 19:10
of a land many are the p thereof...... Prov 28:2
nor for p strong drink .... Prov 31:4
p walking as servants upon the......... Eccl 10:7
and thy p eat in the morning............ Eccl 10:16
thy p eat in due season, for .... Eccl 10:17
Thy p are rebellious, and................. Is 1:23
will give children to be their p.......... Is 3:4
of his people, and the p thereof .... Is 3:14
Are but my p altogether kings.......... Is 10:8
Surely the p of Zoan are fools, ... Is 19:11
The p of Zoan are become fools,...... Is 19:13
the p of Noph are deceived.............. Is 19:13
arise, ye p, and anoint the shield....... Is 21:5
city, whose merchants are p .... Is 23:8
For his p were at Zoan, and his .... Is 30:4
his p shall be afraid of the .... Is 31:9
and p shall rule in judgment............ Is 32:1
all her p shall be nothing................. Is 34:12
That bringeth the p to nothing .... Is 40:23
shall come upon p as upon morter.... Is 41:25
profaned the p of the sanctuary .... Is 43:28
p also shall worship, because of ...... Is 49:7
of Judah, against the p thereof .... Jer 1:18
they, their kings, their p .... Jer 2:26
perish, and the heart of the p........... Jer 4:9
of Judah, and the bones of his p....... Jer 8:1
p sitting upon the throne of .... Jer 17:25
and on horses, they, and their p .... Jer 17:25
and the p of Judah, with the .... Jer 24:8
the king of Judah, and his p .... Jer 24:8
the p thereof, to make them a .... Jer 25:18
Egypt, and his servants, and his p..... Jer 25:19
When the p of Judah heard these ..... Jer 26:10
and the prophets unto the p .... Jer 26:11
spake Jeremiah unto all the p .... Jer 26:12
Then said the p and all the people ... Jer 26:16
all his mighty men, and all the p....... Jer 26:21
the p of Judah and Jerusalem, and ... Jer 29:2
anger, they, their kings, their p .... Jer 32:32
Now when all the p, and all the ...... Jer 34:10
the p of Judah .... Jer 34:19
the p of Jerusalem, the eunuchs, ... Jer 34:19
his p will I give into the hand.......... Jer 34:21
which was by the chamber of the p .. Jer 36:12
all the p sat there, even .... Jer 36:12
the son of Hananeh, and all the p..... Jer 36:12
Therefore all the p sent Jehudi .... Jer 36:14
Then said the p unto Baruch............ Jer 36:19
in the ears of all the p .... Jer 36:21
Jeremiah, and brought it to the .... Jer 37:15
Wherefore the p were wroth with.... Jer 38:4
Therefore the p said unto the .... Jer 38:4
unto the king of Babylon's p .... Jer 38:17
forth to the king of Babylon's p .... Jer 38:18
forth to the king of Babylon's p .... Jer 38:22
But if the p hear that I have .... Jer 38:25
Then came all the p unto Jeremiah ... Jer 38:27

all the p of the king of Babylon....... Jer 39:3
of the p of the king of Babylon........ Jer 39:3
and all the king of Babylon's p .... Jer 39:13
the p of the king, even ten men .... Jer 41:1
our fathers, our kings, and our p ...... Jer 44:17
fathers, your kings, and your p .... Jer 44:21
his priests and his p together .... Jer 48:7
and his priests and his p together...... Jer 49:3
from thence the king and the p .... Jer 49:38
of Babylon, and upon her p .... Jer 50:35
And I will make drunk her p .... Jer 51:57
also all the p of Judah in Riblah...... Jer 52:10
her p are become like harts that ...... Lam 1:6
the kingdom and the p thereof .... Lam 2:2
her p are among the Gentiles .... Lam 2:9
P are hanged up by their hand......... Lam 5:12
son of Beniaiah, p of the people....... Eze 11:1
the p thereof, and led them with ..... Eze 17:12
a lamentation for the p of Israel ...... Eze 19:1
shall be upon all the p of Israel .... Eze 21:12
the p of Israel, every one were......... Eze 22:6
Her p in the midst thereof are .... Eze 22:27
heads, all of them p to look to .... Eze 23:15
Then all the p of the sea shall .... Eze 26:16
all the p of Kedar, they occupied .... Eze 27:21
is Edom, her kings, and all her p ..... Eze 32:29
There be the p of the north .... Eze 32:30
the blood of the p of the earth .... Eze 39:18
my p shall no more oppress my....... Eze 45:8
Let it suffice you, O p of Israel .... Eze 45:9
of the king's seed, and of the p .... Dan 1:3
sent to gather together the p .... Dan 3:2
Then the p, the governors, and........ Dan 3:3
And the p, governors, and captains,.. Dan 3:27
that the king, and his p, his............ Dan 5:2
and the king, and his p, his wives,.... Dan 5:3
kingdom an hundred and twenty p ... Dan 6:1
that the might give accounts............ Dan 6:2
above the presidents and p .... Dan 6:3
p sought to find occasion against...... Dan 6:4
p assembled together to the king, ... Dan 6:6
kingdom, the governors, and the ..... Dan 6:7
stand up against the Prince of p ...... Dan 8:25
in thy name to our kings, our p .... Dan 9:6
of face, to our kings, to our p .... Dan 9:8
lo, Michael, one of the chief p .... Dan 10:13
shall be strong, and one of his p ...... Dan 11:5
Egypt their gods, with their p .... Dan 11:8
The p of Judah were like them. .... Hos 5:10
and the p with their lies. .... Hos 7:3
In the day of our king the p have ..... Hos 7:5
their p shall fall by the sword.......... Hos 7:16
they have made p, and I knew it ...... Hos 8:4
for the burden of the king of p......... Hos 8:10
all their p are revolters.................... Hos 9:15
thou saidst, Give me a king and p .... Hos 13:10
his p together, saith the LORD......... Amos 1:15
slay all the p thereof with him......... Amos 2:3
ye p of the house of Israel .... Mic 3:1
the p of the house of Israel, that ...... Mic 3:9
that I will punish the p .... Hab 1:10
Her p within her are roaring .... Zeph 3:3
not the least among the p of Juda.... Mt 2:6
Ye know that the p of the .... Mt 20:25
nor of the p of this world, that 1Cor 2:6
Which none of the p of this world ... 1Cor 2:8

PRINCESS

p among the provinces, how is she ... Lam 1:1

PRINCESSES

And he had seven hundred wives, p... 1Kin 11:3

PRINCIPAL

Take thou also unto thee p spices .... Ex 30:23
he shall even restore it in the p .... Lev 6:5
his trespass with the p thereof .... Num 5:7
the son of Nathan was p officer 1Kin 4:5
the p scribe of the host, which 2Kin 25:19
one p household being taken for 1Chr 24:6
even the p fathers over against 1Chr 24:31
of Asaph, was the p to begin the...... Neh 11:17
Wisdom is the p thing..................... Prov 4:7
broken down the p plants thereof .... Is 16:8
cummin, and cast in the p wheat ..... Is 28:25
in the ashes, ye p of the flock .... Jer 25:34
nor the p of the flock to escape .... Jer 25:35
an howling of the p of the flock ...... Jer 25:36
the p scribe of the host, who .... Jer 52:25
seven shepherds, and eight p men .... Mic 5:5
p men of the city, at Festus .... Acts 25:23

PRINCIPALITIES

for your p shall come down, even .... Jer 13:18
nor life, nor angels, nor p .... Rom 8:38
To the intent that now unto the p .... Eph 3:10
flesh and blood, but against p .... Eph 6:12
be thrones, or dominions, or p .... Col 1:16
And having spoiled p and powers, he .. Col 2:15
them in mind to be subject to p .... Titus 3:1

PRINCIPALITY

Far above all p, and power, and...... Eph 1:21
him, which is the head of all p......... Col 2:10

PRINCIPLES

the first p of the oracles of God...... Heb 5:12
Therefore leaving the p of the......... Heb 6:1

PRINT

dead, nor p any marks upon you ..... Lev 19:28
thou settest a p upon the heels......... Job 13:27

in his hands the *p* of the nails .... Jn 20:25
my finger into the *p* of the nails .... Jn 20:25

PRINTED
oh that they were *p* in a book .... Job 19:23

PRISCA (pris´-cah) See PRISCILLA. Same as
Priscilla.
Salute *P* and Aquila, and the 2Ti 4:19

PRISCILLA (pris-sil´-lah) See PRISCA. Wife of
Aquila and co-worker of Paul.
come from Italy, with his wife *P* .... Acts 18:2
thence into Syria, and with him *P* .... Acts 18:18
P had heard, they took him unto .... Acts 18:26
Greet *P* and Aquila my helpers in .... Rom 16:3
P salute you much in the Lord, ... 1Cor 16:19

PRISED
price that I was *p* at of them .... Zec 11:13

PRISON
took him, and put him into the *p* .... Gen 39:20
and he was there in the *p* .... Gen 39:20
the sight of the keeper of the *p* .... Gen 39:21
the keeper of the *p* committed to .... Gen 39:22
the prisoners that were in the *p* .... Gen 39:22
The keeper of the *p* looked not to .... Gen 39:23
captain of the guard, into the *p* .... Gen 40:3
Egypt, which were bound in the *p* .... Gen 40:5
brother, and ye shall be kept in *p* .... Gen 42:16
be bound in the house of your *p* .... Gen 42:19
and he did grind in the *p* house .... Judg 16:21
for Samson out of the *p* house .... Judg 16:25
king, Put this fellow in the *p* 1Kin 22:27
shut him up, and bound him in *p* 2Kin 17:4
Jehoiachin king of Judah out of *p* 2Kin 25:27
And changed his *p* garments 2Kin 25:29
the seer, and put him in a *p* house 2Chr 16:10
king, Put this fellow in the *p* 2Chr 18:26
that was by the court of the *p* .... Neh 3:25
and they stood still in the *p* gate .... Neh 12:39
Bring my soul out of *p*, that I .... Ps 142:7
For out of *p* he cometh to reign .... Eccl 4:14
pit, and shall be shut up in the *p* .... Is 24:22
out the prisoners from the *p* .... Is 42:7
in darkness out of the *p* house .... Is 42:7
and they are hid in *p* houses .... Is 42:22
he was taken from a and from .... Is 53:8
the opening of the *p* to them that .... Is 61:1
that thou shouldest put him in *p* .... Jer 29:26
was shut up in the court of the *p* .... Jer 32:2
p according to the word of the .... Jer 32:8
that sat in the court of the *p* .... Jer 32:12
yet shut up in the court of the *p* .... Jer 33:1
for they had not put him into *p* .... Jer 37:4
put him up in the house of .... Jer 37:15
for they had made that the *p* .... Jer 37:15
people, that ye have put me in *p* .... Jer 37:18
Jeremiah into the court of the *p* .... Jer 37:21
remained in the court of the *p* .... Jer 37:21
that was in the court of the *p* .... Jer 38:6
remained in the court of the *p* .... Jer 38:13
abode in the court of the *p* until .... Jer 38:28
out of the court of the *p* .... Jer 39:14
was shut up in the court of the *p* .... Jer 39:15
put him in *p* till the day of his .... Jer 52:11
and brought him forth out of *p* .... Jer 52:31
And changed his *p* garments .... Jer 52:33
heard that John was cast into *p* .... Mt 4:12
officer, and thou be cast into .... Mt 5:25
in the *p* the works of Christ .... Mt 11:2
put him in *p* for Herodias' sake, ... Mt 14:3
sent, and beheaded John in the *p* .... Mt 14:10
but went and cast him into *p* .... Mt 18:30
I was in *p*, and ye came unto me .... Mt 25:36
Or when saw we thee sick, or in *p* .... Mt 25:39
sick, and in *p*, and ye visited me .... Mt 25:43
or naked, or sick, or in *p* .... Mt 25:44
Now after that John was put in *p* .... Mk 1:14
bound him in *p* for Herodias' sake .... Mk 6:17
he went and beheaded him in the *p* .... Mk 6:27
all, that he shut up John in *p* .... Lk 3:20
and the officer cast thee into *p* .... Lk 12:58
to go with thee, both into *p* .... Lk 22:33
and for murder, was cast into *p* .... Lk 23:19
and murder was cast into *p* .... Lk 23:25
For John was not yet cast into *p* .... Jn 3:24
and put them in the common *p* .... Acts 5:18
Lord by night opened the *p* doors .... Acts 5:19
sent to the *p* to have them .... Acts 5:21
came, and found them not in the *p* .... Acts 5:22
The *p* truly found we shut with .... Acts 5:23
the men whom ye put in *p* are .... Acts 5:25
men and women committed them to *p* .... Acts 8:3
apprehended him, he put him in *p* .... Acts 12:4
Peter therefore was kept in *p* .... Acts 12:5
before the door kept the *p* .... Acts 12:6
him, and a light shined in the *p* .... Acts 12:7
Lord had brought him out of the *p* .... Acts 12:17
upon them, they cast them into *p* .... Acts 16:23
thrust them into the inner *p* .... Acts 16:24
foundations of the *p* were shaken .... Acts 16:26
the keeper of the *p* awaking out .... Acts 16:27
sleep, and seeing the *p* doors open .... Acts 16:27
the keeper of the *p* told this .... Acts 16:36
Romans, and have cast us into *p* .... Acts 16:37
And they went out of the *p* .... Acts 16:40
of the saints did I shut up in *p* .... Acts 26:10
and preached unto the spirits in *p* 1Pet 3:19
shall cast some of you into *p* .... Rev 2:10
shall be loosed out of his *p* .... Rev 20:7

PRISONER
sighing of the *p* come before thee .... Ps 79:11
To hear the groaning of the *p* .... Ps 102:20
to release unto the people a *p* .... Mt 27:15
And they had then a notable *p* .... Mt 27:16
feast he released unto them one *p* .... Mk 15:6
Paul the *p* called me unto him, and .... Acts 23:18
to me unreasonable to send a *p* .... Acts 25:27
yet was I delivered *p* from .... Acts 28:17
the *p* of Jesus Christ for you .... Eph 3:1
the *p* of the Lord, beseech you, ... Eph 4:1
of our Lord, nor of me his *p* 2Ti 1:8
a *p* of Jesus Christ, and Timothy, ... Philem 1
now also a *p* of Jesus Christ .... Philem 9

PRISONERS
where the king's *p* were bound. .... Gen 39:20
all the *p* that were in the prison .... Gen 39:22
Israel, and took some of them *p* .... Num 21:1
There the *p* rest together .... Job 3:18
the poor, and despiseth not his *p* .... Ps 69:33
The Lord looseth the *p* .... Ps 146:7
they shall bow down under the *p* .... Is 10:4
opened not the house of his *p* .... Is 14:17
Assyria lead away the Egyptians *p* .... Is 20:4
as *p* are gathered in the pit, and .... Is 24:22
bring out the *p* from the prison .... Is 42:7
That thou mayest say to the *p* .... Is 49:9
his feet all the *p* of the earth .... Lam 3:34
a *p* out of the pit wherein is no .... Zec 9:11
to the strong hold, ye *p* of hope .... Zec 9:12
and the *p* heard them .... Acts 16:25
that the *p* had been fled. .... Acts 16:27
certain other *p* unto one named .... Acts 27:1
counsel was to kill the *p* .... Acts 27:42
the *p* to the captain of the guard .... Acts 28:16

PRISONS
up to the synagogues, and into *p* .... Lk 21:12
and delivering into *p* both men .... Acts 22:4
in *p* more frequent, in deaths oft 2Cor 11:23

PRIVATE
is of any *p* interpretation 2Pet 1:20

PRIVATELY
the disciples came unto him *p* .... Mt 24:3
into a desert place by ship *p* .... Mk 6:32
house, his disciples asked him *p* .... Mk 9:28
and John and Andrew asked him *p* .... Mk 13:3
went aside *p* into a desert place .... Lk 9:10
him unto his disciples, and said *p* .... Lk 10:23
hand, and went with him aside *p* .... Acts 23:19
but *p* to them which were of .... Gal 2:2

PRIVILY
sent messengers unto Abimelech *p* .... Judg 9:31
off the skirt of Saul's robe *p* 1Sa 24:4
his eyes are *p* set against the .... Ps 10:8
that they may *p* shoot at the .... Ps 11:2
net that they have laid *p* for me .... Ps 31:4
they commune of laying snares *p* .... Ps 64:5
Whoso *p* slandereth his neighbour, ... Ps 101:5
have they laid a snare for me .... Ps 142:3
let us lurk *p* for the innocent .... Prov 1:11
they lurk *p* for their own lives .... Prov 1:18
was minded to put her away *p* .... Mt 1:19
when he had called the wise men, ... Mt 2:7
and now do they thrust us out *p* .... Acts 16:37
who came in *p* to spy out our .... Gal 2:4
who *p* shall bring in damnable 2Pet 2:1

PRIVY
or hath his *p* member cut off, ... Deut 23:1
which thine heart is *p* to 1Kin 2:44
entereth into their *p* chambers .... Eze 21:14
his wife also being *p* to it .... Acts 5:2

PRIZE
run all, but one receiveth the *p* 1Cor 9:24
of the high calling of God in *p* .... Phil 3:14

PROCEED
that *p* out of the candlestick .... Ex 25:35
any word *p* out of your mouth. .... Josh 6:10
which shall *p* out of thy bowels, ... 2Sa 7:12
they shall *p* no further .... Job 40:5
I will *p* to do a marvellous work .... Is 29:14
for a law shall *p* from me. .... Is 51:4
for they *p* from evil to evil, and .... Jer 9:3
out of them shall *p* thanksgiving. .... Jer 30:19
their governor shall *p* from the .... Jer 30:21
dignity shall *p* of themselves .... Hab 1:7
But those things which *p* out of .... Mt 15:18
out of the heart *p* evil thoughts, ... Mt 15:19
p evil thoughts, adulteries, ... Mk 7:21
communication *p* out of your mouth. .... Eph 4:29
But they shall *p* no further 2Ti 3:9

PROCEEDED
then whatsoever *p* out of her lips .... Num 30:12
which came *p* out of your mouth. .... Num 32:24
which hath *p* out of thy mouth. .... Judg 11:36
Elihu also *p*, and said, ... Job 36:1
words which *p* out of his mouth .... Lk 4:22
for I *p* forth and came from God. .... Jn 8:42
he *p* further to take Peter also .... Acts 12:3
And out of the throne *p* lightnings .... Rev 4:5
which sword *p* out of his mouth .... Rev 19:21

PROCEEDETH
The thing *p* from the LORD .... Gen 24:50
to all that *p* out of his mouth .... Num 30:2
but by every word that *p* out of .... Deut 8:3
Wickedness *p* from the wicked 1Sa 24:13

PROFANE
an error which *p* from the ruler .... Eccl 10:5
mouth of the most High *p* not evil. .... Lam 3:38
therefore wrong judgment *p* .... Hab 1:4
but by every word that *p* out of .... Mt 4:4
which *p* from the Father, he shall .... Jn 15:26
Out of the same mouth *p* blessing .... Jas 3:10
fire *p* out of their mouth, and .... Rev 11:5

PROCEEDING
p out of the throne of God and of .... Rev 22:1

PROCESS
in *p* of time it came to pass, ... Gen 4:3
in *p* of time the daughter of .... Gen 38:12
And it came to pass in *p* of time .... Ex 2:23
And it came to pass in *p* of time .... Judg 11:4
came to pass, that in *p* of time 2Chr 21:19

PROCHORUS (prok´-o-rus) A leader in the
Jerusalem church.
the Holy Ghost, and Philip, and P...... Acts 6:5

PROCLAIM
I will *p* the name of the LORD .... Ex 33:19
which ye shall *p* to be holy .... Lev 23:2
which ye shall *p* in their seasons. .... Lev 23:4
ye shall *p* on the selfsame day, ... Lev 23:21
which ye shall *p* to be holy. .... Lev 23:37
p liberty throughout all the land .... Lev 25:10
against it, then *p* peace unto it. .... Deut 20:10
in the ears of the people, ... Judg 7:3
say, and set Naboth on high 1Kin 21:9
a solemn assembly for Baal 2Kin 10:20
in all their cities, and in .... Neh 8:15
p before him, Thus shall it be .... Est 6:9
Most men will *p* every one his own .... Prov 20:6
to *p* liberty to the captives, and .... Is 61:1
To *p* the acceptable year of the .... Is 61:2
p these words toward the north, ... Jer 3:12
p there this word, and say, Hear .... Jer 7:2
P all these words in the cities. .... Jer 11:6
p there the words that I shall .... Jer 19:2
Jerusalem, to *p* liberty unto them .... Jer 34:8
p a liberty for you, saith the .... Jer 34:17
P ye this among the Gentiles; .... Joel 3:9
of thanksgiving with leaven, and *p* .... Amos 4:5

PROCLAIMED
there, and *p* the name of the LORD .... Ex 34:5
LORD passed by before him, and *p* .... Ex 34:6
it to be *p* throughout the camp .... Ex 36:6
They *p* a fast, and set Naboth on 1Kin 21:12
And they *p* it 2Kin 10:20
God *p*, who *p* these words 2Kin 23:16
p these things that thou hast 2Kin 23:17
p a fast throughout all Judah. 2Chr 20:3
Then I *p* a fast there, at the .... Ezr 8:21
p before him, Thus shall it be .... Est 6:11
the LORD hath *p* unto the end of .... Is 62:11
that they *p* a fast before the .... Jer 36:9
a fast, and put on sackcloth, ... Jonah 3:5
And he caused it to be *p* and .... Jonah 3:7
shall be *p* upon the housetops .... Lk 12:3

PROCLAIMETH
the heart of fools *p* foolishness. .... Prov 12:23

PROCLAIMING
in *p* liberty every man to his .... Jer 34:15
in *p* liberty, every one to his. .... Jer 34:17
strong angel *p* with a loud voice, ... Rev 5:2

PROCLAMATION
and Aaron made *p*, and said, To .... Ex 32:5
Asa made a *p* throughout all Judah 1Kin 15:22
there went a *p* throughout the 1Kin 22:36
they made a *p* through Judah and 2Chr 24:9
to make *p* throughout all Israel 2Chr 30:5
that he made a *p* throughout all 2Chr 36:22
that he made a *p* throughout all .... Ezr 1:1
they made *p* throughout Judah, and .... Ezr 10:7
made a *p* concerning him, that he .... Dan 5:29

PROCURE
Thus might we *p* great evil. .... Jer 26:19
the prosperity that I *p* unto it. .... Jer 33:9

PROCURED
Hast thou not *p* this unto thyself. .... Jer 2:17
thy doings have *p* these things. .... Jer 4:18

PROCURETH
diligently seeketh good *p* favour .... Prov 11:27

PRODUCE
P your cause, saith the LORD .... Is 41:21

PROFANE
neither shalt thou *p* the name of .... Lev 18:21
neither shalt thou *p* the name of .... Lev 19:12
sanctuary, and to *p* my holy name .... Lev 20:3
among his people, to *p* himself .... Lev 21:4
not *p* the name of their God. .... Lev 21:6
take a wife that is a whore, or *p* .... Lev 21:7
if she *p* herself by playing the .... Lev 21:9
nor *p* the sanctuary of his God. .... Lev 21:12
widow, or a divorced woman, or *p* .... Lev 21:14
Neither shall he *p* his seed among .... Lev 21:15
that he *p* not my sanctuaries .... Lev 21:23
that they *p* not my holy name in .... Lev 22:2
and die therefore, if they *p* it .... Lev 22:9
they shall not *p* the holy things. .... Lev 22:15
Neither shall ye *p* my holy name .... Lev 22:32
that ye do, and *p* the sabbath day .... Neh 13:17
For both prophet and priest are *p* .... Jer 23:11
p wicked prince of Israel, whose .... Eze 21:25

PROFANED

difference between the holy and p..... Eze 22:26
day into my sanctuary to p it..... Eze 23:39
I will p my sanctuary, the..... Eze 24:21
as p out of the mountain of God..... Eze 28:16
the sanctuary and the p placed..... Eze 42:20
difference between the holy and p..... Eze 44:23
shall be a p place for the city,..... Eze 48:15
the same maid, to p my holy name..... Amos 2:7
in the temple p the sabbath..... Mt 12:5
hath gone about to p the temple..... Acts 24:6
and for sinners, for unholy and p..... 1Ti 1:9
But refuse p and old wives' fables..... 1Ti 4:7
to thy trust, avoiding p and vain..... 1Ti 6:20
But shun p and vain babblings..... 2Ti 2:16
or p person, as Esau, who for one..... Heb 12:16

PROFANED

because he hath p the hallowed..... Lev 19:8
thou hast p his crown by casting..... Ps 89:39
Therefore I have p the princes of..... Is 43:28
things, and hast p my sabbaths..... Eze 22:8
law, and have p mine holy things..... Eze 22:26
my sabbaths, and I am p among them..... Eze 22:26
same day, and have p my sabbaths..... Eze 23:38
my sanctuary, when it was p..... Eze 25:3
they p my holy name, when they..... Eze 36:20
of Israel had p among the heathen..... Eze 36:21
which ye have p among the heathen ..... Eze 36:21
which was p among the heathen,..... Eze 36:23
which ye have p in the midst of..... Eze 36:23
But ye have p it, in that ye say,..... Mal 1:12
for Judah hath p the holiness of..... Mal 2:11

PROFANENESS

is p gone forth into all the land..... Jer 23:15

PROFANETH

the whore, she p her father..... Lev 21:9

PROFANING

upon Israel by the sabbath..... Neh 13:18
by p the covenant of our fathers..... Mal 2:10

PROFESS

I p this day unto the LORD thy..... Deut 26:3
And then will I p unto them,..... Mt 7:23
They p that they know God..... Titus 1:16

PROFESSED

they glorify God for your p..... 2Cor 9:13
hast p a good profession before..... 1Ti 6:12

PROFESSING

P themselves to be wise, they..... Rom 1:22
(which becometh women p..... 1Ti 2:10
Which some p have erred..... 1Ti 6:21

PROFESSION

a good p before many witnesses,..... 1Ti 6:12
Apostle and High Priest of our p..... Heb 3:1
of God, let us hold fast our p..... Heb 4:14
Let us hold fast the p of our..... Heb 10:23

PROFIT

what p shall this birthright do..... Gen 25:32
What p is it if we slay our..... Gen 37:26
which cannot p nor deliver..... 1Sa 12:21
for the king's p to suffer them..... Est 3:8
what p should we have, if we pray..... Job 21:15
the strength of their hands p me..... Job 30:2
What p shall I have, if I be..... Job 35:3
may p the son of man..... Job 35:8
What p is there in my blood, when..... Ps 30:9
Treasures of wickedness p nothing..... Prov 10:2
Riches p not in the day of wrath..... Prov 11:4
In all labour there is p..... Prov 14:23
What p hath a man of all his..... Eccl 1:3
there was no p under the sun..... Eccl 2:11
What p hath he that worketh in..... Eccl 3:9
Moreover the p of the earth is..... Eccl 5:9
what p hath he that hath laboured..... Eccl 5:16
by it there is p to them that see..... Eccl 7:11
of a people that could not p them..... Is 30:5
nor be an help nor p..... Is 30:5
to a people that shall not p them..... Is 30:6
delectable things shall not p..... Is 44:9
if so be thou shalt be able to p..... Is 47:12
thy God which teacheth thee to p..... Is 48:17
for they shall not p thee..... Is 57:12
walked after things that do not p..... Jer 2:8
glory for that which doth not p..... Jer 2:11
in lying words, that cannot p..... Jer 7:8
to pain, but shall not p..... Jer 12:13
and things wherein there is no p..... Jer 16:19
shall not p this people at all..... Jer 23:32
what p is it that we have kept..... Mal 3:14
For what shall it p a man..... Mk 8:36
or what p is there of..... Rom 3:1
And this I speak for your own p..... 1Cor 7:35
own p, but the p of many..... 1Cor 10:33
is given to every man to p withal..... 1Cor 12:7
with tongues, what shall I p..... 1Cor 14:6
Christ shall p you nothing..... Gal 5:2
strive not about words to no p..... 2Ti 2:14
the word preached did not p them..... Heb 4:2
but he for our p, that we might..... Heb 12:10
What doth it p, my brethren,..... Jas 2:14
what doth it p..... Jas 2:16

PROFITABLE

Can a man be p unto God, as he..... Job 22:2
is wise may be p unto himself..... Job 22:2
but wisdom is p to direct..... Eccl 10:10
image that is p for nothing..... Is 44:10
was marred, it was p for nothing..... Jer 13:7

for it is p for thee that one of..... Mt 5:29
for it is p for thee that one of..... Mt 5:30
back nothing that was p unto you..... Acts 20:20
godliness is p unto all things..... 1Ti 4:8
is p for doctrine, for reproof,..... 2Ti 3:16
for he is p to me for the..... 2Ti 4:11
things are good and p unto men..... Titus 3:8
unprofitable, but now p to thee..... Philem 11

PROFITED

which was right, and it p me not..... Job 33:27
thou mightest be p by me..... Mt 15:5
For what is a man p, if he shall..... Mt 16:26
thou mightest be p by me..... Mk 7:11
p in the Jews' religion above..... Gal 1:14
which have not p them that have..... Heb 13:9

PROFITETH

It p a man nothing that he should..... Job 34:9
What p the graven image that the..... Hab 2:18
the flesh p nothing..... Jn 6:63
For circumcision verily p..... Rom 2:25
have not charity, it p me nothing..... 1Cor 13:3
For bodily exercise p little..... 1Ti 4:8

PROFITING

that thy p may appear to all..... 1Ti 4:15

PROFOUND

revolters are p to make slaughter..... Hos 5:2

PROGENITORS

above the blessings of my p unto..... Gen 49:26

PROGNOSTICATORS

the stargazers, the monthly p..... Is 47:13

PROLONG

ye shall not p your days upon it,..... Deut 4:26
that thou mayest p thy days upon..... Deut 4:40
that ye may p your days in the..... Deut 5:33
that ye may p your days in the..... Deut 11:9
to the end that he may p his days..... Deut 17:20
and that thou mayest p thy days..... Deut 22:7
that ye shall not p your days,..... Deut 30:18
ye shall p your days in the land..... Deut 32:47
mine end, that I should p my life..... Job 6:11
neither shall he p the perfection..... Job 15:29
Thou wilt p the king's life..... Ps 61:6
covetousness shall p his days..... Prov 28:16
neither shall he p his days..... Eccl 8:13
see his seed, he shall p his days..... Is 53:10

PROLONGED

that thy days may be p, and that..... Deut 5:16
and that thy days may be p..... Deut 6:2
the state thereof shall be p..... Prov 28:2
hundred times, and his days be p..... Eccl 8:12
come, and her days shall not be p..... Is 13:22
of Israel, saying, The days are p..... Eze 12:22
it shall be no more p..... Eze 12:25
none of my words be p any more,..... Eze 12:28
their lives were p for a season..... Dan 7:12

PROLONGETH

The fear of the LORD p days..... Prov 10:27
that p his life in his wickedness..... Eccl 7:15

PROMISE

and he shall know my breach of p..... Num 14:34
failed one word of all his good p..... 1Kin 8:56
let thy p unto David my father be..... 2Chr 1:9
should do according to this p..... Neh 5:12
that performeth not this p..... Neh 5:13
people did according to this p..... Neh 5:13
doth his p fail for evermore..... Ps 77:8
For he remembered his holy p..... Ps 105:42
I send the p of my Father upon..... Lk 24:49
but wait for the p of the Father..... Acts 1:4
Father the p of the Holy Ghost,..... Acts 2:33
For the p is unto you, and to your..... Acts 2:39
when the time of the p drew nigh..... Acts 7:17
p raised unto Israel a Saviour..... Acts 13:23
how that the p which was made..... Acts 13:32
ready, looking for a p from thee..... Acts 23:21
p made of God unto our fathers..... Acts 26:6
Unto which p our twelve tribes,..... Acts 26:7
For the p, that he should be the..... Rom 4:13
he made of none effect..... Rom 4:14
to the end the p might be sure to..... Rom 4:16
at the p of God through unbelief..... Rom 4:20
that children of the p are..... Rom 9:8
For this is the word of p..... Rom 9:9
that we might receive the p of..... Gal 3:14
should make the p of none effect..... Gal 3:17
be of the law, it is no more of p..... Gal 3:18
but God gave it to Abraham by p..... Gal 3:18
come to whom the p was made..... Gal 3:19
that the p by faith of Jesus..... Gal 3:22
seed, and heirs according to the p..... Gal 3:29
but he of the freewoman was by p..... Gal 4:23
Isaac was, are the children of p..... Gal 4:28
sealed with that holy Spirit of p..... Eph 1:13
strangers from the covenants of p..... Eph 2:12
partakers of his p in Christ by..... Eph 3:6
the first commandment with p..... Eph 6:2
having p of the life that now is,..... 1Ti 4:8
according to the p of life which..... 2Ti 1:1
a p being left us of entering..... Heb 4:1
For when God made p to Abraham..... Heb 6:13
endured, he obtained the p..... Heb 6:15
to shew unto the heirs of the p..... Heb 6:17
the p of eternal inheritance..... Heb 9:15
of God, ye might receive the p..... Heb 10:36
he sojourned in the land of p..... Heb 11:9

PRONOUNCE

the heirs with him of the same p..... Heb 11:9
through faith, received not the p..... Heb 11:39
While they p them liberty, they..... 2Pet 2:19
Where is the p of his coming..... 2Pet 3:4
is not slack concerning his p,..... 2Pet 3:9
we, according to his p, look for..... 2Pet 3:13
this is the p that he hath..... 1Jn 2:25

PROMISED

give you, according as he hath p..... Ex 12:25
the place which the LORD hath p..... Num 14:40
and bless you, as he hath p you..... Deut 1:11
God of thy fathers hath p thee..... Deut 6:3
into the land which he p thee..... Deut 9:28
as the LORD thy God p him..... Deut 10:9
thy border, as he hath p thee..... Deut 12:20
God blesseth thee, as he p thee..... Deut 15:6
he p to give unto thy fathers..... Deut 19:8
which thou hast p with thy mouth..... Deut 23:23
people, as he hath p thee..... Deut 26:18
God of thy fathers hath p thee..... Deut 27:3
as the princes had p them..... Josh 9:21
unto your brethren, as he p them..... Josh 22:4
the LORD your God hath p unto you..... Josh 23:5
for you, as he hath p you..... Josh 23:10
which the LORD your God p you,..... Josh 23:15
thou hast p this goodness unto..... 2Sa 7:28
hath made me an house, as he p..... 1Kin 2:24
gave Solomon wisdom, as he p him..... 1Kin 5:12
throne of Israel, as the LORD p..... 1Kin 8:20
according to all that he p..... 1Kin 8:56
which he p by the hand of Moses..... 1Kin 8:56
as I p to David thy father,..... 1Kin 9:5
as he p him to give him always a..... 2Kin 8:19
hast p this goodness unto thy..... 1Chr 17:26
throne of Israel, as the LORD p..... 2Chr 6:10
father that which thou hast p him..... 2Chr 6:15
father that which thou hast p him..... 2Chr 6:16
as he p to give a light to him and..... 2Chr 21:7
thou hadst p to their fathers..... Neh 9:23
to pay to the king's treasuries,..... Est 4:7
all the good that I have p them,..... Jer 32:42
I have p unto the house of Israel..... Jer 33:14
Whereupon he p with an oath to..... Mk 14:7
were glad, and p to give him money..... Mk 14:11
the mercy p to our fathers..... Lk 1:72
And he p, and sought opportunity to..... Lk 22:6
yet he p that he would give it to..... Acts 7:5
(Which he had p afore by his..... Rom 1:2
persuaded that, what he had p..... Rom 4:21
lie, p before the world began..... Titus 1:2
(for he is faithful that p..... Heb 10:23
she judged him faithful who had p..... Heb 11:11
but now he hath p, saying, Yet..... Heb 12:26
which the Lord hath p to them..... Jas 1:12
he hath p to them that love him..... Jas 2:5
is the promise that he hath p us..... 1Jn 2:25

PROMISES

and the service of God, and the p..... Rom 9:4
to confirm the p made unto the..... Rom 15:8
For all the p of God in him are..... 2Cor 1:20
therefore these p dearly beloved..... 2Cor 7:1
and his seed were the p made..... Gal 3:16
the law then against the p of God..... Gal 3:21
faith and patience inherit the p..... Heb 6:12
and blessed him that had the p..... Heb 7:6
was established upon better p..... Heb 8:6
faith, not having received the p..... Heb 11:13
he that had received the p..... Heb 11:17
wrought righteousness, obtained p..... Heb 11:33
us exceeding great and precious p..... 2Pet 1:4

PROMISING

his wicked way, by p him life..... Eze 13:22

PROMOTE

For I will p thee unto very great..... Num 22:17
able indeed to p thee to honour..... Num 22:37
I thought to p thee unto great..... Num 24:11
p Haman the son of Hammedatha the..... Est 3:1
Exalt her, and she shall p thee..... Prov 4:8

PROMOTED

go to be p over the trees..... Judg 9:9
go to be p over the trees..... Judg 9:11
go to be p over the trees..... Judg 9:12
things wherein the king had p him..... Est 5:11
Then the king p Shadrach, Meshach..... Dan 3:30

PROMOTION

p cometh neither from the..... Ps 75:6
but shame shall be the p of fools..... Prov 3:35

PRONOUNCE

that a man shall p with an oath..... Lev 5:4
look on him, and p him unclean..... Lev 13:3
the priest shall p them clean..... Lev 13:6
the priest shall p him unclean..... Lev 13:8
and the priest shall p him unclean..... Lev 13:11
he shall p him clean that hath..... Lev 13:13
raw flesh, and p him to be unclean,..... Lev 13:15
then the priest shall p him unclean..... Lev 13:17
the priest shall p him unclean..... Lev 13:20
and the priest shall p him clean..... Lev 13:23
the priest shall p him unclean..... Lev 13:25
and the priest shall p him clean..... Lev 13:28

P

the priest shall *p* him unclean............ Lev 13:30
then the priest shall *p* him clean........ Lev 13:34
and the priest shall *p* him clean......... Lev 13:37
the priest shall *p* him utterly............ Lev 13:44
to *p* it clean, or to *p* it.................. Lev 13:59
shall *p* him clean, and shall let........ Lev 14:7
priest shall *p* the house clean........... Lev 14:48
he could not frame to *p* it right......... Judg 12:6

PRONOUNCED

but that he *p* this prophecy.............. Neh 6:12
hath *p* evil against thee, for the........ Jer 11:17
Wherefore hath the LORD *p* all.......... Jer 16:10
nation, against whom I have *p*............ Jer 18:8
the evil that I have *p* against it......... Jer 19:15
words which I have *p* against it......... Jer 25:13
evil that he hath *p* against you.......... Jer 26:13
evil which he had *p* against them....... Jer 26:19
for I have *p* the word, saith the......... Jer 34:5
evil that I have *p* against this.......... Jer 36:7
LORD hath *p* against this people........ Jer 36:7
evil that I have *p* against them.......... Jer 36:18
evil that I have *p* against them.......... Jer 36:31
The LORD thy God hath *p* this evil..... Jer 40:2

PRONOUNCING

p with his lips to do evil, or to........... Lev 5:4

PROOF

that I might know the *p* of you........... 2Cor 2:9
the *p* of your love, and of our............ 2Cor 8:24
Since ye seek a *p* of Christ............... 2Cor 13:3
But ye know the *p* of him, that,......... Phil 2:22
make full *p* of thy ministry................ 2Ti 4:5

PROOFS

his passion by many infallible *p*......... Acts 1:3

PROPER

my God, I have of mine own *p* good..... 1Chr 29:3
field is called in their *p* tongue.......... Acts 1:19
every man hath his *p* gift of God........ 1Cor 7:7
because they saw he was a *p* child...... Heb 11:23

PROPHECIES

but whether there be *p*, they,............ 1Cor 13:8
according to the *p* which went........... 1Ti 1:18

PROPHECY

in the *p* of Ahijah the Shilonite,......... 2Chr 9:29
the *p* of Oded the prophet, he........... 2Chr 15:8
he pronounced this *p* against me....... Neh 6:12
Agur the son of Jakeh, even the *p*....... Prov 30:1
the *p* that his mother taught him....... Prov 31:1
and to seal up the vision and *p*.......... Dan 9:24
them is fulfilled the *p* of Esaias........ Mt 13:14
that is given to us, whether *p*............ Rom 12:6
to another *p*................................... 1Cor 12:10
And though I have the gift of *p*........... 1Cor 13:2
thee, which was given thee by *p*......... 1Ti 4:14
have also a more sure word of *p*......... 2Pet 1:19
that no *p* of the scripture is of.......... 2Pet 1:20
For the *p* came not in old time by........ 2Pet 1:21
that hear the words of this *p*............. Rev 1:3
rain not in the days of their *p*............ Rev 11:6
of Jesus is the spirit of *p*................. Rev 19:10
the sayings of the *p* of this book........ Rev 22:7
the sayings of the *p* of this book........ Rev 22:10
the words of the *p* of this book.......... Rev 22:18
the words of the book of this *p*.......... Rev 22:19

PROPHESIED

spirit rested upon them, they *p*......... Num 11:25
and they *p* in the camp.................... Num 11:26
and he *p* among them...................... Num 11:27
he *p* among the prophets, then.......... 1Sa 10:11
he *p* in the midst of the house.......... 1Sa 18:10
of Saul, and they also *p*................... 1Sa 19:20
messengers, and they *p* likewise....... 1Sa 19:21
the third time, and they *p* also.......... 1Sa 19:21
him also, and he went on, and *p*......... 1Sa 19:23
p before Samuel in like manner......... 1Sa 19:24
they *p* until the time of the.............. 1Kin 18:29
and all the prophets *p* before them.... 1Kin 22:10
And all the prophets *p* so, saying,...... 1Kin 22:12
which *p* according to the order of....... 1Chr 25:2
who *p* with a harp, to give thanks...... 1Chr 25:3
for he never *p* good unto me............. 2Chr 18:7
and all the prophets *p* before them.... 2Chr 18:9
And all the prophets *p* so, saying,...... 2Chr 18:11
of Maresha to against Jehoshaphat..... 2Chr 20:37
p unto the Jews that were in.............. Ezr 5:1
me, and the prophets *p* by Baal.......... Jer 2:8
that Jeremiah *p* these things............ Jer 20:1
friends, to whom thou hast *p* lies....... Jer 20:6
they *p* in Baal, and caused my........... Jer 23:13
not spoken to them, yet they *p*.......... Jer 23:21
which Jeremiah hath *p* against all...... Jer 25:13
Why hast thou *p* in the name of......... Jer 26:9
he hath *p* against this city,............... Jer 26:11
Micah the Morasthite *p* in the........... Jer 26:18
that *p* in the name of the LORD.......... Jer 26:20
who *p* against this city, and.............. Jer 26:20
thy words which thou hast *p*............. Jer 28:6
before thee of old *p* both against....... Jer 28:8
that Shemaiah hath *p* unto you......... Jer 29:31
your prophets which *p* unto you........ Jer 37:19
And it came to pass, when I *p*............ Eze 11:13
So I *p* as I was commanded................ Eze 37:7
and as I *p*, there was a noise, and...... Eze 37:7
So I *p* as he commanded me, and the... Eze 37:10
which *p* in those days many years...... Eze 38:17
one of his vision, when he hath *p*....... Zec 13:4
Lord, have we not *p* in thy name........ Mt 7:22

prophets and the law *p* until John...... Mt 11:13
Well hath Esaias *p* of you................. Mk 7:6
filled with the Holy Ghost, and *p*....... Lk 1:67
he *p* that Jesus should die for.......... Jn 11:51
and they spake with tongues, and *p*... Acts 19:6
tongues, but rather that ye *p*............ 1Cor 14:5
who *p* of the grace that should......... 1Pet 1:10
p of these, saying, Behold, the......... Jude 14

PROPHESIETH

The prophet which *p* of peace........... Jer 28:9
he *p* of the times that are far........... Eze 12:27
thrust him through when he *p*........... Zec 13:3
or *p* with her head uncovered........... 1Cor 11:5
But he that *p* speaketh unto men....... 1Cor 14:3
but he that *p* edifieth the church....... 1Cor 14:4
for greater is he that *p* than he......... 1Cor 14:5

PROPHESY

Eldad and Medad do *p* in the camp..... Num 11:27
and they shall *p*............................ 1Sa 10:5
thee, and thou shalt *p* with them....... 1Sa 10:6
for he doth not *p* good concerning..... 1Kin 22:8
he would *p* no good concerning me.... 1Kin 22:18
Jeduthun, who should *p* with harps.... 1Chr 25:1
that he would not *p* good unto me...... 2Chr 18:17
P not unto us right things, speak...... Is 30:10
unto us smooth things, *p* deceits...... Is 30:10
The prophets *p* falsely, and the........ Jer 5:31
P not in the name of the LORD.......... Jer 11:21
The prophets *p* lies in my name........ Jer 14:14
p unto you a false vision and........... Jer 14:14
the prophets that *p* in my name........ Jer 14:15
the people to whom they *p* shall....... Jer 14:16
the LORD had sent him to *p*.............. Jer 19:14
of the prophets that *p* unto you........ Jer 23:16
that *p* lies in my name, saying, I........ Jer 23:25
heart of the prophets that *p* lies....... Jer 23:26
against them that *p* false dreams...... Jer 23:32
Therefore *p* thou against them all..... Jer 25:30
sent me to *p* against this house........ Jer 26:12
For they *p* a lie unto you, to............. Jer 27:10
for they *p* a lie unto you................. Jer 27:14
yet they *p* a lie in my name............. Jer 27:15
and the prophets that *p* unto you....... Jer 27:15
of your prophets that *p* unto you........ Jer 27:16
for they *p* a lie unto you................. Jer 27:16
For they *p* falsely unto you in my....... Jer 29:9
which *p* a lie unto you in my name..... Jer 29:21
up, saying, Wherefore dost thou *p*..... Jer 32:3
and thou shalt *p* against it............... Eze 4:7
of Israel, and *p* against them............ Eze 6:2
p against them, O son.................... Eze 11:4
p against the prophets of Israel........ Eze 13:2
the prophets of Israel that *p*............ Eze 13:2
that *p* out of their own hearts.......... Eze 13:2
which *p* concerning Jerusalem.......... Eze 13:16
which *p* out of their own heart.......... Eze 13:17
and *p* thou against them.................. Eze 13:17
p against the forest of the south...... Eze 20:46
p against the land of Israel.............. Eze 21:2
Son of man, *p*, and say, Thus saith.... Eze 21:9
Thou therefore, son of man, *p*.......... Eze 21:14
And thou, son of man, *p* and say,....... Eze 21:28
the Ammonites, and *p* against them... Eze 25:2
against Zidon, and *p* against it.......... Eze 28:21
p against him, and against all........... Eze 29:2
Son of man, *p* and say, Thus saith..... Eze 30:2
p against the shepherds of Israel....... Eze 34:2
the shepherds of Israel, *p*............... Eze 34:2
mount Seir, and *p* against it,............ Eze 35:2
p unto the mountains of Israel.......... Eze 36:1
Therefore *p* and say, Thus saith........ Eze 36:1
P therefore concerning the land........ Eze 36:6
P upon these bones, and say............ Eze 37:4
P unto the wind, *p*, son of............. Eze 37:9
Therefore *p* and say unto them......... Eze 37:12
and Tubal, and *p* against him,........... Eze 38:2
Therefore, son of man, *p* and say...... Eze 38:14
p against Gog, and say, Thus saith..... Eze 39:1
sons and your daughters shall *p*........ Joel 2:28
the prophets, saying, *P* not.............. Amos 2:12
Gob hath spoken, who can but *p*........ Amos 3:8
and there eat bread, and *p* there....... Amos 7:12
But *p* not again any more at.............. Amos 7:13
me, Go, *p* unto my people Israel......... Amos 7:15
P not against Israel, and drop not...... Amos 7:16
P ye not, say they to them that......... Mic 2:6
ye not, say they to them that *p*......... Mic 2:6
they shall not *p* to them, that.......... Mic 2:6
I will *p* unto thee of wine and............ Mic 2:11
pass, that when any shall yet *p*......... Zec 13:3
well did Esaias *p* of you.................. Mt 15:7
P unto us, thou Christ, Who is he...... Mt 26:68
buffet him, and to say unto him, *P*..... Mk 14:65
the face, and asked him, saying, *P*..... Lk 22:64
sons and your daughters shall *p*........ Acts 2:17
and they shall *p*............................ Acts 2:18
daughters, virgins, which did *p*......... Acts 21:9
let us *p* according to the................. Rom 12:6
we know in part, and we *p* in part...... 1Cor 13:9
gifts, but rather that ye may *p*.......... 1Cor 14:1
But if all *p*, and there come in.......... 1Cor 14:24
For ye may all *p* one by one,............ 1Cor 14:31
Wherefore, brethren, covet to *p*........ 1Cor 14:39
Thou must *p* again before many......... Rev 10:11
they shall *p* a thousand two............ Rev 11:3

PROPHESYING

And when he had made an end of *p*..... 1Sa 10:13
saw the company of the prophets in..... 1Sa 19:20
the *p* of Haggai the prophet.............. Ezr 6:14

Every man praying or *p*, having.......... 1Cor 11:4
or by knowledge, or by *p*................. 1Cor 14:6
but *p* serveth not for them that........ 1Cor 14:22

PROPHESYINGS

Despise not *p*............................... 1Th 5:20

PROPHET

for he is a *p*, and he shall pray.......... Gen 20:7
Aaron thy brother shall be thy *p*........ Ex 7:1
If there be a *p* among you............... Num 12:6
If there arise among you a *p*............. Deut 13:1
hearken unto the words of that *p*....... Deut 13:3
And that *p*, or that dreamer of.......... Deut 13:5
thee a *P* from the midst of thee........ Deut 18:15
I will raise them up a *P* from........... Deut 18:18
But the *p*, which shall presume to..... Deut 18:20
other gods, even that *p* shall die....... Deut 18:20
When a *p* speaketh in the name of..... Deut 18:22
spoken, but the *p* hath spoken it...... Deut 18:22
there arose not a *p* since in............ Deut 34:10
That the LORD sent a *p* unto the........ Judg 6:8
for he that is now called a *P* was...... 1Sa 9:9
the *p* Gad said unto David, Abide...... 1Sa 22:5
the king said unto Nathan the *p*........ 2Sa 7:2
sent by the hand of Nathan the *p*...... 2Sa 12:25
of the LORD came unto the *p* Gad...... 2Sa 24:11
Son of Jehoiada, and Nathan the *p*.... 1Kin 1:8
But Nathan the *p*, and Benaiah, and... 1Kin 1:10
Nathan the *p* also came................. 1Kin 1:22
king, saying, Behold Nathan the *p*..... 1Kin 1:23
Zadok the priest, and Nathan the *p*.... 1Kin 1:32
Nathan the *p* anoint him there......... 1Kin 1:34
Zadok the priest, and Nathan the *p*.... 1Kin 1:38
Zadok the priest, and Nathan the *p*.... 1Kin 1:44
Nathan the *p* have anointed him....... 1Kin 1:45
that the *p* Ahijah the Shilonite.......... 1Kin 11:29
there dwelt an old *p* in Beth-el......... 1Kin 13:11
I am a *p* also as thou art................. 1Kin 13:18
unto the *p* that brought him back....... 1Kin 13:20
for the *p* whom he had brought......... 1Kin 13:23
in the city where the old *p* dwelt....... 1Kin 13:25
when the *p* that brought him back...... 1Kin 13:26
the *p* took up the carcase of the....... 1Kin 13:29
the old *p* came to the city, to.......... 1Kin 13:29
behold, there is Ahijah the *p*,........... 1Kin 14:2
hand of his servant Ahijah the *p*....... 1Kin 14:18
also by the hand of the *p* Ahijah....... 1Kin 16:7
against Baasha by Jehu the *p*........... 1Kin 16:12
I only, remain a *p* of the LORD.......... 1Kin 18:22
that Elijah the *p* came near............. 1Kin 18:36
thou anoint to be *p* in thy room....... 1Kin 19:16
there came a *p* unto Ahab king of...... 1Kin 20:13
the *p* came to the king of Israel........ 1Kin 20:22
So the *p* departed, and waited for..... 1Kin 20:38
not here a *p* of the LORD besides....... 1Kin 22:7
Is there not here a *p* of the LORD....... 2Kin 3:11
with the *p* that is in Samaria........... 2Kin 5:3
know that there is a *p* in Israel......... 2Kin 5:8
if the *p* had bid thee do some......... 2Kin 5:13
the *p* that is in Israel, telleth.......... 2Kin 6:12
Elisha the *p* called one of the.......... 2Kin 9:1
man, even the young man the *p*........ 2Kin 9:4
Jonah, the son of Amittai, the *p*....... 2Kin 14:25
to Isaiah the *p* the son of Amoz....... 2Kin 20:1
the *p* Isaiah the son of Amoz came... 2Kin 20:11
Isaiah the *p* cried unto the LORD....... 2Kin 20:11
Isaiah the *p* unto King Hezekiah....... 2Kin 20:14
with the bones of the *p* that came.... 2Kin 23:18
that David said to Nathan the *p*........ 1Chr 17:1
and in the book of Nathan the *p*........ 1Chr 29:29
in the book of Nathan the *p*............. 2Chr 9:29
came Shemaiah the *p* to Rehoboam... 2Chr 12:5
in the book of Shemaiah the *p*.......... 2Chr 12:15
in the story of the *p* Iddo............... 2Chr 13:22
and the prophecy of Oded the *p*........ 2Chr 15:8
not here a *p* of the LORD besides....... 2Chr 18:6
writing to him from Elijah the *p*......... 2Chr 21:12
Amaziah, and he sent unto him a *p*.... 2Chr 25:15
Then the *p* forbare, and said, I........ 2Chr 25:16
first and last, did Isaiah the *p*.......... 2Chr 26:22
But a *p* of the LORD was there,......... 2Chr 28:9
the king's seer, and Nathan the *p*...... 2Chr 29:25
the *p* Isaiah the son of Amoz,.......... 2Chr 32:20
in the vision of Isaiah the *p*............. 2Chr 32:32
from the days of Samuel the *p*.......... 2Chr 35:18
p speaking from the mouth of the..... 2Chr 36:12
Then the prophets, Haggai the *p*....... Ezr 5:1
the prophesying of Haggai the *p*....... Ezr 6:14
when Nathan the *p* came unto him..... Ps 51:1
there is no more any *p*................... Ps 74:9
man of war, the judge, and the *p*....... Is 3:2
the *p* that teacheth lies, he is........ Is 9:15
the *p* have erred through strong....... Is 28:7
unto Isaiah the *p* the son of Amoz..... Is 37:2
Isaiah the *p* the son of Amoz came... Is 37:2
Isaiah the *p* unto King Hezekiah....... Is 38:1
thee a *p* unto the nations............... Jer 1:5
from the *p* even unto the priest........ Jer 6:13
from the *p* even unto the priest........ Jer 8:10
yea, both the *p* and the priest go..... Jer 14:18
the wise, nor the word from the *p*..... Jer 18:18
Then Pashur smote Jeremiah the *p*.... Jer 20:2
For both *p* and priest are profane...... Jer 23:11
the *p* hath a dream, let him............ Jer 23:28
And when this people, or the *p*......... Jer 23:33
And as for the *p*, and the priest,....... Jer 23:34
Thus shalt thou say to the *p*............ Jer 23:37
The which Jeremiah the *p* spake....... Jer 25:2
Hananiah the son of Azur the *p*........ Jer 28:1

p Jeremiah said unto the p .... Jer 28:5
Even the p Jeremiah said, Amen .... Jer 28:6
The p which prophesieth of peace, ... Jer 28:9
word of the p shall come to pass. .... Jer 28:9
then shall the p be known .... Jer 28:9
Then Hananiah the p took the yoke .... Jer 28:10
from off the p Jeremiah's neck .... Jer 28:10
the p Jeremiah went his way .... Jer 28:11
the LORD came unto Jeremiah the p .... Jer 28:12
after that Hananiah the p had .... Jer 28:12
off the neck of the p Jeremiah .... Jer 28:12
Then said the p Jeremiah unto .... Jer 28:15
Jeremiah unto Hananiah the p .... Jer 28:15
So Hananiah the p died the same. ..... Jer 28:17
p sent from Jerusalem unto the p ..... Jer 29:1
is mad, and maketh himself a p .... Jer 29:26
which maketh himself a p to you. ..... Jer 29:27
in the ears of Jeremiah the p .... Jer 29:29
Jeremiah the p was shut up in the .... Jer 32:2
Then Jeremiah the p spake all .... Jer 34:6
that Jeremiah the p commanded him .... Jer 36:8
the scribe and Jeremiah the p .... Jer 36:26
which he spake by the p Jeremiah ..... Jer 37:2
the priest to the p Jeremiah. .... Jer 37:3
of the LORD unto the p Jeremiah. ..... Jer 37:6
and he took Jeremiah the p .... Jer 37:13
they have done to Jeremiah the p ..... Jer 38:9
Jeremiah the p out of the dungeon .... Jer 38:10
took Jeremiah the p unto him into .... Jer 38:14
And said unto Jeremiah the p .... Jer 42:2
Jeremiah the p said unto them .... Jer 42:4
son of Shaphan, and Jeremiah the p ... Jer 43:6
The word that Jeremiah the p .... Jer 45:1
the p against the Gentiles .... Jer 46:1
the LORD spake to Jeremiah the p...... Jer 46:13
the p against the Philistines .... Jer 47:1
p against Elam in the beginning ...... Jer 49:34
the Chaldeans by Jeremiah the p ...... Jer 50:1
The word which Jeremiah the p .... Jer 51:59
the p be slain in the sanctuary ...... Lam 2:20
there hath been a p among them. ...... Eze 2:5
shall they seek a vision of the p .... Eze 7:26
his face, and cometh to the p .... Eze 14:4
cometh to a p to enquire of him. ..... Eze 14:7
if the p be deceived when he hath .... Eze 14:9
I the LORD have deceived that p ...... Eze 14:9
the punishment of the p shall be. .... Eze 14:10
that a p hath been among them. .... Eze 33:33
the LORD came to Jeremiah the p ...... Dan 9:2
the p also shall fall with him. ...... Hos 4:5
the p is a fool, the spiritual .... Hos 9:7
but the p is a snare of a fowler ..... Hos 9:8
by a p the LORD brought Israel .... Hos 12:13
Egypt, and by a p was he preserved. .. Hos 12:13
and said to Amaziah, I was no p ...... Amos 7:14
even be the p of the people .... Mic 2:11
which Habakkuk the p did see. .... Hab 1:1
of Habakkuk the p upon Shigionoth. ... Hab 3:1
the p unto Zerubbabel the son of ..... Hag 1:1
word of the LORD by Haggai the p ..... Hag 1:3
God, and the words of Haggai the p ... Hag 1:12
word of the LORD by the p Haggai ..... Hag 2:1
word of the LORD by Haggai the p ..... Hag 2:10
Berechiah, the son of Iddo the p ..... Zec 1:1
Berechiah, the son of Iddo the p ..... Zec 1:7
But he shall say, I am no p .... Zec 13:5
I will send you Elijah the p .... Mal 4:5
was spoken of the Lord by the p ...... Mt 1:22
for thus it is written by the p ..... Mt 2:5
was spoken of the Lord by the p ...... Mt 2:15
which was spoken by Jeremy the p ..... Mt 2:17
was spoken of by the p Esaias. .... Mt 3:3
which was spoken by Esaias the p ..... Mt 4:14
which was spoken by Esaias the p ..... Mt 8:17
He that receiveth a p in the name. ... Mt 10:41
of a p shall receive a prophet's. .... Mt 10:41
for to see? A p? .... Mt 11:9
I say unto you, and more than a p .... Mt 11:9
which was spoken by Esaias the p ..... Mt 12:17
it, but the sign of the p Jonas. ..... Mt 12:39
which was spoken by the p Jonas ...... Mt 13:35
A p is not without honour, save ...... Mt 13:57
because they counted him as a p ...... Mt 14:5
it, but the sign of the p Jonas. ..... Mt 16:4
which was spoken by the p .... Mt 21:4
This is Jesus the p of Nazareth ...... Mt 21:11
for all hold John as a p............. Mt 21:26
because they took him for a p .... Mt 21:46
spoken of by Daniel the p .... Mt 24:15
which was spoken by Jeremy the p ..... Mt 27:35
A p is not without honour, but in .... Mk 6:4
And others said, That it is a p ...... Mk 6:15
John, that he was a p indeed. .... Mk 11:32
spoken of by Daniel the p .... Mk 13:14
he called the p of the Highest: ..... Lk 1:76
book of the words of Esaias the p .... Lk 3:4
unto him the book of the p Esaias. ... Lk 4:17
No p is accepted in his own .... Lk 4:24
in the time of Eliseus the p .... Lk 4:27
That a great p is risen up among ..... Lk 7:16
for to see? A p? .... Lk 7:26
unto you, and much more than a p ..... Lk 7:26
a greater p than John the Baptist .... Lk 7:28
saying, This man, if he were a p ..... Lk 7:39
I say unto you, and among the p ...... Lk 11:29
that a p perish out of Jerusalem. .... Lk 13:33
be persuaded that John was a p .... Lk 20:6
which was a p mighty in deed and. .... Lk 24:19
Art thou that p.................. Jn 1:21

of the Lord, as said the p Esaias .... Jn 1:23
Christ, nor Elias, neither that p .... Jn 1:25
Sir, I perceive that thou art a p .... Jn 4:19
that a p hath no honour in his....... Jn 4:44
This is of a truth that p that....... Jn 6:14
said, Of a truth this is the P....... Jn 7:40
for out of Galilee ariseth no p ...... Jn 7:52
He said, He is a p. .... Jn 9:17
Esaias the p might be fulfilled ...... Jn 12:38
which was spoken by the p Joel .... Acts 2:16
Therefore being a p, and knowing. .... Acts 2:30
A p shall the Lord your God raise .... Acts 3:22
soul, which will not hear that p ..... Acts 3:23
A p shall the Lord your God raise .... Acts 7:37
as saith the p, ... Acts 7:48
in his chariot read Esaias the p ..... Acts 8:28
and heard him read the p Esaias. ..... Acts 8:30
the, of whom speaketh the p this..... Acts 8:34
a certain sorcerer, a false p .... Acts 13:6
fifty years, until Samuel the p ...... Acts 13:20
came down from Judaea a certain p. ... Acts 21:10
by Esaias the p unto our fathers. .... Acts 28:25
any man think himself to be a p 1Cor 14:37
even a p of their own, said, The ..... Titus 1:12
voice forbad the madness of the p. ... 2Pet 2:16
out of the mouth of the false p ...... Rev 16:13
with him the false p that wrought .... Rev 19:20
the beast and the false p are........ Rev 20:10

PROPHETESS

And Miriam the p, the sister of ...... Ex 15:20
And Deborah, a p, the wife of........ Judg 4:4
Asahiah, went unto Huldah the p 2Kin 22:14
appointed, went to Huldah the p 2Chr 34:22
on the p Noadiah, and the rest of .... Neh 6:14
And I went unto the p .... Is 8:3
And there was one Anna, a p, ... Lk 2:36
which calleth herself a p .... Rev 2:20

PROPHET'S

prophet, neither was I an p son. ..... Amos 7:14
prophet shall receive a p reward..... Mt 10:41

PROPHETS

that all the LORD's people were p .... Num 11:29
thou shalt meet a company of p 1Sa 10:5
behold, a company of p met him 1Sa 10:10
behold, he prophesied among the 1Sa 10:11
Is Saul also among the p 1Sa 10:11
proverb, Is Saul also among the p 1Sa 10:12
the company of the p prophesying..... 1Sa 19:20
say, Is Saul also among the p 1Sa 19:24
by dreams, nor by Urim, nor by p 1Sa 28:6
me no more, neither by p, nor by..... 1Sa 28:15
Jezebel cut off the p of the LORD 1Kin 18:4
that Obadiah took an hundred p 1Kin 18:4
the p of the LORD by fifty in a 1Kin 18:13
the LORD's p by fifty in a cave 1Kin 18:13
the p of Baal four hundred and 1Kin 18:19
the p of the groves four hundred, ... 1Kin 18:19
gathered the p together unto 1Kin 18:20
but Baal's p are four hundred and. ... 1Kin 18:22
And Elijah said unto the p of Baal ... 1Kin 18:25
unto them, Take the p of Baal........ 1Kin 18:40
slain all the p with the sword. 1Kin 19:1
slain thy p with the sword 1Kin 19:10
slain thy p with the sword 1Kin 19:14
p said unto his neighbour in the. 1Kin 20:35
him that he was of the p 1Kin 20:41
of Israel gathered the p together, .. 1Kin 22:6
all the p prophesied before them. 1Kin 22:10
all the p prophesied so, saying, ... 1Kin 22:12
the words of the p declare good 1Kin 22:13
spirit in the mouth of all his p 1Kin 22:22
in the mouth of all these thy p 1Kin 22:23
the sons of the p that were at. 2Kin 2:3
the sons of the p that were at. 2Kin 2:5
men of the sons of the p went 2Kin 2:7
when the sons of the p which were. ... 2Kin 2:15
get thee to the p of thy father 2Kin 3:13
and to the p of thy mother 2Kin 3:13
of the sons of the p unto Elisha..... 2Kin 4:1
the sons of the p were sitting....... 2Kin 4:38
pottage for the sons of the p 2Kin 4:38
young men of the sons of the p 2Kin 5:22
the sons of the p said unto.......... 2Kin 6:1
one of the children of the p 2Kin 9:1
the blood of my servants the p 2Kin 9:7
call unto me all the p of Baal 2Kin 10:19
and against Judah, by all the p 2Kin 17:13
sent to you by my servants the p 2Kin 17:13
said by all his servants the p 2Kin 17:23
LORD spake by his servants the p 2Kin 21:10
him, and the priests, and the p 2Kin 23:2
he spake by his servants the p 2Kin 24:2
and do my p no harm 1Chr 16:22
together of four hundred men 2Chr 18:5
all the p prophesied before them. 2Chr 18:9
all the p prophesied so, saying, ... 2Chr 18:11
the words of the p declare good 2Chr 18:12
spirit in the mouth of all his p 2Chr 18:21
in the mouth of these thy p 2Chr 18:22
believe his p, so shall ye........... 2Chr 20:20
Yet he sent p to them, to bring a 2Chr 24:19
commandment of the LORD by his p 2Chr 36:16
his words, and misused his p .... Ezr 5:1
Then the p, Haggai the prophet, ... Ezr 5:2
with them were the p of God .... Ezr 5:2
commanded by thy servants the p ..... Neh 6:7
thou hast also appointed p to........ Neh 6:7
Noadiah, and the rest of the p .... Neh 6:14
slew thy p which testified. .... Neh 9:26

them by thy spirit in thy p .... Neh 9:30
and on our priests, and on our p ..... Neh 9:32
mine anointed, and do my p no harm . Ps 105:15
the p and your rulers, the seers ..... Is 29:10
and to the p, Prophesy not unto us ... Is 30:10
the p prophesied by Baal, and........ Jer 2:8
and their priests, and their p .... Jer 2:26
own sword hath devoured your p .... Jer 2:30
astonished, and the p shall wonder... Jer 4:9
the p shall become wind, and the..... Jer 5:13
The p prophesy falsely, and the ...... Jer 5:31
unto you all my servants the p .... Jer 7:25
priests, and the bones of the p ...... Jer 8:1
throne, and the priests, and the p ... Jer 13:13
the p say unto them, Ye shall not. ... Jer 14:13
The p prophesy lies in my name. ...... Jer 14:14
the p that prophesy in my name .... Jer 14:15
famine shall those p be consumed ..... Jer 14:15
me is broken because of the p .... Jer 23:9
seen folly in the p of Samaria .... Jer 23:13
I have seen also in the p of .... Jer 23:14
LORD of hosts concerning the p .... Jer 23:15
for from the p of Jerusalem is....... Jer 23:15
of the p that prophesy unto you...... Jer 23:16
I have not sent these p, yet they.... Jer 23:21
I have heard what the p said......... Jer 23:25
heart of the p that prophesy lies .... Jer 23:26
they are p of the deceit of their.... Jer 23:26
behold, I am against the p .... Jer 23:30
Behold, I am against the p .... Jer 23:31
unto you all his servants the p ...... Jer 25:4
to the words of my servants the p .... Jer 26:5
So the priests and the p and all...... Jer 26:7
people, that the priests and the p ... Jer 26:8
the p unto the princes and to all .... Jer 26:11
unto the priests and to the p........ Jer 26:16
hearken not ye to your p, nor to..... Jer 27:9
of the p that speak unto you......... Jer 27:14
the p that prophesy unto you......... Jer 27:15
of your p that prophesy unto you. .... Jer 27:16
But if they be p, and if the word .... Jer 27:18
The p that have been before me and... Jer 28:8
and to the priests, and to the p ..... Jer 29:1
Let not your p and your diviners..... Jer 29:8
hath raised us up p in Babylon .... Jer 29:15
unto them by my servants the p .... Jer 29:19
their priests, and their p .... Jer 32:32
unto you all my servants the p .... Jer 35:15
her p also find no vision from....... Jer 37:19
unto you all my servants the p .... Jer 44:4
her p also find no vision from....... Lam 2:9
Thy p have seen vain and foolish ..... Lam 2:14
For the sins of her p, and the ...... Lam 4:13
prophesy against the p of Israel ..... Eze 13:2
Woe unto the foolish p, that .... Eze 13:3
thy p are like the foxes in the ..... Eze 13:4
be upon the p that see vanity .... Eze 13:6
the p of Israel that prophesy .... Eze 13:16
of her p in the midst thereof .... Eze 22:25
her p have daubed them with .... Eze 22:28
by my servants the p of Israel ...... Eze 38:17
hearkened unto thy servants the p .... Dan 9:6
before us by his servants the p ...... Dan 9:10
have I hewed them by the p .... Hos 6:5
I have also spoken by the p .... Hos 12:10
by the ministry of the p .... Hos 12:10
And I raised up of your sons for p ... Amos 2:11
and commanded the p, saying, ... Amos 2:12
secret unto his servants the p ...... Amos 3:7
the p that make my people err .... Mic 3:5
the sun shall go down over the p ..... Mic 3:6
the p thereof divine for money ...... Mic 3:11
Her p are light and treacherous ..... Zeph 3:4
unto whom the former p have cried, .. Zec 1:4
and the p, do they live for ever ..... Zec 1:5
I commanded my servants the p .... Zec 1:6
of the LORD of hosts, and to the p ... Zec 7:3
LORD hath cried by the former p ..... Zec 7:7
in his spirit by the former p .... Zec 7:12
these words by the mouth of the p ... Zec 8:9
and also I will cause the p .... Zec 13:2
that the p shall be ashamed every .... Zec 13:4
which was spoken by the p .... Mt 2:23
they the p which were before you. .... Mt 5:12
come to destroy the law, or the ..... Mt 5:17
for this is the law and the p .... Mt 7:12
Beware of false p, which come to ..... Mt 7:15
For all the p and the law .... Mt 11:13
I say unto you, That many p .... Mt 13:17
others, Jeremias, or one of the p .... Mt 16:14
hang all the law and the p .... Mt 22:40
ye build the tombs of the p .... Mt 23:29
with them in the blood of the p ..... Mt 23:30
of them which killed the p .... Mt 23:31
behold, I send unto you p .... Mt 23:34
thou that killest the p, and........ Mt 23:37
And many false p shall rise .... Mt 24:11
arise false Christs, and false p ..... Mt 24:24
of the p might be fulfilled .... Mt 26:56
As it is written in the p .... Mk 1:2
is a prophet, or as one of the p .... Mk 6:15
and others, One of the p .... Mk 8:28
false p shall rise, and shall shew ... Mk 13:22
spake by the mouth of his holy p ..... Lk 1:70
did their fathers unto the p .... Lk 6:23
did their fathers to the false p..... Lk 6:26
one of the old p was risen again..... Lk 9:8
one of the old p is risen again. .... Lk 9:19
For I tell you, that many p .... Lk 10:24
ye build the sepulchres of the p .... Lk 11:47

wisdom of God, I will send them p....... Lk 11:49
That the blood of all the p............... Lk 11:50
and Isaac, and Jacob, and all the p... Lk 13:28
Jerusalem, which killest the p........... Lk 13:34
The law and the p were until John..... Lk 16:16
which have Moses and the p............. Lk 16:29
If they hear not Moses and the p...... Lk 16:31
things that are written by the p........ Lk 18:31
all that the p have spoken.............. Lk 24:25
beginning at Moses and all the p...... Lk 24:27
in the law of Moses, and in the p...... Lk 24:44
whom Moses in the law, and the p.... Jn 1:45
It is written in the p, And they......... Jn 6:45
Abraham is dead, and the p............. Jn 8:52
and the p are dead.......................... Jn 8:53
shewed by the mouth of all his p...... Acts 3:18
his holy p since the world began...... Acts 3:21
all the p from Samuel and those...... Acts 3:24
Ye are the children of the p............. Acts 3:25
is written in the book of the p.......... Acts 7:42
Which of the p have not your........... Acts 7:52
To him give all the p witness........... Acts 10:43
in these days came p from.............. Acts 11:27
that was at Antioch certain p.......... Acts 13:1
the p the rulers of the synagogue.... Acts 13:15
nor yet the voices of the p which..... Acts 13:27
you, which is spoken of in the p...... Acts 13:40
to this agree the words of the p...... Acts 15:15
being p also themselves, exhorted... Acts 15:32
written in the law and in the p........ Acts 24:14
things than those which the p.......... Acts 26:22
Agrippa, believest thou the p........... Acts 26:27
the law of Moses, and out of the p... Acts 28:23
by his p in the holy scriptures........ Rom 1:2
witnessed by the law and the p....... Rom 3:21
Lord, they have killed thy p............. Rom 11:3
and by the scriptures of the p......... Rom 16:26
first apostles, secondarily p............ 1Cor 12:28
are all p?..................................... 1Cor 12:29
Let the p speak two or three, and.... 1Cor 14:29
the p are subject to the p................ 1Cor 14:32
foundation of the apostles and p..... Eph 2:20
holy apostles and p by the Spirit..... Eph 3:5
and some, p.................................. Eph 4:11
the Lord Jesus, and their own p....... 1Th 2:15
past unto the fathers by the p.......... Heb 1:1
also, and Samuel, and of the p, who. Heb 11:32
Take, my brethren, the p, who......... Jas 5:10
salvation the p have enquired.......... 1Pet 1:10
But there were false p also among... 2Pet 2:1
were spoken before by the holy p.... 2Pet 3:2
because many false p are gone out... 1Jn 4:1
declared to his servants the p.......... Rev 10:7
because these two p tormented....... Rev 11:10
reward unto thy servants the p........ Rev 11:18
shed the blood of saints and p........ Rev 16:6
heaven, and ye holy apostles and p. Rev 18:20
in her was found the blood of p....... Rev 18:24
the Lord God of the holy p sent...... Rev 22:6
and of thy brethren the p................ Rev 22:9

PROPITIATION
be a p through faith in his blood...... Rom 3:25
And he is the p for our sins............. 1Jn 2:2
his Son to be the p for our sins....... 1Jn 4:10

PROPORTION
according to the p of every one....... 1Kin 7:36
nor his power, nor his comely p....... Job 41:12
according to the p of faith............... Rom 12:6

PROSELYTE
compass sea and land to make one p.. Mt 23:15
and Nicolas a p of Antioch.............. Acts 6:5

PROSELYTES
and strangers of Rome, Jews and p.. Acts 2:10
religious p followed Paul and.......... Acts 13:43

PROSPECT
their p was toward the south........... Eze 40:44
having the p toward the north......... Eze 40:44
whose p is toward the south, is...... Eze 40:45
the chamber whose p is toward the.. Eze 40:46
gate whose p is toward the east...... Eze 42:15
gate whose p is toward the east...... Eze 43:4

PROSPER
his angel with thee, and p thy way... Gen 24:40
if now thou do p my way which I..... Gen 24:42
all that he did to p in his hand........ Gen 39:3
he did, the Lord made it to p........... Gen 39:23
but it shall not p........................... Num 14:41
and thou shalt not p in thy ways..... Deut 28:29
that ye may p in all that ye do........ Deut 29:9
that thou mayest p whithersoever.... Josh 1:7
that thou mayest p in all that........ 1Kin 2:3
Go up to Ramoth-gilead, and p....... 1Kin 22:12
And he answered him, Go, and p..... 1Kin 22:15
p thou, and build the house of the... 1Chr 22:11
Then shalt thou p, if thou takest..... 1Chr 22:13
for ye shall not p............................ 2Chr 13:12
Go up to Ramoth-gilead, and p....... 2Chr 18:11
And he said, Go ye up, and p.......... 2Chr 18:14
his prophets, so shall ye p............. 2Chr 20:20
of the Lord, that ye cannot p.......... 2Chr 24:20
the Lord, God made him to p.......... 2Chr 26:5
and p, I pray thee, thy servant....... Neh 1:11
The God of heaven, he will p us...... Neh 2:20
The tabernacles of robbers p.......... Job 12:6
and whatsoever he doeth shall p..... Ps 1:3
the ungodly, who p in the world...... Ps 73:12
they shall p that love thee.............. Ps 122:6

coverth his sins shall not p............. Prov 28:13
thou knowest not whether shall p... Eccl 11:6
of the Lord shall p in his hand........ Is 53:10
is formed against thee shall p.......... Is 54:17
it shall p in the thing whereto I...... Is 55:11
and thou shalt not p in them.......... Jer 2:37
of the fatherless, yet they p............ Jer 5:28
therefore they shall not p................ Jer 10:21
doth the way of the wicked p.......... Jer 12:1
for they shall not p........................ Jer 20:11
man that shall not p in his days..... Jer 22:30
for no man of his seed shall p......... Jer 22:30
and a King shall reign and p........... Jer 23:5
the Chaldeans, ye shall not p......... Jer 32:5
are the chief, her enemies p............ Lam 1:5
thou didst p into a kingdom........... Eze 16:13
Shall it p?................................... Eze 17:9
behold, being planted, shall it p...... Eze 17:10
Shall he p?................................... Eze 17:15
destroy wonderfully, and shall p..... Dan 8:24
cause craft to p in his hand............ Dan 8:25
but it shall not p........................... Dan 11:27
shall p till the indignation be.......... Dan 11:36
all things that thou mayest p........... 3Jn 2

PROSPERED
seeing the Lord hath p my way....... Gen 24:56
hand of the children of Israel p...... Judg 4:24
the people did, and how the war p... 2Sa 11:7
he p whithersoever he went forth.... 2Kin 18:7
instead of David his father, and p... 1Chr 29:23
So they built and p....................... 2Chr 14:7
did it with all his heart, and p....... 2Chr 31:21
Hezekiah p in all his works............ 2Chr 32:30
they p through the prophesying of... Ezr 6:14
himself against him, and hath p...... Job 9:4
So this Daniel p in the reign of...... Dan 6:28
and it practised, and p.................. Dan 8:12
him in store, as God hath p............ 1Cor 16:2

PROSPERITY
fast on, and p in their hands.......... Ezr 5:8
because of him who p in his way.... Ps 37:7
whithersoever it turneth, it p......... Prov 17:8
be in health, even as thy soul p...... 3Jn 2

PROSPEROUS
nor their p all thy days for ever...... Deut 23:6
ye say to him that liveth in p......... 1Sa 25:6
p exceedeth the fame which I........ 1Kin 10:7
in p the destroyer shall come......... Job 15:21
they shall spend their days in p...... Job 36:11
in my p I said, I shall never be...... Ps 30:6
pleasure in the p of his servant..... Ps 35:27
when I saw the p of the wicked..... Ps 73:3
Lord, I beseech thee, send now p... Ps 118:25
walls, and p within thy palaces..... Ps 122:7
the p of fools shall destroy them... Prov 1:32
In the day of p be joyful............... Eccl 7:14
I spake unto thee in thy p............. Jer 22:21
for all the p that I procure unto..... Jer 33:9
I forgat p................................... Lam 3:17
My cities through p shall yet be.... Zec 1:17
Jerusalem was inhabited and in p... Zec 7:7

PROSPEROUS
had made his journey p or not....... Gen 24:21
with Joseph, and he was a man...... Gen 39:2
then thou shalt make thy way p...... Josh 1:8
our way which we go shall be p...... Judg 18:5
habitation of thy righteousness p.... Job 8:6
him, and he shall make his way p... Is 48:15
that we length I might have a p...... Rom 1:10

PROSPEROUSLY
in his own house, he p effected...... 2Chr 7:11
majesty ride p because of truth....... Ps 45:4

PROSTITUTE
Do not p thy daughter, to cause..... Lev 19:29

PROTECTION
rise up and help you, and be your p. Deut 32:38

PROTEST
The man did solemnly p unto us..... Gen 43:3
howbeit yet p solemnly unto them... 1Sa 8:9
I p by your rejoicing which I.......... 1Cor 15:31

PROTESTED
p unto thee, saying, Know for a...... 1Kin 2:42
For I earnestly p unto your............ Jer 11:7
angel of the Lord p unto Joshua.... Zec 3:6

PROTESTING
unto this day, rising early and p...... Jer 11:7

PROUD
the p helpers do stoop under him... Job 9:13
he smiteth through the p................ Job 26:12
here shall thy p waves be stayed.... Job 38:11
and behold every one that is p....... Job 40:11
Look on every one that is p............ Job 40:12
the tongue that speaketh p things.. Ps 12:3
plentifully rewardeth the p doer..... Ps 31:23
trust, and respecteth not the p...... Ps 40:4
the p are risen against me, and..... Ps 86:14
render a reward to the p............... Ps 94:2
a p heart will not I suffer.............. Ps 101:5
rebuked the p that are cursed....... Ps 119:21
The p have had me greatly in........ Ps 119:51
The p have forged a lie against..... Ps 119:69
Let the p be ashamed................... Ps 119:78
The p have digged pits for me,...... Ps 119:85

let not the p oppress me................. Ps 119:122
and with the contempt of the p....... Ps 123:4
Then the p waters had gone over.... Ps 124:5
but the p he knoweth afar off........ Ps 138:6
The p have hid a snare for me, and. Ps 140:5
A p look, a lying tongue, and......... Prov 6:17
will destroy the house of the p....... Prov 15:25
Every one that is p in heart is........ Prov 16:5
to divide the spoil with the p.......... Prov 16:19
a p heart, and the plowing of the... Prov 21:4
P and haughty scorner is his name.. Prov 21:24
who dealeth in p wrath................. Prov 21:24
He that is of a p heart stirreth........ Prov 28:25
is better than the p in spirit........... Eccl 7:8
shall be upon every one that is p..... Is 2:12
the arrogancy of the p to cease...... Is 13:11
he is very p................................. Is 16:6
be not p...................................... Jer 13:15
son of Kareah, and all the p men.... Jer 43:2
(he is exceeding p) his loftiness..... Jer 48:29
she hath been p against the Lord.... Jer 50:29
I am against thee, O thou most p.... Jer 50:31
the most p shall stumble and fall,... Jer 50:32
by wine, he is a p man, neither...... Hab 2:5
And now we call the p happy.......... Mal 3:15
and all the p, yea, and all that do... Mal 4:1
he hath scattered the p in the........ Lk 1:51
haters of God, despiteful, p............ Rom 1:30
He is p, knowing nothing, but........ 1Ti 6:4
own selves, covetous, boasters, p... 2Ti 3:2
he saith, God resisteth the p.......... Jas 4:6
for God resisteth the p................... 1Pet 5:5

PROUDLY
they dealt p he was above them..... Ex 18:11
Talk no more so exceeding p.......... 1Sa 2:3
that they dealt p against them........ Neh 9:10
But they and our fathers dealt p..... Neh 9:16
yet they dealt p, and hearkened..... Neh 9:29
with their mouth they speak p........ Ps 17:10
which speak grievous things p........ Ps 31:18
himself p against the ancient.......... Is 3:5
spoken p in the day of distress....... Obad 12

PROVE
rate every day, that I may p them... Ex 16:4
for God is come to p you, and that.. Ex 20:20
to p thee, to know what was in....... Deut 8:2
thee, and that he might p thee........ Deut 8:16
one, whom thou didst p at Massah... Deut 33:8
That through them I may p Israel.... Judg 2:22
to p Israel by them, even as many.. Judg 3:1
they were to p Israel by them, to.... Judg 3:4
let me p, I pray thee, but this........ Judg 6:39
she came to p him with hard........... 1Kin 10:1
she came to p Solomon with hard... 2Chr 9:1
it shall also p me perverse............. Job 9:20
Examine me, O Lord, and p me....... Ps 26:2
I will p thee with mirth.................. Eccl 2:1
P thy servants, I beseech thee,....... Dan 1:12
the now herewith, saith the Lord.... Mal 3:10
yoke of oxen, and I go to p them.... Lk 14:19
And this he said to p him............... Jn 6:6
Neither can they p the things......... Acts 24:13
that which they could not p............ Acts 25:7
that ye may p what is that good,..... Rom 12:2
to p the sincerity of your love........ 2Cor 8:8
p your own selves......................... 2Cor 13:5
But let every man p his own work... Gal 6:4
P all things.................................. 1Th 5:21

PROVED
Hereby ye shall be p..................... Gen 42:15
prison, that your words may be p... Gen 42:16
an ordinance, and there he p them.. Ex 15:25
for he had not p it........................ 1Sa 17:39
for I have not p them.................... 1Sa 17:39
Thou hast p mine heart................. Ps 17:3
For thou, O God, hast p us............ Ps 66:10
I p thee at the waters of Meribah... Ps 81:7
tempted me, p me, and saw my work. Ps 95:9
All this have I p by wisdom............ Eccl 7:23
this matter, and p them ten days.... Dan 1:14
for we have before p both Jews...... Rom 3:9
p diligent in many things............... 2Cor 8:22
And let these also first be p........... 1Ti 3:10
p me, and saw my works forty years. Heb 3:9

PROVENDER
p enough, and room to lodge in...... Gen 24:25
p for the camels, and water to........ Gen 24:32
sack to give his ass p in the inn...... Gen 42:27
and he gave their asses p............... Gen 43:24
is both straw and p for our asses.... Judg 19:19
house, and gave p unto the asses... Judg 19:21
ear the ground shall eat clean p...... Is 30:24

PROVERB
shalt become an astonishment, a p.. Deut 28:37
Therefore it became a p, Is Saul.... 1Sa 10:12
As saith the p of the ancients........ 1Sa 24:13
and Israel shall be a p and a.......... 1Kin 9:7
sight, and will make it to be a p..... 2Chr 7:20
and I became a p to them.............. Ps 69:11
To understand a p, and the............ Prov 1:6
against the king of Babylon............ Is 14:4
hurt, to be a reproach and a p....... Jer 24:9
what is that p that ye have in......... Eze 12:22
I will make this p to cease............. Eze 12:23
no more use it as a p in Israel....... Eze 12:23
and will make him a sign and a p.... Eze 14:8
shall use this p against thee.......... Eze 16:44
that ye use this p concerning the... Eze 18:2

PROVERBS (continued, col 1)

any more to use this *p* in Israel............ Eze 18:3
a taunting *p* against him, and say............ Hab 2:6
Ye will surely say unto me this *p*............ Lk 4:23
thou plainly, and speakest no *p*............ Jn 16:29
unto them according to the true *p*............ 2Pet 2:22

PROVERBS
they that speak in *p* say, Come............ Num 21:27
And he spake three thousand *p*............ 1Kin 4:32
The *P* of Solomon the son of David............ Prov 1:1
The *p* of Solomon............ Prov 10:1
These are also *p* of Solomon............ Prov 25:1
out, and set in order many *p*............ Eccl 12:9
every one that useth *p* shall use............ Eze 16:44
have I spoken unto you in *p*............ Jn 16:25
shall no more speak unto you in *p*............ Jn 16:25

PROVETH
for the LORD your God *p* you............ Deut 13:3

PROVIDE
God will *p* himself a lamb for a............ Gen 22:8
now when shall I *p* for mine own............ Gen 30:30
Moreover thou shalt *p* out of all............ Ex 18:21
P me now a man that can play well............ 1Sa 16:17
when David my father did *p*............ 2Chr 2:7
can he *p* flesh for his people............ Ps 78:20
P neither gold, nor silver, nor............ Mt 10:9
to yourselves bags which wax not............ Lk 12:33
p them beasts, that they may set............ Acts 23:24
P things honest in the sight of............ Rom 12:17
But if any *p* not for his own, and............ 1Ti 5:8

PROVIDED
he *p* the first part for himself,............ Deut 33:21
for I have *p* me a king among his............ 1Sa 16:1
he had *p* the king of sustenance............ 2Sa 19:32
which *p* victuals for the king and............ 1Kin 4:7
those officers *p* victual for king............ 1Kin 4:27
Moreover he *p* him cities, and............ 2Chr 32:29
corn, when thou hast so *p* for it............ Ps 65:9
things be, which thou hast *p*............ Lk 12:20
God having *p* some better thing............ Heb 11:40

PROVIDENCE
done unto this nation by thy............ Acts 24:2

PROVIDETH
Who *p* for the raven his food............ Job 38:41
P her meat in the summer, and............ Prov 6:8

PROVIDING
P for honest things, not only in............ 2Cor 8:21

PROVINCE
of the *p* that went up out of the............ Ezr 2:1
that we went into the *p* of Judea............ Ezr 5:8
that is in the *p* of the Medes............ Ezr 6:2
find in all the *p* of Babylon............ Ezr 7:16
in the *p* are in great affliction............ Neh 1:3
These are the children of the *p*............ Neh 7:6
of the *p* that dwelt in Jerusalem............ Neh 11:3
into every *p* according to the............ Est 3:12
governors that were over every *p*............ Est 3:12
every *p* according to the writing............ Est 3:12
to be given in every *p* was............ Est 3:14
And in every *p*, whithersoever the............ Est 4:3
unto every *p* according to the............ Est 8:9
p that would assault them, both............ Est 8:11
to be given in every *p* was............ Est 8:13
And in every *p*, and in every city............ Est 8:17
generation, every family, every *p*............ Est 9:28
of judgment and justice in a *p*............ Eccl 5:8
ruler over the whole *p* of Babylon............ Dan 2:48
the affairs of the *p* of Babylon............ Dan 2:49
of Dura, in the *p* of Babylon............ Dan 3:1
the affairs of the *p* of Babylon............ Dan 3:12
and Abed-nego, in the *p* of Babylon............ Dan 3:30
palace, which is in the *p* of Elam............ Dan 8:2
upon the fattest places of the *p*............ Dan 11:24
letter, he asked of what *p* he was............ Acts 23:34
when Festus was come into the *p*............ Acts 25:1

PROVINCES
young men of the princes of the *p*............ 1Kin 20:14
young men of the princes of the *p*............ 1Kin 20:15
princes of the *p* went out first............ 1Kin 20:17
of the *p* came out of the city............ 1Kin 20:19
city, and hurtful unto kings and *p*............ Ezr 4:15
an hundred and seven and twenty *p*............ Est 1:1
the nobles and princes of his *p*............ Est 1:3
all the *p* of the king Ahasuerus............ Est 1:16
letters into all the king's *p*............ Est 1:22
in all the *p* of his kingdom............ Est 2:3
and he made a release to the *p*............ Est 2:18
in all the *p* of thy kingdom............ Est 3:8
by posts into all the king's *p*............ Est 3:13
and the people of the king's *p*............ Est 4:11
which are in all the king's *p*............ Est 8:5
rulers of the *p* which are from............ Est 8:9
an hundred twenty and seven *p*............ Est 9:30
in all the *p* of king Ahasuerus............ Est 9:2
all the *p* of the king Ahasuerus............ Est 9:2
And all the rulers of the *p*............ Est 9:3
went out throughout all the *p*............ Est 9:4
done in the rest of the king's *p*............ Est 9:12
p gathered themselves together............ Est 9:16
all the *p* of the king Ahasuerus............ Est 9:16
seven *p* of the kingdom of............ Est 9:30
treasure of kings and of the *p*............ Eccl 2:8
nations, and princess among the *p*............ Lam 1:1
him on every side from the *p*............ Eze 19:8
and all the rulers of the *p*............ Dan 3:2
and all the rulers of the *p*............ Dan 3:3

PROVING (col 2)
p that this is very Christ............ Acts 9:22
P what is acceptable unto the............ Eph 5:10

PROVISION
and to give them *p* for the way............ Gen 42:25
and gave them *p* for the way............ Gen 45:21
all the bread of their *p* was dry............ Josh 9:5
our bread we took hot for our *p*............ Josh 9:12
man his month in a year made *p*............ 1Kin 4:7
Solomon's *p* for one day was............ 1Kin 4:22
And he prepared great *p* for them............ 2Kin 6:23
for the which I have made *p*............ 1Chr 29:19
I will abundantly bless her *p*............ Ps 132:15
them a daily *p* of the king's meat............ Dan 1:5
make not *p* for the flesh, to............ Rom 13:14

PROVOCATION
by his *p* wherewith he provoked............ 1Kin 15:30
for the *p* wherewith thou hast............ 1Kin 21:22
not mine eye continue in their *p*............ Job 17:2
not your heart, as in the *p*............ Ps 95:8
been to me as a *p* of mine anger............ Jer 32:31
presented me of their offering............ Eze 20:28
not your hearts, as in the *p*............ Heb 3:8
not your hearts, as in the *p*............ Heb 3:15

PROVOCATIONS
because of all the *p* that............ 2Kin 23:26
of Egypt, and had wrought great *p*............ Neh 9:18
to thee, and they wrought great *p*............ Neh 9:26

PROVOKE
him, and obey his voice, *p* him not............ Ex 23:21
How long wilt this people *p* me............ Num 14:11
LORD thy God, to *p* him to anger............ Deut 4:25
of the LORD, to *p* him to anger............ Deut 9:18
p me, and break my covenant............ Deut 31:20
to *p* him to anger through the............ Deut 31:29
I will *p* them to anger with a............ Deut 32:21
to *p* me to anger, and hast caused me............ 1Kin 14:9
to *p* me to anger with their sins............ 1Kin 16:2
to *p* the LORD God of Israel to............ 1Kin 16:26
Ahab did more to *p* the LORD God............ 1Kin 16:33
things to *p* the LORD to anger............ 1Kin 17:11
of the LORD, to *p* him to anger............ 2Kin 17:17
of the LORD, to *p* him to anger............ 2Kin 21:6
that they might *p* me to anger............ 2Kin 22:17
had made to *p* the LORD to anger............ 2Kin 23:19
of the LORD, to *p* him to anger............ 2Chr 33:6
that they might *p* me to anger............ 2Chr 34:25
that *p* God are secure............ Job 12:6
How oft did they *p* him in the............ Ps 78:40
to *p* the eyes of his glory............ Is 3:8
gods, that they may *p* me to anger............ Jer 7:18
Do they *p* me to anger............ Jer 7:19
do they not *p* themselves to the............ Jer 7:19
p me to anger in offering incense............ Jer 11:17
p me not to anger with the works............ Jer 25:6
that ye might *p* me to anger............ Jer 25:7
unto other gods, to *p* me to anger............ Jer 32:29
they have done to *p* me to anger............ Jer 32:32
have committed to *p* me to anger............ Jer 44:3
In that ye *p* me unto wrath with............ Jer 44:8
and have returned to *p* me to anger............ Eze 8:17
thy whoredoms, to *p* me to anger............ Eze 16:26
to *p* him to speak of many things............ Lk 11:53
I will *p* you to jealousy by them............ Rom 10:19
for to *p* them to jealousy............ Rom 11:11
If by any means I may *p* to............ Rom 11:14
Do we *p* the Lord to jealousy............ 1Cor 10:22
p not your children to wrath............ Eph 6:4
p not your children to anger,............ Col 3:21
some, when they had heard, did *p*............ Heb 3:16
one another to *p* unto love............ Heb 10:24

PROVOKED
any of them that *p* me see it............ Num 14:23
that these men have *p* the LORD............ Num 16:30
Also in Horeb ye *p* the LORD to............ Deut 9:8
ye *p* the LORD to wrath............ Deut 9:22
They *p* him to jealousy with............ Deut 32:16
abominations *p* they him to anger............ Deut 32:16
they have *p* me to anger with............ Deut 32:21
unto them, and *p* the LORD to anger............ Judg 2:12
And her adversary also *p* her sore............ 1Sa 1:6
house of the LORD, so she *p* her............ 1Sa 1:7
p the LORD to jealousy with their............ 1Kin 14:22
the LORD God of Israel to anger............ 1Kin 15:30
wherewith thou hast *p* me to anger............ 1Kin 21:22
to *p* the LORD God of Israel............ 2Kin 21:53
have *p* me to anger, since the day............ 2Kin 21:15
that Manasseh had *p* him withal............ 2Kin 23:26
and *p* David to number Israel............ 1Chr 21:1
to *p* anger the LORD God of Israel............ 2Chr 28:25
the God of heaven unto anger............ Ezr 5:12
for they have *p* thee to anger............ Neh 4:5
p the most high God, and kept not............ Ps 78:56
For they *p* him to anger with............ Ps 78:58
but *p* him at the sea, even at the............ Ps 106:7
Thus they *p* him to anger with............ Ps 106:29
Because they *p* his spirit............ Ps 106:33
but they *p* him with their counsel............ Ps 106:43
they have *p* the Holy One of............ Is 1:4
Why have they *p* me to anger with............ Jer 8:19
me to anger with the work of............ Jer 25:6
Ephraim *p* him to anger most............ Hos 12:14
when your fathers *p* me to wrath............ Zec 8:14
not her own, is not easily *p*............ 1Cor 13:5
and your zeal hath *p* very many............ 2Cor 9:2

PROVOKEDST (col 3)
how thou *p* the LORD thy God to............ Deut 9:7

PROVOKETH
whoso *p* him to anger sinneth............ Prov 20:2
that *p* me to anger............ Is 65:3
of jealousy, which *p* to jealousy............ Eze 8:3

PROVOKING
because of the *p* of his sons............ Deut 32:19
their groves, to *p* the LORD to anger............ 1Kin 14:15
in *p* him to anger with the work............ 1Kin 16:7
to *p* the LORD God of Israel to............ 1Kin 16:33
sinned yet more against him by *p*............ Ps 78:17
p one another, envying one............ Gal 5:26

PRUDENCE
king a wise son, endued with *p*............ 2Chr 2:12
I wisdom dwell with *p*, and find............ Prov 8:12
toward us in all wisdom and *p*............ Eph 1:8

PRUDENT
p in matters, and a comely person,............ 1Sa 16:18
but a *p* man covereth shame............ Prov 12:16
A *p* man concealeth knowledge............ Prov 12:23
Every *p* man dealeth with............ Prov 13:16
The wisdom of the *p* is to............ Prov 14:8
but the *p* man looketh well to his............ Prov 14:15
but the *p* are crowned with............ Prov 14:18
he that regardeth reproof is *p*............ Prov 15:5
wise in heart shall be called *p*............ Prov 16:21
The heart of the *p* getteth............ Prov 18:15
a *p* wife is from the LORD............ Prov 19:14
A *p* man foreseeth the evil, and............ Prov 22:3
A *p* man foreseeth the evil, and............ Prov 27:12
judge, and the prophet, and the............ Is 3:2
on eyes, and *p* in their own sight............ Is 5:21
for I am *p*............ Is 10:13
of their *p* men shall be hid............ Is 29:14
is counsel perished from the *p*............ Jer 49:7
p, and he shall know them............ Hos 14:9
Therefore the *p* shall keep............ Amos 5:13
these things from the wise and *p*............ Mt 11:25
these things from the wise and *p*............ Lk 10:21
country, Sergius Paulus, a man............ Acts 13:7
the understanding of the *p*............ 1Cor 1:19

PRUDENTLY
Behold, my servant shall deal *p*............ Is 52:13

PRUNE
years thou shalt *p* thy vineyard,............ Lev 25:3
sow thy field, nor *p* thy vineyard............ Lev 25:4

PRUNED
it shall not be *p*, nor digged............ Is 5:6

PRUNINGHOOKS
and their spears into *p*............ Is 2:4
both cut off the sprigs with *p*............ Is 18:5
swords, and your *p* into spears............ Joel 3:10
and their spears into *p*............ Mic 4:3

PSALM
day David delivered first this *p*............ 1Chr 16:7
A *P* of David, when he fled from............ Ps 3:1
on Neginoth, A *P* of David............ Ps 4:1
upon Nehiloth, A *P* of David............ Ps 5:1
upon Sheminith, A *P* of David............ Ps 6:1
upon Gittith, A *P* of David............ Ps 8:1
upon Muth-labben, A *P* of David............ Ps 9:1
the chief Musician, A *P* of David............ Ps 11:1
upon Sheminith, A *P* of David............ Ps 12:1
the chief Musician, A *P* of David............ Ps 13:1
the chief Musician, A *P* of David............ Ps 14:1
A *P* of David............ Ps 15:1
A *P* of David, the servant of the............ Ps 18:1
the chief Musician, A *P* of David............ Ps 19:1
the chief Musician, A *P* of David............ Ps 20:1
the chief Musician, A *P* of David............ Ps 21:1
Aijeleth Shahar, A *P* of David............ Ps 22:1
A *P* of David............ Ps 23:1
A *P* of David............ Ps 24:1
A *P* of David............ Ps 25:1
A *P* of David............ Ps 26:1
A *P* of David............ Ps 27:1
A *P* of David............ Ps 28:1
A *P* of David............ Ps 29:1
A *P* and Song at the dedication of............ Ps 30:1
the chief Musician, A *P* of David............ Ps 31:1
A *P* of David, A Maschil............ Ps 32:1
A *P* of David, when he changed his............ Ps 34:1
the chief Musician, A *P* of David............ Ps 35:1
the chief Musician, A *P* of David............ Ps 36:1
A *P* of David............ Ps 37:1
A *P* of David, to bring to............ Ps 38:1
even to Jeduthun, A *P* of David............ Ps 39:1
the chief Musician, A *P* of David............ Ps 40:1
the chief Musician, A *P* of David............ Ps 41:1
A *P* for the sons of Korah............ Ps 47:1
A Song and *P* for the sons of Korah............ Ps 48:1
A *P* for the sons of Korah............ Ps 49:1
A *P* of Asaph............ Ps 50:1
A *P* of David, when Nathan the............ Ps 51:1
A *P* of David, when Doeg the............ Ps 52:1
Mahalath, Maschil, A *P* of David............ Ps 53:1
A *P* of David, when the Ziphims............ Ps 54:1
Neginoth, Maschil, A *P* of David............ Ps 55:1
upon Neginah, A *P* of David............ Ps 61:1
to Jeduthun, A *P* of David............ Ps 62:1
A *P* of David, when he was in the............ Ps 63:1
the chief Musician, A *P* of David............ Ps 64:1
To the chief Musician, A *P*............ Ps 65:1
the chief Musician, A Song or *P*............ Ps 66:1

PSALMIST

Musician on Neginoth, A P or Song ...... Ps 67:t
Musician, A P or Song of David .... Ps 68:t
upon Shoshannim, A P of David .... Ps 69:t
A P of David, to bring to. .... Ps 70:t
A P for Solomon .... Ps 72:t
A P of David .... Ps 73:t
Altaschith, A P or Song of Asaph .... Ps 75:t
on Neginoth, A P or Song of Asaph ...... Ps 76:t
to Jeduthun, A P of Asaph .... Ps 77:t
A P of Asaph .... Ps 79:t
Shoshannim-Eduth, A P of Asaph. .... Ps 80:t
upon Gittith, A P of Asaph .... Ps 81:t
Take a p, and bring hither the .... Ps 81:2
A P of Asaph .... Ps 82:t
A Song or P of Asaph .... Ps 83:t
A P for the sons of Korah .... Ps 84:t
A P for the sons of Korah .... Ps 85:t
A P or Song for the sons of Korah .... Ps 87:t
A Song or P for the sons of Korah .... Ps 88:t
A P or Song for the sabbath day .... Ps 92:t
A P .... Ps 98:t
the harp, and the voice of a p .... Ps 98:5
A P of praise .... Ps 100:t
A P of David .... Ps 101:t
A P of David .... Ps 103:t
A P of David .... Ps 108:t
the chief Musician, A P of David .... Ps 109:t
A P of David .... Ps 110:t
A P of David .... Ps 138:t
the chief Musician, A P of David .... Ps 139:t
A P of David .... Ps 140:t
A P of David .... Ps 141:t
A P of David .... Ps 143:t
A P of David .... Ps 144:t
David's P of praise .... Ps 145:t
is also written in the second p .... Acts 13:33
he saith also in another p .... Acts 13:35
every one of you hath a p. 1Cor 14:26

PSALMIST

Jacob, and the sweet p of Israel 2Sa 23:1

PSALMS

sing p unto him, talk ye of all. 1Chr 16:9
a joyful noise unto him with p .... Ps 95:2
Sing unto him, sing p unto him .... Ps 105:2
himself saith in the book of P .... Lk 20:42
and in the prophets, and in the P .... Lk 24:44
it is written in the book of P .... Acts 1:20
Speaking to yourselves in p .... Eph 5:19
and admonishing one another in p .... Col 3:16
let him sing p .... Jas 5:13

PSALTERIES

fir wood, even on harps, and on p........ 2Sa 6:5
harps also and p for singers 1Kin 10:12
singing, and with harps, and with p...... 1Chr 13:8
with instruments of musick, p 1Chr 15:16
and Benaiah, with p on Alamoth 1Chr 15:20
cymbals, making a noise with p 1Chr 15:28
and Jeiel with p and with harps 1Chr 16:5
prophesy with harps, with p. 1Chr 25:1
of the LORD, with cymbals, p 1Chr 25:6
white linen, having cymbals and p........ 2Chr 5:12
palace, and harps and p for singers 2Chr 9:11
And they came to Jerusalem with p...... 2Chr 20:28
of the LORD with cymbals, with p. 2Chr 29:25
and with singing, with cymbals, p......... Neh 12:27

PSALTERY

down from the high place with a p. 1Sa 10:5
sing unto him with the p and an .... Ps 33:2
awake, p and harp .... Ps 57:8
will also praise thee with the p .... Ps 71:22
the pleasant harp with the p .... Ps 81:2
on stringed instruments, and upon the p Ps 92:3
Awake, p and harp .... Ps 108:2
upon a p and an instrument of ten .... Ps 144:9
praise him with the p and harp .... Ps 150:3
cornet, flute, harp, sackbut, p. .... Dan 3:5
cornet, flute, harp, sackbut, p. .... Dan 3:7
cornet, flute, harp, sackbut, p .... Dan 3:10
cornet, flute, harp, sackbut, p. .... Dan 3:15

PTOLEMAIS (tol-e-ma'-is) See ACCHO. A
seaport between Carmel and Tyre.
course from Tyre, we came to P. .... Acts 21:7

PUA (pu'-ah) A son of Issachar.
of P, the family of the Punites. .... Num 26:23

PUAH (pu'-ah) See PUAH. A son of Issachar.
1. Same as Pua.
sons of Issachar were, Tola, and P........ 1Chr 7:1
2. Father of Tola.
defend Israel Tola the son of P .... Judg 10:1
3. A Hebrew midwife in Egypt.
and the name of the other P .... Ex 1:15

PUBLICAN

Thomas, and Matthew the p................. Mt 10:3
thee as an heathen man and a p .... Mt 18:17
things he went forth, and saw a p .... Lk 5:27
one a Pharisee, and the other a p .... Lk 18:10
adulterers, or even as this p .... Lk 18:11
And the p, standing afar off................. Lk 18:13

PUBLICANS

do not even the p the same. .... Mt 5:46
do not even the p so .... Mt 5:47
meat in the house, behold, many p ...... Mt 9:10
Why eateth your Master with p .... Mt 9:11
and a winebibber, a friend of p .... Mt 11:19
Verily I say unto you, That the p.......... Mt 21:31

but the p and the harlots believed........ Mt 21:32
sat at meat in his house, many p.......... Mk 2:15
and Pharisees saw him eat with p........ Mk 2:16
that he eateth and drinketh with p .... Mk 2:16
Then came also p to be baptized. .... Lk 3:12
and there was a great company of p..... Lk 5:29
Why do ye eat and drink with p .... Lk 5:30
people that heard him, and the p .... Lk 7:29
and a winebibber, a friend of p............ Lk 7:34
Then drew near unto him all the p........ Lk 15:1
which was the chief among the p .... Lk 19:2

PUBLIC

willing to make her a p example. .... Mt 1:19

PUBLICKLY

convinced the Jews, and that p............ Acts 18:28
shewed you, and have taught you p...... Acts 20:20

PUBLISH

Because I will p the name of the .... Deut 32:3
to p it in the house of their. 1Sa 31:9
p it not in the streets of....................... 2Sa 1:20
And that they should p and proclaim. ... Neh 8:15
That I may p with the voice of.............. Ps 26:7
ye in Judah, and p in Jerusalem .... Jer 4:5
p against Jerusalem, that .... Jer 4:16
Jacob, and p it in Judah, saying .... Jer 5:20
p ye, praise ye, and say, O LORD, ... Jer 31:7
in Migdol, and p in Noph .... Jer 46:14
ye among the nations, and p .... Jer 50:2
p, and conceal not.............................. Jer 50:2
P in the palaces at Ashdod, and in ...... Amos 3:9
proclaim and p the free offerings. .... Amos 4:5
went out, and began to p it much .... Mk 1:45
began to p in Decapolis how great ...... Mk 5:20

PUBLISHED

be p throughout all his empire. .... Est 1:20
that it should be p according to .... Est 1:22
province was p unto all people .... Est 3:14
province was p unto all people .... Est 8:13
the company of those that p it. .... Ps 68:11
p through Nineveh by the decree .... Jonah 3:7
the more a great deal they p it............ Mk 7:36
must first be p among all nations .... Mk 13:10
p throughout the whole city how .... Lk 8:39
which was p throughout all Judaea ...... Acts 10:37
the word of the Lord was p.................. Acts 13:49

PUBLISHETH

good tidings, that p peace .... Is 52:7
tidings of good, that p salvation .... Is 52:7
p affliction from mount Ephraim .... Jer 4:15
good tidings, that p peace .... Nah 1:15

PUBLIUS (pub'-le-us) A chief man on Melita.
of the island, whose name was P......... Acts 28:7
that the father of P lay sick of .... Acts 28:8

PUDENS (pu'-denz) A Christian in Rome.
Eubulus greeteth thee, and P.............. 2Ti 4:21

PUFFED

that no one of you be p up for 1Cor 4:6
Now some are p up, as though I 1Cor 4:18
the speech of them which are p up 1Cor 4:19
And ye are p up, and have not 1Cor 5:2
vaunteth not itself, is not p up 1Cor 13:4
vainly p up by his fleshly mind, ... Col 2:18

PUFFETH

for all his enemies, he p at them.......... Ps 10:5
in safety from him that p at him .... Ps 12:5
Knowledge p up, but charity 1Cor 8:1

PUHITES (pu'-hites) A family descended from
Caleb.
the Ithrites, and the P, and the 1Chr 2:53

PUL (pul)
1. Same as Tiglath-pileser.
P the king of Assyria came.................. 2Kin 15:19
Menahem gave P a thousand talents. ... 2Kin 15:19
the spirit of P king of Assyria 1Chr 5:26
2. A place near Libya.
unto the nations, to Tarshish, P. .... Is 66:19

PULL

he could not p it in again to his. 1Kin 13:4
P me out of the net that they............... Ps 31:4
thy state shall he p them down............ Is 22:19
to p down, and to destroy, and to .... Jer 1:10
p them out like sheep for the .... Jer 12:3
to p down, and to destroy it .... Jer 18:7
build them, and not p them down .... Jer 24:6
not p you down, and I will plant .... Jer 42:10
shall he not p up the roots................... Eze 17:9
ye p off the robe with the .... Mic 2:8
Let me p out the mote out of .... Mt 7:4
let me p out the mote that is in .... Lk 6:42
to p out the mote that is in thy .... Lk 6:42
I will p down my barns, and build .... Lk 12:18
will not straightway p him out .... Lk 14:5

PULLED

p her in unto them into the ark .... Gen 8:9
p Lot into the house to them, and .... Gen 19:10
let timber be p down from his.............. Ezr 6:11
aside my ways, and p me in pieces. ..... Lam 3:11
they shall no more be p up out of .... Amos 9:15
p away the shoulder, and stopped....... Zec 7:11
have been p in pieces of them............. Acts 23:10

PULLING

God to the p down of strong holds....... 2Cor 10:4
with fear, p them out of the fire........... Jude 23

PULPIT

the scribe stood upon a p of wood ...... Neh 8:4

PULSE

beans, and lentiles, and parched p 2Sa 17:28
and let them give us p to eat .... Dan 1:12
and gave them p. .... Dan 1:16

PUNISH

then I will p you seven times .... Lev 26:18
will p you yet seven times for.............. Lev 26:24
Also to p the just is not good, ... Prov 17:26
I will p the fruit of the stout .... Is 10:12
I will p the world for their evil. .... Is 13:11
that the LORD shall p the host of .... Is 24:21
to p the inhabitants of the earth .... Is 26:21
strong sword shall p leviathan .... Is 27:1
I will p all them which are .... Jer 9:25
of hosts, Behold, I will p them .... Jer 11:22
thou say when he shall p thee .... Jer 13:21
But I will p you according to the .... Jer 21:14
the LORD, I will even p that man.......... Jer 23:34
that I will p the king of Babylon .... Jer 25:12
of Babylon, that nation will I p .... Jer 27:8
I will p Shemaiah the Nehelamite, ... Jer 29:32
I will p all that oppress them .... Jer 30:20
And I will p him and his seed and .... Jer 36:31
For I will p them that dwell in .... Jer 44:13
that I will p you in this place, ... Jer 44:29
I will p the multitude of No, and .... Jer 46:25
I will p the king of Babylon and .... Jer 50:18
I will p Bel in Babylon, and I .... Jer 51:44
I will p them for their ways, and .... Hos 4:9
I will not p your daughters when .... Hos 4:14
will p Jacob according to his............... Hos 12:2
therefore I will p you for all .... Amos 3:2
that I will p the princes .... Zeph 1:8
I p all those that leap on the .... Zeph 1:9
the men that are settled on .... Zeph 1:12
As I thought to p you, when your .... Zec 8:14
nothing being thus p them?................. Acts 4:21

PUNISHED

he shall be surely p. .... Ex 21:20
a day or two, he shall not be p .... Ex 21:21
he shall be surely p, according .... Ex 21:22
p us less than our iniquities .... Ezr 9:13
but the simple pass on, and are p .... Job 31:11
an iniquity to be p by the judges .... Job 31:28
When the scorner is p, the simple .... Prov 21:11
but the simple pass on, and are p .... Prov 22:3
but the simple pass on, and are p .... Prov 27:12
of Egypt, as I have p Jerusalem........... Jer 44:13
as I have p the king of Assyria .... Jer 50:18
be cut off, howsoever I p them............ Zeph 3:7
the shepherds, and I p the goats......... Zec 10:3
bound unto Jerusalem, for to be p .... Acts 22:5
I p them oft in every synagogue, ... Acts 26:11
Who shall be p with everlasting........... 2Th 1:9
unto the day of judgment to be p 2Pet 2:9

PUNISHMENT

My p is greater than I can bear............ Gen 4:13
accept of the p of their iniquity............ Lev 26:41
accept of the p of their iniquity............ Lev 26:43
there shall no p happen to thee. 1Sa 28:10
a strange p to the workers of .... Job 31:3
man of great wrath shall suffer p .... Prov 19:19
a man for the p of his sins. .... Lam 3:39
For the p of the iniquity of the .... Lam 4:6
than the p of the sin of Sodom .... Lam 4:6
The p of thine iniquity is .... Lam 4:22
bear the p of their iniquity .... Eze 14:10
the p of the prophet shall be .... Eze 14:10
of him that seeketh unto him............... Eze 14:10
will not turn away the p thereof .... Amos 1:3
will not turn away the p thereof .... Amos 1:6
will not turn away the p thereof .... Amos 1:9
will not turn away the p thereof .... Amos 1:11
will not turn away the p thereof .... Amos 1:13
will not turn away the p thereof .... Amos 2:1
will not turn away the p thereof .... Amos 2:4
will not turn away the p thereof .... Amos 2:6
This shall be the p of Egypt................. Zec 14:19
the p of all nations that come.............. Zec 14:19
shall go away into everlasting p .... Mt 25:46
to such a man is this p, which 2Cor 2:6
Of how much sorer p, suppose ye, ... Heb 10:29
by him for the p of evildoers............... 1Pet 2:14

PUNISHMENTS

wrath bringeth the p of the sword .... Job 19:29
the heathen, and p upon the people..... Ps 149:7

PUNITES (pu'-nites) Descendents of Pua.
of Pua, the family of the P................... Num 26:23

PUNON (pu'-non) An Edomite city.
from Zalmonah, and pitched in P. .... Num 33:42
And they departed from P, and............ Num 33:43

PUR (pur) See PURIM. Same as Purim.
of king Ahasuerus, they cast P .... Est 3:7
to destroy them, and had cast P .... Est 9:24
days Purim after the name of P .... Est 9:26

PURAH See PHURAH.

PURCHASE

The p of the field and of the cave .... Gen 49:32
if a man p of the Levites, then............. Lev 25:33
So I took the evidence of the p .... Jer 32:11
I gave the evidence of the p unto .... Jer 32:12
that subscribed the book of the p .... Jer 32:12
evidences, this evidence of the p .... Jer 32:14

p unto Baruch the son of Neriah........... Jer 32:16
p to themselves a good degree.............. 1Ti 3:13

PURCHASED

Abraham p of the sons of Heth............. Gen 25:10
pass over, which thou hast p.................. Ex 15:16
have I p to be my wife, to raise........... Ruth 4:10
which thou hast p of old........................ Ps 74:2
which his right hand had p..................... Ps 78:54
Now this man p a field with the........... Acts 1:18
gift of God may be p with money.......... Acts 8:20
which he hath p with his own............... Acts 20:28
redemption of the p possession............ Eph 1:14

PURE

thou shalt overlay it with p gold........... Ex 25:11
shalt make a mercy seat of p gold........ Ex 25:17
thou shalt overlay it with p gold........... Ex 25:24
of p gold shalt thou make them............ Ex 25:29
make a candlestick of p gold................ Ex 25:31
be one beaten work of p gold............... Ex 25:36
thereof, shall be of p gold..................... Ex 25:38
Of a talent of p gold shall he.............. Ex 25:39
that they bring thee p oil olive............. Ex 27:20
two chains of p gold at the ends........... Ex 28:14
ends of wreathen work of p gold.......... Ex 28:22
thou shalt make a plate of p gold......... Ex 28:36
thou shalt overlay it with p gold........... Ex 30:3
of p myrrh five hundred shekels........... Ex 30:23
sweet spices with p frankincense.......... Ex 30:34
apothecary, tempered together, p......... Ex 30:35
the p candlestick with all his................ Ex 31:8
he overlaid it with p gold within........... Ex 37:2
he made the mercy seat of p gold......... Ex 37:6
And he overlaid it with p gold.............. Ex 37:11
covers to cover withal, of p gold.......... Ex 37:16
he made the candlestick of p gold......... Ex 37:17
it was one beaten work of p gold......... Ex 37:22
and his snuffdishes, of p gold............... Ex 37:23
Of a talent of p gold made he it,......... Ex 37:24
And he overlaid it with p gold.............. Ex 37:26
the p incense of sweet spices,............... Ex 37:29
ends, of wreathen work of p gold......... Ex 39:15
And they made bells of p gold.............. Ex 39:25
plate of the holy crown of p gold......... Ex 39:30
The p candlestick, with the lamps......... Ex 39:37
that they bring unto thee p oil............. Lev 24:2
the p candlestick before the LORD......... Lev 24:4
upon the p table before the LORD......... Lev 24:6
thou shalt put p frankincense............... Lev 24:7
drink the p blood of the grape............. Deut 32:14
With the p thou wilt shew thyself......... 2Sa 22:27
thou wilt shew thyself p...................... 2Sa 22:27
and twenty measures of p oil................ 1Kin 5:11
and he overlaid it within p gold............ 1Kin 6:20
the house within with p gold................ 1Kin 6:21
And the candlesticks of p gold.............. 1Kin 7:49
spoons, and the censers of p gold........ 1Kin 7:50
forest of Lebanon were of p gold.......... 1Kin 10:21
Also p gold for the fleshhooks,............. 1Chr 28:17
he overlaid it within with p gold.......... 2Chr 3:4
before the oracle, of p gold.................. 2Chr 4:20
spoons, and the censers, of p gold........ 2Chr 4:22
ivory, and overlaid it with p gold......... 2Chr 9:17
forest of Lebanon were of p gold.......... 2Chr 9:20
they in order upon the p table.............. 2Chr 13:11
together, all of them were p.................. Ezr 6:20
a man be more p than his maker.......... Job 4:17
If thou wert p and upright.................... Job 8:6
thou hast said, My doctrine is p............ Job 11:4
also my prayer is p............................... Job 16:17
the stars are not p in his sight............. Job 25:5
shalt it be valued with p gold............... Job 28:19
The words of the LORD are p words...... Ps 12:6
With the p thou wilt shew thyself......... Ps 18:26
thou wilt shew thyself p...................... Ps 18:26
the commandment of the LORD is p...... Ps 19:8
a crown of p gold on his head............. Ps 21:3
hath clean hands, and a p heart........... Ps 24:4
Thy word is very p............................... Ps 119:140
words of the p are pleasant words........ Prov 15:26
heart clean, I am p from my sin........... Prov 20:9
his doings, whether his work be p........ Prov 20:11
but as for the p, his work is................. Prov 21:8
Every word of God is p......................... Prov 30:5
that are p in their own eyes................. Prov 30:12
hair of his head like the p wool............ Dan 7:9
Shall I count them p with the............... Mic 6:11
I turn to the people a p language......... Zeph 3:9
unto my name, and a p offering........... Mal 1:11
Blessed are the p in heart.................... Mt 5:8
that I am p from the blood of all........ Acts 20:26
All things indeed are p.......................... Rom 14:20
are just, whatsoever things are p........... Phil 4:8
is charity out of a p heart.................... 1Ti 1:5
of the faith in a p conscience............... 1Ti 3:9
keep thyself p...................................... 1Ti 5:22
my forefathers with p conscience.......... 2Ti 1:3
call on the Lord out of a p heart......... 2Ti 2:22
Unto the p all things are p................... Titus 1:15
and unbelieving is nothing p................. Titus 1:15
and our bodies washed with p water.... Heb 10:22
P religion and undefiled before............. Jas 1:27
that is from above is first p.................. Jas 3:17
another with a p heart fervently........... 1Pet 1:22
p minds by way of remembrance........... 2Pet 3:1
himself, even as he is p........................ 1Jn 3:3
the seven plagues, clothed in p............ Rev 15:6
and the city was p gold, like unto........ Rev 21:18
the street of the city was p gold.......... Rev 21:21
he shewed me a p river of water......... Rev 22:1

PURELY

p purge away thy dross, and take.......... Is 1:25

PURENESS

delivered by the p of thine hands......... Job 22:30
He that loveth p of heart...................... Prov 22:11
By p, by knowledge, by......................... 2Cor 6:6

PURER

Her Nazarites were p than snow............ Lam 4:7
Thou art of p eyes than to behold........ Hab 1:13

PURGE

twelfth year he began to p Judah.......... 2Chr 34:3
P me with hyssop, and I shall be.......... Ps 51:7
thou shalt p them away........................ Ps 65:3
p away our sins, for thy name's............ Ps 79:9
purely p away thy dross, and take........ Is 1:25
I will p out from among you the.......... Eze 20:38
thou shalt thou cleanse and p it........... Eze 43:20
Seven days shall they p the altar.......... Eze 43:26
shall fall, to try them, and to p........... Dan 11:35
p them as gold and silver, that............ Mal 3:3
and he will throughly p his floor.......... Mt 3:12
and he will throughly p his floor.......... Lk 3:17
but therefore the old leaven,................. 1Cor 5:7
therefore p himself from these............... 2Ti 2:21
p your conscience from dead works....... Heb 9:14

PURGED

of Eli's house shall not be p................. 1Sa 3:14
his reign, when he had p the land....... 2Chr 34:8
By mercy and truth iniquity is p........... Prov 16:6
shall have p the blood of..................... Is 4:4
is taken away, and thy sin p................ Is 6:7
not be p from you till ye die.............. Is 22:14
shall the iniquity of Jacob be p............ Is 27:9
because I have p thee........................... Eze 24:13
and thou wast not p............................ Eze 24:13
thou shalt not be p from thy.............. Eze 24:13
when he had by himself p our sins....... Heb 1:3
are by the law p with blood................ Heb 9:22
once p should have had no more.......... Heb 10:2
that he was p from his old sins........... 2Pet 1:9

PURGETH

that beareth fruit, he p it..................... Jn 15:2

PURGING

out into the draught, p all meats......... Mk 7:19

PURIFICATION

it is a p for sin.................................... Num 19:9
of the burnt heifer of p for sin........... Num 19:17
to the p of the sanctuary..................... 2Chr 30:19
their God, and the ward of the p......... Neh 12:45
their things for p be given them.......... Est 2:3
gave her her things for p..................... Est 2:9
when the days of her p according........ Lk 2:22
accomplishment of the days of p......... Acts 21:26

PURIFICATIONS

the days of their p accomplished.......... Est 2:12

PURIFIED

p the altar, and poured the blood........ Lev 8:15
And the Levites were p, and they......... Num 8:21
nevertheless it shall be p with............. Num 31:23
for she was p from her......................... Num 8:21
and the Levites were p together........... Ezr 6:20
and the Levites p themselves................ Neh 12:30
p the people, and the gates, and......... Neh 12:30
a furnace of earth, p seven times......... Ps 12:6
Many shall be p, and made white,........ Dan 12:10
Asia found me p in the temple............. Acts 24:18
heavens should be p with these........... Heb 9:23
Seeing ye have p your souls in............ 1Pet 1:22

PURIFIER

sit as a refiner and p of silver............. Mal 3:3

PURIFIETH

p not himself, defileth the.................... Num 19:13
hath this hope in him p himself........... 1Jn 3:3

PURIFY

He shall p himself with it on the......... Num 19:12
but if he p not himself the third......... Num 19:12
seventh day he shall p himself............. Num 19:19
unclean, and shall not p himself.......... Num 19:20
p both yourselves and your.................. Num 31:19
p all your raiment, and all that........... Num 31:20
of breakings they p themselves............ Job 41:25
p themselves in the gardens................. Is 66:17
they purge the altar and p it.............. Eze 43:26
he shall p the sons of Levi, and......... Mal 3:3
the passover, to p themselves.............. Jn 11:55
p thyself with them, and be at............ Acts 21:24
p unto himself a peculiar people,......... Titus 2:14
p your hearts, ye double minded......... Jas 4:8

PURIFYING

in the blood of her p three................. Lev 12:4
the days of her p be fulfilled............... Lev 12:4
in the blood of her p threescore........... Lev 12:5
the days of her p are fulfilled.............. Lev 12:6
Sprinkle water of p upon them............ Num 8:7
in the p of all holy things, and........... 1Chr 23:28
things for the p of the women............. Est 2:12
the manner of the p of the Jews.......... Jn 2:6
disciples and the Jews about p............. Jn 3:25
and them, p their hearts by faith........ Acts 15:9
the next day p himself with them........ Acts 21:26
sanctifieth to the p of the flesh........... Heb 9:13

PURIM (pu'-rim) See PUR. A Jewish festival celebrating the deliverance from Haman.

days P after the name of Pur................ Est 9:26
that these days of P should not........... Est 9:28
confirm this second letter of P............. Est 9:29
of P in their times appointed............... Est 9:31
confirmed these matters of P................ Est 9:32

PURITY

in spirit, in faith, in p......................... 1Ti 4:12
younger as sisters, with all p................ 1Ti 5:2

PURLOINING

Not p, but shewing all good................. Titus 2:10

PURPLE

And blue, and p, and scarlet, and........ Ex 25:4
fine twined linen, and blue, and p........ Ex 26:1
shalt make a vail of blue, and p........... Ex 26:31
door of the tent, of blue, and p........... Ex 26:36
of twenty cubits, of blue, and p........... Ex 27:16
shalt take gold, and blue, and p........... Ex 28:5
ephod of gold, of blue, and p.............. Ex 28:6
even of gold, of blue, and p................ Ex 28:8
of gold, of blue, and p........................ Ex 28:15
pomegranates of blue, and of p............ Ex 28:33
And blue, and p, and scarlet, and........ Ex 35:6
with whom was found blue, and p........ Ex 35:23
had spun, both of blue, and of p......... Ex 35:25
the embroiderer, in blue, and in p........ Ex 35:35
fine twined linen, and blue, and.......... Ex 36:8
And he made a vail of blue, and p....... Ex 36:35
the tabernacle door of blue, and p....... Ex 36:37
was needlework, of blue, and p............ Ex 38:18
an embroiderer in blue, and in p.......... Ex 38:23
And of the blue, and p, and scarlet,.... Ex 39:1
the ephod of gold, blue, and p............ Ex 39:2
work it in the blue, and in the p......... Ex 39:3
of gold, blue, and p, and scarlet,........ Ex 39:5
of gold, blue, and p, and scarlet,........ Ex 39:8
robe pomegranates of blue, and p........ Ex 39:24
fine twined linen, and blue, and p....... Ex 39:29
and spread a p cloth thereon............... Num 4:13
p raiment that was on the kings.......... Judg 8:26
and in brass, and in iron, and in p...... 2Chr 2:7
in stone, and in timber, in p............... 2Chr 2:14
And he made the vail of blue, and p.... 2Chr 3:14
p to silver rings and pillars of........... Est 1:6
with a garment of fine linen and p...... Est 8:15
her clothing is silk and p.................... Prov 31:22
of gold, the covering of it of p........... Song 3:10
and the hair of thine head like p........ Song 7:5
blue and p is their clothing................. Jer 10:9
p from the isles of Elishah was........... Eze 27:7
in thy fairs with emeralds, p............... Eze 27:16
And they clothed him with p................ Mk 15:17
him, they took off the p from him....... Mk 15:20
rich man, which was clothed in p......... Lk 16:19
head, and they put on him a p robe..... Jn 19:2
crown of thorns, and the p robe.......... Jn 19:5
woman named Lydia, a seller of p........ Acts 16:14
And the woman was arrayed in p,......... Rev 17:4
and of pearls, and fine linen, and p..... Rev 18:12
was clothed in fine linen, and p.......... Rev 18:16

PURPOSE

some of the handfuls of p for her....... Ruth 2:16
I p to build an house unto the............ 1Kin 5:5
now ye p to keep under the................ 2Chr 28:10
them, to frustrate their p..................... Ezr 4:5
which they had made for the p............ Neh 8:4
he may withdraw man from his p......... Job 33:17
Every p is established by counsel......... Prov 20:18
a time to every p under the................ Eccl 3:1
there is a time there for every p.......... Eccl 3:17
Because to every p there is time........... Eccl 8:6
To what p is the multitude of.............. Is 1:11
This is the p that is purposed............. Is 14:26
shall help in vain, and to no p............ Is 30:7
To what p cometh there to me............ Jer 6:20
which I p to do unto them because...... Jer 26:3
evil which I p to do unto them............ Jer 36:3
and hath conceived a p against you...... Jer 49:30
for every p of the LORD shall be.......... Jer 51:29
that the p might not be changed.......... Dan 6:17
saying, To what p is this waste............ Mt 26:8
that with p of heart they would........... Acts 11:23
appeared unto thee for this p.............. Acts 26:16
that they had obtained their p............. Acts 27:13
save Paul, kept them from their p........ Acts 27:43
are the called according to his p.......... Rom 8:28
that the p of God according to............ Rom 9:11
Even for this same p have I.................. Rom 9:17
or the things that I p.......................... 2Cor 1:17
do I p according to the flesh,.............. 2Cor 1:17
p of him who worketh all things.......... Eph 1:11
According to the eternal p which.......... Eph 3:11
have sent unto you for the same p...... Eph 6:22
have sent unto you for the same p...... Col 4:8
works, but according to his own p........ 2Ti 1:9
my doctrine, manner of life, p.............. 2Ti 3:10
For this p the Son of God was............ 1Jn 3:8

PURPOSED

that he was p to fight against............. 2Chr 32:2
I am p that my mouth shall not.......... Ps 17:3
who have p to overthrow my goings..... Ps 140:4
and as I have p, so shall it stand........ Is 14:24
that is p upon the whole earth............ Is 14:26
LORD of hosts hath p............................ Is 14:27
LORD of hosts hath p it...................... Is 19:12
The LORD of hosts hath p it................. Is 23:9
I have p it, I will also do it............... Is 46:11

I have spoken it, I have *p* it .... Jer 4:28
that he hath *p* against you .... Jer 49:20
that he hath *p* against the land .... Jer 50:45
The LORD hath *p* to destroy the .... Lam 2:8
But Daniel *p* in his heart that he .... Dan 1:8
Paul *p* in the spirit, when he had .... Acts 19:21
he *p* to return through Macedonia .... Acts 20:3
oftentimes I *p* to come unto you .... Rom 1:13
which he hath *p* in himself .... Eph 1:9
he *p* in Christ Jesus our Lord .... Eph 3:11

PURPOSES
my *p* are broken off, even the .... Job 17:11
Without counsel *p* are .... Prov 15:22
shall be broken in the *p* thereof .... Is 19:10
and his *p*, that he hath purposed .... Jer 49:20
and his *p*, that he hath purposed .... Jer 50:45

PURPOSETH
according as he *p* in his heart 2Cor 9:7

PURPOSING
comfort himself, *p* to kill thee .... Gen 27:42

PURSE
let us all have one *p* .... Prov 1:14
no bread, no money in their *p* .... Mk 6:8
Carry neither *p*, nor scrip, nor .... Lk 10:4
them, When I sent you without *p* .... Lk 22:35
them, But now, he that hath a *p* .... Lk 22:36

PURSES
nor silver, nor brass in your *p* .... Mt 10:9

PURSUE
they did not *p* after the sons of .... Gen 35:5
The enemy said, I will *p*, I will .... Ex 15:9
avenger of the blood the slayer .... Deut 19:6
they shall *p* thee until thou .... Deut 28:22
come upon thee, and shall *p* thee .... Deut 28:45
p after them quickly .... Josh 2:5
called together to *p* after them .... Josh 8:16
but *p* after your enemies, and .... Josh 10:19
the avenger of blood *p* after him .... Josh 20:5
after whom dost thou *p* 1Sa 24:14
Yet a man is risen to *p* thee 1Sa 25:29
my lord thus *p* after his servant 1Sa 26:18
Shall I *p* after this troop 1Sa 30:8
And he answered him, *P* 1Sa 30:8
arise and *p* after David this night 2Sa 17:1
p after him, lest he get him 2Sa 20:6
to *p* after Sheba the son of 2Sa 20:7
to *p* after Sheba the son of 2Sa 20:13
thine enemies, while they *p* thee 2Sa 24:13
wilt thou *p* the dry stubble .... Job 13:25
they *p* my soul as the wind .... Job 30:15
seek peace, and *p* it .... Ps 34:14
shall they that *p* you be swift .... Is 30:16
the sword shall *p* thee .... Jer 48:2
unto blood, and blood shall *p* thee .... Eze 35:6
blood, even blood shall *p* thee .... Eze 35:6
the enemy shall *p* him .... Hos 8:3
because he did *p* his brother with .... Amos 1:11
and darkness shall *p* his enemies .... Nah 1:8

PURSUED
and eighteen, and *p* them unto Dan .... Gen 14:14
p them unto Hobah, which is on .... Gen 14:15
p after him seven days' journey .... Gen 31:23
thou hast so hotly *p* after me .... Gen 31:36
he *p* after the children of Israel .... Ex 14:8
But the Egyptians *p* after them .... Ex 14:9
And the Egyptians *p*, and went in .... Ex 14:23
overflow them as they *p* after you .... Deut 11:4
the men *p* after them the way to .... Josh 2:7
as soon as they which *p* after .... Josh 2:7
they *p* after Joshua, and were .... Josh 8:16
the city open, and *p* after Israel .... Josh 8:17
the Egyptians *p* after you .... Josh 24:6
they *p* after him, and caught him, ... Judg 1:6
But Barak *p* after the chariots .... Judg 4:16
And, behold, as Barak *p* Sisera .... Judg 4:22
and *p* after the Midianites .... Judg 7:23
p Midian, and brought the heads of .... Judg 7:25
he *p* after them, and took the two .... Judg 8:12
p hard after them unto Gidom, and .... Judg 20:45
p Philistines, and shout among them, ... 1Sa 7:11
p the Philistines, until thou 1Sa 17:52
that, he *p* after David in the 1Sa 23:25
But David *p*, he and four hundred 1Sa 30:10
And Asahel *p* after Abner 2Sa 2:19
also and Abishai *p* after Abner 2Sa 2:24
p after Israel no more, neither 2Sa 2:28
Abishai his brother *p* after Sheba 2Sa 20:10
and *p* Israel in them 2Sa 22:38
and Israel *p* them 1Kin 20:20
of the Chaldees *p* after the king 2Kin 25:5
Abijah *p* after Jeroboam, and took 2Chr 13:19
were with him *p* them unto Gerar 2Chr 14:13
I have *p* mine enemies, and .... Ps 18:37
He *p* them, and passed safely .... Is 41:3
the Chaldeans' army *p* after them .... Jer 39:5
of the Chaldeans *p* after the king .... Jer 52:8
they *p* us upon the mountains, ... Lam 4:19

PURSUER
without strength before the *p* .... Lam 1:6

PURSUERS
the mountain, lest the *p* meet you .... Josh 2:16
days, until the *p* be returned .... Josh 2:16
until the *p* were returned .... Josh 2:22
the *p* sought them throughout all .... Josh 2:22
wilderness turned back upon the *p* .... Josh 8:20

PURSUETH
and ye shall flee when none *p* you .... Lev 26:17
and they shall fall when none *p* .... Lev 26:36
were before a sword, when none *p* .... Lev 26:37
so he that *p* evil *p* it .... Prov 11:19
evil *p* to his own death .... Prov 11:19
Evil *p* sinners .... Prov 13:21
he *p* them with words, yet they .... Prov 19:7
The wicked flee when no man *p* .... Prov 28:1

PURSUING
were with him, faint, yet *p* them .... Judg 8:4
I am *p* after Zebah and Zalmunna .... Judg 8:5
Saul returned from *p* after David 1Sa 23:28
David and Joab came from *p* a troop 2Sa 3:22
returned from *p* after Israel 2Sa 18:16
either he is talking, or he is *p* 1Kin 18:27
that they turned back from *p* him 1Kin 22:33
they turned back again from *p* him 2Chr 18:32

PURTENANCE
his legs, and with the *p* thereof .... Ex 12:9

PUSH
to *p* with his horn in time past .... Ex 21:29
If the ox shall *p* a manservant or .... Ex 21:32
ox hath used to *p* in time past .... Ex 21:36
with them he shall *p* the people .... Deut 33:17
these shalt thou *p* the Syrians 1Kin 22:11
With these thou shalt *p* Syria 2Chr 18:10
they *p* away my feet, and they .... Job 30:12
the will we *p* down our enemies .... Ps 44:5
the king of the south *p* at him .... Dan 11:40

PUSHED
p all the diseased with your .... Eze 34:21

PUSHING
I saw the ram *p* westward, and .... Dan 8:4

PUT
See PREFACE.

PUTEOLI
(pu-te'-o-li) A seaport in Italy.
and we came the next day to *P* .... Acts 28:13

PUTHITES
See PUHITES.

PUTIEL
(pu'-te-el) Father-in-law of Eleazar.
one of the daughters of *P* to wife .... Ex 6:25

PUTRIFYING
wounds, and bruises, and *p* sores .... Is 1:6

PUTTEST
thou *p* thy nest in a rock .... Num 24:21
all that thou *p* thine hands unto .... Deut 12:18
all that thou *p* thine hand unto .... Deut 15:10
that which thou *p* on me will I 2Kin 18:14
Thou *p* my feet also in the stocks .... Job 13:27
Thou *p* away all the wicked of the .... Ps 119:119
that *p* thy bottle to him, and .... Hab 2:15

PUTTETH
or whosoever *p* any of it upon a .... Ex 30:33
the word that God *p* in my mouth .... Num 22:38
p forth her hand, and taketh him .... Deut 25:11
and *p* it in a secret place .... Deut 27:15
boast himself as he that *p* it off 1Kin 20:11
he *p* no trust in his saints .... Job 15:15
He *p* forth his hand upon the rock .... Job 28:9
He *p* my feet in the stocks, he .... Job 33:11
He that *p* not out his money to .... Ps 15:5
he *p* down one, and setteth up .... Ps 75:7
but he that *p* his trust in the .... Prov 28:25
but whoso *p* his trust in the LORD .... Prov 29:25
The fig tree *p* forth her green .... Song 2:13
but he that *p* his trust in me .... Is 57:13
as a shepherd *p* on his garment .... Jer 43:12
He *p* his mouth in the dust .... Lam 3:29
p the stumblingblock of his .... Eze 14:4
p the stumblingblock of his .... Eze 14:7
he that *p* not into their mouths, ... Mic 3:5
No man *p* a piece of new cloth .... Mt 9:16
p forth leaves, ye know that .... Mt 24:32
no man *p* new wine into old .... Mk 2:22
immediately he *p* in the sickle .... Mk 4:29
p forth leaves, ye know that .... Mk 13:28
No man *p* a piece of a new garment .... Lk 5:36
no man *p* new wine into old .... Lk 5:37
a vessel, or *p* it under a bed .... Lk 8:16
p it in a secret place, neither .... Lk 11:33
Whosoever *p* away his wife, and .... Lk 16:18
when he *p* forth his own sheep, he .... Jn 10:4

PUTTING
p it on her shoulder, and the .... Gen 21:14
p them upon the head of the goat, ... Lev 16:21
p their hand to their mouth, were .... Judg 7:6
the *p* forth of the finger, and .... Is 58:9
saith that he hateth *p* away .... Mal 2:16
p his hand on him, that he might .... Acts 9:12
p his hands on him, said, Brother .... Acts 9:17
multitude, the Jews *p* him forward .... Acts 19:33
as *p* you in mind, because of the .... Rom 15:15
Wherefore *p* away lying, speak .... Eph 4:25
in *p* off the body of the sins of .... Col 2:11
p on the breastplate of faith and 1Th 5:8
faithful, *p* me into the ministry 1Ti 1:12
in thee by the *p* on of my hands 2Ti 1:6
of gold, or of *p* on of apparel 1Pet 3:3
p away of the filth of the flesh 1Pet 3:21
to stir you up by *p* you in 2Pet 1:13

PUVAH
See PUA.

PUVVAH
See PHUVAH.

PYGARG
deer, and the wild goat, and the *p* .... Deut 14:5

PYRRHUS
Not in KJV.

Q

QUAILS
pass, that at even the *q* came up .... Ex 16:13
brought *q* from the sea, and let .... Num 11:31
next day, and they gathered the *q* .... Num 11:32
The people asked, and he brought *q* ...... Ps 105:40

QUAKE
The earth shall *q* before them .... Joel 2:10
The mountains *q* at him, and the .... Nah 1:5
and the earth did *q*, and the rocks .... Mt 27:51
said, I exceedingly fear and *q* .... Heb 12:21

QUAKED
and the whole mount *q* greatly .... Ex 19:18
also trembled, and the earth *q* 1Sa 14:15

QUAKING
Son of man, eat thy bread with *q* .... Eze 12:18
but a great *q* fell upon them, so .... Dan 10:7

QUANTITY
the issue, all vessels of small *q* .... Is 22:24

QUARREL
shall avenge the *q* of my covenant .... Lev 26:25
see how he seeketh a *q* against me 2Kin 5:7
Herodias had a *q* against him .... Mk 6:19
if any man have a *q* against any .... Col 3:13

QUARRIES
from the *q* that were by Gilgal .... Judg 3:19
tarried, and passed beyond the *q* .... Judg 3:26

QUARTER
all the people from every *q* .... Gen 19:4
Then your south *q* shall be from .... Num 34:3
their border in the north *q* was .... Josh 15:5
this was the west *q* .... Josh 18:14
the south *q* was from the end of .... Josh 18:15
shall wander every one to his *q* .... Is 47:15
one for his gain, from his *q* .... Is 56:11
and they came to him from every *q* .... Mk 1:45

QUARTERS
seen with thee in all thy *q* .... Ex 13:7
upon the four *q* of thy vesture .... Deut 22:12
In four *q* were the porters, ... 1Chr 9:24
winds from the four *q* of heaven .... Jer 49:36
house of Togarmah of the north *q* .... Eze 38:6
as Peter passed throughout all *q* .... Acts 9:32
of the Jews which were in those *q* .... Acts 16:3
In the same *q* were possessions of .... Acts 28:7
are in the four *q* of the earth .... Rev 20:8

QUARTUS
(quar'-tus) A Christian in Rome.
city saluteth you, and *Q* a brother .... Rom 16:23

QUATERNIONS
delivered him to four *q* of .... Acts 12:4

QUEEN
when the *q* of Sheba heard of the 1Kin 10:1
when the *q* of Sheba had seen all 1Kin 10:4
of spices as these which the *q* of 1Kin 10:10
the *q* of Sheba all her desire 1Kin 10:13
the sister of Tahpenes the *q* 1Kin 11:19
even her he removed from being *q* 1Kin 15:13
the king and the children of the *q* 2Kin 10:13
when the *q* of Sheba heard of the 2Chr 9:1
when the *q* of Sheba had seen the 2Chr 9:3
the *q* of Sheba saw king Solomon 2Chr 9:9
to the *q* of Sheba all her desire 2Chr 9:12
king, he removed her from being *q* 2Chr 15:16
(the *q* also sitting by him), For .... Neh 2:6
Also Vashti the *q* made a feast .... Est 1:9
To bring Vashti the *q* before the .... Est 1:11
But the *q* Vashti refused to come .... Est 1:12
the *q* Vashti according to law .... Est 1:15
Vashti the *q* hath not done wrong .... Est 1:16
For this deed of the *q* shall come .... Est 1:17
the *q* to be brought in before him .... Est 1:17
have heard of the deed of the *q* .... Est 1:18
the king be *q* instead of Vashti .... Est 1:19
made her *q* instead of Vashti .... Est 2:17
who told it unto Esther the *q* .... Est 2:22
Then was the *q* exceedingly .... Est 4:4
the *q* standing in the court .... Est 5:2
her, What wilt thou, *q* Esther .... Est 5:3
Esther the *q* did let no man come .... Est 5:12
came to banquet with Esther the *q* ...... Est 5:12
What is thy petition, *q* Esther .... Est 7:2
Then Esther the *q* answered .... Est 7:3
Esther the *q* besought him .... Est 7:5
afraid before the king and the *q* .... Est 7:6
for his life to Esther the *q* .... Est 7:7
Will he force the *q* also before .... Est 7:8
the Jews' enemy unto Esther the *q* ...... Est 8:1
Ahasuerus said unto Esther the *q* .... Est 8:7
the king said unto Esther the *q* .... Est 9:12
Then Esther the *q*, the daughter .... Est 9:29
Esther the *q* had enjoined them, ... Est 9:31

did stand the q in gold of Ophir .... Ps 45:9
to make cakes to the q of heaven .... Jer 7:18
Say unto the king and to the q .... Jer 13:18
that Jeconiah the king, and the q .... Jer 29:2
burn incense unto the q of heaven .... Jer 44:17
burn incense to the q of heaven .... Jer 44:18
burned incense to the q of heaven .... Jer 44:19
burn incense to the q of .... Jer 44:25
Now the q, by reason of the words .... Dan 5:10
the q spake and said, O king, live .... Dan 5:10
The q of the south said, O king, live .... Mt 12:42
The q of the south shall rise up .... Lk 11:31
under Candace q of the Ethiopians .... Acts 8:27
she saith in her heart, I sit a q .... Rev 18:7

QUEENS
There are threescore q, and .... Song 6:8
yea, the q and the concubines, and .... Song 6:9
their q thy nursing mothers .... Is 49:23

QUENCH
so they shall q my coal which is 2Sa 14:7
that thou q not the light of 2Sa 21:17
the wild asses q their thirst .... Ps 104:11
Many waters cannot q love .... Song 8:7
together, and none shall q them .... Is 1:31
the smoking flax shall he not q .... Is 42:3
burn that none can q it forever .... Jer 4:4
fire, and burn that none can q it .... Jer 21:12
there be none to q it in Beth-el .... Amos 5:6
and smoking flax shall he not q .... Mt 12:20
to q all the fiery darts of the .... Eph 6:16
Q not the Spirit 1Th 5:19

QUENCHED
unto the LORD, the fire was q .... Num 11:2
this place, and shall not be q 2Kin 22:17
this place, and shall not be q 2Chr 34:25
they are q as the fire of thorns .... Ps 118:12
It shall not be q night nor day .... Is 34:10
are extinct, they are q as tow .... Is 43:17
neither shall their fire be q .... Is 66:24
it shall burn, and shall not be q .... Jer 7:20
Jerusalem, and it shall not be q .... Jer 17:27
the flaming flame shall not be q .... Eze 20:47
it shall not be q .... Eze 20:48
the fire that never shall be q .... Mk 9:43
dieth not, and the fire is not q .... Mk 9:44
the fire that never shall be q .... Mk 9:45
dieth not, and the fire is not q .... Mk 9:46
dieth not, and the fire is not q .... Mk 9:48
Q the violence of fire, escaped .... Heb 11:34

QUESTION
which was a lawyer, asked him a q .... Mt 22:35
forth, and began to q with him .... Mk 8:11
the scribes, What q ye with them .... Mk 9:16
I will also ask of you one q .... Mk 11:29
after that durst ask him any q .... Mk 12:34
durst not ask him any q at all .... Lk 20:40
Then there arose a q between some .... Jn 3:25
apostles and elders about this q .... Acts 15:2
But if it be a q of words .... Acts 18:15
called in q for this day's uproar .... Acts 19:40
of the dead I am called in q .... Acts 23:6
I am called in a q by you this day .... Acts 24:21
asking no q for conscience sake 1Cor 10:25
asking no q for conscience sake 1Cor 10:27

QUESTIONED
Then Hezekiah with the priests 2Chr 31:9
that they q among themselves .... Mk 1:27
Then he q with him in many words .... Lk 23:9

QUESTIONING
q one with another what the .... Mk 9:10
them, and the scribes q with them .... Mk 9:14

QUESTIONS
she came to prove him with hard q 1Kin 10:1
And Solomon told her all her q 1Kin 10:3
Solomon with hard q at Jerusalem 2Chr 9:1
And Solomon told her all her q 2Chr 9:2
that day forth ask him any more q .... Mt 22:46
hearing them, and asking them q .... Lk 2:46
to be accused of q of their law .... Acts 23:29
But had certain q against him of .... Acts 25:19
I doubted of such manner of q .... Acts 25:20
q which are among the Jews .... Acts 26:3
genealogies, which minister q 1Ti 1:4
nothing, but doting about q 1Ti 6:4
But foolish and unlearned q avoid 2Ti 2:23
But avoid foolish q, and .... Titus 3:9

QUICK
there be a q raw flesh in the .... Lev 13:10
the q flesh that burneth have a .... Lev 13:24
and they go down q into the pit .... Num 16:30
and let them go down q into hell .... Ps 55:15
Then they had swallowed us up q .... Ps 124:3
shall make him of q understanding .... Is 11:3
of God to be the Judge of q .... Acts 10:42
Christ, who shall judge the q 2Ti 4:1
For the word of God is q, and .... Heb 4:12
him that is ready to judge the q 1Pet 4:5

QUICKEN
shalt q me again, and shalt bring .... Ps 71:20
q us, and we will call upon thy .... Ps 80:18
q thou me according to thy word .... Ps 119:25
and q thou me in thy way .... Ps 119:37
q me in thy righteousness .... Ps 119:40
Q me after thy lovingkindness .... Ps 119:88
q me, O LORD, according unto thy .... Ps 119:107

q me according to thy judgment .... Ps 119:149
q me according to thy word .... Ps 119:154
q me according to thy judgments .... Ps 119:156
q me, O LORD, according to thy .... Ps 119:159
Q me, O LORD, for thy name's sake .... Ps 143:11
also q your mortal bodies by his .... Rom 8:11

QUICKENED
for thy word hath q me .... Ps 119:50
for with them thou hast q me .... Ps 119:93
that which thou sowest is not q 1Cor 15:36
And you hath he q, who were dead .... Eph 2:1
hath q us together with Christ, (........... Eph 2:5
hath he q together with him, ... Col 2:13
in the flesh, but q by the Spirit 1Pet 3:18

QUICKENETH
raiseth up the dead, and q them .... Jn 5:21
even so the Son q whom he will .... Jn 5:21
It is the spirit that q .... Jn 6:63
who q the dead, and calleth those .... Rom 4:17
who q all things, and before 1Ti 6:13

QUICKENING
the last Adam was made a q spirit 1Cor 15:45

QUICKLY
Make ready q three measures of .... Gen 18:6
it that thou hast found it so q .... Gen 27:20
aside q out of the way which I .... Ex 32:8
go q unto the congregation, and .... Num 16:46
drive them out, and destroy them q .... Deut 9:3
Arise, get thee down q from hence, ... Deut 9:12
they are q turned aside out of .... Deut 9:12
ye had turned aside q out of the .... Deut 9:16
lest ye perish q from off the .... Deut 11:17
destroyed, and until thou perish q .... Deut 28:20
pursue after them q .... Josh 2:5
the ambush arose q out of their .... Josh 8:19
come up to us q, and save us, and .... Josh 10:6
ye shall perish q from off the .... Josh 23:16
they turned q out of the way .... Judg 2:17
days, then thou shalt go down q 1Sa 20:19
Now therefore send q, and tell 2Sa 17:16
but they went both of them away q 2Sa 17:18
Arise, and pass q over the water 2Sa 17:21
Come down q 2Kin 1:11
Fetch q Micaiah the son of Imla 2Chr 18:8
a threefold cord is not q broken .... Eccl 4:12
Agree with thine adversary q .... Mt 5:25
And go q, and tell his disciples .... Mt 28:7
And they departed q from the .... Mt 28:8
And they went out q, and fled from .... Mk 16:8
go out q into the streets and .... Lk 14:21
him, Take thy bill, and sit down q .... Lk 16:6
as she heard that, she arose q .... Jn 11:29
unto him, That thou doest, do q .... Jn 13:27
raised him up, saying, Arise up q .... Acts 12:7
get thee q out of Jerusalem .... Acts 22:18
or else I will come unto thee q .... Rev 2:5
or else I will come unto thee q .... Rev 2:16
Behold, I come q .... Rev 3:11
behold, the third woe cometh q .... Rev 11:14
Behold, I come q .... Rev 22:7
And, behold, I come q .... Rev 22:12
things saith, Surely I come q .... Rev 22:20

QUICKSANDS
lest they should fall into the q .... Acts 27:17

QUIET
were a q all the night, saying, In .... Judg 16:2
the manner of the Zidonians, q .... Judg 18:7
unto a people that were q .... Judg 18:27
rejoiced, and the city was in q 2Kin 11:20
good, and the land was wide, and q 1Chr 4:40
his days the land was q ten years 2Chr 14:1
and the kingdom was q before him 2Chr 14:5
So the realm of Jehoshaphat was q 2Chr 20:30
and the city was q, after that 2Chr 23:21
I have lain still and been q .... Job 3:13
had I rest, neither was I q .... Job 3:26
being wholly at ease and q .... Job 21:23
them that are q in the land .... Ps 35:20
are they glad because they be q .... Ps 107:30
shall be q from fear of evil .... Prov 1:33
a more than the cry of him that .... Eccl 9:17
say unto him, Take heed, and be q .... Is 7:4
whole earth is at rest, and is q .... Is 14:7
dwellings, and in a resting places .... Is 32:18
see Jerusalem a q habitation .... Is 33:20
and shall be in rest, and be q .... Jer 30:10
how long will it be ere thou be q .... Jer 47:6
How can it be q, seeing the LORD .... Jer 47:7
it cannot be q .... Jer 49:23
And this Seraiah was a q prince .... Jer 51:59
depart from thee, and I will be q .... Eze 16:42
Though they be q, and likewise .... Nah 1:12
spoken against, ye ought to be q .... Acts 19:36
And that ye study to be q, and to 1Th 4:11
that we may lead a q and peaceable 1Ti 2:2
a spirit, which is in the sight 1Pet 3:4

QUIETED
q myself, as a child that is .... Ps 131:2
toward the north country have q .... Zec 6:8

QUIETETH
when he q the earth by the south .... Job 37:17

QUIETLY
in the gate to speak with him q 2Sa 3:27
q wait for the salvation of the .... Lam 3:26

QUIETNESS
the country was in q forty years .... Judg 8:28
q unto Israel in his days 1Chr 22:9
he shall not feel q in his belly .... Job 20:20
When he giveth q, who then can .... Job 34:29
q in quietness and to house full .... Prov 17:1
Better is an handful with q .... Eccl 4:6
in q and in confidence shall be .... Is 30:15
and the effect of righteousness q .... Is 32:17
that by thee we enjoy great q .... Acts 24:2
Christ, that with q they work 2Th 3:12

QUIRINIUS See CYRENIUS.

QUIT
then shall he that smote him be q .... Ex 21:19
the owner of the ox shall be q .... Ex 21:28
then we will be q of thine oath .... Josh 2:20
q yourselves like men, O ye 1Sa 4:9
q yourselves like men, and fight 1Sa 4:9
q you like men, be strong 1Cor 16:13

QUITE
hath q devoured also our money .... Gen 31:15
q break down their images .... Ex 23:24
thou shalt q take away their .... Num 17:10
q pluck down all their high .... Num 33:52
sent him away, and he is q gone 2Sa 3:24
and is wisdom driven q from me .... Job 6:13
Thy bow was made q naked, ... Hab 3:9

QUIVER
I pray thee, thy weapons, thy q .... Gen 27:3
The rattleth against him, the q .... Job 39:23
man that hath his q full of them .... Ps 127:5
Elam have the q with chariots of .... Is 22:6
in his q hath he hid me .... Is 49:2
Their q is as an open sepulchre, ... Jer 5:16
of his q to enter into my reins .... Lam 3:13

QUIVERED
my lips q at the voice .... Hab 3:16

R

RAAMA See RAAMAH.

RAAMAH (ra'-a-mah)
  1. A son of Cush.
Seba, and Havilah, and Sabtah, and R ... Gen 10:7
and the sons of R 1Chr 1:9
Seba, and Havilah, and Sabta, and R. 1Chr 1:9
And the sons of R 1Chr 1:9
  2. A place in Arabia.
The merchants of Sheba and R .... Eze 27:22

RAAMIAH (ra-a-mi'-ah) A clan leader in exile.
Jeshua, Nehemiah, Azariah, R .... Neh 7:7

RAAMSES (ra-am'-seze) See RAMESES. An
  Egyptian city.
treasure cities, Pithom and R .... Ex 1:11

RABBAH (rab'-bah) See RABBATH.
  1. An Ammonite city.
unto Aroer that is before R .... Josh 13:25
children of Ammon, and besieged R 2Sa 11:1
Joab fought against R of the 2Sa 12:26
and said, I have fought against R 2Sa 12:27
The people together, and went to R 2Sa 12:29
of R of the children of Ammon 2Sa 17:27
of therewith, and came and besieged R ... 1Chr 20:1
And Joab smote R, and destroyed it...... 1Chr 20:1
to be heard in R of the Ammonites .... Jer 49:2
cry, ye daughters of R, gird you .... Jer 49:3
I will make R a stable for camels .... Eze 25:5
kindle a fire in the wall of R .... Amos 1:14
  2. A city in Judah.
which is Kirjath-jearim, and R .... Josh 15:60

RABBATH (rab'-bath) See RABBAH. Same as
  Rabbah 1.
is it not in R of the children of .... Deut 3:11
may come to R of the Ammonites .... Eze 21:20

RABBI (rab'-bi) See RABBONI. A Jewish title
  meaning 'teacher.'
and to be called of men, R, R .... Mt 23:7
But be not ye called R .... Mt 23:8
They said unto him, R, (which is .... Jn 1:38
answered and saith unto him, R .... Jn 1:49
by night, and said unto him, R .... Jn 3:2
unto John, and said unto him, R .... Jn 3:26
of the sea, they said unto him, R .... Jn 6:25

RABBITH (rab'-bith) A city in Issachar.
And R, and Kishion, and Abez, ... Josh 19:20

RABBONI (rab-bo'-ni) See RABBI. A Jewish
  title of respect.
herself, and saith unto him, R .... Jn 20:16

RAB-MAG A Babylonian prince.
Rab-saris, Nergal-sharezer, R .... Jer 39:3
Rab-saris, and Nergal-sharezer, R .... Jer 39:13

RAB-SARIS
  1. A Babylonian prince.
Samgar-nebo, Sarsechim, R .... Jer 39:3
the guard sent, and Nebushasban, R ..... Jer 39:13
  2. An Assyrian officer.
king of Assyria sent Tartan and R 2Kin 18:17

RAB-SHAKEH (*rab'-sha-keh*) See RABSHAKEH.
An Assyrian officer.
R from Lachish to king Hezekiah 2Kin 18:17
R said unto them, Speak ye now to 2Kin 18:19
and Shebna, and Joah, unto R 2Kin 18:26
But R said unto them, Hath my 2Kin 18:27
Then R stood and cried with a loud .. 2Kin 18:28
rent, and told him the words of R 2Kin 18:37
God will hear all the words of R 2Kin 19:4
So R returned, and found the king 2Kin 19:8

RABSHAKEH (*rab'-sha-keh*) See RAB-SHAKEH.
Same as Rab-shakeh.
the king of Assyria sent R from .... Is 36:2
R said unto them, Say ye now to ...... Is 36:4
Eliakim and Shebna and Joah unto R . Is 36:11
But R said, Hath my master sent ...... Is 36:12
Then R stood, and cried with a .... Is 36:13
rent, and told him the words of R .... Is 36:22
thy God will hear the words of R ...... Is 37:4
So R returned, and found the king .... Is 37:8

RACA (*ra'-cah*) *A Jewish term of disrespect.*
shall say to his brother, R .... Mt 5:22

RACAL See RACHAL.

RACE
as a strong man to run a r .... Ps 19:5
that the r is not to the swift, ... Eccl 9:11
they which run in a r run all 1Cor 9:24
the r that is set before us .... Heb 12:1

RACHAB (*ra'-kab*) See RAHAB. *Same as Rahab;
ancestor of Jesus.*
And Salmon begat Booz of R............. Mt 1:5

RACHAL (*ra'-kal*) *A city in Judah.*
And to them which were in R 1Sa 30:29

RACHEL (*ra'-chel*) See RACHEL's, RAHEL. *Wife
of Jacob.*
R his daughter cometh with the .... Gen 29:6
R came with her father's sheep .... Gen 29:10
when Jacob saw R the daughter of .... Gen 29:10
And Jacob kissed R, and lifted up..... Gen 29:11
Jacob told R that he was her............ Gen 29:12
and the name of the younger was R .. Gen 29:16
but R was beautiful and well .... Gen 29:17
And Jacob loved R .... Gen 29:18
years for R thy younger daughter ..... Gen 29:18
And Jacob served seven years for R... Gen 29:20
did not I serve with thee for R .... Gen 29:25
he gave him R his daughter to.......... Gen 29:28
Laban gave to R his daughter .... Gen 29:29
And he went in also unto R .... Gen 29:30
he loved also R more than Leah, ... Gen 29:30
but R was barren .... Gen 29:31
when R saw that she bare Jacob no ... Gen 30:1
no children, R envied her sister .... Gen 30:1
anger was kindled against R .... Gen 30:2
R said, God hath judged me, and ...... Gen 30:6
R said, With great wrestlings .... Gen 30:8
Then R said to Leah, Give me, I .... Gen 30:14
R said, Therefore he shall lie .... Gen 30:15
And God remembered R, and God ..... Gen 30:22
when R had born Joseph, that .... Gen 30:25
And Jacob sent and called R .... Gen 31:4
And R and Leah answered and said ... Gen 31:14
R had stolen the images that were .... Gen 31:19
knew not that R had stolen them ...... Gen 31:32
Now R had taken the images, and ..... Gen 31:34
the children unto Leah, and unto R .. Gen 33:1
Leah and her children after, and R.... Gen 33:2
and after came Joseph near and R..... Gen 33:7
R travailed, and she had hard .... Gen 35:16
R died, and was buried in the way .... Gen 35:19
The sons of R .... Gen 35:24
The sons of R Jacob's wife .... Gen 46:19
These are the sons of R, which .... Gen 46:22
Laban gave unto R his daughter .... Gen 46:25
R died by me in the land of .... Gen 48:7
is come into thine house like R........ Ruth 4:11
R weeping for her children, and .... Mt 2:18

RACHEL's (*ra'-chelz*)
Bilhah R maid conceived again, and .. Gen 30:7
tent, and entered into R tent............ Gen 31:33
pillar of R grave unto this day .... Gen 35:20
And the sons of Bilhah, R handmaid.. Gen 35:25
by R sepulchre in the border of 1Sa 10:2

RADDAI (*rad'-dahee*) *Son of Jesse.*
the fourth, R the fifth, ... 1Chr 2:14

RAFTERS
house are cedar, and our r of fir .... Song 1:17

RAGAU (*ra'-gaw*) See REU. *Father of Saruch;
ancestor of Jesus.*
of Saruch, which was the son of R..... Lk 3:35

RAGE
So he turned and went away in a r 2Kin 5:12
coming in, and thy r against me....... 2Kin 19:27
Because thy r against me and thy...... 2Kin 19:28
for he was in a r with him 2Chr 16:10
ye have slain them in a r that........... 2Chr 28:9
the ground with fierceness and r ...... Job 39:24
Cast abroad the r of thy wrath .... Job 40:11
Why do the heathen r, and the .... Ps 2:1
because of the r of mine enemies...... Ps 7:6
For jealousy is the r of a man.......... Prov 6:34
man, whether he r or laugh.............. Prov 29:9
coming in, and thy r against me........ Is 37:28
Because thy r against me, and thy..... Is 37:29

and r, ye chariots......................... Jer 46:9
Then Nebuchadnezzar in his r.......... Dan 3:13
sword for the r of their tongue:........ Hos 7:16
chariots shall r in the streets........... Nah 2:4
hast said, Why did the heathen r ...... Acts 4:25

RAGED
The heathen r, the kingdoms were..... Ps 46:6

RAGETH
but the fool r, and is confident......... Prov 14:16

RAGGED
and into the tops of the r rocks .... Is 2:21

RAGING
Thou rulest the r of the sea .... Ps 89:9
is a mocker, strong drink is r .... Prov 20:1
and the sea ceased from her r .... Jonah 1:15
the wind and the r of the water .... Lk 8:24
R waves of the sea, foaming out .... Jude 13

RAGS
shall clothe a man with r .... Prov 23:21
righteousnesses are as filthy r.......... Is 64:6
old cast clouts and old rotten r .... Jer 38:11
rotten r under thine armholes.......... Jer 38:12

RAGUEL (*ra-gu'-el*) *Father-in-law of Moses.*
the son of R the Midianite, ... Num 10:29

RAHAB (*ra'-hab*) See RACHAB.
I. A Jericho woman who befriended the spies.
into an harlot's house, named R .... Josh 2:1
the king of Jericho sent unto R .... Josh 2:3
only R the harlot shall live, she .... Josh 6:17
spies went in, and brought out R ...... Josh 6:23
Joshua saved R the harlot alive, ... Josh 6:25
By faith the harlot R perished. .... Heb 11:31
Likewise also was not R the .... Jas 2:25
2. A symbolic name for Egypt.
I will make mention of R and.......... Ps 87:4
Thou hast broken R in pieces.......... Ps 89:10
Art thou not it that hath cut R .... Is 51:9

RAHAM (*ra'-ham*) *Son of Shema.*
And Shema begat R, the father of 1Chr 2:44

RAHEL (*ra'-hel*) See RACHEL. *Same as Rachel.*
R weeping for her children .... Jer 31:15

RAIL
He wrote also letters to r on the....... 2Chr 32:17

RAILED
and he r on them. 1Sa 25:14
And they that passed by r on him ..... Mk 15:29
which were hanged r on him .... Lk 23:39

RAILER
covetous, or an idolator, or a r 1Cor 5:11

RAILING
evil for evil, or r for r 1Pet 3:9
bring not r accusation against 2Pet 2:11
bring against him a r accusation ...... Jude 9

RAILINGS
whereof cometh envy, strife, r......... 1Ti 6:4

RAIMENT
silver, and jewels of gold, and r .... Gen 24:53
Rebekah took goodly r of her .... Gen 27:15
and he smelled the smell of his r ...... Gen 27:27
me bread to eat, and r to put on, ... Gen 28:20
shaved himself, and changed his r .... Gen 41:14
he gave each man changes of r .... Gen 45:22
of silver, and five changes of r......... Gen 45:22
silver, and jewels of gold, and r .... Ex 3:22
silver, and jewels of gold, and r .... Ex 12:35
her food, her r, and the duty of .... Ex 21:10
for ox, for ass, for sheep, for r .... Ex 22:9
take thy neighbour's r to pledge ...... Ex 22:26
only, it is his r for his skin? .... Ex 22:27
it be any vessel of wood, or r .... Lev 11:32
And purify all your r, and all that..... Num 31:20
Thy r waxed not old upon thee, ... Deut 8:4
stranger in giving him food and r ..... Deut 10:18
she shall put the r of her .... Deut 21:13
and so shalt thou do with his r .... Deut 22:3
that he may sleep in his own r .... Deut 24:13
nor take a widow's r to pledge .... Deut 24:17
and with iron, and with very much r.. Josh 22:8
under his r upon his right thigh .... Judg 3:16
purple r that was on the kings of ..... Judg 8:26
put thy r upon thee, and get thee..... Ruth 3:3
himself, and put on other r 1Sa 28:8
of gold, and ten changes of r 2Kin 5:5
thence silver, and gold, and r 2Kin 7:8
silver, and vessels of gold, and r 2Chr 9:24
she sent r to clothe Mordecai, and ... Est 4:4
dust, and prepare r as the clay .... Job 27:16
unto the king in r of needlework ...... Ps 45:14
as the r of those that are slain, ... Is 14:19
and I will stain all my r .... Is 63:3
thy r was of fine linen, and silk, ... Eze 16:13
will clothe thee with change of r ...... Zec 3:4
John had his r of camel's hair .... Mt 3:4
than meat, and the body than r .... Mt 6:25
And why take ye thought for r .... Mt 6:28
A man clothed in soft r .... Mt 11:8
his r was white as the light .... Mt 17:2
from him, and put his own r on him.. Mt 27:31
lightning, and his r white as snow.... Mt 28:3
his r became shining, exceeding ...... Mk 9:3
A man clothed in soft r .... Lk 7:25
his r was white and glistering.......... Lk 9:29

which stripped him of his r.............. Lk 10:30
meat, and the body is more than r .... Lk 12:23
And they parted his r, and cast .... Lk 23:34
They parted my r among them.......... Jn 19:24
and blasphemed, he shook his r........ Acts 18:6
kept the r of them that slew him...... Acts 22:20
r let us be therewith content........... 1Ti 6:8
come in also a poor man in vile r ...... Jas 2:2
same shall be clothed in white r .... Rev 3:5
and white r, that thou mayest be ...... Rev 3:18
sitting, clothed in white r................ Rev 4:4

RAIN
not caused it to r upon the earth ...... Gen 2:5
I will cause it to r upon the............. Gen 7:4
the r was upon the earth forty......... Gen 7:12
the r from heaven was restrained..... Gen 8:2
it to r a very grievous hail .... Ex 9:18
the r was not poured upon the .... Ex 9:33
And when Pharaoh saw that the r..... Ex 9:34
I will r bread from heaven for .... Ex 16:4
I will give you r in due season .... Lev 26:4
drinketh water of the r of heaven .... Deut 11:11
That I will give you the r of............ Deut 11:14
in his due season, the first r .... Deut 11:14
and the latter r .... Deut 11:14
up the heaven, that there be no r ..... Deut 11:17
the heaven to give the r unto thy..... Deut 28:12
make the r of thy land powder......... Deut 28:24
My doctrine shall drop as the r .... Deut 32:2
as the small r upon the tender........ Deut 32:2
and he shall send thunder and r 1Sa 12:17
LORD sent thunder and r that day.... 1Sa 12:18
be no dew, neither let there be r 2Sa 1:21
earth by clear shining after r 2Sa 23:4
is shut up, and there is no r............. 1Kin 8:35
give r upon thy land, which thou 1Kin 8:36
not be dew nor r these years........... 1Kin 17:1
there had been no r in the land 1Kin 17:7
the LORD sendeth r upon the earth... 1Kin 17:14
I will send r upon the earth............. 1Kin 18:1
is a sound of abundance of r 1Kin 18:41
down, that the r stop thee not 1Kin 18:44
and wind, and there was a great r 1Kin 18:45
see wind, neither shall ye see r 2Kin 3:17
is shut up, and there is no r............. 2Chr 6:26
send r upon thy land, which thou 2Chr 6:27
shut up heaven that there be no r 2Chr 7:13
this matter, and for the great r .... Ezr 10:9
many, and it is a time of much r ...... Ezr 10:13
Who giveth r upon the earth, and.... Job 5:10
shall r it upon him while he is......... Job 20:23
When he made a decree for the r ..... Job 28:26
they waited for me as for the r .... Job 29:23
mouth wide as for the latter r .... Job 29:23
they pour down r according to the ... Job 36:27
likewise to the small r, and to .... Job 37:6
to the great r of his strength .... Job 37:6
To cause it to r on the earth,.......... Job 38:26
Hath the r a father........................ Job 38:28
Upon the wicked he shall r snares.... Ps 11:6
O God, didst send a plentiful r .... Ps 68:9
down like r upon the mown grass..... Ps 72:6
the r also filleth the pools. .... Ps 84:6
He gave them hail for r, and........... Ps 105:32
he maketh lightnings for the r .... Ps 135:7
who prepareth r for the earth.......... Ps 147:8
is as a cloud of the latter r .... Prov 16:15
is like clouds and wind without r ..... Prov 25:14
The north wind driveth away r......... Prov 25:23
as r in harvest, so honour is not ...... Prov 26:1
sweeping r which leaveth no food..... Prov 28:3
If the clouds be full of r, ... Eccl 11:3
nor the clouds return after the r ...... Eccl 12:2
is past, the r is over and gone .... Song 2:11
for a covert from storm and from r .. Is 4:6
that they r no r upon it................... Is 5:6
that they r no r upon it................... Is 5:6
shall he give the r of thy seed .... Is 30:23
an ash, and the r doth nourish it...... Is 44:14
For as the r cometh down, and the ... Is 55:10
and there hath been no latter r .... Jer 3:3
the LORD our God, that giveth r....... Jer 5:24
he maketh lightnings with r............ Jer 10:13
for there was no r in the earth,........ Jer 14:4
of the Gentiles that can cause r .... Jer 14:22
he maketh lightnings with r............ Jer 51:16
in the cloud in the day of r .... Eze 1:28
I will r upon him, and upon his .... Eze 38:22
are with him, and overflowing r ...... Eze 38:22
and he shall come unto us as the r ... Hos 6:3
latter and former r unto the earth.... Hos 6:3
according to the righteousness upon . Hos 10:12
given you the former r moderately.... Joel 2:23
cause to come down for you the r ..... Joel 2:23
the former r, and the latter .... Joel 2:23
the latter r in the first month .... Joel 2:23
I have withholden the r from you...... Amos 4:7
and I caused it to r upon one city..... Amos 4:7
caused it not to r upon another .... Amos 4:7
Ask ye of the LORD r in the time ..... Zec 10:1
in the time of the latter r .... Zec 10:1
clouds, and give them showers of r ... Zec 10:1
even upon them shall be no r .... Zec 14:17
up, and come not, that have no r ...... Zec 14:18
sendeth r on the just and on the ...... Mt 5:45
the r descended, and the floods .... Mt 7:25
the r descended, and the floods .... Mt 7:27
gave us r from heaven, and............. Acts 14:17
one, because of the present r .... Acts 28:2
in the r that cometh upon it............. Heb 6:7

RAINBOW
he receive the early and latter r.......... Jas 5:7
earnestly that it might not r.............. Jas 5:17
again, and the heaven gave r .... Jas 5:18
that it r not in the days of.............. Rev 11:6

RAINBOW
there was a r round about the.......... Rev 4:3
a r was upon his head, and his.......... Rev 10:1

RAINED
Then the LORD r upon Sodom.......... Gen 19:24
the LORD r hail upon the land of........ Ex 9:23
had r down manna upon them to eat.... Ps 78:24
He r flesh also upon them as dust...... Ps 78:27
nor r upon in the day of.................. Eze 22:24
one piece was r upon, and the.......... Amos 4:7
piece whereupon it r not withered...... Amos 4:7
Lot went out of Sodom it r fire.......... Lk 17:29
it r not on the earth by the.............. Jas 5:17

RAINY
dropping in a very r day and a.......... Prov 27:15

RAISE
her, and r up seed to thy brother........ Gen 38:8
Thou shalt not r a false report.......... Ex 23:1
The LORD thy God will r up unto...... Deut 18:15
I will r them up a Prophet from........ Deut 18:18
r up unto his brother a name in........ Deut 25:7
r thereon a great heap of stones........ Josh 8:29
to r up the name of the dead upon...... Ruth 4:5
to r up the name of the dead upon...... Ruth 4:10
I will r me up a faithful priest,........ 1Sa 2:35
I will r up evil against thee out........ 2Sa 12:11
to r him up from the earth.............. 2Sa 12:17
Moreover the LORD shall r him up.... 1Kin 14:14
that I will r up thy seed after.......... 1Chr 17:11
who are ready to r up their.............. Job 3:8
r up their way against me, and........ Job 19:12
they r up against me the ways of...... Job 30:12
r me up, that I may requite them...... Ps 41:10
I will r up a cry of destruction........ Is 15:5
I will r forts against thee................ Is 29:3
I will r up the decayed places.......... Is 44:26
to r up the tribes of Jacob.............. Is 49:6
thou shalt r up the foundations........ Is 58:12
they shall r up the former.............. Is 61:4
that I will r unto David a................ Jer 23:5
whom I will r up unto them............ Jer 30:9
For, lo, I will r and cause to.......... Jer 50:9
and fall, and none shall r him up...... Jer 50:32
I will r up against Babylon, and...... Jer 51:1
I will r up thy lovers against.......... Eze 23:22
I will r up for them a plant of........ Eze 34:29
in the third day he will r us up........ Hos 6:2
I will r them out of the place.......... Joel 3:7
there is none to r her up................ Amos 5:2
I will r up against you a nation,...... Amos 6:14
In that day will I r up the.............. Amos 9:11
I will r up his ruins, and I will........ Amos 9:11
then shall we r against him seven...... Mic 5:5
and there are that r up strife.......... Hab 1:3
I r up the Chaldeans, that bitter...... Hab 1:6
I will r up a shepherd in the.......... Zec 11:16
to r up children unto Abraham........ Mt 3:9
r the dead, cast out devils.............. Mt 10:8
r up seed unto his brother.............. Mt 22:24
r up seed unto his brother.............. Mk 12:19
to r up children unto Abraham........ Lk 3:8
r up seed unto his brother.............. Lk 20:28
and in three days I will r it up........ Jn 2:19
but should r it up again at the........ Jn 6:39
I will r him up at the last day........ Jn 6:40
I will r him up at the last day........ Jn 6:44
I will r him up at the last day........ Jn 6:54
he would r up Christ to sit on........ Acts 2:30
r up unto you of your brethren........ Acts 3:22
r up unto you of your brethren........ Acts 7:37
you, That God should r the dead...... Acts 26:8
will also r up us by his own............ 1Cor 6:14
Jesus shall r up us also by Jesus...... 2Cor 4:14
that God was able to r him up........ Heb 11:19
sick, and the Lord shall r him up...... Jas 5:15

RAISED
for this cause have I r thee up.......... Ex 9:16
whom he r up in their stead, them...... Josh 5:7
they r over him a great heap of........ Josh 7:26
Nevertheless the LORD r up Judges...... Judg 2:16
when the LORD r them up judges,...... Judg 2:18
the LORD r up a deliverer to the...... Judg 3:9
the LORD r them up a deliverer,...... Judg 3:15
and the man who was r up on high...... 2Sa 23:1
king Solomon r a levy out of all...... 1Kin 5:13
of the levy which king Solomon r...... 1Kin 9:15
r it up to the towers, and another...... 2Chr 32:5
r it up a very great height, and........ 2Chr 33:14
all them whose spirit God had r...... Ezr 1:5
nor be r out of their sleep.............. Job 14:12
I r thee up under the apple tree........ Song 8:5
it hath r up from their thrones........ Is 14:9
they r up the palaces thereof.......... Is 23:13
Who r up the righteous man from...... Is 41:2
I have r up one in righteousness,...... Is 45:13
a great nation shall be r from........ Jer 6:22
a great whirlwind shall be r up........ Jer 25:32
The LORD hath r us up prophets in...... Jer 29:15
many kings shall be r up from the...... Jer 50:41
God hath r up by the spirit of........ Jer 51:11
it r up itself on one side, and it...... Dan 7:5
I r up of your sons for prophets, ... Amos 2:11
for he is r up out of his holy............ Zec 2:13

---

r up thy sons, O Zion, against.......... Zec 9:13
Then Joseph being r from sleep........ Mt 1:24
the deaf hear, the dead are r up........ Mt 11:5
and be r again the third day............ Mt 16:21
the third day he shall be r again...... Mt 17:23
hath r up an horn of salvation........ Lk 1:69
the deaf hear, the dead are r.......... Lk 7:22
be slain, and be r the third day........ Lk 9:22
Now that the dead are r, even........ Lk 20:37
dead, whom he r from the dead........ Jn 12:1
whom he had r from the dead.......... Jn 12:9
r him from the dead, bare record...... Jn 12:17
Whom God hath r up, having loosed.... Acts 2:24
This Jesus hath God r up, whereof...... Acts 2:32
whom God hath r from the dead........ Acts 3:15
having r up his Son Jesus, sent........ Acts 3:26
whom God r from the dead, even by...... Acts 4:10
The God of our fathers r up Jesus...... Acts 5:30
Him God r up the third day, and...... Acts 10:40
r him up, saying, Arise up.............. Acts 12:7
he r up unto them David to be.......... Acts 13:22
promise r unto Israel a Saviour........ Acts 13:23
But God r him from the dead.......... Acts 13:30
in that he hath r up Jesus again...... Acts 13:33
that he r him up from the dead........ Acts 13:34
But he, whom God r again, saw no...... Acts 13:37
r persecution against Paul and........ Acts 13:50
in that he hath r him from the........ Acts 17:31
if we believe on him that r up........ Rom 4:24
was r again for our justification...... Rom 4:25
that like as Christ was r up from...... Rom 6:4
Knowing that Christ being r from...... Rom 6:9
to him who is r from the dead.......... Rom 7:4
But if the Spirit of him that r........ Rom 8:11
he that r up Christ from the dead...... Rom 8:11
same purpose have I r thee up........ Rom 9:17
that God hath r him from the dead...... Rom 10:9
And God hath both r up the Lord...... 1Cor 6:14
of God that he r up Christ.............. 1Cor 15:15
whom he r not up, if so be that........ 1Cor 15:15
rise not, then is not Christ r.......... 1Cor 15:16
And if Christ be not r, your faith...... 1Cor 15:17
will say, How are the dead r up?...... 1Cor 15:35
it is r in glory............................ 1Cor 15:43
it is r in power.......................... 1Cor 15:43
it is r a spiritual body.................. 1Cor 15:44
the dead shall be r incorruptible...... 1Cor 15:52
Knowing that he which r up the........ 2Cor 4:14
Father, who r him from the dead...... Gal 1:1
when he r him from the dead, and...... Eph 1:20
hath r us up together, and made us.... Eph 2:6
who hath r him from the dead.......... Col 2:12
whom he r from the dead, even........ 1Th 1:10
r from the dead according to my...... 2Ti 2:8
their dead r to life again.............. Heb 11:35
that r him up from the dead, and...... 1Pet 1:21

RAISER
a r of taxes in the glory of.............. Dan 11:20

RAISETH
He r up the poor out of the dust,...... 1Sa 2:8
When he r up himself, the mighty...... Job 41:25
r the stormy wind, which lifteth...... Ps 107:25
He r up the poor out of the dust...... Ps 113:7
r up all those that be bowed down,...... Ps 145:14
the LORD r them that are bowed...... Ps 146:8
For as the Father r up the dead........ Jn 5:21
but in God which r the dead............ 2Cor 1:9

RAISING
who ceaseth from r after he hath...... Hos 7:4
neither r up the people, neither........ Acts 24:12

RAISINS
corn, and an hundred clusters of r...... 1Sa 25:18
of figs, and two clusters of r.......... 1Sa 30:12
bread, and an hundred bunches of r...... 2Sa 16:1
cakes of figs, and bunches of r........ 1Chr 12:40

RAKEM (ra´-kem) Son of Sheresh.
and his sons were Ulam and R.......... 1Chr 7:16

RAKKATH (rak´-kath) A city in Naphtali.
are Ziddim, Zer, and Hammath, R.... Josh 19:35

RAKKON (rak´-kon) A city in Dan.
And Me-jarkon, and R, with the........ Josh 19:46

RAM (ram)
1. Father of Aminadab.
And Hezron begat R...................... Ruth 4:19
and R begat Amminadab................ Ruth 4:19
Jerahmeel, and R, and Chelubai........ 1Chr 2:9
And R begat Amminadab................ 1Chr 2:10
2. Son of Jerahmeel.
R the firstborn, and Bunah, and...... 1Chr 2:25
the sons of R the firstborn of.......... 1Chr 2:27
3. Head of Elihu's family.
the Buzite, of the kindred of R........ Job 32:2
4. Male sheep.
a r of three years old, and a.......... Gen 15:9
behold behind him a r caught in a...... Gen 22:13
and Abraham went and took the r...... Gen 22:13
Thou shalt also take one r.............. Ex 29:15
hands upon the head of the r.......... Ex 29:15
And thou shalt slay the r, and thou...... Ex 29:16
And thou shalt cut the r in pieces...... Ex 29:17
burn the whole r upon the altar...... Ex 29:18
And thou shalt take the other r........ Ex 29:19
hands upon the head of the r.......... Ex 29:19
Then shalt thou kill the r.............. Ex 29:20
thou shalt take of the r the fat........ Ex 29:22

---

for it is a r of consecration............ Ex 29:22
of the r of Aaron's consecration...... Ex 29:26
of the r of the consecration,.......... Ex 29:27
take the r of the consecration,........ Ex 29:31
sons shall eat the flesh of the r........ Ex 29:32
a r without blemish out of the........ Lev 5:15
the r of the trespass offering.......... Lev 5:16
he shall bring a r without.............. Lev 5:18
a r without blemish out of the........ Lev 6:6
he brought the r for the burnt........ Lev 8:18
hands upon the head of the r.......... Lev 8:18
And he cut the r into pieces............ Lev 8:20
burnt the whole r upon the altar...... Lev 8:21
other ram, the r of consecration...... Lev 8:22
hands upon the head of the r.......... Lev 8:22
for of the r of consecration it........ Lev 8:29
a r for a burnt offering, without...... Lev 9:2
a r for peace offerings, to.............. Lev 9:4
the r for a sacrifice of peace.......... Lev 9:18
fat of the bullock and of the r........ Lev 9:19
and a r for a burnt offering............ Lev 16:3
one r for a burnt offering.............. Lev 16:5
even a r for a trespass offering........ Lev 19:21
an atonement for him with the r...... Lev 19:22
beside the r of the atonement,........ Num 5:8
one r without blemish for peace...... Num 6:14
he shall offer the r for a................ Num 6:17
take the sodden shoulder of the r...... Num 6:19
One young bullock, one r, one.......... Num 7:15
One young bullock, one r, one.......... Num 7:21
One young bullock, one r, one.......... Num 7:27
One young bullock, one r, one.......... Num 7:33
One young bullock, one r, one.......... Num 7:39
One young bullock, one r, one.......... Num 7:45
One young bullock, one r, one.......... Num 7:51
One young bullock, one r, one.......... Num 7:57
One young bullock, one r, one.......... Num 7:63
One young bullock, one r, one.......... Num 7:69
One young bullock, one r, one.......... Num 7:75
One young bullock, one r, one.......... Num 7:81
Or for a r, thou shalt prepare.......... Num 15:6
for one bullock, or for one r.......... Num 15:11
on every altar a bullock and a r...... Num 23:2
upon every altar a bullock and a r.... Num 23:4
a bullock and a r on every altar...... Num 23:14
a bullock and a r on every altar...... Num 23:30
two young bullocks, and one r........ Num 28:11
mingled with oil, for one r............ Num 28:12
the third part of an hin unto a r...... Num 28:14
two young bullocks, and one r........ Num 28:19
and two tenth deals for a r............ Num 28:20
two young bullocks, one r.............. Num 28:27
two tenth deals unto one r............ Num 28:28
one young bullock, one r, and........ Num 29:2
and two tenth deals for a r............ Num 29:3
one young bullock, one r, and........ Num 29:8
and two tenth deals to one r.......... Num 29:9
deals to each r of the two rams...... Num 29:14
one bullock, one r, seven lambs...... Num 29:36
for the bullock, for the r.............. Num 29:37
they offered a r of the flock for...... Ezr 10:19
a r out of the flock without............ Eze 43:23
a r out of the flock, without.......... Eze 43:25
a bullock, and an ephah for a r...... Eze 45:24
blemish, and a r without blemish...... Eze 46:4
shall be an ephah for a r.............. Eze 46:5
blemish, and six lambs, and a r...... Eze 46:6
a bullock, and an ephah for a r...... Eze 46:7
to a bullock, and an ephah to a r.... Eze 46:11
the river a r which had two horns...... Dan 8:3
I saw the r pushing westward, and...... Dan 8:4
he came to the r that had two........ Dan 8:6
I saw him come close unto the r...... Dan 8:7
against him, and smote the r.......... Dan 8:7
in the r to stand before him.......... Dan 8:7
deliver the r out of his hand.......... Dan 8:7
The r which thou sawest having...... Dan 8:20

RAMA (ra´-mah) See RAMAH. Same as Ramah I.
In R was there a voice heard,.......... Mt 2:18

RAMAH (ra´-mah) See RAMA, RAMATH.
1. A city in Benjamin.
Gibeon, and R, and Beeroth,.......... Josh 18:25
palm tree of Deborah between R ...... Judg 4:5
all might, in Gibeah, or in R.......... Judg 19:13
went up against Judah, and built R... 1Kin 15:17
that he left off building of R.......... 1Kin 15:21
and they took away the stones of R... 1Kin 15:22
came up against Judah, and built R... 2Chr 16:1
that he left off building of R.......... 2Chr 16:5
they carried away the stones of R.... 2Chr 16:6
The children of R and Gaba, six...... Ezr 2:26
The men of R and Gaba, six hundred... Neh 7:30
Hazor, R, Gittaim,...................... Neh 11:33
R is afraid............................ Is 10:29
the guard had let him go from R...... Jer 40:1
in Gibeah, and the trumpet in R...... Hos 5:8
2. A city in Naphtali.
And then the coast turneth to R...... Josh 19:29
And Adamah, and R, and Hazor,...... Josh 19:36
3. A city in Ephraim.
and came to their house to R.......... 1Sa 1:19
And Elkanah went to R to his house... 1Sa 2:11
And his return was to R................ 1Sa 7:17
and came to Samuel unto R............ 1Sa 8:4
Then Samuel went to R................ 1Sa 15:34
So Samuel rose up, and went to R.... 1Sa 16:13
escaped, and came to Samuel to R.... 1Sa 19:18
Behold, David is at Naioth in R...... 1Sa 19:19
Then went he also to R, and came.... 1Sa 19:22

R

Behold, they are at Naioth in R............ 1Sa 19:22
And he went thither to Naioth in R 1Sa 19:23
until he came to Naioth in R................ 1Sa 19:23
And David fled from Naioth in R 1Sa 20:1
abode in Gibeah under a tree in R 1Sa 22:6
and buried him in his house at R 1Sa 25:1
lamented him, and buried him in R 1Sa 28:3
A voice was heard in R,....................... Jer 31:15
    4. A short form of Ramoth-Gilead.
the Syrians had given him at R 2Kin 8:29
wounds which were given him at R.... 2Chr 22:6

RAMATH (*ra-math'*) A city in Simeon.
to Baalath-beer, R of the south .... Josh 19:8

RAMATHAIM-ZOPHIM (*ram-a-tha'-im-zo'-fim*) A city on Mt. Ephraim.
Now there was a certain man of R 1Sa 1:1

RAMATHITE (*ra'-math-ite*) An inhabitant of Ramah 1.
the vineyards by Shimei the R 1Chr 27:27

RAMATH-LEHI (*ra'-math-le'-hi*) A place in Judah.
his hand, and called that place R .... Judg 15:17

RAMATH MIZPAH See RAMATH-MIZPEH.

RAMATH-MIZPEH (*ra'-math-miz'-peh*) A city in Gad.
And from Heshbon unto R, and.......... Josh 13:26

RAMESES (*ram'-e-seze*) See RAAMSES. A city in Goshen.
of the land, in the land of R .... Gen 47:11
journeyed from R to Succoth .... Ex 12:37
from R in the first month .... Num 33:3
children of Israel removed from R...... Num 33:5

RAMIAH (*ra'-mi-ah*) Married a foreigner while in exile.
R, and Jeziah, and Malchiah, and........ Ezr 10:25

RAMOTH (*ra'-moth*) See JARMUTH, RAMAH, RAMOTH-GILEAD, REMETH.
  1. A Levitical city in Gad.
R in Gilead, of the Gadites.................. Deut 4:43
R in Gilead out of the tribe of............. Josh 20:8
R in Gilead with her suburbs, to........ Josh 21:38
R in Gilead with her suburbs, and 1Chr 6:80
  2. A Levitical city in Issachar.
R with her suburbs, and Anem with ... 1Chr 6:73
  3. Married a foreigner in exile.
and Adaiah, Jashub, and Sheal, and R.. Ezr 10:29
  4. A city in Simeon.
and to them which were in south R 1Sa 30:27
  5. Same as Ramoth-gilead.
Know ye that R in Gilead is ours,........ 1Kin 22:3

RAMOTH-GILEAD (*ra'-moth-ghil'-e-ad*) A city in Gad.
The son of Geber, in R........................ 1Kin 4:13
thou go with me to battle to R 1Kin 22:4
Shall I go against R to battle 1Kin 22:6
prophesied so, saying, Go up to R..... 1Kin 22:12
shall we go against R to battle 1Kin 22:15
that he may go up and fall at R 1Kin 22:20
the king of Judah went up to R 1Kin 22:29
against Hazael king of Syria in R....... 2Kin 8:28
of oil in thine hand, and go to R 2Kin 9:1
young man the prophet, went to R 2Kin 9:4
(Now Joram had kept R, he and all.... 2Kin 9:14
him to go up with him to R 2Chr 18:2
Judah, Wilt thou go with me to R 2Chr 18:3
them, Shall we go to R to battle 2Chr 18:5
prophesied so, saying, Go up to R..... 2Chr 18:11
shall we go to R to battle 2Chr 18:14
that he may go up and fall at R 2Chr 18:19
the king of Judah went up to R 2Chr 18:28
against Hazael king of Syria at R 2Chr 22:5

RAMOTH NEGEV See RAMOTH-GILEAD.

RAMPART
therefore he made the r and the.......... Lam 2:8
whose r was the sea, and her wall ...... Nah 3:8

RAM'S
make a long blast with the r horn........ Josh 6:5

RAMS
the r which leaped upon the................. Gen 31:10
all the r which leap upon the................ Gen 31:12
the r of thy flock have I not................. Gen 31:38
two hundred ewes, and twenty r .... Gen 32:14
and two r without blemish.................... Ex 29:1
with the bullock and the two r............. Ex 29:3
and goats' hair, and red skins of r ...... Ex 35:23
for the sin offering, and two r .... Lev 8:2
and one young bullock, and two r .... Lev 23:18
peace offerings, two oxen, five r .... Num 7:17
peace offerings, two oxen, five r .... Num 7:23
peace offerings, two oxen, five r .... Num 7:29
peace offerings, two oxen, five r .... Num 7:35
peace offerings, two oxen, five r .... Num 7:41
peace offerings, two oxen, five r .... Num 7:47
peace offerings, two oxen, five r .... Num 7:53
peace offerings, two oxen, five r .... Num 7:59
peace offerings, two oxen, five r .... Num 7:65
peace offerings, two oxen, five r .... Num 7:71
peace offerings, two oxen, five r .... Num 7:77
peace offerings, two oxen, five r .... Num 7:83
the r twelve, the lambs of the............. Num 7:87
the r sixty, the he goats sixty,............ Num 7:88
me here seven oxen and seven r .... Num 23:1
me here seven bullocks and seven r. .. Num 23:29

thirteen young bullocks, two r............ Num 29:13
deals to each ram of the two r .... Num 29:14
twelve young bullocks, two r .... Num 29:17
for the bullocks, for the r .... Num 29:18
thirday eleven bullocks, two r............ Num 29:20
for the bullocks, for the r .... Num 29:21
fourth day ten bullocks, two r............ Num 29:23
for the bullocks, for the r .... Num 29:24
fifth day nine bullocks, two r .... Num 29:26
for the bullocks, for the r .... Num 29:27
sixth day eight bullocks, two r .... Num 29:29
for the bullocks, for the r .... Num 29:30
seventh day seven bullocks, two r ...... Num 29:32
for the bullocks, for the r .... Num 29:33
r of the breed of Bashan, and .... Deut 32:14
and to hearken than the fat of r 1Sa 15:22
lambs, and an hundred thousand r 2Kin 3:4
offered seven bullocks and seven r 1Chr 15:26
a thousand bullocks, a thousand r 1Chr 29:21
with a young bullock and seven r 2Chr 13:9
seven thousand and seven hundred r .. 2Chr 17:11
seven bullocks, and seven r 2Chr 29:21
that they had killed the r 2Chr 29:22
and ten bullocks, an hundred r........... 2Chr 29:32
of both young bullocks, and r .... Ezr 6:9
hundred bullocks, two hundred r....... Ezr 6:17
with this money bullocks, r .... Ezr 7:17
for all Israel, ninety and six r .... Ezr 8:35
you now seven bullocks and seven r .. Job 42:8
fatlings, with the incense of r .... Ps 66:15
The mountains skipped like r .... Ps 114:4
mountains, that ye skipped like r .... Ps 114:6
full of the burnt offerings of r .... Is 1:11
with the fat of the kidneys of r........... Is 34:6
the r of Nebaioth shall minister .... Is 60:7
slaughter, like r with he goats............ Jer 51:40
set fattening r against it round .... Eze 4:2
battering r against the gates............... Eze 21:22
occupied with thee in lambs, and r .... Eze 27:21
cattle and cattle, between the r .... Eze 34:17
of the princes of the earth, of r .... Eze 39:18
seven r without blemish daily the....... Eze 45:23
be pleased with thousands of r .... Mic 6:7

RAMS'
r skins dyed red, and badgers'............ Ex 25:5
for the tent of r skins dyed red........... Ex 26:14
r skins dyed red, and badgers'............ Ex 35:7
for the tent of r skins dyed red........... Ex 36:19
the covering of r skins dyed red .... Ex 39:34
the ark seven trumpets of r horns ...... Josh 6:6
of r horns before the ark of the .... Josh 6:8
bearing the seven trumpets of r .... Josh 6:13
bearing seven trumpets of r horns ...... Josh 6:13

RAN
R to meet them from the tent .... Gen 18:2
Abraham r unto the herd, and .... Gen 18:7
And the servant r to meet her .... Gen 24:17
r again unto the well to draw.............. Gen 24:20
And the damsel r, and told them of .... Gen 24:28
Laban r out unto the man, unto.......... Gen 24:29
and she r and told her father.............. Gen 29:12
that he r to meet him, and................... Gen 29:13
Esau r to meet him, and embraced .... Gen 33:4
the fire r along upon the ground .... Ex 9:23
there r a young man, and told .... Num 11:27
and r into the midst of the................... Num 16:47
and they r unto the tent .... Josh 7:22
and they r as soon as he had............... Josh 8:19
and all the host r, and cried, and........ Judg 7:21
And Jotham r away, and fled, and .... Judg 9:21
the two other companies r upon .... Judg 9:44
And the woman made haste, and r...... Judg 13:10
her r unto Eli, and said, Here am I...... 1Sa 3:5
there r a man of Benjamin out of 1Sa 4:12
And they r and fetched him thence 1Sa 10:23
r toward the army, and came and........ 1Sa 17:22
r toward the army to meet the............. 1Sa 17:48
Therefore David r, and stood upon 1Sa 17:51
And as the lad r, he shot an arrow 1Sa 20:36
bowed himself unto Joab, and r......... 2Sa 18:21
Then Ahimaaz r by the way of the...... 2Sa 18:23
two of the servants of Shimei............. 1Kin 2:39
the water r round about the altar 1Kin 18:35
r before Ahab to the entrance of 1Kin 18:46
r after Elijah, and said, Let me,.......... 1Kin 19:20
the blood r out of the wound into....... 1Kin 22:35
the brook that r through the................ 2Chr 32:4
my sore r in the night, and ceased ...... Ps 77:2
they r in the dry places like a............. Ps 105:41
that r down upon the beard, even .... Ps 133:2
sent these prophets, yet they r .... Jer 23:21
the living creatures r .... Eze 1:14
there r out waters on the right .... Eze 47:2
r unto him in the fury of his .... Dan 8:6
the whole herd of swine r................... Mt 8:32
And straightway one of them r .... Mt 27:48
when he saw Jesus afar off, he .... Mk 5:6
the herd r violently down a steep .... Mk 5:13
r about through that whole region ...... Mk 6:55
And one r and filled a spunge full ...... Mk 15:36
the herd r violently down a steep .... Lk 8:33
saw him, and had compassion, and .... Lk 15:20
he r before, and climbed up into a...... Lk 19:4
Peter, and r unto the sepulchre.......... Lk 24:12
So they r both together........................ Jn 20:4
all the people r together unto............. Acts 3:11
r upon him with one accord,............... Acts 7:57
Philip r thither to him, and heard....... Acts 8:30

the gate for gladness, but r in............. Acts 12:14
r in among the people, crying out ...... Acts 14:14
moved, and the people r together........ Acts 21:30
centurions, and r down unto them...... Acts 21:32
seas met, they r the ship aground ...... Acts 27:41
r greedily after the error of................ Jude 11

RANG
shout, so that the earth r again........... 1Sa 4:5
so that the city r again 1Kin 1:45

RANGE
The r of the mountains is his.............. Job 39:8

RANGES
or r for pots, they shall be.................. Lev 11:35
and he that cometh within the r 2Kin 11:8
Have her forth without the r 2Kin 11:15
them, Have her forth without the r 2Chr 23:14

RANGING
As a roaring lion, and a r bear .... Prov 28:15

RANK
of corn came up upon one stalk, r ...... Gen 41:5
thin ears devoured the seven r .... Gen 41:7
shall set forth in the second r .... Num 2:16
shall go forward in the third r .... Num 2:24
thousand, which could keep r 1Chr 12:33
men of war, that could keep r 1Chr 12:38

RANKS
was against light in three r................. 1Kin 7:4
was against light in three r................. 1Kin 7:5
did not break their r .... Joel 2:7
And they sat down in r, by.................. Mk 6:40

RANSOM
then he shall give for the r of .... Ex 21:30
a r for his soul unto the LORD............. Ex 30:12
I have found a r .... Job 33:24
then a great r cannot deliver .... Job 36:18
nor give to God a r for him .... Ps 49:7
He will not regard any r .... Prov 6:35
The r of a man's life are his................ Prov 13:8
shall be a r for the righteous .... Prov 21:18
I gave Egypt for thy r, Ethiopia .... Is 43:3
I will r them from the power of .... Hos 13:14
and to give his life a r for many .... Mt 20:28
and to give his life a r for many .... Mk 10:45
Who gave himself a r for all............... 1Ti 2:6

RANSOMED
the r of the LORD shall return,............. Is 35:10
sea a way for the r to pass over......... Is 51:10
r him from the hand of him that .... Jer 31:11

RAPHA (*ra'-fah*) See BETH-RAPHA, REPHAIAH.
  1. Son of Benjamin.
Nohah the fourth, and R the fifth........ 1Chr 8:2
  2. A member of Saul's family.
R was his son, Eleasah his son,......... 1Chr 8:37

RAPHAN See REPHA.

RAPHU (*ra'-fu*) A Benjamite spy sent to the Promised Land.
of Benjamin, Palti the son of R .... Num 13:9

RARE
it is a r thing that the king .... Dan 2:11

RASE
R it, r it, even to the............................ Ps 137:7

RASH
Be not r with thy mouth, and let......... Eccl 5:2
The heart also of the r shall................ Is 32:4

RASHLY
to be quiet, and to do nothing r .... Acts 19:36

RASOR
like a sharp r, working........................ Ps 52:2

RATE
and gather a certain r every day.......... Ex 16:4
and mules, a r year by year 1Kin 10:25
a daily r for every day, all the............ 2Kin 25:30
Even after a certain r every day.......... 2Chr 8:13
and mules, a r year by year 2Chr 9:24

RATHER
if we have not r done it for fear.......... Josh 22:24
hath not David r sent his..................... 1Sa 10:3
how much r then, when he saith to..... 2Kin 5:13
and death r than my life .... Job 7:15
he justified himself r than God .... Job 32:2
thou chosen r than affliction.............. Job 36:21
and lying r than to speak.................... Ps 52:3
I had r be a doorkeeper in the .... Ps 84:10
knowledge r than choice gold .... Prov 8:10
to get understanding r to be .... Prov 16:16
r than a fool in his folly..................... Prov 17:12
A good name is r to be chosen .... Prov 22:1
and loving favour r than silver .... Prov 22:1
death shall be chosen r than life........ Jer 8:3
But go r to the lost sheep of the .... Mt 10:6
but r fear him which is able to .... Mt 10:28
but r than having two hands or two ... Mt 18:8
r than having two eyes to be cast ...... Mt 18:9
but go ye r to them that sell, and....... Mt 25:9
better, that r a tumult was made, he ... Mt 27:24
betreed, r a great wrong was............. Mk 5:26
that he should r release Barabbas...... Mk 15:11
but r rejoice, because your names ..... Lk 10:20
But he said, Yea r, blessed are .... Lk 11:28
But r give alms of such things .... Lk 11:41

But r seek ye the kingdom of God...... Lk 12:31
but r division... Lk 12:51
will not r say unto him, Make.............. Lk 17:8
house justified r than the other............ Lk 18:14
men loved darkness r than light........... Jn 3:19
We ought to obey God r than men....... Acts 5:29
And not r, (as we be slanderously........ Rom 3:8
It is Christ that died, yea r.................. Rom 8:34
but r through their fall........................ Rom 11:11
Why give place unto wrath................... Rom 12:19
but judge this r, that no man put.......... Rom 14:13
puffed up, and have not r mourned....... 1Cor 5:2
Why do ye not r take wrong................. 1Cor 6:7
why do ye not r suffer yourselves......... 1Cor 6:7
mayest be made free, use it r............... 1Cor 7:21
this power over you, are not we r......... 1Cor 9:12
but r that ye may prophesy.................. 1Cor 14:1
tongues, but r that ye prophesied......... 1Cor 14:5
Yet in the church I had r speak............ 1Cor 14:19
ye ought r to forgive him..................... 2Cor 2:7
of the spirit be r glorious...................... 2Cor 3:8
willing r to be absent from the............. 2Cor 5:8
will I r glory in my infirmities.............. 2Cor 12:9
or r are known of God, how turn.......... Gal 4:9
but r let him labour, working............... Eph 4:28
but r giving of thanks.......................... Eph 5:4
of darkness, but r reprove them........... Eph 5:11
unto me have fallen out r unto............. Phil 1:12
r than godly edifying which is in.......... 1Ti 1:4
exercise thyself r unto godliness.......... 1Ti 4:7
but r do them service, because............. 1Ti 6:2
for love's sake r forsake...................... Philem 9
Choosing r to suffer affliction.............. Heb 11:25
shall we not much r be in..................... Heb 12:9
but let it r be healed........................... Heb 12:13
I beseech you the r to do this............... Heb 13:19
Wherefore the r, brethren, give............ 2Pet 1:10

RATTLETH

The quiver r against him, the................. Job 39:23

RATTLING

the noise of the r of the wheels............ Nah 3:2

RAVEN

And he sent forth a r, which went......... Gen 8:7
Every r after his kind.......................... Lev 11:15
And every r after his kind, the.............. Deut 14:14
Who provideth for the r his food.......... Job 38:41
locks are bushy, and black as a r.......... Song 5:11
also and the r shall dwell in it.............. Is 34:11

RAVENING

upon with their mouths, as a r............. Ps 22:13
like a roaring lion r the prey................ Eze 22:25
are like wolves r the prey..................... Eze 22:27
but inwardly they are r wolves............. Mt 7:15
but your inward part is full of r............ Lk 11:39

RAVENOUS

nor any r beast shall go up................... Is 35:9
Calling a r bird from the east,............... Is 46:11
unto the r birds of every sort................ Eze 39:4

RAVENS

the r to feed thee there......................... 1Kin 17:4
the r brought him bread and flesh......... 1Kin 17:6
food, and to the young r which cry....... Ps 147:9
the r of the valley shall pick it............. Prov 30:17
Consider the r....................................... Lk 12:24

RAVIN

Benjamin shall r as a wolf.................... Gen 49:27
with prey, and his dens with r.............. Nah 2:12

RAVISHED

be thou r always with her love............. Prov 5:19
be r with a strange woman, and............ Prov 5:20
Thou hast r my heart, my sister,........... Song 4:9
thou hast r my heart with one of.......... Song 4:9
be spoiled, and their wives r................. Is 13:16
They r the women in Zion, and the....... Lam 5:11
the houses rifled, and the women r....... Zec 14:2

RAW

Eat not of it r, nor sodden at................ Ex 12:9
there be quick r flesh in the................. Lev 13:10
But when r flesh appeareth in him....... Lev 13:14
the priest shall see the r flesh.............. Lev 13:15
for the r flesh is unclean..................... Lev 13:15
Or if the r flesh turn again, and........... Lev 13:16
have sodden flesh of thee, but r........... 1Sa 2:15

RAZOR

shall no r come upon his head.............. Num 6:5
no r shall come on his head.................. Judg 13:5
hath not come a r upon mine head....... Judg 16:17
there shall no r come upon his............. 1Sa 1:11
Lord shave with a r that is hired.......... Is 7:20
knife, take thee a barber's r.................. Eze 5:1

REACH

whose top may r unto heaven............... Gen 11:4
boards shall r from end to end.............. Ex 26:28
even unto the thighs they shall r.......... Ex 28:42
shall r unto the vintage....................... Lev 26:5
the vintage shall r unto the................. Lev 26:5
shall r unto the side of the sea............ Num 34:11
shall r from the wall of the city........... Num 35:4
his head r unto the clouds................... Job 20:6
he shall r even to the neck,.................. Is 8:8
shall r to the midst of the neck,........... Is 30:28
they r even to the sea of Jazer............. Jer 48:32
the mountains shall r unto Azal........... Zec 14:5
R hither thy finger, and behold my...... Jn 20:27

r hither thy hand, and thrust in........... Jn 20:27
a measure to r even unto you............... 2Cor 10:13

REACHED

and the top of it r to heaven................ Gen 28:12
r to Dabbasheth, and r to.................... Josh 19:11
he r her parched corn, and she did....... Ruth 2:14
the height thereof r unto heaven.......... Dan 4:11
whose height r unto the heaven,.......... Dan 4:20
as though we r not unto you................. 2Cor 10:14
For her sins have r unto heaven........... Rev 18:5

REACHETH

unto Nophah, which r unto Medeba.... Num 21:30
And the coast r to Tabor, and.............. Josh 19:22
r to Carmel westward, and to.............. Josh 19:26
r to Zebulun, and to the valley of........ Josh 19:27
r to Zebulun on the south side,............ Josh 19:34
r to Asher on the west side, and.......... Josh 19:34
in a rage that r up unto heaven........... 2Chr 28:9
faithfulness r unto the clouds.............. Ps 36:5
thy truth r unto the heavens................ Ps 57:10
she r forth her hands to....................... Prov 31:20
whereas the sword r unto the soul........ Jer 4:10
because it r unto thine heart............... Jer 4:18
for her judgment r unto heaven........... Jer 51:9
r unto heaven, and thy dominion to..... Dan 4:22

REACHING

r to the wall of the house.................... 2Chr 3:11
r to the wing of the other cherub........ 2Chr 3:11
r to the wall of the house.................... 2Chr 3:12
r forth unto those things which........... Phil 3:13

READ

r in the audience of the people............ Ex 24:7
he shall r therein all the days.............. Deut 17:19
thou shalt r this law before all............ Deut 31:11
afterward he r all the words of............ Josh 8:34
which Joshua r not before all.............. Josh 8:35
king of Israel had r the letter.............. 2Kin 5:7
hand of the messengers, and r it.......... 2Kin 19:14
the book to Shaphan, and he r it.......... 2Kin 22:8
Shaphan r it before the king................ 2Kin 22:10
which the king of Judah hath r............ 2Kin 22:16
he r in their ears all the words............ 2Kin 23:2
Shaphan r it before the king................ 2Chr 34:18
have r before the king of Judah........... 2Chr 34:24
he r in their ears all the words............ 2Chr 34:30
us hath been plainly r before me.......... Ezr 4:18
letter was r before Rehum................... Ezr 4:23
he r therein before the street............... Neh 8:3
So they r in the book in the................. Neh 8:8
he r in the book of the law of.............. Neh 8:18
r in the book of the law of the............ Neh 9:3
On that day they r in the book of......... Neh 13:1
they were r before the king................. Esth 6:1
saying, R this, I pray thee.................... Is 29:11
saying, R this, I pray thee.................... Is 29:12
out of the book of the Lord, and r........ Is 34:16
hand of the messengers, and r it.......... Is 37:14
Zephaniah the priest r this.................. Jer 29:29
r in the roll, which thou hast............... Jer 36:6
also thou shalt r them in the............... Jer 36:6
Then r Baruch in the book the............. Jer 36:10
when Baruch r the book in the............ Jer 36:13
hast r in the ears of the people............ Jer 36:14
Sit down now, and r it in our ears....... Jer 36:15
So Baruch r it in their ears.................. Jer 36:15
Jehudi r it in the ears of the................ Jer 36:21
Jehudi had r three or four leaves......... Jer 36:23
see, and shalt r all these words........... Jer 51:61
Whosoever shall r this writing............. Dan 5:7
but they could not r the writing........... Dan 5:8
that they should r this writing............. Dan 5:15
now if thou canst r the writing............ Dan 5:16
yet I will r the writing unto the.......... Dan 5:17
Have ye not r what David did,............. Mt 12:3
Or have ye not r in the........................ Mt 12:5
and said unto them, Have ye not r....... Mt 19:4
have ye never r, Out of the mouth....... Mt 21:16
Did ye never r in the scriptures,.......... Mt 21:42
have ye not r that which was.............. Mt 22:31
Have ye never r what David did,......... Mk 2:25
have ye not r this scripture.................. Mk 12:10
have ye not r in the book of................. Mk 12:26
sabbath day, and stood up for to r........ Lk 4:16
Have ye not r so much as this,............ Lk 6:3
This title then r many of the............... Jn 19:20
his chariot r Esaias the prophet.......... Acts 8:28
heard him r the prophet Esaias............ Acts 8:30
the scripture which he r was this......... Acts 8:32
which are r every sabbath day.............. Acts 13:27
being r in the synagogues every.......... Acts 15:21
Which when they had r, they............... Acts 15:31
the governor had r the letter............... Acts 23:34
than what ye r or acknowledge............ 2Cor 1:13
our hearts, known and r of all men...... 2Cor 3:2
unto this day, when Moses is r............ 2Cor 3:15
Whereby, when ye r, ye may............... Eph 3:4
when this epistle is r among you......... Col 4:16
cause that it be r also in the................ Col 4:16
that ye likewise r the epistle.............. Col 4:16
be r unto all the holy brethren............ 1Th 5:27
to r the book, neither to look.............. Rev 5:4

READEST

how r thou... Lk 10:26
Understandest thou what thou r.......... Acts 8:30

READETH

tables, that he may run that r it.......... Hab 2:2
stand in the holy place, (whoso r........ Mt 24:15

not, (let him that r understand........... Mk 13:14
Blessed is he that r, and they.............. Rev 1:3

READINESS

the word with all r of mind................. Acts 17:11
that as there was a r to will................. 2Cor 8:11
having in a r to revenge all................. 2Cor 10:6

READING

caused them to understand the r......... Neh 8:8
r in the book the words of the............. Jer 36:8
hast made an end of r this book.......... Jer 51:63
after the r of the law and the.............. Acts 13:15
in the r of the old testament.............. 2Cor 3:14
Till I come, give attendance to r......... 1Ti 4:13

READY

Make r quickly three measures of...... Gen 18:6
men home, and slay, and make r......... Gen 43:16
they made r the present against.......... Gen 43:25
And Joseph made r his chariot............ Gen 46:29
he made r his chariot, and took.......... Ex 14:6
they be almost r to stone me.............. Ex 17:4
be r against the third day.................... Ex 19:11
Be r against the third day.................... Ex 19:15
be r in the morning, and come up........ Ex 34:2
But we ourselves will go r armed........ Num 32:17
ye were r to go up into the hill........... Deut 1:41
A Syrian r to perish was my............... Deut 26:5
from the city, but be ye all r............... Josh 8:4
made r a kid, and unleavened cakes.... Judg 6:19
shall have made r a kid for thee......... Judg 13:15
of wine, and five sheep r dressed........ 1Sa 25:18
Behold, thy servants are r to do.......... 2Sa 15:15
that thou hast no tidings r.................. 2Sa 18:22
was built of stone made r before........ 1Kin 6:7
And Joram said, Make r...................... 2Kin 9:21
And his chariot was made r................. 2Kin 9:21
that were r armed to the war.............. 1Chr 12:23
eight hundred, r armed to the war...... 1Chr 12:24
had made r for the building................ 1Chr 28:2
fourscore thousand r prepared for...... 2Chr 17:18
they made r for themselves................ 2Chr 35:14
he was a r scribe in the law of........... Ezr 7:6
but thou art a God r to pardon........... Neh 9:17
they should be r against that day....... Est 3:14
that the Jews should be r against....... Est 8:13
who are r to raise up their................. Job 3:8
He that is r to slip with his................ Job 12:5
day of darkness is r at his hand......... Job 15:23
as a king r to the battle..................... Job 15:24
which are r to become heaps............. Job 15:28
extinct, the graves are r for me......... Job 17:1
shall be r at his side.......................... Job 18:12
that was r to perish came upon me..... Job 29:13
it is r to burst like new bottles.......... Job 32:19
hath bent his bow, and made it r........ Ps 7:12
they make r their arrow upon the....... Ps 11:2
when thou shalt make r thine............. Ps 21:12
For I am r to halt, and my sorrow....... Ps 38:17
tongue is the pen of a r writer........... Ps 45:1
Lord, art good, and r to forgive.......... Ps 86:5
r to die from my youth up.................. Ps 88:15
and those that are r to be slain.......... Prov 24:11
unto him that is r to perish............... Prov 31:6
of God, and be more r to hear............ Eccl 5:1
were r to perish in the land of........... Is 27:13
be to you as a breach r to fall........... Is 30:13
shall be r to speak plainly................. Is 32:4
The LORD was r to save me................ Is 38:20
saying, It is r for the sodering........... Is 41:7
as if he were r to destroy.................. Is 51:13
the trumpet, even to make all r......... Eze 7:14
Now if ye be r that at what time....... Dan 3:15
For they have made r their heart....... Hos 7:6
are killed, and all things are r........... Mt 22:4
to his servants, The wedding is r....... Mt 22:8
Therefore be ye also r........................ Mt 24:44
they that were r went in with him..... Mt 25:10
and they made r the passover............ Mt 26:19
there make r for us............................ Mk 14:15
and they made r the passover............ Mk 14:16
The spirit truly is r, but the.............. Mk 14:38
to make r a people prepared for......... Lk 1:17
unto him, was sick, and r to die......... Lk 7:2
the Samaritans, to make r for him..... Lk 9:52
Be ye therefore r also....................... Lk 12:40
for all things are now r..................... Lk 14:17
Make r wherewith I may sup, and..... Lk 17:8
there make r................................... Lk 22:12
and they made r the passover........... Lk 22:13
I am r to go with thee, both into....... Lk 22:33
but your time is alway r................... Jn 7:6
but while they made r, he fell.......... Acts 10:10
r to depart on the morrow............... Acts 20:7
for I am r not to be bound only........ Acts 21:13
he come near, are r to kill him......... Acts 23:15
and now are they r, looking for a..... Acts 23:21
Make r two hundred soldiers to go... Acts 23:23
I am r to preach the gospel to........... Rom 1:15
and declaration of your r mind......... 2Cor 8:19
that Achaia was a year ago.............. 2Cor 9:2
that, as I said, ye may be r.............. 2Cor 9:3
before, that the same might be r...... 2Cor 9:5
line of things made r to our hand..... 2Cor 10:16
third time I am r to come to you...... 2Cor 12:14
r to distribute, willing to............... 1Ti 6:18
For I am now r to be offered, and..... 2Ti 4:6
to be r to every good work,.............. Titus 3:1
waxeth old is r to vanish away......... Heb 8:13
through faith unto salvation r to....... 1Pet 1:5
be r always to give an answer to...... 1Pet 3:15

R

him that is *r* to judge the quick 1Pet 4:5
for filthy lucre, but of a *r* mind 1Pet 5:2
which remain, that are *r* to die.............. Rev 3:2
woman which was *r* to be delivered.... Rev 12:4
and his wife hath made herself *r* .... Rev 19:7

REAIA (re-ah´-yah) Grandfather of Beerah.
his son, *R* his son, Baal his son,.............. 1Chr 5:5

REAIAH (re-ah´-yah) See REAIA.
1. Son of Shobal.
R the son of Shobal begat Jahath...... 1Chr 4:2
2. A family of exiles.
of Gahar, the children of *R* .... Ezr 2:47
The children of *R*, the children .... Neh 7:50

REALM
So the *r* of Jehoshaphat was quiet.... 2Chr 20:30
his priests and Levites, in my *r* .... Ezr 7:13
wrath against the *r* of the king .... Ezr 7:23
that were in all his *r* .... Dan 1:20
to set him over the whole *r* .... Dan 6:3
king over the *r* of the Chaldeans...... Dan 9:1
up all against the *r* of Grecia.............. Dan 11:2

REAP
when ye *r* the harvest of your .... Lev 19:9
thou shalt not wholly *r* the .... Lev 19:9
shall *r* the harvest thereof, then .... Lev 23:10
when ye *r* the harvest of your .... Lev 23:22
of thy harvest thou shalt not *r* .... Lev 25:5
neither *r* that which groweth of .... Lev 25:11
be on the field that they do *r*.............. Ruth 2:9
to *r* his harvest, and to make his........ 1Sa 8:12
and in the third year sow ye, and *r*.... 2Kin 19:29
and sow wickedness, *r* the same .... Job 4:8
They *r* every one his corn in the........ Job 24:6
that sow in tears shall *r* in joy .... Ps 126:5
soweth iniquity shall *r* vanity .... Prov 22:8
regardeth the clouds shall not *r* .... Eccl 11:4
and in the third year sow ye, and *r*.... Is 37:30
sown wheat, but shall *r* thorns .... Jer 12:13
they shall *r* the whirlwind.............. Hos 8:7
in righteousness, *r* in mercy .... Hos 10:12
shalt sow, but thou shalt not *r*.............. Mic 6:15
they sow not, neither do they........ Mt 6:26
that I *r* where I sowed not.............. Mt 25:26
for they neither sow nor *r* .... Lk 12:24
I sent you to *r* that whereon ye........ Jn 4:38
if we shall *r* your carnal things........ 1Cor 9:11
sparingly shall *r* also sparingly........ 2Cor 9:6
shall *r* also bountifully 2Cor 9:6
man soweth, that shall he also *r* .... Gal 6:7
shall of the flesh *r* corruption........ Gal 6:8
of the Spirit *r* life everlasting........ Gal 6:8
for in due season we shall *r* .... Gal 6:9
cloud, Thrust in thy sickle, and *r*...... Rev 14:15
the time is come for thee to *r* .... Rev 14:15

REAPED
wickedness, ye have *r* iniquity.......... Hos 10:13
who have *r* down your fields .... Jas 5:4
r are entered into the ears of .... Jas 5:4
and the earth was *r* .... Rev 14:16

REAPER
the plowman shall overtake the *r*...... Amos 9:13

REAPERS
gleaned in the field after the *r* .... Ruth 2:3
Beth-lehem, and said unto the *r*........ Ruth 2:4
servant that was set over the *r* .... Ruth 2:5
that was set over the *r* answered........ Ruth 2:6
gather after the *r* among the .... Ruth 2:7
And she sat beside the *r* .... Ruth 2:14
went out to his father to the *r* 2Kin 4:18
of harvest I will say to the *r*.............. Mt 13:30
and the *r* are the angels .... Mt 13:39

REAPEST
corners of thy field when thou *r*........ Lev 23:22
r that thou didst not sow .... Lk 19:21

REAPETH
corn, and *r* the ears with his arm ...... Is 17:5
he that *r* receiveth wages, and .... Jn 4:36
he that *r* may rejoice together .... Jn 4:36
true, One soweth, and another *r*........ Jn 4:37

REAPING
they of Beth-shemesh were *r* their...... 1Sa 6:13
r where thou hast not sown, and........ Mt 25:24
not down, and *r* that I did not sow .... Lk 19:22

REAR
thou shalt *r* up the tabernacle .... Ex 26:30
neither *r* you up a standing image...... Lev 26:1
r an altar unto the LORD in the.......... 2Sa 24:18
wilt thou *r* it up in three days.............. Jn 2:20

REARED
that the tabernacle was *r* up .... Ex 40:17
Moses *r* up the tabernacle, and.......... Ex 40:18
bars thereof, and *r* up his pillars........ Ex 40:18
he *r* up the court round about the...... Ex 40:33
was *r* up the cloud covered the.......... Num 9:15
r up for himself a pillar, which.......... 2Sa 18:18
he *r* up an altar for Baal in the.......... 1Kin 16:32
he *r* up altars for Baal, and made...... 2Kin 21:3
he *r* up the pillars before the 2Chr 3:17
he *r* up altars for Baalim, and.............. 2Chr 33:3

REASON
by *r* of that famine remain .... Gen 41:31
Canaan fainted by *r* of the famine...... Gen 47:13
Israel sighed by *r* of the bondage........ Ex 2:23

---

up unto God by *r* of the bondage........ Ex 2:23
cry by *r* of their taskmasters.............. Ex 3:7
by *r* of the swarm of flies.............. Ex 8:24
be unclean by *r* of a dead body........ Num 9:10
given them by *r* of the anointing........ Num 18:8
ye shall bear no sin by *r* of it .... Num 18:32
ye were afraid by *r* of the fire.......... Deut 5:5
that is not clean by *r* of.............. Deut 23:10
old by *r* of the very long journey...... Josh 9:13
by *r* of them that oppressed them...... Judg 2:18
that I may *r* with you before the........ 1Sa 12:7
this is the *r* of the levy which 1Kin 9:15
his eyes were set by *r* of his age........ 1Kin 14:4
to minister by *r* of the cloud.............. 2Chr 5:14
by *r* of this great multitude................ 2Chr 20:15
by *r* of the sickness day by day.......... 2Chr 21:15
fell out by *r* of his sickness.............. 2Chr 21:19
are blackish by *r* of the ice.............. Job 6:16
choose out my words to *r* with him...... Job 9:14
and I desire to *r* with God.............. Job 13:3
Should he *r* with unprofitable.............. Job 15:3
eye also is dim by *r* of sorrow .... Job 17:7
by *r* of his highness I could not........ Job 31:23
By *r* of the multitude.............. Job 35:9
they cry out by *r* of the arm of.......... Job 35:9
order our speech by *r* of darkness...... Job 37:19
by *r* of breakings they purify.............. Job 41:25
I have roared by *r* of the .... Ps 38:8
by *r* of the enemy and avenger.......... Ps 44:16
man that shouteth by *r* of wine........ Ps 78:65
eye mourneth by *r* of affliction.......... Ps 88:9
if by *r* of strength they be.............. Ps 90:10
By *r* of the voice of my groaning........ Ps 102:5
will not plow by *r* of the cold.............. Prov 20:4
seven men that can render a *r* .... Prov 26:16
the *r* of things, and to know the........ Eccl 7:25
let us *r* together, saith the LORD........ Is 1:18
narrow by *r* of the inhabitants.............. Is 49:19
of branches by *r* of many waters........ Eze 19:10
terrors by *r* of the sword shall............ Eze 21:12
by *r* of the abundance of his.............. Eze 26:10
Syria was thy merchant by *r* of........ Eze 27:16
thy wisdom by *r* of thy brightness...... Eze 28:17
same time my *r* returned unto me........ Dan 4:36
by *r* of the words of the king and........ Dan 5:10
sacrifice by *r* of transgression.............. Dan 8:12
I cried by *r* of mine affliction.............. Jonah 2:2
by *r* of the multitude of men.............. Mic 2:12
why *r* ye among yourselves,.............. Mt 16:8
Why *r* ye these things in your............ Mk 2:8
it, he saith unto them, Why *r* ye........ Mk 8:17
and the Pharisees began to *r*,........ Lk 5:21
them, What *r* ye in your hearts........ Lk 5:22
the sea arose by *r* of a great.............. Jn 6:18
Because that by *r* of him many of........ Jn 12:11
It is not *r* that we should leave........ Acts 6:2
r would that I should bear with .... Acts 18:14
but by *r* of him who hath.............. Rom 8:20
by *r* of the glory that excelleth.......... 2Cor 3:10
by *r* hereof he ought, as for the........ Heb 5:3
even those who by *r* of use have...... Heb 5:14
to continue by *r* of death.............. Heb 7:23
to every man that asketh you a *r* 1Pet 3:15
by *r* of whom the way of.............. 2Pet 2:2
by *r* of the other voices of the.......... Rev 8:13
by *r* of the smoke of the pit.............. Rev 9:2
in the sea by *r* of her costliness........ Rev 18:19

REASONABLE
unto God, which is your *r* service...... Rom 12:1

REASONED
they *r* among themselves, saying,........ Mt 16:7
they *r* with themselves, saying,........ Mt 21:25
that they so *r* within themselves........ Mk 2:8
they *r* among themselves, saying........ Mk 8:16
they *r* with themselves, saying,.......... Mk 11:31
they *r* with themselves, saying,.......... Lk 20:5
they *r* among themselves, saying,........ Lk 20:14
while they communed together and *r*.... Lk 24:15
three sabbath days *r* with them .... Acts 17:2
he *r* in the synagogue every.............. Acts 18:4
the synagogue, and *r* with the Jews .... Acts 18:19
as he *r* of righteousness,.............. Acts 24:25

REASONING
Hear now my *r*, and hearken to the...... Job 13:6
there, and *r* in their hearts,.............. Mk 2:6
and hearing heard them *r* together...... Mk 12:28
Then there arose a *r* among them........ Lk 9:46
had great *r* among themselves .... Acts 28:29

REASONS
I gave ear to your *r*, whilst ye.......... Job 32:11
bring forth your strong *r*.............. Is 41:21

REBA (re´-bah) *A king of Midian.*
. and Rekem, and Zur, and Hur, and *R*.. Num 31:8
and Zur, and Hur, and *R*,.............. Josh 13:21

REBECCA (re-bek´-kah) See REBEKAH. *Greek
form of Rebekah.*
but when *R* also had conceived by ...... Rom 9:10

REBEKAH (re-bek´-kah) See REBECCA,
Rebekah's. Wife of Isaac.
And Bethuel begat *R* .... Gen 22:23
R came out, who was born to.............. Gen 24:15
R had a brother, and his name was...... Gen 24:29
heard the words of *R* his sister.......... Gen 24:30
R came forth with her pitcher on........ Gen 24:45
R is before thee, take her, and go ...... Gen 24:51

---

and raiment, and gave them to *R*........ Gen 24:53
And they called *R*, and said unto........ Gen 24:58
And they sent away *R* their sister...... Gen 24:59
And they blessed *R*, and said unto...... Gen 24:60
R arose, and her damsels, and they...... Gen 24:61
and the servant took *R*, and went...... Gen 24:61
R lifted up her eyes, and when she...... Gen 24:64
mother Sarah's tent, and took *R* .... Gen 24:67
years old when he took *R* to wife........ Gen 25:20
of him, and *R* his wife conceived........ Gen 25:21
but *R* loved Jacob.............. Gen 25:28
of the place should kill me for *R* ...... Gen 26:7
was sporting with *R* his wife.............. Gen 26:8
grief of mind unto Isaac and to *R*........ Gen 26:35
R heard when Isaac spake to Esau...... Gen 27:5
R spake unto Jacob her son,.............. Gen 27:6
And Jacob said to *R* his mother.......... Gen 27:11
R took goodly raiment of her .... Gen 27:15
Esau her elder son were told to *R* ...... Gen 27:42
R said to Isaac, I am weary of my........ Gen 27:46
the Syrian, the brother of *R*,.............. Gen 28:5
they buried Isaac and *R* his wife .... Gen 49:31

REBEKAH'S (re-bek´-kahz)
brother, and that he was *R* son .... Gen 29:12
But Deborah *R* nurse died, and she ...... Gen 35:8

REBEL
Only *r* not ye against the LORD,.......... Num 14:9
doth *r* against my commandment .... Josh 1:18
that ye might *r* this day against.......... Josh 22:16
seeing ye *r* to day against the.............. Josh 22:18
but *r* not against the LORD .... Josh 22:19
ye *r* against us, in building you.......... Josh 22:19
that we should *r* against the LORD...... Josh 22:29
not *r* against the commandment of...... 1Sa 12:14
but *r* against the commandment of...... 1Sa 12:15
will ye *r* against the king.............. Neh 2:19
that thou and the Jews think to *r*........ Neh 6:6
of those that *r* against the light .... Job 24:13
But if ye refuse and *r*, ye shall .... Is 1:20
and wine, and they *r* against me........ Hos 7:14

REBELLED
and in the thirteenth year they *r* .... Gen 14:4
because ye *r* against my word at........ Num 20:24
For ye *r* against my commandment .... Num 27:14
but *r* against the commandment of...... Deut 1:26
but *r* against the commandment of...... Deut 1:43
then ye *r* against the commandment.... Deut 9:23
So Israel *r* against the house of........ 1Kin 12:19
Then Moab *r* against Israel after........ 2Kin 1:1
that the king of Moab *r* against,.......... 2Kin 3:5
king of Moab hath *r* against me.......... 2Kin 3:7
he *r* against the king of Assyria,........ 2Kin 18:7
then he turned and *r* against him........ 2Kin 24:1
that Zedekiah *r* against the king........ 2Kin 24:20
Israel *r* against the house of.............. 2Chr 10:19
up, and hath *r* against his lord.............. 2Chr 13:6
And he also *r* against king.............. 2Chr 36:13
r against thee, and cast thy law.......... Neh 9:26
for they have *r* against thee.............. Ps 5:10
they *r* not against his word.............. Ps 105:28
Because they *r* against the words........ Ps 107:11
and they have *r* against me.............. Is 1:2
But they *r*, and vexed his holy .... Is 63:10
that Zedekiah *r* against the king.......... Jer 52:3
for I have *r* against his.............. Lam 1:18
for I have grievously *r* .... Lam 1:20
We have transgressed and have *r* .... Lam 3:42
nation that hath *r* against me.............. Eze 2:3
But he *r* against him in sending.......... Eze 17:15
But they *r* against me, and would........ Eze 20:8
But the house of Israel *r* against.......... Eze 20:13
the children *r* against me.............. Eze 20:21
and have done wickedly, and have *r*.... Dan 9:5
though we have *r* against him.............. Dan 9:9
for she hath *r* against her God .... Hos 13:16

REBELLEST
trust, that thou *r* against me.............. 2Kin 18:20
trust, that thou *r* against me.............. Is 36:5

REBELLION
For I know thy *r*, and thy stiff .... Deut 31:27
if it be in *r*, or if it .... Josh 22:22
For *r* is as the sin of witchcraft........ 1Sa 15:23
against kings, and hath *r* made.......... Ezr 4:19
in their *r* appointed a captain to........ Neh 9:17
For he addeth unto his sin .... Job 34:37
An evil man seeketh only *r*.............. Prov 17:11
hast taught *r* against the LORD .... Jer 28:16
he hath taught *r* against the LORD...... Jer 29:32

REBELLIOUS
ye have been *r* against the LORD........ Deut 9:7
Ye have been *r* against the LORD........ Deut 9:24
r son, which will not obey the.............. Deut 21:18
This our son is stubborn and *r*............ Deut 21:20
hast been *r* against the LORD.............. Deut 31:27
Thou son of the perverse *r* woman...... 1Sa 20:30
unto Jerusalem, building the *r* .... Ezr 4:12
know that this city is a *r* city .... Ezr 4:15
let not the *r* exalt themselves .... Ps 66:7
but the *r* dwell in a dry land.............. Ps 68:6
yea, for the *r* also, that the.............. Ps 68:18
a stubborn and *r* generation .... Ps 78:8
The princes are *r*, and companions...... Is 1:23
Woe to the *r* children, saith the .... Is 30:1
This is a *r* people, lying .... Is 30:9
opened mine ear, and I was not *r*........ Is 50:5
hands all the day unto a *r* people........ Is 65:2
she hath been *r* against me.............. Jer 4:17

REBELS

hath a revolting and a *r* heart	Jer 5:23
to a *r* nation that hath rebelled	Eze 2:3
forbear, (for they are a *r* house	Eze 2:5
looks, though they be a *r* house	Eze 2:6
for they are most *r*	Eze 2:7
Be not thou *r* like that	Eze 2:8
like that *r* house	Eze 2:8
looks, though they be a *r* house	Eze 3:9
for they are a *r* house	Eze 3:26
for they are a *r* house	Eze 3:27
in the midst of a *r* house	Eze 12:2
for they are a *r* house	Eze 12:2
though they be a *r* house	Eze 12:3
the *r* house, said unto thee, What	Eze 12:9
O *r* house, will I say the word	Eze 12:25
Say now to the *r* house, Know ye	Eze 17:12
utter a parable unto the *r* house	Eze 24:3
And thou shalt say to the *r*	Eze 44:6

REBELS

be kept for a token against the *r*	Num 17:10
he said unto them, Hear now, ye *r*	Num 20:10
purge out from among you the *r*	Eze 20:38

REBUKE

shalt in any wise *r* thy neighbour	Lev 19:17
upon these cursing, vexation, and *r*	Deut 28:20
she may glean them, and *r* her not	Ruth 2:16
day is a day of trouble, and of *r*	2Kin 19:3
our fathers took thereon, and *r*	1Chr 12:17
r me not in thine anger, neither	Ps 6:1
world were discovered at thy *r*	Ps 18:15
O LORD, *r* me not in thy wrath	Ps 38:1
R the company of spearmen, the	Ps 68:30
At thy *r*, O God of Jacob, both	Ps 76:6
at the *r* of thy countenance	Ps 80:16
At thy *r* they fled	Ps 104:7
r a wise man, and he will love	Prov 9:8
but a scorner heareth not *r*	Prov 13:1
but the poor heareth not *r*	Prov 13:8
But to them that *r* him shall be	Prov 24:25
Open *r* is better than secret love	Prov 27:5
better to hear the *r* of the wise	Eccl 7:5
nations, and shall *r* many people	Is 2:4
but God shall *r* them, and they	Is 17:13
the *r* of his people shall he take	Is 25:8
shall flee at the *r* of one	Is 30:17
at the *r* of five shall ye flee	Is 30:17
day is a day of trouble, and of *r*	Is 37:3
at my *r* I dry up the sea, I make	Is 50:2
of the LORD, the *r* of God	Is 51:20
be wroth with thee, nor *r* thee	Is 54:9
his *r* with flames of fire	Is 66:15
for thy sake I have suffered *r*	Jer 15:15
shall be desolate in the day of *r*	Hos 5:9
r strong nations afar off	Mic 4:3
said unto Satan, The LORD *r* thee	Zec 3:2
that hath chosen Jerusalem *r* thee	Zec 3:2
I will *r* the devourer for your	Mal 3:11
Peter took him, and began to *r* him	Mt 16:22
Peter took him, and began to *r* him	Mk 8:32
trespass against thee, *r* him	Lk 17:3
unto him, Master, *r* thy disciples	Lk 19:39
the sons of God, without *r*	Phil 2:15
R not an elder, but intreat him	1Ti 5:1
Them that sin *r* before all	1Ti 5:20
reprove, *r*, exhort with all	2Ti 4:2
Wherefore *r* them sharply, that	Titus 1:13
exhort, and *r* with all authority	Titus 2:15
but said, The Lord *r* thee	Jude 9
As many as I love, I *r* and chasten	Rev 3:19

REBUKED

my hands, and *r* thee yesternight	Gen 31:42
and his father *r* him, and said unto	Gen 37:10
I *r* the nobles, and the rulers, and	Neh 5:7
Thou hast *r* the heathen, thou	Ps 9:5
He *r* the Red sea also, and it was	Ps 106:9
Thou hast *r* the proud that are	Ps 119:21
arose, and *r* the winds and the sea	Mt 8:26
And Jesus *r* the devil	Mt 17:18
and the disciples *r* them	Mt 19:13
And the multitude *r* them, because	Mt 20:31
And Jesus *r* him, saying, Hold thy	Mk 1:25
r the wind, and said unto the sea	Mk 4:39
he *r* Peter, saying, Get thee	Mk 8:33
the foul spirit, saying unto	Mk 9:25
his disciples *r* those that	Mk 10:13
And Jesus *r* him, saying, Hold thy	Lk 4:35
he stood over her, and *r* the fever	Lk 4:39
r the wind and the raging of the	Lk 8:24
Jesus *r* the unclean spirit, and	Lk 9:42
r them, and said, Ye know not what	Lk 9:55
his disciples saw it, they *r* them	Lk 18:15
And they which went before *r* him	Lk 18:39
But the other answering *r* him	Lk 23:40
nor faint when thou art *r* of him	Heb 12:5
But was *r* for his iniquity	2Pet 2:16

REBUKER

I have been a *r* of them all	Hos 5:2

REBUKES

When thou with *r* dost correct man	Ps 39:11
anger and in fury and in furious *r*	Eze 5:15
upon them with furious *r*	Eze 25:17

REBUKETH

he that *r* a wicked man getteth	Prov 9:7
He that *r* a man afterwards shall	Prov 28:23
They hate him that *r* in the gate	Amos 5:10
He *r* the sea, and maketh it dry,	Nah 1:4

REBUKING

at the *r* of the LORD, at the	2Sa 22:16
he *r* them suffered them not to	Lk 4:41

RECALL

This I *r* to my mind, therefore	Lam 3:21

RECEIPT

sitting at the *r* of custom	Mt 9:9
sitting at the *r* of custom	Mk 2:14
Levi, sitting at the *r* of custom	Lk 5:27

RECEIVE

to *r* thy brother's blood from thy	Gen 4:11
then *r* my present at my hand	Gen 33:10
to *r* his pledge from the woman's	Gen 38:20
make his pans to *r* his ashes	Ex 27:3
thou shalt *r* them of their hands,	Ex 29:25
which ye *r* of the children of	Num 18:28
mount to *r* the tables of stone	Deut 9:9
every one shall *r* of thy words	Deut 33:3
which thou shalt *r* of their hands	1Sa 10:4
Though I should *r* a thousand	2Sa 18:12
there, and thou shalt *r* them	1Kin 5:9
little to *r* the burnt offerings	1Kin 8:64
whom I stand, I will *r* none	2Kin 5:16
Is it a time to *r* money	2Kin 5:26
to *r* garments, and oliveyards, and	2Kin 5:26
now therefore *r* no more money of	2Kin 12:7
the priests consented to *r*	2Kin 12:8
not able to *r* the burnt offerings	2Chr 7:7
every one shall *r* of God	Job 2:10
of God, and shall we not *r* evil	Job 2:10
R, I pray thee, the law from his	Job 22:22
they shall *r* of the Almighty	Job 27:13
the LORD will *r* my prayer	Ps 6:10
He shall *r* the blessing from the	Ps 24:5
for he shall *r* me	Ps 49:15
and afterward *r* me to glory	Ps 73:24
When I shall *r* the congregation I	Ps 75:2
To *r* the instruction of wisdom,	Prov 1:3
My son, if thou wilt *r* my words	Prov 2:1
Hear, O my son, and *r* my sayings	Prov 4:10
R my instruction, and not silver	Prov 8:10
wise in heart will *r* commandments	Prov 10:8
r instruction, that thou mayest	Prov 19:20
Should I *r* comfort in these	Is 57:6
they have refused to *r* correction	Jer 5:3
let your ear *r* the word of his	Jer 9:20
might not hear, nor *r* instruction	Jer 17:23
not hearkened to *r* instruction	Jer 32:33
Will ye not *r* instruction to	Jer 35:13
speak unto thee *r* in thine heart	Eze 3:10
when thou shalt *r* thy sisters	Eze 16:61
that ye shall *r* no more reproach	Eze 36:30
ye shall *r* of the gifts and rewards	Dan 2:6
Ephraim shall *r* shame, and Israel	Hos 10:6
all iniquity, and *r* us graciously	Hos 14:2
he shall *r* of you his standing	Mic 1:11
fear me, thou wilt *r* instruction	Zeph 3:7
shall not be room enough to *r* it	Mal 3:10
And whosoever shall not *r* you	Mt 10:14
shall *r* a prophet's reward	Mt 10:41
shall *r* a righteous man's reward	Mt 10:41
The blind *r* their sight, and the	Mt 11:5
And if ye will *r* it, this is Elias	Mt 11:14
whoso shall *r* one such little	Mt 18:5
All men cannot *r* this saying	Mt 19:11
He that is able to *r* it	Mt 19:12
let him *r* it	Mt 19:12
shall *r* an hundredfold, and	Mt 19:29
is right, that shall ye *r*	Mt 20:7
in prayer, believing, ye shall *r*	Mt 21:22
that they might *r* the fruits of	Mt 21:34
therefore ye shall *r* the greater	Mt 23:14
that there was no room to *r* them	Mk 2:2
immediately *r* it with gladness	Mk 4:16
r it, and bring forth fruit, some	Mk 4:20
And whosoever shall not *r* you	Mk 6:11
Whosoever shall *r* one of such	Mk 9:37
and whosoever shall *r* me,	Mk 9:37
Whosoever shall not *r* the kingdom	Mk 10:15
But he shall *r* an hundredfold now	Mk 10:30
Lord, that I might *r* my sight	Mk 10:51
ye pray, believe that ye *r* them	Mk 11:24
servant, that he might *r* from the	Mk 12:2
these shall *r* greater damnation	Mk 12:40
lend to them of whom ye hope to *r*	Lk 6:34
to sinners, to *r* as much again	Lk 6:34
they hear, *r* the word with joy	Lk 8:13
And whosoever will not *r* you	Lk 9:5
Whosoever shall *r* this child in	Lk 9:48
whosoever shall *r* me receiveth	Lk 9:48
And they did not *r* him, because	Lk 9:53
city ye enter, and they *r* you	Lk 10:8
they *r* you not, go your ways out	Lk 10:10
they may *r* me into their houses	Lk 16:4
they may *r* you into everlasting	Lk 16:9
Whosoever shall not *r* the kingdom	Lk 18:17
Who shall not *r* manifold more in	Lk 18:30
said, Lord, that I may *r* my sight	Lk 18:41
Jesus said unto him, R thy sight	Lk 18:42
to *r* for himself a kingdom	Lk 19:12
the same shall *r* greater	Lk 20:47
for we *r* the due reward of our	Lk 23:41
and ye *r* not our witness	Jn 3:11
and said, A man can *r* nothing	Jn 3:27
But I *r* not testimony from man	Jn 5:34
I *r* not honour from men	Jn 5:41
my Father's name, and ye *r* not	Jn 5:43
in his own name, him ye will *r*	Jn 5:43
which ye *r* of the hand of the	Jn 5:44

on the sabbath day *r* circumcision	Jn 7:23
they that believe on him should *r*	Jn 7:39
come again, and *r* you unto myself	Jn 14:3
whom the world cannot *r*, because	Jn 14:17
for he shall *r* of mine, and shall	Jn 16:14
ask, and ye shall *r*, that your joy	Jn 16:24
unto them, R ye the Holy Ghost	Jn 20:22
But ye shall *r* power, after that	Acts 1:8
ye shall *r* the gift of the Holy	Acts 2:38
expecting to *r* something of them	Acts 3:5
Whom the heaven must *r* until the	Acts 3:21
saying, Lord Jesus, *r* my spirit	Acts 7:59
that they might *r* the Holy Ghost	Acts 8:15
hands, he may *r* the Holy Ghost	Acts 8:19
on him, that he might *r* his sight	Acts 9:12
that thou mightest *r* thy sight	Acts 9:17
in him shall *r* remission of sins	Acts 10:43
which are not lawful for us to *r*	Acts 16:21
exhorting the disciples to *r* him	Acts 18:27
is more blessed to give than to *r*	Acts 20:35
me, Brother Saul, *r* thy sight	Acts 22:13
for they will not *r* thy testimony	Acts 22:18
that they may *r* forgiveness of	Acts 26:18
they which *r* abundance of grace	Rom 5:17
that they resist shall *r* to	Rom 13:2
that is weak in the faith *r* ye	Rom 14:1
Wherefore *r* ye one another, as	Rom 15:7
That ye *r* her in the Lord, as	Rom 16:2
every man shall *r* his own reward	1Cor 3:8
thereupon, he shall *r* a reward	1Cor 3:14
hast thou that thou didst not *r*	1Cor 4:7
now if thou didst *r* it, why dost	1Cor 4:7
that the church may *r* edifying	1Cor 14:5
that every one may *r* the things	2Cor 5:10
beseech you also that ye *r* not	2Cor 6:1
and I will *r* you,	2Cor 6:17
R us; we have wronged	2Cor 7:2
that ye might *r* damage by us in	2Cor 7:9
intreaty that we would *r* the gift	2Cor 8:4
or if ye *r* another spirit, which	2Cor 11:4
if otherwise, yet as a fool *r* me	2Cor 11:16
that we might *r* the promise of	Gal 3:14
that we might *r* the adoption of	Gal 4:5
the same shall he *r* of the Lord	Eph 6:8
R him therefore in the Lord with	Phil 2:29
that of the Lord ye shall *r* the	Col 3:24
r for the wrong which he hath	Col 3:25
if he come unto you, *r* him	Col 4:10
Against an elder *r* not an	1Ti 5:19
thou therefore *r* him, that is,	Philem 12
thou shouldest *r* him for ever	Philem 15
a partner, *r* him as myself	Philem 17
of Levi, who *r* the office of the	Heb 7:5
And here men that die *r* tithes	Heb 7:8
might *r* the promise of eternal	Heb 9:15
of God, ye might *r* the promise	Heb 10:36
should after *r* for an inheritance	Heb 11:8
he shall *r* any thing of the Lord	Jas 1:7
he shall *r* the crown of life	Jas 1:12
r with meekness the engrafted	Jas 1:21
knowing that we shall *r* the	Jas 3:1
r not, because ye ask amiss, that	Jas 4:3
until he *r* the early and latter,	Jas 5:7
ye shall *r* a crown of glory that	1Pet 5:4
And shall *r* the reward of	2Pet 2:13
we *r* of him, because we keep his	1Jn 3:22
If we *r* the witness of men, the	1Jn 5:9
but that we *r* a full reward	2Jn 8
r him not into your house,	2Jn 10
We therefore ought to *r* such	3Jn 8
doth he himself *r* the brethren	3Jn 10
to *r* glory and honour and power	Rev 4:11
Lamb that was slain to *r* power	Rev 5:12
to *r* a mark in their right hand,	Rev 13:16
r his mark in his forehead, or in	Rev 14:9
but *r* power as kings one hour	Rev 17:12
that ye *r* not of her plagues	Rev 18:4

RECEIVED

r in the same year an hundredfold	Gen 26:12
he *r* them at their hand, and,	Ex 32:4
they *r* of Moses all the offering,	Ex 36:3
after that let her be *r* in again	Num 12:14
I have *r* commandment to bless	Num 23:20
fathers, have *r* their inheritance	Num 34:14
Manasseh have *r* their inheritance	Num 34:14
the half tribe have *r* their	Num 34:15
of the tribe whereunto they are *r*	Num 36:3
of the tribe whereunto they are *r*	Num 36:4
and the Gadites have *r* their	Josh 13:8
had not yet *r* their inheritance	Josh 18:2
have *r* their inheritance beyond	Josh 18:7
would not have *r* a burnt offering	Judg 13:23
or of whose hand have I *r* any	1Sa 12:3
So David *r* of her hand that which	1Sa 25:35
the king's merchants *r* the linen	1Kin 10:28
Hezekiah *r* the letter of the hand	2Kin 19:14
Then David *r* them, and made them	1Chr 12:18
the king's merchants *r* the linen	2Chr 1:16
and it *r* and held three thousand	2Chr 4:5
and the priests *r* the blood	2Chr 29:22
which they *r* of the hand of the	2Chr 30:16
but he *r* it not	Est 4:4
mine ear *r* a little thereof	Job 4:12
thou hast *r* gifts for men	Ps 68:18
looked upon it, and *r* instruction	Prov 24:32
Hezekiah *r* the letter from the	Is 37:14
for she hath *r* of the LORD's hand	Is 40:2
they *r* no correction	Jer 2:30
that hath not *r* usury nor	Eze 18:17
she *r* not correction	Zeph 3:2

R

freely ye have r, freely give	Mt 10:8
This is he which r seed by the	Mt 13:19
But he that r the seed into story	Mt 13:20
He also that r seed among the	Mt 13:22
But he that r seed into the good	Mt 13:23
they that r tribute money came to	Mt 17:24
hour, they r every man a penny	Mt 20:9
that they should have r more	Mt 20:10
they likewise r every man a penny	Mt 20:10
And when they had r it, they	Mt 20:11
and immediately their eyes r sight	Mt 20:34
Then he that had r the five	Mt 25:16
And likewise he that had r two	Mt 25:17
But he that had r one went	Mt 25:18
so he that had r five talents	Mt 25:20
also that had r two talents came	Mt 25:22
Then he which had r the one	Mt 25:24
should have r mine own with usury	Mt 25:27
be, which they have r to hold	Mk 7:4
And immediately he r his sight	Mk 10:52
but he r it not	Mk 15:23
he was r up into heaven, and sat	Mk 16:19
for ye have r your consolation	Lk 6:24
returned, the people gladly r him	Lk 8:40
he r them, and spake unto them of	Lk 9:11
was come that he should be r up	Lk 9:51
named Martha r him into her house	Lk 10:38
calf, because he hath r him safe	Lk 15:27
And immediately he r his sight	Lk 18:43
and came down, and r him joyfully	Lk 19:6
having r the kingdom, then he	Lk 19:15
his own, and his own r him not	Jn 1:11
But as many as r him, to them	Jn 1:12
And of his fulness have all we r	Jn 1:16
He that hath r his testimony hath	Jn 3:33
Galilee, the Galilaeans r him	Jn 4:45
willingly r him into the ship	Jn 6:21
and I went and washed, and I r sight	Jn 9:11
asked him how he had r his sight	Jn 9:15
r his sight, until they called	Jn 9:18
of him that had r his sight	Jn 9:18
commandment have I of my Father	Jn 10:18
He then having r the sop went	Jn 13:30
and they have r them, and have	Jn 17:8
having r a band of men and	Jn 18:3
Jesus therefore had r the vinegar	Jn 19:30
a cloud r him out of their sight	Acts 1:9
having r of the Father the	Acts 2:33
Then they that gladly r his word	Acts 2:41
feet and ancle bones r strength	Acts 3:7
who r the lively oracles to give	Acts 7:38
Who have r the law by the	Acts 7:53
Samaria had r the word of God	Acts 8:14
on them, and they r the Holy Ghost	Acts 8:17
he r sight forthwith, and arose	Acts 9:18
And when he had r meat, he was	Acts 9:19
the vessel was r up again into	Acts 10:16
which have r the Holy Ghost as	Acts 10:47
had also r the word of God	Acts 11:1
they were r of the church, and of	Acts 15:4
having r such a charge, thrust	Acts 16:24
Whom Jason hath r	Acts 17:7
in that they r the word with all	Acts 17:11
Have ye r the Holy Ghost since ye	Acts 19:2
which I have r of the Lord Jesus	Acts 20:24
the brethren r us gladly	Acts 21:17
from whom also I r letters unto	Acts 22:5
having r authority from the chief	Acts 26:10
r us every one, because of the	Acts 28:2
who r us, and lodged us three days	Acts 28:7
We neither r letters out of	Acts 28:21
r all that came in unto him	Acts 28:30
By whom we have r grace and	Rom 1:5
he r the sign of circumcision, a	Rom 4:11
whom we have now r the atonement	Rom 5:11
For ye have not r the spirit of	Rom 8:15
but ye have r the Spirit of	Rom 8:15
for God hath r him	Rom 14:3
as Christ also r us to the glory	Rom 15:7
Now we have r, not the spirit of	1Cor 2:12
glory, as if thou hadst not r it	1Cor 4:7
For I have r of the Lord that	1Cor 11:23
unto you, which also ye have r	1Cor 15:1
first of all that which I also r	1Cor 15:3
this ministry, as we have r mercy	2Cor 4:1
with fear and trembling ye r him	2Cor 7:15
spirit, which ye have not r	2Cor 11:4
Of the Jews five times r I forty	2Cor 11:24
unto you than that ye have r	Gal 1:9
For I neither r it of man	Gal 1:12
R ye the Spirit by the works of	Gal 3:2
but r me as an angel of God, even	Gal 4:14
which ye have both learned, and r	Phil 4:9
having r of Epaphroditus the	Phil 4:18
As ye have therefore r Christ	Col 2:6
(touching whom ye r commandments	Col 4:10
which thou hast r in the Lord	Col 4:17
having r the word in much	1Th 1:6
when ye r the word of God which	1Th 2:13
ye r it not as the word of men	1Th 2:13
that as ye have r of us how ye	1Th 4:1
because they r not the love of	2Th 2:10
the tradition which he r of us	2Th 3:6
on in the world, r up into glory	1Ti 3:16
which God hath created to be r	1Ti 4:3
if it be r with thanksgiving	1Ti 4:4
disobedience r a just recompence	Heb 2:2
from them r tithes of Abraham	Heb 7:6
for under it the people r the law	Heb 7:11
have r the knowledge of the truth	Heb 10:26
r strength to conceive seed	Heb 11:11
not having r the promises, but	Heb 11:13
he that had r the promises	Heb 11:17
whence also he r him in a figure	Heb 11:19
when she had r the spies with	Heb 11:31
Women r their dead raised to life	Heb 11:35
through faith, r not the promise	Heb 11:39
when she had r the messengers, and	Jas 2:25
from your vain conversation r by	1Pet 1:18
As every man hath r the gift	1Pet 4:10
For he r from God the Father	2Pet 1:17
ye have r of him abideth in you	1Jn 2:27
as we have r a commandment from	2Jn 4
even as I r of my Father	Rev 2:27
therefore how thou hast r	Rev 3:3
which have ro kingdom as yet	Rev 17:12
that had r the mark of the beast	Rev 19:20
neither had r his mark upon their	Rev 20:4

RECEIVEDST

in thy lifetime r thy good things	Lk 16:25

RECEIVER

where is the r	Is 33:18

RECEIVETH

is no man that r me to house	Judg 19:18
or what r he of thine hand	Job 35:7
is instructed, he r knowledge	Prov 21:11
but he that r gifts overthroweth	Prov 29:4
LORD their God, nor r correction	Jer 7:28
or r it with good will at your	Mal 2:13
For every one that asketh r	Mt 7:8
He that r you r me, and he	Mt 10:40
r me r him that sent me	Mt 10:40
He that r a prophet in the name	Mt 10:41
he that r a righteous man in the	Mt 10:41
the word, and anon with joy r it	Mt 13:20
such little child in my name r me	Mt 18:5
of such children in my name, r me	Mk 9:37
r not me, but him that sent me	Mk 9:37
this child in my name r me	Lk 9:48
receive me r him that sent me	Lk 9:48
For every one that asketh r	Lk 11:10
saying, This man r sinners	Lk 15:2
and no man r his testimony	Jn 3:32
And he that reapeth r wages	Jn 4:36
r not my words, hath one that	Jn 12:48
r whomsoever I send r me	Jn 13:20
r me r him that sent me	Jn 13:20
But the natural man r not the	1Cor 2:14
race run all, but one r the prize	1Cor 9:24
is dressed, r blessing from God	Heb 6:7
but there he r them, of whom it	Heb 7:8
who r tithes, payed tithes in	Heb 7:9
and scourgeth every son whom he r	Heb 12:6
preeminence among them, r us not	3Jn 9
man knoweth saving he that r it	Rev 2:17
whosoever r the mark of his name	Rev 14:11

RECEIVING

in not r his hands that which	2Kin 5:20
r a commandment unto Silas and	Acts 17:15
r in themselves that recompence	Rom 1:27
what shall the r of them be but	Rom 11:15
with me as concerning giving and r	Phil 4:15
Wherefore we r a kingdom which	Heb 12:28
R the end of your faith, even the	1Pet 1:9

RECHAB (re'-kab) See RECHABITES.
1. A son of Rimmon.

and the name of the other r	2Sa 4:2
son of Rimmon the Beerothite, r	2Sa 4:5
and R and Baanah his brother	2Sa 4:6
And David answered R and Baanah his	2Sa 4:9

2. Founder of the Rechabites.

the son of R coming to meet him	2Kin 10:15
went, and Jehonadab the son of R	2Kin 10:23
for Jonadab the son of R our	Jer 35:6
R our father in all that he hath	Jer 35:8
The words of Jonadab the son of R	Jer 35:14
R have performed the commandment	Jer 35:16
Jonadab the son of R shall not	Jer 35:19

3. A descendant of Hemath.

the father of the house of R	1Chr 2:55

4. Father of Malchiah.

repaired Malchiah the son of R	Neh 3:14

RECHABITES (rek'-ab-ites) Descendants of Rechab 2.

Go unto the house of the R	Jer 35:2
sons, and the whole house of the R	Jer 35:3
house of the R pots full of wine	Jer 35:5
said unto the house of the R	Jer 35:18

RECHAH A family of Judah.

These are the men of R	1Chr 4:12

RECKON

he shall r with him that bought	Lev 25:50
then the priest shall r unto him	Lev 27:18
Then the priest shall r unto him	Lev 27:23
and by name ye shall r the	Num 4:32
they shall r unto him seven days	Eze 44:26
And when he had begun to r	Mt 18:24
Likewise r ye also yourselves to	Rom 6:11
For I r that the sufferings of	Rom 8:18

RECKONED

offering shall be r unto you	Num 18:27
shall not be r among the nations	Num 23:9
Beeroth also was r to Benjamin	2Sa 4:2
Moreover they r not with the men,	2Kin 12:15
not to be r after the birthright	1Chr 5:1
of their generations was r	1Chr 5:7
All these were r by genealogies	1Chr 5:17
r in all by their genealogies	1Chr 7:5
were r by their genealogies	1Chr 7:7
all Israel were r by genealogies	1Chr 9:1
These were r by their genealogy	1Chr 9:22
to all that were r by genealogies	2Chr 31:19
those that were r by genealogy	Ezr 2:62
with him were r by genealogy of	Ezr 8:3
that they might be r by genealogy	Neh 7:5
those that were r by genealogy	Neh 7:64
they cannot be r up in order unto	Ps 40:5
I r till morning, that, as a lion	Is 38:13
he was r among the transgressors	Lk 22:37
is the reward not r of grace	Rom 4:4
for we say that faith was r to	Rom 4:9
How was it then r	Rom 4:10

RECKONETH

servants cometh, and r with them	Mt 25:19

RECKONING

Howbeit there was no r made with	2Kin 22:7
therefore they were in one r	1Chr 23:11

RECOMMENDED

from whence they had been r to	Acts 14:26
being r by the brethren unto the	Acts 15:40

RECOMPENCE

To me belongeth vengeance, and r	Deut 32:35
for vanity shall be his r	Job 15:31
with vengeance, even God with a r	Is 35:4
his adversaries, r to his enemies	Is 59:18
to the islands he will repay r	Is 59:18
that rendereth r to his enemies	Is 66:6
he will render unto her a r	Jer 51:6
Render unto them a r, O LORD,	Lam 3:64
are come, the days of r are come	Hos 9:7
will ye render me a r	Joel 3:4
return your r upon your own head	Joel 3:4
will return your r upon your own	Joel 3:7
thee again, and a r be made thee	Lk 14:12
receiving in themselves that r of	Rom 1:27
stumblingblock, and a r unto them	Rom 11:9
Now for a r in the same, (I speak	2Cor 6:13
received a just r of reward	Heb 2:2
which hath great r of reward	Heb 10:35
respect unto the r of the reward	Heb 11:26

RECOMPENCES

the year of r for the controversy	Is 34:8
for the LORD God of r shall	Jer 51:56

RECOMPENSE

he shall r his trespass with the	Num 5:7
no kinsman to r the trespass unto	Num 5:8
The LORD r thy work, and a full	Ruth 2:12
why should the king r it me with	2Sa 19:36
he will r it, whether thou refuse	Job 34:33
the r of a man's hands shall be	Prov 12:14
Say not thou, I will r evil	Prov 20:22
will not keep silence, but will r	Is 65:6
even r into their bosom,	Is 65:6
first I will r their iniquity and	Jer 16:18
I will r them according to their	Jer 25:14
r her according to her work	Jer 50:29
will r upon thee all thine	Eze 7:3
but I will r thy ways upon thee,	Eze 7:4
will r thee for all thine	Eze 7:8
I will r thee according to thy	Eze 7:9
but I will r their ways upon their	Eze 9:10
I will r their way upon their own	Eze 11:21
therefore I also will r thy way	Eze 16:43
even it will I r upon his own	Eze 17:19
they shall r your lewdness upon	Eze 23:49
to his doings will he r him	Hos 12:2
and if ye r me, swiftly and	Joel 3:4
for they cannot r thee	Lk 14:14
R to no man evil for evil	Rom 12:17
God to r tribulation to them that	2Th 1:6
belongeth unto me, I will r	Heb 10:30

RECOMPENSED

the trespass be r unto the LORD	Num 5:8
of my hands hath he r me	2Sa 22:21
LORD hath r me according to my	2Sa 22:25
of my hands hath he r me	Ps 18:20
the LORD r me according to my	Ps 18:24
righteous shall be r in the earth	Prov 11:31
Shall evil be r for good	Jer 18:20
own way have I r upon their heads	Eze 22:31
for thou shalt be r at the	Lk 14:14
it shall be r unto him again	Rom 11:35

RECOMPENSEST

r the iniquity of the fathers	Jer 32:18

RECOMPENSING

by r his way upon his own head	2Chr 6:23

RECONCILE

of the congregation to r withal	Lev 6:30
her r himself unto his master	1Sa 29:4
so shall ye r the house	Eze 45:20
that he might r both unto God in	Eph 2:16
by him to r all things unto	Col 1:20

RECONCILED

first be r to thy brother, and	Mt 5:24
we were r to God by the death of	Rom 5:10
of his Son, much more, being r	Rom 5:10
unmarried, or be r to her husband	1Cor 7:11
who hath r us to himself by Jesus	2Cor 5:18
In Christ's stead, be ye r to God	2Cor 5:20

wicked works, yet now hath he r............. Col 1:21

RECONCILIATION
sanctified it, to make r upon it............. Lev 8:15
they made r with their blood upon.... 2Chr 29:24
to make r for them, saith the......... Eze 45:15
to make r for the house of Israel..... Eze 45:17
to make r for iniquity, and to........ Dan 9:24
given to us the ministry of r........... 2Cor 5:18
committed unto us the word of r....... 2Cor 5:19
to make r for the sins of the.......... Heb 2:17

RECONCILING
made an end of r the holy place...... Lev 16:20
of them be the r of the world........ Rom 11:15
r the world unto himself, not........ 2Cor 5:19

RECORD
in all places where I r my name I........ Ex 20:24
earth to r this day against you,....... Deut 30:19
heaven and earth to r against them.. Deut 31:28
the ark of the LORD, and to r......... 1Chr 16:4
and therein was a r thus written..... Ezr 6:2
is in heaven, and my r is on high..... Job 16:19
unto me faithful witnesses to r....... Is 8:2
And this is the r of John, when...... Jn 1:19
And John bare r, saying, I saw the.. Jn 1:32
bare r that this is the Son of....... Jn 1:34
him, Thou bearest r of thyself....... Jn 8:13
thy r is not true...................... Jn 8:13
him, Though I bear r of myself........ Jn 8:14
yet my r is true...................... Jn 8:14
raised him from the dead, bare r..... Jn 12:17
And he that saw it bare r, and his.. Jn 19:35
and his r is true..................... Jn 19:35
I take you to r this day, that I..... Acts 20:26
For I bear them r that they have..... Rom 10:2
I call God for a r upon my soul...... 2Cor 1:23
For to their power, I bear r......... 2Cor 8:3
for I bear you r, that, if it had.... Gal 4:15
For God is my r, how greatly I....... Phil 1:8
For I bear him r, that he hath a..... Col 4:13
are three that bear r in heaven...... 1Jn 5:7
the r that God gave of his Son....... 1Jn 5:10
And this is the r, that God hath..... 1Jn 5:11
yea, and we also bear r.............. 3Jn 12
and ye know that our r is true....... 3Jn 12
Who bare r of the word of God, and.. Rev 1:2

RECORDED
were r chief of the fathers.......... Neh 12:22

RECORDER
the son of Ahilud was r.............. 2Sa 8:16
the son of Ahilud was r.............. 2Sa 20:24
the son of Ahilud, the r............. 1Kin 4:3
and Joah the son of Asaph the r...... 2Kin 18:18
and Joah the son of Asaph the r...... 2Kin 18:37
Jehoshaphat the son of Ahilud, r..... 1Chr 18:15
and Joah the son of Joahaz the r..... 2Chr 34:8
and Joah, Asaph's son, the r......... Is 36:3
and Joah, the son of Asaph, the..... Is 36:22

RECORDS
the book of the r of thy fathers..... Ezr 4:15
thou find in the book of the r....... Ezr 4:15
the book of r of the chronicles..... Est 6:1

RECOUNT
He shall r his worthies.............. Nah 2:5

RECOVER
ye not r them within that time....... Judg 11:26
them, and without fail r all......... 1Sa 30:8
as he went to r his border at the.. 2Sa 8:3
whether I shall r of this disease.... 2Kin 1:2
for he would r him of his leprosy.... 2Kin 5:3
that thou mayest r him of his....... 2Kin 5:6
unto me to r a man of his leprosy... 2Kin 5:7
over the place, and r the leper..... 2Kin 5:11
Shall I r of this disease........... 2Kin 8:8
Shall I r of this disease........... 2Kin 8:9
unto him, Thou mayest certainly r... 2Kin 8:10
me that thou shouldest surely r..... 2Kin 8:14
Neither did Jeroboam r strength..... 2Chr 13:20
that they could not r themselves.... 2Chr 14:13
O spare me, that I may r strength... Ps 39:13
to r the remnant of his people...... Is 11:11
so with thou r me, and make me to.. Is 38:16
upon the bold, and he shall r....... Is 38:21
will r my wool and my flax given.... Hos 2:9
on the sick, and they shall r....... Mk 16:18
that they may r themselves out of... 2Ti 2:26

RECOVERED
David r all that the Amalekites..... 1Sa 30:18
David r all......................... 1Sa 30:19
ought of the spoil that we have r... 1Sa 30:22
him, and r the cities of Israel..... 2Kin 13:25
how he r Damascus, and Hamath...... 2Kin 14:28
king of Syria r Elath to Syria..... 2Kin 16:6
and laid it on the boil, and he r.. 2Kin 20:7
sick, and was r of his sickness..... Is 38:9
that he had been sick, and was r.... Is 39:1
of the daughter of my people r..... Jer 8:22
he had r from Ishmael the son of.... Jer 41:16

RECOVERING
r of sight to the blind, to set...... Lk 4:18

RED *The sea dividing Egypt and Arabia.*
And the first came out r, all over... Gen 25:25
thee, with that same r pottage...... Gen 25:30
His eyes shall be r with wine....... Gen 49:12
and cast them into the R sea........ Ex 10:19

of the wilderness of the R sea...... Ex 13:18
also are showed in the R sea........ Ex 15:4
brought Israel from the R sea....... Ex 15:22
R sea even unto the sea of the...... Ex 23:31
And rams' skins dyed r, and......... Ex 25:5
the tent of rams' skins dyed r...... Ex 26:14
And rams' skins dyed r, and......... Ex 35:7
r skins of rams, and badgers'....... Ex 35:23
the tent of rams' skins dyed r...... Ex 36:19
covering of rams' skins dyed r...... Ex 39:34
by the way of the R sea............. Num 14:25
thee a r heifer without spot........ Num 19:2
mount Hor by the way of the R sea.. Num 21:4
LORD, What he did in the R sea...... Num 21:14
Elim, and encamped by the R sea.... Num 33:10
And they removed from the R sea.... Num 33:11
the plain over against the R sea.... Deut 1:1
by the way of the R sea............. Deut 1:40
by the way of the R sea, as the.... Deut 2:1
R sea to overthrow them as they.... Deut 11:4
up the water of the R sea for you.. Josh 2:10
LORD your God did to the R sea..... Josh 4:23
and horsemen unto the R sea........ Josh 24:6
the wilderness unto the R sea....... Judg 11:16
Eloth, on the shore of the R sea... 1Kin 9:26
on the other side as r as blood.... 2Kin 3:22
heardest their cry by the R sea.... Neh 9:9
and silver, upon a pavement of r... Est 1:6
there is a cup, and the wine is r.. Ps 75:8
him at the sea, even at the R sea.. Ps 106:7
He rebuked the R sea also.......... Ps 106:9
and terrible things by the R sea... Ps 106:22
divided the R sea into parts....... Ps 136:13
Pharaoh and his host in the R sea.. Ps 136:15
thou upon the wine when it is r.... Prov 23:31
though they be r like crimson...... Is 1:18
ye unto her, A vineyard of r wine.. Is 27:2
art thou r in thine apparel........ Is 63:2
thereof was marred in the R sea.... Jer 49:21
of his mighty men is made r........ Nah 2:3
a man riding upon a r horse........ Zec 1:8
and behind him were there r horses. Zec 1:8
the first chariot were r horses.... Zec 6:2
for the sky is r.................... Mt 16:2
for the sky is r and lowering...... Mt 16:3
of Egypt, and in the R sea......... Acts 7:36
through the R sea as by dry land... Heb 11:29
went out another horse that was r.. Rev 6:4
and behold a great r dragon........ Rev 12:3

REDDISH
bright spot, white, and somewhat r.. Lev 13:19
a white bright spot, somewhat r.... Lev 13:24
or bald forehead, a white r sore.... Lev 13:42
sore be white r in his bald head... Lev 13:43
be greenish or r in the garment.... Lev 13:49
hollow streaks, greenish or r...... Lev 14:37

REDEEM
I will r you with a stretched out... Ex 6:6
an ass thou shalt r with a lamb..... Ex 13:13
and if thou wilt not r it, then.... Ex 13:13
among thy children shalt thou r.... Ex 13:13
the firstborn of my children I r... Ex 13:15
an ass thou shalt r with a lamb.... Ex 34:20
and if thou r him not, then shalt.. Ex 34:20
of thy sons thou shalt r........... Ex 34:20
and if any of his kin come to r it. Lev 25:25
then shall he r that which his..... Lev 25:25
And if the man have none to r it... Lev 25:26
and himself be able to r it........ Lev 25:26
then he may r it within a whole.... Lev 25:29
may half year may he r it.......... Lev 25:29
may the Levites r at any time...... Lev 25:32
one of his brethren may r him...... Lev 25:48
or his uncle's son, may r him...... Lev 25:49
unto him of his family may r him... Lev 25:49
if he be able, he may r himself.... Lev 25:49
But if he will at all r it......... Lev 27:13
sanctified it will r his house..... Lev 27:15
the field will in any wise r it.... Lev 27:19
And if he will not r the field..... Lev 27:20
then he shall r it according to.... Lev 27:27
will at all r ought of his tithes.. Lev 27:31
of man shalt thou surely r......... Num 18:15
of unclean beasts shalt thou r..... Num 18:15
from a month old shalt thou r...... Num 18:16
of a goat, thou shalt not r........ Num 18:17
If thou wilt r it.................. Ruth 4:4
r it: but if thou wilt............. Ruth 4:4
but if thou wilt not r it.......... Ruth 4:4
there is none to r it beside thee.. Ruth 4:4
And he said, I will r it........... Ruth 4:4
I cannot r it for myself, lest I... Ruth 4:6
r thou my right to thyself......... Ruth 4:6
for I cannot r it.................. Ruth 4:6
whom God went to r for a people.... 2Sa 7:23
whom God went to r to be his own.. 1Chr 17:21
is it in our power to r them....... Neh 5:5
famine he shall r thee from death.. Job 5:20
R me from the hand of the mighty... Job 6:23
Israel, O God, out of all his...... Ps 25:22
r me, and be merciful unto me...... Ps 26:11
r us for thy mercies' sake......... Ps 44:26
can by any means r his brother..... Ps 49:7
But God will r my soul from the.... Ps 49:15
Draw nigh unto my soul, and r it... Ps 69:18
He shall r their soul from deceit.. Ps 72:14
he shall r Israel from all his..... Ps 130:8
at all, that it cannot r........... Is 50:2
I will r thee out of the hand of.. Jer 15:21

I will r them from death........... Hos 13:14
there the LORD shall r thee from... Mic 4:10
To r them that were under the law.. Gal 4:5
that he might r us from all........ Titus 2:14

REDEEMED
The angel which r me from all...... Gen 48:16
the people which thou hast r....... Ex 15:13
then shall he let her be r......... Ex 21:8
to an husband, and not at all r.... Lev 19:20
if it be not r within the space.... Lev 25:30
they may be r, and they shall go... Lev 25:48
that he is sold he may be r again.. Lev 25:48
if he be not r in these years,..... Lev 25:54
man, it shall not be r any more.... Lev 27:20
or if it be not r, then it shall... Lev 27:27
possession, shall be sold or r..... Lev 27:28
be devoted of men, shall be r...... Lev 27:29
it shall not be r.................. Lev 27:33
are to be r of the two hundred..... Num 3:46
the odd number of them is to be r.. Num 3:48
them that were r by the Levites.... Num 3:49
of them that were r unto Aaron..... Num 3:51
those that are to be r from a...... Num 18:16
r you out of the house of bondmen.. Deut 7:8
which thou hast r through thy...... Deut 9:26
r you out of the house of bondage.. Deut 13:5
Egypt, and the LORD thy God r thee.. Deut 15:15
people Israel, whom thou hast r.... Deut 21:8
and the LORD thy God r thee thence.. Deut 24:18
who hath r my soul out of all...... 2Sa 4:9
that hath r my soul out of all..... 1Kin 1:29
whom thou hast r out of Egypt...... 1Chr 17:21
whom thou hast r by thy great...... Neh 1:10
have r our brethren the Jews....... Neh 5:8
thou hast r me, O LORD God of...... Ps 31:5
and my soul, which thou hast r..... Ps 71:23
inheritance, which thou hast r..... Ps 74:2
hast with thine arm r thy people... Ps 77:15
r them from the hand of the enemy.. Ps 106:10
Let the r of the LORD say so,...... Ps 107:2
whom he hath r from the hand of.... Ps 107:2
hath r us from our enemies......... Ps 136:24
Zion shall be r with judgment...... Is 1:27
who r Abraham, concerning the...... Is 29:22
but the r shall walk there......... Is 35:9
for I have r thee, I have called... Is 43:1
for I have r thee.................. Is 44:22
for the LORD hath r Jacob.......... Is 44:23
The LORD hath r his servant Jacob.. Is 48:20
Therefore the r of the LORD shall.. Is 51:11
ye shall be r without money....... Is 52:3
his people, he hath r Jerusalem.... Is 52:9
holy people, The r of the LORD..... Is 62:12
and the year of my r is come....... Is 63:4
his love and in his pity he r them. Is 63:9
For the LORD hath r Jacob.......... Jer 31:11
thou hast r my life................ Lam 3:58
though I have r them, yet they..... Hos 7:13
r thee out of the house of......... Mic 6:4
for I have r them.................. Zec 10:8
he hath visited and r his people... Lk 1:68
he which should have r Israel...... Lk 24:21
Christ hath r us from the curse.... Gal 3:13
not r with corruptible things...... 1Pet 1:18
hast r us to God by thy blood out. Rev 5:9
which were r from the earth........ Rev 14:3
These were r from among men,....... Rev 14:4

REDEEMEDST
which thou r to thee from Egypt,... 2Sa 7:23

REDEEMER
For I know that my r liveth........ Job 19:25
O LORD, my strength, and my r...... Ps 19:14
rock, and the high God their r..... Ps 78:35
For their r is mighty.............. Prov 23:11
thee, saith the LORD, and thy r.... Is 41:14
Thus saith the LORD, your r........ Is 43:14
and his r the LORD of hosts........ Is 44:6
Thus saith the LORD, the r......... Is 44:24
As for our r, the LORD of hosts.... Is 47:4
Thus saith the LORD, thy R......... Is 48:17
the R of Israel, and his Holy One,. Is 49:7
the LORD am thy Saviour and thy R.. Is 49:26
thy R the Holy One of Israel....... Is 54:5
on thee, saith the LORD thy R...... Is 54:8
the R shall come to Zion, and unto. Is 59:20
the LORD am thy Saviour and thy R.. Is 60:16
O LORD, art our father, our r...... Is 63:16
Their R is strong.................. Jer 50:34

REDEEMETH
The LORD r the soul of his......... Ps 34:22
Who r thy life from destruction.... Ps 103:4

REDEEMING
time in Israel concerning r........ Ruth 4:7
R the time, because the days are... Eph 5:16
them that are without, r the....... Col 4:5

REDEMPTION
ye shall grant a r for the land.... Lev 25:24
give again the price of his r out.. Lev 25:51
give him again the price of his r.. Lev 25:52
Moses took the r money of them..... Num 3:49
(For the r of their soul is........ Ps 49:8
the r cost r unto his people....... Ps 111:9
mercy, and with him is plenteous r. Ps 130:7
for the right of r is thine to.... Jer 32:7
is thine, and the r is thine...... Jer 32:8
that looked for r in Jerusalem.... Lk 2:38
for your r draweth nigh........... Lk 21:28

R

the *r* that is in Christ Jesus .... Rom 3:24
to wit, the *r* of our body .... Rom 8:23
and sanctification, and *r* 1Cor 1:30
In whom we have *r* through his .... Eph 1:7
the *r* of the purchased possession .... Eph 1:14
ye are sealed unto the day of *r* .... Eph 4:30
In whom we have *r* through his .... Col 1:14
having obtained eternal *r* for us ...... Heb 9:12
for the *r* of the transgressions .... Heb 9:15

REDNESS
who hath *r* of eyes .... Prov 23:29

REDOUND
of many *r* to the glory of God 2Cor 4:15

REED
as a *r* is shaken in the water, and 1Kin 14:15
upon the staff of this bruised *r* 2Kin 18:21
trees, in the covert of the *r* .... Job 40:21
in the staff of this broken *r* .... Is 36:6
A bruised *r* shall he not break, ... Is 42:3
staff of *r* to the house of Israel .... Eze 29:6
in his hand, and a measuring *r* .... Eze 40:3
in the man's hand a measuring *r* ...... Eze 40:5
breadth of the building, one *r* .... Eze 40:5
and the height, one *r* .... Eze 40:5
the gate, which was one *r* broad ...... Eze 40:6
the gate, which was one *r* broad ...... Eze 40:6
was one *r* long, and one *r* broad .... Eze 40:7
of the gate within was one *r* .... Eze 40:7
porch of the gate within, one *r* .... Eze 40:8
were a full *r* of six great cubits .... Eze 41:8
east side with the measuring *r* .... Eze 42:16
with the measuring *r* round about .. Eze 42:16
with the measuring *r* round about .. Eze 42:17
reeds, with the measuring *r* .... Eze 42:18
reeds with the measuring *r* .... Eze 42:19
A *r* shaken with the wind .... Mt 11:7
A bruised *r* shall he not break, ... Mt 12:20
head, and a *r* in his right hand .... Mt 27:29
they spit upon him, and took the *r* .. Mt 27:30
it with vinegar, and put it on a *r* .... Mt 27:48
smote him on the head with a *r* .... Mk 15:19
full of vinegar, and put it on a *r* ..... Mk 15:36
A *r* shaken with the wind .... Lk 7:24
was given me a *r* like unto a rod ..... Rev 11:1
a golden *r* to measure the city .... Rev 21:15
he measured the city with the *r* .... Rev 21:16

REEDS
the *r* and flags shall wither .... Is 19:6
The paper *r* by the brooks, by the ... Is 19:7
each lay, shall be grass with *r* .... Is 35:7
the *r* they have burned with fire, ... Jer 51:32
measuring reed, five hundred *r* .... Eze 42:16
the north side, five hundred *r* .... Eze 42:17
the south side, five hundred *r* .... Eze 42:18
measured five hundred *r* with the .. Eze 42:19
round about, five hundred *r* long .... Eze 42:20
of five and twenty thousand *r* .... Eze 45:1
and twenty thousand *r* in breadth ... Eze 48:8

REEL
They *r* to and fro, and stagger like.... Ps 107:27
The earth shall *r* to and fro .... Is 24:20

REELAIAH
(re-el-ah'-yah) A clan leader with
Zerubbabel.
Jeshua, Nehemiah, Seraiah, R .... Ezr 2:2

REFINE
will *r* them as silver is refined, ... Zec 13:9

REFINED
altar of incense *r* gold by weight...... 1Chr 28:18
thousand talents of *r* silver 1Chr 29:4
of wines on the lees well *r* .... Is 25:6
Behold, I have *r* thee, but not .... Is 48:10
will refine them as silver is *r* .... Zec 13:9

REFINER
And he shall sit as a *r* and .... Mal 3:3

REFINER'S
for he is like a *r* fire, and like........... Mal 3:2

REFORMATION
on them until the time of *r* .... Heb 9:10

REFORMED
if ye will not be *r* by me by .... Lev 26:23

REFRAIN
Then Joseph could not *r* himself ...... Gen 45:1
Therefore I will *r* my mouth............. Job 7:11
r thy foot from their path................. Prov 1:15
a time to *r* from embracing............... Eccl 3:5
for my praise will I *r* for thee .... Is 48:9
Wilt thou *r* thyself for these .... Is 64:12
R thy voice from weeping, and .... Jer 31:16
R from these men, and let them .... Acts 5:38
let him *r* his tongue from evil, ... 1Pet 3:10

REFRAINED
r himself, and said, Set on bread ..... Gen 43:31
Nevertheless Haman *r* himself .... Est 5:10
The princes *r* talking, and laid .... Job 29:9
lo, I have not *r* my lips, O LORD,...... Ps 40:9
I have *r* my feet from every evil....... Ps 119:101
I have been still, and *r* myself .... Is 42:14
they have not *r* their feet .... Jer 14:10

REFRAINETH
but he that *r* his lips is wise.............. Prov 10:19

REFRESH
r thyself, and I will give thee a 1Kin 13:7
go unto his friends to *r* himself .... Acts 27:3
r my bowels in the Lord .... Philem 20

REFRESHED
and the stranger, may be *r* .... Ex 23:12
seventh day he rested, and was *r* ..... Ex 31:17
so Saul was *r*, and was well, and 1Sa 16:23
came weary, and *r* themselves there .. 2Sa 16:14
I will speak, that I may be *r* .... Job 32:20
will of God, and may with you be *r* .. Rom 15:32
For they have *r* my spirit 1Cor 16:18
his spirit was *r* by you all. 2Cor 7:13
for he oft *r* me, and was not............. 2Ti 1:16
of the saints are *r* by thee. .... Philem 7

REFRESHETH
for he *r* the soul of his masters. .... Prov 25:13

REFRESHING
and this is the *r* .... Is 28:12
when the times of *r* shall come .... Acts 3:19

REFUGE
there shall be six cities for *r* .... Num 35:6
cities to be cities of *r* for you............ Num 35:11
you cities for *r* from the avenger ...... Num 35:12
six cities shall ye have for *r* .... Num 35:13
which shall be cities of *r* .... Num 35:14
These six cities shall be a *r* .... Num 35:15
restore him to the city of his *r* .... Num 35:25
the border of the city of his *r* .... Num 35:26
the borders of the city of his *r* .... Num 35:27
his *r* until the death of the high .... Num 35:28
that is fled to the city of his *r*. .... Num 35:32
The eternal God is thy *r*, and........... Deut 33:27
Appoint out for you cities of *r* .... Josh 20:2
they shall be your *r* from the............ Josh 20:3
to be a city of *r* for the slayer .... Josh 20:3
to be a city of *r* for the slayer .... Josh 21:21
to be a city of *r* for the slayer .... Josh 21:27
to be a city of *r* for the slayer .... Josh 21:32
to be a city of *r* for the slayer .... Josh 21:38
salvation, my high tower, and my *r*.. 2Sa 22:3
namely, Hebron, the city of *r* 1Chr 6:57
unto them, of the cities of *r* 1Chr 6:67
will be a *r* for the oppressed............. Ps 9:9
a *r* in times of trouble. .... Ps 9:9
poor, because the LORD is his *r* .... Ps 14:6
God is our *r* and strength, a very .... Ps 46:1
the God of Jacob is our *r* .... Ps 46:7
the God of Jacob is our *r* .... Ps 46:11
is known in her palaces for a *r* .... Ps 48:3
of thy wings will I make my *r* .... Ps 57:1
r in the day of my trouble .... Ps 59:16
the rock of my strength, and my *r*.... Ps 62:7
God is a *r* for us .... Ps 62:8
but thou art my strong *r*. .... Ps 71:7
will say of the LORD, He is my *r* ..... Ps 91:2
hast made the LORD, which is my *r* .. Ps 91:9
and my God is the rock of my *r*. ...... Ps 94:22
hills are a *r* for the wild goats .... Ps 104:18
I failed me .... Ps 142:4
I said, Thou art my *r* and my .... Ps 142:5
children shall have a place of *r* .... Prov 14:26
the heat, and for a place of *r* .... Is 4:6
a *r* from the storm, a shadow from ... Is 25:4
for we have made lies our *r* .... Is 28:15
shall sweep away the *r* of lies........... Is 28:17
my *r* in the day of affliction, ... Jer 16:19
whose have fled for *r* to lay hold...... Heb 6:18

REFUSE
if thou *r* to let him go, behold,......... Ex 4:23
if thou *r* to let them go, behold, ... Ex 8:2
For if thou *r* to let them go, and ...... Ex 9:2
How long wilt thou *r* to humble ...... Ex 10:3
if thou *r* to let my people go, ... Ex 10:4
Moses, How long *r* ye to keep my ... Ex 16:28
utterly *r* to give her unto him .... Ex 22:17
every thing that was vile and *r* 1Sa 15:9
recompense it, whether thou *r* .... Job 34:33
and be wise, and *r* it not. .... Prov 8:33
because they *r* to do judgment .... Prov 21:7
for his hands *r* to labour. .... Prov 21:25
But if ye *r* and rebel, ye shall .... Is 1:20
that he may know *r* the evil............. Is 7:15
child shall know to *r* the evil. .... Is 7:16
fast deceit, they *r* to return. .... Jer 8:5
through deceit they *r* to know me .... Jer 9:6
which *r* to hear my words, which .... Jer 13:10
if they *r* to take the cup at .... Jer 25:28
But if thou *r* to go forth .... Jer 38:21
r in the midst of the people.............. Lam 3:45
yea, and sell the *r* of the wheat .... Amos 8:6
worthy of death, I *r* not to die .... Acts 25:11
But *r* profane and old wives' 1Ti 4:7
But the younger widows *r*. 1Ti 5:11
See that ye *r* not him that................. Heb 12:25

REFUSED
but he *r* to be comforted .... Gen 37:35
But he *r*, and said unto his............... Gen 39:8
And his father *r*, and said, I know ... Gen 48:19
Thus Edom *r* to give Israel.............. Num 20:21
Nevertheless the people *r* to obey ... 1Sa 8:19
because I have *r* him 1Sa 16:7
But he *r*, and said, I will not eat 1Sa 28:23
Howbeit he *r* to turn aside. 2Sa 2:23

but he *r* to eat 2Sa 13:9
And the man *r* to smite him. 1Kin 20:35
which he *r* to give thee for money.... 1Kin 21:15
to take it; but he *r* 2Kin 5:16
r to obey, neither were mindful .... Neh 9:17
But the queen Vashti *r* to come at ... Est 1:12
The things that my soul *r* to .... Job 6:7
my soul *r* to be comforted .... Ps 77:2
of God, and *r* to walk in his law ...... Ps 78:10
Moreover he *r* the tabernacle of ...... Ps 78:67
The stone which the builders *r* is ..... Ps 118:22
Because I have called, and ye *r* .... Prov 1:24
a wife of youth, when thou wast *r* ... Is 54:6
but they have *r* to receive .... Jer 5:3
they have *r* to return. .... Jer 5:3
which *r* to hear my words. .... Jer 11:10
r to be comforted for her. .... Jer 31:15
they *r* to let them go .... Jer 50:33
for they have *r* my judgments .... Eze 5:6
king, because they *r* to return .... Hos 11:5
But they *r* to hearken, and pulled ... Zec 7:11
This Moses whom they *r*, saying, ... Acts 7:35
God is good, and nothing to be *r* 1Ti 4:4
r to be called the son of .... Heb 11:24
not who *r* him that spake on earth ... Heb 12:25

REFUSEDST
forehead, thou *r* to be ashamed .... Jer 3:3

REFUSETH
he *r* to let the people go .... Ex 7:14
for the LORD *r* to give me leave .... Num 22:13
and said, Balaam *r* to come with us .. Num 22:14
My husband's brother *r* to raise .... Deut 25:7
but he that *r* reproof erreth. .... Prov 10:17
be to him that *r* instruction .... Prov 13:18
He that *r* instruction despiseth .... Prov 15:32
Forasmuch as this people *r* the .... Is 8:6
incurable, which *r* to be healed .... Jer 15:18

REGARD
Also *r* not your stuff........................ Gen 45:20
and let them not *r* vain words .... Ex 5:9
R not them that have familiar .... Lev 19:31
which shall not *r* the person of .... Deut 28:50
not, neither did she *r* it. 1Sa 4:20
r this man of Belial, even Nabal....... 1Sa 25:25
r not this thing 2Sa 13:20
were it not that I *r* the presence 2Kin 3:14
let not God *r* it from above, ... Job 3:4
neither will the Almighty *r* it. .... Job 35:13
Take heed, *r* not iniquity .... Job 36:21
Because they *r* not the works of .... Ps 28:5
hated them that *r* lying vanities. ...... Ps 31:6
If I *r* iniquity in my heart, the.......... Ps 66:18
shall the God of Jacob *r* it. .... Ps 94:7
He will *r* the prayer of the .... Ps 102:17
That thou mayest *r* discretion .... Prov 5:2
He will not *r* any ransom .... Prov 6:35
that in *r* of the oath of God. .... Eccl 8:2
but they *r* not the work of .... Is 5:12
them, which shall not *r* silver........... Is 13:17
he will no more *r* them. .... Lam 4:16
Neither shall he *r* the God of his ..... Dan 11:37
desire of women, nor *r* any god. ...... Dan 11:37
neither will I *r* the peace. .... Amos 5:22
Behold ye among the heathen, and *r*.. Hab 1:5
will he *r* your persons. .... Mal 1:9
Though I fear not God, nor *r* man.... Lk 18:4
And to him they had *r*, because .... Acts 8:11
day, to the Lord he doth not *r* it .... Rom 14:6

REGARDED
much for the word of the................... Ex 9:21
nor any to answer, nor any that *r* 1Kin 18:29
hast *r* me according to the estate 1Chr 17:17
Nevertheless he *r* their..................... Ps 106:44
out my hand, and no man *r*.............. Prov 1:24
men, O king, have not *r* thee .... Dan 3:12
For he hath *r* the low estate of .... Lk 1:48
feared not God, neither *r* man .... Lk 18:2
I *r* them not, saith the Lord.............. Heb 8:9

REGARDEST
that thou *r* neither princes nor 2Sa 19:6
I stand up, and thou *r* me not .... Job 30:20
for thou *r* not the person of men ..... Mt 22:16
for thou *r* not the person of men,..... Mk 12:14

REGARDETH
which *r* not persons, nor taketh........ Deut 10:17
nor *r* the rich more than the poor ..... Job 34:19
neither *r* he the crying of the. .... Job 39:7
A righteous man *r* the life of his ...... Prov 12:10
but he that *r* reproof shall .... Prov 13:18
but he that *r* reproof is prudent. ...... Prov 15:5
but the wicked *r* not to know it .... Prov 29:7
that is higher than the highest *r* .... Eccl 5:8
he that *r* the clouds shall not .... Eccl 11:4
despised the cities, he *r* no man .... Is 33:8
r not thee, O king, nor the .... Dan 6:13
insomuch that he *r* not the. .... Mal 2:13
He that *r* the day, *r* it. .... Rom 14:6
he that *r* not the day, to the. .... Rom 14:6

REGARDING
perish for ever without any *r* it........ Job 4:20
not *r* his life, to supply your............. Phil 2:30

REGEM
(re'-ghem) A son of Jahdai.
R, and Jotham, and Gesham 1Chr 2:47

REGEM-MELECH
(re''-ghem-me'-lek) A
messenger for Zechariah.
the house of God Sherezer and R .... Zec 7:2

REGENERATION

in the r when the Son of man	Mt 19:28
he saved us, by the washing of r	Titus 3:5

REGION

all the r of Argob, the kingdom	Deut 3:4
all the r of Argob, with all	Deut 3:13
of Abinadab, in all the r of Dor	1Kin 4:11
him also pertained the r of Argob	1Kin 4:13
all the r on this side the river	1Kin 4:24
all the r round about Jordan,	Mt 3:5
and to them which sat in the r	Mt 4:16
all the r round about Galilee	Mk 1:28
through that whole r round about	Mk 6:55
of the r of Trachonitis, and	Lk 3:1
him through all the r round about	Lk 4:14
throughout all the r round about	Lk 7:17
published throughout all the r	Acts 13:49
unto the r that lieth round about	Acts 14:6
the r of Galatia, and were	Acts 16:6

REGIONS

abroad throughout the r of Judaea	Acts 8:1
the gospel in the r beyond you	2Cor 10:16
this boasting in the r of Achaia	2Cor 11:10
I came into the r of Syria	Gal 1:21

REGISTER

These sought their r among those	Ezr 2:62
I found a r of the genealogy of	Neh 7:5
These sought their r among those	Neh 7:64

REHABIAH (re-hab-i´-ah) A son of Eliezer.

sons of Eliezer were, R the chief	1Chr 23:17
but the sons of R were very many	1Chr 24:21
Concerning R	1Chr 24:21
of the sons of R, the first was	1Chr 24:21
R his son, and Jeshaiah his son,	1Chr 26:25

REHEARSE

r it in the ears of Joshua	Ex 17:14
there shall they r the righteous	Judg 5:11

REHEARSED

he r them in the ears of the LORD	1Sa 8:21
spake, they r before Saul	1Sa 17:31
But Peter r the matter from the	Acts 11:4
they r all that God had done with	Acts 14:27

REHOB (re´-hob)

1. A Levitical city in Asher.

from the wilderness of Zin unto R	Num 13:21
and R, and Hammon	Josh 19:28
Ummah also, and Aphek, and R	Josh 19:30
suburbs, and R with her suburbs	Josh 21:31
of Helbah, nor of Aphik, nor of R	Judg 1:31
and the Syrians of Zoba, and of R	2Sa 10:8
suburbs, and R with her suburbs	1Chr 6:75

2. Father of Hadadezer.

also Hadadezer, the son of R	2Sa 8:3
the spoil of Hadadezer, son of R	2Sa 8:12

3. A Levite.

Micha, R, Hashabiah,	Neh 10:11

REHOBOAM (re-ho-bo´-am) See ROBOAM. A son of Solomon and father of Judah.

R his son reigned in his stead	1Kin 11:43
And R went to Shechem	1Kin 12:1
of Israel came, and spake unto R	1Kin 12:3
king R consulted with the old men	1Kin 12:6
people came to the third day	1Kin 12:12
of Judah, R reigned over them	1Kin 12:17
Then king R sent Adoram, who was	1Kin 12:18
Therefore king R made speed to	1Kin 12:18
when R was come to Jerusalem, he	1Kin 12:21
again to R the son of Solomon	1Kin 12:23
Speak unto R, the son of Solomon,	1Kin 12:23
even unto R king of Judah, and	1Kin 12:27
go again to R king of Judah	1Kin 12:27
R the son of Solomon reigned in	1Kin 14:21
R was forty and one years old when	1Kin 14:21
pass in the fifth year of king R	1Kin 14:25
king R made in their stead brasen	1Kin 14:27
Now the rest of the acts of R	1Kin 14:29
And there was war between R	1Kin 14:30
R slept with his fathers, and was	1Kin 14:31
And there was war between R	1Kin 15:6
And Solomon's son was R, Abia his	1Chr 3:10
R his son reigned in his stead	2Chr 9:31
And R went to Shechem	2Chr 10:1
and all Israel came and spake to R	2Chr 10:3
king R took counsel with the old	2Chr 10:6
people came to R on the third day	2Chr 10:12
king R forsook the counsel of the	2Chr 10:13
of Judah, R reigned over them	2Chr 10:17
Then king R sent Hadoram that was	2Chr 10:18
But king R made speed to get him	2Chr 10:18
when R was come to Jerusalem, he	2Chr 11:1
bring the kingdom again to R	2Chr 11:1
Speak unto R the son of Solomon,	2Chr 11:3
R dwelt in Jerusalem, and built	2Chr 11:5
made R the son of Solomon strong,	2Chr 11:17
R took him Mahalath the daughter	2Chr 11:18
R loved Maachah the daughter of	2Chr 11:21
R made Abijah the son of Maachah	2Chr 11:22
when R had established the	2Chr 12:1
R Shishak king of Egypt came up	2Chr 12:2
came Shemaiah the prophet to R	2Chr 12:5
king R made shields of brass	2Chr 12:10
So king R strengthened himself in	2Chr 12:13
for R was one and forty years old	2Chr 12:13
Now the acts of R, first and last,	2Chr 12:15
And there were wars between R	2Chr 12:15
R slept with his fathers, and was	2Chr 12:16
against R the son of Solomon.	2Chr 13:7
when R was young and	2Chr 13:7

REHOBOTH (re´-ho-both)

1. A city in Assyria.

and builded Nineveh, and the city R	Gen 10:11
Saul of R by the river reigned in	Gen 36:37
Shaul of R by the river reigned	1Chr 1:48

2. A well Isaac dug.

And he called the name of it R	Gen 26:22

REHOBOTH-IR See REHOBOTH.

REHUM (re´-hum) See NEHUM.

1. A clan leader with Zerubbabel.

Bilshan, Mizpar, Bigvai, R	Ezr 2:2
Shechaniah, R, Meremoth,	Neh 12:3

2. An officer of King Artaxerxes.

R the chancellor and Shimshai the	Ezr 4:8
Then wrote R the chancellor, and	Ezr 4:9
an answer unto R the chancellor,	Ezr 4:17
letter was read before R, and	Ezr 4:23

3. A Levite rebuilder of Jerusalem's wall.

that was he when he made of Bani	Neh 3:17

4. A sealer of the covenant.

R, Hashabnah, Maaseiah,	Neh 10:25

REI (re´-i) A friend of David.

the prophet, and Shimei, and R	1Kin 1:8

REIGN

him, Shalt thou indeed r over us	Gen 37:8
The LORD shall r for ever	Ex 15:18
that hate you shall r over you	Lev 26:17
thou shalt r over many nations,	Deut 15:6
but they shall not r over thee	Deut 15:6
r over you, or that one	Judg 9:2
the olive tree, R thou over us	Judg 9:8
fig tree, Come thou, and r over us	Judg 9:10
the vine, Come thou, and r over us	Judg 9:12
bramble, Come thou, and r over us	Judg 9:14
me, that I should not r over them	1Sa 8:7
the king that shall r over them	1Sa 8:9
of the king that shall r over you	1Sa 8:11
this same shall r over my people	1Sa 9:17
that said, Shall Saul r over us	1Sa 11:12
but a king shall r over us	1Sa 12:12
when he began to r over Israel	2Sa 2:10
that thou mayest r over all that	2Sa 3:21
years old when he began to r	2Sa 5:4
the son of Haggith do to r	1Kin 1:11
Solomon thy son shall r after me	1Kin 1:13
why then doth Adonijah r	1Kin 1:13
Solomon thy son shall r after me	1Kin 1:17
said, Adonijah shall r after me	1Kin 1:24
Solomon thy son shall r after me	1Kin 1:30
faces on me, that I should r	1Kin 2:15
year of Solomon's r over Israel	1Kin 6:1
thou shalt r according to all	1Kin 11:37
one years old when he began to r	1Kin 14:21
the son of Jeroboam began to r	1Kin 15:25
to r over all Israel in Tirzah	1Kin 15:33
Baasha to r over Israel in Tirzah	1Kin 16:8
came to pass, when he began to r	1Kin 16:11
did Zimri r seven days in Tirzah	1Kin 16:15
Judah began Omri to r over Israel	1Kin 16:23
the son of Omri to r over Israel	1Kin 16:29
the son of Aas began to r over	1Kin 22:41
five years old when he began to r	1Kin 22:42
the son of Ahab began to r over	1Kin 22:51
the son of Ahab began to r over	2Kin 3:1
king of Judah began to r	2Kin 8:16
old was he when he began to r	2Kin 8:17
Jehoram king of Judah begin to r	2Kin 8:25
was Ahaziah when he began to r	2Kin 8:26
began Ahaziah to r over Judah,	2Kin 9:29
Athaliah did r over the land	2Kin 11:3
was Jehoash when he began to r	2Kin 11:21
year of Jehu Jehoash began to r	2Kin 12:1
began to r over Israel in Samaria	2Kin 13:1
to r over Israel in Samaria	2Kin 13:10
five years old when he began to r	2Kin 14:2
of Israel began to r in Samaria	2Kin 14:23
son of Amaziah king of Judah to r	2Kin 15:1
old was he when he began to r	2Kin 15:2
r over Israel in Samaria six	2Kin 15:8
of Jabesh began to r in Samaria	2Kin 15:13
the son of Gadi to r over Israel	2Kin 15:17
began to r over Israel in Samaria	2Kin 15:23
began to r over Israel in Samaria	2Kin 15:27
son of Uzziah king of Judah to r	2Kin 15:32
old was he when he began to r	2Kin 15:33
Jotham king of Judah began to r	2Kin 16:1
old was Ahaz when he began to r	2Kin 16:2
to r in Samaria over Israel nine	2Kin 17:1
of Ahaz king of Judah began to r	2Kin 18:1
old was he when he began to r	2Kin 18:2
years old when he began to r	2Kin 21:1
two years old when he began to r	2Kin 21:19
years old when he began to r	2Kin 22:1
years old when he began to r	2Kin 23:31
that he might not r in Jerusalem	2Kin 23:33
five years old when he began to r	2Kin 23:36
years old when he began to r	2Kin 24:8
him in the eighth year of his r	2Kin 24:12
one years old when he began to r	2Kin 24:18
pass in the ninth year of his r	2Kin 25:1
to r did lift up the head of	2Kin 25:27
their cities unto the r of David	1Chr 4:31
In the fortieth year of the r	1Chr 26:31
With all his r and his might, and	1Chr 29:30
and hast made me to r in his stead	2Chr 1:8
in the fourth year of his r	2Chr 3:2
years old when he began to r	2Chr 12:13
began Abijah to r over Judah	2Chr 13:1
fifteenth year of the r of Asa	2Chr 15:10
and thirtieth year of the r of Asa	2Chr 15:19
thirtieth year of the r of Asa	2Chr 16:1
ninth year of his r was diseased	2Chr 16:12
the one and fortieth year of his r	2Chr 16:13
of his r he sent to his princes	2Chr 17:7
five years old when he began to r	2Chr 20:31
two years old when he began to r	2Chr 21:5
old was he when he began to r	2Chr 21:20
was Ahaziah when he began to r	2Chr 22:2
Behold, the king's son shall r	2Chr 23:3
years old when he began to r	2Chr 24:1
five years old when he began to r	2Chr 25:1
old was Uzziah when he began to r	2Chr 26:3
five years old when he began to r	2Chr 27:1
years old when he began to r	2Chr 27:8
years old when he began to r	2Chr 28:1
began to r when he was five	2Chr 29:1
He in the first year of his r	2Chr 29:3
in his r did cast away in his	2Chr 29:19
years old when he began to r	2Chr 33:1
years old when he began to r	2Chr 33:21
years old when he began to r	2Chr 34:1
For in the eighth year of his r	2Chr 34:3
in the eighteenth year of his r	2Chr 34:8
the r of Josiah was this passover	2Chr 35:19
years old when he began to r	2Chr 36:2
five years old when he began to r	2Chr 36:5
years old when he began to r	2Chr 36:9
his sons until the r of the	2Chr 36:20
even until the r of Darius king	Ezr 4:5
in the r of Ahasuerus, in the	Ezr 4:6
In the beginning of his r	Ezr 4:6
of the r of Darius king of Persia	Ezr 4:24
year of the r of Darius the king	Ezr 6:15
in the r of Artaxerxes king of	Ezr 7:1
in the r of Artaxerxes the king	Ezr 7:7
to the r of Darius the Persian.	Neh 12:22
In third year of his r	Est 1:3
in the seventh year of his r	Est 2:16
That the hypocrite r not, lest	Job 34:30
The LORD shall r for ever	Ps 146:10
By me kings r, and princes decree	Prov 8:15
For out of prison he cometh to r	Eccl 4:14
of hosts shall r in mount Zion	Is 24:23
a king shall r in righteousness,	Is 32:1
in the thirteenth year of his r	Jer 1:2
Shalt thou r, because thou	Jer 22:15
Branch, and a King shall r	Jer 23:5
In the beginning of the r of	Jer 26:1
In the beginning of the r of	Jer 27:1
In the beginning of the r of	Jer 28:1
have a son to r upon his throne	Jer 33:21
the r of Zedekiah king of Judah	Jer 49:34
in the fourth year of his r	Jer 51:59
years old when he began to r	Jer 52:1
pass in the ninth year of his r	Jer 52:4
of his r lifted up the head of	Jer 52:31
In the third year of the r	Dan 1:1
year of the r of Nebuchadnezzar,	Dan 2:1
prospered in the r of Darius	Dan 6:28
in the r of Cyrus the Persian	Dan 6:28
In the first year of his r I	Dan 8:1
In the first year of his r	Dan 9:2
the LORD shall r over them in	Mic 4:7
he heard that Archelaus did r in	Mt 2:22
he shall r over the house of	Lk 1:33
year of the r of Tiberius Caesar	Lk 3:1
not have this man to r over us	Lk 19:14
not that I should r over them	Lk 19:27
shall r in life by one, Jesus	Rom 5:17
even so might grace r through	Rom 5:21
therefore r in your mortal body	Rom 6:12
shall rise to r over the Gentiles	Rom 15:12
and I would to God ye did r	1Cor 4:8
that we also might r with you	1Cor 4:8
For he must r, till he hath put	1Cor 15:25
suffer, we shall also r with him	2Ti 2:12
and we shall r on the earth	Rev 5:10
and he shall r for ever and ever	Rev 11:15
shall r with him a thousand years	Rev 20:6
and they shall r for ever and ever	Rev 22:5

REIGNED

kings that r in the land of Edom	Gen 36:31
before there r any king over the	Gen 36:31
And Bela the son of Beor r in Edom.	Gen 36:32
of Zerah of Bozrah r in his stead.	Gen 36:33
the land of Temani r in his stead.	Gen 36:34
the field of Moab, r in his stead	Gen 36:35
Samlah of Masrekah r in his stead.	Gen 36:36
by the river r in his stead	Gen 36:37
the son of Achbor r in his stead	Gen 36:38
died, and Hadar r in his stead	Gen 36:39
in mount Hermon, and in Salcah,	Josh 12:5
which r in Heshbon, unto the	Josh 13:10
which r in Ashtaroth and in Edrei,	Josh 13:12
which r in Heshbon, whom Moses	Josh 13:21
king of Canaan, that r in Hazor	Judg 4:2
when Abimelech had r three years	Judg 9:22
Saul r one year	1Sa 13:1
when he had r two years over	1Sa 13:1
reign over Israel, and r two years	2Sa 2:10
to reign, and he r forty years	2Sa 5:4
In Hebron he r over Judah seven	2Sa 5:5
and in Jerusalem he r thirty	2Sa 5:5
And David r over all Israel.	2Sa 8:15
and Hanun his son r in his stead.	2Sa 10:1

Saul, in whose stead thou hast r...... 2Sa 16:8
the days that David r over Israel...... 1Kin 2:11
seven years r he in Hebron, and...... 1Kin 2:11
three years r he in Jerusalem...... 1Kin 2:11
Solomon r over all kingdoms from...... 1Kin 4:21
dwelt therein, and r in Damascus...... 1Kin 11:24
abhorred Israel, and r over Syria...... 1Kin 11:25
the time that Solomon r in...... 1Kin 11:42
Rehoboam his son r in his stead...... 1Kin 11:43
of Judah, Rehoboam r over them...... 1Kin 12:17
how he warred, and how he r...... 1Kin 14:19
days which Jeroboam r were two...... 1Kin 14:20
and Nadab his son r in his stead...... 1Kin 14:20
the son of Solomon r in Judah...... 1Kin 14:21
he r seventeen years in Jerusalem...... 1Kin 14:21
And Abijam his son r in his stead...... 1Kin 14:31
son of Nebat r Abijam over Judah...... 1Kin 15:1
Three years r he in Jerusalem...... 1Kin 15:2
Asa his son r in his stead...... 1Kin 15:8
king of Israel r Asa over Judah...... 1Kin 15:9
one years r he in Jerusalem...... 1Kin 15:10
his son r in his stead...... 1Kin 15:24
Judah, and r over Israel two years... 1Kin 15:25
slay him, and r in his stead...... 1Kin 15:28
And it came to pass, when he r...... 1Kin 15:29
and Elah his son r in his stead...... 1Kin 16:6
king of Judah, and r in his stead... 1Kin 16:10
so Tibni died, and Omri r...... 1Kin 16:22
six years r he in Tirzah...... 1Kin 16:23
and Ahab his son r in his stead...... 1Kin 16:28
Ahab the son of Omri r over...... 1Kin 16:29
and Ahaziah his son r in his stead... 1Kin 22:40
he r twenty and five years in...... 1Kin 22:42
and Jehoram his son r in his stead... 1Kin 22:50
Judah, and r two years over Israel... 1Kin 22:51
Jehoram r in his stead in the...... 2Kin 1:17
king of Judah, and r twelve years... 2Kin 3:1
that should have r in his stead...... 2Kin 3:27
and Hazael r in his stead...... 2Kin 8:15
he r eight years in Jerusalem...... 2Kin 8:17
and Ahaziah his son r in his stead... 2Kin 8:24
he r one year in Jerusalem...... 2Kin 8:26
Jehoahaz his son r in his stead...... 2Kin 10:35
the time that Jehu r over Israel...... 2Kin 10:36
forty years r he in Jerusalem...... 2Kin 12:1
and Amaziah his son r in his stead... 2Kin 12:21
in Samaria, and r seventeen years... 2Kin 13:1
and Joash his son r in his stead...... 2Kin 13:9
in Samaria, and r sixteen years...... 2Kin 13:10
Ben-hadad his son r in his stead...... 2Kin 13:24
r Amaziah the son of Joash king... 2Kin 14:1
r twenty and nine years in...... 2Kin 14:2
Jeroboam his son r in his stead...... 2Kin 14:16
Samaria, and r forty and one years... 2Kin 14:23
Zachariah his son r in his stead...... 2Kin 14:29
he r two and fifty years in...... 2Kin 15:2
and Jotham his son r in his stead... 2Kin 15:7
and slew him, and r in his stead...... 2Kin 15:10
he r a full month in Samaria...... 2Kin 15:13
and slew him, and r in his stead...... 2Kin 15:14
Israel, and r ten years in Samaria... 2Kin 15:17
Pekahiah his son r in his stead...... 2Kin 15:22
Israel in Samaria, and r two years... 2Kin 15:23
he killed him, and r in his room...... 2Kin 15:25
in Samaria, and r twenty years...... 2Kin 15:27
r in his stead, in the twentieth...... 2Kin 15:30
he r sixteen years in Jerusalem...... 2Kin 15:33
and Ahaz his son r in his stead...... 2Kin 15:38
r sixteen years in Jerusalem, and... 2Kin 16:2
Hezekiah his son r in his stead...... 2Kin 16:20
he r twenty and nine years in...... 2Kin 18:2
his son r in his stead...... 2Kin 19:37
Manasseh his son r in his stead...... 2Kin 20:21
and r fifty and five years in...... 2Kin 21:1
and Amon his son r in his stead...... 2Kin 21:18
he r two years in Jerusalem...... 2Kin 21:19
and Josiah his son r in his stead... 2Kin 21:26
he r thirty and one years in...... 2Kin 22:1
he r three months in Jerusalem...... 2Kin 23:31
he r eleven years in Jerusalem...... 2Kin 23:36
Jehoiachin his son r in his stead... 2Kin 24:6
he r in Jerusalem three months...... 2Kin 24:8
he r eleven years in Jerusalem...... 2Kin 24:18
Now these are the kings that r...... 1Chr 1:43
r over the children of Israel...... 1Chr 1:43
of Zerah of Bozrah r in his stead... 1Chr 1:44
of the Temanites r in his stead...... 1Chr 1:45
the field of Moab, r in his stead... 1Chr 1:46
Samlah of Masrekah r in his stead... 1Chr 1:47
by the river r in his stead...... 1Chr 1:48
the son of Achbor r in his stead... 1Chr 1:49
was dead, Hadad r in his stead...... 1Chr 1:50
there he r seven years and six...... 1Chr 3:4
and in Jerusalem he r thirty...... 1Chr 3:4
So David r over all Israel, and...... 1Chr 18:14
died, and his son r in his stead... 1Chr 19:1
son of Jesse r over all Israel...... 1Chr 29:26
the time that he r over Israel...... 1Chr 29:27
seven years r he in Hebron, and... 1Chr 29:27
three years r he in Jerusalem...... 1Chr 29:27
and Solomon his son r in his stead... 1Chr 29:28
congregation, and r over Israel...... 2Chr 1:13
he r over all the kings from the... 2Chr 9:26
Solomon r in Jerusalem over all... 2Chr 9:30
Rehoboam his son r in his stead... 2Chr 9:31
of Judah, Rehoboam r over them... 2Chr 10:17
himself in Jerusalem, and r...... 2Chr 12:13
he r seventeen years in Jerusalem... 2Chr 12:13
and Abijah his son r in his stead... 2Chr 12:16
He r three years in Jerusalem...... 2Chr 13:2

Asa his son r in his stead...... 2Chr 14:1
his son r in his stead, and...... 2Chr 17:1
And Jehoshaphat r over Judah...... 2Chr 20:31
he r twenty and five years in...... 2Chr 20:31
and Jehoram his son r in his stead... 2Chr 21:1
he r eight years in Jerusalem...... 2Chr 21:5
he r in Jerusalem eight years, and... 2Chr 21:20
son of Jehoram king of Judah r...... 2Chr 22:1
he r one year in Jerusalem...... 2Chr 22:2
and Athaliah r over the land...... 2Chr 22:12
he r forty years in Jerusalem...... 2Chr 24:1
And Amaziah his son r in his stead... 2Chr 24:27
he r twenty and nine years in...... 2Chr 25:1
he r fifty and two years in...... 2Chr 26:3
and Jotham his son r in his stead... 2Chr 26:23
he r sixteen years in Jerusalem...... 2Chr 27:1
r sixteen years in Jerusalem...... 2Chr 27:8
and Ahaz his son r in his stead...... 2Chr 27:9
he r sixteen years in Jerusalem...... 2Chr 28:1
Hezekiah his son r in his stead...... 2Chr 28:27
he r nine and twenty years in...... 2Chr 29:1
Manasseh his son r in his stead...... 2Chr 32:33
he r fifty and five years in...... 2Chr 33:1
and Amon his son r in his stead...... 2Chr 33:20
and r two years in Jerusalem...... 2Chr 33:21
he r in Jerusalem one and thirty... 2Chr 34:1
he r three months in Jerusalem...... 2Chr 36:2
he r eleven years in Jerusalem...... 2Chr 36:5
he r three months and ten days in... 2Chr 36:9
r eleven years in Jerusalem...... 2Chr 36:11
(this is Ahasuerus which r from...... Est 1:1
his son r in his stead...... Is 37:38
which r instead of Josiah his...... Jer 22:11
r instead of Coniah the son of...... Jer 37:1
he r eleven years in Jerusalem...... Jer 52:1
death r from Adam to Moses...... Rom 5:14
one man's offence death r by one... Rom 5:17
That as sin hath r unto death...... Rom 5:21
ye have r as kings without us...... 1Cor 4:8
thee thy great power, and hast r... Rev 11:17
r with Christ a thousand years...... Rev 20:4

REIGNEST
come of thee, and thou r over all... 1Chr 29:12

REIGNETH
also the king that r over you...... 1Sa 12:14
ye shall say, Absalom r in Hebron... 2Sa 15:10
And now, behold, Adonijah r...... 1Kin 1:18
say among the nations, The LORD r... 1Chr 16:31
God r over the heathen...... Ps 47:8
The LORD r, he is clothed with...... Ps 93:1
among the heathen that the LORD r... Ps 96:10
The LORD r...... Ps 97:1
The LORD r...... Ps 99:1
For a servant when he r...... Prov 30:22
that saith unto Zion, Thy God r...... Is 52:7
which r over the kings of the...... Rev 17:18
for the Lord God omnipotent r...... Rev 19:6

REIGNING
rejected him from r over Israel...... 1Sa 16:1

REINS
about, he cleaveth my r asunder...... Job 16:13
though my r be consumed within me... Job 19:27
God trieth the hearts and r...... Ps 7:9
my r also instruct me in the...... Ps 16:7
try my r and my heart...... Ps 26:2
grieved, and I was pricked in my r... Ps 73:21
For thou hast possessed my r...... Ps 139:13
my r shall rejoice, when thy lips... Prov 23:16
faithfulness the girdle of his r...... Is 11:5
righteously, that triest the r...... Jer 11:20
their mouth, and far from their r... Jer 12:2
search the heart, I try the r...... Jer 17:10
the righteous, and seest the r...... Jer 20:12
of his quiver to enter into my r... Lam 3:13
I am he which searcheth the r...... Rev 2:23

REJECT
knowledge, I will also r thee...... Hos 4:6
sat with him, he would not r her... Mk 6:26
Full well ye r the commandment of... Mk 7:9
the first and second admonition r... Titus 3:10

REJECTED
r thee, but they have r me...... 1Sa 8:7
And ye have this day r your God... 1Sa 10:19
Because thou hast r the word of... 1Sa 15:23
he hath also r thee from being...... 1Sa 15:23
for thou hast r the word of...... 1Sa 15:26
the LORD hath r thee from being... 1Sa 15:26
seeing I have r him from reigning... 1Sa 16:1
they r his statutes, and his...... 2Kin 17:15
the LORD r all the seed of Israel... 2Kin 17:20
He is despised and r of men...... Is 53:3
the LORD hath r thy confidences... Jer 2:37
my words, nor to my law, but r it... Jer 6:19
because the LORD hath r them...... Jer 6:30
for the LORD hath r and forsaken... Jer 7:29
they have r the word of the LORD... Jer 8:9
Hast thou utterly r Judah...... Jer 14:19
the LORD hath r thy...... Lam 5:22
because thou hast r knowledge...... Hos 4:6
The stone which the builders r...... Mt 21:42
be r of the elders, and of the...... Mk 8:31
r is become the head of the...... Mk 12:10
lawyers r the counsel of God...... Lk 7:30
be r of the elders and chief...... Lk 9:22
and be r of this generation...... Lk 17:25
The stone which the builders r...... Lk 20:17

my flesh ye despised not, nor r...... Gal 4:14
beareth thorns and briers is r...... Heb 6:8
inherited the blessing, he was r...... Heb 12:17

REJECTETH
He that r me, and receiveth not my... Jn 12:48

REJOICE
ye shall r before the LORD your...... Lev 23:40
ye shall r in all that ye put...... Deut 12:7
ye shall r before the LORD your...... Deut 12:12
thou shalt r before the LORD thy... Deut 12:18
the LORD thy God, and thou shalt r... Deut 14:26
thou shalt r before the LORD thy... Deut 16:11
thou shalt r in thy feast, thou,... Deut 16:14
therefore thou shalt surely r...... Deut 16:15
thou shalt r in every good thing... Deut 26:11
r before the LORD thy God...... Deut 27:7
so the LORD will r over you to...... Deut 28:63
will again r over thee for good... Deut 30:9
R, O ye nations, with his people... Deut 32:43
And of Zebulun he said, R, Zebulun... Deut 33:18
then r ye in Abimelech...... Judg 9:19
and let him also r in you...... Judg 9:19
unto Dagon their god, and to r...... Judg 16:23
because I r in thy salvation...... 1Sa 2:1
thou sawest it, and didst r...... 1Sa 19:5
daughters of the Philistines r...... 2Sa 1:20
of them r that seek the LORD...... 1Chr 16:10
be glad, and let the earth r...... 1Chr 16:31
let the fields r, and all that is... 1Chr 16:32
and let thy saints r in goodness... 2Chr 6:41
made them to r over their enemies... 2Chr 20:27
had made them r with great joy... Neh 12:43
Which r exceedingly, and are glad... Job 3:22
be, and he shall not r therein...... Job 20:18
r at the sound of the organ...... Job 21:12
with fear, and r with trembling... Ps 2:11
that put their trust in thee r...... Ps 5:11
I will be glad and r in thee...... Ps 9:2
I will r in thy salvation...... Ps 9:14
that trouble me r when I am moved... Ps 13:4
my heart shall r in thy salvation... Ps 13:5
of his people, Jacob shall r...... Ps 14:7
We will r in thy salvation, and in... Ps 20:5
salvation how greatly shall he r... Ps 21:1
not made my foes to r over me...... Ps 30:1
I will be glad and r in thy mercy... Ps 31:7
Be glad in the LORD, and r...... Ps 32:11
R in the LORD, O ye righteous...... Ps 33:1
For our heart shall r in him...... Ps 33:21
it shall r in his salvation...... Ps 35:9
mine enemies wrongfully r over me... Ps 35:19
and let them not r over me...... Ps 35:24
together that r at mine hurt...... Ps 35:26
otherwise they should r over me... Ps 38:16
Let all those that seek thee r...... Ps 40:16
Let mount Zion r, let the...... Ps 48:11
which thou hast broken may r...... Ps 51:8
of his people, Jacob shall r...... Ps 53:6
The righteous shall r when he...... Ps 58:10
I will r, I will divide Shechem... Ps 60:6
the shadow of thy wings will I r... Ps 63:7
But the king shall r in God...... Ps 63:11
of the morning and evening to r... Ps 65:8
the little hills on every side...... Ps 65:12
there did we r in him...... Ps 66:6
let them r before God...... Ps 68:3
yea, let them exceedingly r...... Ps 68:3
by his name JAH, and r before him... Ps 68:4
that seek thee r in thee...... Ps 70:4
greatly r when I sing unto thee... Ps 71:23
that thy people may r in thee...... Ps 85:6
R the soul of thy servant...... Ps 86:4
and Hermon shall r in thy name... Ps 89:12
thy name shall they r all the day... Ps 89:16
hast made all his enemies to r...... Ps 89:42
that we may r and be glad all our... Ps 90:14
Let the heavens r, and let the...... Ps 96:11
shall all the trees of the wood r... Ps 96:12
let the earth r...... Ps 97:1
R in the LORD, ye righteous...... Ps 97:12
make a loud noise, and r, and sing... Ps 98:4
the LORD shall r in his works...... Ps 104:31
of them r that seek the LORD...... Ps 105:3
that I may r in the gladness of... Ps 106:5
The righteous shall see it, and r... Ps 107:42
I will r, I will divide Shechem... Ps 108:7
but let thy servant r...... Ps 109:28
we will r and be glad in it...... Ps 118:24
I r at thy word, as one that...... Ps 119:162
Let Israel r in him that made him... Ps 149:2
Who r to do evil, and delight in... Prov 2:14
r with the wife of thy youth...... Prov 5:18
heart be wise, my heart shall r... Prov 23:15
Yea, my reins shall r, when thy... Prov 23:16
of the righteous shall greatly r... Prov 23:24
and she that bare thee shall r...... Prov 23:25
R not when thine enemy falleth... Prov 24:17
Ointment and perfume r the heart... Prov 27:9
When righteous men do r, there is... Prov 28:12
are in authority, the people r...... Prov 29:2
but the righteous doth sing and r... Prov 29:6
she shall r in time to come...... Prov 31:25
good in them, but for a man to r... Eccl 3:12
a man should r in his own works... Eccl 3:22
come after shall not r in him...... Eccl 4:16
portion, and to r in his labour... Eccl 5:19
live many years, and r in them all... Eccl 11:8
R, O young man, in thy youth...... Eccl 11:9
r in thee, we will remember thy... Song 1:4

REJOICED (column 1 continued)

r in Rezin and Remaliah's son .... Is 8:6
as men r when they divide the .... Is 9:3
even them that r in my highness .... Is 13:3
Yea, the fir trees r at thee .... Is 14:8
R not thou, whole Palestina, ... Is 14:29
And he said, Thou shalt no more r ...... Is 23:12
the noise of them that r endeth .... Is 24:8
be glad and r in his salvation. .... Is 25:9
the poor among men shall r in the ...... Is 29:19
and the desert shall r, and blossom. .... Is 35:1
r even with joy and singing .... Is 35:2
thou shalt r in the LORD, and .... Is 41:16
they shall r in their portion .... Is 61:7
I will greatly r in the LORD .... Is 61:10
so shall thy God r over thee .... Is 62:5
behold, my servants shall r .... Is 65:13
r for ever in that which I create .... Is 65:18
I will r in Jerusalem, and joy in .... Is 65:19
R ye with Jerusalem, and be glad .... Is 66:10
r for joy with her, all ye that .... Is 66:10
ye see this, your heart shall r .... Is 66:14
shall the virgin r in the dance .... Jer 31:13
make them r from their sorrow .... Jer 31:13
I will r over them to do them, ... Jer 32:41
them drunken, that they may r .... Jer 51:39
caused thine enemy to r over thee ...... Lam 2:17
R and be glad, O daughter of Edom, ... Lam 4:21
let not the buyer r, nor the .... Eze 7:12
As thou didst r at the .... Eze 35:15
R not, O Israel, for joy, as .... Hos 9:1
be glad and r .... Joel 2:21
Zion, and r in the LORD your God ...... Joel 2:23
Ye which r in a thing of nought, ... Amos 6:13
R not against me, O mine enemy .... Mic 7:8
therefore they r and are glad. .... Hab 1:15
Yet I will r in the LORD, I will .... Hab 3:18
of thee them that r in thy pride .... Zeph 3:11
r with all the heart, O daughter .... Zeph 3:14
he will r over thee with joy .... Zeph 3:17
Sing and r, O daughter of Zion. .... Zec 2:10
for they shall r, and shall see .... Zec 4:10
R greatly, O daughter of Zion .... Zec 9:9
heart shall r as through wine .... Zec 10:7
their heart shall r in the LORD .... Zec 10:7
R, and be exceeding glad .... Mt 5:12
many shall r at his birth .... Lk 1:14
R ye in that day, and leap for joy .... Lk 6:23
Notwithstanding in this r not .... Lk 10:20
but rather r, because your names .... Lk 10:20
saying unto them, R with me, ... Lk 15:6
together, saying, R with me .... Lk 15:9
of the disciples began to r .... Lk 19:37
and he that reapeth may r together ..... Jn 4:36
for a season to r in his light. .... Jn 5:35
If ye loved me, ye would r .... Jn 14:28
and lament, but the world shall r .... Jn 16:20
you again, and your heart shall r .... Jn 16:22
Therefore did my heart r, and my ...... Acts 2:26
r in hope of the glory of God .... Rom 5:2
R with them that do r .... Rom 12:15
And again he saith, R, ye Gentiles...... Rom 15:10
and they that r, as though they 1Cor 7:30
all the members r with it. 1Cor 12:26
from them of whom I ought to r. 2Cor 2:3
Now I r, not that ye were made 2Cor 7:9
I r therefore that I have 2Cor 7:16
For it is written, R, thou barren .... Gal 4:27
do r, yea, and will r .... Phil 1:18
that I may r in the day of Christ .... Phil 2:16
faith, I joy, and r with you all .... Phil 2:17
also do ye joy, and r with me .... Phil 2:18
when ye see him again, ye may r .... Phil 2:28
my brethren, r in the Lord .... Phil 3:1
r in Christ Jesus, and have no .... Phil 3:3
R in the Lord alway .... Phil 4:4
and again I say, R .... Phil 4:4
Who now r in my sufferings for .... Col 1:24
R evermore 1Th 5:16
degree r in that he is exalted .... Jas 1:9
But now ye r in your boastings .... Jas 4:16
Wherein ye greatly r, though now..... 1Pet 1:6
ye r with joy unspeakable and full 1Pet 1:8
But r, inasmuch as ye are 1Pet 4:13
upon the earth shall r over them .... Rev 11:10
Therefore r, ye heavens, and ye .... Rev 12:12
R over her, thou heaven, and ye .... Rev 18:20
Let us be glad and r, and give .... Rev 19:7

REJOICED

Jethro r for all the goodness .... Ex 18:9
that as the LORD r over you to do ...... Deut 28:63
good, as he r over your fathers .... Deut 30:9
damsel saw him, he r to meet him..... Judg 19:3
and saw the ark, and r to see it. 1Sa 6:13
all the men of Israel greatly 1Sa 11:15
r with great joy, so that the 1Kin 1:40
of Solomon, that he r greatly 1Kin 5:7
and all the people of the land r. 2Kin 11:14
And all the people of the land r. 2Kin 11:20
Then the people r, for that they 1Chr 29:9
the king also r with great joy 1Chr 29:9
And all Judah r at the oath 2Chr 15:15
and all the people of the land r. 2Chr 23:13
And all the people of the land r. 2Chr 23:21
the princes and all the people r 2Chr 24:10
And Hezekiah r, and all the people,..... 2Chr 29:36
Israel, and that dwelt in Judah, r....... 2Chr 30:25
offered great sacrifices, and r. .... Neh 12:43
the wives also and the children r. ...... Neh 12:43
for Judah r for the priests and .... Neh 12:44
and the city of Shushan r and was..... Est 8:15

If I r because my wealth was .... Job 31:25
If I r at the destruction of him, ... Job 31:29
But in mine adversity they r .... Ps 35:15
the daughters of Judah r because .... Ps 97:8
I have r in the way of thy .... Ps 119:14
for my heart r in all my labour. .... Eccl 2:10
assembly of the mockers, nor r........ Jer 15:17
ye were glad, because ye r .... Jer 50:11
r in heart with all thy despite .... Eze 25:6
the priests thereof that r in it. .... Hos 10:5
neither shouldest thou have r .... Obad 12
they r with exceeding great joy .... Mt 2:10
my spirit hath r in God my .... Lk 1:47
and they r with her .... Lk 1:58
In that hour Jesus r in spirit .... Lk 10:21
all the people r for all the .... Lk 13:17
father Abraham r to see my day .... Jn 8:56
r in the works of their own hands...... Acts 7:41
they r for the consolation .... Acts 15:31
he set meat before them, and r .... Acts 16:34
rejoice, as though they r not. 1Cor 7:30
so that I r the more 2Cor 7:7
But I r in the Lord greatly, that .... Phil 4:10
I r greatly that I found of thy 2Jn 4
For I r greatly, when the 3Jn 3

REJOICEST

when thou doest evil, then thou r...... Jer 11:15

REJOICETH

My heart r in the LORD, mine horn 1Sa 2:1
the valley, and r in his strength. .... Job 39:21
my heart is glad, and my glory r. .... Ps 16:9
r as a strong man to run a .... Ps 19:5
therefore my heart greatly r .... Ps 28:7
with the righteous, the city r .... Prov 11:10
The light of the righteous r .... Prov 13:9
The light of the eyes r the heart. .... Prov 15:30
Whoso loveth wisdom r his father ..... Prov 29:3
and their pomp, and he that r .... Is 5:14
the bridegroom r over the bride. .... Is 62:5
Thou meetest him that r and .... Is 64:5
When the whole earth r, I will. .... Eze 35:14
he r more of that sheep, than of .... Mt 18:13
him, r greatly because of the .... Jn 3:29
R not in iniquity 1Cor 13:4
but r in the truth 1Cor 13:6
and mercy r against judgment .... Jas 2:13

REJOICING

and they are come up from thence r... 1Kin 1:45
in the law of Moses, with r 2Chr 23:18
with laughing, and thy lips with r..... Job 8:21
the LORD are right, r the heart .... Ps 19:8
and r shall they be brought. .... Ps 45:15
and declare his works with r .... Ps 107:22
The voice of r and salvation is in .... Ps 118:15
for they are the r of my heart. .... Ps 119:111
shall doubtless come again with r ...... Ps 126:6
his delight, r always before him .... Prov 8:30
R in the habitable part of his .... Prov 8:31
behold, I create Jerusalem a r .... Is 65:18
me the joy and r of mine heart .... Jer 15:16
their r was as to devour the poor....... Hab 3:14
This is the r city that dwelt .... Zeph 2:15
he layeth it on his shoulders, r. .... Lk 15:5
r that they were counted worthy....... Acts 5:41
and he went on his way r .... Acts 8:39
R in hope .... Rom 12:12
I protest by your r which I have 1Cor 15:31
For our r is this, the testimony 2Cor 1:12
us in part, that we are your r 2Cor 1:14
As sorrowful, yet alway r 2Cor 6:10
shall he have r in himself alone .... Gal 6:4
That your r may be more abundant ..... Phil 1:26
our hope, or joy, or crown of r 1Th 2:19
the r of the hope firm unto the .... Heb 3:6
all such r is evil. .... Jas 4:16

REKEM (re'-kem)

1. A prince of Midian.
namely, Evi, and R, and Zur, and Hur Num 31:8
the princes of Midian, Evi, and R ...... Josh 13:21
2. A son of Hebron.
and Tappuah, and R 1Chr 2:43
and R begat Shammai. 1Chr 2:44
3. A city in Benjamin.
And R, and Irpeel, and Taralah, ... Josh 18:27

RELEASE

seven years thou shalt make a r......... Deut 15:1
And this is the manner of the r. .... Deut 15:2
unto his neighbour shall r it. .... Deut 15:2
because it is called the LORD's r. .... Deut 15:2
thy brother thine hand shall r .... Deut 15:3
The seventh year, the year of r .... Deut 15:9
in the solemnity of the year of r........ Deut 31:10
he made a r to the provinces, and ...... Est 2:18
to r unto the people a prisoner. .... Mt 27:15
Whom will ye that I r unto you .... Mt 27:17
that I should r unto you? .... Mt 27:21
Will ye that I r unto you the .... Mk 15:9
rather r Barabbas unto them .... Mk 15:11
therefore chastise him, and r him ...... Lk 23:17
(For of necessity he must r one .... Lk 23:17
this man, and r unto us Barabbas ...... Lk 23:18
therefore, willing to r Jesus .... Lk 23:20
that I should r unto you one at .... Jn 18:39
will ye therefore that I r unto .... Jn 18:39
thee, and have power to r thee .... Jn 19:10
Pilate sought to r him .... Jn 19:12

RELEASED

Then r he Barabbas unto them .... Mt 27:26
Now at that feast he r unto them .... Mk 15:6
people, r Barabbas unto them, and..... Mk 15:15
he r unto them him that for .... Lk 23:25

RELIED

because they r upon the LORD God... 2Chr 13:18
Because thou hast r on the king 2Chr 16:7
not r on the LORD thy God, ... 2Chr 16:7

RELIEF

determined to send r unto the .... Acts 11:29

RELIEVE

then thou shalt r him .... Lev 25:35
r the oppressed, judge the .... Is 1:17
things for meat to r the soul .... Lam 1:11
should r my soul is far from me .... Lam 1:16
their meat to r their souls. .... Lam 1:19
have widows, let them r them, ... 1Ti 5:16
that it may r them that are 1Ti 5:16

RELIEVED

if she have r the afflicted, if 1Ti 5:10

RELIEVETH

he r the fatherless and widow .... Ps 146:9

RELIGION

sect of our r I lived a Pharisee .... Acts 26:5
in time past in the Jews' r .... Gal 1:13
profited in the Jews' r above.......... Gal 1:14
own heart, this man's r is vain .... Jas 1:26
Pure r and undefiled before God and ... Jas 1:27

RELIGIOUS

r proselytes followed Paul and.......... Acts 13:43
If any man among you seem to be r ..... Jas 1:26

RELY

because thou didst r on the LORD 2Chr 16:8

REMAIN

R a widow at thy father's house, ... Gen 38:11
that they may r in the river only .... Ex 8:9
they shall r in the river only .... Ex 8:11
nothing of it r until the morning....... Ex 12:10
my sacrifice r until the morning .... Ex 23:18
r unto the morning, then thou .... Ex 29:34
if ought r until the third day, ... Lev 19:6
r in the hand of him that hath .... Lev 25:28
if there r but few years unto the .... Lev 25:52
according to the years that r. .... Lev 27:18
that those which ye let r of them .... Num 33:55
of every city, we left none to r .... Deut 2:34
r all night until the morning .... Deut 16:4
And those which r shall hear .... Deut 19:20
shall r in thine house, and .... Deut 21:13
His body shall not r all night .... Deut 21:23
shall r in the land which Moses .... Josh 1:14
neither did there r any more .... Josh 2:11
they let none of them r to escape....... Josh 8:22
which r until this very day .... Josh 10:27
he let none r .... Josh 10:28
he let none r in it .... Josh 10:30
you by lot these nations that r .... Josh 23:4
nations, these that r among you .... Josh 23:7
even these that r among you. .... Josh 23:12
and why did Dan r in ships. .... Judg 5:17
we do for wives for them that r........ Judg 21:7
we do for wives for them that r......... Judg 21:16
shalt r by the stone Ezel 1Sa 20:19
did Joab r there with all Israel 1Kin 11:16
I only, r a prophet of the LORD 1Kin 18:22
thee, five of the horses that r 2Kin 7:13
for we r yet escaped, as it is .... Ezr 9:15
the grave, and shall r in the tomb ...... Job 21:32
Those that r of him shall be .... Job 27:15
into dens, and r in their places. .... Job 37:8
far off, and r in the wilderness .... Ps 55:7
and the perfect shall r in it .... Prov 2:21
the way of understanding shall r....... Prov 21:16
As yet shall he r at Nob that day .... Is 10:32
righteousness r in the fruitful .... Is 32:16
that it may r in the house .... Is 44:13
Which r among the graves, and .... Is 65:4
shall r before me, saith the LORD....... Is 66:22
so shall your seed and your name r ..... Is 66:22
them that r of this evil family .... Jer 8:3
which r in all the places whither .... Jer 8:3
and this city shall r for ever .... Jer 17:25
that r in this land, and then that....... Jer 24:8
those will I let r still in their. .... Jer 27:11
the vessels that r in this city .... Jer 27:19
that r in the house of the LORD .... Jer 27:21
the palace shall r after the .... Jer 38:18
men of war that r in this city .... Jer 38:4
none of them shall r or escape......... Jer 42:17
of Judah, to leave you none to r .... Jer 44:7
sojourn there, shall escape or r. .... Jer 44:14
it off, that none shall r in it .... Jer 51:62
none of them shall r, nor of .... Eze 7:11
they that r shall be scattered. .... Eze 17:21
all the fowls of the heaven r .... Eze 31:13
of the heaven to r upon his .... Eze 32:4
that r upon the face of the earth .... Eze 39:14
if there r ten men in one house, ... Amos 6:9
that did r in the day of distress. .... Obad 14
it shall r in the midst of his .... Zec 5:4
All the families that r, every .... Zec 12:14
And in the same house r, eating and ... Lk 10:7
Gather up the fragments that r .... Jn 6:12
you, that my joy might r in you .... Jn 15:11

R

REMAINDER

and that your fruit should r................ Jn 15:16
that the bodies should not r upon ..... Jn 19:31
let her r unmarried, or be............... 1Cor 7:11
greater part r unto this present....... 1Cor 15:6
r unto the coming of the Lord........... 1Th 4:15
r shall be caught up together........... 1Th 4:17
which cannot be shaken may r .... Heb 12:27
from the beginning shall r in you 1Jn 2:24
and strengthen the things which r .... Rev 3:2

REMAINDER

thou shalt burn the r with fire............ Ex 29:34
the r thereof shall Aaron and his .... Lev 6:16
also the r of it shall be eaten.......... Lev 7:16
But the r of the flesh of the............ Lev 7:17
neither name nor r upon the earth 2Sa 14:7
r of wrath shalt thou.................... Ps 76:10

REMAINED

and Noah only r alive, and they.......... Gen 7:23
they that r fled to the mountain......... Gen 14:10
there r not one.......................... Ex 8:31
there r not any green thing in........... Ex 10:15
there r not one locust in all the........ Ex 10:19
there r not so much as one of............ Ex 14:28
But there r two of the men in the........ Num 11:26
Because he should have r in the.......... Num 35:28
their inheritance r in the tribe......... Num 36:12
Bashan r of the remnant of giants........ Deut 3:11
ye shall have r long in the land......... Deut 4:25
that the rest which r of them............ Josh 10:20
in Gath, and in Ashdod, there r......... Josh 11:22
who r of the remnant of the.............. Josh 13:12
there r among the children of............ Josh 18:2
the Levites which r of the............... Josh 21:20
of the children of Kohath that r......... Josh 21:26
and there r ten thousand................. Judg 7:3
that they which r were scattered........ 1Sa 11:11
r in a mountain in the wilderness........ 1Sa 23:14
his men r in the sides of the............ 1Sa 24:3
So Tamar r desolate in her............... 2Sa 13:20
which r in the days of his father....... 1Kin 22:46
So Jehu slew all that r of the.......... 2Kin 10:11
he slew all that r unto Ahab in......... 2Kin 10:17
there r the grove also in Samaria....... 2Kin 13:6
none r, save the poorest sort of........ 2Kin 24:14
that r in the land of Judah............. 2Kin 25:22
the ark of God r with the family........ 1Chr 13:14
also my wisdom r with me................. Eccl 2:9
cities r of the cities of Judah.......... Jer 34:7
there r but wounded men among........... Jer 37:10
Jeremiah had r there many days.......... Jer 37:16
Thus Jeremiah r in the court of......... Jer 37:21
Jeremiah r in the court of the.......... Jer 38:13
of the people that r in the city........ Jer 38:9
the rest of the people that r........... Jer 39:9
all the people that r in Mizpah......... Jer 41:10
therefore his taster r in him........... Jer 48:11
they have r in their holds.............. Jer 51:30
of the people that r in the city........ Jer 52:15
Lord's anger never escaped nor r........ Lam 2:22
r there astonished among them........... Eze 3:15
there r no strength in me................ Dan 10:8
I r there with the kings of............. Dan 10:13
there r no strength in me................ Dan 10:17
it would have r until this day.......... Mt 11:23
that r twelve baskets full.............. Mt 14:20
unto them, and r speechless............. Lk 1:22
that r to them twelve baskets........... Lk 9:17
five barley loaves, which r over........ Jn 6:13
Whiles it r, was it not thine own....... Acts 5:4
r unmoveable, but the hinder part....... Acts 27:41

REMAINEST

Thou, O Lord, r for ever................. Lam 5:19
but thou r................................ Heb 1:11

REMAINETH

While the earth r, seedtime and.......... Gen 8:22
which r unto you from the hail........... Ex 10:5
that which r of it until the............ Ex 12:10
that which r over lay up for you........ Ex 16:23
the remnant that r of the............... Ex 26:12
the tent, the half curtain that r....... Ex 26:12
r in the length of the curtains......... Ex 26:13
that which r of the flesh and of........ Lev 8:32
Take the meat offering that r of........ Lev 10:12
that r among them in midst of........... Lev 16:16
destroy him that r of the city.......... Num 24:19
of stones, that r unto this day......... Josh 8:29
there r yet very much land to be........ Josh 13:1
This is the land that yet r............. Josh 13:2
Then he made him that r have............ Judg 5:13
which stone r unto this day in.......... 1Sa 6:18
There r yet the youngest, and........... 1Sa 16:11
of the Lord r under curtains............ 1Chr 17:1
whosoever r in any place where he....... Ezr 1:4
erred, mine error r with myself......... Job 19:4
in your answers there r falsehood....... Job 21:34
In his neck r strength, and sorrow...... Job 41:22
he that r in Jerusalem, shall be........ Is 4:3
He that r in this city shall die........ Jer 38:2
and Zidon every helper that r........... Jer 47:4
and that r and is besieged shall........ Eze 6:12
Egypt, so my spirit r among you......... Hag 2:5
but he that r, even he, shall be........ Zec 9:7
therefore your sin r.................... Jn 9:41
it r, that both they that have.......... 1Cor 7:29
more that which r is glorious........... 2Cor 3:11
for until this day r the same........... 2Cor 3:14
his righteousness r for ever............ 2Cor 9:9
Seeing therefore it r that some......... Heb 4:6

There r therefore a rest to the......... Heb 4:9
there r no more sacrifice for........... Heb 10:26
for his seed r in him................... 1Jn 3:9

REMAINING

r thereon, the children of Israel....... Num 9:22
him until none was left to him r........ Deut 3:3
until he had left him none r............ Josh 10:33
left none r, according to all........... Josh 10:37
he left none r........................... Josh 10:39
he left none r, but utterly............. Josh 10:40
them, until they left them none r....... Josh 11:8
which were r of the families of......... Josh 21:40
we should be destroyed from r in........ 2Sa 21:5
priests, until he left him none r....... 2Kin 10:11
who r in the chambers were free......... 1Chr 9:33
nor any r in his dwellings.............. Job 18:19
not be any r of the house of Esau....... Obad 18
r on him, the same is he which.......... Jn 1:33

REMALIAH (rem-a-li'-ah) See REMALIAH'S.
Father of Pekah.

But Pekah the son of R, a captain....... 2Kin 15:25
R began to reign over Israel in......... 2Kin 15:27
against Pekah the son of R.............. 2Kin 15:30
R king of Israel began Jotham the....... 2Kin 15:32
of Syria, and Pekah the son of R........ 2Kin 15:37
year of Pekah the son of R Ahaz......... 2Kin 16:1
Pekah son of R king of Israel........... 2Kin 16:5
For Pekah the son of R slew in.......... 2Chr 28:6
of Syria, and Pekah the son of R........ Is 7:1
with Syria, and of the son of R......... Is 7:4
Syria, Ephraim, and the son of R........ Is 7:5

REMALIAH'S (rem-a-li'-ahs)

and the head of Samaria is R son........ Is 7:9
and rejoice in Rezin and R son.......... Is 8:6

REMEDY

his people, till there was no r......... 2Chr 36:16
shall he be broken without r............ Prov 6:15
be destroyed, and that without r........ Prov 29:1

REMEMBER

I will r my covenant, which is.......... Gen 9:15
that I may r the everlasting............ Gen 9:16
did not the chief butler r Joseph....... Gen 40:23
I do r my faults this day............... Gen 41:9
R this day, in which ye came out........ Ex 13:3
the sabbath day, to keep it............. Ex 20:8
R Abraham, Isaac, and Israel, thy....... Ex 32:13
Then will I r my covenant with.......... Lev 26:42
my covenant with Abraham will I r....... Lev 26:42
and I will r the land................... Lev 26:42
But I will for their sakes r them....... Lev 26:45
We r the fish, which we did eat......... Num 11:5
r all the commandments of the........... Num 15:39
That ye may r, and do all my............ Num 15:40
r that thou wast a servant in the....... Deut 5:15
but shalt well r what the Lord.......... Deut 7:18
thou shalt r all the way which......... Deut 8:2
But thou shalt r the Lord thy God....... Deut 8:18
R, and forget not, how thou............ Deut 9:7
R thy servants, Abraham, Isaac......... Deut 9:27
thou shalt r that thou wast a........... Deut 15:15
that thou mayest r the day when........ Deut 16:3
thou shalt r that thou wast a........... Deut 16:12
R what the Lord thy God did unto........ Deut 24:9
But thou shalt r that thou wast a....... Deut 24:18
thou shalt r that thou wast a........... Deut 24:22
R what Amalek did unto thee by.......... Deut 25:17
R the days of old, consider the......... Deut 32:7
R the word which Moses the.............. Josh 1:13
r also that I am your bone and.......... Judg 9:2
r me, I pray thee, and strengthen....... Judg 16:28
r me, and not forget thine.............. 1Sa 1:11
I r that which Amalek did to............ 1Sa 15:2
my lord, then r thine handmaid......... 1Sa 25:31
let the king r the Lord thy God........ 2Sa 14:11
neither do thou r that which thy....... 2Sa 19:19
for r how that, when I and thou........ 2Kin 9:25
r now how I have walked before......... 2Kin 20:3
R his marvellous works that he......... 1Chr 16:12
r the mercies of David thy............. 2Chr 6:42
R, I beseech thee, the word that........ Neh 1:8
r the Lord, which is great and......... Neh 4:14
R me, O my God, concerning this......... Neh 13:14
R me, O my God, concerning this......... Neh 13:22
R them, O my God, because they......... Neh 13:29
R me, O my God, for good............... Neh 13:31
R, I pray thee, who ever perished....... Job 4:7
O r that my life is wind............... Job 7:7
R, I beseech thee, that thou hast....... Job 10:9
it as waters that pass away............ Job 11:16
appoint me a set time, and r me........ Job 14:13
Even when I r I am afraid.............. Job 21:6
R that thou magnify his work........... Job 36:24
him, r the battle, do no more.......... Job 41:8
R all thy offerings, and accept........ Ps 20:3
but we will r the name of the.......... Ps 20:7
All the ends of the world shall r...... Ps 22:27
R, O Lord, thy tender mercies and...... Ps 25:6
R not the sins of my youth, nor........ Ps 25:7
according to thy mercy r thou me....... Ps 25:7
When I r these things, I pour out...... Ps 42:4
therefore will I r thee from the....... Ps 42:6
When I r thee upon my bed, and......... Ps 63:6
R thy congregation, which thou........ Ps 74:2
R this, that the enemy hath............ Ps 74:18
r how the foolish man reproacheth...... Ps 74:22
but I will r the years of the.......... Ps 77:10
I will r the works of the Lord........ Ps 77:11
surely I will r thy wonders of......... Ps 77:11

O r not against us former............... Ps 79:8
R how short my time is.................. Ps 89:47
R, Lord, the reproach of thy........... Ps 89:50
to those that r his commandments....... Ps 103:18
R his marvellous works that he......... Ps 105:5
R me, O Lord, with the favour.......... Ps 106:4
R the word unto thy servant, upon...... Ps 119:49
r David, and all his afflictions....... Ps 132:1
If I do not r thee, let my tongue...... Ps 137:6
R, O Lord, the children of Edom........ Ps 137:7
I r the days of old.................... Ps 143:5
poverty, and r his misery no more...... Prov 31:7
not much r the days of his life........ Eccl 5:20
yet let him r the days of.............. Eccl 11:8
R now thy Creator in the days of....... Eccl 12:1
we will r thy love more than wine...... Song 1:4
R now, O Lord, I beseech thee.......... Is 38:3
R ye not the former things............. Is 43:18
own sake, and will not r thy sins...... Is 43:25
R these, O Jacob and Israel............ Is 44:21
R this, and shew yourselves men........ Is 46:8
R the former things of old............. Is 46:9
neither didst r the latter end of...... Is 47:7
shalt not r the reproach of thy....... Is 54:4
those that r thee in thy ways.......... Is 64:5
neither r iniquity for ever............ Is 64:9
I r thee, the kindness of thy.......... Jer 2:2
neither shall they r it................ Jer 3:16
he will now r their iniquity, and...... Jer 14:10
r, break not thy covenant with us...... Jer 14:21
r me, and visit me, and revenge me..... Jer 15:15
their children r their altars.......... Jer 17:2
R that I stood before thee to.......... Jer 18:20
him, I do earnestly r him still........ Jer 31:20
I will r their sin no more............. Jer 31:34
the land, did not the Lord r them...... Jer 44:21
r the Lord afar off, and let........... Jer 51:50
R, O Lord, what is come upon us........ Lam 5:1
r me among the nations without......... Eze 6:9
Nevertheless I will r my covenant...... Eze 16:60
Then thou shalt r thy ways............. Eze 16:61
That thou mayest r, and be............. Eze 16:63
And there shall ye r your ways......... Eze 20:43
unto them, nor r Egypt any more........ Eze 23:27
Then shall ye r your own evil.......... Eze 36:31
that I r all their wickedness.......... Hos 7:2
now will he r their iniquity, and...... Hos 8:13
he will r their iniquity, he will...... Hos 9:9
r now what Balak king of Moab.......... Mic 6:5
in wrath r mercy...................... Hab 3:2
they shall r me in far countries...... Zec 10:9
R ye the law of Moses my servant...... Mal 4:4
neither r the five loaves of the...... Mt 16:9
we r that that deceiver said.......... Mt 27:63
and do ye not r...................... Mk 8:18
and to r his holy covenant........... Lk 1:72
r that thou in thy lifetime.......... Lk 16:25
R Lot's wife......................... Lk 17:32
r me when thou comest into thy....... Lk 23:42
r how he spake unto you when he...... Lk 24:6
R the word that I said unto you...... Jn 15:20
ye may r that I told you of them..... Jn 16:4
Therefore watch, and r, that by...... Acts 20:31
to r the words of the Lord Jesus..... Acts 20:35
that ye r me in all things, and...... 1Cor 11:2
would that we should r the poor...... Gal 2:10
Wherefore r, that ye being in........ Eph 2:11
my hands. Remember my bonds.......... Col 4:18
For ye r, brethren, our labour and... 1Th 2:9
R ye not, that, when I was yet....... 2Th 2:5
R that Jesus Christ of the seed...... 2Ti 2:8
their iniquities will I r no more.... Heb 8:12
and iniquities will I r no more...... Heb 10:17
R them that are in bonds, as......... Heb 13:3
R them which have the rule over...... Heb 13:7
I will r his deeds which he doeth.... 3Jn 10
r ye the words which were spoken..... Jude 17
R therefore from whence thou art..... Rev 2:5
R therefore how thou hast............ Rev 3:3

REMEMBERED

God r Noah, and every living thing..... Gen 8:1
of the plain, that God r Abraham...... Gen 19:29
God r Rachel, and God hearkened to.... Gen 30:22
Joseph r the dreams which he.......... Gen 42:9
God r his covenant with Abraham...... Ex 2:24
r, neither r ye before............... Ex 6:5
ye shall be r before the Lord........ Num 10:9
Israel r not the Lord their God...... Judg 8:34
and the Lord r..................... 1Sa 1:19
Thus Joash the king r not the........ 2Chr 24:22
he r Vashti, and what she had done... Est 2:1
And that these days should be r...... Est 9:28
he shall be no more r................ Job 24:20
name to be r in all generations..... Ps 45:17
I r God, and was troubled............ Ps 77:3
they r that God was their rock...... Ps 78:35
For he r that they were but flesh.... Ps 78:39
They r not his hand, nor the day..... Ps 78:42
He hath r his mercy and his truth.... Ps 98:3
He hath r his covenant for ever...... Ps 105:8
For he r his holy promise, and....... Ps 105:42
they r not the multitude of thy...... Ps 106:7
he r for them his covenant, and..... Ps 106:45
of his fathers be r with the Lord.... Ps 109:14
Because that he r not to shew........ Ps 109:16
made his wonderful works to be r..... Ps 111:4
r thy judgments of old, O Lord...... Ps 119:52
I have r thy name, O Lord, in the.... Ps 119:55
Who r us in our low estate........... Ps 136:23
yea, we wept, when we r Zion......... Ps 137:1

yet no man *r* that same poor man ...... Eccl 9:15
many songs, that thou mayest be *r* ..... Is 23:16
thou hast lied, and hast not *r* me .... Is 57:11
Then he *r* the days of old, Moses, ... Is 63:11
and the former shall not be *r* .... Is 65:17
that his name may be no more *r* .... Jer 11:19
Jerusalem in the days of her .... Lam 1:7
r not his footstool in the day of .... Lam 2:1
which he hath done shall not be *r* .... Eze 3:20
hast not *r* the days of thy youth .... Eze 16:22
hast not *r* the days of thy youth .... Eze 16:43
have made your iniquity to be *r* .... Eze 21:24
thou shalt be no more *r* .... Eze 21:32
may not be *r* among the nations .... Eze 25:10
righteousnesses shall not be *r* .... Eze 33:13
shall no more be *r* by their name .... Hos 2:17
r not the brotherly covenant .... Amos 1:9
fainted within me I *r* the LORD .... Jonah 2:7
land, and they shall no more be *r* .... Zec 13:2
Peter *r* the word of Jesus, which .... Mt 26:75
Peter *r* the word of the Lord, how ...... Lk 22:61
And they *r* his words, ... Lk 24:8
his disciples *r* that it was .... Jn 2:17
his disciples *r* that he had said .... Jn 2:22
then *r* they that these things .... Jn 12:16
Then *r* I the word of the Lord, ... Acts 11:16
God hath *r* her iniquities .... Rev 18:5

REMEMBEREST

in the grave, who *r* thou *r* no more ..... Ps 88:5
there *r* that thy brother hath .... Mt 5:23

REMEMBERETH

inquisition for blood, he *r* them .... Ps 9:12
he *r* that we are dust .... Ps 103:14
she *r* not her last end .... Lam 1:9
she *r* no more the anguish, for .... Jn 16:21
whilst he *r* the obedience of you 2Cor 7:15

REMEMBERING

R mine affliction and my misery, ... Lam 3:19
R without ceasing your work of 1Th 1:3

REMEMBRANCE

the *r* of Amalek from under heaven ...... Ex 17:14
memorial, bringing iniquity to *r* .... Num 5:15
the *r* of Amalek from under them .... Deut 25:19
I would make the *r* of them to .... Deut 32:26
have no son to keep my name in *r* 2Sa 18:18
come unto me to call my sin to *r* 1Kin 17:18
His *r* shall perish from the earth .... Job 18:17
in death there is no *r* of thee .... Ps 6:5
thanks at the *r* of his holiness .... Ps 30:4
to cut off the *r* of them from the .... Ps 34:16
A Psalm of David, to bring to *r* .... Ps 38:1
A Psalm of David, to bring to *r* .... Ps 70:1
I call to *r* my song in the night .... Ps 77:6
of Israel may be no more in *r* .... Ps 83:4
thanks at the *r* of his holiness .... Ps 97:12
thy *r* unto all generations .... Ps 102:12
shall be in everlasting *r* .... Ps 112:6
There is no *r* of former things, ... Eccl 1:11
neither shall there be any *r* of .... Eccl 2:16
For there is no *r* of the wise .... Eccl 2:16
to thy name, and to the *r* of thee ...... Is 26:8
Put me in *r* .... Is 43:26
the posts hast thou set up thy *r* .... Is 57:8
My soul hath them still in *r* .... Lam 3:20
he will call to *r* the iniquity .... Eze 21:23
I say, that ye are come to *r* .... Eze 21:24
in calling to *r* the days of her .... Eze 23:19
Thus thou calledst to *r* the .... Eze 23:21
bringeth their iniquity to *r* .... Eze 29:16
a book of *r* was written before .... Mal 3:16
Peter calling to *r* saith unto him .... Mk 11:21
servant Israel, in *r* of his mercy .... Lk 1:54
this do in *r* of me .... Lk 22:19
and bring all things to your *r* .... Jn 14:26
are had in *r* in the sight of God .... Acts 10:31
who shall bring you into *r* of my 1Cor 4:17
this do in *r* of me 1Cor 11:24
as oft as ye drink it, in *r* of me 1Cor 11:25
thank my God upon every *r* of you ..... Phil 1:3
that ye have good *r* of us always 1Th 3:6
the brethren in *r* of these things 1Ti 4:6
r of thee in my prayers night 2Ti 1:3
When I call to *r* the unfeigned 2Ti 1:5
Wherefore I put thee in *r* that 2Ti 1:6
Of these things put them in *r* 2Ti 2:14
a *r* again made of sins every year .... Heb 10:3
But call to *r* the former days, in .... Heb 10:32
you always in *r* of these things 2Pet 1:12
stir you up by putting you in *r* 2Pet 1:13
to have these things always in *r* 2Pet 1:15
up your pure minds by way of *r* 2Pet 3:1
I will therefore put you in *r* .... Jude 5
Babylon came in *r* before God .... Rev 16:19

REMEMBRANCES

Your *r* are like unto ashes, your .... Job 13:12

REMETH (re'-meth) See RAMOTH, JARMUTH. A Levitical city in Issachar.

R, and En-gannim, and En-haddah, ... Josh 19:21

REMISSION

shed for many for the *r* of sins .... Mt 26:28
of repentance for the *r* of sins .... Mk 1:4
his people by the *r* of their sins .... Lk 1:77
of repentance for the *r* of sins .... Lk 3:3
r of sins should be preached in .... Lk 24:47
of Jesus Christ for the *r* of sins .... Acts 2:38
in him shall receive *r* of sins .... Acts 10:43

for the *r* of sins that are past .... Rom 3:25
without shedding of blood is no *r* .... Heb 9:22
Now where *r* of these is, there is .... Heb 10:18

REMIT

Whose soever sins ye *r*, they are .... Jn 20:23

REMITTED

ye remit, they are *r* unto them .... Jn 20:23

REMMON (rem'-mon) See RIMMON. A city in Judah.

Ain, R, and Ether, and Ashan. .... Josh 19:7

REMMON-METHOAR (rem''-mon-meth'-o-ar) A city in Zebulun.

and goeth out to R to Neah .... Josh 19:13

REMNANT

the *r* that remaineth of the .... Ex 26:12
the *r* of the meat offerings shall .... Lev 2:3
the *r* shall be the priest's, as a .... Lev 5:13
the *r* of the oil that is in the .... Lev 14:18
remained of the *r* of giants .... Deut 3:11
toward the *r* of his children. .... Deut 28:54
which was of the *r* of the giants .... Josh 12:4
remained of the *r* of the giants .... Josh 13:12
cleave unto the *r* of these .... Josh 23:12
but of the *r* of the Amorites 2Sa 21:2
to the *r* of the people, saying, ... 1Kin 12:23
will take away the *r* of the house 1Kin 14:10
the *r* of the sodomites, which 1Kin 22:46
prayer for the *r* that are left 2Kin 19:4
the *r* that is escaped of the 2Kin 19:30
of Jerusalem shall go forth a *r* 2Kin 19:31
I will forsake the *r* of mine 2Kin 21:14
with the *r* of the multitude, did 2Kin 25:11
of the *r* of the sons of Kohath 1Chr 6:70
and he will return to the *r* of you 2Chr 30:6
and of all the *r* of Israel 2Chr 34:9
the *r* of their brethren the .... Ezr 3:8
God, to leave us a *r* to escape .... Ezr 9:8
there should be no *r* nor escaping ...... Ezr 9:14
The *r* that are left of the .... Neh 1:3
but the *r* of them the flee .... Job 22:20
had left unto us a very small *r* .... Is 1:9
that the *r* of Israel, and such as .... Is 10:20
shall return, even the .... Is 10:21
shall return, even the *r* of Jacob .... Is 10:21
yet a *r* of them shall return .... Is 10:22
to recover the *r* of his people .... Is 11:11
highway for the *r* of his people .... Is 11:16
of from Babylon the name, and *r* .... Is 14:22
famine, and he shall slay thy *r* .... Is 14:30
Moab, and upon the *r* of the land ..... Is 15:9
the *r* shall be very small and, ... Is 16:14
from Damascus, and the *r* of Syria ..... Is 17:3
thy prayer for the *r* that is left. .... Is 37:4
the *r* that is escaped of the .... Is 37:31
of Jerusalem shall go forth a *r* .... Is 37:32
all the *r* of the house of Israel, ... Is 46:3
glean the *r* of Israel as a vine. .... Jer 6:9
And there shall be no *r* of them. .... Jer 11:23
it shall be well with thy *r* .... Jer 15:11
I will gather the *r* of my flock, ... Jer 23:3
and Ekron, and the *r* of Ashdod, ... Jer 25:20
save thy people, the *r* of Israel. .... Jer 31:7
away captive into Babylon the .... Jer 39:9
of Babylon had left a *r* of Judah .... Jer 40:11
and the *r* in Judah perish .... Jer 40:15
all the *r* of the people whom he. .... Jer 41:16
Loro thy God, even for all this *r* .... Jer 42:2
word of the LORD, ye *r* of Judah .... Jer 42:15
concerning you, O ye *r* of Judah .... Jer 42:19
forces, took all the *r* of Judah, ... Jer 43:5
And I will take the *r* of Judah, ... Jer 44:12
So that none of the *r* of Judah. .... Jer 44:14
all the *r* of Judah, that are gone .... Jer 44:28
the *r* of the country of Caphtor. .... Jer 47:4
off with the *r* of their valley .... Jer 47:5
the whole *r* of thee will I .... Eze 5:10
Yet will I leave a *r*, that ye may .... Eze 6:8
a full end of the *r* of Israel .... Eze 11:13
therein shall be left a *r* that, ... Eze 14:22
thy *r* shall fall by the sword. .... Eze 23:25
destroy the *r* of the sea coast .... Eze 25:16
in the *r* whom the LORD shall call .... Joel 2:32
the *r* of the Philistines shall. .... Amos 1:8
be gracious unto the *r* of Joseph .... Amos 5:15
they may possess the *r* of Edom .... Amos 9:12
surely gather the *r* of Israel .... Mic 2:12
I will make her that halted a *r* .... Mic 4:7
then the *r* of his brethren shall .... Mic 5:3
the *r* of Jacob shall be in the .... Mic 5:7
the *r* of Jacob shall be among the. .... Mic 5:8
of the *r* of his heritage .... Mic 7:18
all the *r* of the people shall .... Hab 2:8
I will cut off the *r* of Baal from .... Zeph 1:4
for the *r* of the house of Judah .... Zeph 2:7
the *r* of my people shall possess. .... Zeph 2:9
The *r* of Israel shall not do. .... Zeph 3:13
with all the *r* of the people, ... Hag 1:12
spirit of all the *r* of the people. .... Hag 1:14
of this people in these days. .... Zec 8:6
I will cause the *r* of this people .... Zec 8:12
he *r* took his servants, and .... Mt 22:6
of the sea, a *r* shall be saved .... Rom 9:27
a *r* according to the election of .... Rom 11:5
the *r* were affrighted, and gave .... Rev 11:13
make war with the *r* of her seed, ... Rev 12:17
the *r* were slain with the sword .... Rev 19:21

REMOVE

to *r* it from Ephraim's head unto. .... Gen 48:17
of Israel *r* from tribe to tribe. .... Num 36:7
Neither shall the inheritance *r* .... Num 36:9
Thou shalt not *r* thy neighbour's .... Deut 19:14
then ye shall *r* from your place, ... Josh 3:3
then would I *r* Abimelech. .... Judg 9:29
So David would not *r* the ark of 2Sa 6:10
I will *r* Judah also out of my 2Kin 23:27
to *r* them out of his sight, for. 2Kin 24:3
Neither will I any more *r* the 2Kin 25:8
Some *r* the landmarks .... Job 24:2
till I die I will not *r* mine .... Job 27:5
not the hand of the wicked *r* me .... Ps 36:11
R thy stroke away from me .... Ps 39:10
R from me reproach and contempt ...... Ps 119:22
R from me the way of lying .... Ps 119:29
r thy foot from evil .... Prov 4:27
R thy way far from her, and come .... Prov 5:8
R not the ancient landmark, which ...... Prov 22:28
R not the old landmark. .... Prov 23:10
R far from me vanity and lies .... Prov 30:8
Therefore *r* sorrow from thy heart ..... Eccl 11:10
the earth shall *r* out of her. .... Is 13:13
from his place shall he not *r* .... Is 46:7
my sight, then shalt thou not *r* .... Jer 4:1
to *r* you far from your land. .... Jer 27:10
that I should *r* it from before my ...... Jer 32:31
they shall *r*, they shall depart, ... Jer 50:3
R out of the midst of Babylon, and. ..... Jer 50:8
and *r* by day in their sight .... Eze 12:3
thou shalt *r* from thy place to .... Eze 12:3
they shall *r* and go into captivity. ...... Eze 12:11
R the diadem, and take off the .... Eze 21:26
r violence and spoil, and execute .... Eze 45:9
were like them that *r* the bound. ...... Hos 5:10
But I will *r* far off from you the .... Joel 2:20
that ye might *r* them far from. .... Joel 3:6
which ye shall not *r* your necks. .... Mic 2:3
I will *r* the iniquity of that .... Zec 3:9
mountain shall *r* toward the north .... Zec 14:4
mountain, R hence to yonder place ...... Mt 17:20
and it shall *r* .... Mt 17:20
be willing, *r* this cup from me. .... Lk 22:42
so that I could *r* mountains 1Cor 13:2
will *r* thy candlestick out of his .... Rev 2:5

REMOVED

Noah *r* the covering of the ark, ... Gen 8:13
he *r* thence unto a mountain. .... Gen 12:8
Then Abram *r* his tent .... Gen 13:18
he *r* from thence, and digged .... Gen 26:22
he *r* that day the he goats that .... Gen 30:35
he *r* them to cities from one end ...... Gen 47:21
the *r* the swarms of flies from. .... Ex 8:31
went before the camp of Israel, *r*. ..... Ex 14:19
and when the people saw it, they *r* ... Ex 20:18
the people *r* from Hazeroth .... Num 12:16
From thence they *r*, and pitched in .. Num 21:12
From thence they *r*, and pitched on .. Num 21:13
children of Israel *r* from Rameses. ..... Num 33:5
they *r* from Succoth, and .... Num 33:6
they *r* from Etham, and turned. .... Num 33:8
they *r* from Marah, and came unto .... Num 33:9
they *r* from Elim, and encamped by .. Num 33:10
they *r* from the Red sea, and .... Num 33:11
they *r* from Alush, and encamped at . Num 33:14
they *r* from the desert of Sinai, ... Num 33:16
they *r* from Libnah, and pitched at ... Num 33:21
they *r* from mount Shapher, and ...... Num 33:24
they *r* from Haradah, and pitched ..... Num 33:25
they *r* from Makheloth, and .... Num 33:26
they *r* from Tarah, and pitched in .... Num 33:28
they *r* from Bene-jaakan, and .... Num 33:32
they *r* from Jotbathah, and .... Num 33:34
they *r* from Ezion-gaber, and .... Num 33:36
they *r* from Kadesh, and pitched in .. Num 33:37
they *r* from Dibon-gad, and .... Num 33:46
they *r* from Almon-diblathaim, and .. Num 33:47
shalt be *r* into all the kingdoms ...... Deut 28:25
they *r* from Shittim, and came to ..... Josh 3:1
when the people *r* from their. .... Josh 3:14
why his hand is not *r* from you 1Sa 6:3
Therefore Saul *r* him from him 1Sa 18:13
for a Amasa out of the highway 2Sa 20:12
When he was *r* out of the highway, .. 2Sa 20:13
r all the idols that his fathers. 1Kin 15:12
even her he *r* from being queen, ... 1Kin 15:13
But the high places were not *r* 1Kin 15:14
that the high places were not *r* 2Kin 15:4
the high places were not *r* 2Kin 15:35
r the laver from off them. 2Kin 16:17
and *r* them out of his sight 2Kin 17:18
Until the LORD *r* Israel out of 2Kin 17:23
The nations which thou hast *r* 2Kin 18:4
He *r* the high places, and brake. 2Kin 18:4
of my sight, as I have *r* Israel 2Kin 23:27
Geba, and they *r* to Manahath 1Chr 8:6
he *r* them, and begat Uzza, and 1Chr 8:7
he *r* her from being queen, ... 2Chr 15:16
they *r* the burnt offerings, that 2Chr 35:12
the rock is *r* out of his place .... Job 14:18
the rock be *r* out of his place .... Job 18:4
mine hope hath he *r* like a tree. .... Job 19:10
Even so would he have *r* thee out. .... Job 36:16
we fear, though the earth be *r* .... Ps 46:2
I *r* his shoulder from the burden. ...... Ps 81:6
the west, so far hath he *r* our .... Ps 103:12
that it should not be *r* for ever. .... Ps 104:5
as mount Zion, which cannot be *r*, ... Ps 125:1
The righteous shall never be *r* .... Prov 10:30
And the LORD have *r* men far away ... Is 6:12

R

REMOVETH

I have *r* the bounds of the people .... Is 10:13
Madmenah is *r* .... Is 10:31
fastened in the sure place by *r*.................... Is 22:25
shall be *r* like a cottage............................... Is 24:20
thou hadst *r* it far unto all the .... Is 26:15
but have *r* their heart far from .... Is 29:13
be *r* into a corner any more.......................... Is 30:20
stakes thereof shall ever be *r*...................... Is 33:20
is *r* from me as a shepherd's tent .... Is 38:12
shall depart, and the hills be *r*.................... Is 54:10
the covenant of my peace be *r*.................... Is 54:10
I will cause them to be *r* into.................... Jer 15:4
I will deliver them to be *r* into.................... Jer 24:9
will deliver them to be *r* to all................... Jer 29:18
I will make you to be *r* into all .... Jer 34:17
therefore she is *r* .... Lam 1:8
thou hast *r* my soul far off from .... Lam 3:17
streets, and their gold shall be *r* .... Eze 7:19
them, and will give them to be *r* .... Eze 23:46
as the uncleanness of a *r* woman .... Eze 36:17
stretched themselves forth and .... Amos 6:7
how hath he *r* it from me............................ Mic 2:4
day shall the decree be far *r* .... Mic 7:11
say unto this mountain, Be thou .... Mt 21:21
say unto this mountain, Be thou .... Mk 11:23
he *r* him into this land, wherein................. Acts 7:4
And when he had *r* him, he raised .... Acts 13:22
I marvel that ye are so soon *r* .... Gal 1:6

REMOVETH

Cursed be he that *r* his................................ Deut 27:17
Which *r* the mountains, and they.............. Job 9:5
He *r* away the speech of the........................ Job 12:20
Whoso *r* stones shall be hurt...................... Eccl 10:9
he *r* kings, and setteth up kings................ Dan 2:21

REMOVING

r from thence all the speckled and..... Gen 30:32
a captive, and *r* to and fro.......................... Is 49:21
of man, prepare thee stuff for *r* .... Eze 12:3
in their sight, as stuff for *r* .... Eze 12:4
signifieth the *r* of those things .... Heb 12:27

REMPHAN (rem'-fan) An idol worshipped by
Israel.

Moloch, and the star of your god *R* .... Acts 7:43

REND

the hole, that it should not *r*....................... Ex 39:23
heads, neither *r* your clothes...................... Lev 10:6
then he shall *r* it out of the......................... Lev 13:56
his head, nor *r* his clothes........................... Lev 21:10
R your clothes, and gird you with.............. 2Sa 3:31
I will surely *r* the kingdom from................ 1Kin 11:11
but I will *r* it out of the hand...................... 1Kin 11:12
Howbeit I will not *r* away all the 1Kin 11:13
I will *r* the kingdom out of the 1Kin 11:31
didst *r* thy clothes, and weep.................... 2Chr 34:27
A time to *r*, and a time to sew .... Eccl 3:7
that thou wouldest *r* the heavens.............. Is 64:1
and a stormy wind shall *r* it........................ Eze 13:11
I will even *r* it with a stormy .... Eze 13:13
break, and *r* all their shoulder .... Eze 29:7
will *r* the caul of their heart,...................... Hos 13:8
r your heart, and not your.......................... Joel 2:13
feet, and turn again and *r* you.................... Mt 7:6
among themselves, Let us not *r* it............. Jn 19:24

RENDER

which they shall *r* unto me .... Num 18:9
I will *r* vengeance to mine .... Deut 32:41
and will *r* vengeance to his........................ Deut 32:43
did God *r* upon their heads .... Judg 9:57
The LORD *r* to every man his...................... 1Sa 26:23
r unto every man according unto 2Chr 6:30
for he will *r* unto man his............................ Job 33:26
work of a man shall he *r* unto him .... Job 34:11
r to them their desert .... Ps 28:4
They also that *r* evil for good..................... Ps 38:20
I will *r* praises unto thee............................. Ps 56:12
r unto our neighbours sevenfold............... Ps 79:12
a reward to the proud.................................... Ps 94:2
What shall I *r* unto the LORD for................ Ps 116:12
shalt not he *r* to every man .... Prov 24:12
I will *r* to the man according to .... Prov 24:29
seven men that can *r* a reason................... Prov 26:16
to *r* his anger with fury, and his .... Is 66:15
he will *r* unto her a recompence................ Jer 51:6
I will *r* unto Babylon and to all.................. Jer 51:24
R unto them a recompence, O LORD,.......... Lam 3:64
so will we *r* the calves of our...................... Hos 14:2
will ye *r* me a recompence.......................... Joel 3:4
that I will *r* double unto thee...................... Zec 9:12
which shall *r* him the fruits in.................... Mt 21:41
R therefore unto Caesar the.......................... Mt 22:21
R to Caesar the things that are..................... Mk 12:17
R therefore unto Caesar the......................... Lk 20:25
Who will *r* to every man according .... Rom 2:6
R therefore to all their dues .... Rom 13:7
Let the husband *r* unto the wife................. 1Cor 7:3
can we *r* to God again for you.................... 1Th 3:9
See that none *r* evil for evil........................ 1Th 5:15

RENDERED

Thus God *r* the wickedness of .... Judg 9:56
r unto the king of Israel an......................... 2Kin 3:4
But Hezekiah *r* not again............................ 2Chr 32:25
a man's hands shall be *r* unto him............ Prov 12:14

RENDEREST

for thou *r* to every man according........ Ps 62:12

RENDERETH

a voice of the LORD that *r* .... Is 66:6

RENDERING

Not *r* evil for evil, or railing 1Pet 3:9

RENDING

r it in pieces, while there is .... Ps 7:2

RENEW

to Gilgal, and *r* the kingdom there........ 1Sa 11:14
a right spirit within me................................. Ps 51:10
the LORD shall *r* their strength.................. Is 40:31
let the people *r* their strength.................... Is 41:1
r our days as of old .... Lam 5:21
to *r* them again unto repentance............... Heb 6:6

RENEWED

r the altar of the LORD, that was.............. 2Chr 15:8
in me, and my bow was *r* in my hand...... Job 29:20
thy youth is *r* like the eagle's.................... Ps 103:5
the inward man is *r* day by day................. 2Cor 4:16
be *r* in the spirit of your mind.................... Eph 4:23
which is *r* in knowledge after the............. Col 3:10

RENEWEST

Thou *r* thy witnesses against me,........... Job 10:17
thou *r* the face of the earth....................... Ps 104:30

RENEWING

transformed by the *r* of your mind .... Rom 12:2
and *r* of the Holy Ghost.............................. Titus 3:5

RENOUNCED

But have *r* the hidden things of 2Cor 4:2

RENOWN

men which were of old, men of *r*............... Gen 6:4
in the congregation, men of *r* .... Num 16:2
thy *r* went forth among the......................... Eze 16:14
the harlot because of thy *r* .... Eze 16:15
raise up for them a plant of *r*..................... Eze 34:29
it shall be to them a *r* the day.................... Eze 39:13
hand, and hast gotten thee *r* .... Dan 9:15

RENOWNED

These were the *r* of the.............................. Num 1:16
of evildoers shall never be *r* .... Is 14:20
and rulers, great lords and *r*...................... Eze 23:23
the city, which wast strong in...................... Eze 26:17

RENT

and he *r* his clothes.................................... Gen 37:29
is without doubt *r* in pieces........................ Gen 37:33
Jacob *r* his clothes, and put .... Gen 37:34
Then they *r* their clothes, and .... Gen 44:13
of an habergeon, that it be not *r* .... Ex 28:32
plague is, his clothes shall be *r*.................. Lev 13:45
the land, *r* their clothes.............................. Num 14:6
Joshua *r* his clothes, and fell to................. Josh 7:6
asses, and wine bottles, old, and *r* .... Josh 9:4
and, behold, they be *r* .... Josh 9:13
that he *r* his clothes, and said,.................. Judg 11:35
he *r* him as he would have *r* a .... Judg 14:6
r him as he would have *r* a kid .... Judg 14:6
the same day with his clothes *r* 1Sa 4:12
the skirt of his mantle, and it *r* 1Sa 15:27
The LORD hath *r* the kingdom of 1Sa 15:28
for the LORD hath *r* the kingdom 1Sa 28:17
camp from Saul with his clothes *r* 2Sa 1:2
hold on his clothes, and *r* them................. 2Sa 1:11
r her garment of divers colours.................. 2Sa 13:31
stood by with their clothes *r* 2Sa 13:31
came to meet him with his coat *r* 2Sa 15:32
so that the earth *r* with the......................... 1Kin 1:40
on him, and *r* it in twelve pieces.............. 1Kin 11:30
Behold, the altar shall be *r* 1Kin 13:3
The altar also was *r*, and the 1Kin 13:5
r the kingdom away from the house 1Kin 14:8
strong wind *r* the mountains, and............ 1Kin 19:11
that he *r* his clothes, and put 2Kin 21:27
clothes, and *r* them in two pieces............. 2Kin 2:12
that he *r* his clothes, and said,.................. 2Kin 5:7
king of Israel had *r* his clothes.................. 2Kin 5:8
Wherefore hast thou *r* thy clothes............. 2Kin 5:8
the woman, that he *r* his clothes............... 2Kin 6:30
Athaliah *r* her clothes, and cried,............. 2Kin 11:14
For he *r* Israel from the house of 2Kin 17:21
to Hezekiah with their clothes *r*................ 2Kin 18:37
that he *r* his clothes, and covered............ 2Kin 19:1
of the law, that he *r* his clothes................. 2Kin 22:11
hast *r* thy clothes, and wept...................... 2Kin 22:19
Then Athaliah *r* clothes, and 2Chr 23:13
of the law, that he *r* his clothes................. 2Chr 34:19
I *r* my garment and my mantle, and.......... Ezr 9:3
having *r* my garment and my mantle,....... Ezr 9:5
Mordecai *r* his clothes, and put on........... Est 4:1
r his mantle, and shaved his head............ Job 1:20
they *r* every one his mantle, and .... Job 2:12
and the cloud is not *r* under them............. Job 26:8
and instead of a girdle a *r* .... Is 3:24
to Hezekiah with their clothes *r*................ Is 36:22
that he *r* his clothes, and covered............ Is 37:1
nor *r* their garments, neither he .... Jer 36:24
beards shaven, and their clothes *r* .... Jer 41:5
pain, and No shall be *r* asunder................. Eze 30:16
garment, and the *r* is made worse............. Mt 9:16
the high priest *r* his clothes...................... Mt 26:65
the veil of the temple was *r* in................... Mt 27:51
earth did quake, and the rocks *r*............... Mt 27:51
the old, and the *r* is made worse............... Mk 2:21
r him sore, and came out of him............... Mk 9:26

the high priest *r* his clothes...................... Mk 14:63
the veil of the temple was *r* in................... Mk 15:38
then both the new maketh a *r*.................... Lk 5:36
of the temple was *r* in the midst .... Lk 23:45
they *r* their clothes, and ran in.................. Acts 14:14
the magistrates *r* off their.......................... Acts 16:22

RENTEST

though thou *r* thy face with .... Jer 4:30

REPAID

to the righteous good shall be *r*............. Prov 13:21

REPAIR

let them *r* the breaches of the................... 2Kin 12:5
Why *r* ye not the breaches of the.............. 2Kin 12:7
neither to *r* the breaches of the 2Kin 12:8
hewed stone to *r* the breaches of 2Kin 12:12
laid out for the house to *r* it....................... 2Kin 12:12
to *r* the breaches of the house,.................. 2Kin 22:5
and hewn stone to *r* the house 2Kin 22:6
minded to *r* the house of the LORD........... 2Chr 24:4
gather of all Israel money to *r*.................... 2Chr 24:5
carpenters to *r* the house of the................ 2Chr 24:12
to *r* the house of the LORD his.................. 2Chr 34:8
in the house of the LORD, to *r* 2Chr 34:10
to *r* the desolations thereof, and............... Ezr 9:9
they shall *r* the waste cities,...................... Is 61:4

REPAIRED

r the cities, and dwelt in them.................. Judg 21:23
r the breaches of the city of 1Kin 11:27
he *r* the altar of the LORD that.................. 1Kin 18:30
not *r* the breaches of the house 2Kin 12:6
r therewith the house of the LORD........... 2Kin 12:14
Joab *r* the rest of the city............................ 1Chr 11:8
the house of the LORD, and *r* them.......... 2Chr 29:3
r Millo in the city of David, and................ 2Chr 32:5
he *r* the altar of the LORD, and................. 2Chr 33:16
next unto them *r* Meremoth the son .... Neh 3:4
next unto them *r* Meshullam the .... Neh 3:4
next unto them *r* Zadok the son of .... Neh 3:4
And next unto them the Tekoites *r* .... Neh 3:5
Moreover the old gate *r* Jehoiada............. Neh 3:6
next unto them *r* Melatiah the.................... Neh 3:7
Next unto him *r* Uzziel the son of .... Neh 3:8
Next unto him also *r* Hananiah the .... Neh 3:8
next unto them *r* Rephaiah the son........... Neh 3:9
next unto him *r* Jedaiah the son .... Neh 3:10
next unto him *r* Hattush the son of .... Neh 3:10
r the other piece, and the tower................. Neh 3:11
next unto him *r* Shallum the son............... Neh 3:12
After him *r* Hanun, and the........................ Neh 3:13
But the dung gate *r* Malchiah the.............. Neh 3:14
r Shallun the son of Colhozeh................... Neh 3:15
After him *r* Nehemiah the son of .... Neh 3:16
After him *r* the Levites, Rehum .... Neh 3:17
Next unto him *r* Hashabiah........................ Neh 3:17
After him *r* their brethren, Bavai .... Neh 3:18
next to him *r* Ezer the son of .... Neh 3:19
earnestly *r* the other piece .... Neh 3:20
After him *r* Meremoth the son of .... Neh 3:21
after him *r* the priests, the men................. Neh 3:22
After him *r* Benjamin and Hashub............ Neh 3:23
After him *r* Azariah the son of .... Neh 3:23
After him *r* Binnui the son of .... Neh 3:24
them the Tekoites *r* another piece............. Neh 3:27
After them *r* the priests............................. Neh 3:28
After them *r* Zadok the son of .... Neh 3:29
After him *r* also Shemaiah the son............ Neh 3:29
After him *r* Hananiah the son of .... Neh 3:30
After him *r* Meshullam the son of............. Neh 3:30
After him *r* Malchiah the............................ Neh 3:31
the sheep gate *r* the goldsmiths................ Neh 3:32

REPAIRER

The *r* of the breach, The restorer .... Is 58:12

REPAIRING

the *r* of the house of God, behold 2Chr 24:27

REPAY

he will *r* him to his face............................. Deut 7:10
who shall *r* him what he hath done........... Job 21:31
prevented me, that I should *r* him............. Job 41:11
deeds, accordingly he will *r*....................... Is 59:18
the islands he will *r* recompence............... Is 59:18
when I come again, I will *r* thee................. Lk 10:35
I will *r*, saith the Lord................................ Rom 12:19
with mine own hand, I will *r* it................... Philem 19

REPAYETH

r them that hate him to their..................... Deut 7:10

REPEATETH

but he that *r* a matter separateth............. Prov 17:9

REPENT

the people *r* when they see war .... Ex 13:17
r of this evil against thy people.................. Ex 32:12
the son of man, that he should *r* .... Num 23:19
r himself for his servants, when................ Deut 32:36
of Israel will not lie nor *r* 1Sa 15:29
he is not a man, that he should *r* 1Sa 15:29
they were carried captives, and *r*.............. 1Kin 8:47
myself, and *r* in dust and ashes............... Job 42:6
let it *r* thee concerning thy......................... Ps 90:13
LORD hath sworn, and will not *r*............... Ps 110:4
he will *r* himself concerning his................ Ps 135:14
I have purposed it, and will not *r* .... Jer 4:28
I will *r* of the evil that I.............................. Jer 18:8
voice, then I will *r* of the good.................. Jer 18:10
that I may *r* me of the evil,......................... Jer 26:3

the Lord will r him of the evil...... Jer 26:13
for I r me of the evil that I.............. Jer 42:10
R, and turn yourselves from your ..... Eze 14:6
R, and turn yourselves from all......... Eze 18:30
will I spare, neither will I r............ Eze 24:14
knoweth if he will return and r.......... Joel 2:14
can tell if God will turn and r........... Jonah 3:9
And saying, R ye................................. Mt 3:2
began to preach, and to say, R....... Mt 4:17
r ye, and believe the gospel............. Mk 1:15
and preached that men should r..... Mk 6:12
but, except ye r, ye shall all............. Lk 13:3
but, except ye r, ye shall all............. Lk 13:5
them from the dead, they will r....... Lk 16:30
and if he r, forgive him.................... Lk 17:3
turn again to thee, saying, I r......... Lk 17:4
Then Peter said unto them, R........ Acts 2:38
R ye therefore, and be converted,.. Acts 3:19
R therefore of this thy...................... Acts 8:22
all men every where to r................... Acts 17:30
the Gentiles, that they should r...... Acts 26:20
I do not r, though I did r................... 2Cor 7:8
him, The Lord sware and will not r... Heb 7:21
from whence thou art fallen, and r... Rev 2:5
or I will come unto thee quickly........ Rev 2:5

REPENTANCE

r shall be hid from mine eyes........... Hos 13:14
forth therefore fruits meet for r....... Mt 3:8
baptize you with water unto r........... Mt 3:11
the righteous, but sinners to r.......... Mt 9:13
preach the baptism of r for the........ Mk 1:4
the righteous, but sinners to r.......... Mk 2:17
preaching the baptism of r for........ Lk 3:3
therefore fruits worthy of r.............. Lk 3:8
the righteous, but sinners to r.......... Lk 5:32
just persons, which need no r............ Lk 15:7
And that r and remission of sins..... Lk 24:47
Saviour, for to give r to Israel.......... Acts 5:31
the Gentiles granted r unto life....... Acts 11:18
his coming the baptism of r to......... Acts 13:24
baptized with the baptism of r......... Acts 19:4
r toward God, and faith toward our... Acts 20:21
to God, and do works meet for r....... Acts 26:20
goodness of God leadeth thee to r...... Rom 2:4
and calling of God are without r........ Rom 11:29
sorry, but that ye sorrowed to r........ 2Cor 7:9
For godly sorrow worketh r to........ 2Cor 7:10
r to the acknowledging of the............ 2Ti 2:25
foundation of r from dead works...... Heb 6:1
away, to renew them again unto r..... Heb 6:6
for he found no place of r................. Heb 12:17
but that all should come to r............ 2Pet 3:9

REPENTED

it r the Lord that he had made......... Gen 6:6
the Lord r of the evil which he......... Ex 32:14
for it r the Lord because of............. Judg 2:18
the children of Israel r them for...... Judg 21:6
the people r them for Benjamin,..... Judg 21:15
the Lord r that he had made Saul.... 1Sa 15:35
the Lord r him of the evil, and........ 2Sa 24:16
he r him of the evil, and said to...... 1Chr 21:15
r according to the multitude of....... Ps 106:45
no man r him of his wickedness,...... Jer 8:6
the Lord overthrew, and r not......... Jer 20:16
the Lord r him of the evil which...... Jer 26:19
after that I was turned, I r.............. Jer 31:19
The Lord r for this.......................... Amos 7:3
The Lord r for this.......................... Amos 7:6
God r of the evil, that he had........ Jonah 3:10
the Lord of hosts, and I r not......... Zec 8:14
were done, because they r not......... Mt 11:20
they would have r long ago in......... Mt 11:21
because they r at the preaching....... Mt 12:41
but afterward he r, and went.......... Mt 21:29
r not afterward, that ye might........ Mt 21:32
r himself, and brought again the.... Mt 27:3
you, they had a great while ago r.... Lk 10:13
for they r at the preaching of........ Lk 11:32
to salvation not to be r of.............. 2Cor 7:10
have not r of the uncleanness and.. 2Cor 12:21
and she r not.................................. Rev 2:21
r not of the works of their hands.... Rev 9:20
Neither r they of their murders,...... Rev 9:21
they r not to give him glory........... Rev 16:9
sores, and r not of their deeds........ Rev 16:11

REPENTEST

kindness, and r thee of the evil....... Jonah 4:2

REPENTETH

for it r me that I have made them.... Gen 6:7
It r me that I have set up Saul......... 1Sa 15:11
kindness, and r him of the evil........ Joel 2:13
in heaven over one sinner that r..... Lk 15:7
of God over one sinner that r......... Lk 15:10

REPENTING

I am weary with r............................. Jer 15:6

REPENTINGS

my r are kindled together................. Hos 11:8

REPETITIONS

But when ye pray, use not vain r....... Mt 6:7

REPHAEL (re'-fa-el) A sanctuary servant.
Othni, and R, and Obed, Elzabad,...... 1Chr 26:7

REPHAH (re'-fah) A grandson of Ephraim.
R was his son, also Resheph, and...... 1Chr 7:25

REPHAIAH (ref-a-i'-ah) See Rapha, Rhesa.
  1. Head of a family.
the sons of R, the sons of Arnan,..... 1Chr 3:21
  2. A captain of Simeon.
Pelatiah, and Neariah, and............... 1Chr 4:42
  3. A son of Tola.
Uzzi, and R, and Jeriel, and Jahmai,.. 1Chr 7:2
  4. Son of Binea.
R his son, Eleasah his son, Azel...... 1Chr 9:43
  5. A repairer of Jerusalem's wall.
them repaired R the son of Hur....... Neh 3:9

REPHAIM (re-fa'-im) See Rephaims. A valley
    near Jerusalem.
themselves in the valley of R........... 2Sa 5:18
themselves in the valley of R........... 2Sa 5:22
pitched in the valley of R................. 2Sa 23:13
encamped in the valley of R............. 1Chr 11:15
themselves in the valley of R........... 1Chr 14:9
gathereth ears in the valley of R...... Is 17:5

REPHAIMS (re-fa'-ims) See Rephaim. A tribe
    of Canaanites.
smote the R in Ashteroth Karnaim,.. Gen 14:5
and the Perizzites, and the R........... Gen 15:20

REPHAN See Remphan.

REPHIDIM (ref'-i-dim) An Israelite
    encampment in the wilderness.
of the Lord, and pitched in R........... Ex 17:1
and fought with Israel in R.............. Ex 17:8
For they were departed from R....... Ex 19:2
from Alush, and encamped at R....... Num 33:14
And they departed from R, and....... Num 33:15

REPLENISH
the earth, and subdue it................. Gen 1:28
and multiply, and r the earth........... Gen 9:1

REPLENISHED
because they be r from the east...... Gen 25:6
that pass over the sea, have r......... Is 23:2
I have r every sorrowful soul.......... Jer 31:25
I shall be r, now she is laid............ Eze 26:2
and thou wast r, and made very..... Eze 27:25

REPLIEST
who art thou that r against God...... Rom 9:20

REPORT
unto his father their evil r.............. Gen 37:2
Thou shalt not raise a false r......... Ex 23:1
they brought up an evil r of the...... Num 13:32
bring up the evil r upon the land.... Num 14:37
heaven, who shall hear r of thee.... Deut 2:25
for it is no good r that I hear........ 1Sa 2:24
It was a true r that I heard in........ 1Kin 10:6
It was a true r which I heard in..... 2Chr 9:5
might have matter for an evil r....... Neh 6:13
a good r maketh the bones fat........ Prov 15:30
As at the r concerning Egypt, so.... Is 23:5
be sorely pained at the r of Tyre.... Is 23:5
vexation only to understand the r.. Is 28:19
Who hath believed our r................ Is 53:1
R, say they, and we will r............... Jer 20:10
Babylon hath heard the r of them.. Jer 50:43
Lord, who hath believed our r....... Jn 12:38
among you seven men of honest r.. Acts 6:3
of good r among all the nation of.. Acts 10:22
having a good r of all the Jews...... Acts 22:12
Lord, who hath believed our r....... Rom 10:16
r that God is in you of a truth....... 1Cor 14:25
By honour and dishonour, by evil r. 2Cor 6:8
and good r: as deceivers............... 2Cor 6:8
whatsoever things are of good r..... Phil 4:8
good r of them which are without... 1Ti 3:7
the elders obtained a good r.......... Heb 11:2
obtained a good r through faith..... Heb 11:39
Demetrius hath good r of all men... 3Jn 12

REPORTED
It is r among the heathen, and....... Neh 6:6
now shall it be r to the king.......... Neh 6:7
Also they r his good deeds before... Neh 6:19
in their eyes, when it shall be r...... Est 1:17
the matter, saying, I have done...... Est 9:11
this saying is commonly r among... Mt 28:15
r all that the chief priests and...... Acts 4:23
Which was well r of by the............. Acts 16:2
rather, (as we be slanderously...... Rom 3:8
It is r commonly that there is........ 1Cor 5:1
Well r of for good works............... 1Ti 5:10
which are now r unto you by them... 1Pet 1:12

---

of my r from the hand of Nabal...... 1Sa 25:39
hath sent to r the living God......... 2Kin 19:4
hath sent him to r the living God... 2Kin 19:16
are in great affliction and r......... Neh 2:17
Jerusalem, that we be no more a r... Neh 2:17
turn their r upon their own head,... Neh 4:4
the r of the heathen our enemies... Neh 5:9
evil report, that they might r me..... Neh 6:13
me, and plead against me my r....... Job 19:5
I have heard the check of my r....... Job 20:3
my heart shall not r me so long...... Job 27:6
nor taketh up a r against his......... Ps 15:3
a r of men, and despised of the...... Ps 22:6
I was a r among all mine enemies,.. Ps 31:11
make me not the r of the foolish.... Ps 39:8
in my bones, mine enemies r me.... Ps 42:10
Thou makest us a r to our.............. Ps 44:13
save me from the r of him that..... Ps 57:3
for thy sake I have borne r........... Ps 69:7
with fasting, that was to my r....... Ps 69:10
Thou hast known my r, and my shame Ps 69:19
R hath broken my heart................ Ps 69:20
let them be covered with r............ Ps 71:13
how long shall the adversary r...... Ps 74:10
he put them to a perpetual r......... Ps 78:66
We are become a r to our.............. Ps 79:4
into their bosom their r................ Ps 79:12
he is a r to his neighbours........... Ps 89:41
Lord, the r of thy servants........... Ps 89:50
the r of all the mighty people....... Ps 89:50
Mine enemies r me all the day...... Ps 102:8
I became also a r unto them......... Ps 109:25
Remove from me r and contempt.... Ps 119:22
Turn away my r which I fear......... Ps 119:39
his r shall not be wiped away....... Prov 6:33
but sin is a r to any people.......... Prov 14:34
also contempt, and with ignominy r. Prov 18:3
that causeth shame, and bringeth r.. Prov 19:26
yea, strife and r shall cease......... Prov 22:10
by thy name, to take away our r..... Is 4:1
profit, but a shame, and also a r.... Is 30:5
hath sent to r the living God........ Is 37:4
hath sent to r the living God........ Is 37:17
fear ye not the r of men, neither... Is 51:7
shalt not remember the r of thy.... Is 54:4
word of the Lord is unto them a r.. Jer 6:10
of the Lord was made a r unto me... Jer 20:8
bring an everlasting r upon you..... Jer 23:40
earth for their hurt, to be a r........ Jer 24:9
and an hissing, and a r among all... Jer 29:18
I did bear the r of my youth......... Jer 31:19
astonishment, and a curse, and a r. Jer 42:18
a r among all the nations of the.... Jer 44:8
astonishment, and a curse, and a r. Jer 44:12
shall become a desolation, a r...... Jer 49:13
because we have heard r.............. Jer 51:51
he is filled full with r.................. Lam 3:30
Thou hast heard their r, O Lord,.... Lam 3:61
consider, and behold our r........... Lam 5:1
a r among the nations that are...... Eze 5:14
So it shall be a r and a taunt, an... Eze 5:15
as at the time of thy r of the......... Eze 16:57
Ammonites, and concerning their r.. Eze 21:28
I made thee a r unto the heathen... Eze 22:4
bear the r of the people any more... Eze 36:15
r of famine among the heathen...... Eze 36:30
the people are become a r to all.... Dan 9:16
the r offered by him to cease........ Dan 11:18
without his own r he shall cause.... Dan 11:18
his r shall his Lord return unto..... Hos 12:14
and give not thine heritage to r..... Joel 2:17
make you a r among the heathen.... Joel 2:19
ye shall bear the r of my people.... Mic 6:16
I have heard the r of Moab........... Zeph 2:8
to whom the r of it was a burden... Zeph 3:18
me, to take away my r among men... Lk 1:25
their company, and shall r you...... Lk 6:22
I speak as concerning r, as.......... 2Cor 11:21
lest he fall into r and the snare..... 1Ti 3:7
we both labour and suffer r.......... 1Ti 4:10
Esteeming the r of Christ greater... Heb 11:26
without the camp, bearing his r..... Heb 13:13

REPROACHED
Whom hast thou r and blasphemed... 2Kin 19:22
messengers thou hast r the Lord.... 2Kin 19:23
These ten times have ye r me........ Job 19:3
For it was not an enemy that r me... Ps 55:12
that r thee are fallen upon me....... Ps 69:9
this, that the enemy hath r........... Ps 74:18
wherewith they have r................. Ps 79:12
Wherewith thine enemies have r.... Ps 89:51
wherewith they have r the............ Ps 89:51
Whom hast thou r and blasphemed... Is 37:23
thy servants hast thou r the Lord... Is 37:24
whereby they have r my people..... Zeph 2:8
their pride, because they have r..... Zeph 2:10
of them that r thee fell on me....... Rom 15:3
If ye be r for the name of Christ.... 1Pet 4:14

REPROACHES
the r of them that reproached....... Ps 69:9
to the curse, and Israel to r.......... Is 43:28
The r of them that reproached...... Rom 15:3
pleasure in infirmities, in r.......... 2Cor 12:10
were made a gazingstock both by r.. Heb 10:33

REPROACHEST
thus saying thou r us also............. Lk 11:45

REPROACHETH
a stranger, the same r the Lord..... Num 15:30
For the voice of him that r........... Ps 44:16

R

REPROACHFULLY
how the foolish man *r* thee daily	Ps 74:22
wherewith to answer him that *r* me	Ps 119:42
oppresseth the poor *r* his Maker	Prov 14:31
mocketh the poor *r* his Maker	Prov 17:5
that I may answer him that *r* me	Prov 27:11

REPROACHFULLY
have smitten me upon the cheek *r*	Job 16:10
to the adversary to speak *r*	1Ti 5:14

REPROBATE
R silver shall men call them	Jer 6:30
God gave them over to a *r* mind	Rom 1:28
minds, *r* concerning the faith	2Ti 3:8
and unto every good work *r*	Titus 1:16

REPROBATES
Christ is in you, except ye be *r*	2Cor 13:5
ye shall know that we are not *r*	2Cor 13:6
is honest, though we be as *r*	2Cor 13:7

REPROOF
and are astonished at his *r*	Job 26:11
Turn you at my *r*	Prov 1:23
my counsel, and would none of my *r*	Prov 1:25
they despised all my *r*	Prov 1:30
and my heart despised *r*	Prov 5:12
but he that refuseth *r* erreth	Prov 10:17
but he that hateth *r* is brutish	Prov 12:1
regardeth *r* shall be honoured	Prov 13:18
he that regardeth *r* is prudent	Prov 15:5
and he that hateth *r* shall die	Prov 15:10
The ear that heareth the *r* of	Prov 15:31
but he that heareth *r* getteth	Prov 15:32
A *r* entereth more into a wise man	Prov 17:10
The rod and *r* give wisdom	Prov 29:15
is profitable for doctrine, for *r*	2Ti 3:16

REPROOFS
not, and in whose mouth are no *r*	Ps 38:14
r of instruction are the way of	Prov 6:23

REPROVE
will *r* the words which the LORD	2Kin 19:4
but what doth your arguing *r*	Job 6:25
Do ye imagine to *r* words, and the	Job 6:26
He will surely *r* you, if ye do	Job 13:10
Will he *r* thee for fear of thee	Job 22:4
I will not *r* thee for thy	Ps 50:8
but I will *r* thee, and set them in	Ps 50:21
and let him *r* me	Ps 141:5
R not a scorner, lest he hate	Prov 9:8
r one that hath understanding, and	Prov 19:25
unto his words, lest he *r* thee	Prov 30:6
neither *r* after the hearing of	Is 11:3
r with equity for the meek of the	Is 11:4
will *r* the words which the LORD	Is 37:4
and thy backslidings shall *r* thee	Jer 2:19
let no man strive, nor *r* another	Hos 4:4
he will *r* the world of sin, and of	Jn 16:8
of darkness, but rather *r* them	Eph 5:11
r, rebuke, exhort with all	2Ti 4:2

REPROVED
thus she was *r*	Gen 20:16
Abraham *r* Abimelech because of a	Gen 21:25
he *r* kings for their sakes	1Chr 16:21
he *r* kings for their sakes	Ps 105:14
that being often *r* hardeneth his	Prov 29:1
thou not *r* Jeremiah of Anathoth	Jer 29:27
what I shall answer when I am *r*	Hab 2:1
being *r* by him for Herodias his	Lk 3:19
light, lest his deeds should be *r*	Jn 3:20
But all things that are *r* are	Eph 5:13

REPROVER
so is a wise *r* upon an obedient	Prov 25:12
dumb, and shalt not be to them a *r*	Eze 3:26

REPROVETH
he that *r* God, let him answer it	Job 40:2
He that *r* a scorner getteth to	Prov 9:7
scorner loveth not one that *r* him	Prov 15:12
snare for him that *r* in the gate	Is 29:21

REPUTATION
folly him that is in *r* for wisdom	Eccl 10:1
had in *r* among all the people, and	Acts 5:34
privately to them which were of *r*	Gal 2:2
But made himself of no *r*, and took	Phil 2:7
and hold such in *r*	Phil 2:29

REPUTED
beasts, and *r* vile in your sight	Job 18:3
of the earth are as nothing	Dan 4:35

REQUEST
them, I would desire a *r* of you	Judg 8:24
perform the *r* of his handmaid	2Sa 14:15
fulfilled the *r* of his servant	2Sa 14:22
and the king granted him all his *r*	Ezr 7:6
me, For what dost thou make *r*	Neh 2:4
to make *r* before him for her	Est 4:8
and what is thy *r*	Est 5:3
and what is thy *r*	Est 5:6
and said, My petition and my *r* is	Est 5:7
my petition, and to perform my *r*	Est 5:8
and what is thy *r*	Est 7:2
my petition, and my people at my *r*	Est 7:3
Haman stood up to make *r* for his	Est 7:7
or what is thy *r* further	Est 9:12
Oh that I might have my *r*	Job 6:8
not withholden the *r* of his lips	Ps 21:2
And he gave them their *r*	Ps 106:15
Making *r*, if by any means now at	Rom 1:10

REQUEST
for you all making *r* with joy	Phil 1:4

REQUESTED
earrings that he *r* was a thousand	Judg 8:26
he *r* for himself that he might	1Kin 19:4
God granted him that which he *r*	1Chr 4:10
therefore he *r* of the prince of	Dan 1:8
that Daniel of the king	Dan 2:49

REQUESTS
let your *r* be made known unto God	Phil 4:6

REQUIRE
your blood of your lives will I *r*	Gen 9:5
hand of every beast will I *r* it	Gen 9:5
brother will I *r* the life of man	Gen 9:5
of my hand didst thou *r* it	Gen 31:39
of my hand shalt thou *r* him	Gen 43:9
doth the LORD thy God *r* of thee	Deut 10:12
in my name, I will *r* it of him	Deut 18:19
thy God will surely *r* it of thee	Deut 23:21
let the LORD himself *r* it	Josh 22:23
Let the LORD even *r* it at the	1Sa 20:16
but one thing I *r* of thee	2Sa 3:13
now *r* his blood of your hand	2Sa 4:11
and whatsoever thou shalt *r* of me	2Sa 19:38
at times, as the matter shall *r*	1Kin 8:59
then doth my lord *r* this thing	1Chr 21:3
The LORD look upon it, and *r* it	2Chr 24:22
shall *r* of you, it be done	Ezr 7:21
For I was ashamed to *r* of the	Ezr 8:22
them, and will *r* nothing of them	Neh 5:12
in his heart, Thou wilt not *r* it	Ps 10:13
his blood will I *r* at thine hand	Eze 3:18
his blood will I *r* at thine hand	Eze 3:20
then will I *r* your offerings, and	Eze 20:40
but his blood will I *r* at thine	Eze 33:6
his blood will I *r* at the watchman's	Eze 33:8
I will *r* my flock at their hand	Eze 34:10
and what doth the LORD *r* of thee	Mic 6:8
For the Jews *r* a sign, and the	1Cor 1:22
flower of her age, and need so *r*	1Cor 7:36

REQUIRED
behold, also his blood is *r*	Gen 42:22
unto them such things as they *r*	Ex 12:36
the king's business *r* haste	1Sa 21:8
and when he *r*, they set bread	2Sa 12:20
as every day's work *r*	1Chr 16:37
as the duty of every day *r*	2Chr 8:14
Why hast thou not *r* of me	2Chr 24:6
as the duty of every day *r*	Ezr 3:4
yet for all this *r* not I the	Neh 5:18
she *r* nothing but what Hegai the	Est 2:15
and an offering hast thou not *r*	Ps 40:6
us away captive *r* of us a song	Ps 137:3
they that wasted us *r* of us mirth	Ps 137:3
Two things have I *r* of thee	Prov 30:7
who hath *r* this at your hand, to	Is 1:12
may be *r* of this generation	Lk 11:50
It shall be *r* of this generation	Lk 11:51
night thou soul shall be *r* of thee	Lk 12:20
is given, of him shall be much *r*	Lk 12:48
might have *r* mine own with usury	Lk 19:23
that it should be as they *r*	Lk 23:24
Moreover it is *r* in stewards	1Cor 4:2

REQUIREST
I will do to thee all that thou *r*	Ruth 3:11

REQUIRETH
and God *r* that which is past	Eccl 3:15
is a rare thing that the king *r*	Dan 2:11

REQUIRING
r that he might be crucified	Lk 23:23

REQUITE
will certainly *r* us all the evil	Gen 50:15
Do ye thus *r* the LORD, O foolish	Deut 32:6
I also will *r* you this kindness	2Sa 2:6
that the LORD will *r* me good for	2Sa 16:12
I will *r* thee in this plat, saith	2Kin 9:26
and spite, to *r* it with thy hand	Ps 10:14
and raise me up, that I may *r* them	Ps 41:10
God of recompences shall surely *r*	Jer 51:56
at home, and to *r* their parents	1Ti 5:4

REQUITED
as I have done, so God hath *r* me	Judg 1:7
he hath *r* me evil for good	1Sa 25:21

REQUITING
by *r* the wicked, by recompensing	2Chr 6:23

REREWARD
which was the *r* of all the camps	Num 10:25
the *r* came after the ark, the	Josh 6:9
but the *r* came after the ark of	Josh 6:13
passed on in the *r* with Achish	1Sa 29:2
the God of Israel will be your *r*	Is 52:12
glory of the LORD shall be thy *r*	Is 58:8

RESCUE
and thou shalt have none to *r* them	Deut 28:31
r my soul from their destructions	Ps 35:17
take away, and none shall *r* him	Hos 5:14

RESCUED
So the people *r* Jonathan, that he	1Sa 14:45
and David *r* his two wives	1Sa 30:18
r him, having understood that he	Acts 23:27

RESCUETH
He delivereth and *r*, and he worketh	Dan 6:27

RESEMBLANCE
This is their *r* through all the	Zec 5:6

RESEMBLE
and whereunto shall I *r* it	Lk 13:18

RESEMBLED
each one *r* the children of a king	Judg 8:18

RESEN (re'-zen) A city between Nineveh and Calah.
R between Nineveh and Calah	Gen 10:12

RESERVE
Will he *r* his anger for ever	Jer 3:5
for I will pardon them whom I *r*	Jer 50:20
to *r* the unjust unto the day of	2Pet 2:9

RESERVED
Hast thou not *r* a blessing for me	Gen 27:36
most holy things, *r* from the fire	Num 18:9
because we *r* not to each man his	Judg 21:22
she had *r* after she was sufficed	Ruth 2:18
but *r* of them for an hundred	2Sa 8:4
but *r* of them an hundred chariots	1Chr 18:4
That the wicked is *r* to the day	Job 21:30
Which I have *r* against the time	Job 38:23
be *r* unto the hearing of Augustus	Acts 25:21
I have *r* to myself seven thousand	Rom 11:4
not away, *r* in heaven for you	1Pet 1:4
darkness, to be *r* unto judgment	2Pet 2:4
mist of darkness is *r* for ever	2Pet 2:17
r unto fire against the day of	2Pet 3:7
he hath *r* in everlasting chains	Jude 6
to whom is *r* the blackness of	Jude 13

RESERVETH
he *r* unto us the appointed weeks	Jer 5:24
he *r* wrath for his enemies	Nah 1:2

RESHEPH (re'-shef) A son of Rephah.
and Rephah was his son, also R	1Chr 7:25

RESIDUE
they shall eat the *r* of that	Ex 10:5
the *r* of the families of the sons	1Chr 6:66
the *r* of Israel, of the priests	Neh 11:20
the *r* of the number of archers	Is 21:17
unto the *r* of his people	Is 28:5
am deprived of the *r* of my years	Is 38:10
the *r* thereof he maketh a god	Is 44:17
shall I make the *r* thereof an	Is 44:19
the *r* of them that remain of this	Jer 8:3
the *r* of Jerusalem, that remain	Jer 24:8
concerning the *r* of the vessels	Jer 27:19
the *r* of the elders which were	Jer 29:1
with all the *r* of the princes of	Jer 39:3
the *r* of the people that were in	Jer 41:10
the *r* of the people that remained	Jer 52:15
will thou destroy all the *r* of	Eze 9:8
thy *r* shall be devoured by the	Eze 34:18
your feet the *r* of your pastures	Eze 34:18
ye must foul the *r* with your feet	Eze 34:18
unto the *r* of the heathen	Eze 36:3
derision to the *r* of the heathen	Eze 36:4
against the *r* of the heathen	Eze 36:5
the *r* in length over against the	Eze 48:18
the *r* shall be for the prince, on	Eze 48:21
stamped the *r* with the feet of it	Dan 7:7
stamped the *r* with his feet	Dan 7:19
the *r* of my people shall spoil	Zeph 2:9
to the *r* of the people, saying	Hag 2:2
But now I will not be unto the *r*	Zec 8:11
the *r* of the people shall not be	Zec 14:2
Yet had he the *r* of the spirit	Mal 2:15
they went and told it unto the *r*	Mk 16:13
That the *r* of men might seek	Acts 15:17

RESIST
at his right hand to *r* him	Zec 3:1
say unto you, That ye *r* not evil	Mt 5:39
not be able to gainsay nor *r*	Lk 21:15
were not able to *r* the wisdom	Acts 6:10
ye do always *r* the Holy Ghost	Acts 7:51
they that *r* shall receive to	Rom 13:2
so do these also *r* the truth	2Ti 3:8
R the devil, and he will flee from	Jas 4:7
and he doth not *r* you	Jas 5:6
Whom *r* stedfast in the faith	1Pet 5:9

RESISTED
For who hath *r* his will	Rom 9:19
Ye have not yet *r* unto blood	Heb 12:4

RESISTETH
Whosoever therefore *r* the power	Rom 13:2
the power, *r* the ordinance of God	Rom 13:2
God *r* the proud, but giveth grace	Jas 4:6
for God *r* the proud, and giveth	1Pet 5:5

RESOLVED
I am *r* what to do, that, when I	Lk 16:4

RESORT
the trumpet, *r* ye thither unto us	Neh 4:20
whereunto I may continually *r*	Ps 71:3
the people *r* unto him again, and	Mk 10:1
temple, whither the Jews always *r*	Jn 18:20

RESORTED
r to him out of all their coasts	2Chr 11:13
and all the multitude *r* unto him	Mk 2:13
many *r* unto him, and said, John	Jn 10:41

for Jesus ofttimes r thither with .... Jn 18:2
unto the women which r thither. ...... Acts 16:13

RESPECT

And the LORD had r unto Abel. .... Gen 4:4
and to his offering he had not r .... Gen 4:5
of Israel, and God had r unto them. .... Ex 2:25
thou shalt not r the person of .... Lev 19:15
For I will have r unto you .... Lev 26:9
R not thou their offering. .... Num 16:15
Ye shall not r persons in .... Deut 1:17
thou shalt not r persons, neither. ...... Deut 16:19
neither doth God r any person. 2Sa 14:14
Yet have thou r unto the prayer 1Kin 8:28
had r unto them, because of his 2Kin 13:23
Have r therefore to the prayer of 2Chr 6:19
nor r of persons, nor taking of 2Chr 19:7
Have r unto the covenant. .... Ps 74:20
when I have r unto all thy .... Ps 119:6
precepts, and have r unto thy ways.... Ps 119:15
I will have r unto thy statutes. .... Ps 119:117
yet hath he r unto the lowly .... Ps 138:6
to have r of persons in judgment ...... Prov 24:23
To have r of persons is not good ...... Prov 28:21
his eyes shall have r to the Holy .... Is 17:7
neither shall r that which his .... Is 17:8
neither had r unto that that .... Is 22:11
For there is no r of persons with. ...... Rom 2:11
glorious had no glory in this r 2Cor 3:10
neither is there r of persons .... Eph 6:9
Not that I speak in r of want. .... Phil 4:11
or in r of an holyday, or of the .... Col 2:16
and there is no r of persons .... Col 3:25
for he had r unto the recompence. .... Heb 11:26
Lord of glory, with r of persons .... Jas 2:1
ye have r to him that weareth the. ...... Jas 2:3
But if ye have r to persons .... Jas 2:9
who without r of persons judgeth 1Pet 1:17

RESPECTED

they r not the persons of the .... Lam 4:16

RESPECTER

that God is no r of persons. .... Acts 10:34

RESPECTETH

he r not any that are wise of. .... Job 37:24
r not the proud, nor such as turn .... Ps 40:4

RESPITE

when Pharaoh saw that there was r .... Ex 8:15
unto him, Give us seven days' r. 1Sa 11:3

REST

But the dove found no r for the. .... Gen 8:9
r yourselves under the tree .... Gen 18:4
Jacob fed the r of Laban's flocks. ...... Gen 30:36
And he saw that r was good. .... Gen 49:15
ye make them r from their burdens .... Ex 5:5
To morrow is the r of the holy .... Ex 16:23
seventh year thou shalt let it r .... Ex 23:11
on the seventh day thou shalt r .... Ex 23:12
that thine ox and thine ass may r ...... Ex 23:12
names of the r on the other stone ...... Ex 28:10
the seventh is the sabbath of r .... Ex 31:15
with thee, and I will give thee r .... Ex 33:14
on the seventh day thou shalt r .... Ex 34:21
time and in harvest thou shalt r .... Ex 34:21
day, a sabbath of r to the LORD .... Ex 35:2
the r of the blood shall be wrung ...... Lev 5:9
of the r of the oil that is in .... Lev 14:17
the r of the oil that is in the. .... Lev 14:29
shall be a sabbath of r unto you. ...... Lev 16:31
seventh day is a sabbath of r .... Lev 23:3
shall be unto you a sabbath of r .... Lev 23:32
be a sabbath of r unto the land .... Lev 25:4
it is a year of r unto the land .... Lev 25:5
even then shall the land r .... Lev 26:34
as it lieth desolate it shall r .... Lev 26:35
it did not r in your sabbaths. .... Lev 26:35
beside the r of them that were .... Num 31:8
being the r of the prey which the .... Num 31:32
the r of Gilead, and all Bashan, ... Deut 3:13
have given r unto your brethren ...... Deut 3:20
maidservant may r as well as thou. .... Deut 5:14
ye are not as yet come to the r .... Deut 12:9
when he giveth you r from all. .... Deut 12:10
r from all thine enemies round .... Deut 25:19
shall the sole of thy foot have r .... Deut 28:65
LORD thy God hath given you r .... Josh 1:13
LORD have given your brethren r ...... Josh 1:15
shall r in the waters of Jordan, ... Josh 3:13
that the r which remained of them .... Josh 10:20
the r of the kingdom of Sihon. .... Josh 13:27
And the land had r from war. .... Josh 14:15
There was also a lot for the r of. ...... Josh 17:2
the r of Manasseh's sons had the ...... Josh 17:6
the r of the children of Kohath. .... Josh 21:20
the r of the Levites, out of the. .... Josh 21:34
the LORD gave them r round about .... Josh 21:44
hath given r unto your brethren. ...... Josh 22:4
r unto Israel from all their .... Josh 23:1
And the land had r forty years .... Judg 3:11
the land had r fourscore years .... Judg 3:30
And the land had r forty years .... Judg 5:31
but all the r of the people bowed ...... Judg 7:6
he sent all the r of Israel every .... Judg 7:8
LORD grant you that ye may find r ...... Ruth 1:9
shall I not seek r for thee .... Ruth 3:1
for the man will not be in r. .... Ruth 3:18
the r of the people he sent every........ 1Sa 11:11
the r we have utterly destroyed. 1Sa 15:15
Let it r on the head of Joab, and...... 2Sa 3:29

---

the LORD had given him r round 2Sa 7:1
have caused thee to r from all 2Sa 7:11
the r of the people he delivered 2Sa 10:10
the r of the people together 2Sa 12:28
of the air to r on them by day............ 2Sa 21:10
God hath given me r on every side. 1Kin 5:4
that hath given r unto his people........ 1Kin 8:56
the r of the acts of Solomon, and...... 1Kin 11:41
the r of the acts of Jeroboam, ... 1Kin 14:19
Now the r of the acts of Rehoboam 1Kin 14:29
the r of the acts of Abijam, ... 1Kin 15:7
The r of all the acts of Asa, and. 1Kin 15:23
Now the r of the acts of Nadab, ... 1Kin 15:31
Now the r of the acts of Baasha, ... 1Kin 16:5
Now the r of the acts of Elah, and...... 1Kin 16:14
Now the r of the acts of Zimri, ... 1Kin 16:20
Now the r of the acts of Omri 1Kin 16:27
But the r fled to Aphek, into the. 1Kin 20:30
Now the r of the acts of Ahab, and.... 1Kin 22:39
Now the r of the acts of 1Kin 22:45
Now the r of the acts of Ahaziah. 2Kin 1:18
spirit of Elijah doth r on Elisha. 2Kin 2:15
thou and thy children the r 2Kin 4:7
the r of the acts of Joram, and 2Kin 8:23
Now the r of the acts of Jehu, and.... 2Kin 10:34
the r of the acts of Joash, and 2Kin 12:19
Now the r of the acts of Jehoahaz 2Kin 13:8
the r of the acts of Joash, and 2Kin 13:12
Now the r of the acts of Amaziah, ... 2Kin 14:18
the r of the acts of Jeroboam 2Kin 14:28
Now the r of the acts of Azariah, ... 2Kin 15:6
the r of the acts of Zachariah, ... 2Kin 15:11
the r of the acts of Shallum, and...... 2Kin 15:15
the r of the acts of Menahem, and.... 2Kin 15:21
the r of the acts of Pekahiah, and...... 2Kin 15:26
the r of the acts of Pekah, and 2Kin 15:31
Now the r of the acts of Jotham, ... 2Kin 15:36
Now the r of the acts of Ahaz 2Kin 16:19
Now the r of the acts of Hezekiah, ... 2Kin 20:20
the r of the acts of Manasseh, ... 2Kin 21:17
the r of the acts of Amon 2Kin 21:25
the r of the acts of Josiah, ... 2Kin 23:28
Now the r of the acts of 2Kin 24:5
Now the r of the people that were...... 2Kin 25:11
And they smote the r of the. 1Chr 4:43
LORD, after that the ark had r.......... 1Chr 6:31
Unto the r of the children of 1Chr 6:77
Joab repaired the r of the city 1Chr 11:8
all the r also of Israel were of 1Chr 12:38
the r that were chosen, who were...... 1Chr 16:41
the r of the people he delivered. 1Chr 19:11
to thee, who shall be a man of r 1Chr 22:9
I will give him r from all his 1Chr 22:9
he not given you r on every side. 1Chr 22:18
hath given r unto his people............ 1Chr 23:25
the r of the sons of Levi were 1Chr 24:20
r for the ark of the covenant of 1Chr 28:2
Now the r of the acts of Solomon, ... 2Chr 9:29
the r of the acts of Abijah, and. 2Chr 13:22
for the land had r, and he had no....... 2Chr 14:6
because the LORD had given him r 2Chr 14:6
he hath given us r on every side. 2Chr 14:7
for we r on thee, and in thy name...... 2Chr 14:11
the LORD gave them r round about 2Chr 15:15
his God gave him r round about 2Chr 20:30
Now the r of the acts of 2Chr 20:34
they brought the r of the money. 2Chr 24:14
Now the r of the acts of Amaziah...... 2Chr 25:26
Now the r of the acts of Uzziah, ... 2Chr 26:22
Now the r of the acts of Jotham, ... 2Chr 27:7
Now the r of his acts and of all 2Chr 28:26
Now the r of the acts of Hezekiah, ... 2Chr 32:32
Now the r of the acts of Manasseh 2Chr 33:18
Now the r of the acts of Josiah, ... 2Chr 35:26
Now the r of the acts of 2Chr 36:8
the r of the chief of the fathers. .... Ezr 4:3
the r of their companions, and .... Ezr 4:7
the r of their companions .... Ezr 4:9
the r that are on this side the. .... Ezr 4:10
to the r of their companions that ...... Ezr 4:17
unto the r beyond the river,.............. Ezr 4:17
the r of the children of the .... Ezr 6:16
to do with the r of the silver. .... Ezr 7:18
nor to the r that did the work. .... Neh 2:16
to the r of the people, Be not ye....... Neh 4:14
to the r of the people, The work ...... Neh 4:19
the r of our enemies, heard that. ...... Neh 6:1
the r of the prophets, that would ...... Neh 6:14
that which the r of the people .... Neh 7:72
But after they had r, they did. .... Neh 9:28
the r of the people, the priests, ... Neh 10:28
the r of the people also cast........... Neh 11:1
in the r of the king's provinces. .... Neh 11:3
had r from their enemies, and slew .... Est 9:16
then had I been at r .... Job 3:13
and there the weary be at r .... Job 3:17
There the prisoners r together. .... Job 3:18
not in safety, neither had I r .... Job 3:26
thou shalt take thy r in safety. .... Job 11:18
Turn from him, that he may r .... Job 14:6
when our r together is in the. .... Job 17:16
and my sinews take no r .... Job 30:17
my flesh also shall r in hope .... Ps 16:9
leave the r of their substance to ...... Ps 17:14
R in the LORD, and wait patiently....... Ps 37:7
neither is there any r in my .... Ps 38:3
then would I fly away, and be at r. .... Ps 55:6
That thou mayest give him r from .... Ps 94:13

---

they should not enter into my r. ...... Ps 95:11
Return unto thy r, O my soul. .... Ps 116:7
r upon the lot of the righteous. .... Ps 125:3
Arise, O LORD, into thy r. .... Ps 132:8
This is my r for ever .... Ps 132:14
neither will he r content. .... Prov 6:35
he rage or laugh, there is no r .... Prov 29:9
thy son, and he shall give thee r ...... Prov 29:17
heart taketh not r in the night .... Eccl 2:23
this hath more r than the other. ...... Eccl 6:5
makest thy flock to r at noon. .... Song 1:7
shall r all of them in the. .... Is 7:19
the r of the trees of his forest. .... Is 10:19
the r of the LORD shall r upon him. .... Is 11:2
and his r shall be glorious .... Is 11:10
shall give thee r from thy sorrow ...... Is 14:3
The whole earth is at r, and is .... Is 14:7
said unto me, I will take my r .... Is 18:4
there also shalt thou have no r .... Is 23:12
shall the hand of the LORD r .... Is 25:10
This is the r wherewith ye may .... Is 28:12
ye may cause the weary to r .... Is 28:12
returning and r shall ye be saved ...... Is 30:15
screech owl also shall r there .... Is 34:14
and find for herself a place of r .... Is 34:14
to r for a light of the people .... Is 51:4
they shall r in their beds, each .... Is 57:2
troubled sea, when it cannot r .... Is 57:20
for Jerusalem's sake I will not r ...... Is 62:1
And give him no r, till he .... Is 62:7
of the LORD caused him to r .... Is 63:14
and where is the place of my r .... Is 66:1
ye shall find r for your souls. .... Jer 6:16
shalt return, and shall be in r .... Jer 30:10
when I went to cause him to r .... Jer 31:2
with the r of the people that .... Jer 39:9
in my sighing, and I find no r .... Jer 45:3
and Jacob shall return, and be in r .... Jer 46:27
up thyself into thy scabbard, r .... Jer 47:6
that he may give r to the land .... Jer 50:34
and the r of the multitude. .... Jer 52:15
The heathen, she findeth no r .... Lam 1:3
give thyself no r .... Lam 2:18
we labour, and have no r .... Lam 5:5
will cause my fury to r upon them .... Eze 5:13
I make my fury toward thee to r ...... Eze 16:42
and I will cause my fury to r .... Eze 21:17
caused my fury to r upon thee. .... Eze 24:13
I will go to them that are at r .... Eze 38:11
the blessing to r in thine house ...... Eze 44:30
the r of the land shall they give. ...... Eze 45:8
As for the r of the tribes, from .... Eze 48:23
the r of the wise men of Babylon .... Dan 2:18
was at r in mine house, and.............. Dan 4:4
As concerning the r of the beasts. .... Dan 7:12
for thou shalt r, and stand in thy...... Dan 12:13
for this is not your r .... Mic 2:10
that I might r in the day of .... Hab 3:16
he will r in his love, he will .... Zeph 3:17
earth sitteth still, and is at r. .... Zec 1:11
Damascus shall be the r thereof ...... Zec 9:1
let the r eat every one the flesh. ...... Zec 11:9
heavy laden, and I will give you r ...... Mt 11:28
ye shall find r unto your souls. .... Mt 11:29
through dry places, seeking r .... Mt 12:43
Sleep on now, and take your r .... Mt 26:45
The r said, Let be, let us see .... Mt 27:49
into a desert place, and r a while...... Mk 6:31
Sleep on now, and take your r .... Mk 14:41
there, your peace shall r upon it ...... Lk 10:6
through dry places, seeking r .... Lk 11:24
why take ye thought for the r .... Lk 12:26
unto the eleven, and to all the r. ...... Lk 24:9
spoken of taking of r in sleep .... Jn 11:13
also my flesh shall r in hope .... Acts 2:26
to the r of the apostles, Men and...... Acts 2:37
of the r durst no man join............ Acts 5:13
or what is the place of my r .... Acts 7:49
churches r throughout all Judaea. .... Acts 9:31
the r, some on boards. .... Acts 27:44
it, and the r were blinded. .... Rom 11:7
But to the r speak I, not the. 1Cor 7:12
the r will I set in order when I 1Cor 11:34
I had no r in my spirit, because. 2Cor 2:13
Macedonia, our flesh had no r 2Cor 7:5
the power of Christ may r upon me. 2Cor 12:9
to you who are troubled r with us. 2Th 1:7
They shall not enter into my r .... Heb 3:11
they should not enter into his r ...... Heb 3:18
left us of entering into his r .... Heb 4:1
have believed do enter into r .... Heb 4:3
if they shall enter into my r .... Heb 4:3
God did r the seventh day from ...... Heb 4:4
If they shall enter into my r .... Heb 4:5
If Jesus had given them r .... Heb 4:8
a r to the people of God .... Heb 4:9
For he that is entered into his r ...... Heb 4:10
therefore to enter into that r .... Heb 4:11
he no longer should live the r of 1Pet 4:2
unto the r in Thyatira, as many ...... Rev 2:24
they r not day and night, saying, ... Rev 4:8
that they should r yet for a .... Rev 6:11
the r of the men which were not ...... Rev 9:20
they have no r day nor night, who...... Rev 14:11
that they may r from their. .... Rev 14:13
the r of the dead lived not. .... Rev 20:5

RESTED

he r on the seventh day from all. ...... Gen 2:2
because that in it he had r from. ...... Gen 2:3
the ark r in the seventh month,........ Gen 8:4

r in all the coasts of Egypt ... Ex 10:14
So the people r on the seventh ... Ex 16:30
in them is, and the seventh day ... Ex 20:11
earth, and on the seventh day he r ... Ex 31:17
tabernacle they r in their tents ... Num 9:18
of the LORD they r in the tents ... Num 9:23
the cloud r in the wilderness of ... Num 10:12
And when it r, he said, Return, O ... Num 10:36
that, when the spirit r upon them ... Num 11:25
and the spirit r upon them ... Num 11:26
And the land r from war ... Josh 11:23
they r on the house with timber ... 1Kin 6:10
the people r themselves upon the ... 2Chr 32:8
fourteenth day of the same r they ... Est 9:17
fifteenth day of the same they r ... Est 9:18
the Jews r from their enemies ... Est 9:22
My bowels boiled, and r not ... Job 30:27
r the sabbath day according to ... Lk 23:56

RESTEST
r in the law, and makest thou boast ... Rom 2:17

RESTETH
him to be in safety, whereon he r ... Job 24:23
Wisdom r in the heart of him that ... Prov 14:33
for anger r in the bosom of fools ... Eccl 7:9
of glory and of God r upon you ... 1Pet 4:14

RESTING
to search out a r place for them ... Num 10:33
O LORD God, into thy r place ... 2Chr 6:41
spoil not his r place ... Prov 24:15
dwellings, and in quiet r places ... Is 32:18

RESTINGPLACE
hill, they have forgotten their r ... Jer 50:6

RESTITUTION
for he should make full r ... Ex 22:3
his own vineyard, shall he make r ... Ex 22:5
the fire shall surely make r ... Ex 22:6
he shall make r unto the owner ... Ex 22:12
to his substance shall the r be ... Job 20:18
the times of r of all things ... Acts 3:21

RESTORE
Now therefore r the man his wife ... Gen 20:7
and if thou r her not, know thou ... Gen 20:7
head, and r thee unto thy place ... Gen 40:13
to r every man's money into his ... Gen 42:25
he shall r five oxen for an ox, and ... Ex 22:1
he shall r double ... Ex 22:4
that he shall r that which he ... Lev 6:4
he shall even r it in the ... Lev 6:5
killeth a beast, he shall r it ... Lev 24:21
the overplus unto the man to ... Lev 25:27
if he be not able to r it to him ... Lev 25:28
the congregation shall r him to ... Num 35:25
thou shalt r it to him again ... Deut 22:2
now therefore r those lands again ... Judg 11:13
therefore I will r it unto thee ... Judg 17:3
and I will r it you ... 1Sa 12:3
will r thee all the land of Saul ... 2Sa 9:7
he shall r the lamb fourfold ... 2Sa 12:6
r me the kingdom of my father ... 2Sa 16:3
took from thy father, I will r ... 1Kin 20:34
R all that was hers, and all the ... 2Kin 8:6
R, I pray you, to them, even this ... Neh 5:11
Then said they, We will r them ... Neh 5:12
and his hands shall r their goods ... Job 20:10
which he laboured for shall he r ... Job 20:18
R unto me the joy of thy ... Ps 51:12
he be found, he shall r sevenfold ... Prov 6:31
I will r thy judges as at the ... Is 1:26
for a spoil, and none saith, R ... Is 42:22
to r the preserved of Israel ... Is 49:6
r comforts unto him and to his ... Is 57:18
them up, and r them to this place ... Jer 27:22
For I will r health unto thee, and ... Jer 30:17
if the wicked r the pledge ... Eze 33:15
forth of the commandment to r ... Dan 9:25
I will r to you the years that ... Joel 2:25
shall first come, and r all things ... Mt 17:11
accusation, I r him fourfold ... Lk 19:8
wilt thou at this time r again ... Acts 1:6
r such an one in the spirit of ... Gal 6:1

RESTORED
Abraham, and r him Sarah his wife ... Gen 20:14
he r the chief butler unto his ... Gen 40:21
me he r unto mine office, and him ... Gen 41:13
unto his brethren, My money is r ... Gen 42:28
face, and shall not be r to thee ... Deut 28:31
when he had r the eleven hundred ... Judg 17:3
Yet he r the money unto his ... Judg 17:4
from Israel were r to Israel ... 1Sa 7:14
that my hand may be r me again ... 1Kin 13:6
the king's hand was r him again ... 1Kin 13:6
woman, whose son he had r to life ... 2Kin 8:1
how he had r a dead body to life ... 2Kin 8:5
woman, whose son he had r to life ... 2Kin 8:5
is her son, whom Elisha r to life ... 2Kin 8:5
r it to Judah, after that the ... 2Kin 14:22
He r the coast of Israel from the ... 2Kin 14:25
which Huram had r to Solomon ... 2Chr 8:2
r it to Judah, after that the ... 2Chr 26:2
and brought unto Babylon, be r ... Ezr 6:5
then I r that which I took not ... Ps 69:4
but hath r to the debtor his ... Eze 18:7
hath not r the pledge, and hath ... Eze 18:12
and it was r whole, like as the ... Mt 12:13
his hand was r whole as the other ... Mk 3:5
and he was r, and saw every man ... Mk 8:25

his hand was r whole as the other ... Lk 6:10
that I may be r to you the sooner ... Heb 13:19

RESTORER
be unto thee a r of thy life ... Ruth 4:15
The r of paths to dwell in ... Is 58:12

RESTORETH
He r my soul ... Ps 23:3
cometh first, and r all things ... Mk 9:12

RESTRAIN
dost thou r wisdom to thyself ... Job 15:8
remainder of wrath shalt thou r ... Ps 76:10

RESTRAINED
and the rain from heaven was r ... Gen 8:2
now nothing will be r from them ... Gen 11:6
the LORD hath r me from bearing ... Gen 16:2
the people were r from bringing ... Ex 36:6
themselves vile, and he r them not ... 1Sa 3:13
are they r ... Is 63:15
I r the floods thereof, and the ... Eze 31:15
sayings scarce r they the people ... Acts 14:18

RESTRAINEST
off fear, and r prayer before God ... Job 15:4

RESTRAINT
for there is no r to the LORD to ... 1Sa 14:6

RESTS
he made narrowed r round about ... 1Kin 6:6

RESURRECTION
which say that there is no r ... Mt 22:23
Therefore in the r whose wife ... Mt 22:28
For in the r they neither marry ... Mt 22:30
But as touching the r of the dead ... Mt 22:31
out of the graves after his r ... Mt 27:53
which say there is no r ... Mk 12:18
In the r therefore, when they ... Mk 12:23
recompensed at the r of the just ... Lk 14:14
when deny that there is any r ... Lk 20:27
Therefore in the r whose wife of ... Lk 20:33
the r from the dead, neither ... Lk 20:35
God, being the children of the r ... Lk 20:36
done good, unto the r of life ... Jn 5:29
evil, unto the r of damnation ... Jn 5:29
again in the r at the last day ... Jn 11:24
Jesus said unto her, I am the r ... Jn 11:25
to be a witness with us of his r ... Acts 1:22
before spake of the r of Christ ... Acts 2:31
through Jesus the r from the dead ... Acts 4:2
of the r of the Lord Jesus ... Acts 4:33
unto them Jesus, and the r ... Acts 17:18
they heard of the r of the dead ... Acts 17:32
r of the dead I am called in ... Acts 23:6
Sadducees say that there is no r ... Acts 23:8
there shall be a r of the dead ... Acts 24:15
Touching the r of the dead I am ... Acts 24:21
holiness, by the r from the dead ... Rom 1:4
be also in the likeness of his r ... Rom 6:5
that there is no r of the dead ... 1Cor 15:12
But if there be no r of the dead ... 1Cor 15:13
man came also the r of the dead ... 1Cor 15:21
So also is the r of the dead ... 1Cor 15:42
know him, and the power of his r ... Phil 3:10
attain unto the r of the dead ... Phil 3:11
saying that the r is past already ... 2Ti 2:18
of r of the dead, and of eternal ... Heb 6:2
that they might obtain a better r ... Heb 11:35
r of Jesus Christ from the dead ... 1Pet 1:3
by the r of Jesus Christ ... 1Pet 3:21
This is the first r ... Rev 20:5
he that hath part in the first r ... Rev 20:6

RETAIN
Dost thou still r thine integrity ... Job 2:9
me, Let thine heart r my words ... Prov 4:4
and strong men r riches ... Prov 11:16
over the spirit to r the spirit ... Eccl 8:8
but she shall not r the power of ... Dan 11:6
and whose soever sins ye r ... Jn 20:23
like to r God in their knowledge ... Rom 1:28

RETAINED
r those three hundred men ... Judg 7:8
law, the damsel's father, r him ... Judg 19:4
corruption, and I r no strength ... Dan 10:8
upon me, and I have r no strength ... Dan 10:16
soever sins ye retain, they are r ... Jn 20:23
Whom I would have r with me ... Philem 13

RETAINETH
and happy is every one that r her ... Prov 3:18
A gracious woman r honour ... Prov 11:16
he r not his anger for ever ... Mic 7:18

RETIRE
r ye from him, that he may be ... 2Sa 11:15
r, stay not ... Jer 4:6

RETIRED
the men of Israel r in the battle ... Judg 20:39
they r from the city, every man ... 2Sa 20:22

RETURN
till thou r unto the ground ... Gen 3:19
art, and unto dust shalt thou r ... Gen 3:19
after his r from the slaughter of ... Gen 14:17
R to thy mistress, and submit ... Gen 16:9
I will certainly r unto thee ... Gen 18:10
time appointed I will r unto thee ... Gen 18:14
R unto the land of thy fathers ... Gen 31:3
r unto the land of thy kindred ... Gen 31:13
R unto thy country, and to thy ... Gen 32:9

r unto my brethren which are in ... Ex 4:18
Moses in Midian, Go, r into Egypt ... Ex 4:19
When thou goest to r into Egypt ... Ex 4:21
they see war, and they r to Egypt ... Ex 13:17
they shall r every man unto his ... Lev 25:10
ye shall r every man unto his ... Lev 25:10
year of this jubile ye shall r ... Lev 25:13
that he may r unto his possession ... Lev 25:27
he shall r unto his possession ... Lev 25:28
shall r unto his own family, and ... Lev 25:41
of his fathers shall he r ... Lev 25:41
of the jubile the field shall r ... Lev 27:24
And when it rested, he said, R ... Num 10:36
not better for us to r into Egypt ... Num 14:3
a captain, and let us r into Egypt ... Num 14:4
R unto Balak, and thus thou shalt ... Num 23:5
We will not r unto our houses ... Num 32:18
then afterward ye shall r ... Num 32:22
high priest the slayer shall r ... Num 35:28
then shall ye r every man unto ... Deut 3:20
cause the people to r to Egypt ... Deut 17:16
henceforth r no more that way ... Deut 17:16
r to his house, lest he die in ... Deut 20:5
r unto his house, lest he die in ... Deut 20:6
r unto his house, lest he die in ... Deut 20:7
r unto his house, lest his ... Deut 20:8
shalt r unto the LORD thy God, and ... Deut 30:2
compassion upon thee, and will r ... Deut 30:3
And thou shalt r and obey the voice ... Deut 30:8
then ye shall r unto the land of ... Josh 1:15
then shall the slayer r, and come ... Josh 20:6
therefore now r ye, and get you ... Josh 22:4
R with much riches unto your ... Josh 22:8
is fearful and afraid, let him r ... Judg 7:3
when I r in peace from the ... Judg 11:31
that she might r from the country ... Ruth 1:6
way to r unto the land of Judah ... Ruth 1:7
r each to her mother's house ... Ruth 1:8
Surely we will r with thee unto ... Ruth 1:10
r thou after thy sister in law ... Ruth 1:15
or to r from following after thee ... Ruth 1:16
but in any wise r him a trespass ... 1Sa 6:3
offering which we shall r to him ... 1Sa 6:4
which ye r him for a trespass ... 1Sa 6:8
If ye do r unto the LORD with all ... 1Sa 7:3
And his r was to Ramah ... 1Sa 7:17
was with him, Come, and let us r ... 1Sa 9:5
unto Saul, I will not r with thee ... 1Sa 15:26
r, my son David ... 1Sa 26:21
said unto him, Make this fellow r ... 1Sa 29:4
Wherefore now r, and go in peace ... 1Sa 29:7
to r into the land of the ... 1Sa 29:11
ere thou bid the people r from ... 2Sa 2:26
Then said Abner unto him, Go, r ... 2Sa 3:16
your beards be grown, and then r ... 2Sa 10:5
to him, but he shall not r to me ... 2Sa 12:23
r to thy place, and abide with the ... 2Sa 15:19
r thou, and take back thy brethren ... 2Sa 15:20
r into the city in peace, and your ... 2Sa 15:27
But if thou r to the city ... 2Sa 15:34
R thou, and all thy servants ... 2Sa 19:14
I shall r to him that sent me ... 2Sa 24:13
the LORD shall r his blood upon ... 1Kin 2:32
therefore r upon the head of Joab ... 1Kin 2:33
therefore the LORD shall r thy ... 1Kin 2:44
so r unto thee with all their ... 1Kin 8:48
r every man to his house ... 1Kin 12:24
kingdom r to the house of David ... 1Kin 12:26
And he said, I may not r with thee ... 1Kin 13:16
r on thy way to the wilderness of ... 1Kin 19:15
for at the r of the year the king ... 1Kin 20:22
came to pass at the r of the year ... 1Kin 20:26
let them r every man to his house ... 1Kin 22:17
If thou r at all in peace, the ... 1Kin 22:28
r from me ... 2Kin 18:14
and shall r to his own land ... 2Kin 19:7
he came, by the same shall he r ... 2Kin 19:33
but let the shadow r backward ten ... 2Kin 20:10
your beards be grown, and then r ... 1Chr 19:5
and shall r and confess thy name ... 2Chr 6:24
If they r to thee with all their ... 2Chr 6:38
ye me to r answer to this people ... 2Chr 10:9
we may r answer to this people ... 2Chr 10:9
r every man to his house ... 2Chr 11:4
let them r therefore every man to ... 2Chr 18:16
of affliction, until I r in peace ... 2Chr 18:26
If thou certainly r in peace ... 2Chr 18:27
he will r to the remnant of you ... 2Chr 30:6
face from you, if ye r unto him ... 2Chr 30:9
and when wilt thou r ... Neh 2:6
r unto us they will be upon you ... Neh 4:12
a captain to r to their bondage ... Neh 9:17
bade them r Mordecai this answer ... Est 4:15
should r upon his own head, and ... Est 9:25
womb, and naked shall I r thither ... Job 1:21
R, I pray you, let it not be ... Job 6:29
r again, my righteousness is in ... Job 6:29
He shall r no more to his house ... Job 7:10
Before I go whence I shall not r ... Job 10:21
that he shall r out of darkness ... Job 15:22
go the way whence I shall not r ... Job 16:22
But as for you all, do ye r ... Job 17:10
If thou r to the Almighty, thou ... Job 22:23
he shall r to the days of his ... Job 33:25
that they r from iniquity ... Job 36:10
they go forth, and r not unto them ... Job 39:4
R, O LORD, deliver my soul ... Ps 6:4
let them r and be ashamed suddenly ... Ps 6:10
sakes therefore r thou on high ... Ps 7:7
shall r upon his own head ... Ps 7:16

They r at evening .... Ps 59:6
And at evening let them r.................... Ps 59:14
Therefore his people r hither .... Ps 73:10
O let not the oppressed r ashamed.... Ps 74:21
R, we beseech thee, O God of............ Ps 80:14
and sayest, R, ye children of men ...... Ps 90:3
R, O Lord, how long............................ Ps 90:13
shall r unto righteousness.................. Ps 94:15
they die, and r to their dust .... Ps 104:29
R unto thy rest, O my soul................. Ps 116:7
None that go unto her r again............ Prov 2:19
a stone, it will r upon him.................. Prov 26:27
rivers come, thither they r again........ Eccl 1:7
naked shall he r to go as he came .... Eccl 5:15
nor the clouds r after the rain........... Eccl 12:2
Then shall the dust r to the.............. Eccl 12:7
the spirit shall r unto God who.......... Eccl 12:7
R, r, O Shulamite .... Song 6:13
r, r, that we may look upon .... Song 6:13
shall be a tenth, and it shall r........... Is 6:13
The remnant shall r, even the .... Is 10:21
yet a remnant of them shall r............ Is 10:22
they shall r even to the Lord, and..... Is 19:22
enquire ye: r, come.............................. Is 21:12
the ransomed of the Lord shall r...... Is 35:10
a rumour, and r to his own land........ Is 37:7
he came, by the same shall he r .... Is 37:34
r unto me... Is 44:22
in righteousness, and shall not r....... Is 45:23
the redeemed of the Lord shall r ...... Is 51:11
let him r unto the Lord, and he .... Is 55:7
it shall not r unto me void .... Is 55:11
R for thy servants' sake, the .... Is 63:17
shall he r unto her again .... Jer 3:1
yet r again to me, saith the Lord ..... Jer 3:1
words toward the north, and say, R .. Jer 3:12
R, ye backsliding children, and I ...... Jer 3:22
If thou wilt r, O Israel, saith.......... Jer 4:1
Israel, saith the Lord, r unto me..... Jer 4:1
they have refused to r .... Jer 5:3
shall he turn away, and not r .... Jer 8:4
fast deceit, they refuse to r .... Jer 8:5
I have plucked them out I will r....... Jer 12:15
since they r not from their ways .... Jer 15:7
thus saith the Lord, If thou r .... Jer 15:19
let them r unto thee........................... Jer 15:19
but r not thou unto them................... Jer 15:19
r ye now every one from his evil....... Jer 18:11
for he shall r no more, nor see......... Jer 22:10
He shall not r thither any more .... Jer 22:11
land whereunto they desire to r........ Jer 22:27
thither shall they not r...................... Jer 22:27
that none doth r from his.................. Jer 23:14
The anger of the Lord shall not r..... Jer 23:20
for they shall r unto me with .... Jer 24:7
in causing you to r to this place ...... Jer 29:10
I will cause them to r to the............. Jer 30:3
and Jacob shall r, and shall be in .... Jer 30:10
anger of the Lord shall not r .... Jer 30:24
a great company shall r thither .... Jer 31:8
I will cause their captivity to r .... Jer 32:44
and the captivity of Israel to r .... Jer 33:11
For I will cause to r .... Jer 33:26
I will cause their captivity to r .... Jer 33:26
whom they had let go free, to r........ Jer 34:11
liberty at their pleasure, to r............ Jer 34:16
and cause them to r to this city....... Jer 35:15
R ye now every man from his evil..... Jer 36:3
that they may r every man from...... Jer 36:7
will r every one from his evil............ Jer 36:7
shall r to Egypt from their own........ Jer 37:20
that thou cause me not to r to......... Jer 37:20
cause me to r to Jonathan's house... Jer 38:26
cause you to r to your own land ...... Jer 42:12
that they should r into the land....... Jer 44:14
have a desire to r to the land........... Jer 44:14
for none shall r but such as .... Jer 44:14
that escape the sword shall r out .... Jer 44:28
and Jacob shall r, and be in rest ..... Jer 46:27
none shall r in vain............................ Jer 50:9
shall not r to that which is sold........ Eze 7:13
thereof, which shall not r .... Eze 7:13
that he should not r from his .... Eze 13:22
shall r to their former estate............ Eze 16:55
her daughters shall r to their .... Eze 16:55
thy daughters shall r to your .... Eze 16:55
that he should r from his ways......... Eze 18:23
it shall not r any more .... Eze 21:5
I cause it to r into his sheath .... Eze 21:30
will cause them to r into the .... Eze 29:14
and thy cities shall not r................... Eze 35:9
he shall not r by the way of the....... Eze 46:9
after, it shall r to the prince............ Eze 46:17
caused me to r to the brink of......... Eze 47:6
now will I r to fight with the............ Dan 10:20
shall r into his own land................... Dan 11:9
then shall he r, and be stirred up .... Dan 11:10
For the king of the north shall r ..... Dan 11:13
Then shall he r into his land............ Dan 11:28
do exploits, and r to his own land.... Dan 11:28
At the time appointed he shall r ...... Dan 11:29
he shall be grieved, and r .... Dan 11:30
he shall even r, and have................... Dan 11:30
will go and r to my first husband..... Hos 2:7
Therefore will I r, and take away ..... Hos 2:9
shall the children of Israel r .... Hos 3:5
go and r to my place, till they .... Hos 5:15
Come, and let us r unto the Lord .... Hos 6:1
they do not r to the Lord their......... Hos 7:10
They r, but not to the most High...... Hos 7:16

they shall r to Egypt .... Hos 8:13
but Ephraim shall r to Egypt .... Hos 9:3
He shall not r into the land of......... Hos 11:5
king, because they refused to r .... Hos 11:5
I will not r to destroy Ephraim........ Hos 11:9
shall his Lord r unto him................. Hos 12:14
O Israel, r unto the Lord thy God.... Hos 14:1
dwell under his shadow shall r .... Hos 14:7
Who knoweth if he will r and........... Joel 2:14
speedily will I r your recompence .... Joel 3:4
will r your recompence upon your.... Joel 3:7
thy reward shall r upon thine own... Obad 15
they shall r to the hire of an .... Mic 1:7
r unto the children of Israel .... Mic 5:3
are impoverished, but we will r .... Mal 1:4
R unto me, and I will unto................ Mal 3:7
But ye said, Wherein shall we r .... Mal 3:7
Then shall ye r, and discern............. Mal 3:18
that they should not r to Herod....... Mt 2:12
worthy, let your peace r to you .... Mt 10:13
I will r into my house from............... Mt 12:44
field r back to take his clothes......... Mt 24:18
R to thine own house, and shew how... Lk 8:39
I will r unto my house whence I ...... Lk 11:24
when he will r from the wedding ..... Lk 12:36
let him likewise not r back................ Lk 17:31
for himself a kingdom, and to r .... Lk 19:12
now no more to r to corruption .... Acts 13:34
After this I will r, and will................ Acts 15:16
but I will r again unto you, if .... Acts 18:21
Syria, he purposed to r through........ Acts 20:3

RETURNED
the waters r from off the earth......... Gen 8:3
she r unto him into the ark, for .... Gen 8:9
which r not again unto him any....... Gen 8:12
And they r, and came to En-mishpat,... Gen 14:7
and Abraham r unto his place........... Gen 18:33
they r into the land of the .... Gen 21:32
So Abraham r into his young men,... Gen 22:19
departed, and r into his place .... Gen 31:55
And the messengers r to Jacob......... Gen 32:6
So Esau r that day on his way .... Gen 33:16
And Reuben r unto the pit .... Gen 37:29
he r unto his brethren, and said...... Gen 37:30
he r to Judah, and said, I cannot..... Gen 38:22
r to them again, and communed with... Gen 42:24
now we had r this second time......... Gen 43:10
Because of the money that was r...... Gen 43:18
man his ass, and r to the city .... Gen 44:13
Joseph r into Egypt, he, and his ..... Gen 50:14
r to Jethro his father in law, and ... Ex 4:18
he r to the land of Egypt .... Ex 4:20
Moses r unto the Lord, and said,.... Ex 5:22
the sea r to his strength when .... Ex 14:27
And the waters r, and covered the.... Ex 14:28
Moses r the words of the people....... Ex 19:8
Moses r unto the Lord, and said,.... Ex 32:31
of the congregation r unto him .... Ex 34:31
is r unto her father's house, as ...... Lev 22:13
they r from searching out the land... Num 13:25
sent to search the land, who r .... Num 14:36
Aaron r unto Moses unto the door... Num 16:50
he r unto him and, lo, he stood by.... Num 23:6
up, and went and r to his place .... Num 24:25
And ye r and wept before the Lord... Deut 1:45
days, until the pursuers be r .... Josh 2:16
days, until the pursuers were r .... Josh 2:22
So the two men r, and descended..... Josh 2:23
of Jordan r unto their place............. Josh 4:18
the city once, and r into the camp... Josh 6:11
they r to Joshua, and said unto....... Josh 7:3
that all the Israelites r unto his....... Josh 8:24
And Joshua r, and all Israel with.... Josh 8:15
all the people r to the camp to........ Josh 10:21
and Joshua r, and all Israel with.... Josh 10:38
And Joshua r, and all Israel with.... Josh 10:43
and the half tribe of Manasseh r..... Josh 22:9
r from the children of Reuben, and... Josh 22:32
the judge was dead, that they r ...... Judg 2:19
yea, she r answer to herself............. Judg 5:29
there r of the people twenty and..... Judg 7:3
r into the host of Israel.................... Judg 7:15
Gideon the son of Joash r from........ Judg 8:13
that she r unto her father, who....... Judg 11:39
And after a time he r to take her .... Judg 14:8
r unto their inheritance, and........... Judg 21:23
So Naomi r, and Ruth the Moabitess,... Ruth 1:22
which r out of the country of .... Ruth 1:22
worshipped before the Lord, and..... 1Sa 1:19
they r to Ekron the same day 1Sa 6:16
for a trespass offering unto 1Sa 6:17
r from Saul to feed his father's 1Sa 17:15
Israel r from chasing after the 1Sa 17:53
as David r from the slaughter of 1Sa 17:57
when David was r from the............... 1Sa 18:6
Wherefore Saul r from pursuing....... 1Sa 23:28
when Saul was r from following....... 1Sa 24:1
for the Lord hath r the 1Sa 25:39
his way, and Saul r to his place....... 1Sa 26:25
the camels, and the apparel, and 1Sa 27:9
when David was r from the............... 2Sa 1:1
and the sword of Saul r not empty... 2Sa 1:22
Joab r from following Abner............ 2Sa 3:27
Go, return. And he r.......................... 2Sa 3:16
And when Abner was r to Hebron.... 2Sa 3:26
Then David r to bless his................. 2Sa 6:20
David gat him a name when he r...... 2Sa 8:13
So Joab r from the children of 2Sa 10:14
and she r unto her house.................. 2Sa 11:4
all the people r unto Jerusalem 2Sa 12:31

So Absalom r to his own house, and... 2Sa 14:24
The Lord hath r upon thee all the... 2Sa 16:8
whom thou seekest is as if all r...... 2Sa 17:3
find them, they r to Jerusalem......... 2Sa 17:20
the people r from pursuing after..... 2Sa 18:16
So the king r, and came to Jordan... 2Sa 19:15
and he r unto his own place 2Sa 19:39
Joab r to Jerusalem unto the king... 2Sa 20:22
the people r after him only to 2Sa 23:10
to depart, according to the............... 1Kin 12:24
r not by the way that he came to 1Kin 13:10
Jeroboam r not from his evil way 1Kin 13:33
he r back from him, and took a....... 1Kin 19:21
and from thence he r to Samaria 2Kin 2:25
from him, and r to their own land ... 2Kin 3:27
Then he r, and walked in the house... 2Kin 4:35
he r to the man of God, he and all... 2Kin 5:15
And the messengers r, and told the... 2Kin 7:15
that the woman r out of the land..... 2Kin 8:3
But king Joram was r to be healed... 2Kin 9:15
and hostages, and r to Samaria 2Kin 14:14
So Rab-shakeh r, and found the...... 2Kin 19:8
of Assyria departed, and went and r... 2Kin 19:36
upon them, and r to Jerusalem........ 2Kin 23:20
David r to bless his house................. 1Chr 16:43
and all the people r to Jerusalem ... 1Chr 20:3
it, that Jeroboam r out of Egypt...... 2Chr 10:2
r from going against Jeroboam......... 2Chr 11:4
in abundance, and r to Jerusalem... 2Chr 14:15
Judah r to his house in peace to 2Chr 19:1
when they r to Jerusalem 2Chr 19:8
Then they r, every man of Judah..... 2Chr 20:27
he r to be healed in Jezreel.............. 2Chr 22:6
they r home in great anger 2Chr 25:10
hostages also, and r to Samaria 2Chr 25:24
then they r to Samaria 2Chr 28:15
Then all the children of Israel r...... 2Chr 31:1
So he r with shame of face to his.... 2Chr 32:21
land of Israel, he r to Jerusalem..... 2Chr 34:7
and they r to Jerusalem................... 2Chr 34:9
then they r answer by letter .... Ezr 5:5
And thus they r us answer, saying,... Ezr 5:11
the gate of the valley, and so r........ Neh 2:15
that we r all of us to the wall,......... Neh 4:15
yet when they r, and cried unto ...... Neh 9:28
on the morrow she r into the .... Est 2:14
Then the king r out of the palace.... Est 7:8
my prayer r into mine own bosom ... Ps 35:13
and with Aram-zobah, when Joab r... Ps 60:t
and they r and enquired early after... Ps 78:34
So I r, and considered all the .... Eccl 4:1
Then I r, and I saw vanity under..... Eccl 4:7
I r, and saw under the sun, that...... Eccl 9:11
So Rabshakeh r, and found the king... Is 37:8
of Assyria departed, and went and r... Is 37:37
So the sun r ten degrees, by............ Is 38:8
But she r not.................................... Jer 3:7
they r with their vessels empty........ Jer 14:3
Even all the Jews r out of all.......... Jer 40:12
from Mizpah cast about and r .... Jer 41:14
that were r from all nations,............ Jer 43:5
r as the appearance of a flash of..... Eze 1:14
have r to provoke me to anger......... Eze 8:17
Now when I had r, behold, at the.... Eze 47:7
and mine understanding r unto me... Dan 4:34
the same time my reason r unto me... Dan 4:36
honour and brightness r unto me..... Dan 4:36
when I r the captivity of my............ Hos 6:11
yet have ye not r unto me................ Amos 4:6
yet have ye not r unto me................ Amos 4:8
yet have ye not r unto me................ Amos 4:9
yet have ye not r unto me................ Amos 4:10
yet have ye not r unto me................ Amos 4:11
and they r and said, Like as the...... Zec 1:6
I am r to Jerusalem with mercies..... Zec 1:16
that no man passed through nor r.... Zec 7:14
I am r unto Zion, and will dwell...... Zec 8:3
the morning as he r into the city .... Mt 21:18
And when he r, he found them......... Mk 14:40
months, and r to her own house...... Lk 1:56
And the shepherds r, glorifying and... Lk 2:20
they r into Galilee, to their own...... Lk 2:39
had fulfilled the days, as they r ...... Lk 2:43
of the Holy Ghost r from Jordan..... Lk 4:1
Jesus r in the power of the.............. Lk 4:14
up into the ship, and r back again... Lk 8:37
to pass, that, when Jesus was r....... Lk 8:40
And the apostles, when they were r... Lk 9:10
the seventy r again with joy............. Lk 10:17
found that r to give glory to God .... Lk 17:18
came to pass, that when he was r.... Lk 19:15
done, smote their breasts, and r...... Lk 23:48
And they r, and prepared spices and... Lk 23:56
r from the sepulchre, and told all.... Lk 24:9
to Jerusalem, and found the .... Lk 24:33
r to Jerusalem with great joy........... Lk 24:52
Then r they unto Jerusalem from..... Acts 1:12
them not in the prison, they r .... Acts 5:22
r to Jerusalem, and preached the .... Acts 8:25
Saul r from Jerusalem, when they... Acts 12:25
they r again to Lystra, and to......... Acts 14:21
and they r home again .... Acts 21:6
go with him, and r to the castle....... Acts 23:32
Arabia, and r again unto Damascus... Gal 1:17
have had opportunity to have r .... Heb 11:15
but are now r unto the Shepherd 1Pet 2:25

RETURNETH
goeth forth, he r to his earth .... Ps 146:4
As a dog r to his vomit..................... Prov 26:11

so a fool r to his folly .... Prov 26:11
the wind r again according to his .... Eccl 1:6
r not thither, but watereth the .... Is 55:10
that passeth out and him that r .... Eze 35:7
by, and because of him that r .... Zec 9:8

RETURNING
In r and rest shall ye be saved .... Is 30:15
r to the house, found the servant .... Lk 7:10
Was r, and sitting in his chariot .... Acts 8:28
whom met Abraham from the .... Heb 7:1

REU (re'-u) See RAGAU. *Son of Peleg.*
lived thirty years, and begat R .... Gen 11:18
after he begat R two hundred .... Gen 11:19
R lived two and thirty years, and .... Gen 11:20
R lived after he begat Serug two .... Gen 11:21
Eber, Peleg, R, ... 1Chr 1:25

REUBEN (ru'-ben) See REUBENITE.
1. A son of Jacob and Leah.
a son, and she called his name R..................... Gen 29:32
R went in the days of wheat .... Gen 30:14
dwelt in that land, that R went .... Gen 35:22
R, Jacob's firstborn, and Simeon, ... Gen 35:23
R heard it, and he delivered him .... Gen 37:21
R said unto them, Shed no blood, ... Gen 37:22
And R returned unto the pit .... Gen 37:29
R answered them, saying, Spake I .... Gen 42:22
R spake unto his father, saying, ... Gen 42:37
R, Jacob's firstborn .... Gen 46:8
And the sons of R .... Gen 46:9
as R and Simeon, they shall be .... Gen 48:5
R, thou art my firstborn, my .... Gen 49:3
R, Simeon, Levi, and Judah, ... Ex 1:2
The sons of R the firstborn .... Ex 6:14
these be the families of R, ... Ex 6:14
And the children of R, Israel's, ... Num 1:20
On, the son of Peleth, sons of R, ... Num 16:1
R, the eldest son of Israel .... Num 26:5
the children of R .... Num 26:5
the sons of Eliab, the son of R .... Deut 11:6
the stone of Bohan the son of R .... Josh 15:6
the stone of Bohan the son of R .... Josh 18:17
R, Simeon, Levi, and Judah, ... 1Chr 2:1
Now the sons of R the firstborn 1Chr 5:1
of R the firstborn of Israel were 1Chr 5:3
2. Descendants of Reuben 1.
of the tribe of R, ... Num 1:5
of them, even of the tribe of R .... Num 1:21
of R according to their armies. .... Num 2:10
of R shall be Elizur the son of .... Num 2:10
of R were an hundred thousand. .... Num 2:16
prince of the children of R. .... Num 7:30
the standard of the camp of R set .... Num 10:18
of the tribe of R, Shammua the .... Num 13:4
Now the children of R had a .... Num 32:1
of Gad and the children of R came .... Num 32:2
of Gad and to the children of R .... Num 32:6
the children of R spake unto. .... Num 32:25
the children of R will pass with. .... Num 32:29
Gad and the children of R answered. .... Num 32:31
of Gad, and to the children of R .... Num 32:33
the children of R built Heshbon .... Num 32:37
the tribe of the children of R .... Num 34:14
R, Gad, and Asher. .... Num 34:14
Let R live, and not die .... Deut 33:6
And the children of R, and the .... Josh 4:12
the tribe of the children of R .... Josh 13:15
of the children of R was Jordan. .... Josh 13:23
of R after their families .... Josh 13:23
and Gad, and R, and half the tribe .... Josh 18:7
the plain out of the tribe of R .... Josh 20:8
had out of the tribe of R .... Josh 21:7
And out of the tribe of R, Bezer .... Josh 21:36
And the children of R and the .... Josh 22:9
land of Canaan, the children of R .... Josh 22:10
say, Behold, the children of R .... Josh 22:11
sent unto the children of R .... Josh 22:13
they came unto the children of R .... Josh 22:15
Then the children of R and the .... Josh 22:21
us and you, ye children of R .... Josh 22:25
the words that the children of R .... Josh 22:30
said unto the children of R .... Josh 22:31
returned from the children of R .... Josh 22:32
land wherein the children of R .... Josh 22:33
And the children of R and the .... Josh 22:34
For the divisions of R there were .... Judg 5:15
For the divisions of R there were .... Judg 5:16
The sons of R, and the Gadites, and 1Chr 5:18
families, out of the tribe of R 1Chr 6:63
given them out of the tribe of R 1Chr 6:78
the west side, a portion for R...................... Eze 48:6
And by the border of R, from .... Eze 48:7
one gate of R, one gate of Judah, ... Eze 48:31
Of the tribe of R were sealed .... Rev 7:5

REUBENITE (ru'-ben-ite) See REUBENITES. *A
descendant of Reuben.*
Adina the son of Shiza the R 1Chr 11:42

REUBENITES (ru'-ben-ites)
These are the families of the R..................... Num 26:7
cities thereof, gave I unto the R .... Deut 3:12
And unto the R and unto the Gadites .... Deut 3:16
in the plain country, of the R .... Deut 4:43
it for an inheritance unto the R .... Deut 29:8
And to the R, and to the Gadites, ... Josh 1:12
it for a possession unto the R .... Josh 12:6
With whom the R and the Gadites .... Josh 13:8
Then Joshua called the R, and the .... Josh 22:1
of Gilead, the Gadites, and the R 2Kin 10:33
he was prince of the R. 1Chr 5:6

he carried them away, even the R..................... 1Chr 5:26
the Reubenite, a captain of the R 1Chr 11:42
other side of Jordan, of the R 1Chr 12:37
king David made rulers over the R 1Chr 26:32
the ruler of the R was Eliezer....................... 1Chr 27:16

REUEL (re'u-el) See DEUEL, JETHRO, RAGUEL.
1. A son of Esau.
and Bashemath bare R .... Gen 36:4
R the son of Bashemath the wife .... Gen 36:10
And these are the sons of R .... Gen 36:13
are the sons of R Esau's son .... Gen 36:17
came of R in the land of Edom .... Gen 36:17
Eliphaz, R, and Jeush, and Jaalam. 1Chr 1:35
The sons of R 1Chr 1:37
2. Same as Jethro.
when they came to R their father. .... Ex 2:18
3. Father of Eliasaph.
shall be Eliasaph the son of R .... Num 2:14
4. A Benjamite.
son of Shephatiah, the son of R 1Chr 9:8

REUMAH (re-u'-mah) *Concubine of Nahor.*
his concubine, whose name was R.................. Gen 22:24

REVEAL
The heaven shall r his iniquity .... Job 20:27
will r unto them the abundance of .... Jer 33:6
seeing thou couldst r this secret .... Dan 2:47
to whomsoever the Son will r him .... Mt 11:27
and he to whom the Son will r him .... Lk 10:22
To r his Son in me, that I might .... Gal 1:16
God shall r even this unto you .... Phil 3:15

REVEALED
things which are r belong unto us. .... Deut 29:29
word of the LORD yet r unto him 1Sa 3:7
for the LORD r himself to Samuel 1Sa 3:21
hast r to thy servant, saying, I 2Sa 7:27
it was r in mine ears by the LORD .... Is 22:14
land of Chittim it is r to them .... Is 23:1
the glory of the LORD shall be r .... Is 40:5
to whom is the arm of the LORD r .... Is 53:1
and mine righteousness to be r .... Is 56:1
for unto thee have I r my cause .... Jer 11:20
Then was the secret r unto Daniel .... Dan 2:19
this secret is not r to me for .... Dan 2:30
Persia a thing was r unto Daniel .... Dan 10:1
covered, that shall not be r .... Mt 10:26
and hast r them unto babes .... Mt 11:25
and blood hath not r it unto thee .... Mt 16:17
it was r unto him by the Holy .... Lk 2:26
thoughts of many hearts may be r .... Lk 2:35
and hast r them unto babes .... Lk 10:21
covered, that shall not be r .... Lk 12:2
the day when the Son of man is r .... Lk 17:30
hath the arm of the Lord been r .... Jn 12:38
of God r from faith to faith. .... Rom 1:17
God is r from heaven against all .... Rom 1:18
the glory which shall be r in us. .... Rom 8:18
But God hath r them unto us by 1Cor 2:10
it, because it shall be r by fire 1Cor 3:13
If any thing be r to another that 1Cor 14:30
which should afterwards be r .... Gal 3:23
as it is now r unto his holy .... Eph 3:5
be r from heaven with his mighty 2Th 1:7
first, and that man of sin be r 2Th 2:3
that he might be r in his time. 2Th 2:6
And then shall that Wicked be r 2Th 2:8
ready to be r in the last time 1Pet 1:5
Unto whom it was r, that not unto 1Pet 1:12
that, when his glory shall be r 1Pet 4:13
of the glory that shall be r 1Pet 5:1

REVEALER
a r of secrets, seeing thou .... Dan 2:47

REVEALETH
A talebearer r secrets .... Prov 11:13
about as a talebearer r secrets .... Prov 20:19
He r the deep and secret things. .... Dan 2:22
is a God in heaven that r secrets. .... Dan 2:28
he that r secrets maketh known to .... Dan 2:29
but he r his secret unto his .... Amos 3:7

REVELATION
r of the righteous judgment of .... Rom 2:5
according to the r of the mystery .... Rom 16:25
I shall speak to you either by r 1Cor 14:6
doctrine, hath a tongue, hath a r 1Cor 14:26
but by the r of Jesus Christ .... Gal 1:12
And I went up by r, and .... Gal 2:2
r in the knowledge of him .... Eph 1:17
How that by r he made known unto .... Eph 3:3
unto you at the r of Jesus Christ 1Pet 1:13
The R of Jesus Christ, which God .... Rev 1:1

REVELATIONS
come to visions and r of the Lord 2Cor 12:1
through the abundance of the 2Cor 12:7

REVELLINGS
Envyings, murders, drunkenness, r .... Gal 5:21
lusts, excess of wine, r 1Pet 4:3

REVENGE
me, and r me of my persecutors .... Jer 15:15
and we shall take our r on him .... Jer 20:10
the Philistines have dealt by r .... Eze 25:15
yea, what zeal, yea, what r 2Cor 7:11
a readiness to r all disobedience 2Cor 10:6

REVENGED
offended, and r himself upon them .... Eze 25:12

REVENGER
The r of blood himself shall slay .... Num 35:19
the r of blood shall slay the. .... Num 35:21
the r of blood according to these .... Num 35:24
out of the hand of the r of blood .... Num 35:25
the r of blood find him without .... Num 35:27
the r of blood kill the slayer. .... Num 35:27
a r to execute wrath upon him .... Rom 13:4

REVENGERS
r of blood to destroy any more 2Sa 14:11

REVENGES
the beginning of r upon the enemy .... Deut 32:42

REVENGETH
God is jealous, and the LORD r .... Nah 1:2
the LORD r, and is furious. .... Nah 1:2

REVENGING
r of the blood of thy servants. .... Ps 79:10

REVENUE
shalt endamage the r of the kings .... Ezr 4:13
and my r than choice silver .... Prov 8:19
harvest of the river, is her r .... Is 23:3

REVENUES
but in the r of the wicked is .... Prov 15:6
than great r without right .... Prov 16:8
they shall be ashamed of your r .... Jer 12:13

REVERENCE
my sabbaths, and r my sanctuary .... Lev 19:30
my sabbaths, and r my sanctuary .... Lev 26:2
he fell on his face, and did r 2Sa 9:6
did r to the king, and said, Let 1Kin 1:31
Mordecai bowed not, nor did him r .... Est 3:2
Mordecai bowed not, nor did him r .... Est 3:5
to be had in r of all them that .... Ps 89:7
son, saying, They will r my son .... Mt 21:37
them, saying, They will r my son .... Mk 12:6
it may be they will r him when .... Lk 20:13
wife see that she r her husband .... Eph 5:33
corrected us, and we gave them r .... Heb 12:9
may serve God acceptably with r .... Heb 12:28

REVERENCED
gate's, bowed, and r Haman. .... Est 3:2

REVEREND
holy and r is his name .... Ps 111:9

REVERSE
and I cannot r it .... Num 23:20
let it be written to r the. .... Est 8:5
the king's ring, may no man r .... Est 8:8

REVILE
Thou shalt not r the gods .... Ex 22:28
are ye, when men shall r you .... Mt 5:11

REVILED
And they that passed by r him. .... Mt 27:39
were crucified with him r him .... Mk 15:32
Then they r him, and said, Thou .... Jn 9:28
being r, we bless 1Cor 4:12
when he was r, r not again. 1Pet 2:23

REVILERS
covetous, nor drunkards, nor r 1Cor 6:10

REVILEST
by said, R thou God's high priest................... Acts 23:4

REVILINGS
neither be ye afraid of their r .... Is 51:7
the r of the children of Ammon, ... Zeph 2:8

REVIVE
will they r the stones out of the .... Neh 4:2
Wilt thou not r us again .... Ps 85:6
midst of trouble, thou wilt r me .... Ps 138:7
to r the spirit of the humble, and .... Is 57:15
to r the heart of the contrite .... Is 57:15
After two days will he r us. .... Hos 6:2
they shall r as the corn, and grow .... Hos 14:7
r thy work in the midst of the .... Hab 3:2

REVIVED
spirit of Jacob their father .... Gen 45:27
his spirit came again, and he r .... Judg 15:19
came into him again, and he r 1Kin 17:22
touched the bones of Elisha, he r 2Kin 13:21
when the commandment came, sin r .... Rom 7:9
Christ both died, and rose, and r .... Rom 14:9

REVIVING
give us a little r in our bondage .... Ezr 9:8
kings of Persia, to give us a r .... Ezr 9:9

REVOLT
did Libnah r from under his hand 2Chr 21:10
ye will r more and more.............................. Is 1:5
our God, speaking oppression and r .... Is 59:13

REVOLTED
In his days Edom r from under the 2Kin 8:20
Yet Edom r from under the hand of 2Kin 8:22
Then Libnah r at the same time 2Kin 8:22
In his days the Edomites r from 2Chr 21:8
So the Edomites r from under the 2Chr 21:10
children of Israel have deeply r .... Is 31:6
they are r and gone. .... Jer 5:23

REVOLTERS
They are all grievous r, walking .... Jer 6:28
the r are profound to make .... Hos 5:2
all their princes are r. .... Hos 9:15

REVOLTING
But this people hath a r and a .... Jer 5:23

REWARD
shield, and thy exceeding great r .... Gen 15:1
for it is your r for your service .... Num 18:31
not persons, nor taketh r .... Deut 10:17
Cursed be he that taketh r to .... Deut 27:25
and will r them that hate me .... Deut 32:41
a full r be given thee of the .... Ruth 2:12
wherefore the LORD r thee good 1Sa 24:19
the LORD shall r the doer of evil 2Sa 3:39
given him a r for his tidings 2Sa 4:10
recompense it me with such a r 2Sa 19:36
thyself, and I will give thee a r 1Kin 13:7
Behold, I say, how they r us 2Chr 20:11
Give a r for me of your substance. .... Job 6:22
looketh for the r of his work .... Job 7:2
nor taketh r against the innocent .... Ps 15:5
keeping of them there is great r .... Ps 19:11
Let them be desolate for a r of .... Ps 40:15
He shall r evil unto mine enemies .... Ps 54:5
there is a r for the righteous .... Ps 58:11
for a r of their shame that say .... Ps 70:3
behold and see the r of the wicked .... Ps 91:8
render a r to the proud. .... Ps 94:2
Let this be the r of mine. .... Ps 109:20
and the fruit of the womb is his r. .... Ps 127:3
righteousness shall be a sure r .... Prov 11:18
a r in the bosom strong wrath .... Prov 21:14
found it, then there shall be a r .... Prov 24:14
shall be no r to the evil man. .... Prov 24:20
head, and the LORD shall r thee. .... Prov 25:22
have a good r for their labour .... Eccl 4:9
neither have they any more a r .... Eccl 9:5
for the r of his hands shall be. .... Is 3:11
Which justify the wicked for r .... Is 5:23
his r is with him, and his work .... Is 40:10
my captives, not for price nor r .... Is 45:13
his r is with him, and his work .... Is 62:11
guard gave him victuals and a r .... Eze 16:34
and in that thou givest a r .... Eze 16:34
and no r is given unto them, ... Eze 16:34
ways, and r them their doings .... Hos 4:9
that hath loved a r upon every .... Hos 9:1
thy shall return upon thine own .... Obad 15
The heads thereof judge for r .... Mic 3:11
and the judge asketh for a r .... Mic 7:3
for great is your r in heaven. .... Mt 5:12
which love you, what r have ye .... Mt 5:46
otherwise ye have no r of your .... Mt 6:1
I say unto you, They have their r. .... Mt 6:2
himself shall r thee openly .... Mt 6:4
I say unto you, They have their r. .... Mt 6:5
in secret shall r thee openly .... Mt 6:6
I say unto you, They have their r. .... Mt 6:16
in secret, shall r thee openly .... Mt 6:18
shall receive a prophet's r, ... Mt 10:41
shall receive a righteous man's r .... Mt 10:41
he shall in no wise lose his r. .... Mt 10:42
then he shall r every man. .... Mt 16:27
unto you, he shall not lose his r. .... Mk 9:41
your r is great in heaven. .... Lk 6:23
your r shall be great, and .... Lk 6:35
we receive the due r of our deeds. .... Lk 23:41
a field with the r of iniquity .... Acts 1:18
is the r not reckoned of grace .... Rom 4:4
own r according to his own labour 1Cor 3:8
thereupon, he shall receive a r. 1Cor 3:14
this thing willingly, I have a r. 1Cor 9:17
What is my r then 1Cor 9:18
of your r in a voluntary humility .... Col 2:18
receive the r of the inheritance. .... Col 3:24
The labourer is worthy of his r. 1Ti 5:18
the Lord r him according to his. 2Ti 4:14
received a just recompence of r .... Heb 2:2
which hath great recompence of r .... Heb 10:35
unto the recompence of the r. .... Heb 11:26
And shall receive the r of 2Pet 2:13
but that we receive a full r 2Jn 8
after the error of Balaam for r .... Jude 11
that thou shouldest give r unto .... Rev 11:18
R here even as she rewarded you, ... Rev 18:6
my r is with me, to give every .... Rev 22:12

REWARDED
Wherefore have ye r evil for good .... Gen 44:4
for thou hast r me good, whereas 1Sa 24:17
good, whereas I have r thee evil. 1Sa 24:17
The LORD r me according to my 2Sa 22:21
for your work shall be r. 2Chr 15:7
If I have r evil unto him that .... Ps 7:4
The LORD r me according to my .... Ps 18:20
They r me evil for good to the .... Ps 35:12
nor r us according to our .... Ps 103:10
they have r me evil for good, and .... Ps 109:5
the commandment shall be r. .... Prov 13:13
for they have r evil unto .... Is 3:9
for thy work shall be r, saith .... Jer 31:16
Reward her even as she r you .... Rev 18:6

REWARDER
that he is a r of them that .... Heb 11:6

REWARDETH
he r him, and he shall know it .... Job 21:19
plentifully r the proud doer .... Ps 31:23
that r thee as thou hast served .... Ps 137:8

Whoso r evil for good, evil shall .... Prov 17:13
formed all things both r the fool .... Prov 26:10
and r transgressors. .... Prov 26:10

REWARDS
the r of divination in their hand. .... Num 22:7
gifts, and followeth after r. .... Is 1:23
ye shall receive of the gifts and r .... Dan 2:6
thyself, and give thy r to another .... Dan 5:17
These are my r that my lovers .... Hos 2:12

REZEPH (re'-zef) A fortress near Haran.
Gozan, and Haran, and R 2Kin 19:12
as Gozan, and Haran, and R .... Is 37:12

REZIA (re-zi'-ah) Son of Ulla.
Arah, and Haniel, and R 1Chr 7:39

REZIN (re'-zin)
1. A king of Syria.
against Judah R the king of Syria 2Kin 15:37
Then R king of Syria and Pekah son...... 2Kin 16:5
At that time R king of Syria 2Kin 16:6
of it captive to Kir, and slew R 2Kin 16:9
the fierce anger of R with Syria .... Is 7:4
and the head of Damascus is R .... Is 7:8
that go softly, and rejoice in R .... Is 8:6
the adversaries of R against him .... Is 9:11
2. A family of slaves.
The children of R, the children .... Ezr 2:48
of Reaiah, the children of R .... Neh 7:50

REZON (re'-zon) An enemy of Solomon.
R the son of Eliadah, which fled............ 1Kin 11:23

RHEGIUM (re'-je-um) A port of southern Italy.
fetched a compass, and came to R .... Acts 28:13

RHESA (re'-sah) Son of Zorobabel; an ancestor of Jesus.
of Joanna, which was the son of .... Lk 3:27

RHODA (ro'-dah) A maiden in Mary's house.
a damsel came to hearken, named R. ..... Acts 12:13

RHODES (rodes) A Mediterranean island.
Coos, and the day following unto R....... Acts 21:1

RIB
And the r, which the LORD God had .... Gen 2:22
spear smote him under the fifth r 2Sa 2:23
smote him there under the fifth r 2Sa 3:27
they smote him under the fifth r 2Sa 4:6
him therewith in the fifth r 2Sa 20:10

RIBAI (rib'-ahee) Father of Ittai.
Ittai the son of R out of Gibeah 2Sa 23:29
Ithai the son of R of Gibeah 1Chr 11:31

RIBBAND
fringe of the borders a r of blue .... Num 15:38

RIBLAH (rib'-lah) A city on the Orontes River.
shall go down from Shepham to R .... Num 34:11
put him in bands at R in the land 2Kin 23:33
up to the king of Babylon to R 2Kin 25:6
them to the king of Babylon to R 2Kin 25:20
slew them at R in the land of 2Kin 25:21
king of Babylon to R in the land .... Jer 39:5
of Zedekiah at R before his eyes .... Jer 39:6
to R in the land of Hamath. .... Jer 52:9
all the princes of Judah in R. .... Jer 52:26
king of Babylon to R in the land .... Jer 52:26
put them to death in R in the .... Jer 52:27

RIBS
and he took one of his r, and .... Gen 2:21
it had three r in the mouth of it. .... Dan 7:5

RICH
And Abram was very r in cattle .... Gen 13:2
say, I have made Abram r .... Gen 14:23
The r shall not give more, and the .... Ex 30:15
or stranger wax r the more .... Lev 25:47
not young men, whether poor or r .... Ruth 3:10
The LORD maketh poor, and maketh r . 1Sa 2:7
the one r, and the other poor 2Sa 12:1
The r man had exceeding many 2Sa 12:2
came a traveller unto the r man 2Sa 12:4
He shall not be r, neither shall .... Job 15:29
The r man shall lie down, but he .... Job 27:19
nor regardeth the r more than the .... Job 34:19
came from r even among the people ..... Ps 45:12
Both low and high, r and poor, ... Ps 49:2
thou afraid when one is made r .... Ps 49:16
the hand of the diligent maketh r .... Prov 10:4
The r man's wealth is his strong .... Prov 10:15
blessing of the LORD, it maketh r .... Prov 10:22
There is that maketh himself r .... Prov 13:7
but the r hath many friends .... Prov 14:20
The r man's wealth is his strong .... Prov 18:11
but the r answereth roughly .... Prov 18:23
loveth wine and oil shall not be r .... Prov 21:17
The r and poor meet together. .... Prov 22:2
The r ruleth over the poor, and .... Prov 22:7
and he that giveth to the r .... Prov 22:16
Labour not to be r .... Prov 23:4
in his ways, though he be r .... Prov 28:6
The r man is wise in his own .... Prov 28:11
to be r shall not be innocent. .... Prov 28:20
hasteth to be r hath an evil eye .... Prov 28:22
but the abundance of the r will .... Eccl 5:12
and the r sit in low place. .... Eccl 10:6
curse not the r in thy bedchamber .... Eccl 10:20
and with the r in his death. .... Is 53:9
they are become great, and waxen r ..... Jer 5:27
let not the r man glory in his .... Jer 9:23

work, and in chests of r apparel .... Eze 27:24
Ephraim said, Yet I am become r .... Hos 12:8
For the r men thereof are full of .... Mic 6:12
for I am r .... Zec 11:5
That a r man shall hardly enter .... Mt 19:23
than for a r man to enter into .... Mt 19:24
there came a r man of Arimathaea, ... Mt 27:57
than for a r man to enter into .... Mk 10:25
and many that were r cast in much ...... Mk 12:41
the r he hath sent empty away .... Lk 1:53
But woe unto you that are r .... Lk 6:24
The ground of a certain r man .... Lk 12:16
himself, and is not r toward God .... Lk 12:21
thy kinsmen, nor thy r neighbours .... Lk 14:12
There was a certain r man. .... Lk 16:1
There was a certain r man, ... Lk 16:19
which fell from the r man's table .... Lk 16:21
the r man also died, and was .... Lk 16:22
for he was very r .... Lk 18:23
than for a r man to enter into .... Lk 18:25
among the publicans, and he was r ...... Lk 19:2
saw the r men casting their gifts .... Lk 21:1
Now ye are full, now ye are r 1Cor 4:8
as poor, yet making many r 2Cor 6:10
Christ, that, though he was r 2Cor 8:9
ye through his poverty might be r 2Cor 8:9
who is r in mercy, for his great .... Eph 2:4
will be r fall into temptation. 1Ti 6:9
them that are r in this world. 1Ti 6:17
that they be r in good works, ... 1Ti 6:18
But the r, in that he is made low .... Jas 1:10
so also shall the r man fade away .... Jas 1:11
the poor of this world r in faith .... Jas 2:5
Do not r men oppress you, and draw.... Jas 2:6
ye r men, weep and howl for your .... Jas 5:1
and poverty, (but thou art r) .... Rev 2:9
Because thou sayest, I am r .... Rev 3:17
the fire, that thou mayest be r .... Rev 3:18
and the great men, and the r men .... Rev 6:15
all, both small and great, ... Rev 13:16
of the earth are waxed r through .... Rev 18:3
things, which were made r by her .... Rev 18:15
wherein were made r all that had .... Rev 18:19

RICHER
shall be far r than they all. .... Dan 11:2

RICHES
For all the r which God hath .... Gen 31:16
For their r were more than that .... Gen 36:7
with much r unto your tents .... Josh 22:8
king will enrich him with great r 1Sa 17:25
neither hast asked r for thyself 1Kin 3:11
which thou hast not asked, both r 1Kin 3:13
all the kings of the earth for r 1Kin 10:23
Both r and honour come 1Chr 29:12
a good old age, full of days, r, ... 1Chr 29:28
heart, and thou hast not asked r 2Chr 1:11
and I will give thee r, and wealth, ... 2Chr 1:12
all the kings of the earth in r 2Chr 9:22
and he had r and honour in 2Chr 17:5
Now Jehoshaphat had r and honour 2Chr 18:1
both r with the dead bodies. 2Chr 20:25
had exceeding much r 2Chr 32:27
When he shewed the r of his .... Est 1:4
told them of the glory of his r .... Est 5:11
He hath swallowed down r, and he ...... Job 20:15
Will he esteem thy r .... Job 36:19
better than the r of many wicked. .... Ps 37:16
he heapeth up r, and knoweth not .... Ps 39:6
in the multitude of their r .... Ps 49:6
trusted in the abundance of his r .... Ps 52:7
if r increase, set not your heart. .... Ps 62:10
they increase in r .... Ps 73:12
the earth is full of thy r .... Ps 104:24
Wealth and r shall be in his house ...... Ps 112:3
testimonies, as much as in all r .... Ps 119:14
and in her left hand r and honour .... Prov 3:16
R and honour are with me, ... Prov 8:18
yea, durable r and righteousness .... Prov 8:18
R profit not in the day of wrath .... Prov 11:4
and strong men retain r .... Prov 11:16
that trusteth in his r shall fall .... Prov 11:28
himself poor, yet hath great r .... Prov 13:7
ransom of a man's life are his r .... Prov 13:8
The crown of the wise is their r .... Prov 14:24
r are the inheritance of fathers. .... Prov 19:14
rather to be chosen than great r .... Prov 22:1
and the fear of the LORD are r .... Prov 22:4
the poor to increase his r .... Prov 22:16
for r certainly make themselves .... Prov 23:5
with all precious and pleasant r .... Prov 24:4
For r are not for ever .... Prov 27:24
give me neither poverty nor r .... Prov 30:8
is his eye satisfied with r .... Eccl 4:8
r kept for the owners thereof to. .... Eccl 5:13
But those r perish by evil .... Eccl 5:14
man also to whom God hath given r ..... Eccl 5:19
A man to whom God hath given r .... Eccl 6:2
nor yet r to men of understanding .... Eccl 9:11
the r of Damascus and the spoil of ...... Is 8:4
as a nest the r of the people .... Is 10:14
they will carry their r upon the .... Is 30:6
hidden r of secret places, that .... Is 45:3
shall eat the r of the Gentiles .... Is 61:6
not the rich man glory in his r .... Jer 9:23
so he that getteth r, and not by .... Jer 17:11
because the r that he hath gotten .... Jer 48:36
they shall make a spoil of thy r .... Eze 26:12
of the multitude of all kind of r .... Eze 27:12

for the multitude of all r .... Eze 27:18
Thy r, and thy fairs, thy .... Eze 27:27
earth with the multitude of thy r .... Eze 27:33
thou hast gotten thee r, and hast .... Eze 28:4
hast thou increased thy r .... Eze 28:5
is lifted up because of thy r .... Eze 28:5
by his strength through his r he .... Dan 11:2
with a great army and with much r ...... Dan 11:13
them the prey, and spoil, and r .... Dan 11:24
return into his land with great r ...... Dan 11:28
world, and the deceitfulness of .... Mt 13:22
world, and the deceitfulness of r ...... Mk 4:19
r enter into the kingdom of God .... Mk 10:23
in r to enter into the kingdom of ...... Mk 10:24
and are choked with cares and r .... Lk 8:14
commit to your trust the true r .... Lk 16:11
r enter into the kingdom of God .... Lk 18:24
thou the r of his goodness .... Rom 2:4
that he might make known the r of ...... Rom 9:23
of them be the r of the world .... Rom 11:12
of them the r of the Gentiles .... Rom 11:12
depth of the r both of the wisdom ...... Rom 11:33
unto the r of their liberality 2Cor 8:2
according to the r of his grace .... Eph 1:7
what the r of the glory of his .... Eph 1:18
he might shew the exceeding r of .... Eph 2:7
the unsearchable r of Christ .... Eph 3:8
according to the r of his glory .... Eph 3:16
to his r in glory by Christ Jesus ...... Phil 4:19
r of the glory of this mystery .... Col 1:27
unto all r of the full assurance .... Col 2:2
nor trust in uncertain r 1Ti 6:17
r than the treasures in Egypt .... Heb 11:26
Your r are corrupted, and your .... Jas 5:2
was slain to receive power, and r ...... Rev 5:12
hour so great r is come to nought ...... Rev 18:17

RICHLY

dwell in you r in all wisdom .... Col 3:16
who giveth us r all things to 1Ti 6:17

RID

that he might r him out of their .... Gen 37:22
I will r you out of their bondage ...... Ex 6:6
I will r evil beasts out of the .... Lev 26:6
r them out of the hand of their .... Ps 82:4
r me, and deliver me from the hand ..... Ps 144:7
R me, and deliver me from the hand ..... Ps 144:11

RIDDANCE

thou shalt not make clean r of .... Lev 23:22
r of all them that dwell in the .... Zeph 1:18

RIDDEN

upon which thou hast r ever since ..... Num 22:30

RIDDLE

I will now put forth a r unto you ..... Judg 14:12
said unto him, Put forth thy r .... Judg 14:13
not in three days expound the r .... Judg 14:14
that he may declare unto us the r ..... Judg 14:15
thou hast put forth a r unto the ...... Judg 14:16
she told the r to the children of ..... Judg 14:17
heifer, ye had not found out my r ..... Judg 14:18
unto them which expounded the r .... Judg 14:19
Son of man, put forth a r .... Eze 17:2

RIDE

he made him to r in the second .... Gen 41:43
He made him r on the high places ..... Deut 32:13
ye that r on white asses, ye that ..... Judg 5:10
for the king's household to r on 2Sa 16:2
me an ass, that I may r thereon 2Sa 19:26
my son to r upon mine own mule 1Kin 1:33
caused Solomon to r upon king 1Kin 1:38
him to r upon the king's mule 1Kin 1:44
So they made him r in his chariot 2Kin 10:16
thou causest me to r upon it .... Job 30:22
in thy majesty r prosperously .... Ps 45:4
caused men to r over our heads .... Ps 66:12
and, We will r upon the swift .... Is 30:16
I will cause thee to r upon the ..... Is 58:14
they r upon horses, set in array ..... Jer 6:23
they shall r upon horses, every ..... Jer 50:42
I will make Ephraim to r .... Hos 10:11
thou didst r upon thine .... Hab 3:8
chariots, and those that r in them .. Hag 2:22

RIDER

so that his r shall fall backward .... Gen 49:17
his r hath he thrown into the sea .... Ex 15:1
his r hath he thrown into the sea .... Ex 15:21
she scorneth the horse and his r ..... Job 39:18
in pieces the horse and his r .... Jer 51:21
in pieces the chariot and his r ...... Jer 51:21
and his r with madness .... Zec 12:4

RIDERS

on thy part to set r upon them 2Kin 18:23
r on mules, camels, and young .... Est 8:10
on thy part to set r upon them ...... Is 36:8
their r shall come down, every ...... Hag 2:22
them, and the r on horses shall ..... Zec 10:5

RIDETH

what saddle soever he r upon that .... Lev 15:9
who r upon the heaven in thy help .... Deut 33:26
and the horse that the king r upon ... Est 6:9
extol him that r upon the heavens .... Ps 68:4
To him that r upon the heavens of .... Ps 68:33
the LORD r upon a swift cloud, and ... Is 19:1
neither shall he that r the horse .... Amos 2:15

RIDGES

Thou waterest the r thereof .... Ps 65:10

RIDING

Now he was r upon his ass, and his ... Num 22:22
slack not thy r for me, except I 2Kin 4:24
r in chariots and on horses, they, ... Jer 17:25
r in chariots and on horses, he, ... Jer 22:4
young men, horsemen r upon horses .... Eze 23:6
horsemen r upon horses, all of .... Eze 23:12
all of them r upon horses .... Eze 23:23
thee, all of them r upon horses ...... Eze 38:15
behold a man r upon a red horse, ... Zec 1:8
r upon an ass, and upon a colt the ... Zec 9:9

RIE

wheat and the r were not smitten ..... Ex 9:32
barley and the r in their place ...... Is 28:25

RIFLED

shall be taken, and the houses r ..... Zec 14:2

RIGHT

hand, then I will go to the r .... Gen 13:9
or if thou depart to the r hand ...... Gen 13:9
the Judge of all the earth do r ...... Gen 18:25
in the r way to take my master's ..... Gen 24:48
that I may turn to the r hand .... Gen 24:49
Ephraim in his r hand toward .... Gen 48:13
left hand toward Israel's hand .... Gen 48:13
Israel stretched out his r hand ...... Gen 48:14
saw that his father laid his r .... Gen 48:17
put thy r hand upon his head .... Gen 48:18
a wall unto them on their r hand ..... Ex 14:22
a wall unto them on their r hand ..... Ex 14:29
Thy r hand, O LORD, is become .... Ex 15:6
thy r hand, O LORD, hath dashed ...... Ex 15:6
Thou stretchedst out thy r hand ...... Ex 15:12
do that which is r in his sight ...... Ex 15:26
the tip of the r ear of Aaron .... Ex 29:20
the tip of the r ear of his sons ..... Ex 29:20
and upon the thumb of their r hand ... Ex 29:20
the great toe of their r foot .... Ex 29:20
is upon them, and the r shoulder ..... Ex 29:22
the r shoulder shall ye give unto .... Lev 7:32
shall have the r shoulder for his .... Lev 7:33
it upon the tip of Aaron's r ear ..... Lev 8:23
and upon the thumb of his r hand ..... Lev 8:23
upon the great toe of his r foot ..... Lev 8:23
blood upon the tip of their r ear .... Lev 8:24
upon the thumbs of their r hands ..... Lev 8:24
the great toes of their r feet .... Lev 8:24
and their fat, and the r shoulder .... Lev 8:26
the fat, and upon the r shoulder ..... Lev 8:26
the r shoulder Aaron waved for a ..... Lev 9:21
of the r ear of him that is to be .... Lev 14:14
and upon the thumb of his r hand ..... Lev 14:14
upon the great toe of his r foot ..... Lev 14:14
the priest shall dip his r finger ... Lev 14:16
of the r ear of him that is to ...... Lev 14:17
and upon the thumb of his r hand .... Lev 14:17
upon the great toe of his r foot .... Lev 14:17
of the r ear of him that is to ...... Lev 14:25
and upon the thumb of his r hand .... Lev 14:25
upon the great toe of his r foot .... Lev 14:25
r finger some of the oil that is .... Lev 14:27
of the r ear of him that is to be ... Lev 14:28
and upon the thumb of his r hand .... Lev 14:28
upon the great toe of his r foot .... Lev 14:28
as the r shoulder are thine .... Num 18:18
to the r hand nor to the left .... Num 20:17
to the r hand or to the left .... Num 22:26
daughters of Zelophehad speak r ..... Num 27:7
unto the r hand nor to the left ..... Deut 5:27
to the r hand nor to the left .... Deut 5:32
And thou shalt do that which is r ... Deut 6:18
whatsoever is r in his own eyes ..... Deut 12:8
is r in the sight of the LORD .... Deut 12:25
r in the sight of the LORD thy ...... Deut 12:28
to do that which is r in the eyes ... Deut 13:18
shall shew thee, to the r hand ...... Deut 17:11
the commandment, to the r hand ..... Deut 17:20
is r in the sight of the LORD ...... Deut 21:9
the r of the firstborn is his ...... Deut 21:17
this day, the r hand .... Deut 28:14
without iniquity, just and r is he .. Deut 32:4
from his r hand went a fiery law ... Deut 33:2
it to the r hand or to the left .... Josh 1:7
passed over r against Jericho ...... Josh 3:16
r unto thee to do unto us, do ...... Josh 9:25
r hand unto the inhabitants of ..... Josh 17:7
to the r hand or to the left .... Josh 23:6
his raiment upon his r thigh .... Judg 3:16
took the dagger from his r thigh ... Judg 3:21
her r hand to the workmen's .... Judg 5:26
in their r hands to blow withal ... Judg 7:20
could not frame to pronounce it r .. Judg 12:6
up, of the one with his r hand .... Judg 16:29
that which was r in his own eyes ... Judg 17:6
that which was r in his own eyes ... Judg 21:25
redeem thou my r to thyself .... Ruth 4:6
to the r hand or to the left 1Sa 6:12
I may thrust out all your r eyes .. 1Sa 11:2
teach you the good and the r way .. 1Sa 12:23
the r hand nor to the left 1Sa 12:20
to thy r hand or to thy left 2Sa 2:21
none can turn to the r hand or to . 2Sa 14:19
See, thy matters are good and r ... 2Sa 15:3
the mighty men were on his r hand . 2Sa 16:6
What r therefore have I yet to 2Sa 19:28
have also more r in David than ye . 2Sa 19:43
beard with the r hand to kiss him . 2Sa 20:9

on the r side of the city that 2Sa 24:5
and she sat on his r hand 1Kin 2:19
was in the r side of the house 1Kin 6:8
and he set up the r pillar 1Kin 7:21
bases on the r side of the house ... 1Kin 7:39
he set the sea on the r side of 1Kin 7:39
of pure gold, five on the r side ... 1Kin 7:49
only which was r in mine eyes 1Kin 11:33
do that which is r in mine eyes 1Kin 11:38
do that is r in my sight, to keep .. 1Kin 11:38
only which was r in mine eyes 1Kin 14:8
was r in the eyes of the LORD 1Kin 15:5
Asa did that which was r in the 1Kin 15:11
standing by him on his r hand 1Kin 22:19
doing that which was r in the 1Kin 22:43
and said to him, Is thine heart r .. 2Kin 10:15
that which is r in mine eyes 2Kin 10:30
from the r corner of the temple 2Kin 11:11
Jehoash did that which was r in 2Kin 12:2
on the r side as one cometh into ... 2Kin 12:9
he did that which was r in the 2Kin 14:3
he did that which was r in the 2Kin 15:3
he did that which was r in the 2Kin 15:34
did not that which was r in the 2Kin 16:2
not against the LORD their God 2Kin 17:9
he did that which was r in the 2Kin 18:3
he did that which was r in the 2Kin 22:2
to the r hand or to the left 2Kin 22:2
which were on the r hand of the ... 2Kin 23:13
Asaph, who stood on his r hand 1Chr 6:39
and could use both the r hand 1Chr 12:2
for the thing was r in the eyes .. 1Chr 13:4
the temple, one on the r hand 1Chr 6:39
name of that on the r hand Jachin . 2Chr 3:17
lavers, and put five on the r hand . 2Chr 4:6
in the temple, five on the r hand . 2Chr 4:7
in the temple, five on the r side . 2Chr 4:8
sea on the r side of the east end . 2Chr 4:10
r in the eyes of the LORD his God . 2Chr 14:2
of heaven standing on his r hand . 2Chr 18:18
doing that which was r in the 2Chr 20:32
from the r side of the temple to . 2Chr 23:10
Joash did that which was r in the . 2Chr 24:2
he did that which was r in the ... 2Chr 25:2
he did that which was r in the ... 2Chr 26:4
he did that which was r in the ... 2Chr 27:2
was r in the sight of the LORD ... 2Chr 28:1
was r in the sight of the LORD ... 2Chr 29:2
wrought that which was good and r . 2Chr 31:20
he did that which was r in the ... 2Chr 34:2
and declined neither to the r hand . 2Chr 34:2
to seek of him a r way for us .... Ezr 8:21
but ye have no portion, nor r .... Neh 2:20
and Maaseiah, on his r hand ...... Neh 8:4
and gavest them r judgments ...... Neh 9:13
for thou hast done r, but we have . Neh 9:33
whereof one went on the r hand ... Neh 12:31
the thing seem r before the king, . Est 8:5
How terrible are r words .... Job 6:25
he hideth himself on the r hand .. Job 23:9
Upon my r hand rise the youth .... Job 30:12
and perverted that which was r ... Job 33:27
Should I lie against my r .... Job 34:6
even he that hateth r govern ..... Job 34:17
will not lay upon man more than r . Job 34:23
Thinkest thou this to be r .... Job 35:2
but giveth r to the poor .... Job 36:6
thine own r hand can save thee ... Job 40:14
spoken of me the thing that is r . Job 42:7
spoken of me the thing which is r . Job 42:8
For thou hast maintained my r .... Ps 9:4
satest in the throne judging r ... Ps 9:4
because he is at my r hand .... Ps 16:8
at thy r hand there are pleasures . Ps 16:11
Hear the r, O LORD, attend unto .. Ps 17:1
O thou that savest by thy r hand . Ps 17:7
thy r hand hath holden me up, and . Ps 18:35
The statutes of the LORD are r ... Ps 19:8
the saving strength of his r hand . Ps 20:6
thy r hand shall find out those .. Ps 21:8
their r hand is full of bribes ... Ps 26:10
For the word of the LORD is r .... Ps 33:4
but thy r hand, and thine arm, and . Ps 44:3
thy r hand shall teach thee ...... Ps 45:4
of thy kingdom is a r sceptre .... Ps 45:6
upon thy r hand did stand the .... Ps 45:9
shall help her, and that r early .. Ps 46:5
thy r hand is full of .... Ps 48:10
renew a r spirit within me .... Ps 51:10
save with thy r hand, and hear me . Ps 60:5
thy r hand upholdeth me .... Ps 63:8
thou hast holden me by my r hand . Ps 73:23
thou, thy hand, even thy r hand .. Ps 74:11
of the r hand of the most High ... Ps 77:10
their heart was not r with him ... Ps 78:37
which his r hand had purchased ... Ps 78:54
which thy r hand hath planted .... Ps 80:15
be upon the man of thy r hand, ... Ps 80:17
thy hand, and high is thy r hand . Ps 89:13
sea, and his r hand in the rivers . Ps 89:25
Thou hast set up the r hand of .. Ps 89:42
and ten thousand at thy r hand .. Ps 91:7
his r hand, and his holy arm, hath . Ps 98:1
And he led them forth by the r way . Ps 107:7
save with thy r hand, and answer . Ps 108:6
and let Satan stand at his r hand . Ps 109:6
stand at the r hand of the poor .. Ps 109:31
my Lord, Sit thou at my r hand ... Ps 110:1
The LORD at thy r hand shall .... Ps 110:5
the r hand of the LORD doeth .... Ps 118:15
The r hand of the LORD is exalted . Ps 118:16

the r hand of the LORD doeth .... Ps 118:16
O LORD, that thy judgments are r ..... Ps 119:75
concerning all things to be r .... Ps 119:128
LORD is thy shade upon thy r hand ... Ps 121:5
let my r hand forget her cunning .... Ps 137:5
and thy r hand shall save me .... Ps 138:7
me, and thy r hand shall hold me ..... Ps 139:10
and that my soul knoweth r well .... Ps 139:14
afflicted, and the r of the poor .... Ps 140:12
I looked on my r hand, and beheld, ... Ps 142:4
their r hand is a r hand of .... Ps 144:8
their r hand is a r hand of .... Ps 144:11
Length of days is in her r hand .... Prov 3:16
I have led thee in r paths .... Prov 4:11
Let thine eyes look r on, and let....... Prov 4:25
Turn not to the r hand nor to the ..... Prov 4:27
of my lips shall be r things .... Prov 8:6
r to them that find knowledge .... Prov 8:9
passengers who go r on their ways..... Prov 9:15
thoughts of the righteous are r .... Prov 12:5
of a fool is r in his own eyes............ Prov 12:15
a way which seemeth r unto a man ... Prov 14:12
than great revenues without r .... Prov 16:8
and they love him that speaketh r..... Prov 16:13
a way that seemeth r unto a man ...... Prov 16:25
work be pure, and whether it be r ..... Prov 20:11
way of a man is r in his own eyes...... Prov 21:2
as for the pure, his work is r .... Prov 21:8
when thy lips speak r things .... Prov 23:16
his lips that giveth a r answer .... Prov 24:26
and the ointment of his r hand .... Prov 27:16
all travail, and every r work .... Eccl 4:4
wise man's heart is at his r hand....... Eccl 10:2
his r hand doth embrace me.............. Song 2:6
his r hand should embrace me.......... Song 8:3
And he shall snatch on the r hand ... Is 9:20
to take away the r from the poor........ Is 10:2
Prophesy not unto us r things........... Is 30:10
in it, when ye turn to the r hand....... Is 30:21
even when the needy speaketh r........ Is 32:7
the r hand of my righteousness .... Is 41:10
LORD thy God will hold thy r hand ... Is 41:13
Is there not a lie in my r hand......... Is 44:20
whose r hand I have holden, to .... Is 45:1
I declare things that are r .... Is 45:19
I break, and I have spanned the........ Is 48:13
shalt break forth on the r hand .... Is 54:3
The LORD hath sworn by his r hand .. Is 62:8
That led them by the r hand of .... Is 63:12
a noble vine, wholly a r seed .... Jer 2:21
the r of the needy do they not .... Jer 5:28
that getteth riches, and not by r...... Jer 17:11
out of my lips was r before thee........ Jer 17:16
were the signet upon my r hand....... Jer 22:24
is evil, and their force is not r .... Jer 23:10
for the r of redemption is thine ...... Jer 32:7
for the r of inheritance is thine ...... Jer 32:8
had done r in my sight, in .... Jer 34:15
be driven out every man r forth....... Jer 49:5
he hath drawn back his r hand .... Lam 2:3
he stood with his r hand as an .... Lam 2:4
To turn aside the r of a man .... Lam 3:35
the face of a lion, on the r side....... Eze 1:10
them, lie again on thy r side........... Eze 4:6
stood on the r side of the house ...... Eze 10:3
that dwelleth at thy r hand............. Eze 16:46
and do that which is lawful and r ... Eze 18:5
done that which is lawful and r........ Eze 18:19
and do that which is lawful and r..... Eze 18:21
doeth that which is lawful and r ...... Eze 18:27
or other, either on the r hand......... Eze 21:16
At his r hand was the divination...... Eze 21:22
more, until he come whose r it is ... Eze 21:27
and do that which is lawful and r..... Eze 33:14
done that which is lawful and r........ Eze 33:16
and do that which is lawful and r..... Eze 33:19
arrows to fall out of thy r hand....... Eze 39:3
from the r side of the house .... Eze 47:1
ran out waters on the r side .... Eze 47:2
river, when he held up his r hand.... Dan 12:7
for the ways of the LORD are r .... Hos 14:9
For they know not to do r .... Amos 3:10
the poor in the gate from their r...... Amos 5:12
discern between their r hand.......... Jonah 4:11
the cup of the LORD's r hand.......... Hab 2:16
at his r hand to resist him.............. Zec 3:1
one upon the r side of the bowl....... Zec 4:3
the r side of the candlestick............ Zec 4:11
upon his arm, and upon his r eye..... Zec 11:17
his r eye shall be utterly................. Zec 11:17
people round about, on the r hand... Zec 12:6
aside the stranger from his r .... Mal 3:5
if thy r eye offend thee, pluck......... Mt 5:29
if thy r hand offend thee, cut it ...... Mt 5:30
shall smite thee on thy r cheek........ Mt 5:39
hand know what thy r hand doeth.... Mt 6:3
whatsoever is r I will give you......... Mt 20:4
and whatsoever is r, that shall ye..... Mt 20:7
may sit, the one on thy r hand......... Mt 20:21
but to sit on my r hand, and on my .. Mt 20:23
my Lord, Sit thou on my r hand....... Mt 22:44
shall set the sheep on his r hand..... Mt 25:33
King say unto them on his r hand.... Mt 25:34
sitting on the r hand of power .... Mt 26:64
his head, and a reed in his r hand... Mt 27:29
with him, one on the r hand, ... Mt 27:38
and clothed, and in his r mind........ Mk 5:15
we may sit, one on thy r hand .... Mk 10:37
But to sit on my r hand and on my .. Mk 10:40
to my Lord, Sit thou on my r hand .. Mk 12:36

sitting on the r hand of power .... Mk 14:62
the one on his r hand, and the .... Mk 15:27
a young man sitting on the r side..... Mk 16:5
and sat on the r hand of God.......... Mk 16:19
of the Lord standing on the r .... Lk 1:11
a man whose r hand was withered.... Lk 6:6
Jesus, clothed, and in his r mind...... Lk 8:35
unto him, Thou hast answered r ...... Lk 10:28
yourselves judge ye not what is r ..... Lk 12:57
my Lord, Sit thou on my r hand....... Lk 20:42
high priest, and cut off his r ear...... Lk 22:50
on the r hand of the power of God... Lk 22:69
malefactors, one on the r hand........ Lk 23:33
servant, and cut off his r ear........... Jn 18:10
the net on the r side of the ship...... Jn 21:6
my face, for he is on my r hand....... Acts 2:25
by the r hand of God exalted........... Acts 2:33
my Lord, Sit thou on my r hand....... Acts 2:34
And he took him by the r hand .... Acts 3:7
Whether it be r in the sight of........ Acts 4:19
with his r hand to be a Prince......... Acts 5:31
standing on the r hand of God......... Acts 7:55
man standing on the r hand of God.. Acts 7:56
is not r in the sight of God .... Acts 8:21
to pervert the r ways of the Lord..... Acts 13:10
who is even at the r hand of God ..... Rom 8:34
of righteousness on the r hand........ 2Cor 6:7
to me and Barnabas the r hands of ... Gal 2:9
set him at his own r hand in the ..... Eph 1:20
for this is r .... Eph 6:1
sitteth on the r hand of God .... Col 3:1
sat down on the r hand of the......... Heb 1:3
he at any times, Sit on my r hand.... Heb 1:13
who is set on the r hand of the........ Heb 8:1
sat down on the r hand of the......... Heb 10:12
is set down at the r hand of the....... Heb 12:2
whereof they have no r to eat.......... Heb 13:10
and is on the r hand of God 1Pet 3:22
Which have forsaken the r way 2Pet 2:15
he had in his r hand seven stars...... Rev 1:16
he laid his r hand upon me, ... Rev 1:17
which thou sawest in my r hand....... Rev 2:1
the seven stars in his r hand........... Rev 2:1
I saw in the r hand of him that .... Rev 5:1
took the book out of the r hand ...... Rev 5:7
he set his r foot upon the sea, ... Rev 10:2
to receive a mark in their r hand..... Rev 13:16
that they may have r to the tree ...... Rev 22:14

RIGHTEOUS

thee have I seen r before me .... Gen 7:1
destroy the r with the wicked .... Gen 18:23
there be fifty r within the city .... Gen 18:24
for the fifty r that are therein.......... Gen 18:24
to slay the r with the wicked .... Gen 18:25
that the r should be as the .... Gen 18:25
in Sodom fifty r within the city........ Gen 18:26
shall lack five of the fifty r .... Gen 18:28
wilt thou slay also a r nation........... Gen 20:4
said, She hath been more r than I.... Gen 38:26
The LORD is r, and I and my people . Ex 9:27
the innocent and r slay thou not...... Ex 23:7
and perverteth the words of the r..... Ex 23:8
Let me die the death of the r .... Num 23:10
judgments so r as all this law,......... Deut 4:8
and pervert the words of the r......... Deut 16:19
then they shall justify the r............. Deut 25:1
rehearse the r acts of the LORD .... Judg 5:11
even the r acts toward the .... Judg 5:11
of all the r acts of the LORD 1Sa 12:7
to David, Thou art more r than I 1Sa 24:17
a r person in his own house upon..... 2Sa 4:11
who fell upon two men more r 1Kin 2:32
and justifying the r, to give him...... 1Kin 8:32
said to all the people, Ye be r 2Kin 10:9
and by justifying the r, by giving..... 2Chr 6:23
and they said, The LORD is r 2Chr 12:6
O LORD God of Israel, thou art r....... Ezr 9:15
for thou art r .... Neh 9:8
or where were the r cut off............. Job 4:7
Whom, though I were r, yet would.... Job 9:15
and if I be r, yet will I not lift .... Job 9:15
of a woman, that he should be r....... Job 15:14
The r also shall hold on his way, ... Job 17:9
to the Almighty, that thou art r .... Job 22:3
The r see it, and are glad .... Job 22:19
There the r might dispute with........ Job 23:7
because he was r in his own eyes..... Job 32:1
For Job hath said, I am r .... Job 33:12
If thou be r, what givest thou .... Job 35:7
not his eyes from the r .... Job 36:7
condemn me, that thou mayest be r.. Job 40:8
in the congregation of the r............. Ps 1:5
the LORD knoweth the way of the r... Ps 1:6
For thou, Lord, wilt bless the r........ Ps 5:12
for the r God trieth the hearts......... Ps 7:9
God judgeth the r, and God is......... Ps 7:11
be destroyed, what can the r do ...... Ps 11:3
the LORD trieth the r .... Ps 11:5
For the r LORD loveth .... Ps 11:7
his countenance doth behold the r ... Ps 11:7
God is in the generation of the r...... Ps 14:5
the LORD are true and r altogether... Ps 19:9
and contemptuously against the r..... Ps 31:18
in the LORD, and rejoice, ye r.......... Ps 32:11
Rejoice in the LORD, O ye r .... Ps 33:1
eyes of the LORD are upon the r....... Ps 34:15
The r cry, and the LORD heareth,..... Ps 34:17
Many are the afflictions of the r....... Ps 34:19
that hate the r shall be desolate...... Ps 34:21
be glad, that favour my r cause .... Ps 35:27
A little that a r man hath is .... Ps 37:16

but the LORD upholdeth the r.......... Ps 37:17
but the r sheweth mercy, and.......... Ps 37:21
have I not seen the r forsaken .... Ps 37:25
The r shall inherit the land, and...... Ps 37:29
mouth of the r speaketh wisdom ...... Ps 37:30
The wicked watcheth the r .... Ps 37:32
salvation of the r is of the LORD ...... Ps 37:39
The r also shall see, and fear, and ... Ps 52:6
never suffer the r to be moved......... Ps 55:22
The r shall rejoice when he seeth..... Ps 58:10
there is a reward for the r .... Ps 58:11
The r shall be glad in the LORD,....... Ps 64:10
But let the r be glad .... Ps 68:3
and not be written with the r .... Ps 69:28
In his days shall the r flourish .... Ps 72:7
horns of the r shall be exalted......... Ps 75:10
The r shall flourish like the .... Ps 92:12
against the soul of the r .... Ps 94:21
Light is sown for the r, and............. Ps 97:11
Rejoice in the LORD, ye r .... Ps 97:12
The r shall see it, and rejoice.......... Ps 107:42
and full of compassion, and .... Ps 112:4
the r shall be in everlasting............ Ps 112:6
Gracious is the LORD, and r............. Ps 116:5
is in the tabernacles of the r........... Ps 118:15
into which the r shall enter .... Ps 118:20
have learned thy r judgments.......... Ps 119:7
thee because of thy r judgments...... Ps 119:62
that I will keep thy r judgments...... Ps 119:106
R art thou, O LORD, and upright...... Ps 119:137
that thou hast commanded are r ...... Ps 119:138
every one of thy r judgments.......... Ps 119:160
thee because of thy r judgments...... Ps 119:164
not rest upon the lot of the r .... Ps 125:3
lest the r put forth their hands........ Ps 125:3
The LORD is r .... Ps 129:4
Surely the r shall give thanks.......... Ps 140:13
Let the r smite me .... Ps 141:5
the r shall compass me about.......... Ps 142:7
The LORD is r in all his ways, and ... Ps 145:17
the LORD loveth the r .... Ps 146:8
layeth up sound wisdom for the r..... Prov 2:7
men, and keep the paths of the r...... Prov 2:20
but his secret is with the r .... Prov 3:32
the soul of the r to famish .... Prov 10:3
The mouth of a r man is a well of.... Prov 10:11
labour of the r tendeth to life......... Prov 10:16
The lips of the r feed many............ Prov 10:21
desire of the r shall be granted....... Prov 10:24
but the r is an everlasting............... Prov 10:25
The hope of the r shall be .... Prov 10:28
The r shall never be removed.......... Prov 10:30
The lips of the r know what is .... Prov 10:32
The r is delivered out of trouble...... Prov 11:8
When it goeth well with the r .... Prov 11:10
seed of the r shall be delivered........ Prov 11:21
The desire of the r is only good ...... Prov 11:23
but the r shall flourish as a............ Prov 11:28
The fruit of the r is a tree of .... Prov 11:30
the r shall be recompensed in the ... Prov 11:31
root of the r shall not be moved...... Prov 12:3
The thoughts of the r are right .... Prov 12:5
the house of the r shall stand.......... Prov 12:7
A r man regardeth the life of his ..... Prov 12:10
the root of the r yieldeth fruit......... Prov 12:12
The r is more excellent than his ...... Prov 12:26
A r man hateth lying .... Prov 13:5
The light of the r rejoiceth .... Prov 13:9
but to the r good shall be repaid...... Prov 13:21
The r eateth to the satisfying of...... Prov 13:25
but among the r there is favour ...... Prov 14:9
the wicked at the gates of the r....... Prov 14:19
but the r hath hope in his death..... Prov 14:32
house of the r is much treasure....... Prov 15:6
the way of the r is made plain........ Prov 15:19
The heart of the r studieth to......... Prov 15:28
he heareth the prayer of the r .... Prov 15:29
R lips are the delight of kings......... Prov 16:13
to overthrow the r in judgment....... Prov 18:5
the r runneth into it, and is safe ..... Prov 18:10
The r man wisely considereth the.... Prov 21:12
shall be a ransom for the r .... Prov 21:18
but the r giveth and spareth not ..... Prov 21:26
The father of the r shall greatly ...... Prov 23:24
against the dwelling of the r........... Prov 24:15
saith unto the wicked, Thou art r..... Prov 24:24
A r man falling down before the ...... Prov 25:26
but the r are bold as a lion .... Prov 28:1
Whoso causeth the r to go astray..... Prov 28:10
When r men do rejoice, there is ...... Prov 28:12
when they perish, the r increase...... Prov 28:28
When the r are in authority, the ..... Prov 29:2
but the r doth sing and rejoice .... Prov 29:6
The r considereth the cause of........ Prov 29:7
but the r shall see their fall............ Prov 29:16
mine heart, God shall judge the r.... Eccl 3:17
Be not r over much........................ Eccl 7:16
according to the work of the r.......... Eccl 8:14
to declare all this, that the r .... Eccl 9:1
there is one event to the r .... Eccl 9:2
Say ye to the r, that it shall be .... Is 3:10
righteousness of the r from him ...... Is 5:23
heard songs, even glory to the r ...... Is 24:16
that the r nation which keepeth ...... Is 26:2
raised up the r man from the east ... Is 41:2
that we may say, He is r .... Is 41:26
shall my r servant justify many ...... Is 53:11
The r perisheth, and no man layeth.. Is 57:1
none considering that the r is .... Is 57:1
Thy people also shall be all r .... Is 60:21

R

R art thou, O LORD, when I plead .... Jer 12:1
Lord of hosts, that triest the *r* .... Jer 20:12
will raise unto David a *r* Branch .... Jer 23:5
The LORD is *r* .... Lam 1:18
When a *r* man doth turn from his .... Eze 3:20
if thou warn the *r* man .... Eze 3:21
that the *r* sin not .... Eze 3:21
have made the heart of the *r* sad .... Eze 13:22
they are more *r* than thou .... Eze 16:52
of the *r* shall be upon him .... Eze 18:20
But when the *r* turneth away from .... Eze 18:24
When a *r* man turneth away from .... Eze 18:26
and will cut off from thee the *r* .... Eze 21:3
I will cut off from thee the *r* .... Eze 21:4
And the *r* men, they shall judge .... Eze 23:45
The righteousness of the *r* shall .... Eze 33:12
neither shall the *r* be able to .... Eze 33:12
When I shall say to the *r* .... Eze 33:13
When the *r* turneth from his .... Eze 33:18
for the LORD our God is *r* in all .... Dan 9:14
they sold the *r* for silver .... Amos 2:6
wicked doth compass about the *r* .... Hab 1:4
the man that is more *r* than he .... Hab 1:13
return, and discern between the *r* .... Mal 3:18
for I am not come to call the *r* .... Mt 9:13
the that receiveth a *r* man in the .... Mt 10:41
a *r* man shall receive a *r* .... Mt 10:41
r men have desired to see those .... Mt 13:17
Then shall the *r* shine forth as .... Mt 13:43
also outwardly appear unto men .... Mt 23:28
garnish the sepulchres of the *r* .... Mt 23:29
the *r* blood shed upon the earth .... Mt 23:35
from the blood of *r* Abel unto the .... Mt 23:35
Then shall the *r* answer him .... Mt 25:37
but the *r* into life eternal .... Mt 25:46
I came not to call the *r*, but .... Mk 2:17
And they were both *r* before God .... Lk 1:6
I came not to call the *r*, but .... Lk 5:32
in themselves that they were *r* .... Lk 18:9
Certainly this was a *r* man .... Lk 23:47
appearance, but judge *r* judgment .... Jn 7:24
O *r* Father, the world hath not .... Jn 17:25
of the *r* judgment of God .... Rom 2:5
As it is written, There is none *r* .... Rom 3:10
scarcely for a *r* man will one die .... Rom 5:7
of one shall many be made *r* .... Rom 5:19
token of the *r* judgment of God 2Th 1:5
Seeing it is a *r* thing with God 2Th 1:6
the law is not made for a *r* man 1Ti 1:9
the *r* judge, shall give me at 2Ti 4:8
he obtained witness that he was *r* .... Heb 11:4
prayer of a *r* man availeth much .... Jas 5:16
eyes of the Lord are over the *r* 1Pet 3:12
if the *r* scarcely be saved, where 1Pet 4:18
(For that *r* man dwelling among 2Pet 2:8
vexed his *r* soul from day to day 2Pet 2:8
the Father, Jesus Christ the *r* 1Jn 2:1
If ye know that he is *r*, ye know 1Jn 2:29
he that doeth righteousness is *r* 1Jn 3:7
even as he is *r* 1Jn 3:7
were evil, and his brother's *r* 1Jn 3:12
of the waters say, Thou art *r* .... Rev 16:5
true and *r* are thy judgments .... Rev 16:7
For true and *r* are his judgments .... Rev 19:2
is *r*, let him be *r* still .... Rev 22:11

RIGHTEOUSLY

Judge *r* between every man and his .... Deut 1:16
for thou shalt judge the people *r* .... Ps 67:4
he shall judge the people *r* .... Ps 96:10
Open thy mouth, judge *r*, and plead ...... Prov 31:9
He that walketh *r*, and speaketh .... Is 33:15
O LORD of hosts, that judgest *r* .... Jer 11:20
lusts, we should live soberly, *r* .... Titus 2:12
himself to him that judgeth *r* 1Pet 2:23

RIGHTEOUSNESS

and he counted it to him for *r* .... Gen 15:6
So shall my *r* answer for me in .... Gen 30:33
but in *r* shalt thou judge thy .... Lev 19:15
And it shall be our *r*, if we .... Deut 6:25
For my *r* the LORD hath brought me .... Deut 9:4
Not for thy *r*, or for the .... Deut 9:5
good land to possess it for thy *r* .... Deut 9:6
it shall be *r* unto thee before .... Deut 24:13
they shall offer sacrifices of *r* .... Deut 33:19
LORD render to every man his *r* .... Isa 26:23
rewarded me according to my *r* 2Sa 22:21
recompensed me according to my *r* 2Sa 22:25
before thee in truth, and in *r* 1Kin 3:6
to give him according to his *r* 1Kin 8:32
by giving him according to his *r* 2Chr 6:23
yea, return again, my *r* is in it .... Job 6:29
habitation of thy *r* prosperous .... Job 8:6
My *r* I hold fast, and will not let .... Job 27:6
I put on *r*, and it clothed me .... Job 29:14
for he will render unto man his *r* .... Job 33:26
saidst, My *r* is more than God's .... Job 35:2
thy *r* may profit the son of man .... Job 35:8
and will ascribe *r* to my Maker .... Job 36:3
when I said, O God of my *r* .... Ps 4:1
Offer the sacrifices of *r* .... Ps 4:5
in thy *r* because of mine enemies .... Ps 5:8
me, O LORD, according to my *r* .... Ps 7:8
the LORD according to his *r* .... Ps 7:17
And he shall judge the world in *r* .... Ps 9:8
For the righteous LORD loveth *r* .... Ps 11:7
walketh uprightly, and worketh *r* .... Ps 15:2
me, I will behold thy face in *r* .... Ps 17:15
rewarded me according to my *r* .... Ps 18:20
recompensed me according to my *r* .... Ps 18:24

shall declare his *r* unto a people .... Ps 22:31
paths of *r* for his name's sake .... Ps 23:3
r from the God of his salvation .... Ps 24:5
deliver me in thy *r* .... Ps 31:1
He loveth *r* and judgment .... Ps 33:5
O LORD my God, according to thy *r* .... Ps 35:24
And my tongue shall speak of thy *r* .... Ps 35:28
Thy *r* is like the great mountains .... Ps 36:6
thy *r* to the upright in heart .... Ps 36:10
bring forth thy *r* as the light .... Ps 37:6
I have preached *r* in the great .... Ps 40:9
not hid thy *r* within my heart .... Ps 40:10
because of truth and meekness and *r* ..... Ps 45:4
Thou lovest *r*, and hatest .... Ps 45:7
thy right hand is full of *r* .... Ps 48:10
the heavens shall declare his *r* .... Ps 50:6
tongue shall sing aloud of thy *r* .... Ps 51:14
pleased with the sacrifices of *r* .... Ps 51:19
and lying rather than to speak *r* .... Ps 52:3
Do ye indeed speak *r*, O .... Ps 58:1
things in *r* wilt thou answer us .... Ps 65:5
and let them not come into thy *r* .... Ps 69:27
Deliver me in thy *r*, and cause me .... Ps 71:2
My mouth shall shew forth thy *r* .... Ps 71:15
I will make mention of thy *r* .... Ps 71:16
Thy *r* also, O God, is very high, ... Ps 71:19
talk of thy *r* all the day long .... Ps 71:24
thy *r* unto the king's son .... Ps 72:1
He shall judge thy people with *r* .... Ps 72:2
people, and the little hills, by *r* .... Ps 72:3
r and peace have kissed each other .... Ps 85:10
r shall look down from heaven .... Ps 85:11
R shall go before him .... Ps 85:13
and thy *r* in the land of .... Ps 88:12
in thy *r* shall they be exalted .... Ps 89:16
But judgment shall return unto *r* .... Ps 94:15
he shall judge the world with *r* .... Ps 96:13
and judgment are the habitation .... Ps 97:2
The heavens declare his *r* .... Ps 97:6
his *r* hath he openly shewed in .... Ps 98:2
with *r* shall he judge the world, ... Ps 98:9
executest judgment and *r* in Jacob .... Ps 99:4
The LORD executeth *r* and judgment ...... Ps 103:6
his *r* unto children's children .... Ps 103:17
and he that doeth *r* at all times .... Ps 106:3
for *r* unto all generations for .... Ps 106:31
and his *r* endureth for ever .... Ps 111:3
and his *r* endureth for ever .... Ps 112:3
his *r* endureth for ever .... Ps 112:9
Open to me the gates of *r* .... Ps 118:19
quicken me in thy *r* .... Ps 119:40
and for the word of thy *r* .... Ps 119:123
Thy *r* is an everlasting .... Ps 119:142
r is an everlasting *r* .... Ps 119:142
for the word of thy *r* .... Ps 119:123
for all thy commandments are *r* .... Ps 119:172
Let thy priests be clothed with *r* .... Ps 132:9
answer me, and in thy *r* .... Ps 143:1
goodness, and shall sing of thy *r* .... Ps 145:7
Then shalt thou understand .... Prov 2:9
the words of my mouth are in *r* .... Prov 8:8
r delivereth from death .... Prov 10:2
but *r* delivereth from death .... Prov 11:4
The *r* of the perfect shall direct .... Prov 11:5
The *r* of the upright shall .... Prov 11:6
soweth *r* shall be a sure reward .... Prov 11:18
As *r* tendeth to life .... Prov 11:19
speaketh truth sheweth forth *r* .... Prov 12:17
In the way of *r* is life .... Prov 12:28
R keepeth him that is upright in .... Prov 13:6
R exalteth a nation .... Prov 14:34
loveth him that followeth after *r* .... Prov 15:9
Better is a little with *r* than .... Prov 16:8
the throne is established by *r* .... Prov 16:12
if it be found in the way of *r* .... Prov 16:31
He that followeth after *r* .... Prov 21:21
and mercy findeth life, *r* and .... Prov 21:21
throne shall be established in *r* .... Prov 25:5
and the place of *r*, that iniquity .... Eccl 3:16
just man that perisheth in his *r* .... Eccl 7:15
r lodged in it .... Is 1:21
shall be called, The City of *r* .... Is 1:26
judgment, and her converts with *r* .... Is 1:27
for *r*, but behold a cry .... Is 5:7
he might be sanctified in *r* .... Is 5:16
take away the *r* of the righteous .... Is 5:23
decreed shall overflow with *r* .... Is 10:22
But with *r* shall he judge the .... Is 11:4
r shall be the girdle of his .... Is 11:5
and seeking judgment, and hasting *r* ...... Is 16:5
of the world will learn *r* .... Is 26:9
wicked, yet will he not learn *r* .... Is 26:10
to the line, and *r* to the plummet .... Is 28:17
Behold, a king shall reign in *r* .... Is 32:1
r remain in the fruitful field .... Is 32:16
the work of *r* shall be peace .... Is 32:17
and the effect of *r* quietness .... Is 32:17
filled Zion with judgment and *r* .... Is 33:5
thee with the right hand of my *r* .... Is 41:10
the LORD have called thee in *r* .... Is 42:6
and let the skies pour down *r* .... Is 45:8
and let *r* spring up together .... Is 45:8
I have raised him up in *r* .... Is 45:13
I the LORD speak *r*, I declare .... Is 45:19
word is gone out of my mouth in *r* .... Is 45:23
one say, in the LORD have I *r* .... Is 45:24
stouthearted, that are far from *r* .... Is 46:12
I bring near my *r* .... Is 46:13

but not in truth, nor in *r* .... Is 48:1
thy *r* as the waves of the sea .... Is 48:18
to me, ye that follow after *r* .... Is 51:1
My *r* is near .... Is 51:5
my *r* shall not be abolished .... Is 51:6
Hearken unto me, ye that know *r* .... Is 51:7
but my *r* shall be for ever, and my .... Is 51:8
In *r* shalt thou be established .... Is 54:14
their *r* is of me, saith the LORD .... Is 54:17
to come, and my *r* to be revealed .... Is 56:1
I will declare thy *r*, and thy .... Is 57:12
my ways, as a nation that did *r* .... Is 58:2
thy *r* shall go before thee .... Is 58:8
and his *r*, it sustained him .... Is 59:16
For he put on *r* as a breastplate, ... Is 59:17
peace, and thine exactors *r* .... Is 60:17
they might be called trees of *r* .... Is 61:3
covered me with the robe of *r* .... Is 61:10
so the Lord GOD will cause *r* .... Is 61:11
until the *r* thereof go forth as .... Is 62:1
And the Gentiles shall see thy *r* .... Is 62:2
I that speak in *r*, mighty to save .... Is 63:1
him that rejoiceth and worketh *r* .... Is 64:5
in truth, in judgment, and in *r* .... Jer 4:2
lovingkindness, judgment, and *r* .... Jer 9:24
Execute ye judgment and *r*, and .... Jer 22:3
shall be called, THE LORD OUR *R* .... Jer 23:6
Branch of *r* to grow up unto David ...... Jer 33:15
execute judgment and *r* in the land ...... Jer 33:15
shall be called, The LORD our *r* .... Jer 33:16
The LORD hath brought forth our *r* .... Jer 51:10
man doth turn from his *r*, and .... Eze 3:20
his *r* which he hath done shall .... Eze 3:20
but their own souls by their *r* .... Eze 14:14
their own souls by their *r* .... Eze 14:20
the *r* of the righteous shall be .... Eze 18:20
in his *r* that he hath done he .... Eze 18:22
righteous turneth away from his *r* .... Eze 18:24
All his *r* that he hath done shall .... Eze 18:24
man turneth away from his *r* .... Eze 18:26
The *r* of the righteous shall not .... Eze 33:12
be able to live for his *r* in the .... Eze 33:12
if he trust to his own *r*, and .... Eze 33:13
the righteous turneth from his *r* .... Eze 33:18
thee, and break off thy sins by *r* .... Dan 4:27
r belongeth unto thee, but unto .... Dan 9:7
O Lord, according to all thy *r* .... Dan 9:16
and to bring in everlasting *r* .... Dan 9:24
many to *r* as the stars for ever .... Dan 12:3
I will betroth thee unto me in *r* .... Hos 2:19
Sow to yourselves in *r*, reap in .... Hos 10:12
till he come and rain *r* upon you .... Hos 10:12
leave off *r* in the earth, ... Amos 5:7
waters, and *r* as a mighty stream .... Amos 5:24
and the fruit of *r* into hemlock .... Amos 6:12
ye may know the *r* of the LORD .... Mic 6:5
light, and I shall behold his *r* .... Mic 7:9
seek *r*, seek meekness .... Zeph 2:3
for God, in truth and in *r* .... Zec 8:8
unto the LORD an offering in *r* .... Mal 3:3
fear my name shall the Sun of *r* .... Mal 4:2
it becometh us to fulfil all *r* .... Mt 3:15
which do hunger and thirst after *r* .... Mt 5:6
That except your *r* shall exceed .... Mt 5:20
shall exceed the *r* of the scribes .... Mt 5:20
the kingdom of God, and his *r* .... Mt 6:33
came unto you in the way of *r* .... Mt 21:32
r before him, all the days of our .... Lk 1:75
reprove the world of sin, and of *r* .... Jn 16:8
Of *r*, because I go to my Father, ... Jn 16:10
he that feareth him, and worketh *r* .... Acts 10:35
of the devil, thou enemy of all *r* .... Acts 13:10
in *r* by that man whom he hath .... Acts 17:31
And as he reasoned of *r*, ... Acts 24:25
For therein is the *r* of God .... Rom 1:17
keep the *r* of the law, shall not .... Rom 2:26
commend the *r* of God, what shall .... Rom 3:5
But now the *r* of God without the .... Rom 3:21
Even the *r* of God which is by .... Rom 3:22
blood, to declare his *r* for the .... Rom 3:25
I say, at this time his *r* .... Rom 3:26
and it was counted unto him for *r* .... Rom 4:3
his faith is counted for *r* .... Rom 4:5
whom God imputeth *r* without works .... Rom 4:6
was reckoned to Abraham for *r* .... Rom 4:9
a seal of the *r* of the faith .... Rom 4:11
that *r* might be imputed unto them .... Rom 4:11
law, but through the *r* of faith .... Rom 4:13
it was imputed to him for *r* .... Rom 4:22
the gift of *r* shall reign in .... Rom 5:17
even so by the *r* of the one free .... Rom 5:18
r unto eternal life by Jesus .... Rom 5:21
as instruments of *r* unto God .... Rom 6:13
death, or of obedience unto *r* .... Rom 6:16
sin, ye became the servants of *r* .... Rom 6:18
servants to *r* unto holiness .... Rom 6:19
of sin, ye were free from *r* .... Rom 6:20
That the *r* of the law might be .... Rom 8:4
the Spirit is life because of *r* .... Rom 8:10
the work, and cut it short in *r* .... Rom 9:28
which followed not after *r* .... Rom 9:30
have attained to *r* .... Rom 9:30
even the *r* which is of faith .... Rom 9:30
which followed after the law of *r* .... Rom 9:31
hath not attained to the law of *r* .... Rom 9:31
they being ignorant of God's *r* .... Rom 10:3
about to establish their own *r* .... Rom 10:3
themselves unto the *r* of God .... Rom 10:3
is the end of the law for *r* .... Rom 10:4
the *r* which is of the law .... Rom 10:5

But the r which is of faith................ Rom 10:6
the heart man believeth unto r............. Rom 10:10
but r, and peace, and joy in the.......... Rom 14:17
God is made unto us wisdom, and r....... 1Cor 1:30
Awake to r, and sin not................... 1Cor 15:34
ministration of r exceed in glory......... 2Cor 3:9
might be made the r of God in him........ 2Cor 5:21
by the armour of r on the right........... 2Cor 6:7
hath r with unrighteousness............... 2Cor 6:14
his r remaineth for ever.................. 2Cor 9:9
and increase the fruits of your r......... 2Cor 9:10
transformed as the ministers of r........ 2Cor 11:15
for if r come by the law, then........... Gal 2:21
and it was accounted to him for r......... Gal 3:6
verily r should have been by the......... Gal 3:21
wait for the hope of r by faith.......... Gal 5:5
which after God is created in r........... Eph 4:24
Spirit is in all goodness and r........... Eph 5:9
and having on the breastplate of r........ Phil 1:11
Being filled with the fruits of r........ Phil 1:11
touching the r which is in the........... Phil 3:6
in him, not having mine own r............ Phil 3:9
the r which is of God by faith........... Phil 3:9
and follow after r, godliness............ 1Ti 6:11
but follow r, faith, charity............. 2Ti 2:22
correction, for instruction in r......... 2Ti 3:16
is laid up for me a crown of r........... 2Ti 4:8
Not by works of r which we have.......... Titus 3:5
a sceptre of r is the sceptre of......... Heb 1:8
Thou hast loved r, and hated............. Heb 1:9
is unskilful in the word of r............ Heb 5:13
being by interpretation King of r........ Heb 7:2
heir of the r which is by faith.......... Heb 11:7
faith subdued kingdoms, wrought r........ Heb 11:33
r unto them which are exercised.......... Heb 12:11
of man worketh not the r of God.......... Jas 1:20
and it was imputed unto him for r........ Jas 2:23
the fruit of r is sown in peace.......... Jas 3:18
dead to sins, should live unto r......... 1Pet 2:24
with us through the r of God............. 2Pet 1:1
eighth person, a preacher of r........... 2Pet 2:5
not to have known the way of r........... 2Pet 2:21
a new earth, wherein dwelleth r.......... 2Pet 3:13
one that doeth r is born of him.......... 1Jn 2:29
he that doeth r is righteous............. 1Jn 3:7
doeth not r is not of God................ 1Jn 3:10
the fine linen is the r of saints........ Rev 19:8
in r he doth judge and make war.......... Rev 19:11

RIGHTEOUSNESS'

for thy r sake bring my soul out......... Ps 143:11
is well pleased for his r sake........... Is 42:21
which are persecuted for r sake.......... Mt 5:10
But and if ye suffer for r sake.......... 1Pet 3:14

RIGHTEOUSNESSES

all our r are as filthy rags............. Is 64:6
all his r shall not be remembered........ Eze 33:13
before thee for our r, but for........... Dan 9:18

RIGHTLY

he said, Is not he r named Jacob......... Gen 27:36
said unto him, Thou hast r judged........ Lk 7:43
that thou sayest and teachest r.......... Lk 20:21
r dividing the word of truth............. 2Ti 2:15

RIGOUR

of Israel to serve with r................ Ex 1:13
they made them serve, was with r......... Ex 1:14
shalt not rule over him with r........... Lev 25:43
not rule one over another with r......... Lev 25:46
rule with r over him in thy sight........ Lev 25:53

RIMMON (rim'-mon)

1. A city in Zebulun.
Shilhim, and Ain, and R.................. Josh 15:32
R with her suburbs, Tabor with........... 1Chr 6:77
from Geba to R south of Jerusalem........ Zec 14:10
2. A rock near Gibeah.
the wilderness unto the rock of R........ Judg 20:45
to the wilderness unto the rock of R..... Judg 20:47
abode in the rock R four months.......... Judg 20:47
Benjamin that were in the rock R......... Judg 21:13
3. Father of Baanah and Rechab.
the sons of R a Beerothite, of........... 2Sa 4:2
the sons of R the Beerothite,............ 2Sa 4:5
the sons of R the Beerothite, and........ 2Sa 4:9
4. A Syrian god.
the house of R to worship there.......... 2Kin 5:18
and I bow myself in the house of R....... 2Kin 5:18
bow down myself in the house of R........ 2Kin 5:18
5. A city in Simeon.
villages were, Etam, and Ain, R.......... 1Chr 4:32

RIMMONO See RIMMON.

RIMMON-PAREZ (rim'-mon-pa'-rez) An
Israelite encampment in the wilderness.
from Rithmah, and pitched at R........... Num 33:19
And they departed from R, and............ Num 33:20

RING

took off his r from his hand............. Gen 41:42
above the head of it unto one r.......... Ex 26:24
at the head thereof, to one r............ Ex 36:29
the king took his r from his hand........ Est 3:10
and sealed with the king's r............. Est 3:12
And the king took off his r.............. Est 8:2
and seal it with the king's r........... Est 8:8
name, and sealed with the king's r....... Est 8:8
and sealed it with the king's r......... Est 8:10
put a r on his hand, and shoes on........ Lk 15:22
your assembly a man with a gold r........ Jas 2:2

RINGLEADER

a r of the sect of the Nazarenes......... Acts 24:5

RINGS

shalt cast four r of gold for it......... Ex 25:12
two r shall be in the one side of........ Ex 25:12
two r in the other side of it............ Ex 25:12
the r by the sides of the ark............ Ex 25:14
shall be in the r of the ark............. Ex 25:14
shalt make for it four r of gold......... Ex 25:26
put the r in the four corners............ Ex 25:26
against the border shall the r be........ Ex 25:27
make their r of gold for places.......... Ex 26:29
r in the four corners thereof............ Ex 27:4
staves shall be put into the r........... Ex 27:7
the breastplate two r of gold............ Ex 28:23
shalt put the two r on the two........... Ex 28:23
chains of gold in the two r which........ Ex 28:24
And thou shalt make two r of gold........ Ex 28:26
two other r of gold thou shalt........... Ex 28:27
bind the breastplate by the r............ Ex 28:28
the r of the ephod with a lace of........ Ex 28:28
two golden r that thou make to........... Ex 30:4
bracelets, and earrings, and r........... Ex 35:22
made their r of gold to be places........ Ex 36:34
And he cast for it four r of gold........ Ex 37:3
even two r upon the one side of.......... Ex 37:3
two r upon the other side of it.......... Ex 37:3
the r by the sides of the ark............ Ex 37:5
And he cast for it four r of gold........ Ex 37:13
put the r upon the four corners.......... Ex 37:13
against the border were the r............ Ex 37:14
he made two r of gold for it............. Ex 37:27
he cast four r for the four ends......... Ex 38:5
the r on the sides of the altar.......... Ex 38:7
two ouches of gold, and two gold r....... Ex 39:16
put the two r in the two ends of......... Ex 39:16
chains of gold in the two r.............. Ex 39:17
And they made two r of gold.............. Ex 39:19
And they made two other golden r......... Ex 39:20
his r unto the r of the ephod............ Ex 39:21
of gold, chains, and bracelets, r........ Num 31:50
fine linen and purple to silver r........ Est 1:6
are as gold r set with the beryl......... Song 5:14
The r, and nose jewels................... Is 3:21
As for their r, they were so high........ Eze 1:18
their r were full of eyes round.......... Eze 1:18

RINGSTRAKED

that day the he goats that were r........ Gen 30:35
rods, and brought forth cattle r......... Gen 30:39
faces of the flocks toward the r......... Gen 30:40
thus, The r shall be thy hire............ Gen 31:8
then bare all the cattle r............... Gen 31:8
leaped upon the cattle were r............ Gen 31:10
which leap upon the cattle are r......... Gen 31:12

RINNAH (rin'-nah) A descendant of Caleb.
sons of Shimon were, Amnon, and R........ 1Chr 4:20

RINSED

be both scoured, and r in water.......... Lev 6:28
hath not r his hands in water, he........ Lev 15:11
of wood shall be r in water.............. Lev 15:12

RIOT

not accused of r or unruly............... Titus 1:6
with them to the same excess of r........ 1Pet 4:4
it pleasure to r in the daytime.......... 2Pet 2:13

RIOTING

not in r and drunkenness, not in......... Rom 13:13

RIOTOUS

among r eaters of flesh................. Prov 23:20
of r men shameth his father.............. Prov 28:7
his substance with r living.............. Lk 15:13

RIP

r up their women with child.............. 2Kin 8:12

RIPE

thereof brought forth r grapes.......... Gen 40:10
offer the first of thy r fruits......... Ex 22:29
whatsoever is first r in the land....... Num 18:13
like the figs that are first r.......... Jer 24:2
the sickle, for thy harvest is r........ Joel 3:13
for the harvest of the earth is r....... Rev 14:15
her grapes are fully r.................. Rev 14:18

RIPENING

the sour grape is r in the flower....... Is 18:5

RIPHATH (ri'-fath) A son of Gomer.
Ashkenaz, and R, and Togarmah........... Gen 10:3
Ashchenaz, and R, and Togarmah.......... 1Chr 1:6

RIPPED

that were with child he r up............ 2Kin 15:16
women with child shall be r up.......... Hos 13:16
because they have r up the women........ Amos 1:13

RISE

your feet, and ye shall r up early...... Gen 19:2
that I cannot r up before the........... Gen 31:35
R up early in the morning, and.......... Gen 8:20
R up early in the morning, and.......... Ex 9:13
R up, and get you forth from among...... Ex 12:31
If he r again, and walk abroad.......... Ex 21:19
Thou shalt r up before the hoary........ Lev 19:32
R up, LORD, and let thine enemies....... Num 10:35
call thee, r up, and go with them....... Num 22:20
and said, R up, Balak, and hear......... Num 23:18
the people shall r up as a great........ Num 23:24
a Sceptre shall r out of Israel......... Num 24:17
Now r up, said I, and get you over...... Deut 2:13

R ye up, take your journey, and......... Deut 2:24
r up against him, and smite him......... Deut 19:11
One witness shall not r up.............. Deut 19:15
If a false witness r up against......... Deut 19:16
r up against thee to be smitten......... Deut 28:7
that shall r up after you............... Deut 29:22
and this people will r up, and go a..... Deut 31:16
Let them r up and help you, and be...... Deut 32:38
loins of them that r against him....... Deut 33:11
hate him, that they r not again........ Deut 33:11
Then ye shall r up from the............ Josh 8:7
I will send them, and they shall r..... Josh 18:4
said, R thou, and fall upon us......... Judg 8:21
the sun is up, thou shalt r early...... Judg 9:33
with smoke r up out of the city....... Judg 20:38
him, that he should r against me...... 2Sa 12:13
them not to r against Saul............ 1Sa 24:7
Wherefore now r up early in the....... 1Sa 29:10
the child was dead, thou didst r...... 2Sa 12:21
all that r against thee to do......... 2Sa 18:32
of Israel, which r up against me...... 2Kin 16:7
And they said, Let us r up............. Job 20:27
Upon my right hand r the youth........ Job 30:12
are they that r up against me......... Ps 3:1
from those that r up against them..... Ps 17:7
them that they were not able to r..... Ps 18:38
above those that r up against me...... Ps 18:48
though war should r against me........ Ps 27:3
False witnesses did r up.............. Ps 35:11
down, and shall not be able to r...... Ps 36:12
he lieth he shall r up no more........ Ps 41:8
them under that r up against us....... Ps 44:5
me from them that r up against me..... Ps 74:23
the tumult of those that r........... Ps 74:23
the wicked that r up against me....... Ps 92:11
Who will r up for me against thee..... Ps 94:16
At midnight I will r to give.......... Ps 119:62
It is vain for you to r up early...... Ps 127:2
with those that r up against thee.... Ps 139:21
pits, that they r not up again....... Ps 140:10
their calamity shall r suddenly...... Prov 24:22
but when the wicked r, a man is...... Prov 28:12
When the wicked r, men hide.......... Prov 28:28
of the ruler r up against thee....... Eccl 10:4
he shall r up at the voice of the.... Eccl 12:4
R up, my love, my fair one, and...... Song 2:10
I will r now, and go about the....... Song 3:2
Woe unto them that r up early in..... Is 5:11
that they do not r, nor possess...... Is 14:21
For I will r up against them......... Is 14:22
and it shall fall, and not r again... Is 24:20
are deceased, they shall not r....... Is 26:14
For the LORD shall r up as in........ Is 28:21
R up, ye women that are at ease...... Is 32:9
Now will I r, saith the LORD......... Is 33:10
down together, they shall not r...... Is 43:17
every tongue that shall r against.... Is 54:17
shall thy light r in obscurity....... Is 58:10
r no more, because of the sword...... Jer 25:27
yet should they r up every man in.... Jer 37:10
waters r up out of the north, and.... Jer 47:2
her, and r up to the battle.......... Jer 49:14
of them that r up against me......... Jer 51:1
shall not r from the evil that I..... Jer 51:64
from whom I am not able to r up....... Lam 1:14
and another shall r after them....... Dan 7:24
she shall no more r.................. Amos 5:2
I will r against the house of........ Amos 7:9
it shall r up wholly as a flood...... Amos 8:8
shall fall, and never r up again..... Amos 8:14
it shall r up wholly like a flood.... Amos 9:5
let us r up against her in battle.... Obad 1
shall not r up the second time....... Nah 1:9
Shall they not r up suddenly that.... Hab 2:7
the day that I r up to the prey...... Zeph 3:8
his hand shall r up against thee..... Zec 14:13
maketh his sun to r on the evil...... Mt 5:45
the children shall r up against...... Mt 10:21
shall r in judgment with this........ Mt 12:41
r up in the judgment with this....... Mt 12:42
and the third day he shall r again... Mt 20:19
For nation shall r against nation.... Mt 24:7
And many false prophets shall r...... Mt 24:11
R, let us be going.................. Mt 26:46
After three days I will r again...... Mk 8:31
If Satan r up against himself, and... Mk 3:26
r night and day, and the seed....... Mk 4:27
and after three days r again........ Mk 8:31
killed, he shall r the third day.... Mk 9:31
and the third day he shall r again... Mk 10:49
unto him, Be of good comfort, r..... Mk 10:49
therefore, when they shall r........ Mk 12:23
when they shall r from the dead..... Mk 12:26
as touching the dead, that they r... Mk 12:26
For nation shall r against nation... Mk 13:8
children shall r up against their... Mk 13:12
Christ and false prophets shall r... Mk 13:22
R up, let us go.................... Lk 22:46
or to say, R up and walk........... Lk 5:23
R up, and stand forth in the midst... Lk 6:8
I cannot r and give thee........... Lk 11:7
unto you, Though he will not r..... Lk 11:8
of his importunity he will r....... Lk 11:8
The queen of the south shall r up... Lk 11:31
The men of Nineve shall r up in.... Lk 11:32
ye see a cloud r out of the west... Lk 12:54
and the third day he shall r again.. Lk 18:33
Nation shall r against nation, and.. Lk 21:10
r and pray, lest ye enter into..... Lk 22:46

and the third day r again .... Lk 24:7
to r from the dead the third day .... Lk 24:46
Jesus saith unto him, R, take up........ Jn 5:8
her, Thy brother shall r again........ Jn 11:23
I know that he shall r again in........ Jn 11:24
that he must r again from the........ Jn 20:9
of Jesus Christ of Nazareth r up........ Acts 3:6
And there came a voice to him, R........ Acts 10:13
But r, and stand upon thy feet........ Acts 26:16
first that should r from the dead........ Acts 26:23
he that shall r to reign over the........ Rom 15:12
up, if so be that the dead r not........ 1Cor 15:15
For if the dead r not, then is........ 1Cor 15:16
dead, if the dead r not at all........ 1Cor 15:29
it me, if the dead r not........ 1Cor 15:32
the dead in Christ shall r first........ 1Th 4:16
that another priest should r........ Heb 7:11
and the angel stood, saying, R........ Rev 11:1
saw a beast r up out of the sea........ Rev 13:1

RISEN

The sun was r upon the earth when........ Gen 19:23
If the sun be r upon him, there........ Ex 22:3
ye are r up in your fathers'........ Num 32:14
ye are r up against my father's........ Judg 9:18
And when she was r up to glean........ Ruth 2:15
Yet a man is r to pursue thee, and........ 1Sa 25:29
the whole family is r against........ 2Sa 14:7
I am r up in the room of David my........ 1Kin 8:20
of the man of God was r early........ 2Kin 6:15
for I am r up in the room of........ 2Chr 6:10
Solomon the son of David, is r up........ 2Chr 13:6
Now when Jehoram was r up to the........ 2Chr 21:4
but we are r, and stand upright........ Ps 20:8
witnesses are r up against me........ Ps 27:12
For strangers are r up against me........ Ps 54:3
O God, the proud are r against me........ Ps 86:14
glory of the LORD is r upon thee........ Is 60:1
Violence is r up into a rod of........ Eze 7:11
for the waters were r, waters to........ Eze 47:5
my people is r up as an enemy........ Mic 2:8
born of women there hath not r a........ Mt 11:11
he is r from the dead........ Mt 14:2
of man be r again from the dead........ Mt 17:9
But after I am r again, I will go........ Mt 26:32
the people, He is r from the dead........ Mt 27:64
for he is r, as he said........ Mt 28:6
that he is r from the dead........ Mt 28:7
the Baptist was r from the dead........ Mk 6:14
he is r from the dead........ Mk 6:16
Son of man were r from the........ Mk 9:9
But after that I am r, I will go........ Mk 14:28
he is r........ Mk 16:6
Now when Jesus was r early the........ Mk 16:9
which had seen him after he was r........ Mk 16:14
a great prophet is r up among us........ Lk 7:16
that John was r from the dead........ Lk 9:7
of the old prophets is r again........ Lk 9:8
of the old prophets is r again........ Lk 9:19
the master of the house is r up........ Lk 13:25
He is not here, but is r........ Lk 24:6
Saying, The Lord is r indeed........ Lk 24:34
therefore he was r from the dead........ Jn 2:22
after that he was r from the dead........ Jn 21:14
and r again from the dead........ Acts 17:3
died, yea rather, that is r again........ Rom 8:34
of the dead, then is Christ not r........ 1Cor 15:13
And if Christ be not r, then is........ 1Cor 15:14
But now is Christ r from the dead........ 1Cor 15:20
wherein also ye are r with him........ Col 2:12
If ye then be r with Christ........ Col 3:1
no sooner r with a burning heat........ Jas 1:11

RISEST

liest down, and when thou r up........ Deut 6:7
liest down, and when thou r up........ Deut 11:19

RISETH

for as when a man r against his........ Deut 22:26
man before the LORD, that r up........ Josh 6:26
of the morning, when the sun r........ 2Sa 23:4
commandeth the sun, and it r not........ Job 9:7
So man lieth down, and r not........ Job 14:12
he r up, and no man is sure of........ Job 24:22
he that r up against me as the........ Job 27:7
then shall I do when God r up........ Job 31:14
seven times, and r up again........ Prov 24:16
She r also while it is yet night,........ Prov 31:15
shalt not know from whence it r........ Is 47:11
Egypt r up like a flood, and his........ Jer 46:8
the daughter r up against her........ Mic 7:6
He r from supper, and laid aside........ Jn 13:4

RISING

have in the skin his flesh a r........ Lev 13:2
if the r be white in the skin, and........ Lev 13:10
there be quick raw flesh in the r........ Lev 13:10
of the boil there be a white r........ Lev 13:19
it is a r of the burning, and the........ Lev 13:28
if the r of the sore be white........ Lev 13:43
And for a r, and for a scab, and for........ Lev 14:56
on the east side toward the r of........ Num 2:3
Jordan toward the r of the sun........ Josh 1:15
r up betimes, and sending........ 2Chr 36:15
r of the morning till the stars........ Neh 4:21
my leanness r up in the beareth........ Job 16:8
r betimes for a prey........ Job 24:5
The murderer r with the light........ Job 24:14
called the earth from the r of........ Ps 50:1
From the r of the sun unto the........ Ps 113:3
r early in the morning, it shall........ Prov 27:14
against whom there is no r up........ Prov 30:31

from the r of the sun shall he........ Is 41:25
may know from the r of the sun........ Is 45:6
his glory from the r of the sun........ Is 59:19
kings to the brightness of thy r........ Is 60:3
r up early and speaking, but ye........ Jer 7:13
daily r up early and sending them........ Jer 7:25
r early and protesting, saying,........ Jer 11:7
unto you, r early and speaking........ Jer 25:3
prophets, r early and sending them........ Jer 25:4
both r up early, and sending them,........ Jer 26:5
r up early and sending them........ Jer 29:19
r up early and teaching them, yet........ Jer 32:33
unto you, r early and speaking........ Jer 35:14
r up early and sending them........ Jer 35:15
their sitting down, and their r up........ Lam 3:63
For from the r of the sun even........ Mal 1:11
r up a great while before day, he........ Mk 1:35
the r from the dead should mean........ Mk 9:10
the sepulchre at the r of the sun........ Mk 16:2
r again of many in Israel........ Lk 2:34

RISSAH (ris'-sah) An Israelite encampment in the wilderness.

from Libnah, and pitched at R........ Num 33:21
And they journeyed from R, and........ Num 33:22

RITES

according to all the r of it........ Num 9:3

RITHMAH (rith'-mah) An Israelite encampment in the wilderness.

from Hazeroth, and pitched in R........ Num 33:18
And they departed from R, and........ Num 33:19

RIVER

a r went out of Eden to water the........ Gen 2:10
the name of the second r is Gihon........ Gen 2:13
name of the third r is Hiddekel........ Gen 2:14
the fourth r is Euphrates........ Gen 2:14
from the r of Egypt unto the........ Gen 15:18
the great r, the r Euphrates........ Gen 15:18
he rose up, and passed over the r........ Gen 31:21
by the r reigned in his stead........ Gen 36:37
and, behold, he stood by the r........ Gen 41:1
of the r seven well favoured kine........ Gen 41:2
came up after them out of the r........ Gen 41:3
kine upon the brink of the r........ Gen 41:3
I stood upon the bank of the r........ Gen 41:17
came up out of the r seven kine........ Gen 41:18
is born ye shall cast into the r........ Ex 1:22
down to wash herself at the r........ Ex 2:5
shalt take of the water of the r........ Ex 4:9
which thou takest out of the r........ Ex 4:9
the waters which are in the r........ Ex 7:17
fish that is in the r shall die........ Ex 7:18
and the r shall stink........ Ex 7:18
to drink of the water of the r........ Ex 7:18
the waters that were in the r........ Ex 7:20
in the r were turned to blood........ Ex 7:20
the fish that was in the r died........ Ex 7:21
the r stank, and the Egyptians........ Ex 7:21
not drink of the water of the r........ Ex 7:24
about the r for water to drink........ Ex 7:24
not drink of the water of the r........ Ex 7:24
that the LORD had smitten the r........ Ex 7:25
the r shall bring forth frogs........ Ex 8:3
they may remain in the r only........ Ex 8:9
they shall remain in the r only........ Ex 8:11
rod, wherewith thou smotest the r........ Ex 17:5
and from the desert unto the r........ Ex 23:31
which is by the r of the land of........ Num 22:5
from Admon unto the r of Egypt........ Num 34:5
and unto Lebanon, unto the great r........ Deut 1:7
the great r, the r Euphrates........ Deut 1:7
journey, and pass over the r Arnon........ Deut 2:24
is by the brink of the r Arnon........ Deut 2:36
and from the city that is by the r........ Deut 2:36
unto any place of the r Jabbok........ Deut 2:37
from the r of Arnon unto mount........ Deut 3:8
Aroer, which is by the r Arnon........ Deut 3:12
unto the r Arnon half the valley........ Deut 3:16
the border even unto the r Jabbok........ Deut 3:16
is by the bank of the r Arnon........ Deut 4:48
wilderness and Lebanon, from the r........ Deut 11:24
the r Euphrates, even unto the........ Deut 11:24
Lebanon even unto the great r........ Josh 1:4
the r Euphrates, all the land of........ Josh 1:4
from the r Arnon unto mount........ Josh 12:1
is upon the bank of the r Arnon........ Josh 12:2
and from the middle of the r........ Josh 12:2
Gilead, even unto the r Jabbok........ Josh 12:2
is upon the bank of the r Arnon........ Josh 13:9
that is in the midst of the r........ Josh 13:9
is on the bank of the r Arnon........ Josh 13:16
that is in the midst of the r........ Josh 13:16
and went out unto the r of Egypt........ Josh 15:4
is on the south side of the r........ Josh 15:7
her villages, untc the r of Egypt........ Josh 15:47
Tappuah westward unto the r Kanah........ Josh 16:8
r Kanah, southward of the r........ Josh 17:9
was on the north side of the r........ Josh 17:9
reached to the r that is before........ Josh 19:11
draw unto the r to Kishon........ Judg 4:7
the Gentiles unto the r of Kishon........ Judg 4:13
The r of Kishon swept them away,........ Judg 5:21
that ancient r, the r Kishon........ Judg 5:21
his border at the r Euphrates........ 2Sa 8:3
Syrians that were beyond the r........ 2Sa 10:16
and we will draw it into the r........ 2Sa 17:13
in the midst of the r of Gad........ 2Sa 24:5
from the r unto the land of the........ 1Kin 4:21

all the region on this side the r........ 1Kin 4:24
all the kings on this side the r........ 1Kin 4:24
in of Hamath unto the r of Egypt........ 1Kin 8:65
shalt scatter them beyond the r........ 1Kin 14:15
Aroer, which is by the r Arnon........ 2Kin 10:33
and in Habor by the r of Gozan........ 2Kin 17:6
and in Habor by the r of Gozan........ 2Kin 18:11
of Assyria to the r Euphrates........ 2Kin 23:29
the r of Egypt unto the r........ 2Kin 24:7
by the r reigned in his stead........ 1Chr 1:48
wilderness from the r Euphrates........ 1Chr 5:9
Habor, and Hara, and to the r Gozan........ 1Chr 5:26
his dominion by the r Euphrates........ 1Chr 18:3
Syrians that were beyond the r........ 1Chr 19:16
in of Hamath unto the r of Egypt........ 2Chr 7:8
the r even unto the land of the........ 2Chr 9:26
rest that are on this side the r........ Ezr 4:10
the men on this side the r........ Ezr 4:11
no portion on this side the r........ Ezr 4:16
and unto the rest beyond the r........ Ezr 4:17
over all countries beyond the r........ Ezr 4:20
governor on this side the r........ Ezr 5:3
governor on this side the r........ Ezr 5:6
which were on this side the r........ Ezr 5:6
Tatnai, governor beyond the r........ Ezr 6:6
which are beyond the r, be ye........ Ezr 6:6
even of the tribute beyond the r........ Ezr 6:8
governor on this side the r........ Ezr 6:13
treasurers which are beyond the r........ Ezr 7:21
the people that are beyond the r........ Ezr 7:25
to the r than runneth to Ahava........ Ezr 8:15
at the r of Ahava, that we might........ Ezr 8:21
Then we departed from the r of........ Ezr 8:31
the governors on this side the r........ Ezr 8:36
me to the governors beyond the r........ Neh 2:7
to the governors beyond the r........ Neh 2:9
the governor on this side the r........ Neh 3:7
Behold, he drinketh up a r........ Job 40:23
drink of the r of thy pleasures........ Ps 36:8
There is a r, the streams whereof........ Ps 46:4
enricheth it with the r of God........ Ps 65:9
from the r unto the ends of the........ Ps 72:8
sea, and her branches unto the r........ Ps 80:11
ran in the dry places like a r........ Ps 105:41
namely, by them beyond the r........ Is 7:20
up upon them the waters of the r........ Is 8:7
he shake his hand over the r........ Is 11:15
the r shall be wasted and dried up........ Is 19:5
of Sihor, the harvest of the r........ Is 23:3
Pass through thy land as a r........ Is 23:10
of the r unto the stream of Egypt........ Is 27:12
then had thy peace been as a r........ Is 48:18
will extend peace to her like a r........ Is 66:12
to drink the waters of the r........ Jer 2:18
spreadeth out her roots by the r........ Jer 17:8
which was by the r Euphrates in........ Jer 46:2
the north by the r Euphrates........ Jer 46:6
north country by the r Euphrates........ Jer 46:10
let tears run down like a r day........ Lam 2:18
the captives by the r of Chebar........ Eze 1:1
of the Chaldeans by the r Chebar........ Eze 1:3
that dwelt by the r of Chebar........ Eze 3:15
which I saw by the r of Chebar........ Eze 3:23
that I saw by the r of Chebar........ Eze 10:15
God of Israel by the r of Chebar........ Eze 10:20
which I saw by the r Chebar........ Eze 10:22
My r is mine own, and I have made........ Eze 29:3
The r is mine, and I have made it........ Eze 29:9
vision that I saw by the r Chebar........ Eze 43:3
it was a r that I could not pass........ Eze 47:5
a r that could not be passed over........ Eze 47:5
to return to the brink of the r........ Eze 47:6
at the bank of the r were very........ Eze 47:7
shall live whither the r cometh........ Eze 47:9
by the r upon the bank thereof,........ Eze 47:12
in Kadesh, the r to the great sea........ Eze 47:19
to the r toward the great sea........ Eze 48:28
vision, and I was by the r of Ulai........ Dan 8:2
there stood before me a r: then........ Dan 8:3
I had seen standing before the r........ Dan 8:6
I was by the side of the great r........ Dan 10:4
on this side of the bank of the r........ Dan 12:5
on that side of the bank of the r........ Dan 12:5
was upon the waters of the r........ Dan 12:6
was upon the waters of the r........ Dan 12:7
unto the r of the wilderness........ Amos 6:14
from the fortress even to the r........ Mic 7:12
from the r even to the ends of........ Zec 9:10
the deeps of the r shall dry up........ Zec 10:11
of him in the r of Jordan........ Mk 1:5
went out of the city by a side........ Acts 16:13
bound in the great r Euphrates........ Rev 9:14
vial upon the great r Euphrates........ Rev 16:12
me a pure r of water of life........ Rev 22:1
of it, and on either side of the r........ Rev 22:2

RIVER'S

it in the flags by the r brink........ Ex 2:3
walked along by the r side........ Ex 2:5
by the r brink against he come........ Ex 7:15
forth, as gardens by the r side........ Num 24:6

RIVERS

upon their streams, upon their r........ Ex 7:19
rod over the streams, over the r........ Ex 8:5
waters, in the seas, and in the r........ Lev 11:9
scales in the seas, and in the r........ Lev 11:10
to Jothath, a land of r of waters........ Deut 10:7
r of Damascus, better than all........ 2Kin 5:12
up all the r of besieged places........ 2Kin 19:24
He shall not see the r, the........ Job 20:17

He cutteth out r among the rocks.........Job 28:10
the rock poured me out r of oil............Job 29:6
a tree planted by the r of water...........Ps 1:3
thou driedst up mighty r....................Ps 74:15
caused waters to run down like r.........Ps 78:16
And had turned their r into blood........Ps 78:44
sea, and his right hand in the r...........Ps 89:25
He turneth r into a wilderness.............Ps 107:33
R of waters run down mine eyes,.........Ps 119:136
By the r of Babylon, there we sat........Ps 137:1
r of waters in the streets...................Prov 5:16
of the Lord, as the r of water.............Prov 21:1
All the r run into the sea..................Eccl 1:7
the place from whence the r come........Eccl 1:7
eyes of doves by the r of waters..........Song 5:12
uttermost part of the r of Egypt..........Is 7:18
which is beyond the r of Ethiopia........Is 18:1
whose land the r have spoiled.............Is 18:2
whose land the r have spoiled.............Is 18:7
And they shall turn the r far away........Is 19:6
and upon every high hill, r.................Is 30:25
as r of water in a dry place, as...........Is 32:2
be unto us a place of broad r.............Is 33:21
all the r of the besieged places...........Is 37:25
I will open r in high places, and.........Is 41:18
and I will make the r islands..............Is 42:15
and through the r, they shall not.........Is 43:2
wilderness, and r in the desert...........Is 43:19
r in the desert, to give drink to..........Is 43:20
Be dry, and I will dry up thy r............Is 44:27
the thigh, pass over the r..................Is 47:2
I make the r a wilderness..................Is 50:2
the r of waters in a straight way.........Jer 31:9
whose waters are moved as the r........Jer 46:7
his waters are moved like the r..........Jer 46:8
Mine eye runneth down with r of........Lam 3:48
and to the hills, to the.....................Eze 6:3
that lieth in the midst of his r............Eze 29:3
of thy r to stick unto thy scales..........Eze 29:4
thee up out of the midst of thy r........Eze 29:4
all the fish of thy r shall stick...........Eze 29:4
thee and all the fish of thy r.............Eze 29:5
am against thee, and against thy r......Eze 29:10
And I will make the r dry, and sell......Eze 30:12
set him up on high with her r............Eze 31:4
sent out her little r unto all..............Eze 31:4
broken by all the r of the land..........Eze 31:12
and thou camest forth with thy r........Eze 32:2
thy feet, and fouledst their r..............Eze 32:2
the r shall be full of thee.................Eze 32:6
cause their r to run like oil,.............Eze 32:14
the mountains of Israel by the r.........Eze 34:13
in thy valleys, and in all thy r...........Eze 35:8
and to the hills, to the.....................Eze 36:4
and to the hills, to the.....................Eze 36:6
whithersoever the r shall come...........Eze 47:9
for the r of waters are dried up,.........Joel 1:20
all the r of Judah shall flow...............Joel 3:18
or with ten thousands of r of oil........Mic 6:7
it dry, and drieth up all the r.............Nah 1:4
gates of the r shall be opened............Nah 2:6
No, that was situate among the r........Nah 3:8
the Lord displeased against the r........Hab 3:8
was thine anger against the r.............Hab 3:8
didst cleave the earth with r..............Hab 3:9
From beyond the r of Ethiopia my.......Zeph 3:10
shall flow r of living water.................Jn 7:38
fell upon the third part of the r.........Rev 8:10
poured out his vial upon the r...........Rev 16:4

RIZIA See Rezia.

RIZPAH (riz´-pah) *A concubine of Saul.*
had a concubine, whose name was R......2Sa 3:7
sons of R the daughter of Aiah...........2Sa 21:8
The R daughter of Aiah took..............2Sa 21:10
David what R the daughter of Aiah......2Sa 21:11

ROAD
Whither have ye made a r to day........1Sa 27:10

ROAR
Let the sea r, and the fulness............1Chr 16:32
Though the waters thereof r...............Ps 46:3
Thine enemies in the midst of.............Ps 74:4
Let the sea r, and the fulness............Ps 96:11
Let the sea r, and the fulness............Ps 98:7
The young lions r after their..............Ps 104:21
they shall r like young lions..............Is 5:29
yea, they shall r, and lay hold of........Is 5:29
in that day they shall r against...........Is 5:30
he shall cry, yea, r.........................Is 42:13
We r all like bears, and mourn...........Is 59:11
though they r, yet can they not..........Jer 5:22
The Lord shall r from on high............Jer 25:30
he shall mightily r upon his...............Jer 25:30
the sea when the waves thereof r........Jer 31:35
their voice shall r like the sea............Jer 50:42
They shall r together like lions..........Jer 51:38
her waves do r like great waters.........Jer 51:55
he shall r like a lion.......................Hos 11:10
When he shall r, then the.................Hos 11:10
The Lord also shall r out of Zion........Joel 3:16
said, The Lord will r from Zion..........Amos 1:2
Will a lion r in the forest, when.........Amos 3:4

ROARED
a young lion r against him................Judg 14:5
I have r by reason of the..................Ps 38:8
divided the sea, whose waves r...........Ps 51:15
The young lions r upon him..............Jer 2:15
The lion hath r, who will not.............Amos 3:8

ROARETH
After it a voice r............................Job 37:4
their voice r like the sea..................Jer 6:23
a loud voice, as when a lion r............Rev 10:3

ROARING
The r of the lion, and the voice..........Job 4:10
me, and from the words of my r.........Ps 22:1
mouths, as a ravening and a r lion......Ps 22:13
old through my r all the day long........Ps 32:3
wrath is as the r of a lion.................Prov 19:12
of a king is as the r of a lion............Prov 20:2
As a r lion, and a ranging bear..........Prov 28:15
Their r shall be like a lion................Is 5:29
them like the r of the sea.................Is 5:30
and the young lion r on his prey.........Is 31:4
thereof, by the noise of his r............Eze 19:7
like a r lion ravening the prey...........Eze 22:25
princes within her are r lions............Zeph 3:3
a voice of the r of young lions...........Zec 11:3
the sea and the waves r...................Lk 21:25
adversary the devil, as a r lion..........1Pet 5:8

ROARINGS
my r are poured out like the.............Job 3:24

ROAST
r with fire, and unleavened bread........Ex 12:8
all with water, but r with fire.............Ex 12:9
And thou shalt r and eat it in the........Deut 16:7
Give flesh to r for the priest..............1Sa 2:15
he roasteth r, and is satisfied.............Is 44:16

ROASTED
they r the passover with fire..............2Chr 35:13
I have r flesh, and eaten it................Is 44:19
the king of Babylon r in the fire.........Jer 29:22

ROASTETH
The slothful man r not that which.......Prov 12:27
he r roast, and is satisfied................Is 44:16

ROB
thy neighbour, neither r him.............Lev 19:13
which shall r you of your.................Lev 26:22
they r the threshingfloors.................1Sa 23:1
R not the poor, because he is............Prov 22:22
that they may r the fatherless,...........Is 10:2
us, and the lot of them that r us........Is 17:14
r those that robbed them, saith..........Eze 39:10
Will a man r God...........................Mal 3:8

ROBBED
they r all that came along that...........Judg 9:25
as a bear r of her whelps in the.........Ps 17:8
The bands of the wicked have r me......Ps 119:61
Let a bear r of her whelps meet a.......Prov 17:12
have r their treasures, and I have.......Is 10:13
But this is a people r and spoiled........Is 42:22
and they shall be r........................Jer 50:37
pledge, give again that he had r.........Eze 33:15
them, and rob those that r them........Eze 39:10
Yet ye have r me..........................Mal 3:8
ye say, Wherein have we r thee..........Mal 3:8
for ye have r me, even this whole.......Mal 3:9
I r other churches, taking wages.........2Cor 11:8

ROBBER
the r swalloweth up their.................Job 5:5
that shall prevail against him............Job 18:9
If he beget a son that is a r..............Eze 18:10
way, the same is a thief and a r.........Jn 10:1
Now Barabbas was a r......................Jn 18:40

ROBBERS
The tabernacles of r prosper.............Job 12:6
for a spoil, and Israel to the r...........Is 42:24
become a den of r in your eyes..........Jer 7:11
for the r shall enter into it, and........Jer 7:11
also the r of thy people shall............Dan 11:14
as troops of r wait for a man, so........Hos 6:9
the troop of r spoileth without..........Hos 7:1
if r by night, (how art thou cut..........Obad 5
came before me are thieves and r.......Jn 10:8
which are neither r of churches.........Acts 19:37
perils of waters, in perils of r...........2Cor 11:26

ROBBERY
and become not vain in r.................Ps 62:10
The r of the wicked shall destroy.......Prov 21:7
I hate r for burnt offering................Is 61:8
used oppression, and exercised r.......Eze 22:29
up violence and r in their palaces......Amos 3:10
it is all full of lies and r..................Nah 3:1
thought it not r to be equal with.......Phil 2:6

ROBBETH
Whoso r his father or his mother,......Prov 28:24

ROBE
breastplate, and an ephod, and a r.....Ex 28:4
thou shalt make the r of the.............Ex 28:31
upon the hem of the r round about.....Ex 28:34
the r of the ephod, and the ephod,.....Ex 29:5
he made the r of the ephod of..........Ex 39:22
was an hole in the midst of the r.......Ex 39:23
of the r pomegranates of blue...........Ex 39:24
upon the hem of the r, round............Ex 39:25
the hem of the r to minister in..........Ex 39:26
girdle, and clothed him with the r......Lev 8:7
of the r that was upon him...............1Sa 18:4
off the skirt of Saul's r privily...........1Sa 24:4
see the skirt of thy r in my hand.......1Sa 24:11
that I cut off the skirt of thy r..........1Sa 24:11
clothed with a r of fine linen............1Chr 15:27
my judgment was as a r and a...........Job 29:14

And I will clothe him with thy r.........Is 22:21
me with the r of righteousness..........Is 61:10
throne, and he laid his r from him.....Jonah 3:6
ye pull off the r which.....................Mic 2:8
him, and put on him a scarlet r.........Mt 27:28
him, they took the r off from him......Mt 27:31
servants, Bring forth the best r.........Lk 15:22
and arrayed him in a gorgeous r........Lk 23:11
and they put on him a purple r.........Jn 19:2
crown of thorns, and the purple r......Jn 19:5

ROBES
for with such r were the king's.........2Sa 13:18
his throne, having put on their r........1Kin 22:10
but put thou on thy r.....................1Kin 22:30
on his throne, clothed in their r........2Chr 18:9
but put thou on thy r.....................2Chr 18:29
thrones, and lay away their r............Eze 26:16
which desire to walk in long r..........Lk 20:46
white r were given unto every one.....Rev 6:11
the Lamb, clothed with white r.........Rev 7:9
which are arrayed in white r.............Rev 7:13
and have washed their r, and made....Rev 7:14

ROBOAM (ro-bo´-am) See Rehoboam. *Same as*
Rehoboam; an ancestor of Jesus.
And Solomon begat R......................Mt 1:7
and R begat Abia...........................Mt 1:7

ROCK
thee there upon the r in Horeb..........Ex 17:6
and thou shalt smite the r...............Ex 17:6
me, and thou shalt stand upon a r.....Ex 33:21
will put thee in a clift of the r..........Ex 33:22
ye unto the r before their eyes.........Num 20:8
forth to them water out of the r.......Num 20:8
together before the r, and he said......Num 20:10
we fetch you water out of this r.......Num 20:10
with his rod he smote the r twice......Num 20:11
and thou puttest thy nest in a r.......Num 24:21
forth water out of the r of flint........Deut 8:15
He is the R, his work is perfect.........Deut 32:4
him to suck honey out of the r.........Deut 32:13
and oil out of the flinty r...............Deut 32:13
esteemed the R of his salvation........Deut 32:15
Of the R that begat thee thou art......Deut 32:18
except their R had sold them, and.....Deut 32:30
For their r is not as our R...............Deut 32:31
their r in whom they trusted,..........Deut 32:37
going up to Akrabbim, from the r......Judg 1:36
cakes, and lay them upon this r........Judg 6:20
there rose up fire out of the r.........Judg 6:21
thy God upon the top of this r.........Judg 6:26
and they slew Oreb upon the r Oreb...Judg 7:25
offered it upon a r unto the Lord......Judg 13:19
and dwelt in the top of the r Etam....Judg 15:8
went to the top of the r Etam..........Judg 15:11
and brought him up from the r.........Judg 15:13
wilderness unto the r of Rimmon......Judg 20:45
the wilderness unto the r Rimmon.....Judg 20:47
abode in the r Rimmon four months...Judg 20:47
that were in the r Rimmon..............Judg 21:13
is there any r like our God..............1Sa 2:2
was a sharp r on the one side..........1Sa 14:4
a sharp r on the other side.............1Sa 14:4
wherefore he came down into a r......1Sa 23:25
and spread it for her upon the r.......1Sa 21:10
And he said, The Lord is my r...........2Sa 22:2
The God of my r............................2Sa 22:3
and who is a r, save our God...........2Sa 22:32
and blessed be my r.......................2Sa 22:47
the God of the r of my salvation.......2Sa 22:47
the R of Israel spake to me, He.........2Sa 23:3
went down to the r to David............1Chr 11:15
them unto the top of the r..............2Chr 25:12
them down from the top of the r......2Chr 25:12
out of the r for their thirst.............Neh 9:15
the r is removed out of his place......Job 14:18
shall the r be removed out of his......Job 18:4
pen and lead in the r for ever.........Job 19:24
embrace the r for want of a............Job 24:8
putteth forth his hand upon the r.....Job 28:9
the r poured me out rivers of oil......Job 29:6
wild goats of the r bring forth.........Job 39:1
She dwelleth and abideth on the r....Job 39:28
upon the crag of the r...................Job 39:28
The Lord is my r, and my fortress,....Ps 18:2
or who is a r save our God.............Ps 18:31
and blessed be my r.......................Ps 18:46
he shall set me up upon a r............Ps 27:5
Unto thee will I cry, O Lord my r......Ps 28:1
be thou my strong r, for an house.....Ps 31:2
For thou art my r and my fortress.....Ps 31:3
clay, and set my feet upon a r.........Ps 40:2
I will say unto God my r, Why..........Ps 42:9
lead me to the r that is higher.........Ps 61:2
He only is my r and my salvation.....Ps 62:2
He only is my r and my salvation.....Ps 62:6
the r of my strength, and my..........Ps 62:7
to save me, for thou art my r..........Ps 71:3
brought streams also out of the r.....Ps 78:16
Behold, he smote the r, that the.......Ps 78:20
remembered that God was their r......Ps 78:35
with honey out of the r should I......Ps 81:16
my God, and the r of my salvation....Ps 89:26
he is my r, and there is no.............Ps 92:15
and my God is the r of my refuge.....Ps 94:22
noise to the r of our salvation.........Ps 95:1
He opened the r, and the waters......Ps 105:41
Which turned the r into a...............Ps 114:8
the way of a serpent upon a r.........Prov 30:19
that art in the clefts of the r..........Song 2:14

R

Enter into the r, and hide thee in .... Is 2:10
for a r of offence to both the .... Is 8:14
of Midian at the r of Oreb .... Is 10:26
mindful of the r of thy strength .... Is 17:10
an habitation for himself in a r .... Is 22:16
of a great r in a weary land .... Is 32:2
let the inhabitants of the r sing .... Is 42:11
to flow out of the r for them .... Is 48:21
he clave the r also, and the .... Is 48:21
look unto the r whence ye are .... Is 51:1
made their faces harder than a r .... Jer 5:3
hide it there in a hole of the r .... Jer 13:4
cometh from the r of the field................... Jer 18:14
r of the plain, saith the LORD................... Jer 21:13
that breaketh the r in pieces .... Jer 23:29
the cities, and dwell in the r .... Jer 48:28
dwellest in the clefts of the r................... Jer 49:16
she set it upon the top of a r .... Eze 24:7
set her blood upon the top of a r .... Eze 24:8
and make her like the top of a r .... Eze 26:4
make thee like the top of a r .... Eze 26:14
Shall horses run upon the r .... Amos 6:12
dwellest in the clefts of the r .... Obad 3
which built his house upon a r .... Mt 7:24
for it was founded upon a r .... Mt 7:25
upon this r I will build my .... Mt 16:18
which he had hewn out in the r .... Mt 27:60
which was hewn out of a r .... Mk 15:46
and laid the foundation on a r .... Lk 6:48
for it was founded upon a r .... Lk 6:48
And some fell upon a r .... Lk 8:6
They on the r are they, which, ... Lk 8:13
a stumblingblock and a r of offence .... Rom 9:33
spiritual R that followed them 1Cor 10:4
and that R was Christ 1Cor 10:4
a r of offence, even to them 1Pet 2:8

ROCKS

from the top of the r I see him .... Num 23:9
in caves, and in thickets, and in r 1Sa 13:6
his men upon the r of the sea, ... 1Sa 24:2
in pieces the r before the LORD............... 1Kin 19:11
He cutteth out rivers among the r .... Job 28:10
caves of the earth, and in the r .... Job 30:6
He clave the r in the wilderness, ... Ps 78:15
and the r for the conies.......................... Ps 104:18
make they their houses in the r .... Prov 30:26
shall go into the holes of the r .... Is 2:19
To go into the clefts of the r .... Is 2:21
and into the tops of the ragged r .... Is 2:21
valleys, and in the holes of the r .... Is 7:19
shall be the munitions of r .... Is 33:16
valleys under the clifts of the r .... Is 57:5
thickets, and climb up upon the r .... Jer 4:29
and out of the holes of the r .... Jer 16:16
and roll them down from the r .... Jer 51:25
the r are thrown down by him................. Nah 1:6
earth did quake, and the r rent............... Mt 27:51
lest we should have fallen upon r........... Acts 27:29
in the r of the mountains......................... Rev 6:15
And said to the mountains and r............. Rev 6:16

ROD

And he said, A r .... Ex 4:2
it, and it became a r in his hand............. Ex 4:4
shalt take this r in thine hand .... Ex 4:17
Moses took the r of God in his................ Ex 4:20
shalt say unto Aaron, Take thy r .... Ex 7:9
cast down his r before Pharaoh............... Ex 7:10
they cast down every man his r .... Ex 7:12
but Aaron's r swallowed up their........... Ex 7:12
the r which was turned to a .... Ex 7:15
I will smite with the r that is .... Ex 7:17
Moses, Say unto Aaron, Take thy .... Ex 7:19
and he lifted up the r, and smote........... Ex 7:20
hand with thy r over the streams........... Ex 8:5
Say unto Aaron, Stretch out thy r .... Ex 8:16
stretched out his hand with his r .... Ex 8:17
forth his r toward heaven .... Ex 9:23
his r over the land of Egypt .... Ex 10:13
But lift thou up thy r, and .... Ex 14:16
and thy r, wherewith thou smotest .... Ex 17:5
with the r of God in mine hand............... Ex 17:9
servant, or his maid, with a r .... Ex 21:20
of whatsoever passeth under the r .... Lev 27:32
take of every one of them a r .... Num 17:2
thou every man's name upon his r .... Num 17:2
Aaron's name upon the r of Levi............. Num 17:3
for one r shall be for the head............... Num 17:3
come to pass, that the man's r .... Num 17:5
their princes gave him a r apiece........... Num 17:6
the r of Aaron was among their............. Num 17:6
the r of Aaron for the house of .... Num 17:8
looked, and took every man his r .... Num 17:9
Bring Aaron's r again before the............. Num 17:10
Take the r, and gather thou the............. Num 20:8
Moses took the r from before the .... Num 20:9
with his r he smote the rock................... Num 20:11
end of the r that was in his hand........... 1Sa 14:27
of the r that was in mine hand 1Sa 14:43
chasten him with the r of men................. 2Sa 7:14
Let him take his r away from me........... Job 9:34
neither is the r of God upon them......... Job 21:9
shalt break them with a r of iron .... Ps 2:9
thy r and thy staff they comfort............. Ps 23:4
the r of thine inheritance, which .... Ps 74:2
their transgression with the r .... Ps 89:32
The LORD shall send the r of thy........... Ps 110:2
For the r of the wicked shall not .... Ps 125:3
but a r is for the back of him .... Prov 10:13
that spareth his r hateth his son .... Prov 13:24

of the foolish is a r of pride .... Prov 14:3
the r of his anger shall fail .... Prov 22:8
but the r of correction shall .... Prov 22:15
if thou beatest him with the r .... Prov 23:13
Thou shalt beat him with the r .... Prov 23:14
ass, and a r for the fool's back............. Prov 26:3
The r and reproof give wisdom .... Prov 29:15
the r of his oppressor, as in the .... Is 9:4
the r of mine anger, and the staff......... Is 10:5
as if the r should shake itself .... Is 10:15
he shall smite thee with a r .... Is 10:24
as his r was upon the sea, so .... Is 10:26
a rout of the stem of Jesse .... Is 11:1
the earth with the r of his mouth......... Is 11:4
because the r of him that smote........... Is 14:29
a staff, and the cummin with a r .... Is 28:27
beaten down, which smote with a r....... Is 30:31
I see a r of an almond tree................... Jer 1:11
and Israel is the r of his..................... Jer 10:16
staff broken, and the beautiful r .... Jer 48:17
and Israel is the r of his..................... Jer 51:19
affliction by the r of his wrath............. Lam 3:1
the r hath blossomed, pride hath......... Eze 7:10
risen up into a r of wickedness............. Eze 7:11
gone out of a r of her branches........... Eze 19:14
strong r to be a sceptre to rule .... Eze 19:14
cause you to pass under the r .... Eze 20:37
it contemneth the r of my son .... Eze 21:10
if the sword contemn even the r .... Eze 21:13
of Israel with a r upon the cheek......... Mic 5:1
hear ye the r, and who hath................. Mic 6:9
Feed thy people with thy r .... Mic 7:14
shall I come unto you with a r 1Cor 4:21
rule all nations with a r of iron .... Rev 2:27
shall rule them with a r of iron........... Rev 12:5
shall rule them with a r of iron........... Rev 19:15

RODANIM See DODANIM.

RODE

they r upon the camels, and .... Gen 24:61
sons that r on thirty ass colts .... Judg 10:4
that r on threescore and ten ass .... Judg 12:14
as she r on the ass, that she 1Sa 25:20
r upon an ass, with five damsels 1Sa 30:17
which r upon camels, and fled 1Sa 30:17
Absalom r upon a mule, and the 2Sa 18:9
he r upon a cherub, and did fly........... 2Sa 22:11
and her r thereon.............................. 1Kin 13:13
And Ahab r, and went to Jezreel......... 1Kin 18:45
So Jehu r in a chariot, and went 2Kin 9:16
thou r together after Ahab his........... 2Kin 9:25
me, save the beast that I r upon .... Neh 2:12
So the posts that r upon mules........... Est 8:14
he r upon a cherub, and did fly........... Ps 18:10

RODS

Jacob took him r of green poplar, ... Gen 30:37
white appear which was in the r .... Gen 30:37
he set the r which he had pilled........... Gen 30:38
the flocks conceived before the r .... Gen 30:39
that Jacob laid the r before the........... Gen 30:41
they might conceive among the r .... Gen 30:41
Aaron's r swallowed up their r .... Ex 7:12
house of their fathers twelve r .... Num 17:6
fathers' houses, even twelve r .... Num 17:6
rod of Aaron was among their r .... Num 17:6
Moses laid up the r before the........... Num 17:7
Moses brought out all the r from......... Num 17:9
she had strong r for the sceptres......... Eze 19:11
her strong r were broken and .... Eze 19:12
Thrice was I beaten with r 2Cor 11:25

ROE

was as light of foot as a wild r 2Sa 2:18
as the loving hind and pleasant r .... Prov 5:19
Deliver thyself as a r from the........... Prov 6:5
is like a r or a young hart .... Song 2:9
be thou like a r or a young hart .... Song 2:17
be thou like to a r or to a young......... Song 8:14
And it shall be as the chased r........... Is 13:14

ROEBUCK

may eat thereof, as of the r .... Deut 12:15
Even as the r and the hart is .... Deut 12:22
The hart, and the r, and the fallow ..... Deut 14:5
shalt eat it alike, as the .... Deut 15:22

ROEBUCKS

hundred sheep, beside harts, and r 1Kin 4:23

ROES

swift as the r upon the mountains....... 1Chr 12:8
daughters of Jerusalem, by the r .... Song 2:7
daughters of Jerusalem, by the r .... Song 3:5
like two young r that are twins........... Song 4:5
like two young r that are twins........... Song 7:3

ROGELIM (ro′-chel-im) A city in Gilead.

Barzillai the Gileadite of R 2Sa 17:27
the Gileadite came down from R........... 2Sa 19:31

ROHGAH (ro′-gah) A son of Shamer.

Ahi, and R, Jehubbah, and Aram......... 1Chr 7:34

ROLL

till they r the stone from the .... Gen 29:8
R great stones upon the mouth of .... Josh 10:18
r a great stone unto me this day......... Isa 14:33
in the province of the Medes, a r .... Ezr 6:2
said unto me, Take thee a great r .... Is 8:1
Take thee a r of a book, and write....... Jer 36:2
unto him, upon a r of a book .... Jer 36:4

go thou, and read in the r .... Jer 36:6
Take in thine hand the r wherein......... Jer 36:14
of Neriah took the r in his hand......... Jer 36:14
but they laid up the r in the .... Jer 36:20
king sent Jehudi to fetch the r........... Jer 36:21
until all the r was consumed in........... Jer 36:23
king that he would not burn the r .... Jer 36:25
that the king had burned the r........... Jer 36:27
Take thee again another r................... Jer 36:28
words that were in the first r............. Jer 36:28
Thou hast burned this r, saying,......... Jer 36:29
Then took Jeremiah another r .... Jer 36:32
r thee down from the rocks, and......... Jer 51:25
a r of a book was therein................... Eze 2:9
eat this r, and go speak unto the .... Eze 3:1
and he caused me to eat that r .... Eze 3:2
with this r that I give thee................. Eze 3:3
of Aphrah r thyself in the dust........... Mic 1:10
and looked, and behold a flying r....... Zec 5:1
And I answered, I see a flying r......... Zec 5:2
Who shall r us away the stone .... Mk 16:3

ROLLED

they r the stone from the well's......... Gen 29:3
r the stone from the well's mouth....... Gen 29:10
they have I r away the......................... Josh 5:9
they r themselves upon me .... Job 30:14
noise, and garments r in blood........... Is 9:5
shall be r together as a scroll............. Is 34:4
he r a great stone to the door of .... Mt 27:60
r back the stone from the door,........... Mt 28:2
r a stone unto the door of the........... Mk 15:46
saw that the stone was r away........... Mk 16:4
they found the stone r away from....... Lk 24:2
as a scroll when it is r together......... Rev 6:14

ROLLER

to put a r to bind it, to make it......... Eze 30:21

ROLLETH

and he that r a stone, it will .... Prov 26:27

ROLLING

like a r thing before the..................... Is 17:13

ROLLS

was made in the house of the............. Ezr 6:1

ROMAMTI-EZER (romam′-ti-e′-zur) A
sanctuary servant.
Hanani, Eliathah, Giddalti, and R 1Chr 25:4
The four and twentieth to R 1Chr 25:31

ROMAN (ro′-mun) See ROMANS. A citizen of
Rome.
you to scourge a man that is a R......... Acts 22:25
for this man is a R .... Acts 22:26
unto him, Tell me, art thou a R .... Acts 22:27
after he knew that he was a R........... Acts 22:29
having understood that he was a R ..... Acts 23:27

ROMANS (ro′-muns)
the R shall come and take away......... Jn 11:48
neither to observe, being R .... Acts 16:21
as openly uncondemned, being R....... Acts 16:37
when they heard that they were R ..... Acts 16:38
the R to deliver any man to die......... Acts 25:16
Jerusalem into the hands of the R ..... Acts 28:17
Written to the R from Corinthus......... Rom s

ROME (rome) See ROMAN. Administrative
center of the Roman Empire.
about Cyrene, and strangers of R....... Acts 2:10
all Jews to depart from R................... Acts 18:2
been there, I must also see R .... Acts 19:21
must thou bear witness also at R .... Acts 23:11
and so we went toward R................... Acts 28:14
And when we came to R, the .... Acts 28:16
To all that be in R, beloved of........... Rom 1:7
gospel to you that are at R also......... Rom 1:15
Unto the Galatians written from R ..... Gal s
Written from R unto the Ephesians..... Eph s
from R by Epaphroditus..................... Phil s
Written from R to the Colossians....... Col s
But, when he was in R, he sought....... 2Ti 1:17
the Ephesians, was written from R ..... 2Ti s
Written from R to Philemon .... Philem s

ROMPHA See REMPHAN.

ROOF

they under the shadow of my r........... Gen 19:8
shalt make a battlement for thy r....... Deut 22:8
them up to the r of the house........... Josh 2:6
she had laid in order upon the r .... Josh 2:6
she r′me up unto them upon the r..... Josh 2:8
there were upon the r about three..... Judg 16:27
walked upon the r of the king's......... 2Sa 11:2
from the r he saw a woman washing... 2Sa 11:2
the r over the gate unto the wall....... 2Sa 18:24
every one upon the r of his house..... Neh 8:16
cleaved to the r of their mouth......... Job 29:10
cleave to the r of my mouth .... Ps 137:6
the r of thy mouth like the best......... Song 7:9
to the r of his mouth for thirst......... Lam 4:4
cleave to the r of thy mouth .... Eze 3:26
r of one little chamber to the .... Eze 40:13
chamber to the r of another .... Eze 40:13
thou shouldest come under my r....... Mt 8:8
they uncovered the r where he was..... Mk 2:4
thou shouldest enter under my r....... Lk 7:6

ROOFS

of all the houses upon whose r......... Jer 19:13
upon whose r they have offered......... Jer 32:29

ROOM

is the r in thy father's house.	Gen 24:23
enough, and r to lodge in.	Gen 24:25
the house, and r for the camels.	Gen 24:31
now the LORD hath made r for us.	Gen 26:22
me continually in the r of Joab.	2Sa 19:13
Jehoiada in his r over the host.	1Kin 2:35
the king put in the r of Abiathar.	1Kin 2:35
him king in the r of his father.	1Kin 5:1
will set upon thy throne in thy r.	1Kin 5:5
up in the r of David my father.	1Kin 8:20
anoint to be prophet in thy r.	1Kin 19:16
killed him, and reigned in his r.	2Kin 15:25
in the r of Josiah his father.	2Kin 23:34
up in the r of David my father.	2Chr 6:10
made him king in the r of his.	2Chr 26:1
and set my feet in a large r.	Ps 31:8
Thou preparedst r before it.	Ps 80:9
A man's gift maketh r for him.	Prov 18:16
not be r enough to receive it.	Mal 3:10
in the r of his father Herod.	Mt 2:22
there was no r to receive them.	Mk 2:2
you a large upper r furnished.	Mk 14:15
was no r for them in the inn.	Lk 2:7
because I have no r where to.	Lk 12:17
sit not down in the highest r.	Lk 14:8
with shame to take the lowest r.	Lk 14:9
go and sit down in the lowest r.	Lk 14:10
hast commanded, and yet there is r.	Lk 14:22
you a large upper r furnished.	Lk 22:12
in, they went up into an upper r.	Acts 1:13
Porcius Festus came into Felix' r.	Acts 24:27
r of the unlearned say Amen at.	1Cor 14:16

ROOMS

r shalt thou make in the ark, and.	Gen 6:14
place, and put captains in their r.	1Kin 20:24
this day, and dwelt in their r.	1Chr 4:41
And love the uppermost r at feasts.	Mt 23:6
and the uppermost r at feasts.	Mk 12:39
how they chose out the chief r.	Lk 14:7
and the chief r at feasts.	Lk 20:46

ROOT

among you a r that beareth gall.	Deut 29:18
there a r of them against Amalek.	Judg 5:14
he shall r up Israel out of this.	1Kin 14:15
shall yet again take r downward.	2Kin 19:30
I have seen the foolish taking r.	Job 5:3
Though the r thereof wax old in.	Job 14:8
seeing the r of the matter is.	Job 19:28
My r was spread out by the waters.	Job 29:19
would r out all mine increase.	Job 31:12
r thee out of the land of the.	Ps 52:5
and didst cause it to take deep r.	Ps 80:9
but the r of the righteous shall.	Prov 12:3
but the r of the righteous.	Prov 12:12
so their r shall be as rottenness.	Is 5:24
day there shall be a r of Jesse.	Is 11:10
for out of the serpent's r shall.	Is 14:29
and I will kill thy r with famine.	Is 14:30
them that come of Jacob to take r.	Is 27:6
Judah shall again take r downward.	Is 37:31
shall not take r in the earth.	Is 40:24
as a r out of a dry ground.	Is 53:2
to r out, and to pull down, and to.	Jer 1:10
them, yea, they have taken r.	Jer 12:2
for his r was by great waters.	Eze 31:7
their r is dried up, they shall.	Hos 9:16
leave them neither r nor branch.	Mal 4:1
is laid unto the r of the trees.	Mt 3:10
and because they had no r, they.	Mt 13:6
Yet hath he not r in himself.	Mt 13:21
ye r up also the wheat with them.	Mt 13:29
and because it had no r, it.	Mk 4:6
have no r in themselves, and so.	Mk 4:17
is laid unto the r of the trees.	Lk 3:9
and these have no r, which for a.	Lk 8:13
tree, Be thou plucked up by the r.	Lk 17:6
if the r be holy, so are the.	Rom 11:16
and with them partakest of the r.	Rom 11:17
not the r, but the r thee.	Rom 11:18
There shall be a r of Jesse.	Rom 15:12
of money is the r of all evil.	1Ti 6:10
lest any r of bitterness.	Heb 12:15
the R of David, hath prevailed to.	Rev 5:5
I am the r and the offspring of.	Rev 22:16

ROOTED

the LORD r them out of their land.	Deut 29:28
shall be r out of his tabernacle.	Job 18:14
yea, let my offspring be r out.	Job 31:8
shall be r out of it.	Prov 2:22
noonday, and Ekron shall be r up.	Zeph 2:4
hath not planted, shall be r up.	Mt 15:13
that ye, being r and grounded in.	Eph 3:17
R and built up in him, and.	Col 2:7

ROOTS

the r out of my land which I have.	2Chr 7:20
His r are wrapped about the heap.	Job 8:17
His r shall be dried up beneath.	Job 18:16
the mountains by the r.	Job 28:9
and juniper r for their meat.	Job 30:4
a Branch shall grow out of his r.	Is 11:1
spreadeth out her r by the river.	Jer 17:8
the r thereof were under him.	Eze 17:6
vine did bend her r toward him.	Eze 17:7
he not pull up the r thereof.	Eze 17:9
to pluck it up by the r thereof.	Eze 17:9
the stump of his r in the earth.	Dan 4:15
of the r thereof in the earth.	Dan 4:23

to leave the stump of the tree r.	Dan 4:26
first horns plucked up by the r.	Dan 7:8
her r shall one stand up in his.	Dan 11:7
and cast forth his r as Lebanon.	Hos 14:5
from above, and his r from beneath.	Amos 2:9
the fig tree dried up from the r.	Mk 11:20
twice dead, plucked up by the r.	Jude 12

ROPE

| and sin as it were with a cart r. | Is 5:18 |

ROPES

new r that never were occupied.	Judg 16:11
Delilah therefore took new r.	Judg 16:12
all Israel bring r to that city.	2Sa 17:13
r upon our heads, and go out to.	1Kin 20:31
put r on their heads, and came to.	1Kin 20:32
cut off the r of the boat.	Acts 27:32

ROSE

that Cain r up against Abel his.	Gen 4:8
the men r up from thence, and.	Gen 18:16
Lot seeing them r up to meet them.	Gen 19:1
Therefore Abimelech r early in.	Gen 20:8
Abraham r up early in the morning.	Gen 21:14
then Abimelech r up, and Phichol.	Gen 21:32
Abraham r up early in the morning.	Gen 22:3
r up, and went unto the place of.	Gen 22:3
unto his young men, and they r up.	Gen 22:19
they r up in the morning, and he.	Gen 24:54
drink, and r up, and went his way.	Gen 25:34
they r up betimes in the morning.	Gen 26:31
Jacob r up early in the morning.	Gen 28:18
Then Jacob r up, and set his sons.	Gen 31:17
and he r up, and passed over the.	Gen 31:21
early in the morning Laban r up.	Gen 31:55
he r up that night, and took his.	Gen 32:22
over Penuel the sun r upon him.	Gen 32:31
his daughters r up to comfort him.	Gen 37:35
r up, and went down to Egypt, and.	Gen 43:15
Jacob r up from Beer-sheba.	Gen 46:5
neither r any from his place for.	Ex 10:23
Pharaoh r up in the night, he, and.	Ex 12:30
then that r up against thee.	Ex 15:7
r up early in the morning, and.	Ex 24:4
And Moses r up, and his minister.	Ex 24:13
they r up early on the morrow, and.	Ex 32:6
eat and to drink, and r up to play.	Ex 32:6
that all the people r up.	Ex 33:8
and all the people r up and.	Ex 33:10
Moses r up early in the morning.	Ex 34:4
they r up early in the morning.	Num 14:40
they r up before Moses, with.	Num 16:2
Moses r up and went unto.	Num 16:25
Balaam r up in the morning, and.	Num 22:13
And the princes of Moab r up.	Num 22:14
Balaam r up in the morning, and.	Num 22:21
And Balaam r up, and went and.	Num 24:25
saw it, he r up from among the.	Num 25:7
and r up from Seir unto them.	Deut 33:2
Joshua r early in the morning.	Josh 3:1
r up upon an heap very far from.	Josh 3:16
Joshua r early in the morning, and.	Josh 6:12
that they r early about the.	Josh 6:15
So Joshua r up early in the.	Josh 7:16
Joshua r up early in the morning.	Josh 8:10
r up early, and the men of the.	Josh 8:14
there r up fire out of the rock.	Judg 6:21
for he r up early on the morrow.	Judg 6:38
r up early, and pitched beside the.	Judg 7:1
And Abimelech r up, and all the.	Judg 9:34
And Abimelech r up, and the people.	Judg 9:35
he r up against them, and smote.	Judg 9:43
morning, that he r up to depart.	Judg 19:5
And when the man r up to depart.	Judg 19:7
And when the man r up to depart.	Judg 19:9
not tarry that night, but he r up.	Judg 19:10
her lord r up in the morning, and.	Judg 19:27
up upon an ass, and the man r up.	Judg 19:28
And the men of Gibeah r against me.	Judg 20:5
of Israel r up in the morning.	Judg 20:19
of Israel r up out of their place.	Judg 20:33
morrow, that the people r early.	Judg 21:4
she r up before one could know.	Ruth 3:14
So Hannah r up after they had.	1Sa 1:9
they r up in the morning early.	1Sa 1:19
when Samuel r early to meet Saul.	1Sa 15:12
So Samuel r up, and went to Ramah.	1Sa 16:13
David r up early in the morning.	1Sa 17:20
But Saul r up out of the cave, and.	1Sa 24:7
Then they r up, and went away that.	1Sa 28:25
his men r up early to depart in.	1Sa 29:11
Abishai r up early, and stood.	2Sa 15:2
all them that r up against thee.	2Sa 18:31
them that r up against me hast.	2Sa 22:40
above them that r up against me.	2Sa 22:49
r up, and went every man his way.	1Kin 1:49
the king r up to meet her, and.	1Kin 2:19
when I r in the morning to give.	1Kin 3:21
that Ahab r up to go down to the.	1Kin 21:16
they r up early in the morning.	2Kin 3:22
of Israel, the Israelites r up.	2Kin 3:24
they r up in the twilight, to go.	2Kin 7:5
he r by night, and smote the.	2Kin 8:21
they r early in the morning, and.	2Chr 20:20
he r up by night, and smote the.	2Chr 21:9
the leprosy even r up in his.	2Chr 26:19
which were expressed by name r up.	2Chr 28:15
Then Hezekiah the king r early.	2Chr 29:20
Then r up the chief of the.	Ezr 1:5
Then r up Zerubbabel the son of.	Ezr 5:2
Then Ezra r up from before the.	Ezr 10:6

priest r up with his brethren the.	Neh 3:1
r up, and said unto the nobles, and.	Neh 4:14
r up early in the morning, and.	Job 1:5
me those that r up against me.	Ps 18:39
side, when men r up against us.	Ps 124:2
I am the r of Sharon, and the lily.	Song 2:1
I r up to open to my beloved.	Song 5:5
rejoice, and blossom as the r.	Is 35:1
Then r up certain of the elders.	Jer 26:17
of those that r up against me.	Lam 3:62
r up in haste, and spake, and said.	Dan 3:24
afterward I r up, and did the.	Dan 8:27
But Jonah r up to flee unto.	Jonah 1:3
when the morning r the next day.	Jonah 4:7
but they r early, and corrupted.	Zeph 3:7
he, casting away his garment, r.	Mk 10:50
r up, and thrust him out of the.	Lk 4:29
immediately he r up before them.	Lk 5:25
left all, r up, and followed him.	Lk 5:28
though one r from the dead.	Lk 16:31
when he r up from prayer, and was.	Lk 22:45
they r up the same hour, and.	Lk 24:33
that she r up hastily and went out.	Jn 11:31
Then the high priest r up.	Acts 5:17
before these days r up Theudas.	Acts 5:36
After this man r up Judas of.	Acts 5:37
with him after he r from the dead.	Acts 10:41
stood round about him, he r up.	Acts 14:20
But there r up certain of the.	Acts 15:5
been much disputing, Peter r up.	Acts 15:7
the multitude r up together.	Acts 16:22
he had thus spoken, the king r up.	Acts 26:30
this end Christ both died, and r.	Rom 14:9
to eat and drink, and r up to play.	1Cor 10:7
that he r again the third day.	1Cor 15:4
preached that he r from the dead.	1Cor 15:12
which died for them, and r again.	2Cor 5:15
r again, even so them also which.	1Th 4:14
her smoke r up for ever and ever.	Rev 19:3

ROSH (rosh) A son of Benjamin.

| Gera, and Naaman, Ehi, and R. | Gen 46:21 |

ROT

the LORD doth make thy thigh to r.	Num 5:21
belly to swell, and thy thigh to r.	Num 5:22
shall swell, and her thigh shall r.	Num 5:27
the name of the wicked shall r.	Prov 10:7
chooseth a tree that will not r.	Is 40:20

ROTTEN

as a r thing, consumeth, as a.	Job 13:28
iron as straw, and brass as r wood.	Job 41:27
old r rags, and let them down by.	Jer 38:11
r rags under thine armholes under.	Jer 38:12
The seed is r under their clods.	Joel 1:17

ROTTENNESS

ashamed is as r in his bones.	Prov 12:4
but envy the r of the bones.	Prov 14:30
so their root shall be as r.	Is 5:24
and to the house of Judah as r.	Hos 5:12
r entered into my bones, and I.	Hab 3:16

ROUGH

down the heifer unto a r valley.	Deut 21:4
he stayeth his r wind in the day.	Is 27:8
straight, and the r places plain.	Is 40:4
to come up as the r caterpillers.	Jer 51:27
the r goat is the king of Grecia.	Dan 8:21
they wear a r garment to deceive.	Zec 13:4
the r ways shall be made smooth.	Lk 3:5

ROUGHLY

unto them, and spake r unto them.	Gen 42:7
lord of the land, spake r to us.	Gen 42:30
what if thy father answer thee r.	1Sa 20:10
And the king answered the people r.	1Kin 12:13
And the king answered them r.	2Chr 10:13
but the rich answereth r.	Prov 18:23

ROUND

of Sodom, compassed the house r.	Gen 19:4
were in all the borders r about.	Gen 23:17
the cities that were r about them.	Gen 35:5
your sheaves stood r about.	Gen 37:7
which was r about every city.	Gen 41:48
all the Egyptians digged r about.	Ex 7:24
the dew lay r about the host.	Ex 16:13
there lay a small r thing.	Ex 16:14
bounds unto the people r about.	Ex 19:12
upon it a crown of gold r about.	Ex 25:11
thereto a crown of gold r about.	Ex 25:24
border of an hand breadth r about.	Ex 25:25
to the border thereof r about.	Ex 25:25
All the pillars r about the court.	Ex 27:17
woven work r about the hole of it.	Ex 28:32
scarlet, r about the hem thereof.	Ex 28:33
of gold between them r about.	Ex 28:33
upon the hem of the robe r about.	Ex 28:34
sprinkle it r about upon the.	Ex 29:16
the blood upon the altar r about.	Ex 29:20
and the sides thereof r about.	Ex 30:3
unto it a crown of gold r about.	Ex 30:3
a crown of gold to it r about.	Ex 37:2
thereunto a crown of gold r about.	Ex 37:11
border of an handbreadth r about.	Ex 37:12
for the border thereof r about.	Ex 37:12
it, and the sides thereof r about.	Ex 37:26
unto it a crown of gold r about.	Ex 37:26
All the hangings of the court r.	Ex 38:16
and of the court r about, were of.	Ex 38:20
the sockets of the court r about.	Ex 38:31

R

all the pins of the court r about .... Ex 38:31
with a band r about the hole,................. Ex 39:23
r about between the pomegranates .... Ex 39:25
r about the hem of the robe to .... Ex 39:26
shalt set up the court r about .... Ex 40:8
the court r about the tabernacle .... Ex 40:33
sprinkle the blood r about upon .... Lev 1:5
his blood r about upon the altar .... Lev 1:11
the blood upon the altar r about .... Lev 3:2
thereof r about upon the altar .... Lev 3:8
thereof upon the altar r about .... Lev 3:13
sprinkle r about upon the altar .... Lev 7:2
the altar r about with his finger .... Lev 8:15
the blood upon the altar r about .... Lev 8:19
the blood upon the altar r about .... Lev 8:24
which he sprinkled r about upon .... Lev 9:12
sprinkled upon the altar r about .... Lev 9:18
to be scraped within r about .... Lev 14:41
the horns of the altar r about .... Lev 16:18
Ye shall not r the corners of .... Lev 19:27
r about them shall be counted as ...... Lev 25:31
the heathen that are r about you .... Lev 25:44
it, and shall encamp r about the .... Num 1:50
pitch r about the tabernacle of .... Num 1:53
and by the altar r about, and the ...... Num 3:26
the pillars of the court r about .... Num 3:37
and by the altar r about, and their .... Num 4:26
the pillars of the court r about .... Num 4:32
set them r about the tabernacle .... Num 11:24
r about the camp, and as it were .... Num 11:31
for themselves r about the camp .... Num 11:32
all Israel that were r about them .... Num 16:34
lick up all that are r about us .... Num 22:4
the cities of the country r about .... Num 32:33
with the coasts thereof r about .... Num 34:12
for the cities r about them .... Num 35:2
outward a thousand cubits r about ... Num 35:4
the people which are r about you ...... Deut 6:14
from all your enemies r about .... Deut 12:10
the people which are r about you ...... Deut 13:7
are r about him that is slain .... Deut 21:2
from all thine enemies r about .... Deut 25:19
war, and go r about the city once ..... Josh 6:3
hear of it, and shall environ us r ...... Josh 7:9
Judah r about according to their ...... Josh 15:12
by the coasts thereof r about .... Josh 18:20
that were r about these cities to .... Josh 19:8
the suburbs thereof r about it .... Josh 21:11
with their suburbs r about them, ... Josh 21:42
the LORD gave them rest r about .... Josh 21:44
from all their enemies r about .... Josh 23:1
the people that were r about them .... Judg 2:12
hands of their enemies r about .... Judg 2:14
man in his place r about the camp ... Judg 7:21
Belial, beset the house r about .... Judg 19:22
beset the house r about upon me ...... Judg 20:5
set liers in wait r about Gibeah .... Judg 20:29
inclosed the Benjamites r about .... Judg 20:43
the camp from the country r about ... 1Sa 14:21
his men r about to take them.............. 1Sa 23:26
and the people pitched r about him ... 1Sa 26:5
and the people lay r about him 1Sa 26:7
land of the Philistines r about 1Sa 31:9
David built r about from Millo and ... 2Sa 5:9
rest r about from all his enemies 2Sa 7:1
darkness pavilions r about him 2Sa 22:12
and the wall of Jerusalem r about 1Kin 3:1
peace on all sides r about him 1Kin 4:24
fame was in all nations r about 1Kin 4:31
house he built chambers r about 1Kin 6:5
the walls of the house r about 1Kin 6:5
and he made chambers r about 1Kin 6:5
he made narrowed rests r about 1Kin 6:6
all the walls of the house r 1Kin 6:29
the great court r about was with 1Kin 7:12
two rows r about upon the one 1Kin 7:18
were two hundred in rows r about 1Kin 7:20
it was r all about, and his height 1Kin 7:23
cubits did compass it r about 1Kin 7:23
under the brim of it r about 1Kin 7:24
cubit, compassing the sea r about 1Kin 7:24
but the mouth thereof was r after 1Kin 7:31
their borders, foursquare, not r 1Kin 7:31
a r compass of half a cubit high 1Kin 7:35
every one, and additions r about 1Kin 7:36
top of the throne was r behind 1Kin 10:19
the water ran r about the altar 1Kin 18:35
chariots of fire r about Elisha 2Kin 6:17
ye shall compass the king r about 2Kin 11:8
r about the king, from the right 2Kin 11:11
heathen that were r about them 2Kin 17:15
in the places r about Jerusalem 2Kin 23:5
built forts against it r about 2Kin 25:1
were against the city r about 2Kin 25:4
the walls of Jerusalem r about 2Kin 25:10
upon the chapiter r about 2Kin 25:17
that were r about the same cities 1Chr 4:33
and the suburbs thereof r about it 1Chr 6:55
they lodged r about the house of 1Chr 9:27
land of the Philistines r about 1Chr 10:9
And he built the city r about 1Chr 11:8
about, even from Millo r about 1Chr 11:8
rest from all his enemies r about 1Chr 22:9
and of all the chambers r about 1Chr 28:12
r in compass, and five cubits the 2Chr 4:2
cubits did compass it r about 2Chr 4:2
which did compass it r about 2Chr 4:3
cubit, compassing the sea r about 2Chr 4:3
all the cities r about Gerar................ 2Chr 14:14
the LORD gave them rest r about 2Chr 15:15

the lands that were r about Judah..... 2Chr 17:10
for his God gave him rest r about 2Chr 20:30
shall compass the king r about.......... 2Chr 23:7
the temple, by the king r about......... 2Chr 23:10
with their mattocks r about 2Chr 34:6
plain country r about Jerusalem .... Neh 12:28
them villages r about Jerusalem .... Neh 12:29
and fashioned me together r about .... Job 10:8
His archers compass me r about .... Job 16:13
encamp r about my tabernacle .... Job 19:12
Therefore snares are r about thee ..... Job 22:10
it is turned r about by his .... Job 37:12
his teeth are terrible r about .... Job 41:14
set themselves against me r about ..... Ps 3:6
his pavilion r about him were .... Ps 18:11
bulls of Bashan have beset me r .... Ps 22:12
up above mine enemies r about me ... Ps 27:6
r about them that fear him .... Ps 34:7
to them that are r about us................ Ps 44:13
about Zion, and go r about her .... Ps 48:12
be very tempestuous r about him ...... Ps 50:3
a dog, and go r about the city .... Ps 59:6
a dog, and go r about the city .... Ps 59:14
let all that be r about him bring......... Ps 76:11
r about their habitations .... Ps 78:28
shed like water r about Jerusalem ..... Ps 79:3
to them that are r about us................ Ps 79:4
They came r about me daily like .... Ps 88:17
to thy faithfulness r about thee .... Ps 89:8
and darkness are r about him............. Ps 97:2
and burneth up his enemies r about ... Ps 97:3
mountains are r about Jerusalem .... Ps 125:2
so the LORD is r about his people...... Ps 125:2
olive plants r about thy table............. Ps 128:3
Thy navel is like a goblet.................. Song 7:2
their r tires like the moon,................. Is 3:18
For the cry is gone r about the .... Is 15:8
I will camp against thee r about .... Is 29:3
it hath set him on fire r about............ Is 42:25
Lift up thine eyes r about .... Is 49:18
Lift up thine eyes r about .... Is 60:4
all the walls thereof r about,.............. Jer 1:15
are they against her r about............... Jer 4:17
their tents against her r about .... Jer 6:3
the birds r about are against her .... Jer 12:9
devour all things r about it................ Jer 21:14
against all these nations r about .... Jer 25:9
for fear was r about, saith the .... Jer 46:5
sword shall devour r about thee......... Jer 46:14
in array against Babylon r about .... Jer 50:14
Shout against her r about................... Jer 50:15
the bow, camp against it r about........ Jer 50:29
it shall devour all r about him .... Jer 50:32
they shall be against her r about .... Jer 51:2
and built forts against it r about........ Jer 52:4
were by the city r about..................... Jer 52:7
the walls of Jerusalem r about .... Jer 52:14
upon the chapiters r about................. Jer 52:22
network were an hundred r about ...... Jer 52:23
adversaries should be r about him..... Lam 1:17
fire, which devoureth r about............. Lam 2:3
a solemn day my terrors r about........ Lam 2:22
full of eyes r about them four .... Eze 1:18
of fire r about within it..................... Eze 1:27
and it had brightness r about............. Eze 1:27
of the brightness r about................... Eze 1:28
battering rams against it r about........ Eze 4:2
and countries that are r about her ..... Eze 5:5
countries that are r about her............ Eze 5:6
the nations that are r about you .... Eze 5:7
the nations that are r about you .... Eze 5:7
fall by the sword r about you .... Eze 5:12
the nations that are r about you .... Eze 5:14
the nations that are r about thee .... Eze 5:15
your bones r about your altars .... Eze 6:5
their idols r about their altars........... Eze 6:13
pourtrayed upon the wall r about ...... Eze 8:10
wheels, were full of eyes r about ...... Eze 10:12
the heathen that are r about you .... Eze 11:12
gather them r about against thee .... Eze 16:37
and all that are r about her .... Eze 16:57
which despise thee r about................ Eze 16:57
and shield and helmet r about .... Eze 23:24
army were upon thy walls r about ..... Eze 27:11
shields upon thy walls r about........... Eze 27:11
of all that are r about them .... Eze 28:24
that despise them r about them .... Eze 28:26
rivers running r about his plants........ Eze 31:4
her company is r about her grave ...... Eze 32:23
her multitude r about her are .... Eze 32:24
her graves are r about him .... Eze 32:25
her graves are r about him .... Eze 32:26
the places r about my hill a .... Eze 34:26
of the heathen that are r about .... Eze 36:4
Then the heathen that are left r .... Eze 36:36
caused me to pass by them r about .... Eze 37:2
the outside of the house r about .... Eze 40:5
of the court r about the gate .... Eze 40:14
posts within the gate r about .... Eze 40:16
and windows were r about inward ..... Eze 40:16
made for the court r about .... Eze 40:17
and in the arches thereof r about ...... Eze 40:25
and in the arches thereof r about ...... Eze 40:30
the arches r about were five and .... Eze 40:30
and in the arches thereof r about ...... Eze 40:33
and the windows to it r about .... Eze 40:36
an hand broad, fastened r about .... Eze 40:43
r about the house on every side .... Eze 41:5
for the side chambers r about............ Eze 41:8
still upward r about the house .... Eze 41:7

the height of the house r about.......... Eze 41:8
r about the house on every side .... Eze 41:10
was left was five cubits r about......... Eze 41:11
was five cubits thick r about .... Eze 41:12
the galleries r about on three .... Eze 41:16
door, cieled with wood r about .... Eze 41:16
and by all the wall r about within..... Eze 41:17
through all the house r about .... Eze 42:15
the east, and measured it r about ...... Eze 42:15
with the measuring reed r about .... Eze 42:16
with the measuring reed r about .... Eze 42:17
it had a wall r about, five.................. Eze 42:20
the whole limit thereof r about.......... Eze 43:12
thereof r about shall be a span .... Eze 43:13
and upon the border r about.............. Eze 43:20
all the borders thereof r about .... Eze 45:1
in breadth, square r about................. Eze 45:2
fifty cubits r about for the .... Eze 45:2
a row of building r about in them ..... Eze 46:23
r about them four, and it was made ... Eze 46:23
places under the rows r about .... Eze 46:23
It was r about eighteen thousand ...... Eze 48:35
yourselves together r about .... Joel 3:11
to judge all the heathen r about .... Joel 3:12
shall be even r about the land .... Amos 3:11
the depth closed me r about .... Jonah 2:5
that had the waters r about it............ Nah 3:8
unto her a wall of fire r about .... Zec 2:5
and the cities thereof r about her ..... Zec 7:7
unto all the people r about .... Zec 12:2
devour all the people r about .... Zec 12:6
heathen r about shall be gathered .... Zec 14:14
and all the region r about Jordan ..... Mt 3:5
out into all that country r about ...... Mt 14:35
a vineyard, and hedged it r about ..... Mt 21:33
all the region r about Galilee .... Mk 1:28
when he had looked r about on .... Mk 3:5
he looked r about on them which ..... Mk 3:34
he looked r about to see her that ...... Mk 5:32
he went r about the villages .... Mk 6:6
may go into the country r about .... Mk 6:36
through that whole region r about .... Mk 6:55
when they had looked r about .... Mk 9:8
And Jesus looked r about, and saith ... Mk 10:23
when he had looked r about upon ..... Mk 11:11
on all that dwelt r about them .... Lk 1:65
of the Lord drone r about them .... Lk 2:9
through all the region r about .... Lk 4:14
place of the country r about .... Lk 4:37
looking r about upon them all, he ..... Lk 6:10
throughout all the region r about ..... Lk 7:17
r about besought him to depart .... Lk 8:37
into the towns and country r about ... Lk 9:12
about thee, and compass thee r .... Lk 19:43
Then came the Jews r about him ...... Jn 10:24
the cities r about unto Jerusalem ..... Acts 5:16
suddenly there shined r about him ... Acts 9:3
the region that lieth r about.............. Acts 14:6
the disciples stood r about him .... Acts 14:20
heaven a great light r about me......... Acts 22:6
down from Jerusalem stood r about ... Acts 25:7
shining r about me and them which ... Acts 26:13
r about unto Illyricum, I have .... Rom 15:19
overlaid r about with gold................. Heb 9:4
was a rainbow r about the throne ..... Rev 4:3
r about the throne were four and ...... Rev 4:4
r about the throne, were four............ Rev 4:6
of many angels r about the throne .... Rev 5:11
angels stood r about the throne .... Rev 7:11

ROUSE

who shall r him up.............................. Gen 49:9

ROVERS

David against the band of the r.......... 1Chr 12:21

ROW

the first r shall be a sardius, ... Ex 28:17
this shall be the first r....................... Ex 28:17
the second r shall be an emerald, ... Ex 28:18
And the third r a ligure, an agate ..... Ex 28:19
And the fourth r a beryl, and an .... Ex 28:20
the first r was a sardius, a................ Ex 39:10
this was the first r .... Ex 39:10
And the second r, an emerald, a .... Ex 39:11
And the third r, a ligure, an.............. Ex 39:12
And the fourth r, a beryl, an onyx .... Ex 39:13
set them in two rows, six on a r .... Lev 24:6
put pure frankincense upon each r .... Lev 24:7
stone, and a r of cedar beams 1Kin 6:36
five pillars, fifteen in a r 1Kin 7:3
a r of cedar beams, both for the 1Kin 7:12
stones, and a r of new timber .... Ezr 6:4
there was a r of building round .... Eze 46:23

ROWED

Nevertheless the men r hard to......... Jonah 1:13
So when they had r about five........... Jn 6:19

ROWERS

Thy r have brought thee into............. Eze 27:26

ROWING

And he saw them toiling in r............. Mk 6:48

ROWS

of stones, even four r of stones .... Ex 28:17
they set in it four r of stones .... Ex 39:10
And thou shalt set them in two r ...... Lev 24:6
court with three r of hewed stone 1Kin 6:36
upon four r of cedar pillars, ... 1Kin 7:2
And there were windows in three 1Kin 7:4
was with three r of hewed stones 1Kin 7:12

two *r* round about upon the one 1Kin 7:18
were two hundred in *r* round about 1Kin 7:20
the knops were cast in two *r* 1Kin 7:24
even two *r* of pomegranates for 1Kin 7:42
Two *r* of oxen were cast, when it 2Chr 4:3
two *r* of pomegranates on each 2Chr 4:13
With three *r* of great stones, and .... Ezr 6:4
are comely with *r* of jewels .... Song 1:10
places under the *r* round about .... Eze 46:23

ROYAL

fat, and he shall yield *r* dainties .... Gen 49:20
city, as one of the *r* cities .... Josh 10:2
dwell in the *r* city with thee 1Sa 27:5
of Ammon, and took the *r* city 2Sa 12:26
Solomon gave her of his *r* bounty 1Kin 10:13
arose and destroyed all the seed *r* 2Kin 11:1
son of Elishama, of the seed *r* 2Kin 25:25
bestowed upon him such *r* majesty ... 1Chr 29:25
the seed *r* of the house of Judah 2Chr 22:10
r wine in abundance, according to .... Est 1:7
r house which belonged to king .... Est 1:9
before the king with the crown *r* .... Est 1:11
let there go a *r* commandment from .... Est 1:19
let the king give her *r* estate .... Est 1:19
his house *r* in the tenth month .... Est 2:16
so that he set the *r* crown upon .... Est 2:17
that Esther put on her *r* apparel .... Est 5:1
his *r* throne in the *r* house .... Est 5:1
Let the *r* apparel be brought .... Est 6:8
the crown *r* which is set upon his .... Est 6:8
of the king in *r* apparel of blue .... Est 8:15
a *r* diadem in the hand of thy God ...... Is 62:3
son of Elishama, of the seed *r* .... Jer 41:1
spread his *r* pavilion over them .... Jer 43:10
together to establish a *r* statute .... Dan 6:7
day Herod, arrayed in *r* apparel .... Acts 12:21
If ye fulfil the *r* law according .... Jas 2:8
a *r* priesthood, an holy nation, a 1Pet 2:9

RUBBING

and did eat, *r* them in their hands .... Lk 6:1

RUBBISH

heaps of the *r* which are burned .... Neh 4:2
is decayed, and there is much *r* .... Neh 4:10

RUBIES

the price of wisdom is above *r* .... Job 28:18
She is more precious than *r* .... Prov 3:15
For wisdom is better than *r* .... Prov 8:11
is gold, and a multitude of *r* .... Prov 20:15
for her price is far above *r* .... Prov 31:10
were more ruddy in body than *r* .... Lam 4:7

RUDDER

the sea, and loosed the *r* bands .... Acts 27:40

RUDDY

Now he was *r*, and withal of a 1Sa 16:12
for he was but a youth, and *r* 1Sa 17:42
My beloved is white and *r*, the .... Song 5:10
they were more *r* in body than .... Lam 4:7

RUDE

But though I be *r* in speech 2Cor 11:6

RUDIMENTS

after the *r* of the world, and not .... Col 2:8
Christ from the *r* of the world .... Col 2:20

RUE

for ye tithe mint and *r* and all .... Lk 11:42

RUFUS (ru'-fus)
1. Son of Simon the Cyrenian.
the father of Alexander and R .... Mk 15:21
2. A Christian in Rome.
Salute R chosen in the Lord, and .... Rom 16:13

RUHAMAH (ru-ha'-mah) *A symbolic name of Israel.*
and to your sisters, R .... Hos 2:1

RUIN

But they were the *r* of him 2Chr 28:23
brought his strong holds to *r* .... Ps 89:40
who knoweth the *r* of .... Prov 24:22
and a flattering mouth worketh *r* .... Prov 26:28
let this *r* be under thy hand .... Is 3:6
and he brought it to *r* .... Is 23:13
of a defenced city a *r* .... Is 25:2
so iniquity shall not be your *r* .... Eze 18:30
of the seas in the day of thy *r* .... Eze 27:27
Upon his *r* shall all the fowls of ..... Eze 31:13
the *r* of that house was great .... Lk 6:49

RUINED

For Jerusalem is *r*, and Judah is ...... Is 3:8
r cities are become fenced, and .... Eze 36:35
I the Lord build the *r* places .... Eze 36:36

RUINOUS

waste fenced cities into *r* heaps 2Kin 19:25
a city, and it shall be a *r* heap .... Is 17:1
defenced cities into *r* heaps .... Is 37:26

RUINS

faint, and their *r* be multiplied .... Eze 21:15
and I will raise up his *r*, and I .... Amos 9:11
I will build again the *r* thereof .... Acts 15:16

RULE

the greater light to *r* the day .... Gen 1:16
the lesser light to *r* the night .... Gen 1:16
to *r* over the day and over the .... Gen 1:18
husband, and he shall *r* over thee ... Gen 3:16

---

desire, and thou shalt *r* over him .... Gen 4:7
Thou shalt not *r* over him with .... Lev 25:43
ye shall not *r* one over another .... Lev 25:46
the other shall not *r* with rigour .... Lev 25:53
R thou over us, both thou, and thy .... Judg 8:22
unto them, I will not *r* over you .... Judg 8:23
neither shall my son *r* over you .... Judg 8:23
the Lord shall *r* over you .... Judg 8:23
which bare *r* over the people that 1Kin 9:23
that had *r* over his chariots 1Kin 22:31
that bare *r* over the people 2Chr 8:10
servants bare *r* over the people ...... Neh 5:15
should bear *r* in his own house .... Est 1:22
that the Jews had *r* over them .... Est 9:1
r thou in the midst of thine .... Ps 110:2
The sun to *r* by day .... Ps 136:8
The moon and stars to *r* by night .... Ps 136:9
By me princes *r*, and nobles, even .. Prov 8:16
hand of the diligent shall bear *r* ..... Prov 12:24
A wise servant shall have *r* over ..... Prov 17:2
a servant to have *r* over princes ..... Prov 19:10
He that hath no *r* over his own .... Prov 25:28
but when the wicked beareth *r* .... Prov 29:2
yet shall he have *r* over all my .... Eccl 2:19
and babes shall *r* over them .... Is 3:4
oppressors, and women *r* over them ... Is 3:12
and they shall *r* over their .... Is 14:2
a fierce king shall *r* over them .... Is 19:4
that *r* this people which is in .... Is 28:14
and princes shall *r* in judgment ...... Is 32:1
hand, and his arm shall *r* for him ... Is 40:10
him, and made him *r* over kings ...... Is 41:2
carpenter stretcheth out his *r* .... Is 44:13
they that *r* over them make them .... Is 52:5
thou never barest *r* over them .... Is 63:19
the priests bear *r* by their means ... Jer 5:31
the sceptre of them that bare *r* ...... Eze 19:11
strong rod to be a sceptre to *r* ...... Eze 19:14
poured out, will I *r* over you .... Eze 20:33
shall no more *r* over the nations ..... Eze 29:15
which shall bear *r* over all the .... Dan 2:39
have known that the heavens do *r* .. Dan 4:26
that shall *r* with great dominion ...... Dan 11:3
shall cause them to *r* over many .... Dan 11:39
the heathen should *r* over them ...... Joel 2:17
and shall sit and *r* upon his throne ... Zec 6:13
that shall *r* my people Israel .... Mt 2:6
to *r* over the Gentiles exercise .... Mk 10:42
when he shall have put down all *r* .. 1Cor 15:24
r which God hath distributed to 2Cor 10:13
you according to our *r* abundantly .. 2Cor 10:15
many as walk according to this *r* ... Gal 6:16
let us walk by the same *r* .... Phil 3:16
the peace of God *r* in your hearts ... Col 3:15
know not how to *r* his own house ... 1Ti 3:5
Let the elders that *r* well be 1Ti 5:17
them which have the *r* over you ..... Heb 13:7
them that have the *r* over you .... Heb 13:17
all them that have the *r* over you ... Heb 13:24
he shall *r* them with a rod of .... Rev 2:27
who was to *r* all nations with a ..... Rev 12:5
he shall *r* them with a rod of .... Rev 19:15

RULED

that *r* over all that he had, Put, ... Gen 24:2
thy word shall all my people be *r* ... Gen 41:40
r from Aroer, which is upon the ..... Josh 12:2
in the days when the judges *r* .... Ruth 1:1
which *r* over the people that 1Kin 5:16
that *r* throughout the house of 1Chr 26:6
which have *r* over all countries ..... Ezr 4:20
they that hated them *r* over them .. Ps 106:41
he that *r* the nations in anger, ... Is 14:6
Servants have *r* over us .... Lam 5:8
and with cruelty have ye *r* them .... Eze 34:4
high God *r* in the kingdom of men .. Dan 5:21
to his dominion which he *r* .... Dan 11:4

RULER

he made him *r* over all the land ..... Gen 41:43
he said to the *r* of his house .... Gen 43:16
a *r* throughout all the land of .... Gen 45:8
nor curse the *r* of thy people .... Ex 22:28
When a *r* hath sinned, and done ... Lev 4:22
a man, every one a *r* among them .. Num 13:2
when Zebul the *r* of the city .... Judg 9:30
have appointed thee *r* over Israel .. 1Sa 25:30
to appoint me *r* over the people 2Sa 6:21
to be *r* over my people, over 2Sa 7:8
Jairite was a chief *r* about David 2Sa 20:26
appointed him to be *r* over Israel .. 1Kin 1:35
he made him *r* over all the charge . 1Kin 11:28
of Ahikam, the son of Shaphan, *r* .. 2Kin 25:22
and of him came the chief *r* 1Chr 5:2
the *r* of the house of God 1Chr 9:11
was the *r* over them in time past ... 1Chr 9:20
thou shalt be *r* over my people 1Chr 11:2
be *r* over my people Israel 1Chr 17:7
of Moses, was *r* of the treasures ... 1Chr 26:24
his course was Mikloth also the *r* .. 1Chr 27:4
the *r* of the Reubenites was 1Chr 27:16
he hath chosen Judah to be the *r* .. 1Chr 28:4
to be a *r* over my people Israel 2Chr 6:5
fall thee a man to be *r* in Israel 2Chr 7:18
to be *r* among his brethren 2Chr 11:22
the *r* of the house of Judah, for 2Chr 19:11
the scribe and Maaseiah the *r* 2Chr 26:11
which Conomiah the Levite was *r* .. 2Chr 31:12
Azariah the *r* of the house of God .. 2Chr 31:13
the *r* of the half part of .... Neh 3:9
the *r* of the half part of .... Neh 3:12

---

the *r* of part of Beth-haccerem .... Neh 3:14
Colhozeh, the *r* of part of Mizpah .. Neh 3:15
the *r* of the half part of .... Neh 3:16
the *r* of the half part of Keilah ..... Neh 3:17
the *r* of the half part of Keilah ..... Neh 3:18
the *r* of Mizpah, another piece ..... Neh 3:19
Hananiah the *r* of the palace, ... Neh 7:2
was the *r* of the house of God, ... Neh 11:11
is little Benjamin with their *r* .... Ps 68:27
even the *r* of the people, and let .. Ps 105:20
house, and *r* of all his substance .. Ps 105:21
having no guide, overseer, or *r* .... Prov 6:7
When thou sittest to eat with a *r* .. Prov 23:1
so is a wicked *r* over the poor ..... Prov 28:15
If a *r* hearken to lies, all his .... Prov 29:12
of the *r* rise up against thee .... Eccl 10:4
error which proceedeth from the *r* ... Eccl 10:5
Thou hast clothing, be thou our *r* . Is 3:6
make me not a *r* of the people ..... Is 3:7
Send ye the lamb to the *r* of the ... Is 16:1
in the land, a against *r* .... Jer 51:46
there is no king, nor *r* .... Dan 2:10
and hath made thee *r* over them all ... Dan 2:38
made him *r* over the whole .... Dan 2:48
be the third *r* in the kingdom ...... Dan 5:7
be the third *r* in the kingdom ...... Dan 5:16
be the third *r* in the kingdom ...... Dan 5:29
unto me that is to be *r* in Israel ... Mic 5:2
things, that have no *r* over them ... Hab 1:14
behold, there came a certain *r* ..... Mt 9:18
hath made *r* over his household .... Mt 24:45
make him *r* over all his goods ..... Mt 24:47
will make thee *r* over many things . Mt 25:21
will make thee *r* over many things . Mt 25:23
there came from the *r* of the ...... Mk 5:35
saith unto the *r* of the synagogue .. Mk 5:36
house of the *r* of the synagogue ... Mk 5:38
he was a *r* of the synagogue ...... Lk 8:41
the *r* of the synagogue's house .... Lk 8:49
shall make *r* over his household .... Lk 12:42
make him *r* over all that he hath ... Lk 12:44
the *r* of the synagogue answered .. Lk 13:14
And a certain *r* asked him, saying, .. Lk 18:18
When the *r* of the feast had .... Jn 2:9
named Nicodemus, a *r* of the Jews .. Jn 3:1
away, saying, Who made thee a *r* .. Acts 7:27
saying, Who made thee a *r* .... Acts 7:35
the same did God send to be a *r* .. Acts 7:35
the chief *r* of the synagogue .... Acts 18:8
the chief *r* of the synagogue, and .. Acts 18:17
speak evil of the *r* of thy people .. Acts 23:5

RULER'S

Many seek the *r* favour .... Prov 29:26
when Jesus came into the *r* house .. Mt 9:23

RULERS

then make them *r* over my cattle ... Gen 47:6
all the *r* of the congregation .... Ex 16:22
to be *r* of thousands .... Ex 18:21
r of hundreds, *r* of fifties, ... Ex 18:21
r of fifties, and *r* of tens .... Ex 18:21
r of thousands .... Ex 18:25
r of hundreds, *r* of fifties, ... Ex 18:25
r of fifties, and *r* of tens .... Ex 18:25
all the *r* of the congregation .... Ex 34:31
the *r* brought onyx stones, and .... Ex 35:27
and I will make them *r* over you .... Deut 1:13
the Philistines are *r* over us .... Judg 15:11
and David's sons were chief *r* 2Sa 8:18
r of his chariots, and his 1Kin 9:22
unto the *r* of Jezreel, to the 2Kin 10:1
fetched the *r* over hundreds, with .. 2Kin 11:4
he took the *r* over hundreds, and .. 2Kin 11:19
to the *r* of the people, Go, ... 1Chr 21:2
David made *r* over the Reubenites .. 1Chr 26:32
All these were the *r* of the 1Chr 27:31
with the *r* of the king's work, ... 1Chr 29:6
and gathered the *r* of the city 2Chr 29:20
r of the house of God, gave unto .. 2Chr 35:8
r hath been chief in this .... Ezr 9:2
Let now our *r* of all the .... Ezr 10:14
the *r* knew not whither I went, nor .. Neh 2:16
nor to the nobles, nor to the *r* ..... Neh 2:16
said unto the nobles, and to the *r* .. Neh 4:14
the *r* were behind all the house .... Neh 4:16
said unto the nobles, and to the *r* .. Neh 4:19
and I rebuked the nobles, and the *r* .. Neh 5:7
hundred and fifty of the Jews and *r* .. Neh 5:17
together the nobles, and the *r* ...... Neh 7:5
the *r* of the people dwelt at .... Neh 11:1
I, and the half of the *r* with me .... Neh 12:40
Then contended I with the *r* .... Neh 13:11
to the *r* of every couple of every ... Est 3:12
r of the provinces which are from .. Est 8:9
all the *r* of the provinces, and ..... Est 9:3
the *r* take counsel together, ... Ps 2:2
word of the Lord, ye *r* of Sodom .. Is 1:10
wicked, and the sceptre of the *r* ... Is 14:5
All thy *r* are fled together, they .... Is 22:3
the prophets and your *r*, the seers . Is 29:10
abhorreth, to a servant of *r* .... Is 49:7
to be *r* over the seed of Abraham .. Jer 33:26
I break in pieces captains and *r* ... Jer 51:23
thereof, and all the *r* thereof ...... Jer 51:28
wise men, her captains, and her *r* .. Jer 51:57
clothed with blue, captains and *r* .. Eze 23:6
r clothed most gorgeously, ... Eze 23:12
young men, captains and *r*, great .. Eze 23:23
all the *r* of the provinces, to ...... Dan 3:2
all the *r* of the provinces, were ... Dan 3:3

R

her r with shame do love, Give ye...... Hos 4:18
one of the r of the synagogue...... Mk 5:22
and ye shall be brought before r...... Mk 13:9
kings and r for my name's sake...... Lk 21:12
the chief priests and the r...... Lk 23:13
the r also with them derided him,...... Lk 23:35
our r delivered him to be...... Lk 24:20
Do the r know indeed that this is...... Jn 7:26
Have any of the r or of the...... Jn 7:48
chief r also many believed on him... Jn 12:42
ye did it, as did also your r...... Acts 3:17
pass on the morrow, that their r...... Acts 4:5
Ye r of the people, and elders of...... Acts 4:8
the r were gathered together...... Acts 4:26
the prophets the r of the...... Acts 13:15
dwell at Jerusalem, and their r...... Acts 13:27
and also of the Jews with their r...... Acts 14:5
into the marketplace unto the r...... Acts 16:19
brethren unto the r of the city...... Acts 17:6
the r of the city, when they...... Acts 17:8
For r are not a terror to good...... Rom 13:3
against the r of the darkness of...... Eph 6:12

RULEST
r not thou over all the kingdoms...... 2Chr 20:6
Thou r the raging of the sea...... Ps 89:9

RULETH
He that r over men must be just,...... 2Sa 23:3
let them know that God r in Jacob...... Ps 59:13
He r by his power for ever...... Ps 66:7
and his kingdom r over all...... Ps 103:19
he that r his spirit than he that...... Prov 16:32
The rich r over the poor, and the...... Prov 22:7
r over another to his own hurt...... Eccl 8:9
the cry of him that r among fools... Eccl 9:17
most High r in the kingdom of men... Dan 4:17
most High r in the kingdom of men... Dan 4:25
most High r in the kingdom of men... Dan 4:32
but Judah yet r with God, and is... Hos 11:12
he that r, with diligence...... Rom 12:8
One that r well his own house,...... 1Ti 3:4

RULING
be just, in the fear of God...... 2Sa 23:3
of David, and r any more in Judah ... Jer 22:30
r their children and their own...... 1Ti 3:12

RUMAH (ru'-mah) See ARUMAH. Home of
Jehoiakim's mother.
the daughter of Pedaiah of R...... 2Kin 23:36

RUMBLING
at the r of his wheels, the...... Jer 47:3

RUMOUR
upon him, and he shall hear a r...... 2Kin 19:7
upon him, and he shall hear a r...... Is 37:7
I have heard a r from the LORD...... Jer 49:14
ye fear for the r that shall be...... Jer 51:46
a r shall both come one year, and...... Jer 51:46
in another year shall come a r...... Jer 51:46
and r shall be upon r...... Eze 7:26
We have heard a r from the LORD...... Obad 1
And this r of him went forth...... Lk 7:17

RUMOURS
shall hear of wars and r of wars... Mt 24:6
r of wars, be ye not troubled...... Mk 13:7

RUMP
take of the ram the fat and the r...... Ex 29:22
the fat thereof, and the whole r...... Lev 3:9
the r, and the fat that covereth...... Lev 7:3
And he took the fat, and the r...... Lev 8:25
the bullock and the ram, the r...... Lev 9:19

RUN
whose branches r over the wall...... Gen 49:22
his flesh r with his issue...... Lev 15:3
or if it r beyond the time of her... Lev 15:25
lest angry fellows r upon thee...... Judg 18:25
some shall r before his chariots... 1Sa 8:11
r to the camp to thy brethren...... 1Sa 17:17
he might r to Beth-lehem his city... 1Sa 20:6
And he said unto his lad,...... 1Sa 20:36
and fifty men to r before him...... 2Sa 15:1
the son of Zadok, Let me now r...... 2Sa 18:22
I pray thee, also r after Cushi...... 2Sa 18:22
Joab said, Wherefore wilt thou r...... 2Sa 18:22
But howsoever, said he, let me r... 2Sa 18:23
And he said unto him,...... 2Sa 18:23
by thee I have r through a troop... 2Sa 22:30
and fifty men to r before him...... 1Kin 1:5
that I may r to the man of God,... 2Kin 4:22
R now, I pray thee, to meet her,... 2Kin 4:26
I will r after him, and take...... 2Kin 5:20
For the eyes of the LORD r to...... 2Chr 16:9
by thee I have r through a troop... Ps 18:29
as a strong man to r a race...... Ps 19:5
as waters which r continually,...... Ps 58:7
They r and prepare themselves...... Ps 59:4
waters to r down like rivers...... Ps 78:16
valleys, which r among the hills... Ps 104:10
I will r the way of thy...... Ps 119:32
Rivers of waters r down mine eyes... Ps 119:136
For their feet r to evil, and make... Prov 1:16
All the rivers r into the sea...... Eccl 1:7
Draw me, we will r after thee...... Song 1:4
of locusts shall he r upon them...... Is 33:4
they shall r, and not be weary...... Is 40:31
that knew not thee shall r unto...... Is 55:5
Their feet r to evil, and they...... Is 59:7
R ye to and fro through the...... Jer 5:1

our eyes may r down with tears...... Jer 9:18
If thou hast r with the footmen,... Jer 12:5
r down with tears, because the...... Jer 13:17
Let mine eyes r down with tears... Jer 14:17
r to and fro by the hedges...... Jer 49:3
suddenly make him r away from her... Jer 49:19
them suddenly r away from her...... Jer 50:44
One post shall r to meet another,... Jer 51:31
let tears r down like a river day... Lam 2:18
neither shall thy tears r down...... Eze 24:16
cause their rivers to r like oil...... Eze 32:14
they shall r like mighty men...... Joel 2:4
and as horsemen, so shall they r... Joel 2:4
They shall r like mighty men....... Joel 2:7
They shall r to and fro in the...... Joel 2:9
they shall r upon the wall, they... Joel 2:9
But let judgment r down as waters... Amos 5:24
Shall horses r upon the rock...... Amos 6:12
even to the east, they shall r to... Amos 8:12
they shall r like the lightnings... Nah 2:4
that he may r that readeth it...... Hab 2:2
ye r every man unto his own house... Hag 1:9
And said unto him, R, speak to...... Zec 2:4
the eyes of the LORD, which r to... Zec 4:10
did r to bring his disciples word... Mt 28:8
they which r in a race r all...... 1Cor 9:24
So r, that ye may obtain...... 1Cor 9:24
I therefore so r, not as...... 1Cor 9:26
any means I should r, or had r...... Gal 2:2
Ye did r well...... Gal 5:7
Christ, that I have not r in vain... Phil 2:16
let us r with patience the race...... Heb 12:1
ye r not with them to the same...... 1Pet 4:4

RUNNEST
and when thou r, thou shalt not...... Prov 4:12

RUNNETH
to the river than r to Ahava...... Ezr 8:15
He r upon him, even on his neck,... Job 15:26
he r upon me like a giant...... Job 16:14
my cup r over...... Ps 23:5
his word r very swiftly...... Ps 147:15
the righteous r into it, and is...... Prov 18:10
Mine eye r down with water,...... Lam 1:16
Mine eye r down with rivers of...... Lam 3:48
bottles break, and the wine r out... Mt 9:17
Then she r, and cometh to Simon... Jn 20:2
that willeth, nor of him that r...... Rom 9:16

RUNNING
in an earthen vessel over r water... Lev 14:5
that was killed over the r water... Lev 14:6
in an earthen vessel over r water... Lev 14:50
the slain bird, and in the r water... Lev 14:51
of the bird, and with the r water... Lev 14:52
When any man hath a r issue out... Lev 15:2
and bathe his flesh in r water...... Lev 15:13
is a leper, or hath a r issue....... Lev 22:4
r water shall be put thereto in a... Num 19:17
looked, and behold a man r alone... 2Sa 18:24
watchman saw another man r...... 2Sa 18:26
said, Behold another man r alone... 2Sa 18:26
He thinketh the r of the foremost... 2Sa 18:27
the r of Ahimaaz the son of Zadok... 2Sa 18:27
when Naaman saw him r after him... 2Kin 5:21
heard the noise of the people r...... 2Chr 23:12
r waters out of thine own well...... Prov 5:15
that be swift in r to mischief...... Prov 6:18
as the r to and fro of locusts...... Is 33:4
rivers r round about his plants... Eze 31:4
amazed, and r to him saluted him... Mk 9:15
that the people came r together... Mk 9:25
into the way, there came one r...... Mk 10:17
r over, shall men give into your... Lk 6:38
r under a certain island which is... Acts 27:16
of many horses r to battle...... Rev 9:9

RUSH
Can the r grow up without mire...... Job 8:11
Israel head and tail, branch and r... Is 9:14
The nations shall r like the...... Is 17:13
the head or tail, branch or r...... Is 19:15

RUSHED
r forward, and stood in the...... Judg 9:44
in wait hasted, and r upon Gibeah... Judg 20:37
they r with one accord into the... Acts 19:29

RUSHES
shall be grass with reeds and r...... Is 35:7

RUSHETH
as the horse r into the battle...... Jer 8:6

RUSHING
to the r of nations...... Is 17:12
that make a r like the r of...... Is 17:12
rush like the r of many waters...... Is 17:13
at the r of his chariots, and at... Jer 47:3
behind me a voice of a great r...... Eze 3:12
them, and a noise of a great r...... Eze 3:13
from heaven as of a r mighty wind... Acts 2:2

RUST
r doth corrupt, and where thieves... Mt 6:19
neither moth nor r doth corrupt... Mt 6:20
the r of them shall be a witness... Jas 5:3

RUTH (rooth) Wife of Boaz; an ancestor of
Jesus.
Orpah, and the name of the other R... Ruth 1:4
R clave unto her...... Ruth 1:14
R said, Intreat me not to leave...... Ruth 1:16
R the Moabitess, her daughter in... Ruth 1:22

R the Moabitess said unto Naomi,... Ruth 2:2
Then said Boaz unto R, Hearest... Ruth 2:8
R the Moabitess said, He said...... Ruth 2:21
Naomi said unto R her daughter in... Ruth 2:22
answered, I am R thine handmaid... Ruth 3:9
buy it also of R the Moabitess...... Ruth 4:5
Moreover R the Moabitess, the...... Ruth 4:10
So Booz took R, and she was his... Ruth 4:13
and Booz begat Obed of R...... Mt 1:5

S

SABACHTHANI
voice, saying, Eli, Eli, lama s...... Mt 27:46
voice, saying, Eloi, Eloi, lama s... Mk 15:34

SABAOTH (sab'-a-oth) Title meaning "Lord of
Hosts."
the Lord of S had left us a seed... Rom 9:29
into the ears of the Lord of S...... Jas 5:4

SABBATH
rest of the holy s unto the LORD... Ex 16:23
for to day is a s unto the LORD,... Ex 16:25
the seventh day, which is the s... Ex 16:26
the LORD hath given you the s...... Ex 16:29
Remember the s day, to keep it...... Ex 20:8
day is the s of the LORD thy God... Ex 20:10
the LORD blessed the s day...... Ex 20:11
Ye shall keep the s therefore...... Ex 31:14
in the seventh is the s of rest...... Ex 31:15
doeth any work in the s day...... Ex 31:15
of Israel shall keep the s...... Ex 31:16
to observe the s throughout their... Ex 31:16
holy day, a s of rest to the LORD... Ex 35:2
your habitations upon the s day... Ex 35:3
It shall be a s of rest unto you,... Lev 16:31
the seventh day is the s of rest... Lev 23:3
it is the s of the LORD in all...... Lev 23:3
on the morrow after the s the...... Lev 23:11
you from the morrow after the s... Lev 23:15
a shall ye number fifty days...... Lev 23:16
of the month, shall ye have a s... Lev 23:24
It shall be unto you a s of rest... Lev 23:32
even, shall ye celebrate your s... Lev 23:32
on the first day shall be a s...... Lev 23:39
and on the eighth day shall be a s... Lev 23:39
Every s he shall set it in order... Lev 24:8
the land keep a s unto the LORD... Lev 25:2
be a s of rest unto the land...... Lev 25:4
unto the land, a s for the LORD... Lev 25:4
the s of the land shall be meat... Lev 25:6
gathered sticks upon the s day... Num 15:32
on the s day two lambs of the...... Num 28:9
is the burnt offering of every s... Num 28:10
Keep the s day to sanctify it, as... Deut 5:12
day is the s of the LORD thy God... Deut 5:14
commanded thee to keep the s day... Deut 5:15
it is neither new moon, nor s...... 2Kin 4:23
of you that enter in on the s...... 2Kin 11:5
of all you that go forth on the s... 2Kin 11:7
men that were to come in on the s... 2Kin 11:9
them that should go out on the s... 2Kin 11:9
the covert for the s that they...... 2Kin 16:18
shewbread, to prepare it every s... 1Chr 9:32
part of you entering on the s...... 2Chr 23:4
men that were to come in on the s... 2Chr 23:8
them that were to go out on the s... 2Chr 23:8
as the day desolate she kept s...... 2Chr 36:21
madest known unto them thy holy s... Neh 9:14
any victuals on the s day to sell... Neh 10:31
would not buy it of them on the s... Neh 10:31
treading winepresses on the s...... Neh 13:15
into Jerusalem on the s day...... Neh 13:15
sold on the s unto the children... Neh 13:16
that ye do, and profane the s day... Neh 13:17
upon Israel by profaning the s...... Neh 13:18
began to be dark before the s...... Neh 13:19
not be opened till after the s...... Neh 13:19
burden be brought in on the s day... Neh 13:19
forth came they no more on the s... Neh 13:21
the gates, to sanctify the s day... Neh 13:22
A Psalm or Song for the s day...... Ps 92:1
that keepeth the s from polluting... Is 56:2
keepeth the s from polluting it...... Is 56:6
turn away thy foot from the s...... Is 58:13
call the a delight, the holy of... Is 58:13
from one s to another, shall all... Is 66:23
and bear no burden on the s day... Jer 17:21
out of your houses on the s day... Jer 17:22
any work, but hallow ye the s day... Jer 17:22
gates of this city on the s day... Jer 17:24
but hallow the s day...... Jer 17:24
unto me to hallow the s day,...... Jer 17:24
gates of Jerusalem on the s day... Jer 17:27
but on the s it shall be opened,... Eze 46:1
offer unto the LORD in the s day... Eze 46:12
offerings, as he did on the s day... Eze 46:12
and the s, that we may set forth... Amos 8:5
on the s day through the corn...... Mt 12:1
not lawful to do upon the s day... Mt 12:2
how that on the s days the...... Mt 12:5
in the temple profane the s...... Mt 12:5
of man is Lord even of the s day... Mt 12:8
it lawful to heal on the s days... Mt 12:10
it fall into a pit on the s day... Mt 12:11
lawful to do well on the s days... Mt 12:12

the winter, neither on the s day .... Mt 24:20
In the end of the s, as it began .... Mt 28:1
straightway on the s day he .... Mk 1:21
the corn fields on the s day .... Mk 2:23
why do they on the s day that .... Mk 2:24
The s was made for man .... Mk 2:27
and not man for the s .... Mk 2:27
Son of man is Lord also of the s .... Mk 2:28
he would heal him on the s day .... Mk 3:2
lawful to do good on the s days .... Mk 3:4
when the s day was come, he began ...... Mk 6:2
that is, the day before the s .... Mk 15:42
And when the s was past, Mary .... Mk 16:1
into the synagogue on the s day .... Lk 4:16
and taught them on the s days .... Lk 4:31
on the second s after the first .... Lk 6:1
is not lawful to do on the s days .... Lk 6:2
Son of man is Lord also of the s .... Lk 6:5
it came to pass also on another s .... Lk 6:6
he would heal on the s day .... Lk 6:7
lawful on the s days to do good .... Lk 6:9
in one of the synagogues on the s .... Lk 13:10
Jesus had healed on the s day .... Lk 13:14
and be healed, and not on the s day ...... Lk 13:14
s loose his ox or his ass from .... Lk 13:15
from this bond on the s day .... Lk 13:16
to eat bread on the s day .... Lk 14:1
Is it lawful to heal on the s day .... Lk 14:3
pull him out on the s day .... Lk 14:5
the preparation, and the s drew on .... Lk 23:54
rested the s day according to the .... Lk 23:56
and on the same day was the s .... Jn 5:9
that was cured, It is the s day .... Jn 5:10
done these things on the s day .... Jn 5:16
he not only had broken the s .... Jn 5:18
ye on the s day circumcise a man .... Jn 7:22
If a man on the s day receive .... Jn 7:23
man every whit whole on the s day .... Jn 7:23
it was the s day when Jesus made .... Jn 9:14
because he keepeth not the s day .... Jn 9:16
upon the cross on the s day .... Jn 19:31
(for that s day was an high day,) .... Jn 19:31
from Jerusalem a s day's journey .... Acts 1:12
into the synagogue on the s day .... Acts 13:14
which are read every s day .... Acts 13:27
be preached to them the next s .... Acts 13:42
the next s day came almost the .... Acts 13:44
in the synagogues every s day .... Acts 15:21
on the s we went out of the city .... Acts 16:13
three s days reasoned with them .... Acts 17:2
reasoned in the synagogue every s .... Acts 18:4
of the new moon, or of the s days .... Col 2:16

SABBATHS

Verily my s ye shall keep .... Ex 31:13
and his father, and keep my s .... Lev 19:3
Ye shall keep my s, and reverence .... Lev 19:30
seven s shall be complete .... Lev 23:15
Beside the s of the LORD, and .... Lev 23:38
number seven s of years unto thee .... Lev 25:8
the space of the seven s of years .... Lev 25:8
Ye shall keep my s, and reverence .... Lev 26:2
Then shall the land enjoy her s .... Lev 26:34
the land rest, and enjoy her s .... Lev 26:34
because it did not rest in your s .... Lev 26:35
of them, and shall enjoy her s .... Lev 26:43
sacrifices unto the LORD in the s 1Chr 23:31
morning and evening, on the s 2Chr 2:4
commandment of Moses, on the s 2Chr 8:13
and the burnt offerings for the s 2Chr 31:3
until the land had enjoyed her s 2Chr 36:21
burnt offering, of the s, of the .... Neh 10:33
the new moons and s, the calling .... Is 1:13
unto the eunuchs that keep my s .... Is 56:4
saw her, and did mock at her s .... Lam 1:7
s to be forgotten in Zion, and .... Lam 2:6
Moreover also I gave them my s .... Eze 20:12
my s they greatly polluted .... Eze 20:13
in my statutes, but polluted my s .... Eze 20:16
And hallow my s .... Eze 20:20
they polluted my s .... Eze 20:21
my statutes, and had polluted my s ...... Eze 20:24
things, and hast profaned my s .... Eze 22:8
and have hid their eyes from my s .... Eze 22:26
same day, and have profaned my s .... Eze 23:38
and they shall hallow my s .... Eze 44:24
and in the new moons, and in the s .... Eze 45:17
gate before the LORD in the s .... Eze 46:3
days, her new moons, and her s .... Hos 2:11

SABEANS (sab-e´-uns)

1. Descendants of Sheba.
the S fell upon them, and took .... Job 1:15
and they shall sell them to the S .... Joel 3:8
2. Descendants of Seba.
of Ethiopia and of the S, men of .... Is 45:14
brought S from the wilderness .... Eze 23:42

SABTA (sab´-tah) See SABTAH. A son of Cush.
Seba, and Havilah, and S, and Raamah 1Chr 1:9

SABTAH (sab´-tah) See SABTA. Same as Sabta.
Seba, and Havilah, and S .... Gen 10:7

SABTECA See SABTECHAH.

SABTECHA (sab´-te-kah) See SABTECHAH. A son of Cush.
and Sabta, and Raamah, and S 1Chr 1:9

SABTECHAH (sab´-te-kah) See SABTECHA. Same as Sabtecha.
and Sabtah, and Raamah, and S .... Gen 10:7

SACAR (sa´-kar) See SHARAR.
1. Father of Ahiham.
Ahiam the son of S the Hararite 1Chr 11:35
2. A sanctuary servant.
S the fourth, and Nethaneel the 1Chr 26:4

SACHIA See SHACHIA.

SACK

every man's money into his s .... Gen 42:25
as one of them opened his s to .... Gen 42:27
and, lo, it is even in my s .... Gen 42:28
bundle of money was in his s .... Gen 42:35
money was in the mouth of his s .... Gen 43:21
every man his s to the ground .... Gen 44:11
and opened every man his s .... Gen 44:11
the cup was found in Benjamin's s .... Gen 44:12
wood, or raiment, or skin, or s .... Lev 11:32

SACKBUT

of the cornet, flute, harp, s .... Dan 3:5
of the cornet, flute, harp, s .... Dan 3:7
of the cornet, flute, harp, s .... Dan 3:10
of the cornet, flute, harp, s .... Dan 3:15

SACKCLOTH

put s upon his loins, and mourned .... Gen 37:34
your clothes, and gird you with s 2Sa 3:31
the daughter of Aiah took s 2Sa 21:10
put s on our loins, and ropes upon 1Kin 20:31
So they girded s on their loins 1Kin 20:32
put s upon his flesh, and fasted, ... 1Kin 21:27
his flesh, and fasted, and lay in s 1Kin 21:27
he had s within upon his flesh 2Kin 6:30
and covered himself with s 2Kin 19:1
of the priests, covered with s 2Kin 19:2
of Israel, who were clothed in s 1Chr 21:16
put on s with ashes, and went out .... Est 4:1
the king's gate clothed with s .... Est 4:2
and many lay in s and ashes .... Est 4:3
and to take away his s from him .... Est 4:4
I have sewed s upon my skin .... Job 16:15
thou hast put off my s, and girded .... Ps 30:11
they were sick, my clothing was s .... Ps 35:13
I made s also my garment .... Ps 69:11
of a stomacher a girding of s .... Is 3:24
they shall gird themselves with s .... Is 15:3
loose the s from off thy loins, ... Is 20:2
to baldness, and to girding with s .... Is 22:12
bare, and gird s upon your loins .... Is 32:11
and covered himself with s .... Is 37:1
of the priests covered with s .... Is 37:2
and I make s their covering .... Is 50:3
head as a bulrush, and to spread s .... Is 58:5
For this gird you with s, lament .... Jer 4:8
of my people, gird thee with s .... Jer 6:26
be cuttings, and upon the loins s .... Jer 48:37
of Rabbah, gird you with s .... Jer 49:3
have girded themselves with s .... Lam 2:10
shall also gird themselves with s .... Eze 7:18
for thee, and gird them with s .... Eze 27:31
supplications, with fasting, and s .... Dan 9:3
like a virgin girded with s for .... Joel 1:8
come, lie all night in s, ye .... Joel 1:13
I will bring up s upon all loins .... Amos 8:10
and proclaimed a fast, and put on s ...... Jonah 3:5
from him, and covered him with s .... Jonah 3:6
man and beast be covered with s .... Jonah 3:8
would have repented long ago in s .... Mt 11:21
while ago repented, sitting in s .... Lk 10:13
the sun became black as s of hair .... Rev 6:12
and threescore days, clothed in s .... Rev 11:3

SACKCLOTHES

assembled with fasting, and with s .... Neh 9:1

SACK'S

behold, it was in his s mouth .... Gen 42:27
every man's money in his s mouth .... Gen 44:1
in the s mouth of the youngest, ... Gen 44:2

SACKS

to fill their s with corn .... Gen 42:25
to pass as they emptied their s .... Gen 42:35
again in the mouth of your s .... Gen 43:12
in our s at the first time are we .... Gen 43:18
to the inn, that we opened our s .... Gen 43:21
tell who out our money in our s .... Gen 43:22
hath given you treasure in your s .... Gen 43:23
Fill the men's s with food...................... Gen 44:1
took old s upon their asses, and .... Josh 9:4

SACKS'

which we found in our s mouths .... Gen 44:8

SACRIFICE

Jacob s upon the mount .... Gen 31:54
that we may s to the LORD our God ...... Ex 3:18
and s unto the LORD our God .... Ex 5:3
saying, Let us go and s to our God .... Ex 5:8
Let us go and do s to the LORD .... Ex 5:17
that they may do s unto the LORD .... Ex 8:8
s to your God in the land .... Ex 8:25
for we shall s the abomination of .... Ex 8:26
shall we s the abomination of the .... Ex 8:26
s to the LORD our God, as he .... Ex 8:27
that ye may s to the LORD your .... Ex 8:29
the people go to s to the LORD .... Ex 8:29
that we may s unto the LORD our .... Ex 8:29
It is the s of the LORD's passover .... Ex 12:27
therefore I s to the LORD all .... Ex 13:15
shalt s thereon thy burnt .... Ex 20:24
blood of my s with leavened bread .... Ex 23:18
of my s remain until the morning .... Ex 23:18

of the s of their peace offerings .... Ex 29:28
incense thereon, nor burnt s .... Ex 30:9
do s unto their gods, and one call .... Ex 34:15
call thee, and thou eat of his s .... Ex 34:15
the blood of my s with leaven .... Ex 34:25
neither shall the s of the feast .... Ex 34:25
offering be a burnt s of the herd .... Lev 1:3
all on the altar, to be a burnt s .... Lev 1:9
or of the goats, for a burnt s .... Lev 1:10
it is a burnt s, an offering made .... Lev 1:13
if the burnt s for his offering .... Lev 1:14
it is a burnt s, an offering made .... Lev 1:17
oblation be a s of peace offering, ... Lev 3:1
he shall offer of the s of the .... Lev 3:3
it on the altar upon the burnt s .... Lev 3:5
if his offering for a s of peace .... Lev 3:6
he shall offer of the s of the .... Lev 3:9
of the s of peace offerings .... Lev 4:10
as the fat of the s of peace .... Lev 4:26
from off the s of peace offerings .... Lev 4:31
from the s of the peace offerings .... Lev 4:35
law of the s of peace offerings .... Lev 7:11
the s of thanksgiving unleavened .... Lev 7:12
leavened bread with the s of .... Lev 7:13
the flesh of the s of his being .... Lev 7:15
But if the s of his offering be a .... Lev 7:16
same day that he offereth his s .... Lev 7:16
remainder of the flesh of the s .... Lev 7:17
if any of the flesh of the s of .... Lev 7:18
the s of peace offerings thankful .... Lev 7:20
flesh of the s of peace offerings .... Lev 7:21
He that offereth the s of his .... Lev 7:29
of the s of his peace offerings .... Lev 7:29
of the s of the peace offerings .... Lev 7:37
it was a burnt s for a sweet .... Lev 8:21
offerings, to s before the LORD .... Lev 9:4
beside the burnt s of the morning .... Lev 9:17
and the ram for a s of peace .... Lev 9:18
offereth a burnt offering or s .... Lev 17:8
if they offer a s of peace .... Lev 19:5
whosoever offereth a s of peace .... Lev 22:21
Then ye shall s one kid of the .... Lev 22:29
year for a s of peace offerings .... Lev 23:19
burnt offering, and a meat offering, a .. Lev 23:37
do not offer a s unto the LORD .... Num 6:17
a s of peace offerings unto the .... Num 6:17
the s of the peace offerings .... Num 6:18
for a s of peace offerings, two .... Num 7:17
for a s of peace offerings, two .... Num 7:23
for a s of peace offerings, two .... Num 7:29
for a s of peace offerings, two .... Num 7:35
for a s of peace offerings, two .... Num 7:41
for a s of peace offerings, two .... Num 7:47
for a s of peace offerings, two .... Num 7:53
for a s of peace offerings, two .... Num 7:59
for a s of peace offerings, two .... Num 7:65
for a s of peace offerings, two .... Num 7:71
for a s of peace offerings, two .... Num 7:77
for a s of peace offerings, two .... Num 7:83
all the oxen for the s of .... Num 7:88
or a s in performing a vow, or in .... Num 15:3
with the burnt offering or s .... Num 15:5
or for a s in performing a vow, ... Num 15:8
for a s made by fire, a sweet .... Num 15:25
and, lo, he stood by his burnt s .... Num 23:6
a s made by fire unto the LORD .... Num 28:6
a s made by fire, of a sweet .... Num 28:8
a s made by fire unto the LORD .... Num 28:13
But ye shall offer a s made by .... Num 28:19
the meat of the s made by fire .... Num 28:24
a s made by fire, a sweet .... Num 29:6
a s made by fire, a sweet .... Num 29:13
a s made by fire, of a sweet .... Num 29:36
thou shalt not s it unto the LORD .... Deut 15:21
Thou shalt therefore s the .... Deut 16:2
Thou mayest not s the passover .... Deut 16:5
there thou shalt s the passover .... Deut 16:6
Thou shalt not s unto the LORD .... Deut 17:1
people, from them that offer a s .... Deut 18:3
whole burnt s upon thine altar .... Deut 33:10
not for burnt offering, nor for a s .... Josh 22:26
offer a burnt s with the wood of .... Judg 6:26
a great s unto Dagon their god .... Judg 16:23
to s unto the LORD of hosts in 1Sa 1:3
offer unto the LORD the yearly s 1Sa 1:21
was, that, when any man offered a s ... 1Sa 2:13
her husband for the yearly s 1Sa 2:19
Wherefore kick ye at my s, ... 1Sa 2:29
with s nor offering for ever 1Sa 3:14
for there is a s of the people to 1Sa 9:12
come, because he doth bless the s 1Sa 9:13
and to s sacrifices of peace 1Sa 10:8
to s unto the LORD thy God 1Sa 15:15
to s unto the LORD thy God in 1Sa 15:21
Behold, to obey is better than s 1Sa 15:22
say, I am come to s to the LORD 1Sa 16:2
And call Jesse to the s, and I will 1Sa 16:3
I am come to s unto the LORD 1Sa 16:5
to s, and called them to the s 1Sa 16:5
for there is a yearly s there for 1Sa 20:6
our family hath a s in the city 1Sa 20:29
behold, here be oxen for burnt s 2Sa 24:22
king went to Gibeon to s there 1Kin 3:4
offered a before that altar 1Kin 8:62
Solomon offered a s of peace 1Kin 8:63
If this people go up to do s in 1Kin 12:27
of the offering of the evening s 1Kin 18:29
water, and pour it on the burnt s 1Kin 18:33

of the offering of the evening *s* 1Kin 18:36
fell, and consumed the burnt *s* 1Kin 18:38
offering nor *s* unto other gods 2Kin 5:17
I have a great *s* to do to Baal 2Kin 10:19
as yet the people did *s* and burnt 2Kin 14:4
offering, and the king's burnt *s* 2Kin 16:15
and all the blood of the *s* 2Kin 16:15
nor serve them, nor *s* to them 2Kin 17:35
worship, and to him shall ye do *s* 2Kin 17:36
save only to burn *s* before him 2Chr 2:6
Solomon offered a *s* of twenty 2Chr 7:5
place to myself for an house of *s* 2Chr 7:12
to *s* unto the LORD God of their 2Chr 11:16
them, therefore will I *s* to them 2Chr 28:23
did *s* still in the high places 2Chr 33:17
we do *s* unto him since the days ...... Ezr 4:2
sat astonied until the evening *s* ...... Ezr 9:4
at the evening *s* I arose up from ...... Ezr 9:5
will they *s* ...... Neh 4:2
offerings, and accept thy burnt *s* ...... Ps 20:3
S and offering thou didst not ...... Ps 40:6
have made a covenant with me by *s* ...... Ps 50:5
For thou desirest not *s* ...... Ps 51:16
I will freely *s* unto thee ...... Ps 54:6
let them the *s* sacrifices of ...... Ps 107:22
to thee the *s* of thanksgiving ...... Ps 116:17
bind the *s* with cords, even unto ...... Ps 118:27
up of my hands as the evening *s* ...... Ps 141:2
The *s* of the wicked is an ...... Prov 15:8
acceptable to the LORD than *s* ...... Prov 21:3
The *s* of the wicked is ...... Prov 21:27
hear, than to give the *s* of fools ...... Eccl 5:1
LORD in that day, and shall do a *s* ...... Is 19:21
for the LORD hath a *s* in Bozrah ...... Is 34:6
wentest thou up to offer *s* ...... Is 57:7
of them that bring the *s* of ...... Jer 33:11
offerings, and to do *s* continually ...... Jer 33:18
a *s* in the north country by the ...... Jer 46:10
every side to my *s* ...... Eze 39:17
that I do *s* for you ...... Eze 39:17
even a great *s* upon the mountains ...... Eze 39:17
of my *s* which I have sacrificed ...... Eze 39:19
slew the burnt offering and the *s* ...... Eze 40:42
the *s* for the people, and they ...... Eze 44:11
shall boil the *s* of the people ...... Eze 46:24
by him the daily *s* was taken away ...... Dan 8:11
s by reason of transgression ...... Dan 8:12
the vision concerning the daily *s* ...... Dan 8:13
of the week he shall cause the *s* ...... Dan 9:27
and shall take away the daily *s* ...... Dan 11:31
the daily *s* shall be taken away ...... Dan 12:11
without a prince, and without a *s* ...... Hos 3:4
They *s* upon the tops of the ...... Hos 4:13
whores, and they *s* with harlots ...... Hos 4:14
For I desired mercy, and not *s* ...... Hos 6:6
They *s* flesh for the sacrifices ...... Hos 8:13
they *s* bullocks in Gilgal ...... Hos 12:11
the men that *s* kiss the calves ...... Hos 13:2
offer a *s* of thanksgiving with ...... Amos 4:5
offered a *s* unto the LORD, and ...... Jonah 1:16
But I will *s* unto thee with ...... Jonah 2:9
Therefore they *s* unto their net ...... Hab 1:16
for the LORD hath prepared a *s* ...... Zeph 1:7
pass in the day of the LORD's *s* ...... Zeph 1:8
and all they that *s* shall come ...... Zec 14:21
And if ye offer the blind for *s* ...... Mal 1:8
I will have mercy, and not *s* ...... Mt 9:13
I will have mercy, and not *s* ...... Mt 12:7
every *s* shall be salted with salt ...... Mk 9:49
to offer a *s* according to that ...... Lk 2:24
offered *s* unto the idol, and ...... Acts 7:41
would have done *s* with the people ...... Acts 14:13
they had not done *s* unto the ...... Acts 14:18
ye present your bodies a living *s* ...... Rom 12:1
that are offered in *s* unto idols 1Cor 8:1
in *s* to idols is any thing 1Cor 10:19
the things which the Gentiles *s* 1Cor 10:20
they *s* to devils, and not to God 1Cor 10:20
This is offered in *s* unto idols 1Cor 10:28
a *s* to God for a sweetsmelling ...... Eph 5:2
and if I be offered upon the *s* ...... Phil 2:17
a acceptable, wellpleasing to ...... Phil 4:18
those high priests, to offer up *s* ...... Heb 7:27
put away sin by the *s* of himself ...... Heb 9:26
into the world, he saith, *S* ...... Heb 10:5
Above when he said, *S* and offering ...... Heb 10:8
offered one *s* for sins for ever ...... Heb 10:12
remaineth no more *s* for sins ...... Heb 10:26
God a more excellent than Cain ...... Heb 11:4
of *s* praise to God continually ...... Heb 13:15

SACRIFICED

s peace offerings of oxen unto ...... Ex 24:5
have *s* thereunto, and said, These ...... Ex 32:8
They *s* unto devils, not to God ...... Deut 32:17
the LORD, and *s* peace offerings ...... Josh 8:31
they *s* there unto the LORD ...... Judg 2:5
came, and said to the man that *s* 1Sa 2:15
s sacrifices the same day unto 1Sa 6:15
there they *s* sacrifices of peace 1Sa 11:15
six paces, he *s* oxen and fatlings 2Sa 6:13
Only the people *s* in high places 1Kin 3:2
only he *s* and burnt incense in 1Kin 3:3
incense and *s* unto their gods 1Kin 11:8
the people still *s* and burnt 2Kin 12:3
the people *s* and burnt incense 2Kin 15:4
the people *s* and burned incense 2Kin 15:35
And he *s* and burnt incense in the 2Kin 16:4
which *s* for them in the houses of 2Kin 17:32
the Jebusite, then he *s* there 1Chr 21:28
they *s* sacrifices unto the LORD, ... 1Chr 29:21

SACRIFICEST

which thou *s* the first day at ...... Deut 16:4

SACRIFICES

offered *s* unto the God of his ...... Gen 46:1
said, Thou must give us also *s* ...... Ex 10:25
a burnt offering and *s* for God ...... Ex 18:12
of the *s* of your peace offerings ...... Lev 7:32
the *s* of their peace offerings ...... Lev 7:34
of the *s* of the LORD made by fire ...... Lev 10:13
the *s* of peace offerings of the ...... Lev 10:14
of Israel may bring their *s* ...... Lev 17:5
no more offer their *s* unto devils ...... Lev 17:7
and over the *s* of your peace ...... Num 10:10
people unto the *s* of their gods ...... Num 25:2
and bread for my *s* made by fire ...... Num 28:2
your burnt offerings, and your *s* ...... Deut 12:6
your burnt offerings, and your *s* ...... Deut 12:11
the blood of thy *s* shall be ...... Deut 12:27
Which did eat the fat of their *s* ...... Deut 32:38
shall offer *s* of righteousness ...... Deut 33:19
of the *s* of the LORD God of Israel ...... Josh 13:14
burnt offerings, and with our *s* ...... Josh 22:27
for burnt offerings, nor for *s* ...... Josh 22:28
for meat offerings, or for *s* ...... Josh 22:29
sacrificed *s* the same day unto 1Sa 6:15
to sacrifice *s* of peace offerings 1Sa 10:8
there they sacrificed *s* of peace 1Sa 11:15
delight in burnt offerings and *s* 1Sa 15:22
from Giloh, while he offered *s* 2Sa 15:12
And when they went in to offer *s* 2Kin 10:24
and they offered burnt *s* and peace 1Chr 16:1
to offer all burnt *s* unto the 1Chr 23:31
they sacrificed *s* unto the LORD 1Chr 29:21
s in abundance for all Israel 1Chr 29:21
the burnt offering and the *s* 2Chr 7:1
people offered *s* before the LORD 2Chr 7:4
morning and every evening burnt *s* 2Chr 13:11
the LORD, come near and bring *s* 2Chr 29:31
And the congregation brought in *s* 2Chr 29:31
the place where they offered *s* ...... Ezr 6:3
That they may offer *s* of sweet ...... Ezr 6:10
that day they offered great *s* ...... Neh 12:43
Offer the *s* of righteousness, and ...... Ps 4:5
offer in his tabernacle *s* of joy ...... Ps 27:6
for thy *s* or thy burnt offerings ...... Ps 50:8
The *s* of God are a broken spirit ...... Ps 51:17
with the *s* of righteousness ...... Ps 51:19
unto thee burnt *s* of fatlings ...... Ps 66:15
and ate the *s* of the dead ...... Ps 106:28
sacrifice the *s* of thanksgiving ...... Ps 107:22
an house full of *s* with strife ...... Prov 17:1
the multitude of your *s* unto me ...... Is 1:11
let them kill *s* ...... Is 29:1
hast thou honoured me with thy *s* ...... Is 43:23
filled me with the fat of thy *s* ...... Is 43:24
their *s* shall be accepted upon ...... Is 56:7
nor your *s* sweet unto me ...... Jer 6:20
your burnt offerings unto your *s* ...... Jer 7:21
concerning burnt offerings or *s* ...... Jer 7:22
bringing burnt offerings, and *s* ...... Jer 17:26
bringing *s* of praise, unto the ...... Jer 17:26
and they offered there their *s* ...... Eze 20:28
whereupon they slew their *s* ...... Eze 20:28
be ashamed because of their *s* ...... Hos 4:19
flesh for the *s* of mine offerings ...... Hos 8:13
their *s* shall be unto them as the ...... Hos 9:4
bring your *s* every morning, and ...... Amos 4:4
Have ye offered unto me *s* ...... Amos 5:25
all whole burnt offerings and *s* ...... Mk 12:33
Pilate had mingled with their *s* ...... Lk 13:1
s by the space of forty years in ...... Acts 7:42
of the *s* partakers of the altar 1Cor 10:18
offer both gifts and *s* for sins ...... Heb 5:1
is ordained to offer gifts and *s* ...... Heb 8:3
were offered both gifts and *s* ...... Heb 9:9
with better *s* than these ...... Heb 9:23
can never with those *s* which they ...... Heb 10:1
But in those *s* there is a ...... Heb 10:3
and offering oftentimes the same *s* ...... Heb 10:11
for with such *s* God is well ...... Heb 13:16
to offer up spiritual *s*, ... 1Pet 2:5

SACRIFICETH

He that *s* unto any god, save unto ...... Ex 22:20
to him that *s*, and to him that ...... Eccl 9:2
s, and to him that *s* not ...... Eccl 9:2
that *s* an ox, and killeth a ...... Is 66:3
he that *s* a lamb, as if he cut ...... Is 66:3
unto the LORD a corrupt thing ...... Mal 1:14

SACRIFICING

s sheep and oxen, which could not 1Kin 8:5
unto the calves that he had 1Kin 12:32

sheep and oxen, which could not 2Chr 5:6
He *s* also and burnt incense in the 2Chr 28:4
For he *s* unto the gods of 2Chr 28:23
s thereon peace offerings and 2Chr 33:16
for Amon *s* unto all the carved 2Chr 33:22
of them that had *s* unto them 2Chr 34:4
they *s* there unto, and their ...... Ps 106:37
whom they *s* unto the idols of ...... Ps 106:38
these hast thou *s* unto them to be ...... Eze 16:20
sacrifice which I have *s* for you ...... Eze 39:19
they *s* unto Baalim, and burned ...... Hos 11:2
Christ our passover is *s* for us 1Cor 5:7
to eat things *s* unto idols ...... Rev 2:14
and to eat things *s* unto idols ...... Rev 2:20

SACRILEGE

idols, dost thou commit *s* ...... Rom 2:22

SAD

them, and, behold, they were *s* ...... Gen 40:6
and her countenance was no more *s* 1Sa 1:18
why thy *s* spirit so *s* 1Kin 21:5
been beforetime *s* in his presence ...... Neh 2:1
unto me, Why is thy countenance *s* ...... Neh 2:2
should not my countenance be *s* ...... Neh 2:3
made the heart of the righteous *s* ...... Eze 13:22
s, whom I have not made *s* ...... Eze 13:22
hypocrites, of a *s* countenance ...... Mt 6:16
he was *s* at that saying, and went ...... Mk 10:22
to another, as ye walk, and are *s* ...... Lk 24:17

SADDLE

what *s* soever he rideth upon that ...... Lev 15:9
I will *s* me an ass, that I may 2Sa 19:26
said unto his sons, *S* me the ass 1Kin 13:13
to his sons, saying, *S* me the ass 1Kin 13:27

SADDLED

s his ass, and took two of his ...... Gen 22:3
s his ass, and went with the ...... Num 22:21
there were with him two asses *s* ...... Judg 19:10
met him, with a couple of asses *s* 2Sa 16:1
he *s* his ass, and arose, and gat 2Sa 17:23
s his ass, and went to Gath to 1Kin 2:40
So they *s* him the ass 1Kin 13:13
that he *s* for him the ass, to wit 1Kin 13:23
And they *s* him the ass 1Kin 13:27
Then she *s* an ass, and said to her 2Kin 4:24

SADDUCEES (*sad'-du-sees*) Members of a Jewish sect.

S come to his baptism, he said ...... Mt 3:7
Pharisees also with the *S* came ...... Mt 16:1
of the Pharisees and of the *S* ...... Mt 16:6
of the Pharisees and of the *S* ...... Mt 16:11
of the Pharisees and of the *S* ...... Mt 16:12
The same day came to him the *S* ...... Mt 22:23
that he had put the *S* to silence ...... Mt 22:34
Then come unto him the *S*, which ...... Mk 12:18
Then came to him certain of the *S* ...... Lk 20:27
captain of the temple, and the *S* ...... Acts 4:1
him, (which is the sect of the *S* ...... Acts 5:17
that the one part were *S*, and the ...... Acts 23:6
between the Pharisees and the *S* ...... Acts 23:7
For the *S* say that there is no ...... Acts 23:8

SADLY

Wherefore look ye so *s* to day ...... Gen 40:7

SADNESS

for by the *s* of the countenance ...... Eccl 7:3

SADOC (*sa'-dok*) Father of Achim; an ancestor of Jesus.

And Azor begat *S* ...... Mt 1:14
and *S* begat Achim ...... Mt 1:14

SAFE

on every side, and ye dwelled *s* 1Sa 12:11
said, Is the young man Absalom *s* 2Sa 18:29
Cushi, Is the young man Absalom *s* 2Sa 18:32
Their houses are *s* from fear ...... Job 21:9
Hold thou me up, and I shall be *s* ...... Ps 119:117
runneth into it, and is *s* ...... Prov 18:10
his trust in the LORD shall be *s* ...... Prov 29:25
prey, and shall carry it away *s* ...... Is 5:29
and they shall be *s* in their land ...... Eze 34:27
because he hath received him *s* ...... Lk 15:27
bring him *s* unto Felix the ...... Acts 23:24
that they escaped all *s* to land ...... Acts 27:44
not grievous, but for you it is *s* ...... Phil 3:1

SAFEGUARD

but with me thou shalt be in *s* 1Sa 22:23

SAFELY

the full, and dwell in your land *s* ...... Lev 26:5
And Judah and Israel dwelt *s* 1Kin 4:25
And he led them on *s*, so that they ...... Ps 78:53
hearkeneth unto me shall dwell *s* ...... Prov 1:33
Then shalt thou walk in thy way *s* ...... Prov 3:23
her husband doth *s* trust in her ...... Prov 31:11
He pursued them, and passed *s* ...... Is 41:3
be saved, and Israel shall dwell *s* ...... Jer 23:6
and I will cause them to dwell *s* ...... Jer 32:37
saved, and Jerusalem shall dwell *s* ...... Jer 33:16
And they shall dwell *s* therein ...... Eze 28:26
they shall dwell *s* in the ...... Eze 34:25
but they shall dwell *s*, and none ...... Eze 34:28
and they shall dwell *s* all of them ...... Eze 38:8
that are at rest, that dwell *s* ...... Eze 38:11
my people of Israel dwelleth *s* ...... Eze 38:14
when they dwelt *s* in their land ...... Eze 39:26
and will make them to be down *s* ...... Hos 2:18
Jerusalem shall be *s* inhabited ...... Zec 14:11
take him, and lead him away *s* ...... Mk 14:44
the jailer to keep them *s* ...... Acts 16:23

SAFETY

ye shall dwell in the land in *s* ...... Lev 25:18
your fill, and dwell therein in *s* ...... Lev 25:19
about, so that ye dwell in *s* ...... Deut 12:10
the LORD shall dwell in *s* by him ...... Deut 33:12
then shall dwell in *s* alone ...... Deut 33:28
I was not in *s*, neither had I ...... Job 3:26
His children are far from *s* ...... Job 5:4
which mourn may be exalted to *s* ...... Job 5:11
and thou shalt take thy rest in *s* ...... Job 11:18
Though is be given him to be in *s* ...... Job 24:23
LORD, only makest thou dwell in *s* ...... Ps 4:8

I will set him in s from him that........... Ps 12:5
An horse is a vain thing for s.............. Ps 33:17
of counsellors there is s...................... Prov 11:14
but s is of the LORD.............................. Prov 21:31
of counsellors there is s...................... Prov 24:6
and the needy shall lie down in s......... Is 14:30
truly found we shall with all s.............. Acts 5:23
when they shall say, Peace and s......... 1Th 5:3

SAFFRON
Spikenard and s.................................... Song 4:14

SAID See PREFACE.

SAIDST
Why s thou, She is my sister................ Gen 12:19
how s thou, She is my sister................ Gen 26:9
Isaac, the LORD which s unto me......... Gen 32:9
And thou s, I will surely do these....... Gen 32:12
thou s unto thy servants, Bring........... Gen 44:21
thou s unto thy servants, Except........ Gen 44:23
s unto them, I will multiply your......... Ex 32:13
now thy mouth, wherewith thou s...... Judg 9:38
thou s unto me, The word that I......... 1Kin 2:42
this to be right, that thou s................. Job 35:2
For thou s, What advantage will......... Job 35:3
When thou s, Seek ye my face............. Ps 27:8
in vision to thy holy one, and s.......... Ps 89:19
And thou s, I shall be a lady for......... Is 47:7
yet s thou not, There is no hope......... Is 57:10
but thou s, I will not transgress......... Jer 2:20
but thou s, There is no hope............... Jer 2:25
but thou s, I will not hear.................. Jer 22:21
thou s, Fear not................................... Lam 3:57
Because thou s, Aha, against my....... Eze 25:3
and thy judges of whom thou s.......... Hos 13:10
in that s thou truly............................ Jn 4:18

SAIL
mast, they could not spread the s...... Is 33:23
thou spreadest forth to be thy s......... Acts 27:7
as he was about to s into Syria........... Acts 20:3
had determined to s by Ephesus........ Acts 20:16
that we should s into Italy.................. Acts 27:1
meaning to s by the coasts of............ Acts 27:2
into the quicksands, strake s............. Acts 27:17
the all them that s with thee.............. Acts 27:24

SAILED
But as they s he fell asleep................. Lk 8:23
and from thence they s to Cyprus...... Acts 13:4
thence s to Antioch, from whence...... Acts 14:26
took Mark, and s unto Cyprus............ Acts 15:39
s thence into Syria, and with him...... Acts 18:18
And he s from Ephesus....................... Acts 18:21
we s away from Philippi after the...... Acts 20:6
s unto Assos, there intending to........ Acts 20:13
we s thence, and came the next day.. Acts 20:15
s into Syria, and landed at Tyre......... Acts 21:3
we s under Cyprus, because the........ Acts 27:4
when we had s over the sea of........... Acts 27:5
when we had s slowly many days,..... Acts 27:7
we s under Crete, over against........... Acts 27:7
thence, they s close by Crete.............. Acts 27:13

SAILING
finding a ship s over unto.................. Acts 21:2
a ship of Alexandria s into Italy........ Acts 27:6
when s was now dangerous, because .. Acts 27:9

SAILORS
and all the company in ships, and s.... Rev 18:17

SAINT
camp, and Aaron the s of the LORD ... Ps 106:16
Then I heard one s speaking............... Dan 8:13
another s said unto that certain......... Dan 8:13
unto that certain s which spake......... Dan 8:13
Salute every s in Christ Jesus............ Phil 4:21

SAINTS
he came with ten thousands of s....... Deut 33:2
all his s are in thy hand...................... Deut 33:3
He will keep the feet of his s.............. 1Sa 2:9
let thy s rejoice in goodness.............. 2Chr 6:41
to which of the s wilt thou turn.......... Job 5:1
he putteth no trust in his s................. Job 15:15
But to the s that are in the................ Ps 16:3
O ye s of his, and give thanks at....... Ps 30:4
O love the LORD, all ye his s............. Ps 31:23
O fear the LORD, ye his s.................. Ps 34:9
judgment, and forsaketh not his s..... Ps 37:28
Gather my s together unto me........... Ps 50:5
for it is good before thy s.................. Ps 52:9
the flesh of thy s unto the................. Ps 79:2
unto his people, and to his s............. Ps 85:8
also in the congregation of the s....... Ps 89:5
feared in the assembly of the s......... Ps 89:7
he preserveth the souls of his s......... Ps 97:10
of The LORD is the death of his s..... Ps 116:15
and let thy s shout for joy.................. Ps 132:9
her s shall aloud for joy...................... Ps 132:16
and thy s shall bless thee................... Ps 145:10
people, the praise of all his s............ Ps 148:14
praise in the congregation of s.......... Ps 149:1
Let the s be joyful in glory................. Ps 149:5
this honour have all his s................... Ps 149:9
and preserveth the way of his s......... Prov 2:8
But the s of the most High shall........ Dan 7:18
the same horn made war with the s... Dan 7:21
given to the s of the most High......... Dan 7:22
that the s possessed the kingdom..... Dan 7:22
wear out the s of the most High........ Dan 7:25
people of the s of the most High....... Dan 7:27

God, and is faithful with the s.......... Hos 11:12
come, and all the s with thee............ Zec 14:5
bodies of the s which slept arose...... Mt 27:52
hath done to thy s at Jerusalem........ Acts 9:13
to the s which dwelt at Lydda............ Acts 9:32
up, and when he had called the s...... Acts 9:41
many of the s did I shut up in............ Acts 26:10
beloved of God, called to be s........... Rom 1:7
s according to the will of God............ Rom 8:27
to the necessity of s......................... Rom 12:13
Jerusalem to minister unto the s....... Rom 15:25
the poor s which are at Jerusalem..... Rom 15:26
may be accepted of the s.................. Rom 15:31
her in the Lord, as becometh s.......... Rom 16:2
all the s which are with them............ Rom 16:15
in Christ Jesus, called to be s............ 1Cor 1:2
the unjust, and not before the s........ 1Cor 6:1
that the s shall judge the world......... 1Cor 6:2
as in all churches of the s.................. 1Cor 14:33
the collection for the s, as I.............. 1Cor 16:1
to the ministry of the s,)................... 1Cor 16:15
with all the s which are in all............ 2Cor 1:1
of the ministering to the s................. 2Cor 8:4
touching the ministering to the s....... 2Cor 9:1
only supplieth the want of the s........ 2Cor 9:12
All the s salute you........................... 2Cor 13:13
to the s which are at Ephesus, and... Eph 1:1
Jesus, and love unto all the s........... Eph 1:15
glory of his inheritance in the s........ Eph 1:18
but fellowcitizens with the s.............. Eph 2:19
am less than the least of all s............ Eph 3:8
with all s what is the breadth............ Eph 3:18
For the perfecting of the s.................. Eph 4:12
named among you, as becometh s..... Eph 5:3
and supplication for all s.................... Eph 6:18
to all the s in Christ Jesus................. Phil 1:1
All the s salute you, chiefly............... Phil 4:22
To the s and faithful brethren in....... Col 1:2
love which ye have to all the s.......... Col 1:4
the inheritance of the s in light......... Col 1:12
but now is made manifest to his s..... Col 1:26
Lord Jesus Christ with all his s.......... 1Th 3:13
come to be glorified in his s.............. 2Th 1:10
the Lord Jesus, and toward all s........ Philem 5
of the s are refreshed by thee.......... Philem 7
that ye have ministered to the s....... Heb 6:10
the rule over you, and all the s.......... Heb 13:24
was once delivered unto the s........... Jude 3
with ten thousands of his s............... Jude 14
which are the prayers of s................. Rev 5:8
it with the prayers of all s upon....... Rev 8:3
came with the prayers of the s......... Rev 8:4
the prophets, and to the s................. Rev 11:18
unto him to make war with the s...... Rev 13:7
patience and the faith of the s......... Rev 13:10
Here is the patience of the s............. Rev 14:12
true are thy ways, thou King of s...... Rev 15:3
For they have shed the blood of s..... Rev 16:6
drunken with the blood of the s........ Rev 17:6
the blood of prophets, and of s......... Rev 18:24
linen in the righteousness of s.......... Rev 19:8
compassed the camp of the s about... Rev 20:9

SAINTS'
if she have washed the s feet............ 1Ti 5:10

SAITH See PREFACE.

SAKE
cursed is the ground for thy s........... Gen 3:17
the ground any more for man's s....... Gen 8:21
it may be well with me for thy s........ Gen 12:13
he entreated Abram well for her s..... Gen 12:16
I will not do it for forty's s............... Gen 18:29
not destroy it for twenty's s.............. Gen 18:31
I will not destroy it for ten's s.......... Gen 18:32
they will slay me for my wife's s....... Gen 20:11
seed for my servant Abraham's s...... Gen 26:24
LORD hath blessed me for thy s........ Gen 30:27
Egyptian's house for Joseph's s........ Gen 39:5
to the Egyptians for Israel's s........... Ex 18:8
let him go free for his eye's s.......... Ex 21:26
let him go free for his tooth's s........ Ex 21:27
unto him, Enviest thou for my s........ Num 11:29
was zealous for my s among them..... Num 25:11
day of the plague for Peor's s........... Num 25:18
his people for his great name's s...... 1Sa 12:22
to destroy the city for my s............... 1Sa 23:10
kingdom for his people Israel's s....... 2Sa 5:12
For thy word's s, and according to... 2Sa 7:21
him kindness for Jonathan's s........... 2Sa 9:1
for Jonathan thy father's s............... 2Sa 9:7
for my s with the young man........... 2Sa 18:5
of a far country for thy name's s...... 1Kin 8:41
do it for David thy father's s............ 1Kin 11:12
thy son for David my servant's s...... 1Kin 11:13
for Jerusalem's s which I have.......... 1Kin 11:13
tribe for my servant David's s.......... 1Kin 11:32
and for Jerusalem's s....................... 1Kin 11:32
his life for David my servant's s....... 1Kin 11:34
Nevertheless for David's s did.......... 1Kin 15:4
Judah for David his servant's........... 2Kin 8:19
city, to save it, for mine own s......... 2Kin 19:34
s, and for my servant David's s........ 2Kin 19:34
defend this city for mine own s........ 2Kin 20:6
and for my servant David's s............ 2Kin 20:6
O LORD, for thy servant's s............. 1Chr 17:19
country for thy great name's s......... 2Chr 6:32
for thy great mercies' s thou........... Neh 9:31
the children's s of mine own body.... Job 19:17
oh save me for thy mercies' s........... Ps 6:4
of righteousness for his name's s..... Ps 23:3

thou me for thy goodness' s............. Ps 25:7
For thy name's s, O LORD, pardon... Ps 25:11
for thy name's s lead me, and.......... Ps 31:3
save me for thy mercies' s................ Ps 31:16
for thy s are we killed all the.......... Ps 44:22
for thy s, for thy mercies' s............. Ps 44:26
God of hosts, be ashamed for my s... Ps 69:6
seek thee be confounded for my s.... Ps 69:6
Because for thy s I have borne.......... Ps 69:7
away our sins, for thy name's s........ Ps 79:9
he saved them for his name's s........ Ps 106:8
O God the Lord, for thy name's s..... Ps 109:21
thy mercy, and for thy truth's s........ Ps 115:1
For thy servant David's s turn........... Ps 132:10
me, O LORD, for thy name's s.......... Ps 143:11
for thy righteousness' s bring my..... Ps 143:11
city to save it for mine own s.......... Is 37:35
and for my servant David's s............ Is 37:35
pleased for his righteousness' s....... Is 42:21
For your s I have sent to Babylon..... Is 43:14
thy transgressions for mine own s.... Is 43:25
For Jacob my servant's s, and.......... Is 45:4
For my name's s will I defer mine..... Is 48:9
own s, even for mine own s............. Is 48:11
against thee shall fall for thy s......... Is 54:15
For Zion's s will I not hold my......... Is 62:1
for Jerusalem's s I will not rest........ Is 62:1
Return for thy servants' s................. Is 63:17
that cast you out for my name's s.... Is 66:5
ariseth for the glory of his s............. Jer 14:7
Do not abhor us, for thy name's s.... Jer 14:21
know that for thy s I have................ Jer 15:15
But I wrought for my name's s......... Eze 20:9
But I wrought for my name's s......... Eze 20:14
hand, and wrought for my name's s.. Eze 20:22
wrought with you for my name's s.... Eze 20:44
but for mine holy name's s.............. Eze 36:22
is desolate, for the Lord's s............. Dan 9:17
defer not, for thine own s................ Dan 9:19
for I know that for my s this............ Jonah 1:12
for your s be plowed as a field........ Mic 3:12
persecuted for righteousness' s....... Mt 5:10
against you falsely, for my s............ Mt 5:11
governors and kings for my s........... Mt 10:18
hated of all men for my name's s..... Mt 10:22
his life for my s shall find it............ Mt 10:39
put him in prison for Herodias' s..... Mt 14:3
nevertheless for the oath's s........... Mt 14:9
his life for my s shall find it............ Mt 16:25
for the kingdom of heaven's s......... Mt 19:12
or lands, for my name's s............... Mt 19:29
of all nations for my name's s........ Mt 24:9
but for the elect's s those days....... Mt 24:22
for his oath's s, and for............... Mk 6:26
shall lose his life for my s............... Mk 8:35
or children, or lands, for my s........ Mk 10:29
before rulers and kings for my s...... Mk 13:9
hated of all men for my name's s.... Mk 13:13
but for the elect's s, whom he........ Mk 13:20
as evil, for the Son of man's s........ Lk 6:22
will lose his life for my s................. Lk 9:24
for the kingdom of God's s.............. Lk 18:29
kings and rulers for my name's s..... Lk 21:12
hated of all men for my name's s.... Lk 21:17
they came not for Jesus' s only....... Jn 12:9
I will lay down my life for thy s....... Jn 13:37
thou lay down thy life for my s....... Jn 13:38
believe me for the very works' s...... Jn 14:11
they do unto you for my name's s.... Jn 15:21
he must suffer for my name's s....... Acts 9:16
For which hope's s, king Agrippa..... Acts 26:7
was not written for his s alone....... Rom 4:23
For thy s we are killed all the......... Rom 8:36
wrath, but also for conscience s...... Rom 13:5
for the Lord Jesus Christ's s............ Rom 15:30
We are fools for Christ's s.............. 1Cor 4:10
And this I do for the gospel's s....... 1Cor 9:23
no question for conscience s.......... 1Cor 10:25
no question for conscience s.......... 1Cor 10:27
eat not for his s that shewed it...... 1Cor 10:28
shewed it, and for conscience s...... 1Cor 10:28
your servants for Jesus' s.............. 2Cor 4:5
delivered unto death for Jesus' s.... 2Cor 4:11
in distresses for Christ's s............. 2Cor 12:10
for Christ's s hath forgiven you...... Eph 4:32
him, but also to suffer for his s...... Phil 1:29
in my flesh for his body's s........... Col 1:24
For which things' s the wrath of..... Col 3:6
men we were among you for your s.. 1Th 1:5
highly in love for their work's s...... 1Th 5:13
a little wine for thy stomach's s...... 1Ti 5:23
ought not, for filthy lucre's s......... Titus 1:11
for Yet for love's s I rather beseech.... Philem 9
ordinance of man for the Lord's s.... 1Pet 2:13
if ye suffer for righteousness' s...... 1Pet 3:14
are forgiven you for his name's s.... 1Jn 2:12
For the truth's s, which dwelleth..... 2Jn 2
for his name's s they went forth..... 3Jn 7
and for my name's s hast laboured .. Rev 2:3

SAKES
spare all the place for their s........... Gen 18:26
But I will for their s remember........ Lev 26:45
LORD was angry with me for your s.. Deut 1:37
LORD was wroth with me for your s.. Deut 3:26
LORD was angry with me for your s.. Deut 4:21
Be favourable unto them for our s.... Judg 21:22
s that the hand of the LORD is......... Ruth 1:13
he reproved kings for their s............ 1Chr 16:21

for their *s* therefore return thou .... Ps 7:7
he reproved kings for their *s*............... Ps 105:14
went ill with Moses for their *s* .... Ps 106:32
For my brethren and companions' *s* ..... Ps 122:8
so will I do for my servants' *s* .... Is 65:8
I do not this for your *s*, O house........... Eze 36:22
Not for your *s* do I this, saith .... Eze 36:32
but for their *s* that shall make............. Dan 2:30
rebuke the devourer for your *s*............. Mal 3:11
for their *s* which sat with him,............. Mk 6:26
I am glad for your *s* that I was............. Jn 11:15
not because of me, but for your *s*......... Jn 12:30
for their *s* I sanctify myself,................ Jn 17:19
they are enemies for your *s* .... Rom 11:28
are beloved for the fathers' *s*.............. Rom 11:28
myself and to Apollos for your *s* 1Cor 4:6
saith he it altogether for our *s*.............. 1Cor 9:10
For our *s*, no doubt, this is................... 1Cor 9:10
for your *s* forgave I it in 2Cor 2:10
For all things are for your *s* 2Cor 4:15
yet for your *s* he became poor,............ 2Cor 8:9
we joy for your *s* before our God 1Th 3:9
all things for the elect's *s* 2Ti 2:10

SAKIA See SHACHIA.

SALA (sa'-lah) See SALAH. *Father of Heber; an ancestor of Jesus.*
of Heber, which was the son of Sala .... Lk 3:35

SALAH (sa'-lah) See SALA. *Son of Arphaxad.*
And Arphaxad begat S....................... Gen 10:24
and S begat Eber .... Gen 10:24
five and thirty years, and begat S .... Gen 11:12
after he begat S four hundred............... Gen 11:13
S lived thirty years, and begat.............. Gen 11:14
S lived after he begat Eber four............ Gen 11:15

SALAMIS (sal'-a-mis) *A city on Cyprus.*
And when they were at S, they .... Acts 13:5

SALATHIEL (sa-la'-the-el) See SHEALTIEL. *Descendant of Jehoiakim; an ancestor of Jesus.*
Assir, S his son,................................ 1Chr 3:17
to Babylon, Jechonias begat S .... Mt 1:12
and S begat Zorobabel .... Mt 1:12
Zorobabel, which was the son of S......... Lk 3:27

SALCAH (sal'-kah) See SALCHAH. *A city in Gad.*
reigned in mount Hermon, and in S...... Josh 12:5
Hermon, and all Bashan unto S............ Josh 13:11

SALCHAH (sal'-kah) See SALCAH. *Same as Salcah.*
all Gilead, and all Bashan, unto S .... Deut 3:10
in the land of Bashan unto S 1Chr 5:11

SALE
count the years of the *s* thereof .... Lev 25:27
the price of his *s* shall be.................... Lev 25:50
cometh of the *s* of his patrimony........ Deut 18:8

SALECAH See SALCHAH.

SALEM (sa'-lem) See JERUSALEM. *The city of Melchizedek.*
king of S brought forth bread .... Gen 14:18
In S also is his tabernacle, and .... Ps 76:2
For this Melchisedec, king of S............. Heb 7:1
and after that also King of S .... Heb 7:2

SALIM (sa'-lim) *A city near Aenon.*
was baptizing in Aenon near to S .... Jn 3:23

SALLAI (sal'-lahee) See SALLU.
1. An exile.
And after him Gabbai, S, nine.............. Neh 11:8
2. A priest with Zerubbabel.
Of S, Kallai..................................... Neh 12:20

SALLU (sal'-lu) See SALLAI. *A priest with Zerubbabel.*
S, Amok, Hilkiah, Jedaiah................... Neh 12:7
S the son of Meshullam, the son........... 1Chr 9:7
S the son of Meshullam, the son........... Neh 11:7

SALMA (sal'-mah) See SALMON, ZALMA.
1. Father of Boaz.
And Nahshon begat S, and S................ 1Chr 2:11
2. A son of Caleb.
begat Salma, and S begat Boaz,........... 1Chr 2:11
S the father of Beth-lehem,................. 1Chr 2:51
The sons of S 1Chr 2:54

SALMI See SALMA.

SALMON (sal'-mon) See SALMA.
1. Father of Boaz.
begat Nahshon, and Nahshon begat S .... Ruth 4:20
S begat Boaz, and Boaz begat Obed,..... Ruth 4:21
and Naasson begat S .... Mt 1:4
And S begat Booz of Rachab................ Mt 1:5
of Booz, which was the son of S............ Lk 3:32
2. A mountain near Shechem.
in it, it was white as snow in S............. Ps 68:14

SALMONE (sal-mo'-ne) *A promontory on Crete.*
under Crete, over against S .... Acts 27:7

SALOME (sa-lo'-me) *A woman follower of Jesus.*
James the less and of Joses, and S........ Mk 15:40
and Mary the mother of James, and S .. Mk 16:1

SALT
of Siddim, which is the S Sea.............. Gen 14:3
him, and she became a pillar of *s* ...... Gen 19:26
offering shalt thou season with *s* ...... Lev 2:13
s of the covenant of thy God to .... Lev 2:13
offerings thou shalt offer *s* .... Lev 2:13
it is a covenant of *s* for ever.............. Num 18:19
coast of the *s* sea eastward............... Num 34:3
out of it shall be at the *s* sea........... Num 34:12
sea of the plain, even the *s* sea........ Deut 3:17
land thereof is brimstone, and *s* ...... Deut 29:23
sea of the plain, even the *s* sea......... Josh 3:16
even the *s* sea on the east, the .... Josh 12:3
was from the shore of the *s* sea......... Josh 15:2
And the east border was the *s* sea...... Josh 15:5
And Nibshan, and the city of S .... Josh 15:62
were at the north bay of the *s* .... Josh 18:19
down the city, and sowed it with *s* .... Judg 9:45
of the Syrians in the valley of *s* 2Sa 8:13
me a new cruse, and put *s* therein 2Kin 2:20
waters, and cast the *s* in there.......... 2Kin 2:21
in the valley of *s* ten thousand.......... 2Kin 14:7
The valley of *s* eighteen thousand...... 1Chr 18:12
and to his sons by a covenant of *s* 2Chr 13:5
and went to the valley of *s* 2Chr 25:11
of the God of heaven, wheat, *s* .... Ezr 6:9
s without prescribing how much .... Ezr 7:22
Is unsavoury be eaten without *s* .... Job 6:6
the valley of *s* twelve thousand......... Ps 60:t
in the wilderness, in a *s* land .... Jer 17:6
priests shall cast *s* upon them.......... Eze 43:24
they shall be given to *s* .... Eze 47:11
Ye are the *s* of the earth................... Mt 5:13
but if the *s* have lost his savour......... Mt 5:13
sacrifice shall be salted with *s* .... Mk 9:49
S is good,....................................... Mk 9:50
but if the *s* have lost his .... Mk 9:50
Have *s* in yourselves, and have .... Mk 9:50
S is good.. Lk 14:34
but if the *s* have lost his savour......... Lk 14:34
alway with grace, seasoned with *s* ..... Col 4:6
no fountain both yield *s* water.......... Jas 3:12

SALTED
thou wast not *s* at all, nor.................. Eze 16:4
savour, wherewith shall it be *s*........... Mt 5:13
every one shall be *s* with fire............. Mk 9:49
sacrifice shall be *s* with salt.............. Mk 9:49

SALTPITS
the breeding of nettles, and *s* .... Zeph 2:9

SALU (sa'-lu) *Father of Zimri.*
woman, was Zimri, the son of S .... Num 25:14

SALUTATION
what manner of *s* this should be......... Lk 1:29
Elisabeth heard the *s* of Mary............ Lk 1:41
the babe leaped in my womb for *s* ..... Lk 1:44
The *s* of me Paul with mine own 1Cor 16:21
The *s* by the hand of me Paul .... Col 4:18
The *s* of Paul with mine own hand,..... 2Th 3:17

SALUTATIONS
love *s* in the marketplaces,............... Mk 12:38

SALUTE
And they will *s* thee, and give thee 1Sa 10:4
to meet him, that he might *s* him 1Sa 13:10
of the wilderness to *s* our master 1Sa 25:14
to *s* him, and to bless him,................ 2Sa 8:10
if thou meet any man, *s* him not........ 2Kin 4:29
and if any *s* thee, answer him not....... 2Kin 4:29
we go down to *s* the children of......... 2Kin 10:13
if ye *s* your brethren only, what .... Mt 5:47
when ye come into an house, *s* it .... Mt 10:12
And began to *s* him, Hail, King of ...... Mk 15:18
and *s* no man by the way .... Lk 10:4
came unto Caesarea to *s* Festus .... Acts 25:13
S my wellbeloved Epaenetus, who........ Rom 16:5
S Andronicus and Junia, my kinsmen... Rom 16:7
S Urbane, our helper in Christ,............ Rom 16:9
S Apelles approved in Christ................ Rom 16:10
S them which are of Aristobulus'......... Rom 16:10
S Herodion my kinsman .... Rom 16:11
S Tryphena and Tryphosa, who........... Rom 16:12
S the beloved Persis, which................. Rom 16:12
S Rufus chosen in the Lord, and........... Rom 16:13
S Asyncritus, Phlegon, Hermas,.......... Rom 16:14
S Philologus, and Julia, Nereus,.......... Rom 16:15
S one another with an holy kiss........... Rom 16:16
The churches of Christ *s* you.............. Rom 16:16
and Sosipater, my kinsmen, *s* you...... Rom 16:21
this epistle, *s* you in the Lord............. Rom 16:22
The churches of Asia *s* you................ 1Cor 16:19
Priscilla *s* you much in the Lord,........ 1Cor 16:19
All the saints *s* you 2Cor 13:13
S every saint in Christ Jesus................ Phil 4:21
All the saints *s* you, chiefly .... Phil 4:22
S the brethren which are in................. Col 4:15
S Prisca and Aquila, and the 2Ti 4:19
All that are with me *s* thee................ Titus 3:15
S them there Epaphras, my................. Phlem 23
S all them that have the rule............... Heb 13:24
They of Italy *s* you........................... Heb 13:24
Our friends *s* thee........................... 3Jn 14

SALUTED
unto the house of Micah, and *s* him.... Judg 18:15
army, and came and *s* his brethren..... 1Sa 17:22
near to the people, the *s* them........... 1Sa 30:21

---

he *s* him, and said to him, Is 2Kin 10:15
amazed, and running to him *s* him...... Mk 9:15
of Zacharias, and *s* Elisabeth .... Lk 1:40
s the church, he went down to .... Acts 18:22
s the brethren, and abode with .... Acts 21:7
And when he had *s* them, he............. Acts 21:19

SALUTETH
and of the whole church, *s* you.......... Rom 16:23
the chamberlain of the city *s* you....... Rom 16:23
my fellowprisoner *s* you, and............ Col 4:10
s you, always labouring fervently .... Col 4:12
elected together with you, *s* you......... 1Pet 5:13

SALVATION
I have waited for thy *s*, O LORD .... Gen 49:18
see the *s* of the LORD, which he......... Ex 14:13
and song, and he is become my *s* .... Ex 15:2
esteemed the Rock of his *s*................ Deut 32:15
because I rejoice in thy *s* 1Sa 2:1
the LORD hath wrought *s* in Israel 1Sa 11:13
wrought this great *s* in Israel............. 1Sa 14:45
wrought a great *s* for all Israel 1Sa 19:5
is my shield, and the horn of my *s* 2Sa 22:3
also given me the shield of thy *s* 2Sa 22:36
be the God of the rock of my *s* 2Sa 22:47
He is the tower of *s* for his king 2Sa 22:51
for this is all my *s*, and all my............ 2Sa 23:5
shew forth from day to day his *s* 1Chr 16:23
say ye, Save us, O God of our *s* 1Chr 16:35
O LORD God, be clothed with *s* 2Chr 6:41
see the *s* of the LORD with you, O 2Chr 20:17
He also shall be my *s* .... Job 13:16
S belongeth unto the LORD .... Ps 3:8
I will rejoice in thy *s*........................ Ps 9:14
my heart shall rejoice in thy *s* .... Ps 13:5
Oh that the *s* of Israel were come....... Ps 14:7
my buckler, and the horn of my *s* ...... Ps 18:2
also given me the shield of thy *s* .... Ps 18:35
and let the God of my *s* be exalted ..... Ps 18:46
We will rejoice in thy *s*, and in .... Ps 20:5
in thy *s* how greatly shall he .... Ps 21:1
His glory is great in thy *s* .... Ps 21:5
from the God of his *s* .... Ps 24:5
for thou art the God of my *s* .... Ps 25:5
The LORD is my light and my *s* .... Ps 27:1
neither forsake me, O God of my *s* ..... Ps 27:9
say unto my soul, I am thy *s* .... Ps 35:3
it shall rejoice in his *s* .... Ps 35:9
But the *s* of the righteous is of .... Ps 37:39
haste to help me, O Lord my *s* .... Ps 38:22
thy faithfulness and thy *s* .... Ps 40:10
as love thy *s* say continually............. Ps 40:16
aright will I shew the *s* of God .... Ps 50:23
Restore unto me the joy of thy *s* .... Ps 51:12
O God, thou God of my *s* .... Ps 51:14
Oh that the *s* of Israel were come....... Ps 53:6
from him cometh my *s* .... Ps 62:1
He only is my rock and my *s* .... Ps 62:2
He only is my rock and my *s* .... Ps 62:6
In God is my *s* and my glory.............. Ps 62:7
thou answer us, O God of our *s* .... Ps 65:5
benefits, even the God of our *s* .... Ps 68:19
that is our God is the God of *s* .... Ps 68:20
hear me, in the truth of thy *s* .... Ps 69:13
let thy *s*, O God, set me up on .... Ps 69:29
as love thy *s* say continually............. Ps 70:4
and thy *s* all the day........................ Ps 71:15
working *s* in the midst of the .... Ps 74:12
in God, and trusted not in his *s* .... Ps 78:22
Help us, O God of our *s*, for the .... Ps 79:9
Turn us, O God of our *s*, and cause .... Ps 85:4
mercy, O LORD, and grant us thy *s* .... Ps 85:7
Surely his *s* is nigh them that............ Ps 85:9
O Lord God of my *s*, I have cried .... Ps 88:1
my God, and the rock of my *s* .... Ps 89:26
I satisfy him, and shew him my *s* ...... Ps 91:16
joyful noise to the rock of our *s* .... Ps 95:1
shew forth his *s* from day to day........ Ps 96:2
The LORD hath made known his *s* ...... Ps 98:2
earth have seen the *s* of our God........ Ps 98:3
O visit me with thy *s* .... Ps 106:4
I will take the cup of *s*, and call .... Ps 116:13
and song, and is become my *s* .... Ps 118:14
s is in the tabernacles of the .... Ps 118:15
hast heard me, and art become my *s*... Ps 118:21
also unto me, O LORD, even thy *s* .... Ps 119:41
My soul fainteth for thy *s* .... Ps 119:81
Mine eyes fail for thy *s*, and for......... Ps 119:123
S is far from the wicked .... Ps 119:155
LORD, I have hoped for thy *s* .... Ps 119:166
I have longed for thy *s*, O LORD......... Ps 119:174
also clothe her priests with *s* .... Ps 132:16
the Lord, the strength of my *s* .... Ps 140:7
It is he that giveth *s* unto kings .... Ps 144:10
he will beautify the meek with *s* .... Ps 149:4
Behold, God is my *s*......................... Is 12:2
he also is become my *s* .... Is 12:2
draw water out of the wells of *s* .... Is 12:3
hast forgotten the God of thy *s* .... Is 17:10
will be glad and rejoice in his *s* .... Is 25:9
s will God appoint for walls and......... Is 26:1
our *s* also in the time of trouble........ Is 33:2
of thy times, and strength of *s* .... Is 33:6
open, and let them bring forth *s* .... Is 45:8
in the LORD with an everlasting *s* ...... Is 45:17
far off, and my *s* shall not tarry.......... Is 46:13
I will place *s* in Zion for Israel .... Is 46:13
that thou mayest be my *s* unto the ..... Is 49:6
in a day of *s* have I helped thee.......... Is 49:8
my *s* is gone forth, and mine arms..... Is 51:5

but my s shall be for ever, and my........ Is 51:6
ever, and my s from generation to......... Is 51:8
of good, that publisheth s................ Is 52:7
earth shall see the s of our God......... Is 52:10
for my s is near to come, and my......... Is 56:1
for s, but it is far off from us.......... Is 59:11
his arm brought s unto him............... Is 59:16
an helmet of s upon his head............. Is 59:17
but thou shalt call thy walls S........... Is 60:18
clothed me with the garments of s........ Is 61:10
the s thereof as a lamp that............. Is 62:1
he is just, and having s................. Is 62:11
mine own arm brought s unto me........... Is 63:5
Truly in vain is s hoped for from........ Jer 3:23
LORD our God is the s of Israel.......... Jer 3:23
wait for the s of the LORD............... Lam 3:26
S is of the LORD......................... Jonah 2:9
I will wait for the God of my s.......... Mic 7:7
thine horses and thy chariots of s....... Hab 3:8
forth for the s of thy people............ Hab 3:13
even for s with thine anointed........... Hab 3:13
I will joy in the God of my s............ Hab 3:18
hath raised up an horn of s for.......... Lk 1:69
To give knowledge of s unto his.......... Lk 1:77
For mine eyes have seen thy s............ Lk 2:30
all flesh shall see the s of God......... Lk 3:6
This day is s come to this house......... Lk 19:9
for s is of the Jews..................... Jn 4:22
Neither is there s in any other.......... Acts 4:12
to you is the word of this s sent........ Acts 13:26
for s unto the ends of the earth......... Acts 13:47
which shew unto us the way of s.......... Acts 16:17
that the s of God is sent unto........... Acts 28:28
s to every one that believeth............ Rom 1:16
mouth confession is made unto s.......... Rom 10:10
fall s is come unto the Gentiles......... Rom 11:11
for now is our s nearer than when........ Rom 13:11
it is for your consolation and s......... 2Cor 1:6
it is for your consolation and s......... 2Cor 1:6
in the day of s have I succoured......... 2Cor 6:2
behold, now is the day of s.............. 2Cor 6:2
to s not to be repented of............... 2Cor 7:10
of truth, the gospel of your s........... Eph 1:13
And take the helmet of s, and the........ Eph 6:17
turn to my s through your prayer......... Phil 1:19
of perdition, but to you of s............ Phil 1:28
work out your own s with fear............ Phil 2:12
and for an helmet, the hope of s......... 1Th 5:8
but to obtain s by our Lord Jesus........ 1Th 5:9
the beginning chosen you to s............ 2Th 2:13
s which is in Christ Jesus with.......... 2Ti 2:10
unto s through faith which is in......... 2Ti 3:15
s hath appeared to all men............... Titus 2:11
for them who shall be heirs of s......... Heb 1:14
escape, if we neglect so great s......... Heb 2:3
s perfect through sufferings............. Heb 2:10
s unto all them that obey him............ Heb 5:9
you, and things that accompany s......... Heb 6:9
second time without sin unto s........... Heb 9:28
s ready to be revealed in the............ 1Pet 1:5
faith, even the s of your souls.......... 1Pet 1:9
Of which s the prophets have............. 1Pet 1:10
longsuffering of our Lord is s........... 2Pet 3:15
to write unto you of the common s........ Jude 3
S to our God which sitteth upon.......... Rev 7:10
saying in heaven, Now is come s.......... Rev 12:10
S, and glory, and honour, and power,..... Rev 19:1

SAMARIA (sa-ma're-ah) See SAMARITAN.
1. A city in Ephraim.
he bought the hill S of Shemer........... 1Kin 16:24
of Shemer, owner of the hill, S.......... 1Kin 16:24
his fathers, and was buried in S......... 1Kin 16:28
reigned over Israel in S twenty.......... 1Kin 16:29
of Baal, which he had built in S......... 1Kin 16:32
And there was a sore famine in S......... 1Kin 18:2
and he went up and besieged S............ 1Kin 20:1
if that doubt S shall suffice............ 1Kin 20:10
There are men come out of S.............. 1Kin 20:17
Damascus, as my father made in S......... 1Kin 20:34
heavy and displeased, and came to S...... 1Kin 20:43
king of Israel, which is in S............ 1Kin 21:18
in the entrance of the gate of S......... 1Kin 22:10
king died, and was brought to S.......... 1Kin 22:37
and they buried the king in S............ 1Kin 22:37
the chariot in the pool of S............. 1Kin 22:38
in S the seventeenth year of............. 1Kin 22:51
his upper chamber that was in S.......... 2Kin 1:2
and from thence he returned to S......... 2Kin 2:25
in S the eighteenth year of.............. 2Kin 3:1
went out of S the same time.............. 2Kin 3:6
with the prophet that is in S............ 2Kin 5:3
But he led them to S..................... 2Kin 6:19
pass, when they were come into S......... 2Kin 6:20
they were in the midst of S.............. 2Kin 6:20
host, and went up, and besieged S........ 2Kin 6:24
And there was a great famine in S........ 2Kin 6:25
for a shekel, in the gate of S........... 2Kin 7:1
about this time in the gate of S......... 2Kin 7:18
And Ahab had seventy sons in S........... 2Kin 10:1
Jehu wrote letters, and sent to S........ 2Kin 10:1
arose and departed, and came to S........ 2Kin 10:12
And when he came to S, he slew all....... 2Kin 10:17
all that remained unto Ahab in S......... 2Kin 10:17
and they buried him in S................. 2Kin 10:35
over Israel in S was twenty.............. 2Kin 10:36
began to reign over Israel in S.......... 2Kin 13:1
remained the grove also in S............. 2Kin 13:6
and they buried him in S................. 2Kin 13:9
reign over Israel in S................... 2Kin 13:10

Joash was buried in S with the........... 2Kin 13:13
and hostages, and returned to S.......... 2Kin 14:14
was buried in S with the kings of........ 2Kin 14:16
of Israel began to reign in S............ 2Kin 14:23
reign over Israel in S six months........ 2Kin 15:8
and he reigned a full month in S......... 2Kin 15:13
went up from Tirzah, and came to S....... 2Kin 15:14
Shallum the son of Jabesh in S........... 2Kin 15:14
Israel, and reigned ten years in S....... 2Kin 15:17
began to reign over Israel in S.......... 2Kin 15:23
against him, and smote him in S.......... 2Kin 15:25
began to reign over Israel in S.......... 2Kin 15:27
reign in S over Israel nine years........ 2Kin 17:1
all the land, and went up to S........... 2Kin 17:5
Hoshea the king of Assyria took S........ 2Kin 17:6
king of Assyria came up against S........ 2Kin 18:9
king of Israel, S was taken.............. 2Kin 18:10
they delivered S out of mine hand........ 2Kin 18:34
over Jerusalem the line of S............. 2Kin 21:13
the entering in of the gate of S......... 2Chr 18:9
caught him, (for he was hid in S......... 2Chr 22:9
from S even into Beth-horon, and......... 2Chr 25:13
hostages also, and returned to S......... 2Chr 25:24
them, and brought the spoil to S......... 2Chr 28:8
before the host that came to S........... 2Chr 28:9
then they returned to S.................. 2Chr 28:15
And the head of Ephraim is S............. Is 7:9
the head of S is Remaliah's son.......... Is 7:9
the spoil of S shall be taken............ Is 8:4
Ephraim and the inhabitant of S.......... Is 9:9
is not S as Damascus..................... Is 10:9
excel them of Jerusalem and S............ Is 10:10
I not, as I have done unto S............. Is 10:11
And thine elder sister is S.............. Eze 16:46
Neither hath S committed half of......... Eze 16:51
daughters, and the captivity of S........ Eze 16:53
to their former estate, and S............ Eze 16:55
S is Aholah, and Jerusalem............... Eze 23:4
with the cup of thy sister S............. Eze 23:33
S shall become desolate.................. Hos 13:16
dwell in S in the corner of a bed........ Amos 3:12
Judah, which he saw concerning S......... Mic 1:1
is it not S............................... Mic 1:5
Therefore I will make S as an............ Mic 1:6
Philip went down to the city of S........ Acts 8:5
and bewitched the people of S............ Acts 8:9
S had received the word of God........... Acts 8:14
2. Territory of the northern tribes.
which are in the cities of S............. 1Kin 13:32
by the palace of Ahab king of S.......... 1Kin 21:1
the messengers of the king of S......... 2Kin 1:3
of S instead of the children of......... 2Kin 17:24
and they possessed S, and dwelt in....... 2Kin 17:24
and placed in the cities of S............ 2Kin 17:26
they had carried away from S came........ 2Kin 17:28
of the prophet that came out of S........ 2Kin 23:18
that were in the cities of S............. 2Kin 23:19
years he went down to Ahab to S.......... 2Chr 18:2
over, and set in the cities of S......... Ezr 4:10
their companions that dwell in S......... Ezr 4:17
his brethren and the army of S........... Neh 3:34
they delivered S out of mine hand........ Is 36:19
seen folly in the prophets of S.......... Jer 23:13
vines upon the mountains of S............ Jer 31:5
Shechem, from Shiloh, and from S......... Jer 41:5
and the wickedness of S.................. Hos 7:1
Thy calf, O S, hath cast thee off........ Hos 8:5
but the calf of S shall be broken........ Hos 8:6
The inhabitants of S shall fear.......... Hos 10:5
As for S, her king is cut off as......... Hos 10:7
upon the mountains of S, and............. Amos 3:9
that are in the mountain of S............ Amos 4:1
and trust in the mountain of S........... Amos 6:1
They that swear by the sin of S.......... Amos 8:14
of Ephraim, and the fields of S.......... Obad 19
3. District north of Judah.
he passed through the midst of S......... Lk 17:11
And he must needs go through S........... Jn 4:4
Then cometh he to a city of S............ Jn 4:5
cometh a woman of S to draw water........ Jn 4:7
saith the woman of S unto him............ Jn 4:9
of me, which am a woman of S............. Jn 4:9
and in all Judaea, and in................ Acts 1:8
the regions of Judaea and S.............. Acts 8:1
all Judaea and Galilee and S............. Acts 9:31
they passed through Phenice and S........ Acts 15:3

SAMARITAN (sa-mar'i-tun) See SAMARITANS.
An inhabitant of Samaria.
But a certain S, as he journeyed,........ Lk 10:33
and he was a S............................ Lk 17:16
Say we not well that thou art a S........ Jn 8:48

SAMARITANS (sa-mar'i-tuns)
high places which the S had made......... 2Kin 17:29
any city of the S enter ye not........... Mt 10:5
entered into a village of the S.......... Lk 9:52
Jews have no dealings with the S......... Jn 4:9
many of the S of that city............... Jn 4:39
So when the S were come unto him,........ Jn 4:40
gospel in many villages of the S......... Acts 8:25

SAME See PREFACE.

SAMGAR-NEBO (sam''-gar-ne'-bo) A prince
of Babylon.
gate, even Nergal-sharezer, S............ Jer 39:3

SAMLAH (sam'-lah) A king of Edom.
S of Masrekah reigned in.................. Gen 36:36
S died, and Saul of Rehoboth by.......... Gen 36:37
S of Masrekah reigned in.................. 1Chr 1:47
when S was dead, Shaul of................. 1Chr 1:48

SAMOS (sa'-mos) An island in the Aegean Sea.
and the next day we arrived at S......... Acts 20:15

SAMOTHRACE See SAMOTHRACIA.

SAMOTHRACIA (sam-o-thra'-she-ah) An
island in the Aegean Sea.
came with a straight course to S......... Acts 16:11

SAMSON (sam'-sun) See SAMSON'S. A judge of
Israel.
bare a son, and called his name S........ Judg 13:24
S went down to Timnath, and saw a........ Judg 14:1
S said unto his father, Get her.......... Judg 14:3
Then went S down, and his father......... Judg 14:5
and she pleased S well................... Judg 14:7
and S made them a feast.................. Judg 14:10
S said unto them, I will now put......... Judg 14:12
that S visited his wife with a........... Judg 15:1
S said concerning them, Now shall........ Judg 15:3
S went and caught three hundred.......... Judg 15:4
And they answered, S, the son of......... Judg 15:6
S said unto them, Though ye have......... Judg 15:7
To bind S are we come up, to do.......... Judg 15:10
of the rock Etam, and said to S.......... Judg 15:11
S said unto them, Swear unto me,......... Judg 15:12
S said, With the jawbone of an........... Judg 15:16
Then went S to Gaza, and saw there....... Judg 16:1
Gazites, saying, S is come hither........ Judg 16:2
S lay till midnight, and arose at........ Judg 16:3
And Delilah said to S, Tell me, I........ Judg 16:6
S said unto her, If they bind me,........ Judg 16:7
The Philistines be upon thee, S.......... Judg 16:9
And Delilah said unto S, Behold,......... Judg 16:10
The Philistines be upon thee, S.......... Judg 16:12
And Delilah said unto S, Hitherto........ Judg 16:13
The Philistines be upon thee, S.......... Judg 16:14
The Philistines be upon thee, S.......... Judg 16:20
Our god hath delivered S our............. Judg 16:23
merry, that they said, Call for.......... Judg 16:25
they called for S out of the............. Judg 16:25
S said unto the liar that held him....... Judg 16:26
that beheld while S made sport........... Judg 16:27
S called unto the LORD, and said,........ Judg 16:28
S took hold of the two middle........... Judg 16:29
S said, Let me die with the.............. Judg 16:30
of Gedeon, and of Barak, and of S........ Heb 11:32

SAMSON'S (sam'-suns)
day, that they said unto S wife......... Judg 14:15
S wife wept before him, and said,........ Judg 14:17
But S wife was given to his.............. Judg 14:20

SAMUEL (sam'-u-el) See SHEMUEL. A priest
and judge of Israel.
bare a son, and called his name S........ 1Sa 1:20
But S ministered before the LORD,....... 1Sa 1:24
the child S grew before the LORD........ 1Sa 2:21
And the child S grew on, and was in...... 1Sa 2:26
the child S ministered unto the......... 1Sa 3:1
was, and S was laid down to sleep........ 1Sa 3:3
That the LORD called S................... 1Sa 3:4
And the LORD called yet again, S......... 1Sa 3:6
S arose and went to Eli, and said........ 1Sa 3:6
Now S did not yet know the LORD,......... 1Sa 3:7
the LORD called S again the third........ 1Sa 3:8
Therefore Eli said unto S................ 1Sa 3:9
So S went and lay down in his............ 1Sa 3:9
as at other times, S..................... 1Sa 3:10
Then S answered, Speak................... 1Sa 3:10
And the LORD said to S, Behold, I........ 1Sa 3:11
S lay until the morning, and............. 1Sa 3:15
S feared to shew Eli the vision.......... 1Sa 3:15
Eli called S, and said, S................ 1Sa 3:16
S told him every whit, and hid........... 1Sa 3:18
S grew, and the LORD was with him,....... 1Sa 3:19
even to Beer-sheba knew that S........... 1Sa 3:20
to S in Shiloh by the word of the....... 1Sa 3:21
the word of S came to all Israel......... 1Sa 4:1
S spake unto all the house of............ 1Sa 7:3
S said, Gather all Israel to............. 1Sa 7:5
S judged the children of Israel.......... 1Sa 7:6
the children of Israel said to S......... 1Sa 7:8
S took a sucking lamb, and offered....... 1Sa 7:9
S cried unto the LORD for Israel......... 1Sa 7:9
as S was offering up the burnt.......... 1Sa 7:10
Then S took a stone, and set it.......... 1Sa 7:12
S judged Israel all the days of......... 1Sa 7:15
when S was old, that he made his........ 1Sa 8:1
and came to S unto Ramah,................ 1Sa 8:4
But the thing displeased S............... 1Sa 8:6
And S prayed unto the LORD............... 1Sa 8:6
And the LORD said unto S, Hearken........ 1Sa 8:7
S told all the words of the LORD........ 1Sa 8:10
refused to obey the voice of S........... 1Sa 8:19
S heard all the words of the............. 1Sa 8:21
And the LORD said to S, Hearken.......... 1Sa 8:22
S said unto the men of Israel, Go........ 1Sa 8:22
S came out against them, for to.......... 1Sa 9:14
Now the LORD had told S in his........... 1Sa 9:15
when S saw Saul, the LORD said........... 1Sa 9:17
Saul drew near to S in the gate.......... 1Sa 9:18
S answered Saul, and said, I am.......... 1Sa 9:19
S took Saul and his servant, and......... 1Sa 9:22
S said unto the cook, Bring the.......... 1Sa 9:23
S said, Behold that which is left........ 1Sa 9:24
S commanded with Saul upon the top....... 1Sa 9:25
that S called Saul to the top of........ 1Sa 9:26
went out both of them, he and S......... 1Sa 9:26
S said to Saul, Bid the servant.......... 1Sa 9:27
Then S took a vial of oil, and.......... 1Sa 10:1

had turned his back to go from S 1Sa 10:9
they were no where, we came to S 1Sa 10:14
I pray thee, what S said unto you 1Sa 10:15
of the kingdom, whence S spake 1Sa 10:16
S called the people together unto 1Sa 10:17
when S had caused all the tribes 1Sa 10:20
S said to all the people, See ye 1Sa 10:24
Then S told the people the manner 1Sa 10:25
S sent all the people away, every 1Sa 10:25
not forth after Saul and after S 1Sa 11:7
And the people said unto S 1Sa 11:12
Then said S to the people, Come, ... 1Sa 11:14
S said unto all Israel, Behold, I 1Sa 12:1
S said unto the people, It is the 1Sa 12:6
and Bedan, and Jephthah, and S 1Sa 12:11
So S called unto the LORD 1Sa 12:18
greatly feared the LORD and S 1Sa 12:18
And all the people said unto S 1Sa 12:19
S said unto the people, Fear not 1Sa 12:20
the set time that S had appointed 1Sa 13:8
but S came not to Gilgal 1Sa 13:8
burnt offering, behold, S came 1Sa 13:10
S said, What hast thou done 1Sa 13:11
S said to Saul, Thou hast done 1Sa 13:13
S arose, and gat him up from 1Sa 13:15
S also said unto Saul, The LORD 1Sa 15:1
came the word of the LORD unto S 1Sa 15:10
And it grieved S 1Sa 15:11
when S rose early to meet Saul in 1Sa 15:12
in the morning, it was told S 1Sa 15:12
And S came to Saul 1Sa 15:13
S said, What meaneth then this 1Sa 15:14
Then S said unto Saul, Stay, and I 1Sa 15:16
S said, When thou wast little in 1Sa 15:17
And Saul said unto S, Yea, I have 1Sa 15:20
S said, Hath the LORD as great 1Sa 15:22
And Saul said unto S, I have 1Sa 15:24
S said unto Saul, I will not 1Sa 15:26
as S turned about to go away, he 1Sa 15:27
S said unto him, The LORD hath 1Sa 15:28
So S turned again after Saul 1Sa 15:31
Then said S, Bring ye hither to 1Sa 15:32
S said, As thy sword hath made 1Sa 15:33
S hewed Agag in pieces before the 1Sa 15:33
Then S went to Ramah 1Sa 15:34
S came no more to see Saul until 1Sa 15:35
nevertheless S mourned for Saul 1Sa 15:35
And the LORD said unto S, How long .. 1Sa 16:1
S said, How can I go 1Sa 16:2
S did that which the LORD spake, ... 1Sa 16:4
But the LORD said unto S, Look 1Sa 16:7
and made him pass before S 1Sa 16:8
of his sons to pass before S 1Sa 16:10
S said unto Jesse, The LORD hath 1Sa 16:10
S said unto Jesse, Are here all 1Sa 16:11
S said unto Jesse, Send and fetch 1Sa 16:11
Then S took the horn of oil, and 1Sa 16:13
So S rose up, and went to Ramah. 1Sa 16:13
came to S to Ramah, and told him 1Sa 19:18
S went and dwelt in Naioth 1Sa 19:18
S standing as appointed over them .. 1Sa 19:20
and he asked and said, Where are S. .. 1Sa 19:22
before S in like manner, and lay 1Sa 19:24
And S died. 1Sa 25:1
Now S was dead, and all Israel had 1Sa 28:3
And he said, Bring me up S 1Sa 28:11
And when the woman saw S, she 1Sa 28:12
And Saul perceived that it was S 1Sa 28:14
S said to Saul, Why hast thou 1Sa 28:15
Then said S, Wherefore then dost 1Sa 28:16
afraid, because of the words of S 1Sa 28:20
And the sons of S 1Chr 6:28
S the seer did ordain in their 1Chr 9:22
to the word of the LORD by S 1Chr 11:3
And all that S the seer, and Saul 1Chr 26:28
written in the book of S the seer 1Chr 29:29
from the days of S the prophet 2Chr 35:18
S among them that call upon his. .... Ps 99:6
S stood before me, yet my mind .... Jer 15:1
Yea, and all the prophets from S ...... Acts 3:24
fifty years, until S the prophet .... Acts 13:20
of David also, and S, and of the. .... Heb 11:32

SANBALLAT (san-bal´-lat) An opponent of Nehemiah.
When S the Horonite, and Tobiah .... Neh 2:10
But when S the Horonite, and .... Neh 2:19
that when S heard that we builded.... Neh 4:1
But it came to pass, that when S ...... Neh 4:7
Now it came to pass, when S ...... Neh 6:1
That S and Geshem sent unto me,. .... Neh 6:2
Then sent S his servant unto me,. .... Neh 6:5
for Tobiah and S had hired him. .... Neh 6:12
S according to these their works,. .... Neh 6:14
was son in law to S the Horonite. .... Neh 13:28

SANCTIFICATION
us wisdom, and righteousness, and s.. 1Cor 1:30
is the will of God, even your s 1Th 4:3
how to possess his vessel in s 1Th 4:4
salvation through s of the Spirit 2Th 2:13
through s of the Spirit, unto 1Pet 1:2

SANCTIFIED
blessed the seventh day, and s it .... Gen 2:3
unto the people, and s the people .... Ex 19:14
tabernacle shall be s by my glory .... Ex 29:43
all that was therein, and s them .... Lev 8:10
s it, to make reconciliation upon. .... Lev 8:15
s Aaron, and his garments, and his .... Lev 8:30
I will be s in them that come .... Lev 10:3

if he that s it will redeem his .... Lev 27:15
if he that s the field will in .... Lev 27:19
s it, and all the instruments. .... Num 7:1
And had anointed them, and s them. .... Num 7:1
land of Egypt I s them for myself .... Num 8:17
the LORD, and he was s in them. .... Num 20:13
because ye s me not in the midst. .... Deut 32:51
s Eleazar his son to keep the ark 1Sa 7:1
he s Jesse and his sons, and called. 1Sa 16:5
though it were s this day in the. 1Sa 21:5
the Levites s themselves to bring. 1Chr 15:14
priests that were present were s 2Chr 5:11
s this house, that my name may be. 2Chr 7:16
house, which I have s for my name 2Chr 7:20
s themselves, and came, according 2Chr 29:15
so they s the house of the LORD. 2Chr 29:17
have we prepared and s, and,. 2Chr 29:19
other priests had s themselves. 2Chr 29:34
had not s themselves sufficiently 2Chr 30:3
which he hath s for ever 2Chr 30:8
s themselves, and brought in the 2Chr 30:15
the congregation that were not s 2Chr 30:17
number of priests s themselves. 2Chr 30:24
they s themselves to bring. 2Chr 31:18
they s it, and set up the doors of. .... Neh 3:1
unto the tower of Meah they s it .... Neh 3:1
they s holy things unto the. .... Neh 12:47
the Levites s them unto the. .... Neh 12:47
s them, and rose up early in the .... Job 1:5
holy shall be s in righteousness .... Is 5:16
I have commanded my s ones .... Is 13:3
forth out of the womb I s thee .... Jer 1:5
I will be s in you before the. .... Eze 20:41
in her, and shall be s in her .... Eze 28:22
shall be s in them in the sight. .... Eze 28:25
when I shall be s in you before. .... Eze 36:23
me, when I shall be s in thee. .... Eze 38:16
am s in them in the sight of many. .... Eze 39:27
that are s of the sons of Zadok. .... Eze 48:11
ye of him, whom the Father hath s .. Jn 10:36
also might be s through the truth .... Jn 17:19
among all them which are s. .... Acts 20:32
among them which are s by faith. .... Acts 26:18
being s by the Holy Ghost. .... Rom 15:16
them that are s in Christ Jesus. 1Cor 1:2
but ye are washed, but ye are s. 1Cor 6:11
husband is s by the wife, and the. 1Cor 7:14
wife is s by the husband 1Cor 7:14
For it is s by the word of God and. 1Ti 4:5
shall be a vessel unto honour, s. 2Ti 2:21
they who are s are all of one. .... Heb 2:11
By the which will we are s .... Heb 10:10
for ever them that are s .... Heb 10:14
the covenant, wherewith he was s. .... Heb 10:29
to them that are s by God the. .... Jude 1

SANCTIFIETH
or the temple that s the gold .... Mt 23:17
or the altar that s the gift. .... Mt 23:19
For both he that s and they who. .... Heb 2:11
s to the purifying of the flesh .... Heb 9:13

SANCTIFY
S unto me all the firstborn, ... Ex 13:2
s them to day and to morrow, and .... Ex 19:10
s themselves, lest the LORD break .... Ex 19:22
bounds about the mount, and s it .... Ex 19:23
s them, that they may minister .... Ex 28:41
thou shalt s the breast of the. .... Ex 29:27
made, to consecrate and to s them. .. Ex 29:33
and thou shalt anoint it, to s it. .... Ex 29:36
atonement for the altar, and s it. .... Ex 29:37
I will s the tabernacle of the. .... Ex 29:44
I will s also both Aaron and his .... Ex 29:44
And thou shalt s them, that they. .... Ex 29:37
I am the LORD that doth s you. .... Ex 31:13
all his vessels, and s the altar. .... Ex 40:10
the laver and his foot, and s it. .... Ex 40:11
garments, and anoint him, and s him... Ex 40:13
the laver and his foot, to s them. .... Lev 8:11
head, and anointed him, to s him. .... Lev 8:12
ye shall therefore s yourselves. .... Lev 11:44
S yourselves therefore, and be ye .... Lev 20:7
I am the LORD which s you. .... Lev 20:8
Thou shalt s him therefore .... Lev 21:8
for I the LORD, which s you. .... Lev 21:8
for I the LORD do s them .... Lev 21:15
for I the LORD do s them. .... Lev 21:23
I the LORD do s them. .... Lev 22:9
for I the LORD do s them. .... Lev 22:16
when a man shall s his house to .... Lev 27:14
if a man shall s unto the LORD .... Lev 27:16
If he s his field from the year. .... Lev 27:17
But if he s his field after the. .... Lev 27:18
if a man s unto the LORD a field. .... Lev 27:22
firstling, no man shall s it .... Lev 27:26
S yourselves against to morrow, ... Num 11:18
to s me in the eyes of the. .... Num 20:12
to s me at the water before their. .... Num 27:14
Keep the sabbath day to s it. .... Deut 5:12
shalt s unto the LORD thy God .... Deut 15:19
unto the people. S yourselves. .... Josh 3:5
s the people, and say, S. .... Josh 7:13
s yourselves, and come with me to. .. 1Sa 16:5
s yourselves, both ye and your 1Chr 15:12
that he should s the most holy. 1Chr 23:13
s now yourselves. 2Chr 29:5
s the house of the LORD God of. 2Chr 29:5
first day of the first month to s 2Chr 29:17
to s themselves than the priests 2Chr 29:34

clean, to s them unto the LORD 2Chr 30:17
s yourselves, and prepare your 2Chr 35:6
the gates, to s the sabbath day .... Neh 13:22
S the LORD of hosts himself. .... Is 8:13
of him, they shall s my name. .... Is 29:23
s the Holy One of Jacob, and shall. .. Is 29:23
They that s themselves, and purify. .... Is 66:17
that I am the LORD that s them. .... Eze 20:12
I will s my great name, which was. .. Eze 36:23
know that I the LORD do s Israel. .... Eze 37:28
I magnify myself, and s myself .... Eze 38:23
they shall not s the people with .... Eze 44:19
the utter court, to s the people. .... Eze 46:20
S ye a fast, call a solemn .... Joel 1:14
s a fast, call a solemn assembly. .... Joel 2:15
the congregation, assemble the .... Joel 2:16
S them through thy truth. .... Jn 17:17
And for their sakes I s myself .... Jn 17:19
That he might s and cleanse it .... Eph 5:26
very God of peace s you wholly. 1Th 5:23
that he might s the people with. .... Heb 13:12
But s the Lord God in your hearts 1Pet 3:15

SANCTUARIES
that he profane not my s .... Lev 21:23
bring your s unto desolation, and. .... Lev 26:31
into the s of the LORD's house. .... Jer 51:51
Thou hast defiled thy s by the .... Eze 28:18
the s of Israel shall be laid .... Amos 7:9

SANCTUARY
for thee to dwell in, in the S .... Ex 15:17
And let them make me a s. .... Ex 25:8
shekel after the shekel of the s. .... Ex 30:13
after the shekel of the s. .... Ex 30:24
of work for the service of the s. .... Ex 36:1
the work of the service of the s. .... Ex 36:3
wrought all the work of the s. .... Ex 36:4
work for the offering of the s. .... Ex 36:6
after the shekel of the s. .... Ex 38:24
after the shekel of the s. .... Ex 38:25
shekel, after the shekel of the s. .... Ex 38:26
were cast the sockets of the s. .... Ex 38:27
LORD, before the vail of the s .... Lev 4:6
silver, after the shekel of the s. .... Lev 5:15
from before the s out of the camp. .... Lev 10:4
thing, nor come into the s. .... Lev 12:4
make an atonement for the holy s,. .. Lev 16:33
my sabbaths, and reverence my s .... Lev 19:30
seed unto Molech, to defile my s .... Lev 20:3
Neither shall he go out of the s. .... Lev 21:12
nor profane the s of his God .... Lev 21:12
my sabbaths, and reverence my s .... Lev 26:2
silver, after the shekel of the s. .... Lev 27:3
according to the shekel of the s .... Lev 27:25
keeping the charge of the s .... Num 3:28
the vessels of the s wherewith. .... Num 3:31
that keep the charge of the s. .... Num 3:32
keeping the charge of the s for .... Num 3:38
of the s shall thou take them. .... Num 3:47
after the shekel of the s .... Num 3:50
wherewith they minister in the s .... Num 4:12
made an end of covering the s .... Num 4:15
and all the vessels of the s .... Num 4:15
of all that therein is, in the s .... Num 4:16
because the service of the s. .... Num 7:9
after the shekel of the s .... Num 7:13
after the shekel of the s .... Num 7:19
after the shekel of the s .... Num 7:25
after the shekel of the s .... Num 7:31
after the shekel of the s .... Num 7:37
after the shekel of the s .... Num 7:43
after the shekel of the s .... Num 7:49
after the shekel of the s .... Num 7:55
after the shekel of the s .... Num 7:61
after the shekel of the s .... Num 7:67
after the shekel of the s .... Num 7:73
after the shekel of the s .... Num 7:79
after the shekel of the s .... Num 7:85
apiece, after the shekel of the s. .... Num 7:86
of Israel come nigh unto the s. .... Num 8:19
set forward, bearing the s. .... Num 10:21
shall bear the iniquity of the s .... Num 18:1
come nigh the vessels of the s .... Num 18:3
ye shall keep the charge of the s .... Num 18:5
after the shekel of the s .... Num 18:16
he hath defiled the s of the LORD. .... Num 19:20
that was by the s of the LORD .... Josh 24:26
and all the instruments of the s 1Chr 9:29
build ye the s of the LORD God, ... 1Chr 22:19
for the governors of the s 1Chr 24:5
thee to build an house for the s a 1Chr 28:10
have built thee a s therein for 2Chr 20:8
go out of the s 2Chr 26:18
for the kingdom, and for the s. 2Chr 29:21
the LORD, and enter into his s. 2Chr 30:8
to the purification of the s. 2Chr 30:19
the sword in the house of their s 2Chr 36:17
where are the vessels of the s .... Neh 10:39
Send thee help from the s. .... Ps 20:2
so as I have seen thee in the s .... Ps 63:2
of my God, my King, in the s .... Ps 68:24
Until I went into the s of God. .... Ps 73:17
enemy hath done wickedly in the s .... Ps 74:3
They have cast fire into thy s. .... Ps 74:7
Thy way, O God, is in the s .... Ps 77:13
them to the border of his s. .... Ps 78:54
he built his s like high palaces, ... Ps 78:69
strength and beauty are in his s .... Ps 96:6
down from the height of his s .... Ps 102:19

Judah was his *s*, and Israel his .... Ps 114:2
Lift up your hands in the *s*............................... Ps 134:2
Praise God in his *s*....................................... Ps 150:1
And be built for as *s*...................................... Is 8:14
he shall come to his *s* to pray .... Is 16:12
profaned the princes of the *s*....................... Is 43:28
to beautify the place of my *s*....................... Is 60:13
have trodden down thy *s*............................... Is 63:18
beginning is the place of our *s*.................... Jer 17:12
the heathen entered into her *s*.................... Lam 1:10
his altar, he hath abhorred his *s*................. Lam 2:7
be slain in the *s* of the Lord .... Lam 2:20
the stones of the *s* are poured .... Lam 4:1
because thou hast defiled my *s*.................... Eze 5:11
I should go far off from my *s*........................ Eze 8:6
and begin at my *s*... Eze 9:6
s in the countries where they....................... Eze 11:16
have defiled my *s* in the same day .... Eze 23:38
same day into my *s* to profane it............... Eze 23:39
Behold, I will profane my *s*.......................... Eze 24:21
thou saidst, Aha, against my *s*.................... Eze 25:3
will set my *s* in the midst of....................... Eze 37:26
when my *s* shall be in the midst .... Eze 37:28
squared, and the face of the *s*.................... Eze 41:21
the temple and the *s* had two doors .... Eze 41:23
make a separation between the *s*............... Eze 42:20
place of the house, without the *s*............... Eze 43:21
s which looketh toward the east................. Eze 44:1
with every going forth of the *s*.................. Eze 44:5
have brought into my *s* strangers............. Eze 44:7
in flesh, to be in my *s*, to.......................... Eze 44:7
my charge in my *s* for yourselves.............. Eze 44:8
in flesh, shall enter into my *s*................... Eze 44:9
they shall be ministers in my *s*................ Eze 44:11
that kept the charge of my *s* when .... Eze 44:15
They shall enter into my *s*........................ Eze 44:16
the day that he goeth into the *s*.............. Eze 44:27
inner court, to minister in the *s*.............. Eze 44:27
for the *s* five hundred in length .... Eze 45:2
and in it shall be the *s* and the .... Eze 45:3
priests the ministers of the *s*.................. Eze 45:4
and an holy place for the *s*....................... Eze 45:4
without blemish, and cleanse the *s* .... Eze 45:18
they they issued out of the *s* .... Eze 47:12
the *s* shall be in the midst of it .... Eze 48:8
the *s* of the Lord shall be in the .... Eze 48:10
the *s* of the house shall be in .... Eze 48:21
the place of his *s* was cast down .... Dan 8:11
of desolation, to give both the *s*............. Dan 8:13
then shall the *s* be cleansed.................... Dan 8:14
shine upon thy *s* that is desolate........... Dan 9:17
shall destroy the city and the *s*............. Dan 9:26
shall pollute the *s* of strength .... Dan 11:31
her priests have polluted the *s*............... Zeph 3:4
A minister of the *s*, and of the............... Heb 8:2
of divine service, and a worldly *s*.......... Heb 9:1
which is called the *s*................................. Heb 9:3
the *s* by the high priest for sin .... Heb 13:11

SAND

as the *s* which is upon the sea .... Gen 22:17
make thy seed as the *s* of the sea .... Gen 32:12
gathered corn as the *s* of the sea .... Gen 41:49
the Egyptian, and hid him in the *s* .... Ex 2:12
and of treasures hid in the *s* .... Deut 33:19
even as the *s* that is upon the .... Josh 11:4
as the *s* by the sea side for .... Judg 7:12
people as the *s* which is on the 1Sa 13:5
as the *s* that is by the sea for 2Sa 17:11
as the *s* which is by the sea in 1Kin 4:20
even as the *s* that is on the sea 1Kin 4:29
be heavier than the *s* of the sea .... Job 6:3
I shall multiply my days as the *s* .... Job 29:18
fowls like as the *s* of the sea................... Ps 78:27
are more in number than the *s* .... Ps 139:18
stone is heavy, and the *s* weighty .... Prov 27:3
Israel be as the *s* of the sea .... Is 10:22
Thy seed also had been as the *s* .... Is 48:19
which have placed the *s* for the .... Jer 5:22
to me above the *s* of the seas .... Jer 15:8
neither the *s* of the sea measured .... Jer 33:22
shall be as the *s* of the sea .... Hos 1:10
gather the captivity as the *s* .... Hab 1:9
which built his house upon the *s* .... Mt 7:26
of Israel be as the *s* of the sea .... Rom 9:27
as the *s* which is by the sea .... Rev 20:8
And I stood upon the *s* of the sea .... Rev 13:1
of whom is as the *s* of the sea................. Rev 20:8

SANDALS

But be shod with *s*....................................... Mk 6:9
Gird thyself, and bind on thy *s* .... Acts 12:8

SANG

Then *s* Moses and the children of .... Ex 15:1
Then Israel *s* this song, Spring .... Num 21:17
Then *s* Deborah and Barak the son .... Judg 5:1
of whom they *s* one to another in........... 1Sa 29:5
worshipped, and the singers *s*................. 2Chr 29:28
they *s* praises with gladness, and........... 2Chr 29:30
they *s* together by course in .... Ezr 3:11
And the singers *s* loud, with..................... Neh 12:42
When the morning stars *s* together......... Job 38:7
which he *s* unto the Lord,.......................... Ps 7:t
they *s* his praise... Ps 106:12
prayed, and *s* praises unto God............... Acts 16:25

SANK

they *s* into the bottom as a stone .... Ex 15:5
they *s* as lead in the mighty .... Ex 15:10

SANSANNAH (san-san'-nah) *A city in Judah.*
And Ziklag, and Madmannah, and *S*..... Josh 15:31

SAP

trees of the Lord are full of *s*.................... Ps 104:16

SAPH (saf) See SIPHAI. *A descendant of Rapha.*
Sibbechai the Hushathite slew *s*.............. 2Sa 21:18

SAPHIR (sa'-fur) *A city in Ephraim.*
ye away, thou inhabitant of *S*.................. Mic 1:11

SAPPHIRA (saf-fi'-rah) *Wife of Ananias.*
Ananias, with *S* his wife, sold a............... Acts 5:1

SAPPHIRE

it were a paved work of a *s* stone............ Ex 24:10
row shall be an emerald, a *s*..................... Ex 28:18
the second row, an emerald, a *s* .... Ex 39:11
with the precious onyx, or the *s* .... Job 28:16
rubies, their polishing was of *s* .... Lam 4:7
as the appearance of a *s* stone .... Eze 1:26
over them as it were a *s* stone .... Eze 10:1
the onyx, and the jasper, the *s* .... Eze 28:13
the second, *s*.. Rev 21:19

SAPPHIRES

stones of it are the place of *s* .... Job 28:6
as bright ivory overlaid with *s*............... Song 5:14
and lay thy foundations with *s*.............. Is 54:11

SARA (sa'-rah) See SARAH. *Greek form of
Sarah I.*
Through faith also *S* herself .... Heb 11:11

SARAH (sa'-rah) See SARA, SARAH'S, SARAI,
SERAH.
1. *Wife of Abraham.*
Sarai, but *S* shall her name be .... Gen 17:15
and shall *S*, that is ninety years............. Gen 17:17
S thy wife shall bear thee a son .... Gen 17:19
which *S* shall bear unto thee at............. Gen 17:21
hastened into the tent unto *S*................. Gen 18:6
unto him, Where is *S* thy wife .... Gen 18:9
S thy wife shall have a son .... Gen 18:10
S heard it in the tent door,..................... Gen 18:10
S were old and well stricken in............. Gen 18:11
it ceased to be with *S* after the............. Gen 18:11
Therefore *S* laughed within .... Gen 18:12
Abraham, Wherefore did *S* laugh........... Gen 18:13
of life, and *S* shall have a son .... Gen 18:14
Then *S* denied, saying, I laughed .... Gen 18:15
And Abraham said of *S* his wife............. Gen 20:2
king of Gerar sent, and took *S*.............. Gen 20:2
and restored him *S* his wife .... Gen 20:14
unto *S* he said, Behold, I have .... Gen 20:16
because of *S* Abraham's wife................. Gen 20:18
the Lord visited *S* as he had said .... Gen 21:1
Lord did unto *S* as he had spoken....... Gen 21:1
For *S* conceived, and bare Abraham..... Gen 21:2
whom *S* bare to him, Isaac .... Gen 21:3
S said, God hath made me to laugh..... Gen 21:6
that *S* should have given children .... Gen 21:7
S saw the son of Hagar the .... Gen 21:9
in all that *S* hath said unto thee......... Gen 21:12
S was an hundred and seven and....... Gen 23:1
were the years of the life of *S* .... Gen 23:1
And *S* died in Kirjath-arba .... Gen 23:2
and Abraham came to mourn for *S* ..... Gen 23:2
Abraham buried *S* his wife in the .... Gen 23:19
S my master's wife bare a son to .... Gen 24:36
was Abraham buried, and *S* his wife .. Gen 25:10
they buried Abraham and *S* his wife... Gen 49:31
father, and unto *S* that bare you........ Is 51:2
I come, and *S* shall have a son .... Rom 9:9
Even as *S* obeyed Abraham, calling ... 1Pet 3:6
2. *A daughter of Asher.*
of the daughter of Asher was *S*.......... Num 26:46

SARAH'S (sa'-rahs)
her into his mother *S* tent .... Gen 24:67
S handmaid, bare unto Abraham......... Gen 25:12
yet the deadness of *S* womb................. Rom 4:19

SARAI (sa'-rahee) See SARAH, SARAI'S. *The
original name of Sarah.*
the name of Abram's wife was *S*.......... Gen 11:29
But *S* was barren.. Gen 11:30
S his daughter in law, his son............... Gen 11:31
And Abram took *S* his wife, and Lot..... Gen 12:5
that he said unto *S* his wife .... Gen 12:11
plagues because of *S* Abram's wife ..... Gen 12:17
Now *S* Abram's wife bare him no .... Gen 16:1
S said unto Abram, Behold now,.......... Gen 16:2
Abram hearkened to the voice of *S* .... Gen 16:2
S Abram's wife took Hagar her .... Gen 16:3
S said unto Abram, My wrong be .... Gen 16:5
But Abram said unto *S*, Behold,.......... Gen 16:6
when *S* dealt hardly with her, she ..... Gen 16:6
from the face of my mistress *S*............. Gen 16:8
As for *S* thy wife, thou shalt not,........ Gen 17:15
thou shalt not call her name *S*............. Gen 17:15

SARAI'S (sa'-rahees)
S maid, whence camest thou................ Gen 16:8

SARAPH (sa'-raf) *A descendant of Shelah.*
men of Chozeba, and Joash, and *S* 1Chr 4:22

SARDINE
upon like a jasper and a *s* stone .... Rev 4:3

SARDIS (sar'-dis) *A city in Lydia in Asia
Minor.*
and unto Thyatira, and unto *S*............ Rev 1:11
angel of the church in *S* write.............. Rev 3:1
in *S* which have not defiled their........ Rev 3:4

SARDITES (sar'-dites) *Descendants of Sered.*
of Sered, the family of the *S* .... Num 26:26

SARDIUS
the first row shall be a *s*........................ Ex 28:17
the first row was a *s*, a topaz,.............. Ex 39:10
stone was thy covering, the *s* .... Eze 28:13
the sixth, *s*... Rev 21:20

SARDONYX
The fifth, *s* .... Rev 21:20

SAREPTA (sa-rep'-tah) See ZAREPHATH. *A city
near Sidon.*
them was Elias sent, save unto *S*........ Lk 4:26

SARGON (sar'-gon) *An Assyrian king.*
(when *S* the king of Assyria sent .... Is 20:1

SARID (sa'-rid) *A city in Zebulun.*
of their inheritance was unto *S*........... Josh 19:10
turned from *S* eastward toward the ... Josh 19:12

SARON (sa'-ron) See SHARON. *The area
between Joppa and Caesarea.*
S saw him, and turned to the Lord ..... Acts 9:35

SARSECHIM (sar'-se-kim) *A prince of
Babylon.*
Nergal-sharezer, Samgar-nebo, *S*......... Jer 39:3

SAR-SEKIM See SARSECHIM.

SARUCH (sa'-ruk) See SERUG. *Father of
Nahor; an ancestor of Jesus.*
Which was the son of *S*, which was...... Lk 3:35

SAT

he is in the tent door in the heat............. Gen 18:1
Lot *s* in the gate of Sodom .... Gen 19:1
s her down over against him a .... Gen 21:16
she *s* over against him, and lift............ Gen 21:16
camel's furniture, and *s* upon .... Gen 31:34
And they *s* down to eat bread .... Gen 37:25
s in an open place, which is by .... Gen 38:14
they *s* before him, the firstborn .... Gen 43:33
himself, and *s* upon the bed .... Gen 48:2
and he *s* down by a well.......................... Ex 2:15
that *s* on his throne unto the .... Ex 12:29
when we *s* by the flesh pots, and......... Ex 16:3
put it under him, and he *s* thereon .... Ex 17:12
that Moses *s* to judge the people .... Ex 18:13
the people *s* down to eat and to.......... Ex 32:6
s that hath the issue shall wash .... Lev 15:6
she *s* upon shall wash his clothes ...... Lev 15:22
and they *s* down at thy feet .... Deut 33:3
s under an oak which was in .... Judg 6:11
the woman as she *s* in the field........... Judg 13:9
And they *s* down, and did eat and....... Judg 19:6
he *s* him down in a street of the .... Judg 19:15
s there before the Lord, and .... Judg 20:26
And she *s* beside the reapers .... Ruth 2:14
to the gate, and *s* him down there ...... Ruth 4:1
And he turned aside, and *s* down .... Ruth 4:1
And they *s* down. .... Ruth 4:2
Now Eli the priest *s* upon a seat.......... 1Sa 1:9
Eli *s* upon a seat by the wayside 1Sa 4:13
as he *s* in his house with his 1Sa 19:9
the king *s* him down to eat meat 1Sa 20:24
the king *s* upon his seat, as at 1Sa 20:25
Abner *s* by Saul's side, and................... 1Sa 20:25
from the earth, and *s* upon the bed ... 1Sa 28:23
and they *s* down, the one on the......... 1Sa 25:13
when the king *s* in his house 2Sa 7:1
s before the Lord, and he said, ... 2Sa 7:18
David *s* between the two gates 2Sa 18:24
the king arose, and *s* in the gate 2Sa 19:8
The Tachmonite that *s* in the seat...... 2Sa 23:8
Then *s* Solomon upon the throne of.... 1Kin 2:12
s down on his throne, and caused a .. 1Kin 2:19
and she *s* on his right hand 1Kin 2:19
as they *s* at the table, that the 1Kin 13:20
as soon as he *s* on his throne 1Kin 16:11
s down under a juniper tree 1Kin 19:4
of Belial, and *s* before him 1Kin 21:13
of Judah *s* each on his throne 1Kin 22:10
he *s* on the top of an hill 2Kin 1:9
he *s* on her knees till noon, and......... 2Kin 4:20
But Elisha *s* in his house, and the 2Kin 6:32
house, and the elders *s* with him 2Kin 6:32
he *s* on the throne of the kings 2Kin 11:19
Jeroboam *s* upon his throne 2Kin 13:13
as David *s* in his house, that 1Chr 17:1
s before the Lord, and said, Who 1Chr 17:16
Then Solomon *s* on the throne of 1Chr 29:23
Jehoshaphat king of Judah *s* 2Chr 18:9
they *s* in a void place at the 2Chr 18:9
of my beard, and *s* down astonied ..... Ezr 9:3
I *s* astonied until the evening .... Ezr 9:4
all the people *s* in the street of.......... Ezr 10:9
s down in the first day of the .... Ezr 10:16
heard these words, that I *s* down .... Neh 1:4
booths, and *s* under the booths.......... Neh 8:17
when the king Ahasuerus *s* on the .... Est 1:2
which *s* the first in the kingdom .... Est 1:14
then Mordecai *s* in the king's .... Est 2:19
while Mordecai *s* in the king's............ Est 2:21
the king and Haman *s* down to drink.. Est 3:15
the king *s* upon his royal throne .... Est 5:1
he *s* down among the ashes .... Job 2:8
So they *s* down with him upon the ..... Job 2:13
s chief, and dwelt as a king in .... Job 29:25
I have not *s* with vain persons, ... Ps 26:4
of Babylon, there we *s* down .... Ps 137:1
I *s* down in his shadow with .... Song 2:3

S

In the ways hast thou s for .... Jer 3:2
I s not in the assembly of the .... Jer 15:17
I s alone because of thy hand .... Jer 15:17
s down in the entry of the new .... Jer 26:10
before all the Jews that s in the .... Jer 32:12
and, lo, all the princes s there .... Jer 36:12
Now the king s in the winterhouse ... Jer 36:22
s in the middle gate, even .... Jer 39:3
I s where they s, and remained .... Eze 3:15
of Chebar, and I s where they s .... Eze 3:15
as I s in mine house, and the .... Eze 8:1
the elders of Judah s before me .... Eze 8:1
there s women weeping for Tammuz ... Eze 8:14
of Israel unto me, and s before me .... Eze 14:1
of the LORD, and s before me .... Eze 20:1
but Daniel s in the gate of the .... Dan 2:49
him with sackcloth, and s in ashes .... Jonah 3:6
s on the east side of the city, ... Jonah 4:5
s under it in the shadow, till he .... Jonah 4:5
The people with s in darkness .... Mt 4:16
and to them which s in the region ..... Mt 4:16
as Jesus s at meat in the house, ... Mt 9:10
s down with him and his disciples ..... Mt 9:10
the house, and s by the sea side ..... Mt 13:1
so that he went into a ship, and s .... Mt 13:2
s down, and gathered the good into .. Mt 13:48
them which s with him at meat, he ... Mt 14:9
into a mountain, and s down there .... Mt 15:29
as he s upon the mount of Olives, ... Mt 24:3
it on his head, as he s at meat .... Mt 26:7
he s down with the twelve .... Mt 26:20
I s daily with you teaching in .... Mt 26:55
s with the servants, to see the .... Mt 26:58
Now Peter s without in the palace ..... Mt 26:69
stone from the door, and s upon it .... Mt 28:2
as Jesus s at meat in his house, ... Mk 2:15
sinners s also together with .... Mk 2:15
And the multitude s about him .... Mk 3:32
about on them which s about him ...... Mk 3:34
into a ship, and s in the sea .... Mk 4:1
Herod and them that s with him .... Mk 6:22
for their sakes which s with him ...... Mk 6:26
they s down in ranks, by hundreds .... Mk 6:40
he s down, and called the twelve, ... Mk 9:35
s by the highway side begging .... Mk 10:46
a colt tied, whereon never man s ...... Mk 11:2
and he s upon him .... Mk 11:7
Jesus s over against the treasury ...... Mk 12:41
as he s upon the mount of Olives ...... Mk 13:3
as he s at meat, there came a .... Mk 14:3
And as they s and did eat, Jesus ...... Mk 14:18
he s with the servants, and warmed ... Mk 14:54
unto the eleven as they s at meat ..... Mk 16:14
s on the right hand of God .... Mk 16:19
again to the minister, and s down ..... Lk 4:20
he s down, and taught the people ...... Lk 5:3
of others that s down with them .... Lk 5:29
And he that was dead s up, and .... Lk 7:15
house, and s down to meat .... Lk 7:36
when she knew that Jesus s at .... Lk 7:37
they that s at meat with him .... Lk 7:49
which also s at Jesus' feet, and .... Lk 10:39
and he went in, and s down to meat .. Lk 14:15
when one of them that s at meat ...... Lk 14:15
a certain blind man s by the way ...... Lk 18:35
tied, whereon yet never man s .... Lk 19:30
he s down, and the twelve apostles ... Lk 22:14
together, Peter s down among them .... Lk 22:55
beheld him as he s by the fire .... Lk 22:56
as he s at meat with them, he .... Lk 24:30
his journey, s thus on the well .... Jn 4:6
there he s with his disciples .... Jn 6:3
So the men s down, in number .... Jn 6:10
he s down, and taught them .... Jn 8:2
said, Is not this he that s .... Jn 9:8
but Mary s still in the house .... Jn 11:20
them that s at the table with him .... Jn 12:2
had found a young ass, s thereon ..... Jn 12:14
s down in the judgment seat in a ..... Jn 19:13
fire, and it s upon each of them .... Acts 2:3
s for alms at the Beautiful gate .... Acts 3:10
all that s in the council, ... Acts 6:15
and when she saw Peter, she s up ..... Acts 9:40
s upon his throne, and made an .... Acts 12:21
on the sabbath day, and s down ...... Acts 13:14
there s a certain man at Lystra, ... Acts 14:8
we s down, and spake unto the .... Acts 16:13
there s in a window a certain .... Acts 20:9
morrow I s on the judgment seat ...... Acts 25:17
Bernice, and they that s with them ... Acts 26:30
The people s down to eat and drink ... 1Cor 10:7
s down on the right hand of the ...... Heb 1:3
s down on the right hand of God ...... Heb 10:12
in heaven, and one s on the throne .. Rev 4:2
he that s was to look upon like a ..... Rev 4:3
to him that s on the throne .... Rev 4:9
before him that s on the throne .... Rev 4:10
s on the throne a book written .... Rev 5:1
of him that s upon the throne .... Rev 5:7
he that s on him had a pair of .... Rev 6:5
power was given to him that s .... Rev 6:4
he that s on him had a pair of .... Rev 6:5
his name that s on him was Death .... Rev 6:8
vision, and them that s on them ...... Rev 9:17
which s before God on their seats ..... Rev 11:16
upon the cloud one s like unto. .... Rev 14:14
voice to him that s on the cloud ...... Rev 14:15
he that s on the cloud thrust in .... Rev 14:16
God that s on the throne, saying, ... Rev 19:4
he that s upon him was called .... Rev 19:11

against him that s on the horse .... Rev 19:19
of him that s upon the horse .... Rev 19:21
they s upon them, and judgment was . Rev 20:4
white throne, and him that s on it .... Rev 20:11
he that s upon the throne said, ... Rev 21:5

SATAN (sa´-tun) The adversary.
S stood up against Israel, and 1Chr 21:1
LORD, and S came also among them. ... Job 1:6
And the LORD said unto S, Whence ..... Job 1:7
Then S answered the LORD, and said, .. Job 1:7
And the LORD said unto S, Hast .... Job 1:8
Then S answered the LORD, and said, .. Job 1:9
And the LORD said unto S, Behold, ... Job 1:12
So S went forth from the presence ..... Job 1:12
S came also among them to present ... Job 2:1
And the LORD said unto S, From .... Job 2:2
S answered the LORD, and said .... Job 2:2
And the LORD said unto S, Hast .... Job 2:3
S answered the LORD, and said, ... Job 2:4
And the LORD said unto S, Behold, ... Job 2:6
So went S forth from the presence ..... Job 2:7
let S stand at his right hand .... Ps 109:6
S standing at his right hand to .... Zec 3:1
S, The LORD rebuke thee, O S .... Zec 3:2
Jesus unto him, Get thee hence, S .... Mt 4:10
And if S cast out S, he is .... Mt 12:26
unto Peter, Get thee behind me, S .... Mt 16:23
forty days, tempted of S .... Mk 1:13
How can S cast out S .... Mk 3:23
if S rise up against himself, and ...... Mk 3:26
S cometh immediately, and taketh .... Mk 4:15
saying, Get thee behind me, S .... Mk 8:33
unto him, Get thee behind me, S ...... Lk 4:8
I beheld S as lightning fall from .... Lk 10:18
If S also be divided against .... Lk 11:18
whom S hath bound, lo, these .... Lk 13:16
Then entered S into Judas .... Lk 22:3
S hath desired to have you, that ...... Lk 22:31
after the sop S entered into him ...... Jn 13:27
why hath S filled thine heart to .... Acts 5:3
and from the power of S unto God ..... Acts 26:18
bruise S under your feet shortly. .... Rom 16:20
that S tempt you not for your 1Cor 7:5
Lest S should get an advantage of 2Cor 2:11
for S himself is transformed into 2Cor 11:14
the messenger of S to buffet me. 2Cor 12:7
but S hindered us 1Th 2:18
the working of S with all power 2Th 2:9
whom I have delivered unto S 1Ti 1:20
are already turned aside after S 1Ti 5:15
not, but are the synagogue of S .... Rev 2:9
slain among you, where S dwelleth.. .. Rev 2:13
have not known the depths of S .... Rev 2:24
make them of the synagogue of S ..... Rev 3:9
serpent, called the Devil, and S .... Rev 12:9
serpent, which is the Devil, and S ..... Rev 20:2
S shall be loosed out of his. .... Rev 20:7

SATAN'S (sa´-tuns)
dwellest, even where S seat is .... Rev 2:13

SATEST
thou s in the throne judging .... Ps 9:4
s upon a stately bed, and a table ..... Eze 23:41

SATIATE
I will s the soul of the priests, ... Jer 31:14
shall devour, and it shall be s .... Jer 46:10

SATIATED
For I have s the weary soul, and I ..... Jer 31:25

SATISFACTION
Moreover ye shall take no s for .... Num 35:31
ye shall take no s for him that .... Num 35:32

SATISFIED
my lust shall be s upon them. .... Ex 15:9
and ye shall eat, and not be s .... Lev 26:26
shall come, and shall eat and be s .... Deut 14:29
s with favour, and full with the. .... Deut 33:23
God, and are not s with my flesh ...... Job 19:22
shall not be s with bread .... Job 27:14
we cannot be s .... Job 31:31
I shall be s, when I awake, with. ...... Ps 17:15
The meek shall eat and be s .... Ps 22:26
They shall be abundantly s with. ...... Ps 36:8
days of famine they shall be s .... Ps 37:19
meat, and grudge if they be not s ..... Ps 59:15
My soul shall be s as with marrow .... Ps 63:5
we shall be s with the goodness. ...... Ps 65:4
of the rock should I have s thee. .... Ps 81:16
the earth is s with the fruit of .... Ps 104:13
s them with the bread of heaven ...... Ps 105:40
his land shall be s with bread .... Prov 12:11
A man shall be s with good by the ... Prov 12:14
A man's belly shall be s with the. .... Prov 18:20
and he that hath it shall abide. .... Prov 19:23
and thou shalt be s with bread .... Prov 20:13
so the eyes of man are never s. .... Prov 27:20
are three things that are never s ...... Prov 30:15
the eye is not s with seeing. .... Eccl 1:8
neither is his eye s with riches. .... Eccl 4:8
silver shall not be s with silver .... Eccl 5:10
left hand, and they shall not be s .... Is 9:20
he roasteth roast, and is s .... Is 44:16
of his soul, and shall be s. .... Is 53:11
be s with the breasts of her .... Is 66:11
shall be s with my goodness .... Jer 31:14
all that spoil her shall be s .... Jer 50:10

his soul shall be s upon mount. .... Jer 50:19
the Assyrians, to be s with bread. ..... Lam 5:6
them, and yet couldest not be s .... Eze 16:28
and yet thou wast not s herewith ..... Eze 16:29
oil, and ye shall be s therewith. .... Joel 2:19
ye shall eat in plenty, and be s .... Joel 2:26
but they were not s .... Amos 4:8
Thou shalt eat, but not be s .... Mic 6:14
and is as death, and cannot be s ..... Hab 2:5

SATISFIEST
s the desire of every living .... Ps 145:16

SATISFIETH
Who is thy mouth with good things. ... Ps 103:5
For he s the longing soul, and .... Ps 107:9
your labour for that which s not .... Is 55:2

SATISFY
To s the desolate and waste ground ... Job 38:27
O s us early with thy mercy. .... Ps 90:14
With long life will I s him .... Ps 91:16
I will s her poor with bread .... Ps 132:15
let her breasts s thee at all. .... Prov 5:19
if he steal to s his soul when he ..... Prov 6:30
hungry, and s the afflicted soul. .... Is 58:10
s thy soul in drought, and make. ..... Is 58:11
they shall not s their souls. .... Eze 7:19
From whence can a man s these men .. Mk 8:4

SATISFYING
eateth to the s of his soul. .... Prov 13:25
any honour to the s of the flesh ...... Col 2:23

SATYR
the s shall cry to his fellow .... Is 34:14

SATYRS
there, and s shall dance there. .... Is 13:21

SAUL (sawl) See PAUL, SAUL'S, SHAUL.
I. The first king of Israel.
And he had a son, whose name was S .. 1Sa 9:2
And Kish said to S his son 1Sa 9:3
S said to his servant that was. 1Sa 9:5
Then said S to his servant, But, ... 1Sa 9:7
And the servant answered S again 1Sa 9:8
Then said S to his servant, Well 1Sa 9:10
in his ear a day before S came. 1Sa 9:15
And when Samuel saw S, the LORD 1Sa 9:17
Then S drew near to Samuel in the ... 1Sa 9:18
And Samuel answered S, and said, I .. 1Sa 9:19
S answered and said, Am not I a 1Sa 9:21
And Samuel took S and his servant, .. 1Sa 9:22
was upon it, and set it before S 1Sa 9:24
So S did eat with Samuel that day 1Sa 9:24
Samuel communed with S upon the. ... 1Sa 9:25
that Samuel called S to the top 1Sa 9:26
S arose, and they went out both of ... 1Sa 9:26
end of the city, Samuel said to S. 1Sa 9:27
Is also among the prophets. 1Sa 10:11
Is S also among the prophets 1Sa 10:12
S said unto his uncle, He told us 1Sa 10:16
S the son of Kish was taken 1Sa 10:21
S also went home to Gibeah 1Sa 10:26
the messengers to Gibeah of S 1Sa 11:4
S came after the herd out of the. 1Sa 11:5
S said, What aileth the people. 1Sa 11:5
S when he heard those tidings 1Sa 11:6
cometh not forth after S and after. 1Sa 11:7
that S put the people in three. 1Sa 11:11
that said, Shall S reign over us 1Sa 11:12
S said, There shall not a man be 1Sa 11:13
there they made S king before the ... 1Sa 11:15
and there S and all the men of 1Sa 11:15
S reigned one year 1Sa 13:1
S chose him three thousand men of ... 1Sa 13:2
thousand were with S in Michmash 1Sa 13:2
S blew the trumpet throughout all 1Sa 13:3
all Israel heard say that S had 1Sa 13:4
called together after S to Gilgal 1Sa 13:4
As for S, he was yet in Gilgal 1Sa 13:7
S said, Bring hither a burnt 1Sa 13:9
S went out to meet him, that he 1Sa 13:10
S said, Because I saw that the 1Sa 13:11
And Samuel said to S, Thou hast 1Sa 13:13
S numbered the people that were 1Sa 13:15
And S, and Jonathan his son, and the .. 1Sa 13:16
of the people that were with S. 1Sa 13:22
but with S and with Jonathan his. 1Sa 13:22
that Jonathan the son of S said. 1Sa 14:1
S tarried in the uttermost part. 1Sa 14:2
the watchmen of S in Gibeah of. 1Sa 14:16
Then said S unto the people that 1Sa 14:17
S said unto Ahiah, Bring hither 1Sa 14:18
while S talked unto the priest, ... 1Sa 14:19
S said unto the priest, Withdraw 1Sa 14:19
And S and all the people that were. .. 1Sa 14:20
the Israelites that were with S. 1Sa 14:21
for S had adjured the people, ... 1Sa 14:24
Then they told S, saying, Behold, ... 1Sa 14:33
S said, Disperse yourselves among 1Sa 14:34
S built an altar unto the LORD 1Sa 14:35
S said, Let us go down after the 1Sa 14:36
S asked counsel of God, Shall I 1Sa 14:37
S said, Draw ye near hither, all 1Sa 14:38
And the people said unto S. 1Sa 14:40
Therefore S said unto the LORD. 1Sa 14:41
And S and Jonathan were taken. 1Sa 14:41
S said, Cast lots between me and. 1Sa 14:42
Then S said to Jonathan, Tell me. 1Sa 14:43
S answered, God do so and more. 1Sa 14:44

And the people said unto S............	1Sa 14:45
Then S went up from following the....	1Sa 14:46
So S took the kingdom over Israel.....	1Sa 14:47
Now the sons of S were Jonathan	1Sa 14:49
And Kish was the father of S............	1Sa 14:51
the Philistines all the days of S	1Sa 14:52
when S saw any strong man, or any ...	1Sa 14:52
Samuel also said unto S, The LORD.....	1Sa 15:1
S gathered the people together,.........	1Sa 15:4
S came to a city of Amalek, and	1Sa 15:5
S said unto the Kenites, Go,.............	1Sa 15:6
S smote the Amalekites from	1Sa 15:7
But S and the people spared Agag,.....	1Sa 15:9
that I have set up S to be king,.........	1Sa 15:11
early to meet S in the morning,.........	1Sa 15:12
S came to Carmel, and, behold, he.....	1Sa 15:12
And Samuel came to S......................	1Sa 15:13
S said unto him, Blessed be thou.......	1Sa 15:13
Said, They have brought them............	1Sa 15:15
Then Samuel said unto S, Stay, and...	1Sa 15:16
S said unto Samuel, Yea, I have........	1Sa 15:20
S said unto Samuel, I have sinned.....	1Sa 15:24
And Samuel said unto S, I will not.....	1Sa 15:26
So Samuel turned again after S	1Sa 15:31
and S worshipped the LORD...............	1Sa 15:31
S went up to his house to Gibeah	1Sa 15:34
up to his house to Gibeah of S	1Sa 15:34
see S until the day of his death	1Sa 15:35
nevertheless Samuel mourned for S ...	1Sa 15:35
S also made S king over Israel..........	1Sa 15:35
How long wilt thou mourn for S.........	1Sa 16:1
if S hear it, he will kill me...............	1Sa 16:2
of the LORD departed from S	1Sa 16:14
S said unto his servants, Provide.......	1Sa 16:17
Wherefore S sent messengers unto	1Sa 16:19
sent them by David his son unto S	1Sa 16:20
And David came to S, and stood........	1Sa 16:21
S sent to Jesse, saying, Let	1Sa 16:22
evil spirit from God was upon S	1Sa 16:23
so S was refreshed, and was well,......	1Sa 16:23
And S and the men of Israel were	1Sa 17:2
a Philistine, and ye servants to S	1Sa 17:8
When S and all Israel heard those.....	1Sa 17:11
for an old man in the days of S	1Sa 17:12
went and followed S to the battle	1Sa 17:13
and the three eldest followed S..........	1Sa 17:14
returned from S to feed his..............	1Sa 17:15
Now S, and they, and all the men of...	1Sa 17:19
they rehearsed them before S............	1Sa 17:31
And David said to S, Let no man's	1Sa 17:32
S said to David, Thou art not	1Sa 17:33
And David said unto S, Thy servant....	1Sa 17:34
S said unto David, Go, and the	1Sa 17:37
S armed David with his armour, and...	1Sa 17:38
And David said unto S, I cannot go ...	1Sa 17:39
when S saw David go forth against......	1Sa 17:55
brought him before S with the...........	1Sa 17:57
S said to him, Whose son art thou......	1Sa 17:58
made an end of speaking unto S	1Sa 18:1
S took him that day, and would let	1Sa 18:2
went out whithersoever S sent him......	1Sa 18:5
S set him over the men of war, and....	1Sa 18:5
and dancing, to meet king S.............	1Sa 18:6
S hath slain his thousands, and.........	1Sa 18:7
S was very wroth, and the saying.......	1Sa 18:8
S eyed David from that day and........	1Sa 18:9
evil spirit from God came upon S.......	1Sa 18:10
And S cast the javelin.....................	1Sa 18:11
S was afraid of David, because..........	1Sa 18:12
with him, and was departed from S....	1Sa 18:13
Therefore S removed him from him,....	1Sa 18:13
Wherefore when S saw that he	1Sa 18:15
S said to David, Behold my elder......	1Sa 18:17
For S said, Let not mine hand be	1Sa 18:17
And David said unto S, Who am I	1Sa 18:18
and they told S, and the thing	1Sa 18:20
S said, I will give him her, that........	1Sa 18:21
Wherefore S said to David,..............	1Sa 18:21
S commanded his servants, saying,....	1Sa 18:22
And the servants of S told him..........	1Sa 18:24
S said, Thus shall ye say to.............	1Sa 18:25
But S thought to make David fall.......	1Sa 18:25
S gave him Michal his daughter to.....	1Sa 18:27
S saw and knew that the LORD was ...	1Sa 18:28
S was yet the more afraid of	1Sa 18:29
And S became David's enemy............	1Sa 18:29
wisely than all the servants of S	1Sa 18:30
S spake to Jonathan his son, and......	1Sa 19:1
S my father seeketh to kill thee	1Sa 19:2
good of David unto S his father........	1Sa 19:4
S hearkened unto the voice of	1Sa 19:6
S sware, As the LORD liveth, he	1Sa 19:6
And Jonathan brought David to S.......	1Sa 19:7
spirit from the LORD was upon S	1Sa 19:9
S sought to smite David even to	1Sa 19:10
S also sent messengers unto	1Sa 19:11
when S sent messengers to take	1Sa 19:14
S sent the messengers again to.........	1Sa 19:15
S said unto Michal, Why hast thou	1Sa 19:17
And Michal answered S, He said	1Sa 19:17
him all that S had done to him	1Sa 19:18
And it was told S, saying, Behold,.....	1Sa 19:19
S sent messengers to take David	1Sa 19:20
God was upon the messengers of S	1Sa 19:20
And when it was told S, he sent........	1Sa 19:21
S sent messengers again the third.....	1Sa 19:21
Is S also among the prophets............	1Sa 19:24
Nevertheless Samuel spake not any ...	1Sa 20:26
S said unto Jonathan his son,...........	1Sa 20:27
And Jonathan answered S, David	1Sa 20:28

And Jonathan answered S his father..	1Sa 20:32
S cast a javelin at him to smite........	1Sa 20:33
of the herdmen that belonged to S	1Sa 21:7
and fled that day for fear of S	1Sa 21:10
When S heard that David was	1Sa 22:6
(now S abode in Gibeah under a	1Sa 22:6
Then S said unto his servants	1Sa 22:7
was set over the servants of S	1Sa 22:9
S said, Hear now, thou son of	1Sa 22:12
S said unto him, Why have ye	1Sa 22:13
Abiathar shewed David that S had	1Sa 22:21
that he would surely tell S	1Sa 22:22
it was told S that David was come	1Sa 23:7
S said, God hath delivered him	1Sa 23:7
S called all the people together	1Sa 23:8
David knew that S secretly................	1Sa 23:9
that S seeketh to come to Keilah.......	1Sa 23:10
will S come down, as thy servant......	1Sa 23:11
me and my men into the hand of S	1Sa 23:12
it was told S that David was	1Sa 23:13
S sought him every day, but God.......	1Sa 23:14
David saw that S was come out to......	1Sa 23:15
for the hand of S my father shall.......	1Sa 23:17
that also S my father knoweth	1Sa 23:17
up the Ziphites to S to Gibeah...........	1Sa 23:19
S said, Blessed be ye of the LORD	1Sa 23:21
arose, and went to Ziph before S	1Sa 23:24
S also and his men went to seek........	1Sa 23:25
when S heard that, he pursued..........	1Sa 23:25
S went on this side of the	1Sa 23:26
haste to get away for fear of S	1Sa 23:26
for S and his men compassed David...	1Sa 23:26
But there came a messenger unto S ...	1Sa 23:27
Wherefore S returned from..............	1Sa 23:28
to pass, when S was returned from	1Sa 24:1
Then S took three thousand chosen....	1Sa 24:2
S went in to cover his feet................	1Sa 24:3
them not to rise against S	1Sa 24:7
But S rose up out of the cave, and....	1Sa 24:7
out of the cave, and cried after S	1Sa 24:8
when S looked behind him, David......	1Sa 24:8
And David said to S, Wherefore........	1Sa 24:9
words unto S, that S said	1Sa 24:16
S lifted up his voice, and wept..........	1Sa 24:16
And David sware unto S	1Sa 24:22
And S went home............................	1Sa 24:22
But S had given Michal his..............	1Sa 25:44
Ziphites came unto S to Gibeah........	1Sa 26:1
Then S arose, and went down to the..	1Sa 26:2
S pitched in the hill of Hachilah.......	1Sa 26:3
he saw that S came after him into.....	1Sa 26:3
understood that S was come into	1Sa 26:4
to the place where S had pitched	1Sa 26:5
beheld the place where S lay............	1Sa 26:5
S lay in the trench, and the	1Sa 26:7
go down with me to S to the camp	1Sa 26:6
S lay sleeping within the trench,.......	1Sa 26:7
S knew David's voice, and said, Is....	1Sa 26:17
Then said S, I have sinned..............	1Sa 26:21
Then S said to David, Blessed be	1Sa 26:25
way, and S returned to his place	1Sa 26:25
perish one day by the hand of S	1Sa 27:1
S shall despair of me, to seek me	1Sa 27:1
it was told S that David was............	1Sa 27:4
S had put away those that had	1Sa 28:3
S gathered all Israel together,..........	1Sa 28:4
when S saw the host of the..............	1Sa 28:5
when S enquired of the LORD, the.....	1Sa 28:6
Then said S unto his servants,..........	1Sa 28:7
S disguised himself, and put on........	1Sa 28:8
thou knowest what S hath done	1Sa 28:9
S sware to her by the LORD,.............	1Sa 28:10
and the woman spake to S, saying,....	1Sa 28:12
for thou art S.................................	1Sa 28:12
And the woman said unto S, I saw	1Sa 28:13
S perceived that it was Samuel,........	1Sa 28:14
And Samuel said to S, Why hast	1Sa 28:15
S answered, I am sore distressed......	1Sa 28:15
Then S fell straightway all along.......	1Sa 28:20
the woman came unto S	1Sa 28:21
And she brought it before S	1Sa 28:25
the servant of S the king of.............	1Sa 29:3
S slew his thousands, and David.......	1Sa 29:5
Philistines followed hard upon S	1Sa 31:2
And the battle went sore against S	1Sa 31:3
Then said S unto his armourbearer....	1Sa 31:4
Therefore S took a sword, and fell.....	1Sa 31:4
armourbearer saw that S was dead....	1Sa 31:5
So S died, and his three sons, and....	1Sa 31:6
the men of Israel fled, and that S	1Sa 31:7
the slain, that they found S	1Sa 31:8
the Philistines had done to S	1Sa 31:11
all night, and took the body of S	1Sa 31:12
came to pass after the death of S	2Sa 1:1
camp from S with his clothes rent	2Sa 1:2
and S and Jonathan his son are dead.	2Sa 1:4
told him, How knowest thou that S	2Sa 1:5
behold, S leaned upon his spear.......	2Sa 1:6
wept, and fasted until even, for S	2Sa 1:12
with this lamentation over S	2Sa 1:17
vilely cast away, the shield of S	2Sa 1:21
the sword of S returned not empty.....	2Sa 1:22
S and Jonathan were lovely and........	2Sa 1:23
daughters of Israel, weep over S	2Sa 1:24
were they that buried S...................	2Sa 2:4
your lord, even unto S	2Sa 2:5
for your master S is dead.................	2Sa 2:7
took Ish-bosheth the son of S	2Sa 2:8

of Ish-bosheth the son of S..............	2Sa 2:12
to Ish-bosheth the son of S..............	2Sa 2:15
long war between the house of S.......	2Sa 3:1
and the house of S waxed weaker	2Sa 3:1
was war between the house of S........	2Sa 3:6
himself strong for the house of S	2Sa 3:6
S had a concubine, whose name was .	2Sa 3:7
unto the house of S thy father..........	2Sa 3:8
the kingdom from the house of S	2Sa 3:10
old when the tidings came of S	2Sa 4:4
the son of S thine enemy, which	2Sa 4:8
my lord the king this day of S	2Sa 4:8
S is dead, thinking to have	2Sa 4:10
when S was king over us, thou..........	2Sa 5:2
of S came out to meet David............	2Sa 6:20
Michal the daughter of S had no.......	2Sa 6:23
from him, as I took it from S	2Sa 7:15
that is left of the house of S.............	2Sa 9:1
there was of the house of S a...........	2Sa 9:2
not yet any of the house of S	2Sa 9:3
the son of Jonathan, the son of S	2Sa 9:6
thee all the land of S thy father........	2Sa 9:7
son all that pertained to S	2Sa 9:9
thee out of the hand of S	2Sa 12:7
of the family of the house of S	2Sa 16:5
all the blood of the house of S	2Sa 16:8
the servant of the house of S	2Sa 19:17
Mephibosheth the son of S came	2Sa 19:24
And the LORD answered, It is for S	2Sa 21:1
S sought to slay them in his zeal	2Sa 21:2
will have no silver nor gold of S	2Sa 21:4
up unto the LORD in Gibeah of S	2Sa 21:6
the son of Jonathan the son of S	2Sa 21:7
David and Jonathan the son of S	2Sa 21:7
of Aiah, whom she bare unto S	2Sa 21:8
sons of Michal the daughter of S	2Sa 21:8
of Aiah, the concubine of S	2Sa 21:11
David went and took the bones of S...	2Sa 21:12
Philistines had slain S in Gilboa	2Sa 21:12
up from thence the bones of S	2Sa 21:13
And the bones of S and Jonathan his.	2Sa 21:14
enemies, and out of the hand of S	2Sa 22:1
in the days of S they made war	1Chr 5:10
Ner begat Kish, and Kish begat S	1Chr 8:33
S begat Jonathan, and Malchi-shua,..	1Chr 8:33
and Kish begat S............................	1Chr 9:39
S begat Jonathan, and Malchi-shua,..	1Chr 9:39
Philistines followed hard after S	1Chr 10:2
and Malchi-shua, the sons of S	1Chr 10:2
And the battle went sore against S	1Chr 10:3
Then said S to his armourbearer,......	1Chr 10:4
So S took a sword, and fell upon	1Chr 10:4
armourbearer saw that S was dead....	1Chr 10:5
So S died, and his three sons, and....	1Chr 10:6
saw that they fled, and that S	1Chr 10:7
the slain, that they found S	1Chr 10:8
the Philistines had done to S	1Chr 10:11
men, and took away the body of S	1Chr 10:12
So S died for his transgression	1Chr 10:13
time past, even when S was king.......	1Chr 11:2
because of S the son of Kish	1Chr 12:1
Philistines against S to battle...........	1Chr 12:19
He will fall to his master S to	1Chr 12:19
to turn the kingdom of S to him........	1Chr 12:23
of Benjamin, the kindred of S...........	1Chr 12:29
kept the ward of the house of S	1Chr 12:29
not at it in the days of S	1Chr 13:3
of S looking out at a window saw	1Chr 15:29
S the son of Kish, and Abner the	1Chr 26:28
enemies, and from the hand of S	Ps 18:t
Doeg the Edomite came and told S	Ps 52:t
the Ziphims came and said to S	Ps 54:t
when he fled from S in the cave	Ps 57:t
when S sent, and they watched the ...	Ps 59:t
Gibeah of S is fled	Is 10:29
gave unto them S the son of Cis	Acts 13:21

2. An Edomite king.

S of Rehoboth by the river	Gen 36:37
S died, and Baal-hanan the son of....	Gen 36:38

3. Original name of Paul.

man's feet, whose name was S..........	Acts 7:58
S was consenting unto his death	Acts 8:1
As for S, he made havock of the	Acts 8:3
And S, yet breathing out	Acts 9:1
a voice saying unto him, Saul, S.......	Acts 9:4
And S arose from the earth	Acts 9:8
house of Judas for one called S	Acts 9:11
his hands on him said, Brother S.......	Acts 9:17
Then was S certain days with the	Acts 9:19
But S increased the more in.............	Acts 9:22
their laying await was known of S	Acts 9:24
when S was come to Jerusalem, he	Acts 9:26
Barnabas to Tarsus, for to seek S	Acts 11:25
by the hands of Barnabas and S	Acts 11:30
S returned from Jerusalem, when......	Acts 12:25
up with Herod the tetrarch, and S	Acts 13:1
S for the work whereunto I have	Acts 13:2
who called for Barnabas and S	Acts 13:7
Then S, (who also is called Paul,......	Acts 13:9
a voice saying unto me, Saul, S	Acts 22:7
stood, and said unto me, Brother S....	Acts 22:13
in the Hebrew tongue, Saul, S..........	Acts 26:14

SAUL'S

asses of Kish S father were lost.........	1Sa 9:3
S uncle said unto him and to his.......	1Sa 10:14
S uncle said, Tell me, I pray	1Sa 10:15
the name of S wife was Ahinoam,.....	1Sa 14:50
Abner, the son of Ner, S uncle..........	1Sa 14:50
S servants said unto him, Behold......	1Sa 16:15
also in the sight of S servants..........	1Sa 18:5

and there was a javelin in *S* hand 1Sa 18:10
to pass at the time when Merab *S* 1Sa 18:19
Michal *S* daughter loved David 1Sa 18:20
S servants spake those words in 1Sa 18:23
that Michal *S* daughter loved him 1Sa 18:28
But Jonathan *S* son delighted much 1Sa 19:2
he slipped away out of *S* presence 1Sa 19:10
arose, and Abner sat by *S* side 1Sa 20:25
Then *S* anger was kindled against 1Sa 20:30
Jonathan *S* son arose, and went to 1Sa 23:16
off the skirt of *S* robe privily 1Sa 24:4
because he had cut off *S* skirt 1Sa 24:5
the cruse of water from *S* bolster 1Sa 26:12
Abinadab, and Melchi-shua, *S* sons 1Sa 31:2
the son of Ner, captain of *S* host 2Sa 2:8
Ish-bosheth *S* son was forty years 2Sa 2:10
first bring Michal *S* daughter 2Sa 3:13
messengers to Ish-bosheth *S* son 2Sa 3:14
when *S* son heard that Abner was 2Sa 4:1
S son had two men that were 2Sa 4:2
S son, had a son that was lame of 2Sa 4:4
Michal *S* daughter looked through 2Sa 6:16
S servant, and said unto him, ... 2Sa 9:9
even of *S* brethren of Benjamin 1Chr 12:2

SAVE

me, but they will *s* thee alive .... Gen 12:12
S only that which the young men .... Gen 14:24
s the bread which he did eat .... Gen 39:6
to *s* your lives by a great .... Gen 45:7
this day, to *s* much people alive .... Gen 50:20
every daughter ye shall *s* alive .... Ex 1:22
s that which every man must eat, ... Ex 12:16
s unto the LORD only, he shall be .... Ex 22:20
s Caleb the son of Jephunneh, and ...... Num 14:30
s Caleb the son of Jephunneh, ... Num 26:65
S Caleb the son of Jephunneh, ... Num 32:12
s Caleb the son of Jephunneh .... Deut 1:36
S when there shall be no poor .... Deut 15:4
against your enemies, to *s* you .... Deut 20:4
thou shalt *s* alive nothing that .... Deut 20:16
cried, and there was none to *s* her ...... Deut 22:27
evermore, and no man shall *s* thee ...... Deut 28:29
that ye will *s* alive my father, ... Josh 2:13
us quickly, and *s* us, and help us .... Josh 10:6
burned none of them, *s* Hazor only. ..... Josh 11:13
s the Hivites the inhabitants of .... Josh 11:19
s cities to dwell in, with their .... Josh 14:4
the LORD, (*s* us not this day,) .... Josh 22:22
thou shalt *s* Israel from the hand, ... Judg 6:14
Lord, wherewith shall I *s* Israel? .... Judg 6:15
will ye *s* him .... Judg 6:31
If thou wilt *s* Israel by mine hand, ... Judg 6:36
thou wilt *s* Israel by mine hand, ... Judg 6:37
men that lapped will I *s* you. .... Judg 7:7
This is nothing else *s* the sword .... Judg 7:14
it may *s* us out of the hand of 1Sa 4:3
that he will *s* us out of the hand 1Sa 7:8
that he may *s* my people out of 1Sa 9:16
shouted, and said, God *s* the king 1Sa 10:24
said, How shall this man *s* us 1Sa 10:27
then, if there be no man to *s* us 1Sa 11:3
the LORD to *s* by many or by few 1Sa 14:6
If thou *s* not thy to night, to 1Sa 19:11
for there is no other *s* that here 1Sa 21:9
the Philistines, and *s* Keilah. 1Sa 23:2
s four hundred young men, which 1Sa 30:17
s to every man his wife and his 1Sa 30:22
s my people Israel out of the. 2Sa 3:18
s one little ewe lamb, which he 2Sa 12:3
God *s* the king, God *s* the king 2Sa 16:16
God *s* the king, God *s* the king 2Sa 16:16
the afflicted people thou wilt *s* 2Sa 22:28
For who is God, *s* the LORD 2Sa 22:32
and who is a rock, *s* our God 2Sa 22:32
looked, but there was none to *s* 2Sa 22:42
that thou mayest *s* thine own life 1Kin 1:12
him, and say, God *s* king Adonijah. 1Kin 1:25
and say, God *s* king Solomon. 1Kin 1:34
people said, God *s* king Solomon. 1Kin 1:39
the house, *s* we two in the house 1Kin 3:18
the ark *s* the two tables of stone. 1Kin 8:9
s only in the matter of Uriah the 1Kin 15:5
we may find grass to *s* the horses 1Kin 18:5
peradventure he will *s* thy life 1Kin 20:31
s only with the king of Israel 1Kin 22:31
in the house, *s* a pot of oil 2Kin 4:2
if they *s* us alive, we shall live 2Kin 7:4
hands, and said, God *s* the king 2Kin 11:12
S that the high places were not. 2Kin 15:4
s me out of the hand of the king 2Kin 16:7
s thou us out of his hand, that 2Kin 19:19
I will defend this city, to *s* it 2Kin 19:34
s the poorest sort of the people 2Kin 24:14
S us, O God of our salvation, and 1Chr 16:35
s only to burn sacrifice before 2Chr 2:6
There was nothing in the ark *s* 2Chr 5:10
s only with the king of Israel 2Chr 18:30
s Jehoahaz, the youngest of his 2Chr 21:17
s the priests, and they *that* 2Chr 23:6
him, and said, God *s* the king 2Chr 23:11
s the beast that I rode upon. .... Neh 2:12
go into the temple to *s* his life. .... Neh 6:11
but *s* his life .... Job 2:6
he shall not *s* of that which he .... Job 20:20
he shall *s* the humble person. .... Job 22:29
thine own right hand can *s* thee. .... Job 40:14
s me, O my God .... Ps 3:7
oh *s* me for thy mercies' sake .... Ps 6:4
s me from all them that persecute ..... Ps 7:1
For thou wilt *s* the afflicted. .... Ps 18:27

For who is God *s* the LORD .... Ps 18:31
or who is a rock *s* our God .... Ps 18:31
but there was none to *s* them, ... Ps 18:41
S, LORD .... Ps 28:9
S me from the lion's mouth .... Ps 22:21
S thy people, and bless thine .... Ps 28:9
for an house of defence to *s* me .... Ps 31:2
s me for thy mercies' sake .... Ps 31:16
s them, because they trust in them ... Ps 37:40
neither did their own arm *s* them, ... Ps 44:3
bow, neither shall my sword *s* me ...... Ps 44:6
S me, O God, by thy name, and .... Ps 54:1
and the LORD shall *s* me .... Ps 55:16
s me from the reproach of him .... Ps 57:3
iniquity, and *s* me from bloody men ... Ps 59:2
s with thy right hand, and hear me. ... Ps 60:5
S me, O God .... Ps 69:1
For God will *s* Zion, and will .... Ps 69:35
thine ear unto me, and *s* me .... Ps 71:2
hast given commandment to *s* me ...... Ps 71:3
he shall *s* the children of the .... Ps 72:4
shall *s* the souls of the needy. .... Ps 72:13
to *s* all the meek of the earth .... Ps 76:9
up thy strength, and come and *s* us. ... Ps 80:2
s thy servant that trusteth in .... Ps 86:2
the son of thine handmaid .... Ps 86:16
S us, O LORD our God, and gather .... Ps 106:47
s with thy right hand, and answer ...... Ps 108:6
O s me according to thy mercy .... Ps 109:26
to *s* him from those that condemn, ... Ps 109:31
S now, I beseech thee, O LORD .... Ps 118:25
I am thine, *s* me .... Ps 119:94
s me, and I shall keep thy .... Ps 119:146
and thy right hand shall *s* me. .... Ps 138:7
hear their cry, and will *s* them. .... Ps 145:19
on the LORD, and he shall *s* thee .... Prov 20:22
waited for him, and he will *s* us. .... Is 25:9
he will *s* us .... Is 33:22
he will come and *s* you .... Is 35:4
s us from his hand, that all the .... Is 37:20
city to *s* it for mine own sake .... Is 37:35
The LORD was ready to *s* me .... Is 38:20
and pray unto a god that cannot *s*...... Is 45:20
nor *s* him out of his trouble. .... Is 46:7
s thee from these things that .... Is 47:13
none shall *s* thee. .... Is 47:15
thee, and I will *s* thy children .... Is 49:25
not shortened, that it cannot *s* .... Is 59:1
in righteousness, mighty to *s*. .... Is 63:1
they will say, Arise, and *s* us. .... Jer 2:27
if they can *s* thee in the time of .... Jer 2:28
but they shall not *s* them at all .... Jer 11:12
as a mighty man that cannot *s* .... Jer 14:9
for I am with thee to *s* thee .... Jer 15:20
s me, and I shall be saved .... Jer 17:14
I will *s* thee from afar, and thy .... Jer 30:10
thee, saith the LORD, to *s* thee .... Jer 30:11
s thy people, the remnant of .... Jer 31:7
for I am with you to *s* you. .... Jer 42:11
I will *s* them from afar off, and .... Jer 46:27
s your lives, and be like the .... Jer 48:6
for a nation that could not *s* us .... Lam 4:17
his wicked way, to *s* his life. .... Eze 3:18
will ye *s* the souls alive that .... Eze 13:18
to *s* the souls alive that should .... Eze 13:19
he shall *s* his soul alive .... Eze 18:27
Therefore will I *s* my flock, ... Eze 34:22
I will also *s* you from all your .... Eze 36:29
but I will *s* them out of all .... Eze 37:23
s of thee, O king, he shall be .... Dan 6:7
s of thee, O king, shall be cast .... Dan 6:12
will *s* them by the LORD their God ..... Hos 1:7
will not *s* them by bow, nor by .... Hos 1:7
that may *s* thee in all thy cities. .... Hos 13:10
Asshur shall not *s* us. .... Hos 14:3
of violence, and thou wilt not *s* .... Hab 1:2
he will *s*, he will rejoice over .... Zeph 3:17
I will *s* her that halteth, and .... Zeph 3:19
I will *s* my people from the east .... Zec 8:7
so will I *s* you, and ye shall be a .... Zec 8:13
the LORD their God shall *s* them .... Zec 9:16
I will *s* the house of Joseph, and .... Zec 10:6
The LORD also shall *s* the tents .... Zec 12:7
for he shall *s* his people from. .... Mt 1:21
and awoke him, saying, Lord, *s* us. ..... Mt 8:25
s the Son, and he to whomsoever. ..... Mt 11:27
s in his own country, and in his. .... Mt 13:57
he cried, saying, Lord, *s* me. .... Mt 14:30
For whosoever will *s* his life .... Mt 16:25
they saw no man, *s* Jesus only. .... Mt 17:8
is come to *s* that which was lost. .... Mt 18:11
s they to whom it is given .... Mt 19:11
it in three days, *s* thyself .... Mt 27:40
himself he cannot *s*. .... Mt 27:42
whether Elias will come to *s* him. .... Mt 27:49
to *s* life, or to kill .... Mk 3:4
s Peter, and James, and John the ...... Mk 5:37
s that he laid his hands upon a .... Mk 6:5
for their journey, *s* a staff only. .... Mk 6:8
For whosoever will *s* his life .... Mk 8:35
the gospel's, the same shall *s* it .... Mk 8:35
s Jesus only with themselves. .... Mk 9:8
S thyself, and come down from the ..... Mk 15:30
himself he cannot *s* .... Mk 15:31
s unto Sarepta, a city of Sidon, ... Lk 4:26
to *s* life, or to destroy it .... Lk 6:9
s Peter, and James, and John, and..... Lk 8:51
For whosoever will *s* his life............... Lk 9:24
for my sake, the same shall *s* it .... Lk 9:24
men's lives, but to *s* them .... Lk 9:56

glory to God, *s* this stranger .... Lk 17:18
seek to *s* his life shall lose it .... Lk 17:33
none is good, *s* one, that is, God .... Lk 18:19
seek and to *s* that which was lost ...... Lk 19:10
let him *s* himself, if he be .... Lk 23:35
the king of the Jews, *s* thyself .... Lk 23:37
thou be Christ, *s* thyself and us. .... Lk 23:39
there, *s* that one whereinto his .... Jn 6:22
s he which is of God, he hath .... Jn 6:46
Father, *s* me from this hour .... Jn 12:27
the world, but to *s* the world .... Jn 12:47
needeth not *s* to wash his feet .... Jn 13:10
S yourselves from this untoward .... Acts 2:40
S that the Holy Ghost witnesseth .... Acts 20:23
s only that they keep themselves .... Acts 21:25
the centurion, willing to *s* Paul .... Acts 27:43
my flesh, and might *s* some of them. ... Rom 11:14
preaching to *s* them that believe 1Cor 1:21
s Jesus Christ, and him crucified 1Cor 2:2
s the spirit of man which is in 1Cor 2:11
whether thou shalt *s* thy husband 1Cor 7:16
whether thou shalt *s* thy wife 1Cor 7:16
that I might by all means *s* some 1Cor 9:22
received I forty stripes *s* one 2Cor 11:24
s James the Lord's brother .... Gal 1:19
s in the cross of our Lord Jesus .... Gal 6:14
came into the world to *s* sinners 1Ti 1:15
this thou shalt both *s* thyself 1Ti 4:16
that was able to *s* him from death ...... Heb 5:7
Wherefore he is able also to *s* .... Heb 7:25
which is able to *s* your souls .... Jas 1:21
can faith *s* him .... Jas 2:14
is one lawgiver, who is able to *s*. .... Jas 4:12
prayer of faith shall *s* the sick .... Jas 5:15
his way shall *s* a soul from death .... Jas 5:20
even baptism doth also now *s* us (..... 1Pet 3:21
others *s* with fear, pulling them .... Jude 23
s he that had the mark, or the .... Rev 13:17

SAVED

they said, Thou hast *s* our lives. .... Gen 47:25
but *s* the men children alive .... Ex 1:17
have *s* the men children alive .... Ex 1:18
Thus the LORD *s* Israel that day .... Ex 14:30
ye shall be *s* from your enemies. .... Num 10:9
I had slain then, and *s* her alive. .... Num 22:33
Have ye *s* all the women alive. .... Num 31:15
O people *s* by the LORD, the .... Deut 33:29
Joshua *s* Rahab the harlot alive, ... Josh 6:25
saying, Mine own hand hath *s* me. ..... Judg 7:2
if ye had *s* them alive, I would .... Judg 8:19
they had *s* alive of the women of .... Judg 21:14
who himself *s* you out of all your 1Sa 10:19
s the LORD's Israel that day 1Sa 14:23
So David's the inhabitants of 1Sa 23:5
David's neither man nor woman 1Sa 27:11
which this day have *s* thy life 2Sa 19:5
The King *s* us out of the hand of 2Sa 19:9
so shall I be *s* from mine enemies 2Sa 22:4
s himself there, not once nor 2Kin 6:10
but he *s* them by the hand of 2Kin 14:27
the LORD *s* them by a great 1Chr 11:14
Thus the LORD *s* Hezekiah and the 2Chr 32:22
who *s* them out of the hand of .... Neh 9:27
so shall I be *s* from mine enemies ...... Ps 18:3
There is no king *s* by the .... Ps 33:16
s him out of all his troubles .... Ps 34:6
But thou hast *s* us from our.............. Ps 44:7
and we shall be *s* .... Ps 80:3
and we shall be *s* .... Ps 80:7
and we shall be *s* .... Ps 80:19
Nevertheless he *s* them for his.......... Ps 106:8
he *s* them from the hand of him. .... Ps 106:10
he *s* them out of their distresses. ...... Ps 107:13
walketh uprightly shall be *s*. .... Prov 28:18
returning and rest shall ye be *s*. .... Is 30:15
I have declared, and have *s* .... Is 43:12
But Israel shall be *s* in the LORD .... Is 45:17
Look unto me, and be ye *s*, all the ...... Is 45:22
the angel of his presence *s* them .... Is 63:9
is continuance, and we shall be *s*. ...... Is 64:5
wickedness, that thou mayest be *s* ..... Jer 4:14
summer is ended, and we are not *s*. .... Jer 8:20
save me, and I shall be *s* .... Jer 17:14
In his days Judah shall be *s*, ... Jer 23:6
but he shall be *s* out of it .... Jer 30:7
In those days shall Judah be *s*, ... Jer 33:16
endureth to the end shall be *s*. .... Mt 10:22
amazed, saying, Who then can be *s* .... Mt 19:25
unto the end, the same shall be *s*. ...... Mt 24:13
there should no flesh be *s*: .... Mt 24:22
He *s* others, himself he .... Mt 27:42
themselves, Who then can be *s*. .... Mk 10:26
unto the end, the same shall be *s*. ...... Mk 13:13
those days, no flesh should be *s*. .... Mk 13:20
with the scribes, He *s* others. .... Mk 15:31
and is baptized shall be *s*. .... Mk 16:16
we should be *s* from our enemies. ...... Lk 1:71
the woman, Thy faith hath *s* thee ...... Lk 7:50
lest they should believe and be *s*. ...... Lk 8:12
Lord, are there few that be *s* .... Lk 13:23
heard it said, Who then can be *s*......... Lk 18:26
thy faith hath *s* thee .... Lk 18:42
derided him, saying, He *s* others. .... Lk 23:35
the world through him might be *s*. ...... Jn 3:17
things I say, that ye might be *s*. .... Jn 5:34
any man enter in, he shall be *s* .... Jn 10:9
the name of the Lord shall be *s*. .... Acts 2:21
church daily such as should be *s*. .... Acts 2:47
among men, whereby we must be *s*. .... Acts 4:12
thou and all thy house shall be *s* .... Acts 11:14

manner of Moses, ye cannot be s ...... Acts 15:1
Lord Jesus Christ we shall be s ...... Acts 15:11
Sirs, what must I do to be s ...... Acts 16:30
Jesus Christ, and thou shalt be s ...... Acts 16:31
should be s was then taken away ...... Acts 27:20
abide in the ship, ye cannot be s ...... Acts 27:31
we shall be s from wrath through ...... Rom 5:9
we shall be s by his life ...... Rom 5:10
For we are s by hope ...... Rom 8:24
of the sea, a remnant shall be s ...... Rom 9:27
Israel is, that they might be s ...... Rom 10:1
from the dead, thou shalt be s ...... Rom 10:9
the name of the Lord shall be s ...... Rom 10:13
And so all Israel shall be s ...... Rom 11:26
but unto us which are s it is the 1Cor 1:18
but he himself shall be s 1Cor 3:15
that the spirit may be s in the 1Cor 5:5
of many, that they may be s 1Cor 10:33
By which also ye are s, if ye 1Cor 15:2
of Christ, in them that are s 2Cor 2:15
with Christ, (by grace ye are s ...... Eph 2:5
by grace are ye s through faith ...... Eph 2:8
the Gentiles that they might be s 1Th 2:16
the truth, that they might be s 2Th 2:10
Who will have all men to be s 1Ti 2:4
she shall be s in childbearing 1Ti 2:15
Who hath s us, and called us with 2Ti 1:9
according to his mercy he s us ...... Titus 3:5
is, eight souls were s by water 1Pet 3:20
And if the righteous scarcely be s 1Pet 4:18
but s Noah the eighth person, a 2Pet 2:5
having s the people out of the ...... Jude 5
s shall walk in the light of it ...... Rev 21:24

SAVEST
thou s me from violence 2Sa 22:3
how s thou the arm that hath no ...... Job 26:2
O thou that s by thy right hand ...... Ps 17:7

SAVETH
which s Israel, though it be in 1Sa 14:39
that the Lord s not with sword 1Sa 17:47
But he s the poor from the sword, ... Job 5:15
which s the upright in heart ...... Ps 7:10
I that the Lord s his anointed ...... Ps 20:6
s such as be of a contrite spirit ...... Ps 34:18
he s them out of their distresses ...... Ps 107:19

SAVING
hast shewed unto me in s my life ...... Gen 19:19
s that every one put them off for ...... Neh 4:23
the s strength of his right hand ...... Ps 20:6
he is the s strength of his ...... Ps 28:8
thy s health among all nations ...... Ps 67:2
s the beholding of them with ...... Eccl 5:11
s that I will not utterly destroy ...... Amos 9:8
s for the cause of fornication, ... Mt 5:32
was cleansed, s Naaman the Syrian ...... Lk 4:27
that believe to the s of the soul ...... Heb 10:39
an ark to the s of his house ...... Heb 11:7
knoweth s he that receiveth it ...... Rev 2:17

SAVIOUR
my high tower, and my refuge, my s 2Sa 22:3
(And the Lord gave Israel a s 2Kin 13:5
They forgat God their s, which ...... Ps 106:21
and he shall send them a s ...... Is 19:20
the Holy One of Israel, thy S ...... Is 43:3
and beside me there is no s ...... Is 43:11
thyself, O God of Israel, the S ...... Is 45:15
a just God and a S ...... Is 45:21
know that I the Lord am thy S ...... Is 49:26
know that I the Lord am thy S ...... Is 60:16
so he was their S ...... Is 63:8
the s thereof in time of trouble, ... Jer 14:8
for there is no s beside me ...... Hos 13:4
spirit hath rejoiced in God my S ...... Lk 1:47
this day in the city of David a S ...... Lk 2:11
the Christ, the S of the world ...... Jn 4:42
right hand to be a Prince and a S ...... Acts 5:31
promise raised unto Israel a S ...... Acts 13:23
and he is the s of the body ...... Eph 5:23
whence also we look for the S ...... Phil 3:20
by the commandment of God our S 1Ti 1:1
in the sight of God our S 1Ti 2:3
God, who is the S of all men 1Ti 4:10
appearing of our S Jesus Christ 2Ti 1:10
to the commandment of God our S ...... Titus 1:3
and the Lord Jesus Christ our S ...... Titus 1:4
of God our S in all things ...... Titus 2:10
great God and our S Jesus Christ ...... Titus 2:13
love of God our S toward man ...... Titus 3:4
through Jesus Christ our S ...... Titus 3:6
of God and our S Jesus Christ 2Pet 1:1
of our Lord and S Jesus Christ 2Pet 1:11
S Jesus Christ, they are again 2Pet 2:20
us the apostles of the Lord and S 2Pet 3:2
of our Lord and S Jesus Christ 2Pet 3:18
the Son to be the S of the world 1Jn 4:14
To the only wise God our S ...... Jude 25

SAVIOURS
mercies thou gavest them s ...... Neh 9:27
s shall come up on mount Zion to ...... Obad 21

SAVOUR
And the Lord smelled a sweet s ...... Gen 8:21
because ye have made our s to be ...... Ex 5:21
it is a sweet s, an offering made ...... Ex 29:18
for a sweet s before the Lord ...... Ex 29:25
offering thereof, for a sweet s ...... Ex 29:41
of a sweet s unto the Lord ...... Lev 1:9
of a sweet s unto the Lord ...... Lev 1:13

of a sweet s unto the Lord ...... Lev 1:17
of a sweet s unto the Lord ...... Lev 2:2
of a sweet s unto the Lord ...... Lev 2:9
burnt on the altar for a sweet s ...... Lev 2:12
of a sweet s unto the Lord ...... Lev 3:5
made by fire for a sweet s ...... Lev 3:16
altar for a sweet s unto the Lord ...... Lev 4:31
it upon the altar for a sweet s ...... Lev 6:15
of a sweet s unto the Lord ...... Lev 6:21
a burnt sacrifice for a sweet s ...... Lev 8:21
were consecrations for a sweet s ...... Lev 8:28
fat for a sweet s unto the Lord ...... Lev 17:6
fire unto the Lord for a sweet s ...... Lev 23:13
by fire, of sweet s unto the Lord ...... Lev 23:18
smell the s of your sweet odours ...... Lev 26:31
to make a sweet s unto the Lord ...... Num 15:7
for a sweet s unto the Lord ...... Num 15:13
of a sweet s unto the Lord ...... Num 15:13
of a sweet s unto the Lord ...... Num 15:14
for a sweet s unto the Lord, with ...... Num 15:24
for a sweet s unto the Lord ...... Num 18:17
by fire, for a sweet s unto me ...... Num 28:2
in mount Sinai for a sweet s ...... Num 28:6
of a sweet s unto the Lord ...... Num 28:8
for a burnt offering of a sweet s ...... Num 28:24
unto the Lord for a sweet s ...... Num 28:27
for a sweet s unto the Lord ...... Num 29:2
unto their manner, for a sweet s ...... Num 29:6
unto the Lord for a sweet s ...... Num 29:8
of a sweet s unto the Lord ...... Num 29:13
of a sweet s unto the Lord ...... Num 29:36
to send forth a stinking s ...... Eccl 10:1
Because of the s of thy good ...... SS 1:3
offer sweet s to all their idols ...... Eze 6:13
set it before them for a sweet s ...... Eze 16:19
also they made their sweet s ...... Eze 20:28
will accept you with your sweet s ...... Eze 20:41
his ill a shall come up, because ...... Joel 2:20
but if the salt have lost his s ...... Mt 5:13
but if the salt have lost his s ...... Lk 14:34
maketh manifest the s of his 2Cor 2:14
are unto God a sweet s of Christ 2Cor 2:15
we are the s of death unto death 2Cor 2:16
to the other the s of life unto 2Cor 2:16
to God for a sweetsmelling s ...... Eph 5:2

SAVOUREST
for thou s not the things that be ...... Mt 16:23
for thou s not the things that be ...... Mk 8:33

SAVOURS
of sweet s unto the God of heaven ...... Ezr 6:10

SAVOURY
And make me s meat, such as I love ...... Gen 27:4
me venison, and make me s meat ...... Gen 27:7
I will make them s meat for thy ...... Gen 27:9
and his mother made s meat ...... Gen 27:14
And she gave the s meat and the ...... Gen 27:17
And he also had made s meat ...... Gen 27:31

SAW See PREFACE.

SAWED
s with saws, within and without, ... 1Kin 7:9

SAWEST
said unto Abraham, What s thou ...... Gen 20:10
thou s it, and didst rejoice 1Sa 19:5
for what s thou 1Sa 28:13
told him, And, behold, thou s him 2Sa 18:11
When thou s a thief, then thou ...... Ps 50:18
lovest their bed where thou s it ...... Is 57:8
Thou, O king, s, and behold a ...... Dan 2:31
Thou s till that a stone was cut ...... Dan 2:34
And whereas thou s the feet ...... Dan 2:41
forasmuch as thou s the iron ...... Dan 2:41
whereas thou s iron mixed with ...... Dan 2:43
Forasmuch as thou s that the ...... Dan 2:45
The tree that thou s, which grew, ... Dan 4:20
The ram which thou s having two ...... Dan 8:20
which thou s in my right hand ...... Rev 1:20
thou s are the seven churches ...... Rev 1:20
The beast that thou s was ...... Rev 17:8
horns which thou s are ten kings ...... Rev 17:12
unto me. The waters which thou s ...... Rev 17:15
horns which thou s upon the beast ...... Rev 17:16
which thou s is that great city ...... Rev 17:18

SAWN
were stoned, they were s asunder ...... Heb 11:37

SAWS
were therein, and put them under s 2Sa 12:31
of hewed stones, sawed with s 1Kin 7:9
were in it, and cut them with s 1Chr 20:3

SAY See PREFACE.

SAYEST
thou s unto me, Bring up this ...... Ex 33:12
will do whatsoever thou s unto me ...... Num 22:17
All that thou s unto me I will do ...... Ruth 3:5
And now thou s, Go, tell thy lord, ... 1Kin 18:11
And now thou s, Go, tell thy lord, ... 1Kin 18:14
Thou s, (but they are but vain 2Kin 18:20
Thou s, Lo, thou hast smitten the 2Chr 25:19
so will we do as thou s ...... Neh 6:3
are no such things done as thou s ...... Neh 6:8
And thou s, How doth God know ...... Job 22:13
and s, Return, ye children of men ...... Ps 90:3
If thou s, Behold, we knew it not ...... Prov 24:12

s thou, (but they are but vain ...... Is 36:5
Why s thou, O Jacob, and speakest, ... Is 40:27
that s in thine heart, I am, and ...... Is 47:8
Yet thou s, Because I am innocent ...... Jer 2:35
plead with thee, because thou s ...... Jer 2:35
Thou s, Prophesy not against ...... Amos 7:16
saying, I know not what thou s ...... Mt 26:70
And Jesus said unto him, Thou s ...... Mt 27:11
thee, and s thou, Who touched me ...... Mk 5:31
neither understand I what thou s ...... Mk 14:68
said unto him, Thou s it ...... Mk 15:2
thee, and s thou, Who touched me ...... Lk 8:45
Master, we know that thou s ...... Lk 20:21
said, Man, I know not what thou s ...... Lk 22:60
answered him and said, Thou s it ...... Lk 23:3
What s thou of thyself ...... Jn 1:22
but what s thou ...... Jn 8:5
how s thou, Ye shall be made free ...... Jn 8:33
and thou s, If a man keep my ...... Jn 8:52
What s thou of him, that he hath ...... Jn 9:17
how s thou, The Son of man must ...... Jn 12:34
how s thou then, Shew us the ...... Jn 14:9
S thou this thing of thyself, or ...... Jn 18:34
answered, Thou s that I am a king ...... Jn 18:37
Thou that s a man should not ...... Rom 2:22
he understandeth not what thou s 1Cor 14:16
Because thou s, I am rich, and ...... Rev 3:17

SAYING See PREFACE.

SAYINGS
Moses told these s unto all the ...... Num 14:39
that when thy s come to pass we ...... Judg 13:17
and came and told him all those s 1Sa 19:7
Of Abijah, and his ways, and his s 2Chr 13:22
written among the s of the seers 2Chr 33:19
their posterity approve their s ...... Ps 49:13
I will utter dark s of old ...... Ps 78:2
of the wise, and their dark s ...... Prov 1:6
Hear, O my son, and receive, my s ...... Prov 4:10
incline thine ear unto my s ...... Prov 4:20
whosoever heareth these s of mine ...... Mt 7:24
one that heareth these s of mine ...... Mt 7:26
when Jesus had ended these s ...... Mt 7:28
when Jesus had finished these s ...... Mt 19:1
Jesus had finished all these s ...... Mt 26:1
all these s were noised abroad ...... Lk 1:65
kept all these s in her heart ...... Lk 2:51
cometh to me, and heareth my s ...... Lk 6:47
s in the audience of the people ...... Lk 7:1
about an eight days after these s ...... Lk 9:28
Let these s sink down into your ...... Lk 9:44
again among the Jews for these s ...... Jn 10:19
loveth me not keepeth not my s ...... Jn 14:24
with these s scarce restrained ...... Acts 14:18
And when they heard these s ...... Acts 19:28
mightest be justified in thy s ...... Rom 3:4
me, These are the true s of God ...... Rev 19:9
These are faithful and true s ...... Rev 22:6
s of the prophecy of this book ...... Rev 22:7
which keep the s of this book ...... Rev 22:9
Seal not the s of the prophecy of ...... Rev 22:10

SCAB
skin of his flesh a rising, a s ...... Lev 13:2
the Lord with a s ...... Lev 13:6
But if the s spread much abroad ...... Lev 13:7
the s spreadeth in the skin, then ...... Lev 13:8
And for a rising, and for a s ...... Lev 14:56
with the emerods, and with the s ...... Deut 28:27
the Lord will smite with a s the ...... Is 3:17

SCABBARD
put up thyself into thy s ...... Jer 47:6

SCABBED
in his eye, or be scurvy, or s ...... Lev 21:20
or having a wen, or scurvy, or s ...... Lev 22:22

SCAFFOLD
For Solomon had made a brasen s 2Chr 6:13

SCALES
s in the waters, in the seas, and ...... Lev 11:9
s in the seas, and in the rivers, ... Lev 11:10
hath no fins nor s in the waters ...... Lev 11:12
that have fins and s shall ye eat ...... Deut 14:9
that hath fins and a ye may not eat ...... Deut 14:10
His s are his pride, shut up ...... Job 41:15
and weighed the mountains in s ...... Is 40:12
of thy rivers to stick unto thy s ...... Eze 29:4
thy rivers shall stick unto thy s ...... Eze 29:4
from his eyes as it had been s ...... Acts 9:18

SCALETH
A wise man s the city of the ...... Prov 21:22

SCALL
it is a dry s, even a leprosy ...... Lev 13:30
look on the plague of the s ...... Lev 13:31
the plague of the s seven days ...... Lev 13:31
if the s spread not, and there be ...... Lev 13:32
the s be not in sight deeper than ...... Lev 13:32
but the s shall he not shave ...... Lev 13:33
that hath the s seven days more ...... Lev 13:33
the priest shall look on the s ...... Lev 13:34
if the s be not spread in the ...... Lev 13:34
But if the s spread much in the ...... Lev 13:35
if the s be spread in the skin, ... Lev 13:36
But if the s be in his sight at a ...... Lev 13:37
the s is healed, he is clean ...... Lev 13:37
manner of plague of leprosy, and s ...... Lev 14:54

S

SCALP
the hairy *s* of such an one as.................... Ps 68:21

SCANT
the *s* measure that is abominable........... Mic 6:10

SCAPEGOAT
LORD, and the other lot for the *s*............ Lev 16:8
on which the lot fell to be the *s*.............. Lev 16:10
go for a *s* into the wilderness................. Lev 16:10
for the *s* shall wash his clothes............. Lev 16:26

SCARCE
Jacob was yet *s* gone out from the..... Gen 27:30
with these sayings *s* restrained............ Acts 14:18
s were come over against Cnidus,..... Acts 27:7

SCARCELY
For *s* for a righteous man will............ Rom 5:7
And if the righteous be *s* saved......... 1Pet 4:18

SCARCENESS
thou shalt eat bread without *s* .... Deut 8:9

SCAREST
Then thou *s* me with dreams, and.......... Job 7:14

SCARLET
and bound upon his hand a *s* thread... Gen 38:28
that had the a thread upon his.............. Gen 38:30
And blue, and purple, and *s*, and fine..... Ex 25:4
linen, and blue, and purple, and *s* ..... Ex 26:1
a vail of blue, and purple, and *s* .... Ex 26:31
tent, of blue, and purple, and *s* .... Ex 26:36
cubits, of blue, and purple, and *s* ...... Ex 27:16
gold, and blue, and purple, and *s*......... Ex 28:5
gold, of blue, and of purple, of *s*.......... Ex 28:6
of gold, of blue, and of purple, and *s*... Ex 28:8
of blue, and of purple, and of *s* .... Ex 28:15
of blue, and of purple, and of *s* .... Ex 28:33
And blue, and purple, and *s*, and fine.... Ex 35:6
was found blue, and purple, and *s*...... Ex 35:23
of blue, and of purple, and of *s* .... Ex 35:25
in blue, and in purple, in *s*................... Ex 35:35
linen, and blue, and purple, and *s* ...... Ex 36:8
a vail of blue, and purple, and *s* .... Ex 36:35
door of blue, and purple, and *s*........... Ex 36:37
of blue, and purple, and *s*................... Ex 38:18
in blue, and in purple, and in *s* .... Ex 38:23
And of the blue, and purple, and *s*...... Ex 39:1
of gold, blue, and purple, and *s*........... Ex 39:2
and in the purple, and in the *s*............ Ex 39:3
of gold, blue, and purple, and *s*........... Ex 39:5
of gold, blue, and purple, and *s*........... Ex 39:8
of blue, and purple, and *s*, and........... Ex 39:24
linen, and blue, and purple, and *s* ...... Ex 39:29
and clean, and cedar wood, and *s* ...... Lev 14:4
it, and the cedar wood, and the *s*........ Lev 14:6
two birds, and cedar wood, and *s* ...... Lev 14:49
wood, and the hyssop, and the *s* .... Lev 14:51
and with the hyssop, and with the *s* ... Lev 14:52
spread upon them a cloth of *s* .... Num 4:8
take cedar wood, and hyssop, and *s*... Num 19:6
thou shalt bind this line of *s* .... Josh 2:18
she bound the *s* line in the................... Josh 2:21
over Saul, who clothed you in *s* 2Sa 1:24
her household are clothed with *s*......... Prov 31:21
Thy lips are like a thread of *s*.............. Song 4:3
though your sins be as *s*, they............. Is 1:18
brought up in *s* embrace dunghills...... Lam 4:5
thereof, shall be clothed with *s* .... Dan 5:7
thou shalt be clothed with *s* .... Dan 5:16
and they clothed Daniel with *s* .... Dan 5:29
red, the valiant men are in *s*................ Nah 2:3
him, and put on him a *s* robe............... Mt 27:28
s wool, and hyssop, and sprinkled...... Heb 9:19
woman sit upon a *s* coloured beast..... Rev 17:3
s colour, and decked with gold and.... Rev 17:4
linen, and purple, and silk, and *s* .... Rev 18:12
in fine linen, and purple, and *s*........... Rev 18:16

SCATTER
from thence did the LORD *s* them......... Gen 11:9
in Jacob, and *s* them in Israel.............. Gen 49:7
I will *s* you among the heathen,........... Lev 26:33
and *s* thou the fire yonder.................... Num 16:37
the LORD shall *s* you among the.......... Deut 4:27
the LORD shall *s* thee among all.......... Deut 28:64
I would *s* them into corners, I............. Deut 32:26
shall *s* them beyond the river,............. 1Kin 14:15
I will *s* you abroad among the............. Neh 1:8
s them by thy power........................... Ps 59:11
s thou the people that delight in....... Ps 68:30
and to *s* them in the lands................... Ps 106:27
Cast forth lightning, and *s* them......... Ps 144:6
s the cummin, and cast in the............. Is 28:25
and the whirlwind shall *s* them........... Is 41:16
I will *s* them also among the............... Jer 9:16
Therefore will I *s* them as the............. Jer 13:24
I will *s* them as with an east............... Jer 18:17
s the sheep of my pasture.................. Jer 23:1
I will *s* into all winds them that.......... Jer 49:32
will *s* them toward all those............... Jer 49:36
part thou shalt *s* in the wind............... Eze 5:2
thee will I *s* into all the winds............ Eze 5:10
I will *s* a third part into all................. Eze 5:12
I will *s* your bones round about........... Eze 6:5
and *s* them over the city...................... Eze 10:2
I will *s* toward every wind all.............. Eze 12:14
when I shall *s* them among the........... Eze 12:15
that I would *s* them among the........... Eze 20:23
I will *s* thee among the heathen,......... Eze 22:15
I will *s* the Egyptians among the......... Eze 29:12
I will *s* the Egyptians among the......... Eze 30:23

I will *s* the Egyptians among the .... Ps 30:26
off his leaves, and *s* his fruit............... Dan 4:14
he shall *s* among them the prey,......... Dan 11:24
to *s* the power of the holy people........ Dan 12:7
came out as a whirlwind to *s* me......... Hab 3:14
over the land of Judah to *s* it.............. Zec 1:21

SCATTERED
lest we be *s* abroad upon the face....... Gen 11:4
So the LORD *s* them abroad from.......... Gen 11:8
So the people were *s* abroad............... Ex 5:12
LORD, and let thine enemies be *s*......... Num 10:35
that they which remained were *s* 1Sa 11:11
and the people were *s* from him.......... 1Sa 13:8
that the people were *s* from me........... 1Sa 13:11
there *s* over the face of all the............ 2Sa 18:8
And he sent out arrows, and *s* them.... 2Sa 22:15
I saw all Israel *s* upon the hills.......... 1Kin 22:17
and all his army were *s* from him........ 2Kin 25:5
all Israel *s* upon the mountains.......... 2Chr 18:16
is a certain people *s* abroad............... Est 3:8
stout lion's whelps are *s* abroad......... Job 4:11
brimstone shall be *s* upon his............. Job 18:15
he sent out his arrows, and *s* them..... Ps 18:14
hast *s* us among the heathen.............. Ps 44:11
for God hath *s* the bones of him......... Ps 53:5
hast cast us off, thou hast *s* us........... Ps 60:1
God arise, let his enemies be *s*........... Ps 68:1
When the Almighty *s* kings in it........... Ps 68:14
thou hast *s* thine enemies with.......... Ps 89:10
workers of iniquity shall be *s*.............. Ps 92:9
Our bones are *s* at the grave's........... Ps 141:7
swift messengers, to a nation *s* .... Is 18:2
the LORD of hosts of a people *s*.......... Is 18:7
up of thyself the nations were *s* .... Is 33:3
hast *s* thy ways to the strangers........ Jer 3:13
and all their flocks shall be *s* .... Jer 10:21
Ye have *s* my flock, and driven........... Jer 23:2
all nations whither I have *s* them....... Jer 30:11
He that *s* Israel will gather him,.......... Jer 31:10
gathered unto thee should be *s* .... Jer 40:15
Israel is a *s* sheep............................. Jer 50:17
and all his army was *s* from him......... Jer 52:8
when ye shall be *s* through the........... Eze 6:8
although I have *s* them among the...... Eze 11:16
countries where ye have been *s*.......... Eze 11:17
shall be *s* toward all winds................. Eze 17:21
of the countries wherein ye are *s*....... Eze 20:34
countries wherein ye have been *s* ...... Eze 20:41
the people among whom they are *s*..... Eze 28:25
the people whither they were *s* .... Eze 29:13
And they were *s*, because there is...... Eze 34:5
of the field, when they were *s* .... Eze 34:5
my flock was *s* upon all the face......... Eze 34:6
he is among his sheep that are *s* .... Eze 34:12
they have been *s* in the cloudy........... Eze 34:12
horns, till ye have *s* them abroad........ Eze 34:21
I *s* them among the heathen, and........ Eze 36:19
that my people be not *s* every man..... Eze 46:18
whom they have *s* among the.............. Joel 3:2
thy people is *s* upon the..................... Nah 3:18
the everlasting mountains were *s* ...... Hab 3:6
are the horns which have *s* Judah....... Zec 1:19
are the horns which have *s* Judah....... Zec 1:21
But I *s* them with a whirlwind.............. Zec 7:14
shepherd, and the sheep shall be *s* .... Zec 13:7
were *s* abroad, as sheep having no..... Mt 9:36
of the flock shall be *s* abroad............. Mt 26:31
shepherd, and the sheep shall be *s* .... Mk 14:27
he hath *s* the proud in the.................. Lk 1:51
of God that were *s* abroad.................. Jn 11:52
is now come, that ye shall be *s* .... Jn 16:32
as many as obeyed him, were *s* .... Acts 5:36
they were all *s* abroad throughout...... Acts 8:1
were *s* abroad went every where........ Acts 8:4
Now they which were *s* abroad upon... Acts 11:19
twelve tribes which are *s* abroad........ Jas 1:1
to the strangers *s* throughout............. 1Pet 1:1

SCATTERETH
he *s* his bright cloud......................... Job 37:11
which *s* the east wind upon the.......... Job 38:24
he *s* the hoar frost like ashes............. Ps 147:16
There is that *s*, and yet...................... Prov 11:24
in the throne of judgment *s* away....... Prov 20:8
A wise king *s* the wicked, and............. Prov 20:26
s abroad the inhabitants thereof......... Is 24:1
gathereth not with me *s* abroad......... Mt 12:30
he that gathereth not with me *s* .... Lk 11:23
catcheth them, and *s* the sheep......... Jn 10:12

SCATTERING
flame of a devouring fire, with *s*......... Is 30:30

SCENT
Yet through the *s* of water it............... Job 14:9
in him, and his *s* is not changed......... Jer 48:11
the *s* thereof shall be as the.............. Hos 14:7

SCEPTRE
The *s* shall not depart from Judah....... Gen 49:10
a *s* shall rise out of Israel, and........... Num 24:17
king shall hold out the golden *s* .... Est 4:11
the golden *s* that was in his hand,....... Est 5:2
near, and touched the top of the *s*...... Est 5:2
out the golden *s* toward Esther........... Est 8:4
the *s* of thy kingdom is a right............ Ps 45:6
of thy kingdom is a right *s*.................. Ps 45:6
wicked, and the *s* of the rulers............ Is 14:5
no strong rod to be a *s* to rule............ Eze 19:14
him that holdeth the *s* from the.......... Amos 1:5
that holdeth the *s* from Ashkelon........ Amos 1:8

the *s* of Egypt shall depart away......... Zec 10:11
a *s* of righteousness is the.................. Heb 1:8
is the *s* of thy kingdom...................... Heb 1:8

SCEPTRES
for the *s* of them that bare rule........... Eze 19:11

SCEVA (*see'-vah*) *A Jewish priest at Ephesus.*
And there were seven sons of one *S.*.. Acts 19:14

SCHISM
there should be no *s* in the body......... 1Cor 12:25

SCHOLAR
the great, the teacher as the *s*........... 1Chr 25:8
doeth this, the master and the *s*......... Mal 2:12

SCHOOL
daily in the *s* of one Tyrannus............ Acts 19:9

SCHOOLMASTER
was our *s* to bring us unto Christ......... Gal 3:24
come, we are no longer under a *s* .... Gal 3:25

SCIENCE
in knowledge, and understanding *s* .... Dan 1:4
oppositions of *s* falsely so.................. 1Ti 6:20

SCOFF
they shall *s* at the kings, and.............. Hab 1:10

SCOFFERS
shall come in the last days *s*............... 2Pet 3:3

SCORCH
given unto him to *s* men with fire........ Rev 16:8

SCORCHED
when the sun was up, they were *s*....... Mt 13:6
But when the sun was up, it was *s*....... Mk 4:6
men were *s* with great heat, and......... Rev 16:9

SCORN
they laughed thee to *s*...................... 2Kin 19:21
but they laughed them to *s*................ 2Chr 30:10
heard it, they laughed us to *s*............. Neh 2:19
he thought *s* to lay hands on.............. Est 3:6
just upright man is laughed to *s*......... Job 12:4
My friends *s* me............................... Job 16:20
and the innocent laugh them to *s*....... Job 22:19
they that see me laugh me to *s*.......... Ps 22:7
a reproach to our neighbours, a *s*....... Ps 44:13
a reproach to our neighbours, a *s*....... Ps 79:4
thee, and laughed thee to *s*............... Is 37:22
thou shalt be laughed to *s*................. Eze 23:32
princes shall be a *s* unto them........... Hab 1:10
And they laughed him to *s*................. Mt 9:24
And they laughed him to *s*................. Mk 5:40
And they laughed him to *s*, knowing.... Lk 8:53

SCORNER
He that reproveth a *s* getteth to......... Prov 9:7
Reprove not a *s*, lest he hate.............. Prov 9:8
but a *s* heareth not rebuke................. Prov 13:1
A *s* seeketh wisdom, and findeth it..... Prov 14:6
A *s* loveth not one that reproveth....... Prov 15:12
Smite a *s*, and the simple will............. Prov 19:25
When the *s* is punished, the................ Prov 21:11
haughty *s* is his name, who................ Prov 21:24
Cast out the *s*, and contention........... Prov 22:10
the *s* is an abomination to men.......... Prov 24:9
the *s* is consumed, and all that.......... Is 29:20

SCORNERS
the *s* delight in their scorning............. Prov 1:22
Surely he scorneth the *s*.................... Prov 3:34
Judgments are prepared for *s* .... Prov 19:29
he stretched out his hand with *s*........ Hos 7:5

SCORNEST
but if thou *s*, thou alone shalt............. Prov 9:12
as an harlot, in that thou *s* hire.......... Eze 16:31

SCORNETH
He is the multitude of the city,............. Job 39:7
she *s* the horse and his rider.............. Job 39:18
Surely he *s* the scorners.................... Prov 3:34
An ungodly witness *s* judgment.......... Prov 19:28

SCORNFUL
nor sitteth in the seat of the *s* .... Ps 1:1
bring a city into a snare....................... Prov 29:8
ye *s* men, that rule this people........... Is 28:14

SCORNING
Job, who drinketh up *s* like water........ Job 34:7
the *s* of those that are at ease............ Ps 123:4
the scorners delight in their *s* .... Prov 1:22

SCORPION
ask an egg, will he offer him a *s* .... Lk 11:12
torment was as the torment of a *s* ..... Rev 9:5

SCORPION PASS See MAALEH-ACRABBIM.

SCORPIONS
wherein were fiery serpents, and *s* ..... Deut 8:15
but I will chastise you with *s* 1Kin 12:11
but I will chastise you with *s* 1Kin 12:14
but I will chastise you with *s* 2Chr 10:11
but I will chastise you with *s* 2Chr 10:14
thee, and thou dost dwell among *s*..... Eze 2:6
power to tread on serpents and *s* .... Lk 10:19
as the *s* of the earth have power........ Rev 9:3
And they had tails like unto *s* .... Rev 9:10

SCOURED
a brasen pot, it shall be both s............ Lev 6:28

SCOURGE
be hid from the s of the tongue........... Job 5:21
If the s slay suddenly, he will.............. Job 9:23
up a s for him according to the............ Is 10:26
overflowing s shall pass through.......... Is 28:15
overflowing s shall pass through.......... Is 28:18
and they will s you in their................. Mt 10:17
to the Gentiles to mock, and to s......... Mt 20:19
shall ye s in your synagogues.............. Mt 23:34
shall mock him, and shall s him........... Mk 10:34
And they shall s him, and put him....... Lk 18:33
he had made a s of small cords........... Jn 2:15
you to s a man that is a Roman........... Acts 22:25

SCOURGED
she shall be s................................... Lev 19:20
and when he had s Jesus, he............... Mt 27:26
Jesus, when he had s him, to be......... Mk 15:15
therefore took Jesus, and s him.......... Jn 19:1

SCOURGES
s in your sides, and thorns in............. Josh 23:13

SCOURGETH
s every son whom he receiveth........... Heb 12:6

SCOURGING
that he should be examined by s......... Acts 22:24

SCOURGINGS
had trial of cruel mockings and s........ Heb 11:36

SCRABBLED
s on the doors of the gate, and.......... 1Sa 21:13

SCRAPE
pour out the dust that they s off........ Lev 14:41
a potsherd to s himself withal............ Job 2:8
I will also s her dust from her,........... Eze 26:4

SCRAPED
he be s within round about............... Lev 14:41
and after he hath s the house............ Lev 14:43

SCREECH
the s owl also shall rest there,........... Is 34:14

SCRIBE
and Seraiah was the s...................... 2Sa 8:17
And Sheva was a s........................... 2Sa 20:25
in the chest, that the king's s........... 2Kin 12:10
the household, and Shebna the s....... 2Kin 18:18
the household, and Shebna the s....... 2Kin 18:37
the household, and Shebna the s....... 2Kin 19:2
the son of Meshullam, the s.............. 2Kin 22:3
priest said unto Shaphan the s.......... 2Kin 22:8
Shaphan the s came to the king,....... 2Kin 22:9
Shaphan the s shewed the king,........ 2Kin 22:10
son of Michaiah, and Shaphan the s... 2Kin 22:12
and the principal s of the host.......... 2Kin 25:19
and Shavsha was s.......................... 1Chr 18:16
the son of Nethaneel the s............... 1Chr 24:6
a counsellour, a wise man, and a s.... 1Chr 27:32
was much money, the king's s........... 2Chr 24:11
by the hand of Jeiel the s................. 2Chr 26:11
answered and said to Shaphan the s.. 2Chr 34:15
Then Shaphan the s told the king,..... 2Chr 34:18
son of Micah, and Shaphan the s....... 2Chr 34:20
Shimshai the s wrote a letter............ Ezr 4:8
the chancellor, and Shimshai the s..... Ezr 4:9
chancellor, and to Shimshai the s...... Ezr 4:17
before Rehum, and Shimshai the s...... Ezr 4:23
he was a ready s in the law of.......... Ezr 7:6
gave unto Ezra the priest, the s........ Ezr 7:11
even a s of the words of the............. Ezr 7:11
a s of the law of the God of............. Ezr 7:12
the s of the law of the God of.......... Ezr 7:21
they spake unto Ezra the s to........... Neh 8:1
Ezra the s stood upon a pulpit of...... Neh 8:4
and Ezra the priest the s.................. Neh 8:9
the Levites, unto Ezra the s.............. Neh 8:13
and of Ezra the priest, the s............. Neh 12:26
of God, and Ezra the s before them... Neh 12:36
the priest, and Zadok the s............... Neh 13:13
Where is the s................................ Is 33:18
over the house, and Shebna the s....... Is 36:3
the household, and Shebna the s........ Is 36:22
the household, and Shebna the s........ Is 37:2
Gemariah the son of Shaphan the s.... Jer 36:10
sat there, even Elishama the s........... Jer 36:12
in the chamber of Elishama the s....... Jer 36:20
of Abdeel, to take Baruch the s......... Jer 36:26
roll, and gave to Baruch the s........... Jer 36:32
in the house of Jonathan the s.......... Jer 37:15
to the house of Jonathan the s.......... Jer 37:20
and the principal s of the host.......... Jer 52:25
And a certain s came, and said unto... Mt 8:19
Therefore every s which is................ Mt 13:52
the s said unto him, Well, Master...... Mk 12:32
where is the s................................. 1Cor 1:20

SCRIBE'S
king's house, into the s chamber....... Jer 36:12
it out of Elishama the s chamber....... Jer 36:21

SCRIBES
and Ahiah, the sons of Shisha, s....... 1Kin 4:3
the families of the s which dwelt....... 1Chr 2:55
and of the Levites there were s......... 2Chr 34:13
Then were the king's s called on....... Est 3:12
Then were the king's s called at........ Est 8:9
the pen of the s is in vain................ Jer 8:8
s of the people together, he.............. Mt 2:4

exceed the righteousness of the s..... Mt 5:20
having authority, and not as the s..... Mt 7:29
certain of the s said within............... Mt 9:3
Then certain of the s and of.............. Mt 12:38
Then came to Jesus s and Pharisees... Mt 15:1
the elders and chief priests and s...... Mt 16:21
Why then say the s that Elias........... Mt 17:10
the chief priests and unto the s........ Mt 20:18
s saw the wonderful things that....... Mt 21:15
Saying, The s and the Pharisees........ Mt 23:2
But woe unto you, s and Pharisees,... Mt 23:13
Woe unto you, s and Pharisees,........ Mt 23:14
Woe unto you, s and Pharisees,........ Mt 23:15
Woe unto you, s and Pharisees,........ Mt 23:23
Woe unto you, s and Pharisees,........ Mt 23:25
Woe unto you, s and Pharisees,........ Mt 23:27
Woe unto you, s and Pharisees,........ Mt 23:29
you prophets, and wise men, and s.... Mt 23:34
the chief priests, and the s............... Mt 26:3
the high priest, where the s............. Mt 26:57
priests mocking him, with the s........ Mt 27:41
had authority, and not as the s........ Mk 1:22
certain of the s sitting there............ Mk 2:6
And when the s and Pharisees saw.... Mk 2:16
the s which came down from............ Mk 3:22
Pharisees, and certain of the s......... Mk 7:1
s asked him, Why walk not thy......... Mk 7:5
and of the chief priests, and s.......... Mk 8:31
Why say the s that Elias must.......... Mk 9:11
the s questioning with them............. Mk 9:14
And he asked the s, What question.... Mk 9:16
the chief priests, and unto the s....... Mk 10:33
And the s and chief priests heard...... Mk 11:18
him the chief priests, and the s........ Mk 11:27
and of the s came, and having.......... Mk 12:28
How say the s that Christ is the....... Mk 12:35
in his doctrine, Beware of the s........ Mk 12:38
the s sought how they might take..... Mk 14:1
from the chief priest and the s......... Mk 14:43
priests and the elders and the s....... Mk 14:53
consultation with the elders and s.... Mk 15:1
said among themselves with the s..... Mk 15:31
And the s and the Pharisees began.... Lk 5:21
But their s and Pharisees murmured.. Lk 5:30
And the s and Pharisees watched him.. Lk 6:7
the elders and chief priests and........ Lk 9:22
Woe unto you, s and Pharisees,........ Lk 11:44
these things unto them, the s........... Lk 11:53
a murmured, saying, This man.......... Lk 15:2
But the chief priests and the s......... Lk 19:47
the s came upon him with the.......... Lk 20:1
the s the same hour sought to lay.... Lk 20:19
certain of the s answering said........ Lk 20:39
Beware of the s, which desire to....... Lk 20:46
s sought how they might kill him...... Lk 22:2
the s came together, and led him..... Lk 22:66
s stood and vehemently accused him.. Lk 23:10
And the s and Pharisees brought...... Jn 8:3
their rulers, and elders, and s.......... Acts 4:5
people, and the elders, and the s...... Acts 6:12
the s that were of the Pharisees'...... Acts 23:9

SCRIP
bag which he had, even in a s........... 1Sa 17:40
Nor s for your journey, neither......... Mt 10:10
no s, no bread, no money in their...... Mk 6:8
journey, neither staves, nor s........... Lk 9:3
Carry neither purse, nor s................ Lk 10:4
I sent you without purse, and s......... Lk 22:35
him take it, and likewise his s........... Lk 22:36

SCRIPTURE
which is noted in the s of truth......... Dan 10:21
And have ye not read this s.............. Mk 12:10
the s was fulfilled, which saith,........ Mk 15:28
This day is this s fulfilled in............. Lk 4:21
and they believed the s, and the...... Jn 2:22
as the s hath said, out of his........... Jn 7:38
Hath not the s said, That Christ....... Jn 7:42
came, and the s cannot be broken..... Jn 10:35
but that the s may be fulfilled,......... Jn 13:18
that the s might be fulfilled.............. Jn 17:12
that the s might be fulfilled............. Jn 19:24
that the s might be fulfilled,............ Jn 19:28
that the s should be fulfilled, A........ Jn 19:36
And again another s saith, They....... Jn 19:37
For as yet they knew not the s......... Jn 20:9
this s must needs have been............ Acts 1:16
The place of the s which he read...... Acts 8:32
his mouth, and began at the same s.. Acts 8:35
For what saith the s........................ Rom 4:3
For the s saith unto Pharaoh,........... Rom 9:17
For the s saith, Whosoever.............. Rom 10:11
ye not what the s saith of Elias....... Rom 11:2
And the s, foreseeing that God........ Gal 3:8
But the s hath concluded all............ Gal 3:22
Nevertheless what saith the s.......... Gal 4:30
For the s saith, Thou shalt not........ 1Ti 5:18
All s is given by inspiration of......... 2Ti 3:16
the royal law according to the s....... Jas 2:8
the s was fulfilled which saith,........ Jas 2:23
ye think that the s saith in vain....... Jas 4:5
also it is contained in the s,............. 1Pet 2:6
of the s is of any private.................. 2Pet 1:20

SCRIPTURES
them, Did ye never read in the s....... Mt 21:42
Ye do err, not knowing the s............ Mt 22:29
how then shall the s be fulfilled....... Mt 26:54
that the s of the prophets might...... Mt 26:56
err, because ye know not the s......... Mk 12:24
but the s must be fulfilled............... Mk 14:49

s the things concerning himself......... Lk 24:27
and while he opened to us the s....... Lk 24:32
that they might understand the s...... Lk 24:45
Search the s.................................. Jn 5:39
reasoned with them out of the s...... Acts 17:2
of mind, and searched the s daily..... Acts 17:11
eloquent man, and mighty in the s... Acts 18:24
shewing by the s that Jesus was...... Acts 18:28
by his prophets in the holy s........... Rom 1:2
comfort of the s might have hope..... Rom 15:4
by the s of the prophets,................. Rom 16:26
for our sins according to the s......... 1Cor 15:3
the third day according to the s....... 1Cor 15:4
child thou hast known the holy s...... 2Ti 3:15
as they do also the other s.............. 2Pet 3:16

SCROLL
shall be rolled together as a s........... Is 34:4
the heaven departed as a s when...... Rev 6:14

SCUM
to the pot whose s is therein........... Eze 24:6
whose s is not gone out of it........... Eze 24:6
that the s of it may be consumed..... Eze 24:11
her great s went not forth out of..... Eze 24:12
her s shall be in the fire................... Eze 24:12

SCURVY
a blemish in his eye, or be s............ Lev 21:20
or maimed, or having a wen, or s...... Lev 22:22

SCYTHIAN (sith´-e-un) A barbarous people
north of the Black Sea.
nor uncircumcision, Barbarian, S........ Col 3:11

SEA
dominion over the fish of the s......... Gen 1:26
dominion over the fish of the s......... Gen 1:28
and upon all the fishes of the s........ Gen 9:2
of Siddim, which is the Salt S........... Gen 14:3
sand which is upon the s shore......... Gen 22:17
thy seed as the sand of the s........... Gen 32:12
corn as the sand of the s................ Gen 41:49
shall dwell at the haven of the s...... Gen 49:13
and cast them into the Red s........... Ex 10:19
between Migdol and the s, over........ Ex 14:2
it shall ye encamp by the s.............. Ex 14:2
overtook them encamping by the s.... Ex 14:9
stretch out thine hand over the s..... Ex 14:16
ground through the midst of the s..... Ex 14:16
stretched out his hand over the s..... Ex 14:21
the Lord caused the s to go back...... Ex 14:21
night, and made the s dry land........ Ex 14:21
of the s upon the dry ground........... Ex 14:22
after them to the midst of the s....... Ex 14:23
Stretch out thine hand over the s..... Ex 14:26
forth his hand over the s................. Ex 14:27
the s returned to his strength.......... Ex 14:27
Egyptians in the midst of the s........ Ex 14:27
that came into the s after them,...... Ex 14:28
dry land in the midst of the s.......... Ex 14:29
Egyptians dead upon the s shore...... Ex 14:30
rider hath he thrown into the s......... Ex 15:1
his host hath he cast into the s........ Ex 15:4
also are drowned in the Red s.......... Ex 15:4
congealed in the heart of the s........ Ex 15:8
with thy wind, the s covered them,... Ex 15:10
and with his horsemen into the s...... Ex 15:19
the waters of the s upon them......... Ex 15:19
on dry land in the midst of the s...... Ex 15:19
rider hath he thrown into the s........ Ex 15:21
brought Israel from the Red s........... Ex 15:22
Lord made heaven and earth, the s... Ex 20:11
Red s even unto the s of the........... Ex 23:31
or shall all the fish of the s be........ Num 11:22
and brought quails from the s.......... Num 11:31
and the Canaanites dwell by the s.... Num 13:29
by the way of the Red s.................. Num 14:25
mount Hor by the way of the Red s.. Num 21:4
Lord, What he did in the Red s......... Num 21:14
of the s unto the wilderness............ Num 33:8
Elim, and encamped by the Red s..... Num 33:10
And they removed from the Red s..... Num 33:11
coast of the salt s eastward............. Num 34:3
out of it shall be at the s................ Num 34:5
have the great s for a border........... Num 34:6
from the great s ye shall point......... Num 34:7
of the s of Chinnereth eastward....... Num 34:11
out of it shall be at the salt s.......... Num 34:12
the plain over against the Red s....... Deut 1:1
and in the south, and by the s side... Deut 1:7
by the way of the Red s.................. Deut 1:40
by the way of the Red s, as the...... Deut 2:1
s of the plain, even the salt s........... Deut 3:17
even unto the s of the plain............. Deut 4:49
Red s to overflow them as they....... Deut 11:4
uttermost s shall your coast be....... Deut 11:24
Neither is it beyond the s............... Deut 30:13
Who shall go over the s for us........ Deut 30:13
land of Judah, unto the utmost s..... Deut 34:2
unto the great s toward the going.... Josh 1:4
up the water of the Red s for you.... Josh 2:10
s of the plain, even the salt s.......... Josh 3:16
Lord your God did to the Red s........ Josh 4:23
Canaanites, which were by the s....... Josh 5:1
the great s over against Lebanon...... Josh 9:1
is upon the s shore in multitude...... Josh 11:4
from the plain to the s of.............. Josh 12:3
unto the s of the plain................... Josh 12:3
even the salt s on the east............. Josh 12:3

even unto the edge of the s of .... Josh 13:27
was from the shore of the salt s .... Josh 15:2
out of that coast were at the s .... Josh 15:4
And the east border was the salt s ...... Josh 15:5
s at the uttermost part of Jordan .... Josh 15:5
out of the border were at the s .... Josh 15:11
west border was to the great s .... Josh 15:12
From Ekron even unto the s .... Josh 15:46
river of Egypt, and the great s .... Josh 15:47
goings out thereof are at the s .... Josh 16:3
the border went out toward the s .... Josh 16:6
goings out thereof were at the s .... Josh 16:8
the outgoings of it were at the s .... Josh 17:9
and The s is his border .... Josh 17:10
the corner of the s southward .... Josh 18:14
salt s at the south end of Jordan .... Josh 18:19
their border went up toward the s .... Josh 19:11
at the s from the coast to Achzib .... Josh 19:29
even unto the great s westward .... Josh 23:4
and ye came unto the s .... Josh 24:6
and horsemen unto the Red s .... Josh 24:6
and brought the s upon them .... Josh 24:7
Asher continued on the s shore .... Judg 5:17
sand by the s side for multitude .... Judg 7:12
the wilderness unto the Red s .... Judg 11:16
is on the s shore in multitude 1Sa 13:5
that is by the s for multitude 2Sa 17:11
And the channels of the s appeared 2Sa 22:16
which is by the s in multitude 1Kin 4:20
the sand that is on the s shore 1Kin 4:29
them down from Lebanon unto the s 1Kin 5:9
I will convey them by s in floats 1Kin 5:9
And he made a molten s, ten cubits 1Kin 7:23
compassing the s round about 1Kin 7:23
the s was set above upon them, and 1Kin 7:25
he set the s on the right side of 1Kin 7:39
And one s, and twelve oxen under 1Kin 7:44
s, and twelve oxen under the s 1Kin 7:44
Eloth, on the shore of the Red s 1Kin 9:26
that had knowledge of the s 1Kin 9:27
For the king had at s a navy of 1Kin 10:22
Go up now, look toward the s 1Kin 18:43
a little cloud out of the s 1Kin 18:44
of Hamath unto the s of the plain 2Kin 14:25
took down the s from off the 2Kin 16:17
the brasen s that was in the 2Kin 25:13
The two pillars, one s, and the 2Kin 25:16
Let the s roar, and the fulness 1Chr 16:32
Solomon made the brasen s 1Chr 18:8
to thee in floties by s to Joppa 2Chr 2:16
Also he made a molten s of ten 2Chr 4:2
compassing the s round about 2Chr 4:3
the s was set above upon them, and .. 2Chr 4:4
but the s was for the priests to 2Chr 4:6
he set the s on the right side of ... 2Chr 4:10
One s, and twelve oxen under it 2Chr 4:15
at the s side in the land of Edom ... 2Chr 8:17
that had knowledge of the s 2Chr 8:18
beyond the s on this side Syria 2Chr 20:2
from Lebanon to the s of Joppa ...... Ezr 3:7
heardest their cry by the Red s ..... Neh 9:9
didst divide the s before them ...... Neh 9:11
midst of the s on the dry land ...... Neh 9:11
land, and upon the isles of the s ... Est 10:1
be heavier than the sand of the s ... Job 6:3
Am I a s, or a whale, thou .... Job 7:12
treadeth upon the waves of the s .... Job 9:8
the earth, and broader than the s ... Job 11:9
the fishes of the s shall declare ... Job 12:8
As the waters fail from the s .... Job 14:11
He divideth the s with his power .... Job 26:12
the s saith, It is not with me ...... Job 28:14
and covereth the bottom of the s .... Job 38:30
Or who shut up the s with doors ..... Job 38:8
entered into the springs of the s ... Job 38:16
he maketh the s like a pot of ...... Job 41:31
of the air, and the fish of the s ... Ps 8:8
of the s together as an heap .... Ps 33:7
carried into the midst of the s .... Ps 46:2
them that are afar off upon the s .. Ps 65:5
He turned the s into dry land ...... Ps 66:6
again from the depths of the s ..... Ps 68:22
have dominion also from s to s ..... Ps 72:8
divide the s by thy strength .... Ps 74:13
Thy way is in the s, and thy path .. Ps 77:19
He divided the s, and caused them .. Ps 78:13
fowls like as the sand of the s .... Ps 78:27
but the s overwhelmed their .... Ps 78:53
sent out her boughs unto the s ..... Ps 80:11
Thou rulest the raging of the s .... Ps 89:9
I will set his hand also in the s .. Ps 89:25
than the mighty waves of the s ..... Ps 93:4
The s is his, and he made it .... Ps 95:5
let the s roar, and the fulness .... Ps 96:11
Let the s roar, and the fulness .... Ps 98:7
So is this great and wide s .... Ps 104:25
him at the s, even at the Red s .... Ps 106:7
He rebuked the Red s also .... Ps 106:9
and terrible things by the Red s ... Ps 106:22
that go down to the s in ships ..... Ps 107:23
The s saw it, and fled .... Ps 114:3
What ailed thee, O thou s .... Ps 114:5
divided the Red s into parts .... Ps 136:13
Pharaoh and his host in the Red s .. Ps 136:15
in the uttermost parts of the s .... Ps 139:9
made heaven, and earth, the s ...... Ps 146:6
When he gave to the s his decree ... Prov 8:29
lieth down in the midst of the s ... Prov 23:34
of a ship in the midst of the s .... Prov 30:19
All the rivers run into the s ...... Eccl 1:7

yet the s is not full .... Eccl 1:7
them like the roaring of the s .... Is 5:30
afflict her by the way of the s .... Is 9:1
Israel be as the sand of the s .... Is 10:22
and as his rod was upon the s .... Is 10:26
LORD, as the waters cover the s .... Is 11:9
and from the islands of the s .... Is 11:11
the tongue of the Egyptian s .... Is 11:15
out, they are gone over the s .... Is 16:8
That sendeth ambassadors by the s ...... Is 18:2
the waters shall fail from the s .... Is 19:5
The burden of the desert of the s ...... Is 21:1
of Zidon, that pass over the s .... Is 23:2
for the s hath spoken, even the .... Is 23:4
even the strength of the s .... Is 23:4
stretched out his hand over the s ...... Is 23:11
they shall cry aloud from the s .... Is 24:14
of Israel in the isles of the s .... Is 24:15
slay the dragon that is in the s .... Is 27:1
earth, ye that go down to the s .... Is 42:10
LORD, which maketh a way in the s ...... Is 43:16
as the waves of the s .... Is 48:18
at my rebuke I dry up the s .... Is 50:2
not it which hath dried the s .... Is 51:10
hath made the depths of the s a .... Is 51:10
LORD thy God, that divided the s .... Is 51:15
wicked are like the troubled s .... Is 57:20
s shall be converted unto thee .... Is 60:5
s with the shepherd of his flock .... Is 63:11
of the s by a perpetual decree .... Jer 5:22
their voice roareth like the s .... Jer 6:23
the isles which are beyond the s .... Jer 25:22
the pillars, and concerning the s ...... Jer 27:19
which divideth the s when the .... Jer 31:35
the sand of the s measured .... Jer 33:22
mountains, and as Carmel by the s ...... Jer 46:18
Ashkelon, and against the s shore ...... Jer 47:7
thy plants are gone over the s .... Jer 48:32
they reach even to the s of Jazer ...... Jer 48:32
thereof was heard in the Red s .... Jer 49:21
there is sorrow on the s .... Jer 49:23
their voice shall roar like the s ...... Jer 50:42
and I will dry up her s, and make ...... Jer 51:36
The s is come up upon Babylon .... Jer 51:42
the brasen s that was in the .... Jer 52:17
The two pillars, one s, and twelve ..... Jer 52:20
thy breach is great like the s .... Lam 2:13
Even the s monsters draw out the .... Lam 4:3
the remnant of the s coast .... Eze 25:16
as the s causeth his waves to .... Eze 26:3
of nets in the midst of the s .... Eze 26:5
the s shall come down from their .... Eze 26:16
city, which wast strong in the s .... Eze 26:17
in the s shall be troubled at .... Eze 26:18
art situate at the entry of the s ...... Eze 27:3
all the ships of the s with their ...... Eze 27:9
and all the pilots of the s .... Eze 27:29
destroyed in the midst of the s .... Eze 27:32
So that the fishes of the s .... Eze 38:20
passengers on the east of the s .... Eze 39:11
into the desert, and go into the s ..... Eze 47:8
being brought forth into the s .... Eze 47:8
kinds, as the fish of the great s ...... Eze 47:10
the north side, from the great s .... Eze 47:17
from the s shall be Hazar-enan .... Eze 47:17
from the border unto the east s .... Eze 47:18
Kadesh, the river to the great s .... Eze 47:19
be the great s from the border .... Eze 47:20
to the river toward the great s .... Eze 48:28
heaven strove upon the great s .... Dan 7:2
great beasts came up from the s .... Dan 7:3
shall be as the sand of the s .... Hos 1:10
the fishes of the s also shall be ...... Hos 4:3
with his face toward the east s .... Joel 2:20
hinder part toward the utmost s .... Joel 2:20
calleth for the waters of the s .... Amos 5:8
they shall wander from s to s .... Amos 8:12
my sight in the bottom of the s .... Amos 9:3
calleth for the waters of the s .... Amos 9:6
sent out a great wind into the s .... Jonah 1:4
was a mighty tempest in the s .... Jonah 1:4
that were in the ship into the s .... Jonah 1:5
of heaven, which hath made the s .... Jonah 1:9
that the s may be calm unto us .... Jonah 1:11
for the s wrought, and was .... Jonah 1:11
up, and cast me forth into the s .... Jonah 1:12
so shall the s be calm unto you .... Jonah 1:12
for the s wrought, and was .... Jonah 1:13
and cast him forth into the s .... Jonah 1:15
the s ceased from her raging .... Jonah 1:15
from s to s, and from mountain .... Mic 7:12
that toucheth the s .... Mic 7:19
He rebuketh the s, and maketh it .... Nah 1:4
about it, whose rampart was the s ...... Nah 3:8
and her wall was from the s .... Nah 3:8
makest men as the fishes of the s ...... Hab 1:14
as the waters cover the s .... Hab 2:14
was thy wrath against the s .... Hab 3:8
through the s with thine horses .... Hab 3:15
heaven, and the fishes of the s .... Zeph 1:3
the inhabitants of the s coast .... Zeph 2:5
the s coast shall be dwellings and ..... Zeph 2:6
heavens, and the earth, and the s ...... Hag 2:6
he will smite her power in the s .... Zec 9:4
shall he from s even to s .... Zec 9:10
through the s with affliction .... Zec 10:11
and shall smite the waves in the s ..... Zec 10:11
half of them toward the former s .... Zec 14:8
half of them toward the hinder s .... Zec 14:8
which is upon the s coast .... Mt 4:13

Nephthalim, by the way of the s .... Mt 4:15
walking by the s of Galilee .... Mt 4:18
brother, casting a net into the s ...... Mt 4:18
arose a great tempest in the s .... Mt 8:24
and rebuked the winds and the s .... Mt 8:26
even the winds and the s obey him ...... Mt 8:27
down a steep place into the s .... Mt 8:32
the house, and sat by the s side .... Mt 13:1
a net, that was cast into the s .... Mt 13:47
was now in the midst of the s .... Mt 14:24
went unto them, walking on the s .... Mt 14:25
saw him walking on the s, they .... Mt 14:26
came nigh unto the s of Galilee .... Mt 15:29
offend them, go thou to the s .... Mt 17:27
drowned in the depth of the s .... Mt 18:6
and be thou cast into the s .... Mt 21:21
for ye compass s and land to make ..... Mt 23:15
as he walked by the s of Galilee ...... Mk 1:16
brother casting a net into the s ...... Mk 1:16
he went forth again by the s side ..... Mk 2:13
with his disciples to the s .... Mk 3:7
again to teach by the s side .... Mk 4:1
into a ship, and sat in the s .... Mk 4:1
was by the s on the land .... Mk 4:1
the wind, and said unto the s .... Mk 4:39
even the wind and the s obey him ...... Mk 4:41
over unto the other side of the s ..... Mk 5:1
down a steep place into the s .... Mk 5:13
and were choked in the s .... Mk 5:13
and he was nigh unto the s .... Mk 5:21
ship was in the midst of the s .... Mk 6:47
unto them, walking upon the s .... Mk 6:48
they saw him walking upon the s .... Mk 6:49
he came unto the s of Galilee .... Mk 7:31
neck, and he were cast into the s ..... Mk 9:42
and be thou cast into the s .... Mk 11:23
from the s coast of Tyre and Sidon .... Lk 6:17
his neck, and he cast into the s ...... Lk 17:2
root, and be thou planted in the s .... Lk 17:6
the s and the waves roaring .... Lk 21:25
Jesus went over the s of Galilee ...... Jn 6:1
which is the s of Tiberias .... Jn 6:1
disciples went down unto the s .... Jn 6:16
went over the s toward Capernaum ...... Jn 6:17
the s arose by reason of a great ...... Jn 6:18
they see Jesus walking on the s .... Jn 6:19
s saw that there was none other .... Jn 6:22
him on the other side of the s .... Jn 6:25
disciples at the s of Tiberias .... Jn 21:1
and did cast himself into the s .... Jn 21:7
made heaven, and earth, and the s ..... Acts 4:24
land of Egypt, and in the Red s .... Acts 7:36
whose house is by the s side .... Acts 10:6
one Simon a tanner by the s side ...... Acts 10:32
made heaven, and earth, and the s .... Acts 14:15
Paul to go as it were to the s .... Acts 17:14
had sailed over the s of Cilicia ..... Acts 27:5
had let down the boat into the s ..... Acts 27:30
and cast out the wheat into the s .... Acts 27:38
committed themselves unto the s ...... Acts 27:40
cast themselves first into the s ..... Acts 27:43
though he hath escaped the s .... Acts 28:4
of Israel be as the sand of the s .... Rom 9:27
and all passed through the s 1Cor 10:1
Moses in the cloud and in the s 1Cor 10:2
wilderness, in perils in the s 2Cor 11:26
is by the s shore innumerable .... Heb 11:12
through the Red s as by dry land ..... Heb 11:29
of the s driven with the wind .... Jas 1:6
serpents, and of things in the s ..... Jas 3:7
Raging waves of the s, foaming .... Jude 13
a s of glass like unto crystal .... Rev 4:6
earth, and such as are in the s ...... Rev 5:13
blow on the earth, nor on the s ...... Rev 7:1
given to hurt the earth and the s .... Rev 7:2
Hurt not the earth, neither the s .... Rev 7:3
with fire was cast into the s .... Rev 8:8
third part of the s became blood ..... Rev 8:8
the creatures which were in the s .... Rev 8:9
he set his right foot upon the s ..... Rev 10:2
which I saw stand upon the s .... Rev 10:5
things that therein are, and the s ... Rev 10:6
angel which standeth upon the s ...... Rev 10:8
of the earth and of the s .... Rev 12:12
And I stood upon the sand of the s ... Rev 13:1
saw a beast rise up out of the s ..... Rev 13:1
made heaven, and earth, and the s .... Rev 14:7
I saw as it were a s of glass .... Rev 15:2
his name, stand on the s of glass .... Rev 15:2
poured out his vial upon the s .... Rev 16:3
every living soul died in the s ...... Rev 16:3
sailors, and as many as trade by s ... Rev 18:17
the s by reason of her costliness .... Rev 18:19
millstone, and cast it into the s .... Rev 18:21
of whom is as the sand of the s ...... Rev 20:8
the s gave up the dead which were .... Rev 20:13
and there was no more s .... Rev 21:1

SEAFARING
that was inhabited of s men .... Eze 26:17

SEAL
name, and sealed them with his s 1Kin 21:8
Levites, and priests, s unto it .... Neh 9:38
s it with the king's ring .... Est 8:8
It is turned as clay to the s .... Job 38:14
up together as with a close s .... Job 41:15
Set me as a s upon thine heart .... Song 8:6
heart, as a s upon thine arm .... Song 8:6
the s law among my disciples .... Is 8:16
s them, and take witnesses in the ...... Jer 32:44

SEALED

to s up the vision and prophecy,	Dan 9:24
s the book, even to the time of	Dan 12:4
set to his s that God is true	Jn 3:33
a s of the righteousness of the	Rom 4:11
for the s of mine apostleship are	1Cor 9:2
God standeth sure, having this s	2Ti 2:19
when he had opened the second s	Rev 6:3
And when he had opened the third s	Rev 6:5
when he had opened the fourth s	Rev 6:7
And when he had opened the fifth s	Rev 6:9
when he had opened the sixth s	Rev 6:12
having the s of the living God	Rev 7:2
when he had opened the seventh s	Rev 8:1
the s of God in their foreheads.	Rev 9:4
S up those things which the seven	Rev 10:4
set a s upon him, that he should	Rev 20:3
S not the sayings of the prophecy.	Rev 22:10

SEALED

me, and s up among my treasures	Deut 32:34
s them with his seal, and sent the.	1Kin 21:8
Now those that s were, Nehemiah,	Neh 10:1
and s with the king's ring	Est 3:12
s with the king's ring, may no	Est 8:8
s it with the king's ring, and	Est 8:10
My transgression is s up in a bag	Job 14:17
a spring shut up, a fountain s	Song 4:12
as the words of a book that is s	Is 29:11
for it is s	Is 29:11
s it, and took witnesses, and	Jer 32:10
both that which was s according	Jer 32:11
of the purchase, both which is s	Jer 32:14
the king s it with his own signet	Dan 6:17
s till the time of the end	Dan 12:9
for him hath God the Father s	Jn 6:27
have s to them this fruit, I will	Rom 15:28
Who hath also s us, and given the.	2Cor 1:22
ye were s with that holy Spirit	Eph 1:13
whereby ye are s unto the day of	Eph 4:30
the backside, s with seven seals	Rev 5:1
till we have s the servants of	Rev 7:3
the number of them which were s	Rev 7:4
and there were s an hundred	Rev 7:4
of Juda were s twelve thousand	Rev 7:5
of Reuben were s twelve thousand	Rev 7:5
of Gad were s twelve thousand	Rev 7:5
of Aser were s twelve thousand	Rev 7:6
Nephtalim were s twelve thousand	Rev 7:6
Manasses were s twelve thousand	Rev 7:6
of Simeon were s twelve thousand	Rev 7:7
of Levi were s twelve thousand	Rev 7:7
Issachar were s twelve thousand	Rev 7:7
of Zabulon were s twelve thousand	Rev 7:8
of Joseph were s twelve thousand	Rev 7:8
Benjamin were s twelve thousand	Rev 7:8

SEALEST

Thou s up the sum, full of wisdom	Eze 28:12

SEALETH

and s up the stars	Job 9:7
of men, and s their instruction,	Job 33:16
He s up the hand of every man	Job 37:7

SEALING

s the stone, and setting a watch	Mt 27:66

SEALS

the backside, sealed with seven s	Rev 5:1
book, and to loose the s thereof	Rev 5:2
and to loose the seven s thereof	Rev 5:5
book, and to open the s	Rev 5:9
when the Lamb opened one of the s	Rev 6:1

SEAM

now the coat was without s	Jn 19:23

SEARCH

He shall not s whether it be good	Lev 27:33
to s out a resting place for them.	Num 10:33
that they may s the land of	Num 13:2
which we have gone to it	Num 13:32
which we passed through to s it	Num 14:7
which Moses sent to s the land	Num 14:36
the men that went to s the land	Num 14:38
they shall s us out the land, and	Deut 1:22
to s you out a place to pitch	Deut 1:33
shalt thou enquire, and make s	Deut 13:14
of Israel to s out the country	Josh 2:2
be come to s out all the country	Josh 2:3
to spy out the land, and to s it	Judg 18:2
said unto them, Go, s the land	Judg 18:2
that I will s him out throughout	1Sa 23:23
to s the city, and to spy it out,	2Sa 10:3
they shall s thine house, and the	1Kin 20:6
unto the worshippers of Baal, S	2Kin 10:23
servants come unto thee for to s	1Chr 19:3
That s may be made in the book of	Ezr 4:15
s hath been made, and it is found	Ezr 4:19
let there be s made in the king's	Ezr 5:17
s was made in the house of the	Ezr 6:1
thyself to the s of their fathers	Job 8:8
it good that he should s you out.	Job 13:9
thou walked in the s of the depth	Job 38:16
Shall not God s this out	Ps 44:21
that our iniquities	Ps 64:6
they accomplish a diligent s	Ps 64:6
and my spirit made diligent s	Ps 77:6
S me, O God, and know my heart	Ps 139:23
of kings is to s out a matter	Prov 25:2
so for men to s their own glory	Prov 25:27
s out by wisdom concerning all	Eccl 1:13
mine heart to know, and to s	Eccl 7:25

I have not found it by secret s	Jer 2:34
the Lord s the heart, I try the	Jer 17:10
when ye shall s for me with all	Jer 29:13
Let us s and try our ways, and turn.	Lam 3:40
none did s or seek after them	Eze 34:6
did my shepherds s for my flock	Eze 34:8
I, even I, will both s my sheep	Eze 34:11
end of seven months shall they s	Eze 39:14
in the top of Carmel, I will s	Amos 9:3
that I will s Jerusalem with	Zeph 1:12
s diligently for the young child	Mt 2:8
S the scriptures	Jn 5:39
S, and look	Jn 7:52

SEARCHED

Laban s all the tent, but found	Gen 31:34
And he s, but found not the images	Gen 31:35
Whereas thou hast s all my stuff	Gen 31:37
And he s, and began at the eldest,	Gen 44:12
s the land from the wilderness of	Num 13:21
of the land which they had s unto	Num 13:32
were of them that s the land	Num 14:6
the days in which ye s the land	Num 14:34
To this, we have s it, so it is	Job 5:27
be prepared it, yea, and s it out	Job 28:27
cause which I knew not I s out	Job 29:16
whilst ye s out what to say	Job 32:11
the number of his years he s out	Job 36:26
O Lord, thou hast s me, and known.	Ps 139:1
of the earth s out beneath	Jer 31:37
the Lord, though it cannot be s	Jer 46:23
How are the things of Esau s out	Obad 6
s the scriptures daily, whether	Acts 17:11
s diligently, who prophesied of	1Pet 1:10

SEARCHEST

mine iniquity, and s after my sin	Job 10:6
s for her as for hid treasures	Prov 2:4

SEARCHETH

for the Lord s all hearts, and	1Chr 28:9
darkness, and s out all perfection.	Job 28:3
he s after every green thing	Job 39:8
but his neighbour cometh and s him.	Prov 18:17
that hath understanding s him out.	Prov 28:11
he that s the hearts knoweth what.	Rom 8:27
for the Spirit s all things	1Cor 2:10
that I am he which s the reins	Rev 2:23

SEARCHING

they returned from s of the land	Num 13:25
Canst thou by s find out God	Job 11:7
s all the inward parts of the	Prov 20:27
there is no s of his	Is 40:28
S what, or what manner of time	1Pet 1:11

SEARCHINGS

there were great s of heart	Judg 5:16

SEARED

conscience with a hot iron	1Ti 4:2

SEAS

of the waters called he S	Gen 1:10
and fill the waters in the s	Gen 1:22
and scales in the waters, in the s	Lev 11:9
have not fins and scales in the s	Lev 11:10
suck of the abundance of the s	Deut 33:19
things that are therein, the s	Neh 9:6
through the paths of the s	Ps 8:8
For he hath founded it upon the s	Ps 24:2
Which stilleth the noise of the s	Ps 65:7
heaven and earth praise him, the s	Ps 69:34
in heaven, and in earth, in the s	Ps 135:6
a noise like the noise of the s	Is 17:12
to me above the sand of the s	Jer 15:8
borders are in the midst of the s	Eze 27:4
glorious in the midst of the s	Eze 27:25
broken thee in the midst of the s	Eze 27:26
of the s in the day of thy ruin	Eze 27:27
thy wares went forth out of the s	Eze 27:33
thou shalt be broken by the s in	Eze 27:34
of God, in the midst of the s	Eze 28:2
are slain in the midst of the s	Eze 28:8
and thou art as a whale in the s	Eze 32:2
of his palace between the s in	Dan 11:45
the deep, in the midst of the s	Jonah 2:3
into a place where two s met	Acts 27:41

SEASON

and they continued a s in ward	Gen 40:4
in his s from year to year	Ex 13:10
offering shalt thou s with salt	Lev 2:13
I will give you rain in due s	Lev 26:4
the passover at his appointed s	Num 9:2
shall keep it in his appointed s	Num 9:3
s among the children of Israel	Num 9:7
of the Lord in his appointed s	Num 9:13
to offer unto me in their due s	Num 28:2
rain of your land in his due s	Deut 11:14
at the s that chasu cometh forth	Deut 16:6
the rain unto thy land in his s	Deut 28:12
dwelt in the wilderness a long s	Josh 24:7
And he said, About this s	2Kin 4:16
bare a son at that s that Elisha	2Kin 4:17
were at that s in the high place	1Chr 21:29
Now for a long s Israel hath been	2Chr 15:3
shock of corn cometh in in his s	Job 5:26
are pierced in me in the night s	Job 30:17
bring forth Mazzaroth in his s	Job 38:32
bringeth forth his fruit in his s	Ps 1:3
and in the night s, and am not	Ps 22:2
give them their meat in due s	Ps 104:27

givest them their meat in due s	Ps 145:15
and a word spoken in due s	Prov 15:23
To every thing there is a s	Eccl 3:1
and they princes eat in due s	Eccl 10:17
a word in s to him that is weary	Is 50:4
former and the latter, in his s	Jer 5:24
not be day and night in their s	Jer 33:20
the shower to come down in his s	Eze 34:26
lives were prolonged for a s	Dan 7:12
and my wine in the s thereof	Hos 2:9
to give them meat in due s	Mt 24:45
saltness, wherewith will ye s it	Mk 9:50
And at the s he sent to the	Mk 12:2
shall be fulfilled in their s	Lk 1:20
he departed from him for a s	Lk 4:13
their portion of meat in due s	Lk 12:42
season that told him of the	Lk 13:1
at the s he sent a servant to the	Lk 20:10
desirous to see him of a long s	Lk 23:8
down at a certain s into the pool.	Jn 5:4
ye were willing for a s to	Jn 5:35
blind, not seeing the sun for a s.	Acts 13:11
he himself stayed in Asia for a s.	Acts 19:22
when I have a convenient s	Acts 24:25
sorry, though it were but for a s	2Cor 7:8
for in due s we shall reap, if we	Gal 6:9
be instant in s	2Ti 4:2
out of s; reprove	2Ti 4:2
he therefore departed for a s	Philem 15
the pleasures of sin for a s	Heb 11:25
rejoice, though now for a s	1Pet 1:6
should rest yet for a little s	Rev 6:11
that he must be loosed a little s	Rev 20:3

SEASONED

savour, wherewith shall it be s	Lk 14:34
s with salt, that ye may know how	Col 4:6

SEASONS

let them be for signs, and for s	Gen 1:14
them judge the people at all s	Ex 18:22
they judged the people at all s	Ex 18:26
ye shall proclaim in their s	Lev 23:4
also instruct me in the night s	Ps 16:7
He appointed the moon for s	Ps 104:19
And he changeth the times and the s	Dan 2:21
render him the fruits in their s	Mt 21:41
you to know the times or the s	Acts 1:7
rain from heaven, and fruitful s	Acts 14:17
I have been with you at all s	Acts 20:18
But of the times and the s	1Th 5:1

SEAT

shalt make a mercy s of pure gold.	Ex 25:17
in the two ends of the mercy s	Ex 25:18
even of the mercy s shall ye make	Ex 25:19
the mercy s with their wings	Ex 25:20
toward the mercy s shall the	Ex 25:20
the mercy s above upon the ark	Ex 25:21
with thee from above the mercy s	Ex 25:22
thou shalt put the mercy s upon	Ex 26:34
before the mercy s that is over	Ex 30:6
the mercy s that is thereupon, and	Ex 31:7
staves thereof, with the mercy s	Ex 35:12
he made the mercy s of pure gold	Ex 37:6
on the two ends of the mercy s	Ex 37:7
out of the mercy s made he the	Ex 37:8
with their wings over the mercy s	Ex 37:9
staves thereof, and the mercy s	Ex 39:35
put the mercy s above upon the	Ex 40:20
the vail before the mercy s	Lev 16:2
in the cloud upon the mercy s	Lev 16:2
s that is upon the testimony	Lev 16:13
finger upon the mercy s eastward	Lev 16:14
before the mercy s shall he	Lev 16:14
and sprinkle it upon the mercy s	Lev 16:15
and before the mercy s	Lev 16:15
mercy s that was upon the ark of	Num 7:89
And he arose out of his s	Judg 3:20
Now Eli the priest sat upon a s	1Sa 1:9
Eli sat upon a s by the wayside	1Sa 4:13
that he fell from off the s	1Sa 4:18
because thy s will be empty	1Sa 20:18
And the king sat upon his s	1Sa 20:25
times, even upon a s by the wall.	1Sa 20:25
The Tachmonite that sat in the s	2Sa 23:8
caused a s to be set for the	1Kin 2:19
either side on the place of the s	1Kin 10:19
and of the place of the mercy s	1Chr 28:11
set his s above all the princes	Est 3:1
that I might come even to his s	Job 23:3
I prepared my s in the street	Job 29:7
sitteth in the s of the scornful	Ps 1:1
on a s in the high places of the	Prov 9:14
where was the s of the image of	Eze 8:3
I am a God, I sit in the s of God	Eze 28:2
cause the s of violence to come	Amos 6:3
and the Pharisees sit in Moses' s	Mt 23:2
he was set down on the judgment s	Mt 27:19
sat down in the judgment s in a	Jn 19:13
and brought him to the judgment s	Acts 18:12
he drave them from the judgment s	Acts 18:16
and beat him before the judgment s	Acts 18:17
day sitting on the judgment s	Acts 25:6
I stand at Caesar's judgment s	Acts 25:10
sat on the judgment s	Acts 25:17
before the judgment s of Christ	Rom 14:10
before the judgment s of Christ	2Cor 5:10
dwellest, even where Satan's s is	Rev 2:13
gave him his power, and his s	Rev 13:2
his vial upon the s of the beast	Rev 16:10

S

SEATED
portion of the lawgiver, was he s...... Deut 33:21

SEATS
the s of them that sold doves,............... Mt 21:12
the chief s in the synagogues,............... Mt 23:6
the s of them that sold doves.............. Mk 11:15
the chief s in the synagogues, and .... Mk 12:39
put down the mighty from their s .... Lk 1:52
the uppermost s in the synagogues ... Lk 11:43
the highest s in the synagogues, ... Lk 20:46
and draw you before the judgment s .... Jas 2:6
the throne were four and twenty s ...... Rev 4:4
upon the s I saw four and twenty .... Rev 4:4
which sat before God on their s......... Rev 11:16

SEATWARD
even to the mercy s were the .... Ex 37:9

SEBA (se´-bah) See SABEANS, SHEBA.
I. A son of Cush.
S, and Havilah, and Sabtah, and......... Gen 10:7
S, and Havilah, and Sabta, and.......... 1Chr 1:9
2. The land.
of Sheba and S shall offer gifts .... Ps 72:10
ransom, Ethiopia and S for thee .... Is 43:3

SEBAM See SHEBAM.

SEBAT (se´-bat) *The eleventh month of the Hebrew year.*
month, which is the month S................ Zec 1:7

SECACAH (se-ca´-cah) *A village in Judah.*
Beth-arabah, Middin, and S........... Josh 15:61

SECHU (se´-ku) *A city in Benjamin.*
came to a great well that is in S......... 1Sa 19:22

SECOND
and the morning were the s day .... Gen 1:8
the name of the s river is Gihon........ Gen 2:13
with lower, s, and third stories........... Gen 6:16
of Noah's life, in the s month............. Gen 7:11
And in the s month, on the seven ...... Gen 8:14
Abraham out of heaven the s time ... Gen 22:15
again, and bare Jacob a s son........... Gen 30:7
Leah's maid bare Jacob a s son......... Gen 30:12
And so commanded he the s, and the Gen 32:19
And he slept and dreamed the s time... Gen 41:5
in the s chariot which he had............. Gen 41:43
the name of the s called he.............. Gen 41:52
now we had returned this s time.... Gen 43:10
they came unto him the s year........... Gen 47:18
And when he went out the s day .... Ex 2:13
on the fifteenth day of the s .... Ex 16:1
curtain, in the coupling of the s......... Ex 26:4
that is in the coupling of the s......... Ex 26:10
the curtain which coupleth the s .... Ex 26:10
for the s side of the tabernacle .... Ex 26:20
the s row shall be an emerald, a ...... Ex 28:18
curtain, in the coupling of the s........ Ex 36:11
was in the coupling of the s .... Ex 36:12
the curtain which coupleth the s .... Ex 36:17
And the s row, an emerald, a.............. Ex 39:11
in the first month in the s year .... Ex 40:17
he shall offer the s for a burnt .... Lev 5:10
it shall be washed the s time .... Lev 13:58
on the first day of the s month .... Num 1:1
in the s year after they were............. Num 1:1
on the first day of the s month .... Num 1:18
shall set forth in the s rank............... Num 2:16
On the s day Nethaneel the son of .... Num 7:18
in the first month of the s year........... Num 9:1
The fourteenth day of the s month.... Num 9:11
When ye blow an alarm the s time..... Num 10:6
the s month, in the s year................. Num 10:11
on the s day ye shall offer .... Num 29:17
the children of Israel the s time........ Josh 5:2
the s day they compassed the city .... Josh 6:14
which took it on the s day .... Josh 10:32
the s lot came forth to Simeon,........ Josh 19:1
even the s bullock of seven years .... Judg 6:25
place, and take the s bullock .... Judg 6:26
the s bullock was offered upon .... Judg 6:28
children of Benjamin the s day .... Judg 20:24
them out of Gibeah the s day .... Judg 20:25
and the name of his s, Abiah........... 1Sa 8:2
which was the s day of the month, ... 1Sa 20:27
no meat the s day of the month 1Sa 20:34
I will not smite him the s time........... 1Sa 26:8
And his s, Chileab, of Abigail the 2Sa 3:3
and when he sent again the s time ... 2Sa 14:29
month Zif, which is the s month......... 1Kin 6:1
appeared to Solomon the s time 1Kin 9:2
the s year of Asa king of Judah........ 1Kin 15:25
And he said, Do it the s time,............ 1Kin 18:34
And they did it the s time 1Kin 18:34
Of the LORD came again the s time ... 1Kin 19:7
the s year of Jehoram the son of 2Kin 1:17
Then he sent out a s on horseback ... 2Kin 9:19
wrote a letter the s time to them 2Kin 10:6
In the s year of Joash son of............ 2Kin 14:1
In the s year of Pekah the son of 2Kin 15:32
and in the s year that which............. 2Kin 19:29
and the priests of the s order 2Kin 23:4
like unto these had the s pillar 2Kin 25:17
priest, and Zephaniah the s priest.... 2Kin 25:18
Eliab, and Abinadab the s, and.......... 1Chr 2:13
the s Daniel, of Abigail the 1Chr 3:1
the s Jehoiakim, the third 1Chr 3:15
the name of the s was Zelophehad.... 1Chr 7:15
Bela his firstborn, Ashbel the s 1Chr 8:1
Ulam his firstborn, Jehush the s........ 1Chr 8:39

Ezer the first, Obadiah the s............. 1Chr 12:9
their brethren of the s degree 1Chr 15:18
was the chief, and Zizah the s........... 1Chr 23:11
Jeriah the first, Amariah the s 1Chr 23:19
Micah the first, and Jesiah the s 1Chr 23:20
to Jehoiarib, the s to Jedaiah,........... 1Chr 24:7
Jeriah the first, Amariah the s 1Chr 24:23
the s to Gedaliah, who with his......... 1Chr 25:9
the firstborn, Jediael the s 1Chr 26:2
the firstborn, Jehozabad the s 1Chr 26:4
Hilkiah the s, Tebaliah the third 1Chr 26:11
over the course of the s month 1Chr 27:4
the son of David king the s time....... 1Chr 29:22
in the s day of the s month 2Chr 3:2
pay unto him, both the s year 2Chr 8:13
keep the passover in the s month..... 2Chr 30:2
unleavened bread in the s month...... 2Chr 30:13
the fourteenth day of the s month..... 2Chr 30:15
put him in the s chariot that he........ 2Chr 35:24
basons of a s sort hundred .... Ezr 1:10
Now in the s year of their coming ..... Ezr 3:8
God at Jerusalem, in the s month ..... Ezr 3:8
So it ceased unto the s year of......... Ezr 4:24
on the s day were gathered .... Neh 8:13
son of Senuah was s over the city .... Neh 11:9
Bakbukiah the s among his .... Neh 11:17
into the s house of the women.......... Est 2:14
were gathered together the s time .... Est 2:19
the s day at the banquet of wine ...... Est 7:2
to confirm this s letter of Purim......... Est 9:29
and the name of the s, Kezia............ Job 42:14
is one alone, and there is not a s ...... Eccl 4:8
with the s child that shall stand .... Eccl 4:15
shall set his hand again the s .... Is 11:11
the s year that which springeth .... Is 37:30
the LORD came unto me the s time..... Jer 1:13
the LORD came unto me the s time..... Jer 13:3
came unto Jeremiah the s time.......... Jer 33:1
it came to pass the s day after .... Jer 41:4
The s pillar also and the .... Jer 52:22
priest, and Zephaniah the s priest.... Jer 52:24
the s face was the face of a man,..... Eze 10:14
on the s day thou shalt offer .... Eze 43:22
in the s year of the reign of .... Dan 2:1
And behold another beast, a s.......... Dan 7:5
LORD came unto Jonah the s time ..... Jonah 3:1
shall not rise up the s time .... Nah 1:9
in the s year of Darius the king,........ Hag 1:1
In the s year of Darius the king......... Hag 1:15
In the s year of Darius, came the ..... Hag 2:10
in the s year of Darius, came the ..... Zec 1:1
in the s year of Darius, came the ..... Zec 1:7
in the s chariot black horses .... Zec 6:2
And he came to the s, and said .... Mt 21:30
Likewise the s also, and the third...... Mt 22:26
the s is like unto it, Thou shalt .... Mt 22:39
He went away again the s time.......... Mt 26:42
the took her, and died, neither .... Mk 12:21
the s is like, namely this, Thou .... Mk 12:31
And the s time the cock crew............ Mk 14:72
it came to pass on the s sabbath ..... Lk 6:1
if he shall come in the s watch......... Lk 12:38
the s came, saying, Lord, thy .... Lk 19:18
the s took her to wife, and he .... Lk 20:30
can be enter the s time into his .... Jn 3:4
This is again the s miracle that......... Jn 4:54
He saith to him again the s time....... Jn 21:16
at the s time Joseph was made .... Acts 7:13
spake unto him again the s time ...... Acts 10:15
the s ward, they came unto the .... Acts 12:10
it is also written in the s psalm......... Acts 13:33
the s man is the Lord from heaven.... 1Cor 15:47
that ye might have a s benefit........... 2Cor 1:15
as if I were present, the s time 2Cor 13:2
The s epistle to the Corinthians .... 2Cor s
The s epistle to the .... 2Th s
The s epistle unto Timotheus,.......... 2Ti s
brought before Nero the s time .... 2Ti s
the first and s admonition reject ...... Titus 3:10
place have been sought for the s ..... Heb 8:7
And after the s veil, the .... Heb 9:3
But into the s went the high .... Heb 9:7
for him shall he appear the s .... Heb 9:28
that he may establish the s .... Heb 10:9
This s epistle, beloved, I now............ 2Pet 3:1
shall not be hurt of the s death........ Rev 2:11
the s beast like a calf, and the.......... Rev 4:7
And when he had opened the s seal... Rev 6:5
I heard the s beast say .... Rev 6:3
the s angel sounded, and as it .... Rev 8:8
The s woe is past .... Rev 11:14
the s angel poured out his vial.......... Rev 16:3
on such the s death hath no power.... Rev 20:6
This is the s death .... Rev 20:14
which is the s death.......................... Rev 21:8
the s, sapphire................................. Rev 21:19

SECONDARILY
s prophets, thirdly teachers, ... 1Cor 12:28

SECRET
soul, come not thou into their s .... Gen 49:6
and putteth it in a s place................. Deut 27:15
The s things belong unto the LORD ... Deut 29:29
I have a s errand unto thee, O.......... Judg 3:19
after my name, seeing it is s .... Judg 13:18
they had emerods in their s parts..... 1Sa 5:9
morning, and abide in a s place 1Sa 19:2
that thou wouldest keep me s............ Job 14:13
Hast thou heard the s of God............ Job 15:8

is there any s thing with thee .... Job 15:11
shall be hid in his s places .... Job 20:26
when the s of God was upon my .... Job 29:4
and bind their faces in s.................. Job 40:13
in the s places doth he murder......... Ps 10:8
a young lion lurking in a s places ..... Ps 17:12
He made darkness his s place .... Ps 18:11
cleanse thou me from s faults .... Ps 19:12
The s of the LORD is with them.......... Ps 25:14
in the s of his tabernacle shall.......... Ps 27:5
Thou shalt hide them in the s of....... Ps 31:20
Hide me from the s counsel of the ... Ps 64:2
may shoot in a s at the perfect......... Ps 64:4
thee in the s place of thunder........... Ps 81:7
our s sins in the light of thy .... Ps 90:8
He that dwelleth in the s place......... Ps 91:1
from thee, when I was made in s ...... Ps 139:15
but his s is with the righteous.......... Prov 3:32
and bread eaten in s is pleasant...... Prov 9:17
A gift in s pacifieth anger................. Prov 21:14
and discover not a s to another .... Prov 25:9
Open rebuke is better than s love .... Prov 27:5
into judgment, with every s thing ..... Eccl 12:14
in the s places of the stairs,............. Song 2:14
LORD will discover their s parts......... Is 3:17
and hidden riches of s places,......... Is 45:3
I have not spoken in s, in a dark ...... Is 45:19
spoken in s from the beginning .... Is 48:16
I have not found it by s search .... Jer 2:34
Can any hide himself in s places ..... Jer 23:24
I have uncovered his s places.......... Jer 49:10
in wait, and as a lion in s places ..... Lam 3:10
and they shall pollute my s place ..... Eze 7:22
there is no s that they can hide........ Eze 28:3
God of heaven concerning this s ..... Dan 2:18
Then was the s revealed unto .... Dan 2:19
He revealeth the deep and a things... Dan 2:22
The s which the king hath .... Dan 2:27
this s is not revealed to me for .... Dan 2:30
seeing thou couldest reveal this s ... Dan 2:47
no s troubleth thee, tell me the........ Dan 4:9
but he revealeth his s unto his......... Amos 3:7
That thine aims may be in s .... Mt 6:4
in s himself shall reward thee........... Mt 6:4
pray to thy Father which is in s .... Mt 6:6
in s shall reward thee openly............ Mt 6:6
but unto thy Father which is in s ...... Mt 6:18
and thy Father, which seeth in s ...... Mt 6:18
kept s from the foundation of the ..... Mt 13:35
behold, he is in the s chambers....... Mt 24:26
neither was any thing kept s .... Mk 4:22
For nothing is s, that shall not......... Lk 8:17
a candle, putteth it in a s place........ Lk 11:33
no man that doeth any thing in s ..... Jn 7:4
not openly, but as it were in s .... Jn 7:10
and in s have I said nothing.............. Jn 18:20
which was kept s since the world ..... Rom 16:25
which are done of them in s .... Eph 5:12

SECRETLY
Wherefore didst thou flee away s ..... Gen 31:27
as thine own soul, entice thee s ...... Deut 13:6
he that smiteth his neighbour s .... Deut 27:24
want of all things s in the siege .... Deut 28:57
out of Shittim two men to spy s .... Josh 2:1
saying, Commune with David s 1Sa 18:22
David knew that Saul s practised 1Sa 23:9
For thou didst it s 2Sa 12:12
did s those things that were not....... 2Kin 17:9
Now a thing was s brought to me...... Job 4:12
if ye do s accept persons................. Job 13:10
And my heart hath been s enticed.... Job 31:27
He lieth in wait s as a lion in .... Ps 10:9
thou shalt keep them s in a .... Ps 31:20
the king asked him s in his house .... Jer 37:17
the king sware s unto Jeremiah........ Jer 38:16
spake to Gedaliah in Mizpah s .... Jer 40:15
was as to devour the poor s .... Hab 3:14
way, and called Mary her sister s ..... Jn 11:28
but s for fear of the Jews,................. Jn 19:38

SECRETS
her hand, and taketh him by the s .... Deut 25:11
would shew thee the s of wisdom ..... Job 11:6
he for knoweth the s of the heart ..... Ps 44:21
A talebearer revealeth s .... Prov 11:13
about as a talebearer revealeth s .... Prov 20:19
a God in heaven that revealeth s ..... Dan 2:28
he that revealeth s maketh known.... Dan 2:29
LORD of kings, and a revealer of s .... Dan 2:47
the s of men by Jesus Christ .... Rom 2:16
thus are the s of his heart made...... 1Cor 14:25

SECT
(which is the s of the Sadducees,.... Acts 5:17
there rose up certain of the s of....... Acts 15:5
of the s of the Nazarenes................. Acts 24:5
s of our religion I lived a .... Acts 26:5
for as concerning this s, we know.... Acts 28:22

SECU See SECHU.

SECUNDUS (se-cun´-dus) *A Christian in Thessalonica.*
Thessalonians, Aristarchus and S .... Acts 20:4

SECURE
for the host was s............................ Judg 8:11
of the Zidonians, quiet and s .... Judg 18:7
go, ye shall come unto a people s .... Judg 18:10
a people that were at quiet and s,..... Judg 18:27
And thou shalt be s, because there .. Job 11:18

and they that provoke God are s............ Job 12:6
we will persuade him, and s you........... Mt 28:14

SECURELY
seeing he dwelleth s by thee.................. Prov 3:29
pass by as men averse from war........... Mic 2:8

SECURITY
And when they had taken s of Jason ... Acts 17:9

SEDITION
that they have moved s within the........ Ezr 4:15
and s have been made therein.............. Ezr 4:19
for a certain s made in the city............ Lk 23:19
released unto them him that for s .... Lk 23:25
a mover of s among all the Jews .... Acts 24:5

SEDITIONS
emulations, wrath, strife, s................... Gal 5:20

SEDUCE
shall shew signs and wonders, to s...... Mk 13:22
you concerning them that s you........... 1Jn 2:26
to s my servants to commit................... Rev 2:20

SEDUCED
Manasseh s them to do more evil 2Kin 21:9
they have also s Egypt, even they....... Is 19:13
because they have s my people........... Eze 13:10

SEDUCERS
s shall wax worse and worse,................ 2Ti 3:13

SEDUCETH
but the way of the wicked s them .... Prov 12:26

SEDUCING
faith, giving heed to s spirits................ 1Ti 4:1

SEE See PREFACE.

SEED
forth grass, the herb yielding s............ Gen 1:11
whose s is in itself, upon the............... Gen 1:11
herb yielding s after his kind,.............. Gen 1:12
whose s was in itself, after his .... Gen 1:12
given you every herb bearing s............ Gen 1:29
is the fruit of a tree yielding s .... Gen 1:29
and between thy s and her s .... Gen 3:15
me another s instead of Abel................ Gen 4:25
to keep s alive upon the face of .... Gen 7:3
you, and with your s after you............. Gen 9:9
Unto thy s will I give this land .... Gen 12:7
I give it, and to thy s for ever............. Gen 13:15
I will make thy s as the dust of .... Gen 13:16
then shall thy s also be numbered....... Gen 13:16
to me thou hast given no s................... Gen 15:3
said unto him, So shall thy s be.......... Gen 15:5
Know of a surety that thy s shall........ Gen 15:13
Unto thy s have I given this land....... Gen 15:18
I will multiply thy s exceedingly......... Gen 16:10
thy s after thee in their....................... Gen 17:7
unto thee, and to thy s after thee........ Gen 17:7
to thy s after thee, the land................ Gen 17:8
thy s after thee in their....................... Gen 17:9
me and you and thy s after thee .... Gen 17:10
stranger, which is not of thy s .... Gen 17:12
covenant, and with thy s after him ..... Gen 17:19
we may preserve s of our father.......... Gen 19:32
we may preserve s of our father.......... Gen 19:34
in Isaac shall thy s be called............... Gen 21:12
a nation, because he is thy s................ Gen 21:13
thy s as the stars of the heaven........... Gen 22:17
thy s shall possess the gate of .... Gen 22:17
shall all the nations of................. Gen 22:18
Unto thy s will I give this land .... Gen 24:7
let thy s possess the gate of .... Gen 24:60
for unto thee, and unto thy s .... Gen 26:3
I will make thy s to multiply as.......... Gen 26:4
will give unto thy s all these .... Gen 26:4
in thy s shall all the nations of .... Gen 26:4
multiply thy s for my servant............. Gen 26:24
to thee, and to thy s with thee............ Gen 28:4
thee will I give it, and to thy s .... Gen 28:13
thy s shall be as the dust of the.......... Gen 28:14
in thy s shall all the families.............. Gen 28:14
make thy s as the sand of the sea .... Gen 32:12
to thy s after thee will I give.............. Gen 35:12
raise up s to thy brother...................... Gen 38:8
knew that the s should not be his........ Gen 38:9
he should give s to his brother............ Gen 38:9
Jacob, and all his s with him.............. Gen 46:6
all his s brought he with him.............. Gen 46:7
and give us s, that we may live,.......... Gen 47:19
lo, here is s for you, and ye................. Gen 47:23
for s of the field, and for your............ Gen 47:24
will give this land to thy s.................. Gen 48:4
lo, God hath shewed me also thy s...... Gen 48:11
his s shall become a multitude of........ Gen 48:19
and it was like coriander s.................. Ex 16:31
ever unto him and his s after him........ Ex 28:43
to his s throughout their...................... Ex 30:21
I will multiply your s as the............... Ex 32:13
spoken of will I give unto your s......... Ex 32:13
Unto thy s will I give it........................ Ex 33:1
any sowing s which is to be sown .... Lev 11:37
if any water be put upon the s .... Lev 11:38
If a woman have conceived s............... Lev 12:2
if any man's s of copulation go........... Lev 15:16
whereon is the s of copulation............ Lev 15:17
shall lie with s of copulation .... Lev 15:18
of him whose s goeth from him, and... Lev 15:32
thou shalt not let any of thy s .... Lev 18:21
not sow thy field with mingled s........ Lev 19:19
giveth any of his s unto Molech.......... Lev 20:2

hath given of his s unto Molech.......... Lev 20:3
he giveth of his s unto Molech .... Lev 20:4
he profane his s among his people....... Lev 21:17
Whosoever he be of thy s in their....... Lev 22:3
s of Aaron the priest shall come......... Lev 22:4
all your s among your generations....... Lev 22:3
of the s of Aaron is a leper................. Lev 22:4
or a man whose s goeth from him .... Lev 22:4
and ye shall sow your s in vain........... Lev 26:16
be according to the s thereof .... Lev 27:16
a homer of barley s shall be................ Lev 27:16
whether of the s of the land............... Lev 27:30
be free, and shall conceive s............... Num 5:28
And the manna was as coriander s...... Num 11:7
and his s shall possess it...................... Num 14:24
which is not of the s of Aaron............. Num 16:40
unto thee and to thy s with thee......... Num 18:19
it is no place of s, or of figs,.............. Num 20:5
his s shall be in many waters, and...... Num 24:7
his s after him, even the..................... Num 25:13
them and to their s after them............ Deut 1:8
he chose their s after them.................. Deut 4:37
and he chose their s after them........... Deut 10:15
to give unto them and to their s .... Deut 11:9
out, where thou sowedst thy s .... Deut 11:10
tithe all the increase of thy s .... Deut 14:22
of thy s which thou hast sown............ Deut 22:9
carry much s out into the field .... Deut 28:38
a wonder, and upon thy s for ever ...... Deut 28:46
and the plagues of thy s, even............ Deut 28:59
heart, and the heart of thy s .... Deut 30:6
that both thou and thy s may live....... Deut 30:19
out of the mouths of their s................ Deut 31:21
saying, I will give it unto thy s .... Deut 34:4
of Canaan, and multiplied his s .... Josh 24:3
of the s which the LORD shall.............. Ruth 4:12
The LORD give thee s of this............... 1Sa 2:20
he will take the tenth of your s 1Sa 8:15
between my s and thy s for ever 1Sa 20:42
wit not cut off my s after me.............. 1Sa 24:21
this day of Saul, and of his s 2Sa 4:8
I will set up thy s after thee............... 2Sa 7:12
David, and to his s for evermore......... 2Sa 22:51
upon the head of his s for ever........... 1Kin 2:33
but upon David, and upon his s 1Kin 2:33
he was of the king's s in Edom........... 1Kin 11:14
for this afflict the s of David.............. 1Kin 11:39
would contain two measures of s........ 1Kin 18:32
unto thee, and unto thy s for ever 2Kin 5:27
and destroyed all the s royal 2Kin 11:1
LORD rejected all the s of Israel.......... 2Kin 17:20
son of Elishama, of the s royal............ 2Kin 25:25
O ye s of Israel his servant, ye........... 1Chr 16:13
I will raise up thy s after thee............ 1Chr 17:11
gavest it to the s of Abraham thy....... 2Chr 20:7
destroyed all the s royal of the........... 2Chr 22:10
their father's house, and their s.......... Ezr 2:59
so that the holy s have mingled.......... Ezr 9:2
their father's house, nor their s .... Neh 7:61
the s of Israel separated...................... Neh 9:2
to give it, I say, to his s...................... Neh 9:8
Mordecai be of the s of the Jews........ Esth 6:13
took upon them, and upon their s .... Esth 9:27
of them perish from their s .... Esth 9:28
for themselves and for their s .... Esth 9:31
and speaking peace to all his s .... Esth 10:3
also that thy s shall be great .... Job 5:25
Their s is established in their.............. Job 21:8
that he will bring home thy s .... Job 39:12
David, and to his s for evermore......... Ps 18:50
their s from among the children.......... Ps 21:10
all ye the s of Jacob, glorify............... Ps 22:23
fear him, all ye the s of Israel............. Ps 22:23
A s shall serve him............................ Ps 22:30
his s shall inherit the earth................. Ps 25:13
forsaken, nor his s begging bread....... Ps 37:25
and his s is blessed............................ Ps 37:26
but the s of the wicked shall be.......... Ps 37:28
The s also of his servants shall........... Ps 69:36
Thy s will I establish for ever............. Ps 89:4
His s also will I make to endure.......... Ps 89:29
His s shall endure for ever, and.......... Ps 89:36
his s shall be established...................... Ps 102:28
O ye s of Abraham his servant, ye...... Ps 105:6
To overthrow their s also among......... Ps 106:27
His s shall be mighty upon earth........ Ps 112:2
and weepeth, bearing precious s......... Ps 126:6
but the s of the righteous shall........... Prov 11:21
In the morning sow thy s, and in........ Eccl 11:6
a s of evildoers, children that............. Is 1:4
the s of an homer shall yield an.......... Is 5:10
so the holy s shall be the..................... Is 6:13
the s of evildoers shall never be......... Is 14:20
shalt thou make thy s to flourish .... Is 17:11
And by great waters the s of Sihor...... Is 23:3
shall he give the rain of thy s .... Is 30:23
the s of Abraham my friend................. Is 41:8
I will bring thy s from the east........... Is 43:5
I will pour my spirit upon thy s .... Is 44:3
I said not unto the s of Jacob.............. Is 45:19
all the s of Israel be justified............. Is 45:25
Thy s also had been as the sand,........ Is 48:19
for sin, he shall see his s..................... Is 53:10
thy s shall inherit the Gentiles.......... Is 54:3
that it may give s to the sower........... Is 55:10
the s of the adulterer and the............. Is 57:3
transgression, a s of falsehood,.......... Is 57:4
nor out of the mouth of thy s .... Is 59:21
out of the mouth of thy seed's s......... Is 59:21
their s shall be known among the....... Is 61:9

that they are the s which the............. Is 61:9
will bring forth a s out of Jacob .... Is 65:9
for they are the s of the blessed......... Is 65:23
saith the LORD, so shall your s .... Is 66:22
a noble vine, wholly a right s .... Jer 2:21
even the whole s of Ephraim.............. Jer 7:15
are they cast out, he and his s............ Jer 22:28
for no man of his s shall prosper........ Jer 22:30
which led the s of the house of.......... Jer 23:8
Shemaiah the Nehelamite, and his s... Jer 29:32
thy s from the land of their................ Jer 30:10
house of Judah with the s of man...... Jer 31:27
of man, and with the s of beast......... Jer 31:27
then the s of Israel also shall............. Jer 31:36
the s of Israel for all that they.......... Jer 31:37
the s of David my servant.................. Jer 33:22
will I cast away the s of Jacob........... Jer 33:26
s to be rulers over the s of .... Jer 33:26
be rulers over the s of David.............. Jer 33:26
shall ye build house, nor sow s .... Jer 35:7
we vineyard, nor field, nor s .... Jer 35:9
And I will punish him and his s .... Jer 36:31
son of Elishama, of the s royal.......... Jer 41:1
thy s from the land of their................ Jer 46:27
his s is spoiled, and his brethren....... Jer 49:10
He took also of the s of the land........ Eze 17:5
And hath taken of the king's s .... Eze 17:13
unto the s of the house of Jacob........ Eze 20:5
Levites that be of the s of Zadok....... Eze 43:19
of the s of the house of Israel........... Eze 44:22
of Israel, and of the king's s.............. Dan 1:3
themselves with the s of men............ Dan 2:43
of the s of the Medes, which was....... Dan 9:1
The s is rotten under their clods........ Joel 1:17
of grapes him that soweth s .... Amos 9:13
Is the s yet in the barn...................... Hag 2:19
For the s shall be prosperous............. Zec 8:12
Behold, I will corrupt your s............. Mal 2:3
That he might seek a godly s.............. Mal 2:15
which received s by the way side....... Mt 13:19
received the s into stony places......... Mt 13:20
He also that received s among the...... Mt 13:22
But he that received s into the........... Mt 13:23
which sowed good s in his field......... Mt 13:24
not thou sow good s in thy field........ Mt 13:27
is like to a grain of mustard s........... Mt 13:31
the good s is the Son of man............. Mt 13:37
the good s are the children of............ Mt 13:38
faith as a grain of mustard s............. Mt 17:20
raise up s unto his brother................ Mt 22:24
man should cast s into the ground..... Mk 4:26
the s should spring and grow up,....... Mk 4:27
It is like a grain of mustard s .... Mk 4:31
raise up s unto his brother................ Mk 12:19
took a wife, and dying left no s......... Mk 12:20
and died, neither left he any s........... Mk 12:21
the seven had her, and left no s......... Mk 12:22
to Abraham, and to his s for ever...... Lk 1:55
A sower went out to sow his s........... Lk 8:5
The s is the word of God.................... Lk 8:11
It is like a grain of mustard s .... Lk 13:19
had faith as a grain of mustard s...... Lk 17:6
raise up s unto his brother................ Lk 20:28
Christ cometh of the s of David......... Jn 7:42
answered him, We be Abraham's s ..... Jn 8:33
I know that ye are Abraham's............ Jn 8:37
in thy s shall all the kindreds........... Acts 3:25
to his s after him, when as yet.......... Acts 7:5
That his s should sojourn in a........... Acts 7:6
Of this man's s hath God................... Acts 13:23
which was made of the s of David..... Rom 1:3
was not to Abraham, or to his s .... Rom 4:13
might be sure to all the s .... Rom 4:16
as spoken, So shall thy s be.............. Rom 4:18
because they are the s of Abraham .... Rom 9:7
In Isaac shall thy s be called............. Rom 9:7
the promise are counted for the s ...... Rom 9:29
Lord of Sabaoth had left us a s.......... Rom 9:29
of the s of Abraham, of the tribe....... Rom 11:1
him, and to every s his own body 1Cor 15:38
Now he that ministereth s to the....... 2Cor 9:10
food, and multiply your s sown 2Cor 9:10
Are they the s of Abraham................. 2Cor 11:22
his s were the promises made............ Gal 3:16
but as of one, And to thy s .... Gal 3:16
till the s should come to whom.......... Gal 3:19
Christ's, then are ye Abraham's s ...... Gal 3:29
that Jesus Christ of the s of 2Ti 2:8
he took on him the s of Abraham....... Heb 2:16
received strength to conceive s.......... Heb 11:11
in Isaac shall thy s be called............. Heb 11:18
born again, not of corruptible s......... 1Pet 1:23
for his s remaineth in him................. 1Jn 3:9
war with the remnant of her s........... Rev 12:17

SEED'S
out of the mouth of thy s seed........... Is 59:21

SEEDS
sow thy vineyard with divers s.......... Deut 22:9
some s fell by the way side, and........ Mt 13:4
indeed is the least of all s................. Mt 13:32
all the s that be in the earth............. Mk 4:31
He saith not, And to s, as of many..... Gal 3:16

SEEDTIME
While the earth remaineth, s............. Gen 8:22

SEED
s I go childless, and the steward........ Gen 15:2
S that Abram shall surely.................. Gen 18:18
Lot s them rose up to meet them....... Gen 19:1

S

s thou hast not withheld thy son, ... Gen 22:12
s the LORD hath prospered my way ... Gen 24:56
s ye hate me, and have sent me ...... Gen 26:27
Esau s that the daughters of ...... Gen 28:8
s that his life is bound up in ...... Gen 44:30
the dumb, or deaf, or the s ...... Ex 4:11
s he hath dealt deceitfully with ...... Ex 21:8
hurt, or driven away, no man s it ...... Ex 22:10
s ye were strangers in the land ...... Ex 23:9
s it is most holy, and God hath ...... Lev 10:17
s all the people were in ...... Num 15:26
s all the congregation are holy, ... Num 16:3
s him not, and cast it upon him, ... Num 35:23
s I am a great people, forasmuch ...... Josh 17:14
s ye rebel to day against the ...... Josh 22:18
after my name, s it is secret ...... Judg 13:18
s I have a Levite to my priest ...... Judg 17:13
s that this man is come into mine ...... Judg 19:23
s we have sworn by the LORD that ...... Judg 21:7
s all the women are destroyed out of ...... Judg 21:16
s the LORD hath testified against ...... Ruth 1:21
of me, s I am a stranger ...... Ruth 2:10
s I have rejected him from 1Sa 16:1
s he hath defiled the armies of 1Sa 17:36
s that I am a poor man, and, ... 1Sa 18:23
s he is the anointed of the LORD 1Sa 24:6
s the LORD hath withholden thee 1Sa 25:26
s the LORD is departed from 1Sa 28:16
concerning Amnon, s he was dead 2Sa 13:39
s I go whither I may, return thou. 2Sa 15:20
s that thou hast no tidings ready 2Sa 18:22
s the speech of all Israel is 2Sa 19:11
this day, thine eyes even s it 1Kin 1:48
Solomon s the young man that he. 1Kin 11:28
s your master's sons are with you 2Kin 10:2
s there is no wrong in mine hands 1Chr 12:17
s the heaven and heaven of heaven 2Chr 2:6
s that thou our God hast punished ...... Ezr 9:13
sad, s thou art not sick ...... Neh 2:2
S his days are determined, ... Job 14:5
s the root of the matter is found ...... Job 19:28
s he judgeth those that are high, ... Job 21:22
s in your answers there remaineth ...... Job 21:34
s times are not hidden from the ...... Job 24:1
S it is hid from the eyes of all ...... Job 28:21
him, s he delighted in him ...... Ps 22:8
S thou hatest instruction, and ...... Ps 50:17
s he dwelleth securely by thee ...... Prov 3:29
wisdom, s he hath no heart to it ...... Prov 17:16
The hearing ear, and the s eye ...... Prov 20:12
the eye is not satisfied with s ...... Eccl 1:8
s hath been in the days. ...... Eccl 2:16
S there be many things that ...... Eccl 6:11
I was dismayed at the s of it ...... Is 21:3
and shutteth his eyes from s evil. ...... Is 33:15
S many things, but thou observest ...... Is 42:20
s I have lost my children, and am, ... Is 49:21
s she hath wrought lewdness with ...... Jer 11:15
s the LORD hath given s a charge. ...... Jer 47:7
S thou doest all these things, ... Eze 16:30
S he despised the oath by ...... Eze 17:18
S then that I will cut off from ...... Eze 21:4
s vanity, and divining lies unto ...... Eze 22:28
s thou couldest reveal this secret. ...... Dan 2:47
s thou hast forgotten the law of ...... Hos 4:6
s the multitudes, he went up into. ...... Mt 5:1
Jesus s their faith said unto the ...... Mt 9:2
because they s see not ...... Mt 13:13
s ye shall see, and shall not ...... Mt 13:14
That s they may see, and not ...... Mk 4:12
s a fig tree afar off having ...... Mk 11:13
shall this be, s I know not a man ...... Lk 1:34
who s Jesus fell on his face, and ...... Lk 5:12
that s they might not see, and ...... Lk 8:10
fear God, s thou art in the same ...... Lk 23:40
s that thou doest these things ...... Jn 2:18
therefore, and washed, and came s. ...... Jn 9:7
Peter s him saith to Jesus, Lord, ... Jn 21:21
s it is but the third hour of the ...... Acts 2:15
He s this before spake of the ...... Acts 2:31
Who s Peter and John about to go ...... Acts 3:3
s one of them suffer wrong, he ...... Acts 7:24
s the miracles which he did ...... Acts 8:6
hearing a voice, but s no man ...... Acts 9:7
not s the sun for a season ...... Acts 13:11
but s ye put it from you, and ...... Acts 13:46
s the prison doors open, he drew ...... Acts 16:27
s that he is Lord of heaven and ...... Acts 17:24
s he giveth to all life, and ...... Acts 17:25
S then that these things cannot ...... Acts 19:36
S that by thee we enjoy great ...... Acts 24:2
s ye shall see, and not perceive. ...... Acts 28:26
S it is one God, which shall ...... Rom 3:30
s he understandeth not what thou. 1Cor 14:16
S then that we have such hope, we 2Cor 3:12
s we have this ministry, as we 2Cor 4:1
S that many glory after the flesh 2Cor 11:18
gladly, s ye yourselves are wise 2Cor 11:19
s that ye have put off the old ...... Col 3:9
S it is a righteous thing with 2Th 1:6
S therefore it remaineth that ...... Heb 4:6
S then that we have a great high ...... Heb 4:14
uttered, s ye are dull of hearing ...... Heb 5:11
s they crucify to themselves the ...... Heb 6:6
by him, s he ever liveth to make ...... Heb 7:25
s that there are priests that ...... Heb 8:4
as s him who is invisible ...... Heb 11:27
Wherefore s we also are compassed ...... Heb 12:1
S ye have purified your souls in 1Pet 1:22
man dwelling among them, in s 2Pet 2:8

S then that all these things 2Pet 3:11
s that ye look for such things, ... 2Pet 3:14
S ye know these things before, ... 2Pet 3:17

SEEK

And he said, I s my brethren ...... Gen 37:16
that he may s occasion against us ...... Gen 43:18
shall not s for yellow hair ...... Lev 13:36
neither s after wizards, to be ...... Lev 19:31
that ye s not after your own ...... Num 15:39
and s ye the priesthood also ...... Num 16:10
to s for enchantments, but he set ...... Num 24:1
thou shalt s the LORD thy God ...... Deut 4:29
if thou s him with all thy heart ...... Deut 4:29
unto his habitation shall ye s ...... Deut 12:5
thee until thy brother s after it ...... Deut 22:2
Thou shalt not s their peace nor ...... Deut 23:6
shall I not s rest for thee, that ...... Ruth 3:1
thee, and arise, go s the asses 1Sa 9:3
which thou wentest to s are found 1Sa 10:2
And he said, To s the asses 1Sa 10:14
to s out a man, who is a cunning 1Sa 16:16
Saul was come out to s his life 1Sa 23:15
also and his men went to s him 1Sa 23:25
of all Israel, and went to s David 1Sa 24:2
they that s evil to my lord, be 1Sa 25:26
to pursue thee, and to s thy soul 1Sa 25:29
to s David in the wilderness of 1Sa 26:2
of Israel is come out to s a flea 1Sa 26:20
to s me any more in any coast of 1Sa 27:1
S me a woman that hath a familiar 1Sa 28:7
Philistines came up to s David 2Sa 5:17
Gath to Achish to s his servants 1Kin 2:40
my lord hath not sent to s thee 1Kin 18:10
they s my life, to take it away 1Kin 19:10
they s my life, to take it away 1Kin 19:14
go, we pray thee, and s thy master. 2Kin 2:16
bring you to the man whom ye s 2Kin 6:19
to s pasture for their flocks 1Chr 4:39
Philistines went up to s David 1Chr 14:8
S the LORD and his strength. 1Chr 16:10
s his face continually 1Chr 16:11
your soul to s the LORD your God 1Chr 22:19
s for all the commandments of the 1Chr 28:8
If thou s him, he will be found. 1Chr 28:9
s my face, and turn from their. 2Chr 7:14
such as set their hearts to s the 2Chr 11:16
not his heart to s the LORD 2Chr 12:14
commanded Judah to s the LORD God 2Chr 14:4
and if ye s him, he will be found. 2Chr 15:2
s the LORD God of their fathers 2Chr 15:12
That whosoever would not s the. 2Chr 15:13
prepared thine heart to s God 2Chr 19:3
and set himself to s the LORD 2Chr 20:3
of Judah they came to s the LORD 2Chr 20:4
That prepareth his heart to s God 2Chr 30:19
to s his God, he did it with all 2Chr 31:21
he began to s after the God of 2Chr 34:3
for we s your God, as ye do ...... Ezr 4:2
to s the LORD God of Israel, did ...... Ezr 6:21
heart to s the law of the LORD ...... Ezr 7:10
to s of him a right way for us ...... Ezr 8:21
upon all them for good that s him ...... Ezr 8:22
nor s their peace or their wealth ...... Ezr 9:12
that there was come a man to s ...... Neh 2:10
I would s unto God, and unto God ...... Job 5:8
thou shalt s me in the morning, ... Job 7:21
thou wouldest s unto God betimes. ...... Job 8:5
shall s to please the poor ...... Job 20:10
love vanity, and s after leasing ...... Ps 4:2
not forsaken them that s thee ...... Ps 9:10
countenance, will not s after God ...... Ps 10:4
s out his wickedness till thou ...... Ps 10:15
any that did understand, and s God ...... Ps 14:2
shall praise the LORD that s him. ...... Ps 22:26
the generation of them that s him, ... Ps 24:6
him, that s thy face, O Jacob ...... Ps 24:6
of the LORD, that will I s after ...... Ps 27:4
When thou saidst, S ye my face ...... Ps 27:8
thee, Thy face, LORD, will I s ...... Ps 27:8
but they that s the LORD shall ...... Ps 34:10
s peace, and pursue it ...... Ps 34:14
put to shame that s after my soul ...... Ps 35:4
They also that s after my life ...... Ps 38:12
they that s my hurt speak ...... Ps 38:12
confounded together that s after ...... Ps 40:14
Let all those that s thee rejoice ...... Ps 40:16
did understand, that did s God ...... Ps 53:2
oppressors s after my soul ...... Ps 54:3
early will I s thee ...... Ps 63:1
But those that s my soul, to ...... Ps 63:9
let not those that s thee be ...... Ps 69:6
your heart shall live that s God ...... Ps 69:32
confounded that s after my soul ...... Ps 70:2
Let all those that s thee rejoice ...... Ps 70:4
and dishonour that s my hurt ...... Ps 71:13
unto shame, that s my hurt. ...... Ps 71:24
that they may s thy name, O LORD ...... Ps 83:16
prey, and s their meat from God ...... Ps 104:21
that s their rejoice that s the LORD ...... Ps 105:3
S the LORD, and his strength. ...... Ps 105:4
s his face evermore ...... Ps 105:4
let them s their bread also out ...... Ps 109:10
that s him with the whole heart ...... Ps 119:2
for I s thy precepts ...... Ps 119:45
for they s not thy statutes ...... Ps 119:155
s thy servant ...... Ps 119:176
LORD our God I will s thy good ...... Ps 122:9
they shall s me early, but they. ...... Prov 1:28
thee, diligently to s thy face ...... Prov 7:15

those that s me early shall find. ...... Prov 8:17
to and fro of them that s death ...... Prov 21:6
they that go to s mixed wine ...... Prov 23:30
I will s it yet again ...... Prov 23:35
but they that s the LORD ...... Prov 28:5
but the just s his soul ...... Prov 29:10
Many s the ruler's favour ...... Prov 29:26
And I gave my heart to s and search ...... Eccl 1:13
to s out wisdom, and the reason of ...... Eccl 1:17
though a man labour to s it out. ...... Eccl 8:17
I will s him whom my soul loveth ...... Song 3:2
that we may s him with thee. ...... Song 6:1
s judgment, relieve the oppressed ...... Is 1:17
S unto them that have familiar ...... Is 8:19
not a people s unto their God. ...... Is 8:19
neither do they s the LORD of. ...... Is 9:13
to it shall the Gentiles s ...... Is 11:10
they shall s to the idols, and to. ...... Is 19:3
within me will I s thee early. ...... Is 26:9
Woe unto them that s deep to hide ...... Is 29:15
One of Israel, neither s the LORD. ...... Is 31:1
S ye out of the book of the LORD, ... Is 34:16
Thou shalt s them, and shalt not. ...... Is 41:12
When the poor and needy s water ...... Is 41:17
seed of Jacob, S ye me in vain. ...... Is 45:19
righteousness, ye that s the LORD ...... Is 51:1
S ye the LORD while he may be. ...... Is 55:6
Yet they s me daily, and delight. ...... Is 58:2
all they that s her will not ...... Jer 2:24
trimmed thou thy way to s love ...... Jer 2:33
thee, they will s thy life ...... Jer 4:30
s in the broad places thereof, if. ...... Jer 5:1
that s thy life, saying, Prophesy. ...... Jer 11:21
hands of them that s their lives ...... Jer 19:7
they that s their lives, and ...... Jer 19:9
hand of those that s their life. ...... Jer 21:7
the hand of them that s thy life ...... Jer 22:25
s the peace of the city whither I ...... Jer 29:7
And ye shall s me, and find me, ... Jer 29:13
they s thee not ...... Jer 30:14
hand of them that s their life. ...... Jer 34:20
hand of them that s their life. ...... Jer 34:21
hand of these men that s thy life ...... Jer 38:16
the hand of them that s his life. ...... Jer 44:30
s them not ...... Jer 45:5
hand of those that s their lives. ...... Jer 46:26
and before them that s their life. ...... Jer 49:37
shall go, and s the LORD their God. ...... Jer 50:4
All her people sigh, they s bread. ...... Lam 1:11
and they shall s peace, and there. ...... Eze 7:25
then shall they s a vision of the. ...... Eze 7:26
none did search or s after them. ...... Eze 34:6
search my sheep, and s them out. ...... Eze 34:11
so will I s out my sheep, and will ...... Eze 34:12
I will s that which was lost, and. ...... Eze 34:16
to s by prayer and supplications, ... Dan 9:3
and she shall s them, but shall. ...... Hos 2:7
s the LORD their God, and David ...... Hos 3:5
and with their herds to s the LORD ...... Hos 5:6
their offence, and s my face. ...... Hos 5:15
affliction they will s me early. ...... Hos 5:15
their God, nor s him for all this. ...... Hos 7:10
for it is time to s the LORD ...... Hos 10:12
S ye me, and ye shall live ...... Amos 5:4
But s not Beth-el, nor enter into. ...... Amos 5:5
S the LORD, and ye shall live ...... Amos 5:6
S him that maketh the seven stars ...... Amos 5:8
S good, and not evil, that ye may. ...... Amos 5:14
fro to s the word of the LORD, and. ...... Amos 8:12
whence shall I s comforters for. ...... Nah 3:7
thou also shalt s strength. ...... Nah 3:11
S ye the LORD, all ye meek of the ...... Zeph 2:3
s righteousness, s meekness. ...... Zeph 2:3
LORD, and to s the LORD of hosts ...... Zec 8:21
strong nations shall come to s ...... Zec 8:22
neither shall s the young one. ...... Zec 11:16
that I will s to destroy all the ...... Zec 12:9
they should s the law at his ...... Mal 2:7
That he might s a godly seed. ...... Mal 2:15
and the Lord, whom ye s, shall ...... Mal 3:1
for Herod will s the young child ...... Mt 2:13
these things do the Gentiles s ...... Mt 6:32
But s ye first the kingdom of God ...... Mt 6:33
s, and ye shall find ...... Mt 7:7
for I know that ye s Jesus ...... Mt 28:5
said unto him, All men s for thee ...... Mk 1:37
thy brethren without s for thee ...... Mk 3:32
this generation s after a sign ...... Mk 8:12
S ye Jesus of Nazareth, which was. ...... Mk 16:6
s, and ye shall find ...... Lk 11:9
they s a sign ...... Lk 11:29
s not ye what ye shall eat, or. ...... Lk 12:29
the nations of the world s after ...... Lk 12:30
But rather s ye the kingdom of ...... Lk 12:31
will s to enter in, and shall not ...... Lk 13:24
s diligently till she find it ...... Lk 15:8
Whosoever shall s to save his ...... Lk 17:33
For the Son of man is come to s ...... Lk 19:10
Why s ye the living among the ...... Lk 24:5
and saith unto them, What s ye ...... Jn 1:38
because s not mine own will, ... Jn 5:30
s not the honour that cometh from ...... Jn 5:44
verily, I say unto you, Ye s me ...... Jn 6:26
not this he, whom they s to kill. ...... Jn 7:25
Ye shall s me, and shall not find ...... Jn 7:34
that he said, Ye shall s me ...... Jn 7:36
I go my way, and ye shall s me ...... Jn 8:21
but ye s to kill me, because my ...... Jn 8:37
But now ye s to kill me, a man ...... Jn 8:40
And I s not mine own glory. ...... Jn 8:50

Ye shall s me................................. Jn 13:33
and said unto them, Whom s ye........ Jn 18:4
asked he them again, Whom s ye...... Jn 18:7
if therefore ye s me, let these........... Jn 18:8
him, Behold, three men s thee.......... Acts 10:19
said, Behold, I am he whom ye s...... Acts 10:21
Barnabas to Tarsus, for to s Saul...... Acts 11:25
of men might s after the Lord.......... Acts 15:17
That they should s the Lord............. Acts 17:27
in well doing s for glory.................. Rom 2:7
am left alone, and they s my life....... Rom 11:3
the Greeks s after wisdom............... 1Cor 1:22
s not to be loosed........................... 1Cor 7:27
s not a wife................................... 1Cor 7:27
Let no man s his own, but every...... 1Cor 10:24
s that ye may excel to the............... 1Cor 14:12
for I s not yours, but you................ 2Cor 12:14
Since ye s a proof of Christ.............. 2Cor 13:3
or do I s to please men................... Gal 1:10
while we s to be justified by............ Gal 2:17
For all s their own, not the.............. Phil 2:21
s those things which are above,........ Col 3:1
of them that diligently s him........... Heb 11:6
plainly that they s a country............ Heb 11:14
city, but we s one to come............... Heb 13:14
let him s peace, and ensue it............ 1Pet 3:11
in those days shall men s death......... Rev 9:6

SEEKEST

asked him, saying, What s thou........ Gen 37:15
shew thee the man whom thou s...... Judg 4:22
the man whom thou s is as if all....... 2Sa 17:3
thou s to destroy a city and a.......... 2Sa 20:19
thou s to go to thine own country... 1Kin 11:22
If thou s her as silver, and............... Prov 2:4
s thou great things for thyself.......... Jer 45:5
yet no man said, What s thou........... Jn 4:27
whom s thou.................................. Jn 20:15

SEEKETH

Saul my father s to kill thee............. 1Sa 19:2
thy father, that he s my life.............. 1Sa 20:1
for he that s my life s thy................ 1Sa 22:23
that s my life s thy life................... 1Sa 22:23
that Saul s to come to Keilah........... 1Sa 23:10
saying, Behold, David s thy hurt...... 1Sa 24:9
forth of my bowels, s my life........... 2Sa 16:11
and see how this man s mischief...... 1Kin 20:7
see how he s a quarrel against me.... 2Kin 5:7
From thence she s the prey.............. Job 39:29
the righteous, and s to slay him....... Ps 37:32
He that diligently s good................. Prov 11:27
but he that s mischief, it shall........... Prov 11:27
A scorner s wisdom, and findeth it.. Prov 14:6
hath understanding s knowledge...... Prov 15:14
covereth a transgression s love........ Prov 17:9
An evil man s only rebellion............. Prov 17:11
exalteth his gate s destruction......... Prov 17:19
man, having separated himself, s.... Prov 18:1
the ear of the wise s knowledge....... Prov 18:15
She s wool, and flax, and worketh... Prov 31:13
Which yet my soul s, but I find........ Eccl 7:28
he s unto him a cunning workman... Is 40:20
judgment, that s the truth................ Jer 5:1
This is Zion, whom no man s after.... Jer 30:17
for this man s not the welfare of...... Jer 38:4
for him, to the soul that s him......... Lam 3:25
punishment of him that s unto him... Eze 14:10
As a shepherd s out his flock in....... Eze 34:12
and he that s findeth........................ Mt 7:8
generation s after a sign.................. Mt 12:39
generation s after a sign.................. Mt 16:4
s that which is gone astray............... Mt 18:12
and he that s findeth........................ Lk 11:10
for the Father s such to worship...... Jn 4:23
he himself s to be known openly...... Jn 7:4
of himself s his own glory............... Jn 7:18
but he that s his glory that sent....... Jn 7:18
there is one that s and judgeth......... Jn 8:50
there is none that s after God.......... Rom 3:11
not obtained that which he s for...... Rom 11:7
s not her own, is not easily.............. 1Cor 13:5

SEEKING

s the wealth of his people, and........ Est 10:3
and s judgment, and hasting............. Is 16:5
places, s rest, and findeth none........ Mt 12:43
a merchant man, s goodly pearls...... Mt 13:45
s of him a sign from heaven,........... Mk 8:11
back again to Jerusalem, s him........ Lk 2:45
through dry places, s rest................ Lk 11:24
s to catch something out of his........ Lk 11:54
I come s fruit on this fig tree........... Lk 13:7
and came to Capernaum, s for Jesus. Jn 6:24
s to turn away the deputy from....... Acts 13:8
he went about s some to lead him.... Acts 13:11
not s mine own profit, but the......... 1Cor 10:33
about, s whom he may devour......... 1Pet 5:8

SEEM

I shall s to him as a deceiver............ Gen 27:12
It shall not s hard unto thee,........... Deut 15:18
brother should s vile unto thee........ Deut 25:3
if it s evil unto you to serve............. Josh 24:15
him as it shall s good unto you........ 1Sa 24:4
him what shall s good unto thee...... 2Sa 19:37
that which shall s good unto thee..... 2Sa 19:38
if it s good to thee, I will give.......... 1Kin 21:2
if it s good unto you, and that I...... 1Chr 13:2
if it s good to the king, let.............. Ezr 5:17
whatsoever shall s good unto.......... Ezr 7:18
the trouble s little before thee......... Neh 9:32

If it s good unto the king, let........... Est 5:4
the thing is right before the king..... Est 8:5
If it s good unto thee to come......... Jer 40:4
but if it s ill unto thee to come....... Jer 40:4
they shall s like torches, they.......... Nah 2:4
But if any man s to be...................... 1Cor 11:16
which s to be more feeble, are......... 1Cor 12:22
That I may not s as if I would......... 2Cor 10:9
any of you should s to come short... Heb 4:1
man among you s to be religious...... Jas 1:26

SEEMED

But he s as one that mocked unto.... Gen 19:14
they s unto him but a few days,........ Gen 29:20
Hebron all that s good to Israel........ 2Sa 3:19
that s good to the whole house of.... 2Sa 3:19
the sun, and it s great unto me......... Eccl 9:13
as s good to the potter to make....... Jer 18:4
it unto whom it s meet unto me....... Jer 27:5
for so it s good in thy sight.............. Mt 11:26
it s good to me also, having had....... Lk 10:1
for so it s good in thy sight.............. Lk 10:21
their words to them as idle............... Lk 24:11
it s good unto us, being.................... Acts 15:25
For it s good to the Holy Ghost,...... Acts 15:28
But of these who s to be somewhat.. Gal 2:6
for they who s to be somewhat in.... Gal 2:6
who s to be pillars, perceived.......... Gal 2:9

SEEMETH

It s to me there is as it were a.......... Lev 14:35
S it but a small thing unto you,....... Num 16:9
as it s good and right unto thee........ Josh 9:25
us whatsoever s good unto thee....... Judg 10:15
do with them what s good unto you. Judg 19:24
unto her, Do what s thee good......... 1Sa 1:23
let him do what s him good............. 1Sa 3:18
with us all that s good unto you...... 1Sa 11:10
Do whatsoever s good unto thee...... 1Sa 14:36
Saul, Do what s good unto thee...... 1Sa 14:40
S it to you a light thing to be a....... 1Sa 18:23
the LORD do that which s him good.. 1Sa 10:12
him do to me as s good unto him..... 2Sa 15:26
What s you best I will do................. 2Sa 18:4
and offer up what s good unto thee.. 2Sa 24:22
do with them as it s good to thee..... Est 3:11
is a way which s right unto a man.... Prov 14:12
is a way that s right unto a man....... Prov 16:25
is first in his own cause s just.......... Prov 18:17
do with me as s good and meet unto. Jer 26:14
whither it s good and convenient..... Jer 40:4
or go wheresoever it s convenient.... Jer 40:5
S it a small thing unto you to.......... Eze 34:18
even that which he s to hate............. Lk 8:18
He s to be a setter forth of.............. Acts 17:18
For it s to the unreasonable to......... Acts 25:27
If any man among you s to be wise... 1Cor 3:18
for the present s to be joyous,.......... Heb 12:11

SEEMLY

Delight is not s for a fool................. Prov 19:10
so honour is not s for a fool............ Prov 26:1

SEEN

for thee have I s righteous................ Gen 7:1
were the tops of the mountains s...... Gen 8:5
the bow shall be s in the cloud......... Gen 9:14
mount of the LORD it shall be s....... Gen 22:14
for I have s all that Laban doeth....... Gen 31:12
God hath s mine affliction and the... Gen 31:42
for I have s God face to face, and.... Gen 32:30
for therefore I have s thy face......... Gen 33:10
as though I had s the face of God..... Gen 33:10
Egypt, and of all that ye have s........ Gen 45:13
me die, since I have s thy face.......... Gen 46:30
I have surely s the affliction of........ Ex 3:7
I have also s the oppression............. Ex 3:9
s that which is done to you in.......... Ex 3:16
nor thy fathers' fathers have s......... Ex 10:6
no leavened bread be s with thee..... Ex 13:7
s with them in all thy quarters......... Ex 13:7
Egyptians whom ye have s to day.... Ex 14:13
Ye have s what I did unto the.......... Ex 19:4
Ye have s that I have talked with...... Ex 20:22
I have s this people, and, behold,..... Ex 32:9
but my face shall not be s................. Ex 33:23
thee, neither let any man be s........... Ex 34:3
whether he hath s or known of it..... Lev 5:1
after that he hath been s of the........ Lev 13:7
he shall be s of the priest again........ Lev 13:7
that thou LORD art s face to face..... Num 14:14
those men which have s my glory..... Num 14:22
neither hath he s perverseness in..... Num 23:21
And when thou hast s it, thou also... Num 27:13
moreover we have s the sons of....... Deut 1:28
where thou hast s how that the........ Deut 1:31
Thine eyes have s all that the.......... Deut 3:21
Your eyes have s what the LORD...... Deut 4:3
things which thine eyes have s......... Deut 4:9
we have s this day that God doth..... Deut 5:24
I have s this people, and, behold,..... Deut 9:13
things, which thine eyes have s........ Deut 10:21
which have not s the chastisement.... Deut 11:2
But your eyes have s all the............. Deut 11:7
s with them in all thy coasts............ Deut 16:4
blood, neither have our eyes s it...... Deut 21:7
Ye have s all that the LORD did....... Deut 29:2
which thine eyes have s.................... Deut 29:3
ye have s their abominations, and.... Deut 29:17
to his mother, I have not s him........ Deut 33:9
ye have s all that the LORD your..... Josh 23:3
your eyes have s what I have done... Josh 24:7

who had s all the great works of...... Judg 2:7
was there a shield or spear s............ Judg 5:8
for because I have s an angel of....... Judg 6:22
with him, What ye have s me do...... Judg 9:48
surely die, because we have s God.... Judg 13:22
I have s a woman in Timnah of........ Judg 14:2
for we have s the land, and,............. Judg 18:9
s from the day that the children....... Judg 19:30
lords of the Philistines had s it........ 1Sa 6:16
I have s a son of Jesse the............... 1Sa 16:18
Have ye s this man that is come....... 1Sa 17:25
haunt is, and who hath s him there... 1Sa 23:22
this day thine eyes have s how........ 1Sa 24:10
not be s to come into the city.......... 1Sa 27:17
Go tell the king what thou hast s..... 2Sa 18:21
he was s upon the wings of the........ 2Sa 22:11
there was no stone s........................ 1Kin 6:18
the ends of the staves were s out...... 1Kin 8:8
and they were not s without............ 1Kin 8:8
Sheba had s all Solomon's wisdom... 1Kin 10:4
I came, and mine eyes had s it.......... 1Kin 10:7
trees, nor were s unto this day......... 1Kin 10:12
For his sons had s what way the...... 1Kin 13:12
Hast thou s all this great................. 1Kin 20:13
Surely I have s yesterday the........... 2Kin 9:26
thy prayer, I have s thy tears.......... 2Kin 20:5
What have they s in thine house...... 2Kin 20:15
are in mine house have they s.......... 2Kin 20:15
him at Megiddo, when they had s..... 2Kin 23:29
now have I s with joy thy people,.... 1Chr 29:17
the ends of the staves were s............ 2Chr 5:9
but they were not s without............. 2Chr 5:9
Sheba had s the wisdom of Solomon. 2Chr 9:3
I came, and mine eyes had s it.......... 2Chr 9:6
there were none such s before in..... 2Chr 9:11
that had s the first house, when....... Ezr 3:12
they had s concerning this matter.... Est 9:26
Even as I have s, they that plow...... Job 4:8
I have s the foolish taking root........ Job 5:3
hath s me shall see me no more....... Job 7:8
him, saying, I have not s thee.......... Job 8:18
up the ghost, and no eye had s me... Job 10:18
Lo, mine eye hath s all this............. Job 13:1
which I have s I will declare............ Job 15:17
they which have s him shall say....... Job 20:7
all ye yourselves have s it............... Job 27:12
the vulture's eye hath not s............. Job 28:7
If I have s any perish for want........ Job 31:19
away, that it cannot be s................. Job 33:21
bones that were not s stick out........ Job 33:21
or hast thou s the doors of.............. Job 38:17
or hast thou s the treasures of......... Job 38:22
Thou hast s it................................. Ps 10:14
the channels of waters were s.......... Ps 18:15
said, Aha, aha, our eye hath s it...... Ps 35:21
This thou hast s, O LORD................ Ps 35:22
yet have I not s the righteous.......... Ps 37:25
I have s the wicked in great............. Ps 37:35
so have we s in the city of the......... Ps 48:8
mine eye hath s his desire upon....... Ps 54:7
for I have s violence and strife......... Ps 55:9
so as I have s thee in the................. Ps 63:2
They have s thy goings, O God........ Ps 68:24
the years wherein we have s evil...... Ps 90:15
have s the salvation of our God....... Ps 98:3
I have s an end of all perfection....... Ps 119:96
the prince whom thine eyes have s... Prov 25:7
I have s all the works that are.......... Eccl 1:14
I have s the travail, which God........ Eccl 3:10
who hath not s the evil work that.... Eccl 4:3
evil which I have s under the sun..... Eccl 5:13
Behold that which I have s............... Eccl 5:18
evil which I have s under the sun..... Eccl 6:1
Moreover he hath not s the sun....... Eccl 6:5
twice told, yet hath he s no good..... Eccl 6:6
All things have I s in the days.......... Eccl 7:15
All this have I s, and applied my...... Eccl 8:9
have I s also under the sun.............. Eccl 9:13
evil which I have s under the sun..... Eccl 10:5
I have s servants upon horses, and... Eccl 10:7
for mine eyes have s the King.......... Is 6:5
in darkness have s a great light........ Is 9:2
when it is that Moab is weary......... Is 16:12
Ye have s also the breaches of......... Is 22:9
thy prayer, I have s thy tears.......... Is 38:5
What have they s in thine house...... Is 39:4
that is in mine house have they s..... Is 39:4
Aha, I am warm, I have s the fire..... Is 44:16
yea, thy shame shall be s................. Is 47:3
I have s his ways, and will heal....... Is 57:18
and his glory shall be s upon thee.... Is 60:2
the ear, neither hath the eye s.......... Is 64:4
who hath s such things.................... Is 66:19
my fame, neither have s my glory.... Is 66:19
LORD unto me, Thou hast well s...... Jer 1:12
the king, Hast thou s that which...... Jer 36:23
Behold, even I have s it, saith.......... Jer 7:11
thou hast s me, and tried mine........ Jer 12:3
I have s thine adulteries, and thy..... Jer 13:27
I have s folly in the prophets of....... Jer 23:13
I have s also in the prophets of....... Jer 23:14
Ye have s all the evil that I............. Jer 44:2
Wherefore have I s them dismayed... Jer 46:5
because they have s her nakedness... Lam 1:8
for she hath s that the heathen........ Lam 1:10
Thy prophets have s vain and.......... Lam 2:14
but have s for thee false burdens...... Lam 2:14
we have found, we have s it............. Lam 3:1
I am the man that hath s................. Lam 3:1
O LORD, thou hast s my wrong....... Lam 3:59

S

Thou hast *s* all their vengeance .... Lam 3:60
hast thou *s* what the ancients of .... Eze 8:12
said he unto me, Hast thou *s* this .... Eze 8:15
he said unto me, Hast thou *s* this .... Eze 8:17
that I had *s* went up from me .... Eze 11:24
own spirit, and have *s* nothing .... Eze 13:3
They have *s* vanity and lying .... Eze 13:6
Have ye not *s* a vain vision, and .... Eze 13:7
a lies, therefore, behold, I am .... Eze 13:8
me, Son of man, hast thou *s* this .... Eze 47:6
unto me the dream which I have *s* .... Dan 2:26
visions of my dream that I have *s* .... Dan 4:9
I king Nebuchadnezzar have *s* .... Dan 4:18
which I had *s* standing before the .... Dan 8:6
had *s* the vision, and sought for .... Dan 8:15
whom I had *s* in the vision at the .... Dan 9:21
I have *s* an horrible thing in the .... Hos 6:10
for now have I *s* with mine eyes .... Zec 9:8
And the LORD shall be *s* over them .... Zec 9:14
and the diviners have *s* a lie .... Zec 10:2
for we have a his star in the .... Mt 2:2
alms before men, to be *s* of them .... Mt 6:1
that they may be *s* of men .... Mt 6:5
It was never so *s* in Israel .... Mt 9:33
which ye see, and have not *s* them .... Mt 13:17
and ye, when ye had *s* it, repented .... Mt 21:32
works they do for to be *s* of men .... Mt 23:5
till they have *s* the kingdom of .... Mk 9:1
no man what things they had *s* .... Mk 9:9
was alive, and had been *s* of her .... Mk 16:11
had *s* him after he was risen .... Mk 16:14
he had *s* a vision in the temple .... Lk 1:22
And when they had *s* it, they made .... Lk 2:17
things that they had heard and *s* .... Lk 2:20
before he had *s* the Lord's Christ .... Lk 2:26
mine eyes have *s* thy salvation .... Lk 2:30
We have a strange things to day .... Lk 5:26
tell John what things ye have *s* .... Lk 7:22
of those things which they had *s* .... Lk 9:36
which ye see, and have not *s* them .... Lk 10:24
the mighty works that they had *s* .... Lk 19:37
he hoped to have *s* some miracle .... Lk 23:8
had also a vision of angels .... Lk 24:23
supposed that they had *s* a spirit .... Lk 24:37
No man hath *s* God at any time .... Jn 1:18
know, and testify that we have *s* .... Jn 3:11
And what he hath *s* and heard, that .... Jn 3:32
having *s* all the things that he .... Jn 4:45
at any time, nor *s* his shape .... Jn 5:37
when they had *s* the miracle that .... Jn 6:14
unto you, That ye also have *s* me .... Jn 6:36
that any man hath *s* the Father .... Jn 6:46
is of God, he hath *s* the Father .... Jn 6:46
which I have *s* with my Father .... Jn 8:38
which ye have *s* with your Father .... Jn 8:38
years old, and hast thou *s* Abraham .... Jn 8:57
had *s* him that he was blind .... Jn 9:8
unto him, Thou hast both *s* him .... Jn 9:37
had *s* the things which Jesus did, ... Jn 11:45
ye know him, and have *s* him .... Jn 14:7
hath *s* me hath *s* the Father .... Jn 14:9
but now have they both *s* and hated .... Jn 15:24
disciples that she had *s* the Lord .... Jn 20:18
said unto him, We have *s* the Lord .... Jn 20:25
Thomas, because thou hast *s* me .... Jn 20:29
blessed are they that have not *s* .... Jn 20:29
being *s* of them forty days, and .... Acts 1:3
as ye have *s* him go into heaven .... Acts 1:11
speak the things which we have *s* .... Acts 4:20
I have *s*, I have *s* the .... Acts 7:34
to the fashion that he had *s* .... Acts 7:44
hath *s* in a vision a man named .... Acts 9:12
how he had *s* the Lord in the way .... Acts 9:27
vision which he had *s* should mean .... Acts 10:17
he had *s* an angel in his house .... Acts 11:13
had *s* the grace of God, was glad, ... Acts 11:23
he was *s* many days of them which .... Acts 13:31
And after he had *s* the vision .... Acts 16:10
and when they had *s* the brethren .... Acts 16:40
(For they had *s* before with him .... Acts 21:29
unto all men of what thou hast *s* .... Acts 22:15
of these things which thou hast *s* .... Acts 26:16
of the world are clearly *s* .... Rom 1:20
but hope that is *s* is not hope .... Rom 8:24
as it is written, Eye hath not *s* 1Cor 2:9
have I not *s* Jesus Christ our 1Cor 9:1
And that he was *s* of Cephas 1Cor 15:5
he was *s* of above five hundred 1Cor 15:6
After that, he was *s* of James 1Cor 15:7
last of all he was *s* of me also 1Cor 15:8
not at the things which are *s* 2Cor 4:18
but at the things which are not *s* 2Cor 4:18
things which are *s* are temporal 2Cor 4:18
which are not *s* are eternal 2Cor 4:18
and heard, and *s* in me, do .... Phil 4:9
have not *s* my face in the flesh .... Col 2:1
those things which he hath not *s* .... Col 2:18
s of angels, preached unto the 1Ti 3:16
whom no man hath *s*, nor can see 1Ti 6:16
for, the evidence of things not *s* .... Heb 11:1
so that things which are *s* were .... Heb 11:3
of God of things not *s* as yet .... Heb 11:7
but having *s* them afar off, and .... Heb 11:13
have *s* the end of the Lord .... Jas 5:11
Whom having not *s*, ye love 1Pet 1:8
which we have *s* with our eyes, ... 1Jn 1:1
was manifested, and we have *s* it 1Jn 1:2
That which we have *s* and heard, ... 1Jn 1:3
whosoever sinneth hath not *s* him 1Jn 3:6
No man hath *s* God at any time 1Jn 4:12

And we have *s* and do testify that 1Jn 4:14
not his brother whom he hath *s* 1Jn 4:20
he love God whom he hath not *s* 1Jn 4:20
he that doeth evil hath not *s* God 3Jn 1:11
the things which thou hast *s* .... Rev 1:19
there was *s* in his temple the ark, ... Rev 11:19
And when I had heard and *s*, I fell .... Rev 22:8

SEER

Come, and let us go to the *s* 1Sa 9:9
Prophet was beforetime called a S 1Sa 9:9
and said unto them, Is the *s* here 1Sa 9:11
Saul, and said, I am the *s* 1Sa 9:19
the priest, Art not thou a *s* 2Sa 15:27
unto the prophet Gad's, David's 2Sa 24:11
Samuel the *s* did ordain in their 1Chr 9:22
LORD spake unto Gad, David's 1Chr 21:9
the king's a in the words of God 1Chr 25:5
And all that Samuel the *s*, and Saul 1Chr 26:28
in the book of Samuel the *s* 1Chr 29:29
and in the book of Gad the *s* 1Chr 29:29
in the visions of Iddo the *s* 2Chr 9:29
and of Iddo the *s* concerning 2Chr 12:15
at that time Hanani the *s* came to 2Chr 16:7
Then Asa was wroth with the *s* 2Chr 16:10
Hanani the *s* went out to meet him 2Chr 19:2
of David, and Gad the king's *s* 2Chr 29:25
words of David, and of Asaph the *s* 2Chr 29:30
Heman, and Jeduthun the king's *s* 2Chr 35:15
Amaziah said unto Amos, O thou *s* .... Amos 7:12

SEER'S

I pray there, where the *s* house is 1Sa 9:18

SEERS

all the prophets, and by all the *s* 2Kin 17:13
the words of the *s* that spake to 2Chr 33:18
among the sayings of the *s* 2Chr 33:19
rulers, the *s* hath he covered .... Is 29:10
Which say to the *s*, See not .... Is 30:10
Then shall the *s* be ashamed .... Mic 3:7

SEEST

For all the land which thou *s* .... Gen 13:15
spake unto her, Thou God *s* me .... Gen 16:13
and all that thou *s* is mine .... Gen 31:43
for in that day thou *s* my face .... Ex 10:28
heaven, and when thou *s* the sun .... Deut 4:19
in every place that thou *s* .... Deut 12:13
s horses, and chariots, and a .... Deut 20:1
s among the captives a beautiful .... Deut 21:11
him, Thou *s* the shadow of the .... Judg 9:36
S thou how Ahab humbleth himself . 1Kin 21:29
or *s* thou as man seeth .... Job 10:4
S thou a man diligent in his .... Prov 22:29
S thou a man wise in his own .... Prov 26:12
S thou a man that is hasty in his .... Prov 29:20
If thou *s* the oppression of the .... Eccl 5:8
fasted, say they, and thou *s* not .... Is 58:3
when thou *s* the naked, that thou .... Is 58:7
me, saying, Jeremiah, what *s* thou .... Jer 1:11
second time, saying, What *s* thou .... Jer 1:13
S thou not what they do in the .... Jer 7:17
s the reins and the heart, let me .... Jer 20:12
the Lord unto me, What *s* thou .... Jer 24:3
and, behold, thou *s* it .... Jer 32:24
Son of man, *s* thou what they do .... Eze 8:6
declare all that thou *s* to the .... Eze 40:4
and as thou *s*, deal with thy .... Dan 1:13
said unto me, Amos, what *s* thou .... Amos 7:8
And he said, Amos, what *s* thou .... Amos 8:2
And said unto me, What *s* thou .... Zec 4:2
And he said unto me, What *s* thou .... Zec 5:2
Thou *s* the multitude thronging .... Mk 5:31
Thou seest these great buildings .... Mk 13:2
unto Simon, S thou this woman .... Lk 7:44
Lord, and said unto him, Thou *s* .... Acts 21:20
S thou how faith wrought with his .... Jas 2:22
and, What thou *s*, write in a book, ... Rev 1:11

SEETH

here looked after him that *s* me .... Gen 16:13
when he *s* that the lad is not .... Gen 44:31
and when he *s* thee, he will be .... Ex 4:14
when he *s* the blood upon the .... Ex 12:23
And if, when the priest *s* it .... Lev 13:20
when he *s* that their power is .... Deut 32:36
for the LORD *s* not as man *s* 1Sa 16:7
city is pleasant, as my lord *s* 2Kin 2:19
heap, and *s* the place of stones .... Job 8:17
or seest thou as man *s* .... Job 10:4
he *s* wickedness also .... Job 11:11
a covering to him, that he *s* not .... Job 22:14
his eye *s* every precious thing .... Job 28:10
and *s* under the whole heaven .... Job 28:24
of man, and he *s* all his goings .... Job 34:21
but now mine eye *s* thee .... Job 42:5
for he *s* that his day is coming .... Ps 37:13
For he *s* that wise men die, ... Ps 49:10
rejoice when he *s* the vengeance .... Ps 58:10
nor night *s* sleep with his eyes .... Eccl 8:16
let him declare what he *s* .... Is 21:6
when he that looketh upon it *s* .... Is 28:4
the dark, and they say, Who *s* us .... Is 29:15
thou hast said, None *s* me .... Is 47:10
for they say, The LORD *s* us not .... Eze 8:12
the earth, and the LORD *s* not .... Eze 9:9
because the *s* that he is many .... Eze 12:27
that *s* all his father's sins .... Eze 18:14
If when he *s* the sword come upon .... Eze 33:3
when any *s* a man's bone, then .... Eze 39:15
thy Father which *s* in secret .... Mt 6:4

thy Father which *s* in secret .... Mt 6:6
which *s* in secret, shall reward .... Mt 6:18
s the tumult, and them that wept .... Mk 5:38
s Abraham afar off, and Lazarus in . Lk 16:23
The next day John *s* Jesus coming .... Jn 1:29
but what he *s* the Father do .... Jn 5:19
that every one which *s* the Son .... Jn 6:40
But by what means he now *s* .... Jn 9:21
s the wolf coming, and leaveth the . Jn 10:12
because he *s* the light of this .... Jn 11:9
that *s* me *s* him that sent me .... Jn 12:45
receive, because it *s* him not .... Jn 14:17
while, and the world *s* me no more .... Jn 14:19
the stone taken away from the .... Jn 20:1
and *s* the linen clothes lie, ... Jn 20:6
s two angels in white sitting .... Jn 20:12
s the disciple whom Jesus loved .... Jn 21:20
for what a man *s*, why doth he yet .... Rom 8:24
me above that which he *s* me to be 2Cor 12:6
s his brother have need, and 1Jn 3:17

SEETHE

to day, and *s* that ye will *s* .... Ex 16:23
Thou shalt not *s* a kid in his .... Ex 23:19
s his flesh in the holy place .... Eze 29:31
Thou shalt not *s* a kid in his .... Ex 34:26
Thou shalt not *s* a kid in his .... Deut 14:21
s pottage for the sons of the 2Kin 4:38
let them *s* the bones of it .... Eze 24:5
and take of them, and *s* therein .... Zec 14:21

SEETHING

came, while the flesh was in *s* 1Sa 2:13
as out of a *s* pot or caldron .... Job 41:20
and I said, I see a *s* pot .... Jer 1:13

SEGUB (se'-gub)

1. A son of Hiel.
thereof in his youngest son S 1Kin 16:34
2. A son of Hezron.
and she bare him S 1Chr 2:21
S begat Jair, who had three and 1Chr 2:22

SEIR (se'-ur)

1. A region south of the Dead Sea.
And the Horites in their mount S .... Gen 14:6
his brother unto the land of S .... Gen 32:3
until I come unto my lord unto S .... Gen 33:14
that day on his way unto S .... Gen 33:16
Thus dwelt Esau in mount S .... Gen 36:8
father of the Edomites in mount S .... Gen 36:9
the children of S in the land of .... Gen 36:21
their dukes in the land of S .... Gen 36:30
S also shall be a possession for .... Num 24:18
way of mount S unto Kadesh-barnea .. Deut 1:2
as bees do, and destroyed you in S .... Deut 1:44
and we compassed mount S .... Deut 2:1
of Esau, which dwell in S .... Deut 2:4
S unto Esau for a possession .... Deut 2:5
of Esau, which dwell in S .... Deut 2:8
Horims also dwelt in S beforetime ..... Deut 2:12
of Esau, when they *s* .... Deut 2:22
children of Esau which dwell in S .... Deut 2:29
and rose up from S unto them .... Deut 33:2
mount Halak, that goeth up to S .... Josh 11:17
mount Halak, that goeth up to S .... Josh 12:7
from Baalah westward unto mount S Josh 15:10
and I gave unto Esau mount S .... Josh 24:4
LORD, when thou wentest out of S .... Judg 5:4
five hundred men, went to mount S .. 1Chr 4:42
of Ammon and Moab and mount S 2Chr 20:10
of Ammon, Moab, and mount S 2Chr 20:22
the inhabitants of mount S 2Chr 20:23
an end of the inhabitants of S 2Chr 20:23
of the children of S ten thousand 2Chr 25:11
the gods of the children of S 2Chr 25:14
He calleth to me out of S .... Is 21:11
S do say, Behold, the house of .... Eze 25:8
man, set thy face against mount S ..... Eze 35:2
Behold, O mount S, I am against .... Eze 35:3
will I make mount S most desolate ..... Eze 35:7
thou shalt be desolate, O mount S ..... Eze 35:15
2. Grandfather of Hori.
are the sons of S the Horite .... Gen 36:20
And the sons of S 1Chr 1:38

SEIRAH See SEIRATH.

SEIRATH (se'-ur-ath) A city in Ephraim.

the quarries, and escaped unto S .... Judg 3:26

SEIZE

the ambush, and *s* upon the city .... Josh 8:7
night, let darkness upon it .... Job 3:6
Let death *s* upon them, and let .... Ps 55:15
let us *s* on his inheritance .... Mt 21:38

SEIZED

to flee, and fear hath *s* on her .... Jer 49:24

SELA (se'-lah) See SELAH. *Same as Selah 1.*

the land from S to the wilderness .... Is 16:1

SELAH (se'-lah) See JOKTHEEL, SELA.

1. Capital of Edom.
took S by war, and called the name 2Kin 14:7
2. A musical notation.
no help for him in God. S .... Ps 3:2
me out of his holy hill. S .... Ps 3:4
blessing is upon thy people. S .... Ps 3:8
vanity, and seek after leasing? S .... Ps 4:2
your bed, and be still. S .... Ps 4:4
mine honour in thee. S .... Ps 7:5
his own hands. Higgaion. S .... Ps 9:16
themselves to be but men. S .... Ps 9:20

accept thy burnt sacrifice; S................ Ps 20:3
the request of his lips. S.................... Ps 21:2
thy face, O Jacob. S.......................... Ps 24:6
he is the King of glory. S................... Ps 24:10
the drought of summer. S.................... Ps 32:4
the iniquity of my sin. S.................... Ps 32:5
songs of deliverance. S...................... Ps 32:7
state is altogether vanity. S................ Ps 39:5
every man is vanity. S........................ Ps 39:11
thy name for ever. S.......................... Ps 44:8
with the swelling thereof. S................ Ps 46:3
Jacob is our refuge. S........................ Ps 46:7
Jacob is our refuge. S........................ Ps 46:11
Jacob whom he loved. S....................... Ps 47:4
establish it for ever. S...................... Ps 48:8
approve their sayings. S...................... Ps 49:13
he shall receive me. S......................... Ps 49:15
God is judge himself. S........................ Ps 50:6
to speak righteousness. S..................... Ps 52:3
land of the living. S.......................... Ps 52:5
set God before them. S........................ Ps 54:3
remain in the wilderness. S.................. Ps 55:7
that abideth of old. S......................... Ps 55:19
swallow me up. S............................... Ps 57:3
are fallen themselves. S....................... Ps 57:6
wicked transgressors. S....................... Ps 59:5
ends of the earth. S........................... Ps 59:13
because of the truth. S........................ Ps 60:4
the covert of thy wings S..................... Ps 61:4
but they curse inwardly. S.................... Ps 62:4
is a refuge for us. S.......................... Ps 62:8
sing to thy name. S............................ Ps 66:4
exalt themselves. S............................ Ps 66:7
offer bullocks with goats. S................. Ps 66:15
face to shine upon us; S...................... Ps 67:1
the nations upon earth. S..................... Ps 67:4
through the wilderness. S..................... Ps 68:7
the God of our salvation. S.................. Ps 68:19
praises unto the Lord. S...................... Ps 68:32
up the pillars of it. S........................ Ps 75:3
sword, and the battle. S....................... Ps 76:3
the meek of the earth. S...................... Ps 76:9
was overwhelmed. S............................. Ps 77:3
up his tender mercies? S...................... Ps 77:9
of Jacob and Joseph. S......................... Ps 77:15
the waters of Meribah. S...................... Ps 81:7
persons of the wicked? S...................... Ps 82:2
the children of Lot. S......................... Ps 83:8
be still praising thee. S...................... Ps 84:4
O God of Jacob. S.............................. Ps 84:8
covered all their sin. S....................... Ps 85:2
of city of God. S.............................. Ps 87:3
man was born there. S.......................... Ps 87:6
me with all thy waves. S...................... Ps 88:7
dead arise and praise thee? S................ Ps 88:10
throne to all generations. S................. Ps 89:4
witness in heaven. S........................... Ps 89:37
him with shame. S.............................. Ps 89:45
hand of the grave? S........................... Ps 89:48
is under their lips. S......................... Ps 140:3
have set gins for me. S........................ Ps 140:5
they exalt themselves. S....................... Ps 140:8
as a thirsty land. S........................... Ps 143:6
from mount Paran. S............................ Hab 3:3
even thy word. S............................... Hab 3:9
foundation unto the neck. S.................. Hab 3:13

SELA-HAMMAHLEKOTH (se''-lah-ham-
mah'-le-koth) A hill in the wilderness of
Maon.
they called that place S...................... 1Sa 23:28

SELED (se'-led) A descendant of Jerahmeel.
S, and Appaim: but S died..................... 1Chr 2:30

SELEUCIA (sel-u-si'-ah) A city in Syria.
the Holy Ghost, departed unto S............. Acts 13:4

SELF
whom thou swarest by thine own s........... Ex 32:13
I can of mine own s do nothing............... Jn 5:30
glorify thou me with thine own s............ Jn 17:5
me, I judge not mine own s................... 1Cor 4:3
unto me even thine own s besides........... Philem 19
Who his own s bare our sins in............... 1Pet 2:24

SELFSAME
In the s day entered Noah, and.............. Gen 7:13
of their foreskin in the s day............... Gen 17:23
In the s day was Abraham...................... Gen 17:26
for in this s day have I brought............. Ex 12:17
even the s day it came to pass,.............. Ex 12:41
And it came to pass the s day................ Ex 12:51
until the s day that ye have................. Lev 23:14
And ye shall proclaim on the s day......... Lev 23:21
LORD spake unto Moses that s day............ Deut 32:48
and parched corn in the s day............... Josh 5:11
in the s day the hand of the LORD.......... Eze 40:1
servant was healed in the s hour........... Mt 8:13
the s Spirit, dividing to every............... 1Cor 12:11
wrought us for the s thing is God.......... 2Cor 5:5
For behold this s thing, that ye............ 2Cor 7:11

SELFWILL
in their s they digged down a............... Gen 49:6

SELFWILLED
not s, not soon angry, not given............. Titus 1:7
Presumptuous are they, s, they............... 2Pet 2:10

SELL
S me this day thy birthright................. Gen 25:31
let us s him to the Ishmeelites,............ Gen 37:27
if a man s his daughter to be a............. Ex 21:7

to s her unto a strange nation he........... Ex 21:8
then they shall s the live ox............... Ex 21:35
or a sheep, and kill it, or s it............ Ex 22:1
And if thou s ought unto thy............... Lev 25:14
the fruits he shall s unto thee............. Lev 25:16
of the fruits doth he s unto thee.......... Lev 25:16
if a man s a dwelling house in a........... Lev 25:29
s himself unto the stranger or............. Lev 25:47
Thou shalt s me meat for money,........... Deut 2:28
or thou mayest s it unto an alien......... Deut 14:21
but thou shalt not s her at all............. Deut 21:14
for the LORD had s Sisera into............. Judg 4:9
which did s himself to work................. 1Kin 21:25
s the oil, and pay thy debt, and.......... 2Kin 4:7
will ye even s your brethren............... Neh 5:8
victuals on the sabbath day to s.......... Neh 10:31
Buy the truth, and s it not................ Prov 23:23
s the land into the hand of the........... Eze 30:12
And they shall not s of it................. Eze 48:14
I will s your sons and your................ Joel 3:8
they shall s them to the Sabeans.......... Joel 3:8
moon be gone, that we may s corn.......... Amos 8:5
s the refuse of the wheat.................. Amos 8:6
and they that s them say, Blessed......... Zec 11:5
s that thou hast, and give to the......... Mt 19:21
but go ye rather to them that s............ Mt 25:9
s whatsoever thou hast, and give.......... Mk 10:21
S that ye have, and give alms.............. Lk 12:33
s all that thou hast, and............... Lk 18:22
let him s his garment, and buy one...... Lk 22:36
there a year, and buy and s............... Jas 4:13
And that no man might buy or s........... Rev 13:17

SELLER
as with the buyer, so with the s.......... Is 24:2
buyer rejoice, nor the s mourn............ Eze 7:12
For the s shall not return to............... Eze 7:13
a s of purple, of the city of............... Acts 16:14

SELLERS
of all kind of ware lodged................. Neh 13:20

SELLEST
Thou s thy people for nought, and........ Ps 44:12

SELLETH
s him, or if he be found in his........... Ex 21:16
merchandise of him, or s him............. Deut 24:7
s a parcel of land, which was our........ Ruth 4:3
be upon the head of him that s it......... Prov 11:26
She maketh fine linen, and s it........... Prov 31:24
that s nations through her............... Nah 3:4
s all that he hath, and buyeth............ Mt 13:44

SELVEDGE
from the s in the coupling................ Ex 26:4
from the s in the coupling................ Ex 36:11

SELVES
know of your own s that summer is...... Lk 21:30
of your own s shall men arise,........... Acts 20:30
gave their own s to the Lord............. 2Cor 8:5
prove your own s.......................... 2Cor 13:5
Know ye not your own s, how that........ 2Cor 13:5
shall be lovers of their own s............ 2Ti 3:2
only, deceiving your own s............... Jas 1:22

SEM (sem) See SHEM. Greek form of Shem.
Arphaxad, which was the son of S.......... Lk 3:36

SEMACHIAH (sem-a-ki'-ah) A sanctuary
servant.
were strong men, Elihu, and S............ 1Chr 26:7

SEMEI (sem'-e-i) See SHEMAIAH. A son of
Joseph; an ancestor of Jesus.
which was the son of S, which............. Lk 3:26

SEMEIN See SEMEI.

SENAAH (sen'-a-ah) See HASSENAAH. A city in
Judah.
The children of S, three thousand........ Ezr 2:35
The children of S, three thousand........ Neh 7:38

SENATE
all the s of the children of.............. Acts 5:21

SENATORS
and teach his wisdom..................... Ps 105:22

SEND
he shall s his angel before thee.......... Gen 24:7
s me good speed this day, and shew....... Gen 24:12
will s his angel with thee, and.......... Gen 24:40
he said, S me away unto my master...... Gen 24:54
s me away that I may go to my........... Gen 24:56
then I will s, and fetch thee from........ Gen 27:45
S me away, that I may go unto............ Gen 30:25
come, and I will s thee unto them........ Gen 37:13
I will s thee a kid from the.............. Gen 38:17
give me a pledge, till thou s it......... Gen 38:17
S one of you, and let him fetch.......... Gen 42:16
If thou wilt s our brother with.......... Gen 43:4
But if thou wilt not s him.............. Gen 43:5
S the lad with me, and we will.......... Gen 43:8
that he may s away your other.......... Gen 43:14
for God did s me before you to........... Gen 45:5
I will s thee unto Pharaoh, that....... Ex 3:10
And he said, O my Lord, s, I pray........ Ex 4:13
the hand of him whom thou wilt s........ Ex 4:13
that he s the children of Israel......... Ex 8:21
I will s swarms of flies upon.......... Ex 8:21
For I will at this time s all my......... Ex 9:14
S therefore now, and gather thy......... Ex 9:19
that they might s them out of the...... Ex 12:33
I s an Angel before thee, to keep....... Ex 23:20

I will s my fear before thee, and........ Ex 23:27
I will s hornets before thee,............ Ex 23:28
I will s an angel before thee............ Ex 33:2
me know whom thou wilt s with me....... Ex 33:12
shall s him away by the hand of a...... Lev 16:21
I will also s wild beasts among......... Lev 26:22
I will s the pestilence among you...... Lev 26:25
are left alive of you I will s a........ Lev 26:36
S thou men, that they may search........ Num 13:2
of their fathers shall ye s a man...... Num 13:2
Did I not earnestly s unto thee........ Num 22:37
of Israel, shall ye s to the war........ Num 31:4
We will s men before us, and they...... Deut 1:22
God will s the hornet among them....... Deut 7:20
I will s grass in thy fields for........ Deut 11:15
the elders of his city shall s......... Deut 19:12
hand, and s her out of his house....... Deut 24:1
The LORD shall s upon thee............ Deut 28:20
the LORD shall s against thee.......... Deut 28:48
I will also s the teeth of beasts..... Deut 32:24
and I will s them, and they shall...... Josh 18:4
thou didst s come again unto us....... Judg 13:8
S away the ark of the God of........... 1Sa 5:11
we shall s it to his place............ 1Sa 6:2
If ye s away the ark of the God...... 1Sa 6:3
the God of Israel, s it not empty..... 1Sa 6:3
s it away, that it may go............. 1Sa 6:8
s thee a man out of the land of...... 1Sa 9:16
Up, that I may s thee away............ 1Sa 11:3
that we may s messengers unto all.... 1Sa 11:3
the LORD, and he shall s thunder...... 1Sa 12:17
I will s thee to Jesse the............ 1Sa 16:1
And Samuel said unto Jesse, S........ 1Sa 16:11
S me David thy son, which is with..... 1Sa 16:19
I then s not unto thee, and shew...... 1Sa 20:12
s thee away, that thou mayest go...... 1Sa 20:13
And, behold, I will s a lad........... 1Sa 20:21
Wherefore now s and fetch him unto.... 1Sa 20:31
the business whereabout I s thee....... 1Sa 21:2
men of my lord, whom thou didst s..... 1Sa 25:25
saying, S me Uriah the Hittite......... 2Sa 11:6
that I may s thee to the king, to...... 2Sa 14:32
by them ye shall s unto me every...... 2Sa 15:36
Now therefore s quickly, and tell..... 2Sa 17:16
whithersoever thou shalt s them....... 1Kin 8:44
I will rain upon the earth........... 1Kin 18:1
Now therefore s, and gather to me..... 1Kin 18:19
Yet I will s my servants unto......... 1Kin 20:6
All that thou didst s for to thy...... 1Kin 20:9
I will s thee away with this.......... 1Kin 20:34
And he said, Ye shall not s.......... 2Kin 2:16
till he was ashamed, he said, S....... 2Kin 2:17
S me, I pray thee, one of the......... 2Kin 4:22
I will s a letter unto the king...... 2Kin 5:5
that this man doth s unto me to....... 2Kin 5:7
and spy where he is, that I may s..... 2Kin 6:13
and let us s and see................ 2Kin 7:13
s to meet them, and let him say,..... 2Kin 9:17
s against Judah Rezin the king of.... 2Kin 15:37
I will s a blast upon him, and he.... 2Kin 19:7
let us s abroad unto our brethren.... 1Chr 13:2
didst s him cedars to build him...... 2Chr 2:3
S me now therefore a man cunning..... 2Chr 2:7
S me also cedar trees, fir trees,.... 2Chr 2:8
let him s unto his servants.......... 2Chr 2:15
s rain upon thy land, which thou..... 2Chr 6:27
by the way that thou shalt s them.... 2Chr 6:34
or if I s pestilence among my........ 2Chr 7:13
At that time did king Ahaz s unto.... 2Chr 28:16
s his servants to Jerusalem.......... 2Chr 32:9
let the king s his pleasure to us.... Ezr 5:17
thou wouldest s me unto Judah........ Neh 2:5
So it pleased the king to s me....... Neh 2:6
s portions unto them for whom........ Neh 8:10
to s portions, and to make great..... Neh 8:12
They s forth their little ones....... Job 21:11
Canst thou s lightnings, that........ Job 38:35
S thee help from the sanctuary,...... Ps 20:2
O s out thy light and thy truth...... Ps 43:3
He shall s from heaven, and save..... Ps 57:3
God shall s forth his mercy and...... Ps 57:3
didst s a plentiful rain, whereby.... Ps 68:9
he doth s out his voice, and that.... Ps 68:33
The LORD shall s the rod of thy...... Ps 110:2
I beseech thee, s now prosperity.... Ps 118:25
S thine hand from above,............ Ps 144:7
the sluggard to them that s him..... Prov 10:26
of truth to them that s him......... Prov 22:21
messenger to them that s him........ Prov 25:13
to s forth a stinking savour........ Eccl 10:1
the Lord, saying, Whom shall I s.... Is 6:8
Here am I; s me.................... Is 6:8
I will s him against an............ Is 9:16
s among his fat ones leanness...... Is 10:16
S ye the lamb to the ruler of the.. Is 16:1
he shall s them a saviour, and a... Is 19:20
that s forth thither the feet of... Is 32:20
I will s a blast upon him, and he.. Is 37:7
didst s thy messengers far off,.... Is 57:9
I will s those that escape of...... Is 66:19
go to all that I shall s thee...... Jer 1:7
s unto Kedar, and consider......... Jer 2:10
I will s serpents, cockatrices,.... Jer 8:17
I will s a sword after them, till.. Jer 9:16
for cunning women, that they may... Jer 9:17
I will s for many fishers, saith... Jer 16:16
after will I s for many hunters,... Jer 16:16
I will s the sword, the famine,.... Jer 24:10
Behold, I will s and take all the.. Jer 25:9
all the nations, to whom I s thee.. Jer 25:15

S

sword that I will s among them........... Jer 25:16
sword which I will s among you............ Jer 25:27
s them to the king of Edom, and to...... Jer 27:3
I will s upon them the sword, the......... Jer 29:17
S to all them of the captivity, the....... Jer 29:31
LORD thy God shall s thee to us.......... Jer 42:5
LORD our God, to whom we s thee ...... Jer 42:6
Behold, I will s and take .... Jer 43:10
that I will s unto him wanderers,......... Jer 48:12
I will s the sword after them,.............. Jer 48:37
will s unto Babylon fanners, that......... Jer 51:2
I s thee to the children of .... Eze 2:3
I do s thee unto them .... Eze 2:4
When I shall s upon them the evil........ Eze 5:16
which I will s to destroy you................ Eze 5:16
So will I s upon you famine and,.......... Eze 5:17
I will s mine anger upon thee, and........ Eze 7:3
will s famine upon it, and will............. Eze 14:13
Or if I s a pestilence into that............ Eze 14:19
How much more when I s my four....... Eze 14:21
For I will s into her pestilence,............ Eze 28:23
I will s a fire on Magog, and .... Eze 39:6
but I will s a fire upon his.................. Hos 8:14
I will s you corn, and wine, and........... Joel 2:19
But I will s a fire into the.................. Amos 1:4
But I will s a fire on the wall.............. Amos 1:7
But I will s a fire on the wall.............. Amos 1:10
But I will s a fire upon the wall........... Amos 1:12
But I will s a fire upon Moab, and........ Amos 2:2
But I will s a fire upon Judah,............. Amos 2:5
that I will s a famine in the................ Amos 8:11
I will even s a curse upon you,............ Mal 2:2
I will s my messenger, and he............. Mal 3:1
I will s you Elijah the prophet............. Mal 4:5
that he will s forth labourers.............. Mt 9:38
I s you forth as sheep in the.............. Mt 10:16
I am come to s peace on earth .... Mt 10:34
I came not to s peace, but a............... Mt 10:34
I s my messenger before thy face,........ Mt 11:10
till he s forth judgment unto .... Mt 12:20
of man shall s forth his angels............ Mt 13:41
s the multitude away, that they.......... Mt 14:15
besought him, saying, S her away......... Mt 15:23
I will not s them away fasting,............ Mt 15:32
and straightway he will s them............ Mt 21:3
I s unto you prophets, and wise........... Mt 23:34
he shall s his angels with a .... Mt 24:31
I s my messenger before thy face,........ Mk 1:2
that he might s them forth to .... Mk 3:14
him much that he would not s them..... Mk 5:10
S us into the swine, that we may......... Mk 5:12
began to s them forth by two,............. Mk 6:7
S them away, that they may go........... Mk 6:36
if I s them away fasting to their.......... Mk 8:3
straightway he will s him hither........... Mk 11:3
they s unto him certain of the............ Mk 12:13
And then shall he s his angels............. Mk 13:27
I s my messenger before thy face,........ Lk 7:27
S the multitude away, that they.......... Lk 9:12
that he would s forth labourers........... Lk 10:2
I s you forth as lambs among.............. Lk 10:3
I will s them prophets and .... Lk 11:49
I am come to s fire on the earth .... Lk 12:49
s Lazarus, that he may dip the............ Lk 16:24
that thou wouldest s him to my.......... Lk 16:27
I will s my beloved son .... Lk 20:13
I s the promise of my Father upon....... Lk 24:49
whomsoever I s receiveth me............... Jn 13:20
whom the Father will s in my name...... Jn 14:26
whom I will s unto you from the.......... Jn 15:26
I depart, I will s him unto you............. Jn 16:7
believed that thou didst s me.............. Jn 17:8
hath sent me, even so s I you............. Jn 20:21
he shall s Jesus Christ, which............. Acts 3:20
come, I will s thee into Egypt.............. Acts 7:34
the same did God s to be a ruler......... Acts 7:35
now s men to Joppa, and call for......... Acts 10:5
to s for thee into his house............... Acts 10:22
S therefore to Joppa, and call............. Acts 10:32
S men to Joppa, and call for Simon...... Acts 11:13
determined to s relief unto the........... Acts 11:29
to s chosen men of their own.............. Acts 15:22
brethren s greeting unto the.............. Acts 15:23
to s chosen men unto you with our...... Acts 15:25
for I will s thee far hence unto........... Acts 22:21
that he would s for him to .... Acts 25:3
kept till I might s him to Caesar......... Acts 25:21
I have determined to s him .... Acts 25:25
me unreasonable to s a prisoner......... Acts 25:27
Gentiles, unto whom now I s thee ...... Acts 26:17
them will I s to bring your 1Cor 16:3
to s Timotheus shortly unto .... Phil 2:19
therefore I hope to s presently........... Phil 2:23
to s to you Epaphroditus, my .... Phil 2:25
God shall s them strong delusion......... 2Th 2:11
When I shall s Artemas unto thee,....... Titus 3:12
Doth a fountain s forth at the............ Jas 3:11
s it unto the seven churches............... Rev 1:11
shall s gifts one to another............... Rev 11:10

SENDEST

when thou s him out free from .... Deut 15:13
when thou s him away free from......... Deut 15:18
do, and whithersoever thou s us.......... Josh 1:16
that thou s to enquire of.................. 2Kin 1:6
his countenance, and s him away......... Job 14:20
Thou s forth thy spirit, they are.......... Ps 104:30

SENDETH

hand, and s her out of his house......... Deut 24:3
the LORD s rain upon the earth.......... 1Kin 17:14

and s waters upon the fields.............. Job 5:10
also he s them out, and they.............. Job 12:15
He s the springs into the valleys......... Ps 104:10
He s forth his commandment upon....... Ps 147:15
He s out his word, and melteth........... Ps 147:18
He that s a message by the hand........ Prov 26:6
my spikenard s forth the smell............ Song 1:12
That s ambassadors by the sea,.......... Is 18:2
s rain on the just and on the............. Mt 5:45
he s forth two of his disciples............ Mk 11:1
he s forth two of his disciples............ Mk 14:13
he s an ambassage, and desireth .... Lk 14:32
governor Felix s greeting.................... Acts 23:26

SENDING

this evil in s me away is greater 2Sa 13:16
rising up betimes, and s.................... 2Chr 36:15
of s portions one to another.............. Est 9:19
of s portions one to another, and........ Est 9:22
by s evil angels among them.............. Ps 78:49
shall be for the s forth of oxen.......... Is 7:25
daily rising up early and s them.......... Jer 7:25
prophets, rising early and s them........ Jer 25:4
s them, but ye have not hearkened ..... Jer 26:5
rising up early and s them................. Jer 29:19
s them, saying, Return ye now............ Jer 35:15
s them, saying, Oh, do not this .... Jer 44:4
in s his ambassadors into Egypt.......... Eze 17:15
God s his own Son in the likeness...... Rom 8:3

SENEH (se'-neh) A rock in Benjamin.

Bozez, and the name of the other S..... 1Sa 14:4

SENIR (se'-nur) See SHENIR. A mountain
between Amana and Hermon.

from Bashan unto Baal-hermon and S.. 1Chr 5:23
the ship masts of fir trees of S........... Eze 27:5

SENNACHERIB (sen-nak'-er-ib) An Assyrian
king.

year of king Hezekiah did S king........ 2Kin 18:13
and hear the words of S, which 2Kin 19:16
S king of Assyria I have heard 2Kin 19:20
So S king of Assyria departed, and...... 2Kin 19:36
S king of Assyria came, and 2Chr 32:1
when Hezekiah saw that S was come.... 2Chr 32:2
After this did S king of Assyria........... 2Chr 32:9
S king of Assyria, saying,................... 2Chr 32:10
the hand of S the king of Assyria........ 2Chr 32:22
that S king of Assyria came up........... Is 36:1
and hear all the words of S................ Is 37:17
to me against S king of Assyria........... Is 37:21
So S king of Assyria departed, and...... Is 37:37

SENSE

of God distinctly, and gave the s........ Neh 8:8

SENSES

s exercised to discern both good......... Heb 5:14

SENSUAL

not from above, but is earthly, s......... Jas 3:15
they who separate themselves, s.......... Jude 19

SENT See PREFACE.

SENTENCE

shall shew thee the s of judgment...... Deut 17:9
thou shalt do according to the s .... Deut 17:10
According to the s of the law............. Deut 17:11
the s which they shall shew thee......... Deut 17:11
Let my s come forth from thy............ Ps 17:2
a divine s is in the lips of the .... Prov 16:10
Because s against an evil work is......... Eccl 8:11
also will I give s against them............. Jer 4:12
Pilate gave s that it should be .... Lk 23:24
Wherefore my s is, that we .... Acts 15:19
But we had the s of death in............. 2Cor 1:9

SENTENCES

of dreams, and shewing of hard s ...... Dan 5:12
and understanding dark s, shall........... Dan 8:23

SENTEST

thou s forth thy wrath, which............. Ex 15:7
unto the land whither thou s us,......... Num 13:27
messengers which thou s unto me ...... Num 24:12
the things which thou s to me for....... Josh 5:8

SENUAH (sen'-u-ah) See HASSENUAH. Father of
Judah.

Judah the son of S was second........... Neh 11:9

SEORIM (se-o'-rim) A sanctuary servant.

third to Harim, the fourth to S.......... 1Chr 24:8

SEPARATE

s thyself, I pray thee, from me........... Gen 13:9
And Jacob did s the lambs, and set..... Gen 30:40
him that was s from his brethren........ Gen 49:26
Thus shall ye s the children of........... Lev 15:31
that they s themselves from the .... Lev 22:2
s themselves to vow a vow of a.......... Num 6:2
to s themselves unto the LORD........... Num 6:2
He shall s himself from wine and........ Num 6:3
Thus shalt thou s the Levites............. Num 8:14
S yourselves from among this .... Num 16:21
Thou shalt s three cities for .... Deut 19:2
Thou shalt s three cities for .... Deut 19:7
the LORD shalt s him unto evil........... Deut 29:21
the cities for the children of .... Deut 19:9
For thou didst s them from among...... 1Kin 8:53
s yourselves from the people of.......... Ezr 10:11
to s himself thence in the midst .... Jer 37:12
the s place at the end toward the ...... Eze 41:12
the s place, and the building,............. Eze 41:13
of the s place toward the east,........... Eze 41:14

the s place which was behind it.......... Eze 41:15
that was over against the s place........ Eze 42:1
east, over against the s place .... Eze 42:10
which are before the s place............... Eze 42:13
he shall s them one from another,....... Mt 25:32
when they shall s you from their........ Lk 6:22
S me Barnabas and Saul for the .... Acts 13:2
Who shall s us from the love of......... Rom 8:35
shall be able to s us from the............ Rom 8:39
out from among them, and be ye s...... 2Cor 6:17
s from sinners, and made higher.......... Heb 7:26
These be they who s themselves......... Jude 19

SEPARATED

they s themselves the one from........... Gen 13:11
after that Lot was s from him............. Gen 13:14
people shall be s from thy bowels........ Gen 25:23
so shall we be s, I and thy people....... Ex 33:16
which have s you from other .... Lev 20:24
which I have s from you as clean......... Lev 20:25
that the God of Israel hath s you....... Num 16:9
time the LORD s the tribe of Levi....... Deut 10:8
when he s the sons of Adam, he......... Deut 32:8
him that was s from his brethren........ Deut 33:16
of the Gadites there s themselves 1Chr 12:8
and Aaron was s, that he should......... 1Chr 23:13
the captains of the host s to the 1Chr 25:1
Then Amaziah s them, to wit, the....... 2Chr 25:10
all such as had s themselves unto ...... Ezr 6:21
Then I s twelve of the chief of .... Ezr 8:24
have not s themselves from the.......... Ezr 9:1
himself s from the congregation.......... Ezr 10:8
of them by their names, were s........... Ezr 10:16
we are s upon the wall, one far.......... Neh 4:19
the seed of Israel s themselves.......... Neh 9:2
all they that had s themselves........... Neh 10:28
that they s from Israel all the .... Neh 13:3
having s himself, seeketh and .... Prov 18:1
but the poor is s from................... Prov 19:4
hath utterly s me from his people....... Is 56:3
iniquities have s between you............. Is 59:2
for themselves are s with whores........ Hos 4:14
s themselves unto that shame .... Hos 9:10
the s disciples, disputing daily........... Acts 19:9
s unto the gospel of God,................. Rom 1:1
who s me from my mother's womb,....... Gal 1:15
s himself, fearing them which............ Gal 2:12

SEPARATETH

in the which he s himself unto........... Num 6:5
All the days that he s himself............. Num 6:6
a whisperer s chief friends................ Prov 16:28
repeateth a matter s very friends....... Prov 17:9
which s himself from me, and............. Eze 14:7

SEPARATING

s myself, as I have done these so ...... Zec 7:3

SEPARATION

according to the days of the s........... Lev 12:2
be unclean two weeks, as in her s...... Lev 12:5
upon in her s shall be unclean.......... Lev 15:20
days out of the time of her s .... Lev 15:25
it run beyond the time of her s......... Lev 15:25
shall be as the days of her s............. Lev 15:25
be unto her as the bed of her s........ Lev 15:26
as the uncleanness of her s............... Lev 15:26
All the days of his s shall he .... Num 6:4
s there shall no razor come upon....... Num 6:5
All the days of his s he is holy.......... Num 6:5
unto the LORD the days of his s........ Num 6:12
lost, because his s was defiled........... Num 6:12
the days of his s are fulfilled............ Num 6:13
shall shave the head of his s at........ Num 6:18
the hair of the head of his s............ Num 6:18
after the hair of his s is shaven........ Num 6:19
offering unto the LORD for his s........ Num 6:21
he must do after the law of his s...... Num 6:21
of Israel for a water of s .... Num 19:9
because the water of s was not .... Num 19:13
the water s hath not been................ Num 19:20
water of s shall wash his clothes....... Num 19:21
of s shall be unclean until even......... Num 19:21
be purified with the water of s......... Num 31:23
to make a s between the sanctuary..... Eze 42:20

SEPHAR (se'-far) A mountain in Arabia.

as thou goest unto S a mount of....... Gen 10:30

SEPHARAD (sef'-a-rad) A city in Media.

of Jerusalem, which is in S............... Obad 20

SEPHARVAIM (sef-ar-va'-im) See
SEPHAVITES. A city in Mesopotamia.

Ava, and from Hamath, and from S..... 2Kin 17:24
and Anammelech, the gods of S 2Kin 17:31
where are the gods of S, Hena, and.... 2Kin 18:34
and the king of the city of S............ 2Kin 19:13
where are the gods of S .... Is 36:19
and the king of the city of S............ Is 37:13

SEPHARVITES (sef'-ar-vites) Inhabitants of
Sepharvaim.

the S burnt their children in............. 2Kin 17:31

SEPULCHRE

us shall withhold from thee his s........ Gen 23:6
shalt thou bury in this day............... Deut 34:6
was buried in the s of Joash his .... Judg 8:32
s in the border of Benjamin at.......... 1Sa 10:2
buried him in the s of his father....... 2Sa 2:32
buried it in the s of Abner in........... 2Sa 4:12
was buried in the s of his father....... 2Sa 17:23
in the s of Kish his father............... 2Sa 21:14

come unto the s of thy fathers ... 1Kin 13:22
then bury me in the s wherein the ... 1Kin 13:31
buried him in his s with his ... 2Kin 9:28
cast the man into the s of Elisha ... 2Kin 13:21
he was buried in his s in the ... 2Kin 21:26
It is the s of the man of God ... 2Kin 23:17
and buried him in his own s ... 2Kin 23:30
their throat is an open s ... Ps 5:9
thou hast hewed thee out a s here ... Is 22:16
that heweth him out an s on high ... Is 22:16
Their quiver is as an open s ... Jer 5:16
great stone to the door of the s ... Mt 27:60
Mary, sitting over against the s ... Mt 27:61
Command therefore that the s be ... Mt 27:64
So they went, and made the s sure ... Mt 27:66
and the other Mary to see the s ... Mt 28:1
quickly from the s with fear ... Mt 28:8
laid him in a s which was hewn ... Mk 15:46
a stone unto the door of the s ... Mk 15:46
they came unto the s at the ... Mk 16:2
the stone from the door of the s ... Mk 16:3
And entering into the s, they saw ... Mk 16:5
out quickly, and fled from the s ... Mk 16:8
laid it in a s that was hewn in ... Lk 23:53
followed after, and beheld the s ... Lk 23:55
the morning, they came unto the s ... Lk 24:1
the stone rolled away from the s ... Lk 24:2
And returned from the s, and told ... Lk 24:9
arose Peter, and ran unto the s ... Lk 24:12
which were early at the s ... Lk 24:22
which were with went to the s a ... Lk 24:24
and in the garden a new s, wherein ... Jn 19:41
for the s was nigh at hand ... Jn 19:42
when it was yet dark, unto the s ... Jn 20:1
the stone taken away from the s ... Jn 20:1
taken away the Lord out of the s ... Jn 20:2
other disciple, and came to the s ... Jn 20:3
Peter, and came first to the s ... Jn 20:4
following him, and went into the s ... Jn 20:6
which came first to the s ... Jn 20:8
stood without at the s weeping ... Jn 20:11
down, and looked into the s ... Jn 20:11
his s is with us unto this day ... Acts 2:29
laid in the s that Abraham bought ... Acts 7:16
from the tree, and laid him in a s ... Acts 13:29
Their throat is an open s ... Rom 3:13

SEPULCHRES
the choice of our s bury thee dead ... Gen 23:6
he spied the s that were there in ... Gen 23:6
and took the bones out of the s ... 2Chr 16:14
And they buried him in his own s ... 2Chr 16:14
but not in the s of the kings ... 2Chr 21:20
him not in the s of the kings ... 2Chr 24:25
into the s of the kings of Israel ... 2Chr 28:27
of the s of the sons of David ... 2Chr 32:33
in one of the s of his fathers ... 2Chr 35:24
city, the place of my fathers' s ... Neh 2:3
unto the city of my fathers' s ... Neh 2:5
place over against the s of David ... Neh 3:16
for ye are like unto whited s ... Mt 23:27
garnish the s of the righteous ... Mt 23:29
ye build the s of the prophets ... Lk 11:47
killed them, and ye build their s ... Lk 11:48

SERAH (se'-rah) See SARAH. *A daughter of Asher.*
and Beriah, and S their sister ... Gen 46:17
and Beriah, and S their sister ... 1Chr 7:30

SERAIAH (se-ra-i'-ah) See SHAVSHA.
1. David's scribe.
and S was the scribe ... 2Sa 8:17
2. High priest in Zedekiah's time.
the guard took S the chief priest ... 2Kin 25:18
And Azariah begat S, and Seraiah ... 1Chr 6:14
Seraiah, and S begat Jehozadak ... 1Chr 6:14
king of Persia, Ezra the son of S ... Ezr 7:1
the guard took S the chief priest ... Jer 52:24
3. Son of Tanhumeth.
S the son of Tanhumeth the ... 2Kin 25:23
S the son of Tanhumeth, and the ... Jer 40:8
4. A son of Kenaz.
Othniel, and S ... 1Chr 4:13
S begat Joab, the father of the ... 1Chr 4:14
5. Son of Asiel.
the son of Josibiah, the son of S ... 1Chr 4:35
6. A priest with Zerubbabel.
Jeshua, Nehemiah, S, Reelaiah, ... Ezr 2:2
S, Azariah, Jeremiah, ... Neh 10:2
S, Jeremiah, Ezra, ... Neh 12:1
of S, Meraiah, ... Neh 12:12
7. An exile.
S the son of Hilkiah, the son of ... Neh 11:11
8. Son of Azriel.
S the son of Azriel, and Shelemiah ... Jer 36:26
9. Son of Neriah.
commanded S the son of Neriah ... Jer 51:59
this S was a quiet prince ... Jer 51:59
And Jeremiah said to S, When thou ... Jer 51:61

SERAPHIMS
Above it stood the s ... Is 6:2
Then flew one of the s unto me ... Is 6:6

SERED (se'-red) See SARDITES. *A son of Zebulun.*
S, and Elon, and Jahleel ... Gen 46:14
of S, the family of the Sardites ... Num 26:26

SEREDITES See SARDITES.

SERGIUS (sur'-je-us) *Roman governor of Cyprus.*
country, S Paulus, a prudent man ... Acts 13:7

SERJEANTS
day, the magistrates sent the s ... Acts 16:35
the s told these words unto the ... Acts 16:38

SERPENT
Now the s was more subtil than ... Gen 3:1
And the woman said unto the s ... Gen 3:2
the s said unto the woman, Ye ... Gen 3:4
The s beguiled me, and I did eat ... Gen 3:13
And the Lord God said unto the s ... Gen 3:14
Dan shall be a s by the way ... Gen 49:17
on the ground, and it became a s ... Ex 4:3
Pharaoh, and it shall become a s ... Ex 7:9
his servants, and it became a s ... Ex 7:10
aught a thou take in thine hand ... Ex 7:15
unto Moses, Make thee a fiery s ... Num 21:8
And Moses made a s of brass ... Num 21:9
that if a s had bitten any man ... Num 21:9
when he beheld the s of brass ... Num 21:9
the brasen s that Moses had made ... 2Kin 18:4
hand hath formed the crooked s ... Job 26:13
poison is like the poison of a s ... Ps 58:4
sharpened their tongues like a s ... Ps 140:3
At the last it biteth like a s ... Prov 23:32
the way of a s upon a rock ... Prov 30:19
an hedge, a s shall bite him ... Eccl 10:8
Surely the s will bite without ... Eccl 10:11
fruit shall be a fiery flying s ... Is 14:29
punish leviathan the piercing s ... Is 27:1
even leviathan that crooked s ... Is 27:1
lion, the viper and fiery flying s ... Is 30:6
voice thereof shall go like a s ... Jer 46:22
hand on the wall, and a s bit him ... Amos 5:19
sea, thence will I command the s ... Amos 9:3
They shall lick the dust like a s ... Mic 7:17
ask a fish, will he give him a s ... Mt 7:10
will he for a fish give him a s ... Lk 11:11
lifted up the s in the wilderness ... Jn 3:14
as the s beguiled Eve through his ... 2Cor 11:3
dragon was cast out, that old s ... Rev 12:9
a time, from the face of the s ... Rev 12:14
the s cast out of his mouth water ... Rev 12:15
hold on the dragon, that old s ... Rev 20:2

SERPENT'S
for out of the s root shall come ... Is 14:29
and dust shall be the s meat ... Is 65:25

SERPENTS
man his rod, and they became s ... Ex 7:12
sent fiery s among the people ... Num 21:6
that he take away the s from us ... Num 21:7
wilderness, wherein were fiery s ... Deut 8:15
with the poison of s of the dust ... Deut 32:24
For, behold, I will send s ... Jer 8:17
be ye therefore wise as s ... Mt 10:16
Ye s, ye generation of vipers, ... Mt 23:33
They shall take up s ... Mk 16:18
give unto you power to tread on s ... Lk 10:19
tempted, and were destroyed of s ... 1Cor 10:9
of beasts, and of birds, and of s ... Jas 3:7
for their tails were like unto s ... Rev 9:19

SERUG (se'-rug) See SARUCH. *Father of Nahor.*
two and thirty years, and begat S ... Gen 11:20
after he begat S two hundred ... Gen 11:21
S lived thirty years, and begat ... Gen 11:22
S lived after he begat Nahor two ... Gen 11:23
S, Nahor, Terah, ... 1Chr 1:26

SERVANT See PREFACE.
for thy s heareth ... 1Sa 3:9
Give therefore thy s an ... 1Kin 3:9
O ye seed of Israel his s ... 1Chr 16:13
I called my s, and he gave me no ... Job 19:16
put not thy s away in anger ... Ps 27:9
O Lord, truly I am thy s ... Ps 116:16
I am thy s, and the son of thine ... Ps 116:16
Deal bountifully with thy s ... Ps 119:17
the borrower is s to the lender ... Prov 22:7
as with the s, so with his master ... Is 24:2
and said unto thee, Thou art my s ... Is 41:9
shall my righteous s justify many ... Is 53:11
Is Israel a s ... Jer 2:14
his s was healed in the selfsame ... Mt 8:13
master, nor the s above his lord ... Mt 10:24
his master, and the s as his lord ... Mt 10:25
Who then is a faithful and wise s ... Mt 24:45
done, thou good and faithful s ... Mt 25:21
shall he last of all, and s of all ... Mk 9:35
the chiefest, shall be s of all ... Mk 10:44
And that s, which knew his lord's ... Lk 12:47
No s can serve two masters ... Lk 16:13
The s is not greater than his ... Jn 13:16
for the s knoweth not what his ... Jn 15:15
The s is not greater than his ... Jn 15:20
Art thou called being a s ... 1Cor 7:21
and took upon him the form of a s ... Phil 2:7

SERVANT'S
in, I pray you, into your s house ... Gen 19:2
thou hast spoken also of thy s ... 2Sa 7:19
to thy son for David my s sake ... 1Kin 11:13
of his life for David my s sake ... 1Kin 11:34
Judah for David his s sake ... 2Kin 8:19
thou hast also spoken of thy s ... 1Chr 17:17
O Lord, for thy s sake, and ... 1Chr 17:19
For Jacob my s sake, and Israel ... Is 45:4
The s name was Malchus ... Jn 18:10

SERVANTS See PREFACE.
my s shall be with thy ... 2Chr 2:8
Lord redeemeth the soul of his s ... Ps 34:22
it, and my s shall dwell among ... Is 65:9

unto you all my s the prophets ... Jer 35:15
How many hired s of my father's ... Lk 15:17
Henceforth I call you not s ... Jn 15:15
ye yield yourselves s to obey ... Rom 6:16
his s ye are to whom ye obey ... Rom 6:16
be not ye the s of men ... 1Cor 7:23
but as the s of God ... 1Pet 2:16
Praise our God, all ye his s ... Rev 19:5

SERVANTS'
Thy s trade hath been about ... Gen 46:34
of Pharaoh, and into his s houses ... Ex 8:24
Return for thy s sake, the tribes ... Is 63:17
so will I do for my s sakes ... Is 65:8

SERVE
is not theirs, and shall s them ... Gen 15:13
that nation, whom they shall s ... Gen 15:14
and the elder shall s the younger ... Gen 25:23
Let people s thee, and nations bow ... Gen 27:29
thou live, and shalt s thy brother ... Gen 27:40
thou therefore s me for nought ... Gen 29:15
I will s thee seven years for ... Gen 29:18
did not I s with thee for Rachel ... Gen 29:25
the service which thou didst s ... Gen 29:27
of Israel to s with rigour ... Ex 1:13
service, wherein they made them s ... Ex 1:14
ye shall s God upon this mountain ... Ex 3:12
Let my son go, that he may s me ... Ex 4:23
that they may s me in the ... Ex 7:16
my people go, that they may s me ... Ex 8:1
my people go, that they may s me ... Ex 8:20
my people go, that they may s me ... Ex 9:1
my people go, that they may s me ... Ex 9:13
my people go, that they may s me ... Ex 10:3
that they may s the Lord their ... Ex 10:7
them, Go, s the Lord your God ... Ex 10:8
ye that are men, and s the Lord ... Ex 10:11
Moses, and said, Go ye, s the Lord ... Ex 10:24
we take to s the Lord our God ... Ex 10:26
not with what we must s the Lord ... Ex 10:26
s the Lord, as ye have said ... Ex 12:31
that we may s the Egyptians ... Ex 14:12
better for us to s the Egyptians ... Ex 14:12
down thyself to them, nor s them ... Ex 20:5
servant, six years he shall s ... Ex 21:2
and he shall s him for ever ... Ex 21:6
nor s them, nor do after their ... Ex 23:24
ye shall s the Lord your God, and ... Ex 23:25
for if thou s their gods, it will ... Ex 23:33
compel him to s a bondservant ... Lev 25:39
shall s thee unto the year of ... Lev 25:40
families of the Gershonites, to s ... Num 4:24
so shall they s ... Num 4:26
thereof, and shall s no more ... Num 8:25
and ye shall s ... Num 18:7
for their service which they s ... Num 18:21
s them, which the Lord thy God ... Deut 4:19
And there ye shall s gods, the ... Deut 4:28
thyself unto them, nor s them ... Deut 5:9
s him, and shalt swear by his name ... Deut 6:13
me, that they may s other gods ... Deut 7:4
neither shalt thou s their gods ... Deut 7:16
s them, and worship them, I ... Deut 8:19
to s the Lord thy God with all ... Deut 10:12
him shalt thou s, and to him shalt ... Deut 10:20
and s other gods, and worship ... Deut 11:13
s other gods, and worship them ... Deut 11:16
did these nations s their gods ... Deut 12:30
hast not known, and let us s them ... Deut 13:2
obey his voice, and ye shall s him ... Deut 13:4
s other gods, which thou hast not ... Deut 13:6
s other gods, which ye have not ... Deut 13:13
unto thee, and s thee six years ... Deut 15:12
unto thee, and they shall s thee ... Deut 20:11
to go after other gods to s them ... Deut 28:14
and there shalt thou s other gods ... Deut 28:36
Therefore shalt thou s thine ... Deut 28:48
and there thou shalt s other gods ... Deut 28:64
the s the gods of these nations ... Deut 29:18
and worship other gods, and s them ... Deut 29:26
s them, and provoke me, and break ... Deut 31:20
unto this day, and s under tribute ... Josh 16:10
to s him with all your heart and ... Josh 22:5
to swear by them, neither s them ... Josh 23:7
s him in sincerity and in truth ... Josh 24:14
and s ye the Lord ... Josh 24:14
seem evil unto you to s the Lord ... Josh 24:15
you this day whom ye will s ... Josh 24:15
and my house, we will s the Lord ... Josh 24:15
forsake the Lord, to s other gods ... Josh 24:16
therefore will we also s the Lord ... Josh 24:18
the people, Ye cannot s the Lord ... Josh 24:19
s strange gods, then he will turn ... Josh 24:20
but we will s the Lord ... Josh 24:21
chosen you the Lord, to s him ... Josh 24:22
The Lord our God will we s ... Josh 24:24
in following other gods s them ... Judg 2:19
is Shechem, that we should s him ... Judg 9:28
s the men of Hamor the father of ... Judg 9:28
for why should we s him ... Judg 9:28
Abimelech, that we should s him ... Judg 9:38
unto the Lord, and s him only ... 1Sa 7:3
that thou do as occasion s thee ... 1Sa 11:10
with us, and we will s thee ... 1Sa 11:1
of our enemies, and we will s them ... 1Sa 12:10
s him, and obey his voice, and not ... 1Sa 12:14
but s the Lord with all your ... 1Sa 12:24
s him in truth with all your ... 1Sa 12:24
shall ye be our servants, and s us ... 1Sa 17:9
Lord, saying, Go, s other gods ... 1Sa 26:19
Jerusalem, then I will s the Lord ... 2Sa 15:8

S

And again, whom should I s.............. 2Sa 16:19
should I not s in the presence of...... 2Sa 16:19
which I knew not shall s me............ 2Sa 22:44
s other gods, and worship them....... 1Kin 9:6
us, lighter, and we will s them........ 1Kin 12:4
people this day, and will s them...... 1Kin 12:7
but Jehu shall s him much............. 2Kin 10:18
nor s them, nor sacrifice to them.... 2Kin 17:35
land, and s the king of Babylon...... 2Kin 25:24
s him with a perfect heart and....... 1Chr 28:9
s other gods, and worship them...... 2Chr 7:19
he put upon us, and we will s thee... 2Chr 10:4
to s him, and that ye should......... 2Chr 29:11
s the LORD your God, that their...... 2Chr 30:8
commanded Judah to s the........... 2Chr 33:16
that were present in Israel to s...... 2Chr 34:33
even to s the LORD their God........ 2Chr 34:33
s now the LORD your God, and his... 2Chr 35:3
Almighty, that we should s him...... Job 21:15
s him, they shall spend their........ Job 36:11
the unicorn be willing to s thee..... Job 39:9
S the LORD with fear, and rejoice.... Ps 2:11
whom I have not known shall s me... Ps 18:43
A seed shall s him..................... Ps 22:30
all nations shall s him................. Ps 72:11
be all they that s graven images..... Ps 97:7
S the LORD with gladness.............. Ps 100:2
in a perfect way, he shall s me....... Ps 101:6
and the kingdoms, to s the LORD..... Ps 102:22
wherein thou wast made to s......... Is 14:3
shall s with the Assyrians............. Is 19:23
caused thee to s with an offering.... Is 43:23
hast made me to s with thy sins..... Is 43:24
to s him, and to love the name of... Is 56:6
that will not s thee shall perish...... Is 60:12
so shall ye s strangers in a land..... Jer 5:19
went after other gods to s them..... Jer 11:10
to s them, and to worship them...... Jer 13:10
there shall ye s other gods day...... Jer 16:13
I will cause thee to s thine........... Jer 17:4
go not after other gods to s them... Jer 25:6
these nations shall s the king of..... Jer 25:11
great kings shall s themselves of.... Jer 25:14
field have I given also to s him....... Jer 27:6
And all nations shall s................ Jer 27:7
kings shall s themselves of him....... Jer 27:7
kingdom which will not s the same... Jer 27:8
Ye shall not s the king of............ Jer 27:9
s him, those will I let remain........ Jer 27:11
s him and his people, and live........ Jer 27:12
will not s the king of Babylon........ Jer 27:13
Ye shall not s the king of............ Jer 27:14
s the king of Babylon, and live...... Jer 27:17
that they may s Nebuchadnezzar... Jer 28:14
and they shall s him................. Jer 28:14
shall no more s themselves of him.. Jer 30:8
But they shall s the LORD their...... Jer 30:9
none should s himself of them....... Jer 34:9
that none should s themselves of... Jer 34:10
go not after other gods to s them... Jer 35:15
Fear not to s the Chaldeans......... Jer 40:9
s the king of Babylon, and it........ Jer 40:9
at Mizpah to s the Chaldeans....... Jer 40:10
to s other gods, whom they knew.... Jer 44:3
the countries, to s wood and stone.. Eze 20:32
s ye every one his idols, and......... Eze 20:39
all of them in the land, s me......... Eze 20:40
s a great service against Tyrus...... Eze 29:18
food unto them that s the city...... Eze 48:18
they that s the city shall s.......... Eze 48:19
they s not thy gods, nor worship.... Dan 3:12
and Abed-nego, do not ye s my gods. Dan 3:14
our God whom we is able to......... Dan 3:17
king, that we will not s thy gods.... Dan 3:18
might not s nor worship any god.... Dan 3:28
and languages, should s him........ Dan 7:14
kingdom, and all dominions shall s.. Dan 7:27
to s him with one consent........... Zeph 3:9
Ye have said, It is vain to s God..... Mal 3:14
thy God, and him only shalt thou s.. Mt 4:10
No man can s two masters............ Mt 6:24
Ye cannot s God and mammon....... Mt 6:24
enemies might s him without fear... Lk 1:74
thy God, and him only shalt thou s.. Lk 4:8
my sister hath left me to s alone.... Lk 10:40
and will come forth and s them...... Lk 12:37
Lo, these many years do I s thee.... Lk 15:29
No servant can s two masters....... Lk 16:13
Ye cannot s God and mammon....... Lk 16:13
s me, till I have eaten and.......... Lk 17:8
that is chief, as he that doth s...... Lk 22:26
If any man s me, let him follow...... Jn 12:26
if any man s me, him will my......... Jn 12:26
the word of God, and s tables....... Acts 6:2
come forth, and s me in this place.. Acts 7:7
of God, whose I am, and whom I s... Acts 27:23
whom I s with my spirit in the....... Rom 1:9
henceforth we should not s sin...... Rom 6:6
that we should s in newness of...... Rom 7:6
mind I myself s the law of God...... Rom 7:25
The elder shall s the younger....... Rom 9:12
For they that are such s not our.... Rom 16:18
flesh, but by love s one another..... Gal 5:13
for ye s the Lord Christ.............. Col 3:24
to God from idols to s the living.... 1Th 1:9
whom I s from my forefathers with.. 2Ti 1:3
Who s unto the example and shadow. Heb 8:5
dead works to s the living God...... Heb 9:14
whereby we may s God acceptably.. Heb 12:28
to eat which s the tabernacle....... Heb 13:10

s him day and night in his temple.... Rev 7:15
and his servants shall s him......... Rev 22:3

SERVED

Twelve years they s Chedorlaomer.. Gen 14:4
Jacob s seven years for Rachel...... Gen 29:20
s with him yet seven other years.... Gen 29:30
children, for whom I have s thee.... Gen 29:30
Thou knowest how I have s thee.... Gen 29:29
all my power I have s your father... Gen 31:6
I s thee fourteen years for thy...... Gen 31:41
grace in his sight, and he s him..... Gen 39:4
Joseph with them, and he s them... Gen 40:4
ye shall possess s their gods........ Deut 12:2
s other gods, and worshiped them.. Deut 17:3
s other gods, and worshipped them. Deut 29:26
s other gods, and bowed yourselves. Josh 23:16
and they s other gods............... Josh 24:2
the gods which your fathers s on... Josh 24:14
the gods which your fathers s....... Josh 24:15
Israel s the LORD all the days of.... Josh 24:31
the people s the LORD all the....... Judg 2:7
sight of the LORD, and s Baalim...... Judg 2:11
the LORD, and s Baal and Ashtaroth. Judg 2:13
to their sons, and s their gods...... Judg 3:6
God, and s Baalim and the groves.. Judg 3:7
and the children of Israel s.......... Judg 3:8
So the children of Israel s Eglon.... Judg 3:14
unto him, Why hast thou s us thus.. Judg 4:1
s Baalim, and Ashtaroth, and the... Judg 10:6
and forsook the LORD, and s not him. Judg 10:6
our God, and also s Baalim.......... Judg 10:10
have forsaken me, and s other gods. Judg 10:13
from among them, and s the LORD... Judg 10:16
and Ashtaroth, and s the LORD only. 1Sa 7:4
s other gods, so do they also........ 1Sa 8:8
have s Baalim and Ashtaroth....... 1Sa 12:10
made peace with Israel, and s them. 2Sa 10:19
as I have s in thy Father's.......... 2Sa 16:19
s Solomon all the days of his........ 1Kin 4:21
have worshipped them, and s them.. 1Kin 9:9
s Baal, and worshiped him.......... 1Kin 16:31
For he s Baal, and worshipped him,. 1Kin 22:53
unto them, Ahab s Baal a little..... 2Kin 10:18
For they s idols, whereof the....... 2Kin 17:12
all the host of heaven, and s Baal... 2Kin 17:16
s their own gods, after the.......... 2Kin 17:33
s their graven images, both their... 2Kin 17:41
the king of Assyria, and s him not... 2Kin 18:7
all the host of heaven, and s them.. 2Kin 21:3
s the idols that his father.......... 2Kin 21:21
the idols that his father s.......... 2Kin 21:21
and told David how the men were s. 1Chr 19:5
their officers that s the king in..... 1Chr 27:1
and worshipped them, and s them... 2Chr 7:22
fathers, and s groves and idols...... 2Chr 24:18
all the host of heaven, and s them.. 2Chr 33:3
his father had made, and s them... 2Chr 33:22
For they have not s thee in their... Neh 9:35
the seven chamberlains that s in... Est 1:10
And they s their idols............... Ps 106:36
rewardeth thee as thou hast s us... Ps 137:8
king himself s s for the field....... Eccl 5:9
s strange gods in your land, so..... Jer 5:19
have loved, and whom they have s.. Jer 8:2
after other gods, and have s them.. Jer 16:11
worshipped other gods, and s them.. Jer 22:9
when he hath s thee six years,...... Jer 34:14
which s the king of Babylon, into... Jer 52:12
service that he had s against it..... Eze 29:18
labour wherewith he s against it.... Eze 29:20
those that s themselves of them... Eze 34:27
Israel s for a wife, and for a........ Hos 12:12
but s God with fastings and.......... Lk 2:37
and Martha s...................... Jn 12:2
after he had s his own generation... Acts 13:36
s the creature more than the........ Rom 1:25
he hath s with me in the gospel..... Phil 2:22

SERVEDST

Because thou s not the LORD thy.... Deut 28:47

SERVEST

Thy God whom thou s continually... Dan 6:16
whom thou s continually, able to.... Dan 6:20

SERVETH

thereof, and all that s thereto...... Num 3:36
spareth his own son that s him...... Mal 3:17
s God and him that s him not....... Mal 3:18
sitteth at meat, or he that s........ Lk 22:27
but I am among you as he that s.... Lk 22:27
s Christ is acceptable to God....... Rom 14:18
but prophesying s not for them..... 1Cor 14:22
Wherefore then s the law........... Gal 3:19

SERVICE

give thee this also for the s......... Gen 29:27
for thou knowest my s which I...... Gen 30:26
in all manner of s in the field....... Ex 1:14
all their s, wherein they made...... Ex 1:14
that ye shall keep this s............ Ex 12:25
unto you, What mean ye by this s... Ex 12:26
shalt keep this s in this month..... Ex 13:5
tabernacle in all the s thereof...... Ex 27:19
the s of the tabernacle of.......... Ex 30:16
And the cloths of s, and the holy... Ex 31:10
The cloths of s, to do s in.......... Ex 35:19
to do s in the holy place, and....... Ex 35:19
congregation, and for all his s...... Ex 35:21
wood for any work of the s.......... Ex 35:24
work for the s of the sanctuary.... Ex 36:1
work of the s of the sanctuary..... Ex 36:3

than enough for the s of the work.. Ex 36:5
for the s of the Levites, by the..... Ex 38:21
and scarlet, they made cloths of s.. Ex 39:1
to do s in the holy place, and....... Ex 39:1
of the s of the tabernacle.......... Ex 39:40
The cloths of s to do................ Ex 39:41
to do s in the holy place............ Ex 39:41
to do the s of the tabernacle....... Num 3:7
to do the s of the tabernacle....... Num 3:8
cords of it for all the s thereof..... Num 3:26
the hanging, and all the s thereof... Num 3:31
This shall be the s of the sons...... Num 4:4
appoint them every one to his s..... Num 4:19
that enter in to perform the s....... Num 4:23
This is the s of the families of...... Num 4:24
and all the instruments of their s... Num 4:26
his sons shall be all the s of........ Num 4:27
their burdens, and in all their s..... Num 4:27
This is the s of the families of...... Num 4:28
one that entereth into the s........ Num 4:30
according to all their s in the...... Num 4:31
instruments, and with all their s.... Num 4:32
This is the s of the families of...... Num 4:33
Merari, according to all their s...... Num 4:33
one that entereth into the s........ Num 4:35
all that might do s in the........... Num 4:37
one that entereth into the s........ Num 4:39
of all that might do s in the........ Num 4:41
one that entereth into the s........ Num 4:43
came to do the s of the ministry.... Num 4:47
the s of the burden in the.......... Num 4:47
every one according to his s......... Num 4:49
do the s of the tabernacle of the... Num 7:5
to every man according to his s..... Num 7:5
of Gershon, according to their s..... Num 7:7
have s Baalim according to their s.. Num 7:7
of Merari, according unto their s.... Num 7:8
because the s of the sanctuary..... Num 7:9
may execute the s of the LORD...... Num 8:11
do the s of the tabernacle of the... Num 8:15
to do the s of the children of....... Num 8:19
their s in the tabernacle of the..... Num 8:22
the s of the tabernacle of the...... Num 8:24
cease waiting upon the s thereof... Num 8:25
keep the charge, and shall do no s.. Num 8:26
s of the tabernacle of the LORD..... Num 16:9
for all the s of the tabernacle...... Num 18:4
to do the s of the tabernacle of.... Num 18:6
office unto you as a s of a gift..... Num 18:7
for their s which they serve,........ Num 18:21
even the s of the tabernacle of..... Num 18:21
do the s of the tabernacle of....... Num 18:23
your s in the tabernacle of the..... Num 18:31
that we might do the s of the...... Josh 22:27
thou the grievous s of thy father... 1Kin 12:4
the s of song in the house of the... 1Chr 6:31
appointed unto all manner of s of... 1Chr 6:48
work of the s of the house of God.. 1Chr 9:13
were over the work of the s........ 1Chr 9:19
the s of the house of the LORD...... 1Chr 23:24
vessels of it for the s thereof...... 1Chr 23:26
the s of the house of the LORD...... 1Chr 23:28
the work of the s of the house of... 1Chr 23:28
in the s of the house of God........ 1Chr 23:32
to their offices in their s........... 1Chr 24:3
s to come into the house of the.... 1Chr 24:19
to the s of the sons of Asaph....... 1Chr 25:1
workmen according to their s was... 1Chr 25:1
for the s of the house of God,....... 1Chr 25:6
able men for strength for the s...... 1Chr 26:8
the LORD, and in the s of the king... 1Chr 26:30
for all the work of the s of......... 1Chr 28:13
for all the vessels of s in the....... 1Chr 28:13
instruments of all manner of s...... 1Chr 28:14
instruments of every kind of s...... 1Chr 28:14
for all the s of the house of God.... 1Chr 28:20
for all the s of the house of God.... 1Chr 28:21
skilful man, for any manner of s..... 1Chr 28:21
his s this day unto the LORD........ 1Chr 29:5
gave for the s of the house of...... 1Chr 29:7
courses of the priests to their s..... 2Chr 8:14
that they may know my s, and the.. 2Chr 12:8
the s of the kingdoms of the........ 2Chr 12:8
the s of the house of the LORD...... 2Chr 24:12
So the s of the house of the LORD... 2Chr 29:35
every man according to his s........ 2Chr 31:2
his daily portion for their s in...... 2Chr 31:16
in the s of the house of God........ 2Chr 31:21
the work in any manner of s........ 2Chr 34:13
encouraged them to the s of the.... 2Chr 35:2
So the s was prepared, and the..... 2Chr 35:10
might not depart from their s....... 2Chr 35:15
So all the s of the LORD was........ 2Chr 35:16
their courses, for the s of God...... Ezr 6:18
for the s of the house of thy God... Ezr 7:19
for the s of the Levites, two........ Ezr 8:20
for the s of the house of our God... Neh 10:32
cattle, and herbs for the s of man.. Ps 104:14
his neighbour's s without wages.... Jer 22:13
to serve a great s against Tyrus.... Eze 29:18
for the s that he had served........ Eze 29:18
the house, for all the s thereof..... Eze 44:14
will think that he doeth God s...... Jn 16:2
the s of God, and the promises..... Rom 9:4
God, which is your reasonable s..... Rom 12:1
that my s which I have for.......... Rom 15:31
s not only supplieth the want of... 2Cor 9:12
taking wages of them, to do you s... 2Cor 11:8
ye did s unto them which by........ Gal 4:8
With good will doing s, as to the.... Eph 6:7
s of your faith, I joy, and........... Phil 2:17

supply your lack of s toward me............ Phil 2:30
but rather do them a, because.................... 1Ti 6:2
had also ordinances of divine s................... Heb 9:1
accomplishing the s of God...................... Heb 9:6
make him that did the s perfect................... Heb 9:9
know thy works, and charity, and s............ Rev 2:19

SERVILE
ye shall do no s work therein................. Lev 23:7
ye shall do no s work therein................. Lev 23:8
ye shall do no s work therein................ Lev 23:21
ye shall do no s work therein................ Lev 23:25
ye shall do no s work therein................ Lev 23:35
and ye shall do no s work therein.......... Lev 23:36
do no manner of s work therein............... Num 28:18
ye shall do no s work......................... Num 28:25
ye shall do no s work......................... Num 28:26
ye shall do no s work.......................... Num 29:1
ye shall do no s work, and ye................. Num 29:12
ye shall do no s work........................ Num 29:35

SERVING
we have let Israel go from s us.................... Ex 14:5
to thee, in s thee six years.................... Deut 15:18
Martha was cumbered about much s .... Lk 10:40
s the Lord with all humility of.............. Acts 20:19
tribes, instantly s God day..................... Acts 26:7
fervent in spirit; s the Lord................... Rom 12:11
a divers lusts and pleasures,................. Titus 3:3

SERVITOR
his s said, What, should I set................... 2Kin 4:43

SERVITUDE
the grievous s of thy father................. 2Chr 10:4
affliction, and because of great s........... Lam 1:3

SET See PREFACE.

SETH (seth) See SHETH. A son of Adam and Eve.
bare a son, and called his name S........... Gen 4:25
And to S, to him also there was............... Gen 4:26
and called his name S.......................... Gen 5:3
S were eight hundred years................... Gen 5:4
S lived an hundred and five years,......... Gen 5:6
S lived after he begat Enos eight........... Gen 5:7
all the days of S were nine................... Gen 5:8
of Enos, which was the son of S........... Lk 3:38

SETHUR (se'-thur) A spy sent to the Promised Land.
of Asher, the son of Michael............... Num 13:13

SETTER
He seemeth to be a s forth of................. Acts 17:18

SETTEST
thou s thine hand to in the land......... Deut 23:20
all that thou s thine hand unto............ Deut 28:8
in all that thou s thine hand................ Deut 28:20
that thou s a watch over me.................... Job 7:12
thou s a print upon the heels of............. Job 13:27
thou s a crown of pure gold on............... Ps 21:3
s me before thy face for ever.................. Ps 41:12

SETTETH
And when the tabernacle s forward....... Num 1:51
And when the camp s forward............... Num 2:17
is poor, and s his heart upon it............. Deut 24:15
Cursed be he that s light by his......... Deut 27:16
and s me upon my high places............ Ps 18:33
He s an end to darkness, and.................. Job 28:3
feet, and s me upon my high places...... Ps 18:33
he s himself in a way that is not.............. Ps 36:4
his strength s fast the mountains........... Ps 65:6
God s the solitary in families.................. Ps 68:6
putteth down one, and s up another....... Ps 75:7
as the flame s the mountains on............ Ps 83:14
Yet s he the poor on high from............. Ps 107:41
lay wait, as he that s snares.................... Jer 5:26
of Neriah s thee on against us................ Jer 43:3
that s up his idols in his heart.............. Eze 14:4
s up his idols in his heart, and............. Eze 14:7
he removeth kings, and s up kings........ Dan 2:21
s up over it the basest of men................ Dan 4:17
s him on a pinnacle of the temple.......... Mt 4:5
but s it on a candlestick, that................ Lk 8:16
s on fire the course of nature.................. Jas 3:6

SETTING
In their s of their threshold by............. Eze 43:8
sealing the stone, and s a watch............ Mt 27:66
Now when the sun was s, all they......... Lk 4:40

SETTINGS
thou shalt set in it s of stones.............. Ex 28:17

SETTLE
But I will s him in mine house and....... 1Chr 17:14
I will s you after your old.................. Eze 36:11
the lower s shall be two cubits............ Eze 43:14
from the lesser s even to the.............. Eze 43:14
greater s shall be four cubits.............. Eze 43:14
the s shall be fourteen cubits............. Eze 43:17
and on the four corners of the s.......... Eze 43:20
corners of the s of the altar............... Eze 45:19
S it therefore in your hearts,............... Lk 21:14
stablish, strengthen, s you.................. 1Pet 5:10

SETTLED
a s place for thee to abide in............... 1Kin 8:13
he s his countenance stedfastly,......... 2Kin 8:11
O Lord, thy word is s in heaven........... Ps 119:89
Before the mountains were s................. Prov 8:25
he hath s on his lees, and hath......... Jer 48:11
the men that are s on their lees........... Zeph 1:12

in the faith grounded and s.................... Col 1:23

SETTLEST
thou s the furrows thereof.................... Ps 65:10

SEVEN
s years, and begat sons and.................... Gen 5:7
and s years, and begat Lamech............... Gen 5:25
he begat Lamech a hundred eighty...... Gen 5:26
s hundred seventy and s years............ Gen 5:31
For yet s days, and I will cause............ Gen 7:4
And it came to pass after s days........... Gen 7:10
And he stayed yet other s days............. Gen 8:10
And he stayed yet other s days............. Gen 8:12
And in the second month, on the s....... Gen 8:14
s years, and begat sons and.................. Gen 11:21
Abraham set a ewe lambs of the........... Gen 21:28
What mean these s ewe lambs which..... Gen 21:29
For these s ewe lambs shalt thou.......... Gen 21:30
And Sarah was an hundred and s....... Gen 23:1
an hundred and thirty and s years...... Gen 25:17
I will serve thee s years for................. Gen 29:18
Jacob served s years for Rachel............ Gen 29:20
serve with me yet s other years............ Gen 29:27
served with him yet s other years........ Gen 29:30
pursued after him s days' journey........ Gen 31:23
himself to the ground s times.............. Gen 33:3
of the river s well favoured kine.......... Gen 41:2
s other kine came up after them........... Gen 41:3
did eat up the s well favoured............. Gen 41:4
s ears of corn came up upon one.......... Gen 41:5
s thin ears and blasted with the........... Gen 41:6
the s thin ears devoured the................ Gen 41:7
thin ears devoured the s rank............... Gen 41:7
came up out of the river s kine.......... Gen 41:18
s other kine came up after them,......... Gen 41:19
did eat up the first s fat kine............... Gen 41:20
s ears came up in one stalk, full......... Gen 41:22
s ears, withered, thin, and................. Gen 41:24
ears devoured the s good ears........... Gen 41:24
The s good kine are s years............... Gen 41:26
the s good ears are s years............... Gen 41:26
the s thin and ill favoured kine......... Gen 41:27
came up after them are s years.......... Gen 41:27
the s empty ears blasted with the....... Gen 41:27
wind shall be s years of famine......... Gen 41:27
there come s years of great.............. Gen 41:29
And there shall arise after them......... Gen 41:30
after them s years of famine............ Gen 41:34
of Egypt in the s plenteous years....... Gen 41:34
against the s years of famine........... Gen 41:36
in the s plenteous years the............. Gen 41:47
up all the food of the s years............ Gen 41:48
the s years of plenteousness,........... Gen 41:53
the s years of dearth began to.......... Gen 41:54
all the souls were s..................... Gen 46:25
was an hundred forty and s years....... Gen 47:28
a mourning for his father s days........ Gen 50:10
priest of Midian had s daughters........ Ex 2:16
were an hundred thirty and s years...... Ex 6:16
an hundred and thirty and s years...... Ex 6:20
s days were fulfilled, after that.......... Ex 7:25
S days shall ye eat unleavened........... Ex 12:15
S days shalt there be no leaven......... Ex 12:19
S days thou shalt eat unleavened....... Ex 13:6
bread shall be eaten s days............... Ex 13:7
s days it shall be with his dam......... Ex 22:30
shalt eat unleavened bread s days..... Ex 23:15
shalt make the s lamps thereof.......... Ex 25:37
stead shalt put them on s days......... Ex 29:30
s days shalt thou consecrate them..... Ex 29:35
S days thou shalt make an................ Ex 29:37
S days thou shalt eat unleavened...... Ex 34:18
And he made his s lamps, and his..... Ex 37:23
s hundred and thirty shekels,.......... Ex 38:25
talents, and a thousand s hundred..... Ex 38:28
of the thousand s hundred seventy..... Ex 38:28
the blood s times before the Lord........ Lev 4:6
sprinkle it s times before the........... Lev 4:17
thereof upon the altar s times............ Lev 8:11
of the congregation in s days.......... Lev 8:33
for s days shall he consecrate........... Lev 8:33
congregation day and night s days..... Lev 8:35
then she shall be unclean s days...... Lev 12:2
him that hath the plague s days....... Lev 13:4
shall shut him up s days more.......... Lev 13:5
priest shall shut him up s days......... Lev 13:21
priest shall shut him up s days......... Lev 13:31
the plague of the scall s days........... Lev 13:31
that hath the scall s days more........ Lev 13:33
up it that hath the plague s days...... Lev 13:50
he shall shut it up s days more........ Lev 13:54
cleansed from the leprosy s times..... Lev 14:7
abroad out of his tent s days........... Lev 14:8
finger s times before the Lord.......... Lev 14:16
left hand s times before the Lord...... Lev 14:27
and shut up the house s days........... Lev 14:38
and sprinkle the house s times........ Lev 14:51
himself s days for his cleansing....... Lev 15:13
she shall be put apart s days.......... Lev 15:19
him, he shall be unclean s days...... Lev 15:24
shall number to herself s days........ Lev 15:28
the blood with his finger s times..... Lev 16:14
upon it with his finger s times....... Lev 16:19
then it shall be s days under the..... Lev 22:27
s days ye must eat unleavened........ Lev 23:6
made by fire unto the Lord s days..... Lev 23:8
s sabbaths shall be complete.......... Lev 23:15
s lambs without blemish of the....... Lev 23:18
for s days unto the Lord............... Lev 23:34
S days ye shall offer an offering...... Lev 23:36
keep a feast unto the Lord s days..... Lev 23:39

before the Lord your God s days...... Lev 23:40
unto the Lord s days in the year..... Lev 23:41
Ye shall dwell in booths s days....... Lev 23:42
thou shalt number s sabbaths of...... Lev 25:8
unto thee, s times s years............. Lev 25:8
the space of the s sabbaths of......... Lev 25:8
then I will punish you s times......... Lev 26:18
I will bring s times more plagues..... Lev 26:21
you yet s times for your sins......... Lev 26:24
will chastise you s times for.......... Lev 26:28
s thousand and four hundred......... Num 1:31
and two thousand and s hundred..... Num 1:39
s thousand and four hundred......... Num 2:28
and two thousand and s hundred..... Num 2:26
s thousand and six hundred.......... Num 2:31
numbered of them were s thousand... Num 3:22
were two thousand s hundred........ Num 3:34
the s lamps shall give light over..... Num 8:2
should she not be ashamed s days... Num 12:14
be shut out from the camp s days.... Num 12:14
was shut out from the camp s days.. Num 12:15
(Now Hebron was built s years....... Num 13:22
s hundred, beside them that died.... Num 16:49
of the congregation s times.......... Num 19:4
any man shall be unclean s days.... Num 19:11
the tent, shall be unclean s days.... Num 19:14
a grave, shall be unclean s days.... Num 19:16
Balak, Build me here s altars........ Num 23:1
me here s oxen and s rams........... Num 23:1
him, I have prepared s altars........ Num 23:4
built s altars, and offered a......... Num 23:14
Balak, Build me here s altars........ Num 23:29
me here s bullocks and s rams...... Num 23:29
an hundred and threescore and thirty... Num 26:7
two thousand and a hundred......... Num 26:34
thousand and a thousand s hundred... Num 26:51
s lambs of the first year without.... Num 28:11
s days shall unleavened bread be.... Num 28:17
s lambs of the first year............. Num 28:19
lamb, throughout the s lambs........ Num 28:21
daily, throughout the s lambs....... Num 28:24
s lambs of the first year............. Num 28:27
one lamb, throughout the s lambs... Num 28:29
s lambs of the first year without.... Num 29:2
one lamb, throughout the s lambs... Num 29:4
s lambs of the first year............. Num 29:8
one lamb, throughout the s lambs... Num 29:10
keep a feast unto the Lord s days... Num 29:12
And on the seventh day s bullocks... Num 29:32
s lambs of the first year without.... Num 29:36
ye abide without the camp s days... Num 31:19
three hundred thousand and s....... Num 31:36
s thousand and five hundred sheep,... Num 31:43
was sixteen thousand s hundred.... Num 31:52
s nations greater and mightier...... Deut 7:1
At the end of every s years thou..... Deut 15:1
s days shalt thou eat unleavened.... Deut 16:3
with thee in all thy coast s days.... Deut 16:4
S weeks shalt thou number unto..... Deut 16:9
begin to number the s weeks from... Deut 16:13
the feast of tabernacles s days....... Deut 16:13
S days shalt thou keep a solemn..... Deut 16:15
way, and flee before thee s ways.... Deut 28:7
them, and flee s ways before them... Deut 28:25
At the end of every s years.......... Deut 31:10
s priests shall bear before the...... Josh 6:4
the ark s trumpets of rams' horns... Josh 6:4
ye shall compass the city s times.... Josh 6:4
let s priests bear s trumpets......... Josh 6:6
the s priests bearing the s......... Josh 6:6
s priests bearing s trumpets........ Josh 6:13
after the same manner s times...... Josh 6:15
they compassed the city s times.... Josh 6:15
the children of Israel s parts....... Josh 18:2
they shall divide it into s parts.... Josh 18:5
describe the land into s parts....... Josh 18:9
by cities into s parts in a book.... Josh 18:9
into the hand of Midian s years.... Judg 6:1
the second bullock of s years old... Judg 6:25
s hundred shekels of gold.......... Judg 12:9
And he judged Israel s years....... Judg 12:9
me within the s days of the feast... Judg 14:12
And she wept before him the s days.. Judg 14:17
If they bind me with s green....... Judg 16:8
Philistines brought up to her s..... Judg 16:13
If thou weavest the s locks of my... Judg 16:13
shave off the s locks of his head... Judg 16:19
numbered s hundred chosen men... Judg 20:15
all this people there were s........ Ruth 4:15
is better to thee than s sons........ Ruth 4:15
so that the barren hath born s..... 1Sa 2:5
of the Philistines s months........ 1Sa 6:1
s days shalt thou tarry, till I..... 1Sa 10:8
Give us s days' respite, that we... 1Sa 11:3
And he tarried s days, according... 1Sa 13:8
Jesse made s of his sons to pass... 1Sa 16:10
tree at Jabesh, and fasted s days.. 1Sa 31:13
the house of Judah was s years.... 2Sa 2:11
he reigned over Judah s years..... 2Sa 5:5
s hundred horsemen, and twenty.. 2Sa 8:4
David slew the men of s hundred... 2Sa 10:18
Let s men of his sons be......... 2Sa 21:6
and they fell all s together........ 2Sa 21:9
thirty and s in all............... 2Sa 23:39
Shall s years of famine come unto... 2Sa 24:13
s years reigned he in Hebron, and... 1Kin 2:11
and the third was s cubits broad... 1Kin 6:6
So was he s years in building it... 1Kin 6:38
s for the one chapter............ 1Kin 7:17
and s for the other chapter....... 1Kin 7:17

s days and days, even............1Kin 8:65
And he had a hundred wives,............1Kin 11:3
did Zimri reign s days in Tirzah............1Kin 16:15
And he said, Go again s times............1Kin 18:43
have left me s thousand in Israel............1Kin 19:18
of Israel, being s thousand............1Kin 20:15
one over against the other s days............1Kin 20:29
s thousand of the men that were............1Kin 20:30
a compass of s days' journey............2Kin 3:9
he took with him s hundred men............2Kin 3:26
and the child sneezed s times............2Kin 4:35
Go and wash in Jordan s times............2Kin 5:10
dipped himself s times in Jordan,............2Kin 5:14
also come upon the land s years............2Kin 8:1
land of the Philistines s years............2Kin 8:2
came to pass at the s years' end............2Kin 8:3
S years old was Jehoash when he............2Kin 11:21
even s thousand, and craftsmen and............2Kin 24:16
And it came to pass in the s............2Kin 25:27
in the twelfth month, on the s............2Kin 25:27
and there he reigned s years............1Chr 3:4
Johanan, and Dalaiah, and Anani, s............1Chr 3:24
and Jachan, and Zia, and Heber, s............1Chr 5:13
four and forty thousand s hundred............1Chr 5:18
fourscore and s thousand............1Chr 7:5
and s hundred and threescore............1Chr 9:13
were to come after s days from............1Chr 9:25
oak in Jabesh, and fasted s days............1Chr 10:12
s thousand and one hundred............1Chr 12:25
were three thousand and s hundred............1Chr 12:27
and spear thirty and s thousand............1Chr 12:34
offered s bullocks and s rams............1Chr 15:26
s thousand horsemen, and twenty............1Chr 18:4
David slew of the Syrians s............1Chr 19:18
s hundred, were chosen among............1Chr 26:30
s hundred chief fathers, whom............1Chr 26:32
s thousand talents of refined............1Chr 29:4
s years reigned he in Hebron, and............1Chr 29:27
Solomon kept the feast s days............2Chr 7:8
dedication of the altar s days............2Chr 7:9
s days, and the feast s days............2Chr 7:9
s rams, the same may be a priest............2Chr 13:9
s hundred oxen and s thousand,............2Chr 15:11
s thousand and s hundred rams,............2Chr 17:11
s thousand and s hundred he............2Chr 17:11
Joash was s years old when he............2Chr 24:1
s thousand and five hundred, that............2Chr 26:13
And they brought s bullocks............2Chr 29:21
s rams, and s lambs............2Chr 29:21
s he goats, for a sin offering............2Chr 29:21
bread s days with great gladness............2Chr 30:21
eat throughout the feast s days............2Chr 30:22
took counsel to keep other s days............2Chr 30:23
they kept other s days with............2Chr 30:23
bullocks and s thousand sheep............2Chr 30:24
feast of unleavened bread s days............2Chr 35:17
s hundred seventy and five............Ezr 2:9
Zaccai, s hundred and threescore............Ezr 2:9
s hundred and forty and three............Ezr 2:25
and Ono, s hundred twenty and five............Ezr 2:33
a thousand two hundred forty and s............Ezr 2:38
of whom there were s thousand............Ezr 2:65
three hundred thirty and s............Ezr 2:65
horses were s hundred thirty............Ezr 2:66
asses, six thousand s hundred............Ezr 2:67
unleavened bread s days with joy............Ezr 6:22
of his s counsellors, to enquire............Ezr 7:14
s lambs, twelve he goats for a............Ezr 8:35
Zaccai, s hundred and threescore............Neh 7:14
six hundred threescore and s............Neh 7:18
two thousand threescore and s............Neh 7:19
Beeroth, s hundred forty and three............Neh 7:29
and Ono, s hundred twenty and five............Neh 7:37
a thousand two hundred forty and s............Neh 7:41
of whom there were s thousand............Neh 7:67
three hundred thirty and s............Neh 7:67
horses, s hundred thirty and six............Neh 7:68
six thousand s hundred and twenty............Neh 7:69
threescore and s priests' garments............Neh 7:72
And they kept the feast s days............Neh 8:18
Ethiopia, over an hundred and s............Est 1:1
s days, in the court of the............Est 1:5
the s chamberlains that served in............Est 1:10
the s princes of Persia and Media,............Est 1:14
s maidens, which were meet to be............Est 2:9
s provinces, unto every province............Est 8:9
s provinces of the kingdom of............Est 9:30
there were born unto him s sons............Job 1:2
also was s thousand sheep............Job 1:3
with him upon the ground s days............Job 2:13
s nights, and none spake a word............Job 2:13
in s there shall no evil touch............Job 5:19
take unto you now s bullocks............Job 42:8
s rams, and go to my servant Job,............Job 42:8
He had also s sons and three............Job 42:13
of earth, purified s times............Ps 12:6
S times a day do I praise thee............Ps 119:164
s are an abomination unto him............Prov 6:16
she hath hewn out her s pillars............Prov 9:1
For a just man falleth s times............Prov 24:16
s men that can render a reason............Prov 26:16
for there are s abominations in............Prov 26:25
Give a portion to s, and also to............Eccl 11:2
in that day s women shall take............Is 4:1
shall smite it in the s streams............Is 11:15
sevenfold, as the light of s days............Is 30:26
She that hath borne s languisheth............Jer 15:9
At the end of s years let ye go............Jer 34:14
s men of them that were near the............Jer 52:25
of the Jews s hundred forty............Jer 52:30

And it came to pass in the s............Jer 52:31
astonished among them s days............Eze 3:15
came to pass at the end of s days............Eze 3:16
And it came to pass in the s............Eze 29:17
shall burn them with fire s years............Eze 39:9
s months shall the house of............Eze 39:12
after the end of s months shall............Eze 39:14
they went up unto it by s steps............Eze 40:22
there were s steps to go up to it............Eze 40:26
the breadth of the door, s cubits............Eze 41:3
S days shall they prepare every............Eze 43:25
S days shall they purge the altar............Eze 43:26
they shall reckon unto him s days............Eze 44:26
the passover, a feast of s days............Eze 45:21
s days of the feast he shall............Eze 45:23
s bullocks and s rams without............Eze 45:23
s rams without blemish daily the............Eze 45:23
without blemish daily the s days............Eze 45:23
like in the feast of the s days............Eze 45:25
should heat the furnace one s............Dan 3:19
let s times pass over him............Dan 4:16
till s times pass over him............Dan 4:23
s times shall pass over thee,............Dan 4:25
s times shall pass over thee,............Dan 4:32
the Prince shall be s weeks............Dan 9:25
Seek him that maketh the s stars............Amos 5:8
we raise against him s shepherds............Mic 5:5
upon one stone shall be s eyes............Zec 3:9
his s lamps thereon............Zec 4:2
and s pipes to the s lamps............Zec 4:2
hand of Zerubbabel with those s............Zec 4:10
taketh with himself s other............Mt 12:45
And they said, S, and a few little............Mt 15:34
And he took the s loaves and the............Mt 15:36
meat that was left s baskets full............Mt 15:37
Neither the s loaves of the four............Mt 16:10
till s times............Mt 18:21
say not unto thee, Until s times,............Mt 18:22
but, Until seventy times s............Mt 18:22
Now there were with us s brethren............Mt 22:25
whose wife shall she be of the s............Mt 22:28
And they said, S............Mk 8:5
and he took the s loaves, and gave............Mk 8:6
meat that was left s baskets............Mk 8:8
when the s among four thousand,............Mk 8:8
And they said, S............Mk 8:20
Now there were s brethren............Mk 12:20
the s had her, and left no seed............Mk 12:22
for the s had her to wife............Mk 12:23
out of whom he had cast s devils............Mk 16:9
s years from her virginity............Lk 2:36
out of whom went s devils............Lk 8:2
taketh to him s other spirits............Lk 11:26
against thee s times in a day............Lk 17:4
s times in a day turn again to............Lk 17:4
There were therefore s brethren............Lk 20:29
and in like manner the s also............Lk 20:31
for s had her to wife............Lk 20:33
among you s men of honest report............Acts 6:3
when he had destroyed s nations............Acts 13:19
there were s sons of one Sceva, a............Acts 19:14
where we abode s days............Acts 20:6
we tarried there s days............Acts 21:4
which was one of the s............Acts 21:8
when the s days were almost ended............Acts 21:27
desired to tarry with them s days............Acts 28:14
reserved to myself s thousand men............Rom 11:4
they were compassed about s days............Heb 11:30
John to the s churches which are............Rev 1:4
from the s Spirits which are............Rev 1:4
send it unto the s churches which............Rev 1:11
I saw s golden candlesticks............Rev 1:12
And in the midst of the s............Rev 1:13
his head in his right hand s stars............Rev 1:16
The mystery of the s stars which............Rev 1:20
s golden candlesticks............Rev 1:20
The s stars are the angels of the............Rev 1:20
are the angels of the s churches............Rev 1:20
the s candlesticks which thou............Rev 1:20
thou sawest are the s churches............Rev 1:20
the s stars in his right hand............Rev 2:1
of the s golden candlesticks............Rev 2:1
he that hath the s Spirits of God............Rev 3:1
Spirits of God, and the s stars............Rev 3:1
there were s lamps of fire............Rev 4:5
which are the s Spirits of God............Rev 4:5
the backside, sealed with s seals............Rev 5:1
to loose the s seals thereof............Rev 5:5
it had been slain, having s horns............Rev 5:6
horns and s eyes, which are............Rev 5:6
which are the s Spirits of God............Rev 5:6
I saw the s angels which stood............Rev 8:2
and to them were given s trumpets............Rev 8:2
the s angels which had the............Rev 8:6
s thunders uttered their voices............Rev 10:3
when the s thunders had uttered............Rev 10:4
which the s thunders uttered............Rev 10:4
were slain of men s thousand............Rev 11:13
great red dragon, having s heads............Rev 12:3
horns, and s crowns upon his heads............Rev 12:3
up out of the sea, having s heads............Rev 13:1
s angels having the s last............Rev 15:1
the s angels came out of the............Rev 15:6
the temple, having the s plagues............Rev 15:6
gave unto the s angels............Rev 15:7
fill the s vials of the wrath............Rev 16:1
the temple saying to the s angels............Rev 16:1
there came one of the s angels............Rev 17:1
angels which had the s vials............Rev 17:1
of blasphemy, having s heads............Rev 17:3

her, which hath the s heads............Rev 17:7
The s heads are s mountains,............Rev 17:9
And there are s kings............Rev 17:10
he is the eighth, and is of the s............Rev 17:11
the s angels which had the............Rev 21:9
s vials full of the s last............Rev 21:9

SEVENFOLD

vengeance shall be taken on him s............Gen 4:15
If Cain shall be avenged s............Gen 4:24
truly Lamech seventy and s............Gen 4:24
render unto our neighbours s into............Ps 79:12
he be found, he shall restore s............Prov 6:31
the light of the sun shall be s............Is 30:26

SEVENS

thou shalt take to thee by s............Gen 7:2
Of fowls also of the air by s............Gen 7:3

SEVENTEEN

being s years old, was feeding............Gen 37:2
in the land of Egypt s years............Gen 47:28
thereof, even threescore and s men............Judg 8:14
he reigned s years in Jerusalem,............1Kin 14:21
in Samaria, and reigned s years............2Kin 13:1
were s thousand and two hundred............1Chr 7:11
he reigned s years in Jerusalem,............2Chr 12:13
of Harim, a thousand and s............Ezr 2:39
of Harim, a thousand and s............Neh 7:42
money, even s shekels of silver............Jer 32:9

SEVENTEENTH

the s day of the month, the same............Gen 7:11
on the s day of the month, upon............Gen 8:4
over Israel in Samaria the s year............1Kin 22:51
In the s year of Pekah the son of............2Kin 16:1
The s to Hezir, the eighteenth to............1Chr 24:15
The s to Joshbekashah, he his............1Chr 25:24

SEVENTH

on the s day God ended his work............Gen 2:2
he rested on the s day from all............Gen 2:2
And God blessed the s day, and............Gen 2:3
And the ark rested in the s month............Gen 8:4
the first day until the s day............Ex 12:15
in the s day there shall be an............Ex 12:16
in the s day shall be a feast to............Ex 13:6
but on the s day, which is the............Ex 16:26
people on the s day for to gather............Ex 16:27
go out of his place on the s day............Ex 16:29
So the people rested on the s day............Ex 16:30
But the s day is the sabbath of............Ex 20:10
in them is, and rested the s day............Ex 20:11
in the s he shall go out free for............Ex 21:2
But the s year thou shalt let it............Ex 23:11
on the s day thou shalt............Ex 23:12
the s day he called unto Moses............Ex 24:16
but in the s is the sabbath of............Ex 31:15
on the s day he rested, and was............Ex 31:17
but on the s day thou shalt rest............Ex 34:21
but on the s day there shall be............Ex 35:2
shall look on him the s day............Lev 13:5
shall look on him again the s day............Lev 13:6
shall look upon him the s day............Lev 13:27
in the s day the priest shall............Lev 13:32
in the s day the priest shall............Lev 13:34
look on the plague on the s day............Lev 13:51
But it shall be on the s day............Lev 14:9
priest shall come again the s day............Lev 14:39
that in the s month, on the first............Lev 16:29
but the s day is the sabbath of............Lev 23:3
in the s day is an holy............Lev 23:8
s sabbath shall ye number fifty............Lev 23:16
of Israel, saying, In the s month............Lev 23:24
s month there shall be a day of............Lev 23:27
The fifteenth day of this s month............Lev 23:34
the fifteenth day of the s month............Lev 23:34
shall celebrate it in the s month............Lev 23:41
But in the s year shall be a............Lev 25:4
on the tenth day of the s month............Lev 25:9
say, What shall we eat the s year............Lev 25:20
on the s day shall he shave it............Num 6:9
On the s day Elishama the son of............Num 7:48
on the s day he shall be clean............Num 19:12
then the s day he shall not be............Num 19:12
on the third day, and on the s day............Num 19:19
on the s day he shall purify............Num 19:19
on the s day ye shall have an............Num 28:25
And in the s month, on the first............Num 29:1
this s month an holy convocation............Num 29:12
the month ye shall have an holy............Num 29:12
on the s day seven bullocks, two............Num 29:32
on the third day, and on the s day............Num 31:19
wash your clothes on the s day............Num 31:24
But the s day is the sabbath of............Deut 5:14
The s year, the year of release,............Deut 15:9
then in the s year thou shalt let............Deut 15:12
on the s day shall be a solemn............Deut 16:8
the s day shall compass the............Josh 6:4
And it came to pass on the s day,............Josh 6:15
And it came to pass at the s time............Josh 6:16
the s lot came out for the tribe............Josh 19:40
And it came to pass on the s day............Judg 14:15
and it came to pass on the s day............Judg 14:17
s day before the sun went down............Judg 14:18
And it came to pass on the s day............2Sa 12:18
Ethanim, which is the s month............1Kin 8:2
s year of Asa king of Judah, and............1Kin 16:10
s year of Asa king of Judah did............1Kin 16:15
And it came to pass at the s time............1Kin 18:44
that in the s day the battle was............1Kin 20:29
the s year Jehoiada sent and............2Kin 11:4

In the s year of Jehu Jehoash 2Kin 12:1
s year of Joash king of Judah 2Kin 13:10
s year of Jeroboam king of Israel 2Kin 15:1
which was the s year of Hoshea 2Kin 18:9
on the s day of the month, which 2Kin 25:8
it came to pass in the s month 2Kin 25:25
Ozem the sixth, David the s 1Chr 2:15
Attai the sixth, Eliel the s 1Chr 12:11
The s to Hakkoz, the eighth to 1Chr 24:10
The s to Jesharelah, he, his sons 1Chr 25:14
the sixth, Elioenai the s 1Chr 26:3
Ammiel the sixth, Issachar the s 1Chr 26:5
The s captain for the s 1Chr 27:10
feast which was in the s month 2Chr 5:3
twentieth day of the s month he 2Chr 7:10
And in the s year Jehoiada 2Chr 23:1
and finished them in the s month 2Chr 31:7
when the s month was come, and the ..... Ezr 3:1
From the first day of the s month ...... Ezr 3:6
in the s year of Artaxerxes the .... Ezr 7:7
was in the s year of the king .... Ezr 7:8
when the s month came, the .... Neh 7:73
upon the first day of the s month ...... Neh 8:2
in the feast of the s month month ...... Neh 8:14
and that we would leave the s year ..... Neh 10:31
On the s day, when the heart of .... Est 1:10
in the s year of his reign .... Est 2:16
died the same year in the s month ...... Jer 28:17
it came to pass in the s month .... Jer 41:1
in the s year three thousand Jews ...... Jer 52:28
And it came to pass in the s year ...... Eze 20:1
in the s day of the month, that .... Eze 30:20
so thou shalt do the s day of the ...... Eze 45:20
In the s month, in the fifteenth .... Eze 45:25
In the s month, in the one and .... Eze 45:25
s month, even those seventy years ...... Hag 2:1
the fifth, and the fast of the s .... Zec 7:5
also, and the third, unto the s .... Zec 8:19
Yesterday at the s hour the fever ...... Mt 22:26
place of the s day on this wise .... Jn 4:52
God did rest the s day from all .... Heb 4:4
the s from Adam, prophesied of .... Heb 4:4
And when he had opened the s seal ...... Jude 14
days of the voice of the s angel .... Rev 8:1
And the s angel sounded .... Rev 10:7
the s angel poured out his vial .... Rev 11:15
the s, chrysolite .... Rev 16:17
                                         Rev 21:20

SEVENTY

avenged sevenfold, truly Lamech s ...... Gen 4:24
And Cainan lived s years, and begat .... Gen 5:12
of Lamech were seven hundred s .... Gen 5:31
And Terah lived s years, and begat ..... Gen 11:26
and Abram was s and five years old ..... Gen 12:4
the loins of Jacob were s souls .... Ex 1:5
s of the elders of Israel .... Ex 24:1
s of the elders of Israel .... Ex 24:9
of the thousand seven hundred s .... Ex 38:28
of the offering was s talents .... Ex 38:29
one silver bowl of s shekels .... Num 7:13
one silver bowl of s shekels .... Num 7:19
one silver bowl of s shekels .... Num 7:25
one silver bowl of s shekels .... Num 7:31
one silver bowl of s shekels .... Num 7:37
a silver bowl of s shekels .... Num 7:43
one silver bowl of s shekels .... Num 7:49
one silver bowl of s shekels .... Num 7:55
one silver bowl of s shekels .... Num 7:61
one silver bowl of s shekels .... Num 7:67
one silver bowl of s shekels .... Num 7:73
one silver bowl of s shekels .... Num 7:79
and thirty shekels, each bowl s .... Num 7:85
Gather unto me s men of the .... Num 11:16
gathered the s men of the elders .... Num 11:24
him, and gave it unto the s elders ..... Num 11:25
s thousand and five thousand sheep ..... Num 31:32
father, in slaying his s brethren ...... Judg 9:56
even to Beer-sheba s thousand men 2Sa 24:15
Ahab had s sons in Samaria 2Kin 10:1
being s persons, were with the 2Kin 10:6
slew s persons, and put their 2Kin 10:7
fell of Israel s thousand men 1Chr 21:14
Parosh, two thousand an hundred s ...... Ezr 2:3
of Shephatiah, three hundred s .... Ezr 2:4
children of Arah, seven hundred s ...... Ezr 2:5
house of Jeshua, nine hundred s .... Ezr 2:36
the children of Hodaviah, s .... Ezr 2:40
of Athalah, and with him s males .... Ezr 8:7
and Zabbud, and with him s males .... Ezr 8:14
all Israel, ninety and six rams, s ..... Ezr 8:35
Parosh, two thousand an hundred s ...... Neh 7:8
of Shephatiah, three hundred s .... Neh 7:9
house of Jeshua, nine hundred s .... Neh 7:39
and of the children of Hodevah, s ...... Neh 7:43
kept the gates, were an hundred s ...... Neh 11:19
enemies, and slew of their foes s ...... Est 9:16
Tyre shall be forgotten s years .... Is 23:15
after the end of s years shall .... Is 23:15
to pass after the end of s years ...... Is 23:17
serve the king of Babylon s years ..... Jer 25:11
when s years are accomplished, ... Jer 25:12
the LORD, That after s years be .... Jer 29:10
there stood before them s men of ...... Eze 8:11
the west was s cubits broad .... Eze 41:12
that he would accomplish s years ...... Dan 9:2
S weeks are determined upon thy .... Dan 9:24
seventh month, even those s years ..... Zec 7:5
but, Until s times seven .... Mt 18:22
the Lord appointed other s also .... Lk 10:1
the s returned again with joy, ... Lk 10:17

SEVER

I will s in that day the land of ...... Ex 8:22
the LORD shall s between the .... Ex 9:4
they shall s out men of continual .... Eze 39:14
s the wicked from among the just, ... Mt 13:49

SEVERAL

a s tenth deal of flour mingled .... Num 28:13
A s tenth deal shalt thou offer .... Num 28:21
A s tenth deal unto one lamb, ... Num 28:29
A s tenth deal for one lamb, ... Num 29:10
a s tenth deal to each lamb of .... Num 29:15
his death, and dwelt in a house 2Kin 15:5
in every s city he put shields and ... 2Chr 11:12
his death, and dwelt in a s house 2Chr 26:21
in every s city of Judah he made 2Chr 28:25
of their cities, in every s city 2Chr 31:19
man according to his s ability .... Mt 25:15
every s gate was of one pearl .... Rev 21:21

SEVERALLY

to every man a s as he will 1Cor 12:11

SEVERED

have s you from other people, ... Lev 20:26
Then Moses s three cities on this .... Deut 4:41
had s himself from the Kenites, ... Judg 4:11

SEVERITY

the goodness and s of God .... Rom 11:22
on them which fell, s .... Rom 11:22

SEW

A time to rend, and a time to s ...... Eccl 3:7
Woe to the women that s pillows ...... Eze 13:18

SEWED

they s fig leaves together, and ...... Gen 3:7
I have s sackcloth upon my skin, ... Job 16:15

SEWEST

a bag, and thou s up mine iniquity ... Job 14:17

SEWETH

No man also s a piece of new .... Mk 2:21

SHAALABBIN (sha-al-ab´-bin) See SHAALBIM.
A city in Dan.
And S, and Ajalon, and Jethlah, ... Josh 19:42

SHAALBIM (sha-al´-bim) See SHAALABBIN,
SHAALBONITE. Same as Shaalabbin.
mount Heres in Aijalon, and in s ..... Judg 1:35
son of Dekar, in Makaz, and in S 1Kin 4:9

SHAALBON See SHAALBONITE.

SHAALBONITE (sha-al´-bo-nite) A native of
Shaalabbin.
Eliahba the S, of the sons of 2Sa 23:32
the Baharumite, Eliahba the S 1Chr 11:33

SHAALIM See SHALIM.

SHAAPH (sha´-af) A son of Jahdai.
Gesham, and Pelet, and Ephah, and S . 1Chr 2:47
She bare also S the father of 1Chr 2:49

SHAARAIM (sha-a-ra´-im) See SHARAIM,
SHARUHEN. A city in Judah.
fell down by the way to S 1Sa 17:52
and at Beth-birei, and at S 1Chr 4:31

SHAASHGAZ (sha-ash´-gaz) A servant of King
Ahasuerus.
of the women, to the custody of S .... Est 2:14

SHABBETHAI (shab´-be-thahee)
  1. A Levite who dealt with the foreign wife
  problem.
  and S the Levite helped them, ... Ezr 10:15
  2. A Levite who aided Ezra.
  and Sherebiah, Jamin, Akkub, S ...... Neh 8:7
  3. A family of exiles.
  and S and Jozabad, of the chief of .. Neh 11:16

SHACHIA (sha-ki´-ah) A son of Shaharaim.
And Jeuz, and S, and Mirma 1Chr 8:10

SHADE
the LORD is thy s upon thy right ..... Ps 121:5

SHADOW
came they under the s of my roof ..... Gen 19:8
come and put your trust in my s ...... Judg 9:15
Thou seest the s of the mountains .... Judg 9:36
shall the s go forward ten 2Kin 20:9
for the s to go down ten degrees 2Kin 20:10
but let the s return backward ten 2Kin 20:11
he brought the s ten degrees 2Kin 20:11
our days on the earth are as a s 1Chr 29:15
and the s of death is in .... Job 3:5
servant earnestly desireth the s ..... Job 7:2
our days upon earth are a s .... Job 8:9
of darkness and the s of death .... Job 10:21
of the s of death, without any .... Job 10:22
out to light the s of death .... Job 14:2
he fleeth also as a s, and .... Job 14:2
on my eyelids is the s of death ...... Job 16:16
and all my members are as a s .... Job 17:7
is to them even as the s of death .... Job 24:17
in the terrors of the s of death .... Job 24:17
of darkness, and the s of death ...... Job 28:3
nor s of death, where the workers ... Job 34:22
seen the doors of the s of death .... Job 38:17
trees cover him with their s .... Job 40:22
hide me under the s of thy wings .... Ps 17:8
the valley of the s of death .... Ps 23:4
trust under the s of thy wings ...... Ps 36:7

and covered us with the s of death ... Ps 44:19
in the s of thy wings will I make .... Ps 57:1
therefore in the s of thy wings ...... Ps 63:7
were covered with the s of thy .... Ps 80:10
abide under the s of the Almighty .... Ps 91:1
days are like as a s that declineth . Ps 102:11
in the s of death, being bound in .... Ps 107:10
the s of death, and brake their ...... Ps 107:14
gone like the s when it declineth ... Ps 109:23
days are as a s that passeth away ... Ps 144:4
life which he spendeth as a s .... Eccl 6:12
his days, which are as a s .... Eccl 8:13
under his s with great delight ...... Song 2:3
shall be a tabernacle for a s in .... Is 4:6
in the land of the s of death .... Is 9:2
make thy s as the night in the ..... Is 16:3
a s from the heat, when the blast ... Is 25:4
the heat with the s of a cloud ...... Is 25:5
and to trust in the s of Egypt ...... Is 30:2
the trust in the s of Egypt your .... Is 30:3
as the s of a great rock in a .... Is 32:2
and hatch, and gather under her s ... Is 34:15
bring again the s of the degrees .... Is 38:8
in the s of his hand hath he hid .... Is 49:2
thee in the s of mine hand .... Is 51:16
of the s of death, through a land ... Jer 2:6
the turn it into the s of death ..... Jer 13:16
They that fled stood under the s .... Jer 48:45
Under his s we shall live among ..... Lam 4:20
in the s of the branches thereof ... Eze 17:23
under his s dwell all great .... Eze 31:6
earth are gone down from his s ...... Eze 31:12
that dwelt under his s in the .... Eze 31:17
of the field had s under it .... Dan 4:12
because the s thereof is good .... Hos 4:13
dwell under his s shall return ...... Hos 14:7
turneth the s of death into the .... Amos 5:8
a booth, and sat under it in the s .. Jonah 4:5
it might be a s over his head .... Jonah 4:6
s of death light is sprung up .... Mt 4:16
air may lodge under the s of it ..... Mk 4:32
in the s of death, to guide our .... Lk 1:79
that at the least the s of Peter .... Acts 5:15
Which are a s of things to come .... Col 2:17
s of heavenly things, as Moses ..... Heb 8:5
For the law having a s of good ..... Heb 10:1
neither s of turning .... Jas 1:17

SHADOWING
Woe to the land s with wings .... Is 18:1
fair branches, and with a shroud .... Eze 31:3
of glory s the mercyseat .... Heb 9:5

SHADOWS
the s flee away, turn, my beloved ... Song 2:17
the s flee away, I will get me to ... Song 4:6
for the s of the evening are .... Jer 6:4

SHADRACH (sha´-drak) See HANANIAH. A
companion of Daniel.
and to Hananiah, of S .... Dan 1:7
of the king, and he set S, Meshach .. Dan 2:49
of the province of Babylon, S .... Dan 2:49
rage and fury commanded to bring S .. Dan 3:13
said unto them, Is it true, O S ..... Dan 3:14
S, Meshach, and Abed-nego, ... Dan 3:16
his visage was changed against S .... Dan 3:19
that were in his army to bind S ..... Dan 3:20
slew those men that took up S .... Dan 3:22
And these three men, S, Meshach, ... Dan 3:23
furnace, and spake, and said, S ..... Dan 3:26
Then S, Meshach, and Abed-nego, ... Dan 3:26
and said, Blessed be the God of S ... Dan 3:28
thing amiss against the God of S ... Dan 3:29
Then the king promoted S, Meshach ... Dan 3:30

SHADY
He lieth under the s trees .... Job 40:21
The s trees cover him with their ... Job 40:22

SHAFT
his s and his branches, his bowls ... Ex 25:31
his s, and his branch, his bowls, ... Ex 37:17
beaten gold, unto the s thereof ..... Num 8:4
hid me, and made me a polished s .... Is 49:2

SHAGE (sha´-ghe) A 'mighty man' of David.
the son of S the Hararite 1Chr 11:34

SHAGEE See SHAGE.

SHAGEH See SHAGE.

SHAHAR (sha´-har) A musical notation.
chief Musician upon Aijeleth S ...... Ps 22:t

SHAHARAIM (sha-ha-ra´-im) A Benjamite
from Moab.
S begat children in the country 1Chr 8:8

SHAHAZIMAH (sha-haz´-i-mah) A city in
Issachar.
the coast reacheth to Tabor, and S .. Josh 19:22

SHAHAZUMAH See SHAHAZIMAH.

SHAKE
other times before, and s myself .... Judg 16:20
So God s out every mean from his .... Neh 5:13
which made all my bones to s .... Job 4:14
He shall s off his unripe grape ..... Job 15:33
you, and s mine head at you .... Job 16:4
the lip, they s the head, saying, ... Ps 22:7
though the mountains s with the ..... Ps 46:3
make their loins continually to s ... Ps 69:23
thereof shall s like Lebanon .... Ps 72:16

ariseth to s terribly the earth .... Is 2:19
ariseth to s terribly the earth .... Is 2:21
as if the rod should s itself .... Is 10:15
he shall s his hand against the .... Is 10:32
he s his hand over the river .... Is 11:15
s the hand, that they go into .... Is 13:2
Therefore I will s the heavens .... Is 13:13
to tremble, that did s kingdoms .... Is 14:16
the foundations of the earth do s .... Is 24:18
Carmel s off their fruits .... Is 33:9
S thyself from the dust .... Is 52:2
all my bones s .... Jer 23:9
thy walls shall s at the noise of .... Eze 26:10
Shall not the isles s at the .... Eze 26:15
The suburbs shall s at the sound .... Eze 27:28
I made the nations to s at the .... Eze 31:16
shalt s at my presence, and the .... Eze 32:10
s off his leaves, and scatter his .... Dan 4:14
the heavens and the earth shall s .... Joel 3:16
of the door, that the posts may s .... Amos 9:1
I will s the heavens, and the .... Hag 2:6
I will s all nations, and the .... Hag 2:7
I will s the heavens and the earth .... Hag 2:21
I will s mine hand upon them, and .... Zec 2:9
s off the dust of your feet .... Mt 10:14
for fear of him the keepers did s .... Mt 28:4
s off the dust under your feet .... Mk 6:11
that house, and could not s it .... Lk 6:48
s off the very dust from your .... Lk 9:5
Yet once more I s not the earth .... Heb 12:26

SHAKED

looked upon me they s their heads .... Ps 109:25

SHAKEN

the sound of a s leaf shall chase .... Lev 26:36
as a reed is s in the water 1Kin 14:15
Jerusalem hath s her head at thee 2Kin 19:21
promise, even thus he he s out .... Neh 5:13
s me to pieces, and set me up for .... Job 16:12
the wicked might be s out of it .... Job 38:13
also of the hills moved and were s .... Ps 18:7
Jerusalem hath s her head at thee .... Is 37:22
the fir trees shall be terribly s .... Nah 2:3
if they be s, they shall even .... Nah 3:12
A reed s with the wind .... Mt 11:7
powers of the heavens shall be s .... Mt 24:29
that are in heaven shall be s .... Mk 13:25
s together, and running over, ... Lk 6:38
A reed s with the wind .... Lk 7:24
the powers of heaven shall be s .... Lk 21:26
the place was s where they were .... Acts 4:31
foundations of the prison were s .... Acts 16:26
That ye be not soon s in mind 2Th 2:2
of those things that are s .... Heb 12:27
which cannot be s may remain .... Heb 12:27
when she is s of a mighty wind .... Rev 6:13

SHAKETH

Which s the earth out of her .... Job 9:6
of the LORD s the wilderness .... Ps 29:8
the LORD s the wilderness of .... Ps 29:8
thereof; for it s .... Ps 60:2
itself against him that s it .... Is 10:15
LORD of hosts, which he s over it .... Is 19:16
that s his hands from holding of .... Is 33:15

SHAKING

he laugheth at the s of a spear .... Job 41:29
a s of the head among the people .... Ps 44:14
as the s of an olive tree, two or .... Is 17:6
fear because of the s of the hand .... Is 19:16
be as the s of an olive tree .... Is 24:13
in battles of s will he fight .... Is 30:32
there was a noise, and behold a s .... Eze 37:7
a great s in the land of Israel .... Eze 38:19

SHALEM

And Jacob came to S, a city of .... Gen 33:18

SHALIM

a s (shal'-lim) A district in Dan.
they passed through the land of S 1Sa 9:4

SHALISHA

a s (shal'-i-shah) A district in Ephraim.
and passed through the land of S 1Sa 9:4

SHALISHAH See SHALISHA.

SHALL See PREFACE.

SHALLECHETH

a s (shal'-le-keth) A gate of the
First Temple.
forth westward, with the gate S 1Chr 26:16

SHALLUM See SHALUM.

SHALLUN

a s (shal'-lun) See JEHOAHAZ,
MESHELEMIAH, SHILLEM.
1. A king of Israel.
S the son of Jabesh conspired 2Kin 15:10
the son of Jabesh began to 2Kin 15:13
smote S the son of Jabesh in 2Kin 15:14
And the rest of the acts of S 2Kin 15:15
2. Husband of Huldah.
the wife of S the son of Tikvah 2Kin 22:14
the wife of S the son of Tikvah, ... 2Chr 34:22
3. A descendant of Jerahmeel.
begat Sisamai, and Sisamai begat S 1Chr 2:40
S begat Jekamiah, and Jekamiah 1Chr 2:41
4. A son of King Josiah.
the third Zedekiah, the fourth S 1Chr 3:15
thus saith the LORD touching S .... Jer 22:11
5. Grandson of Simeon.
S his son, Mibsam his son, Mishma 1Chr 4:25
6. Father of Hilkiah.
begat Zadok, and Zadok begat S 1Chr 6:12

S begat Hilkiah, and Hilkiah begat 1Chr 6:13
The son of S, the son of Zadok, ... Ezr 7:2
7. Son of Naphtali.
Jahziel, and Guni, and Jezer, and S 1Chr 7:13
8. A family of exiles.
And the porters were, S, and Akkub, ... 1Chr 9:17
S was the chief 1Chr 9:17
S the son of Kore, the son of 1Chr 9:19
the firstborn of S the Korahite 1Chr 9:31
the children of S, the children .... Ezr 2:42
the children of S, the children .... Neh 7:45
9. Father of Jehizkiah.
and Jehizkiah the son of S 2Chr 28:12
10. A gatekeeper who married a foreigner.
and Telem, and Uri .... Ezr 10:24
11. A son of Bani who married a foreigner.
S, Amariah, and Joseph .... Ezr 10:42
12. A rebuilder of Jerusalem's wall.
repaired S the son of Halohesh .... Neh 3:12
13. Father of Hanameel.
Hanameel the son of S thine uncle .... Jer 32:7
14. Father of Maaseiah.
chamber of Maaseiah the son of S .... Jer 35:4

SHALLUN

a s (shal'-lun) A rebuilder of
Jerusalem's wall.
repaired S the son of Colhozeh .... Neh 3:15

SHALMAI

a s (shal'-mahee) A family of exiles.
of Hagab, the children of S .... Ezr 2:46
of Hagaba, the children of S .... Neh 7:48

SHALMAN

a s (shal'-man) See SHALMANESER. A
king of Assyria.
as S spoiled Beth-arbel in the .... Hos 10:14

SHALMANESER

a s (shal-man-e'-zer) See
SHALMAN. A king of Assyria.
him came up S king of Assyria 2Kin 17:3
that S king of Assyria came up 2Kin 18:9

SHALT See PREFACE.

SHAMA

a s (sha'-mah) A "mighty man" of David.
Uzzia the Ashterathite, S 1Chr 11:44

SHAMARIAH

a s Son of Rehoboam.
Jeush, and S, and Zaham 2Chr 11:19

SHAMBLES

Whatsoever is sold in the s 1Cor 10:25

SHAME

unto their s among their enemies .... Ex 32:25
might put them to s in any thing .... Judg 18:7
because his father had done him s 1Sa 20:34
whither shall I cause my s to go 2Sa 13:13
So he returned with s of face on 2Chr 32:21
hate thee shall be clothed with s .... Job 8:22
long will ye turn my glory into s .... Ps 4:2
put to s that seek after my soul .... Ps 35:4
let them be clothed with s .... Ps 35:26
put to s that wish me evil .... Ps 40:14
of their s that say unto me .... Ps 40:15
hast put them to s that hated us .... Ps 44:7
hast cast off, and put us to s .... Ps 44:9
the s of my face hath covered me, ... Ps 44:15
thou hast put them to s, because .... Ps 53:5
hath covered my face .... Ps 69:7
hast known my reproach, and my s .... Ps 69:19
for a reward of their s that say .... Ps 70:3
for they are brought unto s .... Ps 71:24
Fill their faces with s .... Ps 83:16
yea, let them be put to s .... Ps 83:17
thou hast covered him with s .... Ps 89:45
adversaries be clothed with s .... Ps 109:29
O LORD, put me not to s .... Ps 119:31
His enemies will I clothe with s .... Ps 132:18
but s shall be the promotion of .... Prov 3:35
a scorner getteth to himself s .... Prov 9:7
harvest is a son that causeth s .... Prov 10:5
When pride cometh, then cometh s .... Prov 11:2
but a prudent man covereth s .... Prov 12:16
man is loathsome, and cometh to s .... Prov 13:5
s shall be to him that refuseth .... Prov 13:18
is against him that causeth s .... Prov 14:35
rule over a son that causeth s .... Prov 17:2
it, it is folly and s unto him .... Prov 18:13
mother, is a son that causeth s .... Prov 19:26
thy neighbour hath put thee to s .... Prov 25:8
he that heareth it put thee to s .... Prov 25:10
himself bringeth his mother to s .... Prov 29:15
uncovered, to the s of Egypt .... Is 20:4
be the s of thy lord's house .... Is 22:18
the strength of Pharaoh be your s .... Is 30:3
be an help nor profit, but a s .... Is 30:5
yea, thy s shall be seen .... Is 47:3
I hid not my face from s and .... Is 50:6
for thou shalt not be put to s .... Is 54:4
shalt forget the s of thy youth .... Is 54:4
For your s ye shall have double .... Is 61:7
For s hath devoured the labour of .... Jer 3:24
We lie down in our s, and our .... Jer 3:25
thy face, that thy s may appear .... Jer 13:26
my days should be consumed with s .... Jer 20:18
upon you, and a perpetual s .... Jer 23:40
the reproach have I heard of thy s .... Jer 46:12
hath Moab turned the back with s .... Jer 48:39
s hath covered our faces .... Jer 51:51
s shall be upon all flesh, and .... Eze 7:18
bear thine own s for thy sins .... Eze 16:52
confounded also, and bear thy s .... Eze 16:52
That thou mayest bear thine own s .... Eze 16:54
mouth any more because of thy s .... Eze 16:63

yet have they borne their s with .... Eze 32:24
yet have they borne their s with .... Eze 32:25
bear their s with them that go .... Eze 32:30
neither bear the s of the heathen .... Eze 34:29
have borne the s of the heathen .... Eze 36:6
you, they shall bear their s .... Eze 36:7
the s of the heathen any more .... Eze 36:15
that they have borne their s .... Eze 39:26
but they shall bear their s .... Eze 44:13
to everlasting life, and some to s .... Dan 12:2
will I change their glory into s .... Hos 4:7
her rulers with s do love .... Hos 4:18
separated themselves unto that s .... Hos 9:10
Ephraim shall receive s, and .... Hos 10:6
brother Jacob s shall cover thee .... Obad 10
of Saphir, having thy s naked .... Mic 1:11
them, that they shall not take s .... Mic 2:6
s shall cover her which said unto .... Mic 7:10
nakedness, and the kingdoms thy s .... Nah 3:5
Thou hast consulted s to thy .... Hab 2:10
Thou art filled with s for glory .... Hab 2:16
but the unjust knoweth no s .... Zeph 3:5
where they have been put to s .... Zeph 3:19
thou begin with s to take the .... Lk 14:9
worthy to suffer s for his name .... Acts 5:41
I write not these things to s you 1Cor 4:14
I speak to your s 1Cor 6:5
but if it be a s for a woman to 1Cor 11:6
long hair, it is a s unto him 1Cor 11:14
of God, and s them that have not 1Cor 11:22
for it is a s for women to speak 1Cor 14:35
I speak this to your s 1Cor 15:34
For it is a s even to speak of .... Eph 5:12
and whose glory is in their s .... Phil 3:19
afresh, and put him to an open s .... Heb 6:6
the cross, despising the s .... Heb 12:2
the sea, foaming out their own s .... Jude 13
that the s of thy nakedness do .... Rev 3:18
he walk naked, and they see his s .... Rev 16:15

SHAMED

her take it to her, lest we be s .... Gen 38:23
said Thou hast s this day the 2Sa 19:5
Eber, and Misham, and S, who built 1Chr 8:12
Ye have s the counsel of the poor .... Ps 14:6

SHAMEFACEDNESS

in modest apparel, with s 1Ti 2:9

SHAMEFUL

ye set up altars to that s thing .... Jer 11:13
s spewing shall be on thy glory .... Hab 2:16

SHAMEFULLY

that conceived them hath done s .... Hos 2:5
head, and sent him away s handled .... Mk 12:4
beat him also, and entreated him s .... Lk 20:11
were s entreated, as ye know, at 1Th 2:2

SHAMELESSLY

vain fellows s uncovereth himself 2Sa 6:20

SHAMER

a s (sha'-mur) See SHOMER.
1. Son of Mahli.
the son of Bani, the son of S 1Chr 6:46
2. Son of Heber.
And the sons of S 1Chr 7:34

SHAMETH

of riotous men s his father .... Prov 28:7

SHAMGAR

a s (sham'-gar) A judge of Israel.
after him was S the son of Anath .... Judg 3:31
In the days of S the son of Anath .... Judg 5:6

SHAMHUTH

a s (sham'-huth) See SHAMMOTH. A
captain in David's army.
fifth month was S the Izrahite 1Chr 27:8

SHAMIR

a s (sham'-mur)
1. A city in Judah.
And in the mountains, S, and Jattir .... Josh 15:48
2. A city near Mt. Ephraim.
he dwelt in S in mount Ephraim .... Judg 10:1
and died, and was buried in S .... Judg 10:2
3. Son of Micah the Levite.
the sons of Michah; S 1Chr 24:24

SHAMLAI See SAMLAH.

SHAMMA

a s (sham'-mah) See SHAMMAH. A son
of Zophah.
Bezer, and Hod, and S, and Shilshah, . 1Chr 7:37

SHAMMAH

a s (sham'-mah) See SHAMMA,
SHAMMOTH, SHIMEA, SHIMMA.
1. A son of Reuel.
Nahath, and Zerah, S, and Mizzah .... Gen 36:13
duke Nahath, duke Zerah, duke S .... Gen 36:17
Nahath, Zerah, S, and Mizzah 1Chr 1:37
2. A son of Jesse.
Then Jesse made S to pass by 1Sa 16:9
unto him Abinadab, and the third S 1Sa 17:13
3. A "mighty man" of David.
after him was S the son of Agee 2Sa 23:11
4. A Hararite "mighty man" of David.
S the Hararite, Ahiam the son of 2Sa 23:33
5. A Harodite "mighty man" of David.
S the Harodite, Elika the 2Sa 23:25

SHAMMAI

a s (sham'-mahee)
1. A son of Onan.
And the sons of Onam were, S 1Chr 2:28
And the sons of S 1Chr 2:28
the sons of Jada the brother of S 1Chr 2:32
2. Father of Maon.
and Rekem begat S 1Chr 2:44

And the son of S was Maon 1Chr 2:45
3. A descendant of Caleb.
and she bare Miriam, and S, and.......... 1Chr 4:17

SHAMMOTH (sham'-moth) See SHAMHAH,
SHAMMUTH. *A "mighty man" of David.*
S the Harorite, Helez the 1Chr 11:27

SHAMMUA (sham-mu'-ah) See SHAMMUAH,
SHEMAIAH, SHIMEA.
1. A spy sent to the Promised Land.
of Reuben, S the son of Zaccur............... Num 13:4
2. A son of David.
S, and Shobab, Nathan, and Solomon, 1Chr 14:4
3. A family of exiles.
brethren, and Abda the son of S........... Neh 11:17
4. A priest with Zerubbabel.
Of Bilgah, S .... Neh 12:18

SHAMMUAH (sham-mu'-ah) See SHAMMUA.
Same as Shammua 2.
S, and Shobab, and Nathan, and 2Sa 5:14

SHAMSHERAI (sham'-she-rahee) *A son of
Jeroham.*
And S, and Shehariah, and Athaliah, .. 1Chr 8:26

SHAPE
a bodily s like a dove upon him .... Lk 3:22
voice at any time, nor seen his s .... Jn 5:37

SHAPEN
Behold, I was s in iniquity .... Ps 51:5

SHAPES
the s of the locusts were like................... Rev 9:7

SHAPHAM (sha'-fam) *A Gadite chief.*
S the next, and Jaanai, and Shaphat.... 1Chr 5:12

SHAPHAN (sha'-fan)
1. A scribe in Josiah's time.
king sent S into Josiah's time.
priest said unto S the scribe 2Kin 22:3
And Hilkiah gave the book to S 2Kin 22:8
S the scribe came to the king, and 2Kin 22:9
S the scribe shewed the king, ... 2Kin 22:10
S read it before the king, ... 2Kin 22:10
S the scribe, and Asahiah a 2Kin 22:12
and Ahikam, and Achbor, and S 2Kin 22:12
he sent S the son of Azaliah, and 2Chr 34:8
said to S the scribe, I have 2Chr 34:15
Hilkiah delivered the book to S............. 2Chr 34:16
S carried the book to the king, ... 2Chr 34:16
Then S the scribe told the king, ... 2Chr 34:18
S read it before the king 2Chr 34:18
S the scribe, and Asaiah a servant....... 2Chr 34:20
Gemariah the son of S the scribe .... Jer 36:10
the son of Gemariah, the son of S .... Jer 36:11
Achbor, and Gemariah the son of S ...... Jer 36:12
2. Father of Ahikam.
priest, and Ahikam the son of S 2Kin 22:12
the son of Ahikam, the son of S 2Kin 25:22
Hilkiah, and Ahikam the son of S 2Chr 34:20
the son of S was with Jeremiah .... Jer 26:24
the son of Ahikam the son of S .... Jer 39:14
the son of Ahikam the son of S .... Jer 40:5
the son of S sware unto them .... Jer 40:9
the son of Ahikam the son of S .... Jer 40:11
the son of S with the sword .... Jer 41:2
the son of Ahikam the son of S .... Jer 43:6
3. Messenger for Jeremiah.
the hand of Elasah the son of S............. Jer 29:3
4. Father of Jaazaniah.
them stood Jaazaniah the son of S .... Eze 8:11

SHAPHAT (sha'-fat)
1. A spy sent to the Promised Land.
of Simeon, S the son of Hori .... Num 13:5
2. Father of Elisha the prophet.
and Elisha the son of S of 1Kin 19:16
and found Elisha the son of S 1Kin 19:19
said, Here is Elisha the son of S 2Kin 3:11
of S shall stand on him this day 2Kin 6:31
3. A grandson of Shechaniah.
and Bariah, and Neariah, and S 1Chr 3:22
4. A chief Gadite.
next, and Jaanai, and S in Bashan....... 1Chr 5:12
5. A shepherd of David's herds.
valleys was S the son of Adlai 1Chr 27:29

SHAPHER (sha'-fur) *An Israelite encampment
in the wilderness.*
Kehelathah, and pitched in mount S .... Num 33:23
And they removed from mount S .... Num 33:24

SHAPHIR See SHAPHER.

SHARAI (sha'-rahee) *Married a foreigner in
exile.*
Machnadebai, Shashai, S, ... Ezr 10:40

SHARAIM (sha-ra'-im) See SHAARAIM. *Same as
Shaaraim.*
S, and Adithaim, and Gederah .... Josh 15:36

SHARAR (sha'-rar) See SACAR. *A "mighty
man" of David.*
Ahiam the son of S the Hararite 2Sa 23:33

SHARE
to sharpen every man his s 1Sa 13:20

SHAREZER (sha-re'-zur) See SHEREZER. *Son of
Sennacherib.*
S his sons smote him with the 2Kin 19:37
S his sons smote him with the .... Is 37:38

SHARON (sha'-run) See SARON, SHARONITE.
1. A plain of Ephraim.
in S was Shitrai the Sharonite 1Chr 27:29
I am the rose of S, and the lily .... Song 2:1
S is like a wilderness .... Is 33:9
it, the excellency of Carmel and S .... Is 35:2
S shall be a fold of flocks, and .... Is 65:10
2. A plain or city in Gad.
towns, and in all the suburbs of S 1Chr 5:16

SHARONITE (sha'-run-ite) *An inhabitant of
Sharon 1.*
fed in Sharon was Shitrai the S............. 1Chr 27:29

SHARP
Then Zipporah took a s stone .... Ex 4:25
unto Joshua, Make thee s knives.......... Josh 5:2
And Joshua made him s knives.............. Josh 5:3
there was a s rock on the one................. 1Sa 14:4
a s rock on the other side 1Sa 14:4
S stones are under him .... Job 41:30
he spreadeth s pointed things............... Job 41:30
Thine arrows are s in the heart............. Ps 45:5
like a s razor, working .... Ps 52:2
arrows, and their tongue a s sword....... Ps 57:4
S arrows of the mighty, with .... Ps 120:4
wormwood, as a twoedged sword .... Prov 5:4
a maul, and a sword, and a s arrow..... Prov 25:18
Whose arrows are s, and all their .... Is 5:28
Behold, I will make thee a new s .... Is 41:15
hath made my mouth like a s sword ..... Is 49:2
son of man, take thee a s knife .... Eze 5:1
contention was so s between them .... Acts 15:39
his mouth went a s twoedged sword ..... Rev 1:16
hath the s sword with two edges........... Rev 2:12
crown, and in his hand a s sickle........... Rev 14:14
heaven, he also having a s sickle.......... Rev 14:14
cry to him that had the s sickle .... Rev 14:18
saying, Thrust in thy s sickle................ Rev 14:18
out of his mouth goeth a s sword .... Rev 19:15

SHARPEN
to s every man his share, and his.......... 1Sa 13:20
for the axes, and to s the goads............. 1Sa 13:21

SHARPENED
They have s their tongues like a............ Ps 140:3
Say, A sword, a sword is s .... Eze 21:9
It is s to make a sore slaughter .... Eze 21:10
this sword is s, and it is .... Eze 21:11

SHARPENETH
mine enemy his eyes upon me .... Job 16:9
Iron s iron .... Prov 27:17
so a man s the countenance of his........ Prov 27:17

SHARPER
upright is s than a thorn hedge .... Mic 7:4
s than any twoedged sword,................. Heb 4:12

SHARPLY
And they did chide with him s .... Judg 8:1
Wherefore rebuke them s, that .... Titus 1:13

SHARPNESS
lest being present I should use s 2Cor 13:10

SHARUHEN (sha-ru'-hen) See SHAARAIM,
SHILHIM. *A city in Simeon.*
And Beth-lebaoth, and S........................ Josh 19:6

SHASHAI (sha'-shahee) *Married a foreigner in
exile.*
Machnadebai, S, Sharai,...................... Ezr 10:40

SHASHAK (sha'-shak) *A son of Elpaal.*
And Ishpan, and Heber........................... 1Chr 8:14
and Penuel, the sons of S...................... 1Chr 8:25

SHAUL (sha'-ul) See SAUL, SHAULITES.
1. A son of Simeon.
S the son of a Canaanitish woman .... Gen 46:10
S the son of a Canaanitish woman .... Ex 6:15
of S, the family of the Shaulites............ Num 26:13
and Jamin, Jarib, Zerah, and S............ 1Chr 4:24
2. A king of Edom.
S of Rehoboth by the river 1Chr 1:48
when S was dead, Baal-hanan the 1Chr 1:49
3. Son of Kohath.
son, Uzziah his son, and S his son....... 1Chr 6:24

SHAULITES (sha'-ul-ites) *Descendants of
Shaul 1.*
of Shaul, the family of the S.................. Num 26:13

SHAVE
but the scall shall he not s.................... Lev 13:33
s off all his hair, and wash .... Lev 14:8
that he shall s all his hair off............... Lev 14:9
even all his hair he shall s off .... Lev 14:9
neither shall they s off the .... Lev 21:5
then he shall s his head in the .... Num 6:9
on the seventh day shall he s it .... Num 6:9
the Nazarite shall s the head of .... Num 6:18
let them s all their flesh, and .... Num 8:7
and she shall s her head, and pare...... Deut 21:12
she caused him to s off the seven .... Judg 16:19
Lord s with a razor that is hired .... Is 7:20
Neither shall they s their heads .... Eze 44:20
them, that they may s their heads .... Acts 21:24

SHAVED
he s himself, and changed his............... Gen 41:14
s off the one half of their..................... 2Sa 10:4
s them, and cut off their garments...... 1Chr 19:4
s his head, and fell down upon the ...... Job 1:20

SHAVEH (sha'-veh) *A valley near Aenon.*
Ham, and the Emims in S Kiriathaim .. Gen 14:5
were with him, at the valley of S .... Gen 14:17

SHAVEN
He s beard s, but the scall .... Lev 13:33
the hair of his separation is s .... Num 6:19
if I be s, then my strength will .... Judg 16:17
to grow again after he was s .... Judg 16:22
men, having their beards s .... Jer 41:5
is even all one as if she were s............. 1Cor 11:5
for a woman to be shorn or s 1Cor 11:6

SHEAF
my s arose, and also stood upright .... Gen 37:7
about, and made obeisance to my s ..... Gen 37:7
then ye shall bring a s of the .... Lev 23:10
shall wave the s before the LORD .... Lev 23:11
s an he lamb without blemish of .... Lev 23:12
the s of the wave offering .... Lev 23:15
and hast forgot a s in the field .... Deut 24:19
take away the s from the hungry.......... Job 24:10
and like a torch of fire in a s .... Zec 12:6

SHEAL (she'-al) *Married a foreigner in exile.*
Malluch, and Adaiah, Jashub, and S ... Ezr 10:29

SHEALTIEL (she-al'-te-el) See SALATHIEL.
Father of Zerubbabel.
and Zerubbabel the son of S.................. Ezr 3:2
began Zerubbabel the son of S.............. Ezr 3:8
rose up Zerubbabel the son of S .... Ezr 5:2
up with Zerubbabel the son of S .... Neh 12:1
unto Zerubbabel the son of S .... Hag 1:1
Then Zerubbabel the son of S .... Hag 1:12
spirit of Zerubbabel the son of S........... Hag 1:14
now to Zerubbabel the son of S .... Hag 2:2
my servant, the son of S .... Hag 2:23

SHEAR
And Laban went to s his sheep............. Gen 31:19
up to Timnath to s his sheep................ Gen 38:13
nor s the firstling of thy sheep............. Deut 15:19
that Nabal did s his sheep 1Sa 25:4

SHEARER
and like a lamb dumb before his s........ Acts 8:32

SHEARERS
now I have heard that thou hast s 1Sa 25:7
flesh that I have killed for my s 1Sa 25:11
as a sheep before her s is dumb........... Is 53:7

SHEARIAH (she-a-ri'-ah) *Son of Azel.*
Bocheru, and Ishmael, and S 1Chr 8:38
Bocheru, and Ishmael, and S 1Chr 9:44

SHEARING
he was s his sheep in Carmel 1Sa 25:2
he was at the s house in the way......... 2Kin 10:12
them at the pit of the s house............... 2Kin 10:14

SHEAR-JASHUB (she'-ar-ja'-shub) *Symbolic
name of a son of Isaiah.*
S thy son, at the end of the .... Is 7:3

SHEATH
and drew it out of the s thereof............. 1Sa 17:51
upon his loins in the s thereof 2Sa 20:8
sword again into the s thereof 1Chr 21:27
draw forth my sword out of his s.......... Eze 21:3
his s against all flesh from the .... Eze 21:4
drawn forth my sword out of his s........ Eze 21:5
I cause it to return into his s .... Eze 21:30
Put up thy sword into the s .... Jn 18:11

SHEAVES
we were binding s in the field .... Gen 37:7
your s stood round about, and made.... Gen 37:7
after the reapers among the s............... Ruth 2:7
Let her glean even among the s............. Ruth 2:15
on the sabbath, and bringing in s........ Neh 13:15
bringing his s with him .... Ps 126:6
nor he that bindeth s his bosom .... Ps 129:7
cart is pressed that is full of s .... Amos 2:13
them as the s into the floor .... Mic 4:12

SHEBA (she'-bah) See BATH-SHEBA, BEERSHEBA,
SHEBAH.
1. Son of Raamah.
Raamah; S, and Dedan.......................... Gen 10:7
Raamah; S, and Dedan.......................... 1Chr 1:9
2. Son of Yoktan.
And Obal, and Abimael, and S .... Gen 10:28
And Ebal, and Abimael, and S 1Chr 1:22
3. Son of Yoktan.
And Jokshan begat S, and Dedan .... Gen 25:3
Jokshan; S, and Dedan 1Chr 1:32
4. A region in southwestern Arabia.
when the queen of S heard of the......... 1Kin 10:1
when the queen of S had seen all 1Kin 10:4
queen of S gave to king Solomon 1Kin 10:10
the queen of S all her desire 1Kin 10:13
when the queen of S heard of the......... 2Chr 9:1
when the queen of S had seen the 2Chr 9:3
the queen of S gave king Solomon 2Chr 9:9
to the queen of S all her desire 2Chr 9:12
companies of S waited for them .... Job 6:19
the kings of S and Seba shall .... Ps 72:10
shall be given of the gold of S .... Ps 72:15
all they from S shall come .... Is 60:6

S

cometh there to me incense from S........ Jer 6:20
The merchants of S and Raamah,......... Eze 27:22
and Eden, the merchants of S............. Eze 27:23
S, and Dedan, and the merchants of ... Eze 38:13
5. A city in Simeon.
inheritance Beer-sheba, or S............. Josh 19:2
6. A son of Bichri.
a man of Belial, whose name was S...... 2Sa 20:1
followed S the son of Bichri............. 2Sa 20:2
Now shall S the son of Bichri do....... 2Sa 20:6
to pursue after S the son of............ 2Sa 20:7
pursued after S the son of Bichri...... 2Sa 20:10
to pursue after S the son of............ 2Sa 20:13
S the son of Bichri by name, hath..... 2Sa 20:21
the head of S the son of Bichri........ 2Sa 20:22
7. A chief Gadite.
were, Michael, and Meshullam, and. S. 1Chr 5:13

SHEBAH (she´-bah) See SHEBA. *A well at Beersheba.*
And he called it S.......................... Gen 26:33

SHEBAM (she´-bam) See SHIBMAH. *A city in Reuben.*
and Heshbon, and Elealeh, and S....... Num 32:3

SHEBANIAH (sheb-a-ni´-ah) See SHECHANIAH.
1. A priest who moved the Ark.
And S, and Jehoshaphat, and.......... 1Chr 15:24
2. A Levite who aided Ezra.
Jeshua, and Bani, Kadmiel, S.......... Neh 9:4
Hashabniah, Sherebiah, Hodijah, S.... Neh 9:5
And their brethren, S, Hodijah,........ Neh 10:10
3. A priest who renewed the covenant.
Hattush, S, Malluch,..................... Neh 10:4
of S, Joseph................................ Neh 12:14
4. A Levite who renewed the covenant.
Zaccur, Sherebiah, S,.................... Neh 10:12

SHEBARIM (sheb´-a-rim) *A place near Jericho.*
from before the gate even unto S...... Josh 7:5

SHEBAT See SEBAT.

SHEBER (she´-bur) *A son of Caleb.*
Caleb's concubine, bare S................ 1Chr 2:48

SHEBNA (sheb´-nah)
1. King Hezekiah's scribe.
S the scribe, and Joah the son of 2Kin 18:18
Eliakim the son of Hilkiah, and S 2Kin 18:26
S the scribe, and Joah the son of 2Kin 18:37
S the scribe, and the elders of........ 2Kin 19:2
S the scribe, and Joah, Asaph's........ Is 36:3
Then said Eliakim and S and Joah...... Is 36:11
S the scribe, and Joah, the son of ... Is 36:22
S the scribe, and the elders of........ Is 37:2
2. An unspecified treasurer.
unto this treasurer, even unto S....... Is 22:15

SHEBNAH See SHEBNA.

SHEBUEL (she-bu´-el) See SHUBAEL.
1. A son of Gershom.
sons of Gershom, S was the chief..... 1Chr 23:16
S the son of Gershom, the son of 1Chr 26:24
2. A son of Haman.
Bukkiah, Mattaniah, Uzziel, S 1Chr 25:4

SHECANIAH (shek-a-ni´-ah) See SHEBANIAH, SHECHANIAH.
1. A priest in David's time.
ninth to Jeshua, the tenth to S........ 1Chr 24:11
2. A priest in Hezekiah's time.
and Shemaiah, Amariah, and S 2Chr 31:15

SHECHANIAH (shek-a-ni´-ah) See SHEBANIAH, SHECANIAH.
1. Head of a Davidic family.
sons of Obadiah, the sons of S......... 1Chr 3:21
And the sons of S 1Chr 3:22
2. A family of exiles.
Of the sons of S, of the sons of....... Ezr 8:3
3. Another family of exiles.
Of the sons of S .... Ezr 8:5
4. Married a foreigner in exile.
S the son of Jehiel, one of the........ Ezr 10:2
also Shemaiah the son of S.............. Neh 3:29
6. Son of Arah.
son in law of S the son of Arah........ Neh 6:18
7. A priest with Zerubbabel.
S, Rehum, Meremoth,..................... Neh 12:3

SHECHEM (she´-kem) See SHECHEMITES, SHECHEM's, SICHEM, SYCHEM.
1. A Levitical city near Mt. Ephraim.
Jacob came to Shalem, a city of S..... Gen 33:18
them under the oak which was by S... Gen 35:4
to feed their father's flock in S .... Gen 37:12
thy brethren feed the flock in S........ Gen 37:13
vale of Hebron, and he came to S...... Gen 37:14
Michmethah, that lieth before S........ Josh 17:7
and S in mount Ephraim, and........... Josh 20:7
For they gave them S with her......... Josh 21:21
all the tribes of Israel to S.............. Josh 24:1
a statute and an ordinance in S........ Josh 24:25
And his concubine that was in S........ Judg 8:31
to S unto his mother's brethren........ Judg 9:1
in the ears of all the men of S.......... Judg 9:2
all the men of S all these words....... Judg 9:3
all the men of S gathered............... Judg 9:6
plain of the pillar that was in S........ Judg 9:6
Hearken unto me, ye men of S.......... Judg 9:7
king over the men of S, because....... Judg 9:18

Abimelech, and devour the men of S . Judg 9:20
fire come out from the men of S........ Judg 9:20
between Abimelech and the men of S . Judg 9:23
the men of S dealt treacherously...... Judg 9:23
and upon the men of S, which aided.. Judg 9:24
the men of S set liers in wait........... Judg 9:25
his brethren, and went over to S...... Judg 9:26
the men of S put their confidence .... Judg 9:26
Ebed and his brethren be come to S . Judg 9:31
wait against S in four companies...... Judg 9:34
Gaal went out before the men of S ... Judg 9:39
that they should not dwell in S........ Judg 9:41
men of the tower of S heard that..... Judg 9:46
tower of S were gathered together.... Judg 9:47
men of the tower of S died also........ Judg 9:49
all the evil of the men of S did........ Judg 9:57
that goeth up from Beth-el to S .... Judg 21:19
And Rehoboam went to S................. 1Kin 12:1
were come to S to make him king..... 1Kin 12:1
Jeroboam built S in mount Ephraim . 1Kin 12:25
S in mount Ephraim with her........... 1Chr 6:67
S also and the towns thereof, unto... 1Chr 7:28
And Rehoboam went to S................. 2Chr 10:1
for to S were all Israel come to........ 2Chr 10:1
I will rejoice, I will divide S............. Ps 60:6
I will rejoice, I will divide S............. Ps 108:7
That there came certain from S........ Jer 41:5
2. Son of Hamor.
when S the son of Hamor the.......... Gen 34:2
S spake unto his father Hamor,........ Gen 34:4
Hamor the father of S went out....... Gen 34:6
The soul of my son S longeth for...... Gen 34:8
S said unto her father and unto....... Gen 34:11
And the sons of Jacob answered S .... Gen 34:13
pleased Hamor, and S Hamor's son ... Gen 34:18
S his son came unto the gate of ...... Gen 34:20
unto S his son hearkened all that .... Gen 34:24
S his son with the edge of the......... Gen 34:26
up out of Egypt, buried they in S ..... Josh 24:32
S for an hundred pieces of silver...... Josh 24:32
Who is Abimelech, and who is S .... Judg 9:28
the men of Hamor the father of S .... Judg 9:28
3. Son of Gilead.
and of S, the family of the............. Num 26:31
Asriel, and for the children of S....... Josh 17:2
4. A son of Shemidah.
of Shemidah were, Ahian, and S ...... Chr 7:19

SHECHEMITES (she´-kem-ites) *Descendants of Shechem.*
of Shechem, the family of the S....... Num 26:31

SHECHEM'S (she´-kems) *Refers to Shechem 2*
S father, for an hundred pieces........ Gen 33:19
and took Dinah out of S house......... Gen 34:26

SHED
by man shall his blood be s............. Gen 9:6
S no blood, but cast him into........... Gen 37:22
there shall no blood be s for him...... Ex 22:2
there shall be blood s for him.......... Ex 22:3
he hath s blood............................ Lev 17:4
of the blood that is s therein.......... Num 35:33
but by the blood of him that s it...... Num 35:33
blood be not s in thy land.............. Deut 19:10
Our hands have not s this blood....... Deut 21:7
thee from coming to s blood........... 1Sa 25:26
that thou hast s blood causeless...... 1Sa 25:31
this day from coming to s blood....... 1Sa 25:33
s out his bowels to the ground,....... 2Sa 20:10
s the blood of war in peace, and 1Kin 2:5
the innocent blood, which Joab s 1Kin 2:31
Moreover Manasseh s innocent........ 2Kin 21:16
for the innocent blood that he s 2Kin 24:4
Thou hast s blood abundantly, and .. 1Chr 22:8
because thou hast s much blood....... 1Chr 22:8
a man of war, and hast s blood....... 1Chr 28:3
Their blood have they s like............ Ps 79:3
blood of thy servants which is s ...... Ps 79:10
s innocent blood, even the blood..... Ps 106:38
to evil, and make haste to s blood ... Prov 1:16
hands that s innocent blood,........... Prov 6:17
make haste to s innocent blood....... Is 59:7
s not innocent blood in this............ Jer 7:6
neither s innocent blood in this....... Jer 22:3
for to s innocent blood, and for....... Jer 22:17
that have s the blood of the just...... Lam 4:13
wedlock and a blood are judged....... Eze 16:38
in thy blood that thou hast s.......... Eze 22:4
in thee to their power to s blood..... Eze 22:6
men that carry tales to s blood....... Eze 22:9
have they taken gifts to s blood...... Eze 22:12
to s blood, and to destroy souls,..... Eze 22:27
the manner of women that s blood... Eze 23:45
toward your idols, and s blood........ Eze 23:37
hast s the blood of the children....... Eze 35:5
that they had s upon the land......... Eze 36:18
because they have s innocent.......... Joel 3:19
righteousness s upon the earth........ Mt 26:28
which is s for many for the............. Mt 26:28
testament, which is s for many........ Mk 14:24
which was s from the foundation ..... Lk 11:50
in my blood, which is s for you........ Lk 22:20
he hath s forth this, which ye .... Acts 2:33
blood of thy martyr Stephen was s .. Acts 22:20
Their feet are swift to s blood......... Rom 3:15
because the love of God is s............ Rom 5:5
Which he s on us abundantly........... Titus 3:6
For they have s the blood of........... Rev 16:6

SHEDDER
a s of blood, and that doeth the ...... Eze 18:10

SHEDDETH
Whoso s man's blood, by man shall.... Gen 9:6
The city s blood in the midst of....... Eze 22:3

SHEDDING
and without s of blood is no............ Heb 9:22

SHEDEUR (shed´-e-ur) *A Reubenite who counted the people.*
Elizur the son of S .... Num 1:5
shall be Elizur the son of S............. Num 2:10
fourth day Elizur the son of S .... Num 7:30
offering of Elizur the son of S .... Num 7:35
his host was Elizur the son of S .... Num 10:18

SHEEP
And Abel was a keeper of s............. Gen 4:2
and he had s, and oxen, and he asses. Gen 12:16
And Abimelech took s, and oxen, and. Gen 20:14
and Abraham took s and oxen, and... Gen 21:27
three flocks of s lying by it............. Gen 29:2
well's mouth, and watered the s ...... Gen 29:3
his daughter cometh with the s........ Gen 29:6
water ye the s, and go and feed....... Gen 29:7
then we water the s .... Gen 29:8
Rachel came with her father's s .... Gen 29:9
the s of Laban his mother's............ Gen 29:10
all the brown cattle among the s ..... Gen 30:32
the goats, and brown among the s ... Gen 30:33
it, and all the brown among the s .... Gen 30:35
And Laban went to shear his s .... Gen 31:19
They took their s, and their oxen,.... Gen 34:28
up to Timnath to shear his s .... Gen 38:13
upon the oxen, and upon the s .... Ex 9:3
ye shall take it out from the s .... Ex 12:5
and thy peace offerings, thy s .... Ex 20:24
a man shall steal an ox, or a s .... Ex 22:1
for an ox, and four s for a s............ Ex 22:1
whether it be ox, or ass, or s.......... Ex 22:4
it be for ox, for ass, for s............... Ex 22:9
an ass, or an ox, or a s, or any........ Ex 22:10
do with thine oxen, and with thy s .. Ex 22:30
among thy cattle, whether ox or s ... Ex 34:19
of the flocks, namely, of the s......... Lev 1:10
no manner of fat, of ox, or of s .... Lev 7:23
blemish, of the beeves, of the s ...... Lev 22:19
freewill offering in beeves or s .... Lev 22:21
When a bullock, or a s, or a goat..... Lev 22:27
whether it be ox, or s .... Lev 27:26
of a cow, or the firstling of a s........ Num 18:17
And Balak offered oxen and s.......... Num 22:40
of the LORD be not as a s which....... Num 27:17
and of the asses, and of the s .... Num 31:28
thousand and five thousand s........... Num 31:32
thirty thousand and five hundred s .. Num 31:36
tribute of the s was six hundred...... Num 31:37
seven thousand and five hundred s .. Num 31:43
little ones, and folds for your s .... Num 32:24
and folds of s .... Num 32:36
thy kine, and the flocks of thy s ...... Deut 7:13
the ox, the s, and the goat,............ Deut 14:4
lusteth after, for oxen, or for s .... Deut 14:26
nor shear the firstling of thy s......... Deut 15:19
LORD thy God any bullock, or s .... Deut 17:1
sacrifice, whether it be ox or s .... Deut 18:3
the first of the fleece of thy s.......... Deut 18:4
brother's ox or his s go astray......... Deut 22:1
thy kine, and the flocks of thy s ...... Deut 28:4
thy kine, and the flocks of thy s ...... Deut 28:18
thy s shall be given unto thine......... Deut 28:31
of thy kine, or flocks of thy s .... Deut 28:51
Butter of kine, and milk of s .... Deut 32:14
woman, young and old, and ox, and s. Josh 6:21
his oxen, and his asses, and his s ..... Josh 7:24
sustenance for Israel, neither s........ Judg 6:4
He will take the tenth of your s 1Sa 8:17
flew upon the spoil, and took s 1Sa 14:32
man his ox, and every man his s 1Sa 14:34
infant and suckling, ox and s 1Sa 15:3
spared Agag, and the best of the s ... 1Sa 15:9
bleating of the s in mine ears.......... 1Sa 15:14
people spared the best of the s 1Sa 15:15
the people took of the spoil, s......... 1Sa 15:21
and, behold, he keepeth the s 1Sa 16:11
thy son, which is with the s 1Sa 16:19
feed his father's s at Beth-lehem 1Sa 17:15
left the s with a keeper, and took ... 1Sa 17:20
those few s in the wilderness.......... 1Sa 17:28
Thy servant kept his father's s 1Sa 17:34
and oxen, and asses, and s, with...... 1Sa 22:19
great, and he had three thousand s .. 1Sa 25:2
he was shearing his s in Carmel....... 1Sa 25:4
that Nabal did shear his s 1Sa 25:4
we were with them keeping the s 1Sa 25:16
five s ready dressed, and five.......... 1Sa 25:18
woman alive, and took away the s 1Sa 27:9
sheepcote, from following the s 2Sa 7:8
And honey, and butter, and s 2Sa 17:29
but these s, what have they done 2Sa 24:17
And Adonijah slew s and oxen and fat. 1Kin 1:9
s in abundance, and hath called....... 1Kin 1:19
s in abundance, and hath called....... 1Kin 1:25
of the pastures, and an hundred s ... 1Kin 4:23
him before the ark, sacrificing s 1Kin 8:5
an hundred and twenty thousand s ... 1Kin 8:63
as s that have not a shepherd......... 1Kin 22:17
and oliveyards, and vineyards, and s . 2Kin 5:26

SHEEPCOTE *(continued)*

of *s* two hundred and fifty	1Chr 5:21
and oil, and oxen, and *s* abundantly.	1Chr 12:40
even from following the *s*	1Chr 17:7
but as for these *s*, what have	1Chr 21:17
him before the ark, sacrificed a *s*	2Chr 5:6
an hundred and twenty thousand *s*	2Chr 7:5
of cattle, and carried away *s*	2Chr 14:15
hundred oxen and seven thousand *s*.	2Chr 15:11
And Ahab killed *s* and oxen for	2Chr 18:2
as *s* that have no shepherd	2Chr 18:16
hundred oxen and three thousand *s*.	2Chr 29:33
bullocks and seven thousand *s*	2Chr 30:24
bullocks and ten thousand *s*	2Chr 30:24
brought in the tithe of oxen and *s*.	2Chr 31:6
and they builded the *s* gate	Neh 3:1
s gate repaired the goldsmiths	Neh 3:32
daily was one ox and six choice *s*.	Neh 5:18
of Meah, even unto the *s* gate	Neh 12:39
also was seven thousand *s*	Job 1:3
heaven, and hath burned up the *s*	Job 1:16
warmed with the fleece of my *s*	Job 31:20
for he had fourteen thousand *s*	Job 42:12
All *s* and oxen, yea, and the beasts.	Ps 8:7
us like *s* appointed for meat	Ps 44:11
counted as *s* for the slaughter	Ps 44:22
Like *s* they are laid in the grave	Ps 49:14
against the *s* of thy pasture	Ps 74:1
his own people to go forth like *s*	Ps 78:52
s of thy pasture will give thee	Ps 79:13
his pasture, and the *s* of his hand	Ps 95:7
people, and the *s* of his pasture	Ps 100:3
I have gone astray like a lost *s*	Ps 119:176
that our *s* may bring forth	Ps 144:13
a flock of *s* that are even shorn	Song 4:2
Thy teeth are as a flock of *s*	Song 6:6
nourish a young cow, and two *s*	Is 7:21
as a *s* that no man taketh up	Is 13:14
slaying oxen, and killing *s*	Is 22:13
All we like *s* have gone astray	Is 53:6
as a *s* before her shearers is	Is 53:7
them out like *s* for the slaughter	Jer 12:3
scatter the *s* of my pasture	Jer 23:1
My people hath been lost *s*	Jer 50:6
Israel is a scattered *s*	Jer 50:17
My *s* wandered through all the	Eze 34:6
I, even I, will both search my *s*	Eze 34:11
is among his *s* that are scattered	Eze 34:12
so will I seek out my *s*, and will	Eze 34:12
a wife, and for a wife he kept *s*	Hos 12:12
the flocks of *s* are made desolate	Joel 1:18
then together as the *s* of Bozrah	Mic 2:12
young lion among the flocks of *s*	Mic 5:8
and the *s* shall be scattered	Zec 13:7
abroad, as *s* having no shepherd	Mt 9:36
the lost *s* of the house of Israel	Mt 10:6
I send you forth as *s* in the	Mt 10:16
among you, that shall have one *s*	Mt 12:11
then is a man better than a *s*	Mt 12:12
the lost *s* of the house of Israel	Mt 15:24
if a man have an hundred *s*	Mt 18:12
you, he rejoiceth more of that *s*	Mt 18:13
divideth his *s* from the goats	Mt 25:32
he shall set the *s* on his right	Mt 25:33
the *s* of the flock shall be	Mt 26:31
because they were as *s* not having.	Mk 6:34
and the *s* shall be scattered	Mk 14:27
man of you, having an hundred *s*	Lk 15:4
I have found my *s* which was lost	Lk 15:6
temple those that sold oxen and *s*.	Jn 2:14
all out of the temple, and the *s*	Jn 2:15
Jerusalem by the *s* market a pool	Jn 5:2
the door is the shepherd of the *s*	Jn 10:2
and the *s* hear his voice	Jn 10:3
and he calleth his own *s* by name	Jn 10:3
when he putteth forth his own *s*	Jn 10:4
before them, and the *s* follow him.	Jn 10:4
unto you, I am the door of the *s*	Jn 10:7
that he did not hear them	Jn 10:8
giveth his life for the *s*	Jn 10:11
shepherd, whose own the *s* are not.	Jn 10:12
the wolf coming, and leaveth the *s*.	Jn 10:12
them, and scattereth the *s*	Jn 10:12
hireling, and careth not for the *s*.	Jn 10:13
the good shepherd, and know my *s*.	Jn 10:14
and I lay down my life for the *s*	Jn 10:15
know me, which are not of this	Jn 10:16
not, because ye are not of my *s*	Jn 10:26
My *s* hear my voice, and I know	Jn 10:27
He saith unto him, Feed my *s*	Jn 21:16
Jesus saith unto him, Feed my *s*	Jn 21:17
this, He was led as a *s* to the	Acts 8:32
accounted as *s* for the slaughter	Rom 8:36
that great shepherd of the *s*	Heb 13:20
For ye were as *s* going astray	1Pet 2:25
flour, and wheat, and beasts, and *s*.	Rev 18:13

SHEEPCOTE

of hosts, I took thee from the *s*	2Sa 7:8
of hosts, I took thee from the *s*	1Chr 17:7

SHEEPCOTES

And he came to the *s* by the way	1Sa 24:3

SHEEPFOLD

not by the door into the *s*	Jn 10:1

SHEEPFOLDS

We will build *s* here for our	Num 32:16
Why abodest thou among the *s*	Judg 5:16
servant, and took him from the *s*	Ps 78:70

SHEEPMASTER

And Mesha king of Moab was a *s*	2Kin 3:4

SHEEP'S

which come to you in *s* clothing	Mt 7:15

SHEEPSHEARERS

and went up unto his *s* to Timnath.	Gen 38:12
that Absalom had *s* in Baal-hazor	2Sa 13:23
Behold now, thy servant hath *s*	2Sa 13:24

SHEEPSKINS

they wandered about in *s* and	Heb 11:37

SHEERAH See SHERAH.

SHEET

as it had been a great *s* knit at	Acts 10:11
descend, as it had been a great *s*	Acts 11:5

SHEETS

then I will give you thirty *s*	Judg 14:12
then shall ye give me thirty *s*	Judg 14:13

SHEHARIAH *(she-ha-ri'-ah)* A son of Jeroham.

and S, and Athaliah	1Chr 8:26

SHEKEL

golden earring of half a *s* weight	Gen 24:22
half a *s* after the *s* of the	Ex 30:13
(a *s* is twenty gerahs	Ex 30:13
an half *s* shall be the offering	Ex 30:13
shalt not give less than half a *s*	Ex 30:15
after the *s* of the sanctuary, and	Ex 38:24
after the *s* of the sanctuary	Ex 38:24
after the *s* of the sanctuary	Ex 38:25
for every man, that is, half a *s*	Ex 38:26
after the *s* of the sanctuary, for	Lev 5:15
after the *s* of the sanctuary	Lev 27:3
to the *s* of the sanctuary	Lev 27:25
twenty gerahs shall be the *s*	Num 3:47
after the *s* of the sanctuary	Num 3:47
(the *s* is twenty gerahs	Num 3:47
after the *s* of the sanctuary	Num 3:50
after the *s* of the sanctuary	Num 7:13
after the *s* of the sanctuary	Num 7:19
after the *s* of the sanctuary	Num 7:25
after the *s* of the sanctuary	Num 7:31
after the *s* of the sanctuary	Num 7:37
after the *s* of the sanctuary	Num 7:43
after the *s* of the sanctuary	Num 7:49
after the *s* of the sanctuary	Num 7:55
after the *s* of the sanctuary	Num 7:61
after the *s* of the sanctuary	Num 7:67
after the *s* of the sanctuary	Num 7:73
after the *s* of the sanctuary	Num 7:79
after the *s* of the sanctuary	Num 7:85
after the *s* of the sanctuary	Num 7:86
after the *s* of the sanctuary	Num 18:16
the fourth part of a *s* of silver	1Sa 9:8
of fine flour be sold for a *s*	2Kin 7:1
and two measures of barley for a *s*.	2Kin 7:1
of fine flour was sold for a *s*	2Kin 7:16
and two measures of barley for a *s*.	2Kin 7:16
Two measures of barley for a *s*	2Kin 7:18
a measure of fine flour for a *s*	2Kin 7:18
for the service of the house of	Neh 10:32
the *s* shall be twenty gerahs	Eze 45:12
the *s* great, and falsifying the	Amos 8:5

SHEKELS

is worth four hundred *s* of silver	Gen 23:15
of Heth, four hundred *s* of silver	Gen 23:16
her hands of ten *s* weight of gold	Gen 24:22
their master thirty *s* of silver	Ex 21:32
of pure myrrh five hundred *s*	Ex 30:23
much, even two hundred and fifty *s*.	Ex 30:23
calamus two hundred and fifty *s*	Ex 30:23
And of cassia five hundred *s*	Ex 30:24
and seven hundred and thirty *s*	Ex 38:25
five *s* be made hooks for the	Ex 38:28
and two thousand and four hundred *s*.	Ex 38:29
thy estimation by *s* of silver	Lev 5:15
shall be fifty *s* of silver	Lev 27:3
thy estimation shall be thirty *s*	Lev 27:4
shall be of the male twenty *s*	Lev 27:5
and for the female ten *s*	Lev 27:6
be of the male five *s* of silver	Lev 27:6
shall be three *s* of silver	Lev 27:6
thy estimation shall be fifteen *s*	Lev 27:7
and for the female ten *s*	Lev 27:7
be valued at fifty *s* of silver	Lev 27:16
take five *s* apiece for the poll	Num 3:47
hundred and threescore and five *s*.	Num 3:50
was an hundred and thirty *s*	Num 7:13
one silver bowl of seventy *s*	Num 7:13
One spoon of ten *s* of gold	Num 7:14
was an hundred and thirty *s*	Num 7:19
one silver bowl of seventy *s*	Num 7:19
One spoon of gold of ten *s*	Num 7:20
was an hundred and thirty *s*	Num 7:25
one silver bowl of seventy *s*	Num 7:25
One golden spoon of ten *s*	Num 7:26
weight of an hundred and thirty *s*.	Num 7:31
one silver bowl of seventy *s*	Num 7:31
One golden spoon of ten *s*	Num 7:32
was an hundred and thirty *s*	Num 7:37
one silver bowl of seventy *s*	Num 7:37
One golden spoon of ten *s*	Num 7:38
weight of an hundred and thirty *s*.	Num 7:43
a silver bowl of seventy *s*	Num 7:43
One golden spoon of ten *s*	Num 7:44
was an hundred and thirty *s*	Num 7:49
one silver bowl of seventy *s*	Num 7:49
One golden spoon of ten *s*	Num 7:50
weight of an hundred and thirty *s*.	Num 7:55
one silver bowl of seventy *s*	Num 7:55
one silver bowl of seventy *s*	Num 7:56
One golden spoon of ten *s*	Num 7:56
was an hundred and thirty *s*	Num 7:61
one silver bowl of seventy *s*	Num 7:61
One golden spoon of ten *s*	Num 7:62
one silver bowl of seventy *s*	Num 7:67
One golden spoon of ten *s*	Num 7:68
was an hundred and thirty *s*	Num 7:73
one silver bowl of seventy *s*	Num 7:73
One golden spoon of ten *s*	Num 7:74
was an hundred and thirty *s*	Num 7:79
one silver bowl of seventy *s*	Num 7:79
One golden spoon of ten *s*	Num 7:80
weighing an hundred and thirty *s*.	Num 7:85
two thousand and four hundred *s*	Num 7:85
of incense, weighing ten *s* apiece	Num 7:86
spoons was an hundred and twenty *s*.	Num 7:86
for the money of five *s*, after	Num 18:16
thousand seven hundred and fifty *s*.	Num 31:52
him in an hundred *s* of silver	Deut 22:19
damsel's father fifty *s* of silver	Deut 22:29
and two hundred *s* of silver	Josh 7:21
a wedge of gold of fifty *s* weight	Josh 7:21
and seven hundred *s* of gold	Judg 8:26
The eleven hundred *s* of silver	Judg 17:2
hundred *s* of silver to his mother	Judg 17:3
took two hundred *s* of silver	Judg 17:4
I will give thee ten *s* of silver	Judg 17:10
coat was five thousand *s* of brass	1Sa 17:5
weighed six hundred *s* of iron	1Sa 17:7
hundred *s* after the king's weight	2Sa 14:26
have given thee ten *s* of silver	2Sa 18:11
thousand *s* of silver in mine hand.	2Sa 18:12
hundred *s* of brass in weight	2Sa 21:16
the oxen for fifty *s* of silver	2Sa 24:24
six hundred *s* of gold went to one.	1Kin 10:16
Egypt for six hundred *s* of silver	1Kin 10:29
of each man fifty *s* of silver	2Kin 15:20
six hundred *s* of gold by weight	1Chr 21:25
for six hundred *s* of silver	1Chr 21:25
of the nails was fifty *s* of gold	2Chr 3:9
six hundred *s* of beaten gold went.	2Chr 9:15
hundred *s* of gold went to	2Chr 9:16
and wine, beside forty *s* of silver	Neh 5:15
money, even seventeen *s* of silver	Jer 32:9
by weight, twenty *s* a day	Eze 4:10
twenty *s*, five and twenty	Eze 45:12
five and twenty *s*, fifteen	Eze 45:12

SHELAH *(she'-lah)* See SALAH, SHELANITES.

1. Son of Judah.

and called his name S	Gen 38:5
house, till S my son be grown	Gen 38:11
for she saw that S was grown	Gen 38:14
that I gave her not to S my son	Gen 38:26
and Onan, and S, and Pharez	Gen 46:12
of S, the family of the	Num 26:20
Er, and Onan, and S	1Chr 2:3

2. Son of Arphaxad.

And Arphaxad begat S, and Shelah.	1Chr 1:18
begat Shelah, and S begat Eber	1Chr 1:18
Shem, Arphaxad, S	1Chr 1:24

SHELANITE See SHELANITES.

SHELANITES *(she'-lan-ites)* Descendants of Shelah.

of Shelah, the family of the S	Num 26:20

SHELEMIAH *(shel-e-mi'-ah)* See MESHELEMIAH, SHALLUM.

1. A sanctuary servant.

And the lot eastward fell to S	1Chr 26:14

2. A son of Bani who married a foreigner.

And S, and Nathan, and Adaiah	Ezr 10:39

3. Another son of Bani.

Azareel, and S, Shemariah	Ezr 10:41

4. Father of Hananiah.

repaired Hananiah the son of S	Neh 3:30

5. A treasury servant.

S the priest, and Zadok the scribe.	Neh 13:13

6. Son of Cushi.

son of Nethaniah, the son of S	Jer 36:14

7. Son of Abdeel.

S the son of Abdeel, to take	Jer 36:26

8. Father of Jehucal.

king sent Jehucal the son of S	Jer 37:3
of Pashur, and Jucal the son of S	Jer 38:1

9. Father of Irijah.

name was Irijah the son of S	Jer 37:13

SHELEPH *(she'-lef)* A son of Joktan.

And Joktan begat Almodad, and S.	Gen 10:26
And Joktan begat Almodad, and S	1Chr 1:20

SHELESH *(she'-lesh)* A son of Helem.

Zophah, and Imna, and S, and Amal	1Chr 7:35

SHELOMI *(shel-o'-mi)* Father of Ahihud.

of Asher, Ahihud the son of S	Num 34:27

SHELOMITH *(shel'-o-mith)*

1. Daughter of Debri.

(and his mother's name was S	Lev 24:11

2. Daughter of Zerubbabel.

and Hananiah, and S their sister	1Chr 3:19

3. A son of Shimei.

S, and Haziel, and Haran, three	1Chr 23:9

S

4. A son of Izhar.
S the chief..1Chr 23:18
5. A descendant of Eliezer.
and Zichri his son, and S his son 1Chr 26:25
Which S and his brethren were over   1Chr 26:26
thing, it was under the hand of S 1Chr 26:28
6. A child of King Rehoboam.
Abijah, and Attai, and Ziza, and S 2Chr 11:20
7. A family of exiles.
And of the sons of S ....Ezr 8:10

SHELOMOTH (shel´-o-moth) See SHELOMITH.
A descendant of Izhar.
S: of the sons of 1Chr 24:22

SHELTER
embrace the rock for want of a s ....Job 24:8
For thou hast been a s for me ....Ps 61:3

SHELUMIEL
The son of Zurishaddai ....Num 1:6
shall be S the son of Zurishaddai ......Num 2:12
On the fifth day S the son of ....Num 7:36
of S the son of Zurishaddai ....Num 7:41
was S the son of Zurishaddai ....Num 10:19

SHEM (shem) See SEM. A son of Noah.
and Noah begat S, Ham, and Japheth...Gen 5:32
And Noah begat three sons, S.............. Gen 6:10
selfsame day entered Noah, and S ......Gen 7:13
went forth of the ark, were S..............Gen 9:18
And S and Japheth took a garment,...... Gen 9:23
Blessed be the LORD God of S ....Gen 9:26
he shall dwell in the tents of S ....Gen 9:27
of the sons of Noah, S, Ham, and.........Gen 10:1
Unto S also, the father of all ....Gen 10:21
The children of S ....Gen 10:22
These are the sons of S, after ....Gen 10:31
These are the generations of S ....Gen 11:10
S was an hundred years old, and..........Gen 11:10
S lived after he begat Arphaxad ....Gen 11:11
Noah, S, Ham, and Japheth 1Chr 1:4
The sons of S 1Chr 1:17
S, Arphaxad, Shelah, ...1Chr 1:24

SHEMA (she´-mah) See SHEMAIAH, SHIMHI.
1. A city in Judah.
Amam, and S, and Moladah, ...Josh 15:26
2. A son of Hebron.
Tappuah, and Rekem, and S 1Chr 2:43
S begat Raham, the father of 1Chr 2:44
3. Father of Azaz.
the son of Azaz, the son of S 1Chr 5:8
4. A Benjamite Chief.
Beriah also, and S, who were heads ...1Chr 8:13
5. A priest who aided Ezra.
beside him stood Mattithiah, and S ...Neh 8:4

SHEMAAH (she´-a-ah) Father of two
warriors in David's army.
the sons of S the Gibeathite..............1Chr 12:3

SHEMAIAH (she-ma-i´-ah) See SHAMMUA,
SHEMA, SHIMEI, SIMEI.
1. A prophet in King Rehoboam's time.
of God came unto S the man of God 1Kin 12:22
the LORD came to S the man of God....2Chr 11:2
Then came S the prophet to.................. 2Chr 12:5
the word of the LORD came to S 2Chr 12:7
in the book of S the prophet 2Chr 12:15
2. Son of Shechaniah.
S: and the son of Shemaiah 1Chr 3:22
3. Father of Shimri.
the son of Shimri, the son of S 1Chr 4:37
4. Son of Joel.
S his son, Gog his son, Shimei 1Chr 5:4
5. Son of Hasshub.
the son of Hasshub, the son of 1Chr 9:14
S the son of Hasshub, the son of ....Neh 11:15
6. Father of Obadiah.
And Obadiah the son of S, the son......1Chr 9:16
7. A priest who moved the Ark.
S the chief, and his brethren two.........1Chr 15:8
for Uriel, Asaiah, and Joel, S..............1Chr 15:11
8. Son of Nethaneel.
S the son of Nethaneel the scribe 1Chr 24:6
9. A sanctuary servant.
S the firstborn, Jehozabad the 1Chr 26:4
Also unto S his son were sons.............. 1Chr 26:6
The sons of S 1Chr 26:7
10. A Levite teacher of the people.
with them he sent Levites, even S 2Chr 17:8
11. A Levite who cleansed the temple.
S, and Uzziel 2Chr 29:14
12. A Levite in Hezekiah's time.
and Miniamin, and Jeshua, and S 2Chr 31:15
13. A Levite in Josiah's time.
Conaniah also, and S and Nethaneel, . 2Chr 35:9
14. A family of exiles.
are these, Eliphelet, Jeiel, and S ....Ezr 8:13
15. A messenger of Ezra.
I for Eliezer, for Ariel, for S ....Ezr 8:16
16. A priest who married a foreigner.
Maaseiah, and Elijah, and S ....Ezr 10:21
17. A son of Harim.
Eliezer, Ishijah, Malchijah, S ....Ezr 10:31
18. A rebuilder of Jerusalem's wall.
also S the son of Shechaniah ....Neh 3:29
19. Son of Delaiah.
I came unto the house of S the ....Neh 6:10
20. A priest who renewed the covenant.
Maaziah, Bilgai, S, ...Neh 10:8
S, and Joiarib, Jedaiah,........................Neh 12:6

of S, Jehonathan................................Neh 12:18
Judah, and Benjamin, and S, and........Neh 12:34
the son of Jonathan, the son of S ......Neh 12:35
21. A priest who dedicated the wall.
And his brethren, S, and Azarael,........Neh 12:36
22. A priest who gave thanks at the wall.
Maaseiah, and S, and Eleazar,............Neh 12:42
23. Father of Urijah.
the son of S of Kirjath-jearim...............Jer 26:20
24. A false prophet.
also speak to the Nehelamites ....Jer 29:24
LORD concerning S the Nehelamite ....Jer 29:31
Because that S hath prophesied............Jer 29:31
I will punish S the Nehelamite,............Jer 29:32
25. Father of Delaiah.
scribe, and Delaiah the son of S ....Jer 36:12

SHEPHELAH See PLAIN.

SHEPHER See SHAPHER.

SHEPHERD
for every s is an abomination ....Gen 46:34
(from thence is the s, the stone..........Gen 49:24
be not as sheep which have no s ....Num 27:17
hills, as sheep that have not a s 1Kin 22:17
as sheep that have no s 2Chr 18:16
The LORD is my s ....Ps 23:1
O S of Israel, thou that leadest ....Ps 80:1
which are given from one s ....Eccl 12:11
He shall feed his flock like a s ....Is 40:11
That saith of Cyrus, He is my s ....Is 44:28
the sea with the s of his flock ....Is 63:11
keep him, as a s doth his flock............Jer 31:10
as a s putteth on his garment ....Jer 43:12
who is that s that will stand ....Jer 49:19
who is that s that will stand ....Jer 50:44
break in pieces with thee the s............Jer 51:23
scattered, because there is no s............Eze 34:5
the field, because there was no s ....Eze 34:8
As a s seeketh out his flock in ....Eze 34:12
And I will set up one o'ver them..........Eze 34:23
feed them, and he shall be their s ......Eze 34:23
and they all shall have one s ....Eze 37:24
As the s taketh out of the mouth ....Amos 3:12
troubled, because there was no s ....Zec 10:2
the instruments of a foolish s..............Zec 11:15
I will raise up a s in the land ....Zec 11:16
Woe to the idol s that leaveth ....Zec 11:17
Awake, O sword, against my s ....Zec 13:7
smite the s, and the sheep shall ....Zec 13:7
abroad, as sheep having no s ....Mt 9:36
as a s divideth his sheep from ....Mt 25:32
it is written, I will smite the s ....Mt 26:31
they were as sheep not having a s ......Mk 6:34
it is written, I will smite the s ....Mk 14:27
by the door is the s of the sheep ....Jn 10:2
I am the good s ....Jn 10:11
the good s giveth his life for ....Jn 10:11
that is an hireling, and not the s ....Jn 10:12
I am the good s, and know my sheep....Jn 10:14
there shall be one fold, and one s........Jn 10:16
that great s of the sheep, ...Heb 13:20
but are now returned unto the s 1Pet 2:25
And when the chief S shall appear......1Pet 5:4

SHEPHERDS
put them in a bag which he had, ...1Sa 17:40
and is removed from me as a s ....Is 38:12

SHEPHERDS
And the men are s, for their trade ......Gen 46:32
unto Pharaoh, Thy servants are s ......Gen 47:3
the s came and drove them away ....Ex 2:17
us out of the hand of the s ....Ex 2:19
now thy s which were with us, we......1Sa 25:7
neither shall the s make their..............Is 13:20
when a multitude of s is called ....Is 31:4
they are s that cannot understand ......Is 56:11
The s with their flocks shall ....Jer 6:3
I will set up o'ver them which ....Jer 23:4
Howl, ye s, and cry ....Jer 25:34
the s shall have no way to flee,............Jer 25:35
A voice of the cry of the s ....Jer 25:36
shall be an habitation of s ....Jer 33:12
their s have caused them to go............Jer 50:6
prophesy against the s of Israel..........Eze 34:2
saith the Lord GOD unto the s ....Eze 34:2
Woe be to the s of Israel that do ....Eze 34:2
should not the s feed the flocks ....Eze 34:2
Therefore, ye s, hear the word of........Eze 34:7
neither did my s search for my ....Eze 34:8
but the s fed themselves, and fed ....Eze 34:8
Therefore, O ye s, hear the word, ...Eze 34:9
Behold, I am against the s ....Eze 34:10
neither shall the s feed ....Eze 34:10
habitations of the s shall mourn..........Amos 1:2
we raise against him seven s ....Mic 5:5
Thy s slumber, O king of Assyria........Nah 3:18
be dwellings and cottages for s ....Zeph 2:6
anger was kindled against the s............Zec 10:3
a voice of the howling of the s..............Zec 11:3
their own s pity them not ....Zec 11:5
Three s also I cut off in one ....Zec 11:8
country s abiding in the field ....Lk 2:8
the s said one to another, Let us..........Lk 2:15
the s returned, glorifying and ....Lk 2:20

SHEPHERDS'
feed thy kids beside the s tents ....Song 1:8

SHEPHI (she´-fi) See SHEPHO. A son of Shobal.
Alian, and Manahath, and Ebal, S 1Chr 1:40

SHEPHO (she´-fo) See SHEPHI. Same as
Shephi.
Alvan, and Manahath, and Ebal, S......Gen 36:23

SHEPHUPHAM See SHUPHAM.

SHEPHUPHAN (shef´-u-fan) See SHUPHAM,
SHUPPIM. A son of Bela.
And Gera, and S, and Huram............1Chr 8:5

SHERAH (she´-rah) Daughter of Beriah.
(And his daughter was S, who built....1Chr 7:24

SHERD
a s to take fire from the hearth ....Is 30:14

SHERDS
and thou shalt break the s thereof......Eze 23:34

SHEREBIAH (sher-e-bi´-ah)
1. A family of exiles.
and S, with his sons and his ....Ezr 8:18

of the chief of the priests, S.............. Ezr 8:24
Also Jeshua, and Bani, and S............... Neh 8:7
Zaccur, S, Shebaniah,.......................... Neh 10:12
and Kadmiel, Bani, Hashabniah, S....... Neh 9:5
2. A Levite who renewed the covenant.
Zaccur, S, Shebaniah,.......................... Neh 10:12
Jeshua, Binnui, Kadmiel, S................... Neh 12:8
Hashabiah, S, and Jeshua the son...... Neh 12:24

SHERESH (she'-resh) Son of Machir.
and the name of his brother was S...... 1Chr 7:16

SHEREZER (she-re'-zur) See SHAREZER. A
messenger in Zechariah's time.
had sent unto the house of God S...... Zec 7:2

SHERIFFS
the counsellors, the s, and all............. Dan 3:2
the counsellors, the s, and all............. Dan 3:3

SHESHACH (she'-shak) See BABYLON. Another
name for Babylon.
the king of S shall drink after............ Jer 25:26
How is S taken.................................... Jer 51:41

SHESHAI (she'-shahee) A son of Anak.
where Ahiman, S, and Talmai, the .... Num 13:22
thence the three sons of Anak, S........ Josh 15:14
and they slew S, and Ahiman, and .... Judg 1:10

SHESHAK See SHESHACH.

SHESHAN (she'-shan) A descendant of
Jerahmeel.
S. And the children of S...................... 1Chr 2:31
Now S had no sons, but daughters..... 1Chr 2:34
S had a servant, an Egyptian,.............. 1Chr 2:34
S gave his daughter to Jarha his....... 1Chr 2:35

SHESHBAZZAR (shesh-baz'-zur) See
ZERUBBABEL. Same as Zerubbabel.
and numbered them unto S, the.......... Ezr 1:8
All these did S bring up with.............. Ezr 1:11
unto one, whose name was S.............. Ezr 5:14
Then came the same S, and laid the... Ezr 5:16

SHETH (sheth) See SETH.
1. A Moabite chief.
and destroy all the children of S....... Num 24:17
2. Same as Seth.
Adam, S, Enosh,................................... 1Chr 1:1

SHETHAR (she'-thar) A prince of Media and
Persia.
the next unto him was Carshena, S.... Est 1:14

SHETHAR-BOZENAI See SHETHAR-BOZNAI.

SHETHAR-BOZNAI (she''-thar-boz'-nahee) A
Persian official.
on this side the river, and S............... Ezr 5:3
on this side the river, and S............... Ezr 5:6
governor beyond the river, S............... Ezr 6:6
on this side the river, S...................... Ezr 6:13

SHETHER BAZNAI See SHETHAR BOZNAI.

SHEVA (she'-vah) See SHAVSHA.
1. David's scribe.
And S was scribe..................................... 2Sa 20:25
2. Son of Maachah.
S the father of Machbenah, and the.... 1Chr 2:49

SHEW
unto a land that I will s thee............. Gen 12:1
which thou shalt s unto me................. Gen 20:13
s kindness unto my master Abraham.. Gen 24:12
s kindness, I pray thee, unto me,........ Gen 40:14
s Pharaoh, and say unto him, My....... Gen 46:31
you, saying, S a miracle for you.......... Ex 7:9
for to s in thee my power.................... Ex 10:16
that I might s thee my signs.............. Ex 10:1
thou shalt s thy son in that day,........ Ex 13:8
which he will s to you to day............. Ex 14:13
shalt s them the way wherein they... Ex 18:20
According to all that I s thee............. Ex 25:9
s me now thy way, that I may know... Ex 33:13
I beseech thee, s me thy glory........... Ex 33:18
s mercy on whom I will s mercy......... Ex 33:19
the LORD will s who are his................ Num 16:5
to s you by what way ye should go... Deut 1:33
thou hast begun to s thy servant....... Deut 3:24
to s you the word of the LORD............ Deut 5:5
with them, nor s mercy unto them,.... Deut 7:2
s thee mercy, and have compassion... Deut 13:17
they shall s thee the sentence of...... Deut 17:9
LORD shall choose shall s thee............ Deut 17:10
sentence which they shall s thee....... Deut 17:11
nor s favour to the young................... Deut 28:50
ask thy father, and he will s thee..... Deut 32:7
that ye will also s kindness unto....... Josh 2:12
that he would not s them the land... Josh 5:6
S us, we pray thee, the entrance....... Judg 1:24
the city, and we will s thee mercy..... Judg 1:24
I will s thee the man whom thou...... Judg 4:22
then s me a sign that thou................. Judg 6:17
Samuel feared to s Eli the vision....... 1Sa 3:15
s them the manner of the king.......... 1Sa 8:9
peradventure he can s us our way...... 1Sa 9:6
that I may s thee the word of God.... 1Sa 9:27
s thee what thou shalt do................... 1Sa 10:8
to us, and we will s you a thing......... 1Sa 14:12
I will s thee what thou shalt do........ 1Sa 14:12
small, but that he will s it................. 1Sa 20:2
send not unto thee, and s it thee...... 1Sa 20:12
thee evil, then I will s it thee............. 1Sa 20:13
s me the kindness of the LORD........... 1Sa 20:14
he fled, and did not s it to me.......... 1Sa 22:17

young men, and they will s thee......... 1Sa 25:8
And now the LORD s kindness............... 2Sa 2:6
which against Judah do s kindness..... 2Sa 3:8
that I may s him kindness for............. 2Sa 9:1
that I may s the kindness of God....... 2Sa 9:3
for I will surely s thee kindness......... 2Sa 9:7
I will s kindness unto Hanun the........ 2Sa 10:2
s me both it, and his habitation......... 2Sa 15:25
thou wilt s thyself merciful................. 2Sa 22:26
man thou wilt s thyself upright.......... 2Sa 22:26
the pure thou wilt s thyself pure....... 2Sa 22:27
thou wilt s thyself unsavoury.............. 2Sa 22:27
If he will s himself a worthy man...... 1Kin 1:52
therefore, and s thyself a man........... 1Kin 2:2
But s kindness unto the sons of......... 1Kin 2:7
saying, Go, s thyself unto Ahab.......... 1Kin 18:1
Elijah went to s himself unto............. 1Kin 18:2
I will surely s myself unto him........... 1Kin 18:15
Will ye not s me which of us is......... 2Kin 6:11
I will now s you what the Syrians...... 2Kin 7:12
s forth them day to his.......................... 1Chr 16:23
s kindness unto Hanun the................. 1Chr 19:2
to s himself strong in the behalf........ 2Chr 16:9
but they could not s their................... Ezr 2:59
but they could not s their................... Neh 7:61
to s them light, and the way.............. Neh 9:19
to s the people and the princes......... Est 1:11
her that she should not s it............... Est 2:10
to s it unto Esther, and to................. Est 4:8
s me wherefore thou contendest......... Job 10:2
that he would s thee the secrets........ Job 11:6
I will s thee, hear me........................... Job 15:17
durst not s you mine opinion............. Job 32:6
I also will s mine opinion.................... Job 32:10
I also will s mine opinion.................... Job 32:17
to s unto man his uprightness........... Job 33:23
I will s thee that I have yet to.......... Job 36:2
that say, Who will s us any good...... Ps 4:6
I will s forth all thy marvellous......... Ps 9:1
That I may s forth all thy praise....... Ps 9:14
Thou wilt s me the path of life.......... Ps 16:11
S thy marvellous lovingkindness,......... Ps 17:7
thou wilt s thyself merciful................. Ps 18:25
man thou wilt s thyself upright.......... Ps 18:25
the pure thou wilt s thyself pure....... Ps 18:26
thou wilt s thyself froward................. Ps 18:26
S me thy ways, O LORD........................ Ps 25:4
he will s them his covenant................ Ps 25:14
every man walketh in a vain s............ Ps 39:6
will I s the salvation of God............... Ps 50:23
my mouth shall s forth thy praise...... Ps 51:15
My mouth shall s forth thy.................. Ps 71:15
we will s forth thy praise to all......... Ps 79:13
S us thy mercy, O LORD, and grant.... Ps 85:7
S me a token for good......................... Ps 86:17
Wilt thou s wonders to the dead........ Ps 88:10
him, and s him my salvation............... Ps 91:16
To s forth thy lovingkindness in......... Ps 92:2
To s that the LORD is upright.............. Ps 92:15
vengeance belongeth, s thyself............ Ps 94:1
s forth his salvation from day to....... Ps 96:2
who can s forth all his praise............ Ps 106:2
that he remembered not to s mercy.... Ps 109:16
friends that s himself friendly............ Prov 18:24
The s of their countenance doth......... Is 3:9
formed them will s them no favour.... Is 27:11
shall s the lighting down of his......... Is 30:30
forth, and s us what shall happen..... Is 41:22
let them s the former things,............ Is 41:22
S the things that are to come.......... Is 41:23
this, and s us former things.............. Is 43:9
they shall s forth my praise............... Is 43:21
shall come, let them s unto them..... Is 44:7
this, and s yourselves men.................. Is 46:8
thou didst s them no mercy............... Is 47:6
are in darkness, S yourselves.............. Is 49:9
s my people their transgression.......... Is 58:1
they shall s forth the praises of........ Is 60:6
when thou shalt s this people all...... Jer 16:10
where I will not s you favour............. Jer 16:13
I will s them the back, and not......... Jer 18:17
s thee great and mighty things,......... Jer 33:3
That the LORD thy God may s us....... Jer 42:3
I will s mercies unto you, that.......... Jer 42:12
are cruel, and will not s mercy.......... Jer 50:42
to s the king of Babylon that his...... Jer 51:31
yea, thou shalt s her all her............. Eze 22:2
with their mouth they s much love... Eze 33:31
Wilt thou not s us what thou............ Eze 37:18
upon all that I shall s thee............... Eze 40:4
for to the intent that I might s.......... Eze 40:4
s the house to the house of.............. Eze 43:10
s them the form of the house, and.. Eze 43:11
for to s the king his dreams.............. Dan 2:2
we will s the interpretation................ Dan 2:4
But if ye s the dream, and the.......... Dan 2:6
therefore s me the dream, and the.... Dan 2:6
we will s the interpretation of........... Dan 2:7
I shall know that ye can s me the..... Dan 2:9
that can s the king's matter............... Dan 2:10
that can s it before the king,............ Dan 2:11
that he would s the king the............ Dan 2:16
I will s unto the king the.................. Dan 2:24
the soothsayers, s unto the king........ Dan 2:27
I thought it good to s the signs........ Dan 4:2
s me the interpretation thereof.......... Dan 5:7
he will s the interpretation................ Dan 5:12
but they could not s the.................... Dan 5:15
forth, and I am come to s thee......... Dan 9:23
But I will s thee that which is.......... Dan 10:21

now will I s thee the truth............... Dan 11:2
I will s wonders in the heavens......... Joel 2:30
s unto him marvellous things,............ Mic 7:15
face, and I will s the nations thy...... Nah 3:5
Why dost thou s me iniquity.............. Hab 1:3
I will s thee what these............... Zec 1:9
s mercy and compassions every man... Zec 7:9
s thyself unto the priest, and offer.... Mt 8:4
s John again those things which........ Mt 11:4
he shall s judgment to the................ Mt 12:18
do s forth themselves in him............. Mt 14:2
would s them a sign from heaven...... Mt 16:1
Jesus to s unto his disciples.............. Mt 16:21
S me the tribute money..................... Mt 22:19
disciples came to him for to s........... Mt 24:1
shall s great signs and wonders.......... Mt 24:24
s thyself to the priest, and offer....... Mk 1:44
do s forth themselves in him............. Mk 6:14
shall rise, and shall s signs................ Mk 13:22
being you a large upper room........... Mk 14:15
to s thee these glad tidings............... Lk 1:19
s thyself to the priest, and offer....... Lk 5:14
I will s you to whom he is like.......... Lk 6:47
s how great things God hath done.... Lk 8:39
Go s yourselves unto the priests....... Lk 17:14
S me a penny.................................... Lk 20:24
for a s make long prayers.................. Lk 20:47
he shall s you a large upper room..... Lk 22:12
things, s thyself to the world............. Jn 5:20
where he were, he should s it............ Jn 11:57
s us the Father, and it sufficeth......... Jn 14:8
sayest thou then, S us the Father...... Jn 14:9
he will s you things to come............. Jn 16:13
of mine, and shall s it unto you........ Jn 16:14
of mine, and shall s it unto you........ Jn 16:15
but I shall s you plainly of the.......... Jn 16:25
s whether of these two thou hast...... Acts 1:24
I will s wonders in heaven above,...... Acts 2:19
the land which I shall s thee............. Acts 7:3
For I will s him how great things...... Acts 9:16
Go s these things unto James, and.... Acts 12:17
which s unto us the way of............... Acts 16:17
willing to s the Jews a pleasure,........ Acts 24:27
should s light unto the people,.......... Acts 26:23
Which s the work of the law............. Rom 2:15
that I might s my power in thee,....... Rom 9:17
if God, willing to s his wrath............ Rom 9:22
ye do s the Lord's death till he......... 1Cor 11:26
yet s I unto you a more excellent..... 1Cor 12:31
Behold, I s you a mystery................. 1Cor 15:51
Wherefore s ye to them, and before... 2Cor 8:24
to make a fair s in the flesh............. Gal 6:12
the exceeding riches of his................ Eph 2:7
he made a s of them openly............. Col 2:15
a s of wisdom in will worship............ Col 2:23
For they themselves s of us what...... 1Th 1:9
might s forth all longsuffering............ 1Ti 1:16
learn first to s piety at home............ 1Ti 5:4
Which in his times he shall s............. 1Ti 6:15
Study to s thyself approved unto....... 2Ti 2:15
the same diligence to the full............ Heb 6:11
willing more abundantly to s unto..... Heb 6:17
s me thy faith without thy works,...... Jas 2:18
I will s thee my faith by my............. Jas 2:18
let him s out of a good..................... Jas 3:13
that ye should s forth the................. 1Pet 2:9
s unto you that eternal life,.............. 1Jn 1:2
to s unto his servants things............ Rev 1:1
I will s thee things which must........ Rev 4:1
I will s unto thee the judgment........ Rev 17:1
I will s thee the bride,...................... Rev 21:9
to s unto his servants things............ Rev 22:6

SHEWBREAD
upon the table s before me alway...... Ex 25:30
and all his vessels, and the s............. Ex 35:13
all the vessels thereof, and the s....... Ex 39:36
upon the table of s they shall............ Num 4:7
was no bread there but the s............ 1Sa 21:6
of gold, whereupon the s was............ 1Kin 7:48
the Kohathites, were over the s......... 1Chr 9:32
Both for the s, and for the fine........ 1Chr 23:29
he gave gold for the tables of s........ 1Chr 28:16
incense, and for the continual s......... 2Chr 2:4
the tables whereon the s was set...... 2Chr 4:19
the s also set they in order upon...... 2Chr 13:11
the s table, with all the vessels......... 2Chr 29:18
For the s, and for the continual........ Neh 10:33
house of God, and did eat the s........ Mt 12:4
the high priest, and did eat the s...... Mk 2:26
of God, and did take and eat the s.... Lk 6:4
and the table, and the s................... Heb 9:2

SHEWED
which thou hast s unto me in.......... Gen 19:19
hast s kindness unto my master....... Gen 24:14
hath s me all his work...................... Gen 32:10
s him mercy, and gave him favour..... Gen 39:21
God hath s Pharaoh what he is......... Gen 41:25
as God hath s thee all this............... Gen 41:39
God hath s me also thy seed............ Gen 48:11
the Lomb s him a tree, which when.. Ex 15:25
which was s thee in the mount......... Ex 25:40
which was s thee in the mount......... Ex 26:30
as it was s thee in the mount, so.... Ex 27:8
reddish, and it be s to the priest...... Lev 13:19
shall be s unto the priest................. Lev 13:49
mind of the LORD might be s them.... Lev 24:12
which the LORD had s Moses.............. Num 8:4
s them the fruit of the land............. Num 13:26

signs which I have s among them ..... Num 14:11
Unto thee it was s, that thou............... Deut 4:35
upon earth he s thee his great............. Deut 4:36
LORD our God hath s us his glory .... Deut 5:24
And the LORD s signs and wonders,... Deut 6:22
the LORD s him all the land of .... Deut 34:1
s in the sight of all Israel................... Deut 34:12
LORD, since I have s you kindness ...... Josh 2:12
when he s them the entrance into....... Judg 1:25
they s Sisera that Barak the son .... Judg 4:12
Neither s they kindness to the........... Judg 8:35
which he had s unto Israel .... Judg 8:35
s her husband, and said unto him,...... Judg 13:10
he have s us all these things .... Judg 13:23
for he hath s me all his heart.............. Judg 16:18
unto her, It hath fully been s me......... Ruth 2:11
she s her mother in law with whom ... Ruth 2:19
for thou hast s more kindness in .... Ruth 3:10
s it to the men of Jabesh.................... 1Sa 11:9
for ye s kindness to all the................. 1Sa 15:6
Jonathan s all those things 1Sa 19:7
Abiathar s David that Saul had........... 1Sa 22:21
thou hast s this day how that 1Sa 24:18
that ye have s this kindness unto 2Sa 2:5
as his father s kindness unto me........ 2Sa 10:2
s David all that Joab had sent............. 2Sa 11:22
thou hast not s it unto thy 1Kin 1:27
Thou hast s unto thy servant............. 1Kin 3:6
he did, and his might that he s 1Kin 16:27
and his might that he s, and how 1Kin 22:45
And he s him the place 2Kin 6:6
howbeit the LORD hath s me that....... 2Kin 8:10
The LORD hath s me that..................... 2Kin 8:13
LORD, and s them the king's son 2Kin 11:4
s them all the house of his................ 2Kin 20:13
that Hezekiah s them not................... 2Kin 20:13
treasures that I have not s them........ 2Kin 20:15
And Shaphan the scribe s the king 2Kin 22:10
his father s kindness to me................ 1Chr 19:2
Thou hast s great mercy unto 2Chr 1:8
that the LORD had s unto David 2Chr 7:10
hath been s from the LORD our God .. Ezr 9:8
When he s the riches of his............... Est 1:4
Esther had not s her people nor .... Est 2:10
Esther had not yet s her kindred ...... Est 2:20
for they had s him the people of ..... Est 3:6
pity should be s from his friend ...... Job 6:14
for he hath s me his marvellous....... Ps 31:21
Thou hast s thy people hard .... Ps 60:3
until I have s thy strength unto........ Ps 71:18
Thou, which hast s me great .... Ps 71:20
and his wonders that he had s them.. Ps 78:11
s in the sight of the heathen............ Ps 98:2
They s his signs among them, and.... Ps 105:27
He hath s his people the power of.... Ps 111:6
the LORD, which hath s us light .... Ps 118:27
I s before him my trouble................. Ps 142:2
his wickedness shall be s before ..... Prov 26:26
wherein I have s myself wise .... Eccl 2:19
Let favour be s to the wicked .... Is 26:10
s them the house of his precious...... Is 39:2
that Hezekiah s them not.................. Is 39:2
treasures that I have not s them....... Is 39:4
s to him the way of understanding ... Is 40:14
and have saved, and I have s .... Is 43:12
out of my mouth, and I s them......... Is 48:5
it came to pass I s it thee .... Is 48:5
I have s thee new things from .... Is 48:6
The LORD s me, and, behold, two .... Jer 24:1
the word that the LORD hath s me.... Jer 38:21
the things that the LORD had s me.... Eze 11:25
s them my judgments, which if a...... Eze 20:11
neither have they s difference .... Eze 22:26
Thus hath the Lord GOD s unto me... Amos 7:1
Thus hath the Lord GOD s unto me... Amos 7:4
Thus he s me .... Amos 7:7
Thus hath the Lord GOD s unto me... Amos 8:1
He hath s thee, O man, what is .... Mic 6:8
the LORD s me four carpenters........ Zec 1:20
he s me Joshua the high priest .... Zec 3:1
s unto the chief priests all the........ Mt 28:11
He hath s strength with his arm ...... Lk 1:51
Lord had s great mercy upon her ... Lk 1:58
s unto him all the kingdoms of ...... Lk 4:5
the disciples of John s him of .... Lk 7:18
he said, He that s mercy on him...... Lk 10:37
came, and s his Lord these things ... Lk 14:21
even Moses s at the bush, when he.. Lk 20:37
he s them his hands and his feet..... Lk 24:40
works have I s you from my Father .. Jn 10:32
he s unto them his hands and his ... Jn 20:20
After these things Jesus s .... Jn 21:1
and on this wise s he himself.......... Jn 21:1
Jesus s himself to his disciples....... Jn 21:14
To whom also he s himself alive...... Acts 1:3
which God before had s by the........ Acts 3:18
this miracle of healing was s........... Acts 4:22
the next day he s himself unto........ Acts 7:26
out, after that he had s wonders..... Acts 7:36
they have slain them which s.......... Acts 7:52
but God hath s me that I should ..... Acts 10:28
up the third day, and s him openly.. Acts 10:40
he s us how he had seen an angel... Acts 11:13
and confessed, and s their deeds.... Acts 19:18
unto you, but have s you, and have.. Acts 20:35
I have s you all things, how that ..... Acts 20:35
thou hast s these things to me .... Acts 23:22
But s first unto them of Damascus .. Acts 26:20
the barbarous people s us no .... Acts 28:2
came s or spake any harm of thee... Acts 28:21

for God hath s it unto them............. Rom 1:19
eat not for his sake that s it........... 1Cor 10:28
which ye have s toward his name,... Heb 6:10
pattern s to thee in the mount......... Heb 8:5
mercy, that hath s no mercy............. Jas 2:13
our Lord Jesus Christ hath s me....... 2Pet 1:14
s me that great city, the holy .... Rev 21:10
he s me a pure river of water of ..... Rev 22:1
the angel which s me these things .. Rev 22:8

SHEWEDST

s signs and wonders upon Pharaoh,... Neh 9:10
then thou s me their doings.............. Jer 11:18

SHEWEST

s mercy unto thy servants, that 2Chr 6:14
again thou s thyself marvellous....... Job 10:16
Thou s lovingkindness unto .... Jer 32:18
What sign s thou unto us, seeing ..... Jn 2:18
unto him, What sign s thou then ..... Jn 6:30

SHEWETH

is about to do he s unto Pharaoh ..... Gen 41:28
whatsoever he s me I will tell.......... Num 23:3
there is none that s me that my...... 1Sa 22:8
or s unto me that my son hath........ 1Sa 22:8
s mercy to his anointed, unto......... 2Sa 22:51
Then he s them their work, and....... Job 36:9
The noise thereof s concerning it.... Job 36:33
s mercy to his anointed, to David... Ps 18:50
and the firmament s his handywork. Ps 19:1
and night unto night s knowledge ... Ps 19:2
but the righteous s mercy............... Ps 37:21
A good man s favour, and lendeth ... Ps 112:5
He s his word unto Jacob, his......... Ps 147:19
truth s forth righteousness............. Prov 12:17
and the tender grass s itself .... Prov 27:25
yea, there is none that s .... Is 41:26
s him all the kingdoms of the......... Mt 4:8
s him all things that himself .... Jn 5:20
runneth, but of God that s mercy ... Rom 9:16
he that s mercy, with........................ Rom 12:8

SHEWING

s mercy unto thousands of them ...... Ex 20:6
s mercy unto thousands of them ..... Deut 5:10
s to the generation to come the...... Ps 78:4
s himself through the lattice .... Song 2:9
iniquities by s mercy to the poor..... Dan 4:27
and s of hard sentences, and.......... Dan 5:12
till the day of his s unto Israel....... Lk 1:80
the glad tidings of the kingdom ..... Lk 8:1
the coats and garments which .... Acts 9:39
s by the scriptures that Jesus........ Acts 18:28
of God, s himself that he is God..... 2Th 2:4
In all things s thyself a pattern...... Titus 2:7
in doctrine s uncorruptness,.......... Titus 2:7
but s all good fidelity..................... Titus 2:10
s all meekness unto all men........... Titus 3:2

SHIBAH See SHEBAH.

SHIBBOLETH (shib´-bo-leth) See SIBBOLETH.
Password that distinguished Gileadites from Ephraimites.
said they unto him, Say now S.......... Judg 12:6

SHIBMAH (shib´-mah) See SHEBAM, SIBMAH. A city in Reuben.
(their names being changed,) and S.. Num 32:38

SHICRON (shi´-cron) A city in Judah.
and the border was drawn to S........ Josh 15:11

SHIELD

I am thy s, and thy exceeding .... Gen 15:1
the s of thy help, and who is the .... Deut 33:29
was there a s or spear seen among .. Judg 5:8
one bearing a s went before him 1Sa 17:7
that bare the s went before him 1Sa 17:41
and with a spear, and with a s 1Sa 17:45
for there the s of the mighty is....... 2Sa 1:21
the s of Saul, as though he had 2Sa 1:21
he is my s, and the horn of my....... 2Sa 22:3
given me the s of thy salvation....... 2Sa 22:36
three pound of gold went to one s... 1Kin 10:17
there, nor come before it with s 2Kin 19:32
the battle, that could handle s 1Chr 12:8
The children of Judah that bare s.... 1Chr 12:24
captains, and with them with s 1Chr 12:34
shekels of gold went to one s.......... 2Chr 9:16
bow and s two hundred thousand,... 2Chr 17:17
war, that could handle spear and s .. 2Chr 25:5
the glittering spear and the s.......... Job 39:23
But thou, O LORD, art s for me .... Ps 3:3
wilt thou compass him as with a s... Ps 5:12
given me the s of thy salvation....... Ps 18:35
The LORD is my strength and my s ... Ps 28:7
he is our help and our s .... Ps 33:20
Take hold of s and buckler, and...... Ps 35:2
and bring them down, O Lord our s.. Ps 59:11
he the arrows of the bow, the s...... Ps 76:3
Behold, O God our s, and look upon.. Ps 84:9
For the LORD God is a sun and s...... Ps 84:11
his truth shall be thy s................... Ps 91:4
he is their help and their s............. Ps 115:9
he is their help and their s............. Ps 115:10
he is their help and their s............. Ps 115:11
Thou art my hiding place and my s.. Ps 119:114
my s, and he in whom I trust.......... Ps 144:2
he is a s unto them that put........... Prov 30:5
ye princes, and anoint the s........... Is 21:5
horsemen, and Kir uncovered the s .. Is 22:6
Order ye the buckler and s.............. Jer 46:3

and the Libyans, that handle the s... Jer 46:9
set against thee buckler and s......... Eze 23:24
they hanged the s and helmet in..... Eze 27:10
all of them with s and helmet......... Eze 38:5
The s of his mighty men is made .... Nah 2:3
Above all, taking the s of faith....... Eph 6:16

SHIELDS

David took the s of gold that.......... 2Sa 8:7
three hundred s of beaten gold....... 1Kin 10:17
he took away all the s of gold......... 1Kin 14:26
made in their stead brazen s 1Kin 14:27
give king David's spears and s 2Kin 11:10
out of the house of the LORD,.......... 1Kin 14:28
three hundred s made he of beaten... 2Chr 9:16
And in every several city he put s.... 2Chr 11:12
he carried away also the s of 2Chr 12:9
king Rehoboam made s of brass...... 2Chr 12:10
and out of Benjamin, that bare s 2Chr 14:8
spears, and bucklers, and s 2Chr 23:9
them throughout all the host s 2Chr 26:14
and made darts and s in abundance.. 2Chr 32:5
stones, and for spices, and for s 2Chr 32:27
them held both the spears, the s..... Neh 4:16
for the s of the earth belong .... Ps 47:9
bucklers, all s of mighty men.......... Song 4:4
there, nor come before it with s ..... Is 37:33
gather the s .... Jer 51:11
they hanged their s upon thy .... Eze 27:11
great company with bucklers and s.. Eze 38:4
and burn the weapons, both the s ... Eze 39:9

SHIGGAION (shig-gah´-yon) See SHIGIONOTH.
A musical notation.
S of David, which he sang unto .... Ps 7:t

SHIGIONOTH (shig-i´-o-noth) See SHIGGAION.
A musical notation.
of Habakkuk the prophet upon S....... Hab 3:1

SHIHON (shi´-hon) A city in Issachar.
and S, and Anaharath........................ Josh 19:19

SHIHOR (shi´-hor) See SHIHOR-LIBNATH. Same as Sihor.
from S of Egypt even unto the.......... 1Chr 13:5

SHIHOR-LIBNATH (shi´´-hor-lib´-nath) A small river in Asher.
to Carmel westward, and to S........... Josh 19:26

SHIKKERON See SHICRON.

SHILHI (shil´-hi) Father of Azubah.
name was Azubah the daughter of S.. 1Kin 22:42
name was Azubah the daughter of S.. 2Chr 20:31

SHILHIM (shil´-him) See SHAARAIM, SHARUHEN. A city in Judah.
And Lebaoth, and S, and Ain, and ..... Josh 15:32

SHILLEM (shil´-lem) See SHALLUM, SHILLEMITES. A son of Naphtali.
Jahzeel, and Guni, and Jezer, and S... Gen 46:24
of S, the family of the..................... Num 26:49

SHILLEMITES (shil´-lem-ites) Descendants of Shillem.
of Shillem, the family of the............ Num 26:49

SHILOAH (shi-lo´-ah) See SILOAH, SILOAM. A fountain in Jerusalem.
the waters of S that go softly............ Is 8:6

SHILOH (shi´-loh) See SHILONITE.
1. Symbolic name for the Ruler from Judah.
between his feet, until S come............ Gen 49:10
2. A city in Ephraim.
of Israel assembled together at S...... Josh 18:1
lots for you before the LORD in S...... Josh 18:8
again to Joshua to the host at S........ Josh 18:9
for them in S before the LORD........... Josh 18:10
by lot in S before the LORD............... Josh 19:51
them at S in the land of Canaan .... Josh 21:2
the children of Israel out of S .... Josh 22:9
gathered themselves together at S ... Josh 22:12
that the house of God was in S .... Judg 18:31
brought them unto the camp to S ..... Judg 21:12
S yearly in a place which is on .... Judg 21:19
if the daughters of S come out to..... Judg 21:21
his wife of the daughters of S.......... Judg 21:21
unto the Lord of hosts in S 1Sa 1:3
rose up after they had eaten in S 1Sa 1:9
unto the house of the LORD in S 1Sa 1:24
So they did in S unto all the............. 1Sa 1:24
And the LORD appeared again in S 1Sa 3:21
in S by the word of the LORD 1Sa 3:21
of the LORD out of S unto us............ 1Sa 4:3
So the people sent to S, that 1Sa 4:4
came to S the same day with his...... 1Sa 4:12
of Eli, the LORD's priest in S 1Sa 14:3
concerning the house of Eli in S 1Kin 2:27
and get thee to S 1Kin 14:2
did so, and arose, and went to S 1Kin 14:4
he forsook the tabernacle of S .... Ps 78:60
even my place which was in S .... Jer 7:12
your fathers, as I have done to S ...... Jer 7:14
will I make this house like S............. Jer 26:6
This house shall be like S................. Jer 26:9
came certain from Shechem, from S... Jer 41:5

SHILONI (shi-lo´-ni) See SHILONITE. Father of Zechariah.
son of Zechariah, the son of S........... Neh 11:5

SHILONITE (shi'-lon-ite) See SHILONI,
SHILONITES. *An inhabitant of Shiloh.*
Ahijah the *S* found him in the way 1Kin 11:29
the LORD spake by Ahijah the *S* 1Kin 12:15
spake by his servant Ahijah the *S* 1Kin 15:29
in the prophecy of Ahijah the *S* 2Chr 9:29
S to Jeroboam the son of Nebat 2Chr 10:15

SHILONITES (shi'-lon-ites)
And of the *S* 1Chr 9:5

SHILSHAH (shil'-shah) *Son of Zophah.*
Bezer, and Hod, and Shamma, and *S*.. 1Chr 7:37

SHIMEA (shim'-e-ah) See SHAMMAH, SHAMMUA,
SHAMMUAH, SHIMEAH, SHIMEATHITES, SHIMMA.
1. David's brother.
Jonathan the son of *S* David's 1Chr 20:7
2. A son of David.
S, and Shobab, and Nathan, and 1Chr 3:5
3. Father of Haggiah.
S his son, Haggiah his son, ... 1Chr 6:30
4. Father of Berachiah.
son of Berachiah, the son of *S* 1Chr 6:39

SHIMEAH (shim'-e-ah) See SHIMEA, SHIMEAM.
1. Same as Shimea I.
the son of *S* David's brother 2Sa 13:3
the son of *S* David's brother 2Sa 13:32
Jonathan the son of *S* the brother 2Sa 21:21
2. A relative of King Saul.
And Mikloth begat *S* 1Chr 8:32

SHIMEAM (shim'-e-am) See SHIMEA. *Son of
Mikloth.*
And Mikloth begat *S* 1Chr 9:38

SHIMEATH (shim'-e-ath) *Mother of Jozachar.*
For Jozachar the son of *S* 2Kin 12:21
Zabad the son of *S* an Ammonitess... 2Chr 24:26

SHIMEATHITES (shim'-e-ath-ites) *A family
of scribes.*
the Tirathites, the *S* and 1Chr 2:55

SHIMEI (shim'-e-i) See SHEMAIAH, SHIMHI,
SHIMI, SHIMITES.
1. A son of Gershon.
families; Libni, and *S* .... Num 3:18
Gershom; Libni, and *S* 1Chr 6:17
the son of Zimmah, the son of *S*........ 1Chr 6:42
Gershonites were, Laadan, and *S* 1Chr 23:7
And the sons of *S* were, Jahath, ... 1Chr 23:10
These four were the sons of *S* 1Chr 23:10
2. A son of Gera.
house of Saul, whose name was *S* 2Sa 16:5
thus said *S* when he cursed, Come 2Sa 16:7
S went along on the hill's side 2Sa 16:13
the son of Gera, a Benjamite, ... 2Sa 19:16
the son of Gera fell down 2Sa 19:18
Shall not *S* be put to death for 2Sa 19:21
Therefore the king said unto *S* 2Sa 19:23
hast with thee *S* the son of Gera 1Kin 2:8
And the king sent and called for *S* 1Kin 2:36
S said unto the king, The saying 1Kin 2:38
S dwelt in Jerusalem many days 1Kin 2:38
of *S* ran away unto Achish son of 1Kin 2:39
and they told *S*, saying, Behold, ... 1Kin 2:39
S arose, and saddled his ass, and 1Kin 2:40
S went, and brought his servants 1Kin 2:40
it was told Solomon that *S* had 1Kin 2:41
And the king sent and called for *S* 1Kin 2:42
The king said moreover to *S* 1Kin 2:44
3. An officer of David.
and Nathan the prophet, and *S* 1Kin 1:8
4. An officer of Solomon.
S the son of Elah, in Benjamin 1Kin 4:18
5. A descendant of King Jehoiakim.
of Pediaah were, Zerubbabel, and *S*.. 1Chr 3:19
6. Son of Zacchur.
son, Zacchur his son, *S* his son, ... 1Chr 4:26
S had sixteen sons and six................. 1Chr 4:27
7. Son of Gog.
his son, Gog his son, *S* his son, ... 1Chr 5:4
8. Son of Libni.
his son, *S* his son, Uzza his son, ... 1Chr 6:29
9. A Levite of the Libnan family.
The sons of *S* 1Chr 6:42
10. A sanctuary servant.
The tenth to *S*, he, his sons, and....... 1Chr 25:17
11. A vineyard keeper.
the vineyards was *S* the Ramathite.... 1Chr 27:27
12. A Levite who cleansed the Temple.
Jehiel, and *S* 2Chr 29:14
13. A Temple servant in Hezekiah's time.
S his brother was the next 2Chr 31:12
S his brother, at the commandment.. 2Chr 31:13
14. A Levite who married a foreigner.
Jozabad, and *S*, and Kelaiah, (the .... Ezr 10:23
15. A Hashumite who married a foreigner.
Jeremai, Manasseh, and *S*................. Ezr 10:33
16. A Banite who married a foreigner.
And Bani, and Binnui, *S* .... Ezr 10:38
17. Grandfather of Mordecai.
the son of Jair, the son of *S* .... Est 2:5
18. A representative of the Gershonites.
the family of *S* apart, and their .... Zec 12:13

SHIMEITES (shim'-e-ites) See SHIMEI. *A member
of the Harim family.*
Ishijah, Malchiah, Shemaiah, *S*......... Ezr 10:31

SHIMHI (shim'-hi) See SHEMA, SHIMEI. *Father
of a chief family in Judah.*
and Shimrath, the sons of *S* 1Chr 8:21

SHIMI (shim'-mi) See SHIMEI, SHIMITES. *Same as
Shimei I.*
Libni, and *S*, according to their .... Ex 6:17

SHIMITES (shi'-mites) *Descendants of Shimei
I.*
Libnites, and the family of the *S* .... Num 3:21

SHIMMA (shim'-mah) See SHAMMAH. *Same as
Shamma.*
the second, and *S* the third, ... 1Chr 2:13

SHIMON (shi'-mon) *A descendant of Caleb.*
And the sons of *S* were, Amnon, and.. 1Chr 4:20

SHIMRATH (shim'-rath) *A son of Shimri.*
And Adaiah, and Beraiah, and *S* 1Chr 8:21

SHIMRI (shim'-ri) See SHIMRI.
1. Head of a family in Simeon.
the son of Jedaiah, the son of *S* 1Chr 4:37
2. Father of Jediael.
Jediael the son of *S*, and Joha his..... 1Chr 11:45
3. A Levite who cleansed the Temple.
S, and Jeiel 2Chr 29:13

SHIMRITH (shim'-rith) See SHOMER. *Mother of
Jehozabad.*
the son of *S* a Moabitess................... 2Chr 24:26

SHIMROM (shim'-rom) See SHIMRON. *A son of
Issachar.*
were, Tola, and Puah, Jashub, and *S*.. 1Chr 7:1

SHIMRON (shim'-ron) See SHIMROM,
SHIMRONITES. *Same as Shimron.*
Tola, and Phuvah, and Job, and *S*...... Gen 46:13
of *S*, the family of the .... Num 26:24
of Madon, and to the king of *S* .... Josh 11:1
And Kattath, and Nahallal, and .... Josh 19:15

SHIMRONITE See SHIMRONITES.

SHIMRONITES (shim'-ron-ites) *Descendants
of Shimron.*
of Shimron, the family of the *S*........... Num 26:24

SHIMRON-MERON (shim''-ron-me'-ron) *A
city in Galilee.*
The king of *S*, one............................... Josh 12:20

SHIMSHAI (shim'-shahee) *An opponent of
Nehemiah.*
S the scribe wrote a letter .... Ezr 4:8
S the scribe, and the rest of .... Ezr 4:9
to *S* the scribe, and to the rest .... Ezr 4:17
S the scribe, and their companions .... Ezr 4:23

SHINAB (shi'-nab) *King of Admah.*
S king of Admah, and Shemeber king . Gen 14:2

SHINAR (shi'-nar) *A nation in Babylonia.*
and Calneh, in the land of *S*............... Gen 10:10
found a plain in the land of *S*............. Gen 11:2
in the days of Amraphel king of *S*...... Gen 14:1
of nations, and Amraphel king of *S*.... Gen 14:9
Cush, and from Elam, and from *S*...... Is 11:11
land of *S* to the house of his god .... Dan 1:2
it an house in the land of *S* .... Zec 5:11

SHINE
LORD make his face *s* upon thee........ Num 6:25
neither let the light *s* upon it .... Job 3:4
s upon the counsel of the wicked........ Job 10:3
thou shalt *s* forth, thou shalt be .... Job 11:17
the spark of his fire shall not *s* .... Job 18:5
the light shall *s* upon thy ways.......... Job 22:28
commandeth it not to *s* by the .... Job 36:32
the light of his cloud to *s* .... Job 37:15
By his messings a light doth *s*........... Job 41:18
He maketh a path to *s* after him .... Job 41:32
thy face to *s* upon thy servant........... Ps 31:16
and cause his face to *s* upon us .... Ps 67:1
between the cherubims, *s* forth .... Ps 80:1
O God, and cause thy face to *s* .... Ps 80:3
of hosts, and cause thy face to *s* .... Ps 80:7
God of hosts, cause thy face to *s* ...... Ps 80:19
man, and oil to make his face to *s* .... Ps 104:15
thy face to *s* upon thy servant........... Ps 119:135
man's wisdom maketh his face to *s*... Eccl 8:1
shall not cause her light to *s* .... Is 13:10
Arise, *s*; for thy light is .... Is 60:1
They are waxen fat, they *s*................. Jer 5:28
cause thy face to *s* upon thy .... Dan 9:17
they that be wise shall *s* as the.......... Dan 12:3
Let your light so *s* before men........... Mt 5:16
Then shall the righteous shine .... Mt 13:43
and his face did *s* as the sun .... Mt 17:2
image of God, should *s* unto them..... 2Cor 4:4
the light to *s* out of darkness............. 2Cor 4:6
among whom ye *s* as lights in the...... Phil 2:15
shall *s* no more at all in thee .... Rev 18:23
neither of the moon, to *s* in it .... Rev 21:23

SHINED
he *s* forth from mount Paran, and ..... Deut 33:2
When his candle *s* upon my head....... Job 29:3
If I beheld the sun when it *s* .... Job 31:26
perfection of beauty, God hath *s* .... Ps 50:2
death, upon them hath the light *s* ..... Is 9:2
the earth *s* with his glory................... Eze 43:2
suddenly there *s* round about him .... Acts 9:3
him, and a light *s* in the prison .... Acts 12:7
hath *s* in our hearts, to give the........ 2Cor 4:6

---

even to the moon, and it *s* not .... Job 25:5
but the night *s* as the day .... Ps 139:12
as the shining light, that *s* more........ Prov 4:18
the east, and *s* even unto the west..... Mt 24:27
s unto the other part under .... Lk 17:24
And the light *s* in darkness .... Jn 1:5
a light that *s* in a dark place.............. 2Pet 1:19
is past, and the true light now *s* 1Jn 2:8
was as the sun *s* in his strength .... Rev 1:16

SHINING
the earth by clear *s* after rain 2Sa 23:4
of the just is as the light .... Prov 4:18
the *s* of a flaming fire by night .... Is 4:5
the stars shall withdraw their *s* .... Joel 2:10
the stars shall withdraw their *s* .... Joel 3:15
at the *s* of thy glittering spear .... Hab 3:11
And his raiment became *s*, ... Mk 9:3
as when the bright *s* of a candle .... Lk 11:36
men stood by them in *s* garments...... Lk 24:4
He was a burning and a *s* light .... Jn 5:35
s round about me and them which .... Acts 26:13

SHION See SHIHON.

SHIP
the way of a *s* in the midst of .... Prov 30:19
shall gallant *s* pass thereby .... Is 33:21
They have made all thy *s* boards....... Eze 27:5
he found a *s* going to Tarshish.......... Jonah 1:3
so that the *s* was like to be .... Jonah 1:4
that were in the *s* into the sea............ Jonah 1:5
gone down into the sides of the *s* ...... Jonah 1:5
in a *s* with Zebedee their father,........ Mt 4:21
And they immediately left the *s* .... Mt 4:22
And when he was entered into a *s* ..... Mt 8:23
insomuch that the *s* was covered....... Mt 8:24
And he entered into a *s*, and passed .. Mt 9:1
him, so that he went into a *s* .... Mt 13:2
he departed thence by a *s* into a .... Mt 14:13
his disciples to get into a *s* .... Mt 14:22
But the *s* was now in the midst of ..... Mt 14:24
Peter was come down out of the *s* ..... Mt 14:29
And when they were come into the *s* .. Mt 14:32
Then they that were in the *s* came ..... Mt 14:33
away the multitude, and took *s* .... Mt 15:39
were in the *s* mending their nets .... Mk 1:19
in the *s* with the hired servants .... Mk 1:20
that a small *s* should wait on him ..... Mk 3:9
so that he entered into a *s* .... Mk 4:1
took him even as he was in the *s* ...... Mk 4:36
and the waves beat into the *s* .... Mk 4:37
he was in the hinder part of the *s* ..... Mk 4:38
And when he was come out of the *s* .. Mk 5:2
And when he was come into the *s* ..... Mk 5:18
again by *s* unto the other side........... Mk 5:21
a desert place by a *s* privately........... Mk 6:32
his disciples to get into the *s* .... Mk 6:45
the *s* was in the midst of the sea....... Mk 6:47
he went up unto them into the *s* .... Mk 6:51
when they were come out of the *s* ..... Mk 6:54
into a *s* with his disciples .... Mk 8:10
entering into the *s* again.................... Mk 8:13
neither had they in the *s* with .... Mk 8:14
and taught the people out of the *s* .... Lk 5:3
which were in the other *s* .... Lk 5:7
went into a *s* with his disciples.......... Lk 8:22
and he went up into the *s*, and.......... Lk 8:37
And entered into a *s*, and went over ... Jn 6:17
sea, and drawing nigh unto the *s* ...... Jn 6:19
willingly received him into the *s* .... Jn 6:21
immediately the *s* was at the land..... Jn 6:21
and entered into a *s* immediately ...... Jn 21:3
net on the right side of the *s* .... Jn 21:6
disciples came in a little *s* .... Jn 21:8
And we went before to *s*, and sailed... Acts 20:13
they accompanied him unto the *s* ..... Acts 20:38
finding a *s* sailing over unto............. Acts 21:2
for there the *s* was to unlade her .... Acts 21:3
leave one of another, we took *s* .... Acts 21:6
entering into a *s* of Adramyttium....... Acts 27:2
a *s* of Alexandria sailing into............ Acts 27:6
not only of the lading and a .... Acts 27:10
the master and the owner of the *s* ..... Acts 27:11
when the *s* was caught, and could .... Acts 27:15
used helps, undergirding the *s* .... Acts 27:17
the next day they lightened the *s* ...... Acts 27:18
own hands the tackling of the *s* .... Acts 27:19
life among you, but of the *s* .... Acts 27:22
were about to flee out of the *s* .... Acts 27:30
Except these abide in the *s* .... Acts 27:31
we were in all in the *s* two .... Acts 27:37
enough, they lightened the *s* .... Acts 27:38
were possible, to thrust in the *s* .... Acts 27:39
sea met, they ran the *s* a ground....... Acts 27:41
and some on broken pieces of the *s*... Acts 27:44
we departed in a *s* of Alexandria ...... Acts 28:11

SHIPHI (shi'-fi) *Father of Ziza.*
And Ziza the son of *S*, the son of....... 1Chr 4:37

SHIPHMITE (shif'-mite) *Family name of
Zabdi.*
the wine cellars was Zabdi the *S*....... 1Chr 27:27

SHIPHRAH (shif'-rah) *A Hebrew midwife in
Egypt.*
which the name of the one was *S*....... Ex 1:15

SHIPHTAN (shif'-tan) *Father of Kemuel.*
of Ephraim, Kemuel the son of *S* .... Num 34:24

SHIPMASTER
So the *s* came to him, and said.......... Jonah 1:6
And every *s*, and all the company in .. Rev 18:17

SHIPMEN

s that had knowledge of the sea,....... 1Kin 9:27
about midnight the s deemed that ..... Acts 27:27
as the s were about to flee out......... Acts 27:30

SHIPPING

his disciples, they also took s............ Jn 6:24

SHIPS

and he shall be for an haven of s....... Gen 49:13
s shall come come from the coast....... Num 24:24
thee into Egypt again with s .... Deut 28:68
and why did Dan remain in s............. Judg 5:17
made a navy of s in Ezion-gaber 1Kin 9:26
Jehoshaphat made s of Tharshish 1Kin 22:48
for the s were broken at............... 1Kin 22:48
go with thy servants in the s........... 1Kin 22:49
by the hands of his servants s.......... 2Chr 8:18
For the king's s went to Tarshish 2Chr 9:21
the s of Tarshish bringing gold......... 2Chr 9:21
him to make s to go to Tarshish 2Chr 20:36
they made the s in Ezion-gaber 2Chr 20:36
the s were broken, that they were.... 2Chr 20:37
are passed away as the swift s .... Job 9:26
Thou breakest the s of Tarshish....... Ps 48:7
There go the s .... Ps 104:26
They that go down to the sea in s...... Ps 107:23
She is like the merchants' s .... Prov 31:14
And upon all the s of Tarshish .... Is 2:16
Howl, ye s of Tarshish..................... Is 23:1
Howl, ye s of Tarshish..................... Is 23:14
Chaldeans, whose cry is in the s....... Is 43:14
the s of Tarshish first, to bring......... Is 60:9
all the s of the sea with their .... Eze 27:9
The s of Tarshish did sing of .... Eze 27:25
sea, shall come down from their s..... Eze 27:29
messengers go forth from me in s..... Eze 30:9
For the s of Chittim shall come .... Dan 11:30
and with horsemen, and with many s Dan 11:40
were also with him other little s........ Mk 4:36
saw two s standing by the lake .... Lk 5:2
And he entered into one of the s....... Lk 5:3
they came, and filled both the s........ Lk 5:7
they had brought their s to land .... Lk 5:11
Behold also the s, which though .... Jas 3:4
part of the s were destroyed .... Rev 8:9
and all the company in s, and........... Rev 18:17
had s in the sea by reason of her....... Rev 18:19

SHIPWRECK

was I stoned, thrice I suffered s 2Cor 11:25
away concerning faith have made s ... 1Ti 1:19

SHISHA (shi'-shah) See SHAVSHA. Father of
Elihoreph and Ahiah.
Elihoreph and Ahiah, the sons of S 1Kin 4:3

SHISHAK (shi'-shak) A king of Egypt.
unto S king of Egypt, and was in...... 1Kin 11:40
that S king of Egypt came up 1Kin 14:25
S king of Egypt came up against 2Chr 12:2
to Jerusalem because of S................ 2Chr 12:5
I also left you in the hand of S 2Chr 12:7
upon Jerusalem by the hand of S 2Chr 12:7
So S king of Egypt came up 2Chr 12:9

SHITRAI (shit'-ra-i) A herdsman in David's
court.
fed in Sharon was S the Sharonite 1Chr 27:29

SHITTAH
the s tree, and the myrtle, and the.... Is 41:19

SHITTIM (shit'-tim) A place in Moab.
and badgers' skins, and s wood,........ Ex 25:5
they shall make an ark of s wood ...... Ex 25:10
thou shalt make staves of s wood...... Ex 25:13
shalt also make a table of s wood...... Ex 25:23
shalt make the staves of s wood .... Ex 25:28
tabernacle of s wood standing up...... Ex 26:15
And thou shalt make bars of s wood .. Ex 26:26
and wood overlaid with gold............. Ex 26:32
hanging five pillars of s wood........... Ex 26:37
shalt make an altar of s wood........... Ex 27:1
for the altar, staves of s wood.......... Ex 27:6
of s wood shalt thou make it .... Ex 30:1
shalt make the staves of s wood .... Ex 30:5
and badgers' skins, and s wood,........ Ex 35:7
with whom was found s wood for ...... Ex 35:24
for the tabernacle of s wood............. Ex 36:20
And he made bars of s wood............. Ex 36:31
thereunto four pillars of s wood........ Ex 36:36
Bezaleel made the ark of s wood....... Ex 37:1
And he made staves of s wood .... Ex 37:4
And he made the table of s wood ...... Ex 37:10
And he made the staves of s wood .... Ex 37:15
made the incense altar of s wood ..... Ex 37:25
And he made the staves of s wood .... Ex 37:28
altar of burnt offering of s wood....... Ex 38:1
And he made staves of s wood .... Ex 38:6
And israel abode in S, and the .... Num 25:1
And I made an ark of s wood............ Deut 10:3
out of S two men to spy secretly .... Josh 2:1
and they removed from S, and came.. Josh 3:1
and shall water the valley of S.......... Joel 3:18
answered him from S unto Gilgal....... Mic 6:5

SHIVERS
potter shall they be broken to s .... Rev 2:27

SHIZA (shi'-zah) A 'mighty man' of David.
Adina the son of S the Reubenite 1Chr 11:42

SHOA (sho'-ah) A tribal enemy of Israel.
and all the Chaldeans, Pekod, and S .. Eze 23:23

SHOBAB (sho'-bab)
1. A son of David.
Shammuah, and S, and Nathan, and.. 2Sa 5:14

Shimea, and S, and Nathan, and....... 1Chr 3:5
and S, Nathan, and Solomon............ 1Chr 14:4
2. A son of Caleb.
Jesher, and S, and Ardon................. 1Chr 2:18

SHOBACH (sho'-bak) See SHOPHACH. A Syrian
defeated by David.
S the captain of the host of............. 2Sa 10:16
smote S the captain of their host 2Sa 10:18

SHOBAI (sho'-bahee) A family of exiles.
of Hatita, the children of S .... Ezr 2:42
of Hatita, the children of S .... Neh 7:45

SHOBAL (sho'-bal)
1. A son of Seir.
Lotan, and S, and Zibeon, and Anah,. Gen 36:20
And the children of S were these...... Gen 36:23
duke Lotan, duke S, duke Zibeon,.... Gen 36:29
Lotan, and S, and Zibeon, and Anah,. 1Chr 1:38
The sons of S 1Chr 1:40
2. A son of Caleb.
S the father of Kirjath-jearim,.......... 1Chr 2:50
S the father of Kirjath-jearim,.......... 1Chr 2:52
3. A son of Judah.
Hezron, and Carmi, and Hur, and S... 1Chr 4:1
Reaiah the son of S begat Jahath...... 1Chr 4:2

SHOBEK (sho'-bek) A clan leader who
renewed the covenant.
Hallohesh, Pileha, S .... Neh 10:24

SHOBI (sho'-bi) A son of Nahash.
that S the son of Nahash of............. 2Sa 17:27

SHOCHO (sho'-ko) See SHOCHOH. A city in
Judah.
S with the villages thereof, and........ 2Chr 28:18

SHOCHOH (sho'-ko) See SHOCHO, SHOCO,
SOCHOH, SOCO, SOCOH. Same as Shocho.
and were gathered together at S 1Sa 17:1
to Judah, and pitched between S 1Sa 17:1

SHOCK
like as a s of corn cometh in........... Job 5:26

SHOCKS
and burnt up both the s, and also..... Judg 15:5

SHOCO (sho'-ko) See SHOCHOH. Same as
Shocho.
And Beth-zur, and S, and Adullam,.... 2Chr 11:7

SHOD
s them, and gave them to eat and to .. 2Chr 28:15
s thee with badgers' skin, and I......... Eze 16:10
But be s with sandals...................... Mk 6:9
your feet s with the preparation......... Eph 6:15

SHOE
loose his s from off his foot, and....... Deut 25:9
of him that hath his s loosed .... Deut 25:10
thy s is not waxen old upon thy......... Deut 29:5
Loose thy s from off thy foot............ Josh 5:15
a man plucked off his s, and gave ..... Ruth 4:7
So he drew off his s .... Ruth 4:8
over Edom will I cast out my s .... Ps 60:8
over Edom will I cast out my s .... Ps 108:9
put off thy s from thy foot .... Is 20:2

SHOELATCHET
take from a thread even to a s........... Gen 14:23

SHOE'S
whose s latchet I am not worthy........ Jn 1:27

SHOES
put off thy s from off thy................. Ex 3:5
your s on your feet, and your .... Ex 12:11
Thy s shall be iron and brass............ Deut 33:25
And old s and clouted upon their....... Josh 9:5
our s are become old by reason of .... Josh 9:13
in his s that were on his feet............ 1Kin 2:5
How beautiful are thy feet with s...... Song 7:1
the latchet of their s be broken .... Is 5:27
put on thy s upon thy feet, and .... Eze 24:17
heads, and your s upon your feet ...... Eze 24:23
and the poor for a pair of s .... Amos 2:6
and the needy for a pair of s............ Amos 8:6
whose s I am not worthy to bear........ Mt 3:11
neither two coats, neither s .... Mt 10:10
the latchet of whose s I am not .... Mk 1:7
the latchet of whose s I am not .... Lk 3:16
neither purse, nor scrip, nor s .... Lk 10:4
on his hand, and s on his feet........... Lk 15:22
you without purse, and scrip, and s ... Lk 22:35
Put off thy s from thy feet .... Acts 7:33
whose s of his feet I am not .... Acts 13:25

SHOHAM (sho'-ham) A Merarite.
Beno, and S, and Zaccur, and Ibri..... 1Chr 24:27

SHOMER (sho'-mur) See SHAMER, SHIMRITH.
Same as Shimrith.
and Jehozabad the son of S 2Kin 12:21
Son of Heber.
and Heber and Japhlet, and S........... 1Chr 7:32

SHONE
face s while he talked with him .... Ex 34:29
behold, the skin of his face.............. Ex 34:30
the skin of Moses' face s .... Ex 34:35
the sun s upon the water, and the..... 2Kin 3:22
of the Lord s round about them........ Lk 2:9
suddenly there s from heaven a .... Acts 22:6
the day s not for a third part of........ Rev 8:12

SHOOK
for the oxen s it 2Sa 6:6
Then the earth s and trembled.......... 2Sa 22:8

---

foundations of heaven moved and s ... 2Sa 22:8
Also I s my lap, and said, So God ...... Neh 5:13
Then the earth s and trembled.......... Ps 18:7
The earth s, the heavens also........... Ps 68:8
the earth trembled and s .... Ps 77:18
over the sea, he s the kingdoms........ Is 23:11
But they s off the dust of their .... Acts 13:51
he s his raiment, and said unto .... Acts 18:6
he s off the beast into the fire,......... Acts 28:5
Whose voice then s the earth............ Heb 12:26

SHOOT
he made the middle bar to s .... Ex 36:33
I will s three arrows on the side........ 1Sa 20:20
find out now the arrows which I s...... 1Sa 20:36
that they would s from the wall 2Sa 11:20
Then Elisha said, S......................... 2Kin 13:17
nor s an arrow there, nor come 2Kin 19:32
to s with bow, and skilful in war,...... 2Chr 17:17
to s arrows and great stones 2Chr 26:15
that they may privily s at .... Ps 11:2
they s out the lip, they shake........... Ps 22:7
bendeth his bow to s his arrows........ Ps 58:7
bend their bows to s their arrows...... Ps 64:3
That they may s in secret at the....... Ps 64:4
suddenly do they s at him .... Ps 64:4
But God shall s at them with an........ Ps 64:7
s out thine arrows, and destroy .... Ps 144:6
nor s an arrow there, nor come .... Is 37:33
s at her, spare no arrows .... Jer 50:14
neither s up their top among the ...... Eze 31:14
ye shall s forth your branches,......... Eze 36:8
When they now s forth, ye see and.... Lk 21:30

SHOOTERS
the s shot from off the wall upon...... 2Sa 11:24

SHOOTETH
his branch s forth in his garden........ Job 8:16
In measure, when it s forth.............. Is 27:8
herbs, and s out greater branches ..... Mk 4:32

SHOOTING
s arrows out of a bow, even of......... 1Chr 12:2
of the s up of the latter growth .... Amos 7:1

SHOPHACH (sho'-fak) See SHOBACH. Same as
Shobach.
S the captain of the host of............. 1Chr 19:16
killed S the captain of the host 1Chr 19:18

SHOPHAN (sho'-fan) See ZAPHON. A city in
Gad.
And Atroth, S, and Jaazer, and .... Num 32:35

SHORE
the sand which is upon the sea s....... Gen 22:17
The Egyptians dead upon the sea s 1a 14:30
is upon the sea s in multitude .... Josh 11:4
was from the s of the salt sea.......... Josh 15:2
Asher continued on the sea s........... Judg 5:17
is on the sea s in multitude 1Sa 13:5
as the sand that is on the sea s........ 1Kin 4:29
on the s of the Red sea, in the 1Kin 9:26
Ashkelon, and against the sea s........ Jer 47:7
whole multitude stood on the s .... Mt 13:2
when it was full, they drew to s........ Mt 13:48
of Gennesaret, and drew to the s...... Mk 6:53
now come, Jesus stood on the s........ Jn 21:4
and we kneeled down on the s .... Acts 21:5
a certain creek with a s, into........... Acts 27:39
to the wind, and made toward s .... Acts 27:40
which is by the sea s innumerable .... Heb 11:12

SHORN
a flock of sheep that are even s........ Song 4:2
having s his head in Cenchrea .... Acts 18:18
be not covered, let her also be s 1Cor 11:6
for a woman to be s or shaven.......... 1Cor 11:6

SHORT
Moses, Is the LORD's hand waxed s... Num 11:23
the LORD began to cut Israel s......... 2Kin 10:32
the light is s because of................. Job 17:12
the triumphing of the wicked is s...... Job 20:5
Remember how s my time is.............. Ps 89:47
come s of the glory of God............... Rom 3:23
cut it s in righteousness.................. Rom 9:28
because a s work will the Lord .... Rom 9:28
I say, brethren, the time is s............ 1Cor 7:29
from you for a s time in presence 1Th 2:17
you should seem to come s of it .... Heb 4:1
knoweth that he hath but a s time .... Rev 12:12
he must continue a s space .... Rev 17:10

SHORTENED
The days of his youth hast thou s...... Ps 89:45
he s my days.................................. Ps 102:23
years of the wicked shall be s .... Prov 10:27
Is my hand s at all, that it .... Is 50:2
Behold, the LORD's hand is not s ...... Is 59:1
And except those days should be s .... Mt 24:22
sake those days shall be s .... Mt 24:22
that the Lord had s those days......... Mk 13:20
hath chosen, he hath s the days....... Mk 13:20

SHORTER
For the bed is s than that a man....... Is 28:20
Now the upper chambers were s .... Eze 42:5

SHORTLY
God will s bring it to pass............... Gen 41:32
s be brought again from Babylon ..... Jer 27:16
Now will I s pour out my fury .... Eze 7:8
he himself would depart s thither..... Acts 25:4
bruise Satan under your feet s .... Rom 16:20
But I will come to you s, if the 1Cor 4:19

SHOSHANNIM

to send Timotheus s unto you ...... Phil 2:19
that I also myself shall come s ...... Phil 2:24
thee, hoping to come unto thee s 1Ti 3:14
thy diligence to come s unto me 2Ti 4:9
with whom, if he come s, I will ...... Heb 13:23
Knowing that s I trust out off 2Pet 1:14
But I trust I shall s see thee 3Jn 14
things which must s come to pass ...... Rev 1:1
the things which must s be done ...... Rev 22:6

SHOSHANNIM (sho-shan'-nim) A musical notation.

To the chief Musician upon S .... Ps 45:t
To the chief Musician upon S .... Ps 69:t

SHOSHANNIM-EDUTH (sho-shan''-nim-e'-duth) A musical notation.

To the chief Musician upon S .... Ps 80:t

SHOT

budded, and her blossoms s forth ...... Gen 40:10
him, and s at him, and hated him ...... Gen 49:23
surely be stoned, or s through ...... Ex 19:13
We have s at them ...... Num 21:30
thereof, as though I s at a mark 1Sa 20:20
lad ran, he s an arrow beyond him 1Sa 20:36
of the arrow which Jonathan had s 1Sa 20:37
the shooters s from off the wall 2Sa 11:24
said, Shoot. And he s 2Kin 13:17
the archers s at king Josiah 2Chr 35:23
and he s out lightnings, and ...... Ps 18:14
Their tongue is as an arrow s out ...... Jer 9:8
forth branches, and s forth uppas ...... Eze 17:6
s forth her branches toward him ...... Eze 17:7
of waters, when he s forth ...... Eze 31:5
he hath s up his top among the ...... Eze 31:10

SHOULD See PREFACE.

SHOULDER

unto Hagar, putting it on her s ...... Gen 21:14
with her pitcher upon her s ...... Gen 24:15
forth with her pitcher on her s ...... Gen 24:45
let down her pitcher from her s ...... Gen 24:46
and bowed his s to bear, and became ...... Gen 49:15
that is upon them, and the right s ...... Ex 29:22
the s of the heave offering ...... Ex 29:27
the right s shall ye give unto ...... Lev 7:32
have the right s for his part ...... Lev 7:33
the heave s have I taken of the ...... Lev 7:34
and their fat, and the right s ...... Lev 8:25
on the fat, and upon the right s ...... Lev 9:21
the right s Aaron waved for a ...... Lev 9:21
heave s shall ye eat in a clean ...... Lev 10:14
The heave s and the wave breast ...... Lev 10:15
take the sodden s of the ram ...... Num 6:19
with the wave breast and heave s ...... Num 6:20
and as the right s are thine ...... Num 18:18
shall give unto the priest the s ...... Deut 18:3
man of you a stone upon his s ...... Josh 4:5
and took it, and laid it on his s ...... Judg 9:48
And the cook took up the s 1Sa 9:24
and withdrew the s, and hardened ...... Neh 9:29
let mine arm fall from my s blade ...... Job 31:22
Surely I would take it upon my s ...... Job 31:36
I removed his s from the burden ...... Ps 81:6
his burden, and the staff of his s ...... Is 9:4
government shall be upon his s ...... Is 9:6
be taken away from off thy s ...... Is 10:27
of David will I lay upon his s ...... Is 22:22
They bear him upon the s, they ...... Is 46:7
bare it upon my s in their sight ...... Eze 12:7
bear upon his s in the twilight ...... Eze 12:12
good piece, the thigh, and the s ...... Eze 24:4
didst break, and rend all their s ...... Eze 29:7
made bald, and every s was peeled ...... Eze 29:18
have thrust with side and with s ...... Eze 34:21
to hearken, and pulled away the s ...... Zec 7:11

SHOULDERPIECES

It shall have the two s thereof ...... Ex 28:7
put them on the s of the ephod ...... Ex 28:25
They made s for it, to couple it ...... Ex 39:4
and put them on the s of the ephod ...... Ex 39:18

SHOULDERS

and laid it upon both their s ...... Gen 9:23
up in their clothes upon their s ...... Ex 12:34
the s of the ephod for stones of ...... Ex 28:12
upon his two s for a memorial ...... Ex 28:12
he put them on the s of the ephod ...... Ex 39:7
they should bear upon their s ...... Num 7:9
and he shall dwell between his s ...... Deut 33:12
and all, and put them upon his s ...... Judg 16:3
from his s and upward he was 1Sa 9:2
than any of the people from his s 1Sa 10:23
a target of brass between his s 1Sa 17:6
their s with the staves thereon 1Chr 15:15
shall not be a burden upon your s 2Chr 35:3
But they shall fly upon the s of ...... Is 11:14
burden depart from off their s ...... Is 14:25
riches upon the s of young asses ...... Is 30:6
shall be carried upon their s ...... Is 49:22
shalt thou bear it upon thy s ...... Eze 12:6
be borne, and lay them on men's s ...... Mt 23:4
found it, he layeth it on his s ...... Lk 15:5

SHOULDEST

thee that thou s not eat ...... Gen 3:11
that is thine, lest thou s say ...... Gen 14:23
thou s have brought guiltiness ...... Gen 26:10
s thou therefore serve me for ...... Gen 29:15
that thou s say unto me, Carry ...... Num 11:12
s be driven to worship them, and ...... Deut 4:19
thee, and that thou s keep all his ...... Deut 26:18

That thou s enter into covenant ...... Deut 29:12
is not in heaven, that thou s say ...... Deut 30:12
beyond the sea, that thou s say ...... Deut 30:13
Israel, and s thou possess it ...... Judg 11:23
that thou s take knowledge of me ...... Ruth 2:10
for why s thou bring me to thy 1Sa 20:8
that thou s look upon such a dead 2Sa 9:8
that thou s tell them who shall 1Kin 1:20
me that thou s surely recover 2Kin 8:14
Thou s have smitten five or six 2Kin 13:19
for why s thou meddle to thy hurt 2Kin 14:10
to thy hurt, that thou s fall 2Kin 14:10
that thou s be to lay waste 2Kin 19:25
that thou s be ruler over my 1Chr 17:7
S thou help the ungodly, and love 2Chr 19:2
why s thou be smitten 2Chr 25:16
why s thou meddle to thine hurt 2Chr 25:19
to thine hurt, that thou s fall 2Chr 25:19
is man, that thou s magnify him ...... Job 7:17
that thou s set thine heart upon ...... Job 7:17
that thou s visit him every ...... Job 7:18
unto thee that thou s oppress ...... Job 10:3
that thou s despise the work of ...... Job 10:3
That thou s take it to the bound ...... Job 38:20
that thou s know the paths to the ...... Job 38:20
or that thou s take my covenant ...... Ps 50:16
s mark iniquities, O Lord, who ...... Ps 130:3
Lest thou s ponder the path of ...... Prov 5:6
than that thou s be put lower in ...... Prov 25:7
Though thou s bray a fool in a ...... Prov 27:22
Better is it that thou s not vow ...... Eccl 5:5
than that thou s vow ...... Eccl 5:5
why s thou destroy thyself ...... Eccl 7:16
why s thou die before thy time ...... Eccl 7:17
that thou s take hold of this ...... Eccl 7:18
that thou s be to lay waste ...... Is 37:26
lest thou s say, Mine idol hath ...... Is 48:5
lest thou s say, Behold, I knew ...... Is 48:7
thee by the way that thou s go ...... Is 48:17
s me my servant to raise up the ...... Is 49:6
that thou s be afraid of a man ...... Is 51:12
why s thou be as a stranger in ...... Jer 14:8
Why s thou be as a man astonied ...... Jer 14:9
that thou s put him in prison, and ...... Jer 29:26
though thou s make thy nest as ...... Jer 49:16
But thou s not have looked on the ...... Obad 12
neither s thou have rejoiced over ...... Obad 12
neither s thou have spoken ...... Obad 12
Thou s not have entered into the ...... Obad 13
thou s not have looked on their ...... Obad 13
Neither s thou have stood in the ...... Obad 14
neither s thou have delivered up ...... Obad 14
that thou s come under my roof ...... Mt 8:8
S not thou also have had ...... Mt 18:33
we would that thou s do for us ...... Mk 10:35
that thou s enter under my roof ...... Lk 7:6
thou s see the glory of God ...... Jn 11:40
I pray not that thou s take them ...... Jn 17:15
but that thou s keep them from ...... Jn 17:15
that thou s be for salvation unto ...... Acts 13:47
that thou s know his will, and see ...... Acts 22:14
s hear the voice of his mouth ...... Acts 22:14
that thou s set in order the ...... Titus 1:5
that thou s receive him for ever ...... Philem 15
that thou s give reward unto thy ...... Rev 11:18
s destroy them which destroy the ...... Rev 11:18

SHOUT

voice of them that s for mastery ...... Ex 32:18
the s of a king is among them ...... Num 23:21
people shall s with a great ...... Josh 6:5
people, saying, s with a great ...... Josh 6:5
people, saying, Ye shall not s ...... Josh 6:10
mouth, until the day I bid you s ...... Josh 6:10
then shall ye s ...... Josh 6:10
Joshua said unto the people, S ...... Josh 6:16
the people shouted with a great s ...... Josh 6:20
all Israel shouted with a great s 1Sa 4:5
heard the noise of the s, they 1Sa 4:6
s in the camp of the Hebrews 1Sa 4:6
Then the men of Judah gave a s 2Chr 13:15
the people shouted with a great s ...... Ezr 3:11
s of joy from the noise of the ...... Ezr 3:13
the people shouted with a loud s ...... Ezr 3:13
let them ever s for joy, because ...... Ps 5:11
s for joy, all ye that are ...... Ps 32:11
Let them s for joy, and be glad ...... Ps 35:27
s unto God with the voice of ...... Ps 47:1
God is gone up with a s, the LORD ...... Ps 47:5
they s for joy, they also sing ...... Ps 65:13
and let thy saints s for joy ...... Ps 132:9
her saints shall s aloud for joy ...... Ps 132:16
Cry out and s, thou inhabitant of ...... Is 12:6
let them s from the top of the ...... Is 42:11
s, ye lower parts of the earth ...... Is 44:23
he shall give a s, as they that ...... Jer 25:30
s among the chief of the nations ...... Jer 31:7
S against her round about ...... Jer 50:15
shall lift up a s against thee ...... Jer 51:14
Also when I cry and s, he shutteth ...... Lam 3:8
s, O Israel ...... Zeph 3:14
s, O daughter of Jerusalem ...... Zec 9:9
And the people gave a s, saying ...... Acts 12:22
descend from heaven with a s 1Th 4:16

SHOUTED

the noise of the people as they s ...... Ex 32:17
when all the people saw, they s ...... Lev 9:24
So the people s when the priests ...... Josh 6:20
the people s with a great shout ...... Josh 6:20
the Philistines s against him ...... Judg 15:14
all Israel s with a great shout 1Sa 4:5

And all the people s, and said, God 1Sa 10:24
to the fight, and s for the battle 1Sa 17:20
of Israel and of Judah arose, and s 1Sa 17:52
and as the men of Judah s, it came 2Chr 13:15
all the people s with a great ...... Ezr 3:11
and many s aloud for joy ...... Ezr 3:12
for the people s with a loud ...... Ezr 3:13
and all the sons of God s for joy ...... Job 38:7

SHOUTETH

man that s by reason of wine ...... Ps 78:65

SHOUTING

up the ark of the LORD with s 2Sa 6:15
the covenant of the LORD with s 1Chr 15:28
LORD with a loud voice, and with s 2Chr 15:14
thunder of the captains, and the s ...... Job 39:25
the wicked perish, there is s ...... Prov 11:10
for the s for thy summer fruits ...... Is 16:9
singing, neither shall there be s ...... Is 16:10
made their vintage s to cease ...... Is 16:10
the morning, and the s at noontide ...... Jer 20:16
none shall tread with s ...... Jer 48:33
their s shall be no s ...... Jer 48:33
to lift up the voice with s ...... Jer 21:22
with s in the day of battle, with ...... Amos 1:14
shall die with tumult, with s ...... Amos 2:2

SHOUTINGS

the headstone thereof with s ...... Zec 4:7

SHOVEL

hath been winnowed with the s ...... Is 30:24

SHOVELS

to receive his ashes, and his s ...... Ex 27:3
of the altar, the pots, and the s ...... Ex 38:3
censers, the fleshhooks, and the s ...... Num 4:14
Hiram made the lavers, and the s 1Kin 7:40
And the pots, and the s, and the 1Kin 7:45
And the pots, and the s, and the 2Kin 25:14
And Huram made the pots, and the s 2Chr 4:11
The pots also, and the s, and the 2Chr 4:16
The caldrons also, and the s ...... Jer 52:18

SHOWER

there shall be an overflowing s ...... Eze 13:11
be an overflowing s in mine anger ...... Eze 13:13
I will cause the s to come down ...... Eze 34:26
ye say, There cometh a s ...... Lk 12:54

SHOWERS

herb, and as the s upon the grass ...... Deut 32:2
wet with the s of the mountains ...... Job 24:8
thou makest it soft with s ...... Ps 65:10
as that water the earth ...... Ps 72:6
Therefore the s have been ...... Jer 3:3
or can the heavens give s ...... Jer 14:22
there shall be s of blessing ...... Eze 34:26
as the s upon the grass, that ...... Mic 5:7
clouds, and give them s of rain ...... Zec 10:1

SHRANK

eat not of the sinew which s ...... Gen 32:32
Jacob's thigh in the sinew that s ...... Gen 32:32

SHRED

s them into the pot of pottage 2Kin 4:39

SHRINES

which made silver s for Diana ...... Acts 19:24

SHROUD

branches, and with a shadowing s ...... Eze 31:3

SHRUBS

cast the child under one of the s ...... Gen 21:15

SHUA (shu'-ah) See SHUAH.
1. Daughter of Judah.
the daughter of S the Canaanitess 1Chr 2:3
2. Daughter of Heber.
and Hotham, and S their sister 1Chr 7:32

SHUAH (shu'-ah)
1. A son of Abraham.
Medan, and Midian, and Ishbak, and S ...... Gen 25:2
and Midian, and Ishbak, and S 1Chr 1:32
2. Same as Shua 1.
Canaanite, whose name was S ...... Gen 38:2
daughter of S Judah's wife died ...... Gen 38:12
3. A descendant of Caleb.
the brother of S begat Mehir 1Chr 4:11

SHUAL (shu'-al)
1. A district in Benjamin.
to Ophrah, unto the land of S 1Sa 13:17
2. Son of Zophah.
Suah, and Harnepher, and S, and Beri 1Chr 7:36

SHUBAEL (shu-ba-el) See SHEBUEL.
1. Son of Amram.
sons of Amram: S 1Chr 24:20
of the sons of S 1Chr 24:20
2. A sanctuary servant.
The thirteenth to S, he, his sons 1Chr 25:20

SHUHAH See SHUAH.

SHUHAM (shu'-ham) See HUSHIM.
SHUHAMITES. A son of Dan.
of S, the family of the ...... Num 26:42

SHUHAMITES (shu'-ham-ites) Descendants of Shuham.
of Shuham, the family of the S ...... Num 26:42
All the families of the S ...... Num 26:43

SHUHITE (shu'-hite) A descendant of Shuah.
the Temanite, and Bildad the S ...... Job 2:11
Then answered Bildad the S ...... Job 8:1

S

Then answered Bildad the S .... Job 18:1
Then answered Bildad the S .... Job 25:1
the Temanite and Bildad the S............. Job 42:9

SHULAMITE (*shu'-lam-ite*) *An inhabitant of Shulam.*
Return, return, O S .... Song 6:13
What will ye see in the S .... Song 6:13

SHULAMMITE See SHULAMITE.

SHUMATHITES (*shu'-math-ites*) *Descendants of Shobal.*
and the Puhites, and the S 1Chr 2:53

SHUN
But s profane and vain babblings........ 2Ti 2:16

SHUNAMMITE (*shu'-nam-mite*) *An inhabitant of Shunem.*
of Israel, and found Abishag a S 1Kin 1:3
Abishag the S ministered unto the 1Kin 1:15
he give me Abishag the S to wife 1Kin 2:17
Let Abishag the S be given to............. 1Kin 2:21
ask Abishag the S for Adonijah........... 1Kin 2:22
Gehazi his servant, Call this S 2Kin 4:12
servant, Behold, yonder is that S 2Kin 4:25
Gehazi, and said, Call this S 2Kin 4:36

SHUNEM (*shu'-nem*) See SHUNAMMITE. *A city in Issachar.*
Jezreel, and Chesulloth, and S .... Josh 19:18
together, and came and pitched in S ... 1Sa 28:4
on a day, that Elisha passed to S 2Kin 4:8

SHUNI (*shu'-ni*) See SHUNITES. *A son of Gad.*
Ziphion, and Haggi, S, and Ezbon, ... Gen 46:16
of S, the family of the Shunites........... Num 26:15

SHUNITES (*shu'-nites*) *Descendants of Shuni.*
of Shuni, the family of the S .... Num 26:15

SHUNNED
For I have not s to declare unto......... Acts 20:27

SHUPHAM (*shu'-fam*) See SHEPHUPHAN, SHUPHAMITES. *A son of Benjamin.*
Of S, the family of the .... Num 26:39

SHUPHAMITES (*shu'-fam-ites*) *Descendants of Shupham.*
Of Shupham, the family of the S .... Num 26:39

SHUPPIM (*shup'-pim*) See MUPPIM, SHEPHUPHAN.
1. A Benjamite.
S also, and Huppim, the children........ 1Chr 7:12
to wife the sister of Huppim and S...... 1Chr 7:15
2. A Levite gatekeeper.
To S and Hosah the lot came forth 1Chr 26:16

SHUR (*shur*) *A wilderness east of Egypt.*
by the fountain in the way to S........... Gen 16:7
and dwelled between Kadesh and S .... Gen 20:1
And they dwelt from Havilah unto S .. Gen 25:18
went out into the wilderness of S .... Ex 15:22
Havilah until thou comest to S 1Sa 15:7
of the land, as thou goest to S 1Sa 27:8

SHUSHAN (*shu'-shan*) See SHOSHANNIM. *Capital of Persia.*
year, as I was in S the palace............. Neh 1:1
which was in S the palace.................... Est 1:2
that were present in S the palace........ Est 1:5
young virgins unto S the palace.......... Est 2:3
Now in S the palace there was a......... Est 2:5
together unto S the palace................... Est 2:8
decree was given in S the palace........ Est 3:15
but the city S was perplexed............... Est 3:15
was given at S to destroy them .... Est 4:8
the Jews that are present in S .... Est 4:16
decree was given at S the palace........ Est 8:14
and the city of S rejoiced.................... Est 8:15
in S the palace the Jews slew and ..... Est 9:6
of those that were slain in S the......... Est 9:11
five hundred men in S the palace .... Est 9:12
to the Jews which are in S to do .... Est 9:13
and the decree was given at S .... Est 9:14
For the Jews that were in S .... Est 9:15
and slew three hundred men at S .... Est 9:15
at S assembled together on the .... Est 9:18
that I was at S in the palace .... Dan 8:2

SHUSHAN-EDUTH (*shu'-shan-e'-duth*) *shu''-shan-e'-duth*
To the chief Musician upon S .... Ps 60:t

SHUT
and the LORD s him in......................... Gen 7:16
them, and s the door after him, ... Gen 19:6
house to them, and s to the door .... Gen 19:10
the wilderness hath s them in .... Ex 14:3
then the priest shall s up him.............. Lev 13:4
then the priest shall s him up .... Lev 13:5
unclean, and shall not s him up.......... Lev 13:11
priest shall s him seven days.............. Lev 13:21
priest shall s him up seven days......... Lev 13:26
then the priest shall s up him .... Lev 13:31
the priest shall s up him that .... Lev 13:33
s up it that hath the plague................. Lev 13:50
he shall s it up seven days more........ Lev 13:54
s up the house seven days .... Lev 14:38
s up shall be unclean until the .... Lev 14:46
let her be s out from the camp........... Num 12:14
Miriam was s out from the camp........ Num 12:15
he s up the heaven, that there be .... Deut 11:17
nor s thine hand from thy poor.......... Deut 15:7

them, and the LORD had s them up... Deut 32:30
is gone, and there is none s up .... Deut 32:36
were gone out, they s the gate............ Josh 2:7
Now Jericho was straitly s up .... Josh 6:1
s the doors of the parlour upon .... Judg 3:23
s it to them, and gat them up to .... Judg 9:51
but the LORD had s her womb............ 1Sa 1:5
the LORD had s up her womb............. 1Sa 1:6
s up their calves at home 1Sa 6:10
for he is s in, by entering into............ 1Sa 23:7
So they were s up unto the day of 2Sa 20:3
When heaven is s up, and there is 1Kin 8:35
the wall, and him that is s up............. 1Kin 14:10
the wall, and him that is s up............. 1Kin 21:21
thou shalt s the door upon thee 2Kin 4:4
s the door upon her and upon her...... 2Kin 4:5
s the door upon him, and went out ... 2Kin 4:21
s the door upon them twain, and....... 2Kin 4:33
s the door, and hold him fast at 2Kin 6:32
the wall, and him that is s up............. 2Kin 9:8
for there was not any s up.................. 2Kin 14:26
the king of Assyria s him up 2Kin 17:4
When the heaven is s up, and then 2Chr 6:26
If I s up heaven that there be no........ 2Chr 7:13
s up the doors of the house of 2Chr 28:24
Also they have s up the doors of 2Chr 29:7
son of Mehetabeel, who was s up....... Neh 6:10
let us s the doors of the temple.......... Neh 6:10
let them s the doors, and bar them .... Neh 7:3
that the gates should be s .... Neh 13:19
Because it s not up the doors of .... Job 3:10
s up, or gather together, then............. Job 11:10
Or who s up the sea with doors,......... Job 38:8
s up together as with a close.............. Job 41:15
hast not s me up into the hand of...... Ps 31:8
let not the pit s her mouth upon........ Ps 69:15
hath he in anger s up his tender .... Ps 77:9
I am s up, and I cannot come forth .... Ps 88:8
doors shall be s in the streets............. Eccl 12:4
a spring s up, a fountain sealed.......... Song 4:12
their ears heavy, and s their eyes....... Is 6:10
so he shall open, and none shall s ..... Is 22:22
and he shall s, and none shall open ... Is 22:22
every house is s up, that no man...... Is 24:10
shall be s up in the prison, and.......... Is 24:22
and s thy doors about thee .... Is 26:20
for he hath s their eyes, that.............. Is 44:18
and the gates shall not be s .... Is 45:1
the kings shall s their mouths at .... Is 52:15
they shall not be s day nor night........ Is 60:11
to bring forth, and s the womb?......... Is 66:9
cities of the south shall be s up .... Jer 13:19
a burning fire s up in my bones .... Jer 20:9
Jeremiah the prophet was s up in ...... Jer 32:2
king of Judah had s him up................ Jer 32:3
while he was yet s up in the............... Jer 33:1
Baruch, saying, I am s up,.................. Jer 36:5
while he was s up in the court of....... Jer 39:15
s thyself within thine house............... Eze 3:24
and it was s .... Eze 44:1
This gate shall be s, it shall............... Eze 44:2
in by it, therefore it shall be s .... Eze 44:2
shall be s the six working days.......... Eze 46:1
shall not be s until the evening .... Eze 46:2
going forth one shall s the gate .... Eze 46:12
hath s the lions' mouths, that .... Dan 6:22
wherefore s thou up the vision .... Dan 8:26
s up the words, and seal the book,..... Dan 12:4
that would s the doors for nought...... Mal 1:10
and when thou hast s thy door .... Mt 6:6
for ye s up the kingdom of heaven .... Mt 23:13
and the door was s .... Mt 25:10
that he s up John in prison................. Lk 3:20
the heaven was s up three years........ Lk 4:25
the door is now s, and my children ... Lk 11:7
hath s to the door, and ye begin......... Lk 13:25
when the doors were s where the....... Jn 20:19
came Jesus, the doors being s .... Jn 20:26
truly found we s with all safety.......... Acts 5:23
and forthwith the doors were s .... Acts 21:30
the saints did I s up in prison .... Acts 26:10
s up unto the faith which God............ Gal 3:23
an open door, and no man can s it .... Rev 3:8
These have power to s heaven............ Rev 11:6
s him up, and set a seal upon him,.... Rev 20:3
it shall not be s at all by day .... Rev 21:25

SHUTHALHITES (*shu'-thal-hites*) *Descendants of Shuthelah.*
Shuthelahites, the family of the S ...... Num 26:35

SHUTHELAH (*shu'-the-lah*) See SHUTHALHITES.
1. A son of Ephraim.
of S, the family of the .... Num 26:35
And these are the sons of S .... Num 26:36
S, and Bered his son, and Tahath 1Chr 7:20
2. Son of Zabad.
S his son, and Ezer, and Elead,......... 1Chr 7:21

SHUTHELAHITES See SHUTHALHITES.

SHUTTETH
is up a man, and there can be no....... Job 12:14
He s his eyes to devise froward .... Prov 16:30
he that s his lips is esteemed a .... Prov 17:28
s his eyes from seeing evil.................. Is 33:15
cry and shout, he s out my prayer ..... Lam 3:8
s up his bowels of compassion 1Jn 3:17
he that openeth, and no man s .... Rev 3:7
and s, and no man openeth .... Rev 3:7

SHUTTING
about the time of s of the gate............ Josh 2:5

SHUTTLE
are swifter than a weaver's s .... Job 7:6

SIA (*si'-ah*) See SIAHA. *A family of exiles.*
of Keros, the children of S................... Neh 7:47

SIAHA (*si'a-hah*) See SIA. *Same as Sia.*
of Keros, the children of S................... Ezr 2:44

SIBBECAI (*sib'-be-cahee*) See SIBBECHAI. *A "mighty man" of David.*
the Hushathite, Ilai the....................... 1Chr 11:29
eighth month was S the Hushathite.. 1Chr 27:11

SIBBECHAI (*sib'-be-khahee*) See SIBBECAI.
Same as Sibbecai.
then S the Hushathite slew Saph,....... 2Sa 21:18
at which time S the Hushathite.......... 1Chr 20:4

SIBBOLETH (*sib'-bo-leth*) See SHIBBOLETH. *The Ephraimite pronunciation of Shibboleth.*
and he said S...................................... Judg 12:6

SIBMAH (*sib'-mah*) *A city in Reuben.*
And Kirjathaim, and S, and............... Josh 13:19
languish, and the vine of S .... Is 16:8
weeping of Jazer the vine of S .... Is 16:9
O vine of S, I will weep for thee,....... Jer 48:32

SIBRAIM (*sib'-ra-im*) *A city in Syria between Damascus and Hamath.*
Hamath, Berothah, S, which is .... Eze 47:16

SICHEM (*si'-kem*) See SHECHEM, SYCHEM. *A place on the plain of Moreh.*
unto the place of S .... Gen 12:6

SICK
Joseph, Behold, thy father is s .... Gen 48:1
of her that is s of her flowers............. Lev 15:33
to take David, she said, He is s 1Sa 19:14
because three days agone I fell s 1Sa 30:13
bare unto David, and it was very s 2Sa 12:15
that he fell s for his sister.................. 2Sa 13:2
on thy bed, and make thyself s 2Sa 13:5
Amnon lay down, and made himself s 2Sa 13:6
Abijah the son of Jeroboam fell s 1Kin 14:1
for he is s 1Kin 14:5
the mistress of the house, fell s 1Kin 17:17
that was in Samaria, and was s 2Kin 1:2
Ben-hadad the king of Syria was s 2Kin 8:7
Ahab in Jezreel, because he was s 2Kin 8:29
Ahab was fallen s of his 2Kin 13:14
days was Hezekiah s unto death........ 2Kin 20:1
heard that Hezekiah had been s 2Kin 20:12
Ahab at Jezreel, because he was s 2Chr 22:6
days Hezekiah was s to the death 2Chr 32:24
sad, seeing thou art not s .... Neh 2:2
But as for me, when they were s .... Ps 35:13
Hope deferred maketh the heart s ..... Prov 13:12
shalt thou say, and I was not s .... Prov 23:35
for I am s of love .... Song 2:5
ye tell him, that I am s of love........... Song 5:8
the whole head is s, and the whole ... Is 1:5
inhabitant shall not say, I am s .... Is 33:24
days was Hezekiah s unto death........ Is 38:1
king of Judah, when he had been s ... Is 38:9
he had heard that he had been s .... Is 39:1
them that are s with famine............... Jer 14:18
have ye healed that which was s .... Eze 34:4
will strengthen that which was s .... Eze 34:16
fainted, and was a certain days .... Dan 8:27
made him s with bottles of wine........ Hos 7:5
I make thee s in smiting thee............. Mic 6:13
and if ye offer the lame and s .... Mal 1:8
was torn, and the lame, and the s..... Mal 1:13
they brought unto him all s .... Mt 4:24
lieth at home s of the palsy............... Mt 8:6
mother laid, and s of a fever............. Mt 8:14
word, and healed all that were s .... Mt 8:16
to him a man s of the palsy.............. Mt 9:2
said unto the s of the palsy.............. Mt 9:2
saith he to the s of the palsy............ Mt 9:6
a physician, but they that are s .... Mt 9:12
Heal the s, cleanse the lepers............ Mt 10:8
toward them, and he healed their s... Mt 14:14
I was s, and ye visited me .... Mt 25:36
Or when saw we thee s, or in .... Mt 25:39
s, and in prison, and ye visited me.... Mt 25:43
or a stranger, or naked, or s .... Mt 25:44
wife's mother lay s of a fever .... Mk 1:30
that were s of divers diseases .... Mk 1:34
him, bringing one s of the palsy........ Mk 2:3
wherein the s of the palsy lay............ Mk 2:4
he said unto the s of the palsy.......... Mk 2:5
to say to the s of the palsy............... Mk 2:9
(he saith to the s of the palsy.......... Mk 2:10
physician, but they that are s .... Mk 2:17
laid his hands upon a few s folk .... Mk 6:5
with oil many that were s .... Mk 6:13
about in beds those that were s .... Mk 6:55
they laid the s in the streets,............. Mk 6:56
they shall lay hands on the s .... Mk 16:18
all they that had any s with .... Lk 4:40
(he said unto the s of the palsy........ Lk 5:24
but they that are s .... Lk 5:31
who was dear unto him, was s .... Lk 7:2
the servant which had been s .... Lk 7:10
kingdom of God, and to heal the s .... Lk 9:2
heal the s that are therein, and......... Lk 10:9
whose son was s at Capernaum........ Jn 4:46
Now a certain man was s, named..... Jn 11:1

hair, whose brother Lazarus was s............ Jn 11:2
behold, he whom thou lovest is s............. Jn 11:3
had heard therefore that he was s............. Jn 11:6
forth the s into the streets........................ Acts 5:15
unto Jerusalem, bringing s folks............... Acts 5:16
years, and was s of the palsy..................... Acts 9:33
in those days, that she was s..................... Acts 9:37
the s handkerchiefs or aprons................. Acts 19:12
of Publius lay s of a fever......................... Acts 28:8
ye had heard that he had been s............... Phil 2:26
indeed he was s nigh unto death............... Phil 2:27
have I left at Miletum s........................... 2Ti 4:20
Is any s among you.................................. Jas 5:14
prayer of faith shall save the s................ Jas 5:15

SICKLE
to put the s to the corn........................... Deut 16:9
but thou shalt not move a s unto.............. Deut 23:25
him that handleth the s in the.................. Jer 50:16
Put ye in the s, for the harvest................. Joel 3:13
immediately he putteth in the s................ Mk 4:29
crown, and in his hand a sharp s............... Rev 14:14
sat on the cloud, Thrust in thy s............... Rev 14:16
thrust in his s on the earth...................... Rev 14:16
heaven, he also having a sharp s............... Rev 14:17
cry to him that had the sharp s................. Rev 14:18
saying, Thrust in thy sharp s.................... Rev 14:18
thrust in his s into the earth.................... Rev 14:19

SICKLY
s among you, and many sleep................... 1Cor 11:30

SICKNESS
will s take away from the midst............... Ex 23:25
lie with a woman having her s.................. Lev 20:18
will take away from thee all s................... Deut 7:15
Also every s, and every plague,................. Deut 28:61
plague, whatsoever s there be.................. 1Kin 8:37
his s was so sore, that there was............... 1Kin 17:17
sick of his s whereof he died.................... 2Kin 13:14
sore or whatsoever s there be.................. 2Chr 6:28
thou shalt have great s by....................... 2Chr 21:15
out by reason of the s day by day............. 2Chr 21:15
fell out by reason of his s......................... 2Chr 21:19
with make all his bed in his s................... Ps 41:3
much sorrow and wrath with his s........... Eccl 5:17
sick, and was recovered of his s............... Is 38:9
he will cut me off with pining s................ Is 38:12
When Ephraim saw his s, and Judah........ Hos 5:13
and healing all manner of s...................... Mt 4:23
the kingdom, and healing every s............. Mt 9:35
out, and to heal all manner of s............... Mt 10:1
This s is not unto death, but for............... Jn 11:4

SICKNESSES
and of long continuance, and sore s......... Deut 28:59
the s which the LORD hath laid................. Deut 29:22
our infirmities, and bare our s................. Mt 8:17
And to have power to heal s..................... Mk 3:15

SIDDIM (sid´-dim) *Area of Sodom and Gomorrah*
joined together in the vale of S................ Gen 14:3
battle with them in the vale of S.............. Gen 14:8
the vale of S was full of........................... Gen 14:10

SIDE
shalt thou set in the s thereof.................. Gen 6:16
that was openly by the way s.................... Gen 38:21
walked along by the river's s.................... Ex 2:5
and strike it on the two s posts................. Ex 12:7
the two s posts with the blood.................. Ex 12:22
the lintel, and on the two s posts............. Ex 12:23
his hands, the one on the one.................... Ex 17:12
and the other on the other s..................... Ex 17:12
rings shall be in the one s of it................. Ex 25:12
and two rings in the other s of it.............. Ex 25:12
the candlestick out of the one s................ Ex 25:32
candlestick out of the other s................... Ex 25:32
And a cubit on the one s........................... Ex 26:13
a cubit on the other s of that.................... Ex 26:13
on this s and on that s.............................. Ex 26:13
boards on the south s southward.............. Ex 26:18
And for the second s of the....................... Ex 26:20
s there shall be twenty boards.................. Ex 26:20
of the one s of the tabernacle................... Ex 26:26
of the other s of the tabernacle................ Ex 26:27
boards of the s of the tabernacle.............. Ex 26:27
s of the tabernacle toward the.................. Ex 26:35
put the table on the north s...................... Ex 26:35
for the south s southward the................... Ex 27:9
an hundred cubits long for one s.............. Ex 27:9
likewise for the north s............................. Ex 27:11
of the court on the west s shall................ Ex 27:12
of the court on the east s.......................... Ex 27:13
The hangings of one s of the gate............. Ex 27:14
on the other s shall be hangings.............. Ex 27:15
which is in the s of the ephod................... Ex 28:26
on the one s and on the other were.......... Ex 32:15
and said, Who is on the LORD's s............... Ex 32:26
Put every man his sword by his s.............. Ex 32:27
uttermost s of another curtain................. Ex 36:11
boards for the south s southward............. Ex 36:23
for the other s of the tabernacle.............. Ex 36:25
of the one s of the tabernacle................... Ex 36:31
of the other s of the tabernacle................ Ex 36:32
two rings upon the one s of it................... Ex 37:3
two rings upon the other s of it................ Ex 37:3
One cherub on the end on this s................ Ex 37:8
cherub on the other end on that s............. Ex 37:8
out of the one s thereof, and.................... Ex 37:18
out of the other s thereof......................... Ex 37:18
on the south s southward the................... Ex 38:9

for the north s the hangings were............ Ex 38:11
for the west s were hangings of................ Ex 38:12
for the east s eastward fifty..................... Ex 38:13
The hangings of the one s of the.............. Ex 38:14
for the other s of the court gate............... Ex 38:14
which was on the s of the ephod.............. Ex 39:19
upon the s of the tabernacle..................... Ex 40:22
on the s of the tabernacle........................ Ex 40:24
he shall kill it on the s of the.................... Lev 1:11
wrung out at the s of the altar.................. Lev 1:15
offering upon the s of the altar................ Lev 5:9
on the east s toward the rising.................. Num 2:3
On the south s shall be........................... Num 2:10
On the west s shall be the....................... Num 2:18
be on the north s by their armies............. Num 2:25
the s of the tabernacle southward............ Num 3:29
these shall pitch on the s of the............... Num 3:35
south s shall take their journey................ Num 10:6
it were a day's journey on this s............... Num 11:31
a day's journey on the other s.................. Num 11:31
Dathan, and Abiram, on every s............... Num 16:27
pitched on the other s of Arnon............... Num 21:13
Moab on this s Jordan by Jericho............. Num 22:1
on this s, and a wall on that s................... Num 22:24
as gardens by the river's s........................ Num 24:6
with them on yonder s Jordan................. Num 32:19
to us on this s Jordan eastward............... Num 32:19
on this s Jordan may be ours.................... Num 32:32
to Ribiah, on the east s of Ain................. Num 34:11
shall reach unto the s of the sea.............. Num 34:11
their inheritance on this s........................ Num 34:15
on the east s two thousand cubits............ Num 35:5
on the south s two thousand.................... Num 35:5
on the west s two thousand cubits........... Num 35:5
on the north s two thousand.................... Num 35:5
three cities on this s Jordan..................... Num 35:14
this s Jordan in the wilderness................. Deut 1:1
On this s Jordan, in the land of................ Deut 1:5
and in the south, and by the sea s............ Deut 1:7
land that was on this s Jordan.................. Deut 3:8
ask from the one s of heaven unto........... Deut 4:32
s Jordan toward the sunrising.................. Deut 4:41
On this s Jordan, in the valley.................. Deut 4:46
which were on this s Jordan...................... Deut 4:47
plain on this s Jordan eastward................ Deut 4:49
they not on the other s Jordan................. Deut 11:30
put it in the s of the ark of the................. Deut 31:26
Moses gave you on this s Jordan............... Josh 1:14
s Jordan toward the sunrising.................. Josh 1:15
that were on the other s Jordan................ Josh 2:10
which were on this s of Jordan.................. Josh 5:1
on the east s of Beth-el............................ Josh 7:2
and dwelt on the other s Jordan.............. Josh 7:7
and Ai, on the west s of Ai....................... Josh 8:9
and pitched on the north s of Ai.............. Josh 8:11
and Ai, on the west s of the city.............. Josh 8:12
on this s, and some on that s.................... Josh 8:22
judges, stood on this s the ark................. Josh 8:33
on that s before the priests the............... Josh 8:33
kings which were on this s Jordan............ Josh 9:1
their land on the other s Jordan............... Josh 12:1
on this s Jordan on the west..................... Josh 12:7
on the other s Jordan eastward................ Josh 13:27
of Moab, on the other s Jordan................ Josh 13:32
half tribe on the other s Jordan............... Josh 13:32
to the south s to Maaleh-acrabbim.......... Josh 15:3
on the south s unto Kadesh-barnea.......... Josh 15:3
is on the south s of the river.................... Josh 15:8
unto the south s of the Jebusite............... Josh 15:8
along unto the s of mount Jearim............. Josh 15:10
which is Chesalon, on the north s............. Josh 15:10
out unto the s of Ekron northward........... Josh 15:11
the east s was Ataroth-addar.................... Josh 16:5
sea to Michmethah on the north s............ Josh 16:6
which were on the other s Jordan............. Josh 17:5
was on the north s of the river................. Josh 17:9
on the north s was from Jordan............... Josh 18:12
the border went up to the s of.................. Josh 18:12
of Jericho on the north s.......................... Josh 18:12
toward Luz, to the s of Luz....................... Josh 18:13
south s of the nether Beth-horon............. Josh 18:13
to the s of Jebusi on the south,................ Josh 18:16
passed along toward the s over................ Josh 18:18
to the s of Beth-hoglah northward........... Josh 18:19
the border of it on the east s.................... Josh 18:20
it on the north s to Hannathon................ Josh 19:14
toward the north s of Beth-emek............. Josh 19:27
to Zebulun on the south s......................... Josh 19:34
reacheth to Asher on the west s................ Josh 19:34
on the other s Jordan by Jericho.............. Josh 20:8
gave you on the other s Jordan................. Josh 22:4
on this s Jordan westward........................ Josh 22:7
other s of the flood in old time................ Josh 24:2
from the other s of the flood.................... Josh 24:3
which dwelt on the other s Jordan............ Josh 24:8
on the other s of the flood....................... Josh 24:14
were on the other s of the flood............... Josh 24:15
on the north s of the hill.......................... Josh 24:30
on the north s of the hill Gaash.............. Judg 2:9
were on the north s of them.................... Judg 7:1
sand by the sea s for multitude............... Judg 7:12
also on every s of all the camp............... Judg 7:18
to Gideon on the other s Jordan.............. Judg 7:25
of all their enemies on every s................ Judg 8:34
other s Jordan in the land of................... Judg 10:8
came by the east s of the land of............. Judg 11:18
pitched on the other s of Arnon.............. Judg 11:18
on the s of mount Ephraim...................... Judg 19:1
toward the s of mount Ephraim............... Judg 19:18
is on the north s of Beth-el...................... Judg 21:19

on the east s of the highway that....... Judg 21:19
backward by the s of the gate.................. 1Sa 4:18
in a coffer by the s thereof....................... 1Sa 6:8
hand of your enemies on the other s........ 1Sa 12:11
garrison, that is on the other s.................. 1Sa 14:1
was a sharp rock on the one s................... 1Sa 14:4
and a sharp rock on the other s................ 1Sa 14:4
unto all Israel, Be ye on one s.................. 1Sa 14:40
my son will be on the other s.................... 1Sa 14:40
all his enemies on every s......................... 1Sa 14:47
stood on a mountain on the one s............. 1Sa 17:3
on a mountain on the other s.................... 1Sa 17:3
three arrows on the s thereof................... 1Sa 20:20
the arrows are on this s of thee................ 1Sa 20:21
arose, and Abner sat by Saul's s................ 1Sa 20:25
went on this s of the mountain................. 1Sa 23:26
his men on that s of the mountain............ 1Sa 23:26
David went over to the other s.................. 1Sa 26:13
were on the other s of the valley.............. 1Sa 31:7
that were on the other s Jordan............... 1Sa 31:7
the one on the one s of the pool............... 2Sa 2:13
other on the other s of the pool................ 2Sa 2:13
his sword in his fellow's s.......................... 2Sa 2:16
the way of the hill s behind him............... 2Sa 13:34
on the hill's s over against him................. 2Sa 16:13
And the king stood by the gate s............... 2Sa 18:4
on the right s of the city that.................... 2Sa 24:5
the region on this s the river..................... 1Kin 4:24
in all the kings on this s the river............. 1Kin 4:24
which were about him on every s.............. 1Kin 5:3
God hath given me rest on every s............ 1Kin 5:4
was in the right s of the house.................. 1Kin 6:8
s posts were a fifth part of the.................. 1Kin 6:31
one s of the floor to the other.................. 1Kin 7:7
at the s of every addition......................... 1Kin 7:30
bases on the right s of the house.............. 1Kin 7:39
five on the left s of the house.................. 1Kin 7:39
s of the house eastward over.................... 1Kin 7:39
of pure gold, five on the right s................ 1Kin 7:49
either s on the place of the seat............... 1Kin 10:19
lions stood there on the one s................... 1Kin 10:20
on the other s as red as blood.................. 2Kin 3:22
window, and said, Who is on my s............. 2Kin 9:32
on the right s as one cometh into............ 2Kin 12:9
it on the north s of the altar.................... 2Kin 16:14
unto the east s of the valley..................... 1Chr 4:39
on the other s Jordan by Jericho.............. 1Chr 6:78
on the east s of Jordan............................. 1Chr 6:78
Thine are we, David, and on thy s............ 1Chr 12:18
And on the other s of Jordan.................... 1Chr 12:37
he not given you rest on every s................ 1Chr 22:18
this s Jordan westward in all the.............. 1Chr 26:30
the temple, five on the right s................... 2Chr 4:6
on the right s of the east end................... 2Chr 4:10
at the sea s in the land of Edom.............. 2Chr 8:17
stays on each s of the sitting.................... 2Chr 9:18
lions stood there on the one s................... 2Chr 9:19
having Judah and Benjamin on his s......... 2Chr 11:12
he hath given us rest on every s................ 2Chr 14:7
beyond the sea on this s Syria................... 2Chr 20:2
from the right s of the temple to.............. 2Chr 23:10
to the left s of the temple........................ 2Chr 23:10
other, and guided them on every s............ 2Chr 23:30
the west s of the city of David.................. 2Chr 32:30
of David, on the west s of Gihon.............. 2Chr 33:14
rest that are on this s the river................. Ezr 4:10
the men on this s the river....................... Ezr 4:11
no portion on this s the river................... Ezr 4:16
governor on this s the river....................... Ezr 5:3
governor on this s the river....................... Ezr 5:6
which were on this s the river................... Ezr 6:6
governor on this s the river....................... Ezr 6:13
the governors on this s the river.............. Ezr 8:36
the governor on this s the river................ Neh 3:7
one had his sword girded by his s............. Neh 4:18
about all that he hath on every s.............. Job 1:10
shall make him afraid on every s.............. Job 18:11
shall be ready at his s.............................. Job 18:12
He hath destroyed me on every s............. Job 19:10
The wicked walk on every s...................... Ps 12:8
fear was on every s.................................. Ps 31:13
little hills rejoice on every s..................... Ps 65:12
and comfort me on every s....................... Ps 71:21
A thousand shall fall at thy s.................... Ps 91:7
The LORD is on my s.................................. Ps 118:6
been the LORD who was on our s............... Ps 124:1
been the LORD who was on our s............... Ps 124:2
on the s of their oppressors...................... Eccl 4:1
shall be nursed at thy s............................ Is 60:4
the enemy and fear is on every s............. Jer 6:25
defaming of many, fear on every s........... Jer 20:10
cry unto them, Fear is on every s............. Jer 49:29
ninety and six pomegranates on a s......... Jer 52:23
face of a lion, on the right s..................... Eze 1:10
the face of an ox on the left s................... Eze 1:10
had two, which covered on this s.............. Eze 1:23
them, which covered on this s.................. Eze 1:23
Lie thou also upon thy left s..................... Eze 4:4
them, lie again on thy right s................... Eze 4:6
turn thee from one s to another.............. Eze 4:8
that thou shalt lie upon thy s.................. Eze 4:9
with a writer's inkhorn by his s............... Eze 9:2
had the writer's inkhorn by his s............. Eze 9:3
which had the inkhorn by his s................ Eze 9:11
stood on the right s of the house............. Eze 10:3
is on the east s of the city........................ Eze 11:23
thee on every s for thy whoredom........... Eze 16:33
him on every s from the provinces........... Eze 16:33
them against thee on every s.................... Eze 23:22
I will open the s of Moab from.................. Eze 25:9

S

by the sword upon her on every s...... Eze 28:23
Because ye have thrust with a .... Eze 34:21
and swallowed you up on every s ...... Eze 36:3
and will gather them on every s........ Eze 37:21
every s to my sacrifice that I do........ Eze 39:17
on this s, and three on that s............. Eze 40:10
measure on this s and on that s........ Eze 40:10
chambers was one cubit on this s...... Eze 40:12
the space was one cubit on that s..... Eze 40:12
were six cubits on this s .... Eze 40:12
and six cubits on that s..................... Eze 40:12
the pavement by the s of the .... Eze 40:18
on this s and three on that s .... Eze 40:21
this s, and another on that s .... Eze 40:26
on this s, and on that s..................... Eze 40:34
on this s, and on that s..................... Eze 40:37
gate were two tables on this s .... Eze 40:39
and two tables on that s .... Eze 40:39
at the s without, as one goeth up ..... Eze 40:40
and on the other s, which was at ...... Eze 40:40
Four tables were on this s................. Eze 40:41
that s, by the s of the gate............... Eze 40:41
which was at the s of the north .... Eze 40:44
one at the s of the east gate .... Eze 40:44
the porch, five cubits on this s .... Eze 40:48
and five cubits on that s .... Eze 40:48
gate was three cubits on this s .... Eze 40:48
and three cubits on that s .... Eze 40:48
this s, and another on that s .... Eze 40:49
six cubits broad on the one s .... Eze 41:1
six cubits broad on the other s .... Eze 41:1
were five cubits on the one s .... Eze 41:2
and five cubits on the other s .... Eze 41:2
and the breadth of every s chamber.. Eze 41:5
round about the house on every s ..... Eze 41:6
the s chambers where three, one ...... Eze 41:6
for the s chambers round about .... Eze 41:6
still upward to the s chambers.......... Eze 41:7
the foundations of the s chambers.... Eze 41:8
was for the s chamber without .... Eze 41:9
the s chambers that were within ...... Eze 41:9
round about the house on every s ..... Eze 41:10
the doors of the s chambers were ..... Eze 41:11
on the one s and on the other s .... Eze 41:11
toward the palm tree on the one s .... Eze 41:19
the palm tree on the other s .... Eze 41:19
on the one s and on the other s .... Eze 41:26
upon the s chambers of the house,.... Eze 41:26
was the entry on the east s .... Eze 42:9
He measured the east s with the ...... Eze 42:16
He measured the north s, five .... Eze 42:17
He measured the south s, five .... Eze 42:18
He turned about to the west s .... Eze 42:19
be for the prince on the one s .... Eze 45:7
on the other s of the oblation of the. Eze 45:7
city, from the west s westward .... Eze 45:7
and from the east s eastward............ Eze 45:7
which was at the s of the gate.......... Eze 46:19
from the right s of the house .... Eze 47:1
at the south s of the altar .... Eze 47:1
ran out waters on the right s .... Eze 47:2
were very many trees on the one s.... Eze 47:7
on this s and on that s..................... Eze 47:12
of the land toward the north s.......... Eze 47:15
And this is the north s .... Eze 47:17
the east s ye shall measure from ...... Eze 47:18
And this is the east s .... Eze 47:18
And the south s southward, from .... Eze 47:19
And this is the south s southward .... Eze 47:19
The west s also shall be the .... Eze 47:20
This is the west s .... Eze 47:20
the east s unto the west s .... Eze 48:2
east s even unto the west s .... Eze 48:3
the east s unto the west s .... Eze 48:4
the east s unto the west s .... Eze 48:5
east s even unto the west s .... Eze 48:6
the east s unto the west s .... Eze 48:7
the east s unto the west s .... Eze 48:8
the east s unto the west s .... Eze 48:8
the north s four thousand and five... Eze 48:16
the south s four thousand and.......... Eze 48:16
on the east s four thousand and....... Eze 48:16
the west s four thousand and five.... Eze 48:16
be for the prince, on the one s .... Eze 48:21
the east s four thousand and............ Eze 48:23
the east s four thousand and............ Eze 48:24
the east s four thousand and............ Eze 48:25
the east s four thousand and............ Eze 48:26
the east s unto the west s .... Eze 48:27
of Gad, at the south s southward...... Eze 48:28
out of the city on the north s .... Eze 48:30
at the east s four thousand and........ Eze 48:32
at the south s four thousand and...... Eze 48:33
At the west s four thousand and...... Eze 48:34
and it raised up itself on one s .... Dan 7:5
as I was by the s of the great .... Dan 10:4
but she shall not stand on his s .... Dan 11:17
the one on this s of the bank of .... Dan 12:5
the other on that s of the bank .... Dan 12:5
that thou stoodest on the other s ..... Obad 11
and sat on the east s of the city .... Jonah 4:5
one upon the right s of the bowl....... Zec 4:3
the other upon the left s thereof....... Zec 4:3
the right s of the candlestick .... Zec 4:11
and upon the left s thereof .... Zec 4:11
off as on this s according to it.......... Zec 5:3
off as on that s according to it......... Zec 5:3
to depart unto the other s................ Mt 8:18
other s into the country of the.......... Mt 8:28
of the house, and sat by the sea s .... Mt 13:1

some seeds fell by the way s........... Mt 13:4
which received seed by the way s .... Mt 13:19
to go before him unto the other s .... Mt 14:22
were come to the other s, they .... Mt 16:5
blind men sitting by the way s......... Mt 20:30
he went forth again by the sea s ..... Mk 2:13
began again to teach by the sea s .... Mk 4:1
he sowed, some fell by the way s ..... Mk 4:4
And these are they by the way s ...... Mk 4:15
Let us pass over unto the other s..... Mk 4:35
over unto the other s of the sea........ Mk 5:1
again by ship unto the other s......... Mk 5:21
to go to the other s before unto....... Mk 6:45
again departed to the other s........... Mk 8:13
Judaea by the farther s of Jordan.... Mk 10:1
sat by the highway s begging........... Mk 10:46
young man sitting on the right s ..... Mk 16:5
right s of the altar of incense .... Lk 1:11
he sowed, some fell by the way s ..... Lk 8:5
Those by the way s are they that ..... Lk 8:12
over unto the other s of the lake ...... Lk 8:22
him, he passed by on the other s ...... Lk 10:31
him, and passed by on the other s.... Lk 10:32
man sat by the way s begging.......... Lk 18:35
round, and keep thee in on every s .. Lk 19:43
s of the sea saw that there was........ Jn 6:22
him on the other s of the sea .... Jn 6:25
others with him, on either s one...... Jn 19:18
with a spear pierced his s .... Jn 19:34
unto them his hands and his s .... Jn 20:20
and thrust my hand into his s .... Jn 20:25
thy hand, and thrust it into my s .... Jn 20:27
net on the right s of the ship........... Jn 21:6
whose house is by the sea s .... Acts 10:6
one Simon a tanner by the sea s...... Acts 10:32
and he smote Peter on the s .... Acts 12:7
went out of the city by a river s ...... Acts 16:13
We are troubled on every s 2Cor 4:8
but we were troubled on every s 2Cor 7:5
on either s of the river, was............ Rev 22:2

SIDES

the rings by the s of the ark............ Ex 25:14
shall come out of the s of it .... Ex 25:32
it shall hang over the s of the.......... Ex 26:13
for the s of the tabernacle .... Ex 26:22
of the tabernacle in the two s .... Ex 26:23
for the two s westward..................... Ex 26:27
be upon the two s of the altar .... Ex 27:7
the two s of the ephod underneath ... Ex 28:27
the s thereof round about, and the .. Ex 30:3
upon the two s of it shalt thou........ Ex 30:4
were written on both their s .... Ex 32:15
for the s of the tabernacle .... Ex 36:27
of the tabernacle in the two s .... Ex 36:28
the tabernacle for the s westward .... Ex 36:32
the rings by the s of the ark............ Ex 37:5
going out of the s thereof................ Ex 37:18
the s thereof round about, and the .. Ex 37:26
of it, upon the two s thereof .... Ex 37:27
the rings on the s of the altar .... Ex 38:7
put them on the two s of the .... Ex 38:7
in your eyes, and thorns in your s .. Num 33:55
unto you, and scourges in your s ..... Josh 23:13
they shall be as thorns in your s ..... Judg 2:3
colours of needlework on both s .... Judg 5:30
men remained in the s of the cave.... 1Sa 24:3
peace on all s round about him 1Kin 4:24
cubits on the s of the house............. 1Kin 6:16
to the s of Lebanon, and will cut...... 2Kin 19:23
on the s of the north, the city .... Ps 48:2
vine by the s of thine house............. Ps 128:3
in the s of the north......................... Is 14:13
down to hell, to the s of the pit .... Is 14:15
mountains, to the s of Lebanon........ Is 37:24
ye shall be borne upon her s............. Is 66:12
be raised from the s of the earth...... Jer 6:22
nest in the s of the hole's mouth ..... Jer 48:28
their calamity from all s thereof ...... Jer 49:32
under their wings on their four s ..... Eze 1:8
went, they went upon their four s ... Eze 1:17
went, they went upon their four s ... Eze 10:11
are set in the s of the gate............... Eze 32:23
the s of the door were five .... Eze 41:2
on the s of the porch, and upon........ Eze 42:20
He measured it by the four s............ Eze 42:20
was a place on the two s westward ... Eze 46:19
for these are his s east and west...... Eze 48:1
him that is by the s of the house...... Amos 6:10
gone down into the s of the ship ...... Jonah 1:5

SIDON (si´-don) See SIDONIANS, ZIDON.
1. Son of Canaan.
Canaan begat S his firstborn, and... Gen 10:15
2. Phoenician city north of Tyre.
of the Canaanites was from S .... Gen 10:19
you, had been done in Tyre and S..... Mt 11:21
S at the day of judgment, than .... Mt 11:22
into the coasts of Tyre and S .... Mt 15:21
and they about Tyre and S, a great.. Mk 3:8
into the borders of Tyre and S .... Mk 7:24
from the coasts of Tyre and S .... Mk 7:31
save unto Sarepta, a city of S .... Lk 4:26
from the sea coast of Tyre and S ..... Lk 6:17
works had been done in Tyre and S.. Lk 10:13
S at the judgment, than for you ...... Lk 10:14
displeased with them of Tyre and S.. Lk 12:20
And the next day we touched at S..... Acts 27:3

SIDONIANS (si-do´-ne-uns) See ZIDONIANS.
Inhabitants of Sidon.
(Which Hermon the S call Sirion...... Deut 3:9

and Mearah that is beside the S ...... Josh 13:4
Misrephoth-maim, and all the S ...... Josh 13:6
and all the Canaanites, and the S .... Judg 3:3
to hew timber like unto the S.......... 1Kin 5:6

SIEGE

life) to employ them in the s........... Deut 20:19
thy God hath given thee, in the s..... Deut 28:53
he hath nothing left him in the s ..... Deut 28:55
of all things secretly in the s .... Deut 28:57
and all Israel laid s to Gibbethon 1Kin 15:27
he himself laid s against Lachish 2Chr 32:9
ye abide in the s in Jerusalem......... 2Chr 32:10
will lay s against thee with a .... Is 29:3
the flesh of his friend in the s......... Jer 19:9
lay s against it, and build a fort...... Eze 4:2
and thou shalt lay s against it .... Eze 4:3
face toward the s of Jerusalem .... Eze 4:7
thou hast ended the days of thy s .... Eze 4:8
the days of the s are fulfilled........... Eze 5:2
he hath laid s against us................. Mic 5:1
Draw thee waters for the s .... Nah 3:14
for she is in both against Judah...... Zec 12:2

SIEVE

the nations with the s of vanity....... Is 30:28
like as corn is sifted in a s .... Amos 9:9

SIFT

to s the nations with the sieve......... Is 30:28
I will s the house of Israel .... Amos 9:9
that he may s you as wheat............. Lk 22:31

SIFTED

like as corn is s in a sieve............... Amos 9:9

SIGH

all the merryhearted do s .... Is 24:7
her priests s, her virgins are........... Lam 1:4
All her people s, they seek bread..... Lam 1:11
They have heard that I s .... Lam 1:21
the foreheads of the men that s .... Eze 9:4
S therefore, thou son of man,.......... Eze 21:6
with bitterness before their............. Eze 21:6

SIGHED

the children of Israel s by .... Ex 2:23
And looking up to heaven, he s .... Mk 7:34
he s deeply in his spirit, and........... Mk 8:12

SIGHEST

say unto thee, Wherefore s thou...... Eze 21:7

SIGHETH

yea, she s, and turneth backward..... Lam 1:8

SIGHING

For my s cometh before I eat, and.... Job 3:24
for the s of the needy, now will....... Ps 12:5
with grief, and my years with s .... Ps 31:10
Let the s of the prisoner come .... Ps 79:11
all the s thereof have I made to........ Is 21:2
and sorrow and s shall flee away..... Is 35:10
I fainted in my s, and I find no....... Jer 45:3

SIGHS

for my s are many, and my heart is.. Lam 1:22

SIGHT

tree that is pleasant to the s........... Gen 2:9
now I have found favour in thy s .... Gen 18:3
servant hath found grace in thy s ... Gen 19:19
in Abraham's s because of his son ... Gen 21:11
in thy s because of the lad.............. Gen 21:12
I may bury my dead out of my s ..... Gen 23:4
I should bury my dead out of my s .. Gen 23:8
that I may find grace in thy s .... Gen 32:5
to find grace in the s of my lord...... Gen 33:8
now I have found grace in thy s ...... Gen 33:10
me find grace in the s of my lord..... Gen 33:15
was wicked in the s of the LORD...... Gen 38:7
And Joseph found grace in his s ...... Gen 39:4
gave him favour in the s of the .... Gen 39:21
ought left in the s of my lord .... Gen 47:18
us find grace in the s of my lord ..... Gen 47:25
now I have found grace in thy s ...... Gen 47:29
turn aside, and see this great s .... Ex 3:3
favour in the s of the Egyptians...... Ex 3:21
the signs in the s of the people........ Ex 4:30
in the s of Pharaoh, and in the .... Ex 7:20
and in the s of his servants............. Ex 7:20
the heaven in the s of Pharaoh .... Ex 9:8
favour in the s of the Egyptians...... Ex 11:3
in the s of Pharaoh's servants,........ Ex 11:3
and in the s of the people .... Ex 11:3
favour in the s of the Egyptians...... Ex 12:36
do that which is right in his s .... Ex 15:26
Moses did so in the s of the .... Ex 17:6
s of all the people upon mount .... Ex 19:11
the s of the glory of the LORD......... Ex 24:17
hast also found grace in my s .... Ex 33:12
if I have found grace in thy s .... Ex 33:13
that I may find grace in thy s .... Ex 33:13
people have found grace in thy s .... Ex 33:13
for thou hast found grace in my s ... Ex 33:17
now I have found grace in thy s ...... Ex 34:9
in the s of all the house of.............. Ex 40:38
accepted in the s of the LORD.......... Lev 1:3
the plague in s be deeper than......... Lev 13:3
in s be not deeper than the skin,..... Lev 13:4
the plague in his s be at a stay .... Lev 13:5
it be in s lower than the skin.......... Lev 13:20
it be in s deeper than the skin .... Lev 13:25
if it be in s deeper than the .... Lev 13:30
it be not in s deeper than the.......... Lev 13:31

the scall be not in s deeper than .... Lev 13:32
nor be in s deeper than the skin........... Lev 13:34
the scall be in his s at a stay .... Lev 13:37
which in s are lower than the .... Lev 14:37
cut off in the s of their people .... Lev 20:17
with rigour over him in thy s .... Lev 25:53
of Egypt in the s of the heathen .... Lev 26:45
in the s of Aaron their father........... Num 3:4
have I not found favour in thy s........... Num 11:11
if I have found favour in thy s........... Num 11:15
were in our own s as grasshoppers........... Num 13:33
and so we were in their s .... Num 13:33
shall burn the heifer in his s .... Num 19:5
in the s of all the congregation .... Num 20:27
woman in the s of Moses, and in .... Num 25:6
in the s of all the congregation .... Num 25:6
and give him a charge in their s........... Num 27:19
if we have found grace in thy s........... Num 32:5
done evil in the s of the LORD........... Num 32:13
in the s of all the Egyptians .... Num 33:3
of the nations, which .... Deut 4:6
evil in the s of the LORD thy God .... Deut 4:25
brought thee out in his s with .... Deut 4:37
and good in the s of the LORD .... Deut 6:18
wickedly in the s of the LORD........... Deut 9:18
is right in the s of the LORD........... Deut 12:25
right in the s of the LORD thy .... Deut 12:28
in the s of the LORD thy God .... Deut 17:2
is right in the s of the LORD........... Deut 21:9
s of thine eyes which thou shalt .... Deut 28:34
for the s of thine eyes which .... Deut 28:67
unto him in the s of all Israel........... Deut 31:7
will do evil in the s of the LORD .... Deut 31:29
shewed in the s of all Israel........... Deut 34:12
then in the s of all Israel........... Josh 3:7
Joshua in the s of all Israel........... Josh 4:14
and he said in the s of Israel........... Josh 10:12
and drive them from out of your s........... Josh 23:5
did those great signs in our s........... Josh 24:17
did evil in the s of the LORD........... Judg 2:11
did evil in the s of the LORD........... Judg 3:7
evil again in the s of the LORD........... Judg 3:12
done evil in the s of the LORD........... Judg 4:1
did evil in the s of the LORD........... Judg 6:1
now I have found grace in thy s........... Judg 6:17
of the LORD departed out of his s........... Judg 6:21
evil again in the s of the LORD........... Judg 10:6
evil again in the s of the LORD........... Judg 13:1
him in whose s I shall find grace........... Ruth 2:13
said, Let me find favour in thy s........... 1Sa 1:18
handmaid find grace in thy s........... 1Sa 1:18
ye have done in the s of the LORD........... 1Sa 12:17
thou wast little in thine own s........... 1Sa 15:17
didst evil in the s of the LORD........... 1Sa 15:19
for he hath found favour in my s........... 1Sa 16:22
in the s of all the people 1Sa 18:5
also in the s of Saul's servants........... 1Sa 18:5
me in the host is good in my s........... 1Sa 29:6
I know that thou art good in my s........... 1Sa 29:9
and will be base in mine own s........... 2Sa 6:22
all thine enemies out of thy s........... 2Sa 7:9
was yet a small thing in thy s........... 2Sa 7:19
of the LORD, to do evil in his s........... 2Sa 12:9
thy wives in the s of this sun........... 2Sa 12:11
meat, and dress the meat in my s........... 2Sa 13:5
make me a couple of cakes in my s........... 2Sa 13:6
it, and made cakes in his s........... 2Sa 13:8
that I have found grace in thy s........... 2Sa 14:22
that I may find grace in thy s........... 2Sa 16:4
concubines in the s of all Israel........... 2Sa 16:22
to my cleanness in his eye s........... 2Sa 22:25
s to sit on the throne of Israel........... 1Kin 8:25
my name, will I cast out of my s........... 1Kin 9:7
did evil in the s of the LORD........... 1Kin 11:6
great favour in the s of Pharaoh........... 1Kin 11:19
ways, and do that is right in my s........... 1Kin 11:38
did evil in the s of the LORD........... 1Kin 14:22
he did evil in the s of the LORD........... 1Kin 15:26
he did evil in the s of the LORD........... 1Kin 15:34
that he did in the s of the LORD........... 1Kin 16:7
doing evil in the s of the LORD........... 1Kin 16:19
s of the LORD above all that were........... 1Kin 16:30
to work evil in the s of the LORD........... 1Kin 21:25
wickedness in the s of the LORD........... 1Kin 21:25
he did evil in the s of the LORD........... 1Kin 22:52
servants, be precious in thy s........... 2Kin 1:13
my life now be precious in thy s........... 2Kin 1:14
wrought evil in the s of the LORD........... 2Kin 3:2
light thing in the s of the LORD........... 2Kin 3:18
he did evil in the s of the LORD........... 2Kin 8:18
and did evil in the s of the LORD........... 2Kin 8:27
in the s of the LORD all his days........... 2Kin 12:2
did evil in the s of the LORD........... 2Kin 13:2
was evil in the s of the LORD........... 2Kin 13:11
was right in the s of the LORD........... 2Kin 14:3
was evil in the s of the LORD........... 2Kin 14:24
was right in the s of the LORD........... 2Kin 15:3
was evil in the s of the LORD........... 2Kin 15:9
was evil in the s of the LORD........... 2Kin 15:18
was evil in the s of the LORD........... 2Kin 15:24
was evil in the s of the LORD........... 2Kin 15:28
was right in the s of the LORD........... 2Kin 15:34
in the s of the LORD his God........... 2Kin 16:2
was evil in the s of the LORD........... 2Kin 17:2
to do evil in the s of the LORD........... 2Kin 17:17
and removed them out of his s........... 2Kin 17:18
he had cast them out of his s........... 2Kin 17:20
LORD removed Israel out of his s........... 2Kin 17:23
was right in the s of the LORD........... 2Kin 18:3

done that which is good in thy s........... 2Kin 20:3
was evil in the s of the LORD........... 2Kin 21:2
wickedness in the s of the LORD........... 2Kin 21:6
done that which was evil in my s........... 2Kin 21:15
was evil in the s of the LORD........... 2Kin 21:16
was evil in the s of the LORD........... 2Kin 21:20
was right in the s of the LORD........... 2Kin 22:2
remove Judah also out of my s........... 2Kin 23:27
was evil in the s of the LORD........... 2Kin 23:32
was evil in the s of the LORD........... 2Kin 23:37
to remove them out of his s........... 2Kin 24:3
was evil in the s of the LORD........... 2Kin 24:9
was evil in the s of the LORD........... 2Kin 24:19
do that which is good in his s........... 1Chr 2:3
much blood upon the earth in my s........... 1Chr 22:8
in the s of all Israel........... 1Chr 28:8
in the s of all Israel, and the........... 1Chr 29:25
in my s to sit upon the throne of........... 2Chr 6:16
name, will I cast out of my s........... 2Chr 7:20
was right in the s of the LORD........... 2Chr 20:32
Wherefore he did evil in the s of........... 2Chr 22:4
the s of the LORD all the days of........... 2Chr 24:2
was right in the s of the LORD........... 2Chr 25:2
was right in the s of the LORD........... 2Chr 26:4
was right in the s of the LORD........... 2Chr 27:2
was right in the s of the LORD........... 2Chr 28:1
s of all nations from thenceforth........... 2Chr 32:23
was evil in the s of the LORD........... 2Chr 33:2
much evil in the s of the LORD........... 2Chr 33:6
was evil in the s of the LORD........... 2Chr 33:22
was evil in the s of the LORD........... 2Chr 34:2
evil in the s of the LORD his God........... 2Chr 36:5
was evil in the s of the LORD........... 2Chr 36:9
evil in the s of the LORD his God........... 2Chr 36:12
in the s of the kings of Persia........... Ezr 9:9
him mercy in the s of this man........... Neh 1:11
have found favour in thy s........... Neh 2:5
the book in the s of all people........... Neh 8:5
s of all them that looked upon........... Est 2:15
favour in his s more than all........... Est 2:17
that she obtained favour in his s........... Est 5:2
found favour in the s of the king........... Est 5:8
If I have found favour in thy s........... Est 7:3
if I have found favour in his s........... Est 8:5
heavens are not clean in his s........... Job 15:15
beasts, and reputed vile in your s........... Job 18:3
I am an alien in their s........... Job 19:15
established in their s with them........... Job 21:8
the stars are not pure in his s........... Job 25:5
men in the open s of others........... Job 34:26
be cast down even at the s of him........... Job 41:9
foolish shall not stand in thy s........... Ps 5:5
the heathen be judged in thy s........... Ps 9:19
are far above out of his s........... Ps 10:5
my heart, be acceptable in thy s........... Ps 19:14
and done this evil in thy s........... Ps 51:4
shall their blood be in his s........... Ps 72:14
who may stand in thy s when once........... Ps 76:7
did he in the s of their fathers........... Ps 78:12
s by the revenging of the blood........... Ps 79:10
For a thousand years in thy s are........... Ps 90:4
shewed in the s of the heathen........... Ps 98:2
lies shall not tarry in my s........... Ps 101:7
Precious in the s of the LORD is........... Ps 116:15
for in thy s shall no man living........... Ps 143:2
is spread in the s of any bird........... Prov 1:17
understanding in the s of God........... Prov 3:4
beloved in the s of my mother........... Prov 4:3
man that is good in his s........... Eccl 2:26
Better is the s of the eyes than........... Eccl 6:9
Be not hasty to go out of his s........... Eccl 8:3
heart, and in the s of thine eyes........... Eccl 11:9
eyes, and prudent in their own s........... Is 5:21
not judge after the s of his eyes........... Is 11:3
so have we been in thy s, O LORD........... Is 26:17
done that which is good in thy s........... Is 38:3
Since thou wast precious in my s........... Is 43:4
thine abominations out of my s........... Jer 4:1
And I will cast you out of my s........... Jer 7:15
of Judah have done evil in my s........... Jer 7:30
cast them out of my s, and let........... Jer 15:1
If it do evil in my s, that it........... Jer 18:10
blot out their sin from thy s........... Jer 18:23
s of the men that go with them........... Jer 19:10
in the s of Hanameel mine uncle's........... Jer 32:12
turned, and had done right in my s........... Jer 34:15
in the s of the men of Judah........... Jer 43:9
they have done in Zion in your s........... Jer 51:24
cometh out of man, in their s........... Eze 4:12
of thee in the s of the nations........... Eze 5:8
in the s of all that pass by........... Eze 5:14
And he went in in my s........... Eze 10:2
mounted up from the earth in my s........... Eze 10:19
and remove by day in their s........... Eze 12:3
place to another place in their s........... Eze 12:3
forth thyself by day in their s........... Eze 12:4
shalt go forth at even in their s........... Eze 12:4
thou through the wall in their s........... Eze 12:5
In their s shalt thou bear it........... Eze 12:6
it upon my shoulder in their s........... Eze 12:7
upon thee in the s of all many women........... Eze 16:41
in whose s I made myself known........... Eze 20:9
in whose s I brought them out........... Eze 20:14
polluted in the s of the heathen........... Eze 20:22
in whose s I brought them forth........... Eze 20:22
lothe yourselves in your own s........... Eze 20:43
as a false divination in their s........... Eze 21:23
thyself in the s of the heathen........... Eze 22:16

s of all them that behold thee........... Eze 28:18
in them in the s of the heathen........... Eze 28:25
in your own s for your iniquities........... Eze 36:31
in the s of all that passed by........... Eze 36:34
in them in the s of many nations........... Eze 39:27
and write it in their s, that they........... Eze 43:11
the s thereof to the end of all........... Dan 4:11
the s thereof to all the earth........... Dan 4:20
away her whoredoms out of her s........... Hos 2:2
lewdness in the s of her lovers........... Hos 2:10
us up, and we shall live in his s........... Hos 6:2
my s in the bottom of the sea........... Amos 9:3
I said, I am cast out of thy s........... Jonah 2:4
evil is good in the s of the LORD........... Mal 2:17
The blind receive their s........... Mt 11:5
for so it seemed good in thy s........... Mt 11:26
immediately their eyes received s........... Mt 20:34
Lord, that I might receive my s........... Mk 10:51
And immediately he received his s........... Mk 10:52
be great in the s of the Lord........... Lk 1:15
and recovering of s to the blind........... Lk 4:18
many that were blind he gave s........... Lk 7:21
for so it seemed good in thy s........... Lk 10:21
against heaven, and in thy s........... Lk 15:21
is abomination in the s of God........... Lk 16:15
Lord, that I may receive my s........... Lk 18:41
said unto him, Receive thy s........... Lk 18:42
And immediately he received his s........... Lk 18:43
that came together to that s........... Lk 23:48
and he vanished out of their s........... Lk 24:31
I went and washed, and I received s........... Jn 9:11
him how he had received his s........... Jn 9:15
had been blind, and received his s........... Jn 9:18
of him that had received his s........... Jn 9:18
cloud received him out of their s........... Acts 1:9
man's conscience in the s of God........... Acts 4:19
wisdom in the s of Pharaoh king........... Acts 7:10
saw it, he wondered at the s........... Acts 7:31
is not right in the s of God........... Acts 8:21
And he was three days without s........... Acts 9:9
him, that he might receive his s........... Acts 9:12
that thou mightest receive thy s........... Acts 9:17
and he received s forthwith........... Acts 9:18
in remembrance in the s of God........... Acts 10:31
me, Brother Saul, receive thy s........... Acts 22:13
no flesh be justified in his s........... Rom 3:20
things honest in the s of all men........... Rom 12:17
in the s of God speak we in........... 2Cor 2:17
man's conscience in the s of God........... 2Cor 4:2
(For we walk by faith, not by s........... 2Cor 5:7
s of God might appear unto you........... 2Cor 7:12
not only in the s of the Lord........... 2Cor 8:21
but also in the s of men........... 2Cor 8:21
by the law in the s of God........... Gal 3:11
and unreproveable in his s........... Col 1:22
Jesus Christ, in the s of God........... 1Th 1:3
acceptable in the s of God our........... 1Ti 2:3
give thee charge in the s of God........... 1Ti 6:13
that is not manifest in his s........... Heb 4:13
and so terrible was the s, that........... Heb 12:21
which is wellpleasing in his s........... Heb 13:21
yourselves in the s of the Lord........... Jas 4:10
which is in the s of God of great........... 1Pet 3:4
things that are pleasing in his s........... 1Jn 3:22
in like sight an emerald........... Rev 4:3
on the earth in the s of men........... Rev 13:13
power to do in the s of the beast........... Rev 13:14

SIGHTS

and fearful s and great signs shall ..... Lk 21:11

SIGN

to the voice of the first s........... Ex 4:8
believe the voice of the latter s........... Ex 4:8
to morrow shall this s be........... Ex 8:23
it shall be for a s unto thee........... Ex 13:9
for it is a s between me and you........... Ex 31:13
It is a s between me and the........... Ex 31:17
they shall be a s unto the........... Num 16:38
and they became a s........... Num 26:10
bind them for a s upon thine hand........... Deut 6:8
bind them for a s upon your hand........... Deut 11:18
and giveth thee a s or a wonder........... Deut 13:1
the s or the wonder come to pass........... Deut 13:2
they shall be upon thee for a s........... Deut 28:46
That this may be a s among you........... Josh 4:6
then shew me a s that thou........... Judg 6:17
s between the men of Israel........... Judg 20:38
And this shall be a s unto thee........... 1Sa 2:34
and this shall be a s unto us........... 1Sa 14:10
he gave a s the same day, saying........... 1Kin 13:3
This is the s which the LORD hath........... 1Kin 13:3
according to the s which the man........... 1Kin 13:5
And this shall be a s unto thee........... 2Kin 19:29
What shall be the s that the LORD........... 2Kin 20:8
This s shalt thou have of the........... 2Kin 20:9
unto him, and he gave him a s........... 2Chr 32:24
Ask thee a s of the LORD thy God........... Is 7:11
Lord himself shall give you a s........... Is 7:14
And it shall be for a s and for a........... Is 19:20
and barefoot three years for a s........... Is 20:3
And this shall be a s unto thee........... Is 37:30
this shall be a s unto thee from........... Is 38:7
What is the s that I shall go up........... Is 38:22
for an everlasting s that shall........... Is 55:13
And I will set a s among them........... Is 66:19
Tekoa, and set up a s of fire in........... Jer 6:1
And this shall be a s unto you........... Jer 44:29
This shall be a s to the house of........... Eze 4:3
for a s unto the house of Israel........... Eze 12:6
Say, I am your s........... Eze 12:11

S

that man, and will make him a s....... Eze 14:8
to be a s between me and them,....... Eze 20:12
and they shall be a s between me... Eze 20:20
Thus Ezekiel is unto you a s........... Eze 24:24
and thou shalt be a s unto them... Eze 24:27
then shall he set up a s by it........ Eze 39:15
s the writing, that he not.............. Dan 6:8
we would see a s from thee.......... Mt 12:38
generation seeketh after a s......... Mt 12:39
there shall no s be given to it...... Mt 12:39
but the s of the prophet Jonas..... Mt 12:39
would shew them a s from heaven.. Mt 16:1
generation seeketh after a s......... Mt 16:4
there shall no s be given unto it... Mt 16:4
but the s of the prophet Jonas..... Mt 16:4
what shall the s be of thy coming... Mt 24:3
then shall appear the s of the...... Mt 24:30
that betrayed him gave them a s.. Mt 26:48
seeking of him a s from heaven.... Mk 8:11
this generation seek after a s....... Mk 8:12
There shall no s be given unto..... Mk 8:12
what shall be the s when all......... Mk 13:4
And this shall be a s unto you...... Lk 2:12
for a s which shall be spoken........ Lk 2:34
sought of him a s from heaven...... Lk 11:16
they seek a s............................. Lk 11:29
and there shall no s be given it.... Lk 11:29
but the s of Jonas the prophet...... Lk 11:29
Jonas was a s unto the Ninevites.. Lk 11:30
what s wilt there be when these.... Lk 21:7
What s shewest thou unto us,....... Jn 2:18
What s shewest thou then, that we.. Jn 6:30
whose s was Castor and Pollux..... Acts 28:11
he received the s of circumcision.. Rom 4:11
For the Jews require a s, and the.. 1Cor 1:22
Wherefore tongues are for a s...... 1Cor 14:22
And I saw another s in heaven..... Rev 15:1

SIGNED
king Darius s the writing.............. Dan 6:9
knew that the writing was s........... Dan 6:10
Hast thou not s a decree, that...... Dan 6:12
nor the decree that thou hast s..... Dan 6:13

SIGNET
And she said, Thy s, and thy........ Gen 38:18
pray thee, whose are these, the s.. Gen 38:25
stone, like the engravings of a s... Ex 28:11
names, like the engravings of a s.. Ex 28:21
it, like the engravings of a s......... Ex 28:36
names, like the engravings of a s.. Ex 39:14
like to the engravings of a s......... Ex 39:30
were the s upon my right hand..... Jer 22:24
the king sealed it with his own s... Dan 6:17
and with the s of his lords............ Dan 6:17
LORD, and will make thee as a s... Hag 2:23

SIGNETS
as s are graven, with the names.... Ex 39:6

SIGNIFICATION
and none of them is without s........ 1Cor 14:10

SIGNIFIED
s by the Spirit that there should.... Acts 11:28
s it by his angel unto his............... Rev 1:1

SIGNIFIETH
s the removing of those things....... Heb 12:27

SIGNIFY
to s the accomplishment of the..... Acts 21:26
s to the chief captain that he......... Acts 23:15
not withal to s the crimes laid...... Acts 25:27
of Christ which was in them did s.. 1Pet 1:11

SIGNIFYING
s what death he should die............ Jn 12:33
s what death he should die............ Jn 18:32
s by what death he should glorify... Jn 21:19
The Holy Ghost this s, that........... Heb 9:8

SIGNS
and let them be for s, and for....... Gen 1:14
will not believe also these two s... Ex 4:9
hand, wherewith thou shalt do s... Ex 4:17
all the s which he had commanded.. Ex 4:28
did the s in the sight of the......... Ex 4:30
Pharaoh's heart, and multiply my s.. Ex 7:3
might shew these my s before him.. Ex 10:1
my s which I have done among them... Ex 10:2
for all the s which I have shewed... Num 14:11
nation, by temptations, by s......... Deut 4:34
And the LORD shewed s and wonders.. Deut 6:22
which thine eyes saw, and the s.... Deut 7:19
great terribleness, and with s....... Deut 26:8
which thine eyes have seen, the s.. Deut 29:3
In all the s and the wonders........ Deut 34:11
did those great s in our sight........ Josh 24:17
when these s are come unto thee... 1Sa 10:7
all those s came to pass that day... 1Sa 10:9
And shewedst s and wonders upon.. Neh 9:10
they set up their ensigns for s...... Ps 74:4
We see not our s........................... Ps 74:9
How he had wrought his s in Egypt... Ps 78:43
They shewed his s among them..... Ps 105:27
The LORD hath given me are for s.. Is 8:18
not dismayed at the s of heaven... Jer 10:2
Which hast set s and wonders in... Jer 32:20
out of the land of Egypt with s.... Jer 32:21
I thought it good to shew the s..... Dan 4:2
How great are his s...................... Dan 4:3
and rescueth, and he worketh s..... Dan 6:27
ye not discern the s of the times... Mt 16:3

prophets, and shall shew great s... Mt 24:24
shall rise, and shall shew s........... Mk 13:22
these s shall follow them that....... Mk 16:17
the word with s following.............. Mk 16:20
they made s to his father, how he.. Lk 1:62
great s shall there be from............ Lk 21:11
And there shall be s in the sun..... Lk 21:25
Jesus unto him, Except ye see s.... Jn 4:48
many other s truly did Jesus in.... Jn 20:30
above, and s in the earth beneath... Acts 2:19
you by miracles and wonders and s.. Acts 2:22
s were done by the apostles.......... Acts 2:43
and that s and wonders may be done.. Acts 4:30
hands of the apostles were many s.. Acts 5:12
s in the land of Egypt, and in the... Acts 7:36
the miracles and s which were done.. Acts 8:13
word of his grace, and granted s... Acts 14:3
Through mighty s and wonders, by... Rom 15:19
Truly the s of an apostle were....... 2Cor 12:12
among you in all patience, in s..... 2Cor 12:12
of Satan with all power and s....... 2Th 2:9
bearing them witness, both with s.. Heb 2:4

SIHON (si'-hon) An Amorite king.
unto S king of the Amorites.......... Num 21:21
S would not suffer Israel to pass... Num 21:23
but S gathered all his people........ Num 21:23
of S the king of the Amorites........ Num 21:26
let the city of S be built............... Num 21:27
a flame from the city of S............. Num 21:28
into captivity unto S king of the.... Num 21:29
didst unto S king of the Amorites... Num 21:34
the kingdom of S king of the........ Num 32:33
After he had slain S the king of.... Deut 1:4
into thine hand S the Amorite........ Deut 2:24
S king of Heshbon with words of... Deut 2:26
But S king of Heshbon would not... Deut 2:30
Behold, I have begun to give S...... Deut 2:31
Then S came out against us, he and.. Deut 2:32
didst unto S king of the Amorites... Deut 3:2
as we did unto S king of Heshbon,.. Deut 3:6
in the land of S king of the.......... Deut 4:46
S the king of Heshbon, and Og the.. Deut 29:7
shall do unto them as he did to S... Deut 31:4
were on the other side Jordan, S... Josh 2:10
to S king of Heshbon, and to Og... Josh 9:10
S king of the Amorites, who dwelt... Josh 12:2
the border of S king of Heshbon... Josh 12:5
all the cities of S king of the....... Josh 13:10
all the kingdom of S king of the.... Josh 13:21
and Reba, which were dukes of S.. Josh 13:21
the kingdom of S king of Heshbon... Josh 13:27
unto S king of the Amorites.......... Judg 11:19
But S trusted not Israel to pass..... Judg 11:20
but S gathered all his people........ Judg 11:20
LORD God of Israel delivered S...... Judg 11:21
in the country of S king of the...... 1Kin 4:19
so they possessed the land of S..... Neh 9:22
S king of the Amorites, and Og..... Ps 135:11
S king of the Amorites................. Ps 136:19
and a flame from the midst of S.... Jer 48:45

SIHOR (si'-hor) See SHIHOR. A river in southern Canaan.
From S, which is before Egypt,...... Josh 13:3
And by great waters the seed of S... Is 23:3
Egypt, to drink the waters of S..... Jer 2:18

SIKKUTH See MOLOCH.

SILAS (si'-las) See SILVANUS. A co-worker with Paul.
Judas surnamed Barsabas, and S.... Acts 15:22
We have sent therefore Judas and S.. Acts 15:27
And Judas and S, being prophets... Acts 15:32
it pleased S to abide there still..... Acts 15:34
And Paul chose S, and departed,.... Acts 15:40
was gone, they caught Paul and S.. Acts 16:19
S prayed, and sang praises unto.... Acts 16:25
and fell down before Paul and S.... Acts 16:29
and consorted with Paul and S....... Acts 17:4
Paul and S by night unto Berea..... Acts 17:10
but S and Timotheus abode there... Acts 17:14
a commandment unto S................. Acts 17:15
S and Timotheus were come.......... Acts 18:5

SILENCE
who said, Keep s........................... Judg 3:19
was before mine eyes, there was s.. Job 4:16
waited, and kept s at my counsel... Job 29:21
terrify me, that I kept s................ Job 31:34
Let the king lay his put to s.......... Ps 31:18
When I kept s, my bones waxed old.. Ps 32:3
keep not s.................................... Ps 35:22
I was dumb with s, I held my....... Ps 39:2
shall come, and shall not keep s.... Ps 50:3
hast thou done, and I kept s.......... Ps 50:21
Keep not thou s, O God................ Ps 83:1
my soul had almost dwelt in s....... Ps 94:17
neither any that go down into s..... Ps 115:17
a time to keep s, and a time to..... Eccl 3:7
is laid waste, and brought to s....... Is 15:1
is laid waste, and brought to s....... Is 15:1
Keep s before me, O islands......... Is 41:1
mention of the LORD, keep not s.... Is 62:6
I will not keep s, but will.............. Is 65:6
the LORD our God hath put us to s.. Jer 8:14
sit upon the ground, and keep s..... Lam 2:10
He sitteth alone and keepeth s....... Lam 3:28
prudent shall keep s in that time... Amos 5:13
they shall cast them forth with s.... Amos 8:3
all the earth keep s before him..... Hab 2:20
he had put the Sadducees to s....... Mt 22:34

Then all the multitude kept s......... Acts 15:12
And when there was made a great s.. Acts 21:40
to them, they kept the more s........ Acts 22:2
let him keep s in the church.......... 1Cor 14:28
your women keep s in the churches.. 1Cor 14:34
learn in s with all subjection........ 1Ti 2:11
over the man, but to be in s.......... 1Ti 2:12
to s the ignorance of foolish men... 1Pet 2:15
there was s in heaven about the.... Rev 8:1

SILENT
The wicked shall be s in darkness... 1Sa 2:9
in the night season, and am not s... Ps 22:2
be not s to me............................. Ps 28:1
lest, if thou be s to me, I.............. Ps 28:1
sing praise to thee, and not be s.... Ps 30:12
let them be s in the grave............. Ps 31:17
Sit thou s, and get thee into......... Is 47:5
cities, and let us be s there........... Jer 8:14
Be s, O all flesh, before the.......... Zec 2:13

SILK
her clothing is s and purple........... Prov 31:22
linen, and I covered thee with s..... Eze 16:10
raiment was of fine linen, and s.... Eze 16:13
and fine linen, and purple, and s... Rev 18:12

SILLA (sil'-lah) A place near Jerusalem.
of Millo, which goeth down to S.... 2Kin 12:20

SILLY
man, and envy slayeth the s one.... Job 5:2
is like a s dove without heart........ Hos 7:11
lead captive s women laden with.... 2Ti 3:6

SILOAH (si-lo'-ah) See SHILOAH, SILOAM. Same as Siloam.
pool of S by the king's garden....... Neh 3:15

SILOAM (si'-lo-am) See SILOAH. A pool south of Jerusalem.
upon whom the tower in S fell....... Lk 13:4
him, Go, wash in the pool of S...... Jn 9:7
said unto me, Go to the pool of S... Jn 9:11

SILVANUS (sil-va'-nus) See SILAS.
1. A co-worker with Paul.
among you by us, even by me and S.. 2Cor 1:19
Paul, and S, and Timotheus, unto.. 1Th 1:1
Paul, and S, and Timotheus, unto.. 2Th 1:1
2. A messenger for Peter.
By S, a faithful brother unto you.... 1Pet 5:12

SILVER
was very rich in cattle, in s........... Gen 13:2
brother a thousand pieces of s....... Gen 20:16
worth four hundred shekels of s..... Gen 23:15
Abraham weighed to Ephron the s.. Gen 23:16
Heth, four hundred shekels of s..... Gen 23:16
given him flocks, and herds, and s.. Gen 24:35
servant brought forth jewels of s.... Gen 24:53
for twenty pieces of s.................... Gen 37:28
And put my cup, the s cup, in the... Gen 44:2
out of thy lord's house s or gold.... Gen 44:8
he gave three hundred pieces of s... Gen 45:22
in her house, jewels of s............... Ex 3:22
of her neighbour, jewels of s......... Ex 11:2
of the Egyptians jewels of s.......... Ex 12:35
shall not make with me gods of s... Ex 20:23
their master thirty shekels of s...... Ex 21:32
gold, and s, and brass,.................. Ex 25:3
of s under the twenty boards......... Ex 26:19
And their forty sockets of s........... Ex 26:21
boards, and their sockets of s........ Ex 26:25
gold, upon the four sockets of s..... Ex 26:32
and their fillets shall be of s......... Ex 27:10
the pillars and their fillets of s...... Ex 27:11
court shall be filleted with s.......... Ex 27:17
their hooks shall be of s................ Ex 27:17
works, to work in gold, and in s.... Ex 31:4
gold, and s, and brass,.................. Ex 35:5
that did offer an offering of s........ Ex 35:24
works, to work in gold, and in s.... Ex 35:32
forty sockets of s he made under... Ex 36:24
And their forty sockets of s........... Ex 36:26
sockets were sixteen sockets of s.... Ex 36:30
cast for them four sockets of s....... Ex 36:36
and their fillets were of s.............. Ex 38:10
the pillars and their fillets of s...... Ex 38:11
the pillars and their fillets of s...... Ex 38:12
the pillars and their fillets of s...... Ex 38:17
of their chapiters of s.................... Ex 38:17
of the court were filleted with s..... Ex 38:17
their hooks of s, and the............... Ex 38:19
chapiters and their fillets of s........ Ex 38:19
the s of them that were numbered... Ex 38:25
of the hundred talents of s were.... Ex 38:27
thy estimation by shekels of s........ Lev 5:15
shall be fifty shekels of s.............. Lev 27:3
be of the male five shekels of s..... Lev 27:6
shall be three shekels of s............. Lev 27:6
be valued at fifty shekels of s....... Lev 27:16
And his offering was one s charger... Num 7:13
one s bowl of seventy shekels,....... Num 7:13
for his offering one s charger........ Num 7:19
one s bowl of seventy shekels,....... Num 7:19
His offering was one s charger...... Num 7:25
one s bowl of seventy shekels,....... Num 7:25
His offering was one s charger...... Num 7:31
one s bowl of seventy shekels,....... Num 7:31
His offering was one s charger...... Num 7:37
one s bowl of seventy shekels,....... Num 7:37
His offering was one s charger of... Num 7:43
a s bowl of seventy shekels,.......... Num 7:43

His offering was one s charger...... Num 7:49
one s bowl of seventy shekels........ Num 7:49
His offering was one s charger of.... Num 7:55
one s bowl of seventy shekels........ Num 7:55
His offering was one s charger....... Num 7:61
one s bowl of seventy shekels........ Num 7:61
His offering was one s charger....... Num 7:67
one s bowl of seventy shekels........ Num 7:67
His offering was one s charger....... Num 7:73
one s bowl of seventy shekels........ Num 7:73
His offering was one s charger....... Num 7:79
one s bowl of seventy shekels........ Num 7:79
of s, twelve s bowls.................. Num 7:84
Each charger of s weighing an........ Num 7:85
all the s vessels weighed two........ Num 7:85
Make thee two trumpets of s.......... Num 10:2
would give me his house full of s.... Num 22:18
would give me his house full of s.... Num 24:13
Only the gold, and the s, the........ Num 31:22
the s or gold that is on them........ Deut 7:25
and thy flocks multiply, and thy s... Deut 8:13
he greatly multiply to himself s..... Deut 17:17
him in an hundred shekels of s....... Deut 22:19
father fifty shekels of s............ Deut 22:29
and their idols, wood and stone, s... Deut 29:17
But all the s, and gold, and......... Josh 6:19
only the s, and the gold, and the.... Josh 6:24
and two hundred shekels of s......... Josh 7:21
of my tent, and the s under it....... Josh 7:21
in his tent, and the s under it...... Josh 7:22
Achan the son of Zerah, and the s.... Josh 7:24
and with very much cattle, with s.... Josh 22:8
for an hundred pieces of s........... Josh 24:32
ten pieces of s out of the house..... Judg 9:4
of us eleven hundred pieces of s..... Judg 16:5
of s that were taken from thee....... Judg 17:2
ears, behold, the s is with me....... Judg 17:3
shekels of s to his mother........... Judg 17:3
I had wholly dedicated the s unto.... Judg 17:3
took two hundred shekels of s........ Judg 17:4
thee ten shekels of s by the year.... Judg 17:10
and crouch to him for a piece of s... 1Sa 2:36
the fourth part of a shekel of s..... 1Sa 9:8
brought with him vessels of s........ 2Sa 8:10
unto the LORD, with the s............ 2Sa 8:11
have given thee ten shekels of s..... 2Sa 18:11
shekels of s in mine hand............ 2Sa 18:12
We will have no s nor gold of s...... 2Sa 21:4
the oxen for fifty shekels of s...... 2Sa 24:24
even the s, and the gold, and the.... 1Kin 7:51
none were of s....................... 1Kin 10:21
of Tharshish, bringing gold, and s... 1Kin 10:22
man his present, vessels of s........ 1Kin 10:25
And the king made s to be in......... 1Kin 10:27
for six hundred shekels of s......... 1Kin 10:29
into the house of the LORD, s........ 1Kin 15:15
Then Asa took all the s and the...... 1Kin 15:18
sent unto thee a present of s........ 1Kin 15:19
of Shemer two talents of s........... 1Kin 16:24
Thy s and thy gold is mine........... 1Kin 20:3
Thou shalt deliver me thy s.......... 1Kin 20:5
and for my children, and for my s.... 1Kin 20:7
else thou shalt pay a talent of s.... 1Kin 20:39
and took with him ten talents of s... 2Kin 5:5
them, I pray thee, a talent of s..... 2Kin 5:22
two talents of s in two bags......... 2Kin 5:23
sold for fourscore pieces of s....... 2Kin 6:25
dove's dung for five pieces of s..... 2Kin 6:25
eat and drink, and carried thence s.. 2Kin 7:8
the house of the LORD bowls of s..... 2Kin 12:13
vessels of gold, or vessels of s..... 2Kin 12:13
And he took all the gold and s....... 2Kin 14:14
gave Pul a thousand talents of s..... 2Kin 15:19
of each man fifty shekels of s....... 2Kin 15:20
And Ahaz took the s and the gold that 2Kin 16:8
Judah three hundred talents of s..... 2Kin 18:14
Hezekiah gave him all the s that..... 2Kin 18:15
of his precious things, the s........ 2Kin 20:13
that he may sum the s which is....... 2Kin 22:4
of an hundred talents of s........... 2Kin 23:33
And Jehoiakim gave the s and the..... 2Kin 23:35
he exacted the s and the gold of..... 2Kin 23:35
gold, in gold, and of s, in s........ 2Kin 25:15
manner of vessels of gold and s...... 1Chr 18:10
unto the LORD, with the s............ 1Chr 18:11
of s to hire them chariots.......... 1Chr 19:6
a thousand thousand talents of s..... 1Chr 22:14
Of the gold, the s, and the brass,... 1Chr 22:16
s also for all instruments of........ 1Chr 28:14
all instruments of s by weight....... 1Chr 28:14
the candlesticks of s by weight...... 1Chr 28:15
s for the tables of s................ 1Chr 28:16
likewise s by weight for every....... 1Chr 28:17
by weight for every bason of s....... 1Chr 28:17
the s for things of s................ 1Chr 29:2
own proper good, of gold and s....... 1Chr 29:3
thousand talents of refined s........ 1Chr 29:4
and the s for things of s............ 1Chr 29:5
of s ten thousand talents, and of.... 1Chr 29:7
And the king made s and gold at...... 2Chr 1:15
for six hundred shekels of s......... 2Chr 1:17
cunning to work in gold, and in s.... 2Chr 2:7
skilful to work in gold, and in s.... 2Chr 2:14
and the s, and the gold, and all the. 2Chr 5:1
brought gold and s to Solomon........ 2Chr 9:14
none were of s....................... 2Chr 9:20
of Tarshish bringing gold, and s..... 2Chr 9:21
man his present, vessels of s........ 2Chr 9:24
the king made s in Jerusalem as...... 2Chr 9:27
that he himself had dedicated, s..... 2Chr 15:18

Then Asa brought out s and gold...... 2Chr 16:2
behold, I have sent thee s........... 2Chr 16:3
presents, and tribute s.............. 2Chr 17:11
father gave them great gifts of s.... 2Chr 21:3
spoons, and vessels of gold and s.... 2Chr 24:14
for an hundred talents of s.......... 2Chr 25:6
same year an hundred talents of s.... 2Chr 27:5
he made himself treasuries for s..... 2Chr 32:27
land in an hundred talents of s...... 2Chr 36:3
men of his place help him with s..... Ezr 1:4
their hands with vessels of s........ Ezr 1:6
of gold, a thousand chargers of s.... Ezr 1:9
s basons of a second sort four....... Ezr 1:10
of s were five thousand and four..... Ezr 1:11
gold, and five thousand pound of s... Ezr 2:69
s of the house of God, which........ Ezr 5:14
s vessels of the house of God,....... Ezr 6:5
And to carry the s and gold, which... Ezr 7:15
And all the s and gold that thou..... Ezr 7:16
to do with the rest of the s......... Ezr 7:18
Unto an hundred talents of s......... Ezr 7:22
And weighed unto them the s.......... Ezr 8:25
six hundred and fifty talents of s... Ezr 8:26
s vessels an hundred talents, and.... Ezr 8:26
and the s and the gold are s......... Ezr 8:28
the Levites the weight of the s...... Ezr 8:30
Now on the fourth day was the s...... Ezr 8:33
wine, beside forty shekels of s...... Neh 5:15
and two hundred pound of s........... Neh 7:71
gold, and two thousand pounds of s... Neh 7:72
fine linen and purple to s rings..... Est 1:6
the beds were of gold and s.......... Est 1:6
pay ten thousand talents of s to..... Est 3:9
The s is given to thee, the.......... Est 3:11
who filled their houses with s....... Job 3:15
and thou shalt have plenty of s...... Job 22:25
Though he heap up s as the dust...... Job 27:16
the innocent shall divide the s...... Job 27:17
Surely there is a vein for the s..... Job 28:1
neither shall s be weighed for....... Job 28:15
as s tried in a furnace of earth,.... Ps 12:6
thou hast tried us, as s is tried.... Ps 66:10
wings of a dove covered with s....... Ps 68:13
submit himself with pieces of s...... Ps 68:30
received from him talents of s....... Ps 105:37
Their idols are s and gold,.......... Ps 115:4
me than thousands of gold and s...... Ps 119:72
The idols of the heathen are s....... Ps 135:15
If thou seekest her as s, and........ Prov 2:4
better than the merchandise of s..... Prov 3:14
Receive my instruction, and not s.... Prov 8:10
and my revenue than choice s......... Prov 8:19
tongue of the just is as choice s.... Prov 10:20
rather to be chosen than s........... Prov 16:16
The fining pot is for s, and the..... Prov 17:3
and loving favour rather than s...... Prov 22:1
Take away the dross from the s....... Prov 25:4
apples of gold in pictures of s...... Prov 25:11
a potsherd covered with s dross...... Prov 26:23
As the fining pot for s, and the..... Prov 27:21
He that loveth s shall not be........ Eccl 5:10
shall not be satisfied with s........ Eccl 5:10
Or ever the s cord be loosed, or..... Eccl 12:6
borders of gold with studs of s...... Song 1:11
He made the pillars thereof of s..... Song 3:10
will build upon her a palace of s.... Song 8:9
to bring a thousand pieces of s...... Is 7:23
Thy s is become dross, thy wine,..... Is 1:22
Their land also is full of s......... Is 2:7
a man shall cast his idols of s...... Is 2:20
them, which shall not regard s....... Is 13:17
of thy graven images of s............ Is 30:22
shall cast away his idols of s....... Is 31:7
of his precious things, the s........ Is 39:2
with gold, and casteth s chains...... Is 40:19
weigh s in the balance, and hire a... Is 46:6
have refined thee, but not with s.... Is 48:10
bring thy sons from far, their s..... Is 60:9
gold, and for iron I will bring s.... Is 60:17
Reprobate s shall men call them,..... Jer 6:30
They deck it with s and with gold.... Jer 10:4
S spread into plates is brought...... Jer 10:9
are seventeen shekels of s........... Jer 32:9
and that which was of s in s......... Jer 52:19
shall cast their s in the streets.... Eze 7:19
their s and their gold shall not..... Eze 7:19
wast thou decked with gold and s..... Eze 16:13
fair jewels of my gold and of my s... Eze 16:17
they are even the dross of s......... Eze 22:18
As they gather s, and brass, and..... Eze 22:20
As s is melted in the midst of....... Eze 22:22
with s, iron, tin, and lead, they.... Eze 27:12
gold and s into thy treasures........ Eze 28:4
to carry away s and gold, to take.... Eze 38:13
gold, his breast and his arms of s... Dan 2:32
iron, the clay, the brass, the s..... Dan 2:35
iron, the brass, the clay, the s..... Dan 2:45
s vessels which his father........... Dan 5:2
praised the gods of gold, and of s... Dan 5:4
thou hast praised the gods of s...... Dan 5:23
with their precious vessels of s..... Dan 11:8
shall he honour with gold, and s..... Dan 11:38
the treasures of gold and of s....... Dan 11:43
wine, and oil, and multiplied her s.. Hos 2:8
her to me for fifteen pieces of s.... Hos 3:2
of their s and their gold have....... Hos 8:4
the pleasant places for their s...... Hos 9:6
them molten images of their s........ Hos 13:2
Because ye have taken my s........... Joel 3:5

they sold the righteous for s........ Amos 2:6
That we may buy the poor for s....... Amos 8:6
Take ye the spoil of s, take the..... Nah 2:9
it is laid over with gold and s...... Hab 2:19
all they that bear s are cut off..... Zeph 1:11
Neither their s nor their gold....... Zeph 1:18
The s is mine, and the gold is....... Hag 2:8
Then take s and gold, and make....... Zec 6:11
heaped up s as the dust, and fine.... Zec 9:3
for my price thirty pieces of s...... Zec 11:12
And I took the thirty pieces of s.... Zec 11:13
will refine them as s is refined..... Zec 13:9
be gathered together, gold, and s.... Zec 14:14
sit as a refiner and purifier of s... Mal 3:3
and purge them as gold and s......... Mal 3:3
Provide neither gold, nor s.......... Mt 10:9
with him for thirty pieces of s...... Mt 26:15
pieces of s to the chief priests..... Mt 27:3
the pieces of s in the temple........ Mt 27:5
chief priests took the s pieces...... Mt 27:6
they took the thirty pieces of s..... Mt 27:9
what woman having ten pieces of s.... Lk 15:8
Then Peter said, S and gold have I... Acts 3:6
Godhead is like unto gold, or s...... Acts 17:29
it fifty thousand pieces of s........ Acts 19:19
which made s shrines for Diana,...... Acts 19:24
I have coveted no man's s............ Acts 20:33
upon this foundation gold, s......... 1Cor 3:12
not only vessels of gold and of s.... 2Ti 2:20
Your gold and s is cankered......... Jas 5:3
with corruptible things, as s........ 1Pet 1:18
devils, and idols of gold, and s..... Rev 9:20
The merchandise of gold, and s....... Rev 18:12

SILVERLINGS
a thousand vines at a thousand s..... Is 7:23

SILVERSMITH
certain man named Demetrius, a s..... Acts 19:24

SIMEON (sim'-e-un) See SHIMEON, SIMEONITES,
Simon.
1. A son of Jacob.
and she called his name S........... Gen 29:33
that two of the sons of Jacob, S..... Gen 34:25
And Jacob said to S and Levi, Ye..... Gen 34:30
Reuben, Jacob's firstborn, and S..... Gen 42:24
with them, and took from them S...... Gen 42:24
S is not, and ye will take........... Gen 42:36
he brought S out unto them.......... Gen 43:23
And the sons of S.................... Gen 46:10
as Reuben and S, they shall be....... Gen 48:5
S and Levi are brethren.............. Gen 49:5
Reuben, S, Levi, and Judah,.......... Ex 1:2
And the sons of S.................... Ex 6:15
these are the families of S.......... Ex 6:15
2. Descendants of Simeon 1 and their land.
of S.................................Num 1:6
Of the children of S, by their....... Num 1:22
of them, even of the tribe of S...... Num 1:23
by him shall be the tribe of S....... Num 2:12
S shall be Shelumiel the son of...... Num 2:12
prince of the children of S.......... Num 7:36
Of S was Shelumiel the son of........ Num 10:19
Of the tribe of S, Shaphat the....... Num 13:5
The sons of S after their............ Num 26:12
of the tribe of the children of S.... Num 34:20
S, and Levi, and Judah, and Issachar. Deut 27:12
And the second lot came forth to S... Josh 19:1
of S according to their families..... Josh 19:1
of S according to their families..... Josh 19:8
inheritance of the children of S..... Josh 19:9
therefore the children of S had...... Josh 19:9
Judah, and out of the tribe of S..... Josh 21:4
of the tribe of the children of S.... Josh 21:9
And Judah said unto S his brother.... Judg 1:3
So S went with him................... Judg 1:3
and Judah went with S his brother.... Judg 1:17
Reuben, S, Levi, and Judah,.......... 1Chr 2:1
The sons of S were, Nemuel,.......... 1Chr 4:24
of them, even of the sons of S....... 1Chr 4:42
of the tribe of the children of S.... 1Chr 6:65
Of the children of S, mighty men..... 1Chr 12:25
Ephraim and Manasseh, and out of S... 2Chr 15:9
of Manasseh, and Ephraim, and S...... 2Chr 34:6
west side, S shall have a portion.... Eze 48:24
And by the border of S, from the..... Eze 48:25
one gate of S, one gate of........... Eze 48:33
of the tribe of S were sealed........ Rev 7:7
3. A devout man who blessed Jesus.
In Jerusalem, whose name was S....... Lk 2:25
S blessed them, and said unto Mary... Lk 2:34
father of Levi, an ancestor of Jesus.
Which was the son of S, which was.... Lk 3:30
5. A prophet of Antioch.
S that was called Niger, and......... Acts 13:1
6. Same as Simon Peter.
S hath declared how God at the....... Acts 15:14

SIMEONITES (sim'-e-un-ites) Descendants of
Simeon 1.
of a chief house among the S......... Num 25:14
These are the families of the S...... Num 26:14
of the S, Shephatiah the son of...... 1Chr 27:16

SIMILITUDE
the s of the LORD shall he behold.... Num 12:8
voice of the words, but saw no s..... Deut 4:12
for ye saw no manner of s on the..... Deut 4:15
the s of any figure, the likeness... Deut 4:16
And under it was the s of oxen....... 2Chr 4:3
the s of an ox that eateth grass..... Ps 106:20
polished after the s of a palace..... Ps 144:12

one like the *s* of the sons of men ...... Dan 10:16
the *s* of Adam's transgression .... Rom 5:14
for that after the *s* of .... Heb 7:15
which are made after the *s* of God ...... Jas 3:9

SIMILITUDES

multiplied visions, and used *s* .... Hos 12:10

SIMON (si'mun) See BAR-JONA, NIGER, PETER, SIMEON, SIMON'S, ZELOTES.

1. Same as Peter.

S called Peter, and Andrew his .... Mt 4:18
The first, *S*, who is called Peter .... Mt 10:2
S Peter answered and said, Thou .... Mt 16:16
him, Blessed art thou, *S* Bar-jona .... Mt 16:17
saying, What thinkest thou, *S* .... Mt 17:25
by the sea of Galilee, he saw *S* .... Mk 1:16
they entered into the house of *S* .... Mk 1:29
And *S* and they that were with him ...... Mk 1:36
And *S* he surnamed Peter .... Mk 3:16
sleeping, and saith unto Peter, *S* .... Mk 14:37
had left speaking, he said unto .... Lk 5:4
S answering said unto him, Master .... Lk 5:5
When *S* Peter saw it, he fell down .... Lk 5:8
which were partners with *S* .... Lk 5:10
And Jesus said unto *S*, Fear not .... Lk 5:10
S, (whom he also named Peter,) and .... Lk 6:14
And the Lord said, *S*, *S*, ... Lk 22:31
indeed, and hath appeared to *S* .... Lk 24:34
was Andrew, *S* Peter's brother .... Jn 1:40
first findeth his own brother *S* .... Jn 1:41
Thou art *S* the son of Jona .... Jn 1:42
S Peter's brother, saith unto him .... Jn 6:8
Then *S* Peter answered him, Lord, ... Jn 6:68
Then cometh he to *S* Peter .... Jn 13:6
S Peter saith unto him, Lord, not .... Jn 13:9
S Peter therefore beckoned to him ...... Jn 13:24
S Peter said unto him, Lord, ... Jn 13:36
Then *S* Peter having a sword drew ...... Jn 18:10
S Peter followed Jesus, and so did .... Jn 18:15
S Peter stood and warmed himself .... Jn 18:25
she runneth, and cometh to *S* Peter .... Jn 20:2
Then cometh *S* Peter following him .... Jn 20:6
There were together *S* Peter .... Jn 21:2
S Peter saith unto them, I go a .... Jn 21:3
Now when *S* Peter heard that it .... Jn 21:7
S Peter went up, and drew the net .... Jn 21:11
Jesus saith to *S* Peter, *S*, ... Jn 21:15
to him saith the second time, *S* .... Jn 21:16
saith unto him the third time, *S* .... Jn 21:17
men to Joppa, and call for one *S* .... Acts 10:5
And called, and asked whether *S*, ... Acts 10:18
to Joppa, and call hither *S* .... Acts 10:32
Send men to Joppa, and call for *S* ...... Acts 11:13
S Peter, a servant and an apostle 2Pet 1:1

2. A Canaanite disciple of Jesus.

the Canaanite, and Judas .... Mt 10:4
and Thaddaeus, and *S* the Canaanite, ... Mk 3:18
of Alphaeus, and *S* called Zelotes, ... Lk 6:15
S Zelotes, and Judas the brother .... Acts 1:13

3. A brother of Jesus.

brethren, James, and Joses, and *S* ...... Mt 13:55
James, and Joses, and of Juda, and *S* .... Mk 6:3

4. A leper in Bethany.

in the house of *S* the leper .... Mt 26:6
in the house of *S* the leper .... Mk 14:3

5. A Cyrenian who bore Jesus' cross.

found a man of Cyrene, *S* by name ...... Mt 27:32
and they compel one *S* a Cyrenian.... Mk 15:21
away, they laid hold upon one *S* .... Lk 23:26

6. A Pharisee.

Jesus answering said unto him, *S* .... Lk 7:40
S answered and said, I suppose .... Lk 7:43
to the woman, and said unto *S*, ... Lk 7:44

7. Father of Judas Iscariot.

of Judas Iscariot the son of *S* .... Jn 6:71
to Judas Iscariot, the son of *S*, ... Jn 13:26

8. A Samaritan sorcerer.

there was a certain man, called *S* ...... Acts 8:9
Then *S* himself believed also .... Acts 8:13
when *S* saw that through laying on .... Acts 8:18
Then answered *S*, and said, Pray ye .... Acts 8:24

9. A tanner at Joppa.

days in Joppa with one *S* a tanner .... Acts 9:43
He lodgeth with one *S* a tanner .... Acts 10:6
of one *S* a tanner by the sea side ...... Acts 10:32

SIMON'S (si'-muns)

1. Refers to Simon I.

But *S* wife's mother lay sick of a .... Mk 1:30
and entered into *S* house .... Lk 4:38
S wife's mother was taken with a.......... Lk 4:38
one of the ships, which was *S*, ... Lk 5:3

2. Refers to Simon 7.

S son, which should betray him, ... Jn 12:4
Iscariot, *S* son, to betray him .... Jn 13:2

3. Refers to Simon 9.

had made enquiry for *S* house............ Acts 10:17

SIMPLE

LORD is sure, making wise the *s* .... Ps 19:7
The LORD preserveth the *s* .... Ps 116:6
giveth understanding unto the *s* .... Ps 119:130
To give subtilty to the *s* .... Prov 1:4
How long, ye *s* ones, will ye love .... Prov 1:22
away of the *s* shall slay them .... Prov 1:32
And beheld among the *s* ones .... Prov 7:7
O ye *s*, understand wisdom .... Prov 8:5
Whoso is *s*, let him turn in.................. Prov 9:4
she is *s*, and knoweth nothing .... Prov 9:13
Whoso is *s*, let him turn in.................. Prov 9:16
The *s* believeth every word.................. Prov 14:15

The *s* inherit folly .... Prov 14:18
a scorner, and the *s* will beware.......... Prov 19:25
is punished, the *s* is made wise .... Prov 21:11
but the *s* pass on, and are .... Prov 22:3
but the *s* pass on, and are .... Prov 27:12
that erreth, and for him that is *s* .... Eze 45:20
deceive the hearts of the *s* .... Rom 16:18
is good, and *s* concerning evil .... Rom 16:19

SIMPLICITY

and they went in their *s*, and they 2Sa 15:11
ye simple ones, will ye love *s* .... Prov 1:22
that giveth, let him do it with *s* .... Rom 12:8
of our conscience, that in *s* 2Cor 1:12
from the *s* that is in Christ 2Cor 11:3

SIMRI (sim'-ri) See SHIMRI. A sanctuary servant.

S the chief, (for though he was.......... 1Chr 26:10

SIN (sin)

1. A transgression.

not well, *s* lieth at the door .... Gen 4:7
because their *s* is very grievous .... Gen 18:20
on me and on my kingdom a great *s* .... Gen 20:9
what is my *s*, that thou hast so .... Gen 31:36
wickedness, and *s* against God .... Gen 39:9
Do not *s* against the child .... Gen 42:22
of thy brethren, and their *s* .... Gen 50:17
my *s* only this once, and intreat .... Ex 10:17
before your faces, that ye *s* not .... Ex 20:20
lest they make thee *s* against me........ Ex 23:33
it is a *s* offering .... Ex 29:14
for a *s* offering for atonement .... Ex 29:36
of the *s* offering of atonements .... Ex 30:10
brought so great a *s* upon them .... Ex 32:21
people, Ye have sinned a great *s* .... Ex 32:30
make an atonement for your *s* .... Ex 32:30
this people have sinned a great *s* .... Ex 32:31
now, if thou wilt forgive their *s* .... Ex 32:32
I will visit their *s* upon them.............. Ex 32:34
iniquity and transgression and *s* .... Ex 34:7
and pardon our iniquity and our *s* ...... Ex 34:9
If a soul shall *s* through .... Lev 4:2
do *s* according to the .... Lev 4:3
according to the *s* of the people .... Lev 4:3
then let him bring for his *s* .... Lev 4:3
unto the LORD for a *s* offering .... Lev 4:8
of the bullock for the *s* offering .... Lev 4:8
of Israel *s* through ignorance .... Lev 4:13
When the *s*, which they have .... Lev 4:14
offer a young bullock for the *s* .... Lev 4:14
with the bullock for a *s* offering.......... Lev 4:20
it is a *s* offering for the .... Lev 4:21
Or if his *s*, wherein he hath .... Lev 4:23
it is a *s* offering .... Lev 4:24
of the *s* offering with his finger .... Lev 4:25
for him as concerning his *s* .... Lev 4:26
common people *s* through ignorance.... Lev 4:27
Or if his *s*, which he hath sinned .... Lev 4:28
for his *s* which he hath sinned .... Lev 4:28
upon the head of the *s* offering .... Lev 4:29
slay the *s* offering in the place .... Lev 4:29
he bring a lamb for a *s* offering.......... Lev 4:32
upon the head of the *s* offering .... Lev 4:33
slay it for a *s* offering in the .... Lev 4:33
of the *s* offering with his finger .... Lev 4:34
for his *s* that he hath committed .... Lev 4:35
And if a soul *s*, and hear the voice .... Lev 5:1
for his *s* which he hath sinned .... Lev 5:6
the goats, for a *s* offering .... Lev 5:6
for him concerning his *s* .... Lev 5:6
one for a *s* offering, and the .... Lev 5:7
which is for the *s* offering first............ Lev 5:8
sprinkle of the blood of the *s* .... Lev 5:9
it is a *s* offering .... Lev 5:9
for his *s* which he hath sinned .... Lev 5:10
of fine flour for a *s* offering .... Lev 5:11
for it is a *s* offering .... Lev 5:11
it is a *s* offering .... Lev 5:12
for him as touching his *s* that he .... Lev 5:13
a *s* through ignorance, in the holy .... Lev 5:15
And if a soul *s*, and commit any of .... Lev 5:17
If a soul *s*, and commit a trespass .... Lev 6:2
most holy, as is the *s* offering .... Lev 6:17
This is the law of the *s* offering.......... Lev 6:25
offering is killed shall the *s* .... Lev 6:25
offereth it for a shall eat it .... Lev 6:26
no *s* offering, whereof any of the ...... Lev 6:30
As the *s* offering is, so is the .... Lev 7:7
of the *s* offering, and of the .... Lev 7:37
and a bullock for the *s* offering .... Lev 8:2
the bullock for the *s* offering.............. Lev 8:14
of the bullock for the *s* offering .... Lev 8:14
a young calf for a *s* offering .... Lev 9:2
kid of the goats for a *s* offering .... Lev 9:3
altar, and offer thy *s* offering .... Lev 9:7
slew the calf of the *s* offering .... Lev 9:8
above the liver of the *s* offering .... Lev 9:10
which was the *s* offering for the .... Lev 9:15
and slew it, and offered it for *s* .... Lev 9:15
from offering of the *s* offering .... Lev 9:15
sought the goat of the *s* offering .... Lev 10:16
the *s* offering in the holy place .... Lev 10:17
they offered their *s* offering .... Lev 10:19
I had eaten the *s* offering to day .... Lev 10:19
for a *s* offering, unto the door............ Lev 12:6
and the other for a *s* offering .... Lev 12:8
he shall kill the *s* offering .... Lev 14:13
for as the *s* offering is, the .... Lev 14:13
priest shall offer the *s* offering .... Lev 14:19
and the one shall be a *s* offering .... Lev 14:22

to get, the one for a *s* offering .... Lev 14:31
them, the one for a *s* offering .... Lev 15:15
offer the one for a *s* offering .... Lev 15:30
a young bullock for a *s* offering .... Lev 16:3
of the goats for a *s* offering .... Lev 16:5
his bullock of the *s* offering................ Lev 16:6
and offer him for a *s* offering .... Lev 16:9
the bullock of the *s* offering................ Lev 16:11
s offering which is for himself .... Lev 16:11
kill the goat of the *s* offering .... Lev 16:15
the fat of the *s* offering shall .... Lev 16:25
And the bullock for the *s* offering ...... Lev 16:27
and the goat for the *s* offering .... Lev 16:27
and not suffer *s* upon him.................. Lev 19:17
LORD for his *s* which he hath done .... Lev 19:22
the *s* which he hath done shall be .... Lev 19:22
they shall bear their *s* .... Lev 20:20
lest they bear *s* for it, and die .... Num 22:9
kid of the goats for a *s* offering.......... Lev 23:19
curseth his God shall bear his *s* .... Lev 24:15
commit any *s* that men commit .... Num 5:6
their *s* which they have done.............. Num 5:7
offer the one for a *s* offering .... Num 6:11
without blemish for a *s* offering.......... Num 6:14
and shall offer his *s* offering .... Num 6:16
kid of the goats for a *s* offering .... Num 7:16
kid of the goats for a *s* offering .... Num 7:22
kid of the goats for a *s* offering .... Num 7:28
kid of the goats for a *s* offering .... Num 7:34
kid of the goats for a *s* offering .... Num 7:40
kid of the goats for a *s* offering .... Num 7:46
kid of the goats for a *s* offering .... Num 7:52
kid of the goats for a *s* offering .... Num 7:58
kid of the goats for a *s* offering .... Num 7:64
kid of the goats for a *s* offering .... Num 7:70
kid of the goats for a *s* offering .... Num 7:76
kid of the goats for a *s* offering .... Num 7:82
the goats for a *s* offering twelve .... Num 7:87
shalt thou take for a *s* offering .... Num 8:8
offer the one for a *s* offering .... Num 8:12
season, that man shall bear his *s* ...... Num 9:13
thee, lay not the *s* upon us.................. Num 12:11
kid of the goats for a *s* offering .... Num 15:24
their *s* offering before the LORD,........ Num 15:25
if any soul *s* through ignorance, ... Num 15:27
the first year for a *s* offering .... Num 15:27
of all flesh, shall one man *s* .... Num 16:22
every *s* offering of theirs, and............ Num 18:9
congregation, lest they bear *s* .... Num 18:22
shall bear no *s* by reason of it............ Num 18:32
it is a purification for *s* .... Num 19:9
heifer of purification for *s* .... Num 19:17
but died in his own *s*, and had no...... Num 27:3
one kid of the goats for a *s* .... Num 28:15
And one goat for a *s* offering.............. Num 28:22
kid of the goats for a *s* offering .... Num 29:5
kid of the goats for a *s* offering .... Num 29:11
beside the *s* offering of .... Num 29:11
kid of the goats for a *s* offering .... Num 29:16
kid of the goats for a *s* offering .... Num 29:19
And one goat for a *s* offering .... Num 29:22
kid of the goats for a *s* offering .... Num 29:25
And one goat for a *s* offering .... Num 29:28
And one goat for a *s* offering .... Num 29:31
And one goat for a *s* offering .... Num 29:34
And one goat for a *s* offering .... Num 29:38
be sure your *s* will find you out .... Num 32:23
And I took your *s*, the calf which........ Deut 9:21
their wickedness, nor to their *s* .... Deut 9:27
thee, and it be *s* unto thee.................. Deut 15:9
for any iniquity, or for any *s* .... Deut 19:15
in any *s* that he sinneth .... Deut 19:15
so should ye *s* against the LORD.......... Deut 20:18
committed a *s* worthy of death .... Deut 21:22
the damsel no *s* worthy of death .... Deut 22:26
and it would be *s* in thee .... Deut 23:21
to vow, it shall be no *s* in thee .... Deut 23:22
shalt not cause the land to *s* .... Deut 24:4
the LORD, and it be *s* unto thee .... Deut 24:15
be put to death for his own *s* .... Deut 24:16
Wherefore the *s* of the young men 1Sa 2:17
if one man *s* against another, the 1Sa 2:25
but if a man *s* against the LORD, ... 1Sa 2:25
God forbid that I should *s* 1Sa 12:23
the people *s* against the LORD, in 1Sa 14:33
s not against the LORD in eating.......... 1Sa 14:34
see wherein this *s* hath been this 1Sa 14:38
is as the *s* of witchcraft 1Sa 15:23
I pray thee, pardon my *s* 1Sa 15:25
Let not the king *s* against his.............. 1Sa 19:4
thou *s* against innocent blood............ 1Sa 19:5
what is my *s* before my father,.......... 1Sa 20:1
The LORD also hath put away thy *s* 2Sa 12:13
forgive the *s* of thy people 1Kin 8:34
thy name, and turn from their *s* 1Kin 8:35
forgive the *s* of thy servants, and...... 1Kin 8:36
If they *s* against thee, (for 1Kin 8:46
And this thing became a *s* 1Kin 12:30
this thing became a *s* unto the 1Kin 13:34
the sins of Jeroboam, who did *s* 1Kin 14:16
and who made Israel to *s* 1Kin 14:16
in his *s* wherewith he made 1Kin 14:16
wherewith he made Israel to *s* 1Kin 15:30
sinned, and which he made Israel *s* 1Kin 15:34
in his *s* wherewith he made Israel 1Kin 16:13
wherewith he made Israel to *s* 1Kin 16:19
hast made my people Israel to *s* 1Kin 16:2
and by which they made Israel to *s* 1Kin 16:13
in his *s* which he did, to make 1Kin 16:19
which he did, to make Israel to *s* 1Kin 16:19

SINA (continued)

in his s wherewith he made Israel 1Kin 16:26
wherewith he made Israel to s 1Kin 16:26
me to call my s to remembrance 1Kin 17:18
me to anger, and made Israel to s 1Kin 21:22
of Nebat, who made Israel to s 1Kin 22:52
of Nebat, which made Israel to s 2Kin 3:3
of Nebat, who made Israel to s 2Kin 10:29
Jeroboam, which made Israel to s 2Kin 10:31
s money was not brought into the 2Kin 12:16
of Nebat, which made Israel to s 2Kin 13:2
Jeroboam, who made israel s 2Kin 13:6
son of Nebat, which made Israel s 2Kin 13:11
be put to death for his own s 2Kin 14:6
of Nebat, who made Israel to s 2Kin 14:24
of Nebat, who made Israel to s 2Kin 15:9
of Nebat, who made Israel to s 2Kin 15:18
of Nebat, who made Israel to s 2Kin 15:24
of Nebat, who made Israel to s 2Kin 15:28
Lord, and made them s 2Kin 17:21
a great s 2Kin 17:21
Judah also to s with his idols 2Kin 21:11
beside his s wherewith he made 2Kin 21:16
wherewith he made Judah to s 2Kin 21:16
his s that he sinned, are they 2Kin 21:17
of Nebat, who made Israel to s 2Kin 23:15
If a man s against his neighbour,.......... 2Chr 6:22
forgive the s of thy people 2Chr 6:25
thy name, and turn from their s 2Chr 6:26
forgive the s of thy servants, and 2Chr 6:27
If they s against thee, (for 2Chr 6:36
heaven, and will forgive their s 2Chr 7:14
every man shall die for his own s 2Chr 25:4
for a s offering for the kingdom, ... 2Chr 29:21
the s offering before the king,............ 2Chr 29:23
the s offering should be made for 2Chr 29:24
intreated of him, and all his s 2Chr 33:19
for a s offering for all Israel, ... Ezr 6:17
twelve he goats for a s offering........... Ezr 8:35
let not their s be blotted out,............. Neh 4:5
should be afraid, and do so, and s .... Neh 6:13
the s offerings to make an .... Neh 10:33
king of Israel s by these things,........... Neh 13:26
did outlandish women cause to s .... Neh 13:26
this did not Job s with his lips............ Job 2:10
thy habitation, and shalt not s .... Job 5:24
iniquity, and searchest after my s .... Job 10:6
If I s, then thou markest me, and .... Job 10:14
to know my transgression and my s .... Job 13:23
dost thou not watch over my s .... Job 14:16
are full of the s of his youth .... Job 20:11
have I suffered my mouth to s by .... Job 31:30
he asketh rebellion unto his s .... Job 34:37
have, if I be cleansed from my s .... Job 35:3
Stand in awe, and s not .... Ps 4:4
is forgiven, whose s is covered............ Ps 32:1
I acknowledged my s unto thee........... Ps 32:5
forgavest the iniquity of my s .... Ps 32:5
rest in my bones because of my s .... Ps 38:3
I will be sorry for my s .... Ps 38:18
that I s not with my tongue .... Ps 39:1
s offering hast thou not required .... Ps 40:6
iniquity, and cleanse me from my s .... Ps 51:2
and my s is ever before me .... Ps 51:3
in s did my mother conceive me .... Ps 51:5
my transgression, nor for my s .... Ps 59:3
For the s of their mouth and the .... Ps 59:12
thou hast covered all their s .... Ps 85:2
and let his prayer become s .... Ps 109:7
let not the s of his mother be .... Ps 109:14
that I might not s against thee .... Ps 119:11
the fruit of the wicked to s .... Prov 10:16
of words there wanteth not s .... Prov 10:19
Fools make a mock at s .... Prov 14:9
but s is a reproach to any people .... Prov 14:34
heart clean, I am pure from my s .... Prov 20:9
the plowing of the wicked, is s .... Prov 21:4
The thought of foolishness is s .... Prov 24:9
thy mouth to cause thy flesh to s .... Eccl 5:6
and they declare their s as Sodom .... Is 3:9
s as it were with a cart rope.............. Is 5:18
is taken away, and thy s purged........... Is 6:7
all the fruit to take away his s .... Is 27:9
that they may add s to s .... Is 30:1
hands have made upon you for a s .... Is 31:7
make his soul an offering for s .... Is 53:10
and he bare the s of many, and made ..... Is 53:12
or what is our s that we have .... Jer 16:10
their iniquity and their s double .... Jer 16:18
The s of Judah is written with a .... Jer 17:1
spoil, and thy high places for s .... Jer 17:3
blot out their s from thy sight............ Jer 18:23
I will remember their s no more .... Jer 31:34
abomination, to cause Judah to s .... Jer 32:35
forgive their iniquity and their s .... Jer 36:3
their land was filled with s .... Jer 51:5
the punishment of the s of Sodom .... Lam 4:6
warning, he shall die in his s .... Eze 3:20
s not, and he doth not .... Eze 3:21
in his s that he hath sinned, in .... Eze 18:24
if he turn from his s, and do that .... Eze 33:14
the s offering and the trespass .... Eze 40:39
the s offering, and the trespass .... Eze 42:13
a young bullock for a s offering .... Eze 43:19
bullock also of the s offering............. Eze 43:21
without blemish for a s offering .... Eze 43:22
every day a goat for a s offering .... Eze 43:25
he shall offer his s offering,.............. Eze 44:27
the s offering, and the trespass .... Eze 44:29
shall prepare the s offering............... Eze 45:17
of the blood of the s offering .... Eze 45:19

land a bullock for a s offering............. Eze 45:22
the goats daily for a s offering .... Eze 45:23
days, according to the s offering .... Eze 45:25
the s offering, where they shall .... Eze 46:20
and praying, and confessing my s .... Dan 9:20
the s of my people Israel, and .... Dan 9:20
They eat up the s of my people .... Hos 4:8
hath made many altars to s .... Hos 8:11
altars shall be unto him to s .... Hos 8:11
the s of Israel, shall be .... Hos 12:8
none iniquity in me that were s .... Hos 12:8
And now they s more and more, and...... Hos 13:2
his s is hid............................... Hos 13:12
that swear by the s of Samaria .... Amos 8:14
of the s to the daughter of Zion .... Mic 1:13
transgression, and to Israel his s .... Mic 3:8
of my body for the s of my soul .... Mic 6:7
inhabitants of Jerusalem for s .... Zec 13:1
I say unto you, All manner of s .... Mt 12:31
oft shall my brother s against me .... Mt 18:21
taketh away the s of the world .... Jn 1:29
s no more, lest a worse thing............. Jn 5:14
He that is without s among you .... Jn 8:7
go, and s no more .... Jn 8:11
Whosoever committeth s is the .... Jn 8:34
is the servant of s .... Jn 8:34
Which of you convinceth me of s .... Jn 8:46
him, saying, Master, who did s .... Jn 9:2
were blind, ye should have no s .... Jn 9:41
therefore your s remaineth .... Jn 9:41
unto them, they had not had s .... Jn 15:22
they have no cloke for their s .... Jn 15:22
other man did, they had not had s .... Jn 15:24
he will reprove the world of s .... Jn 16:8
Of s, because they believe not on .... Jn 16:9
me unto thee hath the greater s .... Jn 19:11
lay not this s to their charge .... Acts 7:60
that they are all under s .... Rom 3:9
by the law is the knowledge of s .... Rom 3:20
whom the Lord will not impute s .... Rom 4:8
as by one man s entered into the .... Rom 5:12
into the world, and death by s .... Rom 5:12
until the law s was in the world .... Rom 5:13
but s is not imputed when there .... Rom 5:13
But where s abounded, grace did .... Rom 5:20
That as s hath reigned unto death .... Rom 5:21
Shall we continue in s, that .... Rom 6:1
How shall we, that are dead to s .... Rom 6:2
the body of s might be .... Rom 6:6
henceforth we should not serve s .... Rom 6:6
he that is dead is freed from s .... Rom 6:7
that he died, he died unto s once .... Rom 6:10
to be dead indeed unto s, but .... Rom 6:11
Let not s therefore reign in your .... Rom 6:12
of unrighteousness unto s .... Rom 6:13
For s shall not have dominion............ Rom 6:14
shall we s, because we are not........... Rom 6:15
whether of s unto death, or of .... Rom 6:16
that ye were the servants of s .... Rom 6:17
Being then made free from s .... Rom 6:18
when ye were the servants of s .... Rom 6:20
But now being made free from s .... Rom 6:22
For the wages of s is death .... Rom 6:23
Is the law s .... Rom 7:7
Nay, I had not known s, but by .... Rom 7:7
But s, taking occasion by the .... Rom 7:8
For without the law s was dead .... Rom 7:8
came, s revived, and I died .... Rom 7:9
For s, taking occasion by the .... Rom 7:11
But s, that it might appear s,........... Rom 7:13
by the commandment might............ Rom 7:13
but I am carnal, sold under s .... Rom 7:14
but s that dwelleth in me .... Rom 7:17
but s that dwelleth in me .... Rom 7:20
law of s which is in my members .... Rom 7:23
but with the flesh the law of s .... Rom 7:25
made me free from the law of s .... Rom 8:2
for s, condemned s in the flesh .... Rom 8:3
the body is dead because of s .... Rom 8:10
whatsoever is not of faith is s .... Rom 14:23
Every s that a man doeth is 1Cor 6:18
But when ye s against the 1Cor 8:12
conscience, ye s against Christ 1Cor 8:12
Awake to righteousness, and s not 1Cor 15:34
The sting of death is s 1Cor 15:56
and the strength of s is the law 1Cor 15:56
to be s for us, who knew no s 2Cor 5:21
Christ the minister of s .... Gal 2:17
hath concluded all under s .... Gal 3:22
Be ye angry, and s not .... Eph 4:26
and that man of s be revealed 2Th 2:3
Them that s rebuke before all 1Ti 5:20
through the deceitfulness of s .... Heb 3:13
like as we are, yet without s .... Heb 4:15
by the sacrifice of himself............ Heb 9:26
time without s unto salvation .... Heb 9:28
sacrifices for s thou hast not .... Heb 10:6
Offering for s thou wouldest not, ... Heb 10:8
there is no more offering for s .... Heb 10:18
For if we s wilfully after that .... Heb 10:26
the pleasures of s for a season ...... Heb 11:25
the s which doth so easily beset ..... Heb 12:1
unto blood, striving against s .... Heb 12:4
by the high priest for s, are .... Heb 13:11
conceived, it bringeth forth s .... Jas 1:15
and s, when it is finished,........... Jas 1:15
respect to persons, ye commit s .... Jas 2:9
and doeth it not, to him it is s ...... Jas 4:17
Who did no s, neither was guile 1Pet 2:22
in the flesh hath ceased from s 1Pet 4:1

and that cannot cease from s........... 2Pet 2:14
his Son cleanseth us from all s 1Jn 1:7
If we say that we have no s 1Jn 1:8
write I unto you, that ye s not 1Jn 2:1
And if any man s, we have an 1Jn 2:1
Whosoever committeth s 1Jn 3:4
for s is the transgression of the 1Jn 3:4
and in him is no s 1Jn 3:5
that committeth s is of the devil 1Jn 3:8
is born of God doth not commit s 1Jn 3:9
and he cannot s, because he is 1Jn 3:9
a s s which is not unto death 1Jn 5:16
for them that s not unto death 1Jn 5:16
There is a s unto death 1Jn 5:16
All unrighteousness is s 1Jn 5:17
there is a s not unto death 1Jn 5:17

2. Eastern border of Egypt.

came unto the wilderness of S........... Ex 16:1
from the wilderness of S, after .... Num 33:11
encamped in the wilderness of S .... Num 33:11
out of the wilderness of S .... Num 33:12

SINA (si'-nah) See SINAI. *Greek form of Sinai.*

him in the wilderness of mount S........ Acts 7:30
which spake to him in the mount S....... Acts 7:38

SINAI (si'-nahee) See HOREB, SINA.
Mountainous district in the southern Sinai peninsula.

Sin, which is between Elim and S .... Ex 16:1
they into the wilderness of S .... Ex 19:1
and were come to the desert of S .... Ex 19:2
of all the people upon mount S .... Ex 19:11
mount S was altogether on a smoke..... Ex 19:18
the Lord came down upon mount S ...... Ex 19:20
people cannot come up to mount S ...... Ex 19:23
of the Lord abode upon mount S .... Ex 24:16
communing with him upon mount S ...... Ex 31:18
up in the morning unto mount S .... Ex 34:2
morning, and went up unto mount S .... Ex 34:4
mount S with the two tables of .... Ex 34:29
had spoken with him in mount S .... Ex 34:32
Lord commanded Moses in mount S ..... Lev 7:38
the Lord, in the wilderness of S .... Lev 7:38
Lord spake unto Moses in mount S ..... Lev 25:1
in mount S by the hand of Moses........ Lev 26:46
the children of Israel in mount S ...... Lev 27:34
unto Moses in the wilderness of S ..... Num 1:1
them in the wilderness of S .... Num 1:19
Lord spake with Moses in mount S ..... Num 3:1
the Lord, in the wilderness of S ...... Num 3:4
unto Moses in the wilderness of S .... Num 3:14
the Lord, in the wilderness of S ...... Num 9:1
at even in the wilderness of S .... Num 9:5
out of the wilderness of S .... Num 10:12
of Israel in the wilderness of S ...... Num 26:64
in mount S for a sweet savour .... Num 28:6
and pitched in the wilderness of S .. Num 33:15
they removed from the desert of S ... Num 33:16
And he said, The Lord came from S ... Deut 33:2
even that S itself was moved .... Judg 5:5
camest down also upon mount S ...... Neh 9:13
even S itself was moved at the .... Ps 68:8
the Lord is among them, as in S ...... Ps 68:17
the one from the mount S, which ..... Gal 4:24
this Agar is mount S in Arabia .... Gal 4:25

SINCE

hath blessed thee s my coming......... Gen 30:30
and I saw him not a .... Gen 44:28
s I have seen thy face, because....... Gen 46:30
nor s thou hast spoken unto thy ...... Ex 4:10
For s I came to Pharaoh to speak,..... Ex 5:23
s the foundation thereof even .... Ex 9:18
of Egypt s it became a nation .... Ex 9:24
s the day that they were upon the .... Ex 10:6
ever s I was thine unto this day ...... Num 22:30
s the day that God created man....... Deut 4:32
s Israel like unto Moses............. Deut 34:10
s I have shewed you kindness,........ Josh 2:12
even s the Lord spake this word ...... Josh 14:10
law s the death of thine husband .... Ruth 2:11
s the day that I brought them up 1Sa 8:8
it been kept for thee s I said 1Sa 9:24
s I came out, and the vessels of 1Sa 21:5
I have found no fault in him s he 1Sa 29:3
s the day of thy coming unto me 1Sa 29:6
I have not dwelt in any house s 2Sa 7:6
as s the time that I commanded...... 2Sa 7:11
S the day that I brought forth my 1Kin 8:16
all the fruits of the field s the 2Kin 8:6
s the day their fathers came 2Kin 21:15
house s the day that I brought up 1Chr 17:5
s the time that I commanded........ 1Chr 17:10
S the day that I brought forth my 2Chr 6:5
for s the time of Solomon the son ... 2Chr 30:26
S the people began to bring the 2Chr 31:10
we do sacrifice unto him s the ...... Ezr 4:2
s that time even until now hath ..... Ezr 5:16
S the days of our fathers have we ... Ezr 9:7
for s the days of Joshua the son .... Neh 8:17
s the time of the kings of .... Neh 9:32
a man was placed upon earth,....... Job 20:4
commanded the morning s thy days.. Job 38:12
S thou art laid down, no feller ..... Is 14:8
concerning Moab s that time....... Is 16:13
S thou wast precious in my sight,... Is 43:4
s I appointed the ancient people ... Is 44:7
For s the beginning of the world ... Is 64:4

S the day that your fathers came............ Jer 7:25
s they return not from their ways............ Jer 15:7
For *s* I spake, I cried out, I................... Jer 20:8
But *s* ye say, The burden of the............. Jer 23:36
for *s* I spake against him, I do............... Jer 31:20
But *s* we left off to burn incense .... Jer 44:18
for *s* thou spakest of him, thou............. Jer 48:27
such as never was a there was .... Dan 12:1
S those days were, when one came .... Hag 2:16
such as was not *s* the beginning............ Mt 24:21
is it ago *s* this came into him .... Mk 9:21
which have been *s* the world began .... Lk 1:70
but this woman *s* the time I came......... Lk 7:45
s that time the kingdom of God is....... Lk 16:16
day *s* these things were done................. Lk 24:21
S the world began was it not.................. Jn 9:32
holy prophets *s* the world began .... Acts 3:21
the Holy Ghost *s* ye believed................ Acts 19:2
s I went up to Jerusalem for to .... Acts 24:11
was kept secret *s* the world began........ Rom 16:25
For *s* by man came death, by man....... 1Cor 15:21
S ye seek a proof of Christ 2Cor 13:3
S we heard of your faith in................. Col 1:4
s the day ye heard of it, and knew....... Col 1:6
s the day we heard it, do not............... Col 1:9
of the oath, which was *s* the law.......... Heb 7:28
s the foundation of the world............... Heb 9:26
for *s* the fathers fell asleep,................. 2Pet 3:4
such as was not *s* men were upon........ Rev 16:18

SINCERE

that ye may be *s* and without............... Phil 1:10
desire the *s* milk of the word,................ 1Pet 2:2

SINCERELY

if ye have done truly and *s*................... Judg 9:16
s with Jerubbaal and with his .... Judg 9:19
Christ of contention, not *s*.................... Phil 1:16

SINCERITY

fear the LORD, and serve him in *s*........ Josh 24:14
with the unleavened bread of *s*............ 1Cor 5:8
that in simplicity and godly *s*............... 2Cor 1:12
but as of *s*, but as of God, in.............. 2Cor 2:17
and to prove the *s* of your love 2Cor 8:8
love our Lord Jesus Christ in *s*............ Eph 6:24
shewing uncorruptness, gravity, *s*.......... Titus 2:7

SINEW

eat not of the *s* which shrank .... Gen 32:32
thigh in the *s* that shrank.................... Gen 32:32
and thy neck is an iron *s*..................... Is 48:4

SINEWS

and hast fenced me with bones and *s*... Job 10:11
and my *s* take no rest.......................... Job 30:17
the *s* of his stones are wrapped............ Job 40:17
And I will lay *s* upon you, and will....... Eze 37:6
And when I beheld, lo, the *s*................. Eze 37:8

SINFUL

stead, an increase of *s* men .... Num 32:14
Ah *s* nation, a people laden with........... Is 1:4
Lord GOD are upon the *s* kingdom........ Amos 9:8
this adulterous and *s* generation.......... Mk 8:38
for I am a *s* man, O Lord...................... Lk 5:8
delivered into the hands of *s* men .... Lk 24:7
might become exceeding *s*.................... Rom 7:13
Son in the likeness of *s* flesh............... Rom 8:3

SING

I will *s* unto the LORD, for he.............. Ex 15:1
S ye to the LORD, for he hath............... Ex 15:21
noise of them that *s* do I hear .... Ex 32:18
s ye unto it .... Num 21:17
I, even I, will *s* unto the LORD,............ Judg 5:3
I will *s* praise to the LORD God........... Judg 5:3
did they not *s* one to another of 1Sa 21:11
S unto him, *s* psalms unto him,........... 1Chr 16:9
I will *s* unto the LORD, all the earth 1Chr 16:23
shall the trees of the wood *s* out 1Chr 16:33
And when they began to *s* and to........ 2Chr 20:22
and such as taught to *s* praise............. 2Chr 23:13
commanded the Levites to *s* praise 2Chr 29:30
the widow's heart to *s* for joy............. Job 29:13
will *s* praise to the name of the......... Ps 7:17
I will *s* praise to thy name, O.............. Ps 9:2
S praises to the LORD, which............... Ps 9:11
I will *s* unto the LORD, because........... Ps 13:6
and *s* praises unto thy name................. Ps 18:49
so will we *s* and praise thy power .... Ps 21:13
I will *s*, yea,....................................... Ps 27:6
I will *s* praises unto the LORD............. Ps 27:6
S unto the LORD, O ye saints of .... Ps 30:4
my glory may *s* praise to thee.............. Ps 30:12
s unto him with the psaltery and.......... Ps 33:2
S unto him a new song....................... Ps 33:3
S praises to God, *s* praises............... Ps 47:6
s praises unto our King, *s*.................. Ps 47:6
s ye praises with understanding........... Ps 47:7
my tongue shall *s* aloud of thy............ Ps 51:14
I will *s* and give praise........................ Ps 57:7
I will *s* unto thee among the................ Ps 57:9
But I will *s* of thy power...................... Ps 59:16
I will *s* aloud of thy mercy in............... Ps 59:16
thee, O my strength, will I *s*................. Ps 59:17
So will I *s* praise unto thy name.......... Ps 61:8
they shout for joy, they also *s*............. Ps 65:13
S forth the honour of his name............ Ps 66:2
thee, and shall *s* unto thee................... Ps 66:4
they shall *s* to thy name...................... Ps 66:4
the nations be glad and *s* for joy......... Ps 67:4
S unto God....................................... Ps 68:4

s praises to his name.......................... Ps 68:4
S unto God, ye kingdoms of the .... Ps 68:32
O s praises unto the Lord..................... Ps 68:32
sing unto the *s* with the harp .... Ps 71:22
rejoice when I *s* unto thee................... Ps 71:23
I will *s* praises to the God of............... Ps 75:9
S aloud unto God our strength............. Ps 81:1
I will *s* of the mercies of the............... Ps 89:1
to *s* praises unto thy name, O.............. Ps 92:1
O come, let us *s* unto the LORD .... Ps 95:1
S unto the LORD a new song................ Ps 96:1
s unto the LORD, all the earth.............. Ps 96:1
S unto the LORD, bless his name......... Ps 96:2
O s unto the LORD a new song............. Ps 98:1
noise, and rejoice, and *s* praise............ Ps 98:4
S unto the LORD with the harp .... Ps 98:5
I will *s* of mercy and judgment............ Ps 101:1
unto thee, O LORD, will I *s*.................. Ps 101:1
which *s* among the branches................ Ps 104:12
I will *s* unto the LORD as long as........ Ps 104:33
I will *s* praise to my God while I .... Ps 104:33
S unto him .... Ps 105:2
s psalms unto him............................... Ps 105:2
I will *s* and give praise, even .... Ps 108:1
I will *s* praises unto thee among.......... Ps 108:3
s praises unto his name....................... Ps 135:3
S us one of the songs of Zion............. Ps 137:3
How shall we *s* the Lord's song in .... Ps 137:4
gods will I *s* praise unto thee,.............. Ps 138:1
they shall *s* in the ways of the .... Ps 138:5
I will *s* a new song unto thee, O.......... Ps 144:9
will I *s* praises unto thee..................... Ps 144:9
shall *s* of thy righteousness................. Ps 145:7
I will *s* praises unto the LORD............. Ps 146:2
for it is good to *s* praises unto........... Ps 147:1
S unto the LORD with thanksgiving....... Ps 147:7
s praise upon the harp unto our .... Ps 147:7
S unto the LORD a new song, and......... Ps 149:1
let them *s* praises unto him with........ Ps 149:3
let them *s* aloud upon their beds......... Ps 149:5
but the righteous doth *s* and .... Prov 29:6
Now will I *s* to my wellbeloved a......... Is 5:1
S, O barren,...................................... Is 12:5
years shall Tyre *s* as an harlot .... Is 23:15
s many songs, that thou mayest be ..... Is 23:16
they shall *s* for the majesty of .... Is 24:14
Awake and *s*, ye that dwell in dust...... Is 26:19
In that day *s* ye unto her.................... Is 27:2
hart, and the tongue of the dumb *s* .... Is 35:6
therefore we will *s* my songs to............ Is 38:20
S unto the LORD a new song, and......... Is 42:10
let the inhabitants of the rock *s*.......... Is 42:11
S, O ye heavens................................. Is 44:23
S, O heavens...................................... Is 49:13
the voice together shall they *s*............. Is 52:8
s together, ye waste places of.............. Is 52:9
S, O barren, thou that didst not.......... Is 54:1
servants shall *s* for joy of heart.......... Is 65:14
S unto the LORD, praise ye the............. Jer 20:13
S with gladness for Jacob, and............ Jer 31:7
s in the height of Zion, and shall........ Jer 31:12
s therein, shall a for Babylon.............. Jer 51:48
did *s* of thee in thy market.................. Eze 27:25
and she shall *s* there, as in the............ Hos 2:15
voice shall *s* in the windows................ Zeph 2:14
S, O daughter of Zion.......................... Zeph 3:14
S and rejoice, O daughter of Zion......... Zec 2:10
the Gentiles, and *s* unto thy name....... Rom 15:9
I will *s* with the spirit........................ 1Cor 14:15
I will *s* with the understanding............ 1Cor 14:15
church will I *s* praise unto thee........... Heb 2:12
let him *s* psalms................................. Jas 5:13
they *s* the song of Moses the.............. Rev 15:3

SINGED

nor was an hair of their head *s*........... Dan 3:27

SINGER

Heman a *s*, the son of Joel, the........... 1Chr 6:33
To the chief *s* on my stringed.............. Hab 3:19

SINGERS

harps also and psalteries for *s*............. 1Kin 10:12
And these are the *s*, chief of the.......... 1Chr 9:33
their brethren to be the *s* with 1Chr 15:16
So the *s*, Heman, Asaph, and Ethan,.... 1Chr 15:19
that bare the ark, and the *s*................ 1Chr 15:27
the master of the song with the *s*....... 1Chr 15:27
Also the Levites which were the *s* 2Chr 5:12
s were as one, to make one sound....... 2Chr 5:13
and harps and psalteries for *s*............. 2Chr 9:11
he appointed *s* unto the LORD, and...... 2Chr 20:21
also the *s* with instruments of 2Chr 23:13
the *s* sang, and the trumpeters............ 2Chr 29:28
the *s* the sons of Asaph were in.......... 2Chr 35:15
The *s*: the children of Asaph............... Ezr 2:41
and some of the people, and the *s*...... Ezr 2:70
priests, and the Levites, and the *s* ...... Ezr 7:7
any of the priests and Levites, *s*.......... Ezr 7:24
Of the *s* also...................................... Ezr 10:24
doors, and the porters and the *s*......... Neh 7:1
The *s*: the children of Asaph............... Neh 7:44
Levites, and the porters, and the *s*...... Neh 7:73
the Levites, the porters, the *s*.............. Neh 10:28
and the porters, and the *s*................... Neh 10:39
the *s* were over the business of........... Neh 11:22
portion should be for the *s*.................. Neh 11:23
the sons of the *s* gathered.................. Neh 12:28
for the *s* had builded them.................. Neh 12:29
the sang loud, with Jezrahiah................ Neh 12:42
And both the *s* and the porters kept .... Neh 12:45
of old there were chief of the *s*........... Neh 12:46

gave the portions of the *s*................... Neh 12:47
be given to the Levites, and the *s*........ Neh 13:5
for the Levites and the *s*, that............. Neh 13:10
The *s* went before, the players on........ Ps 68:25
As well the *s* as the players on............ Ps 87:7
I gat me men *s* and women *s*............ Eccl 2:8
of the *s* in the inner court................... Eze 40:44

SINGETH

so is he that *s* songs to an heavy........ Prov 25:20

SINGING

out of all cities of Israel, with.............. 1Sa 18:6
voice of *s* men and women 2Sa 19:35
of the congregation with *s*................... 1Chr 6:32
with all their might, and with *s*............ 1Chr 13:8
Moses, with rejoicing and with *s*.......... 2Chr 23:18
s with loud instruments unto the 2Chr 30:21
and all the *s* men and the *s* 2Chr 35:25
hundred *s* men and women................... Ezr 2:65
and five *s* men and women .... Neh 7:67
with thanksgivings, and with *s*............. Neh 12:27
come before his presence with *s* .... Ps 100:2
laughter, and our tongue with *s*........... Ps 126:2
the time of the *s* of birds is................ Song 2:12
they break forth into *s*......................... Is 14:7
the vineyards there shall be no *s*.......... Is 16:10
and rejoice even with joy and *s*............ Is 35:2
break forth into *s*, ye mountains,......... Is 44:23
with a voice of *s* declare ye................. Is 48:20
and break forth into *s*, O....................... Is 49:13
return, and come with *s* unto Zion....... Is 51:11
break forth into *s*, and cry aloud,......... Is 54:1
break forth before you into *s*................ Is 55:12
he will joy over thee with *s*................. Zeph 3:17
and hymns and spiritual songs, *s* .... Eph 5:19
s with grace in your hearts to.............. Col 3:16

SINGLE

if therefore thine eye be *s*.................... Mt 6:22
therefore when thine eye is *s*................ Lk 11:34

SINGLENESS

meat with gladness and *s* of heart,...... Acts 2:46
in *s* of your heart, as unto................... Eph 6:5
but in *s* of heart, fearing God.............. Col 3:22

SINGULAR

When a man shall make a *s* vow .... Lev 27:2

SINIM

SINIM (si'-nim) *An unspecified people.*
and these from the land of *S*............... Is 49:12

SINITE

SINITE (si'-nite) *A tribe of Canaanites.*
Hivite, and the Arkite, and the *S*......... Gen 10:17
Hivite, and the Arkite, and the *S*......... 1Chr 1:15

SINK

I is in deep mire, where there is........... Ps 69:2
out of the mire, and let me not *s*........ Ps 69:14
shalt say, Thus shall Babylon *s*............ Jer 51:64
and beginning to *s*, he cried,................ Mt 14:30
ships, so that they began to *s* .... Lk 5:7
Let these sayings *s* down into............... Lk 9:44

SINNED

unto them, I have *s* this time.............. Ex 9:27
he *s* yet more, and hardened his .... Ex 9:34
I have *s* against the LORD your............ Ex 10:16
the people, Ye have *s* a great sin........ Ex 32:30
this people have *s* a great sin.............. Ex 32:31
Whosoever hath *s* against me.............. Ex 32:33
for his sin, which he hath *s*................. Lev 4:3
sin, which they have *s* against it.......... Lev 4:14
When a ruler hath *s*, and done............ Lev 4:22
Or if his sin, wherein he hath *s* .... Lev 4:23
Or if his sin, which he hath *s*.............. Lev 4:28
for his sin which he hath *s*.................. Lev 4:28
he hath *s* in that thing........................ Lev 5:5
LORD for his sin which he hath *s*........ Lev 5:6
him for his sin which he hath *s*........... Lev 5:10
then he that *s* shall bring for.............. Lev 5:11
that he hath *s* in one of these............ Lev 5:13
it shall be, because he hath *s*............. Lev 6:4
him, for that he *s* by the dead............ Num 6:11
foolishly, and wherein we have *s* .... Num 12:11
for we have *s* .... Num 14:40
came to Moses, and said, We have *s*... Num 21:7
the angel of the LORD, I have *s*........... Num 22:34
ye have *s* against the LORD .... Num 32:23
We have *s* against the LORD, and........ Deut 1:41
ye had *s* against the LORD your.......... Deut 9:16
of all your sins which ye *s*................... Deut 9:18
Israel hath *s*, and they have also......... Josh 7:11
Indeed I have *s* against the LORD........ Josh 7:20
We have *s* against thee, both .... Judg 10:10
said unto the LORD, We have *s* .... Judg 10:15
I have not *s* against thee..................... Judg 11:27
We have *s* against the LORD................. 1Sa 7:6
unto the LORD, and said, We have *s* ... 1Sa 12:10
Saul said unto Samuel, I have *s*........... 1Sa 15:24
Then he said, I have *s* 1Sa 15:30
he hath not *s* against thee.................. 1Sa 19:4
I have not *s* against thee..................... 1Sa 24:11
Then said Saul, I have *s* 1Sa 26:21
have *s* against the LORD 2Sa 12:13
servant doth know that I have *s*.......... 2Sa 19:20
I have *s* greatly in that I have 2Sa 24:10
the people, and said, Lo, I have *s* 2Sa 24:17
because they have *s* against thee......... 1Kin 8:33
because they have *s* against thee......... 1Kin 8:35
them captives, saying, We have *s* 1Kin 8:47
people that have *s* against thee........... 1Kin 8:50
the sins of Jeroboam which he *s* 1Kin 15:30

of Elah his son, by which they *s*...... 1Kin 16:13
For his sins which he *s* in doing...... 1Kin 16:19
And he said, What have I *s*........... 1Kin 18:9
had *s* against the LORD their God........ 2Kin 17:7
that he did, and his sin that he *s*...... 2Kin 21:17
I have *s* greatly, because I have....... 1Chr 21:8
even I it is that have *s* and done....... 1Chr 21:17
because they have *s* against thee....... 2Chr 6:24
because they have *s* against thee....... 2Chr 6:26
captivity, saying, We have *s*.......... 2Chr 6:37
people which have *s* against thee....... 2Chr 6:39
which we have *s* against thee.......... Neh 1:6
I and my father's house have *s*........ Neh 1:6
but *s* against thy judgments, (......... Neh 9:29
It may be that my sons have *s*......... Job 1:5
In all this Job *s* not, nor........... Job 1:22
I have *s*..................... Job 7:20
thy children have *s* against him........ Job 8:4
doth the grave those which have *s*...... Job 24:19
upon men, and if any say, I have *s*..... Job 33:27
for I have *s* against thee............ Job 33:27
Against thee, thee only, have I *s*...... Ps 51:4
they a yet more against him by.......... Ps 78:17
For all this they *s* still............ Ps 78:32
We have *s* with our fathers, we........ Ps 106:6
Lord, be against whom we have *s*....... Is 42:24
Thy first father hath *s*, and thy....... Is 43:27
for we have *s*................. Is 64:5
because thou sayest, I have not *s*...... Jer 2:35
for we have *s* against the LORD........ Jer 3:25
because we have *s* against the......... Jer 8:14
we have *s* against thee.............. Jer 14:7
for we have *s* against thee........... Jer 14:20
whereby they have *s* against me........ Jer 33:8
iniquities, whereby they have *s*........ Jer 33:8
because ye have *s* against the......... Jer 44:23
they have *s* against the LORD.......... Jer 50:7
for she hath *s* against the LORD....... Jer 50:14
Jerusalem hath grievously *s*........... Lam 1:8
Our fathers have *s*, and are not........ Lam 5:7
woe unto us, that we have *s*.......... Lam 5:16
and in his sin that he hath *s*......... Eze 18:24
with violence, and thou hast *s*........ Eze 28:16
wherein they have *s*, and will......... Eze 37:23
We have *s*, and have committed......... Dan 9:5
because we have *s* against thee........ Dan 9:8
because we have *s* against him......... Dan 9:11
we have *s*, we have done wickedly....... Dan 9:15
increased, so they *s* against me....... Hos 4:7
thou hast *s* from the days of......... Hos 10:9
because I have *s* against him.......... Mic 7:9
and hast *s* against thy soul.......... Hab 2:10
they have *s* against the LORD.......... Zeph 1:17
I have *s* in that I have betrayed....... Mt 27:4
I have *s* against heaven, and.......... Lk 15:18
I have *s* against heaven, and in........ Lk 15:21
answered, Neither hath this man *s*...... Jn 9:3
For as many as have *s* without law...... Rom 2:12
as many as have *s* in the law......... Rom 2:12
upon all men, for that all have *s*...... Rom 5:12
even over them that had not *s*......... Rom 5:14
And not as it was by one that *s*....... 1Cor 15:16
and if thou marry, thou hast not *s*..... 1Cor 7:28
if a virgin marry, she hath not *s*..... 1Cor 7:28
bewail many which have already....... 2Cor 12:21
to them which heretofore have *s*....... 2Cor 13:2
was it not with them that had *s*....... Heb 3:17
God spared not the angels that *s*....... 2Pet 2:4
If we say that we have not *s*.......... 1Jn 1:10

SINNER

much more the wicked and the *s*........ Prov 11:31
but wickedness overthroweth the *s*...... Prov 13:6
the wealth of the *s* is laid up........ Prov 13:22
but to the *s* he giveth travail........ Eccl 2:26
but the *s* shall be taken by her........ Eccl 7:26
Though a *s* do evil an hundred......... Eccl 8:12
as is the good, so is the *s*.......... Eccl 9:2
but one *s* destroyeth much good........ Eccl 9:18
but the *s* being an hundred years...... Is 65:20
woman in the city, which was a *s*...... Lk 7:37
for she is a *s*.................. Lk 7:39
heaven over one *s* that repenteth...... Lk 15:7
of God over one *s* that repenteth...... Lk 15:10
saying, God be merciful to me a *s*..... Lk 18:13
be guest with a man that is a *s*....... Lk 19:7
man that is a *s* do such miracles...... Jn 9:16
we know that this man is a *s*......... Jn 9:24
and said, Whether he be a *s* or no...... Jn 9:25
why yet am I also judged as a *s*....... Rom 3:7
that he which converteth the *s*........ Jas 5:20
shall the ungodly and the *s* appear..... 1Pet 4:18

SINNERS

s before the LORD exceedingly......... Gen 13:13
The censers of these *s* against........ Num 16:38
destroy the *s* the Amalekites......... 1Sa 15:18
nor standeth in the way of *s*.......... Ps 1:1
nor *s* in the congregation of the....... Ps 1:5
will he teach *s* in the way........... Ps 25:8
Gather not my soul with *s*........... Ps 26:9
s shall be converted unto thee........ Ps 51:13
Let the *s* be consumed out of thou..... Ps 104:35
if *s* entice thee, consent thou........ Prov 1:10
Evil pursueth *s*.................. Prov 13:21
Let not thine heart envy *s*.......... Prov 23:17
of the *s* shall be together, and....... Is 1:28
destroy the *s* thereof out of it....... Is 13:9
The *s* in Zion are afraid............ Is 33:14

All the *s* of my people shall die...... Amos 9:10
s came and sat down with him and....... Mt 9:10
your Master with publicans and *s*...... Mt 9:11
righteous, but *s* to repentance........ Mt 9:13
a friend of publicans and *s*.......... Mt 11:19
is betrayed into the hands of *s*....... Mt 26:45
s sat also together with Jesus and..... Mk 2:15
saw him eat with publicans and *s*...... Mk 2:16
and drinketh with publicans and *s*..... Mk 2:16
righteous, but *s* to repentance........ Mk 2:17
is betrayed into the hands of *s*....... Mk 14:41
eat and drink with publicans and *s*.... Lk 5:30
righteous, but *s* to repentance........ Lk 5:32
for *s* also love those that love....... Lk 6:32
for *s* also do even the same.......... Lk 6:33
for *s* also lend to *s*............. Lk 6:34
a friend of publicans and *s*.......... Lk 7:34
were *s* above all the Galileans........ Lk 13:2
think ye that they were *s* above....... Lk 13:4
publicans and *s* for to hear him....... Lk 15:1
saying, This man receiveth *s*......... Lk 15:2
we know that God heareth not *s*........ Jn 9:31
us, in that, while we were yet *s*...... Rom 5:8
disobedience many were made *s*........ Rom 5:19
nature, and not *s* of the Gentiles..... Gal 2:15
we ourselves also are found *s*......... Gal 2:17
for the ungodly and for *s*........... 1Ti 1:9
came into the world to save *s*......... 1Ti 1:15
undefiled, separate from *s*........... Heb 7:26
of *s* against himself, lest ye be...... Heb 12:3
Cleanse your hands, ye *s*............ Jas 4:8
ungodly have spoken against him........ Jude 15

SINNEST

If thou *s*, what doest thou........... Job 35:6

SINNETH

for the soul that *s* ignorantly........ Num 15:28
when he *s* by ignorance before the..... Num 15:28
for him that *s* through ignorance...... Num 15:29
for any sin, in any sin that he *s*..... Deut 19:15
(for there is no man that *s* not....... 1Kin 8:46
(for there is no man which *s* not...... 2Chr 6:36
But he that *s* against me wrongeth..... Prov 8:36
He that despiseth his neighbour *s*..... Prov 14:21
he that hasteth with his feet *s*....... Prov 19:2
to anger *s* against his own soul....... Prov 20:2
earth, that doeth good, and *s* not..... Eccl 7:20
when the land *s* against me by........ Eze 14:13
the soul that *s*, it shall die......... Eze 18:4
The soul that *s*, it shall die........ Eze 18:20
in the day that he *s*.............. Eze 33:12
s against his own body.............. 1Cor 6:18
let him do what he will, he *s* not..... 1Cor 7:36
that is such is subverted, and *s*...... Titus 3:11
Whosoever abideth in him *s* not........ 1Jn 3:6
whosoever *s* hath not seen him......... 1Jn 3:6
for the devil's from the............ 1Jn 3:8
whosoever is born of God *s* not........ 1Jn 5:18

SINNING

withheld thee from *s* against me....... Gen 20:6
these that a man doeth, *s* therein..... Lev 6:3

SINS

transgressions in all their *s*........ Lev 16:16
transgressions in all their *s*........ Lev 16:21
from all your *s* before the LORD....... Lev 16:30
for all their *s* once a year.......... Lev 16:34
you seven times more for your *s*....... Lev 26:18
upon you according to your *s*......... Lev 26:21
you yet seven times for your *s*....... Lev 26:24
you seven times for your *s*.......... Lev 26:28
ye be consumed in all their *s*........ Num 16:26
of all your *s* which ye sinned......... Deut 9:18
your transgressions nor your *s*........ Josh 24:19
added unto all our *s* this evil........ 1Sa 12:19
up because of the *s* of Jeroboam....... 1Kin 14:16
their *s* which they had committed...... 1Kin 14:22
walked in all the *s* of his father..... 1Kin 15:3
Because of the *s* of Jeroboam......... 1Kin 15:30
provoke me to anger with their *s*...... 1Kin 16:2
For all the *s* of Baasha, and the...... 1Kin 16:13
the *s* of Elah his son, by which....... 1Kin 16:13
For his *s* which he sinned in......... 1Kin 16:19
of Jeroboam the son of Nebat.......... 1Kin 16:31
he cleaved unto the *s* of Jeroboam..... 2Kin 3:3
Howbeit from the *s* of Jeroboam....... 2Kin 10:29
not from the *s* of Jeroboam.......... 2Kin 10:31
followed the *s* of Jeroboam.......... 2Kin 13:2
the *s* of the house of Jeroboam....... 2Kin 13:6
of Jeroboam the son of Nebat.......... 2Kin 13:11
s of Jeroboam the son of Nebat........ 2Kin 14:24
he departed not from the *s* of........ 2Kin 15:9
not all his days from the *s* of....... 2Kin 15:18
he departed not from the *s* of........ 2Kin 15:24
he departed not from the *s* of........ 2Kin 15:28
the *s* of Jeroboam which he did........ 2Kin 17:22
of the *s* of Manasseh, according....... 2Kin 24:3
s against the LORD your God.......... 2Chr 28:10
ye intend to add more to our *s*....... 2Chr 28:13
confess the *s* of the children of...... Neh 1:6
and stood and confessed their *s*...... Neh 9:2
hast set over us because of our *s*..... Neh 9:37
How many are mine iniquities and *s*.... Job 13:23
servant also from presumptuous *s*...... Ps 19:13
Remember not the *s* of my youth....... Ps 25:7
and forgive all my *s*.............. Ps 25:18
Hide thy face from my *s*, and blot..... Ps 51:9
my *s* are not hid from thee.......... Ps 69:5
deliver us, and purge away our *s*...... Ps 79:9
our secret *s* in the light of thy...... Ps 90:8

not dealt with us after our *s*......... Ps 103:10
be holden with the cords of his *s*..... Prov 5:22
but love covereth all *s*............. Prov 10:12
covereth his *s* shall not prosper...... Prov 28:13
though your *s* be as scarlet, they..... Is 1:18
cast all my *s* behind thy back........ Is 38:17
Lord's hand double for all her *s*...... Is 40:2
hast made me to serve with thy *s*...... Is 43:24
sake, and will not remember thy *s*..... Is 43:25
and, as a cloud, thy *s*............. Is 44:22
and the house of Jacob their *s*........ Is 58:1
your *s* have hid his face from you..... Is 59:2
thee, and our *s* testify against us.... Is 59:12
your *s* have withholden good.......... Jer 5:25
their iniquity, and visit their *s*..... Jer 14:10
price, and that for all thy *s*........ Jer 15:13
because thy *s* were increased......... Jer 30:14
because thy *s* were increased, I....... Jer 30:15
the *s* of Judah, and they shall not.... Jer 50:20
a man for the punishment of his *s*..... Lam 3:39
For the *s* of her prophets, and the.... Lam 4:13
he will discover thy *s*............. Lam 4:22
Samaria committed half of thy *s*...... Eze 16:51
bear thine own shame for thy *s*....... Eze 16:52
his father's *s* which he hath done..... Eze 18:14
all his *s* that he hath committed...... Eze 18:21
all your doings your *s* do appear...... Eze 21:24
ye shall bear the *s* of your idols..... Eze 23:49
our *s* be upon us, and we pine away.... Eze 33:10
None of his *s* that he hath.......... Eze 33:16
break off thy *s* by righteousness...... Dan 4:27
because for our *s*, and for the....... Dan 9:16
and to make an end of *s*, and to...... Dan 9:24
their iniquity, and visit their *s*..... Hos 8:13
iniquity, he will visit their *s*....... Hos 9:9
transgressions and your mighty *s*...... Amos 5:12
for the *s* of the house of Israel...... Mic 1:5
thee desolate because of thy *s*....... Mic 6:13
thou wilt cast all their *s* into...... Mic 7:19
save his people from their *s*......... Mt 1:21
him in Jordan, confessing their *s*..... Mt 3:6
thy *s* be forgiven thee............. Mt 9:2
to say, Thy *s* be forgiven thee....... Mt 9:5
hath power on earth to forgive *s*...... Mt 9:6
for many for the remission of *s*...... Mt 26:28
repentance for the remission of *s*.... Mk 1:5
of Jordan, confessing their *s*........ Mk 1:5
Son, thy *s* be forgiven thee.......... Mk 2:5
who can forgive *s* but God only........ Mk 2:7
the palsy, Thy *s* be forgiven thee..... Mk 2:9
hath power on earth to forgive *s*...... Mk 2:10
All *s* shall be forgiven unto the...... Mk 3:28
their *s* should be forgiven them....... Mk 4:12
by the remission of their *s*......... Lk 1:77
repentance for the remission of *s*.... Lk 3:3
him, Man, thy *s* are forgiven thee..... Lk 5:20
Who can forgive *s*, but God alone...... Lk 5:21
to say, Thy *s* be forgiven thee....... Lk 5:23
power upon earth to forgive *s*........ Lk 5:24
Wherefore I say unto thee, Her *s*...... Lk 7:47
said unto her, Thy *s* are forgiven..... Lk 7:48
Who is this that forgiveth *s* also..... Lk 7:49
And forgive us our *s*.............. Lk 11:4
remission of *s* should be preached..... Lk 24:47
seek me, and shall die in your *s*...... Jn 8:21
you, that ye shall die in your *s*...... Jn 8:24
I am he, ye shall die in your *s*...... Jn 8:24
Thou wast altogether born in *s*....... Jn 9:34
Whose soever *s* ye remit, they are..... Jn 20:23
and whose soever *s* ye retain........ Jn 20:23
Christ for the remission of *s*........ Acts 2:38
that your *s* may be blotted out....... Acts 3:19
to Israel, and forgiveness of *s*...... Acts 5:31
him shall receive remission of *s*..... Acts 10:43
unto you the forgiveness of *s*........ Acts 13:38
be baptized, and wash away thy *s*...... Acts 22:16
they may receive forgiveness of *s*.... Acts 26:18
the remission of *s* that are past...... Rom 3:25
forgiven, and whose *s* are covered..... Rom 4:7
in the flesh, the motions of *s*....... Rom 7:5
when I shall take away their *s*....... Rom 11:27
our *s* according to the scriptures..... 1Cor 15:3
ye are yet in your *s*.............. 1Cor 15:17
Who gave himself for our *s*.......... Gal 1:4
his blood, the forgiveness of *s*...... Eph 1:7
who were dead in trespasses and *s*..... Eph 2:1
Even when we were dead in *s*......... Eph 2:5
blood, even the forgiveness of *s*...... Col 1:14
body of the *s* of the flesh by........ Col 2:11
And you, being dead in your *s*........ Col 2:13
saved, to fill up their *s* alway...... 1Th 2:16
be partaker of other men's *s*......... 1Ti 5:22
Some men's *s* are open beforehand..... 1Ti 5:24
captive silly women laden with *s*..... 2Ti 3:6
he had by himself purged our *s*....... Heb 1:3
for the *s* of the people............ Heb 2:17
both gifts and sacrifices for *s*...... Heb 5:1
also for himself, to offer for *s*..... Heb 5:3
up sacrifice, first for his own *s*..... Heb 7:27
their unrighteousness, and their *s*.... Heb 8:12
offered to bear the *s* of many........ Heb 9:28
have had no more conscience of *s*..... Heb 10:2
again made of *s* every year.......... Heb 10:3
and goats should take away *s*......... Heb 10:4
which can never take away *s*......... Heb 10:11
one sacrifice for *s* for ever........ Heb 10:12
And their *s* and iniquities will I..... Heb 10:17
remaineth no more sacrifice for *s*.... Heb 10:26
and if he have committed *s*.......... Jas 5:15
and shall hide a multitude of *s*...... Jas 5:20

S

Who his own self bare our *s* in...... 1Pet 2:24
tree, that we, being dead to *s*........ 1Pet 2:24
also hath once suffered for *s*......... 1Pet 3:18
shall cover the multitude of *s*........ 1Pet 4:8
that he was purged from his old *s*.... 2Pet 1:9
If we confess our *s*, he is........... 1Jn 1:9
and just to forgive us our *s*.......... 1Jn 1:9
he is the propitiation for our *s*...... 1Jn 2:2
but also for the *s* of the whole...... 1Jn 2:2
because your *s* are forgiven you...... 1Jn 2:12
was manifested to take away our *s*.... 1Jn 3:5
to be the propitiation for our *s*..... 1Jn 4:10
us from our *s* in his own blood....... Rev 1:5
that ye be not partakers of her *s*.... Rev 18:4
For her *s* have reached unto......... Rev 18:5

SION (sī′-on) See SHENIR, SIRION, ZION.
1. The peak of Mount Hermon.
even unto mount *S* which is Hermon. Deut 4:48
2. A district of Jerusalem.
waiteth for thee, O God in *S*......... Ps 65:1
Tell ye the daughter of *S*........... Mt 21:5
Fear not, daughter of *S*............. Jn 12:15
I say *S* a stumblingstone and......... Rom 9:33
shall come out of *S* the Deliverer.... Rom 11:26
But ye are come unto mount *S*........ Heb 12:22
I lay in *S* a chief corner stone,..... 1Pet 2:6
lo, a Lamb stood on the mount *S*..... Rev 14:1

SIPHMOTH (sif′-moth) *A city in Judah.*
Aroer, and to them which were in *S*.. 1Sa 30:28

SIPPAI (sip′-pahee) See SAPH. *Son of Rapha.*
Sibbechai the Hushathite slew *S*..... 1Chr 20:4

SIR
And said, O *s*, we came indeed down. Gen 43:20
came and said unto him, *S*, didst.... Mt 13:27
And he answered and said, I go *s*.... Mt 21:30
Saying, *S*, we remember that that.... Mt 27:63
The woman saith unto him, *S*........ Jn 4:11
The woman saith unto him, *S*........ Jn 4:15
The woman saith unto him, *S*........ Jn 4:19
the nobleman saith unto him, *S*...... Jn 4:49
The impotent man answered him, *S*... Jn 5:7
and desired him, saying, *S*.......... Jn 12:21
the gardener, saith unto him, *S*..... Jn 20:15
And I said unto him, *S*, thou....... Rev 7:14

SIRAH (sī′-rah) *A well near Hebron.*
him again from the well of *S*........ 2Sa 3:26

SIRION (sir′-e-on) See HERMON. *A Sidonian name for Mount Hermon.*
Which Hermon the Sidonians call *S*... Deut 3:9
Lebanon and *S* like a young unicorn... Ps 29:6

SIRS
set them at one again, saying, *S*.... Acts 7:26
And saying, *S*, why do ye these...... Acts 14:15
And brought them out, and said, *S*... Acts 16:30
of like occupation, and said, *S*..... Acts 19:25
And said unto them, *S*, I perceive... Acts 27:10
in the midst of them, and said, *S*... Acts 27:21
Wherefore, be of good cheer......... Acts 27:25

SISAMAI (sis′-a-mahee) *Son of Eleasah.*
And Eleasah begat *S*................ 1Chr 2:40
and *S* begat Shallum................ 1Chr 2:40

SISERA (sis′-e-rah)
1. A captain in the Canaanite army.
the captain of whose host was *S*..... Judg 4:2
unto thee to the river Kishon, *S*.... Judg 4:7
for the LORD shall sell *S* into...... Judg 4:9
they shewed *S* that Barak the son.... Judg 4:12
S gathered together all his......... Judg 4:13
hath delivered *S* into thine hand.... Judg 4:14
And the LORD discomfited *S*.......... Judg 4:15
so that *S* lighted down off his...... Judg 4:15
all the host of *S* fell upon the..... Judg 4:16
Howbeit *S* fled away on his feet..... Judg 4:17
And Jael went out to meet *S*........ Judg 4:18
And, behold, as Barak pursued *S*..... Judg 4:22
S lay dead, and the nail was in..... Judg 4:22
in their courses fought against *S*... Judg 5:20
and with the hammer she smote *S*..... Judg 5:26
The mother of *S* looked out at a..... Judg 5:28
to *S* a prey of divers colours, a.... Judg 5:30
he sold them into the hand of *S*.... 1Sa 12:9
as to *S*, as to Jabin, at the....... Ps 83:9
2. A family of exiles.
of Barkos, the children of *S*....... Ezr 2:53
of Barkos, the children of *S*....... Neh 7:55

SISMAI See SISAMAI.

SISTER
the *s* of Tubal-cain was Naamah...... Gen 4:22
Say, I pray thee, thou art my *s*..... Gen 12:13
Why saidst thou, She is my *s*........ Gen 12:19
of Sarah his wife, She is my *s*...... Gen 20:2
Said he not unto me, She is my *s*.... Gen 20:5
And yet indeed she is my *s*.......... Gen 20:12
heard the words of Rebekah his *s*.... Gen 24:30
And they sent away Rebekah their *s*.. Gen 24:59
and said unto her, Thou art our *s*... Gen 24:60
the *s* to Laban the Syrian......... Gen 25:20
and he said, She is my *s*........... Gen 26:7
and how saidst thou, She is my *s*.... Gen 26:9
the *s* of Nebajoth, to be his wife... Gen 28:9
no children, Rachel envied her *s*.... Gen 30:1
have I wrestled with my *s*.......... Gen 30:8
he had defiled Dinah their *s*....... Gen 34:13
to give our *s* to one that is....... Gen 34:14

because they had defiled their *s*.... Gen 34:27
deal with our *s* as with an harlot... Gen 34:31
Ishmael's daughter, *s* of Nebajoth... Gen 36:3
and Lotan's *s* was Timna............ Gen 36:22
Isui, and Beriah, and Serah their *s*. Gen 46:17
his *s* stood afar off, to wit what... Ex 2:4
Then said his *s* to Pharaoh's....... Ex 2:7
Jochebed his father's *s* to wife.... Ex 6:20
Amminadab, *s* of Naashon, to wife.... Ex 6:23
of Aaron, took a timbrel in........ Ex 15:20
The nakedness of thy *s*, the......... Lev 18:9
of thy father, she is thy *s*........ Lev 18:11
the nakedness of thy father's *s*.... Lev 18:12
the nakedness of thy mother's *s*.... Lev 18:13
shalt thou take a wife to her *s*..... Lev 18:18
And if a man shall take his *s*....... Lev 20:17
the nakedness of thy mother's *s*.... Lev 20:19
nor of thy father's *s*.............. Lev 20:19
for his *s* a virgin, that is nigh.... Lev 21:3
for his brother, or for his *s*...... Num 6:7
of a prince of Midian, their *s*..... Num 25:18
and Miriam their *s*................. Num 26:59
be that liketh with his *s*.......... Deut 27:22
not her younger *s* fairer than the... Judg 15:2
thy *s* in law is gone back unto..... Ruth 1:15
return thou after thy *s* in law..... Ruth 1:15
the son of David had a fair *s*...... 2Sa 13:1
that he fell sick for his *s* Tamar... 2Sa 13:2
Tamar, my brother Absalom's *s*...... 2Sa 13:4
let my *s* Tamar come, and give me.... 2Sa 13:5
I pray thee, let Tamar my *s* come.... 2Sa 13:6
unto her, Come lie with me, my *s*.... 2Sa 13:11
but hold now thy peace, my *s*....... 2Sa 13:20
because he had forced his *s* Tamar... 2Sa 13:22
day that he forced his *s* Tamar..... 2Sa 13:32
to Zeruiah Joab's mother............ 2Sa 17:25
him to wife the *s* of his own wife... 1Kin 11:19
the *s* of Tahpenes the queen........ 1Kin 11:20
the *s* of Tahpenes bare him......... 1Kin 11:20
s of Ahaziah, took Joash the....... 2Kin 11:2
and Timna was Lotan's *s*............ 1Chr 1:39
the concubines, and Tamar their *s*... 1Chr 3:9
and Hananiah, and Shelomith their *s*. 1Chr 3:19
name of their *s* was Hazelelponi.... 1Chr 4:3
of his wife Hodiah the *s* of Naham... 1Chr 4:19
took to wife the *s* of Huppim....... 1Chr 7:15
his *s* Hammoleketh bare Ishod, and... 1Chr 7:18
and Beriah, and Serah their *s*...... 1Chr 7:30
and Hosham, and Shua their *s*........ 1Chr 7:32
(for she was the *s* of Ahaziah...... 2Chr 22:11
worm, Thou art my mother, and my *s*. Job 17:14
Say unto wisdom, Thou art my *s*..... Prov 7:4
Thou hast ravished my heart, my *s*... Song 4:9
Hove fair is thy love, my *s*........ Song 4:10
A garden inclosed is my *s*.......... Song 4:12
I am come into my garden, my *s*..... Song 5:1
saying, Open to me, my *s*.......... Song 5:2
We have a little *s*, and she hath.... Song 8:8
what shall we do for our *s* in the... Song 8:8
And her treacherous *s* Judah saw it.. Jer 3:7
treacherous *s* Judah feared not..... Jer 3:8
for all this her treacherous *s*..... Jer 3:10
my brother! or, Ah *s*............... Jer 22:18
thou art the *s* of thy sisters...... Eze 16:45
And thine elder *s* is Samaria....... Eze 16:46
and thy younger *s*, that dwelleth... Eze 16:46
Sodom thy *s* hath not done, she..... Eze 16:48
was the iniquity of thy *s* Sodom.... Eze 16:49
For thy *s* Sodom was not mentioned... Eze 16:56
in thee hath humbled his *s*......... Eze 22:11
the elder, and Aholibah her *s*...... Eze 23:4
when her *s* Aholibah saw this, she... Eze 23:11
more than her *s* in her whoredoms... Eze 23:11
my mind was alienated from her *s*.... Eze 23:18
hast walked in the way of thy *s*.... Eze 23:31
with the cup of thy *s* Samaria...... Eze 23:33
or for *s* that hath had no husband... Eze 44:25
the same is my brother, and *s*...... Mt 12:50
the same is my brother, and *s*...... Mk 3:35
she had a *s* called Mary, which..... Lk 10:39
dost thou not care that my *s* hath... Lk 10:40
the town of Mary and her *s* Martha... Jn 11:1
Now Jesus loved Martha, and her *s*... Jn 11:5
and called Mary her *s* secretly..... Jn 11:28
the *s* of him that was dead, saith... Jn 11:39
his mother, and his mother's *s*..... Jn 19:25
I commend unto you Phebe our *s*..... Rom 16:1
and Julia, Nereus, and his *s*....... Rom 16:15
A brother or a *s* is not under...... 1Cor 7:15
we not power to lead about a *s*..... 1Cor 9:5
If a brother or *s* be naked........ Jas 2:15
of the elect's greet thee.......... 2Jn 13

SISTER'S
and bracelets upon his *s* hands..... Gen 24:30
the tidings of Jacob his *s* son..... Gen 29:13
he hath uncovered his *s* nakedness... Lev 20:17
Shuppim, whose a name.............. 1Chr 7:15
shalt drink of thy *s* cup deep...... Eze 23:32
when Paul's *s* son heard of this.... Acts 23:16
a son to Barnabas, (touching whom.... Col 4:10

SISTERS
my brethren, and my *s*, and my...... Josh 2:13
Whose *s* were Zeruiah, and Abigail.. 1Chr 2:16
called for their three *s* to eat.... Job 1:4
all his brethren, and all his *s*.... Job 42:11
and thou art the sister of thy *s*.... Eze 16:45
hast justified thy *s* in all thine... Eze 16:51
also, which hast judged thy *s*...... Eze 16:52
in that thou hast justified thy *s*... Eze 16:52

When thy *s*, Sodom and her.......... Eze 16:55
when thou shalt receive thy *s*...... Eze 16:61
and to your *s*, Ruhamah............. Hos 2:1
are not his *s* here with us......... Mt 13:56
houses, or brethren, or *s*.......... Mt 19:29
are not his *s* here with us......... Mk 6:3
left house, or brethren, or *s*...... Mk 10:29
time, houses, and brethren, and *s*.. Mk 10:30
and children, and brethren, and *s*.. Lk 14:26
Therefore his *s* sent unto him...... Jn 11:3
the younger as *s*, with all purity... 1Ti 5:2

SIT
arise, I pray thee, and eat of...... Gen 27:19
go to war, and shall ye *s* here..... Num 32:6
ye that *s* in judgment, and walk by.. Judg 5:10
S still, my daughter, until thou... Ruth 3:18
turn aside, *s* down here............ Ruth 4:1
the city, and said, *S* down here..... Ruth 4:2
made them a *s* in the chiefest place. 1Sa 9:22
for we will not *s* down till he..... 1Sa 16:11
I should not fail to *s* with the.... 1Sa 20:5
the king doth *s* in the gate........ 2Sa 19:8
he shall *s* upon my throne.......... 1Kin 1:13
he shall *s* upon my throne.......... 1Kin 1:17
s on the throne of my lord the..... 1Kin 1:20
he shall *s* upon my throne.......... 1Kin 1:24
who should *s* on the throne of my... 1Kin 1:27
he shall *s* upon my throne in my.... 1Kin 1:30
he may come and *s* upon my throne... 1Kin 1:35
one to *s* on my throne this day..... 1Kin 1:48
him a son to *s* on his throne....... 1Kin 3:6
s on the throne of Israel, as the... 1Kin 8:20
to *s* on the throne of Israel....... 1Kin 8:25
Why *s* we here until we die......... 2Kin 7:3
if we *s* still here, we die also.... 2Kin 7:4
shall *s* on the throne of Israel.... 2Kin 10:30
Thy sons shall *s* on the throne of.. 2Kin 15:12
me to the men which *s* on the wall... 2Kin 18:27
hath chosen Solomon my son to *s*.... 1Chr 28:5
to *s* upon the throne of Israel..... 2Chr 6:16
will not *s* with the wicked......... Ps 26:5
They that *s* in the gate speak...... Ps 69:12
Such as *s* in darkness and in the... Ps 107:10
S thou at my right hand, until I... Ps 110:1
Princes also did *s* and speak....... Ps 119:23
to *s* up late, to eat the bread of.. Ps 127:2
their children shall also *s* upon... Ps 132:12
and the rich *s* in low place........ Eccl 10:6
desolate shall *s* upon the ground... Is 3:26
I will *s* also upon the mount of.... Is 14:13
he shall *s* upon it in truth in..... Is 16:5
Thy strength is to *s* still......... Is 30:7
to the men that *s* upon the wall.... Is 36:12
them that *s* in darkness out of the. Is 42:7
s in the dust, O virgin daughter... Is 47:1
of Babylon, *s* on the ground....... Is 47:1
S thou silent, and get thee into... Is 47:5
I shall not *s* as a widow, neither... Is 47:8
warm at, nor fire to *s* before it... Is 47:14
arise, and *s* down, O Jerusalem..... Is 52:2
Why do we *s* still................. Jer 8:14
kings that *s* upon David's throne... Jer 13:13
queen, Humble yourselves, *s* down... Jer 13:18
to *s* with them to eat and to drink. Jer 16:8
s upon the throne of the house of.. Jer 33:17
S down now, and read it in our..... Jer 36:15
He shall have none to *s* upon the... Jer 36:30
from thy glory, and *s* in thirst.... Jer 48:18
How doth the city *s* solitary....... Lam 1:1
of Zion *s* upon the ground......... Lam 2:10
they shall *s* upon the ground, and.. Eze 26:16
I *s* in the seat of God, in the..... Eze 28:2
they a before thee as my people..... Eze 33:31
he shall *s* in it to eat bread...... Eze 44:3
and the Ancient of days did *s*...... Dan 7:9
But the judgment shall *s*, and they. Dan 7:26
for there will I *s* to judge all.... Joel 3:12
But they shall *s* every man under... Mic 4:4
when I *s* in darkness, the LORD..... Mic 7:8
and thy fellows that *s* before thee. Zec 3:8
shall bear the glory, and shall *s*.. Zec 6:13
he shall *s* as a refiner and....... Mal 3:3
shall *s* down with Abraham, and..... Mt 8:11
multitude *s* down on the grass...... Mt 14:19
multitude to *s* down on the ground... Mt 15:35
when the Son of man shall *s* in..... Mt 19:28
ye also shall *s* upon twelve....... Mt 19:28
that these my two sons may *s*....... Mt 20:21
but to *s* on my right hand, and on... Mt 20:23
S thou on my right hand, till I.... Mt 22:44
The Pharisees in Moses' seat........ Mt 23:2
then shall he *s* upon the throne.... Mt 25:31
S ye here, while I go and pray..... Mt 26:36
all *s* down by companies upon the... Mk 6:39
people to *s* down on the ground..... Mk 8:6
him, Grant unto us that we may *s*... Mk 10:37
But to *s* on my right hand and on... Mk 10:40
S thou on my right hand, till I.... Mk 12:36
S ye here, while I shall pray...... Mk 14:32
light to them that *s* in darkness... Lk 1:79
Make them a down by fifties in a.... Lk 9:14
did so, and made them all *s* down... Lk 9:15
and make them to *s* down to meat.... Lk 12:37
shall *s* down in the kingdom of..... Lk 13:29
s not down in the highest room..... Lk 14:8
s down in the lowest room......... Lk 14:10
of them that *s* at meat with thee... Lk 14:10
s down quickly, and write fifty.... Lk 16:6
the field, Go and *s* down to meat... Lk 17:7
my lord, *S* thou on my right hand,.. Lk 20:42

s on thrones judging the twelve............ Lk 22:30
s on the right hand of the power.......... Lk 22:69
Jesus said, Make the men s down .... Jn 6:10
up Christ to s on his throne................ Acts 2:30
my Lord, S thou on my right hand,...... Acts 2:34
he would come up and s with him .... Acts 8:31
s at meat in the idol's temple............. 1Cor 8:10
made us s together in heavenly .... Eph 2:6
S on my right hand, until I make.......... Heb 1:13
S thou here in a good place.................. Jas 2:3
or s here under my footstool................ Jas 2:3
I grant to s with me in my throne,...... Rev 3:21
I saw a woman s upon a scarlet .... Rev 17:3
I s a queen, and am no widow, and..... Rev 18:7
horses, and of them that s on them..... Rev 19:18

SITH

s thou hast not hated blood, even....... Eze 35:6

SITHRI See ZITHRI.

SITNAH (sit'-nah) A well near Gerar.

and he called the name of it S .... Gen 26:21

SITTEST

why s thou thyself alone, and all.......... Ex 18:14
them when thou s in thine house .... Deut 6:7
them when thou s in thine house .... Deut 11:19
Thou s and speakest against thy.......... Ps 50:20
When thou s to eat with a ruler,......... Prov 23:1
that s upon the throne of David,......... Jer 22:2
for s thou to judge me after the .... Acts 23:3

SITTETH

of Pharaoh that s upon his throne........ Ex 11:5
and every thing, whereon he s.............. Lev 15:4
he that s on any thing whereon he ...... Lev 15:6
that she s upon shall be unclean.......... Lev 15:20
or on any thing whereon she s .... Lev 15:23
whatsoever she s upon shall be .... Lev 15:26
when he s upon the throne of his......... Deut 17:18
also Solomon s on the throne of 1Kin 1:46
that s at the king's gate .... Est 6:10
nor s in the seat of the scornful.......... Ps 1:1
He that s in the heavens shall .... Ps 2:4
He s in the lurking places of the......... Ps 10:8
The LORD s upon the flood.................... Ps 29:10
yea, the LORD s King for ever.............. Ps 29:10
God s upon the throne of his............... Ps 47:8
he s between the cherubims................. Ps 99:1
For she s at the door of her................. Prov 9:14
A king that s in the throne of .... Prov 20:8
when he s among the elders of the...... Prov 31:23
While the king s at his table............... Song 1:12
to him that s in judgment .... Is 28:6
It is he that s upon the circle............. Is 40:22
As the partridge s on eggs.................. Jer 17:11
that s upon the throne of David......... Jer 29:16
He alone and keepeth silence,.............. Lam 3:28
and, behold, all the earth s still.......... Zec 1:11
this is a woman that s in the .... Zec 5:7
of God, and by him that s thereon...... Mt 23:22
s not down first, and counteth the ...... Lk 14:28
s not down first, and consulteth.......... Lk 14:31
is greater, he that s at meat .... Lk 22:27
is not he that s at meat .... Lk 22:27
be revealed to another that s by 1Cor 14:30
where Christ s on the right hand .... Col 3:1
so that he as God s in the temple........ 2Th 2:4
unto him that s upon the throne .... Rev 4:9
face of him that s on the throne......... Rev 6:16
our God which s upon the throne .... Rev 7:10
he that s on the throne .... Rev 7:15
whore that s upon many waters .... Rev 17:1
mountains, on which the woman s .... Rev 17:9
thou sawest, where the whore s .... Rev 17:15

SITTING

the dam s upon the young, or upon .... Deut 22:6
he was s in a summer parlour,............. Judg 3:20
the s of his servants, and the 1Kin 10:5
God, and found him s under an oak..... 1Kin 13:14
I saw the LORD s on his throne 1Kin 22:19
of the prophets were s before him...... 2Kin 4:38
the captains of the host were s 2Kin 9:5
the s of his servants, and the 2Chr 9:4
stays on each side of the s place......... 2Chr 9:18
I saw the LORD s upon his throne........ 2Chr 18:18
unto me, (the queen also s by him...... Neh 2:6
the Jew s at the king's gate............... Est 5:13
saw also the Lord s upon a throne...... Is 6:1
princes s upon the throne of............... Jer 17:25
kings s upon the throne of David....... Jer 22:4
s upon the throne of David, and.......... Jer 22:30
the king then s in the gate of .... Jer 38:7
Behold their s down, and their .... Lam 3:63
s at the receipt of custom .... Mt 9:9
unto children s in the markets............ Mt 11:16
two blind men s by the way side,........ Mt 20:30
s upon an ass, and a colt the foal....... Mt 21:5
man s on the right hand of power...... Mt 26:64
s down they watched him there.......... Mt 27:36
s over against the sepulchre................ Mt 27:61
certain of the scribes s there.............. Mk 2:6
s at the receipt of custom .... Mk 2:14
the devil, and had the legion, s.......... Mk 5:15
man s on the right hand of power...... Mk 14:62
a young man s on the right side.......... Mk 16:5
s in the midst of the doctors,.............. Lk 2:46
and doctors of the law s by .... Lk 5:17
s at the receipt of custom .... Lk 5:27
children s in the marketplace.............. Lk 7:32
s at the feet of Jesus, clothed,............ Lk 8:35

repented, s in sackcloth and ashes ..... Lk 10:13
doves, and the changers of money s ... Jn 2:14
King cometh, s on an ass's colt........... Jn 12:15
And seeth two angels in white s .... Jn 20:12
all the house where they were s .... Acts 2:2
s in his chariot read Esaias the .... Acts 8:28
the next day s on the judgment.......... Acts 25:6
I saw four and twenty elders s .... Rev 4:4

SITUATE

The forefront of the one was s........... 1Sa 14:5
O thou that art s at the entry of ...... Eze 27:3
that was s among the rivers, that ...... Nah 3:8

SITUATION

the s of this city is pleasant,.............. 2Kin 2:19
Beautiful for situation, the joy of the .... Ps 48:2

SIVAN (si'-van) Third month of the Hebrew year.

third month, that is, the month S....... Est 8:9

SIX

Noah was s hundred years old when.... Gen 7:6
In the s hundredth year of Noah's...... Gen 7:11
came to pass in the s hundredth .... Gen 8:13
s years old, when Hagar bare............. Gen 16:16
because I have born him s sons............ Gen 30:20
and s years for thy cattle.................... Gen 31:41
the souls were threescore and s .... Gen 46:26
about s hundred thousand on foot...... Ex 12:37
he took s hundred chosen chariots ..... Ex 14:7
S days ye shall gather it .... Ex 16:26
S days shalt thou labour, and do .... Ex 20:9
For in s days the LORD made............... Ex 20:11
servant, s years he shall serve............ Ex 21:2
s years thou shalt sow thy land,......... Ex 23:10
S days thou shalt do thy work, and ... Ex 23:12
and the cloud covered it s days .... Ex 24:16
s branches shall come out of the .... Ex 25:32
so in the s branches that come........... Ex 25:33
according to the s branches that .... Ex 25:35
s curtains by themselves, and.............. Ex 26:9
westward thou shalt make s boards..... Ex 26:22
S of their names on one stone, and..... Ex 28:10
the other s names of the rest on......... Ex 28:10
S days may work be done .... Ex 31:15
for in s days the LORD made............... Ex 31:17
S days thou shalt work, but on .... Ex 34:21
S days shall work be done, but on ...... Ex 35:2
and s curtains by themselves............... Ex 36:16
westward he made s boards .... Ex 36:27
s branches going out of the sides........ Ex 37:18
so throughout the s branches .... Ex 37:21
according to the s branches going....... Ex 37:21
for s hundred thousand and three ...... Ex 38:26
purifying threescore and s days........... Lev 12:5
s on a row, upon the pure table .... Lev 24:6
S years thou shalt sow thy field,........ Lev 25:3
s years thou shalt prune thy .... Lev 25:3
s thousand and five hundred.............. Num 1:21
forty and five thousand and hundred ... Num 1:25
and fourteen thousand and s hundred ... Num 1:27
numbered were s hundred thousand... Num 2:4
and fourteen thousand and s hundred ... Num 2:4
s thousand and four hundred,.............. Num 2:9
s thousand and five hundred............... Num 2:11
thousand and s hundred and fifty ...... Num 2:15
and seven thousand and s hundred..... Num 2:31
hosts were s hundred thousand.......... Num 3:28
s hundred, keeping the charge of........ Num 3:34
thousand and s hundred and fifty........ Num 4:40
thousand and s hundred and thirty .... Num 4:48
s covered wagons, and twelve oxen ..... Num 7:3
are s hundred thousand footmen......... Num 11:21
and five thousand and s hundred........ Num 26:41
s hundred thousand and a thousand ... Num 26:51
was s hundred thousand .... Num 31:36
of the sheep was s hundred................. Num 31:37
beeves were thirty and s thousand...... Num 31:38
And thirty and s thousand beeves,...... Num 31:44
shall be s cities for refuge .... Num 35:6
cities which ye shall give s.................. Num 35:13
These s cities shall be a refuge,.......... Num 35:15
S days thou shalt labour, and do........ Deut 5:13
unto thee, and serve thee s years .... Deut 15:12
to thee, in serving thee s years .... Deut 15:18
S days thou shalt eat unleavened....... Deut 16:8
Thus shalt thou do s days.................. Josh 6:3
so they did s days .... Josh 6:14
of them about thirty and s men.......... Josh 7:5
s cities with their villages .... Josh 15:59
s cities with their villages .... Josh 15:62
s hundred men with an ox ephod .... Judg 3:31
And Jephthah judged Israel s years .... Judg 12:7
s hundred men appointed with .... Judg 18:11
the s hundred men appointed with .... Judg 18:16
entering of the gate with the s .... Judg 18:17
s thousand men that drew sword,....... Judg 20:15
But s hundred men turned and fled .... Judg 20:47
he measured s measures of barley...... Ruth 3:15
These s measures of barley gave........ Ruth 3:17
thousand horsemen, and people as 1Sa 13:5
bowes were thirty and s thousand...... 1Sa 13:15
with him were about s hundred men... 1Sa 14:2
Gath, whose height was s cubits 1Sa 17:4
weighed s hundred shekels of iron...... 1Sa 17:7
men, which were about s hundred....... 1Sa 23:13
he passed over with the s hundred..... 1Sa 27:2
the s hundred men that were with..... 1Sa 30:9
Judah was seven years and s months... 2Sa 2:11

Judah seven years and s months......... 2Sa 5:5
ark of the LORD had gone s paces...... 2Sa 6:13
s hundred men which came after......... 2Sa 15:18
that had on every hand s fingers........ 2Sa 21:20
fingers, and on every foot s toes......... 2Sa 21:20
and the middle was s cubits broad...... 1Kin 6:6
one year was s hundred threescore 1Kin 10:14
threescore and s talents of gold,........ 1Kin 10:14
s hundred shekels of gold went to 1Kin 10:16
The throne had s steps, and the 1Kin 10:19
and on the other upon the s steps 1Kin 10:20
went out of Egypt for s hundred........ 1Kin 10:29
(For s months did Joab remain 1Kin 11:16
s years reigned he in Tirzah 1Kin 16:23
s thousand pieces of gold, and ten 2Kin 5:5
in the house of the LORD s years........ 2Kin 11:3
have smitten five or s times................ 2Kin 13:19
over Israel in Samaria s months 2Kin 15:8
These s were born unto him in 1Chr 3:4
reigned seven years and s months 1Chr 3:4
Bariah, and Neariah, and Shaphat, s ... 1Chr 3:22
had sixteen sons and s daughters 1Chr 4:27
and twenty thousand and s hundred... 1Chr 7:4
were bands of soldiers for war, s........ 1Chr 7:4
was twenty and s thousand names..... 1Chr 7:40
And Azel had s sons, whose names..... 1Chr 8:38
brethren, s hundred and ninety.......... 1Chr 9:6
nine hundred and fifty and s 1Chr 9:9
And Azel had s sons, whose names..... 1Chr 9:44
shield and spear were s thousand 1Chr 12:24
Levi four thousand and s hundred...... 1Chr 12:26
and eight thousand and s hundred...... 1Chr 12:35
s on each hand, and s on each........... 1Chr 20:6
s hundred shekels of gold................... 1Chr 21:25
s thousand were officers and 1Chr 23:4
Hashabiah, and Mattithiah, s 1Chr 25:3
Eastward were s Levites,...................... 1Chr 26:17
for s hundred shekels of silver............ 2Chr 1:17
s hundred to oversee them.................. 2Chr 2:2
and three thousand and s hundred..... 2Chr 2:17
s hundred overseers to set the 2Chr 2:18
amounting to s hundred talents 2Chr 8:18
Solomon in one year was s hundred ... 2Chr 9:13
threescore and s talents of gold......... 2Chr 9:13
s hundred shekels of beaten gold........ 2Chr 9:15
there were s steps to the throne,........ 2Chr 9:18
and on the other upon the s steps 2Chr 9:18
In the s and thirtieth year of the 2Chr 16:1
hid in the house of God s years.......... 2Chr 22:12
were two thousand and s hundred...... 2Chr 26:12
things were s hundred oxen 2Chr 29:33
s hundred small cattle, and three 2Chr 35:8
of Bani, s hundred forty and two...... Ezr 2:10
s hundred twenty and three .... Ezr 2:11
Adonikam, s hundred sixty and s ...... Ezr 2:13
Bigvai, two thousand fifty and s .... Ezr 2:14
The men of Netophah, fifty and s ...... Ezr 2:22
and Gaba, s hundred twenty and one ... Ezr 2:26
of Magbish, an hundred fifty and s .... Ezr 2:30
thousand and s hundred and thirty..... Ezr 2:35
of Nekoda, s hundred fifty and two ... Ezr 2:60
were seven hundred thirty and s .... Ezr 2:67
s thousand seven hundred and .... Ezr 2:67
weighed unto their hand s hundred .... Ezr 8:26
s rams, seventy and seven lambs,....... Ezr 8:35
was one ox, and s choice sheep .... Neh 5:18
of Arah, s hundred fifty and two........ Neh 7:10
Binnui, s hundred forty and eight...... Neh 7:15
s hundred twenty and eight................ Neh 7:16
s hundred threescore and seven.......... Neh 7:17
of Adin, s hundred fifty and five........ Neh 7:20
and Gaba, s hundred twenty and one ... Neh 7:30
of Nekoda, s hundred fifty and two ... Neh 7:62
horses, seven hundred thirty and s ..... Neh 7:68
s thousand seven hundred and .... Neh 7:69
s months with oil of myrrh, and......... Est 2:12
s months with sweet odours, and....... Est 2:12
shall deliver thee in s troubles............ Job 5:19
s thousand camels, and a thousand ... Job 42:12
These s things doth the LORD hate..... Prov 6:16
each one had s wings.......................... Is 6:2
when he hath served thee s years ...... Jer 34:14
and s pomegranates on a side............. Jer 52:23
were four thousand and s hundred..... Jer 52:30
s men came from the way of the .... Eze 9:2
of s cubits long by the cubit.............. Eze 40:5
were s cubits on this side.................... Eze 40:12
and s cubits on that side................... Eze 40:12
s cubits broad on the one side,........... Eze 41:1
and s cubits on the other side,.......... Eze 41:3
and the door, s cubits .... Eze 41:3
the wall of the house, s cubits .... Eze 41:5
a full reed of s great cubits................ Eze 41:8
shall be shut the s working days......... Eze 46:1
shall be s lambs without blemish,....... Eze 46:4
blemish, and s lambs, and a ram .... Eze 46:6
and the breadth thereof s cubits .... Dan 3:1
s times shalt thou take it Peter.......... Mt 17:1
after s days Jesus taketh with .... Mk 9:2
s months, when great famine was....... Lk 4:25
There are s days in which men........... Lk 13:14
set there s waterpots of stone .... Jn 2:6
s years was this temple in .... Jn 2:20
Then Jesus s days before the .... Jn 12:1
Moreover these s brethren .... Acts 11:12
s months, teaching the word of .... Acts 18:11
space of three years and s months...... Jas 5:17
each of them s wings about him......... Rev 4:8
is s hundred threescore and .... Rev 13:18
a thousand and s hundred furlongs.... Rev 14:20

SIXSCORE
to the king s talents of gold................1Kin 9:14
wherein are more than s thousand.... Jonah 4:11

SIXTEEN
she bare unto Jacob, even s souls...... Gen 46:18
sockets of silver, s sockets................. Ex 26:25
sockets were s sockets of silver........... Ex 36:30
s thousand and five hundred............... Num 26:22
And the persons were s thousand....... Num 31:40
And s thousand persons...................... Num 31:46
was s thousand seven hundred and.. Num 31:52
s cities with their villages.................... Josh 15:41
s cities with their villages.................... Josh 19:22
in Samaria, and reigned s years........... 2Kin 13:10
Azariah, which was s years old............ 2Kin 14:21
S years old was he when he began...... 2Kin 15:2
he reigned s years in Jerusalem........... 2Kin 15:33
reigned s years in Jerusalem, and...... 2Kin 16:2
And Shimei had s sons and six............ 1Chr 4:27
the sons of Eleazar there were s........ 1Chr 24:4
and two sons, and s daughters............ 2Chr 13:21
who was s years old, and made him.... 2Chr 26:1
S years old was Uzziah when he........ 2Chr 26:3
he reigned s years in Jerusalem.......... 2Chr 27:1
reigned s years in Jerusalem............... 2Chr 27:8
he reigned s years in Jerusalem.......... 2Chr 28:1
two hundred threescore and s souls.... Acts 27:37

SIXTEENTH
to Bilgah, the s to Immer,.................. 1Chr 24:14
The to Hananiah, he, his sons,........... 1Chr 25:23
in the s day of the first month............. 2Chr 29:17

SIXTH
and the morning were the s day......... Gen 1:31
again, and bare Jacob the s son.......... Gen 30:19
that on the s day they shall................ Ex 16:5
that on the s day they gathered.......... Ex 16:22
the s day the bread of two days.......... Ex 16:29
shalt double the s curtain in the......... Ex 26:9
blessing upon you in the s year........... Lev 25:21
On the s day Eliasaph the son of........ Num 7:42
on the s day eight bullocks, two......... Num 29:29
The s lot came out to the.................... Josh 19:32
And the s, Ithream, by Eglah............... 2Sa 3:5
s year of Asa king of Judah began...... 1Kin 16:8
even in the s year of Hezekiah............ 2Kin 18:10
Ozem the s, David the seventh........... 1Chr 2:15
the s, Ithream by Eglah his wife.......... 1Chr 3:3
Attai the s, Eliel the seventh............... 1Chr 12:11
to Malchijah, the s to Mijamin,.......... 1Chr 24:9
The s to Bukkiah, he, his sons,.......... 1Chr 25:13
Elam the fifth, Jehohanan the s.......... 1Chr 26:3
Ammiel the s, Issachar the................. 1Chr 26:5
The s captain for the s month............ 1Chr 27:9
which was in the s year of the............ Ezr 6:15
Hanun the s son of Zalaph,................ Neh 3:30
by measure, the s part of an hin......... Eze 4:11
in the s year, in the s month............... Eze 8:1
and leave but the s part of thee......... Eze 39:2
the s part of an ephah of an.............. Eze 45:13
ye shall give the s part of an.............. Eze 45:13
the s part of an ephah, and............... Eze 46:14
Darius the king, in the s month.......... Hag 1:1
and twentieth day of the s month...... Hag 1:15
Again he went out about the s........... Mt 20:5
Now from the s hour there was.......... Mt 27:45
when the s hour was come, there....... Mk 15:33
in the s month the angel Gabriel........ Lk 1:26
this is the s month with her, who....... Lk 1:36
And it was about the s hour............... Lk 23:44
and it was about the s hour............... Jn 4:6
the passover, and about the s hour.... Jn 19:14
housetop to pray about the s hour..... Acts 10:9
when he had opened the s seal.......... Rev 6:12
the s angel sounded, and I heard a.... Rev 9:14
Saying to the s angel which had......... Rev 9:14
the s angel poured out his vial.......... Rev 16:12
the s, sardius.................................... Rev 21:20

SIXTY
And Mahalaleel lived s and five......... Gen 5:15
And Jared lived an hundred s............. Gen 5:18
days of Jared were nine hundred s..... Gen 5:20
And Enoch lived s and five years,....... Gen 5:21
of Enoch were threescore and s......... Gen 5:23
of Methuselah were nine hundred s.... Gen 5:27
years old even unto s years old.......... Lev 27:3
And if it be from s years old.............. Lev 27:7
the rams s, the he goats s................. Num 7:88
the lambs of the first year s.............. Num 7:88
of Adonikam, six hundred s.............. Ezr 2:13
some an hundredfold, some s............ Mt 13:23
forth, some thirty, and some s........... Mk 4:8
fruit, some thirtyfold, some s............ Mk 4:20

SIXTYFOLD
some an hundredfold, some s............ Mt 13:8

SIYON See SION.

SIZE
the curtains were all of one s............. Ex 36:9
the eleven curtains were of one s....... Ex 36:15
were of one measure and one s.......... 1Kin 6:25
casting, one measure, and one s........ 1Kin 7:37
and for all manner of measure and s.. 1Chr 23:29

SKIES
waters, and thick clouds of the s........ 2Sa 22:12
waters and thick clouds of the s......... Ps 18:11
the s sent out a sound...................... Ps 77:17
let the s pour down righteousness...... Is 45:8

---

and is lifted up even to the s............. Jer 51:9

SKILFUL
s in war, were four and forty............. 1Chr 5:18
about the song, because he was s...... 1Chr 15:22
workmanship every willing s man 1Chr 28:21
to work in gold, and in silver,........... 2Chr 2:14
of brutish men, and s to destroy....... Eze 21:31
s in all wisdom, and cunning in......... Dan 1:4
such as are s of lamentation to......... Amos 5:16

SKILFULLY
play s with a loud noise.................... Ps 33:3

SKILFULNESS
guided them by the s of his hands ..... Ps 78:72

SKILL
can s to hew timber like unto the...... 1Kin 5:6
that can s to grave with the.............. 2Chr 2:7
can s to cut timber in Lebanon.......... 2Chr 2:8
all that could s of instruments.......... 2Chr 34:12
nor yet favour to men of s................ Eccl 9:11
s in all learning and wisdom,............ Dan 1:17
am now come forth to give thee s..... Dan 9:22

SKIN
only, it is his raiment for his s.......... Ex 22:27
flesh of the bullock, and his s........... Ex 29:14
the s of his face shone while he......... Ex 34:29
behold, the s of his face shone.......... Ex 34:30
that the s of Moses' face shone......... Ex 34:35
the s of the bullock, and all his......... Lev 4:11
shall have to himself the s of............ Lev 7:8
vessel of wood, or raiment, or s........ Lev 11:32
in the s of his flesh a rising.............. Lev 13:2
it be in the s of his flesh like........... Lev 13:2
the plague in the s of the flesh......... Lev 13:3
be deeper than the s of his flesh...... Lev 13:3
be white in the s of his flesh............ Lev 13:4
in sight be not deeper than the s...... Lev 13:4
and the plague spread not in the s.... Lev 13:5
and the plague spread not in the s.... Lev 13:6
scab spread much abroad in the s..... Lev 13:7
the scab spreadeth in the s.............. Lev 13:8
if the rising be white in the s........... Lev 13:10
old leprosy in the s of his flesh........ Lev 13:11
leprosy break out abroad in the s..... Lev 13:12
the leprosy cover all the s of............ Lev 13:12
in which, even in the s thereof......... Lev 13:18
it be in sight lower than the s........... Lev 13:20
and if it be not lower than the s....... Lev 13:21
if it spread much abroad in the s...... Lev 13:22
in the s whereof there is a hot......... Lev 13:24
it be in sight deeper than the s........ Lev 13:25
it be no lower than the other s......... Lev 13:26
it be spread much abroad in the s..... Lev 13:27
his place, and spread not in the s...... Lev 13:28
it be in sight deeper than the s........ Lev 13:30
be not in sight deeper than the s...... Lev 13:31
be not in sight deeper than the s...... Lev 13:32
the scab be not spread in the s......... Lev 13:34
nor be in sight deeper than the s...... Lev 13:34
much in the s after his cleansing...... Lev 13:35
if the scall be spread in the s........... Lev 13:36
the s of their flesh bright spots........ Lev 13:38
if the bright spots in the s of............ Lev 13:39
spot that groweth in the s................ Lev 13:39
appeareth in the s of the flesh......... Lev 13:43
a s, or in any thing made of s........... Lev 13:48
in the garment, or in the s............... Lev 13:49
in the wool, or in any thing of s....... Lev 13:49
warp, or in the woof, or in a s.......... Lev 13:51
or in any work that is made of s....... Lev 13:51
or in linen, or in any thing of s......... Lev 13:52
in the woof, or in any thing of s....... Lev 13:53
of the garment, or out of the s......... Lev 13:56
in the wool, or in any thing of s....... Lev 13:57
or whatsoever thing of s it be........... Lev 13:58
And every garment, and every s........ Lev 15:17
her s, and her flesh, and her blood.... Num 19:5
S for s, yea, all that a man............... Job 2:4
my s is broken, and become............. Job 7:5
Thou hast clothed me with s............. Job 10:11
I have sewed sackcloth upon my s..... Job 16:15
devour the strength of his s............. Job 18:13
My bone cleaveth to my s and to my.. Job 19:20
am escaped with the s of my teeth... Job 19:20
though after my s worms destroy..... Job 19:26
My s is black upon me, and my......... Job 30:30
thou fill his s with barbed irons....... Job 41:7
groaning my bones cleave to my s..... Ps 102:5
Can the Ethiopian change his s......... Jer 13:23
My flesh and my s hath he made old.. Lam 3:4
their s cleaveth to their bones.......... Lam 4:8
Our s was black like an oven............ Lam 5:10
and about thee will builders' s......... Eze 16:10
upon you, and cover you with s........ Eze 37:6
them, and the s covered them above.. Eze 37:8
pluck off their s from off them......... Mic 3:2
flay their s from off them................ Mic 3:3
a girdle of a s about his loins.......... Mk 1:6

SKINS
did the LORD God make coats of s..... Gen 3:21
She put the s of the kids of the........ Gen 27:16
s dyed red, and badgers' s............... Ex 25:5
for the tent of rams' s dyed red........ Ex 26:14
and a covering above of badgers' s... Ex 26:14
s dyed red, and badgers' s............... Ex 35:7
red s of rams, and badgers' s........... Ex 35:23
for the tent of rams' s dyed red....... Ex 36:19
covering of badgers' s above that..... Ex 36:19

---

the covering of rams' s dyed red....... Ex 39:34
and the covering of badgers' s.......... Ex 39:34
warp, or woof, or any thing of s........ Lev 13:59
shall burn in the fire their s............. Lev 16:27
the covering of badgers' s................. Num 4:6
with a covering of badgers' s............ Num 4:8
within a covering of badgers' s......... Num 4:10
it with a covering of badgers' s......... Num 4:11
with a covering of badgers' s............ Num 4:12
upon it a covering of badgers' s........ Num 4:14
badgers' s that is above upon it........ Num 4:25
raiment, and all that is made of s...... Num 31:20

SKIP
maketh them also to s like a calf....... Ps 29:6

SKIPPED
The mountains s like rams................ Ps 114:4
the mountains, that ye s like rams..... Ps 114:6

SKIPPEDST
spakest of him, thou s for joy............ Jer 48:27

SKIPPING
the mountains, s upon the hills......... Song 2:8

SKIRT
wife, nor discover his father's s........ Deut 22:30
he uncovereth his father's s............. Deut 27:20
thy s over thine handmaid................. Ruth 3:9
hold upon the s of his mantle............ 1Sa 15:27
cut off the s of Saul's robe................ 1Sa 24:4
because he had cut off Saul's s.......... 1Sa 24:5
see the s of thy robe in my hand....... 1Sa 24:11
that I cut off the s of thy robe.......... 1Sa 24:11
and I spread my s over thee.............. Eze 16:8
flesh in the s of his garment............. Hag 2:12
with his s do touch bread, or............ Hag 2:12
of the s of him that is a Jew,............. Zec 8:23

SKIRTS
down to the s of his garments........... Ps 133:2
Also in thy s is found the blood......... Jer 2:34
iniquity are thy s discovered............ Jer 13:22
I discover thy s upon thy face........... Jer 13:26
Her filthiness is in her s................... Lam 1:9
in number, and bind them in thy s..... Eze 5:3
will discover thy s upon thy face....... Nah 3:5

SKULL
head, and all to brake his s............... Judg 9:53
found no more of her than the s....... 2Kin 9:35
that is to say, a place of a s.............. Mt 27:33
interpreted, The place of a s............. Mk 15:22
a place called the place of a s........... Jn 19:17

SKY
and in his excellency the s................. Deut 33:26
thou with him spread out the s.......... Job 37:18
for the s is red............................... Mt 16:2
for the s is red and lowring.............. Mt 16:3
ye can discern the face of the s......... Mt 16:3
ye can discern the face of the s......... Lk 12:56
the stars of the s in multitude........... Heb 11:12

SLACK
he will not be s to him that.............. Deut 7:10
God, thou shalt not s to pay it.......... Deut 23:21
S not thy hand from thy servants...... Josh 10:6
How long are ye s to go to............... Josh 18:3
s not thy riding for me, except I....... 2Kin 4:24
poor that dealeth with a s hand........ Prov 10:4
to Zion, Let not thine hands be s...... Zeph 3:16
The Lord is not s concerning his........ 2Pet 3:9

SLACKED
Therefore the law is s, and............... Hab 1:4

SLACKNESS
his promise, as some men count s...... 2Pet 3:9

SLAIN
for I have s a man to my wounding.... Gen 4:23
The sons of Jacob came upon the s.... Gen 34:27
them in the blood of the s kind......... Lev 14:51
ye shall be s before your enemies..... Lev 26:17
flocks and the herds be s for them.... Num 11:22
therefore he hath s them in the........ Num 14:16
whosoever toucheth one that is s...... Num 19:16
him that touched a bone, or one s.... Num 19:18
me, surely now also I had s thee....... Num 22:33
away, pierce the blood of the s......... Num 23:24
name of the Israelite that was s........ Num 25:14
even that was s with the.................. Num 25:14
woman that was s was Cozbi............. Num 25:15
which was s in the day of the........... Num 25:18
the rest of them that were s............. Num 31:8
and whosoever hath touched any s... Num 31:19
After he had s Sihon the king of....... Deut 1:4
If one be found s in the land............ Deut 21:1
and it be not known who hath s him.. Deut 21:1
are round about him that is s............ Deut 21:2
city which is next unto the slain........ Deut 21:3
that are next unto the s man............ Deut 21:6
ox shall be a before thine eyes......... Deut 21:6
and that with the blood of the s........ Deut 21:7
them up all s before Israel............... Josh 11:6
among them that were s by them...... Josh 13:22
have s his sons, threescore and........ Judg 9:18
of an ass have I s a thousand men.... Judg 15:16
husband of the woman that was s..... Judg 20:4
by night, and thought to have s me... Judg 20:5
Eli, Hophni and Phinehas, were s...... 1Sa 4:11
Saul s his thousands, and................. 1Sa 18:7
LORD liveth, he shall not be s........... 1Sa 19:6
night, to morrow thou shalt be s....... 1Sa 19:11

SLANDER (continued)

unto him, Wherefore shall he be s ... 1Sa 20:32
Saul hath s his thousands, and ... 1Sa 21:11
Saul had s the LORD's priests ... 1Sa 22:21
fell down s in mount Gilboa ... 1Sa 31:1
Philistines came to strip the s ... 1Sa 31:8
I have s the LORD's anointed ... 2Sa 1:16
Israel is s upon thy high places ... 2Sa 1:19
From the blood of the s, from the ... 2Sa 1:22
thou wast s in thine high places ... 2Sa 1:25
because he had s their brother ... 2Sa 3:30
more, when wicked men have s a ... 2Sa 4:11
hast s him with the sword of the ... 2Sa 12:9
Absalom hath s all the king's ... 2Sa 13:30
s all the young men the king's ... 2Sa 13:32
s before the servants of David ... 2Sa 18:7
Philistines had s Saul in Gilboa ... 2Sa 21:12
sword, thought to have s David ... 2Sa 21:16
And he hath s oxen and fat cattle ... 1Kin 1:9
down this day, and hath s oxen ... 1Kin 1:25
s the Canaanites that dwelt in ... 1Kin 9:16
host was gone up to bury the s ... 1Kin 11:15
s him, according to the word of ... 1Kin 13:26
and hath also s the king ... 1Kin 16:16
withal how he had s all the ... 1Kin 19:1
s thy prophets with the sword ... 1Kin 19:10
s thy prophets with the sword ... 1Kin 19:14
the kings are surely s, and they ... 2Kin 3:23
the king's sons which were s ... 2Kin 11:2
Athaliah, so that he was not s ... 2Kin 11:2
within the ranges, let him be s ... 2Kin 11:8
Let her not be s in the house of ... 2Kin 11:15
and there was the s ... 2Kin 11:16
which had s the king his father ... 2Kin 14:5
For there fell down many s ... 1Chr 5:22
fell down s in mount Gilboa ... 1Chr 10:1
Philistines came to strip the s ... 1Chr 10:8
hundred s by him at one time ... 1Chr 11:11
so there fell down s of Israel ... 1Chr 11:14
also hast s thy brethren of thy ... 2Chr 21:13
to the camp had s all the eldest ... 2Chr 22:1
and when they had s him, they ... 2Chr 22:9
among the king's sons that were s ... 2Chr 22:11
let him be s with the sword ... 2Chr 23:14
after that they had s Athaliah ... 2Chr 23:21
ye have s them in a rage that ... 2Chr 28:9
people, to be destroyed, to be s ... Est 7:4
were s in Shushan the palace was ... Est 9:11
Esther the queen, The Jews have s ... Est 9:12
they have s the servants with the ... Job 1:15
the servants with the edge of ... Job 1:17
and where the s are, there is she ... Job 39:30
ye shall be s all of you ... Ps 62:3
like the s that lie in the grave ... Ps 88:5
Rahab in pieces, as one that is s ... Ps 89:10
strong men have been s by her ... Prov 7:26
I shall be s in the streets ... Prov 22:13
and those that are ready to be s ... Prov 24:11
they shall fall under the s ... Is 10:4
the raiment of those that are s ... Is 14:19
thy land, and s thy people ... Is 14:20
thy s men are not s with the ... Is 22:2
and shall no more cover her s ... Is 26:21
or is he s according to the ... Is 27:7
of them that are s by him ... Is 27:7
Their s also shall be cast out ... Is 34:3
the s of the LORD shall be many ... Is 66:16
night for the s of the daughter ... Jer 9:1
then behold the s with the sword ... Jer 14:18
men be s by the sword in battle ... Jer 18:21
the s of the LORD shall be ... Jer 25:33
whom I have s in mine anger and in ... Jer 41:4
day after he had s Gedaliah ... Jer 41:4
whom he had s because of Gedaliah ... Jer 41:9
filled it with them that were s ... Jer 41:9
after that he had s Gedaliah the ... Jer 41:16
the son of Nethaniah had s ... Jer 41:18
Thus the s shall fall in the land ... Jer 51:4
all her s shall fall in the midst ... Jer 51:47
caused the s of Israel to fall ... Jer 51:49
shall fall the s of all the earth ... Jer 51:49
the prophet be s in the sanctuary ... Lam 2:20
thou hast s them in the day of ... Lam 2:21
thou hast s, thou hast not pitied ... Lam 3:43
They that be s with the sword are ... Lam 4:9
than they that be s with hunger ... Lam 4:9
down your s men before your idols ... Eze 6:4
the s shall fall in the midst of ... Eze 6:7
when their s men shall be among ... Eze 6:13
and fill the courts with the s ... Eze 9:7
multiplied your s in this city ... Eze 11:6
the streets thereof with the s ... Eze 11:6
Your s whom ye have laid in the ... Eze 11:7
That thou hast s my children ... Eze 16:21
third time, the sword of the s ... Eze 21:14
sword of the great men that are s ... Eze 21:14
upon the necks of them that are s ... Eze 21:29
For when they had s their idols ... Eze 23:39
the field shall be s by the sword ... Eze 26:6
s are in the midst of the seas ... Eze 28:8
when the s shall fall in Egypt ... Eze 30:4
and fill the land with the s ... Eze 30:11
them that be s with the sword ... Eze 31:17
with them that be s by the sword ... Eze 31:18
of them that are s by the sword ... Eze 32:20
lie uncircumcised, s by the sword ... Eze 32:21
all of them s, fallen by the ... Eze 32:22
all of them s, fallen by the ... Eze 32:23
about her grave, all of them s ... Eze 32:24
of the s with all her multitude ... Eze 32:25
uncircumcised, by the sword ... Eze 32:25

in the midst of them that be s ... Eze 32:25
s by the sword, though they ... Eze 32:26
them that are s with the sword ... Eze 32:28
by them that were s by the sword ... Eze 32:29
which are gone down with the s ... Eze 32:30
with them that be s by the sword ... Eze 32:30
and all his army s by the sword ... Eze 32:31
them that are s with the sword ... Eze 32:32
fill his mountains with his s ... Eze 35:8
fall that are s with the sword ... Eze 35:8
O breath, and breathe upon these s ... Eze 37:9
that the wise men should be s ... Dan 2:13
Daniel and his fellows to be s ... Dan 2:13
the king of the Chaldeans ... Dan 5:30
beheld even till the beast was s ... Dan 7:11
and many shall fall down s ... Dan 11:26
I have s them by the words of my ... Hos 6:5
young men have I s with the sword ... Amos 4:10
and there is a multitude of s ... Nah 3:3
also, ye shall be s by my sword ... Zeph 2:12
chief priests and scribes, and he ... Lk 9:22
wicked hands have crucified and s ... Acts 2:23
who was s; and all ... Acts 5:36
have ye offered to me s beasts ... Acts 7:42
they have s them which shewed ... Acts 7:52
they Pilate that he should be s ... Acts 13:28
eat nothing until we have s Paul ... Acts 23:14
having s the enmity thereby ... Eph 2:16
tempted, were s with the sword ... Heb 11:37
who was s among you, where Satan ... Rev 2:13
stood a Lamb as it had been s ... Rev 5:6
for thou wast s, and hast redeemed ... Rev 5:9
Lamb that was s to receive power ... Rev 5:12
that were s for the word of God ... Rev 6:9
were s of men seven thousand ... Rev 11:13
Lamb s from the foundation of the ... Rev 13:8
of all that were s upon the earth ... Rev 18:24
the remnant were s with the sword ... Rev 19:21

SLANDER
by bringing up a s upon the land ... Num 14:36
For I have heard the s of many ... Ps 31:13
lips, and he that uttereth s a ... Prov 10:18

SLANDERED
he hath s thy servant unto my ... 2Sa 19:27

SLANDERERS
must their wives be grave, not s ... 1Ti 3:11

SLANDEREST
thou s thine own mother's son ... Ps 50:20

SLANDERETH
Whoso privily s his neighbour ... Ps 101:5

SLANDEROUSLY
not rather, (as we be s reported ... Rom 3:8

SLANDERS
revolters, walking with s ... Jer 6:28
every neighbour will walk with s ... Jer 9:4

SLANG
s it, and smote the Philistine in ... 1Sa 17:49

SLAUGHTER
return from the s of Chedorlaomer ... Gen 14:17
them with a great s at Gibeon ... Josh 10:10
slaying them with a very great s ... Josh 10:20
vineyards, with a very great s ... Judg 11:33
them hip and thigh with a great s ... Judg 15:8
and there was a very great s ... 1Sa 4:10
also a great s among the people ... 1Sa 4:17
many of the people with a great s ... 1Sa 14:14
And that first s, which Jonathan ... 1Sa 14:14
greater s among the Philistines ... 1Sa 14:30
from the s of the Philistine ... 1Sa 17:57
from the s of the Philistine ... 1Sa 18:6
and slew them with a great s ... 1Sa 19:8
and smote them with a great s ... 1Sa 23:5
from the s of the Amalekites ... 2Sa 1:1
There is a s among the people ... 2Sa 17:9
there was there a great s that ... 2Sa 18:7
slew the Syrians with a great s ... 1Kin 20:21
people slew them with a great s ... 2Chr 13:17
come from the s of the Edomites ... 2Chr 25:14
who smote him with a great s ... 2Chr 28:5
the stroke of the sword, and s ... Est 9:5
we are counted as sheep for the s ... Ps 44:22
as an ox goeth to the s, or as a ... Prov 7:22
for him according to the s of ... Is 10:26
Prepare for his children for ... Is 14:21
s of them that are slain by ... Is 30:25
waters in the day of the great s ... Is 30:25
he hath delivered them to the s ... Is 34:2
a great s in the land of Idumea ... Is 34:6
he is brought as a lamb to the s ... Is 53:7
and ye shall all bow down to the s ... Is 65:12
of Hinnom, but the valley of s ... Jer 7:32
or an ox that is brought to the s ... Jer 11:19
them out like sheep for the s ... Jer 12:3
and prepare them for the day of s ... Jer 12:3
of Hinnom, but The valley of s ... Jer 19:6
for the days of your s and of your ... Jer 25:34
young men are gone down to the s ... Jer 48:15
let them go down to the s ... Jer 50:27
them down like lambs to the s ... Jer 51:40
every man s a weapon in his hand ... Eze 9:2
It is sharpened to make a s ... Eze 21:10
it is wrapped up for the s ... Eze 21:15
to open the mouth in the s ... Eze 21:22
for the s it is furbished, to ... Eze 21:28
when the s is made in the midst ... Eze 26:15

revolters are profound to make s ... Hos 5:2
mount of Esau may be cut off by s ... Obad 9
Feed the flock of the s ... Zec 11:4
And I will feed the flock of s ... Zec 11:7
He was led as a sheep to the s ... Acts 8:32
s against the disciples of the ... Acts 9:1
are accounted as sheep for the s ... Rom 8:36
returning from the s of the kings ... Heb 7:1
your hearts, as in a day of s ... Jas 5:5

SLAVE
is he a homeborn s ... Jer 2:14

SLAVES
and horses, and chariots, and s ... Rev 18:13

SLAY
one that findeth me shall s me ... Gen 4:14
to s the righteous with the ... Gen 18:25
wilt thou s also a righteous ... Gen 20:4
they will s me for my wife's sake ... Gen 20:11
and took the knife to s his son ... Gen 22:10
then will I s my brother Jacob ... Gen 27:41
together against me, and s me ... Gen 34:30
conspired against him to s him ... Gen 37:18
now therefore, and let us s him ... Gen 37:20
profit is it if we s our brother ... Gen 37:26
S my two sons, if I bring him not ... Gen 42:37
house, Bring these men home, and s ... Gen 43:16
this thing, he sought to s Moses ... Ex 2:15
I will s thy son, even thy ... Ex 4:23
put a sword in their hand to s us ... Ex 5:21
neighbour, to s them with guile ... Ex 21:14
innocent and righteous s thou not ... Ex 23:7
And thou shalt s the ram, and thou ... Ex 29:16
to s them in the mountains, and to ... Ex 32:12
s every man his brother, and every ... Lev 4:29
s the sin offering in the place ... Lev 4:33
s it for a sin offering in the ... Lev 14:13
he shall s the lamb in the place ... Lev 14:13
and ye shall s the beast ... Lev 20:15
one shall s her before his face ... Num 19:3
S ye every one his men that were ... Num 25:5
himself shall s the murderer ... Num 35:19
he meeteth him, he shall s him ... Num 35:19
of blood shall s the murderer ... Num 35:21
out to s them in the wilderness ... Deut 9:28
because the way is long, and s him ... Deut 11:6
reward to s an innocent person ... Deut 27:25
did the children of Israel s with ... Judg 13:22
them alive, I would not s you ... Judg 8:19
his firstborn, Up, and s them ... Judg 8:20
s me, that men say not of me, A ... Judg 9:54
because the LORD would s them ... 1Sa 2:25
the God of Israel to us, to s us ... 1Sa 5:10
his own place, that it s us not ... 1Sa 5:11
his sheep, and s them here, and eat ... 1Sa 14:34
but s both man and woman, infant ... 1Sa 15:3
to s David without a cause ... 1Sa 19:5
him, and to s him in the morning ... 1Sa 19:11
me in the bed, that I may s him ... 1Sa 19:15
be in me iniquity, s me thyself ... 1Sa 20:8
of his father to s David ... 1Sa 20:33
s the priests of the LORD ... 1Sa 22:17
I pray thee, upon me, and s me ... 2Sa 1:9
king to s thine the son of Ner ... 2Sa 3:37
Saul sought to s them in his zeal ... 2Sa 21:2
not s his servant with the sword ... 1Kin 1:51
living child, and in no wise s it ... 1Kin 3:26
living child, and in no wise s it ... 1Kin 3:26
king of Judah did Baasha s him ... 1Kin 15:28
to remembrance, and to s my son ... 1Kin 17:18
into the hand of Ahab, to s me ... 1Kin 18:9
cannot find thee, he shall s me ... 1Kin 18:12
and he shall s me ... 1Kin 18:14
the sword of Hazael shall Jehu s ... 1Kin 19:17
the sword of Jehu shall Elisha s ... 1Kin 19:17
from me, a lion shall s thee ... 1Kin 20:36
men wilt thou s with the sword ... 2Kin 8:12
to the captains, Go in, and s them ... 2Kin 10:25
them, and, behold, they s them ... 2Kin 17:26
of mount Seir, utterly to s ... 2Chr 20:23
S her not in the house of the ... 2Chr 23:14
s them, and cause the work to ... Neh 4:11
for they will come to s thee ... Neh 6:10
night will they come to s thee ... Neh 6:10
for their life, to destroy, to s ... Est 8:11
If the scourge s suddenly ... Job 9:23
Though he s me, yet will I trust ... Job 13:15
the viper's tongue shall s him ... Job 20:16
Evil shall s the wicked ... Ps 34:21
to s such as be of upright ... Ps 37:32
righteous, and seeketh to s him ... Ps 37:32
S them not, lest my people forget ... Ps 59:11
They s the widow and the stranger ... Ps 94:6
that he might even s the broken ... Ps 109:16
Surely thou wilt s the wicked ... Ps 139:19
away of the simple shall s them ... Prov 1:32
of his lips shall he s the wicked ... Is 11:4
famine, and he shall s thy remnant ... Is 14:30
he shall s the dragon that is in ... Is 27:1
for the Lord GOD shall s thee ... Is 65:15
out of the forest shall s them ... Jer 5:6
the sword to s, and the dogs to s ... Jer 15:3
their counsel against me to s me ... Jer 18:23
shall s them with the sword ... Jer 20:4
tears than mine s before your eyes ... Jer 29:21
the son of Nethaniah to s thee ... Jer 40:15
I will s Ishmael the son of ... Jer 40:15
wherefore should he s thee ... Jer 40:15
that said unto Ishmael, S us not ... Jer 41:8
S all her bullocks ... Jer 50:27

S

S utterly old and young, both .... Eze 9:6
to s the souls that should sin .... Eze 13:19
they shall s their sons and their .... Eze 23:47
He shall s with the sword thy .... Eze 26:8
he shall s thy people by the .... Eze 26:11
to s thereon the burnt offering .... Eze 40:39
they shall s the burnt offering .... Eze 44:11
to s the wise men of Babylon .... Dan 2:14
a dry land, and s her with thirst .... Hos 2:3
yet will I s even the beloved .... Hos 9:16
will s all the princes thereof .... Amos 2:3
I will s the last of them with .... Amos 9:1
the sword, and it shall s them .... Amos 9:4
continually to s the nations .... Hab 1:17
Whose possessors s them, and hold ...... Zec 11:5
and some of them they shall s .... Lk 11:49
bring hither, and s them before me ...... Lk 19:27
Jesus, and sought to s him .... Jn 11:12
heart, and took counsel to s them .... Acts 5:33
but they went about to s him .... Acts 9:29
s and eat .... Acts 11:7
for to s the third part of men .... Rev 9:15

SLAYER
that the s may flee thither .... Num 35:11
shall judge between the s .... Num 35:24
congregation shall deliver the s .... Num 35:25
But if the s shall at any time .... Num 35:26
the revenger of blood kill the s .... Num 35:27
death of the high priest the s .... Num 35:28
That the s might flee thither .... Deut 4:42
that every s may flee thither .... Deut 19:3
And this is the case of the s .... Deut 19:4
avenger of the blood pursue the s ..... Deut 19:6
That the s that killeth any .... Josh 20:3
deliver the s up into his hand .... Josh 20:5
then shall the s return, and come ..... Josh 20:6
to be a city of refuge for the s ...... Josh 21:13
to be a city of refuge for the s ...... Josh 21:21
to be a city of refuge for the s ...... Josh 21:27
to be a city of refuge for the s ...... Josh 21:32
to be a city of refuge for the s ...... Josh 21:38
to give it into the hand of the s ..... Eze 21:11

SLAYETH
him, Therefore whosoever s Cain .... Gen 4:15
s him, even so is this matter .... Deut 22:26
man, and envy s the silly one .... Job 5:2
yet say before him that s thee .... Eze 28:9
in the hand of him that s thee .... Eze 28:9

SLAYING
of all the inhabitants of Ai in ...... Josh 8:24
end of s them with a very great ...... Josh 10:20
in s his seventy brethren .... Judg 9:56
with whom I sojourn, by s her son 1Kin 17:20
s oxen, and killing sheep, eating .... Is 22:13
s the children in the valleys .... Is 57:5
to pass, while they were s them ...... Eze 9:8

SLEEP
caused a deep s to fall upon Adam .... Gen 2:21
down, a deep s fell upon Abram .... Gen 15:12
and lay down in that place to s ...... Gen 28:11
And Jacob awaked out of his s .... Gen 28:16
my s departed from mine eyes .... Gen 31:40
wherein shall he s .... Ex 22:27
thou shalt not s with his pledge .... Deut 24:12
that he may s in his own raiment, ... Deut 24:13
thou shalt s with thy fathers .... Deut 31:16
And he awaked out of his s .... Judg 16:14
she made him s upon her knees .... Judg 16:19
And he awoke out of his s, and said . Judg 16:20
was, and Samuel was laid down to s .. 1Sa 3:3
because a deep s from the LORD 1Sa 26:12
thou shalt s with thy fathers, I 2Sa 7:12
the king shall s with his fathers ... 1Kin 1:21
that night could not the king s ..... Est 6:1
when deep s falleth on men, ... Job 4:13
for now shall I s in the dust, ... Job 7:21
nor be raised out of their s .... Job 14:12
when deep s falleth upon men, in .... Job 33:15
both lay me down in peace, and s .... Ps 4:8
lest I s the s of death .... Ps 13:3
spoiled, they have slept their s .... Ps 76:5
and horse are cast into a dead s .... Ps 76:6
the Lord awaked as one out of s ..... Ps 78:65
they are as a s .... Ps 90:5
shall neither slumber nor s .... Ps 121:4
for so he giveth his beloved s ...... Ps 127:2
I will not give s to mine eyes ...... Ps 132:4
lie down, and thy s shall be sweet .. Prov 3:24
For they s not, except they have .... Prov 4:16
their s is taken away, unless .... Prov 4:16
Give not s to thine eyes, nor .... Prov 6:4
How long wilt thou s, O sluggard .... Prov 6:9
when wilt thou arise out of thy s ... Prov 6:9
Yet a little s, a little slumber, ... Prov 6:10
little folding of the hands to s .... Prov 6:10
casteth into a deep s .... Prov 19:15
Love not s, lest thou come to .... Prov 20:13
Yet a little s, a little slumber, ... Prov 24:33
little folding of the hands to s .... Prov 24:33
The s of a labouring man is sweet ... Eccl 5:12
the rich will not suffer him to s ... Eccl 5:12
nor night seeth s with his eyes .... Eccl 8:16
I s, but my heart waketh .... Song 5:2
none shall slumber nor s .... Is 5:27
out upon you the spirit of deep s .. Is 29:10
and my s was sweet unto me .... Jer 31:26
they may rejoice, and s .... Jer 51:39
a perpetual s, and not wake .... Jer 51:39

they shall s a perpetual s, ... Jer 51:57
and they shall s a perpetual s ..... Jer 51:57
the wilderness, and s in the woods . Eze 34:25
troubled, and his s brake from him . Dan 2:1
and his s went from him .... Dan 6:18
I was in a deep s on my face .... Dan 8:18
then was I in a deep s on my face .. Dan 10:9
many of them that s in the dust .... Dan 12:2
man that is wakened out of his s ... Zec 4:1
s did as the angel of the Lord ..... Mt 1:24
S now, and take your rest .... Mt 26:45
And should s, and rise night and day Mk 4:27
S on now, and take your rest .... Mk 14:41
were with him were heavy with s .... Lk 9:32
And said unto them, Why s ye .... Lk 22:46
go, that I may awake him out of s .. Jn 11:11
said his disciples, Lord, if he s .. Jn 11:12
had spoken of taking of rest in s .. Jn 11:13
by the will of God, fell on s ...... Acts 13:36
the prison awaking out of his s .... Acts 16:27
being fallen into a deep s .... Acts 20:9
preaching, he sunk down with s ..... Acts 20:9
it is high time to awake out of s .. Rom 13:11
and sickly among you, and many s ... 1Cor 11:30
We shall not all s, but we shall ... 1Cor 15:51
even so them also which s in 1Th 4:14
Therefore let us not s, as do 1Th 5:6
they that s in the night 1Th 5:7
us, that, whether we wake or s 1Th 5:10

SLEEPER
unto him, What meanest thou, O s ... Jonah 1:6

SLEEPEST
Awake, why s thou, O Lord .... Ps 44:23
when thou s, it shall keep thee .... Prov 6:22
saith unto Peter, Simon, s thou .... Mk 14:37
he saith, Awake thou that s .... Eph 5:14

SLEEPETH
a journey, or peradventure he s 1Kin 18:27
but he that s in harvest is a son .. Prov 10:5
their baker s all the night .... Hos 7:6
for the maid is not dead, but s .... Mt 9:24
the damsel is not dead, but s ...... Mk 5:39
she is not dead, but s .... Lk 8:52
unto them, Our friend Lazarus s .... Jn 11:11

SLEEPING
Saul lay s within the trench, and .. 1Sa 26:7
s, lying down, loving to slumber ... Is 56:10
coming suddenly he find you s ...... Mk 13:36
And he cometh, and findeth them s .. Mk 14:37
he found them s for sorrow .... Lk 22:45
Peter was s between two soldiers ... Acts 12:6

SLEIGHT
wind of doctrine, by the s of men .. Eph 4:14

SLEPT
sleep to fall upon Adam, and he s .. Gen 2:21
And he s and dreamed the second .... Gen 41:5
But Uriah s at the door of the 2Sa 11:9
So David s with his fathers, and ... 1Kin 2:10
beside me, while thine handmaid s .. 1Kin 3:20
that David s with his fathers 1Kin 11:21
Solomon s with his fathers, and 1Kin 11:43
he s with his fathers, and Nadab ... 1Kin 14:20
Rehoboam s with his fathers, and ... 1Kin 14:31
Abijam s with his fathers 1Kin 15:8
Asa s with his fathers, and was 1Kin 15:24
So Baasha s with his fathers, and .. 1Kin 16:6
So Omri s with his fathers, and 1Kin 16:28
s under a juniper tree, behold, ... 1Kin 19:5
So Ahab s with his fathers 1Kin 22:40
Jehoshaphat s with his fathers 1Kin 22:50
Joram s with his fathers, and was .. 2Kin 8:24
And Jehu s with his fathers 2Kin 10:35
Jehoahaz s with his fathers 2Kin 13:9
And Joash s with his fathers 2Kin 13:13
Jehoash s with his fathers, and 2Kin 14:16
that the king s with his fathers ... 2Kin 14:22
Jeroboam s with his fathers, even .. 2Kin 14:29
So Azariah s with his fathers 2Kin 15:7
Menahem s with his fathers 2Kin 15:22
Jotham s with his fathers, and was . 2Kin 15:38
Ahaz s with his fathers, and was ... 2Kin 16:20
Hezekiah s with his fathers 2Kin 20:21
Manasseh s with his fathers, and ... 2Kin 21:18
So Jehoiakim s with his fathers 2Kin 24:6
Solomon s with his fathers, and he . 2Chr 9:31
Rehoboam s with his fathers, and ... 2Chr 12:16
So Abijah s with his fathers, and .. 2Chr 14:1
Asa s with his fathers, and died ... 2Chr 16:13
Now Jehoshaphat s with his 2Chr 21:1
that the king s with his fathers ... 2Chr 26:2
So Uzziah s with his fathers, and .. 2Chr 26:23
Jotham s with his fathers, and 2Chr 27:9
Ahaz s with his fathers and they ... 2Chr 28:27
Hezekiah s with his fathers, and ... 2Chr 32:33
So Manasseh s with his fathers, ... 2Chr 33:20
and been quiet, I should have s .... Job 3:13
I laid me down and s .... Ps 3:5
spoiled, they have their sleep ..... Ps 76:5
But while men s, his enemy came .... Mt 13:25
tarried, they all slumbered and s .. Mt 25:5
of the saints which s arose .... Mt 27:52
and stole him away while we s ...... Mt 28:13
the firstfruits of them that s 1Cor 15:20

SLEW
Abel his brother, and s him .... Gen 4:8
seed instead of Abel, whom Cain s . Gen 4:25

city boldly, and s all the males ... Gen 34:25
they s Hamor and Shechem his son ... Gen 34:26
and the LORD s him .... Gen 38:7
wherefore he s him also .... Gen 38:10
for in their anger they s a man .... Gen 49:6
he s the Egyptian, and hid him in .. Ex 2:12
that the LORD s all the firstborn .. Ex 13:15
And he s it .... Lev 8:15
And he s it .... Lev 8:23
s the calf of the sin offering, ... Lev 9:8
And he s the burnt offering, ... Lev 9:12
s it, and offered it for sin, as .. Lev 9:15
He s also the bullock and the ram . Lev 9:18
and they s all the males .... Num 31:7
they s the kings of Midian, ... Num 31:8
son of Beor they s with the sword . Num 31:8
turned again, and s them one of Ai . Josh 8:21
of Israel, that they s them not .... Josh 9:26
s them with a great slaughter at ... Josh 10:10
of Israel s with the sword .... Josh 10:11
s them, and hanged them on five .... Josh 10:26
smote them, and s them .... Josh 11:17
they s of them in Bezek ten .... Judg 1:4
they s the Canaanites and the ..... Judg 1:5
they s Sheshai, and Ahiman, and ... Judg 1:10
they s the Canaanites that .... Judg 1:17
they s of Moab at that time about . Judg 3:29
which s of the Philistines six .... Judg 3:31
they s Oreb upon the rock Oreb, ... Judg 7:25
Zeeb they s at the winepress of ... Judg 7:25
Penuel, and s the men of the city . Judg 8:17
men were they whom ye s at Tabor .. Judg 8:18
s Zebah and Zalmunna .... Judg 8:21
s his brethren the sons of .... Judg 9:5
their brother, which s them .... Judg 9:24
were in the fields, and s them .... Judg 9:44
the s people that was therein, and Judg 9:45
men say not of me, A woman s him .. Judg 9:54
s him at the passages of Jordan ... Judg 12:6
a thirty men of them, and took .... Judg 14:19
s a thousand men therewith .... Judg 15:15
our country, which s many of us ... Judg 16:24
So the dead which he s at his ..... Judg 16:30
than they which he s in his life .. Judg 16:30
s two thousand men of them .... Judg 20:45
they s a bullock, and brought the . 1Sa 1:25
they s of the army in the field, .. 1Sa 4:2
the s Ammonites until the heat of . 1Sa 11:11
and his armourbearer s after him .. 1Sa 14:13
calves, and s them on the ground .. 1Sa 14:32
him that night, and s them there .. 1Sa 14:34
his beard, and smote him, and s him 1Sa 17:35
Thy servant s both the lion and ... 1Sa 17:36
and smote the Philistine, and s him 1Sa 17:50
s him, and cut off his head 1Sa 17:51
s of the Philistines two hundred .. 1Sa 18:27
s the Philistine, and the LORD 1Sa 19:5
s them with a great slaughter 1Sa 19:8
s on that day fourscore and five .. 1Sa 22:18
Saul s his thousands, and David ... 1Sa 29:5
they s not any, either great or ... 1Sa 30:2
and the Philistines s Jonathan 1Sa 31:2
a him, because I was sure that he . 2Sa 1:10
and Abishai his brother s Abner ... 2Sa 3:30
s him, and beheaded him, and took . 2Sa 4:7
s him in Ziklag, who thought that . 2Sa 4:10
his young men, and they s them 2Sa 4:12
David s of the Syrians two and 2Sa 8:5
David s the men of seven hundred .. 2Sa 10:18
the one smote the other, and s him 2Sa 14:6
the life of his brother whom he s . 2Sa 14:7
about and smote Absalom, and s him 2Sa 18:15
because he s the Gibeonites 2Sa 21:1
Sibbechai the Hushathite s Saph ... 2Sa 21:18
s the brother of Goliath the 2Sa 21:19
the brother of David s him 2Sa 21:21
hundred, whom he s at one time 2Sa 23:8
defended it, and s the Philistines 2Sa 23:12
s them, and had the name among 2Sa 23:18
he s two lionlike men of Moab 2Sa 23:20
s a lion in the midst of a pit in . 2Sa 23:20
he s an Egyptian, a goodly man 2Sa 23:21
hand, and s him with his own spear 2Sa 23:21
And Adonijah s sheep and oxen and . 1Kin 1:9
the son of Jether, whom he s 1Kin 2:5
s them with the sword, my father .. 1Kin 2:32
up, and fell upon him, and s him .. 1Kin 2:34
when David s them of Zobah 1Kin 11:24
lion met him by the way, and s him 1Kin 13:24
that he s all the house of Baasha . 1Kin 16:11
s the prophets of the Lord 1Kin 18:13
the brook Kishon, and s them there 1Kin 18:40
s them, and boiled their flesh 1Kin 19:21
And they s every one his man 1Kin 20:20
s the Syrians with a great 1Kin 20:21
the children of Israel s of the ... 1Kin 20:29
him, a lion found him, and s him .. 1Kin 20:36
Had Zimri peace, who s his master . 2Kin 9:31
s seventy persons, and put their .. 2Kin 10:7
against my master, and s him 2Kin 10:9
but who s all these 2Kin 10:9
So Jehu s all that remained of 2Kin 10:11
s them at the pit of the shearing . 2Kin 10:14
he s all that remained unto Ahab .. 2Kin 10:17
s Mattan the priest of Baal 2Kin 11:18
they s Athaliah with the sword 2Kin 11:20
s Joash in the house of Millo, ... 2Kin 12:20
that he s his servants which had .. 2Kin 14:5
the murderers he s not 2Kin 14:6
He s of Edom in the valley of 2Kin 14:7

him to Lachish, and s him there...... 2Kin 14:19
s him, and reigned in his stead...... 2Kin 15:10
s him, and reigned in his stead...... 2Kin 15:14
s him, and reigned in his stead...... 2Kin 15:30
of it captive to Kir, and s Rezin...... 2Kin 16:9
among them, which s some of them.. 2Kin 17:25
s the king in his own house............ 2Kin 21:23
the people of the land s all them...... 2Kin 21:24
he s all the priests of the high........ 2Kin 23:20
he s him at Megiddo, when he had.. 2Kin 23:29
they s the sons of Zedekiah............ 2Kin 25:7
s them at Riblah in the land of........ 2Kin 25:21
and he s him................................ 1Chr 2:3
that were born in that land s.......... 1Chr 7:21
and the Philistines s Jonathan........ 1Chr 10:2
therefore he s him, and turned the.. 1Chr 10:14
it, and s the Philistines.................. 1Chr 11:14
he s them, and had a name among.. 1Chr 11:20
he s two lionlike men of Moab........ 1Chr 11:22
s a lion in a pit in a snowy day........ 1Chr 11:22
he s an Egyptian, a man of great.... 1Chr 11:23
hand, and s him with his own spear.. 1Chr 11:23
David s of the Syrians two and........ 1Chr 18:5
Abishai the son Zeruiah s of the.... 1Chr 18:12
David s of the Syrians seven.......... 1Chr 19:18
Sibbechai the Hushathite s Sippai.. 1Chr 20:4
Elhanan the son of Jair s Lahmi...... 1Chr 20:5
of Shimea David's brother s him...... 1Chr 20:7
his people s them with a great........ 2Chr 13:17
s all his brethren with the sword...... 2Chr 21:4
ministered to Ahaziah, he s them.... 2Chr 22:8
Athaliah, so that she s him not........ 2Chr 22:11
king's house, they s her there.......... 2Chr 23:15
s Mattan the priest of Baal............ 2Chr 23:17
had done to him, but s his son........ 2Chr 24:22
s him on his bed, and he died.......... 2Chr 24:25
that he s his servants that had........ 2Chr 25:3
But he s not their children, but........ 2Chr 25:4
Lachish after him, and s him there.. 2Chr 25:27
of Remaliah s in Judah an hundred.. 2Chr 28:6
s Maaseiah the king's son, and........ 2Chr 28:7
bowels s him there with the sword.. 2Chr 32:21
him, and s him in his own house...... 2Chr 33:24
But the people of the land s all........ 2Chr 33:25
who s their young men with the........ 2Chr 36:17
s thy brothers which testified.......... Neh 9:26
in Shushan the palace the Jews........ Est 9:16
the enemy of the Jews, s they........ Est 9:10
s three hundred men at Shushan...... Est 9:15
s of their foes seventy and five........ Est 9:16
s the fattest of them, and smote...... Ps 78:31
When he s them, then they sought.. Ps 78:34
into blood, and s their fish.............. Ps 105:29
great nations, and s mighty kings.... Ps 135:10
And s famous kings........................ Ps 136:18
killeth an ox is as if he s a man...... Is 66:3
Because he s me not from the womb.. Jer 20:17
who s him with the sword, and cast.. Jer 26:23
Then the king of Babylon s............ Jer 39:6
Babylon s all the nobles of Judah.... Jer 39:6
s him, whom the king of Babylon.... Jer 41:2
Ishmael also s all the Jews that...... Jer 41:3
the son of Nethaniah s them.......... Jer 41:9
s them not among their brethren...... Jer 41:8
the king of Babylon s the sons of.... Jer 52:10
he s also all the princes of............ Jer 52:10
s all that were pleasant to the........ Lam 2:4
they went forth, and s in the city.... Eze 9:7
and s her with the sword................ Eze 23:10
whereupon they s their sacrifices.... Eze 40:41
they s the burnt offering................ Eze 40:42
the flame of the fire s those men.... Dan 3:22
whom he would he s...................... Dan 5:19
s all the children that were in.......... Mt 2:16
him out of the vineyard, and s him.. Mt 21:39
them spitefully, and s them............ Mt 22:6
whom ye s between the temple and.. Mt 23:35
s them, think ye that they were...... Lk 13:4
raised up Jesus, whom ye s............ Acts 5:30
whom they s and hanged on a tree.. Acts 10:39
the raiment of them that s him........ Acts 22:20
deceived me, and by it s me............ Rom 7:11
that wicked one, and s his brother.. 1Jn 3:12
And wherefore s he him.................. 1Jn 3:12

SLEWEST
whom thou s in the valley of Elah.... 1Sa 21:9

SLIDDEN
is this people of Jerusalem s............ Jer 8:5

SLIDE
their foot shall s in due time.......... Deut 32:35
therefore I shall not s...................... Ps 26:1
none of his steps shall s.................. Ps 37:31

SLIDETH
For Israel s back as a.................... Hos 4:16

SLIGHTLY
of the daughter of my people s........ Jer 6:14
of the daughter of my people s........ Jer 8:11

SLIME
stone, and s had they for morter...... Gen 11:3
of bulrushes, and daubed it with s.. Ex 2:3

SLIMEPITS
the vale of Siddim was full of s........ Gen 14:10

SLING
every one could s stones at an........ Judg 20:16
and his s was in his hand................ 1Sa 17:40
over the Philistine with a s.............. 1Sa 17:50

enemies, them shall he s out............ 1Sa 25:29
as out of the middle of a s.............. 1Sa 25:29
As he that bindeth a stone in a s...... Prov 26:8
I will s out the inhabitants of.......... Jer 10:18
devour, and subdue with stones...... Zec 9:15

SLINGERS
howbeit the s went about it, and...... 2Kin 3:25

SLINGS
and bows, and s to cast stones........ 2Chr 26:14

SLINGSTONES
s are turned with him into.............. Job 41:28

SLIP
so that my feet did not s................ 2Sa 22:37
He that is ready to s with his.......... Job 12:5
paths, that my footsteps s not........ Ps 17:5
under me, that my feet did not s...... Ps 18:36
at any time we should let them s...... Heb 2:1

SLIPPED
but he s away out of Saul's............ 1Sa 19:10
my steps had well nigh s................ Ps 73:2

SLIPPERY
Let their way be dark and s............ Ps 35:6
thou didst set them in s places........ Ps 73:18
them as s ways in the darkness...... Jer 23:12

SLIPPETH
the head s from the helve, and........ Deut 19:5
when my foot s, they magnify.......... Ps 38:16
When I said, My foot s.................... Ps 94:18

SLIPS
and shalt set it with strange s........ Is 17:10

SLOTHFUL
be not s to go, and to enter to........ Judg 18:9
but the s shall be under tribute........ Prov 12:24
The s man roasteth not that which.. Prov 12:27
The way of the s man is as an........ Prov 15:19
He also that s in his work is............ Prov 18:9
A s man hideth his hand in his........ Prov 19:24
The desire of the s killeth him........ Prov 21:25
The s man saith, There is a lion...... Prov 22:13
I went by the field of the s.............. Prov 24:30
The s man saith, There is a lion...... Prov 26:13
so doth the s upon his bed.............. Prov 26:14
As vinegar to the teeth, so is........ Prov 26:15
s servant, thou knewest that I........ Mt 25:26
Not s in business............................ Rom 12:11
That ye be not s, but followers...... Heb 6:12

SLOTHFULNESS
S casteth into a deep sleep............ Prov 19:15
By much s the building decayeth.... Eccl 10:18

SLOW
but I am s of speech...................... Ex 4:10
and of a s tongue.......................... Ex 4:10
s to anger, and of great kindness.... Neh 9:17
s to anger, and plenteous in mercy.. Ps 103:8
s to anger, and of great mercy........ Ps 145:8
He that is s to wrath is of great...... Prov 14:29
but he that is s to anger................ Prov 15:18
He that is s to anger is better........ Prov 16:32
s to anger, and of great kindness.... Joel 2:13
The Lord is s to anger, and great.... Nah 1:3
s of heart to believe all that.......... Lk 24:25
liars, evil beasts, s bellies.............. Titus 1:12
to speak, s to wrath...................... Jas 1:19

SLOWLY
And when we had sailed s many days. Acts 27:7

SLUGGARD
Go to the ant, thou s...................... Prov 6:6
How long wilt thou sleep, O s.......... Prov 6:9
so is the s to them that send him.... Prov 10:26
The soul of the s desireth.............. Prov 13:4
The s will not plow by reason of...... Prov 20:4
The s is wiser in his own conceit.... Prov 26:16

SLUICES
purposes thereof, all that make s.... Is 19:10

SLUMBER
He that keepeth thee will not s........ Ps 121:3
Israel shall neither s nor sleep........ Ps 121:4
mine eyes, or s to mine eyelids........ Ps 132:4
eyes, nor s to thine eyelids............ Prov 6:4
Yet a little sleep, a little s.............. Prov 6:10
Yet a little sleep, a little s.............. Prov 24:33
none shall s nor sleep.................... Is 5:27
sleeping, lying down, loving to s...... Is 56:10
Thy shepherds s, O king of............ Nah 3:18
hath given them the spirit of s........ Rom 11:8

SLUMBERED
bridegroom tarried, they all s.......... Mt 25:5

SLUMBERETH
not, and their damnation s not........ 2Pet 2:3

SLUMBERINGS
upon men, in s upon the bed.......... Job 33:15

SMALL
the house with blindness, both s...... Gen 19:11
Is it a s matter that thou hast........ Gen 30:15
it shall become s dust in all the...... Ex 9:9
there lay a round thing.................. Ex 16:14

as s as the hoar frost on the.......... Ex 16:14
but every s matter they shall.......... Ex 18:22
but every s matter they judged...... Ex 18:26
thou shalt beat some of it very s.... Ex 30:36
full of sweet incense beaten s........ Lev 16:12
Seemeth it but a s thing unto you.. Num 16:9
Is it a s thing that thou hast.......... Num 16:13
took the s towns thereof, and........ Num 32:41
hear the s as well as the great........ Deut 1:17
stamped it, and ground it very s...... Deut 9:21
even until it was as s as dust.......... Deut 9:21
divers s weights, a great and a s.... Deut 25:13
divers measures, a great and a s.... Deut 25:14
as the s rain upon the tender.......... Deut 32:2
smote the men of the city, both s.... 1Sa 5:9
will do nothing either great or s...... 1Sa 20:2
slew not any, either great or s........ 1Sa 30:2
neither s nor great, neither sons.... 1Sa 30:19
this was yet a s thing in thy............ 2Sa 7:19
he not one s stone found there...... 2Sa 17:13
Then did I beat them as s as the.... 2Sa 22:43
I desire one s petition of thee........ 1Kin 2:20
and after the fire a still s voice...... 1Kin 19:12
Fight neither with s nor great........ 1Kin 22:31
their inhabitants were of s power.... 2Kin 19:26
and all the people, both s................ 2Kin 23:2
Kidron, and stamped it s to powder.. 2Kin 23:6
place, and stamped it s to powder.. 2Kin 23:15
And all the people, both s................ 2Kin 25:26
yet this was a s thing in thine........ 1Chr 17:17
as well the s as the great, the........ 1Chr 25:8
as well the s as the great, whether.. 1Chr 26:13
whether s or great, whether man.... 2Chr 15:13
Fight ye not with s or great............ 2Chr 18:30
came with a company of men.......... 2Chr 24:24
as well to the great as to the s...... 2Chr 31:15
and all the people, great and s........ 2Chr 34:30
thousand and six hundred s cattle.. 2Chr 35:9
offerings five thousand s cattle...... 2Chr 35:9
of the house of God, great and s.... 2Chr 36:18
the palace, both unto great and s.... Est 1:5
honour, both to great and s............ Est 1:20
The s and great are there.............. Job 3:19
Though thy beginning was s............ Job 8:7
consolations of God s with thee...... Job 15:11
For he maketh s the drops of.......... Job 36:27
likewise to the s rain, and to the.... Job 37:6
Then did I beat them s as the........ Ps 18:42
creeping innumerable, both s.......... Ps 104:25
them that fear the Lord, both s........ Ps 115:13
I am s and despised...................... Ps 119:141
of adversity, thy strength is s........ Prov 24:10
s cattle above all that were in........ Eccl 2:7
had left unto us a very s remnant.. Is 1:9
Is it a s thing for you to weary........ Is 7:13
and the remnant shall be very s...... Is 16:14
issue, all vessels of s quantity........ Is 22:24
strangers shall be like s dust.......... Is 29:5
their inhabitants were of s power.... Is 37:27
are counted as the s dust of the.... Is 40:15
the mountains, and beat them s...... Is 41:15
Thou hast not brought me the s...... Is 43:23
For a s moment have I forsaken...... Is 54:7
and so a strong nation................ Is 60:22
the s shall die in this land.............. Jer 16:6
them, and they shall not be s.......... Jer 30:19
Yet a s number that escape the...... Jer 44:28
I will make thee s among the.......... Jer 49:15
this of thy whoredoms a s matter.... Eze 16:20
Seemeth it a s thing unto you to.... Eze 34:18
become strong with a s people........ Dan 11:23
for he is s.. Amos 7:2
for he is s.. Amos 7:5
forth wheat, making the ephah s.... Amos 8:5
I have made thee s among the........ Obad 2
hath despised the day of s things.... Zec 4:10
that a s ship should wait on him...... Mk 3:9
And they had a few s fishes............ Mk 8:7
he had made a scourge of s cords.. Jn 2:15
barley loaves, and two s fishes........ Jn 6:9
there was no s stir among the........ Acts 12:18
and Barnabas had no s dissension.. Acts 15:2
arose no s stir about that way........ Acts 19:23
brought no s gain unto the............ Acts 19:24
this day, witnessing both to s........ Acts 26:22
no s tempest lay on us, all hope...... Acts 27:20
But with me it is a very s thing...... 1Cor 4:3
turned about with a very s helm...... Jas 3:4
and them that fear thy name, s...... Rev 11:18
And he causeth all, both s.............. Rev 13:16
and ye that fear him, both s............ Rev 19:5
men, both free and bond, both s...... Rev 19:18
And I saw the dead, s and great,.... Rev 20:12

SMALLEST
of the s of the tribes of Israel........ 1Sa 9:21
unworthy to judge the s matters.... 1Cor 6:2

SMART
for a stranger shall be s for it........ Prov 11:15

SMELL
he smelled the s of his raiment...... Gen 27:27
the s of my son is as the................ Gen 27:27
to s thereto, shall even be cut........ Ex 30:38
I will not s the savour of your........ Lev 26:31
see, nor hear, nor eat, nor s............ Deut 4:28
All thy garments s of myrrh............ Ps 45:8
noses have they, but they s not...... Ps 115:6
sendeth forth the s thereof............ Song 1:12
the tender grape give a good s........ Song 2:13
the s of thine ointments than all.... Song 4:10

SMELLED

the s of thy garments is like the...... Song 4:11
garments is like the s of Lebanon.... Song 4:11
the s of thy nose like apples........ Song 7:8
The mandrakes give a s, and at our... Song 7:13
of sweet s there shall be the stink.. Is 3:24
nor the s of fire had passed on...... Dan 3:27
olive tree, and his s as Lebanon.... Hos 14:6
I will not s in your solemn......... Amos 5:21
from you, an odour of a sweet s...... Phil 4:18

SMELLED

the LORD s a sweet savour............ Gen 8:21
he s the smell of his raiment, and.. Gen 27:27

SMELLETH

he s the battle afar off, the........ Job 39:25

SMELLING

and my fingers with sweet s myrrh.... Song 5:5
lilies, dropping sweet s myrrh....... Song 5:13
were hearing, where were the s....... 1Cor 12:17

SMITE

neither will I again s any more...... Gen 8:21
s it, then the other company......... Gen 32:8
s me, and the mother with the........ Gen 32:11
s Egypt with all my wonders which.... Ex 3:20
I will s with the rod that is in.... Ex 7:17
I will s all thy borders with....... Ex 8:2
s the dust of the land, that it..... Ex 8:16
out my hand, that I may s thee....... Ex 9:15
will s all the firstborn in the..... Ex 12:12
when I s the land of Egypt.......... Ex 12:13
pass through to s the Egyptians...... Ex 12:23
come in unto your houses to s you.... Ex 12:23
and thou shalt s the rock, and...... Ex 17:6
one s another with a stone, or...... Ex 21:18
if a man s his servant, or his...... Ex 21:20
if a man s the eye of his servant... Ex 21:26
if he s out his manservant's........ Ex 21:27
I will s them with the pestilence... Num 14:12
shall prevail, that we may s them.... Num 22:6
shall s the corners of Moab, and.... Num 24:17
Vex the Midianites, and s them...... Num 25:17
if he s him with an instrument of... Num 35:16
if he s him with throwing a stone... Num 35:17
Or if he s him with an hand........ Num 35:18
Or in enmity s him with his hand.... Num 35:21
thou shalt s them, and utterly...... Deut 7:2
Thou shalt surely s the............. Deut 13:15
s him mortally that he die, and..... Deut 19:11
thou shalt s every male thereof..... Deut 20:13
The LORD shall s thee with a........ Deut 28:22
The LORD shall s thee with the...... Deut 28:27
The LORD shall s thee with the...... Deut 28:28
The LORD shall s thee in the........ Deut 28:35
s through the loins of them that.... Deut 33:11
three thousand men go up and s Ai... Josh 7:3
and help me, that we may s Gibeon... Josh 10:4
and s the hindmost of them.......... Josh 10:19
LORD and the children of Israel s... Josh 12:6
for these did Moses s, and cast..... Josh 13:12
thou shalt s the Midianites as...... Judg 6:16
and they began to s of the people... Judg 20:31
the battle, Benjamin began to s..... Judg 20:39
Go and s the inhabitants of......... Judg 21:10
s Amalek, and utterly destroy all... 1Sa 15:3
and I will s thee, and take thine... 1Sa 17:46
I will s David even to the.......... 1Sa 18:11
Saul sought to s David even to...... 1Sa 19:10
cast a javelin at him to s him...... 1Sa 20:33
Shall I go and s these Philistines.. 1Sa 23:2
s the Philistines, and save Keilah.. 1Sa 23:2
now therefore let me s him.......... 1Sa 26:8
I will not s him the second time.... 1Sa 26:8
LORD liveth, the LORD shall s him... 1Sa 26:10
should I s thee to the ground....... 2Sa 2:22
to s the host of the Philistines.... 2Sa 5:24
and when I say unto you, S Amnon.... 2Sa 13:28
the city with the edge of the....... 2Sa 15:14
and I will s the king only.......... 2Sa 17:2
why didst thou not s him there to... 2Sa 18:11
For the LORD shall s Israel......... 1Kin 14:15
of the LORD, S me, I pray thee...... 1Kin 20:35
And the man refused to s him........ 1Kin 20:35
man, and said, S me, I pray........ 1Kin 20:37
ye shall s every fenced city, and... 2Kin 3:19
S this people, I pray thee, with.... 2Kin 6:18
them, My father, shall I s them..... 2Kin 6:21
shall I s them.................... 2Kin 6:21
answered, Thou shalt not s them..... 2Kin 6:22
wouldest thou s those whom thou..... 2Kin 6:22
thou shalt s the house of Ahab...... 2Kin 9:7
S him also in the chariot.......... 2Kin 9:27
for thou shalt s the Syrians in..... 2Kin 13:17
king of Israel, S upon the ground... 2Kin 13:18
now thou shalt s Syria but thrice... 2Kin 13:19
to s the host of the Philistines.... 1Chr 14:15
plague with the LORD s thy people... 2Chr 21:14
The sun shall not s thee by day..... Ps 121:6
Let the righteous s me............. Ps 141:5
S a scorner, and the simple will.... Prov 19:25
Therefore the Lord will s with a.... Is 3:17
he shall s thee with a rod, and..... Is 10:24
he shall s the earth with the rod... Is 11:4
shall s it in the seven streams..... Is 11:15
And the Lord shall s Egypt.......... Is 19:22
he shall s and heal it.............. Is 19:22
shall the heat nor sun s them....... Is 49:10
to s with the fist of wickedness.... Is 58:4
let us s him with the tongue, and... Jer 18:18
I will s the inhabitants of this.... Jer 21:6

he shall s them with the edge of.... Jer 21:7
he shall s the land of Egypt, and... Jer 43:11
come and s the land of Egypt........ Jer 46:13
king of Babylon shall s, thus....... Jer 49:28
part, and s about it with a knife... Eze 5:2
S with thine hand, and stamp with... Eze 6:11
after him through the city, and s... Eze 9:5
s therefore upon thy thigh......... Eze 21:12
s thine hands together, and let..... Eze 21:14
I will also s mine hands together... Eze 21:17
when I shall s all them that....... Eze 22:13
I will s thy bow out of thy left.... Eze 39:3
I will s the winter house with...... Amos 3:15
he will s the great house with...... Amos 6:11
S the lintel of the door, that..... Amos 9:1
they shall s the judge of Israel.... Mic 5:1
melteth, and the knees s together... Nah 2:10
he will s her power in the sea...... Zec 9:4
shall s the waves in the sea, and... Zec 10:11
and they shall s the land, and out.. Zec 11:6
I will s every horse with.......... Zec 12:4
will s every horse of the people.... Zec 12:4
s the shepherd, and the sheep....... Zec 13:7
plague wherewith the LORD will s.... Zec 14:12
wherewith the LORD will s the....... Zec 14:18
come and s the earth with a curse... Mal 4:6
but whosoever shall s thee on thy... Mt 5:39
And shall begin to s his........... Mt 24:49
I will s the shepherd, and the..... Mk 14:27
s the shepherd, and the sheep....... Mk 14:27
shall we s with the sword.......... Lk 22:49
by him to s him on the mouth....... Acts 23:2
Paul unto him, God shall s thee..... Acts 23:3
if a man s you on the face......... 2Cor 11:20
to s the earth with all plagues..... Rev 11:6
with it he should s the nations.... Rev 19:15

SMITERS

I gave my back to the s, and my..... Is 50:6

SMITEST

Wherefore s thou thy fellow......... Ex 2:13
but if well, why s thou me.......... Jn 18:23

SMITETH

He that s a man, so that he die,.... Ex 21:12
he that s his father, or his....... Ex 21:15
out of the hand of him that s him... Deut 25:11
Cursed be he that s his neighbour... Deut 27:24
he that s Kirjath-sepher, and...... Josh 15:16
He that s Kirjath-sepher, and...... Judg 1:12
s the Jebusites, and the lame and... 2Sa 5:8
Whosoever s the Jebusites first.... 1Chr 11:6
he s through the proud............. Job 26:12
turneth not unto him that s them.... Is 9:13
his cheek to him that s him........ Lam 3:30
know that I am the LORD that s...... Eze 7:9
unto him that s thee on the one.... Lk 6:29

SMITH

Now there was no s found........... 1Sa 13:19
The s with the tongs both worketh... Is 44:12
I have created the s that bloweth... Is 54:16

SMITHS

and all the craftsmen and s......... 2Kin 24:14
s a thousand, all that were......... 2Kin 24:16
Judah, with the carpenters and s.... Jer 24:1
and the carpenters, and the s....... Jer 29:2

SMITING

he spied an Egyptian s an Hebrew.... Ex 2:11
a name when he returned from s of... 2Sa 8:13
so that in s he wounded him........ 1Kin 20:37
they went forward s the Moabites.... 2Kin 3:24
will I make thee sick in s thee..... Mic 6:13

SMITTEN

that the LORD had s the river....... Ex 7:25
And the flax and the barley was s... Ex 9:31
the wheat and the rie were not s.... Ex 9:32
be s that he die, there shall no... Ex 22:2
that ye be not s before your....... Num 14:42
that thou hast s these three....... Num 22:28
Wherefore hast thou s thine ass..... Num 22:32
which the LORD had s among them..... Num 33:4
lest ye be s before your enemies.... Deut 1:42
thee to be s before thy............ Deut 28:7
thee to be s before thine enemies... Deut 28:25
s it with the edge of the sword.... Judg 1:8
They are s down before us, as a.... Judg 20:32
of Benjamin saw that they were s.... Judg 20:36
Surely they are s down before us... Judg 20:39
battle, Israel was s before the.... 1Sa 4:2
the LORD s us to day before the.... 1Sa 4:3
fought, and Israel was s, and they.. 1Sa 4:10
died not were s with the emerods... 1Sa 5:12
because the LORD had s many of..... 1Sa 6:19
they were s before Israel.......... 1Sa 7:10
s a garrison of t.e Philistines.... 1Sa 13:4
s Ziklag, and burned it with fire... 1Sa 30:1
had s all the host of Hadadezer.... 2Sa 8:9
against Hadadezer, and s.......... 2Sa 8:10
that they were s before Israel..... 2Sa 10:15
that they were s before Israel..... 2Sa 10:19
ye from him, that he may be s...... 2Sa 11:15
Israel be s down before his enemies. 1Kin 8:33
after he had s every male in Edom... 1Kin 11:15
and when he also had s the waters... 2Kin 2:14
slain, and they have s one another.. 2Kin 3:23
have s five or six times.......... 2Kin 13:19
then hadst thou s Syria till thou... 2Kin 13:19

Thou hast indeed s Edom, and thine. 2Kin 14:10
of Hamath heard how David had s..... 1Chr 18:9
against Hadarezer, and s him........ 1Chr 18:10
and they were s.................... 2Chr 20:22
why shouldest thou be s............ 2Chr 25:16
Lo, thou hast s the Edomites....... 2Chr 25:19
out, because the LORD had s him..... 2Chr 26:20
s Judah, and carried away captives.. 2Chr 28:17
they have s me upon the cheek...... Job 16:10
for thou hast s all mine enemies.... Ps 3:7
persecute him whom thou hast s..... Ps 69:26
My heart is s, and withered like.... Ps 102:4
he hath s my life down to the...... Ps 143:3
hand against them, and hath s them.. Is 5:25
the gate is s with destruction..... Is 24:12
Hath he s him, as he smote those.... Is 27:7
stricken, s of God, and afflicted... Is 53:4
In vain have I s your children...... Jer 2:30
why hast thou s us, and there is.... Jer 14:19
For though ye had s the whole....... Jer 37:10
therefore I have s mine hand at..... Eze 22:13
unto me, saying, The city is s...... Eze 33:21
year after that the city was s..... Eze 40:1
he hath s, and he will bind us up... Hos 6:1
Ephraim is s, their root is dried... Hos 9:16
I have s you with blasting and...... Amos 4:9
me to be s contrary to the law..... Acts 23:3
the third part of the sun was s.... Rev 8:12

SMOKE

the s of the country went up as.... Gen 19:28
went up as the s of a furnace...... Gen 19:28
mount Sinai was altogether on a s.. Ex 19:18
the s thereof ascended as the...... Ex 19:18
ascended as the s of a furnace..... Ex 19:18
jealousy shall s against that man... Deut 29:20
the s of the city ascended up to... Josh 8:20
that the s of the city ascended.... Josh 8:21
with s rise up out of the city..... Judg 20:38
of the city with a pillar of s..... Judg 20:40
There went up a s out of his....... 2Sa 22:9
Out of his nostrils goeth s........ Job 11:20
There went up a s out of his....... Ps 18:8
into s shall they consume away..... Ps 37:20
As s is driven away, so drive...... Ps 68:2
why doth thine anger s against..... Ps 74:1
For my days are consumed like s.... Ps 102:3
he toucheth the hills, and they s.. Ps 104:32
am become like a bottle in the s... Ps 119:83
the mountains, and they shall s.... Ps 144:5
as s to the eyes, so is the........ Prov 10:26
the wilderness like pillars of s... Song 3:6
s by day, and the shining of a..... Is 4:5
and the house was filled with s.... Is 6:4
mount up like the lifting up of s.. Is 9:18
shall come from the north s........ Is 14:31
the s thereof shall go up for...... Is 34:10
heavens shall vanish away like s.... Is 51:6
These are a s in my nose, a fire... Is 65:5
as the s out of the chimney........ Hos 13:3
blood, and fire, and pillars of s.. Joel 2:30
I will burn her chariots in the s.. Nah 2:13
blood, and fire, and vapour of s... Acts 2:19
the s of the incense, which came... Rev 8:4
there arose a s out of the pit..... Rev 9:2
as the s of a great furnace....... Rev 9:2
by reason of the s of the pit...... Rev 9:2
there came out of the s locusts.... Rev 9:3
of their mouths issued fire and s.. Rev 9:17
killed, by the fire, and by the s.. Rev 9:18
the s of their torment ascendeth... Rev 14:11
with s from the glory of God....... Rev 15:8
shall see the s of her burning..... Rev 18:9
they saw the s of her burning...... Rev 18:18
her s rose up for ever and ever.... Rev 19:3

SMOKING

it was dark, behold a s furnace.... Gen 15:17
of the trumpet, and the mountain s.. Ex 20:18
two tails of these s firebrands.... Is 7:4
the s flax shall he not quench..... Is 42:3
s flax shall he not quench, till... Mt 12:20

SMOOTH

is a hairy man, and I am a s man... Gen 27:11
hands, and upon the s of his neck... Gen 27:16
chose him five s stones out of..... 1Sa 17:40
things, speak unto us s things..... Is 30:10
Among the s stones of the stream... Is 57:6
and the rough ways shall be made s. Lk 3:5

SMOOTHER

of his mouth were s than butter.... Ps 55:21
and her mouth is s than oil........ Prov 5:3

SMOOTHETH

he that s with the hammer him...... Is 41:7

SMOTE

the Rephaims in Ashteroth.......... Gen 14:5
and s all the country of the....... Gen 14:7
s them, and pursued them unto...... Gen 14:15
they s the men that were at the.... Gen 19:11
who s Midian in the field of Moab.. Gen 36:35
the s waters that were in the...... Ex 7:20
s the dust of the earth, and it.... Ex 8:17
he hath s throughout all the....... Ex 9:25
he hath s every herb of the........ Ex 9:25
when he s the Egyptians, and....... Ex 12:27
that at midnight the LORD s all.... Ex 12:29
then shall he that s him be quit... Ex 21:19

for on the day that I s all the .... Num 3:13
on the day that I s every .... Num 8:17
the LORD s the people with a very ..... Num 11:33
s them, and discomfited them, even... Num 14:45
with his rod he s the rock twice .... Num 20:11
Israel s him with the edge of the ..... Num 21:24
So they s him, and his sons, and......... Num 21:35
Balaam s the ass, to turn her.............. Num 22:25
and he s her again .... Num 22:27
he s the ass with a staff .... Num 22:27
and he s his hands together .... Num 24:10
LORD s before the congregation of ... Num 25:1
he that s him shall surely be put...... Num 35:21
we s him, and his sons, and all his .... Deut 2:33
we s him until none was left to.......... Deut 3:3
Moses and the children of Israel s ... Deut 4:46
the hindmost of thee, even all .... Deut 25:18
us unto battle, and we s them .... Deut 29:7
the men of Ai s them about .... Josh 7:5
and s them in the going down.............. Josh 7:5
and they s them, so that they let...... Josh 8:22
s it with the edge of the sword,......... Josh 8:24
the children of Israel s them not ...... Josh 9:18
s them to Azekah, and slew .... Josh 10:10
And afterward Joshua s them,............. Josh 10:26
s it with the edge of the sword,......... Josh 10:28
the s it with the edge of the sword,.. Josh 10:30
s it with the edge of the sword,......... Josh 10:32
and Joshua s him and his people,...... Josh 10:33
s it with the edge of the sword,......... Josh 10:35
s it with the edge of the sword,......... Josh 10:37
they s them with the edge of the .... Josh 10:39
So Joshua s all the country of.............. Josh 10:40
Joshua s them from Kadesh-barnea.. Josh 10:41
who s them, and chased them unto ... Josh 11:8
and they s them, until they left........... Josh 11:8
s the king thereof with the edge of.... Josh 11:10
they s all the souls that were............... Josh 11:11
s them with the edge of the sword,.... Josh 11:12
but every man they s with the............. Josh 11:14
he took, and s them, and slew them... Josh 11:17
which the children of Israel s............. Josh 12:1
the children of Israel s on this............ Josh 12:7
whom Moses s with the princes of.... Josh 13:21
s it with the edge of the sword,......... Josh 19:47
because he s his neighbour .... Josh 20:5
they s the city with the edge of.......... Judg 1:25
s Israel, and possessed the city .... Judg 3:13
the nail into his temples, and........... Judg 4:21
and with the hammer she s Sisera...... Judg 5:26
she s off his head, when she had......... Judg 5:26
s it that it fell, and overturned.......... Judg 7:13
Nobah and Jogbehah, and s them..... Judg 8:11
rose up against them, and s them...... Judg 9:43
hand of Israel, and they s them,........ Judg 11:21
he s them from Aroer, even till .... Judg 11:33
and the men of Gilead s Ephraim...... Judg 12:4
he s them hip and thigh with a........... Judg 15:8
they s them with the edge of the ...... Judg 18:27
the LORD s Benjamin before Israel... Judg 20:35
s all the city with the edge of............ Judg 20:37
s them with the edge of the sword.... Judg 20:48
these are the Gods that s them 1Sa 4:8
s them with emerods, even Ashdod... 1Sa 5:6
he s the men of the city, both............. 1Sa 5:9
that it is not his hand that s us 1Sa 6:9
he s the men of Beth-shemesh,.......... 1Sa 6:19
even he s of the people fifty 1Sa 6:19
s them, until they came under 1Sa 7:11
Jonathan s the garrison of the........... 1Sa 13:3
they s the Philistines that day............ 1Sa 14:31
the Amalekites, and delivered............ 1Sa 14:48
Saul s the Amalekites from.................. 1Sa 15:7
s him, and delivered it out of his...... 1Sa 17:35
his beard, and s him, and slew him... 1Sa 17:35
s the Philistine in his forehead,........ 1Sa 17:49
s the Philistine, and slew him........... 1Sa 17:50
he s the javelin into the wall............... 1Sa 19:10
s he with the edge of the sword, ... 1Sa 22:19
s them with a great slaughter 1Sa 23:5
David's heart s him 1Sa 24:5
days after, that the LORD s Nabal...... 1Sa 25:38
David s the land, and left neither 1Sa 27:9
David s them from the twilight 1Sa 30:17
And he s him that he died 2Sa 2:23
spear s him under the fifth rib........... 2Sa 2:23
s him there under the fifth rib........... 2Sa 3:27
they s him under the fifth rib............. 2Sa 4:6
in his headchamber, and they s him. 2Sa 4:7
David s them there, and said, The..... 2Sa 5:20
s the Philistines from Geba until...... 2Sa 5:25
God s him there for his error.............. 2Sa 6:7
that David s the Philistines, and....... 2Sa 8:1
he s Moab, and measured them with. 2Sa 8:2
David s also Hadadezer, the son....... 2Sa 8:3
s Shobach the captain of their.......... 2Sa 10:18
Who s Abimelech the son of 2Sa 11:21
them, but the one s the other 2Sa 14:6
Deliver him that s his brother 2Sa 14:7
about and s Absalom, and slew him... 2Sa 18:15
so he s him therewith in the.............. 2Sa 20:10
s the Philistines until his hand 2Sa 23:10
David's heart s him after that he...... 2Sa 24:10
saw the angel that s the people......... 2Sa 24:17
of Israel, and s Ijon, and Dan, and... 1Kin 15:20
Baasha s him at Gibbethon, which ... 1Kin 15:27
that he s all the house of................... 1Kin 15:29
s him, and killed him, in the.............. 1Kin 16:10

s the horses and chariots, and slew .. 1Kin 20:21
And the man s him, so that it 1Kin 20:37
s Micaiah on the cheek, and said,...... 1Kin 22:24
the king of Israel between the............ 1Kin 22:34
s the waters, and they were................ 2Kin 2:8
s the waters, and said, Where is 2Kin 2:14
s the Moabites, so that they fled 2Kin 3:24
slingers went about it, and s it.......... 2Kin 3:25
And he s them with blindness 2Kin 6:18
the Edomites which compassed......... 2Kin 8:21
s Jehoram between his arms, and...... 2Kin 9:24
they s them with the edge of the 2Kin 10:25
Hazael s them in all the coasts 2Kin 10:32
his servants, s him, and he died......... 2Kin 12:21
And he s thrice, and stayed 2Kin 13:18
And the LORD s the king, so that 2Kin 15:5
s him before the people, and slew..... 2Kin 15:10
s Shallum the son of Jabesh in 2Kin 15:14
Then Menahem s Tiphsah, and all..... 2Kin 15:16
not to him, therefore he s it.............. 2Kin 15:16
s him in Samaria, in the space 2Kin 15:25
s him, and slew him, and reigned in. 2Kin 15:30
He s the Philistines, even unto........... 2Kin 18:8
s in the camp of the Assyrians an..... 2Kin 19:35
Sharezer his sons s him with the....... 2Kin 19:37
And the king of Babylon s them 2Kin 25:21
s Gedaliah, that he died, and the...... 2Kin 25:25
which s Midian in the field of 1Chr 1:46
s their tents, and the habitations 1Chr 4:41
they s the rest of the Amalekites....... 1Chr 4:43
s him, because he put his hand.......... 1Chr 13:10
s him, and there he died 1Chr 14:11
and they s the host of the 1Chr 14:16
that David s the Philistines, and 1Chr 18:1
And he s Moab,...................................... 1Chr 18:2
David s Hadarezer king of Zobah 1Chr 18:3
Joab s Rabbah, and destroyed it........ 1Chr 20:1
therefore he s Israel 1Chr 21:7
came to pass, that God s Jeroboam... 2Chr 13:15
So the Lord s the Ethiopians 2Chr 14:12
they s all the cities round about 2Chr 14:14
They s also the tents of cattle,........... 2Chr 14:15
and they s Ijon, and Dan, and............ 2Chr 16:4
s the Edomites which compassed...... 2Chr 21:9
after all this the LORD s him in.......... 2Chr 21:18
and the Syrians s Joram........................ 2Chr 22:5
s of the children of Seir ten................. 2Chr 25:11
s three thousand of them, and took... 2Chr 25:13
and they s him, and carried away a.... 2Chr 28:9
which s him with a great slaughter ... 2Chr 28:5
the gods of Damascus, which s him... 2Chr 28:23
s certain of them, and plucked off..... Neh 13:25
Thus the Jews s all their enemies....... Est 9:5
s the four corners of the house,......... Job 1:19
s Job with sore boils from the .... Job 2:7
of Edom in the valley of salt.............. Ps 60:t
he s the rock, that the waters .... Ps 78:20
s down the chosen men of Israel .... Ps 78:31
s all the firstborn in Egypt,............... Ps 78:51
he s his enemies in the hinder........... Ps 78:66
s them hip and thigh with a............... Ps 105:33
He s also all the firstborn in.............. Ps 105:36
Who s the firstborn of Egypt,............. Ps 135:8
Who s great nations, and slew .... Ps 135:10
To him that s Egypt in their .... Ps 136:10
s down great kings .... Ps 136:17
the city found me, they s me............... Song 5:7
again stay upon him that s them........ Is 10:20
He who s the people in wrath with..... Is 14:6
rod of him that s thee is broken......... Is 14:29
as be s those that .... Is 27:7
those that s him .... Is 27:7
beaten down, which s with a rod .... Is 30:31
s in the camp of the Assyrians an..... Is 37:36
Sharezer his sons s him with the....... Is 37:38
the hammer him that s the anvil....... Is 41:7
was I wroth, and s him .... Is 57:17
for in my wrath I s thee, but in.......... Is 60:10
Then Pashur s Jeremiah the.............. Jer 20:2
was instructed, I s upon my thigh .... Jer 31:19
s him, and put him in prison in......... Jer 37:15
s Gedaliah the son of Ahikam the..... Jer 41:2
Nebuchadrezzar king of Babylon s... Jer 46:2
before that Pharaoh s Gaza .... Jer 47:1
And the king of Babylon s them .... Jer 52:27
which s the image upon his feet........ Dan 2:34
the stone that s the image became... Dan 2:35
his knees s one against another......... Dan 5:6
s the ram, and brake his two horns... Dan 8:7
it s the gourd that it withered............ Jonah 4:7
I s you with blasting and mildew ...... Hag 2:17
high priest's, and s off his ear .... Mt 26:51
others s him with the palms of.......... Mt 26:67
Christ, Who is he that s thee.............. Mt 26:68
the reed, and s him on the head........ Mt 27:30
s a servant of the high priest,............ Mk 14:47
they s him on the head with a........... Mk 15:19
but s upon his breast, saying,........... Lk 18:13
one of them s the servant of the....... Lk 22:50
and Jesus mocked him, and s him..... Lk 22:63
Prophesy, who is it that s thee.......... Lk 22:64
s their breasts, and returned .... Lk 23:48
s the high priest's servant, and........ Jn 18:10
they s him with their hands................ Jn 18:22
was oppressed, and s the Egyptian... Acts 7:24
he s Peter on the side, and raised..... Acts 12:7
the angel of the Lord s him................ Acts 12:23

SMOTEST
rod, wherewith thou s the river........... Ex 17:5

SMYRNA (smir′-na) A city of Ionia in Asia Minor.
unto Ephesus, and unto S, and unto... Rev 1:11
angel of the church in S write............. Rev 2:8

SNAIL
and the lizard, and the s, and the..... Lev 11:30
As a s which melteth, let every........... Ps 58:8

SNARE
shall this man be a s unto us .... Ex 10:7
it will surely be a s unto thee .... Ex 23:33
lest it be for a s in the midst .... Ex 34:12
for that will be a s unto thee .... Deut 7:16
their gods shall be a s unto you .... Judg 2:3
thing became a s unto Gideon .... Judg 8:27
her, that she may be a s to him.......... Isa 18:21
then Jayest thou a s for my life.......... Isa 28:9
own feet, and he walketh upon a s..... Job 18:8
The s is laid for him in the .... Job 18:10
his ways, and get a s to thy soul .... Ps 69:22
thee from the s of the fowler.............. Ps 91:3
which were a s unto them.................... Ps 106:36
The wicked have laid a s for me........ Ps 119:110
bird out of the s of the fowlers.......... Ps 124:7
the s is broken, and we are .... Ps 124:7
The proud have laid a s for me.......... Ps 140:5
have they privily laid a s for me........ Ps 142:3
as a bird hasteth to the s .... Prov 7:23
and his lips are the s of his soul .... Prov 18:7
It is a s to the man who .... Prov 20:25
his ways, and get a s to thy soul ...... Prov 22:25
of an evil man there is a s................ Prov 29:6
men bring a city into a s .... Prov 29:8
The fear of man bringeth a s.............. Prov 29:25
birds that are caught in the s .... Eccl 9:12
for a s to the inhabitants of.............. Is 8:14
Fear, and the pit, and the s............... Is 24:17
the pit shall be taken in the s .... Is 24:18
lay a s for him that reproveth in....... Is 29:21
Fear, and the pit, and the s............... Jer 48:43
the pit shall be taken in the s .... Jer 48:44
I have laid a s for thee, and thou..... Jer 50:24
a s is come upon us, desolation........ Lam 3:47
him, and he shall be taken in my s... Eze 12:13
him, and he shall be taken in my s... Eze 17:20
ye have been a s on Mizpah.............. Hos 5:1
but the prophet is a s of a................ Hos 9:8
a bird fall in a s upon the earth....... Amos 3:5
one take up a s from the earth......... Amos 3:5
For as a s shall it come on all.......... Lk 21:35
Let their table be made a s............... Rom 11:9
not that I may cast a s upon you...... 1Cor 7:35
reproach and the s of the devil........ 1Ti 3:7
rich fall into temptation and s......... 1Ti 6:9
out of the s of the devil.................... 2Ti 2:26

SNARED
unto thee, lest thou be s therein ...... Deut 7:25
thou be not s by following them....... Deut 12:30
the wicked is s in the work of .... Ps 9:16
Thou art s with the words of thy ..... Prov 6:2
The wicked is s by the .... Prov 12:13
the sons of men s in an evil time...... Eccl 9:12
and fall, and be broken, and s.......... Is 8:15
fall backward, and be broken, and s. Is 28:13
they are all of them s in holes.......... Is 42:22

SNARES
but they shall be s and traps unto... Josh 23:13
s be of death prevented me............... 2Sa 22:6
Therefore s are round about thee,.... Job 22:10
his nose pierceth through s .... Job 40:24
Upon the wicked he shall rain s........ Ps 11:6
the s of death prevented me.............. Ps 18:5
seek after my life lay s for me........... Ps 38:12
they commune of laying s privily ..... Ps 64:5
Keep me from the s which they........ Ps 141:9
to depart from the s of death........... Prov 13:14
to depart from the s of death .... Prov 14:27
s are in the way of the froward......... Prov 22:5
death the woman, whose heart is s.. Eccl 7:26
lay wait, as he that setteth s .... Jer 5:26
to take me, and hid s for my feet..... Jer 18:22

SNATCH
he shall s on the right hand, and..... Is 9:20

SNEEZED
the child s seven times, and the 2Kin 4:35

SNORTING
The s of his horses was heard .... Jer 8:16

SNOUT
As a jewel of gold in a swine's s....... Prov 11:22

SNOW
behold, his hand was leprous as s .... Ex 4:6
Miriam became leprous, white as s... Num 12:10
the midst of a pit in time of s 2Sa 23:20
presence a leper as white as s 2Kin 5:27
the ice, and wherein the s is hid...... Job 6:16
If I wash myself with s water .... Job 9:30
and heat consume the s waters......... Job 24:19
For he saith to the s, Be thou on ..... Job 37:6
into the treasures of the s .... Job 38:22
me, and I shall be whiter than s....... Ps 51:7
it, it was white as s in Salmon.......... Ps 68:14
He giveth s like wool .... Ps 147:16
Fire, and hail; s, and vapours........... Ps 148:8
As the cold of s in the time of.......... Prov 25:13

As s in summer, and as rain in .... Prov 26:1
afraid of the s for her household .... Prov 31:21
they shall be as white as s .... Is 1:18
the s from heaven, and returneth .... Is 55:10
Will a man leave the s of Lebanon .... Jer 18:14
Her Nazarites were purer than s .... Lam 4:7
sit, whose garment was white as s .... Dan 7:9
and his raiment white as s .... Mt 28:3
shining, exceeding white as s .... Mk 9:3
white like wool, as white as s .... Rev 1:14

SNOWY
slew a lion in a pit in a s day 1Chr 11:22

SNUFFDISHES
the s thereof, shall be of pure .... Ex 25:38
lamps, and his snuffers, and his s .... Ex 37:23
his lamps, and his tongs, and his s .... Num 4:9

SNUFFED
they s up the wind like dragons .... Jer 14:6
and ye have s at it, saith the .... Mal 1:13

SNUFFERS
he made his seven lamps, and his s .... Ex 37:23
And the bowls, and the s, and the 1Kin 7:50
of the LORD bowls of silver, s 2Kin 12:13
pots, and the shovels, and the s 2Kin 25:14
And the s, and the basons, and the 2Chr 4:22
also, and the shovels, and the s .... Jer 52:18

SNUFFETH
that s up the wind at her .... Jer 2:24

SO See PREFACE.

SOAKED
their land shall be s with blood .... Is 34:7

SOBER
or whether we be s, it is for 2Cor 5:13
but let us watch and be s 1Th 5:6
let us, who are of the day, be s 1Th 5:8
husband of one wife, vigilant, s 1Ti 3:2
wives be grave, not slanderers, s 1Ti 3:11
a lover of good men, s, just .... Titus 1:8
That the aged men be s, grave .... Titus 2:2
may teach the young women to be s .... Titus 2:4
likewise exhort to be s minded .... Titus 2:6
up the loins of your mind, be s 1Pet 1:13
be ye therefore s, and watch unto 1Pet 4:7
Be s, be vigilant 1Pet 5:8

SOBERLY
but to think s, according as God .... Rom 12:3
worldly lusts, we should live s .... Titus 2:12

SOBERNESS
forth the words of truth and s .... Acts 26:25

SOBRIETY
apparel, with shamefacedness and s 1Ti 2:9
and charity and holiness with s 1Ti 2:15

SOCHO (so'-ko) See SOCHOH. A son of Heber.
Gedor, and Heber the father of S 1Chr 4:18

SOCHOH (so'-ko) See SHOCHOH, SOCHO,
SOCOH. A city in Judah near Adullam.
to him pertained S, and all the 1Kin 4:10

SOCKET
hundred talents, a talent for a s .... Ex 38:27

SOCKETS
thou shalt make forty s of silver .... Ex 26:19
two s under one board for his two .... Ex 26:19
two s under another board for his .... Ex 26:19
And their forty s of silver .... Ex 26:21
two s under one board .... Ex 26:21
two s under another board .... Ex 26:21
of silver, sixteen s .... Ex 26:25
two s under one board .... Ex 26:25
two s under another board .... Ex 26:25
gold, upon the four s of silver .... Ex 26:32
cast five s of brass for them .... Ex 26:37
their twenty s shall be of brass .... Ex 27:10
and their twenty s of brass .... Ex 27:11
their forty s ten, and their s ten .... Ex 27:12
pillars three, and their s three .... Ex 27:14
pillars three, and their s three .... Ex 27:15
shall be four, and their s four .... Ex 27:16
be of silver, and their s of brass .... Ex 27:17
twinned linen, and their s of brass .... Ex 27:18
his bars, his pillars, and his s .... Ex 35:11
court, his pillars, and their s .... Ex 35:17
forty s of silver he made under .... Ex 36:24
two s under one board for his two .... Ex 36:24
two s under another board for his .... Ex 36:24
And their forty s of silver .... Ex 36:26
two s under one board .... Ex 36:26
two s under another board .... Ex 36:26
s were sixteen s of silver .... Ex 36:26
under every board two s .... Ex 36:30
he cast for them four s of silver .... Ex 36:36
but their five s were of brass .... Ex 36:38
twenty, and their brasen s twenty .... Ex 38:10
and their s of brass twenty .... Ex 38:11
their pillars ten, and their s ten .... Ex 38:12
pillars three, and their s three .... Ex 38:14
pillars three, and their s three .... Ex 38:15
the s for the pillars were of .... Ex 38:17
four, and their s of brass four .... Ex 38:19
were cast the s of the sanctuary .... Ex 38:27
and the s of the vail .... Ex 38:27
an hundred s of the hundred .... Ex 38:27
therewith he made the s to the .... Ex 38:30

the s of the court round about .... Ex 38:31
the s of the court gate, and all .... Ex 38:31
bars, and his pillars, and his s .... Ex 39:33
the court, his pillars, and his s .... Ex 39:40
the tabernacle, and fastened his s .... Ex 40:18
s thereof, and all the vessels .... Num 3:36
the court round about, and their s .... Num 3:37
pillars thereof, and s thereof .... Num 4:31
the court round about, and their s .... Num 4:32
marble, set upon s of fine gold .... Song 5:15

SOD
And Jacob s pottage .... Gen 25:29
holy offerings s they in pots 2Chr 35:13

SODDEN
nor s at all with water, but .... Ex 12:9
wherein it is s shall be broken .... Lev 6:28
if it be s in a brasen pot, it .... Lev 6:28
take the s shoulder of the ram .... Num 6:19
he will not have s flesh of thee 1Sa 2:15
women have s their own children .... Lam 4:10

SODERING
saying, It is ready for the s .... Is 41:7

SODI (so'-di) A spy sent to the Promised Land.
of Zebulun, Gaddiel the son of S .... Num 13:10

SODOM (sod'-om) See SODOMA, SODOMITE. A
city on the Dead Sea.
as thou goest, unto S, and .... Gen 10:19
before the LORD destroyed S .... Gen 13:10
and pitched his tent toward S .... Gen 13:12
But the men of S were wicked .... Gen 13:13
made war with Bera king of S .... Gen 14:2
And there went out the king of S .... Gen 14:8
and the kings of S and Gomorrah .... Gen 14:10
And they took all the goods of S .... Gen 14:11
brother's son, who dwelt in S .... Gen 14:12
the king of S went out to meet .... Gen 14:17
the king of S said unto Abram .... Gen 14:21
And Abram said to the king of S .... Gen 14:22
from thence, and looked toward S .... Gen 18:16
LORD said, Because the cry of S .... Gen 18:20
from thence, and went toward S .... Gen 18:22
If I find in S fifty righteous .... Gen 18:26
came two angels to S at even .... Gen 19:1
and Lot sat in the gate of S .... Gen 19:1
of the city, even the men of S .... Gen 19:4
Then the LORD rained upon S .... Gen 19:24
toward S and Gomorrah .... Gen 19:28
therein, like the overthrow of S .... Deut 29:23
their vine is of the vine of S .... Deut 32:32
remnant, we should have been as S .... Is 1:9
word of the LORD, ye rulers of S .... Is 1:10
and they declare their sin as S .... Is 3:9
shall be as when God overthrew S .... Is 13:19
they are all of them unto me as S .... Jer 23:14
As in the overthrow of S and .... Jer 49:18
overthrow S and Gomorrah .... Jer 50:40
the punishment of the sin of S .... Lam 4:6
dwelleth at thy right hand, is S .... Eze 16:46
S thy sister hath not done, thee .... Eze 16:48
was the iniquity of thy sister S .... Eze 16:49
captivity, the captivity of S .... Eze 16:53
When thy sisters, S and her .... Eze 16:55
For thy sister S was not .... Eze 16:56
some of you, as God overthrew S .... Amos 4:11
Israel, Surely Moab shall be as S .... Zeph 2:9
more tolerable for the land of S .... Mt 10:15
done in thee, had been done in S .... Mt 11:23
land of S in the day of judgment .... Mt 11:24
It shall be more tolerable for S .... Mk 6:11
more tolerable in that day for S .... Lk 10:12
Lot went out of S it rained fire .... Lk 17:29
And turning the cities of S 2Pet 2:6
Even as S and Gomorrha, and the .... Jude 7
which spiritually is called S .... Rev 11:8

SODOMA
left us a seed, we had been as S .... Rom 9:29

SODOMITE
nor a s of the sons of Israel .... Deut 23:17

SODOMITES
And there were also s in the land 1Kin 14:24
took away the s out of the land 1Kin 15:12
And the remnant of the s, which 1Kin 22:46

SOEVER
what soever s he rideth upon that .... Lev 15:9
What man s there be of the house .... Lev 17:3
What man s of the seed of Aaron .... Lev 22:4
What thing s I command you .... Deut 12:32
that what thing s thou shalt hear 2Sa 15:35
the people, how many s be as 2Sa 24:3
supplication s be made by any man 1Kin 8:38
s shall be made of any man 2Chr 6:29
what cause s shall come to you of 2Chr 19:10
wherewith s they shall blaspheme .... Mk 3:28
In what place s ye enter into a .... Mk 6:10
unto you, What things s ye desire .... Mk 11:24
for what things s he doeth .... Jn 5:19
Whose s sins ye remit, they are .... Jn 20:23
that what things s the law saith .... Rom 3:19

SOFT
For God maketh my heart s .... Job 23:16
will he speak s words unto thee .... Job 41:3
thou makest it with showers .... Ps 65:10
A s answer turneth away wrath .... Prov 15:1
a s tongue breaketh the bone .... Prov 25:15
A man clothed in s raiment .... Mt 11:8
they that wear s clothing are in .... Mt 11:8
A man clothed in s raiment .... Lk 7:25

SOFTER
his words were s than oil .... Ps 55:21

SOFTLY
and I will lead on s, according as .... Gen 33:14
went s unto him, and smote the .... Judg 4:21
and she came s, and uncovered his .... Ruth 3:7
and lay in sackcloth, and went s 1Kin 21:27
the waters of Shiloah that go s .... Is 8:6
I shall go s all my years in the .... Is 38:15
And when the south wind blew s .... Acts 27:13

SOIL
in a good s by great waters .... Eze 17:8

SOJOURN
went down into Egypt to s there .... Gen 12:10
This one fellow came in to s .... Gen 19:9
S in this land, and I will be with .... Gen 26:3
For to s in the land are we come .... Gen 47:4
when a stranger shall s with thee .... Ex 12:48
the strangers which s among you .... Lev 17:8
of the strangers that s among you .... Lev 17:10
of the strangers that s among you .... Lev 17:13
if a stranger s with thee in your .... Lev 19:33
of the strangers that s among you .... Lev 20:2
the strangers that do s among you .... Lev 25:45
if a stranger shall s among you .... Num 9:14
And if a stranger s with you .... Num 15:14
to s where he could find a place .... Judg 17:8
I go to s where I may find a .... Judg 17:9
went to s in the country of Moab .... Ruth 1:1
evil upon the widow with whom I s 1Kin 17:20
s wheresoever thou canst s 2Kin 8:1
that I s in Mesech, that I dwell .... Ps 120:5
shall carry her afar off to s .... Is 23:7
aforetime into Egypt to s there .... Is 52:4
into Egypt, and go to s there .... Jer 42:15
faces to go into Egypt to s there .... Jer 42:17
whither ye desire to go and to s .... Jer 42:22
say, Go not into Egypt to s there .... Jer 43:2
into the land of Egypt to s there .... Jer 44:12
into the land of Egypt to s there .... Jer 44:14
into the land of Egypt to s there .... Jer 44:28
They shall no more s there .... Lam 4:15
out of the country where they s .... Eze 20:38
to the strangers that s among you .... Eze 47:22
seed should s in a strange land .... Acts 7:6

SOJOURNED
Kadesh and Shur, and s in Gerar .... Gen 20:1
to the land wherein thou hast s .... Gen 21:23
Abraham s in the Philistines' .... Gen 21:34
I have s with Laban, and stayed .... Gen 32:4
Hebron, where Abraham and Isaac s .... Gen 35:27
out of all Israel, where he s .... Deut 18:6
s there with a few, and became .... Deut 26:5
who was a Levite, and he s there .... Judg 17:7
and he s in Gibeah .... Judg 19:16
s in the land of the Philistines 2Kin 8:2
Jacob s in the land of Ham .... Ps 105:23
By faith he s in the land of .... Heb 11:9

SOJOURNER
I am a stranger and a s with you .... Gen 23:4
a s of the priest, or an hired .... Lev 22:10
though he be a stranger, or a s .... Lev 25:35
as an hired servant, and as a s .... Lev 25:40
If a s or stranger wax rich by .... Lev 25:47
unto the stranger or s by thee .... Lev 25:47
stranger, and for the s among them .... Num 35:15
I am a stranger with thee, and a s .... Ps 39:12

SOJOURNERS
for ye are strangers and s with me .... Lev 25:23
were a there until this day 2Sa 4:3
are strangers before thee, and s 1Chr 29:15

SOJOURNETH
of her that is in her house .... Ex 3:22
the stranger that s among you .... Ex 12:49
or a stranger that s among you .... Lev 16:29
that s among you eat blood .... Lev 17:12
nor any stranger that s among you .... Lev 18:26
for thy stranger that s with thee .... Lev 25:6
for the stranger that s with you .... Num 15:15
and the stranger that s among them .... Num 15:26
the stranger that s among you .... Num 15:29
the stranger that s among them .... Num 19:10
the stranger that s among them .... Josh 20:9
remaineth in any place where he s .... Ezr 1:4
of the stranger that s in Israel .... Eze 14:7
that in what tribe the stranger s .... Eze 47:23

SOJOURNING
Now the s of the children of .... Ex 12:40
s on the side of mount Ephraim .... Judg 19:1
the time of your s here in fear 1Pet 1:17

SOLACE
let us s ourselves with loves .... Prov 7:18

SOLD
he s his birthright unto Jacob .... Gen 25:33
for he hath s us, and hath quite .... Gen 31:15

s Joseph to the Ishmeelites for .... Gen 37:28
the Midianites s him into Egypt .... Gen 37:36
and s unto the Egyptians .... Gen 41:56
he it was that s to all the .... Gen 42:6
brother, whom ye s into Egypt .... Gen 45:4
yourselves, that ye s me hither .... Gen 45:5
for the Egyptians s every man his .... Gen 47:20
wherefore they s not their lands .... Gen 47:22
then he shall be s for his theft .... Ex 22:3
The land shall not be s for ever .... Lev 25:23
poor, and hath s away some of his .... Lev 25:25
redeem that which his brother s .... Lev 25:25
unto the man to whom he s it .... Lev 25:27
then that which is s shall remain .... Lev 25:28
within a whole year after it is s .... Lev 25:29
then the house that was s .... Lev 25:33
their cities may not be s .... Lev 25:34
be waxen poor, and be s unto thee .... Lev 25:39
they shall not be s as bondmen .... Lev 25:42
After that he is s he may be .... Lev 25:48
him from the year that he was s .... Lev 25:50
or if he have s the field to .... Lev 27:20
then it shall be s according to .... Lev 27:27
shall be s or redeemed .... Lev 27:28
be s unto thee, and serve thee six .... Deut 15:12
there ye shall be s unto your .... Deut 28:68
except their Rock hath s them .... Deut 32:30
he s them into the hands of their .... Judg 2:14
he s them into the hand of .... Judg 3:8
the LORD s them into the hand of .... Judg 4:2
he s them into the hands of the .... Judg 10:7
he s them into the hand of Sisera 1Sa 12:9
because thou hast s thyself to 1Kin 21:20
until an ass's head was s for 2Kin 6:25
of fine flour be s for a shekel 2Kin 7:1
of fine flour was s for a shekel 2Kin 7:16
s themselves to do evil in the 2Kin 17:17
which were s unto the heathen .... Neh 5:8
or shall they be s unto us .... Neh 5:8
the day wherein they s victuals .... Neh 13:15
s on the sabbath unto the .... Neh 13:16
For we are s, I and my people, to .... Est 7:4
But if we had been s for bondmen .... Est 7:4
Joseph, who was s for a servant .... Ps 105:17
is it to whom I have s you .... Is 50:1
iniquities have ye s yourselves .... Is 50:1
Ye have s yourselves for nought .... Is 52:3
which hath been s unto the .... Jer 34:14
our wood is s unto us .... Lam 5:4
not return to that which is s .... Eze 7:13
s a girl for wine, that they .... Joel 3:3
have ye s unto the Grecians .... Joel 3:6
the place whither ye have s them .... Joel 3:7
because they s the righteous for .... Amos 2:6
not two sparrows s for a farthing .... Mt 10:29
s all that he had, and bought it .... Mt 13:46
his lord commanded him to be s .... Mt 18:25
God, and cast out all them that s .... Mt 21:12
and the seats of them that s doves ..... Mt 21:12
might have been s for much .... Mt 26:9
and began to cast out them that s .... Mk 11:15
and the seats of them that s doves ..... Mk 11:15
For it might have been s for more ...... Mk 14:5
five sparrows s for two farthings .... Lk 12:6
they drank, they bought, they s .... Lk 17:28
to cast out them that s therein .... Lk 19:45
in the temple those that s oxen .... Jn 2:14
And said unto them that s doves .... Jn 2:16
s for three hundred pence .... Jn 12:5
s their possessions and goods, and ..... Acts 2:45
of lands or houses s them .... Acts 4:34
prices of the things that were s .... Acts 4:34
s it, and brought the money, and .... Acts 4:37
his wife, s a possession, ... Acts 5:1
and after it was s, was it not in .... Acts 5:4
Tell me whether ye s the land for ...... Acts 5:8
with envy, s Joseph into Egypt .... Acts 7:9
but I am carnal, s under sin .... Rom 7:14
Whatsoever is s in the shambles, ... 1Cor 10:25
morsel of meat s his birthright .... Heb 12:16

SOLDIER
four parts, to every s a part .... Jn 19:23
a devout s of them that waited on .... Acts 10:7
by himself with a s that kept him .... Acts 28:16
companion in labour, and fellow .... Phil 2:25
as a good s of Jesus Christ 2Ti 2:3
him who hath chosen him to be a s 2Ti 2:4

SOLDIERS
fathers, were bands of s for war 1Chr 7:4
thousand and two hundred s 1Chr 7:11
But the s of the army which 2Chr 25:13
require of the king a band of s .... Ezr 8:22
therefore the armed s of Moab .... Is 15:4
authority, having s under me .... Mt 8:9
Then the s of the governor took .... Mt 27:27
unto him the whole band of s .... Mt 27:27
they gave large money unto the s .... Mt 28:12
the s led him away into the hall, ... Mk 15:16
the s likewise demanded of him, ... Lk 3:14
authority, having under me a .... Lk 7:8
the s also mocked him, coming to ...... Lk 23:36
the s platted a crown of thorns, ... Jn 19:2
Then the s, when they had .... Jn 19:23
These things therefore the s did .... Jn 19:24
Then came the s, and brake the .... Jn 19:32
But one of the s with a spear .... Jn 19:34
four quaternions of s to keep him ...... Acts 12:4
Peter was sleeping between two s .... Acts 12:6
was no small stir among the s .... Acts 12:18
Who immediately took s and .... Acts 21:32

saw the chief captain and the s .... Acts 21:32
that he was borne of the s for .... Acts 21:35
them, commanded the s to go down .... Acts 23:10
two hundred s to go to Caesarea .... Acts 23:23
Then the s, as it was commanded ...... Acts 23:31
said to the centurion and to the s .... Acts 27:31
Then the s cut off the ropes of .... Acts 27:32

SOLDIERS'
the s counsel was to kill the .... Acts 27:42

SOLE
no rest for the s of her foot .... Gen 8:9
from the s of thy foot unto the .... Deut 28:35
would not adventure to set the s .... Deut 28:56
neither shall the s of thy foot .... Deut 28:65
Every place that the s of your .... Josh 1:3
from the s of his foot even to 2Sa 14:25
with the s of my feet have I 2Kin 19:24
the s of his foot unto his crown .... Job 2:7
From the s of the foot even unto .... Is 1:6
with the s of my feet have I .... Is 37:25
the s of their feet was like the .... Eze 1:7
was like the s of a calf's foot .... Eze 1:7

SOLEMN
it is a s assembly .... Lev 23:36
your gladness, and in your s days .... Num 10:10
offering, or in your s feasts .... Num 15:3
day ye shall have a s assembly .... Num 29:35
a s assembly to the LORD thy God...... Deut 16:8
Seven days shalt thou keep a s .... Deut 16:15
Proclaim a s assembly for Baal 2Kin 10:20
on the s feasts of the LORD our 2Chr 2:4
eighth day they made a s assembly 2Chr 7:9
the new moons, and on the s feasts 2Chr 8:13
the eighth day was a s assembly .... Neh 8:18
appointed, on our s feast day, ... Ps 81:3
upon the harp with a s sound .... Ps 92:3
is iniquity, even the s meeting .... Is 1:13
because none come to the s feasts .... Lam 1:4
the LORD hath caused the s feasts ...... Lam 2:6
LORD, as in the day of a s feast .... Lam 2:7
Thou hast called as in a s day my ...... Lam 2:22
of Jerusalem in her s feasts .... Eze 36:38
before the LORD in the s feasts .... Eze 46:9
her sabbaths, and all her s feasts .... Hos 2:11
What will ye do in the s day .... Hos 9:5
as in the days of the s feast .... Hos 12:9
call a s assembly, gather the .... Joel 1:14
a fast, call a s assembly .... Joel 2:15
not smell in your s assemblies .... Amos 5:21
O Judah, keep thy s feasts .... Nah 1:15
are sorrowful for the s assembly .... Zeph 3:18
even the dung of your s feasts .... Mal 2:3

SOLEMNITIES
Look upon Zion, the city of our s .... Is 33:20
in all s of the house of Israel .... Eze 45:17
in the s the meat offering shall .... Eze 46:11

SOLEMNITY
in the s of the year of release, ... Deut 31:10
the night when a holy s is kept .... Is 30:29

SOLEMNLY
The man did s protest unto us, ... Gen 43:3
unto thee, and protest s unto them 1Sa 8:9

SOLES
Every place whereon the s of your ..... Deut 11:24
as soon as the s of the feet of .... Josh 3:13
the s of the priests' feet were .... Josh 4:18
put them under the s of his feet 1Kin 5:3
down at the s of thy feet .... Is 60:14
and the place of the s of my feet .... Eze 43:7
they shall be ashes under the s .... Mal 4:3

SOLITARILY
which dwell s in the wood .... Mic 7:14

SOLITARY
Lo, let that night be s .... Job 3:7
For want and famine they were s ...... Job 30:3
God setteth the s in families .... Ps 68:6
in the wilderness in a s way .... Ps 107:4
the s place shall be glad for .... Is 35:1
How doth the city sit s, that was .... Lam 1:1
out, and departed into a s place .... Mk 1:35

SOLOMON (sŏl'-o-mun) See JEDIDIAH
SOLOMON'S. Son of David; king of Israel,
and Shobab, and Nathan, and S 2Sa 5:14
a son, and he called his name S 2Sa 12:24
S his brother, he called not 1Kin 1:10
unto Bath-sheba the mother of S 1Kin 1:11
life, and the life of thy son S 1Kin 1:12
Assuredly S thy son shall reign 1Kin 1:13
Assuredly S thy son shall reign 1Kin 1:17
but S thy servant hath he not 1Kin 1:19
my son S shall be counted 1Kin 1:21
son of Jehoiada, and thy servant S..... 1Kin 1:26
Assuredly S thy son shall reign 1Kin 1:30
cause S my son to ride upon mine 1Kin 1:33
trumpet, and say, God save king S 1Kin 1:34
the king, even so be he with S 1Kin 1:37
caused S to ride upon king 1Kin 1:38
of the tabernacle, and anointed S 1Kin 1:39
the people said, God save king S 1Kin 1:39
lord king David hath made S king 1Kin 1:43
also S sitteth on the throne of 1Kin 1:46
name of S better than thy name 1Kin 1:47
And Adonijah feared because of S 1Kin 1:50
And it was told S, saying, Behold, ... 1Kin 1:51
Behold, Adonijah feareth king S 1Kin 1:51
Let king S swear unto me to day 1Kin 1:51

S said, If he will shew himself a 1Kin 1:52
So king S sent, and they brought 1Kin 1:53
came and bowed himself to king S 1Kin 1:53
S said unto him, Go to thine 1Kin 1:53
and he charged S his son, saying, ... 1Kin 2:1
then S sat upon the throne of 1Kin 2:12
to Bath-sheba the mother of S 1Kin 2:13
unto S the king, (for he will not.......... 1Kin 2:17
therefore went unto king S 1Kin 2:19
king S answered and said unto his 1Kin 2:22
Then king S sware by the LORD, ... 1Kin 2:23
king S sent by the hand of 1Kin 2:25
So S thrust out Abiathar from 1Kin 2:27
it was told king S that Joab was 1Kin 2:29
Then S sent Benaiah the son of 1Kin 2:29
it was told S that Shimei had 1Kin 2:41
king S shall be blessed, and the 1Kin 2:45
was established in the hand of S 1Kin 2:46
S made affinity with Pharaoh king 1Kin 3:1
S loved the LORD, walking in the 1Kin 3:3
did S offer upon that altar 1Kin 3:4
appeared to S in a dream by night 1Kin 3:5
S said, Thou hast shewed unto thy 1Kin 3:6
that S had asked this thing 1Kin 3:10
And S awoke 1Kin 3:15
So king S was king over all 1Kin 4:1
S had twelve officers over all 1Kin 4:7
Taphath the daughter of S to wife 1Kin 4:11
Basmath the daughter of S to wife 1Kin 4:15
S reigned over all kingdoms from 1Kin 4:21
served S all the days of his life 1Kin 4:21
to Beer-sheba, all the days of S 1Kin 4:25
S had forty thousand stalls of 1Kin 4:26
provided victual for king S 1Kin 4:27
And God gave S wisdom and 1Kin 4:29
people to hear the wisdom of S 1Kin 4:34
of Tyre sent his servants unto S 1Kin 5:1
And S sent to Hiram, saying, ... 1Kin 5:2
when Hiram heard the words of S 1Kin 5:7
And Hiram sent to S, saying, I 1Kin 5:8
So Hiram gave S cedar trees 1Kin 5:10
S gave Hiram twenty thousand 1Kin 5:11
thus gave S to Hiram year by year 1Kin 5:11
And the LORD gave S wisdom 1Kin 5:12
was peace between Hiram and S 1Kin 5:12
king S raised a levy out of all 1Kin 5:13
S had threescore and ten thousand 1Kin 5:15
which king S built for the LORD 1Kin 6:1
And the word of the LORD came to S.. 1Kin 6:11
So S built the house, and finished...... 1Kin 6:14
So S overlaid the house within 1Kin 6:21
But S was building his own house 1Kin 7:1
S made also an house for 1Kin 7:8
And king S sent and fetched Hiram ... 1Kin 7:13
And he came to king S, and wrought.. 1Kin 7:14
king S for the house of the LORD 1Kin 7:45
which Hiram made to king S for 1Kin 7:45
S left all the vessels unweighed, ... 1Kin 7:47
S made all the vessels that 1Kin 7:48
ended all the work that king S 1Kin 7:51
S brought in the things which 1Kin 7:51
Then S assembled the elders of 1Kin 8:1
unto king S in Jerusalem, that 1Kin 8:1
king S at the feast in the month 1Kin 8:2
And king S, and all the 1Kin 8:5
Then spake S, The LORD said that 1Kin 8:12
S stood before the altar of the 1Kin 8:22
that when S had made an end of 1Kin 8:54
S offered a sacrifice of peace 1Kin 8:63
And at that time S held a feast 1Kin 8:65
when S had finished the building 1Kin 9:1
appeared to S the second time 1Kin 9:2
when S had built the two houses, ... 1Kin 9:10
had furnished S with cedar trees, ... 1Kin 9:11
that then king S gave Hiram 1Kin 9:11
the cities which S had given him 1Kin 9:12
of the levy which king S raised 1Kin 9:15
S built Gezer, and Beth-horon the 1Kin 9:17
the cities of store that S had 1Kin 9:19
of the levy which king S raised 1Kin 9:21
upon those did S levy a tribute 1Kin 9:21
of Israel did S make no bondmen 1Kin 9:22
house which S had built for her 1Kin 9:24
year did S offer burnt offerings 1Kin 9:25
king S made a navy of ships in 1Kin 9:26
the sea, with the servants of S 1Kin 9:27
talents, and brought it to king S 1Kin 9:28
of Sheba heard the fame of S 1Kin 10:1
and when she was come to S 1Kin 10:2
S told her all her questions 1Kin 10:3
the queen of Sheba gave to king S..... 1Kin 10:10
king S gave unto the queen of 1Kin 10:13
beside that which S gave her of 1Kin 10:13
to S in one year was six hundred 1Kin 10:14
king S made two hundred targets....... 1Kin 10:16
accounted of in the days of S 1Kin 10:21
So king S exceeded all the kings 1Kin 10:23
And all the earth sought to S 1Kin 10:24
S gathered together chariots and 1Kin 10:26
S had horses brought out of Egypt 1Kin 10:28
But king S loved many strange 1Kin 11:1
S clave unto these in love 1Kin 11:2
when S was old, that his wives 1Kin 11:4
For S went after Ashtoreth the 1Kin 11:5
S did evil in the sight of the 1Kin 11:6
Then did S build an high place 1Kin 11:7
And the LORD was angry with S 1Kin 11:9
Wherefore the LORD said unto S 1Kin 11:11
stirred up an adversary unto S 1Kin 11:14
to Israel all the days of S 1Kin 11:25

SOMEBODY

cheer, and they also took s meat...... Acts 27:36
s on boards, and s on broken........ Acts 27:44
s believed the things which were...... Acts 28:24
were spoken, and s believed not...... Acts 28:24
impart unto you s spiritual gift....... Rom 1:11
that I might have s fruit among....... Rom 1:13
For what if s did not believe........ Rom 3:3
as s affirm that we say,) Let us....... Rom 3:8
good man s would even dare to die..... Rom 5:7
my flesh, and might save s of them..... Rom 11:14
if s of the branches be broken........ Rom 11:17
more boldly unto you in a sort....... Rom 15:15
Now s are puffed up, as though I....... 1Cor 4:18
And such were s of you.............. 1Cor 6:11
for s with conscience of the idol....... 1Cor 8:7
that I might by all means save s...... 1Cor 9:22
ye idolaters, as were s of them....... 1Cor 10:7
as s of them committed, and fell...... 1Cor 10:8
as s of them also tempted, and....... 1Cor 10:9
as s of them also murmured, and...... 1Cor 10:10
God hath set s in the church,....... 1Cor 12:28
present, but s are fallen asleep...... 1Cor 15:6
how say s among you that there is..... 1Cor 15:12
for s have not the knowledge of...... 1Cor 15:34
But s man will say, How are the...... 1Cor 15:35
of wheat, or of s other grain....... 1Cor 15:37
need we, as s others, epistles of....... 2Cor 3:1
I think to be bold against s.......... 2Cor 10:2
with s that commend themselves...... 2Cor 10:12
but there be s that trouble you,...... Gal 1:7
And he gave s, apostles............. Eph 4:11
and s, prophets.................... Eph 4:11
and s, evangelists.................. Eph 4:11
and s, pastors and teachers......... Eph 4:11
S indeed preach Christ even of...... Phil 1:15
and s also of good will.............. Phil 1:15
the which ye also walked s time..... Col 3:7
lest by s means the tempter have..... 1Th 3:5
For we hear that there are s........ 2Th 3:11
charge s that they teach no other..... 1Ti 1:3
From which s having swerved have.... 1Ti 1:6
which s having put away............ 1Ti 1:19
that in the latter times s shall...... 1Ti 4:1
For s are already turned aside....... 1Ti 5:15
S men's sins are open beforehand,.... 1Ti 5:24
and s men they follow after......... 1Ti 5:24
of s are manifest beforehand....... 1Ti 5:25
which while s coveted after, they..... 1Ti 6:10
Which s professing have erred....... 1Ti 6:21
and overthrow the faith of s........ 2Ti 2:18
s to honour, and s to dishonour..... 2Ti 2:20
every house is builded by s man..... Heb 3:4
For s, when they had heard, did..... Heb 3:16
that s must enter therein........... Heb 4:6
together, as the manner of s is...... Heb 10:25
provided s better thing for us....... Heb 11:40
for thereby s have entertained...... Heb 13:2
as though s strange thing.......... 1Pet 4:12
promise, as s men count slackness.... 2Pet 3:9
in which are s things hard to be..... 2Pet 3:16
of s have compassion, making a...... Jude 22
shall cast s of you into prison....... Rev 2:10

SOMEBODY

And Jesus said, S hath touched me..... Lk 8:46
Theudas, boasting himself to be s..... Acts 5:36

SOMETHING

S hath befallen him, he is not....... 1Sa 20:26
commanded that s should be given..... Mk 5:43
to catch s out of his mouth........ Lk 11:54
that he should give s to the poor..... Jn 13:29
expecting to receive s of them....... Acts 3:5
as though ye would enquire s more.... Acts 23:15
who hath s to say unto thee......... Acts 23:18
if a man think himself to be s....... Gal 6:3

SOMETIME

And you, that were s alienated...... Col 1:21
Which s were disobedient, when...... 1Pet 3:20

SOMETIMES

s were far off are made nigh by..... Eph 2:13
For ye were s darkness, but now..... Eph 5:8
we ourselves also were s foolish..... Titus 3:3

SOMEWHAT

they have done s against any of..... Lev 4:13
done s through ignorance against..... Lev 4:27
while he doeth s against any of..... Lev 4:27
behold, if the plague be s dark..... Lev 13:6
s reddish, and it be shewed to the.... Lev 13:19
than the skin, but be s dark........ Lev 13:21
bright spot, s reddish, or white..... Lev 13:24
the other skin, but be s dark....... Lev 13:26
not in the skin, but it be s dark.... Lev 13:28
the plague be s dark after the...... Lev 13:56
I have s to say unto thee.......... 1Kin 2:14
run after him, and take s of him..... 2Kin 5:20
now therefore ease thou s the...... 2Chr 10:9
Ease s the yoke that thy father..... 2Chr 10:10
but make thou it s lighter for us..... 2Chr 10:10
I have s to say unto thee.......... Lk 7:40
enquire s of him more perfectly..... Acts 23:20
had, I might have s to write........ Acts 25:26
if first I be s filled with your..... Rom 15:24
that ye may have s to answer them.... 2Cor 5:12
boast s more of our authority...... 2Cor 10:8
But of these who seemed to be s..... Gal 2:6
for they who seemed to be s in...... Gal 2:6
this man have s also to offer....... Heb 8:3
I have s against thee, because...... Rev 2:4

SON (column 2) See PREFACE.

bare Abraham a s in his old age..... Gen 21:2
of his s that was born unto him..... Gen 21:3
in order, and bound Isaac his s..... Gen 22:9
he answered, I called not, my s..... 1Sa 3:6
O Absalom, my s, my s............. 2Sa 19:4
So we boiled my s, and did eat him.... 2Kin 6:29
her on the next day, Give thy s..... 2Kin 6:29
And he said unto me, Solomon thy s.... 1Chr 28:6
for I have chosen him to be my s..... 1Chr 28:6
hath said unto me, Thou art my s..... Ps 2:7
the s of man, that thou visitest...... Ps 8:4
or the s of man, that thou makest..... Ps 144:3
My s, forget not my law............ Prov 3:1
A wise s maketh a glad father...... Prov 15:20
Chasten thy s while there is hope..... Prov 19:18
shall conceive, and bear a s........ Is 7:14
is born, unto us a s is given....... Is 9:6
of the s of man which shall be...... Is 51:12
doth not the s bear the iniquity..... Eze 18:19
the fourth is like the S of God..... Dan 3:25
him, and called my s out of Egypt..... Hos 11:1
his own s that serveth him......... Mal 3:17
saying, This is my beloved S....... Mt 3:17
and no man knoweth the S, but the.... Mt 11:27
any man the Father, save the S..... Mt 11:27
whomsoever the S will reveal him..... Mt 11:27
Of a truth thou art the S of God..... Mt 14:33
which said, This is my beloved S..... Mt 17:5
For the S of man is come to save..... Mt 18:11
whose s is he.................... Mt 22:42
the coming of the S of man be...... Mt 24:37
If thou be the S of God, come...... Mt 27:40
for he said, I am the S of God..... Mt 27:43
Truly this was the S of God....... Mt 27:54
Truly this man was the S of God..... Mk 15:39
thee shall be called the S of God..... Lk 1:35
of Adam, which was the s of God..... Lk 3:38
Thou art Christ the S of God....... Lk 4:41
Jesus, thou S of God most high..... Lk 8:28
saying, This is my beloved S....... Lk 9:35
For the S of man is come to seek..... Lk 19:10
then shall they see the S of man..... Lk 21:27
all, Art thou then the S of God..... Lk 22:70
record that this is the S of God..... Jn 1:34
him, Rabbi, thou art the S of God..... Jn 1:49
that he gave his only begotten S..... Jn 3:16
of the only begotten S of God..... Jn 3:18
The S can do nothing of himself..... Jn 5:19
That all men should honour the S..... Jn 5:23
Christ, the S of the living God..... Jn 6:69
If the S therefore shall make you..... Jn 8:36
his mother, Woman, behold thy s..... Jn 19:26
Jesus is the Christ, the S of God..... Jn 20:31
that Jesus Christ is the S of God..... Acts 8:37
that is the S of God............... Acts 9:20
to be the S of God with power...... Rom 1:4
God sending his own S in the...... Rom 8:3
was come, God sent forth his S..... Gal 4:4
art no more a servant, but a s..... Gal 4:7
and if a s, then an heir of God..... Gal 4:7
as a s with the father, he hath..... Phil 2:22
offered up his only begotten s..... Heb 11:17
for what s is he whom the father..... Heb 12:7
He that hath the S hath life...... 1Jn 5:12
not the S of God hath not life..... 1Jn 5:12

SONG

of Israel this s unto the LORD...... Ex 15:1
The LORD is my strength and s..... Ex 15:2
Then Israel sang this s, Spring..... Num 21:17
therefore write ye this s for you..... Deut 31:19
that this s may be a witness for..... Deut 31:19
that this s shall testify against..... Deut 31:21
wrote this s the same day......... Deut 31:22
of Israel the words of this s...... Deut 31:30
this s in the ears of the people..... Deut 32:44
awake, awake, utter a s............ Judg 5:12
unto the LORD the words of this s..... 2Sa 22:1
of s in the house of the LORD...... 1Chr 6:31
chief of the Levites, was for s..... 1Chr 15:22
he instructed about the s......... 1Chr 15:22
master of the s with the singers..... 1Chr 15:27
for s in the house of God called..... 1Chr 25:6
the s of the LORD began also with.... 2Chr 29:27
And now am I their s, yea, I am..... Job 30:9
this is in the day that the LORD..... Ps 28:7
with my s will I praise him......... Ps 28:7
S at the dedication of the house..... Ps 30:t
Sing unto him a new s............. Ps 33:3
he hath put a new s in my mouth..... Ps 40:3
the night his s shall be with me..... Ps 42:8
of Korah, A Maschil, A S of loves..... Ps 45:t
sons of Korah, A S upon Alamoth..... Ps 46:t
A S and Psalm for the sons of..... Ps 65:t
Musician, A Psalm and s of David..... Ps 65:t
the chief Musician, A S or Psalm..... Ps 66:t
on Neginoth, A Psalm or S........ Ps 67:t
Musician, A Psalm or S of David..... Ps 68:t
I was the s of the drunkards....... Ps 69:12
praise the name of God with a s..... Ps 69:30
Altaschith, A Psalm or S of Asaph..... Ps 75:t
Neginoth, A Psalm or S of Asaph..... Ps 76:t
to remembrance my s in the night..... Ps 77:6
A S or Psalm of Asaph............ Ps 83:t
A Psalm or S for the sons of..... Ps 87:t
A S or Psalm for the sons of..... Ps 88:t
A Psalm or S for the sabbath day..... Ps 92:t
O sing unto the LORD a new s....... Ps 96:1
O sing unto the LORD a new s....... Ps 98:1
A S or Psalm of David............ Ps 108:t

The LORD is my strength and s..... Ps 118:14 (column 3)
A S of degrees.................... Ps 120:t
A S of degrees.................... Ps 121:t
A S of degrees of David........... Ps 122:t
A S of degrees.................... Ps 123:t
A S of degrees.................... Ps 124:t
A S of degrees.................... Ps 125:t
A S of degrees.................... Ps 126:t
A S of degrees for Solomon........ Ps 127:t
A S of degrees.................... Ps 128:t
A S of degrees.................... Ps 129:t
A S of degrees.................... Ps 130:t
A S of degrees.................... Ps 131:t
A S of degrees.................... Ps 132:t
A S of degrees of David........... Ps 133:t
A S of degrees.................... Ps 134:t
away captive required of us a s..... Ps 137:3
the LORD's s in a strange land..... Ps 137:4
I will sing a new s unto thee....... Ps 144:9
Sing unto the LORD a new s........ Ps 149:1
for a man to hear the s of fools..... Eccl 7:5
The s of songs, which is.......... Song 1:1
a s of my beloved touching his..... Is 5:1
JEHOVAH is my strength and my s..... Is 12:2
shall not drink wine with a s..... Is 24:9
In that day shall this s be sung..... Is 26:1
Ye shall have a s, as in the...... Is 30:29
Sing unto the LORD a new s........ Is 42:10
and their s all the day.......... Lam 3:14
s of one that hath a pleasant..... Eze 33:32
And they sang a new s, saying..... Rev 5:9
it were a new s before the throne.... Rev 14:3
learn that s but the hundred...... Rev 14:3
they sing the s of Moses the...... Rev 15:3
the s of the Lamb, saying, Great..... Rev 15:3

SONGS

thee away with mirth, and with s..... Gen 31:27
his s were a thousand and five..... 1Kin 4:32
instructed in the s of the LORD..... 1Chr 25:7
s of praise and thanksgiving unto..... Neh 12:46
who giveth s in the night......... Job 35:10
me about with s of deliverance..... Ps 32:7
Thy statutes have been my s in..... Ps 119:54
Sing us one of the s of Zion....... Ps 137:3
that singeth s to an heavy heart..... Prov 25:20
The song of s, which is Solomon's..... Song 1:1
make sweet melody, sing many s..... Is 23:16
part of the earth have we heard s..... Is 24:16
return, and come to Zion with s..... Is 35:10
therefore we will sing my s to..... Is 38:20
cause the noise of thy s to cease..... Eze 26:13
away from me the noise of thy s..... Amos 5:23
the s of the temple shall be...... Amos 8:3
all your s into lamentation...... Amos 8:10
in psalms and hymns and spiritual s.... Eph 5:19
in psalms and hymns and spiritual s.... Col 3:16

SON'S

and Lot the son of Haran his s..... Gen 11:31
of Abram called his s name....... Gen 16:15
with my son, nor with my s son..... Gen 21:23
and let her be my master's s wife..... Gen 24:51
me, and I will eat of my s venison..... Gen 27:25
arise, and eat of his s venison..... Gen 27:31
I pray thee, of thy s mandrakes..... Gen 30:14
take away my s mandrakes also..... Gen 30:15
thee to night for thy s mandrakes..... Gen 30:16
hired thee with my s mandrakes..... Gen 30:16
whether it be thy s coat or no..... Gen 37:32
knew it, and said, It is my s coat..... Gen 37:33
ears of thy son, and of thy s son..... Ex 10:2
The nakedness of thy s daughter..... Lev 18:10
she is thy s wife.................. Lev 18:15
shalt thou take her s daughter..... Lev 18:17
thou, and thy son, and thy s son..... Deut 6:2
and thy son, and thy s son along..... Judg 8:22
the kingdom out of his s hand..... 1Kin 11:35
but in his s days will I bring..... 1Kin 21:29
his name, and what is his s name..... Prov 30:4
him, and his son, and his s son..... Jer 27:7

SONS See PREFACE.

SONS'

wife, and thy s wives with thee..... Gen 6:18
his s wives with him, into the..... Gen 7:7
son, and thy s wives with thee..... Gen 8:16
his wife, and his s wives with him..... Gen 8:18
sons, and his s sons with him, his..... Gen 46:7
his s daughters, and all his seed..... Gen 46:7
loins, besides Jacob's s wives..... Gen 46:26
sons, and his s garments with him..... Ex 29:21
his s by a statute for ever from..... Ex 29:28
of Aaron shall be his s after him..... Ex 29:29
his s garments, to minister in..... Ex 39:41
shall be Aaron's and his s........ Lev 2:3
shall be Aaron's and his s........ Lev 2:10
breast shall be Aaron's and his s..... Lev 7:31
hands, and upon his s hands...... Lev 8:27
upon his s garments with him..... Lev 8:30
sons, and his s garments with him..... Lev 8:30
it is thy due, and thy s due...... Lev 10:13
for they be thy due, and thy s due..... Lev 10:14
thy s with thee, by a statute for..... Lev 10:15
And it shall be Aaron's and his s..... Lev 24:9
them thy sons, and thy s sons..... Deut 4:9
s sons, an hundred and fifty...... 1Chr 8:40
his s sons, even four generations..... Job 42:16
thereof shall be his s............. Eze 46:16
shall be his s for them.......... Eze 46:17

SOON

as s as he had left communing............ Gen 18:33
as s as Isaac had made an end of........ Gen 27:30
As s as the morning was light,............ Gen 44:3
it that ye are come so s to day............ Ex 2:18
As s as I am gone out of the city.......... Ex 9:29
as s as he came night unto the........... Ex 32:19
that ye shall s utterly perish............. Deut 4:26
as s as they which pursued after......... Josh 2:7
as s as we had heard these things......... Josh 2:11
as s as the soles of the feet of........... Josh 3:13
they ran as s as he had stretched......... Josh 8:19
as s as the sun was down, Joshua......... Josh 8:29
as s as Gideon was dead, that the......... Judg 8:33
as s as the sun is up, thou shalt......... Judg 9:33
As s as ye be come into the city,......... 1Sa 9:13
that as s as he had made an end......... 1Sa 13:10
as s as the lad was gone, David......... 1Sa 20:41
as s as ye be up early in the............ 1Sa 29:10
as s as David had made an end of........ 2Sa 6:18
as s as he had made an end of........... 2Sa 13:36
As s as ye hear the sound of the......... 2Sa 15:10
as s as they hear, they shall be......... 2Sa 22:45
as s as he sat on his throne,............ 1Kin 16:11
as s as I am gone from thee, that........ 1Kin 18:12
as s as thou art departed from me........ 1Kin 20:36
as s as he was departed from him,........ 1Kin 20:36
Now as s as this letter cometh to........ 2Kin 10:2
as s as he had made an end of........... 2Kin 10:25
as s as the kingdom was confirmed....... 2Kin 14:5
as s as the commandment came.......... 2Chr 31:5
my maker would s take me away.......... Job 32:22
As s as they hear of me, they........... Ps 18:44
For they shall s be cut down like......... Ps 37:2
go astray as s as they be born........... Ps 58:3
Ethiopia shall s stretch out her......... Ps 68:31
I should s have subdued their.......... Ps 81:14
for it is s cut off, and we fly............ Ps 90:10
They s forgat his works............... Ps 106:13
He that is s angry dealeth............. Prov 14:17
for as s as Zion travailed, she.......... Is 66:8
as s as she saw them with her.......... Eze 23:16
How s is the fig tree withered.......... Mt 21:20
And as s as he had spoken,............ Mk 1:42
as s as Jesus heard the word that....... Mk 5:36
as s as ye be entered into it, ye........ Mk 14:45
as s as he was come, he goeth......... Mk 14:45
that, as s as the days of his.......... Lk 1:23
For, lo, as s as the voice of thou........ Lk 1:44
as s as it was sprung up, it............ Lk 8:6
But as s as this thy son was come....... Lk 15:30
as s as it was day, the elders of....... Lk 22:66
as s as he knew that he belonged....... Lk 23:7
as s as he heard that Jesus was....... Jn 11:20
As s as she heard that, she arose....... Jn 11:29
but as s as she is delivered of......... Jn 16:21
As s then as he had said unto.......... Jn 18:6
As s then as they were come to....... Jn 21:9
as s as I was sent for............... Acts 10:29
Now as s as it was day, there was....... Acts 12:18
I marvel that ye are s removed......... Gal 1:6
so s as I shall see how it will........... Phil 2:23
That ye be not s shaken in mind....... 2Th 2:2
not s angry, not given to wine,......... Titus 1:7
as s as I had eaten it, my belly........ Rev 10:10
her child as s as it was born........... Rev 12:4

SOONER

I may be restored to you the s........... Heb 13:19
For the sun is no s risen with a......... Jas 1:11

SOOTHSAYER

also the son of Beor, the s............ Josh 13:22

SOOTHSAYERS

are s like the Philistines, and......... Is 2:6
astrologers, the magicians, the s....... Dan 2:27
the Chaldeans, and the s............. Dan 4:7
the Chaldeans, and the s............. Dan 5:7
astrologers, Chaldeans, and s......... Dan 5:11
and thou shalt have no more s......... Mic 5:12

SOOTHSAYING

her masters much gain by s.......... Acts 16:16

SOP

it is, to whom I shall give a s........... Jn 13:26
And when he had dipped the s......... Jn 13:26
after the s Satan entered into.......... Jn 13:27
the s went immediately out............ Jn 13:30

SOPATER (so'-pa-ter) See SOSIPATER. A
Christian from Berea.
him into Asia S of Berea................ Acts 20:4

SOPE

with nitre, and take thee much s......... Jer 2:22
fire, and like fullers' s.............. Mal 3:2

SOPHERETH (so-fe'-reth) A family of exiles.
of Sotai, the children of S............ Ezr 2:55
of Sotai, the children of S............ Neh 7:57

SORCERER

Paphos, they found a certain s......... Acts 13:6
But Elymas the s (for so is his........ Acts 13:8

SORCERERS

also called the wise men and the s....... Ex 7:11
to your enchanters, nor to your s....... Jer 27:9
and the astrologers, and the s......... Dan 2:2
be a swift witness against the s....... Mal 3:5
murderers, and whoremongers, and s... Rev 21:8
For without are dogs, and s.......... Rev 22:15

SORCERESS

near hither, ye sons of the s........... Is 57:3

SORCERIES

for the multitude of thy s............ Is 47:9
and with the multitude of thy s....... Is 47:12
time he had bewitched them with s..... Acts 8:11
of their murders, nor of their s....... Rev 9:21
for by thy s were all nations.......... Rev 18:23

SORCERY

in the same city used s, and.......... Acts 8:9

SORE

And they pressed s upon the man...... Gen 19:9
and the men were s afraid............ Gen 20:8
because thou s longedst after thy...... Gen 31:30
the third day, when they were s........ Gen 34:25
the famine waxed s in the land....... Gen 41:56
the famine was so s in all lands....... Gen 41:57
And the famine was in the land....... Gen 43:1
for the famine is s in the land........ Gen 47:4
for the famine was very s............ Gen 47:13
a great and very s lamentation........ Gen 50:10
and they were s afraid.............. Ex 14:10
bald forehead, a white reddish s....... Lev 13:42
if the rising of the s be white........ Lev 13:43
Moab was s afraid of the people,...... Num 22:3
signs and wonders, great and s........ Deut 6:22
with a s botch that cannot be......... Deut 28:35
and s sicknesses, and of long......... Deut 28:59
therefore we were s afraid of........ Josh 9:24
so that Israel was s distressed....... Judg 10:9
her, because she lay s upon him....... Judg 14:17
he was s athirst, and called on....... Judg 15:18
all Israel, and the battle was s....... Judg 20:34
lifted up their voices, and wept s..... Judg 21:2
her adversary also provoked her s..... 1Sa 1:6
prayed unto the LORD, and wept s..... 1Sa 1:10
for his hand is s upon us............ 1Sa 5:7
there was s war against the.......... 1Sa 14:52
fled from him, and were s afraid....... 1Sa 17:24
was s afraid of Achish the king....... 1Sa 21:12
Saul answered, I am s distressed...... 1Sa 28:15
was s afraid, because of the......... 1Sa 28:20
and saw that he was s troubled....... 1Sa 28:21
And the battle went s against Saul.... 1Sa 31:3
he was s wounded of the archers...... 1Sa 31:3
for he was s afraid................ 1Sa 31:4
was s very a battle that day.......... 2Sa 2:17
and all his servants wept very s....... 2Sa 13:36
and his sickness was so s, that....... 1Kin 17:17
there was s famine in Samaria....... 1Kin 18:2
that the battle was too s for him..... 2Kin 3:26
was s troubled for this thing........ 2Kin 6:11
And Hezekiah wept s................ 2Kin 20:3
And the battle went s against Saul.... 1Chr 10:3
for he was s afraid................ 1Chr 10:4
whatsoever s or whatsoever........ 2Chr 6:28
every one shall know his own s....... 2Chr 6:29
so he died of s diseases............ 2Chr 21:19
transgressed s against the LORD..... 2Chr 26:16
for I am s wounded................ 2Chr 35:23
for the people wept very s.......... Ezr 10:1
Then I was very s afraid,........... Neh 2:2
And it grieved me s................ Neh 13:8
smote Job with s boils from the...... Job 2:7
For he maketh s, and bindeth up...... Job 5:18
and vex them in his s displeasure..... Ps 2:5
My soul is also s vexed............ Ps 6:3
enemies be ashamed and s vexed.... Ps 6:10
in me, and thy hand presseth me s.... Ps 38:2
I am feeble and s broken........... Ps 38:8
my friends stand aloof from my s.... Ps 38:11
Though thou hast s broken us in..... Ps 44:19
My heart is s pained within me....... Ps 55:4
s troubles shall quicken me........ Ps 71:20
my s ran in the night, and ceased.... Ps 77:2
Thou hast thrust s at me that I..... Ps 118:13
The LORD hath chastened me s...... Ps 118:18
this s travail hath God given to..... Eccl 1:13
vanity, yea, it is a s travail........ Eccl 4:8
There is a s evil which I have....... Eccl 5:13
And this also is a s evil, that in..... Eccl 5:16
In that day the LORD with his s..... Is 27:1
And Hezekiah wept s.............. Is 38:3
like bears, and mourn s like doves... Is 59:11
Be not wroth very s, O LORD,....... Is 64:9
thy peace, and afflict us very s..... Is 64:12
and mine eyes shall weep s, and run.. Jer 13:17
but weep s for him that goeth....... Jer 22:10
Your mother shall be s confounded.. Jer 50:12
the famine was s in the city........ Jer 52:6
She weepeth s in the night, and..... Lam 1:2
Mine enemies chased me s, like a... Lam 3:52
four s judgments upon Jerusalem.... Eze 14:21
sharpened to make a s slaughter.... Eze 21:10
and their kings shall be s afraid..... Eze 27:35
was s displeased with himself, and.. Dan 6:14
you, even with a s destruction...... Mic 2:10
The LORD hath been s displeased.... Zec 1:2
I am very s displeased with the..... Zec 1:15
on their face, and were s afraid..... Mt 17:6
for he is lunatick, and s vexed...... Mt 17:15
they were s displeased,............ Mt 21:15
they were s amazed in themselves... Mk 6:51
for they were s afraid............. Mk 9:6
the spirit cried, and rent him s..... Mk 9:26
and John, and began to be s amazed.. Mk 14:33
and they were s afraid............ Lk 2:9
And they all wept s, and fell on.... Acts 20:37
grievous to the men which had..... Rev 16:2

SOREK (so'-rek) A valley between Ashkelon
and Gaza.
loved a woman in the valley of S...... Judg 16:4

SORELY

The archers have s grieved him...... Gen 49:23
so shall they be s pained at the...... Is 23:5

SORER

Of how much s punishment, suppose.. Heb 10:29

SORES

and bruises, and putrifying s........ Is 1:6
was laid at his gate, full of s........ Lk 16:20
the dogs came and licked his s...... Lk 16:21
because of their pains and their s.... Rev 16:11

SORROW

I will greatly multiply thy s......... Gen 3:16
in s thou shalt bring forth........... Gen 3:16
in s shalt thou eat of it all the...... Gen 3:17
my gray hairs with s to the grave.... Gen 42:38
my gray hairs with s to the grave.... Gen 44:29
our father with s to the grave....... Gen 44:31
s shall take hold on the........... Ex 15:14
the eyes, and cause s of heart...... Lev 26:16
and failing of eyes, and s of mind.... Deut 28:65
saying, Because I bare him with s... 1Chr 4:9
is nothing else but s of heart....... Neh 2:2
turned unto them from s to joy...... Est 9:22
womb, nor hid s from mine eyes..... Job 3:10
yea, I would harden myself in s..... Job 6:10
eye also is dim by reason of s...... Job 17:7
s is turned into joy before him..... Job 41:22
having s in my heart daily.......... Ps 13:2
my s is continually before me....... Ps 38:17
and my s was stirred.............. Ps 39:2
also and s are in the midst of it..... Ps 55:10
yet is their strength labour and s.... Ps 90:10
oppression, affliction, and s....... Ps 107:39
I found trouble and s............. Ps 116:3
winketh with the eye causeth s..... Prov 10:10
rich, and he addeth no s with it..... Prov 10:22
but by s of the heart the spirit..... Prov 15:13
a fool doeth it to his s............ Prov 17:21
who hath s.................... Prov 23:29
increaseth knowledge increaseth s.. Eccl 1:18
in darkness, and he hath much s.... Eccl 5:17
S is better than laughter.......... Eccl 7:3
Therefore remove s from thy heart.. Eccl 11:10
the land, behold darkness and s.... Is 5:30
shall give thee rest from thy s..... Is 14:3
day of grief and of desperate s..... Is 17:11
and there shall be heaviness and s.. Is 29:2
obtain joy and gladness, and s..... Is 35:10
ye shall lie down in s............. Is 50:11
and s and mourning shall flee away.. Is 51:11
but ye shall cry for s of heart..... Is 65:14
I would comfort myself against s... Jer 8:18
of the womb to see labour and s.... Jer 20:18
thy s is incurable for the......... Jer 30:15
they shall not s any more at all.... Jer 31:12
and make them rejoice from their s.. Jer 31:13
the LORD hath added grief to my s.. Jer 45:3
there is s on the sea............. Jer 49:23
And the land shall tremble and s.... Jer 51:29
he any s like unto my s........... Lam 1:12
you, all people, and behold my s.... Lam 1:18
Give them s of heart, thy curse.... Lam 3:65
be filled with drunkenness and s... Eze 23:33
they shall s a little for the........ Hos 8:10
he found them sleeping for s...... Lk 22:45
you, s hath filled your heart...... Jn 16:6
but your s shall be turned into..... Jn 16:20
when she is in travail hath s...... Jn 16:21
And ye now therefore have s...... Jn 16:22
and continual s in my heart....... Rom 9:2
I should have s from them of whom.. 2Cor 2:3
be swallowed up with overmuch s... 2Cor 2:7
For godly s worketh repentance to.. 2Cor 7:10
but the s of the world worketh..... 2Cor 7:10
lest I should have s upon s........ Phil 2:27
which are asleep, that ye s not..... 1Th 4:13
so much torment and s give her.... Rev 18:7
and am no widow, and shall see no s.. Rev 18:7
shall be no more death, neither s... Rev 21:4

SORROWED

but that ye s to repentance....... 2Cor 7:9
that ye s after a godly sort,....... 2Cor 7:11

SORROWETH

s for you, saying, What shall I..... 1Sa 10:2

SORROWFUL

lord, I am a woman of a s spirit..... 1Sa 1:15
refused to touch are as my s meat... Job 6:7
But I am poor and s.............. Ps 69:29
Even in laughter the heart is s.... Prov 14:13
I have replenished every s soul.... Jer 31:25
are s for the solemn assembly...... Zeph 3:18
also shall see it, and be very s.... Zec 9:5
heard that saying, he went away s.. Mt 19:22
And they were exceeding s, and... Mt 26:22
sons of Zebedee, and began to be s.. Mt 26:37
unto them, My soul is exceeding s.. Mt 26:38
And they began to be s, and to say.. Mk 14:19
My soul is exceeding s unto death.. Mk 14:34
when he heard this, he was very s.. Lk 18:23
when Jesus saw that he was very s.. Lk 18:24
and ye shall be s, but your sorrow.. Jn 16:20
As s, yet alway rejoicing......... 2Cor 6:10
and that I may be the less s....... Phil 2:28

SORROWING

father and I have sought thee s .... Lk 2:48
S most of all for the words which ...... Acts 20:38

SORROWS

for I know their s .... Ex 3:7
The s of hell compassed me about 2Sa 22:6
I am afraid of all my s, I know .... Job 9:28
God distributeth s in his anger .... Job 21:17
young ones, they cast out their s .... Job 39:3
Their s shall be multiplied that .... Ps 16:4
The s of death compassed me, and..... Ps 18:4
The s of hell compassed me about ...... Ps 18:5
Many s shall be to the wicked .... Ps 32:10
The s of death compassed me, and..... Ps 116:3
up late, to eat the bread of s .... Ps 127:2
For all his days are s, and his .... Eccl 2:23
s shall take hold of them .... Is 13:8
a man of s, and acquainted with .... Is 53:3
our griefs, and carried our s .... Is 53:4
shall not s take thee, as a woman ...... Jer 13:21
s have taken her, as a woman in .... Jer 49:24
by the vision my s are turned .... Dan 10:16
The s of a travailing woman shall ...... Hos 13:13
All these are the beginning of s .... Mt 24:8
these are the beginnings of s .... Mk 13:8
themselves through with many s 1Ti 6:10

SORRY

is none of you that is s for me 1Sa 22:8
neither be ye s .... Neh 8:10
I will be s for my sin .... Ps 38:18
who shall be s for thee .... Is 51:19
And the king was s .... Mt 14:9
And they were exceeding s .... Mt 17:23
what was done, they were very s .... Mt 18:31
And the king was exceeding s .... Mk 6:26
For if I make you s, who is he 2Cor 2:2
the same which is made s by me 2Cor 2:2
though I made you s with a letter 2Cor 7:8
the same epistle hath made you s 2Cor 7:8
rejoice, not that ye were made s 2Cor 7:9
for ye were made s after a godly 2Cor 7:9

SORT

two of every s shalt thou bring .... Gen 6:19
two of every s shall come unto .... Gen 6:20
his kind, every bird of every s .... Gen 7:14
save the poorest s of the people 2Kin 24:14
by lot, one s with another 1Chr 24:5
offer so willingly after this s 1Chr 29:14
time in such a s was written 2Chr 30:5
basons of a second s four hundred .... Ezr 1:10
to Artaxerxes the king in this s .... Ezr 4:8
unto me four times after this s .... Neh 6:4
with the men of the common s were .. Eze 23:42
the ravenous birds of every s .... Eze 39:4
of every s of your oblations, ... Eze 44:30
the children which are of your s .... Dan 1:10
God that can deliver after this s .... Dan 3:29
lewd fellows of the baser s .... Acts 17:5
more boldly unto you in some s .... Rom 15:15
every man's work of what a it is 1Cor 3:13
that ye sorrowed after a godly s 2Cor 7:11
For of this s are they which 2Ti 3:6
on their journey after a godly s 3Jn 6

SORTS

not wear a garment of divers s .... Deut 22:11
ten days store of all s of wine .... Neh 5:18
He sent divers s of flies among .... Ps 78:45
and there came divers s of flies .... Ps 105:31
instruments, and that of all s .... Eccl 2:8
thy merchants in all s of things .... Eze 27:24
them clothed with all s of armour ..... Eze 38:4

SOSIPATER (so-sip´-a-tur) See SOPATER. A
relative of Paul.
and Lucius, and Jason, and S............ Rom 16:21

SOSTHENES (sos´-the-neze)
1. *Chief ruler of a synagogue in Corinth.*
Then all the Greeks took S............... Acts 18:17
2. *A co-worker with Paul.*
will of God, and S our brother,......... 1Cor 1:1

SOTAI (so´-tahee) A family of Temple servants.
the children of S, the children......... Ezr 2:55
the children of S, the children......... Neh 7:57

SOTTISH
they are s children, and they have..... Jer 4:22

SOUGHT See PREFACE.

SOUL

and man became a living s .... Gen 2:7
my s shall live because of thee .... Gen 12:13
that s shall be cut off from his .... Gen 17:14
and my s shall live .... Gen 19:20
that my s may bless thee before I ..... Gen 27:4
venison, that thy s may bless me ...... Gen 27:19
venison, that my s may bless thee .... Gen 27:25
venison, that thy s may bless me ...... Gen 27:31
his s clave unto Dinah the .... Gen 34:3
The s of my son Shechem longeth ..... Gen 34:8
as her s was in departing, (for .... Gen 35:18
that we saw the anguish of his s ...... Gen 42:21
O my s, come not thou into their...... Gen 49:6
that s shall be cut off from .... Ex 12:15
even that s shall be cut off from ...... Ex 12:19
a ransom for his s unto the LORD ..... Ex 30:12
that s shall be cut off from .... Ex 31:14
saying, If a s shall sin through......... Lev 4:2
And if a s sin, and hear the voice .... Lev 5:1

Or if a s touch any unclean thing...... Lev 5:2
Or if a s swear, pronouncing with..... Lev 5:4
If a s commit a trespass, and sin ...... Lev 5:15
And if a s sin, and commit a trespass Lev 5:17
If a s sin, and commit a trespass...... Lev 6:2
the s that eateth of it shall .... Lev 7:18
But the s that eateth of the .... Lev 7:20
even that s shall be cut off from ...... Lev 7:20
Moreover the s that shall touch .... Lev 7:21
even that s shall be cut off from ...... Lev 7:21
even the s that eateth it shall .... Lev 7:25
Whatsoever s it be that eateth .... Lev 7:27
even that s shall be cut off from ...... Lev 7:27
against that s that eateth blood,....... Lev 17:10
maketh an atonement for the s .... Lev 17:11
No s of you shall eat blood,............ Lev 17:12
every s that eateth that which......... Lev 17:15
that s shall be cut off from .... Lev 19:8
the s that turneth after such as .... Lev 20:6
even set my face against that s .... Lev 20:6
that s shall be cut off from my .... Lev 22:3
The s which hath touched any such .. Lev 22:6
priest buy any s with his money ...... Lev 22:11
For whatsoever s it be that shall ..... Lev 23:29
whatsoever s it be that doeth any .... Lev 23:30
the same s will I destroy from .... Lev 23:30
and my s shall not abhor you .... Lev 26:11
or if your s abhor my judgments,..... Lev 26:15
idols, and my s shall abhor you .... Lev 26:30
because their s abhorred my .... Lev 26:43
even the same s shall be cut off ...... Num 9:13
But now our s is dried away............ Num 11:6
if any s sin through ignorance,........ Num 15:27
for the s that sinneth ignorantly ...... Num 15:28
But the s that doeth ought .... Num 15:30
that s shall be cut off from .... Num 15:30
that s shall utterly be cut off .... Num 15:31
that s shall be cut off from .... Num 19:13
that s shall be cut off from .... Num 19:20
the s that toucheth it shall be.......... Num 19:22
our s loatheth this light bread .... Num 21:5
an oath to bind his s with a bond..... Num 30:2
wherewith she hath bound her s....... Num 30:4
she hath bound her s shall stand...... Num 30:4
wherewith she hath bound her s....... Num 30:5
lips, wherewith she bound her s....... Num 30:6
she bound her s shall stand............ Num 30:7
lips, wherewith she bound her s....... Num 30:8
or bound her s by a bond with an ... Num 30:10
she bound her s shall stand............ Num 30:11
or concerning the bond of her s ...... Num 30:12
binding oath to afflict the s .... Num 30:13
one s of five hundred, both of .... Num 31:28
keep thy s diligently, lest thou .... Deut 4:9
all thy heart and with all thy .... Deut 4:29
thine heart, and with all thy s .... Deut 6:5
all thy heart and with all thy s .... Deut 10:12
all your heart and with all your s .... Deut 11:13
words in your heart and in your s .... Deut 11:18
whatsoever thy s lusteth after .... Deut 12:15
because thy s longeth to eat .... Deut 12:20
whatsoever thy s lusteth after .... Deut 12:20
whatsoever thy s lusteth after .... Deut 12:21
all your heart and with all your s .... Deut 13:3
friend, which is as thine own s........ Deut 13:6
whatsoever thy s lusteth after .... Deut 14:26
or for whatsoever thy s desireth ...... Deut 14:26
thine heart, and with all thy s .... Deut 26:16
thine heart, and with all thy s .... Deut 30:2
thine heart, and with all thy s .... Deut 30:10
all your heart and with all your s .... Josh 22:5
O my s, thou hast trodden down...... Judg 5:21
his s was grieved for the misery ...... Judg 10:16
so that his s was vexed unto........... Judg 16:16
And she was in bitterness of s 1Sa 1:10
poured out my s before the LORD...... 1Sa 1:15
said, Oh my lord, as thy s liveth 1Sa 1:26
take as much as thy s desireth 1Sa 2:16
And Abner said, As thy s liveth 1Sa 17:55
that the s of Jonathan was knit........ 1Sa 18:1
was knit with the s of David 1Sa 18:1
Jonathan loved him as his own s 1Sa 18:1
because he loved him as his own s ... 1Sa 18:3
LORD liveth, and as thy s liveth 1Sa 20:3
David, Whatsoever thy s desireth 1Sa 20:4
loved him as he loved his own s 1Sa 20:17
the desire of thy s to come down 1Sa 23:20
yet thou huntest my s to take it 1Sa 24:11
LORD liveth, and as thy s liveth 1Sa 25:26
to pursue thee, and to seek thy s 1Sa 25:29
but the s of my lord shall be.......... 1Sa 25:29
because my s was precious in 1Sa 26:21
because the s of all the people 1Sa 30:6
my s out of all adversity 2Sa 4:9
that are hated of David's s 2Sa 5:8
thou livest, and as thy s liveth 2Sa 11:11
the s of king David longed to go 2Sa 13:39
answered and said, As thy s liveth ... 2Sa 14:19
redeemed my s out of all distress 1Kin 1:29
their heart, and with all their s 1Kin 2:4
their heart, and with all their s 1Kin 8:48
to all that thy s desireth 1Kin 11:37
let this child's s come into him....... 1Kin 17:21
the s of the child came into him..... 1Kin 17:22
LORD liveth, and as thy s liveth 2Kin 2:2
LORD liveth, and as thy s liveth 2Kin 2:4
LORD liveth, and as thy s liveth 2Kin 2:6
for her s is vexed within her........... 2Kin 4:27

LORD liveth, and as thy s liveth 2Kin 4:30
all their heart and all their s 2Kin 23:3
all his heart, and with all his s 2Kin 23:25
your s to seek the LORD your God.... 1Chr 22:19
with all their s in the land of 2Chr 6:38
their heart and with all their s 2Chr 15:12
all his heart, and with all his s 2Chr 34:31
and life unto the bitter in s .... Job 3:20
The things that my s refused to .... Job 6:7
in the bitterness of my s .... Job 7:11
So that my s chooseth strangling,.... Job 7:15
yet would I not know my s .... Job 9:21
My s is weary of my life .... Job 10:1
speak in the bitterness of my s .... Job 10:1
In whose hand is the s of every ...... Job 12:10
his s within him shall mourn .... Job 14:22
if your s were in my soul's stead .... Job 16:4
How long will ye vex my s .... Job 19:2
dieth in the bitterness of his s .... Job 21:25
And what his s desireth, even that.... Job 23:13
the s of the wounded crieth out...... Job 24:12
the Almighty, who hath vexed my s . Job 27:2
when God taketh away his s .... Job 30:15
they pursue my s as the wind .... Job 30:15
now my s is poured out upon me .... Job 30:16
was not my s grieved for the poor .. Job 30:25
sin by wishing a curse to his s .... Job 31:30
keepeth back his s from the pit ...... Job 33:18
bread, and his s dainty meat .... Job 33:20
his s draweth near unto the grave ... Job 33:22
He will deliver his s from going ...... Job 33:28
To bring back his s from the pit ..... Job 33:30
Many there be which say of my s .... Ps 3:2
My s is also sore vexed .... Ps 6:3
Return, O LORD, deliver my s .... Ps 6:4
Lest he tear my s like a lion .... Ps 7:2
Let the enemy persecute my s .... Ps 7:5
how say ye to my s, Flee as a .... Ps 11:1
that loveth violence his s hateth ..... Ps 11:5
long shall I take counsel in my s .... Ps 13:2
O my s, thou hast said unto the ..... Ps 16:2
thou wilt not leave my s in hell ..... Ps 16:10
deliver my s from the wicked,......... Ps 17:13
LORD is perfect, converting the s ..... Ps 19:7
Deliver my s from the sword .... Ps 22:20
and none can keep alive his own s .. Ps 22:29
He restoreth my s .... Ps 23:3
not lifted up his s unto vanity .... Ps 24:4
thee, O LORD, do I lift up my s ...... Ps 25:1
His s shall dwell at ease .... Ps 25:13
O keep my s, and deliver me .... Ps 25:20
Gather not my s with sinners.......... Ps 26:9
brought up my s from the grave...... Ps 30:3
hast known my s in adversities .... Ps 31:7
is consumed with grief, yea, my s ... Ps 31:9
To deliver their s from death .... Ps 33:19
Our s waiteth for the LORD .... Ps 33:20
My s shall make her boast in the .... Ps 34:2
redeemeth the s of his servants .... Ps 34:22
say unto my s, I am thy salvation ... Ps 35:3
put to shame that seek after my s ... Ps 35:4
cause they have digged for my s ..... Ps 35:7
my s shall be joyful in the LORD ..... Ps 35:9
for good to the spoiling of my s ..... Ps 35:12
I humbled my s with fasting........... Ps 35:13
rescue my s from their .... Ps 35:17
seek after my s to destroy it .... Ps 40:14
heal my s .... Ps 41:4
so panteth my s after thee .... Ps 42:1
My s thirsteth for God, for the .... Ps 42:2
things, I pour out my s in me .... Ps 42:4
Why art thou cast down, O my s ..... Ps 42:5
my s is cast down within me .... Ps 42:6
Why art thou cast down, O my s ..... Ps 42:11
Why art thou cast down, O my s ..... Ps 43:5
For our s is bowed down to the ...... Ps 44:25
redemption of their s is precious..... Ps 49:8
But God will redeem my s from the . Ps 49:15
while he lived he blessed his s .... Ps 49:18
me, and oppressors seek after my s . Ps 54:3
is with them that uphold my s .... Ps 54:4
He hath delivered my s in peace ..... Ps 55:18
my steps, when they wait for my s .. Ps 56:6
hast delivered my s from death ...... Ps 56:13
for my s trusteth in thee .... Ps 57:1
My s is among lions .... Ps 57:4
my s is bowed down .... Ps 57:6
lo, they lie in wait for my s .... Ps 59:3
Truly my s waiteth upon God .... Ps 62:1
My s, wait thou only upon God ...... Ps 62:5
my s thirsteth for thee, my flesh,.... Ps 63:1
My s shall be satisfied as with .... Ps 63:5
My s followeth hard after thee........ Ps 63:8
But those that seek my s, to.......... Ps 63:9
Which holdeth our s in life............ Ps 66:9
what he hath done for my s .... Ps 66:16
the waters are come in unto my s.... Ps 69:1
and chastened my s with fasting ..... Ps 69:10
Draw nigh unto my s, and redeem it . Ps 69:18
confounded that seek after my s ..... Ps 70:2
for my s take counsel together .... Ps 71:10
that are adversaries to my s .... Ps 71:13
and my s, which thou hast redeemed . Ps 71:23
shall redeem their s from deceit...... Ps 72:14
O deliver not the s of thy .... Ps 74:19
my s refused to be comforted......... Ps 77:2
he spared not their s from death .... Ps 78:50
My s longeth, yea, even fainteth..... Ps 84:2
Preserve my s .... Ps 86:2
Rejoice the s of thy servant........... Ps 86:4

thee, O LORD, do I lift up my *s*	Ps 86:4
my *s* from the lowest hell	Ps 86:13
men have sought after my *s*	Ps 86:14
For my *s* is full of troubles	Ps 88:3
LORD, why castest thou off my *s*	Ps 88:14
shall he deliver his *s* from the	Ps 89:48
my *s* had almost dwelt in silence	Ps 94:17
me thy comforts delight my *s*	Ps 94:19
against the *s* of the righteous	Ps 94:21
Bless the LORD, O my *s*	Ps 103:1
Bless the LORD, O my *s*, and forget	Ps 103:2
bless the LORD, O my *s*	Ps 103:22
Bless the LORD, O my *s*	Ps 104:1
Bless thou the LORD, O my *s*	Ps 104:35
but sent leanness into their *s*	Ps 106:15
thirsty, their *s* fainted in them	Ps 107:5
For he satisfieth the longing *s*	Ps 107:9
the hungry *s* with goodness	Ps 107:9
Their *s* abhorreth all manner of	Ps 107:18
their *s* is melted because of	Ps 107:26
them that speak evil against my *s*	Ps 109:20
him from those that condemn his *s*	Ps 109:31
I beseech thee, deliver my *s*	Ps 116:4
Return unto thy rest, O my *s*	Ps 116:7
hast delivered my *s* from death	Ps 116:8
My *s* breaketh for the longing	Ps 119:20
My *s* cleaveth unto the dust	Ps 119:25
My *s* melteth for heaviness	Ps 119:28
My *s* fainteth for thy salvation	Ps 119:81
My *s* is continually in my hand	Ps 119:109
therefore doth my *s* keep them	Ps 119:129
My *s* hath kept thy testimonies	Ps 119:167
Let my *s* live, and it shall praise	Ps 119:175
Deliver my *s*, O LORD, from lying	Ps 120:2
My *s* hath long dwelt with him	Ps 120:6
he shall preserve thy *s*	Ps 121:7
Our *s* is exceedingly filled with	Ps 123:4
the stream had gone over our *s*	Ps 124:4
proud waters had gone over our *s*	Ps 124:5
Our *s* is escaped as a bird out of	Ps 124:7
my *s* doth wait, and in his word do	Ps 130:5
My *s* waiteth for the Lord more	Ps 130:6
my *s* is even as a weaned child	Ps 131:2
me with strength in my *s*	Ps 138:3
that my *s* knoweth right well	Ps 139:14
leave not my *s* destitute	Ps 141:8
no man cared for my *s*	Ps 142:4
Bring my *s* out of prison, that I	Ps 142:7
the enemy hath persecuted my *s*	Ps 143:3
my *s* thirsteth after thee, as a	Ps 143:6
for I lift up my *s* unto thee	Ps 143:8
sake bring my *s* out of trouble	Ps 143:11
all them that afflict my *s*	Ps 143:12
Praise the LORD, O my *s*	Ps 146:1
knowledge is pleasant unto thy *s*	Prov 2:10
So shall they be life unto thy *s*	Prov 3:22
satisfy his *s* when he is hungry	Prov 6:30
doeth it destroyeth his own *s*	Prov 6:32
against me wrongeth his own *s*	Prov 8:36
the *s* of the righteous to famish	Prov 10:3
man doeth good to his own *s*	Prov 11:17
The liberal *s* shall be made fat	Prov 11:25
but the *s* of the transgressors	Prov 13:2
The *s* of the sluggard desireth	Prov 13:4
but the *s* of the diligent shall	Prov 13:4
accomplished is sweet to the *s*	Prov 13:19
eateth to the satisfying of his *s*	Prov 13:25
instruction despiseth his own *s*	Prov 15:32
keepeth his way preserveth his *s*	Prov 16:17
as an honeycomb, sweet to the *s*	Prov 16:24
his lips are the snare of his *s*	Prov 18:7
that the *s* be without knowledge	Prov 19:2
getteth wisdom loveth his own *s*	Prov 19:8
an idle *s* shall suffer hunger	Prov 19:15
keepeth his own *s*	Prov 19:16
let not thy *s* spare for his	Prov 19:18
anger sinneth against his own *s*	Prov 20:2
The *s* of the wicked desireth evil	Prov 21:10
keepeth his *s* from troubles	Prov 21:23
he that doth keep his *s* shall be	Prov 22:5
spoil the *s* of those that spoiled	Prov 22:23
his ways, and get a snare to thy *s*	Prov 22:25
and shalt deliver his *s* from hell	Prov 23:14
and he that keepeth thy *s*, doth	Prov 24:12
knowledge of wisdom be unto thy *s*	Prov 24:14
refresheth the *s* of his masters	Prov 25:13
As cold waters to a thirsty *s*	Prov 25:25
The full *s* loatheth an honeycomb	Prov 27:7
but to the hungry *s* every bitter	Prov 27:7
but the just seek his *s*	Prov 29:10
he shall give delight unto thy *s*	Prov 29:17
that he should make his *s* enjoy	Eccl 2:24
I labour, and bereave my *s* of good	Eccl 4:8
for his *s* of all that he desireth	Eccl 6:2
his *s* be not filled with good, and	Eccl 6:3
Which yet my *s* seeketh, but I	Eccl 7:28
Tell me, O thou whom my *s* loveth	Song 1:7
bed I sought him whom my *s* loveth	Song 3:1
I will seek him whom my *s* loveth	Song 3:2
said, Saw ye him whom my *s* loveth	Song 3:3
but I found him whom my *s* loveth	Song 3:4
my *s* failed when he spake	Song 5:6
my *s* made me like the chariots of	Song 6:12
your appointed feasts my *s* hateth	Is 1:14
Woe unto their *s*	Is 3:9
and of his fruitful field, both *s*	Is 10:18
desire of our *s* is to thy name	Is 26:8
With my *s* have I desired thee in	Is 26:9
but he awaketh, and his *s* is empty	Is 29:8

is faint, and his *s* hath appetite	Is 29:8
to make empty the *s* of the hungry	Is 32:6
years in the bitterness of my *s*	Is 38:15
but thou hast in love to my *s*	Is 38:17
elect, in whom my *s* delighteth	Is 42:1
that he cannot deliver his *s*	Is 44:20
which have said to thy *s*, Bow	Is 51:23
make his *s* an offering for sin	Is 53:10
shall see of the travail of his *s*	Is 53:11
hath poured out his *s* unto death	Is 53:12
let your *s* delight itself in	Is 55:2
hear, and your *s* shall live	Is 55:3
wherefore have we afflicted our *s*	Is 58:3
a day for a man to afflict his *s*	Is 58:5
thou draw out thy *s* to the hungry	Is 58:10
and satisfy the afflicted *s*	Is 58:10
and satisfy thy *s* in drought	Is 58:11
my *s* shall be joyful in my God	Is 61:10
their *s* delighteth in their	Is 66:3
the sword reacheth unto the *s*	Jer 4:10
because thou hast heard, O my *s*	Jer 4:19
for my *s* is wearied because of	Jer 4:31
shall not my *s* be avenged on such	Jer 5:9
shall not my *s* be avenged on such	Jer 5:29
lest my *s* depart from thee	Jer 6:8
shall not my *s* be avenged on such	Jer 9:9
my *s* into the hand of her enemies	Jer 12:7
my *s* shall weep in secret places	Jer 13:17
hath thy *s* lothed Zion	Jer 14:19
they have digged a pit for my *s*	Jer 18:20
for he hath delivered the *s* of	Jer 20:13
their *s* shall be as a watered	Jer 31:12
I will satiate the *s* of the	Jer 31:14
For I have satiated the weary *s*	Jer 31:25
replenished every sorrowful *s*	Jer 31:25
my whole heart and with my whole *s*	Jer 32:41
LORD liveth, that made us this *s*	Jer 38:16
then thy *s* shall live, and this	Jer 38:17
unto thee, and thy *s* shall live	Jer 38:20
his *s* shall be satisfied upon	Jer 50:19
and deliver every man his *s*	Jer 51:6
deliver ye every man his *s* from	Jer 51:45
things for meat to relieve the *s*	Lam 1:11
relieve my *s* is far from me	Lam 1:16
when their *s* was poured out into	Lam 2:12
removed my *s* far off from peace	Lam 3:17
My *s* hath them still in	Lam 3:20
LORD is my portion, saith my *s*	Lam 3:24
to the *s* that seeketh him	Lam 3:25
hast pleaded the causes of my *s*	Lam 3:58
but thou hast delivered thy *s*	Eze 3:19
also thou hast delivered thy *s*	Eze 3:21
my *s* hath not been polluted	Eze 4:14
as the *s* of the father, so also	Eze 18:4
so also the *s* of the son is mine	Eze 18:4
the *s* that sinneth, it shall die	Eze 18:4
The *s* that sinneth, it shall die	Eze 18:20
right, he shall save his *s* alive	Eze 18:27
and that which your *s* pitieth	Eze 24:21
warning shall deliver his *s*	Eze 33:5
but thou hast delivered thy *s*	Eze 33:9
for their bread for their *s* shall	Hos 9:4
compassed me about, even to the *s*	Jonah 2:5
When my *s* fainted within me I	Jonah 2:7
of my body for the sin of my *s*	Mic 6:7
my *s* desired the firstripe fruit	Mic 7:1
his *s* which is lifted up is not	Hab 2:4
and hast sinned against thy *s*	Hab 2:10
my *s* lothed them	Zec 11:8
and their *s* also abhorred me	Zec 11:8
but are not able to kill the *s*	Mt 10:28
which is able to destroy both *s*	Mt 10:28
in whom my *s* is well pleased	Mt 12:18
whole world, and lose his own *s*	Mt 16:26
a man give in exchange for his *s*	Mt 16:26
all thy heart, and with all thy *s*	Mt 22:37
My *s* is exceeding sorrowful, even	Mt 26:38
whole world, and lose his own *s*	Mk 8:36
a man give in exchange for his *s*	Mk 8:37
all thy heart, and with all thy *s*	Mk 12:30
understanding, and with all the *s*	Mk 12:33
My *s* is exceeding sorrowful unto	Mk 14:34
My *s* doth magnify the Lord	Lk 1:46
pierce through thy own *s* also	Lk 2:35
all thy heart, and with all thy *s*	Lk 10:27
And I will say to my *s*, S, thou	Lk 12:19
And I will say to my *s*, S	Lk 12:19
this night thy *s* shall be	Lk 12:20
Now is my *s* troubled	Jn 12:27
thou wilt not leave my *s* in hell	Acts 2:27
that his *s* was not left in hell	Acts 2:31
And fear came upon every *s*	Acts 2:43
shall come to pass, that every *s*	Acts 3:23
were of one heart and of one *s*	Acts 4:32
upon every *s* of man that doeth	Rom 2:9
Let every *s* be subject unto the	Rom 13:1
man Adam was made a living *s*	1Cor 15:45
I call God for a record upon my *s*	2Cor 1:23
I pray God your whole spirit and *s*	1Th 5:23
even to the dividing asunder of *s*	Heb 4:12
we have as an anchor of the *s*	Heb 6:19
my *s* shall have no pleasure in	Heb 10:38
believe to the saving of the *s*	Heb 10:39
his way shall save a *s* from death	Jas 5:20
lusts, which war against the *s*	1Pet 2:11
vexed his righteous *s* from day to	2Pet 2:8
health, even as thy *s* prospereth	3Jn 2
every living *s* died in the sea	Rev 16:3
the fruits that thy *s* lusted	Rev 18:14

SOUL'S

if your soul were in my *s* stead	Job 16:4

SOULS

the *s* that they had gotten in	Gen 12:5
all the *s* of his sons and his	Gen 46:15
bare unto Jacob, even sixteen *s*	Gen 46:18
all the *s* were fourteen	Gen 46:22
all the *s* were seven	Gen 46:25
All the *s* that came with Jacob	Gen 46:26
all the *s* were threescore and six	Gen 46:26
born him in Egypt, were two *s*	Gen 46:27
all the *s* of the house of Jacob,	Gen 46:27
all the *s* that came out of the	Ex 1:5
the loins of Jacob were seventy *s*	Ex 1:5
according to the number of the *s*	Ex 12:4
to make an atonement for your *s*	Ex 30:15
to make an atonement for your *s*	Ex 30:16
month, ye shall afflict your *s*	Lev 16:29
you, and ye shall afflict your *s*	Lev 16:31
to make an atonement for your *s*	Lev 17:11
even the *s* that commit them shall	Lev 18:29
make your *s* abominable by beast	Lev 20:25
and ye shall afflict your *s*	Lev 23:27
rest, and ye shall afflict your *s*	Lev 23:32
these sinners against their own *s*	Num 16:38
and ye shall afflict your *s*	Num 29:7
wherewith they have bound their *s*	Num 30:9
for our *s* before the LORD	Num 31:50
all the *s* that were therein	Josh 10:28
all the *s* that were therein	Josh 10:30
all the *s* that were therein	Josh 10:32
all the *s* that were therein, he	Josh 10:35
all the *s* that were therein	Josh 10:37
all the *s* that were therein	Josh 10:39
they smote all the *s* that were	Josh 11:11
all your hearts and in all your *s*	Josh 23:14
the *s* of thine enemies, them	1Sa 25:29
and shall save the *s* of the needy	Ps 72:13
he preserveth the *s* of his saints	Ps 97:10
and he that winneth *s* is wise	Prov 11:30
A true witness delivereth *s*	Prov 14:25
me, and the *s* which I have made	Is 57:16
of the *s* of the poor innocents	Jer 2:34
and ye shall find rest for your *s*	Jer 6:16
procure great evil against our *s*	Jer 26:19
ye this great evil against your *s*	Jer 44:7
their meat to relieve their *s*	Lam 1:19
they shall not satisfy their *s*	Eze 7:19
head of every stature to hunt *s*	Eze 13:18
Will ye hunt the *s* of my people	Eze 13:18
will ye save the *s* alive that	Eze 13:18
to slay the *s* that should not die	Eze 13:19
to save the *s* alive that should	Eze 13:19
there hunt the *s* to make them fly	Eze 13:20
your arms, and will let the *s* go	Eze 13:20
even the *s* that ye hunt to make	Eze 13:20
own *s* by their righteousness	Eze 14:14
own *s* by their righteousness	Eze 14:20
Behold, all *s* are mine	Eze 18:4
they have devoured *s*	Eze 22:25
to shed blood, and to destroy *s*	Eze 22:27
and ye shall find rest unto your *s*	Mt 11:29
your patience possess ye your *s*	Lk 21:19
unto them about three thousand *s*	Acts 2:41
kindred, threescore and fifteen *s*	Acts 7:14
Confirming the *s* of the disciples	Acts 14:22
you with words, subverting your *s*	Acts 15:24
hundred threescore and sixteen *s*	Acts 27:37
of God only, but also our own *s*	1Th 2:8
for they watch for your *s*	Heb 13:17
which is able to save your *s*	Jas 1:21
even the salvation of your *s*	1Pet 1:9
s in obeying the truth through	1Pet 1:22
the Shepherd and Bishop of your *s*	1Pet 2:25
eight *s* were saved by water	1Pet 3:20
of their *s* to him in well doing	1Pet 4:19
beguiling unstable *s*	2Pet 2:14
I saw under the altar the *s* of	Rev 6:9
chariots, and slaves, and *s* of men	Rev 18:13
I saw the *s* of them that were	Rev 20:4

SOUND

his *s* shall be heard when he	Ex 28:35
the trumpet of the jubile to *s* on	Lev 25:9
s throughout all your land	Lev 25:9
the *s* of a shaken leaf shall	Lev 26:36
blow, but ye shall not a sound *s*	Num 10:7
when ye hear the *s* of the trumpet	Josh 6:5
people heard the *s* of the trumpet	Josh 6:20
when thou hearest the *s* of a	2Sa 5:24
with the *s* of the trumpet	2Sa 6:15
as ye hear the *s* of the trumpet	2Sa 15:10
the earth rent with the *s* of them	1Kin 1:40
Joab heard the *s* of the trumpet	1Kin 1:41
Ahijah heard the *s* of her feet	1Kin 14:6
for there is a *s* of abundance of	1Kin 18:41
is not the *s* of his master's feet	2Kin 6:32
when thou shalt hear a *s* of going	1Chr 14:15
were appointed to *s* with cymbals	1Chr 15:19
with *s* of the cornet, and with	1Chr 15:28
but Asaph made a *s* with cymbals	1Chr 16:5
for those that should make a *s*	1Chr 16:42
to make one *s* to be heard in	2Chr 5:13
ye hear the *s* of the trumpet	Neh 4:20
A dreadful *s* is in his ears	Job 15:21
and rejoice at the *s* of the organ	Job 21:12
the *s* that goeth out of his mouth	Job 37:2
that it is the *s* of the trumpet	Job 39:24
the LORD with the *s* of a trumpet	Ps 47:5

the skies sent out a s .... Ps 77:17
the people that know the joyful s .... Ps 89:15
upon the harp with a solemn s .... Ps 92:3
s of cornet make a joyful noise .... Ps 98:6
Let my heart be s in thy statutes .... Ps 119:80
him with the s of the trumpet .... Ps 150:3
He layeth up a wisdom for the .... Prov 2:7
keep s wisdom and discretion .... Prov 3:21
Counsel is mine, and s wisdom .... Prov 8:14
A s heart is the life of the .... Prov 14:30
when the s of the grinding is low .... Eccl 12:4
shall s like an harp for Moab .... Is 16:11
the s of the trumpet, the alarm .... Jer 4:19
hear the s of the trumpet .... Jer 4:21
Hearken to the s of the trumpet .... Jer 6:17
s of the neighing of his strong .... Jer 8:16
the s of the millstones, and the .... Jer 25:10
nor hear the s of the trumpet, ... Jer 42:14
heart shall s for Moab like pipes .... Jer 48:36
mine heart shall s like pipes for .... Jer 48:36
A s of battle is in the land, and, ... Jer 50:22
A s of a cry cometh from Babylon, ... Jer 51:54
the s of the cherubims' wings was .... Eze 10:5
the s of thy harps shall be no .... Eze 26:13
isles shake at the s of thy fall .... Eze 26:15
at the s of the cry of thy pilots .... Eze 27:28
to shake at the s of his fall .... Eze 31:16
heareth the s of the trumpet .... Eze 33:4
He heard the s of the trumpet, and ...... Eze 33:5
time ye hear the s of the cornet .... Dan 3:5
people heard the s of the cornet .... Dan 3:7
shall hear the s of the cornet .... Dan 3:10
time ye hear the s of the cornet .... Dan 3:15
s an alarm in my holy mountain .... Joel 2:1
with the s of the trumpet .... Amos 2:2
That chant to the s of the viol .... Amos 6:5
do not a s trumpet before thee, ... Mt 6:2
with a great s of a trumpet .... Mt 24:31
he hath received him sate and s .... Lk 15:27
and thou hearest the s thereof .... Jn 3:8
suddenly there came a s from .... Acts 2:2
their s went into all the earth, ... Rom 10:18
even things without life giving s 1Cor 14:7
the trumpet give an uncertain s 1Cor 14:8
for the trumpet shall s, and the 1Cor 15:52
that is contrary to s doctrine 1Ti 1:10
power, and of love, and of a mind 2Ti 1:7
Hold fast the form of s words 2Ti 1:13
they will not endure s doctrine 2Ti 4:3
that he may be able by s doctrine .... Titus 1:9
that they may be s in the faith .... Titus 1:13
things which become s doctrine .... Titus 2:1
s in faith, in charity, in .... Titus 2:2
S speech, that cannot be .... Titus 2:8
the s of a trumpet, and the voice .... Heb 12:19
his voice as the s of many waters .... Rev 1:15
trumpets prepared themselves to s ...... Rev 8:6
three angels, which are yet to s .... Rev 8:13
the s of their wings was as the .... Rev 9:9
the s of chariots of many horses .... Rev 9:9
angel, when he shall begin to s .... Rev 10:7
the s of a millstone shall be .... Rev 18:22

SOUNDED
the voice of the trumpet s long .... Ex 19:19
when I have a s my father about to 1Sa 20:12
the priests trumpets before 2Chr 7:6
the priests s with the trumpets 2Chr 13:14
s with trumpets, also the singers 2Chr 23:13
singers sang, and the trumpeters s 2Chr 29:28
he that s the trumpet was by me .... Neh 4:18
of thy salutation s in mine ear .... Luke 1:44
And s, and found it twenty fathoms ..... Acts 27:28
they s again, and found it fifteen .... Acts 27:28
For from you s out the word of 1Th 1:8
The first angel s, and there .... Rev 8:7
And the second angel s, and as it .... Rev 8:8
And the third angel s, and there .... Rev 8:10
And the fourth angel s, and the .... Rev 8:12
And the fifth angel s, and I saw a .... Rev 9:1
And the sixth angel s, and I heard .... Rev 9:13
And the seventh angel s .... Rev 11:15

SOUNDETH
when the trumpet s long, they .... Ex 19:13

SOUNDING
psalteries and harps and cymbals, s 1Chr 15:16
and twenty priests s with trumpets 2Chr 5:12
his priests with s trumpets to 2Chr 13:12
him upon the high s cymbals .... Ps 150:5
the s of thy bowels and of thy .... Is 63:15
not the s again of the mountains .... Eze 7:7
charity, I am become as s brass 1Cor 13:1

SOUNDNESS
There is no s in my flesh because .... Ps 38:3
and there is no s in my flesh .... Ps 38:7
unto the head there is no s in it .... Is 1:6
s in the presence of you all .... Acts 3:16

SOUNDS
they give a distinction in the s 1Cor 14:7

SOUR
the s grape is ripening in the .... Is 18:5
The fathers have eaten a s grape .... Jer 31:29
every man that eateth the s grape .... Jer 31:30
The fathers have eaten s grapes .... Eze 18:2
Their drink is s .... Hos 4:18

SOUTH
going on still toward the s .... Gen 12:9
had, and Lot with him, into the s .... Gen 13:1
from the s even to Beth-el .... Gen 13:3
from thence toward the s country .... Gen 20:1
for he dwelt in the s country .... Gen 24:62
and to the north, and to the s .... Gen 28:14
boards on the s side southward .... Ex 26:18
of the tabernacle toward the s .... Ex 26:35
for the s side southward there .... Ex 27:9
boards for the s side southward .... Ex 36:23
on the s side southward the .... Ex 38:9
On the s side shall be the .... Num 2:10
s side shall take their journey .... Num 10:6
And they ascended by the s .... Num 13:22
dwell in the land of the s .... Num 13:29
Canaanite, which dwelt in the s .... Num 21:1
which dwelt in the s in the land .... Num 33:40
Then your s quarter shall be from .... Num 34:3
your s border shall be the .... Num 34:3
the s to the ascent of Akrabbim .... Num 34:4
be from the s to Kadesh-barnea .... Num 34:4
on the s side two thousand cubits .... Num 35:5
and in the vale, and in the s .... Deut 1:7
possess thou the west and the s .... Deut 33:23
And the s, and the plain of the .... Deut 34:3
country of the hills, and of the .... Josh 10:40
and of the plains s of Chinneroth .... Josh 11:2
the hills, and all the s country .... Josh 11:16
and from the s, under .... Josh 12:3
wilderness, and in the s country .... Josh 12:8
From the s, all the land of the .... Josh 12:8
the uttermost part of the s coast .... Josh 15:1
their s border was from the shore .... Josh 15:2
it went out to the s side to .... Josh 15:3
ascended up on the s side unto .... Josh 15:3
this shall be your s coast .... Josh 15:4
which is on the s side of the .... Josh 15:7
unto the s side of the Jebusite .... Josh 15:8
for thou hast given me a land .... Josh 15:19
side of the nether Beth-horon .... Josh 18:5
the s quarter was from the end of ...... Josh 18:15
to the side of Jebusi on the s .... Josh 18:16
salt sea at the s end of Jordan .... Josh 18:19
this was the s coast .... Josh 18:19
to Baalath-beer, Ramath of the s .... Josh 19:8
reacheth to Zebulun on the s side ...... Josh 19:34
in the mountain, and in the s .... Judg 1:9
for thou hast given me a land .... Judg 1:15
which lieth in the s of Arad .... Judg 1:16
Shechem, and on the s of Lebonah .... Judg 21:19
arose out of a place toward the s 1Sa 20:41
which is on the s of Jeshimon 1Sa 23:19
in the plain on the s of Jeshimon 1Sa 23:24
said, Against the s of Judah 1Sa 27:10
of Judah, and against the s of the 1Sa 27:10
against the s of the Kenites 1Sa 27:10
the Amalekites had invaded the s 1Sa 30:1
upon the s of the Cherethites, ... 1Sa 30:14
to Judah, and upon the s of Caleb 1Sa 30:14
and to them which were in s Ramoth .. 1Sa 30:27

the s side southward, from Tamar .... Eze 47:19
this is the s side southward .... Eze 47:19
in breadth, and toward the s .... Eze 48:10
the s side four thousand and five .... Eze 48:16
toward the s two hundred and fifty ...... Eze 48:17
at the s side southward, the .... Eze 48:28
and four a side four thousand and .... Eze 48:33
exceeding great, toward the s .... Dan 8:9
the king of the s shall be strong .... Dan 11:5
s shall come to the king of the .... Dan 11:6
So the king of the s shall come .... Dan 11:6
the king of the s shall be moved .... Dan 11:11
up against the king of the s .... Dan 11:14
the arms of the s shall not .... Dan 11:15
king of the s with a great army .... Dan 11:25
the king of the s shall be .... Dan 11:25
return, and come toward the s .... Dan 11:29
the king of the s push at him .... Dan 11:40
they of the s shall possess the .... Obad 19
shall possess the cities of the s .... Obad 20
go forth toward the s country .... Zec 6:6
her, when men inhabited the s .... Zec 7:7
shall go with whirlwinds of the s .... Zec 9:14
north, and half of it toward the s .... Zec 14:4
Geba to Rimmon s of Jerusalem .... Zec 14:10
The queen of the s shall rise up .... Mt 12:42
The queen of the s shall rise up .... Lk 11:31
And when ye see the s wind blow .... Lk 12:55
and from the north, and from the s ..... Lk 13:29
go toward the s unto the way that ...... Acts 8:26
Crete, and held toward the s west ...... Acts 27:12
when the s wind blew softly, ... Acts 27:13
and after one day the s wind blew ...... Acts 28:13
on the s three gates .... Rev 21:13

SOUTHWARD
where thou art northward, and s .... Gen 13:14
twenty boards on the south side s .... Ex 26:18
for the south side s there shall .... Ex 26:19
boards for the south side .... Ex 36:23
on the south side the hangings .... Ex 38:9
on the side of the tabernacle s .... Ex 40:24
on the side of the tabernacle s .... Num 3:29
unto them, Get you up this way s .... Num 13:17
eyes westward, and northward, and s . Deut 3:27
s was the uttermost part of the .... Josh 15:1
sea, from the bay that looketh s .... Josh 15:2
the coast of Edom s were Kabzeel ...... Josh 15:21
the river Kanah, s of the river .... Josh 17:9
S it was Ephraim's, and northward ..... Josh 17:10
side of Luz, which is Beth-el, s .... Josh 18:13
compassed the corner of the sea s .... Josh 18:14
that lieth before Beth-horon s .... Josh 18:14
the other s over against Gibeah 1Sa 14:5
To Obed-edom s 1Chr 26:15
s four a day, and toward Asuppim 1Chr 26:17
And the south side s, from Tamar .... Eze 47:19
And this is the south side s .... Eze 47:19
of Gad, at the south side s .... Eze 48:28
westward, and northward, and s .... Dan 8:4

SOW
for you, and ye that s shall reap .... Gen 47:23
six years thou shalt s thy land .... Ex 23:10
thou shalt not s thy field with .... Lev 19:19
Six years thou shalt s thy field .... Lev 25:3
thou shalt neither s thy field .... Lev 25:4
ye shall not s, neither reap that .... Lev 25:11
behold, we shall not s, nor .... Lev 25:20
ye shall s the eighth year, and .... Lev 25:22
ye shall s your seed in vain, for .... Lev 26:16
Thou shalt not s thy vineyard .... Deut 22:9
and in the third year s ye 2Kin 19:29
s wickedness, reap the same .... Job 4:8
Then let me s, and let another eat ..... Job 31:8
s the fields, and plant vineyards, ... Ps 107:37
They that s in tears shall reap .... Ps 126:5
observeth the wind shall not s .... Eccl 11:4
In the morning s thy seed .... Eccl 11:6
the plowman give all day to s .... Is 28:24
that thou shalt s the ground .... Is 30:23
are ye that s beside all waters .... Is 32:20
and in the third year s ye .... Is 37:30
ground, and s not among thorns .... Jer 4:3
that I will s the house of Israel .... Jer 31:27
nor s seed, nor plant vineyard, ... Jer 35:7
I will s her unto me in the earth .... Hos 2:23
S to yourselves in righteousness, ... Hos 10:12
Thou shalt s, but thou shalt not .... Mic 6:15
I will s them among the people .... Zec 10:9
for they s not, neither do they .... Mt 6:26
Behold, a sower went forth to s .... Mt 13:3
didst not thou s good seed in thy ...... Mt 13:27
there went out a sower to s .... Mk 4:3
A sower went out to s his seed .... Lk 8:5
for they neither s nor reap .... Lk 12:24
and reapest that thou didst not s ..... Lk 19:21
down, and reaping that I did not s .... Lk 19:22
the s that was washed to her 2Pet 2:22

SOWED
then Isaac s in that land, and............. Gen 26:12
down the city, and s it with salt .... Judg 9:45
And when he s, some seeds fell by...... Mt 13:4
which s good seed in his field .... Mt 13:24
s tares among the wheat, and went ... Mt 13:25
a man took, and s in his field .... Mt 13:31
The enemy that s them is the .... Mt 13:39
knewest that I reap where I s not...... Mt 25:26
And it came to pass, as he s .... Mk 4:4
and as he s, some fell by the way ..... Lk 8:5

SOWEDST
came out, where thou s thy seed .... Deut 11:10

SOWER
that it may give seed to the s .... Is 55:10
Cut off the s from Babylon, and .... Jer 50:16
Behold, a s went forth to sow .... Mt 13:3
ye therefore the parable of the s .... Mt 13:18
Behold, there went out a s to sow .... Mk 4:3
The s soweth the word .... Mk 4:14
A s went out to sow his seed .... Lk 8:5
s both minister bread for your 2Cor 9:10

SOWEST
fool, that which thou s is not 1Cor 15:36
And that which thou s 1Cor 15:37
thou s not that body that shall 1Cor 15:37

SOWETH
he s discord .... Prov 6:14
he that s discord among brethren .... Prov 6:19
but to him that s righteousness .... Prov 11:18
A froward man s strife .... Prov 16:28
He that s iniquity shall reap .... Prov 22:8
treader of grapes him that s seed .... Amos 9:13
He that s the good seed is the .... Mt 13:37
The sower s the word .... Mk 4:14
that both he that s and he that .... Jn 4:36
herein is that saying true, One s .... Jn 4:37
He which s sparingly shall reap 2Cor 9:6
he which s bountifully shall reap 2Cor 9:6
for whatsoever a man s, that .... Gal 6:7
For he that s to his flesh shall .... Gal 6:8
but he that s to the Spirit shall .... Gal 6:8

SOWING
any s seed which is to be sown .... Lev 11:37
shall reach unto the s time .... Lev 26:5

SOWN
which thou hast s in the field .... Ex 23:16
any sowing seed which is to be s .... Lev 11:37
which is neither eared nor s .... Deut 21:4
of thy seed which thou hast s .... Deut 22:9
and burning, that it is not s .... Deut 29:23
And so it was, when Israel had s .... Judg 6:3
Light is s for the righteous, and .... Ps 97:11
every thing s by the brooks, ... Is 19:7
yea, they shall not be s .... Is 40:24
that are s in it to spring forth .... Is 61:11
in a land that was not s .... Jer 2:2
They have s wheat, but shall reap .... Jer 12:13
you, and ye shall be tilled and s .... Eze 36:9
For they have s the wind, and they .... Hos 8:7
that no more of thy name be s .... Nah 1:14
Ye have s much, and bring in .... Hag 1:6
that which was s in his heart .... Mt 13:19
reaping where thou hast not s .... Mt 25:24
the way side, where the word is s .... Mk 4:15
word that was s in their hearts .... Mk 4:15
which are s on stony ground .... Mk 4:16
are they which are s among thorns, ... Mk 4:18
they which are s on good ground, ... Mk 4:20
when it is s in the earth, is .... Mk 4:31
But when it is s, it groweth up, ... Mk 4:32
If we have s unto you spiritual 1Cor 9:11
It is s in corruption 1Cor 15:42
It is s in dishonour 1Cor 15:43
It is s in weakness 1Cor 15:43
It is s a natural body 1Cor 15:44
food, and multiply your seed s 2Cor 9:10
is s in peace of them that make .... Jas 3:18

SPACE
abode with him the s of a month .... Gen 29:14
put a s betwixt drove and drove .... Gen 32:16
the s of the seven sabbaths of .... Lev 25:8
within the s of a full year .... Lev 25:30
the s in which we came from .... Num 2:14
there shall be a s between you .... Josh 3:4
a great s being between them 1Sa 26:13
now for a little s grace hath .... Ezr 9:8
within the s of two full years .... Jer 28:11
The s also before the little .... Eze 40:12
the s was one cubit on that side .... Eze 40:12
about the s of one hour after .... Lk 22:59
it was about the s of three hours .... Acts 5:7
put the apostles forth a little s .... Acts 5:34
sacrifices by the s of forty .... Acts 7:42
about the s of four hundred .... Acts 13:20
Benjamin, by the s of forty years .... Acts 13:21
after they had tarried there a s .... Acts 15:33
boldly for the s of three months .... Acts 19:8
continued by the s of two years .... Acts 19:10
the s of two hours cried out .... Acts 19:34
that by the s of three years I .... Acts 20:31
the earth by the s of three years .... Jas 5:17
I gave her s to repent of her .... Rev 2:21
about the s of half an hour .... Rev 8:1
by the s of a thousand and six .... Rev 14:20
he must continue a short s .... Rev 17:10

SPAIN (spane) Land at the western extremity
of the Mediterranean Sea.
I take my journey into S, I will .... Rom 15:24
fruit, I will come by you into S .... Rom 15:28

SPAKE See PREFACE.

SPAKEST
the man that s unto the woman .... Judg 13:11
s of also in mine ears, behold, ... Judg 17:2
thy words which thou s unto me 1Sa 28:21
thou s also with thy mouth, and 1Kin 8:24
which thou s unto thy servant 1Kin 8:26
as thou s by the hand of Moses 1Kin 8:53
s with thy mouth, and hast 2Chr 6:15
s with them from heaven, and .... Neh 9:13
Then thou s in vision to thy holy .... Ps 89:19
for since thou s of him, thou .... Jer 48:27

SPAN
a s shall be the length thereof, ... Ex 28:16
a s shall be the breadth thereof .... Ex 28:16
a s was the length thereof, and a .... Ex 39:9
a s the breadth thereof, being .... Ex 39:9
height was six cubits and a 1Sa 17:4
and meted out heaven with the s .... Is 40:12
fruit, and children of a s long .... Lam 2:20
thereof round about shall be a s .... Eze 43:13

SPANNED
my right hand hath s the heavens .... Is 48:13

SPARE
not s the place for the fifty .... Gen 18:24
then I will s all the place for .... Gen 18:26
pity him, neither shalt thou s .... Deut 13:8
The Lord will not s him, but then .... Deut 29:20
all that they have, and s them not 1Sa 15:3
s me according to the greatness .... Neh 13:22
let him not s .... Job 6:10
my reins asunder, and doth not s .... Job 16:13
Though he s it, and forsake it not .... Job 20:13
God shall cast upon him, and not s .... Job 27:22
me, and s not to spit in my face .... Job 30:10
O s me, that I may recover .... Ps 39:13
He shall s the poor and needy, and .... Ps 72:13
therefore he will not s in the .... Prov 6:34
let not thy soul s for his crying .... Prov 19:18
no man shall s his brother .... Is 9:19
their eye shall not s children .... Is 13:18
he shall not s .... Is 30:14
s not, lengthen thy cords, and .... Is 54:2
s not, lift up thy voice like a .... Is 58:1
I will not pity, nor s, nor have .... Jer 13:14
he shall not s them, neither have .... Jer 21:7
bow, shoot at her, s no arrows .... Jer 50:14
and s ye not her young men .... Jer 51:3
neither shall mine eye s, neither .... Eze 5:11
And mine eye shall not s thee .... Eze 7:4
And mine eye shall not s, neither .... Eze 7:9
mine eye shall not s, neither .... Eze 8:18
let not your eye s, neither have .... Eze 9:5
for me also, mine eye shall not s .... Eze 9:10
not go back, neither will I s .... Eze 24:14
S thy people, O Lord, and give not .... Joel 2:17
And should not I s Nineveh .... Jonah 4:11
not s continually to slay the .... Hab 1:17
and I will s them, as a man .... Mal 3:17
have bread enough and to s .... Lk 15:17
take heed lest he also s not thee .... Rom 11:21
but I s you 1Cor 7:28
that to s you I came not as yet 2Cor 1:23
if I come again, I will not s 2Cor 13:2

SPARED
But Saul and the people s Agag 1Sa 15:9
for the people s the best of the 1Sa 15:15
but mine eye s thee 1Sa 24:10
he s to take of his own flock and 2Sa 12:4
But the king s Mephibosheth 2Sa 21:7
my master hath s Naaman this 2Kin 5:20
he s not their soul from death, ... Ps 78:50
Nevertheless mine eye s them from .... Eze 20:17
He that s not his own Son, but .... Rom 8:32
For if God s not the natural .... Rom 11:21
For if God s not the angels that 2Pet 2:4
s not the old world, but saved 2Pet 2:5

SPARETH
He that s his rod hateth his son .... Prov 13:24
that hath knowledge s his words .... Prov 17:27
but the righteous giveth and s not .... Prov 21:26
as a man s his own son that .... Mal 3:17

SPARING
in among you, not s the flock .... Acts 20:29

SPARINGLY
He which soweth s shall reap also 2Cor 9:6
shall reap also s 2Cor 9:6

SPARK
the s of his fire shall not shine .... Job 18:5
as tow, and the maker of it as a s .... Is 1:31

SPARKLED
they s like the colour of .... Eze 1:7

SPARKS
unto trouble, as the s fly upward, ... Job 5:7
lamps, and s of fire leap out .... Job 41:19
compass yourselves about with s .... Is 50:11
in the s that ye have kindled .... Is 50:11

SPARROW
the s hath found an house, and the .... Ps 84:3
am as a s alone upon the house .... Ps 102:7

SPARROWS
Are not two s sold for a farthing .... Mt 10:29
ye are of more value than many s .... Mt 10:31
Are not five s sold for two .... Lk 12:6
ye are of more value than many s .... Lk 12:7

SPAT
he s on the ground, and made clay .... Jn 9:6

SPEAK See PREFACE.

SPEAKER
Let not an evil s be established .... Ps 140:11
because he was the chief s .... Acts 14:12

SPEAKEST
wherefore then s thou so to me 1Sa 9:21
Why s thou any more of thy 2Sa 19:29
that thou s in thy bedchamber 2Kin 6:12
Thou s as one of the foolish .... Job 2:10
sittest and s against thy brother .... Ps 50:20
mightest be justified when thou s .... Ps 51:4
Why sayest thou, O Jacob, and s .... Is 40:27
for thou s falsely of Ishmael .... Jer 40:16
unto Jeremiah, Thou s falsely .... Jer 43:2
nor s to warn the wicked from his .... Eze 3:18
for thou s lies in the name of .... Zec 13:3
Why s thou unto them in parables .... Mt 13:10
s thou this parable unto us, or .... Lk 12:41
now s thou plainly .... Jn 16:29
thou plainly, and s no proverb .... Jn 16:29
unto him, S thou not unto me .... Jn 19:10
this new doctrine, whereof thou s .... Acts 17:19

SPEAKETH
it is my mouth that s unto you .... Gen 45:12
as a man s unto his friend .... Ex 33:11
thee, saying, All that the Lord s .... Num 23:26
When a prophet s in the name of .... Deut 18:22
Thus s Ben-hadad, saying, ... 1Kin 20:5
as one of the foolish women s .... Job 2:10
He that s flattery to his friends .... Job 17:5
For God s once, yea twice, yet .... Job 33:14
and the tongue that s proud things .... Ps 12:3
and s the truth in his heart .... Ps 15:2
mouth of the righteous s wisdom .... Ps 37:30
if he come to see me, he s vanity .... Ps 41:6
Whose mouth s vanity, and their .... Ps 144:8
children, whose mouth s vanity .... Ps 144:11
the man that s froward things .... Prov 2:12
he s with his feet, he teacheth .... Prov 6:13
A false witness that s lies .... Prov 6:19
mouth of the wicked s frowardness .... Prov 10:32
He that s truth sheweth forth .... Prov 12:17
There is that s like the .... Prov 12:18
but a deceitful witness s lies .... Prov 14:25
and they love him that s right .... Prov 16:13
he that s lies shall not escape .... Prov 19:5
he that s lies shall perish .... Prov 19:9
the man that heareth s constantly .... Prov 21:28
When he s fair, believe him not .... Prov 26:25
evildoer, and every mouth s folly .... Is 9:17
even when the needy s right .... Is 32:7
righteously, and s uprightly .... Is 33:15
it s deceit .... Jer 9:8
one s peaceably to his neighbour .... Jer 9:8
word which the Lord s unto you .... Jer 10:1
Thus s the Lord of hosts, the God .... Jer 28:2
Thus s the Lord of hosts, the God .... Jer 28:25
Thus s the Lord God of Israel, ... Jer 30:2
of the Almighty God when he s .... Eze 10:5
they abhor him that s superfluity .... Amos 5:10
Thus s the Lord of hosts, saying, ... Hag 1:2
Thus s the Lord of hosts, saying, ... Zec 6:12
Thus s the Lord of hosts, saying, ... Zec 7:9
of your Father which s in you, ... Mt 10:20
whosoever s a word against the .... Mt 12:32
but whosoever s against the Holy .... Mt 12:32
of the heart the mouth s .... Mt 12:34
Who is this which s blasphemies, ... Lk 5:21
of the heart his mouth s .... Lk 6:45
is earthly, and s of the earth .... Jn 3:31
God hath sent s the words of God .... Jn 3:34
He that s of himself seeketh his .... Jn 7:18
he s boldly, and they say nothing .... Jn 7:26
s a lie, he s of his own .... Jn 8:44
himself a king s against Caesar .... Jn 19:12
For David s concerning him, I .... Acts 2:25
of whom s the prophet this .... Acts 8:34
which is of faith s on this wise .... Rom 10:6
For he that s in an unknown 1Cor 14:2
an unknown tongue s not unto men 1Cor 14:2
in the spirit he s mysteries 1Cor 14:2
s unto men to edification 1Cor 14:3
He that s in an unknown tongue 1Cor 14:4
than he that s with tongues 1Cor 14:5
be unto him that s a barbarian 1Cor 14:11
he that s shall be a barbarian 1Cor 14:11
Wherefore let him that s in an 1Cor 14:13
Now the Spirit s expressly 1Ti 4:1
and by it he being dead yet s .... Heb 11:4
which s unto you as unto children .... Heb 12:5
that s better things than that of .... Heb 12:24
See that ye refuse not him that s .... Heb 12:25
away from him that s from heaven .... Heb 12:25
He that s evil of his brother, and .... Jas 4:11
s evil of the law, and judgeth the .... Jas 4:11
their mouth s great swelling .... Jude 16

SPEAKING
to pass, before he had done s .... Gen 24:15
before I had done s in mine heart .... Gen 24:45
till Moses had done s with them .... Ex 34:33
one s unto him from off the mercy .... Num 7:89
made an end of s all these words .... Num 16:31
s out of the midst of the fire .... Deut 4:33
the voice of the living God s out .... Deut 5:26
s of them when thou sittest in .... Deut 11:19
made an end of s unto the people .... Deut 20:9

Moses made an end of s all these ...... Deut 32:45
when he had made an end of s .... Judg 15:17
her, then she left s unto her .... Ruth 1:18
he had made an end of s unto Saul 1Sa 18:1
an end of s these words unto Saul 1Sa 24:16
soon as he had made an end of s 2Sa 13:36
s from the mouth of the LORD 2Chr 36:12
and s peace to all his seed .... Est 10:3
While he was yet s, there came .... Job 1:16
While he was yet s, there came .... Job 1:17
While he was yet s, there came .... Job 1:18
who can withhold himself from s .... Job 4:2
they left off s .... Job 32:15
evil, and thy lips from s guile .... Ps 34:13
as soon as they be born, s lies .... Ps 58:3
forth of the finger, and s vanity .... Is 58:9
pleasure, nor s thine own words .... Is 58:13
our God, s oppression and revolt, ... Is 59:13
and while they are yet s, I will .... Is 65:24
unto you, rising up early and s .... Jer 7:13
unto you, rising up early and s .... Jer 25:3
all the people heard Jeremiah s .... Jer 26:7
Jeremiah had made an end of s all ...... Jer 26:8
unto you, rising up early and s .... Jer 35:14
in s such words unto them .... Jer 38:4
So they left off s with him .... Jer 38:27
of s unto all the people all the .... Jer 43:1
I heard him s unto me out of the .... Eze 43:6
of man, and s mount a great things .... Dan 7:8
Then I heard one saint s, and .... Dan 8:13
Now as he was s with me, I was in .... Dan 8:18
And whiles I was s, and praying, and .. Dan 9:20
Yea, whiles I was s in prayer .... Dan 9:21
shall be heard for their much s .... Mt 6:7
Now when he had left s, he said .... Lk 5:4
s of the things pertaining to the .... Acts 1:3
s unto Moses, that he should make .... Acts 7:44
s to them, persuaded them to .... Acts 13:43
abode they s boldly in the Lord .... Acts 14:3
s perverse things, to draw away .... Acts 20:30
earth, I heard a voice s unto me .... Acts 26:14
that no man s by the Spirit of 1Cor 12:3
if I come unto you s with tongues...... 1Cor 14:6
ye seek a proof of Christ s in me 2Cor 13:3
But s the truth in love, may grow ...... Eph 4:15
and anger, and clamour, and evil s .... Eph 4:31
s to yourselves in psalms and .... Eph 5:19
S lies in hypocrisy 1Ti 4:2
s things which they ought not............ 1Ti 5:13
excess of riot, s evil of you................ 1Pet 4:4
the dumb ass s with man's voice 2Pet 2:16
s in them of these things 2Pet 3:16
unto him a mouth s great things .... Rev 13:5

SPEAKINGS
and envies, and all evil s 1Pet 2:1

SPEAR
Stretch out the s that is in thy............ Josh 8:18
Joshua stretched out the s that............ Josh 8:26
wherewith he stretched out the s........ Josh 8:26
was there a shield or s seen................ Judg 5:8
there was neither sword nor s............ 1Sa 13:22
the staff of his s was like a 1Sa 17:7
to me with a sword, and with a s........ 1Sa 17:45
LORD saveth not with sword and s...... 1Sa 17:47
here under thine hand s or sword 1Sa 21:8
having his s in his hand, and all 1Sa 22:6
his s stuck in the ground at his 1Sa 26:7
with the s even to the earth at 1Sa 26:7
take thou now the s that is at.............. 1Sa 26:11
So David took the s and the cruse 1Sa 26:12
And now see where the king's s is...... 1Sa 26:16
and said, Behold the king's s 1Sa 26:22
behold, Saul leaned upon his s 2Sa 1:6
with the hinder end of the s 2Sa 2:23
that the s came out behind him 2Sa 2:23
the weight of whose s weighed............ 2Sa 21:16
the staff of whose s was like a 2Sa 21:19
with iron and the staff of a s 2Sa 23:7
he lift up his s against eight 2Sa 23:8
he lifted up his s against three............ 2Sa 23:18
the Egyptian had a s in his hand........ 2Sa 23:21
and plucked the s out of the.............. 2Sa 23:21
hand, and slew him with his own s...... 2Sa 23:21
he lifted up his s against three 1Chr 11:11
for lifting up his s against 1Chr 11:20
hand was a s like a weaver's beam...... 1Chr 11:23
and plucked the s out of the 1Chr 11:23
hand, and slew him with his own s 1Chr 11:23
s were six thousand and eight 1Chr 12:24
s thirty and seven thousand 1Chr 12:34
whose s staff was like a weaver's...... 1Chr 20:5
forth to war, that could handle s 2Chr 25:5
against him, the glittering s .... Job 39:23
the s, the dart, nor the........................ Job 41:26
he laugheth at the shaking of a s ...... Job 41:29
Draw out also the s, and stop the...... Ps 35:3
bow, and cutteth the s in sunder........ Ps 46:9
They shall lay hold on bow and s........ Jer 6:23
bright sword and the glittering s .... Nah 3:3
the shining of thy glittering s.............. Hab 3:11
with a s pierced his side .... Jn 19:34

SPEARMEN
Rebuke the company of s, the............ Ps 68:30
s two hundred, at the third hour .... Acts 23:23

SPEAR'S
his s head weighed six hundred............ 1Sa 17:7

SPEARS
the Hebrews make them swords or s .. 1Sa 13:19
the priest give king David's s 2Kin 11:10

several city he put shields and s........ 2Chr 11:12
of men that bare targets and s............ 2Chr 14:8
to the captains of hundreds s.............. 2Chr 23:9
all the host shields, and s 2Chr 26:14
with their swords, their s.................... Neh 4:13
half of them held both the s................ Neh 4:16
half of them held the s from the.......... Neh 4:21
or his head with fish .... Job 41:7
sons of men, whose teeth are s .... Ps 57:4
their s into pruninghooks.................... Is 2:4
furbish the s, and put on the .... Jer 46:4
and the handstaves, and the .... Eze 39:9
and your pruninghooks into s .... Joel 3:10
their s into pruninghooks.................... Mic 4:3

SPECIAL
to be a s people unto himself .... Deut 7:6
God wrought s miracles by the .... Acts 19:11

SPECIALLY
S the day that thou stoodest................ Deut 4:10
s before thee, O king Agrippa, ... Acts 25:26
all men, s of those that believe.......... 1Ti 4:10
s for those of his own house, he 1Ti 5:8
s they of the circumcision .... Titus 1:10
s to me, but how much more unto ...... Philem 16

SPECKLED
removing from thence all the s............ Gen 30:32
the spotted and s among the goats...... Gen 30:32
every one that is not a s .... Gen 30:33
and all the she goats that were s.......... Gen 30:35
forth cattle ringstraked, ... Gen 30:39
thus, The s shall be thy wages............ Gen 31:8
then all the cattle bare s .... Gen 31:8
the cattle were ringstraked, s .... Gen 31:10
the cattle are ringstraked, s .... Gen 31:12
heritage is unto me as a s bird .... Jer 12:9
him were there red horses, s .... Zec 1:8

SPECTACLE
we are made a s unto the world.......... 1Cor 4:9

SPED
Have they not s .... Judg 5:30

SPEECH
of Lamech, hearken unto my s............ Gen 4:23
was of one language, and of one s...... Gen 11:1
not understand one another's s .... Gen 11:7
but I am slow of s, and of a slow ...... Ex 4:10
give occasions of s against her .... Deut 22:14
given occasions of s against her .... Deut 22:17
my s shall distil as the dew, ... Deut 32:2
To fetch about this form of s 2Sa 14:20
seeing the s of all Israel is.................. 2Sa 19:11
the s pleased the Lord, that................ 1Kin 3:10
s unto the people of Jerusalem 2Chr 32:18
spake half in the s of Ashdod............ Neh 13:24
removeth away the s of the trusty ...... Job 12:20
Hear diligently my s, and my .... Job 13:17
Hear diligently my s, and let this........ Job 21:2
liar, and make my s nothing worth...... Job 24:25
and my s dropped upon them .... Job 29:22
order our s by reason of darkness...... Job 37:19
thine ear unto me, and hear my s ...... Ps 17:6
Day unto day uttereth s, and night...... Ps 19:2
There is no s nor language, where .... Ps 19:3
With her much fair s she caused........ Prov 7:21
Excellent s becometh not a fool .... Prov 17:7
of scarlet, and thy s is comely............ Song 4:3
hearken, and hear my s .... Is 28:23
thy s shall be low out of the................ Is 29:4
thy s shall whisper out of the.............. Is 29:4
give ear unto my s .... Is 32:9
a people of a deeper s than thou .... Is 33:19
use this s in the land of Judah .... Jer 31:23
of the Almighty, the voice of s .... Eze 1:24
sent to a people of a strange s............ Eze 3:5
Not to many people of a strange s...... Eze 3:6
O Lord, I have heard thy s.................. Hab 3:2
for thy s bewrayeth thee...................... Mt 26:73
and had an impediment in his s .... Mk 7:32
and thy s agreeth thereto .... Mk 14:70
Why do ye not understand my s .... Jn 8:43
saying in the s of Lycaonia .... Acts 14:11
continued his s until midnight............ Acts 20:7
with excellency of s or of wisdom...... 1Cor 2:1
And my s and my preaching was not.. 1Cor 2:4
not the s of them which are 1Cor 4:19
hope, we use great plainness of s 2Cor 3:12
is my boldness of s toward you 2Cor 7:4
is weak, and his s contemptible.......... 2Cor 10:10
But though I be rude in s 2Cor 11:6
Let your s be alway with grace,.......... Col 4:6
Sound s, that cannot be condemned.. Titus 2:8

SPEECHES
even apparently, and not in dark s...... Num 12:8
the s of one that is desperate,............ Job 6:26
or with s wherewith he can do no...... Job 15:3
will I answer him with your s .... Job 32:14
Job, I pray thee, hear my s .... Job 33:1
fair s deceive the hearts of the .... Rom 16:18
of all their hard s which ungodly ...... Jude 15

SPEECHLESS
And he was s .... Mt 22:12
beckoned unto them, and remained s.. Lk 1:22
which journeyed with him stood s ...... Acts 9:7

SPEED
thee, send me good s this day .... Gen 24:12
cried after the lad, Make s.................. 1Sa 20:38
make s to depart, lest he 2Sa 15:14

s to get him up to his chariot.............. 1Kin 12:18
But king Rehoboam made s to get...... 2Chr 10:18
let it be done with a s .... Ezr 6:12
That say, Let him make s, and............ Is 5:19
they shall come with s swiftly.............. Is 5:26
for to come to him with all s .... Acts 17:15
your house, neither bid him God s...... 2Jn 10
For he that biddeth him God s............ 2Jn 11

SPEEDILY
Then they s took down every man ...... Gen 44:11
for me than that I should 1Sa 27:1
the wilderness, but s pass over 2Sa 17:16
divided them s among all the.............. 2Chr 35:13
the king had sent, so they did s .... Ezr 6:13
That thou mayest buy s with this........ Ezr 7:17
require of you, it be done s .... Ezr 7:21
judgment be executed s upon him ...... Ezr 7:26
he s gave her her things for .... Est 2:9
deliver me s .... Ps 31:2
hear me s .... Ps 69:17
thy tender mercies s prevent us.......... Ps 79:8
the day when I call answer me s.......... Ps 102:2
Hear me s, O LORD .... Ps 143:7
an evil work is not executed s .... Eccl 8:11
thine health shall spring forth s .... Is 58:8
s will I return your recompence.......... Joel 3:4
Let us go s to pray before the.............. Zec 8:21
you that he will avenge them s............ Lk 18:8

SPEEDY
for he shall make even a s .... Zeph 1:18

SPEND
I will s mine arrows upon them .... Deut 32:23
They s their days in wealth, and........ Job 21:13
they shall s their days in.................... Job 36:11
we s our years as a tale that is............ Ps 90:9
Wherefore do ye s money for that ...... Is 55:2
he would not s the time in Asia.......... Acts 20:16
And I will very gladly s and be.......... 2Cor 12:15

SPENDEST
and whatsoever thou s more .... Lk 10:35

SPENDETH
but a foolish man s it up .... Prov 21:20
with harlots s his substance.............. Prov 29:3
vain life which he s as a shadow........ Eccl 6:12

SPENT
And the water was s in the bottle........ Gen 21:15
my lord, how that our money is s........ Gen 47:18
your strength shall be s in vain .... Lev 26:20
were by Jebus, the day was far s........ Judg 19:11
for the bread is s in our vessels.......... 1Sa 9:7
shuttle, and are s without hope .... Job 7:6
For my life is s with grief .... Ps 31:10
I have s my strength for nought,.......... Is 49:4
all the bread in the city were s .... Jer 37:21
had s all that she had, and was.......... Mk 5:26
And when the day was now far s .... Mk 6:35
which had s all her living upon .... Lk 8:43
And when he had s all, there arose .... Lk 15:14
evening, and the day is far s................ Lk 24:29
s their time in nothing else .... Acts 17:21
after he had s some time there,.......... Acts 18:23
Now when much time was s................ Acts 27:9
The night is far s, the day is at............ Rom 13:12
very gladly spend and be s for you.... 2Cor 12:15

SPEWING
shameful s shall be on thy glory........ Hab 2:16

SPICE
And s, and oil for the light, and.......... Ex 35:28
the traffick of the s merchants............ 1Kin 10:15
neither was there any such s as.......... 2Chr 9:9
have gathered my myrrh with my s.... Song 5:1
s it well, and let the bones be............ Eze 24:10

SPICED
of s wine of the juice of my................ Song 8:2

SPICERY
with their camels bearing s .... Gen 37:25

SPICES
little balm, and a little honey, s .... Gen 43:11
s for anointing oil, and for sweet .... Ex 25:6
s of pure myrrh five hundred.............. Ex 30:23
Moses, Take unto thee sweet s .... Ex 30:34
these sweet s with pure .... Ex 30:34
s for anointing oil, and for the............ Ex 35:8
and the pure incense of sweet s.......... Ex 37:29
train, with camels that bare s 1Kin 10:2
of s very great store, and 1Kin 10:10
of s as these which the queen of 1Kin 10:10
and garments, and armour, and s 1Kin 10:25
the silver, and the gold, and the s 2Kin 20:13
and the frankincense, and the s.......... 1Chr 9:29
made the ointment of the s 1Chr 9:30
company, and camels that bare s 2Chr 9:1
of great abundance, and precious...... 2Chr 9:9
gold, and raiment, harness, and s 2Chr 9:24
divers kinds of s prepared by the 2Chr 16:14
and for precious stones, and for s 2Chr 32:27
of thine ointments than all s .... Song 4:10
and aloes, with all the chief s.............. Song 4:14
that the s thereof may flow out .... Song 4:16
His cheeks are as a bed of s .... Song 5:13
into his garden, to the beds of s.......... Song 6:2
hart upon the mountains of s .... Song 8:14
the silver, and the gold, and the s ...... Is 39:2
in thy fairs with chief of all s .... Eze 27:22
and Salome, had bought sweet s........ Mk 16:1

S

And they returned, and prepared s............ Lk 23:56
bringing the s which they had.................. Lk 24:1
it in linen clothes with the s.................. Jn 19:40

SPIDER
The s taketh hold with her hands,..... Prov 30:28

SPIDER'S
and whose trust shall be a s web.............. Job 8:14
eggs, and weave the s web...................... Is 59:5

SPIED
he s an Egyptian smiting an.................... Ex 2:11
men that had s out the country............... Josh 6:22
he s the company of Jehu as he.............. 2Kin 9:17
behold, they s a band of men................ 2Kin 13:21
he s the sepulchres that were................ 2Kin 23:16
that were s in the land of Judah 2Kin 23:24

SPIES
them, and said unto them, Ye are s...... Gen 42:9
true men, thy servants are no s............ Gen 42:11
spake unto you, saying, Ye are s.......... Gen 42:14
life of Pharaoh surely ye are s............. Gen 42:16
took us for s of the country................ Gen 42:30
we are no s....................................... Gen 42:31
shall I know that ye are no s............... Gen 42:34
Israel came by the way of the s .... Num 21:1
the young men that were s went in....... Josh 6:23
the s saw a man come forth out of....... Judg 1:24
David therefore sent out s.................... 1Sa 26:4
But Absalom sent s throughout all 2Sa 15:10
they watched him, and sent forth s...... Lk 20:20
she had received the s with peace....... Heb 11:31

SPIKENARD
my s sendeth forth the smell .... Song 1:12
camphire, with s............................... Song 4:13
S and saffron.................................... Song 4:14
of ointment of s very precious............... Mk 14:3
Mary a pound of ointment of s............. Jn 12:3

SPILLED
that he s it on the ground, lest .... Gen 38:9
the bottles, and the wine is s .... Mk 2:22
will burst the bottles, and be s............ Lk 5:37

SPILT
are as water s on the ground,............ 2Sa 14:14

SPIN
hearted did s with their hands............ Ex 35:25
they toil not, neither do they s............ Mt 6:28
they toil not, they s not..................... Lk 12:27

SPINDLE
She layeth her hands to the s.......... Prov 31:19

SPIRIT
the S of God moved upon the face .... Gen 1:2
My s shall not always strive with........... Gen 6:3
morning that his s was troubled............ Gen 41:8
is, a man in whom the S of God is....... Gen 41:38
the s of Jacob their father................. Gen 45:27
not unto Moses for anguish of s............. Ex 6:9
have filled with the s of wisdom .... Ex 28:3
have filled him with the s of God.......... Ex 31:3
every one whom his s made willing .... Ex 35:21
hath filled him with the s of God.......... Ex 35:31
or woman that hath a familiar s......... Lev 20:27
the s of jealousy come upon him,......... Num 5:14
or if the s of jealousy come upon .... Num 5:14
Or when the s of jealousy cometh....... Num 5:30
take of the s which is upon thee......... Num 11:17
took of the s that was upon him,....... Num 11:25
when the s rested upon them, they....... Num 11:25
and the s rested upon them................ Num 11:26
LORD would put his s upon them......... Num 11:29
because he had another s with him....... Num 14:24
the s of God came upon him............... Num 24:2
of Nun, a man in whom is the s......... Num 27:18
the LORD thy God hardened his s .... Deut 2:30
Nun was full of the s of wisdom......... Deut 34:9
was there s in them any more........... Josh 5:1
the s of the LORD came upon him,...... Judg 3:10
But the S of the LORD came upon........ Judg 6:34
sent an evil s between Abimelech........ Judg 9:23
Then the S of the LORD came upon...... Judg 11:29
the S of the LORD began to move....... Judg 13:25
the S of the LORD came mightily........ Judg 14:6
the S of the LORD came upon him,...... Judg 14:19
the S of the LORD came mightily........ Judg 15:14
his s came again, and he revived........ Judg 15:19
I am a woman of a sorrowful s......... 1Sa 1:15
the S of the LORD will come upon....... 1Sa 10:6
the S of God came upon him, and he.. 1Sa 10:10
the S of God came upon Saul when..... 1Sa 11:6
the S of the LORD came upon David.... 1Sa 16:13
But the S of the LORD departed......... 1Sa 16:14
an evil s from the LORD troubled........ 1Sa 16:14
an evil s from God troubleth thee........ 1Sa 16:15
when the evil s from God is upon....... 1Sa 16:23
when the evil s from God was upon..... 1Sa 16:23
the evil s departed from him............. 1Sa 16:23
that the evil s from God came on........ 1Sa 18:10
the evil s from the LORD was upon...... 1Sa 19:9
the S of God was upon the............... 1Sa 19:20
the S of God was upon him also,....... 1Sa 19:23
me a woman that hath a familiar s..... 1Sa 28:7
that hath a familiar s at En-dor......... 1Sa 28:7
divine unto me by the familiar s......... 1Sa 28:8
eaten, his s came again to him.......... 1Sa 30:12
The S of the LORD spake by me, and.... 2Sa 23:2
there was no more s in her................ 1Kin 10:5
that the S of the LORD shall............. 1Kin 18:12

unto him, Why is thy s so sad............ 1Kin 21:5
And there came forth a s, and stood... 1Kin 22:21
I will be a lying s in the mouth........... 1Kin 22:22
the LORD hath put a lying s in............ 1Kin 22:23
Which way went the S of the LORD 1Kin 22:24
portion of thy s be upon me............... 2Kin 2:9
The s of Elijah doth rest on................ 2Kin 2:15
lest peradventure the S of the............. 2Kin 2:16
up the s of Pul king of Assyria............ 1Chr 5:26
the s of Tilgath-pilneser king of 1Chr 5:26
of one that had a familiar s 1Chr 10:13
Then the s came upon Amasai, who.... 1Chr 12:18
of all that he had by the s 1Chr 28:12
there was no more s in her................ 2Chr 9:4
the S of God came upon Azariah........ 2Chr 15:1
Then there came out a s, and stood... 2Chr 18:20
be a lying s in the mouth of all 2Chr 18:21
lying s in the mouth of these thy....... 2Chr 18:22
Which way went the S of the LORD 2Chr 18:23
came the S of the LORD in the.......... 2Chr 20:14
Jehoram the s of the Philistines 2Chr 21:16
the S of God came upon Zechariah..... 2Chr 24:20
and dealt with a familiar s................ 2Chr 33:6
up the s of Cyrus king of Persia......... 2Chr 36:22
up the s of Cyrus king of Persia......... Ezr 1:1
all them whose s God had raised......... Ezr 1:5
also thy good s to instruct them........ Neh 9:20
them by thy s in thy prophets........... Neh 9:30
Then a s passed before my face......... Job 4:15
poison whereof drinketh up my s......... Job 6:4
will speak in the anguish of my s....... Job 7:11
visitation hath preserved my s........... Job 10:12
thou turnest thy s against God.......... Job 15:13
the s of my understanding causeth...... Job 20:3
why should not my s be troubled........ Job 21:4
and whose s came from thee............. Job 26:4
By his s he hath garnished the.......... Job 26:13
the s of God is in my nostrils........... Job 27:3
But there is a s in man.................... Job 32:8
the s within me constraineth me........ Job 32:18
The s of God hath made me, and the.. Job 33:4
if he gather unto himself his s........... Job 34:14
Into thine hand I commit my s........... Ps 31:5
in whose s there is no guile.............. Ps 32:2
saveth such as be of a contrite s .... Ps 34:18
and renew a right s within me........... Ps 51:10
and take not thy holy s from me......... Ps 51:11
and uphold me with thy free s .... Ps 51:12
sacrifices of God are a broken s.......... Ps 51:17
He shall cut off the s of princes......... Ps 76:12
and my s was overwhelmed................ Ps 77:3
my s made diligent search................. Ps 77:6
whose s was not stedfast with God...... Ps 78:8
Thou sendest forth thy s, they.......... Ps 104:30
Because they provoked his s,............ Ps 106:33
Whither shall I go from thy s............ Ps 139:7
When my s was overwhelmed within.... Ps 142:3
Therefore is my s overwhelmed.......... Ps 143:4
my s faileth................................... Ps 143:7
thy s is good................................. Ps 143:10
I will pour out my s unto you............ Prov 1:23
faithful s concealeth the matter .... Prov 11:13
that is hasty of s exalteth folly .... Prov 14:29
therein is a breach in the s .... Prov 15:4
of the heart the s is broken.............. Prov 15:13
an haughty s before a fall .... Prov 16:18
be of an humble s with the lowly........ Prov 16:19
he that ruleth his s than he that........ Prov 16:32
but a broken s drieth the bones.......... Prov 17:22
is of an excellent s......................... Prov 17:27
The s of a man will sustain his.......... Prov 18:14
but a wounded s who can bear........... Prov 18:14
The s of man is the candle of the....... Prov 20:27
a s like a city that is broken............. Prov 25:28
shall uphold the humble in s .... Prov 29:23
all is vanity and vexation of s .... Eccl 1:14
that this also is vexation of s............ Eccl 1:17
all was vanity and vexation of s .... Eccl 2:11
all is vanity and vexation of s .... Eccl 2:17
also is vanity and vexation of s .... Eccl 2:26
Who knoweth the s of man that.......... Eccl 3:21
the s of the beast that goeth............ Eccl 3:21
is also vanity and vexation of s .... Eccl 4:4
with travail and vexation of s .... Eccl 4:6
also is vanity and vexation of s .... Eccl 4:16
is also vanity and vexation of s .... Eccl 6:9
the patient in s is better than........... Eccl 7:8
is better than the proud in s............. Eccl 7:8
Be not hasty in thy s to be angry ...... Eccl 7:9
over the s to retain the s .... Eccl 8:8
If the s of the ruler rise up .... Eccl 10:4
not what is the way of the s .... Eccl 11:5
the s shall return unto God who........ Eccl 12:7
thereof by the s of judgment............ Is 4:4
and by the s of burning................... Is 4:4
the s of the LORD shall rest upon...... Is 11:2
the s of wisdom and understanding,.... Is 11:2
the s of counsel and might............... Is 11:2
the s of knowledge and of the fear..... Is 11:2
the s of Egypt shall fail in................ Is 19:3
a perverse s in the midst thereof....... Is 19:14
with my s within me will I seek......... Is 26:9
for a s of judgment to him that .... Is 28:6
as of one that hath a familiar s .... Is 29:4
out upon you the s of deep sleep....... Is 29:10
They also that erred in s shall .... Is 29:24
with a covering, but not of my s .... Is 30:1
and their horses flesh, and not s ...... Is 31:3
Until the s be poured upon us........... Is 32:15
his s it hath gathered them............. Is 34:16

these things is the life of my s .... Is 38:16
because the s of the LORD bloweth...... Is 40:7
hath directed the S of the LORD......... Is 40:13
I have put my s upon him................ Is 42:1
s to them that walk therein.............. Is 42:5
I will pour my s upon thy seed.......... Is 44:3
and vow the Lord Goo, and his S ...... Is 48:16
a woman forsaken and grieved in s .... Is 54:6
that is of a contrite and humble s ..... Is 57:15
to revive the s of the humble .... Is 57:15
for the s should fail before me,.......... Is 57:16
the S of the LORD shall lift up a........ Is 59:19
My s that is upon thee, and my......... Is 59:21
The S of the Lord Goo is upon me...... Is 61:1
of praise for the s of heaviness......... Is 61:3
rebelled, and vexed his holy S .... Is 63:10
he that put his holy S within him...... Is 63:11
the S of the LORD caused him to....... Is 63:14
and shall howl for vexation of s .... Is 65:14
that is poor and of a contrite s .... Is 66:2
the s of the kings of the Medes .... Jer 51:11
whither the s was to go, they........... Eze 1:12
Whithersoever the s was to go .... Eze 1:20
went, thither was their s to go.......... Eze 1:20
for the s of the living creature.......... Eze 1:20
for the s of the living creature.......... Eze 1:21
the s entered into me when he.......... Eze 2:2
Then the s took me up, and I heard... Eze 3:12
So the s lifted me up, and took me.... Eze 3:14
bitterness, in the heat of my s .... Eze 3:14
Then the s entered into me, and....... Eze 3:24
the s lifted me up between the.......... Eze 8:3
for the s of the living creature.......... Eze 10:17
Moreover the s lifted me up .... Eze 11:1
the S of the Lord fell upon me,......... Eze 11:5
and I will put a new s within you....... Eze 11:19
Afterwards the s took me up,............ Eze 11:24
by the S of God into Chaldea............ Eze 11:24
prophets, that follow their own s ...... Eze 13:3
make you a new heart and a new s.... Eze 18:31
every s shall faint, and all knees ...... Eze 21:7
a new s will I put within you............ Eze 36:26
And I will put my s within you .... Eze 36:27
me out in the s of the LORD.............. Eze 37:1
And shall put my s in you, and ye ..... Eze 37:14
out my s upon the house of Israel .... Eze 39:29
So the s took me up, and brought..... Eze 43:5
wherewith his s was troubled............ Dan 2:1
my s was troubled to know the.......... Dan 2:3
in whom is the s of the holy gods..... Dan 4:8
because I know that the s of the........ Dan 4:9
for the s of the holy gods is in......... Dan 4:18
in whom is the s of the holy gods..... Dan 5:11
Forasmuch as an excellent s............. Dan 5:12
that the s of the gods is in them...... Dan 5:14
because an excellent s was in him ..... Dan 6:3
in my s in the midst of my body ...... Dan 7:15
for the s of whoredoms hath............ Hos 4:12
for the s of whoredoms is in the....... Hos 5:4
will pour out my s upon all flesh ...... Joel 2:28
those days will I pour out my s .... Joel 2:29
is the s of the LORD straitened......... Mic 2:7
If a man walking in the s .... Mic 2:11
of power by the s of the LORD........... Mic 3:8
the LORD stirred up the s of .... Hag 1:14
the s of Joshua the son of .... Hag 1:14
the s of all the remnant of the......... Hag 1:14
so my s remaineth among you.......... Hag 2:5
might, nor by power, but by my s ...... Zec 4:6
quieted my s in the north country ..... Zec 6:8
in his s by the former prophets........ Zec 7:12
formeth the s of man within him ...... Zec 12:1
Jerusalem, the s of grace and of ...... Zec 12:10
the unclean s to pass out of the....... Zec 13:2
Yet had he the residue of the s .... Mal 2:15
Therefore take heed to your s .... Mal 2:15
therefore take heed to your s .... Mal 2:16
he saw the S of God descending........ Mt 3:16
the s into the wilderness to be .... Mt 4:1
Blessed are the poor in s .... Mt 5:3
but the S of your Father which .... Mt 10:20
I will put my S upon him, and he ...... Mt 12:18
I cast out devils by the S of God....... Mt 12:28
When the unclean s is gone out of .... Mt 12:43
were troubled, saying, It is a s .... Mt 14:26
doth David in s call him Lord............ Mt 22:43
the s indeed is willing, but the......... Mt 26:41
the S like a dove descending upon ..... Mk 1:10
immediately the s driveth him.......... Mk 1:12
synagogue a man with an unclean s... Mk 1:23
when the unclean s had torn him...... Mk 1:26
when Jesus perceived in his s .... Mk 2:8
they said, He hath an unclean s....... Mk 3:30
the tombs a man with an unclean s... Mk 5:2
out of the man, thou unclean s .... Mk 5:8
they supposed it had been a s .... Mk 6:49
young daughter had an unclean s...... Mk 7:25
And he sighed deeply in his s .... Mk 8:12
thee my son, which hath a dumb s ... Mk 9:17
him, straightway the s tare him .... Mk 9:20
together, he rebuked the foul s .... Mk 9:25
unto him, Thou dumb and deaf s ..... Mk 9:25
the s cried, and rent him sore, and... Mk 9:26
The s truly is ready, but the .... Mk 14:38
he shall go before him in the s .... Lk 1:17
my s hath rejoiced in God my .... Lk 1:47
child grew, and waxed strong in s ..... Lk 1:80
he came by the S into the temple..... Lk 2:27
child grew, and waxed strong in s ..... Lk 2:40
was led by the S into the................ Lk 4:1

the power of the S into Galilee......... Lk 4:14
The S of the Lord is upon me,......... Lk 4:18
which had a an unclean devil......... Lk 4:33
unclean s to come out of the man......... Lk 8:29
her s came again, and she arose......... Lk 8:55
a s taketh him, and he suddenly......... Lk 9:39
And Jesus rebuked the unclean s......... Lk 9:42
not what manner of s ye are of......... Lk 9:55
In that hour Jesus rejoiced in s......... Lk 10:21
the Holy S to them that ask him......... Lk 11:13
When the unclean s is gone out of......... Lk 11:24
a s of infirmity eighteen years......... Lk 13:11
into thy hands I commend my s......... Lk 23:46
supposed that they had seen a s......... Lk 24:37
for a s hath not flesh and bones,......... Lk 24:39
I saw the S descending from......... Jn 1:32
thou shalt see the S descending......... Jn 1:33
man be born of water and of the S......... Jn 3:5
which is born of the S is s......... Jn 3:6
every one that is born of the S......... Jn 3:8
not the S by measure unto him......... Jn 3:34
shall worship the Father in s......... Jn 4:23
God is a S;......... Jn 4:24
worship him must worship him in s......... Jn 4:24
It is the s that quickeneth,......... Jn 6:63
that I speak unto you, they are s......... Jn 6:63
(But this spake he of the S,......... Jn 7:39
with her, he groaned in the s......... Jn 11:33
thus said, he was troubled in s......... Jn 13:21
Even the S of truth......... Jn 14:17
The Father, even the S of truth......... Jn 15:26
the S of truth, is come, he will......... Jn 16:13
as the S gave them utterance......... Acts 2:4
pour out of my S upon all flesh......... Acts 2:17
pour out in those days of my S......... Acts 2:18
to tempt the S of the Lord......... Acts 5:9
wisdom and the s by which he spake......... Acts 6:10
saying, Lord Jesus, receive my s......... Acts 7:59
Then the S said unto Philip, Go......... Acts 8:29
the S of the Lord caught away......... Acts 8:39
The S said unto him, Behold,......... Acts 10:19
the S bade me go with them,......... Acts 11:12
signified by the S that there......... Acts 11:28
but the S suffered them not......... Acts 16:7
with a s of divination met us......... Acts 16:16
grieved, turned and said to the s......... Acts 16:18
his s was stirred in him, when he......... Acts 17:16
Paul was pressed in the s......... Acts 18:5
and being fervent in the s......... Acts 18:25
And the evil s answered and said,......... Acts 19:15
the evil s was passed on them......... Acts 19:16
ended, Paul purposed in the s......... Acts 19:21
go bound in the s unto Jerusalem......... Acts 20:22
who said to Paul through the S......... Acts 21:4
neither angel, nor s .... Acts 23:8
but if a s or an angel hath......... Acts 23:9
according to the s of holiness......... Rom 1:4
whom I serve with my s in the......... Rom 1:9
is that of the heart, in the s......... Rom 2:29
we should serve in newness of s......... Rom 7:6
after the flesh, but after the S......... Rom 8:1
For the law of the S of life......... Rom 8:2
after the flesh, but after the S......... Rom 8:4
the S the things of the S......... Rom 8:5
not in the flesh, but in the S......... Rom 8:9
if so be that the S of God dwell......... Rom 8:9
any man have not the S of Christ......... Rom 8:9
but the S is life because of......... Rom 8:10
But if the S of him that raised......... Rom 8:11
by his S that dwelleth in you......... Rom 8:11
but if ye through the S do......... Rom 8:13
many as are led by the S of God......... Rom 8:14
the s of bondage again to fear......... Rom 8:15
have received the S of adoption......... Rom 8:15
The S itself beareth witness with......... Rom 8:16
itself beareth witness with our s......... Rom 8:16
have the firstfruits of the S,......... Rom 8:23
Likewise the S also helpeth our......... Rom 8:26
but the S itself maketh......... Rom 8:26
knoweth what is the mind of the S......... Rom 8:27
hath given them the s of slumber......... Rom 11:8
fervent in s;......... Rom 12:11
by the power of the S of God......... Rom 15:19
sake, and for the love of the S......... Rom 15:30
but in demonstration of the S......... 1Cor 2:4
revealed them unto us by his S......... 1Cor 2:10
for the S searcheth all things,......... 1Cor 2:10
save the s of man which is in him......... 1Cor 2:11
knoweth no man, but the S of God......... 1Cor 2:11
not the s of the world......... 1Cor 2:12
but the s which is of God......... 1Cor 2:12
not the things of the S of God......... 1Cor 2:14
that the S of God dwelleth in you......... 1Cor 3:16
in love, and in the s of meekness......... 1Cor 4:21
absent in body, but present in s......... 1Cor 5:3
ye are gathered together, and my s......... 1Cor 5:4
that the s may be saved in the......... 1Cor 5:5
Jesus, and by the S of our God......... 1Cor 6:11
is joined unto the Lord is one s......... 1Cor 6:17
God in your body, and in your s......... 1Cor 6:20
may be holy both in body and in s......... 1Cor 7:34
also that I have the S of God......... 1Cor 7:40
that no man speaking by the S of......... 1Cor 12:3
of gifts, but the same S......... 1Cor 12:4
But the manifestation of the s......... 1Cor 12:7
given by the S the word of wisdom......... 1Cor 12:8
word of knowledge by the same S......... 1Cor 12:8
To another faith by the same S......... 1Cor 12:9
gifts of healing by the same S......... 1Cor 12:9

that one and the selfsame S......... 1Cor 12:11
For by one S are we all baptized......... 1Cor 12:13
been all made to drink into one S......... 1Cor 12:13
howbeit in the s he speaketh......... 1Cor 14:2
tongue, my s prayeth, but my......... 1Cor 14:14
I will pray with the s, and I will......... 1Cor 14:15
I will sing with the s, and I will......... 1Cor 14:15
when thou shalt bless with the s......... 1Cor 14:16
last Adam was made a quickening s......... 1Cor 15:45
For they have refreshed my s......... 1Cor 16:18
earnest of the S in our hearts......... 2Cor 1:22
I had no rest in my s, because I......... 2Cor 2:13
but with the S of the living God......... 2Cor 3:3
not of the letter, but of the s......... 2Cor 3:6
killeth, but the s giveth life......... 2Cor 3:6
of the s be rather glorious......... 2Cor 3:8
Now the Lord is that S......... 2Cor 3:17
where the S of the Lord is, there......... 2Cor 3:17
even as by the S of the Lord......... 2Cor 3:18
We having the same s of faith......... 2Cor 4:13
unto us the earnest of the S......... 2Cor 5:5
all filthiness of the flesh and s......... 2Cor 7:1
because his s was refreshed by......... 2Cor 7:13
or if ye receive another s......... 2Cor 11:4
walked we not in the same s......... 2Cor 12:18
Received ye the S by the works of......... Gal 3:2
having begun in the S, are ye now......... Gal 3:3
that ministereth to you the S,......... Gal 3:5
promise of the S through faith......... Gal 3:14
God hath sent forth the S of his......... Gal 4:6
him that was born after the S......... Gal 4:29
For we through the S wait for the......... Gal 5:5
This I say then, Walk in the S......... Gal 5:16
the flesh lusteth against the S......... Gal 5:17
and the s against the flesh......... Gal 5:17
But if ye be led of the S......... Gal 5:18
But the fruit of the S is love,......... Gal 5:22
If we live in the S, let us also......... Gal 5:25
let us also walk in the S......... Gal 5:25
such an one in the s of meekness......... Gal 6:1
but he that soweth to the S shall......... Gal 6:8
of the S reap life everlasting......... Gal 6:8
Lord Jesus Christ be with your s......... Gal 6:18
with that holy S of promise......... Eph 1:13
may give unto you the s of wisdom......... Eph 1:17
the s that now worketh in the......... Eph 2:2
access by one S unto the Father......... Eph 2:18
habitation of God through the S......... Eph 2:22
apostles and prophets by the S......... Eph 3:5
might by his S in the inner man......... Eph 3:16
of the S in the bond of peace......... Eph 4:3
There is one body, and one S,......... Eph 4:4
be renewed in the s of your mind......... Eph 4:23
And grieve not the holy S of God......... Eph 4:30
Fruit of the S is in all goodness......... Eph 5:9
but be filled with the S;......... Eph 5:18
salvation, and the sword of the S......... Eph 6:17
prayer and supplication in the S......... Eph 6:18
supply of the S of Jesus Christ......... Phil 1:19
that ye stand fast in one s,......... Phil 1:27
love, if any fellowship of the s......... Phil 2:1
which worship God in the s......... Phil 3:3
unto us your love in the s......... Col 1:8
flesh, yet am I with you in the s......... Col 2:5
also given unto us his holy S......... 1Th 4:8
Quench not the S;......... 1Th 5:19
and I pray God your whole s......... 1Th 5:23
or be troubled, neither by s......... 2Th 2:2
consume with the s of his mouth......... 2Th 2:8
through sanctification of the S......... 2Th 2:13
in the flesh, justified in the S......... 1Ti 3:16
Now the Spirit speaketh expressly,......... 1Ti 4:1
in conversation, in charity, in s......... 1Ti 4:12
hath not given us the s of fear......... 2Ti 1:7
Lord Jesus Christ be with thy s......... 2Ti 4:22
Lord Jesus Christ be with thy s......... Philem 25
the dividing asunder of soul and s......... Heb 4:12
who through the eternal S offered......... Heb 9:14
done despite unto the S of grace......... Heb 10:29
as the body without the s is dead......... Jas 2:26
The s that dwelleth in us lusteth......... Jas 4:5
through sanctification of the S......... 1Pet 1:2
or what manner of time the S of......... 1Pet 1:11
The S unto unfeigned love of the......... 1Pet 1:22
the ornament of a meek and quiet s......... 1Pet 3:4
the flesh, but quickened by the S......... 1Pet 3:18
live according to God in the s......... 1Pet 4:6
for the s of glory and of God......... 1Pet 4:14
by the S which he hath given us......... 1Jn 3:24
Beloved, believe not every s......... 1Jn 4:1
Hereby know ye the S of God......... 1Jn 4:2
Every s that confesseth that......... 1Jn 4:3
every s that confesseth not that......... 1Jn 4:3
this is that s of antichrist,......... 1Jn 4:3
Hereby know we the s of truth,......... 1Jn 4:6
of truth, and the s of error......... 1Jn 4:6
because he hath given us of his S......... 1Jn 4:13
it is the S that beareth witness,......... 1Jn 5:6
witness, because the S is truth......... 1Jn 5:6
that bear witness in earth, the s......... 1Jn 5:8
sensual, having not the S......... Jude 19
I was in the S on the Lord's-day......... Rev 1:10
let him hear what the S saith......... Rev 2:7
let him hear what the S saith......... Rev 2:11
let him hear what the S saith......... Rev 2:17
let him hear what the S saith......... Rev 2:29
let him hear what the S saith......... Rev 3:6
let him hear what the S saith......... Rev 3:13
let him hear what the S saith......... Rev 3:22

And immediately I was in the s......... Rev 4:2
an half the S of life from God......... Rev 11:11
Yea, saith the S, that they may......... Rev 14:13
away in the s into the wilderness......... Rev 17:3
and the hold of every foul s......... Rev 18:2
of Jesus is the s of prophecy......... Rev 19:10
me away in the s to a great......... Rev 21:10
And the S and the bride say, Come......... Rev 22:17

SPIRITS
not them that have familiar s......... Lev 19:31
after such as have familiar s......... Lev 20:6
the God of the s of all flesh......... Num 16:22
the God of the s of all flesh......... Num 27:16
or a consulter with familiar s......... Deut 18:11
away those that had familiar s......... 1Sa 28:3
off those that have familiar s......... 1Sa 28:9
and dealt with familiar s......... 2Kin 21:6
the workers with familiar s......... 2Kin 23:24
Who maketh his angels s......... Ps 104:4
but the LORD weigheth the s......... Prov 16:2
unto them that have familiar s......... Is 8:19
and to them that have familiar s......... Is 19:3
are the four s of the heavens......... Zec 6:5
he cast out the s with his word......... Mt 8:16
gave them power against unclean s......... Mt 10:1
other s more wicked than himself......... Mt 12:45
commandeth he even the unclean s......... Mk 1:27
And unclean s, when they saw him,......... Mk 3:11
And the unclean s went out......... Mk 5:13
and gave them power over unclean s......... Mk 6:7
power he commandeth the unclean s......... Lk 4:36
that were vexed with unclean s......... Lk 6:18
and plagues, and of evil s......... Lk 7:21
which had been healed of evil s......... Lk 8:2
that the s are subject unto you......... Lk 10:20
other s more wicked than himself......... Lk 11:26
which were vexed with unclean s......... Acts 5:16
For unclean s, crying with loud......... Acts 8:7
the evil s went out of them......... Acts 19:12
evil s the name of the Lord Jesus......... Acts 19:13
to another discerning of s......... 1Cor 12:10
the s of the prophets are subject......... 1Cor 14:32
faith, giving heed to seducing s......... 1Ti 4:1
he saith, Who maketh his angels s......... Heb 1:7
Are they not all ministering s......... Heb 1:14
subjection unto the Father of s......... Heb 12:9
to the s of just men made perfect......... Heb 12:23
and preached unto the s in prison......... 1Pet 3:19
but try the s whether they are of......... 1Jn 4:1
from the seven S which are before......... Rev 1:4
he that hath the seven S of God......... Rev 3:1
which are the seven S of God......... Rev 4:5
which are the seven S of God sent......... Rev 5:6
I saw three unclean s like frogs......... Rev 16:13
For they are the s of devils......... Rev 16:14

SPIRITUAL
the s man is mad, for the......... Hos 9:7
I may impart unto you some s gift......... Rom 1:11
For we know that the law is s......... Rom 7:14
made partakers of their s things......... Rom 15:27
comparing s things with s......... 1Cor 2:13
But he that is judgeth all......... 1Cor 2:15
not speak unto you as unto s......... 1Cor 3:1
If we have sown unto you s things......... 1Cor 9:11
And did all eat the same s meat......... 1Cor 10:3
And did all drink the same s drink......... 1Cor 10:4
for they drank of that s Rock......... 1Cor 10:4
Now concerning s gifts, brethren,......... 1Cor 12:1
after charity, and desire s gifts......... 1Cor 14:1
as ye are zealous of s gifts......... 1Cor 14:12
himself to be a prophet, or s,......... 1Cor 14:37
it is raised a s body,......... 1Cor 15:44
body, and there is a s body......... 1Cor 15:44
that was not first which is s,......... 1Cor 15:46
and afterward that which is s......... 1Cor 15:46
in a fault, ye which are s......... Gal 6:1
who hath blessed us with all s......... Eph 1:3
s songs, singing and making melody......... Eph 5:19
against s wickedness in high......... Eph 6:12
in all wisdom and s understanding......... Col 1:9
s songs, singing with grace in......... Col 3:16
stones, are built up a s house......... 1Pet 2:5
to offer up s sacrifices......... 1Pet 2:5

SPIRITUALLY
but to be s minded is life and......... Rom 8:6
because they are s discerned......... 1Cor 2:14
which is called Sodom and Egypt,......... Rev 11:8

SPIT
issue s upon him that is clean......... Lev 15:8
her father had but s in her face......... Num 12:14
a s in his face, and shall answer and......... Deut 25:9
me, and spare not to s in my face......... Job 30:10
Then did they s in his face......... Mt 26:67
they s upon him, and took the reed......... Mt 27:30
fingers into his ears, and he s......... Mk 7:33
and when he had s on his eyes,......... Mk 8:23
shall s upon him, and shall kill......... Mk 10:34
and none began to s on him,......... Mk 14:65
did s upon him, and bowing their......... Mk 15:19

SPITE
for thou beholdest mischief and s......... Ps 10:14

SPITEFULLY
his servants, and entreated them s......... Mt 22:6
s entreated, and spitted on......... Lk 18:32

SPITTED
and spitefully entreated, and s on............ Lk 18:32

SPITTING
I hid not my face from shame and s........ Is 50:6

SPITTLE
let his s fall down upon his................ 1Sa 21:13
me alone till I swallow down my s........ Job 7:19
the ground, and made clay of the s........ Jn 9:6

SPOIL
and at night he shall divide the s .... Gen 49:27
and ye shall s the Egyptians................. Ex 3:22
overtake, I will divide the s................. Ex 15:9
took the s of all their cattle,............. Num 31:9
And they took all the s, and all......... Num 31:11
captives, and the prey, and the s....... Num 31:12
(For the men of war had taken s...... Num 31:53
the s of the cities which we took......... Deut 2:35
the s of the cities, we took for........... Deut 3:7
thou shalt gather all the s of it........ Deut 13:16
all the s thereof every whit, for......... Deut 13:16
the city, even all the s thereof......... Deut 20:14
shalt eat the s of thine enemies......... Deut 20:14
only the s thereof, and the cattle,....... Josh 8:2
the s of that city Israel took............ Josh 8:27
all the s of these cities, and the,........ Josh 11:14
divide the s of your enemies with...... Josh 22:8
the necks of them that take the s...... Judg 5:30
men of them, and took their s........... Judg 14:19
the s of their enemies which they 1Sa 14:30
And the people flew upon the s........ 1Sa 14:32
s them until the morning light,........... 1Sa 14:36
LORD, but didst fly upon the s.......... 1Sa 15:19
But the people took of the s.............. 1Sa 15:21
because of all the great s that........... 1Sa 30:16
sons nor daughters, neither s............. 1Sa 30:19
and said, This is David's 1Sa 30:20
of the s that we have recovered......... 1Sa 30:22
he sent of the s unto the elders......... 1Sa 30:26
the s of the enemies of the LORD.......... 1Sa 30:26
and brought in a great s with them...... 2Sa 3:22
of the s of Hadadezer, son of............. 2Sa 8:12
he brought forth the s of the............. 2Sa 12:30
returned after him only to s.............. 2Sa 23:10
now therefore, Moab, to the s........... 2Kin 3:23
prey and a s to all their enemies....... 2Kin 21:14
exceeding much s out of the city....... 1Chr 20:2
and they carried away very much s 2Chr 14:13
was exceeding much s in them.......... 2Chr 14:14
of the s which they had brought,....... 2Chr 15:11
came to take away the s of them....... 2Chr 20:25
three days in gathering of the s......... 2Chr 20:25
sent all the s of them unto the....... 2Chr 24:23
thousand of them, and took much s 2Chr 25:13
took also away much s from them...... 2Chr 28:8
and brought the s to Samaria............ 2Chr 28:8
the s before the princes and all....... 2Chr 28:14
with the s clothed all that were....... 2Chr 28:15
sword, to captivity, and to a s......... Ezr 9:7
to take the s of them for a prey,........ Est 3:13
to take the s of them for a prey,........ Est 8:11
but on the s laid they not their......... Est 9:10
plucked the s out of his teeth........... Job 29:17
which hate us s for themselves......... Ps 44:10
tarried at home divided the s........... Ps 68:12
All that pass by the way s him.......... Ps 89:41
and let the strangers s his labour...... Ps 109:11
word, as one that findeth great s....... Ps 119:162
we shall fill our houses with s.......... Prov 1:13
to divide the s with the proud......... Prov 16:19
s the soul of those that spoiled......... Prov 22:23
s not his resting place..................... Prov 24:15
that he shall have no need of s......... Prov 31:11
little foxes, that s the vines............ Song 2:15
for the s of the poor is in your......... Is 3:14
the s of Samaria shall be taken........ Is 8:4
rejoice when they divide the s.......... Is 9:3
give him a charge, to take the s....... Is 10:6
they shall s them of the east.......... Is 11:14
is the portion of them that s us........ Is 17:14
when thou shalt cease to s............... Is 33:1
your s shall be gathered like the....... Is 33:4
is the prey of a great s divided........ Is 33:23
for a s, and none saith, Restore....... Is 42:22
Who gave Jacob for a s, and Israel..... Is 42:24
divide the s with the strong............ Is 53:12
wolf of the evenings shall s them...... Jer 5:6
violence and s is heard in her.......... Jer 6:7
I give to the s without price........... Jer 15:13
and all thy treasures to the s.......... Jer 17:3
their enemies, which shall s them...... Jer 20:5
cried out, I cried violence and s....... Jer 20:8
they that s thee shall be a............. Jer 30:16
thee shall be a s.......................... Jer 30:16
cometh to s all the Philistines......... Jer 47:4
the LORD will s the Philistines......... Jer 47:4
Kedar, and s the men of the east....... Jer 49:28
the multitude of their cattle a s........ Jer 49:32
And Chaldea shall be a s................ Jer 50:10
all that s her shall be satisfied........ Jer 50:10
the wicked of the earth for a s....... Eze 7:21
through the land, and they s it........ Eze 14:15
thee for a s to the heathen.............. Eze 25:7
shall become a s to the nations......... Eze 26:5
they shall make s of thy riches......... Eze 26:12
take her multitude, and take her s ...... Eze 29:19
they shall s the pomp of Egypt,....... Eze 32:12
To take a s, and to take a prey......... Eze 38:13
thee, Art thou come to take a s........ Eze 38:13
and goods, to take a great s.......... Eze 38:13

they shall s those that spoiled......... Eze 39:10
remove violence and s, and execute..... Eze 45:9
scatter among them the prey, and s..... Dan 11:24
by flame, by captivity, and by s........ Dan 11:33
altars, he shall s their images......... Hos 10:2
he shall s the treasure of all.......... Hos 13:15
Take ye the s of silver, take the....... Nah 2:9
of silver, take the s of gold........... Nah 2:9
of the people shall s thee.............. Hab 2:8
the s of beasts, which made them...... Hab 2:17
residue of my people shall s them...... Zeph 2:9
they shall be a s to their.............. Zec 2:9
thy s shall be divided in the.......... Zec 14:1
s his goods, except he first bind........ Mt 12:29
and then he will s his house.......... Mt 12:29
s his goods, except he will first....... Mk 3:27
and then he will s his house.......... Mk 3:27
Beware lest any man s you through...... Col 2:8

SPOILED
s the city, because they had.......... Gen 34:27
s even all that was in the house........ Gen 34:29
And they s the Egyptians............... Ex 12:36
s evermore, and no man shall save..... Deut 28:29
the hands of spoilers that s them...... Judg 2:14
of the hand of those that s them....... Judg 2:16
the hands of them that s them......... 1Sa 14:48
and they s their tents................... 1Sa 17:53
s the tents of the Syrians.............. 2Kin 7:16
and they s all the cities................ 2Chr 14:14
He leadeth counsellors away s........... Job 12:17
He leadeth princes away s.............. Job 12:19
The stouthearted are s, they have..... Ps 76:5
the soul of those that s them.......... Prov 22:23
their houses shall be a s, and their.... Is 13:16
whose land the rivers have s............ Is 18:2
whose land the rivers have s............ Is 18:7
be utterly emptied, and utterly s....... Is 24:3
that spoilest, and thou wast not s...... Is 33:1
cease to spoil, thou shalt be s.......... Is 33:1
But this is a people robbed and s....... Is 42:22
why is he s............................. Jer 2:14
for we are s........................... Jer 4:13
for the whole land is s................. Jer 4:20
suddenly are my tents s, and my....... Jer 4:20
And when thou art s, what wilt........ Jer 4:30
heard out of Zion, How are we s........ Jer 9:19
My tabernacle is s, and all my......... Jer 10:20
deliver him that is s out of the........ Jer 21:12
deliver thee s out of the hand of....... Jer 22:3
for the LORD hath s their pasture...... Jer 25:36
for it is s............................. Jer 48:1
Moab is s, and gone up out of her..... Jer 48:15
ye it in Arnon, that Moab is s.......... Jer 48:20
Howl, O Heshbon, for Ai is s........... Jer 49:3
his seed is s, and his brethren,........ Jer 49:10
Because the LORD hath s Babylon....... Jer 51:55
hath s none by violence, hath......... Eze 18:7
hath s by violence, hath................ Eze 18:12
neither hath s by violence............. Eze 18:16
s his brother by violence, and did..... Eze 18:18
will give them to be removed and s..... Eze 23:46
shall spoil those that s them.......... Eze 39:10
and all thy fortresses shall be s....... Hos 10:14
as Shalman s Beth-arbel in the......... Hos 10:14
thee, and thy palaces shall be s........ Amos 3:11
the s against the strong, so that....... Amos 5:9
so that the s shall come against....... Amos 5:9
and say, We be utterly s............... Mic 2:4
Because thou hast s many nations...... Hab 2:8
me unto the nations which s you....... Zec 2:8
because the mighty are s............... Zec 11:2
for their glory is s.................... Zec 11:3
for the pride of Jordan is s............ Zec 11:3
having s principalities and powers...... Col 2:15

SPOILER
to them from the face of the s........ Is 16:4
the s ceaseth, the oppressors are..... Is 16:4
treacherously, and the s spoileth....... Is 21:2
for the s shall suddenly come......... Is 6:26
of the young men a s and bringing...... Jer 15:8
the s shall come upon every city,...... Jer 48:8
for the s of Moab shall come upon..... Jer 48:18
the s is fallen upon thy summer....... Jer 48:32
Because the s is come upon her,....... Jer 51:53

SPOILERS
the hands of s that spoiled them...... Judg 2:14
the s came out of the camp of the..... 1Sa 13:17
the garrison, and the s, they also..... 1Sa 14:15
delivered them into the hand of s..... 2Kin 17:20
The s are come upon all high......... Jer 12:12
for the s shall come unto her......... Jer 51:48
yet from me shall s come unto her..... Jer 51:53

SPOILEST
Woe to thee that s, and thou wast..... Is 33:1

SPOILETH
and the needy from him that s him..... Ps 35:10
treacherously, and the spoiler s........ Is 21:2
and the troop of robbers s without..... Hos 7:1
the cankerworm s, and fleeth away..... Nah 3:16

SPOILING
evil for good to the s of my soul....... Ps 35:12
because of the s of the daughter....... Is 22:4
crying shall be from Horonaim, s....... Jer 48:3
for s and violence are before me....... Hab 1:3
took joyfully the s of your goods...... Heb 10:34

SPOILS
When I saw among the s a goodly...... Josh 7:21
Out of the s won in battles did........ 1Chr 26:27
with the s of their hands................ Is 25:11
he trusted, and divideth his s.......... Lk 11:22
Abraham gave the tenth of the s........ Heb 7:4

SPOKEN
as the LORD had s unto him............ Gen 12:4
that which he hath s of him........... Gen 18:19
city, for the which thou hast s........ Gen 19:21
LORD did unto Sarah as he had s....... Gen 21:1
time of which God had s to him....... Gen 21:2
son's wife, as the LORD hath s......... Gen 24:51
that which I have s to thee of........ Gen 28:15
thing which I have s unto Pharaoh..... Gen 41:28
to the word that Joseph had s......... Gen 44:2
thou hast s unto thy servant.......... Ex 4:10
which the LORD had s unto Moses...... Ex 4:30
as the LORD had s to Moses........... Ex 9:12
as the LORD had s by Moses........... Ex 9:35
And Moses said, Thou hast s well...... Ex 10:29
that the LORD hath s we will do....... Ex 19:8
all this land that I have s of.......... Ex 32:13
place of which I have s unto thee..... Ex 32:34
this thing also that thou hast s........ Ex 33:17
all that the LORD hath s with him..... Ex 34:32
statutes which the LORD hath s......... Lev 10:11
For the LORD had s unto Moses........ Num 1:48
for the LORD hath s good.............. Num 10:29
the LORD indeed s only by Moses...... Num 12:2
hath he not s also by us............... Num 12:2
great, according as thou hast s........ Num 14:17
as ye have s in mine ears, so......... Num 14:28
which the LORD hath s unto Moses..... Num 15:22
for we have s against the LORD,....... Num 21:7
And Balak did as Balaam had s........ Num 23:2
unto him, What hath the LORD s....... Num 23:17
thou hast s is good for us to do....... Deut 1:14
which they have s unto thee.......... Deut 5:28
well said all that they have s......... Deut 5:28
before thee, as the LORD hath s....... Deut 6:19
because he hath s to turn you......... Deut 13:5
They have well s that which they...... Deut 18:17
that which they have s................. Deut 18:17
word which the LORD hath not s....... Deut 18:21
thing which the LORD hath not s,...... Deut 18:22
prophet hath s it presumptuously...... Deut 18:22
the LORD thy God, as he hath s....... Deut 26:19
when Joshua had s unto the people..... Josh 8:35
had s unto the house of Israel......... Josh 21:45
for that thou hast s friendly.......... Ruth 2:13
and grief have I s hitherto............. 1Sa 1:16
I have s concerning thine house........ 1Sa 3:12
matter which thou and I have s of..... 1Sa 20:23
that he hath s concerning thee........ 1Sa 25:30
God liveth, unless thou hadst s........ 2Sa 2:27
for the LORD hath s of David.......... 2Sa 3:18
maidservants which thou hast s of..... 2Sa 6:22
but thou hast s also of thy............ 2Sa 7:19
hast s concerning thy servant......... 2Sa 7:25
for thou, O Lord GOD, hast s it........ 2Sa 7:29
that my lord the king hath s........... 2Sa 14:19
Ahithophel hath s after this........... 2Sa 17:6
if Adonijah have not s this word....... 1Kin 2:23
this people, who have s to me......... 1Kin 12:9
is the sign which the LORD hath s..... 1Kin 13:3
which he had s unto the king......... 1Kin 13:11
for the LORD hath s it................. 1Kin 14:11
answered and said, It is well s......... 1Kin 18:24
the Jezreelite had s to him............ 1Kin 21:6
the LORD hath s evil concerning...... 1Kin 22:23
peace, for the LORD hath not s by me... 1Kin 22:28
of the LORD which Elijah had s........ 2Kin 1:17
thou be s for to the king............. 2Kin 4:13
the man of God had s to the king..... 2Kin 7:18
the LORD hath s concerning him....... 2Kin 19:21
will do the thing that he hath s....... 2Kin 20:9
of the LORD which thou hast s........ 2Kin 20:19
for thou hast also s of thy............ 1Chr 17:17
hast s concerning thy servant......... 1Chr 17:23
the wine, which my lord hath s of..... 2Chr 2:15
performed his word that he hath s..... 2Chr 6:10
which thou hast s unto thy........... 2Chr 6:17
this people, which have s to me....... 2Chr 10:9
the LORD hath s evil against thee..... 2Chr 18:22
then hath not the LORD s by me....... 2Chr 18:27
that the word of the LORD s by....... 2Chr 36:22
because we had s unto the king....... Ezr 8:22
words that he had s unto me.......... Neh 2:18
fail of all that thou hast s............ Est 6:10
who had s good for the king.......... Est 7:9
and after that I have s, mock on...... Job 21:3
Elihu had waited till Job had s........ Job 32:4
my tongue hath s in my mouth........ Job 33:2
thou hast s in mine hearing........... Job 33:8
Job hath s without knowledge, and.... Job 34:35
Once have I s.......................... Job 40:5
LORD had s these words unto Job...... Job 42:7
for ye have not s of me the thing..... Job 42:7
in that ye have not s of me the........ Job 42:8
mighty God, even the LORD, hath s..... Ps 50:1
for he hath s in his holiness.......... Ps 60:6
God hath s once....................... Ps 62:11
have uttered, and my mouth hath s..... Ps 66:14
Glorious things are s of thee........... Ps 87:3
God hath s in his holiness............ Ps 108:7
they have s against me with a........ Ps 109:2
I believed, therefore have I s......... Ps 116:10
a word s in due season, how good..... Prov 15:23
A word fitly is s like apples of....... Prov 25:11

no heed unto all words that are .... Eccl 7:21
the day when she shall be s for......... Song 8:3
for the LORD hath s, I have .... Is 1:2
the mouth of the LORD hath s .... Is 16:13
is the word that the LORD hath s....... Is 16:14
But now the LORD hath s, saying,....... Is 16:14
the LORD God of Israel hath s it .... Is 21:17
for the LORD hath s it .... Is 22:25
for the sea hath s, even the .... Is 23:4
for the LORD hath s this word .... Is 24:3
for the LORD hath s it .... Is 25:8
For thus hath the LORD s unto me..... Is 31:4
the LORD hath s concerning him .... Is 37:22
will do this thing that he hath .... Is 38:7
He hath both s unto me, and............. Is 38:15
of the LORD which thou hast s.......... Is 39:8
the mouth of the LORD hath s it .... Is 40:5
I have not s in secret, in a dark........ Is 45:19
yea, I have s it, I will also................ Is 46:11
I, even I, have s .... Is 48:15
I have not s in secret from the .... Is 48:16
the mouth of the LORD hath s it .... Is 58:14
your lips have s lies, your................. Is 59:3
Behold, thou hast s and done evil .... Jer 3:5
because I have s it, I have .... Jer 4:28
whom the mouth of the LORD hath s .. Jer 9:12
for the LORD hath s................................ Jer 13:15
because I have s it, then they .... Jer 23:21
and, What hath the LORD s .... Jer 23:35
and, What hath the LORD s .... Jer 23:37
I have s unto you, rising early........... Jer 25:3
for he hath s to us in the name........ Jer 26:16
as the LORD hath s against the .... Jer 27:13
have s lying words in my name,........ Jer 29:23
that I have s unto thee in a book ..... Jer 30:2
what thou hast s is come to pass..... Jer 32:24
thou not what this people have s ..... Jer 33:24
notwithstanding I have s unto you... Jer 35:14
because I have s unto them.............. Jer 35:17
I have s unto thee against Israel...... Jer 36:2
the LORD, which he had s unto him.... Jer 36:4
had s unto all the people .... Jer 38:1
As for the word that thou hast s ...... Jer 44:16
have both s with your mouths........... Jer 44:25
be destroyed, as the LORD hath s..... Jer 48:8
thou hast s against this place,......... Jer 51:62
I the LORD have s it in my zeal .... Eze 5:13
I the LORD have s it .... Eze 5:15
I the LORD have s it .... Eze 5:17
word which I have s shall be done ... Eze 12:28
have ye not s a lying divination,...... Eze 13:7
albeit I have not s .... Eze 13:7
Because ye have s vanity, and seen.. Eze 13:8
deceived when he hath s a thing...... Eze 14:9
know that I the LORD have s it .... Eze 17:21
I the LORD have s and have done it .. Eze 17:24
for I the LORD have s it .... Eze 21:32
I the LORD have s it, and so.............. Eze 22:14
GOD, when the LORD hath not s......... Eze 22:28
for I have s it, saith the LORD .... Eze 23:34
I the LORD have s it .... Eze 24:14
for I have s it, saith the Lord............ Eze 26:5
for I the LORD have s it, saith .... Eze 26:14
for I have s it, saith the LORD .... Eze 28:10
I the LORD have s it .... Eze 30:12
for I the LORD have s it .... Eze 34:24
s against the mountains of Israel .... Eze 35:12
I s against the residue of the .... Eze 36:5
I have s in my jealousy and in my .... Eze 36:6
I the LORD have s it, and I will........... Eze 36:36
ye know that I the LORD have s it ..... Eze 37:14
Art thou he of whom I have s in ...... Eze 38:17
in the fire of my wrath have I s .... Eze 38:19
for I have s it, saith the LORD .... Eze 39:5
this is the day whereof I have s .... Eze 39:8
Nebuchadnezzar, to thee it is s .... Dan 4:31
when he had s this word unto me,.... Dan 10:11
when he had s such words unto me,.. Dan 10:15
yet they have s lies against me........ Hos 7:13
They have s words, swearing............. Hos 10:4
I have also s by the prophets, and.... Hos 12:10
for the LORD hath s .... Joel 3:8
that the LORD hath s against you..... Amos 3:1
the LORD God hath s, who can but ... Amos 3:8
shall be with you, as ye have s .... Amos 5:14
neither shouldest thou have s .... Obad 12
for the LORD hath s .... Obad 18
of the LORD of hosts hath s it .... Mic 4:4
inhabitants thereof have s lies .... Mic 6:12
For the idols have s vanity .... Zec 10:2
What have we s so much against...... Mal 3:13
was s of the Lord by the prophet ..... Mt 1:22
was s of the Lord by the prophet ..... Mt 2:15
which was s by Jeremy the prophet .. Mt 2:17
which was s by the prophets............. Mt 2:23
For this is he that was s of by.......... Mt 3:3
which was s by Esaias the prophet .. Mt 4:14
which was s by Esaias the prophet .. Mt 8:17
which was s by the prophet.............. Mt 13:35
which was s by the prophet.............. Mt 21:4
that which was s unto you by God.... Mt 22:31
s of by Daniel the prophet, stand .... Mt 24:15
saying, He hath s blasphemy .... Mt 26:65
which was s by Jeremy the prophet .. Mt 27:9
which was s by the prophet.............. Mt 27:35
And as soon as he had s,.................. Mk 1:42
Jesus heard the word that was s ...... Mk 5:36
he had s the parable against them... Mk 12:12

s of by Daniel the prophet,............... Mk 13:14
be s of for a memorial of them........ Mk 14:9
after the Lord had s unto them........ Mk 16:19
those things which were s of him..... Lk 2:33
a sign which shall be s against......... Lk 2:34
Therefore whatsoever ye have s in.... Lk 12:3
that which ye have s in the ear........ Lk 12:3
knew they the things which were s ... Lk 18:34
And when he had thus s, he went ..... Lk 19:28
had s this parable against them,...... Lk 20:19
all that the prophets have s .... Lk 24:25
And when he had thus s, he shewed.. Lk 24:40
word that Jesus had s unto him....... Jn 4:50
When he had thus s, he spat on....... Jn 9:6
had s of taking of rest in sleep........ Jn 11:13
And when he thus had s, he cried..... Jn 11:43
the word that I have s, the same...... Jn 12:48
For I have not s of myself.................. Jn 12:49
These things have I s unto you......... Jn 14:25
the word which I have s unto you..... Jn 15:3
These things have I s unto you......... Jn 15:11
s unto them, they had not had sin ... Jn 15:22
These things have I s unto you......... Jn 16:1
These things I have s unto you .... Jn 16:25
These things I have s unto you .... Jn 16:33
When Jesus had s these words.......... Jn 18:1
And when he had thus s, one of the.. Jn 18:22
answered him, If I have s evil........... Jn 18:23
that he had s these things unto ...... Jn 20:18
And when he had s this, he saith ..... Jn 21:19
when he had s these things, while ... Acts 1:9
which was s by the prophet Joel....... Acts 2:16
which God hath s by the mouth of.... Acts 3:21
follow after, as many as have s .... Acts 3:24
which ye have s come upon me......... Acts 8:24
the way, and that he had s to him ... Acts 9:27
which is s of in the prophetes.......... Acts 13:40
those things which were s by Paul.... Acts 13:45
should first have been s to you........ Acts 13:46
the things which were s of Paul .... Acts 16:14
these things cannot be s against..... Acts 19:36
And when he had thus s, he .... Acts 19:41
And when he had thus s, he kneeled.. Acts 20:36
spirit or an angel hath s to him .... Acts 23:9
And when he had thus s, the king..... Acts 26:30
those things which were s by Paul.... Acts 27:11
And when he had thus s, he took...... Acts 27:35
that every where it is s against....... Acts 28:22
believed the things which were s ..... Acts 28:24
after that Paul had s one word......... Acts 28:25
you all, that your faith is s of .... Rom 1:8
according to that which was s .... Rom 4:18
not then your good be evil s of........ Rom 14:16
written, To whom he was not s of.... Rom 15:21
why am I evil s of for that 1Cor 10:30
how shall it be known what is s 1Cor 14:9
I believed, and therefore have I s 2Cor 4:13
last days s unto us by his Son......... Heb 1:2
For if the word s by angels was....... Heb 2:2
first began to be s by the Lord .... Heb 2:3
things which were to be s after .... Heb 3:5
afterward have s of another day...... Heb 4:8
are s pertaineth to another tribe....... Heb 7:13
which we have s this is the sum....... Heb 8:1
For when Moses had s every............ Heb 9:19
should not be s to them any more ... Heb 12:19
who have s unto you the word of...... Heb 13:7
who have s in the name of the......... Jas 5:10
on their part he is evil s of 1Pet 4:14
way of truth shall be evil s of 2Pet 2:2
s before by the holy prophets 2Pet 3:2
sinners have s against him .... Jude 15
ye the words which were s before..... Jude 17

SPOKES
and their felloes, and their s 1Kin 7:33

SPOKESMAN
he shall be thy s unto the people .... Ex 4:16

SPOON
One s of ten shekels of gold,............ Num 7:14
One s of gold of ten shekels,............ Num 7:20
One golden s of ten shekels, full...... Num 7:26
One golden s of ten shekels, full...... Num 7:32
One golden s of ten shekels, full...... Num 7:38
One golden s of ten shekels, full...... Num 7:44
One golden s of ten shekels, full...... Num 7:50
One golden s of ten shekels, full...... Num 7:56
One golden s of ten shekels, full...... Num 7:62
One golden s of ten shekels, full...... Num 7:68
One golden s of ten shekels, full...... Num 7:74
One golden s of ten shekels, full...... Num 7:80

SPOONS
s thereof, and covers thereof, and... Ex 25:29
the table, his dishes, and his .... Ex 37:16
put thereon the dishes, and the ...... Num 4:7
silver bowls, twelve s of gold........... Num 7:84
The golden s were twelve, full of..... Num 7:86
the gold of the s was an hundred.... Num 7:86
snuffers, and the basons, and the ... 1Kin 7:50
and the snuffers, and the s............... 2Kin 25:14
snuffers, and the basons, and the s.. 2Chr 4:22
and to offer withal, and s 2Chr 24:14
snuffers, and the bowls, and the ..... Jer 52:18
and the candlesticks, and the s........ Jer 52:19

SPORT
for Samson, that he may make us s .. Judg 16:25
and he made them s upon .... Judg 16:25
that beheld while Samson made s .... Judg 16:27
It is as to a fool to do .... Prov 10:23

and saith, Am not I in s .... Prov 26:19
Against whom do ye s yourselves ..... Is 57:4

SPORTING
Isaac was s with Rebekah his wife ... Gen 26:8
s themselves with their own 2Pet 2:13

SPOT
a rising, a scab, or bright s.............. Lev 13:2
If the bright s be white in the .... Lev 13:4
be a white rising, or a bright s .... Lev 13:19
if the bright s stay in his place........ Lev 13:23
burneth have a white bright s.......... Lev 13:24
in the bright s be turned white........ Lev 13:25
be no white hair in the bright s....... Lev 13:26
if the bright s stay in his place........ Lev 13:28
it is a freckled s that groweth......... Lev 13:39
and for a scab, and for a bright s.... Lev 14:56
bring thee a red heifer without s..... Num 19:2
first year without s day by day........ Num 28:3
lambs of the first year without s ..... Num 28:9
lambs of the first year without s ..... Num 28:11
lambs of the first year without s ..... Num 29:17
lambs of the first year without s ..... Num 29:26
their s is not the s of his................. Deut 32:5
is not the s of his children .... Deut 32:5
thou lift up thy face without s .... Job 11:15
there is no s in thee .... Song 4:7
a glorious church, not having s........ Eph 5:27
keep this commandment without s ... 1Ti 6:14
offered himself without s to God...... Heb 9:14
lamb without blemish and without s.. 1Pet 1:19
found of him in peace, without s 2Pet 3:14

SPOTS
bright s, even white bright s .... Lev 13:38
if the bright s in the skin of............ Lev 13:39
his skin, or the leopard his s .... Jer 13:23
S they are and blemishes, sporting .. 2Pet 2:13
These are s in your feasts of............ Jude 12

SPOTTED
s cattle, and all the brown cattle.... Gen 30:32
cattle among the sheep, and the s ... Gen 30:32
s among the goats............................ Gen 30:33
goats that were ringstraked and s ... Gen 30:35
she goats that were speckled and s.. Gen 30:35
ringstraked, speckled, and s .... Gen 30:39
even the garment s by the flesh....... Jude 23

SPOUSE
Come with me from Lebanon, my s ... Song 4:8
my heart, my sister, my s .... Song 4:9
fair is thy love, my sister, my s........ Song 4:10
Thy lips, O my s, drop as the........... Song 4:11
inclosed is my sister, my s .... Song 4:12
into my garden, my sister, my s ...... Song 5:1

SPOUSES
your s shall commit adultery............ Hos 4:13
nor your s when they commit .... Hos 4:14

SPRANG
and immediately it s up, because..... Mk 4:5
and did yield fruit that s up............. Mk 4:8
and the thorns s up with it .... Lk 8:7
ground, and s up, and bare fruit an.. Lk 8:8
s in, and came trembling, and fell.... Acts 16:29
that our Lord s out of Juda.............. Heb 7:14
Therefore s there even of one, and .. Heb 11:12

SPREAD
of the Canaanites s abroad .... Gen 10:18
thou shalt s abroad to the west,...... Gen 28:14
a field, where he had s his tent .... Gen 33:19
s his tent beyond the tower of......... Gen 35:21
I will s abroad my hands unto the... Ex 9:29
s abroad his hands unto the LORD ... Ex 9:33
the cherubims s out their wings....... Ex 37:9
he s abroad the tent over the.......... Ex 40:19
the plague s not in the skin............ Lev 13:5
the plague s not in the skin, the..... Lev 13:6
But if the scab s much abroad in .... Lev 13:7
if it s much abroad in the skin,....... Lev 13:8
s not, it is a burning boil................. Lev 13:23
if it be s much abroad in the........... Lev 13:27
s not in the skin, but it be .... Lev 13:28
and, behold, if the scall s not .... Lev 13:32
if the scall be not s in the skin .... Lev 13:34
But if the scall s much in the.......... Lev 13:35
if the scall be s in the skin,............. Lev 13:36
if the plague be s in the garment .... Lev 13:51
plague be not s in the garment .... Lev 13:53
colour, and the plague be not s .... Lev 13:55
if the plague be s in the walls .... Lev 14:39
if the plague be s in the house......... Lev 14:44
plague hath not s in the house .... Lev 14:48
shall s over it a cloth wholly of....... Num 4:6
they shall s a cloth of blue .... Num 4:7
they shall s upon them a cloth of.... Num 4:8
they shall s a cloth of blue .... Num 4:11
and s a purple cloth thereon............ Num 4:13
they shall s upon it a covering .... Num 4:14
they s them all abroad for .... Num 11:32
As the valleys are they s forth......... Num 24:6
they shall s the cloth before the...... Deut 22:17
they s a garment, and did cast........ Judg 8:25
in Judah, and s themselves in Lehi .. Judg 15:9
s therefore thy skirt over thine........ Ruth 3:9
they were s abroad upon all the 1Sa 30:16
s themselves in the valley of 2Sa 5:18
s themselves in the valley of 2Sa 5:22
So they s Absalom a tent upon the.. 2Sa 16:22
s a covering over the well's 2Sa 17:19

S

mouth, and s ground corn thereon 2Sa 17:19
s it for her upon the rock, from 2Sa 21:10
the street, and did s them abroad 2Sa 22:43
s gold upon the cherubims, and 1Kin 6:32
For the cherubims s forth their 1Kin 8:7
s forth his hands toward heaven 1Kin 8:22
s forth his hands toward this 1Kin 8:38
with his hands s up to heaven 1Kin 8:54
s it on his face, so that he died 2Kin 8:15
the LORD, and s it before the LORD 2Kin 19:14
s themselves in the valley of 1Chr 14:9
the Philistines yet again s 1Chr 14:13
that s out their wings, and 1Chr 28:18
The wings of these cherubims s 2Chr 5:8
For the cherubims s forth their 2Chr 5:8
of Israel, and s forth his hands 2Chr 6:13
s forth his hands toward heaven 2Chr 6:13
shall s forth his hands in this 2Chr 6:29
his name s abroad even to the 2Chr 26:8
And his name s far abroad 2Chr 26:15
s out my hands unto the LORD my .... Ezr 9:5
My root was s out by the waters .... Job 29:19
Hast thou with him s out the sky .... Job 37:18
He s a cloud for a covering .... Ps 105:39
they have s a net by the wayside .... Ps 140:5
net is s in the sight of any bird .... Prov 1:17
when ye s forth your hands, I .... Is 1:15
the worm is s under thee, and the .... Is 14:11
they that s nets upon the waters .... Is 19:8
vail that is s over all nations .... Is 25:7
he shall s forth his hands in the .... Is 25:11
mast, they could not s the sail .... Is 33:23
the LORD, and s it before the LORD ..... Is 37:14
he that s forth the earth, and .... Is 42:5
to s sackcloth and ashes under him ..... Is 58:5
I have s out my hands all the day .... Is 65:2
they shall s them before the sun, ... Jer 8:2
Silver s into plates is brought .... Jer 10:9
he shall s his royal pavilion .... Jer 43:10
shall s his wings over Moab .... Jer 48:40
eagle, and s his wings over Bozrah ..... Jer 49:22
The adversary hath s out his hand ...... Lam 1:10
he hath s a net for my feet, he .... Lam 1:13
And he s it before me .... Eze 2:10
My net also will I s upon him .... Eze 12:13
I s my skirt over thee, and .... Eze 16:8
I will s my net upon him, and he ...... Eze 17:20
and s their net over him .... Eze 19:8
shalt be a place to s nets upon .... Eze 26:14
I will therefore s out my net .... Eze 32:3
shall be a place to s forth nets .... Eze 47:10
on Mizpah, and a net s upon Tabor .... Hos 5:1
I will s my net upon them .... Hos 7:12
His branches shall s, and his .... Hos 14:6
as the morning s upon the .... Joel 2:2
their horsemen shall s themselves ...... Hab 1:8
prosperity shall yet be s abroad .... Zec 1:17
for I have s you abroad as the .... Zec 2:6
s dung upon your faces, even the .... Mal 2:3
s abroad his fame in all that .... Mt 9:31
a very great multitude s their .... Mt 21:8
immediately his fame s abroad .... Mk 1:28
(for his name was s abroad .... Mk 6:14
many s their garments in the way ...... Mk 11:8
they s their clothes in the way .... Lk 19:36
But that it s no further among .... Acts 4:17
faith to God-ward is s abroad 1Th 1:8

SPREADEST
which thou s forth to be thy sail .... Eze 27:7

SPREADETH
the scab s in the skin, then the .... Lev 13:8
s abroad her wings, taketh them, ... Deut 32:11
Which alone s out the heavens, and .... Job 9:8
throne, and s his cloud upon it .... Job 26:9
he s his light upon it, and .... Job 36:30
he s sharp pointed things upon .... Job 41:30
neighbour s a net for his feet .... Prov 29:5
as he that swimmeth s forth his .... Is 25:11
the goldsmith s it over with gold .... Is 40:19
s them out as a tent to dwell in, ... Is 40:22
that s abroad the earth by myself ...... Is 44:24
that s her hands, saying, Woe is .... Jer 4:31
that s out her roots by the river .... Jer 17:8
Zion s forth her hands, and there ...... Lam 1:17

SPREADING
it is a s plague .... Lev 13:57
s himself like a green bay tree .... Ps 37:35
became a s vine of low stature, ... Eze 17:6
It shall be a place for the s of .... Eze 26:5

SPREADINGS
understand the s of the clouds .... Job 36:29

SPRIGS
cut off the s with pruninghooks .... Is 18:5
forth branches, and shot forth s .... Eze 17:6

SPRING
sang this song, S up, O well .... Num 21:17
depths that s out of valleys and .... Deut 8:7
and when the day began to s .... Judg 19:25
to pass about the s of the day 1Sa 9:26
forth unto the s of the waters 2Kin 2:21
doth trouble s out of the ground .... Job 5:6
bud of the tender herb to s forth ...... Job 38:27
Truth shall s out of the earth .... Ps 85:11
When the wicked s as the grass .... Ps 92:7
troubled fountain, and a corrupt s .... Prov 25:26
a s shut up, a fountain sealed .... Song 4:12
before they s forth I tell you of .... Is 42:9

now it shall s forth .... Is 43:19
they shall s up as among the .... Is 44:4
let righteousness s up together .... Is 45:8
health shall s forth speedily .... Is 58:8
like a s of water, whose waters .... Is 58:11
that are sown in it to s forth .... Is 61:11
praise to s forth before all the .... Is 61:11
wither in all the leaves of her s .... Eze 17:9
his s shall become dry, and his .... Hos 13:15
pastures of the wilderness do s .... Joel 2:22
and day, and the seed should s .... Mk 4:27

SPRINGETH
the hyssop that s out of the wall 1Kin 4:33
year that which s of the same 2Kin 19:29
year that which s of the same .... Is 37:30
thus judgment s up as hemlock in .... Hos 10:4

SPRINGING
and found there a well of s water ...... Gen 26:19
as the tender grass s out of the 2Sa 23:4
thou blessest the s thereof .... Ps 65:10
water s up into everlasting life .... Jn 4:14
of bitterness s up trouble you .... Heb 12:15

SPRINGS
the plain, under the s of Pisgah .... Deut 4:49
and of the vale, and of the s .... Josh 10:40
and in the plains, and in the s .... Josh 12:8
give me also s of water .... Josh 15:19
upper s, and the nether s .... Josh 15:19
give me also s of water .... Judg 1:15
the upper s and the nether s .... Judg 1:15
entered into the s of the sea .... Job 38:16
all my s are in thee .... Ps 87:7
He sendeth the s into the valleys .... Ps 104:10
and the thirsty land s of water .... Is 35:7
water, and the dry land s of water ..... Is 41:18
even by the s of water shall he .... Is 49:10
dry up her sea, and make her s dry ... Jer 51:36

SPRINKLE
let Moses s it toward the heaven .... Ex 9:8
s it round about upon the altar .... Ex 29:16
s the blood upon the altar round .... Ex 29:20
s it upon Aaron, and upon his .... Ex 29:21
s the blood round about upon the ...... Lev 1:5
shall s his blood round about upon .... Lev 1:11
s the blood upon the altar round .... Lev 3:2
Aaron's sons shall s the blood .... Lev 3:8
the sons of Aaron shall s the .... Lev 3:13
s of the blood seven times before ..... Lev 4:6
s it seven times before the LORD, ... Lev 4:17
he shall s of the blood of the .... Lev 5:9
he s round about upon the altar .... Lev 7:2
he shall s upon him that is to be ..... Lev 14:7
shall s of the oil with his .... Lev 14:16
the priest shall s with his right .... Lev 14:27
water, and s the house seven times ... Lev 14:51
s it with his finger upon the .... Lev 16:14
he s of the blood with his finger ..... Lev 16:14
s it upon the mercy seat, and .... Lev 16:15
he shall s of the blood upon it .... Lev 16:19
the priest shall s the blood seven .... Num 8:7
s water of purifying upon them, ... Num 8:7
thou shalt s their blood upon the, ... Num 18:17
of her blood directly before .... Num 19:4
s it upon the tent, and upon all ...... Num 19:18
the clean person shall s upon the .... Num 19:19
s upon it all the blood of the 2Kin 16:15
So shall he s many nations .... Is 52:15
Then will I s clean water upon .... Eze 36:25
thereon, and to s blood thereon .... Eze 43:18

SPRINKLED
Moses s it up toward heaven .... Ex 9:10
of the blood he s on the altar .... Ex 24:6
and on the people, and said, ... Ex 24:8
when there is s of the blood .... Lev 6:27
it was s in the holy place .... Lev 6:27
he s thereof upon the altar seven ..... Lev 8:11
Moses s the blood upon the altar ..... Lev 8:19
Moses s the blood upon the altar ..... Lev 8:24
s it upon Aaron, and upon his .... Lev 8:30
which he s round about upon the ..... Lev 9:12
which he s upon the altar round ...... Lev 9:18
of separation was not s upon him .... Num 19:13
hath not been s upon him .... Num 19:20
of her blood was s on the 2Kin 9:33
and s the blood of his peace 2Kin 16:13
the blood, and s it on the altar 2Chr 29:22
they s the blood upon the altar 2Chr 29:22
they s the blood upon the altar 2Chr 29:22
the priests s the blood, which 2Chr 30:16
the priests s the blood from 2Chr 35:11
s dust upon their heads toward .... Job 2:12
blood shall be s upon thy garments... Is 63:3
s both the book, and all the .... Heb 9:19
Moreover he s with blood both the .. Heb 9:21
having our hearts s from an evil..... Heb 10:22

SPRINKLETH
that s the blood of the peace .... Lev 7:14
that he that s the water of .... Num 19:21

SPRINKLING
ashes of an heifer s the unclean ...... Heb 9:13
the s of blood, lest he that .... Heb 11:28
covenant, and to the blood of s ..... Heb 12:24
s of the blood of Jesus Christ: 1Pet 1:2

SPROUT
be cut down, that it will s again ..... Job 14:7

SPRUNG
the east wind s up after them .... Gen 41:6
the east wind s up after them .... Gen 41:23

it is a leprosy s up in his bald .... Lev 13:42
and shadow of death light is s up ..... Mt 4:16
and forthwith they s up, because ...... Mt 13:5
and the thorns s up, and choked ..... Mt 13:7
But when the blade was s up .... Mt 13:26
and as soon as it was s up .... Lk 8:6

SPUE
That the land s not you out also, ... Lev 18:28
to dwell therein, s you not out .... Lev 20:22
Drink ye, and be drunken, and s ..... Jer 25:27
I will s thee out of my mouth. ...... Rev 3:16

SPUED
as it s out the nations that were ...... Lev 18:28

SPUN
and brought that which they had s ... Ex 35:25
them up in wisdom s goats' hair ...... Ex 35:26

SPUNGE
one of them ran, and took a s .... Mt 27:48
filled a s full of vinegar, and, ... Mk 15:36
and they filled a s with vinegar, ... Jn 19:29

SPY
Moses sent to s out the land .... Num 13:16
Moses sent them to s out the land ... Num 13:17
And Moses sent to s out Jaazer ...... Num 21:32
of Shittim two men to s secretly ...... Josh 2:1
Joshua sent to s out Jericho .... Josh 6:25
to s out the land, and to search ...... Judg 18:2
to s out the country of Laish .... Judg 18:14
went to s out the land went up ...... Judg 18:17
to s it out, and to overthrow it 2Sa 10:3
s where he is, that I may send and ... 2Kin 6:13
overthrow, and to s out the land 1Chr 19:3
who came in privily to s our .... Gal 2:4

SQUARE
And all the doors and posts were s ... 1Kin 7:5
he four s squares thereof .... Eze 43:16
hundred in breadth, s round about ... Eze 45:2

SQUARED
The posts of the temple were s .... Eze 41:21

SQUARES
square in the four s thereof .... Eze 43:16
broad in the four s thereof .... Eze 43:17

STABILITY
shall be the s of thy times .... Is 33:6

STABLE
the world also shall be s 1Chr 16:30
I will make Rabbah a s for camels.... Eze 25:5

STABLISH
I will s the throne of his 2Sa 7:13
I will s his throne for ever 1Chr 17:12
as he went to s his dominion by 1Chr 18:3
Then will I s the throne of thy 2Chr 7:18
To s this among them, that they ..... Est 9:21
S thy word unto thy servant, who ... Ps 119:38
to s you according to my gospel, ... Rom 16:25
To the end he may s your hearts 1Th 3:13
s you in every good word and work... 2Th 2:17
Lord is faithful, who shall s you.... 2Th 3:3
s your hearts .... Jas 5:8
a while, make you perfect, s 1Pet 5:10

STABLISHED
Therefore the LORD s the kingdom 2Chr 17:5
the world also is s, that it .... Ps 93:1
He hath also s them for ever and .... Ps 148:6
s in the faith, as ye have been....... Col 2:7

STABLISHETH
blood, and s a city by iniquity .... Hab 2:12
Now he which is us with you in 2Cor 1:21

STACHYS (sta´-kis) A Christian in Rome.
helper in Christ, and S my beloved... Rom 16:9

STACKS
in thorns, so that the s of corn ...... Ex 22:6

STACTE
Take unto thee sweet spices, s .... Ex 30:34

STAFF
for with my s I passed over this ..... Gen 32:10
thy s that is in thine hand .... Gen 38:18
the signet, and bracelets, and s ..... Gen 38:25
your feet, and your s in your hand... Ex 12:11
again, and walk abroad upon his s ... Ex 21:19
I have broken the s of your bread ... Lev 26:26
they bare it between two upon a s ... Num 13:23
and he smote the ass with a s .... Num 22:27
end of the s that was in his hand ... Judg 6:21
the s of his spear was like a 1Sa 17:7
And he took his s in his hand 1Sa 17:40
a leper, or that leaneth on a s 2Sa 3:29
the s of whose spear was like a 2Sa 21:19
with iron and the s of a spear 2Sa 23:7
but he went down to him with a s ... 2Sa 23:21
take my s in thine hand, and go..... 2Kin 4:29
lay my s upon the face of the 2Kin 4:29
laid the s upon the face of the...... 2Kin 4:31
upon the s of this bruised reed 2Kin 18:21
And he went down to him with a s ... 1Chr 11:23
whose spear s was like a weaver's... 1Chr 20:5
thy rod and thy s they comfort me... Ps 23:4
he brake the whole s of bread .... Ps 105:16
and from Judah the stay and the s .. Is 3:1
the s of his shoulder, the rod of .... Is 9:4
the s in their hand is mine .... Is 10:5
or as if the s should lift up .... Is 10:15

shall lift up his s against them............ Is 10:24
hath broken the s of the wicked............ Is 14:5
fitches are beaten out with a s............ Is 28:27
where the grounded s shall pass............ Is 30:32
in the s of this broken reed.................. Is 36:6
say, How is the strong s broken .... Jer 48:17
I will break the s of bread in .... Eze 4:16
and will break your s of bread .... Eze 5:16
will break the s of the bread.................. Eze 14:13
because they have been a s of .... Eze 29:6
their s declareth unto them................... Hos 4:12
every man with his s in his hand .... Zec 8:4
And I took my s, even Beauty, and ..... Zec 11:10
Then I cut asunder mine other s......... Zec 11:14
for their journey, save a s only .... Mk 6:8
leaning upon the top of his s .... Heb 11:21

STAGGER

he maketh them to s like a.................... Job 12:25
s like a drunken man, and are at........... Ps 107:27
they s, but not with strong drink .... Is 29:9

STAGGERED

He s not at the promise of God .... Rom 4:20

STAGGERETH

as a drunken man s in his vomit............ Is 19:14

STAIN

and the shadow of death s it .... Job 3:5
to s the pride of all glory, and............... Is 23:9
and I will s all my raiment..................... Is 63:3

STAIRS

winding s into the middle chamber.... 1Kin 6:8
it under him on the top of the s 2Kin 9:13
unto the s that go down from the........ Neh 3:15
Then stood up upon the s, of the........ Neh 9:4
they went up by the s of the city......... Neh 12:37
in the secret places of the s .... Song 2:14
east, and went up the s thereof .... Eze 40:6
his s shall look toward the east............ Eze 43:17
And when he came upon the s.............. Acts 21:35
him licence, Paul stood on the s .... Acts 21:40

STAKES

not one of the s thereof shall .... Is 33:20
thy cords, and strengthen thy s .... Is 54:2

STALK

ears of corn came up upon one s .... Gen 41:5
seven ears came up in one s.................. Gen 41:22
it hath no s .... Hos 8:7

STALKS

and hid them with the s of flax .... Josh 2:6

STALL

calves out of the midst of the s .... Amos 6:4
and grow up as calves of the s.............. Mal 4:2
his ox or his ass from the s .... Lk 13:15

STALLED

herbs where love is, than a s ox........... Prov 15:17

STALLS

of horses for his chariots...................... 1Kin 4:26
had four thousand s for horses............. 2Chr 9:25
s for all manner of beasts, and............. 2Chr 32:28
there shall be no herd in the s .... Hab 3:17

STAMMERERS

the tongue of the s shall be .... Is 32:4

STAMMERING

For with s lips and another tongue..... Is 28:11
of a s tongue, that thou canst............... Is 33:19

STAMP

I did s them as the mire of the 2Sa 22:43
s with thy foot, and say, Alas for .... Eze 6:11

STAMPED

s it, and ground it very small,.............. Deut 9:21
s it small to powder, and cast the 2Kin 23:6
s it small to powder, and burned 2Kin 23:15
s it, and burnt it at the brook.............. 2Chr 15:16
s with the feet, and rejoiced in .... Eze 25:6
s the residue with the feet of it .... Dan 7:7
s the residue with his feet................... Dan 7:19
down to the ground, and s upon him.... Dan 8:7
to the ground, and s upon them........... Dan 8:10

STAMPING

At the noise of the s of the.................... Jer 47:3

STANCHED

immediately her issue of blood s .... Lk 8:44

STAND

And they said, s back .... Gen 19:9
I s here by the well of water .... Gen 24:13
Behold, I s by the well of water .... Gen 24:43
thou shalt s by the river's brink .... Ex 7:15
the morning, and s before Pharaoh .... Ex 8:20
the magicians could not s before .... Ex 9:11
s before Pharaoh, and say unto him.... Ex 9:13
s still, and see the salvation of............. Ex 14:13
I will s before thee upon........................ Ex 17:6
to-morrow I will s on the top of........... Ex 17:9
all the people s by thee from .... Ex 18:14
pillar s at the tabernacle door .... Ex 33:10
me, and thou shalt s upon a rock......... Ex 33:21
neither shall any woman s before .... Lev 18:23
neither shalt thou s against the........... Lev 19:16
no power to s before your enemies..... Lev 26:37
shall estimate it, so shall it s .... Lev 27:14
to thy estimation it shall s .... Lev 27:17
of the men that shall s with you........... Num 1:5

S still, and I will hear what he............. Num 9:8
that they may s there with thee........... Num 11:16
to s before the congregation to........... Num 16:9
S by thy burnt offering, and I.............. Num 23:3
S here by thy burnt offering,............... Num 23:15
he shall s before Eleazar the............... Num 27:21
then all her vows shall s .... Num 30:4
she hath bound her soul shall s........... Num 30:4
she hath bound her soul, shall s.......... Num 30:5
then her vows shall s, and her............. Num 30:7
the bound her soul shall s .... Num 30:7
their souls, shall s against her............ Num 30:9
then all her vows shall s .... Num 30:11
she bound her soul shall s .... Num 30:11
the bond of her soul, shall not s.......... Num 30:12
die not, until he s before the............... Num 35:12
s thou here by me, and I will................ Deut 5:31
no man be able to s before thee.......... Deut 7:24
Who can s before the children of........ Deut 9:2
to s before the LORD to minister......... Deut 10:8
no man be able to s before you........... Deut 11:25
to s to minister in the name of .... Deut 18:5
which s there before the LORD .... Deut 18:7
shall s before the LORD, before .... Deut 19:17
Thou shalt s abroad, and the man...... Deut 24:11
and if he s to it, and say, I like............ Deut 25:8
These shall s upon mount Gerizim..... Deut 27:12
these shall s upon mount Ebal to....... Deut 27:13
Ye s this day all of you before............. Deut 29:10
shalt not any man be able to s .... Josh 1:5
ye shall s still in Jordan...................... Josh 3:8
they shall s upon an heap................... Josh 3:13
could not s before their enemies........ Josh 7:12
thou canst not s before thine.............. Josh 7:13
not a man of them s before thee......... Josh 10:8
Sun, s thou still upon Gibeon............. Josh 10:12
s at the entering of the gate of .... Josh 20:4
that city, until he s before the............ Josh 20:6
to s before you unto this day............... Josh 23:9
any longer s before their enemies..... Judg 2:14
S in the door of the tent, and it........... Judg 4:20
Who is able to s before this holy........ 1Sa 6:20
but s thou still a while, that I.............. 1Sa 9:27
Now therefore s still, that I may.......... 1Sa 12:7
Now therefore s and see this great 1Sa 12:16
then we will s still in our place............ 1Sa 14:9
David, I pray thee, s before me............ 1Sa 16:22
s beside my father in the field............. 1Sa 19:3
He said unto me again, S, I pray......... 2Sa 1:9
unto him, Turn aside, and s here........ 2Sa 18:30
let her s before the king, and let........ 1Kin 1:2
not s to minister because of the......... 1Kin 8:11
which s continually before the.......... 1Kin 10:8
of Israel liveth, before whom I s 1Kin 17:1
of hosts liveth, before whom I s........ 1Kin 18:15
s upon the mount before the LORD.... 1Kin 19:11
of hosts liveth, before whom I s........ 2Kin 3:14
will surely come out to me, and s...... 2Kin 5:11
the LORD liveth, before whom I s 2Kin 5:16
Shaphat shall s on him this day......... 2Kin 6:31
how then shall we s 2Kin 10:4
of the LORD s between the earth........ 1Chr 21:16
to s every morning to thank and........ 1Chr 23:30
s to minister by reason of the............ 2Chr 5:14
which s continually before thee,....... 2Chr 9:7
we s before this house, and in thy...... 2Chr 20:9
s ye still, and see the salvation.......... 2Chr 20:17
hath chosen you to s before him......... 2Chr 29:11
Jerusalem and Benjamin to s to it...... 2Chr 34:32
s in the holy place according to.......... 2Chr 35:5
for we cannot s before thee .... Ezr 9:15
and we are not able to s without......... Ezr 10:13
rulers of all the congregation s.......... Neh 7:3
and while they s by, let them shut..... Neh 7:3
S up and bless the LORD your God...... Neh 9:5
Mordecai's matters would s .... Est 3:4
to s for their life, to destroy,............... Est 8:11
his house, but it shall not s .... Job 8:15
that he shall s at the latter day.......... Job 19:25
I s up, and thou regardest me not...... Job 30:20
words in order before me, s up........... Job 33:5
s still, and consider the wondrous.... Job 37:14
and they s as a garment...................... Job 38:14
who then is able to s before me.......... Job 41:10
shall not s in the judgment .... Ps 1:5
S in awe, and sin not .... Ps 4:4
foolish shall not s in thy sight........... Ps 5:5
but we are risen, and s upright .... Ps 20:8
or who shall s in his holy place.......... Ps 24:3
hast made my mountain to s strong.... Ps 30:7
of the world s in awe of him............... Ps 33:8
and buckler, and s up for mine help.... Ps 35:2
my friends s aloof from my sore......... Ps 38:11
and my kinsmen s afar off .... Ps 38:11
upon thy right hand did s the.............. Ps 45:9
Their eyes s out with fatness.............. Ps 73:7
who may s in thy sight when once...... Ps 76:7
made the waters to s as an heap........ Ps 78:13
my covenant shall s fast with him..... Ps 89:28
not made him to s in the battle.......... Ps 89:43
or who will s up for me against........... Ps 94:16
let Satan s at his right hand .... Ps 109:6
For he shall s at the right hand .... Ps 109:31
They s fast for ever and ever, and...... Ps 111:8
Our feet shall s within thy gates....... Ps 122:2
iniquities, O Lord, who shall s .... Ps 130:3
which by night s in the house of .... Ps 134:1
Ye that s in the house of the............... Ps 135:2
who can s before his cold.................... Ps 147:17
house of the righteous shall s............. Prov 12:7

counsel of the LORD, that shall s....... Prov 19:21
he shall s before kings......................... Prov 22:29
he shall not s before mean men.......... Prov 22:29
s not in the place of great men........... Prov 25:6
but who is able to s before envy......... Prov 27:4
that shall s up in his stead.................. Eccl 4:15
s not in an evil thing .... Eccl 8:3
the Lord GOD, It shall not s .... Is 7:7
speak the word, and it shall not s ...... Is 8:10
which shall s for an ensign of............. Is 11:10
as I have purposed, so shall it s .... Is 14:24
My lord, I s continually upon the....... Is 21:8
groves and images shall not s up........ Is 27:9
agreement with hell shall not s .... Is 28:18
and by liberal things shall he s .... Is 32:8
word of our God shall s for ever......... Is 40:8
gathered together, let them s up......... Is 44:11
done, saying, My counsel shall s .... Is 46:10
S now with thine enchantments,....... Is 47:12
s up, and save thee from these........... Is 47:13
unto them, they s up together .... Is 48:13
let us s together.................................... Is 50:8
s up, O Jerusalem, which hast............ Is 51:17
And strangers shall s and feed your .... Is 61:5
S by thyself, come not near to me...... Is 65:5
S ye in the ways, and see, and ask..... Jer 6:16
S in the gate of the LORD's house...... Jer 7:2
s before me in this house, which....... Jer 7:10
asses did s in the high places............. Jer 14:6
again, and thou shalt s before me...... Jer 15:19
s in the gate of the children of .... Jer 17:19
S in the court of the LORD's .... Jer 26:2
a man to s before me for ever............. Jer 35:19
shall know whose words shall s .... Jer 44:28
surely s against you for evil............... Jer 44:29
s forth with your helmets.................... Jer 46:4
say ye, S fast, and prepare thee .... Jer 46:14
they did not s, because the day.......... Jer 46:21
of Aroer, s by the way, and espy........ Jer 48:19
shepherd that will s before me........... Jer 49:19
shepherd that will s before me........... Jer 50:44
the sword, go away, s not still............ Jer 51:50
s upon thy feet, and I will speak........ Eze 2:1
for the house of Israel to s in............. Eze 13:5
of his covenant it might s .... Eze 17:14
s in the gap before me for the............ Eze 22:30
they shall s upon the land................... Eze 27:29
all their loins to be at a s .... Eze 29:7
their trees s up in their height .... Eze 31:14
Ye s upon your sword, ye work .... Eze 33:26
they shall s before them to................ Eze 44:11
they shall s before me to offer........... Eze 44:15
they shall s in judgment .... Eze 44:24
shall s by the post of the gate,.......... Eze 46:2
that the fishers shall s upon it .... Eze 47:10
in them to s in the king's palace....... Dan 1:4
they might s before the king............... Dan 1:5
kingdoms, and it shall s for ever........ Dan 2:44
made s upon the feet as a man, and.... Dan 7:4
that no beasts might s before him...... Dan 8:4
power in the ram to s before him....... Dan 8:7
four kingdoms shall s up out of .... Dan 8:22
dark sentences, shall s up.................. Dan 8:23
he shall also s up against the............. Dan 8:25
I speak unto thee, and s upright......... Dan 10:11
there shall s up three kings .... Dan 11:2
And a mighty king shall s up.............. Dan 11:3
And when he shall s up, his................ Dan 11:4
neither shall he s, nor his arm........... Dan 11:6
shall one s up in his estate................. Dan 11:7
many s up against the king of the...... Dan 11:14
will, and none shall s before him........ Dan 11:16
he shall s in the glorious land,.......... Dan 11:16
but she shall not s on his side........... Dan 11:17
Then shall s up in his estate a.......... Dan 11:20
estate shall s up a vile person .... Dan 11:21
but he shall not s .... Dan 11:25
arms shall s on his part, and they..... Dan 11:31
at that time shall Michael s up .... Dan 12:1
s in thy lot at the end of the.............. Dan 12:13
Neither shall he s that handleth....... Amos 2:15
And he shall s and feed in the........... Mic 5:4
Who can s before his indignation...... Nah 1:6
S, s, shall they cry .... Nah 2:8
I will s upon my watch, and set me.... Hab 2:1
to walk among these that s by............ Zec 3:7
that s by the Lord of the whole......... Zec 4:14
his feet shall s in that day upon........ Zec 14:4
away while they s upon their feet...... Zec 14:12
who shall s when he appeareth .... Mal 3:2
against itself shall not s .... Mt 12:25
how shall then his kingdom s............ Mt 12:26
mother and thy brethren s without.... Mt 12:47
Why s ye here all the day idle........... Mt 20:6
s in the holy place, (whoso............... Mt 24:15
had the withered hand, S forth......... Mk 3:3
itself, that kingdom cannot s .... Mk 3:24
itself, that house cannot s .... Mk 3:25
and be divided, he cannot s .... Mk 3:26
there be some of them that s here..... Mk 9:1
And when ye s praying, forgive, if.... Mk 11:25
that s in the presence of God............ Lk 1:19
Rise up, and s forth in the midst....... Lk 6:8
mother and thy brethren s without.... Lk 8:20
himself, how shall his kingdom s..... Lk 11:18
door, and ye begin to s without......... Lk 13:25
to s before the Son of man .... Lk 21:36
the people which s by I said it.......... Jn 11:42
why s ye gazing up into heaven........ Acts 1:11
this man s here before you whole .... Acts 4:10

S

Go, s and speak in the temple to...... Acts 5:20
commanded the chariot to s still .... Acts 8:38
Peter took him up, saying, S up......... Acts 10:26
loud voice, S upright on thy feet .... Acts 14:10
I s at Caesar's judgment seat............ Acts 25:10
And now I s and am judged for the...... Acts 26:6
But rise, and s upon thy feet .... Acts 26:16
into this grace wherein we s .... Rom 5:2
God according to election might s ...... Rom 9:11
for God is able to make him s .... Rom 14:4
for we shall all s before the .... Rom 14:10
should not s in the wisdom of men 1Cor 2:5
ye have received, and wherein ye s...... 1Cor 15:1
why s we in jeopardy every hour....... 1Cor 15:30
s fast in the faith, quit you 1Cor 16:13
for by faith ye s 2Cor 1:24
for I s in doubt of you....................... Gal 4:20
S fast therefore in the liberty .... Gal 5:1
that ye may be able to s against......... Eph 6:11
day, and having done all, to s............ Eph 6:13
S therefore, having your loins .... Eph 6:14
that ye s fast in one spirit.................. Phil 1:27
so s fast in the Lord, my dearly........... Phil 4:1
in prayers, that ye may s perfect.......... Col 4:12
we live, if ye s fast in the Lord........... 1Th 3:8
s fast, and hold the traditions 2Th 2:15
S thou there, or sit here under .... Jas 2:3
true grace of God wherein ye s 1Pet 5:12
I s at the door, and knock .... Rev 3:20
and who shall be able to s .... Rev 6:17
angel which I saw s upon the sea........ Rev 10:5
s on the sea of glass, having the......... Rev 15:2
shall s afar off for the fear of........... Rev 18:15
small and great, s before God .... Rev 20:12

STANDARD

camp, and every man by his own s ...... Num 1:52
Israel shall pitch by his own s............ Num 2:2
the s of the camp of Judah pitch .... Num 2:3
On the south side shall be the s .... Num 2:10
be the s of the camp of Ephraim........ Num 2:18
The s of the camp of Dan shall be...... Num 2:25
In their first place went the s of........ Num 10:14
the s of the camp of Reuben set......... Num 10:18
the s of the camp of the children...... Num 10:22
the s of the camp of the children...... Num 10:25
set up my s to the people .... Is 49:22
shall lift up s a against him............... Is 59:19
lift up a s for the people .... Is 62:10
Set up the s toward Zion................... Jer 4:6
How long shall I see the s .... Jer 4:21
and publish, and set up a s................ Jer 50:2
Set up the s upon the walls of .... Jer 51:12
Set ye up a s in the land.................... Jer 51:27

STANDARD-BEARER

shall be as when a s fainteth .... Is 10:18

STANDARDS

every man in his place by their s........ Num 2:17
shall go hindmost with their s .... Num 2:31
so they pitched by their s .... Num 2:34

STANDEST

wherefore s thou without................... Gen 24:31
whereon thou s is holy ground............ Ex 3:5
the place whereon thou s is holy .... Josh 5:15
Why s thou afar off, O LORD................ Ps 10:1
place where thou s is holy ground ...... Acts 7:33
broken off, and thou s by faith .... Rom 11:20

STANDETH

and that thy cloud s over them.......... Num 14:14
which s before thee, he shall go......... Deut 1:38
s to minister there before the .... Deut 17:12
But with him that s here with us....... Deut 29:15
the pillars whereupon the house s ...... Judg 16:26
him, Behold, Haman s in the court ...... Est 6:5
the king, s in the house of Haman ...... Est 7:9
nor s in the way of sinners, nor.......... Ps 1:1
My foot s in an even place................. Ps 26:12
counsel of the LORD s for ever .... Ps 33:11
God s in the congregation of the .... Ps 82:1
but my heart s in awe of thy word ...... Ps 119:161
She s in the top of high places,.......... Prov 8:2
he s behind our wall, he looketh........ Song 2:9
The LORD s up to plead .... Is 3:13
and s to judge the people .... Is 3:13
and set him in his place, and he s ...... Is 46:7
backward, and justice s afar off.......... Is 59:14
the great prince which s for the .... Dan 12:1
nor feed that that s falleth................ Zec 11:16
but there s one among you, whom ...... Jn 1:26
friend of the bridegroom, which s ...... Jn 3:29
to his own master he s or falleth....... Rom 14:4
Nevertheless he that s stedfast 1Cor 7:37
eat no flesh while the world s 1Cor 8:13
he s take heed lest he fall 1Cor 10:12
the foundation of God s sure 2Ti 2:19
every priest s daily ministering .... Heb 10:11
the judge s before the door............... Jas 5:9
of the angel which s upon the sea..... Rev 10:8

STANDING

the stacks of corn, or the s corn .... Ex 22:6
tabernacle of shittim wood s up.......... Ex 26:15
tabernacle of shittim wood, s up......... Ex 36:20
neither rear you up a s image............ Lev 26:1
angel of the LORD s in the way .... Num 22:23
angel of the LORD s in the way .... Num 22:31
into the s corn of thy neighbour......... Deut 23:25
unto thy neighbour's s corn................ Deut 23:25
the s corn of the Philistines .... Judg 15:5

---

the shocks, and also the s corn.......... Judg 15:5
Samuel s as appointed over them,...... 1Sa 19:20
all his servants were s about him........ 1Sa 22:6
the lion s by the carcase................... 1Kin 13:25
the lion s by the carcase................... 1Kin 13:28
all the host of heaven s by him 1Kin 22:19
and two lions s by the stays............... 2Chr 9:18
of heaven s on his right hand 2Chr 18:18
Esther the queen s in the court.......... Est 5:2
in deep mire, where there is no s .... Ps 69:2
the wilderness into a s water............. Ps 107:35
turned the rock into a s water .... Ps 114:8
I had seen s before the river............. Dan 8:6
I saw the Lord s upon the altar........ Amos 9:1
he shall receive of you his s .... Mic 1:11
thy s images out of the midst of .... Mic 5:13
he Joshua the high priest s .... Zec 3:1
Satan s at his right hand to.............. Zec 3:1
which go forth from s before the........ Zec 6:5
love to pray s in the synagogues........ Mt 6:5
unto you, There be some s here.......... Mt 16:28
hour, and saw others s idle in the...... Mt 20:3
went out, and found others s idle...... Mt 20:6
s without, sent unto him, calling........ Mk 3:31
s where it ought not, (let him............ Mk 13:14
unto him an angel of the Lord s .... Lk 1:11
And saw two ships s by the lake........ Lk 5:2
of a truth, there be some s here......... Lk 9:27
s afar off, would not lift up so .... Lk 18:13
and the woman s in the midst............ Jn 8:9
his mother, and the disciple s by........ Jn 19:26
herself back, and saw Jesus s .... Jn 20:14
s up with the eleven, lifted up........... Acts 2:14
man which was healed s with them .... Acts 4:14
the keepers s without before the........ Acts 5:23
put in prison are s in the temple........ Acts 5:25
Jesus s on the right hand of God,....... Acts 7:55
the Son of man s on the right .... Acts 7:56
Stephen was slain, I also was s by ..... Acts 22:20
voice, that I cried s among them........ Acts 24:21
as the first tabernacle was yet s .... Heb 9:8
the earth s out of the water and 2Pet 3:5
s on the four corners of the .... Rev 7:1
the two candlesticks s before the .... Rev 11:4
S afar off for the fear of her............. Rev 18:10
And I saw an angel s in the sun .... Rev 19:17

STANK

and the river s, and the Egyptians...... Ex 7:21
and the land s .... Ex 8:14
morning, and it bred worms, and s ..... Ex 16:20
saw that they s before David............. 2Sa 10:6

STAR

there shall come a S out of Jacob........ Num 24:17
the s of your god, which ye made ...... Amos 5:26
we have seen his s in the east .... Mt 2:2
what time the s appeared .... Mt 2:7
and, lo, the s, which they saw in .... Mt 2:9
When they saw the s, they .... Mt 2:10
the s of your god Remphan,.............. Acts 7:43
for one s differeth from another........ 1Cor 15:41
differeth from another s in glory 1Cor 15:41
the day s arise in your hearts 2Pet 1:19
And I will give him the morning s....... Rev 2:28
there fell a great s from heaven......... Rev 8:10
the name of the s is called............... Rev 8:11
I saw a s fall from heaven unto......... Rev 9:1
David, and the bright and morning s... Rev 22:16

STARE

they look and s upon me .... Ps 22:17

STARGAZERS

Let now the astrologers, the s .... Is 47:13

STARS

he made the s also .... Gen 1:16
now toward heaven, and tell the s ...... Gen 15:5
thy seed as the s of the heaven......... Gen 22:17
to multiply as the s of heaven............ Gen 26:4
the eleven s made obeisance to me..... Gen 37:9
your seed as the s of heaven.............. Ex 32:13
ye are this day as the s of................. Deut 1:10
the sun, and the moon, and the s ...... Deut 4:19
as the s of heaven for multitude........ Deut 28:62
whereas ye were as the s of............... Deut 28:62
the s in their courses fought .... Judg 5:20
like to the s of the heavens.............. 1Chr 27:23
the morning till the s appeared.......... Neh 4:21
thou as the s of heaven, and .... Neh 9:23
Let the s of the twilight thereof.......... Job 3:9
and sealeth up the s .... Job 9:7
and behold the height of the s .... Job 22:12
the s are not pure in his sight........... Job 25:5
When the morning s sang together ..... Job 38:7
of thy fingers, the moon and the s ..... Ps 8:3
The moon and s to rule by night .... Ps 136:9
He telleth the number of the s .... Ps 147:4
praise him, all ye s of light .... Ps 148:3
the light, or the moon, or the s.......... Eccl 12:2
For the s of heaven and the .... Is 13:10
my throne above the s of God............ Is 14:13
of the s for a light by night,............. Jer 31:35
and make the s thereof dark.............. Eze 32:7
of the s to the ground, and.............. Dan 8:10
righteousness as the s for ever........... Dan 12:3
the s shall withdraw their................. Joel 2:10
the s shall withdraw their.................. Joel 3:15
Seek him that maketh the seven s ..... Amos 5:8
thou set thy nest among the s .... Obad 4
merchants above the s of heaven....... Nah 3:16
the s shall fall from heaven, and....... Mt 24:29

---

the s of heaven shall fall, and......... Mk 13:25
sun, and in the moon, and in the s ..... Lk 21:25
when neither sun nor s in many......... Acts 27:20
moon, and another glory of the s 1Cor 15:41
so many as the s of the sky in........... Heb 11:12
wandering s, to whom is reserved...... Jude 13
he had in his right hand seven s........ Rev 1:16
The mystery of the seven s which ...... Rev 1:20
The seven s are the angels of the ...... Rev 1:20
the seven s in his right hand............. Rev 2:1
Spirits of God, and the seven s .... Rev 3:1
the s of heaven fell unto the............. Rev 6:13
moon, and the third part of the s ...... Rev 8:12
upon her head a crown of twelve s ..... Rev 12:1
the third part of the s of heaven....... Rev 12:4

STATE

man asked us straitly of our s .... Gen 43:7
set the house of God in his s............. 2Chr 24:13
according to the s of the king........... Est 1:7
according to the s of the king........... Est 2:18
his best s is altogether vanity .... Ps 39:5
to know the s of thy flocks................ Prov 27:23
knowledge the s thereof shall be .... Prov 28:2
from thy s shall he pull thee............. Is 22:19
the last s of that man is worse.......... Mt 12:45
the last s of that man is worse.......... Lk 11:26
good comfort, when I know your s ...... Phil 2:19
will naturally care for your s .... Phil 2:20
learned, in whatsoever s I am............ Phil 4:11
All my s shall Tychicus declare.......... Col 4:7

STATELY

And satest upon a s bed, and a .... Eze 23:41

STATION

And I will drive thee from thy s .... Is 22:19

STATURE

we saw in it are men of a great s ...... Num 13:32
or on the height of his s 1Sa 16:7
Gath, where was a man of great s 2Sa 21:20
an Egyptian, a man of great s 1Chr 11:23
Gath, where was a man of great s 1Chr 20:6
This thy s is like to a palm tree .... Song 7:7
the high ones of s shall be hewn....... Is 10:33
and of the Sabeans, men of s .... Is 45:14
the head of every s to hunt souls...... Eze 13:18
became a spreading vine of low s...... Eze 17:6
treeup s was exalted among the thick .. Eze 19:11
shadowing shroud, and of an high s .... Eze 31:3
can add one cubit unto his s .... Mt 6:27
And Jesus increased in wisdom and s... Lk 2:52
can add to his s one cubit,............... Lk 12:25
press, because he was little of s......... Lk 19:3
unto the measure of the s of the .... Eph 4:13

STATUTE

there he made for them a s .... Ex 15:25
it shall be a s for ever unto .... Ex 27:21
it shall be a s for ever unto him........ Ex 28:43
shall be theirs for a perpetual s .... Ex 29:9
his sons' by a s for ever from .... Ex 29:28
it shall be a s for ever to them,........ Ex 30:21
It shall be a perpetual s for.............. Lev 3:17
It shall be a s for ever in your........... Lev 6:18
it is a s for ever unto the LORD.......... Lev 6:22
unto his sons by a s for ever .... Lev 7:34
by a s for ever throughout their........ Lev 7:36
it shall be a s for ever .... Lev 10:9
sons' with thee, by a s for ever.......... Lev 10:15
this shall be a s for ever unto........... Lev 16:29
your souls, by a s for ever .... Lev 16:31
be an everlasting s unto you .... Lev 16:34
This shall be a s for ever unto........... Lev 16:34
it shall be a s for ever .... Lev 17:7
it shall be a s for ever in all............. Lev 23:14
it shall be a s for ever...................... Lev 23:21
it shall be a s for ever .... Lev 23:31
It shall be a s for ever in your........... Lev 23:41
it shall be a s for ever in your........... Lev 24:3
made by fire by a perpetual s .... Lev 24:9
with thee, by a s for ever .... Num 18:11
with thee, by a s for ever .... Num 18:19
it shall be a s for ever .... Num 18:23
among them, for a s for ever .... Num 19:10
shall be a perpetual s unto them....... Num 19:21
of Israel a s of judgment.................. Num 27:11
So these things shall be for a s .... Num 35:29
people that day, and set them a s ...... Josh 24:25
day forward, that he made it a s........ 1Sa 30:25
For this was a s for Israel................. Ps 81:4
together to establish a royal s........... Dan 6:7
That no decree nor s which the.......... Dan 6:15

STATUTES

my charge, my commandments, my s... Gen 26:5
commandments, and kept all his s ...... Lev 13:26
I do make them know the s of God .... Ex 18:16
the children of Israel all the s .... Lev 10:11
Ye shall therefore keep my s .... Lev 18:5
Ye shall therefore keep my s .... Lev 18:26
Ye shall keep my s .... Lev 19:19
shall ye observe all my s .... Lev 19:37
And ye shall keep my s, and do them . Lev 20:8
Ye shall therefore keep all my s .... Lev 20:22
Wherefore ye shall do my s .... Lev 25:18
If ye walk in my s, and keep my .... Lev 26:3
And if ye shall despise my s .... Lev 26:15
because their soul abhorred my s .... Lev 26:43
These are the s and judgments and .... Lev 26:46
These are the s, which the LORD......... Num 30:16
hearken, O Israel, unto the s .... Deut 4:1
Behold, I have taught you s .... Deut 4:5

which shall hear all these *s* .... Deut 4:6
is there so great, that hath *s* .... Deut 4:8
me at that time to teach you *s* .... Deut 4:14
Thou shalt keep therefore his *s* .... Deut 4:40
are the testimonies, and the *s* .... Deut 4:45
unto them, Hear, O Israel, the *s* .... Deut 5:1
all the commandments, and the *s* .... Deut 5:31
these are the commandments, the *s* .... Deut 6:1
LORD thy God, to keep all his *s* .... Deut 6:2
God, and his testimonies, and his *s* ...... Deut 6:17
mean the testimonies, and the *s* .... Deut 6:20
commanded us to do all these *s* .... Deut 6:24
keep the commandments, and the *s* .... Deut 7:11
and his judgments, and his *s* .... Deut 8:11
of the LORD, and his, which I .... Deut 10:13
God, and keep his charge, and his *s* ..... Deut 11:1
ye shall observe to do all the *s* .... Deut 11:32
These are the *s* and judgments, ... Deut 12:1
thou shalt observe and do these *s* .... Deut 16:12
the words of this law and these *s* .... Deut 17:19
hath commanded thee to do these *s* ...... Deut 26:16
in his ways, and to keep his *s* .... Deut 26:17
and do his commandments and his *s* ...... Deut 27:10
his *s* which I command thee this .... Deut 28:15
his *s* which he commanded thee. .... Deut 28:45
his *s* which are written in this .... Deut 30:10
commandments and his *s* .... Deut 30:16
and as for his *s*, I did not depart 2Sa 22:23
walk in his ways, to keep his *s* 1Kin 2:3
walking in the *s* of David his 1Kin 3:3
walk in my ways, to keep my *s* 1Kin 3:14
if thou wilt walk in my *s* 1Kin 6:12
keep his commandments, and his *s* 1Kin 8:58
LORD our God, to walk in his *s* 1Kin 8:61
commanded thee, and wilt keep my *s* ... 1Kin 9:4
my *s* which I have set before you, ... 1Kin 9:6
hast not kept my covenant and my *s* 1Kin 11:11
in mine eyes, and to keep my *s* 1Kin 11:34
my commandments and my *s* 1Kin 11:34
right in my sight, to keep my *s* 1Kin 11:38
walked in the *s* of the heathen, ... 2Kin 17:8
my commandments and my *s* 2Kin 17:13
And they rejected his *s*, and his 2Kin 17:15
but walked in the *s* of Israel 2Kin 17:19
neither do they after their *s* 2Kin 17:34
And the *s*, and the ordinances, and 2Kin 17:37
his *s* with all their heart and all 2Kin 23:3
thou takest heed to fulfil the *s* 1Chr 22:13
thy testimonies, and thy *s* 1Chr 29:19
thee, and shalt observe my *s* 2Chr 7:17
if ye turn away, and forsake my *s* 2Chr 7:19
between law and commandment, *s* 2Chr 19:10
to the whole law and the *s* 2Chr 33:8
and his testimonies, and his *s* 2Chr 34:31
to do it, and to teach in Israel *s* .... Ezr 7:10
the LORD, and of his *s* to Israel .... Ezr 7:11
kept the commandments, nor the *s* ...... Neh 1:7
judgments, and true laws, good *s* .... Neh 9:13
and commandedst them precepts, *s* ...... Neh 9:14
Lord, and his judgments and his *s* ...... Neh 10:29
I did not pass away his *s* from me .... Ps 18:22
The *s* of the LORD are right, ... Ps 19:8
hast thou to do to declare my *s* .... Ps 50:16
If they break my *s*, and keep not .... Ps 89:31
That they might observe his *s* .... Ps 105:45
ways were directed to keep thy *s* .... Ps 119:5
I will keep thy *s* .... Ps 119:8
teach me thy *s* .... Ps 119:12
I will delight myself in thy *s* .... Ps 119:16
thy servant did meditate in thy *s* .... Ps 119:23
teach me thy *s* .... Ps 119:26
me, O LORD, the way of thy *s* .... Ps 119:33
and I will meditate in thy *s* .... Ps 119:48
Thy *s* have been my songs in the .... Ps 119:54
teach me thy *s* .... Ps 119:64
teach me thy *s* .... Ps 119:68
that I might learn thy *s* .... Ps 119:71
Let my heart be sound in thy *s* .... Ps 119:80
yet do I not forget thy *s* .... Ps 119:83
mine heart to perform thy *s* alway. ..... Ps 119:112
respect unto thy *s* continually. .... Ps 119:117
down all them that err from thy *s* .... Ps 119:118
unto thy mercy, and teach me thy *s* ..... Ps 119:124
and teach me thy *s* .... Ps 119:135
I will keep thy *s* .... Ps 119:145
for they seek not thy *s* .... Ps 119:155
when thou hast taught me thy *s* .... Ps 119:171
the word unto Jacob, his *s* .... Ps 147:19
nor walked in my law, nor in my *s* .... Jer 44:10
walked in his law, nor in his *s* .... Jer 44:23
my *s* more than the countries that .... Eze 5:6
have refused my judgments and my *s* ... Eze 5:6
you, and have not walked in my *s* .... Eze 5:7
for ye have not walked in my *s* .... Eze 11:12
That they may walk in my *s* .... Eze 11:20
Hath walked in my *s*, and hath kept..... Eze 18:9
my judgments, hath walked in my *s* ..... Eze 18:17
and right, and hath kept all my *s* .... Eze 18:19
hath committed, and keep all my *s* .... Eze 18:21
And I gave them my *s*, and shewed ...... Eze 20:11
they walked not in my *s*, and they .... Eze 20:13
judgments, and walked not in my *s* ...... Eze 20:16
ye not in the *s* of your fathers .... Eze 20:18
walk in my *s*, and keep my .... Eze 20:19
they walked not in my *s*, neither .... Eze 20:21
judgments, but had despised my *s* .... Eze 20:24
them also *s* that were not good .... Eze 20:25
had robbed, walk in the *s* of life........... Eze 33:15
you, and cause you to walk in my *s* ..... Eze 36:27
in my judgments, and observe my *s* ..... Eze 37:24

my *s* in all mine assemblies. .... Eze 44:24
For the *s* of Omri are kept, and .... Mic 6:16
But my words and my *s*, which I .... Zec 1:6
Horeb for all Israel, with the *s* .... Mal 4:4

STAVES

thou shalt make *s* of shittim wood .... Ex 25:13
thou shalt put the *s* into the .... Ex 25:14
The *s* shall be in the rings of................. Ex 25:15
places of the *s* to bear the table .... Ex 25:27
shalt make the *s* of shittim wood.......... Ex 25:28
thou shalt make *s* for the altar .... Ex 27:6
s of shittim wood, and overlay.............. Ex 27:6
the *s* shall be put into the rings............ Ex 27:7
the *s* shall be upon the two sides .... Ex 27:7
for the *s* to bear it withal .... Ex 30:4
shalt make the *s* of shittim wood. .... Ex 30:5
the *s* thereof, with the mercy .... Ex 35:12
The table, and his *s*, and all its .... Ex 35:13
And the incense altar, and his *s* .... Ex 35:15
with his brasen grate, his *s* .... Ex 35:16
he made *s* of shittim wood, and .... Ex 37:4
he put the *s* into the rings by .... Ex 37:5
for the *s* to bear the table .... Ex 37:14
he made the *s* of shittim wood, and ..... Ex 37:15
for the *s* to bear it withal .... Ex 37:27
he made the *s* of shittim wood, and ..... Ex 37:28
of brass, to be places for the *s* .... Ex 38:5
he made the *s* of shittim wood, and ..... Ex 38:6
he put the *s* into the rings on .... Ex 38:7
the *s* thereof, and the mercy seat, ... Ex 39:35
and his grate of brass, his *s* .... Ex 39:39
set the *s* on the ark, and put the........... Ex 40:20
and shall put in the *s* thereof .... Num 4:6
and shall put in the *s* thereof .... Num 4:8
and shall put to the *s* thereof .... Num 4:11
skins, and put to the *s* of it .... Num 4:14
of the laught, with their *s* .... Num 21:18
that thou comest to me with *s*.............. 1Sa 17:43
the ark and the *s* thereof above 1Kin 8:7
And they drew out the *s*, that the 1Kin 8:8
that the ends of the *s* were seen 1Kin 8:8
shoulders with the *s* thereon................ 1Chr 15:15
the ark and the *s* thereof above 2Chr 5:8
And they drew out the *s* of the ark. 2Chr 5:9
that the ends of the *s* were seen 2Chr 5:9
his *s* the head of his villages................. Hab 3:14
And I took unto me two *s* .... Zec 11:7
coats, neither shoes, nor yet *s* .... Mt 10:10
great multitude with swords and *s* ...... Mt 26:47
with swords and *s* for to take me. .... Mt 26:55
great multitude with swords and *s* ...... Mk 14:43
with swords and with *s* to take me....... Mk 14:48
for your journey, neither *s* .... Lk 9:3
against a thief, with swords and *s* .... Lk 22:52

STAY

neither *s* thou in all the plain............... Gen 19:17
you go, and ye shall *s* no longer. .... Ex 9:28
the plague in his sight be at a *s* .... Lev 13:5
if the bright spot *s* in his place .... Lev 13:23
if the bright spot *s* in his place .... Lev 13:28
the scall be in his sight at a *s* .... Lev 13:37
s ye not, but pursue after your............. Josh 10:19
would ye *s* for them from having .... Ruth 1:13
then Samuel said unto Saul, S 1Sa 15:16
the lad, Make speed, haste, *s* not. 1Sa 20:38
but the LORD was my *s*......................... 2Sa 22:19
s now thine hand. 2Sa 24:16
It is enough, *s* now thine hand............ 1Chr 21:15
he will not *s* them when his voice .... Job 37:4
or who can *s* the bottles of................... Job 38:37
but the LORD was my *s* .... Ps 18:14
let no man a hum .... Prov 28:17
S me with flagons, comfort me .... Song 2:5
Jerusalem and from Judah the *s* .... Is 3:1
the staff, the whole *s* of bread............. Is 3:1
of bread, and the whole *s* of water ...... Is 3:1
shall no more again *s* upon him. .... Is 10:20
but shall *s* upon the LORD, the .... Is 10:20
are the *s* of the tithes thereof............... Is 19:13
S yourselves, and wonder. .... Is 29:9
and perverseness, and *s* thereon .... Is 30:12
s on horses, and trust in chariots .... Is 31:1
s themselves upon the God of.............. Is 48:2
of the LORD, and *s* upon his God......... Is 50:10
retire, *s* not .... Jer 4:6
with forbearing, and I could not *s*....... Jer 20:9
and none can *s* his hand, or say .... Dan 4:35
for he should not *s* long in the .... Hos 13:13

STAYED

he yet other seven days. .... Gen 8:10
he *s* yet other seven days. .... Gen 8:12
with Laban, and *s* there until now .... Gen 32:4
your flocks and your herds be *s* .... Ex 17:12
Hur *s* up his hands, the one on............ Ex 17:12
and the plague was .... Num 16:48
and the plague was .... Num 16:50
So the plague was *s* from the .... Num 25:8
I *s* in the mount, according to .... Deut 10:10
sun stood still, and the moon *s* .... Josh 10:13
And when thou hast *s* three days 1Sa 20:19
So David *s* his servants with 1Sa 24:7
those that were left behind *s* 1Sa 30:9
Jonathan and Ahimaaz *s* by En-rogel .. 2Sa 17:17
plague may be *s* from the people.......... 2Sa 24:21
and the plague was *s* from Israel 2Sa 24:25
the king was *s* up in his chariot 1Kin 22:35
And the *s* 2Kin 4:6
And he smote thrice, and *s*.................. 2Kin 13:18
back, and *s* not there in the land 2Kin 15:20

plague may be *s* from the people.......... 1Chr 21:22
s himself up in his chariot. 2Chr 18:34
here shall thy proud waves be *s*........... Job 38:11
and so the plague was *s* .... Ps 106:30
peace, whose mind is *s* on thee............ Is 26:3
in a moment, and no hands *s* on her .... Lam 4:6
and the great waters were *s* .... Eze 31:15
the heaven over you is *s* from dew....... Hag 1:10
the earth is *s* from her fruit .... Hag 1:10
s him, that he should not depart .... Lk 4:42
but he himself *s* in Asia for a .... Acts 19:22

STAYETH

he *s* his rough wind in the day of........ Is 27:8

STAYS

there were *s* on either side on.............. 1Kin 10:19
and two lions stood beside the *s* 1Kin 10:19
s on each side of the sitting.................. 2Chr 9:18
and two lions standing by the *s* 2Chr 9:18

STEAD

offering in the *s* of his son .... Gen 22:13
and he said, Am I in God's *s*................. Gen 30:2
Zerah of Bozrah reigned in his *s* .... Gen 36:33
land of Temani reigned in his *s* .... Gen 36:34
field of Moab, reigned in his *s* .... Gen 36:35
of Masrekah reigned in his *s* .... Gen 36:36
by the river reigned in his *s* .... Gen 36:37
son of Achbor reigned in his *s* .... Gen 36:38
died, and Hadar reigned in his *s* .... Gen 36:39
s shall put them on seven days............ Ex 29:30
anointed in his *s* shall offer it. .... Lev 6:22
priest's office in his father's *s* .... Lev 16:32
are risen up in your fathers' *s*.............. Num 32:14
before them, and dwelt in their *s* .... Deut 2:12
them, and dwelt in their *s* .... Deut 2:21
dwelt in their *s* even unto this............. Deut 2:22
them, and dwelt in their *s* .... Deut 2:23
in the priest's office in his *s*................. Deut 10:6
whom he raised up in their *s*............... Josh 5:7
and Hanun his son reigned in his *s*...... 2Sa 10:1
in whose *s* thou hast reigned............... 2Sa 16:8
shalt sit upon my throne in my *s* 1Kin 1:30
for he shall be king in my *s* 1Kin 1:35
Rehoboam his son reigned in his *s* 1Kin 11:43
and Nadab his son reigned in his *s* 1Kin 14:20
made in their *s* brasen shields 1Kin 14:27
Abijam his son reigned in his *s* 1Kin 14:31
and Asa his son reigned in his *s*........... 1Kin 15:8
his son reigned in his *s* 1Kin 15:24
slay him, and reigned in his *s* 1Kin 15:28
and Elah his son reigned in his *s*......... 1Kin 16:6
of Judah, and reigned in his *s* 1Kin 16:10
and Ahab his son reigned in his *s* 1Kin 16:28
Ahaziah his son reigned in his *s* 1Kin 22:40
Jehoram his son reigned in his *s* 1Kin 22:50
Jehoram reigned in his *s* the................ 2Kin 1:17
that should have reigned in his *s* 2Kin 3:27
and Hazael reigned in his *s* 2Kin 8:15
Ahaziah his son reigned in his *s*.......... 2Kin 8:24
Jehoahaz his son reigned in his *s* 2Kin 10:35
Amaziah his son reigned in his *s* 2Kin 12:21
and Joash his son reigned in his *s* 2Kin 13:9
his son reigned in his *s* 2Kin 13:24
Jeroboam his son reigned in his *s* 2Kin 14:16
his son reigned in his *s* 2Kin 14:29
Jotham his son reigned in his *s*............ 2Kin 15:7
and slew him, and reigned in his *s*....... 2Kin 15:10
and slew him, and reigned in his *s* 2Kin 15:14
Pekahiah his son reigned in his *s* 2Kin 15:22
and slew him, and reigned in his *s* 2Kin 15:30
and Ahaz his son reigned in his *s* 2Kin 15:38
Hezekiah his son reigned in his *s* 2Kin 16:20
his son reigned in his *s* 2Kin 19:37
Manasseh his son reigned in his *s* 2Kin 20:21
and Amon his son reigned in his *s*....... 2Kin 21:18
made Josiah his son king in his *s* 2Kin 21:24
Josiah his son reigned in his *s* 2Kin 21:26
made him king in his father's *s*............ 2Kin 23:30
his son reigned in his *s* 2Kin 24:6
father's brother king in his *s*............... 2Kin 24:17
Zerah of Bozrah reigned in his *s* 1Chr 1:44
of the Temanites reigned in his *s*......... 1Chr 1:45
field of Moab, reigned in his *s*............. 1Chr 1:46
of Masrekah reigned in his *s* 1Chr 1:47
by the river reigned in his *s* 1Chr 1:48
son of Achbor reigned in his *s*............. 1Chr 1:49
was dead, Hadad reigned in his *s* 1Chr 1:50
died, and his son reigned in his *s* 1Chr 19:1
Solomon his son reigned in his *s*......... 1Chr 29:28
and hast made me to reign in his *s*...... 2Chr 1:8
Rehoboam his son reigned in his *s* 2Chr 9:31
Abijah his son reigned in his *s* 2Chr 12:16
and Asa his son reigned in his *s* 2Chr 14:1
his son reigned in his *s*, and 2Chr 17:1
Jehoram his son reigned in his *s* 2Chr 21:1
his youngest son king in his *s* 2Chr 22:1
Amaziah his son reigned in his *s*......... 2Chr 24:27
Jotham his son reigned in his *s* 2Chr 26:23
and Ahaz his son reigned in his *s* 2Chr 27:9
Hezekiah his son reigned in his *s* 2Chr 28:27
Manasseh his son reigned in his *s* 2Chr 32:33
and Amon his son reigned in his *s* 2Chr 33:20
made Josiah his son king in his *s* 2Chr 33:25
in his father's *s* in Jerusalem 2Chr 36:1
his son reigned in his *s* 2Chr 36:8
if your soul were in my soul's *s* .... Job 16:4
according to thy wish in God's *s*.......... Job 33:6
number, and set others in their *s*......... Job 34:24
and the wicked cometh in his *s*............ Prov 11:8
that shall stand up in his *s* .... Eccl 4:15

S

STEADS

his son reigned in his s.............................. Is 37:38
in the s of Jehoiada the priest.................. Jer 29:26
we pray you in Christ's s.......................... 2Cor 5:20
that in thy s he might have...................... Philem 13

STEADS

in their s until the captivity...................... 1Chr 5:22

STEADY

his hands were s until the going............... Ex 17:12

STEAL

away secretly, and s away from me......... Gen 31:27
how then should we s out of thy.............. Gen 44:8
Thou shalt not s.. Ex 20:15
If a man shall s an ox, or a....................... Ex 22:1
Ye shall not s, neither deal....................... Lev 19:11
Neither shalt thou s................................... Deut 5:19
as people being ashamed s away............. 2Sa 19:3
if he s to satisfy his soul when................ Prov 6:30
or lest I be poor, and s, and take........... Prov 30:9
Will ye s, murder, and commit................ Jer 7:9
that s my words every one from.............. Jer 23:30
where thieves break through and s......... Mt 6:19
do not break through nor s....................... Mt 6:20
commit adultery, Thou shalt not s........... Mt 19:18
s him away, and say unto the.................. Mt 27:64
adultery, Do not kill, Do not s................. Mk 10:19
adultery, Do not kill, Do not s................. Lk 18:20
thief cometh not, but for to s.................. Jn 10:10
man should not s, dost thou s................. Rom 2:21
shalt not kill, Thou shalt not s................ Rom 13:9
Let him that stole s no more.................... Eph 4:28

STEALETH

And he that s a man, and selleth........... Ex 21:16
a tempest s him away in the night........ Job 27:20
for every one that s shall be cut........... Zec 5:3

STEALING

If a man be found s any of his............... Deut 24:7
and lying, and killing, and s.................... Hos 4:2

STEALTH

them by s that day into the city............. 2Sa 19:3

STEDFAST

yea, thou shalt be s, and shalt............... Job 11:15
whose spirit was not s with God........... Ps 78:8
were they s in his covenant................... Ps 78:37
s for ever, and his kingdom that.......... Dan 6:26
he that standeth s in his heart.............. 1Cor 7:37
my beloved brethren, be ye s................ 1Cor 15:58
And our hope of you is s, knowing....... 2Cor 1:7
the word spoken by angels was s......... Heb 2:2
of our confidence s unto the end........... Heb 3:14
the soul, both sure and s......................... Heb 6:19
Whom resist s in the faith,..................... 1Pet 5:9

STEDFASTLY

she was s minded to go with her......... Ruth 1:18
And he settled his countenance s........ 2Kin 8:11
he s set his face to go to........................ Lk 9:51
while they looked s toward heaven....... Acts 1:10
they continued s in the apostles'.......... Acts 2:42
in the council, looking s on him............ Acts 6:15
looked up s into heaven, and saw........ Acts 7:55
who s beholding him, and....................... Acts 14:9
s behold the face of Moses for.............. 2Cor 3:7
children of Israel could not s................ 2Cor 3:13

STEDFASTNESS

the s of your faith in Christ.................... Col 2:5
the wicked, fall from your own s........... 2Pet 3:17

STEEL

so that a bow of s is broken by............. 2Sa 22:35
the bow of s shall strike him................ Job 20:24
so that a bow of s is broken by............. Ps 18:34
break the northern iron and the s........ Jer 15:12

STEEP

the s places shall fall, and every.......... Eze 38:20
that are poured down a s place............. Mic 1:4
down a s place into the sea.................... Mt 8:32
down a s place into the sea.................... Mk 5:13
down a s place into the lake................. Lk 8:33

STEM

forth a rod out of the s of Jesse........... Is 11:1

STEP

there is but a s between me.................... 1Sa 20:3
If my s hath turned out of the............... Job 31:7

STEPHANAS

*(stef´-a-nas) A convert of Paul
from Achaia.*
baptized also the household of S.......... 1Cor 1:16
brethren, (ye know the house of S....... 1Cor 16:15
I am glad of the coming of S.................. 1Cor 16:17

STEPHANUS

was written from Philippi by S.............. 1Cor s

STEPHEN

*(ste´-ven) A leader of the Jerusalem
church.*
and they chose S, a man full of............. Acts 6:5
And S, full of faith and power, did....... Acts 6:8
of Asia, disputing with S......................... Acts 6:9
men carried S to his burial.................... Acts 7:59
S travelled as far as Phenice................ Acts 8:2
blood of thy martyr S was shed............ Acts 11:19
.... Acts 22:20

STEPPED

the troubling of the water s in.............. Jn 5:4

STEPPETH

coming, another s down before me....... Jn 5:7

STEPS

thou go up by s unto mine altar........... Ex 20:26
Thou hast enlarged my s under me...... 2Sa 22:37
The throne had six s, and the top........ 1Kin 10:19
and on the other upon the six s........... 1Kin 10:20
And there were six s to the throne...... 2Chr 9:18
and on the other upon the six s........... 2Chr 9:19
For now thou numberest my s............... Job 14:16
The s of his strength shall be............... Job 18:7
My foot hath held his s, his way.......... Job 23:11
When I washed my s with butter.......... Job 29:6
he see my ways, and count all my s.... Job 31:4
unto him the number of my s............... Job 31:37
have now compassed us in our s......... Ps 17:11
Thou hast enlarged my s under me...... Ps 18:36
The s of a good man are ordered......... Ps 37:23
none of his s shall slide......................... Ps 37:31
neither have our s declined from........ Ps 44:18
hide themselves, they mark my s........ Ps 56:6
They have prepared a net for my s..... Ps 57:6
my s had well nigh slipped.................... Ps 73:2
shalt set us in the way of his s............ Ps 85:13
Order my s in thy word........................... Ps 119:133
thy s shall not be straitened................ Prov 4:12
her s take hold on hell........................... Prov 5:5
but the Lord directeth his s.................. Prov 16:9
the poor, and the s of the needy......... Is 26:6
man that walketh to direct his s.......... Jer 10:23
They hunt our s, that we cannot.......... Lam 4:18
they went up unto it by seven s.......... Eze 40:22
there were seven s to go up to it........ Eze 40:26
and the going up to it had eight s...... Eze 40:31
and the going up to it had eight s...... Eze 40:34
and the going up to it had eight s...... Eze 40:37
he brought me by the s whereby......... Eze 40:49
the Ethiopians shall be at his s........... Dan 11:43
but who also walk in the s of.............. Rom 4:12
walked we not in the same s............... 2Cor 12:18
that ye should follow his s.................... 1Pet 2:21

STERN

cast four anchors out of the s............. Acts 27:29

STEWARD

the s of my house is this Eliezer......... Gen 15:2
near to the s of Joseph's house........... Gen 43:19
he commanded the s of his house....... Gen 44:1
far off, Joseph said unto his s.............. Gen 44:4
of Arza s of his house in Tirzah.......... 1Kin 16:9
of the vineyard saith unto his s........... Mt 20:8
the wife of Chuza Herod's s.................. Lk 8:3
then is that faithful and wise s............ Lk 12:42
a certain rich man, which had a s........ Lk 16:1
for thou mayest be no longer s........... Lk 16:2
Then the s said within himself............. Lk 16:3
the lord commended the unjust s........ Lk 16:8
be blameless, as the s of God............. Titus 1:7

STEWARDS

s over all the substance and................ 1Chr 28:1
s of the mysteries of God...................... 1Cor 4:1
Moreover it is required in s.................. 1Cor 4:2
as good s of the manifold grace.......... 1Pet 4:10

STEWARDSHIP

give an account of thy s........................ Lk 16:2
my lord taketh away from me the s..... Lk 16:3
that, when I am put out of the s.......... Lk 16:4

STICK

And he cut down a s, and cast it in..... 2Kin 6:6
bones that were not seen s out............ Job 33:21
they s together, that they cannot......... Job 41:17
For thine arrows s fast in me............... Ps 38:2
withered, it is become like a s............. Lam 4:8
thy rivers to s unto thy scales............. Eze 29:4
rivers shall s unto thy scales.............. Eze 29:4
thou son of man, take thee one s........ Eze 37:16
then take another s, and write............. Eze 37:16
the s of Ephraim, and for all the......... Eze 37:16
them one to another into one s............ Eze 37:17
I will take the s of Joseph.................... Eze 37:19
him, even with the s of Judah............. Eze 37:19
of Judah, and make them one s........... Eze 37:19

STICKETH

that s closer than a brother.................. Prov 18:24

STICKS

gathered s upon the sabbath day......... Num 15:32
s brought him unto Moses...................... Num 15:33
woman was there gathering of s.......... 1Kin 17:10
and, behold, I am gathering two s....... 1Kin 17:12
the s whereon thou writest shall........ Eze 37:20
Paul had gathered a bundle of s.......... Acts 28:3

STIFF

know thy rebellion, and thy s neck..... Deut 31:27
speak not with a s neck......................... Ps 75:5
their ear, but made their neck s........... Jer 17:23

STIFFENED

but he s his neck, and hardened.......... 2Chr 36:13

STIFFHEARTED

they are impudent children and s....... Eze 2:4

STIFFNECKED

and, behold, it is a s people................... Ex 32:9
for thou art a s people........................... Ex 33:3

STILL

going on s toward the south.................. Gen 12:9
but they were s ill favoured................. Gen 41:21
let them go, and wilt hold them s........ Ex 9:2
the people, Fear ye not, stand s.......... Ex 14:13
arm they shall be as s as a stone....... Ex 15:16
thou shalt let it rest and lie s.............. Ex 23:11
If it appear s in the garment,.............. Lev 13:57
And Moses said unto them, Stand s.... Num 9:8
went to search the land, lived s.......... Num 14:38
ye shall stand s in Jordan.................... Josh 3:8
Sun, stand thou s upon Gibeon........... Josh 10:12
And the sun stood s, and the moon.... Josh 10:13
So the sun stood s in the midst.......... Josh 10:13
that stood s in their strength.............. Josh 11:13
therefore he blessed you s................... Josh 24:10
and are ye s...................................... Judg 18:9
Then said she, Sit s, my daughter...... Ruth 3:18
on,) but stand thou s a while.............. 1Sa 9:27
Now therefore stand s, that I may...... 1Sa 12:7
But if ye shall s do wickedly............... 1Sa 12:25
then we will stand s in our place....... 1Sa 14:9
things, and also shalt s prevail.......... 1Sa 26:25
Asahel fell down and died stood s..... 2Sa 2:23
and all the people stood s................... 2Sa 2:28
But David tarried s at Jerusalem........ 2Sa 11:1
good for me to have been there s....... 2Sa 14:32
forth, and cursed s as he came.......... 2Sa 16:5
And he turned aside, and stood s....... 2Sa 18:30
saw that all the people stood s.......... 2Sa 20:12
one that came by him stood s............. 2Sa 20:12
and after the fire a small voice......... 1Kin 19:12
in Gilead is ours, and we be s........... 1Kin 22:3
came to pass, as they s went on........ 2Kin 2:11
and if we sit s here, we die also....... 2Kin 7:4
the people s sacrificed and burnt...... 2Kin 15:4
burnt incense s on the high............... 2Kin 15:4
burned incense s in the high............. 2Kin 15:35
set yourselves, stand ye s.................. 2Chr 20:17
no power to keep s the kingdom......... 2Chr 22:9
sacrifice s in the high places............. 2Chr 33:17
they stood s in the prison gate.......... Neh 12:39
s he holdeth fast his integrity,.......... Job 2:3
him, Dost thou s retain thine............. Job 2:9
For now should I have lain s.............. Job 3:13
It stood s, but I could not.................. Job 4:16
but keep it s within his mouth.......... Job 20:13
(for they spake not, but stood s........ Job 32:16
stand s, and consider the wondrous.. Job 37:14
own heart upon your bed, and be s.... Ps 4:4
that thou mightest s the enemy......... Ps 8:2
he leadeth me beside the s waters.... Ps 23:2
Be s, and know that I am God............ Ps 46:10
That he should s live for ever........... Ps 49:9
as goeth on s in his trespasses......... Ps 68:21
the earth feared, and was s............... Ps 76:8
For all this they sinned s.................... Ps 78:32
hold not thy peace, and be not s...... Ps 83:1
they will be s praising thee.............. Ps 84:4
They shall s bring forth fruit in........ Ps 92:14
so that the waves thereof are s......... Ps 107:29
when I awake, I am s with thee.......... Ps 139:18
he s taught the people knowledge..... Eccl 12:9
but his hand is stretched out s.......... Is 5:25
but his hand is stretched out s.......... Is 9:12
but his hand is stretched out s.......... Is 9:17
but his hand is stretched out s.......... Is 9:21
but his hand is stretched out s.......... Is 10:4
Be s, ye inhabitants of the isle.......... Is 23:2
this, Their strength is to sit s............ Is 30:7
I have been s, and refrained.............. Is 42:14
Why do we sit s.............................. Jer 8:14
They say s unto them that despise.... Jer 23:17
I let remain s in their own land........ Jer 27:11
I do earnestly remember him s.......... Jer 31:20
If ye will s abide in this land,.......... Jer 42:10
into thy scabbard, rest, and be s...... Jer 47:6
the sword, go away, stand not s....... Jer 51:50
soul hath them s in remembrance..... Lam 3:20
the children of thy people s are........ Eze 33:30
a winding about s upward to the....... Eze 41:7
s upward round about the house........ Eze 41:7
breadth of the house was s upward... Eze 41:7
moon stood s in their habitation...... Hab 3:11
behold, all the earth sitteth s............ Zec 1:11
nor feed that that standeth s............. Zec 11:16
And Jesus stood s, and called them.. Mt 20:32
and said unto the sea, Peace, be s.... Mk 4:39
And Jesus stood s, and commanded... Mk 10:49
and they that bare him stood s......... Lk 7:14
unto them, he abode s in Galilee...... Jn 7:9
he abode two days s in the same...... Jn 11:6
but Mary sat s in the house.............. Jn 11:20
commanded the chariot to stand s.... Acts 8:38
it pleased Silas to abide there s....... Acts 15:34
Silas and Timotheus abode there s.... Acts 17:14
if they abide not s in unbelief........... Rom 11:23
thee to abide s at Ephesus................ 1Ti 1:3
is unjust, let him be unjust s............ Rev 22:11
is filthy, let him be filthy s.............. Rev 22:11
righteous, let him be righteous s....... Rev 22:11
that is holy, let him be holy s........... Rev 22:11

STILLED

Caleb s the people before Moses,......	Num 13:30
So the Levites s all the people.	Neh 8:11

STILLEST

waves thereof arise, thou s them	Ps 89:9

STILLETH

Which s the noise of the seas,..............	Ps 65:7

STING

O death, where is thy s......................	1Cor 15:55
The s of death is sin.	1Cor 15:56

STINGETH

a serpent, and s like an adder	Prov 23:32

STINGS

there were s in their tails.	Rev 9:10

STINK

to s among the inhabitants of the	Gen 34:30
shall die, and the river shall s	Ex 7:18
and it did not s, neither was.............	Ex 16:24
My wounds s and are corrupt.............	Ps 38:5
of sweet smell there shall be s	Is 3:24
their s shall come up out of	Is 34:3
his s shall come up, and his ill...........	Joel 2:20
I have made the s of your camps.......	Amos 4:10

STINKETH

their fish s, because there is no............	Is 50:2
unto him, Lord, by this time he s	Jn 11:39

STINKING

to send forth a s savour....................	Eccl 10:1

STIR

who shall s him up	Num 24:9
the innocent shall s up himself	Job 17:8
is so fierce that dare s him up	Job 41:10
S up thyself, and awake to my	Ps 35:23
did not s up all his wrath.	Ps 78:38
Manasseh s up the iniquity, strength,...	Ps 80:2
but grievous words s up anger	Prov 15:1
of the field, that ye s not up	Song 2:7
of the field, that ye s not up	Song 3:5
of Jerusalem, that ye s not up...........	Song 8:4
the LORD of hosts shall s up a	Is 10:26
I will s up the Medes against.............	Is 13:17
he shall s up jealousy like a man........	Is 42:13
s up all against the realm of	Dan 11:2
he shall s up his power and his..........	Dan 11:25
was no small s among the soldiers......	Acts 12:18
arose no small s about that way.........	Acts 19:23
that thou s up the gift of God...........	2Ti 1:6
to s you up by putting you in	2Pet 1:13
in both which I s up your pure	2Pet 3:1

STIRRED

every one whose heart s him up	Ex 35:21
all the women whose heart s them.....	Ex 35:26
even every one whose heart s him	Ex 36:2
hath s up my servant against me	1Sa 22:8
If the LORD have s thee up	1Sa 26:19
the LORD s up an adversary unto.......	1Kin 11:14
God s him up another adversary,........	1Kin 11:23
LORD, whom Jezebel his wife s up......	1Kin 21:25
the God of Israel s up the spirit	1Chr 5:26
Moreover the LORD s up against	2Chr 21:16
the LORD s up the spirit of Cyrus.......	2Chr 36:22
the LORD s up the spirit of Cyrus.......	Ezr 1:1
and my sorrow was s	Ps 39:2
But his sons shall be s up...................	Dan 11:10
then shall he return, and be s up	Dan 11:10
s up to battle with a very great..........	Dan 11:25
the LORD s up the spirit of	Hag 1:14
they s up the people, and the	Acts 6:12
But the Jews s up the devout and......	Acts 13:50
Jews s up the Gentiles, and made.......	Acts 14:2
thither also, and s up the people........	Acts 17:13
Athens, his spirit was s in him	Acts 17:16
s up all the people, and laid	Acts 21:27

STIRRETH

As an eagle s up her nest....................	Deut 32:11
Hatred s up strifes............................	Prov 10:12
A wrathful man s up strife..................	Prov 15:18
is of a proud heart s up strife............	Prov 28:25
An angry man s up strife, and a	Prov 29:22
it s up the dead for thee, even	Is 14:9
that s up himself to take hold of........	Is 64:7
He s up the people, teaching.............	Lk 23:5

STIRS

Thou that art full of s, a....................	Is 22:2

STOCK

or to the s of the stranger's..............	Lev 25:47
the s thereof die in the ground	Job 14:8
their s shall not take root in..............	Is 40:24
I fall down to the s of a tree.............	Is 44:19
Saying to a s, Thou art my father	Jer 2:27
the s is a doctrine of vanities	Jer 10:8
children of the s of Abraham..............	Acts 13:26
of the s of Israel, of the tribe............	Phil 3:5

STOCKS

puttest my feet also in the s..............	Job 13:27
He putteth my feet in the s................	Job 33:11
a fool to the correction of the s.........	Prov 7:22
adultery with stones and with s..........	Jer 3:9
put him in the s that were in the	Jer 20:2
forth Jeremiah out of the s	Jer 20:3
put him in prison, and in the s	Jer 29:26
My people ask counsel at their s........	Hos 4:12
and made their feet fast in the s........	Acts 16:24

STOIC

See STOICKS.

STOICKS

(sto′-ics) A sect of Greek
philosophers.

of the Epicureans, and of the S..........	Acts 17:18

STOLE

Jacob s away unawares to Laban........	Gen 31:20
So Absalom s the hearts of the...........	2Sa 15:6
s him from among the king's sons.......	2Kin 11:2
s him from among the king's sons.......	2Chr 22:11
s him away while we slept.	Mt 28:13
Let him that s steal no more	Eph 4:28

STOLEN

that shall be counted s with me	Gen 30:33
Rachel had s the images that were......	Gen 31:19
that thou hast s away unawares to.....	Gen 31:26
yet wherefore hast thou s my gods.....	Gen 31:30
knew not that Rachel had s them........	Gen 31:32
s by day, or s by night.	Gen 31:39
For indeed I was s away out of..........	Gen 40:15
it be s out of the man's house.	Ex 22:7
And if it be s from him, he shall.........	Ex 22:12
accursed thing, and have also s	Josh 7:11
the men of Judah s thee away,...........	2Sa 19:41
which had s them from the street........	2Sa 19:3
S waters are sweet, and bread...........	Prov 9:17
not have s till they had enough	Obad 5

STOMACHER

instead of a s a girding of..................	Is 3:24

STOMACH'S

use a little wine for thy s sake............	1Ti 5:23

STONE

there is bdellium and the onyx s........	Gen 2:12
And they had brick for s, and slime....	Gen 11:3
took the s that he had put for:...........	Gen 28:18
And this s, which I have set for a	Gen 28:22
a great s was upon the well's............	Gen 29:2
they rolled the s from the well's.........	Gen 29:3
put the s again upon the well's...........	Gen 29:3
till they roll the s from the.................	Gen 29:8
rolled the s from the well's	Gen 29:10
And Jacob took a s, and set it up.......	Gen 31:45
with him, even a pillar of s	Gen 35:14
is the shepherd, the s of Israel	Gen 49:24
Then Zipporah took a sharp s...........	Ex 4:25
of wood, and in vessels of s	Ex 7:19
their eyes, and will they not s us	Ex 8:26
they sank into the bottom as a s	Ex 15:5
arm they shall be as still as a s..........	Ex 15:16
they be almost ready to s me	Ex 17:4
and they took a s, and put it under....	Ex 17:12
thou wilt make me an altar of s	Ex 20:25
thou shalt not build it of hewn s........	Ex 20:25
and one smite another with a s...........	Ex 21:18
were a paved work of a sapphire s.....	Ex 24:10
and I will give thee tables of s	Ex 24:12
Six of their names on one s	Ex 28:10
names of the rest on the other s.........	Ex 28:10
With the work of an engraver in s	Ex 28:11
tables of testimony, tables of s	Ex 31:18
tables s like unto the first	Ex 34:1
tables of s like unto the first	Ex 34:4
in his hand the two tables of s	Ex 34:29
the land shall s him with stones.........	Lev 20:2
they shall s them with stones............	Lev 20:27
and let all the congregation s him	Lev 24:14
shall certainly s him	Lev 24:16
of the camp, and s him with stones....	Lev 24:23
up any image of s in your land..........	Lev 26:1
bade s them with stones....................	Num 14:10
all the congregation bade s him.........	Num 15:35
If he smite him with throwing a s	Num 35:17
Or with any s, wherewith a man	Num 35:23
wrote them upon two tables of s	Deut 4:13
work of men's hands, wood and s	Deut 4:28
he wrote them in two tables of s	Deut 5:22
mount to receive the tables of s.........	Deut 9:9
s written with the finger of God.........	Deut 9:10
LORD gave me the two tables of s	Deut 9:11
tables of s like unto the first	Deut 10:1
tables of s like unto the first	Deut 10:3
thou shalt s him with stones,.............	Deut 13:10
shalt s them with stones, till	Deut 17:5
his city shall s him with stones..........	Deut 21:21
the men of her city shall s her............	Deut 22:21
ye shall s them with stones that	Deut 22:24
thou serve other gods, wood and s	Deut 28:36
have known, even wood and s	Deut 28:64
and their idols, wood and s	Deut 29:17
man of you a s upon his shoulder.......	Josh 4:5
the border went up to the s of..........	Josh 15:6
descended to the s of Bohan the.......	Josh 18:17
the law of God, and took a great s.....	Josh 24:26
this s shall be a witness unto us	Josh 24:27
and ten persons, upon one s..............	Judg 9:5
and ten persons, upon one s..............	Judg 9:18
there, where there was a great s.........	1Sa 6:14
and they set on the great s stones,.....	1Sa 6:15
even unto the great s of Abel.............	1Sa 6:18
which s remaineth unto this day.........	1Sa 6:18
Then Samuel took a s, and set it	1Sa 7:12
roll a great s unto me this day...........	1Sa 14:33
in his bag, and took thence a s	1Sa 17:49
that the s sunk into his forehead	1Sa 17:49
with a sling and with a s, and	1Sa 17:50
and shalt remain by the Ezel	1Sa 20:19
within him, and he became as a s	1Sa 25:37
be not one small s found there	2Sa 17:13

at the great s which is in Gibeon	2Sa 20:8
fat cattle by the s of Zoheleth	1Kin 1:9
was built of s made ready before.......	1Kin 6:7
there was no s seen	1Kin 6:18
court with three rows of hewed s	1Kin 6:36
the ark save the two tables of s	1Kin 8:9
out, and s him, that he may die..........	1Kin 21:10
of land cast every man his s	2Kin 3:25
And to masons, and hewers of s	2Kin 12:12
hewed s to repair the breaches of......	2Kin 12:12
work of men's hands, wood and s	2Kin 19:18
hewn s to repair the house	2Kin 22:6
timber also and s have I prepared	1Chr 22:14
abundance, hewers and workers of s ..	1Chr 22:15
silver, in brass, in iron, in s	2Chr 2:14
gave they it, to buy hewn s	2Chr 34:11
even break down their s wall	Neh 4:3
as a s into the mighty waters.............	Neh 9:11
and brass is molten out of the s	Job 28:2
or who laid the corner s thereof	Job 38:6
The waters are hid as with a s	Job 38:30
His heart is as firm as a s	Job 41:24
thou dash thy foot against a s	Ps 91:12
The s which the builders refused	Ps 118:22
become the head s of the corner........	Ps 118:22
A gift is as a precious s in the	Prov 17:8
the s wall thereof was broken............	Prov 24:31
As he that bindeth a s in a sling........	Prov 26:8
and he that rolleth a s, it will	Prov 26:27
A s is heavy, and the sand weighty	Prov 27:3
but for a s of stumbling and for a	Is 8:14
a foundation a s, a tried s	Is 28:16
a precious corner s	Is 28:16
work of men's hands, wood and s	Is 37:19
and to a s, Thou hast brought me	Jer 2:27
not take of thee a s for a corner	Jer 51:26
a corner, nor a s for foundations	Jer 51:26
that thou shalt bind a s to it..............	Jer 51:63
hath inclosed my ways with hewn s	Lam 3:9
the dungeon, and cast a s upon me....	Lam 3:53
as the appearance of a sapphire s	Eze 1:26
over them as it were a sapphire s	Eze 10:1
was as the colour of a beryl s	Eze 10:9
they shall s thee with stones, and......	Eze 16:40
the countries, to serve wood and s	Eze 20:32
company shall s them with stones......	Eze 23:47
every precious s was thy covering.......	Eze 28:13
of hewn s for the burnt offering.........	Eze 40:42
Thou sawest till that a s was cut	Dan 2:34
the s that smote the image became	Dan 2:35
as thou sawest that the s was cut	Dan 2:45
brass, of iron, of wood, and of s	Dan 5:4
gold, of brass, iron, wood, and s	Dan 5:23
a s was brought, and laid upon the....	Dan 6:17
ye have builded houses of hewn s	Amos 5:11
For the s shall cry out of the.............	Hab 2:11
to the dumb s, Arise, it shall.............	Hab 2:19
from before a s was laid upon a........	Hag 2:15
a s in the temple of the LORD	Hag 2:15
For behold the s that I have laid	Zec 3:9
upon one s shall be seven eyes..........	Zec 3:9
made their hearts as an adamant s	Zec 7:12
a burdensome s for all people	Zec 12:3
thou dash thy foot against a s	Mt 4:6
ask bread, will he give him a s	Mt 7:9
The s which the builders rejected.......	Mt 21:42
fall on this s shall be broken.............	Mt 21:44
he left here upon s upon another.......	Mt 24:2
he rolled a great s to the door	Mt 27:60
the sepulchre sure, sealing the s	Mt 27:66
rolled back the s from the door.........	Mt 28:2
The s which the builders rejected.......	Mk 12:10
not be left one s upon another	Mk 13:2
rolled a s unto the door of the..........	Mk 15:46
Who shall roll us away the s from......	Mk 16:3
saw that the s was rolled away..........	Mk 16:4
command this s that it be made	Lk 4:3
thou dash thy foot against a s	Lk 4:11
is a father, will he give him a s	Lk 11:11
leave in thee one s upon another.......	Lk 19:44
all the people will s us......................	Lk 20:6
The s which the builders rejected.......	Lk 20:17
fall upon that s shall be broken.........	Lk 20:18
not be left one s upon another	Lk 21:6
in a sepulchre that was hewn in s	Lk 23:53
they found the s rolled away from......	Lk 24:2
which is by interpretation, A s	Jn 1:42
were set there six waterpots of s	Jn 2:6
let him first cast a s at her	Jn 8:7
took up stones again to s him	Jn 10:31
which of those works do ye s me	Jn 10:32
For a good work we s thee not..........	Jn 10:33
the Jews of late sought to s thee	Jn 11:8
It was a cave, and a s lay upon it......	Jn 11:38
Jesus said, Take ye away the s...........	Jn 11:39
Then they took away the s from........	Jn 11:41
seeth the s taken away from the	Jn 20:1
This is the s which was set at	Acts 4:11
them despitefully, and to s them,.......	Acts 14:5
like unto gold, or silver, or s	Acts 17:29
not in tables of s, but in	2Cor 3:3
himself being the chief corner s	Eph 2:20
whom coming, as unto a living s	1Pet 2:4
I lay in Sion a chief corner s	1Pet 2:6
the s which the builders	1Pet 2:7
a s of stumbling, and a rock of	1Pet 2:8
manna, and will give him a white s	Rev 2:17
in the s a new name written,.............	Rev 2:17
upon like a jasper and a sardine s	Rev 4:3
gold, silver, and brass, and s	Rev 9:20

S

every *s* about the weight of a .... Rev 16:21
up a *s* like a great millstone.......... Rev 18:21
was like unto a *s* most precious.......... Rev 21:11
precious, even like a jasper *s*.......... Rev 21:11

STONED

it, but he shall surely be *s* .... Ex 19:13
then the ox shall be surely *s* .... Ex 21:28
the ox shall be *s*, and his owner .... Ex 21:29
of silver, and the ox shall be *s* .... Ex 21:32
s him with stones, and he died.......... Num 15:36
all Israel *s* him with stones, and.......... Josh 7:25
after they had *s* them with stones.......... Josh 7:25
all Israel *s* him with stones,.......... 1Kin 12:18
all Israel *s* him, that he died.......... 1Kin 21:13
to Jezebel, saying, Naboth is *s* 1Kin 21:14
Jezebel heard that Naboth was *s* 1Kin 21:15
of Israel *s* him with stones 2Chr 10:18
him, and *s* him with stones at the.......... 2Chr 24:21
and killed another, and *s* another.......... Mt 21:35
us, that such should be *s* .... Jn 8:5
lest they should have been *s*.......... Acts 5:26
him out of the city, and *s* him.......... Acts 7:58
they *s* Stephen, calling upon God,.......... Acts 7:59
the people, and, having *s* Paul.......... Acts 14:19
I beaten with rods, once was I *s* 2Cor 11:25
They were *s*, they were sawn .... Heb 11:37
touch the mountain, it shall be *s* .... Heb 12:20

STONE'S

from them about a *s* cast, and.......... Lk 22:41

STONES

and he took of the *s* of that place.......... Gen 28:11
said unto his brethren, Gather *s* .... Gen 31:46
and they took *s*, and made an heap.......... Gen 31:46
Onyx *s*, and *s* to be set in .... Ex 25:7
And thou shalt take two onyx *s* .... Ex 28:9
shalt thou engrave the two *s* with .... Ex 28:11
thou shalt put the two *s* upon the .... Ex 28:12
of memorial unto the children .... Ex 28:12
shalt set in it settings of *s* .... Ex 28:17
even four rows of *s* .... Ex 28:17
the *s* shall be with the names of .... Ex 28:21
And in cutting of *s*, to set them,.......... Ex 31:5
And onyx *s*, and *s* to be set .... Ex 35:9
And the rulers brought onyx *s* .... Ex 35:27
s to be set, for the ephod, and .... Ex 35:27
And in the cutting of *s*, to set .... Ex 35:33
they wrought onyx *s* inclosed in .... Ex 39:6
that they should be *s* for a .... Ex 39:7
And they set in it four rows of *s* .... Ex 39:10
the *s* were according to the names .... Ex 39:14
away the *s* in which the plague is.......... Lev 14:40
And they shall take other *s* .... Lev 14:42
put them in the place of those *s* .... Lev 14:42
that he hath taken away the *s* .... Lev 14:43
the *s* of it, and the timber .... Lev 14:45
the land shall stone him with *s*.......... Lev 20:2
they shall stone them with *s* .... Lev 20:27
or scabbed, or hath his *s* broken .... Lev 21:20
of the camp, and stone him with *s* .... Lev 24:23
bade stone them with *s* .... Num 14:10
stone him with *s* without the camp .... Num 15:35
the camp, and stoned him with *s* .... Num 15:36
a land whose *s* are iron, and out .... Deut 8:9
And thou shalt stone him with *s* .... Deut 13:10
woman, and shalt stone them with *s* .... Deut 17:5
his city shall stone him with *s* .... Deut 21:21
stone her with *s* that she die .... Deut 22:24
stone them with *s* that they die .... Deut 22:24
He that is wounded in the *s* .... Deut 23:1
thou shalt set thee up great *s* .... Deut 27:2
that ye shall set up these *s* .... Deut 27:4
the LORD thy God, an altar of *s* .... Deut 27:5
of the LORD thy God of whole *s* .... Deut 27:6
thou shalt write upon the *s* all .... Deut 27:8
feet stood firm, twelve *s* .... Josh 4:3
saying, What mean ye by these *s* .... Josh 4:6
these *s* shall be for a memorial .... Josh 4:7
took up twelve *s* out of the midst .... Josh 4:8
Joshua set up twelve *s* in the .... Josh 4:9
And those twelve *s*, which they .... Josh 4:20
come, saying, What mean these *s* .... Josh 4:21
And all Israel stoned him with *s* .... Josh 7:25
after they had stoned them with *s* .... Josh 7:25
a great heap of *s* unto this day .... Josh 7:26
raise thereon a great heap of *s* .... Josh 8:29
law of Moses, an altar of whole *s* .... Josh 8:31
he wrote there upon the *s* a copy .... Josh 8:32
s from heaven upon them unto .... Josh 10:11
Roll great *s* upon the mouth of .... Josh 10:18
laid great *s* in the cave's mouth,.......... Josh 10:27
could sling a at an hair breadth .... Judg 20:16
five smooth *s* out of the brook 1Sa 17:40
of gold with the precious *s* 2Sa 12:30
he cast *s* at David, and at the 2Sa 16:6
threw *s* at him, and cast dust.......... 2Sa 16:13
a very great heap of *s* upon him.......... 2Sa 18:17
s, costly *s*, and hewed *s* 1Kin 5:17
timber and *s* to build the house.......... 1Kin 5:18
All these were of costly *s* 1Kin 7:9
to the measures of hewed *s* 1Kin 7:9
of costly *s*, even great *s* 1Kin 7:10
s of ten cubits, and *s* of 1Kin 7:10
And above were costly *s*, after the 1Kin 7:11
after the measures of hewed *s* 1Kin 7:11
was with three rows of hewed *s* 1Kin 7:12
and very much gold, and precious *s* 1Kin 10:2
very great store, and precious *s*.......... 1Kin 10:10
of almug trees, and precious *s*.......... 1Kin 10:11
silver to be in Jerusalem as *s* 1Kin 10:27

and all Israel stoned him with *s* 1Kin 12:18
and they took away the *s* of Ramah 1Kin 15:22
And Elijah took twelve *s*,.......... 1Kin 18:31
with the *s* he built an altar in 1Kin 18:32
sacrifice, and the wood, and the *s* 1Kin 18:38
of the city, and stoned him with *s* 1Kin 21:13
every good piece of land with *s* 2Kin 3:19
left they the *s* thereof.......... 2Kin 3:25
and put it upon a pavement of *s* 2Kin 16:17
hand and the left in hurling *s* 1Chr 12:2
and there were precious *s* in it 1Chr 20:2
s to build the house of God 1Chr 22:2
onyx *s*, and *s* to be set,.......... 1Chr 29:2
to be set, glistering *s* 1Chr 29:2
and all manner of precious *s* 1Chr 29:2
s, and marble *s* in abundance 1Chr 29:2
they with whom precious *s* were 1Chr 29:8
at Jerusalem as plenteous as *s* 1Chr 1:15
house with precious *s* for beauty 2Chr 3:6
gold in abundance, and precious *s* 2Chr 9:1
great abundance, and precious *s* 2Chr 9:9
brought algum trees and precious *s* 2Chr 9:10
made silver in Jerusalem as *s* 2Chr 9:27
of Israel stoned him with *s* 2Chr 10:18
they carried away the *s* of Ramah 2Chr 16:6
him, and stoned him with *s* at the 2Chr 24:21
and bows, and slings to cast *s* 2Chr 26:14
to shoot arrows and great *s* withal 2Chr 26:15
and for gold, and for precious *s* 2Chr 32:27
which is builded with great *s* .... Ezr 5:8
With three rows of great *s* .... Ezr 6:4
will they revive the *s* out of the .... Neh 4:2
in league with the *s* of the field .... Job 5:23
Is my strength the strength of *s* .... Job 6:12
the heap, and seeth the place of *s* .... Job 8:17
The waters wear the *s* .... Job 14:19
of Ophir as the *s* of the brooks .... Job 22:24
the *s* of darkness, and the shadow .... Job 28:3
The *s* of it are the place of .... Job 28:6
the sinews of his *s* are wrapped.......... Job 40:17
Sharp *s* are under him.......... Job 41:30
his thick clouds passed, hail *s* .... Ps 18:12
hail *s* and coals of fire .... Ps 18:13
servants take pleasure in her *s* .... Ps 102:14
thy little ones against the *s* .... Ps 137:9
our daughters may be as corner *s* .... Ps 144:12
A time to cast away *s*, and a time .... Eccl 3:5
and a time to gather *s* together .... Eccl 3:5
Whoso removeth *s* shall be hurt .... Eccl 10:9
it, and gathered out the *s* thereof .... Is 5:2
but we will build with hewn *s* .... Is 9:10
that go down to the *s* of the pit .... Is 14:19
when he maketh all the *s* of the .... Is 27:9
confusion, and the *s* of emptiness .... Is 34:11
I will lay thy *s* with fair colours.......... Is 54:11
and all thy borders of pleasant *s* .... Is 54:12
Among the smooth *s* of the stream .... Is 57:6
and for wood brass, and for *s* iron .... Is 60:17
gather out the *s* .... Is 62:10
and committed adultery with *s* .... Jer 3:9
Take great *s* in thine hand, and .... Jer 43:9
upon these *s* that I have hid .... Jer 43:10
broken my teeth with gravel *s* .... Lam 3:16
the *s* of the sanctuary are poured .... Lam 4:1
and they shall stone thee with *s* .... Eze 16:40
company shall stone them with *s* .... Eze 23:47
and they shall lay thy *s* and thy .... Eze 26:12
spices, and with all precious *s* .... Eze 27:22
in the midst of the *s* of fire .... Eze 28:14
from the midst of the *s* of fire.......... Eze 28:16
and silver, and with precious *s* .... Dan 11:38
I will pour down the *s* thereof .... Mic 1:6
timber thereof and the *s* thereof .... Zec 5:4
devour, and subdue with sling *s* .... Zec 9:15
they shall be as the *s* of a crown.......... Zec 9:16
these *s* to raise up children unto .... Mt 3:9
that these *s* be made bread .... Mt 4:3
crying, and cutting himself with *s* .... Mk 5:5
and at him they cast *s*, and wounded .... Mk 12:4
him, Master, see what manner of *s* .... Mk 13:1
these *s* to raise up children unto .... Lk 3:8
the *s* would immediately cry out......... Lk 19:40
how it was adorned with goodly *s* .... Lk 21:5
took they up *s* to cast at him .... Jn 8:59
Jews took up *s* again to stone him .... Jn 10:31
gold, silver, precious *s*, wood,.......... 1Cor 3:12
death, written and engraven in *s* 2Cor 3:7
Ye also, as lively *s*, are built 1Pet 2:5
and decked with gold and precious *s* .... Rev 17:4
of gold, and silver, and precious *s* .... Rev 18:12
decked with gold, and precious *s* .... Rev 18:16
with all manner of precious *s* .... Rev 21:19

STONESQUARERS

builders did hew them, and the *s* 1Kin 5:18

STONEST

s them which are sent unto thee,.......... Mt 23:37
s them that are sent unto thee .... Lk 13:34

STONING

for the people spake of *s* him 1Sa 30:6

STONY

judges are overthrown in *s* places .... Ps 141:6
I will take the *s* heart out of .... Eze 11:19
I will take away the *s* heart out .... Eze 36:26
Some fell upon *s* places, where.......... Mt 13:5
received the seed into *s* places .... Mt 13:20
And some fell on *s* ground, where.......... Mk 4:5
which are sown on *s* ground .... Mk 4:16

STOOD

and, lo, three men *s* by him .... Gen 18:2
he *s* by them under the tree, and .... Gen 18:8
but Abraham *s* yet before the LORD .... Gen 18:22
place where he *s* before the LORD .... Gen 19:27
Abraham *s* up from before his dead .... Gen 23:3
Abraham *s* up, and bowed.......... Gen 23:7
he *s* by the camels at the well .... Gen 24:30
And, behold, the LORD *s* above it.......... Gen 28:13
my sheaf arose, and also *s* upright .... Gen 37:7
your sheaves *s* round about.......... Gen 37:7
and, behold, he *s* by the river.......... Gen 41:1
s by the other kine upon the .... Gen 41:3
I *s* upon the bank of the river.......... Gen 41:17
he *s* before Pharaoh king of Egypt .... Gen 41:46
down to Egypt, and *s* before Joseph .... Gen 43:15
before all them that *s* by him .... Gen 45:1
there *s* no man with him, while.......... Gen 45:1
And his sister *s* afar off, to wit .... Ex 2:4
but Moses *s* up and helped them, and .... Ex 2:17
who *s* in the way, as they came.......... Ex 5:20
the furnace, and *s* before Pharaoh .... Ex 9:10
their face, and *s* behind them.......... Ex 14:19
the floods *s* upright as an heap.......... Ex 15:8
the people *s* by Moses from the .... Ex 18:13
they *s* at the nether part of the .... Ex 19:17
it, they removed, and *s* afar off .... Ex 20:18
And the people *s* afar off, and.......... Ex 20:21
Then Moses *s* in the gate of the .... Ex 32:26
s every man at his tent door, and .... Ex 33:8
s at the door of the tabernacle,.......... Ex 33:9
s with him there, and proclaimed.......... Ex 34:5
drew near and *s* before the LORD .... Lev 9:5
the people *s* up all that day, and .... Num 11:32
s in the door of the tabernacle,.......... Num 12:5
s in the door of the tabernacle .... Num 16:18
s in the door of their tents, and .... Num 16:27
he *s* between the dead and the .... Num 16:48
the angel of the LORD *s* in the .... Num 22:22
But the angel of the LORD *s* in a .... Num 22:24
s in a narrow place, where was no .... Num 22:26
he *s* by his burnt sacrifice, he .... Num 23:6
he *s* by his burnt offering, and.......... Num 23:17
they *s* before Moses, and before .... Num 27:2
came near and *s* under the mountain .... Deut 4:11
(I *s* between the LORD and you at .... Deut 5:5
the pillar of the cloud *s* over .... Deut 31:15
which came down from above *s* .... Josh 3:16
s firm on dry ground in the midst .... Josh 3:17
where the priests' feet *s* firm .... Josh 4:3
bare the ark of the covenant *s* .... Josh 4:9
the ark *s* in the midst of Jordan.......... Josh 4:10
there *s* a man over against him.......... Josh 5:13
s on this side the ark and on that .... Josh 8:33
And the sun *s* still, and the moon .... Josh 10:13
So the sun *s* still in the midst .... Josh 10:13
that *s* still in their strength .... Josh 11:13
of blood, until he *s* before the .... Josh 20:9
there *s* not a man of all their .... Josh 21:44
all that *s* by him went out from .... Judg 3:19
said unto all that *s* against him .... Judg 6:31
they *s* every man in his place.......... Judg 7:21
s in the top of mount Gerizim, and .... Judg 9:7
s in the entering of the gate .... Judg 9:35
s in the entering of the gate of .... Judg 9:44
pillars upon which the house *s* .... Judg 16:26
s by the entering of the gate.......... Judg 18:16
the priest *s* in the entering of .... Judg 18:17
s before it in those days,).......... Judg 20:28
am the woman that *s* by thee here 1Sa 1:26
And the LORD came, and *s*, and called 1Sa 3:10
women that *s* by her said unto her 1Sa 4:20
s there, where there was a great 1Sa 6:14
when he *s* among the people, he 1Sa 10:23
came to Saul, and *s* before him.......... 1Sa 16:21
The Philistines *s* on a mountain 1Sa 17:3
Israel *s* on a mountain on the 1Sa 17:3
And he *s* and cried unto the armies.......... 1Sa 17:8
spake to the men that *s* by him 1Sa 17:26
s upon the Philistine, and took 1Sa 17:51
his servants that *s* about him 1Sa 22:6
unto the footmen that *s* about him 1Sa 22:17
s on the top of an hill afar off.......... 1Sa 26:13
So I *s* upon him, and slew him,.......... 2Sa 1:10
Asahel fell down and died *s* 2Sa 2:23
troop, and *s* on the top of an hill 2Sa 2:25
and all the people *s* still 2Sa 2:28
all his servants *s* by with their 2Sa 13:31
s beside the way of the gate 2Sa 15:2
the king *s* by the gate side, and 2Sa 18:4
And he turned aside, and *s* still 2Sa 18:30
And one of Joab's men *s* by him 2Sa 20:11
saw that all the people *s* still 2Sa 20:12
one that came by him *s* still 2Sa 20:12
the city, and it *s* in the trench 2Sa 20:15
But he *s* in the midst of the 2Sa 23:12
presence, and *s* before the king 1Kin 1:28
s before the ark of the covenant 1Kin 3:15
unto the king, and *s* before him 1Kin 3:16
It *s* upon twelve oxen, three.......... 1Kin 7:25
all the congregation of Israel *s* 1Kin 8:14
Solomon before the altar of the 1Kin 8:22
And he *s*, and blessed all the 1Kin 8:55
two lions *s* beside the stays 1Kin 10:19
and *s* beside the lions 1Kin 10:20
that *s* before Solomon his father 1Kin 12:6
with him, and which *s* before him 1Kin 12:8
Jeroboam *s* by the altar to burn 1Kin 13:1
in the way, and the ass *s* by it 1Kin 13:24
the lion also *s* by the carcase 1Kin 13:24

s in the entering in of the cave........ 1Kin 19:13
s before the LORD, and said, I........ 1Kin 22:21
went, and s to view afar off........ 2Kin 2:7
and they two s by Jordan........ 2Kin 2:7
back, and s by the bank of Jordan... 2Kin 2:13
and upward, and s in the border........ 2Kin 3:21
had called her, she s before him........ 2Kin 4:12
had called her, she s in the door........ 2Kin 4:15
s at the door of the house of........ 2Kin 5:9
company, and came, and s before him 2Kin 5:15
went in, and s before his master........ 2Kin 5:25
s before him, and said, Thy son........ 2Kin 8:9
there s a watchman on the tower........ 2Kin 9:17
two kings s not before him........ 2Kin 10:4
morning, that he went out, and s........ 2Kin 10:9
And the guard s, every man with........ 2Kin 11:11
he being by a pillar, as the........ 2Kin 11:14
he revived, and s up on his feet........ 2Kin 13:21
s by the conduit of the upper........ 2Kin 18:17
Then Rab-shakeh s and cried with a 2Kin 18:28
the king s by a pillar, and made a.... 2Kin 23:3
all the people s to the covenant........ 2Kin 23:3
who s on his right hand, even........ 1Chr 6:39
sons of Merari s on the left hand...... 1Chr 6:44
Satan s up against Israel, and........ 1Chr 21:1
the angel of the LORD s by the........ 1Chr 21:15
David the king s up upon his feet...... 1Chr 28:2
they s on their feet, and their........ 2Chr 3:13
It s upon twelve oxen, three........ 2Chr 4:4
s at the east end of the altar........ 2Chr 5:12
all the congregation of Israel s........ 2Chr 6:3
he s before the altar of the LORD.... 2Chr 6:12
and upon it he s, and kneeled down.. 2Chr 6:13
before them, and in Israel s........ 2Chr 7:6
twelve lions s there on the one........ 2Chr 9:19
with the old men that had s........ 2Chr 10:6
up with him, that s before him........ 2Chr 10:8
Abijah s up upon mount Zemaraim,.. 2Chr 13:4
s before the LORD, and said, I........ 2Chr 18:20
Jehoshaphat s in the congregation.... 2Chr 20:5
all Judah s before the LORD, with.... 2Chr 20:13
s up to praise the LORD God of........ 2Chr 20:19
as they went forth, Jehoshaphat s.... 2Chr 20:20
Moab s up against the inhabitants.... 2Chr 20:23
the king s at his pillar at the........ 2Chr 23:13
which s above the people, and said.... 2Chr 24:20
s up against them that came from.... 2Chr 28:12
And the Levites s with the........ 2Chr 29:26
they s in their place after their........ 2Chr 30:16
the king s in his place, and made.... 2Chr 34:31
the priests s in their place, and........ 2Chr 35:10
till there s up a priest with........ Ezr 2:63
Then s up Jeshua the son of........ Ezr 3:2
Then s Jeshua with his sons and........ Ezr 3:9
And Ezra the priest s up, and said.... Ezr 10:10
till there s up a priest with........ Neh 7:65
Ezra the scribe s upon a pulpit........ Neh 8:4
and beside him s Mattithiah........ Neh 8:4
he opened it, all the people s up...... Neh 8:5
the people s in their place........ Neh 8:7
from all strangers, and s and........ Neh 9:2
they s up in their place, and read.... Neh 9:3
Then s up upon the stairs, of the.... Neh 9:4
they s still in the prison gate........ Neh 12:39
So s the two companies of them........ Neh 12:40
s in the inner court of the........ Est 5:1
the king's gate, that he s not up...... Est 5:9
Haman s up to make request for...... Est 7:7
arose, and s before the king,........ Est 8:4
s for their lives, and had rest........ Est 9:16
the hair of my flesh s up........ Job 4:15
It s still, but I could not........ Job 4:16
and the aged arose, and s up........ Job 29:8
I s up, and I cried in the........ Job 30:28
but s still, and answered no more.... Job 32:16
he commanded, and it s fast........ Ps 33:9
the waters s above the mountains.... Ps 104:6
chosen s before him in the breach.... Ps 106:23
Then s up Phinehas, and executed.... Ps 106:30
Above it s the seraphims........ Is 6:2
he s by the conduit of the upper...... Is 36:2
Then Rabshakeh s, and cried with a.. Is 36:13
Samuel s before me, yet my mind.... Jer 15:1
Remember that I s before thee to.... Jer 18:20
he s in the court of the Lord's........ Jer 19:14
For who hath s in the counsel of...... Jer 23:18
But if they had s in my counsel...... Jer 23:22
that s in the house of the LORD........ Jer 28:5
princes which s beside the king........ Jer 36:21
gods, and all the women that s by.... Jer 44:15
they s not, because the LORD did.... Jer 46:15
They that fled s under the shadow.... Jer 48:45
he s with his right hand as an........ Lam 2:4
and when those s, these s........ Eze 1:21
when they s, they let down their...... Eze 1:24
was over their heads, when they s.... Eze 1:25
the glory of the LORD s in the........ Eze 3:23
there s before them seventy men...... Eze 8:11
in the midst of them s Jaazaniah.... Eze 8:11
s beside the brasen altar........ Eze 9:2
Now the cherubims s on the right.... Eze 10:3
s over the threshold of the house.... Eze 10:4
went in, and s beside the wheels...... Eze 10:6
When they s, these s........ Eze 10:17
house, and s over the cherubims.... Eze 10:18
every one s at the door of the........ Eze 10:19
s upon the mountain which is on.... Eze 11:23
For the king of Babylon s at the...... Eze 21:21
and s up upon their feet, an........ Eze 37:10
and he s in the gate........ Eze 40:3

and the man s by me........ Eze 43:6
of the house s toward the east........ Eze 47:1
therefore s they before the king...... Dan 1:19
So they came and s before the king.. Dan 2:2
was excellent, s before thee........ Dan 2:31
they s before the image that........ Dan 3:3
times ten thousand s before him...... Dan 7:10
near unto one of them that s by...... Dan 7:16
there s before me a ram........ Dan 8:3
behold, there s before me as the.... Dan 8:15
So he came near where I s........ Dan 8:17
broken, whereas four s up for it...... Dan 8:22
this word unto me, I s trembling.... Dan 10:11
and said unto him that s before me.. Dan 10:16
s to confirm and to strengthen him.. Dan 11:1
there s other two, the one on........ Dan 12:5
there they s........ Hos 10:9
the Lord s upon a wall made by a.... Amos 7:7
thou have s in the crossway........ Obad 14
He s, and measured the earth........ Hab 3:6
moon s still in their habitation........ Hab 3:11
he s among the myrtle trees that.... Zec 1:8
the man that s among the myrtle...... Zec 1:10
that s among the myrtle trees........ Zec 1:11
garments, and s before the angel.... Zec 3:3
unto those that s before him........ Zec 3:4
And the angel of the LORD s by........ Zec 3:5
s over where the young child was.... Mt 2:9
mother and his brethren s without.... Mt 12:46
whole multitude s on the shore........ Mt 13:2
And Jesus s still, and called them.... Mt 20:32
came unto him that they s by........ Mt 26:73
Jesus s before the governor........ Mt 27:11
Some of them that s there........ Mt 27:47
And Jesus s still, and commanded.... Mk 10:49
them that s there said unto them.... Mk 11:5
of them that s by drew a sword........ Mk 14:47
the high priest s up in the midst...... Mk 14:60
and began to say to them that s by.. Mk 14:69
that that s by said again to........ Mk 14:70
And some of them that s by........ Mk 15:35
which s over against him, saw........ Mk 15:39
sabbath day, and s up for to read.... Lk 4:16
he s over her, and rebuked the........ Lk 4:39
he s by the lake of Gennesaret,........ Lk 5:1
And he arose and s forth........ Lk 6:8
s in the plain, and the company of.. Lk 6:17
and they that bare him s still........ Lk 7:14
s at his feet behind him weeping,.... Lk 7:38
and the two men that s with him...... Lk 9:32
And, behold, a certain lawyer s up.. Lk 10:25
were lepers, which s afar off........ Lk 17:12
The Pharisee s and prayed thus...... Lk 18:11
And Jesus s, and commanded him to.. Lk 18:40
And Zacchaeus s, and said unto the.. Lk 19:8
he said unto them that s by........ Lk 19:24
And the chief priests and scribes s.. Lk 23:10
And the people s beholding........ Lk 23:35
s afar off, beholding these........ Lk 23:49
two men s by them in shining........ Lk 24:4
Jesus himself s in the midst of........ Lk 24:36
Again the next day after John s........ Jn 1:35
when the people which s on the...... Jn 6:22
great day of the feast, Jesus s........ Jn 7:37
as they s in the temple, What........ Jn 11:56
The people therefore, that s by........ Jn 12:29
which betrayed him, s with them...... Jn 18:5
But Peter s at the door without........ Jn 18:16
the servants and officers s there...... Jn 18:18
Peter s with them, and warmed........ Jn 18:18
one of the officers which s by........ Jn 18:22
And Simon Peter s and warmed...... Jn 18:25
Now there s by the cross of Jesus.... Jn 19:25
But Mary s without at the........ Jn 20:11
s in the midst, and saith unto........ Jn 20:19
s in the midst, and said, Peace be.. Jn 20:26
now come, Jesus s on the shore........ Jn 21:4
two men s by them in white........ Acts 1:10
in those days Peter s up in the........ Acts 1:15
And he leaping up s, and walked, and.. Acts 3:8
The kings of the earth s up........ Acts 4:26
Then s there up one in the........ Acts 5:34
journeyed with him s speechless...... Acts 9:7
all the widows s by him weeping...... Acts 9:39
house, and s before the gate,........ Acts 10:17
a man s before me in bright........ Acts 10:30
an angel in his house, which s........ Acts 11:13
there s up one of them named........ Acts 11:28
told how Peter s before the gate...... Acts 12:14
Then Paul s up, and beckoning with.. Acts 13:16
the disciples s round about him........ Acts 14:20
There s a man of Macedonia, and.... Acts 16:9
Then Paul s in the midst of Mars'.... Acts 17:22
Paul s on the stairs, and beckoned.. Acts 21:40
Came unto me, and s, and said unto.. Acts 22:13
said unto the centurion that s by.... Acts 23:17
that s by him to smite him on the.... Acts 23:2
And they that s by said, Revilest...... Acts 23:4
night following the Lord s by him.... Acts 23:11
while I s before the council........ Acts 24:20
down from Jerusalem s round about... Acts 25:7
whom when the accusers s up........ Acts 25:18
Paul s forth in the midst of them...... Acts 27:21
For there s by me this night the........ Acts 27:23
my first answer no man s with me.... 2Ti 4:16
the Lord s with me, and........ 2Ti 4:17
Which s only in meats and drinks,.... Heb 9:10
s a Lamb as it had been slain,........ Rev 5:6
s before the throne, and before........ Rev 7:9
all the angels s round about the........ Rev 7:11

seven angels which s before God........ Rev 8:2
s at the altar, having a golden........ Rev 8:3
and the angel s, saying, Rise, and.... Rev 11:1
them, and they s upon their feet...... Rev 11:11
the dragon s before the woman........ Rev 12:4
I s upon the sand of the sea, and.... Rev 13:1
a Lamb s on the mount Sion, and.... Rev 14:1
many as trade by sea, s afar off,...... Rev 18:17

STOODEST
that thou s in the way against me.... Num 22:34
thou s before the LORD thy God in.. Deut 4:10
day that thou s on the other side.... Obad 11

STOOL
there a bed, and a table, and a s.... 2Kin 4:10

STOOLS
women, and see them upon the s...... Ex 1:16

STOOP
the proud helpers do s under him.... Job 9:13
in the heart of man maketh it s...... Prov 12:25
They s, they bow down together...... Is 46:2
shoes I am not worthy to s down...... Mk 1:7

STOOPED
he s down, he couched as a lion,...... Gen 49:9
David s with his face to the........ 1Sa 24:8
he s with his face to the ground,.... 1Sa 28:14
old man, or him that s for age........ 2Chr 36:17
But Jesus s down, and with his........ Jn 8:6
And again he s down, and wrote on.. Jn 8:8
she s down, and looked into the...... Jn 20:11

STOOPETH
Bel boweth down, Nebo s, their........ Is 46:1

STOOPING
s down, he beheld the linen........ Lk 24:12
he s down, and looking in, saw the.. Jn 20:5

STOP
down, that the rain s thee not........ 1Kin 18:44
s all wells of water, and mar........ 2Kin 3:19
his mighty men to s the waters of.... 2Chr 32:3
s the way against them that........ Ps 35:3
and all iniquity shall s her mouth.... Ps 107:42
it shall s the noses of the........ Eze 39:11
no man shall s me of this........ 2Cor 11:10

STOPPED
and the windows of heaven were s.... Gen 8:2
the Philistines had s them........ Gen 26:15
for the Philistines had s them........ Gen 26:18
or his flesh be s from his issue........ Lev 15:3
they s all the wells of water, and.... 2Kin 3:25
who s all the fountains, and the...... 2Chr 32:4
This same Hezekiah also s the........ 2Chr 32:30
that the breaches began to be s...... Neh 4:7
them that speak lies shall be s........ Ps 63:11
And that the passages are s........ Jer 51:32
s their ears, that they should........ Zec 7:11
s their ears, and ran upon him........ Acts 7:57
that every mouth may be s........ Rom 3:19
Whose mouths must be s, who........ Titus 1:11
promises, s the mouths of lions,...... Heb 11:33

STOPPETH
hope, and iniquity s her mouth........ Job 5:16
the deaf adder that s her ear........ Ps 58:4
Whoso s his ears at the cry of........ Prov 21:13
that s his ears from hearing of........ Is 33:15

STORE
of herds, and great s of servants.... Gen 26:14
that food shall be for s to the........ Gen 41:36
come in ye shall eat of the old s...... Lev 25:22
And ye shall eat old s, and bring.... Lev 26:10
shall be thy basket and thy s........ Deut 28:5
shall be thy basket and thy s........ Deut 28:17
Is not this laid up in s with me........ Deut 32:34
the cities of s that Solomon built.... 1Kin 9:19
gold, and of spices very great s........ 1Kin 10:10
have laid up in s unto this day........ 2Kin 20:17
all this s that we have prepared...... 1Chr 29:16
wilderness, and all the cities........ 2Chr 8:4
all the s cities that Solomon had...... 2Chr 8:6
s of victual, and of oil and wine...... 2Chr 11:11
all the s cities of Naphtali........ 2Chr 16:4
in Judah castles, and cities of s...... 2Chr 17:12
which is left in this great s........ 2Chr 31:10
once in ten days s of all sorts........ Neh 5:18
full, affording all manner of s........ Ps 144:13
have laid up in s until this day........ Is 39:6
who s up violence and robbery in.... Amos 3:10
for there is none end of the s........ Nah 2:9
every one of you lay by him in s...... 1Cor 16:2
Laying up in s for themselves a...... 1Ti 6:19
by the same word are kept in s........ 2Pet 3:7

STOREHOUSE
ye all the tithes into the s........ Mal 3:10
which neither have s nor barn........ Lk 12:24

STOREHOUSES
And Joseph opened all the s........ Gen 41:56
the blessing upon thee in thy s........ Deut 28:8
over the s in the fields, in the........ 1Chr 27:25
s also for the increase of corn,...... 2Chr 32:28
he layeth up the depth in s........ Ps 33:7
the uttermost border, open her s.... Jer 50:26

STORIES
third s shalt thou make it........ Gen 6:16
round about on their three s........ Eze 41:16
against gallery in three s........ Eze 42:3

S

For they were in three *s*, but had.......... Eze 42:6
that buildeth his *s* in the heaven.......... Amos 9:6

STORK
And the *s*, the heron after her.......... Lev 11:19
And the *s*, and the heron after her... Deut 14:18
as for the *s*, the fir trees are.......... Ps 104:17
the *s* in the heaven knoweth her.......... Jer 8:7
had wings like the wings of a *s*.......... Zec 5:9

STORM
as chaff that the *s* carrieth away.......... Job 21:18
as a *s* hurleth him out of his.......... Job 27:21
hasten my escape from the windy *s*.......... Ps 55:8
and make them afraid with thy *s*.......... Ps 83:15
He maketh the *s* a calm, so that.......... Ps 107:29
of refuge, and for a covert from *s*.......... Is 4:6
his distress, a refuge from the *s*.......... Is 25:4
ones is as a *s* against the wall.......... Is 25:4
tempest of hail and a destroying *s*.......... Is 28:2
and great noise, with *s* and.......... Is 29:6
shalt ascend and come like a *s*.......... Eze 38:9
way in the whirlwind and in the *s*.......... Nah 1:3
And there arose a great *s* of wind.......... Mk 4:37
there came down a *s* of wind on.......... Lk 8:23

STORMY
commandeth, and raiseth the *s* wind... Ps 107:25
s wind fulfilling his word.......... Ps 148:8
and a *s* wind shall rend it.......... Eze 13:11
rend it with a *s* wind in my fury.......... Eze 13:13

STORY
are written in the *s* of the.......... 2Chr 13:22
they are written in the *s* of the.......... 2Chr 24:27

STOUT
the *s* lion's whelps are scattered.......... Job 4:11
s heart of the king of Assyria.......... Is 10:12
was more *s* than his fellows.......... Dan 7:20
Your words have been *s* against me... Mal 3:13

STOUTHEARTED
The *s* are spoiled, they have.......... Ps 76:5
Hearken unto me, ye *s*, that are.......... Is 46:12

STOUTNESS
say in the pride and *s* of heart.......... Is 9:9

STRAIGHT
ascend up every man *s* before him... Josh 6:5
every man *s* before him, and they.......... Josh 6:20
the kine took the *s* way to the.......... 1Sa 6:12
brought it *s* down to the west.......... 2Chr 32:30
make thy way *s* before my face.......... Ps 5:8
thine eyelids look *s* before thee.......... Prov 4:25
which is crooked cannot be made *s*... Eccl 1:15
for who can make that *s*, which he... Eccl 7:13
make *s* in the desert a highway.......... Is 40:3
and the crooked shall be made *s*.......... Is 40:4
before them, and crooked things a *s*... Is 42:16
and make the crooked places *s*.......... Is 45:2
the rivers of waters in a *s* way.......... Jer 31:9
And their feet were *s* feet.......... Eze 1:7
they went every one *s* forward.......... Eze 1:9
And they went every one *s* forward... Eze 1:12
the firmament were their wings *s*.......... Eze 1:23
they went every one *s* forward.......... Eze 10:22
way of the Lord, make his paths *s*... Mt 3:3
way of the Lord, make his paths *s*... Mk 1:3
way of the Lord, make his paths *s*... Lk 3:4
and the crooked shall be made *s*.......... Lk 3:5
and immediately she was made *s*.......... Lk 13:13
Make *s* the way of the Lord, as.......... Jn 1:23
into the street which is called S....... Acts 9:11
we came with a *s* course to.......... Acts 16:11
we came with a *s* course unto Coos... Acts 21:1
make *s* paths for your feet, lest.......... Heb 12:13

STRAIGHTWAY
the city, ye shall *s* find him.......... 1Sa 9:13
Then Saul fell *s* all along on the.......... 1Sa 28:20
He goeth after her *s*, as an ox.......... Prov 7:22
a there remained no strength in.......... Dan 10:17
went up *s* out of the water.......... Mt 3:16
they *s* left their nets, and.......... Mt 4:20
And a Jesus constrained his.......... Mt 14:22
But *s* Jesus spake unto them.......... Mt 14:27
s ye shall find an ass tied, and a... Mt 21:2
and *s* he will send them.......... Mt 21:3
and *s* took his journey.......... Mt 25:15
s one of them ran, and took a.......... Mt 27:48
s coming up out of the water, he.......... Mk 1:10
s they forsook their nets, and.......... Mk 1:18
And *s* he called them.......... Mk 1:20
s on the sabbath day he entered.......... Mk 1:21
s many were gathered together.......... Mk 2:2
s took counsel with the Herodians... Mk 3:6
s the fountain of her blood was.......... Mk 5:29
s the damsel arose, and walked.......... Mk 5:42
she came in *s* with haste unto the... Mk 6:25
s he constrained his disciples to.......... Mk 6:45
out of the ship, *s* they knew him.......... Mk 6:54
s his ears were opened, and he.......... Mk 7:35
s he entered into a ship with his.......... Mk 8:10
s all the people, when they.......... Mk 9:15
he saw him, *s* the spirit tare him... Mk 9:20
s the father of the child cried.......... Mk 9:24
s he will send him hither.......... Mk 11:3
as he was come, he goeth *s* to him... Mk 14:45
s in the morning the chief.......... Mk 15:1
drunk old wine *s* desireth new.......... Lk 5:39
spirit came again, and she arose *s*... Lk 8:55
s ye say, There cometh a shower... Lk 12:54

will not *s* pull him out on the.......... Lk 14:5
himself, and shall *s* glorify him.......... Jn 13:32
Then fell she down *s* at his feet.......... Acts 5:10
s he preached Christ in the.......... Acts 9:20
and was baptized, he and all his, *s*... Acts 16:33
Then *s* they departed from him.......... Acts 22:29
I sent *s* to thee, and gave.......... Acts 23:30
s forgetteth what manner of man... Jas 1:24

STRAIN
which *s* at a gnat, and swallow a... Mt 23:24

STRAIT
Israel saw that they were in a *s*.......... 1Sa 13:6
said unto Gad, I am in a great *s*.......... 2Sa 24:14
dwell with thee is too *s* for us.......... 2Kin 6:1
said unto Gad, I am in a great *s*.......... 1Chr 21:13
out of the *s* into a broad place.......... Job 36:16
ears, The place is too *s* for me.......... Is 49:20
Enter ye in at the *s* gate.......... Mt 7:13
Because *s* is the gate, and narrow... Mt 7:14
Strive to enter in at the *s* gate.......... Lk 13:24
For I am in a *s* betwixt two.......... Phil 1:23

STRAITEN
seek their lives, shall *s* them.......... Jer 19:9

STRAITENED
steps of his strength shall be *s*.......... Job 18:7
and the breadth of the waters is *s*... Job 37:10
goest, thy steps shall not be *s*.......... Prov 4:12
was *s* more than the lowest.......... Eze 42:6
is the spirit of the Lord *s*.......... Mic 2:7
and how am I *s* till it be.......... Lk 12:50
Ye are not *s* in us, but ye are.......... 2Cor 6:12
but ye are *s* in your own bowels... 2Cor 6:12

STRAITENETH
the nations, and *s* them again.......... Job 12:23

STRAITEST
that after the most *s* sect of our... Acts 26:5

STRAITLY
The man asked us *s* of our state.......... Gen 43:7
for he had *s* sworn the children.......... Ex 13:19
Now Jericho was *s* shut up because... Josh 6:1
Thy father *s* charged the people.......... 1Sa 14:28
Jesus a charged them, saying, See... Mt 9:30
he a charged him, and forthwith.......... Mk 1:43
he *s* charged them that they.......... Mk 3:12
he charged them *s* that no man.......... Mk 5:43
he *s* charged them, and commanded... Lk 8:29
let us *s* threaten them, that they... Acts 4:17
Did not we *s* command you that ye... Acts 5:28

STRAITNESS
thee, in the siege, and in the *s*.......... Deut 28:53
him in the siege, and in the *s*.......... Deut 28:55
things secretly in the siege and *s*... Deut 28:57
broad place, where there is no *s*.......... Job 36:16
of his friend in the siege and *s*.......... Jer 19:9

STRAITS
his sufficiency he shall be in *s*.......... Job 20:22
overtook her between the *s*.......... Lam 1:3

STRAKE
s sail, and so were driven.......... Acts 27:17

STRAKES
and pilled white *s* in them.......... Gen 30:37
walls of the house with hollow *s*... Lev 14:37

STRANGE
Put away the *s* gods that are.......... Gen 35:2
they gave unto Jacob all the *s*.......... Gen 35:4
but made himself *s* unto them.......... Gen 42:7
have been a stranger in a *s* land.......... Ex 2:22
I have been an alien in a *s* land.......... Ex 18:3
to sell her unto a nation he.......... Ex 21:8
shall offer no *s* incense thereon.......... Ex 30:9
offered a fire before the Lord.......... Lev 10:1
when they offered *s* fire before.......... Num 3:4
when they offered a fire before.......... Num 26:61
and there was no *s* god with him.......... Deut 32:12
him to jealousy with *s* gods.......... Deut 32:16
forsake the Lord, and serve *s* gods... Josh 24:20
the *s* gods which are among you.......... Josh 24:23
they put away the *s* gods from.......... Judg 10:16
for thou art the son of a *s* woman... Judg 11:2
hearts, then put away the *s* gods... 1Sa 7:3
king Solomon loved many *s* women... 1Kin 11:1
did he for all his *s* wives.......... 1Kin 11:8
drunk *s* waters, and with the sole... 2Kin 19:24
away the altars of the *s* gods.......... 2Chr 14:3
And he took away the *s* gods.......... 2Chr 33:15
have taken *s* wives of the people... Ezr 10:2
and have taken *s* wives, to.......... Ezr 10:10
of the land, and from the *s* wives... Ezr 10:11
s wives in our cities came at.......... Ezr 10:14
a wives by the first day of the.......... Ezr 10:17
were found that had taken *s* wives... Ezr 10:44
All these had taken *s* wives.......... Ezr 10:44
our God in marrying *s* wives.......... Neh 13:27
that ye make yourselves *s* to me... Job 19:3
My breath is *s* to my wife.......... Job 19:17
a punishment to the workers of.......... Job 31:3
out our hands to a *s* god.......... Ps 44:20
There shall no *s* god be in thee.......... Ps 81:9
shalt thou worship any *s* god.......... Ps 81:9
Jacob from a people of *s* language... Ps 114:1
sing the Lord's song in a *s* land.......... Ps 137:4
from the hand of *s* children.......... Ps 144:7
me from the hand of *s* children.......... Ps 144:11
To deliver them from the *s* woman... Prov 2:16

For the lips of a *s* woman drop as... Prov 5:3
son, be ravished with a *s* woman.......... Prov 5:20
of the tongue of a *s* woman.......... Prov 6:24
may keep thee from the *s* woman... Prov 7:5
a pledge of him for a *s* woman.......... Prov 20:16
The way of man is froward and *s*... Prov 21:8
The mouth of *s* women is a deep.......... Prov 22:14
a woman is a narrow pit.......... Prov 23:27
Thine eyes shall behold *s* women... Prov 23:33
a pledge of him for a *s* woman.......... Prov 27:13
and shalt set it with *s* slips.......... Is 17:10
he may do his work, his *s* work.......... Is 28:21
bring to pass his act, his *s* act.......... Is 28:21
when there was no *s* god among you... Is 43:12
plant of a *s* vine unto me.......... Jer 2:21
served *s* gods in your land, so.......... Jer 5:19
graven images, and with *s* vanities... Jer 8:19
sent to a people of a *s* speech.......... Eze 3:5
Not to many people of a *s* speech... Eze 3:6
most strong holds with a *s* god.......... Dan 11:39
for they have begotten *s* children... Hos 5:7
they were counted as a *s* thing.......... Hos 8:12
as are clothed with *s* apparel.......... Zeph 1:8
married the daughter of a *s* god.......... Mal 2:11
We have seen *s* things to day.......... Lk 5:26
seed should sojourn in a *s* land.......... Acts 7:6
to be a setter forth of *s* gods.......... Acts 17:18
certain *s* things to our ears.......... Acts 17:20
them even unto *s* cities.......... Acts 26:11
of promise, as in a *s* country.......... Heb 11:9
about with divers and *s* doctrines... Heb 13:9
Wherein they think it *s* that ye.......... 1Pet 4:4
think it not *s* concerning the.......... 1Pet 4:12
as though some a thing happened.......... 1Pet 4:12
and going after a flesh, are set.......... Jude 7

STRANGELY
should behave themselves *s*.......... Deut 32:27

STRANGER
a *s* in a land that is not theirs.......... Gen 15:13
the land wherein thou art a *s*.......... Gen 17:8
or bought with money of any *s*.......... Gen 17:12
and bought with money of the *s*.......... Gen 17:27
I am a *s* and a sojourner with you... Gen 23:4
the land wherein thou art a *s*.......... Gen 28:4
land wherein his father was a *s*.......... Gen 37:1
I have been a *s* in a strange land... Ex 2:22
of Israel, whether he be a *s*.......... Ex 12:19
There shall no *s* eat thereof.......... Ex 12:43
when a *s* shall sojourn with thee... Ex 12:48
unto the *s* that sojourneth among... Ex 12:49
nor thy *s* that is within thy.......... Ex 20:10
Thou shalt neither vex a *s*.......... Ex 22:21
Also thou shalt not oppress a *s*.......... Ex 23:9
for ye know the heart of a *s*.......... Ex 23:9
the son of thy handmaid, and the *s*... Ex 23:12
but a *s* shall not eat thereof.......... Ex 29:33
putteth any of it upon a *s*.......... Ex 30:33
or a *s* that sojourneth among you... Lev 16:29
blood, neither shall any *s* that.......... Lev 17:12
one of your own country, or a *s*.......... Lev 17:15
nor any a that sojourneth among.......... Lev 18:26
leave them for the poor and a *s*.......... Lev 19:10
if a *s* sojourn with thee in your.......... Lev 19:33
But the *s* that dwelleth with you... Lev 19:34
There shall no a eat of the holy.......... Lev 22:10
daughter also be married unto a *s*... Lev 22:12
but there shall no a eat thereof.......... Lev 22:13
them unto the poor, and to the *s*... Lev 23:22
as well the *s*, as he that is born... Lev 24:16
manner of law, as well for the *s*... Lev 24:22
for thy a that sojourneth with.......... Lev 25:6
yea, though he be a *s*, or a.......... Lev 25:35
a sojourner or a wax rich by thee... Lev 25:47
unto the *s* or sojourner by thee.......... Lev 25:47
the *s* that cometh nigh shall be.......... Num 1:51
the *s* that cometh nigh shall be.......... Num 3:10
the *s* that cometh nigh shall be.......... Num 3:38
if a *s* shall sojourn among you.......... Num 9:14
one ordinance, both for the *s*.......... Num 9:14
if a *s* sojourn with you, or.......... Num 15:14
also for the *s* that sojourneth.......... Num 15:15
so shall the *s* be before the Lord... Num 15:15
for the *s* that sojourneth with.......... Num 15:16
the *s* that sojourneth among them... Num 15:26
for the *s* that sojourneth among.......... Num 15:29
he be born in the land, or a *s*.......... Num 15:30
the children of Israel, that no *s*... Num 16:40
a shall not come nigh unto you.......... Num 18:4
the *s* that cometh nigh shall be.......... Num 18:7
unto the *s* that sojourneth among... Num 19:10
children of Israel, and for the *s*... Num 35:15
and the *s* that is with him.......... Deut 1:16
nor thy *s* that is within thy.......... Deut 5:14
and widow, and loveth the *s*.......... Deut 10:18
Love ye therefore the *s*.......... Deut 10:19
unto the *s* that is in thy gates.......... Deut 14:21
inheritance with thee,) and the *s*... Deut 14:29
is within thy gates, and the *s*.......... Deut 16:11
maidservant, and the Levite, the *s*... Deut 16:14
thou mayest not set a *s* over thee... Deut 17:15
because thou wast a *s* in his land... Deut 23:7
Unto a *s* thou mayest lend upon.......... Deut 23:20
not pervert the judgment of the *s*... Deut 24:17
it shall be for the *s*, for the.......... Deut 24:19
it shall be for the *s*, for the.......... Deut 24:20
it shall be for the *s*, for the.......... Deut 24:21
shall not marry without unto a *s*... Deut 25:5
and the *s* that is among you.......... Deut 26:11
given it unto the Levite, the *s*.......... Deut 26:12

unto the Levite, and unto the s........ Deut 26:13
peradventure the judgment of the s.... Deut 27:19
The s that is within thee shall.......... Deut 28:43
thy s that is in thy camp, from.......... Deut 29:11
the s that shall come from a far........ Deut 29:22
thy s that is within thy gates,.......... Deut 31:12
the LORD, as well the s.................... Josh 8:33
for the s that sojourneth among........ Josh 20:9
aside hither into the city of a s........ Judg 19:12
knowledge of me, seeing I am a s...... Ruth 2:10
he answered, I am the son of a s...... 2Sa 1:13
for thou art a s, and also an 2Sa 15:19
there was no s with us in the 1Kin 3:18
Moreover concerning a s, that is...... 1Kin 8:41
that the s calleth to thee for.......... 1Kin 8:43
Moreover concerning the s 2Chr 6:32
that the s calleth to thee for.......... 2Chr 6:33
given, and no s passed among them.. Job 15:19
and my maids, count me for a s ...... Job 19:15
The s did not lodge in the street...... Job 31:32
for I am a s with thee, and a .... Ps 39:12
I am become a s unto my brethren,.. Ps 69:8
They slay the widow and the s .... Ps 94:6
I am a s in the earth...................... Ps 119:19
even from the s which flattereth...... Prov 2:16
labours be in the house of a s .... Prov 5:10
and embrace the bosom of a s .... Prov 5:20
hast stricken thy hand with a s ...... Prov 6:1
from the s which flattereth with...... Prov 7:5
surety for a s shall smart for it ...... Prov 11:15
a s doth not intermeddle with his.... Prov 14:10
garment that is surety for a s .... Prov 20:16
a s, and not thine own lips............ Prov 27:2
garment that is surety for a s .... Prov 27:13
to eat thereof, but a s eateth it...... Eccl 6:2
Neither let the son of the s............ Is 56:3
Also the sons of the s, that join...... Is 56:6
the sons of the s shall not drink...... Is 62:8
If ye oppress not the s, the .... Jer 7:6
thou be as a s in the land?............ Jer 14:8
no wrong, do no violence to the s.. Jer 22:3
or of the s that sojourneth in.......... Eze 14:7
dealt by oppression with the s........ Eze 22:29
have oppressed the s wrongfully...... Eze 22:29
No s, uncircumcised in heart, nor.... Eze 44:9
of any s that is among the.............. Eze 44:9
in what tribe the s sojourneth .... Eze 47:23
in the day that he became a s.......... Obad 12
widow, nor the fatherless, the s...... Zec 7:10
turn aside the s from his right........ Mal 3:5
I was a s, and ye took me in............ Mt 25:35
When saw we thee a s, and took...... Mt 25:38
I was a s, and ye took me not in...... Mt 25:43
an hungred, or athirst, or a s.......... Mt 25:44
to give glory to God, save this s...... Lk 17:18
Art thou only a s in Jerusalem........ Lk 24:18
a s will they not follow, but............ Jn 10:5
was a s in the land of Madian,........ Acts 7:29

Neither from a s hand shall ye........ Lev 22:25
or to the stock of the s family .... Lev 25:47

Are we not counted of him s.......... Gen 31:15
the land wherein they were s.......... Gen 36:7
pilgrimage, wherein they were s...... Ex 6:4
for ye were s in the land of............ Ex 22:21
seeing ye were s in the land of ...... Ex 23:9
or of the s which sojourn among...... Lev 17:8
or of the s that sojourn among........ Lev 17:10
or of the s that sojourn among........ Lev 17:13
for ye were s in the land of............ Lev 19:34
or of the s that sojourn in.............. Lev 20:2
of Israel, or of the s in Israel.......... Lev 22:18
for ye are s and sojourners with...... Lev 25:23
the s that do sojourn among you...... Lev 25:45
for ye were s in the land of............ Deut 10:19
or of thy s that are in thy land........ Deut 24:14
the gods of the s of the land.......... Deut 31:16
the s that were conversant among.. Josh 8:35
S shall submit themselves unto me.. 2Sa 22:45
S shall fade away, and they shall.... 2Sa 22:46
but few, even a few, and s in it 1Chr 16:19
to gather together the s that.......... 1Chr 22:2
For we are s before thee, and........ 1Chr 29:15
Solomon numbered all the s that...... 2Chr 2:17
the s with them out of Ephraim and.. 2Chr 15:9
the s that came out of the land...... Neh 9:2
separated themselves from all s ...... Neh 9:2
Thus cleansed I them from all s ...... Neh 13:30
the s shall submit themselves.......... Ps 18:44
The s shall fade away, and the........ Ps 18:45
For s are risen up against me, and.. Ps 54:3
yea, very few, and s in it................ Ps 105:12
let the s spoil his labour................ Ps 109:11
The LORD preserveth the s.............. Ps 146:9
Lest s be filled with thy wealth........ Prov 5:10
s devour it in your presence, and.... Is 1:7
is desolate, as overthrown by s ...... Is 1:7
themselves in the children of s ...... Is 2:6
of the fat ones shall s eat.............. Is 5:17
the s shall be joined with them,...... Is 14:1
a palace of s to be no city.............. Is 25:2
shalt bring down the noise of s ...... Is 25:5
of thy s shall be like small dust...... Is 29:5
the sons of s shall build up thy ...... Is 60:10
s shall stand and feed your flocks.. Is 61:5
for I have loved s, and after them.... Jer 2:25
to the s under every green tree...... Jer 3:13
so shall ye serve s in a land.......... Jer 5:19

s shall no more serve themselves .. Jer 30:8
days in the land where ye be s........ Jer 35:7
for s are come into the.................... Jer 51:51
Our inheritance is turned to s.......... Lam 5:2
the hands of the s for a prey.......... Eze 7:21
deliver you into the hands of s........ Eze 11:9
which taketh s instead of her.......... Eze 16:32
I will bring s upon thee, the............ Eze 28:7
uncircumcised by the hand of s ...... Eze 28:10
that is therein, by the hand of s...... Eze 30:12
And s, the terrible of the nations.... Eze 31:12
have brought into my sanctuary s.... Eze 44:7
to the s that sojourn among you,.... Eze 47:22
S have devoured his strength, and.. Hos 7:9
the s shall swallow it up................ Hos 8:7
there shall no s pass through her.... Joel 3:17
in the day that the s carried............ Obad 11
of their own children, or of s.......... Mt 17:25
Peter saith unto him, Of s................ Mt 17:26
the potter's field, to bury s in........ Mt 27:7
for they know not the voice of s...... Jn 10:5
s of Rome, Jews and proselytes,...... Acts 2:10
dwelt as s in the land of Egypt........ Acts 13:17
s which were spent their.................. Acts 17:21
s from the covenants of promise,.... Eph 2:12
Now therefore ye are no more s ...... Eph 2:19
up children, if she have lodged s 1Ti 5:10
and confessed that they were s ...... Heb 11:13
Be not forgetful to entertain s ...... Heb 13:2
to the s scattered throughout.......... 1Pet 1:1
beloved, I beseech you as s 1Pet 2:11
doest to the brethren, and to s 3Jn 5

thine own, and not s with thee........ Prov 5:17

s for his lionesses, and filled.......... Nah 2:12
fornication, and from things s.......... Acts 15:20
and from blood, and from things s .. Acts 15:29
idols, and from blood, and from s.... Acts 21:25

So that my soul chooseth s.............. Job 7:15

moreover unto him, We have both s.. Gen 24:25
he ungirded his camels, and gave s.. Gen 24:32
give the people s to make brick ...... Ex 5:7
go and gather s for themselves........ Ex 5:7
Pharaoh, I will not give you s.......... Ex 5:10
get you s where ye can find it........ Ex 5:11
to gather stubble instead of s........ Ex 5:12
daily tasks, as when there was s .... Ex 5:13
There is no s given unto thy............ Ex 5:16
for there shall no s be given you.... Ex 5:18
Yet there is both s and provender.. Judg 19:19
s for the horses and dromedaries.... 1Kin 4:28
He esteemeth iron as s, and brass.. Job 41:27
the lion shall eat s like the............ Is 11:7
even as s is trodden down for the.. Is 25:10
lion shall eat s like the bullock...... Is 65:25

s it upon the water, and made the.. Ex 32:20
the trees, and s them in the way...... Mt 21:8
gathering where thou hast not s...... Mt 25:24
not, and gather where I have not s.. Mt 25:26
the trees, and s them in the way...... Mk 11:8

at the s of the brooks that goeth.... Num 21:15
as the s of brooks they pass away.. Job 6:15
the s had gone over our soul.......... Ps 124:4
of the river unto the s of Egypt...... Is 27:12
his breath, as an overflowing s........ Is 30:28
like a s of brimstone, doth.............. Is 30:33
stones of the s is thy portion.......... Is 57:6
of the Gentiles like a flowing s ...... Is 66:12
A fiery s issued and came forth...... Dan 7:10
and righteousness as a mighty s...... Amos 5:24
the s beat vehemently upon that...... Lk 6:48
against which the s did beat .... Lk 6:49

the waters of Egypt, upon their s.... Ex 7:19
hand with thy rod over the s .... Ex 8:5
the s whereof shall make glad the.. Ps 46:4
He brought s also out of the rock.. Ps 78:16
gushed out, and the s overflowed.... Ps 78:20
O LORD, as the s in the south .... Ps 126:4
living waters, and s from Lebanon .. Song 4:15
and shall smite it in the seven s .... Is 11:15
s of waters in the day of.............. Is 30:25
us a place of broad rivers and s .... Is 33:21
the s thereof shall be turned.......... Is 34:9
break out, and s in the desert........ Is 35:6

we will abide in the s all night........ Gen 19:2
into the midst of the s thereof........ Deut 13:16
the doors of thy house into the s.... Josh 2:19
sat him down in a s of the city...... Judg 19:15
man in the s of the city................ Judg 19:17
only lodge not in the s.................. Judg 19:20
them from the s of Beth-shan........ 2Sa 21:12
stamp them as the mire of the s 2Sa 22:43
them together into the s................ 2Chr 29:4
in the s of the gate of the city...... 2Chr 32:6
sat in the s of the house of God.... Ezr 10:9
together as one man into the s........ Neh 8:1
he read therein before the s that.... Neh 8:3
the s of the water gate, and in........ Neh 8:16
in the s of the gate of Ephraim...... Neh 8:16

Mordecai unto the s of the city...... Est 4:6
through the s of the city................ Est 6:9
through the s of the city................ Est 6:11
and he shall have no name in the s.. Job 18:17
when I prepared my seat in the s.... Job 29:7
stranger did not lodge in the s........ Job 31:32
through the s near her corner.......... Prov 7:8
his voice to be heard in the s .... Is 42:2
body as the ground, and as the s .. Is 51:23
for truth is fallen in the s.............. Is 59:14
of bread out of the bakers'............ Jer 37:21
for hunger in the top of every s .... Lam 2:19
poured out in the top of every s .... Lam 4:1
thee an high place in every s.......... Eze 16:24
thine high place in every s.............. Eze 16:31
pestilence, and blood into her s...... Eze 28:23
the s shall be built again, and........ Dan 9:25
go into the s which is called .... Acts 9:11
out, and passed on through one s.... Acts 12:10
lie in the s of that great city.......... Rev 11:8
the s of the city was pure gold,...... Rev 21:21
In the midst of the s of it .... Rev 22:2

it not in the s of Askelon................ 2Sa 1:20
thou shalt make s for thee in.......... 1Kin 20:34
them out as the dirt in the s .... Ps 18:42
and guide depart not from her s...... Ps 55:11
and ten thousands in our s.............. Ps 144:13
there be no complaining in our s...... Ps 144:14
she uttereth her voice in the s........ Prov 1:20
and rivers of waters in the s .... Prov 5:16
Now is she without, now in the s...... Prov 7:12
I shall be slain in the s.................. Prov 22:13
a lion is in the s............................ Prov 26:13
the doors shall be shut in the s ...... Eccl 12:4
and the mourners go about the s .... Eccl 12:5
and go about the city in the s .... Song 3:2
were torn in the midst of the s ...... Is 5:25
them down like the mire of the s .... Is 10:6
In their s they shall gird................ Is 15:3
of their houses, and in their s .... Is 15:3
is a crying for wine in the s .... Is 24:11
they lie at the head of all the s...... Is 51:20
and fro through the s of Jerusalem.. Jer 5:1
of Judah and in the s of Jerusalem.. Jer 7:17
from the s of Jerusalem, the............ Jer 7:34
and the young men from the s.......... Jer 9:21
in the s of Jerusalem, saying,.......... Jer 11:6
the s of Jerusalem have ye set up .. Jer 11:13
shall be cast out in the s of............ Jer 14:16
in the s of Jerusalem, that are........ Jer 33:10
of Judah and in the s of Jerusalem.. Jer 44:6
Judah, and in the s of Jerusalem .... Jer 44:9
Judah, and in the s of Jerusalem .... Jer 44:17
in the s of Jerusalem, ye, and........ Jer 44:21
of Moab, and in the s thereof.......... Jer 48:38
her young men shall fall in her s .... Jer 49:26
shall her young men fall in the s .... Jer 50:30
that are thrust through in her s...... Jer 51:4
swoon in the s of the city.............. Lam 2:11
the wounded in the s of the city .... Lam 2:12
old lie on the ground in the s .... Lam 2:21
delicately are desolate in the s ...... Lam 4:5
they are not known in the s............ Lam 4:8
wandered as blind men in the s...... Lam 4:14
steps, that we cannot go in our s.... Lam 4:18
shall cast their silver in the s .... Eze 7:19
ye have filled the s thereof with .... Eze 11:6
shall be trodden and dirty s .... Eze 26:11
Wailing shall be in all s.................. Amos 5:16
trodden down as the mire of the s.. Mic 7:10
The chariots shall rage in the s...... Nah 2:4
in pieces at the top of all the s ...... Nah 3:10
I made their s waste, that none...... Zeph 3:6
women dwell in the s of Jerusalem.. Zec 8:4
the s of the city shall be full.......... Zec 8:5
and girls playing in the s thereof .. Zec 8:5
and fine gold as the mire of the s .. Zec 9:3
the mire of the s in the battle........ Zec 10:5
do in the synagogues and in the s.. Mt 6:2
and in the corners of the s............ Mt 6:5
any man hear his voice in the s...... Mt 12:19
they laid the sick in the s.............. Mk 6:56
ways out into the s of the same...... Lk 10:10
and thou hast taught in our s .... Lk 13:26
Go out quickly into the s................ Lk 14:21
brought forth the sick into the s .... Acts 5:15

henceforth yield unto thee her s...... Gen 4:12
might, and the beginning of my s .... Gen 49:3
But his bow abode in s, and the .... Gen 49:24
for by s of hand the LORD brought.. Ex 13:3
By s of hand the LORD brought........ Ex 13:14
for by s of hand the LORD brought.. Ex 13:16
the sea returned to his s when........ Ex 14:27
The LORD is my s and song, and he.. Ex 15:2
in thy s unto thy holy habitation .... Ex 15:13
your s shall be spent in vain.......... Lev 26:20
as it were the s of a unicorn.......... Num 23:22
as it were the s of a unicorn.......... Num 24:8
for he is the beginning of his s ...... Deut 21:17
and as thy days, so shall thy s be.. Deut 33:25
that stood still in their s................ Josh 11:13
as my s was then, even so is my.... Josh 14:11
was then, even so is my s now........ Josh 14:11
my soul, thou hast trodden down s.. Judg 5:21
for as the man is, so is his s .... Judg 8:21
and see wherein his great s lieth .... Judg 16:5
thee, wherein thy great s lieth........ Judg 16:6

S

So his s was not known....... Judg 16:9
told me wherein thy great s lieth....... Judg 16:15
then my s will go from me, and I....... Judg 16:17
him, and his s went from him....... Judg 16:19
that stumbled are girded with s....... 1Sa 2:4
for by s shall no man prevail....... 1Sa 2:9
and he shall give s unto his king....... 1Sa 2:10
also the S of Israel will not lie....... 1Sa 15:29
and there was no s in him....... 1Sa 28:20
and eat, that thou mayest have s....... 1Sa 28:22
God is my s and power....... 2Sa 22:33
hast girded me with s to battle....... 2Sa 22:40
went in the s of that meat forty....... 1Kin 19:8
Jehu drew a bow with his full s....... 2Kin 9:24
I have counsel and s for the war....... 2Kin 18:20
there is not s to bring forth....... 2Kin 19:3
Seek the Lord and his s, seek his....... 1Chr 16:11
s and gladness are in his place....... 1Chr 16:27
give unto the Lord glory and s....... 1Chr 16:28
able men for s for the service,....... 1Chr 26:8
make great, and to give s unto all....... 1Chr 29:12
place, thou, and the ark of thy s....... 2Chr 6:41
s again in the days of Abijah....... 2Chr 13:20
The s of the bearers of burdens....... Neh 4:10
for the joy of the Lord is your s....... Neh 8:10
What is my s, that I should hope....... Job 6:11
Is my s the s of stones....... Job 6:12
is wise in heart, and mighty in s....... Job 9:4
If I speak of s, lo, he is strong....... Job 9:19
With him is wisdom and s, he hath....... Job 12:13
With him is s and wisdom....... Job 12:16
and weakeneth the s of the mighty....... Job 12:21
The steps of his s shall be....... Job 18:7
His s shall be hungerbitten, and....... Job 18:12
It shall devour the s of his skin....... Job 18:13
of death shall devour his s....... Job 18:13
One dieth in his full s, being....... Job 21:23
but he would put s in me....... Job 23:6
thou the arm that hath no s....... Job 26:2
whereto might the s of their....... Job 30:2
he is mighty in s and wisdom....... Job 36:5
not gold, nor all the forces of s....... Job 36:19
and to the great rain of his s....... Job 37:6
trust him, because his s is great....... Job 39:11
Hath thou given the horse s....... Job 39:19
the valley, and rejoiceth in his s....... Job 39:21
his s is in his loins, and his....... Job 40:16
In his neck remaineth s, and....... Job 41:22
s because of thine enemies....... Ps 8:2
I will love thee, O Lord, my s....... Ps 18:1
my God, my s, in whom I will....... Ps 18:2
It is God that girdeth me with s....... Ps 18:32
girded me with s unto the battle....... Ps 18:39
in thy sight, O Lord, my....... Ps 19:14
the saving s of his right hand....... Ps 20:6
The king shall joy in thy s....... Ps 21:1
exalted, Lord, in thine own s....... Ps 21:13
My s is dried up like a potsherd....... Ps 22:15
O my s, haste thee to help me....... Ps 22:19
the Lord is the s of my life....... Ps 27:1
The Lord is my s and my shield....... Ps 28:7
The Lord is their s, and he is the....... Ps 28:8
is the saving s of his anointed....... Ps 28:8
give unto the Lord glory and s....... Ps 29:1
Lord will give s unto his people....... Ps 29:11
for thou art my s....... Ps 31:4
my s faileth because of mine....... Ps 31:10
man is not delivered by much s....... Ps 33:16
he deliver any by his great s....... Ps 33:17
he is their s in the time of....... Ps 37:39
My heart panteth, my s faileth me....... Ps 38:10
O spare me, that I may recover s....... Ps 39:13
For thou art the God of my s....... Ps 43:2
God is our refuge and s, a....... Ps 46:1
the man that made not God his s....... Ps 52:7
by thy name, and judge me by thy s....... Ps 54:1
Because of his s will I wait upon....... Ps 59:9
Unto thee, O my s, will I sing....... Ps 59:17
also is the s of mine head....... Ps 60:7
the rock of my s, and my refuge,....... Ps 62:7
Which by his s setteth fast the....... Ps 65:6
Thy God hath commanded thy s....... Ps 68:28
Ascribe ye s unto God....... Ps 68:34
Israel, and his s is in the clouds....... Ps 68:34
God of Israel is he that giveth s....... Ps 68:35
forsake me not when my s faileth....... Ps 71:9
will go in the s of the Lord God....... Ps 71:16
shewed thy s unto this generation....... Ps 71:18
but their s is firm....... Ps 73:4
but God is the s of my heart....... Ps 73:26
didst divide the sea by thy s....... Ps 74:13
declared thy s among the people....... Ps 77:14
the praises of the Lord, and his s....... Ps 78:4
the chief of their s in the....... Ps 78:51
delivered his s into captivity,....... Ps 78:61
and Manasseh stir up thy s....... Ps 80:2
Sing aloud unto God our s....... Ps 81:1
is the man whose s is in thee....... Ps 84:5
They go from s to s....... Ps 84:7
give thy s unto thy servant, and....... Ps 86:16
I am as a man that hath no s....... Ps 88:4
For thou art the glory of their s....... Ps 89:17
if by reason of s they be....... Ps 90:10
years, yet is their s labour....... Ps 90:10
the Lord is clothed with s....... Ps 93:1
the s of the hills is his also....... Ps 95:4
s and beauty are in his sanctuary....... Ps 96:6
give unto the Lord glory and s....... Ps 96:7
The king's s also loveth judgment....... Ps 99:4
He weakened my s in the way....... Ps 102:23

ye his angels, that excel in s....... Ps 103:20
Seek the Lord, and his s....... Ps 105:4
land, the chief of all their s....... Ps 105:36
also is the s of mine head....... Ps 108:8
send the rod of thy s out of Zion....... Ps 110:2
The Lord is my s and song, and is....... Ps 118:14
thou, and the ark of thy s....... Ps 132:8
me with s in my soul....... Ps 138:3
the s of my salvation, thou hast....... Ps 140:7
Blessed be the Lord my s, which....... Ps 144:1
not in the s of the horse....... Ps 147:10
I have s....... Prov 8:14
of the Lord is s to the upright....... Prov 10:29
increase is by the s of the ox....... Prov 14:4
The glory of young men is their s....... Prov 20:29
casteth down the s of the....... Prov 21:22
a man of knowledge increaseth s....... Prov 24:5
day of adversity, thy s is small....... Prov 24:10
Give not thy s unto women....... Prov 31:3
She girdeth her loins with s....... Prov 31:17
S and honour are her clothing....... Prov 31:25
said I, Wisdom is better than s....... Eccl 9:16
edge, then must he put to more s....... Eccl 10:10
princes eat in due season, for s....... Eccl 10:17
men of s to mingle strong drink....... Is 5:22
By the s of my hand I have done....... Is 10:13
for the Lord JEHOVAH is my s....... Is 12:2
been mindful of the rock of thy s....... Is 17:10
even the s of the sea, saying, I....... Is 23:4
there is no more s....... Is 23:10
for your s is laid waste....... Is 23:14
thou hast been a s to the poor....... Is 25:4
a s to the needy in his distress,....... Is 25:4
the Lord JEHOVAH is everlasting s....... Is 26:4
Or let him take hold of my s....... Is 27:5
for s to them that turn the....... Is 28:6
themselves in the s of Pharaoh....... Is 30:2
Therefore shall the s of Pharaoh....... Is 30:3
this, Their s is to sit still....... Is 30:7
and in confidence shall be your s....... Is 30:15
of thy times, and s of salvation....... Is 33:6
I have counsel and s for war....... Is 36:5
there is not s to bring forth....... Is 37:3
tidings, lift up thy voice with s....... Is 40:9
have no might he increaseth s....... Is 40:29
upon the Lord shall renew their s....... Is 40:31
and let the people renew their s....... Is 41:1
of his anger, and the s of battle....... Is 42:25
worketh it with the s of his arms....... Is 44:12
he is hungry, and his s faileth....... Is 44:12
Lord have I righteousness and s....... Is 45:24
I have spent my s for nought....... Is 49:4
the Lord, and my God shall be my s....... Is 49:5
Awake, awake, put on s, O arm of....... Is 51:9
put on thy s, O Zion....... Is 52:1
hand, and by the arm of his s....... Is 62:8
in the greatness of his s....... Is 63:1
bring down their s to the earth....... Is 63:6
where is thy zeal and thy s....... Is 63:15
O Lord, my s, and my fortress, and....... Jer 16:19
deliver all the s of this city....... Jer 20:5
fortify the height of her s....... Jer 51:53
gone without s before the pursuer....... Lam 1:6
he hath made my s to fail....... Lam 1:14
And I said, My s and my hope is....... Lam 3:18
the excellency of your s....... Eze 24:21
day when I take from them their s....... Eze 24:25
my fury upon Sin, the s of Egypt....... Eze 30:15
the pomp of her s shall cease in....... Eze 30:18
and the pomp of her s shall cease....... Eze 33:28
given thee a kingdom, power, and s....... Dan 2:37
be in it of the s of the iron....... Dan 2:41
and there remained no s in me....... Dan 10:8
corruption, and I retained no s....... Dan 10:8
upon me, and I have retained no s....... Dan 10:16
there remained no s in me....... Dan 10:17
by his s through his riches he....... Dan 11:2
shall there be any s to withstand....... Dan 11:15
with the s of his whole kingdom....... Dan 11:17
shall pollute the sanctuary of s....... Dan 11:31
Strangers have devoured his s....... Hos 7:9
by his s he had power with God....... Hos 12:3
tree and the vine do yield their s....... Joel 2:22
the s of the children of Israel....... Joel 3:16
shall bring down thy s from thee....... Amos 3:11
taken to us horns by our own s....... Amos 6:13
and feed in the s of the name of....... Mic 5:4
Ethiopia and Egypt were her s....... Nah 3:9
shall seek a because of the enemy....... Nah 3:11
The Lord God is my s, and he will....... Hab 3:19
I will destroy the s of the....... Hag 2:22
of Jerusalem shall be my s in the....... Zec 12:5
all thy mind, and with all thy s....... Mk 12:30
all the soul, and with all the s....... Mk 12:33
He hath shewed s with his arm....... Lk 1:51
all thy soul, and with all thy s....... Lk 10:27
feet and ancle bones received s....... Acts 3:7
But Saul increased the more in s....... Acts 9:22
For when we were yet without s....... Rom 5:6
and the s of sin is the law....... 1Cor 15:56
pressed out of measure, above s....... 2Cor 1:8
for my s is made perfect in....... 2Cor 12:9
otherwise it is of no s at all....... Heb 9:17
received s to conceive seed....... Heb 11:11
was as the sun shineth in his s....... Rev 1:16
for thou hast a little s, and hast....... Rev 3:8
power, and riches, and wisdom, and s....... Rev 5:12
Now is come salvation, and s....... Rev 12:10
their power and s unto the beast....... Rev 17:13

STRENGTHEN
and encourage him, and s him....... Deut 3:28
s me, I pray thee, only this once....... Judg 16:28
s thyself, and mark, and see what....... 1Kin 20:22
to s their hands in the work of....... Ezr 6:22
Now therefore, O God, s my hands....... Neh 6:9
But I would s you with my mouth,....... Job 16:5
sanctuary, and s thee out of Zion....... Ps 20:2
and he shalt s thine heart....... Ps 27:14
he shall s your heart, all ye....... Ps 31:24
The Lord will s him upon the bed....... Ps 41:3
s, O God, that which thou hast....... Ps 68:28
mine arm also shall s him....... Ps 89:21
s thou me according unto thy word....... Ps 119:28
s him with thy girdle, and I will....... Is 22:21
to s themselves in the strength....... Is 30:2
they could not well s their mast....... Is 33:23
S ye the weak hands, and confirm....... Is 35:3
I will s thee....... Is 41:10
thy cords, and s thy stakes....... Is 54:2
they s also the hands of....... Jer 23:14
neither shall any s himself in....... Eze 7:13
neither did she s the hand of the....... Eze 16:49
I will s the arms of the king of....... Eze 30:24
But I will s the arms of the king....... Eze 30:25
will s that which was sick....... Eze 34:16
I, stood to confirm and to s him....... Dan 11:1
the strong shall not s his force....... Amos 2:14
I will s the house of Judah, and I....... Zec 10:6
I will s them in the Lord....... Zec 10:12
art converted, s thy brethren....... Lk 22:32
make you perfect, stablish, s....... 1Pet 5:10
s the things which remain, that....... Rev 3:2

STRENGTHENED
Israel s himself, and sat upon the....... Gen 48:2
the Lord s Eglon the king of Moab....... Judg 3:12
be s to go down unto the house,....... Judg 7:11
the wood, and s his hand in God....... 1Sa 23:16
Therefore now let your hands be s....... 2Sa 2:7
who s themselves with him in his....... 1Chr 11:10
son of David was s in his kingdom....... 2Chr 1:1
So they s the kingdom of Judah,....... 2Chr 11:17
had s himself, he forsook the law....... 2Chr 12:1
So king Rehoboam s himself in....... 2Chr 12:13
have s themselves against....... 2Chr 13:7
and s himself against Israel....... 2Chr 17:1
he s himself, and slew all his....... 2Chr 21:4
seventh year Jehoiada s himself....... 2Chr 23:1
of God in his state, and s it....... 2Chr 24:13
And Amaziah s himself, and led....... 2Chr 25:11
for he s himself exceedingly....... 2Chr 26:8
and distressed him, but s him not....... 2Chr 28:20
Also he s himself, and built up....... 2Chr 32:5
s their hands with vessels of....... Ezr 1:6
I was a the hand of the Lord....... Ezr 7:28
So they s their hands for this....... Neh 2:18
thou hast s the weak hands....... Job 4:3
thou hast s the feeble knees....... Job 4:4
s himself in his wickedness....... Ps 52:7
For he hath s the bars of thy....... Ps 147:13
when he s the fountains of the....... Prov 8:28
s the hands of the wicked, that....... Eze 13:22
The diseased have ye not s....... Eze 34:4
appearance of a man, and he s me....... Dan 10:18
he had spoken unto me, I was s....... Dan 10:19
for thou hast s me....... Dan 10:19
he that s her in these times....... Dan 11:6
but he shall not be s by it....... Dan 11:12
s their arms, yet do they imagine....... Hos 7:15
he had received meat, he was s....... Acts 9:19
to be s with might by his Spirit....... Eph 3:16
S with all might, according to....... Col 1:11
the Lord stood with me, and s me....... 2Ti 4:17

STRENGTHENEDST
s me with strength in my soul....... Ps 138:3

STRENGTHENETH
s himself against the Almighty....... Job 15:25
and bread which s man's heart....... Ps 104:15
with strength, and s her arms....... Prov 31:17
Wisdom s the wise more than ten....... Eccl 7:19
which he s for himself among the....... Is 44:14
That s the spoiled against the....... Amos 5:9
things through Christ which s me....... Phil 4:13

STRENGTHENING
angel unto him from heaven, s him....... Lk 22:43
in order, s all the disciples....... Acts 18:23

STRETCH
I will s out my hand, and smite....... Ex 3:20
when I s forth mine hand upon....... Ex 7:5
s out thine hand upon the waters....... Ex 7:19
S forth thine hand with thy rod....... Ex 8:5
S out my rod, and smite the dust....... Ex 8:16
For now I will s out my hand,....... Ex 9:15
S forth thine hand toward heaven,....... Ex 10:12
S out thine hand over the land of....... Ex 10:12
S out thine hand toward heaven,....... Ex 10:21
s out thine hand over the sea, and....... Ex 14:16
s out thine hand over the sea,....... Ex 14:26
the cherubim shall s forth their....... Ex 25:20
S out the spear that is in thy....... Josh 8:18
to s forth mine hand against the....... 1Sa 24:6
for who can s forth a hand against....... 1Sa 26:9
s forth mine hand against the....... 1Sa 26:11
but I would not s forth mine hand....... 1Sa 26:23
How wast thou not afraid to s....... 2Sa 1:14
I will s over Jerusalem the line....... 2Kin 21:13
s out thine hands toward him....... Job 11:13
Howbeit he will not s out his....... Job 30:24

s her wings toward the south .... Job 39:26
Ethiopia shall soon s out her .... Ps 68:31
thou shalt s forth thine hand .... Ps 143:6
my hands unto thee .... Ps 143:6
that a man can s himself on it .... Is 28:20
the LORD shall s out his hand .... Is 31:3
he shall s out upon it the line .... Is 34:11
let them s forth the curtains of .... Is 54:2
for I will s out my hand upon the .... Jer 6:12
there is none to s forth my tent .... Jer 10:20
therefore will I s out my hand .... Jer 15:6
I will s out mine hand upon thee, ... Jer 51:25
So will I s out my hand upon them .... Eze 6:14
I will s out my hand upon him and, ... Eze 14:9
then will I s out mine hand upon .... Eze 14:13
therefore I will s out mine hand. .... Eze 25:7
I will also s out mine hand upon .... Eze 25:13
I will s out mine hand upon the .... Eze 25:16
he shall s it out upon the land. .... Eze 30:25
I will s out mine hand against .... Eze 35:3
He shall s forth his hand also. .... Dan 11:42
s themselves upon their couches, ... Amos 6:4
I will also s out mine hand against .... Zeph 1:4
he will s out his hand against. .... Zeph 2:13
he to the man, S forth thine hand .... Mt 12:13
unto the man, S forth thine hand .... Mk 3:5
unto the man, S forth thy hand .... Lk 6:10
thou shalt s forth thy hands, and .... Jn 21:18
For we s not ourselves beyond our ... 2Cor 10:14

STRETCHED
Abraham s forth his hand, and took... Gen 22:10
Israel s out his right hand, and .... Gen 48:14
will redeem you with s out arm .... Ex 6:6
Aaron s out his hand over the .... Ex 8:6
for Aaron s out his hand over the .... Ex 8:17
Moses s forth his rod toward .... Ex 9:23
Moses s forth his rod over the .... Ex 10:13
Moses s forth his hand toward .... Ex 10:22
Moses s out his hand over the sea .... Ex 14:21
Moses s forth his hand over the .... Ex 14:27
by a s out arm, and by great .... Deut 4:34
a mighty hand and by a s out arm .... Deut 5:15
the s out arm, whereby the LORD .... Deut 7:19
mighty power and by thy s out arm .... Deut 9:29
mighty hand, and his s out arm, ... Deut 11:2
Joshua s out the spear that he .... Josh 8:18
as soon as he had s out his hand. .... Josh 8:19
wherewith he s out the spear, ... Josh 8:26
when the angel s out his hand 2Sa 24:16
they s forth the wings of this. 1Kin 6:27
strong hand, and of thy s out arm. 1Kin 8:42
he s himself upon the child three. 1Kin 17:21
he s himself over the child 2Kin 4:34
and went up, and s himself upon him. 2Kin 4:35
a s out arm, him shall ye fear, ... 2Kin 17:36
in his hand s out over Jerusalem ... 1Chr 21:16
thy mighty hand, and thy s out arm 2Chr 6:32
or who hath s the line upon it .... Job 38:5
or s out our hands to a strange .... Ps 44:20
I have s out my hands unto thee. .... Ps 88:9
To him that s out the earth above ... Ps 136:6
strong hand, and with a s out arm. ... Ps 136:12
I have s out my hand, and no man. .... Prov 1:24
walk with s forth necks and wanton. .... Is 3:16
he hath s forth his hand against. .... Is 5:25
away, but his hand is s out still. .... Is 5:25
away, but his hand is s out still. .... Is 9:12
away, but his hand is s out still. .... Is 9:17
away, but his hand is s out still. .... Is 9:21
away, but his hand is s out still .... Is 10:4
is s out upon all the nations .... Is 14:26
and his hand is s out, and who. .... Is 14:27
her branches are s out, they are. .... Is 16:8
He s out his hand over the sea, ... Is 23:11
the heavens, and s them out... .... Is 42:5
have s out the heavens and all... .... Is 45:12
that hath s forth the heavens, and. .... Is 51:13
shadows of the evening are s out .... Jer 6:4
hath s out the heavens by his. .... Jer 10:12
s out arm, and there is nothing .... Jer 32:17
with a s out arm, and with great .... Jer 32:21
hath s out the heaven by his.......... Jer 51:15
he hath s out a line, he hath not .... Lam 2:8
and their wings were s upward. .... Eze 1:11
s forth over their heads above .... Eze 1:22
one cherub s forth his hand from. .... Eze 10:7
therefore I have s out my hand .... Eze 16:27
with a s out arm, and with fury. .... Eze 20:33
with a s out arm, and with fury .... Eze 20:34
he s out his hand with scorners .... Hos 7:5
the banquet of those that s them .... Amos 6:7
a line shall be s forth upon .... Zec 1:16
And he s it forth .... Mt 12:13
he s forth his hand toward his .... Mt 12:49
Jesus s forth his hand, and caught. .... Mt 14:31
were with Jesus s out his hand .... Mt 26:51
And he s it out .... Mk 3:5
put s not his hands against the .... Lk 22:53
s forth his hands to vex certain .... Acts 12:1
Then Paul s forth the hand, and. .... Acts 26:1
All day long I have s forth my .... Rom 10:21

STRETCHEDST
Thou s out thy right hand, the .... Ex 15:12

STRETCHEST
who s out the heavens like a........ Ps 104:2

STRETCHETH
For he s out his hand against God.... Job 15:25
He s out the north over the empty... Job 26:7

She s out her hand to the poor........ Prov 31:20
that s out the heavens as a .... Is 40:22
The carpenter s out his rule.... .... Is 44:13
that s forth the heavens alone .... Is 44:24
which s forth the heavens, and.... .... Zec 12:1

STRETCHING
the s out of his wings shall fill .... Is 8:8
By s forth thine hand to heal. .... Acts 4:30

STRICKEN
Sarah were old and well s in age........ Gen 18:11
Abraham was old, and well s in age... Gen 24:1
Now Joshua was old and s in years ... Josh 13:1
s in years, and there remaineth. .... Josh 13:1
that Joshua waxed old and s in age .... Josh 23:1
unto them, I am old and s in age. .... Josh 23:2
pierced and s through his temples... Judg 5:26
king David was old and s in years 1Kin 1:1
if thou hast s thy hand with a .... Prov 6:1
They have s me, shalt thou say, ... Prov 23:35
Why should ye be s any more .... Is 1:5
surely they are s .... Is 16:7
yet we did esteem him s, smitten .... Is 53:4
of my people was he s .... Is 53:8
thou hast s them, but they have.......... Jer 5:3
s through for want of the fruits... .... Lam 4:9
both were now well s in years. .... Lk 1:7
man, and my wife well s in years. .... Lk 1:18

STRIFE
there was a s between the herdmen ... Gen 13:7
said unto Lot, Let there be no s .... Gen 13:8
in the s of the congregation, to.... .... Num 27:14
and your burden, and your s.... .... Deut 1:12
my people were at great s with .... Judg 12:2
And all the people were at s........ .... 2Sa 19:9
a pavilion from the s of tongues. .... Ps 31:20
seen violence and s in the city .... Ps 55:9
Thou makest us a s unto our. .... Ps 80:6
him also at the waters of s .... Ps 106:32
A wrathful man stirreth up s .... Prov 15:18
that is slow to anger appeaseth s. .... Prov 15:18
A froward man soweth s .... Prov 16:28
house full of sacrifices with s.... .... Prov 17:1
The beginning of s is as when one... Prov 17:14
transgression that loveth s .... Prov 17:19
honour for a man to cease from s.... Prov 20:3
yea, s and reproach shall cease. .... Prov 22:10
meddleth with s belonging not to .... Prov 26:17
so is no talebearer, the s ceaseth.... Prov 26:20
is a contentious man to kindle s........ Prov 26:21
is of a proud heart stirreth up s .... Prov 28:25
An angry man stirreth up s .... Prov 29:22
forcing of wrath bringeth forth s .... Prov 30:33
Behold, ye fast for s and debate, ... Is 58:4
thou hast borne me a man of s........ Jer 15:10
even to the waters of s in Kadesh... Eze 47:19
unto the waters of s in Kadesh... .... Eze 48:28
and there are that raise up s.... .... Hab 1:3
And there was also a s among them.... Num 13:13
and wantonness, not in s and .... Rom 13:13
there is among you envying, and s.... 1Cor 3:3
variance, emulations, wrath, s.... .... Gal 5:20
preach Christ even of envy and s .... Phil 1:15
be done through s or vainglory .... Phil 2:3
of words, whereof cometh envy, s 1Ti 6:4
is to them an end of all s .... Heb 6:16
s in your hearts, glory not, and .... Jas 3:14
s is, there is confusion and every .... Jas 3:16

STRIFES
Hatred stirreth up s .... Prov 10:12
be debates, envyings, wraths, s 2Cor 12:20
s of words, whereof cometh envy 1Ti 6:4
knowing that they do gender s 2Ti 2:23

STRIKE
s it on the two side posts and on .... Ex 12:7
s the lintel and the two side .... Ex 12:22
shall s off the heifer's neck .... Deut 21:4
s his hand over the place, and 2Kin 5:11
is he that will s hands with him. .... Job 17:3
bow of steel shall s him through .... Job 20:24
nor to s princes for equity .... Prov 17:26
not thou one of them that s hands .... Prov 22:26
Thou didst s through with his .... Hab 3:14
the servants did s him with the .... Mk 14:65

STRIKER
Not given to wine, no s, not.......... 1Ti 3:3
angry, not given to wine, no s .... Titus 1:7

STRIKETH
He s them as wicked men in the .... Job 34:26
man void of understanding s hands... Prov 17:18
of a scorpion, when he s a man .... Rev 9:5

STRING
make ready their arrow upon the s........ Ps 11:2
the s of his tongue was loosed, ... Mk 7:35

STRINGED
praise him with s instruments .... Ps 150:4
we will sing my songs to the s .... Is 38:20
chief singer on my s instruments .... Hab 3:19

STRINGS
thy s against the face of them........ Ps 21:12
and an instrument of ten s .... Ps 33:2
Upon an instrument of ten s .... Ps 92:3
an instrument of ten s will I........ Ps 144:9

STRIP
s Aaron of his garments, and put... Num 20:26
Philistines came to s the slain 1Sa 31:8
Philistines came to s the slain 1Chr 10:8
s you, and make you bare, and gird...... Is 32:11
they shall s thee also of thy........ Eze 16:39
They shall also s thee out of thy .... Eze 23:26
Lest I s her naked, and set her as .... Hos 2:3

STRIPE
wound for wound, s for s .... Ex 21:25

STRIPES
Forty s he may give him, and not........ Deut 25:3
beat him above these with many s .... Deut 25:3
with the s of the children of men... 2Sa 7:14
the rod, and their iniquity with s .... Ps 89:32
man than an hundred s into a fool ... Prov 17:10
and s for the back of fools .... Prov 19:29
so do s the inward parts of the .... Prov 20:30
and with his s we are healed .... Is 53:5
will, shall be beaten with many s .... Lk 12:47
and did commit things worthy of s .... Lk 12:48
shall be beaten with few s .... Lk 12:48
they had laid many s upon them .... Acts 16:23
of the night, and washed their s .... Acts 16:33
In s, in imprisonments, in 2Cor 6:5
in s above measure, in prisons 2Cor 11:23
times received I forty s save one... 2Cor 11:24
by whose s ye were healed 1Pet 2:24

STRIPLING
Enquire thou whose son the s is 1Sa 17:56

STRIPPED
And the children of Israel s.... .... Ex 33:6
Moses s Aaron of his garments, and. Num 20:28
Jonathan s himself of the robe. 1Sa 18:4
s off his armour, and sent into.... .... 1Sa 31:9
And when they had s him, they took ... 1Chr 10:9
which they s off for themselves,.... 2Chr 20:25
He hath s me of my glory, and........ Job 19:9
the naked of their clothing.......... Job 22:6
I will wail and howl, I will go s. .... Mic 1:8
And they s him, and put on him a.... Mt 27:28
which s him of his raiment, and. .... Lk 10:30

STRIPT
that they s Joseph out of his........ Gen 37:23
he s off his clothes also, and. 1Sa 19:24

STRIVE
shall not always s with man........ Gen 6:3
Gerar did s with Isaac's herdmen, ... Gen 26:20
if men s together, and one smite.... Ex 21:18
If men s, and hurt a woman with .... Ex 21:22
When men s together one with .... Deut 25:11
with whom thou didst s at the........ Deut 33:8
did he ever s against Israel, or........ Judg 11:25
Why dost thou s against him........ Job 33:13
O LORD, with them that s with me.... Ps 35:1
S not with a man without cause, ... Prov 3:30
Go not forth hastily to s........ .... Prov 25:8
they that s with thee shall........ Is 41:11
Let the potsherd s with the........ Is 45:9
Yet let no man s, nor reprove.... .... Hos 4:4
as they that s with the priest.... .... Hos 4:4
He shall not s, nor cry.......... Mt 12:19
S to enter in at the strait gate, ... Lk 13:24
that ye s together with me in........ Rom 15:30
And if a man also s for masteries.... 2Ti 2:5
not crowned, except he s lawfully.... 2Ti 2:5
s not about words to no profit.......... 2Ti 2:14
servant of the Lord must not s........ 2Ti 2:24

STRIVED
so have I s to preach the gospel,...... Rom 15:20

STRIVEN
thou hast s against the LORD........ Jer 50:24

STRIVETH
unto him that s with his Maker........ Is 45:9
every man that s for the mastery.... 1Cor 9:25

STRIVING
with one mind s together for the........ Phil 1:27
s according to his working, which.... Col 1:29
unto blood, s against sin .... Heb 12:4

STRIVINGS
me from the s of my people........ 2Sa 22:44
me from the s of the people .... Ps 18:43
contentions, and s about the law.... Titus 3:9

STROKE
and plea, and between s and s........ Deut 17:8
his hand fetcheth a s with the .... Deut 19:5
controversy and every s be tried.... Deut 21:5
enemies with the s of the sword........ Est 9:5
my s is heavier than my groaning.... Job 23:2
lest he take thee away with his s.... Job 36:18
Remove thy s away from me........ Ps 39:10
in wrath with a continual s.... .... Is 14:6
healeth the s of their wound........ Is 30:26
the desire of thine eyes with s........ Eze 24:16

STROKES
and his mouth calleth for s........ Prov 18:6

STRONG
Issachar is a s ass couching down... Gen 49:14
s by the hands of the mighty God.... Gen 49:24
for with a s hand shall he let.... .... Ex 6:1
with a s hand shall he drive them.... Ex 6:1
LORD turned a mighty s west wind.... Ex 10:19
for with a s hand hath the LORD.... Ex 13:9

S

by a s east wind all that night .... Ex 14:21
Do not drink wine nor s drink .... Lev 10:9
s drink, and shall drink no .... Num 6:3
of wine, or vinegar of s drink .... Num 6:3
whether they be s or weak .... Num 13:18
whether in tents, or in s holds .... Num 13:19
be s that dwell in the land .... Num 13:28
much people, and with a s hand .... Num 20:20
of the children of Ammon was s .... Num 21:24
S is thy dwellingplace, and thou .... Num 24:21
s wine to be poured unto the LORD .... Num 28:7
was not one city too s for us .... Deut 2:36
you this day, that ye may be s .... Deut 11:8
or for wine, or for s drink .... Deut 14:26
have ye drunk wine or s drink .... Deut 29:6
Be s and of a good courage, fear .... Deut 31:6
in the sight of all Israel, Be s .... Deut 31:7
of Nun a charge, and said, Be s .... Deut 31:23
Be s and of a good courage .... Josh 1:6
Only be thou s and very courageous .... Josh 1:7
Be s and of a good courage .... Josh 1:9
only be a and of a good courage .... Josh 1:18
Fear not, nor be dismayed, be s .... Josh 10:25
As yet I am as s this day as I .... Josh 14:11
children of Israel were waxen s .... Josh 17:13
chariots, and though they be s .... Josh 17:18
to Ramah, and to the s city Tyre .... Josh 19:29
before you great nations and s .... Josh 23:9
came to pass, when Israel was s .... Judg 1:28
mountains, and caves, and s holds .... Judg 6:2
But there was a s tower within .... Judg 9:51
and drink not wine nor s drink .... Judg 13:4
and now drink no wine nor s drink .... Judg 13:7
let her drink wine or s drink .... Judg 13:14
out of the s came forth sweetness .... Judg 14:14
saw that they were too s for him .... Judg 18:26
drunken neither wine nor s drink 1Sa 1:15
Be s, and quit yourselves like men 1Sa 4:9
and when Saul saw any s man 1Sa 14:52
in the wilderness in s holds 1Sa 23:14
with us in s holds in the wood 1Sa 23:19
dwelt in s holds at En-gedi 1Sa 23:29
himself s for the house of Saul 2Sa 3:6
David took the s hold of Zion 2Sa 5:7
If the Syrians be too s for me 2Sa 10:11
of Ammon be too s for thee 2Sa 10:11
battle more s against the city 2Sa 11:25
And the conspiracy was s 2Sa 15:12
of all that are with thee be s 2Sa 16:21
He delivered me from my s enemy 2Sa 22:18
for they were too s for me 2Sa 22:18
came to the s hold of Tyre, and to 2Sa 24:7
be thou s therefore, and shew 1Kin 2:2
thy great name, and of thy s hand 1Kin 8:42
s wind rent the mountains, and 1Kin 19:11
be with thy servants fifty s men 2Kin 2:16
their s holds with thou set on 2Kin 8:12
a thousand, all that were s 2Kin 24:16
If the Syrians be too s for me 1Chr 19:12
of Ammon be too s for thee 1Chr 19:12
Be s and of good courage 1Chr 22:13
whose brethren were s men 1Chr 26:7
sons and brethren, s men, eighteen 1Chr 26:9
be s, and do it 1Chr 28:10
said to Solomon his son, Be s 1Chr 28:20
And he fortified the s holds 2Chr 11:11
spears, and made them exceeding s 2Chr 11:12
Rehoboam the son of Solomon s 2Chr 11:17
Be ye s therefore, and let not 2Chr 15:7
to shew himself s in the behalf 2Chr 16:9
go, do it, be s for the battle 2Chr 25:8
helped, till he was s 2Chr 26:15
But when he was s, his heart was 2Chr 26:16
Be s and courageous, be not afraid 2Chr 32:7
that ye may be s, and eat the good .... Ezr 9:12
thy great power, and by thy s hand .... Neh 1:10
And they took s cities, and a fat .... Neh 9:25
of thy mouth be like a s wind .... Job 8:2
I speak of strength, lo, he is s .... Job 9:19
with thy s hand thou opposest .... Job 30:21
of his bones with a pain .... Job 33:19
spread out the sky, which is s .... Job 37:18
crag of the rock, and the s place .... Job 39:28
bones are as s pieces of brass .... Job 40:18
the poor may fall by his s ones .... Ps 10:10
He delivered me from my s enemy .... Ps 18:17
for they were too s for me .... Ps 18:17
rejoiceth as a man to run a .... Ps 19:5
s bulls of Bashan have beset me .... Ps 22:12
The LORD s and mighty, the LORD .... Ps 24:8
hast made my mountain to stand s .... Ps 30:7
be thou my s rock, for an house .... Ps 31:2
marvellous kindness in a s city .... Ps 31:21
from him that is too s for him .... Ps 35:10
enemies are lively, and they are s .... Ps 38:19
Who will bring me into the s city .... Ps 60:9
me, and a s tower from the enemy .... Ps 61:3
Be thou my s habitation .... Ps 71:3
but thou art my s refuge .... Ps 71:7
that thou madest s for thyself .... Ps 80:15
whom thou madest s for thyself .... Ps 80:17
who is a s LORD like unto thee .... Ps 89:8
thine enemies with thy s arm .... Ps 89:10
s is thy hand, and high is thy .... Ps 89:13
hast brought his s holds to ruin .... Ps 89:40
Who will bring me into the s city .... Ps 108:10
With a s hand, and with a .... Ps 136:12
That our oxen may be s to labour .... Ps 144:14
many s men have been slain by her .... Prov 7:26
rich man's wealth is his s city .... Prov 10:15

and s men retain riches .... Prov 11:16
fear of the LORD is s confidence .... Prov 14:26
The name of the LORD is a tower .... Prov 18:10
rich man's wealth is his s city .... Prov 18:11
is harder to be won than a s city .... Prov 18:19
is a mocker, s drink is raging .... Prov 20:1
and a reward in the bosom s wrath .... Prov 21:14
A wise man is s .... Prov 24:5
The ants are a people not s .... Prov 30:25
nor for princes s drink .... Prov 31:4
Give s drink unto him that is .... Prov 31:6
swift, nor the battle to the s .... Eccl 9:11
the s men shall bow themselves .... Eccl 12:3
for love is as death .... Song 8:6
the s shall be as tow, and the .... Is 1:31
that they may follow s drink .... Is 5:11
men of strength to mingle s drink .... Is 5:22
them the waters of the river, s .... Is 8:7
spake thus to me with a s hand .... Is 8:11
In that day shall is s cities be .... Is 17:9
to destroy the s holds thereof .... Is 23:11
s drink shall be bitter to them .... Is 24:9
shall the s people glorify thee .... Is 25:3
We have a s city .... Is 26:1
s sword shall punish leviathan .... Is 27:1
s one, which as a tempest of hail .... Is 28:2
through s drink are out of the .... Is 28:7
have erred through s drink .... Is 28:7
out of the way through s drink .... Is 28:7
lest your bands be made s .... Is 28:22
stagger, but not with s drink .... Is 29:9
horsemen, because they are very s .... Is 31:1
pass over to his s hold for fear .... Is 31:9
that are of a fearful heart, Be s .... Is 35:4
Lord GOD will come with s hand .... Is 40:10
might, for that he is s in power .... Is 40:26
bring forth your s reasons .... Is 41:21
shall divide the spoil with the s .... Is 53:12
will fill ourselves with s drink .... Is 56:12
and a small one s a nation .... Is 60:22
of the neighing of his s ones .... Jer 8:16
outstretched hand and with a s arm .... Jer 21:5
and with wonders, and with a s hand .... Jer 32:21
of the hoofs of his s horses .... Jer 47:3
are mighty and s men for the war .... Jer 48:14
How is the s staff broken, and the .... Jer 48:17
and he shall destroy thy s holds .... Jer 48:18
the s holds are surprised, and the .... Jer 48:41
against the habitation of the s .... Jer 49:19
Their Redeemer is s .... Jer 50:34
unto the habitation of the s .... Jer 50:44
of Babylon, make the watch s .... Jer 51:12
thrown down in his wrath the s .... Lam 2:2
he hath destroyed his s holds .... Lam 2:5
thy face s against their faces .... Eze 3:8
thy forehead s against their .... Eze 3:9
hand of the LORD was s upon me .... Eze 3:14
make the pomp of the s to cease .... Eze 7:24
she had s rods for the sceptres .... Eze 19:11
her s rods were broken and .... Eze 19:12
so that she hath no s rod to be a .... Eze 19:14
endure, or can thine hands be s .... Eze 22:14
thy s garrisons shall go down to .... Eze 26:11
city, which wast s in the sea .... Eze 26:17
to make it s to hold the sword .... Eze 30:21
will make his arms, the s .... Eze 30:22
The s among the mighty shall .... Eze 32:21
I will destroy the fat and the s .... Eze 34:16
fourth kingdom shall be s as iron .... Dan 2:40
so the kingdom shall be partly s .... Dan 2:42
The tree grew, and was s, and the .... Dan 4:11
thou sawest, which grew, and was s .... Dan 4:20
king, that art grown and become s .... Dan 4:22
and terrible, and s exceedingly .... Dan 7:7
and when he was s, the great horn .... Dan 8:8
unto thee, be s, yea, be s .... Dan 10:19
the king of the south shall be s .... Dan 11:5
and he shall be s above him .... Dan 11:5
shall become s with a small .... Dan 11:23
his devices against the s holds .... Dan 11:24
that do know their God shall be s .... Dan 11:32
most s holds with a strange god .... Dan 11:39
nation is come up upon my land, s .... Joel 1:6
a great people and s .... Joel 2:2
as a s people set in battle array .... Joel 2:5
for he is s that executeth his .... Joel 2:11
let the weak say, I am s .... Joel 3:10
cedars, and he was s as the oaks .... Amos 2:9
he shall not strengthen his .... Amos 2:14
the spoiled against the s .... Amos 5:9
unto thee of wine and of s drink .... Mic 2:11
rebuke s nations afar off .... Mic 4:3
that was cast far off a s nation .... Mic 4:7
the s hold of the daughter of .... Mic 4:8
and throw down all thy s holds .... Mic 5:11
ye s foundations of the earth .... Mic 6:2
a s hold in the day of trouble .... Nah 1:7
watch the way, make thy loins s .... Nah 2:1
All thy s holds shall be like fig .... Nah 3:12
the siege, fortify thy s holds .... Nah 3:14
the mortar, make the brickkiln .... Nah 3:14
they shall deride every s hold .... Hab 1:10
Yet now be s, O Zerubbabel, saith .... Hag 2:4
and be s, O Joshua, son of .... Hag 2:4
and be s, all ye people of the .... Hag 2:4
as many as ye, that hear .... Zec 8:9
fear not, but let your hands be s .... Zec 8:13
s nations shall come to seek the .... Zec 8:22
Tyrus did build herself a s hold .... Zec 9:3
Turn you to the s hold, ye .... Zec 9:12

one enter into a s man's house .... Mt 12:29
except he first bind the s man .... Mt 12:29
can enter into a s man's house .... Mk 3:27
he will first bind the s man .... Mk 3:27
drink neither wine nor s drink .... Lk 1:15
waxed s in spirit, and was in the .... Lk 1:80
waxed s in spirit, filled with .... Lk 2:40
When a s man armed keepeth his .... Lk 11:21
in his name hath made this man s .... Acts 3:16
but was s in faith, giving glory .... Rom 4:20
We then that are s ought to bear .... Rom 15:1
we are weak, but ye are s 1Cor 4:10
faith, quit you like men, be s 1Cor 16:13
to the pulling down of s holds 2Cor 10:4
for when I am weak, then am I s 2Cor 12:10
when we are weak, and ye are s 2Cor 13:9
be s in the Lord, and in the power .... Eph 6:10
God shall send them s delusion 2Th 2:11
be s in the grace that is in 2Ti 2:1
and supplications with s crying .... Heb 5:7
need of milk, and not of s meat .... Heb 5:12
But s meat belongeth to them that .... Heb 5:14
we might have a s consolation .... Heb 6:18
out of weakness were made s .... Heb 11:34
young, young men, because ye are s 1Jn 2:14
I saw a s angel proclaiming with .... Rev 5:2
he cried mightily with a s voice .... Rev 18:2
for s is the Lord God who judgeth .... Rev 18:8

STRONGER

shall be s than the other people .... Gen 25:23
whensoever the s cattle did .... Gen 30:41
were Laban's, and the s Jacob's .... Gen 30:42
for they are s than we .... Num 13:31
And what is s than a lion .... Judg 14:18
eagles, they were s than lions 2Sa 1:23
but David waxed s and s, and 2Sa 3:1
being s than she, forced her, and 2Sa 13:14
therefore they were s than we 1Kin 20:23
and surely we shall be s than they 1Kin 20:23
and surely we shall be s than they 1Kin 20:25
hands shall be s and s .... Judg 7:17
made them s than their enemies .... Ps 105:24
for they are s than I .... Ps 142:6
thou art s than I, and hast .... Jer 20:7
hand of him that was s than he .... Jer 31:11
But when a s than he shall come .... Lk 11:22
the weakness of God is s than men 1Cor 1:25
are we s than he 1Cor 10:22

STRONGEST

A lion which is s among beasts .... Prov 30:30

STRONGLY

the foundations thereof be s laid .... Ezr 6:3

STROVE

because they s with him .... Gen 26:20
another well, and s for that also .... Gen 26:21
and for that they s not .... Gen 26:22
two men of the Hebrews together .... Ex 2:13
a man of Israel s together in the .... Lev 24:10
of Israel s with the LORD .... Num 20:13
who s against Moses and against .... Num 26:9
when they s against the LORD .... Num 26:9
they two s together in the field 2Sa 14:6
when he s with Aram-naharaim and .... Ps 60:ttl
the heaven s upon the great sea .... Dan 7:2
Jews therefore s among themselves .... Jn 6:52
himself unto them as they s .... Acts 7:26
the Pharisees' part arose, and s .... Acts 23:9

STROWED

s it upon the graves of them that 2Chr 34:4

STRUCK

he s it into the pan, or kettle 1Sa 2:14
the LORD s the child that Uriah's 2Sa 12:15
to the ground, and s him not again 2Sa 20:10
and the LORD s him, and he died 2Chr 13:20
s a servant of the high priest's .... Mt 26:51
they s him on the face, and asked .... Lk 22:64
of the officers which stood by s .... Jn 18:22

STRUGGLED

the children s together within .... Gen 25:22

STUBBLE

to gather s instead of straw .... Ex 5:12
wrath, which consumed them as s .... Ex 15:7
and wilt thou pursue the dry s .... Job 13:25
They are as s before the wind, and .... Job 21:18
are turned with him into s .... Job 41:28
Darts are counted as s .... Job 41:29
as the s before the wind .... Ps 83:13
and fire the devoureth the s .... Is 5:24
chaff, ye shall bring forth s .... Is 33:11
shall take them away as s .... Is 40:24
sword, and as driven s to his bow .... Is 41:2
Behold, they shall be as s .... Is 47:14
will I scatter them as the s that .... Jer 13:24
of fire that devoureth the s .... Joel 2:5
flame, and the house of Esau for s .... Obad 18
shall be devoured as s fully dry .... Nah 1:10
all that do wickedly, shall be s .... Mal 4:1
precious stones, wood, hay, s 1Cor 3:12

STUBBORN

If a man have a s and rebellious .... Deut 21:18
of his city, This our son is s .... Deut 21:20
wons doings, nor from their s way .... Judg 2:19
not be as their fathers, a s .... Ps 78:8
(She is loud and s .... Prov 7:11

STUBBORNNESS

not unto the s of this people	Deut 9:27
s is as iniquity and idolatry	1Sa 15:23

STUCK

his spear s in the ground at his	1Sa 26:7
I have s unto thy testimonies	Ps 119:31
and the forepart s fast, and	Acts 27:41

STUDIETH

of the righteous to answer	Prov 15:28
For their heart s destruction	Prov 24:2

STUDS

borders of gold with s of silver	Song 1:11

STUDY

much s is a weariness of the	Eccl 12:12
that ye s to be quiet, and to do	1Th 4:11
S to shew thyself approved unto	2Ti 2:15

STUFF

thou hast searched all my s	Gen 31:37
thou found of all thy household s	Gen 31:37
Also regard not your s	Gen 45:20
his neighbour money or s to keep	Ex 22:7
For the s they had was sufficient	Ex 36:7
put it even among their own s	Josh 7:11
he hath hid himself among the s	1Sa 10:22
and two hundred abode by the s	1Sa 25:13
part be that tarrieth by the s	1Sa 30:24
s of Tobiah out of the chamber	Neh 13:8
man, prepare thee s for removing	Eze 12:3
forth thy s by day in their sight	Eze 12:4
in their sight, as s for removing	Eze 12:4
I brought forth my s by day	Eze 12:7
as s for captivity, and in the	Eze 12:7
his s in the house, let him not	Lk 17:31

STUMBLE

safely, and thy foot shall not s	Prov 3:23
thou runnest, thou shalt not s	Prov 4:12
they know not at what they s	Prov 4:19
shall be weary nor s among them	Is 5:27
And many among them shall s	Is 8:15
err in vision, they s in judgment	Is 28:7
we s at noonday as in the night	Is 59:10
that they should not s	Is 63:13
before your feet s upon the dark	Jer 13:16
they have caused them to s in	Jer 18:15
therefore my persecutors shall s	Jer 20:11
way, wherein they shall not s	Jer 31:9
they shall s, and fall toward the	Jer 46:6
And the most proud shall s	Jer 50:32
but he shall s and fall, and not be	Dan 11:19
they shall s in their walk	Nah 2:5
they s upon their corpses	Nah 3:3
have caused many to s at the law	Mal 2:8
even to them which s at the word	1Pet 2:8

STUMBLED

they that s are girded with	1Sa 2:4
for the oxen s	1Chr 13:9
me to eat up my flesh, they s	Ps 27:2
man hath s against the mighty	Jer 46:12
For they s at that stumblingstone	Rom 9:32
Have they s that they should fall	Rom 11:11

STUMBLETH

not thine heart be glad when he s	Prov 24:17
he s not, because he seeth the	Jn 11:9
if a man walk in the night, he s	Jn 11:10
any thing whereby thy brother s	Rom 14:21

STUMBLING

but for a stone of s and for a	Is 8:14
And a stone of s, and a rock of	1Pet 2:8
is none occasion of s in him	1Jn 2:10

STUMBLINGBLOCK

nor put a s before the blind, but	Lev 19:14
take up the s out of the way of	Is 57:14
I lay a s before him, he shall	Eze 3:20
it is the s of their iniquity	Eze 7:19
put the s of their iniquity	Eze 14:3
putteth the s of his iniquity	Eze 14:4
putteth the s of his iniquity	Eze 14:7
made a snare, and a trap, and a s	Rom 11:9
that no man put a s or an	Rom 14:13
crucified, unto the Jews a s	1Cor 1:23
become a s to them that are weak	1Cor 8:9
who taught Balac to cast a s	Rev 2:14

STUMBLINGBLOCKS

I will lay s before this people	Jer 6:21
the sea, and the s with the wicked	Zeph 1:3

STUMBLINGSTONE

For they stumbled at that s	Rom 9:32
Behold, I lay in Sion a s	Rom 9:33

STUMP

only the s of Dagon was left to	1Sa 5:4
Nevertheless leave the s of his	Dan 4:15
yet leave the s of the roots	Dan 4:23
to leave the s of the tree roots	Dan 4:26

SUAH (su´-ah) *Son of Zophah.*

S, and Harnepher, and Shual, and	1Chr 7:36

SUBDUE

and replenish the earth, and s it	Gen 1:28
Moreover I will s all thine	1Chr 17:10
He shall s the people under us	Ps 47:3
holden, to s nations before him	Is 45:1
first, and he shall s three kings	Dan 7:24
he will s our iniquities	Mic 7:19

SUBDUED

the land be s before the LORD	Num 32:22
and the land shall be s before you	Num 32:29
war with thee, until it be s	Deut 20:20
And the land was s before them	Josh 18:1
So Moab was s that day under the	Judg 3:30
So God s on that day Jabin the	Judg 4:23
Thus was Midian s before the	Judg 8:28
s before the children of Israel	Judg 11:33
So the Philistines were s	1Sa 7:13
smote the Philistines, and s them	2Sa 8:1
of all nations which he s	2Sa 8:11
against me hast thou s under me	2Sa 22:40
s them, and took Gath and her towns	1Chr 18:1
and they were s	1Chr 20:4
the land is s before the LORD, and	1Chr 22:18
thou hast s under me those that	Ps 18:39
should soon have s their enemies	Ps 81:14
all things shall be s unto him	1Cor 15:28
Who through faith s kingdoms	Heb 11:33

SUBDUEDST

land, and thou s before them the	Neh 9:24

SUBDUETH

me, and the people under me	Ps 18:47
who s my people under me	Ps 144:2
in pieces and s all things	Dan 2:40

SUBJECT

to Nazareth, and was s unto them	Lk 2:51
even the devils are s unto us	Lk 10:17
that the spirits are s unto you	Lk 10:20
for it is not s to the law of God	Rom 8:7
the creature was made s to vanity	Rom 8:20
Let every soul be s unto the	Rom 13:1
Wherefore ye must needs be s	Rom 13:5
prophets are s to the prophets	1Cor 14:32
be s unto him that put all things	1Cor 15:28
as the church is s unto Christ	Eph 5:24
world, are ye s to ordinances	Col 2:20
in mind to be s to principalities	Titus 3:1
all their lifetime s to bondage	Heb 2:15
Elias was a man s to like	Jas 5:17
be s to your masters with all	1Pet 2:18
and powers being made s unto him	1Pet 3:22
all of you be s one to another	1Pet 5:5

SUBJECTED

him who hath s the same in hope	Rom 8:20

SUBJECTION

brought into s under their hand	Ps 106:42
brought them into s for servants	Jer 34:11
to return, and brought them into s	Jer 34:16
under my body, and bring it into s	1Cor 9:27
s into the gospel of Christ	2Cor 9:13
To whom we gave place by s	Gal 2:5
woman learn in silence with all s	1Ti 2:11
children in s with all gravity	1Ti 3:4
he not put in s the world to come	Heb 2:5
all things in s under his feet	Heb 2:8
in s unto the Father of spirits	Heb 12:9
be in s to your own husbands	1Pet 3:1
being in s unto their own	1Pet 3:5

SUBMIT

s thyself under her hands	Gen 16:9
Strangers shall s themselves unto	2Sa 22:45
shall s themselves unto me	Ps 18:44
enemies s themselves unto thee	Ps 66:3
till every one s himself with	Ps 68:30
That ye s yourselves unto such,	1Cor 16:16
s yourselves unto your own	Eph 5:22
s yourselves unto your own	Col 3:18
rule over you, and s yourselves	Heb 13:17
S yourselves therefore to God	Jas 4:7
S yourselves to every ordinance	1Pet 2:13
s yourselves unto the elder	1Pet 5:5

SUBMITTED

s themselves unto Solomon the	1Chr 29:24
should have s themselves unto him	Ps 81:15
have not s themselves unto the	Rom 10:3

SUBMITTING

S yourselves one to another in	Eph 5:21

SUBORNED

Then they s men, which said, We	Acts 6:11

SUBSCRIBE

another shall s with his hand	Is 44:5
s evidences, and seal them, and	Jer 32:44

SUBSCRIBED

I s the evidence, and sealed it, in	Jer 32:10
that s the book of the purchase	Jer 32:12

SUBSTANCE

every living s that I have made	Gen 7:4
every living s was destroyed	Gen 7:23
all their s that they had	Gen 12:5
for their s was great, so that	Gen 13:6
shall they come out with great s	Gen 15:14
Shall not their cattle and their s	Gen 34:23
and all his beasts, and all his s	Gen 36:6
all the s that was in their	Deut 11:6
Bless, LORD, his s, and accept the	Deut 33:11
for their cattle and for their s	Josh 14:4
of the s which was king David's	1Chr 27:31
and the stewards over all the s	1Chr 28:1

SUBURBS

carried away all the s that was	2Chr 21:17
of his s for the burnt offerings	2Chr 31:3
for God had given him s very much	2Chr 32:29
these were of the king's s	2Chr 35:7
our little ones, and for all our s	Ezr 8:21
all his s should be forfeited, and	Ezr 10:8
His s also was seven thousand	Job 1:3
his s is increased in the land	Job 1:10
the robber swalloweth up their s	Job 5:5
Give a reward for me of your s	Job 6:22
neither shall his s continue	Job 15:29
according to his s shall the	Job 20:18
Whereas our s is not cut down,	Job 22:20
ride upon it, and dissolvest my s	Job 30:22
rest of their s to their babes	Ps 17:14
his house, and ruler of all his s	Ps 105:21
My s was not hid from thee, when	Ps 139:15
Thine eyes did see my s, yet	Ps 139:16
We shall find all precious s	Prov 1:13
Honour the LORD with thy s	Prov 3:9
shall give all the s of his house	Prov 6:31
those that love me to inherit s	Prov 8:21
casteth away the s of the wicked	Prov 10:3
but the s of a diligent man is	Prov 12:27
and unjust gain increaseth his s	Prov 28:8
with harlots spendeth his s	Prov 29:3
all the s of his house for love	Song 8:7
whose s is in them, when they	Is 6:13
holy seed shall be the s thereof	Is 6:13
Thy s and thy treasures will I	Jer 15:13
in the field, I will give thy s	Jer 17:3
rich, I have found me out s	Hos 12:8
s in the day of their calamity	Obad 13
their s unto the Lord of the	Mic 4:13
ministered unto him of their s	Lk 8:3
there wasted his s with riotous	Lk 15:13
heaven a better and an enduring s	Heb 10:34
Now faith is the s of things	Heb 11:1

SUBTIL

Now the serpent was more s than	Gen 3:1
and Jonadab was a very s man	2Sa 13:3
of an harlot, and s of heart	Prov 7:10

SUBTILLY

is told me that he dealeth very s	1Sa 23:22
to deal s with his servants	Ps 105:25
The same dealt s with our kindred	Acts 7:19

SUBTILTY

he said, Thy brother came with s	Gen 27:35
But Jehu did it in s, to the	2Kin 10:19
To give s to the simple, to the	Prov 1:4
that they might take Jesus by s	Mt 26:4
And said, O full of all s and all	Acts 13:10
beguiled Eve through his s	2Cor 11:3

SUBURBS

But the field of the s	Lev 25:34
give also unto the Levites s for	Num 35:2
the s of them shall be for their	Num 35:3
the s of the cities, which ye	Num 35:4
be to them the s of the cities	Num 35:5
them shall ye give with their s	Num 35:7
with their s for their cattle and	Josh 14:4
with the s thereof for our pasture	Josh 21:2
the LORD, these cities and their s	Josh 21:3
Levites these cities with their s	Josh 21:8
with the s thereof round about it	Josh 21:11
the priest Hebron with her s	Josh 21:13
and Libnah with her s	Josh 21:13
And Jattir with her s, and Eshtemoa	Josh 21:14
and Eshtemoa with her s	Josh 21:14
And Holon with her s, and Debir	Josh 21:15
and Debir with her s	Josh 21:15
And Ain with her s, and Juttah with	Josh 21:16
and Juttah with her s	Josh 21:16
and Beth-shemesh with her s	Josh 21:16
of Benjamin, Gibeon with her s	Josh 21:17
Geba with her s	Josh 21:17
Anathoth with her s, and Almon	Josh 21:18
and Almon with her s	Josh 21:18
nineteen cities with their s	Josh 21:19
with her s in mount Ephraim	Josh 21:21
and Gezer with her s	Josh 21:21
And Kibzaim with her s, and	Josh 21:22
and Beth-horon with her s	Josh 21:22
tribe of Dan, Eltekeh with her s	Josh 21:23
Gibbethon with her s	Josh 21:23
Aijalon with her s, Gath-rimmon	Josh 21:24
Gath-rimmon with her s	Josh 21:24
of Manasseh, Tanach with her s	Josh 21:25
and Gath-rimmon with her s	Josh 21:25
their s for the families of the	Josh 21:26
gave Golan in Bashan with her s	Josh 21:27
and Beesh-terah with her s	Josh 21:27
of Issachar, Kishon with her s	Josh 21:28
Dabareh with her s	Josh 21:28
Jarmuth with her s, En-gannim	Josh 21:29
En-gannim with her s	Josh 21:29
tribe of Asher, Mishal with her s	Josh 21:30
Abdon with her s	Josh 21:30
Helkath with her s, and Rehob with	Josh 21:31
Rehob with her s	Josh 21:31
Kedesh in Galilee with her s	Josh 21:32
and Hammoth-dor with her s	Josh 21:32
and Kartan with her s	Josh 21:32
were thirteen cities with their s	Josh 21:33
of Zebulun, Jokneam with her s	Josh 21:34
and Kartan with her s	Josh 21:34
Dimnah with her s, Nahalal with	Josh 21:35
and Nahalal with her s	Josh 21:35

tribe of Reuben, Bezer with her *s* .... Josh 21:36
and Jahazah with her *s* .... Josh 21:36
Kedemoth with her *s*, and Mephaath ...... Josh 21:37
and Mephaath with her *s* .... Josh 21:37
Gad, Ramoth in Gilead with her *s* .... Josh 21:38
and Mahanaim with her *s*, ... Josh 21:38
Heshbon with her *s*, Jazer with .... Josh 21:39
Jazer with her *s* .... Josh 21:39
and eight cities with their *s*, ... Josh 21:41
one with their *s* round about them .... Josh 21:42
chamberlain, which was in the *s* 2Kin 23:11
towns, and in all the *s* of Sharon 1Chr 5:16
the *s* thereof round about it 1Chr 6:55
of refuge, and Libnah with her *s*, ... 1Chr 6:57
Jattir, and Eshtemoa, with their *s*, ... 1Chr 6:57
And Hilen with her *s*, Debir with 1Chr 6:58
Debir with her *s* 1Chr 6:58
And Ashan with her *s*, ... 1Chr 6:59
and Beth-shemesh with her *s* 1Chr 6:59
Geba with her *s* 1Chr 6:60
and Alemeth with her *s* 1Chr 6:60
and Anathoth with her *s* 1Chr 6:60
Levites these cities with their *s* 1Chr 6:64
in mount Ephraim with her *s* 1Chr 6:67
they gave also Gezer with her *s* 1Chr 6:67
And Jokmeam with her *s*, and 1Chr 6:68
and Beth-horon with her *s* 1Chr 6:68
And Aijalon with her *s*, and 1Chr 6:69
and Gath-rimmon with her *s* 1Chr 6:69
Aner with her *s*, and Bileam with 1Chr 6:70
and Bileam with her *s* 1Chr 6:70
Golan in Bashan with her *s*, ... 1Chr 6:71
and Ashtaroth with her *s* 1Chr 6:71
Kedesh with her *s* 1Chr 6:72
Daberath with her *s* 1Chr 6:72
And Ramoth with her *s*, ... 1Chr 6:73
and Anem with her *s* 1Chr 6:73
Mashal with her *s* 1Chr 6:74
And Abdon with her *s* 1Chr 6:74
And Hukok with her *s* 1Chr 6:75
and Rehob with her *s* 1Chr 6:75
Kedesh in Galilee with her *s* 1Chr 6:76
and Hammon with her *s* 1Chr 6:76
and Kirjathaim with her *s* 1Chr 6:76
of Zebulun, Rimmon with her *s* 1Chr 6:77
Tabor with her *s* 1Chr 6:77
in the wilderness with her *s* 1Chr 6:78
and Jahzah with her *s* 1Chr 6:78
Kedemoth also with her *s*, and 1Chr 6:79
and Mephaath with her *s* 1Chr 6:79
Ramoth in Gilead with her *s* 1Chr 6:80
and Mahanaim with her *s* 1Chr 6:80
And Heshbon with her *s*, and Jazer 1Chr 6:81
and Jazer with her *s* 1Chr 6:81
which are in their cities and *s* 1Chr 13:2
For the Levites left their *s* 2Chr 11:14
fields of the *s* of their cities 2Chr 31:19
The *s* shall shake at the sound of .... Eze 27:28
round about for the *s* thereof .... Eze 45:2
the city, for dwelling, and for *s* .... Eze 48:15
the *s* of the city shall be toward .... Eze 48:17

SUBVERT

To *s* a man in his cause, the Lord .... Lam 3:36
who *s* whole houses, teaching .... Titus 1:11

SUBVERTED

Knowing that he that is such is *s* .... Titus 3:11

SUBVERTING

s your souls, saying, Ye must be............. Acts 15:24
but to the *s* of the hearers 2Ti 2:14

SUCATHITES See SUCHATHITES.

SUCCEED

which she beareth shall *s* in the............. Deut 25:6

SUCCEEDED

but the children of Esau *s* them............. Deut 2:12
and they *s* them, and dwelt in their...... Deut 2:21
and they *s* them, and dwelt in their...... Deut 2:22

SUCCEEDEST

to possess them, and thou *s* them.......... Deut 12:29
God giveth thee, and thou *s* them.......... Deut 19:1

SUCCESS

and then thou shalt have good *s* .... Josh 1:8

SUCCOTH (suc´-coth)
1. A place east of the Jordan.
And Jacob journeyed to *S*, and built....... Gen 33:17
the name of the place is called *S*............ Gen 33:17
2. An Israelite encampment in the wilderness.
journeyed from Rameses to *S* .... Ex 12:37
And they took their journey from *S* .... Ex 13:20
from Rameses, and pitched in *S*.............. Num 33:5
And they departed from *S*, and.............. Num 33:6
3. A place in God.
Beth-aram, and Beth-nimrah, and *S*....... Josh 13:27
And he said unto the men of *S* .... Judg 8:5
And the princes of *S* said, Are the .... Judg 8:6
as the men of *S* had answered him......... Judg 8:8
a young man of the men of *S* .... Judg 8:14
unto him the princes of *S* .... Judg 8:14
And he came unto the men of *S* .... Judg 8:15
with them he taught the men of *S* .... Judg 8:16
4. A city in Ephraim.
in the clay ground between *S* 1Kin 7:46
in the clay ground between *S*................. 2Chr 4:17
and mete out the valley of *S*.................. Ps 60:6
and mete out the valley of *S*.................. Ps 108:7

SUCCOTH-BENOTH (suc´-coth-be´-noth) A
Babylonian god.
And the men of Babylon made *S*............. 2Kin 17:30

SUCCOUR

came to *s* Hadadezer king of Zobah 2Sa 8:5
that thou *s* us out of the city 2Sa 18:3
he is able to *s* them that are .... Heb 2:18

SUCCOURED

Abishai the son of Zeruiah *s* him 2Sa 21:17
day of salvation have I *s* thee 2Cor 6:2

SUCCOURER

for she hath been a *s* of many .... Rom 16:2

SUCH

the father of *s* as dwell in tents............. Gen 4:20
in tents, and of *s* as have cattle.............. Gen 4:20
of all *s* as handle the harp..................... Gen 4:21
as I love, and bring it to me..................... Gen 27:4
for thy father, *s* as he loveth................. Gen 27:9
meat, *s* as his father loved .... Gen 27:14
s as these which are of the .... Gen 27:46
and of *s* shall be my hire........................ Gen 30:32
s as I never saw in all the land............... Gen 41:19
Can we find *s* a one as this is, a............. Gen 41:38
wot ye not that a man as I can................. Gen 44:15
s as hath not been in Egypt since .... Ex 9:18
s as there was none like it in................. Ex 9:24
there were no *s* locusts as they.............. Ex 10:14
neither after them shall be *s* .... Ex 10:14
s as there was none like it, nor.............. Ex 11:6
them *s* things as they required............... Ex 12:36
s as fear God, men of truth, ... Ex 18:21
place *s* over them, to be rulers .... Ex 18:21
s as have not been done in all .... Ex 34:10
s things have befallen me....................... Lev 10:19
that on which *s* water cometh................ Lev 11:34
every *s* vessel shall be unclean.............. Lev 11:34
pigeons, *s* as he is able to get................ Lev 14:22
young pigeons, *s* as he can get............... Lev 14:30
Even *s* as he is able to get, the .... Lev 14:31
after *s* as have familiar spirits............... Lev 20:6
any *s* shall be unclean until even........... Lev 22:6
all that any man giveth of *s* unto........... Lev 27:9
instead of *s* as open every womb,........... Num 8:16
whether there hath been any *s*............... Deut 4:32
there were a *s* heart in them.................. Deut 5:29
shall do no more any *s* wickedness........ Deut 13:11
that *s* abomination is wrought............... Deut 17:4
s time as thou beginnest to put.............. Deut 16:9
that *s* abomination is wrought in........... Deut 17:4
no more any *s* evil among you............... Deut 19:20
For all that do *s* things, and all.............. Deut 25:16
at the least *s* as before knew,................. Judg 3:2
have told us *s* things as these .... Judg 13:23
that thou comest with *s* a company........ Judg 18:23
There was no *s* deed done nor seen........ Judg 19:30
unto whom he said, Ho, *s* a one.............. Ruth 4:1
unto them, Why do ye *s* things 1Sa 2:23
not been a *s* thing heretofore................. 1Sa 4:7
I have appointed my servants to *s*.......... 1Sa 21:2
and *s* a place... 1Sa 21:2
for he is a *s* son of Belial, that............... 1Sa 25:17
look upon *s* a dead dog as I am.............. 2Sa 9:8
given unto thee *s* and *s* things.............. 2Sa 12:8
for no *s* thing ought to be done.............. 2Sa 13:12
for with *s* robes were the king's............. 2Sa 13:18
then hast thou thought *s* a thing............ 2Sa 14:13
that *s* as be faint in the......................... 2Sa 16:2
recompense it me with a reward............... 2Sa 19:36
there came no more *s* abundance of....... 1Kin 10:10
there came no *s* almug trees 1Kin 10:12
with his servants, saying, In *s*............... 2Kin 6:8
a *s* place shall be my camp.................... 2Kin 6:8
that thou pass not a place........................ 2Kin 6:9
in heaven, might a *s* thing be................. 2Kin 7:19
Ye shall eat this year *s* things................ 2Kin 19:29
I am bringing a *s* upon........................... 2Kin 21:12
Surely there was not holden a *s*............. 2Kin 23:22
s things as were of gold, in gold............ 2Kin 25:15
s as went forth to battle, expert 1Chr 12:33
s as went forth to battle, expert 1Chr 12:36
bestowed upon him *s* royal majesty 1Chr 29:25
s as none of the kings have had 2Chr 1:12
s things as they offered for the.............. 2Chr 4:6
neither was there any *s* spice as............ 2Chr 9:9
there were none *s* seen before in........... 2Chr 9:11
s as set their hearts to seek the 2Chr 11:16
s as taught to sing praise...................... 2Chr 23:13
Jehoiada gave it to *s* as did the 2Chr 24:12
also *s* as wrought iron and brass........... 2Chr 24:12
time in *s* sort as it was written.............. 2Chr 30:5
keep a *s* passover as Josiah kept............ 2Chr 35:18
side the river, and at a *s* time .... Ezr 4:10
side the river, and at a *s* time .... Ezr 4:11
the river, Peace, and at a *s* time............ Ezr 4:17
all *s* as had separated themselves.......... Ezr 6:21
perfect peace, and at a *s* time................ Ezr 7:12
all *s* as know the laws of thy God.......... Ezr 7:25
which hath put a *s* thing as this .... Ezr 7:27
of *s* as lay in wait by the way................ Ezr 8:31
hast given us *s* deliverance as .... Ezr 9:13
s as are born of them, according .... Ezr 10:3
There are no *s* things done as .... Neh 6:8
I said, Should *s* a man as I flee.............. Neh 6:11
with *s* things as belonged to her............ Est 2:9
except *s* to whom the king shall............. Est 4:11
the kingdom for *s* a time as this............ Est 4:14
to lay hand on *s* as sought their .... Est 9:2
upon all *s* as joined themselves............. Est 9:27

who knoweth not *s* things as these .... Job 12:3
open thine eyes upon *s* an one............... Job 14:3
lettest *s* words go out of thy.................. Job 15:13
I have heard many *s* things.................... Job 16:2
Surely *s* are the dwellings of the .... Job 18:21
many *s* things are with him................... Job 23:14
truth unto *s* as keep his covenant.......... Ps 25:10
me, and *s* as breathe out cruelty............ Ps 27:12
saveth *s* as be of a contrite.................... Ps 34:18
to slay *s* as be of upright....................... Ps 37:14
For *s* as be blessed of him shall............. Ps 37:22
nor *s* as turn aside to lies...................... Ps 40:4
let *s* as love thy salvation say................ Ps 40:16
altogether *s* an one as thyself................ Ps 50:21
against *s* as be at peace with him.......... Ps 55:20
the hairy scalp of *s* an one as................ Ps 68:21
let *s* as love thy salvation say................ Ps 70:4
even to *s* as are of a clean heart............ Ps 73:1
To *s* as keep his covenant, and to.......... Ps 103:18
S as sit in darkness and in the.............. Ps 107:10
As for *s* as turn aside unto their............ Ps 125:5
S knowledge is too wonderful for........... Ps 139:6
that people, that is in *s* a case............... Ps 144:15
but *s* as are upright in their way........... Prov 11:20
but *s* as keep the law contend............... Prov 28:4
S is the way of an adulterous................ Prov 30:20
the dumb in the cause of all *s* as........... Prov 31:8
the tears of *s* as were oppressed............ Eccl 4:1
not be a *s* was in her vexation .... Is 9:1
s as are escaped of the house of............ Is 10:20
s is our expectation, whither we............ Is 20:6
this year *s* as groweth of itself .... Is 37:30
Is it *s* a fast that I have chosen............. Is 58:5
Who hath heard *s* a thing...................... Is 66:8
who hath seen *s* things.......................... Is 66:8
and see if there be *s* a thing.................. Jer 2:10
be avenged on *s* a nation as this........... Jer 5:9
be avenged on *s* a nation as this........... Jer 5:29
be avenged on *s* a nation as this........... Jer 9:9
S as are for death, to death.................. Jer 15:2
s as are for the sword, to the................ Jer 15:2
s as are for the famine, to the.............. Jer 15:2
s as are for the captivity, to................. Jer 15:2
heathen, who hath heard *s* things.......... Jer 18:13
s as are left in this city from .... Jer 21:7
in speaking *s* words unto them.............. Jer 38:4
deliver *s* as are for death to.................. Jer 43:11
s as are for captivity to........................ Jer 43:11
s as are for the sword to the .... Jer 43:11
return but *s* as shall escape .... Jer 44:14
he escape that doeth *s* things................ Eze 17:15
considereth, and doeth not *s* like.......... Eze 18:14
s as had ability in them to stand.......... Dan 1:4
that asked *s* things at any..................... Dan 2:10
he had spoken *s* words unto me............. Dan 10:15
s as do wickedly against the................. Dan 11:32
s as never was since there was a........... Dan 12:1
s as skilful of lamentation .... Amos 5:16
heathen, *s* as they have not heard......... Mic 5:15
all *s* as are clothed with strange........... Zeph 1:8
which had given *s* power unto men........ Mt 9:8
one *s* little child in my name................. Mt 18:5
for of *s* is the kingdom of heaven......... Mt 19:14
s as was not since the beginning........... Mt 24:21
for in a *s* hour as ye think not.............. Mt 24:44
said, Go into the city to *s* a man .... Mt 26:18
as he hear the word,............................... Mk 4:18
and *s* as receive it, and receive it.......... Mk 4:20
with many *s* parables spake he the .... Mk 4:33
that even *s* mighty works are................ Mk 6:2
many other *s* like things ye do.............. Mk 7:8
and many *s* like things do ye .... Mk 7:13
one of *s* children in my name .... Mk 9:37
for of *s* is the kingdom of God .... Mk 10:14
for *s* things must needs be.................... Mk 13:7
s as was not from the beginning........... Mk 13:19
in this, of whom I hear *s* things............ Lk 9:9
drinking *s* things as they give............... Lk 10:7
eat *s* things as are set before................. Lk 10:8
give alms of *s* things as ye have............ Lk 11:41
because they suffered *s* things.............. Lk 13:2
for of *s* is the kingdom of God............. Lk 18:16
Father seeketh *s* to worship him........... Jn 4:23
murmured *s* things concerning him....... Jn 7:32
us, that *s* should be stoned................... Jn 8:5
that is a sinner do *s* miracles............... Jn 9:16
church daily *s* as should be saved .... Acts 2:47
s as I have give I thee.......................... Acts 3:6
gave no *s* commandment...................... Acts 15:24
Who, having received *s* a charge........... Acts 16:24
I will be no judge of *s* matters............. Acts 18:15
that they observe no *s* thing................. Acts 21:25
Away with a fellow from the .... Acts 22:22
to live after *s* as I supposed.................. Acts 25:18
doubted of *s* manner of questions......... Acts 25:20
almost, and altogether *s* as I am........... Acts 26:29
they laded us with *s* things as............... Acts 28:10
that they which commit *s* things .... Rom 1:32
them which commit *s* things................. Rom 2:2
judgest them which do *s* things............ Rom 2:3
For they that are *s* serve not our.......... Rom 16:18
s fornication as is not so much............. 1Cor 5:1
To deliver a *s* one unto Satan for 1Cor 5:5
hast not *s* a one have I not..................... 1Cor 5:11
And *s* were some of you......................... 1Cor 6:11
is not under bondage in *s* cases............ 1Cor 7:15
Nevertheless *s* shall have trouble.......... 1Cor 7:28
you but *s* as is common to man............ 1Cor 10:13
contentious, we have no *s* custom......... 1Cor 11:16
s are they also that are earthy.............. 1Cor 15:48

s are they also that are heavenly.......1Cor 15:48
That ye submit yourselves unto s.......1Cor 16:16
acknowledge ye them that are s 1Cor 16:18
Sufficient to s a man is this.......2Cor 2:6
lest perhaps s one should be.......2Cor 2:7
s trust have we through Christ to.......2Cor 3:4
Seeing then that we have a hope.......2Cor 3:12
Let s an one think this, that,.......2Cor 10:11
s as we are in word by letters.......2Cor 10:11
s will we be also in deed when we.......2Cor 10:11
For s are false apostles,.......2Cor 11:13
s an one caught up to the third.......2Cor 12:2
And I knew s a man, (whether in.......2Cor 12:3
Of s an one will I glory,.......2Cor 12:5
I shall not find you s as I would.......2Cor 12:20
found unto you s as ye would not.......2Cor 12:20
revellings, and s like.......Gal 5:21
that they which do s things shall.......Gal 5:21
against s there is no law.......Gal 5:23
restore s an one in the spirit of.......Gal 6:1
spot, or wrinkle, or any s thing.......Eph 5:27
and hold s in reputation.......Phil 2:29
the Lord is the avenger of all s.......1Th 4:6
Now them that are s we command.......2Th 3:12
from s withdraw thyself.......2Ti 3:5
from s turn away.......2Ti 3:5
that he that is s is subverted.......Titus 3:11
being s an one as Paul the aged,.......Philem 9
are become s as have need of milk.......Heb 5:12
For s an high priest became us,.......Heb 7:26
We have s an high priest, who is.......Heb 8:1
For they that say s things.......Heb 11:14
s contradiction of sinners.......Heb 12:3
be content with s things as ye.......Heb 13:5
for with s sacrifices God is well.......Heb 13:16
morrow we will go into s a city.......Jas 4:13
all s rejoicing is evil.......Jas 4:16
when there came s a voice to him.......2Pet 1:17
seeing that ye look for s things.......2Pet 3:14
We therefore ought to receive s.......3Jn 8
s as are in the sea, and all that.......Rev 5:13
s as was not since men were upon.......Rev 16:18
on s the second death hath no.......Rev 20:6

SUCHATHITES (soo´-kath-ites) A family of
scribes.
the Shimeathites, and S.......1Chr 2:55

SUCK
should have given children s.......Gen 21:7
he made him to s honey out of the.......Deut 32:13
for they shall s of the abundance.......Deut 33:19
gave her son s until she weaned.......1Sa 1:23
in the morning to give s child.......1Kin 3:21
why the breasts that I should s.......Job 3:12
He shall s the poison of asps.......Job 20:16
Her young ones also s up blood.......Job 39:30
Thou shalt also s the milk of the.......Is 60:16
shalt s the breast of kings.......Is 60:16
That ye may s, and be satisfied.......Is 66:11
then shall ye s, ye shall be.......Is 66:12
they give s to their young ones.......Lam 4:3
s it out, and thou shalt break the.......Eze 23:34
and those that s the breasts.......Joel 2:16
to them that give s in those days.......Mt 24:19
to them that give s in those days.......Mk 13:17
child, and to them that give s.......Lk 21:23
and the paps which never gave s.......Lk 23:29

SUCKED
that s the breasts of my mother.......Song 8:1
and the paps which thou hast s.......Lk 11:27

SUCKING
father beareth the s child.......Num 11:12
And Samuel took a s lamb, and.......1Sa 7:9
the s child shall play on the.......Is 11:8
Can a woman forget her s child.......Is 49:15
The tongue of the s child.......Lam 4:4

SUCKLING
the s also with the man of gray.......Deut 32:25
both man and woman, infant and s.......1Sa 15:3
from you man and woman, child and s.......Jer 44:7

SUCKLINGS
both men and women, children and s.......1Sa 22:19
s hast thou ordained strength.......Ps 8:2
the s swoon in the streets of the.......Lam 2:11
s thou hast perfected praise.......Mt 21:16

SUDDEN
thee, and s fear troubleth thee.......Job 22:10
Be not afraid of s fear, neither.......Prov 3:25
then s destruction cometh upon.......1Th 5:3

SUDDENLY
And if any man die very s by him.......Num 6:9
And the LORD spake s unto Moses.......Num 12:4
if he thrust him s without enmity.......Num 35:22
against you, and destroy thee s.......Deut 7:4
Joshua therefore came unto them s.......Josh 10:9
to depart, lest he overtake us s.......2Sa 15:14
for the thing was done s.......2Chr 29:36
but s I cursed his habitation.......Job 5:3
If the scourge slay s, he will.......Job 9:23
let them return and be ashamed s.......Ps 6:10
s do they shoot at him, and fear.......Ps 64:4
s shall they be wounded.......Ps 64:7
shall his calamity come.......Prov 6:15
s shall he be broken without.......Prov 6:15
For their calamity shall rise s.......Prov 24:22
shall s be destroyed, and that.......Prov 29:1

---

time, when it falleth s upon them.......Eccl 9:12
yea, s it shall be at an instant s.......Is 29:5
breaking cometh s at an instant.......Is 30:13
desolation shall come upon thee s.......Is 47:11
I did them s, and they came.......Is 48:3
s are my tents spoiled, and my.......Jer 4:20
the spoiler shall s come upon us.......Jer 6:26
have caused him to fail upon it s.......Jer 15:8
shall bring a troop s upon them.......Jer 18:22
but I will s shake him from away.......Jer 49:19
make them s run away from her.......Jer 50:44
Babylon is s fallen and destroyed.......Jer 51:8
rise up s that shall bite thee.......Hab 2:7
shall s come to his temple, even.......Mal 3:1
And s, when they had looked round.......Mk 9:8
Lest coming s he find you.......Mk 13:36
s there was with the angel a.......Lk 2:13
taketh him, and he s crieth out.......Lk 9:39
s there came a sound from heaven.......Acts 2:2
s there shined round about him a.......Acts 9:3
s there was a great earthquake,.......Acts 16:26
s there shone from heaven a great.......Acts 22:6
swollen, or fallen down dead s.......Acts 28:6
Lay hands s on no man, neither be.......1Ti 5:22

SUE
if any man will s thee at the law.......Mt 5:40

SUFFER
will not s the destroyer to come.......Ex 12:23
Thou shalt not s a witch to live.......Ex 22:18
neither shalt thou s the salt of.......Lev 2:13
neighbour, and not s sin upon him.......Lev 19:17
Or s them to bear the iniquity of.......Lev 22:16
Sihon would not s Israel to pass.......Num 21:23
s them not to enter into their.......Josh 10:19
for they would not s them to come.......Judg 15:1
father would not s him to go in.......Judg 15:1
S me that I may feel the pillars.......Judg 16:26
that thou wouldest not s the.......2Sa 14:11
that he might not s any to go out.......1Kin 15:17
for the king's profit to s them.......Est 3:8
He will not s me to take my.......Job 9:18
S me that I may speak.......Job 21:3
their winepresses, and s thirst.......Job 24:11
thou s him to dwell in.......Job 36:2
which I s of them that hate me.......Ps 9:13
neither wilt thou s thine Holy.......Ps 16:10
young lions do lack, and s hunger.......Ps 34:10
he shall never s the righteous to.......Ps 55:22
when I s thy terrors I am.......Ps 88:15
nor s my faithfulness to fail.......Ps 89:33
and a proud heart will not s.......Ps 101:5
nor wilt thou s thy foot to be.......Ps 121:3
The LORD will not s the soul of.......Prov 10:3
and an idle soul shall s hunger.......Prov 19:15
of great wrath shall s punishment.......Prov 19:19
S not thy mouth to cause thy.......Eccl 5:6
the rich will not s him to sleep.......Eccl 5:12
nor s their locks to grow long.......Eze 44:20
said unto him, S it to be so now.......Mt 3:15
s me first to go and bury my.......Mt 8:21
s us to go away into the herd of.......Mt 8:31
s many things of the elders and.......Mt 16:21
also the Son of man s of them.......Mt 17:12
how long shall I s you.......Mt 17:17
S little children, and forbid them.......Mt 19:14
neither s ye them that are.......Mt 23:13
ye s him no more to do ought for.......Mk 7:12
the Son of man must s many things.......Mk 8:31
man, that he must s many things.......Mk 9:12
how long shall I s you.......Mk 9:19
S the little children to come.......Mk 10:14
would not s that any man should.......Mk 11:16
would s them to enter into them.......Lk 8:32
The Son of man must s many things.......Lk 9:22
shall I be with you, and s you.......Lk 9:41
s me first to go and bury my.......Lk 9:59
But first must he s many things.......Lk 17:25
S little children to come unto me.......Lk 18:16
this passover with you before I s.......Lk 22:15
answered and said, S ye thus far.......Lk 22:51
and thus it behoved Christ to s.......Lk 24:46
neither wilt thou s thine Holy.......Acts 2:27
prophets, that Christ should s.......Acts 3:18
worthy to s shame for his name.......Acts 5:41
And seeing one of them s wrong.......Acts 7:24
he must s for my name's sake.......Acts 9:16
Thou shalt not s thine Holy One.......Acts 13:35
s me to speak unto the people.......Acts 21:39
That Christ should s, and that he.......Acts 26:23
if so be that we s with him.......Rom 8:17
shall be burned, he shall s loss.......1Cor 3:15
being persecuted, we s it.......1Cor 4:12
why do ye not rather s yourselves.......1Cor 6:7
but s all things, lest we should.......1Cor 9:12
who will not s you to be tempted.......1Cor 10:13
And whether one member s, all the.......1Cor 12:26
s, all the members s with it.......1Cor 12:26
same sufferings which we also s.......2Cor 1:6
For ye s fools gladly, seeing ye.......2Cor 11:19
For ye s, if a man bring you into.......2Cor 11:20
why do I yet s persecution.......Gal 5:11
only lest they should s.......Gal 6:12
but also to s for his sake.......Phil 1:29
both to abound and to s need.......Phil 4:12
that we should s tribulation.......1Th 3:4
of God, for which ye also s.......2Th 1:5
But I s not a woman to teach, nor.......1Ti 2:12
s reproach, because we trust in.......1Ti 4:10
which cause I also s these things.......2Ti 1:12

Wherein I s trouble, as an evil.......2Ti 2:9
If we s, we shall also reign with.......2Ti 2:12
Christ Jesus shall s persecution.......2Ti 3:12
Choosing rather to s affliction.......Heb 11:25
and them which s adversity.......Heb 13:3
the word of exhortation.......Heb 13:22
s for it, ye take it patiently,.......1Pet 2:20
if ye s for righteousness' sake,.......1Pet 3:14
that ye s for well doing, than,.......1Pet 3:17
let none of you s as a murderer.......1Pet 4:15
Yet if any man s as a Christian.......1Pet 4:16
Wherefore let them that s.......1Pet 4:19
those things which thou shalt s.......Rev 2:10
shall not s their dead bodies to.......Rev 11:9

therefore s I thee not to touch.......Gen 20:6
but God s him not to hurt me.......Gen 31:7
hast not s me to kiss my sons and.......Gen 31:28
s thee to hunger, and fed thee.......Deut 8:3
thy God hath not s thee so to do.......Deut 18:14
Moab, and s not a man to pass over.......Judg 3:28
s them not to rise against Saul.......1Sa 24:7
s neither the birds of the air to.......2Sa 21:10
He so man to do them wrong.......1Chr 16:21
(Neither have I s my mouth to sin.......Job 31:30
He s no man to do them wrong.......Ps 105:14
that for thy sake I have s rebuke.......Jer 15:15
Then he s him.......Mt 3:15
s you to put away your wives.......Mt 19:8
would not have s his house to be.......Mt 24:43
for I have s many things this day.......Mt 27:19
s not the devils to speak.......Mk 1:34
Howbeit Jesus s him not, but.......Mk 5:19
had s many things of many.......Mk 5:26
he so man to follow him, save.......Mk 5:37
Moses s to write a bill of.......Mk 10:4
he rebuking them s them not to.......Lk 4:41
And he s them.......Lk 8:32
he so man to go in, save Peter,.......Lk 8:51
not have s his house to be broken.......Lk 12:39
because they s such things.......Lk 13:2
not Christ to have s these things.......Lk 24:26
years s he their manners in the.......Acts 13:18
Who in times past s all nations.......Acts 14:16
but the Spirit s them not.......Acts 16:7
that Christ must needs have s.......Acts 17:3
people, the disciples s him not.......Acts 19:30
but Paul was s to dwell by.......Acts 28:16
nor for his cause that s wrong.......2Cor 7:12
thrice I s shipwreck, a night and.......2Cor 11:25
Have ye so many things in vain.......Gal 3:4
for whom I have s the loss of all.......Phil 3:8
even after that we had s before.......1Th 2:2
for ye also have s like things of.......1Th 2:14
he himself hath s being tempted.......Heb 2:18
by the things which he s.......Heb 5:8
because they were not s to.......Heb 7:23
s since the foundation of the.......Heb 9:26
his own blood, s without the gate.......Heb 13:12
because Christ also s for us.......1Pet 2:21
when he s, he threatened not.......1Pet 2:23
Christ also hath once s for sins.......1Pet 3:18
Christ hath s for us in the flesh.......1Pet 4:1
for he that hath s in the flesh.......1Pet 4:1
after that ye have s a while.......1Pet 5:10

SUFFEREST
because thou s that woman Jezebel.......Rev 2:20

SUFFERETH
s not our feet to be moved.......Ps 66:9
s not their cattle to decrease.......Ps 107:38
the kingdom of heaven s violence.......Mt 11:12
sea, yet vengeance s not to live.......Acts 28:4
Charity s long, and is kind.......1Cor 13:4

SUFFERING
against Cnidus, the wind not s us.......Acts 27:7
the angels for the s of death.......Heb 2:9
for an example of s affliction.......Jas 5:10
God endure grief, s wrongfully.......1Pet 2:19
the vengeance of eternal fire.......Jude 7

SUFFERINGS
For I reckon that the s of this.......Rom 8:18
For as the s of Christ abound in.......2Cor 1:5
the same s which we also suffer.......2Cor 1:6
that as ye are partakers of the s.......2Cor 1:7
and the fellowship of his s.......Phil 3:10
Who now rejoice in my s for you.......Col 1:24
their salvation perfect through s.......Heb 2:10
beforehand the s of Christ.......1Pet 1:11
as ye are partakers of Christ's s.......1Pet 4:13
and a witness of the s of Christ.......1Pet 5:1

SUFFICE
be slain for them, to s them.......Num 11:22
together for them, to s them.......Num 11:22
LORD said unto me, Let it s thee.......Deut 3:26
if the dust of Samaria shall s.......1Kin 20:10
Israel, let it s you of all your.......Eze 44:6
Let it s you, O princes of Israel.......Eze 45:9
the time past of our life may s.......1Pet 4:3

SUFFICED
arfd yet so they s them not.......Judg 21:14
corn, and she did eat, and was s.......Ruth 2:14
she had reserved after she was s.......Ruth 2:18

SUFFICETH
shew us the Father, and it s us.......Jn 14:8

In the fulness of his s he shall.......Job 20:22
but our s is of God.......2Cor 3:5

always having all s in all things 2Cor 9:8

SUFFICIENT
For the stuff they had was s for .... Ex 36:7
surely lend him s for his need .... Deut 15:8
let his hands be s for him .... Deut 33:7
eat so much as is s for thee .... Prov 25:16
And Lebanon is not s to burn .... Is 40:16
thereof s for a burnt offering .... Is 40:16
S unto the day is the evil .... Mt 6:34
whether he have s to finish it .... Lk 14:28
of bread is not s for them .... Jn 6:7
S to such a man is this 2Cor 2:6
who is s for these things 2Cor 2:16
Not that we are s of ourselves to 2Cor 3:5
unto me, My grace is s for thee 2Cor 12:9

SUFFICIENTLY
had not sanctified themselves s 2Chr 30:3
dwell before the LORD, to eat s .... Is 23:18

SUIT
a s of apparel, and thy victuals .... Judg 17:10
any s or cause might come unto me 2Sa 15:4
yea, many shall make s unto thee .... Job 11:19

SUITS
The changeable s of apparel .... Is 3:22

SUKKIIMS (suk´-ke-ims) An Egyptian tribe.
the Lubim, the S, and the 2Chr 12:3

SUM
there be laid on him a s of money .... Ex 21:30
When thou takest the s of the .... Ex 30:12
This is the s of the tabernacle .... Ex 38:21
Take ye the s of all the .... Num 1:2
neither take the s of them among .... Num 1:49
Take the s of the sons of Kohath .... Num 4:2
Take also the s of the sons of .... Num 4:22
Take the s of all the .... Num 26:2
Take the s of the people, from .... Num 26:4
Take the s of the prey that was .... Num 31:26
the s of the men of war which are .... Num 31:49
Joab gave up the s of the number 2Sa 24:9
that he may s the silver which is 2Kin 22:4
Joab gave the s of the number of 1Chr 21:5
of the s of the money that Haman .... Est 4:7
How great is the s of them .... Ps 139:17
Thou sealest up the s, full of .... Eze 28:12
told the s of the matters .... Dan 7:1
that Abraham bought for a s of .... Acts 7:16
With a great s obtained I this .... Acts 22:28
we have spoken this is the s .... Heb 8:1

SUMMER
and harvest, and cold and heat, and s.. .... Gen 8:22
and he was sitting in a s parlour .... Judg 3:20
his feet in his s chamber .... Judg 3:24
and an hundred of s fruits 2Sa 16:1
s fruit for the young men to eat 2Sa 16:2
is turned into the drought of s .... Ps 32:4
thou hast made a s and winter .... Ps 74:17
Provideth her meat in the s .... Prov 6:8
that gathereth in s is a wise son .... Prov 10:5
As snow in s, and as rain in .... Prov 26:1
they prepare their meat in the s .... Prov 30:25
for the shouting for thy s fruits .... Is 16:9
and the fowls shall s upon them .... Is 18:6
as the hasty fruit before the s .... Is 28:4
the s is ended, and we are not .... Jer 8:20
s fruits, and oil, and put them in .... Jer 40:10
wine and s fruits very much .... Jer 40:12
is fallen upon thy s fruits .... Jer 48:32
chaff of the s threshingfloors .... Dan 2:35
the winter house with the s house .... Amos 3:15
and behold a basket of s fruit .... Amos 8:1
And I said, A basket of s fruit .... Amos 8:2
they have gathered the s fruits .... Mic 7:1
in s and in winter shall it be .... Zec 14:8
leaves, ye know that s is nigh .... Mt 24:32
leaves, ye know that s is near .... Mk 13:28
selves that s is now nigh at hand .... Lk 21:30

SUMPTUOUSLY
fine linen, and fared s every day .... Lk 16:19

SUN
when the s was going down, a deep .... Gen 15:12
when the s went down, and it was .... Gen 15:17
The s was risen upon the earth .... Gen 19:23
all night, because the s was set .... Gen 28:11
over Penuel the s rose upon him .... Gen 32:31
and, behold, the s and the moon and .... Gen 37:9
when the s waxed hot, it melted .... Ex 16:21
until the going down of the s .... Ex 17:12
If the s be risen upon him, there .... Ex 22:3
unto him by that the s goeth down .... Ex 22:26
And when the s is down, he shall .... Lev 22:7
s shall they of the standard of .... Num 2:3
up before the LORD against the s .... Num 25:4
heaven, and when they seeth down .... Deut 4:19
by the way where the s goeth down .... Deut 11:30
even, at the going down of the s .... Deut 16:6
and worshipped them, either the s .... Deut 17:3
even, at the s is down, he shall .... Deut 23:11
again when the s goeth down .... Deut 24:13
shall the s go down upon it .... Deut 24:15
fruits brought forth by the s .... Deut 33:14
toward the going down of the s .... Josh 1:4
and as soon as the s was down .... Josh 8:29
he said in the sight of Israel, S .... Josh 10:12
the s stood still, and the moon .... Josh 10:13
So the s stood still in the midst .... Josh 10:13

time of the going down of the s .... Josh 10:27
Jordan toward the rising of the s .... Josh 12:1
the s when he goeth forth in his .... Judg 5:31
from battle before the s was up .... Judg 8:13
morning, as soon as the s is up .... Judg 9:33
day before the s went down .... Judg 14:18
the s went down upon them when .... Judg 19:14
morrow, by that time the s be hot 1Sa 11:9
the s went down when they were 2Sa 2:24
or ought else, till the s be down 2Sa 3:35
thy wives in the sight of this s 2Sa 12:11
all Israel, and before the s 2Sa 12:12
of the morning, when the s riseth 2Sa 23:4
about the going down of the s 1Kin 22:36
the s shone upon the water, and 2Kin 3:22
incense unto Baal, to the s 2Kin 23:5
kings of Judah had given to the s 2Kin 23:11
the chariots of the s with fire 2Kin 23:11
time of the s going down he died 2Chr 18:34
be opened until the s be hot .... Neh 7:3
He is green before the s, and his .... Job 8:16
Which commandeth the s, and it .... Job 9:7
I went mourning without the s .... Job 30:28
If I behold the s when it shined .... Job 31:26
he set a tabernacle for the s .... Ps 19:4
the s unto the going down thereof .... Ps 50:1
that they may not see the s .... Ps 58:8
shall fear thee as long as the s .... Ps 72:5
be continued as long as the s .... Ps 72:17
hast prepared the light and the s .... Ps 74:16
For the LORD God is a s and shield .... Ps 84:11
and his throne as the s before me .... Ps 89:36
the s knoweth his going down .... Ps 104:19
The s ariseth, they gather .... Ps 104:22
From the rising of the s unto the .... Ps 113:3
The s shall not smite thee by day .... Ps 121:6
The s to rule by day .... Ps 136:8
Praise ye him, s and moon .... Ps 148:3
which he taketh under the s .... Eccl 1:3
The s also ariseth .... Eccl 1:5
the s goeth down, and hasteth to .... Eccl 1:5
there is no new thing under the s .... Eccl 1:9
works that are done under the s .... Eccl 1:14
there was no profit under the s .... Eccl 2:11
under the s is grievous unto me .... Eccl 2:17
which I had taken under the s .... Eccl 2:18
shewed myself wise under the s .... Eccl 2:19
labour which I took under the s .... Eccl 2:20
he hath laboured under the s .... Eccl 2:22
under the s the place of judgment .... Eccl 3:16
done under the s .... Eccl 4:1
work that is done under the s .... Eccl 4:3
and I saw vanity under the s .... Eccl 4:7
the living which walk under the s .... Eccl 4:15
which I have seen under the s .... Eccl 5:13
the s all the days of his life .... Eccl 5:18
which I have seen under the s .... Eccl 6:1
Moreover he hath not seen the s .... Eccl 6:5
shall be after him under the s .... Eccl 6:12
is profit to them that see the s .... Eccl 7:11
work that is done under the s .... Eccl 8:9
hath no better thing under the s .... Eccl 8:15
which God giveth him under the s .... Eccl 8:15
the work that is done under the s .... Eccl 8:17
things that are done under the s .... Eccl 9:3
thing that is done under the s .... Eccl 9:6
he hath given thee under the s .... Eccl 9:9
which thou labest under the s .... Eccl 9:9
I returned, and saw under the s .... Eccl 9:11
have I seen also under the s .... Eccl 10:5
which I have seen under the s .... Eccl 10:5
is for the eyes to behold the s .... Eccl 11:7
While the s, or the light, or the .... Eccl 12:2
because the s hath looked upon me .... Song 1:6
fair as the moon, clear as the s .... Song 6:10
the s shall be darkened in his .... Is 13:10
the s ashamed, when the LORD of .... Is 24:23
shall be as the light of the s .... Is 30:26
the light of the s shall be .... Is 30:26
gone down in the s dial of Ahaz .... Is 38:8
So the s returned ten degrees, by .... Is 38:8
from the rising of the s shall he .... Is 41:25
may know from the rising of the s .... Is 45:6
shall the heat nor s smite them .... Is 49:10
glory from the rising of the s .... Is 59:19
The s shall be no more thy light .... Is 60:19
shall no more go down .... Is 60:20
and spread them before the s .... Jer 8:2
her s is gone down while it was .... Jer 15:9
which giveth the s for a light by .... Jer 31:35
worshipped the s toward the east .... Eze 8:16
I will cover the s with a cloud .... Eze 32:7
down of the s to deliver him .... Dan 6:14
and the moon shall be dark, ... Joel 2:10
The s shall be turned into .... Joel 2:31
the s and the moon shall be .... Joel 3:15
cause the s to go down at noon .... Amos 8:9
when the s did rise, that God .... Jonah 4:8
the s beat upon the head of Jonah .... Jonah 4:8
till the s go down over the .... Mic 3:6
but when the s ariseth they flee .... Nah 3:17
The s and moon stood still in .... Hab 3:11
For from the rising of the s even .... Mal 1:11
The S of righteousness arise with .... Mal 4:2
for he maketh his s to rise on .... Mt 5:45
And when the s was up, they were .... Mt 13:6
righteous shine forth as the s in .... Mt 13:43
and his face did shine as the s .... Mt 17:2
days shall the s be darkened .... Mt 24:29
And at even, when the s did set .... Mk 1:32

But when the s was up, it was .... Mk 4:6
the s shall be darkened, and the .... Mk 13:24
sepulchre at the rising of the s .... Mk 16:2
Now when the s was setting .... Lk 4:40
And there shall be signs in the s .... Lk 21:25
the s was darkened, and the veil .... Lk 23:45
The s shall be turned into .... Acts 2:20
not seeing the s for a season .... Acts 13:11
above the brightness of the s .... Acts 26:13
when neither s nor stars in many .... Acts 27:20
There is one glory of the s 1Cor 15:41
let not the s go down upon your .... Eph 4:26
For the s is no sooner risen with .... Jas 1:11
as the s shineth in his strength .... Rev 1:16
the s became black as sackcloth .... Rev 6:12
neither shall the s light on them .... Rev 7:16
third part of the s was smitten .... Rev 8:12
and the s and the air were darkened .... Rev 9:2
and his face was as it were the s .... Rev 10:1
a woman clothed with the s .... Rev 12:1
poured out his vial upon the s .... Rev 16:8
I saw an angel standing in the s .... Rev 19:17
And the city had no need of the s .... Rev 21:23
no candle, neither light of the s .... Rev 22:5

SUNDER
bow, and cutteth the spear in s .... Ps 46:9
death, and brake their bands in s .... Ps 107:14
and cut the bars of iron in s .... Ps 107:16
chalkstones that are beaten in s .... Is 27:9
cut in s the bars of iron .... Is 45:2
and will burst thy bonds in s .... Nah 1:13
not aware, and will cut him in s .... Lk 12:46

SUNDERED
together, that they cannot be s .... Job 41:17

SUNDRY
God, who at s times and in divers .... Heb 1:1

SUNG
song is in the land of Judah .... Is 26:1
And when they had a s an hymn .... Mt 26:30
And when they had a s an hymn .... Mk 14:26
they a new song, saying, Thou .... Rev 5:9
they s as it were a new song .... Rev 14:3

SUNK
that the stone s into his 1Sa 17:49
and he s down in his chariot 2Kin 9:24
The heathen are s down in the pit .... Ps 9:15
so Jeremiah s in the mire .... Jer 38:6
thy feet are s in the mire .... Jer 38:22
Her gates are s into the ground .... Lam 2:9
he s down with sleep, and fell .... Acts 20:9

SUNRISING
is before Moab, toward the s .... Num 21:11
Jericho eastward, toward the s .... Num 34:15
on this side Jordan toward the s .... Deut 4:41
on this side Jordan toward the s .... Deut 4:47
and all Lebanon, toward the s .... Josh 1:15
toward the s unto the border of .... Josh 19:12
toward the s to Beth-dagon .... Josh 19:27
to Judah upon Jordan toward the s .... Josh 19:34
over against Gibeah toward the s .... Judg 20:43

SUP
their faces shall s up as the .... Hab 1:9
him, Make ready wherewith I may s .... Lk 17:8
will s with him, and he with me .... Rev 3:20

SUPERFLUITY
s of naughtiness, and receive with .... Jas 1:21

SUPERFLUOUS
hath a flat nose, or any thing s .... Lev 21:18
thing s or lacking in his parts .... Lev 22:23
it is s for me to write to you 2Cor 9:1

SUPERSCRIPTION
them, Whose is this image and s .... Mt 22:20
them, Whose is this image and s .... Mk 12:16
the s of his accusation was .... Mk 15:26
Whose image and s hath it .... Lk 20:24
a s also was written over him .... Lk 23:38

SUPERSTITION
against him of their own s .... Acts 25:19

SUPERSTITIOUS
that in all things ye are too s .... Acts 17:22

SUPPED
he took the cup, when he had s 1Cor 11:25

SUPPER
birthday made a s to his lords .... Mk 6:21
When thou makest a dinner or a s .... Lk 14:12
man, A certain man made a great s .... Lk 14:16
sent his servant at s time to say .... Lk 14:17
were bidden shall taste of my s .... Lk 14:24
Likewise also the cup after s .... Lk 22:20
There they made him a s .... Jn 12:2
s being ended, the devil having .... Jn 13:2
He riseth from s, and laid aside .... Jn 13:4
also leaned on his breast at s .... Jn 21:20
this is not to eat the Lord's s 1Cor 11:20
one taketh before other his own s 1Cor 11:21
unto the marriage s of the Lamb .... Rev 19:9
unto the s of the great God .... Rev 19:17

SUPPLANT
for every brother will utterly s............... Jer 9:4

SUPPLANTED
for he hath s me these two times........ Gen 27:36

SUPPLE
thou washed in water to s thee............. Eze 16:4

SUPPLIANTS
the rivers of Ethiopia my s................... Zeph 3:10

SUPPLICATION
I have not made s unto the LORD........ 1Sa 13:12
of thy servant, and to his s................... 1Kin 8:28
thou to the s of thy servant................. 1Kin 8:30
make s unto thee in this house........... 1Kin 8:33
s soever be made by any man, or...... 1Kin 8:38
in heaven their prayer and their s...... 1Kin 8:45
make s unto thee in the land of......... 1Kin 8:47
their s in heaven thy dwelling............. 1Kin 8:49
be open unto the s of thy servant...... 1Kin 8:52
unto the s of thy people Israel,........... 1Kin 8:52
s unto the LORD, be arose from.......... 1Kin 8:54
I have made s before the LORD........... 1Kin 8:59
I have heard thy prayer and thy s...... 1Kin 9:3
of thy servant, and to his s................. 2Chr 6:19
make s before thee in this house........ 2Chr 6:24
Then what prayer or what s soever.... 2Chr 6:29
heavens their prayer and their s........ 2Chr 6:35
intreated of him, and heard his s....... 2Chr 33:13
to make s unto him, and to make....... Est 4:8
make thy s to the Almighty................ Job 8:5
but I would make s to my judge......... Job 9:15
The LORD hath heard my s................. Ps 6:9
and unto the LORD I made s............... Ps 30:8
and hide not thyself from my s.......... Ps 55:1
Let my s come before thee................. Ps 119:170
unto the LORD did I make my s.......... Ps 142:1
thee, they shall make s unto thee...... Is 45:14
present their s before the LORD.......... Jer 36:7
let my s, I pray thee, be................... Jer 37:20
I presented my s before the king,...... Jer 38:26
our s be accepted before thee, and.... Jer 42:2
me to present your s before him........ Jer 42:9
and making s before his God.............. Dan 6:11
presenting my s before the LORD........ Dan 9:20
he wept, and made s unto him........... Hos 12:4
with one accord in prayer and s......... Acts 1:14
s in the Spirit, and watching.............. Eph 6:18
perseverance and s for all saints........ Eph 6:18
s with thanksgiving let your.............. Phil 4:6

SUPPLICATIONS
unto the s of thy servant.................. 2Chr 6:21
place, their prayer and their s........... 2Chr 6:39
Will he make many s unto thee.......... Job 41:3
Hear the voice of my s, when I.......... Ps 28:2
he hath heard the voice of my s......... Ps 28:6
of my s when I cried unto thee........... Ps 31:22
and attend to the voice of my s.......... Ps 86:6
he hath heard my voice and my s....... Ps 116:1
be attentive to the voice of my s....... Ps 130:2
hear the voice of my s, O LORD.......... Ps 140:6
prayer, O LORD, give ear to my s........ Ps 143:1
s of the children of Israel................... Jer 3:21
and with s will I lead them................. Jer 31:9
Lord God, to seek by prayer and s...... Dan 9:3
prayer of thy servant, and his s......... Dan 9:17
present our s before thee for our........ Dan 9:18
At the beginning of thy s the............. Dan 9:23
the spirit of grace and of s............... Zec 12:10
therefore, that, first of all, s............. 1Ti 2:1
in God, and continueth in s............... 1Ti 5:5
s with strong crying and tears........... Heb 5:7

SUPPLIED
lacking on your part they have s........ 1Cor 16:17
which came from Macedonia s............. 2Cor 11:9

SUPPLIETH
not only s the want of the saints....... 2Cor 9:12
by that which every joint s................ Eph 4:16

SUPPLY
may be a s for their want.................. 2Cor 8:14
also may be a s for your want........... 2Cor 8:14
the s of the Spirit of Jesus................ Phil 1:19
to s your lack of service toward........ Phil 2:30
But my God shall s all your need....... Phil 4:19

SUPPORT
labouring ye ought to s the weak....... Acts 20:35
s the weak, be patient toward all....... 1Th 5:14

SUPPOSE
Let not my lord s that they have....... 2Sa 13:32
I s that he, to whom he forgave......... Lk 7:43
S ye that I am come to give peace..... Lk 12:51
S ye that these Galilaeans were......... Lk 13:2
I s that even the world itself............. Jn 21:25
these are not drunken, as ye s.......... Acts 2:15
I s therefore that this is good........... 1Cor 7:26
For I s I was not a whit behind.......... 2Cor 11:5
ye, shall he be thought worthy,......... Heb 10:29
faithful brother unto you, as I s........ 1Pet 5:12

SUPPOSED
they s that they should have............. Mt 20:10
they s it had been a spirit, and.......... Mk 6:49
being (as was s) the son of................ Lk 3:23
s that they had seen a vision............. Lk 24:37
For be s his brethren would have....... Acts 7:25
whom they s that Paul had brought... Acts 21:29
accusation of such things as I s......... Acts 25:18

Yet I s it necessary to send to............ Phil 2:25

SUPPOSING
s him to have been in the company.... Lk 2:44
s him to be the gardener, saith......... Jn 20:15
of the city, a he had been dead......... Acts 14:19
s that the prisoners had been............ Acts 16:27
s that they had obtained their........... Acts 27:13
s to add affliction to my bonds......... Phil 1:16
truth, s that gain is godliness............ 1Ti 6:5

SUPREME
whether it be to the king, as s.......... 1Pet 2:13

SUR
SUR (*sur*) *A gate of the Temple.*
part shall be at the gate of S............. 2Kin 11:6

SURE
borders round about, were made s..... Gen 23:17
were made s unto Abraham for a....... Gen 23:20
I am s that the king of Egypt............. Ex 3:19
be s your sin will find you out........... Num 32:23
Only be s that thou eat not the........ Deut 12:23
and I will build him a s house............ 1Sa 2:35
then be s that evil is determined....... 1Sa 20:7
certainly make my lord a s house...... 1Sa 25:28
because I was s that he could not...... 2Sa 1:10
ordered in all things, and s............... 2Sa 23:5
thee, and build thee a s house........... 1Kin 11:38
of all this we make a s covenant........ Neh 9:38
riseth up, and no man is s of life....... Job 24:22
the testimony of the LORD is s........... Ps 19:7
Thy testimonies are very s................ Ps 93:5
all his commandments are s............... Ps 111:7
thyself, and make s thy friend........... Prov 6:3
and he that hateth suretiship is s...... Prov 11:15
righteousness shall be a s reward...... Prov 11:18
fasten him as a nail in a s place........ Is 22:23
in the s place be removed................. Is 22:25
corner stone, a s foundation.............. Is 28:16
in s dwellings, and in quiet............... Is 32:18
his waters shall be s........................ Is 33:16
even the s mercies of David............... Is 55:3
and the interpretation thereof s......... Dan 2:45
thy kingdom shall be s unto thee...... Dan 4:26
be made s until the third day............ Mt 27:64
your way, make it as s as ye can...... Mt 27:65
went, and made the sepulchre s......... Mt 27:66
notwithstanding be ye s of this......... Lk 10:11
are s that thou art Christ.................. Jn 6:69
Now are we s that thou knewest....... Jn 16:30
give you the s mercies of David......... Acts 13:34
But we are s that the judgment of..... Rom 2:2
might be s to all the seed.................. Rom 4:16
and I am s that, when I come s.......... Rom 15:29
the foundation of God standeth s...... 2Ti 2:19
as an anchor of the soul, both s......... Heb 6:19
make your calling and election s........ 2Pet 1:10
also a more s word of prophecy......... 2Pet 1:19

SURELY
eatest thereof thou shalt s die.......... Gen 2:17
the woman, Ye shall not s die............ Gen 3:4
s your blood of your lives will I......... Gen 9:5
Abraham shall s become a great........ Gen 18:18
know that thou shalt s die................ Gen 20:7
S the fear of God is not in this......... Gen 20:11
his wife shall s be put to death......... Gen 26:11
S the LORD is in this place................ Gen 28:16
I will s give the tenth unto thee........ Gen 28:22
S thou art my bone and my flesh...... Gen 29:14
S the LORD hath looked upon my...... Gen 29:32
for s I have hired thee with my......... Gen 30:16
s thou hadst sent me away now........ Gen 31:42
I will s do thee good, and make......... Gen 32:12
life of Pharaoh s ye are spies............ Gen 42:16
s now we had returned this second.... Gen 43:10
and I said, S he is torn in pieces........ Gen 44:28
I will also s bring thee up again........ Gen 46:4
God will s visit you, and bring........... Gen 50:24
God will s visit you, and ye shall....... Gen 50:25
and said, S this thing is known......... Ex 2:14
I have s seen the affliction of........... Ex 3:7
I have s visited you, and seen.......... Ex 3:16
S a bloody husband art thou to me... Ex 4:25
he shall s thrust you out hence......... Ex 11:1
saying, God will s visit you.............. Ex 13:19
Thou wilt s wear away, both thou,.... Ex 18:18
the mount shall be s put to death..... Ex 19:12
it, but he shall s be stoned.............. Ex 19:13
he die, shall be s put to death......... Ex 21:12
mother, shall be s put to death........ Ex 21:15
father, shall be s put to death......... Ex 21:17
the shall be s punished..................... Ex 21:20
he shall be s punished, according...... Ex 21:22
then the ox shall be s stoned............ Ex 21:28
he shall s pay ox for ox.................... Ex 21:36
the fire shall s make restitution........ Ex 22:6
with it, he shall s make it good........ Ex 22:14
shall s endow her to be his.............. Ex 22:16
a beast shall s be put to death......... Ex 22:19
unto me, I will s hear their cry......... Ex 22:23
thou shalt s bring it back to him....... Ex 23:4
shalt s help with him....................... Ex 23:5
it will s be a snare unto thee............ Ex 23:33
it shall s be put to death................. Ex 31:14
he shall s be put to death................ Ex 31:15
for their anointing shall s be an........ Ex 40:15
he shall s be put to death................ Lev 20:2
mother shall be s put to death......... Lev 20:9
shall s be put to death..................... Lev 20:10
of them shall s be put to death......... Lev 20:11

of them shall s be put to death......... Lev 20:12
they shall s be put to death.............. Lev 20:13
he shall s be put to death................ Lev 20:15
they shall s be put to death.............. Lev 20:16
a wizard, shall s be put to death....... Lev 20:27
he shall s be put to death, and......... Lev 24:16
any man shall s be put to death....... Lev 24:17
but shall s be put to death............... Lev 27:29
s it floweth with milk and honey....... Num 13:27
S they shall not see the land............ Num 14:23
I will s do it unto all this evil........... Num 14:35
The man shall be s put to death........ Num 15:35
of man shalt thou s redeem.............. Num 18:15
s now also I had slain thee, and....... Num 22:33
S there is no enchantment against..... Num 23:23
of them, They shall s die the............ Num 26:65
thou shalt s give them a.................. Num 27:7
S none of the men that came up....... Num 32:11
murderer shall s be put to death....... Num 35:16
murderer shall s be put to death....... Num 35:17
murderer shall s be put to death....... Num 35:18
smote him shall s be put to death..... Num 35:21
but he shall be s put to death.......... Num 35:31
S there shall not one of these........... Deut 1:35
S this great nation is a wise and....... Deut 4:6
this day that ye shall s perish........... Deut 8:19
But thou shalt s kill him.................. Deut 13:9
Thou shalt s smite thine................... Deut 13:15
shalt s lend him sufficient for........... Deut 15:8
Thou shalt s give him, and thine....... Deut 15:10
therefore thou shalt s rejoice........... Deut 16:15
thou shalt s help him to lift............. Deut 22:4
thy God will s require it of thee........ Deut 23:21
this day, that ye shall s perish......... Deut 30:18
I will s hide my face in that day....... Deut 31:18
S the land whereon thy feet have..... Josh 14:9
S he covereth his feet in his............. Judg 3:24
she said, I will s go with thee........... Judg 4:9
S I will be with thee, and thou......... Judg 6:16
shall s be the LORD's and, I will........ Judg 11:31
unto his wife, We shall s die............. Judg 13:22
but s we will not kill thee................. Judg 15:13
S they are smitten down before us.... Judg 20:39
He shall s be put to death................ Judg 21:5
S we will return with thee unto........ Ruth 1:10
that he saith cometh s to pass......... 1Sa 9:6
Jonathan my son, he shall s die........ 1Sa 14:39
for thou shalt s die, Jonathan.......... 1Sa 14:44
S the bitterness of death is past....... 1Sa 15:32
S the LORD's anointed is before........ 1Sa 16:6
s to defy Israel is he come up........... 1Sa 17:25
s he is not clean............................. 1Sa 20:26
him unto me, for he shall s die......... 1Sa 20:31
the king said, Thou shalt s die.......... 1Sa 22:16
there, that he would s tell Saul......... 1Sa 23:12
well that thou shalt s be king........... 1Sa 24:20
S in vain have I kept all that............ 1Sa 25:21
s there had not been left unto.......... 1Sa 25:34
S thou shalt know what thy.............. 1Sa 28:2
called David, and said unto him, S.... 1Sa 29:6
for thou shalt s overtake them......... 1Sa 30:8
s then in the morning the people...... 2Sa 2:27
for I will s shew thee kindness......... 2Sa 9:7
S men prevailed against us,............. 2Sa 11:23
hath done this thing shall s die......... 2Sa 12:5
is born onto thee shall s die............. 2Sa 12:14
s in what place my lord the king....... 2Sa 15:21
I will s go forth with you myself....... 2Sa 18:2
They shall s ask counsel at Abel........ 2Sa 20:18
but I will s buy it of thee at a.......... 2Sa 24:24
for certain that thou shalt s die........ 1Kin 2:37
whither, that thou shalt s die........... 1Kin 2:42
I have s built thee an house to......... 1Kin 8:13
for s they will turn away your.......... 1Kin 11:2
I will s rend the kingdom from.......... 1Kin 11:11
of Samaria, shall s come to pass....... 1Kin 13:32
I will s shew myself unto him to....... 1Kin 18:15
s we shall be stronger than they...... 1Kin 20:23
s we shall be stronger than they...... 1Kin 20:25
S it is the king of Israel.................. 1Kin 22:32
thou art gone up, but shalt s die...... 2Kin 1:4
thou art gone up, but shalt s die...... 2Kin 1:6
thou art gone up, but shalt s die...... 2Kin 1:16
liveth, before whom I stand, s.......... 2Kin 3:14
the kings are s slain, and they........ 2Kin 3:23
He will s come out to me, and.......... 2Kin 5:11
shewed me that he shall s die........... 2Kin 8:10
me that thou shouldest s recover...... 2Kin 8:14
S I have seen yesterday the blood.... 2Kin 9:26
The LORD will s deliver us................ 2Kin 18:30
S there was not holden such a......... 2Kin 23:22
S at the commandment of the LORD.. 2Kin 24:3
but shalt s fall before him............... Est 6:13
s now he would awake for thee, and.. Job 8:6
S I would speak to the Almighty,...... Job 13:3
He will s reprove you, if ye do......... Job 13:10
s the mountain falling cometh to...... Job 14:18
S such are the dwellings of the........ Job 18:21
S he shall not feel quietness in........ Job 20:20
S there is a vein for the silver,........ Job 28:1
S I would take it upon my................ Job 31:36
S thou hast spoken in mine............. Job 33:8
S God will not do wickedly,.............. Job 34:12
S it is meet to be said unto God,...... Job 34:31
S God will not hear vanity,.............. Job 35:13
s he shall be swallowed up.............. Job 37:20
S the mountains bring him forth....... Job 40:20
S goodness and mercy shall follow.... Ps 23:6
s in the floods of great waters........ Ps 32:6
S every man walketh in a vain......... Ps 39:6

s they are disquieted in vain .... Ps 39:6
s every man is vanity .... Ps 39:11
S men of low degree are vanity, ... Ps 62:9
S thou didst set them in slippery .... Ps 73:18
S the wrath of man shall praise .... Ps 76:10
s I will remember thy wonders of... .... Ps 77:11
S his salvation is nigh them that .... Ps 85:9
S he shall deliver thee from the .... Ps 91:3
S he shall not be moved for ever .... Ps 112:6
S I have behaved and quieted .... Ps 131:2
S I will not come into the .... Ps 132:3
S the darkness shall cover me .... Ps 139:11
S thou wilt slay the wicked, O .... Ps 139:19
S the righteous shall give thanks .... Ps 140:13
S in vain the net is spread in .... Prov 1:17
S he scorneth the scorners .... Prov 3:34
that walketh uprightly walketh s .... Prov 10:9
to the rich, shall s come to want... .... Prov 22:16
For s there is an end .... Prov 23:18
S I am more brutish than any man... .... Prov 30:2
S the churning of milk bringeth .... Prov 30:33
S this also is vanity and vexation .... Eccl 4:16
S I will be s for him .... Eccl 7:7
yet s I know that it shall be .... Eccl 8:12
S the serpent will bite without .... Eccl 10:11
s ye shall not be established .... Is 7:9
S as I have thought, so shall it .... Is 14:24
s they are stricken .... Is 16:7
S the princes of Zoan are fools, ... Is 19:11
S this iniquity shall not be .... Is 22:14
captivity, and will s cover thee... .... Is 22:17
He will s violently turn and toss .... Is 22:18
S your turning of things upside .... Is 29:16
The LORD will s deliver us .... Is 36:15
s the people is grass .... Is 40:7
thee, saying, S God is in thee .... Is 45:14
S, shall one say, in the LORD .... Is 45:24
yet s my judgment is with the .... Is 49:4
thou shalt s clothe thee with .... Is 49:18
S he hath borne our griefs, and .... Is 53:4
they shall s gather together, but .... Is 54:15
S the isles shall wait for me, and... .... Is 60:9
S I will no more give thy corn to .... Is 62:8
S they are my people, children .... Is 63:8
s his anger shall turn from me .... Jer 2:35
S as a wife treacherously .... Jer 3:20
s thou hast greatly deceived this. .... Jer 4:10
s they swear falsely .... Jer 5:2
I said, S these are poor .... Jer 5:4
S I will s consume them, saith the .... Jer 8:13
S our fathers have inherited lies .... Jer 16:19
yet s I will make thee a .... Jer 22:6
S then shalt thou be ashamed and .... Jer 22:22
s thus saith the LORD, So will I... .... Jer 24:8
him, saying, Thou shalt s die .... Jer 26:8
ye shall s bring innocent blood ... . Jer 26:15
I have s heard Ephraim bemoaning.. .... Jer 31:18
S after that I was turned, I .... Jer 31:19
I will s have mercy upon him .... Jer 31:20
but shalt s be delivered into the .... Jer 32:4
of his hand, but shalt s be taken .... Jer 34:3
We will s tell the king of all ... . Jer 36:16
Chaldeans shall s depart from us. .... Jer 37:9
This city shall s be given into.... .... Jer 38:3
wilt thou not s put me to death ... . Jer 38:15
For I will s deliver thee, and .... Jer 39:18
We will s perform our vows that .... Jer 44:25
ye will s accomplish your vows,.... .... Jer 44:25
your vows, and s perform your vows ... . Jer 44:25
s stand against you for evil .... Jer 44:29
S as Tabor is among the mountains ... . Jer 46:18
but thou shalt s drink of it .... Jer 49:12
S the least of the flock shall .... Jer 49:20
s he shall make their habitations .... Jer 49:20
S the least of the flock shall .... Jer 50:45
s he shall make their habitation .... Jer 50:45
S I will fill them with men, as .... Jer 51:14
of recompences shall s requite .... Jer 51:56
S against me is he turned .... Lam 3:3
S, had I sent thee to them, they .... Eze 3:6
unto the wicked, Thou shalt s die .... Eze 3:18
he doth not sin, he shall s live .... Eze 3:21
S, because thou hast defiled my .... Eze 5:11
s in the place where the king .... Eze 17:16
s mine oath that he hath despised .... Eze 17:19
he is just, he shall s live .... Eze 18:9
he shall s die... .... Eze 18:13
of his father, he shall s live .... Eze 18:17
hath done them, he shall s live .... Eze 18:19
lawful and right, he shall s live .... Eze 18:21
hath committed, he shall s live .... Eze 18:28
s with a mighty hand, and with a .... Eze 20:33
he shall s deal with them .... Eze 31:11
O wicked man, thou shalt s die .... Eze 33:8
righteous, that he shall s live .... Eze 33:13
unto the wicked, Thou shalt s die .... Eze 33:14
he shall s live, he shall not die .... Eze 33:15
he shall s live... .... Eze 33:16
s they that are in the wastes... .... Eze 33:27
s because my flock became a prey,. .... Eze 34:8
S in the fire of my jealousy have ... . Eze 36:5
S the heathen that are about you,. .... Eze 36:7
S in that day there shall be a .... Eze 38:19
made known that which shall s be .. .. Hos 5:9
s they are vanity .... Hos 12:11
S the Lord GOD will do nothing,.. .... Amos 3:7
for Gilgal shall s go into .... Amos 5:5
Israel shall s be led away .... Amos 7:11
Israel shall s go into captivity .... Amos 7:17
S I will never forget any of .... Amos 8:7

I will s assemble, O Jacob, all .... Mic 2:12
I will s gather the remnant of... .... Mic 2:12
because it will s come, it will .... Hab 2:3
S Moab shall be as Sodom, and the ... . Zeph 2:9
S thou wilt fear me, thou wilt .... Zeph 3:7
S thou also art one of them ... . Mt 26:73
to Peter, S thou art one of them... .... Mk 14:70
are most s believed among us .... Lk 1:1
Ye will s say unto me this .... Lk 4:23
have known s that I came out from ... . Jn 17:8
S blessing I will bless thee, and ... . Heb 6:14
things saith, S I come quickly .... Rev 22:20

SURETIES
or of them that are s for debts.......... Prov 22:26

SURETISHIP
and he that hateth s is sure.......... Prov 11:15

SURETY
Know of a s that thy seed shall .... Gen 15:13
Shall I of a s bear a child .... Gen 18:13
Behold, of a s she is thy wife.......... Gen 26:9
I will be s for him .... Gen 43:9
For thy servant became s for the ... . Gen 44:32
down now, put me in a s with thee ... . Job 17:3
Be s for thy servant for good,.......... Ps 119:122
if thou be s for thy friend, if .... Prov 6:1
He that is s for a stranger shall ... . Prov 11:15
becometh s in the presence of his ... . Prov 17:18
garment that is s for a stranger.......... Prov 20:16
garment that is s for a stranger... .... Prov 27:13
he said, Now I know of a s... .... Acts 12:11
made a s of a better testament.......... Heb 7:22

SURFEITING
your hearts be overcharged with s ... . Lk 21:34

SURMISINGS
envy, strife, railings, evil s.......... 1Ti 6:4

SURNAME
himself by the name of Israel.......... Is 44:5
Lebbaeus, whose was Thaddaeus ... . Mt 10:3
for one Simon, whose s is Peter.......... Acts 10:5
hither Simon, whose s is Peter.......... Acts 10:32
call for Simon, whose s is Peter... .... Acts 11:13
mother of John, whose s was Mark ... . Acts 12:12
with them John, whose s was Mark .. .. Acts 12:25
with them John, whose s was Mark .. .. Acts 15:37

SURNAMED
I have s thee, though thou hast.......... Is 45:4
And Simon he s Peter.......... Mk 3:16
he s them Boanerges, which is,.......... Mk 3:17
Satan into Judas s Iscariot.......... Lk 22:3
called Barsabas, who was s Justus ... . Acts 1:23
by the apostles was s Barnabas.......... Acts 4:36
whether Simon, which was s Peter ... . Acts 10:18
Judas s Barsabas, and Silas, chief... .... Acts 15:22

SURPRISED
fearfulness hath s the hypocrites.......... Is 33:14
taken, and the strong holds are s... .... Jer 48:41
the praise of the whole earth s .... Jer 51:41

SUSA See SHUSHAN.

SUSANCHITES (su´-san-kites) Resettled
foreigners in Israel.
The Babylonians, the S, the .... Ezr 4:9

SUSANNA (su´-zan-nah) A woman follower of
Jesus.
of Chuza Herod's steward, and S.......... Lk 8:3

SUSI (su´-si) Father of Gaddi
of Manasseh, Gaddi the son of S .... Num 13:11

SUSTAIN
a widow woman there to s thee 1Kin 17:9
thou s them in the wilderness ..... Neh 9:21
upon the LORD, and he shall s thee .... Ps 55:22
of a man with s his infirmity............ Prov 18:14

SUSTAINED
and with corn and wine have I s him ... Gen 27:37
for the LORD s me .... Ps 3:5
and his righteousness, it s him.......... Is 59:16

SUSTENANCE
left no s for Israel, neither .... Judg 6:4
of s while he lay at Mahanaim.......... 2Sa 19:32
and our fathers found no s.......... Acts 7:11

SWADDLED
those that I have s and brought up... .... Lam 2:22
not salted at all, nor s at all....... Eze 16:4

SWADDLING
son, and wrapped him in s clothes... .... Lk 2:7
the babe wrapped in s clothes.......... Lk 2:12

SWADDLINGBAND
and thick darkness a s for it.......... Job 38:9

SWALLOW
and s them up, with all that .... Num 16:30
and seal. The earth s us up also .... Num 16:34
why wilt thou s up the 2Sa 20:19
me, that I should s up or destroy 2Sa 20:20
me alone till I s down my spittle... .... Job 7:19
restore, and shall not s it down .... Job 20:18
the LORD shall s them up in his .... Ps 21:9
for man would s me up .... Ps 56:1
Mine enemies would daily s me up... .... Ps 56:2
of him that would s me up .... Ps 57:3
me, neither let the deep s me up.......... Ps 69:15
the s a nest for herself, where.......... Ps 84:3

Let us s them up alive as the .... Prov 1:12
as the s by flying, so the curse.......... Prov 26:2
lips of a fool will s up himself ... . Eccl 10:12
He will s up death in victory .... Is 25:8
Like a crane or a s, so did I .... Is 38:14
the s observe the time of their... .... Jer 8:7
the strangers shall s it up .... Hos 8:7
O ye that s up the needy, even to ... . Amos 8:4
shall drink, and they shall s down. .... Obad 16
a great fish to s up Jonah .... Jonah 1:17
strain at a gnat, and s a camel .... Mt 23:24

SWALLOWED
but Aaron's rod s up their rods,.......... Ex 7:12
thy right hand, the earth s them... .... Ex 15:12
s them up, and their houses, and .... Num 16:32
s them up together with Korah.......... Num 26:10
s them up, and their households, ... Deut 11:6
lest the king be s up, and all the 2Sa 17:16
therefore my words are s up .... Job 6:3
He hath s down riches, and he .... Job 20:15
speak, surely he shall be s up .... Job 37:20
them not say, We have s him up ... . Ps 35:25
s up Dathan, and covered the.......... Ps 106:17
Then they had s us up quick .... Ps 124:3
they are s up of wine, they are .... Is 28:7
they that s thee up shall be far... .... Is 49:19
he hath s me up like a dragon, he... .... Jer 51:34
his mouth that which he hath s up... .... Jer 51:44
The Lord hath s up all the .... Lam 2:2
he hath s up Israel, he hath .... Lam 2:5
he hath s up all her palaces .... Lam 2:5
they say, We have s her up .... Lam 2:16
s you up on every side, that ye...... .... Eze 36:3
Israel is s up... .... Hos 8:8
written, Death is s up in victory... .... 1Cor 15:54
be s up with overmuch sorrow.......... 2Cor 2:7
mortality might be s up of life 2Cor 5:4
s up the flood which the dragon ... . Rev 12:16

SWALLOWETH
the robber s up their substance.......... Job 5:5
He s the ground with fierceness.......... Job 39:24

SWAN
And the s, and the pelican, and the ... Lev 11:18
owl, and the great owl, and the s ... Deut 14:16

SWARE
because there they s both of them... Gen 21:31
that s unto me, saying, Unto thy ... Gen 24:7
s to him concerning that matter.......... Gen 24:9
and he s unto him .... Gen 25:33
which I s unto Abraham thy father ... Gen 26:3
the morning, and s one to another... Gen 26:31
Jacob s by the fear of his father ... Gen 31:53
And he s unto him .... Gen 47:31
the land which he s to Abraham .... Gen 50:24
which he s unto thy fathers to .... Ex 13:5
as he s unto thee and to thy .... Ex 13:11
the land which I s unto Abraham.......... Ex 33:1
the land which he s unto them .... Num 14:16
land which I s unto their fathers .... Num 14:23
concerning which I s to make you... Num 14:30
kindled the same time, and he s .... Num 32:10
the land which I s unto Abraham.......... Num 32:11
S unto Jabesh unto your fathers .... Deut 1:8
of your words, and was wroth, and s... Deut 1:34
which I s to give unto your .... Deut 1:35
the host, as the LORD s unto them ... Deut 2:14
s that I should not go over .... Deut 4:21
thy fathers which he s unto them ... Deut 4:31
land which he s unto thy fathers .... Deut 6:10
which the LORD s unto thy fathers... Deut 6:18
land which he s unto our fathers,.......... Deut 6:23
mercy which he s unto thy fathers... Deut 7:12
in the land which he s unto thy .... Deut 7:13
the LORD s unto your fathers .... Deut 8:1
which he s unto thy fathers .... Deut 8:18
which the LORD s unto thy fathers... Deut 9:5
which I s unto their fathers to .... Deut 10:11
which the LORD s unto your .... Deut 11:9
in the land which the LORD s unto... Deut 11:21
s unto our fathers for to give us... Deut 26:3
in the land which the LORD s unto... Deut 28:11
which the LORD s unto thy fathers... Deut 30:20
land which I s unto their fathers... Deut 31:20
them into the land which I s .... Deut 31:21
into the land which I s unto them... Deut 31:23
the land which I s unto Abraham... Deut 34:4
which I s unto their fathers to .... Josh 1:6
unto whom the LORD s that he .... Josh 5:6
which the LORD s unto them .... Josh 5:6
that she hath, as ye s unto her... Josh 6:22
of the congregation s unto them .... Josh 9:15
of the oath which we s unto them... Josh 9:20
Moses s on that day, saying,.......... Josh 14:9
he s to give unto their fathers .... Josh 21:43
all that he s unto their fathers .... Josh 21:44
land which I s unto your fathers... Judg 2:1
and Saul s, As the LORD liveth, he ... 1Sa 19:6
David s moreover, and said, Thy 1Sa 20:3
And David s unto Saul... .... 1Sa 24:22
Saul s to her by the LORD, saying ... 1Sa 28:10
while it was yet day, David s 2Sa 3:35
And the king s unto him 2Sa 19:23
Then the men of David s unto him... 2Sa 21:17
And the king s, and said, As the... 1Kin 1:29
Even as I s unto thee by the LORD ... 1Kin 1:30
I s to him by the LORD, saying, I... 1Kin 2:8
Then king Solomon s by the LORD... 1Kin 2:23
And Gedaliah s to them, and to.......... 2Kin 25:24

they s unto the Lord with a loud...... 2Chr 15:14
And they s .... Ezr 10:5
Unto whom I s in my wrath that ...... Ps 95:11
How he s unto the Lord, and vowed.... Ps 132:2
So Zedekiah the king s secretly.......... Jer 38:16
the son of Shaphan s unto them .... Jer 40:9
I s unto thee, and entered into a .... Eze 16:8
s by him that liveth for ever.............. Dan 12:7
he s unto her, Whatsoever thou.......... Mk 6:23
The oath which he s to our father ...... Lk 1:73
So I s in my wrath, They shall............ Heb 3:11
to whom s he that they should not...... Heb 3:18
by no greater, he s by himself,............ Heb 6:13
that said unto him, The Lord s .... Heb 7:21
s by him that liveth for ever and ...... Rev 10:6

SWAREST
to whom thou s by thine own self,...... Ex 32:13
which thou s unto their fathers .... Num 11:12
as thou s unto our fathers, a.............. Deut 26:15
thou s by the Lord thy God unto 1Kin 1:17
which thou s unto David in thy .... Ps 89:49

SWARM
there came a grievous s of flies .... Ex 8:24
by reason of the s of flies .... Ex 8:24
and, behold, there was a s of bees ...... Judg 14:8

SWARMS
I will send a s of flies upon thee,........ Ex 8:21
shall be full of s of flies .... Ex 8:21
that no s of flies shall be there .... Ex 8:22
the s of flies may depart from............ Ex 8:29
he removed the s of flies from .... Ex 8:31

SWEAR
Now therefore s unto me here by .... Gen 21:23
And Abraham said, I will s .... Gen 21:24
And I will make thee s by the Lord .... Gen 24:3
And my master made me s, saying...... Gen 24:37
And Jacob said, S to me this day .... Gen 25:33
And he said, S unto me.................... Gen 47:31
My father made me s, saying, Lo,........ Gen 50:5
according as he made thee s .... Gen 50:6
I did s to give it to Abraham.............. Ex 13:5
Or if a soul s, pronouncing with .... Lev 5:4
ye shall not s by my name falsely........ Lev 19:12
or s an oath to bind his soul .... Num 30:2
serve him, and shalt s by his name .... Deut 6:13
thou cleave, and s by his name .... Deut 10:20
s unto me by the Lord, since I .... Josh 2:12
oath which thou hast made us s.......... Josh 2:17
oath which thou hast made us to s ...... Josh 2:20
gods, nor cause to s by them .... Josh 23:7
S unto me, that ye will not fail.......... Judg 15:12
Jonathan caused David to s again........ 1Sa 20:17
S now therefore unto me by the 1Sa 24:21
the S unto me by God, that thou wilt .. 1Sa 30:15
for I s by the Lord, if thou go............ 2Sa 19:7
s unto thine handmaid, saying,.......... 1Kin 1:13
Let king Solomon s unto me to day 1Kin 1:51
I not make thee to s by the Lord 1Kin 2:42
laid upon him to cause him to s 1Kin 8:31
be laid upon him to make him s 2Chr 6:22
who had made him s by God 2Chr 36:13
Israel, to s that they should do .... Ezr 10:5
their hair, and made them s by God .... Neh 13:25
In that day shall he s, saying, I .... Is 3:7
Canaan, and s to the Lord of hosts .... Is 19:18
shall bow, every tongue shall s .... Is 45:23
which s by the name of the Lord, ... Is 48:1
earth shall s by the God of truth ...... Is 65:16
And thou shalt s, The Lord liveth, ... Jer 4:2
surely they s falsely........................ Jer 5:2
s falsely, and burn incense unto .... Jer 7:9
to s by my name, The Lord liveth ...... Jer 12:16
taught my people to s by Baal .... Jer 12:16
I s by myself, saith the Lord,.............. Jer 22:5
which thou didst s to their................ Jer 32:22
go ye up to Beth-aven, nor s .... Hos 4:15
They that s by the sin of Samaria...... Amos 8:14
that s by the Lord............................ Zeph 1:5
and that s by Malcham........................ Zeph 1:5
But I say unto you, S not at all.......... Mt 5:34
Neither shalt thou s by thy head........ Mt 5:36
Whosoever shall s by the temple .... Mt 23:16
but whosoever shall s by the gold ...... Mt 23:16
Whosoever shall s by the altar.......... Mt 23:18
therefore shall s by the altar.............. Mt 23:20
whoso shall s by the temple,.............. Mt 23:21
And he that shall s by heaven............ Mt 23:22
Then began he to curse and to s .... Mt 26:74
But he began to curse and to s .... Mk 14:71
because he could s by no greater .... Heb 6:13
For men verily s by the greater.......... Heb 6:16
s not, neither by heaven,.................... Jas 5:12

SWEARERS
adulterers, and against false s............ Mal 3:5

SWEARETH
lieth concerning it, and s falsely........ Lev 6:3
He that s to his own hurt, and.......... Ps 15:4
every one that s by him shall.............. Ps 63:11
and he that s, as he that feareth .... Eccl 9:2
he that s in the earth shall................ Is 65:16
every one that s shall be cut off .... Zec 5:3
of him that s falsely by my name........ Zec 5:4
but whosoever s by the altar.............. Mt 23:18
s by it, and by all things thereon........ Mt 23:20
s by it, and by him that dwelleth........ Mt 23:21
s by the throne of God, and by him.... Mt 23:22

SWEARING
soul sin, and hear the voice of s .... Lev 5:1
for because of s the land .... Jer 23:10
By s, and lying, and killing, and........ Hos 4:2
s falsely in making a covenant............ Hos 10:4

SWEAT
In the s of thy face shalt thou .... Gen 3:19
with any thing that causeth s .... Eze 44:18
his s was as it were great drops.......... Lk 22:44

SWEEP
I will s it with the besom of.............. Is 14:23
the hail shall s away the refuge .... Is 28:17
s the house, and seek diligently.......... Lk 15:8

SWEEPING
a rain which leaveth no food.............. Prov 28:3

SWEET
And the Lord smelled a s savour .... Gen 8:21
waters, the waters were made s .... Ex 15:25
anointing oil, and for s incense,........ Ex 25:6
it is a s savour, an offering .... Ex 29:18
for a s savour before the Lord .... Ex 29:25
for a s savour, an offering made........ Ex 29:41
thereon s incense every morning .... Ex 30:7
of s cinnamon half so much, even ...... Ex 30:23
of s calamus two hundred and fifty .... Ex 30:23
Moses, Take unto thee s spices .... Ex 30:34
these s spices with pure...................... Ex 30:34
s incense for the holy place................ Ex 31:11
oil, and for the s incense .... Ex 35:8
the s incense, and the hanging for...... Ex 35:15
oil, and for the s incense .... Ex 35:28
and the pure incense of s spices.......... Ex 37:29
the s incense, and the hanging for...... Ex 39:38
he burnt s incense thereon .... Ex 40:27
of a s savour unto the Lord .... Lev 1:9
of a s savour unto the Lord .... Lev 1:13
of a s savour unto the Lord .... Lev 1:17
of a s savour unto the Lord .... Lev 2:2
of a s savour unto the Lord .... Lev 2:9
burnt on the altar for a s savour .... Lev 2:12
of a s savour unto the Lord .... Lev 3:5
made by fire for a s savour .... Lev 3:16
of a s savour unto the Lord .... Lev 4:31
for a s savour unto the Lord .... Lev 6:15
it upon the altar for a s savour .... Lev 6:21
for a s savour unto the Lord .... Lev 8:21
a burnt sacrifice for a s savour .... Lev 8:28
were consecrations for a s savour........ Lev 8:28
his hands full of s incense.................. Lev 16:12
burn the fat for a s savour .... Lev 17:6
fire unto the Lord for a s savour .... Lev 23:13
smell the savour of your s odours ...... Lev 26:31
the s incense, and the daily meat........ Num 4:16
to make a s savour unto the Lord,...... Num 15:3
for a s savour unto the Lord .... Num 15:7
of a s savour to the Lord .... Num 15:10
of a s savour unto the Lord .... Num 15:13
of a s savour unto the Lord .... Num 15:14
for a s savour unto the Lord .... Num 15:24
for a s savour unto the Lord .... Num 18:17
for a s savour unto me, shall ye .... Num 28:2
in mount Sinai for a s savour .... Num 28:6
of a s savour unto the Lord .... Num 28:8
a burnt offering of a s savour .... Num 28:13
of a s savour unto the Lord .... Num 28:24
of a s savour unto the Lord .... Num 28:27
for a s savour unto the Lord .... Num 29:2
for a s savour, a sacrifice made.......... Num 29:6
unto the Lord for a s savour .... Num 29:8
of a s savour unto the Lord .... Num 29:13
of a s savour unto the Lord .... Num 29:36
the s psalmist of Israel, said,.............. 2Sa 23:1
and to burn before him s incense........ 2Chr 2:4
burnt sacrifices and s incense............ 2Chr 13:11
which was filled with s odours 2Chr 16:14
they may offer sacrifices of s.............. Ezr 6:10
way, eat the fat, and drink the s........ Neh 8:10
and six months with s odours............ Est 2:12
wickedness be s in his mouth.............. Job 20:12
of the valley shall be s unto him........ Job 21:33
Canst thou bind the s influences........ Job 38:31
We took s counsel together, and .... Ps 55:14
My meditation of him shall be s .... Ps 104:34
How s are thy words unto my taste.... Ps 119:103
for they are s .... Ps 141:6
lie down, and thy sleep shall be s ...... Prov 3:24
Stolen waters are s, and bread .... Prov 9:17
accomplished is s to the soul.............. Prov 13:19
s to the soul, and health to the .... Prov 16:24
Bread of deceit is s to a man.............. Prov 20:17
vomit up, and lose thy s words .... Prov 23:8
which is s to thy taste........................ Prov 24:13
soul every bitter thing is s .... Prov 27:7
The sleep of a labouring man is s........ Eccl 5:12
Truly the light is s, and a .... Eccl 11:7
and his fruit was s to my taste............ Song 2:3
for s is thy voice, and thy.................. Song 2:14
my fingers with s smelling myrrh........ Song 5:5
as a bed of spices, as s flowers............ Song 5:13
dropping s smelling myrrh.................. Song 5:13
His mouth is most s .... Song 5:16
that instead of s smell there .... Is 3:24
bitter for s, and s for bitter................ Is 5:20
make s melody, sing many songs,........ Is 23:16
bought me no s cane with money .... Is 43:24
their own blood, as with s wine.......... Is 49:26
the s cane from a far country .... Jer 6:20

---

nor your sacrifices s unto me.............. Jer 6:20
and my sleep was s unto me................ Jer 31:26
offer s savour to all their idols............ Eze 6:13
set it before them for a s savour .... Eze 16:19
also they made their s savour .... Eze 20:28
accept you with your s savour .... Eze 20:41
an oblation and s odours unto him...... Dan 2:46
the mountains shall drop s wine,........ Amos 9:13
s wine, but shall not drink wine.......... Mic 6:15
and Salome, had bought s spices.......... Mk 16:1
are unto God a s savour of Christ........ 2Cor 2:15
from you, an odour of a s smell .... Phil 4:18
forth at the same place s water .... Jas 3:11
shall be in thy mouth s as honey .... Rev 10:9
and it was in my mouth s as honey...... Rev 10:10

SWEETER
went down, What is s than honey ...... Judg 14:18
s also than honey and the .... Ps 19:10
yea, s than honey to my mouth .... Ps 119:103

SWEETLY
the worm shall feed s on him .... Job 24:20
for my beloved, that goeth down s ...... Song 7:9

SWEETNESS
unto them, Should I forsake my s ...... Judg 9:11
and out of the strong came forth s ...... Judg 14:14
the s of the lips increaseth .... Prov 16:21
so doth the s of a man's friend .... Prov 27:9
it was in my mouth as honey for s ...... Eze 3:3

SWEETSMELLING
a sacrifice to God for a s savour .... Eph 5:2

SWELL
thigh to rot, and thy belly to s .... Num 5:21
bowels, to make thy belly to s .... Num 5:22
bitter, and her belly shall s .... Num 5:27
upon thee, neither did thy foot s .... Deut 8:4

SWELLED
not old, and their feet s not................ Neh 9:21

SWELLING
shake with the s thereof .... Ps 46:3
s out in a high wall, whose................ Is 30:13
wilt thou do in the s of Jordan .... Jer 12:5
from the s of Jordan against the .... Jer 49:19
come up like a lion from the s of ...... Jer 50:44
speak great s words of vanity............ 2Pet 2:18
mouth speaketh great s words .... Jude 16

SWELLINGS
backbitings, whisperings, s 2Cor 12:20

SWEPT
The river of Kishon s them away........ Judg 5:21
Why are thy valiant men s away .... Jer 46:15
is come, he findeth it empty, s .... Mt 12:44
when he cometh, he findeth it s .... Lk 11:25

SWERVED
From which some having s have.......... 1Ti 1:6

SWIFT
earth, as s as the eagle flieth.............. Deut 28:49
were as s as the roes upon the............ 1Chr 12:8
are passed away as the s ships .... Job 9:26
He is s as the waters.......................... Job 24:18
feet that be s in running to................ Prov 6:18
that the race is not to the s .... Eccl 9:11
ye s messengers, to a nation................ Is 18:2
the Lord rideth upon a s cloud .... Is 19:1
And, We will ride upon the s .... Is 30:16
shall they that pursue you be s .... Is 30:16
upon s beasts, to my holy .... Is 66:20
thou art s a dromedary traversing ...... Jer 2:23
Let not the s flee away, nor the .... Amos 2:14
flight shall perish from the s .... Amos 2:15
he that is s of foot shall not.............. Amos 2:15
bind the chariot to the s beast............ Mic 1:13
I will be a s witness against the .... Mal 3:5
Their feet are s to shed blood............ Rom 3:15
let every man be s to hear.................. Jas 1:19
upon themselves s destruction............ 2Pet 2:1

SWIFTER
they were s than eagles, they............ 2Sa 1:23
My days are s than a weaver's............ Job 7:6
Now my days are s than a post .... Job 9:25
his horses are s than eagles................ Jer 4:13
Our persecutors are s than the .... Lam 4:19
also are s than the leopards................ Hab 1:8

SWIFTLY
his word runneth very s .... Ps 147:15
they shall come with speed s .... Is 5:26
beginning, being caused to fly s.......... Dan 9:21
and if ye recompense me, s .... Joel 3:4

SWIM
and the iron did s 2Kin 6:6
all the night make I my bed to s .... Ps 6:6
spreadeth forth his hands to s .... Is 25:11
waters were risen, waters to s in .... Eze 47:5
lest any of them should s out.............. Acts 27:42
s should cast themselves first .... Acts 27:43

SWIMMEST
thou blood the land wherein thou s .... Eze 32:6

SWIMMETH
as he that s spreadeth forth his .... Is 25:11

SWINE
And the s, though he divide the .... Lev 11:7
And the s, because it divideth the ...... Deut 14:8

S

cast ye your pearls before *s*	Mt 7:6
them an herd of many *s* feeding	Mt 8:30
us to go away into the herd of *s*	Mt 8:31
out, they went into the herd of *s*	Mt 8:32
the whole herd of *s* ran violently	Mt 8:32
a great herd of *s* feeding	Mk 5:11
him, saying, Send us into the *s*	Mk 5:12
went out, and entered into the *s*	Mk 5:13
And they that fed the *s* fled	Mk 5:14
devil, and also concerning the *s*	Mk 5:16
of many *s* feeding on the mountain	Lk 8:32
of the man, and entered into the *s*	Lk 8:33
him into his fields to feed *s*	Lk 15:15
with the husks that the *s* did eat	Lk 15:16

SWINE'S

As a jewel of gold in a *s* snout	Prov 11:22
the monuments, which eat *s* flesh	Is 65:4
as if he offered *s* blood	Is 66:3
tree in the midst, eating *s* flesh	Is 66:17

SWOLLEN

they looked when he should have *s*	Acts 28:6

SWOON

the sucklings *s* in the streets of	Lam 2:11

SWOONED

when they *s* as the wounded in	Lam 2:12

SWORD

a flaming *s* which turned every	Gen 3:24
by thy *s* shalt thou live, and	Gen 27:40
as captives taken with the *s*	Gen 31:26
brethren, took each man his *s*	Gen 34:25
his son with the edge of the *s*	Gen 34:26
the hand of the Amorite with my *s*	Gen 48:22
us with pestilence, or with the *s*	Ex 5:3
to put a *s* in their hand to slay	Ex 5:21
I will draw my *s*, my hand shall	Ex 15:9
his people with the edge of the *s*	Ex 17:13
me from the *s* of Pharaoh	Ex 18:4
and I will kill you with the *s*	Ex 22:24
Put every man his *s* by his side	Ex 32:27
neither shall the *s* go through	Lev 26:6
shall fall before you by the *s*	Lev 26:7
shall fall before you by the *s*	Lev 26:8
And I will bring a *s* upon you	Lev 26:25
and will draw out a *s* after you	Lev 26:33
shall flee, as fleeing from a *s*	Lev 26:36
another, as it were before a *s*	Lev 26:37
unto this land, to fall by the *s*	Num 14:3
you, and ye shall fall by the *s*	Num 14:43
slain with a *s* in the open fields	Num 19:16
come out against thee with the *s*	Num 20:18
smote him with the edge of the *s*	Num 21:24
way, and his *s* drawn in his hand	Num 22:23
would there were a *s* in mine hand	Num 22:29
way, and his *s* drawn in his hand	Num 22:31
son of Beor they slew with the *s*	Num 31:8
that city with the edge of the *s*	Deut 13:15
thereof, with the edge of the *s*	Deut 13:15
thereof with the edge of the *s*	Deut 20:13
an extreme burning, and with the *s*	Deut 28:22
The *s* without, and terror within	Deut 32:25
If I whet my glittering *s*	Deut 32:41
blood, and my *s* shall devour flesh	Deut 32:42
who is the *s* of thy excellency	Deut 33:29
him with his *s* drawn in his hand	Josh 5:13
and ass, with the edge of the *s*	Josh 6:21
all fallen on the edge of the *s*	Josh 8:24
smote it with the edge of the *s*	Josh 8:24
of Israel slew with the *s*	Josh 10:11
smote it with the edge of the *s*	Josh 10:28
smote it with the edge of the *s*	Josh 10:30
smote it with the edge of the *s*	Josh 10:32
smote it with the edge of the *s*	Josh 10:35
smote it with the edge of the *s*	Josh 10:37
smote them with the edge of the *s*	Josh 10:39
smote the king thereof with the *s*	Josh 11:10
therein with the edge of the *s*	Josh 11:11
smote them with the edge of the *s*	Josh 11:12
they smote with the edge of the *s*	Josh 11:14
of Israel slay with the *s* among	Josh 13:22
smote it with the edge of the *s*	Josh 19:47
but not with thy *s*, nor with thy	Josh 24:12
smitten it with the edge of the *s*	Judg 1:8
the city with the edge of the *s*	Judg 1:25
the edge of the *s* before Barak	Judg 4:15
fell upon the edge of the *s*	Judg 4:16
the *s* of Gideon the son of Joash	Judg 7:14
The *s* of the LORD, and of Gideon	Judg 7:18
The *s* of the LORD, and of Gideon	Judg 7:20
every man's *s* against his fellow	Judg 7:22
twenty thousand men that drew *s*	Judg 8:10
But the youth drew not his *s*	Judg 8:20
and said unto him, Draw thy *s*	Judg 9:54
the *s* with the edge of the *s*	Judg 18:27
thousand footmen that drew *s*	Judg 20:2
and six thousand men that drew *s*	Judg 20:15
hundred thousand men that drew *s*	Judg 20:17
all these drew the *s*	Judg 20:25
all these drew the *s*	Judg 20:35
the city with the edge of the *s*	Judg 20:37
five thousand men that drew the *s*	Judg 20:46
smote them with the edge of the *s*	Judg 20:48
with the edge of the *s*, with the	Judg 21:10
that there was neither *s* nor	1Sa 13:22
every man's *s* was against his	1Sa 14:20
the people with the edge of the *s*	1Sa 15:8
said, As thy *s* hath made women	1Sa 15:33
girded his *s* upon his armour	1Sa 17:39
Thou comest to me with a *s*	1Sa 17:45
that the LORD saveth not with *s*	1Sa 17:47
but there was no *s* in the hand of	1Sa 17:50
the Philistine, and took his *s*	1Sa 17:51
and his garments, even to his *s*	1Sa 18:4
here under thine hand spear or *s*	1Sa 21:8
my *s* nor my weapons with me	1Sa 21:8
The *s* of Goliath the Philistine	1Sa 21:9
gave him the *s* of Goliath the	1Sa 22:10
thou hast given him bread, and a *s*	1Sa 22:13
smote he with the edge of the *s*	1Sa 22:19
and sheep, with the edge of the *s*	1Sa 22:19
men, Gird ye on every man his *s*	1Sa 25:13
And they girded on every man his *s*	1Sa 25:13
and David also girded on his *s*	1Sa 25:13
unto his armourbearer, Draw thy *s*	1Sa 31:4
Therefore Saul took a *s*, and fell	1Sa 31:4
dead, he fell likewise upon his *s*	1Sa 31:5
because they were fallen by the *s*	2Sa 1:12
the *s* of Saul returned not empty	2Sa 1:22
thrust his *s* in his fellow's side	2Sa 2:16
Shall the *s* devour for ever	2Sa 2:26
a staff, or that falleth on the *s*	2Sa 3:29
for the *s* devoureth one as well	2Sa 11:25
Uriah the Hittite with the *s*	2Sa 12:9
hast slain him with the *s* of the	2Sa 12:9
Now therefore the *s* shall never	2Sa 12:10
the city with the edge of the *s*	2Sa 15:14
that day than the *s* devoured	2Sa 18:8
upon it a girdle with a *s*	2Sa 20:8
to the *s* that was in Joab's hand	2Sa 20:10
he being girded with a *s*	2Sa 21:16
and his hand clave unto the *s*	2Sa 23:10
valiant men that drew the *s*	2Sa 24:9
not slay his servant with the *s*	1Kin 1:51
not put thee to death with the *s*	1Kin 2:8
than he, and slew them with the *s*	1Kin 2:32
And the king said, Bring me a *s*	1Kin 3:24
they brought a *s* before the king	1Kin 3:24
slain all the prophets with the *s*	1Kin 19:1
and slain thy prophets with the *s*	1Kin 19:10
and slain thy prophets with the *s*	1Kin 19:14
the *s* of Hazael shall Jehu slay	1Kin 19:17
the *s* of Jehu shall Elisha slay	1Kin 19:17
hast taken captive with thy *s*	2Kin 6:22
men wilt thou slay with the *s*	2Kin 6:22
smote them with the edge of the *s*	2Kin 10:25
followeth her kill with the *s*	2Kin 11:15
the *s* beside the king's house	2Kin 11:20
to fall by the *s* in his own land	2Kin 19:7
his sons smote him with the *s*	2Kin 19:37
men able to bear buckler and *s*	1Chr 5:18
to his armourbearer, Draw thy *s*	1Chr 10:4
So Saul took a *s*, and fell upon it	1Chr 10:4
dead, he fell likewise on the *s*	1Chr 10:5
hundred thousand men that drew *s*	1Chr 21:5
and ten thousand men that drew *s*	1Chr 21:5
while that the *s* of their enemies	1Chr 21:12
else three days the *s* of the LORD	1Chr 21:12
having a drawn *s* in his hand	1Chr 21:16
he put up his *s* again into the	1Chr 21:27
of the *s* of the angel of the LORD	1Chr 21:30
evil cometh upon us, as the *s*	2Chr 20:9
slew all his brethren with the *s*	2Chr 21:4
her, let him be slain with the *s*	2Chr 23:14
had slain Athaliah with the *s*	2Chr 23:21
our fathers have fallen by the *s*	2Chr 29:9
bowels slew him there with the *s*	2Chr 32:21
slew their young men with the *s*	2Chr 36:17
the *s* carried he away to Babylon	2Chr 36:20
the kings of the lands, to the *s*	Ezr 9:7
every one had his *s* girded by his	Neh 4:18
enemies with the stroke of the *s*	Est 9:5
servants with the edge of the *s*	Job 1:15
servants with the edge of the *s*	Job 1:17
But he saveth the poor from the *s*	Job 5:15
and in war from the power of the *s*	Job 5:20
and he is waited for of the *s*	Job 15:22
Be ye afraid of the *s*	Job 19:29
bringeth the punishments of the *s*	Job 19:29
the glittering *s* cometh out of	Job 20:25
be multiplied, it is for the *s*	Job 27:14
his life from perishing by the *s*	Job 33:18
not, they shall perish by the *s*	Job 36:12
turneth he back from the *s*	Job 39:22
make his *s* to approach unto him	Job 40:19
The *s* of him that layeth at his	Job 41:26
he turn not, he will whet his *s*	Ps 7:12
from the wicked, which is thy *s*	Ps 17:13
Deliver my soul from the *s*	Ps 22:20
The wicked have drawn out the *s*	Ps 37:14
Their *s* shall enter into their	Ps 37:15
As with a *s* in my bones, mine	Ps 42:10
land in possession by their own *s*	Ps 44:3
bow, neither shall my *s* save me	Ps 44:6
Gird thy *s* upon thy thigh, O most	Ps 45:3
arrows, and their tongue a sharp *s*	Ps 57:4
They shall fall by the *s*	Ps 63:10
Who whet their tongue like a *s*	Ps 64:3
of the bow, the shield, and the *s*	Ps 76:3
his people over also unto the *s*	Ps 78:62
Their priests fell by the *s*	Ps 78:64
also turned the edge of the *s*	Ps 89:43
his servant from the hurtful *s*	Ps 144:10
a twoedged *s* in their hand	Ps 149:6
wormwood, sharp as a twoedged *s*	Prov 5:4
like the piercings of a *s*	Prov 12:18
his neighbour is a maul, and a *s*	Prov 25:18
every man hath his *s* upon his	Song 3:8
ye shall be devoured with the *s*	Is 1:20
not lift up *s* against nation	Is 2:4
Thy men shall fall by the *s*	Is 3:25
unto them shall fall by the *s*	Is 13:15
slain, thrust through with a *s*	Is 14:19
from the swords, from the drawn *s*	Is 21:15
men are not slain with the *s*	Is 22:2
strong *s* shall punish leviathan	Is 27:1
the Assyrian fall with the *s*	Is 31:8
and the *s*, not of a mean man	Is 31:8
but he shall flee from the *s*	Is 31:8
For my *s* shall be bathed in	Is 34:5
The *s* of the LORD is filled with	Is 34:6
to fall by the *s* in his own land	Is 37:7
his sons smote him with the *s*	Is 37:38
he gave them as the dust to his *s*	Is 41:2
hath made my mouth like a sharp *s*	Is 49:2
and the famine, and the *s*	Is 51:19
will I number you to the *s*	Is 65:12
by his *s* will the LORD plead with	Is 66:16
your own *s* hath devoured your	Jer 2:30
whereas the *s* reacheth unto the	Jer 4:10
neither shall we see *s* nor famine	Jer 5:12
thou trustedst, with the *s*	Jer 5:17
for the *s* of the enemy and fear is	Jer 6:25
and I will send a *s* after them	Jer 9:16
the young men shall die by the *s*	Jer 11:22
for the *s* of the Lord shall	Jer 12:12
but I will consume them by the *s*	Jer 14:12
unto them, Ye shall not see the *s*	Jer 14:13
I sent them not, yet they say, *S*	Jer 14:15
By *s* and famine shall those	Jer 14:15
because of the famine and the *s*	Jer 14:16
then behold the slain with the *s*	Jer 14:18
as are for the *s*, to the *s*	Jer 15:2
the *s* to slay, and the dogs to	Jer 15:3
to the *s* before their enemies	Jer 15:9
they shall be consumed by the *s*	Jer 16:4
their blood by the force of the *s*	Jer 18:21
men be slain by the *s* in battle	Jer 18:21
by the *s* before their enemies	Jer 19:7
fall by the *s* of their enemies	Jer 19:7
and shall slay them with the *s*	Jer 20:4
from the pestilence, from the *s*	Jer 21:7
smite them with the edge of the *s*	Jer 21:7
in this city shall die by the *s*	Jer 21:9
And I will send the *s*, the famine	Jer 24:10
because of the *s* that I will send	Jer 25:16
because of the *s* which I will	Jer 25:27
for I will call for a *s* upon all	Jer 25:29
them that are wicked to the *s*	Jer 25:31
who slew him with a *s*, and cast	Jer 26:23
saith the LORD, with the *s*	Jer 27:8
die, thou and thy people, by the *s*	Jer 27:13
I will send upon them the *s*	Jer 29:17
I will persecute them with the *s*	Jer 29:18
s found grace in the wilderness	Jer 31:2
against it, because of the *s*	Jer 32:24
of the king of Babylon by the *s*	Jer 32:36
down by the mounts, and by the *s*	Jer 33:4
thee, Thou shalt not die by the *s*	Jer 34:4
for you, saith the LORD, to the *s*	Jer 34:17
in this city shall die by the *s*	Jer 38:2
and thou shalt not fall by the *s*	Jer 39:18
the son of Shaphan with the *s*	Jer 41:2
it shall come to pass, that the *s*	Jer 42:16
they shall die by the *s*, by the	Jer 42:17
that ye shall die by the *s*	Jer 42:22
as are for the *s* to the *s*	Jer 43:11
shall even be consumed by the *s*	Jer 44:12
even unto the greatest, by the *s*	Jer 44:12
have punished Jerusalem, by the *s*	Jer 44:13
and have been consumed by the *s*	Jer 44:18
Egypt shall be consumed by the *s*	Jer 44:27
a small number that escape the *s*	Jer 44:28
the *s* shall devour, and it shall	Jer 46:10
for the *s* shall found round	Jer 46:14
nativity, from the oppressing *s*	Jer 46:16
O thou *s* of the LORD, how long	Jer 47:6
the *s* shall pursue thee	Jer 48:2
keepeth back his *s* from blood	Jer 48:10
and I will send the *s* after them	Jer 49:37
for fear of the oppressing *s* they	Jer 50:16
A *s* is upon the Chaldeans, saith	Jer 50:35
A *s* is upon the liars	Jer 50:36
A *s* is upon her mighty men	Jer 50:36
A *s* is upon their horses, and upon	Jer 50:37
a *s* is upon her treasures	Jer 50:37
Ye that have escaped the *s*	Jer 51:50
abroad the *s* bereaveth, at home	Lam 1:20
my young men are fallen by the *s*	Lam 2:21
They that be slain with the *s* are	Lam 4:9
of the *s* of the wilderness	Lam 5:9
and I will draw out a *s* after them	Eze 5:2
fall by the *s* round about thee	Eze 5:12
and I will draw out a *s* after them	Eze 5:12
and I will bring the *s* upon thee	Eze 5:17
even I, will bring a *s* upon you	Eze 6:3
escape the *s* among the nations	Eze 6:8
they shall fall by the *s*	Eze 6:11
that is near shall fall by the *s*	Eze 6:12
The *s* is without, and the	Eze 7:15
in the field shall die with the *s*	Eze 7:15
Ye have feared the *s*	Eze 11:8
and I will bring a *s* upon you	Eze 11:8
Ye shall fall by the *s*	Eze 11:10
I will draw out the *s* after them	Eze 12:14
a few men of them from the *s*	Eze 12:16
a *s* upon that land, and say, *S*	Eze 14:17
judgments upon Jerusalem, the *s*	Eze 14:21
all his bands shall fall by the *s*	Eze 17:21
draw forth my *s* out of his sheath	Eze 21:3

therefore shall my s go forth out .... Eze 21:4
forth my s out of his sheath .... Eze 21:5
Say, A s, a s is sharpened, ... Eze 21:9
this s is sharpened, and it is.. .... Eze 21:9
of the s shall be upon my people .... Eze 21:12
what if the s of contemn even the .... Eze 21:13
let the s be doubled the third .... Eze 21:14
third time, the s of the slain .... Eze 21:14
it is the s of the great men that .... Eze 21:14
of the s against all their gates.. .... Eze 21:15
that the s of the king of Babylon .... Eze 21:19
that the s may come to Rabbath of .... Eze 21:20
thou, The s, the s is drawn .... Eze 21:28
daughters, and slew her with the s .... Eze 23:10
thy remnant shall fall by the s .... Eze 23:25
ye have left shall fall by the s .... Eze 24:21
they of Dedan shall fall by the s .... Eze 25:13
the field shall be slain by the s .... Eze 26:6
He shall slay with the s thy .... Eze 26:8
he shall slay thy people by the s .... Eze 26:11
by the s upon her on every side .... Eze 28:23
I will bring a s upon thee.. .... Eze 29:8
the s shall come upon Egypt, and.. .... Eze 30:4
shall fall with them by the s .... Eze 30:6
shall they fall in it by the s.. .... Eze 30:6
of Pi-beseth shall fall by the s .... Eze 30:17
to make it strong to hold the s .... Eze 30:21
I will cause the s to fall out of .... Eze 30:22
Babylon, and put my s in his hand .... Eze 30:24
when I shall put my s into the.. .... Eze 30:25
them that be slain with the s .... Eze 31:17
them that be slain by the s.. .... Eze 31:18
I shall brandish my s before them.. .... Eze 32:10
The s of the king of Babylon .... Eze 32:11
of them that are slain by the s .... Eze 32:20
is delivered to the s .... Eze 32:20
lie uncircumcised, slain by the s .... Eze 32:21
of them slain, fallen by the s .... Eze 32:22
of them slain, fallen by the s .... Eze 32:23
of them slain, fallen by the s .... Eze 32:24
uncircumcised, slain by the s .... Eze 32:25
uncircumcised, slain by the s .... Eze 32:26
them that are slain with the s .... Eze 32:28
by them that were slain by the s .... Eze 32:29
with them that be slain by the s .... Eze 32:30
and all his army slain by the s .... Eze 32:31
them that are slain with the s .... Eze 32:32
When I bring the s upon a land .... Eze 33:2
he seeth the s come upon the land .... Eze 33:3
if the s come, and take him away,.. .... Eze 33:4
if the watchman see the s come .... Eze 33:6
if the s come, and take any person .... Eze 33:6
Ye stand upon your s, ye work.. .... Eze 33:26
in the wastes shall fall by the s .... Eze 33:27
s in the time of their calamity.. .... Eze 35:5
fall that are slain with the s .... Eze 35:8
that is brought back from the s .... Eze 38:8
I will call for a s against him.. .... Eze 38:21
every man's s shall be against.. .... Eze 38:21
so fell they all by the s.. .... Eze 39:23
yet they shall fall by the s .... Dan 11:33
not save them by bow, nor by s .... Hos 1:7
and I will break the bow and the s .... Hos 2:18
s for the rage of their tongue.. .... Hos 7:16
the s shall abide on his cities, ... Hos 11:6
they shall fall by the s .... Hos 13:16
and when they fall upon the s .... Joel 2:8
did pursue his brother with the s .... Amos 1:11
young men have I slain with the s .... Amos 4:10
the house of Jeroboam with the s .... Amos 7:9
Jeroboam shall die by the s .... Amos 7:11
thy daughters shall fall by the s .... Amos 7:17
slay the last of them with the s .... Amos 9:1
thence will I command the s .... Amos 9:4
of my people shall die by the s .... Amos 9:10
not lift up a s against nation.. .... Mic 4:3
the land of Assyria with the s .... Mic 5:6
will I give up to the s .... Mic 6:14
the s shall devour thy young.. .... Nah 2:13
lifteth up both the bright s .... Nah 3:3
the s shall cut thee off, it.. .... Nah 3:15
also, ye shall be slain by my s .... Zeph 2:12
every one by the s of his brother .... Hag 2:22
thee as the s of a mighty man .... Zec 9:13
the s shall be upon him arm, and.. .... Zec 11:17
Awake, O s, against my shepherd, ... Zec 13:7
I came not to send peace, but a s .... Mt 10:34
out his hand, and drew his s.. .... Mt 26:51
Put up again thy s into his place.. .... Mt 26:52
the s shall perish with the s .... Mt 26:52
of them that stood by drew a s .... Mk 14:47
a s shall pierce through thy own.. .... Lk 2:35
shall fall by the edge of the s .... Lk 21:24
and he that hath no s, let him .... Lk 22:36
Lord, shall we smite with the s.. .... Lk 22:49
Simon Peter having a s drew it.. .... Jn 18:10
Put up thy s into the sheath.. .... Jn 18:11
the brother of John with the s .... Acts 12:2
doors open, he drew out his s .... Acts 16:27
or nakedness, or peril, or s.. .... Rom 8:35
for he beareth not the s in vain.. .... Rom 13:4
the s of the Spirit, which is the.. .... Eph 6:17
and sharper than any twoedged s .... Heb 4:12
fire, escaped the edge of the s .... Heb 11:34
tempted, were slain with the s .... Heb 11:37
his mouth went a sharp twoedged s .... Rev 1:16
hath the sharp s with two edges .... Rev 2:12
them with the s of my mouth.. .... Rev 2:16
was given unto him a great s .... Rev 6:4
part of the earth, to kill with s .... Rev 6:8

---

he that killeth with the s must.. .... Rev 13:10
must be killed with the s .... Rev 13:10
beast, which had the wound by a s .... Rev 13:14
out of his mouth goeth a sharp s.. .... Rev 19:15
s of him that sat upon the horse.. .... Rev 19:21
which s proceeded out of his .... Rev 19:21

SWORDS

the Hebrews make them s or spears.. .... 1Sa 13:19
him seven hundred men that drew s 2Kin 3:26
after their families with their s .... Neh 4:13
than oil, yet were they drawn s .... Ps 55:21
s are in their lips.. .... Ps 59:7
generation, whose teeth are as s .... Prov 30:14
They all hold s, being expert in .... Song 3:8
beat their s into plowshares .... Is 2:4
For they fled from the s, from.. .... Is 21:15
thrust thee through with their s .... Eze 16:40
and dispatch them with their s .... Eze 23:47
they shall draw their s against.. .... Eze 28:7
shall draw their s against Egypt .... Eze 30:11
By the s of the mighty will I .... Eze 32:12
laid their s under their heads .... Eze 32:27
shields, all of them handling s................... Eze 38:4
Beat your plowshares into s .... Joel 3:10
beat their s into plowshares .... Mic 4:3
with him a great multitude with s .... Mt 26:47
out as against a thief with s .... Mt 26:55
with him a great multitude with s .... Mk 14:43
out, as against a thief, with s .... Mk 14:48
Lord, behold, here are two s .... Lk 22:38
out, as against a thief, with s .... Lk 22:52

SWORN

And said, By myself have I s .... Gen 22:16
for he had straitly s the.. .... Ex 13:19
Because the LORD hath s that the.. .... Ex 17:16
about which he hath s falsely.. .... Lev 6:5
which he had s unto your fathers, ... Deut 7:8
as he hath s unto thy fathers.. .... Deut 13:17
as he hath s unto thy fathers, and.. .... Deut 19:8
himself, as he hath s unto the.. .... Deut 28:9
as he hath s unto thy fathers, to.. .... Deut 29:13
the land which the LORD hath s .... Deut 31:7
s unto them by the LORD God of .... Josh 9:18
We have s unto them by the LORD .... Josh 9:19
and as the LORD had s unto them .... Judg 2:15
the men of Israel had s in Mizpeh .... Judg 21:1
seeing we have s by the LORD that.. .... Judg 21:7
for the children of Israel have s .... Judg 21:18
therefore I have s unto the house.. .... 1Sa 3:14
forasmuch as we have s both of us.. .... 1Sa 20:42
as the LORD hath s to David 2Sa 3:9
of Israel had s unto them.. .... 2Sa 21:2
for they had s with all their.. .... 2Chr 15:15
were many in Judah s unto him .... Neh 6:18
which thou hadst s to give them .... Neh 9:15
unto vanity, nor s deceitfully.. .... Ps 24:4
I have s unto David my servant,.. .... Ps 89:3
Once have I s by my holiness that .... Ps 89:35
mad against me are s against me .... Ps 102:8
The LORD hath s, and will not .... Ps 110:4
I have s, and I will perform it,.. .... Ps 119:106
The LORD hath s in truth unto .... Ps 132:11
The LORD of hosts hath s, saying, ... Is 14:24
I have s by myself, the word is.. .... Is 45:23
for as I have s that the waters .... Is 54:9
so have I s that I would not be.. .... Is 54:9
The LORD hath s by his right hand.. .... Is 62:8
s by them that are no gods .... Jer 5:7
which I have s unto your fathers.. .... Jer 11:5
I have s by my great name, saith.. .... Jer 44:26
For I have s by myself, saith the.. .... Jer 49:13
Lord of hosts hath s by himself .... Jer 51:14
sight, to them that have s oaths.. .... Eze 21:23
Lord God hath s by his holiness.. .... Amos 4:2
The Lord God hath s by himself .... Amos 6:8
The LORD hath s by the excellency.. .... Amos 8:7
which thou hast s unto our .... Mic 7:20
God had s with an oath to him.. .... Acts 2:30
nigh, which God had s to Abraham.. .... Acts 7:17
As I have s in my wrath, If they.. .... Heb 4:3

SYCAMINE

ye might say unto this s tree .... Lk 17:6

SYCHAR (si'-kar) See SHECHEM. A city in Samaria.

of Samaria, which is called S .... Jn 4:5

SYCHEM (si'-kem) See SHECHEM. Same as Shechem.

were carried over into S.. .... Acts 7:16
the sons of Emmor the father of S.. .... Acts 7:16

SYCOMORE

the s trees that are in the vale.. .... 1Kin 10:27
the s trees that were in the low 1Chr 27:28
cedar trees made he as the s 2Chr 1:15
the s trees that are in the low 2Chr 9:27
hail, and their s trees with frost.. .... Ps 78:47
herdman, and a gatherer of s fruit.. .... Amos 7:14
up into a s tree to see him .... Lk 19:4

SYCOMORES

the s are cut down, but we will .... Is 9:10

SYENE (si-e'-ne) An Egyptian city.

from the tower of S even unto the.. .... Eze 29:10
from the tower of S shall they .... Eze 30:6

SYNAGOGUE

thence, he went into their s .... Mt 12:9
he taught them into their s .... Mt 13:54

---

sabbath day he entered into the s.. .... Mk 1:21
there was in their s a man with.. .... Mk 1:23
when they were come out of the s .... Mk 1:29
And he entered again into the s .... Mk 3:1
cometh one of the rulers of the s.. .... Mk 5:22
he saith unto the ruler of the s .... Mk 5:38
the house of the ruler of the s .... Mk 5:38
come, he began to teach in the s.. .... Mk 6:2
he went into the s on the sabbath .... Lk 4:16
in the s were fastened on him.. .... Lk 4:20
And all they in the s, when they .... Lk 4:28
in the s there was a man, which .... Lk 4:33
And he arose out of the s, and.. .... Lk 4:38
that he entered into the s .... Lk 6:6
nation, and he hath built us a s .... Lk 7:5
and he was a ruler of the s.. .... Lk 8:41
the ruler of the s answered with.. .... Lk 13:14
These things said he in the s .... Jn 6:59
he should be put out of the s .... Jn 9:22
they should be put out of the s .... Jn 12:42
I ever taught in the s, and in the.. .... Jn 18:20
Then there arose certain of the s.. .... Acts 6:9
is called the s of the Libertines .... Acts 6:9
went into the s on the sabbath .... Acts 13:14
rulers of the s sent unto them.. .... Acts 13:15
the Jews were gone out of the s .... Acts 13:42
together into the s of the Jews.. .... Acts 14:1
where was a s of the Jews.. .... Acts 17:1
went into the s of the Jews, ... Acts 17:10
he in the s with the Jews.. .... Acts 17:17
reasoned in the s every sabbath.. .... Acts 18:4
whose house joined hard to the s .... Acts 18:7
Crispus, the chief ruler of the s.. .... Acts 18:8
the chief ruler of the s.. .... Acts 18:17
but he himself entered into the s .... Acts 18:19
he began to speak boldly in the s.. .... Acts 18:26
And he went into the s, and spake.. .... Acts 19:8
beat in every s them that.. .... Acts 22:19
And I punished them in every s.. .... Acts 26:11
are not, but are the s of Satan .... Rev 2:9
will make them of the s of Satan.. .... Rev 3:9

SYNAGOGUE'S

of the s house certain which said.. .... Mk 5:35
one from the ruler of the s house .... Lk 8:49

SYNAGOGUES

up all the s of God in the land .... Ps 74:8
all Galilee, teaching in their s.. .... Mt 4:23
as the hypocrites do in the s .... Mt 6:2
love to pray standing in the s .... Mt 6:5
and villages, teaching in their s .... Mt 9:35
they will scourge you in their s .... Mt 10:17
and the chief seats in the s .... Mt 23:6
them shall ye scourge in your s.. .... Mk 13:9
he preached in their s throughout.. .... Mk 1:39
And the chief seats in the s .... Mk 12:39
in the s ye shall be beaten.. .... Mk 13:9
And he taught in their s, being.. .... Lk 4:15
he preached in the s of Galilee .... Lk 4:44
love the uppermost seats in the s .... Lk 11:43
And when they bring you unto the s.. .... Lk 12:11
in one of the s on the sabbath .... Lk 13:10
and the highest seats in the s.. .... Lk 20:46
you, delivering you up to the s.. .... Lk 21:12
They shall put you out of the s.. .... Jn 16:2
him letters to Damascus to the s.. .... Acts 9:2
he preached Christ in the s .... Acts 9:20
word of God in the s of the Jews.. .... Acts 13:5
read in the s every sabbath day.. .... Acts 15:21
up the people, neither in the s.. .... Acts 24:12

SYNTYCHE (sin'-ti-ke) A Christian at Philippi.

I beseech Euodias, and beseech S.. .... Phil 4:2

SYRACUSE (sir'-a-cuse) A city on Sicily.

And landing at S, we tarried there.. .... Acts 28:12

SYRIA (sir'-e-ah) See ARAM, SYRIA-DAMASCUS, SYRIA-MAACHAH, SYRIAN. Nation north of Israel.

and Ashtaroth, and the gods of S .... Judg 10:6
put garrisons in S of Damascus.. .... 2Sa 8:6
Of S, and of Moab, and of the 2Sa 8:12
vow while I abode at Geshur in S 2Sa 15:8
Hittites, and for the kings of S 1Kin 10:29
Israel, and reigned over S 1Kin 11:25
the son of Hezion, king of S 1Kin 15:18
anoint Hazael to be king over S 1Kin 19:15
Ben-hadad the king of S gathered 1Kin 20:1
Ben-hadad the king of S escaped 1Kin 20:20
of S will come up against thee 1Kin 20:22
of the king of S said unto him 1Kin 20:23
three years without war between S 1Kin 22:1
out of the hand of the king of S.. .... 1Kin 22:3
But the king of S commanded his.. .... 1Kin 22:31
of the host of the king of S 2Kin 5:1
the king of S deliverance unto S 2Kin 5:1
And the king of S said, Go to, go, ... 2Kin 5:5
Then the king of S warred against.. .... 2Kin 6:8
the heart of the king of S was.. .... 2Kin 6:11
So the bands of S came no more.. .... 2Kin 6:23
king of S gathered all his host 2Kin 6:24
uttermost part of the camp of S.. .... 2Kin 7:5
Ben-hadad the king of S was sick.. .... 2Kin 8:7
king of S hath sent me to thee.. .... 2Kin 8:9
me that thou shalt be king over S.. .... 2Kin 8:13
Hazael king of S in Ramoth-gilead 2Kin 8:28
fought against Hazael king of S 2Kin 8:29
because of Hazael king of S 2Kin 9:14
he fought with Hazael king of S 2Kin 9:15
Then Hazael king of S went up.. .... 2Kin 12:17
and sent it to Hazael king of S.. .... 2Kin 12:18

S

into the hand of Hazael king of *S*........ 2Kin 13:3
the king of *S* oppressed them............... 2Kin 13:4
for the king of *S* had destroyed.......... 2Kin 13:7
the arrow of deliverance from *S*........ 2Kin 13:17
then hadst thou smitten *S* till............ 2Kin 13:19
now thou shalt smite *S* but thrice....... 2Kin 13:19
But Hazael king of *S* oppressed......... 2Kin 13:22
So Hazael king of *S* died.................... 2Kin 13:24
against Judah Rezin the king of *S*....... 2Kin 15:37
But the *S* Rezin king of *S* and Pekah son... 2Kin 16:5
of *S* recovered Elath to *S*.................... 2Kin 16:6
out of the hand of the king of *S*.......... 2Kin 16:7
Hittites, and for the kings of *S*.......... 2Chr 1:17
and sent to Ben-hadad king of *S*........ 2Chr 16:2
thou hast relied on the king of *S*........ 2Chr 16:7
of *S* escaped out of thine hand............ 2Chr 16:7
push *S* until they be consumed............ 2Chr 18:10
Now the king of *S* had commanded..... 2Chr 18:30
beyond the sea on this side *S*.............. 2Chr 20:2
Hazael king of *S* at Ramoth-gilead..... 2Chr 22:5
he fought with Hazael king of *S*........... 2Chr 22:6
that the host of *S* came up................... 2Chr 24:23
into the hand of the king of *S*............ 2Chr 28:5
gods of the kings of *S* help them........ 2Chr 28:23
Judah, that Rezin the king of *S*........... Is 7:1
S is confederate with Ephraim............ Is 7:2
the fierce anger of Rezin with *S*.......... Is 7:4
Because *S*, Ephraim, and the son of.... Is 7:5
For the head of *S* is Damascus............ Is 7:8
Damascus, and the remnant of *S*........ Is 17:3
reproach of the daughters of *S*........... Eze 16:57
S was thy merchant by reason of......... Eze 27:16
Jacob fled into the country of *S*.......... Hos 12:12
the people of *S* shall go into.............. Amos 1:5
And his fame went throughout all *S*.... Mt 4:24
when Cyrenius was governor of *S*........ Lk 2:2
of the Gentiles in Antioch and *S*......... Acts 15:23
And he went through *S* and Cilicia,..... Acts 15:41
brethren, and sailed thence into *S*...... Acts 18:18
as he was about to sail into *S*............. Acts 20:3
the left hand, and sailed into *S*.......... Acts 21:3
I came into the regions of *S*............... Gal 1:21

SYRIACK (*sir'-e-ak*) See SYRIAN. *Language of the Syrians.*
the Chaldeans to the king in *S*............ Dan 2:4

SYRIA-DAMASCUS (*sir'-e-ah-da-mas'-cus*) See SYRIA, DAMASCUS. *Same as Damascus.*
Then David put garrisons in *S*............ 1Chr 18:6

SYRIA-MAACHAH (*sir'-e-ah-ma-a-kah*) A *Syrian city-state.*
out of Mesopotamia, and out of *S*....... 1Chr 19:6

SYRIAN (*sir'-e-un*) See ARAMITES, SYRIANS, SYROPHENICIAN.
  1. *An inhabitant of Syria.*
of Bethuel the *S* of Padan-aram............ Gen 25:20
the sister to Laban the *S*..................... Gen 25:20
unto Laban, son of Bethuel the *S*......... Gen 28:5
away unawares to Laban the *S*............. Gen 31:20
Laban the *S* in a dream by night.......... Gen 31:24
A *S* ready to perish was my father........ Deut 26:5
master hath spared Naaman this *S*....... 2Kin 5:20
was cleansed, saving Naaman the *S*..... Lk 4:27
  2. *The language of Syria.*
to thy servants in the *S* language......... 2Kin 18:26
was written in the *S* tongue................. Ezra 4:7
and interpreted in the *S* tongue.......... Ezra 4:7
thy servants in the *S* language............. Is 36:11

SYRIANS
when the *S* of Damascus came to........ 2Sa 8:5
of Zobah, David slew of the *S* two....... 2Sa 8:5
the *S* became servants to David,......... 2Sa 8:6
of the *S* in the valley of salt............... 2Sa 8:13
hired the *S* of Beth-rehob, and the...... 2Sa 10:6
the *S* of Zoba, twenty thousand........... 2Sa 10:6
the *S* of Zoba, and of Rehob, and........ 2Sa 10:6
put them in array against the *S*........... 2Sa 10:9
If the *S* be too strong for me,............. 2Sa 10:11
unto the battle against the *S*.............. 2Sa 10:13
of Ammon saw that the *S* were fled..... 2Sa 10:14
when the *S* saw that they were............ 2Sa 10:15
brought out the *S* that were................ 2Sa 10:16
the *S* set themselves in array............. 2Sa 10:16
And the *S* fled before Israel............... 2Sa 10:18
seven hundred chariots of the *S*......... 2Sa 10:18
So the *S* feared to help the................. 2Sa 10:19
and the *S* fled................................. 1Kin 20:20
slew the *S* with a great slaughter........ 1Kin 20:21
that Ben-hadad numbered the *S*......... 1Kin 20:26
but the *S* filled the country................ 1Kin 20:27
the Lord, Because the *S* have said...... 1Kin 20:28
S an hundred thousand footmen in..... 1Kin 20:29
With these shalt thou push the *S*........ 1Kin 22:11
up in his chariot against the *S*............ 1Kin 22:35
the *S* had gone out by companies........ 2Kin 5:2
for thither the *S* are come down.......... 2Kin 6:9
us fall unto the host of the *S*.............. 2Kin 7:4
to go unto the camp of the *S*.............. 2Kin 7:5
the *S* to hear a noise of chariots......... 2Kin 7:6
We came to the camp of the *S*............ 2Kin 7:10
you what the *S* have done to us........... 2Kin 7:12
king sent after the host of the *S*......... 2Kin 7:14
which the *S* had cast away in.............. 2Kin 7:15
and spoiled the tents of the *S*............ 2Kin 7:16
of Hazael king of the *S*..................... 2Kin 8:28
the *S* bound wounded Joram............... 2Kin 8:29
the *S* had given him at Ramah............. 2Kin 8:29
wounds which the *S* had given him..... 2Kin 9:15
out from under the hand of the *S*........ 2Kin 13:5
thou shalt smite the *S* in Aphek.......... 2Kin 13:17

---

the *S* came to Elath, and dwelt............ 2Kin 16:6
the Chaldees, and bands of the *S*........ 2Kin 24:2
when the *S* of Damascus came to........ 1Chr 18:5
of Zobah, David slew of the *S* two....... 1Chr 18:5
the *S* became David's servants, and.... 1Chr 18:6
put them in array against the *S*........... 1Chr 19:10
If the *S* be too strong for me,............. 1Chr 19:12
nigh before the *S* unto the battle......... 1Chr 19:14
of Ammon saw that the *S* were fled...... 1Chr 19:15
when the *S* saw that they were put...... 1Chr 19:16
drew forth the *S* that were beyond 1Chr 19:16
the battle in array against the *S* 1Chr 19:17
But the *S* fled before Israel............... 1Chr 19:18
David slew of the *S* seven................. 1Chr 19:18
neither would the *S* help the.............. 1Chr 19:19
against the *S* until the even............... 2Chr 18:34
and the *S* smote Joram..................... 2Chr 22:5
For the army of the *S* came with a...... 2Chr 24:24
The *S* before, and the Philistines....... Is 9:12
and for fear of the army of the *S* .... Jer 35:11
from Caphtor, and the *S* from Kir....... Amos 9:7

SYROPHENICIAN (*sy'-ro-fe-ne'-she-un*) A *citizen of Phenicia in Syria.*
woman was a Greek, a *S* by nation ...... Mk 7:26

SYRTIS

T

TAANACH (*ta'-a-nak*) See TANACH. *A Levitical city in Manasseh.*
The king of *T*, one......................... Josh 12:21
towns, and the inhabitants of *T*.......... Josh 17:11
of Beth-shean and her towns, nor *T*.... Judg 1:27
in *T* by the waters of Megiddo............ Judg 5:19
to him pertained *T* and Megiddo, and.. 1Kin 4:12
Beth-shean and her towns, *T*............. 1Chr 7:29

TAANATH-SHILOH (*ta'-a-nath-shi'-lo*) A *city on the border of Benjamin.*
border went about unto *T*................. Josh 16:6

TABALIAH See TEBALIAH.

TABBAOTH (*tab-ba-oth*) A *family of exiles.*
of Hasupha, the children of *T*............ Ezra 2:43
of Hasupha, the children of *T*............ Neh 7:46

TABBATH (*tab'-bath*) A *city in Issachar.*
border of Abel-meholah, unto *T*......... Judg 7:22

TABEAL (*tab'-e-al*) See TABEEL. *Father of a would-be king of Israel.*
midst of it, even the son of *T*............. Is 7:6

TABEEL (*tab'-e-el*) See TABEAL. *A Persian official in Samaria.*
wrote Bishlam, Mithredath, *T*............ Ezra 4:7

TABERAH (*tab'-e-rah*) A *place in the wilderness of Paran.*
he called the name of the place *T*....... Num 11:3
And at *T*, and at Massah, and at......... Deut 9:22

TABERING
of doves, *t* upon their breasts............ Nah 2:7

TABERNACLE
thee, after the pattern of the *t*........... Ex 25:9
the *t* with ten curtains of fine........... Ex 26:1
and it shall be one *t* .... Ex 26:6
hair to be a covering upon the *t*......... Ex 26:7
curtain in the forefront of the *t*......... Ex 26:9
hang over the backside of the *t*......... Ex 26:12
the sides of the *t* on this side........... Ex 26:13
the *t* of shittim wood standing up...... Ex 26:15
make for all the boards of the *t* .... Ex 26:18
shalt make the boards for the *t* .... Ex 26:18
for the second side of the *t* on .... Ex 26:20
for the sides of the *t* westward .... Ex 26:22
corners of the *t* in the two sides....... Ex 26:23
boards of the one side of the *t*......... Ex 26:26
boards of the other side of the *t*....... Ex 26:27
the boards of the side of the *t*.......... Ex 26:27
And thou shalt rear up the *t*............. Ex 26:30
side of the *t* toward the south .... Ex 26:35
shalt make the court of the *t*............ Ex 27:9
All the vessels of the *t* in all........... Ex 27:19
In the *t* of the congregation............ Ex 27:21
in unto the *t* of the congregation...... Ex 28:43
door of the *t* of the congregation...... Ex 29:4
by the door of the *t* of the.............. Ex 29:10
when he cometh into the *t* of the ..... Ex 29:30
by the door of the *t* of the.............. Ex 29:32
t of the congregation before the....... Ex 29:42
the *t* shall be sanctified by my .... Ex 29:43
the *t* of the congregation............... Ex 29:44
of the *t* of the congregation............ Ex 30:16
between the *t* of the congregation..... Ex 30:18
go into the *t* of the congregation...... Ex 30:20
thou shalt anoint the *t* of the........... Ex 30:26
in the *t* of the congregation............ Ex 30:36
The *t* of the congregation, and the.... Ex 31:7
and all the furniture of the *t*........... Ex 31:7
And Moses took the *t*, and pitched.... Ex 33:7
camp, and called it the *T* of the........ Ex 33:7
unto the *t* of the congregation......... Ex 33:7
when Moses went out unto the *t*....... Ex 33:8
until he was gone into the *t*............. Ex 33:8

---

pass, as Moses entered into the *t*...... Ex 33:9
and stood at the door of the *t*.......... Ex 33:9
cloudy pillar stand at the *t* door....... Ex 33:10
man, departed not out of the *t*.......... Ex 33:11
The *t*, his tent, and his covering,...... Ex 35:11
door at the entering in of the *t*......... Ex 35:15
The pins of the *t*, and the pins of..... Ex 35:18
work of the *t* of the congregation..... Ex 35:21
the *t* made ten curtains of fine......... Ex 36:8
so it became one *t* .... Ex 36:13
hair for the tent over the *t* .... Ex 36:14
boards for the *t* of shittim wood ...... Ex 36:20
make for all the boards of the *t*........ Ex 36:22
And he made boards for the *t*........... Ex 36:23
And for the other side of the *t*......... Ex 36:25
for the sides of the *t* westward......... Ex 36:27
corners of the *t* in the two sides....... Ex 36:28
boards of the one side of the *t*......... Ex 36:31
boards of the other side of the *t*....... Ex 36:32
of the *t* for the sides westward .... Ex 36:32
an hanging for the *t* door of Moses... Ex 36:37
door of the *t* of the congregation...... Ex 38:8
And all the pins of the *t*, and of........ Ex 38:20
This is the sum of the *t*, even of ...... Ex 38:21
even of the *t* of testimony, as it .... Ex 38:21
door of the *t* of the congregation...... Ex 38:30
gate, and all the pins of the *t*........... Ex 38:31
Thus was all the work of the *t* of...... Ex 39:32
And they brought the *t* unto Moses.... Ex 39:33
and the hanging for the *t* door .... Ex 39:38
vessels of the service of the *t*.......... Ex 39:40
month shalt thou set up the *t* of .... Ex 40:2
the hanging of the door to the *t*........ Ex 40:5
t of the tent of the congregation....... Ex 40:6
anointing oil, and anoint the *t* .... Ex 40:9
door of the *t* of the congregation...... Ex 40:12
month, that the *t* was reared up........ Ex 40:17
And Moses reared up the *t*, and....... Ex 40:18
spread abroad the tent over the *t*...... Ex 40:19
And he brought the ark into the *t*...... Ex 40:21
upon the side of the *t* northward....... Ex 40:22
on the side of the *t* southward.......... Ex 40:24
the hanging at the door of the *t*........ Ex 40:28
offering by the door of the *t* of .... Ex 40:29
up the court round about the *t*......... Ex 40:33
glory of the LORD filled the *t*............ Ex 40:34
glory of the LORD filled the *t*............ Ex 40:35
was taken up from over the *t*............ Ex 40:36
of the LORD was upon the *t* by day.... Ex 40:38
out of the *t* of the congregation........ Lev 1:1
will at the door of the *t* of the.......... Lev 1:3
door of the *t* of the congregation...... Lev 1:5
door of the *t* of the congregation...... Lev 3:2
kill it before the *t* of the.................. Lev 3:8
kill it before the *t* of the.................. Lev 3:13
bullock unto the door of the *t* of....... Lev 4:4
and bring it to the *t* of the.............. Lev 4:5
LORD, which is in the *t* of the .... Lev 4:7
door of the *t* of the congregation...... Lev 4:7
door of the *t* of the congregation...... Lev 4:14
to the *t* of the congregation............ Lev 4:16
the LORD, that is in the *t* of the........ Lev 4:18
door of the *t* of the congregation...... Lev 4:18
in the court of the *t* of the.............. Lev 6:16
of the *t* of the congregation............ Lev 6:26
into the *t* of the congregation to...... Lev 6:30
door of the *t* of the congregation...... Lev 8:3
door of the *t* of the congregation...... Lev 8:4
anointing oil, and anointed the *t* ...... Lev 8:10
door of the *t* of the congregation...... Lev 8:31
t of the congregation in seven.......... Lev 8:33
of the *t* of the congregation day....... Lev 8:35
before the *t* of the congregation....... Lev 9:5
into the *t* of the congregation.......... Lev 9:23
door of the *t* of the congregation...... Lev 10:7
go into the *t* of the congregation...... Lev 10:9
door of the *t* of the congregation...... Lev 12:6
at the door of the *t* of the............... Lev 14:11
door of the *t* of the congregation...... Lev 14:23
door of the *t* of the congregation...... Lev 15:14
to the door of the *t* of.................... Lev 15:29
defile my *t* that is among them......... Lev 15:31
door of the *t* of the congregation...... Lev 16:7
do for the *t* of the congregation....... Lev 16:16
the *t* of the congregation when he..... Lev 16:17
the *t* of the congregation, and the.... Lev 16:20
into the *t* of the congregation.......... Lev 16:23
for the *t* of the congregation........... Lev 17:4
door of the *t* of the congregation...... Lev 17:4
the LORD before the *t* of the LORD..... Lev 17:4
door of the *t* of the congregation...... Lev 17:5
door of the *t* of the congregation...... Lev 17:6
door of the *t* of the congregation...... Lev 17:9
in the *t* of the congregation,........... Lev 19:21
in the *t* of the congregation,........... Lev 24:3
And I will set my *t* among you........... Lev 26:11
in the *t* of the congregation, on........ Num 1:1
Levites over the *t* of testimony......... Num 1:50
they shall bear the *t*, and all the....... Num 1:50
and shall encamp round about the *t*... Num 1:50
when the *t* setteth forward, the........ Num 1:51
when the *t* is to be pitched, the........ Num 1:51
round about the *t* of testimony......... Num 1:53
the charge of the *t* of testimony....... Num 1:53
far off about the *t* of the................ Num 2:2
Then the *t* of the congregation........ Num 2:17
before the *t* of the congregation....... Num 3:7
to do the service of the *t*................. Num 3:7
of the *t* of the congregation............ Num 3:8
to do the service of the *t*................. Num 3:8

shall pitch behind the *t* westward....... Num 3:23
t the congregation shall be .... Num 3:25
the congregation shall be the *t*....... Num 3:25
door of the *t* of the congregation....... Num 3:25
of the court, which is by the *t*....... Num 3:25
on the side of the *t* southward....... Num 3:29
on the side of the *t* northward....... Num 3:35
shall be the boards of the *t*....... Num 3:36
before the *t* toward the east....... Num 3:38
even before the *t* of the....... Num 3:38
work in the *t* of the congregation....... Num 4:3
in the *t* of the congregation....... Num 4:4
the oversight of all the *t*....... Num 4:16
and the oversight of all the *t*....... Num 4:16
work in the *t* of the congregation....... Num 4:23
shall bear the curtains of the *t*....... Num 4:25
the *t* of the congregation, his....... Num 4:25
door of the *t* of the congregation....... Num 4:25
of the court, which is by the *t*....... Num 4:26
in the *t* of the congregation....... Num 4:28
work of the *t* of the congregation....... Num 4:31
in the *t* of the congregation....... Num 4:31
the boards of the *t*, and the bars....... Num 4:31
work in the *t* of the congregation....... Num 4:33
in the *t* of the congregation....... Num 4:35
work in the *t* of the congregation....... Num 4:37
work in the *t* of the congregation....... Num 4:39
in the *t* of the congregation....... Num 4:41
work in the *t* of the congregation....... Num 4:43
in the *t* of the congregation....... Num 4:47
of the *t* the priest shall take....... Num 5:17
to the door of the *t* of the....... Num 6:10
door of the *t* of the congregation....... Num 6:13
door of the *t* of the congregation....... Num 6:18
that Moses had fully set up the *t*....... Num 7:1
and they brought before the *t*....... Num 7:3
of the *t* of the congregation....... Num 7:5
t of the congregation to speak....... Num 7:89
before the *t* of the congregation....... Num 8:9
of the *t* of the congregation....... Num 8:15
in the *t* of the congregation....... Num 8:19
in the *t* of the congregation....... Num 8:19
the *t* of the congregation before....... Num 8:22
of the *t* of the congregation....... Num 8:24
in the *t* of the congregation....... Num 8:26
on the day that the *t* was reared....... Num 9:15
reared up the cloud covered the *t*....... Num 9:15
at even there was upon the *t* as....... Num 9:15
the cloud was taken up from the *t*....... Num 9:17
the *t* they rested in their tents....... Num 9:18
tarried long upon the *t* many days....... Num 9:19
cloud was a few days upon the *t*....... Num 9:20
that the cloud tarried upon the *t*....... Num 9:22
door of the *t* of the congregation....... Num 10:3
from off the *t* of the testimony....... Num 10:11
And the *t* was taken down....... Num 10:17
Merari set forward, bearing the *t*....... Num 10:17
set up the *t* against they came....... Num 10:21
unto the *t* of the congregation....... Num 11:16
and set them round about the *t*....... Num 11:24
but went not out unto the *t*....... Num 11:26
unto the *t* of the congregation....... Num 12:4
and stood in the door of the *t*....... Num 12:5
the cloud departed from off the *t*....... Num 12:10
of the LORD appeared in the *t* of....... Num 14:10
the service of the *t* of the LORD....... Num 16:9
stood in the door of the *t* of the....... Num 16:18
door of the *t* of the congregation....... Num 16:19
you up from about the *t* of Korah....... Num 16:24
they gat up from the *t* of Korah....... Num 16:27
toward the *t* of the congregation....... Num 16:42
before the *t* of the congregation....... Num 16:43
door of the *t* of the congregation....... Num 16:50
thou shalt lay them up in the *t*....... Num 17:4
the LORD in the *t* of witness....... Num 17:7
Moses went into the *t* of witness....... Num 17:8
unto the *t* of the LORD shall die....... Num 17:13
minister before the *t* of witness....... Num 18:2
and the charge of all the *t*....... Num 18:3
of the *t* of the congregation....... Num 18:4
for all the service of the *t*....... Num 18:4
of the *t* of the congregation....... Num 18:6
of the *t* of the congregation....... Num 18:21
nigh the *t* of the congregation....... Num 18:22
of the *t* of the congregation....... Num 18:23
in the *t* of the congregation....... Num 18:31
her blood directly before the *t*....... Num 19:4
defileth the *t* of the LORD....... Num 19:13
door of the *t* of the congregation....... Num 20:6
of the *t* of the congregation....... Num 25:6
by the door of the *t* of the....... Num 27:2
the charge of the *t* of the LORD....... Num 31:30
the charge of the *t* of the LORD....... Num 31:47
it into the *t* of the congregation....... Num 31:54
in the *t* of the congregation....... Deut 31:14
in the *t* in a pillar of a cloud....... Deut 31:15
stood over the door of the *t*....... Deut 31:15
set up the *t* of the congregation....... Josh 18:1
at the door of the *t* of the....... Josh 19:51
wherein the LORD's *t* dwelleth....... Josh 22:19
LORD our God that is before his *t*....... Josh 22:29
door of the *t* of the congregation....... 1Sa 2:22
in the midst of the *t* that David....... 2Sa 6:17
have walked in a tent and in a *t*....... 2Sa 7:6
took an horn of oil out of the *t*....... 1Kin 1:39
Joab fled unto the *t* of the LORD....... 1Kin 2:28
was fled unto the *t* of the LORD....... 1Kin 2:29
Benaiah came to the *t* of the LORD....... 1Kin 2:30
the *t* of the congregation, and all....... 1Kin 8:4
holy vessels that were in the *t*....... 1Kin 8:4

of the *t* of the congregation with....... 1Chr 6:32
of the *t* of the house of God....... 1Chr 6:48
keepers of the gates of the *t*....... 1Chr 9:19
door of the *t* of the congregation....... 1Chr 9:21
LORD, namely, the house of the *t*....... 1Chr 9:23
before the *t* of the LORD in the....... 1Chr 16:39
to tent, and from one *t* to another....... 1Chr 17:5
For the *t* of the LORD, which....... 1Chr 21:29
they shall no more carry the *t*....... 1Chr 23:26
of the *t* of the congregation....... 1Chr 23:32
for there was the *t* of the....... 2Chr 1:3
he put before the *t* of the LORD....... 2Chr 1:5
which was at the *t* of the....... 2Chr 1:6
from before the *t* of the....... 2Chr 1:13
the *t* of the congregation, and all....... 2Chr 5:5
holy vessels that were in the *t*....... 2Chr 5:5
of Israel, for the *t* of witness....... 2Chr 24:6
know that thy *t* shall be in peace....... Job 5:24
The light shall be dark in his *t*....... Job 18:6
shall be rooted out of his *t*....... Job 18:14
It shall dwell in his *t*, because....... Job 18:15
me, and among round about my *t*....... Job 19:12
with him that is left in his *t*....... Job 20:26
the secret of God was upon my *t*....... Job 29:4
If the men of my *t* said not....... Job 31:31
the clouds, or the noise of his *t*....... Job 36:29
Lord, who shall abide in thy *t*....... Ps 15:1
them hath he set a *t* for the sun....... Ps 19:4
secret of his I shall he hide me....... Ps 27:5
offer in his *t* sacrifices of joy....... Ps 27:6
I will abide in thy *t* for ever....... Ps 61:4
In Salem also in his *t*, and his....... Ps 76:2
that he forsook the *t* of Shiloh....... Ps 78:60
he refused the *t* of Joseph....... Ps 78:67
not come into the *t* of my house....... Ps 132:3
but the *t* of the upright shall....... Prov 14:11
there shall be a *t* for a shadow....... Is 4:6
it in truth in the *t* of David....... Is 16:5
a *t* that shall not be taken down....... Is 33:20
My *t* is spoiled, and all my cords....... Jer 10:20
in the *t* of the daughter of Zion....... Lam 2:4
hath violently taken away his *t*....... Lam 2:6
My *t* also shall be with them....... Eze 37:27
which was the breadth of the *t*....... Eze 41:1
have borne the *t* of your Moloch....... Amos 5:26
up the *t* of David that is fallen....... Amos 9:11
Yea, ye took up the *t* of Moloch....... Acts 7:43
Our fathers had the *t* of witness....... Acts 7:44
desired to find a *t* for the God....... Acts 7:46
will build again the *t* of David....... Acts 15:16
house of this *t* were dissolved....... 2Cor 5:1
we that are in this *t* do groan....... 2Cor 5:4
the sanctuary, and the true *t*....... Heb 8:2
when he was about to make the *t*....... Heb 8:5
For there was a *t* made....... Heb 9:2
the *t* which is called the Holiest....... Heb 9:3
went always into the first *t*....... Heb 9:6
as the first *t* was yet standing....... Heb 9:8
by a greater and more perfect *t*....... Heb 9:11
sprinkled with blood both the *t*....... Heb 9:21
no right to eat which serve the *t*....... Heb 13:10
meet, as long as I am in this *t*....... 2Pet 1:13
shortly I must put off this my *t*....... 2Pet 1:14
to blaspheme his name, and his *t*....... Rev 13:6
the temple of the *t*....... Rev 15:5
the *t* of God is with men, and he....... Rev 21:3

TABERNACLES

month shall be the feast of *t* for....... Lev 23:34
are thy tents, O Jacob, and thy *t*....... Num 24:5
observe the feast of *t* seven days....... Deut 16:13
of weeks, and in the feast of *t*....... Deut 16:16
of release, in the feast of *t*....... Deut 31:10
of weeks, and in the feast of *t*....... 2Chr 8:13
They kept also the feast of *t*....... Ezr 3:4
let not wickedness dwell in thy *t*....... Job 11:14
The *t* of robbers prosper, and they....... Job 12:6
shall consume the *t* of bribery....... Job 15:34
put away iniquity far from thy *t*....... Job 22:23
unto thy holy hill, and to thy *t*....... Ps 43:3
place of the *t* of the most High....... Ps 46:4
of their strength in the *t* of Ham....... Ps 78:51
The *t* of Edom, and the Ishmaelites....... Ps 83:6
How amiable are thy *t*, O LORD of....... Ps 84:1
is in the *t* of the righteous....... Ps 118:15
We will go into his *t*....... Ps 132:7
he shall plant the *t* of his....... Dan 11:45
thorns shall be in their *t*....... Hos 9:6
will yet make thee to dwell in *t*....... Hos 12:9
hosts, and to keep the feast of *t*....... Zec 14:16
not up to keep the feast of *t*....... Zec 14:18
not up to keep the feast of *t*....... Zec 14:19
scholar, out of the *t* of Jacob....... Mal 2:12
wilt, let us make here three *t*....... Mt 17:4
and let us make three *t*....... Mk 9:5
and let us make three *t*....... Lk 9:33
the Jews' feast of *t* was at hand....... Jn 7:2
country, dwelling in *t* with Isaac....... Heb 11:9

TABITHA

TABITHA (tab´-ith-ah) *Woman raised from the dead by Peter.*

Joppa a certain disciple named *T*....... Acts 9:36
turning him to the body said, *T*....... Acts 9:40

TABLE

also make a *t* of shittim wood....... Ex 25:23
of the staves to bear the *t*....... Ex 25:28
that the *t* may be borne with them....... Ex 25:28
thou shalt set upon the *t*....... Ex 25:30
shalt set the *t* without the vail....... Ex 26:35
candlestick over against the *t* on....... Ex 26:35
shalt put the *t* on the north side....... Ex 26:35

And the *t* and all his vessels, and....... Ex 30:27
And the *t* and his furniture, and the....... Ex 31:8
The *t*, and his staves, and all his....... Ex 35:13
he made the *t* of shittim wood....... Ex 37:10
for the staves to bear the *t*....... Ex 37:14
them with gold, to bear the *t*....... Ex 37:15
the vessels which were upon the *t*....... Ex 37:16
The *t*, and all the vessels thereof....... Ex 39:36
And thou shalt bring in the *t*....... Ex 40:4
he put the *t* in the tent of the....... Ex 40:22
congregation, over against the *t*....... Ex 40:24
upon the pure *t* before the LORD....... Lev 24:6
charge shall be the ark, and the *t*....... Num 3:31
upon the *t* of shewbread they....... Num 4:7
gathered their meat under my *t*....... Judg 1:7
he cometh not unto the king's *t*....... 1Sa 20:29
arose from the *t* in fierce anger....... 1Sa 20:34
eat bread at my *t* continually....... 2Sa 9:7
son shall eat bread alway at my *t*....... 2Sa 9:10
the king, he shall eat at my *t*....... 2Sa 9:11
eat continually at the king's *t*....... 2Sa 9:13
them that did eat at their own *t*....... 1Kin 2:7
be of those that eat at thy *t*....... 1Kin 2:7
that came unto king Solomon's *t*....... 1Kin 4:27
the *t* of gold, whereupon the....... 1Kin 7:48
And the meat of his *t*, and the....... 1Kin 10:5
to pass, as they sat at the *t*....... 1Kin 13:20
hundred, which eat at Jezebel's *t*....... 1Kin 18:19
set for him there a bed, and a *t*....... 2Kin 4:10
tables of shewbread, for every *t*....... 1Chr 28:16
And the meat of his *t*, and the....... 2Chr 9:4
set they in order upon the pure *t*....... 2Chr 13:11
thereof, and the shewbread *t*....... 2Chr 29:18
there were at my *t* an hundred....... Neh 5:17
thy *t* should be full of fatness....... Job 36:16
Thou preparest a *t* before me....... Ps 23:5
Let their *t* become a snare before....... Ps 69:22
God furnish a *t* in the wilderness....... Ps 78:19
olive plants round about thy *t*....... Ps 128:3
them upon the *t* of thine heart....... Prov 3:3
them upon the *t* of thine heart....... Prov 7:3
she hath also furnished her *t*....... Prov 9:2
While the king sitteth at his *t*....... Song 1:12
Prepare the *t*, watch in the....... Is 21:5
go, write it before them in a *t*....... Is 30:8
that prepare a *t* for that troop....... Is 65:11
graven upon the *t* of their heart....... Jer 17:1
a *t* prepared before it, whereupon....... Eze 23:41
be filled at my *t* with horses....... Eze 39:20
This is the *t* that is before the....... Eze 41:22
and they shall come near to my *t*....... Eze 44:16
and they shall speak lies at one *t*....... Dan 11:27
The *t* of the LORD is contemptible....... Mal 1:7
The *t* of the LORD is polluted....... Mal 1:12
which fall from their masters'....... Mt 15:27
yet the dogs under the *t* eat of....... Mk 7:28
And he asked for a writing *t*....... Lk 1:63
which fell from the rich man's *t*....... Lk 16:21
betrayeth me is with me on the *t*....... Lk 22:21
drink at my *t* in my kingdom, and....... Lk 22:30
them that sat at the *t* with him....... Jn 12:2
Now no man at the *t* knew for what....... Jn 13:28
Let their *t* be made a snare, and a....... Rom 11:9
be partakers of the Lord's *t*....... 1Cor 10:21
and of the *t* of devils....... 1Cor 10:21
was the candlestick, and the *t*....... Heb 9:2

TABLES

and I will give thee *t* of stone....... Ex 24:12
two *t* of testimony, *t* of....... Ex 31:18
t of stone, written with the....... Ex 31:18
the two *t* of the testimony were....... Ex 32:15
the *t* were written on both their....... Ex 32:15
the *t* were the work of God, and....... Ex 32:16
writing of God, graven upon the *t*....... Ex 32:16
he cast the *t* out of his hands....... Ex 32:19
Hew thee two *t* of stone like unto....... Ex 34:1
I will write upon these *t* the....... Ex 34:1
words that were in the first *t*....... Ex 34:1
he hewed two *t* of stone like unto....... Ex 34:4
in his hand the two *t* of stone....... Ex 34:4
he wrote upon the *t* the words of....... Ex 34:28
two *t* of testimony in Moses' hand....... Ex 34:29
he wrote them upon two *t* of stone....... Deut 4:13
he wrote them in two *t* of stone....... Deut 5:22
mount to receive the *t* of stone....... Deut 9:9
even the *t* of the covenant which....... Deut 9:9
two *t* of stone written with the....... Deut 9:10
LORD gave me the two *t* of stone....... Deut 9:11
even the *t* of the covenant....... Deut 9:11
the two *t* of the covenant were in....... Deut 9:15
And I took the two *t*, and cast them....... Deut 9:17
Hew thee two *t* of stone like unto....... Deut 10:1
I will write on the *t* the words....... Deut 10:2
in the first *t* which thou brakest....... Deut 10:2
hewed two *t* of stone like unto....... Deut 10:3
having the two *t* in mine hand....... Deut 10:3
And he wrote on the *t*, according....... Deut 10:4
put the *t* in the ark which I had....... Deut 10:5
the ark save the two *t* of stone....... 1Kin 8:9
gave gold for the *t* of shewbread....... 1Chr 28:16
silver for the *t* of silver....... 1Chr 28:16
He made also ten *t*, and placed....... 2Chr 4:8
the *t* whereon the shewbread was....... 2Chr 4:19
two *t* which Moses put therein at....... 2Chr 5:10
For all *t* are full of vomit and....... Is 28:8
the gate were two *t* on this side....... Eze 40:39
two *t* on that side, to slay....... Eze 40:39
of the north gate, were two *t*....... Eze 40:40
the porch of the gate, were two *t*....... Eze 40:40
Four *t* were on this side, and four....... Eze 40:41

T

four t on that side, by the side .... Eze 40:41
eight t, whereupon they slew .... Eze 40:41
the four t were of hewn stone for....... Eze 40:42
upon the t was the flesh of the............ Eze 40:43
vision, and make it plain upon t .... Hab 2:2
temple, and overthrew the t of the ...... Mt 21:12
and pots, brasen vessels, and of t .... Mk 7:4
temple, and overthrew the t of the....... Mk 11:15
money, and overthrew the t .... Jn 2:15
leave the word of God, and serve t ..... Acts 6:2
not in t of stone, but in fleshly 2Cor 3:3
but in fleshly t of the heart 2Cor 3:3
budded, and the t of the covenant .... Heb 9:4

TABLETS
and earrings, and rings, and t .... Ex 35:22
bracelets, rings, earrings, and t .... Num 31:50
legs, and the headbands, and the t ...... Is 3:20

TABOR (ta'-bor)
  1. A mountain in Issachar and Zebulun.
And the coast reacheth to T .... Josh 19:22
saying, Go and draw toward mount T .. Judg 4:6
of Abinoam was gone up to mount T ... Judg 4:12
So Barak went down from mount T ..... Judg 4:14
men were they whom ye slew at T .... Judg 8:18
T and Hermon shall rejoice in thy....... Ps 89:12
hosts, Surely as T is among the .... Jer 46:18
on Mizpah, and a net spread upon T ... Hos 5:1
  2. A plain in Benjamin.
thou shalt come to the plain of T......... 1Sa 10:3
  3. A Levitical city in Zebulun.
her suburbs, T with her suburbs.......... 1Chr 6:77

TABRET
with mirth, and with songs, with t ...... Gen 31:27
place with a psaltery, and a t .... Job 17:6
and aforetime I was as a t .... Job 17:6
And the harp, and the viol, the t .... Is 5:12

TABRETS
to meet king Saul, with t 1Sa 18:6
The mirth of t ceaseth, the noise.......... Is 24:8
lay upon him, it shall be with t .... Is 30:32
shalt again be adorned with thy t .... Jer 31:4
the workmanship of thy t and............. Eze 28:13

TABRIMMON See TABRIMON.

TABRIMON (tab'-rim-on) *Father of Benhadad,
  king of Syria.*
them to Ben-hadad, the son of T......... 1Kin 15:18

TACHES
thou shalt make fifty t of gold............. Ex 26:6
the curtains together with the t .... Ex 26:6
thou shalt make fifty t of brass .... Ex 26:11
put the t into the loops, and................ Ex 26:11
hang up the vail under the t .... Ex 26:33
his tent, and his covering, his t .... Ex 35:11
And he made fifty t of gold .... Ex 36:13
one unto another with the t .... Ex 36:13
he made fifty t of brass to................... Ex 36:18
tent, and all his furniture, his t .... Ex 39:33

TACHMONITE (tak'-mun-ite) See
  HACHMONITE. *Family name of a 'mighty man'
  of David.*
The T that sat in the seat, chief 2Sa 23:8

TACKLING
our own hands the t of the ship .... Acts 27:19

TACKLINGS
Thy t are loosed .... Is 33:23

TADMOR (tad'-mor) *A city rebuilt by
  Solomon.*
T in the wilderness, in the land,.......... 1Kin 9:18
he built T in the wilderness, and......... 2Chr 8:4

TAHAN (ta'-han) See TAHANITES.
  1. A son of Ephraim.
of T, the family of the Tahanites .... Num 26:35
  2. A descendant of Ephraim.
and Telah his son, and T his son,........ 1Chr 7:25

TAHANITES (ta'-han-ites) *Descendants of
  Tahan 1.*
of Tahan, the family of the T............... Num 26:35

TAHAPANES (ta-hap'-a-neze) See
  TAHPANHES. *A city in Egypt.*
T have broken the crown of thy .... Jer 2:16

TAHASH See THAHASH.

TAHATH (ta'-hath)
  1. An Israelite encampment in the wilderness.
from Makheloth, and encamped at T ... Num 33:26
And they departed from T, and .... Num 33:27
  2. Father of Uriel.
T his son, Uriel his son, Uzziah 1Chr 6:24
The son of T, the son of Assir,............ 1Chr 6:37
  3. Father of Eladah.
T his son, and Eladah his son, and...... 1Chr 7:20
  4. Son of Eladah.
and Eladah his son, and T his son,...... 1Chr 7:20

TAHCHEMONITE See TACHMONITE.

TAHKEMONITE See TACHMONITE.

TAHPANHES (tah'-pan-heze) See TAHPANES,
  TAHPENES, TEHAPHNEHES. *Same as
  Tahapanes.*
thus came they even to .... Jer 43:7
of the LORD unto Jeremiah in T........... Jer 43:8
the entry of Pharaoh's house in T........ Jer 43:9

which dwell at Migdol, and at T........... Jer 44:1
and publish in Noph and in T .... Jer 46:14

TAHPENES (tah'-pe-neze) See TAHPANHES.
  Queen of a pharaoh.
wife, the sister of T the queen 1Kin 11:19
the sister of T bare him Genubath....... 1Kin 11:20
whom T weaned in Pharaoh's house 1Kin 11:20

TAHREA (tah'-re-ah) See TAREA. *Son of
  Micah.*
were, Pithon, and Melech, and T......... 1Chr 9:41

TAHTIM-HODSHI (tah'-'tim-hod'shi) *A
  district north of Gilead in Bashan.*
to Gilead, and to the land of T 2Sa 24:6

TAIL
thine hand, and take it by the t .... Ex 4:4
make thee the head, and not the t .... Deut 28:13
the head, and thou shalt be the t .... Deut 28:44
firebrands, and turned t to t .... Judg 15:4
He moveth his t like a cedar................ Job 40:17
cut off from Israel head and t .... Is 9:14
that teacheth lies, he is the t .... Is 9:15
for Egypt, which the head or t .... Is 19:15
his t drew the third part of the .... Rev 12:4

TAILS
in the midst between two t .... Judg 15:4
two t of these smoking firebrands .... Is 7:4
they had t like unto scorpions,............ Rev 9:10
and there were stings in their t .... Rev 9:10
is in their mouth, and in their t .... Rev 9:19
for their t were like unto .... Rev 9:19

TAKE See PREFACE.

TAKEN
which the LORD God had t from man... Gen 2:22
because she was t out of Man.............. Gen 2:23
for out of it wast thou t .... Gen 3:19
the ground from whence he was t .... Gen 3:23
shall be t on him sevenfold................. Gen 4:15
the woman was t into Pharaoh's .... Gen 12:15
so I might have t her to me.................. Gen 12:19
that his brother was t captive .... Gen 14:14
I have t upon me to speak unto .... Gen 18:27
I have t upon me to speak unto .... Gen 18:31
for the woman which thou hast t .... Gen 20:3
servants had violently t away.............. Gen 21:25
where is he that hath t venison .... Gen 27:33
and hath t away thy blessing............... Gen 27:35
now he hath t away my blessing.......... Gen 27:36
that thou hast t my husband................ Gen 30:15
God hath t away my reproach.............. Gen 30:23
Jacob hath t away all that was............ Gen 31:1
Thus God hath t away the cattle.......... Gen 31:9
which God hath t from our father .... Gen 31:16
as captives t with the sword .... Gen 31:26
Now Rachel had t the images .... Gen 31:34
hast thou t us away to die in the .... Ex 14:11
they shall not be t from it .... Ex 25:15
when the cloud was t up from over ..... Ex 40:36
But if the cloud were not t up .... Ex 40:37
not till the day that it was t up............. Ex 40:37
As it was t off from the bullock .... Lev 4:10
as the fat is t away from off the .... Lev 4:31
as the fat of the lamb is t away............ Lev 4:35
or in a thing t away by violence,......... Lev 6:2
the heave shoulder have I t of .... Lev 7:34
that he hath t of the stones.................. Lev 14:43
being t from the children of .... Lev 24:8
I have t the Levites from among .... Num 3:12
neither she be t with the manner .... Num 5:13
of Israel, have I t them unto me.......... Num 8:16
I have t the Levites for all the .... Num 8:18
when the cloud was t up from the .... Num 9:17
the cloud was t up in the morning....... Num 9:21
by night that the cloud was t up .... Num 9:21
but when it was t up, they .... Num 9:22
that the cloud was t up from off.......... Num 10:11
And the tabernacle was t down........... Num 10:17
I have not t one ass from them,.......... Num 16:15
I have t your brethren the .... Num 18:6
t all his land out of his hand,.............. Num 21:26
the sum of the prey that was t .... Num 31:26
Thy servants have t the sum of .... Num 31:49
(For the men of war had t spoil .... Num 31:53
be t from the inheritance of our .... Num 36:3
so shall it be t from the lot of .... Num 36:3
be t away from the inheritance of ...... Num 36:4
But the LORD hath t you, and .... Deut 4:20
a wife, and hath not t her.................... Deut 20:7
thou hast t them captive,.................... Deut 21:10
When a man hath t a wife, and........... Deut 24:1
When a man hath t a new wife .... Deut 24:5
cheer up his wife which he hath t .... Deut 24:5
neither have I t away ought .... Deut 26:14
t away from before thy face............... Deut 28:31
for they have even t of the .... Josh 7:11
that he that is t with the .... Josh 7:15
for the tribe of Judah was t .... Josh 7:16
and Zabdi was t .... Josh 7:17
of the tribe of Judah, was t................ Josh 7:18
shall be, when ye have t the city .... Josh 8:8
that the ambush had t the city .... Josh 8:21
had heard how Joshua had t Ai .... Josh 10:1
against Jerusalem, and had t .... Josh 10:5
forasmuch as the LORD hath t .... Judg 11:36
he told not them that he had t .... Judg 14:6
because he had t his wife .... Judg 15:6
of silver that were t from thee .... Judg 17:2

Ye have t away my gods which I......... Judg 18:24
And the ark of God was t 1Sa 4:11
are dead, and the ark of God is t 1Sa 4:17
tidings that the ark of God was t 1Sa 4:19
because the ark of God is t 1Sa 4:21
for the ark of God is t 1Sa 4:22
which the Philistines had t from.......... 1Sa 7:14
near, the tribe of Benjamin was t 1Sa 10:20
the family of Matri was t.................... 1Sa 10:21
and Saul the son of Kish was t............ 1Sa 10:21
whose ox have I t 1Sa 12:3
or whose ass have I t 1Sa 12:3
neither have thou t ought of any.......... 1Sa 12:4
And Saul and Jonathan were t 1Sa 14:41
And Jonathan was t 1Sa 14:42
that was t from before the LORD,......... 1Sa 21:6
the day when it was t away,................. 1Sa 21:6
had t the women captives, that 1Sa 30:2
their daughters, were t captives........... 1Sa 30:3
David's two wives were t captives 1Sa 30:5
they had t out of the land of the 1Sa 30:16
any thing that they had t to them 1Sa 30:19
hast t his wife to be thy wife,.............. 2Sa 12:9
hast t the wife of Uriah the 2Sa 12:10
have t the city of waters 2Sa 12:27
thou art t in thy mischief,................... 2Sa 16:8
he was t up between the heaven and.... 2Sa 18:9
Now Absalom in his lifetime had t 2Sa 18:18
they cannot be t with hands,.............. 2Sa 23:6
daughter, whom he had t to wife 1Kin 7:8
have t hold upon other gods, and....... 1Kin 9:9
t Gezer, and burnt it with fire,........... 1Kin 9:16
Zimri saw that the city was t 1Kin 16:18
thou killed, and also t possession 1Kin 21:19
the high places were not t away 1Kin 22:43
before I be t away from thee 2Kin 2:9
thou see when I am t from thee 2Kin 2:10
Spirit of the LORD hath t him up......... 2Kin 2:16
And when he had t him, and brought.. 2Kin 4:20
hast t captive with thy sword 2Kin 6:22
the high places were not t away 2Kin 12:3
which he had t out of the hand of 2Kin 13:25
the high places were not t away 2Kin 14:4
king of Israel, Samaria was t 2Kin 18:10
whose altars Hezekiah hath t away 2Kin 18:22
for the king of Babylon had t 2Kin 24:7
household being t for Eleazar............ 1Chr 24:6
for Eleazar, and one t for Ithamar...... 1Chr 24:6
which he had t from mount Ephraim .. 2Chr 15:8
were not t away out of Israel 2Chr 15:17
which Asa his father had t 2Chr 17:2
in that thou hast t away the 2Chr 19:3
the high places were not t away 2Chr 20:33
which ye have t captive of your 2Chr 28:11
had t Beth-shemesh............................ 2Chr 28:18
For the king had t counsel 2Chr 30:2
Hezekiah t away his high places 2Chr 32:12
For they have t of their...................... Ezr 9:2
have t strange wives of the .... Ezr 10:2
have t strange wives, to increase....... Ezr 10:10
let all them which have t strange........ Ezr 10:14
end with all the men that had t .... Ezr 10:17
found that had t strange wives........... Ezr 10:18
All these had t strange wives............. Ezr 10:44
had t of them bread and wine,............ Neh 5:15
his son Johanan had t the................... Neh 6:18
who had t her for his daughter,.......... Est 2:15
So Esther was t unto king.................. Est 2:16
ring, which he had t from Haman....... Est 8:2
gave, and the LORD hath t away......... Job 1:21
he hath also t me by my neck, and..... Job 16:12
and t the crown from my head........... Job 19:9
because he hath violently t away .... Job 20:19
For thou hast t a pledge from thy ...... Job 22:6
they are t out of the way as all.......... Job 24:24
who hath t away my judgment .... Job 27:2
Iron is t out of the earth, and............ Job 28:2
of affliction have t hold upon me....... Job 30:16
God hath t away my judgment .... Job 34:5
shall be t away without hand .... Job 34:20
they had is their own foot t............... Ps 9:15
let them be t in the devices that......... Ps 10:2
iniquities have t hold upon me .... Ps 40:12
let them even be t in their pride .... Ps 59:12
They have t crafty counsel................ Ps 83:3
Thou hast t away all thy wrath .... Ps 85:3
Horror hath t hold upon me............... Ps 119:53
Thy testimonies have I t as an........... Ps 119:111
and anguish have t hold on me.......... Ps 119:143
shall keep thy foot from being t .... Prov 3:26
and their sleep is t away, unless......... Prov 4:16
thou art t with the words of thy .... Prov 6:2
He hath t a bag of money with him... Prov 7:20
be t in their own naughtiness............. Prov 11:6
which I had t under the sun............... Eccl 2:18
to it, nor any thing t from it.............. Eccl 3:14
but the sinner shall be t by her .... Eccl 7:26
fishes that are t in an evil net .... Eccl 9:12
which he had t with the tongs........... Is 6:6
shame their iniquity is t away .... Is 14:2
have t evil counsel against thee,...... Is 7:5
the spoil of Samaria shall be t .... Is 8:4
be broken, and be snared, and be t ... Is 8:15
that his burden shall be t away .... Is 10:27
they have t up their lodging at .... Is 10:29
And gladness is t away, and joy out .. Is 16:10
Damascus is t away from being a..... Is 17:1
pangs have t hold upon me, as the .... Is 21:3
Who hath t this counsel against........ Is 23:8
the pit shall be t in the snare............ Is 24:18

and be broken, and snared, and *t* .... Is 28:13
that shall not be *t* down .... Is 33:20
whose altars Hezekiah hath *t* away.... Is 36:7
Thou whom I have *t* from the ends.... Is 41:9
the prey be *t* from the mighty........... Is 49:24
of the mighty shall be *t* away .... Is 49:25
I have *t* out of thine hand the........... Is 51:22
my people is *t* away for nought .... Is 52:5
He was *t* from prison and from......... Is 53:8
and merciful men are *t* away.............. Is 57:1
that the righteous is *t* away from...... Is 57:1
like the wind, have *t* us away............ Is 64:6
husband with the wife shall be *t* ...... Jer 6:11
anguish hath *t* hold of us .... Jer 6:24
ashamed, they are dismayed and *t* .... Jer 8:9
astonishment hath *t* hold on me........ Jer 8:21
them, yea, they have *t* root.............. Jer 12:2
for I have *t* away my peace from ...... Jer 16:5
of them shall be *t* up a curse by........ Jer 29:22
his hand, but shalt surely be *t* .... Jer 34:3
but shalt be *t* by the hand of the...... Jer 38:23
the day that Jerusalem was *t* .... Jer 38:28
he was there when Jerusalem was *t* .. Jer 38:28
and when they had *t* him, they......... Jer 39:5
when he had *t* him being bound in .... Jer 40:1
in your cities that ye have *t* .... Jer 40:10
Kiriathaim is confounded and *t* .... Jer 48:1
treasures, thou shalt also be *t* .... Jer 48:7
gladness is *t* from the plentiful......... Jer 48:33
Kerioth is *t*, and the strong holds..... Jer 48:41
the pit shall be *t* in the snare........... Jer 48:44
for thy sons are *t* captives............... Jer 48:46
Lord, that he hath *t* against Edom..... Jer 49:20
anguish and sorrows have *t* her......... Jer 49:24
hath *t* counsel against you .... Jer 49:30
say, Babylon is *t*, Bel is................... Jer 50:2
from thence she shall be *t* .... Jer 50:9
for thee, and thou art also *t* .... Jer 50:24
that he hath *t* against Babylon .... Jer 50:45
that his city is *t* at one end.............. Jer 51:31
How is Sheshach *t* .... Jer 51:41
Babylon, and her mighty men are *t* ... Jer 51:56
he hath violently *t* away his............. Lam 2:6
was *t* in their pits, of whom we......... Lam 4:20
him, and he shall be *t* in my snare.... Eze 12:13
Shall wood be *t* thereof to do any..... Eze 15:3
Thou hast also *t* thy fair jewels........ Eze 16:17
Moreover thou hast *t* thy sons.......... Eze 16:20
with whom thou hast *t* pleasure........ Eze 16:37
hath *t* the king thereof, and the....... Eze 17:12
hath *t* of the king's seed, and.......... Eze 17:13
him, and hath *t* an oath of him .... Eze 17:13
he hath also *t* the mighty of the....... Eze 17:13
him, and he shall be *t* in my snare.... Eze 17:20
neither hath *t* any increase.............. Eze 18:8
upon usury, and hath *t* increase....... Eze 18:13
That hath *t* off his hand from the ..... Eze 18:17
he was *t* in their pit, and they......... Eze 19:4
he was *t* in their pit .... Eze 19:8
the iniquity, that they may be *t* .... Eze 21:23
ye shall be *t* with the hand .... Eze 21:24
In thee have they *t* gifts to shed ...... Eze 22:12
thou hast *t* usury and increase, and.. Eze 22:12
they have *t* the treasure and .... Eze 22:25
and have *t* vengeance with a............ Eze 25:15
they have *t* cedars from Lebanon...... Eze 27:5
he is *t* away in his iniquity............... Eze 33:6
ye are *t* up in the lips of .... Eze 36:3
his father Nebuchadnezzar had *t* ...... Dan 5:2
the golden vessels that were *t* .... Dan 5:3
So Daniel was *t* up out of the den..... Dan 6:23
they had their dominion *t* away........ Dan 7:12
the daily sacrifice was *t* away .... Dan 8:11
when he hath *t* away the multitude... Dan 11:12
daily sacrifice shall be *t* away .... Dan 12:11
of the sea also shall be *t* away.......... Hos 4:3
Because ye have *t* my silver.............. Joel 3:5
of his den, if he have *t* nothing......... Amos 3:4
earth, and have *t* nothing at all........ Amos 3:5
be *t* out that dwell in Samaria in ...... Amos 3:12
sword, and have *t* away your horses... Amos 4:10
Have we not *t* to us horns by our...... Amos 6:13
have ye *t* away my glory for ever....... Mic 2:9
for kings have *t* thee as a woman...... Mic 4:9
The Lord hath *t* away thy .... Zeph 3:15
and thy city shall be *t*, and the......... Zec 14:2
that were *t* with divers diseases........ Mt 4:24
bridegroom shall be *t* from them....... Mt 9:15
from him shall be *t* away even........... Mt 13:12
It is because we have *t* no bread........ Mt 16:7
of God shall be *t* from you .... Mt 21:43
the one shall be *t*, and the other....... Mt 24:40
the one shall be *t*, and the other....... Mt 24:41
be *t* away even that which he hath .... Mt 25:29
And when Joseph had *t* the body....... Mt 27:59
had *t* counsel, they gave large.......... Mt 28:12
shall be *t* away from them................ Mk 2:20
from him shall be *t* even than .... Mk 4:25
when he had *t* the five loaves and..... Mk 6:41
when he had *t* him in his arms, he..... Mk 9:36
Forasmuch as many have *t* in hand ... Lk 1:1
mother was *t* with a great fever........ Lk 4:38
all the night, and have *t* nothing ...... Lk 5:5
of the fishes which they had *t* .... Lk 5:9
a man which was *t* with a palsy .... Lk 5:18
shall be *t* away from them................ Lk 5:35
the piece that was *t* out of the .... Lk 5:36
from him shall be *t* even .... Lk 8:18
for they were *t* with great fear......... Lk 8:37
there was *t* up of fragments that ...... Lk 9:17

---

shall not be *t* away from her............. Lk 10:42
for ye have *t* away the key of............ Lk 11:52
the one shall be *t*, and the other....... Lk 17:34
the one shall be *t*, and the other....... Lk 17:35
the one shall be *t*, and the other....... Lk 17:36
if I have *t* any thing from any........... Lk 19:8
he hath shall be *t* away from him...... Lk 19:26
And some of them would have *t* him .. Jn 7:44
unto him a woman *t* in adultery........ Jn 8:3
this woman was *t* in adultery............ Jn 8:4
had *t* his garments, and was set........ Jn 13:12
and that they might be *t* away.......... Jn 19:31
seeth the stone *t* away from the........ Jn 20:1
They have *t* away the Lord out of ..... Jn 20:2
Because they have *t* away my Lord .... Jn 20:13
the day in which he was *t* up .... Acts 1:2
while they beheld, he was *t* up.......... Acts 1:9
which is *t* up from you into .... Acts 1:11
same day that he was *t* up from......... Acts 1:22
foreknowledge of God, ye have *t* ...... Acts 2:23
many *t* with palsies, and that were ... Acts 8:7
his judgment was *t* away.................. Acts 8:33
for his life is *t* from the earth........... Acts 8:33
when they had *t* security of Jason .... Acts 17:9
the third loft, and was *t* up dead ...... Acts 20:9
when we had *t* our leave one of........ Acts 21:6
This man was *t* of the Jews .... Acts 23:27
Which when they had *t* up, they .... Acts 27:17
should be saved was then *t* away....... Acts 27:20
fasting, having *t* nothing.................. Acts 27:33
when they had *t* up the anchors, ... Acts 27:40
word of God hath *t* none effect......... Rom 9:6
might be *t* away from among you....... 1Cor 5:2
There hath no temptation *t* you 1Cor 10:13
Lord, the vail shall be *t* away............ 2Cor 3:16
being *t* from you for a short time 1Th 2:17
until he be *t* out of the way.............. 2Th 2:7
Let not a widow be *t* into the 1Ti 5:9
who are *t* captive by him at his......... 2Ti 2:26
For every high priest *t* from............. Heb 5:1
brute beasts, made to be *t* 2Pet 2:12
And when he had *t* the book.............. Rev 5:8
because thou hast *t* to thee thy .... Rev 11:17
And the beast was *t*, and with him .... Rev 19:20

TAKER

as with the *t* of usury, so with.......... Is 24:2

TAKEST

the water which thou *t* out of the ..... Ex 4:9
When thou *t* the sum of the .... Ex 30:12
the journey that thou *t* shall not...... Judg 4:9
if thou *t* heed to fulfil the 1Chr 22:13
thou *t* away their breath, they......... Ps 104:29
that thou *t* knowledge of him........... Ps 144:3
labour which thou *t* under the sun.... Eccl 9:9
our soul, and thou *t* no knowledge .... Is 58:3
thou *t* up that thou layedst not....... Lk 19:21

TAKETH

guiltless that *t* his name in vain .... Ex 20:7
guiltless that *t* his name in vain .... Deut 5:11
not persons, nor *t* reward................. Deut 10:17
for he *t* a man's life to pledge.......... Deut 24:6
her hand, and *t* him by the secrets ... Deut 25:11
Cursed be he that *t* reward to .... Deut 27:25
t them, beareth them on her wings... Deut 32:11
I shall come according to the .... Josh 7:14
t it, to him will I give Achsah .... Josh 15:16
t it, to him will I give Achsah .... Judg 1:12
t away the reproach from Israel 1Sa 17:26
as a man *t* away dung, till it be 1Kin 14:10
it even out of the thorns, and............ Job 5:5
He *t* the wise in their own............... Job 5:13
he *t* away, who can hinder him......... Job 9:12
t away the understanding of the ...... Job 12:20
He *t* away the heart of the chief ...... Job 12:24
trembling *t* hold on my flesh............ Job 21:6
gained, when God *t* away his............ Job 27:8
He *t* it with his eyes....................... Job 40:24
nor *t* up a reproach against his .... Ps 15:3
nor *t* reward against the innocent..... Ps 15:5
The Lord *t* my part with them .... Ps 118:7
Happy shall he be, that *t* .... Ps 137:9
he *t* not pleasure in the legs of........ Ps 147:10
The Lord *t* pleasure in them that...... Ps 147:11
For the Lord *t* pleasure in his .... Ps 149:4
which *t* away the life of the............. Prov 1:19
his spirit than he that *t* a city.......... Prov 16:32
A wicked man *t* a gift out of the ...... Prov 17:23
As he that *t* away a garment in......... Prov 25:20
is like one that *t* a dog by the.......... Prov 26:17
The Spider *t* hold with her hands,.... Prov 30:28
labour which he *t* under the sun .... Eccl 1:3
his heart *t* not rest in the night .... Eccl 2:23
t under the sun all the days of......... Eccl 5:18
and as a sheep that no man *t* up .... Is 13:14
he *t* up the isles as a very................ Is 40:15
t the cypress and the oak, which...... Is 44:14
neither is there any that *t* her.......... Is 51:18
it, and *t* hold of my covenant........... Is 56:6
which *t* strangers instead of her .... Eze 16:32
of the trumpet, and *t* not warning .... Eze 33:4
But he that *t* warning shall............... Eze 33:5
As the shepherd *t* out of the............ Amos 3:12
Then the devil *t* him up into the...... Mt 4:5
the devil *t* him up into an................ Mt 4:8
to fill it up *t* from the garment .... Mt 9:16
he that *t* not his cross, and .... Mt 10:38
t with himself seven other .... Mt 12:45
And after six days Jesus *t* Peter........ Mt 17:1
filled it up *t* away from the old .... Mk 2:21

---

t away the word that was sown in..... Mk 4:15
he *t* the father and the mother of..... Mk 5:40
six days Jesus *t* with him Peter......... Mk 9:2
And wheresoever he *t* him, he.......... Mk 9:18
he *t* with him Peter and James and ... Mk 14:33
him that *t* away thy cloke forbid ...... Lk 6:29
of him that *t* away thy goods ask...... Lk 6:30
t away the word out of their .... Lk 8:12
And, lo, a spirit *t* him, and he .... Lk 9:39
he *t* from him all his armour .... Lk 11:22
t to him seven other spirits more ..... Lk 11:26
for my lord *t* away from me the......... Lk 16:3
which *t* away the sin of the world ..... Jn 1:29
No man *t* it from me, but I lay it .... Jn 10:18
that beareth not fruit he *t* away .... Jn 15:2
and your joy no man *t* from you........ Jn 16:22
t bread, and giveth them, and fish.... Jn 21:13
God unrighteous who *t* vengeance .... Rom 3:5
He *t* the wise in their own............... 1Cor 3:19
For in eating every one *t* before....... 1Cor 11:21
no man *t* this honour unto himself .... Heb 5:4
he *t* away the first, that he may....... Heb 10:9

TAKING

of persons, nor *t* of gifts.................. 2Chr 19:7
I have seen the foolish *t* root .... Job 5:3
by *t* heed thereto according to .... Ps 119:9
At the noise of the *t* of Babylon........ Jer 50:46
the house of Judah by *t* vengeance ... Eze 25:12
also to go, *t* them by their arms........ Hos 11:3
Which of you by *t* thought can add ... Mt 6:27
man is as a man *t* a far journey......... Mk 13:34
t him up into an high mountain,........ Lk 4:5
which of you with *t* thought can .... Lk 12:25
t up that I laid not down, and .... Lk 19:22
had spoken of *t* of rest in sleep........ Jn 11:13
t occasion by the commandment,...... Rom 7:8
t occasion by the commandment,...... Rom 7:11
but *t* my leave of them, I went......... 2Cor 2:13
t wages of them, to do you.............. 2Cor 11:8
t the shield of faith, wherewith .... Eph 6:16
In flaming fire *t* vengeance on 2Th 1:8
t the oversight thereof, not by 1Pet 5:2
t nothing of the Gentiles................. 3Jn 7

TALE

the *t* of the bricks, which they .... Ex 5:8
shall ye deliver the *t* of bricks.......... Ex 5:18
gave them in full *t* to the king 1Sa 18:27
should bring them in and out by *t* 1Chr 9:28
our years as a *t* that is told .... Ps 90:9

TALEBEARER

down as a *t* among thy people.......... Lev 19:16
A *t* revealeth secrets....................... Prov 11:13
The words of a *t* are as wounds......... Prov 18:8
about as a *t* revealeth secrets .... Prov 20:19
so where there is no *t*, the .... Prov 26:20
The words of a *t* are as wounds......... Prov 26:22

TALENT

Of a *t* of pure gold shall he make...... Ex 25:39
Of a *t* of pure gold made he it,......... Ex 37:24
hundred talents, a *t* for a socket ...... Ex 38:27
the weight whereof was a *t* of.......... 2Sa 12:30
else thou shalt pay a *t* of silver........ 1Kin 20:39
a *t* of silver, and two changes of 2Kin 5:22
talents of silver, and a *t* of gold....... 2Kin 23:33
and found it to weigh a *t* of gold 1Chr 20:2
talents of silver and a *t* of gold........ 2Chr 36:3
there was lifted up a *t* of lead.......... Zec 5:7
which had received the one *t* came.... Mt 25:24
and went and hid thy *t* in the earth... Mt 25:25
Take therefore the *t* from him.......... Mt 25:28
stone about the weight of a *t* .... Rev 16:21

TALENTS

offering, was twenty and nine *t* .... Ex 38:24
the congregation was an hundred *t* ... Ex 38:25
of the hundred *t* of silver were......... Ex 38:27
hundred sockets of the hundred *t* .... Ex 38:27
of the offering was seventy *t* .... Ex 38:29
to the king sixscore *t* of gold............ 1Kin 9:14
gold, four hundred and twenty *t* 1Kin 9:28
twenty *t* of gold, and of spices......... 1Kin 10:10
threescore and six *t* of gold............. 1Kin 10:14
of Shemer for two *t* of silver............ 1Kin 16:24
and took with him ten *t* of silver...... 2Kin 5:5
said, Be content, take two *t* 2Kin 5:23
bound two *t* of silver in two bags...... 2Kin 5:23
gave Pul a thousand *t* of silver......... 2Kin 15:19
Judah three hundred *t* of silver 2Kin 18:14
of silver and thirty *t* of gold............ 2Kin 18:14
tribute of an hundred *t* of silver 2Kin 23:33
of Ammon seven a thousand *t* of 1Chr 19:6
an hundred thousand *t* of gold.......... 1Chr 22:14
a thousand thousand *t* of silver........ 1Chr 22:14
Even three thousand *t* of gold........... 1Chr 29:4
seven thousand *t* of refined 1Chr 29:4
of God of gold five thousand *t* 1Chr 29:7
and of silver ten thousand *t* 1Chr 29:7
and of brass eighteen thousand 1Chr 29:7
and one hundred thousand *t* of iron... 1Chr 29:7
gold, amounting to six hundred *t* 2Chr 3:8
fifty *t* of gold, and brought them on .. 2Chr 8:18
twenty *t* of gold, and of spices......... 2Chr 9:9
and threescore and six *t* of gold 2Chr 9:13
Israel for an hundred *t* of silver 2Chr 25:6
shall we do for the hundred *t*........... 2Chr 25:9
same year an hundred *t* of silver....... 2Chr 27:5
land in an hundred *t* of silver........... 2Chr 36:3
Unto an hundred *t* of silver.............. Ezr 7:22
fifty *t* of silver, and silver.............. Ezr 8:26

TALES (continued)

and silver vessels an hundred *t* .... Ezr 8:26
and of gold an hundred *t* .... Ezr 8:26
I will pay ten thousand *t* of .... Est 3:9
which owed him ten thousand *t* .... Mt 18:24
And unto one he gave five *t* .... Mt 25:15
that had received the five *t* went .... Mt 25:16
same, and made them other five *t* .... Mt 25:16
he that had received five *t* came .... Mt 25:20
came and brought other five *t* .... Mt 25:20
thou deliveredst unto me five *t* .... Mt 25:20
gained beside then five *t* more .... Mt 25:20
also that had received two *t* came .... Mt 25:22
thou deliveredst unto me two *t* .... Mt 25:22
gained two other *t* beside them .... Mt 25:22
give it unto him which hath ten *t* .... Mt 25:28

TALES

men that carry *t* to shed blood .... Eze 22:9
words seemed to them as idle *t* .... Lk 24:11

TALITHA (tal'-ith-ah) *Aramaic for damsel.*

hand, and said unto her, T cumi .... Mk 5:41

TALK

come down and talk there .... Num 11:17
this day that God doth *t* with man......... Deut 5:24
shalt *t* of them when thou sittest .... Deut 6:7
T no more so exceeding proudly.............. 1Sa 2:3
t not with us in the Jews' 2Kin 18:26
t ye of all his wondrous works 1Chr 16:9
a man full of *t* be justified .... Job 11:2
and *t* deceitfully for him .... Job 13:7
he reason with unprofitable *t* .... Job 15:3
they *t* to the grief of those whom .... Ps 69:26
My tongue also shall *t* of thy .... Ps 71:24
all thy work, and *t* of thy doings .... Ps 77:12
t ye of all his wondrous works .... Ps 105:2
so shall I *t* of thy wondrous.................. Ps 119:27
of thy kingdom, and *t* of thy power...... Ps 145:11
awakest, it shall *t* with thee .... Prov 6:22
but the *t* of the lips tendeth.................. Prov 14:23
and their lips *t* of mischief .... Prov 10:13
the end of his *t* is mischievous............. Eccl 10:13
yet let me *t* with thee of thy .... Jer 12:1
and I will there *t* with thee.................... Eze 3:22
this my lord *t* with this my lord .... Dan 10:17
they might entangle him in his *t* .... Mt 22:15
I will not *t* much with you .... Jn 14:30

TALKED

Cain *t* with Abel his brother................... Gen 4:8
and God *t* with him, saying, ... Gen 17:3
in the place where he *t* with him .... Gen 35:13
in the place where he *t* with him .... Gen 35:14
that his brethren *t* with him .... Gen 45:15
I have *t* with you from heaven.............. Ex 20:22
and the Lord *t* with Moses .... Ex 33:9
face showe while he *t* with him .... Ex 34:29
and Moses *t* with them .... Ex 34:31
The Lord *t* with you face to face .... Deut 5:4
he went down, and *t* with the woman .. Judg 14:7
while Saul *t* unto the priest, ... 1Sa 14:19
as he *t* with them, behold, there 1Sa 17:23
lo, while she yet *t* with the king............ 1Kin 1:22
pass, as they still went on, and *t* 2Kin 2:11
And while he yet *t* with them 2Kin 6:33
the king *t* with Gehazi the 2Kin 8:4
as he *t* with him, that the king............. 2Chr 25:16
hear that I have *t* with thee .... Jer 38:25
t with me, and said, O Daniel, I .... Dan 9:22
the angel that *t* with me .... Zec 1:9
that *t* with me with good words............ Zec 1:13
unto the angel that *t* with me............... Zec 1:19
the angel that *t* with me went .... Zec 2:3
the angel that *t* with me came .... Zec 4:1
spake to the angel that *t* with .... Zec 4:4
the angel that *t* with me answered .... Zec 4:5
angel that *t* with me went forth .... Zec 5:5
I to the angel that *t* with me .... Zec 5:10
there *t* with me the angel .... Zec 6:4
While he yet *t* to the people, ... Mt 12:46
And immediately he *t* with them .... Mk 6:50
they *t* with him two men, which .... Lk 9:30
they *t* together of all these .... Lk 24:14
while he *t* with us by the way, and ...... Lk 24:32
that he *t* with the woman .... Jn 4:27
as he *t* with him, he went in, and......... Acts 10:27
t a long while, even till break .... Acts 20:11
they *t* between themselves, saying .... Acts 26:31
t with me, saying unto me, Come.......... Rev 17:1
t with me, saying, Come hither, I .... Rev 21:9
he that *t* with me had a golden .... Rev 21:15

TALKERS

ye are taken up in the lips of *t* .... Eze 36:3
there are many unruly and vain *t* .... Titus 1:10

TALKEST

me a sign that thou *t* with me............... Judg 6:17
while thou yet *t* there with the............. 1Kin 1:14
or, Why *t* thou with her......................... Jn 4:27

TALKETH

and his tongue *t* of judgment .... Ps 37:30
him, and it is he that *t* with thee.......... Jn 9:37

TALKING

And he left off *t* with him .... Gen 17:22
either he is *t*, or he is pursuing 1Kin 18:27
And while they were yet *t* with him ...... Est 6:14
The princes refrained *t*, and laid.......... Job 29:9
of thy people still are *t* against .... Eze 33:30
them Moses and Elias *t* with .... Mt 17:3
and they were *t* with Jesus .... Mk 9:4

Neither filthiness, nor foolish *t* .... Eph 5:4
as it were of a trumpet *t* with me .... Rev 4:1

TALL

a people great, and many, and *t* .... Deut 2:10
A people great, and many, and .... Deut 2:21
A people great and *t*, the children .... Deut 9:2
will cut down the *t* cedar trees 2Kin 19:23
cut down the *t* cedars thereof .... Is 37:24

TALLER

people is greater and *t* than we .... Deut 1:28

TALMAI (tal'-mahee)

1. A son of Anak.

where Ahiman, Sheshai, and T .... Num 13:22
Sheshai, and Ahiman, and T .... Josh 15:14
slew Sheshai, and Ahiman, and T .... Judg 1:10

2. A king of Geshur.

the daughter of T king of Geshur 2Sa 3:3
But Absalom fled, and went to T 2Sa 13:37
the daughter of T king of Geshur 1Chr 3:2

TALMON (tal'-mon) *A Levite in Jerusalem.*

were, Shallum, and Akkub, and T 1Chr 9:17
of Ater, the children of T........................ Ezr 2:42
of Ater, the children of T........................ Neh 7:45
Moreover the porters, Akkub, T .... Neh 11:19
Bakbukiah, Obadiah, Meshullam, T .... Neh 12:25

TAMAH (ta'-mah) See THAMAH. *A family of exiles.*

of Sisera, the children of T...................... Neh 7:55

TAMAR (ta'-mar) See THAMAR.

1. Wife of Er.

his firstborn, whose name was T............. Gen 38:6
Then said Judah to T his daughter .... Gen 38:11
T went and dwelt in her father's .... Gen 38:11
And it was told T, saying, Behold........... Gen 38:13
T thy daughter in law hath played......... Gen 38:24
whom T bare unto Judah, of the .... Ruth 4:12
T his daughter in law bare him............... 1Chr 2:4

2. A daughter of Absalom.

a fair sister, whose name was T.............. 2Sa 13:1
he fell sick for his sister T 2Sa 13:2
And Amnon said unto him, I love T 2Sa 13:4
I pray thee, let my sister T come 2Sa 13:5
let T my sister come, and make me 2Sa 13:6
Then David sent home to T...................... 2Sa 13:7
So T went to her brother Amnon's.......... 2Sa 13:8
And Amnon said unto T, Bring the 2Sa 13:10
T took the cakes which she had 2Sa 13:10
T put ashes on her head, and rent 2Sa 13:19
So T remained desolate in her 2Sa 13:20
he had forced his sister T 2Sa 13:22
day that he forced his sister T 2Sa 13:32
the concubines, and T their sister 1Chr 3:9

3. A daughter of Absalom.

and one daughter, whose name was T 2Sa 14:27

4. A city in Judah.

from T even to the waters of................... Eze 47:19
T unto the waters of strife in.................. Eze 48:28

TAME

neither could any man *t* him .... Mk 5:4
But the tongue can no man *t* .... Jas 3:8

TAMED

and of things in the sea, is *t* .... Jas 3:7
and hath been *t* of mankind .... Jas 3:7

TAMMUZ (tam'-muz) *A Syrian god.*

there sat women weeping for T................ Eze 8:14

TANACH (ta'-nak) See TAANACH. *Same as Taanach.*

Manasseh, T with her suburbs, and........ Josh 21:25

TANHUMETH (tan'-hu-meth) *Father of Seraiah.*

the son of T the Netophathite................. 2Kin 25:23
Kareah, and Seraiah the son of T .... Jer 40:8

TANNER

days in Joppa with one Simon a *t* .... Acts 9:43
He lodgeth with one Simon a *t* .... Acts 10:6
of one Simon a *t* by the sea side........... Acts 10:32

TAPESTRY

decked my bed with coverings of *t* .... Prov 7:16
She maketh herself coverings of *t*......... Prov 31:22

TAPHATH (ta'-fath) *A daughter of Solomon.*

which had T the daughter of 1Kin 4:11

TAPPUAH (tap'-pu-ah)

1. A city in Judah.

The king of T, one............................... Josh 12:17
and Zanoah, and En-gannim, T .... Josh 15:34

2. A city in Ephraim.

The border went out from T.................. Josh 16:8
Now Manasseh had the land of T .... Josh 17:8
but T on the border of Manasseh .... Josh 17:8

3. A son of Hebron.

Korah, and T, and......................... 1Chr 2:43

TARAH (ta'-rah) *An Israelite encampment in the wilderness.*

from Tahath, and pitched at T............... Num 33:27
And they removed from T, and .... Num 33:28

TARALAH (tar'-a-lah) *A city in Benjamin.*

And Rekem, and Irpeel, and T.............. Josh 18:27

TARE

t his garments, and lay on the.............. 2Sa 13:31
t forty and two children of them.......... 2Kin 2:24

---

him, straightway the spirit *t* him .... Mk 9:20
devil threw him down, and *t* him.......... Lk 9:42

TAREA (ta'-reah) See TAHREA. *A son of Micah.*

were, Pithon, and Melech, and T............ 1Chr 8:35

TARES

sowed *t* among the wheat, and went..... Mt 13:25
fruit, then appeared the *t* also.............. Mt 13:26
from whence then hath it *t* .... Mt 13:27
lest while ye gather up the *t* .... Mt 13:29
Gather ye together first the *t* .... Mt 13:30
the parable of the *t* of the field .... Mt 13:36
but the *t* are the children of the .... Mt 13:38
As therefore the *t* are gathered............. Mt 13:40

TARGET

legs, and a *t* of brass between his......... 1Sa 17:6
shekels of gold went to one *t*................ 1Kin 10:16
of beaten gold went to one *t* 2Chr 9:15

TARGETS

made two hundred *t* of beaten gold...... 1Kin 10:16
made two hundred *t* of beaten gold...... 2Chr 9:15
had an army of men that bare *t*............ 2Chr 14:8

TARPELITES (tar'-pel-ites) *Foreigners resettled in Israel.*

the Apharsathchites, the T .... Ezr 4:9

TARRIED

were with him, and *t* all night............... Gen 24:54
t there all night, because the .... Gen 28:11
and *t* all night in the mount .... Gen 31:54
when the cloud *t* long upon the............ Num 9:19
that the cloud *t* upon the...................... Num 9:22
they *t* till they were ashamed............... Judg 3:25
And Ehud escaped while they *t* .... Judg 3:26
they *t* until afternoon, and they .... Judg 19:8
that she *t* a little in the house .... Ruth 2:7
he *t* seven days, according to the 1Sa 13:8
Saul *t* in the uttermost part of 1Sa 14:2
But David *t* still at Jerusalem 2Sa 11:1
t in a place that was far off 2Sa 15:17
and they *t* there...................................... 2Sa 15:29
but he *t* longer than the set time.......... 2Sa 20:5
(for he *t* at Jericho,) he said 2Kin 2:18
But David *t* at Jerusalem 1Chr 20:1
she that *t* at home divided the .... Ps 68:12
While the bridegroom *t*, they all........... Mt 25:5
marvelled that he *t* so long in .... Lk 1:21
the child Jesus *t* behind in .... Lk 2:43
there he *t* with them, and baptized ..... Jn 3:22
that he *t* many days in Joppa with........ Acts 9:43
And after they had *t* there a space....... Acts 15:33
Paul after this *t* there yet a .... Acts 18:18
going before *t* for us at Troas .... Acts 20:5
at Samos, and *t* at Trogyllium .... Acts 20:15
disciples, we *t* there seven days .... Acts 21:4
as we *t* there many days, there............. Acts 21:10
when he had *t* among them more .... Acts 25:6
the fourteenth day that ye have *t* .... Acts 27:33
Syracuse, we *t* there three days .... Acts 28:12

TARRIEST

And now why *t* thou .... Acts 22:16

TARRIETH

his part be that *t* by the stuff 1Sa 30:24
that *t* not for man, nor waiteth .... Mic 5:7

TARRY

all night, and wash your feet, ... Gen 19:2
t with him a few days, until thy .... Gen 27:44
found favour in thine eyes, *t* .... Gen 30:27
come down unto me, *t* not................... Gen 45:9
out of Egypt, and could not *t* .... Ex 12:39
T ye here for us, until we come............. Ex 24:14
shall *t* abroad out of his tent .... Lev 14:8
t ye also here this night, that I .... Num 22:19
Why *t* the wheels of his chariots........ Judg 5:28
I will *t* until thou come again .... Judg 6:18
t all night, and let thine heart .... Judg 19:6
evening, I pray you *t* all night............ Judg 19:9
the man would not *t* that night .... Judg 19:10
Would ye *t* for them till they .... Ruth 1:13
T this night, and it shall be in.............. Ruth 3:13
t until thou have weaned him 1Sa 1:23
seven days shalt thou *t*, till I 1Sa 10:8
unto us, T until we come to you........... 1Sa 14:9
T at Jericho until your beards be 2Sa 10:5
T here to day also, and to morrow 2Sa 11:12
I will *t* in the plain of the 2Sa 15:28
I may not *t* thus with thee.................. 2Sa 18:14
there will not *t* one with thee............. 2Sa 19:7
unto Elisha, T here, I pray thee 2Kin 2:2
him, Elisha, T here, I pray thee 2Kin 2:4
And Elijah said unto him, T................. 2Kin 2:6
if we *t* till the morning light, ... 2Kin 7:9
open the door, and fled, and *t* not 2Kin 9:3
glory of this, and *t* at home 2Kin 14:10
T at Jericho until your beards be 1Chr 19:5
lies shall not *t* in my sight .... Ps 101:7
They that *t* long at the wine .... Prov 23:30
off, and my salvation shall not *t* .... Is 46:13
turneth aside to *t* for a night............. Jer 14:8
though it *t*, wait for it .... Hab 2:3
will surely come, it will not *t* .... Hab 2:3
ye here, and watch with me.................. Mt 26:38
t ye here, and watch .... Mk 14:34
And he went in to *t* with them.......... Lk 24:29
but *t* ye in the city of Jerusalem .... Lk 24:49
him that he would *t* with them .... Jn 4:40

TARRYING

If I will that he *t* till I come	Jn 21:22
If I will that he *t* till I come	Jn 21:23
prayed they him to *t* certain days	Acts 10:48
him to *t* longer time with them	Acts 18:20
were desired to *t* with them seven	Acts 28:14
to eat, *t* one for another	1Cor 11:33
but I trust to *t* a while with you	1Cor 16:7
But I will *t* at Ephesus until	1Cor 16:8
But if I *t* long, that thou mayest	1Ti 3:15
come will come, and will not *t*	Heb 10:37

TARRYING

make no *t*, O my God	Ps 40:17
O Lord, make no *t*	Ps 70:5

TARSHISH (*tar′-shish*) See **THARSHISH**.

1. A son of Javan.

Elishah, and *T*, Kittim, and Dodanim	Gen 10:4
Elishah, and *T*, Kittim, and Dodanim	1Chr 1:7

2. Spain.

to *T* with the servants of Huram	2Chr 9:21
came the ships of *T* bringing gold	2Chr 9:21
with him to make ships to go to *T*	2Chr 20:36
they were not able to go to *T*	2Chr 20:37
the ships of *T* with an east wind	Ps 48:7
The kings of *T* and of the isles	Ps 72:10
And upon all the ships of *T*	Is 2:16
Howl, ye ships of *T*	Is 23:1
Pass ye over to *T*	Is 23:6
land as a river, O daughter of *T*	Is 23:10
Howl, ye ships of *T*	Is 23:14
for me, and the ships of *T* first	Is 60:9
of them unto the nations, to *T*	Is 66:19
into plates is brought from *T*	Jer 10:9
T was thy merchant by reason of	Eze 27:12
The ships of *T* did sing of thee	Eze 27:25
and Dedan, and the merchants of *T*	Eze 38:13
T from the presence of the Lord	Jonah 1:3
and he found a ship going to *T*	Jonah 1:3
to go with them unto *T* from the	Jonah 1:3
Therefore I fled before unto *T*	Jonah 4:2

3. A prince of Persia.

was Carshena, Shethar, Admatha, *T*	Est 1:14

TARSHISHAH See **TARSHISH**.

TARSUS (*tar′-sus*) *Capital of Roman province of Cilicia.*

Judas for one called Saul, of *T*	Acts 9:11
Caesarea, and sent him forth to *T*	Acts 9:30
then departed Barnabas to *T*	Acts 11:25
I am a man which am a Jew of *T*	Acts 21:39
a man which am a Jew, born in *T*	Acts 22:3

TARTAK (*tar′-tak*) *A god of the Avites.*

And the Avites made Nibhaz and *T*	2Kin 17:31

TARTAN (*tar′-tan*) *The commander of the Assyrian army.*

And the king of Assyria sent *T*	2Kin 18:17
the year that *T* came unto Ashdod	Is 20:1

TASK

have ye not fulfilled your *t* in	Ex 5:14
from your bricks of your daily *t*	Ex 5:19

TASKMASTERS

they did set over them *t* to	Ex 1:11
their cry by reason of their *t*	Ex 3:7
the same day the *t* of the people	Ex 5:6
the *t* of the people went out, and	Ex 5:10
the *t* hasted them, saying, Fulfil	Ex 5:13
which Pharaoh's *t* had set over	Ex 5:14

TASKS

Fulfil your works, your daily *t*	Ex 5:13

TASTE

the *t* of it was like wafers made	Ex 16:31
the *t* of it was as the	Num 11:8
of it was as the *t* of fresh oil	Num 11:8
I did but *t* a little honey with	1Sa 14:43
if I t bread, or ought else, till	2Sa 3:35
can thy servant *t* what I eat or	2Sa 19:35
or is there any *t* in the white of	Job 6:6
cannot my *t* discern perverse	Job 6:30
and the mouth *t* his meat	Job 12:11
O *t* and see that the Lord is good	Ps 34:8
How sweet are thy words unto my *t*	Ps 119:103
which is sweet to thy *t*	Prov 24:13
and his fruit was sweet to my *t*	Song 2:3
therefore his *t* remained in him,	Jer 48:11
herd nor flock, *t* any thing	Jonah 3:7
here, which shall not *t* of death	Mt 16:28
here, which shall not *t* of death	Mk 9:1
here, which shall not *t* of death	Lk 9:27
were bidden shall *t* of my supper	Lk 14:24
saying, he shall never *t* of death	Jn 8:52
t not	Col 2:21
God should *t* death for every man	Heb 2:9

TASTED

So none of the people *t* any food	1Sa 14:24
because I *t* a little of this	1Sa 14:29
Belshazzar, whiles he *t* the wine	Dan 5:2
and when he had *t* thereof, he	Mt 27:34
t the water that was made wine	Jn 2:9
have *t* of the heavenly gift, and	Heb 6:4
have *t* the good word of God, and	Heb 6:5
If so be ye have *t* that the Lord	1Pet 2:3

TASTETH

trieth words, as the mouth *t* meat	Job 34:3

TATNAI (*tat′-nahee*) *Persian governor of Samaria.*

At the same time came to them *T*	Ezr 5:3

The copy of the letter that *T*	Ezr 5:6
Now therefore, *T*, governor beyond	Ezr 6:6
Then *T*, governor on this side the	Ezr 6:13

TATTENAI See **TATNAI**.

TATTLERS

but *t* also and busybodies,	1Ti 5:13

TAUGHT

Behold, I have *t* you statutes and	Deut 4:5
t it the children of Israel	Deut 31:22
with them he *t* the men of Succoth	Judg 8:16
t them how they should fear the	2Kin 17:28
when thou hast *t* them the good	2Chr 6:27
they *t* in Judah, and had the book	2Chr 17:9
cities of Judah, and *t* the people	2Chr 17:9
and such as *t* to sing praise	2Chr 23:13
unto all the Levites that *t* the	2Chr 30:22
the Levites that *t* all Israel	2Chr 35:3
and the Levites that *t* the people	Neh 8:9
thou hast *t* me from my youth	Ps 71:17
when thou hast *t* me thy statutes	Ps 119:102
when thou hast *t* me thy statutes	Ps 119:171
He *t* me also, and said unto me,	Prov 4:4
I have *t* thee in the way of	Prov 4:11
prophecy that his mother *t* him	Prov 31:1
he still *t* the people knowledge	Eccl 12:9
me is *t* by the precept of men	Is 29:13
being his counsellor hath *t* him	Is 40:13
t him in the path of judgment, and	Is 40:14
t him knowledge, and shewed to him	Is 40:14
children shall be *t* of the Lord	Is 54:13
also *t* the wicked ones thy ways	Jer 2:33
have *t* their tongue to speak	Jer 9:5
which their fathers *t* them	Jer 9:14
as they *t* my people to swear by	Jer 12:16
for thou hast *t* them to be	Jer 13:21
because thou hast *t* rebellion	Jer 28:16
because he hath *t* rebellion	Jer 29:32
though I *t* them, rising up early	Jer 32:33
that all women may be *t* not to do	Eze 23:48
Ephraim is as an heifer that is *t*	Hos 10:11
I *t* Ephraim also to go, taking	Hos 11:3
for man *t* me to keep cattle from	Zec 13:5
his mouth, and *t* them, saying,	Mt 5:2
For he *t* them as one having	Mt 7:29
he *t* them in their synagogue,	Mt 13:54
the money, and did as they were *t*	Mt 28:15
entered into the synagogue, and *t*	Mk 1:21
for he *t* them as one that had	Mk 1:22
resorted unto him, and he *t* them	Mk 2:13
he *t* them many things by parables	Mk 4:2
they had done, and what they had *t*	Mk 6:30
For he *t* his disciples, and said	Mk 9:31
as he was wont, he *t* them again	Mk 10:1
And he *t*, saying unto them, Is it	Mk 11:17
while he *t* in the temple, How say	Mk 12:35
he *t* in their synagogues, being	Lk 4:15
t them on the sabbath days	Lk 4:31
t the people out of the ship,	Lk 5:3
entered into the synagogue and *t*	Lk 6:6
as John also *t* his disciples	Lk 11:1
thou hast *t* in our streets	Lk 13:26
and *t* daily in the temple	Lk 19:47
as he *t* the people in the temple,	Lk 20:1
And they shall be all *t* of God	Jn 6:45
synagogue, as he *t* in Capernaum	Jn 6:59
went up into the temple, and *t*	Jn 7:14
cried Jesus in the temple as he *t*	Jn 7:28
and he sat down, and *t* them	Jn 8:2
treasury, as he *t* in the temple	Jn 8:20
but as my Father hath *t* me	Jn 8:28
I ever *t* in the synagogue, and in	Jn 18:20
grieved that they *t* the people	Acts 4:2
temple early in the morning, and *t*	Acts 5:21
with the church, and *t* much people	Acts 11:26
had *t* many, they returned again	Acts 14:21
down from Judaea *t* the brethren,	Acts 15:1
t diligently the things of the	Acts 18:25
have *t* you publickly, and from	Acts 20:20
t according to the perfect manner,	Acts 22:3
t of man, neither was I *t* it,	Gal 1:12
Let him that is *t* in the word	Gal 6:6
heard him, and have been *t* by him	Eph 4:21
in the faith, as ye have been *t*	Col 2:7
for yourselves are *t* of God to	1Th 4:9
traditions which ye have been *t*	2Th 2:15
faithful word as he hath been *t*	Titus 1:9
no lie, and even as it hath *t* you,	1Jn 2:27
of Balaam, who *t* Balac to cast a	Rev 2:14

TAUNT

be a reproach and a proverb, a *t*	Jer 24:9
So it shall be a reproach and a *t*	Eze 5:15

TAUNTING

a *t* proverb against him, and say,	Hab 2:6

TAVERNS

as Appii forum, and The three *t*	Acts 28:15

TAXATION

of every one according to his *t*	2Kin 23:35

TAXED

but he *t* the land to give the	2Kin 23:35
that all the world should be *t*	Lk 2:1
And all went to be *t*, every one	Lk 2:3
To be *t* with Mary his espoused	Lk 2:5

TAXES

of *t* in the glory of the kingdom	Dan 11:20

TAXING

this *t* was first made when	Lk 2:2
of Galilee in the days of the *t*	Acts 5:37

TEACH

t thee what thou shalt say	Ex 4:12
will *t* you what ye shall do	Ex 4:15
thou shalt *t* them ordinances and	Ex 18:20
that thou mayest *t* them	Ex 24:12
put in his heart that he may *t*	Ex 35:34
that ye may *t* the children of	Lev 10:11
To *t* when it is unclean, and when	Lev 14:57
unto the judgments, which I *t* you	Deut 4:1
but *t* them thy sons, and thy sons'	Deut 4:9
that they may *t* their children	Deut 4:10
me at that time to *t* you statutes	Deut 4:14
which thou shalt *t* them, that	Deut 5:31
Lord our God commanded to *t* you	Deut 6:1
thou shalt *t* them diligently unto	Deut 6:7
ye shall *t* them your children,	Deut 11:19
the law which they shall *t* thee	Deut 17:11
That they *t* you not to do after	Deut 20:18
priests the Levites shall *t* you	Deut 24:8
t it the children of Israel	Deut 31:19
They shall *t* Jacob thy judgments,	Deut 33:10
to *t* them war, at the least such	Judg 3:2
t us what we shall do unto the	Judg 13:8
but I will *t* you the good and the	1Sa 12:23
(Also he bade them *t* the children	2Sa 1:18
that thou *t* them the good way	1Kin 8:36
let him *t* them the manner of the	1Kin 8:36*
t in the cities of Judah	2Chr 17:7
to *t* in Israel statutes and	Ezr 7:10
t ye them that know them not	Ezr 7:25
T me, and I will hold my tongue	Job 6:24
Shall not they *t* thee, and tell	Job 8:10
he beasts, and they shall *t* thee	Job 12:7
to the earth, and it shall *t* thee	Job 12:8
Shall any *t* God knowledge	Job 21:22
I will *t* you by the hand of God	Job 27:11
of years should *t* wisdom	Job 32:7
peace, and I shall *t* thee wisdom	Job 33:33
That which I see not *t* thou me	Job 34:32
T us what we shall say unto him	Job 37:19
t me thy paths	Ps 25:4
Lead me in thy truth, and *t* me	Ps 25:5
therefore will he *t* sinners in	Ps 25:8
and the meek will he *t* his way	Ps 25:9
him shall he *t* in the way that he	Ps 25:12
T me thy way, O Lord, and lead me	Ps 27:11
t thee in the way which thou	Ps 32:8
I will *t* you the fear of the Lord	Ps 34:11
hand shall *t* thee terrible things	Ps 45:4
Then will I *t* transgressors thy	Ps 51:13
Mictham of David, to *t*	Ps 60:t
T me thy way, O Lord	Ps 86:11
So *t* us to number our days, that	Ps 90:12
and *t* his senators wisdom	Ps 105:22
t me thy statutes	Ps 119:12
t me thy statutes	Ps 119:26
T me, O Lord, the way of thy	Ps 119:33
t me thy judgments	Ps 119:64
T me good judgment and knowledge	Ps 119:66
t me thy statutes	Ps 119:68
O Lord, and *t* me thy judgments	Ps 119:108
thy mercy, and *t* me thy statutes	Ps 119:124
and *t* me thy statutes	Ps 119:135
my testimony that I shall *t* them	Ps 132:12
T me to do thy will	Ps 143:10
a just man, and he will increase	Prov 9:9
he will *t* us of his ways, and we	Is 2:3
Whom shall he *t* knowledge	Is 28:9
him to discretion, and doth *t* him	Is 28:26
t your daughters wailing, and	Jer 9:20
they shall *t* no more every man	Jer 31:34
they shall *t* my people the	Eze 44:23
and whom they might *t* the learning	Dan 1:4
and the priests thereof *t* for hire	Mic 3:11
he will *t* us of his ways, and we	Mic 4:2
the dumb stone, Arise, it shall *t*	Hab 2:19
shall *t* men so, he shall be	Mt 5:19
t them, the same shall be called	Mt 5:19
he departed thence to *t* and	Mt 11:1
t all nations, baptizing them in	Mt 28:19
began again to *t* by the sea side.	Mk 4:1
he began to *t* in the synagogue	Mk 6:2
he began to *t* them many things.	Mk 6:34
And he began to *t* them, that the	Mk 8:31
t us to pray, as John also *t*	Lk 11:1
For the Holy Ghost shall *t* you in	Lk 12:12
the Gentiles, and *t* the Gentiles?	Jn 7:35
born in sins, and dost thou *t* us	Jn 9:34
he shall *t* you all things, and	Jn 14:26
that Jesus began both to do and *t*	Acts 1:1
at all nor *t* in the name of Jesus	Acts 4:18
that ye should not *t* in this name	Acts 5:28
every house, they ceased not to *t*	Acts 5:42
t customs, which are not lawful	Acts 16:21
as I *t* every where in every	1Cor 4:17
Doth not even nature itself *t* you	1Cor 11:14
by my voice I might *t* others also	1Cor 14:19
that they *t* no other doctrine	1Ti 1:3
But I suffer not a woman to *t*	1Ti 2:12
given to hospitality, apt to *t*	1Ti 3:2
These things command and *t*	1Ti 4:11
These things *t* and exhort	1Ti 6:2
If any man *t* otherwise, and	1Ti 6:3
shall be able to *t* others also	2Ti 2:2
be gentle unto all men, apt to *t*	2Ti 2:24
That they may *t* the young women	Titus 2:4
ye have need that one *t* you again	Heb 5:12
they shall not *t* every man his	Heb 8:11
and ye need not that any man *t* you	1Jn 2:27
herself a prophetess, to *t*	Rev 2:20

T

TEACHER

the great, the *t* as the scholar.............. 1Chr 25:8
a *t* of lies, that the maker of............... Hab 2:18
that thou art a *t* come from God........... Jn 3:2
a *t* of babes, which hast the form......... Rom 2:20
a *t* of the Gentiles in faith and............. 1Ti 2:7
apostle, and a *t* of the Gentiles........... 2Ti 1:11

TEACHERS

more understanding than all my *t*........ Ps 119:99
have not obeyed the voice of my *t*........ Prov 5:13
yet shall not thy *t* be removed............. Is 30:20
but thine eyes shall see thy *t*.............. Is 30:20
thy *t* have transgressed against.......... Is 43:27
At Antioch certain prophets and *t*........ Acts 13:1
secondarily prophets, thirdly *t*........... 1Cor 12:28
are all *t*?...................................... 1Cor 12:29
and some, pastors and *t*..................... Eph 4:11
Desiring to be *t* of the law................. 1Ti 1:7
shall they heap to themselves *t*........... 2Ti 4:3
to much wine, *t* of good things........... Titus 2:3
for the time ye ought to be *t*............... Heb 5:12
there shall be false *t* among you........... 2Pet 2:1

TEACHEST

O LORD, and *t* him out of thy law......... Ps 94:12
t the way of God in truth.................... Mt 22:16
but *t* the way of God in truth.............. Mk 12:14
t rightly, neither acceptest thou........... Lk 20:21
but *t* the way of God truly.................. Lk 20:21
that thou *t* all the Jews which............. Acts 21:21
Thou therefore which *t* another........... Rom 2:21
t thou not thyself?.......................... Rom 2:21

TEACHETH

He *t* my hands to war........................ 2Sa 22:35
Who *t* us more than the beasts of......... Job 35:11
who *t* like him................................. Job 36:22
He *t* my hands to war, so that a........... Ps 18:34
he that *t* man knowledge, shall........... Ps 94:10
which *t* my hands to war, and my......... Ps 144:1
his feet, he *t* with his fingers.............. Prov 6:13
The heart of the wise *t* his mouth........ Prov 16:23
and the prophet that *t* lies.................. Is 9:15
thy God which *t* thee to profit............ Is 48:17
that *t* all men every where................. Acts 21:28
or he that *t*, on teaching................... Rom 12:7
in the words which man's wisdom *t*...... 1Cor 2:13
but which the Holy Ghost *t*................. 1Cor 2:13
him that *t* in all good things............... Gal 6:6
anointing *t* you of all things.............. 1Jn 2:27

TEACHING

true God, and without a *t* priest.......... 2Chr 15:3
t them, yet they have not.................... Jer 32:33
t in their synagogues, and................. Mt 4:23
t in their synagogues, and................. Mt 9:35
t for doctrines the commandments...... Mt 15:9
people came unto him as he was *t*........ Mt 21:23
daily with you *t* in the temple............. Mt 26:55
t them to observe all things............... Mt 28:20
went round about the villages, *t*.......... Mk 6:6
t for doctrines the commandments...... Mk 7:7
daily with you in the temple *t*............. Mk 14:49
on a certain day, as he was *t*............... Lk 5:17
he was *t* in one of the synagogues....... Lk 13:10
through the cities and villages, *t*.......... Lk 13:22
day time he was *t* in the temple.......... Lk 21:37
t throughout all Jewry, beginning........ Lk 23:5
in the temple, and *t* the people............ Acts 5:25
Barnabas continued in Antioch, *t*........ Acts 15:35
the word of God among them .... Acts 18:11
t those things which concern the......... Acts 28:31
or he that teacheth, on *t*.................... Rom 12:7
t every man in all wisdom.................. Col 1:28
t and admonishing one another in....... Col 3:16
t things which they ought not............. Titus 1:11
T us that, denying ungodliness and...... Titus 2:12

TEAR

then I will *t* your flesh with the........... Judg 8:7
Lest he *t* my soul like a lion,............... Ps 7:2
they did *t* me, and ceased not............. Ps 35:15
lest I *t* you in pieces, and there........... Ps 50:22
sword to slay, and the dogs to *t*.......... Jer 15:3
Neither shall men *t* themselves........... Jer 16:7
I will *t* them from your arms, and........ Eze 13:20
Your kerchiefs also will I *t*................. Eze 13:21
I, even I, will *t* and go away............... Hos 5:14
the wild beast shall *t* them................. Hos 13:8
and his anger did *t* perpetually........... Amos 1:11
The lion did *t* in pieces enough........... Nah 2:12
fat, and their claws in pieces................. Zec 11:16

TEARETH

t the arm with the crown of the........... Deut 33:20
He *t* me in his wrath, who hateth......... Job 16:9
He *t* himself in his anger.................... Job 18:4
t in pieces, and none can deliver.......... Mic 5:8
he taketh him, he *t* him...................... Mk 9:18
it *t* him that he foameth again,............ Lk 9:39

TEARS

thy prayer, I have seen thy *t*............... 2Kin 20:5
besought him with *t* to put away......... Est 8:3
mine eye poureth out *t* unto God......... Job 16:20
I water my couch with my *t*................ Ps 6:6
hold not thy peace at my *t*................. Ps 39:12
My *t* have been my meat day and......... Ps 42:3
put thou my *t* into thy bottle.............. Ps 56:8
feedest them with the bread of *t*.......... Ps 80:5
givest them *t* to drink in great............ Ps 80:5
soul from death, mine eyes from *t*........ Ps 116:8

They that sow in *t* shall reap in........... Ps 126:5
behold the *t* of such as were............... Eccl 4:1
I will water thee with my *t*................. Is 16:9
wipe away *t* from off all faces............. Is 25:8
thy prayer, I have seen thy *t*............... Is 38:5
and mine eyes a fountain of *t*.............. Jer 9:1
that our eyes may run down with *t*....... Jer 9:18
weep sore, and run down with *t*.......... Jer 13:17
mine eyes run down with *t* night........ Jer 14:17
weeping, and thine eyes from *t*........... Jer 31:16
night, and her *t* are on her cheeks....... Lam 1:2
Mine eyes do fail with *t*, my............... Lam 2:11
let *t* run down like a river day............. Lam 2:18
neither shall thy *t* run down............... Eze 24:16
the altar of the LORD with *t*................ Mal 2:13
child cried out, and said with *t*........... Mk 9:24
and began to wash his feet with *t*........ Lk 7:38
she hath washed my feet with *t*........... Lk 7:44
humility of mind, and with many *t*....... Acts 20:19
every one night and day with *t*............ Acts 20:31
I wrote unto you with many *t*............. 2Cor 2:4
see thee, being mindful of thy *t*........... 2Ti 1:4
t unto him that was able to save.......... Heb 5:7
he sought it carefully with *t*............... Heb 12:17
wipe away all *t* from their eyes........... Rev 7:17
wipe away all *t* from their eyes........... Rev 21:4

TEATS

They shall lament for the *t*................. Is 32:12
bruised the *t* of their virginity............ Eze 23:3
youth, in bruising thy *t* by the............ Eze 23:21

TEBAH

TEBAH (te′-bah) A son of Nahor.
name was Reumah, she bare also *T*...... Gen 22:24

TEBALIAH

TEBALIAH (teb-a-li′-ah) A sanctuary servant.
T the third, Zechariah the fourth......... 1Chr 26:11

TEBETH

TEBETH (te′-beth) Tenth month of the
Hebrew year.
tenth month, which is the month *T*....... Est 2:16

TEDIOUS

that I be not further *t* unto thee.......... Acts 24:4

TEETH

wine, and his *t* white with milk............ Gen 49:12
the flesh was yet between their *t*.......... Num 11:33
send the *t* of beasts upon them........... Deut 32:24
fleshhook of three *t* in his hand.......... 1Sa 2:13
the *t* of the young lions, are................. Job 4:10
do I take my flesh in my *t*................... Job 13:14
he gnasheth upon me with his *t*.......... Job 16:9
am escaped with the skin of my *t*........ Job 19:20
and plucked the spoil out of his *t*........ Job 29:17
his *t* are terrible round about.............. Job 41:14
hast broken the *t* of the ungodly.......... Ps 3:7
they gnashed upon me with their *t*....... Ps 35:16
and gnasheth upon him with his *t*........ Ps 37:12
whose *t* are spears and arrows, and...... Ps 57:4
Break their *t*, O God, in their............... Ps 58:6
the great *t* of the young lions.............. Ps 58:6
he shall gnash with his *t*, and............. Ps 112:10
not given us as a prey to their *t*........... Ps 124:6
As vinegar to the *t*, and as smoke........ Prov 10:26
whose *t* are as swords, and their......... Prov 30:14
swords, and their *t* as knives.............. Prov 30:14
Thy *t* are like a flock of sheep............ Song 4:2
Thy *t* are as a flock of sheep.............. Song 6:6
threshing instrument having *t*............. Is 41:15
the children's *t* are set on edge........... Jer 31:29
his *t* shall be set on edge................... Jer 31:30
they hiss and gnash the *t*................... Lam 2:16
whose *t* with gravel stones............... Lam 3:16
the children's *t* are set on edge........... Eze 18:2
mouth of *t* between the *t* of them....... Dan 7:5
and it had great iron *t*...................... Dan 7:7
whose *t* were of iron, and his.............. Dan 7:19
whose *t* are the....................... Joel 1:6
are the *t* of a lion........................ Joel 1:6
hath the cheek of a great lion.............. Joel 1:6
cleanness of *t* in all your cities........... Amos 4:6
err, that bite with their *t*................... Mic 3:5
abominations from between his *t*......... Zec 9:7
shall be weeping and gnashing of *t*...... Mt 8:12
shall be wailing and gnashing of *t*....... Mt 13:42
shall be wailing and gnashing of *t*....... Mt 13:50
shall be weeping and gnashing of *t*...... Mt 22:13
shall be weeping and gnashing of *t*...... Mt 24:51
shall be weeping and gnashing of *t*...... Mt 25:30
with him, cast the same in his *t*.......... Mt 27:44
foameth, and gnasheth with his *t*........ Mk 9:18
shall be weeping and gnashing of *t*...... Lk 13:28
they gnashed on him with their *t*......... Acts 7:54
their *t* were as the............................ Rev 9:8
were as the *t* of lions........................ Rev 9:8

TEHAPHNEHES

TEHAPHNEHES (te-haf′-ne-heze) Same as
Tahpanhes.
At *T* also the day shall be.................. Eze 30:18

TEHINNAH

TEHINNAH (te-hin′-nah) A descendant of
Judah.
T the father of Ir-nahash.................... 1Chr 4:12

TEIL

as a *t* tree, and as an oak, whose.......... Is 6:13

TEKEL

TEKEL (te′-kel) Part of the "handwriting of the
wall."
that was written, MENE, MENE, *T*........ Dan 5:25
T; Thou art weighed......................... Dan 5:27

TEKOA

TEKOA (te′-ko-ah) See TEKOAH, TEKOITE.
1. Son of Ashur.
bare him Ashur the father of *T*............ 1Chr 2:24
the father of *T* had two wives............. 1Chr 4:5
2. A city in Judah.
even Beth-lehem, and Etam, and *T*....... 2Chr 11:6
and blow the wilderness of *T*............... 2Chr 20:20
and blow the trumpet in *T*................. Jer 6:1
who was among the herdmen of *T*........ Amos 1:1

TEKOAH

TEKOAH (te′-ko-ah) See TEKOA. Same as
Tekoa 2.
And Joab sent to *T*, and fetched.......... 2Sa 14:2
the woman of *T* spake to the king........ 2Sa 14:4
the woman of *T* said unto the king....... 2Sa 14:9

TEKOITE

TEKOITE (te′-ko-ite) See TEKOITES. An
inhabitant of Tekoa.
Ira the son of Ikkesh the *T*................. 2Sa 23:26
Ira the son of Ikkesh the *T*................. 1Chr 11:28
was Ira the son of Ikkesh the *T*........... 1Chr 27:9

TEKOITES

TEKOITES (te′-ko-ites)
And next unto them the *T* repaired...... Neh 3:5
After them the *T* repaired another........ Neh 3:27

TEL-ABIB

TEL-ABIB (tel-a′-bib) Town of the River
Chebar.
to them of the captivity at *T*............... Eze 3:15

TELAH

TELAH (te′-lah) Father of Tahan.
T his son, and Tahan his son,.............. 1Chr 7:25

TELAIM

TELAIM (tel′-a-im) See TELEM. A place in
Judah.
together, and numbered them in *T*........ 1Sa 15:4

TELASSAR

TELASSAR (te-las′-sar) See THELASAR. A city
in Mesopotamia.
children of Eden which were in *T*......... Is 37:12

TELEM

TELEM (te′-lem) See TELAIM.
1. A city in Judah.
Ziph, and *T*, and Bealoth,.................. Josh 15:24
2. Married a foreigner in exile.
Shallum, and *T*, and Uri.................... Ezr 10:24

TEL-HARESHA

TEL-HARESHA (tel-ha-re′-sha) See TEL-
HARSA. A Babylonian settlement of exiles.
went up also from Tel-melah, *T*............ Neh 7:61

TEL-HARSA

TEL-HARSA (tel′-har-sah) See TEL-HARESHA.
Same as Tel-haresha.
which went up from Tel-melah, *T*......... Ezr 2:59

TELL

why didst thou not *t* me that she......... Gen 12:18
the *t* stars, if thou be able to............... Gen 15:5
neither didst thou *t* me, neither........... Gen 21:26
mountains which I will *t* thee of.......... Gen 22:2
t me, I pray thee............................... Gen 24:23
and truly with my master, *t* me........... Gen 24:49
and if not, *t* me............................... Gen 24:49
the land which I shall *t* thee of............ Gen 26:2
t me, what shall thy wages be............. Gen 29:15
and didst not *t* me, that I might........... Gen 31:27
and I have sent to *t* my lord............... Gen 32:5
T me, I pray thee, thy name................ Gen 32:29
t me, I pray thee, where they.............. Gen 37:16
T me them, I pray........................... Gen 40:8
as to *t* the man whether ye had........... Gen 43:6
we cannot *t* who put our money in...... Gen 43:22
ye shall *t* my father of all my.............. Gen 45:13
that I may *t* you that which shall......... Gen 49:1
t him, Thus saith the LORD God of...... Ex 9:1
that thou mayest *t* in the ears of......... Ex 10:2
word that we did *t* thee in Egypt......... Ex 14:12
and *t* the children of Israel................. Ex 19:3
t the priest, saying, It seemeth........... Lev 14:35
they will *t* it to the inhabitants........... Num 14:14
heard I that Israel came by the............. Num 21:1
he sheweth me I will *t* thee................ Num 23:3
judgment which they shall *t* thee......... Deut 17:11
thy elders, and they will *t* thee........... Deut 32:7
t me now what thou hast done........... Josh 7:19
my mother, and shall I *t* thee.............. Judg 14:16
T me, I pray thee, wherein thy............. Judg 16:6
now I me, I pray thee, wherewith........... Judg 16:10
I me wherewith thou mightest be.......... Judg 16:13
T us, how was this wickedness............ Judg 20:3
he will *t* thee what thou shalt do......... Ruth 3:4
wilt not redeem it, then I me................. Ruth 4:4
I us wherewith we shall send it............. 1Sa 6:2
the man of God, to *t* us our way.......... 1Sa 9:8
t me, I pray thee, where the................ 1Sa 9:18
wilt thou *t* all that is in thine.............. 1Sa 9:19
T me, I pray thee, what Samuel........... 1Sa 10:15
T me what thou hast done.................. 1Sa 14:43
I will *t* thee what the LORD hath.......... 1Sa 15:16
soul liveth, O king, I cannot *t*............. 1Sa 17:55
and what I see, that I will *t* thee......... 1Sa 19:3
thee, then would not I *t* thee.............. 1Sa 20:9
David to Jonathan, Who shall I me........ 1Sa 20:10
that he would surely *t* Saul................ 1Sa 22:22
I beseech thee, *t* thy servant.............. 1Sa 23:11
saying, Lest they should *t* on us......... 1Sa 27:11
I pray thee, *t* me............................. 2Sa 1:4
T it not in Gath, publish it not........... 2Sa 1:20
t my servant David, Thus saith.......... 2Sa 7:5
to *t* him that the child was dead......... 2Sa 12:18
if we *t* him that the child is............... 2Sa 12:18
Who can *t* whether God will be.......... 2Sa 12:22
wilt thou not *t* me........................... 2Sa 13:4
thou shalt *t* it to Zadok and.............. 2Sa 15:35

t David, saying, Lodge not this.......... 2Sa 17:16
Go t the king what thou hast seen.... 2Sa 18:21
that thou shouldest t them who......... 1Kin 1:20
he shall t thee what shall become..... 1Kin 14:3
t Jeroboam, Thus saith the LORD 1Kin 14:7
t thy lord, Behold, Elijah is............... 1Kin 18:8
thy lord, Behold, Elijah is................. 1Kin 18:11
t Ahab, and he cannot find thee,...... 1Kin 18:12
t thy lord, Behold, Elijah is.............. 1Kin 18:14
T my lord the king, All that thou...... 1Kin 20:9
T him, Let not him that girdeth........ 1Kin 20:11
t me nothing but that which is.......... 1Kin 22:16
Did I not t thee that he would.......... 1Kin 22:18
t me, what hast thou in the house.... 2Kin 4:2
may go and t the king's household.... 2Kin 7:9
T me, I pray thee, all the great........ 2Kin 8:4
t us now....................................... 2Kin 9:12
the city to go to t it in Jezreel........ 2Kin 9:15
t Hezekiah the captain of my........... 2Kin 20:5
The man that sent you to me,........... 2Kin 22:15
t David my servant, Thus saith........ 1Chr 17:4
Furthermore I t thee that the.......... 1Chr 17:10
t David, saying, Thus saith the........ 1Chr 21:10
Did I not t thee that he would.......... 2Chr 18:17
T ye the man that sent you to me,.... 2Chr 34:23
I only am escaped alone to t thee .... Job 1:15
I only am escaped alone to t thee .... Job 1:16
I only am escaped alone to t thee .... Job 1:17
I only am escaped alone to t thee .... Job 1:19
t thee, and utter words out of.......... Job 8:10
of the air, and they shall t thee....... Job 12:7
Let men of understanding t me........ Job 34:34
I may t all my bones....................... Ps 22:17
t of all thy wondrous works............. Ps 26:7
t the towers thereof........................ Ps 48:12
that ye may t it to the.................... Ps 48:13
I were hungry, I would not t thee..... Ps 50:12
his son's name, if thou canst t........ Prov 30:4
for who can t a man what shall be... Eccl 6:12
for who can t him when it shall....... Eccl 8:7
a man cannot t what shall be.......... Eccl 10:14
shall be after him, who can t him.... Eccl 10:14
hath wings shall t the matter.......... Eccl 10:20
T me, O thou whom my soul loveth,.. Song 1:7
ye find my beloved, that ye t him,... Song 5:8
I will t you what I will do to my...... Is 5:5
t this people, Hear ye indeed,.......... Is 6:9
and let them t thee now, and let..... Is 19:12
they spring forth I t you of them ... Is 42:9
T ye, and bring them near.............. Is 45:21
t this, utter it even to the end........ Is 48:20
then thou shalt t them, Thus.......... Jer 15:2
the words that I shall t thee........... Jer 19:2
they t every man to his neighbour... Jer 23:27
hath a dream, let him t a dream..... Jer 23:28
do t them, and cause my people to... Jer 23:32
t Hananiah, saying, Thus saith........ Jer 28:13
t him, Thus saith the LORD .... Jer 34:2
t the men of Judah and the............ Jer 35:13
We will surely t the king of all........ Jer 36:16
T us now, How didst thou write....... Jer 36:17
t ye it in Arnon, that Moab is......... Jer 48:20
t them, Thus saith the LORD God .... Jer 50:2
T them therefore, Thus saith the..... Eze 12:23
t them, Behold, the king of............. Eze 17:12
Wilt thou not t us what these.......... Eze 24:19
t thy servants the dream, and we.... Dan 2:4
Let the king t his servants the........ Dan 2:7
therefore t me the dream, and I...... Dan 2:9
we will t the interpretation............. Dan 2:36
t me the visions of my dream that... Dan 4:9
T ye your children of it, and set...... Joel 1:3
your children t their children........... Joel 1:3
T us, we pray thee, for whose......... Jonah 1:8
Who can t if God will turn and........ Jonah 3:9
saith unto him, See thou t no man... Mt 8:4
What I t you in darkness, that........ Mt 10:27
t no man that he was Jesus the...... Mt 16:20
T the vision to no man, until the..... Mt 17:9
t him his fault between thee and..... Mt 18:15
hear them, t it unto the church...... Mt 18:17
T ye the daughter of Sion, Behold... Mt 21:5
you one thing, which if ye t me....... Mt 21:24
In like wise will t you by what........ Mt 21:27
Jesus, and said, We cannot t........... Mt 21:27
Neither t I you by what authority.... Mt 21:27
T them which are bidden, Behold,.... Mt 22:4
T us therefore, What thinkest.......... Mt 22:17
T us, when shall these things be..... Mt 24:3
that thou t us whether thou be....... Mt 26:63
t his disciples that he is risen......... Mt 28:7
as they went to t his disciples........ Mt 28:9
go t my brethren that they go......... Mt 28:10
fever, and anon they t him of her.... Mk 1:30
t them how great things the Lord.... Mk 5:19
them that they should t no man...... Mk 7:36
nor t it to any in the town............. Mk 8:26
that they should t no man of him.... Mk 8:30
t no man what things they had........ Mk 9:9
began to t them what things.......... Mk 10:32
I will t you by what authority I....... Mk 11:29
and said unto Jesus, We cannot t.... Mk 11:33
Neither do I t you by what............. Mk 11:33
T us, when shall these things be..... Mk 13:4
t his disciples and Peter that he...... Mk 16:7
But I t you of a truth, many........... Lk 4:25
And he charged him to t no man..... Lk 5:14
t John what things ye have seen..... Lk 7:22
T me therefore, which of them........ Lk 7:42

should t no man what was done........ Lk 8:56
them to t no man that thing............ Lk 9:21
But I t you of a truth, there be........ Lk 9:27
For I t you, that many prophets....... Lk 10:24
I t you, Nay................................... Lk 12:51
I t thee, thou shalt not depart......... Lk 12:59
I t you, Nay................................... Lk 13:3
I t you, Nay................................... Lk 13:5
I t you, I know you not whence ye.... Lk 13:27
t that Fox, Behold, I cast out........... Lk 13:32
I t you, in that night there.............. Lk 17:34
I t you that he will avenge them...... Lk 18:8
I t you, this man went down to....... Lk 18:14
I t you that, if these should............ Lk 19:40
T us, by what authority doest.......... Lk 20:2
they could not t whence it was........ Lk 20:7
Neither t I you by what authority..... Lk 20:8
I t thee, Peter, the cock shall.......... Lk 22:34
Art thou the Christ? t us................. Lk 22:67
And he said unto them, If I t you..... Lk 22:67
but canst not t whence it cometh,.... Jn 3:8
if I t you of heavenly things............ Jn 3:12
is come, he will t us all things......... Jn 4:25
but ye cannot t whence I come........ Jn 8:14
because I t you the truth, ye............ Jn 8:45
thou be the Christ, t us plainly........ Jn 10:24
and again Andrew and Philip t Jesus. Jn 12:22
Now I t you before it come, that,.... Jn 13:19
Nevertheless I t you the truth......... Jn 16:7
we cannot t what he saith.............. Jn 16:18
or did others t it thee of me........... Jn 18:34
t me where thou hast laid him, and.. Jn 20:15
T me whether ye sold the land for... Acts 5:8
he shall t thee what thou............... Acts 10:6
Who shall t thee words, whereby..... Acts 11:14
who shall also t you the same......... Acts 15:27
in nothing else, but either to t........ Acts 17:21
unto him, T me, art thou a Roman... Acts 22:27
he hath a certain thing to t thee..... Acts 23:17
What is that thou hast to t me........ Acts 23:19
See thou t no man that thou hast.... Acts 23:22
(whether in the body, I cannot t...... 2Cor 12:2
out of the body, I cannot t............. 2Cor 12:2
or out of the body, I cannot t......... 2Cor 12:3
because I t you the truth................ Gal 4:16
T me, ye that desire to be under..... Gal 4:21
of the which I t you before............. Gal 5:21
now I t you even weeping, that they.. Phil 3:18
time would fail me to t of Gedeon.... Heb 11:32
I will t thee the mystery of the........ Rev 17:7

TELLEST
Thou t my wanderings.................... Ps 56:8

TELLETH
Also the LORD t thee that he will..... 2Sa 7:11
t the king of Israel the words......... 2Kin 6:12
when he goeth abroad, he t it......... Ps 41:6
he that t lies shall not tarry in........ Ps 101:7
He t the number of the stars.......... Ps 147:4
the hands of him that t them......... Jer 33:13
Philip cometh and t Andrew............ Jn 12:22

TELLING
Gideon heard the t of the dream..... Judg 7:15
When thou hast made an end of t.... 2Sa 11:19
as he was t the king how he had..... 2Kin 8:5

TEL-MELAH (tel-me'-lah) A place where the exiles lived.
were they which went up from T...... Ezr 2:59
they which went up also from T....... Neh 7:61

TEMA (te'-mah)
1. A son of Ishmael.
Hadar, and T, Jetur, Naphish, and... Gen 25:15
and Dumah, Massa, Hadad, and T.... 1Chr 1:30
T brought water to him that was..... Is 21:14
Dedan, and T, and Buz, and all that.. Jer 25:23
2. A city in northern Arabia.
The troops of T looked, the........... Job 6:19

TEMAH See THAMAH.

TEMAN (te'-man) See TEMANITE.
1. A son of Eliphaz.
And the sons of Eliphaz were T....... Gen 36:11
duke T, duke Omar, duke Zepho,...... Gen 36:15
Duke Kenaz, duke T, duke Mibzar,... Gen 36:42
T, and Omar, Zephi, and Gatam,...... 1Chr 1:36
Duke Kenaz, duke T, duke Mibzar,... 1Chr 1:53
2. A near and district of Edom.
Is wisdom no more in T.................. Jer 49:7
against the inhabitants of T............ Jer 49:20
and I will make it desolate from T.... Eze 25:13
But I will send a fire upon T........... Amos 1:12
And thy mighty men, O T, shall be.. Obad 9
God came from T, and the Holy One. Hab 3:3

TEMANI (te'-ma-ni) See TEMANITE. A son of Ashur.
land of T reigned in his stead......... Gen 36:34

TEMANITE (te'-man-ite) See TEMANI, TEMANITES. An inhabitant of Teman 3.
Eliphaz the T, and Bildad the.......... Job 2:11
Then Eliphaz the T answered........... Job 4:1
Then answered Eliphaz the T........... Job 15:1
Then Eliphaz the T answered........... Job 22:1
the LORD said to Eliphaz the T........ Job 42:7
So Eliphaz the T and Bildad the...... Job 42:9

TEMANITES (te'-man-ites)................. 1Chr 1:45

TEMENI (tem'-e-ni) A descendant of Caleb.
bare him Ahuzam, and Hepher, and T.. 1Chr 4:6

TEMPER
of oil, to t with the fine flour........... Eze 46:14

TEMPERANCE
he reasoned of righteousness, t....... Acts 24:25
Meekness, t.................................. Gal 5:23
And to knowledge t........................ 2Pet 1:6
and to t patience........................... 2Pet 1:6

TEMPERATE
the mastery is in all things............. 1Cor 9:25
of good men, sober, just, holy, t...... Titus 1:8
the aged men be sober, grave, t...... Titus 2:2

TEMPERED
and cakes unleavened t with oil....... Ex 29:2
t together, pure and holy................ Ex 30:35
but God hath t the body together,... 1Cor 12:24

TEMPEST
For he breaketh me with a t............ Job 9:17
a t stealeth him away in the........... Job 27:20
and brimstone, and an horrible t..... Ps 11:6
escape from the windy storm and t.. Ps 55:8
So persecute them with thy t.......... Ps 83:15
strong one, which as a t of hail...... Is 28:2
and great noise, with storm and t.... Is 29:6
fire, with scattering, and t............. Is 30:30
the wind, and a covert from the t.... Is 32:2
O thou afflicted, tossed with t........ Is 54:11
with a t in the day of the.............. Amos 1:14
there was a mighty t in the sea...... Jonah 1:4
my sake this great t is upon you..... Jonah 1:12
there arose a great t in the sea...... Mt 8:24
being exceedingly tossed with a t.... Acts 27:18
no small t lay on us, all hope......... Acts 27:20
unto blackness, and darkness, and t.. Heb 12:18
clouds that are carried with a t....... 2Pet 2:17

TEMPESTUOUS
shall be very t round about him....... Ps 50:3
for the sea wrought, and was t....... Jonah 1:11
wrought, and was t against them..... Jonah 1:13
there arose against it a t wind........ Acts 27:14

TEMPLE
by a post of the t of the LORD 1Sa 1:9
God went out in the t of the LORD... 1Sa 3:3
he did hear my voice out of his t..... 2Sa 22:7
porch before the t of the house...... 1Kin 6:3
house round about, both of the t..... 1Kin 6:5
the t before it, was forty cubits...... 1Kin 6:17
door of the t posts of olive tree...... 1Kin 6:33
the pillars in the porch of the t....... 1Kin 7:21
of the house, to wit, of the t.......... 1Kin 7:50
that were in the t of the LORD 2Kin 11:10
the t to the left corner of the.......... 2Kin 11:11
to the left corner of the t............... 2Kin 11:11
along by the altar and the t........... 2Kin 11:11
the people into the t of the LORD ... 2Kin 11:13
the doors of the t of the LORD 2Kin 18:16
to bring forth out of the t of........... 2Kin 23:4
and made in the t of the LORD 2Kin 23:11
the priest's office in the t that........ 1Chr 6:10
his head in the t of Dagon.............. 1Chr 10:10
up the pillars before the t.............. 2Chr 3:17
their form, and set them in the t..... 2Chr 4:7
tables, and placed them in the t...... 2Chr 4:8
the doors of the house of the t....... 2Chr 4:22
from the right side of the t to......... 2Chr 23:10
to the left side of the t.................. 2Chr 23:10
along by the altar and the t........... 2Chr 23:10
went into the t of the LORD to........ 2Chr 26:16
not into the t of the LORD 2Chr 27:2
that they found in the t of the........ 2Chr 29:16
when Josiah had prepared the t....... 2Chr 35:20
and put them in his t at Babylon..... 2Chr 36:7
But the foundation of the t of......... Ezr 3:6
foundation of the t of the LORD ...... Ezr 3:10
the t unto the LORD God of Israel.... Ezr 4:1
of the t that was in Jerusalem........ Ezr 5:14
them into the t of Babylon............. Ezr 5:14
king take out of the t of Babylon.... Ezr 5:14
carry them into the t that is in....... Ezr 5:15
of the t which is at Jerusalem........ Ezr 6:5
unto the t which is at Jerusalem..... Ezr 6:5
in the house of God, within the t..... Neh 6:10
and let us shut the doors of the t.... Neh 6:10
go into the t to save his life........... Neh 6:11
will I worship toward thy holy t...... Ps 5:7
The LORD is in his holy t............... Ps 11:4
he heard my voice out of his t........ Ps 18:6
the LORD, and to enquire in his t..... Ps 27:4
in his t doth every one speak of...... Ps 29:9
O God, in the midst of thy t........... Ps 48:9
of thy house, even of thy holy t...... Ps 65:4
Because of thy t at Jerusalem........ Ps 68:29
thy holy t have they defiled............ Ps 79:1
I will worship toward thy holy t...... Ps 138:2
up, and his train filled the t........... Is 6:1
and to the t, Thy foundation shall... Is 44:28
from the city, a voice from the t..... Is 66:6
The t of the LORD .... Jer 7:4
The t of the LORD .... Jer 7:4
The t of the LORD, are these.......... Jer 7:4
were set before the t of the LORD... Jer 24:1
our God, the vengeance of his t...... Jer 50:28
the LORD, the vengeance of his t.... Jer 51:11

T

at the door of the *t* of the LORD .... Eze 8:16
backs toward the *t* of the LORD .... Eze 8:16
Afterward he brought me to the *t*........... Eze 41:1
twenty cubits, before the *t* .... Eze 41:4
hundred cubits, with the inner *t*........... Eze 41:15
made, and on the wall of the *t*........... Eze 41:20
The posts of the *t* were squared .... Eze 41:21
And the *t* and the sanctuary had two. ... Eze 41:23
on them, on the doors of the *t*........... Eze 41:25
before the *t* were an hundred........... Eze 42:8
had taken out of the *t* which was .... Dan 5:2
that were taken out of the *t* of........... Dan 5:3
the songs of the *t* shall be .... Amos 8:3
will look again toward thy holy *t* .... Jonah 2:4
in unto thee, into thine holy *t* .... Jonah 2:7
you, the Lord from his holy *t*........... Mic 1:2
But the LORD is in his holy *t*........... Hab 2:20
upon a stone in the *t* of the LORD .... Hag 2:15
of the LORD's *t* was laid, ... Hag 2:18
he shall build the *t* of the LORD .... Zec 6:12
he shall build the *t* of the LORD .... Zec 6:13
a memorial in the *t* of the LORD .... Zec 6:14
and build in the *t* of the LORD........... Zec 6:15
that the *t* might be built. .... Zec 8:9
shall suddenly come to his *t*........... Mal 3:1
him on a pinnacle of the *t* .... Mt 4:5
in the *t* profane the sabbath .... Mt 12:5
place is one greater than the *t* .... Mt 12:6
And Jesus went into the *t* of God........... Mt 21:12
them that sold and bought in the *t* .... Mt 21:12
and the lame came to him in the *t*........... Mt 21:14
and the children crying in the *t*........... Mt 21:15
And when he was come into the *t* .... Mt 21:23
Whosoever shall swear by the *t*........... Mt 23:16
shall swear by the gold of the *t* .... Mt 23:16
or the *t* that sanctifieth the........... Mt 23:17
And whoso shall swear by the *t* .... Mt 23:21
whom ye slew between the *t* .... Mt 23:35
went out, and departed from the *t* .... Mt 24:1
shew him the buildings of the *t* .... Mt 24:1
daily with you teaching in the *t* .... Mt 26:55
I am able to destroy the *t* of God........... Mt 26:61
the pieces of silver in the *t* .... Mt 27:5
Thou that destroyest the *t* .... Mt 27:40
the veil of the *t* was rent in .... Mt 27:51
into Jerusalem, and into the *t* .... Mk 11:11
and Jesus went into the *t*, and........... Mk 11:15
them that sold and bought in the *t* .... Mk 11:15
carry any vessel through the *t* .... Mk 11:16
and as he was walking in the *t* .... Mk 11:27
and said, while he taught in the *t* .... Mk 12:35
And as he went out of the *t* .... Mk 13:1
of Olives over against the *t* .... Mk 13:3
daily with you in the *t* teaching .... Mk 14:49
I will destroy this *t* and, ... Mk 14:58
Ah, thou that destroyest the *t* .... Mk 15:29
the veil of the *t* was rent in. .... Mk 15:38
he went into the *t* of the Lord .... Lk 1:9
that he tarried so long in the *t* .... Lk 1:21
he had seen a vision in the *t* .... Lk 1:22
he came by the Spirit into the *t* .... Lk 2:27
which departed not from the *t* .... Lk 2:37
days they found him in the *t*, ... Lk 2:46
and set him on a pinnacle of the *t* .... Lk 4:9
between the altar and the *t* .... Lk 11:51
men went up into the *t* to pray .... Lk 18:10
And he went into the *t*, and began........... Lk 19:45
And he taught daily in the *t* .... Lk 19:47
as he taught the people in the *t* .... Lk 20:1
And as some spake of the *t*........... Lk 21:5
day time he was teaching in the *t* .... Lk 21:37
in the morning to him in the *t* .... Lk 21:38
priests, and captains of the *t* .... Lk 22:52
I was daily with you in the *t* .... Lk 22:53
the veil of the *t* was rent in the........... Lk 23:45
And were continually in the *t* .... Lk 24:53
found in the *t* those that sold .... Jn 2:14
he drove them all out of the *t* .... Jn 2:15
and said unto them, Destroy this *t* .... Jn 2:19
six years was this *t* in building .... Jn 2:20
But he spake of the *t* of his body .... Jn 2:21
Jesus findeth him in the *t*........... Jn 5:14
feast Jesus went up into the *t* .... Jn 7:14
cried Jesus in the *t* as he taught .... Jn 7:28
morning he came again into the *t* .... Jn 8:2
treasury, as he taught in the *t* .... Jn 8:20
hid himself, and went out of the *t* .... Jn 8:59
in the *t* in Solomon's porch .... Jn 10:23
as they stood in the *t*. What .... Jn 11:56
in the synagogue, and in the *t* .... Jn 18:20
daily with one accord in the *t* .... Acts 2:46
into the *t* at the hour of prayer........... Acts 3:1
the *t* which is called Beautiful........... Acts 3:2
of them that entered into the *t* .... Acts 3:2
to go into the *t* asked an alms........... Acts 3:3
and entered with them into the *t* .... Acts 3:8
at the Beautiful gate of the *t* .... Acts 3:10
priests, and the captain of the *t* .... Acts 4:1
speak in the *t* to the people all........... Acts 5:20
into the *t* early in the morning........... Acts 5:21
priest and the captain of the *t* .... Acts 5:24
in prison were standing in the *t* .... Acts 5:25
And daily in the *t*, and in every .... Acts 5:42
but also that the *t* of the great........... Acts 19:27
with them entered into the *t* .... Acts 21:26
Asia, when they saw him in the *t* .... Acts 21:27
brought Greeks also into the *t* .... Acts 21:28
that Paul had brought into the *t* .... Acts 21:29
Paul, and drew him out of the *t* .... Acts 21:30
even while I prayed in the *t*........... Acts 22:17

hath gone about to profane the *t* .... Acts 24:6
in the *t* disputing with any man .... Acts 24:12
Asia found me purified in the *t* .... Acts 24:18
the Jews, neither against the *t* .... Acts 25:8
the Jews caught me in the *t* .... Acts 26:21
ye not that ye are the *t* of God........... 1Cor 3:16
If any man defile the *t* of God 1Cor 3:17
for the *t* of God is holy, which........... 1Cor 3:17
of God is holy, which *t* ye are........... 1Cor 3:17
ye not that your body is the *t* of........... 1Cor 6:19
sit at meat in the idol's *t*........... 1Cor 8:10
live of the things of the *t* 1Cor 9:13
hath the *t* of God with idols........... 2Cor 6:16
for ye are the *t* of the living 2Cor 6:16
unto an holy *t* in the Lord........... Eph 2:21
he as God sitteth in the *t* of God........... 2Th 2:4
make a pillar in the *t* of my God .... Rev 3:12
serve him day and night in his *t* .... Rev 7:15
Rise, and measure the *t* of God .... Rev 11:1
which is without the *t* leave out........... Rev 11:2
the *t* of God was opened in heaven .... Rev 11:19
there was seen in his *t* the ark .... Rev 11:19
another angel came out of the *t* .... Rev 14:15
out of the *t* which is in heaven .... Rev 14:17
the *t* of the tabernacle of the .... Rev 15:5
seven angels came out of the *t* .... Rev 15:6
the *t* was filled with smoke from .... Rev 15:8
man was able to enter into the *t* .... Rev 15:8
the *t* saying to the seven angels........... Rev 16:1
voice out of the *t* of heaven........... Rev 16:17
And I saw no *t* therein........... Rev 21:22
and the Lamb are the *t* of it. .... Rev 21:22

TEMPLES

him, and smote the nail into his *t* .... Judg 4:21
dead, and the nail was in his *t*........... Judg 4:22
pierced and stricken through his *t* .... Judg 5:26
thy *t* are like a piece of a. .... Song 4:3
are thy *t* within thy locks........... Song 6:7
his Maker, and buildeth *t*........... Hos 8:14
have carried into your *t* my .... Joel 3:5
dwelleth not in *t* made with hands........... Acts 7:48
dwelleth not in *t* made with hands........... Acts 17:24

TEMPORAL

the things which are seen are *t*........... 2Cor 4:18

TEMPT

things, that God did *t* Abraham .... Gen 22:1
wherefore do ye *t* the LORD?........... Ex 17:2
Ye shall not *t* the LORD your God, ... Deut 6:16
ask, neither will I *t* the LORD........... Is 7:12
yea, they that *t* God are even .... Mal 3:15
Thou shalt not *t* the Lord thy God........... Mt 4:7
Why *t* ye me, ye hypocrites .... Mt 22:18
said unto them, Why *t* ye me........... Mk 12:15
Thou shalt not *t* the Lord thy God........... Lk 4:12
and said unto them, Why *t* ye me .... Lk 20:23
to *t* the Spirit of the Lord .... Acts 5:9
Now therefore why *t* ye God .... Acts 15:10
that Satan *t* you not for your........... 1Cor 7:5
Neither let us *t* Christ, as some 1Cor 10:9

TEMPTATION

as in the day of *t* in the........... Ps 95:8
And lead us not into *t*, but .... Mt 6:13
and pray, that ye enter not into *t*........... Mt 26:41
ye and pray, lest ye enter into *t*........... Mk 14:38
the devil had ended all the *t* .... Lk 4:13
and in time of *t* fall away........... Lk 8:13
And lead us not into *t*........... Lk 11:4
Pray that ye enter not into *t* .... Lk 22:40
and pray, lest ye enter into *t* .... Lk 22:46
There hath no *t* taken you but 1Cor 10:13
but will with the *t* also make a 1Cor 10:13
my *t* which was in my flesh ye .... Gal 4:14
that will be rich fall into *t*........... 1Ti 6:9
in the day of *t* in the wilderness........... Heb 3:8
is the man that endureth *t* .... Jas 1:12
will keep thee from the hour of *t*........... Rev 3:10

TEMPTATIONS

the midst of another nation, by *t* .... Deut 4:34
The great *t* which thine eyes saw........... Deut 7:19
The great *t* which thine eyes have .... Deut 29:3
have continued with me in my *t* .... Lk 22:28
of mind, and with many tears, and *t*........... Acts 20:19
joy when ye fall into divers *t* .... Jas 1:2
in heaviness through manifold *t* 1Pet 1:6
how to deliver the godly out of *t* 2Pet 2:9

TEMPTED

and because they *t* the LORD........... Ex 17:7
have *t* me now these ten times, and .... Num 14:22
your God, as ye *t* him in Massah .... Deut 6:16
they *t* God in their heart by........... Ps 78:18
t God, and limited the Holy One of........... Ps 78:41
Yet they *t* and provoked the most .... Ps 78:56
When your fathers *t* me, proved me........... Ps 95:9
and *t* God in the desert .... Ps 106:14
wilderness to be *t* of the devil........... Mt 4:1
wilderness forty days, *t* of Satan........... Mk 1:13
Being forty days *t* of the devil........... Lk 4:2
t him, saying, Master, what shall........... Lk 4:22
Christ, as some of them also *t*........... 1Cor 10:9
to be *t* above that ye are able........... 1Cor 10:13
thyself, lest thou also be *t* .... Gal 6:1
some means the tempter have *t* you........... 1Th 3:5
he himself hath suffered being *t*........... Heb 2:18
able to succour them that are *t* .... Heb 2:18
When your fathers *t* me, proved me........... Heb 3:9
in all points like as we are........... Heb 4:15
they were sawn asunder, were *t*........... Heb 11:37

when he is *t*, I am *t* of God .... Jas 1:13
for God cannot be *t* with evil........... Jas 1:13
But every man is *t*, when he is .... Jas 1:14

TEMPTER

when the *t* came to him, he said, ... Mt 4:3
some means the *t* have tempted you 1Th 3:5

TEMPTETH

with evil, neither *t* he any man .... Jas 1:13

TEMPTING

I desired him that he would shew .... Mt 16:1
t him, and saying unto him, Is it .... Mt 19:3
him a question, *t* him, and saying,........... Mt 22:35
of him a sign from heaven, *t* him .... Mk 8:11
put away his wife? *t* him .... Mk 10:2
t him, sought of him a sign from .... Lk 11:16
t him, that they might have to........... Jn 8:6

TEN

were nine hundred and *t* years .... Gen 5:14
after Abram had dwelt *t* years in .... Gen 16:3
Peradventure *t* shall be found........... Gen 18:32
the servant took *t* camels of the........... Gen 24:10
hands of *t* shekels weight of gold........... Gen 24:22
us a few days, at the least *t*........... Gen 24:55
me, and changed my wages *t* times .... Gen 31:7
hast changed my wages *t* times........... Gen 31:41
t bulls, twenty she asses .... Gen 32:15
twenty she asses, and *t* foals........... Gen 32:15
Joseph's *t* brethren went down to .... Gen 42:3
t asses laden with the good........... Gen 45:23
t she asses laden with corn and .... Gen 45:23
into Egypt, were threescore and *t*........... Gen 46:27
for him threescore and *t* days .... Gen 50:3
lived an hundred and *t* years .... Gen 50:22
being an hundred and *t* years old........... Gen 50:26
and threescore and *t* palm trees .... Ex 15:27
t curtains of fine twined linen........... Ex 26:1
t cubits shall be the length of a........... Ex 26:16
pillars *t*, and their sockets *t* .... Ex 27:12
the covenant, the *t* commandments........... Ex 34:28
t curtains of fine twined linen........... Ex 36:8
length of a board was *t* cubits .... Ex 36:21
pillars *t*, and their sockets *t*........... Ex 38:12
shall put *t* thousand to flight........... Lev 26:8
t women shall bake your bread in........... Lev 26:26
and for the female *t* shekels........... Lev 27:5
and for the female *t* shekels........... Lev 27:7
One spoon of *t* shekels of gold,........... Num 7:14
One spoon of gold of *t* shekels........... Num 7:20
One golden spoon of *t* shekels .... Num 7:26
One golden spoon of *t* shekels .... Num 7:32
One golden spoon of *t* shekels .... Num 7:38
One golden spoon of *t* shekels .... Num 7:44
One golden spoon of *t* shekels .... Num 7:50
One golden spoon of *t* shekels .... Num 7:56
One golden spoon of *t* shekels .... Num 7:62
One golden spoon of *t* shekels .... Num 7:68
One golden spoon of *t* shekels .... Num 7:74
One golden spoon of *t* shekels .... Num 7:80
weighing *t* shekels apiece, after .... Num 7:86
nor five days, neither *t* days........... Num 11:19
gathered least gathered *t* homers........... Num 11:32
have tempted me now these *t* times........... Num 14:22
And on the fourth day *t* bullocks........... Num 29:23
and threescore and *t* palm trees........... Num 33:9
to perform, even *t* commandments........... Deut 4:13
the *t* commandments, which he........... Deut 10:4
with threescore and *t* persons........... Deut 10:22
two put *t* thousand to flight........... Deut 32:30
he came with *t* thousands of........... Deut 33:2
they are the *t* thousands of........... Josh 33:17
t cities with their villages........... Josh 15:57
there fell *t* portions to Manasseh........... Josh 17:5
half tribe of Manasseh, *t* cities........... Josh 21:5
All the cities were *t* with their .... Josh 21:26
And with him *t* princes, of each........... Josh 22:14
being an hundred and *t* years old........... Josh 24:29
of them in Bezek *t* thousand men........... Judg 1:4
t kings, having their thumbs and........... Judg 1:7
being an hundred and *t* years old........... Judg 2:8
at that time about *t* thousand men........... Judg 3:29
take with thee *t* thousand men of .... Judg 4:6
he went up with *t* thousand men at........... Judg 4:10
and *t* thousand men after him........... Judg 4:14
Then Gideon took *t* men of his........... Judg 6:27
and there remained *t* thousand........... Judg 7:3
t sons of his body begotten........... Judg 8:30
t persons, reign over you, or .... Judg 9:2
t pieces of silver out of the .... Judg 9:4
t persons, upon one stone........... Judg 9:5
t persons, upon one stone, and........... Judg 9:18
t sons of Jerubbaal might come,........... Judg 9:24
and he judged Israel *t* years........... Judg 12:11
rode on threescore and *t* ass colts........... Judg 12:14
I will give thee *t* shekels of .... Judg 17:10
we will take *t* men of an hundred........... Judg 20:10
and a thousand out of *t* thousand .... Judg 20:10
there came against Gibeah *t*........... Judg 20:34
they dwelled there about *t* years........... Ruth 1:4
he took *t* men of the elders of........... Ruth 4:2
not *t* better to thee than *t* sons........... 1Sa 1:8
thousand and threescore and *t* men 1Sa 6:19
and *t* thousand men of Judah........... 1Sa 15:4
these *t* loaves, and run to the........... 1Sa 17:17
carry these *t* cheeses unto the 1Sa 17:18
and David his *t* thousands........... 1Sa 18:7
ascribed unto David *t* thousands........... 1Sa 18:8
and David his *t* thousands........... 1Sa 21:11
And David sent out *t* young men........... 1Sa 25:5

came to pass about *t* days after........ 1Sa 25:38
and David his *t* thousands................ 1Sa 29:5
And the king left *t* women, which 2Sa 15:16
thou art worth *t* thousand of us........ 2Sa 18:3
given thee *t* shekels of silver........... 2Sa 18:11
t young men that bare Joab's.......... 2Sa 18:15
We have *t* parts in the king, and...... 2Sa 19:43
the king took the *t* women his........ 2Sa 20:3
T fat oxen, and twenty oxen out of .. 1Kin 4:23
t thousand a month by courses......... 1Kin 5:14
t thousand that bare burdens, and.... 1Kin 5:15
t cubits was the breadth thereof....... 1Kin 6:3
of olive tree, each *t* cubits high....... 1Kin 6:23
part of the other were *t* cubits......... 1Kin 6:24
And the other cherub was *t* cubits.... 1Kin 6:25
of the one cherub was *t* cubits......... 1Kin 6:26
great stones, stones of *t* cubits......... 1Kin 7:10
t cubits from the one brim to the..... 1Kin 7:23
t in a cubit, compassing the sea 1Kin 7:24
And he made *t* bases of brass........... 1Kin 7:27
this manner he made the *t* bases....... 1Kin 7:37
Then made he *t* lavers of brass........ 1Kin 7:38
one of the *t* bases one laver............. 1Kin 7:38
bases, and *t* lavers on the bases....... 1Kin 7:43
to Jeroboam, Take thee *t* pieces...... 1Kin 11:31
will give *t* tribes to thee................. 1Kin 11:31
give *t* unto thee, even *t* tribes......... 1Kin 11:35
And take with thee *t* loaves............. 1Kin 14:3
took with him *t* talents of silver........ 2Kin 5:5
of gold, and *t* changes of raiment..... 2Kin 5:5
t chariots, and *t* thousand.............. 2Kin 13:7
in the valley of salt *t* thousand......... 2Kin 14:7
reigned *t* years in Samaria.............. 2Kin 15:17
t degrees, or go back *t* degrees....... 2Kin 20:9
the shadow to go down *t* degrees..... 2Kin 20:10
shadow return backward *t* degrees.... 2Kin 20:10
the shadow *t* degrees backward........ 2Kin 20:11
even *t* thousand captives, and all..... 2Kin 24:14
t men with him, and smote Gedaliah 1Chr 6:61
of Manasseh, by lot, *t* cities............. 1Chr 6:61
t thousand men that drew sword....... 1Chr 21:5
t thousand drams, and of silver........ 1Chr 29:7
of silver *t* thousand talents, and....... 1Chr 29:7
t thousand men to bear burdens,...... 2Chr 2:2
t thousand of them to be bearers...... 2Chr 2:18
t cubits the height thereof................ 2Chr 4:1
sea of *t* cubits from brim to brim...... 2Chr 4:2
t in a cubit, compassing the sea 2Chr 4:3
He made also *t* lavers, and put........ 2Chr 4:6
he made *t* candlesticks of gold......... 2Chr 4:7
He made also *t* tables, and placed.... 2Chr 4:8
days the land was quiet *t* years........ 2Chr 14:1
the children of Seir *t* thousand......... 2Chr 25:11
other *t* thousand left alive did......... 2Chr 25:12
t thousand measures of wheat.......... 2Chr 27:5
and *t* thousand of barley................. 2Chr 27:5
t bullocks, an hundred rams, and..... 2Chr 29:32
bullocks and *t* thousand sheep......... 2Chr 30:24
months and *t* days in Jerusalem....... 2Chr 36:9
to fulfil threescore and *t* years......... 2Chr 36:21
a second sort four hundred and *t* .... Ezr 1:10
and with him an hundred and *t* males . Ezr 8:12
t of their brethren with them,.......... Neh 4:12
came, they said unto us *t* times........ Neh 4:12
once in *t* days store of all sorts......... Neh 5:18
to bring one of *t* to dwell in.............. Neh 11:1
I will pay *t* thousand talents of........ Est 3:9
The *t* sons of Haman the son of........ Est 9:10
palace, and the *t* sons of Haman...... Est 9:12
let Haman's *t* sons be hanged upon.. Est 9:13
and they hanged Haman's *t* sons...... Est 9:14
These *t* times have ye reproached..... Job 19:3
afraid of *t* thousands of people......... Ps 3:6
and an instrument of *t* strings........... Ps 33:2
years are threescore years and *t* ...... Ps 90:10
t thousand at thy right hand............. Ps 91:7
Upon an instrument of *t* strings......... Ps 92:3
an instrument of *t* strings will I........ Ps 144:9
t thousands in our streets................. Ps 144:13
the wise more than *t* mighty men..... Eccl 7:19
the chiefest among *t* thousand.......... Song 5:10
t acres of vineyard shall yield.......... Is 5:10
dial of Ahaz, *t* degrees backward...... Is 38:8
So the sun returned *t* degrees.......... Is 38:8
even *t* men with him, came unto....... Jer 41:1
the *t* men that were with him, and.... Jer 41:2
But *t* men were found among them.... Jer 41:8
And it came to pass after *t* days....... Jer 42:7
the entry of the gate, *t* cubits.......... Eze 40:11
breadth of the door was *t* cubits....... Eze 41:2
a walk of *t* cubits breadth inward..... Eze 42:4
the breadth shall be *t* thousand........ Eze 45:1
and the breadth of *t* thousand.......... Eze 45:3
the *t* thousand of breadth, shall........ Eze 45:5
cor, which is an homer of *t* baths...... Eze 45:14
for *t* baths are an homer................. Eze 45:14
and of *t* thousand in breadth............ Eze 48:9
toward the west *t* thousand.............. Eze 48:10
toward the east *t* thousand.............. Eze 48:10
length, and *t* thousand in breadth..... Eze 48:13
and the breadth *t* thousand.............. Eze 48:13
shall be *t* thousand eastward........... Eze 48:18
and *t* thousand westward................ Eze 48:18
servants, *t* between, the *t* days....... Dan 1:12
matter, and proved them *t* days........ Dan 1:14
at the end of *t* days their................ Dan 1:15
he found them *t* times better than..... Dan 1:20
and it had *t* horns........................ Dan 7:7
unto him, and *t* thousand times........ Dan 7:10
t thousand stood before him............. Dan 7:10

of the *t* horns that were in his.......... Dan 7:20
the *t* horns out of this kingdom........ Dan 7:24
are *t* kings that shall arise.............. Dan 7:24
shall cast down many *t* thousands.... Dan 11:12
forth by an hundred shall leave *t* ..... Amos 5:3
if there remain *t* men in one............ Amos 6:9
or with *t* thousands of rivers of........ Mic 6:7
twenty measures, there were but *t* .... Hag 2:16
these threescore and *t* years............ Zec 1:12
and the breadth thereof *t* cubits....... Zec 5:2
that *t* men shall take hold out of ...... Zec 8:23
which owed him *t* thousand talents.... Mt 18:24
And when the *t* heard it, they were... Mt 20:24
heaven be likened unto *t* virgins....... Mt 25:1
it unto him which hath *t* talents....... Mt 25:28
And when the *t* heard it, they.......... Mk 10:41
whether he be able with *t* .... Lk 14:31
woman having *t* pieces of silver........ Lk 15:8
there met him *t* men that were......... Lk 17:12
said, Were there not *t* cleansed........ Lk 17:17
And he called his *t* servants............ Lk 19:13
and delivered them *t* pounds........... Lk 19:13
thy pound hath gained *t* pounds....... Lk 19:16
have thou authority over *t* cities....... Lk 19:17
give it to him that hath *t* pounds...... Lk 19:24
unto him, Lord, he hath *t* pounds..... Lk 19:25
and horsemen threescore and *t* .... Acts 23:23
among them more than *t* days.......... Acts 25:6
For though ye have *t* thousand........ 1Cor 4:15
than *t* thousand words in an............ 1Cor 14:19
the Lord cometh with *t* thousands..... Jude 14
ye shall have tribulation *t* days........ Rev 2:10
the number of them was *t* thousand... Rev 5:11
thousand times *t* thousand.............. Rev 5:11
t horns, and seven crowns upon his... Rev 12:3
t horns, and upon his horns............. Rev 13:1
and upon his horns *t* crowns............ Rev 13:1
having seven heads and *t* horns........ Rev 17:3
hath the seven heads and *t* horns..... Rev 17:7
the *t* horns which thou sawest are..... Rev 17:12
which thou sawest are *t* kings.......... Rev 17:12
the *t* horns which thou sawest......... Rev 17:16

TEND

diligent *t* only to plenteousness........ Prov 21:5

TENDER

unto the herd, and fetch a calf *t* ...... Gen 18:7
Leah was *t* eyed........................... Gen 29:17
knoweth that the children are *t* .... Gen 33:13
that the man that is *t* among you..... Deut 28:54
The *t* and delicate woman............... Deut 28:56
as the small rain upon the *t* herb...... Deut 32:2
as the *t* grass springing out of......... 2Sa 23:4
Because thine heart was *t* .... Kin 22:19
Solomon my son is young and *t* 1Chr 22:5
hath chosen, is yet young and *t* 1Chr 29:1
Because thine heart was *t* 2Chr 34:27
that the *t* branch thereof will........... Job 14:7
bud of the *t* herb to spring forth....... Job 38:27
O Lord, thy *t* mercies and thy.......... Ps 25:6
not thou thy *t* mercies from me........ Ps 40:11
of thy *t* mercies blot out my............ Ps 51:1
to the multitude of thy *t* mercies...... Ps 69:16
he in anger shut up his *t* mercies...... Ps 77:9
let thy *t* mercies speedily............... Ps 79:8
with lovingkindness and *t* mercies.... Ps 103:4
Let thy *t* mercies come unto me,....... Ps 119:77
Great are thy *t* mercies, O LORD...... Ps 119:156
his *t* mercies are over all his........... Ps 145:9
For I was my father's son, *t* .... Prov 4:3
but the *t* mercies of the wicked........ Prov 12:10
the *t* grass sheweth itself, and.......... Prov 27:25
the vines with the *t* grape give a...... Song 2:13
for our vines have *t* grapes.............. Song 2:15
whether the *t* grape appear, and....... Song 7:12
thou shalt no more be called *t* .... Is 47:1
grow up before him as a *t* plant....... Is 53:2
top of his young twigs a *t* one.......... Eze 17:22
t love with the prince of the............ Dan 1:9
in the *t* grass of the field................ Dan 4:15
in the *t* grass of the field................ Dan 4:23
When his branch is yet *t*, and.......... Mt 24:32
When her branch is yet *t*, and.......... Mk 13:28
Through the *t* mercy of our God....... Lk 1:78
is very pitiful, and of *t* mercy.......... Jas 5:11

TENDERHEARTED

when Rehoboam was young and *t* 2Chr 13:7
And be ye kind one to another, *t* ..... Eph 4:32

TENDERNESS

the ground for delicateness and *t* ..... Deut 28:56

TENDETH

labour of the righteous *t* to life......... Prov 10:16
As righteousness *t* to life................ Prov 11:19
than is meet, but it *t* to poverty........ Prov 11:24
talk of the lips *t* only to penury........ Prov 14:23
The fear of the LORD *t* to life........... Prov 19:23

TENONS

Two *t* shall there be in one board..... Ex 26:17
under one board for his two *t* .... Ex 26:19
under another board for his two *t* .... Ex 26:19
One board had two *t*, equally........... Ex 36:22
under one board for his two *t* .... Ex 36:24
under another board for his two *t* .... Ex 36:24

TENOR

according to the *t* of these words...... Gen 43:7
for after the *t* of these words I......... Gen 34:27

TEN'S

I will not destroy it for *t* sake.......... Gen 18:32

TENS

rulers of fifties, and rulers of *t* .... Ex 18:21
rulers of fifties, and rulers of *t* .... Ex 18:25
over fifties, and captains over *t* .... Deut 1:15

TENT

and he was uncovered within his *t* ... Gen 9:21
east of Beth-el, and pitched his *t* ..... Gen 12:8
unto the place where his *t* had......... Gen 13:3
pitched his *t* toward Sodom............ Gen 13:12
Abram removed his *t* .... Gen 13:18
he sat in the *t* door in the heat........ Gen 18:1
ran to meet them from the *t* door..... Gen 18:2
hastened into the *t* unto Sarah........ Gen 18:6
And he said, Behold, in the *t* .... Gen 18:9
And Sarah heard it in the *t* door...... Gen 18:10
her into his mother Sarah's *t* .... Gen 24:67
pitched his *t* in the valley of........... Gen 26:17
the Lord, and pitched his *t* there...... Gen 26:25
had pitched his *t* in the mount......... Gen 31:25
Jacob's *t*, and into Leah's *t* .... Gen 31:33
Then went he out of Leah's *t* .... Gen 31:33
and entered into Rachel's *t* .... Gen 31:33
And Laban searched all the *t* .... Gen 31:34
pitched his *t* before the city............ Gen 33:18
field, where he had spread his *t* ...... Gen 33:19
spread his *t* beyond the tower of...... Gen 35:21
and they came into the *t* .... Ex 18:7
loops, and couple the *t* together....... Ex 26:11
of the curtains of the *t*, the............ Ex 26:12
length of the curtains of the *t* .... Ex 26:13
for the *t* of rams' skins dyed red...... Ex 26:14
an hanging for the door of the *t* ...... Ex 26:36
and stood every man at his *t* door.... Ex 33:8
every man in his *t* door................. Ex 33:10
The tabernacle, his *t*, and his......... Ex 35:11
for the *t* over the tabernacle........... Ex 36:14
of brass to couple the *t* together....... Ex 36:18
for the *t* of rams' skins dyed red...... Ex 36:19
of the congregation finished.............. Ex 39:32
the tabernacle unto Moses, the *t* ..... Ex 39:33
for the *t* of the congregation,.......... Ex 39:40
of the *t* of the congregation............ Ex 40:2
of the *t* of the congregation............ Ex 40:6
of the *t* of the congregation............ Ex 40:7
between the *t* of the congregation..... Ex 40:12
abroad the *t* over the tabernacle...... Ex 40:19
covering of the *t* above upon it........ Ex 40:19
in the *t* of the congregation............ Ex 40:22
in the *t* of the congregation............ Ex 40:24
of the congregation before the........... Ex 40:26
of the *t* of the congregation............ Ex 40:29
between the *t* of the congregation..... Ex 40:30
into the *t* of the congregation.......... Ex 40:32
covered the *t* of the congregation..... Ex 40:34
into the *t* of the congregation.......... Ex 40:35
abroad out of his *t* every man.......... Lev 14:8
shall be the tabernacle, and the *t* .... Num 3:25
namely, the *t* of the testimony........ Num 9:15
every man in the door of his *t* .... Num 11:10
the law, when a man dieth in a *t* ..... Num 19:14
all that come into the *t*, and all....... Num 19:14
and all that is in the *t* .... Num 19:14
water, and sprinkle it upon the *t* ..... Num 19:18
the man of Israel into the *t* .... Num 25:8
in the earth in the midst of my *t* ..... Josh 7:21
and they ran unto the *t* .... Josh 7:22
and, behold, it was hid in his *t* .... Josh 7:22
them out of the midst of the *t* .... Josh 7:23
his asses, and his sheep, and his *t* ... Josh 7:24
pitched his *t* unto the plain of......... Judg 4:11
fled away on his feet to the *t* of ...... Judg 4:17
had turned in unto her into the *t* ..... Judg 4:18
her, Stand in the door of the *t* .... Judg 4:20
Heber's wife took a nail of the *t* ...... Judg 4:21
And when he came into her *t* .... Judg 5:24
shall she be above women in the *t* ... Judg 5:24
of Israel every man unto his *t* .... Judg 7:8
host of Midian, and came unto a *t* ... Judg 7:13
it, that the *t* lay along.................. Judg 7:13
We will not any of us go to his *t* ...... Judg 20:8
and they fled every man into his *t* ... 1Sa 4:10
people he sent every man to his *t* 1Sa 13:2
but he put his armour in his *t* 1Sa 17:54
this day, but have walked in a *t* 2Sa 7:6
So they spread Absalom a *t* upon..... 2Sa 16:22
Israel fled every one to his *t* 2Sa 18:17
had fled every man to his *t* 2Sa 19:8
from the city, every man to his *t* 2Sa 20:22
of the camp, they went into one *t* 2Kin 7:8
again, and entered into another *t* 2Kin 7:8
ark of God, and pitched for it a *t* 1Chr 15:1
set it in the midst of the *t* that........ 1Chr 16:1
but have gone from *t* to *t* 1Chr 17:5
pitched a *t* for it at Jerusalem......... 2Chr 1:4
and they fled every man to his *t* 2Chr 25:22
the which he placed among men......... Ps 78:60
shall the Arabian pitch *t* there......... Is 13:20
removed from me as a shepherd's *t* .. Is 38:12
them out as a *t* to dwell in............. Is 40:22
Enlarge the place of thy *t* .... Is 54:2
to stretch forth my *t* any more........ Jer 10:20
they rise up every man in his *t* .... Jer 37:10

TENTH

continually, until the *t* month.......... Gen 8:5
in the *t* month, on the first day....... Gen 8:5
will surely give the *t* unto thee........ Gen 28:22
In the *t* day of this month they........ Ex 12:3
an omer is the *t* part of an ephah.... Ex 16:36

with the one lamb a *t* deal of	Ex 29:40
bring for his offering the *t* part	Lev 5:11
the *t* part of an ephah of fine	Lev 6:20
three *t* deals of fine flour for a	Lev 14:10
one *t* deal of fine flour mingled	Lev 14:21
on the *t* day of the month, ye	Lev 16:29
two *t* deals of fine flour mingled	Lev 23:13
two wave loaves of two *t* deals	Lev 23:17
Also on the *t* day of this seventh	Lev 23:27
two *t* deals shall be in one cake	Lev 24:5
on the *t* day of the seventh month	Lev 25:9
the *t* shall be holy unto the LORD	Lev 27:32
the *t* part of an ephah of barley	Num 5:15
On the *t* day Ahiezer the son of	Num 7:66
t deal of flour mingled with the	Num 15:4
t deals of flour mingled with the	Num 15:6
a meat offering of three *t* deals	Num 15:9
t in Israel for an inheritance	Num 18:21
even a *t* part of the tithe	Num 18:26
a *t* part of an ephah of flour for	Num 28:5
two *t* deals of flour for a meat	Num 28:9
three *t* deals of flour for a meat	Num 28:12
two *t* deals of flour for a meat	Num 28:12
a several *t* deal of flour mingled	Num 28:13
three *t* deals shall ye offer for	Num 28:20
bullock, and two *t* deals for a ram	Num 28:20
A several *t* deal shalt thou offer	Num 28:21
three *t* deals unto one bullock,	Num 28:28
two *t* deals unto one ram,	Num 28:28
A several *t* deal unto one lamb,	Num 28:29
three *t* deals for a bullock	Num 29:3
and two *t* deals for a ram,	Num 29:3
And one *t* deal for one lamb,	Num 29:4
ye shall have on the *t* day	Num 29:7
three *t* deals to a bullock	Num 29:9
and two *t* deals for one ram,	Num 29:9
A several *t* deal for one lamb,	Num 29:10
three *t* deals unto every bullock,	Num 29:14
two *t* deals to each ram of the	Num 29:14
a several *t* deal to each lamb of	Num 29:15
even to his *t* generation shall he	Deut 23:2
even to their *t* generation shall	Deut 23:3
on the *t* day of the first month,	Josh 4:19
he will take the *t* of your seed	1Sa 8:15
He will take the *t* of your sheep	1Sa 8:17
year of his reign, in the *t* month	2Kin 25:1
in the *t* day of the month, that	2Kin 25:1
Jeremiah the *t*, Machbanai the	1Chr 12:13
to Jeshua, the *t* to Shecaniah,	1Chr 24:11
The *t* to Shimei, he, his sons, and	1Chr 25:17
The *t* captain for the *t* month	1Chr 27:13
the *t* month to examine the matter	Ezr 10:16
his house royal in the *t* month	Est 2:16
But yet in it shall be a *t*	Is 6:13
Jeremiah from the LORD in the *t*	Jer 32:1
king of Judah, in the *t* month	Jer 39:1
year of his reign, in the *t* month	Jer 52:4
in the *t* day of the month, that	Jer 52:4
in the *t* day of the month, which	Jer 52:12
the *t* day of the month, that	Eze 20:1
in the ninth year, in the *t* month	Eze 24:1
in the *t* day of the month, the	Eze 24:1
In the *t* year, in the *t* month	Eze 29:1
of our captivity, in the *t* month	Eze 33:21
in the *t* day of the month, in the	Eze 40:1
contain the *t* part of an homer	Eze 45:11
the ephah the *t* part of an homer	Eze 45:14
ye shall offer the *t* part of a	Eze 45:14
the seventh, and the fast of the *t*	Zec 8:19
for it was about the *t* hour	Jn 1:39
also Abraham gave a *t* part of all	Heb 7:2
Abraham gave the *t* of the spoils	Heb 7:4
the *t* part of the city fell, and	Rev 11:13
the *t*, a chrysoprasus	Rev 21:20

TENTMAKERS

by their occupation they were *t*	Acts 18:3

TENTS

the father of such as dwell in *t*	Gen 4:20
he shall dwell in the *t* of Shem,	Gen 9:27
Abram, had flocks, and herds, and *t*	Gen 13:5
was a plain man, dwelling in *t*	Gen 25:27
and into the two maidservants' *t*	Gen 31:33
man for them which are in his *t*	Ex 16:16
of Israel shall pitch their *t*	Num 1:52
of Israel pitched their *t*	Num 9:17
tabernacle they rested in their *t*	Num 9:18
of the LORD they abode in their *t*	Num 9:20
of Israel abode in their *t*	Num 9:22
of the LORD they rested in the *t*	Num 9:23
that they dwell in, whether in *t*	Num 13:19
from the *t* of these wicked men,	Num 16:26
and stood in the door of their *t*	Num 16:27
his *t* according to their tribes	Num 24:2
How goodly are thy *t*, O Jacob, and	Num 24:5
And ye murmured in your *t*, and said	Deut 1:27
out a place to pitch your *t* in	Deut 1:33
them, Get you into your *t* again	Deut 5:30
and their households, and their *t*	Deut 11:6
in the morning, and go unto thy *t*	Deut 16:7
and, Issachar, in thy *t*	Deut 33:18
the people removed from their *t*	Josh 3:14
return ye, and get you unto your *t*	Josh 22:4
and they went unto their *t*	Josh 22:6
sent them away also unto their *t*	Josh 22:7
with much riches unto your *t*	Josh 22:8
up with their cattle and their *t*	Judg 6:5
dwelt in *t* on the east of Nobah	Judg 8:11
and they spoiled their *t*	1Sa 17:53
and Israel, and Judah, abide in *t*	2Sa 11:11

every man to his *t*, O Israel	2Sa 20:1
king, and went unto their *t* joyful	1Kin 8:66
to your *t*, O Israel	1Kin 12:16
So Israel departed unto their *t*	1Kin 12:16
in the twilight, and left their *t*	2Kin 7:7
asses tied, and the *t* as they were	2Kin 7:10
spoiled the *t* of the Syrians	2Kin 7:16
and the people fled into their *t*	2Kin 8:21
of Israel dwelt in their *t*	2Kin 13:5
and they fled every man to their *t*	2Kin 14:12
king of Judah, and smote their *t*	1Chr 4:41
they dwelt in their *t* throughout	1Chr 5:10
sent the people away into their *t*	2Chr 7:10
every man to your *t*, O Israel, and	2Chr 10:16
So all Israel went to their *t*	2Chr 10:16
They smote also the *t* of cattle	2Chr 14:15
in the gates of the *t* of the LORD	2Chr 31:2
and there abode we in *t* three days	Ezr 8:15
and let none dwell in their *t*	Ps 69:25
of Israel to dwell in their *t*	Ps 78:55
to dwell in the *t* of wickedness	Ps 84:10
But murmured in their *t*, and	Ps 106:25
that I dwell in the *t* of Kedar	Ps 120:5
as the *t* of Kedar, as the	Song 1:5
thy kids beside the shepherds' *t*	Song 1:8
suddenly are my *t* spoiled	Jer 4:20
they shall pitch their *t* against	Jer 6:3
again the captivity of Jacob's *t*	Jer 30:18
all your days ye shall dwell in *t*	Jer 35:7
But we have dwelt in *t*, and have	Jer 35:10
Their *t* and their flocks shall	Jer 49:29
I saw the *t* of Cushan in	Hab 3:7
shall save the *t* of Judah first	Zec 12:7
beasts that shall be in these *t*	Zec 14:15

TERAH (te'-rah) See THARA. *Father of Abraham.*

nine and twenty years, and begat *T*	Gen 11:24
lived after he begat *T* an hundred	Gen 11:25
T lived seventy years, and begat	Gen 11:26
these are the generations of *T*	Gen 11:27
T begat Abram, Nahor, and Haran,	Gen 11:27
T in the land of his nativity	Gen 11:28
T took Abram his son, and Lot the	Gen 11:31
the days of *T* were two hundred and	Gen 11:32
and *T* died in Haran	Gen 11:32
of the flood in old time, even *T*	Josh 24:2
Serug, Nahor, *T*,	1Chr 1:26

TERAPHIM

of gods, and made an ephod, and *t*	Judg 17:5
is in these houses an ephod, and *t*	Judg 18:14
image, and the ephod, and the *t*	Judg 18:17
carved image, the ephod, and the *t*	Judg 18:18
and he took the ephod, and the *t*	Judg 18:20
and without an ephod, and without *t*	Hos 3:4

TERESH (te'-resh) *A servant of King Ahasuerus.*

king's chamberlains, Bigthan and *T*	Est 2:21
had told of Bigthana and *T*	Est 6:2

TERMED

Thou shalt no more be *t* Forsaken	Is 62:4
thy land any more be *t* Desolate	Is 62:4

TERRACES

trees to the house of the LORD	2Chr 9:11

TERRESTRIAL

celestial bodies, and bodies *t*	1Cor 15:40
and the glory of the *t* is another	1Cor 15:40

TERRIBLE

for it is a *t* thing that I will	Ex 34:10
t wilderness, which ye saw by the	Deut 1:19
is among you, a mighty God and *t*	Deut 7:21
t wilderness, wherein were fiery	Deut 8:15
a great God, a mighty, and a *t*	Deut 10:17
t things, which thine eyes have	Deut 10:21
of an angel of God, very *t*	Judg 13:6
to do for you great things, and *t*	2Sa 7:23
t God, that keepeth covenant and	Neh 1:5
the LORD, which is great and *t*	Neh 4:14
great, the mighty, and the *t* God	Neh 9:32
with God is *t* majesty	Job 37:22
the glory of his nostrils is *t*	Job 39:20
his teeth are *t* round about	Job 41:14
hand shall teach thee *t* things	Ps 45:4
For the LORD most high is *t*	Ps 47:2
By *t* things in righteousness wilt	Ps 65:5
How *t* art thou in thy works	Ps 66:3
he is *t* in his doing toward the	Ps 66:5
thou art *t* out of thy holy places	Ps 68:35
he is *t* to the kings of the earth	Ps 76:12
them praise thy great and *t* name	Ps 99:3
Ham, and *t* things by the Red sea	Ps 106:22
speak of the might of thy *t* acts	Ps 145:6
t as an army with banners	Song 6:4
t as an army with banners	Song 6:10
lay low the haughtiness of the *t*	Is 13:11
peeled, to a people *t* from their	Is 18:2
from a people *t* from their	Is 18:7
the city of the *t* nations shall	Is 25:3
when the blast of the *t* ones is	Is 25:4
the branch of the *t* ones shall be	Is 25:5
the multitude of the *t* ones shall	Is 29:5
For the *t* one is brought to	Is 29:20
the prey of the *t* shall be	Is 49:25
When thou didst *t* things which we	Is 64:3
out of the hand of the *t*	Jer 15:21
LORD is with me as a mighty *t* one	Jer 20:11

an oven because of the *t* famine	Lam 5:10
as the colour of the *t* crystal	Eze 1:22
upon thee, the *t* of the nations	Eze 28:7
the *t* of the nations, shall be	Eze 30:11
the *t* of the nations, have cut	Eze 31:12
the *t* of the nations, all of them	Eze 32:12
and the form thereof was *t*	Dan 2:31
a fourth beast, dreadful and *t*	Dan 7:7
of the LORD is great and very *t*	Joel 2:11
the *t* day of the LORD come	Joel 2:31
They are *t* and dreadful	Hab 1:7
The LORD will be *t* unto them	Zeph 2:11
so *t* was the sight, that Moses	Heb 12:21

TERRIBLENESS

outstretched arm, and with great *t*	Deut 26:8
thee a name of greatness and *t*	1Chr 17:21
Thy *t* hath deceived thee, and the	Jer 49:16

TERRIBLY

he ariseth to shake *t* the earth	Is 2:19
he ariseth to shake *t* the earth	Is 2:21
the fir trees shall be *t* shaken	Nah 2:3

TERRIFIED

neither be ye *t* because of them	Deut 20:3
of wars and commotions, be not *t*	Lk 21:9
But they were *t* and affrighted, and	Lk 24:37
in nothing *t* by your adversaries	Phil 1:28

TERRIFIEST

dreams, and *t* me through visions	Job 7:14

TERRIFY

let the blackness of the day *t* it	Job 3:5
from me, and let not his fear *t* me	Job 9:34
did the contempt of families *t* me	Job 31:34
as if I would *t* you by letters	2Cor 10:9

TERROR

the *t* of God was upon the cities	Gen 35:5
I will even appoint over you *t*	Lev 26:16
t within, shall destroy both the	Deut 32:25
in all the great *t* which Moses	Deut 34:12
that your *t* is fallen upon us, and	Josh 2:9
from God was a *t* to me, and by	Job 31:23
my *t* shall not make thee afraid,	Job 33:7
not be afraid for the *t* by night	Ps 91:5
hosts, shall lop the bough with *t*	Is 10:33
of Judah shall be a *t* unto Egypt	Is 19:17
Thine heart shall meditate *t*	Is 54:14
and from *t*	Is 54:14
Be not a *t* unto me	Jer 17:17
I will make thee a *t* to thyself	Jer 20:4
out arm, and with great *t*	Jer 32:21
which cause their *t* to be on all	Eze 26:17
I will make thee a *t*, and thou	Eze 26:21
thou shalt be a *t*, and never shalt	Eze 27:36
thou shalt be a *t*, and never shalt	Eze 28:19
which caused *t* in the land of the	Eze 32:23
which caused their *t* in the land	Eze 32:24
though their *t* was caused in the	Eze 32:25
though they caused their *t* in the	Eze 32:26
though they were the *t* of the	Eze 32:27
with their *t* they are ashamed of	Eze 32:30
For I have caused my *t* in the	Eze 32:32
rulers are not a *t* to good works	Rom 13:3
therefore the *t* of the Lord	2Cor 5:11
and be not afraid of their *t*	1Pet 3:14

TERRORS

stretched out arm, and by great *t*	Deut 4:34
the *t* of God do set themselves in	Job 6:4
T shall make him afraid on every	Job 18:11
shall bring him to the king of *t*	Job 18:14
t are upon him	Job 20:25
they are in the *t* of the shadow	Job 24:17
T take hold on him as waters, a	Job 27:20
T are turned upon me	Job 30:15
the *t* of death are fallen upon me	Ps 55:4
they are utterly consumed with *t*	Ps 73:19
I suffer thy *t* I am distracted	Ps 88:15
thy *t* have cut me off	Ps 88:16
it suddenly, and I spoke thy *t*	Jer 15:8
in a solemn day my *t* round about	Lam 2:22
t by reason of the sword shall be	Eze 21:12

TERTIUS (tur'-she-us) *An assistant of Paul.*

I *T*, who wrote this epistle,	Rom 16:22

TERTULLUS (tur-tul'-lus) *An orator who opposed Paul.*

and with a certain orator named *T*	Acts 24:1
T began to accuse him, saying,	Acts 24:2

TESTAMENT

For this is my blood of the new *t*	Mt 26:28
This is my blood of the new *t*	Mk 14:24
This cup is the new *t* in my blood	Lk 22:20
This cup is the new *t* in my blood	1Cor 11:25
us able ministers of the new *t*	2Cor 3:6
away in the reading of the old *t*	2Cor 3:14
Jesus made a surety of a better *t*	Heb 7:22
he is the mediator of the new *t*	Heb 9:15
that were under the first *t*	Heb 9:15
For where a *t* is, there must also	Heb 9:16
For a *t* is of force after men are	Heb 9:17
t was dedicated without blood	Heb 9:18
This is the blood of the *t* which	Heb 9:20
in his temple the ark of his *t*	Rev 11:19

TESTATOR

necessity be the death of the *t*	Heb 9:16
at all while the *t* liveth	Heb 9:17

TESTIFIED

and it hath been t to its owner	Ex 21:29
hath t falsely against his	Deut 19:18
seeing the LORD hath t against me	Ruth 1:21
for thy much hath t against thee	2Sa 1:16
Yet the LORD t against Israel, and	2Kin 17:13
which he t against them	2Kin 17:15
and they t against them	2Chr 24:19
slew thy prophets which t against	Neh 9:26
I t against them in the day	Neh 13:15
Then I t against them, and said	Neh 13:21
the saying of the woman, which t	Jn 4:39
For Jesus himself t, that a	Jn 4:44
he was troubled in spirit, and t	Jn 13:21
And they, when they had t and	Acts 8:25
t to the Jews that Jesus was	Acts 18:5
for as thou hast t of me in	Acts 23:11
t the kingdom of God, persuading	Acts 28:23
because we have t of God that he	1Cor 15:15
we also have forewarned you and t	1Th 4:6
for all, to be t in due time	1Ti 2:6
But one in a certain place t	Heb 2:6
signify, when it t beforehand the	1Pet 1:11
of God which he hath t of his Son	1Jn 5:9
t of the truth that is in thee	3Jn 3

TESTIFIEDST

t against them, that thou	Neh 9:29
t against them by thy spirit in	Neh 9:30

TESTIFIETH

the pride of Israel t to his face	Hos 7:10
he hath seen and heard, that he t	Jn 3:32
disciple which t of these things	Jn 21:24
For he t, Thou art a priest for	Heb 7:17
He which t these things saith	Rev 22:20

TESTIFY

but one witness shall not t	Num 35:30
I t against you this day that ye	Deut 8:19
rise up against any that t	Deut 19:16
that this song shall t against	Deut 31:21
which I t among you this day	Deut 32:46
thou didst t against them	Neh 9:34
thine own lips t against thee	Job 15:6
Israel, and I will t against thee	Ps 50:7
my people, and I will t unto thee	Ps 81:8
thee, and our sins t against us	Is 59:12
our iniquities t against us	Jer 14:7
of Israel doth t to his face	Hos 5:5
t in the house of Jacob, saith	Amos 3:13
t against me	Mic 6:3
that he may t unto them, lest	Lk 16:28
not that any should t of man	Jn 2:25
do know, and t that we have seen	Jn 3:11
and they are they which t of me	Jn 5:39
me it testifieth, because I t	Jn 7:7
from the Father, he shall t of me	Jn 15:26
And with many other words did he t	Acts 2:40
to t that it is he which was	Acts 10:42
to t the gospel of the grace of	Acts 20:24
the beginning, if they would t	Acts 26:5
For I t again to every man that	Gal 5:3
t in the Lord, that ye henceforth	Eph 4:17
do t that the Father sent the Son	1Jn 4:14
to t unto you these things in the	Rev 22:16
For I t unto every man that	Rev 22:18

TESTIFYING

T both to the Jews, and also to	Acts 20:21
was righteous, God t of his gifts	Heb 11:4
t that this is the true grace of	1Pet 5:12

TESTIMONIES

These are the t, and the statutes,	Deut 4:45
of the LORD your God, and his t	Deut 6:17
to come, saying, What mean the t	Deut 6:20
and his judgments, and his t	1Kin 2:3
his t which he testified against	2Kin 17:15
to keep his commandments and his t	2Kin 23:3
to keep thy commandments, and thy t	1Chr 29:19
keep his commandments, and his t	2Chr 34:31
unto thy commandments and thy t	Neh 9:34
as keep his covenant and thy t	Ps 25:10
most high God, and kept not his t	Ps 78:56
Thy t are very sure	Ps 93:5
they kept his t, and the ordinance	Ps 99:7
Blessed are they that keep his t	Ps 119:2
have rejoiced in the way of thy t	Ps 119:14
for I have kept thy t	Ps 119:22
Thy t also are my delight, and my	Ps 119:24
I have stuck unto thy t	Ps 119:31
Incline my heart unto thy t	Ps 119:36
speak of thy t also before kings	Ps 119:46
and turned my feet unto thy t	Ps 119:59
and those that have known thy t	Ps 119:79
but I will consider thy t	Ps 119:95
for thy t are my meditation	Ps 119:99
Thy t have I taken as an heritage	Ps 119:111
therefore I love thy t	Ps 119:119
that I may know thy t	Ps 119:125
Thy t are wonderful	Ps 119:129
Thy t that thou hast commanded	Ps 119:138
of thy t is everlasting	Ps 119:144
save me, and I shall keep thy t	Ps 119:146
Concerning thy t, I have known of	Ps 119:152
yet do I not decline from thy t	Ps 119:157
My soul hath kept thy t	Ps 119:167
I have kept thy precepts and thy t	Ps 119:168
nor in his statutes, nor in his t	Jer 44:23

TESTIMONY

so Aaron laid it up before the T	Ex 16:34
ark the t which I shall give thee	Ex 25:16
put the t that I shall give thee	Ex 25:21
which are upon the ark of the t	Ex 25:22
within the vail the ark of the t	Ex 26:33
of the t in the most holy place	Ex 26:34
the vail, which is before the t	Ex 27:21
vail that is by the ark of the t	Ex 30:6
the mercy seat that is over the t	Ex 30:6
therewith, and the ark of the t	Ex 30:26
put of it before the t in the	Ex 30:36
congregation, and the ark of the t	Ex 31:7
upon mount Sinai, two tables of t	Ex 31:18
tables of the t were in his hand	Ex 32:15
two tables of t in Moses' hand	Ex 34:29
even of the tabernacle of t	Ex 38:21
The Ark of the t, and the staves	Ex 39:35
put therein the ark of the t	Ex 40:3
incense before the ark of the t	Ex 40:5
put the t into the ark, and set	Ex 40:20
and covered the ark of the t	Ex 40:21
the mercy seat that is upon the t	Lev 16:13
Without the vail of the t	Lev 24:3
Levites over the tabernacle of t	Num 1:50
round about the tabernacle of t	Num 1:53
the charge of the tabernacle of t	Num 1:53
and cover the ark of t with it	Num 4:5
seat that was upon the ark of t	Num 7:89
namely, the tent of the t	Num 9:15
from off the tabernacle of the t	Num 10:11
of the congregation before the t	Num 17:4
Aaron's rod again before the t	Num 17:10
that bear the ark of the t	Josh 4:16
and this was a t in Israel	Ruth 4:7
crown upon him, and gave him the t	2Chr 23:11
the t of the LORD is sure, making	Ps 19:7
For he established a t in Jacob	Ps 78:5
he ordained in Joseph for a t	Ps 81:5
shall I keep the t of thy mouth	Ps 119:88
unto the t of Israel, to give	Ps 122:4
my t that I shall teach them	Ps 132:12
Bind up the t, seal the law among	Is 8:16
To the law and to the t	Is 8:20
commanded, for a t unto them	Mt 8:4
for a t against them and the	Mt 10:18
commanded, for a t unto them	Mk 1:44
your feet for a t against them	Mk 6:11
for my sake, for a t against them	Mk 13:9
commanded, for a t unto them	Lk 5:14
your feet for a t against them	Lk 9:5
And it shall turn to you for a t	Lk 21:13
and no man receiveth his t	Jn 3:32
He that hath received his t hath	Jn 3:33
But I receive not t from man	Jn 5:34
that the t of two men is true	Jn 8:17
and we know that his t is true	Jn 21:24
to whom also he gave it, and said,	Acts 13:22
which gave t unto the word of his	Acts 14:3
not receive thy t concerning me	Acts 22:18
Even as the t of Christ was	1Cor 1:6
declaring unto you the t of God	1Cor 2:1
the t of our conscience, that in	2Cor 1:12
them that believe (because our t	2Th 1:10
ashamed of the t of our Lord	2Ti 1:8
for a t of those things which	Heb 3:5
his translation he had this t	Heb 11:5
of the t of Jesus Christ, and of	Rev 1:2
for the t of Jesus Christ	Rev 1:9
for the t which they held	Rev 6:9
they shall have finished their t	Rev 11:7
Lamb, and by the word of their t	Rev 12:11
have the t of Jesus Christ	Rev 12:17
of the t in heaven was opened	Rev 15:5
brethren that have the t of Jesus	Rev 19:10
for the t of Jesus is the spirit	Rev 19:10

TETRARCH

At that time Herod the t heard of	Mt 14:1
and Herod being t of Galilee	Lk 3:1
his brother Philip t of Ituraea	Lk 3:1
and Lysanias the t of Abilene	Lk 3:1
But Herod the t, being reproved	Lk 3:19
Now Herod the t heard of all that	Lk 9:7
been brought up with Herod the t	Acts 13:1

THADDAEUS (thad-de'-us) See JUDE, LEBBAEUS. A disciple of Jesus.

and Lebbaeus, whose surname was T	Mt 10:3
James the son of Alphaeus, and T	Mk 3:18

THAHASH (tha'-hash) A son of Reumah.

bare also Tebah, and Gaham, and T	Gen 22:24

THAMAH (tha'-mah) See TAMAH. A family of exiles.

of Sisera, the children of T	Ezr 2:53

THAMAR (tha'-mar) See TAMAR. Mother of Phares and Zaraian; ancestor of Jesus.

Judas begat Phares and Zara of T	Mt 1:3

THAN See PREFACE.

THANK

the LORD, and to record, and to t	1Chr 16:4
delivered first this psalm to t	1Chr 16:7
And to stand every morning to t	1Chr 23:30
we t thee, and praise thy glorious	1Chr 29:13
t offerings into the house of the	2Chr 29:31
in sacrifices and t offerings	2Chr 29:31
t offerings, and commanded Judah	2Chr 29:31
I t, and praise thee, O thou	Dan 2:23
I t thee, O Father, Lord of	Mt 11:25
which love you, what t have ye	Lk 6:32
do good to you, what t have ye	Lk 6:33
hope to receive, what t have ye	Lk 6:34
I t thee, O Father, Lord of	Lk 10:21
Doth he t that servant because he	Lk 17:9
I t thee, that I am not as other	Lk 18:11
I t thee that thou hast heard me	Jn 11:41
t my God through Jesus Christ	Rom 1:8
I God through Jesus Christ our	Rom 7:25
I t my God always on your behalf	1Cor 1:4
I t God that I baptized none of	1Cor 1:14
I t my God, I speak with tongues	1Cor 14:18
I t my God upon every remembrance	Phil 1:3
For this cause also I t God	1Th 2:13
We are bound to t God always for	2Th 1:3
t Christ Jesus our Lord, who	1Ti 1:12
I God, whom I serve from my	2Ti 1:3
t my God, making mention of	Philem 4

THANKED

and bowed himself, and t the king	2Sa 14:22
he t God, and took courage	Acts 28:15
But God be t, that ye were the	Rom 6:17

THANKFUL

be t unto him, and bless his name	Ps 100:4
him not as God, neither were t	Rom 1:21
and be ye t	Col 3:15

THANKFULNESS

most noble Felix, with all t	Acts 24:3

THANKING

heard in praising and t the LORD	2Chr 5:13

THANKS

Therefore I will give t unto thee	2Sa 22:50
Give t unto the LORD, call upon	1Chr 16:8
O give t unto the LORD	1Chr 16:34
we may give t to thy holy name	1Chr 16:35
to give t to the LORD, because	1Chr 16:41
prophesied with a harp, to give t	1Chr 25:3
to minister, and to give t	1Chr 23:30
and giving t unto the LORD	Ezr 3:11
them, to praise and to give t	Neh 12:24
companies of them that gave t	Neh 12:31
gave t went over against them	Neh 12:38
that gave t in the house of God	Neh 12:40
the grave who shall give thee t	Ps 6:5
Therefore will I give t unto thee	Ps 18:49
give t at the remembrance of his	Ps 30:4
I will give t unto thee for ever	Ps 30:12
I will give thee t in the great	Ps 35:18
Unto thee, O God, do we give t	Ps 75:1
unto thee do we give t	Ps 75:1
pasture will give thee t for ever	Ps 79:13
thing to give t unto the LORD	Ps 92:1
give t at the remembrance of his	Ps 97:12
O give t unto the LORD	Ps 105:1
O give t unto the LORD	Ps 106:1
to give t unto thy holy name, and	Ps 106:47
O give t unto the LORD, for he is	Ps 107:1
O give t unto the LORD	Ps 118:1
O give t unto the LORD	Ps 118:29
give t unto thee because of thy	Ps 119:62
to give t unto the name of the	Ps 122:4
O give t unto the LORD	Ps 136:1
O give t unto the God of gods	Ps 136:2
O give t to the Lord of lords	Ps 136:3
O give t unto the God of heaven	Ps 136:26
shall give t unto thy name	Ps 140:13
gave t before his God, as he did	Dan 6:10
loaves and the fishes, and gave t	Mt 15:36
And he took the cup, and gave t	Mt 26:27
took the seven loaves, and gave t	Mk 8:6
the cup, and when he had given t	Mk 14:23
gave t likewise unto the Lord	Lk 2:38
face at his feet, giving him t	Lk 17:16
And he took the cup, and gave t	Lk 22:17
And he took bread, and gave t	Lk 22:19
and when he had given t, he	Jn 6:11
after that the Lord had given t	Jn 6:23
gave t to God in presence of them	Acts 27:35
to the Lord, for he giveth God t	Rom 14:6
he eateth not, and giveth God t	Rom 14:6
unto whom not only I give t	Rom 16:4
of for that for which I give t	1Cor 10:30
And when he had given t, he brake	1Cor 11:24
say Amen at thy giving of t	1Cor 14:16
For thou verily givest t well	1Cor 14:17
But I be to God, which giveth us	1Cor 15:57
t may be given by many on our	2Cor 1:11
Now t be unto God, which always	2Cor 2:14
But t be to God, which put the	2Cor 8:16
T be unto God for his unspeakable	2Cor 9:15
Cease not to give t for you	Eph 1:16
but rather giving of t	Eph 5:4
Giving t always for all things	Eph 5:20
We give t to God and the Father of	Col 1:3
Giving t unto the Father, which	Col 1:12
the Lord Jesus, giving t to God	Col 3:17
We give t to God always for you	1Th 1:2
For what t can we render to God	1Th 3:9
In every thing give t	1Th 5:18
to give t alway to God for	2Th 2:13
intercessions, and giving of t	1Ti 2:1
of our lips giving t to his name	Heb 13:15
to him that sat on the throne,	Rev 4:9
Saying, We give thee t, O Lord	Rev 11:17

THANKSGIVING

If he offer it for a *t*, then he .... Lev 7:12
offer with the sacrifice of *t* .... Lev 7:12
of *t* of his peace offerings .... Lev 7:13
of his peace offerings for *t* .... Lev 7:15
a sacrifice of *t* unto the LORD .... Lev 22:29
to begin the *t* in prayer .... Neh 11:17
Mattaniah, who was over the *t* .... Neh 12:8
I may publish with the voice of *t* .... Ps 26:7
Offer unto God *t* .... Ps 50:14
song, and will magnify him with *t* .... Ps 69:30
come before his presence with *t* .... Ps 95:2
Enter into his gates with *t* .... Ps 100:4
sacrifice the sacrifices of *t* .... Ps 107:22
offer to thee the sacrifice of *t* .... Ps 116:17
Sing unto the LORD with *t* .... Ps 147:7
shall be found therein, *t* .... Is 51:3
And out of them shall proceed *t* .... Jer 30:19
a sacrifice of *t* with leaven .... Amos 4:5
unto thee with the voice of *t* .... Jonah 2:9
grace might through the *t* of many 2Cor 4:15
which causeth through us *t* to God 2Cor 9:11
supplication with *t* let your .... Phil 4:6
taught, abounding therein with *t* .... Col 2:7
and watch in the same with *t* .... Col 4:2
with *t* of them which believe 1Ti 4:3
refused, if it be received with *t* 1Ti 4:4
and glory, and wisdom, and *t* .... Rev 7:12

THANKSGIVINGS

with gladness, both with *t* .... Neh 12:27
abundant also by many *t* unto God 2Cor 9:12

THANKWORTHY

For this is *t*, if a man for 1Pet 2:19

THANKS

and songs of praise and *t* unto God .... Neh 12:46

THARA (tha'-*bez*) See TERAH. *Greek form of Terah.*
Abraham, which was the son of T .... Lk 3:34

THARSHISH (thar'-shish) See TARSHISH.

I. Ships fitted for long voyages.
navy of T with the navy of Hiram 1Kin 10:22
in three years came the navy of T 1Kin 10:22
to Ophir for gold 1Kin 22:48
2. Son of Bilhan.
and Chenaanah, and Zethan, and T 1Chr 7:10

THAT See PREFACE.

THE See PREFACE.

THEATRE

rushed with one accord into the *t* .... Acts 19:29
not adventure himself into the *t* .... Acts 19:31

THEBES See THEBEZ.

THEBEZ (the'-bez) A city in Ephraim.

Then went Abimelech to T, and .... Judg 9:50
to T, and encamped against T .... Judg 9:50
from the wall, that he died in T 2Sa 11:21

THEE See PREFACE.

THEE-WARD

works have been to *t* very good 1Sa 19:4

THEFT

then he shall be sold for his *t* .... Ex 22:3
If the *t* be certainly found in .... Ex 22:4

THEFTS

adulteries, fornications, *t* .... Mt 15:19
T, covetousness, wickedness, ... Mk 7:22
their fornication, nor of their *t* .... Rev 9:21

THEIR See PREFACE.

THEIR'S

thing in Israel shall be *t* .... Eze 44:29

THEIRS

stranger in a land that is not *t* .... Gen 15:13
and every beast of *t* be ours .... Gen 34:23
five times so much as any of *t* .... Gen 43:34
be *t* for a perpetual statute .... Ex 29:9
for *t* is thine own nakedness .... Lev 18:10
wicked men, and touch nothing of *t*. Num 16:26
t, every meat offering of *t* .... Num 18:9
and every sin offering of *t* .... Num 18:9
and every trespass offering of *t* .... Num 18:9
for *t* was the first lot .... Josh 21:10
for *t* was the lot 1Chr 6:54
I pray thee, be like one of *t* 2Chr 18:12
words shall stand, mine, or *t* .... Jer 44:28
their multitude, nor of any of *t* .... Eze 7:11
the dwellingplaces that were *t* .... Hab 1:6
for *t* is the kingdom of heaven .... Mt 5:3
for *t* is the kingdom of heaven .... Mt 5:10
of Jesus Christ our Lord, both *t* 1Cor 1:2
unto all men, as *t* also was 2Ti 3:9

THELASAR (the-la'-sar) See TELASSAR. *Same as Telassar.*
children of Eden which were in T 2Kin 19:12

THEM See PREFACE.

THEMSELVES See PREFACE.

THEN See PREFACE.

THENCE

from *t* it was parted, and became .... Gen 2:10
t upon the face of all the earth .... Gen 11:8
from *t* did the LORD scatter them .... Gen 11:9

---

he removed from *t* unto a mountain ... Gen 12:8
And the men rose up from *t* .... Gen 18:16
the men turned their faces from *t* .... Gen 18:22
Abraham journeyed from *t* toward .... Gen 20:1
take a wife unto my son from *t* .... Gen 24:7
And Isaac departed *t*, and pitched .... Gen 26:17
And he removed from *t*, and digged .... Gen 26:22
he went up from *t* to Beer-sheba. .... Gen 26:23
fetch me from *t* two good kids of .... Gen 27:9
I will send, and fetch thee from *t* .... Gen 27:45
take thee a wife from *t* of the .... Gen 28:2
to take him a wife from *t* .... Gen 28:6
removing from *t* all the speckled. .... Gen 30:32
thither, and buy for us from *t* .... Gen 42:2
with the corn, and departed .... Gen 42:26
(from *t* is the shepherd, the .... Gen 49:24
cut down from *t* a branch with one. ... Num 13:23
of Israel cut down from *t* .... Num 13:24
From *t* they removed, and pitched .... Num 21:12
From *t* they removed, and pitched .... Num 21:13
And from *t* they went to Beer .... Num 21:16
that *t* he might see the utmost .... Num 22:41
and curse me them from *t* .... Num 23:13
thou mayest curse me them from *t*. ... Num 23:27
But if from *t* thou shalt seek the .... Deut 4:29
the out *t* through a mighty hand .... Deut 5:15
And he brought us out from *t* .... Deut 6:23
From *t* they journeyed unto .... Deut 10:7
city shall send and fetch him *t* .... Deut 19:12
house, if any man fail from *t* .... Deut 22:8
the LORD thy God redeemed thee *t*. ... Deut 24:18
from *t* will the LORD thy God .... Deut 30:4
from *t* will he fetch thee .... Deut 30:4
house, and bring out *t* the woman .... Josh 6:22
From *t* it passed toward Azmon, and. ... Josh 15:4
Caleb drove *t* the three sons of .... Josh 15:14
he went up *t* to the inhabitants .... Josh 15:15
went over from *t* toward Luz .... Josh 18:13
And the border was drawn *t* .... Josh 18:14
t, passeth on along on the .... Josh 18:19
and goeth out from *t* to Hukkok. ... Josh 19:34
from *t* he went against the .... Judg 1:11
he expelled *t* the three sons of .... Judg 1:20
And he went up *t* to Penuel .... Judg 8:8
there went from *t* of the family. .... Judg 18:11
they passed *t* unto mount Ephraim. ... Judg 18:13
from *t* am I .... Judg 19:18
David departed *t* at that time .... Judg 21:24
they went out from *t* every man to .... Judg 21:24
that they might bring from *t* the 1Sa 4:4
shalt thou go on forward from *t* 1Sa 10:3
And they ran and fetched him *t* 1Sa 10:23
took *t* a stone, and slang it, and 1Sa 17:49
David therefore departed *t* 1Sa 22:1
David went *t* to Mizpeh of Moab 1Sa 22:3
And David went up from *t*, and dwelt .. 1Sa 23:29
to bring up from *t* the ark of God. ... 2Sa 6:2
fetched *t* a wise woman, and said 2Sa 14:2
I came out a man of the family of 2Sa 16:5
up from *t* the bones of Saul 2Sa 21:13
they are come up from *t* rejoicing ... 1Kin 1:45
and go not forth *t* any whither 1Kin 2:36
to Ophir, and fetched from *t* gold. ... 1Kin 9:28
and went out from *t*, and found Elisha. ... 1Kin 19:19
So he departed *t*, and found Elisha. ... 1Kin 19:19
there shall not be from *t* any 2Kin 2:21
And he went up from *t* unto Beth-el. ... 2Kin 2:23
he went from *t* to mount Carmel, ... 2Kin 2:25
from *t* he returned to Samaria. 2Kin 2:25
take *t* every man a beam, and let 2Kin 6:2
eat and drink, and carried *t* silver. ... 2Kin 7:8
another tent, and carried *t* also 2Kin 7:8
And when he was departed *t*. 2Kin 10:15
priests whom ye brought from *t* 2Kin 17:27
whom they carried away from *t* 2Kin 17:33
down, and brake them down from *t*. ... 2Kin 23:12
And he carried out *t* all the 2Kin 24:13
to bring up *t* the ark of God the 1Chr 13:6
took *t* four hundred and fifty 2Chr 8:18
and they thrust him out from *t* 2Chr 26:20
the river, be ye far from *t* .... Ezr 6:6
yet will I gather them from *t* .... Neh 1:9
From *t* she seeketh the prey, and .... Job 39:29
ye, depart ye, go ye out from *t* .... Is 52:11
be no more *t* an infant of days .... Is 65:20
out *t* shall be torn in pieces .... Jer 5:6
and take the girdle from *t* .... Jer 13:6
hand, yet would I pluck thee *t* .... Jer 22:24
shall cause to cease from *t* man .... Jer 36:29
to separate himself *t* in the .... Jer 37:12
took *t* old cast clouts and old .... Jer 38:11
he shall go forth from *t* in peace. .... Jer 43:12
I will bring thee down from *t* .... Jer 49:16
and will destroy from *t* the king .... Jer 49:38
from *t* shall be taken .... Jer 50:9
the abominations thereof from *t*. .... Eze 11:18
give her her vineyards from *t* .... Hos 2:15
from *t* go ye to Hamath the great. .... Amos 6:2
t shall mine hand take them. .... Amos 9:2
heaven, *t* will I bring them down. .... Amos 9:2
I will search and take them out *t*. .... Amos 9:3
t will I command the serpent, and. ... Amos 9:3
t will I command the sword, and it. ... Amos 9:4
t will I bring them down, saith. .... Obad 4
And going on from *t*, he saw other .... Mt 4:21
Thou shalt by no means come out *t* ... Mt 5:26
And as Jesus passed forth from *t*. .... Mt 9:9
And when Jesus departed *t*, two. .... Mt 9:27
and there abide till ye go *t*. .... Mt 10:11
disciples, he departed *t* to teach. .... Mt 11:1

And when he was departed *t* .... Mt 12:9
it, he withdrew himself from *t* .... Mt 12:15
these parables, he departed *t* .... Mt 13:53
he departed *t* by ship into a .... Mt 14:13
Then Jesus went *t*, and departed. .... Mt 15:21
And Jesus departed from *t*, and came. ... Mt 15:29
his hands on them, and departed *t*. ... Mt 19:15
he had gone a little farther *t* .... Mk 1:19
And he went out from *t*, and came .... Mk 6:1
nor hear you, when ye depart *t*. .... Mk 6:11
from *t* he arose, and went into the. ... Mk 7:24
And they departed *t*, and passed. .... Mk 9:30
And he arose from *t*, and cometh .... Mk 10:1
into, there abide, and *t* depart. .... Lk 9:4
thee, thou shalt not depart *t* .... Lk 12:59
to us, that would come from *t* .... Lk 16:26
Now after two days he departed *t* .... Jn 4:43
but went *t* unto a country near to. ... Jn 11:54
and from *t*, when his father was. .... Acts 7:4
from *t* they sailed to Cyprus .... Acts 13:4
I sailed to Antioch, from whence. .... Acts 14:26
from *t* to Philippi, which is the. .... Acts 16:12
And he departed *t*, and entered into. ... Acts 18:7
sailed I into Syria, and with him. .... Acts 18:18
And we sailed *t*, and came the next. ... Acts 20:15
Rhodes, and from *t* unto Patara. .... Acts 21:1
And when we had launched from *t*. ... Acts 27:4
part advised to depart *t* also .... Acts 27:12
obtained their purpose, loosing *t*. ... Acts 27:13
from *t* we fetched a compass, and. ... Acts 28:13
And from *t*, when the brethren. .... Acts 28:15
I went from *t* into Macedonia. 2Cor 2:13

THENCEFORTH

t it shall be accepted for an .... Lev 22:27
the sight of all nations from *t* 2Chr 32:23
it is *t* good for nothing, but to .... Mt 5:13
from *t* Pilate sought to release .... Jn 19:12

THEOPHILUS (the-of'-il-us) To whom the gospel of Luke and the Acts of the Apostles are addressed.

thee in order, most excellent T .... Lk 1:3
former treatise have I made, O T .... Acts 1:1

THERE See PREFACE.

THEREABOUT

as they were much perplexed *t* .... Lk 24:4

THEREAT

wash their hands and their feet *t* .... Ex 30:19
their hands and their feet *t* .... Ex 40:31
and many there be which go in *t* .... Mt 7:13

THEREBY

t shall I know that thou hast .... Gen 24:14
them, that ye should be defiled *t*. .... Lev 11:43
I good shall come unto thee .... Job 22:21
is deceived *t* is not wise .... Prov 20:1
wood shall be endangered *t* .... Eccl 10:9
neither shall gallant ship pass *t* .... Is 33:21
passeth *t* shall be astonished .... Jer 18:16
passeth *t* shall be astonished .... Jer 19:8
doth any son of man pass *t* .... Jer 51:43
in their sight, and carry out *t* .... Eze 12:5
through the wall to carry out *t* .... Eze 12:12
he shall not fall *t* in the day .... Eze 33:12
iniquity, he shall even die *t* .... Eze 33:18
lawful and right, he shall live *t* .... Eze 33:19
And Hamath also shall border *t*. .... Zec 9:2
Son of God might be glorified *t* .... Jn 11:4
cross, having slain the enmity *t*. .... Eph 2:16
unto them which are exercised *t*. .... Heb 12:11
trouble you, and *t* many be defiled. .... Heb 12:15
for *t* some have entertained .... Heb 13:2
of the word, that ye may grow *t* 1Pet 2:2

THEREFORE

T shall a man leave his father and .... Gen 2:24
T the LORD God sent him forth. .... Gen 3:23
T whosoever slayeth Cain. .... Gen 4:15
T is the name of it called Babel .... Gen 11:9
T it shall come to pass, when the. .... Gen 12:12
now I behold thy wife, take her. .... Gen 12:19
Thou shalt keep my covenant *t* .... Gen 17:9
for *t* are ye come to your servant .... Gen 18:5
T Sarah laughed within herself. .... Gen 18:12
for I came they under the shadow. .... Gen 19:8
T the name of the city was called. .... Gen 19:22
I suffered I thee not to touch. .... Gen 20:6
Now I restore the man his wife .... Gen 20:7
T Abimelech rose early in the .... Gen 20:8
Now I swear unto me here by God. .... Gen 21:23
bury I they dead .... Gen 23:15
I she took a vail, and covered. .... Gen 24:65
I was his name called Edom. .... Gen 25:30
the name of the city is .... Gen 26:33
Now I take, I pray thee, thy. .... Gen 27:3
Now I, my son, obey my voice .... Gen 27:8
T God give thee of the dew of .... Gen 27:28
Now I, my son, obey my voice .... Gen 27:43
shouldest thou I serve me for .... Gen 29:15
now I my husband will love me. .... Gen 29:32
he hath I given me this son also. .... Gen 29:33
I was his name called Levi. .... Gen 29:34
I she called his name Judah. .... Gen 29:35
I called she his name Dan. .... Gen 30:6
T he shall lie with thee to night. .... Gen 30:15
Now I come thou, let us make a .... Gen 31:44
T was the name of it called. .... Gen 31:48
T the children of Israel eat not. .... Gen 32:32
for I have seen thy face, as. .... Gen 33:10

t the name of the place is called...... Gen 33:17
t let them dwell in the land, and...... Gen 34:21
Come now t, and let us slay him,...... Gen 37:20
t his name was called Pharez .... Gen 38:29
Now t let Pharaoh look out a man .... Gen 41:33
t is this distress come upon us........ Gen 42:21
t, behold, also his blood is .... Gen 42:22
Now t when I come to thy servant.... Gen 44:30
Now t, I pray thee, let thy .... Gen 44:33
Now t be not grieved, nor angry ..... Gen 45:5
now t, we pray thee, let thy........... Gen 47:4
Now t let me go up, I pray thee,...... Gen 50:5
Now t fear ye not.................... Gen 50:21
T they did set over them .... Ex 1:11
T God dealt well with the .... Ex 1:20
Now t, behold, the cry of the .... Ex 3:9
Come now t, and I will send thee .... Ex 3:10
Now t go, and I will be with thy ..... Ex 4:12
t they cry, saying, Let us go and ..... Ex 5:8
t say, Let us go and do............... Ex 5:17
Go t now, and work.................. Ex 5:18
Send t now, and gather thy cattle,... Ex 9:19
Now t forgive, I pray thee, my .... Ex 10:17
t shall ye observe this day in......... Ex 12:17
Thou shalt t keep this ordinance..... Ex 13:10
t I sacrifice to the LORD all.......... Ex 13:15
t the name of it was called Marah ... Ex 15:23
t he giveth you on the sixth day ..... Ex 16:29
Now t, if ye will obey my voice ...... Ex 19:5
Ye shall keep the sabbath t........... Ex 31:14
Now t let me alone, that my wrath... Ex 32:10
T now go, lead the people unto .... Ex 32:34
t now put off thy ornaments from.... Ex 33:5
Now t, I pray thee, if I have.......... Ex 33:13
T shall ye abide at the door of........ Lev 8:35
Aaron t went unto the altar, and..... Lev 9:8
ye shall t sanctify yourselves, ... Lev 11:44
ye shall t be holy, for I am holy ..... Lev 11:45
He shall t burn that garment,......... Lev 13:52
t shall he wash his flesh in........... Lev 16:4
T I also said unto the children of .... Lev 17:12
t I said unto the children of .... Lev 17:14
Ye shall t keep my statutes, and ..... Lev 18:5
t I do visit the iniquity thereof ...... Lev 18:25
Ye shall t keep my statutes and my.. Lev 18:26
Ye shall t keep mine ordinance,...... Lev 18:30
t every one that eateth it shall .... Lev 19:8
t shall ye observe all my............. Lev 20:7
Sanctify yourselves t, and be ye ..... Lev 20:7
Ye shall t keep all my statutes,...... Lev 20:22
things, and t I abhorred them....... Lev 20:23
Ye shall t put difference between..... Lev 20:25
t they shall be holy................. Lev 21:6
Thou shalt sanctify him t............. Lev 21:8
They shall t keep mine ordinance,... Lev 22:9
they bear sin for it, and die t......... Lev 22:9
t shall ye keep my commandments,.. Lev 22:31
Ye shall not t oppress one............ Num 3:12
t the Levites shall be mine............ Num 3:12
t the LORD will give you flesh,....... Num 11:18
t he hath slain them in the........... Num 14:16
t the LORD will not be with you ..... Num 14:43
the LORD, t they are hallowed........ Num 16:38
T thou and thy sons with thee .... Num 18:2
t I have said unto them, Among...... Num 18:24
T thou shalt say unto them, When... Num 18:30
t ye shall not bring this.............. Num 20:12
T the people came to Moses, and..... Num 21:7
He sent messengers t unto Balaam... Num 22:5
Come now t, I pray thee, curse me... Num 22:6
come t, I pray thee, curse me......... Num 22:11
Now t, I pray you, tarry ye also...... Num 22:19
now t, if it displease thee, I.......... Num 22:34
T now flee thou to thy place......... Num 24:11
come t, and I will advertise thee..... Num 24:14
Give unto us t a possession among... Num 32:5
Now t kill every male among the .... Num 31:17
We have t brought an oblation for... Num 31:50
Defile not t the land which ye .... Num 35:34
ye good heed unto yourselves t .... Deut 2:4
Now t hearken, O Israel, unto the... Deut 4:1
Keep t and do them................. Deut 4:6
Take ye t good heed unto............ Deut 4:15
t he chose their seed after them,..... Deut 4:37
Know t this day, and consider it..... Deut 4:39
Thou shalt keep t his statutes .... Deut 4:40
t the LORD thy God commanded thee. Deut 5:15
Now t why should we die .... Deut 5:25
Ye shall observe to do t as the .... Deut 5:32
Hear t, O Israel, and observe to..... Deut 6:3
Know t that the LORD thy God, he.. Deut 7:9
Thou shalt t keep the................ Deut 7:11
T thou shalt keep the............... Deut 8:6
Understand t this day, that the ..... Deut 9:3
Understand t, that the LORD thy.... Deut 9:6
I prayed t unto the LORD, and said. Deut 9:26
Circumcise t the foreskin of your... Deut 10:16
Love ye t the stranger.............. Deut 10:19
t thou shalt love the LORD thy ...... Deut 11:1
t shall ye keep all the............... Deut 11:8
t shall ye lay up these my words ... Deut 11:18
t they are unclean unto you.......... Deut 14:7
t I command thee, saying, Thou ..... Deut 15:11
t I command thee this thing to...... Deut 15:15
Thou shalt t sacrifice the............ Deut 16:2
t thou shalt surely rejoice............ Deut 16:15
t shall they have no inheritance ..... Deut 18:2
t shall thy camp be holy............. Deut 23:14
t I command thee to do this thing,.. Deut 24:18
t I command thee to do this thing,.. Deut 24:22
T it shall be, when the LORD .... Deut 25:19

thou shalt t keep and do them with.. Deut 26:16
T it shall be when ye be gone .... Deut 27:4
Thou shalt t obey the voice of........ Deut 27:10
T shalt thou serve thine enemies .... Deut 28:48
Keep t the words of this covenant ... Deut 29:9
t choose life, that both thou and.... Deut 30:19
Now t write ye this song for you,.... Deut 31:19
Moses t wrote this song the same ... Deut 31:22
now t arise, go over this Jordan,..... Josh 1:2
Now t, I pray you, swear unto me ... Josh 2:12
Now t take you twelve men out of ... Josh 3:12
Joshua t commanded the priests,..... Josh 4:17
T the children of Israel could .... Josh 7:12
In the morning t ye shall be .... Josh 7:14
t we will flee before them............ Josh 8:6
Joshua t sent them forth .... Josh 8:9
now t make ye a league with us ..... Josh 9:6
t now make ye a league with us ..... Josh 9:8
now t we may not touch them........ Josh 9:19
Now t ye are cursed, and there ...... Josh 9:23
t we were sore afraid of our.......... Josh 9:24
The five kings of the Amorites,...... Josh 10:5
Joshua t came unto them suddenly,.. Josh 10:9
Now t divide this land for an......... Josh 13:7
t they gave no part unto the.......... Josh 14:4
Now t give me this mountain,........ Josh 14:12
Hebron t became the inheritance .... Josh 14:14
t he had Gilead and Bashan .... Josh 17:1
T according to the commandment of. Josh 17:4
Ye shall t describe the land into..... Josh 18:6
t the children of Simeon had .... Josh 19:9
the children of Dan went up to ...... Josh 19:47
t now return ye, and get you unto ... Josh 22:4
T we said, Let us now prepare to .... Josh 22:26
T said we, that it shall be, when .... Josh 22:28
Be ye t very courageous to keep..... Josh 23:6
Take good heed t unto yourselves,... Josh 23:11
T it shall come to pass, that as,..... Josh 23:15
t he blessed you still................ Josh 24:10
Now t fear the LORD, and serve him. Josh 24:14
t will we also serve the LORD .... Josh 24:18
Now t put away, said he, the .... Josh 24:23
t it shall be t a witness unto you,.... Josh 24:27
The LORD left those nations,......... Judg 2:23
the anger of the LORD was hot .... Judg 3:8
t they took a key, and opened them.. Judg 3:25
T on that day he called him.......... Judg 6:32
Now t go to, proclaim in the ears... Judg 7:3
T when the LORD had delivered..... Judg 8:7
Now t, if ye have done truly and .... Judg 9:16
Now t up by night, thou and the .... Judg 9:32
Now t war again to thee now, that .. Judg 11:8
now t restore those lands again...... Judg 11:13
why t did ye not recover them........ Judg 11:26
Now t beware, I pray thee, and ..... Judg 13:4
now t get her for me to wife......... Judg 14:2
t I gave her to thy companion........ Judg 15:2
Delilah t took new ropes, and........ Judg 16:12
now t I will restore it unto thee .... Judg 17:3
now t consider what I have to do ... Judg 18:14
t he lodged there again............... Judg 19:7
Now t deliver us the men, the....... Judg 20:13
T they turned their backs before .... Judg 20:42
T they commanded the children of .. Judg 21:20
Wash thyself t, and anoint thee,..... Ruth 3:3
spread t thy skirt over thine......... Ruth 3:9
T the kinsman said unto Boaz, Buy.. Ruth 4:8
T she wept, and did not eat........... 1Sa 1:7
t Eli thought she had been............ 1Sa 1:13
T also I have lent him to the......... 1Sa 1:28
T Eli said unto Samuel, Go, lie...... 1Sa 3:9
t I have sworn unto the house of 1Sa 3:14
t neither the priests of Dagon,....... 1Sa 5:5
They sent t and gathered all the 1Sa 5:11
T they sent the ark of God to........ 1Sa 5:8 (?)
Now t make a new cart, and take.... 1Sa 6:7
Now t hearken unto their voice...... 1Sa 8:9
Now t get you up................... 1Sa 9:13
T it became a proverb, Is Saul....... 1Sa 10:12
Now t present yourselves before 1Sa 10:19
T they enquired of the LORD......... 1Sa 10:22
T the men of Jabesh said, To........ 1Sa 11:10
Now t stand still, that I may......... 1Sa 12:7
Now t behold the king whom ye 1Sa 12:13
Now t stand and see this great....... 1Sa 12:16
T said I, The Philistines will......... 1Sa 13:12
I forced myself t, and offered a 1Sa 13:12
T Saul said unto the Lord God of... 1Sa 14:41
now t hearken thou unto the voice.. 1Sa 15:1
Now t, I pray thee, pardon my sin .. 1Sa 15:25
T David ran, and stood upon the 1Sa 17:51
T Saul removed him from him, and.. 1Sa 18:13
now t be the king's son in law 1Sa 18:22
now t, I pray thee, take heed to..... 1Sa 19:2
T thou shalt deal kindly with thy ... 1Sa 20:8
T he cometh not unto the king's 1Sa 20:29
Now t what is under thine hand..... 1Sa 21:3
David t departed thence, and......... 1Sa 22:1
David t enquired of the LORD,........ 1Sa 23:2
Now t, O king, come down........... 1Sa 23:20
See t, and take knowledge of all..... 1Sa 23:23
t they called that place.............. 1Sa 23:28
The LORD t be judge, and judge 1Sa 24:15
Swear t now unto me by the LORD... 1Sa 24:21
Now t know and consider what thou. 1Sa 25:17
Now t, my lord, as the LORD......... 1Sa 25:26
David t sent out spies, and........... 1Sa 26:4
Now t let me smite him, I pray....... 1Sa 26:8
Now t, I pray thee, let my lord 1Sa 26:19
Now t, let not my blood fall to....... 1Sa 26:20
t he shall be my servant for ever.... 1Sa 27:12

T will I make thee keeper of mine.... 1Sa 28:2
t I have called thee, that thou....... 1Sa 28:15
t hath the LORD done this thing 1Sa 28:18
Now t, I pray thee, hearken thou.... 1Sa 28:22
T Saul took a sword, and fell upon .. 1Sa 31:4
T now let your hands be.............. 2Sa 2:7
shall I not t now require his......... 2Sa 4:11
T he called the name of that 2Sa 5:20
t will I play before the LORD......... 2Sa 6:21
T Michal the daughter of Saul had.. 2Sa 6:23
Now t so shalt thou say unto my 2Sa 7:8
t hath thy servant found in his...... 2Sa 7:27
T now let it please thee to bless 2Sa 7:29
Thou t, and thy sons, and thy 2Sa 9:10
Now t the sword shall never.......... 2Sa 12:10
David t besought God for the 2Sa 12:16
t David said unto his servants,....... 2Sa 12:19
Now t gather the rest of the.......... 2Sa 12:28
Now t, I pray thee, speak unto 2Sa 13:13
Now t let not my lord the king 2Sa 13:33
Now t that I am come to speak of ... 2Sa 14:15
t the LORD thy God will be with..... 2Sa 14:17
go t, bring the young man Absalom.. 2Sa 14:21
was heavy on him, t he polled it..... 2Sa 14:26
T Absalom sent for Joab, to have.... 2Sa 14:29
T he said unto his servants, See,..... 2Sa 14:30
now t let me see the king's face...... 2Sa 14:32
Zadok t and Abiathar carried the ... 2Sa 15:29
t it shall be, that what thing......... 2Sa 15:35
T I counsel that all Israel be......... 2Sa 17:11
Now t send quickly, and tell David.. 2Sa 17:16
t now it is better that thou.......... 2Sa 18:3
Now t arise, go forth, and speak 2Sa 19:7
Now t why speak ye not a word of .. 2Sa 19:10
t, behold, I am come the first........ 2Sa 19:20
T the king said unto Shimei, Thou.. 2Sa 19:23
do t what is good in thine eyes 2Sa 19:27
What right t have I yet to cry 2Sa 19:28
T the LORD hath recompensed me.... 2Sa 22:25
T I will give thanks unto thee, O ... 2Sa 22:50
t he would not drink it.............. 2Sa 23:17
t he was their captain............... 2Sa 23:19
Now t come, let me, I pray thee,..... 1Kin 1:12
be thou strong t, and shew thyself .. 1Kin 2:2
Do t according to thy wisdom, and.. 1Kin 2:6
Now t hold him not guiltless......... 1Kin 2:9
Bath-sheba t went unto king......... 1Kin 2:19
Now t, as the LORD liveth, which ... 1Kin 2:24
Their blood shall t return upon...... 1Kin 2:33
t the LORD shall return thy 1Kin 2:44
Give t thy servant an................ 1Kin 3:9
Now t command thou that they hew. 1Kin 5:6
T now, LORD God of Israel, keep 1Kin 8:25
Let your heart t be perfect with..... 1Kin 8:61
t hath the LORD brought upon them. 1Kin 9:9
t made he thee king, to do........... 1Kin 10:9
Solomon sought t to kill Jeroboam .. 1Kin 11:40
now t make thou the grievous........ 1Kin 12:4
T king Rehoboam made speed to get. 1Kin 12:18
They hearkened t to the word of 1Kin 12:24
t the LORD hath delivered him .... 1Kin 14:10 (?)
T, behold, I will bring evil upon..... 1Kin 14:10
Arise thou t, get thee to thine....... 1Kin 14:12
Now t send, and gather to me all ... 1Kin 18:19
Let them t give us two bullocks...... 1Kin 18:23
t they were stronger than we 1Kin 20:23
t will I deliver all this great......... 1Kin 20:42
t thy life shall go for his life,........ 1Kin 20:42
Hear thou t the word of the LORD... 1Kin 22:19
Now t, behold, the LORD hath put... 1Kin 22:23
Now t thus saith the LORD, Thou.... 2Kin 1:4
t thou shalt not come down from.... 2Kin 1:6
t let my life now be precious in...... 2Kin 1:14
t thou shalt not come down off 2Kin 1:16
They sent t fifty men................ 2Kin 2:17
now t, Moab, to the spoil............. 2Kin 3:23
He went in t, and shut the door 2Kin 4:33
now t, I pray thee, take a............ 2Kin 5:15
The leprosy t of Naaman shall....... 2Kin 5:27
T said he, Take it up to thee......... 2Kin 6:7
The heart of the king of Syria....... 2Kin 6:11
T sent he thither horses, and........ 2Kin 6:14
Now t come, and let us fall unto 2Kin 7:4
now t come, that we may go and 2Kin 7:9
t are they gone out of the camp 2Kin 7:12
They took t two chariot horses 2Kin 7:14
Now t take and cast him into the.... 2Kin 9:26
Now t call unto me all the........... 2Kin 10:19
t I Jehoash king of Israel went up... 2Kin 14:11
opened not to him, t he smote it 2Kin 15:16
t the king of Assyria shut him up ... 2Kin 17:4
T the LORD was very angry with 2Kin 17:18
t the LORD sent lions among them,.. 2Kin 17:25
t he hath sent lions among them,.... 2Kin 17:26
Now t, I pray thee, give pledges..... 2Kin 18:23
t they have destroyed them.......... 2Kin 19:18
Now t, O LORD our God, I beseech .. 2Kin 19:19
T their inhabitants were of small ... 2Kin 19:26
t I will put my hook in thy nose,.... 2Kin 19:28
T thus saith the LORD concerning ... 2Kin 19:32
T thus saith the LORD God of........ 2Kin 21:12
t my wrath shall be kindled.......... 2Kin 22:13
Behold t, I will gather thee unto 2Kin 22:20
t he slew him, and turned the........ 1Chr 10:14
T came all the elders of Israel....... 1Chr 11:3
t they called it the city of........... 1Chr 11:7
t he would not drink it.............. 1Chr 11:19
T David enquired again of God 1Chr 14:14
David t did as God commanded him. 1Chr 14:16

Now t thus shalt thou say unto my 1Chr 17:7
T now, LORD, let the thing that 1Chr 17:23
t thy servant hath found in his. 1Chr 17:25
Now I let it please thee to bless 1Chr 17:27
t he smote Israel 1Chr 21:7
Now t advise thyself what word I..... 1Chr 21:12
I will t now make preparation for 1Chr 22:5
Arise t, and be doing, and the LORD .. 1Chr 22:16
arise t, and build ye the 1Chr 22:19
t they were in one reckoning. 1Chr 23:11
t Eleazar and Ithamar executed the ... 1Chr 24:2
Now t, in the sight of all Israel 1Chr 28:8
Now t, our God, we thank thee, and. .. 1Chr 29:13
Send me now t a man cunning to....... 2Chr 2:7
Now t the wheat, and the barley, ... 2Chr 2:15
The LORD t hath performed his 2Chr 6:10
Now t, O LORD God of Israel, keep.... 2Chr 6:16
Have respect t to the prayer of 2Chr 6:19
Hearken t unto the supplications...... 2Chr 6:21
Now t arise, O LORD God, into thy 2Chr 6:41
t hath he brought all this evil 2Chr 7:22
t made he the king over them, to 2Chr 9:8
Now t hast thou somewhat the......... 2Chr 10:4
t have I also sent you in the 2Chr 12:5
t I will not destroy them, but I 2Chr 12:7
T he said unto Judah, Let us 2Chr 14:7
Be ye strong t, and let not your 2Chr 15:7
t is the host of the king of 2Chr 16:7
t from henceforth thou shalt have..... 2Chr 16:9
Hearken t unto the supplications...... 2Chr 17:5
The LORD stablished the kingdom 2Chr 17:5
T the king of Israel gathered........ 2Chr 18:5
let thy word t, I pray thee, be 2Chr 18:12
let them return t every man to 2Chr 18:16
T hear the word of the LORD. 2Chr 18:18
Now t, behold, the LORD hath put 2Chr 18:22
T they compassed about him to 2Chr 18:31
t he said to his chariot man,......... 2Chr 18:33
t is wrath upon thee from before..... 2Chr 19:2
t the name of the same place was 2Chr 20:26
Now hear me t, and deliver the 2Chr 28:11
t will I sacrifice to them, that 2Chr 28:23
who t gave them up to desolation, ... 2Chr 30:7
the Levites had the charge of 2Chr 30:17
Now t let not Hezekiah deceive 2Chr 32:15
t there was wrath upon him, and 2Chr 32:25
t my wrath shall be poured out....... 2Chr 34:25
t the Levites prepared for 2Chr 35:14
His servants t took him out of 2Chr 35:24
T he brought upon them the king 2Chr 36:17
t were they, as polluted, put. .... Ezr 2:62
t have we sent and certified the ..... Ezr 4:14
Now t, if it seem good to the .... Ezr 5:17
Now t, Tatnai, governor beyond .... Ezr 6:6
Now t give not your daughters .... Ezr 9:12
Now t let us make a covenant with .... Ezr 10:3
Now t make confession unto the ...... Ezr 10:11
t we his servants will arise and..... Neh 2:20
T set I in the lower places. .... Neh 4:13
In what place t ye hear the sound .... Neh 4:20
t we take up corn for them, that. .... Neh 5:2
Come now t, and let us take .... Neh 6:7
Now t, O God, strengthen my hands. ... Neh 6:9
T was he hired, that I should be ..... Neh 6:13
t were they, as polluted, put. .... Neh 7:64
T thou deliveredst them into the ..... Neh 9:27
t leftest thou them in the hand. ..... Neh 9:28
t gavest thou them into the hand .... Neh 9:30
Now t, our God, the great, the....... Neh 9:32
T I cast forth all the household ..... Neh 13:8
t chased him from the .... Neh 13:28
t was the king very wroth, and his... Est 1:12
t they were both hanged on a tree .... Est 2:23
t it is not for the king's profit .... Est 3:8
T the Jews of the villages, that. .... Est 9:19
T for all the words of this .... Est 9:26
t despise not thou the chastening.... Job 5:17
t my words are swallowed up.......... Job 6:3
Now t be content, look upon me .... Job 6:28
T I will not refrain my mouth .... Job 7:11
t I said it, He destroyeth the .... Job 9:22
t see thou mine affliction .... Job 10:15
Know t that God exacteth of thee ..... Job 11:6
t shalt thou not exalt them .... Job 17:4
T do my thoughts cause me to .... Job 20:2
t shall no man look for his goods .... Job 20:21
T they say unto God, Depart from. .... Job 21:14
T snares are round about thee, and ... Job 22:10
T am I troubled at his presence ...... Job 23:15
T I said, Hearken to me. .... Job 32:10
T hearken unto me, ye men of .... Job 34:10
T he knoweth their works, and he ..... Job 34:25
t speak what thou knowest. .... Job 34:33
t trust thou in him .... Job 35:14
T doth Job open his mouth in vain .... Job 35:16
Men do t fear him. .... Job 37:24
t have I uttered that I .... Job 42:3
T take unto you now seven .... Job 42:8
T the ungodly shall not stand in ..... Ps 1:5
Be wise now t, O ye kings .... Ps 2:10
for their sakes t return thou on ..... Ps 7:7
T my heart is glad, and my glory ..... Ps 16:9
T hath the LORD recompensed me .... Ps 18:24
T will I give thanks unto thee, O.... Ps 18:49
T shalt thou make them turn their .... Ps 21:12
t will he teach sinners in the .... Ps 25:8
t I shall not slide .... Ps 26:1
t will I offer in his tabernacle ..... Ps 27:6
t my heart greatly rejoiceth......... Ps 28:7
t for thy name's sake lead me, and ... Ps 31:3
t the children of men put their ..... Ps 36:7
t my heart faileth me .... Ps 40:12

t will I remember thee from the ...... Ps 42:6
t God hath blessed thee for ever...... Ps 45:2
t God, thy God, hath anointed .... Ps 45:7
t shall the people praise thee .... Ps 45:17
T will not we fear, though the .... Ps 46:2
no changes, t they fear not God ...... Ps 55:19
Thou t, O LORD God of hosts, the ..... Ps 59:5
t in the shadow of thy wings will .... Ps 63:7
T pride compasseth them about as ..... Ps 73:6
T his people return hither .... Ps 73:10
T the LORD heard this, and was .... Ps 78:21
T their days did he consume in....... Ps 78:33
upon me, t will I deliver him. .... Ps 91:14
T he said that he would destroy...... Ps 106:23
T he lifted up his hand against ...... Ps 106:26
T was the wrath of the LORD. .... Ps 106:40
T he brought down their heart .... Ps 107:12
t shall he lift up the head .... Ps 110:7
t will I call upon him as long as .... Ps 116:2
I believed, t have I spoken.......... Ps 116:10
t shall I see my desire upon them .... Ps 118:7
t I hate every false way .... Ps 119:104
t I love thy testimonies .... Ps 119:119
T I love thy commandments above ..... Ps 119:127
T I esteem all thy precepts .... Ps 119:128
t doth my soul keep them .... Ps 119:129
t thy servant loveth it .... Ps 119:140
depart from me t, ye bloody men ...... Ps 139:19
T is my spirit overwhelmed within .... Ps 143:4
T shall they eat of the fruit of ..... Prov 1:31
t get wisdom .... Prov 4:7
Hear me now t, O ye children, and .... Prov 5:7
T shall his calamity come .... Prov 6:15
t be will not spare in the day of .... Prov 6:34
T came I forth to meet thee, ... Prov 7:15
Hearken unto me now t, O ye .... Prov 7:24
Now t hearken unto me, O ye .... Prov 8:32
t a cruel messenger shall be sent .... Prov 17:11
t leave off contention, before it .... Prov 17:14
t shall he beg in harvest, and. ...... Prov 20:4
t meddle not with them that .... Prov 20:19
thee with mirth, t enjoy pleasure.... Eccl 2:1
T I hated life. .... Eccl 2:17
T I went about to cause my heart .... Eccl 2:20
t let thy words be few .... Eccl 5:2
t the misery of man is great upon.... Eccl 8:6
t the heart of the sons of men is .... Eccl 8:11
T remove sorrow from thy heart, ... Eccl 11:10
t do the virgins love thee. .... Song 1:3
T saith the Lord, the LORD of .... Is 1:24
T thou hast forsaken thy people...... Is 2:6
t forgive them not .... Is 2:9
T the Lord will smite with a scab .... Is 3:17
T my people are gone into............ Is 5:13
t hell hath enlarged herself, and ... Is 5:14
T as the fire devoureth the.......... Is 5:24
T is the anger of the LORD .... Is 5:25
T the Lord himself shall give you.... Is 7:14
Now t, behold, the Lord bringeth ..... Is 8:7
T the LORD shall set up the .... Is 9:11
t the LORD will cut off from.......... Is 9:14
T the Lord shall have no joy in ...... Is 9:17
T shall the Lord, the Lord of .... Is 10:16
T thus saith the Lord GOD of .... Is 10:24
T with joy shall ye draw water ...... Is 12:3
T shall all hands be faint, and ...... Is 13:7
T I will shake the heavens, and ...... Is 13:13
t the armed soldiers of Moab .... Is 15:4
T the abundance they have gotten, ... Is 15:7
T shall Moab howl for Moab, every .... Is 16:7
T I will bewail with the weeping ..... Is 16:9
t shalt thou plant pleasant .... Is 17:10
T are my loins filled with pain ...... Is 21:3
t said I, Look away from me. .... Is 22:4
T hath the curse devoured the .... Is 24:6
t the inhabitants of the earth .... Is 24:6
T shall the strong people glorify .... Is 25:3
t hast thou visited and destroyed.... Is 26:14
By this t shall the iniquity of ...... Is 27:9
t he that made them will not have.... Is 27:11
T thus saith the Lord GOD, Behold.... Is 28:16
Now t be ye not mockers, lest. ...... Is 28:22
T, behold, I will proceed to do a .... Is 29:14
T thus saith the LORD, who. .... Is 29:22
T shall the strength of Pharaoh ...... Is 30:3
t have I cried concerning this, ... Is 30:7
T this iniquity shall be to you, ... Is 30:13
t shall ye flee .... Is 30:16
t shall they that pursue you be ..... Is 30:16
t will the LORD wait, that he may .... Is 30:18
t will he be exalted, that he may .... Is 30:18
Now t give pledges, I pray thee, ... Is 36:8
t they have destroyed them .... Is 37:19
Now t, O LORD our God, save us .... Is 37:20
T their inhabitants were of small.... Is 37:27
t will I put my hook in thy nose, ... Is 37:29
T thus saith the LORD concerning .... Is 37:33
t we will sing my songs to the .... Is 38:20
T he hath poured upon him the .... Is 42:25
t will I give over thee, and. .... Is 43:4
T ye are my witnesses, saith the .... Is 43:12
T I have profaned the princes of .... Is 43:28
T hear now this, thou that art .... Is 47:8
T shall evil come upon thee .... Is 47:11
t shall I not be confounded. .... Is 50:7
t have I set my face like a flint .... Is 50:7
T the redeemed of the LORD shall ..... Is 51:11
T hear now this, thou afflicted, ... Is 51:21
Now t, what have I here, saith .... Is 52:5
T my people shall know my name .... Is 52:6
t they shall know in that day........ Is 52:6

T will I divide him a portion .... Is 53:12
t thou wast not grieved .... Is 57:10
T is judgment far from us, ... Is 59:9
t his arm brought salvation unto ..... Is 59:16
T thy gates shall be open............ Is 60:11
t in their land they shall .... Is 61:7
t mine own arm brought salvation..... Is 63:5
t he was turned to be their enemy .... Is 63:10
t will I measure their former .... Is 65:7
T will I number you to the sword, ... Is 65:12
T thus saith the Lord GOD, Behold.... Is 65:13
Thou t gird up thy loins, and........ Jer 1:17
Know t and see that it is an evil .... Jer 2:19
t hast thou also taught the .... Jer 2:33
T the showers have been .... Jer 3:3
T I said, Surely these are poor ..... Jer 5:4
t they are become great, and waxen .. Jer 5:27
T I am full of the fury of the....... Jer 6:11
t they shall fall among them that .... Jer 6:15
T hear, ye nations, and know, O ..... Jer 6:18
T thus saith the LORD, Behold, I ..... Jer 6:21
T will I do unto this house, ... Jer 7:14
t pray not thou for this people, ... Jer 7:16
T thus saith the Lord GOD .... Jer 7:20
t thou shalt speak all these .... Jer 7:27
T, behold, the days come, saith ...... Jer 7:32
t will I give their wives unto .... Jer 8:10
t shall they fall among them that .... Jer 8:12
T thus saith the LORD of hosts, ... Jer 9:7
T thus saith the LORD of hosts, ... Jer 9:15
t they shall not prosper, and all .... Jer 10:21
t I will bring upon them all the ..... Jer 11:8
T thus saith the LORD, Behold I ...... Jer 11:11
T pray not thou for this people, ... Jer 11:14
T thus saith the LORD of the men .... Jer 11:21
T thus saith the LORD of hosts, ... Jer 11:22
t have I hated it. .... Jer 12:8
T thou shalt speak unto them this.... Jer 13:12
T will I scatter them as the .... Jer 13:24
t will I discover thy skirts upon .... Jer 13:26
T the LORD doth not accept them ..... Jer 14:10
T thus saith the LORD concerning .... Jer 14:15
T thou shalt say this word unto ..... Jer 14:17
t we will wait upon them. .... Jer 14:22
t will I stretch out my hand .... Jer 15:6
T thus saith the LORD, If thou .... Jer 15:19
T will I cast you out of this .... Jer 16:13
T, behold, the days come, saith ...... Jer 16:14
T, behold, I will this once cause .... Jer 16:21
Now t go to, speak to the men of .... Jer 18:11
T thus saith the LORD .... Jer 18:13
T deliver up their children to....... Jer 18:21
T, behold, the days come, saith ...... Jer 19:6
t my persecutors shall stumble, ... Jer 20:11
T thus saith the LORD concerning .... Jer 22:18
T thus saith the LORD God of .... Jer 23:2
T, behold, the days come, saith ...... Jer 23:7
T thus saith the LORD of hosts ...... Jer 23:15
T, behold, I am against the .... Jer 23:30
t they shall not profit this .... Jer 23:32
t thus saith the LORD................ Jer 23:38
T, behold, I, even I, will .... Jer 23:39
T thus saith the LORD of hosts....... Jer 25:8
t thou shalt say unto them, Thus .... Jer 25:27
T prophesy thou against them all .... Jer 25:30
T now amend your ways and your ...... Jer 26:13
T hearken not ye to your prophets ... Jer 27:9
T hearken not unto the words of ..... Jer 27:14
T thus saith the LORD .... Jer 28:16
Hear ye t the word of the LORD, ... Jer 29:20
Now t why hast thou not reproved..... Jer 29:27
For t he sent unto us in Babylon, ... Jer 29:28
T thus saith the LORD................ Jer 29:32
T fear thou not, O my servant .... Jer 30:10
t all they that devour thee shall ... Jer 30:16
t with lovingkindness have I .... Jer 31:3
T they shall come and sing in the ... Jer 31:12
t my bowels are troubled for him. ... Jer 31:20
t thou hast caused all this evil .... Jer 32:23
T thus saith the LORD................ Jer 32:28
now t thus saith the LORD, the ...... Jer 32:36
T the word of the LORD came to....... Jer 34:12
T thus saith the LORD................ Jer 34:17
T thus saith the LORD God of .... Jer 35:19
t go thou, and read in the roll, ... Jer 36:6
T all the princes sent Jehudi the ... Jer 36:14
T thus saith the LORD................ Jer 36:30
T hear now, I pray thee, O my........ Jer 37:20
T the princes said unto the king .... Jer 38:4
T thus saith the LORD................ Jer 40:3
now t hear the word of the LORD, ... Jer 42:15
Now t know certainly that ye .... Jer 42:22
T now thus saith the LORD, the ...... Jer 44:7
T thus saith the LORD of hosts, ... Jer 44:11
t is your land a desolation, and.... Jer 44:22
t this evil is happened unto you, ... Jer 44:23
T hear ye the word of the LORD ...... Jer 44:24
t his taste remained in him, and.... Jer 48:11
T, behold, the days come, saith ...... Jer 48:12
T will I howl for Moab, and I will ... Jer 48:31
t their heart shall sound for Moab .. Jer 48:36
T, behold, the days come, saith ...... Jer 49:2
T hear the counsel of the LORD, ... Jer 49:20
T hear young men shall fall in her .. Jer 49:26
T thus saith the LORD of hosts, ... Jer 50:18
t shall her young men fall in the ... Jer 50:30
T the wild beasts of the desert ..... Jer 50:39
T hear ye the counsel of the LORD ... Jer 50:45
t the nations are mad .... Jer 51:7
T thus saith the LORD .... Jer 51:36

T, behold, the days come, that I......	Jer 51:47
t she is removed......	Lam 1:8
t she came down wonderfully......	Lam 1:9
t he made the rampart and the wall......	Lam 2:8
recall to my mind, t have I hope......	Lam 3:21
t will I hope in him......	Lam 3:24
t hear the word at my mouth, and......	Eze 3:17
T thou shalt set thy face toward......	Eze 4:7
T thus saith the Lord God......	Eze 5:7
T thus saith the Lord God......	Eze 5:8
T the fathers shall eat the sons......	Eze 5:10
t will I also diminish thee......	Eze 5:11
t have I set it far from them......	Eze 5:16
T will I also deal in fury......	Eze 8:18
t prophesy against them, prophesy......	Eze 11:4
T thus saith the Lord God......	Eze 11:7
T say, Thus saith the Lord God......	Eze 11:16
T say, Thus saith the Lord God......	Eze 11:17
T, thou son of man, prepare thee......	Eze 12:3
Tell them t, Thus saith the Lord......	Eze 12:23
T say unto them, Thus saith the......	Eze 12:28
T thus saith the Lord God......	Eze 13:8
spoken vanity, and seen lies, t......	Eze 13:8
T thus saith the Lord God......	Eze 13:13
T ye shall see no more vanity,......	Eze 13:23
T speak unto them, and say unto......	Eze 14:4
T say unto the house of Israel,......	Eze 14:6
T thus saith the Lord God......	Eze 15:6
t I have stretched out my hand......	Eze 16:27
unto thee, t thou art contrary,......	Eze 16:37
t I will gather all thy lovers,......	Eze 16:37
t I also will recompense thy way,......	Eze 16:43
t I took them away as I saw good......	Eze 16:50
T thus saith the Lord God......	Eze 17:19
T will judge you, O house of......	Eze 18:30
T, son of man, speak unto the......	Eze 20:27
t shall my sword go forth out of......	Eze 21:4
Sigh t, thou son of man, with the......	Eze 21:6
smite t upon thy thigh......	Eze 21:12
Thou t, son of man, prophesy, and......	Eze 21:14
T thus saith the Lord God......	Eze 21:24
t have I made thee a reproach......	Eze 22:4
t I have smitten mine hand at thy......	Eze 22:13
T thus saith the Lord God......	Eze 22:19
t I will gather you into the......	Eze 22:19
T have I poured out mine......	Eze 22:31
T, O Aholibah, thus saith the......	Eze 23:22
t will I give her cup into thine......	Eze 23:31
T thus saith the Lord God......	Eze 23:35
t bear thou also thy lewdness and......	Eze 23:35
T thus saith the Lord God......	Eze 23:35
T I will deliver thee to the men......	Eze 25:4
T I will stretch out mine hand......	Eze 25:7
T, behold, I will open the side......	Eze 25:9
T thus saith the Lord God......	Eze 25:13
T thus saith the Lord God......	Eze 25:16
T thus saith the Lord God......	Eze 26:3
T thus saith the Lord God......	Eze 26:7
t I will bring strangers upon......	Eze 28:7
T will cast thee as profane out......	Eze 28:16
T thus saith the Lord God......	Eze 28:18
T I am against thee, and against......	Eze 29:10
T thus saith the Lord God......	Eze 29:19
T thus saith the Lord God......	Eze 29:32
T his height was exalted above......	Eze 31:5
T thus saith the Lord God......	Eze 31:10
I have t delivered him into the......	Eze 31:11
t will I spread out my net over......	Eze 32:3
t thou shalt hear the word at my......	Eze 33:7
T, O thou son of man, speak unto......	Eze 33:10
T, thou son of man, say unto the......	Eze 33:12
T, ye shepherds, hear the word of......	Eze 34:7
T, O ye shepherds, hear the word......	Eze 34:9
T thus saith the Lord God unto......	Eze 34:20
T will I save my flock, and they......	Eze 34:22
T, as I live, saith the Lord God,......	Eze 35:6
T, as I live, saith the Lord God,......	Eze 35:11
T prophesy and say, Thus saith the......	Eze 36:3
T, ye mountains of Israel, hear......	Eze 36:4
T thus saith the Lord God......	Eze 36:5
Prophesy t concerning the land of......	Eze 36:6
T thus saith the Lord God......	Eze 36:7
T thou shalt devour men no more,......	Eze 36:14
T say unto the house of Israel,......	Eze 36:22
T prophesy and say unto them, Thus......	Eze 37:12
T, son of man, prophesy and say......	Eze 38:14
T, thou son of man, prophesy,......	Eze 39:1
t hid I my face from them, and......	Eze 39:23
T thus saith the Lord God......	Eze 39:25
t the breadth of the house was......	Eze 41:7
t the building was straitened......	Eze 42:5
in by t, t it shall be shut......	Eze 44:2
t have I lifted up mine hand......	Eze 44:12
t he requested of the prince of......	Dan 1:8
t stood they before the king......	Dan 1:19
t shew me the dream, and the......	Dan 2:6
t tell me the dream, and I shall......	Dan 2:9
t there is no king, lord, nor......	Dan 2:10
T Daniel went in unto Arioch,......	Dan 2:24
T at that time, when all the......	Dan 3:7
t he spake, and commanded that......	Dan 3:13
T because the king's commandment......	Dan 3:22
T I make a decree, That every......	Dan 3:29
T I made a decree to bring in all......	Dan 4:6
T the he goat waxed very great......	Dan 8:8
t the curse is poured upon us, and......	Dan 9:11
T the Lord watched upon the......	Dan 9:14
Now t, O our God, hear the prayer......	Dan 9:17
t understand the matter, and......	Dan 9:23
Know t and understand, that from......	Dan 9:25
T I was left alone, and saw this......	Dan 10:8
t he shall be grieved, and return,......	Dan 11:30
t he shall go forth with great......	Dan 11:44
let her t put away her whoredoms......	Hos 2:2
T, behold, I will hedge up thy......	Hos 2:6
T will I return, and take away my......	Hos 2:9
T, behold, I will allure her, and......	Hos 2:14
T shall the land mourn, and every......	Hos 4:3
T shalt thou fall in the day, and......	Hos 4:5
t will I change their glory into......	Hos 4:7
t your daughters shall commit......	Hos 4:13
t the people that doth not......	Hos 4:14
t shall Israel and Ephraim fall in......	Hos 5:5
T will I pour out my wrath upon......	Hos 5:10
T will I be unto Ephraim as a......	Hos 5:12
t have I hewed them by the......	Hos 6:5
t it is not God......	Hos 8:6
T he will remember their iniquity......	Hos 9:9
T shall a tumult arise among thy......	Hos 10:14
T turn thou to thy God......	Hos 12:6
t shall he leave his blood upon......	Hos 12:14
T they shall be as the morning......	Hos 13:3
t have they forgotten me......	Hos 13:6
T I will be unto them as a lion......	Hos 13:7
T also now, saith the Lord, turn......	Joel 2:12
T the flight shall perish from......	Amos 2:14
t I will punish you for all your......	Amos 3:2
T thus saith the Lord God......	Amos 3:11
T thus will I do unto thee, O......	Amos 4:12
Forasmuch t as your treading is......	Amos 5:11
T the prudent shall keep silence......	Amos 5:13
T the Lord, the God of hosts, the......	Amos 5:16
T will I cause you to go into......	Amos 5:27
T now shall they go captive with......	Amos 6:7
t will I deliver up the city which......	Amos 6:8
Now t hear thou the word of the......	Amos 7:16
T thus saith the Lord......	Amos 7:17
T I fled before unto Tarshish......	Jonah 4:2
T now, O Lord, take, I beseech......	Jonah 4:3
T will I make Samaria as an heap......	Mic 1:6
T I will wail and howl, I will go......	Mic 1:8
T shalt thou give presents to......	Mic 1:14
T thus saith the Lord......	Mic 2:3
T thou shalt have none that shall......	Mic 2:5
T night shall be unto you, that......	Mic 3:6
T shall Zion for your sake be......	Mic 3:12
T will he give them up, until the......	Mic 5:3
T also will I make thee sick in......	Mic 6:13
t ye shall bear the reproach of......	Mic 6:16
T I will look unto the Lord......	Mic 7:7
T the law is slacked, and judgment......	Hab 1:4
t wrong judgment proceedeth......	Hab 1:4
t they rejoice and are glad......	Hab 1:15
T they sacrifice unto their net,......	Hab 1:16
Shall they t empty their net, and......	Hab 1:17
T their goods shall become a......	Zeph 1:13
T as I live, saith the Lord God......	Zeph 2:9
T wait ye upon me, saith the Lord......	Zeph 3:8
Now t thus saith the Lord of......	Hag 1:5
T the heaven over you is stayed......	Hag 1:10
T say thou unto them, Thus saith......	Zec 1:3
T thus saith the Lord......	Zec 1:16
t came a great wrath from the......	Zec 7:12
T it is come to pass, that as he......	Zec 7:13
t love the truth and peace......	Zec 8:19
t they went their way as a flock,......	Zec 10:2
T have I also made you......	Mal 2:9
T take heed to your spirit, and......	Mal 2:15
t take heed to your spirit, that......	Mal 2:16
t ye sons of Jacob are not......	Mal 3:6
Bring forth t fruits meet for......	Mt 3:8
t every tree which bringeth not......	Mt 3:10
Whosoever t shall break one of......	Mt 5:19
T if thou bring thy gift to the......	Mt 5:23
Be ye t perfect, even as your......	Mt 5:48
T when thou doest thine alms, do......	Mt 6:2
Be not ye t like unto them......	Mt 6:8
After this manner t pray ye......	Mt 6:9
if t thine eye be single, thy......	Mt 6:22
If t the light that is in thee be......	Mt 6:23
T I say unto you, Take no thought......	Mt 6:25
T take no thought, saying, What......	Mt 6:31
Take t no thought for the morrow......	Mt 6:34
T all things whatsoever ye would......	Mt 7:12
t whosoever heareth these sayings......	Mt 7:24
Pray ye t the Lord of the harvest......	Mt 9:38
be ye t wise as serpents, and......	Mt 10:16
Fear them not t......	Mt 10:26
Fear ye not t, ye are of more......	Mt 10:31
Whosoever t shall confess me......	Mt 10:32
t they shall be your judges......	Mt 12:27
T speak I to them in parables......	Mt 13:13
Hear ye t the parable of the......	Mt 13:18
As t the tares are gathered and......	Mt 13:40
them, T every scribe which is......	Mt 13:52
t mighty works do shew forth......	Mt 13:54
Whosoever t shall humble himself......	Mt 18:4
T is the kingdom of heaven......	Mt 18:23
The servant t fell down, and......	Mt 18:26
What t God hath joined together,......	Mt 19:6
what shall we have t......	Mt 19:27
When the lord t of the vineyard......	Mt 21:40
T say I unto you, The kingdom of......	Mt 21:43
t ye in the highways, and as......	Mt 22:9
Tell us t, What thinkest thou......	Mt 22:17
Render t unto Caesar the things......	Mt 22:21
T in the resurrection whose wife......	Mt 22:23
All t whatsoever they bid you......	Mt 23:3
t ye shall receive the greater......	Mt 23:14
Whoso t shall swear by the altar,......	Mt 23:20
When ye t shall see the......	Mt 24:15
Watch t: for ye know not......	Mt 24:42
T be ye also ready......	Mt 24:44
Watch t, for ye know neither the......	Mt 25:13
Thou oughtest t to have put my......	Mt 25:27
Take t the talent from him, and......	Mt 25:28
T when they were gathered......	Mt 27:17
Command t that the sepulchre be......	Mt 27:64
Go ye t, and teach all nations,......	Mt 28:19
for t came I forth......	Mk 1:38
T the Son of man is Lord also of......	Mk 2:28
t mighty works do shew forth......	Mk 6:14
T Herodias had a quarrel against......	Mk 6:19
Whosoever t shall be ashamed of......	Mk 8:38
What t God hath joined together,......	Mk 10:9
T I say unto you, What things......	Mk 11:24
Having yet t one son, his......	Mk 12:6
What shall t the lord of the......	Mk 12:9
In the resurrection t, when they......	Mk 12:23
said unto them, Do ye not t err......	Mk 12:24
ye t do greatly err......	Mk 12:27
David t himself calleth him Lord......	Mk 12:37
Watch ye t......	Mk 13:35
t also that holy thing which......	Lk 1:35
Bring forth t fruits worthy of......	Lk 3:8
every tree t which bringeth not......	Lk 3:9
If thou t wilt worship me, all......	Lk 4:7
for t am I sent......	Lk 4:43
Be ye t merciful, as your Father......	Lk 6:36
Tell me t, which of them will......	Lk 7:42
Take heed t how ye hear......	Lk 8:18
T said he unto them, The harvest......	Lk 10:2
pray ye t the Lord of the harvest......	Lk 10:2
bid her t that she help me......	Lk 10:40
t shall they be your judges......	Lk 11:19
t when thine eye is single, thy......	Lk 11:34
Take heed t that the light which......	Lk 11:35
thy whole body t be full of light......	Lk 11:36
T also said the wisdom of God, I......	Lk 11:49
T whatsoever ye have spoken in......	Lk 12:3
Fear not t......	Lk 12:7
T I say unto you, Take no thought......	Lk 12:22
Be ye t ready also......	Lk 12:40
in them t come and be healed, and......	Lk 13:14
a wife, and t I cannot come......	Lk 14:20
t came his father out, and......	Lk 15:28
If t ye have not been faithful in......	Lk 16:11
Then he said, I pray thee t......	Lk 16:27
He said t, A certain nobleman......	Lk 19:12
What t shall the lord of the......	Lk 20:15
Render t unto Caesar the things......	Lk 20:25
There were t seven brethren......	Lk 20:29
T in the resurrection whose wife......	Lk 20:33
David t calleth him Lord, how is......	Lk 20:44
go ye not t after them......	Lk 21:8
Settle it t in your hearts, not......	Lk 21:14
Watch ye t, and pray always, that......	Lk 21:36
I will t chastise him, and release......	Lk 23:16
Pilate t, willing to release......	Lk 23:20
I will t chastise him, and let him......	Lk 23:22
t am I come baptizing with water......	Jn 1:31
When t he was risen from the dead......	Jn 2:22
this my joy t is fulfilled......	Jn 3:29
When t the Lord knew how the......	Jn 4:1
Jesus t, being wearied with his......	Jn 4:6
T said the disciples one to......	Jn 4:33
The Jews t said unto him that was......	Jn 5:10
t did the Jews persecute Jesus,......	Jn 5:16
The Jews sought the more to......	Jn 5:18
T they gathered them together, and......	Jn 6:13
When Jesus t perceived that they......	Jn 6:15
When the people t saw that Jesus......	Jn 6:24
They said t unto him, What sign......	Jn 6:30
Jesus t answered and said unto......	Jn 6:43
Every man t that hath heard, and......	Jn 6:45
The Jews t strove among......	Jn 6:52
Many t of his disciples, when......	Jn 6:60
T said I unto you, that no man......	Jn 6:65
His brethren t said unto him,......	Jn 7:3
Moses t gave unto you......	Jn 7:22
Many of the people t, when they......	Jn 7:40
The Pharisees t said unto him......	Jn 8:13
I said t unto you, that ye shall......	Jn 8:24
If the Son t shall make you free,......	Jn 8:36
ye t hear them not, because ye......	Jn 8:47
He went his way t, and washed, and......	Jn 9:7
The neighbours t, and they which......	Jn 9:8
T said they unto him, How were......	Jn 9:10
T said some of the Pharisees,......	Jn 9:16
T said his parents, He is of age......	Jn 9:23
t your sin remaineth......	Jn 9:41
T doth my Father love me, because......	Jn 10:17
There was a division t again......	Jn 10:19
T they sought again to take him......	Jn 10:39
T his sisters sent unto him,......	Jn 11:3
he had heard t that he was sick......	Jn 11:6
When Jesus t saw her weeping, and......	Jn 11:33
Jesus t again groaning in himself......	Jn 11:38
Jesus t walked no more openly......	Jn 11:54
the Jews t knew that he was there......	Jn 12:9
The people t that was with him......	Jn 12:17
The Pharisees t said among......	Jn 12:19
The same came t to Philip......	Jn 12:21
The people t, that stood by, and......	Jn 12:29
T they could not believe, because......	Jn 12:39
whatsoever I speak t, even as the......	Jn 12:50
t said he, Ye are not all clean......	Jn 13:11
Simon Peter t beckoned to him,......	Jn 13:24
T, when he was gone out, Jesus......	Jn 13:31
the world, t the world hateth you......	Jn 15:19
t said I, that he shall take of......	Jn 16:15
They said t, What is this that he......	Jn 16:18

And ye now t have sorrow .... Jn 16:22
Jesus t, knowing all things that .... Jn 18:4
if t ye seek me, let these go .... Jn 18:8
They said t unto him, Art not .... Jn 18:25
The Jews t said unto him, It is .... Jn 18:31
Pilate t said unto him, Art thou .... Jn 18:37
will ye t that I release unto you .... Jn 18:39
Then Pilate t took Jesus, and .... Jn 19:1
Pilate t went forth again, and .... Jn 19:4
When the chief priests t and .... Jn 19:6
When Pilate t heard that saying, ... Jn 19:8
t he that delivered me unto thee .... Jn 19:11
When Pilate t heard that saying, ... Jn 19:13
Then delivered he him t unto them .... Jn 19:16
They said t among themselves, Let .... Jn 19:24
These things t the soldiers did .... Jn 19:24
When Jesus t saw his mother, and .... Jn 19:26
When Jesus t had received the .... Jn 19:30
The Jews t, because it was the .... Jn 19:31
He came t, and took the body of .... Jn 19:38
they Jesus t because of the Jews' .... Jn 19:42
Peter t went forth, and that other .... Jn 20:3
other disciples t said unto him .... Jn 20:25
They cast t, and now they were not ...... Jn 21:6
t that disciple whom Jesus loved .... Jn 21:7
When they t were come together, ... Acts 1:6
T did my heart rejoice, and my .... Acts 2:26
T being a prophet, and knowing .... Acts 2:30
T being by the right hand of God .... Acts 2:33
T let all the house of Israel .... Acts 2:36
Repent ye t, and be converted, ... Acts 3:19
T they that were scattered abroad .... Acts 8:4
Repent t of this thy wickedness, ... Acts 8:22
Arise t, and get thee down, and go ...... Acts 10:20
T came I unto you without .... Acts 10:29
I ask t for what intent ye have .... Acts 10:29
Send t to Joppa, and call hither .... Acts 10:32
Immediately t I sent to thee .... Acts 10:33
Now t are we all here present .... Acts 10:33
Peter t was kept in prison .... Acts 12:5
Be it known unto you t, men and .... Acts 13:38
Beware t, lest that come upon you .... Acts 13:40
Long time t abode they speaking .... Acts 14:3
When t Paul and Barnabas had no .... Acts 15:2
Now t why tempt ye God, to put a ...... Acts 15:10
We have sent t Judas and Silas, ... Acts 15:27
T loosing from Troas, we came .... Acts 16:11
now t depart, and go in peace .... Acts 16:36
T many of them believed .... Acts 17:12
T disputed he in the synagogue .... Acts 17:17
we would know t what these things... ... Acts 17:20
Whom t ye ignorantly worship, him ...... Acts 17:23
Some t cried one thing, and some .... Acts 19:32
When he t was come up again, and ...... Acts 20:11
Take heed t unto yourselves, and .... Acts 20:28
T watch, and remember, that by the .... Acts 20:31
What is it t .... Acts 21:22
Do t this that we say to thee .... Acts 21:23
Now t ye with the council signify .... Acts 23:15
Let them t, said he, which among .... Acts 25:5
T, when they were come hither, ... Acts 25:17
Having t obtained help of God, I .... Acts 26:22
For this cause I have t called .... Acts 28:20
Be it known t unto you, that the .... Acts 28:28
T thou art inexcusable, O man, ... Rom 2:1
Thou t which teachest another .... Rom 2:21
T if the uncircumcision keep the .... Rom 2:26
T by the deeds of the law there .... Rom 3:20
T we conclude that a man is .... Rom 3:28
T it is of faith, that it might .... Rom 4:16
t it was imputed to him for .... Rom 4:22
T being justified by faith, we .... Rom 5:1
T as by the offence of one .... Rom 5:18
We are buried with him by .... Rom 6:4
Let not sin t reign in your .... Rom 6:12
There is t now no condemnation to ...... Rom 8:1
T, brethren, we are debtors, not .... Rom 8:12
T hath he mercy on whom he will........ Rom 9:18
Behold t the goodness and severity ...... Rom 11:22
I beseech you t, brethren, by the .... Rom 12:1
T if thine enemy hunger, feed him .... Rom 12:20
Whosoever t resisteth the power, ... Rom 13:2
Render t to all their dues .... Rom 13:7
t love is the fulfilling of the .... Rom 13:10
let us cast off the works of .... Rom 13:12
whether we live t, or die, we are .... Rom 14:8
Let us not t judge one another .... Rom 14:13
Let us t follow after the things .... Rom 14:19
I have t whereof I may glory .... Rom 15:17
When t I have performed this, and ...... Rom 15:28
I am glad t on your behalf .... Rom 16:19
T let no man glory in men 1Cor 3:21
T judge nothing before the 1Cor 4:5
Purge out t the old leaven, that 1Cor 5:7
T let us keep the feast, not with, ... 1Cor 5:8
T put away from among yourselves 1Cor 5:13
Now t there is utterly a fault 1Cor 6:7
t glorify God in your body, and in 1Cor 6:20
I say t to the unmarried and 1Cor 7:8
I suppose t that this is good for 1Cor 7:26
As concerning t the eating of 1Cor 8:4
I t so run, not as uncertainly 1Cor 9:26
Whether t ye eat, or drink, or 1Cor 10:31
ye come together t into one place 1Cor 11:20
is it t not of the body 1Cor 12:15
is it t not of the body 1Cor 12:16
T if I know not the meaning of 1Cor 14:11
If t the whole church be come.............. 1Cor 14:23
T whether it were I or they, so 1Cor 15:11
T, my beloved brethren, be ye 1Cor 15:58
Let no man t despise him 1Cor 16:11

---

t acknowledge ye them that are.......... 1Cor 16:18
When I t was thus minded, did I.......... 2Cor 1:17
T, seeing we have this ministry, ... 2Cor 4:1
I believed, and t have I spoken, ... 2Cor 4:13
we also believe, and t speak 2Cor 4:13
T we are always confident, ... 2Cor 5:6
Knowing t the terror of the Lord, ... 2Cor 5:11
T if any man be in Christ, he is 2Cor 5:17
Having t these promises dearly 2Cor 7:1
T we were comforted in your 2Cor 7:13
I rejoice t that I have 2Cor 7:16
T, as ye abound in every thing, ... 2Cor 8:7
Now t perform the doing of it............... 2Cor 8:11
T thought it necessary to 2Cor 9:5
T it is no great thing if his................... 2Cor 11:15
Most gladly t will I rather glory 2Cor 12:9
T I take pleasure in infirmities, ... 2Cor 12:10
T I write these things being 2Cor 13:10
is t Christ the minister of sin .... Gal 2:17
He t that ministereth to you the .... Gal 3:5
Know ye t that they which are of .... Gal 3:7
Am I t become your enemy, because .... Gal 4:16
Stand fast t in the liberty .... Gal 5:1
As we have t opportunity, let us .... Gal 6:10
Now t ye are no more strangers and ... Eph 2:19
I t, the prisoner of the Lord, ... Eph 4:1
This I say t, and testify in the .... Eph 4:17
Be ye t followers of God, as dear ...... Eph 5:1
Be not ye t partakers with them .... Eph 5:7
T as the church is subject unto, ... Eph 5:24
Stand t, having your loins girt .... Eph 6:14
If there be t any consolation in .... Phil 2:1
Him t I hope to send presently, ... Phil 2:23
I sent him t the more carefully, ... Phil 2:28
Receive him t in the Lord with .... Phil 2:29
Let us t, as many as be perfect, ... Phil 3:15
T, my brethren dearly beloved and ...... Phil 4:1
As ye have t received Christ .... Col 2:6
Let no man t judge you in meat, ... Col 2:16
Mortify t your members which are ...... Col 3:5
Put on t, as the elect of God, ... Col 3:12
T, brethren, we were comforted 1Th 3:7
He t that despiseth, despiseth.............. 1Th 4:8
T let us not sleep, as do others 1Th 5:6
T, brethren, stand fast, and hold 2Th 2:15
I exhort t, that, first of all, ... 1Ti 2:1
I will t that men pray every 1Ti 2:8
For t we both labour and suffer............ 1Ti 4:10
I will t that the younger women 1Ti 5:14
Be not thou t ashamed of the 2Ti 1:8
Thou t, my son, be strong in the 2Ti 2:1
Thou t endure hardness, as a good 2Ti 2:3
T endure all things for the 2Ti 2:10
If a man t purge himself from 2Ti 2:21
I charge thee t before God................... 2Ti 4:1
thou t receive him, that is, mine......... Philem 12
For perhaps he t departed for a .... Philem 15
If thou count me t a partner .... Philem 17
t God, even thy God, hath.................... Heb 1:9
T we ought to give the more .... Heb 2:1
Let us t fear, lest a promise .... Heb 4:1
Seeing t it remaineth that some .... Heb 4:6
There remaineth t a rest to the .... Heb 4:9
Let us labour t to enter into .... Heb 4:11
Let us t come boldly unto the .... Heb 4:16
T leaving the principles of the .... Heb 6:1
If t perfection were by the .... Heb 7:11
It was t necessary that the .... Heb 9:23
Having t, brethren, boldness to .... Heb 10:19
Cast not away t your confidence,......... Heb 10:35
T sprang there even of one, and .... Heb 11:12
Let us go forth t unto him .... Heb 13:13
By him t let us offer the .... Heb 13:15
whosoever t will be a friend of .... Jas 4:4
Submit yourselves t to God .... Jas 4:7
T to him that knoweth to do good, ... Jas 4:17
Be patient t, brethren, unto the .... Jas 5:7
Unto you t which believe he is 1Pet 2:7
be ye t sober, and watch unto 1Pet 4:7
Humble yourselves t under the 1Pet 5:6
Ye t, beloved, seeing ye know 2Pet 3:17
Let that t abide in you, which ye 1Jn 2:24
t the world knoweth us not, ... 1Jn 3:1
t speak they of the world, and the 1Jn 4:5
We t ought to receive such, that 3Jn 8
I will t put you in remembrance, ... Jude 5
Remember t from whence thou art...... Rev 2:5
Remember t how thou hast received ... Rev 3:3
If t thou shalt not watch, I will .... Rev 3:3
be zealous t, and repent .... Rev 3:19
T are they before the throne of .... Rev 7:15
T rejoice, ye heavens, and ye that ..... Rev 12:12
T shall her plagues come in one......... Rev 18:8

THEREFROM

that ye turn not aside t to the .... Josh 23:6
he departed not t 2Kin 3:3
he departed not t 2Kin 13:2

THEREIN See PREFACE.

THEREINTO

that are in the countries enter t .... Lk 21:21

THEREOF See PREFACE.

THEREON See PREFACE.

THEREOUT

he shall take t his handful of .... Lev 2:2
in the jaw, and there came water t ... Judg 15:19

THERETO See PREFACE.

THEREUNTO

it, and have sacrificed t, and said......... Ex 32:8
he made t four pillars of shittim .... Ex 36:36
made t a crown of gold round .... Ex 37:11
Also he made t a border of an .... Ex 37:12
and unto all the places nigh t............... Deut 1:7
watching t with all perseverance.......... Eph 6:18
know that we are appointed t 1Th 3:3
make the comers t perfect..................... Heb 10:1
knowing that ye are t called 1Pet 3:9

THEREUPON

and the mercy seat that is t .... Ex 31:7
colours, and playedst the harlot t.......... Eze 16:16
they shall feed t .... Zeph 2:7
man take heed how he buildeth t 1Cor 3:10
work abide which he hath built t......... 1Cor 3:14

THEREWITH

corn, or the field, be consumed t........... Ex 22:6
tabernacle of the congregation t .... Ex 30:26
t he made the sockets to the door .... Ex 38:30
maketh atonement t shall have it .... Lev 7:7
the ephod, and bound it unto him t ..... Lev 8:7
goeth from him, and is defiled t........... Lev 15:32
any beast so defile thyself t .... Lev 18:23
shall not eat to defile himself t .... Lev 22:8
shalt thou eat unleavened bread t .... Deut 16:3
thyself abroad, thou shalt dig t .... Deut 23:13
took it, and slew a thousand men t ..... Judg 15:15
took new ropes, and bound him t.......... Judg 16:12
any bribe to blind mine eyes t 1Sa 12:3
slew him, and cut off his head t.......... 1Sa 17:51
thy sword, and thrust me through t 1Sa 31:4
so he smote him t in the fifth 2Sa 20:10
I have t sent Naaman my servant 2Kin 5:6
repaired t the house of the LORD.......... 2Kin 12:14
thy sword, and thrust me through t 1Chr 10:4
I made, said David, to praise t 1Chr 23:5
and he built t Geba and Mizpah 2Chr 16:6
than great treasure and trouble t .... Prov 15:16
is, than a stalled ox and hatred t .... Prov 15:17
is a dry morsel, and quietness t .... Prov 17:1
for thee, lest thou be filled t .... Prov 25:16
the sons of man to be exercised t .... Eccl 1:13
to water t the wood that bringeth .... Eccl 2:6
removeth stones shall be hurt t .... Eccl 10:9
itself against him that heweth t .... Isa 10:15
and thou shalt prepare thy bread t ...... Eze 4:15
oil, and ye shall be satisfied t .... Joel 2:19
state I am, t to be content .... Phil 4:11
and raiment let us be t content............ 1Ti 6:8
T bless we God, even the Father .... Jas 3:9
t curse we men, which are made........... Jas 3:9
and not content t, neither doth he 3Jn 10

THESE See PREFACE.

THESSALONIANS (thes-sa-lo´-ne-uns) The
inhabitants of Thessalonica.

and of the T, Aristarchus and .... Acts 20:4
unto the church of the T which is 1Th 1:1
the T was written from Athens .... 1Th s
church of the T in God our Father....... 2Th 1:1
to the T was written from Athens........ 2Th s

THESSALONICA (thes-sa-lo-ni´-cah) A city in
Macedonia.

and Apollonia, they came to T .... Acts 17:1
were more noble than those in T .... Acts 17:11
But when the Jews of T had................. Acts 17:13
Aristarchus, a Macedonian of T .... Acts 27:2
For even in T ye sent once and............ Phil 4:16
world, and is departed unto T 2Ti 4:10

THEUDAS (thew´-das) A false Jewish Messiah.

For before these days rose up T.......... Acts 5:36

THEY See PREFACE.

THICK

there was a t darkness in all the .... Ex 10:22
Lo, I come unto thee in a t cloud .... Ex 19:9
a t cloud upon the mount, and the .... Ex 19:16
unto the t darkness where God was..... Ex 20:21
trees, and the boughs of t trees.......... Lev 23:40
darkness, clouds, and t darkness .... Deut 4:11
of the t darkness, with a great .... Deut 5:22
art waxen fat, thou art grown t .... Deut 32:15
under the t boughs of a great oak 2Sa 18:9
waters, and t clouds of the skies 2Sa 22:12
the t beam were before them 1Kin 7:6
And it was an hand breadth t.............. 1Kin 7:26
he would dwell in the t darkness 1Kin 8:12
morrow, that he took a t cloth 2Kin 8:15
he would dwell in the t darkness 2Chr 6:1
branches, and branches of t trees......... Neh 8:15
upon the t bosses of his bucklers........ Job 15:26
T clouds are a covering to him, ... Job 22:14
up the waters in his t clouds .... Job 26:8
watering he wearieth the t cloud......... Job 37:11
t darkness a swaddlingband for it .... Job 38:9
waters and t clouds of the skies .... Ps 18:11
before him his t clouds passed............ Ps 18:12
lifted up axes upon the t trees .... Ps 74:5
as a t cloud, thy transgressions, ... Is 44:22
green tree, and under every t oak....... Eze 6:13
a t cloud of incense went up .... Eze 8:11
was exalted among the t branches ...... Eze 19:11
high hill, and all the t trees............... Eze 20:28
and his top was among the t boughs... Eze 31:3
up his top among the t boughs........... Eze 31:10

THICKER

up their top among the t boughs........ Eze 31:14
was five cubits t round about............ Eze 41:12
there were t planks upon the face ...... Eze 41:25
of the house, and t planks................ Eze 41:26
of t darkness, as the morning............ Joel 2:2
that ladeth himself with t clay.......... Hab 2:6
a day of clouds and t darkness,......... Zeph 1:15
people were gathered t together........ Lk 11:29

THICKER

shall be t than my father's loins........ 1Kin 12:10
shall be t than my father's loins........ 2Chr 10:10

THICKET

a ram caught in a t by his horns........ Gen 22:13
The lion is come up from his t .... Jer 4:7

THICKETS

hide themselves in caves, and in t...... 1Sa 13:6
kindle in the t of the forest................ Is 9:18
he shall cut down the t of the............ Is 10:34
they shall go into t, and climb up...... Jer 4:29

THICKNESS

the t of it was an handbreadth,.......... 2Chr 4:5
the t thereof was four fingers............ Jer 52:21
The t of the wall, which was for .... Eze 41:9
The chambers were in the t of the...... Eze 42:10

THIEF

If a t be found breaking up, and........ Ex 22:2
if the t be found, let him pay .... Ex 22:7
If the t be not found, then the........... Ex 22:8
then that t shall die....................... Deut 24:7
needy, and in the night is as a t .... Job 24:14
cried after them as after a t .... Job 30:5
When thou sawest a t, then thou........ Ps 50:18
Men do not despise a t, if he............ Prov 6:30
with a t hateth his own soul.............. Prov 29:24
As the t is ashamed when he is .... Jer 2:26
the t cometh in, and the troop of...... Hos 7:1
enter in at the windows like a t .... Joel 2:9
enter into the house of the t .... Zec 5:4
in what watch the t would come......... Mt 24:43
out as against a t with swords........... Mt 26:55
Are ye come out, as against a t .... Mk 14:48
where no t approacheth, neither .... Lk 12:33
known what hour the t would come.... Lk 12:39
Be ye come out, as against a t .... Lk 22:52
some other way, the same is a t .... Jn 10:1
The t cometh not, but for to............. Jn 10:10
but because he was a t, and had........ Jn 12:6
so cometh as a t in the night............ 1Th 5:2
day should overtake you as a t 1Th 5:4
suffer as a murderer, or as a t 1Pet 4:15
will come as a t in the night 2Pet 3:10
watch, I will come on thee as a t ...... Rev 3:3
Behold, I come as a t .... Rev 16:15

THIEVES

rebellious, and companions of t .... Is 1:23
was he found among t....................... Jer 48:27
if t by night, they will destroy........... Jer 49:9
If t came to thee, if robbers by .... Obad 5
where t break through and steal......... Mt 6:19
where t do not break through nor...... Mt 6:20
but ye have made it a den of t .... Mt 21:13
there two t crucified with him........... Mt 27:38
The t also, which were crucified........ Mt 27:44
but ye have made it a den of t .... Mk 11:17
And with him they crucify two t .... Mk 15:27
to Jericho, and fell among t .... Lk 10:30
unto him that fell among the t .... Lk 10:36
but ye have made it a den of t .... Lk 19:46
that ever came before me are t .... Jn 10:8
Nor t, nor covetous, nor 1Cor 6:10

THIGH

I pray thee, thy hand under my t........ Gen 24:2
under the t of Abraham his master..... Gen 24:9
he touched the hollow of his t .... Gen 32:25
of Jacob's t was out of joint .... Gen 32:25
upon him, and he halted upon his t .... Gen 32:31
which is upon the hollow of the t ...... Gen 32:32
t in the sinew that shrank................. Gen 32:32
I pray thee, thy hand under my t........ Gen 47:29
the LORD did make thy t to rot.......... Num 5:21
belly to swell, and thy t to rot........... Num 5:22
shall swell, and her t shall rot........... Num 5:27
his raiment upon his right t .... Judg 3:16
took the dagger from his right t .... Judg 3:21
hip and with a great slaughter........... Judg 15:8
Gird thy sword upon thy t .... Ps 45:3
man hath his sword upon his t .... Song 3:8
make bare the leg, uncover the t .... Is 47:2
was instructed, I smote upon my t ..... Jer 31:19
smite therefore upon thy t .... Eze 21:12
it, even every good piece, the t .... Eze 24:4
on his t a name written, KING OF..... Rev 19:16

THIGHS

even unto the t they shall reach .... Eze 28:42
joints of thy t are like jewels............ Song 7:1
his belly and his t of brass,............... Dan 2:32

THIMNATHAH (thim'-nath-ah) See TIMNAH.
A city in Dan.
And Elon, and T, and Ekron,............ Josh 19:43

THIN

And, behold, seven t ears and .... Gen 41:6
the seven t ears devoured the .... Gen 41:7
behold, seven ears, withered, t .... Gen 41:23
the t ears devoured the seven .... Gen 41:24
And the seven t and ill favoured........ Gen 41:27

did beat the gold into t plates............ Ex 39:3
and there be in it a yellow t hair........ Lev 13:30
certain additions made of t work....... 1Kin 7:29
glory of Jacob shall be made t........... Is 17:4

THINE See PREFACE.

THING

his kind, cattle, and creeping t .... Gen 1:24
every t that creepeth upon the.......... Gen 1:25
over every creeping t that .... Gen 1:26
over every living t that moveth......... Gen 1:28
to every t that creepeth upon the ...... Gen 1:30
God saw every t that he had made,.... Gen 1:31
man, and beast, and the creeping t.... Gen 6:7
every t that is in the earth............... Gen 6:17
And of every living t of all flesh .... Gen 6:19
of every creeping t of the earth........ Gen 6:20
of every t that creepeth upon the ...... Gen 7:8
every creeping t that creepeth .... Gen 7:14
of every creeping t that creepeth ..... Gen 7:21
Noah, and every living t, and all....... Gen 8:1
every living t that is with thee.......... Gen 8:17
of every creeping t that creepeth ..... Gen 8:17
Every beast, every creeping t .... Gen 8:19
smite any more every t living........... Gen 8:21
Every moving t that liveth shall .... Gen 9:3
will not take any t that is thine......... Gen 14:23
Is any t too hard for the LORD .... Gen 18:14
from Abraham that t which I do .... Gen 18:17
the concerning this I also................. Gen 19:21
for I cannot do any t till thou........... Gen 19:22
thou, that thou hast done this t......... Gen 20:10
the t was very grievous in............... Gen 21:11
I wot not who hath done this t.......... Gen 21:26
neither do thou any t unto him......... Gen 22:12
for because thou hast done this t....... Gen 22:16
The proceedeth from the LORD .... Gen 24:50
Thou shalt not give me any t .... Gen 30:31
if thou wilt do this t for me.............. Gen 30:31
which t ought not to be done........... Gen 34:7
unto them, We cannot do this t .... Gen 34:14
man deferred not to do the t .... Gen 34:19
the t which he did displeased the...... Gen 38:10
kept back any t from me but thee...... Gen 39:9
to any t that was under his hand ...... Gen 39:23
This is the t which I have spoken...... Gen 41:28
it is because the t is .... Gen 41:32
the t was good in the eyes of........... Gen 41:37
should do according to this t .... Gen 44:7
them, Why have ye done this t .... Gen 43:18
and said, Surely this t is known ...... Ex 2:14
Now when Pharaoh heard this t ...... Ex 2:15
LORD shall do this t in the land........ Ex 9:5
the LORD did that t on the morrow.... Ex 9:6
not any green t in the trees............. Ex 10:15
ye shall observe this t for an........... Ex 12:24
there lay a small round t .... Ex 16:14
This is the t which the LORD hath..... Ex 16:16
This is the t which the LORD............ Ex 16:32
for in the t wherein they dealt......... Ex 18:11
What is this t that thou doest to....... Ex 18:14
The t that thou doest is not good...... Ex 18:17
for this t is too heavy for thee......... Ex 18:18
If thou shalt do this t, and God........ Ex 18:23
any likeness of any t that is .... Ex 20:4
nor any t that is thy neighbour's...... Ex 20:17
or for any manner of lost t .... Ex 22:9
if it be an hired t, it came for.......... Ex 22:15
this is the t that thou shalt do.......... Ex 29:1
I will do this t also that thou........... Ex 33:17
for it is a terrible t that I................. Ex 34:10
This is the t which the LORD............ Ex 35:4
it is a t most holy of the .... Lev 2:3
it is a t most holy of the .... Lev 2:10
the t be hid from the eyes of the....... Lev 4:13
Or if a soul touch any unclean t .... Lev 5:2
that he hath sinned in that t .... Lev 5:5
that he hath done in the holy t .... Lev 5:16
or in a t taken away by violence,...... Lev 6:2
away, or the t which he hath .... Lev 6:4
or the lost t which he found,............ Lev 6:4
any t of all that he hath done in ...... Lev 6:7
any unclean t shall not be eaten ...... Lev 7:19
that shall touch any unclean t.......... Lev 7:21
or any abominable unclean t .... Lev 7:21
This is the t which the LORD............ Lev 8:5
This is the t which the LORD............ Lev 9:6
of any living t which is the.............. Lev 11:10
t that goeth upon all four................ Lev 11:21
every t whereupon any part of .... Lev 11:24
every creeping t that creepeth .... Lev 11:41
any t whereby t that creepeth.......... Lev 11:43
with any manner of creeping t .... Lev 11:44
she shall touch no hallowed t .... Lev 12:4
a skin, or in any t made of skin........ Lev 13:48
in the woof, or in any t of skin......... Lev 13:49
or any t of skin, wherein the............ Lev 13:52
in the woof, or in any t of skin......... Lev 13:53
wash the t wherein the plague is ...... Lev 13:54
in the woof, or in any t of skin......... Lev 13:57
or whatsoever t of skin it be .... Lev 13:58
or any t of skins, to pronounce........ Lev 13:59
and every t, whereon he sitteth,....... Lev 15:4
he that sitteth on any t whereon....... Lev 15:6
whosoever toucheth any t that was ... Lev 15:10
every t that she lieth upon in........... Lev 15:20
every t also that she sitteth............. Lev 15:20
whosoever toucheth any t that she ... Lev 15:22
or on any t whereon she sitteth,....... Lev 15:23
This is the t which the LORD hath..... Lev 17:2

the hallowed t of the LORD.............. Lev 19:8
not eat any t with the blood............. Lev 19:26
it is a wicked t .... Lev 20:17
wife, it is an unclean t .... Lev 20:21
or by any manner of living t that...... Lev 20:25
flat nose, or any t superfluous,........ Lev 21:18
whoso toucheth any t that is .... Lev 22:4
whosoever toucheth any creeping t... Lev 22:5
no stranger eat of the holy t .... Lev 22:10
shall not eat of the holy t .... Lev 22:10
man eat of the holy t unwittingly..... Lev 22:14
unto the priest with the holy t .... Lev 22:14
t superfluous or lacking in his.......... Lev 22:23
offerings, every t upon his day......... Lev 23:37
as a holy t unto the LORD................ Lev 27:23
Notwithstanding no devoted t .... Lev 27:28
every devoted t is most holy unto .... Lev 27:28
they shall not touch any holy t .... Num 4:15
Seemeth it but a small t unto you .... Num 16:9
Is it a small t that thou hast............ Num 16:13
But if the LORD make a new t .... Num 16:30
Whosoever cometh any t near unto... Num 17:13
office for every t of the altar............ Num 18:7
Every t devoted in Israel shall......... Num 18:14
Every t that openeth the matrix........ Num 18:15
only, without doing any t else .... Num 20:19
now any power at all to say any t ..... Num 22:38
This is the t which the LORD hath..... Num 30:1
Every t that may abide the fire,........ Num 31:23
unto them, If ye will do this t .... Num 32:20
him any t without laying of wait ..... Num 35:22
This is the t which the LORD doth .... Num 36:6
The t which thou hast spoken is....... Deut 1:14
Yet in this t ye did not believe......... Deut 1:32
The likeness of any t that................ Deut 4:18
image, or the likeness of any t .... Deut 4:23
image, or the likeness of any t .... Deut 4:25
any such t as this great t is.............. Deut 4:32
or any likeness of any t that is .... Deut 5:8
or any t that is thy neighbour's........ Deut 5:21
lest thou be a cursed t like it .... Deut 7:26
for it is a cursed t .... Deut 7:26
thou shalt not lack any t in it .... Deut 8:9
What t soever I command you,......... Deut 12:32
and the t certain, that it................. Deut 13:14
of the cursed t to thine hand........... Deut 13:17
shalt not eat any abominable t .... Deut 14:3
every creeping t that flieth is.......... Deut 14:19
eat of any t that dieth of itself .... Deut 14:21
because that for this t the LORD....... Deut 15:10
I command thee this t to day........... Deut 15:15
shall there any t of the flesh........... Deut 16:4
true, and the t certain, that such..... Deut 17:4
have committed that wicked t .... Deut 17:5
if the t follow not, nor come to....... Deut 18:22
that is the t which the LORD hath .... Deut 18:22
But if this t be true, and the........... Deut 22:20
keep thee from every wicked t .... Deut 23:9
that he see no unclean t in thee....... Deut 23:14
usury of any t that is lent upon....... Deut 23:19
thou dost lend thy brother any t ..... Deut 23:19
I command thee to do this t .... Deut 24:18
I command thee to do this t .... Deut 24:22
t which the LORD thy God hath........ Deut 26:11
which have not known any t .... Deut 31:13
For it is not a vain t for you........... Deut 32:47
through this t ye shall prolong......... Deut 32:47
until every t was finished that......... Josh 4:10
yourselves from the accursed t .... Josh 6:18
when ye take of the accursed t .... Josh 6:18
a trespass in the accursed t .... Josh 7:1
of Judah, took of the accursed t ..... Josh 7:1
have even taken of the accursed t ... Josh 7:11
accursed t in the midst of thee........ Josh 7:13
the accursed t from among you....... Josh 7:13
t shall be burnt with fire............... Josh 7:15
of you, and have done this t .... Josh 9:24
Thou knowest the t that the LORD.... Josh 14:6
failed not ought of any good t .... Josh 21:45
a trespass in the accursed t .... Josh 22:20
rather done it for fear of this t .... Josh 22:24
the t pleased the children of .... Josh 22:33
that not one t hath failed of all....... Josh 23:14
not one t hath failed thereof........... Josh 23:14
to another, Who hath done this t..... Judg 6:29
the son of Joash hath done this t..... Judg 6:29
which t became a snare unto .... Judg 8:27
now art thou any t better than........ Judg 11:25
Let this t be done for me............... Judg 11:37
drink, and eat not any unclean t ..... Judg 13:4
drink, neither eat any unclean t ...... Judg 13:7
She may not eat of any t that.......... Judg 13:14
drink, nor eat any unclean t .... Judg 13:14
might put them to shame in any t .... Judg 18:7
of any t that is in the earth............ Judg 18:10
there is no want of any t .... Judg 19:19
unto this man do not so vile a t ...... Judg 19:24
But now this shall be the t which .... Judg 20:9
this is the t that ye shall do,........... Judg 21:11
he have finished the t this day........ Ruth 3:18
Behold, I will do a t in Israel.......... 1Sa 3:11
What is the t that the LORD hath 1Sa 3:17
if thou hide any t from me of all 1Sa 3:17
hath not been such a t heretofore.... 1Sa 4:7
But the t displeased Samuel, when .. 1Sa 8:6
stand and see this great t 1Sa 12:16
up to us, and we will shew you a t ... 1Sa 14:12
but every t that was vile and........... 1Sa 15:9
told Saul, and the t pleased him 1Sa 18:20
light t to be a king's son in law 1Sa 18:23

my father hide this *t* from me 1Sa 20:2
Saul spake not any *t* that day 1Sa 20:26
But the lad knew not any *t* 1Sa 20:39
Let no man know any *t* of the 1Sa 21:2
impute any *t* unto his servant 1Sa 22:15
I should do this *t* unto my master 1Sa 24:6
not hurt, neither missed we any *t* 1Sa 25:15
This *t* is not good that thou hast 1Sa 26:16
happen to thee for this *t* 1Sa 28:10
done this *t* unto thee this day 1Sa 28:18
nor any *t* that they had taken to 1Sa 30:19
because ye have done this *t* 2Sa 2:6
but one *t* I require of thee, that 2Sa 3:13
was yet a small *t* in thy sight 2Sa 7:19
soul liveth, I will not do this *t* 2Sa 11:11
Let not this *t* displease thee, ... 2Sa 11:25
But the *t* that David had done 2Sa 11:27
hath done this *t* shall surely die 2Sa 12:5
fourfold, because he did this *t* 2Sa 12:6
will do this *t* before all Israel 2Sa 12:12
What *t* is this that thou hast 2Sa 12:21
hard for him to do any *t* to her 2Sa 13:2
for no such *t* ought to be done in 2Sa 13:12
regard not this *t* 2Sa 13:20
the king take the *t* to his heart 2Sa 13:33
a *t* against the people of God 2Sa 14:13
this *t* as one which is faulty 2Sa 14:13
of this *t* unto my lord the king 2Sa 14:15
the *t* that I shall ask thee 2Sa 14:18
hath thy servant Joab done this *t* 2Sa 14:20
Behold now, I have done this *t* 2Sa 14:21
and they knew not any *t* 2Sa 15:11
that what *t* soever thou shalt 2Sa 15:35
unto me every *t* that ye can hear 2Sa 15:36
and the *t* was not known 2Sa 17:19
lord the king delight in this *t* 2Sa 24:3
Is this *t* done by my lord the 1Kin 1:27
that Solomon had asked this *t* 1Kin 3:10
Because thou hast asked this *t* 1Kin 3:11
was not any *t* hid from the king 1Kin 10:3
commanded him concerning this *t* 1Kin 11:10
for this *t* is from me 1Kin 12:24
And this *t* became a sin 1Kin 12:30
After this *t* Jeroboam returned 1Kin 13:33
this *t* became sin unto the house 1Kin 13:34
to ask a *t* of thee for her son 1Kin 14:5
t toward the LORD God of Israel 1Kin 14:13
turned not aside from any *t* that 1Kin 15:5
as if it had been a light *t* for 1Kin 16:31
but this *t* I may not do 1Kin 20:9
And do this *t*, Take the kings away 1Kin 20:24
whether any *t* would come from him 1Kin 20:33
he said, Thou hast asked a hard *t* 2Kin 2:10
this is but a light *t* in the 2Kin 3:18
hath not any *t* in the house 2Kin 4:2
had bid thee do some great 2Kin 5:13
this *t* the LORD pardon thy 2Kin 5:18
LORD pardon thy servant in this *t* 2Kin 5:18
was sore troubled for this *t* 2Kin 6:11
in heaven, might this *t* be 2Kin 7:2
in heaven, might such a *t* be 2Kin 7:19
even of every good *t* of Damascus 2Kin 8:9
that he should do this great *t* 2Kin 8:13
This is the *t* that ye shall do 2Kin 11:5
unto them, Ye shall not do this *t* 2Kin 17:12
will do the *t* that he hath spoken 2Kin 20:9
It is a light *t* for the shadow to 2Kin 20:10
transgressed in the *t* accursed 1Chr 2:7
it me, that I should do this *t* 1Chr 21:8
for the *t* was right in the eyes 1Chr 13:4
this was a small *t* in thine eyes 1Chr 17:17
let the *t* that thou hast spoken 1Chr 17:23
then doth my lord require this *t* 1Chr 21:3
And God was displeased with this *t* 1Chr 21:7
because I have done this *t* 1Chr 21:8
and whosoever had dedicated any *t* 1Chr 26:28
it was not any *t* accounted of in 2Chr 9:20
for this *t* is done of me 2Chr 11:4
a rage with him because of this *t* 2Chr 16:10
This is the *t* that ye shall do 2Chr 23:4
unclean in any *t* should enter in 2Chr 23:19
for the *t* was done suddenly 2Chr 29:36
the *t* pleased the king and all the 2Chr 30:4
which hath put such a *t* as this .... Ezr 7:27
And when I heard this *t*, I rent my .... Ezr 9:3
hope in Israel concerning this *t* .... Ezr 10:2
that have transgressed in this *t* .... Ezr 10:13
said, What is this *t* that ye do .... Neh 2:19
What evil *t* is this that ye do .... Neh 13:17
And the *t* pleased the king .... Est 2:4
the *t* was known to Mordecai, who .... Est 2:22
And the *t* pleased Haman .... Est 5:14
every *t* that had befallen him .... Est 6:13
the *t* seem right before the king .... Est 8:5
For the *t* which I greatly feared .... Job 3:25
Now a *t* was secretly brought to .... Job 4:12
grant me the *t* that I long for .... Job 6:8
For now ye are no *t* .... Job 6:21
This is one *t*, therefore I said .... Job 9:22
is the soul of every living *t* .... Job 12:10
And he, as a rotten *t*, consumeth .... Job 13:28
bring a clean *t* out of an unclean .... Job 14:4
is there any secret *t* with thee .... Job 15:11
Thou shalt also decree a *t* .... Job 22:28
For he performeth the *t* that is .... Job 23:14
declared the *t* as it is .... Job 26:3
and his eye seeth every precious *t* .... Job 28:10
the *t* that is hid bringeth he .... Job 28:11
If thou hast any *t* to say .... Job 33:32
he searcheth after every green *t* .... Job 39:8

I know that thou canst do every *t* .... Job 42:2
spoken of me the *t* that is right .... Job 42:7
spoken of me the *t* which is right .... Job 42:8
and the people imagine a vain *t* .... Ps 2:1
One *t* have I desired of the LORD, ... Ps 27:4
An horse is a vain *t* for safety .... Ps 33:17
LORD shalt not want any good *t* .... Ps 34:10
I follow the *t* that good is .... Ps 38:20
every *t* that moveth therein .... Ps 69:34
no good *t* will he withhold from .... Ps 84:11
nor alter the *t* that is gone out .... Ps 89:34
It is a good *t* to give thanks .... Ps 92:1
set no wicked *t* before mine eyes .... Ps 101:3
not my heart to any evil *t* .... Ps 141:4
the desire of every living *t* .... Ps 145:16
Let every *t* that hath breath .... Ps 150:6
Wisdom is the principal *t* .... Prov 4:7
findeth a wife findeth a good *t* .... Prov 18:22
For it is a pleasant *t* if thou .... Prov 22:18
the glory of God to conceal a *t* .... Prov 25:2
soul every bitter *t* is sweet .... Prov 27:7
The *t* that hath been, it is that .... Eccl 1:9
there is no new *t* under the sun .... Eccl 1:9
Is there any *t* whereof it may be .... Eccl 1:10
To every *t* there is a season, and .... Eccl 3:1
He hath made every *t* beautiful in .... Eccl 3:11
to it, nor any *t* taken from it .... Eccl 3:14
even one *t* befalleth them .... Eccl 3:19
hasty to utter any *t* before God .... Eccl 5:2
not seen the sun, nor known any *t* .... Eccl 6:5
Better is the end of a *t* than the .... Eccl 7:8
knoweth the interpretation of a *t* .... Eccl 8:1
stand not in an evil *t* .... Eccl 8:3
commandment shall feel no evil *t* .... Eccl 8:5
hath no better *t* under the sun .... Eccl 8:15
but the dead know not any *t* .... Eccl 9:5
any *t* that is done under the sun .... Eccl 9:6
a pleasant *t* it is for thine eyes .... Eccl 11:7
judgment, with every secret *t* .... Eccl 12:14
Is it a small *t* for you to weary .... Is 7:13
faileth, there is no green *t* .... Is 15:6
like a rolling *t* before the .... Is 17:13
every *t* sown by the brooks, shall .... Is 19:7
or shall the *t* framed say of him .... Is 29:16
aside the just for a *t* of nought .... Is 29:21
do this *t* that he hath spoken .... Is 38:7
up the isles as a very little *t* .... Is 40:15
as nothing, and as a *t* of nought .... Is 41:12
Behold, I will do a new *t* .... Is 43:19
It is a light *t* that thou .... Is 49:6
from thence, touch no unclean *t* .... Is 52:11
in the *t* whereto I sent it .... Is 55:11
But we are all as an unclean *t* .... Is 64:6
Who hath heard such a *t* .... Is 66:8
and see if there be such a *t* .... Jer 2:10
and see that it is an evil *t* .... Jer 2:19
horrible *t* is committed in the .... Jer 5:30
But this *t* commanded I them, ... Jer 7:23
set up altars to that shameful *t* .... Jer 11:13
a *t* of nought, and the deceit of .... Jer 14:14
hath done a very horrible *t* .... Jer 18:13
For if ye do this *t* indeed .... Jer 22:4
of Jerusalem an horrible *t* .... Jer 23:14
hath created a new *t* in the earth .... Jer 31:22
is there any *t* too hard for me .... Jer 32:27
that I will perform that good *t* .... Jer 33:14
he that can do any *t* against you .... Jer 38:5
Jeremiah, I will ask thee a *t* .... Jer 38:14
therefore this *t* is come upon you .... Jer 40:3
Kareah, Thou shalt not do this *t* .... Jer 40:16
may walk, and the *t* that we may do .... Jer 42:3
that whatsoever *t* the LORD shall .... Jer 42:4
nor any *t* for the which he hath .... Jer 42:21
not this abominable *t* that I hate .... Jer 44:4
t goeth forth out of our own .... Jer 44:17
What *t* shall I take to witness .... Lam 2:13
what *t* shall I liken to thee, O .... Lam 2:13
Is it a light *t* to the house of .... Eze 8:17
deceived when he hath spoken a *t* .... Eze 14:9
as if there were a very little *t* .... Eze 16:47
Seemeth it a small *t* unto you to .... Eze 34:18
with any *t* that causeth swine .... Eze 44:18
every dedicated *t* in Israel shall .... Eze 44:29
of any *t* that is dead of itself .... Eze 44:31
that every *t* that liveth, which .... Eze 47:9
every *t* shall live whither the .... Eze 47:9
t most holy by the border of the .... Eze 48:12
Chaldeans, The *t* is gone from me .... Dan 2:5
ye see the *t* is gone from me .... Dan 2:8
it is a rare *t* that the king .... Dan 2:11
Arioch made the *t* known to Daniel .... Dan 2:15
made the *t* known to Hananiah, ... Dan 2:17
which speak any *t* amiss against .... Dan 3:29
The same hour was the *t* fulfilled .... Dan 4:33
shew the interpretation of the *t* .... Dan 5:15
is the interpretation of the *t* .... Dan 5:26
The *t* is true, according to the .... Dan 6:12
a *t* was revealed unto Daniel .... Dan 10:1
the *t* was true, but the time .... Dan 10:1
and he understood the *t*, and had .... Dan 10:1
horrible *t* in the house of Israel .... Hos 6:10
hath cast off the *t* that is good .... Hos 8:3
they were counted as a strange *t* .... Hos 8:12
Ye which rejoice in a *t* of nought .... Amos 6:13
herd nor flock, taste any *t* .... Jonah 3:7
unto the Lord a corrupt *t* .... Mal 1:14
into the city, and told every *t* .... Mt 8:33
any *t* that they shall ask .... Mt 18:19
what good *t* shall I do, that I .... Mt 19:16
and desiring a certain *t* of him .... Mt 20:20

them, I also will ask you one *t* .... Mt 21:24
to take any *t* out of his house .... Mt 24:17
saying, What *t* is this .... Mk 1:27
neither was any *t* kept secret .... Mk 4:22
to see her that had done this *t* .... Mk 5:32
that whatsoever *t* from without .... Mk 7:18
but if thou canst do any *t* .... Mk 9:22
said unto him, One *t* thou lackest .... Mk 10:21
haply he might find any *t* thereon .... Mk 11:13
to take any *t* out of his house .... Mk 13:15
neither said they any *t* to any .... Mk 16:8
and if they drink any deadly *t* .... Mk 16:18
therefore also that holy *t* which .... Lk 1:35
see this *t* which is come to pass, ... Lk 2:15
unto them, I will ask you one *t* .... Lk 6:9
neither any *t* hid, that shall not .... Lk 8:17
them to tell no man that *t* .... Lk 9:21
But one *t* is needful .... Lk 10:42
how or what *t* ye shall answer .... Lk 12:11
able to do that *t* which is least .... Lk 12:26
unto him, Yet lackest thou one *t* .... Lk 18:22
if I have taken any *t* from any .... Lk 19:8
them, I will also ask you one *t* .... Lk 20:3
them it was that should do this *t* .... Lk 22:23
scrip, and shoes, lacked ye any *t* .... Lk 22:35
was not any *t* made that was made .... Jn 1:3
Can there any good *t* come out of .... Jn 1:46
lest a worse *t* come unto thee .... Jn 5:14
no man that doeth any *t* in secret .... Jn 7:4
one *t* I know, that, whereas I was .... Jn 9:25
Why herein is a marvellous *t* .... Jn 9:30
If ye shall ask any *t* in my name .... Jn 14:14
Sayest thou this *t* of thyself .... Jn 18:34
conceived this *t* in thine heart .... Acts 5:4
any *t* that is common or unclean .... Acts 10:14
t for a man that is a Jew to keep .... Acts 10:28
And when he had considered the *t* .... Acts 12:12
to tell, or to hear some new *t* .... Acts 17:21
hands, as though he needed any *t* .... Acts 17:25
Some therefore cried one *t* .... Acts 19:32
But if ye enquire any *t* .... Acts 19:39
that they observe no such *t* .... Acts 21:25
And some cried one *t*, some another .... Acts 21:34
he hath a certain *t* to tell him .... Acts 23:17
have I offended any *t* at all .... Acts 25:8
committed any *t* worthy of death .... Acts 25:11
certain *t* to write unto my lord .... Acts 25:26
thought a *t* incredible with you .... Acts 26:8
Which *t* I also did in Jerusalem .... Acts 26:10
for this *t* was not done in .... Acts 26:26
in my flesh,) dwelleth no good *t* .... Rom 7:18
Shall the *t* formed say to him .... Rom 9:20
continually upon this very *t* .... Rom 13:6
Owe no man any *t*, but to love one .... Rom 13:8
esteemeth any *t* to be unclean .... Rom 14:14
nor any *t* whereby thy brother .... Rom 14:21
in that *t* which he alloweth .... Rom 14:22
That in every *t* ye are enriched 1Cor 1:5
that ye all speak the same *t* 1Cor 1:10
not to know any *t* among you 1Cor 2:2
neither is he that planteth any *t* 1Cor 3:7
t that I should be judged of you 1Cor 4:3
man think that he knoweth any *t* 1Cor 8:2
it as a *t* offered unto an idol 1Cor 8:7
is it a great *t* if we shall reap 1Cor 9:11
For if I do this *t* willingly 1Cor 9:17
that the idol is any *t*, or that 1Cor 10:19
in sacrifice to idols is any *t* 1Cor 10:19
If any *t* be revealed to another 1Cor 14:30
And if they will learn any *t* 1Cor 14:35
To whom ye forgive any *t*, I, ... 2Cor 2:10
for if I forgave any *t*, to whom I 2Cor 2:10
to think any *t* as of ourselves 2Cor 3:5
us for the selfsame *t* is God 2Cor 5:5
Giving no offence in any *t* 2Cor 6:3
Lord, and touch not the unclean *t* 2Cor 6:17
For behold this selfsame *t* 2Cor 7:11
have boasted any *t* to him of you 2Cor 7:14
as ye abound in every *t*, in 2Cor 8:7
in every *t* to all bountifulness 2Cor 9:11
every high *t* that exalteth itself 2Cor 10:5
great *t* if his ministers also be 2Cor 11:15
For this *t* I besought the Lord 2Cor 12:8
affected always in a good *t* .... Gal 4:18
circumcision availeth any *t* .... Gal 5:6
circumcision availeth any *t* .... Gal 6:15
his hands the *t* which is good .... Eph 4:28
to their own husbands in every *t* .... Eph 5:24
spot, or wrinkle, or any such *t* .... Eph 5:27
whatsoever good *t* any man doeth .... Eph 6:8
Being confident of this very *t* .... Phil 1:6
but this one *t* I do, forgetting .... Phil 3:13
if in any *t* ye be otherwise .... Phil 3:15
same rule, let us mind the same *t* .... Phil 3:16
but in every *t* by prayer and .... Phil 4:6
that we need not to speak any *t* 1Th 1:8
In every *t* give thanks 1Th 5:18
t with God to recompense 2Th 1:6
if there be any other *t* that is 1Ti 1:10
That good *t* which was committed 2Ti 1:14
having no evil *t* to say of you .... Titus 2:8
t which is in you in Christ Jesus .... Philem 6
he was sanctified, an unholy *t* .... Heb 10:29
It is a fearful *t* to fall into .... Heb 10:31
provided some better *t* for us .... Heb 11:40
For it is a good *t* that the heart .... Heb 13:9
shall receive any *t* of the Lord .... Jas 1:7
some strange *t* happened unto you 1Pet 4:12
be not ignorant of this one *t* 2Pet 3:8

which *t* is true in him and in you.... 1Jn 2:8
if we ask any *t* according to his........ 1Jn 5:14
the Nicolaitanes, which *t* I hate........ Rev 2:15
of the earth, neither any green *t*........ Rev 9:4
enter into it any *t* that defileth......... Rev 21:27

THINGS See PREFACE.

THINGS'
For which *t* sake the wrath of God........ Col 3:6

THINK
But *t* on me when it shall be well....... Gen 40:14
them marry to whom they *t* best....... Num 36:6
to *t* that all the king's sons are........ 2Sa 13:33
now ye *t* to withstand the kingdom.... 2Chr 13:8
T upon me, my God, for good,.......... Neh 5:19
that thou and the Jews to rebel........... Neh 6:6
t thou upon Tobiah and Sanballat..... Neh 6:14
T not with thyself that thou............. Est 4:13
why then should I *t* upon a maid....... Job 31:1
one would *t* the deep to be hoary...... Job 41:32
though a wise man *t* to know it.......... Eccl 8:17
so, neither doth his heart *t* so........... Is 10:7
Which *t* to cause my people to......... Jer 23:27
the thoughts that I *t* toward you....... Jer 29:11
thou shalt *t* an evil thought............. Eze 38:10
t to change times and laws.............. Dan 7:25
if so be that God will *t* upon us........ Jonah 1:6
And I said unto them, If ye *t* good..... Zec 11:12
I not to say within yourselves,.......... Mt 3:9
T not that I am come to destroy........ Mt 5:17
for they *t* that they shall be............. Mt 6:7
Wherefore *t* ye evil in your.............. Mt 9:4
T not that I am come to send........... Mt 10:34
How *t* ye?.................................... Mt 18:12
But what *t* ye............................... Mt 21:28
Saying, What *t* ye of Christ............. Mt 22:42
as ye *t* not the Son of man cometh.... Mt 24:44
What *t* ye?................................. Mt 26:66
what *t* ye?.................................. Mk 14:64
cometh at an hour when ye *t* not...... Lk 12:40
t ye that they were sinners above..... Lk 13:4
for in them ye *t* ye have eternal........ Jn 5:39
Do not I that I will accuse you.......... Jn 5:45
stood in the temple, What *t* ye......... Jn 11:56
will I that he doeth God service........... Jn 16:2
he said, Whom *t* ye that I am............ Acts 13:25
we ought not to *t* that the............... Acts 17:29
I *t* myself happy, king Agrippa,........ Acts 26:2
not to *t* of himself more highly......... Rom 12:3
more highly than he ought to *t*......... Rom 12:3
but to *t* soberly, according as.......... Rom 12:3
to *t* of men above that which is......... 1Cor 4:6
For I *t* that God hath set forth.......... 1Cor 4:9
But if any man *t* that he behaveth...... 1Cor 7:36
I *t* also that I have the Spirit............. 1Cor 7:40
if any man *t* that he knoweth any....... 1Cor 8:2
which we *t* to be less honourable,...... 1Cor 12:23
If any man *t* himself to be a............. 1Cor 14:37
to *t* any thing as of ourselves........... 2Cor 3:5
wherewith I *t* to be bold against....... 2Cor 10:2
which *t* of us as if we walked........... 2Cor 10:2
let him of himself *t* this again........... 2Cor 10:7
Let such an one *t* this, that,............. 2Cor 10:11
say again, Let no man *t* me a fool...... 2Cor 11:16
lest any man should *t* of me above..... 2Cor 12:6
t ye that we excuse ourselves........... 2Cor 12:19
For if a man *t* himself to be............. Gal 6:3
above all that we ask or *t*............... Eph 3:20
meet for me to *t* this of you all........ Phil 1:7
be any praise, *t* on these things........ Phil 4:8
For let not that man *t* that he.......... Jas 1:7
Do ye *t* that the scripture saith........ Jas 4:5
Wherein they *t* it strange that ye...... 1Pet 4:4
t it not strange concerning the......... 1Pet 4:12
I *t* it meet, as long as I am in........... 2Pet 1:13

THINKEST
T thou that David doth honour thy..... 2Sa 10:3
T thou that David doth honour thy..... 1Chr 19:3
T thou this to be right, that............. Job 35:2
him, saying, What *t* thou, Simon....... Mt 17:25
Tell us therefore, What *t* thou.......... Mt 22:17
T thou that I cannot now pray to...... Mt 26:53
t thou, was neighbour unto him........ Lk 10:36
to hear of thee what thou *t*.............. Acts 28:22
t thou this, O man, that judgest........ Rom 2:3

THINKETH
Me *t* the running of the foremost....... 2Sa 18:27
yet the Lord *t* upon me................... Ps 40:17
For as he *t* in his heart, so is............ Prov 23:7
Wherefore let him that *t* he............. 1Cor 10:12
is not easily provoked, *t* no evil........ 1Cor 13:5
If any other man *t* that he hath......... Phil 3:4

THINKING
t to have brought good tidings, I....... 2Sa 4:10
t, David cannot come in.................. 2Sa 5:6

THIRD
and the morning were the *t* day........ Gen 1:13
the name of the *t* river is................ Gen 2:14
t stories shall thou make it.............. Gen 6:16
Then on the *t* day Abraham lifted...... Gen 22:4
on the *t* day that Jacob was fled........ Gen 31:22
commanded he the second, and the *t*... Gen 32:19
And it came to pass on the *t* day....... Gen 34:25
And it came to pass the *t* day........... Gen 40:20
Joseph said unto them the *t* day....... Gen 42:18
children of the *t* generation............. Gen 50:23
In the *t* month, when the children...... Ex 19:1

And be ready against the *t* day......... Ex 19:11
for the *t* day the LORD will come....... Ex 19:11
Be ready against the *t* day............... Ex 19:15
pass on the *t* day in the morning....... Ex 19:16
upon the children unto the *t*............ Ex 20:5
the *t* row a ligure, an agate, and....... Ex 28:19
children's children, unto the *t*.......... Ex 34:7
And the *t* row, a ligure, an agate,...... Ex 39:12
t day shall be burnt with fire........... Lev 7:17
be eaten at all on the *t* day............. Lev 7:18
if ought remain until the *t* day......... Lev 19:6
it be eaten at all on the *t* day........... Lev 19:7
shall go forward in the *t* rank.......... Num 2:24
On the *t* day Elah the son of........... Num 7:24
upon the children unto the *t*............ Num 14:18
with the *t* part of an hin of oil......... Num 15:6
the *t* part of an hin of wine............. Num 15:7
himself with it on the *t* day............ Num 19:12
he purify not himself the *t* day......... Num 19:12
upon the unclean on the *t* day.......... Num 19:19
the *t* part of an hin unto a ram......... Num 28:14
on the *t* day eleven bullocks, two...... Num 29:20
and your captives on the *t* day.......... Num 31:19
upon the children unto the *t*............ Deut 5:9
the part of the LORD's in their *t* generation.... Deut 23:8
of thine increase the *t* year............ Deut 26:12
unto their cities on the *t* day............ Josh 9:17
the *t* lot came up for the................. Josh 19:10
children of Benjamin on the *t* day..... Judg 20:30
called Samuel again the *t* time.......... 1Sa 3:8
him Abinadab, and the *t* Shammah.... 1Sa 17:13
sent messengers again the *t* time....... 1Sa 19:21
the field unto the *t* day at even........ 1Sa 20:5
to morrow any time, or the *t* day...... 1Sa 20:12
were come to Ziklag on the *t* day...... 1Sa 30:1
It came even to pass on the *t* day...... 2Sa 1:2
and the *t*, Absalom the son of.......... 2Sa 3:3
David sent forth a *t* company of....... 2Sa 18:2
a *t* part under the hand of............... 2Sa 18:2
and the *t* under the hand of Ittai...... 2Sa 18:2
it came to pass the *t* day after.......... 1Kin 3:18
the *t* was seven cubits broad............ 1Kin 6:6
and out of the middle into the *t*........ 1Kin 6:8
people came to Rehoboam the *t* day... 1Kin 12:12
Come to me again the *t* day............. 1Kin 12:12
Even in the *t* year of Asa king of....... 1Kin 15:28
In the *t* year of Asa king of............. 1Kin 15:33
LORD came to Elijah in the *t* year...... 1Kin 18:1
And he said, Do it the *t* time............ 1Kin 18:34
And they did it the *t* time............... 1Kin 18:34
And it came to pass in the *t* year...... 1Kin 22:2
of the *t* fifty with his fifty.............. 2Kin 1:13
the *t* captain of fifty went up.......... 2Kin 1:13
a *t* part of you that enter in on......... 2Kin 11:5
a *t* part shall be at the gate of.......... 2Kin 11:6
a *t* part at the gate behind the.......... 2Kin 11:6
Now it came to pass in the *t* year..... 2Kin 18:1
in the *t* year saw ye, and reap, and... 2Kin 19:29
on the *t* day thou shalt go up........... 2Kin 20:5
the house of the LORD the *t* day....... 2Kin 20:8
the second, and Shimma the *t*.......... 1Chr 2:13
the *t*, Absalom the son of Maachah.... 1Chr 3:2
the *t* Zedekiah, the fourth.............. 1Chr 3:15
the second, and Aharah the *t*........... 1Chr 8:1
the second, and Eliphelet the *t*........ 1Chr 8:39
Obadiah the second, Eliab the *t*....... 1Chr 12:9
the second, Jahaziel the *t*............... 1Chr 23:19
The *t* to Harim, the fourth to.......... 1Chr 24:8
the second, Jahaziel the *t*............... 1Chr 24:23
The *t* to Zaccur, the his, sons, and... 1Chr 25:10
the second, Zebadiah the *t*.............. 1Chr 26:2
Jehozabad the second, Joah the *t*...... 1Chr 26:4
the second, Tebaliah the *t*.............. 1Chr 26:11
The *t* captain of the host for the...... 1Chr 27:5
captain of the host for the *t*............ 1Chr 27:5
came to Rehoboam on the *t* day....... 2Chr 10:12
Come again to me on the *t* day......... 2Chr 10:12
at Jerusalem in the *t* month............ 2Chr 15:10
Also in the *t* year of his reign.......... 2Chr 17:7
A *t* part of you entering on the......... 2Chr 23:4
a *t* part shall be at the king's.......... 2Chr 23:5
a *t* part at the gate of the............... 2Chr 23:5
both the second year, and the *t*........ 2Chr 31:7
In the *t* month they began to lay...... 2Chr 31:7
on the *t* day of the month Adar........ Ezra 6:15
the part of a shekel for the................ Neh 10:32
In the *t* year of his reign, he........... Est 1:3
Now it came to pass on the *t* day...... Est 5:1
at that time in the *t* month............. Est 8:9
and the name of the *t*,................... Job 42:14
shall Israel be the *t* with Egypt........ Is 19:24
In the *t* year sow ye, and reap, and... Is 37:30
I entry that is in the house of........... Eze 5:2
Thou shalt burn with fire a *t*........... Eze 5:2
and thou shalt take a *t* part............ Eze 5:2
a *t* part thou shalt scatter in........... Eze 5:2
A *t* part of thee shalt die with......... Eze 5:12
a *t* part shall fall by the sword........ Eze 5:12
I will scatter a *t* part into all........... Eze 5:12
the *t* the face of a lion, and the........ Eze 10:14
the sword be doubled the *t* time....... Eze 21:14
the eleventh year, in the *t* month..... Eze 31:1
the *t* part of an hin of oil, to.......... Eze 46:14
In the *t* year of the reign of............ Dan 1:1
another *t* kingdom of brass, which.... Dan 2:39
shall be the *t* ruler in the.............. Dan 5:7
shall be the *t* ruler in the.............. Dan 5:16
be the *t* ruler in the kingdom.......... Dan 5:29
In the *t* year of the reign of............ Dan 8:1
In the *t* year of Cyrus king of......... Dan 10:1

in the *t* day he will raise us up,........ Hos 6:2
in the *t* chariot white horses........... Zec 6:3
but the *t* shall be left therein........... Zec 13:8
I will bring the *t* part through......... Zec 13:9
and be raised again the *t* day........... Mt 16:21
the *t* day he shall be raised.............. Mt 17:23
And he went out about the *t* hour..... Mt 20:3
the *t* day he shall rise again............ Mt 20:19
the second also, and the *t*.............. Mt 22:26
away again, and prayed the *t* time..... Mt 26:44
be made sure until the *t* day............ Mt 27:64
killed, be shall rise the *t* day........... Mk 9:31
the *t* day he shall rise again............ Mk 10:34
and the *t* likewise....................... Mk 12:21
And he cometh the *t* time, and saith... Mk 14:41
And it was the *t* hour, and they........ Mk 15:25
be slain, and be raised the *t* day....... Lk 9:22
watch, or come in the *t* watch.......... Lk 12:38
the *t* day I shall be perfected........... Lk 13:32
the *t* day he shall rise again............ Lk 18:33
And again he sent a *t*................... Lk 20:12
And the *t* took her....................... Lk 20:31
And he said unto them the *t* time...... Lk 23:22
and the *t* day rise again................. Lk 24:7
to day is the *t* day since these.......... Lk 24:21
to rise from the dead the *t* day........ Lk 24:46
the *t* day there was a marriage in...... Jn 2:1
This is now the *t* time that Jesus...... Jn 21:14
He saith unto him the *t* time............ Jn 21:17
he said unto him the *t* time............. Jn 21:17
it is but the *t* hour of the day.......... Acts 2:15
Him God raised up the *t* day............ Acts 10:40
and fell down from the *t* loft........... Acts 20:9
at the *t* hour of the night............... Acts 23:23
the *t* day we cast out with our......... Acts 27:19
that he rose again the *t* day............. 1Cor 15:4
an one caught up to the *t* heaven...... 2Cor 12:2
the time I am ready to come to.......... 2Cor 12:14
This is the *t* time I am coming to...... 2Cor 13:1
the beast had a face as a man,........... Rev 4:7
And when he had opened the *t* seal.... Rev 6:5
I heard the *t* beast say.................. Rev 6:5
the *t* part of trees was burnt up,....... Rev 8:7
the *t* part of the sea became............ Rev 8:9
the *t* part of the creatures which...... Rev 8:9
the *t* part of the ships were............. Rev 8:9
the angel sounded, and there............ Rev 8:10
it fell upon the *t* part of the............ Rev 8:10
the *t* part of the waters became........ Rev 8:11
the *t* part of the sun was smitten...... Rev 8:12
the *t* part of the moon, and the........ Rev 8:12
moon, and the *t* part of the stars....... Rev 8:12
so as the *t* part of them was............ Rev 8:12
for the two woe for a *t* part of it...... Rev 8:13
for to slay the *t* part of men........... Rev 9:15
was the *t* part of men killed............ Rev 9:18
behold, the *t* woe cometh quickly..... Rev 11:14
his tail drew the *t* part of the.......... Rev 12:4
the *t* angel followed them, saying..... Rev 14:9
the *t* angel poured out his vial......... Rev 16:4
the *t*, a chalcedony.................... Rev 21:19

THIRDLY
t teachers, after that miracles,........ 1Cor 12:28

THIRST
our children and our cattle with *t*...... Deut 25:18
against thee, in hunger, and in *t*....... Deut 28:48
heart, to add drunkenness to *t*......... Deut 29:19
and now shall I die for *t*, and fall...... Judg 15:18
to die by famine and by *t*, saying,..... 2Chr 32:11
them out of the rock for their *t*........ Neh 9:15
and gavest them water for their *t*...... Neh 9:20
their winepresses, and suffer *t*......... Job 24:11
in my *t* they gave me vinegar to....... Ps 69:21
the wild asses quench their *t*.......... Ps 104:11
their multitude dried up with *t*........ Is 5:13
and their tongue faileth for *t*.......... Is 41:17
They shall not hunger nor *t*............ Is 49:10
there is no water, and dieth for *t*..... Is 50:2
unshod, and thy throat from *t*......... Jer 2:25
down from thy glory, and sit in *t*..... Jer 48:18
to the roof of his mouth for *t*......... Lam 4:4
a dry land, and slay her with *t*........ Hos 2:3
nor a *t* for water, but of hearing...... Amos 8:11
virgins and young men faint for *t*..... Amos 8:13
hunger and *t* after righteousness...... Mt 5:6
of this water shall *t* again.............. Jn 4:13
I shall give him shall never *t*........... Jn 4:14
give me this water, that I *t* not........ Jn 4:15
believeth on me shall never *t*.......... Jn 6:35
and cried, saying, If any man *t*........ Jn 7:37
might be fulfilled, saith, I............... Jn 19:28
if he *t*, give him drink................. Rom 12:20
present hour we both hunger, and *t*... 1Cor 4:11
watchings often, in hunger and *t*...... 2Cor 11:27
no more, neither *t* any more........... Rev 7:16

THIRSTED
the people *t* there for water........... Ex 17:3
they *t* not when he led them........... Is 48:21

THIRSTETH
My soul *t* for God, for the living...... Ps 42:2
my soul *t* for thee, my flesh........... Ps 63:1
my soul *t* after thee, as a.............. Ps 143:6
Ho, every one that *t*, come ye to...... Is 55:1

THIRSTY
for I am *t*.............................. Judg 4:19
people is hungry, and weary, and *t*.... 2Sa 17:29
land, where no water is.................. Ps 63:1
Hungry and *t*, their soul fainted...... Ps 107:5

thirsteth after thee, as a *t* land............. Ps 143:6
and if he be *t*, give him water to ...... Prov 25:21
As cold waters to a *t* soul............... Prov 25:25
brought water to him that was *t* .... Is 21:14
or as when a *t* man dreameth .... Is 29:8
cause the drink of the *t* to fail .... Is 32:6
the *t* land springs of water.............. Is 35:7
pour water upon him that is *t* .... Is 44:3
shall drink, but ye shall be *t* .... Is 65:13
wilderness, in a dry and *t* ground.... Eze 19:13
I was *t*, and ye gave me drink............ Mt 25:35
or *t*, and gave thee drink.................. Mt 25:37
I was *t*, and ye gave me no drink........ Mt 25:42

THIRTEEN

Ishmael his son was *t* years old........ Gen 17:25
two hundred and threescore and *t* ..... Num 3:43
t of the firstborn of the..................... Num 3:46
t young bullocks, two rams, and .... Num 29:13
every bullock of the *t* bullocks......... Num 29:14
t cities and their villages................. Josh 19:6
the tribe of Benjamin, *t* cities......... Josh 21:4
of Manasseh in Bashan, *t* cities....... Josh 21:6
were *t* cities with their suburbs......... Josh 21:19
to their families were *t* cities........... Josh 21:33
building his own house *t* years 1Kin 7:1
their families were *t* cities............... 1Chr 6:60
of Manasseh in Bashan, *t* cities........ 1Chr 6:62
sons and brethren of Hosah were *t* ... 1Chr 26:11
the length of the gate, *t* cubits .... Eze 40:11

THIRTEENTH

in the *t* year they rebelled................. Gen 14:4
the *t* to Huppah, the fourteenth........ 1Chr 24:13
The *t* to Shubael, he, his sons,......... 1Chr 25:20
on the *t* day of the first month.......... Est 3:12
even upon the *t* day of the................ Est 3:13
upon the *t* day of the twelfth............. Est 8:12
on the *t* day of the same, when........ Est 9:1
On the *t* day of the month Adar........ Est 9:17
together on the *t* day thereof............ Est 9:18
in the *t* year of his reign................... Jer 1:2
From the *t* year of Josiah the son...... Jer 25:3

THIRTIETH

t year of Uzziah king of Judah.......... 2Kin 15:13
t year of Azariah king of Judah......... 2Kin 15:17
t year of the captivity....................... 2Kin 25:27
t year of the reign of Asa................. 2Chr 15:19
t year of the reign of Asa Baasha 2Chr 16:1
t year of Artaxerxes the king,........... Neh 5:14
t year of Artaxerxes king of .... Neh 13:6
t year of the captivity....................... Jer 52:31
Now it came to pass in the *t* year...... Eze 1:1

THIRTY

t years, and begat a son in his .... Gen 5:3
were nine hundred and *t* years .... Gen 5:5
t years, and begat sons and .... Gen 5:16
and the height of it *t* cubits.............. Gen 6:15
five and *t* years, and begat Salah ..... Gen 11:12
And Salah lived *t* years, and begat ... Gen 11:14
four and *t* years, and begat Peleg ..... Gen 11:16
t years, and begat sons and .... Gen 11:17
And Peleg lived *t* years, and begat ... Gen 11:18
two and *t* years, and begat Serug ..... Gen 11:20
And Serug lived *t* years, and begat ... Gen 11:22
there shall *t* be found there .... Gen 18:30
will not do it, if I find *t* there .... Gen 18:30
life of Ishmael, an hundred and *t* ..... Gen 25:17
t milch camels with their colts,......... Gen 32:15
Joseph was *t* years old when he........ Gen 41:46
his sons and his daughters were *t* ..... Gen 46:15
are an hundred and *t* years............... Gen 47:9
life of Levi were an hundred and *t* .... Ex 6:16
life of Kohath were an hundred *t* ...... Ex 6:18
of Amram were an hundred and *t* ...... Ex 6:20
was four hundred and *t* years........... Ex 12:40
t years, even the selfsame day it ...... Ex 12:41
their master *t* shekels of silver......... Ex 21:32
of one curtain shall be *t* cubits......... Ex 26:8
of one curtain was *t* cubits............... Ex 36:15
t shekels, after the shekel of .... Ex 38:24
of her purifying three and *t* days ...... Lev 12:4
thy estimation shall be *t* shekels ...... Lev 27:4
of the tribe of Manasseh, were *t* ...... Num 1:35
of the tribe of Benjamin, were *t* .... Num 1:37
were numbered of them, were *t* .... Num 2:21
were numbered of them, were *t* .... Num 2:23
From *t* years old and upward even ..... Num 4:3
From *t* years old and upward until..... Num 4:23
From *t* years old and upward even ..... Num 4:30
From *t* years old and upward even ..... Num 4:35
From *t* years old and upward even ..... Num 4:39
two thousand and six hundred and *t* .. Num 4:40
From *t* years old and upward even ..... Num 4:43
From *t* years old and upward even ..... Num 4:47
t shekels, one silver bowl of .... Num 7:13
t shekels, one silver bowl of .... Num 7:19
t shekels, one silver bowl of .... Num 7:25
t shekels, one silver bowl of .... Num 7:31
t shekels, one silver bowl of .... Num 7:37
t shekels, a silver bowl of................ Num 7:43
t shekels, one silver bowl of .... Num 7:49
t shekels, one silver bowl of .... Num 7:55
t shekels, one silver bowl of .... Num 7:61
t shekels, one silver bowl of .... Num 7:67
t shekels, one silver bowl of .... Num 7:73
t shekels, one silver bowl of .... Num 7:79
t shekels, each bowl seventy............ Num 7:85
they mourned for Aaron *t* days.......... Num 20:29
thousand and seven hundred and *t* .... Num 26:7

that were numbered of them, *t*......... Num 26:37
and a thousand seven hundred and *t* . Num 26:51
And *t* and two thousand persons in ... Num 31:35
t thousand and five hundred sheep ... Num 31:36
And the beeves were *t* and six.......... Num 31:38
And the asses were *t* thousand......... Num 31:39
of which the LORD's tribute was *t* ...... Num 31:40
t thousand and seven thousand and.. Num 31:43
And *t* and six thousand beeves,......... Num 31:44
t thousand asses and five hundred,... Num 31:45
come over the brook Zered, was *t* ..... Deut 2:14
in the plains of Moab *t* days............. Deut 34:8
men of Ai smote of them about *t*....... Josh 7:5
Joshua chose out *t* thousand .... Josh 8:3
all the kings *t* and one.................... Josh 12:24
he had *t* sons that rode................... Judg 10:4
sons that rode on *t* ass colts........... Judg 10:4
ass colts, and they had *t* cities........ Judg 10:4
And he had *t* sons........................... Judg 12:9
t daughters, whom he sent abroad,... Judg 12:9
took in *t* daughters from abroad .... Judg 12:9
sons and *t* nephews, that rode on ..... Judg 12:14
that they brought *t* companions to .... Judg 14:11
then I will give you *t* sheets............. Judg 14:12
sheets and *t* change of garments...... Judg 14:12
then shall ye give me *t* sheets.......... Judg 14:13
sheets and *t* change of garments...... Judg 14:13
slew *t* men of them, and took their ... Judg 14:19
the field, about *t* men of Israel......... Judg 20:31
the men of Israel about *t* persons .... Judg 20:39
fell of Israel *t* thousand footmen 1Sa 4:10
which were about *t* persons............... 1Sa 9:22
and the men of Judah *t* thousand 1Sa 11:8
t thousand chariots, and six............ 1Sa 13:5
David was *t* years old when he......... 2Sa 5:4
and in Jerusalem he reigned *t* 2Sa 5:5
chosen men of Israel, *t* thousand 2Sa 6:1
three of the *t* chief went down,......... 2Sa 23:13
He was more honourable than the *t*... 2Sa 23:23
brother of Joab was one of the *t* 2Sa 23:24
t and seven in all 2Sa 23:39
years reigned he in Hebron, and *t* 1Kin 2:11
day was *t* measures of fine flour 1Kin 4:22
and the key was *t* thousand men 1Kin 5:13
and the height thereof *t* cubits 1Kin 6:2
and the height thereof *t* cubits 1Kin 7:2
and the breadth thereof *t* cubits 1Kin 7:6
a line of *t* cubits did compass it 1Kin 7:23
In the *t* and first year of Asa........... 1Kin 16:23
And in the *t* and eighth year of Asa.. 1Kin 16:29
and there were *t* and two kings with . 1Kin 20:1
they were two hundred and *t*............ 1Kin 20:15
pavilions, he and the kings, the *t* 1Kin 20:16
the king of Syria commanded his *t* ... 1Kin 22:31
Jehoshaphat was *t* and five years..... 1Kin 22:42
t and two years old was he when he . 2Kin 8:17
In the *t* and seventh year of Joash ... 2Kin 13:10
In the *t* and eighth year of 2Kin 15:8
of silver and *t* talents of gold.......... 2Kin 18:14
began to reign, and he reigned *t* 2Kin 22:1
and in Jerusalem he reigned *t* 1Chr 3:4
for war, six and *t* thousand men....... 1Chr 7:4
twenty and two thousand and *t* 1Chr 7:7
Now three of the *t* captains went 1Chr 11:15
he was honourable among the *t* 1Chr 11:25
of the Reubenites, and with him,......... 1Chr 11:42
among the *t*, and over the *t* 1Chr 12:4
with them with shield and spear *t* 1Chr 12:34
and his brethren an hundred and *t* ... 1Chr 15:7
So they hired *t* and two thousand 1Chr 19:7
numbered from the age of *t* years 1Chr 23:3
by their polls, man by man, was *t* 1Chr 23:3
among the *t*, and above the *t* 1Chr 27:6
years reigned he in Hebron, and *t* 1Chr 29:27
before the house two pillars of *t* 2Chr 3:15
a line of *t* cubits did compass it 2Chr 4:2
And Asa in the *t* and ninth year of ... 2Chr 16:12
he was *t* and five years old when 2Chr 20:31
Jehoram was *t* and two years old...... 2Chr 21:5
t and two years old was he when he . 2Chr 22:2
t years old was he when he died 2Chr 24:15
in Jerusalem one and *t* years........... 2Chr 34:1
to the number of *t* thousand 2Chr 35:7
t chargers of gold, a thousand.......... Ezr 1:9
t basons of gold, silver basons......... Ezr 1:10
thousand and six hundred and *t* .... Ezr 2:35
of Shobai, in all an hundred *t* .... Ezr 2:42
seven thousand three hundred *t* .... Ezr 2:65
Their horses were seven hundred *t* ... Ezr 2:66
Their camels, four hundred *t* .... Ezr 2:67
three thousand nine hundred and *t* ... Neh 7:38
children of Shobai, an hundred *t* ...... Neh 7:45
seven thousand three hundred *t* .... Neh 7:67
Their horses, seven hundred *t* .... Neh 7:68
Their camels, four hundred *t* .... Neh 7:69
hundred and *t* priests' garments....... Neh 7:70
in unto the king their *t* days............ Est 4:11
Take from hence *t* men with thee ...... Jer 38:10
from Jerusalem eight hundred *t* .... Jer 52:29
t chambers were upon the pavement . Eze 40:17
one over another, and *t* in order .... Eze 41:6
of forty cubits long and *t* broad........ Eze 46:22
of any God or man for *t* days............ Dan 6:7
of any God or man within *t* days .... Dan 6:12
three hundred and five and *t* days .... Dan 12:12
for my price *t* pieces of silver........... Zec 11:12
I took the *t* pieces of silver, and ...... Zec 11:13
hundredfold, some sixty, some *t* .... Mt 13:23
with him for *t* pieces of silver........... Mt 26:15
brought again the *t* pieces of .... Mt 27:3

they took the *t* pieces of silver,........ Mt 27:9
and brought forth, some *t*, and some. Mk 4:20
began to be about *t* years of age...... Lk 3:23
there, which had an infirmity *t* .... Jn 5:5
five and twenty or *t* furlongs............. Jn 6:19
t years after, cannot disannul,......... Gal 3:17

THIRTYFOLD

some sixtyfold, some *t*..................... Mt 13:8
it, and bring forth fruit, some *t* .... Mk 4:20

THIS See PREFACE.

THISTLE

The *t* that was in Lebanon sent to..... 2Kin 14:9
in Lebanon, and trode down the *t* 2Kin 14:9
The *t* that was in Lebanon sent to..... 2Chr 25:18
in Lebanon, and trode down the *t* 2Chr 25:18
the *t* shall come up on their............. Hos 10:8

THISTLES

t shall it bring forth to thee............. Gen 3:18
Let *t* grow instead of wheat, and...... Job 31:40
grapes of thorns, or figs of *t*............ Mt 7:16

THITHER

Oh, let me escape *t*, (is it not a .... Gen 19:20
Haste thee, escape *t* .... Gen 19:22
do any thing till thou be come *t* .... Gen 19:22
thou bring not my son *t* again.......... Gen 24:6
only bring not my son *t* again........... Gen 24:8
I were all the flocks gathered............. Gen 29:3
which had brought him down *t* .... Gen 39:1
get you down *t*, and buy for us......... Gen 42:2
serve the LORD, until we come *t* .... Ex 10:26
that thou mayest bring in *t* .... Ex 26:33
the manslayer, that he may flee *t* ..... Num 35:6
that the slayer may flee *t* .... Num 35:11
any person unawares may flee *t*........ Num 35:15
Thou also shalt not go in *t* .... Deut 1:37
before thee, he shall go in *t* .... Deut 1:38
good and evil, they shall go in *t* .... Deut 1:39
That the slayer might flee *t* .... Deut 4:42
ye seek, and *t* thou shalt come .... Deut 12:5
ye shall bring your burnt .... Deut 12:6
t shall ye bring all that I .... Deut 12:11
that every slayer may flee *t* .... Deut 19:3
of the slayer, which shall flee *t* .... Deut 19:4
but thou shalt not go *t* unto the........ Deut 32:52
but thou shalt not go over *t* .... Deut 34:4
not all the people to labour *t* .... Josh 7:3
So there went up *t* of the people ...... Josh 7:4
and unwittingly may flee *t* .... Josh 20:3
person at unawares might flee *t* .... Josh 20:9
all Israel went *t* a whoring after........ Judg 8:27
t fled all the men and women, and.... Judg 9:51
and they turned in *t*, and said unto .. Judg 18:3
the land went up, and came *t* .... Judg 18:17
And they turned aside *t*, to go in ...... Judg 18:15
the congregation meet *t* twelve .... Judg 21:10
all the Israelites that came *t*............. 1Sa 2:14
ark of the God of Israel about *t* 1Sa 3:3
now let us go *t* 1Sa 9:6
when thou art come *t* to the city 1Sa 10:5
And when they came *t* to the hill 1Sa 10:10
if the man should yet come *t* 1Sa 10:22
he went *t* to Naioth in Ramah 1Sa 19:23
heard it, they went down *t* to him 1Sa 22:1
Abiathar brought *t* the ephod to 1Sa 30:7
So David went up *t*, and his two........ 2Sa 2:2
they came *t* into the midst of the...... 2Sa 4:6
ready before it was brought *t*............ 1Kin 6:7
he came *t* unto a cave, and lodged ... 1Kin 19:9
and they were divided hither and *t*.... 2Kin 2:8
waters, they parted hither and *t* 2Kin 2:14
by, he turned in *t* to eat bread.......... 2Kin 4:8
to us, that he shall turn in *t* 2Kin 4:10
it fell on a day, that he came *t* 2Kin 4:11
cut down a stick, and cast it in *t* 2Kin 6:6
for *t* the Syrians are come down 2Kin 6:9
Therefore sent he *t* horses 2Kin 6:14
And when thou comest *t*, look out 2Kin 9:2
Carry *t* one of the priests whom 2Kin 17:27
Solomon went up *t* to the brasen...... 2Chr 1:6
and when he came *t*, he did eat no ... Ezr 10:6
the trumpet, resort ye *t* unto us........ Neh 4:20
were gathered *t* unto the work.......... Neh 5:16
I brought *t* again the vessels of........ Neh 13:9
womb, and naked shall I return *t* ...... Job 1:21
they came *t*, and were ashamed........ Job 6:20
rivers come, *t* they return again........ Eccl 1:7
and with bows shall men come *t* .... Is 7:24
not come *t* the fear of briers............. Is 7:25
that send forth *t* the feet of the .... Is 32:20
from heaven, and returneth not *t* ...... Is 55:10
even I western thou up to offer .... Is 57:7
He shall not return *t* any more.......... Jer 22:11
return, *t* shall they not return .... Jer 22:27
a great company shall return *t* .... Jer 31:8
convenient for thee to go, *t* go .... Jer 40:4
went, *t* was their spirit to go .... Eze 1:20
And they shall come *t*, and they,...... Eze 11:18
was upon me, and brought me, *t* ...... Eze 40:1
And he brought me *t*, and, behold,.... Eze 40:3
because these waters shall come *t* ... Eze 47:9
I cause thy mighty ones to come......... Joel 3:11
Herod, he was afraid to go *t* .... Mt 2:22
ran afoot *t* out of all cities, and........ Mk 6:33
it will the eagles be gathered .... Lk 17:37
poor widow casting in *t* two mites ..... Lk 21:2
and where I am, *t* ye cannot come..... Jn 7:34
and where I am, *t* ye cannot come..... Jn 7:36
and goest thou *t* again.................... Jn 11:8

THITHERWARD

resorted *t* with his disciples............. Jn 18:2
cometh *t* with lanterns and torches...... Jn 18:3
And Philip ran *t* to him, and heard..... Acts 8:30
there came *t* certain Jews from......... Acts 14:19
unto the women which resorted *t*........ Acts 16:13
who coming *t* went into the........... Acts 17:10
Paul at Berea, they came *t* also........ Acts 17:13
he himself would depart shortly *t*....... Acts 25:4

THITHERWARD

And they turned *t*, and came to the .... Judg 18:15
way to Zion with their faces *t*.......... Jer 50:5
to be brought on my way *t* by you..... Rom 15:24

THOMAS (tom′-us) See DIDYMUS. One of the
twelve apostles.

T, and Matthew the publican............. Mt 10:3
and Bartholomew, and Matthew, and *T* .. Mk 3:18
Matthew and *T*, James the son of........ Lk 6:15
Then said *T*, which is called............ Jn 11:16
T saith unto him, Lord, we know....... Jn 14:5
But *T*, one of the twelve, called.......... Jn 20:24
were within, and *T* with them........... Jn 20:26
Then saith he to *T*, Reach hither........ Jn 20:27
T answered and said unto him, My....... Jn 20:28
Jesus saith unto him, *T*, because........ Jn 20:29
T called Didymus, and Nathanael of..... Jn 21:2
and John, and Andrew, Philip, and *T*.... Acts 1:13

THONGS

And as they bound him with *t* .... Acts 22:25

THORN

or bore his jaw through with a *t* .... Job 41:2
As a *t* goeth up into the hand of........ Prov 26:9
Instead of the the *t* shall come.......... Is 55:13
nor any grieving *t* of all that........... Eze 28:24
the *t* and the thistle shall come......... Hos 10:8
upright is sharper than a *t* hedge........ Mic 7:4
was given to me a *t* in the flesh........ 2Cor 12:7

THORNS

T also and thistles shall it bring........ Gen 3:18
If fire break out, and catch in *t* .... Ex 22:6
t in your sides, and shall vex you ...... Num 33:55
t in your eyes, until ye perish.......... Josh 23:13
they shall be as *t* in your sides......... Judg 2:3
with the *t* of the wilderness............ Judg 8:7
t of the wilderness and briers, and..... Judg 8:16
be all of them as *t* thrust away......... 2Sa 23:6
which took Manasseh among the *t* 2Chr 33:11
and taketh it even out of the *t* .... Job 5:5
Before your pots can feel the *t* .... Ps 58:9
are quenched as the fire of *t* .... Ps 118:12
slothful man is as an hedge of *t* .... Prov 15:19
T and snares are in the way of the...... Prov 22:5
lo, it was all grown over with *t* .... Prov 24:31
as the crackling of *t* under a pot....... Eccl 7:6
As the lily among *t*, so is my.......... Song 2:2
there shall come up briers and *t* .... Is 5:6
holes of the rocks, and upon all *t* ...... Is 7:19
it shall even be for briers and *t* .... Is 7:23
the land shall become briers and *t* ..... Is 7:24
thither the fear of briers and *t* .... Is 7:25
it shall devour the briers and *t* .... Is 9:18
and it shall burn and devour his *t* ..... Is 10:17
briers and *t* against me in battle....... Is 27:4
land of my people shall come up *t* ..... Is 32:13
as *t* cut up shall they be burned........ Is 33:12
t shall come up in her palaces.......... Is 34:13
fallow ground, and sow not among *t* .... Jer 4:3
have sown wheat, but shall reap *t* ..... Jer 12:13
I be with thee, and thou dost............ Eze 2:6
I will hedge up thy way with *t* .... Hos 2:6
t shall be in their tabernacles.......... Hos 9:6
they be folden together as *t* .... Nah 1:10
Do men gather grapes of *t* .... Mt 7:16
And some fell among *t* .... Mt 13:7
the *t* sprung up, and choked them...... Mt 13:7
the *t* is he that heareth the word....... Mt 13:22
they had platted a crown of *t* .... Mt 27:29
And some fell among *t*, and the........ Mk 4:7
the *t* grew up, and choked it, and...... Mk 4:7
are they which are sown among *t* ...... Mk 4:18
purple, and platted a crown of *t* .... Mk 15:17
For of *t* men do not gather figs......... Lk 6:44
And some fell among *t* .... Lk 8:7
the *t* sprang up with it, and........... Lk 8:7
that which fell among *t* are they........ Lk 8:14
the soldiers platted a crown of *t* .... Jn 19:2
forth, wearing the crown of *t* .... Jn 19:5
But that which beareth *t* and........... Heb 6:8

THOROUGHLY
and shall cause him to be *t* healed...... Ex 21:19
his images brake they in pieces *t* 2Kin 11:18

THOSE See PREFACE.

THOU See PREFACE.

THOUGH
t thou wouldest needs be gone.......... Gen 31:30
as *t* I had seen the face of God......... Gen 33:10
and it was as *t* it budded, and her..... Gen 40:10
t he wist it not, yet is............... Lev 5:17
t he divide the hoof, and be.......... Lev 11:7
yea, *t* he be a stranger, or a........... Lev 25:35
as *t* it were the corn of the........... Num 18:27
t I walk in the imagination of......... Deut 29:19
t they have iron chariots, and......... Josh 17:18
chariots, and *t* they be strong......... Josh 17:18
T thou detain me, I will not eat....... Judg 13:16
t I do them a displeasure............. Judg 15:3

T ye have done this, yet will I........ Judg 15:7
t I be not like unto one of thine....... Ruth 2:13
t it be in Jonathan my son, he........ 1Sa 14:39
thereof, as *t* I shot at a mark......... 1Sa 20:20
t it were sanctified this day in....... 1Sa 21:5
as *t* he had not been anointed........ 2Sa 1:21
am this day weak, *t* anointed king.... 2Sa 3:39
as *t* they would have fetched......... 2Sa 14:20
t I should receive a thousand......... 2Sa 18:12
he turned not after Absalom............ 1Kin 2:28
(for *t* he was not the firstborn....... 1Chr 26:10
t he be not cleansed according to..... 2Chr 30:19
t there were of you cast out unto..... Neh 1:9
(at that time I had not sat............ Neh 6:1
t it was turned to the contrary....... Est 9:1
T thy beginning was small, yet....... Job 8:7
t I were righteous, yet would I....... Job 9:15
have been as *t* I had not been......... Job 10:19
t man be born like a wild ass′s....... Job 11:12
t the slay me, yet will I trust in...... Job 13:15
the root thereof wax old in the......... Job 14:8
t I speak, my grief is not........... Job 16:6
t I forbear, what am I eased......... Job 16:6
t I entreated for the children′s....... Job 19:17
t after my skin worms destroy....... Job 19:26
t my reins be consumed within me... Job 19:27
T his excellency mount up to the..... Job 20:6
t wickedness be sweet in his......... Job 20:12
he hide it under his tongue............ Job 20:12
T he spare it, and forsake it not..... Job 20:13
t it be given him to be in safety..... Job 24:23
t he hath gained, when God taketh.. Job 27:8
t he heap up silver as the dust....... Job 27:16
t they cry in his destruction......... Job 30:24
ones, as *t* they were not born........ Job 39:16
t I walk through the valley of....... Ps 23:4
t an host should encamp against me.. Ps 27:3
t war should rise against me, in...... Ps 27:3
I behaved myself as *t* he had been... Ps 35:14
the fall, he shall not be............. Ps 37:24
t thou hast sore broken us in the.... Ps 44:19
t the earth be removed............ Ps 46:2
the mountains be carried into........ Ps 46:2
t the waters thereof roar and be.... Ps 46:3
t the mountains shake with the..... Ps 46:3
t while he lived he blessed his...... Ps 49:18
t ye have lien among the pots...... Ps 68:13
t he had commanded the clouds..... Ps 78:23
t thou tookest vengeance of their.... Ps 99:8
t the LORD be high, yet hath he.... Ps 138:7
T I walk in the midst of trouble..... Prov 6:35
content, *t* thou givest many gifts.... Prov 11:21
t hand join in hand, the wicked..... Prov 16:5
t hand join in hand, he shall not.... Prov 16:5
T thou shouldest bray a fool in a.... Prov 27:22
in his ways, *t* he be.............. Prov 29:19
for *t* he understand he will not...... Eccl 6:6
t it would not come to you......... Eccl 8:11
T a sinner do evil an hundred....... Eccl 8:12
because *t* a man labour to seek it.... Eccl 8:17
t a wise man think to know it,...... Eccl 8:17
t your sins be as scarlet, they...... Is 1:18
t they be red like crimson, they.... Is 1:18
For *t* thy people Israel be as the.... Is 10:22
t thou wast angry with me, thine... Is 12:1
the Lord give you the bread of...... Is 30:20
t fools, shall not err therein....... Is 35:8
thee, *t* thou hast not known me..... Is 45:4
thee, *t* thou hast not known me..... Is 45:5
T Israel be not gathered, yet....... Is 49:5
t Abraham be ignorant of us, and... Is 63:16
For *t* thou wash with nitre,........ Jer 2:22
T Moses and Samuel stood before me.. Jer 15:1
t they roar, yet can they not...... Jer 6:23
t they shall cry unto me, I will..... Jer 11:11
t they speak fair words unto thee... Jer 12:6
t our iniquities testify against...... Jer 14:7
t Moses and Samuel stood before me.. Jer 15:1
t Coniah the son of Jehoiakim..... Jer 22:24
t I make a full end of all.......... Jer 30:11
t ye fight with the Chaldeans, ye... Jer 32:5
t I taught them, rising up early.... Jer 32:33
For *t* ye had smitten the whole..... Jer 37:10
the LORD, *t* it cannot be searched... Jer 46:23
t thou shouldest make thy nest as... Jer 49:16
their land was filled with sin....... Jer 51:5
T Babylon should mount up to..... Jer 51:53
t she should fortify the height..... Jer 51:53
But *t* he cause grief, yet will he.... Lam 3:32
t briers and thorns be with thee.... Eze 2:6
t they be a rebellious house....... Eze 2:6
t they be a rebellious house....... Eze 2:5
t they cry in mine ears with a..... Eze 8:18
t they be a rebellious house....... Eze 12:2
not see it, *t* he die there.......... Eze 12:13
T these three men, Noah, Daniel.... Eze 14:14
T these three men were in it, as... Eze 14:16
T these three men were in it, as... Eze 14:18
T these three men were in it, as... Eze 14:20
t Noah, Daniel, and Job, were in... Eze 14:20
t thou be sought for, yet shalt..... Eze 26:21
t thou set thine heart as the...... Eze 28:6
t their terror was caused in the.... Eze 32:25
t they caused their terror in the... Eze 32:30
t they were the terror of the...... Eze 32:27
heart, *t* thou knewest all this...... Dan 5:22

---

t we have rebelled against him...... Dan 9:9
T thou, Israel, play the harlot...... Hos 4:15
t I have been a rebuker of them.... Hos 5:2
t I have redeemed them, yet they... Hos 7:13
T I have bound and strengthened... Hos 7:15
t they have hired among the........ Hos 8:10
T they bring up their children...... Hos 9:12
t they bring forth, yet will I....... Hos 9:16
t they called them to the most..... Hos 11:7
t he be fruitful among his......... Hos 13:15
t ye offer me burnt offerings and... Amos 5:22
T they dig into hell, thence....... Amos 9:2
t they climb up to heaven, thence.. Amos 9:2
t they hide themselves in the top... Amos 9:3
t they be hid from my sight in..... Amos 9:3
t they go into captivity before..... Amos 9:4
T thou exalt thyself as the eagle... Obad 4
t thou set thy nest among the...... Obad 4
they shall be as *t* they had not..... Obad 16
t thou be little among the......... Mic 5:2
T they be quiet, and likewise many.. Nah 1:12
t I have afflicted thee, I will...... Nah 1:12
not believe, *t* it be told you....... Hab 1:5
t it tarry, wait for it............ Hab 2:3
and Zidon, *t* it be very wise...... Zec 9:2
t they shall be as *t* I had not cast.. Zec 10:6
t all the people of the earth be.... Zec 12:3
t all men shall be offended....... Mt 26:33
T I should die with thee, I........ Mt 26:35
t many false witnesses came, yet... Mt 26:60
because his face was as *t* he....... Lk 9:53
The will not rise and give him...... Lk 11:8
t one rose from the dead.......... Lk 16:31
T I fear not God, nor regard man... Lk 18:7
him, *t* he bear long with them..... Lk 18:7
t he made as *t* he would have gone.. Lk 24:28
(*T* Jesus himself baptized not..... Jn 4:2
ground, as *t* he heard them not.... Jn 8:6
T I bear record of myself, yet my... Jn 8:14
t ye believe not me, believe the.... Jn 10:38
t he were dead, yet shall he live.... Jn 11:25
But *t* he had done so many........ Jn 12:37
as *t* by our own power or holiness... Acts 3:12
t they found no cause of death in... Acts 13:28
t a man declare it unto you....... Acts 13:41
as *t* he needed any thing, seeing.... Acts 17:25
t he be not far from every one of... Acts 17:27
as *t* ye would enquire something.... Acts 23:15
as *t* they would enquire somewhat.. Acts 23:20
under colour as *t* they would have... Acts 23:30
t he hath escaped the sea, yet...... Acts 28:4
t I commanded nothing........... Acts 28:17
t they be not circumcised......... Rom 4:11
which be not as *t* they were........ Rom 4:17
t she be married to another man.... Rom 7:3
Not as *t* the word of God hath..... Rom 9:6
The number of the children of...... Rom 9:27
For *t* ye have ten thousand........ 1Cor 4:15
t I would not come to you......... 1Cor 4:18
as *t* I were present, concerning..... 1Cor 5:3
have wives be as *t* they had none... 1Cor 7:29
that weep, as *t* they wept not..... 1Cor 7:30
rejoice, as *t* they rejoiced not...... 1Cor 7:30
that buy, as *t* they possessed not... 1Cor 7:30
For *t* there be that are called...... 1Cor 8:5
For *t* I preach the gospel, I have... 1Cor 9:16
For *t* I be free from all men, yet.... 1Cor 9:19
T I speak with the tongues of men.. 1Cor 13:1
t I have the gift of prophecy, and... 1Cor 13:2
t I have all faith, so that I....... 1Cor 13:2
t I bestow all my goods to feed.... 1Cor 13:3
t I give my body to be burned, and.. 1Cor 13:3
but *t* our outward man perish, yet... 2Cor 4:16
t we have known Christ after the... 2Cor 5:16
t God did beseech you by us...... 2Cor 5:20
For *t* I made you sorry with a..... 2Cor 7:8
I do not repent, *t* I did repent.... 2Cor 7:8
it were but for a season.............. 2Cor 7:8
t I wrote unto you, I did it not.... 2Cor 7:12
he was rich, yet for your sakes...... 2Cor 8:9
For *t* we walk in the flesh, we do... 2Cor 10:3
For *t* I should boast somewhat..... 2Cor 10:8
as *t* we reached not unto you...... 2Cor 10:14
But *t* I be rude in speech, yet...... 2Cor 11:6
reproach, as *t* we had been weak.... 2Cor 11:21
For *t* I would desire to glory, I.... 2Cor 12:6
chiefest apostles, *t* I be nothing.... 2Cor 12:11
the more abundantly I love you,..... 2Cor 12:15
For *t* he was crucified through..... 2Cor 13:4
is honest, *t* we be as reprobates.... 2Cor 13:7
But I we, or an angel from heaven... Gal 1:8
t it be but a man′s covenant, though.. Gal 3:15
a servant, *t* he be lord of all....... Gal 4:1
T I might also have confidence in... Phil 3:4
Not as *t* I had already attained..... Phil 3:12
For *t* be absent in the flesh,...... Col 2:5
as *t* living in the world, are ye.... Col 2:20
I might be much bold in Christ...... Philem 8
The were a Son, yet learned he...... Heb 5:8
t cannot speak, *t* thus speak...... Heb 6:9
t they come out of the loins of.... Heb 7:5
t he taught it carefully with...... Heb 12:17
a man say he hath faith, and....... Jas 2:14
which *t* they be so great, and are... Jas 3:4
t now for a season, if need be,.... 1Pet 1:6
t it be tried with fire, might be.... 1Pet 1:7
t now ye see him not, yet......... 1Pet 1:8
some strange thing happened....... 1Pet 4:12
t ye know them, and be established... 2Pet 1:12
lady, not as *t* I wrote a new....... 2Jn 5

T

t ye once knew this, how that the .... Jude 5

THOUGHT
And Abraham said, Because I *t* .... Gen 20:11
saw her, he *t* her to be an harlot......... Gen 38:15
I had not *t* to see thy face .... Gen 48:11
as for you, ye *t* evil against me........... Gen 50:20
which he *t* to do unto his people .... Ex 32:14
I *t* to promote thee unto great.............. Num 24:11
unto you, as I *t* to do unto them .... Num 33:56
be not a *t* in thy wicked heart............... Deut 15:9
as he had to have done unto his .... Deut 19:19
I verily *t* that thou hadst...................... Judg 15:2
by night, and *t* to have slain me........... Judg 20:5
I *t* to advertise thee, saying................. Ruth 4:4
therefore Eli *t* she had been................. 1Sa 1:13
for the asses, and take *t* for us............ 1Sa 9:5
But Saul *t* to make David fall by 1Sa 18:25
for he *t*, Something hath befallen......... 1Sa 20:26
who *t* that I would have given him 2Sa 4:10
Amnon *t* it hard for him to do any 2Sa 13:2
Wherefore then hast thou *t* such a 2Sa 14:13
and to do what he *t* good 2Sa 19:18
new sword, *t* to have slain David 2Sa 21:16
went away, and said, Behold, I *t* 2Kin 5:11
for he *t* to make him king 2Chr 11:22
t to win them for himself 2Chr 32:1
But they *t* to do me mischief................ Neh 6:2
he *t* scorn to lay hands on................... Est 3:6
Now Haman *t* in his heart, To whom .... Est 6:6
in the *t* of him that is at ease.............. Job 12:5
that no *t* can be withholden from .... Job 42:2
We have *t* of thy lovingkindness,......... Ps 48:9
Their inward *t* is, that their.................. Ps 49:11
both the inward *t* of every one of......... Ps 64:6
When I *t* to know this, it was too .... Ps 73:16
I *t* on my ways, and turned my feet ...... Ps 119:59
thou understandest my *t* afar off .... Ps 139:2
The *t* of foolishness is sin .... Prov 24:9
thyself, or if thou hast *t* evil................ Prov 30:32
not the king, no not in thy *t* .... Eccl 10:20
sworn, saying, Surely as I have *t*......... Is 14:24
the evil that I *t* to do unto them .... Jer 18:8
and thou shalt think an evil *t* .... Eze 38:10
I *t* it good to shew the signs and.......... Dan 4:2
the king *t* to set him over the.............. Dan 6:3
declareth unto man what is his *t*........... Amos 4:13
the LORD of hosts *t* to do unto us......... Zec 1:6
As I *t* to punish you, when your........... Zec 8:14
So again have I *t* in these days........... Zec 8:15
the LORD, and that *t* upon his name..... Mal 3:16
But while he *t* on these things,............ Mt 1:20
Take no *t* for your life, what ye .... Mt 6:25
Which of you by taking *t* can add......... Mt 6:27
And why take ye *t* for raiment............. Mt 6:28
Therefore take no *t*, saying, What....... Mt 6:31
therefore no *t* for the morrow.............. Mt 6:34
take *t* for the things of itself............... Mt 6:34
take no *t* how or what ye shall .... Mt 10:19
take no *t* beforehand what ye .... Mk 13:11
And when he *t* thereon, he wept .... Mk 14:72
Wherefore neither *t* I myself .... Lk 7:7
perceiving the *t* of their heart .... Lk 9:47
take ye no *t* how or what thing ye........ Lk 12:11
he *t* within himself, saying, What .... Lk 12:17
Take no *t* for your life, what ye .... Lk 12:22
which of you with taking *t* can .... Lk 12:25
why take ye *t* for the rest .... Lk 12:26
because they *t* that the kingdom .... Lk 19:11
but they *t* that he had spoken of.......... Jn 11:13
For some of them *t*, because Judas .... Jn 13:29
because thou hast *t* that the gift .... Acts 8:20
if perhaps the *t* of thine heart .... Acts 8:22
While Peter *t* on the vision, the .... Acts 10:19
but I *t* he saw a vision......................... Acts 12:9
But Paul *t* not good to take him .... Acts 15:38
Why should it be *t* a thing .... Acts 26:8
I verily *t* with myself, that I .... Acts 26:9
as a child, I *t* as a child..................... 1Cor 13:11
Therefore I *t* it necessary to 2Cor 9:5
t to the obedience of Christ................ 2Cor 10:5
t it not robbery to be equal with......... Phil 2:6
we *t* it good to be left at Athens 1Th 3:1
suppose ye, shall he be *t* worthy......... Heb 10:29

THOUGHTEST
thou *t* that I was altogether such.......... Ps 50:21

THOUGHTS
the *t* of his heart was only evil............. Gen 6:5
there were great *t* of heart.................. Judg 5:15
all the imaginations of the *t* 1Chr 28:9
the *t* of the heart of thy people 1Chr 29:18
In *t* from the visions of the................. Job 4:13
off, even the *t* of my heart .... Job 17:11
Therefore do my *t* cause me to .... Job 20:2
Behold, I know your *t*, and the............ Job 21:27
God is not in all his *t* .... Ps 10:4
the *t* of his heart to all .... Ps 33:11
thy *t* which are to us-ward.................. Ps 40:5
all their *t* are against me for.............. Ps 56:5
and thy *t* are very deep...................... Ps 92:5
The LORD knoweth the *t* of man.......... Ps 94:11
In the multitude of my *t* within........... Ps 94:19
I hate vain *t* .... Ps 119:113
precious also are thy *t* unto me .... Ps 139:17
try me, and know my *t*........................ Ps 139:23
in that very day I *t* perish .... Ps 146:4
The *t* of the righteous are right .... Prov 12:5
The *t* of the wicked are an .... Prov 15:26
thy *t* shall be established .... Prov 16:3
The *t* of the diligent tend only .... Prov 21:5

way, and the unrighteous man his *t* .... Is 55:7
For my *t* are not your *t* .... Is 55:8
ways, and my *t* than your *t* .... Is 55:9
their *t* are *t* of iniquity...................... Is 59:7
was not good, after their own *t* .... Is 65:2
For I know their works and their *t* .... Is 66:18
thy vain *t* lodge within thee................ Jer 4:14
people, even the fruit of their *t* .... Jer 6:19
have performed the *t* of his heart....... Jer 23:20
For I know the *t* that I think .... Jer 29:11
of peace, and not of evil, to .... Jer 29:11
thy *t* came into thy mind upon thy ...... Dan 2:29
mightest know the *t* of thy heart......... Dan 2:30
the *t* upon my bed and the visions...... Dan 4:5
one hour, and his *t* troubled him .... Dan 4:19
his *t* troubled him, so that the .... Dan 5:6
let not thy *t* trouble thee, nor .... Dan 5:10
they know not the *t* of the LORD .... Mic 4:12
And Jesus knowing their *t* said.......... Mt 9:4
And Jesus knew their *t*, and said .... Mt 12:25
out of the heart proceed evil *t* .... Mt 15:19
the heart of men, proceed evil *t*......... Mk 7:21
that the *t* of many hearts may be........ Lk 2:35
But when Jesus perceived their *t* .... Lk 5:22
But he knew their *t*, and said to .... Lk 6:8
But he, knowing their *t*, said .... Lk 11:17
why do *t* arise in your hearts............. Lk 24:38
their *t* the mean while accusing .... Rom 2:15
Lord knoweth the *t* of the wise 1Cor 3:20
and is a discerner of the *t* .... Heb 4:12
and are become judges of evil *t* .... Jas 2:4

THOUSAND
thy brother a *t* pieces of silver............ Gen 20:16
about six hundred *t* on foot that .... Ex 12:37
people that day about three *t* men....... Ex 32:28
a *t* seven hundred and threescore .... Ex 38:25
six hundred *t* and three *t* .... Ex 38:26
of the *t* seven hundred seventy and..... Ex 38:28
was seventy talents, and two *t* .... Ex 38:29
of you shall put ten *t* to flight .... Lev 26:8
of Reuben, were forty and six *t* .... Num 1:21
of Simeon, were fifty and nine *t* .... Num 1:23
five *t* six hundred and fifty................... Num 1:25
were threescore and fourteen *t*........... Num 1:27
of Issachar, were fifty and four *t*......... Num 1:29
of Zebulun, were fifty and seven *t*....... Num 1:31
tribe of Ephraim, were forty *t* .... Num 1:33
of Manasseh, were thirty and two *t* ..... Num 1:35
Benjamin, were thirty and five *t*.......... Num 1:37
of Dan, were threescore and two *t* ...... Num 1:39
of Asher, were forty and one *t* .... Num 1:41
Naphtali, were fifty and three *t* .... Num 1:43
were numbered were six hundred *t*...... Num 1:46
six hundred *t* and three *t* .... Num 1:46
were threescore and fourteen *t* .... Num 2:4
thereof, were fifty and four *t* .... Num 2:6
thereof, were fifty and seven *t* .... Num 2:8
camp of Judah were an hundred *t* .... Num 2:9
and fourscore *t* and six *t* .... Num 2:9
thereof, were forty and six *t* .... Num 2:11
of them, were fifty and nine *t* .... Num 2:13
of them, were forty and five *t* .... Num 2:15
camp of Reuben were an hundred *t* ..... Num 2:16
and fifty and one *t* .... Num 2:16
numbered of them, were forty *t* .... Num 2:19
of them, were thirty and two *t* .... Num 2:21
of them, were thirty and five *t* .... Num 2:23
an hundred *t* and eight *t* .... Num 2:24
of them, were threescore and two *t* ..... Num 2:26
of them, were forty and one *t* .... Num 2:28
of them, were fifty and three *t* .... Num 2:30
the camp of Dan were an hundred *t* .... Num 2:31
and fifty and seven *t* .... Num 2:31
six hundred *t* and three *t* .... Num 2:32
numbered of them were forty *t* .... Num 3:22
month old and upward, were eight *t* .... Num 3:28
a month old and upward, were six *t* ..... Num 3:34
and upward, were twenty and two *t* ..... Num 3:39
two *t* two hundred and threescore .... Num 3:43
a *t* three hundred and threescore........ Num 3:50
families were two *t* seven hundred ...... Num 4:40
of their fathers, were two *t* .... Num 4:44
their families, were three *t* .... Num 4:44
numbered of them, were eight *t* .... Num 4:48
the silver vessels weighed two *t*.......... Num 7:85
I am, are six hundred *t* footmen .... Num 11:21
in the plague were fourteen *t* .... Num 16:49
the plague were twenty and four *t* .... Num 25:9
of them were forty and three *t* .... Num 26:7
the Simeonites, twenty and two *t*......... Num 26:14
were numbered of them, forty *t* .... Num 26:18
of them, threescore and sixteen *t* .... Num 26:22
of them, threescore and four *t* .... Num 26:25
numbered of them, threescore *t* .... Num 26:27
numbered of them, fifty and two *t* .... Num 26:34
numbered of them, thirty and two *t* ..... Num 26:37
of them were forty and five *t* .... Num 26:41
them, were threescore and four *t* .... Num 26:43
who were fifty and three *t* .... Num 26:47
of them were forty and five *t* .... Num 26:50
children of Israel, six hundred *t* .... Num 26:51
a *t* seven hundred and thirty .... Num 26:51
of them were twenty and three *t* .... Num 26:62
of every tribe a *t*, throughout .... Num 31:4
a *t* of every tribe, were war .... Num 31:5
tribe, twelve *t* armed for war .... Num 31:5
a *t* of every tribe, them and .... Num 31:6
war had caught, was six hundred *t* ...... Num 31:32
seventy *t* and five *t* sheep................ Num 31:32
And threescore and twelve *t* beeves.... Num 31:33

And threescore and one *t* asses........... Num 31:34
two *t* persons in all, of women .... Num 31:35
was in number three hundred *t*............ Num 31:36
and seven and thirty *t* .... Num 31:36
the beeves were thirty and six *t* .... Num 31:38
And the asses were thirty *t* .... Num 31:39
And the persons were sixteen *t* .... Num 31:40
congregation was three hundred *t*........ Num 31:43
and thirty *t* and seven *t* .... Num 31:43
And thirty and six *t* beeves................. Num 31:44
And thirty *t* asses and five hundred..... Num 31:45
And sixteen *t* persons .... Num 31:46
was sixteen *t* seven hundred and......... Num 31:52
outward a *t* cubits round about............ Num 35:4
on the east side two *t* cubits .... Num 35:5
and on the south side two *t* cubits .... Num 35:5
and on the west side two *t* cubits......... Num 35:5
and on the north side two *t* cubits .... Num 35:5
a *t* times so many more as ye are .... Deut 1:11
commandments to a *t* generations .... Deut 7:9
How should one chase a *t*, and two ..... Deut 32:30
and two put ten *t* to flight .... Deut 32:30
about two *t* cubits by measure .... Josh 3:4
About forty *t* prepared for war .... Josh 4:13
about two or three *t* men go up .... Josh 7:3
of the people about three *t* men.......... Josh 7:4
out thirty *t* mighty men of valour......... Josh 8:3
And he took about five *t* men.............. Josh 8:12
of men and women, were twelve *t* .... Josh 8:25
One man of you shall chase a *t* .... Josh 23:10
slew of them in Bezek ten *t* men......... Judg 1:4
Moab at that time about ten *t* men....... Judg 3:29
take with thee ten *t* men of the........... Judg 4:6
up with ten *t* men at his feet .... Judg 4:14
Tabor, and ten *t* men after him .... Judg 4:14
seen among forty *t* in Israel .... Judg 5:8
of the people twenty and two *t*........... Judg 7:3
and there remained ten *t* .... Judg 7:3
with them, about fifteen *t* men .... Judg 8:10
twenty *t* men that drew sword .... Judg 8:10
that he requested was a *t* .... Judg 8:26
Shechem died also, about a *t* men ...... Judg 9:49
of the Ephraimites forty and two *t* ...... Judg 12:6
Then three *t* men of Judah went to...... Judg 15:11
it, and slew a *t* men therewith .... Judg 15:15
of an ass have I slain a *t* men............. Judg 15:16
upon the roof about three *t* men.......... Judg 16:27
four hundred *t* footmen that drew .... Judg 20:2
of Israel, and an hundred *t* of............. Judg 20:10
and a *t* out of ten *t* .... Judg 20:10
six *t* men that drew sword, beside ...... Judg 20:15
hundred *t* men that drew sword........... Judg 20:17
that day twenty and two *t* men .... Judg 20:21
of Israel again eighteen *t* men............ Judg 20:25
t chosen men out of all Israel .... Judg 20:34
that day twenty and five *t* .... Judg 20:35
fell of Benjamin eighteen *t* men.......... Judg 20:44
them in the highways five *t* men.......... Judg 20:45
Gidom, and slew two *t* men of them .... Judg 20:45
five *t* men that drew the sword .... Judg 20:46
sent thither twelve *t* men of the.......... Judg 21:10
in the field about four *t* men............... 1Sa 4:2
fell of Israel thirty *t* footmen.............. 1Sa 4:10
the smote of the people fifty *t* 1Sa 6:19
of Israel were three hundred *t*............ 1Sa 11:8
and the men of Judah thirty *t* 1Sa 11:8
chosen him three *t* men of Israel 1Sa 13:2
whereof two *t* were with Saul in.......... 1Sa 13:2
a *t* were with Jonathan in Gibeah 1Sa 13:2
thirty *t* chariots, and six 1Sa 13:5
six *t* horsemen, and people as the 1Sa 13:5
in Telaim, two hundred *t* footmen 1Sa 15:4
footmen, and ten *t* men of Judah 1Sa 15:4
coat was five *t* shekels of brass.......... 1Sa 17:5
unto the captain of their......................... 1Sa 17:18
and made him his captain over a *t*....... 1Sa 18:13
Then Saul took three *t* chosen men..... 1Sa 24:2
great, and he had three *t* sheep 1Sa 25:2
sheep, and a *t* goats 1Sa 25:2
having three *t* chosen men of 1Sa 26:2
chosen men of Israel, thirty *t* 2Sa 6:1
David took from him a *t* chariots......... 2Sa 8:4
horsemen, and twenty *t* footmen 2Sa 8:4
the Syrians two and twenty *t* men........ 2Sa 8:5
of salt, being eighteen *t* men.............. 2Sa 8:13
twenty *t* footmen, and of king 2Sa 10:6
and of king Maacah a *t* men 2Sa 10:6
and of Ish-tob twelve *t* men 2Sa 10:6
forty *t* horsemen, and smote................ 2Sa 10:18
me now choose out twelve *t* men 2Sa 17:1
now thou art worth ten *t* of us 2Sa 18:3
that day of twenty *t* men 2Sa 18:7
Though I should receive a *t* 2Sa 18:12
there were a *t* men of Benjamin 2Sa 19:17
were in Israel eight hundred *t* 2Sa 24:9
of Judah were five hundred *t* men....... 2Sa 24:9
even to Beer-sheba seventy *t* men 2Sa 24:15
a burnt offerings did Solomon 1Kin 3:4
Solomon had forty *t* stalls of............... 1Kin 4:26
chariots, and twelve *t* horsemen 1Kin 4:26
And he spake three *t* proverbs............ 1Kin 4:32
and his songs were a *t* and five........... 1Kin 4:32
Solomon gave Hiram twenty *t* 1Kin 5:11
and the levy was thirty *t* men 1Kin 5:13
Lebanon, ten *t* a month by courses..... 1Kin 5:14
ten *t* bare burdens, and...................... 1Kin 5:15
fourscore *t* hewers in the 1Kin 5:15
which were over the work, three *t* 1Kin 5:16
it contained two *t* baths 1Kin 7:26
the LORD, two and twenty *t* oxen 1Kin 8:63

and an hundred and twenty t sheep	1Kin 8:63
and he had a t and four hundred	1Kin 10:26
twelve t horsemen, whom he	1Kin 10:26
fourscore t chosen men, which	1Kin 12:21
I have left me seven t in Israel	1Kin 19:18
children of Israel, being seven t	1Kin 20:15
an hundred t footmen in one day	1Kin 20:29
seven t of the men that were left	1Kin 20:30
king of Israel an hundred t lambs	2Kin 3:4
lambs, and an hundred t rams	2Kin 3:4
six t pieces of gold, and ten	2Kin 5:5
and ten chariots, and ten t footmen	2Kin 13:7
Edom in the valley of salt ten t	2Kin 14:7
gave Pul a t talents of silver	2Kin 15:19
I will deliver thee two t horses	2Kin 18:23
an hundred fourscore and five t	2Kin 19:35
of valour, even ten t captives	2Kin 24:14
the men of might, even seven t	2Kin 24:16
and craftsmen and smiths a t	2Kin 24:16
four and forty t seven hundred and	1Chr 5:18
of their camels fifty t, and of	1Chr 5:21
fifty t, and of asses two t	1Chr 5:21
and of men an hundred t	1Chr 5:21
the days of David two and twenty t	1Chr 7:2
for war, six and thirty t men	1Chr 7:4
genealogies fourscore and six t	1Chr 7:7
their genealogies twenty and two t	1Chr 7:9
men of valour, was twenty t	1Chr 7:9
men of valour, were seventeen t	1Chr 7:11
to battle was twenty and six t men	1Chr 7:40
the house of their fathers, a t	1Chr 9:13
hundred, and the greatest over a t	1Chr 12:14
bare shield and spear were six t	1Chr 12:24
of valour for the war, seven t	1Chr 12:25
Of the children of Levi four t	1Chr 12:26
and with him were three t	1Chr 12:27
the kindred of Saul, three t	1Chr 12:29
the children of Ephraim twenty t	1Chr 12:30
half tribe of Manasseh eighteen t	1Chr 12:31
all instruments of war, fifty t	1Chr 12:33
And of Naphtali a t captains	1Chr 12:34
shield and spear thirty and seven t	1Chr 12:34
expert in war twenty and eight t	1Chr 12:35
to battle, expert in war, forty t	1Chr 12:36
battle, an hundred and twenty t	1Chr 12:37
he commanded to a t generations	1Chr 16:15
David took from him a t chariots	1Chr 18:4
seven t horsemen, and twenty	1Chr 18:4
horsemen, and twenty t footmen	1Chr 18:4
the Syrians two and forty t	1Chr 18:5
in the valley of salt eighteen t	1Chr 18:12
the children of Ammon sent a t	1Chr 19:6
two t chariots, and the king of	1Chr 19:7
t men which fought in chariots	1Chr 19:18
forty t footmen, and killed	1Chr 19:18
they of Israel were a t	1Chr 21:5
an hundred t men that drew sword	1Chr 21:5
ten t men that drew sword	1Chr 21:5
fell of Israel seventy t	1Chr 21:14
LORD an hundred t talents of gold	1Chr 22:14
a t t talents of silver	1Chr 22:14
man by man, was thirty and eight t	1Chr 23:3
four t were to set forward the	1Chr 23:4
six t were officers and judges	1Chr 23:4
Moreover four t were porters	1Chr 23:5
four t praised the LORD with the	1Chr 23:5
his brethren, men of valour, a t	1Chr 26:30
men of valour, two t and seven	1Chr 26:32
course were twenty and four t	1Chr 27:1
his course were twenty and four t	1Chr 27:2
likewise were twenty and four t	1Chr 27:4
his course were twenty and four t	1Chr 27:5
his course were twenty and four t	1Chr 27:7
his course were twenty and four t	1Chr 27:8
his course were twenty and four t	1Chr 27:9
his course were twenty and four t	1Chr 27:10
his course were twenty and four t	1Chr 27:11
his course were twenty and four t	1Chr 27:12
his course were twenty and four t	1Chr 27:13
his course were twenty and four t	1Chr 27:15
Even thee t talents of gold, of	1Chr 29:4
seven t talents of refined silver	1Chr 29:4
of God of gold five t talents	1Chr 29:7
ten t drams, and of silver ten	1Chr 29:7
drams, and of silver ten t talents	1Chr 29:7
and of brass eighteen t talents	1Chr 29:7
one hundred t talents of iron	1Chr 29:7
even a t bullocks, a t	1Chr 29:21
a t rams, and a t lambs	1Chr 29:21
offered a t burnt offerings upon	2Chr 1:6
and he had a t and four hundred	2Chr 1:14
twelve t horsemen, which he	2Chr 1:14
hew in the mountain, and three t	2Chr 2:2
ten t men to bear burdens, and	2Chr 2:2
fourscore t to hew in the	2Chr 2:2
twenty t measures of beaten wheat	2Chr 2:10
twenty t measures of barley, and	2Chr 2:10
twenty t baths of wine, and twenty	2Chr 2:10
of wine, and twenty t baths of oil	2Chr 2:10
and fifty t and three t	2Chr 2:17
ten t of them to be hewers in the	2Chr 2:18
fourscore t to be hewers in the	2Chr 2:18
in the mountain, and three t	2Chr 2:18
it received and held three t baths	2Chr 4:5
two t oxen, and an hundred and	2Chr 7:5
and an hundred and twenty t sheep	2Chr 7:5
Solomon had four t stalls for	2Chr 9:25
and chariots, and twelve t horsemen	2Chr 9:25
fourscore t chosen men, which	2Chr 11:1

and threescore t horsemen	2Chr 12:3
even four hundred t chosen men	2Chr 13:3
with eight hundred t chosen men	2Chr 13:3
Israel five hundred t chosen men	2Chr 13:17
out of Judah three hundred t	2Chr 14:8
bows, two hundred and fourscore t	2Chr 14:8
with an host of a t t	2Chr 14:9
hundred oxen and seven t sheep	2Chr 15:11
brought him flocks, seven t	2Chr 17:11
hundred rams, and seven t	2Chr 17:11
men of valour three hundred t	2Chr 17:14
him two hundred and fourscore t	2Chr 17:15
hundred t mighty men of valour	2Chr 17:16
with bow and shield two hundred t	2Chr 17:17
fourscore t ready prepared for	2Chr 17:18
them three hundred t choice men	2Chr 25:5
He hired also an hundred t mighty	2Chr 25:6
of the children of Seir ten t	2Chr 25:11
other ten t left alive did the	2Chr 25:12
and smote three t of them	2Chr 25:13
mighty men of valour were two t	2Chr 26:12
three hundred t and seven t	2Chr 26:13
ten t measures of wheat, and ten	2Chr 27:5
of wheat, and ten t of barley	2Chr 27:5
twenty t in one day, which were	2Chr 28:6
of their brethren two hundred t	2Chr 28:8
six hundred oxen and three t sheep	2Chr 29:33
to the congregation a t bullocks	2Chr 30:24
bullocks and seven t sheep	2Chr 30:24
to the congregation a t bullocks	2Chr 30:24
t bullocks and ten t sheep	2Chr 30:24
to the number of thirty t	2Chr 35:7
and three t bullocks	2Chr 35:7
for the passover offerings two t	2Chr 35:9
offerings five t small cattle	2Chr 35:9
a t chargers of silver, nine and	Ezr 1:9
and ten, and other vessels a t	Ezr 1:10
of gold and of silver were five t	Ezr 1:11
two t an hundred seventy and two	Ezr 2:3
two t eight hundred and twelve	Ezr 2:6
a two hundred fifty and six	Ezr 2:7
a two hundred twenty and two t	Ezr 2:10
of Bigvai, two t fifty and six	Ezr 2:14
a two hundred fifty and four	Ezr 2:31
The children of Senaah, three t	Ezr 2:35
of Immer, a t fifty and two	Ezr 2:37
a two hundred forty and seven	Ezr 2:38
The children of Harim, a t	Ezr 2:39
two hundred fourscore and threescore	Ezr 2:64
were seven t three hundred thirty	Ezr 2:65
six t seven hundred and twenty	Ezr 2:66
one t drams of gold, and five	Ezr 2:69
five t pound of silver, and one	Ezr 2:69
basons of gold, of a t drams	Ezr 8:27
a t cubits on the wall unto the	Neh 7:3
children of Jeshua and Joab, two t	Neh 7:11
a t two hundred fifty and four	Neh 7:13
a t two hundred twenty and two	Neh 7:19
two t threescore and seven	Neh 7:34
a two hundred fifty and four	Neh 7:36
three t nine hundred and thirty	Neh 7:38
of Immer, a t fifty and two	Neh 7:40
a two hundred forty and seven	Neh 7:41
The children of Harim, a t	Neh 7:42
two t three hundred and threescore	Neh 7:66
were seven t three hundred thirty	Neh 7:67
six t seven hundred and twenty	Neh 7:69
to the treasure a t drams of gold	Neh 7:70
the work twenty t drams of gold	Neh 7:71
of gold, and two t	Neh 7:71
gave was twenty t drams of gold	Neh 7:72
two t pounds of silver, and	Neh 7:72
I will pay ten t talents of	Est 3:9
of their foes seventy and five t	Est 9:16
substance also was seven t sheep	Job 1:3
three t camels, and five hundred	Job 1:3
he cannot answer him one of a t	Job 9:3
an interpreter, one among a t	Job 33:23
for he had fourteen t sheep	Job 42:12
six t camels, and a t yoke	Job 42:12
yoke of oxen, and a t she asses	Job 42:12
and the cattle upon a t hills	Ps 50:10
in the valley of salt twelve t	Ps 60:t
The chariots of God are twenty t	Ps 68:17
in thy courts is better than a t	Ps 84:10
For a t years in thy sight are	Ps 90:4
A t shall fall at thy side, and	Ps 91:7
side, and ten t at thy right hand	Ps 91:7
he commanded to a t generations	Ps 105:8
he live a t years twice told	Eccl 6:6
one man among a t have I found	Eccl 7:28
whereon there hang a t bucklers	Song 4:4
ruddy, the chiefest among ten t	Song 5:10
was to bring a t pieces of silver	Song 8:11
thou, O Solomon, must have a t	Song 8:12
t vines at a t silverlings	Is 7:23
One t shall flee at the rebuke of	Is 30:17
and I will give thee two t horses	Is 36:8
an hundred and fourscore and five t	Is 37:36
A little one shall become a t	Is 60:22
in the seventh year three t Jews	Jer 52:28
all the persons were four t	Jer 52:30
length of five and twenty t reeds	Eze 45:1
and the breadth shall be ten t	Eze 45:1
the length of five and twenty t	Eze 45:3
the breadth of ten t	Eze 45:3
the ten t of breadth, shall also	Eze 45:5
of the city five t broad, and five	Eze 45:6

broad, and five and twenty t long	Eze 45:6
eastward, he measured a t cubits	Eze 47:3
Again he measured a t, and brought	Eze 47:4
Again he measured a t, and brought	Eze 47:4
Afterward he measured a t	Eze 47:5
twenty t reeds in breadth, and in	Eze 48:8
twenty t in length, and of ten	Eze 48:9
in length, and of ten t in breadth	Eze 48:9
twenty t in length, and toward the	Eze 48:10
toward the west ten t in breadth	Eze 48:10
toward the east ten t in breadth	Eze 48:10
south five and twenty t in length	Eze 48:10
twenty t in length, and ten	Eze 48:13
in length, and ten t in breadth	Eze 48:13
length shall be five and twenty t	Eze 48:13
and the breadth ten t	Eze 48:13
And the five t, that are left in	Eze 48:15
over against the five and twenty t	Eze 48:15
the north side four t and five	Eze 48:16
hundred, and the south side four t	Eze 48:16
and on the east side four t and	Eze 48:16
hundred, and the west side four t	Eze 48:16
portion shall be ten t eastward	Eze 48:18
eastward, and ten t westward	Eze 48:18
twenty t by five and twenty	Eze 48:20
by five and twenty t	Eze 48:20
twenty t of the oblation toward	Eze 48:21
twenty t toward the west border,	Eze 48:21
city on the north side, four t	Eze 48:30
And at the east side four t	Eze 48:32
And at the south side four t	Eze 48:33
At the west side four t and five	Eze 48:34
round about eighteen t measures	Eze 48:35
a great beast to a t of his lords	Dan 5:1
lords, and drank wine before the t	Dan 5:1
t thousands ministered unto him,	Dan 7:10
ten t times ten t stood	Dan 7:10
And he said unto me, Unto two t	Dan 8:14
there shall be a t two hundred	Dan 12:11
and cometh to the a three hundred	Dan 12:12
out by a t shall leave an hundred	Amos 5:3
t persons that cannot discern	Jonah 4:11
had eaten were about five t men	Mt 14:21
they that did eat were four t men	Mt 15:38
the five loaves of the five t	Mt 16:9
the seven loaves of the four t	Mt 16:10
him, which owed him ten t talents	Mt 18:24
the sea, (they were about two t	Mk 5:13
the loaves were about five t men	Mk 6:44
that had eaten were about four t	Mk 8:9
the five loaves among five t	Mk 8:19
And when the seven among four t	Mk 8:20
For they were about five t men,	Lk 9:14
whether he be able with ten t to	Lk 14:31
cometh against him with twenty t	Lk 14:31
sat down, in number about five t	Jn 6:10
unto them about three t souls	Acts 2:41
of the men was about five t	Acts 4:4
found it fifty t pieces of silver	Acts 19:19
four t men that were murderers	Acts 21:38
reserved to myself seven t men	Rom 11:4
have ten t instructers in Christ	1Cor 4:15
fell in one day three and twenty t	1Cor 10:8
than ten t words in an unknown	1Cor 14:19
day is with the Lord as a t years	2Pet 3:8
years, and a t years as one day	2Pet 3:8
them was ten t times ten t,	Rev 5:11
four t of all the tribes of	Rev 7:4
of Juda were sealed twelve t	Rev 7:5
of Reuben were sealed twelve t	Rev 7:5
tribe of Gad were sealed twelve t	Rev 7:5
of Aser were sealed twelve t	Rev 7:6
of Nephtalim were sealed twelve t	Rev 7:6
of Manasses were sealed twelve t	Rev 7:6
of Simeon were sealed twelve t	Rev 7:7
of Levi were sealed twelve t	Rev 7:7
of Issachar were sealed twelve t	Rev 7:7
of Zabulon were sealed twelve t	Rev 7:8
of Joseph were sealed twelve t	Rev 7:8
of Benjamin were sealed twelve t	Rev 7:8
were two hundred t	Rev 9:16
shall prophesy a t two hundred	Rev 11:3
were slain of men seven t	Rev 11:13
feed her there a t two hundred	Rev 12:6
him an hundred forty and four t	Rev 14:1
the hundred and forty and four t	Rev 14:3
bridles, by the space of a t	Rev 14:20
and Satan, and bound him a t years	Rev 20:2
till the t years should be	Rev 20:3
and reigned with Christ a t years	Rev 20:4
until the t years were finished	Rev 20:5
and shall reign with him a t years	Rev 20:6
when the t years are expired,	Rev 20:7
with the reed, twelve t furlongs	Rev 21:16

THOUSANDS

thou the mother of t of millions	Gen 24:60
such over them, to be rulers of t	Ex 18:21
over the people, rulers of t	Ex 18:25
shewing mercy unto t of them that	Ex 20:6
Keeping mercy for t, forgiving	Ex 34:7
fathers, heads of t in Israel	Num 1:16
are heads of the t of Israel	Num 10:4
O LORD, unto the many t of Israel	Num 10:36
delivered out of the t of Israel	Num 31:5
host, with the captains over t	Num 31:14
which were over t of the host	Num 31:48
of the host, the captains of t	Num 31:48
to the LORD, the captains of t	Num 31:52
the gold of the captains of t	Num 31:54
heads over you, captains over t	Deut 1:15

T

shewing mercy unto *t* of them that ...... Deut 5:10
and he came with ten *t* of saints .... Deut 33:2
and they are the ten *t* of Ephraim .... Deut 33:17
and they are the *t* of Manasseh .... Deut 33:17
fathers among the *t* of Israel .... Josh 22:14
unto the heads of the *t* of Israel .... Josh 22:21
heads of the *t* of Israel which .... Josh 22:30
will appoint him captains over *t* 1Sa 8:12
LORD by your tribes, and by your *t* 1Sa 10:19
his *t*, and David his ten *t* 1Sa 18:7
have ascribed unto David ten *t* 1Sa 18:8
and to me they have ascribed but *t* 1Sa 18:8
saying, Saul hath slain his *t* 1Sa 21:11
and David his ten *t* 1Sa 21:11
and make you all captains of *t* 1Sa 22:7
out throughout all the *t* of Judah 1Sa 23:23
passed on by hundreds, and by *t* 1Sa 29:2
dances, saying, Saul slew his *t* 1Sa 29:5
and David his ten *t* 1Sa 29:5
with him, and set captains of *t* 2Sa 18:1
came out by hundreds and by *t* 2Sa 18:4
captains of the *t* that were of 1Chr 12:20
consulted with the captains of *t* 1Chr 13:1
of Israel, and the captains over *t* 1Chr 15:25
fathers, the captains over *t* 1Chr 26:26
chief fathers and captains of *t* 1Chr 27:1
and the captains over the *t* 1Chr 28:1
of Israel, and the captains of *t* 1Chr 29:6
all Israel, to the captains of *t* 2Chr 1:2
Of Judah, the captains of *t* 2Chr 17:14
and made them captains over *t* 2Chr 25:5
not be afraid of ten *t* of people .... Ps 3:6
twenty thousand, even *t* of angels .... Ps 68:17
is better unto me than *t* of gold .... Ps 119:72
that our sheep may bring forth *t* .... Ps 144:13
and ten *t* in our streets .... Ps 144:13
shewest lovingkindness unto *t* .... Jer 32:18
thousand *t* ministered unto him .... Dan 7:10
and he shall cast down many ten *t* .... Dan 11:12
be little among the *t* of Judah .... Mic 5:2
LORD be pleased with *t* of rams .... Mic 6:7
or with ten *t* of rivers of oil .... Mic 6:7
how many *t* of Jews there are .... Acts 21:20
cometh with ten *t* of his saints .... Jude 14
ten thousand, and *t* of *t* .... Rev 5:11

THREAD

from a *t* even to a shoelatchet .... Gen 14:23
bound upon his hand a scarlet *t* .... Gen 38:28
had the scarlet *t* upon his hand .... Gen 38:30
t in the window which thou didst .... Josh 2:18
as a *t* of tow is broken when it .... Judg 16:9
them from off his arms like a *t* .... Judg 16:12
Thy lips are like a *t* of scarlet .... Song 4:3

THREATEN

people, let us straitly *t* them .... Acts 4:17

THREATENED

So when they had further *t* them .... Acts 4:21
when he suffered, he *t* not 1Pet 2:23

THREATENING

things unto them, forbearing *t* .... Eph 6:9

THREATENINGS

And now, Lord, behold their *t* .... Acts 4:29
And Saul, yet breathing out *t* .... Acts 9:1

THREE

begat Methuselah *t* hundred years .... Gen 5:22
of Enoch were *t* hundred sixty .... Gen 5:23
And Noah begat *t* sons, Shem, Ham, ... Gen 6:10
the ark shall be *t* hundred cubits .... Gen 6:15
the *t* wives of his sons with them .... Gen 7:13
These are the *t* sons of Noah .... Gen 9:19
lived after the flood *t* hundred .... Gen 9:28
t years, and begat sons and .... Gen 11:13
t years, and begat sons and .... Gen 11:15
t hundred and eighteen, and pursued ... Gen 14:14
Take me an heifer of *t* years old .... Gen 15:9
old, and a she goat of *t* years old .... Gen 15:9
a ram of *t* years old, and a .... Gen 15:9
and, lo, *t* men stood by him .... Gen 18:2
Make ready quickly *t* measures of .... Gen 18:6
there were *t* flocks of sheep .... Gen 29:2
because I have born him *t* sons .... Gen 29:34
he set *t* days' journey betwixt .... Gen 30:36
came to pass about *t* months after .... Gen 38:24
And in the vine were *t* branches .... Gen 40:10
The *t* branches are *t* days .... Gen 40:12
Yet within *t* days shall Pharaoh .... Gen 40:13
I had *t* white baskets on my head .... Gen 40:16
The *t* baskets are *t* days .... Gen 40:18
Yet within *t* days shall Pharaoh .... Gen 40:19
all together into ward *t* days .... Gen 42:17
but to Benjamin he gave *t* hundred ...... Gen 45:22
and his daughters were thirty and *t* ...... Gen 46:15
child, she hid him *t* months .... Ex 2:2
thee, *t* days' journey into the .... Ex 3:18
t days' journey into the desert .... Ex 5:3
were an hundred thirty and *t* years .... Ex 6:18
t years old, when they spake unto .... Ex 7:7
We will go *t* days' journey into .... Ex 8:27
in all the land of Egypt *t* days .... Ex 10:22
any from his place for *t* days .... Ex 10:23
and they went *t* days in the .... Ex 15:22
And if he do not these *t* unto her .... Ex 21:11
t times thou shalt keep a feast .... Ex 23:14
t times in the year all thy males .... Ex 23:17
t branches of the candlestick out .... Ex 25:32
t branches of the candlestick out .... Ex 25:32
t bowls made like unto almonds, ... Ex 25:33

t bowls made like almonds in the .... Ex 25:33
height thereof shall be *t* cubits .... Ex 27:1
pillars *t*, and their sockets *t* .... Ex 27:14
pillars *t*, and their sockets *t* .... Ex 27:15
that day about *t* thousand men .... Ex 32:28
t branches of the candlestick out .... Ex 37:18
t branches of the candlestick out .... Ex 37:18
t bowls made after the fashion of .... Ex 37:19
t bowls made like almonds in .... Ex 37:19
t cubits the height thereof .... Ex 38:1
pillars *t*, and their sockets *t* .... Ex 38:14
pillars *t*, and their sockets *t* .... Ex 38:15
t thousand and five hundred and .... Ex 38:26
in the blood of her purifying *t* .... Ex 38:26
t tenth deals of fine flour for a .... Lev 14:10
t years shall it be as .... Lev 19:23
bring forth fruit for *t* years .... Lev 25:21
shall be *t* sheekels of silver .... Lev 27:6
and nine thousand and *t* hundred .... Num 1:23
t thousand and four hundred .... Num 1:43
t thousand and four hundred and .... Num 1:46
and nine thousand and *t* hundred .... Num 2:13
t thousand and four hundred .... Num 2:30
t thousand and five hundred and .... Num 2:32
a thousand *t* hundred and .... Num 3:50
were *t* thousand and two hundred .... Num 4:44
mount of the LORD *t* days' journey ...... Num 10:33
them in the *t* days' journey .... Num 10:33
Come out ye *t* unto the tabernacle .... Num 12:4
And they *t* came out .... Num 12:4
of *t* tenth deals of flour mingled .... Num 15:9
hast smitten me these *t* times .... Num 22:28
smitten thine ass these *t* times .... Num 22:32
and turned from me these *t* times .... Num 22:33
blessed them these *t* times .... Num 24:10
t thousand and seven hundred and ...... Num 26:7
and four thousand and *t* hundred .... Num 26:25
t thousand and four hundred .... Num 26:47
t thousand, all males from a .... Num 26:62
t tenth deals of flour for a meat .... Num 28:12
t tenth deals shall ye offer for .... Num 28:20
t tenth deals unto one bullock .... Num 28:28
t tenth deals of a bullock, and .... Num 29:3
t tenth deals to a bullock, and .... Num 29:9
was in number *t* hundred thousand ...... Num 31:36
was *t* hundred thousand and thirty ...... Num 31:43
went *t* days' journey in the .... Num 33:8
t years old when he died in mount .... Num 33:39
Ye shall give *t* cities on this .... Num 35:14
t cities shall ye give in the .... Num 35:14
Then Moses severed *t* cities on .... Deut 4:41
At the end of *t* years thou shalt .... Deut 14:28
t times in a year shall all thy .... Deut 16:16
or *t* witnesses, shall he that is .... Deut 17:6
Thou shalt separate *t* cities for .... Deut 19:2
into *t* parts, that every slayer .... Deut 19:3
shalt separate *t* cities for thee .... Deut 19:7
then shalt thou add *t* cities more .... Deut 19:9
more for thee, beside these .... Deut 19:9
or at the mouth of *t* witnesses .... Deut 19:15
for within *t* days ye shall pass .... Josh 1:11
and hide yourselves there *t* days .... Josh 2:16
mountain, and abode there *t* days .... Josh 2:22
And it came to pass after *t* days .... Josh 3:2
about two or *t* thousand men go up ...... Josh 7:3
the people about *t* thousand .... Josh 7:4
of *t* days after they had made a .... Josh 9:16
drove thence the *t* sons of Anak .... Josh 15:14
and her towns, even *t* countries .... Josh 17:11
among you *t* men for each tribe .... Josh 18:4
with her suburbs; *t* cities .... Josh 21:32
thence the *t* sons of Anak .... Judg 1:20
their mouth, were *t* hundred men .... Judg 7:6
By the *t* hundred men that lapped .... Judg 7:7
and retained those *t* hundred men .... Judg 7:8
he divided the *t* hundred men into .... Judg 7:16
hundred men into *t* companies .... Judg 7:16
the *t* companies blew the trumpets ...... Judg 7:20
the *t* hundred blew the trumpets .... Judg 7:22
the *t* hundred men that were with .... Judg 8:4
had reigned *t* years over Israel .... Judg 9:22
and divided them into *t* companies ...... Judg 9:43
t years, and died, and was buried .... Judg 10:2
coasts of Arnon, *t* hundred years .... Judg 11:26
they could not in *t* days expound .... Judg 14:14
caught *t* hundred foxes, and took .... Judg 15:4
Then *t* thousand men of Judah went ..... Judg 15:11
thou hast mocked me these *t* times ...... Judg 16:15
the roof about *t* thousand men .... Judg 16:27
and he abode with him *t* days .... Judg 19:4
with *t* bullocks, and one ephah of 1Sa 1:24
fleshhook of *t* teeth in his hand 1Sa 2:13
she conceived, and bare *t* 1Sa 2:21
asses that were lost *t* days ago 1Sa 9:20
there shall meet thee *t* men going 1Sa 10:3
to Beth-el, one carrying *t* kids 1Sa 10:3
carrying *t* loaves of bread 1Sa 10:3
of Israel were *t* hundred thousand 1Sa 11:8
put the people in *t* companies 1Sa 11:11
Saul chose him *t* thousand men of 1Sa 13:2
of the Philistines in *t* companies 1Sa 13:17
the eldest sons of Jesse went 1Sa 17:13
the names of his *t* sons that went 1Sa 17:13
the eldest followed Saul 1Sa 17:14
And when thou hast stayed *t* days 1Sa 20:19
I will shoot *t* arrows on the side 1Sa 20:20
ground, and bowed himself *t* times 1Sa 20:41
kept from us about these *t* days 1Sa 21:5
Then Saul took *t* thousand chosen 1Sa 24:2

he had *t* thousand sheep, and a 1Sa 25:2
having *t* thousand chosen men of 1Sa 26:2
any water, *t* days and *t* nights 1Sa 30:12
because *t* days agone I fell sick 1Sa 30:13
his *t* sons, and his armourbearer 1Sa 31:6
his *t* sons fallen in mount Gilboa 1Sa 31:8
there were *t* sons of Zeruiah 2Sa 2:18
of Abner's ribs, so that *t* hundred 2Sa 2:31
t years over all Israel and Judah 2Sa 5:5
of Obed-edom the Gittite *t* months 2Sa 6:11
to Geshur, and was there *t* years 2Sa 13:38
Absalom there were born *t* sons 2Sa 14:27
he took *t* darts in his hand, and 2Sa 18:14
me the men of Judah within *t* days 2Sa 20:4
in the days of David *t* years 2Sa 21:1
t hundred sheekels of brass in 2Sa 21:16
one of the *t* mighty men went down 2Sa 23:13
the *t* mighty men brake through 2Sa 23:16
things did these *t* mighty men 2Sa 23:17
son of Zeruiah, was chief among *t* 2Sa 23:18
up his spear against *t* hundred 2Sa 23:18
them, and had the name among *t* 2Sa 23:18
Was he not most honourable of *t* 2Sa 23:19
he attained not unto the first *t* 2Sa 23:19
had the name among *t* mighty men 2Sa 23:22
he attained not to the first *t* 2Sa 23:23
the LORD, I offer thee *t* things 2Sa 24:12
or wilt thou flee *t* months before 2Sa 24:13
or that there be *t* days 2Sa 24:13
t years reigned he in Jerusalem 1Kin 2:11
to pass at the end of *t* years 1Kin 2:39
he spake *t* thousand proverbs 1Kin 4:32
t thousand and *t* hundred 1Kin 5:16
court with *t* rows of hewed stone 1Kin 6:36
And there were windows in *t* rows 1Kin 7:4
was against light in *t* ranks 1Kin 7:4
was against light in *t* ranks 1Kin 7:5
was with *t* rows of hewed stones 1Kin 7:12
t looking toward the north, and 1Kin 7:25
t looking toward the west, and 1Kin 7:25
t looking toward the south, and 1Kin 7:25
t looking toward the east 1Kin 7:25
t cubits the height of it 1Kin 7:25
t times in a year did Solomon 1Kin 9:25
he made *t* hundred shields of 1Kin 10:17
t pound of gold went to one 1Kin 10:17
once in *t* years came the navy of 1Kin 10:22
and *t* hundred concubines 1Kin 11:3
unto them, Depart yet for *t* days 1Kin 12:5
t years reigned he in Jerusalem 1Kin 15:2
himself upon the child *t* times 1Kin 17:21
they continued *t* years without 1Kin 22:1
and they sought *t* days, but found 2Kin 2:17
called these *t* kings together 2Kin 3:10
called these *t* kings together 2Kin 3:13
out to him two or *t* eunuchs 2Kin 9:32
But it was so, that in the *t* 2Kin 12:6
In the *t* and twentieth year of 2Kin 13:1
T times did Joash beat him, and 2Kin 13:25
Samaria, and besieged it *t* years 2Kin 17:5
at the end of *t* years they took 2Kin 18:10
Judah *t* hundred talents of silver 2Kin 18:14
t years old when he began to 2Kin 23:31
he reigned *t* months in Jerusalem 2Kin 23:31
became his servant *t* years 2Kin 24:1
he reigned in Jerusalem *t* months 2Kin 24:8
height of the chapiter *t* cubits 2Kin 25:17
the *t* keepers of the door 2Kin 25:18
which *t* were born unto him of 1Chr 2:3
Abishai, and Joab, and Asahel, *t* 1Chr 2:16
And Segub begat Jair, who had *t* 1Chr 2:22
he reigned thirty and *t* years 1Chr 3:4
and Hezekiah, and Azrikam, *t* 1Chr 3:23
Bela, and Becher, and Jediael, *t* 1Chr 7:6
Jeush, and *t* sons, and all his house 1Chr 10:6
t hundred slain by him at one 1Chr 11:11
who was one of the *t* mighties 1Chr 11:12
Now *t* of the thirty captains went 1Chr 11:15
the *t* brake through the host of 1Chr 11:18
things did these *t* mightiest 1Chr 11:19
of Joab, he was chief of the *t* 1Chr 11:20
up his spear against *t* hundred 1Chr 11:20
them, and had a name among the *t* 1Chr 11:20
Of the *t*, he was more honourable 1Chr 11:21
he attained not to the first *t* 1Chr 11:21
had the name among the *t* mighties 1Chr 11:24
but attained not to the first *t* 1Chr 11:25
and with him were *t* thousand 1Chr 12:27
the kindred of Saul, *t* thousand 1Chr 12:29
there they were with David *t* days 1Chr 12:39
Obed-edom in his house *t* months 1Chr 13:14
the LORD, I offer thee *t* things 1Chr 21:10
t years' famine 1Chr 21:12
or *t* months to be destroyed 1Chr 21:12
or else *t* days the sword of the 1Chr 21:12
was Jehiel, and Zetham, and Joel, *t* 1Chr 23:8
Shelomith, and Haziel, and Haran, *t* ... 1Chr 23:9
Mahli, and Eder, and Jeremoth, *t* 1Chr 23:23
the *t* and twentieth to Delaiah, ... 1Chr 24:18
fourteen sons and *t* daughters 1Chr 25:5
The *t* and twentieth to Mahazioth, ... 1Chr 25:30
t thousand talents of gold, ... 1Chr 29:4
t years reigned he in Jerusalem 1Chr 29:27
t thousand six hundred to 2Chr 2:2
t thousand and six hundred 2Chr 2:17
t thousand and six hundred 2Chr 2:18
t looking toward the north, and 2Chr 4:4
t looking toward the west, and 2Chr 4:4
t looking toward the south, and 2Chr 4:4

t looking toward the east ... 2Chr 4:4
received and held t thousand baths ... 2Chr 4:5
t cubits high, and had set it in ... 2Chr 6:13
And on the t and twentieth day of ... 2Chr 7:10
t times in the year, even in the ... 2Chr 8:13
t hundred shields made he of ... 2Chr 9:16
t hundred shekels of gold went to ... 2Chr 9:16
every t years once came the ships ... 2Chr 9:21
Come again unto me after t days ... 2Chr 10:5
son of Solomon strong, t years ... 2Chr 11:17
for t years they walked in the ... 2Chr 11:17
He reigned t years in Jerusalem ... 2Chr 13:2
out of Judah t hundred thousand ... 2Chr 14:8
thousand, and t hundred chariots ... 2Chr 14:9
men of valour t hundred thousand ... 2Chr 17:14
they were t days in gathering of ... 2Chr 20:25
found them t hundred thousand ... 2Chr 25:5
smote t thousand of them, and took ... 2Chr 25:13
t hundred thousand and seven ... 2Chr 26:13
hundred oxen and t thousand sheep ... 2Chr 29:33
from t years old and upward, even ... 2Chr 31:16
thousand, and t thousand bullocks ... 2Chr 35:7
small cattle, and t hundred oxen ... 2Chr 35:8
t years old when he began to ... 2Chr 36:2
he reigned t months in Jerusalem ... 2Chr 36:9
to reign, and he reigned t months ... 2Chr 36:9
t hundred seventy and two ... Ezr 2:3
of Bebai, six hundred twenty and t ... Ezr 2:11
Bezai, t hundred twenty and t ... Ezr 2:17
Hashum, two hundred twenty and t ... Ezr 2:19
an hundred twenty and t ... Ezr 2:21
seven hundred and forty and t ... Ezr 2:25
and Ai, two hundred twenty and t ... Ezr 2:28
of Harim, t hundred and twenty ... Ezr 2:32
Jericho, t hundred forty and five ... Ezr 2:34
t thousand and six hundred and ... Ezr 2:35
Jeshua, nine hundred seventy and t ... Ezr 2:36
t hundred ninety and two ... Ezr 2:58
forty and two thousand t hundred ... Ezr 2:64
seven thousand t hundred thirty ... Ezr 2:65
With t rows of great stones, and a ... Ezr 6:4
and with him t hundred males ... Ezr 8:5
and there abode us in tents t days ... Ezr 8:15
Jerusalem, and abode there t days ... Ezr 8:32
would not come within t days ... Ezr 10:8
unto Jerusalem within t days ... Ezr 10:9
to Jerusalem, and was there t days ... Neh 2:11
t hundred seventy and two ... Neh 7:9
two thousand t hundred twenty and ... Neh 7:17
t hundred twenty and eight ... Neh 7:22
Bezai, t hundred twenty and four ... Neh 7:23
Beeroth, seven hundred forty and t ... Neh 7:29
and Ai, an hundred twenty and t ... Neh 7:32
of Harim, t hundred and twenty ... Neh 7:35
Jericho, t hundred forty and five ... Neh 7:36
t thousand nine hundred and thirty ... Neh 7:38
Jeshua, nine hundred seventy and t ... Neh 7:39
were t hundred ninety and two ... Neh 7:60
forty and two thousand t hundred ... Neh 7:66
seven thousand t hundred thirty ... Neh 7:67
and neither eat nor drink t days ... Est 4:16
is, the month Sivan, on the t ... Est 8:9
slew t hundred men at Shushan ... Est 9:15
him seven sons and t daughters ... Job 1:2
t thousand camels, and five ... Job 1:3
called for their t sisters to eat ... Job 1:4
The Chaldeans made out t bands ... Job 1:17
Now when Job's t friends heard of ... Job 2:11
So these t men ceased to answer ... Job 32:1
Also against his t friends was ... Job 32:3
in the mouth of these t men ... Job 32:5
also seven sons and t daughters ... Job 42:13
There are t things that are never ... Prov 30:15
There be t things which are too ... Prov 30:21
For t things the earth is ... Prov 30:21
There be t things do well, yea ... Prov 30:29
Zoar, an heifer of t years old ... Is 15:5
spoken, saying, Within t years ... Is 16:14
two or t berries in the top of ... Is 17:6
barefoot t years for a sign and ... Is 20:3
even unto this day, that is the t ... Jer 25:3
Jehudi had read t or four leaves ... Jer 36:23
as an heifer of t years old ... Jer 48:34
the t keepers of the door ... Jer 52:24
year t thousand Jews and t ... Jer 52:28
In the t and twentieth year of ... Jer 52:30
days, t hundred and ninety days ... Eze 4:5
t hundred and ninety days shall ... Eze 4:9
Though these t men, Noah, Daniel ... Eze 14:14
Though these t men were in it, as ... Eze 14:16
Though these t men were in it, as ... Eze 14:18
gate eastward were t on this side ... Eze 40:10
on this side, and t on that side ... Eze 40:10
they t were of one measure ... Eze 40:10
thereof were t on this side ... Eze 40:21
on this side and t on that side ... Eze 40:21
gate was t cubits on this side ... Eze 40:48
side, and t cubits on that side ... Eze 40:48
And the side chambers were t ... Eze 41:6
round about on their t stories ... Eze 41:6
altar of wood was t cubits high ... Eze 41:22
against gallery in t stories ... Eze 42:3
For they were in t stories ... Eze 42:6
t gates northward ... Eze 48:31
hundred measures; and t gates ... Eze 48:32
five hundred, and t gates ... Eze 48:34
so nourishing them t years ... Dan 1:5
And these t men, Shadrach, Meshach ... Dan 3:23
Did not we cast t men bound into ... Dan 3:24

And over these t presidents ... Dan 6:2
upon his knees t times a day ... Dan 6:10
maketh his petition t times a day ... Dan 6:13
it had t ribs in the mouth of it ... Dan 7:5
before whom there were t of the ... Dan 7:8
came up, and before whom t fell ... Dan 7:20
first, and he shall subdue t kings ... Dan 7:24
two thousand and t hundred days ... Dan 8:14
Daniel was mourning t full weeks ... Dan 10:2
till t whole weeks were fulfilled ... Dan 10:3
stand up yet t kings in Persia ... Dan 11:2
cometh to the thousand t hundred ... Dan 12:12
For t transgressions of Damascus ... Amos 1:3
For t transgressions of Gaza, and ... Amos 1:6
For t transgressions of Tyrus, and ... Amos 1:9
For t transgressions of Edom, and ... Amos 1:11
For t transgressions of the ... Amos 1:13
For t transgressions of Moab, and ... Amos 2:1
For t transgressions of Judah, and ... Amos 2:4
For t transgressions of Israel ... Amos 2:6
and your tithes after t years ... Amos 4:4
when there were yet t months to ... Amos 4:7
So two or t cities wandered unto ... Amos 4:8
the fish t days and t nights ... Jonah 1:17
great city of t days' journey ... Jonah 3:3
t shepherds also I cut off in one ... Zec 11:8
For as Jonas was t days and ... Mt 12:40
t nights in the whale's belly ... Mt 12:40
so shall the Son of man be t days ... Mt 12:40
t nights in the heart of the ... Mt 12:40
hid in t measures of meal, till ... Mt 13:33
they continue with me now t days ... Mt 15:32
let us make here t tabernacles ... Mt 17:4
or t witnesses every word may be ... Mt 18:16
For where two or t are gathered ... Mt 18:20
of God, and to build it in t days ... Mt 26:61
and buildest it in t days ... Mt 27:40
After t days I will rise again ... Mt 27:63
they have now been with me t days ... Mk 8:2
and after t days rise again ... Mk 8:31
and let us make t tabernacles ... Mk 9:5
for more than t hundred pence ... Mk 14:5
within t days I will build ... Mk 15:29
temple, and buildest it in t days ... Lk 1:56
abode with her about t months ... Lk 2:46
that after t days they found him ... Lk 4:25
the heaven was shut up t years ... Lk 9:33
and let us make t tabernacles ... Lk 10:36
Which now of these t, thinkest ... Lk 11:5
him, Friend, lend me t loaves ... Lk 12:52
t against two, and two against ... Lk 13:7
against two, and two against t ... Lk 13:21
hid in t measures of meal, till ... Jn 2:6
two or t firkins apiece ... Jn 2:19
in t days I will raise it up ... Jn 12:5
and wilt thou rear it up in t days ... Jn 21:11
ointment sold for t hundred pence ... Acts 2:41
unto them about t thousand souls ... Acts 5:7
about the space of t hours after ... Acts 7:20
up in his father's house t months ... Acts 9:9
he was t days without sight, and ... Acts 10:19
unto him, Behold, t men seek thee ... Acts 11:11
And this was done t times ... Acts 17:2
immediately there were t men ... Acts 17:2
t sabbath days reasoned with them ... Acts 19:8
boldly for the space of t months ... Acts 20:3
And there abode t months ... Acts 25:1
that by the space of t years I ... Acts 28:7
after t days he ascended from ... Acts 28:11
lodged us t days courteously ... Acts 28:12
after t months we departed in a ... Acts 28:12
Syracuse, we tarried there t days ... Acts 28:12
as Appii forum, and The t taverns ... Acts 28:15
that after t days Paul called the ... 1Cor 13:8
committed, and fell in one day t ... 1Cor 13:13
it be by two, or at the most by t ... 1Cor 14:27
Let the prophets speak two or t ... 2Cor 13:1
In the mouth of two or t ... Gal 1:18
Then after t years I went up to ... Heb 10:28
but before two or t witnesses ... Heb 11:23
mercy under two or t witnesses ... Jas 5:17
was hid t months of his parents ... 1Jn 5:7
the earth by the space of t years ... 1Jn 5:7
For there are t that bear record ... 1Jn 5:8
and these t are one ... 1Jn 5:8
there are t that bear witness in ... Rev 6:6
and these t agree in one ... Rev 8:13
t measures of barley for a penny ... Rev 9:18
the trumpet of the t angels ... Rev 16:13
By these t was the third part of ... Rev 16:19
see their dead bodies t days ... Rev 21:13
And after t days and a half the ... Rev 21:13
I saw t unclean spirits like ... Rev 21:13
city was divided into t parts ... Rev 21:13
On the east t gates ... Rev 21:13
on the north t gates ... Rev 21:13
on the south t gates ... Rev 21:13
and on the west t gates ... Rev 21:13

THREEFOLD

a t cord is not quickly broken ... Eccl 4:12

THREESCORE

life which he lived, an hundred t ... Gen 25:7
Isaac was t years old when she ... Gen 25:26
sons' wives, all the souls were t ... Gen 46:26
which came into Egypt, were t ... Gen 46:27
the Egyptians mourned for him t ... Gen 50:3

were twelve wells of water, and t ... Ex 15:27
and a thousand seven hundred and t ... Ex 38:25
in the blood of her purifying t ... Lev 12:5
of the tribe of Judah, were t ... Num 1:27
even of the tribe of Dan, were t ... Num 1:39
were numbered of them, were t ... Num 2:4
were numbered of them, were t ... Num 2:26
and two thousand two hundred and t ... Num 3:43
redeemed of the two hundred and t ... Num 3:46
a thousand three hundred and t ... Num 3:50
that were numbered of them, t ... Num 26:22
that were numbered of them, t ... Num 26:25
t thousand and five hundred ... Num 26:27
were numbered of them, were t ... Num 26:43
And t and twelve thousand beeves ... Num 31:33
And t and one thousand asses ... Num 31:34
of the sheep was six hundred and t ... Num 31:37
of which the LORD's tribute was t ... Num 31:38
of which the LORD's tribute was t ... Num 31:39
twelve fountains of water, and t ... Deut 3:4
t cities, all the region of Argob ... Deut 3:4
went down into Egypt with t ... Deut 10:22
which are in Bashan, t cities ... Josh 13:30
And Adoni-bezek said, T and ten ... Judg 1:7
and the elders thereof, even t ... Judg 8:14
And Gideon had t and ten sons of ... Judg 8:30
sons of Jerubbaal, which are t ... Judg 9:2
And they gave him t and ten pieces ... Judg 9:4
the sons of Jerubbaal, being t ... Judg 9:5
day, and have slain his sons, t ... Judg 9:18
That the cruelty done to the t ... Judg 9:24
and thirty nephews, that rode on t ... Judg 12:14
of the people fifty thousand and t ... 1Sa 6:19
that three hundred and t men died ... 2Sa 2:31
t great cities with walls and ... 1Kin 4:13
flour, and t measures of meal ... 1Kin 4:22
And Solomon had t and ten thousand ... 1Kin 5:15
the length thereof was t cubits ... 1Kin 6:2
in one year was six hundred t ... 1Kin 10:14
t men of the people of the land ... 2Kin 25:19
married when he was t years old ... 1Chr 2:21
the towns thereof, even t cities ... 1Chr 2:23
forty thousand seven hundred and t ... 1Chr 5:18
a thousand and seven hundred and t ... 1Chr 9:13
Obed-edom with their brethren, t ... 1Chr 16:38
and Judah was four hundred and t ... 1Chr 21:5
strength for the service, were t ... 1Chr 26:8
And Solomon told out t and ten ... 2Chr 2:2
And he set t and ten thousand of ... 2Chr 2:18
the first measure was t cubits ... 2Chr 3:3
in one year was six hundred and t ... 2Chr 9:13
eighteen wives, and t concubines ... 2Chr 11:21
and eight sons, and t daughters ... 2Chr 11:21
chariots, and t thousand horsemen ... 2Chr 12:3
the congregation brought, was t ... 2Chr 29:32
she kept sabbath, to fulfil t ... 2Chr 36:21
of Zaccai, seven hundred and t ... Ezr 2:14
two thousand three hundred and t ... Ezr 2:69
unto the treasure of the work t ... Ezr 2:69
the height thereof t cubits ... Ezr 6:3
and the breadth thereof t cubits ... Ezr 6:3
with him an hundred and t males ... Ezr 8:10
and Shemaiah, and with them t males ... Ezr 8:13
of Zaccai, seven hundred and t ... Neh 7:14
of Adonikam, six hundred t ... Neh 7:18
of Bigvai, two thousand t ... Neh 7:19
two thousand three hundred and t ... Neh 7:66
thousand pounds of silver, and t ... Neh 7:72
at Jerusalem seven four hundred t ... Neh 11:6
The days of our years are t years ... Ps 90:10
t valiant men are about it, of ... Song 3:7
There are t queens, and fourscore ... Song 6:8
and within t and five years shall ... Is 7:8
t men of the people of the land ... Jer 52:25
He made also posts of t cubits ... Eze 40:14
gold, whose height was t cubits ... Dan 3:1
took the kingdom, being about t ... Dan 5:31
Prince shall be seven weeks, and t ... Dan 9:25
And after t and two weeks shall ... Dan 9:26
thou hast had indignation these t ... Zec 1:12
from Jerusalem about t furlongs ... Lk 24:13
to him, and all his kindred, t ... Acts 7:14
to go to Caesarea, and horsemen t ... Acts 23:23
in all in the ship two hundred t ... Acts 27:37
into the number under t years old ... 1Ti 5:9
t days, clothed in sackcloth ... Rev 11:3
and his number is six hundred t ... Rev 13:18

THRESH

thou shalt t the mountains, and ... Is 41:15
it is time to t her ... Jer 51:33
Arise and t, O daughter of Zion ... Mic 4:13
thou didst t the heathen in anger ... Hab 3:12

THRESHED

his son Gideon t wheat by the ... Judg 6:11
For the fitches are not t with a ... Is 28:27
because they have t Gilead with ... Amos 1:3

THRESHETH

that he that t in hope should be ... 1Cor 9:10

THRESHING

your t shall reach unto the ... Lev 26:5
and t instruments and other ... 2Sa 24:22
had made them like the dust by t ... 2Kin 13:7
Now Ornan was t wheat ... 1Chr 21:20
the t instruments for wood, and ... 1Chr 21:23
O my t, and the corn of my floor ... Is 21:10
not threshed with a t instrument ... Is 28:27
because he will not ever be t it ... Is 28:28

THRESHINGFLOOR

And they came to the t of Atad .... Gen 50:10
ye do the heave offering of the t .... Num 15:20
though it were the corn of the t .... Num 18:27
Levites as the increase of the t .... Num 18:30
barley to night in the t .... Ruth 3:2
And when they came to Nachon's t 2Sa 6:6
in the t of Araunah the Jebusite 2Sa 24:16
David said, To buy the t of these 2Sa 24:21
So David bought the t and the oxen 2Sa 24:24
they came unto the t of Chidon 1Chr 13:9
by the t of Ornan the Jebusite 1Chr 21:15
in the t of Ornan the Jebusite 1Chr 21:18
saw David, and went out of the t 1Chr 21:21
Grant me the place of this t 1Chr 21:22
in the t of Ornan the Jebusite 1Chr 21:28
in the t of Ornan the Jebusite 2Chr 3:1
daughter of Babylon is like a t .... Jer 51:33

THRESHINGFLOORS

against Keilah, and they rob the t 1Sa 23:1
like the chaff of the summer t .... Dan 2:35

THRESHINGPLACE

by the t of Araunah the Jebusite 2Sa 24:16

THRESHOLD

and her hands were upon the t .... Judg 19:27
his hands were cut off upon the t 1Sa 5:4
tread on the t of Dagon in Ashdod 1Sa 5:5
she came to the t of the door 1Kin 14:17
he was, to the t of the house .... Eze 9:3
and stood over the t of the house .... Eze 10:4
from off the t of the house .... Eze 10:18
and measured the t of the gate .... Eze 40:6
the other t of the gate, which .... Eze 40:7
the t of the gate by the porch of .... Eze 40:7
their t by my thresholds .... Eze 43:8
worship at the t of the same .... Eze 46:2
under the t of the house eastward .... Eze 47:1
all those that leap on the t .... Zeph 1:9

THRESHOLDS

the ward at the t of the gates .... Neh 12:25
of their threshold by my t .... Eze 43:8
desolation shall be in the t .... Zeph 2:14

THREW

t stones at him, and cast dust 2Sa 16:13
So they t her down 2Kin 9:33
t down his high places and the 2Chr 31:1
she t in two mites, which make a .... Mk 12:42
a coming, the devil t him down .... Lk 9:42
clothes, and t dust into the air .... Acts 22:23

THREWEST

persecutors thou t into the deeps .... Neh 9:11

THRICE

T in the year shall all your men .... Ex 34:23
the Lord thy God t in the year .... Ex 34:24
And he smote t, and stayed 2Kin 13:18
now thou shalt smite Syria but t 2Kin 13:19
cock crow, thou shalt deny me t .... Mt 26:34
cock crow, thou shalt deny me t .... Mt 26:75
crow twice, thou shalt deny me t .... Mk 14:30
crow twice, thou shalt deny me t .... Mk 14:72
before that thou shalt t deny .... Lk 22:34
cock crow, thou shalt deny me t .... Lk 22:61
crow, till thou hast denied me t .... Jn 13:38
This was done t .... Acts 10:16
I was t beaten with rods, once 2Cor 11:25
t I suffered shipwreck, a night 2Cor 11:25
this thing I besought the Lord t 2Cor 12:8

THROAT

their t is an open sepulchre .... Ps 5:9
my t is dried .... Ps 69:3
speak they through their t .... Ps 115:7
And put a knife to thy t, if thou .... Prov 23:2
unshod, and thy t from thirst .... Jer 2:25
on him, and took him by the t .... Mt 18:28
their t is an open sepulchre .... Rom 3:13

THRONE

only in the t will I be greater .... Gen 41:40
Pharaoh that sitteth upon his t .... Ex 11:5
his t unto the firstborn of the .... Ex 12:29
sitteth upon the t of his kingdom .... Deut 17:18
make them inherit the t of glory 1Sa 2:8
to set up the t of David over 2Sa 3:10
I will stablish the t of his 2Sa 7:13
thy t shall be established for 2Sa 7:16
and the king and his t be guiltless 2Sa 14:9
me, and he shall sit upon my t 1Kin 1:13
me, and he shall sit upon my t 1Kin 1:17
t of my lord the king after 1Kin 1:20
me, and he shall sit upon my t 1Kin 1:24
who should sit on the t of my 1Kin 1:27
shall sit upon my t in my stead 1Kin 1:30
that he may come and sit upon my t 1Kin 1:35
make his t greater than the 1Kin 1:37
than the t of my lord king David 1Kin 1:47
sitteth on the t of the kingdom 1Kin 1:46
his t greater than thy t 1Kin 1:47
given one to sit on my t this day 1Kin 1:48
said he) a man on the t of Israel 1Kin 2:4
upon the t of David his father 1Kin 2:12
unto her, and sat down on his t 1Kin 2:19
set me on the t of David my 1Kin 2:24
and upon his house, and upon his t 1Kin 2:33
and the t of David shall be 1Kin 2:45

given him a son to sit on his t 1Kin 3:6
I will set upon thy t in thy room 1Kin 5:5
for the t where he might judge 1Kin 7:7
father, and sit on the t of Israel 1Kin 8:20
sight to sit on the t of Israel 1Kin 8:25
Then I will establish the t of 1Kin 9:5
thee a man upon the t of Israel 1Kin 9:5
to set thee on the t of Israel 1Kin 10:9
the king made a great t of ivory 1Kin 10:18
The t had six steps, and the top 1Kin 10:19
the top of the t was round behind 1Kin 10:19
reign, as soon as he sat on his t 1Kin 16:11
king of Judah sat each on his t 1Kin 22:10
I saw the LORD sitting on his t 1Kin 22:19
and set him on his father's t 2Kin 10:3
shall sit on the t of Israel 2Kin 10:30
And he sat on the t of the kings 2Kin 11:19
and Jeroboam sat upon his t 2Kin 13:13
the t of Israel unto the fourth 2Kin 15:12
set his t above the t of the 2Kin 25:28
and I will stablish his t for ever 1Chr 17:12
his t shall be established for 1Chr 17:14
I will establish the t of his 1Chr 22:10
Solomon my son to sit upon the t 1Chr 28:5
Then Solomon sat on the t of the 1Chr 29:23
and am set on the t of Israel 2Chr 6:10
sight to sit upon the t of Israel 2Chr 6:16
I stablish the t of thy kingdom 2Chr 7:18
in thee to set thee on his t 2Chr 9:8
the king made a great t of ivory 2Chr 9:17
And there were six steps to the t 2Chr 9:18
which were fastened to the t 2Chr 9:18
Judah sat either of them on his t 2Chr 18:9
I saw the LORD sitting upon his t 2Chr 18:18
king upon the t of the kingdom 2Chr 23:20
unto the t of the governor on .... Neh 3:7
sat on the t of his kingdom .... Est 1:2
his royal t in the royal house .... Est 5:1
He holdeth back the face of his t .... Job 26:9
but with kings are they on the t .... Job 36:7
satest in the t judging right .... Ps 9:4
hath prepared his t for judgment .... Ps 9:7
the LORD's t is in heaven .... Ps 11:4
Thy t, O God, is for ever and ever .... Ps 45:6
upon the t of his holiness .... Ps 47:8
build up thy t to all generations .... Ps 89:4
are the habitation of thy t .... Ps 89:14
his t as the days of heaven .... Ps 89:29
make his t to endure as the .... Ps 89:36
cast his t down to the ground .... Ps 89:44
Thy t is established of old .... Ps 93:2
Shall the t of iniquity have .... Ps 94:20
are the habitation of his t .... Ps 97:2
prepared his t in the heavens .... Ps 103:19
of thy body will I set upon thy t .... Ps 132:11
also sit upon thy t for evermore .... Ps 132:12
for the t is established by .... Prov 16:12
A king that sitteth in the t of .... Prov 20:8
his t is upholden by mercy .... Prov 20:28
his t shall be established in .... Prov 25:5
also the Lord sitting upon a t .... Prov 29:14
be no end, upon the t of David .... Is 6:1
I will exalt my t above the stars .... Is 9:7
mercy shall the t be established .... Is 14:13
glorious t to his father's house .... Is 16:5
there is no t, O daughter of the .... Is 22:23
the LORD, The heaven is my t .... Is 66:1
they shall set every one his t at .... Jer 1:15
call Jerusalem the t of the LORD .... Jer 3:17
the kings that sit upon David's t .... Jer 13:13
not disgrace the t of thy glory .... Jer 14:21
A glorious high t from the .... Jer 17:12
sitting upon the t of David .... Jer 17:25
that sittest upon the t of David .... Jer 22:2
kings sitting upon the t of David .... Jer 22:4
sitting upon the t of David .... Jer 22:30
that sitteth upon the t of David .... Jer 29:16
upon the t of the house of Israel .... Jer 33:17
have a son to reign upon his t .... Jer 33:21
none to sit upon the t of David .... Jer 36:30
will set his t upon these stones .... Jer 43:10
And I will set my t in Elam .... Jer 49:38
set his t above the t of the .... Jer 52:32
thy t from generation to .... Lam 5:19
heads was the likeness of a t .... Eze 1:26
of the t was the likeness as the .... Eze 1:26
appearance of the likeness of a t .... Eze 10:1
me, Son of man, the place of my t .... Eze 43:7
he was deposed from his kingly t .... Dan 5:20
his t was like the fiery flame .... Dan 7:9
Nineveh, and he arose from his t .... Jonah 3:6
will overthrow the t of kingdoms .... Hag 2:22
and shall sit and rule upon his t .... Zec 6:13
he shall be a priest upon his t .... Zec 6:13
for it is God's t .... Mt 5:34
shall sit in the t of his glory .... Mt 19:28
heaven, sweareth by the t of God .... Mt 23:22
he sit upon the t of his glory .... Mt 25:31
him the t of his father David .... Lk 1:32
raise up Christ to sit on his t .... Acts 2:30
Heaven is my t, and earth is my .... Acts 7:49
in royal apparel, sat upon his t .... Acts 12:21
But unto the Son he saith, Thy t .... Heb 1:8
boldly unto the t of grace .... Heb 4:16
t of the Majesty in the heavens .... Heb 8:1
at the right hand of the t of God .... Heb 12:2
Spirits which are before his t .... Rev 1:4
I grant to sit with me in my t .... Rev 3:21
set down with my Father in his t .... Rev 3:21

a t was set in heaven, and one sat .... Rev 4:2
in heaven, and one sat on the t .... Rev 4:2
was a rainbow round about the t .... Rev 4:3
And round about the t were four .... Rev 4:4
out of the t proceeded lightnings .... Rev 4:5
of fire burning before the t .... Rev 4:5
before the t there was a sea of .... Rev 4:6
and in the midst of the t, and .... Rev 4:6
and round about the t .... Rev 4:6
thanks to him that sat on the t .... Rev 4:9
down before him that sat on the t .... Rev 4:10
and cast their crowns before the t .... Rev 4:10
on the t a book written within .... Rev 5:1
and, lo, in the midst of the t .... Rev 5:6
hand of him that sat upon the t .... Rev 5:7
of many angels round about the t .... Rev 5:11
unto him that sitteth upon the t .... Rev 5:13
face of him that sitteth on the t .... Rev 6:16
and tongues, stood before the t .... Rev 7:9
our God which sitteth upon the t .... Rev 7:10
angels stood round about the t .... Rev 7:11
fell before the t on their faces .... Rev 7:11
are they before the t of God .... Rev 7:15
on the t shall dwell among them .... Rev 7:15
midst of the t shall feed them .... Rev 7:17
altar which was before the t .... Rev 8:3
caught up unto God, and to his t .... Rev 12:5
it were a new song before the t .... Rev 14:3
without fault before the t of God .... Rev 14:5
the temple of heaven, from the t .... Rev 16:17
worshipped God that sat on the t .... Rev 19:4
And a voice came out of the t .... Rev 19:5
And I saw a great white t, and him .... Rev 20:11
And he that sat upon the t said .... Rev 21:5
proceeding out of the t of God .... Rev 22:1
the t of God and of the Lamb .... Rev 22:3

THRONES

For there are set t of judgment .... Ps 122:5
the t of the house of David .... Ps 122:5
t all the kings of the nations .... Is 14:9
sea shall come down from their t .... Eze 26:16
behold till the t were cast down .... Dan 7:9
ye also shall sit upon twelve t .... Mt 19:28
sit t judging the twelve .... Lk 22:30
and invisible, whether they be t .... Col 1:16
And I saw t, and they sat upon them .... Rev 20:4

THRONG

multitude, lest they should t him .... Mk 3:9
Master, the multitude t thee .... Lk 8:45

THRONGED

people followed him, and t him .... Mk 5:24
But as he went the people t him .... Lk 8:42

THRONGING

Thou seest the multitude t .... Mk 5:31

THROUGH

is filled with violence t thee .... Gen 6:13
Abram passed t the land unto the .... Gen 12:6
walk t the land in the length of .... Gen 13:17
I will pass t all thy flock to .... Gen 30:32
the land perish not t the famine .... Gen 41:36
field, t all the land of Egypt .... Ex 10:15
For I will pass t the land of .... Ex 12:12
pass t to smite the Egyptians .... Ex 12:23
that God led them not t the way .... Ex 13:17
the way of the wilderness of .... Ex 13:18
dry ground t the midst of the sea .... Ex 14:16
Egyptians t the pillar of fire .... Ex 14:24
shall surely be stoned, or shot t .... Ex 19:13
lest they break t unto the LORD .... Ex 19:21
the people break t to come up .... Ex 19:24
shall bore his ear t with an aul .... Ex 21:6
the boards from the one end to .... Ex 36:33
If a soul shall sin t ignorance .... Lev 4:2
of Israel sin t ignorance .... Lev 4:13
done somewhat t ignorance against .... Lev 4:22
the common people sin t ignorance .... Lev 4:27
sin t ignorance, in the holy .... Lev 5:15
seed pass t the fire to Molech .... Lev 18:21
shalt the sword go t your land .... Lev 26:6
t which we have gone to search it .... Num 13:32
which we passed t to search it .... Num 14:7
And if any soul sin t ignorance .... Num 15:27
for him that sinneth t ignorance .... Num 15:28
pass, I pray thee, t thy country .... Num 20:17
we will not pass t the fields .... Num 20:17
or t the vineyards, neither will .... Num 20:17
any thing else, go t on my feet .... Num 20:19
And he said, Thou shalt not go t .... Num 20:20
give Israel passage t his border .... Num 21:22
Let us pass t thy land .... Num 21:22
Israel to pass t his border .... Num 21:23
pierce them t with his arrows .... Num 24:8
tent, and thrust both of them t .... Num 25:8
Israel, and the woman t her belly .... Num 25:8
t the counsel of Balaam, to .... Num 31:16
ye shall make it go t the fire .... Num 31:23
fire ye shall make go t the water .... Num 31:23
passed t the midst of the sea .... Num 33:8
we went t all that great and .... Deut 1:19
Ye are to pass t the coast of .... Deut 2:4
walking t this great wilderness .... Deut 2:7
the way of the plain from Elath .... Deut 2:8
Thou shalt pass t over t Ar .... Deut 2:18
Let me pass t thy land .... Deut 2:27
only I will pass t on my feet .... Deut 2:28
thee out thence t a mighty hand .... Deut 5:15
Who led thee t that great .... Deut 8:15
hast redeemed t thy greatness .... Deut 9:26

thrust it *t* thy ear unto the door	Deut 15:17
his daughter to pass *t* the fire	Deut 18:10
how we came *t* the nations which	Deut 29:16
to anger *t* the work of your hands	Deut 31:29
t this thing ye shall prolong	Deut 32:47
smite *t* the loins of them that	Deut 33:11
Pass *t* the host, and command the	Josh 1:11
them down by a cord *t* the window	Josh 2:15
that the officers went *t* the host	Josh 3:2
go *t* the land, and describe it	Josh 18:4
walk *t* the land, and describe it	Josh 18:8
passed *t* the land, and described	Josh 18:9
went up *t* the mountains westward	Josh 17:18
all the people *t* whom we passed	Josh 24:17
That *t* them I may prove Israel,	Judg 2:22
Then Ehud went forth *t* the porch	Judg 3:23
and the travellers walked *t* byways	Judg 5:6
pierced and stricken *t* his temples	Judg 5:26
cried *t* the lattice, Why is his	Judg 5:28
And his young man thrust him *t*	Judg 9:54
walked *t* the wilderness unto the	Judg 11:16
me, I pray thee, pass *t* thy land	Judg 11:17
went along *t* the wilderness	Judg 11:18
thee, *t* thy land into my place	Judg 11:19
not Israel to pass *t* his coast	Judg 11:20
men *t* all the tribe of Benjamin	Judg 20:12
he passed *t* mount Ephraim, and	1Sa 9:4
passed *t* the land of Shalisha,	1Sa 9:4
then they passed *t* the land of	1Sa 9:4
he passed *t* the land of	1Sa 9:4
Michal let David down *t* a window	1Sa 19:12
sword, and thrust me *t* therewith	1Sa 31:4
uncircumcised come and thrust me *t*	1Sa 31:4
walked all that night *t* the plain	2Sa 2:29
went *t* all Bithron, and they came	2Sa 2:29
gat them away *t* the plain all	2Sa 4:7
Saul's daughter looked *t* a window	2Sa 6:16
and made them pass *t* the brickkiln	2Sa 12:31
thrust them *t* the heart of	2Sa 18:14
he went *t* all the tribes of	2Sa 20:14
T the brightness before him were	2Sa 22:13
For by thee I have run *t* a troop	2Sa 22:30
the three mighty men brake *t* the	2Sa 23:16
Go now *t* all the tribes of Israel	2Sa 24:2
when they had gone *t* all the land	2Sa 24:8
Ahaziah fell down *t* a lattice in	2Kin 1:2
The way *t* the wilderness of Edom	2Kin 3:8
to break *t* even unto the king of	2Kin 3:26
And Jehu sent *t* all Israel	2Kin 10:21
made his son to pass *t* the fire	2Kin 16:3
daughters to pass *t* the fire	2Kin 17:17
he made his son pass *t* the fire	2Kin 21:6
to pass *t* the fire to Molech	2Kin 23:10
For *t* the anger of the Lord it	2Kin 24:20
sword, and thrust me *t* therewith	1Chr 10:4
the three brake *t* the host of the	1Chr 11:18
he went out again *t* the people	2Chr 19:4
they came *t* the high gate into	2Chr 23:20
they made a proclamation *t* Judah	2Chr 24:9
to city *t* the country of Ephraim	2Chr 30:10
daughters, *t* all the congregation	2Chr 31:18
the brook that ran *t* the midst of	2Chr 32:4
t the fire in the valley of the	2Chr 33:6
they prospered *t* the prophesying	Ezr 6:14
so that they went *t* the midst of	Neh 9:11
t the street of the city, and	Est 6:9
t the street of the city, and	Est 6:11
and terrifiest me *t* visions	Job 7:14
Yet *t* the scent of water it will	Job 14:9
bow of steel shall strike him *t*	Job 20:24
can he judge *t* the dark cloud	Job 22:13
In the dark they dig *t* houses	Job 24:16
he smiteth *t* the proud	Job 26:12
by his light I walked *t* darkness	Job 29:3
I went out to the gate *t* the city	Job 29:7
his nose pierceth *t* snares	Job 40:24
or bore his jaw *t* with a thorn	Job 41:2
whatsoever passeth *t* the paths of	Ps 8:8
the pride of his countenance	Ps 10:4
For by thee I have run *t* a troop	Ps 18:29
line is gone out *t* all the earth	Ps 19:4
t the mercy of the most High he	Ps 21:7
though I walk *t* the valley of the	Ps 23:4
my bones waxed old *t* my roaring	Ps 32:3
T thee will we push down our	Ps 44:5
t thy name will we tread down	Ps 44:5
T God we shall do valiantly	Ps 60:12
t the greatness of thy power	Ps 66:3
they went *t* the flood on foot	Ps 66:6
we went *t* fire and *t* water	Ps 66:12
thou didst march *t* the wilderness	Ps 68:7
their tongue walketh *t* the earth	Ps 73:9
the sea, and caused them to pass *t*	Ps 78:13
when he went out *t* the land of	Ps 81:5
Who passing *t* the valley of Baca	Ps 84:6
hast made me glad *t* thy work	Ps 92:4
so he led them *t* the depths	Ps 106:9
the depths, as *t* the wilderness	Ps 106:9
and brought low *t* oppression	Ps 107:39
T God we shall do valiantly	Ps 108:13
My knees are weak *t* fasting	Ps 109:24
t kings in the day of his wrath	Ps 110:5
neither speak they *t* their throat	Ps 115:7
Thou *t* thy commandments hast made	Ps 119:98
T thy precepts I	Ps 119:104
Israel to pass *t* the midst of it	Ps 136:14
led his people *t* the wilderness	Ps 136:16
my house I looked *t* my casement	Prov 7:6
Passing *t* the street near her	Prov 7:8
Till a dart strike *t* his liver	Prov 7:23

but *t* knowledge shall the just be	Prov 11:9
T desire a man, having separated	Prov 18:1
T wisdom is an house builded	Prov 24:3
For a dream cometh *t* the	Eccl 5:3
t idleness of the hands the house	Eccl 10:18
of the hands the house droppeth *t*	Eccl 10:18
shewing himself *t* the lattice	Song 2:9
And he shall pass *t* Judah	Is 8:8
And they shall pass *t* it, hardly	Is 8:21
T the wrath of the Lord of hosts	Is 9:19
that is found shall be thrust *t*	Is 13:15
thrust *t* with a sword, that go	Is 14:19
they wandered *t* the wilderness	Is 16:8
As whirlwinds in the south pass *t*	Is 21:1
Pass *t* thy land as a river, O	Is 23:10
I would go *t* them, I would burn	Is 27:4
But they also have erred *t* wine	Is 28:7
t strong drink are out of the way	Is 28:7
prophet have erred *t* strong drink	Is 28:7
are out of the way *t* strong drink	Is 28:7
overflowing scourge shall pass *t*	Is 28:15
overflowing scourge shall pass *t*	Is 28:18
For *t* the voice of the Lord shall	Is 30:31
none shall pass *t* it for ever	Is 34:10
When thou passest *t* the waters	Is 43:2
t the rivers, they shall not	Is 43:2
when thou walkest *t* the fire	Is 43:2
when he led them *t* the deserts	Is 48:21
hated, so that no man went *t* thee	Is 60:15
Go *t*, go *t* the gates	Is 62:10
That led them *t* the deep, as an	Is 63:13
that led us *t* the wilderness,	Jer 2:6
t a land of deserts and of pits,	Jer 2:6
t a land of drought, and of the	Jer 2:6
t a land that no man passed	Jer 2:6
a land that no man passed	Jer 2:6
t came to pass *t* the lightness	Jer 3:9
fro *t* the streets of Jerusalem,	Jer 5:1
t deceit they refuse to know me,	Jer 9:6
up, so that none can pass *t* them	Jer 9:10
a wilderness, that none passeth *t*	Jer 9:12
all high places *t* the wilderness	Jer 12:12
to bring in no burden *t* the gates	Jer 17:24
to pass *t* the fire unto Molech	Jer 32:35
that are thrust *t* in her streets	Jer 51:4
t all her land the wounded shall	Jer 51:52
For *t* the anger of the Lord it	Lam 4:9
that our prayer should not pass *t*	Lam 3:44
stricken *t* for want of the fruits	Lam 4:9
cup also shall pass *t* unto thee	Lam 4:21
and blood shall pass *t* thee	Eze 5:17
be scattered *t* the countries	Eze 6:8
Go *t* the midst of the city,	Eze 9:4
t the midst of Jerusalem, and set	Eze 9:4
Go ye after him *t* the city	Eze 9:5
Dig thou *t* the wall in their	Eze 12:5
in the even I digged *t* the wall	Eze 12:7
they shall dig *t* the wall to	Eze 12:12
estranged from me *t* their idols	Eze 14:5
noisome beasts to pass *t* the land	Eze 14:15
that no man may pass *t* because of	Eze 14:15
and say, Sword, go *t* the land	Eze 14:17
it was perfect *t* my comeliness	Eze 16:14
them to pass *t* the fire for them	Eze 16:21
hast discovered *t* thy	Eze 16:36
thrust thee *t* with their swords	Eze 16:40
and disperse them *t* the countries	Eze 20:23
in that they caused to pass *t* the	Eze 20:26
make your sons to pass *t* the fire	Eze 20:31
me, to pass for them *t* the fire	Eze 23:37
No foot of man shall pass *t* it	Eze 29:11
nor foot of beast shall pass *t* it	Eze 29:11
disperse them *t* the countries	Eze 29:12
disperse them *t* the countries	Eze 30:23
desolate, that none shall pass *t*	Eze 33:28
wandered *t* all the mountains	Eze 34:6
were dispersed *t* the countries	Eze 36:19
passing *t* the land to bury with	Eze 39:14
passengers that pass *t* the land	Eze 39:15
it was made *t* all the house round	Eze 41:19
After he brought me *t* the entry	Eze 46:19
and he brought me *t* the waters	Eze 47:3
and brought me *t* the waters	Eze 47:4
a thousand, and brought me *t*	Eze 47:4
t his policy also he shall cause	Dan 8:25
by his strength *t* his riches he	Dan 11:2
come, and overflow, and pass *t*	Dan 11:10
no strangers pass *t* her any more	Joel 3:17
you forty years *t* the wilderness	Amos 2:10
for I will pass *t* thee, saith the	Amos 5:17
published *t* Nineveh by the decree	Jonah 3:7
up, and have passed *t* the gate	Mic 2:13
who, if he go *t*, both treadeth	Nah 1:12
be cut down, when he shall pass *t*	Nah 1:12
wicked shall no more pass *t* thee	Nah 1:15
selleth nations *t* her whoredoms	Nah 3:4
families *t* her witchcrafts	Nah 3:4
which shall march *t* the breadth	Hab 1:6
Thou didst march *t* the land in	Hab 3:12
Thou didst strike *t* with his	Hab 3:14
Thou didst walk *t* the sea with	Hab 3:15
t the heap of great waters	Hab 3:15
to walk to and fro *t* the earth	Zec 1:10
fro *t* the earth, and, behold, all	Zec 1:11
My cities *t* prosperity shall yet	Zec 1:17
run to and fro *t* the whole earth	Zec 4:10
the two golden pipes empty the	Zec 4:12
their resemblance *t* all the earth	Zec 5:6
might walk to and fro *t* the earth	Zec 6:7

hence, walk to and fro *t* the earth	Zec 6:7
they walked to and fro *t* the earth	Zec 6:7
that no man passed *t* nor returned	Zec 7:14
shall pass *t* them any more	Zec 9:8
drink, and make a noise as *t* wine	Zec 9:15
heart shall rejoice as *t* wine	Zec 10:7
he shall pass *t* the sea with	Zec 10:11
thrust him *t* when he prophesieth	Zec 13:3
bring the third part *t* the fire	Zec 13:9
corrupt, and where thieves break *t*	Mt 6:19
thieves do not break *t* nor steal	Mt 6:20
He casteth out devils *t* the	Mt 9:34
on the sabbath day *t* the corn	Mt 12:1
of a man, he walketh *t* dry places	Mt 12:43
camel to go *t* the eye of a needle	Mt 19:24
that he went *t* the corn fields on	Mk 2:23
ran *t* that whole region round	Mk 6:55
of none effect *t* your tradition	Mk 7:13
t the midst of the coasts of	Mk 7:31
thence, and passed *t* Galilee	Mk 9:30
camel to go *t* the eye of a needle	Mk 10:25
carry any vessel *t* the temple	Mk 11:16
T the tender mercy of our God	Lk 1:78
shall pierce *t* thy own soul also	Lk 2:35
him *t* all the region round about	Lk 4:14
But he passing *t* the midst of	Lk 4:30
let him down *t* the tiling with	Lk 5:19
that he went *t* the corn fields	Lk 6:1
went *t* the towns, preaching the	Lk 9:6
are subject unto us *t* thy name	Lk 10:17
He casteth out devils *t* Beelzebub	Lk 11:15
I cast out devils *t* Beelzebub	Lk 11:18
of man, he walketh *t* dry places	Lk 11:24
suffered his house to be broken *t*	Lk 12:39
he went *t* the cities and villages	Lk 13:22
woe unto him, *t* whom they come	Lk 17:1
that he passed *t* the midst of	Lk 17:11
a camel to go *t* a needle's eye	Lk 18:25
Jesus entered and passed *t* Jericho	Lk 19:1
that all men *t* him might believe	Jn 1:7
the world *t* him might be saved	Jn 3:17
And he must needs go *t* Samaria	Jn 4:4
going *t* the midst of them, and so	Jn 8:59
Now ye are clean *t* the word which	Jn 15:3
keep *t* thine own name those whom	Jn 17:11
Sanctify them *t* thy truth	Jn 17:17
might be sanctified *t* the truth	Jn 17:19
shall believe on me *t* their word	Jn 17:20
ye might have life *t* his name	Jn 20:31
after that he *t* the Holy Ghost	Acts 1:2
his name *t* faith in his name hath	Acts 3:16
I wot that *t* ignorance ye did it,	Acts 3:17
preached *t* Jesus the resurrection	Acts 4:2
when Simon saw that *t* laying on	Acts 8:18
passing *t* he preached in all the	Acts 8:40
that *t* his name whosoever	Acts 10:43
out, and passed on *t* one street	Acts 12:10
when they had gone *t* the isle	Acts 13:6
that *t* this man is preached unto	Acts 13:38
that we must *t* much tribulation	Acts 14:22
the church, they passed *t* Phenice	Acts 15:3
But we believe that *t* the grace	Acts 15:11
And he went *t* Syria and Cilicia,	Acts 15:41
And as they went *t* the cities	Acts 16:4
when they had passed *t* Amphipolis	Acts 17:1
much which had believed *t* grace	Acts 18:27
Paul having passed *t* the upper	Acts 19:1
when he had passed *t* Macedonia	Acts 20:3
he purposed to return *t* Macedonia	Acts 20:3
who said to Paul *t* the Spirit	Acts 21:4
I thank my God *t* Jesus Christ for	Rom 1:8
gave them up to uncleanness *t* the	Rom 1:24
t breaking the law dishonourest	Rom 2:23
among the Gentiles *t* you, as it	Rom 2:24
abounded *t* my lie unto his glory	Rom 3:7
grace *t* the redemption that is in	Rom 3:24
propitiation *t* faith in his blood	Rom 3:25
righteousness of God	Rom 3:30
faith, and uncircumcision *t* faith	Rom 3:30
we then make void the law *t* faith	Rom 3:31
t the law, but *t* the	Rom 4:13
at the promise of God *t* unbelief	Rom 4:20
with God *t* our Lord Jesus Christ	Rom 5:1
shall be saved from wrath *t* him	Rom 5:9
in God *t* our Lord Jesus Christ	Rom 5:11
For if *t* the offence of one many	Rom 5:15
even so might grace reign *t*	Rom 5:21
but alive unto God *t* Jesus Christ	Rom 6:11
life *t* Jesus Christ our Lord	Rom 6:23
I thank God *t* Jesus Christ our	Rom 7:25
in that it was weak *t* the flesh	Rom 8:3
but if ye *t* the Spirit do mortify	Rom 8:13
conquerors *t* him that loved us	Rom 8:37
but rather *t* their fall salvation	Rom 11:11
obtained mercy *t* their unbelief	Rom 11:30
that *t* your mercy they also may	Rom 11:31
t him, and to him, are all things	Rom 11:36
t the grace given unto me, to	Rom 12:3
that we *t* patience and comfort of	Rom 15:4
t the power of the Holy Ghost	Rom 15:13
t Jesus Christ in those things	Rom 15:17
t mighty signs and wonders, by the	Rom 15:19
be glory *t* Jesus Christ for ever	Rom 16:27
to you in Jesus Christ *t* the will of God	1Cor 1:1
have begotten you *t* the gospel	1Cor 4:15
t thy knowledge shall the weak	1Cor 8:11
cloud, and all passed *t* the sea	1Cor 10:1
t a glass, darkly	1Cor 13:12
For now we see *t* a glass, darkly	1Cor 13:12
victory *t* our Lord Jesus Christ	1Cor 15:57
when I shall pass *t* Macedonia	1Cor 16:5

T

for I do pass t Macedonia 1Cor 16:5
have we t Christ to God-ward 2Cor 3:4
might t the thanksgiving of many 2Cor 4:15
that ye t his poverty might be 2Cor 8:9
which causeth t us thanksgiving 2Cor 9:11
but mighty t God to the pulling 2Cor 10:4
beguiled Eve t his subtilty 2Cor 11:3
t a window in a basket was I let 2Cor 11:33
measure t the abundance of the 2Cor 12:7
he was crucified t weakness 2Cor 13:4
For I t the law am dead to the .... Gal 2:19
would justify the heathen t faith .... Gal 3:8
on the Gentiles t Jesus Christ .... Gal 3:14
the promise of the Spirit t faith .... Gal 3:14
son, then an heir of God t Christ .... Gal 4:7
Ye know how t infirmity of the .... Gal 4:13
For we t the Spirit wait for the .... Gal 5:5
have confidence in you t the Lord .... Gal 5:10
we have redemption t his blood .... Eph 1:7
kindness toward us t Christ Jesus .... Eph 2:7
For by grace are ye saved t faith .... Eph 2:8
For t him we both have access by .... Eph 2:18
an habitation of God t the Spirit .... Eph 2:22
all, and t all, and in you all .... Eph 4:6
t the ignorance that is in them .... Eph 4:18
to my salvation t your prayer .... Phil 1:19
be done t strife or vainglory .... Phil 2:3
but that which is t the faith of .... Phil 3:9
hearts and minds t Christ Jesus .... Phil 4:7
I can do all things t Christ .... Phil 4:13
we have redemption t his blood .... Col 1:14
having made peace t the blood of .... Col 1:20
In the body of his flesh t death .... Col 1:22
any man spoil you t philosophy .... Col 2:8
also ye are risen with him t the .... Col 2:12
chosen you to salvation t 2Th 2:13
consolation and good hope t grace 2Th 2:16
themselves t with many sorrows 1Ti 6:10
immortality to light t the gospel 2Ti 1:10
make thee wise unto salvation t 2Ti 3:15
manifested his word t preaching .... Titus 1:3
t Jesus Christ our Saviour .... Titus 3:6
for I trust that t your prayers I .... Philem 22
salvation perfect t sufferings .... Heb 2:10
that t death he might destroy him .... Heb 2:14
deliver them who t fear of death .... Heb 2:15
the deceitfulness of sin .... Heb 3:13
but followers of them who t faith .... Heb 6:12
who t the eternal Spirit offered .... Heb 9:14
t the offering of the body of .... Heb 10:10
the veil, that is to say, his... .... Heb 10:20
he understand that the .... Heb 11:3
t faith also Sara herself .... Heb 11:11
t faith he kept the passover, and .... Heb 11:28
By faith they passed t the Red .... Heb 11:29
Who t faith subdued kingdoms, ... Heb 11:33
obtained a good report t faith .... Heb 11:39
stoned, or thrust t with a dart .... Heb 12:20
t the blood of the everlasting .... Heb 13:20
in his sight, t Jesus Christ .... Heb 13:21
t sanctification of the Spirit 1Pet 1:2
are kept by the power of God t 1Pet 1:5
ye are in heaviness t manifold 1Pet 1:6
t the Spirit unto unfeigned love 1Pet 1:22
may be glorified t Jesus Christ 1Pet 4:11
us t the righteousness of God 2Pet 1:1
unto you t the knowledge of God 2Pet 1:2
t the knowledge of him that hath 2Pet 1:3
that is in the world t lust 2Pet 1:4
t covetousness shall they with 2Pet 2:3
they allure t the lusts of the 2Pet 2:18
t much wantonness, those that 2Pet 2:18
world t the knowledge of the Lord 2Pet 2:20
world, that we might live t him 1Jn 4:9
flying t the midst of heaven .... Rev 8:13
of the earth are waxed rich t the .... Rev 18:3
may enter in t the gates into the .... Rev 22:14

THROUGHLY

let us make brick, and burn them t ..... Gen 11:3
O that my grief were t weighed .... Job 6:2
Wash me t from mine iniquity, and ..... Ps 51:2
They shall t glean the remnant of ...... Jer 6:9
For if ye t amend your ways and .... Jer 7:5
if ye t execute judgment between .... Jer 7:5
he shall t plead their cause, ... Jer 50:34
t I washed away thy blood from .... Eze 16:9
he will t purge his floor, and... .... Mt 3:12
he will t purge his floor, and .... Lk 3:17
but we have been t made manifest 2Cor 11:6
t furnished unto all good works 2Ti 3:17

THROUGHOUT

plenty t all the land of Egypt .... Gen 41:29
went t all the land of Egypt .... Gen 41:46
a ruler t all the land of Egypt .... Gen 45:8
people were scattered abroad t .... Ex 5:12
be blood t all the land of Egypt ...... Ex 7:19
there was blood t all the land of ...... Ex 7:21
lice t all the land of Egypt .... Ex 8:16
lice t all the land of Egypt .... Ex 8:17
beast, t all the land of Egypt .... Ex 9:9
may be declared t all the earth .... Ex 9:16
of the field, t the land of Egypt ..... Ex 9:22
the hail smote t all the land of ...... Ex 9:25
great cry t all the land of .... Ex 11:6
to the LORD t your generations ...... Ex 12:14
be a continual burnt offering t .... Ex 29:42
the LORD t your generations .... Ex 30:8
upon it t your generations .... Ex 30:10
to his seed t their generations .... Ex 30:21

oil unto me t your generations .... Ex 30:31
me and you t your generations .... Ex 31:13
the sabbath t their generations .... Ex 31:16
out from gate to gate t the camp .... Ex 32:27
any man be seen t all the mount ..... Ex 34:3
Ye shall kindle no fire t your .... Ex 35:3
it to be proclaimed t the camp .... Ex 36:6
so t the six branches going out ...... Ex 37:19
priesthood t their generations .... Ex 40:15
of Israel, t all their journeys .... Ex 40:38
generations t all your dwellings ..... Lev 3:17
for ever t their generations .... Lev 7:36
for ever t your generations .... Lev 10:9
unto them t their generations .... Lev 17:7
t your generations in all your .... Lev 23:14
your dwellings t your generations .. Lev 23:21
t your generations in all your .... Lev 23:31
the trumpet sound t all your land ... Lev 25:9
proclaim liberty t all the land .... Lev 25:10
that bought it t his generations ..... Lev 25:30
t their generations, after their ...... Num 1:42
his own standard, t their hosts ...... Num 1:52
of Judah pitch t their armies .... Num 2:3
be our four hundred, t their armies . Num 2:9
hundred and fifty, t their armies .... Num 2:16
and an hundred, t their armies .... Num 2:24
t their hosts were six hundred... .... Num 2:32
t their families, all the males, ... Num 3:39
the houses of their fathers, by ...... Num 4:22
t their families, and by the house .. Num 4:38
t their families, by the house of ... Num 4:40
t their families, by the house of ... Num 4:42
for ever t your generations .... Num 10:8
of all the camps t their families .... Num 10:25
the people weep t their families ..... Num 11:10
garments t their generations .... Num 15:38
for ever t your generations .... Num 15:38
t their fathers' house, all that ...... Num 26:2
month t the months of the year ..... Num 28:14
for every lamb, t the seven lambs .. Num 28:21
t the seven days, the meat of the ... Num 28:24
unto one lamb, t the seven lambs ... Num 28:29
for one lamb, t the seven lambs .... Num 29:4
for one lamb, t the seven lambs .... Num 29:10
t all the tribes of Israel, shall .... Num 31:4
t your generations in all your ...... Num 35:29
thy God giveth thee, t thy tribes .. Deut 16:18
have olive trees t all thy coasts ... Deut 28:40
thou trustedst, t all thy land ...... Deut 28:52
in all thy gates t all thy land .... Deut 28:52
sought them t all the way .... Josh 2:22
fame was noised t all the country . Josh 6:27
up from Jericho t mount Beth-el ... Josh 16:1
prince t all the tribes of Israel ... Josh 18:4
led him t all the land of Canaan, .. Josh 24:3
he sent messengers t all Manasseh . Judg 6:35
his fellow, even t all the host .... Judg 7:22
messengers t all mount Ephraim ... Judg 7:24
sent her t all the country of the .. Judg 20:6
t all the tribes of Israel .... Judg 20:10
deadly destruction t all the city . 1Sa 5:11
sent them t all the coasts of 1Sa 7:14
blew the trumpet t all the land .. 1Sa 13:3
found t all the land of Israel 1Sa 13:19
out t all the thousands of Judah .. 1Sa 23:23
t Edom put he garrisons, and 2Sa 8:14
But Absalom sent spies t all the .. 2Sa 15:10
strife t all the tribes of Israel .. 2Sa 19:9
damsel t all the coasts of Israel . 1Kin 1:3
finished t all the parts thereof .. 1Kin 6:9
made a proclamation t Judah 1Kin 15:22
there went a proclamation t the .. 1Kin 18:6
of Assyria came up t all the land . 2Kin 17:5
they dwelt in their tents t all .. 1Chr 5:10
t their castles in their families . 1Chr 6:54
All their cities t their families . 1Chr 6:54
to the sons of Gershom t their ... 1Chr 6:62
t their families, out of the 1Chr 6:63
the number t the genealogy of ... 1Chr 7:40
were chief t their generations ... 1Chr 7:40
famous t the house of their 1Chr 9:34
went t all Israel, and came to .. 1Chr 13:2
to all the coasts of Israel 1Chr 21:4
fame and of glory t all countries . 1Chr 22:5
that ruled t the house of their .. 1Chr 26:6
went out month by month t all .. 1Chr 27:1
t all the land of his dominion .. 2Chr 9:26
t all the countries of Judah 2Chr 11:23
fro t the whole earth, to shew .. 2Chr 16:9
went about t all the cities of .. 2Chr 17:9
in the fenced cities t all Judah . 2Chr 17:19
he set judges in the land t all . 2Chr 19:5
and proclaimed a fast t all Judah . 2Chr 20:3
fathers, t all Judah and Benjamin . 2Chr 25:5
for them t all their shields 2Chr 26:14
to make proclamation t all Israel . 2Chr 30:5
king and his princes t all Israel . 2Chr 30:6
they did eat t the feast seven .. 2Chr 30:22
And thus did Hezekiah t all Judah . 2Chr 31:20
idols t all the land of Israel .. 2Chr 34:7
a proclamation t his kingdom ... 2Chr 36:22
a proclamation t all his kingdom . Ezr 1:1
And they made proclamation t Judah . Ezr 10:7
be published t all his empire ... Est 1:20
the whole kingdom of Ahasuerus .. Est 3:6
together in their cities t all .. Est 8:11
fame went out t all the provinces . Est 9:4
kept t every generation, every .. Est 9:28
and moon endure, t all generations . Ps 72:5

thy years are t all generations ...... Ps 102:24
O LORD, t all generations .... Ps 135:13
endureth t all generations .... Ps 145:13
places for him, t all thy borders ... Ps 147:14
against him t all my mountains .... Eze 38:21
And his fame went t all Syria .... Mt 4:24
his fame spread abroad t all the .... Mk 1:28
in their synagogues t all Galilee ... Mk 1:39
be preached t the whole world .... Mk 14:9
sayings were noised abroad t all .... Lk 1:65
great famine was t all the land ..... Lk 4:25
of him went forth t all Judaea ...... Lk 4:25 (?)
t all the region round about .... Lk 7:17
that he went t every city .... Lk 8:1
published t the whole city how ..... Lk 8:39
teaching t all Jewry, beginning .... Lk 23:5
seam, woven from the top t .... Jn 19:23
abroad t the regions of Judaea .... Acts 8:1
the churches rest t all Judaea .... Acts 9:31
as Peter passed t all quarters .... Acts 9:32
And it was known t all Joppa ..... Acts 9:42
which was published t all Judaea .. Acts 10:37
be great dearth t all the world ... Acts 11:28
was published t all the region ... Acts 13:49
after they had passed t Pisidia .. Acts 14:24
Now when they had gone t Phrygia . Acts 16:6
at Ephesus, but almost t all Asia . Acts 19:26
among all the Jews t the world ... Acts 24:5
t all the coasts of Judaea, and .. Acts 26:20
is spoken of t the whole world ... Rom 1:8
might be declared t all the earth . Rom 9:17
in the gospel t all the churches .. 2Cor 8:18
church by Christ Jesus t all ages . Eph 3:21
the strangers scattered t Pontus .. 1Pet 1:1

THROW

ye shall t down their altars .... Judg 2:2
t down the altar of Baal that thy .. Judg 6:25
battered the wall, to t it down 2Sa 20:15
And he said, T her down 2Kin 9:33
to t down, to build, and to plant .. Jer 1:10
to t down, and to destroy, and to .. Jer 31:28
they shall t down thine eminent ... Eze 16:39
t down all thy strong holds... .... Mic 5:11
shall build, but I will t down .... Mal 1:4

THROWING

And if he smite him with t a stone .. Num 35:17

THROWN

his rider hath he t into the sea .... Ex 15:1
his rider hath he t into the sea .... Ex 15:21
because he hath t down his altar ... Judg 6:32
his head shall be t to thee over ... 2Sa 20:21
t down thine altars, and slain thy . 1Kin 19:10
t down thine altars, and slain thy . 1Kin 19:14
nor t down any more for ever ..... Jer 31:40
which are t down by the mounts, .. Jer 33:4
are fallen, her walls are t down .. Jer 50:15
he hath t down in his wrath the .. Lam 2:2
he hath t down, and hath not .... Lam 2:17
I will leave thee t into the .... Eze 29:5
and the mountains shall be t down . Eze 38:20
and the rocks are t down by him .. Nah 1:6
another, that shall not be t down . Mt 24:2
another, that shall not be t down . Mk 13:2
the devil hath t him in the midst . Lk 4:35
another, that shall not be t down . Lk 21:6
that great city Babylon be t down . Rev 18:21

THRUST

he shall surely t you out hence .... Ex 11:1
because they were t out of Egypt, .. Ex 12:39
she t herself unto the wall, and ... Num 22:25
t both of them through, the man ... Num 25:8
But if he t him of hatred, or ..... Num 35:20
But if he t him suddenly without .. Num 35:22
to t thee out of the way which .... Deut 13:5
because he hath sought to t thee .. Deut 13:10
t it through his ear unto the .... Deut 15:17
he shall t out the enemy from ... Deut 33:27
thigh, and t it into his belly ... Judg 3:21
t the fleece together, and wringed . Judg 6:38
Zebul t out Gaal and his brethren . Judg 9:41
And his young man t him through .. Judg 9:54
they t out Jephthah, and said unto . Judg 11:2
that I may t out all your right .. 1Sa 11:2
sword, and t me through therewith . 1Sa 31:4
t me through, and abuse me 1Sa 31:4
t his sword in his fellow's side .. 2Sa 2:16
t them through the heart of 2Sa 18:14
but all drawn a thorns t away 2Sa 23:6
So Solomon t out Abiathar from ... 1Kin 2:27
Gehazi came near to t her away ... 2Kin 4:27
sword, and t me through therewith . 1Chr 10:4
they t him out from thence 2Chr 26:20
Thou hast t sore at me that I ... Ps 118:13
that is found shall be t through .. Is 13:15
t through with a sword, that go .. Is 14:19
they that are t through in her .. Jer 51:4
t thee through with their swords . Eze 16:40
Because ye have t with side .... Eze 34:21
to t them out of their possession . Eze 46:18
Neither shall one t another .... Joel 2:8
t him through when he prophesieth . Zec 13:3
t him out of the city, and led him . Lk 4:29
prayed him that he would t out a .. Lk 5:3
heaven, shalt be t down to hell .. Lk 10:15
of God, and you yourselves t out . Lk 13:28
t my hand into his side, I will .. Jn 20:25
thy hand, and t it into my side .. Jn 20:27
his neighbour wrong t him away .. Acts 7:27

THRUSTETH
but *t* him from them, and in their.......... Acts 7:39
t them into the inner prison, and........... Acts 16:24
now do they *t* us out privily.................. Acts 16:37
were possible, to *t* in the ship............... Acts 27:39
stoned, or *t* through with a dart.............. Heb 12:20
cloud, T in thy sickle, and reap.............. Rev 14:15
he that sat on the cloud *t* in his............. Rev 14:16
T in thy sharp sickle, and gather............ Rev 14:18
the angel *t* in his sickle into................ Rev 14:19

THRUSTETH
God *t* him down, not man..................... Job 32:13

THUMB
upon the *t* of their right hand,............... Ex 29:20
upon the *t* of his right hand, and........... Lev 8:23
upon the *t* of his right hand, and........... Lev 14:14
upon the *t* of his right hand, and........... Lev 14:17
upon the *t* of his right hand, and........... Lev 14:25
upon the *t* of his right hand, and........... Lev 14:28

THUMBS
upon the *t* of their right hands,.............. Lev 8:24
and caught him, and cut off his *t*............ Judg 1:6
and ten kings, having their *t*................. Judg 1:7

THUMMIM (thum'-mim) A symbolic object in
the High Priest's breastplate.
of judgment the Urim and the T............ Ex 28:30
the breastplate the Urim and the T......... Lev 8:8
And of Levi he said, Let thy T................ Deut 33:8
up a priest with Urim and with T........... Ezr 2:63
stood up a priest with Urim and T.......... Neh 7:65

THUNDER
and the LORD sent *t* and hail, and........... Ex 9:23
the *t* shall cease, neither shall.............. Ex 9:29
of heaven shall he *t* upon them............. 1Sa 2:10
a great *t* on that day upon the............... 1Sa 7:10
unto the LORD, and he shall send *t*......... 1Sa 12:17
and the LORD sent *t* and rain that.......... 1Sa 12:18
but the *t* of his power who can.............. Job 26:14
a way for the lightning of the *t*.............. Job 28:26
or a way for the lightning of *t*,.............. Job 38:25
hast thou clothed his neck with *t*........... Job 39:19
the *t* of the captains, and the............... Job 39:25
or canst thou *t* with a voice like............ Job 40:9
The voice of thy *t* was in the................ Ps 77:18
thee in the secret place of *t*................. Ps 81:7
voice of thy *t* they hasted away............. Ps 104:7
of the LORD of hosts with *t*.................. Is 29:6
which is, The sons of *t*....................... Mk 3:17
heard, as it were the noise of *t*............. Rev 6:1
and as the voice of a great *t*................ Rev 14:2

THUNDERBOLTS
hail, and their flocks to hot *t*................ Ps 78:48

THUNDERED
but the LORD *t* with a great................... 1Sa 7:10
The LORD *t* from heaven, and the........... 2Sa 22:14
The LORD also *t* in the heavens,............ Ps 18:13
by, and heard it, said that it T............... Jn 12:29

THUNDERETH
he *t* with the voice of his..................... Job 37:4
God *t* marvellously with his voice.......... Job 37:5
the God of glory *t*........................... Ps 29:3

THUNDERINGS
that there be no more mighty *t*.............. Ex 9:28
And all the people saw the *t*................ Ex 20:18
throne proceeded lightnings and *t*......... Rev 4:5
and there were voices, and *t*................ Rev 8:5
were lightnings, and voices, and *t*......... Rev 11:19
and as the voice of mighty *t*................ Rev 19:6

THUNDERS
and the *t* and hail ceased, and the......... Ex 9:33
the *t* were ceased, he sinned yet........... Ex 9:34
in the morning, that there were *t*........... Ex 19:16
seven *t* uttered their voices................. Rev 10:3
when the seven *t* had uttered................ Rev 10:4
things which the seven *t* uttered........... Rev 10:4
And there were voices, and *t*................ Rev 16:18

THUS
T the heavens and the earth were.......... Gen 2:1
T did Noah.................................. Gen 6:22
T were both the daughters of Lot........... Gen 19:36
t she was reproved........................ Gen 20:16
T they made a covenant at................. Gen 21:32
saying, T spake the man unto me........... Gen 24:30
she said, If it be so, why am I.............. Gen 25:22
t Esau despised his birthright............. Gen 25:34
If he said *t*, The speckled shall........... Gen 31:8
and if he said *t*, The ringstreaked......... Gen 31:8
T God hath taken away the cattle........... Gen 31:9
T I was.................................... Gen 31:40
T have I been twenty years in thy........... Gen 31:41
T shall ye speak unto my lord.............. Gen 32:4
Thy servant Jacob saith.................... Gen 32:4
T dwelt Esau in mount Seir................. Gen 36:8
T his father wept for him................... Gen 37:35
and *t* did he unto them..................... Gen 42:25
T saith thy son Joseph, God hath.......... Gen 45:9
T shalt thou say unto the................... Ex 3:14
T shalt thou say unto the................... Ex 3:15
T saith the LORD, Israel is my.............. Ex 4:22
T saith the LORD God of Israel.............. Ex 5:1
T saith Pharaoh, I will not give............ Ex 5:10
dealest thou *t* with thy servants............ Ex 5:15
T saith the LORD, In this thou.............. Ex 7:17
T saith the LORD, Let my people........... Ex 8:1
T saith the LORD, Let my people........... Ex 8:20

T saith the LORD God of the................. Ex 9:1
T saith the LORD God of the................. Ex 9:13
T saith the LORD God of the................. Ex 10:3
T saith the LORD, About midnight........... Ex 11:4
And *t* shall ye eat it........................ Ex 12:11
T did all the children of Israel............. Ex 12:50
hast thou dealt *t* with us................... Ex 14:11
T the LORD saved Israel that day...... Ex 14:30
T shalt thou say to the house of........... Ex 19:3
T thou shalt say unto the.................. Ex 20:22
t shalt thou make for all the............... Ex 26:17
t shall it be for them both................. Ex 26:24
t shalt thou do unto Aaron, and............ Ex 29:35
T saith the LORD God of Israel,............. Ex 32:27
t did he make for all the boards........... Ex 36:22
t he did to both of them in both........... Ex 36:29
T was all the work of the.................. Ex 39:32
t did Moses............................... Ex 40:16
T shall ye separate the children........... Lev 15:31
T shall Aaron come into the holy........... Lev 16:3
But *t* do unto them, that they may......... Num 4:19
t were they numbered of him, as........... Num 4:49
t shalt thou do unto them, to.............. Num 8:7
T shalt thou separate the Levites.......... Num 8:14
T shalt thou do unto the Levites........... Num 8:26
T were the journeyings of the............. Num 11:15
And if thou deal *t* with me................. Num 11:15
t shall it be done for one................. Num 15:11
T speak unto the Levites, and say.......... Num 18:26
T ye also shall offer an heave............. Num 18:28
T saith thy brother Israel, Thou........... Num 20:14
Edom refused to give Israel............... Num 20:21
T Israel dwelt in the land of the.......... Num 21:31
T saith Balak the son of Zippor,........... Num 22:16
unto Balak, and *t* thou shalt speak........ Num 23:5
Go again unto Balak, and speak............ Num 23:16
T did your fathers, when I sent............ Num 32:8
But *t* shall ye deal with them.............. Deut 7:5
t I fell down before the LORD............... Deut 9:25
T shalt thou do unto this............... Deut 20:15
the LORD done *t* unto this land............ Deut 29:24
Do ye *t* require the LORD, O................ Deut 32:6
two men, and hid them, and said *t*......... Josh 2:4
T shalt thou do six days................... Josh 6:3
liest thou *t* upon thy face.................. Josh 7:10
for *t* saith the LORD God of................ Josh 7:13
the LORD God of Israel, and *t*.............. Josh 7:20
and I have *t* done.......................... Josh 7:20
for *t* shall the LORD do to all.............. Josh 10:25
according to their families was *t*.......... Josh 16:5
T they gave to the children of............. Josh 21:3
t were all the cities...................... Josh 21:41
T saith the whole congregation of.......... Josh 22:16
T saith the LORD God of the................ Judg 6:8
T saith the LORD God of Israel,............. Judg 6:8
him, Why hast thou served us *t*............ Judg 8:1
T was Midian subdued before the.......... Judg 8:28
T God rendered the wickedness of......... Judg 9:56
T saith Jephthah, Israel took not........... Judg 11:15
The children of Ammon unto............... Judg 11:33
Why askest thou *t* after my name.......... Judg 13:18
And he said unto them, T and.............. Judg 18:4
t dealeth Micah with me, and hath......... Judg 18:4
T they inclosed the Benjamites............ Judg 20:43
T saith the LORD, Did I plainly............. 1Sa 2:27
t he spake, Come, and let us go to......... 1Sa 10:14
T saith the LORD God of Israel,............. 1Sa 10:18
T shall ye say unto the men of............. 1Sa 14:9
If they say *t* unto us, Tarry................ 1Sa 14:9
But if they say *t*, Come up unto............ 1Sa 14:10
T saith the LORD, Behold, I will............ 1Sa 15:2
T shall ye say to David, The king.......... 1Sa 18:25
T did he unto all the cities............... 1Sa 20:7
Say *t*, It is well........................... 1Sa 20:7
But if I say *t* unto the young man.......... 1Sa 20:22
t shall ye say to him that liveth........... 1Sa 25:6
Wherefore doth my lord *t* pursue.......... 1Sa 26:18
And I will yet be more vile than *t*.......... 2Sa 6:22
T saith the LORD, Shalt thou.............. 2Sa 7:5
T saith the LORD of hosts, I took.......... 2Sa 7:8
t shalt thou say unto Joab, Let............ 2Sa 11:25
T saith the LORD God of Israel,............. 2Sa 12:7
T saith the LORD, Behold, I will............ 2Sa 12:11
t did he unto all the cities of............. 2Sa 12:31
But if he *t* say, I have no................. 2Sa 15:26
t said Shimei when he cursed,............. 2Sa 16:7
and to Abiathar the priest, *t*.............. 2Sa 17:15
T did Ahithophel counsel Absalom......... 2Sa 17:15
and *t* and *t* have I counselled............. 2Sa 17:15
for *t* hath Ahithophel counselled.......... 2Sa 17:15
Joab, I may not tarry *t* with thee.......... 2Sa 18:14
t he said, O my son Absalom, my.......... 2Sa 18:33
T saith the LORD, I offer thee.............. 2Sa 24:12
also *t* said the king, Blessed be........... 1Kin 1:48
T saith the king, Come forth............... 1Kin 2:30
T said Joab, and *t* he answered............ 1Kin 2:30
T they spake before the king.............. 1Kin 3:22
t gave Solomon to Hiram year by.......... 1Kin 5:11
T had done *t* unto this land............... 1Kin 9:8
for *t* saith the LORD, the God of........... 1Kin 11:31
T shalt thou speak unto this,.............. 1Kin 12:10
t shalt thou say unto them, My............ 1Kin 12:10
T saith the LORD, Ye shall not go.......... 1Kin 12:24
O altar, altar, *t* saith the LORD............ 1Kin 13:2
T saith the LORD, Forasmuch as........... 1Kin 13:21
t and *t* shalt thou say unto her............ 1Kin 14:5
t shalt thou say unto her.................. 1Kin 14:5
T saith the LORD God of Israel,............ 1Kin 14:7
T did Zimri destroy all the house.......... 1Kin 16:12
T saith the LORD God of................... 1Kin 17:14
said unto him, T saith Ben-hadad,......... 1Kin 20:2

T speaketh Ben-hadad, saying,.............. 1Kin 20:5
T saith the LORD, Hast thou seen.......... 1Kin 20:13
T saith the LORD, Even by the.............. 1Kin 20:14
T saith the LORD, Because the.............. 1Kin 20:28
T saith the LORD, Because thou............ 1Kin 21:19
T saith the LORD, In the place............. 1Kin 21:19
T saith the LORD, With these............... 1Kin 22:11
T saith the king, Put this fellow........... 1Kin 22:27
Now therefore I saith the LORD............. 2Kin 1:4
T saith the LORD, Is it not................. 2Kin 1:6
man of God, *t* hath the king said........... 2Kin 1:16
T saith the LORD, Forasmuch as........... 2Kin 1:16
T saith the LORD, I have healed............ 2Kin 2:21
T saith the LORD, Make this............... 2Kin 3:16
For *t* saith the LORD, Ye shall............. 2Kin 3:17
for *t* saith the LORD, They shall........... 2Kin 4:43
in, and told his lord, saying, T........... 2Kin 5:4
t said the maid that is of................. 2Kin 5:4
T saith the LORD, To morrow about......... 2Kin 7:1
T saith the LORD, I have anointed......... 2Kin 9:3
T saith the LORD God of Israel, I.......... 2Kin 9:6
And he said, T and *t* spake he to.......... 2Kin 9:12
T saith the LORD, I have anointed......... 2Kin 9:12
T saith the king, Is it peace.............. 2Kin 9:18
T saith the king, Is it peace.............. 2Kin 9:19
T Jehu destroyed Baal out of.............. 2Kin 10:28
T did Jehu: howbeit.......................... 2Kin 10:31
T saith the great king, the king........... 2Kin 18:19
T saith the king, Let not................. 2Kin 18:29
for *t* saith the king of Assyria,............ 2Kin 18:31
T saith Hezekiah, This day is a........... 2Kin 19:3
T shall ye say to your master............. 2Kin 19:6
T saith the LORD, Be not afraid............ 2Kin 19:6
T shall ye speak to Hezekiah king......... 2Kin 19:10
T saith the LORD God of Israel,............ 2Kin 19:15
Therefore *t* saith the LORD................ 2Kin 19:32
T saith the LORD, Set thine house......... 2Kin 20:1
t saith the LORD, the God of.............. 2Kin 20:5
Therefore *t* saith the LORD God of......... 2Kin 21:12
T saith the LORD God of Israel,............ 2Kin 22:15
T saith the LORD, Behold, I will........... 2Kin 22:16
t shall ye say to him, T saith............. 2Kin 22:18
T saith the LORD God of Israel,............ 2Kin 22:18
T all Israel brought up the ark............ 1Chr 15:28
T saith the LORD, Thou shalt not........... 1Chr 17:4
Now therefore *t* shalt thou say............. 1Chr 17:7
T saith the LORD of hosts, I took.......... 1Chr 17:7
The LORD preserved David................. 1Chr 18:6
T saith the LORD, I offer thee.............. 1Chr 21:10
T saith the LORD, Choose thee............. 1Chr 21:11
and *t* were they divided................... 1Chr 24:5
T were they divided by lot, one............ 1Chr 24:5
T David the son of Jesse reigned........... 2Chr 1:8
T Solomon made all these vessels.......... 2Chr 4:18
T all the work that Solomon made.......... 2Chr 5:1
T Solomon finished the house of........... 2Chr 7:11
the LORD done *t* unto this land............ 2Chr 7:21
T shalt thou say unto them................ 2Chr 10:10
t shalt thou say unto them, My............ 2Chr 10:14
T saith the LORD, Ye shall not go.......... 2Chr 11:4
T saith the LORD, Ye have................. 2Chr 12:5
The children of Israel were................ 2Chr 13:18
T saith the LORD, These make thou......... 2Chr 18:10
T saith the king, Put this fellow........... 2Chr 18:26
T shall ye do in the fear of the............ 2Chr 19:9
T saith the LORD unto you, Be not......... 2Chr 20:15
T saith the LORD God of David thy......... 2Chr 21:12
T they did day by day, and................ 2Chr 24:11
T saith God, Why transgress ye............ 2Chr 24:20
T Joash the king remembered not.......... 2Chr 24:22
t did Hezekiah throughout all............. 2Chr 31:20
T saith Sennacherib king of............... 2Chr 32:10
T the LORD saved Hezekiah and the....... 2Chr 32:22
T saith the LORD God of Israel,............ 2Chr 34:23
T saith the LORD, Behold, I will........... 2Chr 34:24
T saith the LORD God of Israel............. 2Chr 34:26
T saith Cyrus king of Persia, All.......... 2Chr 36:23
T saith Cyrus king of Persia, The......... Ezr 1:2
said *t* unto them, Who hath............... Ezr 5:3
unto him, wherein was written *t*........... Ezr 5:7
those elders, and said unto them *t*........ Ezr 5:9
t they returned us answer, saying......... Ezr 5:11
and therein was a record *t* written........ Ezr 6:2
even *t* be he shaken out, and.............. Neh 5:13
Did not your fathers *t*, and did............ Neh 13:18
t cleansed I them from all................ Neh 13:30
For the Lord spake *t* to me............... Est 1:18
Then *t* came every maiden unto the........ Est 2:13
T shall it be done to the man............. Est 6:9
T shall it be done unto the man........... Est 6:11
The Jews smote at their.................... Est 9:5
T did Job continually...................... Job 1:5
why then are ye *t* altogether vain.......... Job 27:12
T I was as a man that heareth not......... Ps 63:4
T will I bless thee while I live............ Ps 63:4
If I say, I will speak *t*.................... Ps 73:15
T my heart was grieved, and I was......... Ps 73:21
They changed their glory into............. Ps 106:20
T they provoked him to anger with......... Ps 106:29
t were they defiled with their............ Ps 106:39
that *t* shall the man be blessed............ Ps 128:4
T saith the Lord GOD, It shall............. Is 7:7
For the LORD spake *t* to me with a.......... Is 8:11
Therefore *t* saith the Lord God of.......... Is 10:24
For *t* hath the Lord said unto me,......... Is 21:6
For *t* hath the Lord said unto me,......... Is 21:16
T saith the LORD God of hosts, Go.......... Is 22:15
When *t* it shall be in the midst............ Is 24:13

Say thou t unto them, I saith .... Eze 33:27
T saith the Lord God unto the .... Eze 34:2
T saith the Lord God .... Eze 34:10
For t saith the Lord God .... Eze 34:11
O my flock, t saith the Lord God .... Eze 34:17
Therefore t saith the Lord God .... Eze 34:20
T shall they know that I the Lord. .... Eze 35:4
say unto it, T saith the Lord God .... Eze 35:7
T will I make mount Seir most .... Eze 35:13
T with your mouth ye have boasted .... Eze 35:14
T saith the Lord God .... Eze 35:14
T saith the Lord God .... Eze 36:2
and say, T saith the Lord God .... Eze 36:3
Therefore t saith the Lord God .... Eze 36:4
the valleys, T saith the Lord God .... Eze 36:6
Therefore t saith the Lord God .... Eze 36:7
T saith the Lord God .... Eze 36:13
of Israel, T saith the Lord God .... Eze 36:22
T saith the Lord God .... Eze 36:33
T saith the Lord God .... Eze 36:37
T saith the Lord God unto these .... Eze 37:5
to the wind, T saith the Lord God .... Eze 37:9
unto them, T saith the Lord God .... Eze 37:12
unto them, T saith the Lord God .... Eze 37:19
unto them, T saith the Lord God .... Eze 37:21
And say, T saith the Lord God .... Eze 38:3
T saith the Lord God .... Eze 38:10
unto Gog, T saith the Lord God .... Eze 38:14
T saith the Lord God .... Eze 38:17
T will I magnify myself, and .... Eze 38:23
Gog, and say, T saith the Lord God .... Eze 39:1
T shall they cleanse the land .... Eze 39:16
son of man, t saith the Lord God .... Eze 39:17
T ye shall be filled at my table .... Eze 39:20
Therefore t saith the Lord God .... Eze 39:25
Son of man, t saith the Lord God .... Eze 43:18
t shalt thou cleanse and purge it .... Eze 43:20
of Israel, T saith the Lord God .... Eze 44:6
T saith the Lord God .... Eze 44:9
T saith the Lord God .... Eze 45:9
T saith the Lord God .... Eze 45:18
T saith the Lord God .... Eze 46:1
T shall they prepare the lamb, and .... Eze 46:13
T saith the Lord God .... Eze 46:16
T saith the Lord God .... Eze 47:13
T Melzar took away the portion of .... Dan 1:16
he went and said t unto him .... Dan 2:24
said t unto him, I have found a .... Dan 2:25
T were the visions of mine head .... Dan 4:10
He cried aloud, and said .... Dan 4:14
said t unto him, King Darius .... Dan 6:6
and they said t unto it, Arise .... Dan 7:5
T he said, The fourth beast shall .... Dan 7:23
t shall he do .... Dan 11:17
T shall he do in the most strong .... Dan 11:30
t judgment springeth up as .... Hos 10:4
T saith the Lord .... Amos 1:3
T saith the Lord .... Amos 1:6
T saith the Lord .... Amos 1:9
T saith the Lord .... Amos 1:11
T saith the Lord .... Amos 1:13
T saith the Lord .... Amos 2:1
T saith the Lord .... Amos 2:4
T saith the Lord .... Amos 2:6
Is it not even I, O ye children .... Amos 2:11
Therefore t saith the Lord God .... Amos 3:11
T saith the Lord .... Amos 3:12
Therefore t will I do unto thee .... Amos 4:12
For t saith the Lord God .... Amos 5:3
For t saith the Lord unto the .... Amos 5:4
God of hosts, the Lord, saith t .... Amos 5:16
T hath the Lord God shewed unto .... Amos 7:1
T hath the Lord God shewed unto .... Amos 7:4
T he shewed me .... Amos 7:7
For t Amos saith, Jeroboam shall .... Amos 7:11
Therefore t saith the Lord .... Amos 7:17
T hath the Lord God shewed unto .... Amos 8:1
Therefore t saith the Lord God .... Obad 1
Therefore t will I do unto .... Mic 2:3
T saith the Lord concerning the .... Mic 3:5
t shall he deliver us from the .... Mic 5:6
T saith the Lord .... Nah 1:12
yet t shall they be cut down .... Nah 1:12
T speaketh the Lord of hosts .... Hag 1:2
Now therefore t saith the Lord of .... Hag 1:5
For t saith the Lord of hosts .... Hag 1:7
For t saith the Lord of hosts .... Hag 2:6
T saith the Lord of hosts .... Hag 2:11
T saith the Lord of hosts .... Zec 1:3
T saith the Lord .... Zec 1:4
T saith the Lord .... Zec 1:14
T saith the Lord .... Zec 1:16
T saith the Lord .... Zec 1:17
Therefore t saith the Lord .... Zec 3:7
For t saith the Lord of hosts .... Zec 6:12
T speaketh the Lord of hosts .... Zec 7:9
the land was desolate after .... Zec 7:14
T saith the Lord of hosts .... Zec 8:2
T saith the Lord of hosts .... Zec 8:3
T saith the Lord of hosts .... Zec 8:4
T saith the Lord of hosts .... Zec 8:6
T saith the Lord of hosts .... Zec 8:7
T saith the Lord of hosts .... Zec 8:9
For t saith the Lord of hosts .... Zec 8:14
T saith the Lord of hosts .... Zec 8:19
T saith the Lord of hosts .... Zec 8:20
T saith the Lord of hosts .... Zec 8:23
T saith the Lord my God .... Zec 11:4

t saith the Lord of hosts, They .... Mal 1:4
t ye brought an offering .... Mal 1:13
for t it is written by the .... Mt 2:5
for t it becometh us to fulfil .... Mt 3:15
T have ye made the commandment of .... Mt 15:6
be fulfilled, that t it must be .... Mt 26:54
doth this man t speak blasphemies .... Mk 2:7
T hath the Lord dealt with me in .... Lk 1:25
why hast thou t dealt with us .... Lk 2:48
While he t spake, there came a .... Lk 9:34
t saying thou reproachest us also .... Lk 11:45
Even t shall it be in the day .... Lk 17:30
prayed t with himself, God .... Lk 18:11
And when he had t spoken, he went .... Lk 19:28
t shall ye say unto him, Because .... Lk 19:31
answered and said, Suffer ye t far .... Lk 22:51
and having said t, he gave up the .... Lk 23:46
And as they t spake, Jesus himself .... Lk 24:36
And when he had t spoken, he .... Lk 24:40
T it is written, and I .... Lk 24:46
his journey, sat t on the well .... Jn 4:6
When he had t spoken, he spat on .... Jn 9:6
when he t had spoken, he cried .... Jn 11:43
If we let him t alone, all men .... Jn 11:48
When Jesus had t said, he was .... Jn 13:21
And when he had t spoken, one of .... Jn 18:22
And when she had t said, she .... Jn 20:14
And when he had t spoken, he .... Acts 19:41
And when he had t spoken, he .... Acts 20:36
T saith the Holy Ghost, So shall .... Acts 21:11
as he t spake for himself, Festus .... Acts 26:24
And when he had t spoken, the king .... Acts 26:30
And when he had t spoken, he took .... Acts 27:35
t are the secrets of his heart .... Rom 9:20
When I therefore was t minded 1Cor 14:25
because we t judge, that if one 2Cor 1:17
many as be perfect, be t minded 2Cor 5:14
salvation, though we t speak .... Phil 3:15
when these things were t ordained .... Heb 6:9
t I saw the horses in the vision .... Heb 9:6
be, because thou hast judged t .... Rev 16:5
T with violence shall that great .... Rev 18:21

THY See PREFACE.

THYATIRA (thi-a-ti'-rah) A city in Lydia in Asia Minor

of purple, of the city of T .... Acts 16:14
and unto Pergamos, and unto T .... Rev 1:11
angel of the church in T write .... Rev 2:18
you I say, and unto the rest in T .... Rev 2:24

THYINE

all t wood, and all manner vessels .... Rev 18:12

THYSELF

separate t, I pray thee, from me .... Gen 13:9
persons, and take the goods to t .... Gen 14:21
and submit t under her hands .... Gen 16:9
keep that thou hast unto t .... Gen 33:9
exaltest thou t against my people .... Ex 9:17
thou refuse to humble t before me .... Ex 10:3
Get thee from me, take heed to t .... Ex 10:28
why sittest thou t alone, and all .... Ex 18:14
not able to perform it t alone .... Ex 18:18
so shall it be easier for t .... Ex 18:22
Thou shalt not bow down t to them .... Ex 20:5
present t there to me in the top .... Ex 34:2
Take heed to t, lest thou make a .... Ex 34:12
and make an atonement for t .... Lev 9:7
wife, to defile t with her .... Lev 18:23
any beast to defile t therewith .... Lev 18:23
shalt love thy neighbour as t .... Lev 19:18
you, and thou shalt love him as t .... Lev 19:34
that thou bear it not t alone .... Num 11:17
except thou make t altogether a .... Num 16:13
Only take heed to t, and keep thy .... Deut 4:9
shalt not bow down t unto them .... Deut 5:9
greater and mightier than t .... Deut 9:1
Take heed to t that thou offer .... Deut 12:13
Take heed to t that thou forsake .... Deut 12:19
Take heed to t that thou be not .... Deut 12:30
thereof, shalt thou take unto t .... Deut 20:14
go astray, and hide t from them .... Deut 22:1
thou mayest not hide t .... Deut 22:3
by the way, and hide t from them .... Deut 22:4
wherewith thou coverest t .... Deut 22:12
be, when thou wilt ease t abroad .... Deut 23:13
shalt not anoint t with the oil .... Deut 28:40
cut down for t there in the wood .... Josh 17:15
Wash t therefore, and anoint thee .... Ruth 3:3
but make not t known unto the man .... Ruth 3:3
redeem thou my right to t .... Ruth 4:6
take heed to t until the morning 1Sa 19:2
in a secret place, and hide t 1Sa 20:5
be in the iniquity, slay me t 1Sa 20:8
t when the business was in hand 1Sa 20:19
from avenging t with thine own 1Sa 25:26
that then thou shalt bestir t 2Sa 5:24
to t thy people Israel to be a 2Sa 7:24
down on thy bed, and make t sick 2Sa 13:5
feign t to be a mourner, and put 2Sa 14:2
apparel, and anoint not t with oil 2Sa 14:2
thou t wouldest have set t 2Sa 18:13
wouldest have set t against me 2Sa 18:13
thou wilt shew t merciful 2Sa 22:26
man thou wilt shew t upright 2Sa 22:26
the pure thou wilt shew t pure 2Sa 22:27
thou wilt shew t unsavoury 2Sa 22:27
strong therefore, and shew t a man 1Kin 2:2
and whithersoever thou turnest t 1Kin 2:3

and hast not asked for t long life 1Kin 3:11
neither hast asked riches for t 1Kin 3:11
but hast asked for t 1Kin 3:11
Come home with me, and refresh t 1Kin 13:7
Arise, I pray thee, and disguise t 1Kin 14:2
why feignest thou t to be another 1Kin 14:6
hide t by the brook Cherith, that 1Kin 17:3
saying, Go, shew t unto Ahab 1Kin 18:1
said unto him, Go, strengthen t 1Kin 20:40
t hast decided it 1Kin 20:40
because thou hast sold t to work 1Kin 21:20
into an inner chamber to hide t 1Kin 22:25
hast humbled t before the Lord 2Kin 22:19
Now therefore advise t what reward 1Chr 21:3
asked wisdom and knowledge for t 2Chr 1:11
into an inner chamber to hide t 2Chr 18:24
thou hast joined t with Ahaziah 2Chr 20:37
house, which were better than t 2Chr 21:13
and thou didst humble t before God 2Chr 34:27
thereof, and humbledst t before me 2Chr 34:27
Think not with t that thou shalt .... Est 4:13
prepare t to the search of their .... Job 8:8
thou shewest t marvellous upon me .... Job 10:16
and dost thou restrain wisdom to t .... Job 15:8
Acquaint now t with him, and be at .... Job 22:21
hand thou opposest t against me .... Job 30:21
Deck t now with majesty and .... Job 40:10
array t with glory and beauty .... Job 40:10
lift up t because of the rage of .... Ps 7:6
why hidest thou t in times of .... Ps 10:1
thou wilt shew t merciful .... Ps 18:25
man thou wilt shew t upright .... Ps 18:25
the pure thou wilt shew t pure .... Ps 18:26
froward thou wilt shew t froward .... Ps 18:26
Stir up t, and awake to my .... Ps 35:23
Fret not t because of evildoers, ... Ps 37:1
Delight t also in the Lord .... Ps 37:4
fret not t because of him who .... Ps 37:7
fret not t in any wise to do evil .... Ps 37:8
thee, when thou doest well to t .... Ps 49:18
I was altogether such an one as t .... Ps 50:21
Why boastest thou t in mischief .... Ps 52:1
hide not t from my supplication .... Ps 55:1
O turn t to us again .... Ps 60:1
that thou madest strong for t .... Ps 80:15
man whom thou madest strong for t .... Ps 80:17
thou hast turned t from the .... Ps 85:3
wilt thou hide t for ever .... Ps 89:46
whom vengeance belongeth, shew t .... Ps 94:1
Lift up t, thou judge of the .... Ps 94:2
Who coverest t with light as with .... Ps 104:2
Do this now, my son, and deliver t .... Prov 6:3
go, humble t, and make sure thy .... Prov 6:3
Deliver t as a roe from the hand .... Prov 6:5
be wise, thou shalt be wise for t .... Prov 9:12
Fret not t because of evil men, ... Prov 24:19
and make it fit for t in the field .... Prov 24:27
Put not forth t in the presence .... Prov 25:6
Boast not t of to morrow .... Prov 27:1
done foolishly in lifting up t .... Prov 30:32
neither make t over wise .... Eccl 7:16
why shouldest thou destroy t .... Eccl 7:16
t likewise hast cursed others .... Eccl 7:22
hide t as it were for a little .... Is 26:20
at the lifting up of thine .... Is 33:3
thou art a God that hidest t .... Is 45:15
Shake t from the dust .... Is 52:2
loose t from the bands of thy .... Is 52:2
discovered t to another than me .... Is 57:8
didst debase t even unto hell .... Is 57:9
that thou hide not t from thine .... Is 58:7
shalt thou delight t in the Lord .... Is 58:14
to make t a glorious name .... Is 63:14
thou refrain t for these things .... Is 64:12
Which say, Stand by t, come not .... Is 65:5
thou not procured this unto t .... Jer 2:17
thou clothest t with crimson .... Jer 4:30
in vain shalt thou make t fair .... Jer 4:30
sackcloth, and wallow t in ashes .... Jer 6:26
And thou, even t, shalt .... Jer 17:4
I will make thee a terror to t .... Jer 20:4
because thou closest t in cedar .... Jer 22:15
buy it for t .... Jer 32:8
seekest thou great things for t .... Jer 45:5
furnish t to go into captivity .... Jer 46:19
how long wilt thou cut t .... Jer 47:5
put up t into thy scabbard, rest .... Jer 47:6
give t no rest .... Lam 2:18
Thou hast covered t with a cloud .... Lam 3:44
be drunken, and shalt make t naked .... Lam 4:21
shut t within thine house .... Eze 3:24
madest to t images of men, and .... Eze 16:17
hast defiled t in thine idols .... Eze 22:4
in t in the sight of the heathen .... Eze 22:16
for whom thou didst wash t .... Eze 23:40
deckedst t with ornaments .... Eze 23:40
thou hast lifted up t in height .... Eze 31:10
thou preparest, and prepare for t .... Eze 38:7
the king, Let thy gifts be to t .... Dan 5:17
But hast lifted up t against the .... Dan 5:23
to chasten t before thy God, thy .... Dan 10:12
O Israel, thou hast destroyed t .... Hos 13:9
Though thou exalt t as the eagle .... Obad 4
of Aphrah roll t in the dust .... Mic 1:10
thou, O Zion, that dwellest .... Mic 5:1
Now gather t in troops, O .... Mic 5:1
make t many as the cankerworm .... Nah 3:15
make t many as the locusts .... Nah 3:15
Deliver t, O Zion, that dwellest .... Zec 2:7
be the Son of God, cast t down .... Mt 4:6
time, Thou shalt not forswear t .... Mt 5:33

T

shew t to the priest, and offer .... Mt 8:4
shalt love thy neighbour as t .... Mt 19:19
shalt love thy neighbour as t .... Mt 22:39
buildest it in three days, save t .... Mt 27:40
shew t to the priest, and offer .... Mk 1:44
shalt love thy neighbour as t .... Mk 12:31
Save t, and come down from the .... Mk 15:30
of God, cast t down from hence .... Lk 4:9
this proverb, Physician, heal t .... Lk 4:23
shew t to the priest, and offer .... Lk 5:14
when thou t beholdest not the .... Lk 6:42
unto him, Lord, trouble not t .... Lk 7:6
and thy neighbour as t .... Lk 10:27
wherewith I may aup, and gird t .... Lk 17:8
be the king of the Jews, save t .... Lk 23:37
shall by the Christ, save t .... Lk 23:39
What sayest thou of t .... Jn 1:22
these things, shew t to the world .... Jn 7:4
him, Thou bearest record of t .... Jn 8:13
whom makest thou t .... Jn 8:53
thou, being a man, makest t God .... Jn 10:33
that thou wilt manifest t unto us .... Jn 14:22
him, Sayest thou this thing of t .... Jn 18:34
thou wast young, thou girdedst t .... Jn 21:18
near, and join t to this chariot .... Acts 8:29
the angel said unto him, Gird t .... Acts 12:8
loud voice, saying, Do t no harm .... Acts 16:28
purify t with them, and be at .... Acts 21:24
but that thou t also walkest .... Acts 21:24
by examining of whom t mayest .... Acts 24:8
Thou art permitted to speak for t .... Acts 26:1
voice, Paul, thou art beside t .... Acts 26:24
another, thou condemnest t .... Rom 2:1
heart treasurest up unto t wrath .... Rom 2:5
art confident that thou art a .... Rom 2:19
another, teachest thou not t .... Rom 2:21
shalt love thy neighbour as t .... Rom 13:9
have it to t before God .... Rom 14:22
shalt love thy neighbour as t .... Gal 5:14
considering t, lest thou also be .... Gal 6:1
to behave t in the house of God 1Ti 3:15
exercise t rather unto godliness 1Ti 4:7
give t wholly to them 1Ti 4:15
Take heed unto t, and unto the 1Ti 4:16
doing this thou shalt both save t 1Ti 4:16
keep t pure 1Ti 5:22
from such withdraw t 1Ti 6:5
Study to shew t approved unto God ... 2Ti 2:15
In all things shewing t a pattern .... Titus 2:7
shalt love thy neighbour as t .... Jas 2:8

TIARAS See HOODS.

TIBERIAS (ti-be'-re-as) A city on the Sea of
Galilee.
of Galilee, which is the sea of T .... Jn 6:1
there came other boats from T .... Jn 6:23
to the disciples at the sea of T .... Jn 21:1

TIBERIUS (ti-be'-re-us) See CAESAR. A Roman
emperor.
year of the reign of T Caesar .... Lk 3:1

TIBHATH (tib'-hath) A city in Aram Zobah.
Likewise from T, and from Chun, ... 1Chr 18:8

TIBNI (tib'-ni) Son of Ginath.
followed T the son of Ginath 1Kin 16:21
that followed T the son of Ginath 1Kin 16:22
so T died, and Omri reigned. 1Kin 16:22

TIDAL (ti'-dal) A king of Goyim.
of Elam, and T king of nations, ... Gen 14:1
with T king of nations, and .... Gen 14:9

TIDINGS
when Laban heard the t of Jacob, ... Gen 29:13
the people heard these evil t .... Ex 33:4
when she heard the t that the ark 1Sa 4:19
told the t in the ears of the 1Sa 11:4
they told him the t of the men of 1Sa 11:5
upon Saul when he heard those t 1Sa 11:6
woman alive, to bring t to Gath 1Sa 27:11
years old when the t came of Saul 2Sa 4:4
thinking to have brought good t 2Sa 4:10
have given him a reward for his t 2Sa 4:10
that t came to David, saying, ... 2Sa 13:30
me now run, and bear the king t 2Sa 18:19
Thou shalt not bear t this day 2Sa 18:20
but thou shalt bear t another day 2Sa 18:20
but this day thou shalt bear no t 2Sa 18:20
seeing that thou hast no t ready 2Sa 18:22
be alone, there is t in his mouth 2Sa 18:25
the king said, He also bringeth t 2Sa 18:26
a good man, and cometh with good t .. 2Sa 18:27
and Cushi said, T, my lord the 2Sa 18:31
a valiant man, and bringest good t 1Kin 1:42
Then t came to Joab. 1Kin 2:28
I am sent to thee with heavy t 1Kin 14:6
this day is a day of good t 2Kin 7:9
to carry t unto their idols, and 1Chr 10:9
He shall not be afraid of evil t .... Ps 112:7
O Zion, that bringest good t .... Is 40:9
O Jerusalem, that bringest good t .... Is 40:9
one that bringeth good t .... Is 41:27
feet of him that bringeth good t .... Is 52:7
that bringeth good t of good .... Is 52:7
me to preach good t unto the meek ..... Is 61:1
good t of health to my fellows .... Jer 20:15
Jerusalem heard t of them .... Jer 37:5
for they have heard evil t .... Jer 49:23
thou that shalt answer, For the t .... Eze 21:7
But t out of the east and out of .... Dan 11:44

feet of him that bringeth good t .... Nah 1:15
and to shew thee these glad t .... Lk 1:19
I bring you good t of great joy .... Lk 2:10
shewing the glad t of the kingdom .... Lk 8:1
Then t of these things came unto .... Acts 11:22
And we declare unto you glad t .... Acts 13:32
t came unto the chief captain of .... Acts 21:31
bring glad t of good things. .... Rom 10:15
brought us good t of your faith. 1Th 3:6

TIE
t the kine to the cart, and bring 1Sa 6:7
heart, and t them about thy neck .... Prov 6:21

TIED
they t unto it a lace of blue, to .... Ex 39:31
t them to the cart, and shut up 1Sa 6:10
voice of man, but horses t 2Kin 7:10
man, but horses t, and asses t 2Kin 7:10
ye shall find an ass t, and a colt. .... Mt 21:2
into it, ye shall find a colt t .... Mk 11:2
found the colt t by the door .... Mk 11:4
entering ye shall find a colt t .... Lk 19:30

TIGLATH-PILESER (tig'-lath-pi-le'-zur) See
TILGATH-PILNESER. An Assyrian king.
of Israel came T king of Assyria 2Kin 15:29
messengers to T king of Assyria 2Kin 16:7
to meet T king of Assyria. 2Kin 16:10

TIGRIS See HIDDEKEL.

TIKVAH (tik'-vah) See TIKVATH.
1. Father-in-law of Huldah.
the wife of Shallum the son of T 2Kin 22:14
2. Father of Jahaziah.
Jahaziah the son of T were .... Ezr 10:15

TIKVATH (tik'-vath) See TIKVAH. Same as
Tikvah 1.
the wife of Shallum the son of T 2Chr 34:22

TIL
t the Assyrian founded it for .... Is 23:13

TILE
also, son of man, take thee a t .... Eze 4:1

TILGATH-PILNESER (til'-gath-pil-ne'-zur)
See TIGLATH-PILESER. Same as Tiglath-pileser.
whom T king of Assyria carried 1Chr 5:6
the spirit of T king of Assyria, ... 1Chr 5:26
T king of Assyria came unto him, ... 2Chr 28:20

TILING
let him down through the t with .... Lk 5:19

TILL
was not a man to t the ground .... Gen 2:5
t thou return unto the ground .... Gen 3:19
to t the ground from whence he .... Gen 3:23
any thing t thou be come thither .... Gen 19:22
t they roll the stone from the .... Gen 29:8
house, t Shelah my son be grown ...... Gen 38:11
give me a pledge, t thou send it. .... Gen 38:17
t thy people pass over, O LORD, ... Ex 15:16
the people pass over, which .... Ex 15:16
no man leave of it t the morning .... Ex 16:19
And they laid it up t the morning ...... Ex 16:24
t Moses had done speaking with .... Ex 34:33
then they journeyed not t the day ...... Ex 40:37
the people journeyed not t Miriam ..... Num 12:15
them with stones, t they die. .... Deut 17:5
thee, t thou be destroyed. .... Deut 28:45
t all the people that were men of .... Josh 5:6
in the camp, t they were whole. .... Josh 5:8
us t we have drawn them from the ..... Josh 8:6
t they were consumed in the .... Josh 10:20
they tarried t they were ashamed ...... Judg 3:25
t thou come unto Gaza, and left no .... Judg 6:4
even t thou come to Minnith, even .... Judg 11:33
And Samson lay t midnight, and .... Judg 16:3
her lord was, t it was light. .... Judg 19:26
abode there t even before God, and ... Judg 21:2
tarry for them t they were grown ...... Ruth 1:13
t I come to thee, and shew you 1Sa 10:8
not sit down t he come hither 1Sa 16:11
t I know what God will do for me 1Sa 22:3
or ought else, t the sun be down. 1Sa 25:36
shalt t the land for him, and thou 2Sa 9:10
away dung, t it be all gone 1Kin 14:10
t the blood gushed out upon them 1Kin 18:28
they urged him t he was ashamed 2Kin 2:17
he sat on her knees t noon 2Kin 4:20
if we tarry t the morning light, ... 2Kin 7:9
t he had destroyed them, according ... 2Kin 10:17
t thou have consumed them. 2Kin 13:17
Syria t thou hadst consumed it. 2Kin 13:19
t he had killed Jerusalem from 2Kin 21:16
helped, t he was strong. 2Chr 26:15
t the work was ended, and until 2Chr 29:34
his people, t there was no remedy. 2Chr 36:16
t there stood up a priest with .... Ezr 2:63
the matter came to Darius .... Ezr 5:5
with us t thou hadst consumed us ..... Ezr 9:14
me over t I come into Judah .... Neh 2:7
t we come in the midst among them. .. Neh 4:11
the morning t the stars appeared .... Neh 4:21
t there stood up a priest with .... Neh 7:65
not be opened t after the sabbath ...... Neh 13:19
nor let me alone t I swallow down. .... Job 7:19
The fill thy mouth with laughing ...... Job 8:21
t he shall accomplish, as an .... Job 14:6
the heavens be no more, they .... Job 14:12
will I wait, t my change come. .... Job 14:14

t I die I will not remove mine .... Job 27:5
Elihu had waited t Job had spoken .... Job 32:4
his wickedness t thou find none .... Ps 10:15
t turn again t they were consumed. ... Ps 18:37
t every one submit himself with .... Ps 68:30
T a dart strike through his liver .... Prov 7:23
man keepeth it in t afterwards. .... Prov 7:23
t I might see what was that good .... Eccl 2:3
nor awake my love, t he please. .... Song 2:7
nor awake my love, t he please. .... Song 3:5
t there be no place, that they .... Is 5:8
until night, t wine inflame them .... Is 5:11
not be purged from you t ye die. .... Is 6:11
t ye be left as a beacon upon the ...... Is 22:14
t reckoned t morning, that, as a .... Is 30:17
t he have set judgment in the .... Is 42:4
t the establish, and t he make. .... Is 62:7
in Tophet, t there be no place .... Jer 7:32
them, t I have consumed them .... Jer 9:16
t there be no place to bury .... Jer 19:11
t he have performed the thoughts. .... Jer 23:20
t they be consumed from off the .... Jer 24:10
and they shall t it, and dwell .... Jer 27:11
will destroy t they have enough .... Jer 49:9
them, t I have consumed them .... Jer 49:37
t he had cast them out from his .... Jer 52:3
put him in prison t the day of .... Jer 52:11
T the LORD look down, and behold ... Lam 3:50
t thou hast ended the days of thy ...... Eze 4:8
for from my youth up even t now ..... Eze 4:14
t I have caused my fury to rest .... Eze 24:13
t iniquity was found in thee. .... Eze 28:15
t ye have scattered them abroad .... Eze 34:21
t the buriers have buried it in .... Eze 39:15
And ye shall eat fat t ye be full .... Eze 39:19
drink blood t ye be drunken, of .... Eze 39:19
t a man come over against Hamath .... Eze 47:20
before me, t the time be changed. ..... Dan 2:9
Thou sawest t that a stone was .... Dan 2:34
t seven times pass over him .... Dan 4:23
t thou know that the most High .... Dan 4:25
t his hairs were grown like .... Dan 4:33
t he knew that the most high God ..... Dan 5:21
he laboured t the going down of ...... Dan 6:14
I beheld t the wings thereof were ..... Dan 7:4
I beheld t the thrones were cast .... Dan 7:9
I beheld even t the beast was, ... Dan 7:11
at all, t three whole weeks were .... Dan 10:3
shall prosper t the indignation .... Dan 11:36
sealed t the time of the end. .... Dan 12:9
But go thou thy way t the end be ...... Dan 12:13
t they acknowledge their offence, ... Hos 5:15
t he come and rain righteousness. ..... Hos 10:12
not have stolen t they had enough .... Obad 5
t he might see what would become. ... Jonah 4:5
gnaw out the bones t the morrow ..... Zeph 3:3
knew her not t she had brought .... Mt 1:25
t it came and stood over where the .... Mt 2:9
T heaven and earth pass, one jot .... Mt 5:18
from the law, t all be fulfilled. .... Mt 5:18
t thou hast paid the uttermost .... Mt 5:26
there abide t ye go thence: .... Mt 10:11
Israel, t the Son of man be come. ..... Mt 10:23
he send forth judgment unto .... Mt 12:20
of meal, t the whole was leavened ... Mt 13:33
t they see the Son of man coming. ... Mt 16:28
t seven times? .... Mt 18:21
prison, t he should pay the debt. ...... Mt 18:30
he should pay all that was due. .... Mt 18:34
t I make thine enemies thy .... Mt 22:44
t ye shall say, Blessed is he. .... Mt 23:39
t all these things be fulfilled. .... Mt 24:34
there abide t ye depart from that ...... Mk 6:10
t they have seen the kingdom of ...... Mk 9:1
the Son of man were risen from .... Mk 9:9
t I make thine enemies thy .... Mk 12:36
t all these things be done .... Mk 13:30
was in the deserts t the day of .... Lk 1:80
t they see the kingdom of God. .... Lk 9:27
t straitened t it be accomplished. .... Lk 12:50
t thou hast paid the very last .... Lk 12:59
t I shall dig about it, and dung. ...... Lk 13:8
of meal, t the whole was leavened. ... Lk 13:21
and seek diligently t she find it .... Lk 15:8
t I have eaten and drunken .... Lk 17:8
said unto them, Occupy t I come. .... Lk 19:13
T I make thine enemies thy .... Lk 20:43
not pass away, t all be fulfilled .... Lk 21:32
t thou hast denied me thrice .... Lk 22:34
If I will that he tarry t I come .... Jn 21:22
If I will that he tarry t I come .... Jn 21:23
T an: her king arose, which knew .... Acts 7:18
the cities, t he came to Caesarea. .... Acts 8:40
even t break of day, so he .... Acts 20:11
t we were out of the city .... Acts 21:5
nor drink t they had killed Paul. ..... Acts 23:12
nor drink t they have killed him. .... Acts 23:14
kept t I might send him to Caesar .... Acts 25:21
prophets, from morning t evening. ... Acts 28:23
where the Lord's people t he come 1Cor 11:26
t he hath put all enemies under 1Cor 15:25
the seed should come to whom .... Gal 3:19
T we all come in the unity of the ..... Eph 4:13
without offence t the day of .... Phil 1:10
T I come, give attendance to 1Ti 4:13
t his enemies be made his. .... Heb 10:13
have already hold fast t I come. .... Rev 2:25
t we have sealed the servants of ...... Rev 7:3
t the seven plagues of the seven ...... Rev 15:8
t the thousand years should be .... Rev 20:3

TILLAGE
did the work of the field for t 1Chr 27:26
tithes in all the cities of our t .... Neh 10:37
Much food is in the t of the poor .... Prov 13:23

TILLED
turn unto you, and ye shall be t .... Eze 36:9
And the desolate land shall be t .... Eze 36:34

TILLER
but Cain was a t of the ground.............. Gen 4:2

TILLEST
When thou t the ground, it shall .... Gen 4:12

TILLETH
He that t his land shall be.................. Prov 12:11
He that t his land shall have .... Prov 28:19

TILON (ti´-lon) A descendant of Judah.
Rinnah, Ben-hanan, and T 1Chr 4:20

TIMAEUS (ti-me´-us) See BARTIMAEUS. Father
of Bartimaeus.
blind Bartimaeus, the son of T .... Mk 10:46

TIMBER
to set them, and in carving of t.......... Ezr 31:5
the t thereof, and all the morter......... Lev 14:45
to hew t like unto the Sidonians 1Kin 5:6
thy desire concerning t of cedar 1Kin 5:8
of cedar, and concerning t of fir 1Kin 5:8
so they prepared t and stones to 1Kin 5:18
on the house with t of cedar 1Kin 6:10
the t thereof, wherewith Baasha 1Kin 15:22
and hewers of stone, and to buy t 2Kin 12:12
builders, and masons, and to buy t ... 2Kin 22:6
t of cedars, with masons and 1Chr 14:1
t also and stone have I prepared 1Chr 22:14
hewers and workers of stone and t ... 1Chr 22:15
can skill to cut t in Lebanon 2Chr 2:8
Even to prepare me t in abundance 2Chr 2:9
servants, the hewers that cut t 2Chr 2:10
brass, in iron, in stone, and in t 2Chr 2:14
the t thereof, wherewith Baasha 2Chr 16:6
t for couplings, and to floor the 2Chr 34:11
t is laid in the walls, and this .... Ezr 5:8
great stones, and a row of new t .... Ezr 6:4
let t be pulled down from his............ Ezr 6:11
that he may give me t to make........... Neh 2:8
shall lay thy stones and thy t .... Eze 26:12
beam out of the t shall answer it........ Hab 2:11
consume it with the t thereof .... Zec 5:4

TIMBREL
of Aaron, took a t in her hand............. Ex 15:20
They take the t and harp, and............ Job 21:12
a psalm, and bring hither the t .... Ps 81:2
sing praises unto him with the t .... Ps 149:3
Praise him with the t and dance.......... Ps 150:4

TIMBRELS
women went out after her with t.......... Ex 15:20
came out to meet him with t .... Judg 11:34
harps, and on psalteries, and on t 2Sa 6:5
and with psalteries, and with t 1Chr 13:8
were the damsels playing with t .... Ps 68:25

TIME See PREFACE.

TIMES
he hath supplanted me these two t ...... Gen 27:36
me, and changed my wages ten t .... Gen 31:7
thou hast changed my wages ten t ...... Gen 31:41
himself to the ground seven t .... Gen 33:3
five t so much as any of theirs........... Gen 43:34
Three t thou shalt keep a feast .... Ex 23:14
Three t in the year all thy males........ Ex 23:17
the blood seven t before the LORD....... Lev 4:6
it seven t before the LORD................. Lev 4:17
thereof upon the altar seven t .... Lev 8:11
cleansed from the leprosy seven t .... Lev 14:7
finger seven t before the LORD........... Lev 14:16
left hand seven t before the LORD ...... Lev 14:27
and sprinkle the house seven t .... Lev 14:51
that he come not at all t into .... Lev 16:2
the blood with his finger seven t .... Lev 16:14
upon it with his finger seven t .... Lev 16:19
ye use enchantment, nor observe t ...... Lev 19:26
unto thee, seven t seven years............ Lev 25:8
seven t more for your sins .... Lev 26:18
I will bring seven t more plagues .... Lev 26:21
yo yet seven t for your sins .... Lev 26:24
you seven t for your sins .... Lev 26:28
have tempted me now these ten t .... Num 14:22
of the congregation seven t .... Num 19:4
hast smitten me these three t .... Num 22:28
smitten thee these three t .... Num 22:32
and turned from me these three t .... Num 22:33
he went not, as at other t .... Num 24:1
blessed them these three t .... Num 24:10
thousand t so many more as ye are .... Deut 1:11
The Emims dwelt therein in t past ...... Deut 2:10
and hated him not in t past.............. Deut 4:42
Three t in a year shall all thy .... Deut 16:16
divination, or an observer of t .... Deut 18:10
hearkened unto observers of t .... Deut 18:14
ye shall compass the city seven t .... Josh 6:4
after the same manner seven t .... Josh 6:15
they compassed the city seven t .... Josh 6:15
at t in the camp of Dan between .... Judg 13:25
thou hast mocked me these three t .... Judg 16:15
will go out as at other t before.......... Judg 20:30
against Gibeah, as at other t .... Judg 20:31
people, and kill, as at other t .... Judg 20:31

and stood, and called as at other t 1Sa 3:10
with his hand, as at other t 1Sa 18:10
was in his presence, as in t past 1Sa 19:7
sat upon his seat, as at other t 1Sa 20:25
ground, and bowed himself three t 1Sa 20:41
Ye sought for David in t past to 2Sa 3:17
of his people Israel at all t 1Kin 8:59
three t in a year did Solomon 1Kin 9:25
himself upon the child three t 1Kin 17:21
And he said, Go again seven t 1Kin 18:43
How many t shall I adjure thee 1Kin 22:16
of ancient t have I formed 2Kin 4:35
Go and wash in Jordan seven t 2Kin 5:10
dipped himself seven t in Jordan 2Kin 5:14
have smitten five or six t 2Kin 13:19
Three t did Joash beat him, and 2Kin 13:25
of ancient t that I have formed 2Kin 19:25
through the fire, and observed t 2Kin 21:6
that had understanding of the t 1Chr 12:32
hundred t so many more as they be... 1Chr 21:3
the t that went over him, and over 1Chr 29:30
three t in the year, even in the 2Chr 8:13
in those t there was no peace to 2Chr 15:5
How many t shall I adjure thee 2Chr 18:15
also he observed t, and used 2Chr 33:6
in our cities come at appointed t .... Ezr 10:14
came, they said unto us ten t .... Neh 4:12
unto me four t after this sort .... Neh 6:4
many t didst thou deliver them .... Neh 9:28
at t appointed year by year, to .... Neh 10:34
at t appointed, and for the .... Neh 13:31
to the wise men, which knew the t ..... Est 1:13
of Purim in their t appointed .... Est 9:31
These ten t have ye reproached me ..... Job 19:3
seeing t are not hidden from the .... Job 24:1
a refuge in t of trouble .... Ps 9:9
thou thyself in t of trouble.............. Ps 10:1
of earth, purified seven t .... Ps 12:6
My t are in thy hand..................... Ps 31:15
I will bless the LORD at all t .... Ps 34:1
in their days, in the t of old .... Ps 44:1
Trust in him at all t .... Ps 62:8
of old, the years of ancient t .... Ps 77:5
that doeth righteousness at all t .... Ps 106:3
Many t did he deliver them .... Ps 106:43
hath unto thy judgments at all t .... Ps 119:20
Seven t a day do I praise thee........... Ps 119:164
her breasts satisfy thee at all t .... Prov 5:19
A friend loveth at all t, and a .... Prov 17:17
For a just man falleth seven t .... Prov 24:16
a sinner do evil an hundred t .... Eccl 8:12
shall be alone in his appointed t .... Is 14:31
shall be the stability of thy .... Is 33:6
and of ancient t, that I have .... Is 37:26
from ancient t the things that .... Is 46:10
heaven knoweth her appointed t .... Jer 8:7
of the t that are far off................. Eze 12:27
he found them ten t better than........ Dan 1:20
And he changeth the t and the.......... Dan 2:21
heat the furnace seven t more .... Dan 3:19
let seven t pass over him .... Dan 4:16
till seven t pass over him .... Dan 4:23
seven t shall pass over thee, ... Dan 4:25
seven t shall pass over thee, ... Dan 4:32
upon his knees three t a day .... Dan 6:10
maketh his petition three t a day ...... Dan 6:13
ten thousand t ten thousand stood ..... Dan 7:10
most High, and think to change t ...... Dan 7:25
into his hand until a time and t .... Dan 7:25
and the wall, even in troublous t ...... Dan 9:25
that strengthened her in these t .... Dan 11:6
in those t there shall many stand...... Dan 11:14
that it shall be for a time, t .... Dan 12:7
ye not discern the signs of the t .... Mt 16:3
till seven t .... Mt 18:21
say not unto thee, Until seven t .... Mt 18:22
but, Until seventy t seven............... Mt 18:22
against thee seven t in a day .... Lk 17:4
seven t in a day turn again to .... Lk 17:4
until the t of the Gentiles be .... Lk 21:24
you to know the t of the seasons .... Acts 1:7
when the t of refreshing shall .... Acts 3:19
t of restitution of all things............ Acts 3:21
And this was done three t .... Acts 11:10
Who in t past suffered all .... Acts 14:16
determined the t before appointed ..... Acts 17:26
the t of this ignorance God .... Acts 17:30
For as ye in t past have not .... Rom 11:30
Of the Jews five t received I 2Cor 11:24
in t past now preacheth the faith ...... Gal 1:23
Ye observe days, and months, and t ... Gal 4:10
dispensation of the fulness of t .... Eph 1:10
t past in the lusts of our flesh.......... Eph 2:3
But of the t and the seasons............ 1Th 5:1
that in the latter t some shall 1Ti 4:1
Which in his t he shall shew, who 1Ti 6:15
last days perilous t shall come 2Ti 3:1
But hath in due t manifested his ...... Titus 1:3
God, who at sundry t and in divers..... Heb 1:1
of the angels said he at any t .... Heb 1:13
manifest in these last t 1Pet 1:20
was ten thousand t ten thousand ...... Rev 5:11
she is nourished for a time, and t ...... Rev 12:14

TIMNA (tim´-nah) See TIMNATH.
1. Concubine of Eliphaz.
T was concubine to Eliphaz Esau's..... Gen 36:12
2. Daughter of Seir.
and Lotan's sister was T .... Gen 36:22
and T was Lotan's sister................. 1Chr 1:39
3. A son of Eliphaz.

Zephi, and Gatam, Kenaz, and T 1Chr 1:36

TIMNAH (tim´-nah) See TIMNA, TIMNATH.
1. A chief of Edom.
duke T, duke Alvah, duke Jetheth, ... Gen 36:40
duke T, duke Aliah, duke Jetheth,..... 1Chr 1:51
2. A city in Judah.
Cain, Gibeah, and T .... Josh 15:57
3. A city in Dan.
Beth-shemesh, and passed on to T ..... Josh 15:10
T with the villages thereof,.............. 2Chr 28:18

TIMNATH (tim´-nah) See TIMNATHNAH,
TIMNAH.
1. Same as Timnah 2.
up unto his sheepshearers to T .... Gen 38:12
goeth up to T to shear his sheep .... Gen 38:13
place, which is by the way to T .... Gen 38:14
2. Same as Timnah 3.
And Samson went down to T .... Judg 14:1
saw a woman in T of the daughters .... Judg 14:1
I have seen a woman in T of the .... Judg 14:2
and his father and his mother, to T .... Judg 14:5
and came to the vineyards of T .... Judg 14:5

TIMNATH-HERES (tim´-nath-he´-rez) See
TIMNATH-SERAH. Land near Mount Ephraim.
border of his inheritance in T .... Judg 2:9

TIMNATH-SERAH (tim´-nath-se´-rah) See
TIMNATH-HERES. Same as Timnath-heres.
he asked, even T in mount Ephraim .... Josh 19:50
border of his inheritance in T .... Josh 24:30

TIMNITE (tim´-nite) An inhabitant of Timnath.
Samson, the son in law of the T .... Judg 15:6

TIMON (ti´-mon) A leader in the Jerusalem
church.
and Prochorus, and Nicanor, and T .... Acts 6:5

TIMOTHEOUS
and Fortunatus, and Achaicus, and T ... 1Cor s

TIMOTHEUS (ti-mo´-the-us) See TIMOTHY.
Same as Timothy.
disciple was there, named T .... Acts 16:1
but Silas and T abode there still........ Acts 17:14
For to come to him with all .... Acts 17:15
T were come from Macedonia, Paul .... Acts 18:5
them that ministered unto him, T ...... Acts 19:22
and Gaius of Derbe, and T .... Acts 20:4
T my workfellow, and Lucius, and ...... Rom 16:21
this cause have I sent unto you T 1Cor 4:17
Now if T come, see that he may be 1Cor 16:10
us, even by me and Silvanus and T 2Cor 1:19
Paul and T, the servants of Jesus ...... Phil 1:1
Jesus to send T shortly unto you .... Phil 2:19
will of God, and T our brother,.......... Col 1:1
Paul, and Silvanus, and T, unto the ... 1Th 1:1
And sent T, our brother, and 1Th 3:2
But now when T came from you unto... 1Th 3:6
Paul, and Silvanus, and T, unto the ... 2Th 1:1
The second epistle unto T .... 2Ti s

TIMOTHY (tim´-o-thy) See TIMOTHEUS. A co-
worker with Paul.
T our brother, unto the church of 2Cor 1:1
Unto T, my own son in the faith 1Ti 1:2
charge I commit unto thee, son T....... 1Ti 1:18
O T, keep that which is committed...... 1Ti 6:20
The first to T was written from .... 1Ti s
To T, my dearly beloved son 2Ti 1:2
T our brother, unto Philemon our .... Philem 1
our brother T is set at liberty .... Heb 13:23
to the Hebrews from Italy by T .... Heb s

TIN
the brass, the iron, the t .... Num 31:22
thy dross, and take away all thy t ...... Is 1:25
all they are brass, and t, and iron...... Eze 22:18
and brass, and iron, and lead, and t ... Eze 22:20
with silver, iron, t, and lead,........... Eze 27:12

TINGLE
every one that heareth it shall t 1Sa 3:11
of it, both his ears shall t............... 2Kin 21:12
heareth, his ears shall t .... Jer 19:3

TINKLING
making a t with their feet .... Is 3:16
t ornaments about their feet .... Is 3:18
as sounding brass, or a t cymbal 1Cor 13:1

TIP
put it upon the t of the right........... Ex 29:20
upon the t of the right ear of .... Ex 29:20
put it upon the t of Aaron's............. Lev 8:23
upon the t of their right ear .... Lev 8:24
priest shall put it upon the t of .... Lev 14:14
shall the priest put upon the t .... Lev 14:17
put it upon the t of the right........... Lev 14:25
that is in his hand upon the t of .... Lev 14:28
in water, and dip the t of his .... Lk 16:24

TIPHSAH (tif´-sah)
1. A city on the Euphrates River.
from T even to Azzah, over all 1Kin 4:24
2. A city in Judah.
then Menahem smote T 2Kin 15:16

TIRAS (Ti´-ras) A son of Japheth.
Javan, and Tubal, and Meshech, and T .. Gen 10:2
Javan, and Tubal, and Meshech, and T .. 1Chr 1:5

TIRATHITES (ti′-rath-ites) *A family of scribes.*
the T, the Shimeathites, and 1Chr 2:55

TIRE
bind the t of thine head upon .... Eze 24:17

TIRED
t her head, and looked out at a 2Kin 9:30

TIRES
their round t like the moon, ... Is 3:18
your t shall be upon your heads, ... Eze 24:23

TIRHAKAH (tur-ha′-kah) *A king of Ethiopia.*
heard say of T king of Ethiopia 2Kin 19:9
say concerning T king of Ethiopia ... Is 37:9

TIRHANAH (tur-ha′-nah) *A son of Caleb.*
concubine, bare Sheber, and, T 1Chr 2:48

TIRIA (tir′-e-ah) *A descendant of Judah.*
Ziph, and Ziphah, T, and Asareel 1Chr 4:16

TIRSHATHA (tur′-sha-thah) *Persian governors of Judah.*
the T said unto them, that they ...... Ezr 2:63
the T said unto them, that they ...... Neh 7:65
The T gave to the treasure a .... Neh 7:70
And Nehemiah, which is the T .... Neh 8:9
that sealed were, Nehemiah, the T ... Neh 10:1

TIRZAH (tur′-zah)
1. A daughter of Zelophehad.
and Noah, Hoglah, Milcah, and T ... Num 26:33
Noah, and Hoglah, and Milcah, and T Num 27:1
For Mahlah, T, and Hoglah, and ...... Num 36:11
and Noah, Hoglah, Milcah, and T ... Josh 17:3
2. A city in Ephraim.
The king of T, one .... Josh 12:24
arose, and departed, and came to T ... 1Kin 14:17
building of Ramah, and dwelt in T ... 1Kin 15:21
to reign over all Israel in T 1Kin 15:33
his fathers, and was buried in T 1Kin 16:6
Baasha to reign over Israel in T 1Kin 16:8
against him, as he was in T 1Kin 16:9
of Arza steward of his house in T ... 1Kin 16:9
did Zimri reign seven days in T 1Kin 16:15
with him, and they besieged T 1Kin 16:17
six years reigned he in T 1Kin 16:23
the son of Gadi went up from T 2Kin 15:14
and the coasts thereof from T 2Kin 15:16
art beautiful, O my love, as T .... Song 6:4

TISHBE See TISHBITE.

TISHBITE (tish′-bite) *An inhabitant of Tishbe.*
And Elijah the T, who was of the ... 1Kin 17:1
of the LORD came to Elijah the T 1Kin 21:17
of the LORD came to Elijah the T 1Kin 21:28
of the LORD said to Elijah the T 2Kin 1:3
And he said, It is Elijah the T 2Kin 1:8
spake by his servant Elijah the T ... 2Kin 9:36

TITHE
all the t of the land, whether of.... Lev 27:30
And concerning the t of the herd ..... Lev 27:32
LORD, even a tenth part of the t ..... Num 18:26
thy gates the t of thy corn .... Deut 12:17
Thou shalt truly t all the .... Deut 14:22
the t of thy corn, of thy wine, ... Deut 14:23
thou shalt bring forth all the t ..... Deut 14:28
the t of all things brought they 2Chr 31:5
also brought in the t of oxen 2Chr 31:6
the t of holy things which were 2Chr 31:6
the Levites shall bring up the t ..... Neh 10:38
all Judah the t of the corn .... Neh 13:12
for ye pay t of mint and anise and.. Mt 23:23
for ye t mint and rue and all ...... Lk 11:42

TITHES
And he gave him t of all .... Gen 14:20
will at all redeem ought of his t .... Lev 27:31
But the t of the children of.......... Num 18:24
the t which I have given you from .. Num 18:26
unto the LORD of all your t .... Num 18:28
and your sacrifices, and your t ..... Deut 12:6
and your sacrifices, your t .... Deut 12:11
the t of thine increase the third ... Deut 26:12
brought in the offerings and the t .. 2Chr 31:12
the t of our ground unto the .... Neh 10:37
the t in all the cities of our .... Neh 10:37
Levites, when the Levites take t .... Neh 10:38
the t unto the house of our God .... Neh 10:38
for the firstfruits, and for the t ... Neh 12:44
the t of corn, the new wine, ... Neh 13:5
and your t after three years....... Amos 4:4
in t and offerings .... Mal 3:8
Bring ye all the t into the .... Mal 3:10
I give t of all that I possess....... Lk 18:12
have a commandment to take t of .. Heb 7:5
from them received t of Abraham ... Heb 7:6
And here men that die receive t .... Heb 7:8
say, Levi also, who receiveth t .... Heb 7:9
payed t in Abraham .... Heb 7:9

TITHING
end of t all the tithes of thine...... Deut 26:12
year, which is the year of t........ Deut 26:12

TITUS See JUSTUS.

TITUS JUSTUS See JUSTUS.

TITLE
What t is that that I see 2Kin 23:17
And Pilate wrote a t, and put it on .. Jn 19:19

This t then read many of the Jews..... Jn 19:20

TITLES
let me give flattering t unto man.... Job 32:21
I know not to give flattering t ...... Job 32:22

TITTLE
one jot or one t shall in no wise..... Mt 5:18
than one t of the law to fail .... Lk 16:17

TITUS (ti′-tus) *A co-worker with Paul.*
because I found not T my brother 2Cor 2:13
comforted us by the coming of T 2Cor 7:6
more joyed we for the joy of T 2Cor 7:13
boasting, which I made before T 2Cor 7:14
Insomuch that we desired T 2Cor 8:6
care into the heart of T for you..... 2Cor 8:16
Whether any do enquire of T 2Cor 8:23
I desired T, and with him I sent a ... 2Cor 12:18
Did T make a gain of you 2Cor 12:18
a city of Macedonia, by T .... 2Cor ?
Barnabas, and took T with me also.. Gal 2:1
But neither T, who was with me, ... Gal 2:3
to Galatia, T unto Dalmatia......... 2Ti 4:10
To T, mine own son after the .... Titus 1:4
It was written to T, ordained the ... Titus s

TIZITE (ti′-zite) *Family name of Joha.*
and Joha his brother, the T 1Chr 11:45

TO See PREFACE.

TOAH (to′-ah) See NAHATH, TOHU. *An ancestor of Samuel.*
the son of Eliel, the son of T........ 1Chr 6:34

TOB (tob) *A district in Syria.*
and dwelt in the land of T .... Judg 11:3
Jephthah out of the land of T .... Judg 11:5

TOB-ADONIJAH (tob′′-ad-o-ni′-jah) *A Levite messenger of King Jehoshaphat.*
and Adonijah, and Tobijah, and T ... 2Chr 17:8

TOBIAH (to-bi′-ah) See TOBIJAH.
1. A family of exiles.
of Delaiah, the children of T .... Ezr 2:60
of Delaiah, the children of T .... Neh 7:62
2. An Ammonite who opposed Nehemiah.
T the servant, the Ammonite, ... Neh 2:10
the servant, the Ammonite, and ..... Neh 2:19
Now T the Ammonite was by him, and Neh 4:3
pass, that when Sanballat, and T .... Neh 4:7
to pass, when Sanballat, and T ..... Neh 6:1
for T and Sanballat had hired men .. Neh 6:12
My God, think thou upon T .... Neh 6:14
of Judah sent many letters unto T ... Neh 6:17
the letters of T came unto them..... Neh 6:17
T sent letters to put me in fear ..... Neh 6:19
of our God, was allied unto T ...... Neh 13:4
the evil that Eliashib did for T ..... Neh 13:7
stuff of T out of the chamber ...... Neh 13:8

TOBIJAH (to-bi′-jah) See TOBIAH.
1. A Levite messenger of King Jehoshaphat.
and Jehonathan, and Adonijah, and T 2Chr 17:8
2. A clan leader of exiles.
captivity, even of Heldai, of T ...... Zec 6:10
crowns shall be to Helem, and to T .. Zec 6:14

TOCHEN (to′-ken) *A city in Simeon.*
were, Etam, and Ain, Rimmon, and T 1Chr 4:32

TODAY
glorious was the king of Israel t..... 2Sa 6:20
T thy servant knoweth that I have... 2Sa 14:22
T shall the house of Israel......... 2Sa 16:3

TOE
upon the great t of their right ...... Ex 29:20
upon the great t of his right .... Lev 8:23
upon the great t of his right .... Lev 14:14
upon the great t of his right .... Lev 14:17
upon the great t of his right .... Lev 14:25
upon the great t of his right .... Lev 14:28

TOES
upon the great t of their right....... Lev 8:24
cut off his thumbs and his great t ... Judg 1:6
thumbs and their great t cut off..... Judg 1:7
fingers, and on every foot six t ..... Dan 21:20
t were four and twenty, six on 1Chr 20:6
whereas thou sawest the feet and t .. Dan 2:41
as the t of the feet were part ...... Dan 2:42

TOGARMAH (to-gar′-mah) *A son of Gomer.*
Ashkenaz, and Riphath, and T ...... Gen 10:3
Ashchenaz, and Riphath, and T 1Chr 1:6
They of the house of T traded in .... Eze 27:14
the house of T of the north .... Eze 38:6

TOGETHER See PREFACE.
The rich and poor meet t .... Prov 22:2
three are gathered t in my name .... Mt 18:20
I have gathered thy children t ...... Mt 23:37
What therefore God hath joined t ... Mk 10:9
And all that believed were t .... Acts 2:44
and had gathered the church t ...... Acts 14:27
we know that all things work t ...... Rom 8:28
We then, as workers t with him 2Cor 6:1
yoked t with unbelievers........... 2Cor 6:14
the assembling of ourselves t ...... Heb 10:25

TOHU (to′-hu) See NAHATH, TOAH. *An ancestor of Samuel.*
the son of Elihu, the son of T........ 1Sa 1:1

TOI (to′-i) See TOU. *King of Hamath.*
When T king of Hamath heard that ... 2Sa 8:9
Then T sent Joram his son unto 2Sa 8:10

for Hadadezer had wars with T 2Sa 8:10

TOIL
of our hands, because of the .... Gen 5:29
he, hath made me forget all my t .... Gen 41:51
they t not, neither do they spin .... Mt 6:28
they t not, they spin not .... Lk 12:27

TOILED
we have t all the night, and have ... Lk 5:5

TOILING
And he saw them t in rowing .... Mk 6:48

TOKEN
This is the t of the covenant .... Gen 9:12
it shall be for a t of a covenant .... Gen 9:13
This is the t of the covenant .... Gen 9:17
it shall be a t of the covenant ..... Gen 17:11
and this shall be a t unto thee ..... Ex 3:12
a t upon the houses where ye are ... Ex 12:13
shall be for a t upon thine hand .... Ex 13:16
to be kept for a t against the ...... Num 17:10
house, and give me a true t .... Josh 2:12
Shew me a t for good .... Ps 86:17
betrayed him had given them a t .... Mk 14:44
to them an evident t of perdition ... Phil 1:28
Which is a manifest t of the 2Th 1:5
which is the t in every epistle 2Th 3:17

TOKENS
bring forth the t of the damsel's .... Deut 22:15
yet these are the t of my........... Deut 22:17
the t of virginity be not found...... Deut 22:20
and do ye not know their t .... Job 21:29
parts are afraid as thy t .... Ps 65:8
Who sent t and wonders into the .... Ps 135:9
frustrateth the t of the liars....... Is 44:25

TOKHATH See TIKVATH.

TOLA (to′-lah) See TOLAITES.
1. A son of Issachar.
and Phuvah, and Job .... Gen 46:13
of T, the family of the Tolaites .... Num 26:23
Now the sons of Issachar were, T ... 1Chr 7:1
And the sons of T 1Chr 7:2
father's house, to wit, of T 1Chr 7:2
2. A judge of Israel.
defend Israel T the son of Puah .... Judg 10:1

TOLAD (to′-lad) See EL-TOLAD. *A city in Simeon.*
And at Bilhah, and at Ezem, and at T. 1Chr 4:29

TOLAITES (to′-lah-ites) *Descendants of Tola.*
of Tola, the family of the T .... Num 26:23

TOLD
Who t thee that thou wast naked .... Gen 3:11
t his two brethren without........... Gen 9:22
escaped, and t Abram the Hebrew ... Gen 14:13
t all these things in their ears...... Gen 20:8
the place of which God had t him .... Gen 22:3
the place which God had t him of .... Gen 22:9
things, that it was t Abraham ...... Gen 22:20
t them of her mother's house....... Gen 24:28
eat, until I have t mine errand ..... Gen 24:33
the servant t Isaac all things....... Gen 24:66
him t concerning the well which ..... Gen 26:32
her older son were t to Rebekah..... Gen 27:42
Jacob t Rachel that he was her ..... Gen 29:12
and she ran and t her father........ Gen 29:12
he t Laban all these things .... Gen 29:13
in that he t him not that he fled .... Gen 31:20
it was t Laban on the third day ..... Gen 31:22
a dream, and he t it his brethren ... Gen 37:5
t it his brethren, and said.......... Gen 37:9
he t it to his father, and to his ..... Gen 37:10
And it was t Tamar, saying, Behold.. Gen 38:13
months after, that it was t Judah .... Gen 38:24
the chief butler t his dream to ..... Gen 40:9
and Pharaoh t them his dream....... Gen 41:8
we t him, and he interpreted to us... Gen 41:12
t him all that befell unto them...... Gen 42:29
we t him according to the tenor .... Gen 43:7
we t him the words of my lord ...... Gen 44:24
t him, saying, Joseph is yet .... Gen 45:26
they t him all the words of .... Gen 45:27
t Pharaoh, and said, My father and . Gen 47:1
these things, that one t Joseph ..... Gen 48:1
one t Jacob, and said, Behold, thy .. Gen 48:2
Moses t Aaron all the words of ..... Ex 4:28
t Pharaoh, Thus saith the LORD .... Ex 5:1
it was t the king of Egypt that...... Ex 14:5
the congregation came and t Moses... Ex 16:22
Moses t his father in law all .... Ex 18:8
Moses t the words of the people .... Ex 19:9
t the people all the words of the ... Ex 24:3
Moses t it unto Aaron, and to his ... Lev 21:24
t the people the words of the ...... Num 11:24
t Moses, and said, Eldad and Medad . Num 11:27
And they t him, and said, We came .. Num 13:27
Moses t these sayings unto all ..... Num 14:39
T not I thee, saying, All that ...... Num 23:26
Moses t the children of Israel ...... Num 29:40
And it be t thee, and thou hast ..... Deut 17:4
it was t the king of Jericho,....... Josh 2:2
t him all things that befell them .... Josh 2:23
it was certainly t thy servants...... Josh 9:24
And it was t Joshua, saying, The ... Josh 10:17
which our fathers t us of .... Judg 6:13
there was a man that t a dream ..... Judg 7:13
when they t it to Jotham, he went ... Judg 9:7
and it was t Abimelech .... Judg 9:25

and they *t* Abimelech........................... Judg 9:42
it was *t* Abimelech, that all the .... Judg 9:47
t her husband, saying, A man of .... Judg 13:6
he was, neither *t* he me his name .... Judg 13:6
have *t* us such things as these .... Judg 13:23
t his father and his mother, and......... Judg 14:2
but he *t* not his father or his .... Judg 14:6
but he *t* not them that he had .... Judg 14:9
of my people, and hast not *t* it me...... Judg 14:16
I have not *t* it my father nor my........... Judg 14:16
on the seventh day, that he *t* her....... Judg 14:17
she *t* the riddle to the children .... Judg 14:17
it was *t* the Gazites, saying,............... Judg 16:2
thou hast mocked me, and *t* me lies. .. Judg 16:10
thou hast mocked me, and *t* me lies. .. Judg 16:13
hast not *t* me wherein thy great........ Judg 16:15
That he *t* her all his heart, and........... Judg 16:17
that he had *t* her all his heart .... Judg 16:18
she *t* her all that the man had........... Ruth 3:16
For I have *t* him that I will................... 1Sa 3:13
Samuel *t* him every whit, and hid 1Sa 3:18
it, all the city cried out........................ 1Sa 4:13
the man came in hastily, and *t* Eli 1Sa 4:14
Samuel *t* all the words of the 1Sa 8:10
Now the LORD had *t* Samuel in his 1Sa 9:15
He *t* us plainly that the asses 1Sa 10:16
Samuel spake, he *t* him not 1Sa 10:16
Then Samuel *t* the people the 1Sa 10:25
t the tidings in the ears of the........... 1Sa 11:4
they *t* him the tidings of the men 1Sa 11:5
But he *t* not his father 1Sa 14:1
Then they *t* Saul, saying, Behold,....... 1Sa 14:33
And Jonathan *t* him, and said, I did.... 1Sa 14:43
in the morning, it was *t* Samuel.......... 1Sa 15:12
and they *t* Saul, and the thing 1Sa 18:20
And the servants of Saul *t* him........... 1Sa 18:24
his servants *t* David these words........ 1Sa 18:26
and Jonathan *t* David, saying, Saul 1Sa 19:2
and Michal David's wife *t* him 1Sa 19:11
t him all that Saul had done to 1Sa 19:18
And it was *t* Saul, saying, Behold,....... 1Sa 19:19
And when it was *t* Saul, he sent......... 1Sa 19:21
Then they *t* David, saying, Behold 1Sa 19:21
it was *t* Saul that David was come..... 1Sa 23:7
it was *t* Saul that David was............... 1Sa 23:13
for it is I me that he dealeth................ 1Sa 23:22
And they *t* David.............................. 1Sa 23:25
Philistines, that it was *t* him............. 1Sa 24:1
came and *t* him all those sayings 1Sa 25:12
one of the young men *t* Abigail........... 1Sa 25:14
But she *t* not her husband Nabal........ 1Sa 25:19
wherefore she *t* him nothing.............. 1Sa 25:36
his wife had *t* him these things,......... 1Sa 25:37
it was *t* Saul that David was fled 1Sa 27:4
unto the young man that *t* him........... 2Sa 1:5
And the young man that *t* him said 2Sa 1:6
unto the young man that *t* him 2Sa 1:13
they *t* David, saying, That the........... 2Sa 2:4
with him were come, they *t* Joab....... 2Sa 3:23
When one *t* me, saying, Behold,......... 2Sa 4:10
it was *t* king David, saying, The......... 2Sa 6:12
When they *t* it unto David, he............ 2Sa 10:5
And when it was *t* David, he............... 2Sa 10:17
t David, and said, I am with child....... 2Sa 11:5
And when they had *t* David, saying, ... 2Sa 11:10
t David all the things concerning 2Sa 11:18
Joab came to the king, and *t* him....... 2Sa 14:33
one *t* David, saying, Ahithophel......... 2Sa 15:31
and a wench went and *t* them 2Sa 17:17
and they went and *t* king David......... 2Sa 17:17
a lad saw them, and *t* Absalom.......... 2Sa 17:18
t king David, and said unto David,..... 2Sa 18:10
t Joab, and said, Behold, I saw 2Sa 18:10
Joab said unto the man that *t* him..... 2Sa 18:11
the watchman cried, and *t* the king... 2Sa 18:25
And it was *t* Joab, Behold, the 2Sa 19:1
they *t* unto all the people.................. 2Sa 19:8
it was *t* David what Rizpah the 2Sa 21:11
t him, and said unto him, Shall 2Sa 24:13
they *t* the king, saying, Behold 1Kin 1:23
it was *t* Solomon, Saying, Behold,...... 1Kin 1:51
it was *t* king Solomon that Joab........ 1Kin 2:29
they *t* Shimei, saying, Behold,........... 1Kin 2:39
it was *t* Solomon that Shimei had...... 1Kin 2:41
that could not be *t* nor numbered...... 1Kin 8:5
Solomon *t* her all her questions......... 1Kin 10:3
from the king, which he *t* her not...... 1Kin 10:3
and, behold, the half was not *t* me 1Kin 10:7
t him all the works that the man....... 1Kin 13:11
then they *t* also to their father.......... 1Kin 13:11
t it in the city where the old 1Kin 13:25
which *t* me that I should be king....... 1Kin 14:2
Was it not *t* my lord what I did 1Kin 18:13
went to meet Ahab, and *t* him........... 1Kin 18:16
Ahab *t* Jezebel all that Elijah............ 1Kin 19:1
Ben-hadad sent out, and they *t* him.. 1Kin 20:17
to meet you, and *t* you these words.... 2Kin 1:7
Then she came and *t* the man of God.. 2Kin 4:7
hid it from me, and hath not *t* me 2Kin 4:27
t him, saying, The child is not........... 2Kin 4:31
t his lord, saying, Thus and thus 2Kin 5:4
place which the man of God *t* him...... 2Kin 6:10
And it was *t* him, saying, Behold,....... 2Kin 6:13
and they *t* them, saying, We came..... 2Kin 7:10
they *t* it to the king's house............... 2Kin 7:11
returned, and *t* the king 2Kin 7:15
king asked the woman, she *t* him 2Kin 8:6
and it was *t* him, saying, The man..... 2Kin 8:7
He *t* me that thou shouldest............... 2Kin 8:14
And the watchman said, saying, The 2Kin 9:18

And the watchman *t*, saying, He........ 2Kin 9:20
they came again, and *t* him 2Kin 9:36
t him, saying, They have brought 2Kin 10:8
the money that was found in the 2Kin 12:10
And they gave the money, being *t* 2Kin 12:11
t him the words of Rab-shakeh.......... 2Kin 18:37
And the men of the city *t* him........... 2Kin 23:17
hast *t* thy servant that thou wilt....... 1Chr 17:25
t David how the men were served 1Chr 19:17
And it was *t* David............................ 1Chr 19:17
Solomon *t* out threescore and ten 2Chr 2:2
which could not be *t* nor numbered ... 2Chr 5:6
Solomon *t* her all her questions......... 2Chr 9:2
from Solomon which he *t* her not....... 2Chr 9:2
of thy wisdom was not *t* me.............. 2Chr 9:6
came some that *t* Jehoshaphat.......... 2Chr 20:2
Shaphan the scribe *t* the king........... 2Chr 34:18
I *t* them what they should say .... Ezr 8:17
neither I *t* any man what my God ...... Neh 2:12
had I as yet *t* it to the Jews.............. Neh 2:16
Then I *t* them of the hand of my .... Neh 2:18
who *t* it unto Esther the queen .... Est 2:22
not unto them, that they *t* Haman ..... Est 3:4
for he had *t* them that he was a......... Est 3:4
her chamberlains came and *t* it her ... Est 4:4
Mordecai *t* him of all that had.......... Est 4:7
t Esther the words of Mordecai .... Est 4:9
they *t* to Mordecai Esther's words...... Est 4:12
Haman *t* them of the glory of his ...... Est 5:11
that Mordecai had *t* of Bigthana .... Est 6:2
Haman *t* Zeresh his wife and all .... Est 6:13
for Esther had *t* what he was unto..... Est 8:1
men have *t* from their fathers........... Job 15:18
Shall it be *t* him that I speak............ Job 37:20
O God, our fathers have *t* us............. Ps 44:1
t Saul, and said unto him, David....... Ps 52:t
known, and our fathers have *t* us....... Ps 78:3
our years as a tale that is *t*.............. Ps 90:9
he live a thousand years twice *t*....... Eccl 6:6
it was *t* the house of David 1s 7:2
t him the words of Rabshakeh........... 1s 36:22
hath it not been *t* you from the 1s 40:21
have not I *t* thee from that time,....... 1s 44:8
who hath it *t* from that time 1s 45:21
not been *t* them shall they see.......... 1s 52:15
t all the words in the ears of............. Jer 36:20
he *t* them according to all these .... Jer 38:27
I *t* the dream before them................. Dan 4:8
and before him I *t* the dream .... Dan 4:8
and I the sum of the matters............... Dan 7:1
So he *t* me, and made me know the .. Dan 7:16
the morning which was *t* is true .... Dan 8:26
the LORD, because he had *t* them...... Jonah 1:10
not believe, though it be *t* you.......... Hab 1:5
a lie, and have *t* false dreams;.......... Zec 10:2
I every thing, and what was................ Mt 8:33
and said unto him that *t* him............. Mt 12:48
and buried it, and went and *t* Jesus .. Mt 14:12
t unto their lord all that was .... Mt 18:31
Behold, I have *t* you before.............. Mt 24:25
for a memorial of her........................ Mt 26:13
lo, I have *t* you................................ Mt 28:7
t it in the city, and in the .... Mk 5:14
they that saw it *t* them how it.......... Mk 5:16
him, and *t* him all the truth.............. Mk 5:33
t him all things, both what they .... Mk 6:30
t them, Elias verily cometh first .... Mk 9:12
t them that had been with him, as .... Mk 16:10
went and *t* it unto the residue.......... Mk 16:13
which were *t* her from the Lord .... Lk 1:45
was *t* them concerning this child....... Lk 2:17
were *t* them by the shepherds .... Lk 2:18
and seen, as it was *t* unto them .... Lk 2:20
it was *t* him by certain which,........... Lk 8:20
it it in the city and in the .... Lk 8:34
They also which saw it *t* them by...... Lk 8:36
t him all that they had done............ Lk 9:10
I no man in those days any of............. Lk 9:21
some that *t* him of the Galilaeans..... Lk 13:1
And they *t* him, that Jesus of........... Lk 18:37
t all these things unto the............... Lk 24:10
they *t* what things were done in the.. Lk 24:35
If I have *t* you earthly things,........... Jn 3:12
which I me all things that ever I........ Jn 4:29
He *t* me all that ever I did................. Jn 4:39
t him, saying, Thy son liveth............ Jn 4:51
the Jews that it was Jesus.................. Jn 5:15
a man that hath *t* you the truth......... Jn 8:40
I have *t* you already, and ye............ Jn 9:27
I *t* you, and ye believed not .... Jn 10:25
t them what things Jesus had done ... Jn 11:46
were not so, I would have *t* you .... Jn 14:2
now I have *t* you before it come .... Jn 14:29
But these things have I *t* you............ Jn 16:4
may remember that I *t* you of them.... Jn 16:4
I have *t* you that I am he .... Jn 18:8
the disciples that she had seen........... Jn 20:18
the prison, they returned, and I......... Acts 5:22
t them, saying, Behold, the men .... Acts 5:25
it shall be *t* thee what thou must ...... Acts 9:6
t how Peter stood before the gate .... Acts 12:14
the prison *t* this saying to Paul......... Acts 16:36
the serjeants *t* these words unto ...... Acts 16:38
then it shall be *t* thee of all .... Acts 22:10
the chief captain, saying, Take.......... Acts 22:26
into the castle, and *t* Paul................ Acts 23:16
when it was *t* how that the............... Acts 23:30
it shall be even as it was *t* me........... Acts 27:25
when he *t* us your earnest desire,..... 2Cor 7:7

t you before, and foretell you,........... 2Cor 13:2
as I have also *t* you in time past .... Gal 5:21
walk, of whom I have *t* you often ...... Phil 3:18
we *t* you before that we should.......... 1Th 3:4
with you, I *t* you these things............. 2Th 2:5
How that they *t* you there should ...... Jude 18

TOLERABLE

It shall be more *t* for the land .... Mt 10:15
you, It shall be more *t* for Tyre........... Mt 11:22
That it shall be more *t* for the .... Mt 11:24
you, It shall be more *t* for Sodom....... Mk 6:11
be more *t* in that day for Sodom .... Lk 10:12
But it shall be more *t* for Tyre........... Lk 10:14

TOLL

again, then will they not pay *t* .... Ezr 4:13
and *t*, tribute, and custom, was......... Ezr 4:20
shall not be lawful to impose *t* .... Ezr 7:24

TOMB

grave, and shall remain in the *t*........ Job 21:32
And laid it in his own new *t*............... Mt 27:60
up his corpse, and laid it in a *t*......... Mk 6:29

TOMBS

with devils, coming out of the *t*......... Mt 8:28
ye build the *t* of the prophets............ Mt 23:29
there met him out of the *t* a man....... Mk 5:2
Who had his dwelling among the *t*..... Mk 5:3
was in the mountains, and in the *t*.... Mk 5:5
abode in any house, but in the *t*....... Lk 8:27

TONGS

the *t* thereof, and the snuffdishes ..... Ex 25:38
the light, and his lamps, and his *t*...... Num 4:9
and the lamps, and the *t* of gold,....... 1Kin 7:49
flowers, and the lamps, and the *t*...... 2Chr 4:21
with the *t* from off the altar 1s 6:6
The smith with the *t* both worketh 1s 44:12

TONGUE

every one after his *t*, after .... Gen 10:5
am slow of speech, and of a slow *t*.... Ex 4:10
Israel shalt not a dog move his *t* .... Ex 11:7
a nation whose *t* thou shalt not......... Deut 28:49
none moved his *t* against any of........ Josh 10:21
lappeth of the water with his *t* .... Judg 7:5
by me, and his word was in my *t*....... 2Sa 23:2
was written in the Syrian *t*............... Ezr 4:7
and interpreted in the Syrian *t*......... Ezr 4:7
and bondwomen, I had held my *t*...... Est 7:4
be hid from the scourge of the *t*....... Job 5:21
Teach me, and I will hold my *t*......... Job 6:24
Is there iniquity in my *t*................... Job 6:30
for now, if I hold my *t*, I shall.......... Job 13:19
thou choosest the *t* of the crafty...... Job 15:5
though he hide it under his *t*............ Job 20:12
the viper's *t* shall slay him .... Job 20:16
wickedness, nor my *t* utter deceit ..... Job 27:4
their *t* cleaved to the roof of .... Job 29:10
my *t* hath spoken in my mouth......... Job 33:2
or his *t* with a cord which thou......... Job 41:1
they flatter with their *t*................... Ps 5:9
under his *t* is mischief and vanity ..... Ps 10:7
the *t* that speaketh proud things ...... Ps 12:3
With our *t* will we prevail................. Ps 12:4
He that backbiteth not with his *t*...... Ps 15:3
and my *t* cleaveth to my jaws........... Ps 22:15
Keep thy *t* from evil, and thy lips...... Ps 34:13
And my *t* shall speak of thy .... Ps 35:28
his *t* talketh of judgment................. Ps 37:30
my ways, that I sin not with my *t*...... Ps 39:1
then spake I with my *t*..................... Ps 39:3
my *t* the pen of a ready writer .... Ps 45:1
to evil, and thy *t* frameth deceit ...... Ps 50:19
my *t* shall sing aloud of thy .... Ps 51:14
Thy *t* deviseth mischiefs .... Ps 52:2
O thou deceitful *t*............................ Ps 52:4
arrows, and their *t* a sharp sword...... Ps 57:4
Who whet their *t* like a sword........... Ps 64:3
own *t* to fall upon themselves .... Ps 64:8
and he was extolled with my *t* .... Ps 66:17
the *t* of thy dogs in the same........... Ps 68:23
My *t* also shall talk of thy .... Ps 71:24
their waketh through the earth .... Ps 73:9
spoken against me with a lying *t*....... Ps 109:2
My *t* shall speak of thy word............ Ps 119:172
lying lips, and from a deceitful *t*....... Ps 120:2
be done unto thee, thou false *t* .... Ps 120:3
laughter, and our *t* with singing .... Ps 126:2
let my *t* cleave to the roof of my....... Ps 137:6
For there is not a word in my *t*......... Ps 139:4
A proud look, a lying *t*, and hands..... Prov 6:17
of the *t* of a strange woman............. Prov 6:24
The *t* of the just is as choice............ Prov 10:20
but the froward *t* shall be cut .... Prov 10:31
but the *t* of the wise is health.......... Prov 12:18
but a lying *t* is but for a moment....... Prov 12:19
The *t* of the wise useth knowledge.... Prov 15:2
A wholesome *t* is a tree of life.......... Prov 15:4
in man, and the answer of the *t*........ Prov 16:1
a liar giveth ear to a naughty *t*........ Prov 17:4
perverse falleth into mischief............. Prov 17:20
and life are in the power of the *t*....... Prov 18:21
a lying *t* is a vanity tossed to........... Prov 21:6
his *t* keepeth his soul from.............. Prov 21:23
a soft *t* breaketh the bone............... Prov 25:15
angry countenance a backbiting *t*..... Prov 25:23
A lying *t* hateth those that are .... Prov 26:28
he that flattereth with his *t*............. Prov 28:23
in her *t* is the law of kindness.......... Prov 31:26
honey and milk are under thy *t*......... Song 4:11

T

because their *t* and their doings............ Is 3:8
destroy the *t* of the Egyptian sea...... Is 11:15
another *t* will he speak to this............. Is 28:11
his *t* as a devouring fire...................... Is 30:27
the *t* of the stammerers shall be........... Is 32:4
of a stammering *t*, that thou .... Is 33:19
hart, and the *t* of the dumb sing......... Is 35:6
their *t* faileth for thirst, I the............. Is 41:17
shall bow, every *t* shall swear.............. Is 45:23
given me the *t* of the learned............... Is 50:4
every *t* that shall rise against.............. Is 54:17
a wide mouth, and draw out the *t*........ Is 57:4
your *t* hath muttered perverseness........ Is 59:3
have taught their *t* to speak lies........... Jer 9:5
Their *t* is an arrow shot out............... Jer 9:8
and let us smite him with the *t*............ Jer 18:18
The *t* of the sucking child.................... Lam 4:4
I will make thy *t* cleave to the .... Eze 3:26
and the *t* of the Chaldeans.................. Dan 1:4
the sword for the rage of their *t* .... Hos 7:16
Then shall he say, Hold thy *t*............... Amos 6:10
their *t* is deceitful in their................... Mic 6:12
holdest thy *t* when the wicked.............. Hab 1:13
t be found in their mouth..................... Zeph 3:13
their *t* shall consume away in .... Zec 14:12
and he spit, and touched his *t* .... Mk 7:33
and the string of his *t* was loosed......... Mk 7:35
his *t* loosed, and he spake, and .... Lk 1:64
his finger in water, and cool my *t* .... Lk 16:24
called in the Hebrew *t* Bethesda........... Jn 5:2
field is called in their proper *t* .... Acts 1:19
hear we every man in our own *t* .... Acts 2:8
heart rejoice, and my *t* was glad......... Acts 2:26
spake unto them in the Hebrew *t* .... Acts 21:40
he spake in the Hebrew *t* to them........ Acts 22:2
me, and saying in the Hebrew *t* .... Acts 26:14
every *t* shall confess to God................. Rom 14:11
unknown *t* speaketh not unto men....... 1Cor 14:2
in an unknown *t* edifieth himself.......... 1Cor 14:4
except ye utter by the *t* words.............. 1Cor 14:9
t pray that he may interpret.................. 1Cor 14:13
For if I pray in an unknown *t* 1Cor 14:14
thousand words in an unknown *t* 1Cor 14:19
psalm, hath a doctrine, hath a *t* 1Cor 14:26
if any man speak in an unknown *t* 1Cor 14:27
that every *t* should confess that............ Phil 2:11
religious, and bridleth not his *t* .... Jas 1:26
Even so the *t* is a little member,........... Jas 3:5
the *t* is a fire, a world of....................... Jas 3:6
so is the *t* among our members,............ Jas 3:6
But the *t* can no man tame.................... Jas 3:8
let him refrain his *t* from evil................ 1Pet 3:10
us not love in word, neither in *t* 1Jn 3:18
blood out of every kindred, and *t* .... Rev 5:9
name in the Hebrew *t* is Abaddon......... Rev 9:11
but in the Greek *t* hath his name......... Rev 9:11
to every nation, and kindred, and *t* ..... Rev 14:6
called in the Hebrew *t* Armageddon...... Rev 16:16

TONGUES

their families, after their *t*.................... Gen 10:20
their families, after their *t*.................... Gen 10:31
a pavilion from the strife of *t* .... Ps 31:20
O Lord, and divide their *t* .... Ps 55:9
they lied unto him with their *t* .... Ps 78:36
sharpened their *t* like a serpent........... Ps 140:3
I will gather all nations and *t* .... Is 66:18
they bend their *t* like their bow........... Jer 9:3
saith the Lord, that use their *t* .... Jer 23:31
they shall speak with new *t* .... Mk 16:17
them cloven *t* like as of fire.................. Acts 2:3
and began to speak with other *t* .... Acts 2:4
our *t* the wonderful works of God......... Acts 2:11
For they heard them speak with *t* .... Acts 10:46
and they spake with *t*, and .... Acts 19:6
with their *t* they have used................... Rom 3:13
to another divers kinds of *t* 1Cor 12:10
another the interpretation of *t* 1Cor 12:10
governments, diversities of *t* 1Cor 12:28
do all speak with *t* 1Cor 12:30
Though I speak with the *t* of men......... 1Cor 13:1
whether there be *t*, they shall.............. 1Cor 13:8
I would that ye all spake with *t* 1Cor 14:5
than he that speaketh with *t* 1Cor 14:5
I come unto you speaking with *t* 1Cor 14:6
I speak with *t* more than ye all............ 1Cor 14:18
is written, With men of other *t* 1Cor 14:21
Wherefore *t* are for a sign, not............. 1Cor 14:22
one place, and all speak with *t* 1Cor 14:23
and forbid not to speak with *t* 1Cor 14:39
and kindreds, and people, and *t* .... Rev 7:9
many peoples, and nations, and *t* .... Rev 10:11
of the people and kindreds and *t* .... Rev 11:9
given him over all kindreds, and *t* .... Rev 13:7
and they gnawed their *t* for pain.......... Rev 16:10
and multitudes, and nations, and *t* .... Rev 17:15

TOO

is any thing *t* hard for the Lord........... Gen 18:14
be *t* little for the lamb, let him............. Ex 12:4
this thing is *t* heavy for thee................. Ex 18:18
the work to make it, and *t* much........... Ex 36:7
because it is *t* heavy for me .... Num 11:14
Ye take *t* much upon you, seeing........... Num 16:3
ye take *t* much upon you, ye sons......... Num 16:7
for they are *t* mighty for me................. Num 22:6
the cause that is *t* hard for you............ Deut 1:17
was not one city *t* strong for us............ Deut 2:36
his name there be *t* far from thee.......... Deut 12:21
And if the way be *t* long for thee.......... Deut 14:24
if the place be *t* far from thee.............. Deut 14:24

If there arise a matter *t* hard............... Deut 17:8
Ephraim be *t* narrow for them.............. Josh 17:15
of Judah was *t* much for them.............. Josh 19:9
of Dan went out *t* little for them......... Josh 19:47
iniquity of Peor *t* little for us.............. Josh 22:17
are *t* many for me to give the.............. Judg 7:2
Gideon, The people are yet *t* many....... Judg 7:4
that they were *t* strong for him............ Judg 18:26
for I am *t* old to have an husband....... Ruth 1:12
sons of Zeruiah be *t* hard for me......... 2Sa 3:39
If the Syrians be *t* strong for me.......... 2Sa 10:11
of Ammon be *t* strong for thee............ 2Sa 10:11
and if that had been *t* little.................. 2Sa 12:8
for they were *t* strong for me 2Sa 22:18
God of my lord the king say so *t* 1Kin 1:36
was *t* little to receive the burnt............ 1Kin 8:64
It is *t* much for you to go up to.......... 1Kin 12:28
the journey is *t* great for thee.............. 1Kin 19:7
the battle was *t* sore for him................ 2Kin 3:26
with thee is *t* strait for us................... 2Kin 6:1
If the Syrians be *t* strong for me.......... 1Chr 19:12
of Ammon be *t* strong for them............ 1Chr 19:12
But the priests were *t* few.................... 2Chr 29:34
shall there arise *t* much contempt......... Est 1:18
wonderful for me, which I knew.............. Ps 35:10
for they were *t* strong for me .... Ps 18:17
from him that is *t* strong for him......... Ps 35:10
burden they are *t* heavy for me........... Ps 38:4
this, it was *t* painful for me................. Ps 73:16
or in things *t* high for me.................... Ps 131:1
knowledge is *t* wonderful for me.......... Ps 139:6
Wisdom is *t* high for a fool................. Prov 24:7
which are *t* wonderful for me............... Prov 30:18
shall even now be *t* narrow by............. Is 49:19
The place is *t* strait for me................. Is 49:20
there is nothing *t* hard for thee........... Jer 32:17
is there any thing *t* hard for me.......... Jer 32:27
all things ye are *t* superstitious............ Acts 17:22

TOOK See PREFACE.

TOOKEST

though thou *t* vengeance of their........... Ps 99:8
t thy broidered garments, and.............. Eze 16:18

TOOL

for if thou lift up thy *t* upon it........... Ex 20:25
and fashioned it with a graving *t* .... Ex 32:4
not lift up any iron *t* upon them.......... Deut 27:5
any *t* of iron heard in the house.......... 1Kin 6:7

TOOTH

Eye for eye, *t* for *t*, hand.................... Ex 21:24
he smite out his manservant's *t* .... Ex 21:27
or his maidservant's *t* .... Ex 21:27
breach, eye for eye, *t* for *t* .... Lev 24:20
life, eye for eye, *t* for *t* .... Deut 19:21
of trouble is like a broken *t* .... Prov 25:19
for an eye, and a *t* for a *t* .... Mt 5:38

TOOTH'S

let him go free for his *t* sake............... Ex 21:27

TOP

whose *t* may reach unto heaven............ Gen 11:4
the *t* of it reached to heaven............... Gen 28:12
and poured oil upon the *t* of it............ Gen 28:18
to morrow I will stand on the *t* .... Ex 17:9
Hur went up to the *t* of the hill.......... Ex 17:10
Sinai, on the *t* of the mount............... Ex 19:20
Moses up to the *t* of the mount........... Ex 19:20
was like devouring fire on the *t* .... Ex 24:17
shall be an hole in the *t* of it.............. Ex 28:32
the *t* thereof, and the sides.................. Ex 30:3
there to me in the *t* of the mount........ Ex 34:2
with pure gold, both the *t* of it........... Ex 37:26
up into the *t* of the mountain.............. Num 14:40
presumed to go up unto the hill *t* .... Num 14:44
died there in the *t* of the mount.......... Num 20:28
to the *t* of Pisgah, which looketh......... Num 21:20
For from the *t* of the rocks I see......... Num 23:9
to the *t* of Pisgah, and built............... Num 23:14
brought Balaam unto the *t* of Peor....... Num 23:28
Get thee up into the *t* of Pisgah.......... Deut 3:27
thy foot unto the *t* of thy head............ Deut 28:35
upon the *t* of the head of him............. Deut 33:16
to the *t* of Pisgah, that is over............ Deut 34:1
the border went up to the *t* of............ Josh 15:8
of the hill unto the fountain.................. Josh 15:9
thy God upon the *t* of this rock........... Judg 6:26
stood in the *t* of mount Gerizim......... Judg 9:7
for him in the *t* of the mountains........ Judg 9:25
down from the *t* of the mountains........ Judg 9:36
gat them up to the *t* of the tower........ Judg 9:51
dwelt in the *t* of the rock Etam........... Judg 15:8
went to the *t* of the rock Etam............ Judg 15:11
carried them up to the *t* of an............ Judg 16:3
with Saul upon the *t* of the house........ 1Sa 9:25
called Saul to the *t* of the house.......... 1Sa 9:26
stood on the *t* of an hill afar............... 1Sa 26:13
and stood on the *t* of an hill............... 2Sa 2:25
was come to the *t* of the mount........... 2Sa 15:32
a little past the *t* of the hill............... 2Sa 16:1
a tent upon the *t* of the house............. 2Sa 16:22
were upon the *t* of the pillars............. 1Kin 7:17
chapiters that were upon the *t* 1Kin 7:18
the *t* of the pillars were of lily........... 1Kin 7:19
upon the *t* of the pillars was.............. 1Kin 7:22
in the *t* of the base was there a.......... 1Kin 7:35
on the *t* of the base the ledges............ 1Kin 7:35
were on the *t* of the two pillars.......... 1Kin 7:41
were upon the *t* of the pillars............. 1Kin 7:41
the *t* of the throne was round............. 1Kin 10:19

Elijah went up to the *t* of Carmel........ 1Kin 18:42
he sat on the *t* of an hill.................... 2Kin 1:9
under him on the *t* of the stairs.......... 2Kin 9:13
the altars that were on the *t* 2Kin 23:12
the chapiter that was on the *t* 2Chr 3:15
were on the *t* of the two pillars.......... 2Chr 4:12
were on the *t* of the pillars................. 2Chr 4:12
them unto the *t* of the rock................ 2Chr 25:12
them down from the *t* of the rock....... 2Chr 25:12
touched the *t* of the sceptre................ Esth 5:2
earth upon the *t* of the mountains....... Ps 72:16
a sparrow alone upon the house *t* .... Ps 102:7
standeth in the *t* of high places.......... Prov 8:2
that lieth upon the *t* of a mast........... Prov 23:34
look from the *t* of Amana, from........... Song 4:8
from the *t* of Shenir and Hermon,....... Song 4:8
in the *t* of the mountains.................... Is 2:2
in the *t* of the uppermost bough.......... Is 17:6
a beacon upon the *t* of a mountain...... Is 30:17
shout from the *t* of the mountains........ Is 42:11
hunger in the *t* of every street............ Lam 2:19
out in the *t* of every street................. Lam 4:1
off the *t* of his young twigs................. Eze 17:4
I will crop off from the *t* of his.......... Eze 17:22
she set it upon the *t* of a rock............ Eze 24:7
her blood upon the *t* of a rock............ Eze 24:8
and make her like the *t* of a rock........ Eze 26:4
make thee like the *t* of a rock............. Eze 26:14
his *t* was among the thick boughs........ Eze 31:3
he hath shot up his *t* among the.......... Eze 31:10
up their *t* among the thick boughs........ Eze 31:14
Upon the *t* of the mountain the........... Eze 43:12
the *t* of Carmel shall wither............... Amos 1:2
themselves in the *t* of Carmel.............. Amos 9:3
in the *t* of the mountains................... Mic 4:1
at the *t* of all the streets................... Nah 3:10
with a bowl upon the *t* of it............... Zec 4:2
which are upon the *t* thereof.............. Zec 4:2
in twain from the *t* to the bottom....... Mt 27:51
in twain from the *t* to the bottom....... Mk 15:38
seam, woven from the *t* throughout...... Jn 19:23
leaning upon the *t* of his staff............ Heb 11:21

TOPAZ

first row shall be a sardius, a *t* .... Ex 28:17
the first row was a sardius, a *t* .... Ex 39:10
The *t* of Ethiopia shall not equal........ Job 28:19
was thy covering, the sardius, *t* .... Eze 28:13
the ninth, a *t* .... Rev 21:20

TOPHEL (to'-fel) A place in the Sinai wilderness.
the Red sea, between Paran, and T......... Deut 1:1

TOPHET (to'-fet) See TOPHETH. A place in the valley of Hinnom.
For T is ordained of old........................ Is 30:33
have built the high places of T.............. Jer 7:31
that it shall no more be called T........... Jer 7:32
for they shall bury in T, till................. Jer 7:32
place shall no more be called T............. Jer 19:6
and they shall bury them in T............... Jer 19:11
even them make this city as T............... Jer 19:12
be defiled as the place of T................... Jer 19:13
Then came Jeremiah from T................... Jer 19:14

TOPHETH (to'-feth) See TOPHET. Same as Tophet.
And he defiled T, which is in the.......... 2Kin 23:10

TOPS

were the *t* of the mountains seen......... Gen 8:5
in the *t* of the mulberry trees............. 2Sa 5:24
to set upon the *t* of the pillars........... 1Kin 7:16
herb, as the grass on the house *t* 2Kin 19:26
in the *t* of the mulberry trees............. 1Chr 14:15
cut off as the *t* of the ears of............. Job 24:24
into the *t* of the ragged rocks,............ Is 2:21
in all the *t* of the mountains, and....... Is 15:3
upon the *t* of the mountains............... Eze 6:13
t of mountains shall they leap.............. Joel 2:5

TORCH
like a *t* of fire in a sheaf .... Zec 12:6

TORCHES
t in the day of his preparation............ Nah 2:3
they shall seem like *t*, they................. Nah 2:4
cometh thither with lanterns and *t* ...... Jn 18:3

TORMENT
hither to *t* us before the time.............. Mt 8:29
thee by God, that thou *t* me not.......... Mk 5:7
I beseech thee, *t* me not..................... Lk 8:28
also come into this place of *t* .... Lk 16:28
because fear hath *t* 1Jn 4:18
their *t* was as the *t* of .... Rev 9:5
was as the *t* of a scorpion.................. Rev 9:5
the smoke of their *t* ascendeth up....... Rev 14:11
and lived deliciously, so much *t* .... Rev 18:7
afar off for the fear of her *t* .... Rev 18:10
afar off for the fear of her *t* .... Rev 18:15

TORMENTED
sick of the palsy, grievously *t* .... Mt 8:6
for I am *t* in this flame..................... Lk 16:24
he is comforted, and thou art *t* .... Lk 16:25
being destitute, afflicted, *t* .... Heb 11:37
that they should be *t* five months........ Rev 9:5
because these two prophets *t* them....... Rev 11:10
and he shall be *t* with fire.................. Rev 14:10
prophet are, and shall be *t* day............ Rev 20:10

TORMENTORS

wroth, and delivered him to the t....... Mt 18:34

TORMENTS

taken with divers diseases and t .... Mt 4:24
he lift up his eyes, being in t............. Lk 16:23

TORN

That which was t of beasts I........... Gen 31:39
I said, Surely he is t in pieces........... Gen 44:28
If it be t in pieces, then let .... Ex 22:13
not make good that which was t .... Ex 22:13
that is t of beasts in the field .... Ex 22:31
that of which is t with beasts .... Lev 7:24
or that which was t with beasts .... Lev 17:15
or is t with beasts, he shall not........ Lev 22:8
unto the lion, which hath t him....... 1Kin 13:26
eaten the carcase, nor t the ass....... 1Kin 13:28
their carcases were t in the........... Is 5:25
out thence shall be t in pieces......... Jer 5:6
of itself, or is t in pieces............... Eze 4:14
that is dead of itself, or t.............. Eze 44:31
for he hath t, and he will heal us...... Hos 6:1
and ye brought that which was t..... Mal 1:13
when the unclean spirit had t him..... Mk 1:26

TORTOISE

mouse, and the t after his kind,....... Lev 11:29

TORTURED

and others were t, not accepting...... Heb 11:35

TOSS

t thee like a ball into a large........... Is 22:18
the waves thereof t themselves........ Jer 5:22

TOSSED

I am t up and down as the locust...... Ps 109:23
a lying tongue is a vanity t to......... Prov 21:6
t with tempest, and not comforted,.... Is 54:11
midst of the sea, t with waves.......... Mt 14:24
exceedingly t with a tempest.......... Acts 27:18
t to and fro, and carried about....... Eph 4:14
the sea driven with the wind and t.... Jas 1:6

TOSSINGS

and I am full of t to and fro unto..... Job 7:4

TOTTERING

wall shall ye be, and as a t fence...... Ps 62:3

TOU

(to'-u) See Toi. *Same as* Toi.
Now when T king of Hamath heard.... 1Chr 18:9
(for Hadarezer had war with T......... 1Chr 18:10

TOUCH

eat of it, neither shall ye t it .... Gen 3:3
suffered I thee not to t her............ Gen 20:6
the mount, or t the border of it .... Ex 19:12
There shall not an hand t it .... Ex 19:13
Or if a soul t any unclean thing........ Lev 5:2
Or if he t the uncleanness of man..... Lev 5:3
Whatsoever shall t the flesh........... Lev 6:27
that shall t any unclean thing,......... Lev 7:21
and their carcase shall ye not t .... Lev 11:8
whosoever doth t them, when they..... Lev 11:31
she shall t no hallowed thing,......... Lev 12:4
they shall not t any holy thing........ Num 4:15
t nothing of theirs, lest ye be........ Num 16:26
flesh, nor t their dead carcase......... Deut 14:8
now therefore we may not t them..... Josh 9:19
men that they shall not t thee......... Ruth 2:9
he shall not t thee any more........... 2Sa 14:10
Beware that none t the young man..... 2Sa 18:12
But the man that shall t them......... 2Sa 23:7
T not mine anointed, and do my....... 1Chr 16:22
t all that he hath, and he will.......... Job 1:11
t his bone and his flesh, and he........ Job 2:5
seven there shall no evil t thee........ Job 5:19
to t are as my sorrowful meat.......... Job 6:7
T not mine anointed, and do my....... Ps 105:15
t the mountains, and they shall........ Ps 144:5
from thence, t no unclean thing........ Is 52:11
that t the inheritance which I.......... Jer 12:14
men could not t their garments........ Lam 4:14
depart, depart, t not........................ Lam 4:15
and with his skirt do t bread............ Hag 2:12
by a dead body t any of these.......... Hag 2:13
If I may but t his garment............... Mt 9:21
only t the hem of his garment......... Mt 14:36
pressed upon him for to t him......... Mk 3:10
If I may t but his clothes,................ Mk 5:28
t if it were but the border of......... Mk 6:56
him, and besought him to t him........ Mk 8:22
to him, that he should t them........... Mk 10:13
whole multitude sought to t him...... Lk 6:19
ye yourselves t not the burdens....... Lk 11:46
that they would t him .... Lk 18:15
Jesus saith unto her, T me not......... Jn 20:17
good for a man not to t a woman..... 1Cor 7:1
Lord, and t not the unclean thing..... 2Cor 6:17
T not; taste not............................. Col 2:21
the firstborn should t them............ Heb 11:28
so much as a beast t the mountain.... Heb 12:20

TOUCHED

us no hurt, as we have not t thee...... Gen 26:29
he t the hollow of his thigh............ Gen 32:25
because he t the hollow of............. Gen 32:32
The soul which hath t any such........ Lev 22:6
there, and upon him that t a bone.... Num 19:18
and whosoever hath t any slain........ Num 31:19
t the flesh and the unleavened........ Judg 6:21
of men, whose hearts God had t....... 1Sa 10:26
wing of the one t the one wall.......... 1Kin 6:27

the other cherub t the other wall...... 1Kin 6:27
their wings t one another in the........ 1Kin 6:27
tree, behold, then an angel t him...... 1Kin 19:5
t him, and said, Arise and eat.......... 1Kin 19:7
the bones of Elisha, he revived......... 2Kin 13:21
near, and t the top of the sceptre..... Est 5:2
for the hand of God hath t me.......... Job 19:21
and said, Lo, this hath t thy lips........ Is 6:7
put forth his hand, and t my mouth... Jer 1:9
creatures that t one another............ Eze 3:13
whole earth, and t not the ground..... Dan 8:5
but he t me, and set me upright........ Dan 8:18
t me about the time of the............. Dan 9:21
And, behold, an hand t me, which..... Dan 10:10
of the sons of men t my lips.......... Dan 10:16
t me one like the appearance of a..... Dan 10:18
hand, and t him, saying, I will......... Mt 8:3
he t her hand, and the fever left...... Mt 8:15
him, and t the hem of his garment.... Mt 9:20
Then t he their eyes, saying,........... Mt 9:29
as many as t were made perfectly..... Mt 14:36
t them, and said, Arise, and be not.... Mt 17:7
on them, and t their eyes............... Mt 20:34
t him, and saith unto him, I will....... Mk 1:41
press behind, and t his garment....... Mk 5:27
press, and said, Who t my clothes..... Mk 5:30
thee, and sayest thou, Who t me....... Mk 5:31
as many as t him were made whole.... Mk 6:56
ears, and he spit, and t his tongue.... Mk 7:33
hand, and t him, saying, I will......... Lk 5:13
And he came and t the bier............. Lk 7:14
t the border of his garment............ Lk 8:44
And Jesus said, Who t me............... Lk 8:45
thee, and sayest thou, Who t me....... Lk 8:45
And Jesus said, Somebody hath t me.. Lk 8:46
for what cause she had t him........... Lk 8:47
he t his ear, and healed him........... Lk 22:51
And the next day we t at Sidon......... Acts 27:3
be t with the feeling of our............. Heb 4:15
unto the mount that might be t....... Heb 12:18

TOUCHETH

He that t this man or his wife.......... Gen 26:11
whosoever t the mount shall be....... Ex 19:12
whatsoever t the altar shall be......... Ex 29:37
whatsoever t them shall be holy....... Ex 30:29
every one that t them shall be......... Lev 6:18
the flesh that t any unclean........... Lev 7:19
whosoever t the carcase of them ..... Lev 11:24
every one that t them shall be......... Lev 11:26
whoso t their carcase shall be........ Lev 11:27
but that which t their carcase......... Lev 11:31
he that t the carcase thereof.......... Lev 11:39
whosoever t his bed shall wash........ Lev 15:5
he that t the flesh of him that......... Lev 15:7
whosoever t any thing that was on.... Lev 15:10
whomsoever he t that hath the........ Lev 15:11
that he t which hath the issue........ Lev 15:12
whosoever t her bed shall be unclean. Lev 15:21
whosoever t her bed shall wash....... Lev 15:22
whosoever t any thing that she........ Lev 15:22
whereon she sitteth, when he t it...... Lev 15:23
whosoever t those things shall be..... Lev 15:27
whoso t any thing that is unclean..... Lev 22:4
Or whosoever t any creeping thing.... Lev 22:5
He that t the dead body of any........ Num 19:11
Whosoever t the dead body of any.... Num 19:13
whosoever t one that is slain........... Num 19:16
he that t the water of separation...... Num 19:21
unclean person t shall be unclean..... Num 19:22
the soul that t it shall be............... Num 19:22
tow is broken when it t the fire....... Judg 16:9
it t thee, and thou art troubled........ Job 4:5
he t the hills, and they smoke......... Ps 104:32
whosoever t her shall not be........... Prov 6:29
wither, when the east wind t it........ Eze 17:10
they break out, and blood t blood..... Hos 4:2
of hosts as the t the land.............. Amos 9:5
for he that t you........................... Zec 2:8
you t the apple of his eye............... Zec 2:8
of woman this is that t her.............. Lk 7:39
and that wicked one t him not......... 1Jn 5:18

TOUCHING

as t them, doth comfort himself,....... Gen 27:42
make an atonement for him as t....... Lev 5:13
unto the Levites t their charge......... Num 8:26
as t the matter which thou and I...... 1Sa 20:23
As t the words which thou hast....... 2Kin 22:18
that t any of the priests and.......... Ezr 7:24
The Almighty, we cannot find.......... Job 37:23
which I have made t the king......... Ps 45:1
song of my beloved t his vineyard.... Is 5:1
them t all their wickedness............. Jer 1:16
t the house of the king of Judah,...... Jer 21:11
For thus saith the LORD t Shallum.... Jer 22:11
for the vision is t the multitude....... Eze 7:13
t any thing that they shall ask........ Mt 18:19
But as t the resurrection of the....... Mt 22:31
as the dead, that they rise............. Mk 12:26
t those things whereof ye accuse..... Lk 23:14
ye intend to do as t these men........ Acts 5:35
As t the Gentiles which believe,...... Acts 21:25
T the resurrection of the dead I...... Acts 24:21
t all the things whereof I am.......... Acts 26:2
but as t the election, they are........ Rom 11:28
Now as t things offered unto.......... 1Cor 8:1
As t our brother Apollos, I............. 1Cor 16:12
For as t the ministering to the........ 2Cor 9:1
as t the law, a Pharisee................ Phil 3:5
t the righteousness which is in........ Phil 3:6

(t whom ye received commandments... Col 4:10
But as t brotherly love ye need....... 1Th 4:9
have confidence in the Lord t you..... 2Th 3:4

TOW

as a thread of t is broken when....... Judg 16:9
And the strong shall be as t............ Is 1:31
extinct, they are quenched as t........ Is 43:17

TOWARD

which goeth t the east of Assyria..... Gen 2:14
going on still t the south............... Gen 12:9
and pitched his tent t Sodom.......... Gen 13:12
and said, Look now t heaven.......... Gen 15:5
and bowed himself t the ground...... Gen 18:2
up from thence, and looked t Sodom.. Gen 18:16
from thence, and went t Sodom....... Gen 18:22
with his face t the ground.............. Gen 19:1
looked t Sodom and Gomorrah........ Gen 19:28
t all the land of the plain, and........ Gen 19:28
from thence t the south country...... Gen 20:1
Egypt, as thou goest t Assyria........ Gen 25:18
from Beer-sheba, and went t Haran... Gen 28:10
of the flocks t the ringstraked........ Gen 30:40
it was not t him as before............ Gen 31:2
that it is not t me as before.......... Gen 31:5
set his face t the mount Gilead........ Gen 31:21
right hand t Israel's left hand......... Gen 48:13
left hand t Israel's right hand........ Gen 48:13
let Moses sprinkle it t he.............. Ex 9:8
and Moses sprinkled it up t heaven... Ex 9:10
Stretch forth thine hand t heaven..... Ex 9:22
stretched forth his rod t heaven...... Ex 9:23
Stretch out thine hand t heaven...... Ex 10:21
stretched forth his hand t heaven.... Ex 10:22
that they looked t the wilderness..... Ex 16:10
t the mercy seat shall the faces....... Ex 25:20
of the tabernacle t the south......... Ex 26:35
t the forepart thereof, over........... Ex 26:27
and bowed his head t the earth....... Ex 34:8
which is t the north corner, he........ Ex 36:25
t the forepart of it, over............... Ex 39:20
lifted up his hand t the people........ Lev 9:22
the part of his head t his face........ Lev 13:41
on the east side t the rising of....... Num 2:3
before the tabernacle t the east....... Num 3:38
that they looked t the tabernacle.... Num 16:42
is before Moab, t the sunrising....... Num 21:11
Pisgah, which looketh t Jeshimon.... Num 21:20
of Peor, that looketh t Jeshimon..... Num 23:28
he set his face t the wilderness...... Num 24:1
fierce anger of the LORD t Israel..... Num 32:14
Jericho eastward, t the sunrising..... Num 34:15
this side Jordan t the sunrising....... Deut 4:41
this side Jordan t the sunrising....... Deut 4:47
eye shall be evil t his brother......... Deut 28:54
t the wife of his bosom, and.......... Deut 28:54
the remnant of his children........... Deut 28:54
her eye shall be evil t the............. Deut 28:56
t her son, and t her daughter......... Deut 28:56
t her young one that cometh out..... Deut 28:57
t her children which she shall......... Deut 28:57
unto the great sea t the going........ Josh 1:4
this side Jordan t the sunrising....... Josh 1:15
came down t the sea of the plain..... Josh 3:16
spear that is in thy hand t Ai.......... Josh 8:18
he had in his hand t the city.......... Josh 8:18
Jordan t the rising of the sun......... Josh 12:1
t the sunrising, from Baal-gad......... Josh 13:5
From thence it passed t Aznon....... Josh 15:4
the border went up t Debir from..... Josh 15:7
and so northward, looking t Gilgal.... Josh 15:7
the border passed t the waters of.... Josh 15:7
t the coast of Edom southward....... Josh 15:21
the border went out t the sea to..... Josh 16:3
went over from thence t Luz.......... Josh 18:13
and went forth t Gelioth............... Josh 18:17
passed along t the side over.......... Josh 18:18
And their border went up t the sea... Josh 19:11
turned from Sarid eastward t the..... Josh 19:12
And their border was t Jezreel........ Josh 19:18
turneth t the sunrising to.............. Josh 19:27
t the north side of Beth-emek........ Josh 19:27
Judah upon Jordan t the sunrising... Josh 19:34
took the fords of Jordan t Moab...... Judg 3:28
draw t mount Tabor, and take with... Judg 4:6
and they set the governors of......... Judg 5:9
even the righteous acts t the.......... Judg 5:11
Then their anger was abated t him... Judg 8:3
when the flame went up t heaven.... Judg 13:20
now the day draweth t evening....... Judg 19:9
t the side of mount Ephraim.......... Judg 19:18
against Gibeah t the sunrising........ Judg 20:43
fled t the wilderness unto the......... Judg 20:45
valley of Zeboim t the wilderness.... 1Sa 13:18
And he turned from him t another.... 1Sa 17:30
ran t the army to meet the............ 1Sa 17:48
behold, if there be good t David...... 1Sa 20:12
arose out of a place t the south...... 1Sa 20:41
the king's heart was t Absalom....... 2Sa 14:1
t the way of the wilderness............ 2Sa 15:23
of the river of Gad, and t Jazer...... 2Sa 24:5
and his servants came t the king..... 2Sa 24:20
on the outside t the great court...... 1Kin 7:9
oxen, three looking t the north....... 1Kin 7:25
and three looking t the west.......... 1Kin 7:25
and three looking t the south........ 1Kin 7:25
and three looking t the east.......... 1Kin 7:25
spread forth his hands t heaven...... 1Kin 8:22
may be open t this house night...... 1Kin 8:29
even t the place of which thou....... 1Kin 8:29

T

servant shall make *t* this place 1Kin 8:29
when they shall pray *t* this place 1Kin 8:30
if they pray *t* this place 1Kin 8:35
forth his hands *t* this house 1Kin 8:38
shall come and pray *t* this house 1Kin 8:42
shall pray unto the LORD *t* the 1Kin 8:44
t the house that I have built for 1Kin 8:44
and pray unto thee *t* their land 1Kin 8:48
t the LORD God of Israel in the 1Kin 14:13
Go up now, look *t* the sea 1Kin 18:43
of Judah, I would not look *t* thee 2Kin 3:14
the king went the way *t* the plain 2Kin 25:4
t the east, west, north, and south 1Chr 9:24
both *t* the east, and *t* the 1Chr 12:15
t the east, and *t* the west 1Chr 12:15
a day, and *t* Asuppim two and two 1Chr 26:17
oxen, three looking *t* the north 2Chr 4:4
and three looking *t* the west 2Chr 4:4
and three looking *t* the south 2Chr 4:4
and three looking *t* the east 2Chr 4:4
spread forth his hands *t* heaven 2Chr 6:13
thy servant prayeth *t* this place 2Chr 6:20
they shall make *t* this place 2Chr 6:21
yet if they pray *t* this place 2Chr 6:26
they pray unto thee *t* this city 2Chr 6:34
pray *t* their land, which thou 2Chr 6:38
the city which thou hast chosen 2Chr 6:38
t the house which I have built 2Chr 6:38
them whose heart is perfect *t* him 2Chr 16:9
when Judah came *t* the watch tower ... 2Chr 20:24
done good in Israel, both *t* God 2Chr 24:16
God, and *t* his house 2Chr 24:16
the Levite, the porter *t* the east 2Chr 31:14
mercy endureth for ever *t* Israel .... Ezr 3:11
against the water gate *t* the east .... Neh 3:26
upon the wall *t* the dung gate .... Neh 12:31
king's manner *t* all that knew law .... Est 1:13
out the golden sceptre *t* Esther .... Est 8:4
dust upon their heads *t* heaven .... Job 2:12
and stretch out thine hands *t* him .... Job 11:13
and stretch her wings *t* the south .... Job 39:26
will I worship *t* thy holy temple .... Ps 5:7
Mine eyes are ever *t* the LORD .... Ps 25:15
up my hands *t* thy holy oracle .... Ps 28:2
his doing *t* the children of men .... Ps 66:5
cause thine anger *t* us to cease .... Ps 85:4
For great is thy mercy *t* me .... Ps 86:13
his truth *t* the house of Israel .... Ps 98:3
is his mercy *t* them that fear him .... Ps 103:11
LORD for all his benefits *t* me .... Ps 116:12
merciful kindness is great *t* us .... Ps 117:2
I will worship *t* thy holy temple .... Ps 138:2
king's favour is *t* a wise servant .... Prov 14:35
fly away as an eagle *t* heaven .... Prov 23:5
The wind goeth *t* the south .... Eccl 1:6
and if the tree fall *t* the south .... Eccl 11:3
or *t* the north, in the place .... Eccl 11:3
Lebanon which looketh *t* Damascus ..... Song 7:4
beloved's, and his desire is *t* me .... Song 7:10
went up *t* Jerusalem to war .... Is 7:1
of the Philistines *t* the west .... Is 11:14
their fear *t* me is taught by the .... Is 29:13
turned his face *t* the wall .... Is 38:2
thee with their face *t* the earth .... Is 49:23
the great goodness *t* the house of .... Is 63:7
thy bowels and of thy mercies *t* me ..... Is 63:15
shall be known *t* his servants .... Is 66:14
and his indignation *t* his enemies .... Is 66:14
the face thereof is *t* the north .... Jer 1:13
proclaim these words *t* the north .... Jer 3:12
Set up the standard *t* Zion .... Jer 4:6
t the daughter of my people .... Jer 4:11
me, and tried mine heart *t* thee .... Jer 12:3
mind could not be *t* this people .... Jer 15:1
and perform my good word *t* you .... Jer 29:10
the thoughts that I think *t* you .... Jer 29:11
set thine heart *t* the highway .... Jer 31:21
of the horse gate *t* the east .... Jer 31:40
fall *t* the north by the river .... Jer 46:6
scatter them *t* all those winds .... Jer 49:36
lift up thy hands *t* him for the .... Lam 2:19
straight, the one *t* the other .... Eze 1:23
thy face *t* the siege of Jerusalem .... Eze 4:7
set thy face *t* the mountains of .... Eze 6:2
than the wilderness *t* Diblath .... Eze 6:14
gate, that looketh *t* the north .... Eze 8:3
eyes now the way *t* the north .... Eze 8:5
up mine eyes the way *t* the north .... Eze 8:5
house which was *t* the north .... Eze 8:14
with their backs *t* the temple of .... Eze 8:16
LORD, and their faces *t* the east .... Eze 8:16
worshipped the sun *t* the east .... Eze 8:16
gate, which lieth *t* the north .... Eze 9:2
I will scatter *t* every wind all .... Eze 12:14
I make my fury *t* thee to rest .... Eze 16:42
when I am pacified *t* thee for all .... Eze 16:63
whose branches turned *t* him .... Eze 17:6
vine did bend her roots *t* him .... Eze 17:7
and shot forth her branches *t* him .... Eze 17:7
shall be scattered *t* all winds .... Eze 17:21
of man, set thy face *t* the south .... Eze 20:46
and drop thy word *t* the south .... Eze 20:46
of man, set thy face *t* Jerusalem .... Eze 21:2
drop thy word *t* the holy places, ... Eze 21:2
and mourn one *t* another .... Eze 24:23
and lift up your eyes *t* your idols .... Eze 33:25
the gate which looketh *t* the east .... Eze 40:6
court that looketh *t* the north .... Eze 40:20
the gate that looketh *t* the east .... Eze 40:22
t the north, and *t* the east .... Eze 40:23

that he brought me *t* the south .... Eze 40:24
and behold a gate *t* the south .... Eze 40:24
in the inner court *t* the south .... Eze 40:27
t the south an hundred cubits .... Eze 40:27
thereof were *t* the utter court .... Eze 40:31
into the inner court *t* the east .... Eze 40:32
thereof were *t* the outward court .... Eze 40:34
thereof were *t* the utter court .... Eze 40:37
and their prospect was *t* the north .... Eze 42:44
having the prospect *t* the north .... Eze 40:44
whose prospect is *t* the south .... Eze 40:45
is *t* the north is for the priests .... Eze 40:46
were *t* the place that was left .... Eze 41:11
one door *t* the north, and another .... Eze 41:11
and another door *t* the south .... Eze 41:11
end *t* the west was seventy cubits .... Eze 41:12
of the separate place *t* the east .... Eze 41:14
t the palm tree on the one side .... Eze 41:19
the face of a young lion *t* the .... Eze 41:19
utter court, the way *t* the north .... Eze 42:1
before the building *t* the north .... Eze 42:1
and their doors *t* the north .... Eze 42:4
t the utter court on the forepart .... Eze 42:7
the wall of the court *t* the east .... Eze 42:10
chambers which were *t* the north .... Eze 42:11
t the south was a door in the .... Eze 42:12
before the wall *t* the east .... Eze 42:12
he brought me forth *t* the gate .... Eze 42:15
gate whose prospect is *t* the east .... Eze 42:15
the gate that looketh *t* the east .... Eze 43:1
gate whose prospect is *t* the east .... Eze 43:4
his stairs shall look *t* the east .... Eze 43:17
which looketh *t* the east .... Eze 44:1
the east shall be shut the six .... Eze 46:1
the gate that looketh *t* the east .... Eze 46:12
priests, which looked *t* the north .... Eze 46:19
of the house stood *t* the east: .... Eze 47:1
issue out *t* the east downward .... Eze 47:8
of the land *t* the north side, ... Eze 47:15
t the north five and twenty .... Eze 48:10
t the west ten thousand in .... Eze 48:10
t the east ten thousand in .... Eze 48:10
t the south five and twenty .... Eze 48:10
shall be *t* the north two hundred .... Eze 48:16
t the south two hundred and fifty, ... Eze 48:17
t the east two hundred and fifty, ... Eze 48:17
t the west two hundred and fifty, ... Eze 48:17
of the oblation *t* the east border .... Eze 48:21
twenty thousand *t* the west border ...... Eze 48:21
to the river *t* the great sea .... Eze 48:28
the high God hath wrought *t* me .... Dan 4:2
open in his chamber *t* Jerusalem .... Dan 6:10
ones *t* the four winds of heaven .... Dan 8:8
t the south, and *t* the east, ... Dan 8:9
the east, and *t* the pleasant land .... Dan 8:9
sleep on my face *t* the ground .... Dan 8:18
my face, and my face *t* the ground....... Dan 10:9
me, I set my face *t* the ground .... Dan 10:15
shall be divided *t* the four winds .... Dan 11:4
face *t* the fort of his own land .... Dan 11:19
shall return, and come *t* the south .... Dan 11:29
the LORD *t* the children of Israel .... Hos 3:1
for judgment is *t* you, because ye .... Hos 5:1
with his face *t* the east sea .... Joel 2:20
his hinder part *t* the utmost sea .... Joel 2:20
will look again *t* thy holy temple .... Jonah 2:4
go forth *t* the south country .... Zec 6:6
these that go *t* the north country .... Zec 6:8
of Israel, shall be *t* the LORD .... Zec 9:1
in the midst thereof *t* the east .... Zec 14:4
t the west, and there shall be a .... Zec 14:4
mountain shall remove *t* the north ...... Zec 14:4
north, and half of it *t* the south .... Zec 14:4
half of them *t* the former sea, and ...... Zec 14:8
half of them *t* the hinder sea .... Zec 14:8
forth his hand *t* his disciples .... Mt 12:49
was moved with compassion *t* them .... Mt 14:14
as it began to dawn *t* the first .... Mt 28:1
was moved with compassion *t* them .... Mk 6:34
on earth peace, good will *t* men .... Lk 2:14
for himself, and is not rich *t* God .... Lk 12:21
and journeying *t* Jerusalem .... Lk 13:22
for it is *t* evening, and the day .... Lk 24:29
and went over the sea *t* Capernaum .... Jn 6:17
stedfastly *t* heaven as he went up .... Acts 1:10
go *t* the south unto the way that .... Acts 8:26
to the Greeks, repentance *t* God .... Acts 20:21
faith *t* our Lord Jesus Christ .... Acts 20:21
the fathers, and was zealous *t* God ..... Acts 22:3
And have hope *t* God, which they .... Acts 24:15
conscience void of offence *t* God .... Acts 24:16
God, and *t* men .... Acts 24:16
lieth *t* the south west and north .... Acts 27:12
the wind, and made *t* shore, ... Acts 27:40
and so we went *t* Rome .... Acts 28:14
in their lust one *t* another .... Rom 1:27
But God commendeth his love *t* us, ... Rom 5:8
but *t* thee, goodness, if thou .... Rom 11:22
Be of the same mind one *t* another ..... Rom 12:16
one *t* another according to Christ .... Rom 15:5
himself uncomely *t* his virgin 1Cor 7:36
to be brought on my way *t* Judaea 2Cor 1:16
our word *t* you was not yea and nay ... 2Cor 1:18
ye would confirm your love *t* him 2Cor 2:8
is my boldness of speech *t* you 2Cor 7:4
mourning, your fervent mind *t* me 2Cor 7:7
affection is more abundant *t* you 2Cor 7:15
to make all grace abound *t* you 2Cor 9:8
but being absent am bold *t* you 2Cor 10:1
him by the power of God *t* you 2Cor 13:4

was mighty in me *t* the Gentiles .... Gal 2:8
hath abounded *t* us in all wisdom .... Eph 1:8
t us through Christ Jesus...................... Eph 2:7
supply your lack of service *t* me .... Phil 2:30
I press *t* the mark for the prize .... Phil 3:14
Walk in wisdom *t* them that are .... Col 4:5
and abound in love one *t* another......... 1Th 3:12
t all men, even as we do *t* 1Th 3:12
all men, even as we do *t* you 1Th 3:12
indeed ye do it *t* all the 1Th 4:10
honestly *t* them that are without 1Th 4:12
the weak, be patient *t* all men 1Th 5:14
of you all *t* each other aboundeth 2Th 1:3
of God our Saviour *t* man appeared .... Titus 3:4
which thou hast *t* the Lord Jesus......... Philem 5
the Lord Jesus, and *t* all saints .... Philem 5
dead works, and of faith *t* God .... Heb 6:1
which ye have shewed *t* his name .... Heb 6:10
for conscience *t* God endure grief 1Pet 2:19
answer of a good conscience *t* God 1Pet 3:21
then have we confidence *t* God 1Jn 3:21
manifested the love of God *t* us 1Jn 4:9

TOWEL

and took a *t*, and girded himself .... Jn 13:4
to wipe them with the *t* wherewith .... Jn 13:5

TOWER

to, let us build us a city and a *t* .... Gen 11:4
down to see the city and the *t* .... Gen 11:5
his tent beyond the *t* of Edar .... Gen 35:21
peace, I will break down this *t* .... Judg 8:9
And he beat down the *t* of Penuel .... Judg 8:17
of the *t* of Shechem heard that .... Judg 9:46
that all the men of the *t* of .... Judg 9:47
men of the *t* of Shechem died also ..... Judg 9:49
was a strong *t* within the city .... Judg 9:51
gat them up to the top of the *t* .... Judg 9:51
And Abimelech came unto the *t* .... Judg 9:52
of the *t* to burn it with fire .... Judg 9:52
horn of my salvation, my high *t* 2Sa 22:3
He is the *t* of salvation for his 2Sa 22:51
And when he came to the *t*, he took 2Kin 5:24
a watchman on the *t* in Jezreel 2Kin 9:17
from the *t* of the watchmen to the 2Kin 17:9
from the *t* of the watchmen to the 2Kin 18:8
the watch *t* in the wilderness 2Chr 20:24
even unto the *t* of Meah they .... Neh 3:1
it, unto the *t* of Hananeel .... Neh 3:1
piece, and the *t* of the furnaces .... Neh 3:11
the *t* which lieth out from the .... Neh 3:25
the east, and the *t* that lieth out .... Neh 3:27
the great *t* that lieth out .... Neh 3:27
from beyond the *t* of the furnaces ...... Neh 12:38
the *t* of Hananeel .... Neh 12:39
the *t* of Meah, even unto the .... Neh 12:39
of my salvation, and my high *t* .... Ps 18:2
a strong *t* from the enemy .... Ps 61:3
my high *t*, and my deliverer .... Ps 144:2
name of the LORD is a strong *t* .... Prov 18:10
Thy neck is like the *t* of David .... Song 4:4
Thy neck is as a *t* of ivory .... Song 7:4
thy nose is as the *t* of Lebanon .... Song 7:4
And upon every high *t*, and upon .... Is 2:15
built a *t* in the midst of it, and .... Is 5:2
I have set thee for a *t* and a .... Jer 6:27
t of Hananeel unto the gate of .... Jer 31:38
from the *t* of Syene even unto the ...... Eze 29:10
from the *t* of Syene shall they .... Eze 30:6
O *t* of the flock, the strong hold .... Mic 4:8
my watch, and set me upon the *t* .... Hab 2:1
from the *t* of Hananeel unto the .... Zec 14:10
a winepress in it, and built a *t* .... Mt 21:33
for the winefat, and built a *t* .... Mk 12:1
upon whom the *t* in Siloam fell, ... Lk 13:4
of you, intending to build a *t* .... Lk 14:28

TOWERS

and make about them walls, and *t* 2Chr 14:7
Moreover Uzziah built *t* in 2Chr 26:9
Also he built *t* in the desert 2Chr 26:10
by cunning men, to be on the *t* 2Chr 26:15
the forests he built castles and *t* 2Chr 27:4
broken, and raised it up to the *t* 2Chr 32:5
tell the *t* thereof .... Ps 48:12
I am a wall, and my breasts like *t* ...... Song 8:10
they set up the *t* thereof .... Is 23:13
great slaughter, when the *t* fall .... Is 30:25
t shall be for dens for ever, a .... Is 32:14
where is he that counted the *t* .... Is 33:18
of Tyrus, and break down her *t* .... Eze 26:4
axes he shall break down thy *t* .... Eze 26:9
and the Gammadims were in thy *t* ...... Eze 27:11
cities, and against the high *t* .... Zeph 1:16
their *t* are desolate .... Zeph 3:6

TOWN

for her house was upon the *t* wall ...... Josh 2:15
the elders of the *t* trembled at 1Sa 16:4
entering into a *t* that hath gates 1Sa 23:7
a place in some *t* in the country 1Sa 27:5
him that buildeth a *t* with blood .... Hab 2:12
city or *t* ye shall enter, enquire .... Mt 10:11
the hand, and led him out of the *t* ..... Mk 8:23
saying, Neither go into the *t*, ... Mk 8:26
nor tell it to any in the *t* .... Mk 8:26
come out of every *t* of Galilee .... Lk 5:17
out of the *t* of Bethlehem, where— ..... Jn 7:42
the *t* of Mary and her sister .... Jn 11:1
Jesus was not yet come into the *t* ...... Jn 11:30

TOWNCLERK
when the *t* had appeased the .... Acts 19:35

TOWNS
these are their names, by their *t* .... Gen 25:16
went and took the small *t* thereof ...... Num 32:41
beside unwalled *t* a great many .... Deut 3:5
of Bashan, and all the *t* of Jair .... Josh 13:30
Ekron, with her *t* and her villages ...... Josh 15:45
Ashdod with her *t* and her villages ..... Josh 15:47
and her villages, Gaza with her *t* .... Josh 15:47
in Asher Beth-shean and her *t* .... Josh 17:11
and Ibleam and her *t* .... Josh 17:11
the inhabitants of Dor and her *t* .... Josh 17:11
inhabitants of En-dor and her *t* .... Josh 17:11
inhabitants of Taanach and her *t* .... Josh 17:11
inhabitants of Megiddo and her *t* .... Josh 17:11
who are of Beth-shean and her *t* .... Josh 17:16
of Beth-shean and her *t*, nor .... Judg 1:27
nor Taanach and her *t* .... Judg 1:27
the inhabitants of Dor and her *t* .... Judg 1:27
inhabitants of Ibleam and her *t* .... Judg 1:27
inhabitants of Megiddo and her *t* .... Judg 1:27
Israel dwelt in Heshbon and her *t* .... Judg 11:26
and in Aroer and her *t* .... Judg 11:26
to him pertained the *t* of Jair 1Kin 4:13
and Aram, with the *t* of Jair 1Chr 2:23
the *t* thereof, even threescore 1Chr 2:23
in Gilead in Bashan, and in her *t* 1Chr 5:16
the *t* thereof, and eastward Naaran 1Chr 7:28
Gezer, with the *t* thereof 1Chr 7:28
unto Gaza and the *t* thereof 1Chr 7:28
of Manasseh, Beth-shean and her *t* 1Chr 7:29
Taanach and her *t* 1Chr 7:29
Megiddo and her *t* 1Chr 7:29
Dor and her *t* 1Chr 7:29
Ono, and Lod, with the *t* thereof 1Chr 8:12
her *t* out of the hand of the 1Chr 18:1
him, Beth-el with the *t* thereof 2Chr 13:19
and Jeshanah with the *t* thereof 2Chr 13:19
and Ephraim with the *t* thereof 2Chr 13:19
that dwelt in the unwalled *t* .... Est 9:19
upon all her *t* all the evil that .... Jer 19:15
t without walls for the multitude .... Zec 2:4
them, Let us go into the *t* .... Mk 1:38
into the *t* of Caesarea Philippi .... Mk 8:27
departed, and went through the *t* .... Lk 9:6
away, that they may go into the *t* .... Lk 9:12

TRACHONITIS (*trak-o-ni'-tis*) A rocky district
east of the Jordan.
of Ituraea and of the region of *T* .... Lk 3:1

TRADE
dwell and *t* ye therein, and get you .... Gen 34:10
dwell in the land, and *t* therein .... Gen 34:21
for their *t* hath been to feed .... Gen 46:32
Thy servants' *t* hath been about... .... Gen 46:34
sailors, and as many as by sea... .... Rev 18:17

TRADED
tin, and lead, they *t* in thy fairs .... Eze 27:12
they *t* the persons of men and .... Eze 27:13
t in thy fairs with horses .... Eze 27:14
they *t* in thy market wheat of .... Eze 27:17
t with the same, and made them .... Mt 25:16

TRADING
much every man had gained by *t* .... Lk 19:15

TRADITION
transgress the *t* of the elders .... Mt 15:2
the commandment of God by your *t* ... Mt 15:3
of God of none effect by your *t* .... Mt 15:6
holding the *t* of the elders .... Mk 7:3
according to the *t* of the elders .... Mk 7:5
of God, ye hold the *t* of men .... Mk 7:8
God, that ye may keep your own *t* ...... Mk 7:9
God of none effect through your *t* ...... Mk 7:13
vain deceit, after the *t* of .... Col 2:8
not after the *t* which he received........ 2Th 3:6
received by *t* from your fathers... .... 1Pet 1:18

TRADITIONS
zealous of the *t* of my fathers .... Gal 1:14
hold the *t* which ye have been 2Th 2:15

TRAFFIC
and ye shall *t* in the land.................... Gen 42:34
of the *t* of the spice merchants,........... 1Kin 10:15
and carried it into a land of *t* .... Eze 17:4
by thy *t* hast thou increased thy .... Eze 28:5
by the iniquity of thy *t* .... Eze 28:18

TRAFFICKERS
whose *t* are the honourable of the .... Is 23:8

TRAIN
to Jerusalem with a very great *t* 1Kin 10:2
up a child in the way he should .... Prov 22:6
up, and his *t* filled the temple .... Is 6:1

TRAINED
captive, he armed his *t* servants .... Gen 14:14

TRAITOR
Iscariot, which also was the *t* .... Lk 6:16

TRAITORS
T, heady, highminded, lovers of 2Ti 3:4

TRAMPLE
dragon shalt thou *t* under feet .... Ps 91:13
mine anger, and *t* them in my fury ...... Is 63:3
lest they *t* them under their feet......... Mt 7:6

TRANCE
of the Almighty, falling into a *t* .... Num 24:4
of the Almighty, falling into a *t* .... Num 24:16
they made ready, he fell into a *t* .... Acts 10:10
in a *t* I saw a vision, A certain .... Acts 11:5
in the temple, I was in a *t* .... Acts 22:17

TRANQUILITY
it may be a lengthening of thy *t* .... Dan 4:27

TRANSFERRED
I have in a figure to myself.................. 1Cor 4:6

TRANSFIGURED
And was *t* before them .... Mt 17:2
and he was *t* before them................... Mk 9:2

TRANSFORMED
but be ye *t* by the renewing of .... Rom 12:2
for Satan himself is *t* into an............. 2Cor 11:14
also be *t* as the ministers of 2Cor 11:15

TRANSFORMING
t themselves into the apostles of 2Cor 11:13

TRANSGRESS
Wherefore now do ye *t* the .... Num 14:41
ye make the LORD's people to *t* 1Sa 2:24
Why *t* ye the commandments of the ... 2Chr 24:20
servant Moses, saying, If ye *t* .... Neh 1:8
to *t* against our God in marrying .... Neh 13:27
that my mouth shall not *t* .... Ps 17:3
be ashamed which *t* without cause ..... Ps 25:3
a piece of bread that man will *t* .... Prov 28:21
and thou saidst, I will not *t* .... Jer 2:20
rebels, and them that *t* against me ..... Eze 20:38
Come to Beth-el, and *t* .... Amos 4:4
Why do thy disciples *t* the .... Mt 15:2
Why do ye also *t* the commandment ... Mt 15:3
and circumcision dost *t* the law......... Rom 2:27

TRANSGRESSED
I have not *t* thy commandments,........ Deut 26:13
they have also *t* my covenant........... Josh 7:11
because he hath *t* the covenant of ..... Josh 7:15
When ye have *t* the covenant of .... Josh 23:16
t my covenant which I commanded.... Judg 2:20
And he said, Ye have *t* 1Sa 14:33
for I have *t* the commandment of 1Sa 15:24
wherein they have *t* against me......... 1Kin 8:50
but *t* his covenant, and that 2Kin 18:12
who *t* in the thing accursed 1Chr 2:7
they *t* against the God of their 1Chr 5:25
they had *t* against the LORD,............. 2Chr 12:2
for he *t* against the LORD his God.... 2Chr 26:16
naked, and *t* sore against the LORD ... 2Chr 28:19
t very much after all the 2Chr 36:14
up, and said unto them, Ye have *t* .... Ezr 10:10
many that have *t* in this thing .... Ezr 10:13
because they have *t* the laws .... Is 24:5
and thy teachers have *t* against me.... Is 43:27
of the men that have *t* against me ..... Is 66:24
the pastors also *t* against me............ Jer 2:8
ye all have *t* against me, saith.......... Jer 2:29
that thou hast *t* against the LORD..... Jer 3:13
and whereby they have *t* against me ... Jer 33:8
the men that have *t* my covenant...... Jer 34:18
We have *t* and have rebelled............. Lam 3:42
their fathers have *t* against me.......... Eze 2:3
transgressors, whereby ye have *t* ...... Eze 18:31
Yea, all Israel have *t* thy law............ Dan 9:11
they like men have *t* the covenant..... Hos 6:7
because they have *t* against me.......... Hos 7:13
because they have *t* my covenant...... Hos 8:1
wherein thou hast *t* against me .... Zeph 3:11
neither I *t* at any time thy .... Lk 15:29

TRANSGRESSEST
Why *t* thou the king's commandment .... Est 3:3

TRANSGRESSETH
his mouth *t* not in judgment .... Prov 16:10
Yea also, because he *t* by wine......... Hab 2:5
committeth sin *t* also the law 1Jn 3:4
Whosoever *t*, and abideth not in........ 2Jn 9

TRANSGRESSING
LORD thy God, in *t* his covenant,....... Deut 17:2
In *t* and lying against the LORD,........ Is 59:13

TRANSGRESSION
forgiving iniquity and *t* and sin,........ Ex 34:7
mercy, forgiving iniquity and *t* .... Num 14:18
or if in *t* against the LORD, (............ Josh 22:22
neither evil nor *t* in mine hand.......... 1Sa 24:11
away to Babylon for their *t* 1Chr 9:1
So Saul died for his *t* which he......... 1Chr 10:13
his reign did cast away in his *t* 2Chr 29:19
because of the *t* of those that........... Ezr 9:4
of them that had been carried .... Ezr 10:6
And why dost thou not pardon my *t* ... Job 7:21
have cast them away for their *t* .... Job 8:4
make me to know my *t* and my sin .... Job 13:23
My *t* is sealed up in a bag, and,........ Job 14:17
I am clean without *t*, I am................ Job 33:9
my wound is incurable without *t* .... Job 34:6
be innocent from the great *t* .... Ps 19:13
Blessed is he whose *t* is forgiven ...... Ps 32:1
The *t* of the wicked saith within........ Ps 36:1
not for my *t*, nor for my sin, O.......... Ps 59:3
will I visit their *t* with the rod........... Ps 89:32
Fools, because of their *t* .... Ps 107:17
is snared by the *t* of his lips.............. Prov 12:13
He that covereth a *t* seeketh love...... Prov 17:9
he loveth *t* that loveth strife............. Prov 17:19

it is his glory to pass over a *t*............ Prov 19:11
For the *t* of a land many are the .... Prov 28:2
his mother, and saith, It is no *t* .... Prov 28:24
In the *t* of an evil man there is .... Prov 29:6
are multiplied, *t* increaseth .... Prov 29:16
and a furious man aboundeth in *t* ...... Prov 29:22
the *t* thereof shall be heavy upon...... Is 24:20
for the *t* of my people was he .... Is 53:8
are ye not children of *t*, a seed......... Is 57:4
and shew my people their *t*, ... Is 58:1
them that turn from *t* in Jacob.......... Is 59:20
deliver him in the day of his *t*........... Eze 33:12
daily sacrifice by reason of *t*............. Dan 8:12
of desolation, to give both............... Dan 8:13
thy holy city, to finish the *t* .... Dan 9:24
at Gilgal multiply *t* .... Amos 4:4
For the *t* of Jacob is all this,............. Mic 1:5
What is the *t* of Jacob .... Mic 1:5
to declare unto Jacob his *t* .... Mic 3:8
I give my firstborn for my *t* .... Mic 6:7
passeth by the *t* of the remnant......... Mic 7:18
from which Judas by *t* fell................. Acts 1:25
where no law is, there is no *t*............ Rom 4:15
after the similitude of Adam's *t* .... Rom 5:14
woman being deceived was in the *t* ... 1Ti 2:14
angels was stedfast, and every *t* .... Heb 2:2
for sin is the *t* of the law 1Jn 3:4

TRANSGRESSIONS
for he will not pardon your *t* .... Ex 23:21
because of their *t* in all their .... Lev 16:16
all their *t* in all their sins,................ Lev 16:21
not forgive your *t* nor your sins......... Josh 24:19
all their *t* wherein they have 1Kin 8:50
If I covered my *t* as Adam .... Job 31:33
or if thy *t* be multiplied, what........... Job 35:6
their *t* that they have exceeded .... Job 36:9
out in the multitude of their *t* .... Ps 5:10
the sins of my youth, nor my *t* .... Ps 25:7
I will confess my *t* unto the LORD ..... Ps 32:5
Deliver me from all my *t*................... Ps 39:8
thy tender mercies blot out my *t* .... Ps 51:1
For I acknowledge my *t* .... Ps 51:3
as for our *t*, thou shalt purge............ Ps 65:3
hath he removed our *t* from us.......... Ps 103:12
out thy *t* for mine own sake.............. Is 43:25
out, as a thick cloud, thy *t* .... Is 44:22
for your *t* is your mother put .... Is 50:1
But he was wounded for our *t* .... Is 53:5
For our *t* are multiplied before .... Is 59:12
for our *t* are with us .... Is 59:12
because their *t* are many, and .... Jer 5:6
her for the multitude of her *t* .... Lam 1:5
The yoke of my *t* is bound by his...... Lam 1:14
hast done unto me for all my *t* .... Lam 1:22
any more with all their *t* .... Eze 14:11
All his *t* that he hath committed,....... Eze 18:22
all his *t* that he hath committed........ Eze 18:28
turn yourselves from all your *t* .... Eze 18:30
Cast away from you all your *t* .... Eze 18:31
in that your *t* are discovered, so .... Eze 21:24
Thus ye speak, saying, If our *t* .... Eze 33:10
things, nor with any of their *t* .... Eze 37:23
according to their *t* have I done......... Eze 39:24
For three *t* of Damascus, and for....... Amos 1:3
For three *t* of Gaza, and for four,....... Amos 1:6
For three *t* of Tyrus, and for four...... Amos 1:9
For three *t* of Edom, and for four,...... Amos 1:11
For three *t* of the children of .... Amos 1:13
For three *t* of Moab, and for four,...... Amos 2:1
For three *t* of Judah, and for four ...... Amos 2:4
For three *t* of Israel, and for.............. Amos 2:6
of Israel upon him I will also............... Amos 3:14
For I know your manifold *t* .... Amos 5:12
for the *t* of Israel were found in .... Mic 1:13
It was added because of *t* .... Gal 3:19
the *t* that were under the first............ Heb 9:15

TRANSGRESSOR
and the *t* for the upright .... Prov 21:18
overthroweth the words of the *t* .... Prov 22:12
and wast called a *t* from the womb .... Is 48:8
I destroyed, I make myself a *t* .... Gal 2:18
thou art become a *t* of the law .... Jas 2:11

TRANSGRESSORS
But the *t* shall be destroyed .... Ps 37:38
Then will I teach *t* thy ways,............. Ps 51:13
be not merciful to any wicked *t* .... Ps 59:5
I beheld the *t*, and was grieved.......... Ps 119:158
the *t* shall be rooted out of it .... Prov 2:22
of *t* shall destroy them..................... Prov 11:3
but *t* shall be taken in their own .... Prov 11:6
soul of the *t* shall eat violence .... Prov 13:2
but the way of *t* is hard .... Prov 13:15
and increaseth the *t* among men .... Prov 23:28
the fool, and rewardeth *t* .... Prov 26:10
And the destruction of the *t* .... Is 1:28
bring it again to mind, O ye *t* .... Is 46:8
and he was numbered with the *t* .... Is 53:12
and made intercession for the *t* .... Is 53:12
when the *t* are come to the full,........ Dan 8:23
but the *t* shall fall therein .... Hos 14:9
And he was numbered with the *t* .... Mk 15:28
And he was reckoned among the *t* ..... Lk 22:37
and are convinced of the law as *t* ..... Jas 2:9

TRANSLATE
To *t* the kingdom from the house 2Sa 3:10

TRANSLATED
hath *t* us into the kingdom of his ...... Col 1:13
By faith Enoch was *t* that he............. Heb 11:5

T

not found, because God had *t* him .... Heb 11:5

TRANSLATION
for before his *t* he had this .... Heb 11:5

TRANSPARENT
was pure gold, as it were *t* glass .... Rev 21:21

TRAP
ground, and a *t* for him in the way .... Job 18:10
their welfare, let it become a *t* .... Ps 69:22
they set a *t*, they catch men .... Jer 5:26
table be made a snare, and a *t* .... Rom 11:9

TRAPS
t unto you, and scourges in your .... Josh 23:13

TRAVAIL
came to pass in the time of her *t* .... Gen 38:27
all the *t* that had come upon them ...... Ex 18:8
and pain, as of a woman in *t* .... Ps 48:6
this sore *t* hath God given to the .... Eccl 1:13
days are sorrows, and his *t* grief ...... Eccl 2:23
but to the sinner he giveth *t* .... Eccl 2:26
I have seen the *t*, which God hath .... Eccl 3:10
Again, I considered all *t* .... Eccl 4:4
than both the hands full with *t* .... Eccl 4:6
also vanity, yea, it is a sore *t* .... Eccl 4:8
But those riches perish by evil *t* .... Eccl 5:14
I *t* not, nor bring forth children .... Is 23:4
He shall see of the *t* of his soul .... Is 53:11
thou that didst not *t* with child .... Is 54:1
heard a voice as of a woman in *t* .... Jer 4:31
us, and pain, as of a woman in *t* .... Jer 6:24
take thee, as a woman in *t* .... Jer 13:21
thee, the pain as of a woman in *t* .... Jer 22:23
whether a man doth *t* with child .... Jer 30:6
on his loins, as a woman in *t* .... Jer 30:6
have taken her, as a woman in *t* .... Jer 49:24
him, and pangs as of a woman in *t* ...... Jer 50:43
have taken thee as a woman in *t* .... Mic 4:9
of Zion, like a woman in *t* .... Mic 4:10
when she is in *t* hath sorrow .... Jn 16:21
of whom I *t* in birth again until .... Gal 4:19
brethren, our labour and *t* 1Th 2:9
as I upon a woman with child 1Th 5:3
t night and day, that we might not 2Th 3:8

TRAVAILED
and Rachel *t*, and she had hard .... Gen 35:16
And it came to pass, when she *t* .... Gen 38:28
were dead, she bowed herself and *t* 1Sa 4:19
Before she *t*, she brought forth .... Is 66:7
for as soon as Zion *t*, she .... Is 66:8

TRAVAILEST
forth and cry, thou that *t* not .... Gal 4:27

TRAVAILETH
The wicked man *t* with pain all .... Job 15:20
he *t* with iniquity, and hath .... Ps 7:14
be in pain as a woman that *t* .... Is 13:8
as the pangs of a woman that *t* .... Is 21:3
her that *t* with child together .... Jer 31:8
she which *t* hath brought forth .... Mic 5:3
in pain together until now .... Rom 8:22

TRAVAILING
now will I cry like a woman *t* .... Is 42:14
The sorrows of a *t* woman shall .... Hos 13:13
t in birth, and pained to be .... Rev 12:2

TRAVEL
Thou knowest all the *t* that hath .... Num 20:14
and compassed me with gall and *t* ...... Lam 3:5
Macedonia, Paul's companions in *t* .... Acts 19:29
to *t* with us with this grace 2Cor 8:19

TRAVELERS
the *t* walked through byways .... Judg 5:6

TRAVELLED
about Stephen *t* as far as Phenice ...... Acts 11:19

TRAVELLER
there came a *t* unto the rich man 2Sa 12:4
but I opened my doors to the *t* .... Job 31:32

TRAVELLETH
thy poverty come as one that *t* .... Prov 6:11
thy poverty come as one that *t* .... Prov 24:34

TRAVELLING
O ye *t* companies of Dedanim .... Is 21:13
t in the greatness of his .... Is 63:1
is as a man *t* into a far country .... Mt 25:14

TRAVERSING
art a swift dromedary *t* her ways .... Jer 2:23

TREACHEROUS
the *t* dealer dealeth .... Is 21:2
the *t* dealers have dealt .... Is 24:16
the *t* dealers have dealt very .... Is 24:16
her *t* sister Judah saw it .... Jer 3:7
yet her *t* sister Judah feared not .... Jer 3:8
yet for all this her *t* sister .... Jer 3:10
herself more than *t* Judah .... Jer 3:11
adulterers, an assembly of *t* men .... Jer 9:2
prophets are light and *t* persons .... Zeph 3:4

TREACHEROUSLY
of Shechem dealt *t* with Abimelech .... Judg 9:23
the treacherous dealer dealeth *t* .... Is 21:2
treacherous dealers have dealt *t* .... Is 24:16
dealers have dealt very *t* .... Is 24:16
and dealest *t*, and they dealt not .... Is 33:1
and they dealt not *t* with thee .... Is 33:1

thou shalt make an end to deal *t* .... Is 33:1
they shall deal *t* with thee .... Is 33:1
that thou wouldest deal very *t* .... Is 48:8
Surely as a wife *t* departeth from .... Jer 3:20
so have ye dealt *t* with me .... Jer 3:20
have dealt very *t* against me .... Jer 5:11
all they happy that deal very *t* .... Jer 12:1
even they have dealt *t* with thee .... Jer 12:6
her friends have dealt *t* with her .... Lam 1:2
They have dealt *t* against the .... Hos 5:7
have they dealt *t* against me .... Hos 6:7
thou upon them that deal *t* .... Hab 1:13
why do we deal *t* every man .... Mal 2:10
Judah hath dealt *t*, and an .... Mal 2:11
against whom thou hast dealt *t* .... Mal 2:14
let none deal *t* against the wife .... Mal 2:15
your spirit, that ye deal not *t* .... Mal 2:16

TREADER
the *t* of grapes him that soweth .... Amos 9:13

TREADERS
the *t* shall tread out no wine in .... Is 16:10

TREADETH
the ox when he *t* out the corn .... Deut 25:4
t upon the waves of the sea .... Job 9:8
mortar, and as the potter *t* clay .... Is 41:25
like him that *t* in the winefat .... Is 63:2
t upon the high places of the .... Amos 4:13
when he *t* within our borders .... Mic 5:6
if he go through, both *t* down .... Mic 5:8
of the ox that *t* out the corn 1Cor 9:9
muzzle the ox that *t* out the corn 1Ti 5:18
he *t* the winepress of the .... Rev 19:15

TREADING
some *t* winepresses on the sabbath .... Neh 13:15
for the *t* of lesser cattle .... Is 7:25
of *t* down, and of perplexity by .... Is 22:5
as your *t* is upon the poor .... Amos 5:11

TREASON
his *t* that he wrought, are they 1Kin 16:20
rent her clothes, and cried, *T* 2Kin 11:14
her clothes, and cried, *T, T* 2Kin 11:14
rent her clothes, and said, *T* 2Chr 23:13
her clothes, and said, *T, T* 2Chr 23:13

TREASURE
hath given you *t* in your sacks .... Gen 43:23
they built for Pharaoh *t* cities .... Ex 1:11
t unto me above all people .... Ex 19:5
shall open unto thee his good *t* .... Deut 28:12
to the *t* of the house of the LORD 1Chr 29:8
unto the *t* of the work threescore ...... Ezr 2:69
search made in the king's *t* house ...... Ezr 5:17
it out of the king's *t* house .... Ezr 7:20
to the *t* a thousand drams of gold ...... Neh 7:70
of the fathers gave to the *t* .... Neh 7:71
to the chambers, into the *t* house ...... Neh 10:38
belly thou fillest with thy hid *t* .... Ps 17:14
and Israel for his peculiar *t* .... Ps 135:4
house of the righteous is much *t* .... Prov 15:6
the fear of the LORD than great *t* .... Prov 15:16
There is *t* to be desired and oil .... Prov 21:20
gold, and the peculiar *t* of kings .... Eccl 2:8
the fear of the LORD is his *t* .... Is 33:6
have taken the *t* and precious .... Eze 22:25
into the *t* house of his god .... Dan 1:2
he shall spoil the *t* of all .... Hos 13:15
For where your *t* is, there will .... Mt 6:21
A good man out of the good *t* of .... Mt 12:35
evil *t* bringeth forth evil things .... Mt 12:35
is like unto *t* hid in a field .... Mt 13:44
forth out of his *t* things new .... Mt 13:52

and thou shalt have *t* in heaven .... Mt 19:21
and thou shalt have *t* in heaven .... Mk 10:21
A good man out of the good *t* of .... Lk 6:45
t of his heart bringeth forth .... Lk 6:45
he that layeth up *t* for himself .... Lk 12:21
a *t* in the heavens that faileth .... Lk 12:33
For where your *t* is, there will .... Lk 12:34
and thou shalt have *t* in heaven .... Lk 18:22
who had the charge of all her *t* .... Acts 8:27
But we have this *t* in earthen 2Cor 4:7
Ye have heaped *t* together for the ...... Jas 5:3

TREASURED
it shall not be *t* nor laid up .... Is 23:18

TREASURER
by the hand of Mithredath the *t* .... Ezr 1:8
hosts, Go, get thee unto this *t* .... Is 22:15

TREASURERS
the *t* which are beyond the river .... Ezr 7:21
I made *t* over the treasuries .... Neh 13:13
the captains, the judges, the *t* .... Dan 3:2
and captains, the judges, the *t* .... Dan 3:3

TREASURES
with me, and sealed up among my *t* .... Deut 32:34
the seas, and of *t* hid in the sand .... Deut 33:19
did he put among the *t* of the 1Kin 7:51
he took away the *t* of the house 1Kin 14:26
the *t* of the king's house 1Kin 14:26
in the *t* of the house of the LORD 1Kin 15:18
the *t* of the king's house 1Kin 15:18
in the *t* of the house of the LORD 2Kin 12:18
in the *t* of the king's house, and 2Kin 14:14
in the *t* of the king's house, and 2Kin 16:8
in the *t* of the king's house 2Kin 18:15
and all that was found in his *t* 2Kin 20:13
there is nothing among my *t* that 2Kin 20:15
in the *t* of the house of the LORD 2Kin 24:13
the *t* of the king's house, and cut 2Kin 24:13
over the *t* of the house of God 1Chr 26:20
over the *t* of the dedicated 1Chr 26:20
which were over the *t* of the 1Chr 26:22
son of Moses, was ruler of the *t* 1Chr 26:24
all the *t* of the dedicated things 1Chr 26:26
over the king's *t* was Azmaveth 1Chr 27:25
put he among the *t* of the house 2Chr 5:1
any matter, or concerning the *t* 2Chr 8:15
took away the *t* of the house of 2Chr 12:9
the *t* of the king's house 2Chr 12:9
gold out of the *t* of the house of 2Chr 16:2
the *t* of the king's house, the 2Chr 25:24
the *t* of the house of the LORD 2Chr 36:18
the *t* of the king, and of his 2Chr 36:18
where the *t* were laid up in .... Ezr 6:1
over the chambers for the *t* .... Neh 12:44
and dig for it more than for hid *t* .... Job 3:21
entered into the *t* of the snow .... Job 38:22
hast thou seen the *t* of the hail .... Job 38:22
and searchest for her as for hid *t* .... Prov 2:4
and I will fill their *t* .... Prov 8:21
T of wickedness profit nothing .... Prov 10:2
The getting of *t* by a lying .... Prov 21:6
is there any end of their *t* .... Is 2:7
people, and have robbed their *t* .... Is 10:13
their *t* upon the bunches of .... Is 30:6
and all that was found in his *t* .... Is 39:2
there is nothing among my *t* that ...... Is 39:4
will give thee the *t* of darkness .... Is 45:3
forth the wind out of his *t* .... Jer 10:13
thy *t* will I give to the spoil .... Jer 15:13
all thy *t* to the spoil, and thy .... Jer 17:3
all the *t* of the kings of Judah .... Jer 20:5
for we have *t* in the field, of .... Jer 41:8
trusted in thy works and in thy *t* .... Jer 48:7
that trusted in her *t*, saying .... Jer 49:4
a sword is upon her *t* .... Jer 50:37
upon many waters, abundant in *t* ...... Jer 51:13
forth the wind out of his *t* .... Jer 51:16
gotten gold and silver into thy *t* .... Eze 28:4
have power over the *t* of gold .... Dan 11:43
Are there yet the *t* of wickedness ...... Mic 6:10
and when they had opened their *t* ...... Mt 2:11
up for yourselves *t* upon earth .... Mt 6:19
lay up for yourselves *t* in heaven ...... Mt 6:20
whom are hid all the *t* of wisdom ...... Col 2:3
riches that the *t* in Egypt .... Heb 11:26

TREASUREST
impenitent heart *t* up unto .... Rom 2:5

TREASURIES
chambers and *t* of the house of God... 1Chr 9:26
of the *t* thereof, and of the upper 1Chr 28:11
of the *t* of the house of God, and 1Chr 28:12
of the *t* of the dedicated things 1Chr 28:12
and he made himself *t* for silver 2Chr 32:27
new wine and the oil unto the *t* .... Neh 13:12
And I made treasurers over the *t* .... Neh 13:13
to bring it into the king's *t* .... Est 3:9
pay to the king's *t* for the Jews .... Est 4:7
he bringeth the wind out of his *t* .... Ps 135:7

TREASURY
shall come into the *t* of the LORD .... Josh 6:19
they put into the *t* of the house .... Josh 6:24
and brought it into the *t* of .... Josh 6:24
lawful for to put them into the *t* .... Mt 27:6
And Jesus sat over against the *t* .... Mk 12:41
the people cast money into the *t* .... Mk 12:41
they which have cast into the *t* .... Mk 12:43
casting their gifts into the *t* .... Lk 21:1

These words spake Jesus in the *t* .... Jn 8:20

TREATISE
The former *t* have I made, O .... Acts 1:1

TREE
the fruit *t* yielding fruit after .... Gen 1:11
the *t* yielding fruit, whose seed .... Gen 1:12
face of all the earth, and every *t* .... Gen 1:29
is the fruit of a *t* yielding seed .... Gen 1:29
the *t* of knowledge of good and .... Gen 2:9
t that is pleasant to the sight .... Gen 2:9
the *t* of life also in the midst .... Gen 2:9
the *t* of knowledge of good and .... Gen 2:9
Of every *t* of the garden thou .... Gen 2:16
But of the *t* of the knowledge of .... Gen 2:17
not eat of every *t* of the garden .... Gen 3:1
But of the fruit of the *t* which .... Gen 3:3
saw that the *t* was good for food .... Gen 3:6
a *t* to be desired to make one .... Gen 3:6
Hast thou eaten of the *t*, whereof .... Gen 3:11
be with me, she gave me of the *t* .... Gen 3:12
thy wife, and hast eaten of the *t* .... Gen 3:17
and take also of the *t* of life .... Gen 3:22
to keep the way of the *t* of life .... Gen 3:24
and rest yourselves under the *t* .... Gen 18:4
and he stood by them under the *t* .... Gen 18:8
and of the hazel and chesnut *t* .... Gen 30:37
thee, and shalt hang thee on a *t* .... Gen 40:19
brake every *t* of the field .... Ex 9:25
shall eat every *t* which groweth .... Ex 10:5
and the LORD shewed him a *t* .... Ex 15:25
land, or of the fruit of the *t* .... Lev 27:30
that is made of the vine *t* .... Num 6:4
the hills, and under every green *t* .... Deut 12:2
with the axe to cut down the *t* .... Deut 19:5
not cut them down (for the *t* of .... Deut 20:19
to death, and thou hang him on a *t* .... Deut 21:22
not remain all night upon the *t* .... Deut 21:23
before thee in the way in any *t* .... Deut 22:6
When thou beatest thine olive *t* .... Deut 24:20
he hanged on a *t* until eventide .... Josh 8:29
take his carcase down from the *t* .... Josh 8:29
palm *t* of Deborah between Ramah .... Judg 4:5
and they said unto the olive *t* .... Judg 9:8
But the olive *t* said unto them, ... Judg 9:9
And the trees said to the fig *t* .... Judg 9:10
But the fig *t* said unto them, ... Judg 9:11
pomegranate *t* which is in Migron 1Sa 14:2
in Gibeah under a *t* in Ramah 1Sa 22:6
buried them under a *t* at Jabesh 1Sa 31:13
under his vine and under his fig *t* 1Kin 4:25
from the cedar *t* that is in 1Kin 4:33
he made two cherubims of olive *t* 1Kin 6:23
oracle he made doors of olive *t* 1Kin 6:31
two doors also were of olive *t* 1Kin 6:33
of the temple posts of olive *t* 1Kin 6:33
And the two doors were of fir *t* 1Kin 6:34
high hill, and under every green *t* 1Kin 14:23
and sat down under a juniper *t* 1Kin 19:4
he lay and slept under a juniper *t* 1Kin 19:5
city, and shall fell every good *t* 2Kin 3:19
the hills, and under every green *t* 2Kin 16:4
high hill, and under every green *t* 2Kin 17:10
vine, and every one of his fig *t* 2Kin 18:31
house me cieled with fir *t* 2Chr 3:5
the hills, and under every green *t* 2Chr 28:4
they were both hanged on a *t* .... Esth 2:23
For there is hope of a *t*, if it .... Job 14:7
hope hath he removed like a *t* .... Job 19:10
wickedness shall be broken as a *t* .... Job 24:20
he shall be like a *t* planted by .... Ps 1:3
himself like a green bay *t* .... Ps 37:35
green olive *t* in the house of God .... Ps 52:8
shall flourish like the palm *t* .... Ps 92:12
She is a *t* of life to them that .... Prov 3:18
of the righteous is a *t* of life .... Prov 11:30
desire cometh, it is a *t* of life .... Prov 13:12
A wholesome tongue is a *t* of life .... Prov 15:4
Whoso keepeth the fig *t* shall eat .... Prov 27:18
if the *t* fall toward the south, ... Eccl 11:3
in the place where the *t* falleth .... Eccl 11:3
the almond *t* shall flourish, and .... Eccl 12:5
As the apple *t* among the trees of .... Song 2:3
The fig *t* putteth forth her green .... Song 2:13
thy stature is like to a palm *t* .... Song 7:7
said, I will go up to the palm *t* .... Song 7:8
raised thee up under the apple *t* .... Song 8:5
as a teil *t*, and as an oak, whose .... Is 6:13
it, as the shaking of an olive *t* .... Is 17:6
be as the shaking of an olive *t* .... Is 24:13
as a falling fig from the fig *t* .... Is 34:4
vine, and every one of his fig *t* .... Is 36:16
chooseth a *t* that will not rot .... Is 40:20
the cedar, the shittah *t*, and the .... Is 41:19
t, and the myrtle, and the oil *t* .... Is 41:19
will set in the desert the fir *t* .... Is 41:19
the pine, and the box *t* together .... Is 41:19
I fall down to the stock of a *t* .... Is 44:19
O forest, and every *t* therein. .... Is 44:23
the thorn shall come up the fir *t* .... Is 55:13
brier shall come up the myrtle *t* .... Is 55:13
eunuch say, Behold, I am a dry *t* .... Is 56:3
with idols under every green *t* .... Is 57:5
shall come unto thee, the fir *t* .... Is 60:13
thee, the fir *t*, the pine .... Is 60:13
for as the days of a *t* are the .... Is 65:22
gardens behind one *t* in the midst .... Is 66:17
said, I saw a rod of an almond *t* .... Jer 1:11
every green *t* thou wanderest .... Jer 2:20
mountain and under every green *t* .... Jer 3:6
the strangers under every green *t* .... Jer 3:13

the vine, nor figs on the fig *t* .... Jer 8:13
one cutteth a *t* out of the forest .... Jer 10:3
They are upright as the palm *t* .... Jer 10:5
called thy name, A green olive *t* .... Jer 11:16
Let us destroy the *t* with the .... Jer 11:19
For he shall be as a *t* planted by .... Jer 17:8
mountains, and under every green *t* .... Eze 6:13
is the vine *t* more than any .... Eze 15:2
As the vine *t* among the trees of .... Eze 15:6
waters, and set it as a willow *t* .... Eze 17:5
LORD have brought down the high *t* .... Eze 17:24
have exalted the low *t* .... Eze 17:24
t, have dried up the green *t* .... Eze 17:24
have made the dry *t* to flourish .... Eze 17:24
devour every green *t* in thee .... Eze 20:47
and every dry *t* .... Eze 20:47
the rod of my son, as every *t* .... Eze 21:10
nor any *t* in the garden of God .... Eze 31:8
the *t* of the field shall yield .... Eze 34:27
will multiply the fruit of the *t* .... Eze 36:30
so that a palm *t* was between a .... Eze 41:18
toward the palm *t* on the one side .... Eze 41:19
the palm *t* on the other side .... Eze 41:19
behold a *t* in the midst of the .... Dan 4:10
The *t* grew, and was strong, and the .... Dan 4:11
and said thus, Hew down the *t* .... Dan 4:14
The *t* that thou sawest, which .... Dan 4:20
heaven, and saying, Hew the *t* down .... Dan 4:23
to leave the stump of the *t* roots .... Dan 4:26
in the fig *t* at her first time .... Hos 9:10
beauty shall be as the olive *t* .... Hos 14:6
I am like a green fir *t* .... Hos 14:8
my vine waste, and barked my fig *t* .... Joel 1:7
up, and the fig *t* languisheth .... Joel 1:12
pomegranate *t*, the palm *t* also .... Joel 1:12
also, and the apple *t* .... Joel 1:12
for the *t* beareth her fruit, the .... Joel 2:22
beareth her fruit, the fig *t* .... Joel 2:22
under his vine and under his fig *t* .... Mic 4:4
Although the fig *t* shall not .... Hab 3:17
as yet the vine, and the fig *t* .... Hag 2:19
the pomegranate, and the olive *t* .... Hag 2:19
under the vine and under the fig *t* .... Zec 3:10
Howl, fir *t* .... Zec 11:2
therefore every *t* which bringeth .... Mt 3:10
Even so every good *t* bringeth .... Mt 7:17
but a corrupt *t* bringeth forth .... Mt 7:17
A good *t* cannot bring forth evil .... Mt 7:18
neither can a corrupt *t* bring .... Mt 7:18
Every *t* that bringeth not forth .... Mt 7:19
Either make the *t* good, and his .... Mt 12:33
or else make the *t* corrupt .... Mt 12:33
for the *t* is known by his fruit .... Mt 12:33
among herbs, and becometh a *t* .... Mt 13:32
And when he saw a fig *t* in the way .... Mt 21:19
presently the fig *t* withered away .... Mt 21:19
soon is the fig *t* withered away .... Mt 21:20
this which is done to the fig *t* .... Mt 21:21
Now learn a parable of the fig *t* .... Mt 24:32
seeing a fig *t* afar off having .... Mk 11:13
they saw the fig *t* dried up from .... Mk 11:20
the fig *t* which thou cursedst is. .... Mk 11:21
Now learn a parable of the fig *t* .... Mk 13:28
every *t* therefore which bringeth .... Lk 3:9
For a good *t* bringeth not forth .... Lk 6:43
corrupt *t* bring forth good fruit. .... Lk 6:43
For every *t* is known by his own .... Lk 6:44
a fig *t* planted in his vineyard .... Lk 13:6
come seeking fruit on this fig *t* .... Lk 13:7
and it grew, and waxed a great *t* .... Lk 13:19
ye might say unto this sycamine *t* .... Lk 17:6
up into a sycomore *t* to see him .... Lk 19:4
Behold the fig *t*, and all the .... Lk 21:29
they do these things in a green *t* .... Lk 23:31
when thou wast under the fig *t* .... Jn 1:48
thee, I saw thee under the fig *t* .... Jn 1:50
whom ye slew and hanged on a *t* .... Acts 5:30
whom they slew and hanged on a *t* .... Acts 10:39
they took him down from the *t* .... Acts 13:29
and thou, being a wild olive *t* .... Rom 11:17
root and fatness of the olive *t* .... Rom 11:17
olive *t* which is wild by nature. .... Rom 11:24
to nature into a good olive *t* .... Rom 11:24
be graffed into their own olive *t* .... Rom 11:24
is every one that hangeth on a *t* .... Gal 3:13
Can the fig *t*, my brethren, bear .... Jas 3:12
our sins in his own body on the *t* 1Pet 2:24
I give to eat of the *t* of life .... Rev 2:7
even as a fig *t* casteth her .... Rev 6:13
nor on the sea, nor on any *t* .... Rev 7:1
any green thing, neither any *t* .... Rev 9:4
river, was there the *t* of life .... Rev 22:2
the leaves of the *t* were for the .... Rev 22:2
may have right to the *t* of life .... Rev 22:14

TREES
the fruit of the *t* of the garden .... Gen 3:2
God amongst the *t* of the garden .... Gen 3:8
all the *t* that were in the field, ... Gen 23:17
all the fruit of the *t* which the .... Ex 10:15
not any green thing in the *t* .... Ex 10:15
and threescore and ten palm *t* .... Ex 15:27
planted all manner of *t* for food .... Lev 19:23
first day the boughs of goodly *t* .... Lev 23:40
branches of palm *t* .... Lev 23:40
and the boughs of thick *t* .... Lev 23:40
the *t* of the field shall yield .... Lev 26:4
neither shall the *t* of the land .... Lev 26:20
as the *t* of lign aloes which the .... Num 24:6
as cedar *t* beside the waters .... Num 24:6
and threescore and ten palm *t* .... Num 33:9

not, vineyards and olive *t* .... Deut 6:11
and barley, and vines, and fig *t* .... Deut 8:8
not plant thee a grove of any *t* .... Deut 16:21
the *t* thereof by forcing an ax. .... Deut 20:19
Only the *t* which thou knowest. .... Deut 20:20
that they be not *t* for meat. .... Deut 20:20
Thou shalt have olive *t* .... Deut 28:40
All thy *t* and fruit of thy land .... Deut 28:42
of Jericho, the city of palm *t* .... Deut 34:3
them, and hanged them on five *t* .... Josh 10:26
upon the *t* until the evening .... Josh 10:26
and they took them down off the *t* .... Josh 10:27
t with the children of Judah into .... Judg 1:16
and possessed the city of palm *t* .... Judg 3:13
The *t* went forth on a time to .... Judg 9:8
and go to be promoted over the *t* .... Judg 9:9
the *t* said to the fig tree, Come. .... Judg 9:10
and go to be promoted over the *t* .... Judg 9:11
Then said the *t* unto the vine .... Judg 9:12
and go to be promoted over the *t* .... Judg 9:13
said all the *t* unto the bramble, ... Judg 9:14
And the bramble said unto the *t* .... Judg 9:15
and cut down a bough from the *t* .... Judg 9:48
messengers to David, and cedar *t* 2Sa 5:11
them over against the mulberry *t* 2Sa 5:23
in the tops of the mulberry *t* 2Sa 5:24
And he spake of *t*, from the cedar 1Kin 4:33
hew me cedar *t* out of Lebanon. 1Kin 5:6
So Hiram gave Solomon cedar *t* 1Kin 5:10
fir *t* according to all his desire 1Kin 5:10
figures of cherubims and palm *t* 1Kin 6:29
carvings of cherubims and palm *t* 1Kin 6:32
the cherubims, and upon the palm *t* 1Kin 6:32
thereon cherubims and palm *t* 1Kin 6:32
cherubims, lions, and palm *t* 1Kin 7:36
Solomon with cedar *t* and fir *t* 1Kin 9:11
Ophir great plenty of almug *t* 1Kin 10:11
the king made of the almug *t* 1Kin 10:12
there came no such almug *t* 1Kin 10:12
sycomore *t* that are in the vale. 1Kin 10:27
water, and felled all the good *t* 2Kin 3:25
cut down the tall cedar *t* thereof. 2Kin 19:23
and the choice fir *t* thereof 2Kin 19:23
them over against the mulberry *t* 1Chr 14:14
in the tops of the mulberry *t* 1Chr 14:15
Then shall the *t* of the wood sing 1Chr 16:33
Also cedar *t* in abundance 1Chr 22:4
And over the olive *t* and the 1Chr 27:28
the sycomore *t* that were in the. 1Chr 27:28
cedar *t* made he as the sycomore 2Chr 1:15
t that are in the vale for 2Chr 1:15
Send me also cedar *t* 2Chr 2:8
fir *t*, and algum *t* 2Chr 2:8
fine gold, and set thereon palm *t* 2Chr 3:5
gold from Ophir, brought algum *t* 2Chr 9:10
the king made of the algum *t* 2Chr 9:11
cedar *t* made he as the sycomore 2Chr 9:27
t that are in the low plains in 2Chr 9:27
to Jericho, the city of palm *t* 2Chr 28:15
to bring cedar *t* from Lebanon to .... Ezr 3:7
branches, and branches of thick *t* .... Neh 8:15
and fruit *t* in abundance .... Neh 9:25
firstfruits of all fruit of all *t* .... Neh 10:35
and the fruit of all manner of *t* .... Neh 10:37
He lieth under the shady *t* .... Job 40:21
The shady *t* cover him with their .... Job 40:22
lifted up axes upon the thick *t* .... Ps 74:5
and their sycomore *t* with frost .... Ps 78:47
then shall all the *t* of the wood .... Ps 96:12
The *t* of the LORD are full of sap .... Ps 104:16
stork, the fir *t* are her house. .... Ps 104:17
their vines also and their fig *t* .... Ps 105:33
brake the *t* of their coasts. .... Ps 105:33
fruitful *t*, and all cedars .... Ps 148:9
I planted *t* in them of all kind, ... Eccl 2:5
the wood that bringeth forth *t* .... Eccl 2:6
tree among the *t* of the wood .... Song 2:3
with all *t* of frankincense, ... Song 4:14
as the *t* of the wood are moved .... Is 7:2
the rest of the *t* of his forest. .... Is 10:19
the fir *t* rejoice at thee, and the .... Is 14:8
and the choice fir *t* thereof .... Is 37:24
himself among the *t* of the forest. .... Is 44:14
all the *t* of the field shall clap .... Is 55:12
be called *t* of righteousness. .... Is 61:3
eat up thy vines and thy fig *t* .... Jer 5:17
Loxo of hosts said, Hew ye down *t* .... Jer 6:6
upon the *t* of the field, and upon. .... Jer 7:20
the green *t* upon the high hills. .... Jer 17:2
is among the *t* of the forest .... Eze 15:2
tree among the *t* of the forest. .... Eze 15:6
all the *t* of the field shall know .... Eze 17:24
high hill, and all the thick *t* .... Eze 20:28
thy ship boards of the *t* of Senir. .... Eze 27:5
unto all the *t* of the field .... Eze 31:4
above all the *t* of the field .... Eze 31:5
the fir *t* were not like his. .... Eze 31:8
the chestnut *t* were not like his. .... Eze 31:8
so that all the *t* of Eden. .... Eze 31:9
t by the waters exalt themselves. .... Eze 31:14
neither their *t* stand up in their. .... Eze 31:14
all the *t* of the field fainted. .... Eze 31:15
and all the *t* of Eden, the choice. .... Eze 31:16
in greatness among the *t* of Eden .... Eze 31:18
of Eden unto the nether parts. .... Eze 31:18
and upon each post were palm *t* .... Eze 40:16
and their arches, and their palm *t* .... Eze 40:22
and it had palm *t*, one on this. .... Eze 40:26
palm *t* were upon the posts .... Eze 40:31
palm *t* were upon the posts .... Eze 40:34

T

palm *t* were upon the posts .... Eze 40:37
was made with cherubims and palm *t* . Eze 41:18
were cherubims and palm *t* made .... Eze 41:20
the temple, cherubims and palm *t* ...... Eze 41:25
palm *t* on the one side and on the ...... Eze 41:26
were very many *t* on the one side....... Eze 47:7
side, shall grow all *t* for meat .... Eze 47:12
destroy her vines and her fig *t*.......... Hos 2:12
tree, even all the *t* of the field .... Joel 1:12
burned all the *t* of the field .... Joel 1:19
and your vineyards and your fig *t* ...... Amos 4:9
and your olive *t* increased .... Amos 4:9
the fir *t* shall be terribly................. Nah 2:3
fig *t* with the firstripe figs.............. Nah 3:12
myrtle *t* that were in the bottom .... Zec 1:8
stood among the myrtle *t* answered..... Zec 1:10
that stood among the myrtle *t* .... Zec 1:11
And two olive *t* by it, one upon......... Zec 4:3
What are these two olive *t* upon........ Zec 4:11
ax is laid unto the root of the *t* .... Mt 3:10
cut down branches from the *t* .... Mt 21:8
up, and said, I see men as *t* .... Mk 8:24
cut down branches off the *t* .... Mk 11:8
is laid unto the root of the *t* .... Lk 3:9
Behold the fig tree, and all the *t* .... Lk 21:29
Took branches of palm *t*, and went .... Jn 12:13
t whose fruit withereth, without........ Jude 12
earth, neither the sea, nor the *t* .... Rev 7:3
the third part of *t* was burnt up......... Rev 8:7
These are the two olive *t* .... Rev 11:4

TREMBLE

hear report of thee, and shall *t* .... Deut 2:25
faint, fear not, and do not *t* .... Deut 20:3
lord, and of those that *t* at the .... Ezr 10:3
place, and the pillars thereof *t* .... Job 9:6
The pillars of heaven *t*, and are .... Job 26:11
Thou hast made the earth to *t*........... Ps 60:2
let the people *t* .... Ps 99:1
t, thou earth, at the presence of .... Ps 114:7
the keepers of the house shall *t* .... Eccl 12:3
and the hills did *t*, and their............ Is 5:25
the man that made the earth to *t*........ Is 14:16
T, ye women that are at ease............ Is 32:11
the nations may *t* at thy presence...... Is 64:2
the LORD, ye that *t* at his word......... Is 66:5
will ye not *t* at my presence............ Jer 5:22
at his wrath the earth shall *t* .... Jer 10:10
t for all the goodness and for all....... Jer 33:9
And the land shall *t* and sorrow .... Jer 51:29
shall *t* at every moment, and be .... Eze 26:16
Now shall the isles *t* in the day......... Eze 26:18
they shall *t* at every moment, ... Eze 32:10
dominion of my kingdom men *t* .... Dan 6:26
children shall *t* from the west........... Hos 11:10
They shall *t* as a bird out of............. Hos 11:11
all the inhabitants of the land *t* .... Joel 2:1
the heavens shall *t* .... Joel 2:10
Shall not the land *t* for this............. Amos 8:8
of the land of Midian did *t*.............. Hab 3:7
the devils also believe, and *t*........... Jas 2:19

TREMBLED

Isaac *t* very exceedingly, and said..... Gen 27:33
the people that was in the camp *t* ...... Ex 19:16
of the field of Edom, the earth *t* .... Judg 5:4
for his heart *t* for the ark of 1Sa 4:13
and the spoilers, they also *t* 1Sa 14:15
of the town *t* at his coming 1Sa 16:4
afraid, and his heart greatly *t* 1Sa 28:5
Then the earth shook and *t* 2Sa 22:8
unto me every one that *t* at the .... Ezr 9:4
the earth shook and *t* .... Ps 18:7
the earth *t* and shook .... Ps 77:18
the earth saw, and *t* .... Ps 97:4
the mountains, and, lo, they *t* .... Jer 4:24
the whole land *t* at the sound of........ Jer 8:16
people, nations, and languages, *t* ...... Dan 5:19
The mountains saw thee, and they *t*.... Hab 3:10
When I heard, my belly *t* .... Hab 3:16
I *t* in myself, that I might rest .... Hab 3:16
for they *t* and were astonished.......... Mk 16:8
Then Moses *t*, and durst not behold ... Acts 7:32
and judgment to come, Felix *t* .... Acts 24:25

TREMBLETH

At this also my heart *t*, and is .... Job 37:1
He looketh on the earth, and it *t* .... Ps 104:32
My flesh *t* for fear of thee.............. Ps 119:120
contrite spirit, and *t* at my word........ Is 66:2

TREMBLING

t shall take hold upon them .... Ex 15:15
shall give thee there a *t* heart.......... Deut 28:65
and all the people followed him *t* 1Sa 13:7
there was *t* in the host, in the 1Sa 14:15
so it was a very great *t* 1Sa 14:15
t because of this matter, and for .... Ezr 10:9
Fear came upon me, and *t*, which ...... Job 4:14
t taketh hold on my flesh .... Job 21:6
Rejoice with *t* .... Ps 2:11
t are come upon me, and horror .... Ps 55:5
drunken the dregs of the cup of *t* ...... Is 51:17
out of thine hand the cup of *t* .... Is 51:22
We have heard a voice of *t*.............. Jer 30:5
and drink thy water with *t* .... Eze 12:18
shall clothe themselves with *t* .... Eze 26:16
drink thy water with *t*................... Dan 10:11
When Ephraim spake *t*, he exalted ..... Hos 13:1
I will make Jerusalem a cup of *t*........ Zec 12:2
But the woman fearing and *t*............ Mk 5:33
that she was not hid, she came *t* .... Lk 8:47

And he *t* and astonished said, Lord,... Acts 9:6
a light, and sprang in, and came *t* ..... Acts 16:29
and in fear, and in much *t* 1Cor 2:3
with fear and *t* ye received him......... 2Cor 7:15
to the flesh, with fear and *t* .... Eph 6:5
your own salvation with fear and *t*.... Phil 2:12

TRENCH

and he came to the *t*, as the host....... 1Sa 17:20
and Saul lay in the *t*, and the 1Sa 26:5
Saul lay sleeping within the *t* 1Sa 26:7
the city, and it stood in the *t* 2Sa 20:15
he made a *t* about the altar, as 1Kin 18:32
he filled the *t* also with water 1Kin 18:35
up the water that was in the *t* 1Kin 18:38
enemies shall cast a *t* about thee .... Lk 19:43

TRESPASS

and said to Laban, What is my *t* .... Gen 31:36
the *t* of thy brethren, and their.......... Gen 50:17
forgive the *t* of the servants of .... Gen 50:17
For all manner of *t*, whether .... Ex 22:9
he shall bring his *t* offering............. Lev 5:6
then he shall bring for his .... Lev 5:7
If a soul commit a *t*, and sin .... Lev 5:15
his *t* unto the LORD a ram without .... Lev 5:15
the sanctuary, for a *t* offering .... Lev 5:15
with the ram of the *t* offering .... Lev 5:16
for a *t* offering, unto the priest .... Lev 5:18
It is a *t* offering .... Lev 5:19
commit a *t* against the LORD, and ...... Lev 6:2
in the day of his *t* offering.............. Lev 6:5
he shall bring his *t* offering............. Lev 6:6
for a *t* offering, unto the priest .... Lev 6:6
offering, and as the *t* offering .... Lev 6:17
this is the law of the *t* offering .... Lev 7:1
shall they kill the *t* offering .... Lev 7:2
it is a *t* offering .... Lev 7:5
offering is, so is the *t* offering .... Lev 7:7
of the *t* offering, and of the .... Lev 7:37
and offer him for a *t* offering.......... Lev 14:12
priest's, so is the *t* offering............ Lev 14:13
of the blood of the *t* offering .... Lev 14:14
upon the blood of the *t* offering ...... Lev 14:17
lamb for a *t* offering to be waved ..... Lev 14:21
take the lamb of the *t* offering......... Lev 14:24
kill the lamb of the *t* offering.......... Lev 14:25
of the blood of the *t* offering .... Lev 14:25
of the blood of the *t* offering .... Lev 14:28
he shall bring his *t* offering............ Lev 19:21
even a ram for a *t* offering .... Lev 19:21
for him with the ram of the *t* .... Lev 19:22
them to bear the iniquity of .... Lev 22:16
fathers, with their *t* which they .... Lev 26:40
to do a *t* against the LORD, and .... Num 5:6
he shall recompense his *t* with......... Num 5:7
kinsman to recompense the *t* unto ..... Num 5:8
let the *t* be recompensed unto the ..... Num 5:8
aside, and commit a *t* against him,..... Num 5:12
have done *t* against her husband,....... Num 5:27
the first year for a *t* offering .... Num 6:12
every *t* offering of theirs, which....... Num 18:9
to commit a *t* against the LORD in ... Num 31:16
a *t* in the accursed thing .... Josh 7:1
What is this that ye have........ .... Josh 22:16
commit a *t* in the accursed thing ...... Josh 22:20
committed this *t* against the LORD ... Josh 22:31
any wise return him a *t* offering....... 1Sa 6:3
What shall be the *t* offering 1Sa 6:4
ye return him for a *t* offering........... 1Sa 6:4
for a *t* offering unto the LORD.......... 1Sa 6:17
forgive the *t* of thine handmaid 1Sa 25:28
If any man *t* against his 1Kin 8:31
The *t* money and sin money was not 2Kin 12:16
will he be a cause of *t* to Israel 1Chr 21:3
that they *t* not against the LORD 2Chr 19:10
this do, and ye shall not *t* 2Chr 19:10
and Jerusalem for this their *t* 2Chr 24:18
add more to our sins and to our *t* 2Chr 28:13
for our *t* is great, and there is 2Chr 28:13
he yet more against the LORD 2Chr 28:22
of him, and all his sin, and his *t* 2Chr 33:19
rulers hath been chief in this *t* .... Ezr 9:2
our *t* is grown up unto the .... Ezr 9:6
been in a great *t* unto this day.......... Ezr 9:7
evil deeds, and for our great *t* .... Ezr 9:13
to increase the *t* of Israel............... Ezr 10:10
a ram of the flock for their *t* .... Ezr 10:19
because they have committed a *t* ...... Eze 15:8
plead with him there for his *t* .... Eze 17:20
in his *t* that he hath trespassed,........ Eze 18:24
have committed a *t* against me......... Eze 20:27
sin offering and the *t* offering.......... Eze 40:39
sin offering, and the *t* offering .... Eze 42:13
sin offering, and for the *t* .... Eze 44:29
priests shall boil the *t* offering........ Eze 46:20
because of their *t* that they have....... Dan 9:7
thy brother shall *t* against thee .... Mt 18:15
If thy brother *t* against thee............ Lk 17:3
if he *t* against thee seven times........ Lk 17:4

TRESPASSED

hath certainly *t* against the LORD ...... Lev 5:19
trespass which they *t* against me....... Lev 26:40
sinned against him, whom he hath *t* ... Num 5:7
Because ye *t* against me among the.... Deut 32:51
for thou hast *t* 2Chr 26:18
For our fathers have *t*, and done 2Chr 29:6
which *t* against the LORD God of....... 2Chr 30:7
but Amon *t* more and more.............. 2Chr 33:23
We have *t* against our God, and .... Ezr 10:2
that he hath *t* against me .... Eze 17:20

in his trespass that he hath *t*............ Eze 18:24
because they *t* against me............... Eze 39:23
whereby they have *t* against me .... Eze 39:26
that they have *t* against them .... Dan 9:7
my covenant, and *t* against my law .... Hos 8:1

TRESPASSES

we are before thee in our *t*.............. Ezr 9:15
an one as goeth on still in his *t* .... Ps 68:21
all their *t* whereby they have........... Eze 39:26
For if ye forgive men their *t* .... Mt 6:14
But if ye forgive not men their *t* .... Mt 6:15
will your Father forgive your *t*......... Mt 6:15
not every one his brother their *t* .... Mt 18:35
in heaven may forgive you your *t* ...... Mk 11:25
which is in heaven forgive your *t* ...... Mk 11:26
not imputing their *t* unto them 2Cor 5:19
he quickened, who were dead in *t* ..... Eph 2:1
him, having forgiven you all *t* .... Col 2:13

TRESPASSING

that he hath done in *t* therein........... Lev 6:7
against me by *t* grievously .... Eze 14:13

TRIAL

laugh at the *t* of the innocent .... Job 9:23
Because it is a *t*, and what if the .... Eze 21:13
How that in a great *t* of 2Cor 8:2
others had *t* of cruel mockings and ... Heb 11:36
That the *t* of your faith, being 1Pet 1:7
the fiery *t* which is to try you.......... 1Pet 4:12

TRIBE

the son of Hur, of the *t* of Judah .... Ex 31:2
son of Ahisamach, of the *t* of Dan ..... Ex 31:6
The son of Hur, of the *t* of Judah ...... Ex 35:30
son of Ahisamach, of the *t* of Dan ..... Ex 35:34
of the *t* of Judah, made all the .... Ex 38:22
son of Ahisamach, of the *t* of Dan ..... Ex 38:23
of Dibri, of the *t* of Dan................. Lev 24:11
there shall be a man of every *t* .... Num 1:4
of the *t* of Reuben .... Num 1:5
of them, even of the *t* of Reuben....... Num 1:21
of them, even of the *t* of Simeon ...... Num 1:23
of them, even of the *t* of Gad .... Num 1:25
of them, even of the *t* of Judah .... Num 1:27
them, every of the *t* of Issachar .... Num 1:29
of them, even of the *t* of Zebulun ..... Num 1:31
of them, even of the *t* of Ephraim ..... Num 1:33
them, even of the *t* of Manasseh .... Num 1:35
them, even of the *t* of Benjamin .... Num 1:37
of them, even of the *t* of Dan .... Num 1:39
of them, even of the *t* of Asher .... Num 1:41
them, even of the *t* of Naphtali .... Num 1:43
the *t* of their fathers were not .... Num 1:47
shalt not number the *t* of Levi .... Num 1:49
him shall be the *t* of Issachar .... Num 2:5
Then the *t* of Zebulun .... Num 2:7
by him shall be the *t* of Simeon .... Num 2:12
Then the *t* of Gad .... Num 2:14
by him shall be the *t* of Manasseh ..... Num 2:20
Then the *t* of Benjamin .... Num 2:22
by him shall be the *t* of Asher .... Num 2:27
Then the *t* of Naphtali .... Num 2:29
Bring the *t* of Levi near, and .... Num 3:6
Cut ye not off the *t* of the .... Num 4:18
of Amminadab, of the *t* of Judah ...... Num 7:12
over the host of the *t* of the .... Num 10:15
over the host of the *t* of the .... Num 10:16
over the host of the *t* of the .... Num 10:19
over the host of the *t* of the .... Num 10:20
over the host of the *t* of the .... Num 10:22
over the host of the *t* of the .... Num 10:23
over the host of the *t* of the .... Num 10:26
over the host of the *t* of the .... Num 10:27
of every *t* of their fathers shall .... Num 13:2
of the *t* of Reuben, Shammua the ...... Num 13:4
of the *t* of Simeon, Shaphat the .... Num 13:5
Of the *t* of Judah, Caleb the son .... Num 13:6
Of the *t* of Issachar, Igal the........... Num 13:7
Of the *t* of Ephraim, Oshea the .... Num 13:8
Of the *t* of Benjamin, Palti the .... Num 13:9
Of the *t* of Zebulun, Gaddiel the ...... Num 13:10
Of the *t* of Joseph, namely, of .... Num 13:11
of the *t* of Manasseh, Gaddi the .... Num 13:11
Of the *t* of Dan, Ammiel the son .... Num 13:12
Of the *t* of Asher, Sethur the son ...... Num 13:13
Of the *t* of Naphtali, Nahbi the .... Num 13:14
Of the *t* of Gad, Geuel the son of ...... Num 13:15
brethren also of the *t* of Levi .... Num 18:2
the *t* of thy father, bring thou .... Num 18:2
Of every *t* a thousand, throughout..... Num 31:4
of Israel, a thousand of every *t* .... Num 31:5
to the war, a thousand of every *t* ...... Num 31:6
unto half the *t* of Manasseh the .... Num 32:33
the nine tribes, and to the half *t* .... Num 34:13
For the *t* of the children of .... Num 34:14
the *t* of the children of Gad............ Num 34:14
half the *t* of Manasseh have .... Num 34:14
the half *t* have received their .... Num 34:15
shalt take one prince of every *t* .... Num 34:18
Of the *t* of Judah, Caleb the son .... Num 34:19
Of the *t* of the children of .... Num 34:20
Of the *t* of Benjamin, Elidad the ...... Num 34:21
the prince of the *t* of the .... Num 34:22
the prince of the *t* of the .... Num 34:23
For the *t* of the children of .... Num 34:24
the prince of the *t* of the .... Num 34:25
the prince of the *t* of the .... Num 34:26
the prince of the *t* of the .... Num 34:27
the prince of the *t* of the .... Num 34:28
the *t* whereunto they are received..... Num 36:3

the t whereunto they are received .... Num 36:4
of the t of our fathers .... Num 36:6
The t of the sons of Joseph hath .... Num 36:5
only to the family of the t of .... Num 36:6
of Israel remove from t to t .... Num 36:7
of the t of his fathers .... Num 36:7
an inheritance in any t of the .... Num 36:8
the family of the t of her father .... Num 36:8
from one t to another t .... Num 36:9
inheritance remained in the t of .... Num 36:12
twelve men of you, one of a t .... Deut 1:23
I unto the half t of Manasseh .... Deut 3:13
the LORD separated the t of Levi .... Deut 10:8
the Levites, and all the t of Levi .... Deut 18:1
and to the half t of Manasseh .... Deut 29:8
man, or woman, or family, or t .... Deut 29:18
and to half the t of Manasseh .... Josh 1:12
of Israel, out of every t a man .... Josh 3:12
the people, out of every t a man .... Josh 4:2
of Israel, out of every t a man .... Josh 4:4
half the t of Manasseh, passed .... Josh 4:12
of the t of Judah, took of the .... Josh 7:1
that the t which the LORD taketh .... Josh 7:14
and the t of Judah was taken .... Josh 7:16
of the t of Judah, was taken .... Josh 7:16
and the half t of Manasseh .... Josh 12:6
and the half t of Manasseh .... Josh 13:7
Only unto the t of Levi he gave .... Josh 13:15
Moses gave unto the t of the .... Josh 13:15
inheritance unto the t of Gad .... Josh 13:24
unto the half t of Manasseh .... Josh 13:29
t of the children of Manasseh by .... Josh 13:29
But unto the t of Levi Moses gave .... Josh 13:33
nine tribes, and for the half t .... Josh 14:2
an half t on the other side .... Josh 14:3
the t of the children of Judah by .... Josh 15:1
of the t of the children of Judah .... Josh 15:20
the uttermost cities of the t of .... Josh 15:21
t of the children of Ephraim by .... Josh 16:8
also a lot for the t of Manasseh .... Josh 17:1
among you three men for each t .... Josh 18:4
half the t of Manasseh, have .... Josh 18:7
the lot of the t of the children .... Josh 18:11
Now the cities of the t of the .... Josh 18:21
even for the t of the children of .... Josh 19:1
the t of the children of Simeon .... Josh 19:8
the t of the children of Issachar .... Josh 19:23
the t of the children of Asher .... Josh 19:24
of the t of the children of Asher .... Josh 19:31
the t of the children of Naphtali .... Josh 19:39
for the t of the children of Dan .... Josh 19:40
of the t of the children of Dan .... Josh 19:48
the plain out of the t of Reuben .... Josh 20:8
in Gilead out of the t of Gad .... Josh 20:8
Bashan out of the t of Manasseh .... Josh 20:8
had by lot out of the t of Judah .... Josh 21:4
Judah, and out of the t of Simeon .... Josh 21:4
out of the t of Benjamin .... Josh 21:4
the families of the t of Ephraim .... Josh 21:5
Ephraim, and out of the t of Dan .... Josh 21:5
and out of the half t of Manasseh .... Josh 21:5
the families of the t of Issachar .... Josh 21:6
and out of the t of Asher .... Josh 21:6
out of the t of Naphtali, and out .... Josh 21:6
out of the half t of Manasseh in .... Josh 21:6
had out of the t of Reuben .... Josh 21:7
of Reuben, and out of the t of Gad .... Josh 21:7
Gad, and out of the t of Zebulun .... Josh 21:7
they gave out of the t of the .... Josh 21:9
out of the t of the children of .... Josh 21:9
out of the t of Benjamin, Gibeon .... Josh 21:17
their lot out of the t of Ephraim .... Josh 21:20
And out of the t of Dan, Eltekeh .... Josh 21:23
And out of the half t of Manasseh .... Josh 21:25
out of the other half t of .... Josh 21:27
out of the t of Issachar, Kishon .... Josh 21:28
And out of the t of Asher, Mishal .... Josh 21:30
out of the t of Naphtali, Kedesh .... Josh 21:32
Levites, out of the t of Zebulun .... Josh 21:34
And out of the t of Reuben .... Josh 21:36
And out of the t of Gad, Ramoth in ...... Josh 21:38
and the half t of Manasseh, ... Josh 22:1
Now to the one half of the t of .... Josh 22:7
the half t of Manasseh returned, ... Josh 22:9
the half t of Manasseh built .... Josh 22:10
the half t of Manasseh have built .... Josh 22:11
Gad, and to the half t of Manasseh .... Josh 22:13
Gad, and to the half t of Manasseh .... Josh 22:15
the half t of Manasseh answered, ... Josh 22:21
in those days the t of .... Judg 18:1
or that thou be a priest unto a t .... Judg 18:19
of the t of Dan until the day of the .... Judg 18:30
men through all the t of Benjamin .... Judg 20:12
be to day one t lacking in Israel? .... Judg 21:3
There is one t cut off from .... Judg 21:6
that a t be not destroyed out of .... Judg 21:17
at that time, every man to his t .... Judg 21:24
the families of the t of Benjamin 1Sa 9:21
the t of Benjamin was taken 1Sa 10:20
When he had caused the t of 1Sa 10:21
widow's son of the t of Naphtali 1Kin 7:14
but will give one t to thy son 1Kin 11:13
(But he shall have one t for my 1Kin 11:32
And unto his son will I give one t 1Kin 11:36
of David, but the t of Judah only 1Kin 12:20
with the t of Benjamin, an 1Kin 12:21
none left but the t of Judah only 2Kin 17:18
half the t of Manasseh, ... 1Chr 5:18
the children of the half t of 1Chr 5:23
the half t of Manasseh, and 1Chr 5:26

TRIBES

people, as one of the t of Israel .... Gen 49:16
these are the twelve t of Israel .... Gen 49:28
to the twelve t of Israel .... Ex 24:4
they be according to the twelve t .... Ex 28:21
name, according to the twelve t .... Ex 39:14
princes of the t of their fathers .... Num 1:16
who were the princes of the t .... Num 7:2
in his tents according to their t .... Num 24:2
the t of their fathers they shall .... Num 26:55
t concerning the children of .... Num 30:1
throughout all the t of Israel .... Num 31:4
the chief fathers of the t of the .... Num 32:28
according to the t of your .... Num 33:54
commanded to give unto the nine t ...... Num 34:13
The two t and the half tribe have .... Num 34:15
other t of the children of Israel .... Num 34:15
but every one of the t of the .... Num 36:9
and known among your t, and I will ...... Deut 1:13
So I took the chief of your t .... Deut 1:15
tens, and officers among your t .... Deut 1:15
me, even all the heads of your t .... Deut 5:23
all your t to put his name there .... Deut 12:5
LORD shall choose in one of thy t .... Deut 12:14
God giveth thee, throughout thy t .... Deut 16:18
hath chosen him out of all thy t .... Deut 18:5
your captains of your t, your .... Deut 29:10
evil out of all the t of Israel .... Deut 29:21
unto me all the elders of your t .... Deut 31:28
the t of Israel were gathered .... Deut 33:5
twelve men out of the t of Israel .... Josh 3:12
unto the number of the t of the .... Josh 4:5
the t of the children of Israel .... Josh 4:8
he brought according to your t .... Josh 7:14
and brought Israel by their t .... Josh 7:16
to their divisions by their t .... Josh 11:23
the t of Israel for a possession .... Josh 12:7
an inheritance unto the nine t .... Josh 13:7
the t of the children of Israel .... Josh 14:1
the hand of Moses, for the nine t .... Josh 14:2
given the inheritance of two t .... Josh 14:3
the children of Joseph were two t .... Josh 14:4
the children of Israel seven t .... Josh 18:2
the children of Israel seven t .... Josh 18:2
the t of the children of Israel .... Josh 19:51
the t of the children of .... Josh 21:1
nine cities out of those two t .... Josh 21:16
throughout all the t of Israel .... Josh 22:14
to be an inheritance for your t .... Josh 23:4
all the t of Israel to Shechem .... Josh 24:1
unto them among the t of Israel .... Judg 18:1
even of all the t of Israel .... Judg 20:2
throughout all the t of Israel .... Judg 20:10
the t of Israel sent men through .... Judg 20:12
Who is there among all the t of .... Judg 21:5
What one is there of the t of .... Judg 21:8
made a breach in the t of Israel .... Judg 21:15
the t of Israel to be my priest 1Sa 2:28
the smallest of the t of Israel? 1Sa 9:21
before the LORD by your t 1Sa 10:19

all the t of Israel to come near 1Sa 10:20
made the head of the t of Israel 1Sa 15:17
Then came all the t of Israel to 2Sa 5:1
word with any of the t of Israel 2Sa 7:7
is of one of the t of Israel 2Sa 15:2
throughout all the t of Israel 2Sa 15:10
throughout all the t of Israel 2Sa 19:9
all the t of Israel unto Abel 2Sa 20:14
now through all the t of Israel 2Sa 24:2
Israel, and all the heads of the 1Kin 8:1
the t of Israel to build an house 1Kin 8:16
and will give ten t to thee 1Kin 11:31
chosen out of all the t of Israel 1Kin 11:32
give it unto thee, even ten t 1Kin 11:35
choose out of all the t of Israel 1Kin 14:21
of the t of the sons of Jacob 1Kin 18:31
chosen out of all t of Israel 2Kin 21:7
Furthermore over the t of Israel 1Chr 27:16
the princes of the t of Israel 1Chr 27:22
of Israel, the princes of the t 1Chr 28:1
and princes of the t of Israel 1Chr 29:6
Israel, and all the heads of the 2Chr 5:2
I chose no city among all the t 2Chr 6:5
after them out of all the t of 2Chr 11:16
chosen out of all the t of Israel 2Chr 12:13
chosen before all the t of Israel 2Chr 33:7
to the number of the t of Israel .... Ezr 6:17
made the t of Israel to dwell in .... Ps 78:55
one feeble person among their t .... Ps 105:37
Whither the t go up, the t .... Ps 122:4
to the LORD, unto the .... Ps 122:4
are the stay of the t thereof .... Is 19:13
to raise up the t of Jacob .... Is 49:6
the t of thine inheritance .... Is 63:17
the t of Israel his fellows, and .... Eze 37:19
of Israel according to their t .... Eze 45:8
to the twelve t of Israel .... Eze 47:13
you according to the t of Israel .... Eze 47:21
with you among the t of Israel .... Eze 47:22
Now these are the names of the .... Eze 48:1
it out of all the t of Israel .... Eze 48:19
As for the rest of the t, from .... Eze 48:23
the t of Israel for inheritance .... Eze 48:29
the names of the t of Israel .... Eze 48:31
among the t of Israel have I made .... Hos 5:9
according to the oaths of the t .... Hab 3:9
of man, as of all the t of Israel .... Zec 9:1
judging the twelve t of Israel .... Mt 19:28
all the t of the earth mourn .... Mt 24:30
judging the twelve t of Israel .... Lk 22:30
Unto which promise our twelve t .... Acts 26:7
to the twelve t which are .... Jas 1:1
four thousand of all the t of the .... Rev 7:4
t of the children of Israel .... Rev 21:12

TRIBULATION

When thou art in t, and all these .... Deut 4:30
deliver you in the time of your t .... Judg 10:14
let him deliver me out of all t 1Sa 26:24
for when t or persecution ariseth .... Mt 13:21
For then shall be great t .... Mt 24:21
Immediately after the t of those .... Mt 24:29
But in those days, after that t .... Mk 13:24
In the world ye shall have t .... Jn 16:33
that we must through much t enter .... Acts 14:22
T and anguish, upon every soul of ...... Rom 2:9
knowing that t worketh patience .... Rom 5:3
shall I, or distress, or .... Rom 8:35
patient in t .... Rom 12:12
Who comforteth us in all our t 2Cor 1:4
am exceeding joyful in all our t 2Cor 7:4
before that we should suffer t 1Th 3:4
t to them that trouble you 2Th 1:6
your brother, and companion in t .... Rev 1:9
I know thy works, and t, and .... Rev 2:9
and ye shall have t ten days .... Rev 2:10
adultery with her into great t .... Rev 2:22
they which came out of great t .... Rev 7:14

TRIBULATIONS

of all your adversities and your t 1Sa 10:19
only so, but we glory in t also .... Rom 5:3
that ye faint not at my t for you .... Eph 3:13
persecutions and t which ye endure 2Th 1:4

TRIBUTARIES

therein shall be t unto thee .... Deut 20:11
dwelt among them, and became t .... Judg 1:30
of Beth-anath became t unto them .... Judg 1:33
prevailed, so that they became t .... Judg 1:35

TRIBUTARY

provinces, how is she become t .... Lam 1:1

TRIBUTE

bear, and became a servant unto .... Gen 49:15
levy a t unto the LORD of the men .... Num 31:28
the LORD's t of the sheep was six .... Num 31:37
which the LORD's t was threescore .... Num 31:38
which the LORD's t was thirty .... Num 31:39
of which the LORD's t was thirty .... Num 31:40
And Moses gave the t, which was .... Num 31:41
unto the LORD thy God with a t of .... Deut 16:10
unto this day, and serve under t .... Josh 16:10
that they put the Canaanites to t .... Josh 17:13
that they put the Canaanites to t .... Judg 1:28
And Adoram was over the t 2Sa 20:24
the son of Abda was over the t 1Kin 4:6
a t of bondservice unto this day 1Kin 9:21
sent Adoram, who was over the t 1Kin 12:18
put the land to a t of an hundred 2Kin 23:33
make to pay t until this day 2Chr 8:8
sent Hadoram that was over the t 2Chr 10:18

Jehoshaphat presents, and t silver 2Chr 17:11
then will they not pay toll, t .... Ezr 4:13
and toll, t, and custom, was paid .... Ezr 4:20
even of the t beyond the river, ... Ezr 6:8
not be lawful to impose toll, t .... Ezr 7:24
borrowed money for the king's t .... Neh 5:4
but the slothful shall be under t .... Est 10:1
but the slothful shall be under t .... Prov 12:24
they that received t money came .... Mt 17:24
said, Doth not your master pay t .... Mt 17:24
of the earth take custom or t .... Mt 17:25
it lawful to give t unto Caesar .... Mt 22:17
Shew me the t money .... Mt 22:19
Is it lawful to give t to Caesar .... Mk 12:14
for us to give t unto Caesar .... Lk 20:22
and forbidding to give t to Caesar ..... Lk 23:2
For for this cause pay ye t also .... Rom 13:6
t to whom t is due .... Rom 13:7

TRICKLETH
Mine eye t down, and ceaseth not, ... Lam 3:49

TRIED
controversy and every stroke be t ...... Deut 21:5
the word of the LORD is t 2Sa 22:31
when he hath t me, I shall come .... Job 23:10
is that Job may be t unto the end .... Job 34:36
as silver t in a furnace of earth .... Ps 12:6
thou hast t me, and shalt find .... Ps 17:3
the word of the LORD is t .... Ps 18:30
hast t us, as silver is t .... Ps 66:10
the word of the LORD hath t .... Ps 105:19
a t stone, a precious corner, ... Is 28:16
me, and t mine heart toward thee ...... Jer 12:3
be purified, and made white, and t .... Dan 12:10
and will try them as gold is t .... Zec 13:9
By faith Abraham, when he was t ...... Heb 11:17
for when he is t, he shall .... Jas 1:12
though it be t with fire 1Pet 1:7
thou hast t them which say they .... Rev 2:2
you into prison, that ye may be t .... Rev 2:10
to buy of me gold t in the fire .... Rev 3:18

TRIEST
my God, that thou t the heart 1Chr 29:17
that t the reins and the heart, ... Jer 11:20
that t the righteous, and seest .... Jer 20:12

TRIETH
For the ear t words, as the mouth .... Job 34:3
the righteous God t the hearts, ... Ps 7:9
The LORD t the righteous .... Ps 11:5
but the LORD t the hearts, ... Prov 17:3
men, but God, which t our hearts, ... 1Th 2:4

TRIMMED
nor t his beard, nor washed his 2Sa 19:24
virgins arose, and t their lamps. .... Mt 25:7

TRIMMEST
Why t thou thy way to seek love, ... Jer 2:33

TRIUMPH
daughters of the uncircumcised t 2Sa 1:20
let not mine enemies t over me. .... Ps 25:2
mine enemy doth not t over me. .... Ps 41:11
unto God with the voice of t .... Ps 47:1
Philistia, t thou because of me .... Ps 60:8
I will t in the works of thy .... Ps 92:4
how long shall the wicked t .... Ps 94:3
holy name, and to t in thy praise. ...... Ps 106:47
over Philistia will I t .... Ps 108:9
always causeth us to t in Christ. 2Cor 2:14

TRIUMPHED
LORD, for he hath t gloriously .... Ex 15:1
LORD, for he hath t gloriously .... Ex 15:21

TRIUMPHING
That the t of the wicked is short .... Job 20:5
of them openly, t over them in it .... Col 2:15

TROAS (tro'-as) A seaport of Phrygia in Asia
Minor.
passing by Mysia came down to T ...... Acts 16:8
Therefore loosing from T, we came... Acts 16:11
going before tarried for us at T .... Acts 20:5
came unto them to T in five days. ...... Acts 20:6
when I came to T to preach 2Cor 2:12
that I left at T with Carpus 2Ti 4:13

TRODDEN
give the land that he hath t upon...... Deut 1:36
have t shall be thine inheritance. ...... Josh 14:9
thou hast t down strength .... Judg 5:21
old way which wicked men have t ..... Job 22:15
The lion's whelps have not t it .... Job 28:8
Thou hast t down all them that .... Ps 119:118
thereof, and it shall be t down .... Is 5:5
as a carcase t under feet. .... Is 14:19
t down, whose land the rivers .... Is 18:2
t under foot, whose land the .... Is 18:7
Moab shall be t down under him, ... Is 25:10
even as straw is t down for the .... Is 25:10
of Ephraim, shall be t under feet ...... Is 28:3
then ye shall be t down by it .... Is 28:18
I have t the winepress alone .... Is 63:3
have t down thy sanctuary .... Is 63:18
they have t my portion under foot ..... Jer 12:10
The Lord hath t under foot all my ..... Lam 1:15
the Lord hath t the virgin. .... Lam 1:15
which ye have t with your feet .... Eze 34:19
and the host to be t under foot? .... Dan 8:13
now shall she be t down as the .... Mic 7:10
to be t under foot of men .... Mt 5:13

and it was t down, and the fowls of .... Lk 8:5
Jerusalem shall be t down of the .... Lk 21:24
who hath t under foot the Son of .... Heb 10:29
winepress was t without the city .... Rev 14:20

TRODE
t the grapes, and made merry, and..... Judg 9:27
t them down with ease over .... Judg 20:43
the people t upon him in the gate 2Kin 7:17
for the people t upon him in the 2Kin 7:20
and he t her under foot....................... 2Kin 9:33
in Lebanon, and t down the thistle..... 2Kin 14:9
in Lebanon, and t down the thistle..... 2Chr 25:18
that they t one upon another............. Lk 12:1

TROGYLLIUM (tro-jil'-le-um) A coastal town
in Ionia in Asia Minor.
arrived at Samos, and tarried at T...... Acts 20:15

TROOP
And Leah said, A t cometh .... Gen 30:11
Gad, a t shall overcome him.............. Gen 49:19
Shall I pursue after this t 1Sa 30:8
after Abner, and became one t........... 2Sa 2:25
and Joab came from pursuing a t 2Sa 3:22
by thee I have run through a t 2Sa 22:30
were gathered together into a t 2Sa 23:11
the t of the Philistines pitched 2Sa 23:13
by thee I have run through a t .... Ps 18:29
that prepare a table for that t............ Is 65:11
bring a t suddenly upon them............ Jer 18:22
the t of robbers spoileth without ...... Hos 7:1
hath founded his t in the earth.......... Amos 9:6

TROOPS
of the t of Tema looked, the .... Job 6:19
His t come together, and raise up...... Job 19:12
by t in the harlots' houses. .... Jer 5:7
as t of robbers wait for a man, ... Hos 6:9
in t, O daughter of t .... Mic 5:1
he will invade them with his t .... Hab 3:16

TROPHIMUS (trof'-im-us) A companion of
Paul.
and of Asia, Tychicus and T.............. Acts 20:4
him in the city T an Ephesian .... Acts 21:29
but T have I left at Miletum sick 2Ti 4:20

TROUBLE
camp of Israel a curse, and it t .... Josh 6:18
the LORD shall t thee this day .... Josh 7:25
and thou art one of them that t me .... Judg 11:35
Hezekiah, This day is a day of 2Kin 19:3
in my t I have prepared for the 1Chr 22:14
But when they in their t did turn 2Chr 15:4
and he hath delivered them to t 2Chr 29:8
to affright them, and to t them 2Chr 32:18
and in the time of their t .... Neh 9:27
let not all the t seem little. .... Neh 9:32
yet t came, ... Job 3:26
neither doth t spring out of the .... Job 5:6
Yet man is born unto t, as the .... Job 5:7
is of few days, and full of t............... Job 14:1
T and anguish shall make him .... Job 15:24
his cry when t cometh upon him. ..... Job 27:9
not I weep for him that was in t .... Job 30:25
quietness, who then can make t .... Job 34:29
reserved against the time of t .... Job 38:23
how are they increased that t me ..... Ps 3:1
oppressed, a refuge in times of t ...... Ps 9:9
consider my t which I suffer of .... Ps 9:13
hidest thou thyself in times of t .... Ps 10:1
those that t me rejoice when I am ..... Ps 13:4
LORD hear thee in the day of t .... Ps 20:1
for t is near .... Ps 22:11
For in the time of t he shall .... Ps 27:5
for thou hast considered my t............ Ps 31:7
upon me, O LORD, for I am in t .... Ps 31:9
thou shalt preserve me from t .... Ps 32:7
their strength in the time of t .... Ps 37:39
will deliver him in time of t .... Ps 41:1
a very present help in t .... Ps 46:1
And call upon me in the day of t....... Ps 50:15
he hath delivered me out of all t ...... Ps 54:7
and refuge in the day of my t .... Ps 59:16
Give us help from t .... Ps 60:11
hath spoken, when I was in t .... Ps 66:14
for I am in t .... Ps 69:17
They are not in t as other men .... Ps 73:5
In the day of my t I sought the .... Ps 77:2
in vanity, and their years in t .... Ps 78:33
wrath, and indignation, and t .... Ps 78:49
Thou calledst in t, and I .... Ps 81:7
In the day of my t I will call.............. Ps 86:7
I will be with him in t .... Ps 91:15
from me in the day when I am in t .... Ps 102:2
cried unto the LORD in their t .... Ps 107:6
cried unto the LORD in their t .... Ps 107:13
they cry unto the LORD in their t ...... Ps 107:19
their soul is melted because of t .... Ps 107:26
they cry unto the LORD in their t ...... Ps 107:28
Give us help from t .... Ps 108:12
I found t and sorrow. .... Ps 116:3
T and anguish have taken hold on..... Ps 119:143
Though I walk in the midst of t.......... Ps 138:7
I shewed before him my t .... Ps 142:2
sake bring my soul out of t .... Ps 143:11
righteous is delivered out of t .... Prov 11:8
but the just shall come out of t.......... Prov 12:13
the revenues of the wicked is t .... Prov 15:6
great treasure and t therewith .... Prov 15:16
time of t is like a broken tooth .... Prov 25:19
they are a t unto me .... Is 1:14

and behold t and darkness, dimness ... Is 8:22
And behold at eveningtide t .... Is 17:14
For it is a day of t, and of .... Is 22:5
in t have they visited thee. .... Is 26:16
into the land of t and anguish, ... Is 30:6
salvation also in the time of t .... Is 33:2
Hezekiah, This day is a day of t......... Is 37:3
answer, nor save him out of his t ...... Is 46:7
in vain, nor bring forth for t .... Is 65:23
the time of their t they will say .... Jer 2:27
save thee in the time of thy t .... Jer 2:28
for a time of health, and behold t...... Jer 8:15
at all in the time of their t .... Jer 11:12
that they cry unto me for their t .... Jer 11:14
the saviour thereof in time of t .... Jer 14:8
the time of healing, and behold t ...... Jer 14:19
it is even the time of Jacob's t .... Jer 30:7
for in the day of t they shall be .... Jer 51:2
mine enemies have heard of my t ..... Lam 1:21
is come, the day of t is near .... Eze 7:7
the foot of man t them any more. ...... Eze 32:13
nor the hoofs of beasts t them .... Eze 32:13
interpretation thereof, t thee. .... Dan 4:19
let not thy thoughts t thee. .... Dan 5:10
and out of the north shall t him .... Dan 11:44
and there shall be a time of t .... Dan 12:1
a strong hold in the day of t .... Nah 1:7
that I might rest in the day of t .... Hab 3:16
day is a day of wrath, a day of t........ Zeph 1:15
unto them, Why t ye the woman .... Mt 26:10
why t ye her. .... Mk 14:6
unto him, Lord, t not thyself.............. Lk 7:6
t not the Master .... Lk 8:49
shall answer and say, T me not .... Lk 11:7
that we t not them, which from .... Acts 15:19
Jews, do exceedingly t our city .... Acts 16:20
him said, T not yourselves .... Acts 20:10
such shall have t in the flesh. 1Cor 7:28
comfort them which are in any t 2Cor 1:4
of our t which came to us in Asia 2Cor 1:8
but there be some that t you .... Gal 1:7
were even cut off which t you .... Gal 5:12
From henceforth let no man t me ...... Gal 6:17
tribulation to them that t you 2Th 1:6
of bitterness springing up t you .... Heb 12:15

TROUBLED
Ye have t me to make me to stink ..... Gen 34:30
the morning that his spirit was t .... Gen 41:8
for they were t at his presence .... Gen 45:3
the host of the Egyptians, ... Ex 14:24
Joshua said, Why hast thou t us. .... Josh 7:25
My father hath t the land 1Sa 14:29
evil spirit from the LORD t him. 1Sa 16:14
Saul, and saw that he was sore t 1Sa 28:21
and all the Israelites were t 2Sa 4:1
he answered, I have not t Israel 1Kin 18:18
Syria was sore t for this thing 2Kin 6:11
of Judah, and t them in building, ... Ezr 4:4
it toucheth thee, and thou art t .... Job 4:5
so, why should not my spirit be t ...... Job 21:4
Therefore am I t at his presence. ...... Job 23:15
the people shall be t at midnight ...... Job 34:20
didst hide thy face, and I was t .... Ps 30:7
I am t .... Ps 38:6
the waters thereof roar and be t .... Ps 46:3
they were t, and hasted away .... Ps 48:5
I remembered God, and was t .... Ps 77:3
I am so t that I cannot speak. .... Ps 77:4
the depths also were t .... Ps 77:16
them be confounded and t for ever ... Ps 83:17
anger, and by thy wrath are we t ..... Ps 90:7
Thou hidest thy face, they are t .... Ps 104:29
the wicked is as a t fountain .... Prov 25:26
Many days and years shall ye be t .... Is 32:10
be t, ye careless ones .... Is 32:11
But the wicked are like the t sea ..... Is 57:20
therefore my bowels are t for him .... Jer 31:20
my bowels are t .... Lam 1:20
fall with tears, my bowels are t .... Lam 2:11
the people of the land shall be t ...... Eze 7:27
sea shall be t at thy departure. .... Eze 26:18
afraid, they shall be t in their .... Eze 27:35
wherewith his spirit was t .... Dan 2:1
my spirit was t to know the dream..... Dan 2:3
and the visions of my head t me ...... Dan 4:5
one hour, and his thoughts t him ..... Dan 4:19
changed, and his thoughts t him ...... Dan 5:6
was king Belshazzar greatly t .... Dan 5:9
and the visions of my head t me ...... Dan 7:15
Daniel, my cogitations much t me .... Dan 7:28
their way as a flock, they were t ...... Zec 10:2
had heard these things, he was t ...... Mt 2:3
walking on the sea, they were t .... Mt 14:26
see that ye be not t .... Mt 24:6
For they all saw him, and were t ..... Mk 6:50
and rumours of wars, be ye not t ..... Mk 13:7
when Zacharias saw him, he was t ... Lk 1:12
she was t at his saying, and cast...... Lk 1:29
careful and t about many things. ..... Lk 10:41
he said unto them, Why are ye t ...... Lk 24:38
into the pool, and t the water. .... Jn 5:4
have no man, when the water is t ..... Jn 5:7
groaned in the spirit, and was t .... Jn 11:33
Now is my soul t .... Jn 12:27
he was t in spirit, and testified, ... Jn 13:21
Let not your heart be t .... Jn 14:1
Let not your heart be t, neither .... Jn 14:27
out from us have t you with words.... Acts 15:24
they t the people and the rulers. ..... Acts 17:8

We are t on every side, yet not ... 2Cor 4:8
but we were t on every side ... 2Cor 7:5
And to you who are t with us in ... 2Th 1:7
not soon shaken in mind, or be t ... 2Th 2:2
of their terror, neither be t ... 1Pet 3:14

TROUBLEDST
t the waters with thy feet, and ... Eze 32:2

TROUBLER
the t of Israel, who transgressed ... 1Chr 2:7

TROUBLES
many evils and t shall befall them ... Deut 31:21
t are befallen them, that this ... Deut 31:21
He shall deliver thee in six t ... Job 5:19
The t of my heart are enlarged ... Ps 25:17
Israel, O God, out of all his t ... Ps 25:22
and saved him out of all his t ... Ps 34:6
them out of all their t ... Ps 34:17
hast shewed me great and sore t ... Ps 71:20
For my soul is full of t ... Ps 88:3
tongue keepeth his soul from t ... Prov 21:23
the former t are forgotten ... Is 65:16
and there shall be famines and ... Mk 13:8

TROUBLEST
why t thou the Master any further ... Mk 5:35

TROUBLETH
an evil spirit from God t thee ... 1Sa 16:15
him, Art thou he that t Israel ... 1Kin 18:17
about thee, and sudden fear t thee ... Job 22:10
heart soft, and the Almighty t me ... Job 23:16
he that is cruel t his own flesh ... Prov 11:17
He that t his own house shall ... Prov 11:29
is greedy of gain t his own house ... Prov 15:27
is in thee, and no secret t thee ... Dan 4:9
Yet because while I live ... Lk 18:5
but he that t you shall bear his ... Gal 5:10

TROUBLING
There the wicked cease from t ... Job 3:17
the t of the water stepped in was ... Jn 5:4

TROUBLOUS
and the wall, even in t times ... Dan 9:25

TROUGH
and emptied her pitcher into the t ... Gen 24:20

TROUGHS
t when the flocks came to drink ... Gen 30:38
filled the t to water their ... Ex 2:16

TROW
It not ... Lk 17:9

TRUCEBREAKERS
Without natural affection, t ... 2Ti 3:3

TRUE
we are t men, thy servants are no ... Gen 42:11
If ye be t men, let one of your ... Gen 42:19
And we said unto him, We are t men ... Gen 42:31
shall I know that ye are t men ... Gen 42:33
no spies, but that we are t men ... Gen 42:34
diligently, and, behold, it be t ... Deut 17:4
But if this thing be t, and the ... Deut 22:20
house, and give me a t token ... Josh 2:12
now it is t that I am thy near ... Ruth 3:12
art that God, and thy words be t ... 2Sa 7:28
It was a t report that I heard in ... 1Kin 10:6
is t in the name of the LORD ... 1Kin 22:16
It was a t report which I heard ... 2Chr 9:5
hath been without the t God ... 2Chr 15:3
and t laws, good statutes and ... Neh 9:13
the judgments of the LORD are t ... Ps 19:9
Thy word is t from the beginning ... Ps 119:160
A t witness delivereth souls ... Prov 14:25
But the LORD is the t God ... Jer 10:10
said to Jeremiah, The LORD be a t ... Jer 42:5
hath executed t judgment between ... Eze 18:8
spake and said unto them, Is it t ... Dan 3:14
answered and said unto the king, T ... Dan 3:24
answered and said, The thing is t ... Dan 6:12
the morning which was told is t ... Dan 8:26
and the thing was t, but the time ... Dan 10:1
Execute t judgment, and shew mercy ... Zec 7:9
Master, we know that thou art t ... Mt 22:16
Master, we know that thou art t ... Mk 12:14
commit to your trust the t riches ... Lk 16:11
That was the t Light, which ... Jn 1:9
set to his seal that God is t ... Jn 3:33
when the t worshippers shall ... Jn 4:23
And herein is that saying ... Jn 4:37
of myself, my witness is not t ... Jn 5:31
which he witnesseth of me is t ... Jn 5:32
you t bread from heaven ... Jn 6:32
that sent me, the same is t ... Jn 7:18
myself, but he that sent me is t ... Jn 7:28
thy record is not t ... Jn 8:13
of myself, yet my record is t ... Jn 8:14
yet if I judge, my judgment is t ... Jn 8:16
the testimony of two men is t ... Jn 8:17
but he that sent me is t ... Jn 8:26
John spake of this man were t ... Jn 10:41
I am the t vine, and my Father is ... Jn 15:1
might know thee the only t God ... Jn 17:3
bare record, and his record is t ... Jn 19:35
and he knoweth that he saith ... Jn 19:35
we know that his testimony is t ... Jn 21:24
wist not that it was t which was ... Acts 12:9
yea, let God be t, but every man ... Rom 3:4
But as God is t, our word toward ... 2Cor 1:18
as deceivers, and yet t ... 2Cor 6:8

in righteousness and t holiness ... Eph 4:24
t yokefellow, help those women ... Phil 4:3
brethren, whatsoever things are t ... Phil 4:8
to serve the living and t God ... 1Th 1:9
This is a t saying, If a man ... 1Ti 3:1
This witness is t ... Titus 1:13
of the t tabernacle, which the ... Heb 8:2
which are the figures of the t ... Heb 9:24
Let us draw near with a t heart ... Heb 10:22
testifying that this is the t ... 1Pet 5:12
them according to the t proverb ... 2Pet 2:22
unto you, which thing is t in him ... 1Jn 2:8
past, and the t light now shineth ... 1Jn 2:8
that we may know him that is t ... 1Jn 5:20
and we are in him that is t ... 1Jn 5:20
This is the t God, and eternal ... 1Jn 5:20
and ye know that our record is t ... 3Jn 12
he that is holy, he that is t ... Rev 3:7
t witness, the beginning of the ... Rev 3:14
How long, O Lord, holy and t ... Rev 6:10
t are thy ways, thou King of ... Rev 15:3
Even so, Lord God Almighty, t ... Rev 16:7
For t and righteous are his ... Rev 19:2
These are the t sayings of God ... Rev 19:9
upon him was called Faithful and T ... Rev 19:11
for these words are t and faithful ... Rev 21:5
These sayings are faithful and t ... Rev 22:6

TRULY
T Lamech seventy and sevenfold ... Gen 4:24
with my master, tell me ... Gen 24:49
and deal kindly and t with my ... Gen 47:29
but t his younger brother shall ... Gen 48:19
But as t as I live, all the earth ... Num 14:21
As t as I live, saith the LORD ... Num 14:28
Thou shalt t tithe all the ... Deut 14:22
will deal kindly and t with thee ... Josh 2:14
The LORD hath delivered into ... Josh 2:24
Now therefore, if ye have done t ... Judg 9:16
If ye then have dealt t and ... Judg 9:19
but t as the LORD liveth, and as ... 1Sa 20:3
For t my words shall not be false ... Job 36:4
t my soul waiteth upon God ... Ps 62:1
T God is good to Israel, even to ... Ps 73:1
O LORD, t I am thy servant ... Ps 116:16
they that deal t are his delight ... Prov 12:22
T the light is sweet, and a ... Eccl 11:7
T in vain is salvation hoped for ... Jer 3:23
t in the LORD our God is the ... Jer 3:23
T this is a grief, and I must bear ... Jer 10:19
that the LORD hath t sent him ... Jer 28:9
hath kept my judgments, to deal t ... Eze 18:9
But t I am full of power by the ... Mic 3:8
The harvest t is plenteous, but ... Mt 9:37
Elias t shall first come, and ... Mt 17:11
T this was the Son of God ... Mt 27:54
The Spirit t is ready; but the ... Mk 14:38
T this man was the Son of God ... Mk 15:39
unto them, The harvest t is ... Lk 10:2
T ye bear witness that ye allow ... Lk 11:48
but teachest the way of God t ... Lk 20:21
t the Son of man goeth, as it was ... Lk 22:22
in that saidst thou ... Jn 4:18
many other signs t did Jesus in ... Jn 20:30
For John t baptized with water ... Acts 1:5
For Moses t said unto the fathers ... Acts 3:22
The prison t found we shut with ... Acts 5:23
T the signs of an apostle were ... 2Cor 12:12
they t were many priests, because ... Heb 7:23
And t, if they had been mindful of ... Heb 11:15
t our fellowship is with the ... 1Jn 1:3

TRUMP
O my soul, the sound of the t ... Jer 4:19
in Gibeah, and the t in Ramah ... Hos 5:8
of an eye, at the last t ... 1Cor 15:52
archangel, and with the t of God ... 1Th 4:16

TRUMPET
when the t soundeth long, they ... Ex 19:13
the voice of the t exceeding loud ... Ex 19:16
the voice of the t sounded long ... Ex 19:19
lightnings, and the noise of the t ... Ex 20:18
Then shalt thou cause the t of ... Lev 25:9
t sound throughout all your land ... Lev 25:9
And if they blow but with one t ... Num 10:4
when ye hear the sound of the t ... Josh 6:5
people heard the sound of the t ... Josh 6:20
that he blew a t in the mountain ... Judg 3:27
came upon Gideon, and he blew a t ... Judg 6:34
he put a t in every man's hand ... Judg 7:16
When I blow with a t, I and all ... Judg 7:18
Saul blew the t throughout all ... 1Sa 13:3
So Joab blew a t, and all the ... 2Sa 2:28
and with the sound of the t ... 2Sa 6:15
as ye hear the sound of the t ... 2Sa 15:10
And Joab blew the t, and the people ... 2Sa 18:16
and he blew a t, and said, We have ... 2Sa 20:1
And he blew a t, and they retired ... 2Sa 20:22
and blow ye with the t, and say ... 1Kin 1:34
And they blew the t ... 1Kin 1:39
Joab heard the sound of the t ... 1Kin 1:41
he that sounded the t was by me ... Neh 4:18
ye hear the sound of the t ... Neh 4:20
he that it is the sound of the t ... Job 39:24
the LORD with the sound of a t ... Ps 47:5
Blow up the t in the new moon ... Ps 81:3
him with the sound of the t ... Ps 150:3
and when he bloweth a t, hear ye ... Is 18:3
that the great t shall be blown ... Is 27:13
not, lift up thy voice like a t ... Is 58:1
and say, Blow ye the t in the land ... Jer 4:5

and hear the sound of the t ... Jer 4:21
Jerusalem, and blow the t in Tekoa ... Jer 6:1
Hearken to the sound of the t ... Jer 6:17
war, nor hear the sound of the t ... Jer 42:14
blow the t among the nations ... Jer 51:27
They have blown the t, even to ... Eze 7:14
come upon the land, he blow the t ... Eze 33:3
heareth the sound of the t ... Eze 33:4
He heard the sound of the t ... Eze 33:5
the sword come, and blow not the t ... Eze 33:6
Set the t to thy mouth ... Hos 8:1
Blow ye the t in Zion, and sound ... Joel 2:1
Blow the t in Zion, sanctify a ... Joel 2:15
and with the sound of the t ... Amos 2:2
Shall a t be blown in the city ... Amos 3:6
A day of the t and alarm against ... Zeph 1:16
and the Lord GOD shall blow the t ... Zec 9:14
do not sound a t before thee ... Mt 6:2
angels with a great sound of a t ... Mt 24:31
For if the t give an uncertain ... 1Cor 14:8
for the t shall sound, and the ... 1Cor 15:52
And the sound of a t, and the voice ... Heb 12:19
me a great voice, as of a t ... Rev 1:10
as it were of a t talking with me ... Rev 4:1
of the t of the three angels ... Rev 8:13
the sixth angel which had the t ... Rev 9:14

TRUMPETERS
the t by the king, and all the ... 2Kin 11:14
It came even to pass, as the t ... 2Chr 5:13
singers sang, and the t sounded ... 2Chr 29:28
and musicians, and of pipers, and t ... Rev 18:22

TRUMPETS
a memorial of blowing of t ... Lev 23:24
Make thee two t of silver ... Num 10:2
priests, shall blow with the t ... Num 10:8
ye shall blow an alarm with the t ... Num 10:9
ye shall blow with the t over ... Num 10:10
a day of blowing the t unto you ... Num 29:1
the t to blow in his hand ... Num 31:6
the ark seven t of rams' horns ... Josh 6:4
the priests shall blow with the t ... Josh 6:4
let seven priests bear seven t of ... Josh 6:6
t of rams' horns passed on before ... Josh 6:8
t of rams' horns, and the LORD ... Josh 6:8
the LORD, and blew with the t ... Josh 6:8
the priests that blew with the t ... Josh 6:9
going on, and blowing with the t ... Josh 6:9
seven priests bearing seven t of ... Josh 6:13
continually, and blew with the t ... Josh 6:13
going on, and blowing with the t ... Josh 6:13
when the priests blew with the t ... Josh 6:16
when the priests blew with the t ... Josh 6:20
in their hand, and their t ... Judg 7:8
then blow ye the t also on every ... Judg 7:18
and they blew the t, and brake the ... Judg 7:19
And the three companies blew the t ... Judg 7:20
the t in their right hands to ... Judg 7:20
And the three hundred blew the t ... Judg 7:22
top of the stairs, and blew with t ... 2Kin 9:13
the land rejoiced, and blew with t ... 2Kin 11:14
of silver, snuffers, basons, t ... 2Kin 12:13
and with cymbals, and with t ... 1Chr 13:8
did blow with the t before the ... 1Chr 15:24
sound of the cornet, and with t ... 1Chr 15:28
Jahaziel the priests with t ... 1Chr 16:6
them Heman and Jeduthun with t ... 1Chr 16:42
and twenty priests sounding with t ... 2Chr 5:12
lifted up their voice with the t ... 2Chr 5:13
the priests sounded t before them ... 2Chr 7:6
t to cry alarm against you ... 2Chr 13:12
and the priests sounded with the t ... 2Chr 13:14
and with shouting, and with t ... 2Chr 15:14
t unto the house of the LORD ... 2Chr 20:28
the princes and the t by the king ... 2Chr 23:13
land rejoiced, and sounded with t ... 2Chr 23:13
David, and the priests with t ... 2Chr 29:26
of the LORD began also with the t ... 2Chr 29:27
priests in their apparel with t ... Ezr 3:10
of the priests' sons with t ... Neh 12:35
Zechariah, and Hananiah, with t ... Neh 12:41
He saith among the t, Ha, ha ... Job 39:25
With t and sound of cornet make a ... Ps 98:6
and to them were given seven t ... Rev 8:2
angels which had the seven t ... Rev 8:6

TRUST
come and put your t in my shadow ... Judg 9:15
whose wings thou art come to t ... Ruth 2:12
in him will I t ... 2Sa 22:3
buckler to all them that t in him ... 2Sa 22:31
Now on whom dost thou t, that ... 2Kin 18:20
of Egypt unto all that t in him ... 2Kin 18:21
unto me, We t in the LORD our God ... 2Kin 18:22
put thy t on Egypt for chariots ... 2Kin 18:24
Hezekiah make you t in the LORD ... 2Kin 18:30
because they put their t in him ... 1Chr 5:20
king of Assyria, Whereon do ye t ... 2Chr 32:10
he put no t in his servants ... Job 4:18
whose t shall be a spider's web ... Job 8:14
he slay me, yet will I t in him ... Job 13:15
he putteth no t in his saints ... Job 15:15
him that is deceived t in vanity ... Job 15:31
therefore t thou in him ... Job 35:14
Wilt thou t him, because his ... Job 39:11
all they that put their t in him ... Ps 2:12
and put your t in the LORD ... Ps 4:5
that put their t in thee rejoice ... Ps 5:11
my God, in thee do I put my t ... Ps 7:1
thy name will put their t in thee ... Ps 9:10
In the LORD put I my t ... Ps 11:1
for in thee do I put my t ... Ps 16:1

T

t in the from those that rise up ... Ps 17:7
my strength, in whom I will t ... Ps 18:2
to all those that t in him ... Ps 18:30
Some t in chariots, and some in ... Ps 20:7
O my God, I t in thee ... Ps 25:2
for I put my t in thee ... Ps 25:20
IN thee, O LORD, do I put my t ... Ps 31:1
but I t in the LORD ... Ps 31:6
t in thee before the sons of men ... Ps 31:19
none of them that t in him shall ... Ps 34:22
t under the shadow of thy wings ... Ps 36:7
T in the LORD, and do good ... Ps 37:3
t also in him ... Ps 37:5
save them, because they t in him ... Ps 37:40
and fear, and shall t in the LORD ... Ps 40:3
man that maketh the LORD his t ... Ps 40:4
For I will not t in my bow ... Ps 44:6
They that t in their wealth, and ... Ps 49:6
t in the mercy of God for ever ... Ps 52:8
but I will t in thee ... Ps 55:23
I am afraid, I will t in thee ... Ps 56:3
his word, in God I have put my t ... Ps 56:4
In God have I put my t ... Ps 56:11
I will t in the covert of thy ... Ps 61:4
T in him at all times ... Ps 62:8
T not in oppression, and become ... Ps 62:10
in the LORD, and shall t in him ... Ps 64:10
In thee, O LORD, do I put my t ... Ps 71:1
thou art my t from my youth ... Ps 71:5
I have put my t in the Lord GOD, ... Ps 73:28
in him will I t ... Ps 91:4
and under his wings shalt thou t ... Ps 91:4
O Israel, t thou in the LORD ... Ps 115:9
O house of Aaron, t in the LORD ... Ps 115:10
that fear the LORD, t in the LORD ... Ps 115:11
It is better to t in the LORD ... Ps 118:8
It is better to t in the LORD ... Ps 118:9
for I t in thy word ... Ps 119:42
They that t in the LORD shall be ... Ps 125:1
in thee is my t ... Ps 141:8
for in thee do I t ... Ps 143:8
my shield, and he in whom I t ... Ps 144:2
Put not your t in princes ... Ps 146:3
T in the LORD with all thine ... Prov 3:5
That thy t may be in the LORD, I ... Prov 22:19
but he that putteth his t in the ... Prov 28:25
but whoso putteth his t in the ... Prov 29:25
unto them that put their t in him ... Prov 30:5
her husband doth safely t in her ... Prov 31:11
I will t, and not be afraid ... Is 12:2
poor of his people shall t in it ... Is 14:32
T ye in the LORD for ever ... Is 26:4
to t in the shadow of Egypt your ... Is 30:2
the t in the shadow of Egypt your ... Is 30:3
t in oppression and perverseness, ... Is 30:12
t in chariots, because they are ... Is 31:1
now on whom dost thou t, ... Is 36:5
of Egypt to all that t in him ... Is 36:6
to me, We t in the LORD our God, ... Is 36:7
put thy t on Egypt for chariots ... Is 36:9
Hezekiah make you t in the LORD ... Is 36:15
that t in graven images, that say ... Is 42:17
let him t in the name of the LORD ... Is 50:10
but he shall t in my name ... Is 51:5
but he that putteth his t in me ... Is 57:13
they t in vanity, and speak lies ... Is 59:4
T ye not in lying words, saying, ... Jer 7:4
ye t in lying words, that cannot ... Jer 7:8
called by my name, wherein ye t ... Jer 7:14
and t ye not in any brother ... Jer 9:4
makest this people to t in a lie ... Jer 28:15
and he caused you to t in a lie ... Jer 29:31
because thou hast put thy t in me ... Jer 39:18
and all them that t in him ... Jer 46:25
and let thy widows t in me ... Jer 49:11
But thou didst t in thine own ... Eze 16:15
if he t to his own righteousness, ... Eze 33:13
because thou didst t in thy way ... Hos 10:13
t in the mountain of Samaria, ... Amos 6:1
T ye not in a friend, put ye not ... Mic 7:5
and he knoweth them that t in him ... Nah 1:7
they shall t in the name of the ... Zeph 3:12
in his name shall the Gentiles t ... Mt 12:21
t in riches to enter into the ... Mk 10:24
commit to your t the true riches ... Lk 16:11
you, even Moses, in whom ye t ... Jn 5:45
in him shall the Gentiles t ... Rom 15:12
for I t to see you in my journey, ... Rom 15:24
but I t to tarry a while with you ... 1Cor 16:7
that we should not t in ourselves ... 2Cor 1:9
in whom we t that he will yet ... 2Cor 1:10
I t ye shall acknowledge even to ... 2Cor 1:13
such t have we through Christ to ... 2Cor 3:4
I also are made manifest in ... 2Cor 5:11
If any man t to himself that he ... 2Cor 10:7
But I t that ye shall know that ... 2Cor 13:6
But I t in the Lord Jesus to send ... Phil 2:19
But I t in the Lord that I also ... Phil 2:24
whereof he might t in the flesh ... Phil 3:4
to be put in t with the gospel ... 1Th 2:4
God, which was committed to my t ... 1Ti 1:11
because we t in the living God, ... 1Ti 4:10
nor in uncertain riches, but in ... 1Ti 6:17
that which is committed to thy t ... 1Ti 6:20
for I t that through your prayers ... Philem 22
And again, I will put my t in him ... Heb 2:13
for we t we have a good ... Heb 13:18
but I t to come unto you, and ... 2Jn 12

But I t I shall shortly see thee, ... 3Jn 14

TRUSTED
gods, their rock in whom they t ... Deut 32:37
But Sihon t not Israel to pass ... Judg 11:20
because they t unto the liers in ... Judg 20:36
He t in the LORD God of Israel ... 2Kin 18:5
But I have t in thy mercy ... Ps 13:5
Our fathers t in thee ... Ps 22:4
they t, and thou didst deliver ... Ps 22:4
they t in thee, and were not ... Ps 22:5
He t on the LORD that he would ... Ps 22:8
I have t also in the LORD ... Ps 26:1
my heart t in him, and I am helped ... Ps 28:7
But I t in thee, O LORD ... Ps 31:14
because we have t in his holy ... Ps 33:21
own familiar friend, in whom I t ... Ps 41:9
but t in the abundance of his ... Ps 52:7
in God, and t not in his salvation ... Ps 78:22
For thou hast t in thy wickedness ... Is 47:10
forgotten me, and t in falsehood ... Jer 13:25
because thou hast t in thy works ... Jer 48:7
that t in her treasures, saying, ... Jer 49:4
his servants that t in him ... Dan 3:28
she t not in the LORD ... Zeph 3:2
He t in God ... Mt 27:43
him all his armour wherein he t ... Lk 11:22
t in themselves that they were ... Lk 18:9
But we t that it had been he ... Lk 24:21
his glory, who first t in Christ ... Eph 1:12
In whom ye also t, after that ye ... Eph 1:13
who t in God, adorned themselves, ... 1Pet 3:5

TRUSTEDST
walls come down, wherein thou t ... Deut 28:52
thy fenced cities, wherein thou t ... Jer 5:17
the land of peace, wherein thou t ... Jer 12:5

TRUSTEST
confidence is this wherein thou t ... 2Kin 18:19
thou t upon the staff of this ... 2Kin 18:21
God in whom thou t deceive thee ... 2Kin 19:10
confidence is this wherein thou t ... Is 36:4
thou t in the staff of this ... Is 36:6
Let not thy God, in whom thou t ... Is 37:10

TRUSTETH
he t that he can draw up Jordan ... Job 40:23
For the king t in the LORD ... Ps 21:7
but he that t in the LORD ... Ps 32:10
blessed is the man that t in him ... Ps 34:8
for my soul t in thee ... Ps 57:1
blessed is the man that t in thee ... Ps 84:12
save thy servant that t in thee ... Ps 86:2
so is every one that t in them ... Ps 115:8
so is every one that t in them ... Ps 135:18
He that t in his riches shall ... Prov 11:28
whoso t in the LORD, happy is he ... Prov 16:20
He that t in his own heart is a ... Prov 28:26
because he t in thee ... Is 26:3
Cursed be the man that t in man ... Jer 17:5
is the man that t in the LORD ... Jer 17:7
the maker of his work t therein ... Hab 2:18
t in God, and continueth in ... 1Ti 5:5

TRUSTING
his heart is fixed, t in the LORD ... Ps 112:7

TRUSTY
removeth away the speech of the t ... Job 12:20

TRUTH
my master of his mercy and his t ... Gen 24:27
all the mercies, and of all the t ... Gen 32:10
whether there be any t in you ... Gen 42:16
men, such as fear God, men of t ... Ex 18:21
and abundant in goodness and t ... Ex 34:6
and, behold, it be t, and the ... Deut 13:14
a God of t and without iniquity, ... Deut 32:4
and serve him in sincerity and in t ... Josh 24:14
If in t ye anoint me king over ... Judg 9:15
serve him in t with all your ... 1Sa 12:24
Of a t women have been kept from ... 1Sa 21:5
LORD shew kindness and t unto you ... 2Sa 2:6
mercy and t be with thee ... 2Sa 15:20
me in t with all their heart ... 1Kin 2:4
as he walked before thee in t ... 1Kin 3:6
of the LORD in thy mouth is t ... 1Kin 17:24
Of a t, LORD, the kings of ... 2Kin 19:17
I have walked before thee in t ... 2Kin 20:3
good, if peace and t be in my days ... 2Kin 20:19
t to me in the name of the LORD ... 2Chr 18:15
t before the LORD his God ... 2Chr 31:20
with words of peace and t ... Est 9:30
I know it is so of a t ... Job 9:2
and speaketh the t in his heart ... Ps 15:2
Lead me in thy t, and teach me ... Ps 25:5
t unto such as keep his covenant ... Ps 25:10
and I have walked in thy t ... Ps 26:3
shall it declare thy t ... Ps 30:9
hast redeemed me, O LORD God of t ... Ps 31:5
and all his works are done in t ... Ps 33:4
thy t from the great congregation ... Ps 40:10
thy t continually preserve me ... Ps 40:11
O send out thy light and thy t ... Ps 43:3
ride prosperously because of t ... Ps 45:4
thou desirest t in the inward ... Ps 51:6
cut them off in thy t ... Ps 54:5
send forth his mercy and his t ... Ps 57:3
heavens, and thy t unto the clouds ... Ps 57:10
may be displayed because of the t ... Ps 60:4
O prepare mercy and t, which may ... Ps 61:7
in the t of thy salvation ... Ps 69:13

with the psaltery, even thy t ... Ps 71:22
Mercy and t are met together ... Ps 85:10
T shall spring out of the earth ... Ps 85:11
I will walk in thy t ... Ps 86:11
and plenteous in mercy and t ... Ps 86:15
t shall go before thy face ... Ps 89:14
thou swarest unto David in thy t ... Ps 89:49
his t shall be thy shield and ... Ps 91:4
and the people with his t ... Ps 96:13
his t toward the house of Israel ... Ps 98:3
his t endureth to all generations ... Ps 100:5
thy t reacheth unto the clouds ... Ps 108:4
ever and ever, and are done in t ... Ps 111:8
the t of the LORD endureth for ... Ps 117:2
I have chosen the way of t ... Ps 119:30
take not the word of t utterly ... Ps 119:43
and thy law is the t ... Ps 119:142
and all thy commandments are t ... Ps 119:151
LORD hath sworn in t unto David ... Ps 132:11
thy lovingkindness and for thy t ... Ps 138:2
to all that call upon him in t ... Ps 145:18
which keepeth t for ever ... Ps 146:6
Let not mercy and t forsake thee ... Prov 3:3
For my mouth shall speak t ... Prov 8:7
He that speaketh t sheweth forth ... Prov 12:17
The lip of t shall be established ... Prov 12:19
t shall be to them that devise ... Prov 14:22
By mercy and t iniquity is purged ... Prov 16:6
Mercy and t preserve the king ... Prov 20:28
the certainty of the words of t ... Prov 22:21
of t to them that send unto thee ... Prov 22:21
Buy the t, and sell it not ... Prov 23:23
was upright, even words of t ... Eccl 12:10
Of a t many houses shall be ... Is 5:9
the Holy One of Israel, in t ... Is 10:20
he shall sit upon it in t in the ... Is 16:5
of old are faithfulness and t ... Is 25:1
which keepeth the t may enter in ... Is 26:2
Of a t, LORD, the kings of ... Is 37:18
I have walked before thee in t ... Is 38:3
the pit cannot hope for thy t ... Is 38:18
children shall make known thy t ... Is 38:19
shall be peace and t in my days ... Is 39:8
shall bring forth judgment unto t ... Is 42:3
or let them hear, and say, It is t ... Is 43:9
The God of Israel, but not in t ... Is 48:1
justice, nor any rejudeeth for t ... Is 59:4
for t is fallen in the street, and ... Is 59:14
Yea, t faileth ... Is 59:15
and I will direct their work in t ... Is 61:8
bless himself in the God of t ... Is 65:16
earth shall swear by the God of t ... Jer 4:2
swear, The LORD liveth, in t ... Jer 4:2
judgment, that seeketh the t ... Jer 5:1
are not thine eyes upon the t ... Jer 5:3
t is perished, and is cut off from ... Jer 7:28
valiant for the t upon the earth ... Jer 9:3
and will not speak the t ... Jer 9:5
for of a t the LORD hath sent me ... Jer 26:15
them the abundance of peace and t ... Jer 33:6
Of a t it is, that your God is a ... Dan 2:47
of heaven, all whose works are ... Dan 4:37
and asked him the t of all this ... Dan 7:16
know the t of the fourth beast ... Dan 7:19
it cast down the t to the ground ... Dan 8:12
iniquities, and understand thy t ... Dan 9:13
is noted in the scripture of t ... Dan 10:21
And now will I shew thee the t ... Dan 11:2
the land, because there is no t ... Hos 4:1
Thou wilt perform the t to Jacob ... Mic 7:20
shall be called a city of t ... Zec 8:3
and I will be their God, in t ... Zec 8:8
every man the t to his neighbour ... Zec 8:16
execute the judgment of t ... Zec 8:16
therefore love the t and peace ... Zec 8:19
The law of t was in his mouth, and ... Mal 2:6
Of a t thou art the Son of God ... Mt 14:33
And she said, T, Lord ... Mt 15:27
and teachest the way of God in t ... Mt 22:16
before him, and told him all the t ... Mk 5:33
but teachest the way of God in t ... Mk 12:14
Master, thou hast said the t ... Mk 12:32
But I tell you of a t, many ... Lk 4:25
But I tell you of a t, there be ... Lk 9:27
Of a t I say unto you, that he ... Lk 12:44
Of a t I say unto you, that this ... Lk 21:3
Of a t this fellow also was with ... Lk 22:59
grace and t came by Jesus Christ ... Jn 1:17
But he that doeth t cometh to the ... Jn 3:21
the Father in spirit and in t ... Jn 4:23
worship him in spirit and in t ... Jn 4:24
and he bare witness unto the t ... Jn 5:33
This is of a t that prophet that ... Jn 6:14
Of a t this is the Prophet ... Jn 7:40
And ye shall know the t, and the ... Jn 8:32
the t shall make you free ... Jn 8:32
a man that hath told you the t ... Jn 8:40
beginning, and abode not in the t ... Jn 8:44
because there is no t in him ... Jn 8:44
And because I tell you the t ... Jn 8:45
And if I say the t, why do ye not ... Jn 8:46
unto him, I am the way, the t ... Jn 14:6
Even the Spirit of t ... Jn 14:17
the Father, even the Spirit of t ... Jn 15:26
Nevertheless I tell you the t ... Jn 16:7
Howbeit when he, the Spirit of t ... Jn 16:13
he will guide you into all t ... Jn 16:13
Sanctify them through thy t ... Jn 17:17

thy word is *t* .... Jn 17:17
might be sanctified through the *t* .... Jn 17:19
I should bear witness unto the *t* .... Jn 18:37
that is of the *t* heareth my voice .... Jn 18:37
Pilate saith unto him, What is *t* .... Jn 18:38
For of a *t* against thy holy child .... Acts 4:27
Of a I perceive that God is no .... Acts 10:34
but speak forth the words of *t* .... Acts 26:25
who hold the *t* in unrighteousness .... Rom 1:18
Who changed the *t* of God into a .... Rom 1:25
t against them which commit such.......... Rom 2:2
contentious, and do not obey the *t* .... Rom 2:8
knowledge and of the *t* in the law .... Rom 2:20
For if the *t* of God hath more .... Rom 3:7
they say in Christ, I lie not................ Rom 9:1
the circumcision for the *t* of God .... Rom 15:8
bread of sincerity and *t* 1Cor 5:8
iniquity, but rejoiceth in the *t* 1Cor 13:6
report that God is in you of a *t* 1Cor 14:25
but by manifestation of the *t* 2Cor 4:2
By the word of *t*, by the power of 2Cor 6:7
we spake all things to you in *t* 2Cor 7:14
I made before Titus, is found a *t* 2Cor 7:14
As the *t* of Christ is in me, no.............. 2Cor 11:10
for I will say the *t* 2Cor 12:6
against the *t*, but for the *t* 2Cor 13:8
that the *t* of the gospel might.............. Gal 2:5
according to the *t* of the gospel .... Gal 2:14
that ye should not obey the *t* .... Gal 3:1
enemy, because I tell you the *t* .... Gal 4:16
you that ye should not obey the *t* .... Gal 5:7
after that ye heard the word of *t* .... Eph 1:13
But speaking the *t* in love.................. Eph 4:15
by him, as the *t* is in Jesus................ Eph 4:21
speak every man *t* with his................ Eph 4:25
goodness and righteousness and *t* .... Eph 5:9
your loins girt about with *t* .... Eph 6:14
way, whether in pretence, or in *t* .... Phil 1:18
the word of the *t* of the gospel............ Col 1:5
it, and knew the grace of God in *t* .... Col 1:6
word of men, but as it is in *t* 1Th 2:13
received not the love of the *t* 2Th 2:10
be damned who believed not the *t* 2Th 2:12
of the Spirit and belief of the *t* 2Th 2:13
come unto the knowledge of the *t* 1Ti 2:4
apostle, (I speak the *t* in Christ 1Ti 2:7
the pillar and ground of the *t* 1Ti 3:15
them which believe and know the *t* 1Ti 4:3
minds, and destitute of the *t* 1Ti 6:5
rightly dividing the word of *t* 2Ti 2:15
Who concerning the *t* have erred 2Ti 2:18
to the acknowledging of the *t* 2Ti 2:25
to come to the knowledge of the *t* 2Ti 3:7
so do these also resist the *t* 2Ti 3:8
turn away their ears from the *t* 2Ti 4:4
of the *t* which is after godliness.......... Titus 1:1
of men, that turn from the *t*.............. Titus 1:14
received the knowledge of the *t*.......... Heb 10:26
begat he us with the word of *t* .... Jas 1:18
not, and lie not against the *t* .... Jas 3:14
if any of you do err from the *t* .... Jas 5:19
the *t* through the Spirit unto 1Pet 1:22
be established in the present *t* 2Pet 1:12
way of *t* shall be evil spoken of.......... 2Pet 2:2
darkness, we lie, and do not the *t* 1Jn 1:6
ourselves, and the *t* is not in us.......... 1Jn 1:8
is a liar, and the *t* is not in him.......... 1Jn 2:4
you because ye know not the *t* 1Jn 2:21
it, and that no lie is of the *t* 1Jn 2:21
you of all things, and is *t* 1Jn 2:27
but in deed and in *t* 1Jn 3:18
we know that we are of the *t* 1Jn 3:19
Hereby know we the spirit of *t* 1Jn 4:6
witness, because the Spirit is *t* 1Jn 5:6
children, whom I love in the *t* 2Jn 1
all they that have known the *t*............ 2Jn 1
the Son of the Father, in *t* 2Jn 3
of thy children walking in *t* 2Jn 4
children, whom I love in the *t* 3Jn 1
of the *t* that is in thee, even as.......... 3Jn 3
even as thou walkest in the *t* 3Jn 3
hear that my children walk in *t* 3Jn 4
might be fellowhelpers to the *t* 3Jn 8
of all men, and of the *t* itself............ 3Jn 12

TRUTH'S
for thy mercy, and for thy *t* sake .... Ps 115:1
For the *t* sake, which dwelleth in 2Jn 2

TRY
I will *t* them for thee there .... Judg 7:4
to *t* him, that he might know all 2Chr 32:31
morning, and *t* him every moment.......... Job 7:18
Doth not the ear *t* words.................. Job 12:11
his eyes behold, his eyelids *t* .... Ps 11:4
t my reins and my heart .... Ps 26:2
t me, and know my thoughts .... Ps 139:23
thou mayest know and *t* their way.......... Jer 6:27
I will melt them, and *t* them .... Jer 9:7
I *t* the reins, even to give every.......... Jer 17:10
for our ways, and turn again to the .... Lam 3:40
to *t* them, and to purge, and to .... Dan 11:35
will *t* them as gold is tried .... Zec 13:9
the fire shall *t* every man's work 1Cor 3:13
the fiery trial which is to *t* you 1Pet 4:12
but *t* the spirits whether they............ 1Jn 4:1
to *t* them that dwell upon the .... Rev 3:10

TRYING
that the *t* of your faith worketh.......... Jas 1:3

TRYPHAENA See TRYPHENA.

TRYPHENA (tri-fe'-nah) A Christian in Rome.
Salute T and Tryphosa, who labour.... Rom 16:12

TRYPHOSA (tri-fo'-sah) A Christian in Rome.
Salute Tryphena and T, who labour.... Rom 16:12

TUBAL (tu'-bal)
1. A son of Japeth.
Magog, and Madai, and Javan, and T... Gen 10:2
Magog, and Madai, and Javan, and T... 1Chr 1:5
2. Migrants to Sicily and Spain.
and Lud, that draw the bow, to T .... Is 66:19
Javan, T, and Meshech, they were.......... Eze 27:13
There is Meshech, T, and all her.......... Eze 32:26
the chief princes of Meshech and T .... Eze 38:2
the chief princes of Meshech and T .... Eze 38:3
the chief princes of Meshech and T .... Eze 39:1

TUBAL-CAIN (tu'-bal-cain) *Son of Lamech.*
And Zillah, she also bare T .... Gen 4:22
and the sister of T was Naamah .... Gen 4:22

TUMBLED
a cake of barley bread *t* into the.......... Judg 7:13

TUMULT
What meaneth the noise of this *t* 1Sa 4:14
me thy servant, I saw a great *t* 2Sa 18:29
thy *t* is come up into mine ears 2Kin 19:28
waves, and the *t* of the people .... Ps 65:7
the *t* of those that rise up.............. Ps 74:23
For, lo, thine enemies make a *t* .... Ps 83:2
noise of the *t* the people fled............ Is 33:3
thy rage against me, and thy *t* .... Is 37:29
with the noise of a great *t* .... Jer 11:16
Therefore shall a *t* arise among.......... Hos 10:14
and Moab shall die with *t*, with.......... Amos 2:2
that a great *t* from the LORD .... Zec 14:13
but that rather a *t* was made .... Mt 27:24
of the synagogue, and seeth the *t* .... Mk 5:38
not know the certainty for the *t* .... Acts 21:34
with multitude, nor with *t* .... Acts 24:18

TUMULTS
behold the great *t* in the midst .... Amos 3:9
stripes, in imprisonments, in *t*.......... 2Cor 6:5
whisperings, swellings, *t* 2Cor 12:20

TUMULTUOUS
a *t* noise of the kingdoms of.............. Is 13:4
of stirs, a *t* city, a joyous city.......... Is 22:2
crown of the head of the *t* ones .... Jer 48:45

TURN
t in, I pray you, into your................ Gen 19:2
that I may *t* to the right hand,.......... Gen 24:49
until thy brother's fury *t* away .... Gen 27:44
brother's anger *t* away from thee.......... Gen 27:45
And Moses said, I will now *t* aside........ Ex 3:3
children of Israel, that they *t* .... Ex 14:2
enemies their backs unto thee.............. Ex 23:27
t from thy fierce wrath, and............ Ex 32:12
Or if the raw flesh *t* again.............. Lev 13:16
T ye not unto idols, nor make to.......... Lev 19:4
To morrow *t* you, and get you into........ Num 14:25
we will not *t* to the right hand.......... Num 20:17
we will not *t* into the fields, or........ Num 20:17
the ass, to *t* him into the way.......... Num 22:23
where was no way to *t* either to.......... Num 22:26
For if ye *t* away from after him,.......... Num 32:15
your border shall *t* from the.............. Num 34:4
T you, and take your journey, and.......... Deut 1:7
t you, and take your journey into .... Deut 1:40
t you northward .... Deut 2:3
I will neither *t* unto the right.......... Deut 2:27
if thou *t* to the LORD thy God, and........ Deut 4:30
ye shall not *t* aside to the right .... Deut 5:32
For they will *t* away thy son from........ Deut 7:4
ye *t* aside, and serve other gods,........ Deut 11:16
but *t* aside of the way which I .... Deut 11:28
because he hath spoken to *t* you.......... Deut 13:5
that the LORD may *t* from the.............. Deut 13:17
Then shalt thou *t* it into money.......... Deut 14:25
thou shalt *t* in the morning, and.......... Deut 16:7
that his heart *t* not away................ Deut 17:17
that he *t* not aside from the.............. Deut 17:20
dig therewith, and shalt *t* back.......... Deut 23:13
in thee, and *t* away from thee .... Deut 23:14
LORD thy God will *t* thy captivity........ Deut 30:3
if thou *t* unto the LORD thy God.......... Deut 30:10
But if thine heart *t* away,.............. Deut 30:17
then will they *t* unto other gods,........ Deut 31:20
t aside from the way which I have........ Deut 31:29
t not from it to the right hand.......... Josh 1:7
to *t* away this day from following........ Josh 22:16
But that ye must *t* away this day.......... Josh 22:18
to *t* from following the LORD .... Josh 22:23
t this day from following the.............. Josh 22:29
that ye *t* not aside therefrom to........ Josh 23:6
strange gods, then he will *t* .... Josh 24:20
T in, my lord, *t* in to me................ Judg 4:18
Therefore we *t* again to thee now,........ Judg 18:3
let us *t* into this city of the............ Judg 19:11
We will not *t* aside hither into.......... Judg 19:12
we any of us *t* into his house.............. Judg 20:8
Naomi said, T again, my daughters.......... Ruth 1:11
T again, my daughters, go your.............. Ruth 1:12
t aside, sit down here...................... Ruth 4:1
yet *t* not aside from following.......... 1Sa 12:20
And *t* ye not aside 1Sa 12:21

---

t thee; behold, I am...................... 1Sa 14:7
t again with me, that I may.............. 1Sa 15:25
t again with me, that I may.............. 1Sa 15:30
footmen that stood about him, T............ 1Sa 22:17
T thou, and fall upon the priests.......... 1Sa 22:18
T thee aside to thy right hand or.......... 2Sa 2:21
But Asahel would not *t* aside from........ 2Sa 2:21
T thee aside from following me.............. 2Sa 2:22
Howbeit he refused to *t* aside 2Sa 2:23
none can *t* to the right hand or.......... 2Sa 14:19
Let him *t* to his own house, and.......... 2Sa 14:24
t the counsel of Ahithophel into........ 2Sa 15:31
unto him, T aside, and stand here.......... 2Sa 18:30
t back again, that I may die in.......... 2Sa 19:37
shall *t* again to thee, and confess........ 1Kin 8:33
t from their sin, when thou.............. 1Kin 8:35
shall at all *t* from following me.......... 1Kin 9:6
for surely they will *t* away your.......... 1Kin 11:2
people *t* again unto their lord............ 1Kin 12:27
nor *t* again by the same way that.......... 1Kin 13:9
nor *t* again to go by the way that........ 1Kin 13:17
t thee eastward, and hide thyself........ 1Kin 17:3
T thine hand, and carry me out of.......... 1Kin 22:34
t again unto the king that sent.......... 2Kin 1:6
to us, that he shall *t* in thither........ 2Kin 4:10
t thee behind me.......................... 2Kin 9:18
t thee behind me.......................... 2Kin 9:19
T ye from your evil ways, and keep 2Kin 17:13
How then wilt thou *t* away the............ 2Kin 18:24
I will *t* thee back by the way by.......... 2Kin 19:28
T again, and tell Hezekiah the.............. 2Kin 20:5
to *t* the kingdom of Saul to him,.......... 1Chr 12:23
t away from them, and come upon.......... 1Chr 14:14
t from their sin, when thou dost.......... 2Chr 6:26
they are carried captive, and *t* 2Chr 6:37
t not away the face of thine.............. 2Chr 6:42
face, and *t* from their wicked ways........ 2Chr 7:14
But if ye *t* away, and forsake my.......... 2Chr 7:19
did *t* unto the LORD God of Israel 2Chr 15:4
T thine hand, that thou mayest.............. 2Chr 18:33
t away from following the LORD............ 2Chr 25:27
fierce wrath may *t* away from us.......... 2Chr 29:10
t again unto the Lord God of 2Chr 30:6
of his wrath may *t* away from you.......... 2Chr 30:8
For if ye *t* again unto the LORD,.......... 2Chr 30:9
will not *t* away his face from you.......... 2Chr 30:9
would not *t* his face from him.............. 2Chr 35:22
But if ye *t* unto me, and keep my.......... Neh 1:9
t their reproach upon their own.......... Neh 4:4
against them to *t* them to thee............ Neh 9:26
Now when every maid's *t* was come.......... Est 2:12
Now when the *t* of Esther, the.............. Est 2:15
which of the saints wilt thou *t* .... Job 5:1
T from him, that he may rest,.............. Job 14:6
is in one mind, and who can *t* him........ Job 23:13
They *t* the needy out of the way.......... Job 24:4
man shall *t* again unto dust .... Job 34:15
how long will ye *t* my glory into.......... Ps 4:2
If he *t* not, he will whet his............ Ps 7:12
neither did I *t* again till they.......... Ps 18:37
shalt thou make them their back.............. Ps 21:12
shall remember and *t* unto the LORD........ Ps 22:27
T thee unto me, and have mercy.............. Ps 25:16
nor such as *t* aside to lies.............. Ps 40:4
Thou makest us to *t* back from the........ Ps 44:10
then shall mine enemies *t* back .... Ps 56:9
O T thyself to us again...................... Ps 60:1
t unto me according to the .... Ps 69:16
T us again, O God, and cause thy.......... Ps 80:3
T us again, O God of hosts, and............ Ps 80:7
T us again, O LORD God of hosts,.......... Ps 80:19
T us, O God of our salvation, and.......... Ps 85:4
but let them not *t* again to folly........ Ps 85:8
O T unto me, and have mercy upon.......... Ps 86:16
the work of them that *t* aside............ Ps 101:3
that they *t* not again to cover .... Ps 104:9
to *t* away his wrath, lest he.............. Ps 106:23
T away my reproach which I fear............ Ps 119:39
T away my reproach which I fear............ Ps 119:39
those that fear thee *t* unto me.......... Ps 119:79
As for such as *t* aside unto their........ Ps 125:5
T again our captivity, O LORD, as.......... Ps 126:4
sake I *t* away the face of thine.......... Ps 132:10
he will not *t* from it........................ Ps 132:11
T you at my reproof .... Prov 1:23
by it, *t* from it, and pass away .... Prov 4:15
T not to the right hand nor to.............. Prov 4:27
is simple, let him *t* in hither.......... Prov 9:4
is simple, let him *t* in hither.......... Prov 9:16
he *t* away his wrath from him .... Prov 24:18
shame, and thine infamy *t* not away........ Prov 25:10
but wise men *t* away wrath................ Prov 29:8
the dust, and all *t* to dust again.......... Eccl 3:20
and the shadows flee away, *t* .... Song 2:17
T away thine eyes from me, for............ Song 6:5
I will *t* my hand upon thee, and.......... Is 1:25
To *t* aside the needy from................ Is 10:2
every man *t* to his own people............ Is 13:14
out, and who shall *t* it back.............. Is 14:27
they shall *t* the rivers far away.......... Is 19:6
He will surely violently *t* .... Is 22:18
he shall *t* for hire, and shall.......... Is 23:17
that *t* the battle to the gate .... Is 28:6
t aside the just for a thing of.......... Is 29:21
T aside out of the path, cause .... Is 30:11
when ye *t* to the right hand, and........ Is 30:21
hand, and when ye *t* to the left.......... Is 30:21
T ye unto him from whom the .... Is 31:6
How then wilt thou *t* away the............ Is 36:9
I will *t* thee back by the way by.......... Is 37:29

If thou *t* away thy foot from the	Is 58:13
to Zion, and unto them that *t* from	Is 59:20
her occasion who can *t* her away	Jer 2:24
surely his anger shall *t* from me	Jer 2:35
all these things, T thou unto me	Jer 3:7
T, O backsliding children, saith	Jer 3:14
and shalt not *t* away from me	Jer 3:19
neither will I *t* back from it	Jer 4:28
t back thine hand as a	Jer 6:9
shall he *t* away, and not return	Jer 8:4
he *t* it into the shadow of death,	Jer 13:16
t from their evil, I will repent	Jer 18:8
to *t* away thy wrath from them	Jer 18:20
I will *t* back the weapons of war	Jer 21:4
T ye again now every one from his	Jer 25:5
t every man from his evil way	Jer 26:3
I will *t* away your captivity, and	Jer 29:14
for I will *t* their mourning into	Jer 31:13
t thou me, and I shall be turned	Jer 31:18
t again, O virgin of Israel	Jer 31:21
t again to these thy cities	Jer 31:21
that I will not *t* away from them	Jer 32:40
ear to *t* from their wickedness	Jer 44:5
t back, dwell deep, O inhabitants	Jer 49:8
shall *t* every one to his own	Jer 50:16
iniquity, to *t* away thy captivity	Lam 2:14
To *t* aside the right of a man	Lam 3:35
our ways, and *t* again to the LORD	Lam 3:40
T thou us unto thee, O LORD, and	Lam 5:21
he *t* not from his wickedness, nor	Eze 3:19
man doth *t* from his righteousness	Eze 3:20
thou shalt not *t* thee from one	Eze 4:8
My face will I *t* also from them	Eze 7:22
but *t* thee yet again, and thou	Eze 8:6
T thee yet again, and thou shalt	Eze 8:13
t thee yet again, and thou shalt	Eze 8:15
t yourselves from your idols	Eze 14:6
t away your faces from all your	Eze 14:6
But if the wicked will *t* from all	Eze 18:21
t yourselves from all your	Eze 18:30
wherefore *t* yourselves, and live	Eze 18:32
wicked of his way to *t* from it	Eze 33:9
if he do not *t* from his way	Eze 33:9
that the wicked *t* from his way	Eze 33:11
t ye, *t* ye from your evil ways	Eze 33:11
if he *t* from his sin, and do that	Eze 33:14
But if the wicked *t* from his	Eze 33:19
I will *t* unto you, and ye shall be	Eze 36:9
I will *t* thee back, and put hooks	Eze 38:4
to *t* thine hand upon the desolate	Eze 38:12
I will *t* thee back, and leave but	Eze 39:2
our God, that we might *t* from our	Dan 9:13
After this shall he *t* his face	Dan 11:18
he shall cause it to *t* upon him	Dan 11:18
Then he shall *t* his face toward	Dan 11:19
they that *t* many to righteousness	Dan 12:3
their doings to *t* unto their God	Hos 5:4
Therefore *t* thou to thy God	Hos 12:6
with you words, and *t* to the LORD	Hos 14:2
T even to me with all your	Joel 2:12
and *t* unto the LORD your God	Joel 2:13
I will not *t* away the punishment	Amos 1:3
I will not *t* away the punishment	Amos 1:6
I will *t* mine hand against Ekron	Amos 1:8
I will not *t* away the punishment	Amos 1:9
I will not *t* away the punishment	Amos 1:11
I will not *t* away the punishment	Amos 1:13
I will not *t* away the punishment	Amos 2:1
I will not *t* away the punishment	Amos 2:4
I will not *t* away the punishment	Amos 2:6
t aside the way of the meek	Amos 2:7
t judgment to wormwood	Amos 5:7
they *t* aside the poor in the gate	Amos 5:12
I will *t* your feasts into	Amos 8:10
let them *t* every one from his	Jonah 3:8
Who can tell if God will *t*	Jonah 3:9
t away from his fierce anger	Jonah 3:9
He will *t* again, he will have	Mic 7:19
them, and *t* away their captivity	Zeph 2:7
For then will I *t* to the people a	Zeph 3:9
when I *t* back your captivity	Zeph 3:20
T ye unto me, saith the LORD of	Zec 1:3
I will *t* unto you, saith the LORD	Zec 1:3
T ye now from your evil ways, and	Zec 1:4
T you to the strong hold, ye	Zec 9:12
with their children, and *t* again	Zec 10:9
I will *t* mine hand upon the	Zec 13:7
did *t* many away from iniquity	Mal 2:6
that *t* aside the stranger from	Mal 3:5
he shall *t* the heart of the	Mal 4:6
cheek, *t* to him the other also	Mt 5:39
borrow of thee *t* not thou away	Mt 5:42
feet, and *t* again and rend you	Mt 7:6
him that is in the field not *t*	Mk 13:16
shall he *t* to the Lord their God	Lk 1:16
to *t* the hearts of the fathers to	Lk 1:17
if not, it shall *t* to you again	Lk 10:6
times in a day *t* again to thee	Lk 17:4
it shall *t* to you for a testimony	Lk 21:13
seeking to *t* away the deputy from	Acts 13:8
life, lo, we *t* to the Gentiles	Acts 13:46
t from these vanities unto the	Acts 14:15
to *t* them from darkness to light,	Acts 26:18
t to God, and do works meet for	Acts 26:20
shall *t* away ungodliness from	Rom 11:26
when it shall *t* to the Lord	2Cor 3:16
how *t* ye again to the weak and	Gal 4:9
For I know that this shall *t* to	Phil 1:19
from such *t* away	2Ti 3:5
they shall *t* away their ears from	2Ti 4:4
of men, that *t* from the truth	Titus 1:14
if we *t* away from him that	Heb 12:25
we *t* about their whole body	Jas 3:3
to *t* from the holy commandment	2Pet 2:21
over waters to *t* them to blood	Rev 11:6

TURNED

a flaming sword which *t* every way	Gen 3:24
the men *t* their faces from thence	Gen 18:22
they *t* in unto him, and entered	Gen 19:3
t in to a certain Adullamite,	Gen 38:1
he *t* unto her by the way, and said	Gen 38:16
he *t* himself about from them, and	Gen 42:24
LORD saw that he *t* aside to see	Ex 3:4
it was *t* again as his other flesh	Ex 4:7
the rod which was *t* to a serpent	Ex 7:15
and they shall be *t* to blood	Ex 7:17
were in the river were *t* to blood	Ex 7:20
And Pharaoh *t* and went into his	Ex 7:23
he *t* himself, and went out from	Ex 10:6
the LORD *t* a mighty strong west	Ex 10:19
servants was *t* against the people	Ex 14:5
they have *t* aside quickly out of	Ex 32:8
And Moses *t*, and went down from the	Ex 32:15
And he *t* again into the camp	Ex 33:11
the hair in the plague is *t* white	Lev 13:3
the hair thereof be not *t* white	Lev 13:4
it have *t* the hair white, and	Lev 13:10
it is all *t* white	Lev 13:13
if the plague be *t* into white	Lev 13:16
and the hair thereof be *t* white	Lev 13:20
in the bright spot be *t* white	Lev 13:25
because ye are *t* away from the	Num 14:43
wherefore Israel *t* away from him	Num 20:21
And they *t* and went up by the way	Num 21:33
the ass *t* aside out of the way,	Num 22:23
t from me these three times	Num 22:33
unless she had *t* from me, surely	Num 22:33
LORD may be *t* away from Israel	Num 25:4
hath *t* my wrath away from the	Num 25:11
t again unto Pi-hahiroth, which	Num 33:7
And they *t* and went up into the	Deut 1:24
Then we *t*, and took our journey	Deut 2:1
Elath, and from Ezion-gaber, we *t*	Deut 2:8
Then we *t*, and went up the way to	Deut 3:1
they are quickly *t* aside out of	Deut 9:12
So I *t* and came down from the	Deut 9:15
ye had *t* aside quickly out of the	Deut 9:16
I *t* myself and came down from the	Deut 10:5
but the LORD thy God *t* the curse	Deut 23:5
that they are *t* unto other gods	Deut 31:18
but *t* their backs before their	Josh 7:12
So the LORD *t* from the fierceness	Josh 7:26
t back upon the pursuers	Josh 8:20
city ascended, then they *t*	Josh 8:21
And Joshua at that time *t* back	Josh 11:10
t from Gilgal eastward toward the	Josh 19:12
they *t* quickly out of the way	Judg 2:17
But he himself *t* again from the	Judg 3:19
when he had *t* in unto her into	Judg 4:18
the children of Israel *t* again	Judg 8:33
he *t* aside to see the carcase of	Judg 14:8
and *t* tail to tail, and put a	Judg 15:4
they *t* in thither, and said unto	Judg 18:3
they *t* thitherward, and came to	Judg 18:15
So they *t* and departed, and put the	Judg 18:21
they *t* their faces, and said unto	Judg 18:23
were too strong for him, he *t*	Judg 18:26
they *t* aside thither, to go in and	Judg 19:15
And when the men of Israel *t* again	Judg 20:41
Therefore they *t* their backs	Judg 20:42
And they *t* and fled toward the	Judg 20:45
But six hundred men *t* and fled to	Judg 20:47
the men of Israel *t* again upon	Judg 20:48
the man was afraid, and *t* himself	Ruth 3:8
And he *t* aside, and sat down	Ruth 4:1
t not aside to the right hand or	1Sa 6:12
but *t* aside after lucre, and took	1Sa 8:3
shalt be *t* into another man	1Sa 10:6
that when he had *t* his back to go	1Sa 10:9
one company *t* unto the way that	1Sa 13:17
another company *t* the way to	1Sa 13:18
another company *t* to the way of	1Sa 13:18
even they also *t* to be with the	1Sa 14:21
and whithersoever he *t* himself	1Sa 14:47
for he is *t* back from following	1Sa 15:11
as Samuel *t* about to go away, he	1Sa 15:27
So Samuel *t* again after Saul	1Sa 15:31
he *t* from him toward another, and	1Sa 17:30
And Doeg the Edomite *t*, and he fell	1Sa 22:18
So David's young men *t* their way	1Sa 25:12
the bow of Jonathan *t* not back	2Sa 1:22
in going he *t* not to the right	2Sa 2:19
he *t* aside, and stood still	2Sa 18:30
the victory that day was *t* into	2Sa 19:2
t not again until I had consumed	2Sa 22:38
howbeit the kingdom is *t* about	1Kin 2:15
for Joab had *t* after Adonijah,	1Kin 2:28
though he *t* not after Absalom	1Kin 2:28
the king *t* his face about, and	1Kin 8:14
So she *t* and went to her own	1Kin 10:13
his wives *t* away his heart	1Kin 11:3
that his wives *t* away his heart	1Kin 11:4
because his heart was *t* from the	1Kin 11:9
t not aside from any thing that	1Kin 15:5
that thou hast *t* their heart back	1Kin 18:37
and, behold, a man *t* aside	1Kin 20:39
t away his face, and would eat no	1Kin 21:4
they *t* aside to fight against him	1Kin 22:32
that they *t* back from pursuing	1Kin 22:33
he *t* not aside from it, doing	1Kin 22:43
the messengers *t* back unto him	1Kin 1:5
unto them, Why are ye now *t* back	2Kin 1:5
he *t* back, and looked on them, and	2Kin 2:24
he *t* in thither to eat bread	2Kin 4:8
he *t* into the chamber, and lay	2Kin 4:11
So he *t* and went away in a rage	2Kin 5:12
when the man *t* again from his	2Kin 5:26
Joram *t* his hands, and fled, and	2Kin 9:23
So the king of Assyria *t* back	2Kin 15:20
t he from the house of the LORD	2Kin 16:18
Then he *t* his face to the wall,	2Kin 20:2
t not aside to the right hand or	2Kin 22:2
And as Josiah *t* himself, he spied	2Kin 23:16
that *t* to the LORD with all his	2Kin 23:25
Notwithstanding the LORD *t* not	2Kin 23:26
t his name to Jehoiakim, and took	2Kin 23:34
then he *t* and rebelled against him	2Kin 24:1
t the kingdom unto David the son	1Chr 10:14
Orman *t* back, and saw the	1Chr 21:20
And the king *t* his face, and	2Chr 6:3
So she *t*, and went away to her own	2Chr 9:12
the wrath of the LORD *t* from him	2Chr 12:12
they *t* back again from pursuing	2Chr 18:32
Egypt, but they *t* from them, and	2Chr 20:10
have *t* away their faces from the	2Chr 29:6
of the LORD, and *t* their backs	2Chr 29:6
and *t* his name to Jehoiakim	2Chr 36:4
t the heart of the king of	Ezr 6:22
God for this matter be *t* from us	Ezr 10:14
t back, and entered by the gate of	Neh 2:15
neither *t* they from their wicked	Neh 9:35
howbeit our God *t* the curse into	Neh 13:2
(though it was *t* to the contrary	Est 9:1
the month which was *t* unto them	Est 9:22
paths of their way are *t* aside	Job 6:18
t me over into the hands of the	Job 16:11
whom I loved are *t* against me	Job 19:19
Yet his meat in his bowels is *t*	Job 20:14
under it is *t* up as it were fire	Job 28:5
Terrors are *t* upon me	Job 30:15
My harp also is *t* to mourning	Job 30:31
If my step hath *t* out of the way	Job 31:7
Because they *t* back from him, and	Job 34:27
it is *t* round about by his	Job 37:12
It is *t* as clay to the seal	Job 38:14
sorrow is *t* into joy before him	Job 41:22
slingstones are *t* with him into	Job 41:28
the LORD *t* the captivity of Job,	Job 42:10
When mine enemies are *t* back	Ps 9:3
The wicked shall be *t* into hell	Ps 9:17
Thou hast *t* for me my mourning	Ps 30:11
my moisture is *t* into the drought	Ps 32:4
let them be *t* back and brought to	Ps 35:4
Our heart is not *t* back, neither	Ps 44:18
He *t* the sea into dry land	Ps 66:6
which hath not *t* away my prayer	Ps 66:20
let them be *t* backward, and put to	Ps 70:2
Let them be *t* back for a reward	Ps 70:3
t back in the day of battle	Ps 78:9
many a time *t* he his anger away,	Ps 78:38
Yea, they *t* back and tempted God,	Ps 78:41
had *t* their rivers into blood	Ps 78:44
But *t* back, and dealt unfaithfully	Ps 78:57
they were *t* aside like a	Ps 78:57
and *t* my hand against their	Ps 81:14
thou hast *t* thyself from the	Ps 85:3
Thou hast also *t* the edge of his	Ps 89:43
He *t* their heart to hate his	Ps 105:25
He *t* their waters into blood, and	Ps 105:29
Which *t* the rock into a standing	Ps 114:8
t my feet unto thy testimonies	Ps 119:59
When the LORD *t* again the	Ps 126:1
and *t* back that hate Zion	Ps 129:5
t myself to behold wisdom, and	Eccl 2:12
whither is thy beloved *t* aside	Song 6:1
all this his anger is not *t* away	Is 5:25
all this his anger is not *t* away	Is 9:12
all this his anger is not *t* away	Is 9:17
all this his anger is not *t* away	Is 9:21
all this his anger is not *t*	Is 10:4
with me, thine anger is *t* away	Is 12:1
hath *t* it into fear unto me	Is 21:4
wheel *t* about upon the cummin	Is 28:27
Lebanon shall be *t* into a	Is 29:17
thereof shall be *t* into pitch,	Is 34:9
Then Hezekiah *t* his face toward	Is 38:2
They shall be *t* back, they shall	Is 42:17
a deceived heart hath *t* him aside	Is 44:20
rebellious, neither *t* away back	Is 50:5
we have *t* every one to his own	Is 53:6
judgment is *t* away backward, and	Is 59:14
therefore he was *t* to be their	Is 63:10
how then art thou *t* into the	Jer 2:21
for they have *t* their back unto	Jer 2:27
sister Judah hath not *t* unto me	Jer 3:10
of the LORD is not *t* back from us	Jer 4:8
have *t* away these things, and your	Jer 5:25
houses shall be *t* unto others	Jer 6:12
every one *t* to his course, as the	Jer 8:6
They are *t* back to the iniquities	Jer 11:10
then they should have *t* them from	Jer 23:22
and all faces are *t* into paleness	Jer 30:6
turn thou me, and I shall be *t*	Jer 31:18
Surely after that I was *t*	Jer 31:19
they have *t* unto me the back, and	Jer 32:33
But afterward they *t*, and caused	Jer 34:11
And ye were now *t*, and had done	Jer 34:15
But ye *t* and polluted my name, and	Jer 34:16
the mire, and they are *t* away back	Jer 38:22
seen them dismayed and *t* away back	Jer 46:5

for they also are t back, and are.......... Jer 46:21
how hath Moab t the back with.......... Jer 48:39
they have t them away on the.......... Jer 50:6
for my feet, he hath t me back.......... Lam 1:13
mine heart is t within me.......... Lam 1:20
Surely against me is he t.......... Lam 3:3
He hath t aside my ways, and.......... Lam 3:11
Our inheritance is t to strangers.......... Lam 5:2
our dance is t into mourning.......... Lam 5:15
thee, O LORD, and we shall be t.......... Lam 5:21
they t not when they went.......... Eze 1:9
they t not when they went.......... Eze 1:12
they t not when they went.......... Eze 1:17
they t not as they went, but to.......... Eze 10:11
they t not as they went.......... Eze 10:11
also t not from beside them.......... Eze 17:6
whose branches t toward him.......... Eze 17:6
she is t unto the.......... Eze 26:2
He t about to the west side, and.......... Eze 42:19
thy fury be t away from thy city.......... Dan 9:16
was I in me into corruption.......... Dan 10:8
vision my sorrows are t upon me.......... Dan 10:16
Ephraim is a cake not t.......... Hos 7:8
mine heart is t within me.......... Hos 11:8
for mine anger is t away from him.......... Hos 14:4
The sun shall be t into darkness.......... Joel 2:31
for ye have t judgment into gall,.......... Amos 6:12
that they t from their evil way.......... Jonah 3:10
For the Lord hath t away the.......... Nah 2:2
right hand shall be t unto thee.......... Hab 2:16
them that are t back from.......... Zeph 1:6
yet ye t not to me, saith the.......... Hag 2:17
Then I t, and lifted up mine eyes,.......... Zec 5:1
And I t, and lifted up mine eyes,.......... Zec 6:1
All the land shall be t as a.......... Zec 14:10
he t aside into the parts of.......... Mt 2:22
But Jesus t him about, and when he,.......... Mt 9:22
But he t, and said unto Peter, Get.......... Mt 16:23
But when he had t about and looked.......... Mk 8:30
they t back again to Jerusalem,.......... Lk 2:45
t him about, and said unto the.......... Lk 7:9
he t to the woman, and said unto.......... Lk 7:44
But he t, and rebuked them, and.......... Lk 9:55
he t him unto his disciples,.......... Lk 10:23
and he t, and said unto them,.......... Lk 17:15
t back, and with a loud voice.......... Lk 17:15
And the Lord t, and looked upon.......... Lk 22:61
Then Jesus t, and saw them.......... Jn 1:38
your sorrow shall be t into joy.......... Jn 16:20
she t herself back, and saw Jesus.......... Jn 20:14
She t herself, and saith unto him,.......... Jn 20:16
The sun shall be t into darkness.......... Acts 2:20
in their hearts t back again into.......... Acts 7:39
Then God t, and gave them up to.......... Acts 7:42
Saron saw him, and t to the Lord.......... Acts 9:35
believed, and t unto the Lord.......... Acts 11:21
among the Gentiles are t to God.......... Acts 15:19
But Paul, being grieved, t.......... Acts 16:18
These that have t the world.......... Acts 17:6
t away much people, saying that.......... Acts 19:26
how ye t to God from idols to.......... 1Th 1:9
have t aside unto vain jangling.......... 1Ti 1:6
are already t aside after Satan.......... 1Ti 5:15
are in Asia be t away from me.......... 2Ti 1:15
truth, and shall be t unto fables.......... 2Ti 4:4
t to flight the armies of the.......... Heb 11:34
which is lame be t out of the way.......... Heb 12:13
yet are they t about with a very.......... Jas 3:4
your laughter be t to mourning.......... Jas 4:9
The dog is t to his own vomit.......... 2Pet 2:22
I t to see the voice that spake.......... Rev 1:12
And being t, I saw seven golden.......... Rev 1:12

TURNEST
and whithersoever thou t thyself.......... 1Kin 2:3
That thou t thy spirit against.......... Job 15:13
Thou t man to destruction.......... Ps 90:3

TURNETH
the soul that t after such as.......... Lev 20:6
whose heart t away this day from.......... Deut 29:18
when Israel t their backs before.......... Josh 7:8
t toward the sunrising to.......... Josh 19:27
And then the coast t to Ramah.......... Josh 19:29
and the coast t to Hosah.......... Josh 19:29
then the coast t westward to.......... Josh 19:34
neither t he back from the sword.......... Job 39:22
He t rivers into a wilderness, and,.......... Ps 107:33
The t the wilderness into a.......... Ps 107:35
of the wicked he t upside down.......... Ps 146:9
A soft answer t away wrath.......... Prov 15:1
whithersoever it t, it prospereth.......... Prov 17:8
he t it whithersoever he will.......... Prov 21:1
As the door t upon his hinges, so.......... Prov 26:14
He that t away his ear from.......... Prov 28:9
beasts, and t not away for any.......... Prov 30:30
south, and t about unto the north.......... Eccl 1:6
that t aside by the flocks of thy.......... Song 1:7
For the people t not unto him.......... Is 9:13
t it upside down, and scattereth.......... Is 24:1
that t wise men backward, and.......... Is 44:25
as a wayfaring man that t aside.......... Jer 14:8
t herself to flee, and fear hath.......... Jer 46:21
yea, she sigheth, and t backward.......... Lam 1:8
he t his hand against me at the.......... Lam 3:3
But when the righteous t away.......... Eze 18:24
When a righteous man t away from,.......... Eze 18:26
when the wicked man t away from.......... Eze 18:27
and t away from all his.......... Eze 18:28
day that he t from his wickedness.......... Eze 33:12

When the righteous t from his.......... Eze 33:18
t the shadow of death into the.......... Amos 5:8

TURNING
wiping it, and t it upside down.......... 2Kin 21:13
gate, and at the t of the wall, and.......... 2Chr 26:9
hardened his heart from t unto.......... 2Chr 36:13
the armoury at the t of the wall.......... Neh 3:19
from the t of the wall unto the.......... Neh 3:20
of Azariah unto the t of the wall.......... Neh 3:24
over against the t of the wall.......... Neh 3:25
For the t away of the simple.......... Prov 1:32
Surely your t of things upside.......... Is 29:16
two leaves apiece, two t leaves.......... Eze 41:24
t away he hath divided our fields.......... Mic 2:4
But Jesus t unto them said,.......... Lk 23:28
t about, seeth the disciple whom.......... Jn 21:20
in t away every one of you from.......... Acts 3:26
t him to the body said, Tabitha,.......... Acts 9:40
variableness, neither shadow of t.......... Jas 1:17
t the cities of Sodom and Gomorrah.......... 2Pet 2:6
t the grace of our God into.......... Jude 4

TURTLE
the voice of the t is heard in.......... Song 2:12
and the t and the crane in the.......... Jer 8:7

TURTLEDOVE
a ram of three years old, and a t.......... Gen 15:9
and a young pigeon, or a t.......... Lev 12:6
thy t unto the multitude of the.......... Ps 74:19

TURTLEDOVES
he shall bring his offering of t.......... Lev 1:14
which he hath committed, two t.......... Lev 5:7
if he be not able to bring two t.......... Lev 5:11
And two t, or two young pigeons,.......... Lev 14:22
he shall offer the one of the t.......... Lev 14:30
he shall take to him two t.......... Lev 15:14
the law of the Lord, A pair of t.......... Lk 2:24

TURTLES
lamb, then she shall bring two t.......... Lev 12:8
day she shall take unto her two t.......... Lev 15:29
eighth day he shall bring two t.......... Num 6:10

TUTORS
But is under t and governors until.......... Gal 4:2

TWAIN
my son in law in the one of the t.......... 1Sa 18:21
and shut the door upon them t.......... 2Kin 4:33
with t he covered his face, and.......... Is 6:2
with t he covered his feet, and.......... Is 6:2
his feet, and with t he did fly.......... Is 6:2
me, when they cut the calf in t.......... Jer 34:18
both t shall come forth out of.......... Eze 21:19
thee to go a mile, go with him t.......... Mt 5:41
they t shall be one flesh.......... Mt 19:5
Wherefore they are no more t.......... Mt 19:6
Whether of them t did the will of.......... Mt 21:31
Whether of the t will ye that I.......... Mt 27:21
in t from the top to the bottom.......... Mt 27:51
they t shall be one flesh.......... Mk 10:8
so then they are no more t.......... Mk 10:8
in t from the top to the bottom.......... Mk 15:38
make in himself of t one new man.......... Eph 2:15

TWELFTH
On the t day Ahira the son of.......... Num 7:78
oxen before him, and he with the t.......... 1Kin 19:19
In the t year of Joram the son of.......... 2Kin 8:25
In the t year of Ahaz king of.......... 2Kin 17:1
king of Judah, in the t month.......... 2Kin 25:27
to Eliashib, the t to Jakim,.......... 1Chr 24:12
The t to Hashabiah, he, his sons,.......... 1Chr 25:19
The t captain for the t.......... 1Chr 27:15
in the t year he began to purge.......... 2Chr 34:3
In the t day of the first month,.......... Ezr 8:31
in the t year of king Ahasuerus,.......... Est 3:7
month to month, to the t month,.......... Est 3:7
the thirteenth day of the t month.......... Est 3:13
the thirteenth day of the t month.......... Est 8:12
Now in the t month, that is, the.......... Est 9:1
king of Judah, in the t month.......... Jer 52:31
in the t day of the month, the.......... Eze 29:1
the t year, in the t month,.......... Eze 32:1
came to pass also in the t year.......... Eze 32:17
in the t year of our captivity.......... Eze 33:21
the t, an amethyst.......... Rev 21:20

TWELVE
Seth were nine hundred and t years.......... Gen 5:8
t years they served Chedorlaomer,.......... Gen 14:4
t princes shall he beget, and I.......... Gen 17:20
t princes according to their.......... Gen 25:16
Now the sons of Jacob were t.......... Gen 35:22
said, Thy servants are t brethren,.......... Gen 42:13
We be t brethren, sons of our.......... Gen 42:32
these are the t tribes of Israel.......... Gen 49:28
where were t wells of water, and.......... Ex 15:27
t pillars, according to the.......... Ex 24:4
to the t tribes of Israel.......... Ex 24:4
the children of Israel, t.......... Ex 28:21
they be according to the t tribes.......... Ex 28:21
of the children of Israel, t.......... Ex 39:14
name, according to the t tribes.......... Ex 39:14
flour, and bake t cakes thereof.......... Lev 24:5
princes of Israel, being t men.......... Num 7:3
six covered wagons, and t oxen.......... Num 7:3
t chargers of silver,.......... Num 7:84
t silver bowls, t spoons of.......... Num 7:84
The golden spoons t, full of.......... Num 7:86
were t bullocks, the rams t.......... Num 7:87

the lambs of the first year t.......... Num 7:87
of the goats for sin offering t.......... Num 7:87
the house of their fathers t rods.......... Num 17:2
fathers' houses, even t rods.......... Num 17:6
ye shall offer t young bullocks.......... Num 29:17
tribe, t thousand armed for war.......... Num 31:5
threescore and t thousand beeves,.......... Num 31:33
tribute was threescore and t.......... Num 31:38
in Elim were t fountains of water.......... Num 33:9
I took t men of you, one of a.......... Deut 1:23
Now therefore take you t men out.......... Josh 3:12
Take you t men out of the people,.......... Josh 3:12
t stones, and ye shall carry them.......... Josh 4:3
Then Joshua called the t men,.......... Josh 4:4
took up t stones out of the midst.......... Josh 4:8
Joshua set up t stones in the.......... Josh 4:9
those t stones, which they took.......... Josh 4:20
were t thousand, even all the men.......... Josh 8:25
t cities with their villages.......... Josh 18:24
t cities with their villages.......... Josh 19:15
of the tribe of Zebulun, t cities.......... Josh 21:7
were by their lot t cities.......... Josh 21:40
into t pieces, and sent her into.......... Judg 19:29
the congregation sent thither t.......... Judg 21:10
went over by number t of Benjamin.......... 2Sa 2:15
t of the servants of David.......... 2Sa 2:15
t of Ish-tobi t thousand men.......... 2Sa 10:6
we now choose out t thousand men,.......... 2Sa 17:1
Solomon had t officers over all.......... 1Kin 4:7
chariots, and t thousand horsemen.......... 1Kin 4:26
a line of t cubits did compass.......... 1Kin 7:15
It stood upon t oxen, three.......... 1Kin 7:25
one sea, and t oxen under the sea.......... 1Kin 7:44
t lions stood there on the one.......... 1Kin 10:20
t thousand horsemen, whom he.......... 1Kin 10:26
on him, and rent it in t pieces.......... 1Kin 11:30
to reign over Israel, t years.......... 1Kin 14:21
And Elijah took t stones,.......... 1Kin 18:31
who was plowing with t yoke of.......... 1Kin 19:19
king of Judah, and reigned t years.......... 2Kin 3:1
Manasseh was t years old when he.......... 2Kin 21:1
of the tribe of Zebulun, t cities.......... 1Chr 6:63
the gates were t hundred and t.......... 1Chr 9:22
and his brethren and sons were t.......... 1Chr 15:10
with his brethren and sons were t.......... 1Chr 25:9
his sons, and his brethren, were t.......... 1Chr 25:10
his sons, and his brethren,.......... 1Chr 25:11
his sons, and his brethren, were t.......... 1Chr 25:12
his sons, and his brethren, were t.......... 1Chr 25:13
his sons, and his brethren, were t.......... 1Chr 25:14
his sons, and his brethren, were t.......... 1Chr 25:15
his sons, and his brethren, were t.......... 1Chr 25:16
his sons, and his brethren, were t.......... 1Chr 25:17
his sons, and his brethren, were t.......... 1Chr 25:18
his sons, and his brethren, were t.......... 1Chr 25:19
his sons, and his brethren, were t.......... 1Chr 25:20
his sons, and his brethren, were t.......... 1Chr 25:21
his sons, and his brethren, were t.......... 1Chr 25:22
his sons, and his brethren, were t.......... 1Chr 25:23
his sons, and his brethren, were t.......... 1Chr 25:24
his sons, and his brethren, were t.......... 1Chr 25:25
his sons, and his brethren, were t.......... 1Chr 25:26
his sons, and his brethren, were t.......... 1Chr 25:29
his sons, and his brethren, were t.......... 1Chr 25:30
his sons, and his brethren, were t.......... 1Chr 25:31
t thousand horsemen, which he.......... 2Chr 1:14
It stood upon t oxen, three.......... 2Chr 4:4
One sea, and t oxen under it.......... 2Chr 4:15
t lions stood there on the one.......... 2Chr 9:19
chariots, and t thousand horsemen.......... 2Chr 9:25
t hundred thousand chariots, and.......... 2Chr 12:3
Manasseh was t years old when he.......... 2Chr 33:1
two thousand eight hundred and t.......... Ezr 2:6
of Jorah, an hundred and t.......... Ezr 2:18
t he goats, according to the.......... Ezr 6:17
Then I separated t of the chief.......... Ezr 8:24
t bullocks for all Israel, ninety.......... Ezr 8:35
t he goats for a sin offering.......... Ezr 8:35
t years, I and my brethren have.......... Neh 5:14
of Harim, an hundred and t.......... Neh 7:24
after that she had been t months.......... Est 2:12
in the valley of salt t thousand.......... Ps 60:t
t brasen bulls that were under.......... Jer 52:20
a fillet of t cubits did compass.......... Jer 52:21
the altar shall be t cubits long,.......... Eze 43:16
t broad, square in the four.......... Eze 43:16
to the t tribes of Israel.......... Eze 47:13
At the end of t months he walked.......... Dan 4:29
with an issue of blood t years,.......... Mt 9:20
called unto him his t disciples.......... Mt 10:1
names of the t apostles are these.......... Mt 10:2
These t Jesus sent forth, and.......... Mt 10:5
end of commanding his t disciples.......... Mt 11:1
that remained t baskets full.......... Mt 14:20
ye also shall sit upon t thrones.......... Mt 19:28
judging the t tribes of Israel.......... Mt 19:28
the t disciples apart in the way.......... Mt 20:17
Then one of the t, called Judas.......... Mt 26:14
was come, he sat down with the t.......... Mt 26:20
spake, lo, Judas, one of the t.......... Mt 26:47
more than t legions of angels.......... Mt 26:53
And he ordained t, that they.......... Mk 3:14
the t asked of him the parable.......... Mk 4:10
had an issue of blood t years.......... Mk 5:25
for she was of the age of t years.......... Mk 5:42
And he called unto him the t.......... Mk 6:7
they took up t baskets full of.......... Mk 6:43
They say unto him, T.......... Mk 8:19

T

And he sat down, and called the t ...... Mk 9:35
And he took again the t, and began ...... Mk 10:32
went out unto Bethany with the t ...... Mk 11:11
And Judas Iscariot, one of the t ...... Mk 14:10
the evening he cometh with the t ...... Mk 14:17
unto them, It is one of the t ...... Mk 14:20
spake, cometh Judas, one of the t ...... Mk 14:43
And when he was t years old ...... Lk 2:42
and of them he chose, whom also ...... Lk 6:13
and the t were with him, ... Lk 8:1
about t years of age, and she lay ...... Lk 8:42
having an issue of blood t years ...... Lk 8:43
called his t disciples together ...... Lk 9:1
to wear away, then came the t ...... Lk 9:12
that remained to them t baskets ...... Lk 9:17
Then he took unto him the t ...... Lk 18:31
being of the number of the t ...... Lk 22:3
down, and the t apostles with him ...... Lk 22:14
judging the t tribes of Israel ...... Lk 22:30
was called Judas, one of the t ...... Lk 22:47
filled t baskets with the ...... Jn 6:13
Then said Jesus unto the t ...... Jn 6:67
them, Have not I chosen you t ...... Jn 6:70
betray him, being one of the t ...... Jn 6:71
Are there not t hours in the day ...... Jn 11:9
But Thomas, one of the t, called ...... Jn 20:24
Then the t called the multitude ...... Acts 6:2
and Jacob begat the t patriarchs ...... Acts 7:8
And all the men were about t ...... Acts 19:7
that there are yet but t days ...... Acts 24:11
Unto which promise our t tribes ...... Acts 26:7
was seen of Cephas, then of the t 1Cor 15:5
to the t tribes which are ...... Jas 1:1
of Juda were sealed t thousand ...... Rev 7:5
of Reuben were sealed t thousand ...... Rev 7:5
of Gad were sealed t thousand ...... Rev 7:5
of Aser were sealed t thousand ...... Rev 7:6
Nephthalim were sealed t thousand ...... Rev 7:6
Manasses were sealed t thousand ...... Rev 7:6
of Simeon were sealed t thousand ...... Rev 7:7
of Levi were sealed t thousand ...... Rev 7:7
Issachar were sealed t thousand ...... Rev 7:7
of Zabulon were sealed t thousand ...... Rev 7:8
of Joseph were sealed t thousand ...... Rev 7:8
Benjamin were sealed t thousand ...... Rev 7:8
upon her head a crown of t stars ...... Rev 12:1
had t gates, and at the gates ...... Rev 21:12
gates, and at the gates t angels ...... Rev 21:12
the t tribes of the children of ...... Rev 21:12
the t city had t foundations ...... Rev 21:14
of the t apostles of the Lamb ...... Rev 21:14
the reed, t thousand furlongs ...... Rev 21:16
the t gates were t pearls ...... Rev 21:21
which bare t manner of fruits, and ...... Rev 22:2

TWENTIETH

t day of the month, was the earth ...... Gen 8:14
t day of the month at even ...... Ex 12:18
it came to pass on the t day of ...... Num 10:11
in the t year of Jeroboam king of 1Kin 15:9
t year of king Jehoash the 2Kin 12:6
t year of Joash the son of 2Kin 13:1
in the t year of Jotham the son 2Kin 15:30
seven and t day of the month, that 2Kin 25:27
to Pethahiah, the t to Jehezekel, ... 1Chr 24:16
to Jachin, the two and 1Chr 24:17
to Jachin, the two and t to Gamul, ... 1Chr 24:17
t to Delaiah, the four and 1Chr 24:18
Delaiah, the four and t to Maaziah 1Chr 24:18
The t to Eliathah, he, his sons, ... 1Chr 25:27
to Hothir, he, his sons, and his 1Chr 25:28
to Giddalti, he, his sons, and 1Chr 25:29
to Mahazioth, he, his sons, and 1Chr 25:30
to Romamti-ezer, he, his sons, ... 1Chr 25:31
t day of the seventh month he 2Chr 7:10
on the t day of the month ...... Ezr 10:9
the month Chisleu, in the t year ...... Neh 1:1
in the t year of Artaxerxes the ...... Neh 2:1
from the t year even unto the two ...... Neh 5:14
on the three and t day thereof ...... Est 8:9
t year, the word of the LORD hath ...... Jer 25:3
three and t year of Nebuchadnezzar ...... Jer 52:30
five and t day of the month, that ...... Jer 52:31
t year, in the first month, in ...... Eze 29:17
t year of our captivity, in the ...... Eze 40:1
t day of the first month, as I ...... Dan 10:4
t day of the sixth month, in the ...... Hag 1:15
t day of the month, came the word ...... Hag 2:1
t day of the ninth month, in the ...... Hag 2:10
t day of the month, even ...... Hag 2:18
t day of the month, saying, ... Hag 2:20
t day of the eleventh month, ... Zec 1:7

TWENTY

shall be an hundred and t years ...... Gen 6:3
nine and t years, and begat Terah ...... Gen 11:24
there shall be t found three ...... Gen 18:31
hundred and seven and t years die ...... Gen 23:1
This t years have I been with ...... Gen 31:38
Thus have I been t years in thy ...... Gen 31:41
t he goats, two hundred ewes, and ...... Gen 32:14
two hundred ewes, and t rams, ... Gen 32:14
t she asses, and ten foals ...... Gen 32:15
for t pieces of silver ...... Gen 37:28
t cubits, and the breadth of one ...... Ex 26:2
t boards on the south side ...... Ex 26:18
of silver under the t boards ...... Ex 26:19
side there shall be t boards ...... Ex 26:20
their t pillars thereof and their ...... Ex 27:10
their t sockets shall be of brass ...... Ex 27:10
his t pillars and their t ...... Ex 27:11

shall be an hanging of t cubits ...... Ex 27:16
(a shekel is t gerahs ...... Ex 30:13
from t years old and above, shall ...... Ex 30:14
The length of one curtain was t ...... Ex 36:9
t boards for the south side ...... Ex 36:23
silver he made under the t boards ...... Ex 36:24
north corner, he made t boards ...... Ex 36:25
Their pillars were t, and their ...... Ex 38:10
and their brasen sockets t ...... Ex 38:10
cubits, their pillars were t ...... Ex 38:11
and their sockets of brass t ...... Ex 38:11
t cubits was the length, and the ...... Ex 38:18
the gold of the offering, was t ...... Ex 38:24
from t years old and upward, for ...... Ex 38:26
shall be of the male from t years ...... Lev 27:3
years old even unto t years old, ... Lev 27:5
shall be of the male t shekels ...... Lev 27:5
t gerahs shall be the shekel ...... Lev 27:25
From t years old and upward, all ...... Num 1:3
from t years old and upward, by ...... Num 1:18
every male from t years old ...... Num 1:20
every male from t years old ...... Num 1:22
from t years old and upward, all ...... Num 1:24
from t years old and upward, all ...... Num 1:26
from t years old and upward, all ...... Num 1:28
from t years old and upward, all ...... Num 1:30
from t years old and upward, all ...... Num 1:32
from t years old and upward, all ...... Num 1:34
from t years old and upward, all ...... Num 1:36
from t years old and upward, all ...... Num 1:38
from t years old and upward, all ...... Num 1:40
from t years old and upward, all ...... Num 1:42
from t years old and upward, all ...... Num 1:45
a month old and upward, were t ...... Num 3:39
were numbered of them, were t ...... Num 3:43
(the shekel is t gerahs ...... Num 3:47
was an hundred and t shekels ...... Num 7:86
of the peace offerings were t ...... Num 7:88
from t and five years old and ...... Num 8:24
neither ten days, nor t days ...... Num 11:19
from t years old and upward, which ...... Num 14:29
the sanctuary, which is t gerahs ...... Num 18:16
that died in the plague were t ...... Num 25:9
from t years old and upward, ... Num 26:2
from t years old and upward ...... Num 26:4
the families of the Simeonites, t ...... Num 26:14
that were numbered of them were t ...... Num 26:62
from t years old and upward, shall ...... Num 32:11
And Aaron was an hundred and t ...... Num 33:39
hundred and t years old this day ...... Deut 31:2
and t years old when he died ...... Deut 34:7
all the cities are t and nine, ... Josh 15:32
and t two cities with their ...... Josh 19:30
t years he mightily oppressed the ...... Judg 4:3
And there returned of the people t ...... Judg 7:3
t thousand men that drew sword ...... Judg 8:10
And he judged Israel t and three ...... Judg 10:2
a Gileadite, and judged Israel t ...... Judg 10:3
even t cities, and unto the plain ...... Judg 11:33
days of the Philistines t years ...... Judg 15:20
And he judged Israel t years ...... Judg 16:31
at that time out of the cities t ...... Judg 20:15
of the Israelites that day t ...... Judg 20:21
of the Benjamites that day t ...... Judg 20:35
fell that day of Benjamin were t ...... Judg 20:46
for it was t years 1Sa 7:2
made, was about t men, within as 1Sa 14:14
to Hebron, and t men with him 2Sa 3:20
horsemen, and t thousand footmen 2Sa 8:4
the Syrians two and t thousand men 2Sa 8:5
had fifteen sons and t servants 2Sa 9:10
t thousand footmen, and of king 2Sa 10:6
that day of t thousand men 2Sa 18:7
sons and his t servants with him, ... 2Sa 19:17
six toes, four and t in number 2Sa 21:20
the end of nine months and t days 2Sa 24:8
t oxen out of the pastures, and an 1Kin 4:23
Solomon gave Hiram t thousand 1Kin 5:11
and t measures of pure oil 1Kin 5:11
and the breadth thereof t cubits 1Kin 6:2
t cubits was the length thereof, ... 1Kin 6:3
he built t cubits on the sides of 1Kin 6:16
forepart was t cubits in length, ... 1Kin 6:20
t cubits in breadth 1Kin 6:20
t cubits in the height thereof 1Kin 6:20
thousand oxen, and an hundred and t 1Kin 8:63
and an hundred and t thousand sheep 1Kin 8:63
to pass at the end of t years 1Kin 9:10
then king Solomon gave Hiram t 1Kin 9:11
t talents, and brought it to king 1Kin 9:28
t talents of gold, and of spices 1Kin 10:10
reigned were two and t years 1Kin 14:20
over all Israel in Tirzah, t 1Kin 15:33
In the t and sixth year of Asa 1Kin 15:33
him, and killed him, in the t 1Kin 16:10
In the t and seventh year of Asa 1Kin 16:15
reigned over Israel in Samaria t 1Kin 16:29
and there a wall felt upon t 1Kin 20:30
and he reigned t and five years in 1Kin 22:42
t loaves of barley, and full ears 2Kin 4:42
t years old was Ahaziah when he 2Kin 8:26
over Israel in Samaria was t 2Kin 10:36
He was t and five years old when 2Kin 14:2
he began to reign, and reigned t 2Kin 14:2
In the t and seventh year of 2Kin 15:1
in Samaria, and reigned t years, ... 2Kin 15:27
t years old was he when he began 2Kin 15:33
T years old was Ahaz when he 2Kin 16:2
T and five years old was he when 2Kin 18:2
and he reigned t and nine years in 2Kin 18:2

Amon was t and two years old when 2Kin 21:19
Jehoahaz was t and three years old 2Kin 23:31
Jehoiakim was t and five years old 2Kin 23:36
Zedekiah was t and one years old 2Kin 24:18
t cities in the land of Gilead 1Chr 2:22
t thousand and six hundred 1Chr 7:2
reckoned by their genealogies t 1Chr 7:7
was t thousand and two hundred 1Chr 7:9
apt to the war and to battle was t 1Chr 7:40
and of his father's house t 1Chr 12:28
children of Ephraim t thousand 1Chr 12:30
And of the Danites expert in war t 1Chr 12:35
battle, an hundred and t thousand 1Chr 12:37
and his brethren an hundred and t 1Chr 15:5
and his brethren two hundred and t 1Chr 15:6
horsemen, and t thousand footmen 1Chr 18:4
the Syrians two and t thousand men 1Chr 18:5
fingers and toes were four and t 1Chr 20:6
Of which, t and four thousand were 1Chr 23:4
the Loab, from the age of t years 1Chr 23:24
were numbered from t years old 1Chr 23:27
the year, of every course were t 1Chr 27:1
and in his course were t and four 1Chr 27:2
in his course likewise were t 1Chr 27:4
and in his course were t and four 1Chr 27:5
and in his course were t and four 1Chr 27:7
and in his course were t and four 1Chr 27:8
and in his course were t and four 1Chr 27:9
and in his course were t and four 1Chr 27:10
and in his course were t and four 1Chr 27:11
and in his course were t and four 1Chr 27:12
and in his course were t and four 1Chr 27:13
and in his course were t and four 1Chr 27:13
and in his course were t and four 1Chr 27:15
number of them from t years old 1Chr 27:23
t thousand measures of beaten 2Chr 2:10
t thousand measures of barley, and 2Chr 2:10
t thousand baths of wine, and 2Chr 2:10
wine, and t thousand baths of oil 2Chr 2:10
cubits, and the breadth t cubits 2Chr 3:3
t cubits, and the height was an 2Chr 3:4
and the height was an hundred and t 2Chr 3:4
t cubits, and the breadth thereof 2Chr 3:8
and the breadth thereof t cubits 2Chr 3:8
the cherubims were t cubits long 2Chr 3:11
spread themselves forth t cubits 2Chr 3:13
t cubits the length thereof, and 2Chr 4:1
t cubits the breadth thereof, and 2Chr 4:1
t priests sounding with trumpets 2Chr 5:12
Solomon offered a sacrifice of t 2Chr 7:5
and an hundred and t thousand sheep 2Chr 7:5
to pass at the end of t years 2Chr 8:1
t talents of gold, and of spices 2Chr 9:9
and begat t and eight sons, and 2Chr 11:21
fourteen wives, and begat t 2Chr 13:21
began to reign, and he reigned t 2Chr 20:31
Amaziah was t and five years old 2Chr 25:1
began to reign, and he reigned t 2Chr 25:5
he numbered them from t years old 2Chr 25:5
Jotham was t and five years old 2Chr 27:1
t years old when he began to 2Chr 27:8
Ahaz was t years old when he 2Chr 28:1
t thousand in one day, which were 2Chr 28:6
t years old, and he reigned nine 2Chr 29:1
nine and t years in Jerusalem 2Chr 29:1
and the Levites from t years old 2Chr 31:17
t years old when he began to 2Chr 33:21
Jehoahaz was t and three years old 2Chr 36:2
Jehoiakim was t and five years old 2Chr 36:5
t years old when he began to 2Chr 36:11
of silver, nine and t knives, ... Ezr 1:9
children of Bebai, six hundred t ...... Ezr 2:11
Azgad, a thousand two hundred t ...... Ezr 2:12
of Bezai, three hundred t ...... Ezr 2:17
children of Hashum, two hundred t ...... Ezr 2:19
of Beth-lehem, an hundred t ...... Ezr 2:21
The men of Anathoth, an hundred t ...... Ezr 2:23
of Ramah and Gaba, six hundred t ...... Ezr 2:26
The men of Michmas, an hundred t ...... Ezr 2:27
of Beth-el and Ai, two hundred t ...... Ezr 2:28
of Harim, three hundred and t ...... Ezr 2:32
Hadid, and Ono, seven hundred t ...... Ezr 2:33
children of Asaph, an hundred t ...... Ezr 2:41
six thousand seven hundred and t ...... Ezr 2:67
from t years old and upward, to ...... Ezr 3:8
the son of Bebai, and with him t ...... Ezr 8:11
his brethren and their sons, t ...... Ezr 8:19
two hundred and t Nethinims ...... Ezr 8:20
Also t basons of gold, of a ...... Ezr 8:27
So the wall was finished in the t ...... Neh 6:15
children of Bebai, six hundred t ...... Neh 7:16
two thousand three hundred t ...... Neh 7:17
of Hashum, three hundred t ...... Neh 7:22
of Bezai, three hundred t ...... Neh 7:23
The men of Anathoth, an hundred t ...... Neh 7:27
of Ramah and Gaba, six hundred t ...... Neh 7:30
men of Michmas, an hundred t ...... Neh 7:31
of Beth-el and Ai, an hundred t ...... Neh 7:32
of Harim, three hundred and t ...... Neh 7:35
Hadid, and Ono, seven hundred t ...... Neh 7:37
thousand seven hundred and t asses ...... Neh 7:69
the work t thousand drams of gold ...... Neh 7:71
gave was t thousand drams of gold ...... Neh 7:72
Now in the t and fourth day of ...... Neh 9:1
Gabbai, Sallai, nine hundred t ...... Neh 11:8
of the house were eight hundred t ...... Neh 11:12
men of valour, an hundred t ...... Neh 11:14
hundred and seven and t provinces ...... Est 1:1
India unto Ethiopia, an hundred t ...... Est 8:9
all the Jews, to the hundred t ...... Est 9:30

chariots of God are *t* thousand .... Ps 68:17
t years old when he began to .... Jer 52:1
three thousand Jews and three and *t* .. Jer 52:28
be by weight, *t* shekels a day .... Eze 4:10
t men, with their backs toward .... Eze 8:16
door of the gate five and *t* men .... Eze 11:1
t cubits, door against door .... Eze 40:13
and the breadth five and *t* cubits ...... Eze 40:21
and the breadth five and *t* cubits ...... Eze 40:25
long, and five and *t* cubits broad ...... Eze 40:29
t cubits long, and five cubits .... Eze 40:33
long, and five and *t* cubits broad ...... Eze 40:33
and the breadth five and *t* cubits ...... Eze 40:36
length of the porch was *t* cubits .... Eze 40:49
and the breadth, *t* cubits .... Eze 41:2
the length thereof, *t* cubits .... Eze 41:4
t cubits, before the temple .... Eze 41:4
chambers was the wideness of *t* .... Eze 41:10
Over against the *t* cubits which .... Eze 42:3
t thousand reeds, and the breadth ...... Eze 45:1
t thousand, and the breadth of ten ..... Eze 45:3
t thousand of length, and the ten ...... Eze 45:5
for a possession for *t* chambers .... Eze 45:5
t thousand long, over against the ...... Eze 45:6
And the shekel shall be *t* gerahs .... Eze 45:12
t shekels, five and *t* shekels .... Eze 45:12
t thousand reeds in breadth, and .... Eze 48:8
t thousand in length, and toward .... Eze 48:9
t thousand in length, and toward .... Eze 48:10
five and *t* thousand in length .... Eze 48:13
t thousand in length, and ten .... Eze 48:13
t thousand, and the breadth ten .... Eze 48:13
t thousand, shall be a profane .... Eze 48:15
t thousand in length toward .... Eze 48:18
thousand by five and *t* thousand .... Eze 48:20
t thousand of the oblation toward ...... Eze 48:21
t thousand toward the west border ...... Eze 48:21
t princes, which should be over .... Dan 6:1
Persia withstood me one and *t* days ..... Dan 10:13
one came to an heap of *t* measures ...... Hag 2:16
of the press, there were but *t* .... Hag 2:16
against him with *t* thousand .... Lk 14:31
t or thirty furlongs, they see .... Jn 6:19
were about an hundred and *t* .... Acts 1:15
And sounded, and found it *t* fathoms .... Acts 27:28
in one day three and *t* thousand 1Cor 10:8
the throne were four and *t* seats .... Rev 4:4
t elders sitting, clothed in .... Rev 4:4
t elders fell down before him .... Rev 4:10
t elders fell down before the .... Rev 5:8
t elders fell down and worshipped ...... Rev 5:14
t elders, which sat before God on ...... Rev 11:16
t elders and the four beasts fell ...... Rev 19:4

TWENTY'S
I will not destroy it for *t* sake .... Gen 18:31

TWICE
dream was doubled unto Pharaoh *t* .... Gen 41:32
it shall be *t* as much as they .... Ex 16:5
day they gathered *t* as much bread ...... Ex 16:22
with his rod he smote the rock *t* .... Num 20:11
avoided out of his presence *t* 1Sa 18:11
which had appeared unto him *t* 1Kin 11:9
himself there, not once nor *t* 2Kin 6:10
without Jerusalem once or *t* .... Neh 13:20
For God speaketh once, yea *t* .... Job 33:14
will not answer: yea, *t* .... Job 40:5
also the LORD gave Job *t* as much .... Job 42:10
I have *t* heard this .... Ps 62:11
he live a thousand years *t* told .... Eccl 6:6
night, before the cock crow *t* .... Mk 14:30
unto him, Before the cock crow *t* .... Mk 14:72
I fast *t* in the week, I give .... Lk 18:12
t dead, plucked up by the roots .... Jude 12

TWIGS
off the top of his young *t* .... Eze 17:4
top of his young *t* a tender one .... Eze 17:22

TWILIGHT
David smote them from the *t* even 1Sa 30:17
And they rose up in the *t*, to go 2Kin 7:5
they arose and fled in the *t* 2Kin 7:7
stars of the *t* thereof be dark .... Job 3:9
the adulterer waiteth for the *t* .... Job 24:15
In the *t*, in the evening, in the .... Prov 7:9
and carry it forth in the *t* .... Eze 12:6
I brought it forth in the *t* .... Eze 12:7
bear upon his shoulder in the *t* .... Eze 12:12

TWINED
with ten curtains of fine *t* linen ..... Ex 26:1
fine *t* linen of cunning work .... Ex 26:31
fine *t* linen, wrought .... Ex 26:36
hangings for the court of fine *t* .... Ex 27:9
fine *t* linen, wrought with .... Ex 27:16
five cubits of fine *t* linen .... Ex 27:18
fine *t* linen, with cunning work .... Ex 28:6
and scarlet, and fine *t* linen .... Ex 28:8
and of scarlet, and of fine *t* linen .... Ex 28:15
made ten curtains of fine *t* linen ...... Ex 36:8
and scarlet, and fine *t* linen .... Ex 36:35
fine *t* linen, of needlework .... Ex 36:37
of the court were of fine *t* linen ...... Ex 38:16
round about were of fine *t* linen .... Ex 38:16
and scarlet, and fine *t* linen .... Ex 38:18
and scarlet, and fine *t* linen .... Ex 39:2
and scarlet, and fine *t* linen .... Ex 39:5
and scarlet, and fine *t* linen .... Ex 39:8
and purple, and scarlet, and *t* linen ... Ex 39:24
and linen breeches of fine *t* linen ..... Ex 39:28

And a girdle of fine *t* linen .... Ex 39:29

TWINKLING
in the *t* of an eye, at the last 1Cor 15:52

TWINS
behold, there were *t* in her womb .... Gen 25:24
that, behold, *t* were in her womb .... Gen 38:27
whereof every one bear *t*, and none ..... Song 4:2
like two young roes that are *t* .... Song 4:5
whereof every one beareth *t* .... Song 6:6
like two young roes that are *t* .... Song 7:3

TWO See PREFACE.

TWOEDGED
mouth, and a *t* sword in their hand ..... Ps 149:6
as wormwood, sharp as a *t* sword .... Prov 5:4
and sharper than any *t* sword .... Heb 4:12
of his mouth went a sharp *t* sword ...... Rev 1:16

TWOFOLD
ye make him *t* more the child of .... Mt 23:15

TYCHICUS (*tik´-ik-us*) A co-worker with Paul.
and of Asia, *T* and Trophimus .... Acts 20:4
know my affairs, and how I do, *T* .... Eph 6:21
from Rome unto the Ephesians by *T* ...... Eph 's
my state shall *T* declare unto you ...... Col 4:7
from Rome to the Colossians by *T* .... Col 's
And *T* have I sent to Ephesus 2Ti 4:12
send Artemas unto thee, or *T* .... Titus 3:12

TYRANNUS (*ti-ran´-nus*) An Ephesian
schoolmaster.
daily in the school of one *T* .... Acts 19:9

TYRE (*tire*) See TYRUS. A coastal city of
Phoenicia.
to Ramah, and to the strong city *T* ..... Josh 19:29
Hiram king of *T* sent messengers 2Sa 5:11
And came to the strong hold of *T* 2Sa 24:7
Hiram king of *T* sent his servants 1Kin 5:1
sent and fetched Hiram out of *T* 1Kin 7:13
and his father was a man of *T* 1Kin 7:14
(Now Hiram the king of *T* had 1Kin 9:11
Hiram came out from *T* to see the 1Kin 9:12
Now Hiram king of *T* sent 1Chr 14:1
they of *T* brought much cedar wood 1Chr 22:4
sent to Huram the king of *T* 2Chr 2:3
the king of *T* answered in writing 2Chr 2:11
Dan, and his father was a man of *T* 2Chr 2:14
them of Zidon, and to them of *T* .... Ezr 3:7
There dwelt men of *T* also therein ...... Neh 13:16
the daughter of *T* shall be there .... Ps 45:12
with the inhabitants of *T* .... Ps 83:7
behold, Philistia, and *T*, with .... Ps 87:4
The burden of *T* .... Is 23:1
sorely pained at the report of *T* .... Is 23:5
hath taken this counsel against *T* ...... Is 23:8
that *T* shall be forgotten seventy ...... Is 23:15
years shall *T* sing as an harlot .... Is 23:15
years, that the LORD will visit *T* ...... Is 23:17
what have ye to do with me, O *T* .... Joel 3:4
done in you, had been done in *T* .... Mt 11:21
It shall be more tolerable for *T* .... Mt 11:22
and departed into the coasts of *T* ...... Mt 15:21
and they about *T* and Sidon, a great .... Mk 3:8
and went into the borders of *T* .... Mk 7:24
departing from the coasts of *T* .... Mk 7:31
and from the sea coast of *T* .... Lk 6:17
mighty works had been done in *T* .... Lk 10:13
it shall be more tolerable for *T* .... Lk 10:14
highly displeased with them of *T* .... Acts 12:20
sailed into Syria, and landed at *T* ..... Acts 21:3
we had finished our course from *T* ...... Acts 21:7

TYRIAN See TYRE.

TYRUS (*ti´-rus*) See TYRE. Same as Tyre.
And all the kings of *T*, and all the .... Jer 25:22
Ammonites, and to the king of *T* .... Jer 27:3
Philistines, and to cut off from *T* ..... Jer 47:4
because that *T* hath said against .... Eze 26:2
Behold, I am against thee, O *T* .... Eze 26:3
they shall destroy the walls of *T* ...... Eze 26:4
Behold, I will bring upon *T* .... Eze 26:7
Thus saith the Lord GOD to *T* .... Eze 26:15
man, take up a lamentation for *T* .... Eze 27:2
And say unto *T*, O thou that art .... Eze 27:3
O *T*, thou hast said, I am of .... Eze 27:3
thy wise men, O *T*, that were in .... Eze 27:8
thee, saying, What city is like *T* ...... Eze 27:32
of man, say unto the prince of *T* .... Eze 28:2
a lamentation upon the king of *T* .... Eze 28:12
serve a great service against *T* .... Eze 29:18
he no wages, nor his army, for *T* .... Eze 29:18
Ephraim, as I saw *T*, is planted .... Hos 9:13
For three transgressions of *T* .... Amos 1:9
will send a fire on the wall of *T* ...... Amos 1:10
and Zidon, though it be very .... Zec 9:2
T did build herself a strong hold ...... Zec 9:3

U

UCAL (*u´-cal*) An obscure name.
Ithiel, even unto Ithiel and U.......... Prov 30:1

UEL (*u´-el*) Married a foreigner in exile.
Maadai, Amram, and U.................... Ezr 10:34

ULAI (*u´-lahee*) A river near Susa.
and I was by the river of U............. Dan 8:2
voice between the banks of U............ Dan 8:16

ULAM (*u´-lam*)
1. A son of Sheresh.
and his sons were U and Rakem 1Chr 7:16
And the sons of U 1Chr 7:17
2. A son of Eshek.
U his firstborn, Jehush the 1Chr 8:39
the sons of U were mighty men of 1Chr 8:40

ULLA (*ul´-lah*)
And the sons of U....................... 1Chr 7:39

UMMAH (*um´-mah*) A city in Asher.
U also, and Aphek, and Rehob .... Josh 19:30

UNACCUSTOMED
as a bullock a *u* to the yoke .... Jer 31:18

UNADVISEDLY
so that he spake *u* with his lips .... Ps 106:33

UNAWARES
Jacob stole away *u* to Laban the .... Gen 31:20
thou hast stolen away *u* to me .... Gen 31:26
which killeth any person at *u* .... Num 35:11
any person *u* may flee thither .... Num 35:15
which should kill his neighbour *u* ...... Deut 4:42
slayer that killeth any person *u* .... Josh 20:3
person at *u* might flee thither .... Josh 20:9
destruction come upon him at *u* .... Ps 35:8
and so that day come upon you *u* .... Lk 21:34
of false brethren *u* brought in .... Gal 2:4
some have entertained angels *u* .... Heb 13:2
there are certain men crept in *u* .... Jude 4

UNBELIEF
works because of their *u* .... Mt 13:58
said unto them, Because of your *u* ...... Mt 17:20
he marvelled because of their *u* .... Mk 6:6
help thou mine *u* .... Mk 9:24
and upbraided them with their *u* .... Mk 16:14
shall their *u* make the faith of .... Rom 3:3
at the promise of God through *u* .... Rom 4:20
because of *u* they were broken off ...... Rom 11:20
if they abide not still in *u* .... Rom 11:23
obtained mercy through their *u* .... Rom 11:30
God hath concluded them all in *u* .... Rom 11:32
because I did it ignorantly in *u* 1Ti 1:13
in any of you an evil heart of *u* .... Heb 3:12
could not enter in because of *u* .... Heb 3:19
entered not in because of *u* .... Heb 4:6
fall after the same example of *u* .... Heb 4:11

UNBELIEVERS
him his portion with the *u* .... Lk 12:46
brother, and that before the *u* 1Cor 6:6
in those that are unlearned, or *u* 1Cor 14:23
unequally yoked together with *u* 2Cor 6:14

UNBELIEVING
But the *u* Jews stirred up the .... Acts 14:2
For the *u* husband is sanctified 1Cor 7:14
the *u* wife is sanctified by the 1Cor 7:14
But if the *u* depart, let him 1Cor 7:15
are defiled and *u* is nothing pure ...... Titus 1:15
But the fearful, and *u*, and the .... Rev 21:8

UNBLAMEABLE
death, to present you holy and *u* .... Col 1:22
hearts *u* in holiness before God 1Th 3:13

UNBLAMEABLY
u we behaved ourselves among you 1Th 2:10

UNCERTAIN
if the trumpet give an *u* sound 1Cor 14:8
highminded, nor trust in *u* riches 1Ti 6:17

UNCERTAINLY
I therefore so run, not as *u* 1Cor 9:26

UNCHANGEABLE
ever, hath an *u* priesthood .... Heb 7:24

UNCIRCUMCISED
the *u* man child whose flesh of .... Gen 17:14
give our sister to one that is *u* .... Gen 34:14
Pharaoh hear me, who am of *u* lips ...... Ex 6:12
the LORD, Behold, I am of *u* lips .... Ex 6:30
for no *u* person shall eat thereof ...... Ex 12:48
count the fruit thereof as *u* .... Lev 19:23
years shall it be as *u* unto you .... Lev 19:23
if then their *u* hearts be humbled ...... Lev 26:41
for they were *u*, because they had ...... Josh 5:7
take a wife of the *u* Philistines .... Judg 14:3
and fall into the hand of the *u* .... Judg 15:18
over unto the garrison of these *u* 1Sa 14:6
for who is this *u* Philistine 1Sa 17:26
this *u* Philistine shall be as one 1Sa 17:36
lest these *u* come and thrust me 1Sa 31:4
the daughters of the *u* triumph 2Sa 1:20
lest these *u* come and abuse me 1Chr 10:4
no more come into thee the *u* .... Is 52:1
behold, their ear is *u*, and they .... Jer 6:10
which are circumcised with the *u* .... Jer 9:25
for all these nations are *u* .... Jer 9:26
of Israel are *u* in the heart .... Jer 9:26
of the *u* by the hand of strangers ...... Eze 28:10
shalt lie in the midst of the *u* .... Eze 31:18
down, and be thou laid with the *u* ...... Eze 32:19
they are gone down, they lie *u* .... Eze 32:21
which are gone down *u*, slain by .... Eze 32:24
all of them *u*, slain by the sword ...... Eze 32:25
all of them *u*, slain by the sword ...... Eze 32:26
mighty that are fallen of the *u* .... Eze 32:27
be broken in the midst of the *u* .... Eze 32:28
they shall lie with the *u* .... Eze 32:29
they lie *u* with them that be .... Eze 32:30
be laid in the midst of the *u* .... Eze 32:32

U

u in heart, and u in flesh .... Eze 44:7
u in heart, nor u in flesh .... Eze 44:9
u in heart and ears, ye do always .... Acts 7:51
Saying, Thou wentest in to men u .... Acts 11:3
faith which he had yet being u .... Rom 4:11
Abraham, which he had being yet u ...... Rom 4:12
let him not become u 1Cor 7:18

UNCIRCUMCISION
law, thy circumcision is made u .... Rom 2:25
Therefore if the u keep the .... Rom 2:26
shall not his u be counted for .... Rom 2:26
shall not u which is by nature, ... Rom 2:27
by faith, and u through faith .... Rom 3:30
only, or upon the u also, ... Rom 4:9
he was in circumcision, or in u .... Rom 4:10
Not in circumcision, but in u .... Rom 4:10
Is any called in u 1Cor 7:18
u is nothing, but the keeping of 1Cor 7:19
of the u was committed unto me. .... Gal 2:7
availeth any thing, nor u .... Gal 5:6
availeth any thing, nor u .... Gal 6:15
who are called U by that which is .... Eph 2:11
the u of your flesh, hath he .... Col 2:13
Greek nor Jew, circumcision nor u .... Col 3:11

UNCLE
the sons of Uzziel the u of Aaron .... Lev 10:4
Either his u, or his uncle's son, ... Lev 25:49
Saul's u said unto him and to his 1Sa 10:14
And Saul's u said, Tell me, I pray 1Sa 10:15
And Saul said unto his u, He told 1Sa 10:16
Abner, the son of Ner, Saul's u 1Sa 14:50
David's u was a counsellor 1Chr 27:32
of Abihail the u of Mordecai .... Est 2:15
thine u shall come unto thee .... Jer 32:7
a man's u shall take him up, and .... Amos 6:10

UNCLEAN
Or if a soul touch any u thing .... Lev 5:2
it be a carcase of an u beast .... Lev 5:2
or a carcase of u cattle .... Lev 5:2
the carcase of u creeping things .... Lev 5:2
he also shall be u, and guilty .... Lev 5:2
any u thing shall not be eaten .... Lev 7:19
soul that shall touch any u thing .... Lev 7:21
of man, or any u beast, or any .... Lev 7:21
or any abominable u thing, ... Lev 7:21
holy and unholy, and between u .... Lev 10:10
he is u unto you .... Lev 11:4
he is u unto you .... Lev 11:5
he is u unto you .... Lev 11:6
he is u to you .... Lev 11:7
they are u to you. .... Lev 11:8
And for these ye shall be u .... Lev 11:24
of them shall be u until the even .... Lev 11:24
clothes, and be u until the even .... Lev 11:25
cheweth the cud, are u unto you .... Lev 11:26
one that toucheth them shall be u .... Lev 11:26
on all four, those are u unto you .... Lev 11:27
carcase shall be u until the even .... Lev 11:27
clothes, and be u until the even .... Lev 11:28
they are u unto you .... Lev 11:28
These also shall be u unto you .... Lev 11:29
These are u to you among all that. .... Lev 11:31
shall be u until the even .... Lev 11:31
dead, doth fall, it shall be u .... Lev 11:32
it shall be u until the even. .... Lev 11:32
whatsoever is in it shall be u .... Lev 11:33
such water cometh shall be u .... Lev 11:34
in every such vessel shall be u .... Lev 11:34
their carcase falleth shall be u .... Lev 11:35
for they are u, and shall be .... Lev 11:35
and shall be u unto you. .... Lev 11:35
toucheth their carcase shall be u .... Lev 11:36
thereon, it shall be u unto you .... Lev 11:38
thereof shall be u until the even .... Lev 11:39
clothes, and be u until the even .... Lev 11:40
clothes, and be u until the even .... Lev 11:40
ye make yourselves with them. .... Lev 11:43
make a difference between the u .... Lev 11:47
then she shall be u seven days .... Lev 12:2
for her infirmity shall she be u .... Lev 12:2
then she shall be u two weeks. .... Lev 12:5
look on him, and pronounce him u .... Lev 13:3
the priest shall pronounce him u .... Lev 13:8
the priest shall pronounce him u .... Lev 13:11
for he is u .... Lev 13:11
appeareth in him, he shall be u .... Lev 13:14
flesh, and pronounce him to be u .... Lev 13:15
for the raw flesh is u .... Lev 13:15
the priest shall pronounce him u .... Lev 13:20
the priest shall pronounce him u .... Lev 13:22
when the u spot had torn him, ... Lev 13:25
the priest shall pronounce him u .... Lev 13:27
the priest shall pronounce him u .... Lev 13:30
He is a leprous man, he is u .... Lev 13:44
shall pronounce him utterly u .... Lev 13:44
lip, and shall cry, U, u, ... Lev 13:45
he is u .... Lev 13:46
it is u .... Lev 13:51
it is u .... Lev 13:55
it clean, or to pronounce it u .... Lev 13:59
is in the house be not made u .... Lev 14:36
into an u place without the city .... Lev 14:40
without the city into an u place .... Lev 14:41
it is u .... Lev 14:44
out of the city into an u place .... Lev 14:45
shut up shall be u until the even .... Lev 14:46
To teach when it is u, and when it .... Lev 14:57
because of his issue he is u .... Lev 15:2

lieth that hath the issue, is u .... Lev 15:4
whereon he sitteth, shall be u .... Lev 15:4
in water, and be u until the even .... Lev 15:5
in water, and be u until the even .... Lev 15:6
in water, and be u until the even .... Lev 15:7
in water, and be u until the even .... Lev 15:8
that hath the issue shall be u .... Lev 15:9
him shall be u until the even. .... Lev 15:10
in water, and be u until the even .... Lev 15:10
in water, and be u until the even .... Lev 15:11
in water, and be u until the even .... Lev 15:16
water, and be u until the even .... Lev 15:17
in water, and be u until the even .... Lev 15:18
her shall be u until the even .... Lev 15:19
upon in her separation shall be u .... Lev 15:20
that she sitteth upon shall be u .... Lev 15:20
in water, and be u until the even .... Lev 15:21
in water, and be u until the even .... Lev 15:22
he shall be u until the even .... Lev 15:23
him, he shall be u seven days. .... Lev 15:24
bed whereon he lieth shall be u .... Lev 15:24
she shall be u .... Lev 15:25
she sitteth upon shall be u .... Lev 15:26
toucheth those things shall be u .... Lev 15:27
in water, and be u until the even .... Lev 15:27
him that lieth with her that is u .... Lev 15:33
in water, and be u until the even .... Lev 17:15
brother's wife, it is an u thing. .... Lev 20:21
between clean beasts and u .... Lev 20:25
and between u fowls. .... Lev 20:25
I have separated from you as u .... Lev 20:25
any thing that is u by the dead .... Lev 22:4
thing, whereby he may be made u .... Lev 22:5
any such shall be u until even .... Lev 22:6
And if it be any u beast, of which. .... Lev 27:11
And if it be of an u beast .... Lev 27:27
not make himself u for his father .... Num 6:7
to be by reason of a dead body .... Num 9:10
the firstling of u beasts shalt .... Num 18:15
priest shall be u until the even .... Num 19:7
shall be u until the even .... Num 19:8
clothes, and be u until the even .... Num 19:10
of any man shall be u seven days .... Num 19:11
sprinkled upon him, he shall be u .... Num 19:13
the tent, shall be u seven days .... Num 19:14
no covering bound upon it, is u .... Num 19:15
or a grave, shall be u seven days .... Num 19:16
for an u person they shall take. .... Num 19:17
upon the u on the third day .... Num 19:19
But the man that shall be u .... Num 19:20
he is u .... Num 19:20
separation shall be u until even. .... Num 19:21
whatsoever the u person toucheth .... Num 19:22
person toucheth shall be u .... Num 19:22
toucheth it shall be u until even .... Num 19:22
the u and the clean may eat .... Deut 12:15
the u and the clean shall eat of .... Deut 12:22
therefore they are u unto you. .... Deut 14:7
not the cud, it is u unto you .... Deut 14:8
it is u unto you. .... Deut 14:10
thing that flieth is u unto you .... Deut 14:19
the u and the clean person shall .... Deut 15:22
that he see no u thing in thee .... Deut 23:14
away ought thereof for any u use .... Deut 26:14
the land of your possession be u .... Josh 22:19
drink, and eat not any u thing .... Judg 13:4
drink, neither eat any u thing .... Judg 13:7
strong drink, nor eat any u thing .... Judg 13:14
that none which was u in any 2Chr 23:19
is an u land with the filthiness .... Ezr 9:11
bring a clean thing out of an u .... Job 14:4
and their life is among the u .... Job 36:14
good and to the clean, and to the u ..... Eccl 9:2
because I am a man of u lips. .... Is 6:5
the midst of a people of u lips .... Is 6:5
the u shall not pass over it. .... Is 35:8
thee the uncircumcised and the u .... Is 52:1
out from thence, touch no u thing. .... Is 52:11
But we are all as an u thing, ... Is 64:6
it is u .... Lam 4:15
shewed difference between the u .... Eze 22:26
them to discern between the u .... Eze 44:23
they shall eat u things in .... Hos 9:3
If one that is u by a dead body .... Hag 2:13
touch any of these, shall it be u .... Hag 2:13
answered and said, It shall be u .... Hag 2:13
that which they offer there is u .... Hag 2:14
the u spirit to pass out of the .... Zec 13:2
gave them power against u spirits. ...... Mt 10:1
When the u spirit is gone out of. .... Mt 12:43
synagogue a man with an u spirit .... Mk 1:23
when the u spirit had torn him, ... Mk 1:26
commandeth he even the u spirits .... Mk 1:27
u spirits, when they saw him, ... Mk 3:11
they said, He hath an u spirit .... Mk 3:30
the tombs a man with an u spirit .... Mk 5:2
out of the man, thou u spirit .... Mk 5:8
the u spirits went out, and .... Mk 5:13
and gave them power over u spirits. .... Mk 6:7
young daughter had an u spirit, ... Mk 7:25
which had a spirit of an u devil .... Lk 4:33
power he commandeth the u spirits ...... Lk 4:36
that were vexed with u spirits .... Lk 6:18
(For he had commanded the u .... Lk 8:29
And Jesus rebuked the u spirit .... Lk 9:42
When the u spirit is gone out of .... Lk 11:24
which were vexed with u spirits .... Acts 5:16
For u spirits, crying with loud .... Acts 8:7
any thing that is common or u .... Acts 10:14
not call any man common or u .... Acts 10:28

for nothing common or u hath at .... Acts 11:8
that there is nothing u of itself .... Rom 14:14
that esteemeth any thing to be u .... Rom 14:14
to him it is u .... Rom 14:14
else were your children u 1Cor 7:14
Lord, and touch not the u thing 2Cor 6:17
nor u person, nor covetous man, ... Eph 5:5
of an heifer sprinkling the u .... Heb 9:13
I saw three u spirits like frogs. .... Rev 16:13
foul spirit, and a cage of every u .... Rev 18:2

UNCLEANNESS
Or if he touch the u of man .... Lev 5:3
whatsoever u it be that a man .... Lev 5:3
the Lord, having his u upon him .... Lev 7:20
unclean thing, as the u of man .... Lev 7:21
that is to be cleansed from his u .... Lev 14:19
this shall be his u in his issue. .... Lev 15:3
from his issue, it is his u .... Lev 15:3
her u shall be as the days of her .... Lev 15:25
as the u of her separation .... Lev 15:26
the Lord for the issue of her u .... Lev 15:30
children of Israel from their u .... Lev 15:31
that they die not in their u .... Lev 15:31
because of the u of the children .... Lev 16:16
them in the midst of their u .... Lev 16:16
hallow it from the u of the .... Lev 16:19
as she is put apart for her u .... Lev 18:19
the Lord, having his u upon him .... Lev 22:3
or a man of whom he may take u .... Lev 22:5
whatsoever u he hath .... Lev 22:5
to u with another instead of thy .... Num 5:19
his u is yet upon him .... Num 19:13
of u that chanceth him by night .... Deut 23:10
he hath found some u in her .... Deut 24:1
for she was purified from her u 2Sa 11:4
brought out all the u that they 2Chr 29:16
one end to another with their u .... Ezr 9:11
me as the u of a removed woman .... Eze 36:17
According to their u and according ...... Eze 39:24
of Jerusalem for sin and for u .... Zec 13:1
of dead men's bones, and of all u .... Mt 23:27
God also gave them up to u .... Rom 1:24
your members servants to u .... Rom 6:19
and have not repented of the u 2Cor 12:21
Adultery, fornication, u, ... Gal 5:19
to work all u with greediness .... Eph 4:19
But fornication, and all u .... Eph 5:3
fornication, u, inordinate .... Col 3:5
was not of deceit, nor of u 1Th 2:3
For God hath not called us unto u 1Th 4:7
after the flesh in the lust of u 2Pet 2:10

UNCLEANNESSES
also save you from all your u .... Eze 36:29

UNCLE'S
a man shall lie with his u wife .... Lev 20:20
hath uncovered his u nakedness. .... Lev 20:20
Either his uncle, or his u son, ... Lev 25:49
that is, Esther, his u daughter .... Est 2:7
So Hanameel mine u son came to me ... Jer 32:8
the field of Hanameel my u son .... Jer 32:9
the sight of Hanameel mine u son .... Jer 32:12

UNCLOTHED
not for that we would be u 2Cor 5:4

UNCOMELY
himself u toward his virgin 1Cor 7:36
our u parts have more abundant. 1Cor 12:23

UNCONDEMNED
They have beaten us openly u .... Acts 16:37
a man that is a Roman, and u .... Acts 22:25

UNCORRUPTIBLE
changed the glory of the u God. .... Rom 1:23

UNCORRUPTNESS
in doctrine shewing u, gravity, ... Titus 2:7

UNCOVER
U not your heads, neither rend. .... Lev 10:6
kin to him, to u their nakedness .... Lev 18:6
of thy mother, shalt thou not u .... Lev 18:7
thou shalt not u her nakedness .... Lev 18:7
father's wife shalt thou not u .... Lev 18:8
their nakedness thou shalt not u. .... Lev 18:9
their nakedness thou shalt not u. .... Lev 18:10
thou shalt not u her nakedness. .... Lev 18:11
Thou shalt not u the nakedness of ...... Lev 18:12
Thou shalt not u the nakedness of ...... Lev 18:13
Thou shalt not u the nakedness of ...... Lev 18:14
thou shalt not u her nakedness. .... Lev 18:15
Thou shalt not u the nakedness .... Lev 18:16
Thou shalt not u her nakedness. .... Lev 18:16
Thou shalt not u the nakedness of ...... Lev 18:17
daughter, to u her nakedness; .... Lev 18:17
to u her nakedness, beside the .... Lev 18:18
unto a woman to u her nakedness. ...... Lev 18:19
and shall u her nakedness. .... Lev 20:18
thou shalt not u the nakedness of .... Lev 20:19
garments, shall not u his head .... Lev 21:10
u the woman's head, and put the .... Num 5:18
u his feet, and lay thee down. .... Ruth 3:4
u thy locks, make bare the leg, ... Is 47:2
u the thigh, pass over the rivers .... Is 47:2
for he shall u the cedar work .... Zeph 2:14

UNCOVERED
and he was u within his tent .... Gen 9:21
hath u his father's nakedness. .... Lev 20:11
he hath u his sister's nakedness .... Lev 20:17
she hath u the fountain of her .... Lev 20:18

he hath *u* his uncle's nakedness......... Lev 20:20
he hath *u* his brother's nakedness..... Lev 20:21
u his feet, and laid her down .... Ruth 3:7
of Israel today, who *u* himself 2Sa 6:20
even with their buttocks *u* .... Is 20:4
and horsemen, and Kir *u* the shield ...... Is 22:6
Thy nakedness shall be *u*, yea,............... Is 47:3
I have *u* his secret places, and he ...... Jer 49:10
and thine arm shall be *u*, and thou....... Eze 4:7
also, and let thy foreskin be *u* .... Hab 2:16
they *u* the roof where he was.................. Mk 2:4
her head *u* dishonoureth her head...... 1Cor 11:5
that a woman pray unto God *u* 1Cor 11:13

UNCOVERETH

for he *u* his near kin................................ Lev 20:19
because he *u* his father's skirt .... Deut 27:20
fellows shamelessly *u* himself 2Sa 6:20

UNCTION

But ye have an *u* from the Holy 1Jn 2:20

UNDEFILED

Blessed are the *u* in the way .... Ps 119:1
my sister, my love, my dove, my *u* ...... Song 5:2
My dove, my *u* is but one .... Song 6:9
us, who is holy, harmless, *u*, ... Heb 7:26
honourable in all, and the bed *u* .... Heb 13:4
u before God and the Father is........... Jas 1:27
inheritance incorruptible, and *u* 1Pet 1:4

UNDER

u the firmament from the waters .... Gen 1:7
Let the waters *u* the heaven be .... Gen 1:9
the breath of life, from *u* heaven......... Gen 6:17
that were *u* the whole heaven,.............. Gen 7:19
and submit thyself *u* her hands .... Gen 16:9
and rest yourselves *u* the tree............ Gen 18:4
and he stood by them *u* the tree .... Gen 18:8
came they *u* the shadow of my roof.... Gen 19:8
the child *u* one of the shrubs.............. Gen 21:15
I pray thee, thy hand *u* my thigh........ Gen 24:2
the servant put his hand *u* the .... Gen 24:9
Jacob hid them *u* the oak which .... Gen 35:4
buried beneath Beth-el *u* an oak .... Gen 35:8
to any thing that was *u* him .... Gen 39:23
lay up corn *u* the hand of Pharaoh .... Gen 41:35
I pray thee, thy hand *u* my thigh .... Gen 47:29
of the deep that lieth *u*,........................ Gen 49:25
I will bring you out from *u* the .... Ex 6:6
which bringeth you out from *u* the ...... Ex 6:7
took a stone, and put it *u* him .... Ex 17:12
of Amalek from *u* heaven .... Ex 17:14
from *u* the hand of the Egyptians .... Ex 18:10
that is in the water *u* the earth .... Ex 20:4
with a rod, and he die *u* his hand ..... Ex 21:20
hateth thee lying *u* his burden............ Ex 23:5
and builded an altar *u* the hill,........... Ex 24:4
there was *u* his feet as it were a .... Ex 24:10
there shall be a knop *u* two,................ Ex 25:35
a knop *u* two branches of the same .. Ex 25:35
a knop *u* two branches of the same .. Ex 25:35
of silver *u* the twenty boards .... Ex 26:19
two sockets *u* one board for his .... Ex 26:19
two sockets *u* another board for......... Ex 26:19
two sockets *u* one board .... Ex 26:21
two sockets *u* another board............... Ex 26:21
two sockets *u* one board .... Ex 26:25
two sockets *u* another board............... Ex 26:25
hang up the vail *u* the taches .... Ex 26:33
thou shalt put it *u* the compass .... Ex 27:5
thou make to it *u* the crown of it....... Ex 30:4
be made *u* the twenty boards .... Ex 36:24
two sockets *u* one board for his .... Ex 36:24
two sockets *u* another board for......... Ex 36:24
two sockets *u* one board .... Ex 36:26
two sockets *u* another board............... Ex 36:26
u every board two sockets .... Ex 36:30
a knop *u* two branches of the same .. Ex 37:21
a knop *u* two branches of the same .. Ex 37:21
a knop *u* two branches of the same .. Ex 37:21
gold for it *u* the crown thereof............ Ex 37:27
u the compass thereof beneath .... Ex 38:4
toucheth any thing that was *u* him ... Lev 15:10
it shall be seven days *u* the dam .... Lev 22:27
of whatsoever passeth *u* the rod......... Lev 27:32
u the custody and charge of the .... Num 3:36
their charge shall be *u* the hand .... Num 4:28
the hand of Ithamar the son of............. Num 4:33
is *u* the sacrifice of the peace .... Num 6:18
u the hand of Ithamar the son of .... Num 7:8
clave asunder that was *u* them .... Num 16:31
the LORD, she fell down *u* Balaam ..... Num 22:27
men of war which are *u* our charge... Num 31:49
their armies *u* the hand of Moses ..... Num 33:1
that are *u* the whole heaven .... Deut 2:25
u Ashdoth-pisgah eastward.................. Deut 3:17
came near and stood *u* the mountain. Deut 4:11
all nations *u* the whole heaven .... Deut 4:19
plain, *u* the springs of Pisgah .... Deut 4:49
destroy their name from *u* heaven ..... Deut 7:24
blot out their name from *u* heaven .... Deut 9:14
the hills, and *u* every green tree....... Deut 12:2
of Amalek from *u* heaven .... Deut 25:19
the earth that is *u* thee shall be .... Deut 28:23
blot out his name from *u* heaven .... Deut 29:20
of my tent, and the silver *u* it .... Josh 7:21
in his tent, and the silver *u* it .... Josh 7:22
to the Hivite *u* Hermon in the............ Josh 11:3
valley of Lebanon *u* mount Hermon .. Josh 11:17
from the south, *u* Ashdoth-pisgah ...... Josh 12:3
from Baal-gad *u* mount Hermon unto. Josh 13:5

unto this day, and serve *u* tribute ...... Josh 16:10
and set it up *u* an oak .... Josh 24:26
gathered their meat *u* my table .... Judg 1:7
he did gird it *u* his raiment upon....... Judg 3:16
that day *u* the hand of Israel .... Judg 3:30
she dwelt *u* the palm tree of .... Judg 4:5
sat *u* an oak which was in Ophrah, ... Judg 6:11
brought it out unto him *u* the oak ..... Judg 6:19
to God this people were *u* my hand ... Judg 9:29
u whose wings thou art come to .... Ruth 2:12
them, until they came *u* Beth-car...... 1Sa 7:11
a pomegranate tree which is in............. 1Sa 14:2
therefore what is *u* thine hand........... 1Sa 21:3
is no common bread a mine hand 1Sa 21:4
is there not here a thine hand............... 1Sa 21:8
abode in Gibeah *u* a tree in Ramah.. 1Sa 22:6
buried them *u* a tree at Jabesh,........ 1Sa 31:13
spear smote him *u* the fifth rib 2Sa 2:23
smote him there *u* the fifth rib........... 2Sa 3:27
and they smote him *u* the fifth rib..... 2Sa 4:6
were therein, and put them *u* saws... 2Sa 12:31
u harrows of iron, and *u* axes 2Sa 12:31
of the people *u* the hand of Joab...... 2Sa 18:2
a third part *u* the hand of 2Sa 18:2
a third part *u* the hand of Ittai 2Sa 18:2
the mule went *u* the thick boughs...... 2Sa 18:9
the mule that was *u* him went away ... 2Sa 18:9
and darkness was *u* his feet............... 2Sa 22:10
Thou hast enlarged my steps *u* me.... 2Sa 22:37
yea, they are fallen *u* my feet 2Sa 22:39
against me hast thou subdued *u* me.. 2Sa 22:40
bringeth down the people *u* me 2Sa 22:48
safely, every man *u* his vine 1Kin 4:25
u his fig tree, from Dan even to 1Kin 4:25
put them *u* the soles of his feet 1Kin 5:3
u the brim of it round about.............. 1Kin 7:24
u the laver were undersetters............ 1Kin 7:30
u the borders were four wheels........... 1Kin 7:32
one sea, and twelve oxen *u* the sea .. 1Kin 7:44
even *u* the wings of the cherubims.... 1Kin 8:6
and found him sitting *u* an oak 1Kin 13:14
high hill, and *u* every green tree........ 1Kin 14:23
lay it on wood, and put no fire *u*....... 1Kin 18:23
lay it on wood, and put no fire *u* 1Kin 18:25
of your gods, but put no fire *u*........... 1Kin 18:25
sat down *u* a juniper tree.................... 1Kin 19:4
slept *u* a juniper tree, behold, ... 1Kin 19:5
revolted from *u* the hand of Judah ... 2Kin 8:20
Yet Edom revolted from *u* the hand... 2Kin 8:22
put it *u* him on the top of the 2Kin 9:13
and he trode her *u* foot 2Kin 9:33
from *u* the hand of the Syrians........... 2Kin 13:5
the name of Israel from *u* heaven 2Kin 14:27
the hills, and *u* every green tree........ 2Kin 16:4
the brasen oxen that were *u* it........... 2Kin 16:17
u the hand of Pharaoh king................ 2Kin 17:7
high hill, and *u* every green tree........ 2Kin 17:10
their bones *u* the oak in Jabesh........ 1Chr 10:12
of the LORD remaineth *u* curtains...... 1Chr 17:1
u Aaron their father, as the LORD..... 1Chr 24:19
the sons of Asaph *u* the hands of 1Chr 25:2
u the hands of their father 1Chr 25:3
All these were *u* the hands of............ 1Chr 25:6
it was *u* the hand of Shelomith,......... 1Chr 26:28
them from twenty years old and *u* 2Chr 31:16
u it was the similitude of oxen, ... 2Chr 4:3
One sea, and twelve oxen *u* it 2Chr 4:15
even *u* the wings of the cherubims.... 2Chr 5:7
were brought *u* at that time 2Chr 13:18
from *u* the dominion of Judah 2Chr 21:8
So the Edomites revolted from *u* 2Chr 21:10
did Libnah revolt from *u* his hand..... 2Chr 21:10
u the hand of Hananiah, one of......... 2Chr 26:11
u their hand was an army, three,........ 2Chr 26:13
the hills, and *u* every green tree........ 2Chr 28:4
to keep *u* the children of Judah 2Chr 28:10
were overseers *u* the hand of............. 2Chr 34:12
the beast that was *u* me to pass........ Neh 2:14
made booths, and sat *u* the booths.... Neh 8:17
the proud helpers do stoop *u* him ..... Job 9:13
though he hide it *u* his tongue .... Job 20:12
are formed from *u* the waters............ Job 26:5
and the cloud is not rent *u* them...... Job 26:8
u it is turned up as it were fire .... Job 28:5
and seeth *u* the whole heaven............ Job 28:24
u the nettles they were gathered ...... Job 30:7
He directeth it *u* the whole.............. Job 37:3
He lieth *u* the shady trees, in............ Job 40:21
whatsoever is *u* the whole heaven ...... Job 41:11
Sharp stones are *u* him .... Job 41:30
hast put all things *u* his feet .... Ps 8:6
u his tongue is mischief and .... Ps 10:7
hide me *u* the shadow of thy wings.... Ps 17:8
and darkness was *u* his feet............... Ps 18:9
Thou hast enlarged my steps *u* me.... Ps 18:36
they are fallen *u* my feet .... Ps 18:38
thou hast subdued *u* me those that... Ps 18:39
me, and subdueth the people *u* me... Ps 18:47
trust *u* the shadow of thy wings........ Ps 36:7
them *u* that rise up against us,.......... Ps 44:5
whereby the people fall *u* thee .... Ps 45:5
He shall subdue the people *u* us....... Ps 47:3
us, and the nations *u* our feet .... Ps 47:3
u the shadow of the Almighty............. Ps 91:1
thine wings shalt thou trust *u* .... Ps 91:4
dragon shalt thou trample *u* feet ...... Ps 91:13
into subjection *u* thine hand............... Ps 106:42
adders' poison is *u* their lips.............. Ps 140:3
who subdueth my people *u* me .... Ps 144:2
the slothful shall be *u* tribute .... Prov 12:24

he take away thy bed from *u* thee...... Prov 22:27
labour which he taketh *u* the sun....... Eccl 1:3
there is no new thing *u* the sun.......... Eccl 1:9
all things that are done *u* heaven....... Eccl 1:13
the works that are done *u* the sun...... Eccl 1:14
which they should do *u* the heaven.... Eccl 2:3
and there was no profit *u* the sun....... Eccl 2:11
the work that is wrought *u* the .... Eccl 2:17
which I had taken *u* the sun............... Eccl 2:18
have shewed myself wise *u* the sun.... Eccl 2:19
the labour which I took *u* the sun ..... Eccl 2:20
he hath laboured *u* the sun................. Eccl 2:22
to every purpose *u* the heaven .... Eccl 3:1
moreover I saw *u* the sun the .... Eccl 3:16
that are done *u* the sun .... Eccl 4:1
evil work that is done *u* the sun......... Eccl 4:3
and I saw vanity *u* the sun.................. Eccl 4:7
the living which walk *u* the sun .... Eccl 4:15
evil which I have seen *u* the sun......... Eccl 5:13
u the sun all the days of his .... Eccl 5:18
evil which I have seen *u* the sun......... Eccl 6:1
what shall be after him *u* the sun....... Eccl 6:12
the crackling of thorns *u* a pot .... Eccl 7:6
every work that is done *u* the sun....... Eccl 8:9
hath no better thing *u* the sun .... Eccl 8:15
which God giveth him *u* the sun......... Eccl 8:15
the work that is done *u* the sun.......... Eccl 8:17
that are done *u* the sun .... Eccl 9:3
any thing that is done *u* the sun........ Eccl 9:6
he hath given thee *u* the sun.............. Eccl 9:9
which thou takest *u* the sun .... Eccl 9:9
saw *u* the sun, that the race is........... Eccl 9:11
wisdom have I seen *u* the sun............. Eccl 9:13
evil which I have seen *u* the sun......... Eccl 10:5
I sat down *u* his shadow with .... Song 2:3
his left hand is *u* my head .... Song 2:6
honey and milk are *u* thy tongue .... Song 4:11
His left hand should be *u* my head..... Song 8:3
I raised thee up *u* the apple tree .... Song 8:5
and let this ruin be *u* thy hand .... Is 3:6
shall bow down *u* the prisoners........... Is 10:4
and they shall fall *u* the slain .... Is 10:4
u his glory he shall kindle a .... Is 10:16
the worm is spread *u* thee,................. Is 14:11
as a carcase trodden *u* feet .... Is 14:19
my mountains tread him *u* foot .... Is 14:25
meted out and trodden *u* foot .... Is 18:7
defiled *u* the inhabitants thereof......... Is 24:5
Moab shall be trodden down *u* him ... Is 25:10
Ephraim, shall be trodden *u* feet .... Is 28:3
a falsehood have we hid ourselves........ Is 28:15
and hatch, and gather *u* her shadow.. Is 34:15
with idols *u* every green tree............. Is 57:5
valleys in the clifts of the rocks........... Is 57:5
spread sackcloth and ashes *u* him ..... Is 58:5
u every green tree thou wanderest ..... Jer 2:20
u every green tree, and there hath .... Jer 3:6
the strangers *u* every green tree .... Jer 3:13
earth, and from *u* these heavens .... Jer 10:11
have trodden my portion *u* foot.......... Jer 12:10
that will not put their neck *u* .... Jer 27:8
nations that bring their neck *u* .... Jer 27:11
Bring your necks *u* the yoke of .... Jer 27:12
shall the flocks pass again *u* the .... Jer 33:13
house of the king *u* the treasury .... Jer 38:11
thine armholes *u* the cords .... Jer 38:12
They that fled stood *u* the shadow .... Jer 48:45
bulls that were *u* the bases .... Lam 1:14
The Lord hath trodden *u* foot all........ Lam 1:15
To crush *u* his feet all the .... Lam 3:34
from *u* the heavens of the LORD .... Lam 3:66
U his shadow we shall live among .... Lam 4:20
Our necks are *u* persecution............... Lam 5:5
the princes fell *u* the wood................. Lam 5:13
they had the hands of a man *u* .... Eze 1:8
u the firmament were their wings........ Eze 1:23
u every green tree .... Eze 6:13
every thick oak, the place .... Eze 6:13
even *u* the cherub, and fill thine........ Eze 10:2
of man's hand *u* their wings................ Eze 10:8
the God of Israel be *u* their .... Eze 10:20
hands of a man was *u* their wings...... Eze 10:21
and the roots thereof were *u* him....... Eze 17:6
it it shall dwell all fowl of...................... Eze 17:23
will cause you to pass *u* the rod........ Eze 20:37
and burn also the bones *u* .... Eze 24:5
u his branches did all the beasts....... Eze 31:6
u his shadow dwelt all great............... Eze 31:17
that dwelt *u* his shadow in................. Eze 31:17
laid their swords *u* their heads........... Eze 32:27
from *u* these chambers was the .... Eze 42:9
places *u* the rows round about........... Eze 46:23
waters issued out from *u* the .... Eze 47:1
the waters came down from *u* from... Eze 47:1
of the field had shadow *u* it .... Dan 4:12
let the beasts get away from *u* it....... Dan 4:14
which *u* the beasts of the field .... Dan 4:21
of the kingdom *u* the whole heaven ... Dan 7:27
and the host to be trodden *u* foot ..... Dan 8:13
for *u* the whole heaven hath not .... Dan 9:12
gone a whoring from *u* their God .... Hos 4:12
u oaks and poplars and elms,............. Hos 4:13
They that dwell *u* his shadow .... Hos 14:7
The seed is rotten *u* their clods......... Joel 1:17
Behold, I am pressed *u* you .... Amos 2:13
bread have laid a wound *u* thee......... Obad 7
sat *u* it in the shadow, till he .... Jonah 4:5
mountains shall be molten *u* him ...... Mic 1:4
u his vine and *u* his fig tree............. Mic 4:4
man his neighbour *u* the vine .... Zec 3:10

u the vine and u the fig tree.	Zec 3:10
for they shall be ashes u the	Mal 4:3
thereof, from two years old and u........	Mt 2:16
and to be trodden u foot of men........	Mt 5:13
put it u a bushel, but on a........	Mt 5:15
they trample them u their feet........	Mt 7:6
thou shouldest come u my roof........	Mt 8:8
For I am a man u authority........	Mt 8:9
authority, having soldiers u me........	Mt 8:9
her chickens u her wings, and ye........	Mt 23:37
be put u a bushel, or u a bed........	Mk 4:21
air may lodge u the shadow of it........	Mk 4:32
shake off the dust u your feet........	Mk 6:11
yet the dogs u the table eat of........	Mk 7:28
thou shouldest enter u my roof........	Lk 7:6
I also am a man set u authority........	Lk 7:8
having u me soldiers, and I say........	Lk 7:8
a vessel, or putteth it u a bed........	Lk 8:16
neither u a bushel, but on a........	Lk 11:33
doth gather her brood u her wings........	Lk 13:34
out of the one part u heaven........	Lk 17:24
unto the other part u heaven........	Lk 17:24
when thou wast u the fig tree........	Jn 1:48
I saw thee u the fig tree........	Jn 1:50
men, out of every nation u heaven........	Acts 2:5
name u heaven given among men........	Acts 4:12
an eunuch of great authority u........	Acts 8:27
and bound themselves u a curse........	Acts 23:12
bound ourselves u a great curse........	Acts 23:14
from thence, we sailed u Cyprus........	Acts 27:4
suffering us, we sailed u Crete........	Acts 27:7
running u a certain island which........	Acts 27:16
u colour as though they would........	Acts 27:30
Gentiles, that they are all u sin........	Rom 3:9
poison of asps is u their lips........	Rom 3:13
saith to them who are u the law........	Rom 3:19
not u the law, but u grace........	Rom 6:14
not u the law, but u grace........	Rom 6:15
but I am carnal, sold u sin........	Rom 7:14
bruise Satan u your feet shortly........	Rom 16:20
not be brought u the power of any........	1Cor 6:12
is not u bondage in such cases........	1Cor 7:15
to them that are u the law........	1Cor 9:20
as u the law, that I might gain........	1Cor 9:20
gain them that are u the law........	1Cor 9:20
but u the law to Christ,) that I........	1Cor 9:21
But I keep u my body, and bring it........	1Cor 9:27
all our fathers were u the cloud........	1Cor 10:1
are commanded to be u obedience........	1Cor 14:34
hath put all enemies u his feet........	1Cor 15:25
he hath put all things u his feet........	1Cor 15:27
he saith all things are put u him........	1Cor 15:27
which did put all things u him........	1Cor 15:27
him that put all things u him........	1Cor 15:27
In Damascus the governor u Aretas........	2Cor 11:32
works of the law are u the curse........	Gal 3:10
hath concluded all u sin, that........	Gal 3:22
came, we were kept u the law........	Gal 3:23
we are no longer u a schoolmaster........	Gal 3:25
But is u tutors and governors........	Gal 4:2
were in bondage u the elements of........	Gal 4:3
made of a woman, made u the law........	Gal 4:4
redeem them that were u the law........	Gal 4:5
ye that desire to be u the law........	Gal 4:21
the Spirit, ye are not u the law........	Gal 5:18
And hath put all things u his feet........	Eph 1:22
in earth, and things u the earth........	Phil 2:10
every creature which is u heaven........	Col 1:23
the number u threescore years old........	1Ti 5:9
as are u the yoke count their own........	1Ti 6:1
things in subjection u his feet........	Heb 2:8
he put all in subjection u him........	Heb 2:8
nothing that is not put u him........	Heb 2:8
see not yet all things put u him........	Heb 2:8
(for u it the people received the........	Heb 7:11
that were u the first testament........	Heb 9:15
mercy u two or three witnesses........	Heb 10:28
who hath trodden u foot the Son........	Heb 10:29
or sit here u my footstool........	Jas 2:3
u the mighty hand of God, that he........	1Pet 5:6
u darkness unto the judgment of........	Jude 6
neither u the earth, was able to........	Rev 5:3
u the earth, and such as are in........	Rev 5:13
I saw u the altar the souls of........	Rev 6:9
shall they tread u foot forty........	Rev 11:2
the sun, and the moon u her feet........	Rev 12:1

UNDERGIRDING
up, they used helps, u the ship........	Acts 27:17

UNDERNEATH
on the two sides of the ephod u........	Ex 28:27
on the two sides of the ephod u........	Ex 39:20
u are the everlasting arms........	Deut 33:27

UNDERSETTERS
and the four corners thereof had u........	1Kin 7:30
under the laver were u molten........	1Kin 7:30
there were four u to the four........	1Kin 7:34
the u were of the very base........	1Kin 7:34

UNDERSTAND
that they may not u one another's........	Gen 11:7
that thou canst u a dream to........	Gen 41:15
then ye shall u that these men........	Num 16:30
U therefore this day, that the........	Deut 9:3
U therefore, that the LORD thy........	Deut 9:6
whose tongue thou shalt not u........	Deut 28:49
for we u it........	2Kin 18:26
the LORD made me u in writing by........	1Chr 28:19
the women, and those that could u........	Neh 8:3
caused the people to u the law........	Neh 8:7

and caused them to u the reading........	Neh 8:8
even to u the words of the law........	Neh 8:13
cause me to u wherein I have........	Job 6:24
u what he would say unto me........	Job 23:5
thunder of his power who can u........	Job 26:14
neither do the aged u judgment........	Job 32:9
Also can any u the spreadings of........	Job 36:29
see if there were any that did u........	Ps 14:2
Who can u his errors........	Ps 19:12
see if there were any that did u........	Ps 53:2
know not, neither will they u........	Ps 82:5
neither doth a fool u this........	Ps 92:6
U, ye brutish among the people........	Ps 94:8
things, even they shall u the........	Ps 107:43
Make me to u the way of thy........	Ps 119:27
I u more than the ancients........	Ps 119:100
To u a proverb, and the........	Prov 1:6
Then shalt thou u the fear of the........	Prov 2:5
Then shalt thou u righteousness........	Prov 2:9
O ye simple, u wisdom........	Prov 8:5
of the prudent is to u his way........	Prov 14:8
and he will u knowledge........	Prov 19:25
how can a man then u his own way........	Prov 20:24
Evil men u not judgment........	Prov 28:5
that seek the LORD u all things........	Prov 28:5
for though he u he will not........	Prov 29:19
people, Hear ye indeed, but u not........	Is 6:9
u with their heart, and convert,........	Is 6:10
whom shall he make to u doctrine........	Is 28:9
a vexation only to u the report........	Is 28:19
of the rash shall u knowledge........	Is 32:4
tongue, that thou canst not u........	Is 33:19
for we u it........	Is 36:11
u together, that the hand of the........	Is 41:20
and believe me, and u that I am he........	Is 43:10
their hearts, that they cannot u........	Is 44:18
they are shepherds that cannot u........	Is 56:11
is the wise man, that may u this........	Jer 9:12
whose words thou canst not u........	Eze 3:6
make this man to u the vision........	Dan 8:16
but he said unto me, U, O son of........	Dan 8:17
our iniquities, and u thy truth........	Dan 9:13
therefore u the matter, and........	Dan 9:23
Know therefore and u, that from........	Dan 9:25
u the words that I speak unto........	Dan 10:11
thou didst set thine heart to u........	Dan 10:12
I am come to make thee u........	Dan 10:14
they that u among the people........	Dan 11:33
and none of the wicked shall u........	Dan 12:10
but the wise shall u........	Dan 12:10
people that doth not u shall fall........	Hos 4:14
wise, and he shall u these things........	Hos 14:9
neither u they his counsel........	Mic 4:12
they hear not, neither do they u........	Mt 13:13
ye shall hear, and shall not u........	Mt 13:14
should u with their heart, and........	Mt 13:15
and said unto them, Hear, and u........	Mt 15:10
Do not ye yet u, that whatsoever........	Mt 15:17
Do ye not yet u, neither........	Mt 16:9
How is it that ye do not u that I........	Mt 16:11
place, (whoso readeth, let him u........	Mt 24:15
hearing they may hear, and not u........	Mk 4:12
unto me every one of you, and u........	Mk 7:14
perceive ye not yet, neither u........	Mk 8:17
them, How is it that ye do not u........	Mk 8:21
not, (let him that readeth u........	Mk 13:14
neither u I what thou sayest........	Mk 14:68
see, and hearing they might not u........	Lk 8:10
that they might u the scriptures........	Lk 24:45
Why do ye not u my speech........	Jn 8:43
nor u with their heart, and be........	Jn 12:40
Because that thou mayest u........	Acts 24:11
ye shall hear, and shall not u........	Acts 28:26
u with their heart, and should be........	Acts 28:27
they that have not heard shall u........	Rom 15:21
Wherefore I give you to u........	1Cor 12:3
all mysteries, and all knowledge........	1Cor 13:2
ye may u my knowledge in the........	Eph 3:4
But I would ye should u, brethren........	Phil 1:12
Through faith we u that the........	Heb 11:3
of the things that they u not........	2Pet 2:12

UNDERSTANDEST
what u thou, which is not in us........	Job 15:9
u my thought afar off........	Ps 139:2
not, neither u what they say........	Jer 5:15
and said, U thou what thou readest........	Acts 8:30

UNDERSTANDETH
u all the imaginations of the........	1Chr 28:9
God u the way thereof, and he........	Job 28:23
u not, is like the beasts that........	Ps 49:20
They are all plain to him that u........	Prov 8:9
knowledge is easy unto him that u........	Prov 14:6
glorieth glory in this, that he u........	Jer 9:24
u it not, then cometh the wicked........	Mt 13:19
he that heareth the word, and u it........	Mt 13:23
There is none that u, there is........	Rom 3:11
for no man u him........	1Cor 14:2
seeing he u not what thou sayest........	1Cor 14:16

UNDERSTANDING
spirit of God, in wisdom, and in u........	Ex 31:3
spirit of God, in wisdom, in u........	Ex 35:31
u to know how to work all manner........	Ex 36:1
Take you wise men, and u........	Deut 1:13
your u in the sight of the........	Deut 4:6
nation is a wise and u people........	Deut 4:6
neither is there any u in them........	Deut 32:28
and she was a woman of good u........	1Sa 25:3
an u heart to judge thy people........	1Kin 3:9
for thyself u to discern judgment........	1Kin 3:11

given thee a wise and an u heart........	1Kin 3:12
u exceeding much, and largeness of........	1Kin 4:29
he was filled with wisdom, and u........	1Kin 7:14
were men that had u of the times........	1Chr 12:32
the LORD give thee wisdom and u........	1Chr 22:12
son, endued with prudence and u........	2Chr 2:12
sent a cunning man, endued with u........	2Chr 2:13
who had u in the visions of God........	2Chr 26:5
and for Elnathan, men of u........	Ezr 8:16
us they brought us a man of u........	Ezr 8:18
and all that could hear with u........	Neh 8:2
one having knowledge, and having u........	Neh 10:28
But I have u as well as you........	Job 12:3
and in length of days u........	Job 12:12
and strength, he hath counsel and u........	Job 12:13
and taketh away the u of the aged........	Job 12:20
thou hast hid their heart from u........	Job 17:4
the spirit of my u causeth me to........	Job 20:3
by his u he smiteth through the........	Job 26:12
and where is the place of u........	Job 28:12
and where is the place of u........	Job 28:20
and to depart from evil is u........	Job 28:28
of the Almighty giveth them u........	Job 32:8
hearken unto me, ye men of u........	Job 34:10
If now thou hast u, hear this........	Job 34:16
Let men of u tell me, and let a........	Job 34:34
declare, if thou hast u........	Job 38:4
or who hath given u to the heart........	Job 38:36
neither hath he imparted to her u........	Job 39:17
or as the mule, which have no u........	Ps 32:9
sing ye praises with u........	Ps 47:7
of my heart shall be of u........	Ps 49:3
a good u have all they that do........	Ps 111:10
Give me u, and I shall keep thy........	Ps 119:34
give me u, that I may learn thy........	Ps 119:73
I have more u than all my........	Ps 119:99
Through thy precepts I get u........	Ps 119:104
give me u, that I may know thy........	Ps 119:125
it giveth u unto the simple........	Ps 119:130
give me u, and I shall live........	Ps 119:144
give me u according to thy word........	Ps 119:169
his u is infinite........	Ps 147:5
to perceive the words of u........	Prov 1:2
a man of u shall attain unto wise........	Prov 1:5
wisdom, and apply thine heart to u........	Prov 2:2
and liftest up thy voice for u........	Prov 2:3
his mouth cometh knowledge and u........	Prov 2:6
preserve thee, u shall keep thee........	Prov 2:11
good u in the sight of God and man........	Prov 3:4
and lean not unto thine own u........	Prov 3:5
wisdom, and the man that getteth u........	Prov 3:13
by u hath he established the........	Prov 3:19
of a father, and attend to know u........	Prov 4:1
Get wisdom, get u........	Prov 4:5
and with all thy getting get u........	Prov 4:7
wisdom, and bow thine ear to my u........	Prov 5:1
adultery with a woman lacketh u........	Prov 6:32
and call u thy kinswoman........	Prov 7:4
the youths, a young man void of u........	Prov 7:7
and u put forth her voice........	Prov 8:1
and, ye fools, be ye of an u heart........	Prov 8:5
I am u........	Prov 8:14
as for him that wanteth u........	Prov 9:4
and go in the way of u........	Prov 9:6
and the knowledge of the holy is u........	Prov 9:10
and as for him that wanteth u........	Prov 9:16
him that hath u wisdom is found........	Prov 10:13
the back of him that is void of u........	Prov 10:13
but a man of u hath wisdom........	Prov 10:23
but a man of a holdeth his peace........	Prov 11:12
vain persons is void of u........	Prov 12:11
Good u giveth favour........	Prov 13:15
is slow to wrath is of great u........	Prov 14:29
in the heart of him that hath u........	Prov 14:33
him that hath u seeketh knowledge........	Prov 15:14
but a man of u walketh uprightly........	Prov 15:21
he that heareth reproof getteth u........	Prov 15:32
to get u rather to be chosen than........	Prov 16:16
U is a wellspring of life unto........	Prov 16:22
A man void of u striketh hands,........	Prov 17:18
Wisdom is before him that hath u........	Prov 17:24
a man of u is of an excellent........	Prov 17:27
his lips is esteemed a man of u........	Prov 17:28
A fool hath no delight in u........	Prov 18:2
he that keepeth u shall find good........	Prov 19:8
and reprove one that hath u........	Prov 19:25
but a man of u will draw it out........	Prov 20:5
the way of u shall remain in the........	Prov 21:16
There is no wisdom nor u nor........	Prov 21:30
also wisdom, and instruction, and u........	Prov 23:23
and by u it is established........	Prov 24:3
the vineyard of the man void of u........	Prov 24:30
but by a man of u and knowledge........	Prov 28:2
that hath u searcheth him out........	Prov 28:11
The prince that wanteth u is also........	Prov 28:16
man, and have not the u of a man........	Prov 30:2
wise, nor yet riches to men of u........	Eccl 9:11
him, the spirit of wisdom and u........	Is 11:2
quick u in the fear of the LORD........	Is 11:3
for it is a people of no u........	Is 27:11
the u of their prudent men shall........	Is 29:14
him that framed it, He had no u........	Is 29:16
erred in spirit shall come to u........	Is 29:24
and shewed to him the way of u........	Is 40:14
there is no searching of his u........	Is 40:28
is there knowledge nor u to say........	Is 44:19
feed you with knowledge and u........	Jer 3:15
children, and they have none u........	Jer 4:22
O foolish people, and without u........	Jer 5:21
stretched out the heaven by his u........	Jer 51:15

UNDERSTOOD

with thine *u* thou hast gotten	Eze 28:4
u science, and such as had ability	Dan 1:4
Daniel had in all visions and	Dan 1:17
And in all matters of wisdom and *u*	Dan 1:20
and knowledge to them that know *u*	Dan 2:21
mine *u* returned unto me, and I	Dan 4:34
the days of thy father light and *u*	Dan 5:11
spirit, and knowledge, and *u*	Dan 5:12
is in thee, and that light and *u*	Dan 5:14
dark sentences, shall stand up	Dan 8:23
forth to give thee skill and *u*	Dan 9:22
the thing, and had *u* of the vision	Dan 10:1
And some of them of *u* shall fall	Dan 11:35
and idols according to their own *u*	Hos 13:2
there is none *u* in him	Obad 7
u out of the mount of Esau	Obad 8
said, Are ye also yet without *u*	Mt 15:16
them, Are ye so without *u* also	Mk 7:18
all the heart, and with all the *u*	Mk 12:33
having had perfect *u* of all	Lk 1:3
him were astonished at his *u*	Lk 2:47
Then opened he their *u*, that they	Lk 24:45
Without *u*, covenantbreakers	Rom 1:31
to nothing the *u* of the prudent	1Cor 1:19
prayeth, but my *u* is unfruitful	1Cor 14:14
and I will pray with the *u* also	1Cor 14:15
and I will sing with the *u* also	1Cor 14:15
rather speak five words with my *u*	1Cor 14:19
Brethren, be not children in *u*	1Cor 14:20
be ye children, but in *u* be men	1Cor 14:20
The eyes of your *u* being	Eph 1:18
Having the *u* darkened, being	Eph 4:18
but *u* what the will of the Lord	Eph 5:17
peace of God, which passeth all *u*	Phil 4:7
will in all wisdom and spiritual *u*	Col 1:9
riches of the full assurance of *u*	Col 2:2
u neither what they say, nor	1Ti 1:7
Lord give thee *u* in all things	2Ti 2:7
is come, and hath given us an *u*	1Jn 5:20
Let him that hath *u* count the	Rev 13:18

UNDERSTOOD

they knew not that Joseph *u* them	Gen 42:23
they were wise, that they *u* this	Deut 32:29
they *u* that the ark of the Lord	1Sa 4:6
u that Saul was come in very deed	1Sa 26:4
all Israel *u* that day that it was	2Sa 3:37
because they had *u* the words that	Neh 8:12
u of the evil Eliashib did	Neh 13:7
this, mine ear hath heard and it	Job 13:1
have I uttered that I *u* not	Job 42:3
then *u* I their end	Ps 73:17
I heard a language that I *u* not	Ps 81:5
Our fathers *u* not thy wonders in	Ps 106:7
have ye not *u* from the	Is 40:21
They have not known nor *u*	Is 44:18
at the vision, but none *u* it	Dan 8:27
u by books the number of the	Dan 9:2
and he *u* the thing, and had	Dan 10:1
And I heard, but I *u* not	Dan 12:8
Have ye *u* all these things	Mt 13:51
Then *u* they how that he bade them	Mt 16:12
Then the disciples *u* that he	Mt 17:13
When Jesus *u* it, he said unto	Mt 26:10
But they *u* not that saying, and	Mk 9:32
they *u* not the saying which he	Lk 2:50
But they *u* not this saying, and it	Lk 9:45
they *u* none of these things	Lk 18:34
They *u* not that he spake to them	Jn 8:27
but they *u* not what things they	Jn 10:6
These things *u* not his disciples	Jn 12:16
his brethren would have *u* how	Acts 7:25
but they *u* not	Acts 7:25
having *u* that he was a Roman	Acts 23:27
when he *u* that he was of Cilicia	Acts 23:34
being *u* by the things that are	Rom 1:20
I *u* as a child, I thought as a	1Cor 13:11
by the tongue words easy to be *u*	1Cor 14:9
are some things hard to be *u*	2Pet 3:16

UNDERTAKE

oppressed; *u* for me	Is 38:14

UNDERTOOK

the Jews to do as they had	Est 9:23

UNDO

to *u* the heavy burdens, and to let	Is 58:6
at that time I will *u* all that	Zeph 3:19

UNDONE

thou art *u*, O people of Chemosh	Num 21:29
he left nothing *u* of all that	Josh 11:15
for I am *u*	Is 6:5
done, and not to leave the other *u*	Mt 23:23
done, and not to leave the other *u*	Lk 11:42

UNDRESSED

gather the grapes of thy vine *u*	Lev 25:5
the grapes in it of thy vine *u*	Lev 25:11

UNEQUAL

are not your ways *u*	Eze 18:25
are not your ways *u*	Eze 18:29

UNEQUALLY

Be ye not *u* yoked together with	2Cor 6:14

UNFAITHFUL

Confidence in an *u* man in time of	Prov 25:19

UNFAITHFULLY

dealt *u* like their fathers	Ps 78:57

UNFEIGNED

by the Holy Ghost, by love *u*	2Cor 6:6
a good conscience, and of faith *u*	1Ti 1:5

---

the *u* faith that is in thee	2Ti 1:5
unto *u* love of the brethren	1Pet 1:22

UNFRUITFUL

choke the word, and he becometh *u*	Mt 13:22
choke the word, and it becometh *u*	Mk 4:19
but my understanding is *u*	1Cor 14:14
with the *u* works of darkness	Eph 5:11
uses, that they be not *u*	Titus 3:14
u in the knowledge of our Lord	2Pet 1:8

UNGIRDED

he *u* his camels, and gave straw and	Gen 24:32

UNGODLINESS

from heaven against all *u*	Rom 1:18
and shall turn away *u* from Jacob	Rom 11:26
they will increase unto more	2Ti 2:16
Teaching us that, denying *u*	Titus 2:12

UNGODLY

The floods of *u* men made me	2Sa 22:5
Shouldest thou help the *u*	2Chr 19:2
God hath delivered me to the *u*	Job 16:11
and to princes, Ye are *u*	Job 34:18
not in the counsel of the *u*	Ps 1:1
The *u* are not so	Ps 1:4
Therefore the *u* shall not stand	Ps 1:5
but the way of the *u* shall perish	Ps 1:6
hast broken the teeth of the *u*	Ps 3:7
the floods of *u* men made me	Ps 18:4
my cause against an *u* nation	Ps 43:1
Behold, these are the *u*, who	Ps 73:12
An *u* man diggeth up evil	Prov 16:27
An *u* witness scorneth judgment	Prov 19:28
on him that justifieth the *u*	Rom 4:5
in due time Christ died for the *u*	Rom 5:6
lawless and disobedient, for the *u*	1Ti 1:9
be saved, where shall the *u*	1Pet 4:18
the flood upon the world of the *u*	2Pet 2:5
those that after should live *u*	2Pet 2:6
of judgment and perdition of *u* men	2Pet 3:7
u men, turning the grace of our	Jude 4
to convince all that are *u* among	Jude 15
u deeds which they have	Jude 15
deeds which they have committed	Jude 15
all their hard speeches which *u*	Jude 15
walk after their own *u* lusts	Jude 18

UNHOLY

put difference between holy and *u*	Lev 10:10
the ungodly and for sinners, for *u*	1Ti 1:9
to parents, unthankful, *u*	2Ti 3:2
an *u* thing, and hath done despite	Heb 10:29

UNICORN

as it were the strength of a *u*	Num 23:22
as it were the strength of a *u*	Num 24:8
Will the *u* be willing to serve	Job 39:9
Canst thou bind the *u* with his	Job 39:10
Lebanon and Sirion like a young *u*	Ps 29:6
thou exalt like the horn of an *u*	Ps 92:10

UNICORNS

his horns are like the horns of *u*	Deut 33:17
heard me from the horns of the *u*	Ps 22:21
u shall come down with them	Is 34:7

UNITE

u my heart to fear thy name	Ps 86:11

UNITED

mine honour, be not thou *u*	Gen 49:6

UNITY

brethren to dwell together in *u*	Ps 133:1
Endeavouring to keep the *u* of the	Eph 4:3
we all come in the *u* of the faith	Eph 4:13

UNJUST

me from the deceitful and *u* man	Ps 43:1
the hope of *u* men perisheth	Prov 11:7
u gain increaseth his substance	Prov 28:8
An *u* man is an abomination to the	Prov 29:27
but the *u* knoweth no shame	Zeph 3:5
rain on the just and on the *u*	Mt 5:45
the lord commended the *u* steward	Lk 16:8
he that is *u* in the least is	Lk 16:10
in the least is *u* also in much	Lk 16:10
said, Hear what the *u* judge saith	Lk 18:6
as other men are, extortioners, *u*	Lk 18:11
the dead, both of the just and *u*	Acts 24:15
another, go to law before the *u*	1Cor 6:1
for sins, the just for the *u*	1Pet 3:18
to reserve the *u* unto the day of	2Pet 2:9
He that is *u*, let him be *u*	Rev 22:11

UNJUSTLY

How long will ye judge *u*, and	Ps 82:2
of uprightness will he deal *u*	Is 26:10

UNKNOWN

this inscription, TO THE *U* GOD	Acts 17:23
For he that speaketh in an *u*	1Cor 14:2
He that speaketh in an *u* tongue	1Cor 14:4
in an *u* tongue pray that he may	1Cor 14:13
For if I pray in an *u* tongue	1Cor 14:14
ten thousand words in an *u* tongue	1Cor 14:19
If any man speak in an *u* tongue	1Cor 14:27
As *u*, and yet well known	2Cor 6:9
was *u* by face unto the churches	Gal 1:22

UNLADE

the ship was to *u* her burden	Acts 21:3

UNLAWFUL

know how that it is an *u* thing	Acts 10:28
day to day with their *u* deeds	2Pet 2:8

UNLEARNED

and perceived that they were *u*	Acts 4:13
the *u* say Amen at thy giving of	1Cor 14:16
and there come in those that are *u*	1Cor 14:23
one that believeth not, or one *u*	1Cor 14:24
u questions avoid, knowing that	2Ti 2:23
understood, which they that are *u*	2Pet 3:16

UNLEAVENED

them a feast, and did bake *u* bread	Gen 19:3
roast with fire, and *u* bread	Ex 12:8
Seven days shall ye eat *u* bread	Ex 12:15
observe the feast of *u* bread	Ex 12:17
at even, ye shall eat *u* bread	Ex 12:18
habitations shall ye eat *u* bread	Ex 12:20
they baked *u* cakes of the dough	Ex 12:39
Seven days thou shalt eat *u* bread	Ex 13:6
U bread shall be eaten seven days	Ex 13:7
shalt keep the feast of *u* bread	Ex 23:15
(thou shalt eat *u* bread seven	Ex 23:15
u bread, and cakes *u*	Ex 29:2
wafers *u* anointed with oil	Ex 29:2
u bread that is before the Lord	Ex 29:23
The feast of *u* bread shalt thou	Ex 34:18
Seven days thou shalt eat *u* bread	Ex 34:18
it shall be *u* cakes of fine flour	Lev 2:4
or *u* wafers anointed with oil	Lev 2:4
pan, it shall be of fine flour *u*	Lev 2:5
with *u* bread shall it be eaten	Lev 6:16
u cakes mingled with oil, and	Lev 7:12
u wafers anointed with oil, and	Lev 7:12
two rams, and a basket of *u* bread	Lev 8:2
And out of the basket of *u* bread	Lev 8:26
the Lord, he took one cake of *u*	Lev 8:26
feast of *u* bread unto the Lord	Lev 23:6
seven days ye must eat *u* bread	Lev 23:6
And a basket of *u* bread, cakes of	Num 6:15
wafers of *u* bread anointed with	Num 6:15
Lord, with the basket of *u* bread	Num 6:17
one *u* cake out of the basket, and	Num 6:19
one *u* wafer, and shall put them	Num 6:19
keep it, and eat it with *u* bread	Num 9:11
seven days shall *u* bread be eaten	Num 28:17
shalt thou eat *u* bread therewith	Deut 16:3
Six days thou shalt eat *u* bread	Deut 16:8
in the feast of *u* bread, and in	Deut 16:16
u cakes, and parched corn in the	Josh 5:11
u cakes of an ephah of flour	Judg 6:19
the *u* cakes, and lay them upon	Judg 6:20
touched the flesh and the *u* cakes	Judg 6:21
consumed the flesh and the *u* cakes	Judg 6:21
it, and did bake *u* bread thereof	1Sa 28:24
but they did eat of the *u* bread	2Kin 23:9
meat offering, and the *u* cakes	1Chr 23:29
even in the feast of *u* bread	2Chr 8:13
of *u* bread in the second month	2Chr 30:13
u bread seven days with great	2Chr 30:21
the feast of *u* bread seven days	2Chr 35:17
kept the feast of *u* bread seven	Ezr 6:22
u bread shall he eaten	Eze 45:21
of *u* bread the disciples came to	Mt 26:17
of the passover, and of *u* bread	Mk 14:1
And the first day of *u* bread	Mk 14:12
the feast of *u* bread drew nigh	Lk 22:1
Then came the day of *u* bread	Lk 22:7
(Then were the days of *u* bread	Acts 12:3
after the days of *u* bread	Acts 20:6
ye may be a new lump, as ye are *u*	1Cor 5:7
but with the *u* bread of sincerity	1Cor 5:8

UNLESS

u he wash his flesh with water	Lev 22:6
u she had turned from me, surely	Num 22:33
u thou hadst spoken, surely then	2Sa 2:27
u I had believed to see the	Ps 27:13
U the Lord had been my help, my	Ps 94:17
U thy law had been my delights, I	Ps 119:92
u they cause some to fall	Prov 4:16
u ye have believed in vain	1Cor 15:2

UNLOOSE

am not worthy to stoop down and *u*	Mk 1:7
whose shoes I am not worthy to *u*	Lk 3:16
latchet I am not worthy to *u*	Jn 1:27

UNMARRIED

I say therefore to the *u* and	1Cor 7:8
if she depart, let her remain *u*	1Cor 7:11
He that is *u* careth for the	1Cor 7:32
The *u* woman careth for the things	1Cor 7:34

UNMERCIFUL

natural affection, implacable, *u*	Rom 1:31

UNMINDFUL

Rock that begat thee thou art *u*	Deut 32:18

UNMOVABLE

brethren, be ye stedfast, *u*	1Cor 15:58

UNMOVEABLE

stuck fast, and remained *u*	Acts 27:41

UNNI

and Shemiramoth, and Jehiel, and *U*	1Chr 15:18
and Shemiramoth, and Jehiel, and *U*	1Chr 15:20
Also Bakbukiah and *U*, their	Neh 12:9

UNOCCUPIED

days of Jael, the highways were *u*	Judg 5:6

UNPERFECT

did see my substance, yet being *u*	Ps 139:16

UNPREPARED

come, and find you *u*	2Cor 9:4

UNPROFITABLE

Should he reason with *u* talk	Job 15:3
cast ye the *u* servant into outer	Mt 25:30

you, say, We are *u* servants .... Lk 17:10
way, they are together become *u* ... Rom 3:12
for they are *u* and vain .... Titus 3:9
Which in time past was to thee *u* .... Philem 11
for that is *u* for you .... Heb 13:17

UNPROFITABLENESS
for the weakness and *u* thereof .... Heb 7:18

UNPUNISHED
hand, the wicked shall not be *u* ...... Prov 11:21
join in hand, he shall not be *u* .... Prov 16:5
glad at calamities shall not be *u* ..... Prov 17:5
A false witness shall not be *u* .... Prov 19:5
A false witness that is not *u* .... Prov 19:9
name, and should ye be utterly *u* .... Jer 25:29
Ye shall not be *u* .... Jer 25:29
will not leave thee altogether *u* .... Jer 30:11
will I not leave thee wholly *u* .... Jer 46:28
he that shall altogether go *u* .... Jer 49:12
thou shalt not go *u*, but thou .... Jer 49:12

UNQUENCHABLE
burn up the chaff with *u* fire .... Mt 3:12
chaff he will burn with fire *u* .... Lk 3:17

UNREASONABLE
to me *u* to send a prisoner .... Acts 25:27
that we may be delivered from *u* 2Th 3:2

UNREBUKEABLE
this commandment without spot, *u*.... 1Ti 6:14

UNREPROVEABLE
and unblameable and *u* in his sight ...... Col 1:22

UNRIGHTEOUS
the wicked to be an *u* witness .... Ex 23:1
riseth up against me as the *u* .... Job 27:7
wicked, out of the hand of the *u* ...... Ps 71:4
unto them that decree *u* decrees ...... Is 10:1
way, and the *u* man his thoughts ...... Is 55:7
hath been faithful in the *u* mammon ... Lk 16:11
Is God *u* who taketh vengeance .... Rom 3:5
Know ye not that the *u* shall not 1Cor 6:9
For God is not *u* to forget your .... Heb 6:10

UNRIGHTEOUSLY
do such things, and all that do *u* ...... Deut 25:16

UNRIGHTEOUSNESS
Ye shall do no *u* in judgment .... Lev 19:15
Ye shall do no *u* in judgment .... Lev 19:35
my rock, and there is no *u* in him ..... Ps 92:15
him that buildeth his house by *u* ...... Jer 22:13
friends of the mammon of *u* .... Lk 16:9
same is true, and no *u* is in him .... Jn 7:18
u of men, who hold the truth in ...... Rom 1:18
of men, who hold the truth in *u* ...... Rom 1:18
Being filled with all *u*, ... Rom 1:29
do not obey the truth, but obey *u* ... Rom 2:8
But if our *u* commend the .... Rom 3:5
as instruments of *u* unto sin .... Rom 6:13
Is there *u* with God .... Rom 9:14
hath righteousness and *u* 2Cor 6:14
of *u* in them that perish 2Th 2:10
the truth, but had pleasure in *u* 2Th 2:12
For I will be merciful to their *u* ...... Heb 8:12
And shall receive the reward of *u* ... 2Pet 2:13
Bosor, who loved the wages of *u* 2Pet 2:15
sins, and to cleanse us from all *u* 1Jn 1:9
All *u* is sin 1Jn 5:17

UNRIPE
shake off his *u* grape as the vine ...... Job 15:33

UNRULY
brethren, warn them that are *u* 1Th 5:14
children not accused of riot or *u* ...... Titus 1:6
For there are many *u* and vain .... Titus 1:10
it is an *u* evil, full of deadly .... Jas 3:8

UNSATIABLE
Assyrians, because thou wast *u* .... Eze 16:28

UNSAVOURY
froward thou wilt shew thyself *u* 2Sa 22:27
Can that which is *u* be eaten .... Job 6:6

UNSEARCHABLE
Which doeth great things and *u* ...... Job 5:9
and his greatness is *u* .... Ps 145:3
depth, and the heart of kings is *u* ..... Prov 25:3
how *u* are his judgments, and his ..... Rom 11:33
Gentiles the *u* riches of Christ.......... Eph 3:8

UNSEEMLY
with men working that which is *u* ..... Rom 1:27
Doth not behave itself *u*, seeketh 1Cor 13:5

UNSHOD
Withhold thy foot from being *u* ...... Jer 2:25

UNSKILFUL
is *u* in the word of righteousness........ Heb 5:13

UNSPEAKABLE
Thanks be unto God for his *u* gift 2Cor 9:15
into paradise, and heard *u* words 2Cor 12:4
believing, ye rejoice with joy *u* 1Pet 1:8

UNSPOTTED
to keep himself *u* from the world........ Jas 1:27

UNSTABLE
U as water, thou shalt not excel........ Gen 49:4
minded man is *u* in all his ways .... Jas 1:8
beguiling *u* souls 2Pet 2:14
u wrest, as they do also the 2Pet 3:16

UNSTOPPED
the ears of the deaf shall be *u* .... Is 35:5

UNTAKEN
day remaineth the same vail *u* 2Cor 3:14

UNTEMPERED
others daubed it with *u* morter........ Eze 13:10
them which daub it with *u* morter.... Eze 13:11
that ye have daubed with *u* morter.... Eze 13:14
that have daubed it with *u* morter.... Eze 13:15
have daubed them with *u* morter..... Eze 22:28

UNTHANKFUL
for he is kind unto the *u* .... Lk 6:35
disobedient to parents, *u* 2Ti 3:2

UNTIL
continually *u* the tenth month .... Gen 8:5
u the waters were dried up from .... Gen 8:7
they have done drinking .... Gen 24:19
u I have told mine errand .... Gen 24:33
grew *u* he became very great .... Gen 26:13
u thy brother's fury turn away .... Gen 27:44
u thy brother's anger turn away .... Gen 27:45
u I have done that which I have .... Gen 28:15
u all the flocks be gathered .... Gen 29:8
with Laban, and stayed there *u* now ... Gen 32:4
him *u* the breaking of the day .... Gen 32:24
u he came near to his brother .... Gen 33:3
u I come unto my lord unto Seir ...... Gen 33:14
held his peace *u* they were come...... Gen 34:5
by her, *u* his lord came home........... Gen 39:16
very much, *u* he left numbering .... Gen 41:49
cattle from our youth even *u* now..... Gen 46:34
between his feet, *u* Shiloh come .... Gen 49:10
the foundation thereof even *u* now ... Ex 9:18
serve the LORD, *u* we come thither ... Ex 10:26
ye shall keep it up *u* the .... Ex 12:6
of it remain *u* the morning .... Ex 12:10
that which remaineth of it *u* the ...... Ex 12:10
the first day *u* the seventh day .... Ex 12:15
u the one and twentieth day of the ... Ex 12:18
door of his house *u* the morning ..... Ex 12:22
of them left of it *u* the morning ...... Ex 12:22
for you to be kept *u* the morning ..... Ex 16:23
u they came to a land inhabited........ Ex 16:35
u they came unto the borders of ...... Ex 16:35
his hands were steady *u* the going .... Ex 17:12
my sacrifice remain *u* the morning ... Ex 23:18
u thou be increased, and inherit ...... Ex 23:30
for us, *u* we come again unto you ..... Ex 24:14
u he was gone into the tabernacle .... Ex 33:8
took the vail off, *u* he came out........ Ex 34:34
u he went in to speak with him .... Ex 34:35
not leave any of it *u* the morning ..... Lev 7:15
u the days of your consecration .... Lev 8:33
them shall be unclean *u* the even ..... Lev 11:24
clothes, and be unclean *u* the even ... Lev 11:25
shall be unclean *u* the even .... Lev 11:27
clothes, and be unclean *u* the even ... Lev 11:28
dead, shall be unclean *u* the even .... Lev 11:31
and it shall be unclean *u* the even .... Lev 11:32
shall be unclean *u* the even .... Lev 11:39
clothes, and be unclean *u* the even ... Lev 11:40
clothes, and be unclean *u* the even ... Lev 11:40
u the days of her purifying be.......... Lev 12:4
up shall be unclean *u* the even .... Lev 14:46
water, and be unclean *u* the even ..... Lev 15:5
water, and be unclean *u* the even ..... Lev 15:6
water, and be unclean *u* the even ..... Lev 15:7
water, and be unclean *u* the even ..... Lev 15:8
him shall be unclean *u* the even ...... Lev 15:10
water, and be unclean *u* the even ..... Lev 15:10
water, and be unclean *u* the even ..... Lev 15:11
water, and be unclean *u* the even ..... Lev 15:16
water, and be unclean *u* the even ..... Lev 15:17
water, and be unclean *u* the even ..... Lev 15:18
her shall be unclean *u* the even .... Lev 15:19
water, and be unclean *u* the even ..... Lev 15:21
water, and be unclean *u* the even ..... Lev 15:22
he shall be unclean *u* the even .... Lev 15:23
water, and be unclean *u* the even ..... Lev 15:27
u he come out, and have made an ..... Lev 16:17
shall be unclean *u* the even .... Lev 17:15
if ought remain *u* the third day .... Lev 19:6
with thee all night *u* the morning ..... Lev 19:13
of the holy things, *u* he be clean...... Lev 22:4
any such shall be unclean *u* even ..... Lev 22:6
leave none of it *u* the morrow.......... Lev 22:30
u the selfsame day that ye have........ Lev 23:14
yet of old fruit *u* the ninth year .... Lev 25:22
u her fruits come in ye shall eat .... Lev 25:22
bought it *u* the year of jubile .... Lev 25:28
upward even *u* fifty years old, ... Num 4:3
upward *u* fifty years old shall .... Num 4:23
u the days be fulfilled, in the .... Num 6:5
appearance of fire, *u* the morning ... Num 9:15
u it come out at your nostrils, ... Num 11:20
people, from Egypt even *u* now .... Num 14:19
u your carcases be wasted in the ..... Num 14:33
shall be unclean *u* the even .... Num 19:7
and shall be unclean *u* the even ...... Num 19:8
clothes, and be unclean *u* the even ... Num 19:10
shall be unclean *u* even .... Num 19:21
u I come unto the .... Num 19:22
u we have passed thy borders.......... Num 20:17
way, *u* we be past thy borders.......... Num 21:22
u there was none left him alive........ Num 21:35
not lie down *u* he eat of the prey ..... Num 23:24
u Asshur shall carry thee away .... Num 24:22
u all the generation, that had .... Num 32:13

u we have brought them unto their... Num 32:17
u the children of Israel have .... Num 32:18
u he hath driven out his enemies..... Num 32:21
die not, *u* he stand before the .... Num 35:12
in the city of his refuge *u* the .... Num 35:28
u the death of the priest.................. Num 35:32
u ye came into this place .... Deut 1:31
u we were come over the brook ...... Deut 2:14
u all the generation of the men .... Deut 2:14
the host, *u* they were consumed ...... Deut 2:15
u I shall pass over Jordan into .... Deut 2:29
we smote him *u* none was left to...... Deut 3:3
U the LORD have given rest unto .... Deut 3:20
u they also possess the land............. Deut 3:20
u they that are left, and hide .... Deut 7:20
destruction, *u* they be destroyed ..... Deut 7:23
u thou have destroyed them .... Deut 7:24
u ye came unto this place, ye .... Deut 9:7
even *u* it was as small as dust .... Deut 9:21
u ye came into this place .... Deut 11:5
remain all night *u* the morning .... Deut 16:4
war with thee, *u* it be subdued......... Deut 20:20
it shall be with thee *u* thy .... Deut 22:2
u thou be destroyed .... Deut 28:20
and *u* thou perish quickly .... Deut 28:20
u he have consumed thee from off ... Deut 28:21
shall pursue thee *u* thou perish .... Deut 28:22
upon thee, *u* thou be destroyed ...... Deut 28:24
neck, *u* he have destroyed thee .... Deut 28:48
of thy land, *u* thou be destroyed ..... Deut 28:51
sheep, *u* he have destroyed thee ..... Deut 28:51
u thy high and fenced walls come .... Deut 28:52
upon thee, *u* thou be destroyed ...... Deut 28:61
in a book, *u* they were finished, ... Deut 31:24
of this song, *u* they were ended .... Deut 31:30
U the LORD have given you .... Josh 1:15
u the pursuers be returned .... Josh 2:16
u the pursuers were returned .... Josh 2:22
u all the people were passed .... Josh 3:17
u every thing was finished that........ Josh 4:10
u ye were passed over, as the .... Josh 4:23
before us, *u* we were gone over........ Josh 4:23
u we were passed over, that their .... Josh 5:1
the day I bid you should .... Josh 6:10
ark of the LORD *u* the eventide .... Josh 7:6
u ye take away the accursed thing ... Josh 7:13
u they were consumed, that all .... Josh 8:24
u he had utterly destroyed all.......... Josh 8:26
Ai he hanged on a tree *u* eventide ... Josh 8:29
stayed, *u* the people had avenged .... Josh 10:13
upon the trees *u* the evening .... Josh 10:26
which remain *u* this very day........... Josh 10:27
u he had left him none remaining .... Josh 10:33
u they left them none remaining ..... Josh 11:8
u they had destroyed them, ... Josh 11:14
among the Israelites *u* this day .... Josh 13:13
that city, *u* he stand before the .... Josh 20:6
u the death of the high priest .... Josh 20:6
of blood, *u* he stood before the .... Josh 20:9
we are not cleansed *u* this day .... Josh 22:17
u ye perish from off this good .... Josh 23:13
u he have destroyed you from off .... Josh 23:15
u they had destroyed Jabin king ...... Judg 4:24
u that I Deborah arose, that I.......... Judg 5:7
u thou come, tell thee, and bring .... Judg 6:18
I will tarry *u* thou come again .... Judg 6:18
u we shall have made ready a kid..... Judg 13:15
priests the tribe of Dan *u* the .... Judg 18:30
And they tarried *u* afternoon .... Judg 19:8
her all the night *u* the morning .... Judg 19:25
up and wept before the LORD *u* even... Judg 20:23
LORD, and fasted that day *u* even ..... Judg 20:26
So they two went *u* they came to ..... Ruth 1:19
even from the morning *u* now.......... Ruth 2:7
she gleaned in the field *u* even .... Ruth 2:17
u they have ended all my harvest...... Ruth 2:21
u he shall have done eating and ...... Ruth 3:3
lie down *u* the morning .... Ruth 3:13
she lay at his feet *u* the morning ..... Ruth 3:14
u thou know how the matter will ..... Ruth 3:18
u he have finished the thing this ..... Ruth 3:18
I will not go up *u* the child be .... Ruth 3:18
tarry *u* thou have weaned him 1Sa 1:23
her son suck *u* she weaned him 1Sa 1:23
Samuel lay *u* the morning, and 1Sa 3:15
a they came under Beth-car 1Sa 7:11
the people will not eat *u* he come 1Sa 9:13
slew the Ammonites *u* the heat of 1Sa 11:11
unto us, Tarry *u* we come to you 1Sa 14:9
that eateth any food *u* evening......... 1Sa 14:24
spoil them *u* the morning light, ... 1Sa 14:36
Havilah *u* thou comest to Shur......... 1Sa 15:7
against them *u* they be consumed 1Sa 15:18
see Saul *u* the day of his death 1Sa 15:35
u thou come to the valley, and to 1Sa 17:52
heed to thyself *u* the morning 1Sa 19:2
u he came to Naioth in Ramah......... 1Sa 19:23
with another, *u* David exceeded 1Sa 20:41
less or more, *u* the morning light 1Sa 25:36
u they had no more power to weep ... 1Sa 30:4
and wept, and fasted *u* even 2Sa 1:12
were sojourners there *u* this day 2Sa 4:3
from Geba *u* thou come to Gazer...... 2Sa 5:25
Tarry at Jericho *u* your beards be 2Sa 10:5
u all the people had done passing 2Sa 15:24
a there come word from you to 2Sa 15:28
u there be not one small stone 2Sa 17:13
befell them from thy youth *u* now 2Sa 19:7
u the day he came again in peace 2Sa 19:24
from the beginning of harvest *u* 2Sa 21:10

turned not again *u* I had consumed 2Sa 22:38
Philistines his hand was weary 2Sa 23:10
u he had made an end of building 1Kin 3:1
name of the LORD, *u* those days 1Kin 5:3
u the LORD put them under the 1Kin 5:3
u he had finished all the house 1Kin 6:22
u I came, and mine eyes had seen 1Kin 10:7
u he had cut off every male in 1Kin 11:16
was in Egypt at the death of 1Kin 11:40
u he had destroyed them, according 1Kin 15:29
u the day that the LORD sendeth 1Kin 17:14
of Baal from morning even *u* noon 1Kin 18:26
they prophesied *u* the time of the 1Kin 18:29
u thou have consumed them 1Kin 22:11
of affliction, I come in peace 1Kin 22:27
u an ass's head was sold for 2Kin 6:25
another, Why sit we here *u* we die 2Kin 7:3
she left the land, even *u* now 2Kin 8:6
stedfastly, *u* he was ashamed 2Kin 8:11
in of the gate *u* the morning 2Kin 10:11
u he left him none remaining 2Kin 10:11
u he had cast them out of his 2Kin 17:20
U the LORD removed Israel out of 2Kin 17:23
U I come and take you away to a 2Kin 18:32
u he had cast them out from his 2Kin 24:20
in their steads *u* the captivity 1Chr 5:22
u Solomon had built the house of 1Chr 6:32
u it was a great host, like the 1Chr 12:22
Tarry at Jericho *u* your beards be 1Chr 19:5
u thou hast finished all the work 1Chr 28:20
make to pay tribute *u* this day 2Chr 8:8
of the LORD, and *u* it was finished 2Chr 8:16
u I came, and mine eyes had seen 2Chr 9:6
u his disease was exceeding great 2Chr 16:12
push Syria *u* they be consumed 2Chr 18:10
affliction, *u* I return in peace 2Chr 18:26
against the Syrians *u* the even 2Chr 18:34
u they bowels fall out by reason 2Chr 21:15
the chest, *u* they had made an end 2Chr 24:10
all this continued *u* the hour 2Chr 29:28
ended, and *u* the other priests had 2Chr 29:34
u they had utterly destroyed them 2Chr 31:1
offerings and the fat *u* night 2Chr 35:14
u the wrath of the LORD arose 2Chr 36:16
his sons *u* the reign of 2Chr 36:20
u he had enjoyed her 2Chr 36:21
even *u* the reign of Darius king .... Ezr 4:5
an another commandment shall be .... Ezr 4:21
since that time even *u* now hath .... Ezr 5:16
u ye weigh them before the chief .... Ezr 8:29
I sat astonied *u* the evening .... Ezr 9:4
u the fierce wrath of our God for .... Ezr 10:14
be opened *u* the sun be hot .... Neh 7:3
gate from the morning *u* midday .... Neh 8:3
even in the days of Johanan the .... Neh 12:23
u thy wrath be past, that thou .... Job 14:13
u the day and night come to an end .... Job 26:10
his iniquity be found to be .... Ps 36:2
u these calamities be overpast .... Ps 57:1
u I have shewed thy strength unto .... Ps 71:18
U I went into the sanctuary of .... Ps 73:17
u the pit be digged for .... Ps 94:13
and to his labour *u* the evening .... Ps 104:23
U the time that his word came .... Ps 105:19
u I have mine enemies thy .... Ps 110:1
u he see his desire upon his .... Ps 112:8
u that he have mercy upon us .... Ps 123:2
U I find out a place for the LORD .... Ps 132:5
our fill of love *u* the morning .... Prov 7:18
U the day break, and the shadows .... Song 2:17
u I had brought him into my .... Song 3:4
U the day break, and the shadows .... Song 4:6
nor awake my love, *u* he please .... Song 8:4
that continue *u* night, till wine .... Is 5:11
U the cities be wasted without .... Is 6:11
the indignation be overpast .... Is 26:20
U the spirit be poured upon us .... Is 32:15
U I come and take you away to a .... Is 36:17
have laid up in store *u* this day .... Is 39:6
the righteousness thereof go .... Is 62:1
u he have executed, and till he .... Jer 23:20
the very time of his land come .... Jer 27:7
u I have consumed them by his .... Jer 27:8
there shall they be *u* the day .... Jer 27:22
u he have done it .... Jer 30:24
u he have performed the intents .... Jer 30:24
there shall he be *u* I visit him .... Jer 32:5
u all the roll was consumed in .... Jer 36:23
u all the bread in the city were .... Jer 37:21
u the day that Jerusalem was .... Jer 38:28
u there be an end of them .... Jer 44:27
every day a portion *u* the day of .... Jer 52:34
u come whose right it is .... Eze 21:27
u he came to me in the morning .... Eze 33:22
shall not be shut *u* the evening .... Eze 46:2
u thou know that the most High .... Dan 4:32
U the Ancient of days came, and .... Dan 7:22
be given into his hand *u* a time .... Dan 7:25
even *u* the consummation, and that .... Dan 9:27
the dough, *u* it be leavened .... Hos 7:4
u the time that she inherit .... Mic 5:3
u he plead my cause, and execute .... Mic 7:9
u the day that I rise up to the .... Zeph 3:8
from David *u* the carrying away .... Mt 1:17
u thou there *u* I bring thee word .... Mt 2:13
was there *u* the death of Herod .... Mt 2:15
u now the kingdom of heaven .... Mt 11:12
and the law prophesied *u* John .... Mt 11:13
it would have remained *u* this day .... Mt 11:23
both grow together *u* the harvest .... Mt 13:30

the Son of man be risen again .... Mt 17:9
say not unto thee, *U* seven times .... Mt 18:22
but, *U* seventy times seven .... Mt 18:22
u the day that Noe entered into .... Mt 24:38
knew not *u* the flood came, and .... Mt 24:39
u that day when I drink it new .... Mt 26:29
be made sure *u* the third day .... Mt 27:64
among the Jews *u* this day .... Mt 28:15
u that day that I drink it new .... Mk 14:25
the whole land *u* the ninth hour .... Mk 15:33
u the day that these things shall .... Lk 1:20
u the time come when ye shall say .... Lk 13:35
that which is lost, *u* he find it .... Lk 15:4
law and the prophets were *u* John .... Lk 16:16
u the day that Noe entered into .... Lk 17:27
u the times of the Gentiles be .... Lk 21:24
u it be fulfilled in the kingdom .... Lk 22:16
the kingdom of God shall come .... Lk 22:18
all the earth *u* the ninth hour .... Lk 23:44
u ye be endued with power from on .... Lk 24:49
hast kept the good wine *u* now .... Jn 2:10
u they called the parents of him .... Jn 9:18
U the day in which he was taken .... Acts 1:2
U I make thy foes thy footstool .... Acts 2:35
Whom the heaven must receive *u* .... Acts 3:21
ago I was fasting *u* this hour .... Acts 10:30
fifty years, a Samuel the prophet .... Acts 13:20
continued his speech *u* midnight .... Acts 20:7
u that an offering should be .... Acts 21:26
conscience before God *u* this day .... Acts 23:1
eat nothing *u* we have slain Paul .... Acts 23:14
(For *u* the law sin was in the .... Rom 5:13
travaileth in pain together *u* now .... Rom 8:22
u the fulness of the Gentiles be .... Rom 11:25
the Lord come, who both will 1Cor 4:5
will tarry at Ephesus *u* Pentecost 1Cor 16:8
for *u* this day remaineth the same 2Cor 3:14
governors *u* the time appointed of .... Gal 4:2
again *u* Christ be formed in you .... Gal 4:19
the earnest of our inheritance *u* .... Eph 1:14
gospel of Christ *u* this day *u* now .... Phil 1:5
it *u* the day of Jesus Christ .... Phil 1:6
u he be taken out of the way 2Th 2:7
the appearing of our Lord Jesus 1Ti 6:14
u I make thine enemies thy .... Heb 1:13
imposed on them *u* the time of .... Heb 9:10
u he receive the early and latter .... Jas 5:7
the day dawn, and the day star 2Pet 1:19
u is in darkness even *u* now 1Jn 2:9
u their fellowservants also and .... Rev 6:11
the words of God shall be .... Rev 17:17
again *u* the thousand years were .... Rev 20:5

UNTIMELY

Or as an *u*ntimely birth I had not .... Job 3:16
like the *u* birth of a woman, that .... Ps 58:8
that an *u* birth is better than he .... Eccl 6:3
as a fig tree casteth her *u* figs .... Rev 6:13

UNTO See PREFACE.

UNTOWARD

yourselves from this *u* generation .... Acts 2:40

UNWALLED

beside *u* towns a great many .... Deut 3:5
that dwelt in the *u* towns .... Est 9:19
go up to the land of *u* villages .... Eze 38:11

UNWASHEN

but to eat with *u* hands defileth .... Mt 15:20
defiled, that is to say, with *u* .... Mk 7:2
but eat bread with *u* hands .... Mk 7:5

UNWEIGHED

And Solomon left all the vessels *u* 1Kin 7:47

UNWISE

the LORD, O foolish people and *u* .... Deut 32:6
he is an *u* son .... Hos 13:13
both to the wise, and to the *u* .... Rom 1:14
Wherefore be ye not *u*, but .... Eph 5:17

UNWITTINGLY

if a man eat of the holy thing *u* .... Lev 22:14
unawares and *u* may flee thither .... Josh 20:3
because he smote his neighbour *u* .... Josh 20:5

UNWORTHILY

and drink this cup of the Lord, *u* 1Cor 11:27
For he that eateth and drinketh *u* 1Cor 11:29

UNWORTHY

judge yourselves *u* of everlasting .... Acts 13:46
are ye *u* to judge the smallest 1Cor 6:2

UP See PREFACE.

UPBRAID

Zalmunna, with whom ye did *u* .... Judg 8:15
Then began he to *u* the cities .... Mt 11:20

UPBRAIDED

u them with their unbelief and .... Mk 16:14

UPBRAIDETH

and to all men liberally, and *u* .... Jas 1:5

UPHARSIN (*u-far'sin*) See PERES. Part of the 'handwriting on the wall.'

MENE, MENE, TEKEL, *U* .... Dan 5:25

UPHAZ (*u'-faz*) A place in southern Arabia.

from Tarshish, and gold from *U* .... Jer 10:9
were girded with fine gold of *U* .... Dan 10:5

UPHELD

and my fury, it *u* me .... Is 63:5

UPHOLD

u me with thy free spirit .... Ps 51:12
Lord is with them that *u* my soul .... Ps 54:4
U me according unto thy word, ... Ps 119:116
but honour shall *u* the humble in .... Prov 29:23
I will *u* thee with the right hand .... Is 41:10
Behold my servant, whom I *u* .... Is 42:1
wondered that there was none to *u* .... Is 63:5
They also that *u* Egypt shall fall .... Eze 30:6

UPHOLDEN

Thy words have *u* him that was .... Job 4:4
and his throne is *u* by mercy .... Prov 20:28

UPHOLDEST

thou *u* me in mine integrity, and .... Ps 41:12

UPHOLDETH

but the LORD *u* the righteous .... Ps 37:17
for the LORD *u* him with his hand .... Ps 37:24
thy right hand *u* me .... Ps 63:8
The LORD *u* all that fall, and .... Ps 145:14

UPHOLDING

u all things by the word of his .... Heb 1:3

UPON See PREFACE.

UPPER

on the *u* door post of the houses, ... Ex 12:7
put a covering upon his *u* lip .... Lev 13:45
or the *u* millstone to pledge .... Deut 24:6
And he gave her the *u* springs .... Josh 15:19
unto Beth-horon the .... Josh 16:5
And Caleb gave her the *u* springs .... Judg 1:15
his *u* chamber that was in Samaria 2Kin 1:2
by the conduit of the *u* pool 2Kin 18:17
the top of the *u* chamber of Ahaz 2Kin 23:12
Beth-horon the nether, and the *u*... .... 1Chr 7:24
of the *u* chambers thereof, and of 1Chr 28:11
he overlaid the *u* chambers with 2Chr 3:9
Also he built Beth-horon the *u* 2Chr 8:5
the watercourse of Gihon, ... 2Chr 32:30
the *u* pool in the highway of the .... Is 7:3
the *u* pool in the highway of the .... Is 36:2
the chambers were shorter .... Eze 42:5
lodge in the *u* lintels of it .... Zeph 2:14
shew you a large *u* room furnished .... Mk 14:15
shew you a large *u* room furnished .... Lk 22:12
in, they went up into an *u* room .... Acts 1:13
they laid her in an *u* chamber .... Acts 9:37
brought him into the *u* chamber .... Acts 9:39
the *u* coasts came to Ephesus .... Acts 19:1
were many lights in the *u* chamber .... Acts 20:8

UPPERMOST

in the *u* basket there was of all .... Gen 40:17
berries in the top of the *u* bough .... Is 17:6
an *u* branch, which they left .... Is 17:9
love the *u* rooms at feasts, and .... Mt 23:6
and the *u* rooms at feasts .... Mk 12:39
for ye love the *u* seats in the .... Lk 11:43

UPRIGHT

my sheaf arose, and also stood *u* .... Gen 37:7
the floods stood *u* as an heap... .... Ex 15:8
of your yoke, and made you go *u* .... Lev 26:13
the LORD liveth, thou hast been *u* 1Sa 29:6
I was also *u* before him, and have 2Sa 22:24
with the *u* man thou wilt shew 2Sa 22:26
man thou wilt shew thyself *u* 2Sa 22:26
for the Levites were more *u* in 2Chr 29:34
and that man was perfect and *u* .... Job 1:1
an *u* man, one that feareth God, ... Job 1:8
an *u* man, one that feareth God, ... Job 2:3
If thou wert pure and *u* .... Job 8:6
the just *u* man is laughed to .... Job 12:4
U men shall be astonied at this, ... Job 17:8
God, which saveth the *u* in heart .... Ps 7:10
privily shoot at the *u* in heart .... Ps 11:2
his countenance doth behold the *u* .... Ps 11:7
I was also *u* before him, and I .... Ps 18:23
with an *u* man thou wilt shew .... Ps 18:25
man thou wilt shew thyself *u* .... Ps 18:25
then shall I be *u*, and I shall be .... Ps 19:13
but we are risen, and stand *u* .... Ps 20:8
Good and *u* is the LORD .... Ps 25:8
joy, all ye that are *u* in heart .... Ps 32:11
for praise is comely for the *u* .... Ps 33:1
righteousness to the *u* in heart .... Ps 36:10
slay such as be of *u* conversation .... Ps 37:14
Look knoweth the days of the *u* .... Ps 37:18
the perfect man, and behold the *u* .... Ps 37:37
the *u* shall have dominion over .... Ps 49:14
all in heart shall glory .... Ps 64:10
To shew that the LORD is *u* .... Ps 92:15
all the *u* in heart shall follow .... Ps 94:15
and gladness for the *u* in heart .... Ps 97:11
heart, in the assembly of the *u* .... Ps 111:1
of the *u* shall be blessed .... Ps 112:2
Unto the *u* there ariseth light in .... Ps 112:4
O LORD, and *u* are thy judgments .... Ps 119:137
than the *u* shall dwell in thy .... Ps 125:4
the *u* shall dwell in thy presence .... Ps 140:13
For the *u* shall dwell in the land .... Prov 2:21
of the LORD is strength to the *u* .... Prov 10:29
of the *u* shall guide them .... Prov 11:3
of the *u* shall deliver them .... Prov 11:6
of the *u* is to depart from .... Prov 11:11
but such as are *u* in their way .... Prov 11:20
mouth of the *u* shall deliver them .... Prov 12:6

keepeth his path is u in the way ...... Prov 13:6
of the u shall flourish ...... Prov 14:11
prayer of the u is his delight. ...... Prov 15:8
The highway of the u is to depart. ...... Prov 16:17
and the transgressor for the u. ...... Prov 21:18
but as for the u, he directeth. ...... Prov 21:29
but the u shall have good things ...... Prov 28:10
The bloodthirsty hate the u. ...... Prov 29:10
he that is u in the way is. ...... Prov 29:27
I found, that God hath made man u. ...... Eccl 7:29
and that which was written was u ...... Eccl 12:10
the u love thee ...... Song 1:4
thou, most. u, dost weigh the path ...... Is 26:7
They are u as the palm tree, but ...... Jer 10:5
but he touched me, and set me u. ...... Dan 8:18
I speak unto thee, and stand u ...... Dan 10:11
whole kingdom, and u ones with him ...... Dan 11:17
and there is none u among men. ...... Mic 7:2
the most u is sharper than a ...... Mic 7:4
is lifted up is not u in him ...... Hab 2:4
a loud voice, Stand u on thy feet ...... Acts 14:10

UPRIGHTLY
He that walketh u, and worketh. ...... Ps 15:2
do ye judge u, O ye sons of men ...... Ps 58:1
the congregation I will judge u. ...... Ps 75:2
he withhold from them that walk u ...... Ps 84:11
is a buckler to them that walk u ...... Prov 2:7
He that walketh u walketh surely ...... Prov 10:9
a man of understanding walketh u. ...... Prov 15:21
Whoso walketh u shall be saved ...... Prov 28:18
righteously, and speaketh u ...... Is 33:15
and they abhor him that speaketh u. ...... Amos 5:10
do good to him that walketh u ...... Mic 2:7
u according to the truth of the ...... Gal 2:14

UPRIGHTNESS
or for the u of thine heart, dost ...... Deut 9:5
and in u of heart with thee 1Kin 3:6
in integrity of heart, and in u 1Kin 9:4
the heart, and hast pleasure in u 1Chr 29:17
in the u of mine heart I have 1Chr 29:17
the hope, and the u of thy ways. ...... Job 4:6
shall be of the u of my heart ...... Job 33:3
thousand, to shew unto man his u ...... Job 33:23
judgment to the people in u ...... Ps 9:8
Let integrity and u preserve me. ...... Ps 25:21
ever, and are done in truth and u ...... Ps 111:8
will praise thee with u of heart ...... Ps 119:7
lead me into the land of u ...... Ps 143:10
Who leave the paths of u, to walk ...... Prov 2:13
walketh in his u feareth the LORD. ...... Prov 14:2
is the poor that walketh in his u ...... Prov 28:6
The way of the just is u ...... Is 26:7
in the land of u will he deal ...... Is 26:10
beds, each one walking in his u ...... Is 57:2

UPRISING
knowest my downsitting and mine u... ...... Ps 139:2

UPROAR
noise of the city being in an u 1Kin 1:41
there be an u among the people ...... Mt 26:5
lest there be an u of the people ...... Mk 14:2
and set all the city on an u ...... Acts 17:5
in question for this day's u ...... Acts 19:40
after the u was ceased, Paul ...... Acts 20:1
that all Jerusalem was in an u ...... Acts 21:31
before these days madest an u ...... Acts 21:38

UPSIDE
wiping it, and turning it u down 2Kin 21:13
of the wicked he turneth u down ...... Ps 146:9
it waste, and turneth it u down ...... Is 24:1
u down shall be esteemed as the ...... Is 29:16
world u down are come hither also... ...... Acts 17:6

UPWARD
Fifteen cubits u did the waters ...... Gen 7:20
from twenty years old and u. ...... Ex 38:26
From twenty years old and u ...... Num 1:3
names, from twenty years old and u ...... Num 1:18
male from twenty years old and u... ...... Num 1:20
male from twenty years old and u ...... Num 1:22
names, from twenty years old and u ...... Num 1:24
names, from twenty years old and u ...... Num 1:26
names, from twenty years old and u ...... Num 1:28
names, from twenty years old and u ...... Num 1:30
names, from twenty years old and u ...... Num 1:32
names, from twenty years old and u ...... Num 1:34
names, from twenty years old and u ...... Num 1:36
names, from twenty years old and u ...... Num 1:38
names, from twenty years old and u ...... Num 1:40
names, from twenty years old and u ...... Num 1:42
from twenty years old and u ...... Num 1:45
old and u shall thou number them ...... Num 3:15
the males, from a month old and u ...... Num 3:22
the males, from a month old and u ...... Num 3:28
the males, from a month old and u ...... Num 3:34
the males from a month old and u ...... Num 3:39
of Israel from a month old and u ...... Num 3:40
of names, from a month old and u ...... Num 3:43
u even until fifty years old, all... ...... Num 4:3
u until fifty years old shall ...... Num 4:23
u even unto fifty years old shall ...... Num 4:30
u even unto fifty years old ...... Num 4:35
u even unto fifty years old, ... Num 4:39
u even unto fifty years old, ... Num 4:43
u even unto fifty years old ...... Num 4:47
u they shall go in to wait upon ...... Num 8:24
from twenty years old and u ...... Num 14:29
from twenty years old and u ...... Num 26:2
from twenty years old and u ...... Num 26:4

all males from a month old and u ...... Num 26:62
Egypt, from twenty years old and u. ...... Num 32:11
to Akrabbim, from the rock, and u ...... Judg 1:36
u he was higher than any of the 1Sa 9:2
people from his shoulders and u 1Sa 10:23
were able to put on armour, and u 2Kin 3:21
root downward, and bear fruit u 2Kin 19:30
from the age of thirty years and u 1Chr 23:3
from the age of twenty years and u 1Chr 23:24
males, from three years old and u 2Chr 31:16
from twenty years old and u 2Chr 31:17
from twenty years old and u ...... Ezr 3:8
unto trouble, as the sparks fly u ...... Job 5:7
the spirit of man that goeth u ...... Eccl 3:21
king and their God, and look u ...... Is 8:21
root downward, and bear fruit u ...... Is 37:31
mine eyes fail with looking u ...... Is 38:14
and their wings were stretched u ...... Eze 1:11
appearance of his loins even u ...... Eze 1:27
and from his loins even u, as the ...... Eze 8:2
still u to the side chambers ...... Eze 41:7
still u round about the house ...... Eze 41:7
breadth of the house was still u ...... Eze 41:7
altar and u shall be four horns ...... Eze 43:15
you, consider from this day and u ...... Hag 2:15
Consider now from this day and u ...... Hag 2:18

UR (ur)
1. A district in Mesopotamia.
nativity, in U of the Chaldees ...... Gen 11:28
with them from U of the Chaldees ...... Gen 11:31
thee out of U of the Chaldees ...... Gen 15:7
forth out of U of the Chaldees ...... Neh 9:7
2. Father of Eliphal.
Hararite, Eliphal the son of U 1Chr 11:35

URBANE (ur'-bane) *A Christian in Rome.*
Salute U, our helper in Christ, ... Rom 16:9

URBANUS See URBANE.

URGE
began to u him vehemently ...... Lk 11:53

URGED
And he u him, and he took it ...... Gen 33:11
u him, so that his soul was vexed ...... Judg 16:16
depart, his father in law u him ...... Judg 19:7
when they u him till he was 2Kin 2:17
And he u him to take it 2Kin 5:16
he u him, and bound two talents of... ...... 2Kin 5:23

URGENT
Egyptians were u upon the people. ...... Ex 12:33
the king's commandment was u ...... Dan 3:22

URI (u'-ri)
1. Father of Bezaleel.
by name Bezaleel the son of U ...... Ex 31:2
by name Bezaleel the son of U ...... Ex 35:30
And Bezaleel the son of U, the son ...... Ex 38:22
And Hur begat U 1Chr 2:20
altar, that Bezaleel the son of U 2Chr 1:5
2. Father of Geber.
Geber the son of U was in the 1Kin 4:19
Shallum, and Telem, and U ...... Ezr 10:24

URIAH (u-ri'-ah) See URIAH'S, URIAS, URIJAH.
1. Husband of Bathsheba.
Eliam, the wife of U the Hittite 2Sa 11:3
saying, Send me U the Hittite 2Sa 11:6
And Joab sent U to David. 2Sa 11:6
when U was come unto him, David... ...... 2Sa 11:7
And David said to U, Go down to 2Sa 11:8
U departed out of the king's 2Sa 11:8
But U slept at the door of the 2Sa 11:9
U went not down unto his house 2Sa 11:10
unto his house, David said unto U 2Sa 11:10
U said unto David, The ark, and 2Sa 11:11
And David said to U, Tarry here to 2Sa 11:12
So U abode in Jerusalem that day... ...... 2Sa 11:12
Joab, and sent it by the hand of U 2Sa 11:14
Set ye U in the forefront of the 2Sa 11:15
that he assigned U unto a place 2Sa 11:16
and U the Hittite died also 2Sa 11:17
The servant U the Hittite is dead. 2Sa 11:21
the servant U the Hittite is dead. 2Sa 11:24
when the wife of U heard that 2Sa 11:26
heard that U her husband was dead. 2Sa 11:26
thou hast killed U the Hittite 2Sa 12:9
hast taken the wife of U the 2Sa 12:10
U the Hittite 2Sa 23:39
in the matter of U the Hittite. 1Kin 15:5
the Hittite, Zabad the son of U 1Chr 11:41
2. A rebuilder of Jerusalem's wall.
Meremoth the son of U the priest ...... Ezr 8:33
3. A priest who aided Isaiah.
U the priest, and Zechariah the ...... Is 8:2

URIAH'S (u-ri'-ahz) *Refers to URIAH 1.*
child that U wife bare unto David 2Sa 12:15

URIAS (u-ri'-as) *Greek form of URIAH 1.*
her that had been the wife of U ...... Mt 1:6

URIEL (u'-ri-el)
1. Son of Tahath.
U his son, Uzziah his son, ... 1Chr 6:24
the chief, and his brethren an 1Chr 15:5
and for the Levites, for U 1Chr 15:11
2. Father of Micaiah.
the daughter of U of Gibeah 2Chr 13:2

URIJAH (u-ri'-jah) See URIAH.
1. A priest in Jerusalem.
king Ahaz sent to U the priest. 2Kin 16:10
U the priest built an altar 2Kin 16:11
so U the priest made it against 2Kin 16:11
king Ahaz commanded U the priest 2Kin 16:15
Thus did U the priest, according 2Kin 16:16
2. A priest who rebuilt the wall.
repaired Meremoth the son of U ...... Neh 3:4
of U the son of Koz another piece ...... Neh 3:21
3. A priest who aided Ezra.
and Shema, and Anaiah, and U ...... Neh 8:4
4. A prophet killed by Jehoiakim.
LORD, U the son of Shemaiah of ...... Jer 26:20
but when U heard it, he was ...... Jer 26:21
they fetched forth U out of Egypt ...... Jer 26:23

URIM (u'-rim) *A symbolic object in the High Priest's breastplate.*
the breastplate of judgment the U... ...... Ex 28:30
he put in the breastplate the U ...... Lev 8:8
the judgment of U before the LORD. ...... Num 27:21
thy U be with thy holy one, whom ...... Deut 33:8
not, neither by dreams, nor by U 1Sa 28:6
there stood up a priest with U ...... Ezr 2:63
he stood up a priest with U ...... Neh 7:65

US See PREFACE.

USE
may be used in any other u ...... Lev 7:24
neither shalt ye u enchantment ...... Lev 19:26
that thou mayest u them for the ...... Num 10:2
after which ye u to go a whoring ...... Num 15:39
sought thereof for any unclean u ...... Deut 26:14
of Judah the u of the bow 2Sa 1:18
could u both the right hand and 1Chr 12:2
according to the u of every 1Chr 28:15
that u their tongues, and say, He ...... Jer 23:31
As yet they shall u this speech ...... Jer 31:23
vain shalt thou u many medicines ...... Jer 46:11
they shall no more u it as a ...... Eze 12:23
shall u this proverb against thee ...... Eze 16:44
that ye u this proverb concerning ...... Eze 18:2
more to u this proverb in Israel. ...... Eze 18:3
of the two ways, to u divination. ...... Eze 21:21
for them which despitefully u you... ...... Mt 5:44
u not vain repetitions, as the ...... Mt 6:7
for them which despitefully u you... ...... Lk 6:28
to them despitefully, and to ...... Acts 14:5
u into that which is against ...... Rom 1:26
the natural u of the woman. ...... Rom 1:27
mayest be made free, u it rather 1Cor 7:21
they that u this world, as not... ...... 1Cor 7:31
thus minded, did I u lightness 2Cor 1:17
we u great plainness of speech 2Cor 3:12
present I should u sharpness 2Cor 13:10
only u not liberty for an ...... Gal 5:13
is good to the u of edifying ...... Eph 4:29
is good, if a man u it lawfully 1Ti 1:8
then let them u the office of a 1Ti 3:10
but u a little wine for thy 1Ti 5:23
and meet for the master's u 2Ti 2:21
even those who by reason of u ...... Heb 5:14
U hospitality one to another 1Pet 4:9

USED
ox hath u to push in time past ...... Ex 21:36
may be u in any other use ...... Lev 7:24
for so u the young men to do ...... Judg 14:10
whom he had u as his friend... ...... Judg 14:20
u divination and enchantments, and 2Kin 17:17
u enchantments, and dealt with 2Chr 33:6
times, and u enchantments, and u 2Chr 33:6
u witchcraft, and dealt with a 2Chr 33:6
A wild ass u to the wilderness, ... Jer 2:24
of the land have u oppression ...... Eze 22:29
to thine envy which thou hast u ...... Eze 35:11
u similitudes, by the ministry of ...... Hos 12:10
of the Pharisees u to fast ...... Mk 2:18
in the same city u sorcery ...... Acts 8:9
Many of them also which u curious... ...... Acts 19:19
they u helps, undergirding the ...... Acts 27:17
their tongues they have u deceit... ...... Rom 3:13
we have not u this power 1Cor 9:12
But I have u none of these things 1Cor 9:15
at any time u we flattering words 1Th 2:5
For they that have u the office... ...... 1Ti 3:13
companions of them that were so u ...... Heb 10:33

USES
good works for necessary u ...... Titus 3:14

USEST
as thou u to do unto those that ...... Ps 119:132

USETH
or that u divination, or an ...... Deut 18:10
brought which the king u to wear ...... Est 6:8
of the wise u knowledge aright ...... Prov 15:2
The poor u intreaties ...... Prov 18:23
that u his neighbour's service ...... Jer 22:13
every one that u proverbs shall ...... Eze 16:44
For every one that u milk is ...... Heb 5:13

USING
all are to perish with the u ...... Col 2:22
not u your liberty for a cloke of 1Pet 2:16

USURER
thou shalt not be to him as a u ...... Ex 22:25

USURP
nor to u authority over the man, ... 1Ti 2:12

USURY
neither shalt thou lay upon him u ...... Ex 22:25
Take thou no u of him, or ...... Lev 25:36

not give him thy money upon u........ Lev 25:37
not lend upon u to thy brother........ Deut 23:19
of money, u of victuals,................ Deut 23:19
u of any thing that is lent upon....... Deut 23:19
of any thing that is lent upon u...... Deut 23:20
stranger thou mayest lend upon u..... Deut 23:20
thou shalt not lend upon u............. Deut 23:20
and said unto them, Ye exact u....... Neh 5:7
pray you, let us leave off this u....... Neh 5:10
putteth out his money to u.............. Ps 15:5
He that by u and unjust gain........... Prov 28:8
as with the taker of u.................... Is 24:2
so with the giver of u to him........... Is 24:2
I have neither lent on u................. Jer 15:10
nor men have lent to me on u.......... Jer 15:10
that hath not given forth upon u...... Eze 18:8
Hath given forth upon u, and hath... Eze 18:13
hath not received u nor increase....... Eze 18:17
thou hast taken u and increase, and.. Eze 22:12
have received mine own with u........ Mt 25:27
have required mine own with u........ Lk 19:23

US-WARD
and thy thoughts which are to u....... Ps 40:5
of his power to u who believe........... Eph 1:19
but is longsuffering to u................ 2Pet 3:9

UTHAI (u'-thahee)
1. *Son of Ammihud.*
U the son of Ammihud, the son of.... 1Chr 9:4
2. *A clan leader with Ezra.*
U, and Zabbud, and with them......... Ezr 8:14

UTMOST
of my progenitors unto the u........... Gen 49:26
of Arnon, which is in the u coast...... Num 22:36
see the u part of the people............ Num 22:41
shalt see but the u part of them....... Num 23:13
the land of Judah, unto the u sea..... Deut 34:2
and all that are in the u corners....... Jer 9:26
and all that are in the u corners....... Jer 25:23
them that are in the u corners......... Jer 49:32
against her from the u border.......... Jer 50:26
his hinder part toward the u sea....... Joel 2:20
for she came from the u parts of...... Lk 11:31

UTTER
if he do not u it, then he shall......... Lev 5:1
if ye u not this our business,........... Josh 2:14
if thou u this our business, then...... Josh 2:20
awake, awake, u a song................. Judg 5:12
whom I appointed to u destruction.. 1Kin 20:42
u words out of their heart.............. Job 8:10
a wise man u vain knowledge.......... Job 15:2
my tongue u deceit....................... Job 27:4
my lips shall u knowledge clearly..... Job 33:3
I will u dark sayings of old............. Ps 78:2
How long shall they u and speak...... Ps 94:4
Who can u the mighty acts of the..... Ps 106:2
My lips shall u praise, when thou..... Ps 119:171
They shall abundantly u the........... Ps 145:7
but a false witness will u lies.......... Prov 14:5
heart shall u perverse things.......... Prov 23:33
man cannot u it........................... Eccl 1:8
hasty to u any thing before God...... Eccl 5:2
to u error against the LORD, to....... Is 32:6
u it even to the end of the earth....... Is 48:20
I will u my judgments against......... Jer 1:16
u his voice from his holy................ Jer 25:30
a parable unto the rebellious........... Eze 24:3
thereof were toward the u court....... Eze 40:31
thereof were toward the u court....... Eze 40:37
brought me forth into the u court..... Eze 42:1
which was for the u court............... Eze 42:3
toward the u court on the............... Eze 42:7
in the u court was fifty cubits......... Eze 42:8
goeth into them from the u court..... Eze 42:9
the holy place into the u court......... Eze 42:14
they go forth into the u court.......... Eze 44:19
even into the u court to the............ Eze 44:19
them not out into the u court.......... Eze 46:20
brought me forth into the u court..... Eze 46:21
u gate by the way that looketh........ Eze 47:2
the LORD shall u his voice before..... Joel 2:11
u his voice from Jerusalem............. Joel 3:16
u his voice from Jerusalem............. Amos 1:2
flood he will make an end of u......... Nah 1:8
he will make an u end................... Nah 1:9
shall be no more u destruction........ Zec 14:11
I will u things which have been....... Mt 13:35
except ye u by the tongue words...... 1Cor 14:9
it is not lawful for a man to........... 2Cor 12:4

UTTERANCE
as the Spirit gave them u............... Acts 2:4
ye are enriched by him, in all u....... 1Cor 1:5
in every thing, in faith, and u......... 2Cor 8:7
that u may be given unto me, that.... Eph 6:19
would open unto us a door of u........ Col 4:3

UTTERED
or u ought out of her lips,.............. Num 30:6
and that which she u with her lips.... Num 30:8
Jephthah u all his words before....... Judg 11:11
and the most High u his voice......... 2Sa 22:14
before me, and u my words to him... Neh 6:19
To whom hast thou u words........... Job 26:4
therefore have I u that I................ Job 42:3
he u his voice, the earth melted...... Ps 46:6
Which my lips have u, and my mouth.. Ps 66:14
have they u these words, from........ Jer 48:34
a noise of their voice is u............... Jer 51:55
the deep is his voice, and lifted....... Hab 3:10
with groanings which cannot be u.... Rom 8:26

things to say, and hard to be u....... Heb 5:11
seven thunders had u their voices.... Rev 10:3
seven thunders had u their voices.... Rev 10:4
things which the seven thunders u.... Rev 10:4

UTTERETH
For thy mouth u thine iniquity,....... Job 15:5
Day unto day u speech, and night.... Ps 19:2
she u her voice in the streets........... Prov 1:20
in the city she u her words............. Prov 1:21
he that u a slander, is a fool........... Prov 10:18
A fool u all his mind..................... Prov 29:11
When he u his voice, there is a........ Jer 10:13
When he u his voice, there is a........ Jer 51:16
he u his mischievous desire............ Mic 7:3

UTTERING
u from the heart words of............... Is 59:13

UTTERLY
for I will u put out the.................. Ex 17:14
If her father u refuse to give.......... Ex 22:17
only, he shall be u destroyed.......... Ex 22:20
but thou shalt u overthrow them..... Ex 23:24
shall pronounce him u unclean....... Lev 13:44
I abhor them, to destroy them u...... Lev 26:44
that soul shall u be cut off.............. Num 15:31
then I will u destroy them.............. Num 21:2
they u destroyed them and their...... Num 21:3
But if her husband hath u made...... Num 30:12
u destroyed the men, and the women. Deut 2:34
we u destroyed them, as we did....... Deut 3:6
u destroying the men, women, and... Deut 3:6
that ye shall soon u perish from...... Deut 4:26
upon it, but shalt u destroy them..... Deut 7:2
smite them, and u destroy them...... Deut 7:2
but thou shalt u detest it............... Deut 7:26
and thou shalt u abhor it.............. Deut 7:26
Ye shall u destroy all the places...... Deut 12:2
of the sword, destroying it u........... Deut 13:15
But thou shalt u destroy them....... Deut 20:17
ye will u corrupt yourselves........... Deut 31:29
Sihon and Og, whom ye u destroyed. Josh 2:10
they u destroyed all that was in...... Josh 6:21
until he had u destroyed all the...... Josh 8:26
taken Ai, and had u destroyed it..... Josh 10:1
the king thereof he u destroyed...... Josh 10:28
but had u destroyed that day........... Josh 10:35
u destroyed it, and all the............. Josh 10:37
u destroyed all the souls that......... Josh 10:39
u destroyed all that breathed......... Josh 10:40
of the sword, u destroying them..... Josh 11:11
he u destroyed them, as Moses the.. Josh 11:12
that he might destroy them u......... Josh 11:20
them u with their cities............... Josh 11:21
but did not u drive them out.......... Josh 17:13
Zephath, and u destroyed it........... Judg 1:17
and did not u drive them out.......... Judg 1:28
that thou hadst u hated her........... Judg 15:2
Ye shall u destroy every male, and.. Judg 21:11
u destroy all that they have, and.... 1Sa 15:3
but destroyed u u, and all the........ 1Sa 15:8
good, and would not u destroy them. 1Sa 15:9
and refuse, that they destroyed u.... 1Sa 15:9
have u destroyed the Amalekites..... 1Sa 15:20
to destroy the sinners from............ 1Sa 15:20
should have been u destroyed........ 1Sa 15:21
his people Israel to abhor him......... 1Sa 27:12
the heart of a lion, shall u melt...... 2Sa 17:10
they shall be u burned with fire...... 2Sa 23:7
also were not able u to destroy....... 1Kin 9:21
all lands, by destroying them u....... 2Kin 19:11
destroyed them u unto this day...... 1Chr 4:41
to slay and destroy them u............ Est 3:13
until they had u destroyed them..... 2Chr 31:1
that my fathers u destroyed them... 2Chr 32:14
thou gavest not u consume them..... Neh 9:31
fall, he shall not be u cast down..... Ps 37:24
they are consumed with terrors....... Ps 73:19
will I not u take from him.............. Ps 89:33
O forsake me not u...................... Ps 119:8
word of truth u out of my mouth..... Ps 119:43
for love, it would u be contemned... Song 8:7
And the idols he shall u abolish....... Is 2:18
man, and the land he u desolate...... Is 6:11
the LORD shall u destroy the.......... Is 11:15
be u emptied, and u spoiled........... Is 24:3
the LORD maketh u empty, and...... Is 24:3
be u broken down....................... Is 24:19
he hath u destroyed them, he hath.. Is 34:2
to all lands by destroying them u.... Is 37:11
and the young men shall u fall........ Is 40:30
The LORD hath u separated me from. Is 56:3
salvation shall be u wasted............ Is 60:12
for every brother will u supplant..... Jer 9:4
will I pluck up and destroy that...... Jer 12:17
Hast thou u rejected Judah............ Jer 14:19
will u forget you, and I will........... Jer 23:39
deliver them, and make them......... Jer 25:9
and should ye be u unpunished....... Jer 25:29
u destroy after them, saith the....... Jer 50:21
her up as heaps, and destroy her u.. Jer 50:26
destroy ye u all her host............... Jer 51:3
of Babylon shall be u broken........... Jer 51:58
But thou hast u rejected us............ Lam 5:22
Slay u old and young, both maids,... Eze 9:6
shall it not u wither, when the....... Eze 17:10
make themselves u bald for thee..... Eze 27:31
make the land of Egypt u waste..... Eze 29:10
destroy, and u to make away many.. Dan 11:44
but I will u take them away........... Hos 1:6
the king of Israel u be cut off........ Hos 10:15
saving that I will not u destroy..... Amos 9:8

and say, We be u spoiled............... Mic 2:4
he is u cut off............................ Nah 1:15
I will u consume all things from..... Zeph 1:2
his right eye shall be u darkened.... Zec 11:17
for a u fault among you................ 1Cor 6:7
shall u perish in their own........... 2Pet 2:12
she shall be u burned with fire...... Rev 18:8

UTTERMOST
in the u edge of another curtain...... Ex 26:4
in the u side of another curtain...... Ex 36:11
the u edge of the curtain in the...... Ex 36:17
were in the u parts of the camp...... Num 11:1
a city in the u of thy border........... Num 20:16
even unto the u sea shall your....... Deut 11:24
was the u part of the south coast.... Josh 15:1
the sea at the u part of Jordan....... Josh 15:5
the u cities of the tribe of the........ Josh 15:21
Saul tarried in the u part of.......... 1Sa 14:2
from the u part of the one wing...... 1Kin 6:24
the u part of the other were ten...... 1Kin 6:24
the u part of the camp of Syria...... 2Kin 7:5
came to the u part of the camp....... 2Kin 7:8
out unto the u part of the heaven.... Neh 1:9
the u parts of the earth for thy...... Ps 2:8
They also that dwell in the u......... Ps 65:8
dwell in the u parts of the sea....... Ps 139:9
the u part of the rivers of Egypt..... Is 7:18
From the u part of the earth have.... Is 24:16
thou hast paid the u farthing......... Mt 5:26
for she came from the u parts of..... Mt 12:42
from the u part of the earth to...... Mk 13:27
the earth to the u part of heaven.... Mk 13:27
unto the u part of the earth.......... Acts 1:8
I will know the u of your matter..... Acts 24:22
wrath is come upon them to the u... 1Th 2:16
that came unto God by him........... Heb 7:25

UZ (uz)
1. *A son of Aram.*
U, and Hul, and Gether, and Mash... Gen 10:23
are these; U, and Aran.................. Gen 36:28
Arphaxad, and Lud, and Aram, and U. 1Chr 1:17
of Dishan; U, and Aran................. 1Chr 1:42
There was a man in the land of U.... Job 1:1
and all the kings of the land of U.... Jer 25:20
that dwellest in the land of U........ Lam 4:21

UZAI (u'-zahee) *Father of Palal.*
Palal the son of U, over against...... Neh 3:25

UZAL (u'-zal) *A son of Joktan.*
And Hadoram, and U, and Diklah,... Gen 10:27
Hadoram also, and U, and Diklah,... 1Chr 1:21

UZZA (uz'-zah) See UZZAH.
1. *Name of the burial ground of Manasseh and Amon.*
his own house, in the garden of U.... 2Kin 21:18
his sepulchre in the garden of U...... 2Kin 21:26
2. *Son of Shimei.*
son, Shimei his son, U his son,....... 1Chr 6:29
3. *A brother of Ahihud.*
Gera, he removed them, and begat U.. 1Chr 8:7
4. *Touched the Ark and died.*
and U and Ahio drave the cart........ 1Chr 13:7
U put forth his hand to hold the..... 1Chr 13:9
of the LORD was kindled against U... 1Chr 13:10
had made a breach upon U............. 1Chr 13:11
5. *A family of Nethinims.*
The children of U, the children....... Ezr 2:49
of Gazzam, the children of U......... Neh 7:51

UZZAH (uz'-zah) See UZZA. Same as UZZA 4.
and U and Ahio, the sons of............ 2Sa 6:3
U put forth his hand to the ark....... 2Sa 6:6
of the LORD was kindled against U... 2Sa 6:7
The LORD had made a breach upon... 2Sa 6:8

UZZEN-SHEERAH See UZZEN-SHERAH.

UZZEN-SHERAH (uz''-zen-she'-rah) *A city in Ephraim.*
the nether, and the upper, and U..... 1Chr 7:24

UZZI (uz'-zi)
1. *A son of Bukki.*
begat Bukki, and Bukki begat U...... 1Chr 6:5
U begat Zerahiah, and Zerahiah..... 1Chr 6:5
U his son, Zerahiah his................. 1Chr 6:51
The son of Zerahiah, the son of U.... Ezr 7:4
2. *Father of Izrahiah.*
U, and Rephaiah, and Jeriel, and.... 1Chr 7:2
And the sons of U....................... 1Chr 7:3
3. *Son of Bela.*
Ezbon, and U, and Uzziel, and....... 1Chr 7:7
4. *A family of exiles.*
of Jeroham, and Elah the son of U.. 1Chr 9:8
5. *An overseer of Levites.*
Jerusalem was U the son of Bani..... Neh 11:22
6. *A priest descended from Jedaiah.*
of Jedaiah, U........................... Neh 12:19
of Shemaiah, and Eleazar, and U.... Neh 12:42

UZZIA (uz-zi'-ah) *A 'mighty man' of David.*
U the Ashterathite, Shama and....... 1Chr 11:44

UZZIAH (uz-zi'-ah)
1. *A king of Judah.*
thirtieth year of U king of Judah.... 2Kin 15:13
year of Jotham the son of U........... 2Kin 15:30
son of U king of Judah to reign....... 2Kin 15:32
to all that his father U had done.... 2Kin 15:34
all the people of Judah took U........ 2Chr 26:1
Sixteen years old was U when he.... 2Chr 26:3
And the Ammonites gave gifts to U.. 2Chr 26:8

Moreover *U* built towers in 2Chr 26:9
Moreover *U* had an host of 2Chr 26:11
U prepared for them throughout 2Chr 26:14
And they withstood *U* the king 2Chr 26:18
It appertaineth not unto thee, *U* 2Chr 26:18
U was wroth, and had 2Chr 26:19
U the king was a leper unto the 2Chr 26:21
Now the rest of the acts of *U* 2Chr 26:22
So *U* slept with his fathers, and 2Chr 26:23
to all that his father *U* did 2Chr 27:2
and Jerusalem in the days of *U* .... Is 1:1
In the year that king *U* died I .... Is 6:1
the son of Jotham, the son of *U* .... Is 7:1
of Beeri, in the days of *U* .... Hos 1:1
in the days of *U* king of Judah .... Amos 1:1
in the days of *U* king of Judah .... Zec 14:5

2. Son of Uriel.
U his son, and Shaul his son 1Chr 6:24

3. Father of Jehonathan.
was Jehonathan the son of *U* 1Chr 27:25

4. Married a foreigner in exile.
and Shemaiah, and Jehiel, and *U* .... Ezr 10:21

5. A family of exiles.
Athaiah the son of *U*, the son of .... Neh 11:4

UZZIEL (uz-zi'-el)
1. A son of Kohath.
Amram, and Izhar, and Hebron, and *U*.. Ex 6:18
And the sons of *U* .... Ex 6:22
the sons of *U* the uncle of Aaron, ... Lev 10:4
Amram, and Izehar, Hebron, and *U* ...... Num 3:19
shall be Elizaphan the son of *U* .... Num 3:30
Amram, Izhar, and Hebron, and *U* 1Chr 6:2
Izhar, and Hebron, and *U* 1Chr 6:18
Of the sons of *U* 1Chr 15:10
Amram, Izhar, Hebron, and *U* 1Chr 23:12
Of the sons of *U* 1Chr 23:20
Of the sons of *U* 1Chr 24:24

2. A son of Ishi.
and Neariah, and Rephaiah, and 1Chr 4:42

3. A son of Bela.
Ezbon, and Uzzi, and *U*, and Jerimoth . 1Chr 7:7

4. A sanctuary servant.
Bukkiah, Mattaniah, *U*, Shebuel, ... 1Chr 25:4

5. A Levite who cleansed the Temple.
Shemaiah, and *U* 2Chr 29:14

6. A repairer of Jerusalem's wall.
repaired *U* the son of Harhaiah .... Neh 3:8

UZZIELITES (uz-zi'-el-ites) Descendants of
Uzziel 1.
and the family of the *U* .... Num 3:27
the Hebronites, and the *U* 1Chr 26:23

V

VAGABOND
a *v* shalt thou be in the earth .... Gen 4:12
be a fugitive and a *v* in the earth ...... Gen 4:14
Then certain of the *v* Jews .... Acts 19:13

VAGABONDS
Let his children be continually *v* ...... Ps 109:10

VAIL
therefore she took a *v*, and .... Gen 24:65
from her, and covered her with a *v* ...... Gen 38:14
away, and laid by her *v* from her .... Gen 38:19
And thou shalt make a *v* of blue, ... Ex 26:31
hang up the *v* under the taches, ... Ex 26:33
the *v* the ark of the testimony .... Ex 26:33
the *v* shall divide unto you .... Ex 26:33
shalt set the table without the *v* ...... Ex 26:35
of the congregation without the *v* ...... Ex 27:21
the *v* that is by the ark of .... Ex 30:6
with them, he put a *v* on his face ...... Ex 34:33
speak with him, he took the *v* off ...... Ex 34:34
Moses put the *v* upon his face .... Ex 34:35
seat, and the *v* of the covering, ... Ex 35:12
And he made a *v* of blue, and purple, ... Ex 36:35
and the sockets of the *v* .... Ex 36:36
skins, and the *v* of the covering, ... Ex 39:34
and cover the ark with the *v* .... Ex 40:3
set up the *v* of the covering, and ...... Ex 40:21
northward, without the *v* .... Ex 40:22
of the congregation before the *v* .... Ex 40:26
before the *v* of the sanctuary .... Lev 4:6
the LORD, even before the *v* .... Lev 4:17
the *v* before the mercy seat .... Lev 16:2
small, and bring it within the *v* .... Lev 16:12
and bring his blood within the *v* .... Lev 16:15
he shall not go in unto the *v* .... Lev 21:23
Without the *v* of the testimony, ... Lev 24:3
shall take down the covering *v* .... Num 4:5
of the altar, and within the *v* .... Num 18:7
Bring the *v* that thou hast upon .... Ruth 3:15
And he made the *v* of blue, and 2Chr 3:14
the *v* that is spread over all .... Is 25:7
which put a *v* over his face, that 2Cor 3:13
this day remaineth the same *v* 2Cor 3:14
which *v* is done away in Christ 2Cor 3:14
the *v* is upon their heart 2Cor 3:15
the *v* shall be taken away 2Cor 3:16

VAILS
linen, and the hoods, and the *v* .... Is 3:23

VAIN
and let them not regard *v* words .... Ex 5:9
the name of the LORD thy God in *v*....... Ex 20:7
that taketh his name in *v* .... Ex 20:7
and ye shall sow your seed in *v*......... Lev 26:16
your strength shall be spent in *v* ...... Lev 26:20
the name of the LORD thy God in *v* ...... Deut 5:11
that taketh his name in *v* .... Deut 5:11
For it is not a *v* thing for you .... Deut 32:47
wherewith Abimelech hired *v* .... Judg 9:4
were gathered *v* men to Jephthah .... Judg 11:3
then should ye go after *v* things 1Sa 12:21
for they are *v* 1Sa 12:21
Surely in *v* have I kept all that 1Sa 25:21
servants, as one of the *v* fellows 2Sa 6:20
they followed vanity, and became *v* 2Kin 17:15
sayest, (but they are but *v* words 2Kin 18:20
there are gathered unto him *v* men 2Chr 13:7
be wicked, why then labour I in *v* ...... Job 9:29
For he knoweth *v* men .... Job 11:11
For *v* man would be wise, though .... Job 11:12
a wise man utter *v* knowledge .... Job 15:2
Shall *v* words have an end .... Job 16:3
How then comfort ye me in *v* .... Job 21:34
why then are ye thus altogether *v* ...... Job 27:12
doth Job open his mouth in *v* .... Job 35:16
her labour is in *v* without fear .... Job 39:16
Behold, the hope of him is in *v* .... Job 41:9
and the people imagine a *v* thing ...... Ps 2:1
I have not sat with *v* persons .... Ps 26:4
An horse is a *v* thing for safety ...... Ps 33:17
every man walketh in a *v* shew .... Ps 39:6
surely they are disquieted in *v* .... Ps 39:6
for *v* is the help of man .... Ps 60:11
and become not *v* in robbery .... Ps 62:10
I have cleansed my heart in *v* .... Ps 73:13
hast thou made all men in *v* .... Ps 89:47
for *v* is the help of man .... Ps 108:12
I hate *v* thoughts .... Ps 119:113
they labour in *v* that build it .... Ps 127:1
the watchman waketh but in *v* .... Ps 127:1
It is *v* for you to rise up early, ... Ps 127:2
thine enemies take thy name in *v* ...... Ps 139:20
Surely in *v* the net is spread in ...... Prov 1:17
followeth *v* persons is void of .... Prov 12:11
v persons shall have poverty .... Prov 28:19
and take the name of my God in *v* ...... Prov 30:9
is deceitful, and beauty is *v* .... Prov 31:30
all the days of his *v* life which ...... Eccl 6:12
Bring no more *v* oblations .... Is 1:13
For the Egyptians shall help in *v* ...... Is 30:7
(but they are but *v* words) I have ...... Is 36:5
it, he created it not in *v* .... Is 45:18
seed of Jacob, Seek ye me in *v* .... Is 45:19
Then I said, I have laboured in *v* ...... Is 49:4
my strength for nought, and in *v* ...... Is 49:4
They shall not labour in *v* .... Is 65:23
after vanity, and are become *v* .... Jer 2:5
In *v* have I smitten your children ...... Jer 2:30
Truly in *v* is salvation hoped for ...... Jer 3:23
How long shall thy *v* thoughts .... Jer 4:14
in *v* shalt thou make thyself fair ...... Jer 4:30
the founder melteth in *v* .... Jer 6:29
Lo, certainly in *v* made he it .... Jer 8:8
the pen of the scribes is in *v* .... Jer 8:8
the customs of the people are *v* .... Jer 10:3
they make you *v* .... Jer 23:16
in *v* shalt thou use many .... Jer 46:11
none shall return in *v* .... Jer 50:9
and the people shall labour in *v*....... Jer 51:58
Thy prophets have seen *v* and .... Lam 2:14
eyes as yet failed for our *v* help ...... Lam 4:17
that I have not said in *v* that I ...... Eze 6:10
more any *v* vision nor flattering ...... Eze 12:24
Have ye not seen a *v* vision .... Eze 13:7
they comfort in *v* .... Zec 10:2
have said, It is *v* to serve God .... Mal 3:14
use not *v* repetitions, as the .... Mt 6:7
But in *v* they do worship me, ... Mt 15:9
Howbeit in *v* do they worship me, ... Mk 7:7
and the people imagine *v* things .... Acts 4:25
but became *v* in their .... Rom 1:21
for he heareth not the sword in *v*...... Rom 13:4
of the wise, that they are *v* 1Cor 3:20
you, unless ye have believed in *v* 1Cor 15:2
was bestowed upon me was not in *v* 1Cor 15:10
risen, then is our preaching *v* 1Cor 15:14
and your faith is also *v* 1Cor 15:14
be not raised, your faith is *v* 1Cor 15:17
labour is not in *v* in the Lord 1Cor 15:58
receive not the grace of God in *v* 2Cor 6:1
you should be in *v* in this behalf 2Cor 9:3
I should run, or had run, in *v* .... Gal 2:2
the law, Christ is dead in *v* .... Gal 2:21
ye suffered so many things in *v* .... Gal 3:4
if it be yet in *v* .... Gal 3:4
bestowed upon you labour in *v* .... Gal 4:11
Let us not be desirous of *v* glory, ... Gal 5:26
no man deceive you with *v* words ...... Eph 5:6
Christ, that I have not run in *v* ...... Phil 2:16
neither laboured in *v* .... Phil 2:16
of deceit, after the tradition of .... Col 2:8
shew thee, O man, that it was not in *v* . 1Th 2:1
you, and our labour be in *v* 1Th 3:5
have turned aside unto *v* jangling 1Ti 1:6
v babblings, and oppositions of 1Ti 6:20
But shun profane and *v* babblings 2Ti 2:16
v talkers and deceivers, specially ...... Titus 1:10

for they are unprofitable and *v* .... Titus 3:9
heart, this man's religion is *v* .... Jas 1:26
O *v* man, that faith without works ...... Jas 2:20
that the scripture saith in *v* .... Jas 4:5
from your *v* conversation received 1Pet 1:18

VAINGLORY
be done through strife or *v* .... Phil 2:3

VAINLY
v puffed up by his fleshly mind, ... Col 2:18

VAIZATHA See VAJEZATHA.

VALE
together in the *v* of Siddim .... Gen 14:3
with them in the *v* of Siddim .... Gen 14:8
the *v* of Siddim was full of .... Gen 14:10
sent him out of the *v* of Hebron ...... Gen 37:14
plain, in the hills, and in the *v*, ... Deut 1:7
and of the south, and of the *v* .... Josh 10:40
sycomore trees that are in the *v* 1Kin 10:27
that are in the *v* for abundance. 2Chr 1:15
mountains, in the cities of the *v*..... Jer 33:13

VALIANT
saw any strong man, or any *v* man 1Sa 14:52
in playing, and a mighty *v* man 1Sa 16:18
only be thou *v* for me, and fight 1Sa 18:17
to Abner, Art not thou a *v* man 1Sa 26:15
All the *v* men arose, and went all. 1Sa 31:12
hands be strengthened, and be ye *v*. ... 2Sa 2:7
where he knew that *v* men were 2Sa 11:16
be courageous, and be *v* 2Sa 13:28
And he also that is *v*, whose heart. ... 2Sa 17:10
they which be with him are *v* men 2Sa 17:10
of Jehoiada, the son of a *v* man 2Sa 23:20
v men that drew the sword 2Sa 24:9
for thou art a *v* man, and bringest ... 1Kin 1:42
of *v* men, men able to bear 1Chr 5:18
they were *v* men of might in their ... 1Chr 7:2
of Issachar were *v* men of might 1Chr 7:5
They arose, all the *v* men 1Chr 10:12
the son of a *v* man of Kabzeel, ... 1Chr 11:22
Also the *v* men of the armies were ... 1Chr 11:26
mighty men, and with all the *v* men ... 1Chr 28:1
with an army of *v* men of war 2Chr 13:3
of the LORD, that were *v* men. 2Chr 26:17
in one day, which were all *v* men 2Chr 28:6
hundred threescore and eight *v* men. ... Neh 11:6
threescore *v* men are about it, of..... Song 3:7
are about it, of the *v* of Israel. .... Song 3:7
down the inhabitants like a *v* man. ... Is 10:13
their *v* ones shall cry without. ...... Is 33:7
but they are not *v* for the truth. .... Jer 9:3
Why are thy *v* men swept away, ... Jer 46:15
red, the *v* men are in scarlet. ...... Nah 2:3
waxed *v* in fight, turned to .... Heb 11:34

VALIANTEST
twelve thousand men of the *v* .... Judg 21:10

VALIANTLY
and Israel shall do *v* .... Num 24:18
behave ourselves *v* for our people ... 1Chr 19:13
Through God we shall do *v* .... Ps 60:12
Through God we shall do *v* .... Ps 108:13
right hand of the LORD doeth *v* ...... Ps 118:15
right hand of the LORD doeth *v* ...... Ps 118:16

VALLEY
at the *v* of Shaveh, which is the ...... Gen 14:17
his tent in the *v* of Gerar .... Gen 26:17
Isaac's servants digged in the *v* ...... Gen 26:19
and the Canaanites dwelt in the *v*, ... Num 14:25
and pitched in the *v* of Zared .... Num 21:12
And from Bamoth in the *v*, that is ... Num 21:20
they went up unto the *v* of Eshcol. ... Num 32:9
and came unto the *v* of Eshcol... ...... Deut 1:24
unto the river Arnon half the *v*, ... Deut 2:36
So we abode in the *v* over against. ... Deut 3:29
in the *v* over against Beth-peor, ... Deut 4:46
down the heifer unto a rough *v* .... Deut 21:4
the heifer's neck there in the *v* ...... Deut 21:4
heifer that is beheaded in the *v*, ... Deut 21:6
and the plain of the *v* of Jericho. .... Deut 34:3
he buried him in a *v* in the land. .... Deut 34:6
brought them unto the *v* of Achor. .... Josh 7:24
The *v* of Achor, unto this day. .... Josh 7:26
now there was a *v* between them. ...... Josh 8:11
night into the midst of the *v* .... Josh 8:13
and Dius, Moon, in the *v* of Ajalon. ... Josh 10:12
south of Chinneroth, and in the *v*..... Josh 11:2
unto the *v* of Mizpeh eastward...... ... Josh 11:8
all the land of Goshen, and the *v* ..... Josh 11:16
of Israel, and the *v* of the same. .... Josh 11:16
even unto Baal-gad in the *v* of ...... Josh 11:17
from Baal-gad in the *v* of Lebanon. ... Josh 12:7
in the mount of the *v*, ... Josh 13:19
toward Debir from the *v* of Achor. .... Josh 15:7
the border went up by the *v* of ...... Josh 15:8
unto the *v* of the son of Hinnom. ...... Josh 15:8
of the *v* of the giants northward. ...... Josh 15:8
And in the *v*, Eshtaol, and Zoreah, ... Josh 15:33
v have chariots of iron. .... Josh 17:16
they who are of the *v* of Jezreel. .... Josh 17:16
before the *v* of the son of Hinnom. ... Josh 18:16
which is in the *v* of the giants. ...... Josh 18:16
and descended to the *v* of Hinnom. .... Josh 18:16
Beth-hoglah, and the *v* of Keziz,. .... Josh 18:21

are in the v of Jiphthah-el .... Josh 19:14
to the v of Jiphthah-el toward ...... Josh 19:27
and in the south, and in the v....... Judg 1:9
out the inhabitants of the v.......... Judg 1:19
suffer them to come down to the v .. Judg 1:34
he was sent on foot into the v .... Judg 5:15
and pitched in the v of Jezreel...... Judg 6:33
by the hill of Moreh, in the v....... Judg 7:1
Midian was beneath him in the v..... Judg 7:8
of the east lay along in the v .... Judg 7:12
loved a woman in the v of Sorek .... Judg 16:4
it was in the v that lieth by.......... Judg 18:28
their wheat harvest in the v......... 1Sa 6:13
the border that looketh to the v..... 1Sa 13:18
of Amalek, and laid wait in the v.... 1Sa 15:5
and pitched by the v of Elah........ 1Sa 17:2
there was a v between them......... 1Sa 17:3
of Israel, were in the v of Elah..... 1Sa 17:19
until thou come to the v............ 1Sa 17:52
thou slewest in the v of Elah........ 1Sa 21:9
were on the other side of the v..... 1Sa 31:7
themselves in the v of Rephaim..... 2Sa 5:18
themselves in the v of Rephaim..... 2Sa 5:22
of the Syrians in the v of salt........ 2Sa 8:13
pitched in the v of Rephaim......... 2Sa 23:13
some mountain, or into some v...... 2Kin 2:16
Make this v full of ditches.......... 2Kin 3:16
in the v of salt ten thousand....... 2Kin 14:7
which is in the v of the children ... 2Kin 23:10
the father of the v of Charashim 1Chr 4:14
even unto the east side of the v..... 1Chr 4:39
were in the v saw that they fled 1Chr 10:7
encamped in the v of Rephaim....... 1Chr 11:15
themselves in the v of Rephaim..... 1Chr 14:9
spread themselves abroad in the v ... 1Chr 14:13
the v of salt eighteen thousand 1Chr 18:12
in the v of Zephathah at Mareshah.. 2Chr 14:10
themselves in the v of Berachah..... 2Chr 20:26
The v of Berachah, unto this day ... 2Chr 20:26
people, and went to the v of salt.... 2Chr 25:11
the corner gate, and at the v gate ... 2Chr 26:9
in the v of the son of Hinnom 2Chr 28:3
in the v of the son of Hinnom 2Chr 33:6
the west side of Gihon, in the v 2Chr 32:30
came to fight in the v of Megiddo .. 2Chr 35:22
out by night by the gate of the v ... Neh 2:13
and entered by the gate of the v .... Neh 2:15
The v gate repaired Hanun, and the .. Neh 3:13
Beer-sheba unto the v of Hinnom ... Neh 11:30
Lod, and Ono, the v of craftsmen... Neh 11:35
The clods of the v shall be sweet.... Job 21:33
He paweth in the v, and rejoiceth... Job 39:21
the v of the shadow of death........ Ps 23:4
smote of Edom in the v of salt....... Ps 60:t
and mete out the v of Succoth...... Ps 60:6
the v of Baca make it a well........ Ps 84:6
and mete out the v of Succoth...... Ps 108:7
ravens of the v shall pick it out.... Prov 30:17
nuts to see the fruits of the v...... Song 6:11
ears in the v of Rephaim........... Is 17:5
The burden of the v of vision...... Is 22:1
God of hosts in the v of vision...... Is 22:5
which is on the head of the fat v .... Is 28:1
be wroth as in the v of Gibeon ..... Is 28:21
Every v shall be exalted, and....... Is 40:4
As a beast goeth down into the v ... Is 63:14
the v of Achor a place for.......... Is 65:10
see thy way in the v, know what .... Jer 2:23
which is in the v of the son of...... Jer 7:31
nor the v of the son of............. Jer 7:32
nor the v of the son of Hinnom ..... Jer 7:32
of Hinnom, but the v of slaughter.. Jer 7:32
go forth unto the v of the son of.... Jer 19:2
nor The v of the son of Hinnom ..... Jer 19:6
of Hinnom, but The v of slaughter.. Jer 19:6
thee, O inhabitant of the v......... Jer 21:13
the whole v of the dead bodies, ... Jer 31:40
which are in the v of the son of..... Jer 32:35
and in the cities of the v.......... Jer 32:44
off with the remnant of their v...... Jer 47:5
the v also shall perish, and the..... Jer 48:8
in the valleys, thy flowing v........ Jer 49:4
of the v which was full of bones ... Eze 37:1
were very many in the open v....... Eze 37:2
the v of the passengers on the..... Eze 39:11
shall call it The v of Hamon-gog.... Eze 39:11
buried it in the v of Hamon-gog ... Eze 39:15
bow of Israel in the v of Jezreel... Hos 1:5
the v of Achor for a door of hope.... Hos 2:15
down into the v of Jehoshaphat..... Joel 3:2
come up to the v of Jehoshaphat.... Joel 3:12
multitudes in the v of decision...... Joel 3:14
LORD is near in the v of decision... Joel 3:14
and shall water the v of Shittim..... Joel 3:18
the stones thereof into the v........ Mic 1:6
Hadadrimmon in the v of Megiddon.. Zec 12:11
and there shall be a very great v... Zec 14:4
flee to the v of the mountains...... Zec 14:5
for the v of the mountains shall..... Zec 14:5
Every v shall be filled, and every ... Lk 3:5

VALLEYS
As the v are they spread forth,..... Num 24:6
and depths that spring out of v...... Deut 8:7
it, is a land of hills and v......... Deut 11:11
Jordan, in the hills, and in the v .... Josh 9:1
In the mountains, and in the v ...... Josh 12:8
hills, but he is not God of the v..... 1Kin 20:28
put to flight all their v............. 1Chr 12:15
v was Shaphat the son of Adlai 1Chr 27:29
To dwell in the cliffs of the v....... Job 30:6

will he harrow the v after thee ..... Job 39:10
the v also are covered over with..... Ps 65:13
they go down by the v unto the ..... Ps 104:8
He sendeth the springs into the v... Ps 104:10
of Sharon, and the lily of the v .... Song 2:1
all of them in the desolate v........ Is 7:19
that thy choicest v shall be full..... Is 22:7
are on the head of the fat v of..... Is 28:1
fountains in the midst of the v ..... Is 41:18
slaying the children in the v .... Is 57:5
Wherefore gloriest thou in the v .... Jer 49:4
hills, to the rivers, and to the v .... Eze 6:3
the mountains like doves of the v... Eze 7:16
in all the v his branches are .... Eze 31:12
fill the v with thy height........... Eze 32:5
in thy hills, and in thy v........... Eze 35:8
hills, to the rivers, and to the v .... Eze 36:4
hills, to the rivers, and to the v .... Eze 36:6
the v shall be cleft, as wax .... Mic 1:4

VALOUR
armed, all the mighty men of v...... Josh 1:14
thereof, and the mighty men of v.... Josh 6:2
thirty thousand mighty men of v .... Josh 8:3
him, and all the mighty men of v.... Josh 10:7
men, all lusty, and all men of v ..... Judg 3:29
with thee, thou mighty man of v .... Judg 6:12
Gileadite was a mighty man of v..... Judg 11:1
men from their coasts, men of v ..... Judg 18:2
all these were men of v............ Judg 20:44
all these were men of v............ Judg 20:46
Jeroboam was a mighty man of v 1Kin 11:28
he was also a mighty man of v...... 2Kin 5:1
and all the mighty men of v........ 2Kin 24:14
of their fathers, mighty men of v ... 1Chr 5:24
of their fathers, mighty men of v ... 1Chr 7:7
of their fathers, mighty men of v ... 1Chr 7:9
of their fathers, mighty men of v ... 1Chr 7:11
house, choice and mighty men of v .. 1Chr 7:40
sons of Ulam were mighty men of v .. 1Chr 8:40
for they were all mighty men of v ... 1Chr 12:21
mighty men of v for the war........ 1Chr 12:25
a young man mighty of v........... 1Chr 12:28
and eight hundred, mighty men of v .. 1Chr 12:30
for they were mighty men of v 1Chr 26:6
and his brethren, men of v.......... 1Chr 26:7
men of v at Jazer of Gilead 1Chr 26:31
And his brethren, men of v.......... 1Chr 26:30
chosen men, being mighty men of v .. 2Chr 13:3
all these were mighty men of v 2Chr 14:8
the men of war, mighty men of v 2Chr 17:13
men of v three hundred thousand ... 2Chr 17:14
hundred thousand mighty men of v .. 2Chr 17:16
Eliada a mighty man of v, and with .. 2Chr 17:17
of v out of Israel for an hundred ... 2Chr 25:6
mighty men of v were two thousand .. 2Chr 26:12
cut off all the mighty men of v 2Chr 32:21
their brethren, mighty men of v ..... Neh 11:14

VALUE
priest, and the priest shall v him ... Lev 27:8
that vowed shall the priest v him.... Lev 27:8
And the priest shall v it, whether.... Lev 27:12
ye are all physicians of no v .... Job 13:4
ye are of more v than many .... Mt 10:31
of the children of Israel did v...... Mt 27:9
ye are of more v than many........ Lk 12:7

VALUED
be v at fifty shekels of silver .... Lev 27:16
It cannot be v with the gold of ..... Job 28:16
shall it be v with pure gold......... Job 28:19
the price of him that was v......... Mt 27:9

VALUEST
as thou v it, who art the priest,..... Lev 27:12

VANIAH (va-ni'-ah) *Married a foreigner in exile.*
V, Meremoth, Eliashib,............ Ezr 10:36

VANISH
What time they wax warm, they v ... Job 6:17
heavens shall v away like smoke..... Is 51:6
be knowledge, it shall v away....... 1Cor 13:8
and waxeth old is ready to v away... Heb 8:13

VANISHED
is their wisdom v.................. Jer 49:7
and he v out of their sight......... Lk 24:31

VANISHETH
The cloud is consumed and v away... Job 7:9
for a little time, and then v away.... Jas 4:14

VANITIES
provoked me to anger with their v... Deut 32:21
of Israel to anger with their v....... 1Kin 16:13
of Israel to anger with their v....... 1Kin 16:26
hated them that regard lying v ..... Ps 31:6
Vanity of v, saith the Preacher,..... Eccl 1:2
saith the Preacher, vanity of v ..... Eccl 1:2
words there are also divers v....... Eccl 5:7
Vanity of v, saith the preacher...... Eccl 12:8
graven images, and with strange v .. Jer 8:19
the stock is a doctrine of v........ Jer 10:8
Are there any among the v of the ... Jer 14:22
lying v forsake their own mercy..... Jonah 2:8
from these v unto the living God..... Acts 14:15

VANITY
they followed v, and became........ 2Kin 17:15
and made to possess months of v ... Job 7:3
for my days are v.................. Job 7:16
him that is deceived trust in v....... Job 15:31

for v shall be his recompense........ Job 15:31
mischief, and bring forth v......... Job 15:35
If I have walked with v, or if my ... Job 31:5
Surely God will not hear v.......... Job 35:13
how long will ye love v, and seek ... Ps 4:2
under his tongue is mischief and v ... Ps 10:7
They speak v every one with his..... Ps 12:2
not lifted up his soul unto v........ Ps 24:4
at his best state is altogether v ..... Ps 39:5
surely every man is v............... Ps 39:11
he come to see me, he speaketh v ... Ps 41:6
Surely men of low degree are v...... Ps 62:9
are altogether lighter than v........ Ps 62:9
their days did he consume in v ..... Ps 78:33
thoughts of man, that they are v ... Ps 94:11
away mine eyes from beholding v ... Ps 119:37
Man is like to v................... Ps 144:4
Whose mouth speaketh v, and their .. Ps 144:8
children, whose mouth speaketh v ... Ps 144:11
Wealth gotten by v shall be......... Prov 13:11
a lying tongue is a v tossed to ...... Prov 21:6
that soweth iniquity shall reap v .... Prov 22:8
Remove far from me v and lies...... Prov 30:8
V of vanities, saith the Preacher .... Eccl 1:2
saith the Preacher, v of vanities .... Eccl 1:2
all is v............................ Eccl 1:2
and, behold, all is v and vexation ... Eccl 1:14
and, behold, this also is v.......... Eccl 2:1
and, behold, all was v and vexation.. Eccl 2:11
in my heart, that this also is v ...... Eccl 2:15
for all is v and vexation of .... Eccl 2:17
This is also v...................... Eccl 2:19
This also is v and a great evil....... Eccl 2:21
This is also v...................... Eccl 2:23
This also is v and vexation of .... Eccl 2:26
for all is v........................ Eccl 3:19
This is also v and vexation of .... Eccl 4:4
and I saw v under the sun.......... Eccl 4:7
This is also v, yea, it is a sore...... Eccl 4:8
Surely this also is v and vexation ... Eccl 4:16
this is also v...................... Eccl 5:10
this is v, and it is an evil.......... Eccl 6:2
For he cometh in with v, and....... Eccl 6:4
this is also v and vexation of .... Eccl 6:9
be many things that increase v ..... Eccl 6:11
this also is v...................... Eccl 7:6
have I seen in the days of my v ..... Eccl 7:15
this is also v...................... Eccl 8:10
There is a v which is done upon..... Eccl 8:14
I said that this also is v............ Eccl 8:14
all the days of the life of thy v ..... Eccl 9:9
the sun, all the days of thy v .... Eccl 9:9
All that cometh is v................ Eccl 11:8
for childhood and youth are v .... Eccl 11:10
V of vanities, saith the preacher..... Eccl 12:8
this is v.......................... Eccl 12:8
draw iniquity with cords of v....... Is 5:18
the nations with the sieve of v...... Is 30:28
to him less than nothing, and v ..... Is 40:17
the judges of the earth as v........ Is 40:23
Behold, they are all v.............. Is 41:29
a graven image are all of them v.... Is 44:9
v shall take them................. Is 57:13
of the finger, and speaking v .... Is 58:9
they trust in v, and speak lies...... Is 59:4
from me, and have walked after v ... Jer 2:5
They are v, and the work of errors... Jer 10:15
fathers have inherited lies, v....... Jer 16:19
me, they have burned incense to v ... Jer 18:15
They are v, the work of errors...... Jer 51:18
They have seen v and lying .... Eze 13:6
Because ye have spoken v, and seen.. Eze 13:8
be upon the prophets that see v .... Eze 13:9
Therefore ye shall see no more v .... Eze 13:23
Have ye not seen a v vision........ Eze 21:29
with untempered mortar, seeing v ... Eze 22:28
surely they are v................. Hos 12:11
shall weary themselves for very v ... Hab 2:13
For the idols have spoken v........ Zec 10:2
creature was made subject to v ..... Rom 8:20
walk, in the v of their mind,........ Eph 4:17
speak great swelling words of v 2Pet 2:18

VAPORS
he causeth the v to ascend from .... Jer 10:13
he causeth the v to ascend from .... Jer 51:16

VAPOUR
rain according to the v thereof...... Job 36:27
the cattle also concerning the v ..... Job 36:33
blood, and fire, and v of smoke...... Acts 2:19
It is even a v, that appeareth....... Jas 4:14

VAPOURS
He causeth the v to ascend from .... Ps 135:7
and hail; snow, and v............. Ps 148:8

VARIABLENESS
of lights, with whom is no v .... Jas 1:17

VARIANCE
set a man at v against his father .... Mt 10:35
Idolatry, witchcraft, hatred, v....... Gal 5:20

VASHNI (vash'-ni) *A son of Samuel.*
the firstborn V, and Abiah 1Chr 6:28

VASHTI (vash'-ti) *A Persian queen, succeeded by Esther.*
Also V the queen made a feast for ... Est 1:9
To bring V the queen before the .... Est 1:11
But the queen V refused to come .... Est 1:12
unto the queen V according to law ... Est 1:15

V

VAUNT

V the queen hath not done wrong ...... Est 1:16
the queen to be brought in .... Est 1:17
That V come no more before king ...... Est 1:19
was appeased, he remembered V ...... Est 2:1
the king be queen instead of V ...... Est 2:4
and made her queen instead of V ...... Est 2:17

VAUNT

lest Israel v themselves against .... Judg 7:2

VAUNTETH

charity v not itself, is not 1Cor 13:4

VEDAN See DAN.

VEHEMENT

fire, which hath a most v flame .... Song 8:6
that God prepared a v east wind ...... Jonah 4:8
what v desire, yea, what zeal, ... 2Cor 7:11

VEHEMENTLY

But he spake the more v, If I .... Mk 14:31
the stream beat v upon that house .... Lk 6:48
which the stream did beat v .... Lk 6:49
the Pharisees began to urge him v .... Lk 11:53
and scribes stood and v accused him .. Lk 23:10

VEIL

the walls took away my v from me .... Song 5:7
the v of the temple was rent in ...... Mt 27:51
the v of the temple was rent in ...... Mk 15:38
the v of the temple was rent in ...... Lk 23:45
entereth into that within the v ...... Heb 6:19
And after the second v, the .... Heb 9:3
consecrated for us, through the v ...... Heb 10:20

VEIN

there is a v for the silver. .... Job 28:1

VENGEANCE

v shall be taken on him sevenfold .... Gen 4:15
To me belongeth v, and recompence ... Deut 32:35
I will render v to mine enemies, ... Deut 32:41
will render v to his adversaries, ... Deut 32:43
as the Lord hath taken v for the .... Judg 11:36
shall rejoice when he seeth the v ..... Ps 58:10
O LORD God, to whom v belongeth ... Ps 94:1
to whom v belongeth, shew thyself, ... Ps 94:1
tookest v of their inventions. .... Ps 99:8
To execute v upon the heathen, and .. Ps 149:7
he will not spare in the day of v ..... Prov 6:34
For it is the day of the LORD's v ..... Is 34:8
behold, your God will come with v ... Is 35:4
I will take v, and I will not meet .... Is 47:3
on the garments of v for clothing .... Is 59:17
LORD, and the day of v of our God .. Is 61:2
For the day of v is in mine heart .... Is 63:4
heart, let me see thy v on them. ..... Jer 11:20
heart, let me see thy v on them. ..... Jer 20:12
the Lord God of hosts, a day of v ... Jer 46:10
for it is the v of the LORD. .... Jer 50:15
take v upon her .... Jer 50:15
in Zion the v of the LORD our God .. Jer 50:28
LORD our God, the v of his temple ... Jer 50:28
this is the time of the LORD's v...... Jer 51:6
because it is the v of the LORD. ...... Jer 51:11
of the LORD, the v of his temple ..... Jer 51:11
thy cause, and take v for thee. ...... Jer 51:36
Thou hast seen all their v .... Lam 3:60
cause fury to come up to take v. .... Eze 24:8
the house of Judah by taking v ...... Eze 25:12
I will lay my v upon Edom by the ... Eze 25:14
and they shall know my v, saith ..... Eze 25:14
have taken v with a despiteful ...... Eze 25:15
I will execute great v upon them .... Eze 25:17
when I shall lay my v upon them .... Eze 25:17
And I will execute v in anger .... Mic 5:15
will take v on his adversaries, ... Nah 1:2
For these be the days of v .... Lk 21:22
yet v suffereth not to live .... Acts 28:4
to God unrighteous who taketh v ..... Rom 3:5
for it is written, V is mine. .... Rom 12:19
In flaming fire taking v on them 2Th 1:8
V belongeth unto me, I will .... Heb 10:30
suffering the v of eternal fire. .... Jude 7

VENISON

Esau, because he did eat of his v .... Gen 25:28
to the field, and take me some v ..... Gen 27:3
went to the field to hunt for v ...... Gen 27:5
Bring me v, and make me savoury ... Gen 27:7
I pray thee, sit and eat of my v ..... Gen 27:19
me, and I will eat of my son's v ..... Gen 27:25
arise, and eat of his son's v .... Gen 27:31
where is he that hath taken v .... Gen 27:33

VENOM

dragons, and the cruel v of asps. .... Deut 32:33

VENOMOUS

saw the v beast hang on his hand .... Acts 28:4

VENT

belly is as wine which hath no v ..... Job 32:19

VENTURE

a certain man drew a bow at a v 1Kin 22:34
a certain man drew a bow at a v 2Chr 18:33

VERIFIED

so shall your words be v, and ye ..... Gen 42:20
let thy word, I pray thee, be v 1Kin 8:26
God of Israel, let thy word be v 2Chr 6:17

VERILY

We are v guilty concerning our ...... Gen 42:21
V my sabbaths ye shall keep .... Ex 31:13

I v thought that thou hadst .... Judg 15:2
V our lord king David hath made 1Kin 1:43
V she hath no child, and her 2Kin 4:14
but I will v buy it for the full 1Chr 21:24
are v estranged from me .... Job 19:13
the land, and v thou shalt be fed .... Ps 37:3
v every man at his best state is, ... Ps 39:5
V there is a reward for the .... Ps 58:11
v he is a God that judgeth in the .... Ps 58:11
But v God hath heard me. .... Ps 66:19
V I have cleansed my heart in .... Ps 73:13
V thou art a God that hidest .... Is 45:15
V it shall be well with thy .... Jer 15:11
I will cause the enemy to .... Jer 15:11
For v I say unto you, Till heaven .... Mt 5:18
V I say unto thee, Thou shalt be .... Mt 5:26
V I say unto you, They have their .... Mt 6:2
V I say unto you, They have their .... Mt 6:5
V I say unto you, They have their .... Mt 6:16
V I say unto you, I have not .... Mt 8:10
V I say unto you, It shall be .... Mt 10:15
for v I say unto you, Ye shall .... Mt 10:23
v I say unto you, he shall in no .... Mt 10:42
V I say unto you, Among them that .. Mt 11:11
For v I say unto you, That many ..... Mt 13:17
V I say unto you, There be some ..... Mt 16:28
for v I say unto you, If ye have ..... Mt 17:20
V I say unto you, Except ye be, ... Mt 18:3
V I say unto you, he rejoiceth .... Mt 18:13
V I say unto you, Whatsoever ye ..... Mt 18:18
V I say unto you, That a rich man ... Mt 19:23
V I say unto you, That ye which, ... Mt 19:28
V I say unto you, If ye have, ... Mt 21:21
V I say unto you, That .... Mt 21:31
V I say unto you, All these .... Mt 23:36
v I say unto you, There shall not ... Mt 24:2
V I say unto you, This generation .... Mt 24:34
V I say unto you, The shall .... Mt 24:47
V I say unto you, I know you not. ... Mt 25:12
V I say unto you, Inasmuch as ye .... Mt 25:40
V I say unto you, Inasmuch as ye .... Mt 25:45
V I say unto you, Wheresoever ...... Mt 26:13
V I say unto you, That one of you ... Mt 26:21
V I say unto you, That this .... Mt 26:34
V I say unto you, All sins shall ..... Mk 3:28
V I say unto you, It shall be .... Mk 6:11
V I say unto you, There shall no .... Mk 8:12
V I say unto you, That there be ...... Mk 9:1
them, Elias v cometh first, and, ... Mk 9:12
v I say unto you, he shall not .... Mk 9:41
V I say unto you, Whosoever shall ... Mk 10:29
V I say unto you, There is no man ... Mk 10:29
For v I say unto you, That .... Mk 11:23
V I say unto you, That this poor ..... Mk 12:43
V I say unto you, that ye shall ...... Mk 13:30
V I say unto you, Wheresoever ...... Mk 14:9
v I say unto you, One of you .... Mk 14:18
v I say unto you, I will drink no .... Mk 14:25
V I say unto thee, That this day, ... Mk 14:30
v I say unto you, No prophet is ..... Lk 4:24
v I say unto you, It shall be .... Lk 11:51
v I say unto you, that he shall ...... Lk 12:37
v I say unto you, He shall .... Lk 13:35
V I say unto you, Whosoever shall ... Lk 18:17
V I say unto you, There is no man ... Lk 18:29
v I say unto you, This generation .... Lk 21:32
V I say unto thee, To day shalt ...... Lk 23:43
And he saith unto him, V, v, ... Jn 1:51
and said unto him, V, v, ... Jn 3:3
Jesus answered, V, v, ... Jn 3:5
V, v, I say unto thee, We .... Jn 3:11
and said unto them, V, v, ... Jn 5:19
V, v, I say unto you, He .... Jn 5:24
V, v, I say unto you, The .... Jn 5:25
answered them and said, V, v, ... Jn 6:26
Jesus said unto them, V, v, ... Jn 6:32
V, v, I say unto you, He .... Jn 6:47
Jesus said unto them, V, v, ... Jn 6:53
Jesus answered them, V, v, ... Jn 8:34
V, v, I say unto you, If a .... Jn 8:51
Jesus said unto them, V, v, ... Jn 8:58
V, v, I say unto you, He .... Jn 10:1
Jesus unto them again, V, v, ... Jn 10:7
V, v, I say unto you, Except .... Jn 12:24
V, v, I say unto you, He .... Jn 13:16
V, v, I say unto you, The .... Jn 13:20
and testified, and said, V, v, ... Jn 13:21
V, v, I say unto thee, The .... Jn 13:38
V, v, I say unto you, He .... Jn 14:12
V, v, I say unto you, That .... Jn 16:20
V, v, I say unto you .... Jn 16:23
V, v, I say unto thee, When .... Jn 21:18
nay v; but let them .... Acts 16:37
John v baptized with the baptism, ... Acts 19:4
I am v a man which am a Jew, born .. Acts 22:3
I v thought with myself, that I ...... Acts 26:9
for circumcision v profiteth .... Rom 2:25
Yes v, their sound went into all ..... Rom 10:18
It hath been shewed unto v .... Rom 15:27
For I v, as absent in body, but 1Cor 5:3
V that, when I preach the gospel, ... 1Cor 9:18
For thou v givest thanks well, ... 1Cor 14:17
V, when we were with you, we ...... Gal 3:21
For v he took not on him the .... Heb 2:16
Moses v was faithful in all his, ... Heb 3:5
For men v swear by the greater ..... Heb 6:16
v they that are of the sons of .... Heb 7:5
For there is v a disannulling of .... Heb 7:18
Then v the first covenant had .... Heb 9:1

For they v for a few days .... Heb 12:10
Who v was foreordained before the ... 1Pet 1:20
in him v is the love of God 1Jn 2:5

VERITY

The works of his hands are v .... Ps 111:7
of the Gentiles in faith and v 1Ti 2:7

VERMILION

with cedar, and painted with v ...... Jer 22:14
the Chaldeans pourtrayed with v .... Eze 23:14

VERY

made, and, behold, it was v good .... Gen 1:31
Now also v was v wroth, and his, ... Gen 4:5
the woman that she was v fair ...... Gen 12:14
Abram was v rich in cattle, in ...... Gen 13:2
because their sin is v grievous ...... Gen 18:20
the thing was v grievous in .... Gen 21:11
the damsel was v fair to look .... Gen 24:16
and grew until he became v great ... Gen 26:13
thou be my v son Esau or not. ...... Gen 27:21
he said, Art thou v son Esau .... Gen 27:24
And Isaac trembled v exceedingly .... Gen 27:33
grieved, and they were v wroth ...... Gen 34:7
v ill favoured and leanfleshed, ... Gen 41:19
for it shall be v grievous .... Gen 41:31
v much, until he left numbering ..... Gen 41:49
for the famine was v sore .... Gen 47:13
and it was a v great company. ...... Gen 50:9
a great and v sore lamentation ...... Gen 50:10
multiplied, and waxed v mighty ..... Ex 1:20
only ye shall not go v far away ..... Ex 8:28
shall be a v grievous murrain. ...... Ex 9:3
in v deed for this cause have I ...... Ex 9:16
it to rain a v grievous hail .... Ex 9:18
v grievous, such as there was .... Ex 9:24
v grievous were they. .... Ex 10:14
was v great in the land of Egypt ... Ex 11:3
and herds, even v much cattle. ...... Ex 12:38
shalt beat some of it v small. ...... Ex 30:36
if any man die v suddenly by him, .. Num 6:9
the people with a v great plague. .... Num 11:33
(Now the man Moses was v meek. .... Num 12:3
the cities are walled, and v great ... Num 13:28
And Moses was v wroth, and said ... Num 16:15
promote them unto v great honour ... Num 22:17
had a v great multitude of cattle ... Num 32:1
the LORD was v angry with Aaron ... Deut 9:20
stamped it, and ground it v small ... Deut 9:21
which are v far off from thee, ... Deut 20:15
the words of this law v plainly. .... Deut 27:8
shall get up above thee v high. ..... Deut 28:43
and thou shalt come down v low. ... Deut 28:43
v delicate, his eye shall be evil, ... Deut 28:54
But the word is v nigh unto thee .... Deut 30:14
for they are a v froward. .... Deut 32:20
v courageous, that thou mayest ..... Josh 1:7
rose up upon an heap v far from .... Josh 3:16
go not v far from the city, but ...... Josh 8:4
From a v far country thy servants ... Josh 9:9
by reason of the v long journey. .... Josh 9:13
us, saying, We are v far from you, .. Josh 9:22
them with a v great slaughter. ...... Josh 10:20
which remain until this v day .... Josh 10:27
with horses and chariots v many ... Josh 11:4
there remaineth yet v much land ... Josh 13:1
with v much cattle, with silver, ... Josh 22:8
with iron, and with v much raiment .. Josh 22:8
Be ye therefore v courageous to ..... Josh 23:6
and Eglon was a v fat man .... Judg 3:17
with a v great slaughter .... Judg 11:33
thou hast brought me v low .... Judg 11:35
of an angel of God, v terrible ...... Judg 13:6
land, and, behold, it is v good ...... Judg 18:9
hath dealt v bitterly with me .... Ruth 1:20
men was v great before the LORD ... 1Sa 2:17
Now Eli was v old, and heard all ... 1Sa 2:22
there was a v great slaughter 1Sa 4:10
city with a v great destruction. 1Sa 5:9
the hand of God was v heavy there ... 1Sa 5:11
so it was a v great trembling. 1Sa 14:15
there was a v great discomfiture 1Sa 14:20
and the people were v faint 1Sa 14:31
And Saul was v wroth, and the 1Sa 18:8
that he behaved himself v wisely. ... 1Sa 18:15
have been to thee-ward v good. 1Sa 19:4
but if he be v wroth, then be 1Sa 20:7
me that he dealeth v subtilly 1Sa 23:22
and the man was v great, and he had ... 1Sa 25:2
But the men were v good unto us. ... 1Sa 25:15
For in v deed, as the LORD God of ... 1Sa 25:34
within him for he was v drunken 1Sa 25:36
that Saul was come v near 1Sa 26:4
v pleasant hast thou been unto me. ... 2Sa 1:26
there was a v sore battle that. 2Sa 2:17
Then was Abner v wroth for the 2Sa 3:8
the woman was v beautiful to look .. 2Sa 11:2
unto David, and it was v sick. 2Sa 12:15
and Jonadab was a v subtil man. 2Sa 13:3
all these things, he was v wroth 2Sa 13:21
and all his servants wept v sore. 2Sa 13:36
laid a v great heap of stones. 2Sa 18:17
Now Barzillai was a v aged man. 2Sa 19:32
for I have done v foolishly— 2Sa 24:10
And the damsel was v fair, and 1Kin 1:4
and he also was a v goodly man. 1Kin 1:6
and he was v old. 1Kin 1:15
were of the v base itself 1Kin 7:34
to Jerusalem with a v great train. ... 1Kin 10:2
v much gold, and precious stones 1Kin 10:2

of spices v great store, and 1Kin 10:10
I have been v jealous for the.............. 1Kin 19:10
I have been v jealous for the.............. 1Kin 19:14
he did v abominably in following ... 1Kin 21:26
of Israel, that it was v bitter............. 2Kin 14:26
the LORD was v angry with Israel 2Kin 17:18
shed innocent blood v much............. 2Kin 21:16
v able men for the work of the......... 1Chr 9:13
brought David v much brass............... 1Chr 18:8
for I have done v foolishly............... 1Chr 21:8
for v great are his mercies................. 1Chr 21:13
the sons of Rehabiah were v many ... 1Chr 23:17
But will God in v deed dwell with.... 2Chr 6:18
a v great congregation, from the 2Chr 7:8
with a v great company, and camels,.. 2Chr 9:1
and they carried away v much spoil .. 2Chr 14:13
with v many chariots and horsemen.. 2Chr 16:8
they made a v great burning for 2Chr 16:14
of Israel, who did v wickedly............ 2Chr 20:35
the LORD delivered a v great host 2Chr 24:24
month, a v great congregation 2Chr 30:13
had given him substance v much 2Chr 32:29
and raised it up a v great height......... 2Chr 33:14
transgressed v much after all the 2Chr 36:14
unto him out of Israel a v great .... Ezr 10:1
for the people were v sore.................. Ezr 10:1
We have dealt v corruptly against ... Neh 1:7
Then I was v sore afraid,................... Neh 2:2
stopped, then they were v wroth........ Neh 4:7
I was v angry when I heard their ...... Neh 5:6
there was v great gladness.................. Neh 8:17
therefore was the king v wroth .... Est 1:12
the asses, and a v great household...... Job 1:3
saw that his grief was v great .... Job 2:13
v aged men, much elder than thy....... Job 15:10
said, I am young, and ye are v old ..... Job 32:6
their inward part is v wickedness ..... Ps 5:9
into that v destruction let him .... Ps 35:8
a v present help in trouble.................. Ps 46:1
it shall be v tempestuous round .... Ps 50:3
is v high, who hast done great .... Ps 71:19
for we are brought v low .... Ps 79:8
thou establish in the v heavens.......... Ps 89:2
and thy thoughts are v deep .... Ps 92:5
Thy testimonies are v sure................. Ps 93:5
O LORD my God, thou art v great ...... Ps 104:1
v few, and strangers in it.................... Ps 105:12
I am afflicted v much........................ Ps 119:107
are righteous and v faithful................ Ps 119:138
Thy word is v pure .... Ps 119:140
for I am brought v low .... Ps 142:6
in that v day his thoughts perish........ Ps 146:4
his word runneth v swiftly................. Ps 147:15
a matter separateth v friends .... Prov 17:9
dropping in a v rainy day .... Prov 27:15
left unto us a v small remnant .... Is 1:9
a vineyard in a v fruitful hill............. Is 5:1
For yet a v little while, and the.......... Is 10:25
he is v proud.................................... Is 16:6
and the remnant shall be v small .... Is 16:14
have dealt v treacherously .... Is 24:16
Is it not yet a v little while .... Is 29:17
he will be v gracious unto thee.......... Is 30:19
because they are v strong................... Is 31:1
behold the land that is v far off.......... Is 33:17
up the isles as a v little thing............. Is 40:15
hast thou v heavily laid thy yoke....... Is 47:6
wouldest deal v treacherously .... Is 48:8
exalted and extolled, and be v high ... Is 52:13
Be not wroth v sore, O LORD,............ Is 64:9
thy peace, and afflict us v sore .... Is 64:12
be ye v desolate, saith the LORD......... Jer 2:12
I am pained at my v heart .... Jer 4:19
dealt v treacherously against me .... Jer 5:11
happy that deal v treacherously .... Jer 12:1
breach, with a v grievous blow .... Jer 14:17
hath done a v horrible thing............... Jer 18:13
making him v glad .... Jer 20:15
One basket had v good figs................ Jer 24:2
other basket had v naughty figs......... Jer 24:2
the good figs, v good .... Jer 24:3
v evil, that cannot be eaten,............... Jer 24:3
until the v time of his land come .... Jer 27:7
wine and summer fruits v much......... Jer 40:12
Egypt is like a v fair heifer................. Jer 46:20
thou art v wroth against us .... Lam 5:22
against me, even unto this v day......... Eze 2:3
as if that were a v little thing............. Eze 16:47
made v glorious in the midst of .... Eze 27:25
thou art unto them as a v lovely .... Eze 33:32
there were v many in the open........... Eze 37:2
and, lo, they were v dry .... Eze 37:2
and set me upon a v high mountain.... Eze 40:2
were v many trees on the one side ..... Eze 47:7
and there shall be a v great................ Eze 47:9
v furious, and commanded to............. Dan 2:12
Then the king arose v early in .... Dan 6:19
a mouth that spake v great things....... Dan 7:20
the he goat waxed v great .... Dan 8:8
up to battle with a v great.................. Dan 11:25
for his camp is v great........................ Joel 2:11
the LORD is great and v terrible.......... Joel 2:11
even v dark, and no brightness in ...... Amos 5:20
exceedingly, and he was v angry .... Jonah 4:1
people shall labour in the v fire .... Hab 2:13
weary themselves for v vanity .... Hab 2:13
I am v sore displeased with the.......... Zec 1:15
his staff in his hand for v age............. Zec 8:4
and Zidon, though it be v wise .... Zec 9:2
it, and be v sorrowful, and Ekron ...... Zec 9:5

there shall be a v great valley............ Zec 14:4
But the v hairs of your head are........ Mt 10:30
was made whole from that v hour ..... Mt 15:28
child was cured from that v hour ...... Mt 17:18
what was done, they were v sorry...... Mt 18:31
a v great multitude spread their......... Mt 21:8
they shall deceive the v elect............. Mt 24:24
box of v precious ointment .... Mt 26:7
began to be sorrowful and v heavy.... Mt 26:37
days the multitude being v great........ Mk 8:1
ointment of spikenard v precious ...... Mk 14:3
be sore amazed, and to be v heavy..... Mk 14:33
v early in the morning the first .... Mk 16:2
for it was v great .... Mk 16:4
of all things from thy v first .... Lk 1:3
shake off the v dust from your .... Lk 9:5
Even the v dust of your city,............. Lk 10:11
But even the v hairs of your head...... Lk 12:7
thou hast paid the v last mite............ Lk 12:59
he heard this, he was v sorrowful ..... Lk 18:23
for he was v rich .... Lk 18:23
Jesus saw that he was v sorrowful..... Lk 18:24
hast been faithful in a v little............ Lk 19:17
were v attentive to hear him.............. Lk 19:48
v early in the morning, they came ..... Lk 24:1
indeed that this is the v Christ .... Jn 7:26
taken in adultery, in the v act............ Jn 8:4
v costly, and anointed the feet of....... Jn 12:3
believe me for the v works' sake .... Jn 14:11
proving that this is v Christ .... Acts 9:22
And he became v hungry, and would.. Acts 10:10
that v worthy deeds are done unto..... Acts 24:2
no wrong, as thou v well knowest ..... Acts 25:10
But Esaias is v bold, and saith, I....... Rom 10:20
continually upon this v thing............. Rom 13:6
But with me it is a v small thing 1Cor 4:3
and your zeal hath provoked v many.. 2Cor 9:2
behind the v chiefest apostles 2Cor 11:5
I behind the v chiefest apostles 2Cor 12:11
I will v gladly spend and be spent..... 2Cor 12:15
Being confident of this v thing......... Phil 1:6
to esteem them v highly in love......... 1Th 5:13
the v God of peace sanctify you........ 1Th 5:23
he sought me out v diligently 2Ti 1:17
at Ephesus, thou knowest v well 2Ti 1:18
not the v image of the things,........... Heb 10:1
turned about with a v small helm...... Jas 3:4
that the Lord is v pitiful .... Jas 5:11

VESSEL
But the earthen v wherein it is......... Lev 6:28
whether it be any v of wood.............. Lev 11:32
skin, or sack, whatsoever v it be .... Lev 11:32
And every earthen v, whereinto any.. Lev 11:33
in every such v shall be unclean........ Lev 11:34
an earthen v over running water....... Lev 14:5
an earthen v over running water....... Lev 14:50
the v of earth, that he toucheth.......... Lev 15:12
every v of wood shall be rinsed .... Lev 15:12
take holy water in an earthen v......... Num 5:17
And every open v, which hath no...... Num 19:15
water shall be put thereto in a v .... Num 19:17
thou shalt not put any in thy v........... Deut 23:24
were sanctified this day in the v 1Sa 21:5
pray thee, a little water in a v 1Kin 17:10
unto her son, Bring me yet a v 2Kin 4:6
unto her, There is not a v more.......... 2Kin 4:6
them in pieces like a potter's v .... Ps 2:9
I am like a broken v .... Ps 31:12
come forth a v for the finer............... Prov 25:4
v that is broken in pieces .... Is 30:14
v into the house of the LORD............. Is 66:20
the v that he made of clay was .... Jer 18:4
so he made it again another v............ Jer 18:4
as one breaketh a potter's v .... Jer 19:11
is he a v wherein is no pleasure......... Jer 22:28
ye shall fall like a pleasant v .... Jer 25:34
and put them in an earthen v............. Jer 32:14
not been emptied from v to v .... Jer 48:11
like a v wherein is no pleasure.......... Jer 48:38
me, hath made me an empty v............ Jer 51:34
and fitches, and put them in one v ..... Eze 4:9
a pin of it to hang any v thereon .... Eze 15:3
as a v wherein is no pleasure............. Hos 8:8
carry any v through the temple .... Mk 11:16
a candle, covereth it with a v .... Lk 8:16
there was set a v full of vinegar........ Jn 19:29
for he is a chosen v unto me .... Acts 9:15
a certain v descending unto him,....... Acts 10:11
the v was received up again into .... Acts 10:16
saw a vision. A certain v descend...... Acts 11:5
lump to make one v unto honour....... Rom 9:21
possess his v in sanctification........... 1Th 4:4
he shall be a v unto honour............... 2Ti 2:21
the wife, as unto the weaker v 1Pet 3:7

VESSELS
best fruits in the land in your v .... Gen 43:11
v of wood, and in v of stone.............. Ex 7:19
he make it, with all these v .... Ex 25:39
all the v thereof thou shalt make,...... Ex 27:3
All the v of the tabernacle in............. Ex 27:19
And the table and all his v .... Ex 30:27
and the candlestick and his v .... Ex 30:27
of burnt offering with all his v .... Ex 30:28
and his staves, and all his v .... Ex 35:13
grate, his staves, and all his v .... Ex 35:16
he made the v which were upon the... Ex 37:16
made he it, and all the v thereof........ Ex 37:24
And he made all the v of the altar...... Ex 38:3
all the v thereof made he of.............. Ex 38:3

it, and all the v of the altar,.............. Ex 38:30
The table, and all the v thereof.......... Ex 39:36
in order, and all the v thereof........... Ex 39:37
brass, his staves, and all his v .... Ex 39:39
all the v of the service of the .... Ex 39:40
hallow it, and all the v thereof.......... Ex 40:9
the burnt offering, and all his v .... Ex 40:10
anointed the altar and all his v .... Lev 8:11
and over all the v of war................... Num 1:50
tabernacle, and all the v thereof........ Num 1:50
the v of the sanctuary wherewith ..... Num 3:31
thereof, and all the v thereof............. Num 3:36
and all the oil v thereof .... Num 4:9
all the v thereof within a .... Num 4:10
put upon it all the v thereof.............. Num 4:14
basons, all the v of the altar.............. Num 4:14
all the v of the sanctuary, as............. Num 4:15
sanctuary, and in the v thereof .... Num 4:16
the altar and all the v thereof............ Num 7:1
all the silver v weighed two .... Num 7:85
come nigh the v of the sanctuary....... Num 18:3
upon the tent, and upon all the v .... Num 19:18
gold, and v of brass and iron, are ...... Josh 6:19
the v of brass and iron, they............. Josh 6:24
thou art athirst, go unto the v .... Ruth 2:9
for the bread is spent in our v............ 1Sa 9:7
the v of the young men are holy,....... 1Sa 21:5
brought with him v of silver 2Sa 8:10
and v of gold, and v of brass 2Sa 8:10
beds, and basons, and earthen v 2Sa 17:28
and all these v, which Hiram made.... 1Kin 7:45
Solomon left all the v unweighed...... 1Kin 7:47
Solomon made all the v that............. 1Kin 7:48
the silver, and the gold, and the v 1Kin 7:51
all the holy v that were in the 1Kin 8:4
Solomon's drinking v were of gold ... 1Kin 10:21
all the v of the house of the 1Kin 10:21
v of silver, and v of gold,.................. 1Kin 10:25
the LORD, silver, and gold, and v 1Kin 15:15
borrow thee v abroad of all thy 2Kin 4:3
all thy neighbours, even empty v 2Kin 4:3
shalt pour out into all those v 2Kin 4:4
sons, who brought the v to her.......... 2Kin 4:5
when the v were full, that she 2Kin 4:6
the way was full of garments and v ... 2Kin 7:15
any v of gold 2Kin 12:13
or v of silver, of the money that........ 2Kin 12:13
all the v that were found in the 2Kin 14:14
all the v that were made for Baal 2Kin 23:4
cut in pieces all the v of gold 2Kin 24:13
all the v of brass wherewith they 2Kin 25:14
of all these v was without weight 2Kin 25:16
the charge of the ministering v 1Chr 9:28
were appointed to oversee the v 1Chr 9:29
and the pillars, and the v of brass 1Chr 18:8
with him all manner of v of gold 1Chr 18:10
of the LORD, and the holy v of God.... 1Chr 22:19
nor any v of it for the service 1Chr 23:26
for all the v of service in the............ 1Chr 28:13
all these v in great abundance........... 2Chr 4:18
Solomon made all the v that were 2Chr 4:19
all the holy v that were in the 2Chr 5:5
all the drinking v of king 2Chr 9:20
all the v of the house of the 2Chr 9:24
v of silver, and v of gold,.................. 2Chr 9:24
dedicated, silver, and gold, and v 2Chr 15:18
whereof were made v for the house... 2Chr 24:14
even v to minister, and to offer 2Chr 24:14
and spoons, and v of gold and silver.. 2Chr 24:14
all the v that were found in the 2Chr 25:24
the v of the house of God 2Chr 28:24
cut in pieces the v of the house 2Chr 28:24
offering, with all the v thereof.......... 2Chr 29:18
table, with all the v thereof 2Chr 29:18
Moreover all the v, which king 2Chr 29:19
also carried of the v of the 2Chr 36:7
with the goodly v of the house of 2Chr 36:10
all the v of the house of God,............ 2Chr 36:18
all the goodly v thereof 2Chr 36:19
their hands with v of silver .... Ezr 1:6
the v of the house of the LORD,......... Ezr 1:7
and ten, and other v a thousand......... Ezr 1:10
All the v of gold and silver .... Ezr 1:11
the v also of gold and silver of.......... Ezr 5:14
And said unto him, Take these v .... Ezr 5:15
silver v of the house of God.............. Ezr 6:5
The v also that are given thee............ Ezr 7:19
the silver, and the gold, and the v ..... Ezr 8:25
silver v an hundred talents, and .... Ezr 8:26
two v of fine copper, precious as ...... Ezr 8:27
the v are holy also.......................... Ezr 8:28
the silver, and the gold, and the v ..... Ezr 8:30
the weighed in the house of our .... Ezr 8:33
where are the v of the sanctuary,....... Neh 10:39
the frankincense, and the v .... Neh 13:5
I again the v of the house of God....... Neh 13:9
they gave them drink in v of gold ..... Est 1:7
(the v being diverse one from........... Est 1:7
even in v of bulrushes upon the .... Is 18:2
all v of small quantity, from the .... Is 22:24
quantity, from the v of cups,............. Is 22:24
even to all the v of flagons .... Is 22:24
that bear the v of the LORD............... Is 52:11
abominable things is in their v .... Is 65:4
they returned with their v empty....... Jer 14:3
the v of the LORD's house shall .... Jer 27:16
that the v which are left in the .... Jer 27:19
of the v that remain in this city .... Jer 27:19
concerning the v that remain in .... Jer 27:21
all the v of the LORD's house............ Jer 28:3

VESTMENTS (cont.)

to bring again the v of the .... Jer 28:6
and oil, and put them in your v .... Jer 40:10
to wander, and shall empty his v .... Jer 48:12
their curtains, and all their v .... Jer 49:29
all the v of brass wherewith they .... Jer 52:18
of all these v was without weight .... Jer 52:20
men and v of brass in they market ...... Eze 27:13
with part of the v of the house .... Dan 1:2
he brought the v into the .... Dan 1:2
silver v which his father .... Dan 5:2
v that were taken out of the .... Dan 5:3
they have brought the v of his .... Dan 5:23
with their precious v of silver .... Dan 11:8
the treasure of all pleasant v .... Hos 13:15
draw out fifty v out of the press .... Hag 2:16
down, and gathered the good into v .... Mt 13:48
oil in their v with their lamps .... Mt 25:4
of cups, and pots, brasen v .... Mk 7:4
with much longsuffering the v of .... Rom 9:22
of his glory on the v of mercy .... Rom 9:23
have this treasure in earthen v 2Cor 4:7
there are not only v of gold 2Ti 2:20
all the v of the ministry .... Heb 9:21
as the v of a potter shall they .... Rev 2:27
wood, and all manner v of ivory .... Rev 18:12
all manner v of most precious .... Rev 18:12

VESTMENTS

Bring forth v for all the 2Kin 10:22
And he brought them forth v 2Kin 10:22

VESTRY

said unto him that was over the v 2Kin 10:22

VESTURE

upon the four quarters of thy v .... Deut 22:12
them, and cast lots upon my v .... Ps 22:18
as a v shalt thou change them, and .... Ps 102:26
upon my v did they cast lots .... Mt 27:35
for my v they did cast lots .... Jn 19:24
as a v shalt thou fold them up, ... Heb 1:12
clothed with a v dipped in blood .... Rev 19:13
And he hath on his v and on his .... Rev 19:16

VESTURES

and arrayed him in v of fine linen ...... Gen 41:42

VEX

Thou shalt neither v a stranger .... Ex 22:21
sister, to v her, to uncover her .... Lev 18:18
in your land, ye shall not v him .... Lev 19:33
V the Midianites, and smite them .... Num 25:17
For they v you with their wiles, ... Num 25:18
shall v you in the land wherein .... Num 33:55
how wilt he then v himself 2Sa 12:18
for God did v them with all 2Chr 15:6
How long will ye v my soul .... Job 19:2
v them in his sore displeasure .... Ps 2:5
v it, and let us make a breach .... Is 7:6
and Judah shall not v Ephraim .... Is 11:13
I will also v the hearts of many .... Eze 32:9
thee, and awake that shall v thee ...... Hab 2:7
hands to v certain of the church .... Acts 12:1

VEXATION

shall send upon thee cursing, ... Deut 28:20
all is vanity and v of spirit .... Eccl 1:14
that this also is v of spirit .... Eccl 1:17
v of spirit, and there was no .... Eccl 2:11
for all is vanity and v of spirit .... Eccl 2:17
of the v of his heart, wherein he .... Eccl 2:22
also is vanity and v of spirit .... Eccl 2:26
is also vanity and v of spirit .... Eccl 4:4
full with travail and v of spirit .... Eccl 4:6
also is vanity and v of spirit .... Eccl 4:16
is also vanity and v of spirit .... Eccl 6:9
shall not be such as was in her v .... Is 9:1
and it shall be a v only to .... Is 28:19
and shall howl for v of spirit .... Is 65:14

VEXATIONS

but great v were upon all the 2Chr 15:5

VEXED

and the Egyptians v us, and our .... Num 20:15
that oppressed them and v them .... Judg 2:18
And that year they v and oppressed .... Judg 10:8
so that his soul was v unto death ...... Judg 16:16
he turned himself, he v them 1Sa 14:47
And Amnon was so v, that he fell 2Sa 13:2
for her soul is v within her 2Kin 4:27
hand of their enemies, who v them .... Neh 9:27
the Almighty, who hath v my soul ...... Job 27:2
for my bones are v .... Ps 6:2
My soul is also sore v .... Ps 6:3
mine enemies be ashamed and sore v .. Ps 6:10
rebelled, and v his holy Spirit .... Is 63:10
which art infamous and much v .... Eze 22:5
thee have they v the fatherless .... Eze 22:7
and have v the poor and needy .... Eze 22:29
is grievously v with a devil .... Mt 15:22
for he is lunatick, and sore v .... Mt 17:15
that that were v with unclean .... Lk 6:18
them which were v with unclean .... Acts 5:16
with the filthy conversation of 2Pet 2:7
v his righteous soul from day to 2Pet 2:8

VIAL

Then Samuel took a v of oil 1Sa 10:1
poured out his v upon the earth .... Rev 16:2
poured out his v upon the sea .... Rev 16:3
poured out his v upon the rivers .... Rev 16:4
poured out his v upon the sun .... Rev 16:8
his v upon the seat of the beast .... Rev 16:10

v upon the great river Euphrates .... Rev 16:12
poured out his v into the air .... Rev 16:17

VIALS

golden v full of odours, which .... Rev 5:8
golden v full of the wrath of God .... Rev 15:7
pour out the v of the wrath of .... Rev 16:1
angels which had the seven .... Rev 17:1
angels which had the seven v full .... Rev 21:9

VICTORY

the v that was turned into 2Sa 19:2
LORD wrought a great v that day 2Sa 23:10
and the LORD wrought a great v 2Sa 23:12
the power, and the glory, and the v 1Chr 29:11
holy arm, hath gotten him the v .... Ps 98:1
He will swallow up death in v .... Is 25:8
he send forth judgment unto v .... Mt 12:20
Death is swallowed up in v 1Cor 15:54
O grave, where is thy v 1Cor 15:55
which giveth us the v through our 1Cor 15:57
this is the v that overcometh the 1Jn 5:4
had gotten the v over the beast .... Rev 15:2

VICTUAL

prepared for themselves any v .... Ex 12:39
to fetch v for the people, that .... Judg 20:10
provided v for king Solomon 1Kin 4:27
captains in them, and store of v 2Chr 11:11
and he gave them v in abundance 2Chr 11:23

VICTUALS

Sodom and Gomorrah, and all their v .. Gen 14:11
nor lend him thy v for increase .... Lev 25:37
usury of money, usury of v .... Deut 23:19
the people, saying, Prepare you v .... Josh 1:11
Take v with you for the journey, ... Josh 9:11
And the men took of their v .... Josh 9:14
the people took v in their hand .... Judg 7:8
and a suit of apparel, and thy v .... Judg 17:10
the LORD for him, and gave him v 1Sa 22:10
which provided v for the king 1Kin 4:7
him an house, and appointed him v 1Kin 11:18
any v on the sabbath day to sell .... Neh 10:31
in the day wherein they sold v .... Neh 13:15
captain of the guard gave him v .... Jer 40:5
for then had we plenty of v .... Jer 44:17
the villages, and buy themselves v ...... Mt 14:15
round about, and lodge, and get v ...... Lk 9:12

VIEW

Go v the land, even Jericho .... Josh 2:1
saying, Go up and v the country .... Josh 7:2
went, and stood to v afar off 2Kin 2:7
were to v at Jericho saw him 2Kin 2:15

VIEWED

And the men went up and v Ai .... Josh 7:2
I v the people, and the priests, ... Ezr 8:15
the walls of Jerusalem, which .... Neh 2:13
v the wall, and turned back, and .... Neh 2:15

VIGILANT

the husband of one wife, v 1Ti 3:2
Be sober, be v 1Pet 5:8

VILE

brother should seem v unto thee .... Deut 25:3
unto this man do not so a thing .... Judg 19:24
his sons made themselves v 1Sa 3:13
but every thing that was v 1Sa 15:9
And I will yet be more v than thus 2Sa 6:22
and reputed v in your sight .... Job 18:3
Behold, I am v .... Job 40:4
In whose eyes a v person is .... Ps 15:4
The v person shall be no more .... Ps 32:5
For the v person will again .... Is 32:6
forth the precious from the v .... Jer 15:19
and will make them like v figs .... Jer 29:17
for I am become v .... Lam 1:11
estate shall stand up a v person .... Dan 11:21
for thou art v .... Nah 1:14
filth upon thee, and make thee v .... Nah 3:6
gave them up unto v affections .... Rom 1:26
Who shall change our v body .... Phil 3:21
in also a poor man in v raiment .... Jas 2:2

VILELY

of the mighty is v cast away 2Sa 1:21

VILER

they were v than the earth .... Job 30:8

VILEST

when the v men are exalted .... Ps 12:8

VILLAGE

Go into the v over against you .... Mt 21:2
way into the v over against you .... Mk 11:2
went throughout every city and v .... Lk 8:1
went, and entered into a v of the ...... Lk 9:52
And they went to another v .... Lk 9:56
that he entered into a certain v .... Lk 10:38
And as he entered into a certain v ...... Lk 17:12
into the v over against you .... Lk 19:30
same day to a v called Emmaus .... Lk 24:13
And they drew nigh unto the v .... Lk 24:28

VILLAGES

out of the houses, out of the v .... Ex 8:13
But the houses of the v which .... Lev 25:31
Heshbon, and in all the v thereof........ Num 21:25
and they took the v thereof .... Num 21:32
the v thereof, and called it Nobah ...... Num 32:42
the cities and the v thereof .... Josh 13:23
families, the cities, and their v .... Josh 13:28

are twenty and nine, with their v .... Josh 15:32
fourteen cities with their v .... Josh 15:36
sixteen cities with their v .... Josh 15:41
nine cities with their v .... Josh 15:44
Ekron, with her towns and her v .... Josh 15:45
lay near Ashdod, with their v .... Josh 15:46
Ashdod with her towns and her v .... Josh 15:47
Gaza with her towns and her v .... Josh 15:47
eleven cities with their v .... Josh 15:51
nine cities with their v .... Josh 15:54
ten cities with their v .... Josh 15:57
six cities with their v .... Josh 15:59
two cities with their v .... Josh 15:60
six cities with their v .... Josh 15:62
all the cities with their v .... Josh 16:9
twelve cities with their v .... Josh 18:24
fourteen cities with their v .... Josh 18:28
thirteen cities and their v .... Josh 19:6
four cities and their v .... Josh 19:7
all the v that were round about .... Josh 19:8
twelve cities with their v .... Josh 19:15
these cities with their v .... Josh 19:16
sixteen cities with their v .... Josh 19:22
families, the cities and their v .... Josh 19:23
twenty and two cities with their v ...... Josh 19:30
these cities with their v .... Josh 19:31
nineteen cities and their v .... Josh 19:38
families, the cities and their v .... Josh 19:39
these cities with their v .... Josh 19:48
the v thereof, gave they to Caleb ...... Josh 21:12
The inhabitants of the v ceased .... Judg 5:7
inhabitants of his v in Israel .... Judg 5:11
of fenced cities, and of country v 1Sa 6:18
And their v were, Etam, and Ain, ... 1Chr 4:32
all their v that were round about 1Chr 4:33
the v thereof, they gave to Caleb 1Chr 6:56
that dwelt in the v of the 1Chr 9:16
by their genealogy in their v 1Chr 9:22
brethren, which were in their v 1Chr 9:25
in the cities, and in the v 1Chr 27:25
and Shocho with the v thereof 2Chr 28:18
and Timnah with the v thereof 2Chr 28:18
Gimzo also and the v thereof 2Chr 28:18
one of the v in the plain of Ono .... Neh 6:2
And for the v, with their fields, ... Neh 11:25
in the v thereof, and at Dibon, and .... Neh 11:25
in the v thereof, and at Jekabzeel ...... Neh 11:25
Jekabzeel, and in the v thereof, ... Neh 11:25
Beer-sheba, and in the v thereof, ... Neh 11:27
at Mekonah, and in the v thereof, ... Neh 11:28
Zanoah, Adullam, and in their v .... Neh 11:30
at Azekah, and in the v thereof, ... Neh 11:30
Aija, and Beth-el, and in their v .... Neh 11:31
and from the v of Netophathi, ... Neh 11:28
them v round about Jerusalem .... Neh 12:29
Therefore the Jews of the v .... Est 9:19
in the lurking places of the v .... Ps 10:8
let us lodge in the v .... Song 7:11
the v that Kedar doth inhabit .... Is 42:11
go up to the land of unwalled v .... Eze 38:11
with his staves the head of his v .... Hab 3:14
went about all the cities and v .... Mt 9:35
away, that they may go into the v ...... Mk 6:36
And he went round about the v .... Mk 6:6
round about, and into the v .... Mk 6:36
whithersoever he entered, into v .... Mk 6:56
he went through the cities and v .... Lk 13:22
in many v of the Samaritans .... Acts 8:25

VILLANY

For the vile person will speak v .... Is 32:6
they have committed v in Israel .... Jer 29:23

VINE

dream, behold, a v was before me ...... Gen 40:9
were three branches .... Gen 40:10
Binding his foal unto the v .... Gen 49:11
his ass's colt unto the choice v .... Gen 49:11
the grapes of thy v undressed .... Lev 25:5
grapes in it of thy v undressed .... Lev 25:11
that is made of the v tree .... Num 6:4
their v is of the v of Sodom................ Deut 32:32
Then said the trees unto the v .... Judg 9:12
the v said unto them, Should I .... Judg 9:13
of any thing that cometh of the v ...... Judg 13:14
safely, every man under his v 1Kin 4:25
gather herbs, and found a wild v 2Kin 4:39
eat ye every man of his own v 2Kin 18:31
v dressers in the mountains, and 2Chr 26:10
off his unripe grape as the v .... Job 15:33
hast brought a v out of Egypt .... Ps 80:8
and behold, and visit this v .... Ps 80:14
v by the sides of thine house .... Ps 128:3
to see whether the v flourished .... Song 6:11
shall be as clusters of the v .... Song 7:8
let us see if the v flourish .... Song 7:12
and planted it with the choicest v ...... Is 5:2
languish, and the v of Sibmah .... Is 16:8
weeping of Jazer the v of Sibmah ...... Is 16:9
the v languisheth, all the .... Is 24:7
fields, for the fruitful v .... Is 32:12
the leaf falleth off from the v .... Is 34:4
and set ye every one of his v .... Is 36:16
Yet I had planted thee a noble v .... Jer 2:21
plant of a strange v unto me .... Jer 2:21
the remnant of Israel as a v .... Jer 6:9
there shall be no grapes on the v ...... Jer 8:13
of Sibmah, I will weep for .... Jer 48:32
What is the v tree more than any ...... Eze 15:2
As the v tree among the trees of .... Eze 15:6
a spreading v of low stature .... Eze 17:6

VINEDRESSERS (cont.)

so it became a v, and brought............ Eze 17:6
this v did bend her roots toward......... Eze 17:7
that it might be a goodly v................. Eze 17:8
mother is like a v in thy blood............ Eze 19:10
Israel is an empty v, he bringeth........ Hos 10:1
as the corn, and grow as the v........... Hos 14:7
He hath laid my v waste, and............. Joel 1:7
The v is dried up, and the fig............. Joel 1:12
the v do yield their strength............... Joel 2:22
shall sit every man under his v........... Mic 4:4
out, and marred their v branches....... Nah 2:2
yea, as yet the v, and the fig............. Hag 2:19
man his neighbour under the v........... Zec 3:10
the v shall give her fruit, and............. Zec 8:12
neither shall your v cast her.............. Mal 3:11
henceforth of this fruit of the v.......... Mt 26:29
no more of the fruit of the v.............. Mk 14:25
not drink of the fruit of the v............. Lk 22:18
I am the true v, and my Father is....... Jn 15:1
itself, except it abide in the v............ Jn 15:4
I am the v, ye are the branches......... Jn 15:5
either a v, figs?................................ Jas 3:12
clusters of the v of the earth............. Rev 14:18
and gathered the v of the earth......... Rev 14:19

VINEDRESSERS

of the poor of the land to be v............ 2Kin 25:12
shall be your plowmen and your v...... Is 61:5
of the poor of the land for v............... Jer 52:16
howl, O ye v, for the wheat and.......... Joel 1:11

VINEGAR

and shall drink no v of wine.............. Num 6:3
or v of strong drink, neither.............. Num 6:3
bread, and dip thy morsel in the v..... Ruth 2:14
my thirst they gave me v to drink....... Ps 69:21
As v to the teeth, and as smoke to.... Prov 10:26
as v upon nitre, so is he that............ Prov 25:20
They gave him v to drink mingled...... Mt 27:34
a spunge, and filled it with v............. Mt 27:48
ran and filled a spunge full of v......... Mk 15:36
coming to him, and offering him v...... Lk 23:36
there was set a vessel full of v.......... Jn 19:29
and they filled a spunge with v.......... Jn 19:29
had received the v........................... Jn 19:30

VINES

of seed, or of figs, or of v................. Num 20:5
A land of wheat, and barley, and v.... Deut 8:8
He destroyed their v with hail............ Ps 78:47
He smote their v also and their......... Ps 105:33
the v with the tender grape gives...... Song 2:13
little foxes, that spoil the v............... Song 2:15
for our v have tender grapes............. Song 2:15
v at a thousand silverlings............... Is 7:23
they shall eat up thy v and thy.......... Jer 5:17
Thou shalt yet plant v upon the......... Jer 31:5
And I will destroy her v and her......... Hos 2:12
neither shall fruit be in the v............. Hab 3:17

VINEYARD

an husbandman, and he planted a v.. Gen 9:20
cause a field or v to be eaten............ Ex 22:5
and of the best of his own v.............. Ex 22:5
manner thou shalt deal with thy v...... Ex 23:11
And thou shalt not glean thy v........... Lev 19:10
thou gather every grape of thy v....... Lev 19:10
six years thou shalt prune thy v......... Lev 25:3
sow thy field, nor prune thy v........... Lev 25:4
man is he that hath planted a v......... Deut 20:6
not sow thy v with divers seeds........ Deut 22:9
hast sown, and the fruit of thy v....... Deut 22:9
comest into thy neighbour's v........... Deut 23:24
gatherest the grapes of thy v........... Deut 24:21
thou shalt plant a v, and shalt.......... Deut 28:30
Naboth the Jezreelite had a v........... 1Kin 21:1
having, Give me thy v.................... 1Kin 21:2
thee for it a better v than it............. 1Kin 21:2
unto him, Give me thy v for money... 1Kin 21:6
I will give thee another v for it.......... 1Kin 21:6
I will not give thee my v................. 1Kin 21:6
I will give thee the v of Naboth......... 1Kin 21:7
take possession of the v of............. 1Kin 21:15
to the v of Naboth the Jezreelite....... 1Kin 21:16
behold, he is in the v of Naboth........ 1Kin 21:18
the v which thy right hand hath........ Ps 80:15
by the v of the man void of............... Prov 24:30
of her hands she planteth a v........... Prov 31:16
but mine own v have I not kept......... Song 1:6
Solomon had a v at Baal-hamon....... Song 8:11
he let out the v unto keepers........... Song 8:11
My v, which is mine, is before me..... Song 8:12
Zion is left as a cottage in a v.......... Is 1:8
for ye have eaten up the v............... Is 3:14
song of my beloved touching his v.... Is 5:1
My wellbeloved hath a v in a very..... Is 5:1
I pray you, betwixt me and my v....... Is 5:3
could have been done more to my v... Is 5:4
tell you what I will do to my v........... Is 5:5
For the v of the LORD of hosts is....... Is 5:7
ten acres of v shall yield one.......... Is 5:10
sing ve unto her, A v of red wine...... Is 27:2
Many pastors have destroyed my v... Jer 12:10
house, nor sow seed, nor plant v...... Jer 35:7
neither have ye v, nor field, nor....... Jer 35:9
the field, and as plantings of a v...... Mic 1:6
to hire labourers into his v............... Mt 20:1
a day, he sent them into his v.......... Mt 20:2
Go ye also into the v, and............... Mt 20:4
unto them, Go ye also into the v....... Mt 20:7
the lord of the v saith unto his......... Mt 20:8
said, Son, go work to day in my v...... Mt 21:28

householder, which planted a v......... Mt 21:33
him, and cast him out of the v.......... Mt 21:39
lord therefore of the v cometh.......... Mt 21:40
will let out his v unto other............... Mt 21:41
A certain man planted a v................ Mk 12:1
husbandman of the fruit of the v....... Mk 12:2
him, and cast him out of the v.......... Mk 12:8
therefore the lord of the v do........... Mk 12:9
and will give the v unto others......... Mk 12:9
had a fig tree planted in his v........... Lk 13:6
said he unto the dresser of his v...... Lk 13:7
A certain man planted a v................ Lk 20:9
give him of the fruit of the v............. Lk 20:10
Then said the lord of the v............... Lk 20:13
So they cast him out of the v........... Lk 20:15
the lord of the v do unto them.......... Lk 20:15
and shall give the v to others.......... Lk 20:16
who planteth a v, and eateth not...... 1Cor 9:7

VINEYARDS

us inheritance of fields and v............ Num 16:14
the fields, or through the v............... Num 20:17
into the fields, or into the v.............. Num 21:22
the LORD stood in a path of the v...... Num 22:24
which thou diggedst not, v............... Deut 6:11
Thou shalt plant v, and dress them... Deut 28:39
of the v and oliveyards which ye....... Josh 24:13
the fields, and gathered their v........ Judg 9:27
and unto the plain of the v.............. Judg 11:33
and came to the v of Timnath.......... Judg 14:5
the standing corn, with the v........... Judg 15:5
Go and lie in wait in the v............... Judg 21:20
dances, then come ye out of the v.... Judg 21:21
will take your fields, and your v........ 1Sa 8:14
tenth of your seed, and of your v..... 1Sa 8:15
give every one of you fields and v.... 1Sa 22:7
hundred, and oliveyards, and v........ 2Kin 5:26
and wine, a land of bread and v...... 2Kin 18:32
year sow ye, and reap, and plant v.. 2Kin 19:29
over the v was Shimei the............... 1Chr 27:27
over the increase of the v for.......... 1Chr 27:27
We have mortgaged our lands, v..... Neh 5:3
and that upon our lands and v........ Neh 5:4
for other men have our lands and v.. Neh 5:5
this day, their lands, their v............ Neh 5:11
of all goods, wells digged, v.......... Neh 9:25
he beholdeth not the way of the v.... Job 24:18
And sow the fields, and plant v....... Ps 107:37
I planted me v................................ Eccl 2:4
they made me the keeper of the v.... Song 1:6
of camphire in the v of En-gedi....... Song 1:14
Let us get up early to the v............ Song 7:12
in the v there shall be no.............. Is 16:10
and wine, a land of bread and v..... Is 36:17
year sow ye, and reap, and plant v.. Is 37:30
over them shall they plant v, and.... Is 65:21
v shall be possessed again in........ Jer 32:15
the land of Judah, and gave them v. Jer 39:10
and shall build houses, and plant v.. Eze 28:26
I will give her her v from thence..... Hos 2:15
when your gardens and your v....... Amos 4:9
ye have planted pleasant v............ Amos 5:11
in all v shall be wailing................. Amos 5:17
and they shall plant v, and drink.... Amos 9:14
and they shall plant v, but not....... Zeph 1:13

VINTAGE

threshing shall reach unto the v...... Lev 26:5
the v shall reach unto the sowing.... Lev 26:5
better than the v of Abi-ezer.......... Judg 8:2
they gather the v of the wicked...... Job 24:6
made their v shouting to cease....... Is 16:10
grapes when the v is done............. Is 24:13
for the v shall fail, the................... Is 32:10
thy summer fruits and upon thy v.... Jer 48:32
as the grapegleanings of the v...... Mic 7:1
the forest of the v is come down..... Zec 11:2

VIOL

And the harp, and the v, the tabret.. Is 5:12
That chant to the sound of the v..... Amos 6:5

VIOLATED

Her priests have v my law............. Eze 22:26

VIOLENCE

and the earth was filled with v........ Gen 6:11
is filled with v through them........... Gen 6:13
or in a thing taken away by v.......... Lev 6:2
thou savest me from v................... 2Sa 22:3
him that loveth v his soul hateth...... Ps 11:5
for I have seen v and strife in......... Ps 55:9
ye weigh the v of your hands in...... Ps 58:2
their soul from deceit and v............ Ps 72:14
v covereth them as a garment........ Ps 73:6
and drink the wine of v.................. Prov 4:17
but v covereth the mouth of the...... Prov 10:6
but v covereth the mouth of the...... Prov 10:11
of the transgressors shall eat v...... Prov 13:2
A man that doeth v to the blood...... Prov 28:17
because he had done no v, neither.. Is 53:9
the act of v is in their hands.......... Is 59:6
V shall no more be heard in thy..... Is 60:18
v and spoil is heard in her............ Jer 6:7
I spake, I cried out, I cried............ Jer 20:8
do no v to the stranger, the........... Jer 22:3
and for oppression, and for v......... Jer 22:17
The v done to me and to my flesh... Jer 51:35
v in the land, ruler against............ Jer 51:46
V risen up into a rod of................. Eze 7:11
because the city is full of v............ Eze 7:23
they have filled the land with v....... Eze 8:17
because of the v of all them that.... Eze 12:19

pledge, hath spoiled none by v........ Eze 18:7
poor and needy, hath spoiled by v.... Eze 18:12
pledge, neither hath spoiled by v..... Eze 18:16
spoiled his brother by v.................. Eze 18:18
filled the midst of thee with v.......... Eze 28:16
remove v and spoil, and execute..... Eze 45:9
for the v against the children of....... Joel 3:19
saith the LORD, who store up v........ Amos 3:10
cause the seat of v to come near.... Amos 6:3
For thy v against thy brother........... Obad 10
from the v that is in their hands..... Jonah 3:8
covet fields, and take them by v...... Mic 2:2
rich men thereof are full of v.......... Mic 6:12
even cry out unto thee of v............ Hab 1:2
for spoiling and v are before me.... Hab 1:3
They shall come all for v............... Hab 1:9
for the v of the land, of the........... Hab 2:8
For the v of Lebanon shall cover.... Hab 2:17
for the v of the land, of the........... Hab 2:17
fill their masters' houses with v..... Zeph 1:9
they have done v to the law.......... Zeph 3:4
one covereth v with his garment.... Mal 2:16
the kingdom of heaven suffereth v.. Mt 11:12
Do v to no man, neither accuse..... Lk 3:14
and brought them without v........... Acts 5:26
soldiers for the v of the people...... Acts 21:35
with great v took him away out of.. Acts 24:7
broken with the v of the waves..... Acts 27:41
Quenched the v of fire, escaped... Heb 11:34
Thus with v shall that great city.... Rev 18:21

VIOLENT

hast delivered me from the v man... 2Sa 22:49
his v dealing shall come down....... Ps 7:16
hast delivered me from the v man... Ps 18:48
the assemblies of v men have....... Ps 86:14
preserve me from the v man......... Ps 140:1
preserve me from the v man......... Ps 140:4
evil shall hunt the v man to.......... Ps 140:11
A v man enticeth his neighbour,... Prov 16:29
v perverting of judgment and....... Eccl 5:8
and the v take it by force............ Mt 11:12

VIOLENTLY

servants had v taken away.......... Gen 21:25
restore that which he took v away.. Lev 6:4
thine ass shall be v taken away.... Deut 28:31
because he hath v taken and an.... Job 20:19
they v take away flocks, and feed.. Job 24:2
He will surely v turn and toss....... Is 22:18
And he hath v taken away his...... Lam 2:6
the whole herd of swine ran v...... Mt 8:32
the herd ran v down a steep place.. Mk 5:13
the herd ran v down a steep place.. Lk 8:33

VIOLS

the grave, and the noise of thy v.. Is 14:11
will not hear the melody of thy v... Amos 5:23

VIPER

come the young and old lion, the v.. Is 30:6
is crushed breaketh out into a v..... Is 59:5
there came a v out of the heat,...... Acts 28:3

VIPER'S

the v tongue shall slay him........... Job 20:16

VIPERS

said unto them, O generation of v.. Mt 3:7
O generation of v, how can ye,...... Mt 12:34
Ye serpents, ye generation of v..... Mt 23:33
of him, O generation of v.............. Lk 3:7

VIRGIN

was very fair to look upon, a v....... Gen 24:16
that when the v cometh forth to...... Gen 24:43
And for his sister a v, that is......... Lev 21:3
but he shall take a v of his own..... Lev 21:14
an evil name upon a v of Israel..... Deut 22:19
If a damsel that is a v be.............. Deut 22:23
a man find a damsel that is a v...... Deut 22:28
both the young man and the v....... Deut 22:25
for she was a v............................ 2Sa 13:2
for my lord the king a young v...... 1Kin 1:2
The v the daughter of Zion hath.... 2Kin 19:21
a v shall conceive, and bear a son. Is 7:14
more rejoice, O thou oppressed v.. Is 23:12
The v, the daughter of Zion,......... Is 37:22
O daughter of Babylon, sit on....... Is 47:1
v daughter of Zion hath done a v... Is 62:5
shalt be built, O v of Israel........... Jer 31:4
Then shall the v rejoice in the...... Jer 31:13
O v of Israel, turn again to.......... Jer 31:21
up into Gilead, and take balm, O v. Jer 46:11
The Lord hath trodden the v.......... Lam 1:15
thee, O v daughter of Zion........... Lam 2:13
Lament like a v girded with.......... Joel 1:8
The v of Israel is fallen............... Amos 5:2
a v shall be with child, and shall... Mt 1:23
To a v espoused to a man whose... Lk 1:27
if a v marry, she hath not sinned... 1Cor 7:28
also between a wife and a v......... 1Cor 7:34
himself unconvey toward his v...... 1Cor 7:36
his heart that he will keep his v.... 1Cor 7:37
you as a chaste v to Christ.......... 2Cor 11:2

VIRGINITY

And he shall take a wife in her v... Lev 21:13
the tokens of the damsel's v unto.. Deut 22:15
are the tokens of my daughter's v.. Deut 22:17
the tokens of v be not found for.... Deut 22:20
the mountains, and bewail my v.... Judg 11:37

bewailed her v upon the mountains .. Judg 11:38
they bruised the teats of their v........ Eze 23:3
they bruised the breasts of her v....... Eze 23:8
an husband seven years from her v...... Lk 2:36

VIRGIN'S
and the v name was Mary.............. Lk 1:27

VIRGINS
money according to the dowry of v.... Ex 22:17
four hundred young v, that had .... Judg 21:12
daughters that were v apparelled 2Sa 13:18
fair young v sought for the king .... Est 2:2
young v unto Shushan the palace....... Est 2:3
in his sight more than all the v .... Est 2:17
when the v were gathered together ... Est 2:19
the v her companions that follow....... Ps 45:14
therefore do the v love thee............ Song 1:3
concubines, and v without number .... Song 6:8
up young men, nor bring up v .... Is 23:4
her v are afflicted, and she is in .... Lam 1:4
my v and my young men are gone...... Lam 1:18
the v of Jerusalem hang down .... Lam 2:10
my v and my young men are fallen .... Lam 2:21
In that day shall the fair v............... Amos 8:13
of heaven be likened unto ten v .... Mt 25:1
Then all those v arose, and .... Mt 25:7
Afterward came also the other v .... Mt 25:11
same man had four daughters, v .... Acts 21:9
Now concerning v I have no............. 1Cor 7:25
for they are v .... Rev 14:4

VIRTUE
that v had gone out of him .... Mk 5:30
for there went v out of him.............. Lk 6:19
perceive that v is gone out of me ...... Lk 8:46
if there be any v, and if there be...... Phil 4:8
that hath called us to glory and v 2Pet 1:3
diligence, add to your faith v 2Pet 1:5
and to v knowledge 2Pet 1:5

VIRTUOUS
doth know that thou art a v woman .. Ruth 3:11
A v woman is a crown to her............. Prov 12:4
Who can find a v woman .... Prov 31:10

VIRTUOUSLY
Many daughters have done v .... Prov 31:29

VISAGE
his v was so marred more than any.... Is 52:14
Their v is blacker than a coal........... Lam 4:8
the form of his v was changed.......... Dan 3:19

VISIBLE
heaven, and that are in earth, v........ Col 1:16

VISION
the LORD came unto Abram in a v..... Gen 15:1
make myself known unto him in a v... Num 12:6
which saw the v of the Almighty,...... Num 24:4
which saw the v of the Almighty,...... Num 24:16
there was no open v 1Sa 3:1
Samuel feared to shew Eli the v 1Sa 3:15
words, and according to all this v...... 2Sa 7:17
words, and according to all this v 1Chr 17:15
in the v of Isaiah the prophet............ 2Chr 32:32
chased away as a v of the night .... Job 20:8
in a v of the night, when deep .... Job 33:15
thou spakest in v to thy holy one....... Ps 89:19
Where there is no v, the people......... Prov 29:18
The v of Isaiah the son of Amoz,........ Is 1:1
A grievous v is declared unto me ...... Is 21:2
The burden of the valley of v .... Is 22:1
God of hosts in the valley of v .... Is 22:5
they err in v, they stumble in........... Is 28:7
shall be as a dream of a night v .... Is 29:7
the v of all is become unto you......... Is 29:11
they prophesy unto you a false v ...... Jer 14:14
they speak a v of their own heart ..... Jer 23:16
also find no v from the LORD .... Lam 2:9
for the v is touching the whole......... Eze 7:13
they seek a v of the prophet............ Eze 7:26
according to the v that I saw in .... Eze 8:4
brought me in a v by the Spirit........ Eze 11:24
So the v that I had seen went up...... Eze 11:24
are prolonged, and every v faileth ... Eze 12:22
at hand, and the effect of every v .... Eze 12:23
vain v nor flattering divination .... Eze 12:24
The v that he seeth is for many .... Eze 12:27
Have ye not seen a vain v .... Eze 13:7
appearance of the v which I saw ...... Eze 43:3
even according to the v that I .... Eze 43:3
the visions were like the v that .... Eze 43:3
revealed unto Daniel in a night v..... Dan 2:19
and said, I saw in my v by night....... Dan 7:2
Belshazzar a v appeared unto me..... Dan 8:1
And I saw in a v .... Dan 8:2
and I saw in a v, and I was by the .... Dan 8:2
spake, How long shall be the v .... Dan 8:13
I, even I Daniel, had seen the v .... Dan 8:15
make this man to understand the v .. Dan 8:16
time of the end shall be the v.......... Dan 8:17
the v of the evening and the .... Dan 8:26
wherefore shut thou up the v........... Dan 8:26
and I was astonished at the v .... Dan 8:27
seen in the v at the beginning......... Dan 9:21
the matter, and consider the v......... Dan 9:23
and to seal up the v and prophecy,... Dan 9:24
and had understanding of the v........ Dan 10:1
And I Daniel alone saw the v........... Dan 10:7
that were with me saw not the v ...... Dan 10:7
left alone, and saw this great v .... Dan 10:8
for yet the v is for many days........... Dan 10:14

by the v my sorrows are turned .... Dan 10:16
themselves to establish the v........... Dan 11:14
The v of Obadiah .... Obad 1
you, that ye shall not have a v .... Mic 3:6
The book of the v of Nahum the........ Nah 1:1
answered me, and said, Write the v... Hab 2:2
For the v is yet for an appointed....... Hab 2:3
be ashamed every one of his v......... Zec 13:4
Tell the v to no man, until the......... Mt 17:9
he had seen a v in the temple......... Lk 1:22
they had also seen a v of angels...... Lk 24:23
and to him said the Lord in a v........ Acts 9:10
hath seen in a v a man named .... Acts 9:12
He saw in a v evidently about the.... Acts 10:3
doubted in himself what this v .... Acts 10:17
While Peter thought on the v .... Acts 10:19
and in a trance I saw a v, A............ Acts 11:5
but thought he saw a v .... Acts 12:9
a v appeared to Paul in the night ... Acts 16:9
And after he had seen the v .... Acts 16:10
Lord to Paul in the night by a v ...... Acts 18:9
disobedient unto the heavenly v..... Acts 26:19
And thus I saw the horses in the .... Rev 9:17

VISIONS
unto Israel in the v of the night ...... Gen 46:2
in the v of Iddo the seer against 2Chr 9:29
had understanding in the v of God.... 2Chr 26:5
thoughts from the v of the night...... Job 4:13
and terrifiest me through v .... Job 7:14
were opened, and I saw v of God...... Eze 1:1
brought me in the v of God to.......... Eze 8:3
which saw v of peace for her, and.... Eze 13:16
In the v of God brought he me......... Eze 40:2
the v were like the vision that I ...... Eze 43:3
Daniel had understanding in all v.... Dan 1:17
the v of thy head upon thy bed,...... Dan 2:28
the v of my head troubled me......... Dan 4:5
tell me the v of my dream that I ..... Dan 4:9
Thus were the v of mine head in..... Dan 4:10
I saw in the v of my head upon my.. Dan 4:13
v of his head upon his bed.............. Dan 7:1
After this I saw in the night v .... Dan 7:7
I saw in the night v, and, behold,.... Dan 7:13
the v of my head troubled me......... Dan 7:15
prophets, and I have multiplied v.... Hos 12:10
your young men shall see .... Joel 2:28
and your young men shall see v ..... Acts 2:17
I will come to v and revelations...... 2Cor 12:1

VISIT
and God will surely v you,............... Gen 50:24
saying, God will surely v you .... Gen 50:25
saying, God will surely v you .... Ex 13:19
I v I will v their sin upon................. Ex 32:34
therefore I do v the iniquity .... Lev 18:25
thou shalt v thy habitation, and...... Job 5:24
shouldest v him every morning....... Job 7:18
awake to v all the heathen.............. Ps 59:5
heaven, and behold, and v this vine... Ps 80:14
Then will I v their transgression...... Ps 89:32
O v me with thy salvation............... Ps 106:4
years, that the LORD will v Tyre...... Is 23:17
neither shall they v it .... Jer 3:16
Shall I not v for these things.......... Jer 5:9
Shall I not v for these things.......... Jer 5:29
at the time that I v them they......... Jer 6:15
Shall I not v them for these........... Jer 9:9
their iniquity, and v their sins........ Jer 14:10
v me, and revenge me of my .... Jer 15:15
I will v upon you the evil of............ Jer 23:2
be until the day that I v them......... Jer 27:22
at Babylon I will v you, and............ Jer 29:10
there shall he be until I v him........ Jer 32:5
him, the time that I will v him,....... Jer 49:8
come, the time that I will v thee..... Jer 50:31
he will v thine iniquity, O.............. Lam 4:22
I will v upon her the days of........... Hos 2:13
their iniquity, and v their sins........ Hos 8:13
iniquity, he will v their sins............ Hos 9:9
v the transgressions of Israel......... Amos 3:14
will also v the altars of Beth-el ...... Amos 3:14
the LORD their God shall v them .... Zeph 2:7
which shall not v those that be...... Zec 11:16
it came into his heart to v his........ Acts 7:23
at the first did v the Gentiles......... Acts 15:14
v our brethren in every city............ Acts 15:36
To v the fatherless and widows in... Jas 1:27

VISITATION
be visited after the v of all men...... Num 16:29
thy v hath preserved my spirit........ Job 10:12
what wilt ye do in the day of v........ Is 10:3
in the time of their v they shall...... Jer 8:12
time of their v they shall perish...... Jer 10:15
even the year of their v .... Jer 11:23
them, even the year of their v........ Jer 23:12
upon them, and the time of their v.. Jer 46:21
upon Moab, the year of their v .... Jer 48:44
day is come, the time of their v...... Jer 50:27
time of their v they shall perish...... Jer 51:18
The days of v are come, the days ... Hos 9:7
of thy watchmen and thy v cometh.. Mic 7:4
knewest not the time of thy v......... Lk 19:44
glorify God in the day of v.............. 1Pet 2:12

VISITED
the LORD v Sarah as he had said,.... Gen 21:1
me, saying, I have surely v you........ Ex 3:16
LORD had v the children of Israel.... Ex 4:31
or if they be v after the .... Num 16:29
that Samson v his wife with a kid.... Judg 15:1

of Moab how that the LORD had v .... Ruth 1:6
And the LORD v Hannah, so that she... 1Sa 2:21
is not so, he hath v in his anger ...... Job 35:15
thou hast v me in the night .... Ps 17:3
he shall not be v with evil.............. Prov 19:23
after many days shall they be v ...... Is 24:22
therefore hast thou v and............. Is 26:14
LORD, in trouble have they v thee... Is 26:16
Thou shalt be v of the LORD of ...... Is 29:6
this is the city to be v.................... Jer 6:6
them away, and have not v them.... Jer 23:2
After many days thou shalt be v...... Eze 38:8
for the LORD of hosts hath v his..... Zec 10:3
I was sick, and ye v me................... Mt 25:36
and in prison, and ye v me not....... Mt 25:43
for he hath v and redeemed his..... Lk 1:68
dayspring from on high hath v us.... Lk 1:78
and, That God hath v his people..... Lk 7:16

VISITEST
the son of man, that thou v him...... Ps 8:4
Thou v the earth, and waterest it.... Ps 65:9
the son of man, that thou v............ Heb 2:6

VISITETH
and when he v, what shall I answer... Job 31:14

VISITING
the iniquity of the fathers............. Ex 20:5
v the iniquity of the fathers........... Ex 34:7
v the iniquity of the fathers........... Num 14:18
v the iniquity of the fathers........... Deut 5:9

VOCATION
of the v wherewith ye are called..... Eph 4:1

VOICE See PREFACE.
the v of thy brother's blood .... Gen 4:10
and said, The v is Jacob's v............ Gen 27:22
Beware of him, and obey his v........ Ex 23:21
the people answered with one v ..... Ex 24:3
ye heard the v of the words............ Deut 4:12
Did ever people hear the v of God... Deut 4:33
and after the fire a still small v...... 1Kin 19:12
into the v of them that weep.......... Job 30:31
After it a v roareth........................ Job 37:4
with the v of his excellency............ Job 37:4
not stay them when his v is heard... Job 37:4
marvellously with his v .... Job 37:5
thou lift up thy v to the clouds....... Job 38:34
My v shalt thou hear in the .... Ps 5:3
house of God, with the v of joy...... Ps 42:4
To day if ye will hear his .... Ps 95:7
my v is to the sons of man .... Prov 8:4
unto thee at the v of thy cry.......... Is 30:19
The v of him that crieth in the ...... Is 40:3
the v of weeping shall be no more... Is 65:19
heard in her, nor the v of crying .... Is 65:19
When he uttereth his v, there is .... Jer 10:13
as the v of the Almighty God when.. Eze 10:5
his v was like a noise of many .... Eze 43:2
The v of one crying in the.............. Mt 3:3
lo a v from heaven, saying, This...... Mt 3:17
behold a v out of the cloud,........... Mt 17:5
The v of one crying in the.............. Mk 1:3
The v of one crying in the.............. Lk 3:4
I am the v of one crying in the ...... Jn 1:23
hear the v of the Son of God .... Jn 5:25
for they know his v .... Jn 10:4
This v came not because of me,...... Jn 12:30
that is of the truth heareth my v.... Jn 18:37
him stood speechless, hearing a v .. Acts 9:7
saying, It is the v of a god.............. Acts 12:22
that by my v I might teach others... 1Cor 14:19
To day if ye will hear his v............. Heb 3:7
To day if ye will hear his v............. Heb 3:15
Whose v then shook the earth........ Heb 12:26
his v as the sound of many waters... Rev 1:15
if any man hear my v, and open the... Rev 3:20

VOICES
before God, and lifted up their v..... Judg 21:2
all the people lifted up their v 1Sa 11:4
When he uttereth his v, there is .... Lk 17:13
And they were instant with loud v .. Lk 23:23
the v of them and of the chief........ Lk 23:23
nor yet the v of the prophets.......... Acts 13:27
had done, they lifted up their v...... Acts 14:11
word, and then lifted up their v ..... Acts 22:22
so many kinds of v in the world...... 1Cor 14:10
lightnings and thunderings and ..... Rev 4:5
and there were v, and thunderings,.. Rev 8:5
v of the trumpet of the three......... Rev 8:13
seven thunders uttered their v ...... Rev 10:3
thunders had uttered their v .... Rev 10:4
and there were great v in heaven... Rev 11:15
and there were lightnings, and v.... Rev 11:19
And there were v, and thunders, and . Rev 16:18

VOID
the earth was without form, and v... Gen 1:2
them v on the day he heard them ... Num 30:12
them v on the day he heard them ... Num 30:12
it, or her husband may make it v ..... Num 30:13
v after that he hath heard them...... Num 30:15
they are a nation v of counsel......... Deut 32:28
in a v place in the entrance of........ 1Kin 22:10
they sat in a v place at the............. 2Chr 18:9
Thou hast made v the covenant of .. Ps 89:39
for they have made v thy law.......... Ps 119:126
a young man v of understanding,..... Prov 7:7
of him that is v of understanding.... Prov 10:13
He that is v of wisdom despiseth.... Prov 11:12

persons is v of understanding............ Prov 12:11
A man v of understanding striketh...... Prov 17:18
of the man v of understanding........... Prov 24:30
it shall not return unto me v.............. Is 55:11
and, lo, it was without form, and v...... Jer 4:23
I will make v the counsel of............... Jer 19:7
She is empty, and v, and waste.......... Nah 2:10
v of offence toward God, and............ Acts 24:16
Do we then make v the law through... Rom 3:31
the law be heirs, faith is made v......... Rom 4:14
any man should make my glorying v... 1Cor 9:15

VOLUME
in the v of the book it is.................... Ps 40:7
I come (in the v of the book it............ Heb 10:7

VOLUNTARILY
peace offerings v unto the LORD....... Eze 46:12

VOLUNTARY
his own v will at the door of the.......... Lev 1:3
or a v offering, it shall be.................. Lev 7:16
a v burnt offering or peace............... Eze 46:12
of your reward in a v humility............ Col 2:18

VOMIT
and he shall v them up again............. Job 20:15
thou hast eaten shalt thou v up........ Prov 23:8
thou be filled therewith, and v it....... Prov 25:16
As a dog returneth to his v............... Prov 26:11
a drunken man staggereth in his v... Is 19:14
For all tables are full of v.................. Is 28:8
Moab also shall wallow in his v......... Jer 48:26
dog is turned to his own v again........ 2Pet 2:22

VOMITED
it v out Jonah upon the dry land......... Jonah 2:10

VOMITETH
the land itself v out her.................... Lev 18:25

VOPHSI
(vof´-si) A spy sent to the Promised Land.
of Naphtali, Nahbi the son of V........ Num 13:14

VOW
And Jacob vowed a v, saying, I........ Gen 28:20
and where thou vowedst a v unto me Gen 31:13
sacrifice of his offering be a v........... Lev 7:16
unto the LORD to accomplish his v... Lev 22:21
but for a v it shall not be................... Lev 22:23
a man shall make a singular v.......... Lev 27:2
separate themselves to v................. Num 6:2
a v of a Nazarite, to.......................... Num 6:2
All the days of the v of his................ Num 6:5
according to the v which he vowed.... Num 6:21
or a sacrifice in performing a v......... Num 15:3
for a sacrifice in performing a v........ Num 15:8
And Israel vowed a v unto the LORD.. Num 21:2
If a man v a.. Num 30:2
a v unto the LORD............................ Num 30:2
If a woman also v a........................... Num 30:3
a v unto the LORD............................ Num 30:3
And her father hear her v, and her... Num 30:4
shall make her v which she vowed.... Num 30:5
But every v of a widow, and of her.... Num 30:9
Every v, and every binding oath to... Num 30:13
vows which ye v unto the LORD....... Deut 12:11
of the LORD thy God for any v.......... Deut 12:26
When thou shalt v a.......................... Deut 23:21
a v unto the LORD thy God............... Deut 23:21
But if thou shalt forbear to v............. Deut 23:22
Jephthah vowed a v unto the LORD... Judg 11:30
to his v which he had vowed............. Judg 11:39
And she vowed a v, and said, O LORD.. 1Sa 1:11
the yearly sacrifice, and his v........... 1Sa 1:21
pray thee, let me go and pay my v..... 2Sa 15:7
For thy servant vowed a v while I..... 2Sa 15:8
thee shall the v be performed............ Ps 65:1
V, and pay unto the LORD your God... Ps 76:11
When thou vowest a v unto God....... Eccl 5:4
is it that thou shouldest not v............ Eccl 5:5
than that thou shouldest v................ Eccl 5:5
oblation; yea, they shall v................ Is 19:21
a v unto the LORD............................ Is 19:21
for he had a v.................................... Acts 18:18
four men which have a v on them..... Acts 21:23

VOWED
And Jacob a vow, saying, If God....... Gen 28:20
that v shalt the priest value him........ Lev 27:8
law of the Nazarite who hath v......... Num 6:21
according to the vow which he v........ Num 6:21
Israel v a vow unto the LORD, and... Num 21:2
had at all an husband, when she v..... Num 30:6
he shall make her vow which she v... Num 30:8
if she v in her husband's house,....... Num 30:10
thou hast v unto the LORD thy God.. Deut 23:23
Jephthah v a vow unto the LORD....... Judg 11:30
to his vow which he had v................. Judg 11:39
she v a vow, and said, O LORD of..... 1Sa 1:11
which I have v unto the LORD, in...... 2Sa 15:8
For thy servant v a vow while I......... 2Sa 15:8
v unto the mighty God of Jacob........ Ps 132:2
pay that which thou hast v............... Eccl 5:4
perform our vows that we have v...... Jonah 2:9
I will pay that that I have v............... Jonah 2:9

VOWEDST
where thou v a vow unto me............. Gen 31:13

VOWEST
nor any of thy vows which thou v...... Deut 12:17
When thou v a vow unto God, defer... Eccl 5:4

VOWETH
hath in his flock a male, and v........... Mal 1:14

VOWS
offer his oblation for all his v............ Lev 22:18
your gifts, and beside all your v....... Lev 23:38
in your set feasts, beside your v...... Num 29:39
then all her v shall stand.................. Num 30:4
not any of her v, or of her bonds....... Num 30:5
then her v shall stand, and her......... Num 30:7
then all her v shall stand.................. Num 30:11
out of her lips concerning her v........ Num 30:12
then he establisheth all her v.......... Num 30:14
offerings of your hand, and your v.... Deut 12:6
all your choice v which ye vow......... Deut 12:11
nor any of thy v which thou............... Deut 12:17
things which thou hast, and thy v..... Deut 12:26
thee, and thou shalt pay thy v.......... Job 22:27
I will pay my v before them that....... Ps 22:25
pay thy v unto the most High............ Ps 50:14
Thy v are upon me, O God................. Ps 56:12
For thou, O God, hast heard my v..... Ps 61:5
that I may daily perform my v........... Ps 61:8
I will pay thee my v.......................... Ps 66:13
I will pay my v unto the LORD now.... Ps 116:14
I will pay my v unto the LORD now.... Ps 116:18
this day have I payed my v.............. Prov 7:14
holy, and after v to make enquiry..... Prov 20:25
and what, the son of my v................ Prov 31:2
perform our v that we have vowed.... Jer 44:25
ye will surely accomplish your v...... Jer 44:25
and surely perform your v................ Jer 44:25
unto the LORD, and perform your v.. Jonah 1:16
the solemn feasts, perform thy v..... Nah 1:15

VOYAGE
that this v will be with hurt............... Acts 27:10

VULTURE
And the v, and the kite after his....... Lev 11:14
kite, and the v after his kind,........... Deut 14:13

VULTURE'S
which the v eye hath not seen.......... Job 28:7

VULTURES
there shall the v also be.................... Is 34:15

W

WADI ZERED See ZERED.

WAFER
one w out of the basket of the.......... Ex 29:23
a cake of oiled bread, and one w....... Lev 8:26
the basket, and one unleavened w... Num 6:19

WAFERS
of it was like w made with honey....... Ex 16:31
w unleavened anointed with oil......... Ex 29:2
or unleavened w anointed with oil.... Lev 2:4
unleavened w anointed with oil,....... Lev 7:12
of unleavened bread anointed.......... Num 6:15

WAG
be astonished, and w his head......... Jer 18:16
w their head at the daughter of........ Lam 2:15
by her shall hiss, and w his hand..... Zeph 2:15

WAGES
tell me, what shall thy w be.............. Gen 29:15
And he said, Appoint me thy v.......... Gen 30:28
me, and changed my w ten times...... Gen 31:7
thus, The speckled shall be thy w... Gen 31:8
thou hast changed my w ten times... Gen 31:41
for me, and I will give thee thy w...... Ex 2:9
the w of him that is hired shall......... Lev 19:13
his neighbour's service without w.... Jer 22:13
yet had he no w, nor his army,.......... Eze 29:18
and it shall be the w for his army..... Eze 29:19
he that earneth w earneth w............ Hag 1:6
oppress the hireling in his w............ Mal 3:5
and be content with your w.............. Lk 3:14
And he that reapeth receiveth w...... Jn 4:36
For the w of sin is death.................... Rom 6:23
taking w of them, to do you.............. 2Cor 11:8
son of Bosor, who loved the w of...... 2Pet 2:15

WAGGING
by reviled him, w their heads,.......... Mt 27:39
w their heads, and saying, Ah,......... Mk 15:29

WAGON
a w for two of the princes, and......... Num 7:3

WAGONS
take you w out of the land of............ Gen 45:19
And Joseph gave them w, according.. Gen 45:21
when he saw the w which Joseph..... Gen 45:27
in the w which Pharaoh had sent...... Gen 46:5
before the LORD, six covered w....... Num 7:3
And Moses took the w and the oxen,.. Num 7:6
Two w and four oxen he gave unto... Num 7:7
And four w and eight oxen he gave... Num 7:8
against thee with chariots, w.......... Eze 23:24

WAIL
w for the multitude of Egypt, and..... Eze 32:18
Therefore I will w and howl, I........... Mic 1:8
the earth shall w because of him...... Rev 1:7

WAILED
and them that wept and w greatly..... Mk 5:38

WAILING
and fasting, and weeping, and w...... Est 4:3
will I take up a weeping and w........... Jer 9:10
make haste, and take up a w for us... Jer 9:18
For a voice of w is heard out of........ Jer 9:19
mouth, and teach your daughters w... Jer 9:20
neither shall there be w for them...... Eze 7:11
bitterness of heart and bitter w........ Eze 27:31
in their w they shall take up a.......... Eze 27:32
W shall be in all streets.................... Amos 5:16
are skilful at lamentation to w.......... Amos 5:16
And in all vineyards shall be w......... Amos 5:17
I will make a w like the dragons,...... Mic 1:8
there shall be w and gnashing of..... Mt 13:42
there shall be w and gnashing of..... Mt 13:50
fear of her torment, weeping and w.. Rev 18:15
heads, and cried, weeping and w..... Rev 18:19

WAIT
And if a man lie not in w, but God..... Ex 21:13
they shall w on their priest's........... Num 3:10
in to w upon the service of the......... Num 8:24
or hurl at him by laying of w............. Num 35:20
him any thing without laying of w..... Num 35:22
lie in w for him, and rise up.............. Deut 19:11
ye shall lie in w against the............. Josh 8:4
their liers in w on the west of........... Josh 8:13
in w for him in the top of the............ Judg 9:25
thee, and lie in w in the field........... Judg 9:32
they laid w against Shechem in....... Judg 9:34
were with him, from lying in w.......... Judg 9:35
laid w in the field, and looked,......... Judg 9:43
laid w for him all night in the........... Judg 16:2
Now there were men lying in w......... Judg 16:9
there were liers in w abiding in........ Judg 16:12
set liers in w round about Gibeah.... Judg 20:29
the liers in w of Israel came............ Judg 20:33
in w which they had set beside........ Judg 20:36
And the liers in w hasted, and......... Judg 20:37
the liers in w drew themselves........ Judg 20:37
men of Israel and the liers in w....... Judg 20:38
lie in w in the vineyards................... Judg 21:20
how he laid w for him in the way,..... 1Sa 15:2
Amalek, and laid w in the valley...... 1Sa 15:5
servant against me, to lie in w......... 1Sa 22:8
rise against me, to lie in w.............. 1Sa 22:13
what should I w for the LORD any.... 2Kin 6:33
Because their office was to w on...... 1Chr 23:28
and did not then w by course........... 2Chr 5:11
the Levites w upon their business.... 2Chr 13:10
and of such as lay in w for their....... Ezr 8:31
of my appointed time will I w........... Job 14:14
If I w, the grave is mine house......... Job 17:13
or if I have laid w at my................... Job 31:9
abide in the covert to lie in w........... Job 38:40
He lieth in w secretly as a lion......... Ps 10:9
he lieth in w to catch the poor......... Ps 10:9
let none that w on thee be............... Ps 25:3
on thee do I w all the day................. Ps 25:5
for I w on thee................................ Ps 25:21
W on the LORD................................ Ps 27:14
I, say, on the LORD.......................... Ps 27:14
W on the LORD, and patiently for him.. Ps 37:7
but those that w upon the LORD....... Ps 37:9
W on the LORD, and keep his way,.... Ps 37:34
And now, LORD, what v I w for.......... Ps 39:7
and I will w on thy name.................. Ps 52:9
my steps, when they w for my soul... Ps 56:6
lo, they lie in w for my soul.............. Ps 59:3
his strength will I w upon thee......... Ps 59:9
My soul, w thou only upon God........ Ps 62:5
eyes fail while I w for my God........... Ps 69:3
Let not them that w on thee............. Ps 69:6
they that lay w for my soul take....... Ps 71:10
These w all upon thee..................... Ps 104:27
so our eyes w upon the LORD our..... Ps 123:2
w for the LORD, my soul doth w....... Ps 130:5
The eyes of all w upon thee............ Ps 145:15
with us, let us lay w for blood.......... Prov 1:11
they lay w for their own blood......... Prov 1:18
lieth in w at every corner................ Prov 7:12
wicked are to lie in w for blood........ Prov 12:6
but w on the LORD, and keep........... Prov 20:22
She also lieth in w as for a prey....... Prov 23:28
Lay not w, O wicked man, against.... Prov 24:15
I will w upon the LORD, that............ Is 8:17
And therefore will the LORD w......... Is 30:18
are all they that w for him............... Is 30:18
But they that w upon the LORD........ Is 40:31
and the isles shall w for his law....... Is 42:4
be not ashamed that w for me......... Is 49:23
that wait on me shall not be............ Is 51:5
we w for light, but behold................ Is 59:9
Surely the isles shall w for me......... Is 60:9
they lay w, as he that setteth.......... Jer 5:26
but in heart he layeth his w............. Jer 9:8
therefore we will w upon thee......... Jer 14:22
was unto me as a bear lying in w...... Lam 3:10
is good unto them that w for him...... Lam 3:25
quietly w for the salvation of.......... Lam 3:26
they laid w for us in the.................. Lam 4:19
as troops of robbers w for a man..... Hos 6:9

an oven, whiles they lie in w .... Hos 7:6
and w on thy God continually .... Hos 12:6
they all lie in w for blood .... Mic 7:2
I will w for the God of my .... Mic 7:7
though it tarry, w for it .... Hab 2:3
Therefore w ye upon me, saith the .... Zeph 3:8
that a small ship should w on him .... Mk 3:9
Laying w for him, and seeking to .... Lk 11:54
unto men that w for their lord .... Lk 12:36
but w for the promise of the .... Acts 1:4
And when the Jews laid w for him .... Acts 20:3
me by the lying in w of the Jews .... Acts 20:19
son heard of their lying in w .... Acts 23:16
for there lie in w for him of .... Acts 23:21
that the Jews laid w for the man .... Acts 23:30
laying w in the way to kill him .... Acts 25:3
then do we with patience w for it .... Rom 8:25
let us w on our ministering .... Rom 12:7
they which w at the altar are 1Cor 9:13
For we through the Spirit w for .... Gal 5:5
whereby they lie in w to deceive .... Eph 4:14
to w for his Son from heaven, ... 1Th 1:10

WAITED
I have w for thy salvation, O .... Gen 49:18
w for the king by the way, and 1Kin 20:38
and she w on Naaman's wife 2Kin 5:2
then they w on their office 1Chr 6:32
that they w with their children 1Chr 6:33
Who hitherto w in the king's gate 1Chr 9:18
the priests w on their offices 2Chr 7:6
These w on the king, beside those 2Chr 17:19
the porters w at every gate 2Chr 35:15
priests and for the Levites that w .... Neh 12:44
the companies of Sheba w for them .... Job 6:19
and he is w for of the sword .... Job 15:22
Unto me men gave ear, and w .... Job 29:21
they w for me as for the rain .... Job 29:23
when I w for light, there came .... Job 30:26
Now Elihu had w till Job had .... Job 32:4
Behold, I w for your words .... Job 32:11
When I had w, (for they spake not .... Job 32:16
I w patiently for the Lord .... Ps 40:1
they w not for his counsel .... Ps 106:13
The wicked have w for me to .... Ps 119:95
we have w for him, and he will .... Is 25:9
we have w for him, we will be .... Is 25:9
O Lord, have we w for thee .... Is 26:8
we have w for thee .... Is 33:2
Now when she saw that she had w .... Eze 19:5
of Maroth w carefully for good .... Mic 1:12
w upon me knew that it was the .... Zec 11:11
which also w for the kingdom of .... Mk 15:43
the people w for Zacharias, and .... Lk 1:21
who also himself w for the .... Lk 23:51
of them that w on him continually .... Acts 10:7
And Cornelius w for them, and had .... Acts 10:24
Now while Paul w for them at .... Acts 17:16
of God w in the days of Noah 1Pet 3:20

WAITETH
the adulterer w for the twilight .... Job 24:15
Our soul w for the Lord .... Ps 33:20
Truly my soul w upon God .... Ps 62:1
Praise w for thee, O God in Sion .... Ps 65:1
My soul w for the Lord more than .... Ps 130:6
so he that w on his master shall .... Prov 27:18
prepared for him that w for him .... Is 64:4
Blessed is he that w, and cometh .... Dan 12:12
nor w for the sons of men .... Mic 5:7
expectation of the creature w for .... Rom 8:19
the husbandman w for the precious .... Jas 5:7

WAITING
cease w upon the service thereof .... Num 8:25
w at the posts of my doors .... Prov 8:34
w for the consolation of Israel .... Lk 2:25
for they were all w for him .... Lk 8:40
w for the moving of the water .... Jn 5:3
w for the adoption, to wit, ... Rom 8:23
w for the coming of our Lord 1Cor 1:7
and into the patient w for Christ 2Th 3:5

WAKE
sleep a perpetual sleep, and not w .... Jer 51:39
sleep a perpetual sleep, and not w .... Jer 51:57
w up the mighty men, let all the .... Joel 3:9
us, that, whether we w or sleep 1Th 5:10

WAKED
w me, as a man that is wakened .... Zec 4:1

WAKENED
Let the heathen be w, and come up .... Joel 3:12
a man that is w out of his sleep .... Zec 4:1

WAKENETH
he w morning by morning .... Is 50:4
he w mine ear to hear as the .... Is 50:4

WAKETH
city, the watchman w but in vain .... Ps 127:1
I sleep, but my heart w .... Song 5:2

WAKING
Thou holdest mine eyes w .... Ps 77:4

WALK
w through the land in the length .... Gen 13:17
w before me, and be thou perfect .... Gen 17:1
me, The Lord, before whom I w .... Gen 24:40
my fathers Abraham and Isaac did w .... Gen 48:15
whether they will w in my law .... Ex 16:4
them the way wherein they must w .... Ex 18:20
w abroad upon thy staff, then .... Ex 21:19

neither shall ye w in their .... Lev 18:3
mine ordinances, to w therein .... Lev 18:4
ye shall not w in the manners of .... Lev 20:23
If ye w in my statutes, and keep .... Lev 26:3
I will w among you, and will be .... Lev 26:12
if ye w contrary unto me, and will .... Lev 26:21
but will w contrary unto me .... Lev 26:23
Then will I also w contrary unto .... Lev 26:24
unto me, but w contrary unto me .... Lev 26:27
Then I will w contrary unto you .... Lev 26:28
Ye shall w in all the ways which .... Deut 5:33
to w in his ways, and to fear him .... Deut 8:6
w after other gods, and serve them .... Deut 8:19
to w in his ways, and to love .... Deut 10:12
to w in all his ways, and to .... Deut 11:22
Ye shall w after the Lord your .... Deut 13:4
thy God commanded thee to w in .... Deut 13:5
thy God, and to w ever in his ways .... Deut 19:9
to w in his ways, and to keep his .... Deut 26:17
Lord thy God, and w in his ways .... Deut 28:9
though I w in the imagination of .... Deut 29:19
to w in his ways, and to keep his .... Deut 30:16
w through the land, and describe .... Josh 18:8
to w in all his ways, and to keep .... Josh 22:5
the way of the Lord to w therein .... Judg 2:22
sit in judgment, and w by the way .... Judg 5:10
should w before me for ever 1Sa 2:30
he shall w before mine anointed 1Sa 2:35
thy sons w not in thy ways 1Sa 8:5
to w in his ways, to keep his 1Kin 2:3
to w before me in truth with all 1Kin 2:4
And if thou wilt w in my ways 1Kin 3:14
as thy father David did w 1Kin 3:14
if thou wilt w in my statutes, and 1Kin 6:12
all my commandments to w in them 1Kin 6:12
that w before thee with all their 1Kin 8:23
that they w before me as thou 1Kin 8:25
good way wherein they should w 1Kin 8:36
to w in all his ways, and to keep 1Kin 8:58
to w in his statutes, and to keep 1Kin 8:61
And if thou wilt w before me 1Kin 9:4
wilt w in my ways, and do that 1Kin 11:38
been a light thing for him to w 1Kin 16:31
But Jehu took no heed to w in the 2Kin 10:31
to w after the Lord, and to keep 2Kin 23:3
that w before them with all their 2Chr 6:14
heed to their way to w in my law 2Chr 6:16
good way, wherein they should w 2Chr 6:27
to w in thy ways, so long as they 2Chr 6:31
thee, if thou wilt w before me 2Chr 7:17
to w after the Lord, and to keep 2Chr 34:31
The wicked w on every side, when .... Ps 12:8
though I w through the valley of .... Ps 23:4
I will w in mine integrity .... Ps 26:11
W about Zion, and go round about .... Ps 48:12
that I may w before God in the .... Ps 56:13
God, and refused to w in his law .... Ps 78:10
they w on in darkness .... Ps 82:5
from them that w uprightly .... Ps 84:11
I will w in thy truth .... Ps 86:11
they shall w, O Lord, in the .... Ps 89:15
my law, and w not in my judgments .... Ps 89:30
I will w within my house with a .... Ps 101:2
feet have they, but they w not .... Ps 115:7
I will w before the Lord in the .... Ps 116:9
who w in the law of the Lord .... Ps 119:1
they w in his ways .... Ps 119:3
And I will w at liberty .... Ps 119:45
Though I w in the midst of .... Ps 138:7
know the way wherein I should w .... Ps 143:8
w not thou in the way with them .... Prov 1:15
buckler to them that w uprightly .... Prov 2:7
to w in the ways of darkness .... Prov 2:13
That thou mayest w in the way of .... Prov 2:20
Then shalt thou w in thy way .... Prov 3:23
the living which w under the sun .... Eccl 4:15
that knoweth to w before the .... Eccl 6:8
w in the ways of thine heart, and .... Eccl 11:9
ways, and we will w in his paths .... Is 2:3
let us w in the light of the Lord .... Is 2:5
w with stretched forth necks and .... Is 3:16
not w in the way of this people .... Is 8:11
That w to go down into Egypt, and .... Is 30:2
w ye in it, when ye turn to the .... Is 30:21
but the redeemed shall w there .... Is 35:9
and they shall w, and not faint .... Is 40:31
and spirit to them that w therein .... Is 42:5
for they would not w in his ways .... Is 42:24
w in the light of your fire, and .... Is 50:11
brightness, but we w in darkness .... Is 59:9
neither shall they w any more .... Jer 3:17
shall w with the house of Israel .... Jer 3:18
w therein, and ye shall find rest .... Jer 6:16
they said, We will not w therein .... Jer 6:16
into the field, nor w by the way .... Jer 6:25
neither w after other gods to .... Jer 7:6
w after other gods whom ye know .... Jer 7:9
w ye in all the ways that I have .... Jer 7:23
neighbour with w with slanders .... Jer 9:4
which w in the imagination of .... Jer 13:10
w after other gods, to serve them .... Jer 13:10
behold, we every one after the .... Jer 16:12
but we will w after our own .... Jer 18:12
to w in paths, in a way not cast .... Jer 18:15
commit adultery, and w in lies .... Jer 23:14
to w in my law, which I have set .... Jer 26:4
I will cause them to w by the .... Jer 31:9

shew us the way wherein we may w .... Jer 42:3
is desolate, the foxes w upon it .... Lam 5:18
That they may w in my statutes .... Eze 11:20
w ye not in the statutes of your .... Eze 20:18
w in my statutes, and keep my .... Eze 20:19
w in the statutes of life, ... Eze 33:15
I will cause men to w upon you .... Eze 36:12
cause you to w in my statutes, and .... Eze 36:27
they shall also w in my judgments .... Eze 37:24
before the chambers was a w of .... Eze 42:4
those that w in pride he is able .... Dan 4:37
to w in his laws, which he set .... Dan 9:10
They shall w after the Lord .... Hos 11:10
and the just shall w in them .... Hos 14:9
they shall w every one in his .... Joel 2:8
Can two w together, except they .... Amos 3:3
ways, and we will w in his paths .... Mic 4:2
For all people will w every one .... Mic 4:5
we will w in the name of the Lord .... Mic 4:5
and to w humbly with thy God .... Mic 6:8
Ahab, and ye w in their counsels .... Mic 6:16
they shall stumble in their w .... Nah 2:5
Thou didst w through the sea with .... Hab 3:15
he will make me to w upon mine .... Hab 3:19
that they shall w like blind men .... Zeph 1:17
whom the Lord hath sent to w to .... Zec 1:10
If thou wilt w in my ways .... Zec 3:7
to w among these that stand by .... Zec 3:7
sought to go that they might w to .... Zec 6:7
w to and fro through the earth .... Zec 6:7
and they shall w up and down in his .... Zec 10:12
or to say, Arise, and w .... Mt 9:5
their saint, and the lame w .... Mt 11:5
maimed to be whole, the lame to w .... Mt 15:31
Arise, and take up thy bed, and w .... Mk 2:9
Why w not thy disciples according .... Mk 7:5
or to say, Rise up and w .... Lk 5:23
that the blind see, the lame w .... Lk 7:22
the men that w over them are not .... Lk 11:44
Nevertheless I must w to day .... Lk 13:33
which desire to w in long robes .... Lk 20:46
ye have one to another, as ye w .... Lk 24:17
Rise, take up thy bed, and w .... Jn 5:8
unto me, Take up thy bed, and w .... Jn 5:11
unto thee, Take up thy bed, and w .... Jn 5:12
for he would not w in Jewry .... Jn 7:1
he shall not w in darkness .... Jn 8:12
If any man w in the day, he .... Jn 11:9
But if a man w in the night .... Jn 11:10
W while ye have the light, lest .... Jn 12:35
Christ of Nazareth rise up and w .... Acts 3:6
we had made this man to w .... Acts 3:12
nations to w in their own ways .... Acts 14:16
neither to w after the customs .... Acts 21:21
but who also w in the steps of .... Rom 4:12
also should w in newness of life .... Rom 6:4
who w not after the flesh, but .... Rom 8:1
who w not after the flesh, but .... Rom 8:4
Let us w honestly, as in the day .... Rom 13:13
are ye not carnal, and w as men 1Cor 3:3
called every one, so let him w 1Cor 7:17
(For we w by faith, not by sight 2Cor 5:7
will dwell in them, and w in them 2Cor 6:16
For though we w in the flesh 2Cor 10:3
W in the Spirit, and ye shall not .... Gal 5:16
let us also w in the Spirit .... Gal 5:25
as many as w according to this .... Gal 6:16
ordained that we should w in them .... Eph 2:10
beseech you that ye w worthy of .... Eph 4:1
w not as other Gentiles w .... Eph 4:17
w in love, as Christ also hath .... Eph 5:2
w as children of light .... Eph 5:8
See then that ye w circumspectly .... Eph 5:15
let us w by the same rule, let us .... Phil 3:16
mark them which so as ye have .... Phil 3:17
(For many w, of whom I have told .... Phil 3:18
That ye might w worthy of the .... Col 1:10
Jesus the Lord, so w ye in him .... Col 2:6
W in wisdom toward them that are .... Col 4:5
That ye would w worthy of God 1Th 2:12
received of us how ye ought to w 1Th 4:1
That ye may w honestly toward 1Th 4:12
some which w among you disorderly 2Th 3:11
But chiefly them that w after the 2Pet 2:10
w in darkness, we lie, and do not 1Jn 1:6
But if we w in the light, as he 1Jn 1:7
in him ought himself also so to w 1Jn 2:6
that we w after his commandments 2Jn 6
the beginning, ye should w in it 2Jn 6
hear that my children w in truth 3Jn 4
who should w after their own .... Jude 18
they shall w with me in white .... Rev 3:4
neither can see, nor hear, nor w .... Rev 9:20
his garments, lest he w naked .... Rev 16:15
saved shall w in the light of it .... Rev 21:24

WALKED
Enoch w with God after he begat .... Gen 5:22
And Enoch w with God .... Gen 5:24
generations, and Noah w with God .... Gen 6:9
her maidens w along by the .... Ex 2:5
for the children of Israel w upon .... Ex 14:29
also they have w contrary unto me .... Lev 26:40
that I also have w contrary unto .... Lev 26:41
For the children of Israel w .... Josh 5:6
the way which their fathers w in .... Judg 2:17
the travellers w through byways .... Judg 5:6
w through the wilderness unto the .... Judg 11:16
his sons w not in his ways, but 1Sa 8:3
I have w before you from my 1Sa 12:2

WALKEDST (column 1 continued)

his men w all that night through ... 2Sa 2:29
but have w in a tent and in a ... 2Sa 7:6
all the places wherein I have w ... 2Sa 7:7
w upon the roof of the king's ... 2Sa 11:2
according as he w before thee in ... 1Kin 3:6
me as thou hast w before me ... 1Kin 8:25
before me, as David thy father w ... 1Kin 9:4
have not w in my ways, to do that ... 1Kin 11:33
he w in all the sins of his ... 1Kin 15:3
w in the way of his father, and in ... 1Kin 15:26
w in the way of Jeroboam, and in ... 1Kin 15:34
thou hast w in the way of ... 1Kin 16:2
For he w in all the way of ... 1Kin 16:26
he w in all the ways of Asa his ... 1Kin 22:43
w in the way of his father, and in ... 1Kin 22:52
and w in the house to and fro ... 2Kin 4:35
he w in the way of the kings of ... 2Kin 8:18
he w in the way of the house of ... 2Kin 8:27
made Israel sin, but w therein ... 2Kin 13:6
but he w therein ... 2Kin 13:11
But he w in the way of the kings ... 2Kin 16:3
w in the statutes of the heathen ... 2Kin 17:8
but w in the statutes of Israel ... 2Kin 17:19
For the children of Israel w in ... 2Kin 17:22
how I have w before thee in truth ... 2Kin 20:3
he w in all the way that his ... 2Kin 21:21
all the way that his father w in ... 2Kin 21:21
w not in the way of the LORD ... 2Kin 21:22
w in all the way of David his ... 2Kin 22:2
I have w with all Israel, spake I ... 1Chr 17:6
thee whithersoever thou hast w ... 1Chr 17:8
my law, as thou hast w before me ... 2Chr 6:16
before me, as David thy father w ... 2Chr 7:17
years they w in the way of David ... 2Chr 11:17
because he w in the first ways of ... 2Chr 17:3
w in his commandments, and not ... 2Chr 17:4
he w in the way of Asa his father ... 2Chr 20:32
he w in the way of the kings of ... 2Chr 21:6
Because thou hast not w in the ... 2Chr 21:12
But hast w in the way of the ... 2Chr 21:13
He also w in the ways of the ... 2Chr 22:3
He w also after their counsel, and ... 2Chr 22:5
For he w in the ways of the kings ... 2Chr 28:2
w in the ways of David his father ... 2Chr 34:2
Mordecai w every day before the ... Est 2:11
by his light I w through darkness ... Job 29:3
If I have w with vanity, or if my ... Job 31:5
mine heart w after mine eyes, and ... Job 31:7
or hast thou w in the search of ... Job 38:16
for I have w in mine integrity ... Ps 26:1
and I have w in thy truth ... Ps 26:3
w unto the house of God in ... Ps 55:14
they w in their own counsels ... Ps 81:12
me, and Israel had w in my ways ... Ps 81:13
In the way wherein I have w ... Ps 142:3
The people that w in darkness ... Is 9:2
as my servant Isaiah hath w naked ... Is 20:3
how I have w before thee in truth ... Is 38:3
have w after vanity, and are ... Jer 2:5
w after things that do not profit ... Jer 2:8
but w in the counsels and in the ... Jer 7:24
served, and after whom they have w ... Jer 8:2
my voice, neither w therein ... Jer 9:13
But have w after the imagination ... Jer 11:8
their ear, but w every one in the ... Jer 11:8
have w after other gods, and have ... Jer 16:11
thy voice, neither w in thy law ... Jer 32:23
nor w in my law, nor in my ... Jer 44:10
nor w in his law, nor in his ... Jer 44:23
statutes, they have not w in them ... Eze 5:6
have not w in my statutes ... Eze 5:7
for ye have not w in my statutes ... Eze 11:12
hast thou not w after their ways ... Eze 16:47
Hath w in my statutes, and hath ... Eze 18:9
judgments, hath w in my statutes ... Eze 18:17
they w not in my statutes, and ... Eze 20:13
w not in my statutes, but ... Eze 20:16
they w not in my statutes ... Eze 20:21
Thou hast w in the way of thy ... Eze 23:31
thou hast w up and down in the ... Eze 28:14
At the end of twelve months he w ... Dan 4:29
because he willingly w after the ... Hos 5:11
the which their fathers have w ... Amos 2:4
the lion, even the old lion, w ... Nah 2:11
trees, and said, We have w to ... Zec 1:11
So they w to and fro through the ... Zec 6:7
he w with me in peace and equity ... Mal 2:6
that we have w mournfully before ... Mal 3:14
he w on the water, to go to Jesus ... Mt 14:29
Now as he w by the sea of Galilee ... Mk 1:16
the damsel arose, and w ... Mk 5:42
form unto two of them, as they w ... Mk 16:12
And looking upon Jesus as he w ... Jn 1:36
whole, and took up his bed, and w ... Jn 5:9
went back, and w no more with him ... Jn 6:66
these things Jesus w in Galilee ... Jn 7:1
And Jesus w in the temple in ... Jn 10:23
Jesus therefore w no more openly ... Jn 11:54
And he leaping up stood, and w ... Acts 3:8
mother's womb, who never had w ... Acts 14:8
And he leaped and w ... Acts 14:10
as if we w according to the flesh ... 2Cor 10:2
w we not in the same spirit ... 2Cor 12:18
w we not in the same steps ... 2Cor 12:18
But when I saw that they w not ... Gal 2:14
Wherein in time past ye w ... Eph 2:2
In the which ye also w some time ... Col 3:7
when we w in lasciviousness ... 1Pet 4:3
also so to walk, even as he w ... 1Jn 2:6

WALKEDST

and w whither thou wouldest ... Jn 21:18

WALKEST

when thou w by the way, and when ... Deut 6:7
thou w by the way ... Deut 11:19
w abroad any whither, that thou ... 1Kin 2:42
when thou w through the fire ... Is 43:2
that thou thyself also w orderly ... Acts 21:24
now w thou not charitably ... Rom 14:15
thee, even as thou w in the truth ... 3Jn 3

WALKETH

What man is this that w in the ... Gen 24:65
For the LORD thy God w in the ... Deut 23:14
behold, the king w before you ... 1Sa 12:2
own feet, and he w upon a snare ... Job 18:8
he w in the circuit of heaven ... Job 22:14
of iniquity, and w with wicked men ... Job 34:8
Blessed is the man that w not in ... Ps 1:1
He that w uprightly, and worketh ... Ps 15:2
Surely every man w in a vain shew ... Ps 39:6
their tongue w through the earth ... Ps 73:9
the pestilence that w in darkness ... Ps 91:6
he that w in a perfect way, he ... Ps 101:6
who w upon the wings of the wind ... Ps 104:3
that w in his ways ... Ps 128:1
man, w with a froward mouth ... Prov 6:12
that w uprightly w surely ... Prov 10:9
He that w with wise men shall be ... Prov 13:20
He that w in his uprightness ... Prov 14:2
man of understanding w uprightly ... Prov 15:21
the poor that w in his integrity ... Prov 19:1
The just man w in his integrity ... Prov 20:7
poor that w in his uprightness ... Prov 28:6
Whoso w uprightly shall be saved ... Prov 28:18
but whoso w wisely, he shall be ... Prov 28:26
but the fool w in darkness ... Eccl 2:14
he that is a fool w by the way ... Eccl 10:3
He that w righteously, and ... Is 33:15
that w in darkness, and hath no ... Is 50:10
which w in a way that was not ... Is 65:2
in man that w to direct his steps ... Jer 10:23
w after the imagination of his ... Jer 13:10
heart w after that which is evil ... Eze 11:21
do good to him that w uprightly ... Mic 2:7
he w through dry places, seeking ... Mt 12:43
he w through dry places, seeking ... Lk 11:24
for he that w in darkness knoweth ... Jn 12:35
every brother that w disorderly ... 2Th 3:6
w about, seeking whom he may ... 1Pet 5:8
w in darkness, and knoweth not ... 1Jn 2:11
who w in the midst of the seven ... Rev 2:1

WALKING

w in the garden in the cool of ... Gen 3:8
he knoweth thy w through this ... Deut 2:7
w in the statutes of David his ... 1Kin 3:3
in w in the way of Jeroboam, and ... 1Kin 16:19
and fro in the earth, and from w up ... Job 1:7
and fro in the earth, and from w up ... Job 2:2
or the moon w in brightness ... Job 31:26
princes w as servants upon the ... Eccl 10:7
forth necks and wanton eyes, w ... Is 3:16
And he did so, w naked and barefoot ... Is 20:2
each one w in his uprightness ... Is 57:2
revolters, w with slanders ... Jer 6:28
w in the midst of the fire, and ... Dan 3:25
If a man w in the spirit and ... Mic 2:11
w by the sea of Galilee, saw two ... Mt 4:18
went unto them, w on the sea ... Mt 14:26
disciples saw him w on the sea ... Mt 14:26
w upon the sea, and would have ... Mk 6:48
when they saw him w upon the sea ... Mk 6:49
and said, I see men as trees, w ... Mk 8:24
as he was w in the temple, there ... Mk 11:27
w in all the commandments, and ... Lk 1:6
they see Jesus w on the sea ... Jn 6:19
with them into the temple, w ... Acts 3:8
And all the people saw him w ... Acts 3:9
w in the fear of the Lord, and in ... Acts 9:31
not w in craftiness, nor handling ... 2Cor 4:2
w after their own lusts ... 2Pet 3:3
found of thy children w in truth ... 2Jn 4
w after their own lusts ... Jude 16

WALL

selfwill they digged down a w ... Gen 49:6
whose branches run over the w ... Gen 49:22
the waters were a w unto them on ... Ex 14:22
the waters were a w unto them on ... Ex 14:29
in sight are lower than the w ... Lev 14:37
no w round about them shall be ... Lev 25:31
a w being on this side, and a w ... Num 22:24
she thrust herself unto the w ... Num 22:25
Balaam's foot against the w ... Num 22:25
reach from the w of the city ... Num 35:4
for her house was upon the town w ... Josh 2:15
and she dwelt upon the w ... Josh 2:15
the w of the city shall fall down ... Josh 6:5
that the w fell down flat, so ... Josh 6:20
smite David even to the w with it ... 1Sa 18:11
even to the w with the javelin ... 1Sa 19:10
he smote the javelin into the w ... 1Sa 19:10
upon a seat by the w ... 1Sa 20:25
They were a w unto us both by ... 1Sa 25:16
any that pisseth against the w ... 1Sa 25:22
any that pisseth against the w ... 1Sa 25:34
his body to the w of Beth-shan ... 1Sa 31:10
his sons from the w of Beth-shan ... 1Sa 31:12
that they would shoot from the w ... 2Sa 11:20
a millstone upon him from the w ... 2Sa 11:21

why went ye nigh the w ... 2Sa 11:21
from off the w upon thy servants ... 2Sa 11:24
the roof over the gate unto the w ... 2Sa 18:24
were with Joab battered the w to ... 2Sa 20:15
be thrown to thee over the w ... 2Sa 20:21
by my God have I leaped over a w ... 2Sa 22:30
the w of Jerusalem round about ... 1Kin 3:1
that springeth out of the w ... 1Kin 4:33
against the w of the house he ... 1Kin 6:5
for without in the w of the house ... 1Kin 6:6
wing of the one touched the one w ... 1Kin 6:27
other cherub touched the other w ... 1Kin 6:27
posts were a fifth part of the w ... 1Kin 6:31
tree, a fourth part of the w ... 1Kin 6:33
the w of Jerusalem, and Hazor, and ... 1Kin 9:15
him that pisseth against the w ... 1Kin 14:10
not one that pisseth against a w ... 1Kin 16:11
there a w fell upon twenty and ... 1Kin 20:30
him that pisseth against the w ... 1Kin 21:21
eat Jezebel by the w of Jezreel ... 1Kin 21:23
for a burnt offering upon the w ... 2Kin 3:27
chamber, I pray thee, on the w ... 2Kin 4:10
Israel was passing by upon the w ... 2Kin 6:26
and he passed by upon the w ... 2Kin 6:30
him that pisseth against the w ... 2Kin 9:8
her blood was sprinkled on the w ... 2Kin 9:33
brake down the w of Jerusalem ... 2Kin 14:13
of the people that are on the w ... 2Kin 18:26
me to the men which sit on the w ... 2Kin 18:27
Then he turned his face to the w ... 2Kin 20:2
reaching to the w of the house ... 2Chr 3:11
reaching to the w of the house ... 2Chr 3:12
brake down the w of Jerusalem ... 2Chr 25:23
and brake down the w of Gath ... 2Chr 26:6
the w of Jabneh, and the ... 2Chr 26:6
the w of Ashdod, and built cities ... 2Chr 26:6
gate, and at the turning of the w ... 2Chr 26:9
on the w of Ophel he built much ... 2Chr 27:3
up all the w that was broken ... 2Chr 32:5
the towers, and another w without ... 2Chr 32:5
of Jerusalem that were on the w ... 2Chr 32:18
a w without the city of David ... 2Chr 33:14
and brake down the w of Jerusalem ... 2Chr 36:19
this house, and to make up this w ... Ezr 5:3
and to give us a w in Judah ... Ezr 9:9
the w of Jerusalem also is broken ... Neh 1:3
for the w of the city, and for the ... Neh 2:8
by the brook, and viewed the w ... Neh 2:15
us build up the w of Jerusalem ... Neh 2:17
Jerusalem unto the broad w ... Neh 3:8
on the w unto the dung gate ... Neh 3:13
the w of the pool of Siloah by ... Neh 3:15
armoury at the turning of the w ... Neh 3:19
from the turning of the w unto ... Neh 3:20
Azariah unto the turning of the w ... Neh 3:24
over against the turning of the w ... Neh 3:25
out, even unto the w of Ophel ... Neh 3:27
heard that we builded the w ... Neh 4:1
even break down their stone w ... Neh 4:3
So built we the w ... Neh 4:6
all the w was joined together ... Neh 4:6
we are not able to build the w ... Neh 4:10
in the lower places behind the w ... Neh 4:13
we returned all of us to the w ... Neh 4:15
They which builded on the w ... Neh 4:17
and we are separated upon the w ... Neh 4:19
I continued in the work of this w ... Neh 5:16
heard that I had builded the w ... Neh 6:1
which cause thou buildest the w ... Neh 6:6
So the w was finished in the ... Neh 6:15
when the w was built, and I had ... Neh 7:1
at the dedication of the w of ... Neh 12:27
people, and the gates, and the w ... Neh 12:30
the princes of Judah upon the w ... Neh 12:31
upon the w toward the dung gate ... Neh 12:31
David, at the going up of the w ... Neh 12:37
the half of the people upon the w ... Neh 12:38
furnaces even unto the broad w ... Neh 12:38
them, Why lodge ye about the w ... Neh 13:21
by my God have I leaped over a w ... Ps 18:29
as a bowing w shall ye be ... Ps 62:3
as an high w in his own conceit ... Prov 18:11
the stone w thereof was broken ... Prov 24:31
behold, he standeth behind our w ... Song 2:9
If she be a w, we will build upon ... Song 8:9
I am a w, and my breasts like ... Song 8:10
tower, and upon every fenced w ... Is 2:15
and break down the w thereof ... Is 5:5
ye broken down to fortify the w ... Is 22:10
ones is as a storm against the w ... Is 25:4
to fall, swelling out in a high w ... Is 30:13
of the people that are on the w ... Is 36:11
me to the men that sit upon the w ... Is 36:12
turned his face toward the w ... Is 38:2
We grope for the w like the blind ... Is 59:10
this people a fenced brasen w ... Jer 15:20
a fire in the w of Damascus ... Jer 49:27
the w of Babylon shall fall ... Jer 51:44
the w of the daughter of Zion ... Lam 2:8
the rampart and the w to lament ... Lam 2:8
O w of the daughter of Zion, let ... Lam 2:18
set it for a w of iron between ... Eze 4:3
I looked, behold a hole in the w ... Eze 8:7
me, Son of man, dig now in the w ... Eze 8:8
and when I had digged in the w ... Eze 8:8
portrayed upon the w round about ... Eze 8:10
thou through the w in their sight ... Eze 12:7
through the w with mine hand ... Eze 12:7
the w to carry out thereby ... Eze 12:12
and one built up a w, and, lo ... Eze 13:10

W

when the w is fallen, shall it .... Eze 13:12
the w that ye have daubed with ...... Eze 13:14
I accomplish my wrath upon the w .... Eze 13:15
The w is no more, neither they .... Eze 13:15
she saw men pourtrayed upon the w .. Eze 23:14
every w shall fall to the ground .... Eze 38:20
behold a w on the outside of the ...... Eze 40:5
he measured the w of the house .... Eze 41:5
they entered into the w which was .... Eze 41:6
not hold in the w of the house .... Eze 41:6
The thickness of the w, which was .... Eze 41:9
the w of the building was five .... Eze 41:12
by all the w round about within .... Eze 41:17
made, and on the w of the temple .... Eze 41:20
the w that was without over .... Eze 42:7
w of the court toward the east .... Eze 42:10
before the w toward the east .... Eze 42:12
it had a w round about, five .... Eze 42:20
the w between the and them, they .... Eze 43:8
of the w of the king's palace .... Dan 5:5
shall be built again, and the w .... Dan 9:25
thy way with thorns, and make a w ... Hos 2:6
shall climb the w like men of war ..... Joel 2:7
they shall run upon the w .... Joel 2:9
will send a fire on the w of Gaza ...... Amos 1:7
send a fire on the w of Tyrus .... Amos 1:10
kindle a fire in the w of Rabbah .... Amos 1:14
and leaned his hand on the w .... Amos 5:19
upon a w made by a plumbline .... Amos 7:7
shalt make haste to the w thereof .... Nah 2:5
sea, and her w was from the sea ...... Nah 3:8
the stone shall cry out of the w .... Hab 2:11
will be unto her a w of fire .... Zec 2:5
let him down by the w in a basket ... Acts 9:25
shall smite thee, thou whited w .... Acts 23:3
a basket was I let down by the w 2Cor 11:33
middle w of partition between us ..... Eph 2:14
And had a w great and high, and had Rev 21:12
the w of the city had twelve .... Rev 21:14
gates thereof, and the w thereof ..... Rev 21:15
And he measured the w thereof .... Rev 21:17
of the w of it was of jasper .... Rev 21:18
the foundations of the w of the .... Rev 21:19

WALLED
sell a dwelling house in a w city ...... Lev 25:29
w city shall be established for .... Lev 25:30
in the land, and the cities are w ...... Num 13:28
are great and up to heaven .... Deut 1:28

WALLOW
sackcloth, and w thyself in ashes ..... Jer 6:26
w yourselves in the ashes, ye .... Jer 25:34
Moab also shall w in his vomit .... Jer 48:26
they shall w themselves in the .... Eze 27:30

WALLOWED
Amasa w in blood in the midst of 2Sa 20:12
fell on the ground, and w foaming .... Mk 9:20

WALLOWING
was washed to her in the mire 2Pet 2:22

WALLS
if the plague be in the w of the .... Lev 14:37
be spread in the w of the house ...... Lev 14:39
cities were fenced with high w .... Deut 3:5
fenced w come down, wherein thou .. Deut 28:52
threescore great cities with w 1Kin 4:13
against the w of the house round 1Kin 6:5
be fastened in the w of the house ... 1Kin 6:6
he built the w of the house 1Kin 6:15
house, and the w of the cieling 1Kin 6:15
the w with boards of cedar 1Kin 6:16
he carved all the w of the house 1Kin 6:29
the way of the gate between two w .. 2Kin 25:4
brake down the w of Jerusalem 2Kin 25:10
to overlay the w of the houses 1Chr 29:4
the w thereof, and the doors 2Chr 3:7
and graved cherubims on the w 2Chr 3:7
the nether, fenced cities, with w 2Chr 8:5
cities, and make about them w 2Chr 14:7
and have set up the w thereof .... Ezr 4:12
the w set up again, then will .... Ezr 4:13
the w thereof set up, by this .... Ezr 4:16
and timber is laid in the w .... Ezr 5:8
this house, and to make up these w . Ezr 5:9
viewed the w of Jerusalem, which ... Neh 2:13
heard that the w of Jerusalem .... Neh 4:7
Which make oil within their w .... Job 24:11
build thou the w of Jerusalem .... Ps 51:18
go about it upon the w thereof .... Ps 55:10
Peace be within thy w, and .... Ps 122:7
that is broken down, and without w . Prov 25:28
the keepers of the w took away my .. Song 5:7
of vision, breaking down the w .... Is 22:5
also a ditch between the two w .... Is 22:11
fort of thy w shall he bring down ..... Is 25:12
salvation will God appoint for w .... Is 26:1
thy w are continually before me ...... Is 49:16
mine house and within my w a place . Is 56:5
of strangers shall build up thy w ...... Is 60:10
thou shalt call thy w Salvation .... Is 60:18
I have set watchmen upon thy w ...... Is 62:6
against all the w thereof round .... Jer 1:15
brazen w against the whole land ...... Jer 1:18
Go ye up upon her w, and destroy .... Jer 5:10
which besiege you without the w ...... Jer 21:4
by the gate betwixt the two w .... Jer 39:4
and brake down the w of Jerusalem .. Jer 39:8
are fallen, her w are thrown down .... Jer 50:15
standard upon the w of Babylon .... Jer 51:12
The broad w of Babylon shall be ...... Jer 51:58

way of the gate between the two w ... Jer 52:7
brake down all the w of Jerusalem .... Jer 52:14
of the enemy the w of her palaces .... Lam 2:7
they shall destroy the w of Tyrus ...... Eze 26:4
set engines of war against thy w .... Eze 26:9
thy w shall shake at the noise of .... Eze 26:10
and they shall break down thy w .... Eze 26:12
army were upon thy w round about ... Eze 27:11
shields upon thy w round about .... Eze 27:11
are talking against thee by the w ...... Eze 33:30
all of them dwelling without w .... Eze 38:11
the building, with the w thereof .... Eze 41:13
the w thereof, were of wood .... Eze 41:22
like as were made upon the w .... Eze 41:25
day that thy w are to be built .... Mic 7:11
w for the multitude of men .... Zec 2:4
By faith the w of Jericho fell .... Heb 11:30

WANDER
when God caused me to w from my ... Gen 20:13
your children shall w in the .... Num 14:33
he made them w in the wilderness .... Num 32:13
the blind to w out of the way .... Deut 27:18
causeth them to w in a wilderness .... Job 12:24
unto God, they w for lack of meat .... Job 38:41
Lo, then would I w far off .... Ps 55:7
Let them w up and down for meat .... Ps 59:15
and causeth them to w in the .... Ps 107:40
O let me not w from thy .... Ps 119:10
they shall w every one to his .... Is 47:15
people, Thus have they loved to w .... Jer 14:10
that shall cause him to w .... Jer 48:12
they shall w from sea to sea, and .... Amos 8:12

WANDERED
w in the wilderness of Beer-sheba .... Gen 21:14
of Israel w in the wilderness .... Josh 14:10
They w in the wilderness in .... Ps 107:4
they w through the wilderness .... Is 16:8
They have w as blind men in the ...... Lam 4:14
when they fled away and w, they ..... Lam 4:15
My sheep w through all the .... Eze 34:6
or three cities w unto one city .... Amos 4:8
they w about in sheepskins and .... Heb 11:37
they w in deserts, and in .... Heb 11:38

WANDERERS
LORD, that I will send unto him w ..... Jer 48:12
they shall be w among the nations ... Hos 9:17

WANDEREST
and under every green tree thou w ... Jer 2:20

WANDERETH
He w abroad for bread, saying .... Job 15:23
The man that w out of the way of ..... Prov 21:16
As a bird that w from her nest .... Prov 27:8
so is a man that w from his place ..... Prov 27:8
bewray not him that w .... Is 16:3
none shall gather up him that w .... Jer 49:5

WANDERING
and, behold, he was w in the field .... Gen 37:15
As the bird by w, as the swallow ...... Prov 26:2
the eyes then w of the desire .... Eccl 6:9
as a w bird cast out of the nest, ... Is 16:2
w about from house to house 1Ti 5:13
w stars, to whom is reserved the ..... Jude 13

WANDERINGS
Thou tellest my w .... Ps 56:8

WANT
nakedness, and in w of all things ...... Deut 28:48
for she shall eat them for w of .... Deut 28:57
a place where there is no w of .... Judg 18:10
there is no w of any thing .... Judg 19:19
the rock for w of a shelter .... Job 24:8
For w and famine they were .... Job 30:3
seen any perish for w of clothing ...... Job 31:19
I shall not w .... Ps 23:1
for there is no w to them that .... Ps 34:9
LORD shall not w any good thing ...... Ps 34:10
and thy w as an armed man .... Prov 6:11
but fools die for w of wisdom .... Prov 10:21
is destroyed for w of judgment .... Prov 13:23
the belly of the wicked shall w .... Prov 13:25
but in the w of people is the .... Prov 14:28
every one that is hasty only to w ..... Prov 21:5
the rich, shall surely come to w .... Prov 22:16
and thy w as an armed man .... Prov 24:34
shall fail, none shall w her .... Is 34:16
David shall never w a man to sit ...... Jer 33:17
shall the priests the Levites w a ...... Jer 33:18
the son of Rechab shall not w a .... Jer 35:19
stricken through for w of the .... Lam 4:9
That they may w bread and water, ... Eze 4:17
w of bread in all your places .... Amos 4:6
but she of her w did cast in all .... Mk 12:44
and he began to be in w .... Lk 15:14
may be a supply for their w 2Cor 8:14
also may be a supply for your w 2Cor 8:14
supplieth the w of the saints 2Cor 9:12
Not that I speak in respect of w .... Phil 4:11

WANTED
we have w all things, and have .... Jer 44:18
And when they w wine, the mother ... Jn 2:3
when I was present with you, and w .. 2Cor 11:9

WANTETH
for his need, in that which he w .... Deut 15:8
as for him that w understanding ...... Prov 9:4
as for him that w understanding ...... Prov 9:16
of words there w not sin .... Prov 10:19

The prince that w understanding ...... Prov 28:16
so that he w nothing for his soul ...... Eccl 6:2
round goblet, which w not liquor ...... Song 7:2

WANTING
let none be w 2Kin 10:19
whosoever shall be w, he shall 2Kin 10:19
with words, yet they are w to him .... Prov 19:7
that which is w cannot be .... Eccl 1:15
in the balances, and art w .... Dan 5:27
in order the things that are w .... Titus 1:5
that nothing be w unto them .... Titus 3:13
be perfect and entire, w nothing ...... Jas 1:4

WANTON
w eyes, walking and mincing as .... Is 3:16
begun to wax w against Christ 1Ti 5:11
pleasure on the earth, and been w ... Jas 5:5

WANTONNESS
not in chambering and w, not in ...... Rom 13:13
of the flesh, through much w 2Pet 2:18

WANTS
let all thy w lie upon me .... Judg 19:20
and he that ministered to my w .... Phil 2:25

WAR
That these made w with Bera king .... Gen 14:2
when there falleth out any w .... Ex 1:10
the people repent when they see w .. Ex 13:17
The LORD is a man of w .... Ex 15:3
sworn that the LORD will have w .... Ex 17:16
There is a noise of w in the camp .... Ex 32:17
able to go forth to w in Israel .... Num 1:3
that were able to go forth to w .... Num 1:20
that were able to go forth to w .... Num 1:22
that were able to go forth to w .... Num 1:24
that were able to go forth to w .... Num 1:26
that were able to go forth to w .... Num 1:28
that were able to go forth to w .... Num 1:30
that were able to go forth to w .... Num 1:32
that were able to go forth to w .... Num 1:34
that were able to go forth to w .... Num 1:36
that were able to go forth to w .... Num 1:38
that were able to go forth to w .... Num 1:40
that were able to go forth to w .... Num 1:45
able to go forth to w in Israel .... Num 1:45
if ye go to w in your land .... Num 10:9
are able to go to w in Israel .... Num 26:2
Arm some of yourselves unto the w .. Num 31:3
of Israel, shall ye send to the w ...... Num 31:4
twelve thousand armed for w .... Num 31:5
And Moses sent them to the w .... Num 31:6
of Eleazar the priest, to the w .... Num 31:6
men of w which went to the battle ... Num 31:21
them that took the w upon them ...... Num 31:27
men of w which went out to battle ... Num 31:27
which the men of w had caught .... Num 31:32
of them that went out to w .... Num 31:36
of w which are under our charge ...... Num 31:49
(For the men of w had taken spoil .... Num 31:53
Shall your brethren go to w .... Num 32:6
go armed before the LORD to w .... Num 32:20
pass over, every man armed for w .... Num 32:27
on every man his weapons of w .... Deut 1:41
the generation of the men of w .... Deut 2:14
all the men of w were consumed ...... Deut 2:16
all that are meet for the w .... Deut 3:18
by signs, and by wonders, and by w . Deut 4:34
but will make w against thee .... Deut 20:12
in making w against it to take it ...... Deut 20:19
the city that maketh w with thee ..... Deut 20:20
forth to w against thine enemies ...... Deut 21:10
wife, he shall not go out to w .... Deut 24:5
for w passed over before the LORD ... Josh 4:13
were males, even all the men of w .... Josh 5:4
all the people that were men of w .... Josh 5:6
compass the city, all ye men of w .... Josh 6:3
all the people of w with them .... Josh 8:1
arose, and all the people of w .... Josh 8:3
people of w that were with him .... Josh 8:11
Gibeon, and made w against it .... Josh 10:5
and all the people of w with him ...... Josh 10:7
the men of w which went with him ... Josh 10:24
and all the people of w with him ...... Josh 11:7
Joshua made w a long time with ...... Josh 11:18
And the land rested from w .... Josh 11:23
even so is my strength now, for w .... Josh 14:11
And the land had rest from w .... Josh 14:15
because he was a man of w .... Josh 17:1
to go up to w against them .... Josh 22:12
might know, to teach them w .... Judg 3:2
judged Israel, and went out to w ...... Judg 3:10
then was w in the gates .... Judg 5:8
of Ammon made w against Israel ...... Judg 11:4
of Ammon made w against Israel ...... Judg 11:5
doest me wrong to w against me ...... Judg 11:27
men appointed with weapons of w .... Judg 18:11
appointed with their weapons of w ... Judg 18:16
were appointed with weapons of w ... Judg 18:17
all these were men of w .... Judg 20:17
not to each man his wife in the w .... Judg 21:22
and to make his instruments of w 1Sa 8:12
there was sore w against the 1Sa 14:52
mighty valiant man, and a man of w . 1Sa 16:18
he a man of w from his youth 1Sa 17:33
and Saul set him over the men of w . 1Sa 18:5
And there was w again 1Sa 19:8
all the people together to w 1Sa 23:8
the Philistines make w against me ... 1Sa 28:15
and the weapons of w perished 2Sa 1:27
Now there was long w between the ... 2Sa 3:1

while there was w between the	2Sa 3:6
did, and how the w prospered	2Sa 11:7
all the things concerning the w	2Sa 11:18
matters of the w unto the king	2Sa 11:19
and thy father is a man of w	2Sa 17:8
had yet w again with Israel	2Sa 21:15
He teacheth my hands to w	2Sa 22:35
and shed the blood of w in peace	1Kin 2:5
put the blood of w upon his	1Kin 2:5
but they were men of w, and his	1Kin 9:22
there was w between Rehoboam and	1Kin 14:30
there was w between Rehoboam and	1Kin 15:6
there was w between Abijam and	1Kin 15:7
there was w between	1Kin 15:16
there was w between	1Kin 15:32
or whether they be come out for w	1Kin 20:18
years without w between Syria	1Kin 22:1
Joram the son of Ahab to the w	2Kin 8:28
hand of Jehoahaz his father by w	2Kin 13:25
ten thousand, and took Selah by w	2Kin 14:7
Israel came up to Jerusalem to w	2Kin 16:5
counsel and strength for the w	2Kin 18:20
all that were strong and apt for w	2Kin 24:16
all the men of w fled by night by	2Kin 25:4
that was set over the men of w	2Kin 25:19
they made w with the Hagarites	1Chr 5:10
shoot with bow, and skilful in w	1Chr 5:18
that went out to the w	1Chr 5:18
they made w with the Hagarites,	1Chr 5:19
slain, because the w was of God	1Chr 5:22
were bands of soldiers for w	1Chr 7:4
soldiers, fit to go out for w	1Chr 7:11
of them that were apt to the w	1Chr 7:40
the mighty men, helpers of the w	1Chr 12:1
men of w fit for the battle, that	1Chr 12:8
that were ready armed to the w	1Chr 12:23
hundred, ready armed to the w	1Chr 12:24
mighty men of valour for the w	1Chr 12:25
went forth to battle, expert in w	1Chr 12:33
with all instruments of w	1Chr 12:33
of the Danites expert in w twenty	1Chr 12:35
went forth to battle, expert in w	1Chr 12:36
instruments of w for the battle,	1Chr 12:37
All these men of w, that could	1Chr 12:38
(for Hadarezer had w with Tou	1Chr 18:10
that there arose w at Gezer with	1Chr 20:4
there was w again with the	1Chr 20:5
And yet again there was w at Gath	1Chr 20:6
because thou hast been a man of w	1Chr 28:3
If thy people go out to w against	2Chr 6:34
but they were men of w, and chief	2Chr 8:9
there was w between Abijah and	2Chr 13:2
with an army of valiant men of w	2Chr 13:3
he had no w in those years	2Chr 14:6
there was no more w unto the five	2Chr 15:19
made no w against Jehoshaphat	2Chr 17:10
and the men of w, mighty men of	2Chr 17:13
thousand ready prepared for the w	2Chr 17:18
and we will be with thee in the w	2Chr 18:5
son of Ahab king of Israel to w	2Chr 22:5
choice men, able to go forth to w	2Chr 25:5
men, that went out to w by bands	2Chr 26:11
that made w with mighty power, to	2Chr 26:13
against them that came from the w	2Chr 28:12
set captains of w over the people	2Chr 32:6
captains of w in all the	2Chr 33:14
the house wherewith I have w	2Chr 35:21
in w from the power of the sword	Job 5:20
changes and w are against me	Job 10:17
against the day of battle and w	Job 38:23
He teacheth my hands to w	Ps 18:34
though w should rise against me,	Ps 27:3
butter, but w was in his heart	Ps 55:21
thou the people that delight in w	Ps 68:30
but when I speak, they are for w	Ps 120:7
are they gathered together for w	Ps 140:2
which teacheth my hands to w	Ps 144:1
and with good advice make w	Prov 20:18
counsel thou shalt make thy w	Prov 24:6
a time of w, and a time of peace	Eccl 3:8
there is no discharge in that w	Eccl 8:8
is better than weapons of w	Eccl 9:18
hold swords, being expert in w	Song 3:8
shall they learn w any more	Is 2:4
The mighty man, and the man of w	Is 3:2
the sword, and thy mighty in the w	Is 3:25
toward Jerusalem to w against it	Is 7:1
and from the grievousness of w	Is 21:15
I have counsel and strength for w	Is 36:5
is come forth to make w with thee	Is 37:9
that that w against thee shall be	Is 41:12
stir up jealousy like a man of w	Is 42:13
of the trumpet, the alarm of w	Jer 4:19
Prepare w against her	Jer 6:4
array as men for w against thee	Jer 6:23
of Babylon maketh w against us	Jer 21:2
of w that are in your hand,	Jer 21:4
and against great kingdoms, of w	Jer 28:8
the hands of the men of w that	Jer 38:4
saw them, and all the men of w	Jer 39:4
were found there, and the men of w	Jer 41:3
of Ahikam, even mighty men of w	Jer 41:16
of Egypt, where we shall see no w	Jer 42:14
mighty and strong men for the w	Jer 48:14
of w to be heard in Rabbah of the	Jer 49:2
all the men of w shall be cut off	Jer 49:26
all her men of w shall be cut off	Jer 50:30
art my battle ax and weapons of w	Jer 51:20
the men of w are affrighted	Jer 51:32
up, and all the men of w fled	Jer 52:7

had the charge of the men of w	Jer 52:25
company make for him in the w	Eze 17:17
engines of w against thy walls	Eze 26:9
were in thine army, thy men of w	Eze 27:10
merchandise, and all thy men of w	Eze 27:27
to hell with their weapons of w	Eze 32:27
mighty men, and all men of w	Eze 39:20
same horn made w with the saints	Dan 7:21
unto the end of the w desolations	Dan 9:26
climb the wall like men of w	Joel 2:7
Prepare w, wake up the mighty men	Joel 3:9
let all the men of w draw near	Joel 3:9
by securely as men averse from w	Mic 2:8
they even prepare w against him	Mic 3:5
shall they learn w any more	Mic 4:3
going to make w against another	Lk 14:31
his men of w set him at nought	Lk 23:11
we do not w after the flesh	2Cor 10:3
by them mightest w a good warfare	1Ti 1:18
your lusts that w in your members	Jas 4:1
w fight and ye, yet ye have not	Jas 4:2
lusts, which w against the soul	1Pet 2:11
pit shall make w against them	Rev 11:7
And there was w in heaven	Rev 12:7
went to make w with the remnant	Rev 12:17
who is able to make w with him	Rev 13:4
him to make w with the saints	Rev 13:7
These shall make w with the Lamb	Rev 17:14
he doth judge and make w	Rev 19:11
gathered together to make w	Rev 19:19

WARD

he put them in w the house of	Gen 40:3
and they continued a season in w	Gen 40:4
him in the w of his lord's house	Gen 40:7
put me in w in the captain of the	Gen 41:10
all together into w three days	Gen 42:17
And they put him in w, that the	Lev 24:12
And they put him in w, because it	Num 15:34
keep the house, and put them in w	2Sa 20:3
kept the w of the house of Saul	1Chr 12:29
And they cast lots, w against	1Chr 25:8
against w, as well	1Chr 26:16
of the going up, w against	1Chr 26:16
man of God, w over against w	Neh 12:24
were porters keeping the w at the	Neh 12:25
porters kept the w of their God	Neh 12:45
the w of the purification,	Neh 12:45
and I am set in my w whole nights	Is 21:8
a captain of the w was there	Jer 37:13
And they put him in w in chains	Eze 19:9
past the first and the second w	Acts 12:10

WARDROBE

son of Harhas, keeper of the w	2Kin 22:14
son of Hasrah, keeper of the w	2Chr 34:22

WARDS

the house of the tabernacle, by w	1Chr 9:23
having w one against another, to	1Chr 26:12
appointed the w of the priests and	Neh 13:30

WARE

w or any victuals on the sabbath	Neh 10:31
brought fish, and all manner of w	Neh 13:16
sellers of all kind of w lodged	Neh 13:20
w no clothes, neither abode in	Lk 8:27
They were w of it, and fled unto	Acts 14:6
Of whom be thou w also	2Ti 4:15

WARES

Gather up thy w out of the land,	Jer 10:17
multitude of the w of thy making	Eze 27:16
multitude of the w of thy making	Eze 27:18
When thy w went forth out of the	Eze 27:33
cast forth the w that were in the	Jonah 1:5

WARFARE

their armies together for w	1Sa 28:1
that her w is accomplished, that	Is 40:2
Who goeth a w any time at his own	1Cor 9:7
weapons of our w are not carnal	2Cor 10:4
by them mightest war a good w	1Ti 1:18

WARM

and the flesh of the child waxed w	2Kin 4:34
What time they wax w, they vanish	Job 6:17
How thy garments are w, when he	Job 37:17
but how can one be w alone	Eccl 4:11
will take thereof, and w himself	Is 44:15
himself, and saith, Aha, I am w	Is 44:16
there shall not be a coal to w at	Is 47:14
clothe you, but there is none w	Hag 1:6

WARMED

if he were not w with the fleece	Job 31:20
and w himself at the fire	Mk 14:54
and they w themselves	Jn 18:18
stood with them, and w himself	Jn 18:18
And Simon Peter stood and w himself	Jn 18:25
them, Depart in peace, be ye w	Jas 2:16

WARMETH

the earth, and w them in the dust,	Job 39:14
he himself, and saith, Aha, I am w	Is 44:16

WARMING

And when she saw Peter w himself	Mk 14:67

WARN

ye shall even w them that they	2Chr 19:10
nor speakest to w the wicked from	Eze 3:18
Yet if thou w the wicked, and he	Eze 3:19
if thou w the righteous man	Eze 3:21
blow the trumpet, and the people	Eze 33:3

at my mouth, and w them from me	Eze 33:7
to w the wicked from his way	Eze 33:8
if thou w the wicked of his way	Eze 33:9
I ceased not to w every one night	Acts 20:31
but as my beloved sons I w you	1Cor 4:14
w them that are unruly, comfort	1Th 5:14

WARNED

w him of, and saved himself there,	2Kin 6:10
Moreover by them is thy servant w	Ps 19:11
surely live, because he is w	Eze 3:21
trumpet, and the people be not w	Eze 33:5
being of God in a dream that	Mt 2:12
being w of God in a dream, he	Mt 2:22
who hath w you to flee from the	Mt 3:7
who hath w you to flee from the	Lk 3:7
was w from God by an holy angel	Acts 10:22
being w of God of things not seen	Heb 11:7

WARNING

To whom shall I speak, and give w	Jer 6:10
my mouth, and give them w from me	Eze 3:17
and thou givest him not w, nor	Eze 3:18
because thou hast not given him w	Eze 3:20
of the trumpet, and taketh not w	Eze 33:4
of the trumpet, and took not w	Eze 33:5
But he that taketh w shall	Eze 33:5
w every man, and teaching every	Col 1:28

WARP

Whether it be in the w, or woof	Lev 13:48
or in the skin, either in the w	Lev 13:49
in the garment, either in the w	Lev 13:51
that garment, whether w or woof	Lev 13:52
in the garment, either in the w	Lev 13:53
out of the skin, or out of the w	Lev 13:56
in the garment, either in the w	Lev 13:57
And the garment, either w, or woof	Lev 13:58
woollen or linen, either in the w	Lev 13:59

WARRED

they w against the Midianites, as	Num 31:7
Moses divided from the men that w	Num 31:42
w against Israel, and sent and	Josh 24:9
of the acts of Jeroboam, how he w	1Kin 14:19
besieged Samaria, and w against it	1Kin 20:1
he shewed, and how he w	1Kin 22:45
king of Syria w against Israel	2Kin 6:8
he did, and his might, how he w	2Kin 14:28
w against the Philistines, and	2Chr 26:6

WARRETH

No man that w entangleth himself	2Ti 2:4

WARRING

king of Assyria w against Libnah	2Kin 19:8
king of Assyria w against Libnah	Is 37:8
w against the law of my mind, and	Rom 7:23

WARRIOR

of the w is with confused noise	Is 9:5

WARRIORS

chosen men, which were w	1Kin 12:21
thousand chosen men, which were w	2Chr 11:1

WARS

in the book of the w of the LORD	Num 21:14
had not known all the w of Canaan	Judg 3:1
for Hadarezer had w with Toi	2Sa 8:10
of the Lord his God for the w	1Kin 5:3
abundantly, and hast made great w	1Chr 22:8
there were w between	2Chr 12:15
from henceforth thou shalt have w	2Chr 16:9
the acts of Jotham, and all his w	2Chr 27:7
He maketh w to cease unto the end	Ps 46:9
hear of w and rumours of w	Mt 24:6
hear of w and rumours of w	Mk 13:7
But when ye shall hear of w	Lk 21:9
From whence come w and fightings	Jas 4:1

WAS See PREFACE.

WASH

w your feet, and rest yourselves	Gen 18:4
w your feet, and ye shall rise up	Gen 19:2
camels, and water to w his feet	Gen 24:32
down to w herself at the river	Ex 2:5
let them w their clothes,	Ex 19:10
and shalt w them with water	Ex 29:4
w the inwards of him, and his legs	Ex 29:17
foot also of brass, to w withal	Ex 30:18
and his sons shall w their hands	Ex 30:19
they shall w with water, that	Ex 30:20
So they shall w their hands	Ex 30:21
and his sons shall w with water	Ex 40:12
and put water there, to w withal	Ex 40:30
and his legs shall he w in water	Lev 1:9
But he shall w the inwards	Lev 1:13
thou shalt w that whereon it was	Lev 6:27
he did w the inwards and the legs,	Lev 9:14
of them shall w his clothes	Lev 11:25
of them shall w his clothes	Lev 11:28
carcase of it shall w his clothes	Lev 11:40
carcase of it shall w his clothes	Lev 11:40
he shall w his clothes, and be	Lev 13:6
he shall w his clothes, and be	Lev 13:34
priest shall command that they w	Lev 13:54
of skin it be, which thou shalt w	Lev 13:58
be cleansed shall w his clothes	Lev 14:8
w himself in water, that he may	Lev 14:8
he shall w his clothes, also he	Lev 14:9
also he shall w his flesh in	Lev 14:9
in the house shall w his clothes	Lev 14:47
in the house shall w his clothes	Lev 14:47

W

his bed shall *w* his clothes .... Lev 15:5
the issue shall *w* his clothes .... Lev 15:6
the issue shall *w* his clothes .... Lev 15:7
then he shall *w* his clothes .... Lev 15:8
those things shall *w* his clothes .... Lev 15:10
he shall *w* his clothes, and bathe .... Lev 15:11
w his clothes, and bathe his flesh .... Lev 15:11
then he shall *w* all his flesh in .... Lev 15:16
her bed shall *w* his clothes .... Lev 15:21
she sat upon shall *w* his clothes .... Lev 15:22
shall *w* his clothes, and bathe .... Lev 15:27
shall he *w* his flesh in water .... Lev 16:4
he shall *w* his flesh with water .... Lev 16:24
the scapegoat shall *w* his clothes .... Lev 16:26
burneth them shall *w* his clothes .... Lev 16:28
he shall both *w* his clothes .... Lev 17:15
But if he *w* them not, nor bathe .... Lev 17:16
unless he *w* his flesh with water .... Lev 22:6
let them *w* their clothes, and so .... Num 8:7
the priest shall *w* his clothes .... Num 19:7
her shall *w* his clothes in water .... Num 19:8
of the heifer shall *w* his clothes .... Num 19:10
w his clothes, and bathe himself .... Num 19:19
of separation shall *w* his clothes .... Num 19:21
ye shall *w* your clothes on the .... Num 31:24
shall *w* their hands over the .... Deut 21:6
he shall *w* himself with water .... Deut 23:11
W thyself therefore, and anoint .... Ruth 3:3
w the feet of the servants of my 1Sa 25:41
down to thy house, and *w* thy feet 2Sa 11:8
w in Jordan seven times, and thy 2Kin 5:10
may I not *w* in them, and be clean 2Kin 5:12
then, when he saith to thee, W 2Kin 5:13
and five on the left, to *w* in them 2Chr 4:6
sea was for the priests to *w* in 2Chr 4:6
If I *w* myself with snow water, and .... Job 9:30
I will *w* mine hands in innocency .... Ps 26:6
W me throughly from mine iniquity .... Ps 51:2
w me, and I shall be whiter than .... Ps 51:7
he shall *w* his feet in the blood .... Ps 58:10
W you, make you clean .... Is 1:16
For though thou *w* thee with nitre .... Jer 2:22
w thine heart from wickedness, ... Jer 4:14
for whom thou didst *w* thyself .... Eze 23:40
anoint thine head, and *w* thy face .... Mt 6:17
for they *w* not their hands when .... Mt 15:2
except they *w* their hands oft, ... Mk 7:3
from the market, except they *w* .... Mk 7:4
began to *w* his feet with tears, ... Lk 7:38
w in the pool of Siloam, (which .... Jn 9:7
Go to the pool of Siloam, and *w* .... Jn 9:11
began to *w* the disciples' feet, ... Jn 13:5
him, Lord, dost thou *w* my feet .... Jn 13:6
him, Thou shalt never *w* my feet .... Jn 13:8
If I *w* thee not, thou hast no .... Jn 13:8
needeth not save to *w* his feet .... Jn 13:10
ye also ought to *w* one another's .... Jn 13:14
w away thy sins, calling on the .... Acts 22:16

WASHED

them water, and they *w* their feet .... Gen 43:24
he *w* his face, and went out, and .... Gen 43:31
he *w* his garments in wine, and his .... Gen 49:11
and they *w* their clothes .... Ex 19:14
his sons *w* their hands and their .... Ex 40:31
came near unto the altar, they *w* .... Ex 40:32
and his sons, and *w* them with water .... Lev 8:6
he *w* the inwards and the legs in .... Lev 8:21
on the plague, after that it is *w* .... Lev 13:55
it shall be *w* the second time, ... Lev 13:58
shall be *w* with water, and be .... Lev 15:17
purified, and they *w* their clothes .... Num 8:21
they *w* their feet, and did eat and .... Judg 19:21
David arose from the earth, and *w* 2Sa 12:20
nor *w* his clothes, from the day 2Sa 19:24
one *w* the chariot in the pool of 1Kin 22:38
and they *w* his armour 1Kin 22:38
the burnt offering they *w* in them 2Chr 4:6
When I *w* my steps with butter, and .... Job 29:6
vain, and *w* my hands in innocency .... Ps 73:13
eyes, and yet is not *w* from their .... Prov 30:12
I have *w* my feet .... Song 5:3
w with milk, and fitly set .... Song 5:12
When the Lord shall have *w* away .... Is 4:4
neither wast thou *w* in water to .... Eze 16:4
Then *w* I thee with water .... Eze 16:9
I throughly *w* away thy blood from .... Eze 16:9
where they *w* the burnt offering .... Eze 40:38
w his hands before the multitude, ... Mt 27:24
but she hath *w* my feet with tears .... Lk 7:44
he had not first *w* before dinner .... Lk 11:38
He went his way therefore, and *w* .... Jn 9:7
and I went and *w*, and I received .... Jn 9:11
put clay upon mine eyes, and I *w* .... Jn 9:15
He that is *w* needeth not save to .... Jn 13:10
So after he had *w* their feet .... Jn 13:12
Lord and Master, have *w* your feet .... Jn 13:14
whom when they had *w*, they laid .... Acts 9:37
of the night, and *w* their stripes .... Acts 16:33
but ye are *w*, but ye are 1Cor 6:11
if she have *w* the saints' feet, ... 1Ti 5:10
our bodies *w* with pure water .... Heb 10:22
the sow that was *w* to her 2Pet 2:22
w us from our sins in his own .... Rev 1:5
have *w* their robes, and made them .... Rev 7:14

WASHEST

thou *w* away the things which grow .... Job 14:19

WASHING

somewhat dark after the *w* of it .... Lev 13:56
the roof he saw a woman *w* herself 2Sa 11:2

that every one put them off for *w* .... Neh 4:23
shorn, which came up from the *w* .... Song 4:2
of sheep which go up from the *w* .... Song 6:6
as the *w* of cups, and pots, brasen .... Mk 7:4
of men, as the *w* of pots and cups .... Mk 7:8
out of them, and were *w* their nets .... Lk 5:2
cleanse it with the *w* of water by .... Eph 5:26
by the *w* of regeneration, and .... Titus 3:5

WASHINGS

in meats and drinks, and divers *w* .... Heb 9:10

WASHPOT

Moab is my *w* .... Ps 60:8
Moab is my *w* .... Ps 108:9

WAST

Who told thee that thou *w* naked .... Gen 3:11
for out of it *w* thou taken .... Gen 3:19
of God, and thou *w* pleased with me .... Gen 33:10
manner when thou *w* his butler .... Gen 40:13
remember that thou *w* a servant in ...... Deut 5:15
thou shalt remember that thou *w* a ..... Deut 15:15
that thou *w* a bondman in Egypt .... Deut 16:12
because thou *w* a stranger in his .... Deut 23:7
that thou *w* a bondman in Egypt, ... Deut 24:18
thou shalt remember that thou *w* a ..... Deut 24:22
behind thee, when thou *w* faint .... Deut 25:18
of Egypt, which thou *w* afraid of .... Deut 28:60
with whose maidens thou *w* .... Ruth 3:2
When thou *w* little in thine own 1Sa 15:17
w thou not made the head of the 1Sa 15:17
How *w* thou not afraid to stretch 2Sa 1:14
thou *w* slain in thine high places 2Sa 1:25
thou *w* that leddest out and 2Sa 5:2
thou *w* he that leddest out and 1Chr 11:2
or *w* thou made before the hills .... Job 15:7
Where *w* thou when I laid the .... Job 38:4
thou it, because thou *w* then born .... Job 38:21
thou *w* a God that forgavest them, ... Ps 99:8
Jordan, that thou *w* driven back .... Ps 114:5
though thou *w* angry with me, ... Is 12:1
wherein thou *w* made to serve .... Is 14:3
spoilest, and thou *w* not spoiled .... Is 33:1
Since thou *w* precious in my sight .... Is 43:4
w called a transgressor from the .... Is 48:8
of youth, when thou *w* refused .... Is 54:6
therefore thou *w* not grieved .... Is 57:10
as thou *w* ashamed of Assyria .... Jer 2:36
O Babylon, and thou *w* not aware .... Jer 50:24
in the day thou *w* born thy navel .... Eze 16:4
neither *w* thou washed in water to ...... Eze 16:4
thou *w* not salted at all, nor .... Eze 16:4
thou *w* cast out in the open .... Eze 16:5
in the day that thou *w* born .... Eze 16:5
thee when thou *w* in thy blood .... Eze 16:6
thee when thou *w* in thy blood .... Eze 16:6
is grown, whereas thou *w* naked .... Eze 16:7
Thus *w* thou decked with gold and ..... Eze 16:13
thou *w* exceeding beautiful, and .... Eze 16:13
of thy youth, when thou *w* naked .... Eze 16:22
bare, and *w* polluted in thy blood .... Eze 16:22
because thou *w* unsatiable .... Eze 16:28
yet thou *w* not satisfied herewith .... Eze 16:29
thou *w* corrupted more than they .... Eze 16:47
in the place where thou *w* created ...... Eze 21:30
thou *w* not purged, thou shalt not ...... Eze 24:13
Thou *w* replenished, and made very .... Eze 27:25
in the day that thou *w* created .... Eze 28:13
thou *w* upon the holy mountain of ..... Eze 28:14
Thou *w* perfect in thy ways from .... Eze 28:15
from the day that thou *w* created .... Eze 28:15
even thou *w* as one of them .... Obad 11
Thou also *w* with Jesus of Galilee .... Mt 26:69
thou also *w* with Jesus of .... Mk 14:67
when thou *w* under the fig tree, I .... Jn 1:48
Thou *w* altogether born in sins, ... Jn 9:34
say unto thee, When thou *w* young ..... Jn 21:18
for thou *w* slain, and hast .... Rev 5:9
God Almighty, which art, and *w* .... Rev 11:17
O Lord, which art, and *w*, and .... Rev 16:5

WASTE

And I will make your cities *w* .... Lev 26:31
be desolate, and your cities *w* .... Lev 26:33
have laid them *w* even unto Nophah ... Num 21:30
in the *w* howling wilderness .... Deut 32:10
The barrel of meal shall not *w* 1Kin 17:14
lay *w* fenced cities into ruinous 2Kin 19:25
of wickedness *w* them any more 1Chr 17:9
my fathers' sepulchres, lieth *w* .... Neh 2:3
we are in, how Jerusalem lieth *w* .... Neh 2:17
in former time desolate and *w* .... Job 30:3
satisfy the desolate and ground .... Job 38:27
laid *w* his dwelling place .... Ps 79:7
boar out of the wood doth *w* it .... Ps 80:13
And I will lay it *w* .... Is 5:6
the *w* places of the fat ones, ... Is 5:17
in the right Ar of Moab is laid *w* .... Is 15:1
the night Kir of Moab is laid *w* .... Is 15:1
for it is laid *w*, so that there .... Is 23:1
for your strength is laid *w* .... Is 23:14
the earth empty, and maketh it *w* ..... Is 24:1
The highways lie *w*, the wayfaring ..... Is 33:8
to generation it shall lie *w* .... Is 34:10
have laid *w* all the nations .... Is 37:18
w defenced cities into ruinous .... Is 37:26
I will make *w* mountains and hills, ... Is 42:15
they that made thee *w* shall go .... Is 49:17
For thy *w* and thy desolate places, ... Is 49:19

he will comfort all her *w* places .... Is 51:3
ye *w* places of Jerusalem .... Is 52:9
thee shall build the old *w* places .... Is 58:12
and they shall repair the *w* cities .... Is 61:4
our pleasant things are laid *w* .... Is 64:11
yelled, and they made his land *w* .... Jer 2:15
and thy cities shall be laid *w* .... Jer 4:7
should this city be laid *w* .... Jer 27:17
for Noph shall be *w* and desolate .... Jer 46:19
a desolation, a reproach, a *w* .... Jer 49:13
w and utterly destroy after them, ... Jer 50:21
Moreover I will make thee *w* .... Eze 5:14
the cities shall be laid *w* .... Eze 6:6
that your altars may be laid *w* .... Eze 6:6
are inhabited shall be laid *w* .... Eze 12:20
and he laid *w* their cities .... Eze 19:7
be replenished, now she is laid *w* ...... Eze 26:2
of Egypt shall be desolate and *w* .... Eze 29:9
make the land of Egypt utterly *w* ...... Eze 29:10
w shall be desolate forty years, ... Eze 29:12
and I will make the land *w* .... Eze 30:12
I will lay thy cities *w*, and thou .... Eze 35:4
and the *w* and desolate and ruined ..... Eze 36:35
so shall the *w* cities be filled .... Eze 36:38
Israel, which have been always *w* .... Eze 38:8
He hath laid thy vine *w*, and barked ... Joel 1:7
of Israel shall be laid *w* .... Amos 7:9
and they shall build the *w* cities .... Amos 9:14
they shall *w* the land of Assyria .... Mic 5:6
She is empty, and void, and *w* .... Nah 2:10
thee, and say, Nineveh is laid *w* .... Nah 3:7
I made their streets *w*, that none .... Zeph 3:6
houses, and this house lie *w* .... Hag 1:4
Because of mine house that is *w* .... Hag 1:9
his heritage *w* for the dragons of .... Mal 1:3
saying, To what purpose is this *w* ...... Mt 26:8
Why was this *w* of the ointment .... Mk 14:4

WASTED

carcases be *w* in the wilderness .... Num 14:33
the Kenite shall be *w*, until .... Num 24:22
of the men of war were *w* out from ... Deut 2:14
And the barrel of meal *w* not 1Kin 17:16
w country of the children of 1Chr 20:1
they that *w* us required of us .... Ps 137:3
cities be *w* without inhabitant .... Is 6:11
the sea, and the river shall be *w* .... Is 19:5
those nations shall be utterly *w* .... Is 60:12
and they are *w* and desolate, as at ..... Jer 44:6
midst of the cities that are *w* .... Eze 30:7
The field is *w*, the land mourneth ...... Joel 1:10
for the corn is *w* .... Joel 1:10
there *w* his substance with .... Lk 15:13
unto him that he had *w* his goods ...... Lk 16:1
the church of God, and *w* it .... Gal 1:13

WASTENESS

trouble and distress, a day of *w* .... Zeph 1:15

WASTER

brother to him that is a great *w* .... Prov 18:9
I have created the *w* to destroy .... Is 54:16

WASTES

And they shall build the old *w* .... Is 61:4
thereof shall be perpetual *w* .... Jer 49:13
they that inhabit those *w* of the .... Eze 33:24
in the *w* shall fall by the sword .... Eze 33:27
to the valleys, to the desolate *w* .... Eze 36:4
and the *w* shall be builded .... Eze 36:10
cities, and the *w* shall be builded .... Eze 36:33

WASTETH

But man dieth, and *w* away .... Job 14:10
the destruction that *w* at noonday ..... Ps 91:6
He that *w* his father, and chaseth ...... Prov 19:26

WASTING

w and destruction are in their .... Is 59:7
w nor destruction within thy .... Is 60:18

WATCH

The LORD *w* between me and thee, ... Gen 31:49
that in the morning *w* the Lord .... Ex 14:24
in the beginning of the middle *w* .... Judg 7:19
and they had but newly set the *w* ...... Judg 7:19
of the host in the morning *w* 1Sa 11:11
to *w* him, and to slay him in the 1Sa 19:11
kept the *w* lifted up his eyes 2Sa 13:34
of the *w* of the king's house 2Kin 11:5
shall *w* keep the *w* of the house 2Kin 11:6
even they shall keep the *w* of the 2Kin 11:7
the *w* tower in the wilderness 2Chr 20:24
shall keep the *w* of the LORD 2Chr 23:6
W ye, and keep them, until ye .... Ezr 8:29
set a *w* against them day and night .... Neh 4:9
of Jerusalem, every one in his *w* .... Neh 7:3
that thou settest a *w* over me .... Job 7:12
dost thou not *w* over my sin .... Job 14:16
is past, and as a *w* in the night .... Ps 90:4
I *w*, and am as a sparrow alone .... Ps 102:7
than they that *w* for the morning ...... Ps 130:6
than they that *w* for the morning ...... Ps 130:6
Set a *w*, O LORD, before my mouth ... Ps 141:3
w in the watchtower, eat, drink .... Is 21:5
all that *w* for iniquity are cut .... Is 29:20
a leopard shall *w* over their .... Jer 5:6
so will I *w* over them, to build, ... Jer 31:28
I will *w* over them for evil, and .... Jer 44:27
of Babylon, make thy *w* strong .... Jer 51:12
w the way, make thy loins strong, ... Nah 2:1
I will stand upon my *w*, and set me ... Hab 2:1
will *w* to see what he will say .... Hab 2:1

in the fourth *w* of the night	Mt 14:25
W therefore	Mt 24:42
in what *w* the thief would come	Mt 24:43
W therefore, for ye know neither	Mt 24:43
tarry ye here, and *w* with me	Mt 26:38
could ye not *w* with me one hour	Mt 26:40
W and pray, that ye enter not into	Mt 26:41
said unto them, Ye have a *w*	Mt 27:65
sealing the stone, and setting a *w*	Mt 27:66
some of the *w* came into the city	Mt 28:11
about the fourth *w* of the night	Mk 6:48
take ye heed, *w* and pray	Mk 13:33
and commanded the porter to *w*	Mk 13:34
W ye therefore	Mk 13:35
I say unto you I say unto all, W	Mk 13:37
tarry ye here, and *w*	Mk 14:34
couldest not thou *w* one hour	Mk 14:37
W ye and pray, lest ye enter into	Mk 14:38
keeping *w* over their flock by	Lk 2:8
if he shall come in the second *w*	Lk 12:38
or come in the third *w*	Lk 12:38
W ye therefore, and pray always	Lk 21:36
Therefore *w*, and remember, that by	Acts 20:31
W ye, stand fast in the faith	1Cor 16:13
w in the same with thanksgiving	Col 4:2
but let us *w* and be sober	1Th 5:6
But *w* thou in all things, endure	2Ti 4:5
for they *w* for your souls, as	Heb 13:17
therefore sober, and *w* unto prayer	1Pet 4:7
If therefore thou shalt not *w*	Rev 3:3

WATCHED

they *w* the house to kill him	Ps 59:f
All my familiars *w* for my halting	Jer 20:10
that like as I have *w* over them	Jer 31:28
in our watching we have *w* for a	Lam 4:17
hath the LORD *w* upon the evil	Dan 9:14
thief would come, he would have *w*	Mt 24:43
And sitting down they *w* him there	Mt 27:36
And they *w* him, whether he would	Mk 3:2
And the scribes and Pharisees *w*	Lk 6:7
thief would come, he would have *w*	Lk 12:39
the sabbath day, that they *w* him	Lk 14:1
And they *w* him, and sent forth	Lk 20:20
they *w* the gates day and night to	Acts 9:24

WATCHER

head upon my bed, and, behold, a *w*	Dan 4:13
And witness the king saw a *w*	Dan 4:23

WATCHERS

that *w* come from a far country	Jer 4:16
matter is by the decree of the *w*	Dan 4:17

WATCHES

appoint *w* of the inhabitants of	Neh 7:3
were over against them in the *w*	Neh 12:9
meditate on thee in the night *w*	Ps 63:6
Mine eyes prevent the night *w*	Ps 119:148
in the beginning of the *w* pour	Lam 2:19

WATCHETH

The wicked *w* the righteous, and	Ps 37:32
it *w* for thee	Eze 7:6
Blessed is he that *w*, and keepeth	Rev 16:15

WATCHFUL

Be *w*, and strengthen the things	Rev 3:2

WATCHING

sat upon a seat by the wayside *w*	1Sa 4:13
w daily at my gates, waiting at	Prov 8:34
in our *w* we have watched for a	Lam 4:17
w Jesus, saw the earthquake, and	Mt 27:54
lord when he cometh shall find *w*	Lk 12:37
w thereunto with all perseverance	Eph 6:18

WATCHINGS

in tumults, in labours, in *w*	2Cor 6:5
in *w* often, in hunger and thirst	2Cor 11:27

WATCHMAN

the *w* went up to the roof over	2Sa 18:24
he cried, and told the king	2Sa 18:25
the *w* saw another man running	2Sa 18:26
the *w* called unto the porter, and	2Sa 18:26
the *w* said, Me thinketh the	2Sa 18:27
there stood a *w* on the tower in	2Kin 9:17
the *w* told, saying, The messenger	2Kin 9:18
the *w* told, saying, He came even	2Kin 9:20
city, the *w* waketh but in vain	Ps 127:1
Lord said unto me, Go, set a *w*	Is 21:6
He calleth to me out of Seir, W	Is 21:11
W, what of the night	Is 21:11
The *w* said, The morning cometh	Is 21:12
I have made thee a *w* unto the	Eze 3:17
coasts, and set him for their *w*	Eze 33:2
But if the *w* see the sword come	Eze 33:6
I have set thee a *w* unto the	Eze 33:7
The *w* of Ephraim was with my God	Hos 9:8

WATCHMAN'S

will I require at the *w* hand	Eze 33:6

WATCHMEN

the *w* of Saul in Gibeah of	1Sa 14:16
tower of the *w* to the fenced city	2Kin 17:9
tower of the *w* to the fenced city	2Kin 18:8
The *w* that go about the city	Song 3:3
The *w* that went about the city	Song 5:7
Thy *w* shall lift up the voice	Is 52:8
His *w* are blind	Is 56:10
I have set *w* upon thy walls, O	Is 62:6
Also I set *w* over you, saying	Jer 6:17
that the *w* upon the mount Ephraim	Jer 31:6

the watch strong, set up the *w*	Jer 51:12
the day of thy *w* and thy	Mic 7:4

WATCHTOWER

Prepare the table, watch in the *w*	Is 21:5
upon the *w* in the daytime	Is 21:8

WATER

went out of Eden to *w* the garden	Gen 2:10
a fountain of *w* in the wilderness	Gen 16:7
Let a little *w*, I pray you, be	Gen 18:4
and took bread, and a bottle of *w*	Gen 21:14
the *w* was spent in the bottle, and	Gen 21:15
her eyes, and she saw a well of *w*	Gen 21:19
went, and filled the bottle with *w*	Gen 21:19
Abimelech because of a well of *w*	Gen 21:25
of *w* at the time of the evening	Gen 24:11
time that women go out to draw *w*	Gen 24:11
I stand here by the well of *w*	Gen 24:13
of the city come out to draw *w*	Gen 24:13
drink a little *w* of thy pitcher	Gen 24:17
I will draw *w* for thy camels also	Gen 24:19
ran again unto the well to draw *w*	Gen 24:20
w to wash his feet, and the men's	Gen 24:32
Behold, I stand by the well of *w*	Gen 24:43
the virgin cometh forth to draw *w*	Gen 24:43
a little *w* of thy pitcher to	Gen 24:43
down unto the well, and drew *w*	Gen 24:45
Isaac digged again the wells of *w*	Gen 26:18
found there a well of springing *w*	Gen 26:19
herdmen, saying, The *w* is ours	Gen 26:20
and said unto him, We have found *w*	Gen 26:32
w ye the sheep, and go and feed	Gen 29:7
then *w* ye the sheep	Gen 29:8
was empty, there was no *w* in it	Gen 37:24
Joseph's house, and gave them *w*	Gen 43:24
Unstable as *w*, thou shalt not	Gen 49:4
Because I drew him out of the *w*	Ex 2:10
and they came and drew *w*, and filled	Ex 2:16
troughs to *w* their father's flock	Ex 2:16
also drew *w* enough for us, and	Ex 2:19
shalt take of the *w* of the river	Ex 4:9
the *w* which thou takest out of	Ex 4:9
lo, he goeth out unto the *w*	Ex 7:15
to drink of the *w* of the river	Ex 7:18
and upon all their pools of *w*	Ex 7:19
not drink of the *w* of the river	Ex 7:21
about the river for *w* to drink	Ex 7:24
not drink of the *w* of the river	Ex 7:24
lo, he cometh forth to the *w*	Ex 8:20
it raw, nor sodden at all with *w*	Ex 12:9
in the wilderness, and found no *w*	Ex 15:22
where were twelve wells of *w*	Ex 15:27
there was no *w* for the people to	Ex 17:1
Give us *w* that we may drink	Ex 17:2
the people thirsted there for *w*	Ex 17:3
and there shall come *w* out of it	Ex 17:6
that is in the *w* under the earth	Ex 20:4
shall bless thy bread, and thy *w*	Ex 23:25
and shalt wash them with *w*	Ex 29:4
and thou shalt put *w* therein	Ex 30:18
they shall wash with *w*, that	Ex 30:20
powder, and strawed it upon the *w*	Ex 32:20
neither eat bread, nor drink *w*	Ex 34:28
the altar, and shalt put *w* therein	Ex 40:7
congregation, and wash them with *w*	Ex 40:12
put *w* there, to wash withal	Ex 40:30
and his legs shall he wash in *w*	Lev 1:9
the inwards and the legs with *w*	Lev 1:13
be both scoured, and rinsed in *w*	Lev 6:28
his sons, and washed them with *w*	Lev 8:6
the inwards and the legs in *w*	Lev 9:14
is done, it must be put into *w*	Lev 11:32
that on which such *w* cometh shall	Lev 11:34
pit, wherein there is plenty of *w*	Lev 11:36
But if any *w* be put upon the seed	Lev 11:38
an earthen vessel over running *w*	Lev 14:5
was killed over the running *w*	Lev 14:6
his hair, and wash himself in *w*	Lev 14:8
also he shall wash his flesh in *w*	Lev 14:9
an earthen vessel over running *w*	Lev 14:50
slain bird, and in the running *w*	Lev 14:51
the bird, and with the running *w*	Lev 14:52
clothes, and bathe himself in *w*	Lev 15:5
clothes, and bathe himself in *w*	Lev 15:6
clothes, and bathe himself in *w*	Lev 15:7
clothes, and bathe himself in *w*	Lev 15:8
clothes, and bathe himself in *w*	Lev 15:10
and hath not rinsed his hands in *w*	Lev 15:11
clothes, and bathe himself in *w*	Lev 15:11
of wood shall be rinsed in *w*	Lev 15:12
and bathe his flesh in running *w*	Lev 15:13
he shall wash all his flesh in *w*	Lev 15:16
shall be washed with *w*, and be	Lev 15:17
shall both bathe themselves in *w*	Lev 15:18
clothes, and bathe himself in *w*	Lev 15:21
clothes, and bathe himself in *w*	Lev 15:22
clothes, and bathe himself in *w*	Lev 15:27
shall he wash his flesh in *w*	Lev 16:4
flesh with *w* in the holy place	Lev 16:24
clothes, and bathe his flesh in *w*	Lev 16:26
clothes, and bathe his flesh in *w*	Lev 16:28
clothes, and bathe himself in *w*	Lev 17:15
unless he wash his flesh with *w*	Lev 22:6
take holy *w* in an earthen vessel	Num 5:17
shalt take, and put it into the *w*	Num 5:17
bitter *w* that causeth the curse	Num 5:18
bitter *w* that causeth the curse	Num 5:19
this *w* that causeth the curse	Num 5:22
blot them out with the bitter *w*	Num 5:23
bitter *w* that causeth the curse	Num 5:24

the *w* that causeth the curse	Num 5:24
cause the woman to drink the *w*	Num 5:26
he hath made her to drink the *w*	Num 5:27
that the *w* that causeth the curse	Num 5:27
Sprinkle *w* of purifying upon them	Num 8:7
and he shall bathe his flesh in *w*	Num 19:7
her shall wash his clothes in *w*	Num 19:8
and bathe his flesh in *w*	Num 19:8
of Israel for a *w* of separation	Num 19:9
because the *w* of separation was	Num 19:13
running *w* shall be put thereto in	Num 19:17
take hyssop, and dip it in the *w*	Num 19:18
clothes, and bathe himself in *w*	Num 19:19
the *w* of separation hath not been	Num 19:20
that he that sprinkleth the *w* of	Num 19:21
he that toucheth the *w* of	Num 19:21
And there was no *w* for the	Num 20:2
neither is there any *w* to drink	Num 20:5
and it shall give forth his *w*	Num 20:8
forth to them *w* out of the rock	Num 20:8
we fetch you *w* out of this rock	Num 20:10
the *w* came out abundantly, and the	Num 20:11
This is the *w* of Meribah	Num 20:13
we drink of the *w* of the wells	Num 20:17
if I and my cattle drink of thy *w*	Num 20:19
my word at the *w* of Meribah	Num 20:24
no bread, neither is there any *w*	Num 21:5
together, and I will give them *w*	Num 21:16
He shall pour the *w* out of his	Num 24:7
me at the *w* before their eyes	Num 27:14
that is the *w* of Meribah in	Num 27:14
purified with the *w* of separation	Num 31:23
ye shall make go through the *w*	Num 31:23
Elim were twelve fountains of *w*	Num 33:9
where was no *w* for the people to	Num 33:14
also buy *w* of them for money	Deut 2:6
give me *w* for money, that I may	Deut 2:28
good land, a land of brooks of *w*	Deut 8:7
and drought, where there was no *w*	Deut 8:15
who brought thee forth *w* out of	Deut 8:15
neither did eat bread nor drink *w*	Deut 9:9
neither eat bread, nor drink *w*	Deut 9:18
how he made the *w* of the Red sea	Deut 11:4
drinketh *w* of the rain of heaven	Deut 11:11
shalt pour it upon the earth as *w*	Deut 12:16
shalt pour it upon the earth as *w*	Deut 12:24
pour it upon the ground as *w*	Deut 15:23
with *w* in the way, when ye came	Deut 23:4
on, he shall wash himself with *w*	Deut 23:11
thy wood unto the drawer of thy *w*	Deut 29:11
up the *w* of the Red sea for you	Josh 2:10
to the brink of the *w* of Jordan	Josh 3:8
were dipped in the brim of the *w*	Josh 3:15
the people melted, and became as *w*	Josh 7:5
drawers of *w* unto all the	Josh 9:21
drawers of *w* for the house of my	Josh 9:23
drawers of *w* for the congregation	Josh 9:27
the fountain of the *w* of Nephtoah	Josh 15:9
give me also springs of *w*	Josh 15:19
unto the *w* of Jericho on the east	Josh 16:1
give me also springs of *w*	Josh 15:19
I pray thee, a little *w* to drink	Judg 4:19
the clouds also dropped *w*	Judg 5:4
in the places of drawing *w*	Judg 5:11
He asked *w*, and she gave him milk	Judg 5:25
of the fleece, a bowl full of *w*	Judg 6:38
bring them down unto the *w*	Judg 7:4
down the people unto the *w*	Judg 7:5
lappeth of the *w* with his tongue	Judg 7:5
down upon their knees to drink *w*	Judg 7:6
the jaw, and there came *w* thereout	Judg 15:19
together to Mizpeh, and drew *w*	1Sa 7:6
young maidens going out to draw *w*	1Sa 9:11
I then take my bread, and my *w*	1Sa 25:11
at his bolster, and the cruse of *w*	1Sa 26:11
the cruse of *w* from Saul's	1Sa 26:12
the cruse of *w* that was at his	1Sa 26:16
and they made him drink *w*	1Sa 30:11
eaten no bread, nor drunk any *w*	1Sa 30:12
are as *w* spilt on the ground	2Sa 14:14
They be gone over the brook of *w*	2Sa 17:20
Arise, and pass quickly over the *w*	2Sa 17:21
the beginning of harvest until *w*	2Sa 21:10
the *w* of the well of Beth-lehem	2Sa 23:15
drew *w* out of the well	2Sa 23:16
bread nor drink *w* in this place	1Kin 13:8
saying, Eat no bread, nor drink *w*	1Kin 13:9
drink *w* with thee in this place	1Kin 13:16
eat no bread nor drink *w* there	1Kin 13:17
that he may eat bread and drink *w*	1Kin 13:18
bread in his house, and drank *w*	1Kin 13:19
drunk *w* in the place, of the	1Kin 13:22
thee, Eat no bread, and drink no *w*	1Kin 13:22
as a reed is shaken in the *w*	1Kin 14:15
a little *w* in a vessel, that I	1Kin 17:10
cave, and fed them with bread and *w*	1Kin 18:4
the land, unto all fountains of *w*	1Kin 18:5
fed them with bread and *w*	1Kin 18:13
and said, Fill four barrels with *w*	1Kin 18:33
drink twice. And they did the *w*	1Kin 18:34
the filled the trench also with *w*	1Kin 18:35
licked up the *w* that was in the	1Kin 18:38
and a cruse of *w* at his head	1Kin 19:6
with *w* of affliction, until I	1Kin 22:27
but the *w* is naught, and the	2Kin 2:19
and there was no *w* for the host	2Kin 3:9
which poured *w* on the hands of	2Kin 3:11
valley shall be filled with *w*	2Kin 3:17
good tree, and stop all wells of *w*	2Kin 3:19
there came *w* by the way of Edom,	2Kin 3:20

and the country was filled with w 2Kin 3:20
and the sun shone upon the w........... 2Kin 3:22
the Moabites saw the w on the........... 2Kin 3:22
they stopped all the wells of w 2Kin 3:25
beam, the ax head fell into the w......... 2Kin 6:5
w before them, that they may eat....... 2Kin 6:22
a thick cloth, and dipped it in w......... 2Kin 8:15
brought w into the city, are they 2Kin 20:20
the w of the well of Beth-lehem......... 1Chr 11:17
drew w out of the well of 1Chr 11:18
with w of affliction, until I............... 2Chr 18:26
of Assyria come, and find much w 2Chr 32:4
he did eat no bread, nor drink w .... Ezr 10:6
the w gate toward the east .... Neh 3:26
street that was before the w gate......... Neh 8:1
the w gate from the morning until....... Neh 8:3
and in the street of the w gate............ Neh 8:16
broughtest forth w for them out .... Neh 9:15
gavest them w for their thirst............. Neh 9:20
even unto the w gate eastward........... Neh 12:37
of Israel with bread and with w .... Neh 13:2
can the flag grow without w .... Job 8:11
If I wash myself with snow w .... Job 9:30
the scent of w it will bud.................... Job 14:9
which drinketh iniquity like w .... Job 15:16
Thou hast not given w to the.............. Job 22:7
who drinketh up scorning like w .... Job 34:7
he maketh small the drops of w .... Job 36:27
a tree planted by the rivers of w .... Ps 1:3
I w my couch with my tears................ Ps 6:6
I am poured out like w, and all my...... Ps 22:14
hart panteth after the w brooks........... Ps 42:1
and thirsty land, where no w is............ Ps 63:1
river of God, which is full of w .... Ps 65:9
we went through fire and through w ... Ps 66:12
as showers that w the earth .... Ps 72:6
The clouds poured out w .... Ps 77:17
shed like w round about Jerusalem..... Ps 79:3
came round about me daily like w ...... Ps 88:17
the wilderness into a standing w .... Ps 107:35
it come into his bowels like w .... Ps 109:18
turned the rock into a standing w....... Ps 114:8
no fountains abounding with w .... Prov 8:24
is as when one letteth out w .... Prov 17:14
the heart of man is like deep w .... Prov 20:5
of the LORD, as the rivers of w............ Prov 21:1
be thirsty, give him w to drink .... Prov 25:21
As in w face answereth to face,........... Prov 27:19
earth that is not filled with w .... Prov 30:16
I made me pools of w .... Eccl 2:6
to w therewith the wood that .... Eccl 2:6
dross, thy wine mixed with w .... Is 1:22
and as a garden that hath no w .... Is 1:30
of bread, and the whole stay of w .... Is 3:1
with joy shall ye draw w out of........... Is 12:3
for the hittern, and pools of w .... Is 14:23
I will w thee with my tears, O............. Is 16:9
brought w to him that was thirsty....... Is 21:14
walls for the w of the old pool .... Is 22:11
I will w it every moment.................... Is 27:3
or to take w withal out of the.............. Is 30:14
the w of affliction, yet shall............... Is 30:20
as rivers of w in a dry place, as.......... Is 32:2
and the thirsty land springs of w .... Is 35:7
I have digged, and drunk w................ Is 37:25
When the poor and needy seek w .... Is 41:17
make the wilderness a pool of w .... Is 41:18
and the dry land springs of w............. Is 41:18
For I will pour w upon him that.......... Is 44:3
as willows by the w courses .... Is 44:4
he drinketh no w, and is faint............. Is 44:12
springs of w shall he guide them....... Is 49:10
stinketh, because there is no w .... Is 50:2
garden, and like a spring of w .... Is 58:11
arm, dividing the w before them .... Is 63:12
cisterns, that can hold no w .... Jer 2:13
given us w of gall to drink,................. Jer 8:14
give them w of gall to drink............... Jer 9:15
thy loins, and put it not in w .... Jer 13:1
came to the pits, and found no w .... Jer 14:3
and make them drink the w of gall .... Jer 23:15
And in the dungeon there was no w ... Jer 38:6
eye, mine eye runneth down with w ... Lam 1:16
pour out thine heart like w................. Lam 2:19
of w for the destruction of the .... Lam 3:48
We have drunken our w for money..... Lam 5:4
shalt drink also w by measure............ Eze 4:11
and they shall drink w by measure ..... Eze 4:16
That they may want bread and w .... Eze 4:17
and all knees shall be weak as w .... Eze 7:17
drink thy w with trembling and......... Eze 12:18
drink their w with astonishment,....... Eze 12:19
thou washed in w to supple thee......... Eze 16:4
Then washed I thee with w................. Eze 16:9
that he might w it by the furrows........ Eze 17:7
and all knees shall be weak as w .... Eze 21:7
set it on, and also pour w into it .... Eze 24:3
and thy dust in the midst of the w ..... Eze 26:12
in their height, all that drink w .... Eze 31:14
best of Lebanon, all that drink w .... Eze 31:16
I will also w with thy blood the.......... Eze 32:6
will I sprinkle clean w upon you........ Eze 36:25
us pulse to eat, and w to drink........... Dan 1:12
that give me thy bread and my w .... Hos 2:5
out my wrath upon them like w .... Hos 5:10
is cut off as the foam upon the w .... Hos 10:7
shall w the valley of Shittim.............. Joel 3:18
unto one city, to drink w.................... Amos 4:8
of bread, nor a thirst for w................. Amos 8:11
let them not feed, nor drink w .... Jonah 3:7

is of old like a pool of w..................... Nah 2:8
overflowing of the w passed by .... Hab 3:10
out of the pit wherein is no w .... Zec 9:11
you with w unto repentance................ Mt 3:11
went up straightway out of the w .... Mt 3:16
w only in the name of a disciple .... Mt 10:42
bid me come unto thee on the w.......... Mt 14:28
of the ship, he walked on the w........... Mt 14:29
into the fire, and oft into the w .... Mt 17:15
a tumult was made, he took w............. Mt 27:24
I indeed have baptized you with w ..... Mk 1:8
coming up out of the w, he saw.......... Mk 1:10
a cup of w to drink in my name.......... Mk 9:41
you a man bearing a pitcher of w .... Mk 14:13
all, I indeed baptize you with w .... Lk 3:16
thou gavest me no w for my feet......... Lk 7:44
and they were filled with w .... Lk 8:23
the wind and the raging of the w .... Lk 8:24
he commandeth even the winds and w .. Lk 8:25
dip the tip of his finger in w .... Lk 16:24
meet you, bearing a pitcher of w .... Lk 22:10
them, saying, I baptize with w .... Jn 1:26
am I come baptizing with w .... Jn 1:31
he that sent me to baptize with w .... Jn 1:33
them, Fill the waterpots with w .... Jn 2:7
tasted the w that was made wine......... Jn 2:9
servants which drew the w knew......... Jn 2:9
thee, Except a man be born of w .... Jn 3:5
because there was much w there .... Jn 3:23
a woman of Samaria to draw w........... Jn 4:7
he would have given thee living w ...... Jn 4:10
then hast thou that living w .... Jn 4:11
of this w shall thirst again.................. Jn 4:13
the w that I shall give him shall......... Jn 4:14
but the w that I shall give him .... Jn 4:14
w springing up into everlasting.......... Jn 4:14
unto him, Sir, give me this w .... Jn 4:15
Galilee, where he made the w wine .... Jn 4:46
waiting for the moving of the w.......... Jn 5:3
into the pool, and troubled the w .... Jn 5:4
after the troubling of the w .... Jn 5:4
when the w is troubled, to put me....... Jn 5:7
shall flow rivers of living w .... Jn 7:38
that he poureth w into a bason........... Jn 13:5
came there out blood and w .... Jn 19:34
For John truly baptized with w .... Acts 1:5
way, they came unto a certain w .... Acts 8:36
the eunuch said, See, here is w .... Acts 8:36
and they went down both into the w ... Acts 8:38
they were come up out of the w .... Acts 8:39
Can any man forbid w, that these....... Acts 10:47
said, John indeed baptized with w ..... Acts 11:16
with the washing of w by the word .... Eph 5:26
Drink no longer w, but use a.............. 1Tim 5:23
of calves and of goats, with w .... Heb 9:19
and our bodies washed with pure w ... Heb 10:22
forth at the same place sweet w .... Jas 3:11
can no fountain both yield salt w .... Jas 3:12
is, eight souls were saved by w 1Pet 3:20
These are wells without w 2Pet 2:17
out of the w and in the w 2Pet 3:5
then was, being overflowed with w 2Pet 3:6
This is he that came by w 1Jn 5:6
not by w only, but by w 1Jn 5:6
in earth, the spirit, and the w 1Jn 5:8
clouds they are without w .... Jude 12
w as a flood after the woman............. Rev 12:15
the w thereof was dried up, that......... Rev 16:12
fountain of the w of life freely............ Rev 21:6
me a pure river of w of life .... Rev 22:1
let him take the w of life freely........... Rev 22:17

WATERCOURSE
also stopped the upper w of Gihon..... 2Chr 32:30
Who hath divided a w for the .... Job 38:25

WATERED
w the whole face of the ground........... Gen 2:6
that it was well w every where............ Gen 13:10
of that well they w the flocks .... Gen 29:2
w the sheep, and put the stone........... Gen 29:3
w the flock of Laban his mother's...... Gen 29:10
and helped them, and w their flock.... Ex 2:17
enough for us, and w the flock........... Ex 2:19
watereth shall be w also himself .... Prov 11:25
and thou shalt be like a w garden ...... Is 58:11
their soul shall be as a w garden .... Jer 31:12
I have planted, Apollos w 1Cor 3:6

WATEREDST
w it with thy foot, as a garden........... Deut 11:10

WATEREST
Thou visitest the earth, and w it......... Ps 65:9
Thou w the ridges thereof.................. Ps 65:10

WATERETH
He w the hills from his chambers....... Ps 104:13
he that w shall be watered also .... Prov 11:25
but w the earth, and maketh it........... Is 55:10
any thing, neither he that w 1Cor 3:7
planteth and he that w are one 1Cor 3:8

WATERFLOOD
Let not the w overflow me.................. Ps 69:15

WATERING
flocks in the gutters in the w.............. Gen 30:38
Also by w he wearieth the thick.......... Job 37:11
the stall, and lead him away to w ...... Lk 13:15

WATERPOT
The woman then left her w .... Jn 4:28

WATERPOTS
were set there six w of stone............... Jn 2:6
unto them, Fill the w with water........ Jn 2:7

WATERS
God moved upon the face of the w ..... Gen 1:2
a firmament in the midst of the w ..... Gen 1:6
it divide the w from the w .... Gen 1:6
divided the w which were under......... Gen 1:7
under the firmament from the w .... Gen 1:7
Let the w under the heaven be............ Gen 1:9
together of the w called he Seas .... Gen 1:10
fill the w in the seas, and let.............. Gen 1:22
bring a flood of w upon the earth ...... Gen 6:17
the flood of w was upon the earth...... Gen 7:6
because of the w of the flood .... Gen 7:7
that the w of the flood were upon....... Gen 7:10
the w increased, and bare up the .... Gen 7:17
And the w prevailed, and were .... Gen 7:18
the w prevailed exceedingly upon...... Gen 7:19
cubits upward did the w prevail .... Gen 7:20
the w prevailed upon the earth an ..... Gen 7:24
over the earth, and the w asswaged ... Gen 8:1
the w returned from off the earth....... Gen 8:3
and fifty days the w were abated .... Gen 8:3
the w decreased continually until....... Gen 8:5
until the w were dried up from .... Gen 8:7
to see if the w were abated from......... Gen 8:8
for the w were on the face of the .... Gen 8:9
so Noah knew that the w were............ Gen 8:11
the w were dried up from off the .... Gen 8:13
off any more by the w of a flood......... Gen 9:11
the w shall no more become a .... Gen 9:15
upon the w which are in the river....... Ex 7:17
thine hand upon the w of Egypt .... Ex 7:19
smote the w that were in the.............. Ex 7:20
all the w that were in the river .... Ex 7:20
out his hand over the w of Egypt .... Ex 8:6
dry land, and the w were divided........ Ex 14:21
the w were a wall unto them on.......... Ex 14:22
that the w may come again upon .... Ex 14:26
the w returned, and covered the .... Ex 14:28
the w were a wall unto them on.......... Ex 14:29
the w were gathered together.............. Ex 15:8
they sank as lead in the mighty w ...... Ex 15:10
again the w of the sea upon them ...... Ex 15:19
could not drink of the w of Marah ..... Ex 15:23
which when he had cast into the w ..... Ex 15:25
the w were made sweet .... Ex 15:25
and they encamped there by the w ..... Ex 15:27
ye eat of all that are in the w .... Lev 11:9
hath fins and scales in the .... Lev 11:9
rivers, of all that move in the w .... Lev 11:10
living thing which is in the w .... Lev 11:10
hath no fins nor scales in the w .... Lev 11:12
creature that moveth in the w .... Lev 11:46
not drink of the w of the well .... Num 20:17
and as cedar trees beside the w .... Num 24:6
and his seed shall be in many w .... Num 24:7
is in the w beneath the earth.............. Deut 4:18
is in the w beneath the earth.............. Deut 5:8
to Jotbath, a land of rivers of w .... Deut 10:7
eat of all that are in the w .... Deut 14:9
Israel at the w of Meribah-kadesh..... Deut 32:51
didst strive at the w of Meribah......... Deut 33:8
shall rest in the w of Jordan .... Josh 3:13
that the w of Jordan shall be cut .... Josh 3:13
the w that come down from above ..... Josh 3:13
That the w which came down from..... Josh 3:16
That the w of Jordan were cut off ...... Josh 4:7
the w of Jordan returned.................... Josh 4:18
the w of Jordan from before you......... Josh 4:23
the w of Jordan from before the .... Josh 5:1
together at the w of Merom .... Josh 11:5
them by the w of Merom suddenly ..... Josh 11:7
passed toward the w of En-shemesh .. Josh 15:7
out to the well of w of Nephtoah....... Josh 18:15
in Taanach by the w of Megiddo .... Judg 5:19
before them the w unto Beth-barah ... Judg 7:24
took the w unto Beth-barah and .... Judg 7:24
before me, as the breach of w 2Sa 5:20
and have taken the city of w 2Sa 12:27
pavilions round about him, dark w 2Sa 22:12
he drew me out of many w 2Sa 22:17
it together, and smote the w 2Kin 2:8
fell from him, and smote the w.......... 2Kin 2:14
and when he also had smitten the w ... 2Kin 2:14
forth unto the spring of the w 2Kin 2:21
the LORD, I have healed these w......... 2Kin 2:21
So the w were healed unto this.......... 2Kin 2:22
better than all the w of Israel 2Kin 5:12
ye every one the w of his cistern 2Kin 18:31
I have digged and drunk strange w 2Kin 19:24
hand like the breaking forth of w 1Chr 14:11
his mighty men to stop the w of 2Chr 32:3
as a stone into the mighty w .... Neh 9:11
are poured out like the w .... Job 3:24
sendeth w upon the fields................... Job 5:10
remember it as that pass away........... Job 11:16
Behold, he withholdeth the w .... Job 12:15
As the w fail from the sea, and .... Job 14:11
The w wear the stones .... Job 14:19
and abundance of w cover thee......... Job 22:11
He is swift as the w .... Job 24:18
and heat consume the snow w .... Job 24:19
are formed from under the w .... Job 26:5
He bindeth up the w in his thick...... Job 26:8
hath compassed the w with bounds ... Job 26:10
Terrors take hold on him as w .... Job 27:20
even the w forgotten of the foot .... Job 28:4

and he weigheth the w by measure	Job 28:25
My root was spread out by the w	Job 29:19
me as a wide breaking in of w	Job 30:14
breadth of the w is straitened	Job 37:10
for the overflowing of w, or a	Job 38:25
The w are hid as with a stone, and	Job 38:30
abundance of w may cover these	Job 38:34
round about him were dark w	Ps 18:11
Then the channels of w were seen	Ps 18:15
took me, he drew me out of many w	Ps 18:16
he leadeth me beside the still w	Ps 23:2
voice of the LORD is upon the w	Ps 29:3
the LORD is upon many w	Ps 29:3
w they shall not come nigh unto	Ps 32:6
He gathereth the w of the sea	Ps 33:7
Though the w thereof roar and be	Ps 46:3
away as w which run continually	Ps 58:7
for the w are come in unto my	Ps 69:1
I am come into deep w, where the	Ps 69:2
hate me, and out of the deep w	Ps 69:14
w of a full cup are wrung out to	Ps 73:10
the heads of the dragons in the w	Ps 74:13
The w saw thee, O God, the w	Ps 77:16
sea, and thy path in the great w	Ps 77:19
he made the w to stand as an heap	Ps 78:13
caused w to run down like rivers	Ps 78:16
that the w gushed out, and the	Ps 78:20
I proved thee at the w of Meribah	Ps 81:7
mightier than the noise of many w	Ps 93:4
beams of his chambers in the w	Ps 104:3
the w stood above the mountains	Ps 104:6
He turned their w into blood	Ps 105:29
the rock, and the w gushed out	Ps 105:41
he w covered their enemies	Ps 106:11
him also at the w of strife	Ps 106:32
that do business in great w	Ps 107:23
the flint into a fountain of w	Ps 114:8
Rivers of w run down mine eyes,	Ps 119:136
Then the w had overwhelmed us,	Ps 124:4
Then the proud w had gone over	Ps 124:5
out the earth above the w	Ps 136:6
me, and deliver me out of great w	Ps 144:7
his wind to blow, and the w flow	Ps 147:18
ye w that be above the heavens	Ps 148:4
Drink w out of thine own cistern,	Prov 5:15
running w out of thine own well	Prov 5:15
rivers of w in the streets	Prov 5:16
that the w should not pass his	Prov 8:29
Stolen w are sweet, and bread	Prov 9:17
of a man's mouth are as deep w	Prov 18:4
As cold w to a thirsty soul, so	Prov 25:25
who hath bound the w in a garment	Prov 30:4
Cast thy bread upon the w	Eccl 11:1
of gardens, a well of living w	Song 4:15
eyes of doves by the rivers of w	Song 5:12
Many w cannot quench love,	Song 8:7
the w of Shiloah that go softly	Is 8:6
up upon them the w of the river	Is 8:7
the LORD, as the w cover the sea	Is 11:9
For the w of Nimrim shall be	Is 15:6
For the w of Dimon shall be full	Is 15:9
like the rushing of mighty w	Is 17:12
rush like the rushing of many w	Is 17:13
vessels of bulrushes upon the w	Is 18:2
the w shall fail from the sea, and	Is 19:5
nets upon the w shall languish	Is 19:8
together the w of the lower pool	Is 22:9
by great w the seed of Sihor, the	Is 23:3
a flood of mighty w overflowing	Is 28:2
the w shall overflow the hiding	Is 28:17
streams of w in the day of the	Is 30:25
are ye that sow beside all w	Is 32:20
his w shall be sure	Is 33:16
the wilderness shall w break out	Is 35:6
one the w of his own cistern	Is 36:16
Who hath measured the w in the	Is 40:12
When thou passest through the w	Is 43:2
sea, and a path in the mighty w	Is 43:16
because I give w in the	Is 43:20
come forth out of the w of Judah	Is 48:1
he caused the w to flow out of	Is 48:21
rock also, and the w gushed out	Is 48:21
the sea, the w of the great deep	Is 51:10
this is as the w of Noah unto me	Is 54:9
for as I have sworn that the w of	Is 54:9
that thirsteth, come ye to the w	Is 55:1
whose w cast up mire and dirt	Is 57:20
spring of water, whose w fail not	Is 58:11
the fire causeth the w to boil	Is 64:2
me the fountain of living w	Jer 2:13
of Egypt, to drink the w of Sihor	Jer 2:18
to drink the w of the river	Jer 2:18
As a fountain casteth out her w	Jer 6:7
Oh that my head were w, and mine	Jer 9:1
and our eyelids gush out with w	Jer 9:18
a multitude of w in the heavens	Jer 10:13
sent their little ones to the w	Jer 14:3
me as a liar, and as w that fail	Jer 15:18
be as a tree planted by the w	Jer 17:8
LORD, the fountain of living w	Jer 17:13
or shall the cold flowing w that	Jer 18:14
the rivers of w in a straight way	Jer 31:9
by the great w that are in Gibeon	Jer 41:12
whose w are moved as the rivers	Jer 46:7
his w are moved like the waters	Jer 46:8
w rise up out of the north, and	Jer 47:2
for the w also of Nimrim shall be	Jer 48:34
A drought is upon her w	Jer 50:38
O thou that dwellest upon many w	Jer 51:13
a multitude of w in the heavens	Jer 51:16

her waves do roar like great w	Jer 51:55
W flowed over mine head	Lam 3:54
wings, like the noise of great w	Eze 1:24
he placed it by great w, and set	Eze 17:5
planted in a good soil by great w	Eze 17:8
in thy blood, planted by the w	Eze 19:10
of branches by reason of many w	Eze 19:10
thee, and great w shall cover thee	Eze 26:19
have brought thee into great w	Eze 27:26
depths of the w thy merchandise	Eze 27:34
The w made him great, the deep	Eze 31:4
because of the multitude of w	Eze 31:5
for his root was by great w	Eze 31:7
the w exalt themselves for their	Eze 31:14
and the great w were stayed	Eze 31:15
and troubledst the w with thy feet	Eze 32:2
thereof from beside the great w	Eze 32:13
Then will I make their w deep	Eze 32:14
and to have drunk of the deep w	Eze 34:18
voice was like a noise of many w	Eze 43:2
w issued out from under the	Eze 47:1
the w came down from under from	Eze 47:1
there ran out w on the right side	Eze 47:2
and he brought me through the w	Eze 47:3
the w were to the ancles	Eze 47:3
and brought me through the w	Eze 47:4
the w were to the knees	Eze 47:4
the w were to the loins	Eze 47:4
for the w were risen	Eze 47:5
w to swim in, a river that could	Eze 47:5
These w issue out toward the east	Eze 47:8
the sea, the w shall be healed	Eze 47:8
because these w shall come	Eze 47:9
because their w they issued	Eze 47:12
even to the w of strife in Kadesh	Eze 47:19
unto the w of strife in Kadesh	Eze 48:28
which was upon the w of the river	Dan 12:6
which was upon the w of the river	Dan 12:7
for the rivers of w are dried up	Joel 1:20
rivers of Judah shall flow with w	Joel 3:18
that calleth for the w of the sea	Amos 5:8
But let judgment run down as w	Amos 5:24
that calleth for the w of the sea	Amos 9:6
The w compassed me about, even to	Jonah 2:5
as the w that are poured down a	Mic 1:4
that had the w round about it,	Nah 3:8
Draw thee w for the siege,	Nah 3:14
the LORD, as the w cover the sea	Hab 2:14
through the heap of great w	Hab 3:15
that living w shall go out from	Zec 14:8
the sea, and perished in the w	Mt 8:32
him into the fire, and into the w	Mk 9:22
journeyings often, in perils of w	2Cor 11:26
his voice as the sound of many w	Rev 1:15
them unto living fountains of w	Rev 7:17
and upon the fountains of w	Rev 8:10
part of the w became wormwood	Rev 8:11
and many men died of the w	Rev 8:11
have power over w to turn them to	Rev 11:6
as the voice of many w	Rev 14:2
and the sea, and the fountains of w	Rev 14:7
upon the rivers and fountains of w	Rev 16:4
And I heard the angel of the w say	Rev 16:5
whore that sitteth upon many w	Rev 17:1
The w which thou sawest, where	Rev 17:15
and as the voice of many w	Rev 19:6

WATERSPOUTS

unto deep at the noise of thy w	Ps 42:7

WATERSPRINGS

and the w into dry ground	Ps 107:33
water, and dry ground into w	Ps 107:35

WAVE

shalt w them for a	Ex 29:24
them for a w offering	Ex 29:24
and w it for a	Ex 29:26
it for a w offering before	Ex 29:26
the breast of the w offering	Ex 29:27
for a w offering before the LORD	Lev 7:30
For the w breast and the heave	Lev 7:34
waved them for a w offering	Lev 8:27
waved it for a w offering before	Lev 8:29
for a w offering before the LORD	Lev 9:21
the w breast and heave shoulder	Lev 10:15
the w breast shall they bring	Lev 10:15
to w it for a w offering	Lev 10:15
w them for a	Lev 14:12
them for a w offering before	Lev 14:12
the priest shall w them for a	Lev 14:24
for a w offering before the LORD	Lev 14:24
he shall w the sheaf before the	Lev 23:11
the sabbath the priest shall w it	Lev 23:11
ye w the sheaf an he lamb without	Lev 23:12
the sheaf of the w offering	Lev 23:15
two w loaves of two tenth deals	Lev 23:17
the priest shall w them with the	Lev 23:20
for a w offering before the LORD	Lev 23:20
shall w the offering before the	Num 5:25
the priest shall w them for a	Num 6:20
for a w offering before the LORD	Num 6:20
for the priest, with the w breast	Num 6:20
with all the w offerings of the	Num 18:11
shall be thine, as the w breast	Num 18:18
For he that waveth is like a w	Jas 1:6

WAVED

of the heave offering, which is w	Ex 29:27
that the breast may be w for a	Lev 7:30
w them for a wave offering before	Lev 8:27
w it for a wave offering before	Lev 8:29

the right shoulder Aaron w for a	Lev 9:21
for a trespass offering to be w	Lev 14:21

WAVERETH

For he that w is like a wave of	Jas 1:6

WAVERING

profession of our faith without w	Heb 10:23
let him ask in faith, nothing w	Jas 1:6

WAVES

When the w of death compassed me,	2Sa 22:5
and treadeth upon the w of the sea	Job 9:8
here shall thy proud w be stayed	Job 38:11
all thy w and thy billows are gone	Ps 42:7
of the seas, the noise of their w	Ps 65:7
hast afflicted me with all thy w	Ps 88:7
when the w thereof arise, thou	Ps 89:9
the floods lift up their w	Ps 93:3
yea, than the mighty w of the sea	Ps 93:4
which lifteth up the w thereof	Ps 107:25
so that the w thereof are still	Ps 107:29
righteousness as the w of the sea	Is 48:18
divided the sea, whose w roared	Is 51:15
though the w thereof toss	Jer 5:22
the sea when the w thereof roar	Jer 31:35
the multitude of the w thereof	Jer 51:42
when her w do roar like great	Jer 51:55
the sea causeth his w to come up	Eze 26:3
billows and thy w passed over me	Jonah 2:3
and shall smite the w in the sea	Zec 10:11
the ship was covered with the w	Mt 8:24
midst of the sea, tossed with w	Mt 14:24
the w beat into the ship, so that	Mk 4:37
the sea and the w roaring	Lk 21:25
broken with the violence of the w	Acts 27:41
Raging w of the sea, foaming out	Jude 13

WAX

And my wrath shall w hot, and I	Ex 22:24
my wrath may w hot against them	Ex 32:10
why doth thy wrath w hot against	Ex 32:11
not the anger of my lord w hot	Ex 32:22
or stranger w rich by thee	Lev 25:47
that dwelleth by him w poor	Lev 25:47
place, and his eyes began to w dim	1Sa 3:2
What time they w warm, they	Job 6:17
root thereof wax old in the earth	Job 14:8
my heart is like w	Ps 22:14
as w melteth before the fire, so	Ps 68:2
The hills melted like w at the	Ps 97:5
all of them shall w old like a	Ps 102:26
fatness of his flesh shall w lean	Is 17:4
neither shall his face now w pale	Is 29:22
they all shall w old as a garment	Is 50:9
the earth shall w old like a	Is 51:6
our hands w feeble	Jer 6:24
as w before the fire, and as the	Mic 1:4
the love of many shall w cold	Mt 24:12
yourselves bags which w not old	Lk 12:33
begun to w wanton against Christ	1Ti 5:11
men and seducers shall w worse	2Ti 3:13
they all shall w old as doth an	Heb 1:11

WAXED

After I am w old shall I have	Gen 18:12
And the man w great, and went	Gen 26:13
the famine was sore in the land of	Gen 41:56
multiplied, and w exceeding mighty	Ex 1:7
multiplied, and w very mighty	Ex 1:20
and when the sun w hot, it melted	Ex 16:21
w louder and louder, Moses spake,	Ex 19:19
and Moses' anger w hot, and he cast	Ex 32:19
Moses, in the LORD's hand w short	Num 11:23
Thy raiment w not old upon thee,	Deut 8:4
But Jeshurun w fat, and kicked	Deut 32:15
round about, that Joshua w old	Josh 23:1
hath many children is w feeble	1Sa 2:5
but David w stronger and stronger,	2Sa 3:1
and the house of Saul w weaker	2Sa 3:1
and David w faint	2Sa 21:15
and the flesh of the child w warm	2Kin 4:34
So David w greater and greater	1Chr 11:9
But Abijah w mighty, and married	2Chr 13:21
Jehoshaphat w great exceedingly	2Chr 17:12
But Jehoiada w old, and was full	2Chr 24:15
their clothes w not old, and their	Neh 9:21
for this man Mordecai w greater	Est 9:4
my bones w old through my roaring	Ps 32:3
Damascus is w feeble, and turneth	Jer 49:24
of them, and his hands w feeble	Jer 50:43
the goat w very great	Dan 8:8
which w exceeding great, toward	Dan 8:9
it w great, even to the host of	Dan 8:10
this people's heart is w gross	Mt 13:15
w strong in spirit, and was in the	Lk 1:80
w strong in spirit, filled with	Lk 2:40
and it grew, and w a great tree	Lk 13:19
Then Paul and Barnabas w bold	Acts 13:46
heart of this people is w gross	Acts 28:27
w valiant in fight, turned to	Heb 11:34
w rich through the abundance of	Rev 18:3

WAXEN

because the cry of them is w	Gen 19:13
If thy brother be w poor, and hath	Lev 25:25
And if thy brother be w poor	Lev 25:35
that dwelleth by thee be w poor	Lev 25:39
clothes are not w old upon you	Deut 29:5
thy shoe is not w old upon thy	Deut 29:5
and filled themselves, and w fat	Deut 31:20
thou art w fat, thou art grown	Deut 32:15
children of Israel were w strong	Josh 17:13

W

they are become great, and *w* rich............ Jer 5:27
They are *w* fat, they shine........................ Jer 5:28
w great, and thou art come to................... Eze 16:7

WAXETH

it *w* old because of all mine....................... Ps 6:7
w old is ready to vanish away.................... Heb 8:13

WAXING

w confident by my bonds, are much.......... Phil 1:14

WAY See PREFACE.

WAYFARING

he saw a *w* man in the street of........... Judg 19:17
to dress for the *w* man that was................ 2Sa 12:4
lie waste, the *w* man ceaseth..................... Is 33:8
the *w* men, though fools, shall................... Is 35:8
a lodging place of *w* men............................ Jer 9:2
as a *w* man that turneth aside to............. Jer 14:8

WAYMARKS

Set thee up *w*, make thee high.............. Jer 31:21

WAYS

rise up early, and go on your *w*................ Gen 19:2
w hide their eyes from the man............... Lev 20:4
your hair shall be desolate......................... Lev 26:22
But if he shall any *w* make them........... Num 30:15
Ye shall walk in all the *w* which............. Deut 5:33
LORD thy God, to walk in his *w*.............. Deut 8:6
thy God, to walk in all his *w*................... Deut 10:12
your God, to walk in all his *w*................. Deut 11:22
thy God, and to walk ever in his *w*........ Deut 19:9
be thy God, and to walk in his *w*............ Deut 26:17
way, and flee before thee seven *w*.......... Deut 28:7
LORD thy God, and walk in his *w*........... Deut 28:9
them, and flee seven *w* before them....... Deut 28:25
thou shalt not prosper in thy *w*.............. Deut 28:29
LORD thy God, to walk in his *w*.............. Deut 30:16
for all his *w* are judgment...................... Deut 32:4
your God, and to walk in all his *w*......... Josh 22:5
And his sons walked not in his *w*............ 1Sa 8:3
and thy sons walk not in thy *w*............... 1Sa 8:5
himself wisely in all his *w*...................... 1Sa 18:14
For I have kept the *w* of the LORD 2Sa 22:22
LORD thy God, to walk in his *w*.............. 1Kin 2:3
And if thou wilt walk in my *w*................ 1Kin 3:14
to every man according to his *w*............. 1Kin 8:39
unto him, to walk in all his *w*................. 1Kin 8:58
have not walked in my *w*......................... 1Kin 11:33
thee, and wilt walk in my *w*.................... 1Kin 11:38
in all the *w* of Asa his father................. 1Kin 22:43
saying, Turn ye from your evil *w*........... 2Kin 17:13
man according unto all his *w*................... 2Chr 6:30
may fear thee, to walk in thy *w*.............. 2Chr 6:31
face, and turn from their wicked *w*......... 2Chr 7:14
of the acts of Abijah, and his *w*............. 2Chr 13:22
the first *w* of his father David................ 2Chr 17:3
lifted up in the *w* of the LORD................ 2Chr 17:6
the *w* of Jehoshaphat his father.............. 2Chr 21:12
nor in the *w* of Asa king of Judah.......... 2Chr 21:12
in the *w* of the house of Ahab................. 2Chr 22:3
his *w* before the LORD his God............... 2Chr 27:6
Jotham, and all his wars, and his *w*........ 2Chr 27:7
For he walked in the *w* of the................. 2Chr 28:2
rest of his acts and of all his *w*............... 2Chr 28:26
the nations of those lands any *w*............. 2Chr 32:13
walked in the *w* of David his.................. 2Chr 34:2
hope, and the uprightness of thy *w*......... Job 4:6
maintain mine own *w* before him............ Job 13:15
desire not the knowledge of thy *w*.......... Job 21:14
that thou makest thy *w* perfect............... Job 22:3
the light shall shine upon thy *w*............. Job 22:28
they know not the *w* thereof................... Job 24:13
yet his eyes are upon their *w*.................. Job 24:23
Lo, these are parts of his *w*..................... Job 26:14
the me *w* of their destruction.................. Job 30:12
Doth not he see my *w*, and count........... Job 31:4
man to find according to his *w*............... Job 34:11
his eyes are upon the *w* of man.............. Job 34:21
would not consider any of his *w*............. Job 34:27
He is the chief of the *w* of God.............. Job 40:19
His *w* are always grievous....................... Ps 10:5
For I have kept the *w* of the LORD .... Ps 18:21
Shew me thy *w*, O LORD........................... Ps 25:4
I said, I will take heed to my *w*.............. Ps 39:1
I will teach transgressors thy *w*............. Ps 51:13
me, and Israel had walked in my *w*......... Ps 81:13
in whose heart are the *w* of them........... Ps 84:5
thee, to keep thee in all thy *w*................ Ps 91:11
and they have not known my *w*............... Ps 95:10
He made known his *w* unto Moses.......... Ps 103:7
they walk in his *w*.................................... Ps 119:3
O that my *w* were directed to keep........ Ps 119:5
and have respect unto thy *w*................... Ps 119:15
I have declared my *w*, and thou............. Ps 119:26
I thought on my *w*, and turned my......... Ps 119:59
for all my *w* are before thee................... Ps 119:168
turn aside unto their crooked *w*............. Ps 125:5
that walketh in his *w*............................... Ps 128:1
shall sing in the *w* of the LORD.............. Ps 138:5
and art acquainted with all my *w*........... Ps 139:3
LORD is righteous in all his *w*................ Ps 145:17
So are the *w* of every one that is........... Prov 1:19
to walk in the *w* of darkness................... Prov 2:13
Whose *w* are crooked, and they.............. Prov 2:15
In all thy *w* acknowledge him, and........ Prov 3:6
Her *w* are *w* of pleasantness.................. Prov 3:17
and choose none of his *w*........................ Prov 3:31
let all thy *w* be established..................... Prov 4:26
her *w* are moveable, that thou................ Prov 5:6
For the *w* of man are before the............. Prov 5:21

consider her *w*, and be wise.................... Prov 6:6
not thine heart decline to her *w*............. Prov 7:25
blessed are they that keep my *w*............. Prov 8:32
who go right on their *w*........................... Prov 9:15
perverteth his *w* shall be known............ Prov 10:9
perverse in his *w* despiseth him............. Prov 14:2
end thereof are the *w* of death............... Prov 14:12
shall be filled with his own *w*................. Prov 14:14
All the *w* of a man are clean in.............. Prov 16:2
When a man's *w* please the LORD.......... Prov 16:7
end thereof are the *w* of death............... Prov 16:25
to pervert the *w* of judgment................. Prov 17:23
he that despiseth his *w* shall die........... Prov 19:16
Lest thou learn his *w*, and get a............. Prov 22:25
and let thine eyes observe my *w*............. Prov 23:26
than he that is perverse in his *w*............ Prov 28:6
in his *w* shall fall at once....................... Prov 28:18
women, nor thy *w* to that which............. Prov 31:3
well to the *w* of her household............... Prov 31:27
walk in the *w* of thine heart, and........... Eccl 11:9
In the broad *w* I will seek him............... Song 3:2
and he will teach us of his *w*.................. Is 2:3
for they would not walk in his *w*............ Is 42:24
and I will direct all his *w*....................... Is 45:13
They shall feed in the *w*, and.................. Is 49:9
neither are your *w* my *w*...................... Is 55:8
so are my *w* higher than your *w*.......... Is 55:9
I have seen his *w*, and will heal.............. Is 57:18
me daily, and delight to know my *w*....... Is 58:2
honour him, not doing thine own *w*........ Is 58:13
thou made us to err from thy *w*.............. Is 63:17
those that remember thee in thy *w*......... Is 64:5
Yea, they have chosen their own *w*......... Is 66:3
swift dromedary traversing her *w*........... Jer 2:23
also taught the wicked ones thy *w*.......... Jer 2:33
In the *w* hast thou sat for them,............ Jer 3:13
hast scattered thy *w* to the..................... Jer 3:13
saith the LORD, Stand ye in the *w*......... Jer 6:16
the God of Israel, Amend your *w*........... Jer 7:3
For if ye throughly amend your *w*.......... Jer 7:5
walk ye in all the *w* that I have............. Jer 7:23
learn the *w* of my people, to.................. Jer 12:16
they return not from their *w*................... Jer 15:7
mine eyes are upon all their *w*............... Jer 16:17
give every man according to his *w*......... Jer 17:10
from his evil way, and make your *w*....... Jer 18:11
in their *w* from the ancient paths........... Jer 18:15
as slippery *w* in the darkness.................. Jer 23:12
Therefore now amend your *w*.................. Jer 26:13
upon all the *w* of the sons of men.......... Jer 32:19
give every one according to his *w*.......... Jer 32:19
The *w* of Zion do mourn, because.......... Lam 1:4
inclosed my *w* with hewn stone............. Lam 3:9
He hath turned aside my *w*..................... Lam 3:11
Let us search and try our *w*.................... Lam 3:40
judge thee according to thy *w*................ Eze 7:3
I will recompense thy *w* upon thee........ Eze 7:4
judge thee according to thy *w*................ Eze 7:8
thee according to thy *w* and thine.......... Eze 7:9
comfort you, when ye see their *w*.......... Eze 14:22
thou not walked after their *w*................. Eze 16:47
more than they in all thy *w*..................... Eze 16:47
Then thou shalt remember thy *w*............ Eze 16:61
that thou should return from his *w*........ Eze 18:23
are not your *w* unequal........................... Eze 18:25
of Israel, are not my *w* equal................. Eze 18:29
are not your *w* unequal........................... Eze 18:29
every one according to his *w*.................. Eze 18:30
And there shall ye remember your *w*...... Eze 20:43
not according to your wicked *w*.............. Eze 20:44
son of man, appoint thee two *w*.............. Eze 21:19
the way, at the head of the two *w*.......... Eze 21:21
according to thy *w*, and according......... Eze 24:14
Thou wast perfect in thy *w* from............ Eze 28:15
turn ye, turn ye from your evil *w*........... Eze 33:11
judge you every one after his *w*............. Eze 33:20
shall ye remember your own evil *w*........ Eze 36:31
and confounded for your own *w*............. Eze 36:32
are truth, and his *w* judgment............... Dan 4:37
breath is, and whose are all thy *w*.......... Dan 5:23
and I will punish them for their *w*......... Hos 4:9
a snare of a fowler in all his *w*.............. Hos 9:8
punish Jacob according to his *w*............ Hos 12:2
for the *w* of the LORD are right,............ Hos 14:9
shall march every one on his *w*.............. Joel 2:7
and he will teach us of his *w*.................. Mic 4:2
against another in the broad *w*................ Nah 2:4
his *w* are everlasting................................ Hab 3:6
Consider your *w*.. Hag 1:5
Consider your *w*.. Hag 1:7
Turn ye now from your evil *w*................ Zec 1:4
to do unto us, according to our *w*........... Zec 1:6
If thou wilt walk in my *w*....................... Zec 3:7
as ye have not kept my *w*, but............... Mal 2:9
went their *w* into the city, and.............. Mt 8:33
made light of it, and went their *w*......... Mt 22:5
in a place where two *w* met.................... Mk 11:4
face of the Lord to prepare his *w*........... Lk 1:76
the rough *w* shall be made smooth......... Lk 3:5
Go your *w*... Lk 10:3
go your *w* out into the streets of............ Lk 10:10
went their *w* to the Pharisees................. Jn 11:46
made known to me the *w* of life............. Acts 2:28
pervert the right *w* of the Lord.............. Acts 13:10
nations to walk in their own *w*............... Acts 14:16
and misery are in their *w*........................ Rom 3:16
his *w* past finding out.............................. Rom 11:33
of my *w* which be in Christ..................... 1Cor 4:17
and they have not known my *w*.............. Heb 3:10
man is unstable in all his *w*.................... Jas 1:8

the rich man fade away in his *w*............. Jas 1:11
shall follow their pernicious *w*................ 2Pet 2:2
just and true are thy *w*, thou King......... Rev 15:3
to the seven angels, Go your *w*............... Rev 16:1

WAYSIDE

sat upon a seat by the *w* watching......... 1Sa 4:13
they have spread a net by the *w*............. Ps 140:5

WE See PREFACE.

WEAK

whether they be strong or *w*................... Num 13:18
never dried, then shall I be *w*................. Judg 16:7
were occupied, then shall I be *w*............ Judg 16:11
go from me, and I shall become *w*.......... Judg 16:17
And I am this day *w*, though................... 2Sa 3:39
w handed, and will make him afraid....... 2Sa 17:2
and let not your hands be *w*.................... 2Chr 15:7
hast strengthened the *w* hands............... Job 4:3
for I am *w*... Ps 6:2
My knees are *w* through fasting.............. Ps 109:24
Art thou also become *w* as we................ Is 14:10
Strengthen ye the *w* hands...................... Is 35:3
and all knees shall be *w* as water........... Eze 7:17
How *w* is thine heart, saith the.............. Eze 16:30
and all knees shall be *w* as water........... Eze 21:7
let the *w* say, I am strong....................... Joel 3:10
is willing, but the flesh is *w*................... Mt 26:41
is ready, but the flesh is *w*..................... Mk 14:38
ye ought to support the *w*....................... Acts 20:35
And being not *w* in faith, he.................. Rom 4:19
in that it was *w* through the................... Rom 8:3
Him that is *w* in the faith....................... Rom 14:1
another, who is *w*, eateth herbs.............. Rom 14:2
or is offended, or is made *w*................... Rom 14:21
to bear the infirmities of the *w*.............. Rom 15:1
God hath chosen the *w* things of............ 1Cor 1:27
we are *w*, but ye are strong.................... 1Cor 4:10
conscience being *w* is defiled................. 1Cor 8:7
stumblingblock to them that are *w*......... 1Cor 8:9
is *w* be emboldened to eat those............ 1Cor 8:10
shall the *w* brother perish....................... 1Cor 8:11
and wound their *w* conscience............... 1Cor 8:12
To the *w* became I as *w*........................ 1Cor 9:22
as *w*, that I might gain the *w*............... 1Cor 9:22
For this cause many are *w*....................... 1Cor 11:30
but his bodily presence is *w*................... 2Cor 10:10
reproach, as though we had been *w*........ 2Cor 11:21
Who is *w*, and I am not *w*..................... 2Cor 11:29
for when I am *w*, then am I strong......... 2Cor 12:10
in me, which to you-ward is not *w*......... 2Cor 13:3
For we also are *w* in him, but we........... 2Cor 13:4
For we are glad, when we are *w*............. 2Cor 13:9
God, how turn ye again to the *w*............ Gal 4:9
the feebleminded, support the *w*............ 1Th 5:14

WEAKEN

ground, which didst *w* the nations......... Is 14:12

WEAKENED

land w the hands of the people of............ Ezr 4:4
hands shall be *w* from the work............. Neh 6:9
He *w* my strength in the way................... Ps 102:23

WEAKENETH

w the strength of the mighty................... Job 12:21
for thus he *w* the hands of the............... Jer 38:4

WEAKER

house of Saul waxed *w* and *w*............... 2Sa 3:1
the wife, as unto the *w* vessel................. 1Pet 3:7

WEAKNESS

the *w* of God is stronger than men......... 1Cor 1:25
And I was with you in *w*, and in............. 1Cor 2:3
it is sown in *w*.. 1Cor 15:43
my strength is made perfect in *w*........... 2Cor 12:9
though he was crucified through *w*......... 2Cor 13:4
going before for the *w* and...................... Heb 7:18
out of *w* were made strong, waxed........ Heb 11:34

WEALTH

And all their *w*, and all their.................. Gen 34:29
mine hand hath gotten me this *w*............ Deut 8:17
that giveth thee power to get *w*.............. Deut 8:18
her husband's, a mighty man of............... Ruth 2:1
in all the *w* which God shall give........... 1Sa 2:32
even of all the mighty men of *w*............ 2Kin 15:20
and thou hast not asked riches, *w*.......... 2Chr 1:11
And I will give thee riches, and *w*......... 2Chr 1:12
their peace or their *w* for ever............... Ezr 9:12
seeking the *w* of his people, and........... Est 10:3
They spend their days in *w*...................... Job 21:13
I rejoiced because my *w* was great......... Job 31:25
not increase thy *w* by their price........... Ps 44:12
They that trust in their *w*....................... Ps 49:6
and leave their *w* to others..................... Ps 49:10
W and riches shall be in his house......... Ps 112:3
strangers be filled with thy *w*............... Prov 5:10
The rich man's *w* is his strong............... Prov 10:15
W gotten by vanity shall be.................... Prov 13:11
the *w* of the sinner is laid up.................. Prov 13:22
The rich man's *w* is his strong............... Prov 18:11
W maketh many friends........................... Prov 19:4
whom God hath given riches and *w*........ Eccl 5:19
to whom God hath given riches, *w*......... Eccl 6:2
the *w* of all the heathen round............... Zec 14:14
that by this craft we have our *w*............. Acts 19:25
own, but every man another's *w*............. 1Cor 10:24

WEALTHY

broughtest us out into a *w* place............. Ps 66:12
get you up unto the *w* nation.................. Jer 49:31

WEANED
And the child grew, and was w............ Gen 21:8
the same day that Isaac was w............ Gen 21:8
not go up until the child be w............ 1Sa 1:22
tarry until thou have w him............ 1Sa 1:23
gave her son suck until she w him............ 1Sa 1:23
And when she had w him, she took............ 1Sa 1:24
whom Tahpenes in Pharaoh's............ 1Kin 11:20
a child that is w of his mother............ Ps 131:2
my soul is even as a w child............ Ps 131:2
the w child shall put his hand on............ Is 11:8
them that are w from the milk............ Is 28:9
Now when she had w Lo-ruhamah............ Hos 1:8

WEAPON
smite him with an hand w of wood............ Num 35:18
shalt have a paddle upon thy w............ Deut 23:13
man having his w in his hand............ 2Chr 23:10
and with the other hand held a w............ Neh 4:17
He shall flee from the iron w............ Job 20:24
No w that is formed against thee............ Is 54:17
with his destroying w in his hand............ Eze 9:1
man a slaughter w in his hand............ Eze 9:2

WEAPONS
take, I pray thee, w, thy............ Gen 27:3
girded on every man his w of war............ Deut 1:41
men appointed with w of war............ Judg 18:11
men appointed with their w of war............ Judg 18:16
that were appointed with w of war............ Judg 18:17
brought my sword nor my w with me............ 1Sa 21:8
fallen, and the w of war perished............ 2Sa 1:27
every man with his w in his hand............ 2Kin 11:8
every man with his w in his hand............ 2Kin 11:11
every man with his w in his hand............ 2Chr 23:7
Wisdom is better than w of war............ Eccl 9:18
the w of his indignation, to............ Is 13:5
I will turn back the w of war............ Jer 21:4
thee, every one with his w............ Jer 22:7
forth the w of his indignation............ Jer 50:25
Thou art my battle ax and w of war............ Jer 51:20
down to hell with their w of war............ Eze 32:27
shall set on fire and burn the w............ Eze 39:9
they shall burn the w with fire............ Eze 39:10
with lanterns and torches and w............ Jn 18:3
(For the w of our warfare are not............ 2Cor 10:4

WEAR
Thou wilt surely w away, both............ Ex 18:18
The woman shall not w that which............ Deut 22:5
Thou shalt not w a garment of............ Deut 22:11
incense, to w an ephod before me............ 1Sa 2:28
persons that did w a linen ephod............ 1Sa 22:18
brought which the king useth to w............ Est 6:8
The waters w the stones............ Job 14:19
own bread, and w our own apparel............ Is 4:1
shall w out the saints of the............ Dan 7:25
neither shall they w a rough............ Zec 13:4
they that w soft clothing are in............ Mt 11:8
And when the day began to w away............ Lk 9:12

WEARETH
to him that w the gay clothing............ Jas 2:3

WEARIED
so that they w themselves to find............ Gen 19:11
offering, nor w thee with incense............ Is 43:23
thou hast w me with thine............ Is 43:24
Thou art w in the multitude of............ Is 47:13
Thou art w in the greatness of............ Is 57:10
for my soul is w because of............ Jer 4:31
the footmen, and they have w thee............ Jer 12:5
thou trustedst, they w thee............ Jer 12:5
She hath w herself with lies, and............ Eze 24:12
and wherein have I w thee............ Mic 6:3
Ye have w the LORD with your............ Mal 2:17
Yet ye say, Wherein have we w him............ Mal 2:17
being w with his journey, sat............ Jn 4:6
against himself, lest ye be w............ Heb 12:3

WEARIETH
by watering he w the thick cloud............ Job 37:11
the foolish w every one of them............ Eccl 10:15

WEARINESS
and much study is a w of the flesh............ Eccl 12:12
said also, Behold, what a w is it............ Mal 1:13
In w and painfulness, in watchings............ 2Cor 11:27

WEARING
priest in Shiloh, an ephod............ 1Sa 14:3
the crown of thorns, and the............ Jn 19:5
of w of gold, or of putting on of............ 1Pet 3:3

WEARISOME
w nights are appointed to me............ Job 7:3

WEARY
I am w of my life because of the............ Gen 27:46
thee, when thou wast faint and w............ Deut 25:18
for he was fast asleep and w............ Judg 4:21
bread unto thy men that are w............ Judg 8:15
people that were with him, came w............ 2Sa 16:14
will come upon him while he is w............ 2Sa 17:2
said, The people is hungry, and w............ 2Sa 23:10
Philistines until his hand was w............ 2Sa 23:10
and there the w be at rest............ Job 3:17
My soul is w of my life............ Job 10:1
But now he hath made me w............ Job 16:7
not given water to the w to drink............ Job 22:7
I am w with my groaning............ Ps 6:6
thine inheritance, when it was w............ Ps 68:9
I am w of my crying............ Ps 69:3
neither be w of his correction............ Prov 3:11
lest he be w of thee, and so hate............ Prov 25:17

I am w to bear them............ Is 1:14
None shall be w nor stumble among............ Is 5:27
it a small thing for you to w men............ Is 7:13
but will ye w my God also............ Is 7:13
that Moab is w on the high place............ Is 16:12
ye may cause the w to rest............ Is 28:12
of a great rock in a w land............ Is 32:2
earth, fainteth not, neither is w............ Is 40:28
the youths shall faint and be w............ Is 40:30
they shall run, and not be w............ Is 40:31
but thou hast been w of me............ Is 43:22
they are a burden to the weary............ Is 46:1
a word in season to him that is w............ Is 50:4
seek her will not w themselves............ Jer 2:24
I am w with holding in............ Jer 6:11
w themselves to commit iniquity............ Jer 9:5
I am w with repenting............ Jer 15:6
I was w with forbearing, and I............ Jer 20:9
For I have satiated the w soul............ Jer 31:25
in the fire, and they shall be w............ Jer 51:58
and they shall be w............ Jer 51:64
the people shall w themselves............ Hab 2:13
by her continual coming she w me............ Lk 18:5
And let us not be w in well doing............ Gal 6:9
brethren, be not w in well doing............ 2Th 3:13

WEASEL
the w, and the mouse, and the............ Lev 11:29

WEATHER
Fair w cometh out of the north............ Job 37:22
taketh away a garment in cold w............ Prov 25:20
ye say, It will be fair w............ Mt 16:2
morning, It will be foul w to day............ Mt 16:3

WEAVE
flax, and they that w networks............ Is 19:9
eggs, and w the spider's web............ Is 59:5

WEAVER
and in fine linen, and of the w............ Ex 35:35
I have cut off like a w my life............ Is 38:12

WEAVER'S
of his spear was like a w beam............ 1Sa 17:7
of whose spear was like a w beam............ 2Sa 21:19
hand was a spear like a w beam............ 1Chr 11:23
spear staff was like a w beam............ 1Chr 20:5
days are swifter than a w shuttle............ Job 7:6

WEAVEST
If thou w the seven locks of my............ Judg 16:13

WEB
seven locks of my head with the w............ Judg 16:13
pin of the beam, and with the w............ Judg 16:14
whose trust shall be a spider's w............ Job 8:14
eggs, and weave the spider's w............ Is 59:5

WEBS
Their w shall not become garments............ Is 59:6

WEDDING
them that were bidden to the w............ Mt 22:3
The w is ready, but they which............ Mt 22:8
man which had not on a w garment............ Mt 22:11
in hither not having a w garment............ Mt 22:12
when he will return from the w............ Lk 12:36
thou art bidden of any man to a w............ Lk 14:8

WEDGE
a w of gold of fifty shekels............ Josh 7:21
the w of gold, and his sons, and............ Josh 7:24
a man than the golden w of Ophir............ Is 13:12

WEDLOCK
judge thee, as women that break w............ Eze 16:38

WEEDS
the w were wrapped about my head............ Jonah 2:5

WEEK
Fulfil her w, and we will give............ Gen 29:27
Jacob did so, and fulfilled her w............ Gen 29:28
the covenant with many for one w............ Dan 9:27
in the midst of the w he shall............ Dan 9:27
toward the first day of the w............ Mt 28:1
morning the first day of the w............ Mk 16:2
early the first day of the w............ Mk 16:9
I fast twice in the w, I give............ Lk 18:12
Now upon the first day of the w............ Lk 24:1
The first day of the w cometh............ Jn 20:1
being the first day of the w............ Jn 20:19
And upon the first day of the w............ Acts 20:7
Upon the first day of the w let............ 1Cor 16:2

WEEKS
thou shalt observe the feast of w............ Ex 34:22
then she shall be unclean two w............ Lev 12:5
the LORD, after your w be out............ Num 28:26
Seven w shalt thou number unto............ Deut 16:9
seven w from such time as thou............ Deut 16:9
of w unto the LORD thy God with a............ Deut 16:10
bread, and in the feast of w............ Deut 16:16
bread, and in the feast of w............ 2Chr 8:13
us the appointed w of the harvest............ Jer 5:24
Seventy w are determined upon thy............ Dan 9:24
the Prince shall be seven w............ Dan 9:25
and threescore and two w............ Dan 9:25
two w shall Messiah be cut off............ Dan 9:26
Daniel was mourning three full w............ Dan 10:2
till three whole w were fulfilled............ Dan 10:3

WEEP
mourn for Sarah, and to w for her............ Gen 23:2
and he sought where to w............ Gen 43:30

w throughout their families............ Num 11:10
for they w unto me, saying, Give............ Num 11:13
aileth the people that they w............ 1Sa 11:5
until they had no more power to w............ 1Sa 30:4
over Saul, who clothed you in............ 2Sa 1:24
w for the child, while it was............ 2Sa 12:21
rend thy clothes, and w before me............ 2Chr 34:27
mourn not, nor w............ Neh 8:9
and his widows shall not w............ Job 27:15
Did not I w for him that was in............ Job 30:25
into the voice of them that w............ Job 30:31
A time to w, and a time to laugh............ Eccl 3:4
to Dibon, the high places, to w............ Is 15:2
I will w bitterly, labour not to............ Is 15:5
thou shalt w no more............ Is 30:19
of peace shall w bitterly............ Is 33:7
of tears, that I might w day............ Jer 9:1
my soul shall w in secret places............ Jer 13:17
and mine eyes shall w sore, and run............ Jer 13:17
W ye not for the dead, neither............ Jer 22:10
but w sore for him that goeth............ Jer 22:10
I will w for thee with the............ Jer 48:32
For these things I w............ Lam 1:16
neither shalt thou mourn nor w............ Eze 24:16
ye shall not mourn nor w............ Eze 24:23
they shall w for thee with............ Eze 27:31
Awake, ye drunkards, and w............ Joel 1:5
w between the porch and the altar............ Joel 2:17
it not at Gath, w ye not at all............ Mic 1:10
Should I w in the fifth month............ Zec 7:3
them, Why make ye this ado, and w............ Mk 5:39
Blessed are ye that w now............ Lk 6:21
for ye shall mourn and w............ Lk 6:25
on her, and said unto her, W not............ Lk 7:13
but he said, W not............ Lk 8:52
w not for me, but w for............ Lk 23:28
goeth unto the grave to w there............ Jn 11:31
I say unto you, That ye shall w............ Jn 16:20
Paul answered, What mean ye to w............ Acts 21:13
rejoice, and w with them that w............ Rom 12:15
And they that w, as though they............ 1Cor 7:30
Be afflicted, and mourn, and w............ Jas 4:9
Go to now, ye rich men, w............ Jas 5:1
the elders saith unto me, W not............ Rev 5:5
merchants of the earth shall w............ Rev 18:11

WEEPEST
to her, Hannah, why w thou............ 1Sa 1:8
say unto her, Woman, why w thou............ Jn 20:13
saith unto her, Woman, why w thou............ Jn 20:15

WEEPETH
was told Joab, Behold, the king w............ 2Sa 19:1
And Hazael said, Why w my lord............ 2Kin 8:12
He that goeth forth and w, bearing............ Ps 126:6
She w sore in the night, and her............ Lam 1:2

WEEPING
who were w before the door of the............ Num 25:6
so the days of w and mourning for............ Deut 34:8
her along w behind her to Bahurim............ 2Sa 3:16
they went up, w as they went up............ 2Sa 15:30
the noise of the w of the people............ Ezr 3:13
and when he had confessed, w............ Ezr 10:1
among the Jews, and fasting, and w............ Est 4:3
My face is foul with w, and on my............ Job 16:16
LORD hath heard the voice of my w............ Ps 6:8
bread, and mingled my drink with w............ Ps 102:9
one shall howl, w abundantly............ Is 15:3
Luhith with w shall they go up............ Is 15:5
I will bewail with the w of Jazer............ Is 16:9
the Lord GOD of hosts call to w............ Is 22:12
the voice of w shall be no more............ Is 65:19
was heard upon the high places, w............ Jer 3:21
the mountains will I take up a w............ Jer 9:10
They shall come with w, and with............ Jer 31:9
Ramah, lamentation, and bitter w............ Jer 31:15
Rahel w for her children refused............ Jer 31:15
Refrain thy voice from w, and............ Jer 31:16
meet them, w all along as he went............ Jer 41:6
of Luhith continual w shall go up............ Jer 48:5
weep for them with the w of Jazer............ Jer 48:32
of Judah together, going and w............ Jer 50:4
sat women w for Tammuz............ Eze 8:14
heart, and with fasting, and w............ Joel 2:12
of the LORD with tears, with w............ Mal 2:13
a voice heard, lamentation, and w............ Mt 2:18
Rachel w for her children, and............ Mt 2:18
there shall be w and gnashing of............ Mt 8:12
there shall be w and gnashing of............ Mt 22:13
there shall be w and gnashing of............ Mt 24:51
there shall be w and gnashing of............ Mt 25:30
And stood at his feet behind him w............ Lk 7:38
There shall be w and gnashing of............ Lk 13:28
When Jesus therefore saw her w............ Jn 11:33
the Jews also w which came with............ Jn 11:33
stood without at the sepulchre w............ Jn 20:11
and all the widows stood by w............ Acts 9:39
you often, and now tell you even w............ Phil 3:18
for the fear of her torment, w............ Rev 18:15
dust on their heads, and cried, w............ Rev 18:19

WEIGH
found it to us a talent of gold............ 1Chr 20:2
until ye w them before the chief............ Ezr 8:29
ye w the violence of your hands............ Ps 58:2
dost w the path of the just............ Is 26:7
w silver in the balance, and hire............ Is 46:6
then take thee balances to w............ Eze 5:1

W

WEIGHED

Abraham w to Ephron the silver,	Gen 23:16
the silver vessels w two thousand	Num 7:85
and by him actions are w	1Sa 2:3
his spear's head w six hundred	1Sa 17:7
he w the hair of his head at two	2Sa 14:26
the weight of whose spear w three	2Sa 21:16
w unto them the silver, and the,	Ezr 8:25
I even w unto their hand six	Ezr 8:26
the vessels w in the house of our	Ezr 8:33
O that my grief were throughly w	Job 6:2
silver be w for the price thereof	Job 28:15
Let me be w in an even balance,	Job 31:6
w the mountains in scales, and the	Is 40:12
w him the money, even seventeen	Jer 32:9
w him the money in the balances,	Jer 32:10
Thou art w in the balances, and	Dan 5:27
So they w for my price thirty	Zec 11:12

WEIGHETH

he w the waters by measure	Job 28:25
but the LORD w the spirits	Prov 16:2

WEIGHING

charger of silver w an hundred	Num 7:85
w ten shekels apiece, after the	Num 7:86

WEIGHT

golden earring of half a shekel w	Gen 24:22
hands of ten shekels w of gold	Gen 24:22
of his sack, our money in full w	Gen 43:21
of each shall there be a like w	Ex 30:34
in judgment, in meteyard, in w	Lev 19:35
deliver you your bread again by w	Lev 26:26
the w whereof was an hundred and,	Num 7:13
the w whereof was an hundred and	Num 7:19
the w whereof was an hundred and	Num 7:25
charger of the w of an hundred	Num 7:31
the w whereof was an hundred and	Num 7:37
charger of the w of an hundred	Num 7:43
the w whereof was an hundred and	Num 7:49
charger of the w of an hundred	Num 7:55
the w whereof was an hundred and	Num 7:61
the w whereof was an hundred and	Num 7:67
the w whereof was an hundred and	Num 7:73
the w whereof was an hundred and	Num 7:79
shalt have a perfect and just w	Deut 25:15
wedge of gold of fifty shekels w	Josh 7:21
w of the golden earrings that	Judg 8:26
the w of the coat was the	1Sa 17:5
the w whereof was a talent of	2Sa 12:30
shekels after the king's w	2Sa 14:26
the w of whose spear weighed	2Sa 21:16
hundred shekels of brass in w	2Sa 21:16
neither was the w of the brass.	1Kin 7:47
Now the w of gold that came to	1Kin 10:14
all these vessels was without w	2Kin 25:16
six hundred shekels of gold by w	1Chr 21:25
and brass in abundance without w	1Chr 22:3
and of brass and iron without w	1Chr 22:14
of gold by w for things of gold	1Chr 28:14
all instruments of silver by w	1Chr 28:14
Even the w for the candlesticks	1Chr 28:15
by w for every candlestick,	1Chr 28:15
the candlesticks of silver by w	1Chr 28:15
by w he gave gold for the tables	1Chr 28:16
he gave gold by w for every bason	1Chr 28:17
likewise silver by w for every	1Chr 28:17
of incense refined gold by w	1Chr 28:18
for the w of the nails were fifty	2Chr 3:9
for the w of the brass could not	2Chr 4:18
Now the w of gold that came to	2Chr 9:13
the Levites the w of the silver	Ezr 8:30
By number and by w of every one	Ezr 8:34
all the w was written at that	Ezr 8:34
To make the w for the winds	Job 28:25
but a just w is his delight	Prov 11:1
A just w and balance are the	Prov 16:11
the diverse vessels was without w	Jer 52:20
thou shalt eat bread by w to	Eze 4:10
and they shall eat bread by w	Eze 4:16
he cast the w of lead upon the	Zec 5:8
aloes, about an hundred pound w	Jn 19:39
exceeding and eternal w of glory	2Cor 4:17
let us lay aside every w	Heb 12:1
stone about the w of a talent	Rev 16:21

WEIGHTIER

have omitted the w matters of the	Mt 23:23

WEIGHTS

Just balances, just w, a just	Lev 19:36
not have in thy bag divers w	Deut 25:13
all the w of the bag are his work	Prov 16:11
Divers w, and divers measures,	Prov 20:10
Divers w are an abomination unto	Prov 20:23
and with the bag of deceitful w	Mic 6:11

WEIGHTY

A stone is heavy, and the sand w	Prov 27:3
For his letters, say they, are w	2Cor 10:10

WELFARE

And he asked them of their w	Gen 43:27
they asked each other of their w	Ex 18:7
king David, to enquire of his w	1Chr 18:10
the w of the children of Israel	Neh 2:10
my w passeth away as a cloud	Job 30:15
should have been for their w	Ps 69:22
seeketh not the w of this people	Jer 38:4

WELL

If thou doest w, shalt thou not	Gen 4:7
and if thou doest not w, sin lieth	Gen 4:7
that it may be w with me for thy	Gen 12:13
he entreated Abram w for her sake	Gen 12:16
that it was w watered every where	Gen 13:10
Wherefore the w was called	Gen 16:14
were old and w stricken in age,	Gen 18:11
her eyes, and she saw a w of water	Gen 21:19
Abimelech because of a w of water	Gen 21:25
me, that I have digged this w	Gen 21:30
was old, and w stricken in age	Gen 24:1
down without the city by a w of	Gen 24:11
I stand here by the w of water	Gen 24:13
and she went down to the w	Gen 24:16
again unto the w to draw water	Gen 24:20
ran out unto the man, unto the w	Gen 24:29
he stood by the camels at the w	Gen 24:30
And I came this day unto the w	Gen 24:42
Behold, I stand by the w of water	Gen 24:43
and she went down unto the w	Gen 24:45
from the way of the w Lahai-roi	Gen 24:62
and Isaac dwelt by the w Lahai-roi	Gen 25:11
found there a w of springing	Gen 26:19
he called the name of the w Esek	Gen 26:20
And they digged another w, and	Gen 26:21
from thence, and digged another w	Gen 26:22
there Isaac's servants digged a w	Gen 26:25
the w which they had digged	Gen 26:32
behold a w in the field, and, lo,	Gen 29:2
for out of that w they watered	Gen 29:2
And he said unto them, Is he w	Gen 29:6
And they said, He is w	Gen 29:6
was beautiful and w favoured	Gen 29:17
and I will deal w with thee	Gen 32:9
whether it be w with thy brethren	Gen 37:14
and w with the flocks	Gen 37:14
a goodly person, and w favoured	Gen 39:6
me when it shall be w with thee	Gen 40:14
the river seven w favoured kine	Gen 41:2
did eat up the seven w favoured	Gen 41:4
kine, fatfleshed and w favoured	Gen 41:18
and said, Is your father w	Gen 43:27
and it pleased Pharaoh w, and his	Gen 45:16
even a fruitful bough by a w	Gen 49:22
God dealt w with the midwives	Ex 1:20
and he sat down by a w	Ex 2:15
I know that he can speak w	Ex 4:14
And Moses said, Thou hast spoken w	Ex 10:29
as w the stranger, as he that is	Ex 12:49
as w for the stranger, as for one	Lev 24:22
for it was w with us in Egypt	Num 11:18
for we are w able to overcome it	Num 13:30
that is the w whereof the LORD	Num 21:16
sang this song, Spring up, O w	Num 21:17
The princes digged the w, the	Num 21:18
not drink of the waters of the w	Num 21:22
of the sons of Joseph hath said w	Num 36:5
hear the small as w as the great	Deut 1:17
And the saying pleased me w	Deut 1:23
as w as unto you, and until they	Deut 3:20
day, that it may go w with thee	Deut 4:40
maidservant may rest as w as thou	Deut 5:14
and that it may go w with thee,	Deut 5:16
they have w said all that they	Deut 5:28
that it might be w with them	Deut 5:29
and that it may be w with thee	Deut 5:33
that it may be w with thee	Deut 6:3
that it may be w with thee	Deut 6:18
but shalt w remember what the	Deut 7:18
that it may go w with thee	Deut 12:25
thee, that it may go w with thee	Deut 12:28
house, because he is w with thee	Deut 15:16
They have w spoken that which	Deut 18:17
that it may go w with thee	Deut 19:13
heart faint as w as his heart	Deut 20:8
that it may be w with thee	Deut 22:7
as w the stranger, as he that was	Josh 8:33
went out to the w of waters of	Josh 18:15
and pitched beside the w of Harod	Judg 7:1
if ye have dealt w with Jerubbaal	Judg 9:16
for she pleaseth me w	Judg 14:3
and she pleased Samson w	Judg 14:7
as w the men of every city, as	Judg 20:48
thee, that it may be w with thee	Ruth 3:1
thee the part of a kinsman, w	Ruth 3:13
said Saul to his servant, W said	1Sa 16:17
with his hand, and thou shalt be w	1Sa 16:16
me now a man that can play w	1Sa 16:17
so Saul was refreshed, and was w	1Sa 16:23
it pleased David w to be the	1Sa 18:26
came to a great w that is in	1Sa 19:22
If he say thus, It is w	1Sa 20:7
that thou hast dealt w with me	1Sa 24:18
enemy, will he let him go w away	1Sa 24:19
I know w that thou shalt surely	1Sa 24:20
shalt have dealt w with my lord	1Sa 25:31
And he said, W	2Sa 3:13
him again from the w of Sirah	2Sa 3:26
as w the women as men, to	2Sa 6:19
devoureth one as w as another	2Sa 11:25
And the saying pleased Absalom w	2Sa 17:4
which had a w in his court	2Sa 17:18
that they came up out of the w	2Sa 17:21
and said unto the king, All is w	2Sa 18:28
day, then it had pleased thee w	2Sa 19:6
the water of the w of Beth-lehem	2Sa 23:15
water out of the w of Beth-lehem	2Sa 23:16
And Bath-sheba said, W	1Kin 1:16
thou didst w that it was in thine	1Kin 8:18
answered and said, It is w spoken	1Kin 18:24
And she said, It shall be w	2Kin 4:23
say unto her, Is it w with thee	2Kin 4:26
is it w with thy husband	2Kin 4:26
is it w with the child	2Kin 4:26
And she answered, It is w	2Kin 4:26
to meet him, and said, Is all w	2Kin 5:21
And he said, All is w	2Kin 5:22
said one to another, We do not w	2Kin 7:9
and one said unto him, Is all w	2Kin 9:11
Because thou hast done w in	2Kin 10:30
and it shall be w with you	2Kin 25:24
the water of the w of Beth-lehem	1Chr 11:17
water out of the w of Beth-lehem,	1Chr 11:18
as w the small as the great, the	1Chr 25:8
as w the small as the great,	1Chr 26:13
thou didst w in that it was in	2Chr 6:8
and also in Judah things were w	2Chr 12:12
as w to the great as to the small	2Chr 31:15
valley, even before the dragon w	Neh 2:13
I have understanding as w as you	Job 12:3
Mark w, O Job, hearken unto me	Job 33:31
Mark ye w her bulwarks, consider	Ps 48:13
when thou doest w to thyself	Ps 49:18
my steps had w nigh slipped	Ps 73:2
So they did eat, and were w filled	Ps 78:29
the valley of Baca make it a w	Ps 84:6
As w the singers as the players	Ps 87:7
Thou hast dealt w with thy	Ps 119:65
be, and it shall be w with thee	Ps 128:2
and that my soul knoweth right w	Ps 139:14
running waters out of thine own w	Prov 5:15
of a righteous man is as w of life	Prov 10:11
When it goeth w with the	Prov 11:10
but with the w advised is wisdom	Prov 13:10
man looketh w to his going	Prov 14:15
Then I saw, and considered it w	Prov 24:32
flocks, and look w to thy herds	Prov 27:23
There be three things which go w	Prov 30:29
She looketh w to the ways of her	Prov 31:27
be w with them that fear God	Eccl 8:12
it shall not be w with the wicked	Eccl 8:13
of a living waters, and streams	Song 4:15
Learn to do w	Is 1:17
that it shall be w with him	Is 3:10
instead of w are hair baldness	Is 3:24
of wines on the lees w refined	Is 25:6
they could not w strengthen their	Is 33:23
The LORD is w pleased for his	Is 42:21
LORD unto me, Thou hast w seen	Jer 1:12
you, that it may be w unto you	Jer 7:23
it shall be w with thy remnant	Jer 15:11
thee w in the time of evil	Jer 15:11
and then it was w with him	Jer 22:15
then it was w with him	Jer 22:16
so it shall be w unto thee	Jer 38:20
look w to him, and do him no harm	Jer 39:12
and I will look w unto thee	Jer 40:4
and it shall be w with you	Jer 40:9
that it may be w with us, when we	Jer 42:6
we plenty of victuals, and were w	Jer 44:17
bones under it, and make it boil w	Eze 24:5
consume the flesh, and spice it w	Eze 24:10
can play w on an instrument	Eze 33:32
said unto me, Son of man, mark w	Eze 44:5
mark w the entering in of the	Eze 44:5
inherit it, one as w as another	Eze 47:14
but favoured, and skilful in all	Dan 1:4
which I have made;	Dan 3:15
LORD, Doest thou w to be angry	Jonah 4:4
Doest thou w to be angry for the	Jonah 4:9
I do w to be angry, even unto	Jonah 4:9
these days to do w unto Jerusalem	Zec 8:15
Son, in whom I am w pleased	Mt 3:17
to do w on the sabbath days	Mt 12:12
in whom my soul is w pleased	Mt 12:18
w did Esaias prophesy of you,	Mt 15:7
Son, in whom I am w pleased	Mt 17:5
W done, thou good and faithful	Mt 25:21
W done, good and faithful servant	Mt 25:23
Son, in whom I am w pleased	Mk 1:11
W hath Esaias prophesied of you	Mk 7:6
Full w ye reject the commandment	Mk 7:9
saying, He hath done all things w	Mk 7:37
that he had answered them w	Mk 12:28
And the scribe said unto him, W	Mk 12:32
both were now w stricken in years	Lk 1:7
my wife w stricken in years	Lk 1:18
in thee I am w pleased	Lk 3:22
when all men shall speak w of you	Lk 6:26
And if it bear fruit, w	Lk 13:9
And he said unto him, W, thou good	Lk 19:17
said, Master, thou hast w said	Lk 20:39
and when men have w drunk, then	Jn 2:10
Now Jacob's w was there	Jn 4:6
his journey, sat thus on the w	Jn 4:6
to draw with, and the w is deep	Jn 4:11
father Jacob, which gave us the w	Jn 4:12
a w of water springing up into	Jn 4:14
said unto her, Thou hast w said	Jn 4:17
for thou hast w said that I have	Jn 4:18
Lord, if he sleep, he shall do w	Jn 11:12
and ye say w	Jn 13:13
but if w, why smitest thou me	Jn 18:23
thou hast w done that thou art	Acts 10:33
the Holy Ghost as w as we	Acts 10:47
ye keep yourselves, ye shall do w	Acts 15:29
Fare ye w	Acts 15:29
Which was w reported of by the	Acts 16:2
so wrong, as thou very w knewest	Acts 25:10
W spake the Holy Ghost by Esaias	Acts 28:25
in w doing seek for glory	Rom 2:7
W; because of unbelief	Rom 11:20

he will keep his virgin, doeth w...... 1Cor 7:37
giveth her in marriage doeth w...... 1Cor 7:38
as w as other apostles, and as the... 1Cor 9:5
of them God was not w pleased 1Cor 10:5
For thou verily givest thanks w 1Cor 14:17
As unknown, and yet w known........ 2Cor 6:9
ye might w bear with him................. 2Cor 11:4
zealously affect you, but not w...... Gal 4:17
Ye did run w..................................... Gal 5:7
And let us not be weary in w doing.. Gal 6:9
That it may be w with thee .... Eph 6:3
Notwithstanding ye have w done .... Phil 4:14
for this is w pleasing unto the......... Col 3:20
brethren, be not weary in w doing .. 2Th 3:13
One that ruleth w his own house 1Ti 3:4
children and their own houses w..... 1Ti 3:12
used the office of a deacon w.......... 1Ti 3:13
W reported of for good works......... 1Ti 5:10
Let the elders that rule w be............ 1Ti 5:17
at Ephesus, thou knowest very w..... 2Ti 1:18
and to please them w in all things.... Titus 2:9
preached, as w as unto them........... Heb 4:2
such sacrifices God is w pleased ..... Heb 13:16
thy neighbour as thyself, ye do w .... Jas 2:8
thou doest w .... Jas 2:19
for the praise of them that do w...... 1Pet 2:14
that with w doing ye may put to...... 1Pet 2:15
but if, when ye do w, and suffer 1Pet 2:20
ye are, as long as ye do w............... 1Pet 3:6
be so, that ye suffer for w doing...... 1Pet 3:17
of their souls to him in w doing....... 1Pet 4:19
Son, in whom I am w pleased.......... 2Pet 1:17
whereunto ye do w that ye take....... 2Pet 1:19
a godly sort, thou shalt do w........... 3Jn 6

WELLBELOVED
A bundle of myrrh is my w unto me.. Song 1:13
Now will I sing to my w a song of .... Is 5:1
My w hath a vineyard in a very .... Is 5:1
yet therefore one son, his w............ Mk 12:6
Salute my w Epaenetus, who is the... Rom 16:5
The elder unto the w Gaius............... 3Jn 1

WELLFAVOURED
of the whoredoms of the w harlot .... Nah 3:4

WELLPLEASING
a sacrifice acceptable, w to God...... Phil 4:18
you that which is w in his sight .... Heb 13:21

WELL'S
great stone was upon the w mouth... Gen 29:2
rolled the stone from the w mouth... Gen 29:3
upon the w mouth in his place......... Gen 29:3
roll the stone from the w mouth...... Gen 29:8
rolled the stone from the w mouth... Gen 29:10
a covering over the w mouth............ 2Sa 17:19

WELLS
For all the w which his father's .... Gen 26:15
Isaac digged again the w of water.... Gen 26:18
where were twelve w of water .... Ex 15:27
we drink of the water of the w .... Num 20:17
w digged, which thou diggedst not .. Deut 6:11
good tree, and stop all w of water ... 2Kin 3:19
they stopped all the w of water 2Kin 3:25
in the desert, and digged many w 2Chr 26:10
goods, w digged, vineyards, and...... Neh 9:25
water out of the w of salvation........ Is 12:3
These are w without water, clouds... 2Pet 2:17

WELLSPRING
Understanding is a w of life unto..... Prov 16:22
the w of wisdom as a flowing.......... Prov 18:4

WEN
broken, or maimed, or having a w.... Lev 22:22

WENCH
and a w went and told them.............. 2Sa 17:17

WENT See PREFACE.

WENTEST
because thou w up to thy father's ... Gen 49:4
when thou w out of Seir, when........ Judg 5:4
when thou w to fight with .... Judg 8:1
which thou w to seek are found 1Sa 10:2
with thee whithersoever thou w 2Sa 7:9
why w thou not with thy friend........ 2Sa 16:17
Wherefore w not thou with me,........ 2Sa 19:25
when thou w forth before thy .... Ps 68:7
even thither w thou up to offer........ Is 57:7
thou w to the king with ointment,... Is 57:9
when thou w after me in the............ Jer 2:2
even the way which thou w .... Jer 31:21
Thou w forth for the salvation of..... Hab 3:13
Thou w in to men uncircumcised,.... Acts 11:3

WEPT
him, and lift up her voice, and w..... Gen 21:16
And Esau lifted up his voice, and w.. Gen 27:38
and lifted up his voice, and w .... Gen 29:11
and they w .... Gen 33:4
Thus his father w for him .... Gen 37:35
himself about from them, and w ..... Gen 42:24
into his chamber, and w there .... Gen 43:30
And he w aloud................................ Gen 45:2
his brother Benjamin's neck, and w.. Gen 45:14
and Benjamin w upon his neck .... Gen 45:14
all his brethren, and w upon them.... Gen 45:15
w on his neck a good while .... Gen 46:29
w upon him, and kissed him............. Gen 50:1
Joseph w when they spake unto him.. Gen 50:17
and, behold, the babe w................... Ex 2:6

children of Israel also w again......... Num 11:4
for ye have w in the ears of the....... Num 11:18
have w before him, saying, Why...... Num 11:20
and the people w that night .... Num 14:1
ye returned and w before the LORD,.. Deut 1:45
the children of Israel w for .... Deut 34:8
lifted up their voice, and w .... Judg 2:4
And Samson's wife w before him..... Judg 14:16
she w before him the seven days,..... Judg 14:17
w before the LORD until even, and... Judg 20:23
came unto the house of God, and w.. Judg 20:26
lifted up their voices, and w .... Judg 21:2
they lifted up their voice, and w ...... Ruth 1:9
lifted up their voice, and w again .... Ruth 1:14
therefore she w, and did not eat...... 1Sa 1:7
prayed unto the LORD, and w sore ... 1Sa 1:10
lifted up their voices, and w 1Sa 11:4
w one with another, until David....... 1Sa 20:41
And Saul lifted up his voice, and w .. 1Sa 24:16
him lifted up their voice and w 1Sa 30:4
And they mourned, and w, and......... 2Sa 1:12
voice, and w at the grave of Abner .. 2Sa 3:32
and all the people w..................... 2Sa 3:32
all the people w again over him....... 2Sa 3:34
was yet alive, I fasted and w 2Sa 12:22
and lifted up their voice and w......... 2Sa 13:36
and all his servants w very sore 2Sa 13:36
all the country w with a loud........... 2Sa 15:23
w as he went up, and had his head... 2Sa 15:30
the chamber over the gate, and w 2Sa 18:33
and the man of God w 2Kin 8:11
w over his face, and said, O my 2Kin 13:14
And Hezekiah w sore 2Kin 20:3
rent thy clothes, and w before me ... 2Kin 22:19
their eyes, w with a loud voice......... Ezr 3:12
for the people w very sore............... Ezr 10:1
these words, that I sat down and w .. Neh 1:4
For all the people w, when they........ Neh 8:9
they lifted up their voice, and w ...... Job 2:12
When I w, and chastened my soul .... Ps 69:10
there we sat down, yea, we w .... Ps 137:1
And Hezekiah w .... Is 38:3
he w, and made supplication unto.... Hos 12:4
And he went out, and w bitterly....... Mt 26:75
seeth the tumult, and them that w ... Mk 5:38
And when he thought thereon, he w.. Mk 14:72
with him, as they mourned and w .... Mk 16:10
mourned to you, and ye have not w .. Lk 7:32
And all w, and bewailed her............. Lk 8:52
he beheld the city, and w over it,..... Lk 19:41
And Peter went out, and w bitterly... Lk 22:62
Jesus w .... Jn 11:35
and as she w, she stooped down, and.. Jn 20:11
And they all w sore, and fell on........ Acts 20:37
that weep, as though they w not 1Cor 7:30
I w much, because no man was........ Rev 5:4

WERE See PREFACE.

WERT
If thou w pure and upright .... Job 8:6
O that thou w as my brother, that .... Song 8:1
w graffed in among them, and with.. Rom 11:17
For if thou w cut out of the .... Rom 11:24
w graffed contrary to nature into .... Rom 11:24
I would thou w cold or hot............... Rev 3:15

WEST
he tent, having Beth-el on the w ...... Gen 12:8
thou shalt spread abroad to the w.... Gen 28:14
turned a mighty strong w wind,....... Ex 10:19
w side shall be hangings of fifty ...... Ex 27:12
for the w side were hangings of........ Ex 38:12
On the w side shall be the................ Num 2:18
this shall be your w border............... Num 34:6
on the w side two thousand cubits... Num 35:5
of the LORD, possess thou the w ...... Deut 33:23
and Ai, on the w side of Ai .... Josh 8:9
on the w side of the city.................. Josh 8:12
in wait on the w of the city .... Josh 8:13
and in the borders of Dor on the w .. Josh 11:2
Canaanite on the east and on the w.. Josh 11:3
on this side Jordan on the w .... Josh 12:7
the w border was to the great sea.... Josh 15:12
this was the w quarter..................... Josh 18:14
and the border went out on the w .... Josh 18:15
reacheth to Asher on the w side....... Josh 19:34
and three looking toward the w........ 1Kin 7:25
the porters, toward the east, w,....... 1Chr 9:24
toward the east, and toward the w.... 1Chr 12:15
and three looking toward the w 2Chr 4:4
w side of the city of David 2Chr 32:30
on the w side of Gihon, in the.......... 2Chr 33:14
from the east, nor from the w .... Ps 75:6
As far as the east is from the w .... Ps 103:12
from the east, and from the w.......... Ps 107:3
of the Philistines toward the w......... Is 11:14
east, and gather them from the w ..... Is 43:5
rising of the sun, and from the w ..... Is 45:6
from the north and from the w......... Is 49:12
the name of the LORD from the w ..... Is 59:19
the w was seventy cubits broad .... Eze 41:12
He turned about to the w side......... Eze 42:19
from the w side westward, and from.. Eze 45:7
from the w border unto the east....... Eze 45:7
The w side shall be the .... Eze 47:20
This is the w side............................ Eze 47:20
for these are his sides east and w .... Eze 48:1
the east side unto the w side........... Eze 48:2
east side even unto the w side......... Eze 48:3
the east side unto the w side........... Eze 48:4

east side even unto the w side......... Eze 48:6
the east side unto the w side........... Eze 48:7
the east side unto the w side........... Eze 48:8
the east side unto the w side........... Eze 48:8
toward the w ten thousand in........... Eze 48:10
the w side four thousand and five.... Eze 48:16
toward the w two hundred and fifty .. Eze 48:17
thousand toward the w border......... Eze 48:21
the east side unto the w side........... Eze 48:23
the east side unto the w side........... Eze 48:24
the east side unto the w side........... Eze 48:25
the east side unto the w side........... Eze 48:26
the east side unto the w side........... Eze 48:27
At the w side four thousand and...... Eze 48:34
an he goat came from the w on the... Dan 8:5
children shall tremble from the w..... Hos 11:10
country, and from the w country...... Zec 8:7
toward the east and toward the w .... Zec 14:4
shall come from the east and w .... Mt 8:11
east, and shineth even unto the w .... Mt 24:27
ye see a cloud rise out of the w .... Lk 12:54
come from the east, and from the w.. Lk 13:29
and lieth toward the south w .... Acts 27:12
and north w................................... Acts 27:12
and on the w three gates.................. Rev 21:13

WESTERN
And as for the w border, ye shall...... Num 34:6

WESTWARD
And southward, and eastward, and w.. Gen 13:14
w thou shalt make six boards .... Ex 26:22
tabernacle, for the two sides w .... Ex 26:27
tabernacle w he made six boards ..... Ex 36:27
of the tabernacle for the sides w ..... Ex 36:32
pitch behind the tabernacle w .... Num 3:23
Pisgah, and lift up thine eyes w .... Deut 3:27
were on the side of Jordan w .... Josh 5:1
before the valley of Hinnom w .... Josh 15:8
from Baalah w unto mount Seir ...... Josh 15:10
goeth down w to the coast of.......... Josh 16:3
Tappuah w unto the river Kanah...... Josh 16:8
went up through the mountains w .... Josh 18:12
and reacheth to Carmel w, and to.... Josh 19:26
coast turneth w to Azmoth-tabor..... Josh 19:34
brethren on this side Jordan w .... Josh 22:7
off, even unto the great sea w .... Josh 23:4
w Gezer, with the towns thereof...... 1Chr 7:28
and Hosah the lot came forth w........ 1Chr 26:16
At Parbar w, four at the causeway 1Chr 26:18
of Israel on this side Jordan w 1Chr 26:30
of the city, from the west side w ...... Eze 45:7
was a place on the two sides w......... Eze 47:17
eastward, and ten thousand w .... Eze 48:18
w over against the five and twenty ... Eze 48:21
save the ram pushing w, and .... Dan 8:4

WET
They are w with the showers of .... Job 24:8
let it be w with the dew of .... Dan 4:15
let it be w with the dew of .... Dan 4:23
they shall w them with the dew of ... Dan 4:25
his body was w with the dew of .... Dan 4:33
his body was w with the dew of .... Dan 5:21

WHALE
Am I a sea, or a w, that thou .... Job 7:12
thou art as a w in the seas .... Eze 32:2

WHALE'S
and three nights in the w belly .... Mt 12:40

WHALES
And God created great w, and every... Gen 1:21

WHAT See PREFACE.

WHATSOEVER
w Adam called every living.............. Gen 2:19
w creepeth upon the earth, after...... Gen 8:19
w thou hast in the city, bring........... Gen 19:12
w God hath said unto thee, do .... Gen 31:16
w they did there, he was the doer .... Gen 39:22
w openeth the womb among the ...... Ex 13:2
of his life w is laid upon him .... Ex 21:30
w toucheth the altar shall be .... Ex 29:37
w toucheth them shall be holy .... Ex 30:29
w uncleanness it be that a man........ Lev 5:3
do good, w it be that a man shall ..... Lev 5:4
W shall touch the flesh thereof .... Lev 6:27
W soul it be that eateth any .... Lev 7:27
W parteth the hoof, and is .... Lev 11:3
w hath fins and scales in the .... Lev 11:9
w hath no fins nor scales in the .... Lev 11:12
w goeth upon his paws, among all.... Lev 11:27
upon w any of them, when they are.. Lev 11:32
w vessel it be, wherein any work,..... Lev 11:32
w is in it shall be unclean .... Lev 11:33
W goeth upon the belly, and .... Lev 11:42
w goeth upon all four, or .... Lev 11:42
or w hath more feet among all .... Lev 11:42
or w thing of skin it be, which .... Lev 13:58
w she sitteth upon shall be .... Lev 15:6
W man there be of the house of....... Lev 17:8
w man there be of the house of....... Lev 17:10
w man there be of the children of .... Lev 17:13
For w man he be that hath a .... Lev 22:5
w uncleanness he hath .... Lev 22:5
W be of the house of Israel, ... Lev 22:18
But w hath a blemish, that shall ...... Lev 22:20
For w soul it be that shall not .... Lev 23:29
w soul it be that doeth any work,..... Lev 23:30
even of w passeth under the rod,..... Num 27:32
w any man giveth the priest, it .... Num 5:10

W

w is first ripe in the land,............... Num 18:13
w the unclean person toucheth....... Num 19:22
I will do as thou sayest unto me..... Num 22:17
w he sheweth me I will tell thee...... Num 23:3
then w proceeded out of her lips..... Num 30:12
nor unto w the LORD our God......... Deut 2:37
every man w is right in his own....... Deut 12:8
w thy soul lusteth after.................. Deut 12:15
flesh, w thy soul lusteth after......... Deut 12:20
gates w thy soul lusteth after......... Deut 12:21
w hath not fins and scales ye may... Deut 14:10
for w thy soul lusteth after............ Deut 14:26
or for w thy soul desireth.............. Deut 14:26
do thou unto us w seemeth good... Judg 10:15
that w cometh forth of the doors.... Judg 11:31
Do w seemeth good unto thee....... 1Sa 14:36
W thy soul desireth, I will even...... 1Sa 20:4
w cometh to thine hand unto thy... 1Sa 25:8
as w the king did pleased all the.... 2Sa 3:36
thy servants are ready to do w may... 2Sa 15:15
w thou shalt require of me, that..... 2Sa 19:38
w plague, w sickness.................... 1Kin 8:37
w she asked, beside that which...... 1Kin 10:13
that w is pleasant in thine eyes,...... 1Kin 20:6
w sore or w sickness.................... 2Chr 6:28
w she asked, beside that which...... 2Chr 9:12
w shall seem good to thee, and to... Ezr 7:18
w more shall be needful for the..... Ezr 7:20
that w Ezra the priest, the............ Ezr 7:21
W is commanded by the God of .... Ezr 7:23
w she desired was given her to go... Ezr 2:13
that they may do w he commandeth... Job 37:12
w is under the whole heaven is...... Job 41:11
and w he doeth shall prosper......... Ps 1:3
w passeth through the paths of ..... Ps 8:8
he hath done w he hath pleased..... Ps 115:3
W the LORD pleased, that did he.... Ps 135:6
w mine eyes desired I kept not...... Eccl 2:10
w God doeth, it shall be for ever.... Eccl 3:14
for w he doeth w pleaseth him....... Eccl 8:3
W thy hand findeth to do, do it.... Eccl 9:10
w I command thee thou shalt speak... Jer 1:7
that w thing the LORD said............ Jer 42:4
But we will certainly do w thing..... Jer 44:17
for w is more than these cometh..... Mt 5:37
Therefore all things w ye would..... Mt 7:12
into w city or town ye shall........... Mt 10:11
oath to give her w she would ask.... Mt 14:7
by w thou mightest be profited by... Mt 15:5
that w entereth in at the mouth...... Mt 15:17
w thou shalt bind on earth shall..... Mt 16:19
w thou shalt loose on earth shall... Mt 16:19
have done unto him w they listed... Mt 17:12
W ye shall bind on earth shall be... Mt 18:18
w ye shall loose on earth shall...... Mt 18:18
w is right I will give you.............. Mt 20:4
w is right, that shall ye receive...... Mt 20:7
w ye shall ask in prayer,............... Mt 21:22
All therefore w they bid you.......... Mt 23:3
all things w I have commanded you... Mt 28:20
the damsel, Ask of me w thou wilt... Mk 6:22
W thou shalt ask of me, I will........ Mk 6:23
by w thou mightest be profited by... Mk 7:11
that w thing from without............. Mk 7:18
have done unto him w they listed... Mk 9:13
sell w thou hast, and give to the.... Mk 10:21
do for us w we shall desire............ Mk 10:35
he shall have w he saith................ Mk 11:23
but w shall be given you in that..... Mk 13:11
we have heard done in Capernaum... Lk 4:23
w house ye enter into, there......... Lk 9:4
into w house ye enter, first say,..... Lk 10:5
into w city ye enter, and they........ Lk 10:8
But into w city ye enter, and they... Lk 10:10
w thou spendest more, when I come... Lk 10:35
Therefore w ye have spoken in...... Lk 12:3
W he saith unto you, do it............ Jn 2:5
made whole of w disease he had.... Jn 5:4
w thou wilt ask of God, God will.... Jn 11:22
w I speak therefore, even as the..... Jn 12:50
w ye shall ask in my name, that..... Jn 14:13
w I have said unto you................. Jn 14:26
friends, if ye do w I command you... Jn 15:14
that w ye shall ask of the Father.... Jn 15:16
but w he shall hear, that shall....... Jn 16:13
W ye shall ask the Father in my..... Jn 16:23
w thou hast given me are of these... Jn 17:7
things w he shall say unto you....... Acts 3:22
For to do w thy hand and thy........ Acts 4:28
for w is not of faith is sin............. Rom 14:23
For w things were written............. Rom 15:4
that ye assist her in w business..... Rom 16:2
W is sold in the shambles, that..... 1Cor 10:25
w is set before you, eat, asking..... 1Cor 10:27
or w ye do, do all to the glory....... 1Cor 10:31
(w they were, it maketh no matter... Gal 2:6
for w a man soweth, that shall he... Gal 6:7
for w doth make manifest is light... Eph 5:13
Knowing that w good thing any man... Eph 6:8
w things are true......................... Phil 4:8
w things are honest...................... Phil 4:8
w things are just.......................... Phil 4:8
w things are pure......................... Phil 4:8
w things are lovely....................... Phil 4:8
w things are of good report.......... Phil 4:8
in w state I am, therewith to be..... Phil 4:11
w ye do in word or deed, do all..... Col 3:17
w ye do, do it heartily, as to......... Col 3:23
w we ask, we receive of him......... 1Jn 3:22
For w is born of God overcometh... 1Jn 5:4

w we ask, we know that we have... 1Jn 5:15
thou doest faithfully w thou.......... 3Jn 5
w craft he be, shall be found......... Rev 18:22
neither w worketh abomination, or... Rev 21:27

WHEAT
went in the days of w harvest........ Gen 30:14
But the w and the w the were not... Ex 9:32
of the firstfruits of w harvest......... Ex 34:22
The best of the wine, and of the w... Num 18:12
A land of w, and barley, and vines,... Deut 8:8
with the fat of kidneys of w........... Deut 32:14
threshed w by the winepress.......... Judg 6:11
after, in the time of w harvest........ Judg 15:1
of barley harvest and of w harvest... Ruth 2:23
their w harvest in the valley........... 1Sa 6:13
Is it not w harvest to day.............. 1Sa 12:17
though they would have fetched w... 2Sa 4:6
basons, and earthen vessels, and w... 2Sa 17:28
of w for food to his household....... 1Kin 5:11
Now Ornan was threshing w........... 1Chr 21:20
the w for the meat offering............ 1Chr 21:23
thousand measures of beaten w..... 2Chr 2:10
Now therefore the w, and the........ 2Chr 2:15
and ten thousand measures of w..... 2Chr 27:5
offerings of the God of heaven, w... Ezr 6:9
and to an hundred measures of w... Ezr 7:22
Let thistles grow instead of w........ Job 31:40
also with the finest of the w.......... Ps 81:16
thee with the finest of the w.......... Ps 147:14
in a mortar among w with a pestle... Prov 27:22
heap of w set about with lilies....... Song 7:2
and cast in the principal w............ Is 28:25
They have sown w, but shall reap... Jer 12:13
What is the chaff to the w............. Jer 23:28
the goodness of the LORD, for w.... Jer 31:12
have creatures in the field, of w..... Jer 41:8
Take thou also unto the w............. Eze 4:9
traded in thy market w of Minnith... Eze 27:17
part of an ephah of an homer of w... Eze 45:13
O ye vinedressers, for the w.......... Joel 1:11
And the floors shall be full of w..... Joel 2:24
and ye take from him burdens of w... Amos 5:11
sabbath, that we may set forth w.... Amos 8:5
yea, and sell the refuse of the w.... Amos 8:6
gather his w into the garner.......... Mt 3:12
came and sowed tares among the w... Mt 13:25
ye root up also the w with them.... Mt 13:29
but gather the w into my barn....... Mt 13:30
will gather the w into his garner.... Lk 3:17
he said, An hundred measures of w... Lk 16:7
you, that he may sift you as w....... Lk 22:31
Except a corn of w fall into the..... Jn 12:24
and cast out the w into the sea..... Acts 27:38
bare grain, it may chance of w...... 1Cor 15:37
say, A measure of w for a penny.... Rev 6:6
wine, and oil, and fine flour, and w... Rev 18:13

WHEATEN
of w flour shalt thou make them.... Ex 29:2

WHEEL
and the height of a w was a cubit... 1Kin 7:32
was like the work of a chariot w.... 1Kin 7:33
O my God, make them like a w...... Ps 83:13
and bringeth the w over them........ Prov 20:26
or the w broken at the cistern....... Eccl 12:6
neither is a cart w turned about..... Is 28:27
break it with the w of his cart....... Is 28:28
behold one w upon the earth by.... Eze 1:15
were a w in the middle of a w....... Eze 1:16
one w by one cherub, and another... Eze 10:9
another w by another cherub......... Eze 10:9
as if a w had been in the midst...... Eze 10:10
had been in the midst of a w......... Eze 10:10
unto them in my hearing, O w....... Eze 10:13

WHEELS
And took off their chariot w........... Ex 14:25
Why tarry the w of his chariots..... Judg 5:28
And every base had four brasen w... 1Kin 7:30
And under the borders were four w... 1Kin 7:32
the axletrees of the w were.......... 1Kin 7:32
the work of the w was like the...... 1Kin 7:33
and their w like a whirlwind.......... Is 5:28
he wrought a work on the w.......... Jer 18:3
and at the rumbling of his w......... Jer 47:3
The appearance of the w and their... Eze 1:16
went, the w went by them............. Eze 1:19
the earth, the w were lifted up...... Eze 1:19
the w were lifted up over against... Eze 1:19
the living creature was in the w..... Eze 1:20
the w were lifted up over against... Eze 1:21
the living creature was in the w..... Eze 1:21
the noise of the w over against...... Eze 3:13
and said, Go in between the w....... Eze 10:6
Take fire from between the w........ Eze 10:6
he went in, and stood beside the w... Eze 10:6
looked, behold the four w by the... Eze 10:9
the appearance of the w was as..... Eze 10:9
hands, and their wings, and the w... Eze 10:16
even the w that they four had....... Eze 10:16
As for the w, it was cried unto..... Eze 10:13
went, the w went by them............. Eze 10:16
the same w also turned not from.... Eze 10:16
the w also were beside them,........ Eze 10:16
their wings, and the w beside them... Eze 11:22
thee with chariots, wagons, and w... Eze 23:24
of the horsemen, and of the.......... Eze 26:10
flame, and his w as burning fire..... Dan 7:9
noise of the rattling of the w........ Nah 3:2

WHELP
Judah is a lion's w...................... Gen 49:9
of Dan he said, Dan is a lion's w... Deut 33:22
old lion, walked, and the lion's w... Nah 2:11

WHELPS
bear robbed of her w in the field... 2Sa 17:8
the stout lion's w are scattered...... Job 4:11
The lion's w have not trodden it.... Job 28:8
a bear robbed of her w meet a man... Prov 17:12
they shall yell as lions'................. Jer 51:38
nourished her w among young lions... Eze 19:2
And she brought up one of her w... Eze 19:3
then she took another of her w...... Eze 19:5
a bear that is bereaved of her w.... Hos 13:8
tear in pieces enough for his w...... Nah 2:12

WHEN See PREFACE.

WHENCE
the ground from w he was taken.... Gen 3:23
Sarai's maid, w camest thou.......... Gen 16:8
unto the land from w thou camest... Gen 24:5
unto them, My brethren, w be ye.... Gen 29:4
and he said unto them, W come ye... Gen 42:7
W should I have flesh to give........ Num 11:13
from w thou mayest see them........ Num 23:13
Lest the land w thou broughtest..... Deut 9:28
from w ye came out, where thou,.... Deut 11:10
me, but I wist not w they were....... Josh 2:4
and from w came ye...................... Josh 9:8
unto the city from w he fled.......... Josh 20:6
but I asked him not w he was........ Judg 13:6
said unto him, W comest thou....... Judg 17:9
and w comest thou....................... Judg 19:17
men, whom I know not w they be... 1Sa 25:11
and w art thou............................ 1Sa 30:13
said unto him, From w comest thou... 2Sa 1:3
man that told him, W art thou....... 2Sa 1:13
unto him, W comest thou, Gehazi... 2Kin 5:25
help thee, w shall I help thee......... 2Kin 6:27
from w came they unto thee.......... 2Kin 20:14
From all places w ye shall return.... Neh 4:12
said unto Satan, W comest thou..... Job 1:7
unto Satan, From w comest thou.... Job 2:2
Before I go w I shall not return...... Job 10:21
go the way w I shall not return...... Job 16:22
W then cometh wisdom................. Job 28:20
the hills, from w cometh my help... Ps 121:1
the place from w the rivers come... Eccl 1:7
from w come the young and old lion... Is 30:6
from w came they unto thee.......... Is 39:3
shalt not know from w it riseth...... Is 47:11
look unto the rock w ye are hewn... Is 51:1
hole of the pit w ye are digged...... Is 51:1
bring you again into the place w.... Jer 29:14
and w comest thou....................... Jonah 1:8
w shall I seek comforters for........ Nah 3:7
into my house from w I came out... Mt 12:44
from w then hath it tares.............. Mt 13:27
W hath this man this wisdom, and... Mt 13:54
W then hath this man all these...... Mt 13:56
W should we have so much bread in... Mt 15:33
The baptism of John, w was it....... Mt 21:25
From w hath this man these things... Mk 6:2
From w can a man satisfy these..... Mk 8:4
and w is he then his son.............. Mk 12:37
w is this to me, that the mother.... Lk 1:43
return unto my house w I came out... Lk 11:24
unto you, I know you not w ye are... Lk 13:25
tell you, I know you not w ye are... Lk 13:27
that they could not tell w it was.... Lk 20:7
saith unto him, W knowest thou me... Jn 1:48
made wine, and knew not w it was... Jn 2:9
but canst not tell w it cometh....... Jn 3:8
from w then hast thou that living... Jn 4:11
W shall we buy bread, that these... Jn 6:5
Howbeit we know this man w he is... Jn 7:27
cometh, no man knoweth w he is... Jn 7:27
both know me, and w know w I am... Jn 7:28
for I know w I came, and whither I... Jn 8:14
but ye cannot tell w I come.......... Jn 8:14
fellow, we know not from w he is... Jn 9:29
that ye know not from w he is....... Jn 9:30
and saith unto Jesus, W art thou.... Jn 19:9
from w they had been recommended... Acts 14:26
from w also we look for the.......... Phil 3:20
that country from w they came out... Heb 11:15
from w also he received him in a... Heb 11:19
From w come wars and fightings.... Jas 4:1
therefore from w thou art fallen..... Rev 2:5
and w came they........................ Rev 7:13

WHENSOEVER
w the stronger cattle did............... Gen 30:41
w ye will ye may do them good..... Mk 14:7
W I take my journey into Spain, I... Rom 15:24

WHERE
land of Havilah, w there is gold..... Gen 2:11
and said unto him, W art thou...... Gen 3:9
unto Cain, W is Abel thy brother... Gen 4:9
unto the place w his tent had....... Gen 13:3
that it was well watered every w.... Gen 13:10
the place w thou art northward..... Gen 13:14
unto him, W is Sarah thy wife....... Gen 18:9
W are the men which came in to... Gen 19:5
place w he stood before the LORD... Gen 19:27
dwell w it pleaseth thee............... Gen 20:15
the voice of the lad w he is.......... Gen 21:17
but w is the lamb for a burnt....... Gen 22:7
w is he that hath taken venison,... Gen 27:33
w thou anointedst the pillar, and... Gen 31:13

w thou vowedst a vow unto me .... Gen 31:13
w he had spread his tent, at the .... Gen 33:19
in the place w he talked with him .... Gen 35:13
in the place w he talked with him .... Gen 35:14
of the place w God spake with him .... Gen 35:15
w Abraham and Isaac sojourned .... Gen 35:27
thee, w they feed their flocks .... Gen 37:16
W is the harlot, that was openly .... Gen 38:21
a place w the king's prisoners .... Gen 39:20
the place w Joseph was bound .... Gen 40:3
and he sought w to weep .... Gen 43:30
unto his daughters, And w is he .... Ex 2:20
get you straw w ye can find it .... Ex 5:11
the children of Israel were .... Ex 9:26
a token upon the houses w ye are .... Ex 12:13
a house w there was not one dead .... Ex 12:30
w were twelve wells of water, and .... Ex 15:27
w he encamped at the mount of God .... Ex 18:5
unto the thick darkness w God was .... Ex 20:21
in all places w I record my name .... Ex 20:24
and the breadth fifty every w .... Ex 27:18
w I will meet you, to speak there .... Ex 29:42
w I will meet with thee .... Ex 30:6
w I will meet with thee .... Ex 30:36
the ashes are poured out, shall .... Lev 4:12
w the ashes are poured out shall .... Lev 4:12
kill it in the place w they kill .... Lev 4:24
w they kill the burnt offering .... Lev 4:33
In the place w the burnt offering .... Lev 6:25
in the place w they kill the .... Lev 7:2
slay the lamb in the place w .... Lev 14:13
in the place w the cloud abode .... Num 9:17
w Ahiman, Sheshai, and Talmai, the .... Num 13:22
testimony, w I will meet with you .... Num 17:4
w was no way to turn either to .... Num 22:26
w was no water for the people to .... Num 33:14
be in the place w his kid faileth .... Num 33:14
w thou hast seen how that the .... Deut 1:31
and drought, w there was no water .... Deut 8:15
w thou sowedst thy seed, and .... Deut 11:10
by the way w the sun goeth down .... Deut 11:30
he sojourned, and came with all .... Deut 18:6
thy gates, w it liketh him best .... Deut 23:16
W are their gods, their rock in .... Deut 32:37
out of the place w the priests' .... Josh 4:3
w ye shall lodge this night .... Josh 4:3
them unto the place w they lodged .... Josh 4:8
in the place w the feet of the .... Josh 4:9
w he bowed, there he fell down .... Judg 5:27
w be all his miracles which our .... Judg 6:13
W is now thy mouth, wherewith .... Judg 9:38
sojourn w he could find a place .... Judg 17:8
I go to sojourn w I may find a .... Judg 17:9
a place w there is no want of any .... Judg 18:10
of the man's house w her lord was .... Judg 19:26
again in array in the place w .... Judg 20:22
forth out of the place w she was .... Ruth 1:7
w thou lodgest, I will lodge .... Ruth 1:16
W thou diest, I will die, and .... Ruth 1:17
W hast thou gleaned to day .... Ruth 2:19
and w wroughtest thou .... Ruth 2:19
mark the place w he shall lie .... Ruth 3:4
w the ark of God was, and Samuel 1Sa 3:3
w there was a great stone 1Sa 6:18
the city w the man of God was 1Sa 9:10
pray thee, w the seer's house is 1Sa 9:18
of God, w is the garrison of the 1Sa 10:5
when we saw that they were no w 1Sa 10:14
holes w they had hid themselves 1Sa 14:11
my father in the field w thou art 1Sa 19:3
and said, W are Samuel and David 1Sa 19:22
come to the place w thou didst 1Sa 23:22
and see his place w his haunt is 1Sa 23:23
places w he hideth himself 1Sa 23:23
by the way, w was a cave 1Sa 24:3
to the place w Saul had pitched 1Sa 26:5
David beheld the place w Saul lay 1Sa 26:5
now see w the king's spear is, and 1Sa 26:16
w those that were left behind 1Sa 30:9
to all the places w David himself 1Sa 30:31
to the place w Asahel fell down 2Sa 2:23
the king said unto him, W is he 2Sa 9:4
w he knew that valiant men were 2Sa 11:16
w he worshipped God, behold 2Sa 15:32
said, And w is thy master's son 2Sa 16:3
in some place w he shall be found 2Sa 17:12
said, W is Ahimaaz and Jonathan 2Sa 17:20
W the people of Israel were slain 2Sa 18:7
the Philistines had hanged them 2Sa 21:12
w Elhanan the son of Jaare-oregim 2Sa 21:19
w was a man of great stature 2Sa 21:20
w was a piece of ground full of 2Sa 23:11
the place w the officers were 1Kin 4:28
for the throne w he might judge 1Kin 7:7
his house w he dwelt had another 1Kin 7:8
told it in the city w the old 1Kin 13:25
w he abode, and laid him upon his 1Kin 17:19
In the place w dogs licked the 1Kin 21:19
W is the LORD God of Elijah 2Kin 2:14
to Shunem, w was a great woman 2Kin 4:8
the place w we dwell with thee is 2Kin 6:1
us a place there, w we may dwell 2Kin 6:2
And the man of God said, W fell it 2Kin 6:6
spy w he is, that I may send and 2Kin 6:13
W are the gods of Hamath, and of 2Kin 18:34
w are the gods of Sepharvaim 2Kin 18:34
W is the king of Hamath, and the 2Kin 19:13
w the women wove hangings for the 2Kin 23:7
defiled the high places w the 2Kin 23:8
w the Jebusites were, the 1Chr 11:4

w was a parcel of ground full of 1Chr 11:13
abroad unto our brethren every w 1Chr 13:2
w was a man of great stature 1Chr 20:6
w the LORD appeared unto David 2Chr 3:1
w the LORD commanded, saying, The 2Chr 25:4
w they were servants to him and 2Chr 36:20
in any place w he sojourneth .... Ezr 1:4
the treasures were laid up in .... Ezr 6:1
builded, the place w the offering .... Ezr 6:3
w are the vessels of the .... Neh 10:39
w aforetime they laid the meat .... Neh 13:5
W were white, green, and blue .... Est 1:6
w is he, that durst presume in .... Est 7:5
or w were the righteous cut off .... Job 4:7
if not, w, and who is he .... Job 9:24
w the light is as darkness .... Job 10:22
in a wilderness w there is no way .... Job 12:24
giveth up the ghost, and w is he .... Job 14:10
abroad for bread, saying, W is it .... Job 15:23
And w is now my hope .... Job 17:15
have seen him shall say, W is he .... Job 20:7
W is the house of the prince .... Job 21:28
w are the dwelling places of the .... Job 21:28
Oh that I knew w I might find him .... Job 23:3
w he doth work, but I cannot .... Job 23:9
a place for gold w they fine it .... Job 28:1
But w shall wisdom be found .... Job 28:12
w is the place of understanding .... Job 28:12
w is the place of understanding .... Job 28:20
the workers of iniquity may .... Job 34:22
W is God my maker, who giveth .... Job 35:10
place, w there is no straitness .... Job 36:16
W wast thou when I laid the .... Job 38:4
W is the way w light dwelleth .... Job 38:19
darkness, w is the place thereof .... Job 38:19
to rain on the earth, w no man is .... Job 38:26
w the slain are, there is she .... Job 39:30
w all the beasts of the field .... Job 40:20
w their voice is not heard .... Ps 19:3
the place w thine honour dwelleth .... Ps 26:8
say unto me, W is thy God .... Ps 42:3
say daily unto me, W is thy God .... Ps 42:10
they in great fear, w no fear was .... Ps 53:5
and thirsty land, w no water is .... Ps 63:1
deep mire, w there is no standing .... Ps 69:2
waters, w the floods overflow me .... Ps 69:2
the heathen say, W is their God .... Ps 79:10
w I heard a language that I .... Ps 81:5
w she may lay her young, even .... Ps 84:3
w are thy former lovingkindnesses .... Ps 89:49
W the birds make their nests .... Ps 104:17
the wilderness, w there is no way .... Ps 107:40
heathen say, W is now their God .... Ps 115:2
W no counsel is, the people fall .... Prov 11:14
W no oxen are, the crib is clean .... Prov 14:4
is a dinner of herbs w love is .... Prov 15:17
W no wood is, there the fire .... Prov 26:20
so w there is no talebearer, the .... Prov 26:20
W there is no vision, the people .... Prov 29:18
hasteth to his place w he arose .... Eccl 1:5
W the word of a king is, there is .... Eccl 8:4
in the city w they had so done .... Eccl 8:10
in the place w the tree falleth .... Eccl 11:3
thou feedest, w thou makest .... Song 1:7
w there were a thousand vines at .... Is 7:23
w will ye leave your glory .... Is 10:3
W are they .... Is 19:12
w are thy wise men .... Is 19:12
to Ariel, the city w David dwelt .... Is 29:1
in every place w the grounded .... Is 30:32
W is the scribe .... Is 33:18
w is the receiver .... Is 33:18
w is he that counted the towers .... Is 33:18
w each lay, shall be grass with .... Is 35:7
W are the gods of Hamath .... Is 36:19
w are the gods of Sepharvaim .... Is 36:19
W is the king of Hamath, and the .... Is 37:13
these, w had they been .... Is 49:21
W is the bill of your mother's .... Is 50:1
w is the fury of the oppressor .... Is 51:13
their bed w thou sawest it .... Is 57:8
W is he that brought them up out .... Is 63:11
w is he that put his holy Spirit .... Is 63:11
w is thy zeal and thy strength .... Is 63:15
w our fathers praised thee, is .... Is 64:11
is the house that ye build unto .... Is 66:1
w is the place of my rest .... Is 66:1
W is the LORD that brought us up .... Jer 2:6
passed through, and w no man dwelt .... Jer 2:6
priests said not, W is the LORD .... Jer 2:8
But w are thy gods that thou hast .... Jer 2:28
see w thou hast not been slain .... Jer 3:2
w is the good way, and walk .... Jer 6:16
w I set my name at the first, and .... Jer 7:12
from the place w I had hid it .... Jer 13:7
w is the flock that was given .... Jer 13:20
w I will not shew you favour .... Jer 16:13
W is the word of the LORD .... Jer 17:15
country, w ye were not born .... Jer 22:26
in the land w ye be strangers .... Jer 35:7
and let no man know w ye be .... Jer 36:19
W are now your prophets which .... Jer 37:19
for hunger in the place w he is .... Jer 38:9
w he gave judgment upon him .... Jer 52:9
w we shall see no war, nor hear .... Jer 42:14
w he gave judgment upon him .... Jer 52:9
their mothers, W is corn and wine .... Lam 2:12
I sat w they sat, and remained .... Eze 3:15
the place w they did offer sweet .... Eze 6:13
w was the seat of the image of .... Eze 8:3

the countries w they shall come .... Eze 11:16
w ye have been scattered, and I .... Eze 11:17
W is the daubing wherewith ye .... Eze 13:12
within in the furrows w it grew .... Eze 17:10
surely in the place w the king .... Eze 17:16
out of the country w they sojourn .... Eze 20:38
in the place w thou wast created .... Eze 21:30
deliver them out of all places w .... Eze 34:12
they washed the burnt offering .... Eze 40:38
w the priests that approach unto .... Eze 42:13
w I will dwell in the midst of .... Eze 43:7
This is the place w the priests .... Eze 46:20
w they shall bake the meat .... Eze 46:20
w the ministers of the house .... Eze 46:24
So he came near w I stood .... Dan 8:17
that in the place w it was said .... Hos 1:10
w is any other that may save thee .... Hos 13:10
among the people, W is their God .... Joel 2:17
the earth, w no gin is for him .... Amos 3:5
unto me, W is the LORD thy God .... Mic 7:10
W is the dwelling of the lions .... Nah 2:11
w the lion, even the old lion .... Nah 2:11
place is not known w they are .... Nah 3:17
fame in every land w they have .... Zeph 3:19
Your fathers, w are they .... Zec 1:5
I be a father, w is mine honour .... Mal 1:6
and if I be a master, w is my fear .... Mal 1:6
or, W is the God of judgment .... Mal 2:17
W is he that is born King of the .... Mt 2:2
he demanded of them w Christ .... Mt 2:4
stood over w the young child was .... Mt 2:9
w moth and rust doth corrupt, and .... Mt 6:19
w thieves break through and steal .... Mt 6:19
w neither moth nor rust doth .... Mt 6:20
w thieves do not break through .... Mt 6:20
For w your treasure is, there .... Mt 6:21
of man hath not w to lay his head .... Mt 8:20
w they had not much earth .... Mt 13:5
For w two or three are gathered .... Mt 18:20
reaping w thou hast not sown, and .... Mt 25:24
gathering w thou hast not strawed .... Mt 25:24
knewest that I reap w I sowed not .... Mt 25:26
gather w I have not strawed .... Mt 25:26
W wilt thou that we prepare for .... Mt 26:17
w the scribes and the elders were .... Mt 26:57
see the place w the Lord lay .... Mt 28:6
into a mountain w Jesus had .... Mt 28:16
they uncovered the roof w he was .... Mk 2:4
ground, w it had not much earth .... Mk 4:5
the way side, w the word is sown .... Mk 4:15
entereth in w the damsel was .... Mk 5:40
were sick, w they heard he was .... Mk 6:55
W their worm dieth not, and the .... Mk 9:44
W their worm dieth not, and the .... Mk 9:46
W their worm dieth not, and the .... Mk 9:48
without in a place w two ways met .... Mk 11:4
standing w it ought not, (let him .... Mk 13:14
W wilt thou that we go and prepare .... Mk 14:12
W is the guestchamber .... Mk 14:14
w I shall eat the passover with .... Mk 14:14
of Joses beheld w he was laid .... Mk 15:47
behold the place w they laid him .... Mk 16:6
went forth, and preached every w .... Mk 16:20
w he had been brought up .... Lk 4:16
found the place w it was written .... Lk 4:17
said unto them, W is your faith .... Lk 8:25
the gospel, and healing every w .... Lk 9:6
of man hath not w to lay his head .... Lk 9:58
as he journeyed, came w he was .... Lk 10:33
no room w to bestow my fruits .... Lk 12:17
w no thief approacheth, neither .... Lk 12:33
For w your treasure is, there .... Lk 12:34
but w are the nine .... Lk 17:17
they answered and said unto him, W ... Lk 17:37
W wilt thou that we prepare .... Lk 22:9
into the house w he entereth in .... Lk 22:10
W is the guestchamber .... Lk 22:11
w I shall eat the passover with .... Lk 22:11
Jordan, w John was baptizing .... Jn 1:28
Master,) w dwellest thou .... Jn 1:38
saw w he dwelt, and abode with him ... Jn 1:39
The wind bloweth w it listeth .... Jn 3:8
the place w men ought to worship .... Jn 4:20
Galilee, w he made the water wine .... Jn 4:46
the place w they did eat bread .... Jn 6:23
of man ascend up w he was before .... Jn 6:62
at the feast, and said, W is he .... Jn 7:11
w I am, thither ye cannot come .... Jn 7:34
w I am, thither ye cannot come .... Jn 7:36
town of Bethlehem, w David was .... Jn 7:42
w are those three accusers .... Jn 8:10
they unto him, W is thy Father .... Jn 8:19
Then said they unto him, W is he .... Jn 9:12
place w John at first baptized .... Jn 10:40
still in the same place w he was .... Jn 11:6
in that place w Martha met him .... Jn 11:30
when Mary was come w Jesus was .... Jn 11:32
And said, W have ye laid him .... Jn 11:34
the place w the dead was laid .... Jn 11:41
that, if any man knew w he were .... Jn 11:57
w Lazarus was which had been dead ...... Jn 12:1
w I am, there also ye be also .... Jn 12:26
that w I am, there ye may be also .... Jn 14:3
hast given me, be with me w I am .... Jn 17:24
was a garden, into the which he .... Jn 18:1
W they crucified him, and two .... Jn 19:18
for the place w Jesus was .... Jn 19:20
Now in the place w he was .... Jn 19:41
we know not w they have laid him .... Jn 20:2
w the body of Jesus had lain .... Jn 20:12

I know not w they have laid him .... Jn 20:13
tell me w thou hast laid him, and .... Jn 20:15
when the doors were shut w the .... Jn 20:19
w abode both Peter, and James, and ...... Acts 1:13
all the house w they were sitting .... Acts 2:2
the place was shaken w they were .... Acts 4:31
of Madian, w he begat two sons .... Acts 7:29
for the place w thou standest is .... Acts 7:33
went every w preaching the word .... Acts 8:4
come unto the house w I was .... Acts 11:11
w many were gathered together .... Acts 12:12
our brethren in every city w we .... Acts 15:36
w prayer was wont to be made .... Acts 16:13
w was a synagogue of the Jews .... Acts 17:1
all men every w to repent .... Acts 17:30
w we abode seven days .... Acts 20:6
w they were gathered together .... Acts 20:8
men every w against the people .... Acts 21:28
seat, w I ought to be judged .... Acts 25:10
into a place w two seas met .... Acts 27:41
W we found brethren, and were .... Acts 28:14
we know that every w it is spoken ...... Acts 28:22
W is boasting then .... Rom 3:27
for w no law is, there is no .... Rom 4:15
But w sin abounded, grace did .... Rom 5:20
that in the place w it was said .... Rom 9:26
not w Christ was named, lest I .... Rom 15:20
W is the wise 1Cor 1:20
w is the scribe 1Cor 1:20
w is the disputer of this world 1Cor 1:20
I teach every w in every church 1Cor 4:17
were an eye, w were the hearing 1Cor 12:17
were hearing, w were the smelling 1Cor 12:17
all one member, w were the body 1Cor 12:19
O death, w is thy sting 1Cor 15:55
O grave, w is thy victory 1Cor 15:55
w the Spirit of the Lord is, ... 2Cor 3:17
W is then the blessedness ye .... Gal 4:15
every w and in all things I am .... Phil 4:12
w Christ sitteth on the right .... Col 3:1
W there is neither Greek nor Jew, ... Col 3:11
therefore that men pray every w 1Ti 2:8
For a w testament is, there must .... Heb 9:16
Now w remission of these is, ... Heb 10:18
For w envying and strife is, there ...... Jas 3:16
w shall the ungodly and the sinner 1Pet 4:18
W is the promise of his coming 2Pet 3:4
w thou dwellest .... Rev 2:13
even w Satan's seat is .... Rev 2:13
slain among you, w Satan dwelleth .... Rev 2:13
w also our Lord was crucified .... Rev 11:8
w she hath a place prepared of .... Rev 12:6
w she is nourished for a time, and .... Rev 12:14
w the whore sitteth, are peoples, ... Rev 17:15
w the beast and the false prophet ...... Rev 20:10

WHEREABOUT

of the business w I send thee.............. 1Sa 21:2

WHEREAS

W thou hast searched all my stuff ...... Gen 31:37
w he was not worthy of death, ... Deut 19:6
w ye were as the stars of heaven........ Deut 28:62
w I have rewarded thee evil 1Sa 24:17
W I have not dwelt in any house 2Sa 7:6
W thou camest but yesterday, ... 2Sa 15:20
W it was in thine heart to build 1Kin 8:18
now w my father did lade you with 1Kin 12:11
w now thou shalt smite Syria but...... 2Kin 13:19
For w my father put a heavy yoke 2Chr 10:11
for w we have offended against 2Chr 28:13
W our substance is not cut down, ... Job 22:20
w that is but in him is .... Eccl 4:14
W thou hast prayed to me against ...... Is 37:21
W thou hast been forsaken and.......... Is 60:15
w the sword reacheth unto the .... Jer 4:10
w ye say, The Lord saith it .... Eze 13:7
w thou wast naked and bare .... Eze 16:7
w none followeth thee to commit ...... Eze 16:34
w the Lord was there .... Eze 35:10
w it lay desolate in the sight of .... Dan 8:27
w thou sawest the feet and toes, ... Dan 2:41
w thou sawest iron mixed with .... Dan 2:43
w the king saw a watcher and an ...... Dan 4:23
w they commanded to leave the .... Dan 4:26
w four stood up for it, four .... Dan 8:22
W Edom saith, We are impoverished .... Mal 1:4
that, w I was blind, now I see .... Jn 9:25
for w there is among you envying........ 1Cor 3:3
W ye know not what shall be on ...... Jas 4:14
w they speak against you as 1Pet 2:12
w they speak evil of you, as of 1Pet 3:16
W angels, which are greater in.......... 2Pet 2:11

WHEREBY

w shall I know that I shall.................. Gen 15:8
drinketh, and w he divineth .... Gen 44:5
w he may be made unclean, or a ...... Lev 22:5
w an atonement shall be made for .... Num 5:8
w they murmur against you............. Num 17:5
w the Lord thy God brought thee........ Deut 7:19
doings, w thou hast forsaken me........ Deut 28:20
w Jonathan knew that it was............ 1Sa 20:33
w the people fall under thee .... Ps 45:5
w they have made thee glad............ Ps 45:8
w thou didst confirm thine .... Ps 68:9
when for all the causes w .... Jer 3:8
w the kings of Judah come in, and .... Jer 17:19
this is his name w he shall be .... Jer 23:6
w they have sinned against me .... Jer 33:8
w they have sinned .... Jer 33:8
w they have transgressed against ...... Jer 33:8

w ye have transgressed, ... Eze 18:31
judgments w they should not live .... Eze 20:25
all their trespasses w they have ...... Eze 39:26
by the steps w they went up to it .... Eze 40:49
the way of the gate w he came in...... Eze 46:9
w ye shall inherit the land .... Eze 47:13
w they have reproached my people, .. Zeph 2:8
the angel, W shall I know this .... Lk 1:18
w the dayspring from on high hath .. Lk 1:78
among men, w we must be saved...... Acts 4:12
w thou and all thy house shall be .... Acts 11:14
there being no cause w we may........ Acts 19:40
adoption, w we cry, Abba, Father .... Rom 8:15
nor any thing w thy brother .... Rom 14:21
W, when ye read, ye may.................. Eph 3:4
w they lie in wait to deceive............ Eph 4:14
w ye are sealed unto the day of .... Eph 4:30
according to the working w he is ...... Phil 3:21
w we may serve God acceptably ...... Heb 12:28
W are given unto us exceeding.......... 2Pet 1:4
W the world that then was, being 2Pet 3:6
w we know that it is the last............ 1Jn 2:18

WHEREFORE

w it is said, Even as Nimrod the........ Gen 10:9
W the well was called .... Gen 16:14
W did Sarah laugh, saying, Shall ...... Gen 18:13
W she said unto Abraham, Cast .... Gen 21:10
W he called that place Beer-sheba..... Gen 26:33
w standest thou without.................... Gen 24:31
W come ye to me, seeing ye hate ...... Gen 26:27
w then hast thou beguiled me .... Gen 29:25
W didst thou flee away secretly, ... Gen 31:27
yet w hast thou stolen my gods .... Gen 31:30
W is it that thou dost ask after .... Gen 32:29
W he slew him also .... Gen 38:10
W look ye so sadly to day................ Gen 40:7
W dealt ye so ill with me, as to ...... Gen 43:6
W have ye rewarded evil for good .... Gen 44:4
W saith my lord these words.......... Gen 44:7
W shall we die before thine eyes, ... Gen 47:19
w they sold not their lands .... Gen 47:22
w the name of it was called .... Gen 50:11
W, smitest thou my fellow .... Ex 2:13
W do ye, Moses and Aaron, let the .. Ex 5:4
W have ye not fulfilled your task .... Ex 5:14
W dealest thou thus with thy .... Ex 5:15
w hast thou so evil entreated .... Ex 5:22
W say unto the children of Israel .... Ex 6:6
w hast thou dealt thus with us, ... Ex 14:11
unto Moses, W criest thou unto me .. Ex 14:15
W the people did chide with Moses .. Ex 17:2
w do ye tempt the Lord .... Ex 17:2
W is this that thou hast brought ...... Ex 17:3
W the Lord blessed the sabbath ...... Ex 20:11
W the children of Israel shall.......... Ex 31:16
W should the Egyptians speak, and .. Ex 32:12
W have ye not eaten the sin .... Lev 10:17
W the priest shall pronounce him .... Lev 13:25
W ye shall do my statutes, and .... Lev 25:18
w are we kept back, that we may...... Num 9:7
W hast thou afflicted thy servant .... Num 11:11
w have I not found favour in thy .... Num 11:11
w then were ye not afraid to .... Num 12:8
w hath the Lord brought us unto...... Num 14:3
W now do ye transgress the .... Num 14:41
w then lift ye up yourselves............ Num 16:3
W have ye made us to come up out .. Num 20:5
w Israel turned away from him........ Num 20:21
W have ye brought us up out of ...... Num 21:5
W it is said in the book of the .... Num 21:14
W they that speak in proverbs say .. Num 21:27
W hast thou smitten thine ass.......... Num 22:32
w camest thou not unto me.............. Num 22:37
W say, Behold, I give unto him my .. Num 25:12
W, said they, if we have found........ Num 32:5
w discourage ye the heart of the .... Num 32:7
W it shall come to pass, if ye .... Deut 7:12
W Levi hath no part nor .... Deut 10:9
W I command thee, saying, Thou...... Deut 19:7
W hath the Lord done this unto ...... Deut 29:24
W the name of the place is called .... Josh 5:9
w the hearts of the people melted .... Josh 7:5
w hast thou at all brought this .... Josh 7:7
w liest thou thus upon thy face .... Josh 7:10
W the name of that place was .... Josh 7:26
W our elders and all the .... Josh 9:11
W have ye beguiled us, saying, We .. Josh 9:22
W Adoni-zedek king of Jerusalem...... Josh 10:3
W I also said, I will not drive.......... Judg 2:3
w I will deliver you no more............ Judg 10:13
W I have not sinned against thee, ... Judg 11:27
W passedst thou over to fight.......... Judg 12:1
w then are ye come up unto me ...... Judg 12:3
w he called the name thereof .... Judg 15:19
w they called that place.................... Judg 18:12
W she went forth out of the place .... Ruth 1:7
W it came to pass, when the 1Sa 1:20
W the sin of the young men was 1Sa 2:17
W kick ye at my sacrifice and a 1Sa 2:29
W the Lord God of Israel saith, I...... 1Sa 2:30
W hath the Lord smitten us to day .. 1Sa 4:3
W ye shall make images of your 1Sa 6:5
W then do ye harden your hearts, ... 1Sa 6:6
w then speakest thou so to me 1Sa 9:21
W he put forth the end of the rod 1Sa 14:27
W then didst thou not obey the 1Sa 15:19
W Saul sent messengers unto Jesse .. 1Sa 16:19
W when Saul saw that he behaved.... 1Sa 18:15
W Saul said to David, Thou shalt...... 1Sa 18:21
W David arose and went, he and his .. 1Sa 18:27

w then wilt thou sin against.............. 1Sa 19:5
W they say, Is Saul also among 1Sa 19:24
W cometh not the son of Jesse to 1Sa 20:27
W now send and fetch him unto me, .. 1Sa 20:31
unto him, W shall he be slain............ 1Sa 20:32
w then have ye brought him to me 1Sa 21:14
w he came down into a rock, and 1Sa 23:25
W Saul returned from pursuing 1Sa 23:28
W hearest thou men's words, ... 1Sa 24:9
W the Lord reward thee good for 1Sa 24:19
W let the young men find favour 1Sa 25:8
w she told him nothing, less or 1Sa 25:36
w then hast thou not kept thy............ 1Sa 26:15
W doth my lord thus pursue after 1Sa 26:18
w Ziklag pertaineth unto the 1Sa 27:6
w then layest thou a snare for my 1Sa 28:9
W then dost thou ask of me,.............. 1Sa 28:16
W now return, and go in peace, ... 1Sa 29:7
W now rise up early in the 1Sa 29:10
w that place was called 2Sa 2:16
w should I smite thee to the 2Sa 2:22
w Abner with the hinder end of 2Sa 2:23
W hast thou gone in unto my 2Sa 3:7
W they said, The blind and the 2Sa 5:8
W thou art great, O Lord God 2Sa 7:22
W Hanun took David's servants, and .. 2Sa 10:4
W approached ye so nigh unto the 2Sa 11:20
W hast thou despised the 2Sa 12:9
now he is dead, w should I fast 2Sa 12:23
W then hast thou thought such a 2Sa 14:13
W have thy servants set my field...... 2Sa 14:31
to say, W am I come from Geshur 2Sa 14:32
W goest thou also with us 2Sa 15:19
then say, W hast thou done so 2Sa 16:10
W wilt thou run, my son, seeing 2Sa 18:22
w then are ye the last to bring 2Sa 19:12
W wentest not thou with me, ... 2Sa 19:25
w then should thy servant be yet...... 2Sa 19:35
w then be ye angry for this 2Sa 19:42
W David said unto the Gibeonites, ... 2Sa 21:3
W is my lord the king come to his 2Sa 24:21
W his servants said unto him, Let 1Kin 1:2
W Nathan spake unto Bath-sheba...... 1Kin 1:11
W is this noise of the city being 1Kin 1:41
W the Lord said unto Solomon, ... 1Kin 11:11
W the king hearkened not unto the .. 1Kin 12:15
w all Israel made Omri, the 1Kin 16:16
W he said unto the messengers of 1Kin 20:9
w he said unto the driver of his 1Kin 22:34
W wilt thou go to him to day 2Kin 4:23
W he went again to meet him, and 2Kin 4:31
w consider, I pray you, and see 2Kin 5:7
W hast thou rent thy clothes............ 2Kin 5:8
W they arose and fled in the 2Kin 7:7
w came this mad fellow to thee 2Kin 9:11
W they came again, and told him 2Kin 9:36
W they spake to the king of.............. 2Kin 17:26
w lift up thy prayer for the.............. 2Kin 19:4
W that place is called Perez-uzza...... 1Chr 13:11
W Hanun took David's servants, and .. 1Chr 19:4
W Joab departed, and went................ 1Chr 21:4
W David blessed the Lord before 1Chr 29:10
W all the men of Israel assembled 2Chr 5:3
W now let the fear of the Lord be 2Chr 19:7
W he did evil in the sight of the 2Chr 21:6
w their anger was greatly kindled 2Chr 25:10
W the anger of the Lord was 2Chr 25:15
W the Lord his God delivered him 2Chr 28:5
W the wrath of the Lord was upon 2Chr 29:8
w their brethren the Levites did 2Chr 29:34
W the Lord brought upon them the .. 2Chr 33:11
W the king said unto me, Why is...... Neh 2:2
w Haman sought to destroy all the .. Est 3:6
W they called these days Purim .... Est 9:26
W is light given to him that is .... Job 3:20
shew me w thou contendest with me .. Job 10:2
W then hast thou brought me forth .. Job 10:18
W do I take my flesh in my teeth, ... Job 13:14
W hidest thou thy face, and .... Job 13:24
W are we counted as beasts, and ...... Job 18:3
W do the wicked live, become old, ... Job 21:7
w I was afraid, and durst not shew .. Job 32:6
W the anger of the Lord was .... Job 33:1
W I abhor myself, and repent in ...... Job 42:6
w doth the wicked contemn God...... Ps 10:13
W hidest thou thy face, and .... Ps 44:24
w should I fear in the days of .... Ps 49:5
W should the heathen say, Where .... Ps 79:10
w hast thou made all men in vain .... Ps 89:47
W should the heathen say, Where .... Ps 115:2
w is there a price in the hand of ...... Prov 17:16
W I perceive that there is nothing .... Eccl 3:22
W I praised the dead which are ...... Eccl 4:2
w should God be angry at thy .... Eccl 5:6
w, when I looked that it should........ Is 5:4
W it shall come to pass, that .... Is 10:12
W my bowels shall sound like an .... Is 16:11
W glorify ye the Lord in the .... Is 24:15
W hear the word of the Lord, ye ...... Is 28:14
W the Lord said, Forasmuch as .... Is 29:13
W thus saith the Holy One of .... Is 30:12
w lift up thy prayer for the.............. Is 37:4
W, when I came, was there no man .. Is 50:2
W do ye spend money for that .... Is 55:2
W have we fasted, say they, and ...... Is 58:3
w have we afflicted our soul, and...... Is 58:3
W art thou red in thine apparel, ... Is 63:2
W I will yet plead with you, ... Jer 2:9
W will ye plead with me.................... Jer 2:29
w say my people, We are lords .... Jer 2:31

W a lion out of the forest shall .... Jer 5:6
W thus saith the Lᴏʀᴅ God of .... Jer 5:14
W doeth the Lᴏʀᴅ our God all............ Jer 5:19
W doth the way of the wicked............ Jer 12:1
w are all they happy that deal .... Jer 12:1
W come these things upon me............ Jer 16:10
W hath the Lᴏʀᴅ pronounced all...... Jer 16:10
W came I forth out of the womb to .... Jer 20:18
W hath the Lᴏʀᴅ done thus unto........ Jer 22:8
w are they cast out, he and his.......... Jer 22:28
W their way shall be unto them as..... Jer 23:12
w should this city be laid waste.......... Jer 27:17
w do I see every man with his............ Jer 30:6
W dost thou prophesy, and say,........... Jer 32:3
W the princes were wroth with .... Jer 37:15
w should he slay thee, that all............ Jer 40:15
W my fury and mine anger was........... Jer 44:6
W commit ye this great evil .... Jer 44:7
W have I seen them dismayed and...... Jer 46:5
W gloriest thou in the valleys,........... Jer 49:4
W, behold, the days come, saith .... Jer 51:52
W doth a living man complain, a......... Lam 3:39
W dost thou forget us for ever,........... Lam 5:20
W, as I live, saith the Lord God......... Eze 5:11
W I will bring the worst of the.......... Eze 7:24
W thus saith the Lord God.................. Eze 13:20
W, O harlot, hear the word of the ..... Eze 16:35
w turn yourselves, and live ye .... Eze 18:32
W I caused them to go forth out .... Eze 20:10
W I gave them also statutes that........ Eze 20:25
W say unto the house of Israel,.......... Eze 20:30
say unto thee, W sighest thou .... Eze 21:7
W I have delivered her into the......... Eze 23:9
W thus saith the Lord God.................. Eze 24:6
W say unto them, Thus saith the .... Eze 33:25
W I poured my fury upon them for .... Eze 36:18
w I have consumed them in mine........ Eze 43:8
W at that time certain Chaldeans....... Dan 3:8
W, O king, let my counsel be.............. Dan 4:27
W king Darius signed the writing...... Dan 6:9
w shut thou up the vision .... Dan 8:26
Knowest thou w I come unto thee....... Dan 10:20
w should they say among the .... Joel 2:17
W they cried unto the Lᴏʀᴅ, and....... Jonah 1:14
w lookest thou upon them that .... Hab 1:13
Yet ye say, W.................................... Mal 2:14
And w one..Mal 2:15
W, if God so clothe the grass of .... Mt 6:30
W by their fruits ye shall know........... Mt 7:20
W think ye evil in your hearts .... Mt 9:4
W it is lawful to do well on the.......... Mt 12:12
W I say unto you, All manner of........ Mt 12:31
little faith, w didst thou doubt............ Mt 14:31
W if thy hand or thy foot offend .... Mt 18:8
W they are no more twain, but one.... Mt 19:6
W ye be witnesses unto yourselves..... Mt 23:31
W, behold, I send unto you................. Mt 23:34
W if they shall say unto you,............. Mt 26:26
unto him, Friend, w art thou come..... Mt 26:50
W that field was called, The .... Mt 27:8
W neither thought I myself worthy .... Lk 7:7
W I say unto thee, Her sins,.............. Lk 7:47
W then gavest not thou my money..... Lk 19:23
w would ye hear it again .... Jn 9:27
W of these men which have .... Acts 1:21
W, brethren, look ye out among.......... Acts 6:3
what is the cause w ye are come......... Acts 10:21
W he saith also in another psalm,....... Acts 13:35
W my sentence is, that we trouble...... Acts 15:19
the more part knew not w they .... Acts 19:32
W if Demetrius, and the craftsmen .... Acts 19:38
W I take you to record this day,......... Acts 20:26
that he might know w they cried........ Acts 22:24
he was accused of the Jews,............... Acts 23:28
the cause w they accused him,........... Acts 23:28
w he sent for him the oftener, and..... Acts 24:26
W I have brought him forth before .... Acts 25:26
w fears be heard to hear me.............. Acts 26:3
W, sirs, be of good cheer .... Acts 27:25
W I pray you to take some meat......... Acts 27:34
W God also gave them up to............... Rom 1:24
W, as by one man sin entered into ..... Rom 5:12
W, my brethren, ye also are............... Rom 7:4
W the law is holy, and the.................. Rom 7:12
W? Because they sought...................... Rom 9:32
W must needs be subject, not............. Rom 13:5
W receive ye one another, as.............. Rom 15:7
W I beseech you, be ye followers........ 1Cor 4:16
W, if meat make my brother to 1Cor 8:13
W let him that thinketh he.................. 1Cor 10:12
W, my dearly beloved, flee from........ 1Cor 10:14
W whosoever shall eat this bread,...... 1Cor 11:27
W, my brethren, when ye come.......... 1Cor 11:33
W I give you to understand that......... 1Cor 12:3
W let him that speaketh in an............ 1Cor 14:13
W tongues are for a sign, not to 1Cor 14:22
W, brethren, covet to prophesy,......... 1Cor 14:39
W I beseech you that ye would........... 2Cor 2:8
W we labour, that, whether................ 2Cor 5:9
W henceforth know we no man after.. 2Cor 5:16
W come out from among them 2Cor 6:17
W, though I wrote unto you, I did 2Cor 7:12
W shew ye to them, and before the ... 2Cor 8:24
W? because I love 2Cor 11:11
W then serveth the law....................... Gal 3:19
W the law was our schoolmaster to ... Gal 3:24
W thou art no more a servant, but..... Gal 4:7
W I also, after I heard of your .... Eph 1:15
W remember, that ye being in time ... Eph 2:11
W I desire ye faint not at .... Eph 3:13

W he saith, When he ascended up ..... Eph 4:8
W putting away lying, speak every..... Eph 4:25
W he saith, Awake thou that .... Eph 5:14
W ye be not unwise, but..................... Eph 5:17
W take unto you the whole armour ... Eph 6:13
W God also hath highly exalted.......... Phil 2:9
W, my beloved, as ye have always..... Phil 2:12
W if ye be dead with Christ from ...... Col 2:20
W we would have come unto you,...... 1Th 2:18
W when we could no longer forbear... 1Th 3:1
W comfort one another with these 1Th 4:18
W comfort yourselves together, and.. 1Th 5:11
W also we pray always for you,.......... 2Th 1:11
W I put thee in remembrance that 2Ti 1:6
W rebuke them sharply, that they ..... Titus 1:13
W, though I might be much bold in .... Philem 8
W in all things it behoved him to....... Heb 2:17
W, holy brethren, partakers of........... Heb 3:1
W (as the Holy Ghost saith, To .... Heb 3:7
W I was grieved with that .... Heb 3:10
W he is able also to save them to ...... Heb 7:25
w it is of necessity that this................ Heb 8:3
W when he cometh into the world,..... Heb 10:5
W God is not ashamed to be called.... Heb 11:16
W seeing we also are compassed........ Heb 12:1
W lift up the hands which hang .... Heb 12:12
W we receiving a kingdom which .... Heb 12:28
W Jesus also, that he might................ Heb 13:12
W, my beloved brethren, let every..... Jas 1:19
W lay apart all filthiness and.............. Jas 1:21
W he saith, God resisteth the.............. Jas 4:6
W unto the loins of your mind,........... 1Pet 1:13
W laying aside all malice, and all....... 1Pet 2:1
W also it is contained in the............... 1Pet 2:6
W let them that suffer according........ 1Pet 4:19
W the rather, brethren, give ye.......... 2Pet 1:10
W I will not be negligent to put 2Pet 1:12
W, beloved, seeing that ye look 2Pet 3:14
And w slew he him 1Jn 3:12
W, if I come, I will remember his 3Jn 10
said unto me, W didst thou marvel .... Rev 17:7

WHEREIN

w there is life, I have given .... Gen 1:30
w is the breath of life, from .... Gen 6:17
flesh, w is the breath of life .... Gen 7:15
the land w thou art a stranger............ Gen 17:8
to the land w thou hast sojourned...... Gen 21:23
the land w thou art a stranger .... Gen 28:4
the land w they were strangers .... Gen 36:7
Jacob dwelt in the land w his............. Gen 37:1
W, made them serve, was with .... Ex 1:14
pilgrimage, w they were strangers..... Ex 6:4
the houses, w they shall eat it .... Ex 12:7
for in the thing w they dealt............... Ex 18:11
them the way w they must walk .... Ex 18:20
w shall he sleep.................................. Ex 22:27
For w shall it be known here that ...... Ex 33:16
w hath sinned, come to his .... Lev 4:23
his ignorance w he erred and wist..... Lev 5:18
But the earthen vessel w it is .... Lev 6:28
w any work is done, it must be .... Lev 11:32
w there is plenty of water, shall......... Lev 11:36
All the days w the plague shall.......... Lev 13:46
thing of skin, w the plague is .... Lev 13:52
wash the thing w the plague is .... Lev 13:57
thou shalt burn that w the plague ..... Lev 13:57
w ye dwell, shall ye not do .... Lev 18:3
w we have done foolishly .... Num 12:11
w we have sinned................................ Num 12:11
w is no blemish, and upon which ...... Num 19:2
all their cities w they dwell................ Num 31:10
vex you in the land w ye dwell .... Num 33:55
not pollute the land w ye are............. Num 35:33
w ye shall inhabit, w I dwell.............. Num 35:34
A land w thou shalt eat bread .... Deut 8:9
w were fiery serpents, and .... Deut 8:15
the nations which w dwelt .... Deut 12:2
w the Lᴏʀᴅ thy God hath blessed....... Deut 12:7
of sheep, w is blemish, or any........... Deut 17:1
w thou trustedst, throughout all........ Deut 28:52
the wilderness w they chased them.... Josh 5:6
into the cave w they had been hid..... Josh 10:27
w the Lᴏʀᴅ's tabernacle dwelleth,..... Josh 22:19
to destroy the land w the.................... Josh 22:33
us in all the way w we went............... Josh 24:17
see w his great strength lieth,............ Judg 16:5
w thy great strength lieth, and.......... Judg 16:6
hast not told me w thy great .... Judg 16:15
the Lᴏʀᴅ is your way w ye go............ Judg 18:6
the jewels of gold were, and put 1Sa 6:15
see w this sin hath been this day....... 1Sa 14:38
In all the places w I have walked 2Sa 7:7
w in all my father was afflicted 1Kin 2:26
w is the covenant of the Lᴏʀᴅ,.......... 1Kin 8:21
the good way w they should walk 1Kin 8:36
all their transgressions w they.......... 1Kin 8:50
w the man of God is buried 1Kin 13:31
w Jehoiada the priest instructed........ 2Kin 12:2
w the Lᴏʀᴅ commanded, saying, The. 2Kin 17:12
in their cities w they dwelt 2Kin 17:29
w this thou trustest 2Kin 18:19
w this passover was holden to the 2Kin 23:23
Now these are the things w 2Chr 3:3
w is the covenant of the Lᴏʀᴅ,.......... 2Chr 6:11
the good way, w they should walk 2Chr 6:27
w Solomon had built the house of 2Chr 8:1
the places w he built high places 2Chr 33:19
unto him, w was written thus .... Ezr 5:7
W was written, It is reported .... Neh 6:6
light in the way w they should go ...... Neh 9:12

and the way w they should go............ Neh 9:19
in the day w they sold victuals .... Neh 13:15
all the things w the king had.............. Est 5:11
W the king granted the Jews which ... Est 8:11
As the days w the Jews rested............ Est 9:22
Let the day perish w I was born......... Job 3:3
of the ice, and w the snow is hid .... Job 6:16
me to understand w I have erred .... Job 6:24
the wilderness, w there is no man ..... Job 38:26
mount Zion, w thou hast dwelt .... Ps 74:2
the days w thou hast afflicted us........ Ps 90:15
the years w we have seen evil............ Ps 90:15
w all the beasts of the forest do........ Ps 104:20
w are things creeping innumerable.... Ps 104:25
In the way w I walked have they .... Ps 142:3
to know the way w I should walk....... Ps 143:8
all my labour w I have laboured......... Eccl 2:19
w I have shewed myself wise under .. Eccl 2:19
w he hath laboured under the sun...... Eccl 2:22
worketh in that w he laboureth.......... Eccl 3:9
there is a time w one man ruleth .... Eccl 8:9
for w is he to be accounted of............ Is 2:22
from the hard bondage w thou wast .. Is 14:3
w shall go to galley with oars,............ Is 33:21
this is w thou trustest .... Is 36:4
w thou hast laboured from thy .... Is 47:12
did choose that w I delighted not ...... Is 65:12
w thou trustedst, with the sword ...... Jer 5:17
w ye trust, and unto the place .... Jer 7:14
w thou trustedst, they wearied.......... Jer 12:5
things w there is no profit.................. Jer 16:19
Cursed be the day w I was born......... Jer 20:14
let not the day w my mother bare ..... Jer 20:14
is he a vessel w is no pleasure........... Jer 22:28
way, w they shall not stumble .... Jer 31:9
Take in thine hand the roll w .... Jer 36:14
Now the pit w Ishmael had cast........ Jer 41:9
may shew us the way w we may walk . Jer 42:3
like a vessel w is no pleasure............ Jer 48:38
a land w no man dwelleth, neither ..... Jer 51:43
the countries w ye are scattered .... Eze 20:34
w ye have been scattered .... Eze 20:41
doings, w ye have been defiled .... Eze 20:43
w she had played the harlot in........... Eze 23:19
into a city w is made a breach .... Eze 26:10
blood the land w thou swimmest .... Eze 32:6
w they have sinned, and will.............. Eze 37:23
w your fathers have dwelt .... Eze 37:25
their garments w they minister.......... Eze 42:14
their garments w they ministered ...... Eze 44:19
w she burned incense to them, and.... Hos 2:13
as a vessel w is no pleasure............... Hos 8:8
w are more than sixscore thousand ... Jonah 4:11
and w have I wearied thee................. Mic 6:3
w thou hast transgressed against....... Zeph 3:11
out of the pit w is no water................ Zec 9:11
Yet ye say, W hast thou loved us....... Mal 1:2
W have we despised thy name .... Mal 1:6
ye say, W have we polluted thee........ Mal 1:7
Yet ye say, W have we wearied him .. Mal 2:17
But ye said, W shall we return .... Mal 3:7
But ye say, W have we robbed thee ... Mal 3:8
w most of his mighty works were ...... Mt 11:20
the hour w the Son of man cometh .... Mt 25:13
they let down the bed w the sick .... Mk 2:4
w thou hast been instructed................ Lk 1:4
me in the days w he looked on me..... Lk 1:25
him all his armour w he trusted......... Lk 11:22
w never man before was laid .... Lk 23:53
w was never man yet laid .... Jn 19:41
in our own tongue, w we were born ... Acts 2:8
into this land, w ye now dwell .... Acts 7:4
W were all manner of fourfooted ...... Acts 10:12
for w thou judgest another, thou .... Rom 2:1
faith into this grace w we stand......... Rom 5:2
that being dead w we were held......... Rom 7:6
the same calling w he was called 1Cor 7:20
w he is called, therein abide.............. 1Cor 7:24
ye have received, and w ye stand 1Cor 15:1
that w they glory, they may be 2Cor 11:12
For what is it w ye were inferior 2Cor 12:13
w he hath made us accepted in the ... Eph 1:6
W he hath abounded toward us in ..... Eph 1:8
W in time past ye walked................... Eph 2:2
not drunk with wine, w is excess ...... Eph 5:18
w ye were also careful, but ye........... Phil 4:10
w also ye are risen with him .... Col 2:12
W I suffer trouble, as an evil............. 2Ti 2:9
W God, willing more abundantly to ... Heb 6:17
w was the candlestick, and the .... Heb 9:2
w was the golden pot that had .... Heb 9:4
W ye greatly rejoice, though now 1Pet 1:6
w few, that is, eight souls were 1Pet 3:20
W they think it strange that ye 1Pet 4:4
the true grace of God w ye stand....... 1Pet 5:12
w the heavens being on fire shall...... 2Pet 3:12
earth, w dwelleth righteousness 2Pet 3:13
even in those days w Antipas was ..... Rev 2:13
w were made rich all that had............ Rev 18:19

WHEREINSOEVER

Howbeit w any is bold, (I speak 2Cor 11:21

WHEREINTO

w any of them falleth, whatsoever ..... Lev 11:33
I bring into the land w he went .... Num 14:24
save that one w his disciples............... Jn 6:22

WHEREOF

W I commanded thee that thou .... Gen 3:11
w any of the blood is brought .... Lev 6:30
in the skin w there is a hot .... Lev 13:24

W

w men bring an offering unto the........ Lev 27:9
camps, in the midst w I dwell........ Num 5:3
the weight w was an hundred and........ Num 7:13
the weight w was an hundred and........ Num 7:19
the weight w was an hundred and........ Num 7:25
the weight w was an hundred and........ Num 7:31
the weight w was an hundred and........ Num 7:49
the weight w was an hundred and........ Num 7:61
the weight w was an hundred and........ Num 7:67
the weight w was an hundred and........ Num 7:73
the weight w was an hundred and........ Num 7:79
that is the well w the LORD spake........ Num 21:16
w he spake unto thee, saying, Let........ Deut 13:2
w thou canst not be healed........ Deut 28:27
by the way w I spake unto thee........ Deut 28:68
the LORD spake in that day........ Josh 14:12
I spake unto you by the hand of........ Josh 20:2
w they were possessed, according........ Josh 22:9
w Samuel spake, he told him not........ 1Sa 10:16
w two thousand were with Saul in........ 1Sa 13:2
the weight w was a talent of gold........ 2Sa 12:30
sick of his sickness w he died........ 2Kin 13:14
w the LORD had said unto them, Ye........ 2Kin 17:12
the length w was according to the........ 2Chr 3:8
upon the place w thou hast said........ 2Chr 6:20
w were made vessels for the house........ 2Chr 24:14
the LORD had said, In Jerusalem........ 2Chr 33:4
w one went on the right hand upon........ Neh 12:31
the poison w drinketh up my........ Job 6:4
the streams w shall make glad the........ Ps 46:4
into the midst w they are fallen........ Ps 57:6
w we are glad........ Ps 126:3
there any thing w it may be said........ Eccl 1:10
w every one bear twins, and none........ Song 4:2
w every one beareth twins, and........ Song 6:6
w ye say, It shall be delivered........ Jer 32:36
w ye say, It is desolate without........ Jer 32:43
w ye were afraid, shall follow........ Jer 42:16
destitute of that w it was full........ Eze 32:15
this is the day w I have spoken........ Eze 39:8
the word of the LORD came to........ Dan 9:2
w she hath said, These are my........ Hos 2:12
those things w ye accuse him........ Lk 23:14
raised up, w we all are witnesses........ Acts 2:32
w we are witnesses........ Acts 3:15
new doctrine, w thou speakest, is........ Acts 17:19
w he hath given assurance unto........ Acts 17:31
w they were informed concerning........ Acts 21:24
all these things, w we accuse him........ Acts 24:8
the things w they now accuse me........ Acts 24:13
of these things w these accuse me........ Acts 25:11
things w I am accused of them........ Acts 26:2
by works, he hath w to glory........ Rom 4:2
those things w ye are now ashamed........ Rom 6:21
I have therefore w I may glory........ Rom 15:17
the things w ye wrote unto me........ 1Cor 7:1
w ye had notice before, that the........ 2Cor 9:5
w I was made a minister........ Eph 3:7
w he might trust in the flesh........ Phil 3:4
w ye heard before in the word of........ Col 1:5
w I Paul am made a minister........ Col 1:23
w I am made a minister, according........ Col 1:25
what they say, nor w they affirm........ 1Ti 1:7
w cometh envy, strife, railings,........ 1Ti 6:4
the world to come, w we speak........ Heb 2:5
w the Holy Ghost also is a........ Heb 10:15
w all are partakers, then are ye........ Heb 12:8
w they, have no right to eat which........ Heb 13:10
w ye have heard that it should........ Jn 4:3

WHEREON

the land w thou liest, to thee........ Gen 28:13
for the place w thou standest is........ Ex 3:5
and also the ground w they are........ Ex 8:21
thou shalt wash that w it was........ Lev 6:27
w lie lieth that hath the unclean........ Lev 15:4
w is the seat of copulation,........ Lev 15:17
or on any thing w she sitteth........ Lev 15:23
all the bed w he lieth shall be........ Lev 15:26
Every bed w she lieth all the........ Lev 15:26
Every place w the soles of your........ Deut 11:24
for the place w thou standest is........ Josh 5:15
Surely the land w thy feet have........ Josh 14:9
w they set down the ark of the........ 1Sa 6:18
the tables w the shewbread was........ 2Chr 4:19
W do ye trust, that ye abide in........ 2Chr 32:10
fallen upon the bed w Esther was........ Est 7:8
him to be in safety, w he resteth........ Job 24:23
w there hang a thousand bucklers,........ Song 4:4
w if a man hear, it will go into........ Is 36:6
the sticks w thou writest shall........ Eze 37:20
find a colt tied, w never man sat........ Mk 11:2
the hill w their city was built........ Lk 4:29
them, and took up that w he lay........ Lk 5:25
a colt tied, w yet never man sat........ Lk 19:30
reap that w ye bestowed no labour........ Jn 4:38

WHERESOEVER

to his foot, w the priest looketh........ Lev 13:12
sojourn w thou canst sojourn........ 2Kin 8:1
w any breach shall be found........ 2Kin 12:5
W I have walked with all Israel,........ 1Chr 17:6
or go w it seemeth convenient........ Jer 40:5
w the children of men dwell, the........ Dan 2:38
For w the carcase is, there will........ Mt 24:28
W this gospel shall be preached........ Mt 26:13
w he taketh him, he teareth him........ Mk 9:18
W this gospel shall be preached........ Mk 14:9
w he shall go in, say ye to the........ Mk 14:14
w the body is, thither will the........ Lk 17:37

WHERETO

w might the strength of their........ Job 30:2
prosper in the thing w I sent it........ Is 55:11
w we have already attained, let........ Phil 3:16

WHEREUNTO

of the tribe w they are received........ Num 36:3
of the tribe w they are received........ Num 36:4
perish from off the land w ye go........ Deut 4:26
of the ark of the LORD hath come........ 2Chr 8:11
w the king advanced him, are the........ Est 10:2
w I may continually resort........ Ps 71:3
But to the land w they desire to........ Jer 22:27
w I will not do any more the like........ Eze 5:9
What is the high place w ye go........ Eze 20:29
But w shall I liken this........ Mt 11:16
W shall we liken the kingdom of........ Mk 4:30
W then shall I liken the men of........ Lk 7:31
and w shall I resemble it........ Lk 13:18
W shall I liken the kingdom of........ Lk 13:20
doubted of them w this would grow........ Acts 5:24
Saul for the work w I have called........ Acts 13:2
nigh w was the city of Lasea........ Acts 27:8
w ye desire again to be in........ Gal 4:9
w I also labour, striving........ Col 1:29
w he called you by our gospel, to........ 2Th 2:14
w I am ordained a preacher, and a........ 1Ti 2:7
doctrine, w thou hast attained........ 1Ti 4:6
w thou art also called, and hast........ 1Ti 6:12
w I am appointed a preacher, and........ 2Ti 1:11
w also they were appointed........ 1Pet 2:8
The like figure w even baptism........ 1Pet 3:21
w ye do well that ye take heed,........ 2Pet 1:19

WHEREUPON

every thing w any part of their........ Lev 11:35
the pillars w the house standeth........ Judg 16:26
of gold, w the shewbread was,........ 1Kin 7:48
W the king took counsel, and made........ 1Kin 12:28
the princes of Israel and the........ 2Chr 12:6
W are the foundations thereof........ Job 38:6
w he was, to the threshold of the........ Eze 9:3
w thou hast set mine incense and........ Eze 23:41
that w they set their sacrifices,........ Eze 24:25
w they slew their sacrifices........ Eze 40:41
w also they laid the instruments........ Eze 40:42
the piece w it rained not........ Amos 4:7
w he promised with an oath to........ Mt 14:7
w certain Jews from Asia found me........ Acts 24:18
W as I went to Damascus with........ Acts 26:12
W, O king Agrippa, I was not........ Acts 26:19
w neither the first testament was........ Heb 9:18

WHEREWITH

blessing w his father blessed him........ Gen 27:41
w the Egyptians oppress them........ Ex 3:9
thine hand, w thou shalt do signs........ Ex 4:17
the bread w I have fed you in the........ Ex 16:32
w thou smotest the river, take in........ Ex 17:5
things w the atonement was made........ Ex 29:33
of the sanctuary w they minister........ Num 3:31
the odd number of them is to be........ Num 3:48
thereof, w they minister unto it........ Num 4:9
w they minister in the sanctuary,........ Num 4:12
w they minister about it, even........ Num 4:14
w they that were burnt had........ Num 16:39
w they beguiled you in the........ Num 25:18
her bond w she hath bound her........ Num 30:4
every bond w she hath bound her........ Num 30:4
of her bonds w she hath bound........ Num 30:5
of her lips, w she bound her soul........ Num 30:6
her bonds w she bound her soul........ Num 30:7
w she bound her soul, of none........ Num 30:8
w they have bound their souls,........ Num 30:9
every bond w she bound her soul........ Num 30:11
w may die, and he die, he is a........ Num 35:17
w he may die, and he die, he is a........ Num 35:18
w a man may die, seeing him not,........ Num 35:23
w the LORD was wroth against you........ Deut 9:19
of that w the LORD thy God hath........ Deut 15:14
vesture, w thou coverest thyself........ Deut 22:12
w thine enemies shall distress........ Deut 28:53
w thine enemies shall distress........ Deut 28:55
w thine enemy shall distress thee........ Deut 28:57
of thine heart w thou shalt fear........ Deut 28:67
w Moses the man of God blessed........ Deut 33:1
w he stretched out the spear........ Josh 8:26
Oh my Lord, w shall I save Israel........ Judg 6:15
w Abimelech hired vain and light........ Judg 9:4
w by me they honour God and man,........ Judg 9:9
w thou saidst, Who is Abimelech,........ Judg 9:38
w thou mightest be bound to........ Judg 16:6
thee, w thou mightest be bound........ Judg 16:10
tell me w thou mightest be bound........ Judg 16:13
tell us w we shall send it to his........ 1Sa 6:2
w they have forsaken me, and........ 1Sa 8:8
for w should he reconcile himself........ 1Sa 29:4
so that the hatred w he hated her........ 2Sa 13:15
than the love w he had loved her........ 2Sa 13:15
w shall I make the atonement,........ 2Sa 21:3
w I have made supplication before........ 1Kin 8:59
thereof, w Baasha had builded........ 1Kin 15:22
in his sin w he made Israel to........ 1Kin 15:26
by his provocation w he provoked........ 1Kin 15:30
in his sins w he made Israel to........ 1Kin 15:30
in his sin w he made Israel to........ 1Kin 16:26
for the provocation w thou hast........ 1Kin 21:22
And the LORD said unto him, W........ 1Kin 22:22
w might w he fought against........ 1Kin 22:45
beside his sin w he made Judah to........ 2Kin 21:16
w his anger was kindled against........ 2Kin 23:26
of brass w they ministered........ 2Kin 25:14

w Solomon made the brasen sea, and........ 1Chr 18:8
after the numbering w David his........ 2Chr 2:17
thereof, w Baasha was building........ 2Chr 16:5
And the LORD said unto him, W........ 2Chr 18:20
against the house w I have war........ 2Chr 35:21
w thou didst testify against them,........ Neh 9:34
or with speeches w he can do no........ Job 15:3
w they have reproached thee, O........ Ps 79:12
w thine enemies have reproached,........ Ps 89:51
w they have reproached the........ Ps 89:51
w he hath girded himself........ Ps 93:1
for a girdle w he is girded........ Ps 109:19
So shall I have w to answer him........ Ps 119:42
W the mower filleth not his hand........ Ps 129:7
king Solomon with the crown w his........ Song 3:11
This is the rest w ye may cause........ Is 28:12
w the servants of the king of........ Is 37:6
w I said I would benefit them........ Jer 18:10
w their enemies, and they that........ Jer 19:9
w ye fight against the king of........ Jer 21:4
this is the name w she shall be........ Jer 33:16
of brass w they ministered........ Jer 52:18
w the LORD hath afflicted me in........ Lam 1:12
the daubing w ye have daubed it........ Eze 13:12
w ye there hunt the souls to make........ Eze 13:20
w I fed thee, thou hast even set........ Eze 16:19
his labour w he served against it........ Eze 29:20
w they shall lament her........ Eze 32:16
for their idols w they had........ Eze 36:18
w they slew the burnt offering........ Eze 40:42
w his spirit was troubled, and his........ Dan 2:1
w shall I come before the LORD,........ Mic 6:6
this shall be the plague w the........ Zec 14:12
w the LORD will smite the heathen........ Zec 14:18
him for the fear w he feared me........ Mal 2:5
his savour, w shall it be salted........ Mt 5:13
blasphemies w soever they shall........ Mk 3:28
his saltness, w will ye season it........ Mk 9:50
savour, w shall it be seasoned........ Lk 14:34
unto him, Make ready w I may sup........ Lk 17:8
with the towel w he was girded........ Jn 13:5
the love w thou hast loved........ Jn 17:26
things w one may edify another........ Rom 14:19
by the comfort w we ourselves are........ 2Cor 1:4
but by the consolation w he was........ 2Cor 7:7
w I think to be bold against some........ 2Cor 10:2
w Christ hath made us free........ Gal 5:1
for his great love w he loved us,........ Eph 2:4
of the vocation w ye are called........ Eph 4:1
w ye shall be able to quench all........ Eph 6:16
for all the joy w we joy for your........ 1Th 3:9
w he was sanctified, an unholy........ Heb 10:29

WHEREWITHAL

W shall a young man cleanse his........ Ps 119:9
or, W shall we be clothed........ Mt 6:31

WHET

If I w my glittering sword, and........ Deut 32:41
he turn not, he will w his sword........ Ps 7:12
Who w their tongue like a sword,........ Ps 64:3
be blunt, and he do not w the edge........ Eccl 10:10

WHETHER

see w they have done altogether........ Gen 18:21
to wit w the LORD had made his........ Gen 24:21
w thou be my very son Esau or not........ Gen 27:21
w stolen by day, or stolen by........ Gen 31:39
see w it be well with thy........ Gen 37:14
know now w it be thy son's coat........ Gen 37:32
w there be any truth in you........ Gen 42:16
as to tell the man w ye had yet a........ Gen 43:6
Egypt, and see w they be yet alive........ Ex 4:18
w he be a stranger, or born in........ Ex 12:19
w they will walk in my law, or no........ Ex 16:4
w it be beast or man, it shall........ Ex 19:13
W he have gored a son, or have........ Ex 21:31
w it be ox, or ass, or sheep........ Ex 22:4
to see w he have put his hand........ Ex 22:8
w it be for ox, for ass, for........ Ex 22:9
w ox or sheep, that it........ Ex 34:19
w it be a male or female, he........ Lev 3:1
w he hath seen or known of it........ Lev 5:1
w it be a carcase of an unclean........ Lev 5:2
w it be of fowl or of beast, in........ Lev 7:26
w it be any vessel of wood, or........ Lev 11:32
w it be oven, or ranges for pots,........ Lev 11:35
w it be a woollen garment, or a........ Lev 13:47
W it be in the warp, or woof.........
w in a skin, or in any thing made........ Lev 13:48
w warp or woof, or woollen or in........ Lev 13:52
w it be bare within or without........ Lev 13:55
w his flesh run with his issue,........ Lev 15:3
w it be one of your own country,........ Lev 16:29
w it be one of your own country,........ Lev 17:15
w she be born at home, or born........ Lev 18:9
w it be cow or ewe, ye shall not........ Lev 22:28
value it, w it be good or bad........ Lev 27:12
estimate it, w it be good or bad........ Lev 27:14
w it be ox, or sheep........ Lev 27:26
w of the seed of the land, or of........ Lev 27:30
not search w it be good or bad........ Lev 27:33
w it was by day or by night that........ Num 9:21
Or w it were two days, or a month........ Num 9:22
thou shalt see now w my word........ Num 11:23
w they be strong or weak, few or........ Num 13:18
dwell in, w it be good or bad........ Num 13:19
w in tents, or in strong holds........ Num 13:19
w it be fat or lean........ Num 13:20
w there be wood therein, or not........ Num 13:20
w he be born in the land, or a........ Num 15:30
w it be of men or beasts, shall........ Num 18:15

WHICH

w there hath been any such thing .... Deut 4:32
heart, w thou wouldest keep his .... Deut 8:2
to know w ye love the LORD your .... Deut 13:3
a sacrifice, w it be ox or sheep .... Deut 18:3
w they be young ones, or eggs, and .... Deut 22:6
w be of thy brethren, or of .... Deut 24:14
w the gods which your fathers........ Josh 24:15
w they will keep the way of the .... Judg 2:22
to know w they would hearken unto .... Judg 3:4
W is better for you, either that........ Judg 9:2
that we may know w our way which .... Judg 18:5
not young men, w poor or rich .... Ruth 3:10
Who can tell w God will be 2Sa 12:22
in death or life, even there 2Sa 15:21
W they be come out for peace, ... 1Kin 20:18
or w they be come out for war, ... 1Kin 20:18
w any thing would come from him........ 1Kin 20:33
of Baal-zebub the god of Ekron w 2Kin 1:2
w with many, or with them that........ 2Chr 14:11
w small or great 2Chr 15:13
w man or woman 2Chr 15:13
their seed, w they were of Israel........ Ezr 2:59
w it be so, that a decree was .... Ezr 5:17
w it be unto death, or to .... Ezr 7:26
their seed, w they were of Israel .... Neh 7:61
to see w Mordecai's matters would .... Est 3:4
w man or woman, shall come unto .... Est 4:11
who knoweth w thou art come to........ Est 4:14
w it be done against a nation, or .... Job 34:29
w thou refuse, or w thou .... Job 34:33
w for correction, or for his land........ Job 37:13
w his work be pure .... Prov 20:11
and w it be right .... Prov 20:11
w he rage or laugh, there is no........ Prov 29:9
who knoweth w he shall be a wise........ Eccl 2:19
is sweet, w he eat little or much .... Eccl 5:12
thou knowest not w shall prosper........ Eccl 11:6
or w they both shall be alike........ Eccl 11:6
w it be good, or w it be .... Eccl 12:14
to see w the vine flourished, and .... Song 6:11
w the tender grape appear, and the .... Song 7:12
see w a man doth travail with .... Jer 30:6
W it be good, or w it be .... Jer 42:6
w they will hear, or w they .... Eze 2:5
w they will hear, or w they .... Eze 2:7
w they will hear, or w they .... Eze 3:11
or torn, w it be fowl or beast .... Eze 44:31
For w is easier, to say, Thy sins be .... Matt 9:5
W of them twain did the will of........ Mt 21:31
for w is greater, the gold, or .... Mt 23:17
for w is greater, the gift, or .... Mt 23:19
that thou tell us w thou be the .... Mt 26:63
W of the twain will ye that I .... Mt 27:21
let us see w Elias will come to........ Mt 27:49
W is it easier to say to the sick .... Mk 2:9
w he would heal him on the .... Mk 3:2
let us see w Elias will come to........ Mk 15:36
he asked him w he had been any .... Mk 15:44
w we be the Christ, or not .... Lk 3:15
W is easier, to say, Thy sins be .... Lk 5:23
w he would heal on the sabbath .... Lk 6:7
w he have sufficient to finish it........ Lk 14:28
consulteth w he be able with ten........ Lk 14:31
For w is greater, he that sitteth .... Lk 22:27
he asked w the man were .... Lk 23:6
w it be of God .... Jn 7:17
or w I speak of myself .... Jn 7:17
W he be a sinner or no, I know........ Jn 9:25
shew w of these two thou hast .... Acts 1:24
W it be right in the sight of God .... Acts 4:19
Tell me w ye sold the land for so .... Acts 5:8
w they were men or women, he .... Acts 9:2
And called, and asked w Simon........ Acts 10:18
daily, w those things were so .... Acts 17:11
heard w there be any Holy Ghost .... Acts 19:2
I asked him w he would go to .... Acts 25:20
w of us unto death, or of .... Rom 6:16
w prophecy, let us prophesy .... Rom 12:6
For w we live, we live unto the........ Rom 14:8
w we die, we die unto the Lord .... Rom 14:8
we live therefore, or die, w .... Rom 14:8
I know not w I baptized any other 1Cor 1:16
W Paul, or Apollos, or Cephas, or 1Cor 3:22
w thou shalt save thy husband 1Cor 7:16
w thou shalt save thy wife 1Cor 7:16
w in heaven or in earth, (as 1Cor 8:5
W therefore ye eat, or drink, or 1Cor 10:31
w we be Jews or Gentiles 1Cor 12:13
we be bond or free 1Cor 12:13
w one member suffer, all the 1Cor 12:26
but w there be prophecies, they........ 1Cor 13:8
w there be tongues, they shall 1Cor 13:8
w there be knowledge, it shall 1Cor 13:8
w pipe or harp, except they give 1Cor 14:7
Therefore w it were I or they, so 1Cor 15:11
w we be afflicted, it is for your 2Cor 1:6
or w we be comforted, it is for 2Cor 1:6
W ye be obedient in all things 2Cor 2:9
w present or absent, we may be........ 2Cor 5:9
he hath done, w it be good or bad 2Cor 5:10
For w we be beside ourselves, it 2Cor 5:13
or w we be sober, it is for your........ 2Cor 5:13
W any do enquire of Titus, he is 2Cor 8:23
(w in the body, I cannot tell........ 2Cor 12:2
or w out of the body, I cannot 2Cor 12:2
(w in the body, or out of the 2Cor 12:3
yourselves, w ye be in the faith 2Cor 13:5
of the Lord, w he be bond or free .... Eph 6:8
w in pretence, or in truth, ... Phil 1:18
w it be by life, or by death .... Phil 1:20

that w I come and see you, or else .... Phil 1:27
w they be thrones, or dominions, ... Col 1:16
w they be things in earth, or .... Col 1:20
w we wake or sleep, we should 1Th 5:10
w by word, or our epistle 2Th 2:15
w it be to the king, as supreme........ 1Pet 2:13
try the spirits w they are of God 1Jn 4:1

WHICH See PREFACE.

WHILE

W the earth remaineth, seedtime........ Gen 8:22
w he lingered, the men laid hold .... Gen 19:16
he yet lived, eastward, unto .... Gen 25:6
w he yet spake with them, Rachel .... Gen 29:9
w Joseph made himself known unto .... Gen 45:1
and wept on his neck a good w .... Gen 46:29
w my glory passeth by, that I .... Ex 33:22
thee with my hand w I pass by .... Ex 33:22
face shone w he talked with him .... Ex 34:29
w he doeth somewhat against any .... Lev 4:27
w the that it is shut up shall be .... Lev 13:46
w she lieth desolate without them.... Lev 26:43
w the flesh was yet between their .... Num 11:33
w the children of Israel were in .... Num 15:32
w I meet the LORD yonder .... Num 23:15
w he was zealous for my sake .... Num 25:11
w his heart is hot, and overtake........ Deut 19:6
w I am yet alive with you this .... Deut 31:27
w the children of Israel wandered .... Josh 5:6
And Ehud escaped w they tarried........ Judg 3:26
W Israel dwelt in Heshbon and her .... Judg 11:26
seven days, w their feast lasted .... Judg 14:17
it came to pass within a w after........ Judg 16:27
that beheld w Samson made sport........ Judg 16:27
w the flesh was in seething, with 1Sa 2:13
w the ark abode in Kirjath-jearim 1Sa 7:2
on,) but stand thou still a w 1Sa 9:27
w Saul talked unto the priest, ... 1Sa 14:19
thou shalt not only w yet I live 1Sa 20:14
that w David was in the hold 1Sa 22:4
all the w they were in Carmel 1Sa 25:16
all the w we were with them 1Sa 25:16
w he dwelleth in the country of 1Sa 27:11
w there was war between the house 2Sa 3:6
to eat meat w it was yet day 2Sa 7:19
house for a great w to come 2Sa 7:19
w the child was yet alive, we 2Sa 12:18
for the child, w it was alive 2Sa 12:21
W the child was yet alive, I 2Sa 12:22
w they were in the way, that 2Sa 13:30
vow w I abode at Geshur in Syria 2Sa 15:8
Giloh, w he offered sacrifices 2Sa 15:12
will come upon him w he is weary 2Sa 17:2
w he was yet alive in the midst 2Sa 18:14
sustenance w he lay at Mahanaim 2Sa 19:32
thine enemies, w they pursue thee 2Sa 24:13
w thou yet talkest there with the 1Kin 1:14
w she yet talked with the king, ... 1Kin 1:22
w he yet spake, behold, Jonathan 1Kin 1:42
w thine handmaid slept, and laid 1Kin 3:20
the house, w it was in building 1Kin 6:7
Solomon has father w he was 1Kin 8:54
And it came to pass after a w 1Kin 17:7
And it came to pass in the mean w 1Kin 18:45
w he yet talked with them, behold 2Kin 6:33
Though w he lived w yet being........ 1Chr 12:1
house for a great w to come 1Chr 17:17
w that the sword of thine enemies 1Chr 21:12
Solomon his father w he was 2Chr 10:6
w the land is yet before us 2Chr 14:7
is with you, w ye be with him 2Chr 15:2
w he was yet young, he began to........ 2Chr 34:3
they stand by, let them shut .... Neh 7:3
w Mordecai sat in the king's gate .... Est 2:21
w they were yet talking with him .... Est 6:14
W he was yet speaking, there came .... Job 1:16
W he was yet speaking, there came .... Job 1:17
W he was yet speaking, there came .... Job 1:18
rain it upon him w he is eating .... Job 20:23
They are exalted for a little w .... Job 24:24
All the w my breath is in me, and .... Job 27:3
w there is none to deliver .... Ps 7:2
w they took counsel together .... Ps 31:13
For yet a little w, and the wicked .... Ps 37:10
of the wicked is before me .... Ps 39:1
w I was musing the fire burned........ Ps 39:3
w they continually say unto me, ... Ps 42:3
w they say daily unto me, Where, ... Ps 42:10
Though w he lived w he blessed his .... Ps 49:18
Thus will I bless thee w I live .... Ps 63:4
mine eyes fail w I wait for my .... Ps 69:3
but w their meat was yet in their .... Ps 78:30
I suffer thy terrors I am .... Ps 88:15
to my God w I have my being .... Ps 104:33
W I live will I praise the LORD .... Ps 146:2
unto my God w I have any being .... Ps 146:2
W as yet he had not made the .... Prov 8:26
Chasten thy son w there is hope........ Prov 19:18
She riseth also w it is yet night .... Prov 31:15
is in their heart w they live .... Eccl 9:3
w the evil days come not, nor the .... Eccl 12:1
W the sun, or the light, or the .... Eccl 12:2
W the king sitteth at his table, ... Song 1:12
For yet a very little w, and the .... Is 10:25
w it is yet in his hand he eateth .... Is 28:4
Is it not yet a very little w .... Is 29:17
ye the LORD w he may be found .... Is 55:6
call ye upon him w he is near .... Is 55:6
have possessed it but a little w .... Is 63:18

w they are yet speaking, I will........ Is 65:24
w ye look for light, we turn it .... Jer 13:16
sun is gone down w it was yet day .... Jer 15:9
w he was yet shut up in the court .... Jer 33:1
w he was shut up in the court of .... Jer 39:15
Now w he was not yet gone back, ... Jer 40:5
yet a little w, and the time of .... Jer 51:33
w they sought their meat to .... Lam 1:19
w they were slaying them, and I .... Eze 9:8
The word was in the king's .... Dan 4:31
for yet a little w, and I will .... Hos 1:4
For w they be folden together as .... Nah 1:10
w they are drunken as drunkards, ... Nah 1:10
Yet once, it is a little w .... Hag 2:6
away w they stand upon their feet .... Zec 14:12
But w he thought on these things, ... Mt 1:20
W he spake these things unto them .... Mt 9:18
W he yet talked to the people, ... Mt 12:46
in himself, but durst for a w .... Mt 13:25
But w men slept, his enemy came .... Mt 13:25
lest w ye gather up the tares, ye .... Mt 13:29
w he sent the multitudes away .... Mt 14:22
W he yet spake, behold, a bright .... Mt 17:5
w they abode in Galilee, Jesus, ... Mt 17:22
W the Pharisees were gathered........ Mt 22:41
W the bridegroom tarried, they .... Mt 25:5
And w they went to buy, the .... Mt 25:10
ye here, w I go and pray yonder .... Mt 26:36
w he yet spake, lo, Judas, one of .... Mt 26:47
after a w came unto him they that .... Mt 26:73
w he was yet alive, After three .... Mt 27:63
and stole him away w we slept .... Mt 28:13
rising up a great w before day........ Mk 1:35
w the bridegroom is with them .... Mk 2:19
W he yet spake, there came from .... Mk 5:35
into a desert place, and rest a w .... Mk 6:31
w he sent away the people .... Mk 6:45
w he taught in the temple, How .... Mk 12:35
Sit ye here, w I shall pray .... Mk 14:32
w he yet spake, cometh Judas, one .... Mk 14:43
whether he had been any w dead .... Mk 15:44
that w he executed the priest's........ Lk 1:8
w they were there, the days were .... Lk 2:6
w the bridegroom is with them .... Lk 5:34
no root, which for a w believe........ Lk 8:13
W he yet spake, there cometh one .... Lk 8:49
W thus spake, there came a .... Lk 9:34
But w they wondered every one at .... Lk 9:43
they had a great w ago repented .... Lk 10:13
w the other is yet a great way........ Lk 14:32
And he would not for a w .... Lk 18:4
And w he yet spake, behold .... Lk 22:47
after a little w another saw him........ Lk 22:58
w he yet spake, the cock crew .... Lk 22:60
w they communed together and .... Lk 24:15
w he talked with us by the way, ... Lk 24:32
w he opened to us the scriptures .... Lk 24:32
w they yet believed not for joy, ... Lk 24:41
w I was yet with you, that all .... Lk 24:44
he blessed them, he was parted .... Lk 24:51
in the mean w his disciples .... Jn 4:31
but w I am coming, another .... Jn 5:7
Yet a little w am I with you, and .... Jn 7:33
of him that sent me, w it is day .... Jn 9:4
Yet a little w is the light with .... Jn 12:35
Walk w ye have the light, lest .... Jn 12:35
W ye have light, believe in the, ... Jn 12:36
yet a little w I am with you .... Jn 13:33
Yet a little w, and the world .... Jn 14:19
A little w, and ye shall not see........ Jn 16:16
and again, a little w, and ye shall .... Jn 16:16
that he saith unto us, A little w, ... Jn 16:17
and again, a little w, and ye shall .... Jn 16:17
is this that he saith, A little w .... Jn 16:18
of that I said, A little w, and ye .... Jn 16:19
and again, a little w, and ye shall .... Jn 16:19
W I was with them in the world, I .... Jn 17:12
w they beheld, he was taken up .... Acts 1:9
w they looked stedfastly toward .... Acts 1:10
Dorcas made, w she was with them .... Acts 9:39
but w they made ready, he fell........ Acts 10:10
Now w Peter doubted in himself........ Acts 10:17
W Peter thought on the vision, ... Acts 10:19
W Peter yet spake these words, ... Acts 10:44
w know how that a good w ago God .... Acts 15:7
Now w Paul waited for them at .... Acts 17:16
this tarried there a good w .... Acts 19:11
w Apollos was at Corinth, Paul .... Acts 19:1
and eaten, and talked a long w .... Acts 20:11
even w I prayed in the temple, I .... Acts 22:17
w I stood before the council, ... Acts 24:20
W he answered for himself, ... Acts 26:1
w the day was coming on, Paul .... Acts 27:33
after they had looked a great w .... Acts 28:6
their thoughts the mean w .... Rom 2:15
w we were yet sinners, Christ .... Rom 5:8
w her husband liveth, she be........ Rom 7:2
For w one saith, I am of Paul 1Cor 3:4
eat no flesh w the world standeth 1Cor 8:13
but I trust to tarry a w with you 1Cor 16:7
W we look not at the things which 2Cor 4:18
w we seek to be justified by........ Gal 2:17
in pleasure is dead w she liveth 1Ti 5:6
W it is said, To day if ye will .... Heb 3:15
w as the first tabernacle was yet .... Heb 9:8
w ye at all w the testators lived .... Heb 10:37
For yet a little w, and he that .... Heb 10:37
W they behold your chaste 1Pet 3:2

W

w the ark was a preparing,.............1Pet 3:20
after that ye have suffered a w.....1Pet 5:10
deceivings by they feast with you...2Pet 2:13
W they promise them liberty, they....2Pet 2:19

WHILES

W they see vanity unto thee,.........Eze 21:29
w they divine a lie unto thee, to....Eze 21:29
w they minister in the gates of......Eze 44:17
w he tasted the wine, commanded......Dan 5:2
w I was speaking, and praying, and...Dan 9:20
w I was speaking in prayer, even.....Dan 9:21
like an oven, w they lie in wait.....Hos 7:6
w thou art in the way with him.......Mt 5:25
W it remained, was it not thine......Acts 5:4
W by the experiment of this..........2Cor 9:13

WHILST

put to death is it yet morning.......Judg 6:31
w I leave it, and come down to you...Neh 6:3
W it is yet in his greenness, and....Job 8:12
w ye searched out what to say........Job 32:11
own nets, w that I withal escape.....Ps 141:10
W their children remember their......Jer 17:2
w we are at home in the body, we.....2Cor 5:6
w he remembereth the obedience of...2Cor 7:15
w ye were made a gazingstock both...Heb 10:33
w ye became companions of them......Heb 10:33

WHIP

A w for the horse, a bridle for......Prov 26:3
The noise of a w, and the noise of...Nah 3:2

WHIPS

father hath chastised you with w.....1Kin 12:11
father also chastised you with w....1Kin 12:14
my father chastised you with w......2Chr 10:11
my father chastised you with w......2Chr 10:14

WHIRLETH

it w about continually, and the.....Eccl 1:6

WHIRLWIND

take up Elijah into heaven by a w....2Kin 2:1
Elijah went up by a w into heaven...2Kin 2:11
Out of the south cometh the w.......Job 37:9
LORD answered Job out of the w.......Job 38:1
the LORD unto Job out of the w......Job 40:6
shall take them away as with a w....Ps 58:9
and your destruction cometh as a w..Prov 1:27
As the w passeth, so is the..........Prov 10:25
flint, and their wheels like a w....Is 5:28
like a rolling thing before the w...Is 17:13
the w shall take them away as.......Is 40:24
away, and the w shall scatter them...Is 41:16
and with his chariots like a w......Is 66:15
and his chariots shall be as a.......Jer 4:13
a w of the LORD is gone forth in....Jer 23:19
forth in fury, even a grievous w....Jer 23:19
a great w shall be raised up from...Jer 25:32
the w of the LORD goeth forth.......Jer 30:23
forth with fury, a continuing w.....Jer 30:23
a w came out of the north, a........Eze 1:4
shall come against him like a w....Dan 11:40
wind, and they shall reap the w....Hos 8:7
with the w out of the floor.........Hos 13:3
a tempest in the day of the w.......Amos 1:14
the LORD hath his way in the w......Nah 1:3
came out as a w to scatter me.......Hab 3:14
But I scattered them with a w.......Zec 7:14

WHIRLWINDS

As in the south pass through.........Is 21:1
and shall go with w of the south....Zec 9:14

WHISPER

All that hate me w together..........Ps 41:7
speech shall w out of the dust......Is 29:4

WHISPERED

David saw that his servants w........2Sa 12:19

WHISPERER

a w separateth chief friends.........Prov 16:28

WHISPERERS

w,...................................Rom 1:29

WHISPERINGS

wraths, strifes, backbitings, w.....2Cor 12:20

WHIT

and all the spoil thereof every w....Deut 13:16
And Samuel told him every w..........1Sa 3:18
every w whole on the sabbath day....Jn 7:23
his feet, but is clean every w......Jn 13:10
not a w behind the very chiefest....2Cor 11:5

WHITE

every one that had some w in it......Gen 30:35
pilled w strakes in them.............Gen 30:37
made the w appear which was in......Gen 30:37
I had three w baskets on my head....Gen 40:16
wine, and his teeth w with milk.....Gen 49:12
and it was like coriander seed, w...Ex 16:31
hair in the plague is turned w......Lev 13:3
If the bright spot be w in the......Lev 13:4
the hair thereof be not turned w....Lev 13:4
if the rising be w in the skin......Lev 13:10
and it have turned the hair w.......Lev 13:10
it is all turned w.................Lev 13:13
turn again, and be changed unto w...Lev 13:16
if the plague be turned into w.....Lev 13:17
of the boil there be a w rising....Lev 13:19
or a bright spot, w..................Lev 13:19
and the hair thereof be turned w...Lev 13:19
there be no w hairs therein, and....Lev 13:21

that burneth have a w bright spot...Lev 13:24
somewhat reddish, or w...............Lev 13:24
in the bright spot be turned w......Lev 13:25
there be no w hair in the place.....Lev 13:26
bright spots, even w bright spots...Lev 13:38
skin of their flesh be darkish w...Lev 13:39
bald forehead, a w reddish sore.....Lev 13:42
be w reddish in his bald head.......Lev 13:42
Miriam became leprous, as snow......Num 12:10
Speak, ye that ride on w asses......Judg 5:10
his presence a leper as w as snow...2Kin 5:27
being arrayed in w linen............2Chr 5:12
Where were w, green, and blue,......Est 1:6
a pavement of red, and blue, and w..Est 1:6
in royal apparel of blue and w.....Est 8:15
any taste in the w of an egg.......Job 6:6
it was w as snow in Salmon..........Ps 68:14
Let thy garments be always w........Eccl 9:8
My beloved is w and ruddy, the......Song 5:10
they shall be as w as snow..........Is 1:18
in the wine of Helbon, and w wool...Eze 27:18
sit, whose garment was w as snow...Dan 7:9
and to purge, and to make them w....Dan 11:35
Many shall be purified, and made w..Dan 12:10
the branches thereof are made w....Joel 1:7
there red horses, speckled, and w...Zec 1:8
And in the third chariot w horses..Zec 6:3
the w go forth after them...........Zec 6:6
not make one hair w or black........Mt 5:36
and his raiment was as the light...Mt 17:2
and his raiment w as snow...........Mt 28:3
shining, exceeding w as snow........Mk 9:3
as no fuller on earth can w them....Mk 9:3
side, clothed in a long w garment...Mk 16:5
was altered, and his raiment was w..Lk 9:29
for they are w already to harvest...Jn 4:35
And seeth two angels in w sitting...Jn 20:12
men stood by them in w apparel.....Acts 1:10
w like wool, as w as snow...........Rev 1:14
manna, and will give him a w stone..Rev 2:17
and they shall walk with me in w...Rev 3:4
shall be clothed in w raiment......Rev 3:5
w raiment, that thou mayest be......Rev 3:18
sitting, clothed in w raiment......Rev 4:4
And I saw, and behold a w horse.....Rev 6:2
w robes were given unto every one...Rev 6:11
the Lamb, clothed with w robes......Rev 7:9
which are arrayed in w robes........Rev 7:13
made them w in the blood of the....Rev 7:14
And I looked, and behold a w cloud..Rev 14:14
w linen, and having their breasts...Rev 15:6
arrayed in fine linen, clean and w..Rev 19:8
opened, and behold a w horse........Rev 19:11
heaven followed him upon w horses...Rev 19:14
clothed in fine linen, w............Rev 19:14
And I saw a great w throne..........Rev 20:11

WHITED

for ye are like unto w sepulchres...Mt 23:27
God shall smite thee, thou w wall...Acts 23:3

WHITER

me, and I shall be w than snow......Ps 51:7
than snow, they were w than milk....Lam 4:7

WHITHER

and w wilt thou go....................Gen 16:8
at every place w we shall come......Gen 20:13
thee in all places w thou goest.....Gen 28:15
and w goest thou...................Gen 32:17
and I, w shall I go..................Gen 37:30
thee a place w he shall flee........Ex 21:13
of the land w thou goest, lest it...Ex 34:12
w I bring you, shall ye not be......Lev 18:3
w I bring you to dwell therein,.....Lev 20:22
unto the land w thou sentest us....Num 13:27
come into the land w I bring you....Num 15:18
city of his refuge, w he was fled...Num 35:25
city of his refuge, w he had fled...Num 35:26
W shall we go up.....................Deut 1:28
all the kingdoms w thou passest....Deut 3:21
in the land w ye go to possess it...Deut 4:5
land w ye go over to possess it....Deut 4:14
w the LORD shall lead you...........Deut 4:27
in the land w ye go to possess it...Deut 6:1
land w thou goest to possess it.....Deut 7:1
the land, w ye go to possess it,....Deut 11:8
w thou goest in to possess it,......Deut 11:10
w ye go to possess it, is a land....Deut 11:11
land w thou goest to possess it.....Deut 11:29
w thou goest to possess them, and...Deut 12:29
thou shalt let go w ye shall will...Deut 21:14
w thou shalt go forth abroad.......Deut 23:12
land w thou goest to possess it.....Deut 23:20
w thou goest to possess it..........Deut 28:21
among all nations w the LORD.......Deut 28:37
land w thou goest to possess it....Deut 28:63
w the LORD thy God hath driven.....Deut 30:1
land w the LORD thy God hath scattered...Deut 30:3
w thou passest over Jordan to go....Deut 30:18
as long as ye live in the land w....Deut 31:13
w they go to be among them, and....Deut 31:16
w ye go over Jordan to possess it...Deut 32:47
die in the mount w thou goest up...Deut 32:50
the men when I wot not..............Josh 2:5
and the old man said, W goest thou..Judg 19:17
for w thou goest, I will go.........Ruth 1:16
him and to his servant, W went we...1Sa 10:14
W have ye made a road to day........1Sa 27:10
And David said, W shall I go up.....2Sa 2:1

w shall I cause my shame to go......2Sa 13:13
seeing I go w I may, return thou,...2Sa 15:20
w they went down.....................2Sa 17:18
and go not forth thence any w.......1Kin 2:36
out, and walkest abroad any w.......1Kin 2:42
land w they were carried captives...1Kin 8:47
w my lord hath not sent to seek....1Kin 18:10
shall carry thee w I know not.......1Kin 18:12
w he is gone down to possess it....1Kin 21:18
And he said, Thy servant went no w..2Kin 5:25
land w they are carried captive....2Chr 6:37
w they have carried them captives..2Chr 6:38
w he had fled from the presence.....2Chr 10:2
And the rulers knew not w I went....Neh 2:16
W the tribes go up, the tribes of...Ps 122:4
W shall I go from thy spirit........Ps 139:7
or w shall I flee from thy..........Ps 139:7
in the grave, w thou goest..........Ps 139:7
W is thy beloved gone, O thou.......Song 6:1
w is thy beloved turned aside.......Song 6:1
w we flee for help to be............Is 20:6
the places w I have driven them....Jer 8:3
unto thee, W shall we go forth......Jer 15:2
the lands w he had driven them......Jer 16:15
w he is gone down to possess it....Jer 18:14
place w they have led him captive..Jer 22:12
countries w I have driven them......Jer 23:3
all countries w I had driven them..Jer 23:8
in all places w I shall drive......Jer 24:9
seek the peace of the city w I.....Jer 29:7
the places w I have driven you......Jer 29:14
the nations w I have driven them...Jer 29:18
nations w I have scattered thee....Jer 30:11
w I have driven them in mine........Jer 32:37
w it seemeth good and convenient....Jer 40:4
of all places w they were driven...Jer 40:12
in the place w ye desire to go and..Jer 42:22
w they had been driven, to dwell...Jer 43:5
w ye be gone to dwell, that ye......Jer 44:8
a prey in all places w thou goest..Jer 45:5
the nations w I have driven thee...Jer 46:28
there shall be no nation w the.....Jer 49:36
w the spirit was to go, they went..Eze 1:12
the Gentiles, w I will drive them..Eze 4:13
remember me among the nations w....Eze 6:9
but to the place w the head........Eze 10:11
among the heathen w they come.......Eze 12:16
the people w they were scattered....Eze 29:13
w they went, they profaned my......Eze 36:20
among the heathen, w they went......Eze 36:21
among the heathen, w we went........Eze 36:22
w they be gone, and will gather....Eze 37:21
shall live w the river cometh......Eze 47:9
countries w thou hast driven them..Dan 9:7
the place w ye have sold them.......Joel 3:7
Then said I, W goest thou...........Zec 2:2
W do these bear the ephah...........Zec 5:10
and place, w he himself would come..Lk 10:1
unto the village, w they went.......Lk 24:28
whence it cometh, and w it goeth....Jn 3:8
ship was at the land w they went....Jn 6:21
W will he go, that we shall not.....Jn 7:35
I know whence I came, and w I go....Jn 8:14
tell whence I come, and w I go......Jn 8:14
w I go, ye cannot come..............Jn 8:21
he saith, W I go, ye cannot come....Jn 8:22
darkness knoweth not w he goeth....Jn 12:35
the Jews, W I go, ye cannot come....Jn 13:33
said unto him, Lord, w goest thou..Jn 13:36
W I go, thou canst not follow me....Jn 13:36
w I go ye know, and the way ye......Jn 14:4
Lord, we know not w thou goest.....Jn 14:5
of you asketh me, W goest thou......Jn 16:5
temple, w the Jews always resort....Jn 18:20
and walkedst w thou wouldest........Jn 21:18
carry thee w thou wouldest not.....Jn 21:18
W the forerunner is for us..........Heb 6:20
went out, not knowing w he went....Heb 11:8
and knoweth not w he goeth..........1Jn 2:11

WHITHERSOEVER

thou mayest prosper w thou goest....Josh 1:7
thy God is with thee w thou goest...Josh 1:9
w thou sendest us, we will go.......Josh 1:16
W they went out, the hand of the...Judg 2:15
w he turned himself, he vexed......1Sa 14:47
And David went out w Saul sent him..1Sa 18:5
Keilah, and went w they could go...1Sa 23:13
And I was with thee w thou wentest...2Sa 7:9
LORD preserved David w he went......2Sa 8:6
Lord preserved David w he went......2Sa 8:14
doest, and w thou turnest thyself...1Kin 2:3
w thou shalt send them, and shall..1Kin 5:44
he prospered w he went forth.......2Kin 18:7
been with thee w thou hast walked..1Chr 17:8
LORD preserved David w he went......1Chr 18:6
LORD preserved David w he went......1Chr 18:13
w the king's commandment and his...Est 4:17
w the king's commandment and his...Est 8:17
w it turneth, it prospereth........Prov 17:8
he turneth it w he will.............Prov 21:1
W the spirit was to go, they went..Eze 1:20
or on the left, w thy face is set..Eze 21:16
w the rivers shall come, shall.....Eze 47:9
I will follow thee w thou goest.....Mt 8:19
w he entered, into villages, or.....Mk 6:56
I will follow thee w thou goest.....Lk 9:57
may bring me on my journey w I go...1Cor 16:6
helm, w the governor listeth........Jas 3:4
which follow the Lamb w he goeth....Rev 14:4

WHO

WHO See PREFACE.

WHOLE

watered the w face of the ground ...... Gen 2:6
compasseth the w land of Havilah ...... Gen 2:11
compasseth the w land of Ethiopia ...... Gen 2:13
that were under the w heaven ...... Gen 7:19
were on the face of the w earth ...... Gen 8:9
and of them was the w earth ...... Gen 9:19
the w earth was of one language, ... Gen 11:1
upon the face of the w earth ...... Gen 11:4
Is not the w land before thee ...... Gen 13:9
so the w age of Jacob was an ...... Gen 47:28
covered the face of the w earth ...... Ex 10:15
and the w assembly of the ...... Ex 12:6
the w congregation of the ...... Ex 16:2
to kill this w assembly with ...... Ex 16:3
as Aaron spake unto the w ...... Ex 16:10
the w mount quaked greatly ...... Ex 19:18
burn the w ram upon the altar ...... Ex 29:18
the w rump, it shall he take of ...... Lev 3:9
Even the w bullock shall he carry ...... Lev 4:12
if the w congregation of Israel ...... Lev 4:13
he shall offer one out of the w ...... Lev 7:14
Moses burnt the w ram upon the ...... Lev 8:21
the w house of Israel, bewail the ...... Lev 10:6
within a w year after it is sold ...... Lev 25:29
the charge of the w congregation ...... Num 3:7
thou shalt gather the w assembly ...... Num 8:9
of a w piece shalt thou make them ...... Num 10:2
But even a w month, until it come ...... Num 11:20
that they may eat a w month ...... Num 11:21
the w congregation said unto them ...... Num 14:2
you, according to your w number ...... Num 14:29
even the w congregation, into the ...... Num 20:22
Israel, even the w congregation, ... Num 20:29
that are under the w heaven ...... Deut 2:25
all nations under the w heaven ...... Deut 4:19
of the LORD thy God of w stones ...... Deut 27:6
that the w land thereof is ...... Deut 29:23
w burnt sacrifice upon thine ...... Deut 33:10
in the camp, till they were w ...... Josh 5:8
of Moses, an altar of w stones ...... Josh 8:31
not to go down about a w day ...... Josh 10:13
So Joshua took the w land ...... Josh 11:23
the w congregation of the ...... Josh 18:1
the w congregation of the ...... Josh 21:1
Thus saith the w congregation of ...... Josh 22:16
with the w congregation of Israel ...... Josh 22:18
and was there four w months ...... Judg 19:2
the w congregation sent some to ...... Judg 21:13
because my life is yet w in me 2Sa 1:9
good to the w house of Benjamin 2Sa 3:19
even among the w multitude of 2Sa 16:22
the w family is risen against 2Sa 14:7
the w house he overlaid with gold 1Kin 6:22
also the w altar that was by the 1Kin 6:22
the w kingdom out of his hand 1Kin 11:34
For the w house of Ahab shall 2Kin 9:8
blessed the w congregation of 2Chr 6:3
and sought him with their w desire 2Chr 15:15
to and fro throughout the w earth 2Chr 16:9
The w number of the chief of the 2Chr 26:12
the w assembly took counsel to 2Chr 30:23
them, according to the w law 2Chr 33:8
The w congregation together was ...... Ezr 2:64
the w congregation together was ...... Neh 7:66
the w kingdom of Ahasuerus ...... Est 3:6
he woundeth, and his hands make w ...... Job 5:18
and seeth under the w heaven ...... Job 28:24
Or who hath disposed the w world ...... Job 34:13
directeth it under the w heaven ...... Job 37:3
is under the w heaven is mine ...... Job 41:11
then, O LORD, with my w heart ...... Ps 9:1
situation, the joy of the w earth ...... Ps 48:2
offering and w burnt offering ...... Ps 51:19
let the w earth be filled with ...... Ps 72:19
of the LORD of the w earth ...... Ps 97:5
he brake the w staff of bread ...... Ps 105:16
praise the LORD with my w heart ...... Ps 111:1
and that seek him with the w heart ...... Ps 119:2
With my w heart have I sought ...... Ps 119:10
shall observe it with my w heart ...... Ps 119:34
thy favour with my w heart ...... Ps 119:58
keep thy precepts with my w heart ...... Ps 119:69
I cried with my w heart ...... Ps 119:145
will praise thee with my w heart ...... Ps 138:1
and w, as those that go down into ...... Prov 1:12
but the w disposing thereof is of ...... Prov 16:33
shewed before the w congregation ...... Prov 26:26
the conclusion of the w matter ...... Eccl 12:13
for this is the w duty of man ...... Eccl 12:13
the w head is sick ...... Is 1:5
and the w heart faint ...... Is 1:5
the w stay of bread ...... Is 3:1
and the w stay of water ...... Is 3:1
the w earth is full of his glory ...... Is 6:3
his w work upon mount Zion ...... Is 10:12
to destroy the w land ...... Is 13:5
The w earth is at rest, and is ...... Is 14:7
that is purposed upon the w earth ...... Is 14:26
w Palestina, because the rod of ...... Is 14:29
w Palestina, art dissolved ...... Is 14:31
and I am set in my w nights ...... Is 21:8
even determined upon the w earth ...... Is 28:22
The God of the w earth shall he ...... Is 54:5
brazen walls against the w land ...... Jer 1:18
turned unto me with her w heart ...... Jer 3:10
for the w land is spoiled ...... Jer 4:20
The w land shall be desolate ...... Jer 4:27
The w city shall flee for the ...... Jer 4:29

even the w seed of Ephraim ...... Jer 7:15
the w land trembled at the sound ...... Jer 8:16
the w land is made desolate, ... Jer 12:11
unto the w house of Israel ...... Jer 13:11
the w house of Judah, saith the ...... Jer 13:11
man of contention to the w ...... Jer 15:10
that cannot be made w again ...... Jer 19:11
return unto me with their w heart ...... Jer 24:7
this w land shall be a desolation ...... Jer 25:11
the w valley of the dead bodies, ... Jer 31:40
my w heart and with my w soul ...... Jer 32:41
the w house of the Rechabites ...... Jer 35:3
the w army of the Chaldeans that ...... Jer 37:10
I will pluck up, even this w land ...... Jer 45:4
the w land cut in asunder ...... Jer 51:41
praise of the w earth surprised ...... Jer 51:41
her w land shall be confounded, ... Jer 51:47
of beauty, The joy of the w earth ...... Lam 2:15
the w remnant of thee will I ...... Eze 5:10
touching the w multitude thereof ...... Eze 7:13
And their w body, and their backs, ... Eze 10:12
Behold, when it was w, it was ...... Eze 15:5
beasts of the w earth with thee ...... Eze 32:4
When the w earth rejoiceth, ... Eze 35:14
bones are the w house of Israel ...... Eze 37:11
mercy upon the w house of Israel ...... Eze 39:25
they may keep the w form thereof ...... Eze 43:11
the top of the mountain the w ...... Eze 43:12
be for the w house of Israel ...... Eze 45:6
mountain, and filled the w earth ...... Dan 2:35
over the w province of Babylon ...... Dan 2:48
should be over the w kingdom ...... Dan 6:1
to set him over the w realm ...... Dan 6:3
and shall devour the w earth ...... Dan 7:23
of the kingdom under the w heaven ...... Dan 7:27
west on the face of the w earth, ... Dan 8:5
for under the w heaven hath not ...... Dan 9:12
till three w weeks were fulfilled ...... Dan 10:3
the strength of his w kingdom ...... Dan 11:17
away captive the w captivity ...... Amos 1:6
up the w captivity to Edom ...... Amos 1:9
against the w family which I ...... Amos 3:1
unto the Lord of the w earth ...... Mic 4:13
but the w land shall be devoured ...... Zeph 1:18
run to and fro through the w earth ...... Zec 4:10
stand by the Lord of the w earth ...... Zec 6:5
over the face of the w earth ...... Zec 5:3
robbed me, even this w nation ...... Mal 3:9
not that thy w body should be ...... Mt 5:29
not that thy w body should be ...... Mt 5:30
thy w body shall be full of light ...... Mt 6:22
thy w body shall be full of ...... Mt 6:23
the w herd of swine ran violently, ... Mt 8:32
touch his garment, I shall be w ...... Mt 9:21
That they w need not a ...... Mt 9:12
faith hath made thee w ...... Mt 9:22
woman was made w from that hour ...... Mt 9:22
and it was restored w, like as the ...... Mt 12:13
the w multitude stood on the ...... Mt 13:2
of meal, till the w was leavened ...... Mt 13:33
as touched were made perfectly w ...... Mt 14:36
was made w from that very hour ...... Mt 15:28
and to speak, the maimed to be w, ... Mt 15:31
if he shall gain the w world ...... Mt 16:26
shall be preached in the w world ...... Mt 26:13
unto him the w band of soldiers ...... Mt 27:27
They that are w have no need of ...... Mk 2:17
hand was restored as the other ...... Mk 3:5
the w multitude was by the sea on ...... Mk 4:1
but his clothes, I shall be w ...... Mk 5:28
thy faith hath made thee w ...... Mk 5:34
in peace, and be w of thy plague ...... Mk 5:34
ran through that w region round ...... Mk 6:55
many as touched him were made w ...... Mk 6:56
man, if he shall gain the w world ...... Mk 8:36
thy faith hath made thee w ...... Mk 10:52
more than all w burnt offerings ...... Mk 12:33
preached throughout the w world ...... Mk 14:9
the w council, and bound Jesus, and ...... Mk 15:1
and they call together the w band ...... Mk 15:16
the w land until the ninth hour ...... Lk 1:10
the w multitude of the people ...... Lk 1:10
They that are w need not a ...... Lk 5:31
hand was restored as the other ...... Lk 6:10
the w multitude sought to touch ...... Lk 6:19
found the servant w that had been ...... Lk 7:10
Then the w multitude of the ...... Lk 8:37
published throughout the w city ...... Lk 8:39
thy faith hath made thee w ...... Lk 8:48
only, and she shall be made w ...... Lk 8:50
if he gain the w world, and lose ...... Lk 9:25
thy w body also is full of light ...... Lk 11:34
If thy w body therefore be full ...... Lk 11:36
the w shall be full of light, as ...... Lk 11:36
of meal, till the w was leavened ...... Lk 13:21
thy faith hath made thee w ...... Lk 17:19
the w multitude of the disciples ...... Lk 19:37
dwell on the face of the w earth ...... Lk 21:35
the w multitude of them arose, and ...... Lk 23:1
himself believed, and his w house ...... Jn 4:53
of w whatsoever disease he had ...... Jn 5:4
unto him, Wilt thou be made w ...... Jn 5:6
And immediately the man was made w ...... Jn 5:9
answered then, He that made me w ...... Jn 5:11
unto him, Behold, thou art made w ...... Jn 5:15
was Jesus, which had made him w ...... Jn 5:15
every w it on the sabbath day ...... Jn 7:23
that the w nation perish not, ... Jn 11:50
man, by what means he is made w ...... Acts 4:9

this man stand here before you w ...... Acts 4:10
saying pleased the w multitude ...... Acts 6:5
Jesus Christ maketh thee w ...... Acts 9:34
that a w year they assembled ...... Acts 11:26
sabbath day came almost the w ...... Acts 13:44
and elders, with the w church ...... Acts 15:22
the w city was filled with ...... Acts 19:29
Paul dwelt two w years in his own ...... Acts 28:30
spoken of throughout the w world ...... Rom 1:8
know that the w creation groaneth ...... Rom 8:22
mine host, and of the w church ...... Rom 16:23
leaven leaveneth the w lump 1Cor 5:6
If the w body were an eye, where 1Cor 12:17
If the w were hearing, where were 1Cor 12:17
If therefore the w church be come 1Cor 14:23
he is a debtor to do the w law ...... Gal 5:3
leaven leaveneth the w lump ...... Gal 5:9
Of whom the w family in heaven and ...... Eph 3:15
From whom the w body fitly joined ...... Eph 4:16
Put on the w armour of God, that ...... Eph 6:11
take unto you the w armour of God ...... Eph 6:13
and I pray God your w spirit 1Th 5:23
be stopped, who subvert w houses ...... Titus 1:11
whosoever shall keep the w law ...... Jas 2:10
and able also to bridle the w body ...... Jas 3:2
and we turn about their w body ...... Jas 3:3
that it defileth the w body ...... Jas 3:6
also for the sins of the w world 1Jn 2:2
the w world lieth in wickedness 1Jn 5:19
which deceiveth the w world ...... Rev 12:9
of the earth and of the w world ...... Rev 16:14

WHOLESOME

A w tongue is a tree of life ...... Prov 15:4
and consent not to w words 1Ti 6:3

WHOLLY

it shall be w burnt ...... Lev 6:22
for the priest shall be w burnt ...... Lev 6:23
thou shalt not w reap the corners ...... Lev 19:9
they are w given unto him out of ...... Num 3:9
spread over it a cloth w of blue ...... Num 4:6
For they are w given unto me from ...... Num 8:16
they have not w followed me ...... Num 32:11
for they have w followed the LORD ...... Num 32:12
because he hath w followed the ...... Deut 1:36
but I w followed the LORD my God, ... Josh 14:8
because thou hast w followed the ...... Josh 14:9
because that he w followed the ...... Josh 14:14
I had w dedicated the silver unto ...... Judg 17:3
a burnt offering w unto the LORD 1Sa 7:9
will be w at thy commandment 1Chr 28:21
being w at ease and quiet ...... Job 21:23
that thou art w gone up to the ...... Is 22:1
thee a noble vine, w a right seed... ...... Jer 2:21
she is w oppression in the midst ...... Jer 6:6
it shall be w carried away ...... Jer 13:19
If ye set your faces to w enter ...... Jer 42:15
I not leave thee w unpunished ...... Jer 46:28
but it shall be w desolate ...... Jer 50:13
and all the house of Israel w ...... Eze 11:15
and it shall rise up w as a flood ...... Amos 8:8
it shall rise up w like a flood ...... Amos 9:5
saw the city w given to idolatry ...... Acts 17:16
very God of peace sanctify you w 1Th 5:23
give thyself w to them 1Ti 4:15

WHOM See PREFACE.

WHOMSOEVER

With w thou findest thy gods, let... ...... Gen 31:32
With w of thy servants it be... ...... Gen 44:9
w he toucheth that hath the issue ...... Lev 15:11
of w I say unto thee, This shall ...... Judg 7:4
So the LORD our God shall drive... ...... Judg 11:24
of men, and giveth it to w he will ...... Dan 4:17
of men, and giveth it to w he will ...... Dan 4:25
of men, and giveth it to w he will ...... Dan 4:32
he appointeth over it w he will ...... Dan 5:21
he to w the Son will reveal him ...... Mt 11:27
but on w it shall fall, it will ...... Mt 21:44
W I shall kiss, that same is he ...... Mt 26:48
W I shall kiss, that same is he ...... Mk 14:44
them one prisoner, w they desired ...... Mk 15:6
and to w I will I give it ...... Lk 4:6
For unto w much is given, of him ...... Lk 12:48
but on w it shall fall, it will ...... Lk 20:18
He that receiveth w I send... ...... Jn 13:20
that on w I lay hands, he may ...... Acts 8:19
w ye shall approve by your 1Cor 16:3

WHORE

daughter, to cause her to be a w ...... Lev 19:29
shall not take a wife that is a w ...... Lev 21:7
profane herself by playing the w ...... Lev 21:9
to play the w in her father's... ...... Deut 22:21
There shall be no w of the... ...... Deut 23:17
shalt not bring the hire of a w ...... Deut 23:18
played the w against him, and went ...... Judg 19:2
For a w is a deep ditch ...... Prov 23:27
seed of the adulterer and the w ...... Is 57:3
Thou hast played the w also with ...... Eze 16:28
w that sitteth upon many waters ...... Rev 17:1
thou sawest, where the w sitteth ...... Rev 17:15
these shall hate the w ...... Rev 17:16
for he hath judged the great w ...... Rev 19:2

WHOREDOM

behold, she is with child by w ...... Gen 38:24
lest the land fall to w, and the... ...... Lev 19:29
to commit w with Molech, from... ...... Lev 20:5
w with the daughters of Moab ...... Num 25:1
through the lightness of her w... ...... Jer 3:9

W

neighings, the lewdness of thy w .... Jer 13:27
men, and didst commit w with them... Eze 16:17
unto thee on every side for thy w...... Eze 16:33
and commit ye w after their........... Eze 20:30
and poured their w upon her........... Eze 23:8
and they defiled her with their w..... Eze 23:17
thy w brought from the land of........ Eze 23:27
they, nor their kings, by their w...... Eze 43:7
Now let them put away their w......... Eze 43:9
the land hath committed great w...... Hos 1:2
they shall commit w, and shall not.... Hos 4:10
W and wine and new wine take away..... Hos 4:11
your daughters shall commit w......... Hos 4:13
your daughters when they commit w.... Hos 4:14
they have committed w continually.... Hos 4:18
now, O Ephraim, thou committest w.... Hos 5:3
there is the w of Ephraim............. Hos 6:10

WHOREDOMS

forty years, and bear your w.......... Num 14:33
so long as the w of thy mother....... 2Kin 9:22
like to the w of the house of........ 2Chr 21:13
hast polluted the land with thy w.... Jer 3:2
Is this of thy w a small matter...... Eze 16:20
thy w thou hast not remembered....... Eze 16:22
passed by, and multiplied thy w...... Eze 16:25
and hast increased thy w, to......... Eze 16:26
in thee from other women in thy w.... Eze 16:34
none followeth thee to commit w...... Eze 16:34
through thy w with thy lovers........ Eze 16:36
And they committed w in Egypt........ Eze 23:3
they committed w in their youth...... Eze 23:3
she committed her w with them........ Eze 23:7
left her her w brought from Egypt.... Eze 23:8
in her w more than her sister in.... Eze 23:11
more than her sister in her w........ Eze 23:11
And that she increased her w......... Eze 23:14
So she discovered her w, and......... Eze 23:18
Yet she multiplied her w, in......... Eze 23:19
of thy w shall be discovered......... Eze 23:29
both thy lewdness and thy w.......... Eze 23:29
thou also thy lewdness and thy w..... Eze 23:35
Will they now commit w with her...... Eze 23:43
Go, take unto thee a wife of w....... Hos 1:2
and children of w.................... Hos 1:2
put away her w out of her sight...... Hos 2:2
for they be the children of w....... Hos 2:4
for the spirit of w hath caused...... Hos 4:12
for the spirit of w is in the....... Hos 5:4
the w of the wellfavoured harlot..... Nah 3:4
selleth nations through her w........ Nah 3:4

WHOREMONGER

For this ye know, that no w.......... Eph 5:5

WHOREMONGERS

For w, for them that defile.......... 1Ti 1:10
but w and adulterers God will........ Heb 13:4
abominable, and murderers, and w..... Rev 21:8
are dogs, and sorcerers, and w....... Rev 22:15

WHORE'S

and thou hadst a w forehead.......... Jer 3:3

WHORES

They give gifts to all w............. Eze 16:33
themselves are separated with w...... Hos 4:14

WHORING

they go a w after their gods, and.... Ex 34:15
daughters go a w after their gods.... Ex 34:16
thy sons go a w after their gods..... Ex 34:16
after whom they have gone a w........ Lev 17:7
off, and all that go a w after him... Lev 20:5
to go a w after them, I will even.... Lev 20:6
after which ye use to go a w......... Num 15:39
go a w after the gods of the......... Deut 31:16
but they went a w after other........ Judg 2:17
Israel went thither a w after it..... Judg 8:27
went a w after Baalim, and made...... Judg 8:33
went a w after the gods of the....... Judg 10:6
of Jerusalem to go a w, like to...... 2Chr 21:13
all them that go a w from thee....... Ps 73:27
works, and went a w with their own... Ps 106:39
which go a w after their idols....... Eze 6:9
hast gone a w after the heathen...... Eze 23:30
they have gone a w from under........ Hos 4:12
thou hast gone a w from thy God...... Hos 9:1

WHORISH

For by means of a w woman a man...... Prov 6:26
I am broken with their w heart....... Eze 6:9
the work of an imperious w woman..... Eze 16:30

WHOSE

w seed is in itself, upon the........ Gen 1:11
w seed was in itself, after his...... Gen 1:12
All in w nostrils was the breath..... Gen 7:22
w top may reach unto heaven.......... Gen 11:4
an Egyptian, w name was Hagar........ Gen 16:1
the uncircumcised man child w........ Gen 17:14
w name was Reumah, she bare also..... Gen 22:24
And said, W daughter art thou........ Gen 24:23
the Canaanites, in w land I dwell.... Gen 24:37
her, and said, W daughter art thou... Gen 24:47
asketh thee, saying, W art thou...... Gen 32:17
and w are these before thee......... Gen 32:17
Adullamite, w name was Hirah........ Gen 38:1
Canaanite, w name was Shuah......... Gen 38:2
his firstborn, w name was Tamar..... Gen 38:6
w these are, am I with child........ Gen 38:25
w are these, the signet, and........ Gen 38:25
but the man in w hand the cup is.... Gen 44:17
w branches run over the wall........ Gen 49:22

w name is Jealous, is a jealous....... Ex 34:14
every one w heart stirred him up...... Ex 35:21
all the women w heart stirred........ Ex 35:26
w heart made them willing to......... Ex 35:29
in w heart the LORD had put.......... Ex 36:2
even every one w heart stirred....... Ex 36:2
the man w hair is fallen off his..... Lev 13:40
w hand is not able to get that....... Lev 14:32
of him w seed goeth from him, and.... Lev 15:32
w blood was brought in to make....... Lev 16:27
upon w head the anointing oil was.... Lev 21:10
or a man w seed goeth from him....... Lev 22:4
w father was an Egyptian, went....... Lev 24:10
the man w eyes are open hath said.... Num 24:3
the man w eyes are open hath said.... Num 24:15
a land w stones are iron............. Deut 8:9
out of w hills thou mayest dig....... Deut 8:9
w land the LORD thy God giveth....... Deut 19:1
a nation w tongue thou shalt not..... Deut 28:49
w heart turneth away this day........ Deut 29:18
the Amorites, in w land ye dwell..... Josh 24:15
the captain of w host was Sisera..... Judg 4:2
the Amorites, in w land ye dwell..... Judg 6:10
w name he called Abimelech.......... Judg 8:31
of the Danites, w name was Manoah.... Judg 13:2
of Sorek, w name was Delilah........ Judg 16:4
mount Ephraim, w name was Micah..... Judg 17:1
him in w sight I shall find grace.... Ruth 2:2
the reapers, W damsel is this....... Ruth 2:5
under w wings thou art come to....... Ruth 2:12
kindred, with w maidens thou wast.... Ruth 3:2
w name was Kish, the son of Abiel.... 1Sa 9:1
w name was Saul, a choice young..... 1Sa 9:2
of men, w hearts God had touched.... 1Sa 10:26
w ox have I taken................... 1Sa 12:3
or w ass have I taken............... 1Sa 12:3
or of w hand have I received any.... 1Sa 12:3
w height was six cubits and a span.. 1Sa 17:4
w name was Jesse.................... 1Sa 17:12
host, Abner, w son is this youth.... 1Sa 17:55
Enquire thou w son the stripling.... 1Sa 17:56
W son art thou, thou young man...... 1Sa 17:58
w possessions were in Carmel........ 1Sa 25:2
w name was Nabal; and the name..... 1Sa 25:3
w name was Rigpah, the daughter.... 2Sa 3:7
behalf, saying, W is the land....... 2Sa 3:12
w name is called by the name of.... 2Sa 6:2
of Saul a servant w name was Ziba... 2Sa 9:2
had a young son, w name was Micha... 2Sa 9:12
a fair sister, w name was Tamar..... 2Sa 13:1
w name was Jonadab, the son of..... 2Sa 13:3
w name was Tamar................... 2Sa 14:27
w name was Shimei, the son of...... 2Sa 16:5
in stead thou hast reigned......... 2Sa 16:8
w heart is as the heart of a lion.. 2Sa 17:10
w name was Ithra an Israelite...... 2Sa 17:25
w name was Sheba, the son of....... 2Sa 20:1
the weight of w spear weighed...... 2Sa 21:16
the staff of w spear was like a.... 2Sa 21:19
Then spake the woman w the living.. 1Kin 3:26
to his ways, w heart thou knowest.. 1Kin 8:39
w mother's name was Zeruah, a...... 1Kin 11:26
Then a lord on w hand the living... 2Kin 7:2
on w hand he leaned to have the.... 2Kin 7:17
w son he had restored to life...... 2Kin 8:1
w son he had restored to life...... 2Kin 8:5
into w hand they delivered the..... 2Kin 12:15
w high places and w altars......... 2Kin 18:22
W sisters were Zeruiah, and........ 1Chr 2:16
another wife, w name was Atarah.... 1Chr 2:26
an Egyptian, w name was Jarha...... 1Chr 2:34
w number was in the days of David.. 1Chr 7:2
w sister's name was Maachah........ 1Chr 7:15
w wife's name was Maachah.......... 1Chr 7:16
w names are these, Azrikam......... 1Chr 8:38
w wife's name was Maachah.......... 1Chr 9:35
w names are these, Azrikam......... 1Chr 9:44
w faces were like the faces of..... 1Chr 12:8
cherubims, w name is called on it.. 1Chr 13:6
w spear staff was like a weaver's.. 1Chr 20:5
w fingers and toes were four and... 1Chr 20:6
w brethren were strong men, Elihu.. 1Chr 26:7
his ways, w heart thou knowest..... 2Chr 6:30
w heart is perfect toward him...... 2Chr 16:9
LORD was there, w name was Oded.... 2Chr 28:9
with all them w spirit God had..... Ezr 1:5
w name was Sheshbazzar, whom he.... Ezr 5:14
w habitation is in Jerusalem....... Ezr 7:15
w names are these, Eliphelet....... Ezr 8:13
w name was Mordecai, the son of.... Est 2:5
the land of Uz, w name was Job..... Job 1:1
light given to a man w way is hid.. Job 3:23
w foundation is in the dust........ Job 4:19
W harvest the hungry eateth up..... Job 5:5
W hope shall he cut off............ Job 8:14
w trust shall be a spider's web.... Job 8:14
into w hand God heapeth............ Job 12:6
In w hand is the soul of every..... Job 12:10
w foundation was overflown with a.. Job 22:16
and w spirit came from thee........ Job 26:4
w fathers I would have disdained... Job 30:1
Out of w womb came the ice......... Job 38:29
W house I have made the............ Job 39:6
In w ears is no life person is..... Job 39:6
w belly thou fillest with thy hid.. Ps 17:14
In w hands is mischief, and their.. Ps 26:10
Blessed is he w transgression is... Ps 32:1
is forgiven, w sin is covered...... Ps 32:1
in w spirit there is no guile...... Ps 32:2
w mouth must be held in with bit... Ps 32:9
is the nation w God is the LORD.... Ps 33:12

in w mouth are no reproofs......... Ps 38:14
w teeth are spears and arrows, and. Ps 57:4
w spirit was not stedfast with.... Ps 78:8
w name alone is JEHOVAH, art the... Ps 83:18
Blessed is the man w strength is... Ps 84:5
in w heart are the ways of them... Ps 84:5
W feet they hurt with fetters...... Ps 105:18
W mouth speaketh vanity, and their. Ps 144:8
w mouth speaketh vanity, and their. Ps 144:11
is that people, w God is the LORD.. Ps 144:15
w hope is in the LORD his God...... Ps 146:5
W ways are crooked, and they....... Prov 2:15
W hatred is covered by deceit...... Prov 26:26
w teeth are as swords, and their... Prov 30:14
For there is a man w labour is in.. Eccl 2:21
w heart is snares and nets, and her Eccl 7:26
shall be as an oak w leaf fadeth... Is 1:30
w breath is in his nostrils........ Is 2:22
W arrows are sharp, and all their.. Is 5:28
w substance is in them, when they.. Is 6:13
w graven images did excel them of.. Is 10:10
captives, w captives they were..... Is 14:2
w land the rivers have spoiled..... Is 18:2
w land the rivers have spoiled..... Is 18:7
w antiquity is of ancient days..... Is 23:7
w merchants are princes............ Is 23:8
w traffickers are the honourable... Is 23:8
peace, w mind is stayed on thee.... Is 26:3
w glorious beauty is a fading...... Is 28:1
w breaking cometh suddenly at an... Is 30:13
w fire is in Zion, and his furnace. Is 31:9
w high places and w altars......... Is 36:7
Chaldeans, w cry is in the ships... Is 43:14
w right hand I have holden, to..... Is 45:1
the people in w heart is my law.... Is 51:7
divided the sea, w waves roared.... Is 51:15
eternity, w name is Holy........... Is 57:15
w waters cast up mire and dirt..... Is 57:20
of water, w waters fail not........ Is 58:11
a nation w language thou knowest... Jer 5:15
w heart departeth from the LORD.... Jer 17:5
the LORD, and w hope the LORD is... Jer 17:7
w roofs they have burned incense... Jer 19:13
hand of them w face thou fearest... Jer 22:25
upon w roofs they have offered..... Jer 32:29
for all w wickedness I have hid.... Jer 33:5
w name was Irijah, the son of...... Jer 37:13
shall know w words shall stand..... Jer 44:28
w waters are moved as the rivers... Jer 46:7
w name is the LORD of hosts........ Jer 46:18
w name is the LORD of hosts........ Jer 48:15
they w judgment was not to drink... Jer 49:12
w name is the LORD of hosts........ Jer 50:34
w words thou canst not understand.. Eze 3:6
But as for them w heart walketh.... Eze 11:21
w branches turned toward him, and.. Eze 17:6
w oath he despised................. Eze 17:16
w covenant he brake, even with..... Eze 17:18
in w sight I made myself known..... Eze 20:9
in w sight I brought them out...... Eze 20:14
in w sight I brought them forth.... Eze 20:22
w day is come, when iniquity...... Eze 21:25
more, until he come w right it is.. Eze 21:27
w day is come, when their.......... Eze 21:29
w flesh is as the flesh of asses... Eze 23:20
w issue is like the issue of....... Eze 23:20
to the pot w scum is therein, and.. Eze 24:6
w scum is not gone out of it....... Eze 24:6
w graves are set in the sides of... Eze 32:23
w appearance was like the.......... Eze 40:3
w prospect is toward the south,.... Eze 40:45
the chamber w prospect is toward... Eze 40:46
the forth toward the east.......... Eze 42:15
w prospect is toward the east...... Eze 43:4
w leaf shall not fade, neither..... Eze 47:12
w dwelling is not with flesh....... Dan 2:11
w name was Belteshazzar, Art thou.. Dan 2:26
w brightness was excellent, stood.. Dan 2:31
w height was threescore cubits,.... Dan 3:1
upon w bodies the fire had no...... Dan 3:27
me, w name was Belteshazzar........ Dan 4:8
w name was Belteshazzar, was....... Dan 4:19
w height reached unto the heaven... Dan 4:20
W leaves were fair, and the fruit.. Dan 4:21
upon w branches the fowls of the... Dan 4:21
w dominion is an everlasting....... Dan 4:34
all w works are truth, and his..... Dan 4:37
the God in w hand thy breath is,... Dan 5:23
w are all thy ways, hast thou not.. Dan 5:23
w garment was white as snow, and... Dan 7:9
w teeth were of iron, and his...... Dan 7:19
w look was more stout than his..... Dan 7:20
w kingdom is an everlasting........ Dan 7:27
w name was called Belteshazzar..... Dan 10:1
w loins were girded with fine...... Dan 10:5
w teeth are the teeth of a lion,... Joel 1:6
w height was like the height of... Amos 2:9
w name is The God of hosts......... Amos 5:27
of the rock, w habitation is high.. Obad 3
that we may know for w cause this.. Jonah 1:7
for w cause this evil is upon us... Jonah 1:8
w goings forth have been from of... Mic 5:2
w rampart was the sea, and her..... Nah 3:8
Behold the man w name is The....... Zec 6:12
W possessors slay them, and hold... Zec 11:5
w shoes I am not worthy to bear.... Mt 3:11
W fan is in his hand, and he will.. Mt 3:12
Lebbaeus, w surname was Thaddaeus.. Mt 10:3
whis image and superscription...... Mt 22:20
Therefore in the resurrection w.... Mt 22:28

w son is he?.................................... Mt 22:42
the latchet of w shoes I am not..... Mk 1:7
w young daughter had an unclean.... Mk 7:25
W is this image and superscription.. Mk 12:16
w wife shall she be of them .... Mk 12:23
to a man w name was Joseph............ Lk 1:27
in Jerusalem, w name was Simeon.... Lk 2:25
the latchet of w shoes I am not ...... Lk 3:16
W fan is in his hand, and he will ..... Lk 3:17
there was a man w right hand was ... Lk 6:6
then w shall those things be, ... Lk 12:20
w blood Pilate had mingled with..... Lk 13:1
W image and superscription hath it .. Lk 20:24
w wife of them is she....................... Lk 20:33
w name was Cleopas, answering,..... Lk 24:18
sent from God, w name was John..... Jn 1:6
w shoe's latchet I am not worthy..... Jn 1:27
w son was sick at Capernaum........... Jn 4:46
w father and mother we know.......... Jn 6:42
w own the sheep are not, seeth........ Jn 10:12
w brother Lazarus was sick .... Jn 11:2
his kinsman w ear Peter cut off .... Jn 18:26
cast lots for it, w it shall be .... Jn 19:24
W soever sins ye remit, they are ..... Jn 20:23
w soever sins ye retain, they are ..... Jn 20:23
young man's feet, w name was Saul.. Acts 7:58
for one Simon, w surname is Peter ... Acts 10:5
w house is by the sea side .... Acts 10:6
hither Simon, w surname is Peter ..... Acts 10:32
for Simon, w surname is Peter .... Acts 11:13
of John, w surname was Mark .... Acts 12:12
them John, w surname was Mark ..... Acts 12:25
a Jew, w name was Bar-jesus .... Acts 13:6
w whoes of his feet I am not .... Acts 13:25
them John, w surname was Mark ..... Acts 15:37
w heart the Lord opened, that she .. Acts 16:14
w house joined hard to the .... Acts 18:7
of God, w I am, and whom I serve,.. Acts 27:23
of the island, w name was Publius .... Acts 28:7
w sign was Castor and Pollux .... Acts 28:11
W praise is not of men, but of .... Rom 2:29
w damnation is just .... Rom 3:8
W mouth is full of cursing and........ Rom 3:14
Blessed are they w iniquities are ..... Rom 4:7
forgiven, and w sins are covered...... Rom 4:7
W are the fathers, and of whom as.. Rom 9:5
w praise is in the gospel 2Cor 8:18
w end shall be according to their 2Cor 11:15
before w eyes Jesus Christ hath .... Gal 3:1
W end is destruction........................ Phil 3:19
W God is their belly......................... Phil 3:19
w glory is in their shame, who........ Phil 3:19
w names are in the book of life....... Phil 4:3
w coming is after the working of 2Th 2:9
W mouths must be stopped, who ..... Titus 1:11
w house are we, if we hold fast ...... Heb 3:6
w carcases fell in the wilderness...... Heb 8:17
w end is to be burned...................... Heb 6:8
But he w descent is not counted ..... Heb 7:6
w builder and maker is God............. Heb 11:10
W voice then shook the earth........... Heb 12:26
w faith follow, considering the .... Heb 13:7
w blood is brought into the.............. Heb 13:11
by w stripes ye were healed............. 1Pet 2:24
W adorning let it not be that 1Pet 3:3
w daughters ye are, as long as ye ... 1Pet 3:6
w judgment now of a long time....... 2Pet 2:3
trees w fruit withereth, without .... Jude 12
w name in the Hebrew tongue is...... Rev 9:11
w names are not written in the .... Rev 13:8
w deadly wound was healed............. Rev 13:12
w names were not written in the ..... Rev 17:8
from w face the earth and the.......... Rev 20:11

WHOSO

W sheddeth man's blood, by man .... Gen 9:6
w toucheth their carcase shall be ..... Lev 11:27
w toucheth any thing that is............. Lev 22:4
W killeth any person, the .... Num 35:30
w killeth his neighbour..................... Deut 19:4
w followeth her, let him be slain...... 2Chr 23:14
W offereth praise glorifieth me........ Ps 50:23
w privily slandereth his..................... Ps 101:5
W keepeth it, shall observe these ..... Ps 107:43
But w hearkeneth unto me shall .... Prov 1:33
But w committeth adultery with a.... Prov 6:32
For w findeth me findeth life, and..... Prov 8:35
W is simple, let him turn in .... Prov 9:4
W is simple, let him turn in .... Prov 9:16
W loveth instruction loveth .... Prov 12:1
W despiseth the word shall be .... Prov 13:13
w trusteth in the Lord, happy is ...... Prov 16:20
W mocketh the poor reproacheth...... Prov 17:5
W rewardeth evil for good, evil........ Prov 17:13
W findeth a wife findeth a good ...... Prov 18:22
w provoketh him to anger sinneth.... Prov 20:2
W stoppeth his ears at the cry of..... Prov 21:13
W keepeth his mouth and .... Prov 21:23
W boasteth himself of a false........... Prov 25:14
W diggeth a pit shall fall .... Prov 26:27
W keepeth the fig tree shall eat........ Prov 27:18
W keepeth the law is a wise son...... Prov 28:7
W causeth the righteous to go.......... Prov 28:10
w w confesseth and forsaketh........... Prov 28:13
W walketh uprightly shall be .... Prov 28:18
W robbeth his father or his .... Prov 28:24
but w walketh wisely, he shall be .... Prov 28:26
W loveth wisdom rejoiceth his .... Prov 29:3
W is partner with a thief hateth....... Prov 29:24
but w putteth his trust in the.......... Prov 29:25

w pleaseth God shall escape from.... Eccl 7:26
W keepeth the commandment shall .. Eccl 8:5
w breaketh an hedge, a serpent....... Eccl 10:8
W removeth stones shall be hurt ...... Eccl 10:9
w falleth not down and worshippeth.. Dan 3:6
w falleth not down and worshippeth.. Dan 3:11
that w will not come up or all.......... Zec 14:17
w shall receive one such little.......... Mt 18:5
But w shall offend one of these........ Mt 18:6
w marrieth her which is put away .... Mt 19:9
W therefore shall swear by the .... Mt 23:20
w curseth father or mother, let .... Mt 23:21
(w readeth, let him understand.......... Mk 7:10
W eateth my flesh, and drinketh my.. Jn 6:54
But w looketh into the perfect.......... Jas 1:25
But w keepeth his word, in him 1Jn 2:5
But w hath this world's good, and ... 1Jn 3:17

WHOSOEVER

Therefore w slayeth Cain, ... Gen 4:15
for w eateth leavened bread from..... Ex 12:15
for w eateth that which is .... Ex 12:19
w toucheth the mount shall be,........ Ex 19:12
W lieth with a beast shall surely...... Ex 22:19
W compoundeth any like it .... Ex 30:33
w or putteth any of it upon a .... Ex 30:33
W shall make like unto that, to........ Ex 30:33
for w doeth any work therein,.......... Ex 31:14
w doeth any work in the sabbath..... Ex 31:15
W hath any gold, let them break...... Ex 32:24
W hath sinned against me, him .... Ex 32:33
w doeth work therein shall be put.... Ex 35:2
is of a willing heart, let him............ Ex 35:5
W w eateth the fat of the beast....... Lev 7:25
w toucheth the carcase of them .... Lev 11:24
w beareth ought of the carcase of ... Lev 11:25
w doth touch them, when they be .... Lev 11:31
w toucheth his bed shall wash his.... Lev 15:5
w toucheth any thing that was .... Lev 15:10
w toucheth her shall be unclean .... Lev 15:19
w toucheth her bed shall wash his ... Lev 15:21
w toucheth any thing that she sat..... Lev 15:27
w toucheth those things shall be ...... Lev 15:27
w eateth it shall be cut off .... Lev 17:14
For w shall commit any of these....... Lev 18:29
w lieth carnally with a woman,......... Lev 19:20
W be of the children of Israel,......... Lev 20:2
W he be of thy seed shall in .... Lev 21:17
Or w toucheth any creeping thing,.... Lev 22:5
w offereth a sacrifice of peace .... Lev 22:21
W curseth his God shall bear his ..... Lev 24:15
and w is defiled by the dead........... Num 5:2
or w be among you in that .... Num 11:3
W toucheth the dead body of any .... Num 19:13
w toucheth one that is slain with ..... Num 19:16
w hath killed any person, and.......... Num 31:19
w hath touched any slain, purify ...... Num 31:19
that w will not hearken unto my...... Deut 18:19
W he be that doth rebel against .... Josh 1:18
that w shall go out of the doors,...... Josh 2:19
w shall be with thee in the house .... Josh 2:19
that w killeth any person at .... Josh 20:9
W is fearful and afraid, let him........ Judg 7:3
W cometh not forth after Saul and .. 1Sa 11:7
W getteth up to the gutter, and........ 2Sa 5:8
w saith ought unto thee, bring 2Sa 14:10
that w heareth it will say, There 2Sa 17:9
w would, he consecrated him, and... 1Kin 13:33
w shall be wanting, he shall lose 2Kin 10:19
that w heareth of it, both his 2Kin 21:12
W smiteth the Jebusites first 1Chr 11:6
w had dedicated any thing, it was.... 1Chr 18:11
so that w cometh to consecrate 2Chr 13:9
That w would not seek the Lord,...... 2Chr 15:13
w else cometh into the house, he..... 2Chr 23:7
w remaineth in any place where he .. Ezr 1:4
that w shall alter this word, let........ Ezr 6:11
w will not do the law of thy God,.... Ezr 7:26
that w would not come within......... Ezr 10:8
W toucheth her shall not be .... Est 4:11
w toucheth her shall not be .... Prov 6:29
w is deceived thereby is not wise .... Prov 20:1
W hideth her hatred the wind, and... Prov 27:16
w shall gather together against .... Is 54:15
w gareth therein shall not know....... Is 59:8
this place, the which w heareth........ Jer 19:3
Then w heareth the sound of the..... Eze 33:4
W shall read this writing, and.......... Dan 5:7
w that shall ask a petition of........... Dan 6:7
that w shall call on the name of...... Joel 2:32
W therefore shall break one of........ Mt 5:19
but w shall do and teach, them, the.. Mt 5:19
w shall kill shall be in danger.......... Mt 5:21
That w is angry with his brother...... Mt 5:22
w shall say to his brother, Raca,...... Mt 5:22
but w shall say, Thou fool, shall...... Mt 5:22
That w looketh on a woman to lust.. Mt 5:28
W shall put away his wife, let.......... Mt 5:31
That w shall put away his wife,........ Mt 5:32
w shall marry her that is .... Mt 5:32
but w shall smite thee on thy .... Mt 5:39
w shall compel thee to go a mile,.... Mt 5:41
Therefore w heareth these sayings.... Mt 10:14
w shall not receive you, nor hear .... Mt 10:32
W therefore shall confess me........... Mt 10:32
But w shall deny me before men,..... Mt 10:33
w shall give to drink unto one of..... Mt 10:42
w shall not be offended in me .... Mt 11:6

w speaketh a word against the Son .. Mt 12:32
but w speaketh against the Holy....... Mt 12:32
For w shall do the will of my.......... Mt 12:50
For w hath, to him shall be given .... Mt 13:12
but w hath not, from him shall be ... Mt 13:12
W shall say to his father or his....... Mt 15:5
For w will save his life shall............ Mt 16:25
w will lose his life for my sake .... Mt 16:25
W therefore shall humble himself..... Mt 18:4
W shall put away his wife, except.... Mt 19:9
but w will be great among you,........ Mt 20:26
w will be chief among you, let......... Mt 20:27
w shall fall on this stone shall.......... Mt 21:44
w shall exalt himself shall be .... Mt 23:12
W shall swear by the temple, it....... Mt 23:16
but w shall swear by the gold of...... Mt 23:16
W shall swear by the altar, it is....... Mt 23:18
but w sweareth by the gift that .... Mt 23:18
For w shall do the will of God,........ Mk 3:35
w shall not receive you, nor hear .... Mk 6:11
W will come after me, let him .... Mk 8:34
For w will save his life shall............ Mk 8:35
but w shall lose his life for my .... Mk 8:35
W therefore shall be ashamed of ..... Mk 8:38
W shall receive one of such .... Mk 9:37
w shall receive me, receiveth not..... Mk 9:37
For w shall give you a cup of .... Mk 9:41
w shall offend one of these.............. Mk 9:42
W shall put away his wife, and........ Mk 10:11
W shall not receive the kingdom ..... Mk 10:15
but w will be great among you,........ Mk 10:43
w of you will be the chiefest........... Mk 10:44
That w shall say unto this .... Mk 11:23
W cometh to me, and heareth my.... Lk 6:47
w shall not be offended in me .... Lk 7:23
for w hath, to him shall be given ..... Lk 8:18
w hath not, from him shall be.......... Lk 8:18
w will not receive you, when ye ...... Lk 9:5
For w will save his life shall............ Lk 9:24
but w will lose his life .... Lk 9:24
For w shall be ashamed of me and .. Lk 9:26
W shall receive this child in my ...... Lk 9:48
w shall receive me receiveth............ Lk 9:48
W shall confess me before men,....... Lk 12:8
w shall speak a word against the ..... Lk 12:10
For w exalteth himself shall be......... Lk 14:11
w doth not bear his cross, and......... Lk 14:27
w he of you that forsaketh not .... Lk 14:33
W putteth away his wife, and........... Lk 16:18
w marrieth her that is put away .... Lk 16:18
W shall seek to save his life .... Lk 17:33
w shall lose his life .... Lk 17:33
W shall not receive the kingdom ..... Lk 18:17
W shall fall upon that stone............. Lk 20:18
that w believeth in him should .... Jn 3:15
that w believeth in him should .... Jn 3:16
W drinketh of this water should .... Jn 4:13
w drinketh of the water that .... Jn 4:14
w then first after the troubling .... Jn 5:4
W committeth sin is the servant ...... Jn 8:34
w liveth and believeth in me shall ... Jn 11:26
that w believeth on me should not ... Jn 12:46
that w killeth you will think .... Jn 16:2
w maketh himself a king speaketh ... Jn 19:12
w shall call on the name of .... Acts 2:21
that through his name w believeth ... Acts 10:43
w among you feareth God, to you ... Acts 13:26
O man, w thou art that judgest .... Rom 2:1
w believeth on him shall not be ...... Rom 9:33
W believeth on him shall not be...... Rom 10:11
For w shall call upon the name of ... Rom 10:13
W therefore resisteth the power,...... Rom 13:2
Wherefore w shall eat this bread,...... 1Cor 11:27
w of you are justified by the law...... Gal 5:4
shall bear his judgment, w he .... Gal 5:10
For w shall keep the whole law,....... Jas 2:10
w therefore will be a friend of .... Jas 4:4
W denieth the Son, the same hath ... 1Jn 2:23
W committeth sin transgresseth 1Jn 3:4
W abideth in him sinneth not........... 1Jn 3:6
w sinneth hath not seen him,........... 1Jn 3:6
he is born of God doth not commit.. 1Jn 3:9
w doeth not righteousness is not 1Jn 3:10
W hateth his brother is a 1Jn 3:15
W shall confess that Jesus is the 1Jn 4:15
W believeth that Jesus is the............ 1Jn 5:1
We know that w is born of God 1Jn 5:18
W transgresseth, and abideth not 2Jn 9
w receiveth the mark of his name ... Rev 14:11
w was not found written in the .... Rev 20:15
and w loveth and maketh a lie .... Rev 22:15
w will, let him take the water of ..... Rev 22:17

WHY

said unto Cain, W art thou wroth..... Gen 4:6
w is thy countenance fallen .... Gen 4:6
W didst thou not tell me that she .... Gen 12:18
W saidst thou, She is my sister......... Gen 12:19
said, If it be so, w am I thus............ Gen 25:22
w should I be deprived also of .... Gen 27:45
W do ye look one upon another ...... Gen 42:1
for w should we die in the .... Gen 47:15
W have ye done this thing, and .... Ex 1:18
w is it that ye have left the man...... Ex 2:20
sight, w the bush is not burnt.......... Ex 3:3
w is it that thou hast sent me.......... Ex 5:22
W have we done this, that we have.. Ex 14:5
unto them, W chide ye with me....... Ex 17:2
w sittest thou thyself alone, and...... Ex 18:14
w doth thy wrath wax hot against.... Ex 32:11
W came ye forth out of Egypt.......... Num 11:20

And w have ye brought us up ...... Num 20:4
W should the name of our father ...... Num 27:4
Now therefore w should we die ...... Deut 5:25
this is the cause w Joshua did ...... Josh 5:4
said, W hast thou troubled us ...... Josh 7:25
W hast thou given me but one lot ...... Josh 17:14
w have ye done this ...... Judg 2:2
W abodest thou among the ...... Judg 5:16
w did Dan remain in ships ...... Judg 5:17
W is his chariot so long in ...... Judg 5:28
W tarry the wheels of his ...... Judg 5:28
w then is all this befallen us ...... Judg 6:13
W hast thou served us thus, that ...... Judg 8:1
for w should we serve him ...... Judg 9:28
w are ye come unto me now when ye ...... Judg 11:7
w therefore did ye not recover ...... Judg 11:26
W askest thou thus after my name ...... Judg 13:18
W are ye come up against us ...... Judg 15:10
w is this come to pass in Israel ...... Judg 21:3
w will ye go with me ...... Ruth 1:11
w then call ye me Naomi, seeing ...... Ruth 1:21
W have I found grace in thine ...... Ruth 2:10
to her, Hannah, w weepest thou 1Sa 1:8
and w eatest thou not 1Sa 1:8
and w is thy heart grieved 1Sa 1:8
unto them, W do ye such things 1Sa 2:23
it shall be known to you w his 1Sa 6:3
W are ye come out to set your 1Sa 6:3
w camest thou down hither 1Sa 17:28
W hast thou deceived me so, and 1Sa 19:17
w should I kill thee 1Sa 19:17
w should my father hide this 1Sa 20:2
for w shouldest thou bring me to 1Sa 20:8
W art thou alone, and no man with 1Sa 21:1
W have ye conspired against me 1Sa 22:13
for w should thy servant dwell in 1Sa 27:5
saying, W hast thou deceived me 1Sa 28:12
W hast thou disquieted me, to 1Sa 28:15
w is it that thou hast sent him 2Sa 3:24
W build ye not me an house of 2Sa 7:7
w then didst thou not go down 2Sa 11:10
w went ye nigh the wall 2Sa 11:20
W art thou, being the king's son 2Sa 13:4
him, W should he go with thee 2Sa 13:26
W should this dead dog curse my 2Sa 16:9
w wentest thou not with thy 2Sa 16:17
w didst thou not smite him there 2Sa 18:11
Now therefore w speak ye not a 2Sa 19:10
W are ye the last to bring the 2Sa 19:11
W speakest thou any more of thy 2Sa 19:29
w should the king recompense it 2Sa 19:36
W have our brethren the men of 2Sa 19:41
w then did ye despise us, that 2Sa 19:43
w will thou swallow up the 2Sa 20:19
but w doth my lord the king 2Sa 24:3
in saying, W hast thou done so 1Kin 1:6
w then doth Adonijah reign 1Kin 1:13
w dost thou ask Abishag the 1Kin 2:22
W then hast thou not kept the 1Kin 2:43
W hath the LORD done this unto 1Kin 9:8
w feignest thou thyself to be 1Kin 14:6
W is thy spirit so sad, that thou 1Kin 21:5
them, W are ye now turned back 2Kin 1:5
W sit we here until we die 2Kin 7:3

And Hazael said, W weepeth my lord 2Kin 8:12
W repair ye not the breaches of 2Kin 12:7
for w shouldest thou meddle to 2Kin 14:10
W have ye not built me an house 1Chr 17:6
w then doth my lord require this 1Chr 21:3
w will he be a cause of trespass 1Chr 21:3
W hath the LORD done this unto 2Chr 7:21
W hast thou not required of me 2Chr 24:6
W transgress ye the commandments 2Chr 24:20
W hast thou sought after the gods 2Chr 25:15
w shouldest thou be smitten 2Chr 25:16
w shouldest thou meddle to thine 2Chr 25:19
W should the kings of Assyria 2Chr 32:4
w should damage grow in the hurt ...... Ezr 4:22
for w should there be wrath ...... Ezr 7:23
W is thy countenance sad, seeing ...... Neh 2:2
w should not my countenance be ...... Neh 2:3
w should the work cease, whilst I ...... Neh 6:3
W is the house of God forsaken ...... Neh 13:11
W lodge ye about the wall ...... Neh 13:21
W transgressest thou the king's ...... Est 3:3
to know what it was, and w it was ...... Est 4:5
W died I not from the womb ...... Job 3:11
w did I not give up the ghost ...... Job 3:11
W did the knees prevent me ...... Job 3:12
or w the breasts that I should ...... Job 3:12
W is light given to a man whose ...... Job 3:23
w hast thou set me as a mark ...... Job 7:20
w dost thou not pardon my ...... Job 7:21
wicked, w then labour I in vain ...... Job 9:29
W doth thine heart carry thee ...... Job 15:12
W do ye persecute me as God, and ...... Job 19:22
W persecute we him, seeing the ...... Job 19:28
w should not my spirit be ...... Job 21:4
W, seeing times are not hidden ...... Job 24:1
w then are ye thus altogether ...... Job 27:12
w then should I think upon a maid ...... Job 31:1
W dost thou strive against him ...... Job 33:13
W do the heathen rage, and the ...... Ps 2:1
W standest thou afar off, O LORD ...... Ps 10:1
w hidest thou thyself in times of ...... Ps 10:1
my God, w hast thou forsaken me ...... Ps 22:1
w art thou so far from helping me ...... Ps 22:1
W art thou cast down, O my soul ...... Ps 42:5
w art thou disquieted in me ...... Ps 42:5
my rock, w hast thou forgotten me ...... Ps 42:9

w go I mourning because of the ...... Ps 42:9
W art thou cast down, O my soul ...... Ps 42:11
w art thou disquieted within me ...... Ps 42:11
w dost thou cast me off ...... Ps 43:2
W go I mourning because of the ...... Ps 43:2
W art thou cast down, O my soul ...... Ps 43:5
w art thou disquieted within me ...... Ps 43:5
Awake, w sleepest thou, O Lord ...... Ps 44:23
W boastest thou thyself in ...... Ps 52:1
W leap ye, ye high hills ...... Ps 68:16
w hast thou cast us off for ever ...... Ps 74:1
w doth thine anger smoke against ...... Ps 74:1
W withdrawest thou thy hand, even ...... Ps 74:11
W hast thou then broken down her ...... Ps 80:12
w castest thou off my soul ...... Ps 88:14
w hidest thou thy face from me ...... Ps 88:14
w with thou, my son, be ravished ...... Prov 5:20
w should he take away thy bed ...... Prov 22:27
and w was I then more wise ...... Eccl 2:15
w shouldest thou destroy thyself ...... Eccl 7:16
w shouldest thou die before thy ...... Eccl 7:17
for w should I be as one that ...... Song 1:7
W should ye be stricken any more ...... Is 1:5
W sayest thou, O Jacob, and ...... Is 40:27
w hast thou made us to err from ...... Is 63:17
w is he spoiled ...... Jer 2:14
W trimmest thou thy way to seek ...... Jer 2:33
W gaddest thou about so much to ...... Jer 2:36
W then is this people of ...... Jer 8:5
W do we sit still ...... Jer 8:14
W have they provoked me to anger ...... Jer 8:19
w then is not the health of the ...... Jer 8:22
w shouldest thou be as a stranger ...... Jer 14:8
W shouldest thou be as a man ...... Jer 14:9
W hast thou smitten us, and there ...... Jer 14:19
W is my pain perpetual, and my ...... Jer 15:18
W hast thou prophesied in the ...... Jer 26:9
W will ye die, thou and thy people ...... Jer 27:13
Now therefore w hast thou not ...... Jer 29:27
W criest thou for thine ...... Jer 30:15
W hast thou written therein ...... Jer 36:29
W are thy valiant men swept away ...... Jer 46:15
w then doth their king inherit ...... Jer 49:1
Yet say ye, W ...... Eze 18:19
for w will ye die, O house of ...... Eze 18:31
for w will ye die, O house of ...... Eze 33:11
for w should he see your faces ...... Dan 1:10
W is the decree so hasty from the ...... Dan 2:15
unto him, W hast thou done this ...... Jonah 1:10
W dost thou cry out aloud ...... Mic 4:9
W dost thou shew me iniquity, and ...... Hab 1:3
W spoilt the Lord ...... Hag 1:9
w do we deal treacherously every ...... Mal 2:10
w take ye thought for raiment ...... Mt 6:28
w beholdest thou the mote that is ...... Mt 7:3
W are ye fearful, O ye of little ...... Mt 8:26
W eateth your Master with ...... Mt 9:11
W do we and the Pharisees fast oft ...... Mt 9:14
w speakest thou unto them in ...... Mt 13:10
W do thy disciples transgress the ...... Mt 15:2
W do ye also transgress the ...... Mt 15:3
w reason ye among yourselves ...... Mt 16:8
W then say the scribes that Elias ...... Mt 17:10
W could not we cast him out ...... Mt 17:19
W did Moses then command to give ...... Mt 19:7
unto him, W callest thou me good ...... Mt 19:17
W stand ye here all the day idle ...... Mt 20:6
W did ye not then believe him ...... Mt 21:25
W tempt ye me, ye hypocrites ...... Mt 22:18
unto them, W trouble ye the woman ...... Mt 26:10
And the governor said, W, what ...... Mt 27:23
W doth this man thus speak ...... Mk 2:7
W reason ye these things in your ...... Mk 2:8
W do the disciples of John and of ...... Mk 2:18
w do they on the sabbath day that ...... Mk 2:24
unto them, W are ye so fearful ...... Mk 4:40
w troublest thou the Master any ...... Mk 5:35
W make ye this ado, and weep ...... Mk 5:39
him, W walk not thy disciples ...... Mk 7:5
W doth this generation seek after ...... Mk 8:12
W reason ye, because ye have no ...... Mk 8:17
W say the scribes that Elias must ...... Mk 9:11
W could not we cast him out ...... Mk 9:28
unto him, W callest thou me good ...... Mk 10:18
man say unto you, W do ye this ...... Mk 11:3
W then do ye not believe him ...... Mk 11:31
said unto them, W tempt ye me ...... Mk 12:15
W was this waste of the ointment ...... Mk 14:4
w trouble ye her ...... Mk 14:6
Then Pilate said unto them, W ...... Mk 15:14
my God, w hast thou forsaken me ...... Mk 15:34
w hast thou thus dealt with us ...... Lk 2:48
W do ye eat and drink with ...... Lk 5:30
W do the disciples of John fast ...... Lk 5:33
W do ye that which is not lawful ...... Lk 6:2
w beholdest thou the mote that is ...... Lk 6:41
w call ye me, Lord, Lord, and do ...... Lk 6:46
w even of yourselves judge ye not ...... Lk 12:57
w cumbereth it the ground ...... Lk 13:7
unto him, W callest thou me good ...... Lk 18:19
man ask you, W do ye loose him ...... Lk 19:31
unto them, W loose ye the colt ...... Lk 19:33
W then believed ye him not ...... Lk 20:5
And said unto them, W tempt ye me ...... Lk 20:23
And said unto them, W sleep ye ...... Lk 22:46
said unto them the third time, W ...... Lk 23:22
W seek ye the living among the ...... Lk 24:5
said unto them, W are ye troubled ...... Lk 24:38

w do thoughts arise in your ...... Lk 24:38
W baptizest thou then, if thou be ...... Jn 1:25
or, W talkest thou with her ...... Jn 4:27
W go ye about to kill me ...... Jn 7:19
W have ye not brought him ...... Jn 7:45
W do ye not understand my speech ...... Jn 8:43
the truth, w do ye not believe me ...... Jn 8:46
W herein is a marvellous thing, ... Jn 9:30
w hear ye him ...... Jn 10:20
W was not this ointment sold for ...... Jn 12:5
w cannot I follow thee now ...... Jn 13:37
W askest thou me ...... Jn 18:21
but if well, w smitest thou me ...... Jn 18:23
unto her, Woman, w weepest thou ...... Jn 20:13
unto her, Woman, w weepest thou ...... Jn 20:15
w stand ye gazing up into heaven ...... Acts 1:11
of Israel, w marvel ye at this ...... Acts 3:12
w look ye so earnestly on us ...... Acts 3:12
W did the heathen rage, and the ...... Acts 4:25
w hath Satan filled thine heart ...... Acts 5:3
w hast thou conceived this thing ...... Acts 5:4
w do ye wrong one to another ...... Acts 7:26
Saul, Saul, w persecutest thou me ...... Acts 9:4
Sirs, w do ye these things ...... Acts 14:15
Now therefore w tempt ye God ...... Acts 15:10
Saul, Saul, w persecutest thou me ...... Acts 22:7
And now w tarriest thou ...... Acts 22:16
w should it be thought a thing ...... Acts 26:8
Saul, Saul, w persecutest thou me ...... Acts 26:14
w yet am I also judged as a ...... Rom 3:7
man seeth, w doth he yet hope for ...... Rom 8:24
unto me, W doth he yet find fault ...... Rom 9:19
it, W hast thou made me thus ...... Rom 9:20
But w dost thou judge thy brother ...... Rom 14:10
or w dost thou set at nought thy ...... Rom 14:10
w dost thou glory, as if thou 1Cor 4:7
W do ye not rather take wrong 1Cor 6:7
w do ye not rather suffer 1Cor 6:7
for w is my liberty judged of 1Cor 10:29
And I even spoken of for that 1Cor 10:30
w are they then baptized for the 1Cor 15:29
w stand we in jeopardy every hour 1Cor 15:30
w compellest thou the Gentiles to ...... Gal 2:14
w do I yet suffer persecution ...... Gal 5:11
the rudiments of the world, w ...... Col 2:20

WICKED

But the men of Sodom were w ...... Gen 13:13
destroy the righteous with the w ...... Gen 18:23
to slay the righteous with the w ...... Gen 18:25
the righteous should be as the w ...... Gen 18:25
was w in the sight of the LORD ...... Gen 38:7
and I and my people are w ...... Ex 9:27
put not thine hand with the w to ...... Ex 23:1
for I will not justify the w ...... Ex 23:7
it is a w thing ...... Lev 20:17
from the tents of these w men ...... Num 16:26
be not a thought in thy w heart ...... Deut 15:9
which have committed that w thing ...... Deut 17:5
then keep thee from every w thing ...... Deut 23:9
the righteous, and condemn the w ...... Deut 25:1
if the w man be worthy to be ...... Deut 25:2
the w shall be silent in darkness 1Sa 2:9
Wickedness proceedeth from the w 1Sa 24:13
Then answered all the w men 1Sa 30:22
as a man falleth before w men 2Sa 3:34
when w men have slain a righteous 2Sa 4:11
wrought w things to provoke the 2Kin 17:11
thy servants, by requiting the w 2Chr 6:23
face, and turn from their w ways 2Chr 7:14
that w woman, had broken up the 2Chr 24:7
turned them from their w works ...... Neh 9:35
and enemy is this w Haman ...... Est 7:6
by letters that his w device ...... Est 9:25
There the w cease from troubling ...... Job 3:17
of the w shall come to nought ...... Job 8:22
destroyeth the perfect and the w ...... Job 9:22
is given into the hand of the w ...... Job 9:24
If I be w, why then labour I in ...... Job 9:29
shine upon the counsel of the w ...... Job 10:3
Thou knowest that I am not w ...... Job 10:7
If I be w, woe unto me ...... Job 10:15
But the eyes of the w shall fail ...... Job 11:20
the over into the hands of the w ...... Job 15:20
the river into the hands of the w ...... Job 16:11
light of the w shall be put out ...... Job 18:5
such are the dwellings of the w ...... Job 18:21
The triumphing of the w is short ...... Job 20:5
every hand of the w shall come ...... Job 20:22
the portion of a w man from God ...... Job 20:29
Wherefore do the w live, become ...... Job 21:7
counsel of the w is far from me ...... Job 21:16
is the candle of the w put out ...... Job 21:17
are the dwelling places of the w ...... Job 21:28
That the w is reserved to the day ...... Job 21:30
old way which w men have trodden ...... Job 22:15
counsel of the w is far from me ...... Job 22:18
they gather the vintage of the w ...... Job 24:6
Let mine enemy be as the w ...... Job 27:7
The portion of a w man with God ...... Job 27:13
And I brake the jaws of the w ...... Job 29:17
Is not destruction to the w ...... Job 31:3
iniquity, and walketh with w men ...... Job 34:8
fit to say to a king, Thou art w ...... Job 34:18
He striketh them as w men in the ...... Job 34:26
because of his anger, lest he ...... Job 34:36
preserveth not the life of the w ...... Job 36:6
fulfilled the judgment of the w ...... Job 36:17
that the w might be shaken out of ...... Job 38:13
from the w their light is ...... Job 38:15

tread down the w in their place ...... Job 40:12
of the w come to an end .... Ps 7:9
God is angry with the w every day .... Ps 7:11
thou hast destroyed the w .... Ps 9:5
the w is snared in the work of .... Ps 9:16
The w shall be turned into hell .... Ps 9:17
The w in his pride doth persecute .... Ps 10:2
For the w boasteth of his heart's.... Ps 10:3
The w, through the pride of his .... Ps 10:4
Wherefore doth the w contemn God .... Ps 10:13
Break thou the arm of the w .... Ps 10:15
the w bend their bow, they make .... Ps 11:2
but the w and him that loveth .... Ps 11:5
Upon the w he shall rain snares, ... Ps 11:6
The w walk on every side, when .... Ps 12:8
From the w that oppress me, from.... Ps 17:9
deliver my soul from the w .... Ps 17:13
of the w have inclosed me........ Ps 22:16
and will not sit with the w .... Ps 26:5
When the w, even mine enemies and.... Ps 27:2
Draw me not away with the w .... Ps 28:3
let the w be ashamed, and let them.... Ps 31:17
Many sorrows shall be to the w ...... Ps 32:10
Evil shall slay the w .... Ps 34:21
of the w saith within my heart .... Ps 36:1
not the hand of the w remove me.... Ps 36:11
who bringeth w devices to pass .... Ps 37:7
while, and the w shall not be ...... Ps 37:10
The w plotteth against the just .... Ps 37:12
The w have drawn out the sword.... Ps 37:14
better than the riches of many w .... Ps 37:16
the arms of the w shall be broken .... Ps 37:17
But the w shall perish, and the .... Ps 37:20
The w borroweth, and payeth not.... Ps 37:21
seed of the w shall be cut off .... Ps 37:28
The w watcheth the righteous, and .... Ps 37:32
when the w are cut off, thou ...... Ps 37:34
I have seen the w in great power .... Ps 37:35
the end of the w shall be cut off .... Ps 37:38
he shall deliver them from the w .... Ps 37:40
bridle, while the w is before me...... Ps 39:1
But unto the w God saith, What .... Ps 50:16
of the oppression of the w .... Ps 55:3
The w are estranged from the womb.... Ps 58:3
his feet in the blood of the w .... Ps 58:10
merciful to any w transgressors .... Ps 59:5
from the secret counsel of the w .... Ps 64:2
so let the w perish at the........ Ps 68:2
my God, out of the hand of the w.... Ps 71:4
I saw the prosperity of the w ...... Ps 73:3
unto the multitude of the w ...... Ps 74:19
and to the w, Lift not up the horn .... Ps 75:4
all the w of the earth shall .... Ps 75:8
of the w also will I cut off........ Ps 75:10
and accept the persons of the w .... Ps 82:2
rid them out of the hand of the w.... Ps 82:4
behold and see the reward of the w.... Ps 91:8
When the w spring as the grass, ... Ps 92:7
of the w that rise up against me.... Ps 92:11
How long shall the w, ... Ps 94:3
how long shall the w triumph ...... Ps 94:3
until the pit be digged for the w .... Ps 94:13
them out of the hand of the w ...... Ps 97:10
I will set no w thing before mine .... Ps 101:3
I will not know a w person........ Ps 101:4
destroy all the w of the land........ Ps 101:8
that I may cut off all w doers...... Ps 101:8
earth, and let the w be no more...... Ps 104:35
the flame burned up the w .... Ps 106:18
For the mouth of the w and the .... Ps 109:2
Set thou a w man over him........ Ps 109:6
The w shall see it, and be grieved.... Ps 112:10
the desire of the w shall perish .... Ps 112:10
of the w that forsake thy law........ Ps 119:53
The hands of the w have robbed me.... Ps 119:61
The w have waited for me to ...... Ps 119:95
The w have laid a snare for me...... Ps 119:110
all the w of the earth like dross...... Ps 119:155
Salvation is far from the w .... Ps 125:3
For the rod of the w shall not ...... Ps 125:3
cut asunder the cords of the w ...... Ps 129:4
Surely thou wilt slay the w .... Ps 139:19
see if there be any w way in me.... Ps 139:24
O LORD, from the hands of the w .... Ps 140:4
not, O LORD, the desires of the w .... Ps 140:8
further not his w device............ Ps 140:8
to practise w works with men that .... Ps 141:4
Let the w fall into their own........ Ps 141:10
but all the w will he destroy ...... Ps 145:20
but the way of the w he turneth .... Ps 146:9
he casteth the w down to the........ Ps 147:6
in the frowardness of the w........ Prov 2:14
But the w shall be cut off from .... Prov 2:22
of the desolation of the w........ Prov 3:25
the LORD is in the house of the w.... Prov 3:33
Enter not into the path of the w .... Prov 4:14
The way of the w is as darkness .... Prov 4:19
shall take the w himself, and he .... Prov 5:22
a w man, walketh with a froward.... Prov 6:12
that deviseth w imaginations ...... Prov 6:18
he that rebuketh a w man getteth.... Prov 9:7
away the substance of the w .... Prov 10:3
covereth the mouth of the w .... Prov 10:6
but the name of the w shall rot .... Prov 10:7
covereth the mouth of the w .... Prov 10:11
the fruit of the w to sin.......... Prov 10:16
heart of the w is little worth...... Prov 10:20
The fear of the w, it shall come .... Prov 10:24
passeth, so is the w no more ...... Prov 10:25
years of the w shall be shortened .... Prov 10:27

expectation of the w shall perish..... Prov 10:28
but the w shall not inhabit the........ Prov 10:30
of the w speaketh frowardness .... Prov 10:32
but the w shall fall by his own........ Prov 11:5
When a w man dieth, his .... Prov 11:7
the w cometh in his stead............ Prov 11:8
and when the w perish, there is...... Prov 11:10
overthrown by the mouth of the w .... Prov 11:11
The w worketh a deceitful work ...... Prov 11:18
the w shall not be unpunished........ Prov 11:21
the expectation of the w is wrath .... Prov 11:23
much more the w and the sinner .... Prov 11:31
but a man of w devices will he ...... Prov 12:2
the counsels of the w are deceit...... Prov 12:5
The words of the w are to lie in .... Prov 12:6
The w are overthrown, and are not.... Prov 12:7
tender mercies of the w are cruel.... Prov 12:10
The w desireth the net of evil........ Prov 12:12
The w is snared by the .... Prov 12:13
but the w shall be filled with........ Prov 12:21
the way of the w seduceth them .... Prov 12:26
but a w man is loathsome, and........ Prov 13:5
lamp of the w shall be put out...... Prov 13:9
A w messenger falleth into .... Prov 13:17
but the belly of the w shall want .... Prov 13:25
The house of the w shall be........ Prov 14:11
a man of w devices is hated .... Prov 14:17
but at the gates of the .... Prov 14:19
The w is driven away in his .... Prov 14:32
the revenues of the w is trouble .... Prov 15:6
The sacrifice of the w is an........ Prov 15:8
The way of the w is an............ Prov 15:9
The thoughts of the w are an ...... Prov 15:26
but the mouth of the w poureth .... Prov 15:28
The LORD is far from the w........ Prov 15:29
even the w for the day of evil........ Prov 16:4
A w doer giveth heed to false ...... Prov 17:4
He that justifieth the w, and he...... Prov 17:15
A w man taketh a gift out of the .... Prov 17:23
When the w cometh, then cometh.... Prov 18:3
to accept the person of the w ...... Prov 18:5
the mouth of the w devoureth........ Prov 19:28
A wise king scattereth the w .... Prov 20:26
heart, and the plowing of the w .... Prov 21:4
of the w shall destroy them........ Prov 21:7
The soul of the w desireth evil...... Prov 21:10
considereth the house of the w ...... Prov 21:12
the w for their wickedness............ Prov 21:12
The w shall be a ransom for the .... Prov 21:18
sacrifice of the w is abomination.... Prov 21:27
when he bringeth it with a w mind .... Prov 21:27
A w man hardeneth his face........ Prov 21:29
O w man, against the dwelling of .... Prov 24:15
but the w shall fall into............ Prov 24:16
neither be thou envious at the w .... Prov 24:19
candle of the w shall be put out .... Prov 24:20
He that saith unto the w, Thou...... Prov 24:24
Take away the w from before the.... Prov 25:5
the w is as a troubled fountain...... Prov 25:26
a heart are like a potsherd .... Prov 26:23
The w flee when no man pursueth.... Prov 28:1
that forsake the law praise the w.... Prov 28:4
but when the w rise, a man is...... Prov 28:12
so is a w ruler over the poor........ Prov 28:15
When the w rise, men hide .... Prov 28:28
but when the w beareth rule........ Prov 29:2
but the w regardeth not to know .... Prov 29:7
to lies, all his servants are w ...... Prov 29:12
When the w are multiplied, ... Prov 29:16
the way is abomination to the w .... Prov 29:27
judge the righteous and the w ...... Eccl 3:17
there is a w man that prolongeth.... Eccl 7:15
Be not over much w, neither be .... Eccl 7:17
And so I saw the w buried, who had .... Eccl 8:10
it shall not be well with the w ...... Eccl 8:13
according to the work of the w...... Eccl 8:14
again, there be w men, to whom it .... Eccl 8:14
to the righteous, and to the w ...... Eccl 9:2
Woe unto the w .... Is 3:11
Which justify the w for reward...... Is 5:23
of his lips shall he slay the w ...... Is 11:4
evil, and the w for their iniquity .... Is 13:11
hath broken the staff of the w ...... Is 14:5
Let favour be shewed to the w ...... Is 26:10
he deviseth w devices to destroy .... Is 32:7
peace, saith the LORD, unto the w .... Is 48:22
And he made his grave with the w.... Is 53:9
Let the w forsake his way, and the .... Is 55:7
But the w are like the troubled .... Is 57:20
no peace, saith my God, to the w .... Is 57:21
also taught the w ones thy ways...... Jer 2:33
among my people are found w men .... Jer 5:26
they overpass the deeds of the w .... Jer 5:28
for the w are not plucked away .... Jer 6:29
doth the way of the w prosper...... Jer 12:1
thee out of the hand of the w ...... Jer 15:21
all things, and desperately w ...... Jer 17:9
grievously upon the head of the w .... Jer 23:19
give them that are w to the sword .... Jer 25:31
with pain upon the head of the w .... Jer 30:23
When I say unto the w, Thou shalt.... Eze 3:18
to warn the w from his w way........ Eze 3:18
the same w man shall die in his .... Eze 3:18
Yet if thou warn the w, and he...... Eze 3:19
wickedness, nor from his w way .... Eze 3:19
to the w of the earth for a spoil .... Eze 7:21
behold the w abominations that .... Eze 8:9
give w counsel in this city........ Eze 11:2
strengthened the hands of the w ...... Eze 13:22
should not return from his w way .... Eze 13:22

of the w shall be upon him........ Eze 18:20
But if the w will turn from all........ Eze 18:21
at all that the w should die............ Eze 18:23
abominations that the w man doeth .... Eze 18:24
when the w man turneth away from.... Eze 18:27
not according to your w ways ...... Eze 20:44
from thee the righteous and the w.... Eze 21:3
from thee the righteous and the w .... Eze 21:4
profane w prince of Israel, whose .... Eze 21:25
of them that are slain, of the w ...... Eze 21:29
the land into the hand of the w ...... Eze 30:12
When I say unto the w............ Eze 33:8
O w man, thou shalt surely die........ Eze 33:8
speak to warn the w from his way .... Eze 33:8
that w man shall die in his .... Eze 33:8
if thou warn the w of his way to ...... Eze 33:9
no pleasure in the death of the w .... Eze 33:11
but that the w turn from his way .... Eze 33:11
as for the wickedness of the w ...... Eze 33:12
Again, when I say unto the w ...... Eze 33:14
If the w restore the pledge, give........ Eze 33:15
But if the w turn from his.......... Eze 33:19
but the w shall do wickedly........ Dan 12:10
none of the w shall understand...... Dan 12:10
wickedness in the house of the w .... Mic 6:10
them pure with the w balances ...... Mic 6:11
and will not at all acquit the w ...... Nah 1:3
against the LORD, a w counsellor .... Nah 1:11
for the w shall no more pass........ Nah 1:15
for the w doth compass about the .... Hab 1:4
holdest thy tongue when the w...... Hab 1:13
head out of the house of the w ...... Hab 3:13
and the stumblingblocks with the w.... Zeph 1:3
between the righteous and the w .... Mal 3:18
And ye shall tread down the w ...... Mal 4:3
other spirits more w than himself .... Mt 12:45
it be also unto this w generation .... Mt 12:45
it not, then cometh the w one ...... Mt 13:19
are the children of the w one........ Mt 13:38
sever the w from among the just,.... Mt 13:49
A w and adulterous generation ...... Mt 16:4
O thou w servant, I forgave thee .... Mt 18:32
miserably destroy those w men........ Mt 21:41
answered and said unto him, Thou w.... Mt 25:26
other spirits more w than himself .... Lk 11:26
will I judge thee, thou w servant .... Lk 19:22
have I have crucified and.......... Acts 2:23
a matter of wrong or w lewdness .... Acts 18:14
among yourselves that w person...... 1Cor 5:13
all the fiery darts of the w.......... Eph 6:16
enemies in your mind by w works .... Col 1:21
And then shall that W be revealed 2Th 2:8
from unreasonable and w men........ 2Th 3:2
the filthy conversation of the w 2Pet 2:7
led away with the error of the w 2Pet 3:17
ye have overcome the w one........ 1Jn 2:13
and ye have overcome the w one 1Jn 2:14
as Cain, who was of that w one........ 1Jn 3:12
that w one toucheth him not........ 1Jn 5:18

WICKEDLY

I pray you, brethren, do not so w .... Gen 19:7
in doing w in the sight of the........ Deut 9:18
Nay, I pray you, do not so w .... Judg 19:23
But if ye shall still do w 1Sa 12:25
have not w departed from my God.... 2Sa 22:22
I have sinned, and I have done w.... 2Sa 24:17
hath done w above all that the........ 2Kin 21:11
have done amiss, and have dealt w.... 2Chr 6:37
king of Israel, who did very w 2Chr 20:35
mother was his counsellor to do w 2Chr 22:3
done right, but we have done w ...... Neh 9:33
Will ye speak w for God .... Job 13:7
Yea, surely God will not do w ...... Job 34:12
have not w departed from my God .... Ps 18:21
speak w concerning oppression........ Ps 73:8
hath done w in the sanctuary........ Ps 74:3
iniquity, we have done w.......... Ps 106:6
For they speak against thee w........ Ps 139:20
iniquity, and have done w, and have.... Dan 9:5
we have sinned, we have done w ...... Dan 9:15
such as do w against the covenant.... Dan 11:32
but the wicked shall do w .... Dan 12:10
the proud, yea, and all that do w .... Mal 4:1

WICKEDNESS

God saw that the w of man was.... Gen 6:5
how then can I do this great w .... Gen 39:9
it is and.......................... Lev 18:17
and the land become full of w ...... Lev 19:29
a wife and her mother, it is w...... Lev 20:14
that there be no w among you ...... Lev 20:14
but for the w of these nations ...... Deut 9:4
but for the w of these nations ...... Deut 9:5
of this people, nor to their w ...... Deut 9:27
any such w as this is among you .... Deut 13:11
that hath wrought w in the sight .... Deut 17:2
because of the w of thy doings...... Deut 28:20
God rendered the w of Abimelech.... Judg 9:56
Israel, Tell us, how was this w........ Judg 20:3
What w is this that is done among .... Judg 20:12
and see that your w is great........ 1Sa 12:17
ye have done all this w 1Sa 12:20
W proceedeth from the wicked........ 1Sa 24:13
the w of Nabal upon his own head 1Sa 25:39
doer of evil according to his w........ 2Sa 3:39
of w afflict them any more.......... 2Sa 7:10
but if w shall be found in him........ 1Kin 1:52
Thou knowest all the w which........ 1Kin 2:44
return thy w upon thine own head 1Kin 2:44
perversely, we have committed w 1Kin 8:47

work *w* in the sight of the LORD 1Kin 21:25
he wrought much *w* in the sight of 2Kin 21:6
children of *w* waste them any more 1Chr 17:9
they that plow iniquity, and sow *w* ..... Job 4:8
he seeth *w* also................................... Job 11:11
away, and let not *w* dwell in thy ...... Job 11:14
Though *w* be sweet in his mouth, ... Job 20:12
Is not thy *w* great .... Job 22:5
w shall be broken as a tree .... Job 24:20
My lips shall not speak *w* .... Job 27:4
it from God, that he should do *w* ..... Job 34:10
Thy *w* may hurt a man as thou art ..... Job 35:8
God that hath pleasure in *w* .... Ps 5:4
their inward part is very *w* .... Ps 5:9
Oh let the *w* of the wicked come .... Ps 7:9
seek out his *w* till thou find .... Ps 10:15
according to the *w* of their .... Ps 28:4
lovest righteousness, and hatest *w* ... Ps 45:7
and strengthened himself in his *w* .... Ps 52:7
W is in the midst thereof .... Ps 55:11
for *w* is in their dwellings, and .... Ps 55:15
Yea, in heart ye work *w* .... Ps 58:2
than to dwell in the tents of *w* .... Ps 84:10
nor the son of *w* afflict him .... Ps 89:22
shall cut them off in their own *w* ...... Ps 94:23
for the *w* of them that dwell .... Ps 107:34
For they eat the bread of *w* .... Prov 4:17
w is an abomination to my lips .... Prov 8:7
Treasures of *w* profit nothing .... Prov 10:2
wicked shall fall by his own *w* .... Prov 11:5
man shall not be established by *w* ..... Prov 12:3
but *w* overthroweth the sinner .... Prov 13:6
wicked is driven away in his *w* .... Prov 14:32
abomination to kings to commit *w* .... Prov 16:12
the wicked for their *w* .... Prov 21:12
his *w* shall be shewed before the ...... Prov 26:26
mouth, and saith, I have done no *w* ... Prov 30:20
of judgment, that *w* was there .... Eccl 3:16
that prolongeth his life in his *w* .... Eccl 7:15
things, and to know the *w* of folly .... Eccl 7:25
neither shall *w* deliver those .... Eccl 8:8
For *w* burneth as the fire .... Is 9:18
For thou hast trusted in thy *w* .... Is 47:10
and to smite with the fist of *w* .... Is 58:4
to loose the bands of *w*, to undo .... Is 58:6
against them touching all their *w* ..... Jer 1:16
Thine own *w* shall correct thee, ... Jer 2:19
with thy whoredoms and with thy *w* .. Jer 3:2
wash thine heart from *w*, that .... Jer 4:14
this is thy *w*, because it is .... Jer 4:18
waters, so she casteth out her *w* ...... Jer 6:7
it for the *w* of my people Israel .... Jer 7:12
no man repented him of his *w* .... Jer 8:6
for the *w* of them that dwell .... Jer 12:4
for I will pour their *w* upon them ..... Jer 14:16
We acknowledge, O LORD, our *w* .... Jer 14:20
and confounded for all thy *w* .... Jer 22:22
in my house have I found their *w* ..... Jer 23:11
that none doth return from his *w* ..... Jer 23:14
for all whose *w* I have hid my .... Jer 33:5
Because of their *w* which they .... Jer 44:3
their ear to turn from their *w* .... Jer 44:5
forgotten the *w* of your fathers .... Jer 44:9
the *w* of the kings of Judah, and ...... Jer 44:9
the *w* of their wives, and your own ... Jer 44:9
of their wives, and your own *w* .... Jer 44:9
the *w* of your wives, which they .... Jer 44:9
Let all their *w* come before thee ...... Lam 1:22
wicked, and he turn not from his *w* .. Eze 3:19
into *w* more than the nations .... Eze 5:6
is risen up into a rod of *w* .... Eze 7:11
it came to pass after all thy *w* .... Eze 16:23
Before thy *w* was discovered, as ...... Eze 16:57
the *w* of the wicked shall be upon .... Eze 18:20
from his *w* that he hath committed ... Eze 18:27
I have driven him out for his *w* .... Eze 31:11
as for the *w* of the wicked, he .... Eze 33:12
day that he turneth from his *w* .... Eze 33:12
But if the wicked turn from his *w* .... Eze 33:19
discovered, and the *w* of Samaria .... Hos 7:1
that I remember all their *w* .... Hos 7:2
make the king glad with their *w* ...... Hos 7:3
All their *w* is in Gilgal .... Hos 9:15
for the *w* of their doings I will .... Hos 9:15
Ye have plowed *w*, ye have reaped .... Hos 10:13
unto you because of your great *w* .... Hos 10:15
for their *w* is great .... Joel 3:13
for their *w* is come up before me ..... Jonah 1:2
of *w* in the house of the wicked .... Mic 6:10
hath not thy *w* passed continually .... Nah 3:19
And he said, This is *w* .... Zec 5:8
shall call them, The border of *w* ...... Mal 1:4
yea, they that work *w* are set up ...... Mal 3:15
But Jesus perceived their *w* .... Mt 22:18
Thefts, covetousness, *w*, deceit, ... Mk 7:22
part is full of ravening and *w* .... Lk 11:39
Repent therefore of this thy *w* .... Acts 8:22
man, if there be any *w* in him .... Acts 25:5
unrighteousness, fornication, *w*, ... Rom 1:29
with the leaven of malice and *w* 1Cor 5:8
spiritual *w* in high places .... Eph 6:12
and the whole world lies in *w* 1Jn 5:19

WIDE

shalt open thine hand *w* unto him ..... Deut 15:8
thine hand *w* unto thy brother .... Deut 15:11
and good, and the land was *w* 1Chr 4:40
mouth *w* as for the latter rain .... Job 29:23
me as a *w* breaking of waters .... Job 30:14
opened their mouth *w* against me ..... Ps 35:21
open thy mouth *w*, and I will fill ...... Ps 81:10

---

w sea, wherein are things .... Ps 104:25
but he that openeth *w* his lips .... Prov 13:3
a brawling woman and in a *w* house .. Prov 21:9
a brawling woman and in a *w* house ... Prov 25:24
against whom make ye a *w* mouth ..... Is 57:4
saith, I will build me a *w* house ...... Jer 22:14
be set *w* open unto thine enemies ..... Nah 3:13
for *w* is the gate, and broad is .... Mt 7:13

WIDENESS

of twenty cubits round about .... Eze 41:10

WIDOW

Remain a *w* at thy father's house, ... Gen 38:11
Ye shall not afflict any *w* .... Ex 22:22
A *w*, or a divorced woman, or .... Lev 21:14
if the priest's daughter be a *w* .... Lev 22:13
But every vow of a *w*, and of her ...... Num 30:9
judgment of the fatherless and *w* .... Deut 10:18
and the fatherless, and the *w* .... Deut 14:29
and the fatherless, and the *w* .... Deut 16:11
and the fatherless, and the *w* .... Deut 16:14
for the fatherless, and for the *w* ...... Deut 24:19
for the fatherless, and for the *w* ...... Deut 24:20
for the fatherless, and for the *w* ...... Deut 24:21
the fatherless, and the *w* .... Deut 26:12
to the fatherless, and to the *w* .... Deut 26:13
of the stranger, fatherless, and *w* .... Deut 27:19
answered, I am indeed a *w* woman 2Sa 14:5
a *w* woman, even he lifted up his 1Kin 11:26
I have commanded a *w* woman there ... 1Kin 17:9
the *w* woman was there gathering 1Kin 17:10
upon the *w* with whom I sojourn 1Kin 17:20
and doeth not good to the *w* .... Job 24:21
caused the eyes of the *w* to fail .... Job 31:16
They slay the *w* and the stranger, ... Ps 94:6
be fatherless, and his wife a *w* .... Ps 109:9
he relieveth the fatherless and *w* ..... Ps 146:9
establish the border of the *w* .... Prov 15:25
the fatherless, plead for the *w* .... Is 1:17
the cause of the *w* come unto them ... Is 1:23
I shall not sit as a *w*, neither .... Is 47:8
the fatherless, and the *w* .... Jer 7:6
the fatherless, nor the *w* .... Jer 22:3
how is she become as a *w* .... Lam 1:1
vexed the fatherless and the *w* .... Eze 22:7
they take for their wives a *w* .... Eze 44:22
or a *w* that had a priest before .... Eze 44:22
And oppress not the *w*, nor the .... Zec 7:10
the hireling in his wages, the *w* .... Mal 3:5
And there came a certain poor *w* ...... Mk 12:42
That this poor *w* hath cast more ...... Mk 12:43
she was a *w* of about fourscore and .. Lk 2:37
Sidon, unto a woman that was a *w* .... Lk 4:26
son of his mother, and she was a *w* ... Lk 7:12
there was a *w* in that city .... Lk 18:3
Yet because this *w* troubleth me ...... Lk 18:5
he saw also a certain poor *w* .... Lk 21:2
this poor *w* hath cast in .... Lk 21:3
But if any *w* have children or 1Ti 5:4
Now she that is a *w* indeed 1Ti 5:5
Let not a *w* be taken into the 1Ti 5:9
heart, I sit a queen, and am no *w* ..... Rev 18:7

WIDOWHOOD

and put on the garments of her *w* .... Gen 38:19
day of their death, living in *w* 2Sa 20:3
day, the loss of children, and *w* .... Is 47:9
the reproach of thy *w* any more .... Is 54:4

WIDOWS

she put her *w* garments off from ...... Gen 38:14
nor take a *w* raiment to pledge .... Deut 24:17
He was a *w* son of the tribe of 1Kin 7:14
they take the *w* ox for a pledge .... Job 24:3
I caused the *w* heart to sing for ...... Job 29:13

WIDOWS

and your wives shall be *w*, and your .. Ex 22:24
Thou hast sent *w* away empty .... Job 22:9
and his *w* shall not weep, ... Job 27:15
fatherless, and a judge of the *w* ...... Ps 68:5
their *w* made no lamentation .... Ps 78:64
mercy on their fatherless and *w* .... Is 9:17
that *w* may be their prey, and that ... Is 10:2
Their *w* are increased to me above ... Jer 15:8
of their children, and be *w* .... Jer 18:21
and let thy *w* trust in me .... Jer 49:11
fatherless, our mothers are as *w* ...... Lam 5:3
he many *w* in the midst thereof .... Eze 22:25
many *w* were in Israel in the days .... Lk 4:25
because their *w* were neglected in .... Acts 6:1
all the *w* stood by him weeping, ... Acts 9:39
he had called the saints and *w* .... Acts 9:41
therefore to the unmarried and *w* 1Cor 7:8
Honour *w* that are *w* indeed 1Ti 5:3
But the younger *w* refuse 1Ti 5:11
of woman that believeth have *w* 1Ti 5:16
relieve them that are *w* indeed 1Ti 5:16
w in their affliction, and to keep ..... Jas 1:27

WIDOWS'

for ye devour *w* houses, and for a .... Mt 23:14
Which devour *w* houses, and for a .... Mk 12:40
Which devour *w* houses, and for a .... Lk 20:47

WIFE

and shall cleave unto his *w* .... Gen 2:24
were both naked, the man and his *w* .. Gen 2:25
his *w* hid themselves from the .... Gen 3:8
hearkened unto the voice of thy *w* .... Gen 3:17
to his *w* did the LORD God make .... Gen 3:21
And Adam knew Eve his *w* .... Gen 4:1

And Cain knew his *w* .... Gen 4:17
And Lamech knew his *w* again .... Gen 4:25
ark, thou, and thy sons, and thy *w* ... Gen 6:18
went in, and his sons, and his *w* ...... Gen 7:7
the sons of Noah, and Noah's *w* .... Gen 7:13
forth of the ark, thou, and thy *w* ..... Gen 8:16
went forth, and his sons, and his *w* .. Gen 8:18
the name of Abram's *w* was Sarai, ... Gen 11:29
and the name of Nahor's *w*, Milcah, .. Gen 11:29
in law, his son Abram's *w* .... Gen 11:31
And Abram took Sarai his *w* .... Gen 12:5
that he said unto Sarai his *w* .... Gen 12:11
they shall say, This is his *w* .... Gen 12:12
because of Sarai Abram's *w* .... Gen 12:17
not tell me that she was thy *w* .... Gen 12:18
I might have taken her for me to *w* ... Gen 12:19
now therefore behold thy *w* .... Gen 12:19
and they sent him away, and his *w* ... Gen 12:20
up out of Egypt, he, and his *w* .... Gen 13:1
Now Sarai Abram's *w* bare him no ..... Gen 16:1
Sarai Abram's *w* took Hagar her .... Gen 16:3
to her husband Abram to be his *w* .... Gen 16:3
unto Abram, As for Sarai thy *w* .... Gen 17:15
Sarah thy *w* shall bear thee a son .... Gen 17:19
unto him, Where is Sarah thy *w* .... Gen 18:9
Sarah thy *w* shall have a son .... Gen 18:10
Lot, saying, Arise, take thy *w* .... Gen 19:15
hand, and upon the hand of his *w* ..... Gen 19:16
But his *w* looked back from behind ... Gen 19:26
And Abraham said of Sarah his *w* ...... Gen 20:2
for she is a man's *w* .... Gen 20:3
therefore restore the man his *w* .... Gen 20:7
and she became thy *w* .... Gen 20:12
and restored him Sarah his *w* .... Gen 20:14
healed Abimelech, and his *w* .... Gen 20:17
because of Sarah Abraham's *w* .... Gen 20:18
his mother took him a *w* out of .... Gen 21:21
Abraham buried Sarah his *w* in the ... Gen 23:19
that thou shalt not take a *w* unto ..... Gen 24:3
take a *w* unto my son Isaac .... Gen 24:4
thou shalt take a *w* unto my son .... Gen 24:7
the *w* of Nahor, Abraham's brother .... Gen 24:15
Sarah my master's *w* bare a son to .... Gen 24:36
Thou shalt not take a *w* to my son ... Gen 24:37
kindred, and take a *w* unto my son ... Gen 24:38
thou shalt take a *w* for my son of ..... Gen 24:40
let her be thy master's son's *w* .... Gen 24:51
took Rebekah, and she became his *w* .. Gen 24:67
Then again Abraham took a *w* .... Gen 25:1
Abraham buried, and Sarah his *w* ...... Gen 25:10
old when he took Rebekah to *w* .... Gen 25:20
intreated the LORD for his *w* .... Gen 25:21
him, and Rebekah his *w* conceived .... Gen 25:21
of the place asked him of his *w* .... Gen 26:7
he feared to say, She is my *w* .... Gen 26:7
was sporting with Rebekah his *w* ...... Gen 26:8
Behold, of a surety she is thy *w* .... Gen 26:9
lightly have lien with thy *w* .... Gen 26:10
w shall surely be put to death .... Gen 26:11
to *w* Judith the daughter of Beeri ..... Gen 26:34
if Jacob take a *w* of the .... Gen 27:46
Thou shalt not take a *w* of the .... Gen 28:1
take thee a *w* from thence of the ...... Gen 28:2
to take him a *w* from thence .... Gen 28:6
Thou shalt not take a *w* of the .... Gen 28:6
sister of Nebaioth, to be his *w* .... Gen 28:9
said unto Laban, Give me my *w* .... Gen 29:21
him Rachel his daughter to *w* also .... Gen 29:28
gave him Bilhah her handmaid to *w* .. Gen 30:4
her maid, and gave her Jacob to *w* ... Gen 30:9
saying, Get me this damsel to *w* .... Gen 34:4
I pray you give her him to *w* .... Gen 34:8
but give me the damsel to *w* .... Gen 34:12
the son of Adah the *w* of Esau .... Gen 36:10
son of Bashemath the *w* of Esau .... Gen 36:10
were the sons of Adah Esau's *w* .... Gen 36:12
the sons of Bashemath Esau's *w* .... Gen 36:13
the daughter of Zibeon, Esau's *w* ..... Gen 36:14
the sons of Bashemath Esau's *w* .... Gen 36:17
the sons of Aholibamah Esau's *w* ...... Gen 36:18
the daughter of Anah, Esau's *w* .... Gen 36:18
Judah took a *w* for Er his .... Gen 38:6
Onan, Go in unto thy brother's *w* ...... Gen 38:8
he went in unto his brother's *w* .... Gen 38:9
daughter of Shuah Judah's *w* died ..... Gen 38:12
she was not given unto him to *w* .... Gen 38:14
that his master's *w* cast her eyes ...... Gen 39:7
and said unto his master's *w* .... Gen 39:8
but thee, because thou art his *w* .... Gen 39:9
master heard the words of his *w* .... Gen 39:19
he gave him to *w* Asenath the .... Gen 41:45
Ye know that my *w* bare me two .... Gen 44:27
The sons of Rachel Jacob's *w* .... Gen 46:19
buried Abraham and Sarah his *w* .... Gen 49:31
buried Isaac and Rebekah his *w* .... Gen 49:31
took to *w* a daughter of Levi .... Ex 2:1
And Moses took his *w* and his sons, ... Ex 4:20
Jochebed his father's sister to *w* .... Ex 6:20
sister of Naashon, to *w* .... Ex 6:23
of the daughters of Putiel to *w* .... Ex 6:25
in law, took Zipporah, Moses' *w* .... Ex 18:2
his *w* unto Moses into the .... Ex 18:5
am come unto thee, and thy *w* .... Ex 18:6
shalt not covet thy neighbour's *w* ..... Ex 20:17
then his *w* shall go out with him ...... Ex 21:3
If his master have given him a *w* ...... Ex 21:4
the *w* and her children shall be .... Ex 21:4
say, I love my master, my *w* .... Ex 21:5
If he take him another *w* .... Ex 21:10
surely endow her to be his *w* .... Ex 22:16

father's w shalt thou not uncover.......... Lev 18:8
thou shalt not approach to his w............ Lev 18:14
she is thy son's w............................ Lev 18:15
the nakedness of thy brother's w............ Lev 18:16
shalt thou take a w to her sister............. Lev 18:18
carnally with thy neighbour's w.............. Lev 20:10
adultery with another man's w................ Lev 20:10
adultery with his neighbour's w.............. Lev 20:10
w hath uncovered his father's................. Lev 20:11
And if a man take a w and her................ Lev 20:14
man shall lie with his uncle's w.............. Lev 20:20
a man shall take his brother's w............. Lev 20:21
not take a w that is a whore................. Lev 21:7
And he shall take a w in her................. Lev 21:13
a virgin of his own people to w.............. Lev 21:14
them, If any man's w go aside............... Num 5:12
him, and he be jealous of his................ Num 5:14
him, and he be jealous of his................ Num 5:14
man bring his w unto the priest.............. Num 5:15
when a w goeth aside to another............. Num 5:29
him, and he be jealous over his w........... Num 5:30
name of Amram's w was Jochebed...... Num 26:59
Moses, between a man and his w........... Num 30:16
shall be w unto one of the family........... Num 36:8
thou desire thy neighbour's w................ Deut 5:21
or the w of thy bosom, or thy............... Deut 13:6
is there that hath betrothed a w............. Deut 20:7
thou wouldest have her to thy w............. Deut 21:11
husband, and she shall be thy w............ Deut 21:13
If any man take a w, and go in............... Deut 22:13
my daughter unto this man to w............. Deut 22:16
and she shall be his w........................ Deut 22:19
he hath humbled his neighbour's w.......... Deut 22:24
of silver, and she shall be his w............. Deut 22:29
man shall not take his father's w............ Deut 22:30
When a man hath taken a w................. Deut 24:1
she may go and be another man's w........ Deut 24:2
die, which took her to be his w.............. Deut 24:4
not take her again to be his w.............. Deut 24:4
When a man hath taken a new w........... Deut 24:5
shall cheer up his w which he............... Deut 24:5
the w of the dead shall not marry........... Deut 25:5
unto her, and take her to him to w......... Deut 25:5
like not to take his brother's w.............. Deut 25:7
then let his brother's w go up to............ Deut 25:7
Then shall his brother's w come............. Deut 25:9
the w of the one draweth near for.......... Deut 25:11
he that lieth with his father's w............. Deut 27:20
Thou shalt betroth a w, and................. Deut 28:30
toward the w of his bosom, and............. Deut 28:54
I give Achsah my daughter to w............. Josh 15:16
gave him Achsah his daughter to w......... Josh 15:17
I give Achsah my daughter to w............. Judg 1:12
gave him Achsah his daughter to w......... Judg 1:13
the w of Lapidoth, she judged.............. Judg 4:4
of Jael the w of Heber the Kenite.......... Judg 4:17
Then Jael Heber's w took a nail............ Judg 4:21
Jael the w of Heber the Kenite be.......... Judg 5:24
And Gilead's w bare him sons............... Judg 11:2
his w was barren, and bare not............. Judg 13:2
Manoah arose, and went after his w....... Judg 13:11
and Manoah and his w looked on........... Judg 13:19
his w looked on it, and fell on.............. Judg 13:20
to Manoah and to his w...................... Judg 13:21
And Manoah said unto his w................ Judg 13:22
But his w said unto him, If the............. Judg 13:23
now therefore get her for me to w......... Judg 14:2
to take a w of the uncircumcised.......... Judg 14:3
that they said unto Samson's w............ Judg 14:15
Samson's w wept before him, and.......... Judg 14:16
But Samson's w was given to his............ Judg 14:20
Samson visited his w with a kid............ Judg 15:1
go in to my w into the chamber............ Judg 15:6
because he had taken his w................. Judg 15:6
his daughter unto Benjamin to w.......... Judg 21:1
be he that giveth a w to Benjamin........ Judg 21:18
catch you every man his w of the.......... Judg 21:21
not to each man his w in the war......... Judg 21:22
the country of Moab, he, and his w........ Ruth 1:1
and the name of his w Naomi.............. Ruth 1:2
the w of the dead, to raise up............. Ruth 4:5
the w of Mahlon, have I purchased........ Ruth 4:10
have I purchased to be my w.............. Ruth 4:10
Boaz took Ruth, and she was his............ Ruth 4:13
he gave to Peninnah his................... 1Sa 1:4
and Elkanah knew Hannah his w........... 1Sa 1:19
And Eli blessed Elkanah and his w......... 1Sa 2:20
his daughter in law, Phinehas'............ 1Sa 4:19
the name of Saul's w was Ahinoam....... 1Sa 14:50
Merab, her will I give thee to w.......... 1Sa 18:17
unto Adriel the Meholathite to w......... 1Sa 18:19
gave him Michal his daughter to w....... 1Sa 18:27
and Michal David's w told him............. 1Sa 19:11
and the name of his w Abigail............. 1Sa 25:3
young men told Abigail, Nabal's w........ 1Sa 25:14
his w had told him these things.......... 1Sa 25:37
Abigail, to take her to him to w........... 1Sa 25:39
thee, to take thee to him to w........... 1Sa 25:40
of David, and became his w............... 1Sa 25:42
Michal his daughter, David's w........... 1Sa 25:44
the Carmelites, Nabal the................ 1Sa 30:5
Abigail the w of Nabal the................ 1Sa 30:5
save to every man his w and his......... 1Sa 30:22
Abigail Nabal's w the Carmelite........... 2Sa 3:3
of Abigail the w of Nabal the.............. 2Sa 3:3
Ithream, by Eglah David's w............... 2Sa 3:5
saying, Deliver me my w Michal............ 2Sa 3:14
the w of Uriah the Hittite.................. 2Sa 11:3
and to drink, and to lie with my w....... 2Sa 11:11
when the w of Uriah heard that........... 2Sa 11:26

to his house, and she became his w....... 2Sa 11:27
hast taken his w to be thy................. 2Sa 12:9
hast taken the w of Uriah the............. 2Sa 12:10
of Uriah the Hittite to be thy............. 2Sa 12:15
that Uriah's w bare unto David............ 2Sa 12:24
David comforted Bath-sheba his w......... 2Sa 12:24
me Abishag the Shunammite to w......... 1Kin 2:17
to Adonijah thy brother to w.............. 1Kin 2:21
the daughter of Solomon to w............. 1Kin 4:11
the daughter of Solomon to w............. 1Kin 4:15
that he took to w Jezebel the............. 1Kin 16:31
But Jezebel his w came to him............ 1Kin 21:5
Jezebel his w said unto him, Dost........ 1Kin 21:7
whom Jezebel his w stirred up............ 1Kin 21:25
and she waited on Naaman's w........... 2Kin 5:2
the daughter of Ahab was his w.......... 2Kin 8:18
Give thy daughter to my son to w........ 2Kin 14:9
the w of Shallum the son of............... 2Kin 22:14
begat children of Azubah his w........... 1Chr 2:18
then Abiah Hezron's w bare him........... 1Chr 2:24
Jerahmeel had also another w............. 1Chr 2:26
the name of the w of Abishur was........ 1Chr 2:29
to Jarha his servant to w................. 1Chr 2:35
the sixth, Ithream by Eglah his............ 1Chr 3:3
his w Jehudijah bare Jered the............ 1Chr 4:18
the sons of his w Hodiah the.............. 1Chr 4:19
Machir took to w the sister of............. 1Chr 7:15
Maachah the w of Machir bare a.......... 1Chr 7:16
And when he went in to his w............. 1Chr 7:23
And he begat of Hodesh his w............. 1Chr 8:9
My w shall not dwell in the house........ 2Chr 8:11
of Jerimoth the son of David to w......... 2Chr 11:18
he had the daughter of Ahab to w........ 2Chr 21:6
the w of Jehoiada the priest, (........... 2Chr 22:11
Give thy daughter to my son to w........ 2Chr 25:18
the w of Shallum the son of............... 2Chr 34:22
which took a w of the daughters........... Ezr 2:61
of Barzillai the Gileadite to w.............. Neh 7:63
for his friends, and Zeresh his w........... Est 5:10
Then said Zeresh his w and all his......... Est 5:14
And Haman told Zeresh his w.............. Est 6:13
wise men and Zeresh his w unto him...... Est 6:13
Then said his w unto him, Dost............. Job 2:9
My breath is strange to my w............... Job 19:17
Then let my w grind unto another.......... Job 31:10
be fatherless, and his w a widow........... Ps 109:9
Thy w shall be as a fruitful vine........... Ps 128:3
rejoice with the w of thy youth............ Prov 5:18
Whoso findeth a w findeth a good.......... Prov 18:22
the contentions of a w are a............... Prov 19:13
a prudent w is from the LORD.............. Prov 19:14
Live joyfully with the w...................... Eccl 9:9
the children of the married w.............. Is 54:1
a w of youth, when thou wast.............. Is 54:6
They say, If a man put away his w......... Jer 3:1
Surely as a w treacherously................ Jer 3:20
neighed after his neighbour's w............ Jer 5:8
husband with the w shall be taken........ Jer 6:11
Thou shalt not take thee a w............... Jer 16:2
But as a w that committeth................. Eze 16:32
hath defiled his neighbour's w.............. Eze 18:6
and defiled his neighbour's w............... Eze 18:11
not defiled his neighbour's w............... Eze 18:15
with his neighbour's w...................... Eze 22:11
and at even my w died..................... Eze 24:18
every one his neighbour's w................ Eze 33:26
take unto thee a w of whoredoms......... Hos 1:2
for she is not my w, neither am I.......... Hos 2:2
Syria, and Israel served for a w............ Hos 12:12
and for a w he kept sheep.................. Hos 12:12
Thy w shall be an harlot in the........... Amos 7:17
the w of thy youth, against whom......... Mal 2:14
and the w of thy covenant................. Mal 2:14
against the w of his youth.................. Mal 2:15
her that had been the w of Urias.......... Mt 1:6
not to take unto thee Mary thy............ Mt 1:20
him, and took unto him his w.............. Mt 1:24
Whosoever shall put away his w........... Mt 5:31
whosoever shall put away his w............ Mt 5:32
sake, his brother Philip's w................. Mt 14:3
him to be sold, and his w, and............. Mt 18:25
to put away his w for every cause......... Mt 19:3
mother, and shall cleave to his w......... Mt 19:5
Whosoever shall put away his w........... Mt 19:10
case of the man be so with his w........ Mt 19:29
or father, or mother, or w................. Mt 22:24
his brother shall marry his w.............. Mt 22:24
first, when he had married a w............ Mt 22:25
left his w unto his brother................. Mt 22:25
whose w shall she be of the seven........ Mt 22:28
his w went unto him, saying, Have........ Mt 27:19
sake, his brother Philip's w................. Mk 6:17
for thee to have thy brother's w.......... Mk 6:18
for a man to put away his w............... Mk 10:2
and mother, and cleave to his w.......... Mk 10:7
Whosoever shall put away his w........... Mk 10:11
or father, or mother, or w................. Mk 10:29
leave his w behind him, and leave........ Mk 12:19
his brother should take his w.............. Mk 12:19

and the first took a w, and dying........... Mk 12:20
whose w shall he be of them............... Mk 12:23
for the seven had her to w................. Mk 12:23
his w was of the daughters of.............. Lk 1:5
thy w Elisabeth shall bear thee a.......... Lk 1:13
my w well stricken in years................. Lk 1:18
days his w Elisabeth conceived............. Lk 1:24
be taxed with Mary his espoused w....... Lk 2:5
Herodias his brother Philip's w............. Lk 3:19
Joanna the w of Chuza Herod's............ Lk 8:3
another said, I have married a w........... Lk 14:20
not his father, and mother, and w........ Lk 14:26
Whosoever putteth away his w............. Lk 16:18
Remember Lot's w.......................... Lk 17:32
or parents, or brethren, or w.............. Lk 18:29
any man's brother die, having a w......... Lk 20:28
his brother should take his w.............. Lk 20:28
and the first took a w, and died........... Lk 20:29
And the second took her to w............. Lk 20:30
whose w of them is she.................... Lk 20:33
for seven had her to w.................... Lk 20:33
Mary the w of Cleophas, and Mary....... Jn 19:25
Ananias, with Sapphira his w.............. Acts 5:1
his w also being privy to it, and.......... Acts 5:2
of three hours after, when his w......... Acts 5:7
from Italy, with his w Priscilla............ Acts 18:2
Felix came with his w Drusilla............ Acts 24:24
one should have his father's w............ 1Cor 5:1
let every man have his own w............. 1Cor 7:2
render unto the w due benevolence...... 1Cor 7:3
also the w unto the husband.............. 1Cor 7:3
The w hath not power of her own........ 1Cor 7:4
power of his own body, but the.......... 1Cor 7:4
Let not the w depart from her........... 1Cor 7:10
not the husband put away his w......... 1Cor 7:11
hath a w that believeth not.............. 1Cor 7:12
husband is sanctified by the w.......... 1Cor 7:14
the unbelieving w is sanctified.......... 1Cor 7:14
For what knowest thou, O w............. 1Cor 7:16
whether thou shalt save thy w........... 1Cor 7:16
Art thou bound unto a w................. 1Cor 7:27
Art thou loosed from a w................ 1Cor 7:27
seek not a w............................. 1Cor 7:27
world, how he may please his w......... 1Cor 7:33
is difference also between a w........... 1Cor 7:34
The w is bound by the law as long...... 1Cor 7:39
power to lead about a sister, a w........ 1Cor 9:5
the husband is the head of the w....... Eph 5:23
that loveth his w loveth himself......... Eph 5:28
and shall be joined unto his w........... Eph 5:31
so love his w even as himself............ Eph 5:33
the w see that she reverence her....... Eph 5:33
blameless, the husband of one w........ 1Ti 3:2
deacons be the husbands of one w...... 1Ti 3:12
old, having been the w of one man...... 1Ti 5:9
blameless, the husband of one w........ Titus 1:6
giving honour unto the w................ 1Pet 3:7
w is for his make hath herself ready.... Rev 19:7
shew thee the bride, the Lamb's w...... Rev 21:9

WIFE'S

And Adam called his w name Eve......... Gen 3:20
they will slay me for my w sake........... Gen 20:11
his w name was Mehetabel................ Gen 36:39
of thy father's w daughter................. Lev 18:11
his w sons grew up, and they............. Judg 11:2
his w name was Mehetabel................ 1Chr 1:50
whose w name was Maachah.............. 1Chr 9:35
Jehiel, whose w name was Maachah...... Mt 8:14
he saw his w mother laid, and sick...... Mt 8:14
But Simon's w mother lay sick of........ Mk 1:30
Simon's w mother was taken with a..... Lk 4:38

WILD

And he will be a w man.................. Gen 16:12
will also send w beasts among you...... Lev 26:22
the w goat, and the pygarg............... Deut 14:5
the pygarg, and the w..................... Deut 14:5
to the w beasts of the earth............. 1Sa 17:46
men upon the rocks of the w goats...... 1Sa 24:2
was as light of foot as a w roe.......... 2Sa 2:18
gather herbs, and found a w vine........ 2Kin 4:39
gathered thereof w gourds his lap....... 2Kin 4:39
there passed by a w beast that........... 2Kin 14:9
there passed by a w beast that........... 2Chr 25:18
Doth the w ass bray when he hath...... Job 6:5
can the bark like a w ass's colt.......... Job 11:12
as w asses in the desert, go they........ Job 24:5
w goats of the rock bring forth........... Job 39:1
Who hath sent out the w ass free....... Job 39:5
loosed the bands of the w ass........... Job 39:5
or that the w beast may break........... Job 39:8
the w beasts of the field are.............. Ps 50:11
the w beast of the field doth............. Ps 80:13
the w asses quench their thirst.......... Ps 104:11
are a refuge for the w goats............. Ps 104:18
and it brought forth w grapes........... Is 5:2
grapes, brought it forth w grapes........ Is 5:4
but w beasts of the desert shall......... Is 13:21
the w beasts of the islands shall........ Is 13:22
dens for ever, a joy of w asses.......... Is 32:14
The w beasts of the desert shall........ Is 34:14
with the w beasts of the island......... Is 34:14
the streets, as a w bull in a net........ Is 51:20
A w ass used to the wilderness......... Jer 2:24
the w asses did stand in the high...... Jer 14:6
Therefore the w beasts of the.......... Jer 50:39
the w beasts of the islands shall....... Jer 50:39
his dwelling was with the w asses..... Dan 5:21
Assyria, a w ass alone by himself...... Hos 8:9
the w beast shall tear them........... Hos 13:8

his meat was locusts and w honey......... Mt 3:4
and he did eat locusts and w honey......... Mk 1:6
and was with the w beasts..................... Mk 1:13
w beasts, and creeping things, and....... Acts 10:12
w beasts, and creeping things, and....... Acts 11:6
being a w olive tree, wert..................... Rom 11:17
olive tree which is w by nature............. Rom 11:24

WILDERNESS

unto El-paran, which is by the w........... Gen 14:6
by a fountain of water in the w............. Gen 16:7
wandered in the w of Beer-sheba......... Gen 21:14
and he grew, and dwelt in the w........... Gen 21:20
And he dwelt in the w of Paran............ Gen 21:21
that found the mules in the w.............. Gen 36:24
into this pit that is in the w.................. Gen 37:22
three days' journey into the w.............. Ex 3:18
Go into the w to meet Moses................ Ex 4:27
may hold a feast unto me in the w........ Ex 5:1
that they may serve me in the w........... Ex 7:16
go three days' journey into the w.......... Ex 8:27
to the Lᴏʀᴅ your God in the w.............. Ex 8:28
the way of the w of the Red sea........... Ex 13:18
in Etham, in the edge of the w............. Ex 13:20
the land, the w hath shut them in......... Ex 14:3
taken us away to die in the w............... Ex 14:11
than that we should die in the w........... Ex 14:12
they went out into the w of Shur........... Ex 15:22
and they went three days in the w........ Ex 15:22
of Israel came unto the w of Sin........... Ex 16:1
against Moses and Aaron in the w........ Ex 16:2
have brought us forth into this w.......... Ex 16:3
that they looked toward the w.............. Ex 16:10
upon the face of the w there lay........... Ex 16:14
wherewith I have fed you in the w........ Ex 16:32
journeyed from the w of Sin................. Ex 17:1
and his wife unto Moses into the w....... Ex 18:5
day came they into the w of Sinai......... Ex 19:1
of Sinai, and had pitched in the w........ Ex 19:2
unto the Lᴏʀᴅ, in the w of Sinai........... Lev 7:38
him go for a scapegoat into the w........ Lev 16:10
the hand of a fit man into the w........... Lev 16:21
he shall let go the goat in the w........... Lev 16:22
unto Moses in the w of Sinai............... Num 1:1
numbered them in the w of Sinai.......... Num 1:19
in the w of Sinai, and they had no....... Num 3:4
unto Moses in the w of Sinai............... Num 3:14
unto Moses in the w of Sinai............... Num 9:1
month at even in the w of Sinai........... Num 9:5
journeys out of the w of Sinai............. Num 10:12
cloud rested in the w of Paran............ Num 10:12
how we are to encamp in the w........... Num 10:31
and pitched in the w of Paran............. Num 12:16
sent them from the w of Paran............ Num 13:3
land from the w of Zin unto Rehob..... Num 13:21
of Israel, unto the w of Paran............. Num 13:26
would God we had died in this w......... Num 14:2
he hath slain them in the w................ Num 14:16
which I did in Egypt and in the w........ Num 14:22
get you into the w by the way of........ Num 14:25
carcases shall fall in this w................ Num 14:29
they shall fall in this w..................... Num 14:32
shall wander in the w forty years........ Num 14:33
your carcases be wasted in the w........ Num 14:33
in this w they shall be consumed,........ Num 14:35
children of Israel were in the w........... Num 15:32
and honey, to kill us in the w............. Num 16:13
of the Lᴏʀᴅ into this w, that we.......... Num 20:4
up out of Egypt to die in the w........... Num 21:5
in the w which is before Moab............ Num 21:11
which is in the w that cometh out....... Num 21:13
from the w they went to Mattanah...... Num 21:18
out against Israel into the w.............. Num 21:23
but he set his face toward the w......... Num 24:1
of Israel in the w of Sinai.................. Num 26:64
They shall surely die in the w............. Num 26:65
Our father died in the w, and he........ Num 27:3
Meribah in Kadesh in the w of Zin..... Num 27:14
them wander in the w forty years....... Num 32:13
yet again leave them in the w............ Num 32:15
is in the edge of the w...................... Num 33:6
the midst of the sea into the w........... Num 33:8
days' journey in the w of Etham........ Num 33:8
sea, and encamped in the w of Sin..... Num 33:11
their journey out of the w of Sin........ Num 33:12
and pitched in the w of Sinai............. Num 33:15
and pitched in the w of Zin................ Num 33:36
w of Zin along by the coast of........... Num 34:3
on this side Jordan in the w.............. Deut 1:1
all that great and terrible w............... Deut 1:19
And in the w, where thou hast seen.... Deut 1:31
the w by the way of the Red sea........ Deut 1:40
the w by the way of the Red sea........ Deut 2:1
thy walking through this great w........ Deut 2:7
by the way of the w of Moab............. Deut 2:8
I sent messengers out of the w of...... Deut 2:26
Namely, Bezer in the w, in the.......... Deut 4:43
these three forty years in the w......... Deut 8:2
through that great and terrible w........ Deut 8:15
Who fed thee in the w with manna..... Deut 8:16
Lᴏʀᴅ thy God to wrath in the w......... Deut 9:7
them out to slay them in the w.......... Deut 9:28
And what he did unto you in the w..... Deut 11:5
from the w and Lebanon, from the..... Deut 11:24
have led you forty years in the w........ Deut 29:5
land, and in the waste howling w....... Deut 32:10
Meribah-kadesh, in the w of Zin....... Deut 32:51
From the w and this Lebanon even..... Josh 1:4
of war, died in the w by the way........ Josh 5:4
people that were born in the w by the. Josh 5:5
walked forty years in the w................ Josh 5:6

---

them, and fled by the way of the w..... Josh 8:15
the people that fled to the w.............. Josh 8:20
in the w wherein they chased them..... Josh 8:24
and in the springs, and in the w......... Josh 12:8
of Israel wandered in the w............... Josh 14:10
the w of Zin southward was the......... Josh 15:1
In the w, Beth-arabah, Middin, and... Josh 15:61
to the w that goeth up from.............. Josh 16:1
were at the w of Beth-aven............... Josh 18:12
they assigned Bezer in the w upon..... Josh 20:8
ye dwelt in the w a long season......... Josh 24:7
of Judah into the w of Judah............ Judg 1:16
flesh with the thorns of the w........... Judg 8:7
of the city, and thorns of the w......... Judg 8:16
through the w unto the Red sea......... Judg 11:16
they went along through the w.......... Judg 11:18
from the w even unto Jordan............ Judg 11:22
of Israel unto the way of the w.......... Judg 20:42
fled toward the w unto the rock......... Judg 20:45
fled to the w unto the rock............... Judg 20:47
with all the plagues in the w............. 1Sa 4:8
the valley of Zeboim toward the w..... 1Sa 13:18
left those few sheep in the w............ 1Sa 17:28
abode in the w in strong holds.......... 1Sa 23:14
in a mountain in the w of Ziph.......... 1Sa 23:14
David was in the w of Ziph in a......... 1Sa 23:14
and his men were in the w of Maon.... 1Sa 23:24
a rock, and abode in the w of Maon... 1Sa 23:25
after David in the w of Maon............ 1Sa 23:25
David is in the w of En-gedi............. 1Sa 24:1
and went down to the w of Paran...... 1Sa 25:1
David heard in the w that Nabal........ 1Sa 25:4
out of the w to salute our master....... 1Sa 25:14
that this fellow hath in the w............. 1Sa 25:21
and went down to the w of Ziph........ 1Sa 26:2
to seek David in the w of Ziph.......... 1Sa 26:2
But David abode in the w, and he...... 1Sa 26:3
Saul came after him into the w.......... 1Sa 26:3
by the way of the w of Gibeon.......... 2Sa 2:24
over, toward the way of the w........... 2Sa 15:23
will tarry in the plain of the w........... 2Sa 15:28
as he faint in the w may drink........... 2Sa 16:2
this night in the plains of the w......... 2Sa 17:16
and weary, and thirsty, in the w........ 2Sa 17:29
buried in his own house in the w....... 1Kin 2:34
And Baalath, and Tadmor in the w..... 1Kin 9:18
went a day's journey into the w......... 1Kin 19:4
on thy way to the w of Damascus...... 1Kin 19:15
The way through the w of Edom........ 2Kin 3:8
of the w from the river Euphrates...... 1Chr 5:9
Bezer in the w with her suburbs,....... 1Chr 6:78
the hold to the w even of might......... 1Chr 12:8
Lᴏʀᴅ, which Moses made in the w...... 1Chr 21:29
of the Lᴏʀᴅ was made in the w.......... 2Chr 1:3
And he built Tadmor in the w............ 2Chr 8:4
the brook, before the w of Jeruel...... 2Chr 20:16
and went forth into the w of Tekoa.... 2Chr 20:20
toward the watch tower in the w........ 2Chr 20:24
of God laid upon Israel in the w........ 2Chr 24:9
forsookest them not in the w........... Neh 9:19
didst thou sustain them in the w....... Neh 9:21
came a great wind from the w........... Job 1:19
in a w where there is no way............. Job 12:24
the w yieldeth food for them and...... Job 24:5
fleeing into the w in former time....... Job 30:3
on the w, wherein there is no man..... Job 38:26
Whose house I have made the w........ Job 39:6
voice of the Lᴏʀᴅ shaketh the w........ Ps 29:8
the Lᴏʀᴅ shaketh the w of Kadesh..... Ps 29:8
far off, and remain in the w............... Ps 55:7
when he was in the w of Judah.......... Ps 63:t
drop upon the pastures of the w........ Ps 65:12
thou didst march through the w......... Ps 68:7
in the w shall bow before him........... Ps 72:9
to the people inhabiting the w........... Ps 74:14
He clave the rocks in the w............... Ps 78:15
provoking the most High in the w...... Ps 78:17
Can God furnish a table in the w....... Ps 78:19
oft did they provoke him in the w...... Ps 78:40
guided them in the w like a flock...... Ps 78:52
in the day of temptation in the w...... Ps 95:8
I am like a pelican of the w............... Ps 102:6
the depths, as through the w............ Ps 106:9
But lusted exceedingly in the w......... Ps 106:14
them, to overthrow them in the w...... Ps 106:26
in the w in a solitary way.................. Ps 107:4
He turneth rivers into a w................. Ps 107:33
He turneth the w into a standing...... Ps 107:35
causeth them to wander in the w....... Ps 107:40
led his people through the w............. Ps 136:16
It is better to dwell in the w.............. Prov 21:19
of the w like pillars of smoke........... Song 3:6
is this that cometh up from the w...... Song 8:5
That made the world as a w.............. Is 14:17
of the land from Sela to the w........... Is 16:1
they wandered through the w........... Is 16:8
it for them that dwell in the w........... Is 23:13
forsaken, and left like a w................ Is 27:10
the w be a fruitful field, and the........ Is 32:15
judgment shall dwell in the w........... Is 32:16
Sharon is like a w............................ Is 33:9
The w and the solitary place shall..... Is 35:1
for in the w shall waters break.......... Is 35:6
voice of him that crieth in the w........ Is 40:3
I will make the w a pool of water....... Is 41:18
will plant in the w the cedar............. Is 41:19
Let the w and the cities thereof........ Is 42:11
I will even make a way in the w.......... Is 43:19
because I give waters in the w........... Is 43:20
up the sea, I make the rivers a w....... Is 50:2

---

and he will make her w like Eden...... Is 51:3
the deep, as an horse in the w.......... Is 63:13
are a w, Zion is a w.......................... Is 64:10
thou wentest after me in the w.......... Jer 2:2
Egypt, that led us through the w........ Jer 2:6
A wild ass used to the w, that........... Jer 2:24
Have I been a w unto Israel............... Jer 2:31
for them, as the Arabian in the w...... Jer 3:2
the w toward the daughter of my....... Jer 4:11
lo, the fruitful place was a w............. Jer 4:26
Oh that I had in the w a lodging........ Jer 9:2
of the w a lamentation, because........ Jer 9:10
and is burned up like a w, that.......... Jer 9:12
corners, that dwell in the w.............. Jer 9:26
my pleasant portion a desolate w...... Jer 12:10
all high places through the w............ Jer 12:12
passeth away by the wind of the w.... Jer 13:24
the parched places in the w.............. Jer 17:6
yet surely I will make thee a w.......... Jer 22:6
places of the w are dried up............ Jer 23:10
of the sword found graze in the w..... Jer 31:2
and be like the heath in the w.......... Jer 48:6
of the nations shall be a w............... Jer 50:12
a desolation, a dry land, and a w...... Jer 51:43
like the ostriches in the w................ Lam 4:3
they laid wait for us in the w............ Lam 4:19
because of the sword of the w........... Lam 5:9
than the w toward Diblath................ Eze 6:14
And now she is planted in the w........ Eze 19:13
Egypt, and brought them into the w... Eze 20:10
rebelled against me in the w............. Eze 20:13
out my fury upon them in the w........ Eze 20:13
up my hand unto them in the w......... Eze 20:15
I make an end of them in the w......... Eze 20:17
said unto their children in the w....... Eze 20:18
my anger against them in the w........ Eze 20:21
mine hand unto them also in the w.... Eze 20:23
you into the w of the people............ Eze 20:35
in the w of the land of Egypt............ Eze 20:36
were brought Sabeans from the w...... Eze 23:42
will leave thee thrown into the w...... Eze 29:5
they shall dwell safely in the w......... Eze 34:25
she was born, and make her as a w.... Hos 2:3
her, and bring her into the w............ Hos 2:14
found Israel like grapes in the w....... Hos 9:10
I did know thee in the w, in the........ Hos 13:5
the Lᴏʀᴅ shall come up from the w.... Hos 13:15
devoured the pastures of the w......... Joel 1:19
devoured the pastures of the w......... Joel 1:20
them, and behind them a desolate w.. Joel 2:3
the pastures of the w do spring........ Joel 2:22
and Edom shall be a desolate w........ Joel 3:19
led you forty years through the w...... Amos 2:10
and offerings in the w forty years...... Amos 5:25
of Hemath unto the river of the w..... Amos 6:14
a desolation, and dry like a w........... Zeph 2:13
waste for the dragons of the w.......... Mal 1:3
preaching in the w of Judaea............ Mt 3:1
The voice of one crying in the w........ Mt 3:3
the w to be tempted of the devil....... Mt 4:1
went ye out into the w to see............ Mt 11:7
we have so much bread in the w........ Mt 15:33
The voice of one crying in the w........ Mk 1:3
John did baptize in the w................. Mk 1:4
the spirit driveth him into the w........ Mk 1:12
he was there in the w forty days........ Mk 1:13
men with bread here in the w............ Mk 8:4
the son of Zacharias in the w........... Lk 3:2
The voice of one crying in the w........ Lk 3:4
was led by the Spirit into the w......... Lk 4:1
And he withdrew himself into the w... Lk 5:16
went ye out into the w for to see....... Lk 7:24
driven of the devil into the w........... Lk 8:29
leave the ninety and nine in the w..... Lk 15:4
the voice of one crying in the w........ Jn 1:23
lifted up the serpent in the w............ Jn 3:14
fathers did eat manna in the w.......... Jn 6:49
unto a country near to the w............ Jn 11:54
there appeared to him in the w of..... Acts 7:30
Red sea, and in the w forty years...... Acts 7:36
w with the angel which spake to....... Acts 7:38
the space of forty years in the w....... Acts 7:42
tabernacle of witness in the w.......... Acts 7:44
be their manners in the w................ Acts 13:18
leddest out into the w four............... Acts 21:38
for they were overthrown in the w..... 1Cor 10:5
in the city, in perils in the w............ 2Cor 11:26
in the day of temptation in the w...... Heb 3:8
whose carcases fell in the w............. Heb 3:17
And the woman fled into the w.......... Rev 12:6
that she might fly into the w............. Rev 12:14
me away in the spirit into the w........ Rev 17:3

WILES

For they vex you with their w............ Num 25:18
stand against the w of the devil......... Eph 6:11

WILFULLY

For if we sin w after that we............. Heb 10:26

WILILY

They did work w, and went and made.. Josh 9:4

WILL See PREFACE.

WILLETH

So then it is not of him that w........... Rom 9:16

WILLING

the woman will not be w to follow..... Gen 24:5
will not be w to follow the................ Gen 24:8
whosoever is of a w heart................. Ex 35:5
every one whom his spirit made w..... Ex 35:21

WILLINGLY

women, as many as were w hearted	Ex 35:22
a w offering unto the LORD	Ex 35:29
whose heart made them to w bring...	Ex 35:29
a perfect heart and with a w mind	1Chr 28:9
workmanship every w skilful man...	1Chr 28:21
who then is w to consecrate his	1Chr 29:5
the unicorn be w to serve thee	Job 39:9
Thy people shall be w in the day	Ps 110:3
If ye be w and obedient, ye shall	Is 1:19
not w to make her a publick	Mt 1:19
the spirit indeed is w, but the	Mt 26:41
w to content the people, released	Mk 15:15
to w justify himself, said unto	Lk 10:29
Saying, Father, if thou be w	Lk 22:42
w to release Jesus, spake again	Lk 23:20
ye were w for a season to rejoice	Jn 5:35
to w shew the Jews a pleasure,	Acts 24:27
to w do the Jews a pleasure,	Acts 25:9
to w save Paul, kept them from...	Acts 27:43
to w shew his wrath, and to make...	Rom 9:22
w rather to be absent from the...	2Cor 5:8
power they were w of themselves.	2Cor 8:3
For if there be first a w mind	2Cor 8:12
we were w to have imparted unto	1Th 2:8
to distribute, w to communicate	1Ti 6:18
w more abundantly to shew unto	Heb 6:17
in all things to live honestly,	Heb 13:18
not w that any should perish, but...	2Pet 3:9

WILLINGLY

of every man that giveth it w	Ex 25:2
when the people w offered	Judg 5:2
themselves w among the people.	Judg 5:9
answered, We will w give them...	Judg 8:25
of the king's work, offered w	1Chr 29:6
rejoiced, for that they offered w	1Chr 29:9
heart they offered w to the LORD	1Chr 29:9
to offer so w after this son...	1Chr 29:17
of mine heart I have w offered	1Chr 29:17
here, to offer w unto thee	1Chr 29:17
who w offered himself unto the	2Chr 17:16
princes gave w unto the people.	2Chr 35:8
beside all that w offered	Ezr 1:4
of every one that w offered a	Ezr 3:5
offering w for the house of their	Ezr 7:16
that w offered themselves to	Neh 11:2
flax, and worketh w with her hands.	Prov 31:13
For he doth not afflict w nor	Lam 3:33
because he w walked after the	Hos 5:11
Then they w received him into the...	Jn 6:21
was made subject to vanity, not w	Rom 8:20
For if I do this thing w, I have	1Cor 9:17
be as it were of necessity, but w	Philem 14
thereof, not by constraint, but w	1Pet 5:2
For this they w are ignorant of,...	2Pet 3:5

WILLOW

waters, and set it as a w tree	Eze 17:5

WILLOWS

of thick trees, and w of the brook	Lev 23:40
the w of the brook compass him	Job 40:22
upon the w in the midst thereof	Ps 137:2
carry away to the brook of the w	Is 15:7
as w by the water courses	Is 44:4

WILT

if thou w take the left hand,	Gen 13:9
what w thou give me, seeing I go	Gen 15:2
and whither w thou go	Gen 16:8
W thou also destroy the righteous...	Gen 18:23
w thou also destroy and not spare	Gen 18:24
w thou destroy all the city for	Gen 18:28
w thou slay also a righteous...	Gen 20:4
thou w not deal falsely with me	Gen 21:23
saying, But if thou w give it	Gen 23:13
unto her, W thou go with this man	Gen 24:58
That thou w do us no hurt, as we	Gen 26:29
if thou w do this thing for me,	Gen 30:31
What w thou give me, that thou	Gen 38:16
Thou w give me a pledge, till	Gen 38:17
If thou w send our brother with	Gen 43:4
But if thou w not send him, we	Gen 43:5
the hand of him whom thou w send	Ex 4:13
if thou w not let my people go,	Ex 8:21
them go, and w hold them still,	Ex 9:2
that thou w not let them go.	Ex 9:17
How long w thou refuse to humble...	Ex 10:3
if thou w not redeem it, then	Ex 13:13
If thou w diligently hearken to	Ex 15:26
w do that which is right in his	Ex 15:26
w give ear to his commandments,	Ex 15:26
Thou w surely wear away, both	Ex 18:18
if thou w make me an altar of	Ex 20:25
if thou w forgive their sin	Ex 32:32
me know whom thou w send with me	Ex 33:12
w thou put out the eyes of these	Num 16:14
w thou be wroth with all the	Num 21:2
if thou w indeed deliver this	Num 21:2
when thou w raise thyself abroad,	Deut 23:13
if thou w not hearken unto the	Deut 28:15
If thou w not observe to do all...	Deut 28:58
away, so that thou w not hear...	Deut 30:17
what w thou do unto thy great	Josh 7:9
Caleb said unto her, What w thou	Judg 1:14
If thou w save Israel by mine	Judg 6:36
but if thou w not go with me,	Judg 4:8
If thou w save Israel by mine hand	Judg 6:37
W not thou possess that which	Judg 11:24
if thou w offer a burnt offering	Judg 13:16
If thou w redeem it, redeem it	Ruth 4:4

but if thou w not redeem it, then	Ruth 4:4
if thou w indeed look on the	1Sa 1:11
but w give unto thine handmaid a	1Sa 1:11
How long w thou be drunken	1Sa 1:14
w thou deliver them into the hand	1Sa 14:37
How long w thou mourn for Saul,	1Sa 16:1
wherefore then w thou sin against	1Sa 19:5
if thou w take that, take it	1Sa 21:9
that thou w not cut off my seed	1Sa 24:21
that thou w not destroy my name	1Sa 24:21
know and consider what thou w do	1Sa 25:17
that thou w neither kill me, nor	1Sa 30:15
w thou deliver them into mine	2Sa 5:19
w thou not tell me	2Sa 13:4
Joab said, Wherefore w thou run	2Sa 18:22
why w thou swallow up the	2Sa 20:19
thou w shew thyself merciful	2Sa 22:26
man thou w shew thyself upright	2Sa 22:26
the pure thou w shew thyself pure	2Sa 22:27
with the froward thou w shew.	2Sa 22:27
the afflicted people thou w save	2Sa 22:28
or w thou flee three months	2Sa 24:13
if thou w walk in my ways, to	1Kin 3:14
if thou w walk in my statutes, and	1Kin 6:12
if thou w walk before me, as	1Kin 9:4
thee, and w keep my statutes and my	1Kin 9:4
if thou w hearken unto all that I	1Kin 11:38
w walk in my ways, and do that is	1Kin 11:38
If thou w be a servant unto this	1Kin 12:7
w serve them, and answer them, and	1Kin 12:7
If thou w give me half thine	1Kin 13:8
W thou go with me to battle to	1Kin 22:4
w thou go with me against Moab to	2Kin 3:7
Wherefore w thou go to him to day	2Kin 4:23
I know the evil that thou w do	2Kin 8:12
strong holds w thou set on fire,	2Kin 8:12
their young men w thou slay with...	2Kin 8:12
w dash their children, and rip up	2Kin 8:12
How then w thou turn away the	2Kin 18:24
w thou deliver them into mine	1Chr 14:10
that thou w build him an house.	1Chr 17:25
if thou w walk before me, as	2Chr 7:17
of Judah, W thou go with me to	2Chr 18:3
thou w not judge them	2Chr 20:12
O our God, w thou not judge them	2Chr 20:12
But if thou w go, do it, be	2Chr 25:8
and when w thou return.	Neh 2:6
the king unto her, What w thou	Est 5:3
with thee, w thou be grieved	Job 4:2
which of the saints w thou turn	Job 5:1
How long w thou not depart from	Job 7:19
How long w thou speak these	Job 8:2
I know that thou w not hold me	Job 9:28
thou bring me into dust again	Job 10:9
thou w not acquit me from mine.	Job 10:14
W thou break a leaf driven to and	Job 13:25
w thou pursue the dry stubble	Job 13:25
thou w have a desire to the work	Job 14:15
that thou w bring me to death	Job 30:23
thou condemn him that is most	Job 34:17
W thou hunt the prey for the lion	Job 38:39
W thou trust him, because his	Job 39:11
or w thou leave thy labour to him	Job 39:11
W thou believe him, that he will	Job 39:12
W thou also disannul my judgment,	Job 40:8
thou condemn me, that thou	Job 40:8
w thou take him for a servant for	Job 41:4
W thou play with him as with a	Job 41:5
or w thou bind him for thy	Job 41:5
thou, LORD, w bless the righteous	Ps 5:12
with favour w thou compass him as	Ps 5:12
his heart, Thou w not require it.	Ps 10:13
thou w prepare their heart	Ps 10:17
thou w cause thine ear to hear	Ps 10:17
How long w thou forget me, O LORD	Ps 13:1
thou w hide thy face	Ps 13:1
For thou w not leave my soul in	Ps 16:10
neither w thou suffer thine Holy	Ps 16:10
Thou w shew me the path of life.	Ps 16:11
upon thee, for thou w hear me	Ps 17:6
thou w shew thyself merciful	Ps 18:25
man thou w shew thyself upright	Ps 18:25
the pure thou w shew thyself pure	Ps 18:26
thou w shew thyself froward.	Ps 18:26
For thou w save the afflicted	Ps 18:27
but w bring down high looks.	Ps 18:27
For thou w light my candle	Ps 18:28
Lord, how long w thou look on	Ps 35:17
thou w hear, O Lord my God	Ps 38:15
thou w not deliver him unto the	Ps 41:2
thou w make all his bed in his	Ps 41:3
heart, O God, thou w not despise	Ps 51:17
w not thou deliver my feet from...	Ps 56:13
W not thou, O God, which hadst...	Ps 60:10
Thou w prolong the king's life	Ps 61:6
in righteousness w thou answer us	Ps 65:5
w thou be angry for ever	Ps 79:5
How long w thou be angry against	Ps 80:4
if thou w hearken unto me	Ps 81:8
W thou be angry with us for ever	Ps 85:5
w thou draw out thine anger to	Ps 85:5
W thou not revive us again	Ps 85:6
W thou shew wonders to the dead?	Ps 88:10
w thou hide thyself for ever.	Ps 89:46
O when w thou come unto me.	Ps 101:2
W not thou, O God, who hast cast	Ps 108:11
w not thou, O God, go forth with	Ps 108:11
saying, When w thou comfort me	Ps 119:82
when w thou execute judgment on	Ps 119:84

of trouble, thou w revive me	Ps 138:7
Surely thou w slay the wicked, O...	Ps 139:19
if thou w receive my words, and	Prov 2:1
why w thou, my son, be ravished...	Prov 5:20
How long w thou sleep, O sluggard	Prov 6:9
when w thou arise out of thy	Prov 6:9
W thou set thine eyes upon that	Prov 23:5
Thou w keep him in perfect peace,	Is 26:3
thou w ordain peace for us	Is 26:12
forth, thou w debate with it	Is 27:8
How then w thou turn away the	Is 36:9
to night w thou make an end of me	Is 38:12
to night w thou make an end of me	Is 38:13
so w thou recover me, and make me.	Is 38:16
w thou call this a fast, and an	Is 58:5
W thou refrain thyself for these	Is 64:12
w thou hold thy peace, and afflict	Is 64:12
W thou not from this time cry	Jer 3:4
If thou w return, O Israel, saith	Jer 4:1
and if thou w put away thine	Jer 4:1
thou art spoiled, what w thou do	Jer 4:30
then how w thou do in the	Jer 12:5
What w thou say when he shall	Jer 13:21
w thou not be made clean.	Jer 13:27
w thou be altogether unto me as a	Jer 15:18
How long w thou go about, O thou	Jer 31:22
w thou not surely put me to death	Jer 38:15
w thou not hearken unto me	Jer 38:15
if thou w assuredly go forth unto	Jer 38:17
But if thou w not go forth to the	Jer 47:5
how long w thou cut thyself	Lam 1:21
thou w bring the day that thou	Lam 1:21
w thou destroy all the residue of	Eze 9:8
w thou make a full end of the	Eze 11:13
W thou judge them, son of man,	Eze 20:4
son of man, w thou judge them	Eze 22:2
w thou judge, w thou judge the	Eze 22:2
w thou judge Aholah and Aholibah	Eze 23:36
W thou not tell us what these	Eze 24:19
W thou yet say before him that	Eze 28:9
W thou not shew us what thou	Eze 37:18
what w thou give	Hos 9:14
thou w cast all their sins into	Mic 7:19
Thou w perform the truth to Jacob.	Mic 7:20
shall I cry, and thou w not hear	Hab 1:2
of violence, and thou w not save.	Hab 1:2
I said, Surely thou w fear me	Zeph 3:7
thou w receive instruction	Zeph 3:7
how long w thou not have mercy on...	Zec 1:12
If thou w walk in my ways	Zec 3:7
if thou w keep my charge, then,	Zec 3:7
if thou w fall down and worship me	Mt 4:9
Or how w thou say to thy brother,	Mt 7:4
him, saying, Lord, if thou w	Mt 8:2
W thou then that we go and gather	Mt 13:28
be it unto thee even as thou w	Mt 15:28
if thou w, let us make here three	Mt 17:4
but if thou w enter into life,	Mt 19:17
If thou w be perfect, go and sell	Mt 19:21
And he said unto her, What w thou	Mt 20:21
Where w thou that we prepare for	Mt 26:17
not as I will, but as thou w	Mt 26:39
and saying unto him, If thou w	Mk 1:40
Ask of me whatsoever thou w,	Mk 6:22
What w thou that I should do unto	Mk 10:51
Where w thou that we go and	Mk 14:12
not what I will, but what thou w	Mk 14:36
If thou w therefore worship me	Lk 4:7
him, saying, Lord, if thou w	Lk 5:12
w thou that we command fire to	Lk 9:54
What w thou that I shall do unto	Lk 18:41
Where w thou that we prepare	Lk 22:9
w thou rear it up in three days	Jn 2:20
unto him, W thou be made whole.	Jn 5:6
now, whatsoever thou w ask of God	Jn 11:22
W thou lay down thy life for my	Jn 13:38
how is it that thou w manifest	Jn 14:22
w thou at this time restore again	Acts 1:6
Because thou w not leave my soul	Acts 2:27
neither w thou suffer thine Holy	Acts 2:27
W thou kill me, as thou diddest	Acts 7:28
what w thou have me to do	Acts 9:6
w thou not cease to pervert the	Acts 13:10
W thou go up to Jerusalem, and	Acts 25:9
Thou w say then unto me, Why doth	Rom 9:19
Thou w say then, The branches	Rom 11:19
W thou then not be afraid of the	Rom 13:3
knowing that thou w also do more	Philem 21
But w thou know, O vain man, that	Jas 2:20

WIMPLES

apparel, and the mantles, and the w...	Is 3:22

WIN

thought to w them for himself	2Chr 32:1
but dung, that I may w Christ	Phil 3:8

WIND

God made a w to pass over the	Gen 8:1
the east w spread up and their...	Gen 41:6
thin, and blasted with the east w	Gen 41:23
ears blasted with the east w	Gen 41:27
the LORD brought an east w upon	Ex 10:13
the east w brought the locusts	Ex 10:13
turned a mighty strong west w	Ex 10:19
by a strong east w all that night	Ex 14:21
Thou didst blow with thy w	Ex 15:10
went forth a w from the LORD,	Num 11:31
was seen upon the wings of the w	2Sa 22:11
heaven was black with clouds and w	1Kin 18:45
strong w rent the mountains, and	1Kin 19:11
but the LORD was not in the w	1Kin 19:11

after the _w_ an earthquake 1Kin 19:11
the LORD, Ye shall not see _w_ 2Kin 3:17
there came a great _w_ from the .... Job 1:19
that is desperate, which are as _w_ ... Job 6:26
O remember that my life is _w_ .... Job 7:7
of thy mouth be like a strong _w_ ...... Job 8:2
and fill his belly with the east _w_ ... Job 15:2
They are as stubble before the _w_ .. Job 21:18
The east _w_ carrieth him away, and.. Job 27:21
they pursue my soul as the _w_ .... Job 30:15
Thou liftest me up to the _w_ .... Job 30:22
quieteth the earth by the south _w_ .. Job 37:17
but the _w_ passeth, and cleanseth ... Job 37:21
the east _w_ upon the earth .... Job 38:24
chaff which the _w_ driveth away ...... Ps 1:4
did fly upon the wings of the _w_ ...... Ps 18:10
small as the dust before the _w_ ...... Ps 18:42
Let them be as chaff before the _w_.. Ps 35:5
ships of Tarshish with an east _w_ .... Ps 48:7
He caused an east _w_ to blow in ...... Ps 78:26
power he brought in the south _w_ .... Ps 78:26
a _w_ that passeth away, and cometh.. Ps 78:39
as the stubble before the _w_ .... Ps 83:13
For the _w_ passeth over it, and it .... Ps 103:16
walketh upon the wings of the _w_ .... Ps 104:3
and raiseth the stormy _w_, which .... Ps 107:25
he bringeth the _w_ out of his .... Ps 135:7
he causeth his _w_ to blow, and the.. Ps 147:18
stormy _w_ fulfilling his word .... Ps 148:8
his own house shall inherit the _w_ .. Prov 11:29
is like clouds and _w_ without rain .. Prov 25:14
The north _w_ driveth away rain........ Prov 25:23
Whosoever hideth her hideth the _w_.. Prov 27:16
hath gathered the _w_ in his fists...... Prov 30:4
The _w_ goeth toward the south, and Eccl 1:6
the _w_ returneth again according .... Eccl 1:6
he that hath laboured for the _w_ .... Eccl 5:16
observeth the _w_ shall not sow .... Eccl 11:4
Awake, O north _w_ .... Song 4:16
of the wood are moved with the _w_.. Is 7:2
with his mighty _w_ shall he shake.... Is 11:15
of the mountains before the _w_ ...... Is 17:13
have as it were brought forth .... Is 26:18
he stayeth his rough in the day .... Is 27:8
the day of the east _w_ .... Is 27:8
be as an hiding place from the _w_ .. Is 32:2
the _w_ shall carry them away, and.... Is 41:16
their molten images are _w_ .... Is 41:29
but the _w_ shall carry them all .... Is 57:13
and our iniquities, like the _w_ .... Is 64:6
snuffeth up the _w_ at her pleasure .. Jer 2:24
A dry _w_ of the high places in the.... Jer 4:11
Even a full _w_ from those places...... Jer 4:12
And the prophets shall become _w_ .. Jer 5:13
bringeth forth the _w_ out of his ...... Jer 10:13
away by the _w_ of the wilderness .... Jer 13:24
snuffed up the _w_ like dragons .... Jer 14:6
with an east _w_ before the enemy .. Jer 18:17
The _w_ shall eat up all thy .... Jer 22:22
up against me, a destroying _w_ .... Jer 51:1
bringeth forth the _w_ out of his ...... Jer 51:16
part thou shalt scatter in the _w_ .... Eze 5:2
will I scatter toward every _w_ all .... Eze 12:14
and a stormy _w_ shall rend it .... Eze 13:11
it with a stormy _w_ in my fury.......... Eze 13:13
when the east _w_ toucheth it............ Eze 17:10
the east _w_ dried up her fruit .... Eze 19:12
the east _w_ hath broken thee in ...... Eze 27:26
he unto me, Prophesy unto the _w_ .. Eze 37:9
son of man, and say to the _w_ .... Eze 37:9
the _w_ carried them away, that no.... Dan 2:35
The _w_ hath bound her up in her...... Hos 4:19
For they have sown the _w_, and they Hos 8:7
Ephraim feedeth on _w_ .... Hos 12:1
and followeth after the east _w_ .... Hos 12:1
an east _w_ shall come .... Hos 13:15
the _w_ of the LORD shall come up .... Hos 13:15
the mountains, and createth the _w_.. Amos 4:13
sent out a great _w_ into the sea........ Jonah 1:4
God prepared a vehement east _w_ .. Jonah 4:8
faces shall sup as the east _w_ .... Hab 1:9
and the _w_ was in their wings .... Zec 5:9
A reed shaken with the _w_ .... Mt 11:7
for the _w_ was contrary .... Mt 14:24
But when he saw the _w_ boisterous.. Mt 14:30
come into the ship, the _w_ ceased.... Mt 14:32
There there arose a great storm of _w_ .. Mk 4:37
And he arose, and rebuked the _w_ .. Mk 4:39
the _w_ ceased, and there was a........ Mk 4:39
of man is this, that even the _w_ ...... Mk 4:41
for the _w_ was contrary unto them.. Mk 6:48
and the _w_ ceased .... Mk 6:51
A reed shaken with the _w_ .... Lk 7:24
down a storm of _w_ on the lake .... Lk 8:23
Then he arose, and rebuked the _w_.. Lk 8:24
And when ye see the south _w_ blow .. Lk 12:55
The _w_ bloweth where it listeth, ... Jn 3:8
by reason of a great _w_ that blew .... Jn 6:18
heaven as of a rushing mighty _w_ .. Acts 2:2
the _w_ not suffering us, we sailed.... Acts 27:7
And when the south _w_ blew softly .. Acts 27:13
arose against it a tempestuous _w_.. Acts 27:14
and could not bear up into the _w_ .. Acts 27:15
hoised up the mainsail to the _w_ .... Acts 27:40
and after one day the south _w_ blew.. Acts 28:13
about with every _w_ of doctrine ...... Eph 4:14
wave of the sea driven with the _w_.. Jas 1:6
when she is shaken of a mighty _w_ .. Rev 6:13
that the _w_ should not blow on the .. Rev 7:1

WINDING

they went up with _w_ stairs into 1Kin 6:8
a _w_ about still upward to the .... Eze 41:7
for the _w_ about of the house went .. Eze 41:7

WINDOW

A _w_ shalt thou make to the ark, ... Gen 6:16
that Noah opened the _w_ of the ark .. Gen 8:6
the Philistines looked out at a _w_ .. Gen 26:8
them down by a cord through the _w_ .. Josh 2:15
line of scarlet thread in the _w_ ...... Josh 2:21
bound the scarlet line in the _w_ .... Josh 2:21
of Sisera looked out at a _w_ .... Judg 5:28
Michal let David down through a _w_ .. 1Sa 19:12
daughter looked through a _w_.......... 2Sa 6:16
her head, and looked out at a _w_.... 2Kin 9:30
And he lifted up his face to the _w_ .. 2Kin 9:32
And he said, Open the _w_ eastward .. 2Kin 13:17
out at a _w_ saw king David dancing.. 1Chr 15:29
For at the _w_ of my house I looked.. Prov 7:6
there sat in a _w_ a certain young.... Acts 20:9
through a _w_ in a basket was I let .. 2Cor 11:33

WINDOWS

the _w_ of heaven were opened .... Gen 7:11
of the heaven were stopped, and...... Gen 8:2
house he made _w_ of narrow lights .. 1Kin 6:4
there were _w_ in three rows, and.... 1Kin 7:4
and posts were square, with the _w_ .. 1Kin 7:5
the LORD would make _w_ in heaven .. 2Kin 7:2
the LORD should make _w_ in heaven .. 2Kin 7:19
look out of the _w_ be darkened .... Eccl 12:3
wall, he looketh forth at the _w_ ...... Song 2:9
for the _w_ from on high are open, .. Is 24:18
And I will make thy _w_ of agates .. Is 54:12
cloud, and as the doves to their _w_ .. Is 60:8
For death is come up into our _w_ .... Jer 9:21
chambers, and cutteth him out _w_ .. Jer 22:14
there were narrow _w_ to the little .. Eze 40:16
_w_ were round about inward .... Eze 40:16
And their _w_, and their arches, and.. Eze 40:25
And there were _w_ in it and in the.. Eze 40:25
thereof round about, like those _w_ .. Eze 40:25
and there were _w_ in it and in the.. Eze 40:29
and there were _w_ therein and in the.. Eze 40:33
and the _w_ to it round about .... Eze 40:36
The door posts, and the narrow _w_ .. Eze 41:16
and from the ground up to the _w_ .. Eze 41:16
and the _w_ were covered .... Eze 41:16
And there were narrow _w_ and palm.. Eze 41:26
his _w_ being open in his chamber.... Dan 6:10
enter in at the _w_ like a thief .... Joel 2:9
their voice shall sing in the _w_ ...... Zeph 2:14
will not open you the _w_ of heaven.. Mal 3:10

WINDS

To make the weight for the _w_ .... Job 28:25
I will scatter into all _w_ them .... Jer 49:32
four _w_ from the four quarters of .... Jer 49:36
scatter them toward all those _w_ .... Jer 49:36
will I scatter into all the _w_ .... Eze 5:10
a third part into all the _w_ .... Eze 5:12
shall be scattered toward all _w_ ...... Eze 17:21
Come from the four _w_, O breath, ... Eze 37:9
the four _w_ of the heaven strove .... Dan 7:2
ones toward the four _w_ of heaven .. Dan 8:8
toward the four _w_ of heaven .... Dan 11:4
as the four _w_ of the heaven .... Zec 2:6
the _w_ blew, and beat upon that ...... Mt 7:25
the _w_ blew, and beat upon that ...... Mt 7:27
Then he arose, and rebuked the _w_ .. Mt 8:26
of man is this, that even the _w_ ...... Mt 8:27
his elect from the four _w_ .... Mt 24:31
his elect from the four _w_ .... Mk 13:27
for the commandeth even the _w_ .... Lk 8:25
because the _w_ were contrary............ Acts 27:4
great, and are driven of fierce _w_ .. Jas 3:4
without water, carried about of _w_ .. Jude 12
holding the four _w_ of the earth ...... Rev 7:1

WINDY

hasten my escape from the _w_ storm.. Ps 55:8

WINE

And he drank of the _w_, and was .... Gen 9:21
Noah awoke from his _w_ .... Gen 9:24
of Salem brought forth bread and _w_ .. Gen 14:18
let us make our father drink _w_ ...... Gen 19:32
their father drink _w_ that night........ Gen 19:33
make him drink _w_ this night also .. Gen 19:34
father drink _w_ that night also .... Gen 19:35
and he brought him _w_, and he drank.. Gen 27:25
the earth, and plenty of corn and _w_ .. Gen 27:28
corn and _w_ have I sustained him .. Gen 27:37
he washed his garments in _w_ .... Gen 49:11
His eyes shall be red with _w_ .... Gen 49:12
an hin of _w_ for a drink offering ...... Ex 29:40
Do not drink _w_ nor strong drink, .. Lev 10:9
offering thereof shall be of _w_ .... Lev 23:13
He shall separate himself from _w_ .. Num 6:3
and shall drink no vinegar of _w_ .... Num 6:3
that the Nazarite may drink _w_ ...... Num 6:20
the fourth part of an hin of _w_ .... Num 15:5
the third part of an hin of _w_ .... Num 15:7
a drink offering half an hin of _w_ .. Num 15:10
the oil, and all the best of the _w_ .. Num 18:12
shalt thou cause the strong _w_ to.... Num 28:7
half an hin of _w_ unto a bullock...... Num 28:14
of thy land, thy corn, and thy _w_ .... Deut 7:13
gather in thy corn, and thy _w_ .... Deut 11:14
tithe of thy corn, or of thy _w_ .... Deut 12:17
the tithe of thy corn, of thy _w_ .... Deut 14:23
for oxen, or for sheep, or for _w_ ...... Deut 14:26

gathered in thy corn and thy _w_ .... Deut 16:13
also of thy corn, of thy _w_ .... Deut 18:4
but shalt neither drink of the _w_ .... Deut 28:39
not leave thee either corn, _w_ .... Deut 28:51
they are drunk _w_ or strong drink .. Deut 29:6
Their _w_ is the poison of dragons, .. Deut 32:33
drank the _w_ of their drink .... Deut 32:38
shall be upon a land of corn and _w_ .. Deut 33:28
_w_ bottles, old, and rent, and bound.. Josh 9:4
And these bottles of _w_, which we .. Josh 9:13
unto them, Should I leave my _w_ .... Judg 9:13
drink not _w_ nor strong drink, and .. Judg 13:4
now drink no _w_ nor strong drink, .. Judg 13:7
let her drink _w_ or strong drink, ... Judg 13:14
_w_ also for me, and for thy .... Judg 19:19
put away thy _w_ from thee 1Sa 1:14
neither have I drunk _w_ nor............ 1Sa 1:15
ephah of flour, and a bottle of _w_ .. 1Sa 1:24
and another carrying a bottle of _w_ .. 1Sa 10:3
with bread, and a bottle of _w_ 1Sa 16:20
loaves, and two bottles of _w_ 1Sa 25:18
when the _w_ was gone out of Nabal,.. 1Sa 25:37
piece of flesh, and a flagon of _w_ .. 2Sa 6:19
Amnon's heart is merry with _w_ 2Sa 13:28
summer fruits, and a bottle of _w_ .. 2Sa 16:1
and the _w_, that such as be faint 2Sa 16:2
own land, a land of corn and _w_ 2Kin 18:32
and the fine flour, and the _w_ 1Chr 9:29
figs, and bunches of raisins, and _w_ .. 1Chr 12:40
piece of flesh, and a flagon of _w_ .. 1Chr 16:3
of the vineyards for the _w_ 1Chr 27:27
and twenty thousand baths of _w_ .. 2Chr 2:10
and the barley, the oil, and the _w_ .. 2Chr 2:15
store of victual, and of oil and _w_ .. 2Chr 11:11
the firstfruits of corn, ... 2Chr 31:5
for the increase of corn, and _w_ 2Chr 32:28
the God of heaven, wheat, salt, _w_ .. Ezr 6:9
and to an hundred baths of _w_ .... Ezr 7:22
the king, that _w_ was before him...... Neh 2:1
and I took up the _w_, and gave it .... Neh 2:1
the money, and of the corn, the _w_.. Neh 5:11
and had taken of them bread and _w_ .. Neh 5:15
ten days store of all sorts of _w_ ...... Neh 5:18
of all manner of trees, of _w_ .... Neh 10:37
of the corn, of the new _w_ .... Neh 10:39
the tithes of the corn, the new _w_ .. Neh 13:5
tithe of the corn and the new _w_ .... Neh 13:12
as also _w_, grapes, and figs, and.... Neh 13:15
royal in abundance, according .... Est 1:7
of the king was merry with _w_ .... Est 1:10
unto Esther at the banquet of _w_ .... Est 5:6
second day at the banquet of _w_ .... Est 7:2
of _w_ in his wrath went into the........ Est 7:7
the place of the banquet of _w_ .... Est 7:8
drinking _w_ in their eldest .... Job 1:13
drinking _w_ in their eldest .... Job 1:18
my belly is as _w_ which hath no...... Job 32:19
their corn and their _w_ increased.... Ps 4:7
us to drink the _w_ of astonishment .. Ps 60:3
there is a cup, and the _w_ is red ...... Ps 75:8
man that shouteth by reason of _w_ .. Ps x:65
_w_ that maketh glad the heart of ...... Ps 104:15
shalt burst out with new _w_ .... Prov 3:10
and drink the _w_ of violence .... Prov 4:17
she hath mingled her _w_ .... Prov 9:2
drink of the _w_ which I have .... Prov 9:5
W is a mocker, strong drink is............ Prov 20:1
he that loveth _w_ and oil shall not .. Prov 21:17
They that tarry long at the _w_ .... Prov 23:30
they that go to seek mixed _w_ .... Prov 23:30
thou upon the _w_ when it is red ...... Prov 23:31
it is not for kings to drink _w_ .... Prov 31:4
_w_ unto those that be of heavy .... Prov 31:6
mine heart to give myself unto _w_ .. Eccl 2:3
drink thy _w_ with a merry heart ...... Eccl 9:7
for laughter, and _w_ maketh merry .. Eccl 10:19
for thy love is better than _w_ .... Song 1:2
remember thy love more than _w_ .... Song 1:4
much better is thy love than _w_ ...... Song 4:10
I have drunk my _w_ with my milk .. Song 5:1
like the best _w_ for my beloved ...... Song 7:9
cause thee to drink of spiced _w_ .... Song 8:2
dross, thy _w_ mixed with water ...... Is 1:22
until night, till _w_ inflame them ...... Is 5:11
viol, the tabret, and pipe, and _w_ .. Is 5:12
them that are mighty to drink _w_ .. Is 5:22
tread out no _w_ in their presses ...... Is 16:10
eating flesh, and drinking _w_ .... Is 22:13
The new _w_ mourneth, the vine ...... Is 24:7
shall not drink _w_ with a song .... Is 24:9
is a crying for _w_ in the streets .... Is 24:11
ye unto her, A vineyard of red _w_ .. Is 27:2
of them that are overcome with _w_ .. Is 28:1
they also have erred through _w_ .... Is 28:7
drink, they are swallowed up of _w_ .. Is 28:7
they are drunken, but not with _w_ .. Is 29:9
own land, a land of corn and _w_ .... Is 36:17
their own blood, as with sweet _w_ .. Is 49:26
and drunken, but not with _w_ .... Is 51:21
yea, come, buy _w_ and milk without .. Is 55:1
Come ye, say they, I will fetch _w_ .. Is 56:12
stranger shall not drink thy _w_ ...... Is 62:8
As the new _w_ is found in the.......... Is 65:8
bottle shall be filled with _w_ .... Jer 13:12
tithe shall be filled with _w_ .... Jer 13:12
like a man whom _w_ hath overcome.. Jer 23:9
Take the _w_ cup of this fury at my .. Jer 25:15
of the LORD, the wine, and for _w_ .... Jer 31:12
chambers, and give them _w_ to drink .. Jer 35:2
of the Rechabites pots full of _w_ .... Jer 35:5

WINEBIBBER (column 1 continued)

and I said unto them, Drink ye w .... Jer 35:5
But they said, We will drink no w .... Jer 35:6
us, saying, Ye shall drink no w .... Jer 35:6
to drink no w all our days, we, ... Jer 35:8
commanded his sons not to drink w .... Jer 35:14
but ye, gather ye w, and summer .... Jer 40:10
unto Mizpah, and gathered w .... Jer 40:12
I have caused w to fail from the .... Jer 51:7
the nations have drunken of her w .... Lam 2:12
their mothers, Where is corn and w .... Lam 2:12
in the w of Helbon, and white wool .... Eze 27:18
Neither shall any priest drink w .... Eze 44:21
meat, and of the w which he drank .... Dan 1:5
nor with the w which he drank .... Dan 1:8
the w that they should drink .... Dan 1:16
drank w before the thousand .... Dan 5:1
whiles he tasted the w, ... Dan 5:2
They drank w, and praised the gods .... Dan 5:4
concubines, have drunk w in them.... Dan 5:23
came flesh nor w in my mouth .... Dan 10:3
know that I gave her corn, and w .... Hos 2:8
my w in the season thereof, and........ Hos 2:9
shall hear the corn, and the w .... Hos 2:22
other gods, and love flagons of w .... Hos 3:1
Whoredom and w and new .... Hos 4:11
new w takes away the heart........ Hos 4:11
made him sick with bottles of w........ Hos 7:5
assemble themselves for corn and w .... Hos 7:14
the new w shall fail in her........ Hos 9:2
They shall not offer w offerings........ Hos 9:4
shall be as the w of Lebanon .... Hos 14:7
and howl, all ye drinkers of w........ Joel 1:5
because of the new w........ Joel 1:5
the new w is dried up, the oil .... Joel 1:10
I will send you corn, and w........ Joel 2:19
and the fats shall overflow with w .... Joel 2:24
an harlot, and sold a girl for w .... Joel 3:3
mountains shall drop down new w .... Joel 3:18
they drink the w of the condemned .... Amos 2:8
ye gave the Nazarites w to drink .... Amos 2:12
but ye shall not drink of w of them.... Amos 5:11
That drink w in bowls, and anoint........ Amos 6:6
the mountains shall drop sweet w........ Amos 9:13
vineyards, and drink the w thereof .... Amos 9:14
I will prophesy unto thee of w .... Mic 2:11
with oil; and sweet w........ Mic 6:15
but shalt not drink w........ Mic 6:15
because he transgresseth by w .... Hab 2:5
but not drink the w thereof .... Zeph 1:13
upon the corn, and upon the new w.... Hag 1:11
do touch bread, or pottage, or w .... Hag 2:12
and make a noise as through w .... Zec 9:15
men cheerful, and new w the maids.... Zec 9:17
heart shall rejoice as through w .... Zec 10:7
do men put new w into old bottles .... Mt 9:17
the w runneth out, and the bottles .... Mt 9:17
they put new w into new bottles........ Mt 9:17
putteth new w into old bottles .... Mk 2:22
else the new w doth burst the........ Mk 2:22
the w is spilled, and the bottles........ Mk 2:22
but new w must be put into new........ Mk 2:22
him to drink w mingled with myrrh .... Mk 15:23
drink neither w nor strong drink........ Lk 1:15
putteth new w into old bottles .... Lk 5:37
else the new w will burst the........ Lk 5:37
But new w must be put into new........ Lk 5:38
old w straightway desireth new .... Lk 5:39
eating bread nor drinking w........ Lk 7:33
his wounds, pouring in oil and w........ Lk 10:34
And when they wanted w, the mother .... Jn 2:3
saith unto him, They have no w .... Jn 2:3
tasted the water that was made w........ Jn 2:9
beginning doth set forth good w........ Jn 2:10
hast kept the good w until now........ Jn 2:10
where he made the water w .... Jn 4:46
said, These men are full of new w .... Acts 2:13
to eat flesh, nor to drink w .... Rom 14:21
And be not drunk with w, wherein .... Eph 5:18
Not given to w, no striker, not 1Ti 3:3
not given to much w, not greedy 1Ti 3:8
but use a little w for thy 1Ti 5:23
not soon angry, not given to w........ Titus 1:7
accusers, not given to much w .... Titus 2:3
lusts, excess of w, revellings........ 1Pet 4:3
thou hurt not the oil and the w .... Rev 6:6
made all nations drink of the w........ Rev 14:8
of the w of the wrath of God........ Rev 14:10
w of the fierceness of his wrath........ Rev 16:19
with the w of her fornication........ Rev 17:2
all nations have drunk of the w........ Rev 18:3
ointments, and frankincense, and w .... Rev 18:13

WINEBIBBER

Behold a man gluttonous, and a w........ Mt 11:19
Behold a gluttonous man, and a w .... Lk 7:34

WINEBIBBERS

Be not among w .... Prov 23:20

WINEFAT

like him that treadeth in the w........ Is 63:2
it, and digged a place for the w........ Mk 12:1

WINEPRESS

and as the fulness of the w .... Num 18:27
and as the increase of the w........ Num 18:30
out of thy floor, and out of thy w........ Deut 15:14
Gideon threshed wheat by the w .... Judg 6:11
Zeeb they slew at the w of Zeeb........ Judg 7:25
of the barnfloor, or out of the w 2Kin 6:27
of it, and also made a w therein........ Is 5:2
I have trodden the w alone........ Is 63:3

WINEPRESSES

some treading w on the sabbath........ Neh 13:15
their walls, and tread their w........ Job 24:11
caused wine to fail from the w .... Jer 48:33
of Hananeel unto the king's w........ Zec 14:10

WINES

a feast of w on the lees, of fat........ Is 25:6
of w on the lees well refined........ Is 25:6

WING

was the one w of the cherub........ 1Kin 6:24
cubits the other w of the cherub.... 1Kin 6:24
the uttermost part of the one w 1Kin 6:24
so that the w of the one touched.... 1Kin 6:27
the w of the other cherub touched 1Kin 6:27
one w of the one cherub was five 2Chr 3:11
the other w was likewise five........ 2Chr 3:11
reaching to the w of the other........ 2Chr 3:11
one w of the other cherub was........ 2Chr 3:12
The other w was five cubits also,........ 2Chr 3:12
joining to the w of the other........ 2Chr 3:12
there was none that moved the w .... Is 10:14
shall dwell all fowl of every w .... Eze 17:23

WINGED

every w fowl after his kind .... Gen 1:21
the likeness of any w fowl that........ Deut 4:17

WINGS

and how I bare you on eagles' w .... Ex 19:4
stretch forth their w on high........ Ex 25:20
the mercy seat with their w........ Ex 25:20
spread out their w on high........ Ex 37:9
covered with their w over the........ Ex 37:9
cleave it with the w thereof........ Lev 1:17
her young, spreadeth abroad her w .... Deut 32:11
them, beareth them on her w........ Deut 32:11
under whose w thou art come to........ Ruth 2:12
was seen upon the w of the wind.... 2Sa 22:11
forth the w of the cherubims........ 1Kin 6:27
their w touched one another in........ 1Kin 6:27
even under the w of the cherubims.... 1Kin 8:6
spread forth their two w over the.... 1Kin 8:7
that spread out their w, and........ 1Chr 28:18
the w of the cherubims were........ 2Chr 3:11
The w of these cherubims spread........ 2Chr 3:13
even under the w of the cherubims.... 2Chr 5:7
their w over the place of the ark.... 2Chr 5:8
the goodly w unto the peacocks........ Job 39:13
or w and feathers unto the ostrich.... Job 39:13
stretch her w toward the south .... Job 39:26
hide me under the shadow of thy w .... Ps 17:8
he did fly upon the w of the wind.... Ps 18:10
trust under the shadow of thy w........ Ps 36:7
said, Oh that I had w like a dove........ Ps 55:6
in the shadow of thy w will I .... Ps 57:1
will trust in the covert of thy w........ Ps 61:4
shadow of thy w will I rejoice........ Ps 63:7
yet shalt ye be as the w of a........ Ps 68:13
under his w shalt thou trust .... Ps 91:4
walketh upon the w of the wind........ Ps 104:3
If I take the w of the morning,........ Ps 139:9
certainly make themselves w .... Prov 23:5
that which hath w shall tell the........ Eccl 10:20
each one had six w........ Is 6:2
the stretching out of his w shall........ Is 8:8
Woe to the land shadowing with w........ Is 18:1
shall mount up with w as eagles........ Is 40:31
Give w unto Moab, that it may........ Jer 48:9
and shall spread his w over Moab........ Jer 48:40
and spread his w over Bozrah........ Jer 49:22
faces, and every one had four w........ Eze 1:6
under their w on their four sides........ Eze 1:8
four had their faces and their w........ Eze 1:8
Their w were joined one to........ Eze 1:9
their w were stretched upward .... Eze 1:11
two w of every one were joined........ Eze 1:11
firmament were their w straight........ Eze 1:23
I heard the noise of their w .... Eze 1:24
they stood, they let down their w........ Eze 1:24
stood, and had let down their w........ Eze 1:25
w of the living creatures that........ Eze 3:13
w was reared even to the outer........ Eze 10:5
of a man's hand under their w........ Eze 10:8
backs, and their hands, and their w .... Eze 10:12
w to mount up from the earth........ Eze 10:16
the cherubims lifted up their w .... Eze 10:19
faces apiece, and every one four w .... Eze 10:21
hands of a man was under their w .... Eze 10:21
did the cherubims lift up their w........ Eze 11:22
A great eagle with great w........ Eze 17:3
another great eagle with great w .... Eze 17:7
was like a lion, and had eagle's w........ Dan 7:4
I beheld till the w thereof were........ Dan 7:4
the back of it four w of a fowl........ Dan 7:6
wind hath bound her up in her w .... Hos 4:19
women, and the wind was in their w .... Zec 5:9
had w like the w of a stork........ Zec 5:9
arise with healing in his w........ Mal 4:2
her chickens under her w, and ye........ Mt 23:37
doth gather her brood under her w .... Lk 13:34
had each of them six w about him........ Rev 4:8
the sound of their w was as the........ Rev 9:9
were given two w of a great eagle...... Rev 12:14

WINK (column 3)

and what do thy eyes w at,........ Job 15:12
neither let them w with the eye........ Ps 35:19

WINKED

times of this ignorance God w at .... Acts 17:30

WINKETH

He w with his eyes, he speaketh........ Prov 6:13
He that w with the eye causeth .... Prov 10:10

WINNETH

and he that w souls is wise........ Prov 11:30

WINNOWED

which hath been w with the shovel.... Is 30:24

WINNOWETH

he w barley to night in the........ Ruth 3:2

WINTER

and cold and heat, and summer and w .... Gen 8:22
thou hast made summer and w .... Ps 74:17
the w is past, the rain is over .... Song 2:11
of the earth shall w upon them........ Is 18:6
I will smite the w house with the........ Amos 3:15
in summer and in w shall it be........ Zec 14:8
that your flight be not in the w........ Mt 24:20
that your flight be not in the w........ Mk 13:18
of the dedication, and it was w........ Jn 10:22
haven was not commodious to w in .... Acts 27:12
attain to Phenice, and there to w........ Acts 27:12
w with you, that ye may bring me........ 1Cor 16:6
Do thy diligence to come before w........ 2Ti 4:21
for I have determined there to w........ Titus 3:12

WINTERED

which had w in the isle, whose........ Acts 28:11

WINTERHOUSE

sat in the w in the ninth month .... Jer 36:22

WIPE

I will w Jerusalem as a man........ 2Kin 21:13
w not out my good deeds that I .... Neh 13:14
the Lord God will w away tears........ Is 25:8
did w them with the hairs of her........ Lk 7:38
on us, we do w off against you........ Lk 10:11
feet, and to w them with the towel........ Jn 13:5
God shall w away all tears from........ Rev 7:17
God shall w away all tears from........ Rev 21:4

WIPED

his reproach shall not be w away........ Prov 6:33
w them with the hairs of her head........ Lk 7:44
w his feet with her hair, whose........ Jn 11:2
and w his feet with her hair........ Jn 12:3

WIPETH

wipe Jerusalem as a man w dish........ 2Kin 21:13
w her mouth, and saith, I have........ Prov 30:20

WIPING

w it, and turning it upside down 2Kin 21:13

WIRES

thin plates, and cut it into w........ Ex 39:3

WISDOM

have filled with the spirit of w........ Ex 28:3
him with the spirit of God, in w .... Ex 31:3
are wise hearted I have put w .... Ex 31:6
them up in w spun goats' hair .... Ex 35:26
him with the spirit of God, in w........ Ex 35:31
hath he filled with w of heart .... Ex 35:35
man, in whom the Lord put w........ Ex 36:1
in whose heart the Lord had put w........ Ex 36:2
for this is your w and your........ Deut 4:6
Nun was full of the spirit of w .... Deut 34:9
according to the w of an angel of........ 2Sa 14:20
went unto all the people in her w........ 2Sa 20:22
Do therefore according to thy w........ 1Kin 2:6
saw that the w of God was in him........ 1Kin 3:28
And God gave Solomon w and 1Kin 4:29
Solomon's w excelled the 1Kin 4:30
country, and all the w of Egypt........ 1Kin 4:30
people to hear the w of Solomon 1Kin 4:34
earth, which had heard of his w 1Kin 4:34
And the Lord gave Solomon w........ 1Kin 5:12
and he was filled with w, and........ 1Kin 7:14
of Sheba had seen all Solomon's w.... 1Kin 10:4
own land of thy acts and of thy w........ 1Kin 10:6
thy w and prosperity exceedeth the 1Kin 10:7
before thee, and that hear thy w........ 1Kin 10:8
of the earth for riches and for w........ 1Kin 10:23
sought to Solomon, to hear his w........ 1Kin 10:24
and all that he did, and his w........ 1Kin 11:41
Only the Loro give thee w........ 1Chr 22:12
Give me now w and knowledge, that 2Chr 1:10
but hast asked w and knowledge for.... 2Chr 1:11
W and knowledge is granted unto........ 2Chr 1:12
Sheba had seen the w of Solomon........ 2Chr 9:3
land of thine acts, and of thy w........ 2Chr 9:5
of thy w was not told me........ 2Chr 9:6
before thee, and hear thy w........ 2Chr 9:7
kings of the earth in riches and w........ 2Chr 9:23
of Solomon, to hear his w........ 2Chr 9:23
after the w of thy God, that is........ Ezr 7:25
they die, even without w........ Job 4:21
is w driven quite from me........ Job 6:13
would shew thee the secrets of w........ Job 11:6
people, and w shall die with you........ Job 12:2
With the ancient is w........ Job 12:12
With him is w and strength, he........ Job 12:13
With him is strength and........ Job 12:16
and it should be your w........ Job 13:5
dost thou restrain w to thyself........ Job 15:8

W

thou counseled him that hath no w...... Job 26:3
But where shall w be found................ Job 28:12
the price of w is above rubies............ Job 28:18
Whence then cometh w.................... Job 28:20
the fear of the LORD, that is w............ Job 28:28
multitude of years should teach w...... Job 32:7
should say, We have found out w........ Job 32:13
peace, and I shall teach thee w.......... Job 33:33
and his words were without w............ Job 34:35
he is mighty in strength and w............ Job 36:5
Who hath put w in the inward.......... Job 38:36
Who can number the clouds in w........ Job 38:37
God hath deprived her of w.............. Job 39:17
Doth the hawk fly by thy w.............. Job 39:26
mouth of the righteous speaketh w.... Ps 37:30
My mouth shall speak of w................ Ps 49:3
part thou shalt make me to know w.... Ps 51:6
we may apply our hearts unto w........ Ps 90:12
In w hast thou made them all.............. Ps 104:24
and teach his senators w.................. Ps 105:22
of the LORD is the beginning of w...... Ps 111:10
To him that by w made the heavens.... Ps 136:5
To know w and instruction................ Prov 1:2
To receive the instruction of w.......... Prov 1:3
but fools despise w and...................... Prov 1:7
W crieth without................................ Prov 1:20
thou incline thine ear unto w.............. Prov 2:2
For the LORD giveth w........................ Prov 2:6
up sound w for the righteous.............. Prov 2:7
When w entereth into thine heart...... Prov 2:10
Happy is the man that findeth w........ Prov 3:13
The LORD by w hath founded the........ Prov 3:19
keep sound w and discretion.............. Prov 3:21
Get w, get understanding.................. Prov 4:5
W is the principal thing...................... Prov 4:7
therefore get w.................................. Prov 4:7
have taught thee in the way of w........ Prov 4:11
My son, attend unto my w, and bow.... Prov 5:1
Say unto w, Thou art my sister............ Prov 7:4
Doth not w cry.................................... Prov 8:1
O ye simple, understand w.................. Prov 8:5
For w is better than rubies.................. Prov 8:11
I w dwell with prudence, and find...... Prov 8:12
Counsel is mine, and sound w............ Prov 8:14
W hath builded her house, she............ Prov 9:1
of the LORD is the beginning of w...... Prov 9:10
hath understanding w is found............ Prov 10:13
but fools die for want of w.................. Prov 10:21
but a man of understanding hath w.... Prov 10:23
of the just bringeth forth w................ Prov 10:31
but with the lowly is w...................... Prov 11:2
He that is void of w despiseth............ Prov 11:12
be commended according to his w...... Prov 12:8
but with the well advised is w............ Prov 13:10
A scorner seeketh w, and findeth........ Prov 14:6
The w of the prudent is to................ Prov 14:8
W resteth in the heart of him............ Prov 14:33
joy to him that is destitute of w........ Prov 15:21
the LORD is the instruction of w........ Prov 15:33
better is it to get w than gold............ Prov 16:16
in the hand of a fool to get w............ Prov 17:16
W is before him that hath.................. Prov 17:24
and intermeddleth with all w.............. Prov 18:1
the wellspring of w as a flowing........ Prov 18:4
He that getteth w loveth his own........ Prov 19:8
There is no w nor understanding........ Prov 21:30
cease from thine own w...................... Prov 23:4
will despise the w of thy words.......... Prov 23:9
also w, and instruction, and.............. Prov 23:23
Through w is an house builded............ Prov 24:3
W is too high for a fool...................... Prov 24:7
knowledge of w be unto thy soul........ Prov 24:14
Whoso loveth w rejoiceth his.............. Prov 29:3
The rod and reproof give w................ Prov 29:15
I neither learned w, nor have the........ Prov 30:3
She openeth her mouth with w.......... Prov 31:26
search out by w concerning all............ Eccl 1:13
have gotten more w than all they........ Eccl 1:16
heart had great experience of w........ Eccl 1:16
And I gave my heart to know w.......... Eccl 1:17
For in much w is much grief................ Eccl 1:18
yet acquainting mine heart with w.... Eccl 2:3
also my w remained with me.............. Eccl 2:9
And I turned myself to behold w........ Eccl 2:12
Then I saw that a excelleth folly........ Eccl 2:13
is a man whose labour is in w............ Eccl 2:21
a man that is good in his sight w........ Eccl 2:26
W is good with an inheritance............ Eccl 7:11
For w is a defence, and money is a...... Eccl 7:12
that w giveth life to them that............ Eccl 7:12
W strengtheneth the wise more.......... Eccl 7:19
All this have I proved by w................ Eccl 7:23
and to search, and to seek out w........ Eccl 7:25
a man's w maketh his face to.............. Eccl 8:1
I applied mine heart to know w.......... Eccl 8:16
nor device, nor knowledge, nor w...... Eccl 9:10
This w have I seen also under the........ Eccl 9:13
he by his w delivered the city.............. Eccl 9:15
W is better than strength.................... Eccl 9:16
the poor man's w is despised.............. Eccl 9:16
W is better than weapons of war........ Eccl 9:18
him that is in reputation for w............ Eccl 10:1
his w faileth him, and he saith to........ Eccl 10:3
but w is profitable to direct................ Eccl 10:10
hand I have done it, and by my w........ Is 10:13
rest upon him, the spirit of w.............. Is 11:2
for the w of their wise men shall........ Is 29:14
And w and knowledge shall be............ Is 33:6
Thy w and thy knowledge, it hath...... Is 47:10
and what w is in them........................ Jer 8:9

not the wise man glory in his w.......... Jer 9:23
established the world by his w............ Jer 10:12
Is w no more in Teman........................ Jer 49:7
is their w vanished.............................. Jer 49:7
established the world by his w............ Jer 51:15
With thy w and thine.......................... Eze 28:4
By thy great w and by thy traffick...... Eze 28:5
against the beauty of thy w................ Eze 28:7
sealest up the sum, full of w.............. Eze 28:12
thou hast corrupted thy w by.............. Eze 28:17
favoured, and skilful in all w.............. Dan 1:4
and skill in all learning and w............ Dan 1:17
And in all matters of w and................ Dan 1:20
w to Arioch the captain of the............ Dan 2:14
for w and might are his...................... Dan 2:20
he giveth w unto the wise, and.......... Dan 2:21
my fathers, who hast given me w........ Dan 2:23
any w that I have more than any........ Dan 2:30
light and understanding and w.......... Dan 5:11
like the w of the gods, was found...... Dan 5:11
excellent w is found in thee................ Dan 5:14
the man of w shall see thy name........ Mic 6:9
But w is justified of her...................... Mt 11:19
earth to hear the w of Solomon.......... Mt 12:42
said, Whence hath this man this w.... Mt 13:54
what w is this which is given.............. Mk 6:2
disobedient to the w of the just........ Lk 1:17
strong in spirit, filled with w.............. Lk 2:40
and Jesus increased in w and.............. Lk 2:52
But w is justified of all her................ Lk 7:35
earth to hear the w of Solomon.......... Lk 11:31
Therefore also said the w of God........ Lk 11:49
For I will give you a mouth and w...... Lk 21:15
full of the Holy Ghost and w.............. Acts 6:3
were not able to resist the w.............. Acts 6:10
w in the sight of Pharaoh king of...... Acts 7:10
in all the w of the Egyptians.............. Acts 7:22
depth of the riches both of the w...... Rom 11:33
not with w of words, lest the.............. 1Cor 1:17
I will destroy the w of the wise.......... 1Cor 1:19
made foolish the w of this world........ 1Cor 1:20
For after that in the w of God............ 1Cor 1:21
God the world by w knew not God.... 1Cor 1:21
sign, and the Greeks seek after w...... 1Cor 1:22
the power of God, and the w of God.. 1Cor 1:24
who of God is made unto us w............ 1Cor 1:30
with excellency of speech of w.......... 1Cor 2:1
with enticing words of man's w.......... 1Cor 2:4
should not stand in the w of men...... 1Cor 2:5
Howbeit we speak w among them........ 1Cor 2:6
yet not the w of this world, nor.......... 1Cor 2:6
But we speak the w of God in a.......... 1Cor 2:7
in a mystery, even the hidden w........ 1Cor 2:7
the words which man's w teacheth...... 1Cor 2:13
For the w of this world is.................... 1Cor 3:19
given by the Spirit the word of w........ 1Cor 12:8
sincerity, not with fleshly w................ 2Cor 1:12
hath abounded toward us in all w...... Eph 1:8
may give unto you the spirit of w...... Eph 1:17
the church the manifold w of God...... Eph 3:10
knowledge of his will in all w............ Col 1:9
and teaching every man in all w........ Col 1:28
are hid all the treasures of w.............. Col 2:3
a shew of w in will worship................ Col 2:23
dwell in you richly in all w................ Col 3:16
Walk in w toward them that are........ Col 4:5
If any of you lack w, let him ask........ Jas 1:5
his works with meekness of w............ Jas 3:13
This w descendeth not from above...... Jas 3:15
But the w that is from above is.......... Jas 3:17
Paul also according to the w.............. 2Pet 3:15
to receive power, and riches, and w.... Rev 5:12
Blessing, and glory, and w, and.......... Rev 7:12
Here is w... Rev 13:18
And here is the mind which hath w.... Rev 17:9

WISE

tree to be desired to make one w........ Gen 3:6
Egypt, and all the w men thereof........ Gen 41:8
look out a man discreet and w............ Gen 41:33
none so discreet and w as thou art...... Gen 41:39
Pharaoh also called the w men............ Ex 7:11
If thou afflict them in any w................ Ex 22:23
for the gift blindeth the w.................. Ex 23:8
speak unto all that are w hearted...... Ex 28:3
are w hearted I have put wisdom........ Ex 31:6
every w hearted among you shall........ Ex 35:10
all the women that were w hearted.... Ex 35:25
every w hearted man, in whom the.... Ex 36:1
every w hearted man, in whose.......... Ex 36:2
And all the w men, that wrought........ Ex 36:4
every w hearted man, among them.... Ex 36:8
but ye shall in no w eat of it.............. Lev 7:24
thou shalt in any w rebuke thy.......... Lev 19:17
the field will in any w redeem it........ Lev 27:19
On this w ye shall bless the................ Num 6:23
Take you w men, and understanding.. Deut 1:13
w men, and known, and made them.... Deut 1:15
Surely this great nation is a w.......... Deut 4:6
gift doth blind the eyes of the w........ Deut 16:19
Thou shalt in any w set him king...... Deut 17:15
shalt in any w bury him that day...... Deut 21:23
shalt in any w let the dam go............ Deut 22:7
O that they were w, that they............ Deut 32:29
in any w keep yourselves from the...... Josh 6:18
Else if ye do in any w go back............ Josh 23:12
Her w ladies answered her, yea.......... Judg 5:29
but in any w return him a.................. 1Sa 6:3
and fetched thence a w woman.......... 2Sa 14:2
and my lord is w, according to the...... 2Sa 14:20
Then cried a w woman out of the........ 2Sa 20:16

for thou art a w man, and knowest.... 1Kin 2:9
lo, I have given thee a w.................... 1Kin 3:12
living child, and in no w slay it.......... 1Kin 3:26
living child, and in no w slay it.......... 1Kin 3:27
a w son over this great people............ 1Kin 5:7
howbeit let me go in any w................ 1Kin 11:22
a w counsellor, they cast lots............ 1Chr 26:14
counsellor, a w man, and a scribe...... 1Chr 27:32
given to David the king a w son........ 2Chr 2:12
Then the king said to the w men........ Est 1:13
Then said his w men and Zeresh his.. Est 6:13
He taketh the w in their own.............. Job 5:13
He is w in heart, and mighty in.......... Job 9:4
For vain man would be w, though...... Job 11:12
Should a w man utter vain.................. Job 15:2
Which w men have told from their...... Job 15:18
I cannot find one w man among you.. Job 17:10
as he that is w may be profitable...... Job 22:2
Great men are not always w................ Job 32:9
Hear my words, O ye w men................ Job 34:34
let a w man hearken unto me.............. Job 34:34
not any that are w of heart................ Job 37:24
Be w now therefore, O ye kings.......... Ps 2:10
LORD is sure, making w the simple...... Ps 19:7
he hath left off to be w, and to.......... Ps 36:3
not thyself in any w to do evil............ Ps 37:8
For he seeth that w men die................ Ps 49:10
and ye fools, when will ye be w.......... Ps 94:8
Whoso is w, and will observe these.... Ps 107:43
A w man will hear, and will................ Prov 1:5
shalt attain unto w counsels.............. Prov 1:5
the words of the w, and their dark...... Prov 1:6
Be not w in thine own eyes................ Prov 3:7
The w shall inherit glory.................... Prov 3:35
consider her ways, and be w.............. Prov 6:6
Hear instruction, and be w................ Prov 8:33
rebuke a w man, and he will love...... Prov 9:8
Give instruction to a w man................ Prov 9:9
If thou be w, thou shalt...................... Prov 9:12
thou shalt be w for thyself.................. Prov 9:12
A w son maketh a glad father............ Prov 10:1
gathereth in summer is a w son........ Prov 10:5
The w in heart will receive.................. Prov 10:8
W men lay up knowledge.................... Prov 10:14
he that refraineth his lips is w............ Prov 10:19
be servant to the w of heart.............. Prov 11:29
and he that winneth souls is w.......... Prov 11:30
that hearkeneth unto counsel is w.... Prov 12:15
but the tongue of the w is health...... Prov 12:18
A w son heareth his father's................ Prov 13:1
The law of the w is a fountain of...... Prov 13:14
walketh with w men shall.................. Prov 13:20
men shall be w.................................. Prov 13:20
Every w woman buildeth her house.... Prov 14:1
lips of the w shall preserve them........ Prov 14:3
A w man feareth, and departeth.......... Prov 14:16
crown of the w is their riches............ Prov 14:24
favour is toward a w servant.............. Prov 14:35
The tongue of the w useth.................. Prov 15:2
The lips of the w disperse.................. Prov 15:7
neither will he go unto the w.............. Prov 15:12
A w son maketh a glad father............ Prov 15:20
The way of life is above to the w........ Prov 15:24
of life abideth among the w................ Prov 15:31
but a w man will pacify it.................. Prov 16:14
The w in heart shall be called............ Prov 16:21
The heart of the w teacheth his........ Prov 16:23
A w servant shall have rule over........ Prov 17:2
a w man than an hundred stripes........ Prov 17:10
holdeth his peace, is counted w.......... Prov 17:28
and the ear of the w seeketh.............. Prov 18:15
mayest be w in thy latter end............ Prov 19:20
is deceived thereby is not w.............. Prov 20:1
A w king scattereth the wicked.......... Prov 20:26
is punished, the simple is made w...... Prov 21:11
when the w is instructed, he.............. Prov 21:11
and oil in the dwelling of the w.......... Prov 21:20
A w man scaleth the city of the.......... Prov 21:22
ear, and hear the words of the w........ Prov 22:17
My son, if thine heart be w................ Prov 23:15
Hear thou, my son, and be w.............. Prov 23:19
he that begetteth a w child shall........ Prov 23:24
A w man is strong.............................. Prov 24:5
For by w counsel thou shalt make...... Prov 24:6
These things also belong to the w...... Prov 24:23
so is a w reprover upon an................ Prov 25:12
lest he be w in his own conceit.......... Prov 26:5
Seest thou a man w in his own.......... Prov 26:12
My son, be w, and make my heart...... Prov 27:11
Whoso keepeth the law is a w son...... Prov 28:7
The rich man is w in his own.............. Prov 28:11
but w men turn away wrath................ Prov 29:8
If a w man contendeth with a............ Prov 29:9
but a w man keepeth it in till............ Prov 29:11
they are exceeding w.......................... Prov 30:24
The w man's eyes are in his head...... Eccl 2:14
and why was I then more w................ Eccl 2:15
w more than of the fool for ever........ Eccl 2:16
And how dieth the w man.................. Eccl 2:16
he shall be a w man or a fool............ Eccl 2:19
shewed myself w under the sun.......... Eccl 2:19
a w child than an old and foolish...... Eccl 4:13
For what hath the w more than the.... Eccl 6:8
The heart of the w is in the................ Eccl 7:4
to hear the rebuke of the w................ Eccl 7:5
oppression maketh a w man mad........ Eccl 7:7
neither make thyself over w................ Eccl 7:16
Wisdom strengtheneth the w more...... Eccl 7:19
I said, I will be w.............................. Eccl 7:23
Who is as the w man.......................... Eccl 8:1

a w man's heart discerneth both ...... Eccl 8:5
though a w man think to know it, ... Eccl 8:17
that the righteous, and the w ...... Eccl 9:1
neither yet bread to the w ...... Eccl 9:11
was found in it a poor w man ...... Eccl 9:15
The words of w men are heard in ...... Eccl 9:17
A w man's heart is at his right ...... Eccl 10:2
The words of a w man's mouth are ...... Eccl 10:12
because the preacher was w ...... Eccl 12:9
The words of the w are as goads ...... Eccl 12:11
them that are w in their own eyes ...... Is 5:21
the counsel of the w counsellors ...... Is 19:11
Pharaoh, I am the son of the w ...... Is 19:11
where are thy w men ...... Is 19:12
of their w men shall perish ...... Is 29:14
Yet he also is w, and will bring ...... Is 31:2
that turneth w men backward ...... Is 44:25
they are w to do evil, but to do ...... Jer 4:22
How do ye say, We are w, and the ...... Jer 8:8
The w men are ashamed, they are ...... Jer 8:9
Who is the w man, that may ...... Jer 9:12
Let not the w man glory in his ...... Jer 9:23
all the w men of the nations ...... Jer 10:7
priest, nor counsel from the w ...... Jer 18:18
her princes, and upon her w men ...... Jer 50:35
drunk her princes, and her w men ...... Jer 51:57
thy w men, O Tyrus, that were in ...... Eze 27:8
the w men thereof were in thee ...... Eze 27:9
destroy all the w men of Babylon ...... Dan 2:12
that the w men should be slain ...... Dan 2:13
to slay the w men of Babylon ...... Dan 2:14
The rest of the w men of Babylon ...... Dan 2:18
he giveth wisdom unto the w ...... Dan 2:21
to destroy the w men of Babylon ...... Dan 2:24
Destroy not the w men of Babylon ...... Dan 2:24
hath demanded cannot the w men ...... Dan 2:27
over all the w men of Babylon ...... Dan 2:48
the w men of Babylon before me ...... Dan 4:6
forasmuch as all the w men of my ...... Dan 4:18
said to the w men of Babylon, ... Dan 5:7
Then came in all the king's w men ...... Dan 5:8
And now the w men, the astrologers ...... Dan 5:15
they that be w shall shine as the ...... Dan 12:3
but the w shall understand ...... Dan 12:10
Who is w, and he shall understand ...... Hos 14:9
destroy the w men out of Edom ...... Obad 8
and Zidon, though it be very w ...... Zec 9:2
of Jesus Christ was on this w ...... Mt 1:18
there came w men from the east to ...... Mt 2:1
he had privily called the w men ...... Mt 2:7
that he was mocked of the w men ...... Mt 2:16
diligently enquired of the w men ...... Mt 2:16
shall in no w pass from the law ...... Mt 5:18
I will liken him unto a w man ...... Mt 7:24
be ye therefore w as serpents ...... Mt 10:16
he shall in no w lose his reward ...... Mt 10:42
hast hid these things from the w ...... Mt 11:25
I in like w will tell you by what ...... Mt 21:24
prophets, and w men, and scribes ...... Mt 23:34
w servant, whom his lord hath ...... Mt 24:45
And five of them were w, and five ...... Mt 25:2
But the w took oil in their ...... Mt 25:4
And the foolish said unto the w ...... Mt 25:8
But the w answered, saying, Not ...... Mt 25:9
I will not deny thee in any w ...... Mk 14:31
hast hid these things from the w ...... Lk 10:21
w steward, whom his lord shall ...... Lk 12:42
could in no w lift up herself ...... Lk 13:11
child shall in no w enter therein ...... Lk 18:17
to me I will in no w cast out ...... Jn 6:37
on this w shewed he himself ...... Jn 21:1
And God spake on this w, That his ...... Acts 7:6
to corruption, he said on this w ...... Acts 13:34
which ye shall in no w believe ...... Acts 13:41
both to the w, and to the unwise ...... Rom 1:14
Professing themselves to be w ...... Rom 1:22
No, in no w ...... Rom 3:9
is of faith speaketh on this w ...... Rom 10:6
lest ye should be w in your own ...... Rom 11:25
Be not w in your own conceits ...... Rom 12:16
you w unto that which is good ...... Rom 16:19
To God only w, be glory through ...... Rom 16:27
will destroy the wisdom of the w 1Cor 1:19
Where is the w 1Cor 1:20
how that not many w men after the 1Cor 1:26
of the world to confound the w 1Cor 1:27
as a w masterbuilder, I have laid 1Cor 3:10
you seemeth to be w in this world 1Cor 3:18
become a fool, that he may be w 1Cor 3:18
He taketh the w in their own 1Cor 3:19
knoweth the thoughts of the w 1Cor 3:20
sake, but ye are w in Christ 1Cor 4:10
there is not a w man among you 1Cor 6:5
I speak as to w men 1Cor 10:15
among themselves, are not w 2Cor 10:12
seeing ye yourselves are w 2Cor 11:19
not as fools, but as w ...... Eph 5:15
invisible, the only w God, ... 1Ti 1:17
which are able to make thee w 2Ti 3:15
of the seventh day on this w ...... Heb 4:4
Who is a w man and endued w ...... Jas 3:13
To the only w God our Saviour, be ...... Jude 25
there shall in no w enter into it ...... Rev 21:27

WISELY
Come on, let us deal w with them ...... Ex 1:10
sent him, and behaved himself w 1Sa 18:5
behaved himself w in all his ways 1Sa 18:14
that he behaved himself very w 1Sa 18:15
w than all the servants of Saul 1Sa 18:30
And he dealt w, and dispersed of 2Chr 11:23

of charmers, charming never so w ...... Ps 58:5
for they shall w consider of his ...... Ps 64:9
behave myself w in a perfect way ...... Ps 101:2
a matter w shall find good ...... Prov 16:20
The righteous man w considereth ...... Prov 21:12
but whoso walketh w, he shall be ...... Prov 28:26
not enquire w concerning this ...... Eccl 7:10
steward, because he had done w ...... Lk 16:8

WISER
For he was w than all men 1Kin 4:31
maketh us w than the fowls of ...... Job 35:11
hast made me w than mine enemies ...... Ps 119:98
a wise man, and he will be yet w ...... Prov 9:9
The sluggard is w in his own ...... Prov 26:16
Behold, thou art w than Daniel ...... Eze 28:3
w than the children of light ...... Lk 16:8
foolishness of God is w than men 1Cor 1:25

WISH
according to thy w in God's stead ...... Job 33:6
and put to shame that w me evil ...... Ps 40:14
they have more than heart could w ...... Ps 73:7
For I could w that myself were ...... Rom 9:3
and this also we w, even your 2Cor 13:9
I w above all things that thou 3Jn 2

WISHED
w in himself to die, and said, It ...... Jonah 4:8
of the stern, and w for the day ...... Acts 27:29

WISHING
to sin by w a curse to his soul ...... Job 31:30

WIST
for they w not what it was ...... Ex 16:15
that Moses w not that the skin of ...... Ex 34:29
though he w it not, yet is he ...... Lev 5:17
w it not, and it shall be forgiven ...... Lev 5:18
but I w not whence they were ...... Josh 2:4
but he w not that there were ...... Josh 8:14
he w not that the LORD was ...... Judg 16:20
For he w not what to say ...... Mk 9:6
neither w they what to answer ...... Mk 14:40
w ye not that I must be about my ...... Lk 2:49
that was healed w not who it was ...... Jn 5:13
w not that it was true which was ...... Acts 12:9
I w not, brethren, that he was ...... Acts 23:5

WIT
to w whether the LORD had made ...... Gen 24:21
to w what would be done to him ...... Ex 2:4
to w, for Machir the firstborn of ...... Josh 17:1
David not knowing thereof, to w 1Kin 2:32
for the doors of the house, to w 1Kin 7:50
he saddled for him the ass, to w 1Kin 13:23
not from after them, to w 2Kin 10:29
of their father's house, to w 1Chr 7:2
Israel after their number, to w 1Chr 27:1
To w, the two pillars, and the 2Chr 4:12
the LORD is with Israel, to w 2Chr 13:8
Then Amaziah separated them, to w 2Chr 25:10
for the burnt offerings, to w 2Chr 31:3
possession in their cities, to w ...... Neh 11:3
purifications accomplished, to w ...... Est 2:12
To w, Jerusalem, and the cities of ...... Jer 25:18
serve himself of them, to w ...... Jer 34:9
To w, the prophets of Israel ...... Eze 13:16
waiting for the adoption, to w ...... Rom 8:23
To w, that God was in Christ, ... 2Cor 5:19
we do you to w of the grace of 2Cor 8:1

WITCH
Thou shalt not suffer a w to live ...... Ex 22:18
of times, or an enchanter, or a w ...... Deut 18:10

WITCHCRAFT
For rebellion is as the sin of w 1Sa 15:23
and used enchantments, and used w 2Chr 33:6
Idolatry, w, hatred, variance, ... Gal 5:20

WITCHCRAFTS
Jezebel and her w are so many 2Kin 9:22
I will cut off w out of thine ...... Mic 5:12
harlot, the mistress of w ...... Nah 3:4
and families through her w ...... Nah 3:4

WITH See PREFACE.

WITHAL
and bowls thereof, to cover w ...... Ex 25:29
for the staves to bear it w ...... Ex 30:4
his foot also of brass, to wash w ...... Ex 30:18
of the sanctuary, to make it w ...... Ex 36:3
bowls, and his covers to cover w ...... Ex 37:16
for the staves to bear it w ...... Ex 37:27
sides of the altar, to bear it w ...... Ex 38:7
and put water there, to wash w ...... Ex 40:30
be that a man shall be defiled w ...... Lev 5:3
to reconcile w in the holy place ...... Lev 6:30
feet, to leap w upon the earth ...... Lev 11:21
be holy to praise the LORD w ...... Lev 19:24
the bowls, and covers to cover w ...... Num 4:7
in their right hands to blow w ...... Judg 7:20
w of a beautiful countenance, and 1Sa 16:12
w how he had slain all the 1Kin 19:1
that Manasseh had provoked him w 2Kin 23:26
overlay the walls of the houses w 1Chr 29:4
to minister, and to offer w 2Chr 24:14
to shoot arrows and great stones w 2Chr 26:15
man w whom the king delighteth to ...... Est 6:9
a potsherd to scrape himself w ...... Job 2:8
own nets, whilst that I w escape ...... Ps 141:10
they shall be fitted in thy ...... Prov 22:18
or to take water w out of the pit ...... Is 30:14

that thou shalt sow the ground w ...... Is 30:23
baptized with that w be baptized ...... Mk 10:39
it shall be measured to you ...... Lk 6:38
not w to signify the crimes laid ...... Acts 25:27
is given to every man to profit w 1Cor 12:7
W praying also for us, that God ...... Col 4:3
And w they learn to be idle, ... 1Ti 5:13
But w prepare me also a lodging ...... Philem 22

WITHDRAW
unto the priest, W thine hand 1Sa 14:19
If God will not w his anger ...... Job 9:13
W thine hand far from me ...... Job 13:21
That he may w man from his ...... Job 33:17
W thy foot from thy neighbour's ...... Prov 25:17
also from this w not thine hand ...... Eccl 7:18
neither shall thy moon w itself ...... Is 60:20
the stars shall w their shining ...... Joel 2:10
the stars shall w their shining ...... Joel 3:15
that ye yourselves from every 2Th 3:6
from such w thyself 1Ti 6:5

WITHDRAWEST
Why w thou thy hand, even thy ...... Ps 74:11

WITHDRAWETH
He w not his eyes from the ...... Job 36:7

WITHDRAWN
have w the inhabitants of their ...... Deut 13:13
but my beloved had w himself ...... Song 5:6
he hath not w his hand from ...... Lam 2:8
that hath w his hand from ...... Eze 18:8
he hath w himself from them ...... Hos 5:6
he was w from them about a ...... Lk 22:41

WITHDREW
the shoulder, and hardened their ...... Neh 9:29
Nevertheless I w mine hand ...... Eze 20:22
knew it, he w himself from thence ...... Mt 12:15
But Jesus w himself with his ...... Mk 3:7
he w himself into the wilderness ...... Lk 5:16
but when they were come, he w ...... Gal 2:12

WITHER
his leaf also shall not w ...... Ps 1:3
the grass, and w as the green herb ...... Ps 37:2
the reeds and flags shall w ...... Is 19:6
thing sown by the brooks, shall w ...... Is 19:7
blow upon them, and they shall w ...... Is 40:24
and the herbs of every field ...... Jer 12:4
off the fruit thereof, that it w ...... Eze 17:9
it shall w in all the leaves of ...... Eze 17:9
shall it not utterly w, when the ...... Eze 17:10
it shall w in the furrows where ...... Eze 17:10
and the top of Carmel shall w ...... Amos 1:2

WITHERED
And, behold, seven ears, w ...... Gen 41:23
heart is smitten, and w like grass ...... Ps 102:4
and I am w like a grass ...... Ps 102:11
for the hay is w away, the grass ...... Is 15:6
When the boughs thereof are w ...... Is 27:11
it is w, it is become like a ...... Lam 4:8
her strong rods were broken and w ...... Eze 19:12
all the trees of the field, are w ...... Joel 1:12
because joy is w away from the ...... Joel 1:12
for the corn is w ...... Joel 1:17
piece withereth, it rained not w ...... Amos 4:7
and it smote the gourd that it w ...... Jonah 4:7
was a man which had his hand w ...... Mt 12:10
they had no root, they w away ...... Mt 13:6
And presently the fig tree w away ...... Mt 21:19
How soon is the fig tree w away ...... Mt 21:20
a man there which had a w hand ...... Mk 3:1
unto the man which had the w hand ...... Mk 3:3
because it had no root, it w away ...... Mk 4:6
which thou cursedst is w away ...... Mk 11:21
was a man whose right hand was w ...... Lk 6:6
to the man which had the w hand ...... Lk 6:8
it w away, because it lacked ...... Lk 8:6
impotent folk, of blind, halt, w ...... Jn 5:3
cast forth as a branch, and is w ...... Jn 15:6

WITHERETH
it w before any other herb ...... Job 8:12
the evening it is cut down, and w ...... Ps 90:6
which w afore it groweth up ...... Ps 129:6
The grass w, the flower fadeth ...... Is 40:7
The grass w, the flower fadeth ...... Is 40:8
but it w the grass, and the flower ...... Jas 1:11
The grass w, and the flower 1Pet 1:24
trees whose fruit w, without ...... Jude 12

WITHHELD
for I also w thee from sinning ...... Gen 20:6
seeing thou hast not w thy son ...... Gen 22:12
this thing, and hast not w thy son ...... Gen 22:16
who hath w from thee the fruit of ...... Gen 30:2
If I have w the poor from their ...... Job 31:16
I w not my heart from any joy ...... Eccl 2:10

WITHHELDEST
w not thy manna from their mouth, ... Neh 9:20

WITHHOLD
none of us shall w from thee his ...... Gen 23:6
for he will not w me from thee 2Sa 13:13
but who can w himself from ...... Job 4:2
W not thou thy tender mercies, ... Ps 40:11
no good thing will he w from them ...... Ps 84:11
W not good from them to whom it ...... Prov 3:27
W not correction from the child ...... Prov 23:13
in the evening w not thine hand ...... Eccl 11:6
W thy foot from being unshod, and ...... Jer 2:25

W

WITHHOLDEN

seeing the LORD hath w thee from...... 1Sa 25:26
thou hast w bread from the hungry...... Job 22:7
from the wicked their light is w...... Job 38:15
no thought can be w from thee...... Job 42:2
hast not w the request of his...... Ps 21:2
Therefore the showers have been w...... Jer 3:3
your sins have w good things from... Jer 5:25
hath not w the pledge, neither...... Eze 18:16
the drink offering is w from the...... Joel 1:13
also I have w the rain from you,...... Amos 4:7

WITHHOLDETH

he w the waters, and they dry up...... Job 12:15
there is that w more than is meet...... Prov 11:24
He that w corn, the people shall...... Prov 11:26
now ye know what w that he might...... 2Th 2:6

WITHIN

in the ark, and shalt pitch it w...... Gen 6:14
and he was uncovered w his tent...... Gen 9:21
Therefore Sarah laughed w herself...... Gen 18:12
be fifty righteous w the city...... Gen 18:26
Sodom fifty righteous w the city...... Gen 18:26
children straggled together w her... Gen 25:22
of the men of the house there w...... Gen 39:11
Yet w three days shall Pharaoh...... Gen 40:13
Yet w three days shall Pharaoh...... Gen 40:19
thy stranger that is w thy gates...... Ex 20:10
overlay it with pure gold, w...... Ex 25:11
thither w the vail the ark of the...... Ex 26:33
he overlaid it with pure gold w...... Ex 37:2
not brought in w the holy place...... Lev 10:18
whether it be bare w or without...... Lev 13:55
house to be scraped w round about... Lev 14:41
all times into the holy place w...... Lev 16:2
small, and bring it w the vail...... Lev 16:12
and bring his blood w the vail...... Lev 16:15
then he may redeem it w a whole... Lev 25:29
w a full year may he redeem it...... Lev 25:29
if it be not redeemed w the space... Lev 25:30
gathered together w your cities...... Lev 26:25
all the vessels thereof w a...... Num 4:10
thing of the altar, and w the vail... Num 18:7
thy stranger that is w thy gates...... Deut 5:14
the Levite that is w your gates...... Deut 12:12
Thou mayest not eat w thy gates...... Deut 12:17
and the Levite that is w thy gates... Deut 12:18
And the Levite that is w thy gates... Deut 14:27
and shalt lay it up w thy gates...... Deut 14:28
the widow, which are w thy gates...... Deut 14:29
w any of thy gates in the land...... Deut 15:7
Thou shalt eat it w thy gates...... Deut 15:22
the passover w any of thy gates...... Deut 16:5
and the Levite that is w thy gates... Deut 16:11
the widow, that are w thy gates...... Deut 16:14
w any of thy gates which the LORD... Deut 17:2
of controversy w thy gates...... Deut 17:8
he shall not come w the camp...... Deut 23:10
that are in thy land w thy gates...... Deut 24:14
that they may eat w thy gates...... Deut 26:12
The stranger that is w thee shall... Deut 28:43
thy stranger that is w thee shall... Deut 31:12
The sword without, and terror w...... Deut 32:25
for w three days ye shall pass...... Josh 1:11
their inheritance was w the...... Josh 19:1
w the inheritance of them...... Josh 19:9
All the cities of the Levites w...... Josh 21:41
pitchers, and lamps w the pitchers... Judg 7:16
was a strong tower w the city...... Judg 9:51
but came not w the border of Moab... Judg 11:18
ye not recover them w that time...... Judg 11:26
me w the seven days of the feast... Judg 14:12
it came to pass w a while after...... Judg 15:1
caniest not w the days appointed... 1Sa 13:11
w as it were as half acre of land... 1Sa 14:14
Nabal's heart was merry w him for... 1Sa 25:36
things, that his heart died w him... 1Sa 25:37
Saul lay sleeping w the trench...... 1Sa 26:7
ark of God dwelleth w curtains...... 2Sa 7:2
me the men of Judah w three days... 2Sa 20:4
the house w with boards of cedar... 1Kin 6:15
he even built them for it w...... 1Kin 6:16
the house w was carved with knops... 1Kin 6:18
oracle he prepared in the house w... 1Kin 6:19
the house w with pure gold...... 1Kin 6:21
And w the oracle he made two...... 1Kin 6:23
the cherubims w the inner house... 1Kin 6:27
and palm trees and open flowers, w... 1Kin 6:29
house he overlaid with gold, w...... 1Kin 6:30
had another court w the porch...... 1Kin 7:8
hewed stones, sawed with saws, w... 1Kin 7:9
And the mouth of it w the chapiter... 1Kin 7:31
for her soul is vexed w her...... 2Kin 4:27
he had sackcloth w upon his flesh... 2Kin 6:30
told it to the king's house w...... 2Kin 7:11
and he that cometh w the ranges...... 2Kin 11:8
he overlaid it w with pure gold...... 2Chr 3:4
sedition w the same of old time...... 2Chr 13:6
would not come w three days...... Ezr 10:8
unto Jerusalem w three days...... Ezr 10:9
his servant lodge w Jerusalem...... Neh 4:22
w the temple, and let us shut the... Neh 6:10
arrows of the Almighty are w me...... Job 6:4
his soul w him shall mourn...... Job 14:22
though my reins be consumed w me... Job 19:27
but keep it still w his mouth...... Job 20:13
it is the gall of asps w him...... Job 20:14
Which make oil w their walls...... Job 24:11
the spirit w me constraineth me...... Job 32:18
of the wicked saith w my heart...... Ps 36:1

My heart was hot w me...... Ps 39:3
yea, thy law is w my heart...... Ps 40:8
hid thy righteousness w my heart... Ps 40:10
my God, my soul is cast down w me... Ps 42:6
and why art thou disquieted w me... Ps 42:11
and why art thou disquieted w me... Ps 43:5
king's daughter is all glorious w... Ps 45:13
and renew a right spirit w me...... Ps 51:10
My heart is sore pained w me...... Ps 55:4
w me thy comforts delight my soul... Ps 94:19
I will walk w my house with a...... Ps 101:2
deceit shall not dwell w my house... Ps 101:7
and all that is w me, bless his...... Ps 103:1
and my heart is wounded w me...... Ps 109:22
Our feet shall stand w thy gates... Ps 122:2
Peace be w thy walls...... Ps 122:7
and prosperity w thy palaces...... Ps 122:7
Peace be w thee. Because w...... Ps 122:8
my spirit was overwhelmed w me...... Ps 142:3
is my spirit overwhelmed w me...... Ps 143:4
my heart w me is desolate...... Ps 143:4
hath blessed thy children w thee... Ps 147:13
thing if thou keep them w thee...... Prov 22:18
lips, and layeth up deceit w him... Prov 26:24
a little city, and few men w it...... Eccl 9:14
thou hast doves' eyes w thy locks... Song 4:1
of a pomegranate w thy locks...... Song 4:3
are thy temples w thy locks...... Song 6:7
w threescore and five years shall... Is 7:8
W three years, as the years of an... Is 16:14
W a year, according to the years... Is 21:16
with my spirit w me will I seek...... Is 26:9
w my walls a place and a name...... Is 56:5
nor destruction w thy borders...... Is 60:18
he that put his Spirit w him...... Is 63:11
thy vain thoughts lodge w thee...... Jer 4:14
Mine heart w me is broken because... Jer 23:9
W two full years will I bring...... Jer 28:3
w the space of two full years...... Jer 28:11
mine heart is turned w me...... Lam 1:20
of fire round about w it, from...... Eze 1:27
and it was written w and without... Eze 2:10
Go, shut thyself w thine house...... Eze 3:24
and the pestilence and the famine w... Eze 7:15
and I will put a new spirit w you... Eze 11:19
divination w the house of Israel... Eze 12:24
and a new spirit will I put w you... Eze 36:26
And I will put my spirit w you...... Eze 36:27
porch of the gate w was nine cubits... Eze 40:7
also the porch of the gate w...... Eze 40:9
to their posts w the gate round... Eze 40:16
w were hooks, an hand broad...... Eze 40:43
of the side chambers that were w... Eze 41:9
and by all the wall round about w... Eze 41:17
gates of the inner court, and w...... Eze 41:17
of any God or man w thirty days... Dan 6:12
but w few days he shall be...... Dan 11:20
mine heart is turned w me...... Hos 11:8
When my soul fainted w me I...... Jonah 2:7
pot, and as flesh w the caldron... Mic 3:3
and when he treadeth w our borders... Mic 5:6
Her princes w her are roaring...... Zeph 3:3
formeth the spirit of man w him... Zec 12:1
And think not to say w yourselves... Mt 3:9
of the scribes said w themselves... Mt 9:3
For she said w herself, If I may... Mt 9:21
but w they are full of extortion... Mt 23:25
first that which is w the cup...... Mt 23:26
but are w full of dead men's...... Mt 23:27
but w ye are full of hypocrisy and... Mt 23:28
they so reasoned w themselves...... Mk 2:8
For from w, out of the heart of... Mk 7:21
but afterward he said w himself... Lk 18:4
that had indignation w themselves... Mk 14:4
w three days I will build another... Mk 14:58
and begin not to say w yourselves... Lk 3:8
him saw it, he spake w himself...... Lk 7:39
him began to say w themselves...... Lk 7:49
he from w shall answer and say,...... Lk 11:7
without make that which is w also... Lk 11:40
And he thought w himself, saying,... Lk 12:17
Then the steward said w himself... Lk 16:3
the kingdom of God is w you...... Lk 17:21
but afterward he said w himself... Lk 18:4
Did not our heart burn w us...... Lk 24:32
days again his disciples were w...... Jn 20:26
we had opened, we found no man w... Acts 5:23
we ourselves groan w ourselves...... Rom 8:23
do not ye judge them that are w... 1Cor 5:12
were fightings, w were fears...... 2Cor 7:5
entereth into that w the veil...... Heb 6:19
and they were full of eyes w...... Rev 4:8
on the throne a book written w...... Rev 5:1

WITHOUT

And the earth was w form, and void... Gen 1:2
pitch it within and w with pitch... Gen 6:14
and told his two brethren w...... Gen 9:22
him forth, and set him w the city... Gen 19:16
made his camels to kneel down w...... Gen 24:11
wherefore standest thou w...... Gen 24:31
Joseph is w doubt rent in pieces... Gen 37:33
w thee shall no man lift up his...... Gen 41:44
for it was w number...... Gen 41:49
Your lamb shall be w blemish...... Ex 12:5
shall ye go out free w money...... Ex 21:11
shalt thou overlay it, and shalt... Ex 25:11
shalt set the table w the vail...... Ex 26:35
of the congregation w the vail...... Ex 27:21
bullock, and two rams w blemish...... Ex 29:1

thou burn with fire w the camp...... Ex 29:14
and pitched it w the camp...... Ex 33:7
which was w the camp...... Ex 33:7
it with pure gold within and w...... Ex 37:2
tabernacle northward, w the vail... Ex 40:22
let him offer a male w blemish...... Lev 1:3
shall bring it a male w blemish...... Lev 1:10
he shall offer it w blemish...... Lev 3:1
he shall offer it w blemish...... Lev 3:6
a young bullock w blemish unto...... Lev 4:3
w the camp unto a clean place...... Lev 4:12
forth the bullock w the camp...... Lev 4:21
of the goats, a male w blemish...... Lev 4:23
of the goats, a female w blemish... Lev 4:28
shall bring it a female w blemish... Lev 4:32
a ram w blemish out of the flocks... Lev 5:15
he shall bring a ram w blemish...... Lev 5:18
a ram w blemish out of the flock,... Lev 6:6
carry forth the ashes w the camp... Lev 6:11
he burnt with fire w the camp...... Lev 8:17
w blemish, and offer them before... Lev 9:2
w blemish, for a burnt offering...... Lev 9:3
he burnt with fire w the camp...... Lev 9:11
eat it w leaven beside the altar... Lev 10:12
w the camp shall his habitation...... Lev 13:46
whether it be bare within or w...... Lev 13:55
shall take two he lambs w blemish... Lev 14:10
lamb of the first year w blemish... Lev 14:10
into an unclean place w the camp... Lev 14:40
the dust that they scrape off w...... Lev 14:41
shall one carry forth w the camp... Lev 16:27
at your own will a male w blemish... Lev 22:19
ye wave the sheaf an he lamb w...... Lev 23:12
lambs w blemish of the first year... Lev 23:18
W the vail of the testimony, in...... Lev 24:3
him that hath cursed w the camp... Lev 24:14
while she lieth desolate w them...... Lev 26:43
w the camp shall ye put them...... Num 5:3
so, and put them out w the camp... Num 5:4
w blemish for a burnt offering...... Num 6:14
year w blemish for a sin offering... Num 6:14
one ram w blemish for peace...... Num 6:14
ignorance w the knowledge of the... Num 15:24
stone him with stones w the camp... Num 15:35
brought him w the camp...... Num 15:36
bring thee a red heifer w spot...... Num 19:2
he may bring her forth w the camp... Num 19:3
lay them up w the camp in a clean... Num 19:9
w doing any thing else, go...... Num 20:19
the first year w spot day by day... Num 28:3
lambs of the first year w spot...... Num 28:9
lambs of the first year w spot...... Num 28:11
they shall be unto you w blemish... Num 28:19
they shall be unto you w blemish... Num 28:31
lambs of the first year w blemish... Num 29:2
they shall be unto you w blemish... Num 29:8
they shall be w blemish...... Num 29:13
lambs of the first year w spot...... Num 29:17
lambs of the first year w spot...... Num 29:20
lambs of the first year w spot...... Num 29:23
lambs of the first year w spot...... Num 29:26
lambs of the first year w spot...... Num 29:29
lambs of the first year w spot...... Num 29:32
lambs of the first year w blemish... Num 29:36
forth to meet them w the camp...... Num 31:13
do ye abide w the camp seven days... Num 31:19
ye shall measure from w the city... Num 35:5
he thrust him suddenly w enmity... Num 35:22
him any thing w laying of wait...... Num 35:22
w the border of the city of his...... Num 35:26
the borders of the city of his...... Num 35:27
that bath eat bread w scarceness... Deut 8:9
have a place also w the camp...... Deut 23:12
shall not marry w unto a stranger... Deut 25:5
w iniquity, just and right is he... Deut 32:4
The sword w, and terror within,...... Deut 32:25
that he will w fail drive out...... Josh 3:10
left them w the camp of Israel...... Josh 6:23
w driving them out hastily...... Judg 2:23
and their camels were w number...... Judg 6:5
and their camels were w number...... Judg 7:12
If thou shalt w fail deliver the... Judg 11:30
left thee this day w a kinsman...... Ruth 4:14
blood, to slay David w a cause...... 1Sa 19:5
them, and w fail recover all...... 1Sa 30:8
riseth, even a morning w clouds... 2Sa 23:4
for w in the wall of the house he... 1Kin 6:6
and open flowers, within and w...... 1Kin 6:29
overlaid with gold, within and w... 1Kin 6:30
sawed with saws, within and w...... 1Kin 7:9
oracle, and they were not seen w... 1Kin 8:8
three years w war between Syria... 1Kin 22:1
Jehu appointed fourscore men w...... 2Kin 10:24
them, Have her forth w the ranges... 2Kin 11:15
the house, and the king's entry w... 2Kin 16:18
Am I now come up w the LORD...... 2Kin 18:25
he burned them w Jerusalem in the... 2Kin 23:4
w Jerusalem, unto the brook...... 2Kin 23:6
of all these vessels was w weight... 2Kin 25:16
but Seled died w children...... 1Chr 2:30
and Jether died w children...... 1Chr 2:32
nor offer burnt offerings w cost... 1Chr 21:24
and brass in abundance w weight... 1Chr 22:3
and of brass and iron w weight...... 1Chr 22:14
but they were not seen w...... 2Chr 5:9
the people were w number that...... 2Chr 12:3
Israel hath been w the true God... 2Chr 15:3
w a teaching priest...... 2Chr 15:3
a teaching priest, and w law...... 2Chr 15:3
and departed w being desired...... 2Chr 21:20

set it w at the gate of the house	2Chr 24:8
fountains which were w the city	2Chr 32:3
to the towers, and another wall w	2Chr 32:5
built a wall w the city of David	2Chr 33:14
be given them day by day w fail	Ezr 6:9
salt w prescribing how much	Ezr 7:22
and we are not able to stand w	Neh 13:20
lodged in Jerusalem once or twice	Neh 13:20
him, to destroy him w cause	Job 2:3
for ever w any regarding it	Job 4:20
they die, even w wisdom	Job 4:21
marvellous things w number	Job 5:9
is unsavoury be eaten w salt	Job 6:6
shuttle, and are spent w hope	Job 7:6
Can the rush grow up w mire	Job 8:11
can the flag grow w water	Job 8:11
yea, and wonders w number	Job 9:10
and multiplieth my wounds w cause	Job 9:17
w any order, and where the light	Job 10:22
thou lift up thy face w spot	Job 11:15
They grope in the dark w light	Job 12:25
the naked to lodge w clothing	Job 24:7
cause him to go naked w clothing	Job 24:10
thou helped him that is w power	Job 26:2
I went mourning w the sun	Job 30:28
clothing, or any poor w covering	Job 31:19
eaten the fruits thereof w money	Job 31:39
I am clean w transgression, I am	Job 33:9
is incurable w transgression	Job 34:6
mighty shall be taken away w hand	Job 34:20
in pieces mighty men w number	Job 34:24
Job hath spoken w knowledge	Job 34:35
and his words were w wisdom	Job 34:35
he multiplieth words w knowledge	Job 35:16
and they shall die w knowledge	Job 36:12
counsel by words w knowledge	Job 38:2
her labour is in vain w fear	Job 39:16
not his like, who is made w fear	Job 41:33
that hideth counsel w knowledge	Job 42:3
him that w cause is mine enemy	Ps 7:4
ashamed which transgress w cause	Ps 25:3
that did see me w fled from me	Ps 31:11
For w cause have they hid me	Ps 35:7
which w cause they have digged	Ps 35:7
the eye that hate me w a cause	Ps 35:19
and prepare themselves w my fault	Ps 59:4
They that hate me w a cause are	Ps 69:4
caterpillars, and that w number,	Ps 105:34
and fought against me w a cause	Ps 109:3
perversely with me w a cause	Ps 109:3
have persecuted me w a cause	Ps 119:78
privily for the innocent w cause	Prov 1:11
Wisdom crieth w	Prov 1:20
Strive not with a man w cause	Prov 3:30
He shall die w instruction	Prov 5:23
shall he be broken w remedy	Prov 6:15
Now is she w, now in the streets,	Prov 7:12
fair woman which is w discretion	Prov 11:22
W counsel purposes are	Prov 15:22
than great revenues w right	Prov 16:8
that the soul be w knowledge	Prov 19:2
man saith, There is a lion w	Prov 22:13
who hath wounds w cause	Prov 23:29
Prepare thy work, and make it	Prov 24:27
against thy neighbour w cause	Prov 24:28
is like clouds and wind w rain	Prov 25:14
that is broken down, and w walls	Prov 25:28
be destroyed, and that w remedy	Prov 29:1
serpent will bite w enchantment	Eccl 10:11
concubines, and virgins w number	Song 6:8
when I should find thee w	Song 8:1
even great and fair, w inhabitant,	Is 5:9
and opened her mouth w measure	Is 5:14
the cities be wasted w inhabitant	Is 6:11
and the houses w man	Is 6:11
W me they shall bow down under	Is 10:4
their valiant ones shall cry w	Is 33:7
am I now come up w the LORD	Is 36:10
nor confounded world w end	Is 45:17
and ye shall be redeemed w money	Is 52:3
Assyrian oppressed them w cause	Is 52:4
milk w money and w price	Is 55:1
cities are burned w inhabitant	Jer 2:15
have forgotten me days w number	Jer 2:32
be laid waste, w an inhabitant	Jer 4:7
the earth, and, lo, it was w form	Jer 4:23
people, and w understanding	Jer 5:21
Judah desolate, w an inhabitant	Jer 9:11
to cut off the children from the	Jer 9:21
will I give to the spoil w price	Jer 15:13
which besiege you w the walls	Jer 21:4
his neighbour's service w wages	Jer 22:13
shall be desolate w an inhabitant	Jer 26:9
It is desolate w man or beast	Jer 33:10
ye say shall be desolate w man	Jer 33:10
w beast, even in the cities of	Jer 33:10
that are desolate, w man	Jer 33:10
w inhabitant, and w beast,	Jer 33:12
place, which is desolate w man	Jer 33:12
w beast, and in all the cities	Jer 33:12
a desolation w an inhabitant	Jer 44:19
offerings unto her, w our men	Jer 44:22
waste and desolate w an inhabitant	Jer 46:19
desolate, w any to dwell therein	Jer 48:9
nation, that dwelleth w care	Jer 49:31
a desolation w an inhabitant	Jer 51:29
and an hissing, w an inhabitant	Jer 51:37
of all these vessels was w weight	Jer 52:20
they are gone w strength before	Lam 1:6
ceaseth not, w any intermission,	Lam 3:49
the sore, like a bird, w cause	Lam 3:52
and it was written within and w	Eze 2:10
The sword is w, and the pestilence	Eze 7:15
w cause all that I have done in	Eze 17:9
even w great power or many people	Eze 17:9
of life, w committing iniquity	Eze 33:15
all of them dwelling w walls	Eze 38:11
forefront of the inner court w	Eze 40:19
And at the side w, as one goeth up	Eze 40:40
w the inner gate were the	Eze 40:44
which was for the side chamber w	Eze 41:9
even unto the inner house, and w	Eze 41:17
the wall round about within and w	Eze 41:17
upon the face of the porch w	Eze 41:25
the wall that was w over against	Eze 42:7
of the house, w the sanctuary	Eze 42:20
w blemish for a sin offering	Eze 43:22
offer a young bullock w blemish	Eze 43:23
a ram out of the flock w blemish	Eze 43:23
a ram out of the flock, w blemish	Eze 43:25
take a young bullock w blemish	Eze 45:18
seven rams w blemish daily the	Eze 45:23
way of the porch of that gate w	Eze 46:2
day shall be six lambs w blemish	Eze 46:4
blemish, and a ram w blemish	Eze 46:6
be a young bullock w blemish	Eze 46:6
they shall be w blemish	Eze 46:6
lamb of the first year w blemish	Eze 46:13
led me about the way w unto the	Eze 47:2
that a stone was cut out w hands	Dan 2:34
cut out of the mountain w hands	Dan 2:45
but he shall be broken w hand	Dan 8:25
w his own reproach w shall cause	Dan 11:18
shall abide many days w a king	Hos 3:4
and w a prince	Hos 3:4
a sacrifice	Hos 3:4
w an image, and w an ephod,	Hos 3:4
and w teraphim	Hos 3:4
the troop of robbers spoileth w	Hos 7:1
also is like a silly dove w heart	Hos 7:11
without number, w teeth are the	Joel 1:6
shall be inhabited as towns w	Zec 2:4
is angry with his brother w a	Mt 5:22
fall on the ground w your Father	Mt 10:29
mother and his brethren stood w	Mt 12:46
mother and thy brethren stand w	Mt 12:47
a parable spake he not unto	Mt 13:34
them, A prophet is not w honour	Mt 13:57
Are ye also yet w understanding	Mt 15:16
Now Peter sat w in the palace	Mt 26:69
but was w in desert places	Mk 1:45
and his mother, and, standing w	Mk 3:31
thy brethren w seek for thee	Mk 3:32
but unto them that are w, all	Mk 4:11
But w a parable spake he not unto	Mk 4:34
them, A prophet is not w honour,	Mk 6:4
There is nothing from w a man	Mk 7:15
Are ye so w understanding also	Mk 7:18
from w entereth into the man	Mk 7:18
w in a place where two ways met	Mk 11:4
I will build another made w hands	Mk 14:58
praying w at the time of incense	Lk 1:10
enemies might serve him w fear	Lk 1:74
is like a man that w a foundation	Lk 6:49
mother and thy brethren stand w	Lk 8:20
w make that which is within also	Lk 11:40
the door, and ye begin to stand w	Lk 13:25
he die w children, that his	Lk 20:28
took a wife, and died w children	Lk 20:29
them, When I sent you w purse	Lk 22:35
w him was not any thing made that	Jn 1:3
He that is w in among you, let	Jn 8:7
for w me ye can do nothing	Jn 15:5
law, They hated me w a cause	Jn 15:25
But Peter stood at the door w	Jn 18:16
now the coat was w seam, woven	Jn 19:23
But Mary stood w at the sepulchre	Jn 20:11
standing w before the doors	Acts 5:23
and brought them w violence	Acts 5:26
And he was three days w sight	Acts 9:9
came I unto you w gainsaying	Acts 10:29
but prayer was made w ceasing of	Acts 12:5
he left not himself w witness	Acts 14:17
w any delay on the morrow I sat	Acts 25:17
that w ceasing I make mention of	Rom 1:9
so that they are w excuse	Rom 1:20
W understanding, covenantbreakers	Rom 1:31
w natural affection, implacable	Rom 1:31
For as many as have sinned w law	Rom 2:12
law shall also perish w law	Rom 2:12
make the faith of God w effect	Rom 3:3
of God w the law is manifested	Rom 3:21
by faith w the deeds of the law	Rom 3:28
imputeth righteousness w works	Rom 4:6
For when we were yet w strength	Rom 5:6
For w the law sin was dead	Rom 7:8
For I was alive w the law once	Rom 7:9
how shall they hear w a preacher	Rom 10:14
calling of God are w repentance	Rom 11:29
Let love be w dissimulation	Rom 12:9
ye have reigned as kings w us	1Cor 4:8
do to judge them also that are w	1Cor 5:12
But them that are w God judgeth	1Cor 5:13
that a man doeth is w the body	1Cor 6:18
I would have you w carefulness	1Cor 7:32
upon the Lord w distraction	1Cor 7:35
the gospel of Christ w charge	1Cor 9:18
To them that are w law	1Cor 9:21
as w law	1Cor 9:21
being w law to God	1Cor 9:21
I might gain them that are w law	1Cor 9:21
neither is the man w the woman	1Cor 11:11
neither the woman w the man	1Cor 11:11
even things w life giving sound,	1Cor 14:7
none of them is w signification	1Cor 14:10
that he may be with you w fear	1Cor 16:10
w were fightings, within were	2Cor 7:5
not boast of things w our measure	2Cor 10:13
boasting of things w our measure	2Cor 10:15
Beside those things that are w	2Cor 11:28
w blame before him in love	Eph 1:4
at that time ye were w Christ	Eph 2:12
no hope, and w God in the world	Eph 2:12
throughout all ages, world w end	Eph 3:21
it should be holy and w blemish	Eph 5:27
w offence till the day of Christ	Phil 1:10
bold to speak the word w fear	Phil 1:14
Do all things w murmurings	Phil 2:14
w rebuke, in the midst of a	Phil 2:15
the circumcision made w hands	Col 2:11
in wisdom toward them that are w	Col 4:5
Remembering w ceasing your work	1Th 1:3
cause also thank we God w ceasing	1Th 2:13
honestly toward them that are w	1Th 4:12
Pray w ceasing	1Th 5:17
holy hands, w wrath and doubting	1Ti 2:8
a good report of them which are w	1Ti 3:7
w controversy great is the	1Ti 3:16
w preferring one before another	1Ti 5:21
thou keep this commandment w spot	1Ti 6:14
that w ceasing I have remembrance	2Ti 1:3
W natural affection,	2Ti 3:3
But w thy mind would I do nothing	Philem 14
tempted like as we are, yet w sin	Heb 4:15
W father	Heb 7:3
w mother, w descent, having	Heb 7:3
w descent	Heb 7:3
w all contradiction the less is	Heb 7:7
inasmuch as not w an oath he was	Heb 7:20
those priests were made w an oath	Heb 7:21
not w blood, which he offered for	Heb 9:7
offered himself w spot to God	Heb 9:14
testament was dedicated w blood	Heb 9:18
w shedding of blood is no	Heb 9:22
second time w sin unto salvation	Heb 9:28
of our faith w wavering	Heb 10:23
died w mercy under two or three	Heb 10:28
But w faith it is impossible to	Heb 11:6
that they w us should not be made	Heb 11:40
But if ye be w chastisement	Heb 12:8
w which no man shall see the Lord	Heb 12:14
conversation be w covetousness	Heb 13:5
for sin, are burned w the camp	Heb 13:11
own blood, suffered w the gate	Heb 13:12
therefore unto him w the camp	Heb 13:13
he shall have judgment w mercy	Jas 2:13
shew me thy faith w thy works	Jas 2:18
that faith w works is dead	Jas 2:20
For as the body w the spirit is	Jas 2:26
so faith w works is dead also	Jas 2:26
fruits, w partiality	Jas 3:17
partiality, and w hypocrisy	Jas 3:17
who w respect of persons judgeth	1Pet 1:17
of Christ, as of a lamb w blemish	1Pet 1:19
blemish and w spot	1Pet 1:19
they also may w the word be won	1Pet 3:1
one to another w grudging	1Pet 4:9
These are wells w water, clouds	2Pet 2:17
in peace, w spot, and blameless	2Pet 3:14
you, feeding themselves w fear	Jude 12
clouds they are w water, carried	Jude 12
w fruit, twice dead, plucked up	Jude 12
which is w the temple leaved out	Rev 11:2
for they are w fault before the	Rev 14:5
which is poured out w mixture	Rev 14:10
winepress was trodden w the city	Rev 14:20
For w are dogs, and sorcerers, and	Rev 22:15

WITHS

green w that were never dried	Judg 16:7
green w which had not been dried	Judg 16:8
And he brake the w, as a thread of	Judg 16:9

WITHSTAND

behold, I went out to w thee	Num 22:32
and could not w them	2Chr 13:7
now ye think to w the kingdom of	2Chr 13:8
so that none is able to w thee,	2Chr 20:6
and no man could w them	Est 9:2
against him, two shall w him,	Eccl 4:12
the arms of the south shall not w	Dan 11:15
shall there be any strength to w	Dan 11:15
what was I, that I could w God	Acts 11:17
may be able to w in the evil day	Eph 6:13

WITHSTOOD

they w Uzziah the king, and said	2Chr 26:18
of the kingdom of Persia w one one	Dan 10:13
name by interpretation) w them	Acts 13:8
I w him to the face, because he	Gal 2:11
Now as Jannes and Jambres w Moses	2Ti 3:8
for he hath greatly w our words	2Ti 4:15

WITNESS

that they may be a w unto me	Gen 31:30
and let it be for a w between me	Gen 31:44
said, This heap is a w between me	Gen 31:48
God is w betwixt me and thee	Gen 31:50
This heap be w	Gen 31:52
and this pillar be w	Gen 31:52
false w against thy neighbour	Ex 20:16

W

then let him bring it for w .... Ex 22:13
the wicked to be an unrighteous w .... Ex 23:1
the voice of swearing, and is a w .... Lev 5:1
and there be no w against her .... Num 5:13
the LORD in the tabernacle of w .... Num 17:7
went into the tabernacle of w .... Num 17:8
before the tabernacle of w .... Num 18:2
but one w shall not testify .... Num 35:30
earth to w against you this day, ... Deut 4:26
false w against thy neighbour .... Deut 5:20
but at the mouth of one w he .... Deut 17:6
One w shall not rise up against a .... Deut 19:15
if a false w rise up against any .... Deut 19:16
if the w be a false .... Deut 19:18
that this song may be a w for me. .... Deut 31:19
shall testify against them as a w .... Deut 31:21
may be there for a w against thee. .... Deut 31:26
But that it may be a w between us. .... Josh 22:27
but it is a w between us and you, ... Josh 22:28
for it shall be a w between us .... Josh 22:34
this stone shall be a w unto us. .... Josh 24:27
shall be therefore a w unto you. .... Josh 24:27
The LORD be w between us .... Judg 11:10
w against me before the LORD, and. 1Sa 12:3
them, The LORD is w against you 1Sa 12:5
and his anointed is w this day 1Sa 12:5
And they answered, He is w. 1Sa 12:5
to bear w against him, saying, ... 1Kin 21:10
Israel, for the tabernacle of w 2Chr 24:6
wrinkles, which is a w against me. .... Job 16:8
up in me beareth w to my face .... Job 16:8
my w is in heaven, and my record .... Job 16:19
the eye saw me, it gave w to me .... Job 29:11
and as a faithful w in heaven .... Ps 89:37
A false w that speaketh lies, and. .... Prov 6:19
but a false w deceit. .... Prov 12:17
A faithful w will not lie .... Prov 14:5
but a false w will utter lies. .... Prov 14:5
A true w delivereth souls .... Prov 14:25
but a deceitful w speaketh lies. .... Prov 14:25
A false w shall not be unpunished .... Prov 19:5
A false w shall not be unpunished .... Prov 19:9
An ungodly w scorneth judgement. .... Prov 19:28
A false w shall perish .... Prov 21:28
Be not a w against thy neighbour .... Prov 24:28
A man that beareth false w .... Prov 25:18
countenance doth w against them .... Is 3:9
for a w unto the LORD of hosts in .... Is 19:20
given him for a w to the people. .... Is 55:4
even I know, and am a w, saith the .... Jer 29:23
faithful w between us, if we do... .... Jer 42:5
thing shall I take to w for thee...... .... Lam 2:13
let the Lord GOD be w against you. .... Mic 1:2
the LORD hath been w between thee... .... Mal 2:14
I will be a swift w against the .... Mal 3:5
fornications, thefts, false w .... Mt 15:19
Thou shalt not bear false w .... Mt 19:18
world for a w unto all nations. .... Mt 24:14
sought false w against Jesus, to. .... Mt 26:59
is it which these w against thee? .... Mt 26:62
many things they w against thee .... Mt 27:13
Do not steal, Do not bear false w .... Mk 10:19
all the council sought for w. .... Mk 14:55
For many bare false w against him. .... Mk 14:56
but their w agreed not together. .... Mk 14:56
bare false w against him, saying, ... Mk 14:57
so did their w agree together. .... Mk 14:59
is it which these w against thee. .... Mk 14:60
many things they w against thee. .... Mk 15:4
And all bare him w, and wondered at. .... Lk 4:22
Truly ye bear w that ye allow the .... Lk 11:48
Do not steal, Do not bear false w .... Lk 18:20
said, What need we any further w .... Lk 22:71
The same came for a w .... Jn 1:7
to bear w of the Light, that all .... Jn 1:7
was sent to bear w of that Light .... Jn 1:8
John bare w of him, and cried, ... Jn 1:15
and ye receive not our w .... Jn 3:11
Jordan, to whom thou barest w .... Jn 3:26
Ye yourselves bear me w, that I .... Jn 3:28
If I bear w of myself .... Jn 5:31
of myself, my w is not true. .... Jn 5:31
is another that beareth w of me .... Jn 5:32
I know that the w which he .... Jn 5:32
John, and he bare w unto the truth. .... Jn 5:33
have greater w than that of John. .... Jn 5:36
bear w of me, that the Father .... Jn 5:36
hath sent me, hath borne w of me .... Jn 5:37
I am one that bear w of myself..................... Jn 8:18
that sent me beareth w of me .... Jn 8:18
Father's name, they bear w of me .... Jn 10:25
And ye also shall bear w, because .... Jn 15:27
spoken evil, bear w of the evil..................... Jn 18:23
I should bear w unto the truth .... Jn 18:37
a w with us of his resurrection .... Acts 1:22
great power gave the apostles w .... Acts 4:33
tabernacle of w in the wilderness .... Acts 7:44
To him give all the prophets w .... Acts 10:43
he left not himself without w .... Acts 14:17
knoweth the hearts, bare them w .... Acts 15:8
the high priest doth bear me w .... Acts 22:5
For thou shalt be his w unto all. .... Acts 22:15
so must thou bear w also at Rome. .... Acts 23:11
a w both of these things which.................... Acts 26:16
For God is my w, whom I serve.................... Rom 1:9
their conscience also bearing w .... Rom 2:15
itself beareth w with our spirit.................... Rom 8:16
bearing me w in the Holy Ghost.................. Rom 9:1
Thou shalt not bear false w .... Rom 13:9
God is w 1Th 2:5

This w is true.. Titus 1:13
God also bearing them w, both................ Heb 2:4
the Holy Ghost also is a w to us. .... Heb 10:15
by which he obtained w that he............. Heb 11:4
of them shall be a w against you.......... Jas 5:3
a w of the sufferings of Christ,.............. 1Pet 5:1
and we have seen it, and bear w............ 1Jn 1:2
it is the Spirit that beareth w................. 1Jn 5:6
are three that bear w in earth............... 1Jn 5:8
If we receive the w of men....................... 1Jn 5:9
the w of God is greater............................. 1Jn 5:9
for this is the w of God which he........... 1Jn 5:9
Son of God hath the w in himself......... 1Jn 5:10
Which have borne w of thy charity........ 3Jn 6
Christ, who is the faithful w.................. Rev 1:5
the Amen, the faithful and true w.......... Rev 3:14
were beheaded for the w of Jesus. .... Rev 20:4

WITNESSED

the men of Belial w against him........... 1Kin 21:13
being w by the law and the.................... Rom 3:21
Pilate w a good confession...................... 1Ti 6:13
of whom it is w that he liveth................. Heb 7:8

WITNESSES

be put to death by the mouth of w......... Num 35:30
of two w, or three w.................................. Deut 17:6
The hands of the w shall be first............ Deut 17:7
at the mouth of two w.............................. Deut 19:15
or at the mouth of three w...................... Deut 19:15
Ye are w against yourselves that............ Josh 24:22
And they said, We are w......................... Josh 24:22
Ye are w this day, that I have.................. Ruth 4:9
ye are w this day.................................... Ruth 4:10
and the elders, said, We are w................ Ruth 4:11
Thou renewest thy w against me .... Job 10:17
for false w are risen up against .... Ps 27:12
False w did rise up................................... Ps 35:11
took unto me faithful w to record........... Is 8:2
let them bring forth their w.................... Is 43:9
Ye are my w, saith the LORD, and......... Is 43:10
therefore ye are my w, saith the.......... Is 43:12
ye are even my w....................................... Is 44:8
and they are their own w....................... Is 44:9
evidence, and sealed it, and took w....... Jer 32:10
in the presence of the w that................ Jer 32:12
the field for money, and take w............. Jer 32:25
take w in the land of Benjamin............. Jer 32:44
in the mouth of two or three w.............. Mt 18:16
Wherefore ye be w unto yourselves........ Mt 23:31
yea, though many false w came.............. Mt 26:60
At the last came two false w.................... Mt 26:60
what further need have we of w............. Mt 26:65
saith, What need we any further w........ Mk 14:63
And ye are w of these things................... Lk 24:48
ye shall be w unto me both in................ Acts 1:8
raised up, whereof we all are w.............. Acts 2:32
whereof we are w....................................... Acts 3:15
we are his w of these things................... Acts 5:32
And set up false w, which said,.............. Acts 6:13
the w laid down their clothes at............. Acts 7:58
we are w of all things which he............. Acts 10:39
but unto w chosen before of God............ Acts 10:41
who are his w unto the people................ Acts 13:31
and we are found false w of God............ 1Cor 15:15
In the mouth of two or three w.............. 2Cor 13:1
Ye are w, and God also, how holily........ 1Th 2:10
but before two or three w........................ 1Ti 5:19
a good profession before many w........... 1Ti 6:12
hast heard of me among many w............ 2Ti 2:2
mercy under two or three w.................... Heb 10:28
I will give power unto my two w............. Rev 11:3

WITNESSETH

witness which he w of me is true............ Jn 5:32
the Holy Ghost w in every city............... Acts 20:23

WITNESSING

w both to small and great, saying......... Acts 26:22

WIT'S

man, and are at their w end..................... Ps 107:27

WITTINGLY

head, guiding his hands w...................... Gen 48:14

WITTY

out knowledge of w inventions.............. Prov 8:12

WIVES

And Lamech took unto him two w......... Gen 4:19
And Lamech said unto his w.................. Gen 4:23
ye w of Lamech, hearken unto my......... Gen 4:23
they took them w of all which................ Gen 6:2
wife, and thy sons' w with him.............. Gen 6:18
his wife, and his sons' w with him........ Gen 7:7
the three w of his sons with them.......... Gen 7:13
sons, and thy sons' w with thee.............. Gen 8:16
his wife, and his sons' w with him........ Gen 8:18
And Abram and Nahor took them w...... Gen 11:29
took unto the w which he had................ Gen 28:9
Give me my w and my children, for...... Gen 30:26
set his sons and his w upon camels...... Gen 31:17
take other w beside my daughters.......... Gen 31:50
up that night, and took his two w.......... Gen 32:22
take their daughters to us for w............. Gen 34:21
their w took they captive, and................ Gen 34:29
Esau took his w of the daughters........... Gen 36:2
And Esau took his w, and his sons,........ Gen 36:6
sons of Zilpah, his father's w................. Gen 37:2
your little ones, and for your w............. Gen 45:19
and their little ones, and their w........... Gen 46:5
loins, besides Jacob's sons' w................ Gen 46:26

come not at your w...................................... Ex 19:15
your w shall be widows, and your.......... Ex 22:24
which are in the ears of your w.............. Ex 32:2
to fall by the sword, that your w............ Num 14:3
door of their tents, and their w.............. Num 16:27
Our little ones, our w, our........................ Num 32:26
But your w, and your little ones,............ Deut 3:19
shall he w multiply w to himself............ Deut 17:17
If a man have two w, one beloved,........ Deut 21:15
Your little ones, your w, and thy........... Deut 29:11
Your w, your little ones, and your......... Josh 1:14
their daughters to their w........................ Judg 3:6
for he had many w.................................... Judg 8:30
How shall we do for w for them............. Judg 21:7
give them of our daughters to w............ Judg 21:7
they gave them w which they had......... Judg 21:14
How shall we do for w for them............. Judg 21:16
not give them w of our daughters.......... Judg 21:18
Benjamin did so, and took them w......... Judg 21:23
they took them w of the women of........ Ruth 1:4
And he had two w.................................... 1Sa 1:2
they were also both of them his w......... 1Sa 25:43
even David with his two w...................... 1Sa 27:3
and their w, and their sons, and............ 1Sa 30:3
David's two w were taken captives......... 1Sa 30:5
and David rescued his two w.................. 1Sa 30:18
up thither, and his two w........................ 2Sa 2:2
w out of Jerusalem, after he was........... 2Sa 5:13
thy master's w into thy bosom, and....... 2Sa 12:8
I will take thy w before thine................. 2Sa 12:11
he shall lie with thy w in the.................. 2Sa 12:11
daughters, and the lives of thy w........... 2Sa 19:5
And he had seven hundred w................. 1Kin 11:3
his w turned away his heart.................... 1Kin 11:3
that his w turned away his heart............ 1Kin 11:4
did he for all his strange w.................... 1Kin 11:8
thy w also and thy children, even.......... 1Kin 20:3
thy silver, and thy gold, and thy w....... 1Kin 20:5
for he sent unto me for my w................. 1Kin 20:7
the w of the sons of the prophets.......... 2Kin 4:1
king's mother, and the king's w............ 2Kin 24:15
the father of Tekoa had two w............... 1Chr 4:5
for they had many w and sons.............. 1Chr 7:4
Hushim and Baara were his w............... 1Chr 8:8
And David took more w at Jerusalem.... 1Chr 14:3
of Absalom above all his w..................... 2Chr 11:21
(for he took eighteen w, and................... 2Chr 11:21
And he desired many w........................... 2Chr 11:23
mighty, and married fourteen w............. 2Chr 13:21
with their little ones, their w................. 2Chr 20:13
people, and thy children, and thy w..... 2Chr 21:14
house, and his sons also, and his w...... 2Chr 21:17
And Jehoiada took for him two w.......... 2Chr 24:3
our w are in captivity for this................ 2Chr 29:9
of all their little ones, their w............... 2Chr 31:18
have taken strange w of the.................... Ezr 10:2
our God to put away all the w............... Ezr 10:10
and have taken strange w, to.................. Ezr 10:10
the land, and from the strange w.......... Ezr 10:11
them which have taken strange w......... Ezr 10:14
w by the first day of the first................. Ezr 10:17
found that had taken strange w............. Ezr 10:18
that they would put away their w.......... Ezr 10:19
All these had taken strange w................ Ezr 10:44
some of them had w by whom they...... Ezr 10:44
sons, and your daughters, your w.......... Neh 4:14
of their w against their brethren........... Neh 5:1
unto the law of God, their w.................. Neh 10:28
the w also and the children.................... Neh 12:43
Jews that had married w of Ashdod...... Neh 13:23
our God in marrying strange w............. Neh 13:27
all the w shall give to their.................... Est 1:20
be spoiled, and their w ravished........... Is 13:16
with their fields and w together............. Jer 6:12
will I give their w unto others............... Jer 8:10
none to bury them, them, their w.......... Jer 14:16
let their w be bereaved of their............. Jer 18:21
Take ye w, and beget sons and.............. Jer 29:6
take w for your sons, and give............... Jer 29:6
adultery with their neighbours' w......... Jer 29:23
no wine all our days, we, our w............. Jer 35:8
So they shall bring out all thy w........... Jer 38:23
and the wickedness of their w............... Jer 44:9
and the wickedness of your w................ Jer 44:9
w had burned incense unto other......... Jer 44:15
your w have both spoken with your...... Jer 44:22
they take for their w a widow................ Eze 44:22
the king, and his princes, his w............ Dan 5:2
the king, and his princes, his w............ Dan 5:3
and thou, and thy lords, thy w.............. Dan 5:23
them, their children, and their w.......... Dan 6:24
of David apart, and their w apart.......... Zec 12:12
of Nathan apart, and their w apart........ Zec 12:12
of Levi apart, and their w apart............ Zec 12:13
of Shimei apart, and their w apart........ Zec 12:13
family apart, and their w apart.............. Zec 12:14
suffered you to put away your w........... Mt 19:8
eat, they drank, they married w............ Lk 17:27
all brought us on our way, with w........ Acts 21:5
that both they that have w be as........... 1Cor 7:29
w, submit yourselves unto your............. Eph 5:22
so let the w be to their own.................... Eph 5:24
Husbands, love your w, even as............ Eph 5:25
love their w as their own bodies............ Eph 5:28
W, submit yourselves unto your............ Col 3:18
Husbands, love your w, and be not...... Col 3:19
no more after their w be grave,............. 1Ti 3:11
Likewise, ye w, be in subjection............ 1Pet 3:1
won by the conversation of the w......... 1Pet 3:1

WIVES'
old w fables, and exercise thyself.............. 1Ti 4:7

WIZARD
a familiar spirit, or that is a w............. Lev 20:27
with familiar spirits, or a w............. Deut 18:11

WIZARDS
spirits, neither seek after w............. Lev 19:31
have familiar spirits, and after w............. Lev 20:6
had familiar spirits, and the w............. 1Sa 28:3
have familiar spirits, and the w............. 1Sa 28:9
dealt with familiar spirits and w............. 2Kin 21:6
with familiar spirits, and the w............. 2Kin 23:24
a familiar spirit, and with w............. 2Chr 33:6
unto w that peep, and that mutter............. Is 8:19
familiar spirits, and to the w............. Is 19:3

WOE
W to thee, Moab............. Num 21:29
And they said, W unto us............. 1Sa 4:7
W unto us............. 1Sa 4:8
If I be wicked, w unto me............. Job 10:15
W is me, that I sojourn in Mesech............. Ps 120:5
Who hath w............. Prov 23:29
but w to him that is alone when............. Eccl 4:10
W to thee, O land, when thy king............. Eccl 10:16
W unto their soul............. Is 3:9
W unto the wicked............. Is 3:11
W unto them that join house to............. Is 5:8
W unto them that rise up early in............. Is 5:11
W unto them that draw iniquity............. Is 5:18
W unto them that call evil good............. Is 5:20
W unto them that are wise in............. Is 5:21
W unto them that are mighty to............. Is 5:22
I said, W is me............. Is 6:5
W unto them that decree............. Is 10:1
W to the multitude of many people............. Is 17:12
W to the land shadowing with............. Is 18:1
leanness, my leanness, w unto me............. Is 24:16
W to the crown of pride, to the............. Is 28:1
W to Ariel, to Ariel, the city............. Is 29:1
W unto them that seek deep to............. Is 29:15
W to the rebellious children............. Is 30:1
W to them that go down to Egypt............. Is 31:1
W to thee that spoilest, and thou............. Is 33:1
W unto him that striveth with his............. Is 45:9
W unto him that saith unto his............. Is 45:10
W unto us............. Jer 4:13
her hands, saying, W is me now............. Jer 4:31
W unto us............. Jer 6:4
W is me for my hurt............. Jer 10:19
W unto thee, O Jerusalem............. Jer 13:27
W is me, my mother, that thou............. Jer 15:10
W unto him that buildeth his............. Jer 22:13
W be unto the pastors that............. Jer 23:1
Thou didst say, W is me now............. Jer 45:3
W unto Nebo............. Jer 48:1
W be unto thee, O Moab............. Jer 48:46
w unto them............. Jer 50:27
w unto us, that we have sinned............. Lam 5:16
lamentations, and mourning, and w............. Eze 2:10
W unto the foolish prophets, that............. Eze 13:3
W to the women that sew pillows............. Eze 13:18
w, w unto thee............. Eze 16:23
W to the bloody city, to the pot............. Eze 24:6
W to the bloody city............. Eze 24:9
Howl ye, W worth the day............. Eze 30:2
W be to the shepherds of Israel............. Eze 34:2
W unto them............. Hos 7:13
w also to them when I depart from............. Hos 9:12
W unto you that desire the day of............. Amos 5:18
W to them that are at ease in............. Amos 6:1
W to them that devise iniquity............. Mic 2:1
W is me............. Mic 7:1
W to the bloody city............. Nah 3:1
W to him that increaseth that............. Hab 2:6
W to him that coveteth an evil............. Hab 2:9
W to him that buildeth a town............. Hab 2:12
W to him that giveth his............. Hab 2:15
W unto him that saith to the wood............. Hab 2:19
W unto the inhabitants of the sea............. Zeph 2:5
W to her that is filthy and............. Zeph 3:1
W to the idol shepherd that............. Zec 11:17
W unto thee, Chorazin............. Mt 11:21
w unto thee, Bethsaida............. Mt 11:21
W unto the world because of............. Mt 18:7
but w to that man by whom the............. Mt 18:7
But w unto you, scribes and............. Mt 23:13
W unto you, scribes and Pharisees............. Mt 23:14
W unto you, scribes and Pharisees............. Mt 23:15
W unto you, ye blind guides............. Mt 23:16
W unto you, scribes and Pharisees............. Mt 23:23
W unto you, scribes and Pharisees............. Mt 23:25
W unto you, scribes and Pharisees............. Mt 23:27
W unto you, scribes and Pharisees............. Mt 23:29
w unto them that are with child............. Mt 24:19
but w unto that man by whom the............. Mt 26:24
But w to them that are with child............. Mk 13:17
but w to that man by whom the Son............. Mk 14:21
But w unto you that are rich............. Lk 6:24
W unto you that are full............. Lk 6:25
W unto you that laugh now............. Lk 6:25
W unto you, when all men shall............. Lk 6:26
W unto thee, Chorazin............. Lk 10:13
w unto thee, Bethsaida............. Lk 10:13
But w unto you, Pharisees............. Lk 11:42
W unto you, scribes............. Lk 11:44
W unto you also, ye lawyers............. Lk 11:46
W unto you for ye build the............. Lk 11:47
W unto you, lawyers............. Lk 11:52

but w unto him, through whom they......... Lk 17:1
W unto them that are with............. Lk 21:23
but w unto that man by whom he is............. Lk 22:22
w is unto me, if I preach not the............. 1Cor 9:16
W unto them............. Jude 11
saying with a loud voice, W, w............. Rev 8:13
with a loud voice, W, w, w............. Rev 8:13
One w is past............. Rev 9:12
The second w is past............. Rev 11:14
the third w cometh quickly............. Rev 11:14
W to the inhabiters of the earth............. Rev 12:12

WOEFUL
neither have I desired the w day............. Jer 17:16

WOES
there come two w more hereafter............. Rev 9:12

WOLF
Benjamin shall ravin as a w............. Gen 49:27
The w also shall dwell with the............. Is 11:6
The w and the lamb shall feed............. Is 65:25
a w of the evenings shall spoil............. Jer 5:6
sheep are not, seeth the w coming............. Jn 10:12
and the w catcheth them, and............. Jn 10:12

WOLVES
are like w ravening the prey............. Eze 22:27
more fierce than the evening w............. Hab 1:8
he judges are evening w............. Zeph 3:3
but inwardly they are ravening w............. Mt 7:15
forth as sheep in the midst of w............. Mt 10:16
I send you forth as lambs among w............. Lk 10:3
grievous w enter in among you............. Acts 20:29

WOMAN
had taken from man, made he a w............. Gen 2:22
she shall be called W, because............. Gen 2:23
And he said unto the w, Yea, hath............. Gen 3:1
the w said unto the serpent, We............. Gen 3:2
And the serpent said unto the w............. Gen 3:4
when the w saw that the tree was............. Gen 3:6
The w whom thou gavest to be with............. Gen 3:12
And the LORD God said unto the w............. Gen 3:13
the w said, The serpent beguiled............. Gen 3:13
put enmity between thee and the w............. Gen 3:15
Unto the w he said, I will............. Gen 3:16
thou art a fair w to look upon............. Gen 12:11
the w that she was very fair............. Gen 12:14
the w was taken into Pharaoh's............. Gen 12:15
for the w which thou hast taken............. Gen 20:3
Peradventure the w will not be............. Gen 24:5
if the w will not be willing to............. Gen 24:8
Peradventure the w will not............. Gen 24:39
let the same be the w whom thou............. Gen 24:44
Shaul the son of a Canaanitish w............. Gen 46:10
the w conceived, and bare a son............. Ex 2:2
the w took the child, and nursed............. Ex 2:9
But every w shall borrow of her............. Ex 3:22
Shaul the son of a Canaanitish w............. Ex 6:15
every w of her neighbour, jewels............. Ex 11:2
hurt a w with child, so that her............. Ex 21:22
If an ox gore a man or a............. Ex 21:28
that he hath killed a man or a w............. Ex 21:29
unto the LORD, every man and w............. Ex 35:29
Let neither man nor w make any............. Ex 36:6
If a w have conceived seed, and............. Lev 12:2
If a man or w have a plague upon............. Lev 13:29
If a man also or a w have in the............. Lev 13:38
The w also with whom man shall............. Lev 15:18
if a w have an issue, and her............. Lev 15:19
if a w have an issue of her blood............. Lev 15:25
an issue, of the man, and of the w............. Lev 15:33
not uncover the nakedness of a w............. Lev 18:17
unto a w to uncover her nakedness............. Lev 18:19
neither shall any w stand before............. Lev 18:23
whosoever lieth carnally with a w............. Lev 19:20
mankind, as he lieth with a w............. Lev 20:13
if a w approach unto any beast,............. Lev 20:16
thereto, thou shalt kill the w............. Lev 20:16
lie with a w having her sickness............. Lev 20:18
A man also or a w that hath a............. Lev 20:27
a w put away from her husband............. Lev 21:7
A widow, or a divorced w, or............. Lev 21:14
And the son of an Israelitish w............. Lev 24:10
and this son of the Israelitish w............. Lev 24:10
When a man or w shall commit any............. Num 5:6
shall set the w before the LORD............. Num 5:16
her by an oath, and say unto the w............. Num 5:19
the w with an oath of cursing............. Num 5:21
the priest shall say unto the w............. Num 5:21
the w shall say, Amen, amen............. Num 5:22
he shall cause the w to drink the............. Num 5:26
cause the w to drink the water............. Num 5:26
the w shall be a curse among her............. Num 5:27
if the w be not defiled, but be............. Num 5:28
shall set the w before the LORD,............. Num 5:30
this w shall bear her iniquity............. Num 5:31
When either man or w shall............. Num 6:2
Ethiopian w whom he had married............. Num 12:1
for he had married an Ethiopian w............. Num 12:1
in the sight of Moses, and in............. Num 25:6
and the w through her belly............. Num 25:8
was slain with the Midianitish w............. Num 25:14
w that was slain was Cozbi............. Num 25:15
If a w also vow a vow unto the............. Num 30:3
kill every w that hath known man............. Num 31:17
an Hebrew man, or an Hebrew w............. Deut 15:12
thy God giveth thee, man or w............. Deut 17:2
bring forth that man or that w............. Deut 17:5
gates, even that man or that w............. Deut 17:5
among the captives a beautiful w............. Deut 21:11
The w shall not wear that which............. Deut 22:5

upon her, and say, I took this w............. Deut 22:14
with a w married to an husband............. Deut 22:22
that lay with the w, and the w............. Deut 22:22
delicate w among you, which would............. Deut 28:56
should be among you man, or w............. Deut 29:18
the w took the two men, and hid............. Josh 2:4
was in the city, both man and w............. Josh 6:21
house, and bring out thence the w............. Josh 6:22
sell Sisera into the hand of a w............. Judg 4:9
a certain w cast a piece of a............. Judg 9:53
men say not of me, A w slew him............. Judg 9:54
thou art the son of a strange w............. Judg 11:2
of the LORD came upon him in the............. Judg 13:3
Then the w came and told her............. Judg 13:9
the w as she sat in the field............. Judg 13:9
the w made haste, and ran, and............. Judg 13:10
the man that spakest unto the w............. Judg 13:11
I said unto the w let her beware............. Judg 13:13
the w bare a son, and called his............. Judg 13:24
saw a w in Timnath of the............. Judg 14:1
I have seen a w in Timnath of the............. Judg 14:2
Is there never a w among the............. Judg 14:3
went down, and talked with the w............. Judg 14:7
his father went down unto the w............. Judg 14:10
that he loved a w in the valley............. Judg 16:4
The came the w in the dawning of............. Judg 19:26
the w his concubine was fallen............. Judg 19:27
husband of the w that was slain............. Judg 20:4
every w that hath lain by man............. Judg 21:11
the w was left of her two sons and............. Ruth 1:5
and, behold, a w lay at his feet............. Ruth 3:8
know that thou art a virtuous w............. Ruth 3:11
that a w came into the floor............. Ruth 3:14
The LORD make the w that is come............. Ruth 4:11
shall give thee of this young w............. Ruth 4:12
I am a w of a sorrowful spirit............. 1Sa 1:15
So the w went her way, and did eat............. 1Sa 1:18
So the w abode, and gave her son............. 1Sa 1:23
I am the w that stood by thee............. 1Sa 1:26
w for the loan which is lent to............. 1Sa 2:20
but slay both man and w, infant and............. 1Sa 15:3
out of the perverse rebellious w............. 1Sa 20:30
she was a w of good understanding............. 1Sa 25:3
and left neither man nor w alive............. 1Sa 27:9
saved neither man nor w alive............. 1Sa 27:11
Seek me a w that hath a familiar............. 1Sa 28:7
there is a w that hath a familiar............. 1Sa 28:7
and they came to the w by night............. 1Sa 28:8
the w said unto him, Behold, thou............. 1Sa 28:9
Then said the w, Whom shall I............. 1Sa 28:11
when the w saw Samuel, she cried............. 1Sa 28:12
the w spake to Saul, saying, Why............. 1Sa 28:12
the w said unto Saul, I saw gods............. 1Sa 28:13
the w came unto Saul, and saw that............. 1Sa 28:21
his servants, together with the w............. 1Sa 28:23
the w had a fat calf in the house............. 1Sa 28:24
with a fault concerning this w............. 2Sa 3:8
roof he saw a w washing herself............. 2Sa 11:2
the w was very beautiful to look............. 2Sa 11:2
sent and enquired after the w............. 2Sa 11:3
the w conceived, and sent and told............. 2Sa 11:5
did not a w cast a piece of a............. 2Sa 11:21
said, Put now this w out from me............. 2Sa 13:17
and fetched thence a wise w............. 2Sa 14:2
but be as a w that had a long............. 2Sa 14:2
when the w of Tekoah spake to the............. 2Sa 14:4
answered, I am indeed a widow w............. 2Sa 14:5
And the king said unto the w............. 2Sa 14:8
the w of Tekoah said unto the............. 2Sa 14:9
Then the w said, Let thine............. 2Sa 14:12
the w said, Wherefore then hast............. 2Sa 14:13
king answered and said unto the w............. 2Sa 14:18
the w said, Let my lord the king............. 2Sa 14:18
the w answered and said, As thy............. 2Sa 14:19
she was a w of a fair countenance............. 2Sa 14:27
the w took and spread a covering............. 2Sa 17:19
came to the w to the house............. 2Sa 17:20
the w said unto them, They be............. 2Sa 17:20
cried a wise w out of the city............. 2Sa 20:16
the w said, Art thou Joab............. 2Sa 20:17
the w said unto Joab, Behold, his............. 2Sa 20:21
Then the w went unto all the............. 2Sa 20:22
And the one w said, O my lord, I............. 1Kin 3:17
this w dwell in one house............. 1Kin 3:17
that this w was delivered also............. 1Kin 3:18
And the other w said, Nay............. 1Kin 3:22
Then spake the w whose the living............. 1Kin 3:26
name was Zeruah, a widow w............. 1Kin 11:26
feign herself to be another w............. 1Kin 14:5
a widow w there to sustain thee............. 1Kin 17:9
the widow w was there gathering............. 1Kin 17:10
things, that the son of the w............. 1Kin 17:17
the w said to Elijah, Now by this............. 1Kin 17:24
Now there cried a certain w of............. 2Kin 4:1
to Shunem, where was a great w............. 2Kin 4:8
the w conceived, and bare a son at............. 2Kin 4:17
wall, there cried a unto him............. 2Kin 6:26
This w said unto me, Give thy son............. 2Kin 6:28
the king heard the words of the w............. 2Kin 6:30
Then spake Elisha unto the w............. 2Kin 8:1
the w arose, and did after the............. 2Kin 8:2
that the w returned out of the............. 2Kin 8:3
body to life, that, behold, the w............. 2Kin 8:5
My lord, O king, this is the w............. 2Kin 8:5
And when the king asked the w............. 2Kin 8:6
said, Go, see now this cursed w............. 2Kin 9:34
one of Israel, both man and w............. 1Chr 16:3
The son of a w of the daughters............. 2Chr 2:14
small or great, whether man or w............. 2Chr 15:13
sons of Athaliah, that wicked w............. 2Chr 24:7

W

that whosoever, whether man or w .... Est 4:11
is born of a w is of few days .... Job 14:1
and he which is born of a w .... Job 15:14
be he clean that is born of a w .... Job 25:4
heart have been deceived by a w .... Job 31:9
and pain, as of a w in travail .... Ps 48:6
like the untimely birth of a w .... Ps 58:8
maketh the barren w to keep house ...... Ps 113:9
deliver thee from the strange w .... Prov 2:16
a strange w drop as an honeycomb .... Prov 5:3
son, be ravished with a strange w .... Prov 5:20
To keep thee from the evil w .... Prov 6:24
of the tongue of a strange w .... Prov 6:24
For by means of a whorish w a man .... Prov 6:26
with a w lacketh understanding .... Prov 6:32
may keep thee from the strange w .... Prov 7:5
there met him a w with the attire .... Prov 7:10
A foolish w is clamorous .... Prov 9:13
A gracious w retaineth honour .... Prov 11:16
so is a fair w which is without .... Prov 11:22
A virtuous w is a crown to her .... Prov 12:4
Every wise w buildeth her house .... Prov 14:1
a pledge of him for a strange w .... Prov 20:16
housetop, than with a brawling w .... Prov 21:9
with a contentious and angry w .... Prov 21:19
a strange w is a narrow pit .... Prov 23:27
housetop, than with a brawling w .... Prov 25:24
a pledge of him for a strange w .... Prov 27:13
day and a contentious w are alike .... Prov 27:15
is the way of an adulterous w .... Prov 30:20
For an odious w when she is .... Prov 30:23
Who can find a virtuous w .... Prov 31:10
but a w that feareth the LORD, ... Prov 31:30
find more bitter than death the w .... Eccl 7:26
but a w among all those have I .... Eccl 7:28
be in pain as a w that travaileth .... Is 13:8
the pangs of a w that travaileth .... Is 21:3
Like as a w with child, that .... Is 26:17
will I cry like a travailing w .... Is 42:14
or to the w, What hast thou .... Is 45:10
Can a w forget her sucking child, ... Is 49:15
hath called thee as a w forsaken .... Is 54:6
a voice as of a w in travail .... Jer 4:31
of Zion to a comely and delicate w .... Jer 6:2
us, and pain, as of a w in travail .... Jer 6:24
take thee, as a w in travail .... Jer 13:21
the pain as of a w in travail .... Jer 22:23
as a w in travail, and all faces .... Jer 30:6
the w with child and her that .... Jer 31:8
earth, A w shall compass a man .... Jer 31:22
to cut off from you man and w .... Jer 44:7
as the heart of a w in her pangs .... Jer 48:41
as the heart of a w in her pangs .... Jer 49:22
have taken her, as a w in travail .... Jer 49:24
and pangs as of a w in travail .... Jer 50:43
will I break in pieces man and w .... Jer 51:22
is as a menstruous w among them .... Lam 1:17
work of an imperious whorish w .... Eze 16:30
hath come near to a menstruous w .... Eze 18:6
thus go in unto a w that .... Eze 23:44
as the uncleanness of a removed w ...... Eze 36:17
love a w beloved of her friend, ... Hos 3:1
travailing w shall come upon him .... Hos 13:13
have taken thee as a w in travail .... Mic 4:9
of Zion, like a w in travail .... Mic 4:10
this is a w that sitteth in the .... Zec 5:7
on a w to lust after her hath .... Mt 5:28
And, behold, a w, which was .... Mt 9:20
the w was made whole from that .... Mt 9:22
like unto leaven, which a w took .... Mt 13:33
a w of Canaan came out of the .... Mt 15:22
answered and said unto her, O w .... Mt 15:28
And last of all the w died also .... Mt 22:27
There came unto him a w having an .... Mt 26:7
unto them, Why trouble ye the w .... Mt 26:10
also this, that this w hath done .... Mt 26:13
And a certain w, which had an .... Mk 5:25
But the w fearing and trembling, ... Mk 5:33
For a certain w, whose young .... Mk 7:25
The w was a Greek, a .... Mk 7:26
if a w shall put away her husband .... Mk 10:12
last of all the w died also .... Mk 12:22
at meat, there came a w having an ...... Mk 14:3
unto a w that was a widow .... Lk 4:26
a w in the city, which was a .... Lk 7:37
what manner of w this is that .... Lk 7:39
And he turned to the w, and said .... Lk 7:44
unto Simon, Seest thou this w .... Lk 7:44
but this w since the time I came .... Lk 7:45
but this w hath anointed my feet .... Lk 7:46
And he said to the w, Thy faith .... Lk 7:50
a w having an issue of blood .... Lk 8:43
when the w saw that she was not .... Lk 8:47
a certain w named Martha received .... Lk 10:38
And he turned to the w of the company lifted .... Lk 11:27
there was a w which had a spirit .... Lk 13:11
her to him, and said unto her, W .... Lk 13:12
And ought not this w, being a .... Lk 13:16
It is like leaven, which a w took .... Lk 13:21
Either what w having ten pieces .... Lk 15:8
Last of all the w died also .... Lk 20:32
And he denied him, saying, W .... Lk 22:57
Jesus saith unto her, W, what .... Jn 2:4
There cometh a w of Samaria to .... Jn 4:7
Then saith the w of Samaria unto .... Jn 4:9
of me, which am a w of Samaria .... Jn 4:9
The w saith unto him, Sir, thou .... Jn 4:11
The w saith unto him, Sir, give .... Jn 4:15
The w answered and said, I have no .... Jn 4:17
The w saith unto him, Sir, I .... Jn 4:19

Jesus saith unto her, W, believe .... Jn 4:21
The w saith unto him, I know that ...... Jn 4:25
that he talked with the w .... Jn 4:27
The w then left her waterpot, and .... Jn 4:28
on him for the saying of the w .... Jn 4:39
And said unto the w, Now we .... Jn 4:42
unto him a w taken in adultery .... Jn 8:3
this w was taken in adultery, in .... Jn 8:4
the w standing in the midst .... Jn 8:9
up himself, and saw none but the w .... Jn 8:10
he said unto her, W .... Jn 8:10
A w when she is in travail hath .... Jn 16:21
he saith unto his mother, W .... Jn 19:26
And they say unto her, W, why .... Jn 20:13
Jesus saith unto her, W, why .... Jn 20:15
this w was full of good works and ...... Acts 9:36
Timotheus, the son of a certain w ...... Acts 16:1
a certain w named Lydia, a seller .... Acts 16:14
a w named Damaris, and others with .. Acts 17:34
leaving the natural use of the .... Rom 1:27
For the w which hath an husband .... Rom 7:2
good for a man not to touch a w 1Cor 7:1
let every w have her own husband 1Cor 7:2
the w which hath an husband that 1Cor 7:13
The unmarried w careth for the 1Cor 7:34
and the head of the w is the man 1Cor 11:3
But every w that prayeth or 1Cor 11:5
For if the w be not covered, let 1Cor 11:6
for a w to be shorn or shaven 1Cor 11:6
but the w is the glory of the man 1Cor 11:7
For the man is not of the w 1Cor 11:8
but the w of the man 1Cor 11:8
was the man created for the w 1Cor 11:9
but the w for the man 1Cor 11:9
For this cause ought the w to 1Cor 11:10
neither is the man without the w 1Cor 11:11
neither the w without the man, in 1Cor 11:11
For as the w is of the man 1Cor 11:12
even so is the man also by the w 1Cor 11:12
is it comely that a w pray unto 1Cor 11:13
But if a w have long hair, it is 1Cor 11:15
sent forth his Son, made of a w .... Gal 4:4
heir with the son of the free w .... Gal 4:30
as travail upon a w with child 1Th 5:3
Let the w learn in silence with 1Ti 2:11
But I suffer not a w to teach, ... 1Ti 2:12
but the w being deceived was in 1Ti 2:14
If any man or w that believeth 1Ti 5:16
thou sufferest that w Jezebel .... Rev 2:20
a w clothed with the sun, and the ...... Rev 12:1
the dragon stood before the w .... Rev 12:4
the w fled into the wilderness, ... Rev 12:6
he persecuted the w which brought .... Rev 12:13
to the w were given two wings of ...... Rev 12:14
water as a flood after the w .... Rev 12:15
And the earth helped the w .... Rev 12:16
the dragon was wroth with the w ...... Rev 12:17
I saw a w sit upon a scarlet .... Rev 17:3
the w was arrayed in purple and .... Rev 17:4
I saw the w drunken with the .... Rev 17:6
tell thee the mystery of the w .... Rev 17:7
mountains, on which the w sitteth ...... Rev 17:9
the w which thou sawest is that .... Rev 17:18

WOMANKIND

not lie with mankind, as with w .... Lev 18:22

WOMAN'S

his pledge from the w hand .... Gen 38:20
according as the w husband will .... Ex 21:22
the Israelitish w son blasphemed .... Lev 24:11
the LORD, and uncover the w head ...... Num 5:18
offering out of the w hand .... Num 5:25
shall a man put on a w garment .... Deut 22:5
this w child died in the night 1Kin 3:19

WOMB

her, Two nations are in thy w .... Gen 25:23
behold, there were twins in her w ...... Gen 25:24
Leah was hated, he opened her w ...... Gen 29:31
from thee the fruit of the w .... Gen 30:2
hearkened to her, and opened her w .. Gen 30:22
that, behold, twins were in her w .... Gen 38:27
of the breasts, and of the w .... Gen 49:25
whatsoever openeth the w among ...... Ex 13:2
instead of such as open every w .... Num 8:16
he cometh out of his mother's w .... Num 12:12
also bless the fruit of thy w .... Deut 7:13
be a Nazarite unto God from the w .... Judg 13:5
the w to the day of his death .... Judg 13:7
unto God from my mother's w .... Judg 16:17
there yet any more sons in my w .... Ruth 1:11
but the LORD had shut up her w 1Sa 1:5
the LORD had shut up her w 1Sa 1:6
Naked came I out of my mother's w .... Job 1:21
not up the doors of my mother's w ...... Job 3:10
Why died I not from the w .... Job 3:11
brought me forth out of the w .... Job 10:18
carried from the w to the grave.......... Job 10:19
The w shall forget him .... Job 24:20
he that made me in the w make him .... Job 31:15
did not one fashion us in the w .... Job 31:15
guided her from my mother's w .... Job 31:18
as if it had issued out of the w .... Job 38:8
Out of whose w came the ice .... Job 38:29
art he that took me out of the w .... Ps 22:9
I was cast upon thee from the w .... Ps 22:10
wicked are estranged from the w .... Ps 58:3
have I been holden up from the w .... Ps 71:6
from the w of the morning .... Ps 110:3
the fruit of the w is his reward .... Ps 127:3
hast covered me in my mother's w ...... Ps 139:13

and the barren w .... Prov 30:16
and what, the son of my w .... Prov 30:2
he came forth of his mother's w .... Eccl 5:15
the w of her that is with child .... Eccl 11:5
no pity on the fruit of the w .... Is 13:18
thee, and formed thee from the w .... Is 44:2
and he that formed thee from the w .... Is 44:24
which are carried from the w .... Is 46:3
called a transgressor from the w .... Is 48:8
LORD hath called me from the w .... Is 49:1
me from the w to be his servant .... Is 49:5
compassion on the son of her w .... Is 49:15
to bring forth, and shut the w .... Is 66:9
out of the w I sanctified thee .... Jer 1:5
Because he slew me not from the w .... Jer 20:17
her w to be always great with me .... Jer 20:17
forth out of the w to see labour .... Jer 20:18
the fire all that openeth the w .... Eze 20:26
from the birth, and from the w .... Hos 9:11
give them a miscarrying w .... Hos 9:14
even the beloved fruit of their w .... Hos 9:16
his brother by the heel in the w .... Hos 12:3
so born from their mother's w .... Mt 19:12
Ghost, even from his mother's w .... Lk 1:15
thou shalt conceive in thy w .... Lk 1:31
of Mary, the babe leaped in her w ...... Lk 1:41
and blessed is the fruit of thy w .... Lk 1:42
the babe leaped in my w for joy .... Lk 1:44
before he was conceived in the w ...... Lk 2:21
the w shall be called holy to the.......... Lk 2:23
Blessed is the w that bare thee............ Lk 11:27
second time into his mother's w .... Jn 3:4
from his mother's w was carried .... Acts 3:2
a cripple from his mother's w .... Acts 14:8
yet the deadness of Sarah's w .... Rom 4:19
separated me from my mother's w ...... Gal 1:15

WOMBS

the w of the house of Abimelech, ... Gen 20:18
the w that never bare, and the .... Lk 23:29

WOMEN

the w also, and the people .... Gen 14:16
with Sarah after the manner of w .... Gen 18:11
even the time that w go out to .... Gen 24:11
for the custom of w is upon me............ Gen 31:35
lifted up his eyes, and saw the w .... Gen 33:5
of a midwife to the Hebrew w .... Ex 1:16
Because the Hebrew w are not as........ Ex 1:19
not as the Egyptian w .... Ex 1:19
to thee a nurse of the Hebrew w .... Ex 2:7
all the w went out after her with .... Ex 15:20
And they came, both men and w .... Ex 35:22
all the w that were wise hearted.......... Ex 35:25
all the w whose heart stirred .... Ex 35:26
of the w assembling, which .... Ex 38:8
ten w shall bake your bread in .... Lev 26:26
took all the w of Midian captives .... Num 31:9
Have ye saved all the w alive .... Num 31:15
But all the w children, that have .... Num 31:18
of w that had not known man by.......... Num 31:35
destroyed the men, and the w .... Deut 2:34
utterly destroying the men, w .... Deut 3:6
But the w, and the little ones, and ...... Deut 20:14
the people together, men, and w .... Deut 31:12
fell that day, both of men and w .... Josh 8:25
of Israel, with the w, and the .... Josh 8:35
Blessed above w shall Jael the .... Judg 5:24
shall she be above w in the tent............ Judg 5:24
also, about a thousand men and w ...... Judg 9:49
and thither fled all the men and w ...... Judg 9:51
the house was full of men and w .... Judg 16:27
about three thousand men and w .... Judg 16:27
the edge of the sword, with the w ...... Judg 21:10
alive of the w of Jabesh-gilead .... Judg 21:14
seeing the w are destroyed out of ...... Judg 21:16
took them wives of the w of Moab ...... Ruth 1:4
the w said unto Naomi, Blessed be...... Ruth 4:14
the w her neighbours gave it a .... Ruth 4:17
how they lay with the w that 1Sa 2:22
w that stood by said unto her 1Sa 4:20
thy sword hath made w childless 1Sa 15:33
thy mother be childless among w 1Sa 15:33
that the w came out of all cities 1Sa 18:6
the w answered one another as 1Sa 18:7
kept themselves at least from w 1Sa 21:4
Of a truth w have been kept from 1Sa 21:5
edge of the sword, both men and w 1Sa 22:19
And had taken the w captives 1Sa 30:2
wonderful, passing the love of w 2Sa 1:26
Israel, as well to the w as men 2Sa 6:19
And the king left ten w, which 2Sa 15:16
voice of singing men and singing w .. 2Sa 19:35
took the ten w his concubines 2Sa 20:3
Then came there two w, that were 1Kin 3:16
king Solomon loved many strange w .. 1Kin 11:1
w of the Moabites, Ammonites, ... 1Kin 11:1
and rip up their w with child................ 2Kin 8:12
all the w therein that were with 2Kin 15:16
where the w wove hangings for the 2Kin 23:7
brethren two hundred thousand, w 2Chr 28:8
the singing w spake of Josiah in 2Chr 35:25
hundred singing men and singing w .. Ezr 2:65
great congregation of men and w ...... Ezr 10:1
and five singing men and singing w .. Neh 7:67
the congregation both of men and w .. Neh 8:2
midday, before the men and the w ...... Neh 8:3
him did outlandish w cause to sin........ Neh 13:26
the w in the royal house which .... Est 1:17
shall come abroad unto all w .... Est 1:17
the palace, to the house of the w .... Est 2:3

chamberlain, keeper of the w............ Est 2:3
custody of Hegai, keeper of the w.......... Est 2:8
best place of the house of the w............ Est 2:9
according to the manner of the w............ Est 2:12
things for the purifying of the w............ Est 2:12
of the w unto the king's house............ Est 2:13
into the second house of the w............ Est 2:14
chamberlain, the keeper of the w........... Est 2:15
king loved Esther above all the w........... Est 2:17
and old, little children and w........... Est 3:13
them, both little ones and w............ Est 8:11
as one of the foolish w speaketh .... Job 2:10
in all the land were no w found............ Job 42:15
were among thy honourable w .... Ps 45:9
mouth of strange w is a deep pit.......... Prov 22:14
Thine eyes shall behold strange w .... Prov 23:33
Give not thy strength unto w .... Prov 31:3
w singers, and the delights of the........... Eccl 2:8
know not, O thou fairest among w .... Song 1:8
beloved, O thou fairest among w .... Song 5:9
gone, O thou fairest among w .... Song 6:1
oppressors, and w rule over them .... Is 3:12
in that day seven w shall take .... Is 4:1
day shall Egypt be like unto w .... Is 19:16
the w come, and set them on fire........... Is 27:11
Rise up, ye w that are at ease........... Is 32:9
ye be troubled, ye careless w........... Is 32:10
Tremble, ye w that are at ease........... Is 32:11
the w knead their dough, to make........... Jer 7:18
ye, and call for the mourning w........... Jer 9:17
and send for cunning w, that they........... Jer 9:17
hear the word of the LORD, O ye w........... Jer 9:20
all the w that are left in the........... Jer 38:22
those w shall say, Thy friends........... Jer 38:22
had committed unto him men, and w........... Jer 40:7
even mighty men of war, and the w........... Jer 41:16
Even men, and w, and children, and........... Jer 43:6
all the w that stood by, a great........... Jer 44:15
people, to the men, and to the w........... Jer 44:20
all the people, and to all the w........... Jer 44:24
and they shall become as w........... Jer 50:37
they became as w........... Jer 51:30
Shall the w eat their fruit, and........... Lam 2:20
The hands of the pitiful w have........... Lam 4:10
They ravished the w in Zion........... Lam 5:11
there sat w weeping for Tammuz........... Eze 8:14
maids, and little children, and w........... Eze 9:6
Woe to the w that sew pillows to........... Eze 13:18
from other w in thy whoredoms........... Eze 16:34
as w that break wedlock and shed........... Eze 16:38
upon thee in the sight of many w........... Eze 16:41
Son of man, there were two w........... Eze 23:2
and she became famous among w........... Eze 23:10
and unto Aholibah, the lewd w........... Eze 23:44
the manner of w that shed blood........... Eze 23:45
that all w may be taught not to........... Eze 23:48
shall give him the daughter of w........... Dan 11:17
his fathers, nor the desire of w........... Dan 11:37
their w with child shall be........... Hos 13:16
up the w with child of Gilead........... Amos 1:13
The w of my people have ye cast........... Mic 2:9
people in the midst of thee are w........... Nah 3:13
and, behold, there came out two w........... Zec 5:9
old w dwell in the streets of........... Zec 8:4
houses rifled, and the w ravished........... Zec 14:2
Among them that are born of w........... Mt 11:11
about five thousand men, beside w........... Mt 14:21
were four thousand men, beside w........... Mt 15:38
Two w shall be grinding at the........... Mt 24:41
many w were there beholding afar........... Mt 27:55
angel answered and said unto the w........... Mt 28:5
There were also w looking on afar........... Mk 15:40
many other w which came up with........... Mk 15:41
blessed art thou among w........... Lk 1:28
and said, Blessed art thou among w........... Lk 1:42
Among those that are born of w........... Lk 7:28
And certain w, which had been........... Lk 8:2
Two w shall be grinding together........... Lk 17:35
great company of people, and of w........... Lk 23:27
the w that followed him from........... Lk 23:49
the w also, which came with him........... Lk 24:10
other w that were with them,........... Lk 24:10
certain w also of our company........... Lk 24:22
it even so as the w had said........... Lk 24:24
and supplication, with the w........... Acts 1:14
Lord, multitudes both of men and w........... Acts 5:14
w committed them to prison........... Acts 8:3
they were baptized, both men and w........... Acts 8:12
way, whether they were men or w........... Acts 9:2
up the devout and honourable w........... Acts 13:50
spake unto the w which resorted........... Acts 16:13
and of the chief w not a few........... Acts 17:4
of honourable w which were Greeks........... Acts 17:12
into prisons both men and w........... Acts 22:4
for even their w did change the........... Rom 1:26
Let your w keep silence in the........... 1Cor 14:34
for it is a shame for w to speak........... 1Cor 14:35
help those w which laboured with........... Phil 4:3
that w adorn themselves in modest........... 1Ti 2:9
But (which becometh w professing........... 1Ti 2:10
The elder w as mothers........... 1Ti 5:2
that the younger w marry, bear........... 1Ti 5:14
captive silly w laden with sins........... 2Ti 3:6
The aged w likewise, that they........... Titus 2:3
may teach the young w to be sober........... Titus 2:4
W received their dead raised to........... Heb 11:35
in the old time the holy w also........... 1Pet 3:5
And they had hair as the hair of w........... Rev 9:8
which were not defiled with w........... Rev 14:4

WOMEN'S

before the court of the w house........... Est 2:11

WOMENSERVANTS

and oxen, and menservants, and w........... Gen 20:14
flocks, and menservants, and w........... Gen 32:5
took his two wives, and his two w........... Gen 32:22

WON

Out of the spoils w in battles........... 1Chr 26:27
harder to be w than a strong city........... Prov 18:19
be w by the conversation of the........... 1Pet 3:1

WONDER

and giveth thee a sign or a w........... Deut 13:1
And the sign or the w come to pass........... Deut 13:2
upon thee for a sign and for a w........... Deut 28:46
the w that was done in the land........... 2Chr 32:31
I am as a w unto many........... Ps 71:7
upon Egypt and upon Ethiopia........... Is 20:3
Stay yourselves, and........... Is 29:9
even a marvellous work and a w........... Is 29:14
and the prophets shall........... Jer 4:9
and regard, and w marvellously........... Hab 1:5
and they were filled with w........... Acts 3:10
Behold, ye despisers, and w........... Acts 13:41
appeared a great w in heaven........... Rev 12:1
appeared another w in heaven........... Rev 12:3
that dwell on the earth shall........... Rev 17:8

WONDERED

w that there was no intercessor........... Is 59:16
I w that there was none to uphold........... Is 63:5
for they are men w at........... Zec 3:8
Insomuch that the multitude w........... Mt 15:31
themselves beyond measure, and w........... Mk 6:51
all they that heard it w at those........... Lk 2:18
w at the gracious words which........... Lk 4:22
And they being afraid w, saying........... Lk 8:25
But while they w every one at all........... Lk 9:43
and the people w........... Lk 11:14
yet believed not for joy, and w........... Lk 24:41
Moses saw it, he w at the sight........... Acts 7:31
he continued with Philip, and w........... Acts 8:13
all the world w after the beast........... Rev 13:3
I w with great admiration........... Rev 17:6

WONDERFUL

the LORD will make thy plagues w........... Deut 28:59
thy love to me was, passing the........... 2Sa 1:26
about to build shall be w great........... 2Chr 2:9
things too w for me, which I knew........... Job 42:3
are thy w works which thou hast........... Ps 40:5
his w works that he hath done........... Ps 78:4
for his w works to the children........... Ps 107:8
for his w works to the children........... Ps 107:15
for his w works to the children........... Ps 107:21
for his w works to the children........... Ps 107:31
He hath made his w works to be........... Ps 111:4
Thy testimonies are w........... Ps 119:129
Such knowledge is too w for me........... Ps 139:6
things which are too w for me........... Prov 30:18
and his name shall be called W........... Is 9:6
for thou hast done w things........... Is 25:1
which is w in counsel, and........... Is 28:29
A w and horrible thing is........... Jer 5:30
and in thy name done many w works........... Mt 7:22
scribes saw the w things that he........... Mt 21:15
in our tongues the w works of God........... Acts 2:11

WONDERFULLY

when he had wrought w among them........... 1Sa 6:6
for I am fearfully and made........... Ps 139:14
therefore she came down w........... Lam 1:9
and he shall destroy w, and shall........... Dan 8:24

WONDERING

the man w at her held his peace,........... Gen 24:21
w in himself at that which was........... Lk 24:12
is called Solomon's, greatly........... Acts 3:11

WONDEROUSLY

and the angel did w........... Judg 13:19

WONDERS

smite Egypt with all my w which I........... Ex 3:20
do all those w before Pharaoh........... Ex 4:21
my w in the land of Egypt........... Ex 7:3
that my w may be multiplied in........... Ex 11:9
did all these w before Pharaoh........... Ex 11:10
fearful in praises, doing w........... Ex 15:11
by temptations, by signs, and by w........... Deut 4:34
And the LORD shewed signs and w........... Deut 6:22
eyes saw, and the signs, and the w........... Deut 7:19
and with signs, and with w........... Deut 26:8
In all the signs and the w........... Deut 34:11
the LORD will do among you........... Josh 3:5
works that he hath done, his w........... 1Chr 16:12
w upon Pharaoh, and on all his........... Neh 9:10
thy w that thou didst among them........... Neh 9:17
yea, and w without number........... Job 9:10
I will remember thy w of old........... Ps 77:11
Thou art the God that doest w........... Ps 77:14
his w that he had shewed them........... Ps 78:11
his w in the field of Zoan........... Ps 78:43
Wilt thou shew w to the dead........... Ps 88:10
Shall thy w be known in the dark........... Ps 88:12
And the heavens shall praise thy w........... Ps 89:5
heathen, his w among all people........... Ps 96:3
his w, and the judgments of his........... Ps 105:5
them, and in the land of Ham........... Ps 105:27
understood not thy w in Egypt........... Ps 106:7
of the LORD, and his w in the deep........... Ps 107:24
w into the midst of thee, O Egypt........... Ps 135:9

To him who alone doeth great w........... Ps 136:4
for w in Israel from the LORD of........... Is 8:18
w in the land of Egypt, even unto........... Jer 32:20
of Egypt with signs, and with w........... Jer 32:21
w that the high God hath wrought........... Dan 4:2
and how mighty are his w........... Dan 4:3
w in heaven and in earth, who hath........... Dan 6:27
shall it be to the end of these w........... Dan 12:6
I will shew w in the heavens and........... Joel 2:30
and shall shew great signs and w........... Mt 24:24
rise, and shall shew signs and w........... Mk 13:22
him, Except ye see signs and w........... Jn 4:48
I will shew w in heaven above, and........... Acts 2:19
of God among you by miracles and w........... Acts 2:22
and many w and signs were done by........... Acts 2:43
w may be done by the name of thy........... Acts 4:30
w wrought among the people........... Acts 5:12
of faith and power, did great w........... Acts 6:8
out, after that he had shewed w........... Acts 7:36
w to be done by their hands........... Acts 14:3
w God had wrought among the........... Acts 15:12
Through mighty signs and w........... Rom 15:19
in all patience, in signs, and w........... 2Cor 12:12
all power and signs and lying w........... 2Th 2:9
witness, both with signs and w........... Heb 2:4
And he doeth great w, so that he........... Rev 13:13

WONDROUS

him, talk ye of all his w works........... 1Chr 16:9
and consider the w works of God........... Job 37:14
the w works of him which is........... Job 37:16
and tell of all thy w works........... Ps 26:7
have I declared thy w works........... Ps 71:17
Israel, who only doeth w things........... Ps 72:18
name is near thy w works declare........... Ps 75:1
and believed not for his w works........... Ps 78:32
thou art great, and doest w things........... Ps 86:10
talk ye of all his w works........... Ps 105:2
W works in the land of Ham, and........... Ps 106:22
that I may behold w things out of........... Ps 119:18
so shall I talk of thy w works........... Ps 119:27
of thy majesty, and of thy w works........... Ps 145:5
as according to all his w works........... Jer 21:2

WONDROUSLY

God, that hath dealt w with you........... Joel 2:26

WONT

But if the ox were w to push with........... Ex 21:29
was I ever w to do so unto thee........... Num 22:30
and his men were w to haunt........... 1Sa 30:31
They were w to speak in old time,........... 2Sa 20:18
more than it was w to be heated........... Dan 3:19
w to release unto the people a........... Mt 27:15
and, as he was w, he taught them........... Mk 10:1
he came out, and went, as he was w........... Lk 22:39
where prayer was w to be made........... Acts 16:13

WOOD

Make thee an ark of gopher w........... Gen 6:14
clave the w for the burnt........... Gen 22:3
Abraham took the w of the burnt........... Gen 22:6
he said, Behold the fire and the w........... Gen 22:7
there, and laid the w in order........... Gen 22:9
laid him on the altar upon the w........... Gen 22:9
of Egypt, both in vessels of w........... Ex 7:19
and badgers' skins, and shittim w........... Ex 25:5
shall make an ark of shittim w........... Ex 25:10
shalt make staves of shittim w........... Ex 25:13
also make a table of shittim w........... Ex 25:23
make the staves of shittim w........... Ex 25:28
of shittim w standing up........... Ex 26:15
thou shalt make bars of shittim w........... Ex 26:26
of shittim w overlaid with gold,........... Ex 26:32
hanging five pillars of shittim w........... Ex 26:37
shalt make an altar of shittim w........... Ex 27:1
the altar, staves of shittim w........... Ex 27:6
of shittim w shalt thou make it........... Ex 30:1
make the staves of shittim w........... Ex 30:5
and badgers' skins, and shittim w........... Ex 35:7
w for any work of the service........... Ex 35:24
to set them, and in carving of w........... Ex 35:33
for the tabernacle of shittim w........... Ex 36:20
And he made bars of shittim w........... Ex 36:31
four pillars of shittim w........... Ex 36:36
made the ark of shittim w........... Ex 37:1
And he made staves of shittim w........... Ex 37:4
And he made the table of shittim w........... Ex 37:10
he made the staves of shittim w........... Ex 37:15
the incense altar of shittim w........... Ex 37:25
he made the staves of shittim w........... Ex 37:28
of burnt offering of shittim w........... Ex 38:1
he made the staves of shittim w........... Ex 38:6
lay the w in order upon the fire........... Lev 1:7
in order upon the w that is on........... Lev 1:12
w that is on the fire which is........... Lev 1:12
upon the w that is upon the fire........... Lev 1:17
which is upon the w that is on........... Lev 3:5
and burn him on the w with fire........... Lev 4:12
shall burn w on it every morning........... Lev 6:12
whether it be any vessel of w........... Lev 11:32
birds alive and clean, and cedar w........... Lev 14:4
he shall take it, and the cedar w........... Lev 14:6
the house two birds, and cedar w........... Lev 14:49
And he shall take the cedar w........... Lev 14:51
living bird, and with the cedar w........... Lev 14:52
every vessel of w shall be rinsed........... Lev 15:12
lean, whether there be w therein........... Num 13:20
And the priest shall take cedar w........... Num 19:6
hair, and all things made of w........... Num 31:20
him with an hand weapon of w........... Num 35:18
gods, the work of men's hands, w........... Deut 4:28

mount, and make thee an ark of w........ Deut 10:1
And I made an ark of shittim w......... Deut 10:3
As when a man goeth into the w......... Deut 19:5
his neighbour to hew w................. Deut 19:5
shalt thou serve other gods, w......... Deut 28:36
thy fathers have known, even w......... Deut 28:64
from the hewer of thy w unto the....... Deut 29:11
abominations, and their idols, w....... Deut 29:17
but let them be hewers of w............ Josh 9:21
being bondmen, and hewers of w......... Josh 9:23
made them that hewers of w............. Josh 9:27
then get thee up to the w country...... Josh 17:15
for it is a w, and thou shalt cut...... Josh 17:18
a burnt sacrifice with the w of........ Judg 6:26
and they clave the w of the cart....... 1Sa 6:14
all they of the land came to a w....... 1Sa 14:25
the people were come into the w........ 1Sa 14:26
in the wilderness of Ziph in a w....... 1Sa 23:15
and went to David into the w........... 1Sa 23:16
and David abode in the w, and.......... 1Sa 23:18
with us in strong holds in the w....... 1Sa 23:19
of instruments made of fir w........... 2Sa 6:5
battle was in the w of Ephraim......... 2Sa 18:6
the w devoured more people that........ 2Sa 18:8
him into a great pit in the w.......... 2Sa 18:17
instruments of the oxen for w.......... 2Sa 24:22
covered them on the inside with w...... 1Kin 6:15
cut it in pieces, and lay it on w...... 1Kin 18:23
the other bullock, and lay it on w..... 1Kin 18:23
And he put the w in order, and cut..... 1Kin 18:33
in pieces, and laid him on the w....... 1Kin 18:33
the burnt sacrifice, and on the w...... 1Kin 18:33
the burnt sacrifice, and the w......... 1Kin 18:38
forth two she bears out of the w....... 2Kin 2:24
came to Jordan, they cut down w........ 2Kin 6:4
but the work of men's hands, w......... 2Kin 19:18
Then shall the trees of the w.......... 1Chr 16:33
the threshing instruments for w........ 1Chr 21:23
brought much cedar w to David.......... 1Chr 22:4
of iron, and w for things of........... 1Chr 29:2
we will cut w out of Lebanon, as....... 2Chr 2:16
scribe stood upon a pulpit of w........ Neh 8:4
for the w offering, to bring to........ Neh 10:34
for the w offering, at times........... Neh 13:31
as straw, and brass as rotten w........ Job 41:27
boar out of the w doth waste it........ Ps 80:13
As the fire burneth a w, and as........ Ps 83:14
all the trees of the w rejoice......... Ps 96:12
found it in the fields of the w........ Ps 132:6
cleaveth w upon the earth.............. Ps 141:7
Where no w is, there the fire.......... Prov 26:20
to burning coals, and w to fire........ Prov 26:21
to water therewith the w that.......... Eccl 2:6
he that cleaveth w shall be............ Eccl 10:9
tree among the trees of the w.......... Song 2:3
a chariot of the w of Lebanon.......... Song 3:9
as the trees of the w are moved........ Is 7:2
up itself, as if it were no w.......... Is 10:15
pile thereof is fire and much w........ Is 30:33
but the work of men's hands, w......... Is 37:19
up the w of their graven image......... Is 45:20
for w brass, and for stones iron....... Is 60:17
thy mouth fire, and this people w...... Jer 5:14
The children gather w, and the......... Jer 7:18
Thou hast broken the yokes of w........ Jer 28:13
her with axes, as hewers of w.......... Jer 46:22
our w is sold unto us.................. Lam 5:4
and the children fell under the w...... Lam 5:13
Shall w be taken thereof to............ Eze 15:3
of the countries, to serve w........... Eze 20:32
Heap on w, kindle the fire,............ Eze 24:10
shalt take no w out of the field....... Eze 39:10
door, cieled with w round about........ Eze 41:16
The altar of w was three cubits........ Eze 41:22
and the walls thereof, were of w....... Eze 41:22
silver, of brass, of iron, of w........ Dan 5:4
and gold, of brass, iron, w............ Dan 5:23
which dwell solitarily in the w........ Mic 7:14
Woe unto him that saith to the w....... Hab 2:19
Go up to the mountain, and bring w..... Hag 1:8
an hearth of fire among the w.......... Zec 12:6
gold, silver, precious stones, w....... 1Cor 3:12
gold and of silver, but also of w...... 2Ti 2:20
and brass, and stone, and of w......... Rev 9:20
silk, and scarlet, and all thyine w.... Rev 18:12
manner vessels of most precious w...... Rev 18:12

WOODS
the wilderness, and sleep in the w..... Eze 34:25

WOOF
Whether it be in the warp, or w........ Lev 13:48
either in the warp, or in the w........ Lev 13:49
either in the warp, or in the w........ Lev 13:51
that garment, whether warp or w........ Lev 13:52
either in the warp, or in the w........ Lev 13:53
out of the warp, or out of the w....... Lev 13:56
either in the warp, or of the w........ Lev 13:57
And the garment, either warp, or w..... Lev 13:58
linen, either in the warp, or w........ Lev 13:59

WOOL
put a fleece of w in the floor......... Judg 6:37
hundred thousand rams, with the w...... 2Kin 3:4
He giveth snow like w.................. Ps 147:16
She seeketh w, and flax, and........... Prov 31:13
like crimson, they shall be as w....... Is 1:18
and the worm shall eat them like w..... Is 51:8
in the wine of Helbon, and white w..... Eze 27:18
fat, and ye clothe you with the w...... Eze 34:3
no w shall come upon them, whiles...... Eze 44:17
hair of his head like the pure w....... Dan 7:9

my bread and my water, my w............ Hos 2:5
thereof, and will recover my w......... Hos 2:9
goats, with water, and scarlet w....... Heb 9:19
and his hairs were white like w........ Rev 1:14

WOOLLEN
is in, whether it be a w garment....... Lev 13:47
of linen, or of a...................... Lev 13:48
in w or in linen, or any thing of...... Lev 13:52
in a garment of w or linen............. Lev 13:59
of linen and w come upon thee.......... Lev 19:19
garment of divers sorts, as of w....... Deut 22:11

WORD See PREFACE.
unto the w which I command you......... Deut 4:2
but by every w that proceedeth......... Deut 8:3
But the w is very nigh unto thee....... Deut 30:14
the w of the LORD was precious in...... Ps 33:6
heed thereto according to thy w........ Ps 119:9
Thy w have I hid in mine heart......... Ps 119:11
Thy w is a lamp unto my feet, and...... Ps 119:105
For there is not a w in my tongue...... Ps 139:4
a w spoken in due season, how.......... Prov 15:23
A w fitly spoken is like apples........ Prov 25:11
Hear the w of the LORD................. Is 66:5
ye that tremble at his w............... Is 66:5
for every man's w shall be his......... Jer 23:36
the w that I shall speak shall......... Eze 12:25
house, will I say the w, and will...... Eze 12:25
dry bones, hear the w of the LORD...... Eze 37:4
but by every w that proceedeth......... Mt 4:4
cast out the spirits with his w........ Mt 8:16
That every idle w that men shall....... Mt 12:36
The sower soweth the w................. Mk 4:14
In the beginning was the W............. Jn 1:1
the W was with God..................... Jn 1:1
and the W was God...................... Jn 1:1
the W was made flesh, and dwelt........ Jn 1:14
the w which ye hear is not mine........ Jn 14:24
a which I have spoken unto you......... Jn 15:3
thy w is truth......................... Jn 17:17
they agate the w of God with........... Acts 4:31
and to the ministry of the w........... Acts 6:4
went every where preaching the w....... Acts 8:4
on all them which heard the w.......... Acts 10:44
But the w of God grew and.............. Acts 12:24
in that they received the w with....... Acts 17:11
The w is nigh thee, even in thy........ Rom 10:8
the kingdom of God is not in w......... 1Cor 4:20
our w toward you was not yea and....... 2Cor 1:18
all the law is fulfilled in one w...... Gal 5:14
the washing of water by the w.......... Eph 5:26
the Spirit, which is the w of God...... Eph 6:17
And whatsoever ye do in w or deed...... Col 3:17
it is sanctified by the w of God....... 1Ti 4:5
Preach the w........................... 2Ti 4:2
For the w of God is quick, and......... Heb 4:12
with meekness the engrafted w.......... Jas 1:21
But be ye doers of the w, and not...... Jas 1:22
desire the sincere milk of the w....... 1Pet 2:2
have handled, of the W of life......... 1Jn 1:1
children, let us not love in w......... 1Jn 3:18
by the w of their testimony............ Rev 12:11

WORD'S
For thy w sake, and according to....... 2Sa 7:21
arisen for thy w sake.................. Mk 4:17

WORDS See PREFACE.
And these w, which I command thee...... Deut 6:6
w that were in the first tables........ Deut 10:2
lay up these my w in your heart........ Deut 11:18
will put my w in his mouth............. Deut 18:18
These are the w of the covenant........ Deut 29:1
Let the w of my mouth, and the......... Ps 19:14
The w of a talebearer are as........... Prov 26:22
Add thou not unto his w, lest he....... Prov 30:6
The w of a wise man's mouth are........ Eccl 10:12
sought to find out acceptable w........ Eccl 12:10
was upright, even w of truth........... Eccl 12:10
Hear ye the w of this covenant,........ Jer 11:2
not the w of this covenant............. Jer 11:3
he shall speak great w against......... Dan 7:25
For by thy w thou shalt be............. Mt 12:37
by thy w thou shalt be condemned....... Mt 12:37
but my w shall not pass away........... Mt 24:35
but my w shall not pass away........... Mk 13:31
shall be ashamed of me and of my w..... Lk 9:26
And they remembered his w.............. Lk 24:8
thou hast the w of eternal life........ Jn 6:68
a man love me, he will keep my w....... Jn 14:23
the w which thou gavest me............. Jn 17:8
five w with my understanding........... 1Cor 14:19
comfort one another with these w....... 1Th 4:18
Hold fast the form of sound w.......... 2Ti 1:13
for these w are true and faithful...... Rev 21:5
w of the prophecy of this book......... Rev 22:18
w of the book of this prophecy......... Rev 22:19

WORK
God endued him w which he had made..... Gen 2:2
from all his w which he had made....... Gen 2:2
from all his w which God created....... Gen 2:3
shall comfort us concerning our w...... Gen 5:29
Let there more w be laid upon the...... Ex 5:9
of your w shall be diminished.......... Ex 5:11
Go therefore now, and w................ Ex 5:18
no manner of w shall be done in........ Ex 12:16
Israel saw that great w which the...... Ex 14:31
walk, and the w that they must do...... Ex 18:20
thou labour, and do all thy w.......... Ex 20:9

in it thou shalt not do any w.......... Ex 20:10
Six days thou shalt do thy w........... Ex 23:12
a paved w of a sapphire stone.......... Ex 24:10
of beaten w shalt thou make them,...... Ex 25:18
of beaten w shall the candlestick...... Ex 25:31
be one beaten w of pure gold........... Ex 25:36
of cunning w shalt thou make them...... Ex 26:1
and fine twined linen of cunning w..... Ex 26:31
fine twined linen, with cunning w...... Ex 28:6
same, according to the w thereof....... Ex 28:8
With the w of an engraver in........... Ex 28:11
of wreathen w shalt thou make.......... Ex 28:14
of judgment with cunning w............. Ex 28:15
after the w of the ephod thou.......... Ex 28:15
ends of wreathen w of pure gold........ Ex 28:22
w round about the hole of it........... Ex 28:32
to w in gold, and in silver, and in.... Ex 31:4
to w in all manner of workmanship...... Ex 31:5
for whosoever doeth any w therein...... Ex 31:14
Six days may w be done................. Ex 31:15
doeth any w in the sabbath day......... Ex 31:15
And the tables were the w of God....... Ex 32:16
art shall see the w of the LORD........ Ex 34:10
Six days thou shalt w, but on the...... Ex 34:21
Six days shall w be done, but on....... Ex 35:2
whosoever doeth w therein shall........ Ex 35:2
to the w of the tabernacle of the...... Ex 35:21
wood for any w of the service.......... Ex 35:24
to bring for all manner of............. Ex 35:29
to w in gold, and in silver, and in.... Ex 35:32
to make any manner of cunning w........ Ex 35:33
to w all manner of..................... Ex 35:35
all manner of w........................ Ex 35:35
even of them that do any w............. Ex 35:35
and of those that devise cunning w..... Ex 35:35
to w all manner of..................... Ex 36:1
of w for the service of the............ Ex 36:1
up to come unto the w to do it......... Ex 36:2
of Israel had brought for the w........ Ex 36:3
all the w of the sanctuary............. Ex 36:4
man from his w therefore they made..... Ex 36:4
enough for the service of the w........ Ex 36:5
more w for the offering of the......... Ex 36:6
for all the w to make it, and too...... Ex 36:7
the w of the tabernacle made ten....... Ex 36:8
of cunning w made he them.............. Ex 36:8
cherubims made he it of cunning w...... Ex 36:35
of beaten w made he the................ Ex 37:17
it was one beaten w of pure gold....... Ex 37:22
according to the w of the.............. Ex 37:29
the w in all the w of the holy......... Ex 38:24
to w it in the blue, and in the........ Ex 39:3
in the fine linen, with cunning w...... Ex 39:3
same, according to the w thereof....... Ex 39:5
made the breastplate of cunning w...... Ex 39:8
like the w of the ephod................ Ex 39:8
of wreathen w of pure gold............. Ex 39:15
the robe of the ephod of woven w....... Ex 39:22
fine linen of woven w for Aaron........ Ex 39:27
Thus was all the w of the.............. Ex 39:32
children of Israel made all the w...... Ex 39:42
And Moses did look upon all the w...... Ex 39:43
So Moses finished the w................ Ex 40:33
it be, wherein any w is done........... Lev 11:32
or in any w that is made of skin....... Lev 13:51
do no w at all, whether it be one...... Lev 16:29
Six days shall w be done............... Lev 23:3
ye shall do no w therein............... Lev 23:3
ye shall do no servile w therein....... Lev 23:7
ye shall do no servile w therein....... Lev 23:8
ye shall do no servile w therein....... Lev 23:21
Ye shall do no servile w therein....... Lev 23:25
ye shall do no w in that same day...... Lev 23:28
that doeth any w in that same day...... Lev 23:30
Ye shall do no manner of w............. Lev 23:31
ye shall do no servile w therein....... Lev 23:35
ye shall do no servile w therein....... Lev 23:36
to do the w in the tabernacle of....... Num 4:3
to do the w in the tabernacle of....... Num 4:23
to do the w of the tabernacle of....... Num 4:30
for the w in the tabernacle of......... Num 4:35
for the w in the tabernacle of......... Num 4:39
for the w in the tabernacle of......... Num 4:43
this w of the candlestick was of....... Num 8:4
the flowers thereof, was beaten w...... Num 8:4
do no manner of servile w therein...... Num 28:18
ye shall do no servile w............... Num 28:25
ye shall do no servile w............... Num 28:26
ye shall do no servile w............... Num 29:1
ye shall do no servile w............... Num 29:7
ye shall do no w therein............... Num 29:12
ye shall do no servile w and ye........ Num 29:12
ye shall do no servile w therein....... Num 29:35
all w of goats' hair, and all.......... Num 31:20
the w of men's hands, wood and......... Deut 4:28
shalt labour, and do all thy w......... Deut 5:13
in it thou shalt not do any w.......... Deut 5:14
God may bless thee in all the w........ Deut 14:29
thou shalt do no w therein............. Deut 15:19
thou shalt do no w therein............. Deut 16:8
thee in all the w of thine hands....... Deut 24:19
the w of the hands of the.............. Deut 27:15
bless thee in all the w of thine....... Deut 28:12
in every w of thine hand, in the...... Deut 30:9
anger through the w of your hands...... Deut 31:29
He is the Rock, his w is perfect....... Deut 32:4
accept the w of his hands.............. Deut 33:11
They did w wilily, and went and........ Josh 9:4
his w out of the field at even......... Judg 19:16
The LORD recompense thy w.............. Ruth 2:12
your asses, and put them to his w...... 1Sa 8:16

be that the LORD will w for us 1Sa 14:6
officers which were over the w 1Kin 5:16
the people that wrought in the w 1Kin 5:16
gold fitted upon the carved w 1Kin 6:35
porch, which was of the like w 1Kin 7:8
cunning to w all works in brass 1Kin 7:14
Solomon, and wrought all his w 1Kin 7:14
And nets of checker w 1Kin 7:17
and wreaths of chain w 1Kin 7:17
were of lily w in the porch 1Kin 7:19
the top of the pillars was lily w 1Kin 7:22
so was the w of the pillars 1Kin 7:22
the w of the bases was on this 1Kin 7:28
certain additions made of thin w 1Kin 7:29
was round after the w of the base 1Kin 7:31
the w of the wheels was like the 1Kin 7:33
was like the w of a chariot wheel 1Kin 7:33
made an end of doing all the w 1Kin 7:40
So was ended all the w that king 1Kin 7:51
that were over Solomon's w 1Kin 9:23
the people that wrought in the w 1Kin 9:23
to anger with the w of his hands 1Kin 16:7
thou hast sold thyself to w evil 1Kin 21:20
which did sell himself to w 1Kin 21:25
the hands of them that did the w 2Kin 12:11
but the w of men's hands, wood and 2Kin 19:18
the hand of the doers of the w 2Kin 22:5
give it to the doers of the w 2Kin 22:5
the hand of them that do the w 2Kin 22:9
and the wreathen w, and 2Kin 25:17
the second pillar with wreathen w 2Kin 25:17
dwelt with the king for his w 1Chr 4:23
all the w of the place most holy 1Chr 6:49
very able men for the w of the 1Chr 9:13
were over the w of the service 1Chr 9:19
they were employed in that w day 1Chr 9:33
as every day's w required 1Chr 16:37
cunning men for every manner of w 1Chr 22:15
were to set forward the w of the 1Chr 23:4
that did the w for the service of 1Chr 23:24
the w of the service of the house 1Chr 23:28
over them that did the w of the 1Chr 27:26
for all the w of the service of 1Chr 28:13
thou hast finished all the w for 1Chr 28:20
and tender, and the w is great 1Chr 29:1
for all manner of w to be made by 1Chr 29:5
with the rulers of the king's w 1Chr 29:6
a man cunning to w in gold 2Chr 2:7
man of Tyre, skilful to w in gold 2Chr 2:14
overseers to set the people a w 2Chr 2:18
he made two cherubims of image w 2Chr 3:10
like the w of the brim of a cup 2Chr 4:5
Huram finished the w that he was 2Chr 4:11
Thus all the w that Solomon made 2Chr 5:1
make no servants for his w 2Chr 8:9
Now all the w of Solomon was 2Chr 8:16
for your w shall be rewarded 2Chr 15:7
of Ramah, and let his w cease 2Chr 16:5
gave it to such as did the w of 2Chr 24:12
the w was perfected by them, and 2Chr 24:13
till the w was ended, and until 2Chr 29:34
in every w that he began in the 2Chr 31:21
which were the w of the hands of 2Chr 32:19
And the men did the w faithfully 2Chr 34:12
of all that wrought the w in any 2Chr 34:13
the treasure of the w therefore .... Ezr 2:69
to set forward the w of the house .... Ezr 3:8
Then ceased the w of the house of .... Ezr 4:24
and this w goeth fast on, and .... Ezr 5:8
Let the w of this house of God .... Ezr 6:7
in the w of the house of God .... Ezr 6:22
is this a w of one day or two .... Ezr 10:13
nor to the rest that did the w .... Neh 3:5
their hands for this good w .... Neh 2:18
necks to the w of their Lord .... Neh 3:5
for the people had a mind to w .... Neh 4:6
them, and cause the w to cease .... Neh 4:11
to the wall, every one unto his w .... Neh 4:15
of my servants wrought in the w .... Neh 4:16
one of his hands wrought in the w .... Neh 4:17
The w is great and large, and we .... Neh 4:19
So we laboured in the w .... Neh 4:21
I continued in the w of this wall .... Neh 5:16
were gathered thither unto the w .... Neh 5:16
saying, I am doing a great w .... Neh 6:3
why should the w cease, whilst I .... Neh 6:3
shall be weakened from the w .... Neh 6:9
this w was wrought of our God .... Neh 6:16
of the fathers gave unto the w .... Neh 7:70
gave to the treasure of the w .... Neh 7:71
for all the w of the house of our .... Neh 10:33
their brethren that did the w of .... Neh 11:12
and the singers, that did the w .... Neh 13:10
hast blessed the w of his hands .... Job 1:10
looketh for the reward of his w .... Job 7:2
despise the w of thine hands .... Job 10:3
a desire to the w of thine hands .... Job 14:15
On the left hand, where he doth w .... Job 23:9
desert, go they forth to their w .... Job 24:5
For the w of a man shall he .... Job 34:11
they all are the w of his hands .... Job 34:19
Then he sheweth them their w .... Job 36:9
Remember that thou magnify his w .... Job 36:24
that all men may know his w .... Job 37:7
the w of thy fingers, the moon and .... Ps 8:3
snared in the w of his own hands .... Ps 9:16
them after the w of their hands .... Ps 28:4
what w thou didst in their days .... Ps 44:1
Yea, in heart y w wickedness .... Ps 58:2
to every man according to his w .... Ps 62:12

and shall declare the w of God .... Ps 64:9
w thereof at once with axes .... Ps 74:6
I will meditate also of all thy w .... Ps 77:12
Let thy w appear unto thy .... Ps 90:16
establish thou the w of our hands .... Ps 90:17
the w of our hands establish thou .... Ps 90:17
hast made me glad through thy w .... Ps 92:4
me, proved me, and saw my w .... Ps 95:9
I hate the w of them that turn .... Ps 101:3
heavens are the w of thy hands .... Ps 102:25
Man goeth forth unto his w .... Ps 104:23
His w is honourable and glorious .... Ps 111:3
and gold, the w of men's hands .... Ps 115:4
It is time for thee, LORD, to w .... Ps 119:126
and gold, the w of men's hands .... Ps 135:15
works with men that w iniquity .... Ps 141:4
I muse on the w of thy hands .... Ps 143:5
The wicked worketh a deceitful w .... Prov 11:18
the weights of the bag are his w .... Prov 16:11
his w is brother to him that is a .... Prov 18:9
his doings, whether his w be pure .... Prov 20:11
as for the pure, his w is right .... Prov 21:8
Prepare thy w without, and make it .... Prov 24:27
to the man according to his w .... Prov 24:29
because the w that is wrought .... Eccl 2:17
the w that God maketh from the .... Eccl 3:11
for every purpose and for every w .... Eccl 3:17
evil w that is done under the sun .... Eccl 4:3
all travail, and every right w .... Eccl 4:4
destroy the w of thine hands .... Eccl 5:6
Consider the w of God .... Eccl 7:13
w that is done under the sun .... Eccl 8:9
evil w is not executed speedily .... Eccl 8:11
according to the w of the wicked .... Eccl 8:14
to the w of the righteous .... Eccl 8:14
Then I beheld all the w of God .... Eccl 8:17
the w that is done under the sun .... Eccl 8:17
for there is no w, nor devices .... Eccl 9:10
shall bring every w into judgment .... Eccl 12:14
the w of the hands of a cunning .... Song 7:1
they worship the w of their own .... Is 2:8
they regard not the w of the Lord .... Is 5:12
him make speed, and hasten his w .... Is 5:19
his whole w upon mount Zion .... Is 10:12
the w of his hands, neither shall .... Is 17:8
Moreover they that w the fine flax .... Is 19:9
Egypt to err in every w thereof .... Is 19:14
shall there be any w for Egypt .... Is 19:15
and Assyria the w of my hands .... Is 19:25
he may do his w, his strange w .... Is 28:21
a marvellous w among this people .... Is 29:14
this people, even a marvellous w .... Is 29:14
for shall the w say of him that .... Is 29:16
the w of mine hands, in the midst .... Is 29:23
the help of them that w iniquity .... Is 31:2
and his heart will w iniquity .... Is 32:6
the w of righteousness shall be .... Is 32:17
but the w of men's hands, wood and .... Is 37:19
is with him, and his w before him .... Is 40:10
of nothing, and your w of nought .... Is 41:24
I will w, and who shall let it .... Is 43:13
or thy w, He hath no hands .... Is 45:9
concerning the w of my hands .... Is 45:11
the LORD, and my w with my God .... Is 49:4
forth an instrument for his w .... Is 54:16
the w of my hands, that I may be .... Is 60:21
and I will direct their w in truth .... Is 61:8
is with him, and his w before him .... Is 62:11
and we all are the w of thy hand .... Is 64:8
their former w into their bosom .... Is 65:7
long enjoy the w of their hands .... Is 65:22
the w of the hands of the workman .... Jer 10:3
the w of the workman, and of the .... Jer 10:9
they are all the w of cunning men .... Jer 10:9
are vanity, and the w of errors .... Jer 10:15
sabbath day, neither do ye any w .... Jer 17:22
sabbath day, to do no w therein .... Jer 17:24
he wrought a w on the wheels .... Jer 18:3
and giveth him not for his w .... Jer 22:13
for thy w shall be rewarded .... Jer 31:16
Great in counsel, and mighty in w .... Jer 32:19
anger with the w of their hands .... Jer 32:30
the w of the LORD deceitfully .... Jer 48:10
for this is the w of the Lord GOD .... Jer 50:25
recompense her according to her w .... Jer 50:29
in Zion the w of the LORD our God .... Jer 51:10
They are vanity, the w of errors .... Jer 51:18
according to the w of their hands .... Lam 3:64
the w of the hands of the potter .... Lam 4:2
their w was like unto the colour .... Eze 1:16
their w was as it were a wheel in .... Eze 1:16
wood be taken thereof to do any w .... Eze 15:3
Is it meet for any w .... Eze 15:4
was whole, it was meet for no w .... Eze 15:5
shall it be meet yet for any w .... Eze 15:5
thee also with broidered w .... Eze 16:10
linen, and silk, and broidered w .... Eze 16:13
the w of an imperious whorish .... Eze 16:30
Fine linen with broidered w from .... Eze 27:7
emeralds, purple, and broidered w .... Eze 27:16
in blue clothes, and broidered w .... Eze 27:24
ye w abomination, and ye defile .... Eze 33:26
with him he shall w deceitfully .... Dan 11:23
is a city of them that w iniquity .... Hos 6:8
all of it the w of the craftsmen .... Hos 13:2
any more to the w of our hands .... Hos 14:3
and w evil upon their beds .... Mic 2:1
more worship the w of thine hands .... Mic 5:13
For I will w a .... Hab 1:5
a w in your days .... Hab 1:5

maker of his w trusteth therein .... Hab 2:18
revive thy w in the midst of the .... Hab 3:2
for he shall uncover the cedar w .... Zeph 2:14
did w in the house of the LORD of .... Hag 1:14
of the land, saith the LORD, and .... Hag 2:4
so is every w of their hands .... Hag 2:14
they that w wickedness are set up .... Mal 3:15
from me, ye that w iniquity .... Mt 7:23
go w to day in my vineyard .... Mt 21:28
she hath wrought a good w upon me .... Mt 26:10
And he could there do no mighty w .... Mk 6:5
servants, and to every man his w .... Mk 13:34
she hath wrought a good w on me .... Mk 14:6
six days in which men ought to w .... Lk 13:14
that sent me, and to finish his w .... Jn 4:34
Father worketh hitherto, and I w .... Jn 5:17
that we might w the works of God .... Jn 6:28
unto them, This is the w of God .... Jn 6:29
what dost thou w .... Jn 6:30
said unto them, I have done one w .... Jn 7:21
I must w the works of him that .... Jn 9:4
night cometh, when no man can w .... Jn 9:4
For a good w we stone thee not .... Jn 10:33
I have finished the w which thou .... Jn 17:4
this counsel or this w be of men .... Acts 5:38
Saul for the w whereunto I have .... Acts 13:2
for I w a .... Acts 13:41
a w in your days .... Acts 13:41
a w which ye shall in no wise .... Acts 13:41
for the w which they fulfilled .... Acts 14:26
and went not with them to the w .... Acts 15:38
we had much w to come by the boat .... Acts 27:16
Which shew the w of the law .... Rom 2:15
did w in our members to bring .... Rom 7:5
we know that all things w .... Rom 8:28
For he will finish the w, and cut .... Rom 9:28
because a short w will the Lord .... Rom 9:28
otherwise w is no more w .... Rom 11:6
For meat destroy not the w of God .... Rom 14:20
Every man's w shall be made 1Cor 3:13
every man's w of what sort it is 1Cor 3:13
If any man's w abide which he 1Cor 3:14
If any man's w shall be burned 1Cor 3:15
are not ye my w in the Lord 1Cor 9:1
abounding in the w of the Lord 1Cor 15:58
for he worketh the w of the Lord 1Cor 16:10
may abound to every good w 2Cor 9:8
But let every man prove his own w .... Gal 6:4
for the w of the ministry, for .... Eph 4:12
to w all uncleanness with .... Eph 4:19
w in you will perform it until .... Phil 1:6
w out your own salvation with .... Phil 2:12
Because for the w of Christ he .... Phil 2:30
being fruitful in every good w .... Col 1:10
without ceasing your w of faith 1Th 1:3
to w with your own hands, as we 1Th 4:11
the w of faith with power 2Th 1:11
of iniquity doth already w 2Th 2:7
you in every good word and w 2Th 2:17
you, that if any would not w 2Th 3:10
that with quietness they w 2Th 3:12
of a bishop, he desireth a good w 1Ti 3:1
diligently followed every good w 1Ti 5:10
and prepared unto every good w 2Ti 2:21
do the w of an evangelist, make 2Ti 4:5
deliver me from every evil w 2Ti 4:18
and unto every good w reprobate .... Titus 1:16
to be ready to every good w .... Titus 3:1
not unrighteous to forget your w .... Heb 6:10
in every good w to do his will .... Heb 13:21
let patience have her perfect w .... Jas 1:4
hearer, but a doer of the w .... Jas 1:25
is confusion and every evil w .... Jas 3:16
according to every man's w 1Pet 1:17
man according as his w shall be .... Rev 22:12

WORKER

was a man of Tyre, a w in brass 1Kin 7:14

WORKERS

Moreover the w with familiar 2Kin 23:24
w of stone and timber, and all 1Chr 22:15
punishment to the w of iniquity .... Job 31:3
in company with the w of iniquity .... Job 34:8
where the w of iniquity may hide .... Job 34:22
thou hatest all w of iniquity .... Ps 5:5
from me, all ye w of iniquity .... Ps 6:8
Have all the w of iniquity no .... Ps 14:4
with the w of iniquity, which .... Ps 28:3
There are the w of iniquity .... Ps 36:12
envious against the w of iniquity .... Ps 37:1
Have the w of iniquity no .... Ps 53:4
Deliver me from the w of iniquity .... Ps 59:2
insurrection of the w of iniquity .... Ps 64:2
when all the w of iniquity do .... Ps 92:7
all the w of iniquity boast .... Ps 92:9
all the w of iniquity boast .... Ps 94:4
for me against the w of iniquity .... Ps 94:16
them forth with the w of iniquity .... Ps 125:5
and the gins of the w of iniquity .... Ps 141:9
shall to the w of iniquity .... Prov 10:29
shall be to the w of iniquity .... Prov 21:15
from me, all ye w of iniquity .... Lk 13:27
for they are w of iniquity 1Cor 13:29
as w together with him, beseech 2Cor 6:1
are false apostles, deceitful w 2Cor 11:13
Beware of dogs, beware of evil w .... Phil 3:2
fellow w unto the kingdom of God .... Col 4:11

WORKETH

all these things w God oftentimes .... Job 33:29
w righteousness, and speaketh the .... Ps 15:2

He that w deceit shall not dwell......Ps 101:7
The wicked w a deceitful work......Prov 11:18
and a flattering mouth w ruin......Prov 26:28
w willingly with her hands......Prov 31:13
What profit hath he that w in......Eccl 3:9
the tongs both w in the coals......Is 44:12
w it with the strength of his......Is 44:12
w righteousness, those that......Is 64:5
he w signs and wonders in heaven......Dan 6:27
them, My Father w hitherto......Jn 5:17
w righteousness, is accepted with......Acts 10:35
peace, to every man that w good......Rom 2:10
Now to him that w is the reward......Rom 4:4
But to him that w not, but......Rom 4:5
Because the law w wrath......Rom 4:15
that tribulation w patience......Rom 5:3
Love w no ill to his neighbour......Rom 13:10
the same God which w all in all......1Cor 12:6
But all these w that one and the......1Cor 12:11
for he w the work of the Lord, as......1Cor 16:10
So then death w in us, but life......2Cor 4:12
w for us a far more exceeding and......2Cor 4:17
For godly sorrow w repentance to......2Cor 7:10
the sorrow of the world w death......2Cor 7:10
w miracles among you, doeth he it......Gal 3:5
but faith which w by love......Gal 5:6
to the purpose of him who w all......Eph 1:11
the spirit that now w in the......Eph 2:2
to the power that w in us......Eph 3:20
God which w in you both to will......Phil 2:13
working, which w in me mightily......Col 1:29
which effectually w also in you......1Th 2:13
trying of your faith w patience......Jas 1:3
For the wrath of man w not the......Jas 1:20
neither whatsoever w abomination......Rev 21:27

WORKFELLOW
Timotheus my w, and Lucius, and......Rom 16:21

WORKING
like a sharp razor, w deceitfully......Ps 52:2
w salvation in the midst of the......Ps 74:12
in counsel, and excellent in w......Is 28:29
east shall be shut the six w days......Eze 46:1
where, the Lord w with them, and......Mk 16:20
men with men w that which is......Rom 1:27
w death in me by that which is......Rom 7:13
And labour, w with our own hands......1Cor 4:12
have not we power to forbear w......1Cor 9:6
To another the w of miracles......1Cor 12:10
according to the w of his mighty......Eph 1:19
by the effectual w of his power......Eph 3:7
according to the effectual w in......Eph 4:16
w with his hands the thing which......Eph 4:28
according to the w whereby he is......Phil 3:21
striving according to his w......Col 1:29
the w of Satan with all power......2Th 2:9
w not at all, but are busybodies......2Th 3:11
his will, w in you that which is......Heb 13:21
w miracles, which go forth unto......Rev 16:14

WORKMAN
the engraver, and of the cunning w......Ex 35:35
Dan, an engraver, and a cunning w......Ex 38:23
work of the hands of a cunning w......Song 7:1
The w melteth a graven image, and......Is 40:19
w to prepare a graven image......Is 40:20
the work of the hands of the w......Jer 10:3
from Uphaz, the work of the w......Jer 10:9
the w made it......Hos 8:6
for the w is worthy of his meat......Mt 10:10
a w that needeth not to be......2Ti 2:15

WORKMANSHIP
knowledge, and in all manner of w......Ex 31:3
to work in all manner of w......Ex 31:5
knowledge, and in all manner of w......Ex 35:31
according to all the w thereof......2Kin 16:10
of w every willing skilful man......1Chr 28:21
the w of thy tablets and of thy......Eze 28:13
For we are his w, created in......Eph 2:10

WORKMEN
But they gave that to the w......2Kin 12:14
the money to be bestowed on w......2Kin 12:15
Moreover there are w with thee in......1Chr 22:15
the number of the w according to......1Chr 25:1
w wrought, and the work......2Chr 24:13
w that had the oversight of the......2Chr 34:10
they gave it to the w that......2Chr 34:10
and to the hand of the w......2Chr 34:17
to set forward the w in the house......Ezr 3:9
and the w, they are of men......Is 44:11
with the w of like occupation......Acts 19:25

WORKMEN'S
and her right hand to the w hammer......Judg 5:26

WORK'S
highly in love for their w sake......1Th 5:13

WORKS
let the people from their w......Ex 5:4
them, saying, Fulfil your w......Ex 5:13
serve them, nor do after their w......Ex 23:24
To devise cunning w, to work in......Ex 31:4
And to devise curious w, to work......Ex 35:32
hath sent me to do all these w......Num 16:28
thee in all the w of thy hand......Deut 2:7
that can do according to thy w......Deut 3:24
God shall bless thee in all thy w......Deut 15:10
in all the w of thine hands......Deut 16:15
had known all the w of the Lord......Josh 24:31
seen all the great w of the Lord......Judg 2:7

nor yet the w which he had done......Judg 2:10
According to all the w which they......1Kin 8:8
because his w have been to......1Sa 19:4
and cunning to work all w in brass......1Kin 7:14
told him all the w that the man......1Kin 13:11
with all the w of their hands......2Kin 22:17
talk ye of all his wondrous w......1Chr 16:9
marvellous w that he hath done......1Chr 16:12
his marvellous w among all......1Chr 16:24
even all the w of this pattern......1Chr 28:19
the Lord hath broken thy w......2Chr 20:37
Hezekiah prospered in all his w......2Chr 32:30
with all the w of their hands......2Chr 34:25
according to these their w......Neh 6:14
turned they from their wicked w......Neh 9:35
Therefore he knoweth their w......Job 34:25
and consider the wondrous w of God......Job 37:14
the wondrous w of him which is......Job 37:16
dominion over the w of thy hands......Ps 8:6
shew forth all thy marvellous w......Ps 9:1
they have done abominable w......Ps 14:1
and tell of all thy wondrous w......Ps 26:7
they regard not the w of the Lord......Ps 28:5
all his w are done in truth......Ps 33:4
he considereth all their w......Ps 33:15
are thy wonderful w which thou......Ps 40:5
behold the w of the Lord, what......Ps 46:8
How terrible art thou in thy w......Ps 66:3
Come and see the w of God......Ps 66:5
have I declared thy wondrous w......Ps 71:17
God, that I may declare all thy w......Ps 73:28
is near thy wondrous w declare......Ps 75:1
I will remember the w of the Lord......Ps 77:11
his wonderful w that he hath done......Ps 78:4
God, and not forget the w of God......Ps 78:7
And forgat his w, and his wonders......Ps 78:11
believed not for his wondrous w......Ps 78:32
there any w like unto thy w......Ps 86:8
triumph in the w of thy hands......Ps 92:4
O Lord, how great are thy w......Ps 92:5
all his w in all places of his......Ps 103:22
satisfied with the fruit of thy w......Ps 104:13
O Lord, how manifold are thy w......Ps 104:24
the Lord shall rejoice in his w......Ps 104:31
talk ye of all his wondrous w......Ps 105:2
marvellous w that he hath done......Ps 105:5
They soon forgat his w......Ps 106:13
Wondrous w in the land of Ham, and......Ps 106:22
the heathen, and learned their w......Ps 106:35
they defiled with their own w......Ps 106:39
for his wonderful w to the......Ps 107:8
for his wonderful w to the......Ps 107:15
for his wonderful w to the......Ps 107:21
declare his w with rejoicing......Ps 107:22
These see the w of the Lord......Ps 107:24
for his wonderful w to the......Ps 107:31
The w of the Lord are great......Ps 111:2
his wonderful w to be remembered......Ps 111:4
his people the power of his w......Ps 111:6
The w of his hands are verity and......Ps 111:7
and declare the w of the Lord......Ps 118:17
so shall I talk of thy wondrous w......Ps 119:27
forsake not the w of thine own......Ps 138:8
marvellous are thy w......Ps 139:14
to practise wicked w with men......Ps 141:4
I meditate on all thy w......Ps 143:5
shall praise thy w to another......Ps 145:4
thy majesty, and of thy wondrous w......Ps 145:5
tender mercies are over all his w......Ps 145:9
All thy w shall praise thee, O......Ps 145:10
his ways, and holy in all his w......Ps 145:17
of tapestry, with carved w......Prov 7:16
of his way, before his w of old......Prov 8:22
Commit thy w unto the Lord, and......Prov 16:3
to every man according to his w......Prov 24:12
let her own w praise her in the......Prov 31:31
I have seen all the w that are......Eccl 1:14
I made me great w......Eccl 2:4
Then I looked on all the w that......Eccl 2:11
a man should rejoice in his own w......Eccl 3:22
and the wise, and their w, are in......Eccl 9:1
for God now accepteth thy w......Eccl 9:7
not the w of God who maketh all......Eccl 11:5
also hast wrought all our w in us......Is 26:12
their w are in the dark, and they......Is 29:15
w there are nothing......Is 41:24
thy righteousness, and thy w......Is 57:12
cover themselves with their w......Is 59:6
their w are w of iniquity......Is 59:6
For I know their w and their......Is 66:18
worshipped the w of their own......Jer 1:16
because ye have done all these w......Jer 7:13
according to all his wondrous w......Jer 21:2
to anger with the w of your hands......Jer 25:6
provoke me to anger with the w of......Jer 25:7
according to the w of their own......Jer 25:14
wrath with the w of your hands......Jer 44:8
thou hast trusted in thy w......Jer 48:7
down, and your w may be abolished......Eze 6:6
of heaven, all whose w are truth......Dan 4:37
in all his w which he doeth......Dan 9:14
will never forget any of their w......Amos 8:7
And God saw their w, that they......Jon 3:10
all the w of the house of Ahab......Mic 6:16
that they may see your good w......Mt 5:16
in thy name done many wonderful w......Mt 7:22
in the prison the w of Christ......Mt 11:2
most of his mighty w were done......Mt 11:20
for if the mighty, which were......Mt 11:21
for if the mighty, which have......Mt 11:23

this wisdom, and these mighty w......Mt 13:54
he did not many mighty w there......Mt 13:58
therefore mighty w do shew forth......Mt 14:2
every man according to his w......Mt 16:27
but do not ye after their w......Mt 23:3
But all their w they do for to be......Mt 23:5
that even such mighty w are......Mk 6:2
therefore mighty w do shew forth......Mk 6:14
for if the mighty w had been done......Lk 10:13
the mighty w that they had seen......Lk 19:37
shew him greater w than these......Jn 5:20
for the w which the Father hath......Jn 5:36
the same w that I do, bear......Jn 5:36
that we might work the w of God......Jn 6:28
may see the w that thou doest......Jn 7:3
that the w thereof are evil......Jn 7:7
ye would do the w of Abraham......Jn 8:39
but that the w of God should be......Jn 9:3
I must work the w of him that......Jn 9:4
the w that I do in my Father's......Jn 10:25
Many good w have I shewed you......Jn 10:32
which of those w do ye stone me......Jn 10:32
If I do not the w of my Father......Jn 10:37
ye believe not me, believe the w......Jn 10:38
dwelleth in me, he doeth the w......Jn 14:10
the w that I do shall he do also......Jn 14:12
greater w than these shall he do......Jn 14:12
the w which none other man did......Jn 15:24
tongues the wonderful w of God......Acts 2:11
rejoiced in the w of their own......Acts 7:41
this woman was full of good w......Acts 9:36
Known unto God are all his w from......Acts 15:18
God, and do w meet for repentance......Acts 26:20
what law? of w?......Rom 3:27
if Abraham were justified by w......Rom 4:2
imputeth righteousness without w......Rom 4:6
to election might stand, not of w......Rom 9:11
as it were by the w of the law......Rom 9:32
by grace, then is it no more of w......Rom 11:6
But if it be of w, then is it no......Rom 11:6
rulers are not a terror to good w......Rom 13:3
cast off the w of darkness......Rom 13:12
end shall be according to their w......2Cor 11:15
not justified by the w of the law......Gal 2:16
and not by the w of the law......Gal 2:16
for by the w of the law shall no......Gal 2:16
ye the Spirit by the w of the law......Gal 3:2
doeth he it by the w of the law......Gal 3:5
For as many as are of the w of......Gal 3:10
Now the w of the flesh are......Gal 5:19
Not of w, lest any man should......Eph 2:9
in Christ Jesus unto good w......Eph 2:10
with the unfruitful w of darkness......Eph 5:11
enemies in your mind by wicked w......Col 1:21
professing godliness) with good w......1Ti 2:10
Well reported of for good w......1Ti 5:10
Likewise also the good w of some......1Ti 5:25
good, that they be rich in good w......1Ti 6:18
calling, not according to our w......2Ti 1:9
furnished unto all good w......2Ti 3:17
reward him according to his w......2Ti 4:14
but in w they deny him, being......Titus 1:16
thyself a pattern of good w......Titus 2:7
people, zealous of good w......Titus 2:14
Not by w of righteousness which......Titus 3:5
be careful to maintain good w......Titus 3:8
good w for necessary uses......Titus 3:14
heavens are the w of thine hands......Heb 1:10
set him over the w of thine hands......Heb 2:7
me, and saw my w forty years......Heb 3:9
although the w were finished from......Heb 4:3
the seventh day from all his w......Heb 4:4
also hath ceased from his own w......Heb 4:10
of repentance from dead w......Heb 6:1
dead w to serve the living God......Heb 9:14
to provoke unto love and to good w......Heb 10:24
say he hath faith, and have not w......Jas 2:14
Even so faith, if it hath not w......Jas 2:17
say, Thou hast faith, and I have w......Jas 2:18
shew me thy faith without thy w......Jas 2:18
I will shew thee my faith by my w......Jas 2:18
man, that faith without w is dead......Jas 2:20
Abraham our father justified by w......Jas 2:21
thou how faith wrought with his w......Jas 2:22
by w was faith made perfect......Jas 2:22
how that by w a man is justified......Jas 2:24
Rahab the harlot justified by w......Jas 2:25
so faith without w is dead also......Jas 2:26
his w with meekness of wisdom......Jas 3:13
they may by your good w, which......1Pet 2:12
the w that are therein shall be......2Pet 3:10
might destroy the w of the devil......1Jn 3:8
Because his own w were evil......1Jn 3:12
I know thy w, and thy labour, and......Rev 2:2
and repent, and do the first w......Rev 2:5
I know thy w, and tribulation, and......Rev 2:9
I know thy w, and where thou......Rev 2:13
I know thy w, and charity, and......Rev 2:19
faith, and thy patience, and thy w......Rev 2:19
one of you according to your w......Rev 2:23
keepeth my w unto the end, to him......Rev 2:26
I know thy w, that thou hast a......Rev 3:1
found thy w perfect before God......Rev 3:2
I know thy w......Rev 3:8
I know thy w, that thou art......Rev 3:15
not of the w of their hands......Rev 9:20
and their w do follow them......Rev 14:13
Great and marvellous are thy w......Rev 15:3
her double according to her w......Rev 18:6
the books, according to their w......Rev 20:12

WORKS'
every man according to their w ...... Rev 20:13

WORKS'
believe me for the very w sake ...... Jn 14:11

WORLD
and he hath set the w upon them 1Sa 2:8
of the w were discovered, at the 2Sa 22:16
the w also shall be stable, that 1Chr 16:30
darkness, and chased out of the w ...... Job 18:18
Or who hath disposed the whole w ...... Job 34:13
the face of the w in the earth ...... Job 37:12
judge the w in righteousness ...... Ps 9:8
hand, O LORD, from men of the w ...... Ps 17:14
the foundations of the w were ...... Ps 18:15
their words to the end of the w ...... Ps 19:4
the ends of the w shall remember ...... Ps 22:27
the w, and they that dwell therein ...... Ps 24:1
of the w stand in awe of him ...... Ps 33:8
ear, all ye inhabitants of the w ...... Ps 49:1
for the w is mine, and the fulness ...... Ps 50:12
the ungodly, who prosper in the w ...... Ps 73:12
the lightnings lightened the w ...... Ps 77:18
as for the w and the fulness ...... Ps 89:11
hadst formed the earth and the w ...... Ps 90:2
the w also is stablished, that ...... Ps 93:1
the w also shall be established ...... Ps 96:10
judge the w with righteousness ...... Ps 96:13
His lightnings enlightened the w ...... Ps 97:4
the w, and they that dwell therein ...... Ps 98:7
shall he judge the w, and the ...... Ps 98:9
highest part of the dust of the w ...... Prov 8:26
he hath set the w in their heart ...... Eccl 3:11
will punish the w for their evil ...... Is 13:11
That made the w as a wilderness ...... Is 14:17
the face of the w with cities ...... Is 14:21
All ye inhabitants of the w ...... Is 18:3
the w upon the face of the earth ...... Is 23:17
the w languisheth and fadeth away, ... Is 24:4
the inhabitants of the w ...... Is 26:9
the inhabitants of the w fallen ...... Is 26:18
fill the face of the w with fruit ...... Is 27:6
the w, and all things that come ...... Is 34:1
with the inhabitants of the w ...... Is 38:11
nor confounded w without end ...... Is 45:17
proclaimed unto the end of the w ...... Is 62:11
of the w men have not heard ...... Is 64:4
established the w by his wisdom ...... Jer 10:12
and all the kingdoms of the w ...... Jer 25:26
established the w by his wisdom ...... Jer 51:15
and all the inhabitants of the w ...... Lam 4:12
at his presence, yea, the w ...... Nah 1:5
him all the kingdoms of the w ...... Mt 4:8
Ye are the light of the w ...... Mt 5:14
forgiven him, neither in this w ...... Mt 12:32
neither in the w to come ...... Mt 12:32
and the care of this w, and the ...... Mt 13:22
from the foundation of the w ...... Mt 13:35
The field is the w ...... Mt 13:38
the harvest is the end of the w ...... Mt 13:39
shall it be in the end of this w ...... Mt 13:40
shall it be at the end of this w ...... Mt 13:49
if he shall gain the whole ...... Mt 16:26
Woe unto the w because of ...... Mt 18:7
coming, and of the end of the w ...... Mt 24:3
shall be preached in all the w ...... Mt 24:14
beginning of the w to this time ...... Mt 24:21
you from the foundation of the w ...... Mt 25:34
shall be preached in the whole w ...... Mt 26:13
alway, even unto the end of the w ...... Mt 28:20
And the cares of this w, and the ...... Mk 4:19
man, if he shall gain the whole w ...... Mk 8:36
in the w to come eternal life ...... Mk 10:30
preached throughout the whole w ...... Mk 14:9
unto them, Go ye into all the w ...... Mk 16:15
which have been since the w began ...... Lk 1:70
that all the w should be taxed ...... Lk 2:1
of the w in a moment of time ...... Lk 4:5
if he gain the whole w, and lose ...... Lk 9:25
shed from the foundation of the w ...... Lk 11:50
the nations of the w seek after ...... Lk 12:30
for the children of this w are in ...... Lk 16:8
in the w to come life everlasting ...... Lk 18:30
The children of this w marry ...... Lk 20:34
accounted worthy to obtain that w ...... Lk 20:35
every man that cometh into the w ...... Jn 1:9
He was in the w ...... Jn 1:10
the w was made by him, and ...... Jn 1:10
by him, and the w knew him not ...... Jn 1:10
taketh away the sin of the w ...... Jn 1:29
For God so loved the w, that he ...... Jn 3:16
into the w to condemn the w ...... Jn 3:17
but that the w through him might ...... Jn 3:17
that light is come into the w ...... Jn 3:19
the Christ, the Saviour of the w ...... Jn 4:42
that should come into the w ...... Jn 6:14
heaven, and giveth life unto the w ...... Jn 6:33
I will give for the life of the w ...... Jn 6:51
things, shew thyself to the w ...... Jn 7:4
The w cannot hate you ...... Jn 7:7
saying, I am the light of the w ...... Jn 8:12
ye are of this w ...... Jn 8:23
I am not of this w ...... Jn 8:23
I speak to the w those things ...... Jn 8:26
As long as I am in the w ...... Jn 9:5
I am the light of the w ...... Jn 9:5
Since the w began was it not ...... Jn 9:32
judgment I am come into this w ...... Jn 9:39
sanctified, and sent into the w ...... Jn 10:36
he seeth the light of this w ...... Jn 11:9
God, which should come into the w ...... Jn 11:27

behold, the w is gone after him ...... Jn 12:19
w shall keep it unto life eternal ...... Jn 12:25
Now is the judgment of this w ...... Jn 12:31
the prince of this w be cast out ...... Jn 12:31
I am come a light into the w ...... Jn 12:46
for I came not to judge the w ...... Jn 12:47
but to save the w ...... Jn 12:47
out of this w unto the Father ...... Jn 13:1
loved his own which were in the w ...... Jn 13:1
whom the w cannot receive ...... Jn 14:17
while, and the w seeth me no more ...... Jn 14:19
unto us, and not unto the w ...... Jn 14:22
not as the w giveth, give I unto ...... Jn 14:27
for the prince of this w cometh ...... Jn 14:30
But that the w may know that I ...... Jn 14:31
If the w hate you, ye know that ...... Jn 15:18
If ye were of the w ...... Jn 15:19
the w would love his own ...... Jn 15:19
but because ye are not of the w ...... Jn 15:19
I have chosen you out of the w ...... Jn 15:19
therefore the w hateth you ...... Jn 15:19
he will reprove the w of sin ...... Jn 16:8
the prince of this w is judged ...... Jn 16:11
lament, but the w shall rejoice ...... Jn 16:20
Joy that a man is born into the w ...... Jn 16:21
the Father, and am come into the w ...... Jn 16:28
again, I leave the w, and go to ...... Jn 16:28
In the w ye shall have ...... Jn 16:33
I have overcome the w ...... Jn 16:33
I had with thee before the w was ...... Jn 17:5
which thou gavest me out of the w ...... Jn 17:6
I pray not for the w, but for ...... Jn 17:9
And now I am no more in the w ...... Jn 17:11
but these are in the w ...... Jn 17:11
While I was with them in the w ...... Jn 17:12
and these things I speak in the w ...... Jn 17:13
the w hath hated them ...... Jn 17:14
because they are not of the w ...... Jn 17:14
even as I am not of the w ...... Jn 17:14
shouldest take them out of the w ...... Jn 17:15
They are not of the w ...... Jn 17:16
even as I am not of the w ...... Jn 17:16
As thou hast sent me into the w ...... Jn 17:18
have I also sent them into the w ...... Jn 17:18
that the w may believe that thou ...... Jn 17:21
that the w may know that thou ...... Jn 17:23
me before the foundation of the w ...... Jn 17:24
the w hath not known thee ...... Jn 17:25
him, I spake openly to the w ...... Jn 18:20
My kingdom is not of this w ...... Jn 18:36
if my kingdom were of this w ...... Jn 18:36
for this cause came I into the w ...... Jn 18:37
I suppose that even the w itself ...... Jn 21:25
holy prophets since the w began ...... Acts 3:21
great dearth throughout all the w ...... Acts 11:28
works from the beginning of the w ...... Acts 15:18
These that have turned the w ...... Acts 17:6
God that made the w and all things ...... Acts 17:24
w in righteousness by that man ...... Acts 17:31
all Asia and the w worshippeth ...... Acts 19:27
all the Jews throughout the w ...... Acts 24:5
spoken of throughout the whole w ...... Rom 1:8
of the w are clearly seen ...... Rom 1:20
then how shall God judge the w ...... Rom 3:6
of the w may become guilty ...... Rom 3:19
he should be the heir of the w ...... Rom 4:13
by one man sin entered into the w ...... Rom 5:12
until the law sin was in the w ...... Rom 5:13
words unto the ends of the w ...... Rom 10:18
of them be the riches of the w ...... Rom 11:12
them be the reconciling of the w ...... Rom 11:15
And be not conformed to this w ...... Rom 12:2
was kept secret since the w began ...... Rom 16:25
where is the disputer of this w 1Cor 1:20
made foolish the wisdom of this w 1Cor 1:20
God the w by wisdom knew not God 1Cor 1:21
of the w to confound the wise 1Cor 1:27
w to confound the things which 1Cor 1:27
And base things of the w, and 1Cor 1:28
yet not the wisdom of this w 1Cor 2:6
nor of the princes of this w 1Cor 2:6
before the w unto our glory 1Cor 2:7
of the princes of this w knew 1Cor 2:8
received, not the spirit of the w 1Cor 2:12
you seemeth to be wise in this w 1Cor 3:18
For the wisdom of this w is 1Cor 3:19
or Apollos, or Cephas, or the w 1Cor 3:22
are made a spectacle unto the w 1Cor 4:9
we are made as the filth of the w 1Cor 4:13
with the fornicators of this w 1Cor 5:10
must ye needs go out of the w 1Cor 5:10
that the saints shall judge the w 1Cor 6:2
if the w shall be judged by you 1Cor 6:2
And they that use this w, as not 1Cor 7:31
fashion of this w passeth away 1Cor 7:31
for the things that are of the w 1Cor 7:33
careth for the things of the w 1Cor 7:34
that an idol is nothing in the w 1Cor 8:4
eat no flesh while the w standeth 1Cor 8:13
whom the ends of the w are come 1Cor 10:11
not be condemned with the w 1Cor 11:32
so many kinds of voices in the w 1Cor 14:10
had our conversation in the w 2Cor 1:12
In whom the god of this w hath 2Cor 4:4
reconciling the w unto himself 2Cor 5:19
the sorrow of the w worketh death 2Cor 7:10
us from this present evil w ...... Gal 1:4
under the elements of the w ...... Gal 4:3
by whom the w is crucified unto ...... Gal 6:14
unto me, and I unto the w ...... Gal 6:14

before the foundation of the w ...... Eph 1:4
that is named, not only in this w ...... Eph 1:21
according to the course of this w ...... Eph 2:2
no hope, and without God in the w ...... Eph 2:12
of the w hath been hid in God ...... Eph 3:9
all ages, w without end ...... Eph 3:21
rulers of the darkness of this w ...... Eph 6:12
whom ye shine as lights in the w ...... Col 1:6
unto you, as it is in all the w ...... Col 1:6
men, after the rudiments of the w ...... Col 2:8
from the rudiments of the w ...... Col 2:20
why, as though living in the w ...... Col 2:20
came into the w to save sinners 1Ti 1:15
Gentiles, believed on in the w 1Ti 3:16
we brought nothing into this w 1Ti 6:7
them that are rich in this w 1Ti 6:17
Christ Jesus before the w began 2Ti 1:9
me, having loved this present w 2Ti 4:10
lie, promised before the w began ...... Titus 1:2
and godly, in this present w ...... Titus 2:12
in the firstbegotten into the w ...... Heb 1:6
put in subjection the w to come ...... Heb 2:5
from the foundation of the w ...... Heb 4:3
and the powers of the w to come ...... Heb 6:5
since the foundation of the w ...... Heb 9:26
w hath he appeared to put away ...... Heb 9:26
when he cometh into the w ...... Heb 10:5
by the which he condemned the w ...... Heb 11:7
(Of whom the w was not worthy ...... Heb 11:38
keep himself unspotted from the w ...... Jas 1:27
the poor of this w rich in faith ...... Jas 2:5
tongue is a fire, a w of iniquity ...... Jas 3:6
of the w is enmity with God ...... Jas 4:4
the w is the enemy of God ...... Jas 4:4
before the foundation of the w 1Pet 1:20
your brethren that are in the w 1Pet 5:9
that is in the w through lust 2Pet 1:4
And spared not the old w, but 2Pet 2:5
flood upon the w of the ungodly 2Pet 2:5
w through the knowledge of the 2Pet 2:20
Whereby the w that then was, ... 2Pet 3:6
also for the sins of the whole w 1Jn 2:2
Love not the w, neither the 1Jn 2:15
the things that are in the w 1Jn 2:15
If any man love the w, the love 1Jn 2:15
For all that is in the w, the 1Jn 2:16
of the Father, but is of the w 1Jn 2:16
the w passeth away, and the lust 1Jn 2:17
therefore the w knoweth us not, ... 1Jn 3:1
my brethren, if the w hate you 1Jn 3:13
prophets are gone out into the w 1Jn 4:1
even now already is it in the w 1Jn 4:3
in you, than he that is in the w 1Jn 4:4
They are of the w 1Jn 4:5
therefore speak they of the w 1Jn 4:5
and the w heareth them 1Jn 4:5
his only begotten Son into the w 1Jn 4:9
Son to be the Saviour of the w 1Jn 4:14
as he is, so are we in this w 1Jn 4:17
is born of God overcometh the w 1Jn 5:4
the victory that overcometh the w 1Jn 5:4
Who is he that overcometh the w 1Jn 5:5
the whole w lieth in wickedness 1Jn 5:19
decievers are entered into the w 2Jn 7
which shall come upon all the w ...... Rev 3:10
The kingdoms of this w are become ...... Rev 11:15
which deceiveth the whole w ...... Rev 12:9
all the w wondered after the ...... Rev 13:3
from the foundation of the w ...... Rev 13:8
of the earth and of the whole w ...... Rev 16:14
life from the foundation of the w ...... Rev 17:8

WORLDLY
w lusts, we should live soberly, ... Titus 2:12
divine service, and a w sanctuary ...... Heb 9:1

WORLD'S
But whoso hath this w good 1Jn 3:17

WORLDS
by whom also he made the w ...... Heb 1:2
faith we understand that the w ...... Heb 11:3

WORM
neither was there any w therein ...... Ex 16:24
to the w, Thou art my mother, ... Job 17:14
the w shall feed sweetly on him ...... Job 24:20
How much less man, that is a w ...... Job 25:6
and the son of man, which is a w ...... Job 25:6
But I am a w, and no man ...... Ps 22:6
the w is spread under thee, and ...... Is 14:11
thou w Jacob, and ye men of Israel ...... Is 41:14
the w shall eat them like wool ...... Is 51:8
for their w shall not die, ... Is 66:24
But God prepared a w when the ...... Jonah 4:7
Where their w dieth not, and the ...... Mk 9:44
Where their w dieth not, and the ...... Mk 9:46
Where their w dieth not, and the ...... Mk 9:48

WORMS
until the morning, and it bred w ...... Ex 16:20
for the w shall eat them ...... Deut 28:39
My flesh is clothed with w ...... Job 7:5
after my skin w destroy this body ...... Job 19:26
dust, and the w shall cover them ...... Job 21:26
under thee, and the w cover thee ...... Is 14:11
their holes like w of the earth ...... Mic 7:17
and he was eaten of w, and gave up... Acts 12:23

WORMWOOD
you a root that beareth gall and ...... Deut 29:18
But her end is bitter as w ...... Prov 5:4
them, even this people, with w ...... Jer 9:15

W

Behold, I will feed them with *w*...... Jer 23:15
he hath made me drunken with *w*..... Lam 3:15
affliction and my misery, the *w*..... Lam 3:19
Ye who turn judgment to *w*........... Amos 5:7
the name of the star is called *W*.... Rev 8:11
third part of the waters became *w*.... Rev 8:11

WORSE

now will we deal *w* with these........ Gen 19:9
that will be *w* unto thee than all.... 2Sa 19:7
did *w* than all that were before..... Judg 2:19
was put to the *w* before Israel...... 2Kin 14:12
were put to the *w* before Israel..... 1Chr 19:16
were put to the *w* before Israel..... 1Chr 19:19
be put to the *w* before the enemy.... 2Chr 6:24
was put to the *w* before Israel...... 2Chr 25:22
to do *w* than the heathen, whom...... 2Chr 33:9
they did *w* than their fathers....... Jer 7:26
ye have done *w* than your fathers.... Jer 16:12
why should ye see your faces *w*...... Dan 1:10
garment, and the rent is made *w*..... Mt 9:16
of that man is *w* than the first..... Mt 12:45
error shall be *w* than the first..... Mt 27:64
the old, and the rent is made *w*..... Mk 2:21
bettered, but rather grew *w*......... Mk 5:26
of that man is *w* than the first..... Lk 11:26
well drunk, then that which is *w*.... Jn 2:10
lest a *w* thing come unto thee....... Jn 5:14
if we eat not, are we the *w*......... 1Cor 8:8
not for the better, but for the *w*... 1Cor 11:17
faith, and is *w* than an infidel..... 1Ti 5:8
and seducers shall wax *w* and........ 2Ti 3:13
the latter end is *w* with them....... 2Pet 2:20

WORSHIP

I and the lad will go yonder and...... Gen 22:5
and *w* ye afar off..................... Ex 24:1
For thou shalt *w* no other god........ Ex 34:14
shouldest be driven to *w* them....... Deut 4:19
w them, I testify against you........ Deut 8:19
and serve other gods, and *w* them.... Deut 11:16
w before the LORD thy God........... Deut 26:10
w other gods, and serve them........ Deut 30:17
his face to the earth, and did *w*.... Josh 5:14
up out of his city yearly to *w*...... 1Sa 1:3
with me, that I may *w* the LORD...... 1Sa 15:25
that I may *w* the LORD thy God....... 1Sa 15:30
go and serve other gods, and *w* them. 1Kin 9:6
people went to *w* before the one..... 1Kin 12:30
the house of Rimmon to *w* there...... 2Kin 5:18
shall ye fear, and him shall ye *w*... 2Kin 17:36
Ye shall *w* before this altar in..... 2Kin 18:22
w the LORD in the beauty of......... 1Chr 16:29
go and serve other gods, and *w* them. 2Chr 7:19
Ye shall *w* before one altar, and.... 2Chr 32:12
in thy fear will I *w* toward thy...... Ps 5:7
the nations shall *w* before thee..... Ps 22:27
be fat upon earth shall eat and *w*... Ps 22:29
w the LORD in the beauty of......... Ps 29:2
and *w* thou him..................... Ps 45:11
All the earth shall *w* thee.......... Ps 66:4
shalt thou *w* any strange god........ Ps 81:9
come and *w* before thee, O Lord...... Ps 86:9
O come, let us *w* and bow down....... Ps 95:6
O *w* the LORD in the beauty of....... Ps 96:9
w him, all ye gods................. Ps 97:7
our God, and *w* at his footstool..... Ps 99:5
our God, and *w* at his holy hill..... Ps 99:9
we will *w* at his footstool.......... Ps 132:7
I will *w* toward thy holy temple..... Ps 138:2
they *w* the work of their own........ Is 2:8
made each one for himself to *w*...... Is 2:20
shall *w* the Loro in the holy........ Is 27:13
Ye shall *w* before this altar in..... Is 36:7
they fall down, yea, they *w*......... Is 44:17
and arise, princes also shall *w*..... Is 49:7
all flesh come to *w* before me....... Is 66:23
in at these gates to *w* the LORD..... Jer 7:2
to *w* them, shall even be as this.... Jer 13:10
to *w* them, and provoke me not to.... Jer 25:6
which come to *w* in the LORD's....... Jer 26:2
did *w* make her cakes to *w* her..... Jer 44:19
he shall *w* at the threshold of...... Eze 46:2
the people of the land shall *w* at... Eze 46:3
w shall go out by the way of........ Eze 46:9
down and *w* the golden image that.... Dan 3:5
fall down and *w* the golden image.... Dan 3:10
nor *w* the golden image which thou... Dan 3:12
nor *w* the golden image which I...... Dan 3:14
w the image which I have made....... Dan 3:15
but if ye *w* not, ye shall be cast... Dan 3:15
nor *w* the golden image which I...... Dan 3:18
might not serve nor *w* any god....... Dan 3:28
thou shalt no more *w* the work of.... Mic 5:13
them that *w* the host of heaven...... Zeph 1:5
and them that *w* and that swear by... Zeph 1:5
and men shall *w* him, every one...... Zeph 2:11
from year to year to *w* the King..... Zec 14:16
unto Jerusalem to *w* the King........ Zec 14:17
in the east, and are come to *w* him.. Mt 2:2
that I may come and *w* him also...... Mt 2:8
if thou wilt fall down and *w* me..... Mt 4:9
Thou shalt *w* the Lord thy God, and.. Mt 4:10
But in vain they do *w* me,........... Mt 15:9
Howbeit in vain do they *w* me........ Mk 7:7
if thou therefore wilt *w* me......... Lk 4:7
Thou shalt *w* the Lord thy God, and.. Lk 4:8
then shalt thou have *w* in the....... Lk 14:10
is the place where men ought to *w*... Jn 4:20
yet at Jerusalem, is the Father....... Jn 4:21
Ye *w* ye know not what............... Jn 4:22

we know what we *w*................... Jn 4:22
shall *w* the Father in spirit........ Jn 4:23
the Father seeketh such to *w* him.... Jn 4:23
they that *w* him must................ Jn 4:24
must *w* him in spirit................ Jn 4:24
that came up to *w* at the feast...... Jn 12:20
gave them up to *w* the host of....... Acts 7:42
figures which ye made to *w* them..... Acts 7:43
and had come to Jerusalem for to *w*.. Acts 8:27
Whom therefore ye ignorantly *w*...... Acts 17:23
men to *w* God contrary to the law.... Acts 18:13
I went up to Jerusalem for to *w*..... Acts 24:11
so *w* I the God of my fathers,....... Acts 24:14
down on his face he will *w* God...... 1Cor 14:25
which *w* God in the spirit, and...... Phil 3:3
indeed a shew of wisdom in will *w*... Col 2:23
let all the angels of God *w* him..... Heb 1:6
w before thy feet, and to know...... Rev 3:9
w him liveth for ever and........... Rev 4:10
that they should not *w* devils....... Rev 9:20
the altar, and them that *w* therein.. Rev 11:1
dwell upon the earth shall *w* him.... Rev 13:8
therein to *w* the first beast........ Rev 13:12
w the image of the beast should..... Rev 13:15
w him that made heaven, and earth,.. Rev 14:7
voice, If any man *w* the beast....... Rev 14:9
who *w* the beast and his image, and.. Rev 14:11
shall come and *w* before thee........ Rev 15:4
And I fell at his feet to *w* him..... Rev 19:10
w God................................ Rev 19:10
I fell down to *w* before the feet.... Rev 22:8
w God................................ Rev 22:9

WORSHIPPED

down his head, and *w* the LORD....... Gen 24:26
w the LORD, and blessed the LORD.... Gen 24:48
he *w* the LORD, bowing himself to.... Gen 24:52
then they bowed their heads and *w*... Ex 4:31
And the people bowed the head and *w*. Ex 12:27
them a molten calf, and have *w* it... Ex 32:8
and all the people rose up and *w*.... Ex 33:10
his head toward the earth, and *w*.... Ex 34:8
w them, either the sun, or moon,.... Deut 17:3
w them, gods whom they knew not,.... Deut 29:26
interpretation thereof, that he *w*... Judg 7:15
w before the LORD, and returned..... 1Sa 1:19
And he *w* the LORD there............. 1Sa 1:28
and Saul *w* the LORD................. 1Sa 15:31
into the house of the LORD, and *w*... 2Sa 12:20
top of the mount, where he *w* God.... 2Sa 15:32
upon other gods, and have *w* them.... 1Kin 9:9
have *w* Ashtoreth the goddess of..... 2Kin 17:16
served Baal, and *w* him.............. 2Kin 16:31
w him, and provoked to anger the.... 1Kin 22:53
w all the host of heaven, and....... 2Kin 17:16
and *w* all the host of heaven,....... 2Kin 21:3
that his father served, and *w* them.. 2Kin 21:21
heads, and *w* the LORD, and the king. 2Chr 7:3
ground upon the pavement, and *w*..... 2Chr 7:3
gods, and *w* them, and served them... 2Chr 7:22
And all the congregation *w*.......... 2Chr 29:28
with him bowed themselves, and *w*.... 2Chr 29:29
and they bowed their heads and *w*.... 2Chr 29:30
w all the host of heaven, and....... 2Chr 33:3
w the LORD with their faces to...... Neh 8:6
and *w* the Lord their God............ Neh 9:3
fell down upon the ground, and *w*.... Job 1:20
in Horeb, and *w* the molten image.... Ps 106:19
the works of their own hands.......... Jer 1:16
have sought, and whom they have *w*... Jer 8:2
have served them, and have *w* them... Jer 16:11
w other gods, and served them....... Jer 22:9
they *w* the sun toward the east...... Eze 8:16
w Daniel, and commanded that they... Dan 2:46
down and *w* the golden image that.... Dan 3:7
mother, and fell down, and *w* him.... Mt 2:11
w him, saying, Lord, if thou wilt... Mt 8:2
w him, saying, My daughter is....... Mt 9:18
w him, saying Of a truth thou....... Mt 14:33
w him, saying, Lord, help me........ Mt 15:25
w him, saying, Lord, have............ Mt 18:26
and held him by the feet, and *w* him. Mt 28:9
And when they saw him, they *w* him... Mt 28:17
Jesus afar off, he ran and *w* him.... Mk 5:6
him, and bowing their knees *w* him... Mk 15:19
And they *w* him, and returned to..... Lk 24:52
Our fathers *w* in this mountain...... Jn 4:20
And he *w* him....................... Jn 9:38
fell down at his feet, and *w* him.... Acts 10:25
the city of Thyatira, which *w* God... Acts 16:14
Neither is *w* with men's hands, as... Acts 17:25
named Justus, one that *w* God........ Acts 18:7
the truth of God unto a lie, and *w*.. Rom 1:25
that is called God, or that is *w*.... 2Th 2:4
and *w*, leaning upon the top of his.. Heb 11:21
w him that liveth for ever and...... Rev 5:14
throne on their faces, and *w* God.... Rev 7:11
fell upon their faces, and *w* God.... Rev 11:16
they *w* the dragon which gave........ Rev 13:4
they *w* the beast, saying, Who is.... Rev 13:4
and upon them which *w* his image..... Rev 16:2
w God that sat on the throne,....... Rev 19:4
beast, and them that *w* his image.... Rev 19:20
God, and which had not *w* the beast.. Rev 20:4

WORSHIPPER

but if any man be a *w* of God........ Jn 9:31
is a *w* of the great goddess Diana... Acts 19:35

WORSHIPPERS

he might destroy the *w* of Baal...... 2Kin 10:19
all the *w* of Baal came, so that..... 2Kin 10:21

vestments for all the *w* of Baal..... 2Kin 10:22
Baal, and said unto the *w* of Baal... 2Kin 10:23
the LORD, but the *w* of Baal only.... 2Kin 10:23
when the true *w* shall worship....... Jn 4:23
because that he *w* once purged....... Heb 10:2

WORSHIPPETH

and the host of heaven *w* thee....... Neh 9:6
yea, he maketh a god, and *w*......... Is 44:15
w it, and prayeth unto it, and...... Is 44:17
w shall the same hour be cast....... Dan 3:6
And whoso falleth not down and *w*.... Dan 3:11
whom all Asia and the world *w*....... Acts 19:27

WORSHIPPING

as he was *w* in the house of......... 2Kin 19:37
fell before the LORD, and the LORD.... 2Chr 20:18
as he was *w* in the house of......... Is 37:38
w him, and desiring a certain....... Mt 20:20
w of angels, intruding into those... Col 2:18

WORST

I will bring the *w* of the heathen... Eze 7:24

WORTH

it is *w* he shall give it me for a... Gen 23:9
the land is *w* four hundred.......... Gen 23:15
unto him the *w* of thy estimation.... Lev 27:23
for he hath been *w* a double hired... Deut 15:18
but now thou art *w* ten thousand..... 2Sa 18:3
give thee the *w* of it in money...... 1Kin 21:2
liar, and make my speech nothing *w*.. Job 24:25
heart of the wicked is little *w*..... Prov 10:20
Howl ye, Woe *w* the day.............. Eze 30:2

WORTHIES

He shall recount his *w*.............. Nah 2:5

WORTHILY

do thou *w* in Ephratah, and be....... Ruth 4:11

WORTHY

I am not *w* of the least of all...... Gen 32:10
shall he that is *w* of death be...... Deut 17:6
whereas he was not *w* of death....... Deut 19:6
have committed a sin *w* of death..... Deut 21:22
in the damsel no sin *w* of death..... Deut 22:26
the wicked man be *w* to be beaten.... Deut 25:2
unto Haman he gave a *w* portion...... 1Sa 1:5
the LORD liveth, ye are *w* to die.... 1Sa 26:16
the LORD, who is *w* to be praised.... 2Sa 22:4
If he will shew himself a *w* man..... 1Kin 1:52
for thou art *w* of death............. 1Kin 2:26
the LORD, who is *w* to be praised.... Ps 18:3
saying, This man is *w* to die........ Jer 26:11
This man is not *w* to die............ Jer 26:16
I, whose shoes I am not *w* to bear... Mt 3:11
I am not *w* that thou shouldest...... Mt 8:8
for the workman is *w* of his meat.... Mt 10:10
enter, enquire who in it is *w*....... Mt 10:11
And if the house be *w*, let your..... Mt 10:13
but if it be not *w*, let your........ Mt 10:13
more than me is not *w* of me......... Mt 10:37
more than me is not *w* of me......... Mt 10:37
after me, is not *w* of me............ Mt 10:38
they which were bidden were not *w*... Mt 22:8
shoes I am not *w* to stoop down...... Mk 1:7
therefore fruits *w* of repentance.... Lk 3:8
whose shoes I am not *w* to unloose... Lk 3:16
That he was *w* for whom he should.... Lk 7:4
for I am not *w* that thou............ Lk 7:6
I myself to come unto thee............ Lk 7:7
for the labourer is *w* of his hire... Lk 10:7
and did commit things *w* of stripes.. Lk 12:48
am no more *w* to be called thy son... Lk 15:19
am no more *w* to be called thy son... Lk 15:21
accounted to obtain that world........ Lk 20:35
that ye may be accounted *w*.......... Lk 21:36
nothing *w* of death is done unto..... Lk 23:15
latchet I am not *w* to unloose....... Jn 1:27
that they were counted *w* to......... Acts 5:41
of his feet I am not *w* to loose..... Acts 13:25
his charge *w* of death or of bonds... Acts 23:29
that very *w* deeds are done unto..... Acts 24:2
committed any thing *w* of death...... Acts 25:11
had committed nothing *w* of death.... Acts 25:25
nothing *w* of death or of bonds...... Acts 26:31
commit such things are *w* of death... Rom 1:32
of this present time are not *w* to... Rom 8:18
beseech you that ye walk *w* of the... Eph 4:1
That ye might walk *w* of the Lord.... Col 1:10
That ye would walk *w* of God......... 1Th 2:12
counted *w* of the kingdom of God..... 2Th 1:5
would count you *w* of this calling... 2Th 1:11
of all acceptation, that Christ....... 1Ti 1:15
saying and *w* of all acceptation..... 1Ti 4:9
be counted *w* of double honour....... 1Ti 5:17
The labourer is *w* of his reward..... 1Ti 5:18
their own masters *w* of all honour... 1Ti 6:1
w of more glory than Moses.......... Heb 3:3
suppose ye, shall he be thought *w*... Heb 10:29
(Of whom the world was not *w*)....... Heb 11:38
Do not they blaspheme that *w* name... Jas 2:7
for they are *w*...................... Rev 3:4
Thou art *w*, O Lord, to receive...... Rev 4:11
Who is *w* to open the book, and to... Rev 5:2
no man was found *w* to open.......... Rev 5:4
Thou art *w* to take the book, and.... Rev 5:9
W is the Lamb that was slain to..... Rev 5:12
for they are *w*...................... Rev 16:6

WOT

I *w* not who hath done this thing.... Gen 21:26
w ye not that such a man as I can... Gen 44:15

we w not what is become of him — Ex 32:1
we w not what is become of him — Ex 32:23
for I w that he whom thou — Num 22:6
whither the men went I w not — Josh 2:5
I w that through ignorance ye did — Acts 3:17
we w not what is become of — Acts 7:40
W ye not what the scripture saith — Rom 11:2
yet what I shall choose I w not — Phil 1:22

WOTTETH
my master w not what is with me — Gen 39:8

WOULD
Adam to see what he w call them — Gen 2:19
Who w have said unto Abraham — Gen 21:7
I w it might be according to thy — Gen 30:34
he besought us, and we w not hear — Gen 42:21
and ye w not hear — Gen 42:22
we certainly know that the w say — Gen 44:22
his father, his father w die — Ex 2:4
to wit what se w be done to him — Ex 2:4
neither w he let the people go — Ex 8:35
neither w he let the children of — Ex 9:35
so that he w not let the children — Ex 10:20
heart, and he w not let them go — Ex 10:27
so that he w not let the children — Ex 11:10
when Pharaoh w hardly let us go — Ex 13:15
W to God we had died by the hand — Ex 16:3
w God that all the LORD's people — Num 11:29
that the LORD w put his spirit — Num 11:29
W God that we had died in the — Num 14:2
the w God we had died in this — Num 14:2
W God that we had died when our — Num 20:3
Sihon w not suffer Israel to pass — Num 21:23
If Balak w give me his house full — Num 22:18
I w there were a sword in mine — Num 22:29
mine hand, for now w I kill thee — Num 22:29
If Balak w give me his house full — Num 24:13
Notwithstanding we w not go up — Deut 1:26
ye w not hear, but rebelled — Deut 1:43
but the LORD w not hearken to — Deut 1:45
Heshbon w not let us pass by him — Deut 2:30
for your sakes, and w not hear me — Deut 3:26
in them, that they w fear me — Deut 5:29
because he w keep the oath which — Deut 7:8
because ye w not be obedient unto — Deut 8:20
Lord had said he w destroy you — Deut 9:25
the LORD w not destroy thee — Deut 10:10
thy God w not hearken unto Balaam — Deut 23:5
and it w be sin in thee — Deut 23:21
which w not adventure to set the — Deut 28:56
shalt say, W God it were even — Deut 28:67
shalt say, W God it were morning — Deut 28:67
I w scatter them into corners — Deut 32:26
I w make the remembrance of them — Deut 32:26
that they w consider their latter — Deut 32:29
that he w not shew them the land — Josh 5:6
their fathers that he w give us — Josh 5:6
w to God we had been content, and — Josh 7:7
Canaanites w dwell in that land — Josh 17:12
But I w not hearken unto Balaam — Josh 24:10
Canaanites w dwell in that land — Judg 1:27
for they w not suffer them to — Judg 1:34
But the Amorites w dwell in mount — Judg 1:35
yet they w not hearken unto their — Judg 2:17
to know whether they w hearken — Judg 3:4
them alive, I w not slay you — Judg 8:19
I w desire a request of you — Judg 8:24
that ye w give me every man the — Judg 8:24
w to God this people were under — Judg 9:29
then w I remove Abimelech — Judg 9:29
of Edom w not hearken thereto — Judg 11:17
but he w not consent — Judg 11:17
he w not have received a burnt — Judg 13:23
neither w he have shewed us all — Judg 13:23
nor w as at this time have told — Judg 13:23
rent him as he w have rent a kid — Judg 14:6
But her father w not suffer him — Judg 15:1
But the man w not tarry that — Judg 19:10
But the men w not hearken to him — Judg 19:25
w not hearken to the voice of — Judg 20:13
W tarry for them till they — Ruth 1:13
w ye stay for them from having — Ruth 1:13
then he w answer him, Nay — 1Sa 2:16
because the LORD w slay them — 1Sa 2:25
for now w the LORD have — 1Sa 13:13
w not utterly destroy them — 1Sa 15:9
w let him go no more home to his — 1Sa 18:2
then w not I tell it thee — 1Sa 20:9
w not put forth their hand to — 1Sa 22:17
that he w surely tell Saul — 1Sa 23:22
but I w not stretch forth mine — 1Sa 26:23
But his armourbearer w not — 1Sa 31:4
But Asahel w not turn aside from — 2Sa 2:21
as though they w have fetched — 2Sa 4:6
who thought that I w have given — 2Sa 4:10
So David w not remove the ark of — 2Sa 6:10
that they w shoot from the wall — 2Sa 11:20
I w moreover have given unto thee — 2Sa 12:8
but he w not, neither did he eat — 2Sa 12:17
he w not hearken unto our voice — 2Sa 13:14
Howbeit he w not hearken unto her — 2Sa 13:14
But he w not hearken unto her — 2Sa 13:16
howbeit he w not go, but blessed — 2Sa 13:25
hand of the man that w destroy me — 2Sa 14:16
But he w not come to him — 2Sa 14:29
the second time, he w not come — 2Sa 14:29
unto me, and I w do him justice — 2Sa 15:4
I w have given thee ten shekels — 2Sa 18:11
yet w I not put forth mine hand — 2Sa 18:12
w God I had died for thee, O — 2Sa 18:33

Oh that one w give me drink of — 2Sa 23:15
nevertheless he w not drink — 2Sa 23:16
therefore he w not drink it — 2Sa 23:17
The LORD said that he w dwell in — 1Kin 8:12
whosoever w, he consecrated him, — 1Kin 13:33
as great as w contain two — 1Kin 18:32
whether any thing w come from him — 1Kin 20:33
away his face, and w eat no bread — 1Kin 21:4
Did I not tell thee that he w — 1Kin 22:18
But Jehoshaphat w not — 1Kin 22:49
when the LORD w take up Elijah — 2Kin 2:1
I w not look toward thee, nor see — 2Kin 3:14
W God my lord were with the — 2Kin 5:3
for he w recover him of his — 2Kin 5:3
if the LORD w make windows in — 2Kin 7:2
Yet the Lord w not destroy Judah — 2Kin 8:19
w not destroy them, neither cast — 2Kin 13:23
But Amaziah w not hear — 2Kin 14:11
the LORD said not that he w blot — 2Kin 14:27
Notwithstanding they w not hear — 2Kin 17:14
w not hear them, nor do them — 2Kin 18:12
which the LORD w not pardon — 2Kin 24:4
But his armourbearer w not — 1Chr 10:4
Oh that one w give me drink of — 1Chr 11:17
but David w not drink of it, but — 1Chr 11:18
Therefore he w not drink it — 1Chr 11:19
said that they w do so — 1Chr 19:19
neither w the Syrians help the — 1Chr 19:19
he w increase Israel like to the — 1Chr 27:23
The LORD hath said that he w — 2Chr 6:1
the king w not hearken unto them — 2Chr 10:16
that he w not destroy him — 2Chr 12:12
That whosoever w not seek the — 2Chr 15:13
he w not prophesy good unto me — 2Chr 18:7
Howbeit the LORD w not destroy — 2Chr 21:7
but they w not give ear — 2Chr 24:19
But Amaziah w not hear — 2Chr 25:20
but they w not hearken — 2Chr 33:10
Nevertheless Josiah w not turn — 2Chr 35:22
that whosoever w not come within — Ezr 10:8
that they w put away their wives — Ezr 10:19
w go into the temple to save his — Neh 6:11
that w have put me in fear — Neh 6:14
they might do with them as they w — Neh 9:24
their neck, and w not hear — Neh 9:29
yet w they not give ear — Neh 9:30
that we w not give our daughters — Neh 10:30
that we w not buy it of them on — Neh 10:31
that we w leave the seventh year — Neh 10:31
Mordecai's matters w stand — Est 3:4
To whom w the king delight to do — Est 6:6
and province that w assault them — Est 8:11
did what they w unto those that — Est 9:5
that they w keep these two days — Est 9:27
I w seek unto God, and unto God — Job 5:8
unto God w I commit my cause — Job 5:8
For now it w be heavier than the — Job 6:3
that God w grant me the thing — Job 6:8
Even that it w please God to — Job 6:9
that he w loose his hand, and — Job 6:9
I w harden myself in sorrow — Job 6:10
I w not live alway — Job 7:16
surely now he w awake for me — Job 9:16
yet w I not answer — Job 9:15
but I w make supplication to my — Job 9:15
yet w I not believe that he had — Job 9:16
perfect, yet w I not know my soul — Job 9:21
I w despise my life — Job 9:21
Then w I speak, and not fear him — Job 9:35
But oh that God w speak, and open — Job 11:5
that he w shew thee the secrets — Job 11:6
For vain man w be wise, though — Job 11:12
Surely I w speak to the Almighty, — Job 13:3
Oh that ye w altogether hold your — Job 13:5
But I w strengthen you with my — Job 16:5
I w order my cause before him, and — Job 23:4
I w know the words which — Job 23:5
the words which he w answer me — Job 23:5
understand what he w say unto me — Job 23:5
but he w put strength in me — Job 23:6
he w fain flee out of his hand — Job 27:22
whose fathers I w have disdained — Job 30:1
w root out all mine increase — Job 31:12
Oh that one w hear me — Job 31:35
is, that the Almighty w answer me — Job 31:35
Surely I w take it upon my — Job 31:37
I w declare unto him the number — Job 31:37
as a prince w I go near unto him — Job 31:37
my maker w soon take me away — Job 32:22
w not consider any of his ways — Job 34:27
Even so w he have removed thee — Job 36:16
one w think the deep to be hoary — Job 41:32
on the LORD that he w deliver him — Ps 22:8
their hearts, Ah, so w we have — Ps 35:25
if I w declare and speak of them, — Ps 40:5
I were hungry, I w not tell thee — Ps 50:12
else w I give it — Ps 51:16
for then w I fly away, and be at — Ps 55:6
then w I wander far off, and — Ps 55:7
I w hasten my escape from the — Ps 55:8
then I w have hid myself from him — Ps 55:12
for man w swallow me up — Ps 56:1
Mine enemies w daily swallow me — Ps 56:2
of him that w swallow me up — Ps 57:3
they that w destroy me, being — Ps 69:4
But my people w not hearken to my — Ps 81:11
and Israel w none of me — Ps 81:11
he said that he w destroy them — Ps 106:23
Oh that men w praise the LORD for — Ps 107:8
Oh that men w praise the LORD for — Ps 107:15

Oh that men w praise the LORD for — Ps 107:21
Oh that men w praise the LORD for — Ps 107:31
have said that I w keep thy words — Ps 119:57
there was no man that w know me — Ps 142:4
counsel, and w none of my reproof — Prov 1:25
They w none of my counsel — Prov 1:30
w not let him go, until I had — Song 3:4
find thee without, I w kiss thee — Song 8:1
I w lead thee, and bring thee into — Song 8:2
mother's house, who w instruct me — Song 8:2
I w cause thee to drink of spiced — Song 8:2
if a man w give all the substance — Song 8:7
it w utterly be contemned — Song 8:7
who w set the briers and thorns — Is 27:4
I w go through them — Is 27:4
I w burn them together — Is 27:4
yet they w not hear — Is 28:12
and ye w not — Is 30:15
for they w not walk in his ways, — Is 42:24
that I w not be wroth with thee — Is 54:9
When I w comfort myself against — Jer 8:18
Who w not fear thee, O King of — Jer 10:7
but they w not hear — Jer 13:11
wherewith I said I w benefit them. — Jer 18:10
yet w I pluck thee thence — Jer 22:24
but ye w not hear, saith the LORD — Jer 29:19
king that he w not burn the roll — Jer 36:25
but he w not hear them — Jer 36:25
that he w not cause me to return — Jer 38:26
w they not leave some gleaning — Jer 51:9
We w have healed Babylon, but she — Jer 51:9
w not have believed that the — Lam 4:12
they w have hearkened unto thee — Eze 3:6
that I w do this evil unto them — Eze 6:10
hope that they w confirm the word — Eze 13:6
me, and w not hearken unto me — Eze 20:8
I w pour out my fury upon them in — Eze 20:13
that I w not bring them into the — Eze 20:15
I w pour out my fury upon them, — Eze 20:21
that I w scatter them among the — Eze 20:23
that I w bring them against them — Eze 38:17
he w not defile himself with the — Dan 1:8
certainly that ye w gain the time — Dan 2:8
the king that he w give him time — Dan 2:16
that he w shew the king the — Dan 2:16
They w desire mercies of the — Dan 2:18
whom he w he slew — Dan 5:19
and whom he w he kept alive — Dan 5:19
and whom he w he set up — Dan 5:19
and whom he w he put down — Dan 5:19
Then I w know the truth of the — Dan 7:19
that he w accomplish seventy — Dan 9:2
When I w have healed Israel, then — Hos 7:1
High, none at all w exalt him — Hos 11:7
w they not have stolen till they — Obad 5
w they not leave some grapes — Obad 5
had said that he w do unto them. — Jonah 3:10
see what w become of the city — Jonah 4:5
as he cried, and they w not hear — Zec 7:13
I w not hear, saith the LORD of — Zec 7:13
that w shut the doors for nought — Mal 1:10
w not be comforted, because they — Mt 2:18
from him that w borrow of thee — Mt 5:42
all things whatsoever ye w that — Mt 7:12
they besought him that he w — Mt 8:34
they w have repented long ago in — Mt 11:21
it w have remained until this day — Mt 11:23
ye w not have condemned the — Mt 12:7
we w see a sign from thee — Mt 12:38
when he w have put him to death, — Mt 14:5
to give her whatsoever she w ask — Mt 14:7
he w shew them a sign from heaven — Mt 16:1
which w take account of his — Mt 18:23
And he w not — Mt 18:30
and they w not come — Mt 22:3
we w not have been partakers with — Mt 23:30
how often w I have gathered thy — Mt 23:37
under her wings, and ye w not — Mt 23:37
in what watch the thief w come — Mt 24:43
he w have watched — Mt 24:43
w not have suffered his house to — Mt 24:43
people a prisoner, whom they w — Mt 27:15
tasted thereof, he w not drink — Mt 27:34
whether he w heal him on the — Mk 3:2
and calleth unto him whom he w — Mk 3:13
he besought him much that he w — Mk 5:10
against him, and w have killed him — Mk 6:19
sat with him, he w not reject her — Mk 6:26
the sea, and w have passed by them. — Mk 6:48
house, and w have no man know it — Mk 7:24
she besought him that he w cast — Mk 7:26
he w not that any man should know — Mk 9:30
we what thou shouldest do for — Mk 10:35
What w ye that I should do for — Mk 10:36
w not suffer that any man should — Mk 11:16
father, how he w have him called — Lk 1:62
That he w grant unto us, that we, — Lk 1:74
prayed him that he w thrust out a — Lk 5:3
whether he w heal on the sabbath — Lk 6:7
as ye w that men should do to you — Lk 6:31
beseeching him that he w come — Lk 7:3
him that he w eat with him — Lk 7:36
w have known who and what manner — Lk 7:39
they besought him that he w not — Lk 8:31
they besought him that he w — Lk 8:32
come into his house — Lk 8:41
as though he w go to Jerusalem — Lk 9:53
place, whither he himself w come — Lk 10:1
that he w send forth labourers — Lk 10:2
known what hour the thief w come — Lk 12:39

W

he *w* have watched, and not have...... Lk 12:39
how often *w* I have gathered thy ...... Lk 13:34
under her wings, and ye *w* not...... Lk 13:34
he *w* fain have filled his belly ...... Lk 15:16
And he was angry, and *w* not go in ... Lk 15:28
so that they which *w* pass from...... Lk 16:26
to us, that *w* come from thence...... Lk 16:26
And he *w* not for a while...... Lk 18:4
w not lift up so much as his eyes...... Lk 18:13
infants, that he *w* touch them ...... Lk 18:15
which *w* not that I should reign ...... Lk 19:27
the stones *w* immediately cry out ...... Lk 19:40
were about him saw what *w* follow ...... Lk 22:49
as though he *w* have gone further ... Lk 24:28
Jesus *w* go forth into Galilee...... Jn 1:43
he *w* have given thee living water ... Jn 4:10
him that he *w* tarry with them ...... Jn 4:40
besought him that he *w* come down ... Jn 4:47
Moses, ye *w* have believed me ...... Jn 5:46
for he himself knew what he *w* do...... Jn 6:6
of the fishes as much as they *w*...... Jn 6:11
perceived that they *w* come...... Jn 6:15
for he *w* not walk in Jewry...... Jn 7:1
some of them *w* have taken him ...... Jn 7:44
ye *w* do the works of Abraham...... Jn 8:39
were your Father, ye *w* love me ...... Jn 8:42
wherefore ye ye hear it again...... Jn 9:27
him, saying, Sir, we *w* see Jesus ...... Jn 12:21
it were not so, I *w* have told you ...... Jn 14:2
ye *w* rejoice, because I said, I ...... Jn 14:28
world, the world *w* love his own...... Jn 15:19
we *w* not have delivered him up...... Jn 18:30
then *w* my servants fight, that I ...... Jn 18:36
he *w* raise up Christ to sit on...... Acts 2:30
of them whereunto this *w* grow...... Acts 5:24
yet he promised that he *w* give it...... Acts 7:5
For he supposed his brethren *w* ...... Acts 7:25
God by his hand *w* deliver them...... Acts 7:25
w have set them at one again, ... Acts 7:26
To whom our fathers *w* not obey...... Acts 7:39
desired Philip that he *w* come up ... Acts 8:31
desiring him that he *w* not delay ... Acts 9:38
very hungry, and *w* have eaten ...... Acts 10:10
heart they *w* cleave unto the Lord... Acts 11:23
when Herod *w* have brought him...... Acts 12:6
w have done sacrifice with the ...... Acts 14:13
Him *w* Paul have to go forth with ... Acts 16:3
w have killed himself, supposing ... Acts 16:27
w know therefore what these...... Acts 17:20
reason *w* that I should bear with ... Acts 18:14
when Paul *w* have entered in unto ... Acts 19:30
desiring him that he *w* not...... Acts 19:31
w have made his defence unto the... Acts 26:1
because he *w* not spend the time ... Acts 20:16
when he *w* not be persuaded, we ... Acts 21:14
because he *w* have known the ...... Acts 22:30
saying that they *w* neither eat ...... Acts 23:12
as though ye *w* enquire something... Acts 23:15
as though they *w* enquire somewhat... Acts 23:20
when I *w* have known the cause...... Acts 23:28
w have judged according to our ... Acts 24:6
that he *w* send for him to...... Acts 25:3
that he himself *w* depart shortly...... Acts 25:4
him whether he *w* go to Jerusalem... Acts 25:20
I *w* also hear the man myself ...... Acts 25:22
the beginning, if they *w* testify ...... Acts 26:5
I *w* to God, that not only thou, ... Acts 26:29
under colour as though they *w* ...... Acts 27:30
we *w* have let me go, because there... Acts 28:18
Now I *w* not have you ignorant...... Rom 1:13
good man some *w* even dare to die ... Rom 5:7
for what I *w*, that do I not...... Rom 7:15
If then I do that which I *w* not...... Rom 7:16
For the good that I *w* I do not...... Rom 7:19
but the evil which I *w* not...... Rom 7:19
Now if I do that I *w* not, it...... Rom 7:20
when I *w* do good, evil is present ... Rom 7:21
For I *w* not, brethren, that ye ...... Rom 11:25
but yet I *w* have you wise unto...... Rom 16:19
they *w* not have crucified the 1Cor 2:8
I *w* to God ye did reign, that we ... 1Cor 4:8
as though I *w* not come to you...... 1Cor 4:18
For I *w* that all men were even as... 1Cor 7:7
But I *w* have you without...... 1Cor 7:32
I *w* not that ye should be...... 1Cor 10:1
I *w* not that ye should have 1Cor 10:20
But I *w* have you know, that the ... 1Cor 11:3
For if we *w* judge ourselves, we ... 1Cor 11:31
I *w* not have you ignorant...... 1Cor 12:1
I *w* that ye all spake with...... 1Cor 14:5
For we *w* not, brethren, have you ... 2Cor 1:8
that I *w* not come again to you in... 2Cor 2:1
ye *w* confirm your love toward him ... 2Cor 2:8
not for that we *w* be unclothed...... 2Cor 5:4
that we *w* receive the gift...... 2Cor 8:4
so he *w* also finish in you the 2Cor 8:6
that they *w* go before unto you, ... 2Cor 9:5
as if I *w* terrify you by letters...... 2Cor 10:9
W to God ye could bear with me as ... 2Cor 11:1
For though I *w* desire to glory, I ... 2Cor 12:6
I shall not find you such as I *w* 2Cor 12:20
found unto you such as ye *w* not ... 2Cor 12:20
w pervert the gospel of Christ ...... Gal 1:7
Only they *w* that we should ...... Gal 2:10
This only *w* I learn of you,...... Gal 3:2
foreseeing that God *w* justify the... Gal 3:8
ye *w* have plucked out your own...... Gal 4:15
they *w* exclude you, that ye might ... Gal 4:17
I *w* they were even cut off which ... Gal 5:12
ye cannot do the things that ye *w* ... Gal 5:17

WOULDEST

w thou take away my son's...... Gen 30:15
though thou *w* needs be gone,...... Gen 31:30
Peradventure thou *w* take by force ... Gen 31:31
behold, hitherto thou *w* not hear... Ex 7:16
w forbear to help him, thou shalt ... Ex 23:5
heart, whether thou *w* keep his ...... Deut 8:2
because thou *w* not obey the voice... Deut 28:62
Caleb said unto her, What *w* thou ... Josh 15:18
that thou *w* not suffer the...... 2Sa 14:11
thou thyself *w* have set thyself 2Sa 18:13
And the king said, What *w* thou ... 1Kin 1:16
that thou *w* deliver thy servant 1Kin 18:9
w thou be spoken for to the king,... 2Kin 4:13
thing, *w* thou not have done it...... 2Kin 5:13
w thou smite those whom thou hast... 2Kin 6:22
Oh that thou *w* bless me indeed,... 1Chr 4:10
that thou *w* keep me from evil,...... 1Chr 4:10
that thou *w* put thy name there...... 2Chr 6:20
whom thou *w* not let Israel invade... 2Chr 20:10
w not thou be angry with us till...... Ezr 9:14
that thou *w* send me unto Judah,... Neh 2:5
If thou *w* seek unto God betimes,... Job 8:5
Oh that thou *w* hide me in the ...... Job 14:13
that thou *w* keep me secret, until ... Job 14:13
that thou *w* appoint me a set time... Job 14:13
for I knew that thou *w* deal very ... Is 48:8
Oh that thou *w* rend the heavens,... Is 64:1
that thou *w* come down...... Is 64:1
that thou *w* send him to thy...... Lk 16:27
thou *w* have asked of him, and he ... Jn 4:10
thee, that, if thou *w* believe,...... Jn 11:40
and walkedst whither thou *w*...... Jn 21:18
and carry thee whither thou *w* not... Jn 21:18
w bring down Paul to morrow into ... Acts 23:20
I pray thee that thou *w* hear us...... Acts 24:4
Sacrifice and offering thou *w* not... Heb 10:5
and offering for sin thou *w* not...... Heb 10:8

WOUND

w for *w*, stripe for stripe...... Ex 21:25
I *w*, and I heal...... Deut 32:39
the blood ran out of the *w* into 1Kin 22:35
my *w* is incurable without...... Job 34:6
But God shall *w* the head of his...... Ps 68:21
he shall *w* the heads over many ...... Ps 110:6
A *w* and dishonour shall he get ...... Prov 6:33
The blueness of a *w* cleanseth...... Prov 20:30
and healeth the stroke of their *w* ... Is 30:26
my *w* is grievous...... Jer 10:19
my *w* incurable, which refuseth to... Jer 15:18
incurable, and thy *w* is grievous,... Jer 30:12
thee with the *w* of an enemy...... Jer 30:14
his sickness, and Judah saw his *w* ... Hos 5:13
heal you, nor cure you of your *w* ... Hos 5:13
bread have laid a *w* under thee...... Obad 7
For her *w* is incurable...... Mic 1:9
thy *w* is grievous...... Nah 3:19
w it linen clothes with the...... Jn 19:40
w him up, and carried him out, and... Acts 5:6
w their weak conscience, ye sin 1Cor 8:12
and his deadly *w* was healed...... Rev 13:3
beast, whose deadly *w* was healed ... Rev 13:12
beast, which had the *w* by a sword... Rev 13:14

WOUNDED

He that is *w* in the stones, or...... Deut 23:1
were overthrown and *w* ...... Judg 9:40
the *w* of the Philistines fell 1Sa 17:52
he was sore *w* of the archers...... 1Sa 31:3
w them, that they could not arise... 2Sa 22:39
him, so that in smiting he *w* him ... 1Kin 20:37
for I am *w*...... 1Kin 22:34
and the Syrians *w* Joram;...... 2Kin 8:28
him, and he was *w* of the archers... 1Chr 10:3
for I am *w*...... 2Chr 18:33
for I am sore *w*...... 2Chr 35:23
and the soul of the *w* crieth out... Job 24:12
I have *w* them that they were not ... Ps 18:38
suddenly shall they be *w*...... Ps 64:7
grief of those whom thou hast *w*,... Ps 69:26
needy, and my heart is *w* within me... Ps 109:22
For she hath cast down many *w*...... Prov 7:26
but a *w* spirit who can bear...... Prov 18:14
me, they smote me, they *w* me...... Song 5:7
hath cut Rahab, and *w* the dragon ... Is 51:9
But he was *w* for our...... Is 53:5

for I have *w* thee with the wound ... Jer 30:14
remained but *w* men among them ...... Jer 37:10
all her land the *w* shall groan...... Jer 51:52
when they swooned as the *w* in the... Lam 2:12
sound of thy fall, when the *w* cry ... Eze 26:15
the *w* shall be judged in the...... Eze 28:23
the groanings of a deadly *w* man ... Eze 30:24
the sword, they shall not be *w*...... Joel 2:8
Those with which I was *w* in the...... Zec 13:6
w him in the head, and sent him ... Mk 12:4
w him, and departed, leaving him... Lk 10:30
they *w* him also, and cast him out... Lk 20:12
fled out of that house naked and *w* ... Acts 19:16
his heads as it were *w* to death...... Rev 13:3

WOUNDEDST

thou *w* the head out of the house... Hab 3:13

WOUNDETH

he *w*, and his hands make whole...... Job 5:18

WOUNDING

for I have slain a man to my *w* ...... Gen 4:23

WOUNDS

to be healed in Jezreel of the *w*...... 2Kin 8:29
to be healed in Jezreel of the *w*...... 2Kin 9:15
in Jezreel because of the *w* which... 2Chr 22:6
and multiplieth my *w* without...... Job 9:17
My *w* stink and are corrupt because... Ps 38:5
in heart, and bindeth up their *w* ... Ps 147:3
words of a talebearer are as *w*...... Prov 18:8
who hath *w* without cause ...... Prov 23:29
words of a talebearer are as *w*...... Prov 26:22
Faithful are the *w* of a friend...... Prov 27:6
but *w*, and bruises, and putrifying,... Is 1:6
me continually is grief and *w*...... Jer 6:7
and I will heal thee of thy *w* ...... Jer 30:17
What are these *w* in thine hands ... Zec 13:6
And went to him, and bound up his *w*... Lk 10:34

WOVE

where the women *w* hangings for...... 2Kin 23:7

WOVEN

it shall have a binding of *w* work ... Ex 28:32
the robe of the ephod of *w* work... Ex 39:22
of fine linen of *w* work for Aaron... Ex 39:27
w from the top throughout...... Jn 19:23

WRAP

than that he can *w* himself in it ... Is 28:20
so they *w* it up...... Mic 7:3

WRAPPED

w herself, and sat in an open...... Gen 38:14
it is here *w* in a cloth behind...... 1Sa 21:9
that he *w* his face in his mantle,... 1Kin 19:13
w it together, and smote the...... 2Kin 2:8
His roots are *w* about the heap...... Job 8:17
of his stones are *w* together...... Job 40:17
it is *w* up for the slaughter ...... Eze 21:15
the weeds were *w* about my head...... Jonah 2:5
he *w* it in a clean linen cloth,...... Mt 27:59
w him in the linen, and laid him...... Mk 15:46
the babe *w* in swaddling clothes,... Lk 2:7
the babe *w* in swaddling clothes...... Lk 2:12
w it in linen, and laid it in a...... Lk 23:53
but *w* together in a place by...... Jn 20:7

WRATH

that his *w* was kindled...... Gen 39:19
and their *w*, for it was cruel...... Gen 49:7
thou sentest forth thy *w*, which...... Ex 15:7
my *w* shall wax hot, and I will...... Ex 22:24
that my *w* may wax hot against...... Ex 32:10
why doth thy *w* wax hot against...... Ex 32:11
Turn from thy fierce *w*, and repent... Ex 32:12
lest *w* come upon all the people ...... Lev 10:6
that there be no *w* upon the...... Num 1:53
the *w* of the Lord was kindled...... Num 11:33
for there is *w* gone out from the ... Num 16:46
that there be no *w* any more upon... Num 18:5
hath turned my *w* away from the...... Num 25:11
thy God to *w* in the wilderness ...... Deut 9:7
Horeb ye provoked the Lord to *w*... Deut 9:8
ye provoked the Lord to *w*...... Deut 9:22
then the Lord's *w* be kindled...... Deut 11:17
in his anger, and in his *w*...... Deut 29:23
of their land in anger, and in *w*,... Deut 29:28
that I feared the *w* of the enemy... Deut 32:27
lest *w* be upon us, because of the... Josh 9:20
w fell on all the congregation of... Josh 22:20
his fierce *w* upon Amalek...... 1Sa 28:18
if so be that the king's *w* arise...... 2Sa 11:20
for great is the *w* of the Lord...... 2Kin 22:13
therefore my *w* shall be kindled ... 2Kin 22:13
the fierceness of his great *w*...... 2Kin 23:26
because there fell *w* for it...... 1Chr 27:24
my *w* shall not be poured out upon... 2Chr 12:7
the *w* of the Lord turned from him... 2Chr 12:12
therefore is *w* upon thee from...... 2Chr 19:2
so *w* came upon you, and upon your... 2Chr 19:10
w came upon Judah and Jerusalem... 2Chr 19:10
for the fierce *w* of the Lord is...... 2Chr 28:11
there is fierce *w* against Israel... 2Chr 28:13
Wherefore the *w* of the Lord was... 2Chr 29:8
that his fierce *w* may turn away... 2Chr 29:10
of his *w* may turn away from you ... 2Chr 30:8
therefore there was *w* upon him... 2Chr 32:25
so that the *w* of the Lord came...... 2Chr 32:26
for great is the *w* of the Lord...... 2Chr 34:21
therefore my *w* shall be poured...... 2Chr 34:25
until the *w* of the Lord arose...... 2Chr 36:16

WRATHFUL

provoked the God of heaven unto w ...... Ezr 5:12
for why should there be w against...... Ezr 7:23
his w is against all them that ...... Ezr 8:22
until the fierce w of our God for ...... Ezr 10:14
yet ye bring more w upon Israel ...... Neh 13:18
arise too much contempt and w ...... Est 1:18
when the w of king Ahasuerus was ...... Est 2:1
then was Haman full of w ...... Est 3:5
his w went into the palace garden. ...... Est 7:7
Then was the king's w pacified ...... Est 7:10
For w killeth the foolish man, and ...... Job 5:2
the secret, until thy w be past ...... Job 14:13
He heareth me in his w, who ...... Job 16:9
also kindled his w against me. ...... Job 19:11
for w bringeth the punishments of ...... Job 19:29
cast the fury of his w upon them. ...... Job 20:23
flow away in the day of his w ...... Job 20:28
drink of the w of the Almighty. ...... Job 21:20
be brought forth to the day of w ...... Job 21:30
Then was kindled the w of Elihu ...... Job 32:2
against Job was his w kindled ...... Job 32:2
three friends was his w kindled ...... Job 32:3
three men, then his w was kindled ...... Job 32:5
the hypocrites in heart heap up w ...... Job 36:13
Because there is w, beware lest ...... Job 36:18
Cast abroad the rage of thy w ...... Job 40:11
My w is kindled against thee, and ...... Job 42:7
shall he speak unto them in his w ...... Ps 2:5
when his w is kindled but a ...... Ps 2:12
shall swallow them up in his w ...... Ps 21:9
Cease from anger, and forsake w ...... Ps 37:8
O LORD, rebuke me not in thy w ...... Ps 38:1
upon me, and in w they hate me...... Ps 55:3
both living, and in his w ...... Ps 58:9
Consume them in w, consume them, ... Ps 59:13
Surely the w of man shall praise ...... Ps 76:10
the remainder of w shalt thou...... Ps 76:10
The w of God came upon them, and ...... Ps 78:31
and did not stir up all his ...... Ps 78:38
the fierceness of his anger, w ...... Ps 78:49
Pour out thy w upon the heathen...... Ps 79:6
Thou hast taken away all thy w...... Ps 85:3
Thy w lieth hard upon me, and thou...... Ps 88:7
Thy fierce w goeth over me...... Ps 88:16
shall thy w burn like fire ...... Ps 89:46
and by thy w are we troubled ...... Ps 90:7
our days are passed away in thy w ...... Ps 90:9
to thy fear, so is thy w ...... Ps 90:11
Unto whom I sware in my w that...... Ps 95:11
of thine indignation and thy w...... Ps 102:10
in the breach, to turn away his w...... Ps 106:23
Therefore was the w of the LORD...... Ps 106:40
through kings in the day of his w...... Ps 110:5
when their w was kindled against...... Ps 124:3
against the w of mine enemies...... Ps 138:7
Riches profit not in the day of w...... Prov 11:4
expectation of the wicked is w...... Prov 11:23
A fool's w is presently known...... Prov 12:16
He that is slow to w is of great...... Prov 14:29
but his w is against him that...... Prov 14:35
A soft answer turneth away w...... Prov 15:1
The w of a king is as messengers...... Prov 16:14
The king's w is as the roaring of...... Prov 19:12
A man of great w shall suffer...... Prov 19:19
and a reward in the bosom strong w...... Prov 21:14
his name, who dealeth in proud w...... Prov 21:24
and he turn away his w from him...... Prov 24:18
but a fool's w is heavier than...... Prov 27:3
W is cruel, and anger is...... Prov 27:4
but wise men turn away w...... Prov 29:8
so the forcing of w bringeth...... Prov 30:33
sorrow and w with his sickness...... Eccl 5:17
Through the w of the LORD...... Is 9:19
of my w will I give him a charge...... Is 10:6
LORD cometh, cruel both with w...... Is 13:9
in the w of the LORD of hosts, and...... Is 13:13
in w with a continual stroke...... Is 14:6
and his pride, and his w...... Is 16:6
In a little w I hid my face from...... Is 54:8
for in my w I smote thee, but in...... Is 60:10
forsaken the generation of his w...... Jer 7:29
at his w the earth shall tremble...... Jer 10:10
and to turn away thy w from them...... Jer 18:20
anger, and in fury, and in great w...... Jer 21:5
and in my fury, and in great w...... Jer 32:37
in that ye provoke me unto w with...... Jer 44:8
I know his w, saith the LORD...... Jer 48:30
Because of the w of the LORD it...... Jer 50:13
in his w the strong holds of the...... Lam 2:2
affliction by the rod of his w...... Lam 3:1
for w is upon all the multitude...... Eze 7:12
for my w is upon all the...... Eze 7:14
in the day of the w of the LORD...... Eze 7:19
I accomplish my w upon the wall...... Eze 13:15
against the w of the fire of my...... Eze 21:31
blow upon you in the fire of my w...... Eze 22:21
them with the fire of my...... Eze 22:31
in the fire of my w have I spoken...... Eze 38:19
out my w upon them like water...... Hos 5:10
anger, and took him away in my w...... Hos 13:11
and he kept his w for ever...... Amos 1:11
he reserveth w for his enemies...... Nah 1:2
in w remember mercy...... Hab 3:2
was thy w against the sea, that...... Hab 3:8
That day is a day of w, a day of...... Zeph 1:15
them in the day of the LORD's w...... Zeph 1:18
a great w from the LORD of hosts...... Zec 7:12
your fathers provoked me to w...... Zec 8:14
you to flee from the w to come...... Mt 3:7
you to flee from the w to come...... Lk 3:7

these things, were filled with w...... Lk 4:28
the land, and w upon this people...... Lk 21:23
but the w of God abideth on him...... Jn 3:36
sayings, they were full of w...... Acts 19:28
For the w of God is revealed from...... Rom 1:18
w against the day of w...... Rom 2:5
w against the day of w...... Rom 2:5
unrighteousness, indignation and w...... Rom 2:8
Because the law worketh w...... Rom 4:15
shall be saved from w through him...... Rom 5:9
if God, willing to shew his w...... Rom 9:22
of w fitted to destruction...... Rom 9:22
but rather give place unto w...... Rom 12:19
a revenger to execute w upon him...... Rom 13:4
needs be subject, not only for w...... Rom 13:5
hatred, variance, emulations, w...... Gal 5:20
were by nature the children of w...... Eph 2:3
not the sun go down upon your w...... Eph 4:26
Let all bitterness, and w, and...... Eph 4:31
of these things cometh the w of...... Eph 5:6
provoke not your children to w...... Eph 6:4
For which things' sake the w of...... Col 3:6
anger, w, malice, blasphemy...... Col 3:8
delivered us from the w to come...... 1Th 1:10
for the w is come upon them to...... 1Th 2:16
God hath not appointed us to w...... 1Th 5:9
lifting up holy hands, without w...... 1Ti 2:8
So I sware in my w, They shall...... Heb 3:11
he said, As I have sworn in my w...... Heb 4:3
not fearing the w of the king...... Heb 11:27
to hear, slow to speak, slow to w...... Jas 1:19
For the w of man worketh not the...... Jas 1:20
throne, and from the w of the Lamb...... Rev 6:16
the great day of his w is come...... Rev 6:17
thy w is come, and the time of the...... Rev 11:18
down unto you, having great w...... Rev 12:12
wine of the w of her fornication...... Rev 14:8
drink of the wine of the w of God...... Rev 14:10
great winepress of the w of God...... Rev 14:19
in them is filled up the w of God...... Rev 15:1
vials full of the w of God...... Rev 15:7
of the w of God upon the earth...... Rev 16:1
wine of the fierceness of his w...... Rev 16:19
wine of the w of her fornication...... Rev 18:3
fierceness and w of Almighty God...... Rev 19:15

WRATHFUL

let thy w anger take hold of them...... Ps 69:24
A w man stirreth up strife...... Prov 15:18

WRATHS

there be debates, envyings, w...... 2Cor 12:20

WREATH

rows of pomegranates on each w...... 2Chr 4:13

WREATHED

they are w, and come up upon my...... Lam 1:14

WREATHEN

of w work shalt thou make them,...... Ex 28:14
fasten the w chains to the ouches...... Ex 28:14
the ends of w work of pure gold...... Ex 28:22
thou shalt put the two w chains...... Ex 28:24
fasten the two chains of w work...... Ex 28:25
the two w chains thou shalt...... Ex 28:25
the ends, of w work of pure gold...... Ex 39:15
they put the two w chains of gold...... Ex 39:17
the two ends of the two w chains...... Ex 39:18
the w work, and pomegranates upon...... 2Kin 25:17
had the second pillar with w work...... 2Kin 25:17

WREATHS

work, and w of chain work, for the...... 1Kin 7:17
the two w to cover the two...... 2Chr 4:12
hundred pomegranates on the two w...... 2Chr 4:13

WREST

decline after many to w judgment...... Ex 23:2
Thou shalt not w the judgment of...... Ex 23:6
Thou shalt not w judgment...... Deut 16:19
Every day they w my words...... Ps 56:5
that are unlearned and unstable w...... 2Pet 3:16

WRESTLE

For we w not against flesh and...... Eph 6:12

WRESTLED

have I w with my sister, and I...... Gen 30:8
there a man with him until the...... Gen 32:24
out of joint, as he w with him...... Gen 32:25

WRESTLINGS

With great w have I wrestled with...... Gen 30:8

WRETCHED

O w man that I am...... Rom 7:24
and knowest not that thou art w...... Rev 3:17

WRETCHEDNESS

and let me not see my w...... Num 11:15

WRING

w off his head, and burn it on the...... Lev 1:15
w off his head from his neck, but...... Lev 5:8
of the earth shall w them out...... Ps 75:8

WRINGED

the w dew out of the fleece, a...... Judg 6:38

WRINGING

the w of the nose bringeth forth...... Prov 30:33

WRINKLE

church, not having spot, or w...... Eph 5:27

WRINKLES

and thou hast filled me with w...... Job 16:8

WRITE

W this for a memorial in a book,...... Ex 17:14
I will w upon these tables...... Ex 34:1

unto Moses, W thou these words......Ex 34:27
the priest shall w these curses......Num 5:23
w thou every man's name upon his......Num 17:2
thou shalt w Aaron's name upon......Num 17:3
thou shalt w them upon the posts......Deut 6:9
I will w on the tables the words......Deut 10:2
thou shalt w them upon the door......Deut 11:20
that he shall w him a copy of......Deut 17:18
then let him w her a bill of......Deut 24:1
w her a bill of divorcement, and......Deut 24:3
thou shalt w upon them all the......Deut 27:3
thou shalt w upon the stones all......Deut 27:8
Now therefore w ye this song for......Deut 31:19
the prophet, the son of Amoz, w......2Chr 26:22
that we might w the names of these......Ezr 5:10
we make a sure covenant, and w it......Neh 9:38
W ye also for the Jews, as it......Est 8:8
w them upon the table of thine......Prov 3:3
w them upon the table of thine......Prov 7:3
roll, and w in it with a man's pen......Is 8:1
that w grievousness which they......Is 10:19
be few, that a child may w them......Is 10:19
w it before them in a table, and......Is 30:8
W ye this man childless, a man......Jer 22:30
W thee all the words that I have......Jer 30:2
parts, and w it in their hearts......Jer 31:33
w therein all the words that I......Jer 36:2
How didst thou w all these words......Jer 36:17
w in it all the former words that......Jer 36:28
the w thee the curse of the day, even......Eze 24:2
w upon it, For Judah, and for the......Eze 37:16
w upon it, For Joseph, the stick......Eze 37:16
w it in their sight, that they......Eze 43:11
W the vision, and make it plain......Mk 10:4
Moses suffered to w a bill of......Mk 10:4
to w unto thee in order, most......Lk 1:3
and sit down quickly, and w fifty......Lk 16:6
Take thy bill, and w fourscore......Lk 16:7
the law, and the prophets, did w......Jn 1:45
W not, The King of the Jews......Jn 19:21
But that we w unto them, that......Acts 15:20
certain thing to w unto my lord......Acts 25:26
had, I might have somewhat to w......Acts 25:26
I w not these things to shame you......1Cor 4:14
that the things that I w unto you......1Cor 14:37
For we w none other things unto......2Cor 1:13
For to this end also did I......2Cor 2:9
is superfluous for me to w you......2Cor 9:1
being absent now I w to them......2Cor 13:2
Therefore I w these things being......2Cor 13:10
Now the things which I w unto you......Gal 1:20
To w the same things to you, to......Phil 3:1
ye need not that I w unto you......1Th 4:9
ye have no need that I w unto you......1Th 5:1
so I w......2Th 3:17
These things w I unto thee......1Ti 3:14
mind, and w them in their hearts......Heb 8:10
and in their minds will I w them......Heb 10:16
beloved, I now w unto you......2Pet 3:1
And these things w we unto you......1Jn 1:4
these things w I unto you......1Jn 2:1
I w no new commandment unto you......1Jn 2:7
a new commandment I w unto you......1Jn 2:8
I w unto you, little children,......1Jn 2:12
I w unto you, fathers, because ye......1Jn 2:13
I w unto you, young men, because......1Jn 2:13
I w unto you, little children,......1Jn 2:13
Having many things to w unto you......2Jn 12
I would not w with paper......2Jn 12
I had many things to w, but I......3Jn 13
not with ink and pen w unto thee......3Jn 13
to w unto you of the common......Jude 3
was needful for me to w unto you......Jude 3
w in a book, and send it unto the......Rev 1:11
W the things which thou hast seen......Rev 1:19
angel of the church of Ephesus w......Rev 2:1
angel of the church in Smyrna w......Rev 2:8
angel of the church in Pergamos w......Rev 2:12
angel of the church in Thyatira w......Rev 2:18
angel of the church in Sardis w......Rev 3:1
of the church in Philadelphia w......Rev 3:7
I will w upon him the name of my......Rev 3:12
I will w upon him my new name......Rev 3:12
of the church of the Laodiceans w......Rev 3:14
their voices, I was about to w......Rev 10:4
thunders uttered, and w them not......Rev 10:4
from heaven saying unto me, W......Rev 14:13
And he saith unto me, W, Blessed......Rev 19:9
And he said unto me, W......Rev 21:5

WRITER

they that handle the pen of the w......Judg 5:14
my tongue is the pen of a ready w......Ps 45:1

WRITER'S

with a w inkhorn by his side......Eze 9:2
which had the w inkhorn by his......Eze 9:11

WRITEST

For thou w bitter things against......Job 13:26
the sticks whereon thou shalt......Eze 37:20

WRITETH

when he w up the people, that......Ps 87:6

WRITING

the w was the w of God,......Ex 32:16
pure gold, and wrote upon it a w......Ex 39:30
tables, according to the first w......Deut 10:4
when Moses had made an end of w......Deut 31:24
in w by his hand upon me, even......1Chr 28:19
the king of Tyre answered in w......2Chr 2:11
there came a w to him from Elijah......2Chr 21:12
according to the w of David king......2Chr 35:4

according to the w of Solomon his...... 2Chr 35:4
his kingdom, and put it also in w...... 2Chr 36:22
his kingdom, and put it also in w...... Ezr 1:1
the w of the letter was written...... Ezr 4:7
according to the w thereof...... Est 1:22
according to the w thereof...... Est 3:12
The copy of the w for a...... Est 3:14
he gave him the copy of the w of...... Est 4:8
for the w which is written in the...... Est 8:8
according to the w thereof...... Est 8:9
to the Jews according to their w...... Est 8:9
The copy of the w for a...... Est 8:13
two days according to their w...... Est 9:27
The w of Hezekiah king of Judah...... Is 38:9
in the w of the house of Israel...... Eze 13:9
Whosoever shall read this w...... Dan 5:7
but they could not read the w...... Dan 5:8
me, that they should read this w...... Dan 5:15
now if thou canst read the w...... Dan 5:16
I will read the w unto the king...... Dan 5:17
and this w was written...... Dan 5:24
this is the w that was written,...... Dan 5:25
the decree, and sign the w...... Dan 6:8
king Darius signed the w and the...... Dan 6:9
Daniel knew that the w was signed...... Dan 6:10
him give her a w of divorcement...... Mt 5:31
to give a w of divorcement...... Mt 19:7
And he asked for a table...... Lk 1:63
the w was, JESUS...... Jn 19:19

WRITINGS
But if ye believe not his w...... Jn 5:47

WRITTEN
and commandments which I have w...... Ex 24:12
stone, with the finger of God...... Ex 31:18
The tables were w on both their...... Ex 32:15
side and on the other were they w...... Ex 32:15
out of thy book which thou hast w...... Ex 32:32
and they were of them that were w...... Num 11:26
of stone w with the finger of God...... Deut 9:10
on them was w according to all...... Deut 9:10
this law that are w in this book...... Deut 28:58
which is not w in the book of...... Deut 28:61
all the curses that are w in this...... Deut 29:20
are w in this book of the law...... Deut 29:21
curses that are w in this book...... Deut 29:27
his statutes which are w in this...... Deut 30:10
to all that is w therein...... Josh 1:8
as it is w in the book of the law...... Josh 8:31
that is w in the book of the law...... Josh 8:34
Is not this w in the book of...... Josh 10:13
to do all that is w in the book...... Josh 23:6
it is w in the book of Jasher...... 2Sa 1:18
as it is w in the law of Moses...... 1Kin 2:3
are they not w in the book of the...... 1Kin 11:41
they are w in the book of the...... 1Kin 14:19
are they not w in the book of the...... 1Kin 14:29
are they not w in the book of the...... 1Kin 15:7
are they not w in the book of the...... 1Kin 15:23
are they not w in the book of the...... 1Kin 15:31
are they not w in the book of the...... 1Kin 16:5
are they not w in the book of the...... 1Kin 16:14
that are w in the book of the...... 1Kin 16:20
are they not w in the book of the...... 1Kin 16:27
as it was w in the letters which...... 1Kin 21:11
are they not w in the book of the...... 1Kin 22:39
are they not w in the book of the...... 1Kin 22:45
are they not w in the book of the...... 2Kin 1:18
are they not w in the book of the...... 2Kin 8:23
are they not w in the book of the...... 2Kin 10:34
are they not w in the book of the...... 2Kin 12:19
are they not w in the book of the...... 2Kin 13:8
are they not w in the book of the...... 2Kin 13:12
according unto that which is w in...... 2Kin 14:6
are they not w in the book of the...... 2Kin 14:15
are they not w in the book of the...... 2Kin 14:18
are they not w in the book of the...... 2Kin 14:28
they are w in the book of the...... 2Kin 15:11
are they not w in the book of the...... 2Kin 15:15
are they not w in the book of the...... 2Kin 15:21
they are w in the book of the...... 2Kin 15:26
are they not w in the book of the...... 2Kin 15:31
are they not w in the book of the...... 2Kin 15:36
are they not w in the book of the...... 2Kin 16:19
are they not w in the book of the...... 2Kin 20:20
are they not w in the book of the...... 2Kin 21:17
are they not w in the book of the...... 2Kin 21:25
all that which is w concerning us...... 2Kin 22:13
covenant that were w in this book...... 2Kin 23:3
are it is w in the book of this...... 2Kin 23:21
w in the book that Hilkiah the...... 2Kin 23:24
are they not w in the book of the...... 2Kin 23:28
are they not w in the book of the...... 2Kin 24:5
these w by name came in the days...... 1Chr 4:41
they were w in the book of the...... 1Chr 9:1
that is w in the law of the LORD...... 1Chr 16:40
they are w in the book of Samuel...... 1Chr 29:29
are they not w in the book of...... 2Chr 9:29
are they not w in the book of...... 2Chr 12:15
are w in the story of the prophet...... 2Chr 13:22
they are w in the book of...... 2Chr 16:11
they are w in the book of Jehu...... 2Chr 20:34
as it is w in the law of Moses...... 2Chr 23:18
they are w in the story of the...... 2Chr 24:27
but did as it is w in the law in...... 2Chr 25:4
are they not w in the book of the...... 2Chr 25:26
they are w in the book of...... 2Chr 27:7
they are w in the book of the...... 2Chr 28:26
time in such sort as it was w...... 2Chr 30:5

passover otherwise than it was w...... 2Chr 30:18
as it is w in the law of the LORD...... 2Chr 31:3
they are w in the vision of...... 2Chr 32:32
they are w in the book of the...... 2Chr 33:18
they are w among the sayings of...... 2Chr 33:19
after all that is w in this book...... 2Chr 34:21
are w in the book which they have...... 2Chr 34:24
covenant which are w in this book...... 2Chr 34:31
as it is w in the book of Moses...... 2Chr 35:12
they are w in the lamentations...... 2Chr 35:25
was in the law of the LORD...... 2Chr 35:26
they are w in the book of the...... 2Chr 35:27
they are w in the book of the...... 2Chr 36:8
as it is w in the law of Moses...... Ezr 3:2
feast of tabernacles, as it is w...... Ezr 3:4
letter was w in the Syrian tongue...... Ezr 4:7
unto him, wherein was w thus...... Ezr 5:7
and therein was a record thus w...... Ezr 6:2
as it is w in the book of Moses...... Ezr 6:18
all the weight was w at that time...... Ezr 8:34
Wherein was w, It is reported...... Neh 6:6
at the first, and found w therein...... Neh 7:5
they found w in the law which the...... Neh 8:14
trees, to make booths, as it is w...... Neh 8:15
our God, as it is w in the law...... Neh 10:34
were w in the book of the...... Neh 10:36
and therein was found w, that the...... Neh 12:23
let it be among the laws of the...... Est 1:19
it was w in the book of the...... Est 2:23
let it be w that they may be...... Est 3:9
there was w according to all that...... Est 3:12
name of king Ahasuerus was it w...... Est 3:12
And it was found w, that Mordecai...... Est 6:2
let it be w to reverse the...... Est 8:5
which is w in the king's name...... Est 8:8
it was w according to all that...... Est 8:9
and as Mordecai had w unto them...... Est 9:23
and it was w in the book...... Est 9:32
are they not w in the book of the...... Est 10:2
On that my words were now w...... Job 19:23
that mine adversary had w a book...... Job 31:35
volume of the book it is w of me...... Ps 40:7
not be w with the righteous...... Ps 69:28
This shall be w for the...... Ps 102:18
in thy book all my members were w...... Ps 139:16
execute upon them the judgment w...... Ps 149:9
Have not I w to thee excellent...... Prov 22:20
and that which was w was upright...... Eccl 12:10
even every one that is w among...... Is 4:3
Behold, it is w before me...... Is 65:6
of Judah is w with a pen of iron...... Jer 17:1
from me shall be w in the earth...... Jer 17:13
even all that is w in this book...... Jer 25:13
which thou hast w from my mouth...... Jer 36:6
saying, Why hast thou w therein...... Jer 36:29
when he had w these words in a...... Jer 45:1
words that are w against Babylon...... Jer 51:60
and it was w within and without...... Eze 2:10
there was w therein lamentations...... Eze 2:10
neither shall they be w in the...... Eze 13:9
and this writing was...... Dan 5:24
And this is the writing that was w...... Dan 5:25
the oath that is w in the law of...... Dan 9:11
As it is w in the law of Moses...... Dan 9:13
that shall be found w in the book...... Dan 12:1
I have w to him the great things...... Hos 8:12
a book of remembrance was w...... Mal 3:16
for that it is w by the prophet...... Mt 2:5
But he answered and said, It is w...... Mt 4:4
for it is w, He shall give his...... Mt 4:6
said unto him, It is w again...... Mt 4:7
for it is w, Thou shalt worship...... Mt 4:10
For this is he, of whom it is w...... Mt 11:10
And said unto them, It is w...... Mt 21:13
of man goeth as it is w of him...... Mt 26:24
for it is w, I will smite the...... Mt 26:31
up over his head his accusation w...... Mt 27:37
As it is w in the prophets...... Mk 1:2
of you hypocrites, as it is w...... Mk 7:6
how it is w of the Son of man...... Mk 9:12
they listed, as it is w of him...... Mk 9:13
saying unto them, Is it not w...... Mk 11:17
indeed goeth, as it is w of him...... Mk 14:21
for it is w, I will smite the...... Mk 14:27
of his accusation was w over...... Mk 15:26
(As it is w in the law of the...... Lk 2:23
As it is w in the book of the...... Lk 3:4
answered him, saying, It is w...... Lk 4:4
for it is w, Thou shalt worship...... Lk 4:8
For it is w, He shall give his...... Lk 4:10
he found the place where it was w...... Lk 4:17
This is he, of whom it is w...... Lk 7:27
your names are w in heaven...... Lk 10:20
unto him, What is w in the law...... Lk 10:26
all things that are w by the...... Lk 18:31
Saying unto them, It is w...... Lk 19:46
said, What is this then that is w...... Lk 20:17
which are w may be fulfilled...... Lk 21:22
that this that is w must yet be...... Lk 22:37
a superscription also was w over...... Lk 23:38
which were w in the law of Moses...... Lk 24:44
And said unto them, Thus it is w...... Lk 24:46
remembered that it was w, The...... Jn 2:17
as it is w, He gave them bread...... Jn 6:31
It is w in the prophets, And they...... Jn 6:45
It is also w in your law, that...... Jn 8:17
Is it not w in your law, I said...... Jn 10:34
as it is w...... Jn 12:14
that these things were w of him...... Jn 12:16

fulfilled that is w in their law...... Jn 15:25
it was w in Hebrew, and Greek, and...... Jn 19:20
What I have w I have w...... Jn 19:22
which are not w in this book...... Jn 20:30
But these are w, that ye might...... Jn 20:31
if they should be w every one...... Jn 21:25
the books that should be w...... Jn 21:25
For it is w in the book of Psalms...... Acts 1:20
as it is w in the book of the...... Acts 7:42
fulfilled all that was w of him...... Acts 13:29
as it is also w in the second...... Acts 13:33
as it is w...... Acts 15:15
Gentiles which believe, we have w...... Acts 21:25
for it is w, Thou shalt not speak...... Acts 23:5
all things which are w in the law...... Acts 24:14
as it is w, The just shall live...... Rom 1:17
work of the law w in their hearts...... Rom 2:15
Gentiles through you, as it is w...... Rom 2:24
as it is w, That thou mightest be...... Rom 3:4
As it is w, There is none...... Rom 3:10
(As it is w, I have made thee a...... Rom 4:17
Now it was not w for his sake...... Rom 4:23
As it is w, For thy sake we are...... Rom 8:36
As it is w, Jacob have I loved...... Rom 9:13
As it is w, Behold, I lay in Sion...... Rom 9:33
as it is w, How beautiful are the...... Rom 10:15
(According as it is w, God hath...... Rom 11:8
as it is w, There shall come out...... Rom 11:26
for it is w, Vengeance is mine...... Rom 12:19
For it is w, As I live, saith the...... Rom 14:11
but, as it is w, The reproaches...... Rom 15:3
For whatsoever things were w...... Rom 15:4
aforetime were w for our learning...... Rom 15:4
as it is w, For this cause I will...... Rom 15:9
I have w the more boldly unto you...... Rom 15:15
But as it is w, To whom he was...... Rom 15:21
W to the Romans from Corinthus,...... Rom s
That, according as it is w...... 1Cor 1:31
But as it is w, Eye hath not seen...... 1Cor 2:9
For it is w, He taketh the wise...... 1Cor 3:19
of men above that which is w...... 1Cor 4:6
But now I have w unto you not to...... 1Cor 5:11
For it is w in the law of Moses,...... 1Cor 9:9
our sakes, no doubt, this is w...... 1Cor 9:10
neither have I w these things...... 1Cor 9:15
as it is w, The people sat down...... 1Cor 10:7
they are w for our admonition,...... 1Cor 10:11
In the law it is w, With them of...... 1Cor 14:21
And so it is w, The first man Adam...... 1Cor 15:45
to pass the saying that is w...... 1Cor 15:54
was w from Philippi by Stephanas...... 1Cor s
are our epistle w in our hearts...... 2Cor 3:2
w not with ink, but with the...... 2Cor 3:3
if the ministration of death, w...... 2Cor 3:7
of faith, according as it is w...... 2Cor 4:13
As it is w, He that had gathered...... 2Cor 8:15
(As it is w, He hath dispersed...... 2Cor 9:9
Corinthians was w from Philippi...... 2Cor s
for it is w, Cursed is every one...... Gal 3:10
not in all things which are w in...... Gal 3:10
for it is w, Cursed is every one...... Gal 3:13
For it is w, that Abraham had two...... Gal 4:22
for it is w, Rejoice, thou barren...... Gal 4:27
w unto you with mine own hand...... Gal 6:11
Unto the Galatians w from Rome...... Gal s
W from Rome unto the Ephesians by...... Eph s
It was w to the Philippians from...... Phil s
W from Rome to the Colossians by...... Col s
Thessalonians was w from Athens...... 1Th s
Thessalonians was w from Athens...... 2Th s
The first to Timothy was w from...... 1Ti s
was w from Rome, when Paul was...... 2Ti s
It was w to Titus, ordained the...... Titus s
I Paul have w it with mine own...... Philem 19
W from Rome to Philemon, by...... Philem s
volume of the book it is w of me...... Heb 10:7
firstborn, which are w in heaven...... Heb 12:23
for I have w a letter unto you in...... Heb 13:22
W to the Hebrews from Italy by...... Heb s
Because it is w, Be ye holy; for I...... 1Pet 1:16
I have w briefly, exhorting, and...... 1Pet 5:12
given unto him hath w unto you...... 2Pet 3:15
I have w unto you, fathers,...... 1Jn 2:14
I have w unto you, young men,...... 1Jn 2:14
I have not w unto you because ye...... 1Jn 2:21
These things have I w unto you...... 1Jn 2:26
These things have I w unto you...... 1Jn 5:13
those things which are w therein...... Rev 1:3
and in the stone a new name w...... Rev 2:17
sat on the throne a book w within...... Rev 5:1
whose names are not w in the book...... Rev 13:8
name w in their foreheads...... Rev 14:1
And upon her forehead was a name w...... Rev 17:5
whose names were not w in the...... Rev 17:8
and he had a name w, that no man...... Rev 19:12
vesture and on his thigh a name w...... Rev 19:16
things which were w in the books...... Rev 20:12
whosoever was not found w in the...... Rev 20:15
names or thereon, which are the...... Rev 21:12
but they which are w in the...... Rev 21:27
plagues that are w in this book...... Rev 22:18
things which are w in this book...... Rev 22:19

WRONG
unto Abram, My w be upon thee...... Gen 16:5
and he said to him that did the w...... Ex 2:13
against him that which is w...... Deut 19:16
thou doest me w to war against me...... Judg 11:27
there is no w in mine hands...... 1Chr 12:17
He suffered no man to do them w...... 1Chr 16:21

WRONGED

hath not done w to the king only ___ Est 1:16
Behold, I cry out of w, but I am ___ Job 19:7
He suffered no man to do them w ___ Ps 105:14
and do no w, do no violence to the ___ Jer 22:3
and his chambers by w ___ Jer 22:13
O LORD, thou hast seen my w ___ Lam 3:59
therefore w judgment proceedeth ___ Hab 1:4
and said, Friend, I do thee no w ___ Mt 20:13
And seeing one of them suffer w ___ Acts 7:24
why do ye one to another? ___ Acts 7:26
his neighbour w thrust him away ___ Acts 7:27
a matter of w or wicked lewdness ___ Acts 18:14
to the Jews have I done no w ___ Acts 25:10
Why do ye not rather take w ___ 1Cor 6:7
Nay, ye do w, and defraud, and that ___ 1Cor 6:8
for his cause that had done the w ___ 2Cor 7:12
nor for his cause that suffered w ___ 2Cor 7:12
forgive me this w ___ 2Cor 12:13
But he that doeth w shall receive ___ Col 3:25
for he w which he hath done ___ Col 3:25

WRONGED

we have w no man, we have ___ 2Cor 7:2
If he hath w thee, or oweth thee ___ Philem 18

WRONGETH

sinneth against me w his own soul ___ Prov 8:36

WRONGFULLY

which ye w imagine against me ___ Job 21:27
mine enemies w rejoice over me ___ Ps 35:19
that hate me w are multiplied ___ Ps 38:19
destroy me, being mine enemies w ___ Ps 69:4
they persecute me w ___ Ps 119:86
have oppressed the stranger w ___ Eze 22:29
God endure grief, suffering w ___ 1Pet 2:19

WROTE

Moses w all the words of the LORD ___ Ex 24:4
he w upon the tables the words of ___ Ex 34:28
w upon it a writing, like to the ___ Ex 39:30
And Moses w their goings out ___ Num 33:2
he w them upon two tables of ___ Deut 4:13
he w them in two tables of stone ___ Deut 5:22
he w on the tables, according to ___ Deut 10:4
Moses w this law, and delivered it ___ Deut 31:9
Moses therefore w this song the ___ Deut 31:22
he w there upon the stones a copy ___ Josh 8:32
which he w in the presence of the ___ Josh 8:32
Joshua w these words in the book ___ Josh 24:26
w it in a book, and laid it up ___ 1Sa 10:25
that David w a letter to Joab, and ___ 2Sa 11:14
he w in the letter, saying, Set ___ 2Sa 11:15
So she w letters in Ahab's name ___ 1Kin 21:8
she w in the letters, saying ___ 1Kin 21:9
Jehu w letters, and sent to ___ 2Kin 10:1
Then he w a letter the second ___ 2Kin 10:6
commandment, which he w for you ___ 2Kin 17:37
w them before the king, and the ___ 1Chr 24:6
w letters also to Ephraim and ___ 2Chr 30:1
He w also letters to rail on the ___ 2Chr 32:17
w they unto him an accusation ___ Ezr 4:6
the days of Artaxerxes w Bishlam ___ Ezr 4:7
Shimshai the scribe w a letter ___ Ezr 4:8
Then w Rehum the chancellor, and ___ Ezr 4:9
which he w to destroy the Jews ___ Est 8:5
he w in the king Ahasuerus' name ___ Est 8:10
Mordecai w these things, and sent ___ Est 9:20
w with all authority, to confirm ___ Est 9:29
Baruch w from the mouth of ___ Jer 36:4
I w them with ink in the book ___ Jer 36:18
the words which Baruch w at the ___ Jer 36:27
who w therein from the mouth of ___ Jer 36:32
So Jeremiah w in a book all the ___ Jer 51:60
w over against the candlestick ___ Dan 5:5
the same part of the hand that ___ Dan 5:5
king Darius w unto all people ___ Dan 6:25
then he w the dream, and told the ___ Dan 7:1
your heart he w you this precept ___ Mk 10:5
Moses w unto us, If a man's ___ Mk 12:19
asked for a writing table, and w ___ Lk 1:63
Moses w unto us, If any man's ___ Lk 20:28
for he w of me ___ Jn 5:46
with his finger w on the ground ___ Jn 8:6
stooped down, and w on the ground ___ Jn 8:8
Pilate w a title, and put it on ___ Jn 19:19
these things, and w these things ___ Jn 21:24
they w letters by them after this ___ Acts 15:23
pass into Achaia, the brethren w ___ Acts 18:27
he w a letter after this manner ___ Acts 23:25
who w this epistle, salute you in ___ Rom 16:22
I w unto you in an epistle not to ___ 1Cor 5:9
the things whereof ye w unto me ___ 1Cor 7:1
I w this same unto you, lest ___ 2Cor 2:3
anguish of heart I w unto you ___ 2Cor 2:4
Wherefore, though I w unto you ___ 2Cor 7:12
(as I w afore in few words ___ Eph 3:3
in thy obedience I w unto thee ___ Philem 21
lady, not as though I w a new ___ 2Jn 5
I w unto the church ___ 3Jn 9

WROTH

And Cain was very w, and his ___ Gen 4:5
said unto Cain, Why art thou w ___ Gen 4:6
And Jacob was w, and chode with ___ Gen 31:36
were grieved, and they were very w ___ Gen 34:7
Pharaoh was w against two of his ___ Gen 40:2
Pharaoh was w with his servants ___ Gen 41:10
and Moses was w with them ___ Ex 16:20
And Moses was very w ___ Num 16:15
wilt thou be w with all the ___ Num 16:22
Moses was w with the officers of ___ Num 31:14
the voice of your words, and was w ___ Deut 1:34
But the LORD was w with me for ___ Deut 3:26
wherewith the LORD was w against ___ Deut 9:19
that to morrow he will be w with ___ Josh 22:18
And Saul was very w, and the saying ___ 1Sa 18:8
but if he be very w, then be sure ___ 1Sa 20:7
the Philistines were w with him ___ 1Sa 29:4
Then was Abner very w for the ___ 2Sa 3:8
these things, he was very w ___ 2Sa 13:21
moved and shook, because he was w ___ 2Sa 22:8
But Naaman was w, and went away ___ 2Kin 5:11
the man of God was w ___ 2Kin 13:19
Then Asa was w with the seer, and ___ 2Chr 16:10
Then Uzziah was w, and had a ___ 2Chr 26:19
while he was w with the priests ___ 2Chr 26:19
of your fathers was w with Judah ___ 2Chr 28:9
he builded the wall, he was w ___ Neh 4:1
he stopped, then they were very w ___ Neh 4:7
wherefore the king very w ___ Est 1:12
those which kept the door, were w ___ Est 2:21
and were shaken, because he was w ___ Ps 18:7
the LORD heard this, and was w ___ Ps 78:21
When God heard this, he was w ___ Ps 78:59
was w with his inheritance ___ Ps 78:62
he was w, and hate him sore ___ Ps 89:38
thou hast been w with thine ___ Is 28:21
he shall be w as in the valley of ___ Is 28:21
I was w with my people, I have ___ Is 47:6
and the LORD hath been w with thee ___ Is 54:9
ever, neither will I be always w ___ Is 57:16
of his covetousness was I w ___ Is 57:17
I hid me, and was w, and he went on ___ Is 57:17
behold, thou art w ___ Is 64:5
Be not w very sore, O LORD ___ Is 64:9
the princes were w with Jeremiah ___ Jer 37:15
thou art very w against us ___ Lam 5:22
of the wise men, was exceeding w ___ Mt 2:16
And his lord was w, and delivered ___ Mt 18:34
the king heard thereof, he was w ___ Mt 22:7
the dragon was w with the woman ___ Rev 12:17

WROUGHT

because he had w folly in Israel ___ Gen 34:7
what things I have w in Egypt ___ Ex 10:2
twined linen, w with needlework ___ Ex 26:36
twined linen, w with needlework ___ Ex 27:16
Then w Bezaleel and Aholiab, and ___ Ex 36:1
that w all the work of the ___ Ex 36:4
hearted man among them that w the ___ Ex 36:8
they w onyx stones inclosed in ___ Ex 39:6
they have w confusion ___ Lev 20:12
and of Israel, What hath God w ___ Num 23:23
gold of them, even all w jewels ___ Num 31:51
such abomination is w among you ___ Deut 13:14
hath w wickedness in the ___ Deut 17:2
which hath not been w before ___ Deut 17:4
which hath not been w with ___ Deut 21:3
she hath w folly in Israel ___ Deut 22:21
the evils which they shall have w ___ Deut 31:18
because he hath w folly in Israel ___ Josh 7:15
folly that they have w in Israel ___ Judg 20:10
mother in law with whom she had w ___ Ruth 2:19
name with whom I w to day is Boaz ___ Ruth 2:19
and hath w wonderfully among ___ 1Sa 6:6
LORD hath w salvation in Israel ___ 1Sa 11:13
who hath w this great salvation ___ 1Sa 14:45
for he hath w with God this day ___ 1Sa 14:45
that w a great salvation for ___ 1Sa 19:5
Otherwise I should have w ___ 2Sa 18:13
the LORD w a great victory that ___ 2Sa 23:10
the LORD w a great victory ___ 2Sa 23:12
the people that w in the work ___ 1Kin 5:16
King Solomon, and w all his work ___ 1Kin 7:14
the brim thereof was w like the ___ 1Kin 7:26
the people that w in the work ___ 1Kin 9:23
Zimri, and his treason that he w ___ 1Kin 16:20
But Omri w evil in the eyes of ___ 1Kin 16:25
he w evil in the sight of the ___ 2Kin 3:2
that w upon the house of the LORD ___ 2Kin 12:11
w wicked things to provoke the ___ 2Kin 17:11
he w much wickedness in the sight ___ 2Kin 21:6
house of them that w fine linen ___ 1Chr 4:21
he set masons to hew w stones to ___ 1Chr 22:2
linen, and w cherubims thereon ___ 2Chr 3:14
he w that which was evil in the ___ 2Chr 22:4
the LORD, and also such as w iron ___ 2Chr 24:12
the workmen, and the work ___ 2Chr 24:13
w that which was good ___ 2Chr 31:20
he w much evil in the sight of ___ 2Chr 33:6
that w in the house of the LORD ___ 2Chr 34:10
that w the work in any manner of ___ 2Chr 34:13
half of my servants w in the work ___ Neh 4:16
one of his hands w in the work ___ Neh 4:17
that this work was of our God ___ Neh 6:16
and had w great provocations ___ Neh 9:26
they w great provocations ___ Neh 9:26
the hand of the LORD hath w this ___ Job 12:9
who can say, Thou hast w iniquity ___ Job 36:23
which thou hast w for them that ___ Ps 31:19
her clothing is of w gold ___ Ps 45:13
that which thou hast w for us ___ Ps 68:28
For he had w his signs in Egypt ___ Ps 78:43
curiously w in the lowest parts ___ Ps 139:15
all the works that my hands had w ___ Eccl 2:11
because the work that is w under ___ Eccl 2:17
for thou also hast w all our ___ Is 26:12
we have not w any deliverance in ___ Is 26:18
Who hath w and done it, calling ___ Is 41:4
seeing she hath w lewdness with ___ Jer 11:15
he w a work on the wheels ___ Jer 18:3
But I w for my name's sake, that ___ Eze 20:9
But I w for my name's sake, that ___ Eze 20:14
w for my name's sake, that it ___ Eze 20:22
when I have w with you for my ___ Eze 20:44
against it, because they w for me ___ Eze 29:20
the high God hath w toward me ___ Dan 4:2
for the sea w, and was tempestuous ___ Jonah 1:11
for the sea w, and was tempestuous ___ Jonah 1:13
which have w his judgment ___ Zeph 2:3
These last have w but one hour ___ Mt 20:12
She that hath w a good work upon ___ Mt 26:10
mighty works are w by his hands ___ Mk 6:2
she hath w a good work on me ___ Mk 14:6
manifest, that they are w in God ___ Jn 3:21
wonders w among the people ___ Acts 5:12
wonders God had w among the ___ Acts 15:12
craft, he abode with them, and w ___ Acts 18:3
God w special miracles by the ___ Acts 19:11
what things God had w among the ___ Acts 21:19
w in me all manner of ___ Rom 7:8
which Christ hath not w by me ___ Rom 15:18
Now he that hath w us for the ___ 2Cor 5:5
what carefulness it w in you ___ 2Cor 7:11
were w among you in all patience ___ 2Cor 12:12
(For he that w effectually in ___ Gal 2:8
Which he w in Christ, when he ___ Eph 1:20
but w with labour and travail ___ 2Th 3:8
w righteousness, obtained ___ Heb 11:33
thou how faith w with his works ___ Jas 2:22
have w the will of the Gentiles ___ 1Pet 4:3
not those things which we have w ___ 2Jn 8
that w miracles before him ___ Rev 19:20

WROUGHTEST

and where w thou ___ Ruth 2:19

WRUNG

the blood thereof shall be w out ___ Lev 1:15
w out at the bottom of the altar ___ Lev 5:9
of a full cup are w out to them ___ Ps 73:10
cup of trembling, and them out ___ Is 51:17

X

XERXES See AHASUERUS.
XERXES' See AHASUERUS'.

Y

YAH See JAH.

YARN

brought out of Egypt, and linen y ___ 1Kin 10:28
received the linen y at a price ___ 1Kin 10:28
brought out of Egypt, and linen y ___ 2Chr 1:16
received the linen y at a price ___ 2Chr 1:16

YE See PREFACE.

YEA See PREFACE.

YEAR

six hundredth y of Noah's life ___ Gen 7:11
in the six hundredth and first y ___ Gen 8:13
in the thirteenth y they rebelled ___ Gen 14:4
fourteenth y came Chedorlaomer ___ Gen 14:5
at this set time in the next y ___ Gen 17:21
in the same y an hundredfold ___ Gen 26:12
for all their cattle for that y ___ Gen 47:17
When that y was ended, they came ___ Gen 47:18
they came unto him the second y ___ Gen 47:18
the first month of the y in his ___ Ex 12:2
blemish, a male of the first y ___ Ex 12:5
in his season from y to y ___ Ex 13:10
in his season from y to y ___ Ex 13:10
But the seventh y thou shalt let ___ Ex 23:11
keep a feast unto me in the y ___ Ex 23:14
which is in the end of the y ___ Ex 23:16
Three times in the y all thy ___ Ex 23:17
out from before thee in one y ___ Ex 23:29
first y day by day continually ___ Ex 29:38
in a y with the blood of the sin ___ Ex 30:10
once in the y shall he make ___ Ex 30:10
Thrice in the y shall all your ___ Ex 34:23
the LORD thy God thrice in the y ___ Ex 34:24
the first month in the second y ___ Ex 40:17
and a lamb, both of the first y ___ Lev 9:3
the first y for a burnt offering ___ Lev 12:6
of the first y without blemish ___ Lev 14:10
for all their sins once a y ___ Lev 16:34
But in the fourth y all the fruit ___ Lev 19:24
in the fifth y shall ye eat of ___ Lev 19:25
without blemish of the first y ___ Lev 23:12
without blemish of the first y ___ Lev 23:18
of the first y for a sacrifice ___ Lev 23:19
lambs of the first y for a ___ Lev 23:19
unto the LORD seven days in the y ___ Lev 23:41
But in the seventh y shall be a ___ Lev 25:4
for it is a y of rest unto the ___ Lev 25:5
And ye shall hallow the fiftieth y ___ Lev 25:10
shall that fiftieth y be unto you ___ Lev 25:11
In the y of this jubile ye shall ___ Lev 25:13
What shall we eat the seventh y ___ Lev 25:20
blessing upon you in the sixth y ___ Lev 25:21
And ye shall sow the eighth y ___ Lev 25:22
of old fruit until the ninth y ___ Lev 25:22
bought it until the y of jubile ___ Lev 25:28

within a whole y after it is sold .... Lev 25:29
within a full y may he redeem it .... Lev 25:29
within the space of a full y .... Lev 25:30
shall go out in the y of jubile .... Lev 25:33
serve the unto the y of jubile .... Lev 25:40
y that he was sold to him unto .... Lev 25:50
sold to him unto the y of jubile .... Lev 25:50
few years unto the y of jubile .... Lev 25:52
shall go out in the y of jubile .... Lev 25:54
his field from the y of jubile .... Lev 27:17
even unto the y of the jubile .... Lev 27:18
even unto the y of the jubile .... Lev 27:23
in the y of the Jubile the field .... Lev 27:24
in the second y after they were .... Num 1:1
first y for a trespass offering .... Num 6:12
one he lamb of the first y .... Num 6:14
first y without blemish for a sin .... Num 6:14
one ram, one lamb of the first y .... Num 7:15
goats, five lambs of the first y .... Num 7:17
one ram, one lamb of the first y .... Num 7:21
goats, five lambs of the first y .... Num 7:23
one ram, one lamb of the first y .... Num 7:27
goats, five lambs of the first y .... Num 7:29
one ram, one lamb of the first y .... Num 7:33
goats, five lambs of the first y .... Num 7:35
one ram, one lamb of the first y .... Num 7:39
goats, five lambs of the first y .... Num 7:41
one ram, one lamb of the first y .... Num 7:45
goats, five lambs of the first y .... Num 7:47
one ram, one lamb of the first y .... Num 7:51
goats, five lambs of the first y .... Num 7:53
one ram, one lamb of the first y .... Num 7:57
goats, five lambs of the first y .... Num 7:59
one ram, one lamb of the first y .... Num 7:63
goats, five lambs of the first y .... Num 7:65
one ram, one lamb of the first y .... Num 7:69
goats, five lambs of the first y .... Num 7:71
one ram, one lamb of the first y .... Num 7:75
goats, five lambs of the first y .... Num 7:77
one ram, one lamb of the first y .... Num 7:81
goats, five lambs of the first y .... Num 7:83
the lambs of the first y twelve .... Num 7:87
the lambs of the first y sixty .... Num 7:88
the first month of the second y .... Num 9:1
were two days, or a month, or a y .... Num 9:22
the second month, in the second y .... Num 10:11
even forty days, each day for a y .... Num 14:34
of the first y for a sin offering .... Num 15:27
two lambs of the first y without .... Num 28:3
lambs of the first y without spot .... Num 28:9
lambs of the first y without spot .... Num 28:11
throughout the months of the y .... Num 28:14
and seven lambs of the first y .... Num 28:19
ram, seven lambs of the first y .... Num 28:27
of the first y without blemish .... Num 29:2
and seven lambs of the first y .... Num 29:8
and fourteen lambs of the first y .... Num 29:13
lambs of the first y without spot .... Num 29:17
of the first y without blemish .... Num 29:20
of the first y without blemish .... Num 29:23
lambs of the first y without spot .... Num 29:26
of the first y without blemish .... Num 29:29
of the first y without blemish .... Num 29:32
in the forty y after the .... Num 29:36
it came to pass in the fortieth y .... Num 33:38
from the beginning of the y even .... Deut 1:3
y even unto the end of the y .... Deut 11:12
field bringeth forth y by y .... Deut 11:12
field bringeth forth y by y .... Deut 14:22
of thine increase the same y .... Deut 14:22
heart, saying, The seventh y .... Deut 14:28
the y of release, is at hand .... Deut 15:9
then in the seventh y thou shalt .... Deut 15:9
y by y in the place which the LORD .... Deut 15:20
by y in the place which the LORD .... Deut 15:20
Three times in a y shall all thy .... Deut 16:16
he shall be free at home one y .... Deut 24:5
of thine increase the third y .... Deut 26:12
which is the y of tithing .... Deut 26:12
the solemnity of the y of release .... Deut 31:10
of the land of Canaan that y .... Josh 5:12
that y they vexed and oppressed .... Judg 10:8
the Gileadite four days in a y .... Judg 11:40
ten shekels of silver by the y .... Judg 17:10
And as he did so y by y 1Sa 1:7
brought it to him from y to y 1Sa 2:19
he went from y to y in circuit 1Sa 7:16
Saul reigned one y 1Sa 13:1
of the Philistines was a full y 1Sa 27:7
after the y was expired, at the 2Sa 11:1
David three years, y after y 2Sa 21:1
ha month in a y made provision 1Kin 4:7
gave Solomon to Hiram y by y 1Kin 5:11
lightly after the children of 1Kin 6:1
in the fourth y of Solomon's 1Kin 6:1
In the fourth y was the 1Kin 6:37
And in the eleventh y, in the 1Kin 6:38
three times in a y did Solomon 1Kin 9:25
one y was six hundred threescore 1Kin 10:14
and mules, a rate y by y 1Kin 10:25
in the fifth y of king Rehoboam 1Kin 14:25
Now in the eighteenth y of king 1Kin 15:1
in the twentieth y of Jeroboam 1Kin 15:9
the second y of Asa king of Judah 1Kin 15:25
Even in the third y of Asa king 1Kin 15:28
In the third y of Asa king of 1Kin 15:33
sixth y of Asa king of Judah 1Kin 16:8
seventh y of Asa king of Judah 1Kin 16:10
seventh y of Asa king of Judah 1Kin 16:15

first y of Asa king of Judah 1Kin 16:23
eighth y of Asa king of Judah 1Kin 16:29
came to Elijah in the third y 1Kin 18:1
for at the return of the y 1Kin 20:22
to pass at the return of the y 1Kin 20:26
And it came to pass in the third y 1Kin 22:2
fourth y of Ahab king of Israel 1Kin 22:41
in Samaria the seventeenth y of 1Kin 22:51
second y of Jehoram the son of 2Kin 1:17
in Samaria the eighteenth y of 2Kin 3:1
in the fifth y of Joram the son 2Kin 8:16
In the twelfth y of Joram the son 2Kin 8:25
and he reigned one y in Jerusalem 2Kin 8:26
in the eleventh y of Joram 2Kin 9:29
the seventh y Jehoiada sent and 2Kin 11:4
In the seventh y of Jehu Jehoash 2Kin 12:1
twentieth y of king Jehoash the 2Kin 12:6
twentieth y of Joash the son of 2Kin 13:1
seventh y of Joash king of Judah 2Kin 13:10
land at the coming in of the y 2Kin 13:20
In the second y of Joash son of 2Kin 14:1
in the fifteenth y of Amaziah the 2Kin 14:23
seventh y of Jeroboam king of 2Kin 15:1
eighth y of Azariah king of Judah 2Kin 15:8
thirtieth y of Uzziah king of 2Kin 15:13
thirtieth y of Azariah king of 2Kin 15:17
In the fiftieth y of Azariah king 2Kin 15:23
fiftieth y of Azariah king of 2Kin 15:27
in the twentieth y of Jotham the 2Kin 15:30
in the second y of Pekah the son 2Kin 15:32
In the seventeenth y of Pekah the 2Kin 16:1
In the twelfth y of Ahaz king of 2Kin 17:1
Assyria, as had done y by y 2Kin 17:4
In the ninth y of Hoshea the king 2Kin 17:6
it came to pass in the third y of 2Kin 18:1
in the fourth y of king Hezekiah 2Kin 18:9
which was the seventh y of Hoshea 2Kin 18:9
even in the sixth y of Hezekiah 2Kin 18:10
that is the ninth y of Hoshea 2Kin 18:10
fourteenth y of king Hezekiah did 2Kin 18:13
Ye shall eat this y such things 2Kin 19:29
in the second y that which 2Kin 19:29
and in the third y sow ye, and reap 2Kin 19:29
the eighteenth y of king Josiah 2Kin 22:3
the eighteenth y of king Josiah 2Kin 23:23
him in the eighth y of his reign 2Kin 24:12
pass in the ninth y of his reign 2Kin 25:1
the eleventh y of king Zedekiah 2Kin 25:2
which is the nineteenth y of king 2Kin 25:8
thirtieth y of the captivity of 2Kin 25:27
king of Babylon in the y that he 2Kin 25:27
that after the y was expired 1Chr 20:1
In the fortieth y of the reign of 1Chr 26:31
all the months of the y, of every 1Chr 27:1
in the fourth y of his reign 2Chr 13:1
feasts, three times in the y 2Chr 8:13
Solomon in one y was six hundred 2Chr 9:13
and mules, a rate y by y 2Chr 9:24
that in the fifth y of king 2Chr 12:2
Now in the eighteenth y of king 2Chr 13:1
In the fifteenth y of the reign 2Chr 15:10
thirtieth y of the reign of Asa 2Chr 15:19
thirtieth y of the reign of Asa 2Chr 16:1
in the ninth y his reign was diseased 2Chr 16:12
and one fortieth y of his reign 2Chr 16:13
Also in the third y of his reign 2Chr 17:7
and he reigned one y in Jerusalem 2Chr 21:20
in the seventh y Jehoiada 2Chr 23:1
house of your God from y to y 2Chr 24:5
came to pass at the end of the y 2Chr 24:23
of Ammon gave him the same y an 2Chr 27:5
pay unto him, both the second y 2Chr 27:5
He in the first y of his reign 2Chr 29:3
For in the eighth y of his reign 2Chr 34:3
in the twelfth y he began to 2Chr 34:3
in the eighteenth y of his reign 2Chr 34:8
in the eighteenth y of the reign 2Chr 35:19
when the y was expired, king 2Chr 36:10
Now in the first y of Cyrus king 2Chr 36:22
Now in the first y of Cyrus king .... Ezr 1:1
Now in the second y of their .... Ezr 3:8
So it ceased unto the second y of .... Ezr 4:24
But in the first y of Cyrus the .... Ezr 5:13
In the first y of Cyrus the king .... Ezr 6:3
which was in the sixth y of the .... Ezr 6:15
in the seventh y of Artaxerxes .... Ezr 7:7
was in the seventh y of the king .... Ezr 7:8
month Chisleu, in the twentieth y .... Neh 1:1
in the twentieth y of Artaxerxes .... Neh 2:1
the twentieth y even unto the two .... Neh 5:14
thirtieth y of Artaxerxes the .... Neh 5:14
that we would leave the seventh y .... Neh 10:31
at times appointed y by y .... Neh 10:34
at times appointed y by y .... Neh 10:34
all fruit of all trees, y by y .... Neh 10:35
thirtieth y of Artaxerxes king of .... Neh 13:6
In the third y of his reign .... Est 1:3
in the seventh y of his reign .... Est 2:16
Nisan, in the twelfth y of king .... Est 3:7
to their appointed time every y .... Est 9:27
be joined unto the days of the y .... Job 3:6
crowned the y with thy goodness .... Ps 65:11
In the y that king Uzziah died I .... Is 6:1
In the y that king Ahaz died was .... Is 14:28
In the y that Tartan came unto .... Is 20:1
the Lord said unto me, Within a y .... Is 21:16
add ye y to y .... Is 29:1
the y of recompences for .... Is 34:8
the fourteenth y of king Hezekiah .... Is 36:1
Ye shall eat this y such as .... Is 37:30

the second y that which springeth .... Is 37:30
and in the third y sow ye, and reap .... Is 37:30
the acceptable y of the LORD .... Is 61:2
the y of my redeemed is come .... Is 63:4
in the thirteenth y of his reign .... Jer 1:2
unto the end of the eleventh y .... Jer 1:3
even the y of their visitation .... Jer 11:23
be careful in the y of drought .... Jer 17:8
even the y of their visitation .... Jer 23:12
people of Judah in the fourth y .... Jer 25:1
of Judah, that was the first y of .... Jer 25:1
From the thirteenth y of Josiah .... Jer 25:3
that is the three and twentieth y .... Jer 25:3
And it came to pass the same y .... Jer 28:1
king of Judah, in the fourth y .... Jer 28:1
this y thou shalt die, because .... Jer 28:16
the same y in the seventh month .... Jer 28:17
tenth y of Zedekiah king of Judah .... Jer 32:1
eighteenth y of Nebuchadrezzar .... Jer 32:1
it came to pass in the fourth y .... Jer 36:1
it came to pass in the fifth y of .... Jer 36:9
In the ninth y of Zedekiah king .... Jer 39:1
And in the eleventh y of Zedekiah .... Jer 39:2
in the fourth y of Jehoiakim the .... Jer 45:1
y of Jehoiakim the son of Josiah .... Jer 46:2
the y of their visitation, saith .... Jer 48:44
a rumour shall both come one y .... Jer 51:46
in another y shall come a rumour .... Jer 51:46
in the fourth y of his reign .... Jer 51:59
pass in the ninth y of his reign .... Jer 52:4
the eleventh y of king Zedekiah .... Jer 52:5
which was the nineteenth y of .... Jer 52:12
in the seventh y three thousand .... Jer 52:28
In the eighteenth y of .... Jer 52:29
twentieth y of Nebuchadrezzar .... Jer 52:30
thirtieth y of the captivity of .... Jer 52:31
king of Babylon in the first y of .... Jer 52:31
came to pass in the thirtieth y .... Eze 1:1
which was the fifth y of king .... Eze 1:2
appointed the each day for a y .... Eze 4:6
And it came to pass in the sixth y .... Eze 8:1
it came to pass in the seventh y .... Eze 20:1
Again in the ninth y, in the .... Eze 24:1
it came to pass in the eleventh y .... Eze 26:1
In the tenth y, in the tenth .... Eze 29:1
pass in the seven and twentieth y .... Eze 29:17
it came to pass in the eleventh y .... Eze 30:20
it came to pass in the eleventh y .... Eze 31:1
it came to pass in the twelfth y .... Eze 32:1
to pass also in the twelfth y .... Eze 32:17
in the twelfth y of our captivity .... Eze 33:21
twentieth y of our captivity, in .... Eze 40:1
in the beginning of the y .... Eze 40:1
in the fourteenth y after that .... Eze 40:1
of the first y without blemish .... Eze 46:13
shall be his to the y of liberty .... Eze 46:17
In the third y of the reign of .... Dan 1:1
unto the first y of king Cyrus .... Dan 1:21
in the second y of the reign of .... Dan 2:1
In the first y of Belshazzar king .... Dan 7:1
In the third y of the reign of .... Dan 8:1
In the first y of Darius the son .... Dan 9:1
In the first y of his reign I .... Dan 9:2
In the third y of Cyrus king of .... Dan 10:1
in the first y of Darius the Mede .... Dan 11:1
offerings, with calves of a y old .... Mic 6:6
In the second y of Darius the .... Hag 1:1
in the second y of Darius the .... Hag 1:15
month, in the second y of Darius .... Hag 2:10
month, in the second y of Darius .... Zec 1:1
Sebat, in the second y of Darius .... Zec 1:7
in the fourth y of king Darius .... Zec 7:1
y to y to worship the King .... Zec 14:16
y at the feast of the passover .... Lk 2:41
Now in the fifteenth y of the .... Lk 3:1
the acceptable y of the Lord .... Lk 4:19
Lord, let it alone this y also .... Lk 13:8
being that high priest that same y .... Jn 11:49
but being high priest that y .... Jn 11:51
was the high priest that same y .... Jn 18:13
that a whole y they assembled .... Acts 11:26
And he continued there a y .... Acts 18:11
but also to be forward a y ago 2Cor 8:10
that Achaia was ready a y ago 2Cor 9:2
high priest alone once every y .... Heb 9:7
every y with blood of others .... Heb 9:25
y by y continually make the .... Heb 10:1
which they offered y by y .... Heb 10:1
again made of sins every y .... Heb 10:3
a city, and continue there a y .... Jas 4:13
and a day, and a month, and a y .... Rev 9:15

YEARLY

as a y hired servant shall he be .... Lev 25:53
went y to lament the daughter of .... Judg 11:40
y in a place which is on the .... Judg 21:19
up out of his city y to worship 1Sa 1:3
unto the LORD thy sacrifice 1Sa 1:21
husband to offer the y sacrifice 1Sa 2:19
for there is a y sacrifice there 1Sa 20:6
to charge ourselves y with the .... Neh 10:32
the fifteenth day of the same, y .... Est 9:21

YEARN

his bowels did y upon his brother .... Gen 43:30

YEARNED

for her bowels y upon her son 1Kin 3:26

YEAR'S

feast of ingathering at the y end .... Ex 34:22
(for it was at every y end that 2Sa 14:26

YEARS See PREFACE.

unto him that is an hundred y old	Gen 17:17
shall Sarah, that is ninety y old	Gen 17:17
I will serve thee seven y for	Gen 29:18
served with him yet seven other y	Gen 29:30
these forty y in the wilderness	Deut 8:2
led you forty y in the wilderness	Deut 29:5
For a thousand y in thy sight are	Ps 90:4
began to be about thirty y of age	Lk 3:23
much goods laid up for many y	Lk 12:19
sea, and in the wilderness forty y	Acts 7:36
days, and months, and times, and y	Gal 4:10
is with the Lord as a thousand y	2Pet 3:8
and a thousand y as one day	2Pet 3:8

YEARS'

came to pass at the seven y end	2Kin 8:3
Either three y famine	1Chr 21:12

YELL

they shall y as lions' whelps	Jer 51:38

YELLED

young lions roared upon him, and y	Jer 2:15

YELLOW

and there be in it a y thin hair	Lev 13:30
not, and there be in it no y hair	Lev 13:32
priest shall not seek for y hair	Lev 13:36
and her feathers with y gold	Ps 68:13

YES

He saith, Y	Mt 17:25
she answered and said unto him, Y	Mk 7:28
Y, of the Gentiles also	Rom 3:29
Y verily, their sound went into	Rom 10:18

YESTERDAY

your task in making brick both y	Ex 5:14
son of Jesse to meat, neither y	1Sa 20:27
Whereas thou camest but y	2Sa 15:20
Surely I have seen y the blood of	2Kin 9:26
(For we are but of y, and know	Job 8:9
are but as y when it is past	Ps 90:4
Y at the seventh hour the fever	Jn 4:52
as thou diddest the Egyptian y	Acts 7:28
Jesus Christ the same y, and to	Heb 13:8

YESTERNIGHT

Behold, I lay y with my father	Gen 19:34
of your father spake unto me y	Gen 31:29
of my hands, and rebuked thee y	Gen 31:42

YET See PREFACE.

YIELD

y unto thee her strength	Gen 4:12
he shall y royal dainties	Gen 49:20
that it may y unto you the	Lev 19:25
And the land shall y her fruit	Lev 25:19
and the land shall y her increase	Lev 26:4
trees of the field shall y their fruit	Lev 26:4
land shall not y her increase	Lev 26:20
trees of the land y their fruits	Lev 26:20
and that the land y not her fruit	Deut 11:17
but y yourselves unto the LORD	2Chr 30:8
shall the earth y her increase	Ps 67:6
and our land shall y her increase	Ps 85:12
which may y fruits of increase	Ps 107:37
fair speech she caused him to y	Prov 7:21
of vineyard shall y one bath	Is 5:10
seed of an homer shall y an ephah	Is 5:10
of the field shall y her fruit	Eze 34:27
and the earth shall y her increase	Eze 34:27
y your fruit to my people of	Eze 36:8
the bud shall y no meal	Hos 8:7
if so be it y, the strangers	Hos 8:7
the vine do y their strength	Joel 2:22
and the fields shall y no meat	Hab 3:17
did y fruit that sprang up and	Mk 4:8
But do not thou y unto them	Acts 23:21
Neither y ye your members as	Rom 6:13
but y yourselves unto God, as	Rom 6:13
that to whom ye y yourselves	Rom 6:16
even so now y your members	Rom 6:19
can no fountain both y salt water	Jas 3:12

YIELDED

y up the ghost, and was gathered	Gen 49:33
blossoms, and y almonds	Num 17:8
y their bodies, that they might	Dan 3:28
with a loud voice, y up the ghost	Mt 27:50
and choked it, and it y no fruit	Mk 4:7
at his feet, and y up the ghost	Acts 5:10
for as ye have y your members	Rom 6:19
and y her fruit every month	Rev 22:2

YIELDETH

it y much increase unto the kings	Neh 9:37
the wilderness y food for them	Job 24:5
the root of the righteous y fruit	Prov 12:12
it y the peaceable fruit of	Heb 12:11

YIELDING

forth grass, the herb y seed	Gen 1:11
the fruit tree y fruit after his	Gen 1:11
herb y seed after his kind, and	Gen 1:12
his kind, and the tree y fruit	Gen 1:12
is the fruit of a tree y seed	Gen 1:29
for y pacifieth great offences	Eccl 10:4
neither shall cease from y fruit	Jer 17:8

YIRON See IRON.

YOKE

break his y from off thy neck	Gen 27:40
I have broken the bands of your y	Lev 26:13

---

and upon which never came y	Num 19:2
and which hath not drawn in the y	Deut 21:3
he shall put a y of iron upon thy	Deut 28:48
on which there hath come no y	1Sa 6:7
And he took a y of oxen, and hewed	1Sa 11:7
which a y of oxen might plow	1Sa 14:14
Thy father made our y grievous	1Kin 12:4
his heavy y which he put upon us	1Kin 12:4
Make the y which thy father did	1Kin 12:9
Thy father made our y heavy	1Kin 12:10
heavy y, I will add to your y	1Kin 12:11
My father made your y heavy	1Kin 12:14
and I will add to your y	1Kin 12:14
with twelve y of oxen before him	1Kin 19:19
took a y of oxen, and slew them	1Kin 19:21
Thy father made our y grievous	2Chr 10:4
his heavy y that he put upon us	2Chr 10:9
Ease somewhat the y that thy	2Chr 10:9
Thy father made our y heavy	2Chr 10:10
my father put a heavy y upon you	2Chr 10:11
you, I will put more to your y	2Chr 10:11
My father made your y heavy	2Chr 10:14
camels, and five hundred y of oxen	Job 1:3
is y from off thy neck, and the	Is 9:4
the y shall be destroyed because	Is 10:27
then shall his y depart from off	Is 10:27
hast thou very heavily laid thy y	Is 47:6
go free, and that ye break every y	Is 58:6
away from the midst of thee the y	Is 58:9
of old time I have broken thy y	Jer 2:20
have altogether broken the y	Jer 5:5
the y of the king of Babylon	Jer 27:8
the y of the king of Babylon	Jer 27:11
the y of the king of Babylon	Jer 27:12
I have broken the y of the king	Jer 28:2
for I will break the y of the	Jer 28:4
Hananiah the prophet took the y	Jer 28:10
Even so will I break the y of	Jer 28:11
the y from off the neck of the	Jer 28:12
I have put a y of iron upon the	Jer 28:14
break his y from off thy neck	Jer 30:8
a bullock unaccustomed to the y	Jer 31:18
the husbandman and his y of oxen	Jer 51:23
The y of my transgressions is	Lam 1:14
that he bear the y in his youth	Lam 3:27
have broken the bands of their y	Eze 34:27
that take off the y on their jaws	Hos 11:4
will I break his y from off thee	Nah 1:13
Take my y upon you, and learn of	Mt 11:29
For my y is easy, and my burden is	Mt 11:30
I have bought five y of oxen	Lk 14:19
to put a y upon the neck of the	Acts 15:10
again with the y of bondage	Gal 5:1
y count their own masters worthy	1Ti 6:1

YOKED

Be ye not unequally y together	2Cor 6:14

YOKEFELLOW

And I entreat thee also, true y	Phil 4:3

YOKES

Make thee bonds and y, and put them	Jer 27:2
Thou hast broken the y of wood	Jer 28:13
shalt make for them y of iron	Jer 28:13
shall break there the y of Egypt	Eze 30:18

YONDER

and I and the lad will go y	Gen 22:5
and scatter thou the fire y	Num 16:37
offering, while I meet the LORD y	Num 23:15
with them on y side Jordan	Num 32:19
Behold, y is that Shunammite	2Kin 4:25
mountain, Remove hence to y place	Mt 17:20
Sit ye here, while I go and pray y	Mt 26:36

YOU See PREFACE.

YOUNG

wounding, and a man to my hurt	Gen 4:23
that which the y men have eaten	Gen 14:24
and a turtledove, and a y pigeon	Gen 15:9
and good, and gave it unto a y man	Gen 18:7
the house round, both old and y	Gen 19:4
and took two of his y men with him	Gen 22:3
And Abraham said unto his y men	Gen 22:5
Abraham returned unto his y men	Gen 22:19
she goats have not cast their y	Gen 31:38
and herds with y are with me	Gen 33:13
the y man deferred not to do the	Gen 34:19
there was there with us a y man	Gen 41:12
Moses said, We will go with our y	Ex 10:9
There shall nothing cast their y	Ex 23:26
he sent y men of the children of	Ex 24:5
Take one y bullock, and two rams	Ex 29:1
a y man, departed not out of the	Ex 33:11
of turtledoves, or of y pigeons	Lev 1:14
a y bullock without blemish unto	Lev 4:3
offer a y bullock for the sin	Lev 4:14
or two y pigeons, unto the LORD	Lev 5:7
or two y pigeons, then he that	Lev 5:11
Take thee a y calf for a sin	Lev 9:2
a y pigeon, or a turtledove, for	Lev 12:6
two turtles, or two y pigeons	Lev 12:8
or two y pigeons, such as he is	Lev 14:22
turtledoves, or of y pigeons	Lev 14:30
two turtles, or two y pigeons	Lev 15:14
or two y pigeons, and come before	Lev 15:29
with a y bullock for a sin	Lev 16:3
kill it and her y both in one day	Lev 22:28
one y bullock, and two rams	Lev 23:18

---

or two y pigeons, to the priest	Num 6:10
One y bullock, one ram, one lamb	Num 7:15
One y bullock, one ram, one lamb	Num 7:21
One y bullock, one ram, one lamb	Num 7:27
One y bullock, one ram, one lamb	Num 7:33
One y bullock, one ram, one lamb	Num 7:39
One y bullock, one ram, one lamb	Num 7:45
One y bullock, one ram, one lamb	Num 7:51
One y bullock, one ram, one lamb	Num 7:57
One y bullock, one ram, one lamb	Num 7:63
One y bullock, one ram, one lamb	Num 7:69
One y bullock, one ram, one lamb	Num 7:75
One y bullock, one ram, one lamb	Num 7:81
Then let them take a y bullock	Num 8:8
another y bullock shalt thou take	Num 8:8
And there ran a y man, and told	Num 11:27
of Moses, one of his y men	Num 11:28
a y bullock for a burnt offering	Num 15:24
and lift up himself as a y lion	Num 23:24
two y bullocks, and one ram, seven	Num 28:11
two y bullocks, and one ram	Num 28:19
two y bullocks, one ram, seven	Num 28:27
one y bullock, one ram, and seven	Num 29:2
one y bullock, one ram, and seven	Num 29:8
thirteen y bullocks, two rams, and	Num 29:13
ye shall offer twelve y bullocks	Num 29:17
ground, whether they be y ones	Deut 22:6
and the dam sitting upon the y	Deut 22:6
shalt not take the dam with the y	Deut 22:6
the dam go, and take the y to thee	Deut 22:7
the old, nor shew favour to the y	Deut 28:50
toward her y one that cometh out	Deut 28:57
her nest, fluttereth over her y	Deut 32:11
shall destroy both the y man	Deut 32:25
in the city, both man and woman, y	Josh 6:21
the y men that were spies went in	Josh 6:23
him, Take thy father's y bullock	Judg 6:25
caught a y man of the men of	Judg 8:14
unto the y man his armourbearer	Judg 9:54
his y man thrust him through, and	Judg 9:54
a y lion roared against him	Judg 14:5
for so used the y men to do	Judg 14:10
And there was a y man out of	Judg 17:7
the y man was unto him as one of	Judg 17:11
the y man became his priest, and	Judg 17:12
the voice of the y man the Levite	Judg 18:3
the house of the y man the Levite	Judg 18:15
for the y man which is with thy	Judg 19:19
four hundred y virgins, that had	Judg 21:12
have I not charged the y men that	Ruth 2:9
that which the y men have drawn	Ruth 2:9
glean, Boaz commanded his y men	Ruth 2:15
Thou shalt keep fast by my y men	Ruth 2:21
as thou followedst not y men	Ruth 3:10
shall give thee of this y woman	Ruth 4:12
and the child was y	1Sa 1:24
Wherefore the sin of the y men	1Sa 2:17
and your goodliest y men, and put	1Sa 8:16
name was Saul, a choice y man	1Sa 9:2
they found y maidens going out to	1Sa 9:11
the y man that bare his armour	1Sa 14:1
Jonathan said to the y man that	1Sa 14:6
Whose son art thou, thou y man	1Sa 17:58
But if I say thus unto the y man	1Sa 20:22
if the y men have kept themselves	1Sa 21:4
the vessels of the y men are holy	1Sa 21:5
And David sent out ten y men	1Sa 25:5
men, and David said unto the y men	1Sa 25:8
Ask thy y men, and they will shew	1Sa 25:8
Wherefore let the y men find	1Sa 25:8
And when David's y men came	1Sa 25:9
So David's y men turned their way	1Sa 25:12
But one of the y men told Abigail	1Sa 25:14
saw not the y men of my lord	1Sa 25:15
the y men that follow my lord	1Sa 25:19
and let one of the y men come over	1Sa 26:22
I am a y man of Egypt, servant to	1Sa 30:13
of them, save four hundred y men	1Sa 30:17
said unto the y man that told him	2Sa 1:5
the y man that told him said, As	2Sa 1:6
said unto the y man that told him	2Sa 1:13
And David called one of the y men	2Sa 1:15
Let the y men now arise, and play	2Sa 2:14
lay thee hold on one of the y men	2Sa 2:21
And David commanded his y men	2Sa 4:12
And Mephibosheth had a y son	2Sa 9:12
all the y men the king's sons	2Sa 13:29
the y man that kept the watch	2Sa 13:34
bring the y man Absalom again	2Sa 14:21
summer fruit for the y men to eat	2Sa 16:2
gently for my sake with the y man	2Sa 18:5
that none touch the y man Absalom	2Sa 18:12
ten y men that bare Joab's armour	2Sa 18:15
Is the y man Absalom safe	2Sa 18:29
Is the y man Absalom safe	2Sa 18:32
do thee hurt, be as that y man is	2Sa 18:32
for my lord the king a y virgin	1Kin 1:2
Solomon seeing the y man that he	1Kin 11:28
consulted with the y men that	1Kin 12:8
the y men that were grown up with	1Kin 12:10
after the counsel of the y men	1Kin 12:14
Even to the y men of the princes	1Kin 20:14
Then he numbered the y men of the	1Kin 20:15
the y men of the princes of the	1Kin 20:17
So these y men of the princes of	1Kin 20:19
me, I pray thee, one of the y men	2Kin 4:22
to the men mount Ephraim two y	2Kin 5:22
LORD opened the eyes of the y man	2Kin 6:17
thy y men with thou slay with	2Kin 8:12
So the y men, even the y man	2Kin 9:4

Y

even the y man the prophet, went...... 2Kin 9:4
a y man mighty of valour, and of 1Chr 12:28
David said, Solomon my son is y 1Chr 22:5
alone God hath chosen, is yet y 1Chr 29:1
took counsel with the y man that 2Chr 10:8
the y men that were brought up 2Chr 10:10
after the advice of the y men 2Chr 10:14
of Solomon, when Rehoboam was y 2Chr 13:7
himself with a y bullock and seven 2Chr 13:9
of his reign, while he was yet 2Chr 34:3
who slew their y men with the 2Chr 36:17
compassion upon y man or maiden 2Chr 36:17
both y bullocks, and rams, and ...... Ezr 6:9
Let there be fair y virgins ...... Est 2:2
gather together all the fair y ...... Est 2:3
cause to perish, all Jews, both y ...... Est 3:13
mules, camels, and y dromedaries ...... Est 8:10
house, and it fell upon the y men ...... Job 1:19
lion, and the teeth of the y lions ...... Job 4:10
Yea, y children despised me ...... Job 19:18
The y men saw me, and hid ...... Job 29:8
Buzite answered and said, I am y ...... Job 32:6
fill the appetite of the y lions ...... Job 38:39
when his y ones cry unto God ...... Job 38:41
they bring forth their y ones ...... Job 39:3
Their y ones are in good liking ...... Job 39:4
is hardened against her y ones ...... Job 39:16
Her y ones also suck up blood ...... Job 39:30
as it were a y lion lurking in ...... Ps 17:12
and Sirion like a y unicorn ...... Ps 29:6
The y lions do lack, and suffer ...... Ps 34:10
I have been y, and now am old ...... Ps 37:25
the great teeth of the y lions ...... Ps 58:6
The fire consumed their y men ...... Ps 78:63
y he brought him to feed Jacob ...... Ps 78:71
herself, where she may lay her y ...... Ps 84:3
the y lion and the dragon shalt ...... Ps 91:13
The y lions roar after their prey ...... Ps 104:21
shall a y man cleanse his way ...... Ps 119:9
to the y ravens which cry ...... Ps 147:9
Both y men, and maidens ...... Ps 148:12
to the y man knowledge and ...... Prov 1:4
a y man void of understanding ...... Prov 7:7
The glory of y men is their ...... Prov 20:29
the y eagles shall eat it ...... Prov 30:17
Rejoice, O y man, in thy youth ...... Eccl 11:9
beloved is like a roe or a y hart ...... Song 2:9
be thou like a roe or a y hart ...... Song 2:17
like two y roes that are twins ...... Song 4:5
like two y roes that are twins ...... Song 7:3
to a y hart upon the mountains of ...... Song 8:14
they shall roar like y lions ...... Is 5:29
that a man shall nourish a y cow ...... Is 7:21
shall have no joy in their y men ...... Is 9:17
the y lion and the fatling ...... Is 11:6
their y ones shall lie down ...... Is 11:7
shall dash the y men to pieces ...... Is 13:18
and the Ethiopians captives, y ...... Is 20:4
neither do I nourish up y men ...... Is 23:4
anguish, from whence come the y ...... Is 30:6
upon the shoulders of y asses ...... Is 30:6
the y asses that ear the ground ...... Is 30:24
the y lion roaring on his prey ...... Is 31:4
his y men shall be discomfited ...... Is 31:8
gently lead those that are with y ...... Is 40:11
thy y men shall utterly fall ...... Is 40:30
For as a y man marrieth a virgin ...... Is 62:5
The y lions roared upon him, and ...... Jer 2:15
the assembly of y men together ...... Jer 6:11
the y men from the streets ...... Jer 9:21
the y men shall die by the sword ...... Jer 11:22
of the y men a spoiler at noonday ...... Jer 15:8
let their y men to slain by the ...... Jer 18:21
for the y of the flock and of the ...... Jer 31:12
rejoice in the dance, both y men ...... Jer 31:13
his chosen y men are gone down to ...... Jer 48:15
Therefore her y men shall fall in ...... Jer 49:26
Therefore shall her y men fall in ...... Jer 50:30
and spare ye not her y men ...... Jer 51:3
will I break in pieces old and y ...... Jer 51:22
will I break in pieces the y man ...... Jer 51:22
against me to crush my y men ...... Lam 1:15
my y men are gone into captivity ...... Lam 1:18
for the life of thy y children ...... Lam 2:19
The y and the old lie on the ...... Lam 2:21
my y men are fallen by the sword ...... Lam 2:21
they give suck to their y ones ...... Lam 4:3
the y children ask bread, and no ...... Lam 4:4
They took the y men to grind ...... Lam 5:13
the y men from their musick ...... Lam 5:14
Slay utterly old and y, both maids ...... Eze 9:6
off the top of his y twigs ...... Eze 17:4
top of his y twigs a tender one ...... Eze 17:22
her whelps among y lions ...... Eze 19:2
it became a y lion, and it learned ...... Eze 19:3
her whelps, and made him a y lion ...... Eze 19:5
the lions, he became a y lion ...... Eze 19:6
of all them desirable y men ...... Eze 23:6
all of them desirable y men ...... Eze 23:12
all of them desirable y men ...... Eze 23:23
The y men of Aven and of Pi-beseth ...... Eze 30:17
of the field bring forth their y ...... Eze 31:6
Thou art like a y lion of the ...... Eze 32:2
with all the y lions thereof ...... Eze 32:2
the face of a y lion toward the ...... Eze 41:19
a y bullock for a sin offering ...... Eze 43:19
that y offers a y bullock ...... Eze 43:23
shall also prepare a y bullock ...... Eze 43:25
thou shalt take a y bullock ...... Eze 45:18
be a y bullock without blemish ...... Eze 46:6

as a y lion to the house of Judah ...... Hos 5:14
your y men shall see visions ...... Joel 2:28
of your y men for Nazarites ...... Amos 2:11
will a y lion cry out of his den ...... Amos 3:4
your y men have I slain with the ...... Amos 4:10
virgins and y men faint for thirst ...... Amos 8:13
as a y lion among the flocks of ...... Mic 5:8
the feeding place of the y lions ...... Nah 2:11
sword shall devour thy y lions ...... Nah 2:13
her y children also were dashed ...... Nah 3:10
him, Run, speak to this y man ...... Zec 2:4
shall make the y men cheerful ...... Zec 9:17
a voice of the roaring of y lions ...... Zec 11:3
off, neither shall seek the y one ...... Zec 11:16
search diligently for the y child ...... Mt 2:8
stood over where the y child was ...... Mt 2:9
they saw the y child with Mary ...... Mt 2:11
Arise, and take the y child ...... Mt 2:13
seek the y child to destroy him ...... Mt 2:13
he arose, he took the y child ...... Mt 2:14
Arise, and take the y child ...... Mt 2:20
which sought the y child's life ...... Mt 2:20
And he arose, and took the y child ...... Mt 2:21
The y man saith unto him, All ...... Mt 19:20
But when the y man heard that ...... Mt 19:22
whose y daughter had an unclean ...... Mk 7:25
they brought y children to him ...... Mk 10:13
followed him a certain y man ...... Mk 14:51
the y men laid hold on him ...... Mk 14:51
they saw a y man sitting on the ...... Mk 16:5
of turtledoves, or two y pigeons ...... Lk 2:24
I say, I say unto thee, Arise ...... Lk 7:14
Jesus, when he found a y ass ...... Jn 12:14
I say unto thee, When thou wast y ...... Jn 21:18
your y men shall see visions, and ...... Acts 2:17
the y men arose, wound him up, and ...... Acts 5:6
the y men came in, and found her ...... Acts 5:10
said to destroy y their children ...... Acts 7:19
their clothes at a y man's feet ...... Acts 7:58
a certain y man named Eutychus ...... Acts 20:9
And they brought the y man alive ...... Acts 20:12
Bring this y man unto the chief ...... Acts 23:17
me to bring this y man unto thee ...... Acts 23:18
captain then let the y man depart ...... Acts 23:22
may teach the y women to be sober ...... Titus 2:4
Y men likewise exhort to be sober ...... Titus 2:6
y men, because ye have overcome 1Jn 2:13
y men, because ye are strong, and 1Jn 2:14

YOUNGER

Knew what his y son had done unto ...... Gen 9:24
And the firstborn said unto the y ...... Gen 19:34
the firstborn said unto the y ...... Gen 19:34
y arose, and lay with him ...... Gen 19:35
And the y, she also bare a son, and ...... Gen 19:38
and the elder shall serve the y ...... Gen 25:23
and put them upon Jacob her y son ...... Gen 27:15
sent and called Jacob her y son ...... Gen 27:42
and the name of the y was Rachel ...... Gen 29:16
years for Rachel thy y daughter ...... Gen 29:18
country, to give the y before the ...... Gen 29:26
and said, Is this your y brother ...... Gen 43:29
Ephraim's head, who was the y ...... Gen 48:14
but truly his y brother shall be ...... Gen 48:19
son of Kenaz, Caleb's y brother ...... Judg 1:13
son of Kenaz, Caleb's y brother ...... Judg 3:9
is not her y sister fairer than ...... Judg 15:2
and the name of the y Michal 1Sa 14:49
over against their y brethren 1Chr 24:31
But now they that are y than I ...... Job 30:1
thy y sister, that dwelleth at ...... Eze 16:46
thy sisters, thine elder and thy y ...... Eze 16:61
the y of them said to his father ...... Lk 15:12
not many days after the y son ...... Lk 15:13
among you, let him be as the y ...... Lk 22:26
her, The elder shall serve the y ...... Rom 9:12
and the y men as brethren 1Ti 5:1
the y as sisters, with all purity 1Ti 5:2
But the y widows refuse 1Ti 5:11
therefore that the y women marry 1Ti 5:14
Likewise, ye y, submit yourselves 1Pet 5:5

YOUNGEST

the y is this day with our father ...... Gen 42:13
except your y brother come hither ...... Gen 42:15
But bring your y brother unto me ...... Gen 42:20
the y is this day with our father ...... Gen 42:32
bring your y brother unto me ...... Gen 42:34
the y according to his youth ...... Gen 43:33
cup, in the sack's mouth of the y ...... Gen 44:2
at the eldest, and left at the y ...... Gen 44:12
Except your y brother come down ...... Gen 44:23
if our y brother be with us, then ...... Gen 44:26
except our y brother he with us ...... Gen 44:26
in his y son shall he set up the ...... Josh 6:26
the y son of Jerubbaal was left ...... Judg 9:5
said, There remaineth yet the y 1Sa 16:11
And David was the y 1Sa 17:14
gates thereof in his y son Segub 1Kin 16:34
save Jehoahaz, the y of his sons 2Chr 21:17
his y son king in his stead 2Chr 22:1

YOUR See PREFACE.

YOURS

of all the land of Egypt is y ...... Gen 45:20
your feet shall tread shall be y ...... Deut 11:24
men answered her, Our life for y ...... Josh 2:14
for the battle is not y, but 2Chr 20:15
strangers in a land that is not y ...... Jer 5:19
for y is the kingdom of God ...... Lk 6:20
my saying, they will keep y also ...... Jn 15:20

For all things are y 1Cor 3:21
all are y 1Cor 3:21
by any means this liberty of y 1Cor 8:9
have refreshed my spirit and y 1Cor 16:18
for I seek not y, but you 2Cor 12:14

YOURSELVES

feet, and rest y under the tree ...... Gen 18:4
be not grieved, nor angry with y ...... Gen 45:5
Gather y together, that I may ...... Gen 49:1
Gather y together, and hear, ye ...... Gen 49:2
about, saying, Take heed to y ...... Ex 19:12
ye shall not make to y according ...... Ex 30:37
Consecrate y to day to the LORD ...... Ex 32:29
Ye shall not make y abominable ...... Lev 11:43
shall ye make y unclean with them ...... Lev 11:43
ye shall therefore sanctify y ...... Lev 11:44
neither shall ye defile y with ...... Lev 11:44
Defile not ye y in any of these ...... Lev 18:24
and that ye defile not y therein ...... Lev 18:30
idols, nor make to y molten gods ...... Lev 19:4
Sanctify y therefore, and be ye ...... Lev 20:7
Sanctify y against to morrow, and ...... Num 11:18
wherefore then lift ye up y above ...... Num 16:3
Separate y from among this ...... Num 16:21
Arm some of y unto the war, and ...... Num 31:3
lying with him, keep alive for y ...... Num 31:18
touched any slain, purify both y ...... Num 31:19
ye good heed unto y therefore ...... Deut 2:4
ye therefore good heed unto y ...... Deut 4:15
Lest ye corrupt y, and make you a ...... Deut 4:16
Take heed unto y, lest ye forget ...... Deut 4:23
in the land, and shall corrupt y ...... Deut 4:25
Take heed to y, that your heart ...... Deut 11:16
nations and mightier than y ...... Deut 11:23
ye shall not cut y, nor make any ...... Deut 14:1
represent y in the tabernacle of ...... Deut 31:14
death ye will utterly corrupt y ...... Deut 31:29
hide y there three days, until ...... Josh 2:16
said unto the people, Sanctify y ...... Josh 3:5
in any wise keep y from the ...... Josh 6:18
thing, lest ye make y accursed ...... Josh 6:18
Sanctify y against to morrow ...... Josh 7:13
shall ye take for a prey unto y ...... Josh 8:2
serve them, nor bow y unto them ...... Josh 23:7
Take good heed therefore unto y ...... Josh 23:11
other gods, and bowed y to them ...... Josh 23:16
Ye are witnesses against y that ...... Josh 24:22
that ye will not fall upon me y ...... Judg 15:12
to make y fat with the chiefest 1Sa 2:29
quit y like men, O y Philistines 1Sa 4:9
quit y like men, and fight 1Sa 4:9
Now therefore present y before 1Sa 10:19
Disperse y among the people, and 1Sa 14:34
sanctify y, and come with me to 1Sa 16:5
Choose you one bullock for y 1Kin 18:25
unto his servants, Set y in array 1Kin 20:12
other gods, nor bow y to them 2Kin 17:35
sanctify y, both ye and your 2Chr 15:12
set y, stand ye still, and see the 2Chr 20:17
me, ye Levites, sanctify now y 2Chr 29:5
have consecrated y unto the LORD 2Chr 29:31
but yield y unto the LORD, and 2Chr 30:8
to give over y to die by famine 2Chr 32:11
prepare y by the houses of your 2Chr 35:4
kill the passover, and sanctify y 2Chr 35:6
separate y from the people of the ...... Ezr 10:11
unto your sons, or for y ...... Neh 13:25
that ye make y strange to me ...... Job 19:3
ye will magnify y against me ...... Job 19:5
Behold, all ye y have seen it ...... Job 27:12
offer up for y a burnt offering ...... Job 42:8
Associate y, O ye people, and ye ...... Is 8:9
gird y, and ye shall be broken in ...... Is 8:9
gird y, and ye shall be broken in ...... Is 8:9
Stay y, and wonder ...... Is 29:9
Assemble y and come ...... Is 45:20
Remember this, and shew y men ...... Is 46:8
All ye, assemble y, and hear ...... Is 48:14
them that are in darkness, Shew y ...... Is 49:9
your iniquities have ye sold y ...... Is 50:1
that compass y about with sparks ...... Is 50:11
LORD, Ye have sold y for nought ...... Is 52:3
Against whom do ye sport y ...... Is 57:4
Enflaming y with idols under ...... Is 57:5
in their glory shall ye boast y ...... Is 61:6
Circumcise y to the LORD, and take ...... Jer 4:4
together, and say, Assemble y ...... Jer 4:5
gather y to flee out of the midst ...... Jer 6:1
assemble y, and let us enter into ...... Jer 8:14
king and to the queen, Humble y ...... Jer 13:18
Take heed to y, and bear no burden ...... Jer 17:21
wallow y in the ashes, ye ...... Jer 25:34
bring innocent blood upon y ...... Jer 26:15
Deceive not y, saying, The ...... Jer 37:9
to dwell, that ye might cut y off ...... Jer 44:8
Put y in array against Babylon ...... Jer 50:14
Repent, and turn y from your idols ...... Eze 14:6
Repent, and turn y from all your ...... Eze 14:30
wherefore turn y, and live ye ...... Eze 18:32
defile not y with the idols of ...... Eze 20:7
nor defile y with their idols ...... Eze 20:18
ye pollute y with all your idols ...... Eze 20:31
ye shall lothe y in your own ...... Eze 20:43
shall lothe y in your own sight ...... Eze 36:31
beast of the field, Assemble y ...... Eze 39:17
gather y on every side to my ...... Eze 39:17
my charge in my sanctuary for y ...... Eze 44:8
Sow to y in righteousness, reap ...... Hos 10:12
Gird y, and lament, ye priests ...... Joel 1:13
Assemble y, and come, all ye ...... Joel 3:11

gather *y* together round about .... Joel 3:11
Assemble *y* upon the mountains of ...... Amos 3:9
of your good, which ye made to *y* .... Zeph 2:1
Gather *y* together, yea, gather .... Zeph 2:1
did drink, did not ye eat for *y* .... Zec 7:6
for *y*, and drink for *y* .... Zec 7:6
And think not to say within *y* .... Mt 3:9
Lay not up for *y* treasures upon .... Mt 6:19
But lay up for *y* treasures in .... Mt 6:20
faith, why reason ye among *y* .... Mt 16:8
for ye neither go in *y*, neither .... Mt 23:13
more the child of hell than *y* .... Mt 23:15
Wherefore be ye witnesses unto *y* .... Mt 23:31
to them that sell, and buy for *y* .... Mt 25:9
Come ye *y* apart into a desert .... Mk 6:31
ye disputed among *y* by the way .... Mk 9:33
Have salt in *y*, and have peace one ...... Mk 9:50
But take heed to *y* .... Mk 13:9
and begin not to say within *y* .... Lk 3:8
ye *y* touch not the burdens with .... Lk 11:46
ye entered not in *y*, and them that ...... Lk 11:52
provide ye bags which wax not old, ... Lk 12:33
ye *y* like unto men that wait for .... Lk 12:36
why even of *y* judge ye not what .... Lk 12:57
of God, and you *y* thrust out .... Lk 13:28
Make to *y* friends of the mammon .... Lk 16:9
they which justify *y* before men .... Lk 16:15
Take heed to *y* .... Lk 17:3
Go shew *y* unto the priests .... Lk 17:14
And take heed to *y*, lest at any .... Lk 21:34
Take this, and divide it among *y* .... Lk 22:17
weep not for me, but weep for *y* .... Lk 23:28
Ye *y* bear me witness, that I said .... Jn 3:28
unto them, Murmur not among *y* .... Jn 6:43
ye enquire among *y* of that I said .... Jn 16:19
midst of you, as ye *y* also know .... Acts 2:22
Save *y* from this untoward .... Acts 2:40
take heed to *y* what ye intend to .... Acts 5:35
judge *y* unworthy of everlasting .... Acts 13:46
from which if ye keep *y*, ye shall .... Acts 15:29
embracing him said, Trouble not *y* ...... Acts 20:10
Take heed therefore unto *y* .... Acts 20:28
ye *y* know, that these hands have .... Acts 20:34
Likewise reckon ye also *y* to be .... Rom 6:11
but yield *y* unto God, as those .... Rom 6:13
whom ye yield *y* servants to obey .... Rom 6:16
Dearly beloved, avenge not *y* .... Rom 12:19
from among *y* that wicked person 1Cor 5:13
rather suffer *y* to be defrauded 1Cor 6:7
that ye may give *y* to fasting 1Cor 7:5
Judge in *y* 1Cor 11:13
That ye submit *y* unto such 1Cor 16:16
in you, yea, what clearing of *y* 2Cor 7:11
y to be clear in this matter 2Cor 7:11
gladly, seeing ye *y* are wise 2Cor 11:19
Examine *y*, whether ye be in the 2Cor 13:5
and that not of *y* .... Eph 2:8
Speaking to *y* in psalms and hymns ...... Eph 5:19
Submitting *y* one to another in .... Eph 5:21
submit *y* unto your own husbands, ... Eph 5:22
submit *y* unto your own husbands, ... Col 3:18
For *y*, brethren, know our 1Th 2:1
for *y* know that we are appointed 1Th 3:3
for ye *y* are taught of God to 1Th 4:9
For *y* know perfectly that the day 1Th 5:2
Wherefore comfort *y* together 1Th 5:11
And be at peace among *y* 1Th 5:13
that which is good, both among *y* 1Th 5:15
that ye withdraw *y* from every 2Th 3:6
For *y* know how ye ought to follow 2Th 3:7
knowing in *y* that ye have in .... Heb 10:34
as being *y* also in the body .... Heb 13:3
the rule over you, and submit *y* .... Heb 13:17
Are ye not then partial in *y* .... Jas 2:4
Submit *y* therefore to God .... Jas 4:7
Humble *y* in the sight of the Lord ...... Jas 4:10
not fashioning *y* according to the 1Pet 1:14
Submit *y* to every ordinance of 1Pet 2:13
arm *y* likewise with the same mind...... 1Pet 4:1
have fervent charity among *y* 1Pet 4:8
younger, submit *y* unto the elder 1Pet 5:5
Humble *y* therefore under the 1Pet 5:6
children, keep *y* from idols 1Jn 5:21
Look to *y*, that we lose not those 2Jn 8
building up *y* on your most holy .... Jude 20
Keep *y* in the love of God, ... Jude 21
gather *y* together unto the supper ...... Rev 19:17

YOUTH

of man's heart is evil from his *y* .... Gen 8:21
the youngest according to his *y* .... Gen 43:33
cattle from our *y* even until now .... Gen 46:34
her father's house, as in her *y* .... Lev 22:13
in her father's house in her *y* .... Num 30:3
being yet in her *y* in her .... Num 30:16
But the *y* drew not his sword .... Judg 8:20
he feared, because he was yet a *y* ...... Judg 8:20
for thou art but a *y*, and he a man 1Sa 17:33
and he a man of war from his *y* 1Sa 17:33
for he was but a *y*, and ruddy, and 1Sa 17:42
host, Abner, whose son is this *y* 1Sa 17:55
befell thee from thy *y* until now 2Sa 19:7
servant fear the Lord from my *y* 1Kin 18:12
to possess the iniquities of my *y* .... Job 13:26
are full of the sin of his *y* .... Job 20:11
As I was in the days of my *y* .... Job 29:4
Upon my right hand rise the *y* .... Job 30:12
(For from my *y* he was brought up,) .... Job 31:18
shall return to the days of his *y* .... Job 33:25
They die in *y*, and their life is............ Job 36:14
Remember not the sins of my *y* .... Ps 25:7

---

thou art my trust from my *y* .... Ps 71:5
thou hast taught me from my *y* .... Ps 71:17
and ready to die from my *y* up .... Ps 88:15
The days of his *y* hast .... Ps 89:45
so that thy *y* is renewed like the .... Ps 103:5
thou hast the dew of thy *y* .... Ps 110:3
are sons of the *y* .... Ps 127:4
have they afflicted me from my *y* .... Ps 129:1
have they afflicted me from my *y* .... Ps 129:2
be as plants grown up in their *y* .... Ps 144:12
forsaketh the guide of her *y* .... Prov 2:17
and rejoice with the wife of thy *y* .... Prov 5:18
Rejoice, O young man, in thy *y* .... Eccl 11:9
cheer thee in the days of thy *y* .... Eccl 11:9
for childhood and *y* are vanity .... Eccl 11:10
thy Creator in the days of thy *y* .... Eccl 12:1
that laboured from thy *y* .... Is 47:12
even thy merchants, from thy *y* .... Is 47:15
shalt forget the shame of thy *y* .... Is 54:4
grieved in spirit, and a wife of *y* .... Is 54:6
thee, the kindness of thy *y* .... Jer 2:2
thou art the guide of my *y* .... Jer 3:4
labour of our fathers from our *y* .... Jer 3:24
from our *y* even unto this day, and .... Jer 3:25
hath been thy manner from thy *y* ...... Jer 22:21
I did bear the reproach of my *y* .... Jer 31:19
remember thee, the kindness of thy ...... Jer 32:30
Moab hath been at ease from his *y* .... Jer 48:11
that he bear the yoke in his *y* .... Lam 3:27
for from my *y* up even till now .... Eze 4:14
not remembered the days of thy *y* ...... Eze 16:22
not remembered the days of thy *y* ...... Eze 16:43
with thee in the days of thy *y* .... Eze 16:60
committed whoredoms in their *y* .... Eze 23:3
for in her *y* they lay with her, ... Eze 23:8
to remembrance the days of her *y* ...... Eze 23:19
remembrance the lewdness of thy *y* .... Eze 23:21
Egyptians for the paps of thy *y* .... Eze 23:21
there, as in the days of her *y* .... Hos 2:15
for the husband of her *y* .... Joel 1:8
me to keep castle from my *y* .... Zec 13:5
between thee and the wife of thy *y* .... Mal 2:14
against the wife of his *y* .... Mal 2:15
things have I kept from my *y* up .... Mt 19:20
these have I observed from my *y* .... Mk 10:20
these have I kept from my *y* up .... Lk 18:21
My manner of life from my *y* .... Acts 26:4
Let no man despise thy *y* 1Ti 4:12

YOUTHFUL

Flee also *y* lusts 2Ti 2:22

YOUTHS

I come, I discerned among the *y* .... Prov 7:7
Even the *y* shall faint and be.............. Is 40:30

YOU-WARD

world, and more abundantly to *y* 2Cor 1:12
which to *y* is not weak, but is.............. 2Cor 13:3
of God which is given me to *y* .... Eph 3:2

Z

ZAANAIM (za-an-a'-im) See ZAANANNIM. A plain in Naphtali.

his tent unto the plain of Z .... Judg 4:11

ZAANAN (za'-an-an) See ZENAN. A city of Judah.

the inhabitant of Z came not .... Mic 1:11

ZA-ANANNIM See ZAANAIM.

ZAANANNIM (za-an-an'-nim) Same as Zaanaim.

was from Heleph, from Allon to Z .... Josh 19:33

ZAAVAN (za'-av-an) See ZAVAN. A son of Ezer.

Bilhan, and Z, and Akan .... Gen 36:27

ZABAD (za'-bad) See JOSABAD, JOZACHAR.
1. A son of Nathan.

begat Nathan, and Nathan begat Z 1Chr 2:36
Z begat Ephlal, and Ephlal begat 1Chr 2:37
2. Son of Tahath.

Z his son, and Shuthelah his son, ... 1Chr 7:21
3. A "mighty man" of David.

the son of Ahlai, ... 1Chr 11:41
4. A son of Shimeath.

the son of Shimeath an 2Chr 24:26
5. A son of Zattu.

Mattaniah, and Jeremoth, and Z .... Ezr 10:27
6. A son of Hashum.

Mattenai, Mattathah, Z, Eliphelet........ Ezr 10:33
7. A son of Nebo.

Jeiel, Mattithiah, Z, Zebina, ... Ezr 10:43

ZABBAI (zab'-bahee) See ZACCAI.
1. Married a foreigner to wife.

Jehohanan, Hananiah, Z, and Athlai .... Ezr 10:28
2. Father of Baruch.

After him Baruch the son of Z .... Neh 3:20

ZABBUD (zab'-bud) See ZACCUR. An exile with Ezra.

Uthai, and Z, and them with seventy.... Ezr 8:14

ZABDI (zab'-di) See ZACCHUR, ZICHRI.
1. Father of Carmi.

the son of Carmi, the son of Z .... Josh 7:1

---

and Z was taken .... Josh 7:17
the son of Carmi, the son of Z .... Josh 7:18
2. Son of Shimhi.

And Jakim, and Zichri, and Z 1Chr 8:19
3. A storekeeper in David's court.

wine cellars was Z the Shiphmite 1Chr 27:27
4. A Levite.

the son of Micha, the son of .... Neh 11:17

ZABDIEL (zab'-de-el)
1. Father of Jashobeam.

month was Jashobeam the son of Z 1Chr 27:2
2. An overseer of priests.

and their overseer was Z, the son .... Neh 11:14

ZABUD (za'-bud) A family of exiles.

Z the son of Nathan was principal........ 1Kin 4:5

ZABULON (zab'-u-lon) See ZEBULUN. Greek form of Zebulun.

sea coast, in the borders of Z................ Mt 4:13
The land of Z, and the land of .... Mt 4:15
Of the tribe of Z were sealed .... Rev 7:8

ZACCAI (zac'-cahee) See ZABBAI. A family of exiles.

The children of Z, seven hundred .... Ezr 2:9
The children of Z, seven hundred .... Neh 7:14

ZACCHAEUS (zak-ke'-us) A tax collector visited by Jesus.

behold, there was a man named Z .... Lk 19:2
and saw him, and said unto him, Z........ Lk 19:5
Z stood, and said unto the Lord............ Lk 19:8

ZACCHUR (zac'-cur) See ZACCUR. Father of Shimei.

Z his son, Shimei his son 1Chr 4:26

ZACCUR (zac'-cur) See ZABBUD, ZABDI, ZACCHUR, ZICHRI.
1. Father of Shammua.

of Reuben, Shammua the son of Z .... Num 13:4
2. A sanctuary servant.

Beno, and Shoham, and Z, and Ibri 1Chr 24:27
3. A son of Asaph.

Z, and Joseph, and Nethaniah, and...... 1Chr 25:2
The third to Z, he, his sons, and.......... 1Chr 25:10
the son of Michaiah, the son of Z .... Neh 12:35
4. A rebuilder of Jerusalem's wall.

to them builded Z the son of Imri .... Neh 3:2
5. A Levite who renewed the covenant.

Z, Sherebiah, Shebaniah, ... Neh 10:12
6. Father of Hanan.

to them was Hanan the son of Z .... Neh 13:13

ZACHARIAH (zak-a-ri'-ah) See ZECHARIAH.
1. A king of Israel.

Z his son reigned in his stead.............. 2Kin 14:29
of Azariah king of Judah did Z 2Kin 15:8
And the rest of the acts of Z 2Kin 15:11
2. Father of Abi.

also was Abi, the daughter of Z............ 2Kin 18:2

ZACHARIAS (zak-a-ri'-as) See ZECHARIAH.
1. Son of Barachias.

the blood of Z son of Barachias .... Mt 23:35
blood of Abel unto the blood of Z .... Lk 11:51
2. Father of John the Baptist.

Judaea, a certain priest named Z .... Lk 1:5
when Z saw him, he was troubled, ... Lk 1:12
angel said unto him, Fear not, Z .... Lk 1:13
Z said unto the angel, Whereby .... Lk 1:18
And the people waited for Z .... Lk 1:21
And entered into the house of Z .... Lk 1:40
and they called him Z, after the............ Lk 1:59
his father Z was filled with the, ... Lk 1:67
the son of Z in the wilderness.............. Lk 3:2

ZACHER (za'-kur) See ZECHARIAH. Father of Gibeon.

And Gedor, and Ahio, and Z 1Chr 8:31

ZADOK (za'-dok) See ZADOK's.
1. A priest in David's time.

Z the son of Ahitub, and Ahimelech...... 2Sa 8:17
And Z, and all the Levites 2Sa 15:24
and the king said unto Z, Carry............ 2Sa 15:25
king said also unto Z the priest 2Sa 15:27
Z therefore and Abiathar carried.......... 2Sa 15:29
hast thou not there with Z the 2Sa 15:35
house, thou shalt tell it to Z 2Sa 15:35
Then said Hushai unto Z and to 2Sa 15:35
Then said Ahimaaz the son of Z 2Sa 18:19
the son of Z yet again to Joab 2Sa 18:22
running of Ahimaaz the son of Z 2Sa 18:27
And king David sent to Z and to 2Sa 19:11
and Z and Abiathar were the priests 2Sa 20:25
But Z the priest, and Benaiah the 1Kin 1:8
Z the priest, and Benaiah the son........ 1Kin 1:26
Call me Z the priest, and Nathan 1Kin 1:32
let Z the priest and Nathan the 1Kin 1:34
So Z the priest, and Nathan the............ 1Kin 1:38
Z the priest took an horn of oil 1Kin 1:39
hast sent with him Z the priest 1Kin 1:44
Z the priest and Nathan the 1Kin 1:45
the priest did the king put in 1Kin 2:35
Azariah the son of Z the priest, ... 1Kin 4:2
and Z and Abiathar were the priests 1Kin 4:4
And Ahitub begat Z 1Chr 6:8
And Z begat Ahimaaz 1Chr 6:8
Z his son, Ahimaaz his son 1Chr 6:53
And David called for Z and Abiathar 1Chr 15:11
Z the priest, and his brethren the 1Chr 16:39
And Z the son of Ahitub, and Abimelech . 1Chr 18:16

both Z of the sons of Eleazar, and...... 1Chr 24:3
Z the priest, and Ahimelech the........ 1Chr 24:6
presence of David the king, and...... 1Chr 24:31
of the Aaronites, Z................................. 1Chr 27:17
chief governor, and Z to be priest...... 1Chr 29:22
of the house of Z answered him....... 2Chr 31:10
The son of Shallum, the son of Z...... Ezr 7:2
these are the sons of Z among the...... Eze 40:46
Levites that be of the seed of Z....... Eze 43:19
the Levites, the sons of Z............... Eze 44:15
are sanctified of the sons of Z......... Eze 48:11
2. Father of Jerusha.
was Jerusha, the daughter of Z........ 2Kin 15:33
was Jerushah, the daughter of Z....... 2Chr 27:1
3. Son of Ahitub.
And Ahitub begat Z........................... 1Chr 6:12
begat Zadok, and Z begat Shallum,...... 1Chr 6:12
son of Meshullam, the son of Z........ 1Chr 9:11
4. A warrior in David's army.
And Z, a young man mighty of........ 1Chr 12:28
5. Son of Baana.
them repaired Z the son of Baana........ Neh 3:4
6. A priest who rebuilt the wall.
After them repaired Z the son of...... Neh 3:29
7. A renewer of the covenant.
Meshezabeel, Z, Jaddua,................... Neh 10:21
8. A son of Meraioth.
son of Meshullam, the son of Z........ Neh 11:11
9. A Temple servant.
Z the scribe, and of the Levites,........ Neh 13:13

ZADOKITES See ZADOK's.

ZADOK's (za´-doks) *Refers to Zadok 1.*
their two sons, Ahimaaz Z son......... 2Sa 15:36

ZAHAM (za´-ham) *A son of Rehoboam.*
Jeush, and Shamariah, and Z.......... 2Chr 11:19

ZAIR (za´-ur) *A city in Edom.*
So Joram went over to Z, and all...... 2Kin 8:21

ZALAPH (za´-laf) *Father of Hanun.*
and Hanun the sixth son of Z.......... Neh 3:30

ZALMON (zal´-mon) See ILAI, SALMON.
1. A hill in Ephraim.
Abimelech gat him up to mount Z...... Judg 9:48
2. A "mighty man" of David.
Z the Ahohite, Maharai the............. 2Sa 23:28

ZALMONAH (zal´-mo-nah) *An Israelite
encampment in the wilderness.*
from mount Hor, and pitched in Z...... Num 33:41
And they departed from Z, and....... Num 33:42

ZALMUNNA (zal-mun´-nah) *A Midianite king.*
and I am pursuing after Zebah and Z.... Judg 8:5
Z now in thine hand, that we.......... Judg 8:6
Z into mine hand, then I will.......... Judg 8:7
Z were in Karkor, and their hosts...... Judg 8:10
Z fled, he pursued after them, and...... Judg 8:12
two kings of Midian, Zebah and Z...... Judg 8:12
and said, Behold Zebah and Z......... Judg 8:15
Z now in thine hand, that we......... Judg 8:15
Then said he unto Zebah and Z....... Judg 8:18
Z said, Rise thou, and fall upon....... Judg 8:21
Gideon arose, and slew Zebah and Z.... Judg 8:21
their princes as Zebah, and as Z....... Ps 83:11

ZAMZUMMIMS (zam-zum´-mims) See
ZUZIMS. *A tribe in Canaan.*
and the Ammonites call them Z......... Deut 2:20

ZAMZUMMIMS See ZAMZUMMIMS.

ZANOAH (za-no´-ah)
1. A city on the plain of Judah.
And Z, and En-gannim.................... Josh 15:34
Hanun, and the inhabitants of Z....... Neh 3:13
Z, Adullam, and in their villages....... Neh 11:30
2. A city in the hills of Judah.
And Jezreel, and Jokdeam, and Z...... Josh 15:56
3. A descendant of Caleb.
and Jekuthiel the father of Z.......... 1Chr 4:18

ZAPHENATH-PANEAH See ZAPHNATH-
PAANEAH.

ZAPHNATH-PAANEAH (zaf´´-nath-pa-a-ne´-
ah) *Name given to Joseph by Pharaoh.*
And Pharaoh called Joseph's name Z.... Gen 41:45

ZAPHON (za´-fon) *A city in Gad.*
and Succoth, and Z....................... Josh 13:27

ZARA (za´-rah) See ZARAH, ZERAH. *Greek form
of Zarah; an ancestor of Jesus.*
Judas begat Phares and Z of Thamar.... Mt 1:3

ZARAH (za´-rah) See ZARA, ZERAH. *A son of
Judah.*
and his name was called Z.............. Gen 38:30
Onan, and Shelah, and Pharez, and Z.... Gen 46:12

ZAREAH (za´-re-ah) See ZAREATHITES, ZORAH.
A city in Judah.
And at En-rimmon, and at Z, and at.... Neh 11:29

ZAREATHITES (za´-re-ath-ites) See
ZORATHITES. *Descendants of Shobal.*
of them came the Z, and the........... 1Chr 2:53

ZARED (za´-red) See ZERED. *A brook near the
Dead Sea.*
and pitched in the valley of Z.......... Num 21:12

ZAREPHATH (zar´-e-fath) See SAREPTA. *A city
in Phoenicia.*
Arise, get thee to Z, which............. 1Kin 17:9
So he arose and went to Z.............. 1Kin 17:10
of the Canaanites, even unto Z......... Obad 20

ZARETAN (zar´-e-tan) See ZARTANAH,
ZEREDATHAH. *A city in Ephraim.*
the city Adam, that is beside Z........ Josh 3:16

ZARETHAN See ZARTHAN.

ZARETH-SHAHAR (za´´-reth-sha´-har) *A city
in Reuben.*
Z in the mount of the valley,.......... Josh 13:19

ZARHITES (zar´-hites)
1. Descendants of Zerah, the Simeonite.
Of Zerah, the family of the Z.......... Num 26:13
and he took the family of the Z....... Josh 7:17
the family of the Z man by man....... Josh 7:17
Sibbecai the Hushathite, of the Z...... 1Chr 27:11
the Netophathite, of the Z............. 1Chr 27:13
2. Descendants of Zerah, son of Judah.
of Zerah, the family of the Z.......... Num 26:20

ZARTANAH (zar´-ta-nah) See ZARETAN,
ZARTHAN. *Same as Zaretan.*
which is by Z beneath Jezreel,......... 1Kin 4:12

ZARTHAN (zar´-than) See ZARETAN,
ZARTANAH. *Same as Zaretan.*
clay ground between Succoth and Z.... 1Kin 7:46

ZATTHU (zath´-u) See ZATTU. *A renewer of
the covenant.*
Parosh, Pahath-moab, Elam, Z........ Neh 10:14

ZATTU (zat´-tu) See ZATTHU. *A family of
exiles.*
The children of Z, nine hundred....... Ezr 2:8
And of the sons of Z..................... Ezr 10:27
The children of Z, eight hundred....... Neh 7:13

ZAVAN (za´-van) See ZAAVAN. *Son of Ezer.*
Bilhan, and Z, and Jakan................. 1Chr 1:42

ZAZA (za´-zah) *A son of Jonathan.*
Peleth, and Z.............................. 1Chr 2:33

ZEAL
his z to the children of Israel......... 2Sa 21:2
with me, and see my z for the LORD.... 2Kin 10:16
the z of the LORD of hosts shall....... 2Kin 19:31
For the z of thine house hath.......... Ps 69:9
My z hath consumed me, because...... Ps 119:139
The z of the LORD of hosts shall....... Is 9:7
the z of the LORD of hosts shall....... Is 37:32
and was clad with z as a cloke........ Is 59:17
where is thy z and thy strength,....... Is 63:15
the LORD have spoken it in my z...... Eze 5:13
The z of thine house hath eaten....... Jn 2:17
record that they have a z of God...... Rom 10:2
what vehement desire, yea, what z.... 2Cor 7:11
your z hath provoked very many....... 2Cor 9:2
Concerning z, persecuting the......... Phil 3:6
that he hath a great z for you......... Col 4:13

ZEALOT See ZELOTES.

ZEALOUS
while he was z for my sake among.... Num 25:11
because he was z for his God........... Num 25:13
and they are all z of the law.......... Acts 21:20
was z toward God, as ye all are....... Acts 22:3
as ye are z of spiritual gifts........... 1Cor 14:12
being more exceedingly z of the....... Gal 1:14
peculiar people, z of good works...... Titus 2:14
be z therefore, and repent............. Rev 3:19

ZEALOUSLY
They z affect you, but not well....... Gal 4:17
But it is good to be z affected........ Gal 4:18

ZEBADIAH (zeb-ad´-i-ah)
1. Grandson of Elpeal.
And Z, and Arad, and Ader,............ 1Chr 8:15
2. A son of Elpeal.
Z, and Meshullam, and Hezeki......... 1Chr 8:17
3. A warrior in David's army.
And Joelah, and Z, the sons of........ 1Chr 12:7
4. A Levite gatekeeper.
Z the third, Jathniel the fourth,....... 1Chr 26:2
5. A son of Asahel.
of Joab, and Z his son after him...... 1Chr 27:7
6. A messenger for King Jehoshaphat.
and Nethaniah, and Z................... 2Chr 17:8
7. Son of Ishmael.
Z the son of Ishmael, the ruler....... 2Chr 19:11
8. A family of exiles.
the son of Michael, and with him...... Ezr 8:8
9. Married a foreigner in exile.
Hanani, and Z............................. Ezr 10:20

ZEBAH (ze´-bah) *A king of Midian.*
faint, and I am pursuing after Z....... Judg 8:5
Succoth said, Are the hands of Z...... Judg 8:6
when the LORD hath delivered Z....... Judg 8:7
Now Z and Zalmunna were............. Judg 8:10
And when Z and Zalmunna fled, he.... Judg 8:12
took the two kings of Midian, Z....... Judg 8:12
men of Succoth, and said, Behold Z.... Judg 8:15
saying, Are the hands of Z............. Judg 8:15
Then said he unto Z and Zalmunna.... Judg 8:18
Then Z and Zalmunna said, Rise....... Judg 8:21
And Gideon arose, and slew Z......... Judg 8:21
yea, all their princes as Z.............. Ps 83:11

ZEBAIM (ze-ba´-im) *Residence of some exiles
in Babylonia.*
the children of Pochereth of Z......... Ezr 2:57
the children of Pochereth of Z......... Neh 7:59

ZEBEDEE (zeb´-e-dee) See ZEBEDEE's. *Father
of James and John.*
two brethren, James the son of Z...... Mt 4:21
in a ship with Z their father.......... Mt 4:21
James the son of Z, and John his...... Mt 10:2
hit Peter and the two sons of Z....... Mt 26:37
thence, he saw James the son of Z.... Mk 1:19
they left their father Z in the......... Mk 1:20
And James the son of Z, and John...... Mk 3:17
And James and John, the sons of Z.... Mk 10:35
James and John, the sons of Z......... Lk 5:10
Cana in Galilee, and the sons of Z.... Jn 21:2

ZEBEDEE's (zeb´-e-dees)
of Z children with her sons............ Mt 20:20
and the mother of Z children.......... Mt 27:56

ZEBINA See ZEBUDAH.

ZEBINA (ze-bi´-nah) *Married a foreigner in
exile.*
Jeiel, Mattithiah, Zabad, Z............. Ezr 10:43

ZEBOIIM (ze-boy´-im) See ZEBOIM. *City
destroyed with Sodom and Gomorrah.*
of Admah, and Shemeber king of Z.... Gen 14:2
king of Admah, and the king of Z..... Gen 14:8

ZEBOIM (ze-bo´-im) See ZEBOIIM.
1. Same as Zeboiim.
and Gomorrah, and Admah, and Z..... Gen 10:19
Gomorrah, Admah, and Z............... Deut 29:23
how shall I set thee as Z.............. Hos 11:8
2. A city in Benjamin.
valley of Z toward the wilderness..... 1Sa 13:18
Hadid, Z, Neballat,....................... Neh 11:34

ZEBUDAH (ze-bu´-dah) *Mother of King
Jehoiakim.*
And his mother's name was Z.......... 2Kin 23:36

ZEBUL (ze´-bul) *A ruler of Shechem.*
and Z his officer.......................... Judg 9:28
when Z the ruler of the city........... Judg 9:30
Gaal saw the people, he said to Z..... Judg 9:36
Z said unto him, Thou seest the....... Judg 9:36
Then said Z unto him, Where is....... Judg 9:38
Z thrust out Gaal and his brethren.... Judg 9:41

ZEBULONITE (zeb´-u-lon-ite) See
ZEBULONITES. *A descendant of Zebulun 1.*
And after him Elon, a Z, judged....... Judg 12:11
And Elon the Z died, and was buried.... Judg 12:12

ZEBULUN (zeb´-u-lun) See ZABULON,
ZEBULONITE, ZEBULONITES.
1. A son of Jacob.
and she called his name Z.............. Gen 30:20
Levi, and Judah, and Issachar, and Z.... Gen 35:23
And the sons of Z........................ Gen 46:14
Z shall dwell at the haven of the..... Gen 49:13
Issachar, Z, and Benjamin,.............. Ex 1:3
Levi, and Judah, and Issachar, and Z.... 1Chr 2:1
2. Descendants of Zebulun.
Of Z; Eliab the........................... Num 1:9
Of the children of Z, by their......... Num 1:30
of them, even of the tribe of Z....... Num 1:31
Then the tribe of Z...................... Num 2:7
be captain of the children of Z....... Num 2:7
prince of the children of Z............. Num 7:24
of Z was Eliab the son of Helon....... Num 10:16
Of the tribe of Z, Gaddiel the......... Num 13:10
Of the sons of Z after their........... Num 26:26
of the tribe of the children of Z...... Num 34:25
Reuben, Gad, and Asher, and Z........ Deut 27:13
And of Zebulun he said, Rejoice, Z.... Deut 33:18
of Z according to their families....... Josh 19:10
of Z according to their families....... Josh 19:16
to Beth-dagon, and reacheth to Z..... Josh 19:27
reacheth to Z on the south side,...... Josh 19:34
of Gad, and out of the tribe of Z..... Josh 21:7
Levites, out of the tribe of Z......... Josh 21:34
Neither did Z drive out the............ Judg 1:30
Naphtali and the children of Z........ Judg 4:6
And Barak called Z and Naphtali to.... Judg 4:10
out of Z they that handle the pen..... Judg 5:14
Z and Naphtali were a people that.... Judg 5:18
messengers unto Asher, and unto Z.... Judg 6:35
in Ajalon in the country of Z.......... Judg 12:12
of Gad, and out of the tribe of Z..... 1Chr 6:63
were given out of the tribe of Z...... 1Chr 6:77
Of Z, such as went forth to............ 1Chr 12:33
them, even unto Issachar and Z....... 1Chr 12:40
Of Z, Ishmaiah the son of Obadiah.... 1Chr 27:19
Ephraim and Manasseh even unto Z.... 2Chr 30:10
of Z humbled themselves, and came.... 2Chr 30:11
and Manasseh, Issachar, and Z......... 2Chr 30:18
their council, the princes of Z......... Ps 68:27
lightly afflicted the land of Z......... Is 9:1
the west side, Z a portion............. Eze 48:26
And by the border of Z, from the..... Eze 48:27
gate of Issachar, one gate of Z........ Eze 48:33

ZEBULUNITES (zeb´-u-lun-ites) *Descendants
of Zebulun.*
Z according to those that were........ Num 26:27

ZECHARIAH (zek-a-ri´-ah) See ZACCUR,
ZACHARIAH, ZACHARIAS, ZACHER.
1. A chief Reubenite.
were the chief, Jeiel, and Z............ 1Chr 5:7

2. *A Levite gatekeeper.*
Z the son of Meshelemiah was 1Chr 9:21
Z the firstborn, Jediael the............... 1Chr 26:2
Then for Z his son, a wise................ 1Chr 26:14
was Abijah, the daughter of Z............ 2Chr 29:1
3. *A Benjamite.*
And Gedor, and Ahio, and Z, and 1Chr 9:37
4. *A Levite musician.*
brethren of the second degree, Z 1Chr 15:18
And Z, and Aziel, and Shemiramoth, 1Chr 15:20
Asaph the chief, and next to him Z ... 1Chr 16:5
5. *A Tabernacle priest.*
and Nethaneel, and Amasai, and Z ... 1Chr 15:24
6. *A son of Isshiah.*
sons of Isshiah; Z 1Chr 24:25
7. *Son of Hosah.*
Tebaliah the third, Z the fourth......... 1Chr 26:11
8. *A chief of Manasseh.*
in Gilead, Iddo the son of Z.............. 1Chr 27:21
9. *A messenger of King Jehoshaphat.*
Ben-hail, and to Obadiah, and to Z .. 2Chr 17:7
10. *Father of Jehaziel.*
Then upon Jahaziel the son of Z 2Chr 20:14
11. *A son of Jehoshaphat.*
Azariah, and Jehiel, and Z.............. 2Chr 21:2
12. *Son of Jehoida.*
the Spirit of God came upon Z the 2Chr 24:20
13. *A prophet in King Uzziah's time.*
And he sought God in the days of Z .. 2Chr 26:5
14. *A Levite who cleansed the Temple.*
and Mattaniah.............................. 2Chr 29:13
15. *An overseer of the Temple repairs.*
and Z and Meshullam, of the sons of 2Chr 34:12
16. *A prince of Judah.*
Hilkiah and Z and Jehiel, rulers of ... 2Chr 35:8
17. *A prophet in Judah.*
Z the son of Iddo, prophesied.......... Ezr 5:1
the prophet and Z the son of Iddo ..... Ezr 6:14
came the word of the LORD unto Z..... Zec 1:1
came the word of the LORD unto Z .... Zec 1:7
in the fourth day of the ninth .... Zec 7:1
the word of the LORD came unto Z .... Zec 7:8
18. *A son of Pharosh.*
sons of Pharosh; Z .... Ezr 8:3
19. *A son of Bebai.*
The son of Bebai, and with him .... Ezr 8:11
Elnathan, and for Nathan, and for Z. Ezr 8:16
20. *Married a foreigner in exile.*
Mattaniah, and Jehiel, and Abdi,...... Ezr 10:26
21. *A descendant of Pharez.*
and Hashum, and Hashbadana, ... Neh 8:4
22. *A descendant of Pharez.*
the son of Uzziah, the son of Z......... Neh 11:4
23. *A son of Shiloni.*
the son of Joiarib, the son of Z......... Neh 11:5
24. *Father of a resettler in Jerusalem.*
the son of Amzi, the son of Z .... Neh 11:12
25. *A priest in Joiakim's time.*
Of Iddo, Z................................... Neh 12:16
26. *A priest who dedicated the wall.*
Z the son of Jonathan, the son of ..... Neh 12:35
Miniamin, Michaiah, Elioenai, Z .... Neh 12:41
27. *Son of Jeberechiah.*
and Z the son of Jeberechiah........... Is 8:2

ZECHER See ZACHER.

ZEDAD (ze'-dad) *A place near Hamath.*
forth of the border shall be to Z .... Num 34:8
way of Hethlon, as men go to Z .... Eze 47:15

ZEDEKIAH (zed-e-ki'-ah) See MATTANIAH,
ZEDEKIAS, ZIDKIJAH.
1. *A false prophet.*
Z the son of Chenaanah made him.... 1Kin 22:11
But Z the son of Chenaanah went 1Kin 22:24
The son of Chenaanah had made...... 2Chr 18:10
Then Z the son of Chenaanah came . 2Chr 18:23
2. *Name given to Mattaniah by
Nebuchadnezzar.*
stead, and changed his name to Z.... 2Kin 24:17
Z was twenty and one years old....... 2Kin 24:18
that Z rebelled against the king 2Kin 24:20
unto the eleventh year of king Z....... 2Kin 25:2
the sons of Z before his eyes........... 2Kin 25:7
eyes, and put out the eyes of Z 2Kin 25:7
the second Jehoiakim, the third Z 1Chr 3:15
made Z his brother king over............ 2Chr 36:10
Z was one and twenty years old........ 2Chr 36:11
Z the son of Josiah king of Judah ..... Jer 1:3
when king Z sent unto him Pashur ... Jer 21:1
unto them, Thus shall ye say to Z ..... Jer 21:3
I will deliver Z king of Judah .... Jer 21:7
So will I give Z the king of .... Jer 24:8
to Jerusalem unto Z king of Judah ... Jer 27:3
I spake also to Z king of Judah .... Jer 27:12
of the reign of Z king of Judah .... Jer 28:1
(whom Z king of Judah sent unto ..... Jer 29:3
the tenth year of Z king of Judah ..... Jer 32:1
For Z king of Judah had shut him ..... Jer 32:3
Z king of Judah shall not escape...... Jer 32:4
And he shall lead Z to Babylon .... Jer 32:5
speak to Z king of Judah, and tell..... Jer 34:2
of the LORD, O Z king of Judah .... Jer 34:4
unto Z king of Judah in Jerusalem ... Jer 34:6
after that the king Z had made a .... Jer 34:8
Z king of Judah and his princes........ Jer 34:21
king Z the son of Josiah reigned ...... Jer 37:1
Z the king sent Jehucal the son........ Jer 37:3
Then Z the king sent, and took him... Jer 37:17
Jeremiah said unto king Z .... Jer 37:18
Then Z the king commanded that...... Jer 37:21

Then Z the king said, Behold, he ...... Jer 38:5
Then Z the king sent, and took .... Jer 38:14
Then Jeremiah said unto Z .... Jer 38:15
So Z the king sware secretly unto..... Jer 38:16
Then said Jeremiah unto Z .... Jer 38:17
the king said unto Jeremiah, I .... Jer 38:19
Then said Z unto Jeremiah, Let no.... Jer 38:24
the ninth year of Z king of Judah ..... Jer 39:1
and in the eleventh year of Z .... Jer 39:2
that when Z the king of Judah saw .... Jer 39:4
overtook Z in the plains of .... Jer 39:5
of Z in Riblah before his eyes .... Jer 39:6
as I gave Z king of Judah .... Jer 44:30
of the reign of Z king of Judah .... Jer 49:34
when he went with Z the king of .... Jer 51:59
Z was one and twenty years old........ Jer 52:1
that Z rebelled against the king .... Jer 52:3
unto the eleventh year of king Z .... Jer 52:5
overtook Z in the plains of .... Jer 52:8
the sons of Z before his eyes .... Jer 52:10
Then he put out the eyes of Z .... Jer 52:11
3. *Grandson of Jehoiakim.*
Jeconiah his son, Z his son 1Chr 3:16
4. *A false prophet denounced by Jeremiah.*
of Z the son of Maaseiah, which....... Jer 29:21
saying, The LORD make thee like Z ... Jer 29:22
5. *A prince of Judah.*
the son of Hananiah, and all the....... Jer 36:12

ZEDEKIAS (zed-e-ki'-ahs) *Refers to*
Zedekiah 2.
Moreover he put out Z eyes.............. Jer 39:7

ZEEB (ze'-eb) *A Midianite prince.*
of the Midianites, Oreb and Z .... Judg 7:25
Z they slew at the winepress of........ Judg 7:25
they slew at the winepress of Z .... Judg 7:25
Z to Gideon on the other side .... Judg 7:25
the princes of Midian, Oreb and Z .... Judg 8:3
their nobles like Oreb, and like Z ...... Ps 83:11

ZELA See ZELAH.

ZELAH (ze'-lah) *A city in Benjamin.*
And Z, Eleph, and Jebusi, which is.... Josh 18:28
in the country of Benjamin in Z 2Sa 21:14

ZELEK (ze'-lek) *A "mighty man" of David.*
Z the Ammonite, Naharai the........... 2Sa 23:37
Z the Ammonite, Naharai the........... 1Chr 11:39

ZELOPHEHAD (ze-lo'-fe-had) *Son of Hepher.*
Z the son of Hepher had no sons....... Num 26:33
of the daughters of Z were Mahlah ... Num 26:33
Then came the daughters of Z .... Num 27:1
The daughters of Z speak right......... Num 27:7
Z our brother unto his daughters ...... Num 36:2
concerning the daughters of Z .... Num 36:6
Moses, so did the daughters of Z ..... Num 36:10
and Noah, the daughters of Z .... Num 36:11
But Z, the son of Hepher, the son ..... Josh 17:3
and the name of the second was Z ... 1Chr 7:15
and Z had daughters 1Chr 7:15

ZELOTES (ze-lo-teze') See CANAANITE, SIMON.
Surname of Simon, disciple of Jesus.
of Alphaeus, and Simon called Z ..... Lk 6:15
the son of Alphaeus, and Simon Z .... Acts 1:13

ZELZAH (zel'-zah) *A city in Benjamin.*
in the border of Benjamin at Z 1Sa 10:2

ZEMARAIM (zem-a-ra'-im) See ZEMARITE.
1. *A city in Benjamin.*
And Beth-arabah, and Z .... Josh 18:22
2. *A mountain in Ephraim.*
And Abijah stood up upon mount Z ... 2Chr 13:4

ZEMARITE *A descendant of Canaan.*
And the Arvadite, and the Z .... Gen 10:18
And the Arvadite, and the Z 1Chr 1:16

ZEMIRA (ze-mi'-rah) *A son of Becher.*
Z, and Joash, and Eliezer, and........ 1Chr 7:8

ZEMIRAH See ZEMIRA.

ZENAN (ze'-nan) See ZAANAN. *A city in Judah.*
Z, and Hadashah, and Migdal-gad, ... Josh 15:37

ZENAS (ze'-nas) *A Christian lawyer.*
Bring Z the lawyer and Apollos on .... Titus 3:13

ZEPHANIAH (zef-a-ni'-ah)
1. *A priest in exile.*
Z the second priest, and the three..... 2Kin 25:18
The son of Maaseiah the priest,........ Jer 21:1
to Z the son of Maaseiah the........... Jer 29:25
Z the priest read this letter in .... Jer 29:29
Z the son of Maaseiah the priest...... Jer 37:3
Z the second priest, and the three..... Jer 52:24
2. *An ancestor of Samuel.*
the son of Azariah, the son of Z 1Chr 6:36
3. *A prophet.*
came unto Z the son of Cushi .... Zeph 1:1
4. *Son of Josiah the priest.*
the house of Josiah the son of Z ...... Zec 6:10
Jedaiah, and to Hen the son of Z ..... Zec 6:14

ZEPHATH (ze'-fath) See HORMAH. *A city in*
Simeon.
the Canaanites that inhabited Z....... Judg 1:17

ZEPHATHAH (zef'-a-thah) *A valley in Judah.*
in the valley of Z at Mareshah 2Chr 14:10

ZEPHI (ze'-fi) See ZEPHO. *Son of Eliphaz.*
Teman, and Omar, Z, and Gatam,..... 1Chr 1:36

ZEPHO (ze'-fo) See ZEPHI. *Same as Zephi.*
of Eliphaz were Teman, Omar, Z,....... Gen 36:11
duke Teman, duke Omar, duke Z ...... Gen 36:15

ZEPHON (ze'-fon) See ZEPHONITES, ZIPHION. *A*
son of Gad.
Z, the family of the........................ Num 26:15

ZEPHONITES (zef'-on-ites) *Descendants of*
Zephon.
of Zephon, the family of the Z .... Num 26:15

ZER (zur) *A city in Naphtali.*
the fenced cities are Ziddim, Z......... Josh 19:35

ZERAH (ze'-rah) See EZRAHITE, ZARAH,
ZARHITES, ZOHAR.
1. *A son of Reuel.*
and Z, Shammah, and Mizzah .... Gen 36:13
duke Z, duke Shammah .... Gen 36:17
Nahath, Z, Shammah, and Mizzah.... 1Chr 1:37
2. *Father of Jobab.*
Jobab the son of Z of Bozrah .... Gen 36:33
Jobab the son of Z of Bozrah 1Chr 1:44
3. *Son of Judah.*
of Z, the family of the Zarhites......... Num 26:20
the son of Zabdi, the son of Z .... Josh 7:1
the son of Zabdi, the son of Z .... Josh 7:18
with him, took Achan the son of Z .... Josh 7:24
son of Z commit a trespass in the 1Chr 2:4
in law bare him Pharez and Z 1Chr 2:6
And the sons of Z 1Chr 2:6
And of the sons of Z 1Chr 9:6
children of Z the son of Judah .... Neh 11:24
4. *Son of Simeon.*
Of Z, the family of the Zarhites .... Num 26:13
were, Nemuel, and Jamin, Jarib, Z.... 1Chr 4:24
5. *Son of Iddo.*
Z his son, Jeaterai his son 1Chr 6:21
6. *Father of Ethni.*
The son of Ethni, the son of Z 1Chr 6:41
7. *An Ethiopian king.*
there came out against them Z the ... 2Chr 14:9

ZERAHIAH (zer-a-hi'-ah)
1. *An ancestor of Ezra.*
And Uzzi begat Z, and Z 1Chr 6:6
duke Z begat Meraioth, ... 1Chr 6:6
his son, Uzzi his son, Z his son,....... 1Chr 6:51
The son of Z, the son of Uzzi,........... Ezr 7:4
2. *Father of Elihoenai.*
Elihoenai the son of Z, and with ...... Ezr 8:4

ZERAHITE See ZARHITES.

ZERED (ze'-red) See ZARED. *Same as Zared.*
I, and get you over the brook Z .... Deut 2:13
And we went over the brook Z .... Deut 2:13
we were come over the brook Z .... Deut 2:14

ZEREDA (zer'-e-dah) *A city north of Mt.*
Ephraim.
son of Nebat, an Ephrathite of Z....... 1Kin 11:26

ZEREDAH See ZEREDATHAH.

ZEREDATHAH (ze-red'-a-thah) See ZARTHAN,
ZERERATH. *A city in Manasseh.*
clay ground between Succoth and Z . 2Chr 4:17

ZERERATH See ZERERATH.

ZERERATH (zer'-e-rath) See ZARTHAN,
ZEREDATHAH. *A district in Manasseh.*
host fled to Beth-shittah in Z .... Judg 7:22

ZERESH (ze'-resh) *Wife of Haman.*
for his friends, and Z his wife .... Est 5:10
Then said Z his wife and all his .... Est 5:14
And Haman told Z his wife and all .... Est 6:13
Z his wife unto him, If Mordecai....... Est 6:13

ZERETH (ze'-reth) *A descendant of Judah.*
And the sons of Helah were, Z 1Chr 4:7

ZERETH-SHAHAR See ZARETH-SHAHAR.

ZERI (ze'-ri) See IZRI. *Son of Jeduthun.*
Gedaliah, and Z, and Jeshaiah,....... 1Chr 25:3

ZEROR (ze'-ror) *Ancestor of King Saul.*
the son of Abiel, the son of Z 1Sa 9:1

ZERUAH (ze-ru'-ah) *Mother of Jeroboam 1.*
whose mother's name was Z 1Kin 11:26

ZERUBBABEL (ze-rub'-ba-bel) See
SHESHBAZZAR, ZOROBABEL. *A leader of a*
group of exiles.
And the sons of Pedaiah were, Z....... 1Chr 3:19
and the sons of Z 1Chr 3:19
Which came with Z .... Ezr 2:2
Z the son of Shealtiel, and his.......... Ezr 3:2
began Z the son of Shealtiel, and ..... Ezr 3:8
Then they came to Z, and to the....... Ezr 4:2
But Z, and Jeshua, and the rest of .... Ezr 4:3
Then rose up Z the son of .... Ezr 5:2
Who came with Z, Jeshua, Nehemiah, Neh 7:7
And all Israel in the days of Z .... Neh 12:47
unto Z the son of Shealtiel .... Hag 1:1
Then Z the son of Shealtiel, and ...... Hag 1:14
spirit of Z the son of Shealtiel.......... Hag 1:14
Speak now to Z the son of .... Hag 2:2

Yet now be strong, O Z, saith the .... Hag 2:4
Speak to Z, governor of Judah, ... Hag 2:21
of hosts, will I take thee, O Z .... Hag 2:23
is the word of the LORD unto Z .... Zec 4:6
before Z thou shalt become a .... Zec 4:7
The hands of Z have laid the .... Zec 4:9
in the hand of Z with those seven .... Zec 4:10

ZERUIAH (ze-ru-i'-ah) Sister of David.
and to Abishai the son of Z 1Sa 26:6
And Joab the son of Z, and 2Sa 2:13
there were three sons of Z there 2Sa 2:18
the sons of Z be too hard for me 2Sa 3:39
Joab the son of Z saw 2Sa 8:16
Now Joab the son of Z perceived 2Sa 14:1
the son of Z unto the king 2Sa 16:9
I to do with you, ye sons of Z 2Sa 16:10
sister to Z Joab's mother 2Sa 17:25
the hand of Abishai the son of Z 2Sa 18:2
But Abishai the son of Z answered 2Sa 19:21
I to do with you, ye sons of Z 2Sa 19:22
the son of Z succoured him 2Sa 21:17
the brother of Joab, the son of Z 2Sa 23:18
armourbearer to Joab the son of Z 2Sa 23:37
conferred with Joab the son of Z 1Kin 1:7
what Joab the son of Z did to me 1Kin 2:5
priest, and for Joab the son of Z 1Kin 2:22
Whose sisters were Z, and Abigail........ 1Chr 2:16
And the sons of Z 1Chr 2:16
Joab the son of Z went first up 1Chr 11:6
armourbearer of Joab the son of Z 1Chr 11:39
Abishai the son Z slew of the............ 1Chr 18:12
Joab the son of Z was over the........... 1Chr 18:15
son of Ner, and Joab the son of Z 1Chr 26:28
Joab the son of Z began to number........ 1Chr 27:24

ZETHAM (ze'-tham) A descendant of Laadan.
the chief was Jehiel, and Z 1Chr 23:8
Z, and Joel his brother, which 1Chr 26:22

ZETHAN (ze'-than) A son of Bilhan.
and Ehud, and Chenaanah, and Z........... 1Chr 7:10

ZETHAR (ze'-thar) A servant of King Ahasuerus.
Harbona, Bigtha, and Abagtha, Z.......... Est 1:10

ZEUS See MERCURIUS.

ZIA (zi'-ah) A Gadite in Bashan.
Sheba, and Jorai, and Jachan, and Z..... 1Chr 5:13

ZIBA (zi'-bah) A servant of King Saul.
Saul a servant whose name was Z 2Sa 9:2
king said unto him, Art thou Z 2Sa 9:2
Z said unto the king, Jonathan 2Sa 9:3
Z said unto the king, Behold, he 2Sa 9:4
Then the king called to Z 2Sa 9:9
Now Z had fifteen sons and twenty 2Sa 9:10
Then said Z unto the king, ... 2Sa 9:11
all that dwelt in the house of Z 2Sa 9:12
The servant of Mephibosheth met 2Sa 16:1
And the king said unto Z, What 2Sa 16:2
Z said, The asses be for the 2Sa 16:2
Z said unto the king, Behold, he 2Sa 16:3
Then said the king to Z, Behold, ... 2Sa 16:4
Z said, I humbly beseech thee 2Sa 16:4
the servant of the house of 2Sa 19:17
said, Thou and Z divide the land 2Sa 19:29

ZIBEON (zib'-e-un)
1. Grandfather of Adah.
Anah the daughter of Z the Hivite........ Gen 36:2
of Anah the daughter of Z .... Gen 36:14
2. A son of Seir.
Lotan, and Shobal, and Z, and Anah,..... Gen 36:20
And these are the children of Z .... Gen 36:24
he fed the asses of Z his father........ Gen 36:24
duke Lotan, duke Shobal, duke Z.......... Gen 36:29
Lotan, and Shobal, and Z, and Anah,..... 1Chr 1:38
And the sons of Z 1Chr 1:40

ZIBIA (zib'-e-ah) Son of Hodesh.
of Hodesh his wife, Jobab, and Z......... 1Chr 8:9

ZIBIAH (zib'-e-ah) Mother of King Jehoash.
mother's name was Z of Beer-sheba,...... 2Kin 12:1
name also was Z of Beer-sheba 2Chr 24:1

ZICHRI (zik'-ri) See ZITHRI.
1. A son of Izhar.
Korah, and Nepheg, and Z .... Ex 6:21
2. A Benjamite.
And Jakim, and Z, and Zabdi,............. 1Chr 8:19
3. Son of Shishak.
And Abdon, and Z, and Hanan,............. 1Chr 8:23
4. Son of Jeroham.
And Jaresiah, and Eliah, and Z........... 1Chr 8:27
5. Son of Asaph.
the son of Micah, the son of Z 1Chr 9:15
6. Descendant of Eliezer.
Z his son, and Shelomith his son,....... 1Chr 26:25
7. Father of Eliezer.
was Eliezer the son of Z 1Chr 27:16
8. Father of Amasiah.
next him was Amasiah the son of Z....... 2Chr 17:16
9. Father of Elishaphat.
and Elishaphat the son of Z 2Chr 23:1
10. A "mighty man" of Ephraim.
And Z, a mighty man of Ephraim,......... 2Chr 28:7
11. Father of Joel.
Joel the son of Z was their .... Neh 11:9
12. A priest with Zerubbabel.
Of Abijah, Z .... Neh 12:17

ZICRI See ZICHRI.

ZIDDIM (zid'-dim) A city in Naphtali.
And the fenced cities are Z .... Josh 19:35

ZIDKIJAH (zid-ki'-jah) See ZEDEKIAH. A clan leader who renewed the covenant.
the son of Hachaliah, and Z .... Neh 10:1

ZIDON (zi'-don)
1. A city in Asher.
and his border shall be unto Z .... Gen 49:13
them, and chased them unto great Z ...... Josh 11:8
and Kanah, even unto great Z .... Josh 19:28
Accho, nor the inhabitants of Z .... Judg 1:31
gods of Syria, and the gods of .... Judg 10:6
because it was far from Z .... Judg 18:28
came to Dan-jaan, and about to Z 2Sa 24:6
Zarephath, which belongeth to Z 1Kin 17:9
and drink, and oil, unto them of Z ...... Ezr 3:7
thou whom the merchants of Z .... Is 23:2
Be thou ashamed, O Z .... Is 23:4
oppressed virgin, daughter of Z .... Is 23:12
of Tyrus, and all the kings of Z .... Jer 25:22
of Tyrus, and to the king of Z .... Jer 27:3
Z every helper that remaineth,.......... Jer 47:4
The inhabitants of Z and Arvad.......... Eze 27:8
of man, set thy face against Z .... Eze 28:21
Behold, I am against thee, O Z .... Eze 28:22
ye to do with me, O Tyre, and Z .... Joel 3:4
Tyrus, and Z, though it be very........ Zec 9:2
2. A son of Canaan.
Canaan begat Z his firstborn, and....... 1Chr 1:13

ZIDONIANS (zi-do'-ne-uns) See SIDONIANS.
Inhabitants of Zidon.
The also, and the Amalekites, the .... Judg 10:12
after the manner of the Z .... Judg 18:7
and they were far from the Z .... Judg 18:7
Moabites, Ammonites, Edomites, Z........ 1Kin 11:1
Ashtoreth the goddess of the Z.......... 1Kin 11:5
Ashtoreth the goddess of the Z.......... 1Kin 11:33
daughter of Ethbaal king of the Z....... 1Kin 16:31
the abomination of the Z, and for....... 2Kin 23:13
for the Z and they of Tyre brought...... 1Chr 22:4
north, all of them, and all the Z....... Eze 32:30

ZIF (zif) Second month of the Hebrew year.
reign over Israel, in the month Z 1Kin 6:1
the LORD laid, in the month Z 1Kin 6:37

ZIHA (zi'-hah)
1. A family of exiles.
the children of Z, the children .... Ezr 2:43
the children of Z, the children .... Neh 7:46
2. An overseer of Temple servants.
and Z and Gispa were over the .... Neh 11:21

ZIKLAG (zik'-lag) A city in Judah.
And Z, and Madmannah, and .... Josh 15:31
And Z, and Beth-marcaboth, and .... Josh 19:5
Then Achish gave him Z that day......... 1Sa 27:6
wherefore Z pertaineth unto the 1Sa 27:6
were come to Z on the third day......... 1Sa 30:1
south, and Z, and smitten 1Sa 30:1
and we burned Z with fire 1Sa 30:14
And when David came to Z, he sent....... 1Sa 30:26
and David had abode two days in Z....... 2Sa 1:1
hold of him, and slew him in Z 2Sa 4:10
at Bethuel, and at Hormah, and at Z..... 1Chr 4:30
are they that came to David to Z........ 1Chr 12:1
As he went to Z, there fell to.......... 1Chr 12:20
And at Z, and at Mekonah .... Neh 11:28

ZILLAH (zil'-lah) A wife of Lamech.
Adah, and the name of the other Z....... Gen 4:19
And Z, she also bare Tubal-cain,........ Gen 4:22
said unto his wives, Adah and Z .... Gen 4:23

ZILLETHAI See ZILTHAI.

ZILPAH (zil'-pah) Handmaid of Leah.
Leah Z his maid for an handmaid .... Gen 29:24
left bearing, she took Z her maid....... Gen 30:9
Z Leah's maid bare Jacob a son......... Gen 30:10
Z Leah's maid bare Jacob a second...... Gen 30:12
And the sons of Z, Leah's handmaid,..... Gen 35:26
of Bilhah, and with the sons of Z....... Gen 37:2
These are the sons of Z, whom .... Gen 46:18

ZILTHAI (zil'-thahee)
1. Son of Shimhi.
And Elienai, and Z, and Eliel,.......... 1Chr 8:20
2. A warrior in David's army.
and Jozabad, and Elihu, and Z 1Chr 12:20

ZIMMAH (zim'-mah)
1. A son of Jahath.
son, Jahath his son, Z his son,......... 1Chr 6:20
2. A Gershonite.
The son of Ethan, the son of Z 1Chr 6:42
3. Father of Joah.
Joah the son of Z, and Eden the 2Chr 29:12

ZIMRAN (zim'-ran) A son of Abraham.
And she bare him Z, and Jokshan, and.... Gen 25:2
she bare Z, and Jokshan, and Medan,..... 1Chr 1:32

ZIMRI (zim'-ri)
1. A Simeonite.
with the Midianitish woman, was Z...... Num 25:14
2. A king of Israel.
And his servant Z, captain of half...... 1Kin 16:9
Z went in and smote him, and killed..... 1Kin 16:10
Thus did Z destroy all the house........ 1Kin 16:11
did Z reign seven days in Tirzah 1Kin 16:15
Z hath conspired, and hath slain 1Kin 16:16

when Z saw that the city was............ 1Kin 16:18
Now the rest of the acts of Z 1Kin 16:20
Had Z peace, who slew his master........ 2Kin 9:31
3. A son of Zerah.
Z, and Ethan, and Heman, and Calcol,.... 1Chr 2:6
4. Son of Jehoadah.
begat Alemeth, and Azmaveth, and Z...... 1Chr 8:36
and Z begat Moza, ... 1Chr 8:36
begat Alemeth, and Azmaveth, and Z...... 1Chr 9:42
and Z begat Moza 1Chr 9:42
5. An unspecified place.
And all the kings of Z, and all the .... Jer 25:25

ZIN (zin) A wilderness south of Judah.
the wilderness of Z unto Rehob .... Num 13:21
desert of Z in the first month.......... Num 20:1
my commandment in the desert of Z....... Num 27:14
in Kadesh in the wilderness of Z........ Num 27:14
and pitched in the wilderness of Z...... Num 33:36
of Z along by the coast of Edom......... Num 34:3
of Akrabbim, and pass on to Z .... Num 34:4
in the wilderness of Z .... Deut 32:51
of Edom the wilderness of Z .... Josh 15:1
and passed along to Z, and .... Josh 15:3

ZINA (zi'-nah) A son of Shimei.
sons of Shimei were, Jahath, Z.......... 1Chr 23:10

ZION (zi'-un) See SION, ZION'S. A term for Jerusalem.
David took the strong hold of Z 2Sa 5:7
of the city of David, which is Z........ 1Kin 8:1
daughter of Z hath despised thee........ 2Kin 19:21
they that escape out of mount Z......... 2Kin 19:31
David took the castle of Z 1Chr 11:5
of the city of David, which is Z 2Chr 5:2
my king upon my holy hill of Z .... Ps 2:6
to the LORD, which dwelleth in Z .... Ps 9:11
in the gates of the daughter of Z....... Ps 9:14
of Israel were come out of Z............ Ps 14:7
and strengthen thee out of Z .... Ps 20:2
of the whole earth, is mount Z.......... Ps 48:2
mount Z rejoice, let the .... Ps 48:11
Walk about Z, and go round about........ Ps 48:12
Out of Z, the perfection of .... Ps 50:2
good in thy good pleasure unto Z........ Ps 51:18
of Israel were come out of Z............ Ps 53:6
For God will save Z, and will .... Ps 69:35
this mount Z, wherein thou hast......... Ps 74:2
and his dwelling place in Z .... Ps 76:2
the mount Z which he loved .... Ps 78:68
of them in Z appeareth before God....... Ps 84:7
The LORD loveth the gates of Z .... Ps 87:2
of Z it shall be said, This and......... Ps 87:5
Z heard, and was glad .... Ps 97:8
The LORD is great in .... Ps 99:2
shalt arise, and have mercy upon Z...... Ps 102:13
When the LORD shall build up Z .... Ps 102:16
declare the name of the LORD in Z....... Ps 102:21
the rod of thy strength out of Z........ Ps 110:2
in the LORD shall be as mount Z......... Ps 125:1
turned again the captivity of Z......... Ps 126:1
LORD shall bless thee out of Z.......... Ps 128:5
and turned back that hate Z............. Ps 129:5
For the LORD hath chosen Z.............. Ps 132:13
descended upon the mountains of Z....... Ps 133:3
and earth bless thee out of Z........... Ps 134:3
Blessed be the LORD out of Z .... Ps 135:21
we wept, when we remembered Z .... Ps 137:1
Sing us one of the songs of Z .... Ps 137:3
reign for ever, even thy God, O Z,...... Ps 146:10
praise thy God, O Z .... Ps 147:12
let the children of Z be joyful......... Ps 149:2
Go forth, O ye daughters of Z .... Song 3:11
the daughter of Z is left as a .... Is 1:8
Z shall be redeemed with judgment....... Is 1:27
for out of Z shall go forth the .... Is 2:3
the daughters of Z are haughty .... Is 3:16
of the head of the daughters of Z....... Is 3:17
pass, that he that is left in .... Is 4:3
the fifth of the daughters of Z .... Is 4:4
every dwelling place of mount Z .... Is 4:5
hosts, which dwelleth in mount Z........ Is 8:18
his whole work upon mount Z............. Is 10:12
O my people that dwellest in Z.......... Is 10:24
the mount of the daughter of Z.......... Is 10:32
and shout, thou inhabitant of Z......... Is 12:6
that the LORD hath founded Z .... Is 14:32
the mount of the daughter of Z .... Is 16:1
the LORD of hosts, the mount Z .... Is 18:7
of hosts shall reign in mount Z......... Is 24:23
I lay in Z for a foundation a .... Is 28:16
be, that fight against mount Z .... Is 29:8
shall dwell in Z at Jerusalem .... Is 30:19
come down to fight for mount Z .... Is 31:4
the LORD, whose fire is in Z............ Is 31:9
he hath filled Z with judgment .... Is 33:5
The sinners in Z are afraid .... Is 33:14
Look upon Z, the city of our .... Is 33:20
for the controversy of Z .... Is 34:8
and come to Z with songs and .... Is 35:10
The virgin, the daughter of Z .... Is 37:22
they that escape out of mount Z .... Is 37:32
O Z, that bringest good tidings......... Is 40:9
The first shall say to Z, Behold, ... Is 41:27
in Z for Israel my glory .... Is 46:13
But Z said, The LORD hath .... Is 49:14
For the LORD shall comfort Z .... Is 51:3
and come with singing unto Z .... Is 51:11
of the earth, and say unto Z .... Is 51:16
put on thy strength, O Z .... Is 52:1
thy neck, O captive daughter of Z....... Is 52:2

that saith unto Z, Thy God .... Is 52:7
when the Lord shall bring again Z .... Is 52:8
And the Redeemer shall come to Z.... Is 59:20
The Z of the Holy One of Israel .... Is 60:14
appoint unto them that mourn in Z .... Is 61:3
Say ye to the daughter of Z .... Is 62:11
Z is a wilderness, Jerusalem a .... Is 64:10
for as soon as Z travailed .... Is 66:8
family, and I will bring you to Z .... Jer 3:14
Set up the standard toward Z............ Jer 4:6
the voice of the daughter of Z............ Jer 4:31
the daughter of Z to a comely .... Jer 6:2
war against thee, O daughter of Z .... Jer 6:23
Is not the Lord in Z .... Jer 8:19
of wailing is heard out of Z................ Jer 9:19
hath thy soul loathed Z .... Jer 14:19
Z shall be plowed like a field, ... Jer 26:18
an Outcast, saying, This is Z............ Jer 30:17
let us go up to Z unto the Lord .... Jer 31:6
come and sing in the height of Z ...... Jer 31:12
They shall ask the way to Z with ...... Jer 50:5
to declare in Z the vengeance of ...... Jer 50:28
let us declare in Z the work of .... Jer 51:10
they have done in Z in your sight ...... Jer 51:24
shall the inhabitant of Z say .... Jer 51:35
The ways of Z do mourn, because .... Lam 1:4
from the daughter of Z all her .... Lam 1:6
Z spreadeth forth her hands, and .... Lam 1:17
of Z with a cloud in his anger .... Lam 2:1
tabernacle of the daughter of Z .... Lam 2:4
and sabbaths to be forgotten in Z .... Lam 2:6
the wall of the daughter of Z............ Lam 2:8
daughter of Z sit upon the ground .... Lam 2:10
thee, O virgin daughter of Z.............. Lam 2:13
Lord, O wall of the daughter of Z .... Lam 2:18
The precious sons of Z .... Lam 4:2
and hath kindled a fire in Z .... Lam 4:11
is accomplished, O daughter of Z .... Lam 4:22
They ravished the women in Z .... Lam 5:11
Because of the mountain of Z............ Lam 5:18
Blow ye the trumpet in Z, and .... Joel 2:1
Blow the trumpet in Z, sanctify a...... Joel 2:15
Be glad then, ye children of Z............ Joel 2:23
for in mount Z and in Jerusalem .... Joel 2:32
The Lord also shall roar out of Z ...... Joel 3:16
the Lord your God dwelling in Z........ Joel 3:17
for the Lord dwelleth in Z .... Joel 3:21
said, The Lord will roar from Z.......... Amos 1:2
Woe to them that are at ease in Z .... Amos 6:1
But upon mount Z shall be .... Obad 17
Z to judge the mount of Esau .... Obad 21
of the sin to the daughter of Z .... Mic 1:13
They build up Z with blood................ Mic 3:10
Therefore shall Z for your sake .... Mic 3:12
for the law shall go forth of Z............ Mic 4:2
them in mount Z from henceforth ...... Mic 4:7
strong hold of the daughter of Z .... Mic 4:8
to bring forth, O daughter of Z .... Mic 4:10
and let our eye look upon Z................ Mic 4:11
Arise and thresh, O daughter of Z .... Mic 4:13
Sing, O daughter of Z .... Zeph 3:14
and to Z, Let not thine hands be .... Zeph 3:16
for Z with a great jealousy .... Zec 1:14
and the Lord shall yet comfort Z........ Zec 1:17
Deliver thyself, O Z, that .... Zec 2:7
Sing and rejoice, O daughter of Z .... Zec 2:10
I was jealous for Z with great............ Zec 8:2
I am returned unto Z, and will .... Zec 8:3
Rejoice greatly, O daughter of Z .... Zec 9:9
and raised up thy sons, O Z................ Zec 9:13

ZION'S (zi'-uns)
For Z sake will I not hold my .... Is 62:1

ZIOR (zi'-or) A city in Judah.
which is Hebron, and Z...................... Josh 15:54

ZIPH (zif') See Ziphites.
1. A city in southeast Judah.
Z, and Telem, and Bealoth, ... Josh 15:24
a mountain in the wilderness of Z...... 1Sa 23:14
in the wilderness of Z in a wood 1Sa 23:15
arose, and went to Z before Saul 1Sa 23:24
went down to the wilderness of Z 1Sa 26:2
seek David in the wilderness of Z...... 1Sa 26:2
And Gath, and Mareshah, and Z........ 2Chr 11:8
2. A city in Judah near Carmel.
Maon, Carmel, and Z, and Juttah, ... Josh 15:55

3. A descendant of Caleb.
which was the father of Z.................... 1Chr 2:42
4. A son of Jehalaleel.
Ziph, and Ziphah, Tiria, and Asareel .. 1Chr 4:16

ZIPHAH (zi'-fah) A son of Jehalaleel.
Ziph, and Z, Tiria, and Asareel 1Chr 4:16

ZIPHIMS (zif'-ims) See Ziphites. Same as *Ziphites.*
A Psalm of David, when the Z came .. Ps 54:t

ZIPHION (zif'-e-on) See Zephon. A son of Gad.
Z, and Haggi, Shuni, and Ezbon, Eri... Gen 46:16

ZIPHITES (zif'-ites) See Ziphims. Inhabitants of Ziph.
Then came up the Z to Saul to 1Sa 23:19
the Z came unto Saul to Gibeah,........ 1Sa 26:1

ZIPHRON (zif'-ron) A place in northern Palestine.
And the border shall go on to Z.......... Num 34:9

ZIPPOR (zip'-por) Father of Balak.
Balak the son of Z saw all that .... Num 22:2
Balak the son of Z was king of .... Num 22:4
said unto God, Balak the son of Z...... Num 22:10
Thus saith Balak the son of Z .... Num 22:16
hearken unto me, thou son of Z .... Num 23:18
Then Balak the son of Z, king of .... Josh 24:9
better than Balak the son of Z .... Judg 11:25

ZIPPORAH (zip-po'-rah) Wife of Moses.
and he gave Moses Z his daughter .... Ex 2:21
And Jethro took Z, Moses' wife, ... Ex 4:25
Moses' father in law, took Z................ Ex 18:2

ZITHRI (zith'-ri) See Zichri. A son of Uzziel.
Mishael, and Elzaphan, and Z, ... Ex 6:22

ZIV See Zif.

ZIZ (ziz) A place in Judah.
come up by the cliff of Z 2Chr 20:16

ZIZA (zi'-zah) See Zizah.
1. Son of Shiphi.
Z the son of Shiphi, the son of 1Chr 4:37
2. A son of Rehoboam.
bare him Abijah, and Attai, and Z 2Chr 11:20

ZIZAH (zi'-zah) See Zina, Ziza. Son of Shimei.
was the chief, and Z the second 1Chr 23:11

ZOAN (zo'-an) An Egyptian city.
seven years before Z in Egypt .... Num 13:22
land of Egypt, in the field of Z .... Ps 78:12
and his wonders in the field of Z .... Ps 78:43
Surely the princes of Z are fools .... Is 19:11
The princes of Z are become fools .... Is 19:13
For his princes were at Z.................... Is 30:4
desolate, and will set fire in Z .... Eze 30:14

ZOAR (zo'-ar) A Canaanite city.
of Egypt, as thou comest unto Z........ Gen 13:10
and the king of Bela, which is Z.......... Gen 14:2
the king of Bela (the same is Z .... Gen 14:8
the name of the city was called Z ...... Gen 19:22
the earth when Lot entered into Z...... Gen 19:23
And Lot went up out of Z, and dwelt .. Gen 19:30
for he feared to dwell in Z.................. Gen 19:30
the city of palm trees, unto Z .... Deut 34:3
his fugitives shall flee unto Z .... Is 15:5
from Z even unto Horonaim, as an.... Jer 48:34

ZOBA (zo'-bah) See Zobah. A district in northern Syria.
Beth-rehob, and the Syrians of Z 2Sa 10:6
and the Syrians of Z, and of Rehob, .. 2Sa 10:8

ZOBAH (zo'-bah) See Zoba. Same as Zoba.
Edom, and against the kings of Z 1Sa 14:47
the son of Rehob, king of Z 2Sa 8:3
to succour Hadadezer king of Z 2Sa 8:5
son of Rehob, king of Z 2Sa 8:12
Igal the son of Nathan of Z................ 2Sa 23:36
from his lord Hadadezer king of Z 1Kin 11:23
a band, when David slew them of Z .. 1Kin 11:24
Hadarezer king of Z unto Hamath...... 1Chr 18:3
came to help Hadarezer king of Z 1Chr 18:5
the host of Hadarezer king of Z 1Chr 18:9
out of Syria-maachah, and out of Z .. 1Chr 19:6

ZOBEBAH (zo-be'-bah) A daughter of Coz.
And Coz begat Anub, and Z, and the.. 1Chr 4:8

ZOHAR (zo'-har) See Zerah, Zeror.
1. Father of Ephron.
for me to Ephron the son of Z .... Gen 23:8
Ephron the son of Z the Hittite .... Gen 25:9
2. Son of Simeon.
Jamin, and Ohad, and Jachin, and Z.. Gen 46:10
Jamin, and Ohad, and Jachin, and Z.. Ex 6:15

ZOHELETH (zo'-he-leth) A stone near Enrogel.
and fat cattle by the stone of Z 1Kin 1:9

ZOHETH (zo'-heth) Son of Ishi.
And the sons of Ishi were, Z................ 1Chr 4:20

ZOPHAH (zo'-fah) Son of Helem.
Z, and Imna, and Shelesh, and Amal .. 1Chr 7:35
The sons of Z 1Chr 7:36

ZOPHAI (zo'-fahee) See Zuph. Brother of Samuel.
Z his son, and Nahath his son,............ 1Chr 6:26

ZOPHAR (zo'-far)
the Shuhite, and the Naamathite .... Job 2:11
Then answered Z the Naamathite, ... Job 11:1
Then answered Z the Naamathite,...... Job 20:1
the Naamathite went, and did .... Job 42:9

ZOPHIM (zo'-fim) A peak on Mt. Pisgah.
brought him into the field of Z .... Num 23:14

ZORAH (zo'-rah) See Zaraah, Zorathites, Zoreah, Zorites. A city in Judah.
coast of their inheritance was Z.......... Josh 19:41
And there was a certain man of Z ...... Judg 13:2
in the camp of Dan between Z............ Judg 13:25
him up, and buried him between Z...... Judg 16:31
coasts, men of valour, from Z .... Judg 18:2
came unto their brethren to Z .... Judg 18:8
family of the Danites, out of Z .... Judg 18:11
And Z, and Aijalon, and Hebron, ... 2Chr 11:10

ZORATHITES (zo'-rath-ites) Descendants of Shobal.
These are the families of the Z............ 1Chr 4:2

ZOREAH (zo'-re-ah) Same as Zorah.
and in the valley, Eshtaol, and Z .... Josh 15:33

ZORITES (zo'-rites) See Zareathites, Zorathites. Descendants of Salma.
half of the Manahethites, the Z 1Chr 2:54

ZOROBABEL (zo-rob'-a-bel) See Zerubbabel. Father of Abiud; ancestor of Jesus.
and Salathiel begat Z........................ Mt 1:12
And Z begat Abiud.............................. Mt 1:13
of Rhesa, which was the son of Z...... Lk 3:27

ZUAR (zu'-ar) Father of Nethaneel.
Nethaneel the son of Z .... Num 1:8
Nethaneel the son of Z shall be.......... Num 2:5
second day Nethaneel the son of Z .... Num 7:18
was Nethaneel the son of Z .... Num 10:15

ZUPH (zuf)
1. An ancestor of Samuel.
The son of Tohu, the son of Z 1Sa 1:1
The son of Z, the son of Elkanah, ... 1Chr 6:35
2. A district in Jerusalem.
came to the land of Z 1Sa 9:5

ZUPHITE See Zuph.

ZUR (zur)
1. Father of Cozbi.
was Cozbi, the daughter of Z.............. Num 25:15
namely, Evi, and Rekem, and Z.......... Num 31:8
of Midian, Evi, and Rekem, and Z, ... Josh 13:21
2. Son of Jehiel.
And his firstborn son Abdon, and Z.... 1Chr 8:30
his firstborn son Abdon, then Z.......... 1Chr 9:36

ZURIEL (zu'-re-el) Son of Abihail.
Merari was Z the son of Abihail.......... Num 3:35

ZURISHADDAI (zu-re-shad'-da-i) Father of Shelumiel.
Shelumiel the son of Z .... Num 1:6
shall be Shelumiel the son of Z .... Num 2:12
fifth day Shelumiel the son of Z.......... Num 7:36
of Shelumiel the son of Z .... Num 7:41
Simeon was Shelumiel the son of Z .. Num 10:19

ZUZIMS (zu'-zims) See Zamzummims. A tribe in the land of Ham.
the Z in Ham, and the Emims in .... Gen 14:5

Z